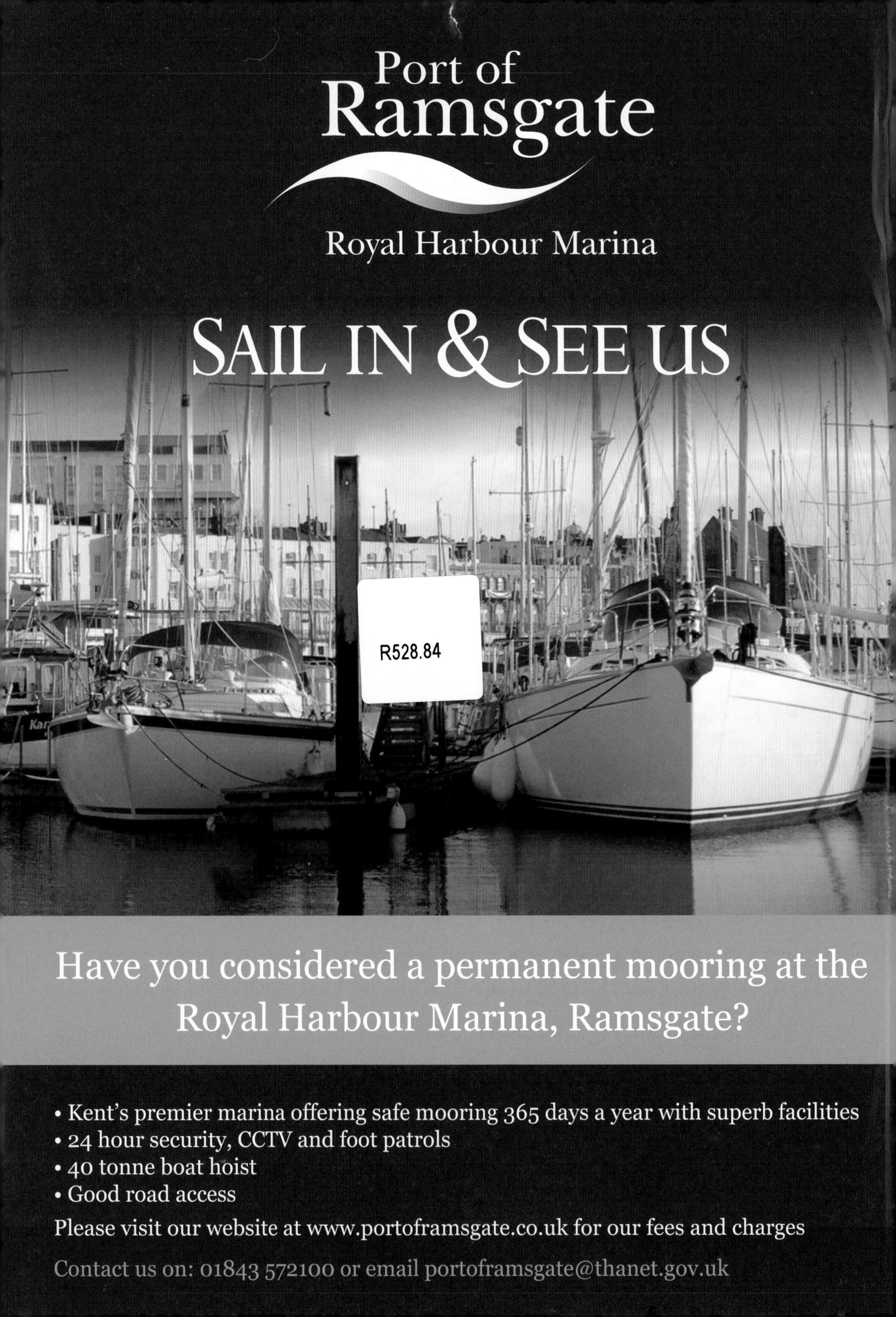
Port of
Ramsgate
Royal Harbour Marina
SAIL IN & SEE US
R528.84
Have you considered a permanent mooring at the
Royal Harbour Marina, Ramsgate?
• Kent's premier marina offering safe mooring 365 days a year with superb facilities
• 24 hour security, CCTV and foot patrols
• 40 tonne boat hoist
• Good road access
Please visit our website at www.portoframsgate.co.uk for our fees and charges
Contact us on: 01843 572100 or email portoframsgate@thanet.gov.uk

REEDS NAUTICAL ALMANAC 2018

EDITORS Perrin Towler and Mark Fishwick

Free updates are available at www.reedsalmanacs.co.uk

IMPORTANT SAFETY NOTE AND LEGAL DISCLAIMER

This Almanac provides basic navigational data for planning and executing passages. The tidal prediction data has been reproduced by permission of national hydrographic offices. Chartlets illustrate items in the text, orientate the user and highlight key features; they should not be relied on for navigational purposes and must always be used in conjunction with a current, corrected navigational chart. Any waypoint or position listed in this Almanac must first be plotted on the appropriate chart to assess its accuracy, safety in the prevailing circumstances and relevance to the Skipper's intentions.

Navigational guidance or suggestions are based on the accumulated experience of editors, agents, harbour masters and users. They are generic and in compiling a passage plan or pilotage notebook all other available publications and information should be consulted. They take no account of the characteristics of individual vessels nor the actual or forecast meteorological conditions, sea or tidal state. These need to be checked with appropriate local authorities for the intended area of operation prior to departure.

While every care has been taken in compiling the Almanac, it is a human endeavour with many contributors. Despite rigorous checking there may be inadvertent errors or inaccuracies, and omissions resulting from the time of notification in relation to the publication date. To the extent that the editors or publishers become aware of these, corrections will be published on the website www.reedsalmanacs.co.uk (requires registration). Readers should therefore regularly check the website between January and June for any such corrections. Data in this Almanac is corrected up to Weekly Edition 25/2017 of Admiralty Notices to Mariners.

The publishers, editors and their agents accept no responsibility for any errors or omissions, or for any accident, loss or damage (including without limitation any indirect, consequential, special or exemplary damages) arising from the use or misuse of, or reliance upon, the information contained in this Almanac.

The use of any data in this Almanac is entirely at the discretion of the Skipper or other individual with responsibility for the command, conduct or navigation of the vessel in which it is relied upon.

Reeds Nautical Almanac

An imprint of Bloomsbury Publishing Plc

50 Bedford Square, London, WC1B 3DP

1385 Broadway, New York, NY 10018, USA

www.bloomsbury.com

Tel: +44 (0)207 631 5600

info@reedsalmanacs.co.uk

editor.britishisles@reedsalmanacs.co.uk

editor.continental@reedsalmanacs.co.uk

www.reedsalmanacs.co.uk

Almanac manager Chris Stevens

Reeds Nautical Almanac 2018 – ISBN 978 1 4729 4801 4

Reeds Looseleaf Almanac 2018 – ISBN 978 1 4729 4650 8

Reeds Looseleaf Update Pk 2018 – ISBN 978 1 4729 4899 1

British Library Cataloguing-in-Publication Data
A catalogue record for this book is available from the British Library.

Library of Congress Cataloguing-in-Publication data has been applied for.

REEDS, ADLARD COLES NAUTICAL and the Buoy logo are trademarks of Bloomsbury Publishing Plc

First published 2017

Bloomsbury Publishing Plc makes every effort to ensure that the papers used in the manufacture of our books are natural, recyclable products made from wood grown in well-managed forests. Our manufacturing processes conform to the environmental regulations of the country of origin.

To find out more about our authors and books visit www.bloomsbury.com. Here you will find extracts, author interviews, details of forthcoming events and the option to sign up for our newsletters.

Printed and bound in the UK by Bell & Bain Ltd, Glasgow

Go the extra mile – we do!
Get a quote today 01752 223656
GER16361 02/2017
PANTAENIUS
Sail & Motor Yacht Insurance
pantaenius.co.uk
Pantaenius UK Limited is authorised and regulated by the Financial Conduct Authority (Authorised No.308688)

Chapter Contents

CHAPTER CONTENTS vii
NAVIGATIONAL CONTENTS ix

Introduction 1

Editorial • Using the almanac • Improvements • Agents wanted • Corrections • Acknowledgements and Permissions

Chapter 1 Reference data 5

Symbols and Abbreviations • Useful addresses (postal and e-mail) and websites • 2017 Calendar • Eclipse notes • Conversion tables • Time • Vocabularies

Chapter 2 Regulations 21

Cruising formalities • HM Revenue and Customs • Foreign Customs • VAT • International Regulations for Preventing Collisions at Sea (COLREGs)

Chapter 3 Navigation 33

Passage planning/SOLAS V • Conduct of the plan • Light characteristics • IALA buoyage • Satellite navigation • Hydrographic surveys • Electronic charts • Waypoints • Chart plotters • Radar and AIS • Racons and ramarks • Navigational warnings • Hazards • Offshore energy installations • Navigational tables: Distance of horizon • Distance, speed and time • Distance off by sextant • True bearing of sun at sunrise/set • Sun's declination • True bearing of sun • Distance off rising/dipping lights • Sunrise/set times • Moonrise/set times • Phases of the Moon

Chapter 4 Tides 53

Introduction • Definitions • Calculating times/heights of tide • Overhead clearances • Computer predictions • Tidal streams • Meteorological effects • Tidal stream rates

Chapter 5 Communications 63

International code of signals • Radio communication • Global communications • Navigational warnings • Gunfacts and subfacts • Coastal radio stations (CRS) • Coastguard contact details for UK • Coast Guard contact details for Republic of Ireland, Denmark, Germany, The Netherlands, Belgium, France, Spain, Portugal, Gibraltar

Chapter 6 Weather 81

Beaufort wind scale • Sea states • Heavy weather warnings • GMDSS weather • NAVTEX • HM Coastguard broadcasts • HF facsimile • BBC broadcasts • Internet weather resources • Sources of foreign weather information

Chapter 7 Safety 105

Introduction • Safety equipment • GMDSS • Definitions of emergencies • Emergency signals • MAYDAY • PAN PAN • SÉCURITÉ • Sound & visual distress signals • Helicopter rescue • Abandon ship • UK SAR • HM CG • RNLI • NCI

Chapter 8 First aid 117

Objectives • Medical care abroad • Medical advice by R/T • Emergency resuscitation • Choking • Drowning • Hypothermia • Shock • Acute illness • Stroke • Bites/stings • Bleeding • Burns • Chest and crush injuries • Cuts • Dental • Eyes • Fish hooks • Fractures • Poison • Sprains • First aid kits • Drugs • Emergency childbirth • Injections • Physiological measurements • Observation form

Chapter 9 Harbours, coasts and tides 129

Map of areas • Area information • Harbour information • Environmental guidance • Distance tables: English Channel, Irish Sea, North Sea, Bay of Biscay

See page ix for details

General index 1047

Gazetteer (index of place names) 1050

Navigational Contents

Chapter 9, Harbours, coasts and tides 129

Map of areas • Harbour details and tide tables • Tidal streams • Lights, buoys and waypoints • Passage information • Ferries • Distance tables • Special notes

Area 1 **South West England, including Isles of Scilly** 137
Isles of Scilly to Anvil Point

Area 2 **Central Southern England** 191
Anvil Point to Selsey Bill

Area 3 **South East England** 247
Selsey Bill to North Foreland

Area 4 **East England** 271
North Foreland to Great Yarmouth

Area 5 **North East England** 331
Winterton to Berwick-upon-Tweed

Area 6 **South East Scotland** 365
Eyemouth to Rattray Head

Area 7 **North East Scotland** 391
Rattray Head to Cape Wrath, incl Orkney and Shetland Islands

Area 8 **North West Scotland** 429
Cape Wrath to Crinan Canal

Area 9 **South West Scotland** 467
Crinan Canal to Mull of Galloway

Area 10 **North West England, Isle of Man and North Wales** 497
Mull of Galloway to Bardsey Island

Area 11 **South Wales and Bristol Channel** 527
Bardsey Island to Land's End

Area 12 **South Ireland** 565
Malahide clockwise to Liscannor Bay

Area 13 **North Ireland** 611
Liscannor Bay clockwise to Lambay Island

Area 14 **West Denmark** 649
Skagen to Romø

Area 15 **Germany** 665
Danish border to Emden

Area 16 **The Netherlands and Belgium** 701
Delfzijl to Nieuwpoort

Area 17 **North France** 749
Dunkerque to Cap de la Hague

Area 18 **Central North France** 797
Cap de la Hague to St Quay-Portrieux

Area 19 **Channel Islands** 821
Alderney to Jersey

Area 20 **North Brittany** 847
Paimpol to Pointe de Penmarc'h

Area 21 **South Brittany** 887
Loctudy to St Nazaire

Area 22 **South Biscay** 917
River Loire to Spanish border

Area 23 **North and North West Spain** 953
Fuenterrabía to Bayona

Area 24 **Portugal** 987
Viana do Castelo to Vila Real de Santo Antonio

Area 25 **South West Spain, Gibraltar and Morocco** 1009
Ayamonte to Europa Point, Tangier and Ceuta

Area 26 **Portuguese Islands** 1027
Azores: Flores, Faial, Pico, São Jorge, Graciosa, Terceira, Santa Maria and São Miguel. **Madeira**: Porto Santo and Madeira

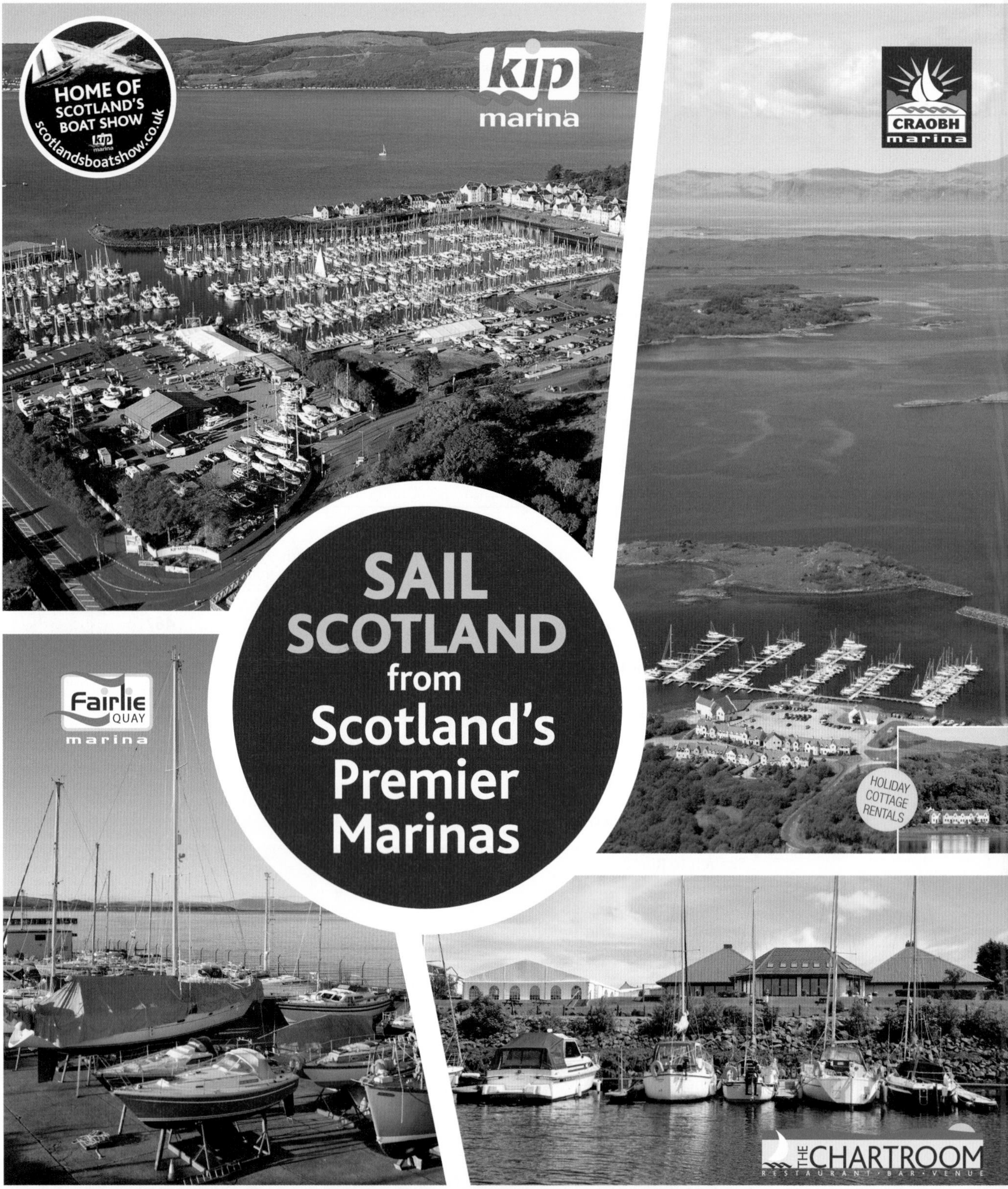
HOME OF SCOTLAND'S BOAT SHOW
scotlandsboatshow.co.uk
kip marina
CRAOBH marina
SAIL SCOTLAND
from
Scotland's
Premier
Marinas
Fairlie QUAY marina
HOLIDAY COTTAGE RENTALS
THE CHARTROOM
RESTAURANT · BAR · VENUE

SWINGING MOORINGS
JET DOCKS
SUPER YACHT BERTHS
PERMANENT BERTHS
POOLE QUAY
VISITOR/PERMANENT BERTHS
Set sail for Poole
with your pride & joy
The Yacht Harbour Association Ltd.
Marina of the Year 2017
UK Coastal
Under 250 Berths
WINNER
PARTNERED BY GJW Insurance
of the Year 2016
Coastal
WINNER
GJW Insurance
PERMANENT BERTHS
Whatever you love to do, you will enjoy our permanent berth marina. It's in a private position that makes the most of the views and gorgeous sunsets, yet it's still close to Poole's historic quay, old town and vibrant shopping centre.
• 75 permanent berths
• Superyacht berths
• Floating docks for jet skis and RIBs up to 6.1m
• 24 hour security
• Showers & toilets, laundry, electric & water
• Deep water: 2.5 - 6m
• Water taxi service, parking
VISITOR MARINA
Use your boat as a holiday home; entertain family, friends, colleagues or customers onboard; sail the stunning Jurassic Coast. Enjoy all the attractions of Poole, Bournemouth and beautiful Dorset. A warm welcome always awaits!
• 125 visitor berths all year for vessels up to 65m in length and up to 4.5m draft
• Swinging moorings
• Floating docks for jet skis and RIBs up to 6.1m
• Showers & toilets, laundry, electric & water
SWINGING MOORINGS
Relax with a glass of wine, on a sunny afternoon, on your own swinging mooring in Poole Harbour overlooking Brownsea Island. Away from the madding crowd, these offer you ultimate privacy, peace & tranquillity.
JET SKI OR RIBS
Keeping your craft on a Jet Ski or RIB Dock has the advantage of 'out-of-water' storage but still offers the convenience of marina berthing and more time for leisure.
POOLE QUAY
Boat Haven
PORT OF POOLE
Marina
Poole Town Quay, Poole, Dorset BH15 1HJ
t: 01202 649488
www.poolequayboathaven.co.uk
VHF Channel 80 call sign "Poole Quay Boat Haven"
POOLE HARBOUR
BOAT SHOW
HOME OF THE
POOLE HARBOUR
BOAT SHOW

www.shop4tanks.com
High quality, marine metalwork, competitively priced
CE marked metal fuel and water tanks
Stainless steel tank accessories
Plastic fuel tanks
BUY ONLINE
www.shop4tanks.com
Bespoke marine metalwork
Bespoke stainless steel & aluminium tanks
Jay Wolfe Metalwork Ltd T: 01604 720988 E: info@shop4tanks.com

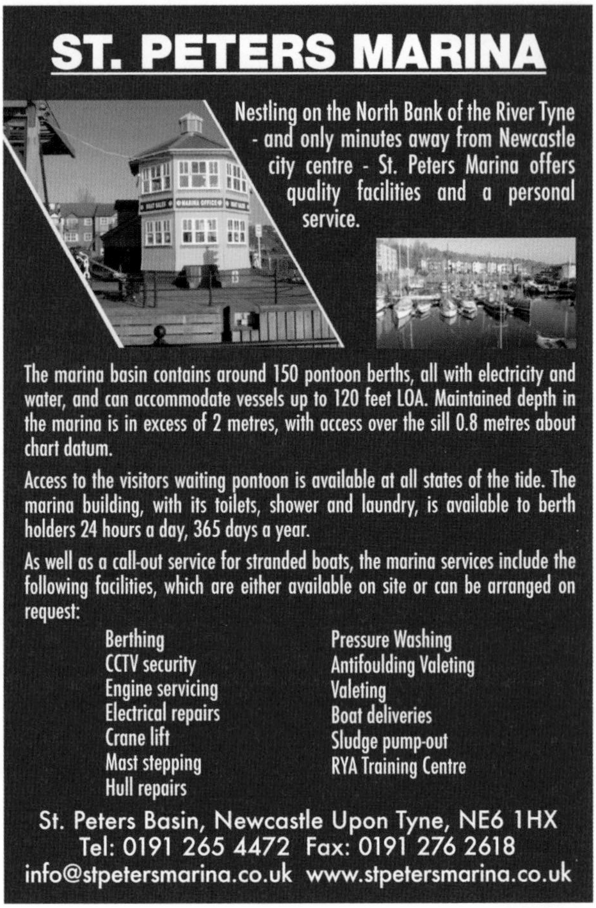
ST. PETERS MARINA
Nestling on the North Bank of the River Tyne - and only minutes away from Newcastle city centre - St. Peters Marina offers quality facilities and a personal service.
The marina basin contains around 150 pontoon berths, all with electricity and water, and can accommodate vessels up to 120 feet LOA. Maintained depth in the marina is in excess of 2 metres, with access over the sill 0.8 metres about chart datum.
Access to the visitors waiting pontoon is available at all states of the tide. The marina building, with its toilets, shower and laundry, is available to berth holders 24 hours a day, 365 days a year.
As well as a call-out service for stranded boats, the marina services include the following facilities, which are either available on site or can be arranged on request:
Berthing
CCTV security
Engine servicing
Electrical repairs
Crane lift
Mast stepping
Hull repairs
Pressure Washing
Antifoulding Valeting
Valeting
Boat deliveries
Sludge pump-out
RYA Training Centre
St. Peters Basin, Newcastle Upon Tyne, NE6 1HX
Tel: 0191 265 4472 Fax: 0191 276 2618
info@stpetersmarina.co.uk www.stpetersmarina.co.uk

"The East Coast's Premier Marina..."
shotleymarina.co.uk
Shotley Marina
The marina is situated where the rivers Stour and Orwell meet in Harwich Harbour. Access to this sheltered marina is via a hydraulically operated lock, manned continually throughout the year, 24 hours a day. The lockmaster listens on VHF CH80. The entrance to the lock is floodlit at night and the outer end of the access channel has lit piles. An "Inogon" guidance light system assists on entering the lock.
350 Ultra Modern Berths
Safe & Secure Mooring
24 Hour Access
Specialist Boat Repairs
Public House & Restaurant
Water, Electricity, Modern Toilets, Showers, Laundry and Disabled Facilities
Ships Stores
WiFi Internet Access
Shotley Marina Ltd. Shotley Gate, Ipswich, Suffolk IP9 1QJ
T: 01473 788982 F: 01473 788868 E: sales@shotleymarina.co.uk

www.yachthavens.com
Neyland Yacht Haven
Visitors Welcome
Full Tidal Access
– Pembrokeshire's Picturesque Marina
– Full tidal access within a well-protected creek
– TransEurope Member – visitor discounts
– Café, Bar/Restaurant & Chandlery
– Full marina services
– Free Wi-Fi
– Bike Hire
HAVEN POD
FLOATING ACCOMMODATION
Neyland Yacht Haven Tel: 01646 601601 VHF Ch 37 & 80
Email: neyland@yachthavens.com

Introduction

0.1	**Introduction**	**2**
	Editorial	
0.2	**Using the Almanac**	**2**
	Numbering system • Contents and Index	
0.3	**Help improve the Almanacs**	**2**
	Improvements and corrections • Harbour Agents • Agents wanted	
0.4	**Corrections and updates**	**2**
	Sources of corrections • Online updates	
0.5	**Acknowledgements & permissions**	**2**
	Acknowledgements • Permissions • Disclaimer	

0.1 INTRODUCTION: USING THE ALMANAC

0.1.1 Editorial

Welcome to the 2018 edition of the Almanac. It continues to encompass the ever-changing seascape and harbours along the coastline of the United Kingdom and Northern Europe. Balancing coverage with its sheer size, there are upwards of 45,000 vital changes to navigation, safety and tidal information. See 0.4.2 below for details of free online monthly updates.

This year sees numerous changes along the UK South Coast. In Portsmouth the fairway has been altered and the leading light moved from Southsea Castle to a new pile ready for the new aircraft carriers. Cowes Breakwater has altered tidal flows, and HW tables reflecting the HM's methodology predict the onset of the strongest tidal streams. Dover is enjoying the renewal of yachting facilities through the Western Docks Revival, and Newhaven is gaining from offshore wind farm investment. The inshore waters of the United Kingdom see continuing development of offshore energy installations. Tidal turbine locations change and generators are replaced. Research buoys and seabed sensors increase in number.

In Scotland the Queensferry Crossing has opened and marina modernisation continues, with new facilities at Loch Boisdale, Ulva Ferry, much work at Dunstaffnage and development at Oban. Ireland has seen the expansion of facilities at Bantry Bay and Knighttown and the rationalisation of lights. The revision of Area 13 has started with Lough Foyle.

In the North Sea the Maas and North Hinder TSS have been altered to increase separation from wind farms and improve routeing to the Westerschelde. The closed Schuitengat-Zuid approach channel to West Terschelling has been reinstated and buoyage renewed. The page layout for the Channel Islands has been modified for clarity and the entry to Courseulles-sur-Mer updated following the removal of inshore shoals. Further south the Tangiers listing now includes the first phase of the 626-berth Tanja Marina Bay.

Important changes to the UK MSI broadcast channels are included as well as updates to the continental weather and safety broadcast routines. The Almanac reflects these developments as they are reported.

Tidal predictions are further updated to maintain clarity and accuracy of printed data to support judicious planning. No matter how good, online prediction is just as susceptible as traditional methods to variation in atmospheric pressure and persistent / strong winds: actual heights and times differ.

The Almanac progressively yet steadily works to retain data most relevant to modern yachtsmen, while remaining rooted in the tradition of good navigation and seamanship.

0.2 USING THE ALMANAC

0.2.1 Numbering system

The nine chapters contain numbered sections. In Chapter 4, for example, sections are numbered 4.1 to 4.9. Within section 4.1 the key paragraphs are numbered 4.1.1 and 4.1.2.

Diagrams are numbered: Fig 4(1) to Fig 4(9). Tables are similarly numbered.

Each main harbour entry in Chapter 9 is shown with the chapter number, the Area number and a sequential number within that Area. Thus Plymouth is shown as 9.1.15.

0.2.2 Contents and Index

Main subject headings and page numbers are listed on the contents page at the start of each section. A General Index and Gazetteer are at the back of the Almanac.

0.3 HELP IMPROVE THE ALMANACS

0.3.1 Improvements and corrections

Corrections or suggestions, however minor, are always welcome. All, especially those based on passages and port visits, will be carefully considered. Please send these to the relevant Editor below, or to info@reedsalmanacs.co.uk. A written note may be forwarded directly to Adlard Coles Nautical (see page v). Please address all queries regarding Reeds Digital to contactus@reedsnauticalalmanac.co.uk

Perrin Towler – editor.britishisles@reedsalmanacs.co.uk
Areas 1 to 13 (*UK and Ireland*) and Chapters 3 (*Navigation*), 4 (*Tides*), 7 (*Safety*) and 8 (*First Aid*).

Mark Fishwick – editor.continental@reedsalmanacs.co.uk
Areas 14 to 26 (*Skagen to Gibraltar*) and Chapters 1 (*Reference Data*), 2 (*Regulations*), 5 (*Communications*) and 6 (*Weather*).

0.3.2 Harbour Agents

Our Harbour Agents provide invaluable local information not always available from official sources. Vacancies are shown below. If you would like to earn a free copy of the Almanac every year, please apply to the relevant Editor.

0.3.3 Agents wanted

We are keen to recruit Agents for the following areas:

UK: London and Thames Estuary.
Continental: River Seine/Paris, Treburden & Lannion, Rade de Brest, Morgat, Raz de Sein, Bénodet/Port-La-Forêt/Concarneau, Lorient, River Étel, Belle Île, Île de Ré/Ars-en-Ré/St Martin-de-Ré.

0.4 CORRECTIONS AND UPDATES

0.4.1 Sources of corrections

This Almanac is corrected to Weekly Edition 25/2017 of Admiralty Notices to Mariners. Where possible, corrections from other sources (Agents, HMs etc) received by 1 June 2017 have also been incorporated.

0.4.2 Online updates

It is important that this Almanac is kept up to date to maintain its accuracy. For free monthly updates from January to June, please register at www.reedsnauticalalmanac.co.uk

Tick the boxes to show which updates have been applied:

Jan ☐ **Feb** ☐ **Mar** ☐ **Apr** ☐ **May** ☐ **Jun** ☐

0.5 ACKNOWLEDGEMENTS & PERMISSIONS

The Editors thank the many authorities which have provided information essential to the preparation of this Almanac.

These include the UK Hydrographic Office, HM Stationery Office and: Trinity House, the Northern Lighthouse Board, HM Nautical Almanac Office, HM Revenue and Customs, the Meteorological Office, the Maritime and Coastguard Agency, the ABP, BBC, IBA, NCI, PLA and RNLI.

Important contributions have also been made by the following authorities in the Republic of Ireland and continental Europe: The Commissioners of Irish Lights, Deutsche Gesellschaft zur Rettung Schiffbrüchiger (DgzRS), Koninklijke Nederlandse Redding Maatschappij (KNRM).

In particular we thank Harbourmasters, Marina Managers, our Harbour Agents and numerous individual yachtsmen who have contributed new ideas and suggestions based on their invaluable local knowledge. As always, Frank Singleton has supported Reeds with information and advice about weather.

0.5.1 Permissions

Information from Admiralty Charts, the Admiralty Lists of Lights, Admiralty Tide Tables and the Admiralty Lists of Radio Signals is reproduced with the permission of the UK Hydrographic Office (Licence No GB DQ – 001 – Adlard Coles) and the Controller of HMSO.

Extracts from the International Code of Signals, 1969 and Meteorological Office Weather Services for Shipping are published by permission of the Controller of HMSO.

Phases of the Moon and Sun/Moon rising and setting times are included by permission of HM Nautical Almanac Office.

Tidal stream diagrams are reproduced from Admiralty charts and tidal stream atlases by permission of the UKHO and the Controller of HMSO.

Tidal stream data in 9.1.5, 9.12.3 and 9.13.3 is printed by kind permission of the Royal Cruising Club and the Irish Cruising Club respectively.

UK and Foreign tidal predictions and curves are supplied by the UK Hydrographic Office, with the permission (and Authorisation Numbers) of the following authorities to use the Standard Port predictions stated:

- Danmarks Meteorologiske Institut, Denmark: Esbjerg.
- SHOM, France: Dunkerque, Boulogne, Dieppe, Le Havre, Cherbourg, St Malo, Brest, Pte de Grave; and tidal coefficients for Calais, St Malo, Brest and Pte de Grave. (2017-238, 2017-255)
- BSH, Germany: Helgoland, Wilhelmshaven and Cuxhaven (11123/2008-07).
- Rijkswaterstaat, The Netherlands: Vlissingen and Hoek van Holland.
- Vlaamse Hydrografie, Belgium: Zeebrugge.
- Marinho Instituto Hidrográfico, Portugal: Lisboa.
- Instituto Hidrográfico de la Marina, Spain: La Coruña (02/17).

0.5.2 Disclaimer

Neither the UK nor any other National Hydrographic Office has verified the information in this product and none accepts liability for the accuracy of reproduction or any modifications made thereafter. No National HO warrants that this product satisfies national or international regulations regarding the use of the appropriate products for navigation.

1

Reference Data

1.1 Symbols and abbreviations 6

Admiralty chart symbols • Symbols and Abbreviations

1.2 Postal and e-mail addresses with websites 9

Listed by countries

1.3 Calendar 2018 and ephemeris 10

Public holidays • Eclipses

1.4 Conversion tables 11

Conversion factors • Feet to metres and vice versa

1.5 Time 12

Zone, UT, Standard, DST • Tide tables • Radio time signals

1.6 Vocabularies 12

English • Deutsch • Nederlands • Français • Español • Português

Fig 1(1) Admiralty chart symbols

Pyl 28 Pyl	Power transmission line with pylons and safe overhead clearance as defined by the responsible authority
20	Vertical clearance above HAT
	Submarine cable
	Buried pipeline
	Overfalls, tide rips and races
3kn	Flood stream Mean spring rate
3kn	Ebb stream Mean spring rate
D	Designated position of tabulated tidal streams
(a) (b)	Examples: (a) fixed beacon; (b) buoy
	Limit of safety zone around offshore installation
	Major light
	Port hand lt bcn (PHM)
V-AIS	Virtual AIS
	Fishing harbour
V	Visitors' berths
	Fuel station (Petrol, Diesel)
	Public slipway
	Water tap
	Public landing, steps, ladder

	Church, chapel
	Radio mast, television mast
	Monument (including column, pillar, obelisk, statue)
	Chimney
	Flare stack (on land)
	Tanks
	Crane
	Bird sanctuary
C G	Coastguard Station
	Woods in general
	Withy - starboard hand
	Withy - port hand
	Floodlit
	Marsh
	Kelp
	Fog signal
	Yacht berths, no facilities
V	Visitor's buoy
	Mooring buoy
	Laundrette
	Yacht Club, Sailing Club

2 0 2 5 1 2 0	Drying contour LW line, Chart Datum Blue ribbon or differing blue tints may be shown
	Anchoring prohibited
	Marine Farm
	Wreck, depth unknown, danger to navigation
	Wreck, depth unknown, no danger to navigation
4 Wk 6	Wreck, depth obtained by sounding
4_6 Wk	Wreck, swept by wire to the depth shown
	Wreck showing any part at level of chart datum
(1_6) (2_7) 3_7	Rock which covers and uncovers, height above chart datum
5 0	Rock awash at level of chart datum
5 0	Dangerous underwater rock of unknown depth
20 (12_2) (5_7) (2_8) 0	Dangerous underwater rock of known depth
	Recommended anchorage
	Rescue station, lifeboat station, rocket station
	Yacht harbour, Marina
	Harbourmaster's Office
	Customs office
	Hospital
	Post office

1.1 SYMBOLS AND ABBREVIATIONS

The following Symbols and Abbreviations feature in Reeds Almanacs and in Admiralty charts and publications. See also Fig 1(1). Admiralty NP 5011 explains Symbols and Abbreviations on printed charts. The symbols in the tinted box immediately below are frequently used within the text describing each port.

	Alongside berth
©	Automatic telling machine (ATM), cashpoint
Ⓑ	Bank
	Bottled gas available, Calor Gas, Camping Gaz,or Kosangas
	Boatyard
	Boat hoist (+tons)
	Crane (+ tons)
	Chandlery
⊖	Customs
	Diesel (supply by hose)
	Diesel (in cans)
	Electrical repairs
Ⓔ	Electronic repairs
	Fresh water supply
	Food shop/supermarket
H	Hospital
≠	In transit with, ie ldg marks/lts
@	Internet café/access
	Landing place/steps/ladder
	Laundry facilities available
LB,	Lifeboat, inshore lifeboat
	Light float, minor
	Lt float, major; Light vessel or Lanby
	Licensed bar, Public house, Inn
©	National Coastwatch Institution (NCI)
	Marine engineering repairs
	Mooring buoy
	Petrol (supply by hose)
	Petrol (in cans)
☒	Post Office
	Pump out facility
✕	Restaurant/café
	Rigger
	Sailmaker
	Shipwright (esp wooden hulls)
	Shower
	Shore power (electrical)
	Slipway
	Visitors' berths
	Visitors' mooring
	Wind turbine
	Weather forecast available
	Yacht Club/(YC), Sailing Club(SC)

abm	Abeam
ABP	Associated British Ports
ACA	Admiralty Chart (AC) Agent
ACN	Adlard Coles Nautical (Publisher)
Aff Mar	Affaires Maritimes
AIS	Automatic Identification System
aka	Also known as
ALL	Admiralty List of Lights
ALRS	Admiralty List of Radio Signals
Al	Alternating light
ANWB	Association of road & waterway users (Dutch)
ATT	Admiralty Tide Tables
ATT	Atterisage (landfall/SWM) buoy
Auto	Météo Répondeur Automatique
B.	Bay, Black
BE	Belgian chart
Bk	Broken (nature of seabed)
Bkwtr	Breakwater
BMS	Bulletin Météorologique Spécial (Strong wind/Gale warning)
Bn, bcn(s)	Beacon, beacon(s)
BSH	German Hydrographic Office/chart(s)
BST	British Summer Time (= DST)
Bu	Blue
By(s)	Buoy, buoys
C.	Cape, Cabo, Cap
c	Coarse (sand; nature of seabed)
ca	Cable (approx 185m long)
Cas	Castle
CD	Chart datum (tidal)
CEVNI	Code Européen de Voies de la Navigation Intérieure (inland waterway signs etc)
cf	Compare, cross-refer to
CG	Coast Guard, HM Coastguard (in the UK)
CGOC	Coast Guard Operations Centre (UK)
chan	Channel (navigational)
Ch	Channel (VHF)
Ch, ✠	Church
Chy	Chimney
Co	Coral (nature of seabed)
Col	Column, pillar, obelisk
CPA	Closest Point of Approach
CROSS	Centre Régional Opérationnel de Surveillance et Sauvetage (= MRCC)
CRS	Coast Radio Station
CRT	Canal and River Trust
C/S	COSPAS/SARSAT (satellite)
Cy	Clay (nature of seabed)
Dec	Declination (of the Sun) abbr: December
Defib	Automated External Defibrillator
D, dest	Destroyed
DF, D/F	Radio Direction Finding
DG	De-gaussing (range)
DGPS	Differential GPS
Dia	Diaphone (fog signal)
Dir Lt	Directional light
discont	Discontinued
DLR	Dockland Light Railway
Dn(s)	Dolphin(s)
DR	Dead Reckoning or Dries (secondary tides)
DSC	Digital Selective Calling
DST	Daylight Saving Time
DW	Deep Water (route)
DYC	Dutch Yacht Chart(s)
DZ	Danger Zone (buoy)
E	East
ECM	East cardinal mark (buoy/beacon)
ED	Existence doubtful. European Datum
EEA	European Economic Area
Elev	Elevation
Ent	Entrance, entry, enter
EP, △	Estimated position
ETA	Estimated Time of Arrival
ETD	Estimated Time of Departure
F	Fixed light
f	Fine (eg sand; nature of seabed)
F&A	Fore and aft (berth/mooring)
FFL	Fixed and Flashing light
Fl	Flashing light
FM	Frequency Modulation
Foc	Free of charge
Fog Det lt	Fog Detector light
Freq, Fx	Frequency
FS	Flagstaff, Flagpole
ft	Foot, feet
Ft,	Fort
FV	Fishing vessel
G	Gravel (nature of seabed), Green
GC	Great Circle
GDOP	Geometric Dilution of Precision (GPS)

GHA	Greenwich Hour Angle
GLA	General Lighthouse Authority
GMDSS	Global Maritime Distress & Safety System
grt	Gross Registered Tonnage
Gy	Grey
H, h, Hrs	Hour(s)
H–, H+	Minutes before, after the whole hour
H24	Continuous
Hd,hd	Headland, head (breakwater/mole)
HAT	Highest Astronomical Tide
HF	High Frequency
HFP	High Focal Plane (buoy)
HIE	Highlands & Islands Enterprise
HJ	Day service only, sunrise to sunset
HM	Harbour Master
HMRC	HM Revenue & Customs
HMSO	Her Majesty's Stationery Office
HN	Night service only, sunset to sunrise
HO	Office hours, Hydrographic Office
(hor)	Horizontally disposed (lights)
hPa	Hectopascal (= 1millibar)
HT	High Tension (overhead electricity line)
HW	High Water
HX	No fixed hours
IALA	International Association of Marine Aids to Navigation and Lighthouse Authorities
iaw	In accordance with
IDM	Isolated Danger Mark (buoy/beacon)
IHO	International Hydrographic Organisation
IMO	International Maritime Organisation
INMARSAT	International Maritime Satellite Organisation
intens	Intensified (light sector)
IPTS	International Port Traffic Signals
IQ	Interrupted quick flashing light
IRPCS	International Regulations for the Prevention of Collisions at Sea
Is, I	Island, Islet
ISAF	International Sailing Federation
Iso	Isophase light
ITU	International Telecommunications Union
ITZ	Inshore Traffic Zone (TSS)
IUQ	Interrupted ultra quick flashing light
IVQ	Interrupted very quick flashing light
kn	Knot(s)
kW	Kilowatts
L	Lake, Loch, Lough
Lat	Latitude
LAT	Lowest Astronomical Tide
Lanby,	Large automatic navigational buoy
Ldg	Leading (light)
LF	Low frequency
L Fl	Long flash
LH	Left hand
LNG	Liquefied Natural Gas
LNTM	Local Notice To Mariners
LOA	Length overall
Long, lng	Longitude
LPG	Liquefied Petroleum Gas
LT	Local time
Lt(s), ☆ ☆	Light(s)
M	Moorings. Nautical (sea) mile(s). Mud
m	Metre(s)
Mag	Magnetic. Magnitude (of star)
Mb, mb	Millibar (= 1 hectopascal, hPa)
MCA	Maritime and Coastguard Agency
Met/Météo	Meteorology/Météorologie (weather)
MHWN	Mean High Water Neaps
MHWS	Mean High Water Springs
MHz	Megahertz
ML	Mean Level (tidal)
MLWN	Mean Low Water Neaps
MLWS	Mean Low Water Springs
MMSI	Maritime Mobile Service Identity
Mo	Morse
Mon	Monument. Abbrev: Monday
MRCC	Maritime Rescue Co-ordination Centre
MRSC	Maritime Rescue Sub-Centre (not in the UK)
MSI	Maritime Safety Information
N	North
Navi	Navicarte (French charts)
NB	Nota Bene. Notice Board
NCM	North Cardinal Mark (buoy/beacon)
ND	No Data (secondary tides)
NGS	Naval Gunfire Support (buoy)
NM	Notice(s) to Mariners
NMOC	National Maritime Operations Centre (HMCG)
np	Neap tides
NP	Naval Publication (plus number)
NRT	Net registered tonnage
NT	National Trust (land/property)
Obscd	Obscured
Obstn	Obstruction
Oc	Occulting light
ODAS	Ocean Data Acquisition System (buoy)
Or	Orange (see also Y)
OT	Other times
P	Pebbles
(P)	Preliminary (NM)
PA	Position approximate
Pax	Passenger(s)
PC	Portuguese chart
PD	Position doubtful
PHM	Port-hand Mark (buoy/beacon)
PLA	Port of London Authority
Pos	Position
Prog	Prognosis (weather charts)
prom	Prominent
PSSA	Particularly Sensitive Sea Area
Pt(e).	Point(e)
Pta	Punta (point)
Q	Quick flashing light
QHM	Queen's Harbour Master
qv	Refer to (quod vide)
R	Red. River.
Racon	Radar transponder beacon
Ramark	Radar beacon
RCD	Recreational Craft Directive
RG	Emergency RDF station
RH	Right hand
Rk, Rky	Rock, Rocky (nature of seabed)
RNLI	Royal National Lifeboat Institution
ROI	Republic of Ireland
R/T	Radiotelephony
Ru	Ruins
RYA	Royal Yachting Association
S	South, Sand (nature of seabed)
S, St, Ste	Saint(s)
SAMU	Service d'Aide Médicale Urgente (ambulance)
SAR	Search and Rescue
SBM	Single buoy mooring
SC	Sailing Club. Spanish chart
SCM	South Cardinal Mark (buoy/beacon)
SD	Sailing Directions,Semi-diameter (of sun) Sounding of doubtful depth
sf	Stiff (nature of seabed)
Sh	Shells (nature of seabed). Shoal
SHM	Starboard-hand Mark (buoy/beacon); Simplified Harmonic Method (tides)
SHOM	Service Hydrographique et Océanographique de la Marine (FrenchHO/Chart)
Si	Silt (nature of seabed)
SIGNI	Signalisation de la Navigation Intérieure
SMS	Short Message Service (mobile texting)
so	Soft (eg mud; nature of seabed)

Reference Data

SOLAS	Safety of Life at Sea (IMO Convention)
Sp	Spire
sp	Spring tides
SPM	Special Mark (buoy/beacon)
SR	Sunrise
SRR	Search and Rescue Region
SS	Sunset. Signal Station
SSB	Single Sideband (radio)
St	Stones (nature of seabed)
Stbd	Starboard
subm	Submerged
SWM	Safe Water Mark (buoy/beacon)
sy	Sticky (eg mud; nature of seabed)
(T), (Temp)	Temporary
tbc	To be confirmed
tbn	To be notified
TD	Temporarily Discontinued (fog signal)
TE	Temporarily Extinguished (light)
tfn	Till further notice
Tr, twr	Tower
T/R	Traffic Report (route notification)
TSS	Traffic Separation Scheme
uncov	Uncovers
UQ	Ultra Quick flashing light
UT	Universal Time (= approx GMT)
Var	Variation (magnetic)
(vert)	Vertically disposed (lights)
Vi	Violet
vis	Visibility, visible
VLCC	Very large crude carrier (Oil tanker)
VNF	Voie Navigable de France (canals)
VQ	Very Quick flashing light
VTS	Vessel Traffic Service
W	West. White
WCM	West Cardinal Mark (buoy/beacon)
Wd	Weed (nature of seabed)
wef	With effect from
WGS	World Geodetic System (GPS datum)
wi-fi	Wireless Fidelity (internet access)
WIG	Wing in ground effect (craft)
WIP	Work in progress
Wk,	Wreck (see also Fig 1(1))
WMO	World Meteorological Organisation
WPT, ⊕	Waypoint
WZ	Code for UK coastal navigation warning
Y	Yellow, Amber, Orange

1.2 POSTAL AND E-MAIL ADDRESSES WITH WEBSITES

Alderney Visitor Information Centre
51 Victoria Street, St Anne, Alderney GY9 3TA. ☎ 01481 823737. www.visitalderney.com

BBC Radio
Broadcasting House, London W1A 1AA. ☎ 020 7580 4468. www.bbc.co.uk

Canal and River Trust
First Floor North, Station House, 500 Elder Gate, Milton Keynes, MK9 1BB. ☎ 0303 040 4040. www.canalrivertrust.org.gov customer.services@canalrivertrust.org.gov

Cruising Association (CA)
CA House, 1 Northey St, Limehouse Basin, London E14 8BT. ☎ 020 7537 2828. 📠 020 7537 2266 www.theca.org.uk office@theca.org.uk

ECMWF (European Centre for Medium-range Weather Forecasts) The Director-General, Shinfield Park, Reading RG2 9AX, UK. ☎ 0118 949 9000. www.ecmwf.int DG@ecmwf.int

Guernsey Tourist Information Centre
North Esplanade, St Peter Port, Guernsey GY1 3AN. ☎ 01481 723552. www.visitguernsey.com enquiries@visitguernsey.com

HM Revenue and Customs (HMRC)
Helpline ☎ 0845 010 9000; www.hmrc.gov.uk

Hydrographic Office, The United Kingdom
Admiralty Way, Taunton, Somerset TA1 2DN. ☎ 01823 337900. 📠 01823 337900. www.ukho.gov.uk customerservices@ukho.gov.uk

International Maritime Organisation (IMO)
4 Albert Embankment, London SE1 7SR. ☎ 020 7735 7611. 📠 020 7587 3210. www.imo.org info@imo.org

Jersey Visitor Services Centre
Liberation Place, St Helier, Jersey JE1 1BB. ☎ 01534 448877. 📠 01534 448899. www.jersey.com info@jersey.com

Lloyd's
One Lime Street, London EC3M 7HA. ☎ 020 73271000; 📠 020 7327 6827. www.lloyds.com enquiries@lloyds.com

Marine Accident Investigation Branch (MAIB)
First Floor, Spring Place, 105 Commercial Road, Southampton SO15 2JU. ☎ 023 8039 5500. 📠 023 8039 5500. www.maib.gov.uk maib@dft.gsi.gov.uk

Maritime and Coastguard Agency (MCA)
Spring Place, 105 Commercial Rd, Southampton SO15 1EG. ☎ 023 8032 9100; Info 0870 6006 505. 📠 023 8032 9105. www.dft.gov.uk/mca infoline@mcga.gov.uk

Meteorological Office
FitzRoy Road, Exeter EX1 3PB. ☎ 0370 900 0100. 📠 0370 900 5050, ☎ +44 1392 885680. 📠 +44 1392 885681 from abroad. www.metoffice.gov.uk enquiries@metoffice.gov.uk

National Coastwatch Institution (NCI)
1 Barras St, Liskeard, Cornwall PL14 6AD. ☎ 0300 111 1202. www.nci.org.uk info@nci.org.uk

Northern Lighthouse Board
84 George St, Edinburgh EH2 3DA. ☎ 0131 473 3100. 📠 0131 220 2093. www.nlb.org.uk enquiries@nlb.org.uk

Registry of Shipping and Seamen/Small Ships Register
Anchor Court, Keen Road,Cardiff CF24 5JW; ☎ 029 2044 8800; www.ukshipregister.co.uk rss@mcga.gov.uk
Part I (Pleasure vessels) ☎ 02920 448 866.part1_registry@mcga.gov.uk SSR ☎ 029 2044 8813.ssr_registry@mcga.gov.uk

Royal Institute of Navigation (RIN)
1 Kensington Gore, London SW7 2AT. ☎ 020 7591 3134. 📠 020 7591 3131. www.rin.org.uk admin@rin.org.uk

Royal National Lifeboat Institution (RNLI)
West Quay Road, Poole, Dorset BH15 1HZ. ☎ 0300 300 9990. www.rnli.org.uk supporter_care@rnli.org.uk

Royal Yachting Association (RYA)
RYA House, Ensign Way, Hamble, SO31 4YA. ☎ 023 8060 4100. 📠 023 8060 4299. www.rya.org.uk info@rya.org.uk

Royal Yachting Association (Scotland)
Caledonia House, 1 Redheughs Rigg, South Gyle, Edinburgh EH12 9DQ.☎ 0131 317 7388. 📠 0844 556 9549. www.ryascotland.org.ukadmin@ryascotland.org.uk

Scottish Canals
Canal House, Applecross St, Glasgow G4 9SP. ☎ 0141 332 6936. www.scottishcanals.co.uk enquiries@scottishcanals.co.uk

Trinity House, Corporation of
Tower Hill, London EC3N 4DH. ☎ 020 7481 6900. 📠 020 7480 7662. www.trinityhouse.co.uk enquiries@thls.org

BELGIUM

Belgian Tourist Information
Unit 6, Cumbrian House, 217 Marsh Wall, London E14 9FJ. ☎ 0207 537 1132 www.belgiumtheplaceto.be info@belgiumtheplace to.be

British Embassy (Consular Services)
Avenue d'Auderghem 10, 1040 Brussels. ☎ +32 2287 6211 consularsection.brussels@fco.gov.uk

Vlaamse Hydrografie
Administratief Centrum, Vrijhavenstraat 3, B-8400 Oostende. ☎ +32 59 554 211. 📠 +32 59 507 037 www.vlaamsehydrografie.be kust@vlaanderen.be.

DENMARK

British Embassy
Kastelsvej 36-40, DK-2100 København Ø.
☎ +45 35 44 52 00. Consular. copenhagen@fco.gov.uk

Danish Hydrographic Office
Kort-og Matrikelstyrelsen, Rentemestervej 8, DK-2400 København. ☎ +45 7254 5000. www.kms.dk gstsfo@gst.dk

Søfartsstyrelsen (Danish Maritime Authority)
Søsportens Sikkerhedsråd (Safety for yachts)
Carl Jacobsens Veg 31, DK-2500 Valby. ☎ +45 72 19 60 00. 📠 +45 72 19 60 01 www.dma.dk sfs@dma.dk

FRANCE

British Embassy (Consular Services)
16 rue d'Anjou, 75008 Paris.
☎ +33 1 44 51 31 00. 📠 +33 1 44 51 31 27.

Service Hydrographique et Océanographique de la Marine
13 rue du Chatellier, CS 92803, 29228 Brest Cedex 2.
☎ +33 2 56 31 23 12. 📠 +33 2 98 22 08 99. www.shom.fr bps@shom.fr

Société Nationale de Sauvetage en Mer (SNSM)
31, cité d'Antin, 75009 Paris.
☎ +33 1 56 02 64 64. 📠 +33 1 56 89 30 01. www.snsm.org

GERMANY

British Embassy (Consular Services)
Wilhelmstrasse 70/71, 10117 Berlin. ☎ +49 30 2045 7-0. 📠 +49 30 204 570. www.ukingermany.fco.gov.uk ukingermany@fco.gov.uk

Bundesamt für Seeschiffahrt und Hydrographie (BSH). (German HO) Bernhard-Nocht-Str 78, 20359 Hamburg.
☎ +49 40 31900. 📠 +49 40 3190 50 00. www.bsh.de posteingang@bsh.de

Deutscher Gesellschaft zur Rettung Schiffbrüchiger (DGzRS = Rescue service). PO Box 10 63 40, 28063 Bremen.
☎ +49 421 53707-0. 📠 +49 421 53707-690. www.dgzrs.de info@seenotretter.de

German National Tourist Board
Beethovenstrasse 69, D-60325 Frankfurt/Main.
☎ +49 0 6997 4640. 📠 +49 0 6975 1903. www.germany-tourism.de info@d-z-t.com

REPUBLIC OF IRELAND

British Embassy
29 Merrion Road, Ballsbridge, Dublin 4. ☎ +353 1 205 3700. 📠 +353 1 205 3885 www.britishembassy.ie consular.dubli@fco.gov.uk

Irish Coast Guard (IRCG)
Department of Transport, Leeson Lane, Dublin 2, ROI.
☎ +353 1 678 3454 www.dttas.ie/maritime/english/irish-coast-guard-ircg sosirishcoastguardgmail.com

Irish Lights, Commissioners of
Harbour Road, Dun Laoghaire, Co Dublin, RoI. ☎ +353 1 2715400; 📠 +353 1 2715564. www.web@irishlights.ie info@irishlightsl.ie

Irish Tourist Board
Nations House,103 Wigmore St, London W1U 1QS. ☎ 020 751 80800. www.ireland.com

MOROCCO

British Embassy
28 Avenue S.A.R. Sidi Mohammed, Rabat 10105 (BP 45), ☎ +212 537 633 333 rabat.consular@fco.gov.uk www.ukinmorocco.fco.gov.uk

Moroccan National Tourist Office
Angle Rue Oued Al Makhazine, Rue Zalaga-BP., 19-Agdal, Rabat ☎ +212 537 27 83 00 www.visitmorocco.com contact@onmt.org.ma

NETHERLANDS

British Embassy (Consular Services)
Koningslaan 44, 1075 AE Amsterdam.☎ +31 20 676 4343. www.ukinnl.fco.gov.uk ukinnl@fco.gov.uk

Dienst der Hydrografie
R.N. Hydrographic Service, PO Box 10000, 1780, CA Den Helder. ☎ +31 70 316 2800. 📠 +31 70 316 2843. www.hydro.nl info@hydro.nl

Stichting Classificatie Waterrecreatiebedrijven
PO Box 93345, 2509 AH Den Haag. ☎ +31 70 328 3807.

PORTUGAL

British Embassy (Consular Services)
Rua de São Bernardo 33, 1249-082 Lisboa. ☎ +351 21 392 4000 📠 +351 21 392 4184. www.ukinportugal.fco.gov.uk portugal.consulate@fco.gov.uk

Hydrographic Office
Instituto Hidrografico, Rua das Trinas 49, 1249-093 Lisboa.
☎ +351 2109 43000. 📠 +351 21 3914 199. www.hidrografico.pt mail@hidrografico.pt

SPAIN

British Embassy (Consular Services)
Torre Espacio, Paseo de la Castellana 259D, 28046 Madrid.
☎ +34 917 146 300 or from inside Spain: 902 109 356. 📠 +34 917 146 301 info.consulate@fco.gov.uk

Instituto Hidrografico de la Marina
Plaza de San Severiano No 3, 11007 Cadiz. ☎ +34 956 54 52 05. www.armada.mde.es/ihm ihmesp@fn.mde.es

Spanish Tourist Office
6th floor, 64 North Row, London W1K 7DE. ☎ 020 7317 2011. www.spain.info/en_GB info.londres@tourspain.es

1.3 2018 CALENDAR AND EPHEMERIS

1.3.1 UK public holidays 2018

Jan 1 New Year
Jan 1 and 2 (Scotland only)
March 19 (St Patrick, N Ireland only)
March 30 (Good Friday)
April 2 (Easter Monday, except Scotland)
May 7 (Early Spring)
May 28 (Spring)
July 12 (Battle of the Boyne, N Ireland only)
Aug 6 (Summer, Scotland only)
Aug 27 (Summer, England, Wales N.Ireland)
Dec 25 (Christmas Day)
Dec 26 (Boxing Day)

Note: Clauses in the *Banking and Financial Dealings Act* allow the Government to alter dates at short notice

1.3.2 Eclipses visible from the British Isles & Europe

A total eclipse of the Moon will occur on July 27 2018 over Europe and the British Isles. The umbral phase begins at 1824 and ends at 2219 UT. Totality lasts from 1930 to 2114 UT.

1.4 CONVERSION TABLES

1.4.1 Conversion factors

To convert	Multiply by	To convert	Multiply by
Area			
sq in to sq mm	645·16	sq mm to sq in	0·00155
sq ft to sq m	0·0929	sq m to sq ft	10·76
Length (See 1.4.2 for feet to metres, and vice versa)			
in to mm	25·4	mm to in	0·0394
yds to m	0·914	m to yds	1·094
fathoms to m	1·8288	m to fathoms	0·5468
nautical miles (M) to kilometres	1·852	kilometres to nautical miles	0·539957
nautical miles to statute miles	1·1515	statute miles to nautical miles	0·8684
(1 cable equals 0·1 M, approx 185m)			
Velocity (See also 6.1.1 for Beaufort scale)			
ft/sec to m/sec	0·3048	m/sec to ft/sec	3·281
ft/sec to miles/hr	0·682	miles/hr to ft/sec	1·467
ft/sec to knots	0·592	knots to ft/sec	1·689
ft/min to m/sec	0·0051	m/sec to ft/min	196·8
knots to miles/hr	1·1515	miles/hr to knots	0·868
knots to km/hr	1·852	km/hr to knots	0·54
knots to m/sec	0·5144	m/sec to knots	1·944
Mass			
oz to grams	28·35	grams to oz	0·0353
lb to kg	0·4536	kg to lb	2·205
tons to tonnes (1000 kg)	1·016	tonnes to tons (2240 lb)	0·9842
Pressure			
inches of mercury to millibars	33·86	millibars to inches of mercury	0·0295
lb/sq in to kg/sq cm	0·0703	kg/sq cm to lb/sq in	14·22
lb/sq in to atmospheres	0·068	atmospheres to lb/sq in	14·7
Volume			
cu in to cu cm (cc or ml)	16·387	cu cm (cc or ml) to cu in	0·061
cu ft to cu metres	0·0283	cu metres to cu ft	35·31
cu ft to galls	6·25	galls to cu ft	0·16
cu ft to litres	28·33	litres to cu ft	0·035
Capacity			
pints to litres	0·568	litres to pints	1·76
Imp galls to litres	4·546	litres to Imp galls	0·22
Imp galls to US galls	1·2	US galls to Imp galls	0·833
Torque			
lbf ft to Nm	1·3558	Nm to lbf ft	0·7376
kgf m to Nm	9·8066	Nm to kgf m	0·102
lbf ft to kgf m	0·1383	kgf m to lbf ft	7·233

1.4.2 Feet to metres, metres to feet

Explanation: The central columns of figures in bold type can be referred to the left to convert metres into feet, or to the right to convert feet into metres, eg, five lines down: 5 metres = 16·40 feet, or 5 feet = 1·52 metres. Alternatively multiply feet by 0·3048 for metres, or multiply metres by 3·2808 for feet.

Feet		Metres	Feet		Metres	Feet		Metres	Feet		Metres
3·28	**1**	0·30	45·93	**14**	4·27	88·58	**27**	8·23	131·23	**40**	12·19
6·56	**2**	0·61	49·21	**15**	4·57	91·86	**28**	8·53	134·51	**41**	12·50
9·84	**3**	0·91	52·49	**16**	4·88	95·14	**29**	8·84	137·80	**42**	12·80
13·12	**4**	1·22	55·77	**17**	5·18	98·43	**30**	9·14	141·08	**43**	13·11
16·40	**5**	1·52	59·06	**18**	5·49	101·71	**31**	9·45	144·36	**44**	13·41
19·69	**6**	1·83	62·34	**19**	5·79	104·99	**32**	9·75	147·64	**45**	13·72
22·97	**7**	2·13	65·62	**20**	6·10	108·27	**33**	10·06	150·92	**46**	14·02
26·25	**8**	2·44	68·90	**21**	6·40	111·55	**34**	10·36	154·20	**47**	14·33
29·53	**9**	2·74	72·18	**22**	6·71	114·83	**35**	10·67	157·48	**48**	14·63
32·81	**10**	3·05	75·46	**23**	7·01	118·11	**36**	10·97	160·76	**49**	14·94
36·09	**11**	3·35	78·74	**24**	7·32	121·39	**37**	11·28	164·04	**50**	15·24
39·37	**12**	3·66	82·02	**25**	7·62	124·67	**38**	11·58	167·32	**51**	15·54
42·65	**13**	3·96	85·30	**26**	7·92	127·95	**39**	11·89	170·60	**52**	15·84

1.5 TIME

Zone Time For timekeeping purposes the world is divided into 24 Time Zones, each 15° of Longitude wide (like orange segments). Zone 0 (7½°E to 7½°W) straddles 0° longitude (the Greenwich Meridian). In the marine world zones E of it (ahead in time, or earlier) are labelled Zone –1, –2 and so on to –11. Zones to the W (later in time) are +1, +2 etc to +11. *Caution: land-based time-zone charts often refer to zones the other way around – be careful which one you are using.*

1.5.1 Universal Time (UT) is a datum to which broadcast times, times of sunrise/set, scientific data etc are referred. UT is also the name of the Standard Time (see below) usually kept in countries wholly or partly within Zone 0.

1.5.2 Standard Time, also called legal time, is that kept in different countries **but is modified by Daylight Saving Time in the summer** (see 1.5.3).

For all practical purposes, Greenwich Mean Time (GMT) is the same as UT.

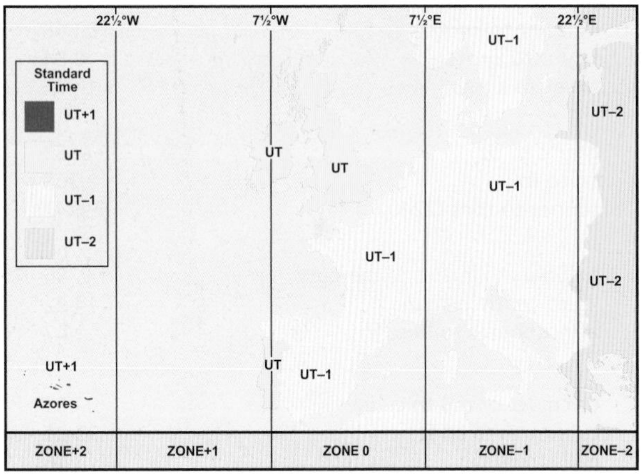

Fig 1(2) Zone Time and Standard Times for Europe

UT is the Standard Time in the UK, including the Channel Islands and Northern Ireland (Zone 0); also the Irish Republic, Portugal and Morocco (Zone 1/2) and Madeira (Zone 2).

UT –1 is the Standard Time in Denmark and Germany (Zone –1); also The Netherlands, Belgium, France, Spain and Gibraltar (Zone 0). Subtract 1 hour from the local Standard Time to give UT, or add 1 hour to UT to give Standard Time in these places.

UT +1 is the Standard Time in the Azores (Zone +2). Add 1 hour to the local Standard Time to give UT, or subtract 1 hour from UT to give Standard Time in these places.

See also Special Notes for each country in Chapter 9.

1.5.3 Daylight Saving Time (DST), or BST in the UK, is an artificial adjustment of 1 hour ahead of Standard Time made during the summer months in most European and many other countries.

In EU countries DST is kept from the last Sunday in March until the last Sunday in October.

1.5.4 Tide Tables Tidal predictions are referred to the Standard Time kept by the port, which is shown to the top left of its tide tables, along with instructions for converting the predicted times to UT; or to local summer time.

In the summer months (no tinted background) add 1 hour to the printed times to convert to local DST.

RADIO TIME SIGNALS

1.5.5 BBC Radio time signals in the UK are broadcast in clock time (ie, in BST during summer; UT in the winter).

	BBC Radio 1	BBC Radio 2	BBC Radio 3
Mainland	97·6–99·8 MHz	88–90·2 MHz	90·2–92·4 MHz
Channel Is	97·1 MHz	89·6 MHz	91·1 MHz
Mon-Thu	0630, 0900, 1000	0700, 0800, 1700	0700, 0800
Fri	0630, 0900 1000, 1900	0700, 0800, 1700	0700, 0800
Sat	No info	0700, 0800	0700, 0800
Sun	No info	0800, 0900	0700

BBC Radio 4 time signals are broadcast on AM (long wave) 198 kHz every hour of every day except 0000 and Mon-Fri: 1800, 2200; Sat: 1500, 1800; Sun: 1000, 1100, 1800, 2200. See 6.10.1 for AM (medium wave) and FM frequencies.

1.5.6 The BBC World Service provides time signals on the following frequencies (kHz) at the times shown below:

A:	198	B:	648	C:	1296	D:	3955
E:	6195	F:	7150	G:	7230	H:	7325
I:	9410	J:	9750	K:	9760	L:	9915
M:	12095	N:	15070	O:	15340	P:	17640
Q:	17705						

Time	A	B	C	D	E	F	G	H	I	J	K	L	M	N	O	P	Q
0000	♦	♦						♦				♦	♦	♦			
0200	♦	♦	♦		♦			♦	♦			♦	♦				
0300	♦	♦	♦		♦		♦	♦	♦			♦	♦				
0400	♦			♦	♦		♦		♦				♦				
0500	♦			♦	♦				♦				♦	♦			
0600		♦	♦	♦	♦	♦			♦				♦	♦			
0700		♦			♦	♦		♦	♦		♦		♦	♦		♦	
0800		♦				♦		♦	♦		♦		♦	♦		♦	♦
0900		♦						♦	♦	♦	♦		♦	♦		♦	♦
1100		♦							♦	♦	♦		♦	♦		♦	♦
1200		♦							♦	♦	♦		♦	♦		♦	♦
1300		♦							♦	♦	♦		♦	♦		♦	♦
1500		♦			♦				♦	♦	♦		♦	♦		♦	♦
1600		♦			♦				♦		♦		♦	♦			♦
1700		♦			♦				♦				♦	♦			
1800					♦				♦				♦	♦			
1900		♦			♦				♦				♦	♦			
2000		♦			♦			♦	♦				♦	♦			
2200		♦	♦		♦			♦	♦			♦	♦	♦	♦		
2300		♦	♦					♦	♦			♦	♦	♦	♦		

1.5.7 Worldwide time signals

Anthorn (54°54'N 03°16'W), UK (MSF) broadcasts UT signals continuously on 60 kHz. This station can be received widely in N and W Europe.

Fort Collins, Colorado (WWV) and Kekaha, Hawaii (WWVH) broadcast UT signals continuously on frequencies 2·5, 5, 10, 15 and 20 (not Kekaha) MHz. The station is identified by voice (English) at every H and H+30. The hour is signalled by a 1500 Hz tone and minutes and seconds by 1200 Hz tones. WWV also broadcasts Atlantic weather in two parts at H+08 and H+09 and weather in the Eastern N. Pacific at H+10.

1.6 VOCABULARIES

English, German, Dutch, French, Spanish and Portuguese vocabularies of useful words are listed, for easy reference, under broad subject headings on the following pages.

English	Deutsch	Nederlands	Français	Español	Português
ON ARRIVAL	**BEI ANKUNFT**	**BIJ AANKOMST**	**À L'ARRIVÉE**	**AL LLEGAR**	**CHEGADA**
Beam	Schiffsbreite	Breedte	Largeur	Manga	Boca
Certificate of competence	Befähigungszeugnis	Getuigschrift	Permis bateau	Titulo	Certificado de competência
Crew list	Besatzungsliste	Bemanningslijst	Liste d'équipage	Lista de tripulación	Lista da tripulação
Customs	Zoll	Douane	Douanes	Aduana	Alfândega
Draught	Tiefgang	Diepgang	Tirant d'eau	Calado	Calado
Insurance certificate	Versicherungspolice	Verzekeringsbewijs	Attestation d'assurance	Certificado de seguro	Certificado de seguro
Length over all (LOA)	Länge über Alles (LüA)	Lengte over alles (LOA)	Longeur hors-tout	Eslora total	Comprimento fora a fora
Passport	Reisepaß	Paspoort	Passeport	Pasaporte	Passaporte
Port of registry	Heimathafen	Thuishaven	Quartier maritime	Puerto de matricula	Porto de registo
Port police	Polizei	Haven politie	Police du port	Policia de puerto	Policia maritima
Pratique	Freie Verkehrserlaubnis	Inklaren	Libre-pratique	Libre prática	Livre prática
Registration certificate	Registierungszertifikat	Zeebrief	Acte de francisation	Certificado de Registro	Certificado de Registro
Ship's logbook	Logbuch	Logboek	Livre de bord	Cuaderno de bitácora	Diário de bordo
Ship's papers	Schiffspapiere	Scheepspapieren	Papiers de bord	Documentación del barco	Documentação do barco
Surveyor	Gutachter	Opzichter, expert	Expert maritime	Inspector	Inspector
VAT certificate	Mehrwertsteuerbescheinigung	BTW-dokument	Attestation de TVA	Certificado IVA	Certificado de IVA
ASHORE	**AN LAND**	**AAN LAND**	**À TERRE**	**A TIERRA**	**A TERRA**
Airport	Flughafen	Vliegveld	Aéroport	Aeropuerto	Aeroporto
Bakery	Bäckerei	Bakkerij	Boulangerie, patisserie	Panaderia	Padaria, Pastelaria
Bank	Bank	Bank	Banque	Banco	Banco
Bus station	Busbahnhof	Busstation	Gare routière	Estación de autobuses	Estação do autocarro
Butcher	Fleischerei	Slagerij	Boucherie	Carniceria	Talho
Chandlery	Yachtausrüster	Scheepswinkel	Shipchandler	Efectos navales	Aprestos
Chemist	Apotheke	Apotheek	Pharmacie	Farmacia	Farmácia
Dentist	Zahnarzt	Tandarts	Dentiste	Dentista	Dentista
Engineer	Motorenservice	Monteur	Mécanicien	Mecánico	Engenheiro
Exchange (money)	Wechselstelle	Geldwisselkantoor	Bureau de change	Cambio	Cambio
Garage	Autowerkstatt	Garage	Garage	Garage	Oficina mecânica
Hospital	Krankenhaus	Ziekenhuis	Hôpital	Hospital	Hospital
Ironmongery	Eisenwarenhandlung	IJzerhandelaar	Quincaillerie	Quincalleria	Loja de ferragens
Launderette	Waschsalon	Wasserette	Laverie	Lavanderia	Lavanderia
Market	Markt	Markt	Marché	Mercado	Mercado
Post office	Postamt	Postkantoor	Bureau de poste, PTT	Correos	Correio, CTT
Railway station	Bahnhof	Station	Gare de chemin de fer	Estación de ferrocanil	Estação de comboios
Sailmaker	Segelmacher	Zeilmaker	Voilier	Velero, veleria	Veleiro
Shops	Geschäfte	Winkels	Boutiques	Tiendas	Lojas
Stamps, postal	Briefmarken	Postzegels	Timbres	Sellos	Selos
Supermarket	Supermarkt	Supermarkt	Supermarché	Supermercado	Supermercado
HARBOUR	**HAFEN**	**HAVEN**	**PORT**	**PUERTO**	**PORTO**
Anchoring, anchorage	Ankern, Ankerplatz	Ankeren, ankerplaats	Mouiller l'ancre	Fondeadero	Fundeadouro
Boathoist	Bootskran	Botenlift	Travelift	Travelift	Portico elevador
Boatyard	Bootswerft	Jachtwerf	Chantier naval	Astilleros	Estaleiro naval
Breakwater, mole	Außenmole	Pier	Brise-lame	Escollera	Quebra-mar, molhe
Bridge, pedestrian	Fußgängerbrücke	Loopbrug	Passerelle	Pasarela	Ponte para peões
Bridge, swing	Drehbrücke	Draaibrug	Pont tournant	Puente giratorio	Ponte giratória
Cable (electrical)	Kabel	Kabel	Câble	Cable	Cabo (electrico)
Commercial port	Handelshafen	Commerciële haven	Port de commerce	Puerto comercial	Porto comercial
Crane	Kran	Kraan	Grue	Grua	Grua
Drying port	Trockenfallender Hafen	Droogvallende haven	Port d'échouage	Puerto seco	Porto secar
Dues, berthing tariff	Hafengebühren	Havengeld	Tarifs portuaire	derechos de puerto	Taxas
Ferry	Fähre	Veerboot	Ferry, bac, transbordeur	Ferry	ferry
Fishing harbour	Fischereihafen	Vissershaven	Port de pêche	Puerto de pesca	Porto de pesca

English	Deutsch	Nederlands	Français	Español	Português
Fuel berth	Tankstelle	Bunkerplaats	Ponton à carburants	Surtidor	Estacão para combustível
Harbour entrance	Hafeneinfahrt	Haveningang	Entrée du port	Entrada de puerto	Entrada
Harbour guide	Hafenhandbuch	Haven gids	Guide du port	Guia del puerto	Guia de Porto
Harbour master	Hafenmeister	Havenmeester	Capitaine du port	Capitán del puerto	Capitão maritímo
Height, headroom	Höhe	Hoogte	Hauteur	Alturas	Altura
Jetty	Steg	Steiger	Jetée	Malecón	Cais
Landing place	Anlegeplatz	Plaats om aan land te gaan	Débarcadère	Desembarcadero	Desembarcadouro
Lock	Schleuse	Sluis	Ecluse	Esclusa	Eclusa
Marina, yacht harbour,	Yachthafen	Jachthaven	Port de plaisance	Puerto deportivo	Doca de recreio
Mast crane	Mastenkran	Mastenkraan	Grue	Grúa	Guindaste (mastro
Mooring (buoy)	Anlegen	Meerplaats	Coffre d'amarrage	Fondeadero	Bólia de atracação
Permitted	Erlaubt	Toegestaan	Autorisé	Permitido	Autorizado
Pier	Pier, Mole	Pier	Appontement/quai	Muelle	Molhe
Prohibited	Verboten	Verboden	Interdit	Prohibido	Proibído
Slip, slipway	Slip, Slipbahn	Helling	Cale	Varadero	Rampa
Water, fresh	Süßwasser	Zoet water	Eau douce	Agua dulce	Água doce
Yacht club	Yachtclub	Jachtclub	Club nautique	Club náutico	Clube nautico
NAVIGATION	**NAVIGATION**	**NAVIGATIE**	**NAVIGATION**	**NAVIGACION**	**NAVEGAÇÃO**
Abeam	Querab	Dwarsscheeps	Par le travers	Por el través	Por de través
Ahead	Voraus	Voor	Par l'avant	Avante	À proa
Astern	Achteraus	Achter	Par l'arrière	Atrás	À popa
Buoy	Tonne	Boei/ton	Bouée	Boya	Bóia
Binoculars	Fernglas	Verrekijker	Jumelles	Prismáticos	Binóculos
Channel (navigational)	Kanal	Kanaal/geul	Chenal	Canal	Canal
Chart	Seekarte	Zeekaart	Carte	Carta náutica	Carta hidrográfica
Compass	**Kompaß**	**Kompas**	**Compas**	**Compás**	**Agulha**
Bearing	Peilung	Peiling	Relèvement	Marcación	Azimute
Compass course	Kompaßkurs	Kompaskoers	Cap du compas	Rumbo de aguja	Rumo do agulha
Course True	Wahrer Kurs	Ware Koers	Cap vrai	Rumbo verdadero	Rumo verdadeiro
Deviation	Ablenkung	Deviatie	Déviation	Desvio	Desvios
East	Ost	Oost	Est	Este	Este
Handbearing compass	Handpeilkompass	Handpeil kompas	Compas de relèvement	Compás de marcaciones	Agulha portátil
North	Nord	Noord	Nord	Norte	Norte
South	Süd	Zuid	Sud	Sur	Sul
Variation	Missweisung	Variatie	Déclinaison magnétique	Variación	Varíação
West	West	West	Ouest	Oeste	Oeste
Current	Strömung	Stroom	Courant	Corriente	Corrente
Dead reckoning	Koppelnavigation	Gegist bestek	Navigation à l'estime	Estima	Navegação estimada
Degree	Grad	Graad	Degré	Grado	Grau
Depth	Wassertiefe	Diepte	Profondeur	Profundidad	Profundidade
Distance	Entfernung	Afstand, verheid	Distance	Distancia	Distância
Downstream	Flußabwärts	Stroomafwaarts	En aval	Río abajo	Jusante
Dredged (channel)	Baggerrinne	Gebaggerd (geul)	Dragué	Dragado	Dragado
Echosounder	Echolot	Dieptemeter	Sondeur	Sonda	Sondador acústica
Estimated position	Geschätzte Position	Gegiste positie	Point estimé	Posición estimada	Posição estimada
Firing range	Schießgebiet	Schietoefeningen	Zone de tir	Zona de tiro	Zone de tiro
Hazard	Gefahr	Gevaar	Danger	Peligro	Perigo
Latitude	Geographische Breite	Breedte	Latitude	Latitud	Latitude
Leeway	Abdrift	Drift	Dérive	Sotavento	Abatimento
Lights list	**Leuchtfeuerverzeichnis**	**Lichtenlijst**	**Liste des feux**	**Libro de faros**	**Lista de faróis**
Leading lights	Richtfeuer	Geleidelichten	Feux d'alignement	Luz de enfilación	Farol de enfiamento
Lighthouse	Leuchtturm	Vuurtoren	Phare	Faro	Farol
Lightship	Feuerschiff	Lichtschip	Bâteau-feu	Buque faro	Barco-farol

English	Deutsch	Nederlands	Français	Español	Português
Log	Log	Log	Loch	Corredera	Odómetro
Longitude	Geographische Länge	Lengte	Longitude	Longitud	Longitude
Nautical mile	Seemeile	Zeemijl	Mille nautique	Milla marina	Milha marítima
Numbers	**Nummern**	**Nummers**	**Nombres**	**Numeros**	**Números**
One	Ein	Een	Un	Uno	Um/uma
Two	Zwei	Twee	Deux	Dos	Dois/duas
Three	Drei	Drie	Trois	Tres	Três
Four	Vier	Vier	Quatre	Cuatro	Quatro
Five	Fünf	Vijf	Cinq	Cinco	Cinco
Six	Sechs	Zes	Six	Seis	Seis
Seven	Sieben	Zeven	Sept	Siete	Sete
Eight	Acht	Acht	Huit	Ocho	Oito
Nine	Neun	Negen	Neuf	Nueve	Nove
Ten	Zehn	Tien	Dix	Diez	Dez
Pilot (guide)	Lotse	Loods, Gids	Pilote	Práctico	Roteiro da costa, Pilôto
Port (side)	Backbord	Bakboord	Bâbord	Babor	Bombordo
Prohibited area	Sperrgebiet	Verboden gebied	Zone interdite	Zona de prohibida	Zonaproibida
River mouth	Flußmündung	Riviermond	Embouchure	Desembocadura	Foz
Starboard	Steuerbord	Stuurboord	Tribord	Estribor	Estibordo
Tide	**Tide, Gezeiten**	**Getijde**	**Marée**	**Marea**	**Maré**
Chart datum (CD)	Kartennull	Reductievlak	Zero des cartes	Datum	Zero hidrográfico
Covers	Deckt	Onderlopend	Couvre	Cubierto	Cobre
Dries	Trockenfallend	Droogvallend	Découvre	Descubierto	Fica em sêco
Ebb	Ebbe	Eb	Jusant	Marea menguante	Corrente evasante
Flood	Flut	Vloed	Flot	Flujo de marea	Corrente de enchente
High water (HW)	Hochwasser	Hoogwater	Pleine mer (PM)	Pleamar	Praia mar
Low water (LW)	Niedrigwasser	Laagwater	Basse mer (BM)	Bajamar	Baixa-mar
Neaps	Nipptide	Doodtij	Morte-eau (ME)	Marea muerta	Mares mortas
Springs	Springtide	Springtij, springvloed	Vive-eau (VE)	Marea viva	Mares vivas
Tidal streams	Gezeitenströme	Getijstromen	Courants de marée	Corrientes de marea	Correntes de maré
Tide tables	Tidenkalender	Getijdetafel	Annuaire des marées	Anuario de mareas	Tabela de marés
Underwater	Unterwasser	Onderwater	Immergé	Debajo del agua	Submerso
Upstream	Flußaufwärts	Stroomopwaarts	En amont	Aguasarriba	Montante
Waypoint	Wegepunkt	Waypoint/Route punt	Point de destination	Waypoint	Ponto de chegada
Wreck	Wrack	Wrak	Epave	Naufragio	Naufrágio
METEOROLOGY	**METEOROLOGIE**	**METEOROLOGIE**	**MÉTÉO**	**METEOROLOGÍA**	**METEOROLOGIA**
Area	Gebiet	Gebied	Zone	Zona	Área
Clouds, cloudy	Wolken	Wolken	Nuages, nuageux	Nublado	Nublado
Cold	Kalt	Koud	Froid	Frio	Frio
Direction	Richtung	Richting	Direction	Dirección	Indicação
Forecast	Vorhersage	Vooruitzicht	Prévision	Previsión	Previsão
Fresh, cool, chilly	Frisch	Fris	Frais	Fresco	Fresco, frio
Local	Örtlich	Plaatselijk	Local	Local	Local
Outlook	Aussichten	Vooruitzicht	Evolution probable	Evolución probable ulterior	Prospecto
Precipitation	**Niederschlag**	**Neerslag**	**Précipitation**	**Precipitación**	**Precipitação**
Drizzle	Niesel	Motregen	Bruine	Llovizna	Chuvisco
Frequent	Häufig	Veelvuldig	Fréquent	Frecuente	Freqüente
Hail	Hagel	Hagel	Grêle	Granizo	Granizo
Heavy	Schwer	Zwaar	Abondant	Abunante	Forte
Isolated	Vereinzelt	Geïsoleerd	Isolé	Aislado	Isolado
Lightning	Blitze	Bliksem	Eclair de foudre	Relampago	Relâmpago
Rain	Regen	Regen	Pluie	lluvia	Chuva
Scattered	Vereinzelt	Verspreid	Esparses	Difuso	Esporádico

English	Deutsch	Nederlands	Français	Español	Português
Shower	Schauer	Bui	Averse	Chubasco	Aguaceiro
Sleet	Schneeregen	Natte sneeuw	Neige fondue	Aguanieve	Geáda miúda
Snow	Schnee	Sneeuw	Neige	Nieve	Neve
Thunder	Donner	Donder	Tonnerre	Trueno	Trovão
Thunderstorm	Gewitter	Onweer	Orage	Tormenta	Trovoada
Pressure systems	**Luftdrucksysteme**	**Druk**	**Pression**	**Presión**	**Pressão**
Air mass	Luftmasse	Luchtmassa	Masse d'air	Masa de aire	Massa de ar
Cold front	Kaltfront	Koufront	Front froid	Frente frio	Frente fria
Decrease	Abnahme	Afnemen	Affaiblissement	Disminuir	Enfraquecer
Deep	Tief	Diep	Profond	Profundo	Profundo
Deepening	Vertiefend	Verdiepend	Se creusant	Ahondamiento	Agravar-se
Disturbance	Störung	Storing	Perturbation	Perturbación	Perturbação
Extending	Ausdehnung	Uitstrekkend	S'étendant	Extendiendose	Alastrando
Falling	Fallend	Dalend	Baissant	Bajando	Descendo
Filling	Auffüllend	Vullend	Se comblant	Rellenandose	Encher-se
Front	Front	Front	Front	Frente	Frente
Gradient	Druckgefälle	Gradiënt	Gradient	Gradiente	Gradiente
High (anticyclone)	Hoch	Hoog, Hogedrukgebied	Anticyclone	Alta presión, Anticiclón	Anticiclone
Isobar	Isobare	Isobaar	Isobare	Isobara	Isóbaro
Low (depression)	Tief,Sturmtief	Laag, Depressie	Dépression	Baja presión, Depresión	Depressão
Moving	Bewegend	Bewegend	Se déplacant	Movimiento, moviendose	Afastar-se
Occlusion, occluded	Okklusion	Occlusie	Occlus	Oclusión	Oclusão
Quickly	Schnell	Snel	Rapidement	Rápidamente	Rápidamente
Ridge	Hochdruckbrücke	Rug	Dorsale, crête	Cresta	Crista
Rising	Ansteigend	Stijgend	Montant	Subiendo	Subindo
Slowly	Langsam	Langzaam	Lentement	Lentamente	Lentamente
Steady	Gleichbleibend	Vast	Stable	Fijo	Constante
Trough	Trog, Tiefausläufer	Trog	Thalweg	Seno	Linha de baixa pressão
Warm front	Warmfront	Warmtefront	Front chaud	Frente calido	Frente quente
Sea/sea state	**See/Seegang**	**Zee**	**Mer**	**Mar**	**Mar**
Breakers	Brecher	Brekende zee	Lames déferlantes	Rompientes	Arrebentação
Calm	Flaute	Kalmte	Calme	Calma	Calma
Choppy	Kabbelig	Kort en steil	Croisée, hachée, clapot	Picada	Mareta
Overfalls (tide race)	Stromkabbelung	Stroomkabbeling	Clapot, brisants	Escarceos, remolino	Bailadeiras
Rough	Rauh	Ruw	Forte	Fuerte marejada	Agitado
Seaway	Seegang	Zeegang	Haute mer	Alta mar	Mare alta
Short, steep	Kurz, steil	Kort, steil	Vagues courtes, creuse	Mar corta, gruesa	Mar curta, cavado
Slight	Leicht	Licht	Legère, peu agitée	Marejadilla	Ligeiramente
Swell	Schwell	Deining	Houle	Mar de fondo	Ondulação
Sun	Sonne	Zon	Soleil	Sol	Sol
Sunrise	Sonnenaufgang	Zonsopgang	Lever du soleil	Orto	Nascer do sol
Sunset	Sonnenuntergang	Zonsondergang	Coucher du soleil	Ocaso	Pôr do sol
Synoptic situation	Wetterlage	Synoptische toestand	Situation générale	Situación sinoptica	Situação sinóptica
Visibility	**Sichtweite**	**Zicht**	**Visibilité**	**Visibilidad**	**Visibilidade**
Dispersing	Auflösend	Oplossend	Se dispersant	Disipación	Limpando
Extensive	Ausgedehnt	Uitgebreid	Etendu	Extenso	Extenso
Fog	Nebel	Mist	Brouillard	Niebla	Nevoeiro
Fog bank	Nebelbank	Mistbank	Banc de brume	Banco de niebla	Banco do nevoeiro
Good	Gut	Goed	Bon	Bueno	Bom/boa
Haze	Diesig	Nevelig	Brume	Calina	Cerração
Mist	Dunst	Nevel	Brume légere	Neblina	Neblina
Moderate	Mäßig	Matig	Médiocre, reduite	Moderardo	Moderada
Poor	Schlecht	Slecht	Mauvais	Malo	Fraca má
Weather	Wetter	Weerraport	Temps	Tiempo	Boletim meteorológico

English	Deutsch	Nederlands	Français	Español	Português
Wind/Beaufort/direction	Wind	Wind	Vent	Viento	Vento
F0, Calm	Windstille	Stil	Calme	Calma	Calma
F1, Light airs	Leiser Zug	Flauw en stil	Très légère brise	Ventolina	Aragem
F2, Light breeze	Leichte Brise	Flauwe koelte	légère brise	Flojito	Fraco
F3, Gentle breeze	Schwache Brise	Lichte koelte	Petite brise	Flojo	Bonançoso
F4, Moderate breeze	Mäßige Brise	Matige koelte	Jolie brise	Bonancible	Moderado
F5, Fresh breeze	Frische Brise	Frisse bries	Bonne brise	Fresquito	Frêsco
F6, Strong breeze	Starker Wind	Stijve bries	Vent frais	Fresco	Muito frêsco
F7, Near gale	Steifer Wind	Harde wind	Grand frais	Freschacón	Forte
F8, Gale	Stürmischer Wind	Stormachtig	Coup de vent	Duro	Muito forte
F9, Strong gale	Sturm	Storm	Fort coup de vent	Muy duro	Tempestuoso
F10, Storm	Schwerer Sturm	Zware storm	Tempête	Temporal	Temporal
Backing	Rückdrehender Wind	Krimpende wind	Vent revenant	Rolar el viento	Sentido retrógrado
Gale warning	Sturmwarnung	Stormwaarschuwing	Avis de coup de vent	Aviso de viento duro	Aviso de vento multo forte
Gust	Windstoß	Windvlaag	Rafale	Ráfaga, racha	Rajada
Increasing	Zunehmend	Toenemend	Augmentant	Aumentar	Aumentando
Land breeze	Landbrise	Landbries	Brise de terre	Brisa de tierra	Brisa da terra
Moderating	Abnehmend	Afnemend	Décroissant	Disminuyendo	Decrescendo
Sea breeze	Seebrise	Zeebries	Brise de mer	Brisa de mar	Brisa do mar
Squall	Bö	Windbui	Grain	Turbonada	Borrasca
Variable	Umlaufend	Veranderlijk	Variable	Variable	Variável
Veering	Rechtdrehend	Ruimende wind	Virant	Cambiar	Sentido horário
SAFETY/EMERGENCY	SICHERHEIT/NOTFALL	VEILIGHEID/NOODGEVAL	SECURITE/URGENCE	SEGURIDAD/EMERGENCIAS	SEGURANCA/EMERGÊNCIAS
Aground	Aufgelaufen	Vastgelopen	Echoué	Encallado	Encalhar
Capsize	Kentern	Omslaan	Sancir, chavirer	Volcó	Virar-se
Coastguard	Küstenwache	Kustwacht	Gendarmerie maritime	Guarda costas	Polícia Marítima
Collision	Kollision	Aanvaring	Abordage	Colisión, abordaje	Colisão abalroamento
Dismasted	Mastbruch	Mastbreuk	Démâté	Desarbolar	Partir o mastro
Distress	Seenot	Nood	Détresse	Socorro	Distress
Distress flares	Signalraketen	Noodvuurwerk	Fusées de détresse	Bengalas	Fachos de socorro
Dragging anchor	Schlierender Anker	Krabbend anker	Chasser sur l'ancre	Ancla garreando	Âncora agarrar
EPIRB	Seenotfunkboje	EPIRB	Balise de détresse	Baliza	EPIRB
Fire extinguisher	Feuerlöscher	Brandblusser	Extincteur	Extintor	Extintor
Harness, safety	Sicherheitsgurt	Harnas	Harnais	Arnés de seguridad	Cinto de segurança
Help!	Hilfe!	Help!	Au secours!	¡Socorro!	Socorro!
Lifeboat	Rettungsboot	Reddingsboot	Canot de sauvetage	Lancha de salvamento	Barco salva-vidas
Lifejacket	Rettungsweste	Reddingsvest	Gilet de sauvetage	Chaleco salvavidas	Colete de salvação
Liferaft	Rettungsinsel	Reddingsvlot	Radeau de sauvetage	Balsa salvavidas	Jangada de salvação
Man overboard	Mann über Bord	Man over boord	Homme à la mer	Hombre al agua	Homem ao mar
Seacock	Seeventil	Afsluiter	Vanne	Grifos de fondo	Torneira de segurança
Seaworthy	Seetüchtig	Zeewaardig	Marin	Marinero	Condição de navegar
Sinking	Sinken	Zinkend	En train de couler	Hundiendose	Afundate
Tow line	Schleppleine	Sleeplijn	Filin de remorque	Cabo remolque	Cabo de rebocador
MEDICAL	MEDIZINISCHES	MEDISCHE	MEDICALE	MEDICO	MÉDICAS
Antibiotic	Antibiotika	Antibiotica	Antibiotique	Antibiotico	Antibiótico
Bandage	Verband	Verband	Pansement	Vendas	Ligadura
Bleeding	Blutend	Bloeden	Saignement	Sangrando	Sangrar
Burns	Verbrennung	Brandwonden	Brûlures	Quemadura	Queimadura
Concussion	Gehirnerschütterung	Hersenschudding	Traumatisme crânien	Conmoción	Traumatismo
Dehydration	Austrocknung	Uitdroging	Déshydratation	Deshidratación	Desidratação
Dentist	Zahnarzt	Tandarts	Dentiste	Dentista	Dentista
Doctor	Doktor	Dokter/arts	Médecin	Médico	Médico
Drown(ing)	Ertrinken	Verdrinken, (verdrinking)	Noyade, (se noyant)	Ahogarse	Afogar-se

Reference Data

English	Deutsch	Nederlands	Français	Español	Português
Exhaustion	Erschöpfung	Uitputting	Epuisement	Agotamiento	Exausto
Fever	Fieber	Koorts	Fièvre	Fiebre	Febre
First aid	Erste Hilfe	Eerste hulp	Premier secours	Primeros auxillos	Primeiros socorros
Fracture	Fraktur	Breuk	Fracture	Fractura	Fractura
Headache	Kopfschmerz	Hoofdpijn	Mal à la tête	Dolor de cabeza	Dor de cabeça
Heart attack	Herzanfall	Hartaanval	Crise cardiaque	Ataque corazón	Ataque cardíaco
Hospital	Krankenhaus	Ziekenhuis	Hôpital	Hospital	Hospital
Hypothermia	Unterkühlung	Onderkoeling	Hypothermie	Hypotermia	Hipotermia
Illness	Krankheit	Ziekte	Maladie	Enfermo	Doença
Injury	Verletzung	Verwonding	Blessure	Lesión	Lesão
Pain	Schmerz	Pijn	Douleur	Dolor	Dôr
Painkiller(s)	Schmerztabletten	Pijnstillers	Analgésique	analgesico	Analgésico
Poisoning	Vergiftung	Vergiftiging	Empoisonnement	Envenenamiento	Envenenamento
Pulse	Puls	Hartslag	Pouls	Pulso	Pulso
Rest	Ruhen	Rust	Repos	Reposo	Descanso
Seasickness	Seekrankheit	Zeeziekte	Mal de mer	Mareo	Enjoar
Shock	Schock	Shock	Choc	Choque	Choque
Splint	Schiene	Spalk	Attelle	Tablilla	Colocar em talas
Sticking plaster	Heftpflaster	Pleister	Pansement adhésif	Esparadrapo	Adesivo
Stomach upset	Bauchbeschwerden	Maag van streek	Indigestion	Mal de estómago	Cólicas
Stretcher	Trage	Draagbaar	Brancard	Camilla	Maca
Sunburn	Sonnenbrand	Zonnebrand	Coup de soleil	Quemadura del sol	Queimadura de sol
Swelling	Schwellung	Zwelling	Enflure	Hinchazón	Inchaço
Toothache	Zahnschmerzen	Tandpijn	Rage de dents	Dolor de muelas	Dôr dos dentes
Unconscious	Bewußtlos	Bewusteloos	Inconscient	Inconsciente	Inconsciente
Wound	Wunde	Wond	Blessure	Herida	Ferida
THE BOAT	**DAS BOOT**	**DE BOOT**	**LE BATEAU**	**EL BARCO**	**DO BARCO**
Rigging and Sails	**Rigg und Segel**	**Tuigage en Zeilen**	**Gréement et Voiles**	**Jarcias y Velas**	**Massame e Velas**
Babystay	Babystag	Baby stag	Bas-étai	Babystay	Babystay
Backstay	Achterstag	Achterstag	Pataras	Estay de popa	Brandal fixo da pôpa
Batten	Segellatte	Zeillat	Latte	Sables	Régua
Beating	Kreuzen	Kruisen	Au prés	Ciñendo	Bolinar
Boom	Baum	Giek	Bôme	Botavara	Retranca
Clevis pin	Schäkelbolzen	Borstbout	Axe à anneau brisé	Pasador de seguridad	Perno com troço de argola
Foresail	Vorsegel	Voorzeil	Voile avant/foc	Foque	Pana de proa
Forestay	Vorstag	Voorstag	Etai	Estay de proa	Estai real
Genoa	Genua	Genua	Génois	Génova	Genoa
Halyard	Fall	Val	Drisse	Driza	Adriça
Jib	Fock	Fok	Foc	Foque	Fiocco
Mainsail	Großsegel	Grootzeil	Grand' voile	Mayor	Vela grande
Mast	Mast	Mast	Mât	Mast	Mastro
Mast track	Mastschiene	Mastrail	Rail	Carril	Calha do mastro
Mizzen	Besan	Bezaan	Artimon	Mesana	Mezena
Reaching	Raumschots	Ruime wind	Au portant	Viento a través	A um largo
Rod kicker	Rod kicker	Giekophouder	Hale-bas rigide	Contra rigido	Rod kicker
Roller reefing foresail	Rollfock	Rolfock	Génois à enrouleur	Enrollador de génova	Genoa de enrolar
Running	Vorm Wind	Voor de wind	Vent arrière	Viento a favor	Vento à pôpa
Sheet	Schot	Schoot	Ecoute	Escota	Escota
Shrouds	Wanten	Wanten	Haubans	Obenques	Enxarcia
Spinnaker	Spinnaker	Spinnaker	Spi	Spi	Spinnaker
Spinnaker boom	Spinnakerbaum	Spinnaker boom	Tangon de spi	Tangon	Pau de spinnaker
Spreader, crosstree	Saling	Zaling	Barre de flèche	Crucetas	Vaus
Staysail	Stagsegel	Stagzeil	Trinquette	Trinqueta	Estai

English	Deutsch	Nederlands	Français	Español	Português
Storm jib	Sturmfock	Stormfok	Tourmentin	Tormentin	Estai de tempo
Topping lift	Dirk	Kraanlijn, Dirk	Balancine	Amantillo	Amantilho
Trysail	Trysegel	Stormzeil, Trysail	Voile de cape	Vela de capa	Cachapana
Upwind	Am Wind	Aan de wind/te loevert	Au vent	Vienta en contra	Bolinando
Whipping twine	Takelgarn	Takelgaren	Fil à surlier	Piolilla	Cordão de pequeña bitola
Working jib	Arbeitsfock	Werkfok	Foc de route	Foque	Estai
On deck	**An Deck**	**Aan dek**	**Sur le pont**	**En cubierta**	**No convés**
Aft	Achtern, achteraus	Achter, achteruit	En arriere	Atrás	À ré
Ahead	Voraus	Vooruit	Par l'avant	Avante	À proa
Anchor	Anker	Anker	Ancre	Ancla	Âncora
Anchor chain	Ankerkette	Ankerketting	Chaîne d'ancre	Cadena	Corrente
Anchor warp	Ankerleine	Ankerlijn	Orin	Cabo de fondeo	Espia da âncora
Astern	achtern	Achteruit, slaan	Par l'arrière	Hacia atrás	À popa
Block	Block	Blok	Poulie	Motón	Moitão
Bow	Bug	Boeg	Etrave	Proa	Proa
Bridgedeck	Brückendeck	Brugdek	Bridgedeck	Cubierta de puente	Pavimento da ponte
Cockpit	Cockpit	Cockpit	Cockpit	Bañera	Cockpit
Deck	Deck	Dek	Pont	Cubierta	Convés
Dinghy, Tender	Jolle, Beiboot	Bijboot	Annexe	Chinchorro, Bote	Escaler, Côco
Fender	Fender	Stootwil	Défense	Defensa	Defensa
Inflatable (dinghy)	Schlauchboot	Opblaasbare boot	Gonflable	Bote hinchable	Inflável
Ladder	Leiter	Ladder, Trap	Echelle	Escala	Escada
Pulpit	Bugkorb	Preekstoel	Balcon avant	Púlpito	Guarda proeiro
Pushpit	Heckkorb	Hekrailing	Balcon arrière	Balcón de popa	Varandim
Railing	Reling	Railing	Filières	Guardamencebos	Balaustrada
Rope	Tauwerk	Touw	Cordage	Cabo, Cuerda, Cabulleria	Cabo, Corda
Rudder	Ruder	Roer	Safran, Gouvernail	Pala de Timón	Leme
Shackle	Schäkel	Sluiting	Manille	Grillete	Manilha
Ship	Schiff	Schip	Navire	Buque	Navio
Stanchion	Seerelingsstütze	Scepter	Chandelier	Candelero	Balaústre
Stern	Heck	Spiegel/hek	Arrière	Popa	Popa
Superstructure	Aufbau	Opbouw	Superstructure	Superestructura	Super-estrutura
Tiller	Pinne	Helmstok	Barre franche	Caña	Cana de leme
Toe rail	Fußleiste	Voetrail	Rail de fargue	Regala	Amurada inferior
Topsides	Rumpfseiten	Bovenwaterschip	Oeuvres mortes	Obra muerta	Costada
Wheel, steering	Steuerrad	Stuurwiel	Barre à roue	Rueda	Roda do leme
Winch	Winsch	Lier	Winch	Winche	Molinete
Windlass, capstan	Ankerwinsch	Ankerlier, Kaapstander	Guindeau	Molinete	Molinete da âncora
Yacht, sailing	Segelyacht	Zeilboot	Voilier	Velero	Veleiro
Below deck	**Unter Deck**	**Onderdeks**	**Sous le pont**	**Bajo cubierta**	**Abaixo do convés**
Bilge	Bilge	Bilge	Galbord	Sentina	Esgôto
Bilge keel	Kimmkiel	Kimkiel	Bi-quilles	Quillas	Quilha dupla
Bilge pump	Bilgepumpe	Bilge pomp	Pompe de cale	Bomba de achique	Bomba de esgoto
Cabin	Kajüte	Kajuit	Cabine	Cabina	Cabine
Calorifier	Wärmespender	Verwarming	Echangeur de chaleur	Calentador	Calorifico
Companionway	Niedergang	Opgang	Descente	Entrada cámera	Escotilha de passagem
Deckhead	Kajütdach	Kajuitdak	Tête de pont	Techo de cabina	Cabeço do convés
Fin keel	Kurzkiel	Vinkiel	Quille courte	Quilla de aleta	Patilhão
Fresh water tank	Frischwassertank	Drinkwatertank	Réservoir d'eau douce	Tanque de agua dulce	Tanque de aguada
Galley	pantry/Kombüse	Kombuis	Cuisine	Cocina	Cozinha
Gas alarm	Gasmelder	Gasalarm	Alarme anti-gaz	Alarma de gas	Alarme de gás
Holding tank	Schmutzwassertank	Vuilwatertank	Réservoir à eaux usées	Tanque aguas negras	Deposito de esgotos
Hull	Rumpf	Romp	Coque	Carena	Casco

English	Deutsch	Nederlands	Français	Español	Português
Keel	Kiel	Kiel	Quille	Quilla	Quilha
Long keel	Langkiel	Langkieler	Quille longue	Quilla corrida	Quilha corrida
Oven	Backofen	Oven	Four	Horno	Forno
Skeg	Skeg	Scheg	Talon	Skeg	Skeg
Underwater hull	Unterwasserschiff	Onderwaterschip	Oeuvres vives	Obra viva	Obras vivas
ELECTRICS	**ELEKTROTECHNIK**	**ELECTRICITEIT**	**ELECTRIQUES**	**ELECTRICOS**	**ELECTRICO**
Alternator	Wechselstromgenerator	Generator	Alternateur	Alternador	Alternador
Battery	Batterie	Accu, batterij	Batterie/accumulateur	Batería	Bateria
Battery charger	Batterieladegerät	Acculader	Chargeur de batterie	Cargador debatería	Carregador debateria
Bulb	Glühbirne	Lamp	Ampoule	Bombilla	Lâmpada
Circuit breaker	Ausschalter	Automaat	Disjoncteur	Disyuntor	Interruptor
Coil	Spule	Spoel	Bobine	Bobina	Bobine
Dynamo	Lichtmaschine	Dynamo	Dynamo	Dinamo	Dinâmo
Electrical wiring	Elektrik	Elektrische bedrading	Réseau électrique	Circuito eléctrico	Circuito electrico
Fuse	Sicherung	(Hoofd)Zekering	Fusible	Fusible	Fusível
Invertor	Wechselrichter	Inverter	Convertisseur	Inverter	Inversor
Regulator (voltage)	Spannungsregler	Spanningsregelaar	Régulateur de tension	Regulador	Regulador
Shore power	Landanschluß	Walstroom	Courant de secteur	Corriente de tierra	Corrente alterna
Solar panel	Solarzellen	Zonnepaneel	Paneau solaire	Placa solar	Painel solar
Soldering iron	Lötkolben	Soldeerbout	fer à souder	Soldador eléctrico	ferro de soldar
Switch	Schalter	Schakelaar	Interrupteur	Interruptor	Interruptor
THE ENGINE	**DER MOTOR**	**DE MOTOR**	**LE MOTEUR**	**EL MOTOR**	**DO MOTOR**
Air filter	Luftfilter	Luchtfilter	Filtre à air	Filtro a aire	Filtro de ar
Carburettor	Vergaser	Carburateur	Carburateur	Carburador	Carburador
Cooling water	Kühlwasser	Koelwater	Eau de refroidissement	Agua refrigerado	Agua fresca
Diesel	Diesel	Dieselolie	Gazole	Gas-oil	Gasóleo
Drive belt	Treibriemen	Aandrijfriem	Courroie d'entrainement	Correa de transmisión	Correia
Engine mount	Motorfundament	Motorsteun	Support moteur	Bancada del motor	Fixe do motor
Engine oil	Motoröl	Motorolie	Huile de moteur	Aceite de motor	Óleo de motor
Exhaust pipe	Auspuff	Uitlaat	Tuyau d'échappement	Tubo de escape	Tubo de escape
Fuel filter	Kraftstoffilter	Brandstoffilter	Filtre de carburant	Filtro de combustible	Filtro de gasóleo
Fuel tank	Tank, Brennstofftank	Brandstof tank	Réservoir à carburant	Tanque de combustible	Tanque de combustivel
Gasket	Dichtung	Pakking	Joint	Empaquetadura junta	Junta
Gearbox	Getriebekasten	Keerkoppeling	Boîte de vitesses	Caja de cambio	Caixa de velocidades
Grease	Fett	Vet	Graisse	Grasa	Massa
Head gasket	Zylinderkopfdichtung	Koppakking	Joint de culasse	Junta de culata	Junta do cabeça
Injector	Einspritzdüse	Injector, Verstuiver	Injecteur	Inyector	Injector
Jubilee clip	Schlauchklemme	Slangklem	Collier de serrage	Abrazadera	Abraçadeira ajustàavel
Methylated spirits	Brennspiritus	Spiritus/Methyalcohol	Alcool à brûler	Alcohol desnaturalizada	Alcool metílico
Oil filter	Ölfilter	Oliefilter	Filtre à huile	Filtro de aceite	Filtro de óleo
Outboard motor	Außenbordmotor	Buitenboordmotor	Moteur hors-bord	Motor fuerabordas	Motor fora de borda
Paraffin	Petroleum	Petroleum, Kerosine	Kérosène, Pétrole	Petróleo, Keroseno	Petróleo
P-bracket	Wellenlagerbock	Schroefas uithouder	Support d'hélice	Casquillo	Polée em P
Petrol	Benzin	Benzine	Essence	Gasolina	Gasolina
Propeller	Propeller, Schraube	Schroef	Hélice	Hélice	Hélice
Propeller shaft	Schraubenwelle	Schroefas	Arbre d'hélice	Eje de la hélice	Veio do hélice
Spark plug	Zündkerze	Bougie	Bougie	Bujia	Vela
Starter	Anlasser	Startmotor	Démarreur	Motor de arranque	Motor de arranque
Stern gland	Stopfbuchse	Schroefasdoorvoer	Presse étoupe	Bocina	Bucim
Throttle	Gas	Gashendel	Accélérateur	Acelerador	Acelerador
Two-stroke	Zweitakt	Tweetakt	A deux temps	Dos tiempos	De dois tempos
Water pump	Wasserpumpe	Waterpomp	Pompe à eau	Bomba de agua	Bomba de água

2 Regulations

2.1 Cruising formalities 22
Documents including ICC • Registration • Insurance

2.2 HM Revenue & Customs 22
The EU • Duty-free stores • Departure/Arrival • Immigration

2.3 Foreign Customs 23
The Schengen Treaty • Red diesel

2.4 EU VAT on vessels 23
VAT • Temporary importation

2.5 e-Borders 23

2.6 Travelling with pets 23

2.7 International Regulations for Preventing Collisions at Sea 24
Rules 2, 5–7, 10 and 12–19 verbatim • Navigation lights and shapes • Learning the Collision Regulations

2.1 CRUISING FORMALITIES

Before your annual cruise, especially beyond UK waters, check that yacht and personal documents are in-date.

Yacht documents

Registration certificate (2.1.1). Marine insurance valid for the intended cruising area, including adequate third-party cover (2.1.2). Proof of VAT status (2.4). Ship's radio licence (5.2.3). Ship's Log, itinerary and a crew list. All must be **originals,** keep them in transparent files for easy inspection; failure to produce them can them can potentially incur fines abroad.

Personal documents

Valid passports and European health insurance card (8.2). Radio Operator's certificate of competence (5.2.3).

International Certificate of Competence

An International Certificate of Competence (ICC) (Pleasure Craft), valid for 5 years, is required in most European countries, especially if inland waterways are part of your cruising plans. It can be endorsed for power or sail, inland or coastal waters, or all four.

The inland waterways endorsement requires a short, written test on CEVNI (ColRegs and buoyage in European inland waterways), but this does not apply to UK inland waterways. If evidence of competence (eg Day Skipper or above) is not held, a practical test must be passed before the ICC is issued. E-mail certification@rya.org.uk or call ☎ 0845 345 0376.

Health regulations

Comply with health regulations (eg report any infectious disease); check if vaccination certificates are needed.

2.1.1 Registration

The Merchant Shipping Act 1995 and related Merchant Shipping (Registration of Ships) Regulations govern the registration of British ships in the UK.

The Register of British Ships is in 4 parts, covering:

Part I	Merchant ships and pleasure vessels.
Part II	Fishing vessels.
Part III	Small ships (Small Ships Register).
Part IV	Bareboat charter ships.

- Registration under Part I is a relatively complex and expensive business (£124), since a yacht has to be surveyed and follows the same procedure as a large merchant vessel. It costs £49 to renew for 5 years. The certificate establishes the ship's nationality and tonnage. Details of registered ownership and mortgages can be obtained from the RSS at Cardiff.
- Part III, *The Small Ships Register (SSR),* is for owners who want a simple registration, to prove the yacht's nationality and meet registration requirement for a privileged ensign, but it registers neither 'Title' nor mortgages. A small ship is defined as < 24m LOA. The cost is £25 for five years, and measurement only requires taking the boat's LOA.

For further details contact: Registry of Shipping and Seamen/ Small Ships Register, Anchor Court, Keen Road, Cardiff CF24 5JW; SSR ☎ 029 2044 8813; rss@mcga.gov.uk

Application forms and the online SSR registration service can be found at www.ukshipregister.com.

2.1.2 Insurance

Every cruising boat should be adequately insured against loss or damage. The insured value should be the cost of replacing the boat and all equipment. Third-party cover for up to £3,000,000 is also needed. Spanish translation needed for Spanish waters. The cruising area must be adjusted and paid for if cruising beyond the usual limits. Failure to disclose all relevant facts may invalidate a policy.

2.2 HM REVENUE & CUSTOMS (HMRC)

2.2.1 The European Union (EU)

EU yachtsmen can move freely within the EU, provided Customs duty, VAT, or any other Customs charges, have been paid in an EU country. Most nations make random checks on yachts and you may be asked for evidence that VAT, or its equivalent, has been paid on your vessel. See 2.3.2 for notes on using UK-bought red diesel overseas.

EU members are listed in Notice No 8. The Channel Islands and the Canary Islands do not operate a VAT system under EU rules, and are therefore treated as outside the EU.

2.2.2 Customs Notice No 8 (Dec 2002)

This Notice *'Sailing your pleasure craft to and from the UK'* (with Update 5 of April 2012) is the UK's interpretation of what the law says about pleasure craft and compliance with HM Revenue & Customs requirements, as summarised below; it is a good idea to have a copy aboard.

This Notice and further information may be obtained from the National Advice Service, ☎ 0845 010 9000 or +44 208 929 0152, which is open M-F, 0800-2000. Or visit HM Revenue & Customs website at: www.hmrc.gov.uk

Yachtsmen are warned that a boat may be searched at any time. Penalties are severe for non-declaration of prohibited or restricted goods, and the carriage and non-declaration of prohibited drugs and firearms. If goods are smuggled the vessel may be seized and the persons concerned may be liable to prosecution, a heavy fine and/or prison sentence.

2.2.3 Duty-free stores

Duty-free stores may be allowed on vessels going south of Brest or north of the N bank of the R. Eider (Denmark), by prior application to a Customs office. Duty-free stores cannot be taken to the Republic of Ireland nor to the Channel Islands. Contact the National Advice Service for details of how to embark stores and the conditions to be satisfied. For more information read Notice 69A *Duty free ship's stores.*

2.2.4 C1331 Pleasure craft departing the UK

To another EU country

No report is needed, unless a Customs Officer asks for one.

To a country which is outside the EU:

You must notify HM Customs of your departure on Form C1331, Part 1 *'Leaving the UK',* available from most YCs, marinas, Customs offices, the National Advice Service or via the HMR&C website.

Before you leave the UK, return the completed Part 1 to a Customs Officer, put it in a Customs post box or take/post it to a Customs office. C1331 is valid for 48 hrs from the stated time of departure. If departure is not notified, delay, inconvenience and possible prosecution may result on return. Keep Part 2 *'Arriving in the UK'* on board for use on your return. If your voyage is abandoned, Part 2, marked 'Voyage abandoned', should be returned to where Part 1 was sent.

2.2.5 Arrival from an EU country

If arriving directly from another EU country there is no need to fly flag 'Q', complete any paperwork, or contact Customs. You must, however, contact the Customs 'Yachtline' (see 2.2.8) if you have goods to declare, or have non-EU nationals on board. You must also declare animals or birds (see 2.6); prohibited or restricted goods, eg controlled drugs, firearms, radio transmitters not accepted in the UK; counterfeit goods; duty-free stores; or the boat itself if duty and VAT are owed on it. Further details are in *Notice No 1*.

2.2.6 Arrival from a non-EU country

If arriving directly from a non-EU country (including the Channel Islands), yachts are subject to Customs control. When inside the 12-mile limit, ie UK Territorial Waters, fly flag 'Q' where most easily seen (lowering it when formalities are complete); and fill in Part 2 of Form C1331.

On arrival, call the Customs 'Yachtline' (see 2.2.8) and inform them if: VAT has not been paid on the vessel; goods in excess of your allowances as detailed in Notice 1, or duty-free stores are on board; you have prohibited or restricted goods; a crew has a notifiable illness or needs immigration clearance; repairs or modifications (not running repairs) have been made since leaving the EU.

Comply with any instructions from the Customs Officer; failure to could incur a penalty. Do not land anybody or goods or transfer to another vessel until a Customs Officer permits.

2.2.7 Immigration

In most yachting centres the Customs Officer also acts as the Immigration Officer. The skipper is responsible for ensuring that any non-EU national aboard gets an Immigration Officer's permission to enter the UK from any country except the Isle of Man, the Channel Islands or ROI.

2.2.8 Customs telephone numbers

The National Yachtline ☎ 0845 723 1110 must only be used by yachtsmen to clear Customs on return to the UK from a non-EU country (2.2.6). Use the National Advice Service ☎ 0845 010 9000 for Customs queries,requests for forms or notices.

2.2.9 Drug smuggling and Project Kraken

Preventing drug smuggling is a key role for HMRC. Public support is very important. If you see or become aware of suspicious activity, call ☎0800 595000. This is a 24-hour, 7/7 free and anonymous hotline. There may be a reward.

Project Kraken is a National Crime Agency/Police and Border Force initiative for the boating public to report unusual or suspicious behaviour on the coast, including illegal entry into the UK by sea. However trivial, if something looks abnormal, phone local police on 101, or, anonymously, Crimestoppers 0800 555 111, quoting 'KRAKEN'. In emergency phone 999.

2.3 FOREIGN CUSTOMS

Other EU countries should apply the regulations outlined in 2.2.1 to 2.2.6 above, and any Customs formalities are likely to be minimal. If boarded by Customs, stay polite and helpful at all times. Before departure, skippers are recommended to check the procedures in force in their destination country.

2.3.1 The Schengen Treaty

In 1985 France, Germany, Luxembourg, Netherlands and Belgium signed a Convention abolishing internal border controls, and created a single external border, around what is sometimes called 'Schengen-land'. Today all 28 EU members (except the UK, Ireland, Romania, Bulgaria, Croatia and Cyprus) are signatories to Schengen as well as the EFTA countries Iceland, Norway, Switzerland and Liechtenstein. Travelling from the UK to a Schengen country, or vice versa, and crossing the external border may incur additional checks. Thus, Belgium and the Netherlands require a vessel to report on arrival *even if coming from another EU country*. Forms can be downloaded from the RYA website (www.rya.org.uk). Select: Information & Advice, then option BOATING ABROAD, Customs Formalities, under Downloads: NL Schengen or B Schengen Crew list, showing names, DOB, place of birth, passport No, nationality, details of vessel and itinerary. These forms are not always requested, but if you have them aboard you may avoid fines which can legally be imposed for not observing Schengen/EU law. On arrival check with the HM whether any Customs or Immigration forms need to be completed.

2.3.2 Red diesel

Problems with UK pleasure craft using red (dyed green in ROI) reduced duty diesel in other EU countries have mostly been resolved using the following guidelines. Carry on board all receipts for red/green diesel (dated, and marked 'UK or ROI duty paid' if possible); keep diesel in the main fuel tank(s) only, *do not carry any red/green diesel in cans*; log engine hours. Although Belgium still maintains its ban on dyed diesel, no fines had been reported by June 2017; but caution is still advised. Check for changes on the RYA website www.rya.org.uk or the free online monthly updates at www.reedsnauticalalmanac.co.uk (January 2018-June 2018).

2.4 EU VAT ON VESSELS

EU residents can move a yacht between member states without restriction, providing VAT has been paid. Documentary evidence supporting a vessel's VAT status should be carried at all times. A leaflet *UK Guide for Yachts,* on the Customs website, gives further advice; see also *Notice 8*, section 6.

2.4.1 Temporary Importation (TI)

TI is a complex process likely to affect few yachtsmen. The maximum stay in the EU is 18 months. See *Notice 8*, Section 5 and *Notice 308*, available on the Customs website or from the National Advice Service. On arrival in the UK fill in Form C108 as well as the usual Form C1331.

2.5 e-BORDERS

The UK Border Force (UKBF) plan for an onerous reporting procedure for private leisure craft on cross-border voyages to and from other EU states remains on hold due to the complexity of finding a practical solution for implementing it. The existing procedures **HMRC C1331 Pleasure craft departing the UK (2.2.4, 2.2.5, 2.2.6 and 2.2.7)** therefore remain unchanged. With the ongoing terrorist threat and growing traffic in illegal immigration by sea, UKBF spot checks on leisure craft will inevitably increase to combat this.

2.6 TRAVELLING WITH PETS

Pets can travel to France from the UK in private leisure craft if they comply with French regulations, see http://www.ambafrance-uk.org/Importing-animals-into-France,2780. Travelling with pets from the EU (and certain non-EU countries) to the UK in private leisure craft is **not** permitted; they can only travel with **'an approved transport company on an approved route'**, see www.gov.uk/take-pet-abroad. Before travel, all pets must be microchipped, with up to date vaccinations, Pet passport and any other paperwork in order (varies according to country). Dogs must also have tapeworm medication administered **by a vet** <120hrs and >24hrs before entering the UK.

2.7 INTERNATIONAL REGULATIONS FOR PREVENTING COLLISIONS AT SEA

The 1972 International Regulations for Preventing Collisions at Sea (IRPCS) are also referred to as the Colregs or Rule of the Road. They should be read as an entity, with the explanatory notes and associated diagrams below. See also *Learning the Rule of the Road* (Basil Mosenthal/ACN), the RYA booklet G2 and *The Mariner's Handbook* NP 100.

Because the exact wording of certain Rules is very important, Rules 2, 3 (in part), 5–10, 12–19 and 25 are quoted verbatim in *blue italics* and then briefly discussed – especially those of specific interest to yachtsmen. This does not imply that this chapter should be consulted in the heat of the moment – since all mariners must have a sound working knowledge of the Rules – but an aide-memoire is sometimes handy.

2.7.1 Part A: General

Rule 1 (Application) is mainly introductory and therefore not quoted verbatim, but note that many harbours have their own local rules – which must be obeyed.

Rule 2 (Responsibility).

(a) Nothing in these Rules shall exonerate any vessel, or the owner, master or crew thereof, from the consequences of any neglect to comply with these Rules or of the neglect of any precaution which may be required by the ordinary practice of seamen, or by the special circumstances of the case.

(b) In construing and applying these Rules due regard shall be had to all dangers of navigation and collision and to all special circumstances, including the limitations of the vessels involved, which may make a departure from these Rules necessary to avoid immediate danger.

The Rules must be interpreted in a seamanlike way. No vessel has a 'right of way' over another regardless of special circumstances – eg other vessels under way or at anchor, shallow water, poor visibility, TSS, fishing fleets, etc – or the handling characteristics of the vessels concerned in the prevailing conditions. Sometimes vessels may need to depart from the Rules to avoid immediate danger (2b).

Rule 3 (Definitions). The following are selected extracts:

(c) 'Sailing vessel' means any vessel under sail provided that propelling machinery, if fitted, is not being used.

(f) 'Vessel not under command' means one which through some exceptional circumstance is unable to manoeuvre as required by these Rules and is therefore unable to keep out of the way of another vessel.

(g) 'Vessel restricted in her ability to manoeuvre' means one which from the nature of her work is thus restricted ... (6 examples are given)

(h) 'Vessel constrained by her draught' means a power-driven vessel which, because of her draught in relation to the available depth and width of navigable water is severely restricted in her ability to deviate from her course.

(i) 'Underway' means that a vessel is not at anchor, or made fast to the shore, or aground. (Note: 'Making way' means progressing through the water, rather than drifting.)

(l) 'Restricted visibility' means any condition in which visibility is restricted by fog, mist, falling snow, heavy rainstorms, sandstorms or any other similar causes.

(m) A 'Wing-in-Ground (WIG) craft' means a multimodal craft which, in its main operational mode, flies in close proximity to the surface by utilising surface-effect action.

2.7.2 Part B: Steering and Sailing Rules Section I – In any condition of visibility

Rule 4 (Application) is self-explanatory. In complying with Rules 4–18 ask yourself, and answer, the following three questions and take action if so required:

- Is there a risk of collision?
- If there is, am I the give-way vessel?
- If I am, what action must I take?

This is not part of the IRPCS, but it concentrates the mind.

Rule 5 (Look-out).

Every vessel shall at all times maintain a proper look-out by sight and hearing as well as by all available means appropriate in the prevailing circumstances and conditions so as to make a full appraisal of the situation and of the risk of collision.

Look-out means not only by eyes and ears, but also by radar and VHF, especially at night or in low visibility. Do not neglect blind arcs, eg look below the genoa and directly to windward. Rule 5 is arguably the most important Rule of all.

Rule 6 (Safe speed).

Every vessel shall at all times proceed at a safe speed so that she can take proper and effective action to avoid collision and be stopped within a distance appropriate to the prevailing circumstances and conditions so as to make a full appraisal of the situation and of the risk of collision. In determining a safe speed the following factors are among those taken into account:

(a) By all vessels:
- *(i) the state of visibility;*
- *(ii) the traffic density including concentrations of fishing vessels or any other vessels;*
- *(iii) the manoeuvrability of the vessel with special reference to stopping distance and turning ability in the prevailing conditions;*
- *(iv) at night the presence of background light such as from shore lights or from back scatter of her own lights;*
- *(v) the state of wind, sea and current, and the proximity of navigational hazards;*
- *(vi) the draught in relation to the available depth of water;*

(b) Additionally, by vessels with operational radar:
- *(i) the characteristics, efficiency and limitations of the radar equipment;*
- *(ii) any constraints imposed by the radar range scale in use;*
- *(iii) the effect on radar detection of the sea state, weather and other sources of interference;*
- *(iv) the possibility that small vessels, ice and other floating objects may not be detected by radar at an adequate range;*
- *(v) the number, location and movement of vessels detected by radar;*
- *(vi) the more exact assessment of the visibility that may be possible when radar is used to determine the range of vessels or other objects in the vicinity.*

The conditions which determine what is a safe speed are clearly listed. Excessive speed gives less time to assess the situation and take avoiding action, and produces a worse collision if such action fails. Even 4 knots may be too fast in a crowded river.

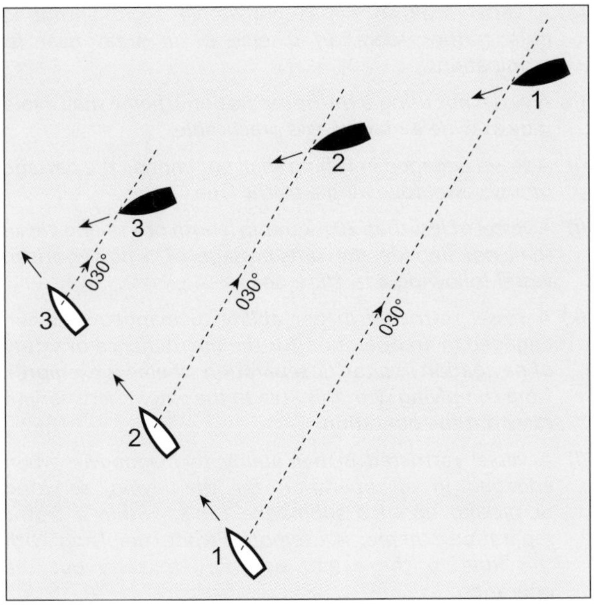

Fig 2(1) Rule 7. The bearing of black from white is steady on 030°. Well before reaching position 2, white should have altered to starboard by at least 45° to pass astern of black.

Rule 7 (Risk of collision).

(a) Every vessel shall use all available means appropriate to the prevailing circumstances and conditions to determine if risk of collision exists. If there is any doubt such risk shall be deemed to exist.

(b) Proper use shall be made of radar equipment if fitted and operational, including long-range scanning to obtain early warning of risk of collision and radar plotting or equivalent systematic observation of detected objects.

(c) Assumptions shall not be made on the basis of scanty information, especially scanty radar information.

(d) In determining if risk of collision exists the following considerations shall be among those taken into account:

(i) such risk shall be deemed to exist if the compass bearing of an approaching vessel does not appreciably change;

(ii) such risk may sometimes exist even when an appreciable bearing change is evident, particularly when approaching a very large vessel or a tow or when approaching a vessel at close range.

A vessel should take a series of compass bearings on a closing ship. Unless the bearings change appreciably, a risk of collision exists; see Fig 2(1). If in doubt, assume that there is a risk. Radar, properly used, offers early warning of risk of collision, but careful systematic plotting of contacts is needed to obtain maximum collision-avoidance data.

Rule 8 (Action to avoid collision).

(a) Any action taken to avoid collision shall be taken in accordance with the Rules of this Part and shall, if the circumstances of the case admit, be positive, made in ample time and with due regard to the observance of good seamanship.

(b) Any alteration of course and/or speed to avoid collision shall, if the circumstances of the case admit, be large enough to be readily apparent to another vessel observing visually or by radar; a succession of small alterations of course and/or speed should be avoided.

(c) If there is sufficient sea room, alteration of course alone may be the most effective action to avoid a close-quarters situation provided that it is made in good time, is substantial and does not result in another close-quarters situation.

(d) Action taken to avoid collision with another vessel shall be such as to result in passing at a safe distance. The effectiveness of the action shall be carefully checked until the other vessel is finally past and clear.

(e) If necessary to avoid collision or allow more time to assess the situation, a vessel shall slacken her speed or take all way off by stopping or reversing her means of propulsion.

(f) (i) A vessel which by any of these Rules is required not to impede the passage or safe passage of another vessel shall, when required by the circumstances of the case, take early action to allow sufficient sea room for the safe passage of the other vessel.

(ii) A vessel required not to impede the passage or safe passage of another vessel is not relieved of this obligation if approaching the other vessel so as to involve risk of collision and shall, when taking action, have full regard to the action which may be required by the Rules of this Part.

(iii) A vessel the passage of which is not to be impeded remains fully obliged to comply with the Rules of this Part when the two vessels are approaching one another so as to involve risk of collision.

Any such actions must be positive, seamanlike and taken early. Large alterations of course and/or speed are more obvious to the other vessel, especially at night or on radar. Turn away (even through 180°), slow down, stop (or go astern). In avoiding one vessel, watch out for others.

Rule 9 (Narrow channels).

(a) A vessel proceeding along the course of a narrow channel or fairway shall keep as near to the outer limit of the channel or fairway which lies on her starboard side as is safe and practicable.

(b) A vessel of less than 20 metres in length or a sailing vessel shall not impede the passage of a vessel which can safely navigate only within a narrow channel or fairway.

(c) A vessel engaged in fishing shall not impede the passage of any other vessel navigating within a narrow channel or fairway.

(d) A vessel shall not cross a narrow channel or fairway if such crossing impedes the passage of a vessel which can safely navigate only within such channel or fairway. The latter vessel may use the sound signal prescribed in Rule 34 (d) if in doubt as to the intention of the crossing vessel.

(e) (i) In a narrow channel or fairway when overtaking can take place only if the vessel to be overtaken has to take action to permit safe passing, the vessel intending to overtake shall indicate her intention by sounding the appropriate signal prescribed in Rule 34 (c) (i). The vessel to be overtaken shall, if in agreement, sound the appropriate signal prescribed in Rule 34 (c) (ii) and take steps to permit safe passing. If in doubt she may sound the signals prescribed in Rule 34 (d).

(ii) This Rule does not relieve the overtaking vessel of her obligation under Rule 13.

(f) A vessel nearing a bend or an area of a narrow channel or fairway where other vessels may be obscured by an

intervening obstruction shall navigate with particular alertness and caution and shall sound the appropriate signal prescribed in Rule 34 (e).

(g) Any vessel shall, if the circumstances of the case admit, avoid anchoring in a narrow channel.

Rule 9 (a) requires a vessel ... to keep as near to the starboard side of a narrow channel as is safe and practicable. Yachts and other small craft can often keep outside the channel altogether, thus ensuring even greater safety.

Rule 10 (Traffic Separation Schemes).

(a) This Rule applies to traffic separation schemes adopted by the Organization (IMO) and does not relieve any vessel of her obligation under any other Rule.

(b) A vessel using a traffic separation scheme shall:

(i) proceed in the appropriate traffic lane in the general direction of traffic flow for that lane;

(ii) so far as practicable keep clear of a traffic separation line or separation zone;

(iii) normally join or leave a traffic lane at the termination of the lane, but when joining or leaving from either side shall do so at as small an angle to the general direction of traffic flow as practicable.

(c) A vessel shall so far as practicable avoid crossing traffic lanes, but if obliged to do so shall cross on a heading as nearly as practicable at right angles to the general direction of traffic flow.

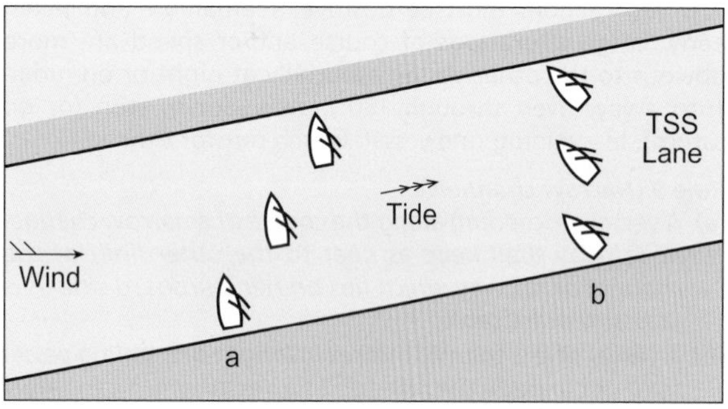

Fig 2(2) Rule 10c. A yacht crossing a TSS lane shall head at right angles to the lane axis, as in (a), regardless of the course made good as a result of wind or tidal streams. Yacht (b) is not heading at right angles and is therefore contravening Rule 10(c).

(d) (i) A vessel shall not use an inshore traffic zone when she can safely use the appropriate traffic lane within the adjacent traffic separation scheme. However, vessels of less than 20 metres in length, sailing vessels and vessels engaged in fishing may use the inshore traffic zone.

(ii) Notwithstanding sub-paragraph (d) (i) a vessel may use an inshore traffic zone when en route to or from a port, offshore installation or structure, pilot station or any other place situated within the traffic zone, or to avoid immediate danger.

(e) A vessel other than a crossing vessel or a vessel joining or leaving a lane shall not normally enter a separation zone or cross a separation line except:

(i) in cases of emergency to avoid immediate danger;

(ii) to engage in fishing within a separation zone.

(f) A vessel navigating in areas near the terminations of traffic separation schemes shall do so with particular caution.

(g) A vessel shall so far as practicable avoid anchoring in a traffic separation scheme or in areas near its terminations.

(h) A vessel not using a traffic separation scheme shall avoid it by as wide a margin as is practicable.

(i) A vessel engaged in fishing shall not impede the passage of any vessel following a traffic lane.

(j) A vessel of less than 20 metres in length or a sailing vessel shall not impede the safe passage of a power-driven vessel following a traffic lane.

(k) A vessel restricted in her ability to manoeuvre when engaged in an operation for the maintenance of safety of navigation in a traffic separation scheme is exempted from complying with this Rule to the extent necessary to carry out the operation.

(l) A vessel restricted in her ability to manoeuvre when engaged in an operation for the laying, servicing or picking up of a submarine cable, within a traffic separation scheme, is exempted from complying with this Rule to the extent necessary to carry out the operation.

TSS are essential to the safety of larger vessels and are shown in Chapter 9 and on most charts. Whilst inconvenient for yachtsmen, TSS shall be avoided where possible, or accepted as another element of passage planning. All vessels, including yachts, must comply with Rule 10.

Fig 2(2) illustrates how to cross a TSS (10c). Note well that craft <20m LOA, and any sailing yacht, shall not impede a power vessel using a traffic lane (10j). However, when two vessels meet or converge in a TSS with a risk of collision, Rule 10 does not modify any other provisions of the IRPCS.

Yachts should use inshore traffic zones (ITZ). It is unusual and certainly undesirable for yachts to use TSS lanes, due to the substantial speed difference between yachts and large vessels. Yachts using TSS lanes may be told by the monitoring radar station (eg Dover CG, CROSS Corsen) to leave asap.

2.7.3 Section II – Vessels in sight of one another

Rule 11 (Application) is self explanatory.

Rule 12 (Sailing vessels).

(a) When two sailing vessels are approaching one another, so as to involve risk of collision, one of them shall keep out of the way of the other as follows:

(i) when each has the wind on a different side, the vessel which has the wind on the port side shall keep out of the way of the other;

(ii) when both have the wind on the same side, the vessel which is to windward shall keep out of the way of the vessel which is to leeward;

(iii) if a vessel with the wind on the port side sees a vessel to windward and cannot determine with certainty whether the other vessel has the wind on the port or on the starboard side, she shall keep out of the way of the other.

(b) For the purposes of this Rule the windward side shall be deemed to be the side opposite to that on which the mainsail is carried or, in the case of a square-rigged vessel, the side opposite to that on which the largest fore-and-aft sail is carried.

Rule 12 does not apply if either yacht is motor sailing. When two yachts under sail are at risk of collision, (a) (i) and (ii) are clear.

(a) (iii) applies where it is unclear which tack a windward yacht is on. Fig 2(3) illustrates the practical application of Rule 12 in these three cases.

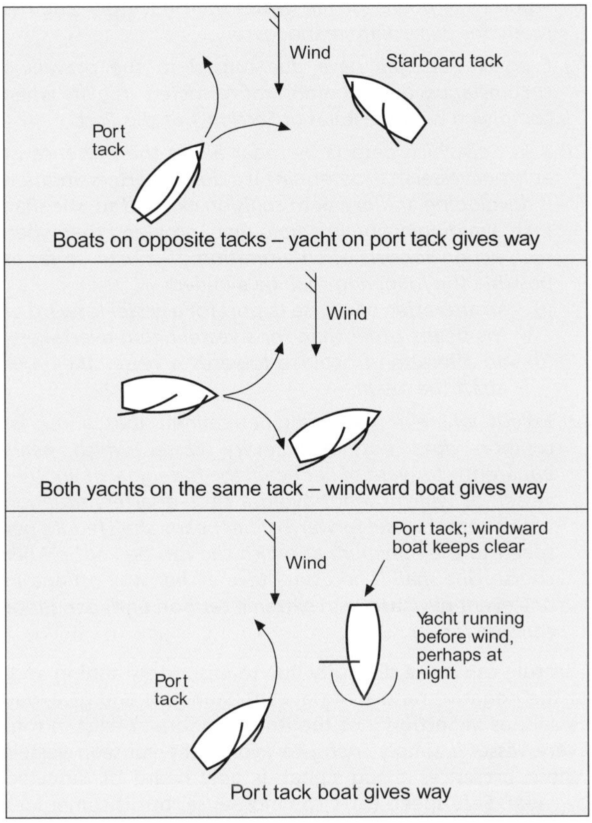
Wind
Starboard tack
Port tack
Boats on opposite tacks – yacht on port tack gives way
Wind
Both yachts on the same tack – windward boat gives way
Wind
Port tack; windward boat keeps clear
Yacht running before wind, perhaps at night
Port tack
Port tack boat gives way

Fig 2(3) Rule 12. A port tack yacht keeps clear. If both yachts are on the same tack the windward boat keeps clear. If in doubt, port tack always keeps clear.

Rule 12 (a) (iii) might cause doubt in 2 other situations:

- The windward side is deemed, Rule 12 (b), to be the side opposite to that on which the mainsail is set or would be set, if sailing under a headsail alone. When sailing under spinnaker alone, windward would be the side on which its boom is set.
- Heaving-to, ideally, set mainsail to port on starboard tack with jib backed to windward. Others (except those with special privileges) will then become the give-way vessel.

Rule 13 (Overtaking).

(a) Notwithstanding anything contained in the Rules of Part B, Sections I & II any vessel overtaking any other shall keep out of the way of the vessel being overtaken.

(b) A vessel shall be deemed to be overtaking when coming up with another vessel from a direction more than 22½° abaft her beam, that is, in such a position with reference to the vessel she is overtaking, that at night she would be able to see only the sternlight of that vessel but neither of her sidelights.

(c) When a vessel is in any doubt as to whether she is overtaking another, she shall assume that this is the case and act accordingly.

(d) Any subsequent alteration of the bearing between the two vessels shall not make the overtaking vessel a crossing vessel within the meaning of these Rules or relieve her of the duty of keeping clear of the overtaken vessel until she is finally past and clear.

An overtaking vessel, whether power or sail, shall keep clear of the vessel being overtaken. It is courteous, but not in the IRPCS, for an overtaking yacht under sail to pass to leeward of the yacht being overtaken.

Rule 14 (Head-on situation).

(a) When two power-driven vessels are meeting on reciprocal or nearly reciprocal courses so as to involve risk of collision each shall alter her course to starboard so that each shall pass on the port side of the other.

(b) Such a situation shall be deemed to exist when a vessel sees the other ahead or nearly ahead and by night she could see the masthead lights of the other in a line or nearly in a line and/or both sidelights and by day she observes the corresponding aspect of the other vessel.

(c) When a vessel is in any doubt as to whether such a situation exists she shall assume that it does exist and act accordingly.

When two power-driven vessels approach head-on, or nearly so, with risk of collision, each must alter course to starboard, to pass port to port. The alteration should be large enough as to be obvious to the other vessel, sounding one short blast, if in audible range, to make intentions clear.

Rule 15 (Crossing situation).

When two power-driven vessels are crossing so as to involve risk of collision, the vessel which has the other on her own starboard side shall keep out of the way and shall, if the circumstances of the case admit, avoid crossing ahead of the other vessel.

The give-way vessel would normally alter to starboard to pass astern of the other. A yacht with limited power and speed should, if possible, avoid crossing ahead of the other. Exceptionally, an alteration to port may be justified (eg shoal water to starboard), in which case a large alteration may be needed to avoid crossing ahead of the other.

Rule 16 (Action by give-way vessel).

Every vessel which is directed to keep out of the way of another vessel shall, so far as possible, take early and substantial action to keep well clear.

'*Early ... substantial ... well clear*' are the key words, ie don't dither or get into a close-quarters situation.

Rule 17 (Action by stand-on vessel).

(a) (i) Where one of two vessels is to keep out of the way, the other shall keep her course and speed.

(ii) The latter vessel may however take action to avoid collision by her manoeuvre alone, as soon as it becomes apparent to her that the vessel required to keep out of the way is not taking appropriate action in compliance with these Rules.

(b) When, from any cause, the vessel required to keep her course and speed finds herself so close that collision cannot be avoided by the action of the give-way vessel alone, she shall take such action as will best aid to avoid collision.

(c) A power-driven vessel which takes action in a crossing situation in accordance with sub-paragraph (a) (ii) of this Rule to avoid collision with another power-driven vessel

shall, if the circumstances of the case admit, not alter course to port for a vessel on her own port side.

(d) This Rule does not relieve the give-way vessel of her obligation to keep out of the way.

This Rule describes a deteriorating sequence of events (**1–3** below) and the actions that a stand-on vessel may or shall (ie must) take if it appears that the give-way vessel is failing to keep clear.

1. At least in the initial stages, the stand-on vessel should maintain her course/speed (17a. i) for fear of inducing a collision by needless avoiding action of her own.

2. The stand-on vessel may manoeuvre to avoid collision (17a. ii) if it appears that the give-way vessel is failing to keep clear. In so manoeuvring a power-driven vessel shall, if possible, not alter course to port for a vessel on her own port side (17c). Usually she would alter substantially to starboard, to reduce the risk of both vessels turning towards each other.

3. When the stand-on vessel finds herself so close that collision cannot be avoided by the action of the give-way vessel alone, the stand-on vessel *shall* take such action (17b), as will best aid to avoid collision. This is likely to be drastic, eg Full astern and/or helm hard over.

Rule 18 (Responsibilities between vessels).

Except where Rules 9, 10 and 13 otherwise require:

(a) A power-driven vessel underway shall keep out of the way of:
- *(i) a vessel not under command;*
- *(ii) a vessel restricted in her ability to manoeuvre;*
- *(iii) a vessel engaged in fishing;*
- *(iv) a sailing vessel.*

(b) A sailing vessel underway shall keep out of the way of:
- *(i) a vessel not under command;*
- *(ii) a vessel restricted in her ability to manoeuvre;*
- *(iii) a vessel engaged in fishing.*

(c) A vessel engaged in fishing when underway shall, so far as possible, keep out of the way of:
- *(i) a vessel not under command;*
- *(ii) a vessel restricted in her ability to manoeuvre.*

(d) (i) Any vessel other than a vessel not under command or a vessel restricted in her ability to manoeuvre shall, if the circumstances of the case admit, avoid impeding the safe passage of a vessel constrained by her draught, exhibiting the signals in Rule 28.

(ii) A vessel constrained by her draught shall navigate with particular caution having full regard to her special condition.

(e) A seaplane on the water shall, in general, keep well clear of all vessels and avoid impeding their navigation. In circumstances, however, where risk of collision exists, she shall comply with the Rules of this Part.

(f) (i) A WIG craft shall, when taking off, landing and in flight near the surface, keep well clear of all other vessels and avoid impeding their navigation.

(ii) A WIG craft operating on the water surface shall comply with the Rules of this Part as a power-driven vessel.

Rule 18 states priorities according to manoeuvrability. The hierarchy is clear and logical: (b) applies to yachts. Para (f) includes Wing in Ground (WIG) craft, defined in Rule 3 (m). These air-cushion vehicles are more aircraft than vessels.

2.7.4 Section III – Vessels in restricted visibility

Rule 19 (Restricted visibility).

(a) This Rule applies to vessels not in sight of one another when navigating in or near an area of restricted visibility.

(b) Every vessel shall proceed at a safe speed adapted to the prevailing circumstances and conditions of restricted visibility. A power-driven vessel shall have her engines ready for immediate manoeuvre.

(c) Every vessel shall have due regard to the prevailing circumstances and conditions of restricted visibility when complying with the Rules of Section 1 of this Part.

(d) A vessel which detects by radar alone the presence of another vessel shall determine if a close-quarters situation is developing and/or risk of collision exists. If so, she shall take avoiding action in ample time, provided that when such action consists of an alteration of course, so far as possible the following shall be avoided:
- *(i) an alteration of course to port for a vessel forward of the beam, other than for a vessel being overtaken;*
- *(ii) an alteration of course towards a vessel abeam or abaft the beam.*

(e) Except where it has been determined that a risk of collision does not exist, every vessel which hears apparently forward of her beam the fog signal of another vessel, or which cannot avoid a close-quarters situation with another vessel forward of her beam, shall reduce her speed to the minimum at which she can be kept on her course. She shall if necessary take all her way off and in any event navigate with extreme caution until danger of collision is over.

This rule can cause difficulty due to misunderstanding and/or the negative nature of para (d). Stand-on and give-way vessels, as in Section II of the Rules, no longer exist in fog. Every vessel is simply trying to avoid other unseen vessels whose presence, ie fog signal, is only heard or detected by radar. Safe speed (b) is commonsense, but is sometimes ignored by commercial ships. Slowing down to maintain steerage way for a fog signal forward of the beam (e) has limited application to an already slow-moving yacht.

Radar can save your life, but only if it is efficiently used and correctly interpreted by an experienced operator. Rule 7c warns against making assumptions based on scanty information, especially radar information. AIS, if fitted and switched on in both vessels, may resolve such assumptions.

If a vessel is detected by radar alone (d), decide whether a collision risk exists and/or a close-quarters situation is developing. If so, take early action to avoid collision.

(d) (i) and (ii) tell you what you should *avoid* doing. Try to envisage the situations which these two clauses address. It may help to transpose their words into more positive terms:

- Turn to starboard in all cases except for a vessel on or abaft your starboard beam, or for a vessel being overtaken.

Safety dictates that you should: sound the appropriate fog signal, keep a good look-out, deploy an efficient radar reflector and use radar if fitted. Consider also using the engine to assist manoeuvrability, especially in light winds. In thick fog it is best to anchor in shallow water; not easy if you are crossing a TSS in mid-Channel. Heaving to in the central separation zone to await better visibility might be an option, but see Rule 10 (b) and (e).

2.7.5 Part C: Lights and shapes

Many of the Rules (20–31) in Part C are semi-technical, not relevant to yachts or can be studied in slow time. The verbatim text is therefore only included for Rule 25 (Lights and shapes for sailing vessels underway).

Rule 20 (Application).
Part C Rules must be complied with in all weathers. All lights and shapes must comply with Annex I. The required lights must be shown from sunset to sunrise, and by day in low visibility. The required shapes must be displayed by day.

Rule 21 (Definitions).
Six types of navigation lights are defined, see Fig 2(4). A vessel <20m LOA may combine her side lights into 1 lantern on the fore and aft centreline, Rule 21 (b). A masthead lt, aka steaming lt, is rarely at the masthead; see Annex 1, para 2.

Rule 22 (Visibility of lights).
This Rule gives the *minimum* visibility range of lights shown by vessels of different LOAs. If <12m: masthead, stern and all-round 2M; side 1M. 12–50m: masthead 5M (but 3M if <20m); stern, side and all-round 2M. See Fig 2(4).

Rule 23 (Power-driven vessels underway).
(a) specifies a masthead light forward and a second, higher light aft if >50m LOA; plus sidelights and sternlight.
(b) refers to the all-round Fl Y light on an air-cushion vessel.
(c) a WIG craft must show a high-intensity all-round Fl R light.
(d) (i) A power-driven vessel <12m LOA may combine her masthead and sternlights into one all-round Ⓦ light.

Rule 24 (Towing and pushing).
This Rule is lengthy and detailed and need not concern yacht owners. However all mariners should know the lights shown by tugs and their tows; see Fig 2(5).

Rule 25 (Sailing vessels underway and vessels under oars).
(a) A sailing vessel underway shall exhibit:
(i) sidelights; (ii) a sternlight.
(b) In a sailing vessel <20m LOA, the lights prescribed in paragraph (a) of this Rule may be combined in one lantern at or near the top of the mast where it can best be seen.
(c) A sailing vessel underway may, in addition to the lights prescribed at (a) of this Rule, exhibit at or near the top of the mast where they can best be seen two all-round lights, in a vertical line, the upper being red and the lower green, but these lights shall not be exhibited in conjunction with the combined lantern permitted by paragraph (b) of this Rule.
(d) (i) A sailing vessel <7m LOA shall, if practicable, exhibit the lights prescribed in paragraphs (a) or (b) of this Rule, but if she does not, she shall have ready at hand an electric torch or lighted lantern showing a white light which shall be exhibited in sufficient time to prevent collision.
(ii) A vessel under oars may exhibit the lights prescribed in this Rule for sailing vessels, but if she does not, she shall have ready at hand an electric torch or lighted lantern showing a white light which shall be exhibited in sufficient time to prevent collision.
(e) A vessel proceeding under sail when also being propelled by machinery shall exhibit forward where it can best be seen a conical shape, apex downwards.

The tricolour light at (b) shall not be switched on at the same time as the normal side and stern lights, and must never be used when under power. It gives max brilliance for minimum battery drain, but note that LED lights easily out-perform conventional lights in power consumption and brilliance, but cost much more. In congested waters or where there are shore lights in the background, the normal side and stern lights are deemed much easier to see from the bridge of a large ship than a masthead tricolour.

Rule 26 (Fishing vessels).
All mariners should know the lights shown by fishing vessels; see Fig 2(5).

Rule 27 (Vessels not under command, or restricted in their ability to manoeuvre).
All mariners should know the lights shown by such vessels. They do not apply to vessels <12m LOA. If engaged in diving operations exhibit a rigid replica of flag 'A' at least 1m high.

Rule 28 (Vessels constrained by their draught).
All mariners should know the lights shown by such vessels; see Fig 2(5).

Rule 29 (Pilot vessels).
All mariners should know the lights shown by such vessels; see Fig 2(5).

Rule 30 (Vessels anchored or aground).
Yachts at ⚓, like other vessels, *shall* show an ⚓ light or ball; see Fig 2(5). This stipulation warns other mariners and has safety and insurance implications. Abroad, especially in the Netherlands and Germany, the ball requirement is often strictly enforced. Rules 30e and 30f grant 2 minor exemptions for yachts <7m LOA and <12m LOA.

Rule 31 (Seaplanes).
This Rule applies to WIG craft as well as seaplanes.

2.7.6 Part D: Sound and light signals

Rule 32 (Definitions).

A whistle in a yacht effectively means a foghorn.
- · A short blast on a foghorn lasts about 1 second.
- – A prolonged blast lasts four to six seconds.

Rule 33 (Equipment for sound signals).
Vessels >12m LOA must have a whistle; plus a bell if >20m. A boat <12m LOA may make an efficient sound signal by other means, judged by audibility within the enclosed bridge of a large ship and against conflicting background noises.

Rule 34 (Manoeuvring and warning signals).
Power-driven vessels in sight of each other:
The following sound signals (short or long blasts on a foghorn) may also be supplemented by light flashes:

·	I am altering course to starboard.
··	I am altering course to port.
···	I am operating astern propulsion.
·····	I do not understand your intentions/actions or I doubt if sufficient action is being taken to avoid collision.

In a narrow channel:

––·	I intend to overtake on your starboard side.
––··	I intend to overtake you on your port side.
–·–·	I agree with your overtaking signal.
–	Warning by vessel nearing a bend where other vessels may not be visible.

Fig 2(4) Navigation lights

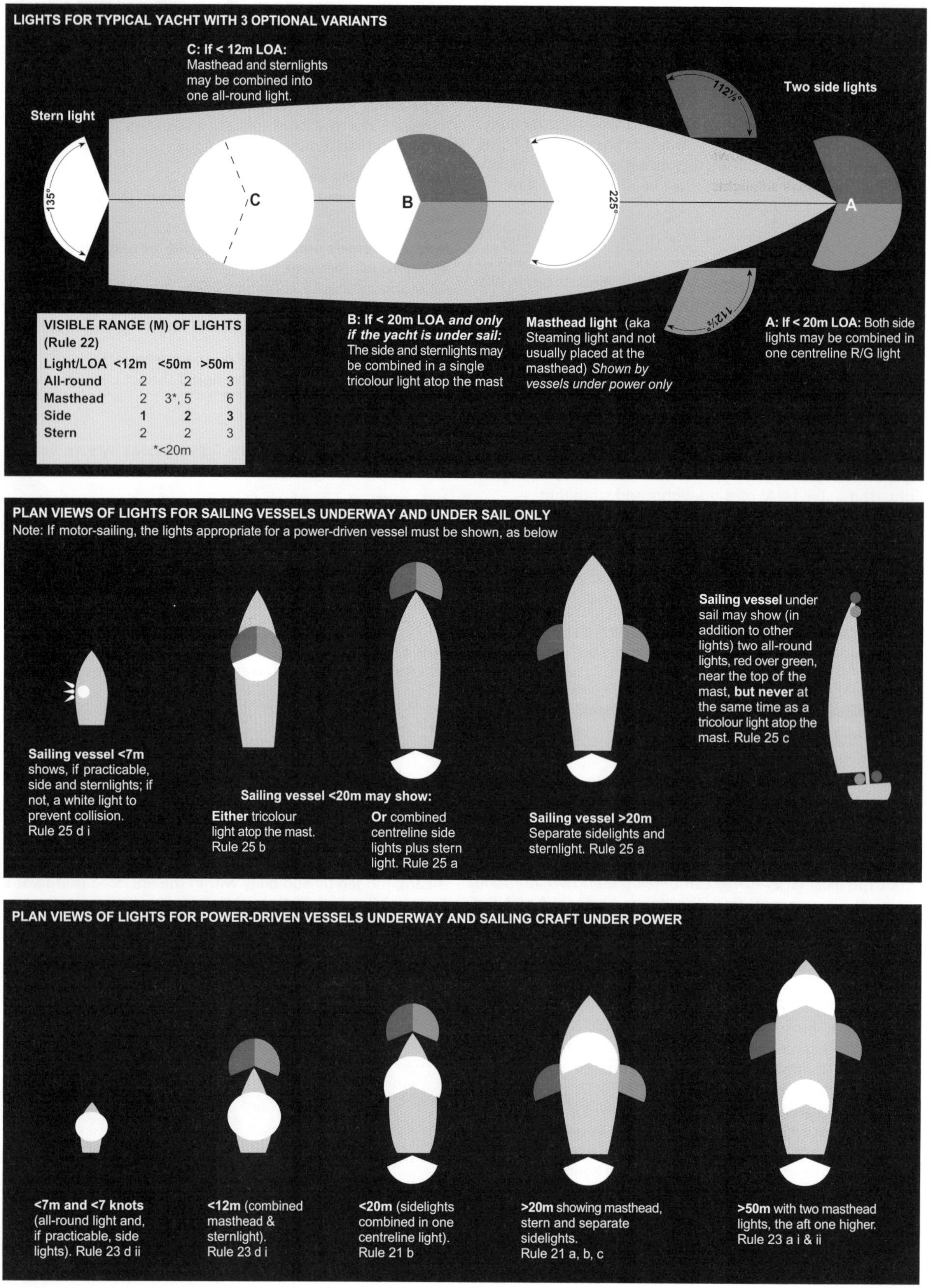
LIGHTS FOR TYPICAL YACHT WITH 3 OPTIONAL VARIANTS
C: If < 12m LOA: Masthead and sternlights may be combined into one all-round light.
Stern light
135°
C
B
225°
112½°
Two side lights
A
112½°
B: If < 20m LOA and only if the yacht is under sail: The side and sternlights may be combined in a single tricolour light atop the mast
Masthead light (aka Steaming light and not usually placed at the masthead) Shown by vessels under power only
A: If < 20m LOA: Both side lights may be combined in one centreline R/G light
VISIBLE RANGE (M) OF LIGHTS (Rule 22)
PLAN VIEWS OF LIGHTS FOR SAILING VESSELS UNDERWAY AND UNDER SAIL ONLY
Note: If motor-sailing, the lights appropriate for a power-driven vessel must be shown, as below
Sailing vessel <7m shows, if practicable, side and sternlights; if not, a white light to prevent collision. Rule 25 d i
Sailing vessel <20m may show:
Either tricolour light atop the mast. Rule 25 b
Or combined centreline side lights plus stern light. Rule 25 a
Sailing vessel >20m Separate sidelights and sternlight. Rule 25 a
Sailing vessel under sail may show (in addition to other lights) two all-round lights, red over green, near the top of the mast, but never at the same time as a tricolour light atop the mast. Rule 25 c
PLAN VIEWS OF LIGHTS FOR POWER-DRIVEN VESSELS UNDERWAY AND SAILING CRAFT UNDER POWER
<7m and <7 knots (all-round light and, if practicable, side lights). Rule 23 d ii
<12m (combined masthead & sternlight). Rule 23 d i
<20m (sidelights combined in one centreline light). Rule 21 b
>20m showing masthead, stern and separate sidelights. Rule 21 a, b, c
>50m with two masthead lights, the aft one higher. Rule 23 a i & ii

Light/LOA	<12m	<50m	>50m
All-round	2	2	3
Masthead	2	3*, 5	6
Side	**1**	**2**	**3**
Stern	2	2	3

*<20m

Fig 2(5) Principal navigation lights and shapes. (Note: All vessels seen from starboard side)

Rule 24

Vessels being towed and towing

Vessel towed shows sidelights (forward) and sternlight

Tug shows two masthead lights, sidelights, sternlight, yellow towing light

Rule 24

Towing by day — Length of tow more than 200m

Towing vessel and tow display diamond shapes. By night, the towing vessel shows three masthead lights instead of two as for shorter tows

---

Rule 25

Motor sailing

Cone point down, forward. At night the lights of a power-driven vessel underway

Rule 26

Vessel fishing

All-round red light over all-round white, plus sidelights and sternlight when making way

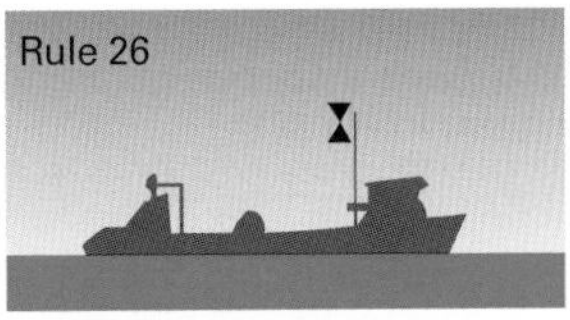
Rule 26

Fishing/Trawling

A shape consisting of two cones point to point in a vertical line one above the other

Rule 26

Vessel trawling

All-round green light over all-round white, plus sidelights and sternlight when making way

---

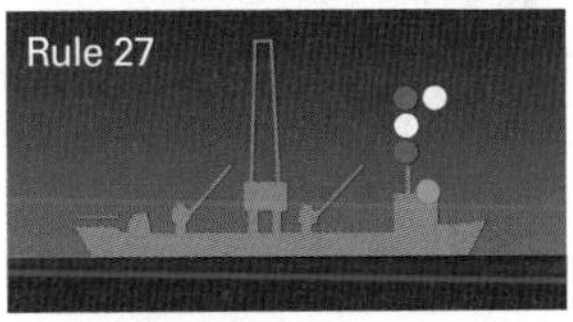
Rule 27

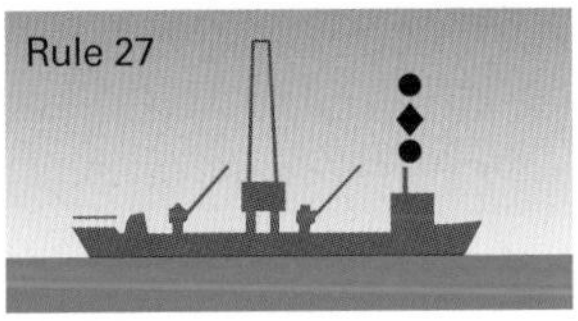
Rule 27

Vessel restricted in her ability to manoeuvre

All-round red, white, red lights vertically, plus normal steaming lights when making way

Three shapes in a vertical line: ball, diamond, ball

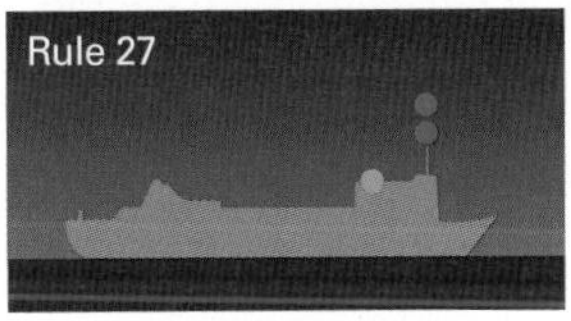
Rule 27

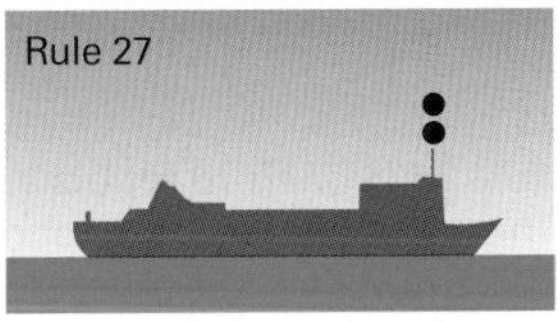
Rule 27

Not under command

Two all-round red lights, plus sidelights and sternlight when making way

Two balls vertically

Rule 27

Dredger

All round red, white, red lights vertically, plus two all-round red lights (or two balls) on foul side, and two all-round green (or two diamonds) on clear side

Rule 27

Divers down

Letter 'A' International Code

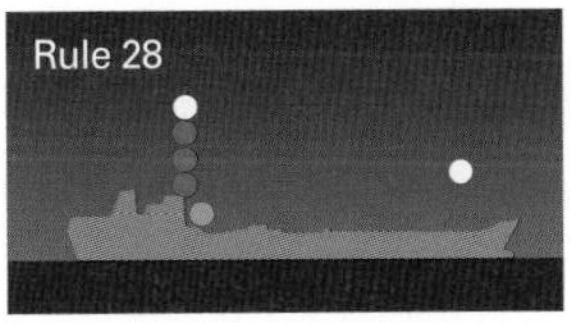
Rule 28

Constrained by draught

Three all-round red lights in a vertical line, plus normal steaming lights. By day — a cylinder

Rule 29

Pilot boat

All-round white light over all-round red, plus sidelights and sternlight when underway, or anchor light

---

Rule 30

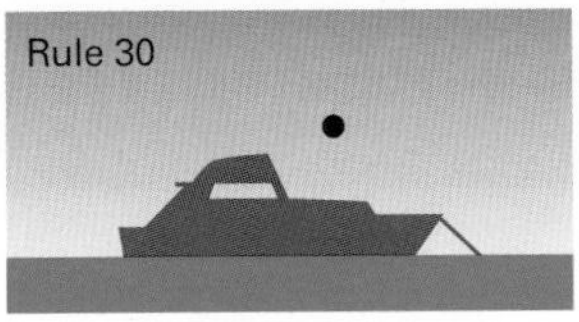
Rule 30

Vessel at anchor

All-round white light; if over 50m, a second light aft and lower

Ball forward

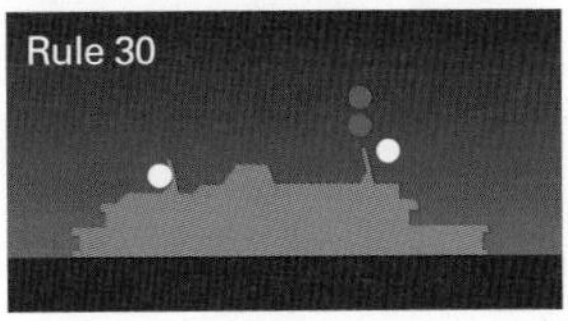
Rule 30

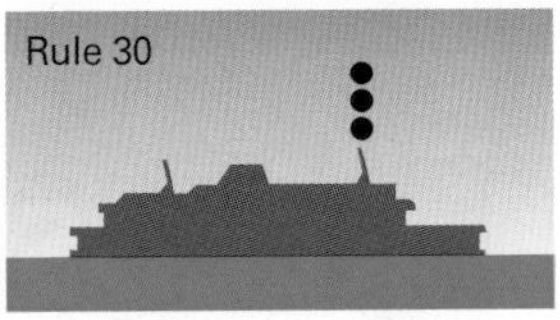
Rule 30

Vessel aground

Anchor light(s), plus two all-round red lights in a vertical line

Three balls in a vertical line

Rule 35 (Sound signals in restricted visibility).

–	Power-driven vessel making way.
– –	Power-driven vessel underway, but stopped and not making way.
–··	Vessel not under command; restricted in her ability to manoeuvre; constrained by her draught; or engaged in fishing, towing or pushing; **or a sailing vessel**.
–···	Vessel being towed, or if more than one vessel is towed, the last vessel in the tow.
····	Pilot vessel engaged on pilotage duties.

The maximum interval between sound signals for vessels underway in restricted visibility is two minutes, but more frequently if other craft are near.

For flag and sound signals which have a special meaning under IRPCS, see the asterisked items in Fig 5(1).

Bell rung rapidly for about 5 seconds, every minute.
= Vessel at anchor.

After the above signal, gong rung rapidly for about 5 seconds every minute; the bell being sounded in the fore part of the vessel and the gong aft
= Vessel of 100m or more in length at anchor.
·–· Vessel at anchor (optional extra sound signal).

Bell rung rapidly for about 5 seconds, with three separate and distinct strokes of the bell before and after the rapid ringing
= Vessel aground.

Rule 36 (Signals to attract attention).
These signals, whether sound or light, must be such as not to be mistaken for other signals in these Rules or an aid to navigation. Avoid using high intensity strobe lights.

Rule 37 (Distress signals).
See Annex IV and Chapter 7, Fig 7(1).

2.7.7 Annexes I to IV

Annex I: vertical/horizontal positioning and technical details of lights and shapes in various vessels.

Annex II: lights which may be shown by fishing vessels working close together.

Annex III: technical details of frequencies, audibility and directional properties of sound signals.

Annex IV: distress signals; see also Chapter 7, Fig 7(1).

2.7.8 Learning the Collision Regulations

Most of this chapter deals with the vitally important Rules of the Collision Regulations (ColRegs). To many people learning these is a chore; something to be swotted up, often parrot-fashion, so as to pass an exam – and then be forgotten. This is not learning, it is simply a memory test without understanding of the subject.

The ColRegs are written by seamen for seamen, unambiguously and in language which leaves little room for misunderstanding. Every word or sentence reflects a real life situation which has occurred at sea. They are steeped in practicality and hard won experience. Above all they exist to prevent collisions and hence save lives.

If we can adopt a better way of learning then what seemed like a chore may turn out to be a pleasure. Start from the Known and move with growing interest towards the Unknown. Grasp the big picture, in this case a site map below, showing how the ColRegs consist of five Parts (A-E), sub-divided, as required, into Sections; thence into the 38 individual Rules; finally 4 Annexes with technical minutiae.

Now for the details: As you study each Rule envisage the scenario which is being described. Ask yourself 'Do I fully understand this Rule?' 'What would I do in this situation?' This is the best way of gaining a sound working knowledge of the Rules – and disposing of that parrot.

PARTS			RULES
A: GENERAL			1–3
B: STEERING & SAILING	I	In any visibility	4–10
	II	In sight of each other	11–18
	III	In restricted visibility	19
C: LIGHTS & SHAPES			20–31 Annexes I/II
D: SOUND & LIGHT SIGNALS			32–37 Annexes III/IV
E: EXEMPTIONS			38

3 Navigation

3.1	**Passage planning and SOLAS V** Passage planning form • Planning considerations	**34**
3.2	**Conduct of the plan** Estimating position • Navigational wrinkles	**35**
3.3	**Lights** Light characteristics • Light sectors and arcs of visibility	**36**
3.4	**IALA buoyage (Region A)**	**38**
3.5	**Satellite navigation** GPS • EGNOS • GLONASS • Galileo • Horizontal datums	**39**
3.6	**Hydrographic surveys**	**40**
3.7	**Electronic charts** Raster charts • Vector charts	**40**
3.8	**Waypoints** Waypoint navigation • Loading waypoints	**40**
3.9	**Chartplotters**	**41**
3.10	**Radar and AIS** Display modes • Radar as an aid to navigation • Collision avoidance • Radar in fog • AIS	**41**
3.11	**Racons and Ramarks**	**43**
3.12	**Navigational warnings**	**43**
3.13	**Hazards** Submarines • Gunfacts • Mines	**43**
3.14	**Offshore energy installations** Gas and oil rigs • Wind farms • Wave and tidal installations	**44**
3.15	**Navigational tables** Notes on Tables 3(1) to 3(6) • Checking a compass for accuracy	**44**
3.16	**Sunrise/set times** Notes on table for Lats 56°N, 48°N and 40°N	**49**
3.17	**Moonrise/set times** Notes on table for Lats 56°N, 48°N and 40°N	**51**
3.18	**Phases of the Moon**	**52**

Fig 3(1) Passage planning form

DATE:............................ FROM: .... TO:.. DIST: ....M

ALTERNATIVE DESTINATION(S): ....

WEATHER FORECAST: ....

....

FORECASTS AVAILABLE DURING PASSAGE: ....

....

TIDES

DATE:.. DATE:.. DATE:..

PLACE:.. PLACE:.. PLACE:..

HW .... HW .... HW ....

LW .... LW .... LW ....

HW .... HW .... HW ....

LW .... LW .... LW ....

COEFFICIENT: ....

HEIGHT OF TIDE AT: ....

..........................hrs ....m ....hrs ....m ....hrs ....m

DEPTH CONSTRAINTS: ....

TIDAL STREAMS AT: ....

TURNS .... AT .... TOTAL SET (FM .... TO ....): ....° ....M

TURNS .... AT .... TOTAL SET (FM .... TO ....): ....° ....M

NET TIDAL STREAM FOR PASSAGE: ....° .... M

ESTIMATED TIME: ....hrs ETD: .... ETA: ....

SUN/MOON SUNRISE: .... SUNSET: ....

MOONRISE: .... MOONSET: .... PHASE: ....

WAYPOINTS

NO	NAME	TRACK/DISTANCE (TO NEXT WAYPOINT)
....	....	.... / ....
....	....	.... / ....
....	....	.... / ....
....	....	.... / ....
....	....	.... / ....

DANGERS CLEARING BEARINGS/RANGES/DEPTHS

....

....

LIGHTS/MARKS EXPECTED ....

....

....

COMMUNICATIONS PORT/MARINA .... VHF .... ☎ ....

PORT/MARINA .... VHF .... ☎ ....

NOTES (CHARTS PREPARED & PAGE NUMBERS OF RELEVANT PILOTS/ALMANACS/ETC): ....

....

....

3.1 PASSAGE PLANNING AND SOLAS V

All passages by any vessel that goes to sea *must* be planned. 'Going to sea' is defined as proceeding beyond sheltered waters. Even in very familiar waters every passage, however short, should be properly planned. Before you set sail you need to determine where you are going, how to get there and what factors may influence the plan.

Passage planning is mandated in the International Convention for Safety of Life at Sea (SOLAS), Chapter V. Guidance for small craft is in the MCA's Pleasure Craft Information Pack: **https://www.gov.uk/government/uploads/system/uploads/attachment_data/file/282631/pleasure_craft_information_packdec07-2.pdf**

Although the passage plan does not have to be recorded on paper, in the event of legal action a written plan is clear proof that the required planning has been completed; it can also be referred to during the passage. A suggested passage planning form is at Fig 3(1) opposite. When completed this would constitute, with due consideration of the points at 3.1.1 below, a reasonable passage plan. The blank form may be photocopied and modified to suit individual needs.

Although spot checks on small craft are unlikely, the MCA could, following an accident or incident, take action under the Merchant Shipping Act if it could be proved that the skipper did not have a reasonable passage plan.

3.1.1 Passage planning considerations

All passage plans should at least consider the following:

- **Weather.** Before setting out check the weather forecast and know how to get regular updates during the passage.
- **Tides.** Check tidal predictions and determine if there are any limiting depths at your port of departure, during the passage and at the port of arrival (and at alternative ports, if applicable). Tidal streams will almost certainly affect the plan.
- **Vessel.** Confirm she is suitable for the intended trip, is properly equipped, and has sufficient fuel, water and food on board.
- **Crew.** Take into account the size of crew, their experience, expertise and stamina. Cold, tiredness and seasickness can be debilitating – and skippers are not immune.
- **Navigation.** Make sure you are aware of all navigational dangers by consulting up to date charts, pilot books and this Almanac. Never *rely* on GPS for fixing your position.
- **Contingency plan.** Consider bolt holes which can be entered *safely* in an emergency, if the weather deteriorates or mutiny threatens.
- **Information ashore.** Make sure someone ashore knows your plans, when they should become concerned and what action to take if necessary. Be sure to join the Coastguard Voluntary Safety Identification Scheme (see 7.11.2).

'The winds and waves are always on the side of the ablest navigators' (Edward Gibbon).

3.1.2 Passage planning form

The following notes amplify some of the items on the form:

- The height of tide affects the depth, and tidal streams may hinder sensible progress – off headlands or in narrow passages, for example. On longer passages, which cross main tidal streams, determine the net effect of the streams and calculate a course to steer – more efficient than trying to maintain a track.
- Note which harbours and marinas have restricted times of access due to bars, sills or locks. These may affect your ETA and, probably, your ETD.
- Prepare a detailed pilotage plan for entry/exit of any unfamiliar harbour; a sketch is invaluable.
- Squinting into the setting sun can make pilotage very difficult. At night, light from a full moon can help enormously.
- Know when you expect to see lights at night – a good check on progress. See Table 3(6).
- Look up and note relevant VHF channels and/or phone numbers for ports of departure and arrival.

3.2 CONDUCT OF THE PLAN

Take every opportunity to fix your position by all available means – visual bearings and electronic aids. Although GPS normally gives accurate positional information 24 hours a day, the system is very vulnerable to external interference. Onboard, the equipment depends on a steady power supply and is susceptible to moisture or accidental damage. It is therefore essential to maintain a written record of positions, headings and distances run at regular intervals. From this an updated position may be established if a fix is unobtainable.

A dead reckoning (DR) plot must be started as soon as there is any doubt about your ability to fix your position.

3.2.1 Estimating position

A well adjusted compass, an accurate timepiece and a log to measure distance run through the water are the essential tools of dead reckoning (DR) navigation. A DR plot starts from your last known or estimated position. After a certain interval, depending on your proximity to dangers, the time, log reading, distance run and course steered are noted. These are then plotted on the chart to obtain an updated position.

This will be more accurate if leeway is applied to the course steered. For example, a yacht steering 090° with a northerly wind might make 5° of leeway; 095° would therefore be the course plotted. To refine this position still further, include the tidal stream rate and direction experienced since the last plotted position. This results in an estimated position (EP), which is the most accurate position in the absence of a fix.

By using conventional symbols on the chart (Fig 3(2)), others can immediately appreciate what they see and check the accuracy of the navigator's work. A sensible navigator always welcomes a second opinion.

Fig 3(2) DR/EP plot

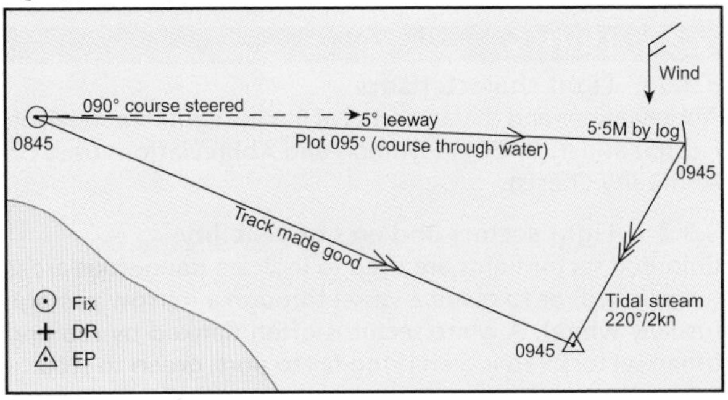

The DR or EP should always be extrapolated to ensure that the vessel will not run into danger. When plotting an EP include possible inaccuracies in the log (for distance run), the tidal stream and the course made good. Leeway, for example, is usually only an inspired guess. From this, instead of a range and bearing from your last position, you will construct a 'lozenge of probability'. Always assume your position is on that part of the lozenge which is closest to danger.

3.2.2 Navigational wrinkles

Distance, speed and time equations (see also Table 3(2)):

Distance (M)	=	Speed (kn) x time (hours)
Speed	=	Distance ÷ time
Time	=	Distance ÷ Speed

Tidal streams. Look at the stream flowing past fishing floats, buoys or any other fixed objects to better estimate the *actual* direction and rate – often significantly different from those obtained from tidal stream atlases or the chart.

Running fix. This is particularly useful at night when only one suitable light is visible. Take a bearing and plot the position line (PL) from the mark; note the time. When the angle has changed by about 45°, take a second bearing and plot the PL. Transfer the first PL by the distance and direction the boat has travelled *over the ground* in the interval between the two bearings. Your position at the time of the second bearing is where the first PL crosses the second.

Pilotage. A detailed sketch of the pilotage passage in a notebook saves constant trips to the chart table. Be very wary of having charts in the cockpit where they can get wet or blow away.

Blind pilotage. In 6 minutes (1/10 hour) you will cover 1/10 of your speed in miles. So at 6 knots you will cover 0·6 miles (6 cables); at 12 knots you will cover 1·2 miles. In 3 minutes you will cover half that distance; in 12 minutes, twice the distance. Remember to allow for any tidal stream.

Distance off track is easily calculated by knowing that 1° at 6 miles subtends an arc of 1 cable; 5° at 60 miles = 5 miles.

A Dutchman's log can be used when the ship's log has failed. Time how long it takes for an object dropped at the bows to pass the stern. Speed (kn) = (0·592 x LOA (ft)) ÷ T (seconds). Thus for an LOA of 34ft and a time of 5 seconds, the speed will be 34 x 0·592 ÷ 5 = 4 knots. A table can be drawn up for your boat for various speeds.

Distances. Although the term Nautical Mile (NM) is commonly used, the strictly correct unit for distance at sea is the Sea Mile. This is the length of one minute of latitude at any particular place. It varies from about 1843m at the equator to about 1862m at the poles. A NM is defined as 1852m.

3.3 LIGHTS

3.3.1 Light characteristics

Abbreviations and characteristics of marine lights are shown in Fig 3(5) and in NP 5011 (Symbols and Abbreviations used on Admiralty Charts).

3.3.2 Light sectors and arcs of visibility

Coloured sector lights are used to indicate dangerous areas (usually red) or to guide a vessel through a narrow passage (usually white). A white sector is often flanked by red and green sectors: red is seen if too far to port; green to stbd.

The limits of light sectors, arcs of visibility and the alignment of directional and leading lights are shown **as seen from your vessel**. All bearings are True, clockwise from north, and are shown for selected lights in Chapter 9 – either in the Lights, buoys and waypoints sections or in individual harbour entries under Lights and Marks.

Fig 3(3) shows a simple sectored light listed as *Oc WR 4s 37m* **W17M**, *R13M; 151°-W-115°-R-151°.*

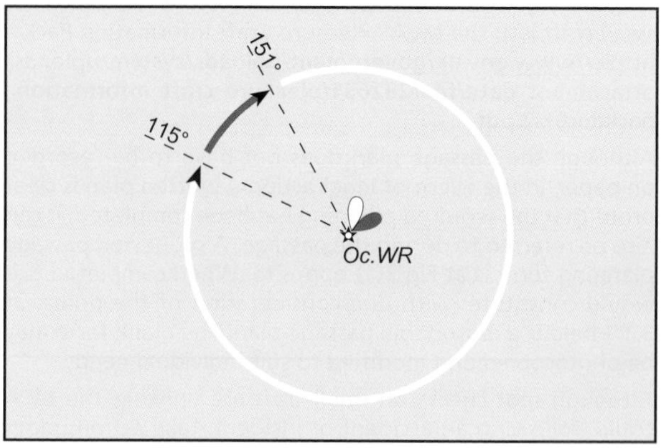

Fig 3(3) A simple sectored light

The light, showing white and red sectors, occults every 4s, is 37 metres above the level of MHWS, its white sector has a nominal range of 17 miles (ranges greater than 15 miles are in **bold**) and the red light's range is 13 miles. The white sector is visible when it bears 151° clockwise to 115°, an arc of 324°; the red sector is visible when it bears 115° to 151°, an arc of 36°.

In Fig 3(4) is a slightly more complex sectored light listed as: *Q WRG 9m 10M; 015°-G-058°-W-065°-R-103°-G-143·5°-W-146·5°-R-015°.*

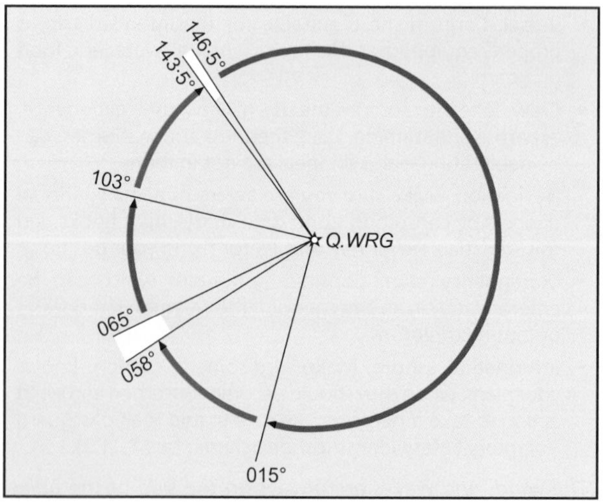

Fig 3(4) A more complex sectored light

This quick flashing light has white, red and green sectors, is 9m above MHWS and has a nominal range of 10M. By inspection there are two sets of WRG sectors providing directional guidance to vessels approaching from SW and NW. In each case a narrow (7° and 3°) white sector is flanked by a red sector to port and a green sector to starboard.

Fig 3(5) Light characteristics

CLASS OF LIGHT		International abbreviations	National abbreviations
FIXED*		F	
OCCULTING *(duration of light longer than dark)*			
Single-occulting		Oc	Occ
Group-occulting	eg	Oc(2)	Gp Occ(2)
Composite group-occulting	eg	Oc(2+3)	Gp Occ(2+3)
ISOPHASE *(light and dark equal duration)*		Iso	
FLASHING *(duration of light shorter than dark)*			
Single-flashing		Fl	
Long-flashing *(flash 2s or longer)*		LFl	L Fl
Group-flashing	eg	Fl(3)	Gp Fl(3)
Composite group-flashing	eg	Fl(2+1)	Gp Fl(2+1)
QUICK *(50 to 79 flashes per minute, usually 50 or 60)*			
Continuous quick		Q	Qk Fl
Group quick	eg	Q(3)	Qk Fl(3)
Interrupted quick		IQ	Int Qk Fl
VERY QUICK *(80 to 159 flashes per minute, usually 100 or 120)*			
Continuous very quick		VQ	V Qk Fl
Group very quick	eg	VQ(3)	V Qk Fl(3)
Interrupted very quick		IVQ	Int V Qk Fl
ULTRA QUICK *(160 or more flashes per minute, usually 240 to 300)*			
Continuous ultra quick		UQ	
Interrupted ultra quick		IUQ	
MORSE CODE	eg	Mo (K)	
FIXED AND FLASHING		F Fl	
ALTERNATING	eg	Al. WR	Alt. WR

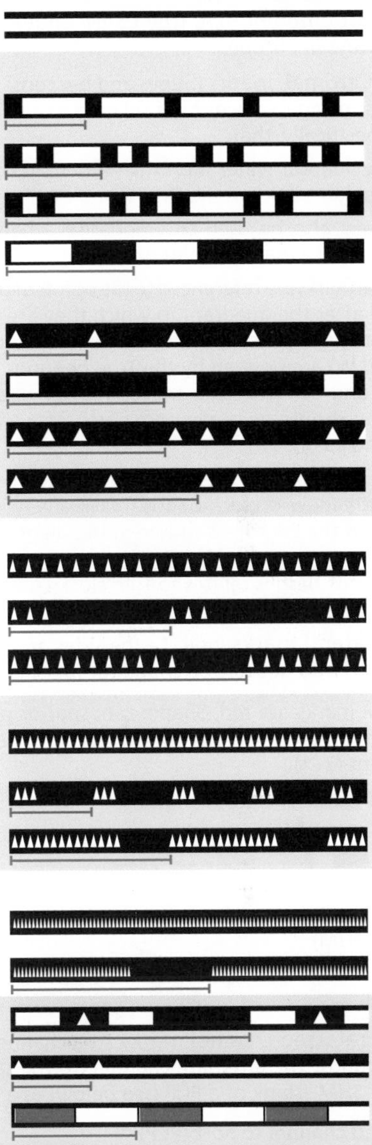
Illustration
Period shown

COLOUR	International abbreviations	NOMINAL RANGE in miles		International abbreviations
White	W *(may be omitted)*	Light with single range	eg	**15M**
Red	R	Light with two different ranges	eg	**15**/10M
Green	G	Light with three or more ranges	eg	**15**-7M
Blue	Bu	**PERIOD** is given in seconds	eg	90s
Violet	Vi	**DISPOSITION** Horizontally disposed		(hor)
Yellow	Y	Vertically disposed		(vert)
Orange	Or **or** Y	Synchronised with (an)other light(s)		(sync)
Amber	Amb **or**Y	**ELEVATION** is given in metres (m) above the level of MHWS		

*NB: Although rarely used in the UK Fixed lights may be shown with Flashing lights in which case the abbreviation FFl is used

3.4 IALA BUOYAGE (REGION A)

IALA buoyage system – Regions
Region A, shown here, includes Europe; Region B covers the Americas and the Pacific.
Note that different rules (the CEVNI Code) apply on Inland Waterways in Europe.

3.4.1 Cardinal marks (buoys and beacons) indicate where the best navigable water lies relative to a danger or hazard and, specifically, that:

- The deepest water is on the named side of the mark
- The named side is the safe side on which to pass

They may also be used to emphasise a bend or fork in a channel, or to mark the end of a shoal.

Cardinal marks are referenced to the points of the compass and named after the quadrant in which they are placed relative to the danger or hazard they mark. The four quadrants (N, E, S and W) are defined by the True bearings NW-NE, NE-SE, SE-SW and SW-NW from the danger or hazard. It follows that you should normally pass north of a NCM, east of an ECM and so on.

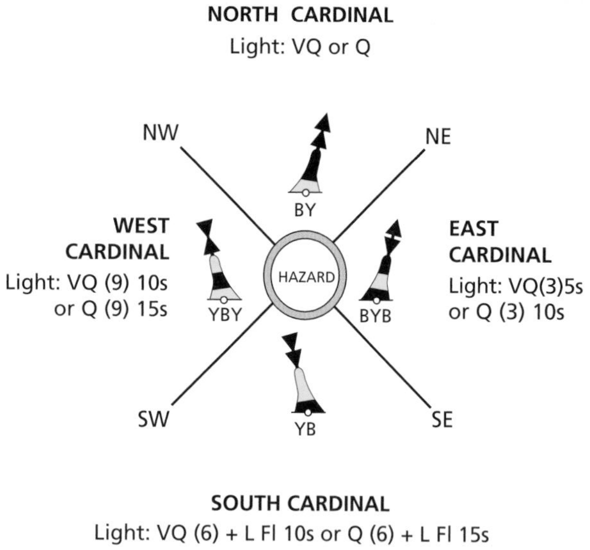
NORTH CARDINAL
Light: VQ or Q
NW
NE
BY
WEST CARDINAL
Light: VQ (9) 10s or Q (9) 15s
YBY
HAZARD
BYB
EAST CARDINAL
Light: VQ(3)5s or Q (3) 10s
SW
YB
SE
SOUTH CARDINAL
Light: VQ (6) + L Fl 10s or Q (6) + L Fl 15s

Topmarks: 2 black cones in various unique combinations.
Colour: yellow & black bands (black always relates to the points of the cones), as shown in the diagram.
Lights: always white, Q or VQ, as defined in Fig 3(5). The number of flashes relates to the 'clock code': a NCM at 12 o'clock flashes continuously; an ECM at 3 o'clock flashes groups of 3; a SCM flashes groups of 6 + a long flash (at least 2 secs duration); and a WCM flashes groups of 9.

3.4.2 Lateral marks indicate the sides of a well-defined channel according to the direction of buoyage (3.4.8). If PHM or SHM marks do not rely on shape for identification, they carry the appropriate topmarks where practicable. In Region A:

- PHM marks are red. Shape: can, spar or pillar. Topmark, if fitted: red can. Even numbering. Light: red; any rhythm except (2+1).
- SHM marks are green (exceptionally, black). Shape: conical, spar or pillar. Topmark, if fitted: green cone, point up. Odd numbering. Light: green; any rhythm except (2+1).

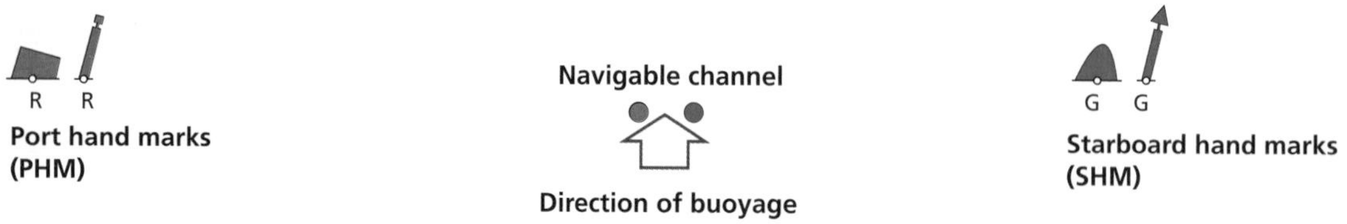
R R
Port hand marks (PHM)
Navigable channel
Direction of buoyage
G G
Starboard hand marks (SHM)

3.4.3 Preferred channel marks At a channel junction the preferred channel may be shown by a lateral mark with red or green bands. The alternate channel (to the same destination) lies on the other side of this mark. Topmarks are those of a PHM or SHM. Think of a PCP (see below) as a SHM modified by a R band, and the PCS as a PHM modified by a G band.

Preferred channel to port (PCP)
SHM mark, green with red band. Light (if fitted): Fl (2+1) G.

Preferred channel to starboard (PCS)
PHM mark, red with green band. Light (if fitted): Fl (2+1) R.

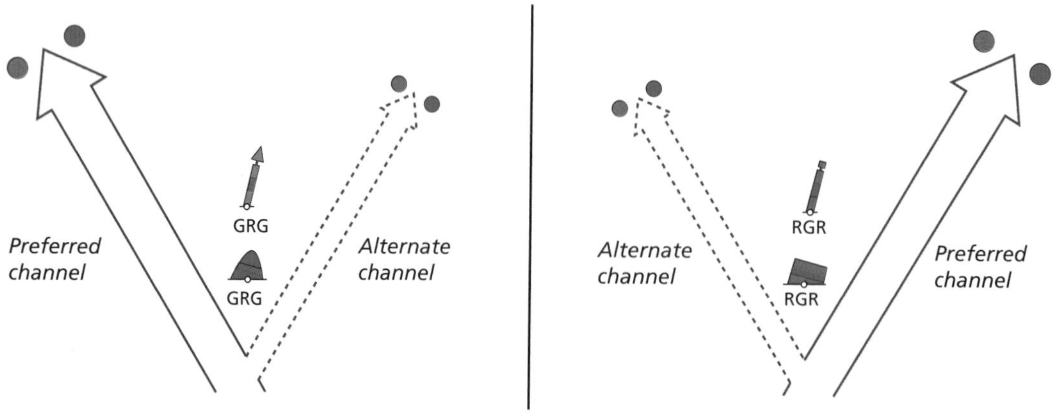
GRG
Preferred channel
GRG
Alternate channel
RGR
Alternate channel
RGR
Preferred channel

3.4.4 Isolated danger marks (IDM) are placed on or above an isolated danger of limited extent, eg a rock or a wreck, which has navigable water all around it.

BRB
BRB

Colour: black with red band(s). Topmark: 2 black balls (vert). Light, if any, is a group of two white flashes, Fl (2).

3.4.5 Safe water marks (SWM) indicate that there is navigable water all round the mark. They are used as centreline, mid-channel or landfall marks.

RW
RW

Shape: spherical, pillar or spar. Colour: red & white vertical stripes. Topmark: 1 R ball, but only on pillar or spar buoys. Light, if any, is white, occulting, isophase, L Fl 10s or Morse code 'A' (• –)

3.4.6 Special marks are not of navigational significance but indicate a special area usually depicted on the chart, eg spoil grounds, naval exercise areas, water-ski and bathing areas. Other features include yacht racing marks, cables or pipelines, outfalls, ODAS buoys and TSS marks (where conventional channel marks might cause confusion).

Y
Y
Y
Y

Colour: yellow. Shape: optional, but not conflicting with lateral or safe water marks. If can or conical buoys are used they indicate the side on which to pass. Topmark if fitted: yellow X. Light if fitted: yellow, any rhythm not used for Cardinal, IDM and SWM marks.

3.4.7 New dangers Emergency wreck-marking buoys are used before other marks can be deployed. They are pillar or spar shaped with blue & yellow vert stripes; WRECK is painted vert in black on yellow; optional topmark yellow +; light Al Bu/Y 3s 4M; Racon 'D' (–••) and/or AIS are optional.

YBu
YBu

Newly discovered hazards – wrecks, obstructions, rocks or shoals – are marked by IALA cardinal or lateral buoys, often 4 or more where the risk to other vessels is high. For emphasis one of the marks may be duplicated until the hazard has been adequately publicised. A Racon coded 'D' (–••) and/or an AIS transducer may also be fitted.

3.4.8 Conventional direction of buoyage

This is defined as either: the **Local** direction when entering estuaries and large waterways from seaward.

Or elsewhere as the **General** direction of buoyage which in principle is clockwise around continents.

Around the UK the general direction is N up the W coast and the Irish Sea, E up the English Channel, thence N up the North Sea (necessitated by the clockwise direction around mainland Europe).

If there is doubt, the direction is marked on charts by a broad arrowhead as shown in 3.4.2. Off Orfordness, Suffolk, for example, the local direction into the Thames Estuary is SW but the general direction is N.

3.5 SATELLITE NAVIGATION

3.5.1 GPS

The NAVSTAR Global Positioning System (GPS) is owned and operated by the United States Department of Defense (DoD). It provides world-wide, 24 hours a day, precise position, velocity and time information to anyone with a suitable receiver. The system consists of at least 24 operational satellites, orbiting 10,900M (20,200km) above the earth, in 6 orbital planes inclined at 55° to the equator. Positional accuracy is within 33m for 95% of the time; for the remaining 5% of the time errors of up to 100m are theoretically possible. Signal propagation delays can cause errors of up to 5m; other system errors are up to 2·5m.

GPS accuracy can be enhanced by Differential GPS (DGPS). An additional MF diferential signal in the 283.5-315 Khz band is transmitted from terrestrial beacons to provide overlapping coverage out to 50M from the coast. The accuracy obtainable from the Standard Positioning Service is generally quite adequate for yachting purposes. Errors may occur when used with charts drawn from surveys which pre-date GPS. Source diagrams on Admiralty charts show survey dates. Corrections must be made before plotting GPS positions on charts not yet referenced to the WGS84 datum (see 3.5.5).

When choosing a GPS receiver, consider size (handheld, portable or fixed installation); check that it has multi-channels (12+ is the norm) and can receive EGNOS. Compatibility with Galileo (see 3.5.4) may also influence your choice.

3.5.2 EGNOS

EGNOS is a Wide Area Augmentation System (WAAS). It consists of 3 geostationary satellites a network of 34 ground stations for ranging and monitoring, 4 master control centres and 6 up-link stations. The 'Wide Area' is bounded by Iceland, Murmansk, Greece and Marrakesh. Many receivers now display a 'WAAS operating' indication. Measured performance (99% accuracy of 1–2m) far exceeds expectations. It is due to cease operating when Galileo is fully established.

3.5.3 GPS integrity monitoring

Urgent information is given in MSI broadcasts by HM CG on VHF or MF, and by Navtex message category J (see Ch 6).

The US CG issues daily status information which may be found on www.navcen.uscg.gov. The US Government states that, although GPS is primarily for military use, it is committed to provide the best possible service to civil and commercial users worldwide – both in times of peace and conflict.

3.5.4 Other satellite-based systems

The *Global Navigation Satellite System* (GLONASS) operated by the Russian Federation is similar to GPS with 27 satellites in orbit to support a need for an operational cluster of 24. Completed in Dec 2015, it is available to users of enabled tablets, smart phones and some navigational systems.

Galileo is a European satellite system, compatible with GPS and GLONASS but promising greater accuracy. The constellation will consist of 27 satellites, plus 3 in-orbit spares. Orbits will be in 3 planes inclined at 56° to the equator and at a height of 23,616km, giving coverage in latitudes up to 75°N or S. Initial operating status has been achieved with 18 satellites and with full capability projected by 2020.

More details are in ALRS Vol 2, NP 282.

3.5.5 Horizontal datums

Spheroids are mathematical models of the earths surface from which horizontal datums are derived for specifying position on the Earth's surface. GPS uses the World Geodetic System 84 (WGS84). With the exception of much of the coast of Ireland and the Western Scotland, Admiralty charts of UK waters have now been converted to the ETRS 89 datum, as have most charts of NW Europe. This is WGS84 compatible. Many charts of Iberia are still to ED 50 but progress is being made. Chartlets in this Almanac are referenced to WGS84.

GPS fixes can be plotted directly onto charts which are referenced to WGS84, but on other charts the coordinates read from the GPS receiver must be converted to the datum of the chart in use. The datum used is always printed on the chart, normally under 'SATELLITE-DERIVED POSITIONS'. This gives the latitude and longitude corrections to be applied to satellite positions before plotting them on the chart. The difference between WGS84 and other horizontal datums varies with location and can vary from tens of metres, up to a maximum of 7 miles in the Pacific. There are 2 options:

- Set the receiver to WGS84 and manually apply the adjustment given on the chart before plotting the position. Take care to apply the adjustment accurately; there is a worked example on each chart.
- Set your receiver to the datum of the chart in use. The corrections will automatically be applied by the receiver's software. This method is convenient but not necessarily very accurate due to the random nature of the differences and software limitations.

The first option is advised by UKHO. Always check the datum of your chart. Do not assume that an adjacent chart will use the same datum. See ALRS Vol 2 for further information.

3.6 HYDROGRAPHIC SURVEYS

3.6.1 Types of Survey

In busy waterways, coastal areas and regions of undersea exploration and exploitation, multibeam and towed sidescan sonars have recorded almost continuous underwater data. These greatly improve seabed definition and plot hydrographic feature such as reefs accurately through satellite geolocation. Less frequented areas rely on older surveys and small scale charts still use passage soundings and lead line surveys. It is imperative to know the nature and quality of source data.

3.6.2 Inshore Surveys

Conducted regularly in the vicinity of ports, but less frequently elsewhere these are limited in water less than 5m in depth. Here surveys using ships and is difficult and hazardous. Along this coastal strip of very shallow water, aircraft overflights use Light Detection and Ranging (LIDAR) to compare returns from coloured lasers shone into shallow water from above. These identify shallow water features, but conditions can adversely effect results, changing the extent of charted rocks and drying ground. Traditional visual transits shown on paper charts may appear impassable on digital vector systems.

3.7 ELECTRONIC CHARTS

Electronic charts fall into two main types: raster and vector. They are produced as a cartridge-type chip for use in chartplotters, as CDs for PCs and laptops or can be downloaded. Coverage is virtually worldwide. It is advisable to ascertain what updating service is provided; for many it is a simple part-exchange of old for new for a reasonable fee.

ARCS (Admiralty Raster Chart Service) has a licence system with update discs supplied weekly, quarterly or annually.

Electronic charts are excellent value for money but are depending on a reliable power source. There needs to be a provision in the event of failureand they need to be supplemented by a suitabel battery powered device or paper charts. Ultimately it is wise to carry a selection of paper charts as an ultimate fallback.

3.7.1 Raster charts

Raster charts are produced by scanning the paper chart. They are selective but exact electronic copies of originals. Admiralty raster charts are ARCS; Maptech is the US equivalent.

Adjacent charts can be automatically linked (known as quilting) to prevent 'sailing off the edge' of the previous one.

Zooming in on a raster chart does not produce more detail, it enlarges the image. The lack of visual clarity associated indicates the need to use a larger scale chart, details of which are included in the folio and may be selected digitally.

3.7.2 Vector charts

Vector charts are produced by digitising paper charts. They are used in most dedicated chartplotters and build the information up in layers, such as seabed detail, depth contours, buoyage, and topographic features. Layers can be de-selected to increase the clarity of the plotter display.

The data seamlessly covers an area such as the Central English Channel rather than using a folio of separate charts. It provides cartographic coverage right down to harbour details. Zooming in provides large scale coverage with more detail, rather than a simple enlargement of the chart.

However, all information displayed is scale dependent. Some detail including hazards is only shown once the appropriate scale is selected. Incidents have shown the need to access detail on larger scale layers to provide advanced warning.

Vector charts are 'intelligent' and interact with their host systems which allows the user to interrogate chart symbols or be warned of impending dangers. Blue Charts, C-Map, and Navionics are all examples.

3.8 WAYPOINTS

3.8.1 Waypoint navigation

- Waypoints (WPT or ⊕) are any geographical positions, usually associated with electronic navigation, and normally expressed as a latitude and longitude. They may be used as departure or arrival points, route turning points, or any other chosen positions to aid navigation.
- In Chapter 9 the waypoint for each harbour under the Navigation sub-heading is a safe position from which to begin the approach. The WPT below the title is usually the harbour entrance or final WPT.
- Section 4 of each Area (Lights, buoys and waypoints) lists the positions of selected lights and buoys which may be used as waypoints, but see 3.8.2 below. The Lat/Long, taken from a large scale chart, is usually stated to 0'·01 of a minute.
- Discrepancies in position may result from different horizontal datums, incomplete data or survey data deemed inadequate by modern standards. Charts may also contain very small integral errors.

- 'Track' means track over the ground, not heading. For example, if required to approach a harbour (or waypoint) on a track of 090°, the waypoint should be kept on a constant bearing of 090°. Any significant deviation from that track could stand you into danger.

3.8.2 Loading waypoints

It is very easy to make mistakes when loading waypoints. The following measures may prevent errors:

- Try to work without interruption.
- While planning your route, plot intended waypoints on the chart(s) before loading them into electronic memories. This ensures that the track(s) between waypoints will not lead you into danger, across shoals, rocks or even over dry land.
- Published waypoints (including those in this Almanac) should be verified by first plotting them on the chart. It helps to label each waypoint with a number or name.
- Undetected errors in lat/long values can cause major navigational problems, usually at the most awkward moment.
- Ensure that positions have been accurately extracted from the paper chart.
- Use the correct format for entering data. Check in the equipment's handbook.
- Check that tracks and distances between waypoints, as computed by the equipment, agree with those measured directly off the paper chart.
- Check longitude for E or W, especially when near the Greenwich Meridian.
- Ask another crew member to double-check your work.

3.9 CHARTPLOTTERS

Chartplotters, linked to GPS receivers, fall into three main categories: handheld/portable, fixed and PC-based. Their greatest benefit is that they continuously display the boat's position on an electronic chart; many also give tidal data. The downside is that they may make you navigationally lazy, to the extent that a total GPS failure could leave some navigators literally lost. See 3.2 and 3.2.1.

Some plotters can be interfaced with an autopilot, engine data, instrument data and even video/live-cam coverage of remote onboard areas. They may display depth and radar overlays on the same screen as the chart. There are many available options, and choice depends on what you want and what you wish to spend. However:

- Although a chartplotter greatly assists the navigator, it is only an *aid* to navigation. It is excellent for pilotage in narrow waters, but is no substitute for a good lookout.
- Be particularly wary if the GPS is coupled with an autopilot – not recommended in confined waters.
- GPS can easily be interrupted; it may even fail completely. It is therefore essential to maintain a written log of the boat's positions, courses and speeds. From this a reliable and reasonably accurate DR/EP plot may be drawn up.

3.9.1 Handheld and portable chartplotters

Modern handheld plotters offer electronic chart displays with all the usual GPS features. Although they are capable of chart overview, they have very limited screen size. They are ideal as an independent battery powered back-up to the boat's primary GPS receiver and plotter.

Portable plotters have a screen at least 3" x 4" (75 x 103mm), about the smallest practical size to avoid excessive zooming. They are ideal for use in smaller craft or as a cockpit display and back-up in larger craft. They can be removed in harbour for security and used ashore for passage planning.

3.9.2 Fixed plotters

Fixed plotters are permanently mounted, at the chart table, on the pedestal or at the wheel on a bridge or fly-bridge, with optional repeaters elsewhere. Many plotters have split or multiple screens and may, with professional installation, allow much onboard data to be displayed. Increasingly they perform additional functions with dedicated power supplies, ruggedised build and water resistance.

3.9.3 PC based plotters

PCs and laptops are used at sea with navigational software and electronic charts linked to a GPS receiver to provide real-time navigation. Software add-ons include tidal stream data, forecasts, communication links, autopilot controls and, for the racing yachtsman, tactical features such as tacking and gybing angles, instrument displays, countdown timing and startline overview. If not fitted with an integral or USB GPS receiver, they require linking to the vessel's GPS NMEA output. Mounting, shock resistance, configuration and a reliable power supply may pose problems. Laptops have many other uses onboard and can, of course, be taken ashore for security and passage planning.

3.9.4 Tablets and mobile phones

Tablets and mobile phones are increasingly being used as handheld and portable plotters. Electronic chart packages are cheap, with the GPS receiver normally integrated in the device which is readily carried everywhere. They can, with appropriate applications, be used effectively. However, their ease of use and familiarity can lead to poor practice. All advice as to origin and accuracy of data applies. Battery life can be a problem as can reliability in the marine environment, and they should not be relied on as the sole navigational aid.

3.10 RADAR AND AIS

3.10.1 Radar

Radar (**Ra**dio **D**irection **a**nd **R**ange) is used for both collision avoidance and navigation. To realise its full potential a sound understanding of its operation and limitations is required. The manufacturer's instruction book should be read carefully; time spent practising with the set to obtain optimum performance in different conditions will build confidence. Many controls have automatic default settings, but the best results can often be obtained by manual tuning. Correct interpretation of the displayed information is fundamental to success.

Small craft radars transmit very short concentrated pulses of microwaves at a frequency of about 9500 MHz (X-band) and 3cm wavelength. Each pulse lasts less than a microsecond (pulse length) and the number of pulses transmitted per second (pulse repetition frequency or PRF) is normally between 800 and 3000. The reflected pulses are displayed on a screen.

3.10.2 Radar display modes

Typical small craft radars can be interfaced with a flux gate compass to give three heading modes:

- **North-up:** North is at the top of the display, the same as the chart. This mode helps general orientation.
- **Head-up**: Ship's current heading is at the top of the display. As the heading changes, the picture rotates; all bearings of radar returns are relative to the ship's head.
- **Course-up:** The selected course is at the top of the display. If a new course is selected, the picture rotates. As heading alters, the heading marker moves in unison. *This is arguably the best mode for use in collision avoidance.*

In *relative motion* mode the ship is usually at the centre of the display, and the land appears to move in the opposite direction to the vessel. The display can be offset so that a larger area of the screen is ahead, astern or abeam of the vessel. In *true motion* mode the vessel moves across the screen, and the land stays still. This may seem ideal, but there are disadvantages: it is not obvious if a contact is closing on a steady bearing; precise speed input is essential; and the image must be reset when close to the edge of the screen.

Some radar sets have split screens for simultaneous displays of, for example, radar picture, chartplotter and echosounder data.The ability to overlay the radar picture on the electronic chart can be invaluable when trying to distinguish charted objects from other contacts.

3.10.3 Radar as an aid to navigation

When used properly radar is a very useful aid to navigation, but it does have limitations:

- Radar cannot see behind objects or around corners; it may not detect small objects and it may not differentiate between two targets that are close together.
- Objects with flat surfaces, such as buildings or cliffs, reflect better than those with curved or sloping surfaces. A low coastline which is below the radar horizon will not be detected, but returns from more distant high ground may be received, giving a false impression of the range of the nearest land.
- Radar beams do not discriminate bearing accurately: 3 ranges will give a better fix than 3 radar bearings.
- The distance of the radar horizon is slightly greater than that of the visible horizon under average atmospheric conditions. It is given by $R = 2{\cdot}2 \times \sqrt{H^s}$ where R = Range (M) and H^s scanner height (m). Most small craft radars have a maximum range of 16 to 24M depending upon power output and scanner and target heights.

3.10.4 Radar for collision avoidance

To determine if a risk of collision exists individual contacts need to be tracked in order to, assess their courses, speeds and closest point of approach (CPA). Practice makes perfect; you should be able to track, plot and assess up to 3 contacts simultaneously. Modern digital radar plotters automate this. In relative motion mode another vessel's course and speed are not obvious from the radar display; it needs to be worked out by resolving the relative velocity triangle.

- A vessel moving in the same direction and at the same speed as you is stationary relative to your boat.
- A risk of collision exists if another contact is on a steady bearing with its range decreasing. If the bearing changes appreciably, assess whether the vessel will cross ahead or astern of you.
- To decide the correct action to take, plot the contact at regular intervals on a plotting sheet and determine its course, speed, CPA and time to CPA.
- Plotting intervals depend on the contact's rate of closure. Keep plotting until all risk of collision is over.

3.10.5 Radar in fog

When navigating in poor visibility a thorough working knowledge of Rule 19 of the Colregs is absolutely essential. Rule 19 is unusual in that:

- It differs markedly from Rules 11–18 (Conduct of vessels in sight of one another) which clearly distinguish between stand-on and give-way vessels. Rule 19 contains no such distinction; every vessel is responsible for keeping clear of others.
- It states what avoiding actions should **not** be taken, leaving you to infer what positive options are open to you. These boil down to:
- Alter to *starboard* for a vessel forward of the beam (unless you are overtaking) and alter *away* from a vessel abeam or abaft the beam.
- In practice this means that you should always alter your course to starboard **except** for a vessel on your own starboard quarter – or if you are overtaking.
- Some commercial vessels greatly exceed the safe speed stipulated by the Colregs. Small craft skippers should be aware of this when deciding what avoiding action to take in restricted visibility.

GRP yachts produce a poor radar return; an effective radar reflector is essential to enable detection by other vessels.

3.10.6 AIS

Automatic Identification System (AIS) transmits information to other ships and shore authorities. SOLAS requires it to be fitted to vessels over 300 GRT. In addition to vessel tracking AIS data is widely used to augment collision avoidance by presenting position, course, speed and identity information continuously in near real-time.

Each ship's course and speed vector is shown by a symbol on an AIS screen or overlaid on radar, chart plotter or PC. This data may also appear in a text box as heading, COG & SOG, range, CPA, position, ship's name (derived from its MMSI), and her status – under power or sail, anchored, constrained by draught, restricted in ability to manoeuvre, not under command.

Increasingly lights, buoys and other aids to navigation (AtoN) are now fitted with AIS. On Admiralty charts, these are shown by a magenta circle around the A2N and the notation 'AIS'. Information available depends on the display system fitted onboard. Not all (esp early) receivers are A2N capable.

Caveats: Many small vessels are not fitted with AIS, and some may not have it switched on; some only display 3 lines of text, not a plot; in busy areas only the strongest signals may be shown; AIS may distract a bridge watchkeeper or lookout from his visual and radar watch; GPS/electronic failures invalidate AIS and it does not yet feature in the Colregs.

AIS is not mandatory for leisure craft, but Class B transmitters/transceivers for non-SOLAS vessels are available. Receivers, either standalone, or integrated in a plotter or computer, will provide accurate and continuous display of other ships' courses and speeds (over the ground) and identity. In areas of traffic concentration Class B transmitters may be excluded from the network if there are no available time slots.

Note: AIS is to some extent dependent on user inputs, and it is not a radar despite what some advertisements may imply.

3.11 RACONS AND RAMARKS

3.11.1 Racons

A Racon is a transponder beacon often fitted to light vessels, lighthouses and important buoys. It appears on charts as a magenta circle marked *Racon*. When triggered by a vessel's radar transmission it emits a distinctive coded return, much more easily recognised than a normal radar return.

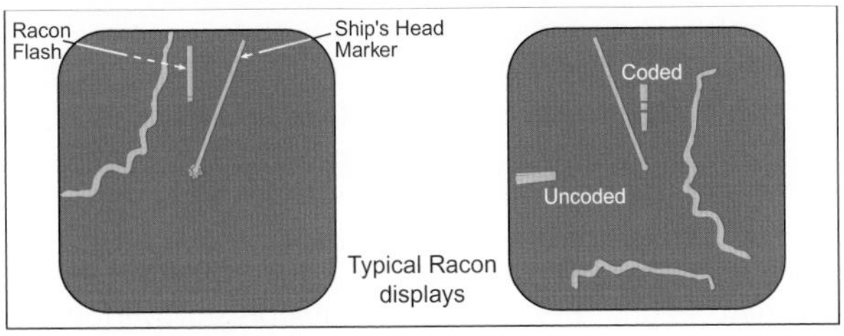

Fig 3(6) Radar beacon responses

A Racon's return or 'flash' appears on the radar display as a line or narrow sector radiating outwards from a point slightly beyond the Racon's actual position. Thus a vessel's distance from the Racon, measured from where the flash begins, is slightly more than the actual distance. This is due to the slight response delay in the Racon apparatus. The coded identification flash is usually a Morse Code letter whose dashes/dots form a bold tail; see Fig 3(6). Racons fitted to temporary 'new danger' buoys are coded 'D', have a 10M range and are 'frequency agile'.

Racon's maximum range is typically 10M but may be greater. In practice, range depends on the power and elevation of both the Racon and vessel's radar. Thus a 2–3kW radar with a scanner height of 5m might not receive a buoy-mounted Racon, height also 5m, until only 6M from it.

Abnormal radio propagation may cause a spurious flash to be seen far beyond the quoted range, appearing along the correct bearing but at random ranges. A flash can only be relied upon if it seems to be stable and is within its quoted range. At short ranges a Racon can cause unwanted interference on the radar which may be reduced by adjusting the rain clutter control on the radar receiver.

3.11.2 Racon details

Racons are shown under 'Lights, buoys and waypoints' for each Area in Chapter 9 of this Almanac. Details given are:

- The Morse identification signal.
- Approximate maximum reception range (M).
- The angular sector (if other than 360°) within which the Racon signal can be received.

Most Racons respond through 360° and scan the 3cm (X-band) frequency range. Frequency agile Racons respond automatically to both 3cm and 10cm (S-band) emissions. But the agile response is switched off for a few seconds every minute, so that the Racon response does not obscure any radar echoes which are needed.

3.11.3 Ramarks

Ramarks are similar to Racons but are not triggered by a ship's radar. Their continuous transmission forms a line of Morse characters which radiates from the centre of the radar display to its edge, and cannot therefore give range. There are very few, if any, in the area covered by this Almanac.

3.12 NAVIGATIONAL WARNINGS

Navigational warnings are promulgated for 16 NavAreas (I–XVI) worldwide. An Area co-ordinator oversees each NavArea and handles inputs from national and other authorities. The 3 types of navigational warnings are:

NavArea warnings which deal with Oceanic matters and are transmitted by SafetyNet and Navtex at scheduled times in English and other languages.

Coastal warnings, up to 250M offshore, are issued by a national authority and broadcast in English or the local language by Navtex, SafetyNet or VHF Coast radio stations. These warnings cover navaids, lights, buoys, rocks, wrecks, naval exercises, SAR operations, cable laying, piracy, etc.

Local warnings supplement the above for inshore waters and within port limits. They are issued by port, pilotage or CG authorities in English and/or the local language.

Full details for all the Areas covered by this Almanac, including broadcast times, are in Chapter 5.

3.13 HAZARDS

3.13.1 Submarines

Fishing vessels, and occasionally yachts, have been snagged or hit by submarines operating just below the surface. The risk is greatest in the western English Channel, Irish Sea, Firth of Clyde, North Channel and West Scotland, especially at night. Submarine exercise areas are shown by name and/or number in 9.8.23 and 9.9.16.

Listen to and take heed of Subfacts (see Chapter 5). If possible avoid areas of known submarine activity, but when in an exercise area the best advice is:

- Keep clear of any vessel flying Code flags 'NE2' which indicate that submarines are in the vicinity.
- Run the engine and operate the echo sounder, which may indicate your presence to the submarine.
- At night show navigation lights low down, on pulpit and stern. They are more likely to be seen by a submarine at periscope depth than a tricolour at the masthead.

3.13.2 Gunfacts

Gunfacts are warnings of intended naval gunnery and missile practice firings, and underwater explosions. They do not restrict the passage of any vessel, and the onus for safety is on the firing warship. For further details see Chapter 5.

3.13.3 Mines

In the very unlikely event of coming across a mine at sea:

- Keep well clear, and do not prod it with a boathook.
- Do not try to tow it to port. Financial rewards for such action have been discontinued.
- Inform the Coastguard on Ch 16 immediately, and make an 'All Ships' Sécurité broadcast so that ships in the vicinity are aware of the situation.

3.14 OFFSHORE ENERGY INSTALLATIONS

In addition to well-established offshore oil and gas platforms, Offshore Renewable Energy Installations (OREIs) may be encountered across the area covered by the Almanac. OREIs include wind farms, operational and under construction; wave and tidal/current generators are also being trialled inshore and offshore posing new challenges to navigation. There is no right of access to any OREI and any approach should only be made in controlled circumstances by trained personnel. The visibility of offshore wind, wave and tidal energy installations depends on the device type; some are totally submerged while others protrude slightly above the sea surface. The marking of offshore wave and tidal energy installations is based on IALA's recommendations.

3.14.1 Gas and oil rigs

Gas and oil field structures are found mainly in the North Sea, Liverpool Bay and Morecambe Bay. There are also numerous installations off the west coasts of Denmark, Germany and the Netherlands. With careful passage planning and study of the relevant charts they can usually be passed at a safe distance without undue detours. Most are protected by Safety Zones, usually 500m radius, in which it is an offence for unauthorised vessels to enter, anchor or fish. Small craft must ***stay well clear of all such installations at all times.***

3.14.2 Wind farms

Wind farms are proliferating, mostly in the shallow waters over coastal banks. Around the UK they are especially prevalent in the Thames Estuary, from the north Norfolk coast to Flamborough Head, in Liverpool Bay and Morecambe Bay. The turbines give early visual warning of where the intervening navigable channels lie, thus they may assist rather than hinder navigation. Spacing between turbines is generally at least 500m, and the lowest point of the rotor sweep is at least 22m above MHWS. The number of wind turbines worldwide rising, and they will tend to move into deeper waters (20–25m) and further offshore.

More information is in the relevant Areas of this Almanac and at: www.mcga.gov.uk; www.bwea.com/offshore; and www.thecrownestate.co.uk.

3.14.3 Effects on navaids

Trials show that wind farms have no adverse effects on GPS, magnetic compasses and VHF. Predictably, however, radar performance is affected by blind or shadow areas, and by large or spurious echoes. This will inevitably lead to increasingly confused radar pictures in areas of multiple wind farms; small craft may be 'lost' on other vessels' radars. Mariners should report any unusual effects found in or near wind farms to the MCA and/or the RYA.

3.14.4 Navigating within a wind farm

It is often impracticable to avoid wind farms without making unacceptable detours. Unlike gas and oil installations, the majority of existing wind farms have Safety Zones. During construction a 500m safety zone, which is applicable to all unauthorised craft, usually exists around the works area.

Mariners should exercise caution navigating in close proximity to wind farms being aware that underwater obstructions may exist. Particular care should be taken passing structures with vessels in attendance and in any event avoid closing within 50m of individual turbines or associated structures.

When planning a voyage, mariners should assess hazards and associated risks in proximity to wind farms and turbines:

- Spacing – wind farm turbines are usually spaced 500m or more apart depending on the size of the turbine
- Depth of water – most wind turbines operate in shallow water, possibly restricting navigable channels
- Seabed changes – wind farm structures may affect the depth of water through silting/scouring of the seabed making adjacent depth information unreliable
- Tidal streams – wind farm structures may obstruct tidal streams locally, creating eddies nearby
- Small craft – vessels involved in turbine maintenance and safety duties may be encountered or obscured within or around a wind farm
- Shore marks – in coastal areas shore marks may also be obscured by wind farm structures
- Electrical transformer stations – can be found in or adjacent to larger wind farms
- Rotor effects – can change the flow of the wind
- No anchoring is possible due to submarine cables.

3.14.5 Wave and tidal installations

There are also many devices that may have unique and very different designs. They vary from attenuators and overtopping devices on or near the surface to submerged turbines. It is important to identify the hazard and its means of attachment to the seabed. Some may be seabed mounted; others may be tethered by floating flexible moorings allowing considerable lateral movement. Great care should be taken in the vicinity of these installations, which should whenever possible be kept well clear.

A new underwater array is proposed SW of St Catherine's Pt.

3.15 NAVIGATIONAL TABLES

Table 3 (1) – Distance of horizon

Enter with height (m/ft) of eye, and extract the theoretical distance (M) of horizon. Actual distance could be reduced by abnormal refraction. Maximum height of eye is desirable; climbing onto the boom may double your height of eye.

TABLE 3(1) DISTANCE OF HORIZON

Height of eye		Horizon distance	Height of eye		Horizon distance
metres	feet	M	metres	feet	M
1	3·3	2·1	21	68·9	9·5
2	6·6	2·9	22	72·2	9·8
3	9·8	3·6	23	75·5	10·0
4	13·1	4·1	24	78·7	10·2
5	16·4	4·7	25	82·0	10·4
6	19·7	5·1	26	85·3	10·6
7	23·0	5·5	27	88·6	10·8
8	26·2	5·9	28	91·9	11·0
9	29·6	6·2	29	95·1	11·2
10	32·8	6·6	30	98·4	11·4
11	36·1	6·9	31	101·7	11·6
12	39·4	7·2	32	105·0	11·8
13	42·7	7·5	33	108·3	12·0
14	45·9	7·8	34	111·6	12·1
15	49·2	8·1	35	114·8	12·3
16	52·5	8·3	36	118·1	12·5
17	55·8	8·6	37	121·4	12·7
18	59·1	8·8	38	124·7	12·8
19	62·3	9·1	39	128·0	13·0
20	65·6	9·3	40	131·2	13·2

Table 3(2) – Distance, speed and time
Enter with time (minutes or decimals of an hour, if using a calculator) and speed (kn) to determine distance run (M). Or extract speed or time as a function of the other two variables; for example speed over a measured mile. For speeds >20kn, use multiples of lesser speeds.

TIME		SPEED IN KNOTS																		TIME	
Decimal of hr	Mins	3·0	4·0	5·0	6·0	7·0	8·0	9·0	10·0	11·0	12·0	13·0	14·0	15·0	16·0	17·0	18·0	19·0	20·0	Mins	Decimal of hr
·0167	1		0·1	0·1	0·1	0·1	0·1	0·2	0·2	0·2	0·2	0·2	0·2	0·3	0·3	0·3	0·3	0·3	0·3	1	·0167
·0333	2	0·1	0·1	0·2	0·2	0·2	0·3	0·3	0·3	0·4	0·4	0·4	0·5	0·5	0·5	0·6	0·6	0·6	0·7	2	·0333
·0500	3	0·1	0·2	0·2	0·3	0·3	0·4	0·4	0·5	0·5	0·6	0·6	0·7	0·7	0·8	0·8	0·8	0·9	1·0	3	·0500
·0667	4	0·2	0·3	0·3	0·4	0·5	0·5	0·6	0·7	0·7	0·8	0·9	0·9	1·0	1·1	1·1	1·2	1·3	1·3	4	·0667
·0833	5	0·2	0·3	0·4	0·5	0·6	0·7	0·7	0·8	0·9	1·0	1·1	1·2	1·2	1·3	1·4	1·5	1·6	1·7	5	·0833
·1000	6	0·3	0·4	0·5	0·6	0·7	0·8	0·9	1·0	1·1	1·2	1·3	1·4	1·5	1·6	1·7	1·8	1·9	2·0	6	·1000
·1167	7	0·4	0·5	0·6	0·7	0·8	0·9	1·1	1·2	1·3	1·4	1·5	1·6	1·8	1·9	2·0	2·1	2·2	2·3	7	·1167
·1333	8	0·4	0·5	0·7	0·8	0·9	1·1	1·2	1·3	1·5	1·6	1·7	1·9	2·0	2·1	2·3	2·4	2·5	2·7	8	·1333
·1500	9	0·4	0·6	0·7	0·9	1·0	1·2	1·3	1·5	1·6	1·8	1·9	2·1	2·2	2·4	2·5	2·7	2·8	3·0	9	·1500
·1667	10	0·5	0·7	0·8	1·0	1·2	1·3	1·5	1·7	1·8	2·0	2·2	2·3	2·5	2·7	2·8	3·0	3·2	3·3	10	·1667
·1833	11	0·5	0·7	0·9	1·1	1·3	1·5	1·6	1·8	2·0	2·2	2·4	2·6	2·7	2·9	3·1	3·3	3·5	3·7	11	·1833
·2000	12	0·6	0·8	1·0	1·2	1·4	1·6	1·8	2·0	2·2	2·4	2·6	2·8	3·0	3·2	3·4	3·6	3·8	4·0	12	·2000
·2167	13	0·6	0·9	1·1	1·3	1·5	1·7	2·0	2·2	2·4	2·6	2·8	3·0	3·2	3·5	3·7	3·9	4·1	4·3	13	·2167
·2333	14	0·7	0·9	1·2	1·4	1·6	1·9	2·1	2·3	2·6	2·8	3·0	3·3	3·5	3·7	4·0	4·2	4·4	4·7	14	·2333
·2500	15	0·7	1·0	1·2	1·5	1·8	2·0	2·2	2·5	2·7	3·0	3·2	3·5	3·7	4·0	4·2	4·5	4·7	5·0	15	·2500
·2667	16	0·8	1·1	1·3	1·6	1·9	2·1	2·4	2·7	2·9	3·2	3·5	3·7	4·0	4·3	4·5	4·8	5·1	5·3	16	·2667
·2833	17	0·8	1·1	1·4	1·7	2·0	2·3	2·5	2·8	3·1	3·4	3·7	4·0	4·2	4·5	4·8	5·1	5·4	5·7	17	·2833
·3000	18	0·9	1·2	1·5	1·8	2·1	2·4	2·7	3·0	3·3	3·6	3·9	4·2	4·5	4·8	5·1	5·4	5·7	6·0	18	·3000
·3167	19	1·0	1·3	1·6	1·9	2·1	2·5	2·9	3·2	3·5	3·8	4·1	4·4	4·8	5·1	5·4	5·7	6·0	6·3	19	·3167
·3333	20	1·0	1·3	1·7	2·0	2·3	2·7	3·0	3·3	3·7	4·0	4·3	4·7	5·0	5·3	5·7	6·0	6·3	6·7	20	·3333
·3500	21	1·0	1·4	1·7	2·1	2·4	2·8	3·1	3·5	3·8	4·2	4·5	4·9	5·2	5·6	5·9	6·3	6·6	7·0	21	·3500
·3667	22	1·1	1·5	1·8	2·2	2·6	2·9	3·3	3·7	4·0	4·4	4·8	5·1	5·5	5·9	6·2	6·6	7·0	7·3	22	·3667
·3833	23	1·1	1·5	1·9	2·3	2·7	3·1	3·4	3·8	4·2	4·6	5·0	5·4	5·7	6·1	6·5	6·9	7·3	7·7	23	·3833
·4000	24	1·2	1·6	2·0	2·4	2·8	3·2	3·6	4·0	4·4	4·8	5·2	5·6	6·0	6·4	6·8	7·2	7·6	8·0	24	·4000
·4167	25	1·3	1·7	2·1	2·5	2·9	3·3	3·8	4·2	4·6	5·0	5·4	5·8	6·3	6·7	7·1	7·5	7·9	8·3	25	·4167
·4333	26	1·3	1·7	2·2	2·6	3·0	3·5	3·9	4·3	4·8	5·2	5·6	6·1	6·5	6·9	7·4	7·8	8·2	8·7	26	·4333
·4500	27	1·3	1·8	2·2	2·7	3·1	3·6	4·0	4·5	4·9	5·4	5·8	6·3	6·7	7·2	7·6	8·1	8·5	9·0	27	·4500
·4667	28	1·4	1·9	2·3	2·8	3·3	3·7	4·2	4·7	5·1	5·6	6·1	6·5	7·0	7·5	7·9	8·4	8·9	9·3	28	·4667
·4833	29	1·5	1·9	2·4	2·9	3·4	3·9	4·3	4·8	5·3	5·8	6·3	6·8	7·2	7·7	8·2	8·7	9·2	9·7	29	·4833
·5000	30	1·5	2·0	2·5	3·0	3·5	4·0	4·5	5·0	5·5	6·0	6·5	7·0	7·5	8·0	8·5	9·0	9·5	10·0	30	·5000
·5167	31	1·6	2·1	2·6	3·1	3·6	4·1	4·7	5·2	5·7	6·2	6·7	7·2	7·8	8·3	8·8	9·3	9·8	10·3	31	·5167
·5333	32	1·6	2·1	2·7	3·2	3·7	4·3	4·8	5·3	5·9	6·4	6·9	7·5	8·0	8·5	9·1	9·6	10·1	10·7	32	·5333
·5500	33	1·6	2·2	2·7	3·3	3·8	4·4	4·9	5·5	6·0	6·6	7·1	7·7	8·2	8·8	9·3	9·9	10·4	11·0	33	·5500
·5667	34	1·7	2·3	2·8	3·4	4·0	4·5	5·1	5·7	6·2	6·8	7·4	7·9	8·5	9·1	9·6	10·2	10·8	11·3	34	·5667
·5833	35	1·7	2·3	2·9	3·5	4·1	4·7	5·2	5·8	6·4	7·0	7·6	8·2	8·7	9·3	9·9	10·5	11·1	11·7	35	·5833
·6000	36	1·8	2·4	3·0	3·6	4·2	4·8	5·4	6·0	6·6	7·2	7·8	8·4	9·0	9·6	10·2	10·8	11·4	12·0	36	·6000
·6117	37	1·8	2·4	3·1	3·7	4·3	4·9	5·5	6·1	6·7	7·3	8·0	8·6	9·2	9·8	10·4	11·0	11·6	12·2	37	·6117
·6333	38	1·9	2·5	3·2	3·8	4·4	5·1	5·7	6·3	7·0	7·6	8·2	8·9	9·5	10·1	10·8	11·4	12·0	12·7	38	·6333
·6500	39	1·9	2·6	3·2	3·9	4·5	5·2	5·8	6·5	7·1	7·8	8·4	9·1	9·7	10·4	11·0	11·7	12·3	13·0	39	·6500
·6667	40	2·0	2·7	3·3	4·0	4·7	5·3	6·0	6·7	7·3	8·0	8·7	9·3	10·0	10·7	11·3	12·0	12·7	13·3	40	·6667
·6833	41	2·0	2·7	3·4	4·1	4·8	5·5	6·1	6·8	7·5	8·2	8·9	9·6	10·2	10·9	11·6	12·3	13·0	13·7	41	·6833
·7000	42	2·1	2·8	3·5	4·2	4·9	5·6	6·3	7·0	7·7	8·4	9·1	9·8	10·5	11·2	11·9	12·6	13·3	14·0	42	·7000
·7167	43	2·2	2·9	3·6	4·3	5·0	5·7	6·5	7·2	7·9	8·6	9·3	10·0	10·8	11·5	12·2	12·9	13·6	14·3	43	·7167
·7333	44	2·2	2·9	3·7	4·4	5·1	5·9	6·6	7·3	8·1	8·8	9·5	10·3	11·0	11·7	12·5	13·2	13·9	14·7	44	·7333
·7500	45	2·2	3·0	3·7	4·5	5·2	6·0	6·7	7·5	8·2	9·0	9·7	10·5	11·2	12·0	12·7	13·5	14·2	15·0	45	·7500
·7667	46	2·3	3·1	3·8	4·6	5·4	6·1	6·9	7·7	8·4	9·2	10·0	10·7	11·5	12·3	13·0	13·8	14·6	15·3	46	·7667
·7833	47	2·3	3·1	3·9	4·7	5·5	6·3	7·0	7·8	8·6	9·4	10·2	11·0	11·7	12·5	13·3	14·1	14·9	15·7	47	·7833
·8000	48	2·4	3·2	4·0	4·8	5·6	6·4	7·2	8·0	8·8	9·6	10·4	11·2	12·0	12·8	13·6	14·4	15·2	16·0	48	·8000
·8167	49	2·5	3·3	4·1	4·9	5·7	6·5	7·4	8·2	9·0	9·8	10·6	11·4	12·2	13·1	13·9	14·7	15·5	16·3	49	·8167
·8333	50	2·5	3·3	4·2	5·0	5·8	6·7	7·5	8·3	9·2	10·0	10·8	11·7	12·5	13·3	14·2	15·0	15·8	16·7	50	·8333
·8500	51	2·5	3·4	4·2	5·1	5·9	6·8	7·6	8·5	9·3	10·2	11·0	11·9	12·7	13·6	14·4	15·3	16·1	17·0	51	·8500
·8667	52	2·6	3·5	4·3	5·2	6·1	6·9	7·8	8·7	9·5	10·4	11·3	12·1	13·0	13·9	14·7	15·6	16·5	17·3	52	·8667
·8833	53	2·6	3·5	4·4	5·3	6·2	7·1	7·9	8·8	9·7	10·6	11·5	12·4	13·2	14·1	15·0	15·9	16·8	17·7	53	·8833
·9000	54	2·7	3·6	4·5	5·4	6·3	7·2	8·1	9·0	9·9	10·8	11·7	12·6	13·5	14·4	15·3	16·2	17·1	18·0	54	·9000
·9167	55	2·8	3·7	4·6	5·5	6·4	7·3	8·3	9·2	10·1	11·0	11·9	12·8	13·8	14·7	15·6	16·5	17·4	18·3	55	·9167
·9333	56	2·8	3·7	4·7	5·6	6·5	7·5	8·4	9·3	10·3	11·2	12·1	13·1	14·0	14·9	15·9	16·8	17·7	18·7	56	·9333
·9500	57	2·8	3·8	4·7	5·7	6·6	7·6	8·5	9·5	10·4	11·4	12·3	13·3	14·2	15·2	16·1	17·1	18·0	19·0	57	·9500
·9667	58	2·9	3·9	4·8	5·8	6·8	7·7	8·7	9·7	10·6	11·6	12·6	13·5	14·5	15·5	16·4	17·4	18·4	19·3	58	·9667
·9833	59	2·9	3·9	4·9	5·9	6·9	7·9	8·8	9·8	10·8	11·8	12·8	13·8	14·7	15·7	16·7	17·7	18·7	19·7	59	·9833
1·0000	60	3·0	4·0	5·0	6·0	7·0	8·0	9·0	10·0	11·0	12·0	13·0	14·0	15·0	16·0	17·0	18·0	19·0	20·0	60	1·0000

Caption: TABLE 3(2) DISTANCE, SPEED AND TIME

Table 3(3) – Distance off by vertical sextant angle (VSA)
From height (m/ft) of the object read across to the VSA obtained (corrected for index error). At the top of the table read off the distance (M) of the object.

If the base of, say, a lighthouse is below the horizon, the VSA will over-read the distance. For very precise ranges, add the amount by which sea level is below MHWS to the height of the object (above MHWS) – before entering the table.

TABLE 3(3) DISTANCE OFF BY VERTICAL SEXTANT ANGLE

HEIGHT OF OBJECT		DISTANCE OF OBJECT (NAUTICAL MILES)															
ft	m	0·2	0·4	0·6	0·8	1·0	1·2	1·4	1·6	1·8	2·0	2·4	2·8	3·2	3·6	4·0	5·0
		° ′	° ′	° ′	° ′	° ′	° ′	° ′	° ′	° ′	° ′	° ′	° ′	° ′	° ′	° ′	° ′
33	**10**	1 33	0 46	0 31	0 23	0 19	0 15	0 13	0 12	0 10							
39	**12**	1 51	0 56	0 37	0 28	0 22	0 19	0 16	0 14	0 12	0 11	0 10					
46	**14**	2 10	1 05	0 43	0 32	0 26	0 22	0 19	0 16	0 14	0 13	0 11					
53	**16**	2 28	1 14	0 49	0 37	0 30	0 25	0 21	0 19	0 16	0 15	0 12	0 11				
59	**18**	2 47	1 24	0 56	0 42	0 33	0 28	0 24	0 21	0 19	0 17	0 14	0 12	0 10			
66	**20**	3 05	1 33	1 02	0 46	0 37	0 31	0 27	0 23	0 21	0 19	0 15	0 13	0 12	0 10		
72	**22**	3 24	1 42	1 08	0 51	0 41	0 34	0 29	0 26	0 23	0 20	0 17	0 15	0 13	0 11	0 10	
79	**24**	3 42	1 51	1 14	0 56	0 45	0 37	0 32	0 28	0 25	0 22	0 19	0 16	0 14	0 12	0 11	
85	**26**	4 01	2 01	1 20	1 00	0 48	0 40	0 34	0 30	0 27	0 24	0 20	0 17	0 15	0 13	0 12	
92	**28**	4 19	2 10	1 27	1 05	0 52	0 43	0 37	0 32	0 29	0 26	0 22	0 19	0 16	0 14	0 13	0 10
98	**30**	4 38	2 19	1 33	1 10	0 56	0 46	0 40	0 35	0 31	0 28	0 23	0 20	0 17	0 15	0 14	0 11
105	**32**	4 56	2 28	1 39	1 14	0 59	0 49	0 42	0 37	0 33	0 30	0 25	0 21	0 19	0 16	0 15	0 12
112	**34**	5 15	2 38	1 45	1 19	1 03	0 53	0 45	0 39	0 35	0 31	0 26	0 23	0 20	0 17	0 16	0 13
118	**36**	5 33	2 47	1 51	1 24	1 07	0 56	0 48	0 42	0 37	0 33	0 28	0 24	0 21	0 19	0 17	0 13
125	**38**	5 41	2 56	1 58	1 28	1 11	0 59	0 50	0 44	0 39	0 35	0 29	0 25	0 22	0 20	0 18	0 14
131	**40**	6 10	3 05	2 04	1 33	1 14	1 02	0 53	0 46	0 41	0 37	0 31	0 27	0 23	0 21	0 19	0 15
138	**42**	6 28	3 15	2 10	1 37	1 18	1 05	0 56	0 49	0 43	0 40	0 32	0 28	0 24	0 22	0 19	0 16
144	**44**	6 46	3 24	2 16	1 42	1 22	1 08	0 58	0 51	0 45	0 41	0 34	0 29	0 25	0 23	0 20	0 16
151	**46**	7 05	3 33	2 22	1 47	1 25	1 11	1 01	0 53	0 47	0 43	0 36	0 30	0 27	0 24	0 21	0 17
157	**48**	7 23	3 42	2 28	1 51	1 29	1 14	1 04	0 56	0 49	0 45	0 37	0 32	0 28	0 25	0 22	0 18
164	**50**	7 41	3 52	2 35	1 56	1 33	1 17	1 06	0 58	0 52	0 46	0 39	0 33	0 29	0 26	0 23	0 19
171	**52**	7 59	4 01	2 41	2 01	1 36	1 20	1 09	1 00	0 54	0 48	0 40	0 34	0 30	0 27	0 24	0 19
177	**54**	8 18	4 10	2 47	2 05	1 40	1 23	1 12	1 03	0 56	0 50	0 42	0 36	0 31	0 28	0 25	0 20
184	**56**	8 36	4 19	2 53	2 10	1 44	1 27	1 14	1 05	0 58	0 52	0 43	0 37	0 32	0 29	0 26	0 21
190	**58**	8 54	4 29	2 59	2 15	1 48	1 30	1 17	1 07	1 00	0 54	0 45	0 38	0 34	0 30	0 27	0 21
197	**60**	9 12	4 38	3 05	2 19	1 51	1 33	1 20	1 10	1 02	0 56	0 46	0 40	0 35	0 31	0 28	0 22
203	**62**	9 30	4 47	3 12	2 24	1 55	1 36	1 22	1 12	1 04	0 58	0 48	0 41	0 36	0 32	0 29	0 23
210	**64**	9 48	4 56	3 18	2 28	1 59	1 39	1 25	1 14	1 06	0 59	0 49	0 42	0 37	0 33	0 30	0 24
217	**66**	10 06	5 05	3 24	2 33	2 02	1 42	1 27	1 17	1 08	1 01	0 51	0 44	0 38	0 34	0 31	0 25
223	**68**	10 24	5 15	3 30	2 38	2 06	1 45	1 30	1 19	1 10	1 03	0 53	0 45	0 39	0 35	0 32	0 25
230	**70**	10 42	5 24	3 36	2 42	2 09	1 48	1 33	1 21	1 12	1 05	0 54	0 46	0 41	0 36	0 32	0 26
236	**72**	11 00	5 33	3 42	2 47	2 14	1 51	1 35	1 24	1 14	1 07	0 56	0 48	0 42	0 37	0 33	0 27
246	**75**	11 27	5 47	3 52	2 54	2 19	1 56	1 39	1 27	1 17	1 10	0 58	0 50	0 44	0 39	0 35	0 28
256	**78**	11 54	6 01	4 01	3 01	2 24	2 01	1 43	1 30	1 20	1 12	1 00	0 52	0 45	0 40	0 36	0 29
266	**81**	12 20	6 14	4 10	3 08	2 30	2 05	1 47	1 34	1 23	1 15	1 03	0 54	0 47	0 42	0 38	0 30
276	**84**	12 47	6 28	4 19	3 15	2 36	2 10	1 51	1 37	1 27	1 18	1 05	0 56	0 49	0 43	0 39	0 31
289	**88**	13 22	6 46	4 32	3 24	2 43	2 16	1 57	1 42	1 31	1 22	1 08	0 58	0 51	0 45	0 41	0 33
302	**92**	13 57	7 05	4 44	3 33	2 51	2 22	2 02	1 47	1 35	1 25	1 11	1 01	0 53	0 47	0 43	0 34
315	**96**	14 32	7 23	4 56	3 42	2 58	2 28	2 07	1 51	1 39	1 29	1 14	1 04	0 56	0 49	0 45	0 36
328	**100**	15 07	7 41	5 09	3 52	3 05	2 35	2 13	1 56	1 43	1 33	1 17	1 06	0 58	0 52	0 46	0 37
341	**104**	15 41	7 59	5 21	4 01	3 13	2 41	2 18	2 01	1 47	1 36	1 20	1 09	1 00	0 54	0 48	0 39
358	**109**	16 24	8 22	5 36	4 12	3 22	2 48	2 24	2 06	1 52	1 41	1 24	1 12	1 03	0 56	0 51	0 40
374	**114**	17 06	8 45	5 51	4 24	3 31	2 56	2 31	2 12	1 58	1 46	1 28	1 16	1 06	0 59	0 53	0 42
394	**120**	17 57	9 12	6 10	4 38	3 42	3 05	2 39	2 19	2 04	1 51	1 33	1 20	1 10	1 02	0 56	0 45
427	**130**	19 20	9 57	6 40	5 01	4 01	3 21	2 52	2 31	2 14	2 01	1 41	1 26	1 15	1 07	1 00	0 48
459	**140**	20 42	10 42	7 11	5 24	4 19	3 36	3 05	2 42	2 24	2 10	1 48	1 33	1 21	1 12	1 05	0 52
492	**150**	22 03	11 27	7 41	5 47	4 38	3 52	3 19	2 54	2 35	2 19	1 56	1 39	1 27	1 17	1 10	0 56
574	**175**	25 17	13 17	8 57	6 44	5 24	4 30	3 52	3 23	3 00	2 42	2 15	1 56	1 41	1 30	1 21	1 05
656	**200**	28 22	15 07	10 12	7 41	6 10	5 09	4 25	3 52	3 26	3 05	2 35	2 13	1 56	1 43	1 33	1 14
738	**225**		16 54	11 27	8 38	6 56	5 47	4 58	4 21	3 52	3 29	2 54	2 29	2 10	1 56	1 44	1 24
820	**250**		18 39	12 41	9 35	7 41	6 25	5 30	4 49	4 17	3 52	3 13	2 46	2 25	2 09	1 56	1 33
902	**275**		20 22	13 54	10 31	8 27	7 03	6 03	5 18	4 43	4 15	3 32	3 02	2 39	2 22	2 08	1 42
984	**300**		22 03	15 07	11 27	9 12	7 41	6 36	5 47	5 09	4 38	3 52	3 19	2 54	2 35	2 19	1 51
1148	**350**			17 29	13 17	10 42	8 57	7 41	6 44	6 00	5 24	4 30	3 52	3 23	3 00	2 42	2 10
1312	**400**			19 48	15 07	12 11	10 12	8 46	7 41	6 51	6 10	5 09	4 25	3 52	3 26	3 05	2 28

Tables 3(4) and 3(5) – Checking a compass for accuracy
The accuracy of a boat's magnetic compass can be checked against the true bearing of the sun at sunrise or sunset. The sun's declination and the boat's approximate latitude are all that are needed; no sextant or sight reduction tables.

Since bearings probably cannot be taken with the steering compass, steer the boat directly towards or away from the rising or setting sun, aligning it with the mast.

Due to refraction, which is about 34' when observing bodies on the horizon, the sun's bearing should be taken when its lower limb is just over half a diameter above the horizon.

Table 3(4) – Sun's declination
Enter with the appropriate date band and read across to the centre column.

Extract and record declination (bold type), noting whether it is North or South.

Table 3(5) – True bearing of sun at sunrise and sunset
Enter with the approximate latitude and declination, obtained from Table 3(4). Extract the tabulated bearing.

The True bearing is measured from North if declination is North, or from South if declination is South; towards the East if rising or towards the West if setting.

For example on 26 Aug, declination 10°N and latitude 45°N: the tabulated bearing is 75·8°, say 76°. If the sun is rising the True bearing will be N76°E, ie 076°T.

Apply local magnetic variation to 076°T and compare the result with the compass reading to determine deviation on the course steered.

3 examples of different Dec N/S and whether rising/setting:

Lat	Dec	SR/SS	Tab brg	True bearing
45°	10°N	Setting	76°	N76°W = 284°
45°	10°S	Rising	76°	S76°E = 104°
45°	10°S	Setting	76°	S76°W = 256°

Table 3(4) Sun's declination for 2018

SOUTH		DECLINATION	NORTH	
Dec 06 - Jan 05		**23°**	Jun 05 - Jul 07	
Jan 06 - Jan 12	Nov 29 - Dec 05	**22°**	May 29 - Jun 04	Jul 08 - Jul 14
Jan 13 - Jan 17	Nov 24 - Nov 28	**21°**	May 23 - May 28	Jul 15 - Jul 20
Jan 18 - Jan 22	Nov 19 - Nov 23	**20°**	May 18 - May 22	Jul 21 - Jul 25
Jan 23 - Jan 26	Nov 15 - Nov 18	**19°**	May 14 - May 17	Jul 26 - Jul 29
Jan 27 - Jan 30	Nov 12 - Nov 14	**18°**	May 10 - May 13	Jul 30 - Aug 02
Jan 31 - Feb 02	Nov 08 - Nov 11	**17°**	May 06 - May 09	Aug 03 - Aug 06
Feb 03 - Feb 06	Nov 05 - Nov 07	**16°**	May 03 - May 05	Aug 07 - Aug 09
Feb 07 - Feb 09	Nov 02 - Nov 04	**15°**	Apr 29 - May 02	Aug 10 - Aug 13
Feb 10 - Feb 12	Oct 29 - Nov 01	**14°**	Apr 26 - Apr 28	Aug 14 - Aug 16
Feb 13 - Feb 15	Oct 26 - Oct 28	**13°**	Apr 23 - Apr 25	Aug 17 - Aug 19
Feb 16 - Feb 18	Oct 24 - Oct 25	**12°**	Apr 20 - Apr 22	Aug 20 - Aug 22
Feb 19 - Feb 20	Oct 21 - Oct 23	**11°**	Apr 17 - Apr 19	Aug 23 - Aug 25
Feb 21 - Feb 23	Oct 18 - Oct 20	**10°**	Apr 15 - Apr 16	Aug 26 - Aug 28
Feb 24 - Feb 26	Oct 15 - Oct 17	**9°**	Apr 12 - Apr 14	Aug 29 - Aug 31
Feb 27 - Feb 28	Oct 13 - Oct 14	**8°**	Apr 09 - Apr 11	Sep 01 - Sep 02
Mar 01 - Mar 03	Oct 10 - Oct 12	**7°**	Apr 06 - Apr 08	Sep 03 - Sep 05
Mar 04 - Mar 06	Oct 07 - Oct 09	**6°**	Apr 04 - Apr 05	Sep 06 - Sep 08
Mar 07 - Mar 08	Oct 05 - Oct 06	**5°**	Apr 01 - Apr 03	Sep 09 - Sep 10
Mar 09 - Mar 11	Oct 02 - Oct 04	**4°**	Mar 30 - Mar 31	Sep 11 - Sep 13
Mar 12 - Mar 13	Sep 30 - Oct 01	**3°**	Mar 27 - Mar 29	Sep 14 - Sep 16
Mar 14 - Mar 16	Sep 27 - Sep 29	**2°**	Mar 24 - Mar 26	Sep 17 - Sep 18
Mar 17 - Mar 18	Sep 24 - Sep 26	**1°**	Mar 22 - Mar 23	Sep 19 - Sep 21
Mar 19 - Mar 21	Sep 22 - Sep 23	**0°**	Mar 19 - Mar 21	Sep 22 - Sep 23

TABLE 3(5) TRUE BEARING OF SUN AT SUNRISE AND SUNSET

LAT	DECLINATION 0°	1°	2°	3°	4°	5°	6°	7°	8°	9°	10°	11°	LAT
	°	°	°	°	°	°	°	°	°	°	°	°	
30°	90	88·8	87·7	86·5	85·4	84·2	83·1	81·9	80·7	79·6	78·4	77·3	30°
31°	90	88·8	87·7	86·5	85·3	84·2	83·0	81·9	80·6	79·5	78·3	77·1	31°
32°	90	88·8	87·6	86·5	85·3	84·1	82·9	81·7	80·5	79·4	78·2	77·0	32°
33°	90	88·8	87·6	86·4	85·2	84·0	82·8	81·6	80·4	79·2	78·0	76·8	33°
34°	90	88·8	87·6	86·4	85·2	84·0	82·7	81·5	80·3	79·1	77·9	76·7	34°
35°	90	88·8	87·5	86·3	85·1	83·9	82·7	81·4	80·2	79·0	77·8	76·5	35°
36°	90	88·8	87·5	86·3	85·0	83·8	82·6	81·3	80·1	78·8	77·6	76·3	36°
37°	90	88·7	87·5	86·2	85·0	83·7	82·5	81·2	80·0	78·7	77·4	76·2	37°
38°	90	88·7	87·5	86·2	84·9	83·6	82·4	81·1	79·8	78·5	77·3	76·0	38°
39°	90	88·7	87·4	86·1	84·8	83·6	82·3	81·0	79·7	78·4	77·1	75·8	39°
40°	90	88·7	87·4	86·1	84·8	83·5	82·1	80·8	79·5	78·2	76·9	75·6	40°
41°	90	88·7	87·3	86·0	84·7	83·4	82·0	80·7	79·4	78·0	76·7	75·3	41°
42°	90	88·6	87·3	86·0	84·6	83·3	81·9	80·6	79·2	77·8	76·5	75·1	42°
43°	90	88·6	87·3	85·9	84·5	83·1	81·8	80·4	79·0	77·6	76·3	74·9	43°
44°	90	88·6	87·2	85·8	84·4	83·0	81·6	80·2	78·8	77·4	76·0	74·6	44°
45°	90	88·6	87·2	85·7	84·3	82·9	81·5	80·1	78·6	77·2	75·8	74·3	45°
46°	90	88·6	87·1	85·7	84·2	82·8	81·3	79·9	78·4	77·0	75·5	74·0	46°
47°	90	88·5	87·1	85·6	84·1	82·6	81·2	79·7	78·2	76·7	75·2	73·7	47°
48°	90	88·5	87·0	85·5	84·0	82·5	81·0	79·5	78·0	76·5	75·0	73·4	48°
49°	90	88·5	86·9	85·4	83·9	82·4	80·8	79·3	77·7	76·2	74·6	73·1	49°
50°	90	88·4	86·9	85·3	83·8	82·2	80·6	79·1	77·5	75·9	74·3	72·7	50°
51°	90	88·4	86·8	85·2	83·6	82·0	80·4	78·8	77·2	75·6	74·0	72·4	51°
52°	90	88·4	86·7	85·1	83·5	81·9	80·2	78·6	76·9	75·3	73·6	71·9	52°
53°	90	88·3	86·7	85·0	83·3	81·7	80·0	78·3	76·6	74·9	73·2	71·5	53°
54°	90	88·3	86·6	84·9	83·2	81·5	79·8	78·0	76·3	74·6	72·8	71·1	54°
55°	90	88·2	86·5	84·8	83·0	81·3	79·5	77·7	76·0	74·2	72·4	70·6	55°
56°	90	88·2	86·4	84·6	82·8	81·0	79·2	77·4	75·6	73·8	71·9	70·0	56°
57°	90	88·2	86·3	84·5	82·6	80·8	78·9	77·0	75·2	73·3	71·4	69·5	57°
58°	90	88·1	86·2	84·3	82·4	80·5	78·6	76·7	74·8	72·8	70·9	68·9	58°
59°	90	88·1	86·1	84·2	82·2	80·3	78·3	76·3	74·3	72·3	70·3	68·3	59°
60°	90	88·0	86·0	84·0	82·0	80·0	77·9	75·9	73·8	71·8	69·7	67·6	60°

LAT	DECLINATION 12°	13°	14°	15°	16°	17°	18°	19°	20°	21°	22°	23°	LAT
	°	°	°	°	°	°	°	°	°	°	°	°	
30°	76·1	74·9	73·8	72·6	71·4	70·3	69·1	67·9	66·7	65·5	64·4	63·2	30°
31°	76·0	74·8	73·6	72·4	71·2	70·0	68·9	67·7	66·5	65·3	64·1	62·9	31°
32°	75·8	74·6	73·4	72·2	71·0	69·8	68·6	67·4	66·2	65·0	63·8	62·6	32°
33°	75·6	74·4	73·2	72·1	70·8	69·6	68·4	67·1	65·9	64·7	63·5	62·2	33°
34°	75·5	74·2	73·0	71·8	70·6	69·3	68·1	66·9	65·6	64·4	63·1	61·9	34°
35°	75·3	74·1	72·8	71·6	70·3	69·1	67·8	66·6	65·3	64·1	62·8	61·5	35°
36°	75·1	73·8	72·6	71·3	70·1	68·8	67·5	66·3	65·0	63·7	62·4	61·1	36°
37°	74·9	73·6	72·4	71·1	69·8	68·5	67·2	65·9	64·6	63·3	62·0	60·7	37°
38°	74·7	73·4	72·0	70·8	69·5	68·2	66·9	65·6	64·3	62·9	61·6	60·3	38°
39°	74·5	73·2	71·9	70·5	69·2	67·9	66·6	65·2	63·9	62·5	61·2	59·8	39°
40°	74·2	72·9	71·6	70·2	68·9	67·6	66·2	64·8	63·5	62·1	60·7	59·3	40°
41°	74·0	72·7	71·3	69·9	68·6	67·2	65·8	64·4	63·0	61·6	60·2	58·8	41°
42°	73·7	72·4	71·0	69·6	68·2	66·8	65·4	64·0	62·6	61·2	59·7	58·3	42°
43°	73·5	72·1	70·7	69·3	67·9	66·4	65·0	63·6	62·1	60·7	59·2	57·7	43°
44°	73·2	71·8	70·3	68·9	67·5	66·0	64·6	63·1	61·6	60·1	58·6	57·1	44°
45°	72·9	71·4	70·0	68·5	67·0	65·6	64·1	62·6	61·1	59·5	58·0	56·4	45°
46°	72·6	71·1	69·6	68·1	66·6	65·1	63·6	62·0	60·5	58·9	57·4	55·8	46°
47°	72·2	70·7	69·2	67·7	66·2	64·6	63·1	61·5	59·9	58·3	56·7	55·0	47°
48°	71·9	70·3	68·8	67·2	65·7	64·1	62·5	60·9	59·3	57·6	55·9	54·3	48°
49°	71·5	69·9	68·4	66·8	65·1	63·5	61·9	60·2	58·6	56·9	55·2	53·4	49°
50°	71·1	69·5	67·9	66·2	64·6	62·9	61·3	59·6	57·8	56·1	54·3	52·6	50°
51°	70·7	69·1	67·4	65·7	64·0	62·3	60·6	58·8	57·1	55·3	53·5	51·6	51°
52°	70·3	68·6	66·9	65·1	63·4	61·6	59·9	58·1	56·3	54·4	52·5	50·6	52°
53°	69·8	68·1	66·3	64·5	62·7	60·9	59·1	57·3	55·4	53·5	51·5	49·5	53°
54°	69·3	67·5	65·7	63·9	62·0	60·2	58·3	56·4	54·4	52·4	50·4	48·3	54°
55°	68·7	66·9	65·1	63·2	61·3	59·4	57·4	55·4	53·4	51·3	49·2	47·1	55°
56°	68·2	66·3	64·4	62·4	60·5	58·5	56·5	54·4	52·3	50·1	47·9	45·7	56°
57°	67·6	65·6	63·6	61·6	59·6	57·5	55·4	53·3	51·1	48·9	46·5	44·2	57°
58°	66·9	64·9	62·8	60·8	58·7	56·5	54·3	52·1	49·8	47·4	45·0	42·5	58°
59°	66·2	64·1	62·0	59·8	57·6	55·4	53·1	50·8	48·4	45·9	43·3	40·7	59°
60°	65·4	63·3	61·1	58·8	56·5	54·2	51·8	49·4	46·8	44·2	41·5	38·6	60°

Table 3(6) – Distance off lights when rising or dipping
Enter with height of eye and height of light to extract the range (M) of a light when it first rises above, or finally dips below, the horizon. This range, with a bearing, gives a fix.

TABLE 3(6) LIGHTS – DISTANCE OFF (M) WHEN RISING OR DIPPING

HEIGHT OF LIGHT metres	HEIGHT OF LIGHT feet	HEIGHT OF EYE metres 1 / feet 3	2 / 7	3 / 10	4 / 13	5 / 16	6 / 20	7 / 23	8 / 26	9 / 30	10 / 33
10	33	8·7	9·5	10·2	10·8	11·3	11·7	12·1	12·5	12·8	13·2
12	39	9·3	10·1	10·8	11·4	11·9	12·3	12·7	13·1	13·4	13·8
14	46	9·9	10·7	11·4	12·0	12·5	12·9	13·3	13·7	14·0	14·4
16	53	10·4	11·2	11·9	12·5	13·0	13·4	13·8	14·2	14·5	14·9
18	59	10·9	11·7	12·4	13·0	13·5	13·9	14·3	14·7	15·0	15·4
20	66	11·4	12·2	12·9	13·5	14·0	14·4	14·8	15·2	15·5	15·9
22	72	11·9	12·7	13·4	14·0	14·5	14·9	15·3	15·7	16·0	16·4
24	79	12·3	13·1	13·8	14·4	14·9	15·3	15·7	16·1	16·4	17·0
26	85	12·7	13·5	14·2	14·8	15·3	15·7	16·1	16·5	16·8	17·2
28	92	13·1	13·9	14·6	15·2	15·7	16·1	16·5	16·9	17·2	17·6
30	98	13·5	14·3	15·0	15·6	16·1	16·5	16·9	17·3	17·6	18·0
32	105	13·9	14·7	15·4	16·0	16·5	16·9	17·3	17·7	18·0	18·4
34	112	14·2	15·0	15·7	16·3	16·8	17·2	17·6	18·0	18·3	18·7
36	118	14·6	15·4	16·1	16·7	17·2	17·6	18·0	18·4	18·7	19·1
38	125	14·9	15·7	16·4	17·0	17·5	17·9	18·3	18·7	19·0	19·4
40	131	15·3	16·1	16·8	17·4	17·9	18·3	18·7	19·1	19·4	19·8
42	138	15·6	16·4	17·1	17·7	18·2	18·6	19·0	19·4	19·7	20·1
44	144	15·9	16·7	17·4	18·0	18·5	18·9	19·3	19·7	20·0	20·4
46	151	16·2	17·0	17·7	18·3	18·8	19·2	19·6	20·0	20·3	20·7
48	157	16·5	17·3	18·0	18·6	19·1	19·5	19·9	20·3	20·6	21·0
50	164	16·8	17·6	18·3	18·9	19·4	19·8	20·2	20·6	20·9	21·3
55	180	17·5	18·3	19·0	19·6	20·1	20·5	20·9	21·3	21·6	22·0
60	197	18·2	19·0	19·7	20·3	20·8	21·2	21·6	22·0	22·3	22·7
65	213	18·9	19·7	20·4	21·0	21·5	21·9	22·3	22·7	23·0	23·4
70	230	19·5	20·3	21·0	21·6	22·1	22·5	22·9	23·2	23·6	24·0
80	262	20·7	21·5	22·2	22·8	23·3	23·7	24·1	24·5	24·8	25·2

3.16 SUNRISE/SET TIMES 2018

Showing times of Sunrise (SR) and Sunset (SS) for every 3rd day, the table below is much simpler than in earlier editions.

This does not imply any lack of accuracy since the times of Sunrise and Sunset never change by more than 8 minutes (and often by only 1–3 minutes) between the given dates.

The tables are based on Longitude 0°, so longitude corrections are required: add 4 minutes of time for every degree West of Greenwich; subtract if East.

Latitudes 56°N, 48°N and 40°N are chosen so as to split into 3 equal bands the 24° span of latitude from Shetland 60°N to Gibraltar 36°N. Be sure to enter the correct table.

Times are in UT – add 1 hour in non-shaded months to convert to BST

LATITUDE 56°N

	JANUARY Rise	JANUARY Set	FEBRUARY Rise	FEBRUARY Set	MARCH Rise	MARCH Set	APRIL Rise	APRIL Set	MAY Rise	MAY Set	JUNE Rise	JUNE Set
1	08 31	15 36	07 55	16 33	06 52	17 34	05 31	18 38	04 16	19 39	03 22	20 34
4	08 30	15 40	07 49	16 39	06 44	17 40	05 23	18 44	04 10	19 45	03 19	20 38
7	08 28	15 44	07 43	16 46	06 36	17 47	05 15	18 50	04 03	19 51	03 17	20 42
10	08 26	15 49	07 37	16 53	06 29	17 53	05 08	18 56	03 57	19 57	03 15	20 44
13	08 23	15 54	07 30	16 59	06 21	17 59	05 00	19 02	03 51	20 03	03 14	20 47
16	08 20	16 00	07 23	17 06	06 13	18 05	04 52	19 09	03 46	20 08	03 13	20 49
19	08 16	16 06	07 16	17 12	06 05	18 11	04 45	19 15	03 40	20 14	03 13	20 50
22	08 12	16 12	07 09	17 19	05 57	18 18	04 38	19 21	03 35	20 19	03 13	20 51
25	08 07	16 18	07 02	17 25	05 49	18 24	04 30	19 27	03 31	20 24	03 14	20 51
28	08 02	16 24	06 54	17 32	05 41	18 30	04 23	19 33	03 27	20 29	03 16	20 50
31	07 57	16 31			05 34	18 36			03 23	20 33		

	JULY Rise	JULY Set	AUGUST Rise	AUGUST Set	SEPTEMBER Rise	SEPTEMBER Set	OCTOBER Rise	OCTOBER Set	NOVEMBER Rise	NOVEMBER Set	DECEMBER Rise	DECEMBER Set
1	03 18	20 49	04 04	20 08	05 04	18 55	06 03	17 36	07 07	16 20	08 07	15 31
4	03 21	20 47	04 09	20 02	05 10	18 47	06 09	17 28	07 13	16 13	08 11	15 29
7	03 24	20 45	04 15	19 55	05 16	18 39	06 15	17 20	07 19	16 07	08 16	15 27
10	03 28	20 42	04 21	19 48	05 22	18 31	06 21	17 12	07 26	16 01	08 20	15 26
13	03 32	20 39	04 27	19 42	05 27	18 23	06 27	17 05	07 32	15 56	08 23	15 25
16	03 36	20 35	04 33	19 35	05 33	18 15	06 33	16 57	07 38	15 51	08 26	15 25
19	03 41	20 31	04 38	19 27	05 39	18 07	06 39	16 50	07 44	15 46	08 28	15 26
22	03 46	20 26	04 44	19 20	05 45	17 59	06 45	16 42	07 50	15 41	08 30	15 27
25	03 51	20 21	04 50	19 13	05 51	17 51	06 52	16 35	07 56	15 37	08 31	15 29
28	03 56	20 15	04 56	19 05	05 57	17 43	06 58	16 29	08 01	15 34	08 32	15 32
31	04 02	20 10	05 02	18 57			07 05	16 22			08 31	15 35

Times are in UT – add 1 hour in non-shaded months to convert to BST

LATITUDE 48°N

	Rise	Set	Rise	Set	Rise	Set	Rise	Set	Rise	Set	Rise	Set
	JANUARY		FEBRUARY		MARCH		APRIL		MAY		JUNE	
1	07 50	16 17	07 28	17 00	06 41	17 44	05 39	18 30	04 42	19 13	04 05	19 51
4	07 50	16 21	07 24	17 05	06 35	17 49	05 33	18 34	04 37	19 17	04 03	19 54
7	07 49	16 24	07 19	17 09	06 30	17 53	05 27	18 39	04 33	19 21	04 02	19 56
10	07 48	16 28	07 15	17 14	06 24	17 58	05 21	18 43	04 28	19 25	04 01	19 58
13	07 46	16 31	07 10	17 19	06 18	18 02	05 15	18 47	04 24	19 29	04 00	20 00
16	07 44	16 36	07 05	17 24	06 11	18 07	05 09	18 51	04 20	19 33	04 00	20 02
19	07 42	16 40	07 00	17 29	06 05	18 11	05 03	18 56	04 17	19 37	04 00	20 03
22	07 39	16 44	06 54	17 33	05 59	18 15	04 58	19 00	04 13	19 41	04 01	20 03
25	07 36	16 49	06 49	17 38	05 53	18 20	04 52	19 04	04 10	19 44	04 02	20 04
28	07 33	16 54	06 43	17 43	05 47	18 24	04 47	19 09	04 08	19 47	04 03	20 04
31	07 29	16 58			05 41	18 28			04 06	19 50		

	JULY		AUGUST		SEPTEMBER		OCTOBER		NOVEMBER		DECEMBER	
1	04 04	20 03	04 36	19 36	05 18	18 41	05 59	17 40	06 45	16 42	07 28	16 09
4	04 06	20 02	04 40	19 31	05 22	18 35	06 03	17 33	06 49	16 37	07 32	16 08
7	04 09	20 01	04 44	19 27	05 26	18 29	06 07	17 27	06 54	16 33	07 35	16 07
10	04 11	19 59	04 48	19 22	05 30	18 23	06 12	17 21	06 58	16 29	07 39	16 07
13	04 14	19 57	04 52	19 17	05 34	18 17	06 16	17 16	07 03	16 25	07 41	16 07
16	04 17	19 55	04 56	19 12	05 38	18 11	06 20	17 10	07 08	16 21	07 44	16 07
19	04 20	19 52	05 00	19 06	05 42	18 04	06 25	17 04	07 12	16 18	07 46	16 08
22	04 24	19 49	05 04	19 01	05 46	17 58	06 29	16 59	07 16	16 15	07 47	16 10
25	04 27	19 45	05 08	18 55	05 51	17 52	06 34	16 53	07 21	16 13	07 49	16 11
28	04 31	19 41	05 12	18 49	05 55	17 46	06 38	16 48	07 25	16 11	07 49	16 14
31	04 35	19 37	05 16	18 43			06 43	16 43			07 50	16 16

LATITUDE 40°N

	Rise	Set	Rise	Set	Rise	Set	Rise	Set	Rise	Set	Rise	Set
	JANUARY		FEBRUARY		MARCH		APRIL		MAY		JUNE	
1	07 22	16 45	07 09	17 19	06 34	17 52	05 44	18 24	05 00	18 55	04 33	19 23
4	07 22	16 48	07 06	17 23	06 29	17 55	05 40	18 27	04 57	18 58	04 32	19 25
7	07 22	16 51	07 03	17 26	06 24	17 58	05 35	18 30	04 53	19 01	04 31	19 27
10	07 22	16 54	06 59	17 30	06 20	18 01	05 30	18 33	04 50	19 03	04 31	19 28
13	07 21	16 57	06 56	17 33	06 15	18 05	05 25	18 36	04 47	19 06	04 31	19 30
16	07 20	17 00	06 52	17 37	06 10	18 08	05 21	18 39	04 44	19 09	04 31	19 31
19	07 18	17 04	06 48	17 40	06 05	18 11	05 17	18 42	04 41	19 12	04 31	19 32
22	07 16	17 07	06 44	17 44	06 01	18 14	05 12	18 45	04 39	19 15	04 32	19 32
25	07 14	17 11	06 39	17 47	05 56	18 17	05 08	18 48	04 37	19 17	04 32	19 33
28	07 12	17 14	06 35	17 51	05 51	18 20	05 04	18 51	04 35	19 20	04 33	19 33
31	07 10	17 18			05 46	18 23			04 34	19 22		

	JULY		AUGUST		SEPTEMBER		OCTOBER		NOVEMBER		DECEMBER	
1	04 35	19 33	04 58	19 14	05 28	18 32	05 56	17 43	06 29	16 58	07 02	16 35
4	04 36	19 32	05 01	19 11	05 30	18 27	05 59	17 38	06 32	16 54	07 05	16 35
7	04 38	19 31	05 04	19 07	05 33	18 22	06 02	17 33	06 36	16 51	07 08	16 35
10	04 40	19 30	05 07	19 03	05 36	18 17	06 05	17 28	06 39	16 48	07 11	16 35
13	04 42	19 29	05 10	19 00	05 39	18 12	06 08	17 24	06 43	16 45	07 13	16 35
16	04 44	19 27	05 12	18 56	05 42	18 07	06 11	17 19	06 46	16 43	07 15	16 36
19	04 47	19 25	05 15	18 51	05 45	18 02	06 14	17 15	06 49	16 41	07 17	16 37
22	04 49	19 23	05 18	18 47	05 47	17 57	06 18	17 11	06 53	16 39	07 19	16 38
25	04 52	19 21	05 21	18 43	05 50	17 52	06 21	17 07	06 56	16 37	07 20	16 40
28	04 55	19 18	05 24	18 38	05 53	17 48	06 24	17 03	06 59	16 36	07 21	16 42
31	04 57	19 15	05 27	18 33			06 28	16 59			07 22	16 44

3.17 MOONRISE/SET TIMES 2018

The table below gives the times of Moonrise (MR) and Moonset (MS) for every 3rd day; interpolation is necessary for other days. The aim is simply to indicate whether the night in question will be brightly moonlit, partially moonlit or pitch black – depending, of course, on cloud cover.

The table is based on Longitude 0°. To correct for longitude, add 4 minutes of time for every degree West; subtract if East.

Latitudes 56°N, 48°N and 40°N are chosen so as to split into three equal bands the 24° span of latitude from Shetland 60°N to Gibraltar 36°N. Be sure to enter the correct table.

** Indicates that the phenomenon does not occur.

The phase of the Moon, ie New Moon, 1st Quarter, Full Moon and Last Quarter, are shown on Tide tables and in detail on the penultimate page of Chapter 4 (Tides).

Times are in UT – add 1 hour in non-shaded months to convert to BST

LATITUDE 56°N

	JANUARY		FEBRUARY		MARCH		APRIL		MAY		JUNE	
	Rise	Set	Rise	Set	Rise	Set	Rise	Set	Rise	Set	Rise	Set
1	15 26	07 21	18 01	08 27	16 53	06 53	19 50	06 22	21 12	05 29	22 54	05 47
4	19 11	10 00	22 06	09 39	20 57	08 01	23 28	07 29	** **	07 08	00 04	08 42
7	23 12	11 16	00 34	10 39	** **	09 04	01 28	09 16	01 31	09 51	01 10	12 12
10	01 38	12 13	03 53	12 04	02 42	10 40	03 29	12 08	02 45	13 18	02 04	16 02
13	05 01	13 29	06 22	14 29	04 57	13 19	04 40	15 41	03 41	17 09	03 26	20 09
16	07 43	15 40	07 50	17 49	06 16	16 47	05 38	19 35	04 56	21 16	06 21	23 03
19	09 22	18 50	08 49	21 30	07 14	20 34	07 00	23 34	07 28	** **	10 28	00 03
22	10 24	22 25	09 54	00 04	08 26	** **	09 41	01 39	11 22	01 32	14 22	01 01
25	11 25	00 57	11 52	03 49	10 43	02 46	13 34	03 25	15 17	02 35	17 57	02 02
28	13 09	04 54	15 29	06 21	14 29	04 53	17 30	04 27	18 58	03 33	20 51	03 43
31	16 37	07 50			18 32	06 03			22 06	05 03		

	JULY		AUGUST		SEPTEMBER		OCTOBER		NOVEMBER		DECEMBER	
1	22 35	06 32	21 59	08 57	21 22	11 44	21 10	13 20	23 42	14 33	00 15	13 49
4	23 35	09 57	22 54	12 39	23 17	15 27	** **	15 56	02 29	15 40	04 15	14 42
7	00 09	13 38	** **	16 32	01 36	17 57	03 25	17 16	06 33	16 37	08 00	16 00
10	01 20	17 40	02 43	19 26	05 55	19 13	07 36	18 14	10 15	18 04	10 45	18 23
13	03 55	20 54	07 00	20 52	10 02	20 13	11 24	19 33	12 47	20 37	12 12	21 40
16	08 05	22 29	11 07	21 51	13 38	21 38	14 10	21 51	14 06	23 58	13 03	00 01
19	12 09	23 27	14 45	23 05	16 11	** **	15 40	** **	14 57	02 22	13 55	03 46
22	15 48	00 08	17 32	00 24	17 35	02 14	16 35	03 30	15 55	06 15	15 36	07 48
25	18 48	01 42	19 08	03 19	18 29	05 48	17 30	07 19	17 50	10 11	19 08	10 39
28	20 39	04 23	20 06	06 48	19 26	09 34	19 06	11 13	21 29	12 39	23 24	11 57
31	21 42	07 46	20 59	10 28			22 21	14 00			02 04	12 50

LATITUDE 48°N

	JANUARY		FEBRUARY		MARCH		APRIL		MAY		JUNE	
	Rise	Set	Rise	Set	Rise	Set	Rise	Set	Rise	Set	Rise	Set
1	16 02	06 45	18 23	08 03	17 11	06 32	19 40	06 28	20 44	05 53	22 16	06 26
4	19 36	09 33	22 04	09 38	20 51	08 03	22 57	07 55	23 34	07 45	** **	09 11
7	23 14	11 11	00 18	10 58	** **	09 26	00 50	09 53	00 58	10 23	00 59	12 20
10	01 26	12 28	03 20	12 38	02 06	11 16	02 59	12 37	02 30	13 31	02 14	15 48
13	04 30	14 01	05 47	15 03	04 24	13 50	04 28	15 50	03 47	16 59	03 58	19 33
16	07 07	16 15	07 31	18 07	06 00	17 00	05 47	19 21	05 24	20 43	06 57	22 31
19	08 59	19 12	08 50	21 26	07 19	20 25	07 30	22 59	08 06	23 50	10 42	** **
22	10 20	22 26	10 15	** **	08 52	23 59	10 17	01 02	11 41	01 11	14 12	01 06
25	11 41	00 44	12 28	03 13	11 20	02 09	13 50	03 06	15 13	02 35	17 27	02 27
28	13 44	04 20	15 55	05 54	14 50	04 30	17 23	04 30	18 32	03 54	20 13	04 22
31	17 06	07 20			18 30	06 01			21 28	05 40		

	JULY		AUGUST		SEPTEMBER		OCTOBER		NOVEMBER		DECEMBER	
1	22 08	07 03	21 56	09 04	21 45	11 23	21 48	12 43	** **	14 06	00 26	13 42
4	23 27	10 08	23 12	12 23	23 55	14 50	** **	15 25	02 37	15 37	04 02	14 58
7	00 15	13 28	00 23	15 57	02 09	17 29	03 39	17 07	06 16	16 56	07 25	16 36
10	01 49	17 07	03 19	18 55	06 04	19 09	07 24	18 29	09 38	18 41	10 06	19 02
13	04 33	20 20	07 14	20 43	09 47	20 32	10 50	20 08	12 09	21 13	11 48	22 02
16	08 22	22 16	10 56	22 05	13 03	22 14	13 31	22 29	13 46	** **	13 00	00 08
19	12 02	23 36	14 13	23 38	15 34	** **	15 16	00 26	14 57	02 25	14 14	03 30
22	15 20	00 31	16 54	01 03	17 14	02 39	16 31	03 37	16 17	05 55	16 15	07 09
25	18 10	02 20	18 43	03 48	18 28	05 52	17 48	07 03	18 30	09 31	19 40	10 06
28	20 10	04 56	20 01	06 57	19 47	09 16	19 44	10 36	21 56	12 09	23 29	11 48
31	21 32	08 00	21 15	10 15			22 53	13 26			01 53	13 04

Times are in UT – add 1 hour in non-shaded months to convert to BST

LATITUDE 40°N

	JANUARY Rise	JANUARY Set	FEBRUARY Rise	FEBRUARY Set	MARCH Rise	MARCH Set	APRIL Rise	APRIL Set	MAY Rise	MAY Set	JUNE Rise	JUNE Set
1	16 27	06 20	18 38	07 46	17 24	06 18	19 33	06 32	20 24	06 09	21 50	06 52
4	19 54	09 14	22 02	09 36	20 47	08 04	22 36	08 13	23 07	08 11	23 48	09 31
7	23 15	11 07	00 06	11 11	23 51	09 42	00 25	10 19	00 35	10 45	00 50	12 27
10	01 17	12 39	02 57	13 02	01 42	11 40	02 38	12 57	02 19	13 40	02 21	15 38
13	04 09	14 23	05 23	15 27	04 01	14 12	04 20	15 56	03 51	16 51	04 20	19 08
16	06 42	16 40	07 17	18 19	05 49	17 09	05 54	19 11	05 44	20 20	07 22	22 09
19	08 42	19 27	08 50	21 23	07 23	20 18	07 52	22 35	08 31	23 26	10 52	** **
22	10 17	22 27	10 31	** **	09 11	23 37	10 41	00 37	11 54	00 55	14 06	01 10
25	11 53	00 34	12 53	02 49	11 45	01 43	14 02	02 53	15 10	02 35	17 06	02 46
28	14 08	03 57	16 13	05 35	15 05	04 13	17 18	04 32	18 14	04 09	19 46	04 48
31	17 26	06 59			18 28	06 00			21 02	06 06		

	JULY Rise	JULY Set	AUGUST Rise	AUGUST Set	SEPTEMBER Rise	SEPTEMBER Set	OCTOBER Rise	OCTOBER Set	NOVEMBER Rise	NOVEMBER Set	DECEMBER Rise	DECEMBER Set
1	21 49	07 24	21 53	09 09	22 01	11 09	22 15	12 17	** **	13 47	00 34	13 37
4	23 22	10 17	23 25	12 12	** **	14 24	00 17	15 03	02 43	15 34	03 52	15 10
7	00 20	13 20	00 46	15 32	02 32	17 09	03 48	17 01	06 04	17 10	07 01	17 01
10	02 08	16 44	03 44	18 33	06 10	19 06	07 16	18 40	09 12	19 07	09 39	19 28
13	04 59	19 56	07 23	20 37	09 36	20 45	10 27	20 32	11 44	21 38	11 32	22 17
16	08 35	22 07	10 48	22 15	12 39	22 39	13 05	22 55	13 31	** **	12 58	00 13
19	11 57	23 43	13 51	** **	15 09	00 13	14 59	00 46	14 57	02 28	14 28	03 18
22	15 00	00 48	16 27	01 29	16 59	02 57	16 29	03 43	16 34	05 40	16 41	06 43
25	17 43	02 46	18 26	04 08	18 28	05 55	18 01	06 51	18 57	09 04	20 01	09 43
28	19 50	05 19	19 57	07 03	20 02	09 02	20 10	10 11	22 16	11 48	23 33	11 41
31	21 25	08 10	21 26	10 05			23 16	13 02			01 45	13 14

3.18 PHASES OF THE MOON 2018 which principally determine Springs, Neaps and tide times (UT)

New Moon ●	d	h	m	First Quarter ◐	d	h	m	Full Moon ○	d	h	m	Last Quarter ◑	d	h	m
								Jan	2	02	24	Jan	8	22	25
Jan	17	02	17	Jan	24	22	20	Jan	31	13	27	Feb	7	15	54
Feb	15	21	05	Feb	23	08	09	Mar	2	00	51	Mar	9	11	20
Mar	17	13	12	Mar	24	15	35	Mar	31	12	37	Apr	8	07	18
Apr	16	01	57	Apr	22	21	46	Apr	30	00	58	May	8	02	09
May	15	11	48	May	22	03	49	May	29	14	20	June	6	18	32
June	13	19	43	June	20	10	51	June	28	04	53	July	6	07	51
July	13	02	48	July	19	19	52	July	27	20	20	Aug	4	18	18
Aug	11	09	58	Aug	18	07	49	Aug	26	11	56	Sept	3	02	37
Sept	9	18	01	Sept	16	23	15	Sept	25	02	52	Oct	2	09	45
Oct	9	03	47	Oct	16	18	02	Oct	24	16	45	Oct	31	16	40
Nov	7	16	02	Nov	15	14	54	Nov	23	05	39	Nov	30	00	19
Dec	7	07	20	Dec	15	11	49	Dec	22	17	49	Dec	29	09	34

4
Tides

4.1	**Introduction** Tide tables • Spanish Secondary Ports	54
4.2	**Definitions** CD • LAT • HAT • OD (Newlyn) • Charted depth • Drying height • Vertical clearances • Elevation of lights • Height of tide • Rise and Fall of tide • Duration • Interval • Springs and Neaps • MHWS, MHWN • MLWS, MLWN • MSL/ML • Range • Standard and Secondary Ports • Tidal Coefficients	54
4.3	**Calculating times and heights of High and Low Water** Standard and Secondary Ports: times of HW and LW • Secondary Ports: heights of HW and LW • Graphical interpolation	55
4.4	**Calculating intermediate times and heights of tide** Standard and Secondary Ports • Factors • The Rule of Twelfths • Co-Tidal and Co-Range charts	56
4.5	**Calculating clearances below overhead objects**	58
4.6	**Tidal prediction by computer** EasyTide • TotalTide • Commercial software	58
4.7	**Tidal streams** Tidal stream atlases • Tidal stream diamonds • Flood streams around UK • Calculating rates • Tidal streams in rivers	59
4.8	**Meteorological effects** Wind • Barometric pressure • Storm warning services	61
	Graph for calculating tidal stream rates	62

4.1 INTRODUCTION

This chapter provides background information on the tidal data in Chapter 9 of this Almanac, where times and heights of HW and LW are shown for Standard Ports, and time and height differences for their associated Secondary Ports. Tides are predicted for average meteorological conditions. In the UK the average pressure is about 1013mb. A difference of 34mb can cause the tide to rise (lower pressure) or fall (higher pressure) by about 0·3m. See 4.8 for more details.

4.1.1 Admiralty Tide Tables (ATT) Vol I and Vol II

These are the source for all tidal data in this Almanac.

- Vol 1 (NP201) UK and Ireland (including Channel ports from Hoek van Holland to Brest)
- Vol 2 (NP202) Europe (excluding UK, Ireland and Channel ports), Mediterranean and the Atlantic

Standard Port predictions are replacing some established Secondary Ports in ATT to better support offshore activity. The Almanac continues to replicate the existing differences to provide the data in a compact format for planning. These are in italics where alternative information is available.

4.1.2 Spanish Secondary Ports referenced to Lisboa

In Areas 23 and 25, some Spanish secondary ports have Lisboa as Standard Port. Time differences for these ports, when applied to the printed times of HW and LW for Lisboa (UT), automatically give HW and LW times in the Zone Time for Spain (ie UT –1), *not* Portugal (UT). No other corrections are required, except for DST when applicable.

4.2 DEFINITIONS

Chart Datum (CD)

CD is the reference level from which heights of tide are predicted and charted depths are measured. In the UK it normally approximates to LAT, and the tide will not frequently fall below it. The actual depth of water in any particular position is the charted depth plus the height of tide.

Lowest Astronomical Tide (LAT)

LAT is the lowest level which can be predicted under average meteorological, and any combination of astronomical, conditions. This level will not be reached every year. Storm surges can cause even lower levels to be reached.

Highest Astronomical Tide (HAT)

HAT is the highest level which can be predicted to occur under average meteorological conditions and under any combination of astronomical conditions, except storm surges. It is the level above which vertical clearances under bridges and power lines are measured; see 4.5.

Ordnance Datum (Newlyn)

Ordnance Datum (Newlyn) is the datum of the land levelling system on mainland England, Scotland and Wales, and to which all features on UK land maps are referred. The difference between Ordnance Datum (Newlyn) and CD is shown at the foot of each page of tide tables in this Almanac. Differences between CD and foreign land levelling datums are similarly quoted.

Charted depth

Charted depths are printed on charts in metres and decimetres (0·1m) and show the depth of water below CD. (Not to be confused with a sounding which is the actual depth of water (charted depth + height of tide) in a particular position.)

Drying height

A drying height is the height above CD of any feature which at times is covered by water. The figures, in metres and decimetres, are underlined on the chart. The depth of water over a drying feature is the height of tide minus the drying height. If the result is negative, then the feature is uncovered at that time.

Vertical clearances under bridges and power lines

These are measured above HAT. Some older charts may still show clearances above MHWS; see 4.5.

Elevation of lights

The charted height of a light (its elevation) is measured above MHWS.

Height of tide

The height of the tide is the vertical distance of the sea level above (or very occasionally below) CD. Predicted heights are given in metres and decimetres.

Rise/Fall of tide

The Rise of the tide is the amount the tide has risen since the earlier Low Water. The Fall of a tide is the amount the tide has fallen since the last High Water.

Duration

Duration is the time between LW and the next HW, normally slightly over six hours. It can be used to find the approximate time of LW when only the time of HW is known.

Interval

The interval is a period of time quoted in hours and minutes before (–) or after (+) HW. Intervals are printed in hourly increments (–6hrs to +6hrs) along the bottom of each tidal curve diagram in Chapter 9.

Spring tides

Spring tides occur roughly every 16 days, near to Full ○ and New ● Moon, when the tide-raising forces of Sun and Moon are at a maximum. See 3.18, for phases of the Moon.

Neap tides

Neaps occur roughly every 16 days, near the Moon's first ◐ and last ◑ quarters, when the tide-raising forces of Sun and Moon are at a minimum. See 3.18 for phases of the Moon.

Mean High Water and Low Water Springs/Neaps

MHWS and MHWN are the means of predicted HW heights of Sp or Np tides over a period of 18·6 years. Similarly, MLWS and MLWN are the means of LW heights for Sp and Np tides respectively. Mean tide level (MTL) is the mean of the above values.

Mean Sea Level (MSL or ML)

This is the average level of the sea's surface over a long period, preferably 18·6 years.

Range

The range of a tide is the difference between the heights of successive HWs and LWs. Spring range is the difference between MHWS and MLWS, and Neap range is the difference between MHWN and MLWN.

Standard Ports have tidal characteristics observed over a long period and are suitable as a reference for secondary ports on the adjacent coasts.

Secondary Ports have similar tidal characteristics to those of their Standard Port. Time and height differences are applied to the Standard Port predictions. 'Secondary' does not imply lesser importance.

Tidal Coefficients indicate the range of a tide. Daily values are listed and explained in Area 17 Calais and Cherbourg, Area 18 St Malo, Area 20 Brest, and Area 22 Pte de Grave.

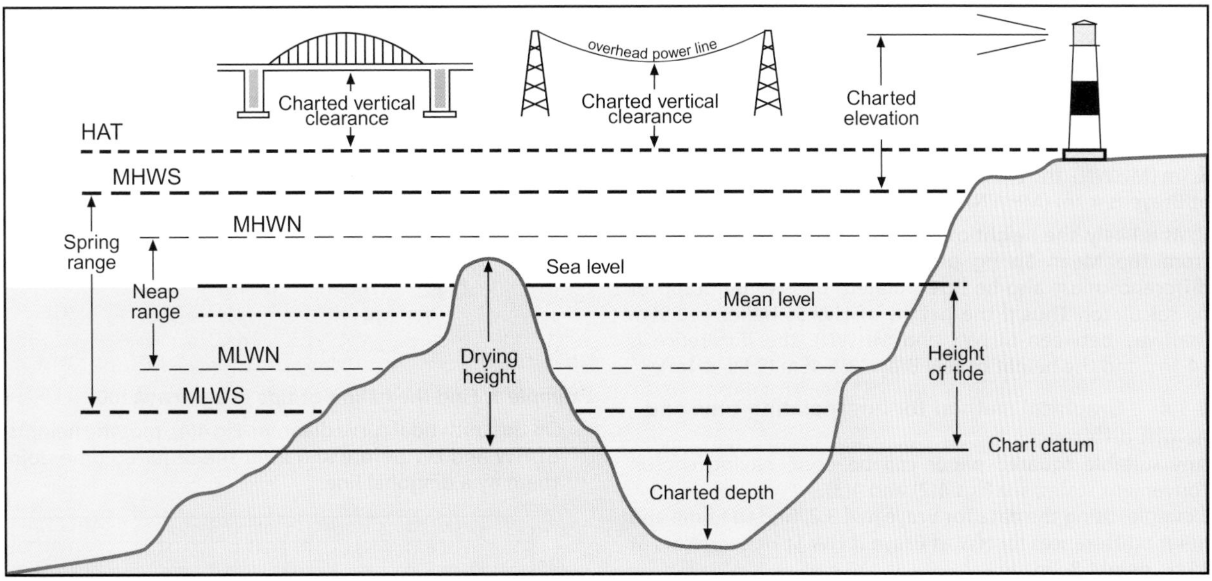

Fig 4(1) Tidal definitions

4.3 CALCULATING TIMES AND HEIGHTS OF HIGH AND LOW WATER

4.3.1 Standard Ports

The Standard Ports for which daily predictions are given in this Almanac are listed below by geographic Areas. Not all ports shown in the ATTs are included, but adjustments have been made to Secondary Port differences where necessary.

1	Falmouth, Plymouth, Dartmouth, Portland.
2	Poole, Southampton, Portsmouth, Chichester.
3	Shoreham, Dover.
4	Margate, Sheerness, London Bridge, Walton-on-the-Naze, Harwich, Lowestoft.
5	Immingham, R Tees, Tyne (North Shields).
6	Leith, Aberdeen.
7	Invergordon, Wick, Lerwick.
8	Stornoway, Ullapool, Oban.
9	Greenock.
10	Liverpool, Holyhead.
11	Milford Haven, Bristol (Avonmouth).
12	Dublin, Cobh, Tarbert Island.
13	Galway, River Foyle, Galway.
14	Esbjerg.
15	Helgoland, Cuxhaven and Wilhelmshaven.
16	Hoek van Holland, Vlissingen, Zeebrugge.
17	Dunkerque, Dieppe, Le Havre, Cherbourg.
18	St Malo.
19	St Peter Port, St Helier.
20	Brest.
22	Pointe de Grave.
23	La Coruña.
24	Lisboa.
25	Gibraltar.
26	Ponta Delgada, Casablanca.

Predicted times and heights of HW and LW are tabulated for each Standard Port. Note that these are only predictions and take no account of the effects of wind and barometric pressure (see 4.8). See 1.5 for Zone times and Daylight Saving Time (DST).

4.3.2 Secondary Ports – times of HW and LW

Each Secondary Port listed in Chapter 9 has a data block for calculating times of HW and LW. The following example is for Braye (Alderney):

TIDES –0400 Dover; ML 3·5; Duration 0545
Standard Port ST HELIER (⟶)

Times				**Height (metres)**			
High Water		Low Water		MHWS	MHWN	MLWN	MLWS
0300	0900	0200	0900	11·0	8·1	4·0	1·4
1500	2100	1400	2100				
Differences BRAYE							
+0050	+0040	+0025	+0105	–4·8	–3·4	–1·5	–0·5

In this example –0400 Dover means that, on average, HW Braye is 4 hours 00 minutes before HW Dover (the Range and times of HW Dover are in Area 3 and on the bookmark).

ML (or MSL) is defined in 4.2.

Duration 0545 means that LW Braye occurs 5 hours and 45 minutes before the next HW.

The arrow (⟶) after the Standard Port's name points to where the tide tables are in the book.

The most accurate method of prediction uses Standard Port times and Secondary Port time differences as in the block. When HW at St Helier occurs at 0300 and 1500, the difference is +0050, and thus HW at Braye occurs at 0350 and 1550. When HW at St Helier occurs at 0900 and 2100, the difference is +0040, and HW at Braye occurs at 0940 and 2140.

If, as will usually be the case, HW St Helier occurs at some other time, then the difference for Braye must be found by interpolation, either by eye, by the graphical method or by calculator.

So when HW St Helier occurs at 1200 (midway between 0900 and 1500), the difference is +0045 (midway between +0040 and +0050), and therefore HW Braye is 1245.

The same method is used for calculating the times of LW. Times thus obtained are in the Secondary Port's Zone Time. For calculating heights of HW and LW see 4.3.3.

4.3.3 Secondary Ports – heights of HW and LW

The Secondary Port data block also contains height differences which are applied to the heights of HW and LW at the Standard Port. When the height of HW at St Helier is 11·0m (MHWS), the difference is –4·8m, so the height of HW Braye is 6·2m (MHWS). When the height of HW St Helier is 8·1m (MHWN), the difference is –3·4m, and the height of HW at Braye is 4·7m (MHWN).

If, as is likely, the height of tide at the Standard Port differs from the Mean Spring or Neap level, then the height difference must also be interpolated: by eye, by graph or by calculator. Thus if the height of HW St Helier is 9·55m (halfway between MHWS and MHWN), the difference is –4·1m, and the height of HW Braye is 5·45m (9·55–4·1m).

4.3.4 Graphical method for interpolating time and height differences

Any suitable squared paper can be used, having chosen convenient scales; see Figs 4(2) and 4(3).
Example: using the data for Braye in 4.3.2, find the time and height differences for HW at Braye if HW St Helier occurs at 1126, height 8·9m.

Time difference

On the horizontal axis of Fig 4(2) select a scale for the time at St Helier covering 0900 to 1500 (for which the relevant time differences for Braye are known). On the vertical axis the scale must cover +0040 to +0050, the time differences given for 0900 and 1500.

Plot point A, the time difference (+0040) for HW St Helier at 0900; and point B, the time difference (+0050) for HW St Helier at 1500. Join AB. Enter the graph at time 1126 (HW St Helier); intersect AB at C then go horizontally to read +0044 on the vertical axis. On that morning HW Braye is 44 minutes after HW St Helier, ie 1210.

Height difference

In Fig 4(3) the horizontal axis covers the height of HW at St Helier (ie 8·1 to 11·0m) and the vertical axis shows the relevant height differences (–3·4 to –4·8m).

Plot point D, the height difference (–3·4m) at Neaps when the height of HW St Helier is 8·1m; and E, the height difference (–4·8m) at Springs when the height of HW St Helier is 11·0m. Join DE.

Enter the graph at 8·9m (the height of HW St Helier that morning) and mark F where that height meets DE. From F follow the horizontal line to read off the corresponding height difference: –3·8m. So that morning the height of HW Braye is 5·1m.

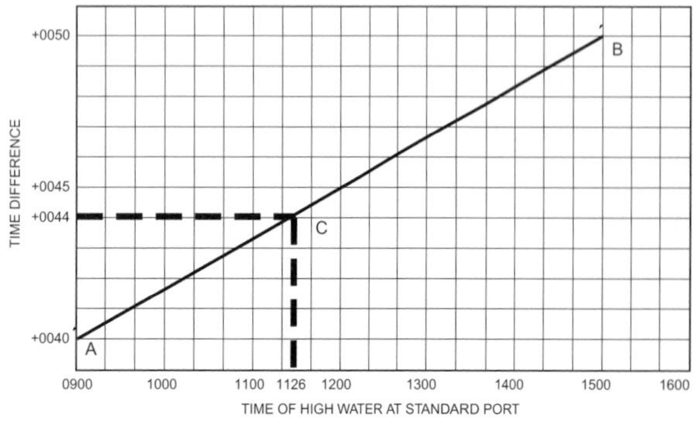

Fig 4(2)

4.4 CALCULATING INTERMEDIATE TIMES AND HEIGHTS OF TIDE

4.4.1 Standard Ports

Intermediate heights and times are best calculated from the Mean Spring and Neap Curves for Standard Ports in Chapter 9. Examples below are for Leith, on a day when the predictions are:

	UT	Ht (m)
22	0202	5·3
	0752	1·0
TU	1417	5·4
	2025	0·5

Example 1: Find the height of tide at Leith at 1200.

- On the Leith tidal curve diagram, Fig 4(4), plot the heights of HW and LW before and after the required time. Join them by a diagonal line.

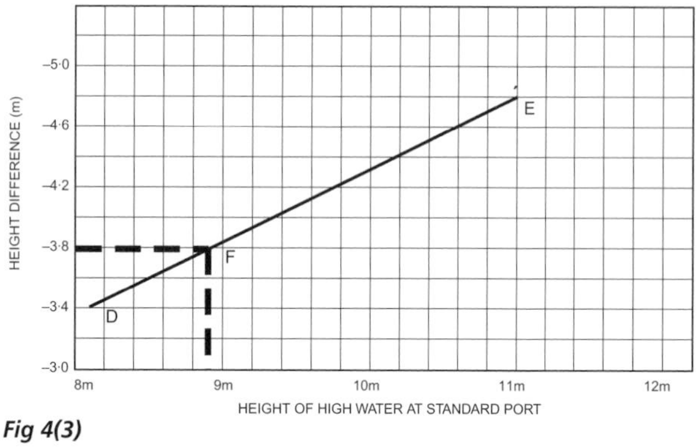

Fig 4(3)

- Enter the HW time and other times as necessary in the boxes below the curves.
- From the required time, go vertically to the curves. The Spring curve is red, and the Neap curve (where it differs) is blue. Interpolate between the curves by comparing the actual range, in this example 4·4m, with the Mean Ranges printed beside the curves. Never extrapolate. Here the Spring curve applies.
- Go horizontally to the diagonal line first plotted, thence vertically to the height scale, to extract 4·2m.

Example 2: Find the time in the afternoon when the height of tide has fallen to 3·7m.

- On Fig 4(5) plot the heights of HW and LW above and below the required height of tide. Join them by a sloping line.
- In the boxes below the curves enter HW time and other hourly times to cover the required timescale.
- From the required height, drop vertically to the diagonal line and thence horizontally to the curves. Interpolate between them as in Example 1; do not extrapolate. In this example the actual range is 4·9m, so the Spring curve applies.
- Drop vertically to the timescale, and read off the time required: 1637.

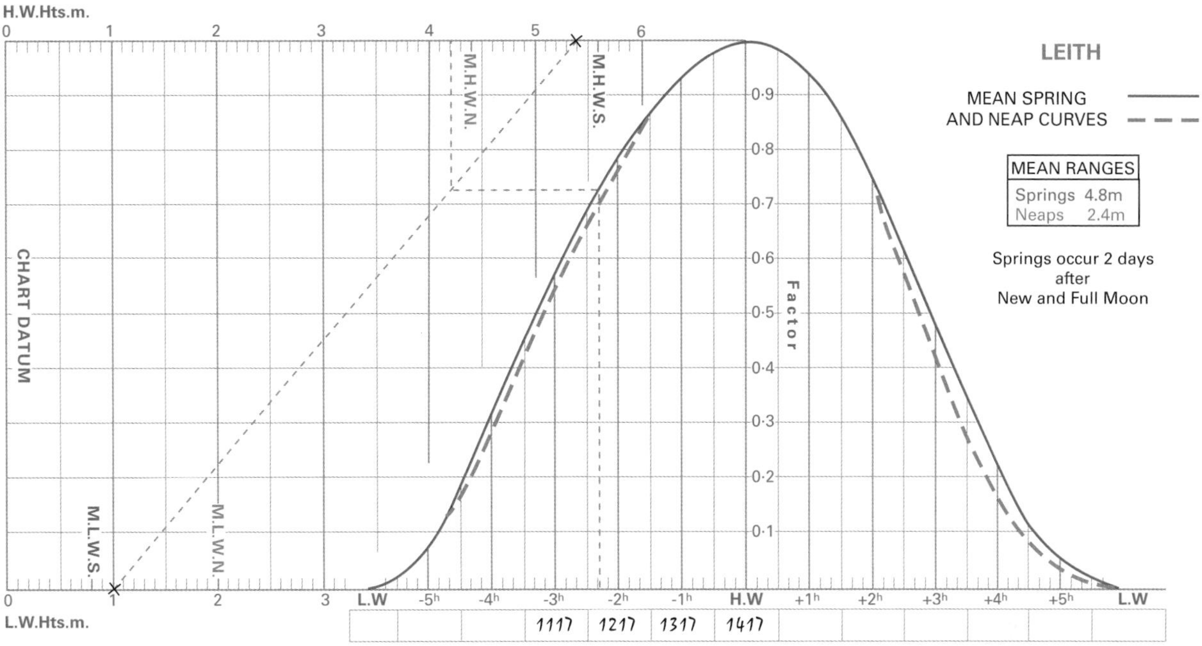

Fig 4(4) Curve for example 1

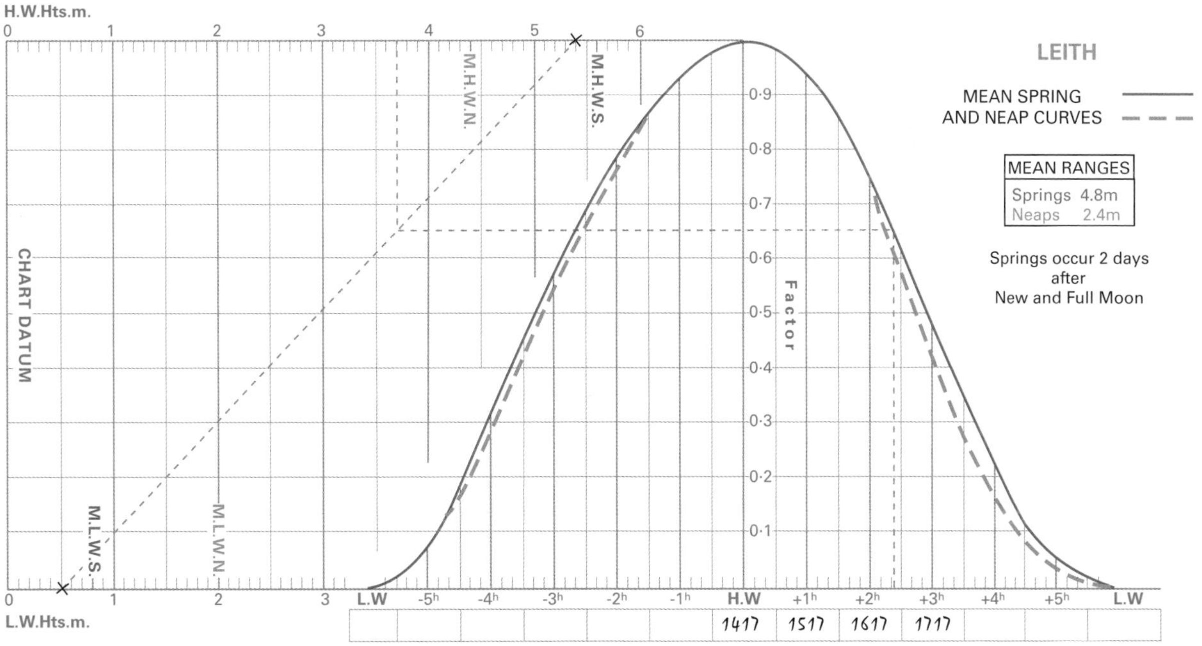

Fig 4(5) Curve for example 2

4.4.2 Secondary Ports

On coasts where the tidal curves for adjacent Standard Ports change little in shape, and where the duration of rise or fall at the Secondary Port is similar to its relevant Standard Port (ie where HW and LW time differences are nearly the same), intermediate times and heights are calculated from the tidal curves for the Standard Port in a similar manner to 4.4.1. The curves are entered with the times and heights of HW and LW at the Secondary Port, calculated as in 4.3.2 and 4.3.3.

Interpolate by eye between the curves, using the range at the Standard Port as argument. Do not extrapolate – use the Spring curve for ranges greater than Springs, and the Neap curve for ranges less than Neaps. With a large change in duration between Springs and Neaps the results may have a slight error, greater near LW.

For places between Christchurch and Selsey Bill (where the tidal regime is complex) special curves are given in 9.2.17.

4.4.3 The use of factors

Factors (in green on tidal curves) are another method of tidal calculation, but the Admiralty tidal prediction form (see 9.2.9) no longer contains the relevant fields. A factor of 1 = HW, and 0 = LW. Tidal curve diagrams show the factor of the range attained at times before and after HW. Thus the factor represents the percentage of the mean range (for the day in question) which has been reached at any particular time. Simple equations used are:

	Range x Factor = Rise
or	Factor = Rise ÷ Range

In determining or using the factor it may be necessary to interpolate between the Spring and Neap curves as described in 4.4.2.

Factors are particularly useful when calculating hourly height predictions for ports with special tidal problems (9.2.17).

4.4.4 The Rule of Twelfths

The Rule of Twelfths estimates by mental arithmetic the height of the tide between HW and LW. It assumes that the duration of rise or fall is 6 hours, the curve is symmetrical and approximates to a sine curve. *Thus the rule is invalid in the Solent, for example, where these conditions do not apply, nor should it be used if accuracy is critical.*

The rule states that from one LW to the next HW, and vice versa, the tide rises or falls by:

1/12th of its range in the 1st hour
2/12ths of its range in the 2nd hour
3/12ths of its range in the 3rd hour
3/12ths of its range in the 4th hour
2/12ths of its range in the 5th hour
1/12th of its range in the 6th hour

4.4.5 Co-Tidal and Co-Range charts

These charts are used to predict tidal times and heights for an offshore position, as distinct from port or coastal locations which are covered by tide tables. There are Admiralty charts for the following offshore areas of NW Europe:

5057	Dungeness to Hoek van Holland
5058	British Isles and adjacent waters
5059	Southern North Sea

They depict Co-Range and Co-Tidal lines, as defined below, with detailed instructions for use.

A Co-Range line joins points of equal Mean Sp (or Np) Range which are simply the difference in level between MHWS and MLWS (or MHWN and MLWN).

A Co-Tidal line joins points of equal Mean HW (or LW) Time Interval. This is defined as the mean time interval between the passage of the Moon over the Greenwich Meridian and the time of the next HW (or LW) at the place concerned.

To find times and heights of tide at an offshore location, say in the Thames Estuary, needs some pre-planning especially if intending to navigate through a shallow gap. The *Tidal Stream Atlas for the Thames Estuary* (NP 249) also contains Co-Tidal and Co-Range charts. These are more clearly arranged and described than charts 5057–5059, but prior study is still necessary. The calculations require predictions for Sheerness, Walton-on-the-Naze or Margate, as relevant to the vessel's position.

4.5 CALCULATING CLEARANCES BELOW OVERHEAD OBJECTS

A diagram often helps when calculating vertical clearances below bridges, power cables etc. Fig 4(6) shows the relationship to CD. The height of such objects as shown on the chart is usually measured above HAT, so the actual clearance will almost always be more. The height of HAT above CD is given at the foot of each page of the tide tables. Most Admiralty charts now show clearances above HAT, but check the **Heights** block below the chart Title.

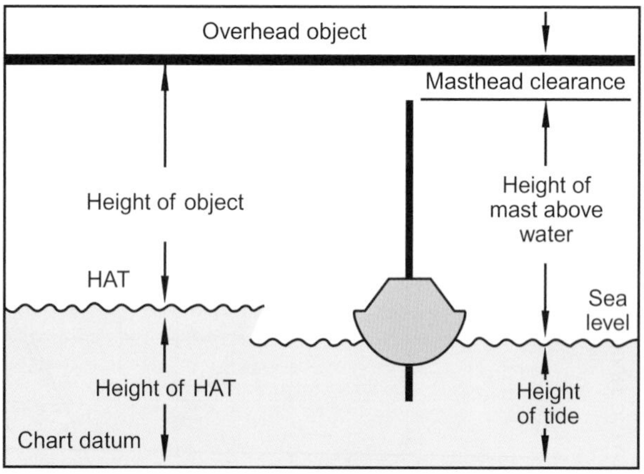

Fig 4(6) Calculating masthead clearance

Insert the dimensions into the following formula, carefully observing the conventions for brackets:

Masthead clearance = (Height of object above HAT + height of HAT above CD) minus (height of tide at the time + height of the masthead above waterline)

4.6 TIDAL PREDICTION BY COMPUTER

The Almanac uses UKHO Standard Port tide prediction curves prepared for Admiralty Tide Tables. The printed tidal curve is drawn to a mean Spring curve and, in dashed line, a mean Neap line, with boxes for the associated times of HW and LW. The curve does not take account of the differing arguments (geometrical positions) of the sun, moon and planets on a daily basis. Nor does it take account of differences which owe to the differing volume passing constrictions or obstructions.

The printed tables give condensed planning information, which is refinable from computer generated predictions, which have proved increasingly reliable and easy to use.

4.6.1 EasyTide - www.ukho.gov.uk/easytide

EasyTide is an on-line UKHO tidal prediction service, which provides free tidal predictions for the current day, and the 6 consecutive days. Times and heights of HW and LW for the required port are presented in tabular and graphical formats. Over 6,000 standard and secondary ports are available worldwide. In this model the arguments are used to adjust the shape of the curve on a daily basis resulting in a more accurate prediction regime than available in the tables, and the times of HW and LW often vary from those in ATT. The predictions may differ markedly at times of extremely flattened (usually Np) curves with little change of gradient.

4.6.2 TotalTide

TotalTide (DP 550) is claimed to be the world's most comprehensive tidal prediction system. It is aimed primarily at commercial shipping and satisfies SOLAS Regulations and the UK Merchant Shipping Safety of Navigation Regulations 2002. It may thus be carried in lieu of paper tide tables.

TotalTide gives fast and accurate tidal predictions for over 7,000 ports and tidal stream data for more than 3,000 locations worldwide. The CD contains a free calculation programme. There are 10 Area Data Sets (ADS), with world-wide coverage. Areas 1–4 (see below) are in one ADS.

Access is via a permit system. Annual updates are available, and are essential to satisfy safety regulations, although TotalTide will still run without them but less accurately.

The ten ADS cover:

1–4. Europe, Mediterranean and northern waters
5. Red Sea, the Gulf and Indian Ocean (north)
6. Singapore to Japan and Philippines
7. Australia and Borneo
8. Pacific Ocean, New Zealand and America (west)
9. North America (east coast) and Caribbean
10. South Atlantic and Indian Ocean (southern part)

TotalTide displays 7 days of times and heights of HW and LW in both tabular and graphical formats. Other useful facilities include: a display of heights at specified times and time intervals; a continuous plot of height against time; indications of periods of daylight and twilight, moon phases, springs/neaps; the option to insert the yacht's draft; calculations of under-keel and overhead clearances.

TotalTide will run on most versions of Microsoft Windows, but check your system is compatible before buying.

4.6.3 Commercial software

Various commercial firms sell tidal prediction software for use on computers or calculators. Such software is mostly based on NP 159 and can often predict many years ahead. It remains essential to install annual updates.

Many chart plotters incorporate a tidal prediction facility. These are embedded in the software, and their accuracy depends on age and edition. Following a lay-up, at the start of the season or if the power has been disconnected it is necessary to check the date–time to which the plotter is set. If on an unfamiliar boat it is prudent to confirm the prediction against another known data source.

Tablet computer and smart phone applications should be selected on the basis of reputation, accuracy and reliability. A secondary method of prediction should be carried on board to cover eventualities such as equipment or power failure. Do not rely solely upon mobile signal dependent options.

4.7 TIDAL STREAMS

Tidal streams are the horizontal movement of water caused by the vertical rise and fall of the tide; see Fig 4(8). They normally change direction about every six hours. They are quite different from ocean currents, such as the Gulf Stream, which run indefinitely in the same direction.

The direction (set) of a tidal stream is always that towards which it is running. The speed (rate) of tidal streams is important to yachtsmen: about 2kn is common, 6–8kn is not unusual in some areas at springs; 16kn has been recorded in the Pentland Firth.

4.7.1 Tidal stream atlases

Admiralty Tidal Stream Atlases, listed below, show the rate and set of tidal streams in the more important areas around the UK and NW Europe.

The set is shown by arrows graded in weight and, where possible, in length to indicate the rate. Thus ⟶ is a weak stream and ⟶ a strong stream. The figures against the arrows give the mean Np and Sp rates in tenths of a knot; thus 19,34 indicates a mean Np rate of 1·9kn and a mean Sp rate of 3·4kn. The comma between 19 and 34 is roughly where the observations were made. Inshore eddies are rarely shown in detail due to limitations of scale.

Tidal stream chartlets in this Almanac are derived from the following Admiralty Tidal Stream Atlases.

NP	Title
209	Orkney and Shetland Islands
218	North Coast of Ireland, West Coast of Scotland
219	Portsmouth Harbour and Approaches
220	Rosyth Harbour and Approaches
221	Plymouth Harbour and Approaches
222	Firth of Clyde and Approaches
233	Dover Strait
249	Thames Estuary (with co-tidal charts)
250	The English Channel
251	North Sea, Southern Part
252	North Sea, North Western Part
253	North Sea, Eastern Part
254	The West Country, Falmouth to Teignmouth
255	Falmouth to Padstow, including the Isles of Scilly
256	Irish Sea and Bristol Channel
257	Approaches to Portland
258	Bristol Channel (Lundy to Avonmouth)
259	Irish Sea, Eastern part
263	Lyme Bay
264	The Channel Islands and adjacent Coast of France
265	France, West Coast
337	The Solent and adjacent waters

Useful information is also given in Admiralty Sailing Directions: times of slack water, when the tide turns, overfalls, races etc.

Along open coasts the tidal stream does not necessarily turn at HW and LW; it often occurs at about half tide. The tidal stream usually turns earlier inshore than offshore. In larger bays the tide often sets inshore towards the coast.

Tidal streams referred to HW Aberdeen

Hours		◇	Geographical Position	
		Direction of streams (degrees)	Rates at spring tides (knots)	Rates at neap tides (knots)
Before High Water	6			
	5			
	4			
	3			
	2			
	1			
High Water				
After High Water	1			
	2			
	3			
	4			
	5			
	6			

	◇A		59°13'·0N 2°43'·0W	◇B		59°12'·0N 2°52'·1W
−6	204	5·0	2·0	148	2·5	1·0
−5	205	5·2	2·1	149	4·7	1·9
−4	207	4·0	1·5	137	3·7	1·5
−3	205	2·5	1·0	129	2·2	0·9
−2		0·0	0·0	118	1·1	0·5
−1	026	2·9	1·1	065	0·6	0·2
0	023	4·1	1·6	347	1·1	0·5
+1	024	4·5	1·8	330	2·4	1·0
+2	025	4·0	1·6	320	4·2	1·7
+3	026	3·0	1·2	310	4·0	1·6
+4	034	1·2	0·5	309	2·4	1·0
+5	209	1·7	0·7	328	1·3	0·5
+6	204	4·8	2·0	145	1·2	0·5

Fig 4(7) Tidal stream diamonds

4.7.2 Tidal stream diamonds

Lettered diamonds (◊) on many medium scale charts refer to tables on the chart giving the most accurate tidal stream set and rate (for springs and neaps) at hourly intervals before and after HW at a convenient Standard Port. See Fig 4(7).

The tidal stream diamonds above are extracted from the table on AC 2250 which covers the eastern part of the Orkney Islands. The streams are referred to HW Aberdeen.

Diamond 'A' is located in the 1M wide Sound of Eday (between the islands of Eday and Sanday).

By inspection the first slack water is sharply defined at HW –2. The stream then sets NNE until a much less obvious slack water occurs between HW +4 and +5. The stream turns at about HW +4½, but rates are still between 1·2 and 1·7kn at springs (0·5 and 0·7kn at neaps).

The SSW-going stream reaches a max spring rate of 5·2kn at HW –5; neap rates are less than half these values.

There is considerable detail in these tables. Careful study enables accurate planning and timing for the transit of narrow waters and best use of the tidal streams.

4.7.3 Flood stream around UK

The main flood stream sets ENE up the English Channel, NE into the Bristol Channel and N up the W coasts of Ireland and Scotland (Fig 4(8)). The ebb stream is the reverse.

Two variations are worth noting:

The flood flows NE-N through St George's Channel. However the flood also sets SE through the North Channel and S into the Irish Sea. Both streams meet off the Isle of Man.

Off the E coasts of Scotland and England the stream sets S all the way from Orkney to the Thames Estuary, finally meeting the N-going stream which has curled round North Foreland and up towards London.

Fig 4(8) The main flood stream around the British Isles

4.7.4 Calculating tidal stream rates

The tidal stream rate at any time may be calculated, assuming that it varies with the range of the tide at Dover. In tidal stream atlases, and on the tidal stream chartlets in this Almanac, the rates are shown in tenths of a knot. Thus '05,27' translates as 0·5 knots at Neaps and 2·7 knots at Springs.

Example: Calculate the tidal stream rate off the north tip of Skye at 0420 UT on a day when the tide at Dover is:

UT	Ht (m)	
0328	1·4	By inspection the mean Range
0819	6·3	at Dover is:
1602	1·1	$\frac{(4·9 + 5·2 + 5·3)}{3} = 5·1m$
2054	6·4	

In 9.8.3 the tidal stream chartlet for HW Dover –4 shows '08,18': a mean Neap rate of 0·8 knots and a Spring rate of 1·8 knots.

On Fig 4(9) overleaf, from the horizontal Rates axis mark 08 on the horizontal blue Neaps line; likewise 18 on the Springs line. Join these two marks with a diagonal. From the range 5·1 on the vertical axis go horizontally to cut the diagonal just drawn. From this point go vertically to the Rates axis, top or bottom, and read off the predicted rate of 15 (1·5 knots).

4.7.5 Tidal streams in rivers

Tidal streams in rivers are influenced by the local topography of the river bed as well as solar and lunar forces. At or near Springs, in a river which is obstructed, for example by a bar, the time of HW gets later going up the river. The time of LW also gets later, but more rapidly so the duration of the flood becomes shorter, and duration of ebb becomes longer. At the entrance the flood stream starts at an interval after LW which increases with the degree of obstruction of the channel; this interval between local LW and the start of the flood increases with the distance upriver. The ebb begins soon after local HW along the length of the river. Hence the duration of flood is less than that of the ebb and the difference increases with distance upriver.

The flood stream is normally stronger than the ebb, and runs harder during the first half of the rise of tide. At Neaps the flood and ebb both start soon after local LW and HW respectively, and their durations and rates are about equal.

The Yachtsman's Manual of Tides by Michael Reeve-Fowkes (ACN) covers all theoretical and practical aspects of tides. It includes four regional **Tidal Atlases**: *Western Channel; Central Channel and the Solent; Southern North Sea and Eastern Channel; Channel Ports and Approaches.* These are also available separately. The atlases are referenced to HW Cherbourg and include annual Cherbourg tide tables (which are downloadable free from www.adlardcoles.com).

4.8 METEOROLOGICAL EFFECTS

Prolonged strong winds and unusually high/low pressure significantly affect tidal heights. Early or late times of HW or LW are principally caused by the wind. The effects of wind or pressure individually may not be great, but the combined effect, which is more likely, may be much greater.

4.8.1 Wind

Wind >Force 5 raises the sea level on a lee shore and lowers it on a windward, but there are wide variations due to topography. Strong on/offshore winds may affect the predicted times of HW or LW by up to 1 hour.

Strong winds blowing parallel to a coast tend to set up long waves, which travel along the coast. Sea level is raised at the crest of these waves (positive surge) and lowered in the troughs (negative surge). A storm surge is an unusually severe positive surge. Under exceptional conditions this can raise the height of HW by >1m; a negative surge can lower the height of LW by the same amount – clearly more serious for yachtsmen and other mariners.

The southern North Sea and Thames Estuary are prone to such surges. In Jan 1953 a deep depression and an exceptionally severe and prolonged northerly storm caused a storm surge which raised sea level by almost 3m on the UK's E coast and by even more on the Dutch coast – with heavy loss of life.

4.8.2 Barometric pressure

Over a period of time and across a wide area sea levels are lowered by high pressure and raised by low. The former is of more practical concern to mariners. Mean sea level pressures are quoted in Admiralty Pilots: 1017mb, for example, along the UK south coast in July; 1014mb in January. 1013mb at Wick in July; 1007mb in January.

Intense minor depressions, line squalls or other abrupt changes in the weather can cause wave oscillations, a phenomenon known as a *seiche*. The wave period can vary from a few minutes up to two hours, with heights up to a metre – usually less, rarely more. Certain harbours, eg Wick and Fishguard, due to their shape or size, are particularly prone to *seiches* especially in winter.

4.8.3 Storm Warning Services

These warn of possible coastal flooding caused by abnormal meteorological conditions. A negative storm surge causes abnormally low tidal levels in the Dover Strait, Thames Estuary and Southern North Sea. 6–12 hrs warning is given, Sept–April, when tidal levels at Dover, Sheerness or Lowestoft are forecast to be >1m below predicted levels.

Warnings are broadcast by Navtex, HM Coastguard and the Channel Navigation Information Service (CNIS) on VHF and MF as normally used for navigation warnings.

Fig 4(9) Graph for calculating tidal stream rates

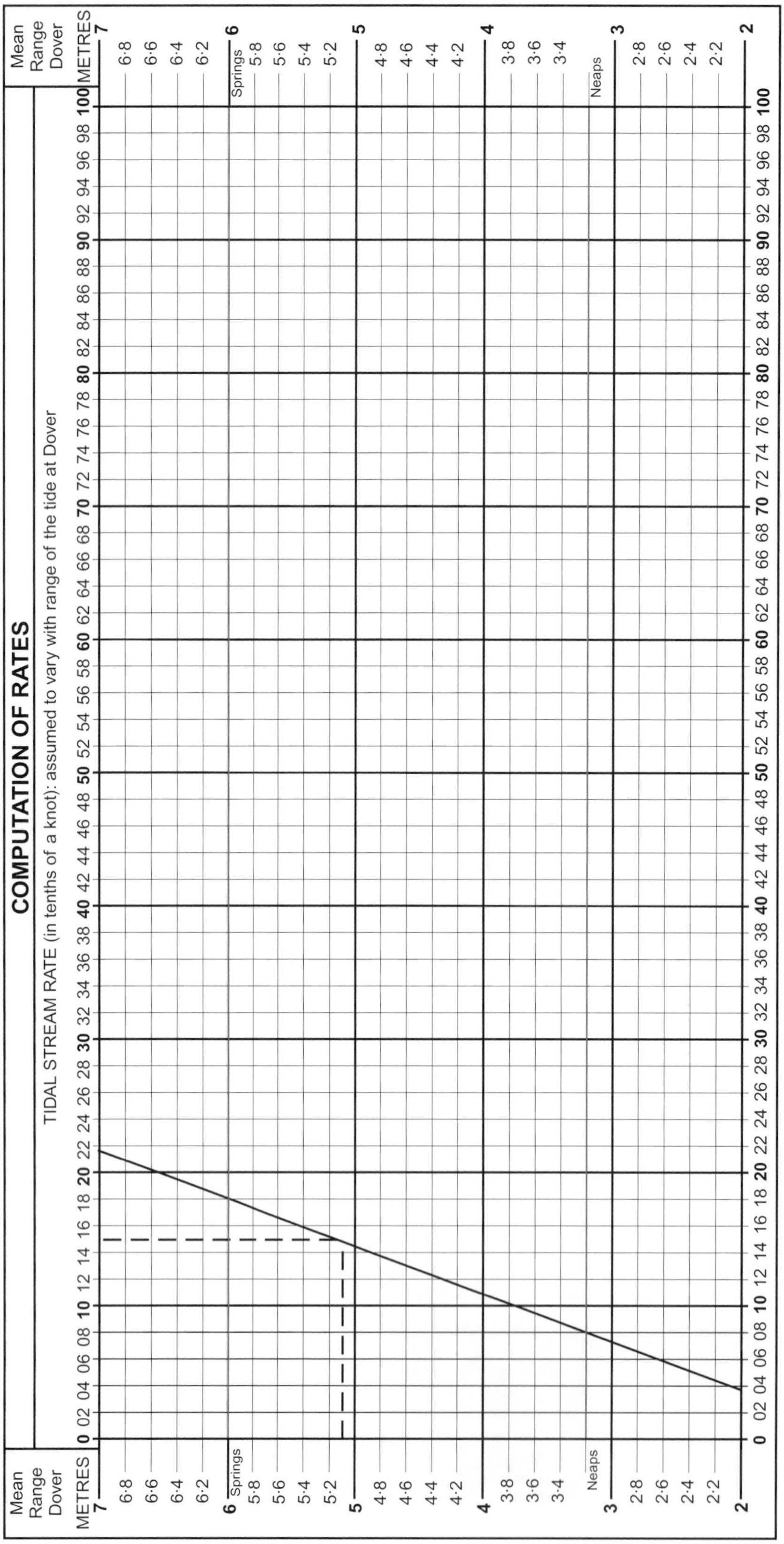

5 Communications

5.1 The International Code of Signals 64
Using the International code

5.2 Operating a radio 65
Frequency bands • Regulations • Licences • R/T procedures • Prowords

5.3 Radio communications systems 65
VHF radio • MF radio • Mobile phones • VOIP • wi-fi/Wi-MAX

5.4 Global communication systems 66
HF radio (SSB) • Satellite communications (Satcoms)

5.5 Navigational warnings 68

5.6 Gunfacts and subfacts 68

5.7 Coast radio stations (CRS) 68
Functions • Track reports • Link calls

5.8 United Kingdom (excluding the Channel Islands) 69

5.9 The Channel Islands 70

5.10 Republic of Ireland 70

5.11 West Denmark 71

5.12 Germany 72

5.13 The Netherlands 73

5.14 Belgium 74

5.15 France 74

5.16 Spain 76

5.17 Mainland Portugal 77

5.18 Portuguese Islands, Gibraltar & Morocco 77

5.19 Vessel Traffic Services (VTS) 78

5.20 International Port Traffic Signals (IPTS) 78

5.21 Flag etiquette 79
Ensigns • Burgees • Salutes • Dressing ship • Ensigns and flags

5.1 THE INTERNATIONAL CODE OF SIGNALS

Marine communication is rooted in the International Code of Signals (2005 edition published by IMO) which provides for safety of navigation and of persons, especially where there are language problems. The present Code came into force in 1969 and is available in nine languages: English, French, German, Greek, Italian, Japanese, Norwegian, Russian and Spanish. Ships, aircraft and shore stations can communicate in these languages without knowing a foreign tongue, provided they have the relevant Code. The English language edition is published by HMSO.

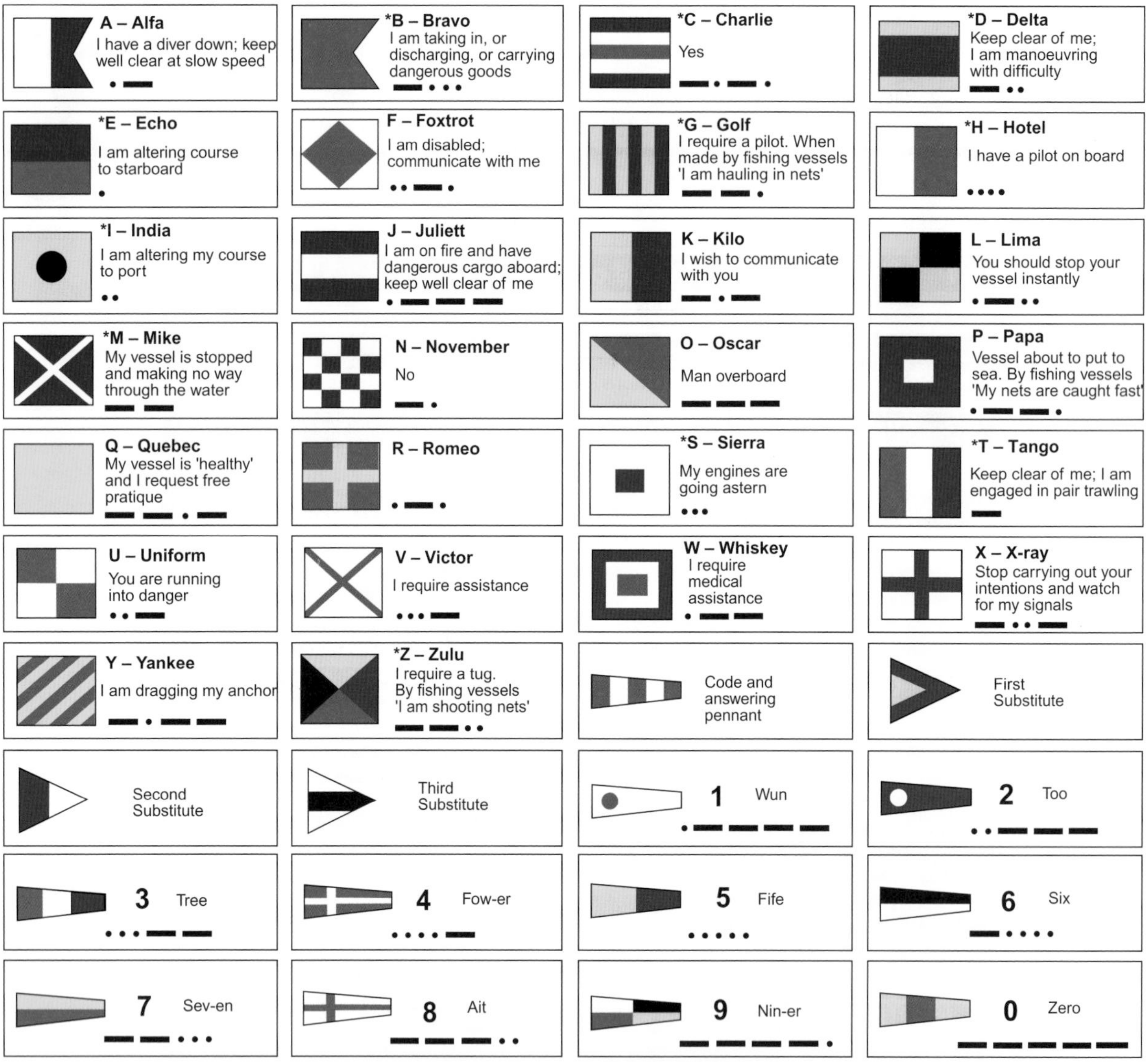

Fig 5(1) International Code of Signals: code flags, single letter meanings, phonetic alphabet (NATO/ITU) and Morse code symbols

5.1.1 Using the International Code

The Code can be used to convey information by: voice, using R/T or loud-hailer; Morse by flashing light and sound signals; alphabetical flags and numeral pendants; or by hand flags.

Signals consist of: single-letter signals which are urgent or much used; two-letter signals in the General Section; and three-letter signals starting with the letter 'M' in the Medical Section. Fig 5(1) above shows the Code flags for letters and numerals, the alphanumeric phonetic alphabet, Morse code for letters and numerals, and the meanings of important or common single-letter signals. **Signals marked with * when made by sound may only be used in compliance with COLREGs Rules 34 and 35.**

You may also see or hear the following important two-letter signals (there are many others):

NC	I am in distress and require immediate assistance.
NE2	You should proceed with great caution; submarines are exercising in this area.
RY	You should proceed at slow speed when passing me (or vessels making signals).
YG	You appear to be contravening the rules of a Traffic Separation Scheme.

5.2 OPERATING A RADIO

5.2.1 Frequency bands

For convenience radio frequencies with similar ranges and transmission characteristics are grouped into different 'bands', such as MF, HF, VHF and UHF (meaning 'medium', 'high', 'very high' and 'ultra-high' frequencies, respectively). Their ranges and characteristics are described below.

5.2.2 Regulations

The regulations for using R/T communications are in the *Handbook for Marine Radio Communication* (Lloyd's of London Press). They are lengthy and form part of the syllabus and examination for certificates of competence.

Some of the more important stipulations are:

Operators must not divulge the contents of messages heard; distress calls have priority; Coast radio stations, or MRCCs as appropriate, control communications in their respective areas. Check that the channel is free before transmitting; unnecessary or superfluous messages are prohibited, as is bad language. In harbour a yacht may not use inter-ship channels except for safety; a radio log must be used to record all messages sent and received.

Communications between CGOCs and second parties are tape recorded, as are intercepted communications with a third party. The following statement is included at the request of the MCA:

'Radio & telephone calls to/from CGOCs are recorded for public safety, prevention/detection of crime and to maintain the operational standards of HM Coastguard'.

5.2.3 Radio licences

- The **vessel** requires a Ship Radio Licence for any VHF, UHF, MF, HF, satellite or EPIRB equipment on board. It is valid 'for life' and is issued free of charge by: Ofcom, Riverside House, 2a Southwark Bridge Rd, London SE1 9HA. ☎ 020 7981 3040; 📠 020 7981 3235. www.ofcom.org.uk.

  This allows the use of international maritime channels, Ch M for communications between yachts, marinas and clubs, and M2 for race control.

- The **person** in charge of a set requires a Certificate of Competence (Pt 1) and Authority to Operate (Pt 2). This will usually be the Short Range Certificate (SRC), incorporating VHF DSC procedures. The syllabus and conduct of examinations are the RYA's responsibility; see RYA booklet G26. The former Restricted Certificate of Competence (VHF only) is no longer issued, but remains valid for VHF-only radios.

  The Long Range Certificate (LRC) covers MF, HF, Satellite communications and EPIRBs, as does the professional seafarers' General Operator's Certificate (GOC).

- Citizen's Band (CB) and Amateur (Ham) Radio can be useful means of communication for other than safety matters, but only supplement maritime radio on VHF, MF or HF. CB no longer requires a licence in the UK, but Amateur Radio licences are issued by: Ofcom, see contact details above.

- ATIS (Automatic Transmission Identification System) is compulsory on European inland waters. An ATIS capable VHF radio must be used. Ofcom issues a Notice of Variation (NOV) to your exisiting VHF licence on request to licencingcentre@ofcom.org.uk

5.2.4 R/T procedures

Communications between a vessel and a Coast radio station are controlled by the latter, except for Distress, Urgency or Safety messages. Between two vessels, the vessel which is called nominates the working channel.

Before calling, decide exactly what you wish to say; it may help to write the message down. Speak slowly and distinctly. Repeat (or spell phonetically) names or important words; see below for the use and meanings of common prowords.

Your position should be given as Lat/Long or the vessel's bearing and distance *from* a charted object, eg 'My position 225° Isle of May 4M' means you are 4M SW of the Isle of May (*not* 4M NE). Use the 360° True bearing notation and the 24 hours clock (0001–2359), specifying UT or LT.

5.2.5 Prowords

These simplify and expedite communications:

ACKNOWLEDGE	Have you received and understood?
CONFIRM	My version is ... is that correct?
CORRECTION	An error has been made; the correct version is ...
I SAY AGAIN	I repeat ... (eg vital words)
I SPELL	What follows is spelled phonetically.
OUT	End of working.
OVER	I have completed this part of my message, and am inviting you to reply.
RECEIVED	Receipt acknowledged.
SAY AGAIN	Repeat your message (or part of it, ie: All after/before ...).
STATION CALLING	Used when a station is unsure of the identity of the calling station.

5.3 RADIO COMMUNICATIONS SYSTEMS

5.3.1 VHF radio

VHF radio (Marine band 156·00–174·00 MHz) is used by most vessels. Range is slightly better than the line of sight between aerials, typically about 20M between yachts and up to 65M to a shore station depending on aerial heights. It always pays to fit a good aerial, as high as possible.

VHF sets may be **Simplex**, ie transmit and receive on the same frequency, so only one person can talk at a time. However, most modern sets transmit and receive simultaneously on different frequencies (full Duplex) so conversation is normal, but two aerials are needed.

Marine VHF frequencies are known by their international channel number (Ch), as shown below.

Channels are grouped according to three main purposes, but some have more than one purpose.

Public correspondence: **(via Coast radio stations).**
Ch 26, 27, 25, 24, 23, 28, 04, 01, 03, 02, 07, 05, 84, 87, 86, 83, 85, 88, 61, 64, 65, 62, 66, 63, 60, 82, 78, 81.
All channels can be used for Duplex.

Inter-ship:
Ch 06*, 08*, 10, 13, 09, 72*, 73, 69, 77*, 15, 17.
These are all Simplex channels. * for use in UK.

Port Operations:
Simplex: Ch 12, 14, 11, 13, 09, 68, 71, 74, 69, 73, 17, 15.
Duplex: Ch 20, 22, 18, 19, 21, 05, 07, 02, 03, 01, 04, 78, 82, 79, 81, 80, 60, 63, 66, 62, 65, 64, 61, 84.

The following channels have one specific purpose:

Ch 0 (156·00 MHz): SAR ops, not available to yachts.

Ch 10 (156·50 MHz), **62** (160·725 MHz), **63** (160·775 MHz) and **64** (160·825 MHz): MSI broadcasts. The optimum channel number is stated on Ch 16 in the announcement prior to the broadcast itself.

Ch 13 (156·650 MHz): Inter-ship communications relating to safety of navigation; a possible channel for calling a merchant ship if no contact on Ch 16.

Ch 16 (156·80 MHz): Distress, Safety and calling. Ch 16, in parallel with DSC Ch 70, will be monitored by ships, CG rescue centres (and, in some areas, any remaining Coast Radio Stations) for Distress and Safety until further notice. Yachts should monitor Ch 16. After an initial call, stations concerned **must** switch to a working channel, except for Distress and Safety matters.

Ch 67 (156·375 MHz): Small craft safety channel used by all UK CG centres, accessed via Ch 16.

Note: For routine (non-emergency) traffic contact NMOC Fareham on Ch 67 using call-sign Solent Coastguard.

Ch 70 (156·525 MHz): Digital Selective Calling for Distress and Safety purposes under GMDSS.

Ch 80 (157·025 MHz): Primary working channel between yachts and UK marinas.

Ch M (157·85 MHz): Secondary working channel, formerly known as Ch 37. For use in UK territorial waters only.

Ch M2 (161·425 MHz): for race control, with Ch M as stand-by. YCs often use Ch M2. For use in UK waters only.

5.3.2 MF radio

MF radios operate in the 1605–4200 kHz wavebands giving typical ranges of 100–300M using the Single Sideband (SSB) mode of transmission. Double sideband (DSB) mode transmissions are prohibited except for emergency transmissions on the marine Distress frequency (2182 kHz).

MF transmissions tend to follow the earth's curvature, which makes them suitable for direction-finding equipment. The GMDSS DSC Distress alerting frequency is 2187·5 kHz.

5.3.3 Mobile phones (GSM/GPRS/3G/4G broadband)

Mobile phones are not suitable for emergency situations, except in extremis (see 7.6.6), but permit low cost messaging as well as roaming when in different countries. Many smartphones now incorporate GPS and mapping functionality as well as wi-fi (see 5.3.5).

Ordinary GSM (Global System for Mobile Communications) wireless telephony allows a PC to connect wirelessly to the Internet at a speed of 9.6kbps (thousand bits per second); slow, but sufficient for sending and receiving basic emails and browsing text-only websites; GSM is more likely to be available than faster, enhanced services (see below), particularly in less populated areas.

Enhancements: many data services may be available, depending upon where you sail and if you have a compatible handset. These include Global Packet Radio Service (GPRS), boosting GSM download rates to around 36–48kbps. Wireless Broadband services such as 3G delivered increasingly better speeds, theoretically up to 14 mbps. The latest Generation, 4G, is about 5–7 times faster than 3G, with a maximum potential speed of around 80 mbps, providing rapid mobile broadband internet access for large downloads like films, mobile TV, connections to laptops with wireless modems, smartphones and other mobile devices.

The connection is 'always on'; charges are according to the amount of data transmitted, not the duration of the call. Availability of each service from base stations varies and range offshore cannot be relied upon, especially off sparsely populated coasts where only a limited service is provided.

5.3.4 Voice over IP (VOIP)

Internet Protocol, or IP, is the 'language' that drives the Internet, and VOIP (Voice over IP) is a system where voice communication is encoded and transmitted very efficiently as computer data. Free to join VOIP services such as Skype provide free voice communication between 'members', and also (for a small charge) with normal land-line telephones. VOIP will work over mobile broadband, but network charges will be high if roaming, so wired broadband connection is required, often available on the marina pontoons.

5.3.5 Wi-fi/Wi-MAX

Basic wireless telephony services such as GSM handle voice communications; 3G/4G wireless broadband service adds data capability that may be used with an on board PC (or Macintosh) to send and receive email, browse websites and download updates and chart corrections, in exactly the same way as from a home PC.

Wi-fi, on the other hand, is an increasingly common wireless system, independent of the phone operators' networks, that provides broadband Internet access via 'hotspots', or 'wireless access points', often located at marinas. Even with special antennae, range is limited and this prevents wi-fi being useful to yachts while at sea, but speeds of up to 10,000kbps in the marina are typical and are perfectly suited to normal Internet use like web browsing and downloading Notices to Mariners or Almanac updates.

The next big thing, Wi-MAX, is an emerging technology that promises Internet access at up to 40mbps over much greater ranges than wi-fi. Services are appearing but its onset has been slower than anticipated.

5.4 GLOBAL COMMUNICATION SYSTEMS

Once out of range of VHF/MF or wireless telephony/ broadband service, the yachtsman's communications options are limited to MF/HF radio and satellite systems (Satcoms).

A yachtsman embarking on an extended offshore venture would usually choose a mix of equipment for sensible reasons of redundancy, this will allow a choice of listening and transmitting, via terrestrial and satellite radio systems, to meet his needs at various times and in different circumstances. A typical setup might include a fixed or handheld satcoms transceiver, a HF SSB transceiver and receiver. For data capability, these would be interfaced to an on-board PC or Mac.

5.4.1 HF/single sideband radio (HF-SSB)

HF SSB radios use frequencies in the 4, 8, 12, 16 and 22 MHz bands (short wave), provide worldwide coverage and usually include MF frequencies as well.

Despite rapid growth in marine satellite communications, HF SSB remains a popular choice amongst long-distance cruisers, providing a cost-free voice (and limited email) capability for cruisers, sometimes operating over vast distances. Operators have the Long Range Certificate (LRC; see 5.2.3) or General Operators Certificate (GOC). To use Amateur (ham) bands (giving more frequencies and higher power, therefore range) operators must take the ham examination.

Using HF SSB radio for email requires a radio modem, often proprietary to the supplier. Though slow and requiring some skill to operate effectively, the almost-nil operating costs appeal to many and SSB radio has a strong following amongst blue-water cruisers. Established suppliers include Sailmail and Globe Wireless.

HF SSB radio is also extensively used for receipt of weatherfax images (see Chapter 6), although a receive-only SSB radio (with an adequate, grounded antenna installation) may be used rather than a full transceiver. Though declining in popularity, several useful weatherfax transmitting stations remain, including Northwood, UK and Offenbach, Germany.

5.4.2 Satellite Communications (Satcoms)

Satellite communications systems operate over **Ultra High Frequency (UHF)** radio using digital technology that makes them easier and more reliable to use than SSB radio; they operate with either a dedicated ship installation or a standalone handset.

Ongoing costs usually include a monthly service fee and usage charges that will be related to either the amount of satellite time used, or the volume of data transmitted and received.

For two-way voice communications, the 'Ship Station' (aka 'Mobile Earth Station') transmits to a visible satellite that is simultaneously in sight of a 'Land Earth Station', eg Goonhilly, Cornwall. From there, the call is routed to its destination through the normal terrestrial telephone network.

The satellite 'constellations' have different architectures. Inmarsat for example has several geostationary (GEO) satellites, each positioned over the equator. Because they are comparatively high up 19,400M (36,000km), each satellite has a large signal 'footprint', overlapping the next one and thus world-wide coverage is provided (although not in the polar regions above about 70°N and 70°S).

[1] typical, if in coverage area [2] using VOIP [3] Likely to be expensive	Wired Broadband	Wi-fi	Cellular GSM	Cellular GPRS	Cellular 3G	Wi-Max
Range offshore[1] (NM)	0	0-1	0-15	0-15	0-15	0-30
Voice communication	Y[2]	Y[2]	Y	Y	Y	Y[2]
Text messages	Y	Y	Y	Y	Y	Y
Light email traffic	Y	Y	Y[3]	Y	Y	Y
Text weather forecasts	Y	Y	Y[3]	Y	Y	Y
Heavy email traffic	Y	Y	×	Y[3]	Y	Y
Graphical weather forecasts	Y	Y	×	Y[3]	Y	Y
Full web browsing	Y	Y	×	Y[3]	Y	Y

Other systems employ many more Low Earth Orbit (LEO) satellites orbiting the Earth about 540M (1,000km) up.

The smaller, low-data rate, handheld voice terminals incorporate an omni-directional antenna that works best with an unobstructed view of the satellite. Fixed installations use an external gyro-stabilised antenna (to keep it pointing at the satellite as the boat moves); more powerful systems that support higher data rates employ antenna radomes that are really too large for installation aboard a 10–15m yacht.

The GMDSS provides automatic distress, urgency and safety communications, with some satcom systems (eg Inmarsat C) providing a red button that alerts a Coastguard Operations Centre (CGOC) when pressed.

There are several service providers, each offering an array of capabilities. Table 5(1) below provides a useful summary of systems that might be used aboard a 10–20m yacht.

This is a fast moving field: check with manufacturers/retailers for up-to-date specifications and prices.

TABLE 5(1) Satellite Communications (Satcoms)

System	Antenna	Satellites	Coverage	GMDSS	Phone (voice)	Fax	SMS text	Position tracking	Data rate
INMARSAT C	Omnidirectional	GEO	Global excepting polar regions	Yes	No	Yes	Yes	Yes (GPS)	Very low, uneconomic for email
INMARSAT Mini-M	Gyrostabilised 40cms diameter	GEO	Global excepting polar regions	No	Yes	Yes	No	No	2.4kbps
INMARSAT D+	Omnidirectional	GEO	Global excepting polar regions	No	No	No	No	Yes (GPS)	Very low, uneconomic for email
Fleet 33	Gyrostabilised 40cms diameter	GEO	Global excepting polar regions	No	Yes	Yes	Yes	No	9.6kbps uncompressed
Iridium	Omnidirectional	66 LEO	Global	No	Yes	Out only	Yes	No	Data kit required 2.4kbps (higher with compression)
Globalstar	Omnidirectional	40 LEO	Global excepting polar regions	No	Yes	Yes	Yes	To 10km	9.6kbps uncompressed, 38.6kbps compressed, 56k with data kit
Thuraya	Omnidirectional	1 GEO	Europe, N Africa & Middle East, India	No	Yes	Yes	Yes	Yes (GPS)	9.6kbps (144kbps possible with land *DSL receiver)

*DSL (Digital Subscriber Line) allows broadband Internet over normal copper telephone lines. It is used in the wireless/Satcoms arena to denote 'broadband-like speeds' over the wireless link and usually means speeds of 5 to 24mbps which is relatively fast for Satcoms.

5.5 NAVIGATIONAL WARNINGS

Navigational warnings are promulgated for 16 NavAreas (I-XVI) worldwide. An Area co-ordinator oversees each NavArea and handles inputs from national and other authorities. The 3 types of navigational warnings are:

NavArea warnings which deal with Oceanic matters and are transmitted over satcoms by SafetyNet and via NAVTEX at scheduled times in English and other languages.

Coastal warnings, up to 250M offshore, are issued by a national authority and broadcast in English or the local langauge by NAVTEX, SafetyNet or VHF Coast radio stations. These warnings cover navaids, lights, buoys, rocks, wrecks, naval exercises, SAR operations, cable laying, piracy etc.

Local warnings supplement the above for inshore waters and within port limits. They are issued by port, pilotage or CG authorities in English and/or the local language.

Details of country by country navwarning provision are given in the relevant country listing.

5.6 GUNFACTS AND SUBFACTS

5.6.1 Gunfacts

Gunfacts are warnings of intended naval firing practice, broadcast on Ch 16. They include gunnery and missile firings and underwater explosions. (For the latter only, broadcasts are made 1 hour, 30 mins and immediately before detonation.) They do not restrict the passage of any vessel. The onus for safety is on the firing warship. The broadcasts include:

- Time (LT) and approximate location of firings, with a declared safe distance in nautical miles.
- Whether illuminants, ie flares etc, are to be fired.

Gunfacts (S Coast) are issued from Plymouth for English Channel exercise areas (9.1.16). See Subfacts (below) for details.

Gunfacts (Ship) are issued by a nominated warship and cover activity in any UK areas. An initial announcement is made on VHF 16.

5.6.2 Subfacts

Are warnings of planned or known submarine activity.

Subfacts (South Coast) give details for the English Channel; see 9.1.16. They are broadcast on NAVTEX (see Chapter 6) and, after an announcement on Ch 16, by Falmouth CGOC every 4 hours from 0140 UT on VHF. The VHF channels are shown on Fig 6(4). For any queries regarding Subfacts and Gunfacts contact FOST (Flag Officer Sea Training) Plymouth ☎01752 557550, or call 'FOST Ops' VHF Ch 74.

Subfacts (Clyde) give details for the W coast of Scotland (see 9.8.22 and 9.9.16). They are broadcast on NAVTEX (see Chapter 6) and, after announcements on Ch 16, by Stornoway CGOC every 4 hours from 0410 UT; and by Belfast CGOC every 4 hours from 0410 UT. The VHF channels are shown on Fig 6(4). For any queries regarding Subfacts and Gunfacts contact Fleet Operations Northwood ☎01923 846371 or 846366.

NAVTEX transmits Subfacts and Gunfacts twice daily: Niton (E) 0440 and 1640 UT; Portpatrick (O) 0620 and 1820 UT.

5.7 COAST RADIO STATIONS (CRS)

Many European nations have closed, or plan to close, their coast radio stations due in part to the popularity of mobile phones. **The UK, France and the Netherlands have no CRS.** Ireland (but see 5.10.4), Denmark, Belgium, Spain and Portugal still operate CRS. In Germany a commercial company, DP07 Seefunk, provides a limited link call service. Details of national CRS are given below in the country by country listing.

5.7.1 Functions

CRS functions include:

- Control of ship-shore communications; see 5.2.4.
- Providing link calls; see 5.7.3. **Note: The Coastguard, or foreign equivalent, do not handle link calls.**
- Broadcasting at scheduled times traffic lists (messages awaiting ships at sea); navigational warnings; weather bulletins and gale warnings (Chapter 6). Note: Do not transmit on a designated broadcast channel when a broadcast is scheduled.
- Handling Distress and Urgency calls in some countries.

5.7.2 Track Reports

A Track Report (TR) may be passed to a CRS or Coastguard centre, as appropriate, stating a yacht's point of departure, destination, ETA and number of people onboard. This is an obvious safety measure, especially in more remote regions, should a yacht subsequently become overdue. On arrival be sure to inform the local CRS or CG and ask that your TR be cancelled with the original CRS/CG. See also Chapter 7.

5.7.3 Making a VHF link call

- Within range (up to 40M), select a 'clear' channel, ie no transmissions. A busy channel will have carrier noise, speech or the engaged signal (a series of pips).
- Call the CRS on a working channel related to the position of the yacht. Calls should state the calling channel and last at least 6 seconds in order to activate the response equipment at the CRS.

For example:

Bilbao Radio, this is Yacht Seabird, Yacht Seabird, Golf Oscar Romeo India Fower, Channel 27, Over.

A four-tone signal or pips indicate a temporary delay, but you will be answered when an operator is free.

- When the call is accepted you will hear pips, indicating that the channel has been engaged. Wait for the operator to speak. If no response, do not change channel since you may lose your turn.

  If the pips are not heard, the station's transmitter has not been activated or may be out of range. Try another station or call again when closer.
- The operator will request: Vessel's callsign (eg Golf Oscar Romeo India Fower), name, accounting code (see 5.7.4), type of message (eg telegram, telephone call) and the telephone number required (and in the case of a personal call the name of the person called).

5.7.4 Paying for a link call

Calls are accounted for worldwide by quoting an 'Accounting Authority Indicator Code' (AAIC). This must previously have been arranged with an ITU-recognised authority such as Cable and Wireless, who use GB 02 as their AAIC. All CRS hold the complete ITU listing of ship stations and their AAICs.

5.7.5 MF link calls

Calls should be initiated on 2182 kHz or the nominated working frequency. The Coast station will allocate a working channel, and cue you into the system.

5.8 UNITED KINGDOM (EXCLUDING THE CHANNEL ISLANDS)

5.8.1 HM Coastguard Communications

Contact details for UK Coastguard Operations Centres are shown below:

SCOTLAND & NORTHERN IRELAND REGION

†ABERDEEN COASTGUARD 57°08'N 02°05'W MMSI 002320004 ☎ 01224 592334 📠 01224 575920
Marine House, Blaikies Quay, Aberdeen AB11 5PB. Area: English border to Cape Wrath, incl Pentland Firth.

†SHETLAND COASTGUARD 60°09'N 01°08'W MMSI 002320001 ☎ 01595 692976 📠 01595 693634
Knab Road, Lerwick ZE1 0AX. Area: Orkney, Fair Isle and Shetland.

†*STORNOWAY COASTGUARD 58°12'N 06°22'W MMSI 002320024 ☎ 01851 702013 📠 01851 706796
Battery Point, Stornoway, Isle of Lewis H51 2RT. Area: Cape Wrath to Mull, Western Isles and St Kilda.

†*BELFAST COASTGUARD 54°40'N 05°40'W MMSI 002320021 ☎ 02891 463933 📠 02891 469854
Bregenz House, Quay St, Bangor, Co Down BT20 5ED.
Area: Carlingford Lough to Lough Foyle and Firth of Clyde, inc islands.

EASTERN REGION

NATIONAL MARITIME OPERATIONS CENTRE (NMOC) 50°51'·50N 01°14'·90W DSC MMSI, 002320011
☎ 02392 552100 📠 02392 554131/01305 760451. Kites Croft, Fareham PO14 4LW.
Area: South Coast: Topsham (River Exe) to Beachy Head (Note: in this area make initial contact using callsign *Solent Coastguard* on Ch 67 (H24) to avoid congestion on Ch 16). East coast: Reculver Towers to Southwold, use callsigns *Thames Coastguard* or *Dover Coastguard*, both on Ch 16.

DOVER COASTGUARD 50°08'N 01°20'E DSC MMSI 002320010 ☎ 01304 210008 📠 01304 225762
Langdon Battery, Swingate, Dover CT15 5NA. Area: Beachy Head to Reculver Towers
Operates Channel Navigation Information Service (CNIS); see 9.3.13.

LONDON COASTGUARD 51°30'N 00°03'E MMSI 002320063 ☎ 0208 3127380 📠 0208 3098196. Thames Barrier Navigation Centre, Unit 28, 34 Bowater Road, Woolwich, London SE18 5TF.
Area: River Thames from Shell Haven Pt (N bank) and Egypt Bay (S bank), upriver to Teddington Lock

†HUMBER COASTGUARD 54°06'N 00°11'W MMSI 002320007 ☎ 01262 672317 📠 01262 400779
Lime Kiln Lane, Bridlington, Yorks E Riding YO15 2LX. Area: Southwold to the Scottish border.

WESTERN REGION

†HOLYHEAD COASTGUARD 53°19'N 04°38'W MMSI 002320018 ☎ 01407 762051 📠 01407 761613
Prince of Wales Rd, Holyhead, Anglesey LL65 1ET. Area: Mull of Galloway to Friog (1·6M S of Barmouth).

†MILFORD HAVEN COASTGUARD 51°42'N 05°03'W MMSI 002320017 ☎ 01646 690909 📠 01646 697287
Gorsewood Drive, Hakin, Milford Haven, SA73 2HD. Area: Friog to Marsland Mouth (near Bude).

†*FALMOUTH COASTGUARD 50°09'N 05°03'W MMSI 002320014 ☎ 01326 317575 📠 01326 315610
Pendennis Point, Castle Drive, Falmouth TR11 4WZ.
Area: Marsland Mouth (near Bude) to Topsham (River Exe) falmouthcoastguard@mcga.gov.uk

NOTES: † Monitors DSC MF 2187.5 kHz.
* Broadcasts Gunfacts/Subfacts; see 5.6.
The 3 Regions above are Search and Rescue Regions.

THE NATIONAL COASTWATCH INSTITUTION (NCI) operates on dedicated VHF Ch 65. Callsign: use name of selected station (see Safety, 7.12) plus abbreviation NCI, eg: *Froward Point NCI.* Do **not** call on Ch 16 or use call-sign *National Coastwatch* which can potentially be confused with Coastguard. There are 50 operational stations (2017) around the English and Welsh coast. Manned by volunteers keeping a visual watch during daylight hours throughout the year, they are able to provide, on request, details of actual weather conditions and sea state at their individual coastal locations, radio checks, and local knowledge, from visitors' moorings to local hazards.

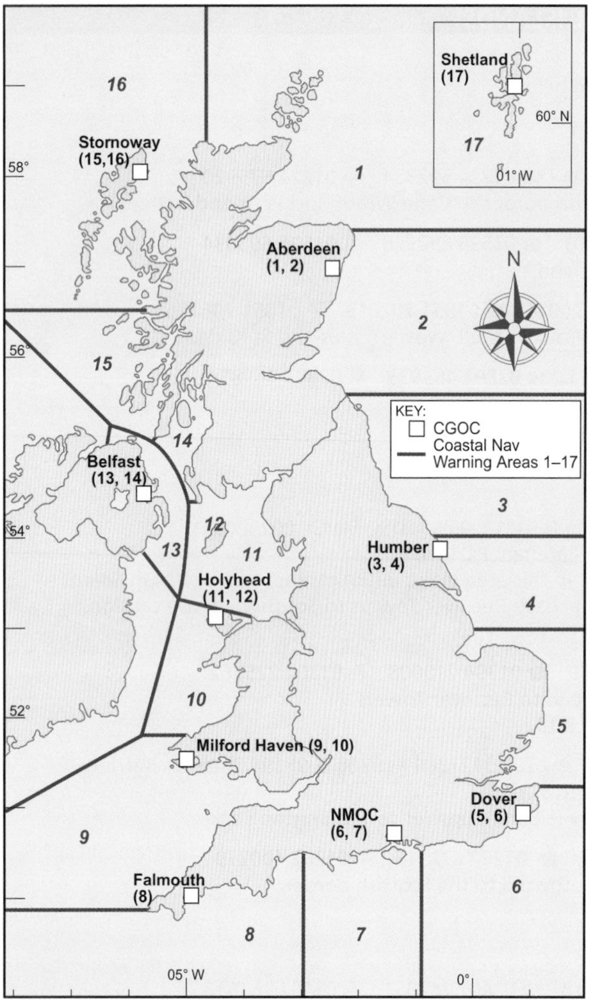

Fig 5(2) UK Coastal (WZ) Navwarning areas 1–17. The area(s) for which each CGOC is responsible are in brackets

5.8.2 Navwarnings (NavArea I Co-ordinator)

After an announcement on Ch 16, HMCG broadcasts coastal navigational warnings (WZ) on receipt and every 12 hours at the same times and on the same frequencies as the Group A MSI broadcasts. See Table 6(2) for details. WZs are also broadcast by NAVTEX at the times shown in Table 6(1), and by SafetyNET at 1730 UT daily for areas not covered by NAVTEX. See also weekly *Notices to Mariners* which include a list of warnings in force.

Urgent warnings are broadcast as soon as possible after receipt on Ch 16 and on 2182 kHz. New dangers to navigation should be notified to other craft and the nearest MRCC by a *Sécurité* call. More details at www.mcga.gov.uk (see Safety Information/Navigational Safety).

5.9 THE CHANNEL ISLANDS

5.9.1 Coastguard communications

Guernsey and Jersey Coastguard stations direct SAR operations in the North and South of the CI area respectively, they also provide communications on VHF and DSC.

Close liaison is maintained with French SAR authorities and a distress situation may be controlled by whichever is more appropriate. For example a British yacht in difficulty in French waters may be handled by St Peter Port or Jersey so as to avoid language problems; and vice versa for a French yacht.

GUERNSEY COASTGUARD (CRS)
49°27'N 02°32'W DSC MMSI 002320064
☎ 01481 720672 📠 01481 256432
VHF Ch 16, 20, 62, 67. guernsey.coastguard@gov.gg
Area: The Channel Islands Northern area.

JERSEY COASTGUARD (CRS)
49°10'·90N 02°06'·80W DSC MMSI 002320060
☎ 01534 447705/04 📠 01534 447799
VHF Ch 16, 25, 67 82, H24. jersey.coastguard@ports.je
Area: The Channel Islands Southern area.

5.9.2 Emergency VHF D/F

In the Channel Islands a yacht in distress should call on Ch 16; expect to be switched to Ch 20 for Guernsey or Ch 82 for Jersey. The emergency D/F sites, *from* which the true bearing of the yacht in distress is given, are: VHF D/F stations, ◉ RG.

Site	Lat/Long	Controlled via
Guernsey	49°26'·27N 02°35'·77W	*Guernsey Coastguard*
Jersey	49°10'·85N 02°14'·30W	*Jersey Coastguard*

5.9.3 Coast Radio Stations

Guernsey Coastguard and Jersey Coastguard are operated by the States of Guernsey and Jersey respectively. They handle Distress and Urgency situations as well as providing link calls (in emergencies only).

Guernsey Coastguard
VHF 16, **20** (primary working Ch, call direct for safety traffic), 16, small craft distress/emergency. Ch 62 available for link calls. Ch 67 on request for yacht safety messages.
DSC Ch 70: **MMSI** 002320064.
Traffic lists: Vessels are called individually on Ch 16.

Jersey Coastguard
VHF 16, **82,** primary working Ch, call direct for safety traffic, 16, small craft distress/emergency. (Ch 25, no continuous listening watch, link calls for emergencies only.)
DSC Ch 70 and 16 H24: **MMSI** 002320060.
Navigational warnings, weather bulletins and traffic lists are broadcast on Ch 82 at times in Chapter 6.

5.10 REPUBLIC OF IRELAND

5.10.1 Coast Guard communications

DUBLIN (MRCC)
53°20'N 06°15W DSC MMSI 002500300 (+2187·5 kHz)
☎ +353 1 662 0922/3 📠 +353 1 662 0795
Area: Carlingford Lough to Youghal.

VALENTIA (MRSC)
51°56'N 10°21'W DSC MMSI 002500200 (+2187·5 kHz)
☎ +353 669 476 109 📠 +353 669 476 289
Area: Youghal to Slyne Head.

MALIN HEAD (MRSC)
55°22'N 07°20W DSC MMSI 002500100 (+2187·5 kHz)
☎ +353 74 9370103 📠 +353 74 9370221
Area: Slyne Head to Lough Foyle

Co-ordinates SAR operations around ROI via Dublin MRCC, Malin Head and Valentia MRSCs and remote sites. It may liaise with the UK and France during any rescue operation

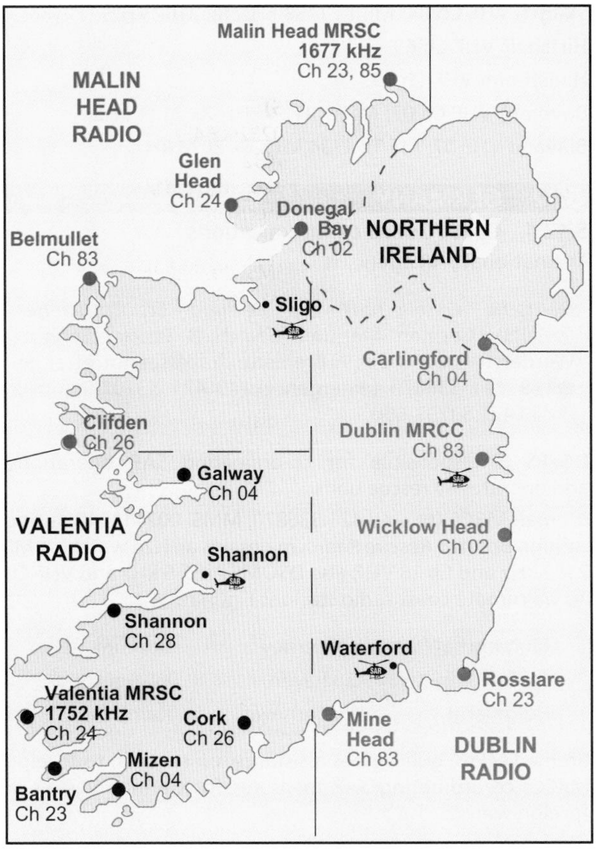

Fig 5(3) Irish coast radio stations, CG centres and boundaries

within 100M of the Irish coast. Dept of Transport, Leeson Lane, Dublin 2. ☎ (01) 6620922; admin@irishcoastguard.ie The Irish EPIRB Registry is also at this address.

The MRCC/MRSCs are co-located with the Coast radio stations of the same name and manned by the same staff. All stations keep watch H24 on VHF Ch 16 and DSC Ch 70. If ashore dial 999 or 112 in an emergency and ask for Marine Rescue.

5.10.2 SAR resources

The Irish Coast Guard provides some 50 units around the coast and is on call H24. The RNLI maintains four stations around the coast and operates 42 lifeboats. Additionally, six community-run inshore rescue boats are available.

Helicopters, based at Dublin, Waterford, Shannon and Sligo, can respond within 15 to 45 minutes and operate to a radius of 200M. They are equipped with infrared search equipment and can uplift 30 survivors.

Military and civilian aircraft and vessels, together with the Garda (Police) and lighthouse service, can also be involved.

Some stations provide specialist cliff climbing services. They are manned by volunteers, who are trained in first aid and equipped with inflatables, breeches buoys, cliff ladders etc. Their ☎ numbers (the Leader's residence) are given, where appropriate, under each port.

5.10.3 Navwarnings

Navwarnings are broadcast by Malin Hd and Valentia NAVTEX 518 kHz, see Table 6(1) and by MRCCs/MRSCs every 4 hours on VHF: Dublin and Malin Head from 0033 UT; Valentia from 0233 UT.

5.10.4 Coast Radio Stations

The main CRS at Malin Head, Dublin and Valentia are co-located with Coast Guard centres. Remote CRS sites, as listed below, ensure full coastal coverage in the three regions (NW, SE and SW Ireland). Callsign is station name and Radio.

All monitor Ch 16 (H24). Broadcasts are made on a working channel after pre-warning on Ch 16 and 2182 kHz. Ch 67 is only used for Safety messages. See Chapter 6 for times and details of gale warnings and weather bulletins.

Commercial link calls, ship to shore, are not available, but Medico link calls can be made on both VHF and MF. Call CRS on a working channel; only call Ch 16 if in difficulty or emergency.

Ships should pass their intended voyage or position to Malin Head Coast Guard, Dublin Coast Guard or Valentia Coast Guard, as appropriate. Update voyage details by TR.

NW Ireland (clockwise from the west)

Clifden Coast Guard Radio	26
Belmullet Coast Guard Radio	83
Donegal Bay Coast Guard Radio	02
Glen Head Coast Guard Radio	24
MALIN HEAD Coast Guard RADIO	23, 85
	MF: Tx 1677 kHz, Rx 2102

SE Ireland

Carlingford Coast Guard Radio	04
DUBLIN Coast Guard RADIO	(No MF) 83
Wicklow Head Coast Guard Radio	02
Rosslare Coast Guard Radio	23
Mine Head Coast Guard Radio	83

SW Ireland

Cork Coast Guard Radio	26
Mizen Coast Guard Head Radio	04
Bantry Coast Guard Radio	23
VALENTIA Coast Guard RADIO	24
	MF: Tx 1752 kHz, Rx 2045
Shannon Coast Guard Radio	28
Galway Coast Guard Radio	04

5.11 WEST DENMARK

5.11.1 Coast Guard communications

The national SAR agency is:

JRCC Admiral Danish Fleet, PO Box 1483, DK-8220 Brabrand, Denmark. ☎+45 894 33099 📠+45 728 50384.

The SAR coordinator is:

JRCC Denmark, ☎+45 728 50000 switchboard; 📠+45 728 50384; jrcc@sok.dk

MMSI 002191000

MF DSC 2187·5 kHz TX/RX (Routine national traffic TX 1624·5 kHz, RX 2159·5 kHz; Routine international TX 2177·0 kHz, RX 2189·5 kHz).

JRCC Denmark has no direct communications with vessels in distress, but operates via two Maritime Operations Centres (MOCs) and Coast Radio Station (CRS) Lyngby Radio.

MOC North (MRSC) ☎+45 992 21520; 📠+45 992 21538, mocn-orum@mil.dk, covers the W coast of Denmark.

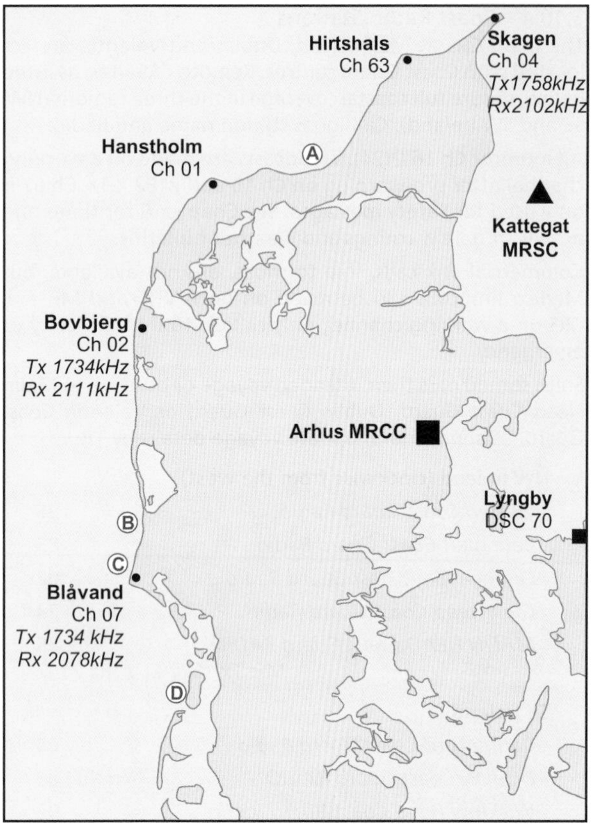

Fig 5(4) Danish Coast Guard and Coast Radio Stations

5.11.2 SAR resources
There are at least 12 lifeboats stationed at the major harbours along this west-facing coast. They double up as Pilot boats.

5.11.3 Navwarnings
Navwarnings are broadcast by Lyngby Radio on VHF and MF 1734 kHz, 1738 kHz every 4 hours from 0133 UT.

5.11.4 Firing practice areas
There are 4 such areas on the W coast as in Fig 5(4) and listed below. Firing times are broadcast daily by Danmarks Radio (243 kHz LW) at 1745 LT after the weather. Times are available from the Range office by ☎ or Ch 16, using callsigns below.

A	Tranum & Blokhus ☎ +45 72839699 or call *Tranum*
B	Nymindegab ☎ +4572839550 or call *Nymindegab*
C	Oksbøl ☎ +45 72839550, call *Oksbøl* or see *www.forsvaret.dk/oksbl*
D	Rømø E ☎ +45 72839550 (☎ +45 73755219 during firing) or call *Fly Rømø*. Rømø W ☎ +45 72848121

5.11.5 Coast Radio Stations
All Danish VHF/MF CRS are remotely controlled by **Lyngby** and use the callsign *Lyngby Radio*.

The stations in the the following list all monitor Ch 16 and DSC Ch 70, H24. Call on working frequencies, to keep Ch 16 clear. MF stations do not monitor 2182 kHz. Traffic lists are broadcast on all VHF channels every odd H+05.

Skagen VHF Ch 04; MF Tx 1758 kHz, Rx 2102 kHz.
Hirtshals VHF Ch 63.
Hanstholm VHF Ch 01.
Bovbjerg VHF Ch 02; MF Tx 1734 kHz, Rx 2111 kHz.
Blåvand VHF 07; MF Tx 1734 kHz, Rx 2078 kHz.

5.12 GERMANY

5.12.1 Coast Guard communications
The national SAR agency is:

Deutsche Gesellschaft zur Rettung Schiffbrüchiger (DGzRS), German Maritime Search & Rescue Service. Werderstrasse 2, D-28199 Bremen. info@seenotretter.de ☎+49 421 536870 (emergency),+49 421 53707-0 (ops); 📠+49 421 53707-690.

DGzRS is responsible for co-ordinating SAR operations, and operates 60 rescue units.

Bremen MRCC (☎ + 49 421 536870; MMSI 002111240), using callsign *Bremen Rescue Radio,* maintains an H24 watch on MF 2182 kHz and Ch 16 VHF, also DSC MF 2187·5 kHz and VHF Ch 70 via remote coast radio stations Fig(5)at:

Blumenthal	Norderney	Borkum
Stade	Cuxhaven	Wangerooge
Helgoland	Westerhever	Kampen

Bremen MRCC guarantees assistance, on request, to foreign MRCCs co-ordinating SAR measures for German vessels in foreign waters.

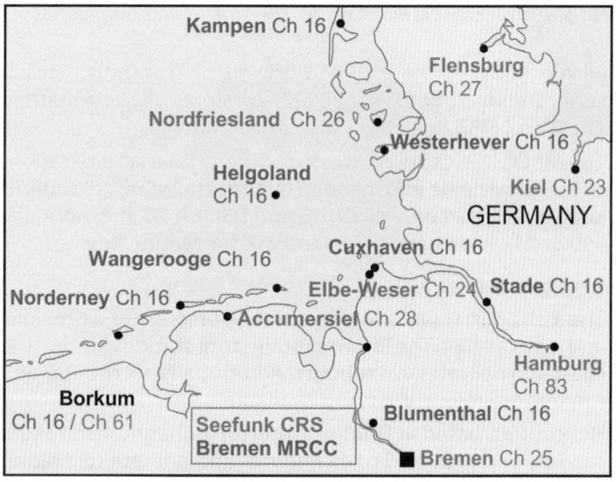

Fig 5(5) German Coastal Radio Stations

5.12.2 SAR resources
DGzRS has a total of 20 offshore lifeboats 20–26m LOA, and 40 <11m LOA along the German seaboard, with 12 large and 16 small based on their North Sea coast at:

Borkum, Juist, Norderney, Norddeich, Baltrum, Langeoog, Neuharlingersiel, Wangerooge, Horumersiel, Hooksiel, Wilhelmshaven, Fedderwardersiel, Bremerhaven, Cuxhaven, Brunsbüttel, Helgoland, Büsum Eiderdamm, Nordstrand, Amrum, Hörnum and List.

There are also many inshore lifeboats.

5.12.3 Navwarnings

Navwarnings *(Nautische Warnnachricht)* are broadcast in English by Pinneberg NAVTEX 518 kHz (see Table 6(1)) every 4 hours from 0300 UT. Bremen MRCC broadcasts vital Navwarnings for the North Sea Coast on VHF 16 on receipt of a warning and every H and H+30 until cancelled.

5.12.4 Coast Radio Stations

DP07 – Seefunk, Estedeich 84, 21129 Hamburg. ☎+49 040 23855782. ℻+49 040 74134242. info@dp07.com www.dp07.com MMSI 002113100

This company operates six CRS on the North Sea coast and five on the Baltic coast as shown on Fig 5(5) and listed below. The Coast Guard CRS monitor Ch 16 and DSC Ch 70.

Traffic Lists: at 0745, 0945, 1245, 1645 and 1945LT. Callsign is the name of the remote station.

Nordfriesland	26	**Baltic coast**	
Elbe-Weser	24	**Kiel**	23
Hamburg	83	**Flensburg**	27
Bremen	25		
Accumersiel	28		
Borkum	61		

5.13 THE NETHERLANDS

5.13.1 Coast Guard communications

The national SAR agency is:

SAR Commission Maritime, Ministry of Infrastructure and the Environment, PO Box 5807, 2280 HV The Hague, The Netherlands.

The Netherlands CG at Den Helder, co-located with the Navy HQ, co-ordinates SAR operations as the Dutch JRCC for A1 and A2 Sea Areas. (JRCC = Joint Rescue Coordination Centre – marine & aeronautical.) Callsign is *Netherlands Coast Guard*, but *Den Helder Rescue* during SAR operations.

The JRCC keeps a listening watch H24 on DSC Ch 70, and MF DSC 2187·5 kHz (but not on 2182 kHz); MMSI 002442000.

Coast Guard Operations can be contacted H24 via:

Emergency and Operations telephone number:

☎+31 223 542300 ℻+31 223 658358 ccc@kustwacht.nl

Admin/info (HO):

☎+31 223 658300 ℻+31 223 658303

info@kustwacht.nl www. kustwacht.nl PO Box 10.000/ MPC 10A, 1780 CA Den Helder.

Remote CG stations are shown on Fig 5(6). Working channels are VHF 23 and 83.

5.13.2 Medical advice

Call initially on Ch 16, DSC Ch 70 or 2187·5 kHz (MMSI 002442000). Working chans are VHF Ch 23 & 83 or MF 2824 kHz (transmit), 2520 kHz (receive).

5.13.3 SAR resources

The Dutch Lifeboat Ass'n (KNRM) manages 45 all-weather lifeboat stations and 13 inshore lifeboat stations along the coast. The 75 lifeboats include 13m LOA water-jet, rigid inflatables capable of 36kn. Helicopters, fixed wing aircraft and ships of the RNN can be called upon; also Air Force helicopters at Leeuwarden. The area of activity extends across the Dutch Continental Shelf and into the Waddenzee, IJsselmeer and estuaries of Zuid Holland and Zeeland.

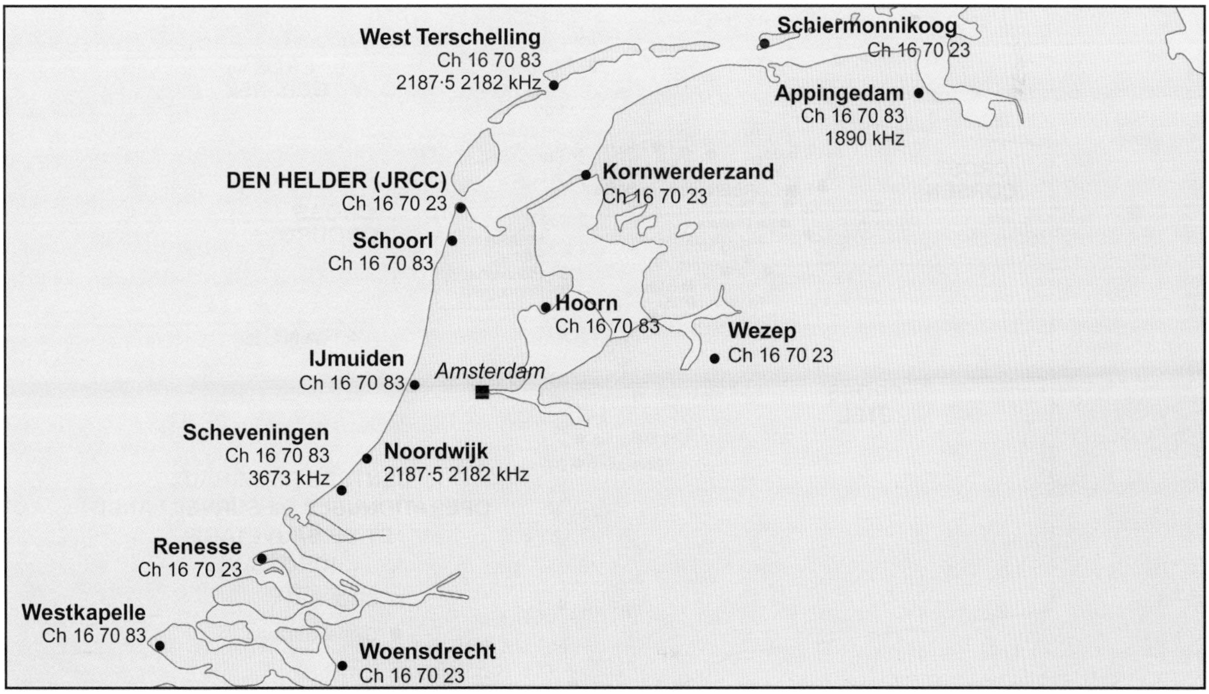

Fig 5(6) Netherlands Coast Guard and Radio stations

5.13.4 Navwarnings

Navwarnings are broadcast by Netherlands Coast Guard on NAVTEX 518 kHz (see Table 6(1)) every 4 hours from 0230 UT, and in English on VHF Ch 23 or Ch 83 and MF 3673 kHz every 4 hours from 0333 UT.

5.14 BELGIUM

5.14.1 Coast Guard communications

The Belgian Coast Guard co-ordinates SAR operations from Oostende MRCC, callsign *Coast Guard Oostende*. The MRCC and *Oostende Radio* (CRS, see below) both keep listening watch H24 on Ch 16, 67, 2182kHz and DSC Ch 70 and 2187·5kHz.

Coast Guard stations

MRCC OOSTENDE
☎ +32 59 701000 📠 +32 59 703605
MMSI 002059981
mrcc@mrcc.be

RCC BRUSSELS (Point of contact for COSPAS/SARSAT)
☎ +32 (0)2 751 4615 📠 +32 (0)2 7524201
rcc@mil.be

5.14.2 SAR resources

Offshore and inshore lifeboats are based at Nieuwpoort, Oostende and Blankenberge.

The Belgian Air Force provides helicopters from Koksijde near the French border. The Belgian Navy also participates in SAR operations as required, ☎ +32 2 4430350 📠 +32 2 4439658 mik@mil.be

5.14.3 Navwarnings

Navwarnings are broadcast by Oostende on NAVTEX 518 kHz (see Chapter 6, Table 6(1)), and in English every 4 hrs on VHF 27 and MF 2761 kHz on receipt, every H+03 and H+33, and every 4 hours from 0233 UT. Local messages are broadcast on 490 kHz. Navwarnings are broadcast for the Schelde on VHF 24 on receipt and every H+55.

5.14.4 Coast Radio Stations

OOSTENDE RADIO
☎ +32 59 255493 📠 +32 59 255467 rmd@mil.be
MMSI 002050480 Ch 16, MF 2182 kHz, DSC Ch 70 and 2187·5 kHz (H24)
MF: Tx 2484, Rx 3178 kHz. VHF Ch 07, 24, 27, 63, 78, 81 85

Zeebrugge	Ch 27, 63
Middelkerke (Oostende)	Ch 27
De Panne (French border)	Ch 78
Antwerp	Ch 07, 27
Ghent	Ch 81
Rest of Belgium	Ch 24.

5.15 FRANCE

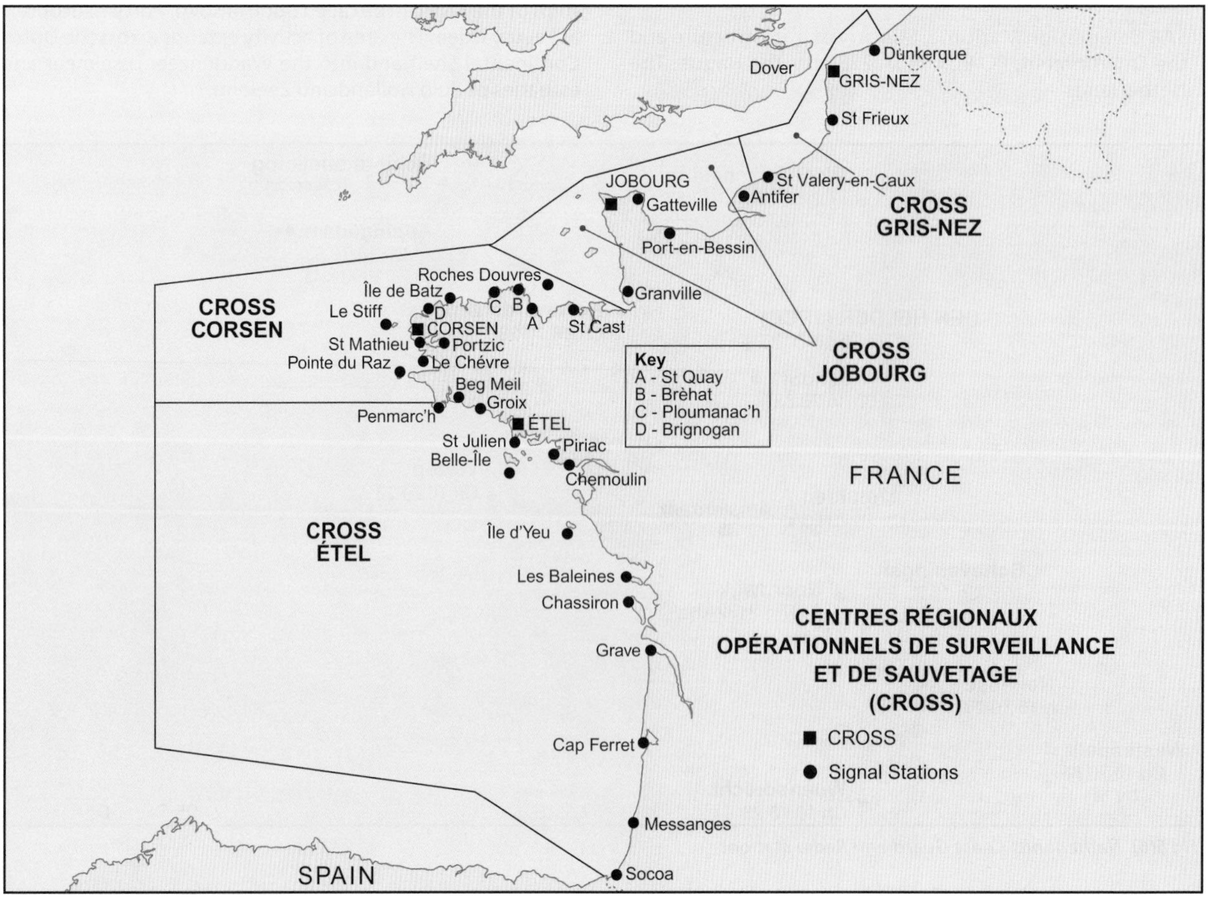

Fig 5(7) CROSS centres and signal stations (for remote stations see 6(12))

5.15.1 French CROSS infrastructure

CROSS (Centres Régionaux Opérationnels de Surveillance et de Sauvetage) provide an all-weather presence H24 along the French coast in liaison with foreign CGs. CROSS is an MRCC. The main functions include:

- Co-ordinating SAR operations
- Navigational surveillance
- Broadcasting navigational warnings (5.5)
- Broadcasting weather information (6.20)
- Anti-pollution control
- Marine and fishery surveillance

All centres monitor VHF Ch 16 and DSC Ch 70 and co-ordinate SAR on Ch 10, 13, 15, **67**, **68**, 73; DSC Ch 70, Corsen MRCC additionally monitors MF DSC (2187·5 kHz). They can be contacted by phone 112; via the National Gendarmerie, Affaires Maritimes or a Semaphore station. If a nautical emergency *is witnessed from the land*, phone direct on 196. CROSS also monitors the TSS in the Dover Strait, off Casquets and off Ouessant using, for example, callsign *Ushant Traffic.*

For medical advice at sea call the appropriate CROSS which will contact the French TMAS (Telemedical Maritime Assistance Service) and co-ordinate an evacuation if necessary. ⚠ Note: SAMU (Ambulance) will respond more quickly to an emergency onshore than calling a doctor. Simply dial 15.

5.15.2 CROSS locations/contact details

Any CROSS can be telephoned simply by dialling **112.**

CROSS Gris-Nez 50°52'N 01°35'E
MMSI 002275100 ☎ 03·21·87·21·87 Fax 03·21·87·78·55
gris-nez@mrccfr.eu Area: Belgian border–Cap d'Antifer. CROSS Gris-Nez responds to COSPAS/SARSAT alerts.

CROSS Jobourg 49°41'N 01°54'W
MMSI 002275200 ☎ 02·33·52·16·16 Fax 02·33·52·78·23.
jobourg@mrccfr.eu Area: Cap d'Antifer–Mt St Michel

CROSS Corsen 48°24'N 04°47'W
MMSI 002275300 ☎ 02·98·89·31·31 Fax 02·98·89·65·75
corsen@mrccfr.eu Area: Mt St Michel–Pointe de Penmarc'h

CROSS Étel 47°39'N 03°12'W
MMSI 002275000 ☎ 02·97·55·35·35 Fax 02·97·55·49·34
etel@mrccfr.eu Area: Pointe de Penmarc'h to the Spanish border.

5.15.3 Lifeboats

Société National de Sauvetage en Mer (SNSM; lifeboat service) comes under CROSS. At sea, all vessels must contact CROSS to call upon the services of SNSM, they should not be contacted directly in an emergency. A hefty charge may be levied for a false call-out.

5.15.4 Navwarnings (NavArea II Co-ordinator)

Navwarnings are of two types: **Long-range** for NavArea II issued by SHOM and broadcast by SafetyNet.

AvurNavs include Coastal and Local warnings. They are issued by Cherbourg for the coast from the Belgian border to Mont St Michel, and by Brest from Mont St Michel to the Spanish border. They are broadcast by CROSS (Corsen) NAVTEX in English every 4 hours from 0000 UT, and in French every 4 hours from 0040 UT. CROSS also broadcasts Navwarnings on VHF 79/80 after initial call on VHF 16 (Jobourg rarely).

5.15.5 Semaphore (signal) stations

These keep visual, radar and radio watch (VHF Ch 16) around the coast and are manned by the French Navy. They relay emergency calls to CROSS and are equipped with VHF DF. They show gale warning signals, repeat forecasts and offer local weather reports. They are listed below.

Semaphore (Signal) stations

Dunkerque	03·28·66·86·18
Boulogne	03·21·31·32·10
Ault	03·22·60·47·33
Dieppe	02·35·84·23·82
Fécamp	02·35·28·00·91
La Hève	02·35·46·07·81
Villerville	02·31·88·11·13
Port-en-Bessin	02·31·21·81·51
St Vaast	02·33·54·44·50
Barfleur	02·33·54·04·37
Le Homet	02·33·92·60·08
La Hague	02·33·52·71·07
Barneville-Carteret	02·33·53·85·08
Granville Le Roc	02·33·50·05·85
* St Cast	02·96·41·85·30
St Quay-Portrieux	02·96.70.42.18
* Bréhat	02·96·20·00·12
Ploumanac'h	02·96·91·46·51
* Batz	02·98·61·76·06
Brignogan	02·98·83·50·84
Ouessant Stiff	02·98·48·81·50
St-Mathieu	02·98·89·01·59
Portzic (Ch 08)	02·98·22·21·47
* Toulinguet	02·98·27·90·02
* Cap-de-la-Chèvre	02·98·27·09·55
Pointe-du-Raz	02·98·70·66·57
Penmarc'h	02·98·58·61·00
* Beg Meil	02·98·94·98·92
Étel Mât Fenoux (HW-3 to HW+2)	02·97·55·35·39
Beg Melen (Groix)	02·97·86·80·13
* Talut (Belle-Île)	02·97·31·85·07
St Julien	02·97·50·09·35
* Piriac-sur-Mer	02·40·23·59·87
Chemoulin	02·40·91·99·00
St Sauveur (Yeu)	02·51·58·31·01
* Les Baleines (Ré)	05·46·29·42·06
Chassiron (Oléron)	05·46·47·85·43
Pointe-de-Grave	05·56·09·60·03
Cap Ferret	05·56·60·60·03
* Messanges	05·58·48·94·10
Socoa	05·59·47·18·54

*Operates sunrise to sunset only. Remainder are H24

5.15.6 Emergency VHF DF stations – France

A vessel in emergency can obtain its true bearing *from* a DF station. DF stations are remotely controlled by a semaphore (signal) station, a †Naval lookout station or a *CROSS, all of which keep primary watch on Ch 16.

To obtain a true bearing from asterisked DF stations, call CROSS on Ch 16, 11 or 67. Also available are seven continuously scanned frequencies from among Ch 1–29, 36, 39, 48, 50, 52, 55, 56 and 60–88.

VHF DF stations are listed below (NE to NW then S):

Dunkerque	51°03′·40N 02°20′·40E
*Gris-Nez	50°52′·20N 01°35′·01E
Boulogne	50°44′·00N 01°36′·00E
Ault	50°06′·50N 01°27′·50E
Dieppe	49°56′·00N 01°05′·20E
Fécamp	49°46′·10N 00°22′·20E
La Hève	49°30′·60N 00°04′·20E
Villerville	49°23′·20N 00°06′·50E
Port-en-Bessin	49°21′·10N 00°46′·30W
St Vaast	49°34′·50N 01°16′·50W
Barfleur	49°41′·90N 01°15′·90W
Levy	49°41′·70N 01°28′·20W
†Homet	49°39′·50N 01°37′·90W
*Jobourg	49°41′·50N 01°54′·50W
La Hague	49°43′·60N 01°56′·30W
Carteret (Barneville)	49°22′·40N 01°48′·30W
Le Roc (Granville)	48°50′·10N 01°36′·90W
Grouin (Cancale) (HJ)	48°42′·60N 01°50′·60W
St Cast	48°38′·60N 02°14′·70W
St Quay-Portrieux (HJ)	48°39′·30N 02°49′·50W
Bréhat	48°51′·30N 03°00′·10W
Ploumanac'h (HJ)	48°49′·50N 03°28′·20W
Batz	48°44′·80N 04°00′·60W
Brignogan (HJ)	48°40′·60N 04°19′·70W
Creac'h (Ouessant)	48°27′·60N 05°07′·70W
*Creac'h (Ouessant)	48°27′·60N 05°07′·80W
†St Mathieu	48°19′·80N 04°46′·20W
Toulinguet (HJ)	48°16′·80N 04°37′·50W
Cap de la Chèvre (HJ)	48°10′·20N 04°33′·00W
Pointe du Raz	48°02′·30N 04°43′·80W
Penmarc'h	47°47′·90N 04°22′·40W
Beg-Meil (HJ)	47°51′·30N 03°58′·40W
Beg Melen	47°39′·20N 03°30′·10W
*Etel	47°39′·80N 03°12′·00W
St Julien (HJ)	47°29′·70N 03°07′·50W
Taillefer	47°21′·80N 03°09′·00W
Le Talut	47°17′·70N 03°13′·00W
Piriac	47°22′·50N 02°33′·40W
Chemoulin	47°14′·10N 02°17′·80W
St Sauveur	46°41′·70N 02°18′·80W
Les Baleines (HJ)	46°14′·60N 01°33′·70W
Chassiron	46°02′·80N 01°24′·50W
La Coubre	45°41′·90N 01°13′·40W
Pointe de Grave	45°34′·30N 01°03′·90W
Cap Ferret	44°37′·50N 01°15′·00W
Messanges (HJ)	43°48′·80N 01°23′·90W
Socoa	43°23′·30N 01°41′·10W

5.16 SPAIN

5.16.1 Coast Guard communications

The Society for Maritime Rescue and Safety (Sociedad de Salvamento y Seguridad Maritima – SASEMAR) is the national agency for SAR operations (and the prevention of pollution); akin to MCA in the UK.

MRCC Madrid co-ordinates SAR operations via 3 MRCCs (Coruña, Gijon and Finisterre) on the N coast and Tarifa MRCC on the SW coast – as listed below.

All facilities monitor (H24) VHF Ch 16, MF 2182 kHz and DSC Ch 70, 2187·5 kHz. They broadcast weather as shown in Chapter 6 and Nav warnings, Chapter 3; they do not handle link calls.

North and North West Spain

In N and NW Spain CG Centres do not keep continuous watch on Ch 16, so call on a working channel; see Fig 5(8).

Madrid MRCC MMSI, 002241022.
☎917 559 132 ℻915 261 440. cncs@sasemar.es

Bilbao MRCC
43°21′N 03°02′W MMSI 002240996
☎944 839 411 ℻944 839 161 bilbao@sasemar.es

Santander MRSC
43°28′N 03°43′W MMSI 002241009
☎942 213 030 ℻942 213 638 santander@sasemar.es

Gijón MRCC
43°34′N 05°42′W MMSI 002240997
☎985 326 050 ℻ 985 320 908 gijon@sasemar.es

Finisterre MRCC
42°42′N 08°59′W MMSI 002240993
☎981 767 320 ℻981 767 740 finisterre@sasemar.es

Coruña MRSC
43°22′N 08°23′W MMSI 002240992
☎981 209 541 ℻981 209 518 coruna@sasemar.es

Vigo MRSC
42°10′N 08°41′W MMSI 002240998
☎986 222 230 ℻986 228 957 vigo@sasemar.es

South West Spain

Tarifa MRCC co-ordinates SAR in SW Spain and the Gibraltar Strait, thus accepts Distress, Urgency and Safety traffic only.

Tarifa MRCC
36°01′N 05°35′W MMSI 002240994
☎956 684 740 ℻956 680 606 tarifa@sasemar.es

Huelva MRSC
37°13′N 07°07′W MMSI 002241012
☎959 243 000 ℻959 242 103 algeciras@sasemar.es
huelva@sasemar.es

Cádiz MRSC
36°32′N 06°18′W MMSI 002241011
☎956 214 253 ℻956 226 091 cadiz@sasemar.es

Algeciras MRSC (controlled by Malaga MRCC)
36°08′N 05°26′W MMSI 002241001
☎956 580 930 ℻956 581 951 algeciras@sasemar.es

5.16.2 Navwarnings (NavArea III Co-ordinator)

Long-range Navwarnings for NavArea III are broadcast by SafetyNet. Coastal warnings are broadcast in English and Spanish by Coast radio stations on NAVTEX 518 kHz (see Table 6(1)) and on VHF; monitor VHF Ch 16 or MF 2182 kHz.

5.16.3 Coast Radio Stations (CRS)

CRS monitor (H24) Ch 16, 2182 kHz and DSC (VHF & MF) call Ch 16, then switch to a working channel. Traffic lists not broadcast on VHF, but passed on a working VHF channel; or on MF at every odd H +33, except 0133 and 2133.

North Spain (Callsign for all: *Bilbao Radio*)
Remote stations controlled by Bilbao Comms Centre are:

Pasajes	Ch 27
Machichaco	*MF: Tx 1677 & 2182; Rx 2102 & 2182.* No VHF or DF
Bilbao	Ch 26
Santander	Ch 24

North West Spain (Callsign for all: *Coruña Radio*)
Remote stations controlled by Coruña Comms Centre are:

Cabo Ortegal	Ch 02
Coruña	*MF: Tx 1707 & 2182; Rx 2132 & 2182.* Ch 26
Finisterre	*MF: Tx 1698 & 2182; Rx 2123 & 2182.* Ch 22
Vigo	Ch 20
La Guardia	Ch 82
Cabo Peñas	Ch 27
Navia	Ch 62

South West Spain
Remote stations controlled by Malaga Comms Centre include:

Chipiona Radio	*MF: Tx 1656; Rx 2081.* No VHF
Cádiz Radio	Ch 28
Tarifa Radio	*MF: Tx 1704; Rx 2129.* Ch 83

5.17 MAINLAND PORTUGAL

5.17.1 Coast Guard communications

The Portuguese Navy co-ordinates SAR in two regions, Lisboa and Santa Maria (Azores), via MRCCs at Lisboa, Ponta Delgada (Azores) and Funchal MRSC (Madeira). A network of CRS maintains an H24 listening watch on all distress frequencies; see Fig 5(8).

Their HQ (Ministério da Defensa Nacional – Marinha) is at:

Estado-Maior da Armada, Rua do Arsenal, 1149-001 Lisboa
☎+351 210 984450 (HO); 📠+351 214 401954

Lisboa MRCC
38°41'N 09°19'W MMSI 002630100
☎+351 214 401919 (Emergency), +351 214 401950;
📠+351 214 401954
mrcc.lisboa@marinha.pt comar.dir@marinha.pt;
Full DSC Ch70 2187.5 kHz coverage not complete but 7 stations remotely controlled by Lisboa MRCC now operational, DSC Ch70/ Voice, VHF Ch16/ 2182 kHz.

5.17.2 Coast Radio Stations (CRS)

Lisboa Radio controls all remote stations.
☎+351 214 190424 📠+351 214 199900
lisboa.radio@telecom.pt

All CRS, Ch 16 (H24). Call name, (see Fig 5(8)) plus 'Radio'.

5.18 PORTUGUESE ISLANDS

5.18.1 Coast Guard communications

Ponta Delgada MRCC
37°45'N 25°38'W MMSI 002040100 VHF Ch 16 2182 kHz
Planned DSC Ch 70; 2182 kHz ☎+351 296 281777;
(Emergency) +351 917 777461; 📠+351 296 205239
mrcc.delgada@marinha.pt mrcc.delgada@gmail.com

Horta MRSC
38°32'N 28°38'W MMSI 002040200 VHF Ch 16
2057 kHz Remotely controlled from Lisbon

Fig 5(8) Spanish and Portuguese CG radio stations

Funchal MRSC
38°38'N 16°54'W MMSI 002550100 VHF Ch 11
2182 kHz ☎+351 291 213112 (Emergency) +351 919 678140 📠+351 291 228232 mrsc.funchal@marinha.pt

5.18.2 Coast Radio Stations (CRS)

All CRS monitor Ch 16 (H24) and are remotely controlled by Lisboa Radio. The following MF frequencies and VHF channels are used:

Flores Radio	23
Faial Radio MF: Tx 2741 & Rx 2237 kHz.	25 (H24), 26, 28
Pico Radio	24 (H24), 26, 28
São Miguel Radio MF: Tx & Rx 2182 kHz.	23 (H24), 26, 27
Porto Santo Radio	23, 28 (H24)

GIBRALTAR

SAR communications

Gibraltar VTS
36°09'N 5°22'W MMSI 002361001 VHF & MF DSC
☎ +350 200 462 54 📠 +350 200 770 11
ops@port.gov.gi

MOROCCO

Coast Guard communications

Rabat MRCC
33°49'N 07°09'W MMSI 002424133 VHF & MF DSC
☎+212 537 625897 emergency +212 537 625877
mrcc.rabat@mpm.gov.ma

Agadir MRSC
30°25'N 09°38'W MMSI 002424136 VHF & MF DSC;
Ch 16 ☎+212 528 842964 mrsc.agadir@mpm.gov.ma

5.19 VESSEL TRAFFIC SERVICES (VTS)

VTS primarily assist commercial shipping and depend on correct sequential use of communications. VTS usually exist in areas of high traffic density with complex routeing and/or navigational constraints, eg shoal water, narrow channels and tight bends. Such conditions are stressful and demanding even for the professional mariner. Small craft must therefore keep clear of big ships, eg by navigating just outside buoyed channels.

VTS both formalises, and is shorthand for, services which have existed for years. These include: Position reporting; radar surveillance; procedural control of traffic (not to be confused with TSS, although the two may exist in close proximity to each other); traffic, weather, navigational and tidal information; pilotage advice; and berthing instructions.

Monitoring of VHF radio channels is therefore compulsory for big ships, but yachts can benefit by:

- Being aware of what commercial ships are doing
- Thereby being better able to avoid them
- Making use of radar assistance if the need arises
- Hearing any constraints on their own movements
- Being readily contactable by the VTS authority.

It is rarely necessary (and often undesirable) for yachts to transmit on a busy VTS channel; indeed many marine authorities discourage this. In Dutch and German waters the letter of the law is often more rigidly enforced than elsewhere; violations may incur on-the-spot fines.

VTS diagrams appear in the relevant geographic area of Chapter 9, with detailed notes in the harbour text.

5.20 INTERNATIONAL PORT TRAFFIC SIGNALS (IPTS)

The International system (IPTS) is now widely used on the Continent, but its universal adoption may take some years. Obsolescent national signals may occasionally be seen in a few minor ports. In some major ports, eg Calais, these important signals are the primary means of controlling traffic, thereby much reducing or even eliminating VHF radio 'chatter'.

- The main movement message always comprises three lights, vertically disposed. No additional light shall be added to the column carrying the main message.

  Thus the main message is always recognisable as IPTS, and not as lights of navigational significance. IPTS may also be used to control traffic at locks and bridges.
- Red lights indicate ***Do not proceed***.
- Green lights indicate ***Proceed, subject to the conditions stipulated***. Red and green lights are never displayed together, to avoid confusion.
- Signals may be omni-directional, ie seen by all vessels simultaneously; or directional, ie seen only by vessels entering or by vessels leaving harbour.
- Signal 1 ***Serious Emergency*** must show at least 60 flashes/minute. All other signals may be fixed or slow occulting (useful when background glare is a problem). A mixture of fixed and occulting lights must not be used.
- Signal No 5 assumes that VHF, signal lamp, loud-hailer, auxiliary signal or other means of communication will specifically inform a vessel that she may proceed.
- Exemption signals. A single yellow light, displayed to the left of the column carrying main messages Nos 2 or 5 and level with the upper light, means ***Vessels which can safely navigate outside the main channel need not comply with the main message***. This signal, shown as Nos 2a and 5a, is obviously important to small craft.
- Signals which are auxiliary to the main message may be devised by local authorities. Such auxiliary signals should show only white and/or yellow lights, and be displayed to the right of the column carrying the main message. Ports with complex entrances and much traffic may need many auxiliary signals, which will have to be documented. Smaller harbours with less traffic may only need the basic signals, such as Nos 2 and 3.

No	Lights		Main message
1		Flashing	Serious emergency – all vessels to stop or divert according to instructions
2		Fixed or Slow Occulting	Vessels shall not proceed (*Note:* Some ports may use an exemption signal, as in 2a below)
3			Vessels may proceed. One-way traffic
4			Vessels may proceed. Two-way traffic
5			A vessel may proceed only when she has received specific orders to do so. (*Note:* Some ports may use an exemption signal, as in 5a below)
			Exemption signals and messages
2a	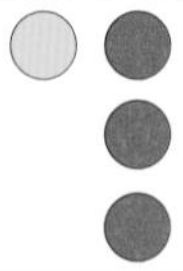	Fixed or Slow Occulting	Vessels shall not proceed, except that vessels which navigate outside the main channel need not comply with the main message
5a			A vessel may proceed when she has received specific orders to do so, except that vessels which navigate outside the main channel need not comply with the main message
			Auxiliary signals and messages
White and/or yellow lights, displayed with the main lights			Local meanings, as promulgated in local port orders

5.21 FLAG ETIQUETTE

Flags are still used to express identity – by national ensigns, club burgees, etc. Brief guidance on their use is given below and in *Reeds Maritime Flag Handbook* (ACN).

5.21.1 Ensign

A yacht's ensign is the national maritime flag corresponding to the nationality of her owner; Fig 5(9). Thus a British yacht should wear the Red Ensign unless she qualifies for a Special ensign (5.21.2). The national ensign should be kept clean and in good repair. It should normally be worn at the stern, or if that's not possible the nearest position should be used, eg at the peak in a gaffer, at the mizzen masthead in a ketch or yawl, or about two-thirds up the leech of the mainsail. In harbour or at anchor the proper position is at the stern.

In British harbours by custom the ensign is hoisted at 0800 (0900 between 1 Nov and 14 Feb) or as soon after that time as people come on board; and lowered when the crew leaves the boat for the evening, at sunset or at 2100LT, whichever occurs first.

Abroad the ensign (and burgee) are increasingly left flying at all times, to identify nationality – even at night in harbour, unless the boat is unattended.

At sea the ensign must be worn when meeting other vessels, when entering or leaving foreign ports, or when approaching forts, Signal and CG stations – ie virtually at all times.

When racing the ensign should not be worn after the five minute gun. It should be hoisted on finishing or retiring.

5.21.2 Special ensigns

Members of certain clubs may apply for a permit to wear a special ensign (eg Blue Ensign, defaced Blue Ensign, or defaced Red Ensign). The yacht must either be registered under Part I of the Merchant Shipping Act 1995 and of at least 2 tons gross tonnage, or be registered on the Small Ships Register and of at least 7m LOA. The owner(s) must be British subjects, and the yacht must not be used for any professional, business or commercial purpose. Full details can be obtained from Secretaries of the clubs concerned. The permit must be carried on board.

A special ensign must only be worn when the owner is on board or ashore in the vicinity, and only when the yacht is flying the burgee (or a Flag Officer's flag) of the club concerned. When the yacht is sold, or the owner ceases to be a member of the club, the permit must be returned to the Secretary of the club.

5.21.3 Courtesy ensign

It is customary when abroad to fly a small maritime ensign of the country concerned at the starboard spreader. *A courtesy ensign must not be worn below any other flag on the same halyard.* Thus a club burgee, if usually flown at the starboard spreader, must be shifted to the port spreader when abroad, permitting the courtesy ensign to be close up at the starboard spreader. The correct courtesy flag for a foreign yacht in British waters is the Red Ensign. British yachts do not need to fly a courtesy flag in the Channel Islands.

5.21.4 Burgee

A burgee shows that a yacht is in the charge of a member of the club indicated, and does not necessarily indicate ownership. It should be flown at the masthead.

If this is impossible due to wind sensors, radio aerials etc, the burgee may be flown at the starboard spreader, but this should be avoided unless strictly necessary. A long bamboo cane can readily be hoisted to the masthead as a staff, keeping the burgee clear above sensors and aerials.

A yacht should not fly more than one burgee. A burgee is not flown when a yacht is racing. If the yacht is on loan, or is chartered, it is correct to use the burgee of the skipper or charterer – not that of the absent owner. Normal practice has been to lower the burgee at night, at the same time as the ensign, but nowadays many owners leave the burgee flying if they are on board or ashore in the vicinity.

5.21.5 Choice of burgee

An owner who is not a Flag Officer, and who belongs to more than one club, should normally fly the burgee (and if authorised the special ensign) of the senior club in the harbour where the yacht is lying. An exception may be if another club is staging a regatta or similar function.

5.21.6 Flag Officer's flag

Clubs authorise their Flag Officers to fly special swallow-tailed flags, with the same design as the club burgee and in place of it. The flags of a vice-commodore and a rear-commodore carry one and two balls respectively. A Flag Officer's flag is flown day and night while he is on board, or ashore nearby. A Flag Officer should fly his flag with the Red Ensign (or special ensign, where authorised) in preference to the burgee of some other club.

It is customary for a Flag Officer to be saluted (not more than once a day) by a yacht flying the burgee of that club.

5.21.7 House flag

An owner may fly his personal flag when he is on board in harbour. It must not conflict with the design of an existing flag. A house flag is normally rectangular, and is flown at the crosstrees in a sloop or cutter, at the mizzen masthead in a ketch or yawl, or at the foremast head in a schooner.

5.21.8 St George's Flag

This is predominantly a land flag, commonly misused afloat. It may only be flown at sea by admirals on duty and members of the Association of Dunkirk Little Ships (in conjunction with their burgee).

5.21.9 Q Flag

Vessels requiring customs' clearance should fly the yellow Q flag. This declares that 'my vessel is healthy and I request free pratique' ie to clear in and come ashore. This is not required for vessels from, and sailing within, the EU.

5.21.10 Salutes

Yachts should salute all Royal Yachts, and all warships of whatever nationality. A salute is made by dipping the ensign (only). The vessel saluted responds by dipping her ensign, and then re-hoisting it, whereupon the vessel saluting re-hoists hers.

5.21.11 Dressing ship

Dressing overall (as opposed to dressing with masthead flags) is normally only done in harbour to mark national festivals. The international code flags and pennants (Fig 5(1)) are flown in the following order from stem to masthead(s) to stern:

E, Q, p 3, G, p 8, Z, p 4, W, p 6, P, p 1, I, Code, T, Y, B, X, 1st Sub, H, 3rd Sub, (masthead) D, F, 2nd Sub, U, A, O, M, R, p 2, J, p 0, N, p 9, K, p 7, V, p 5, L, C, S. (Total = 40).

Fig 5(9) Ensigns and flags

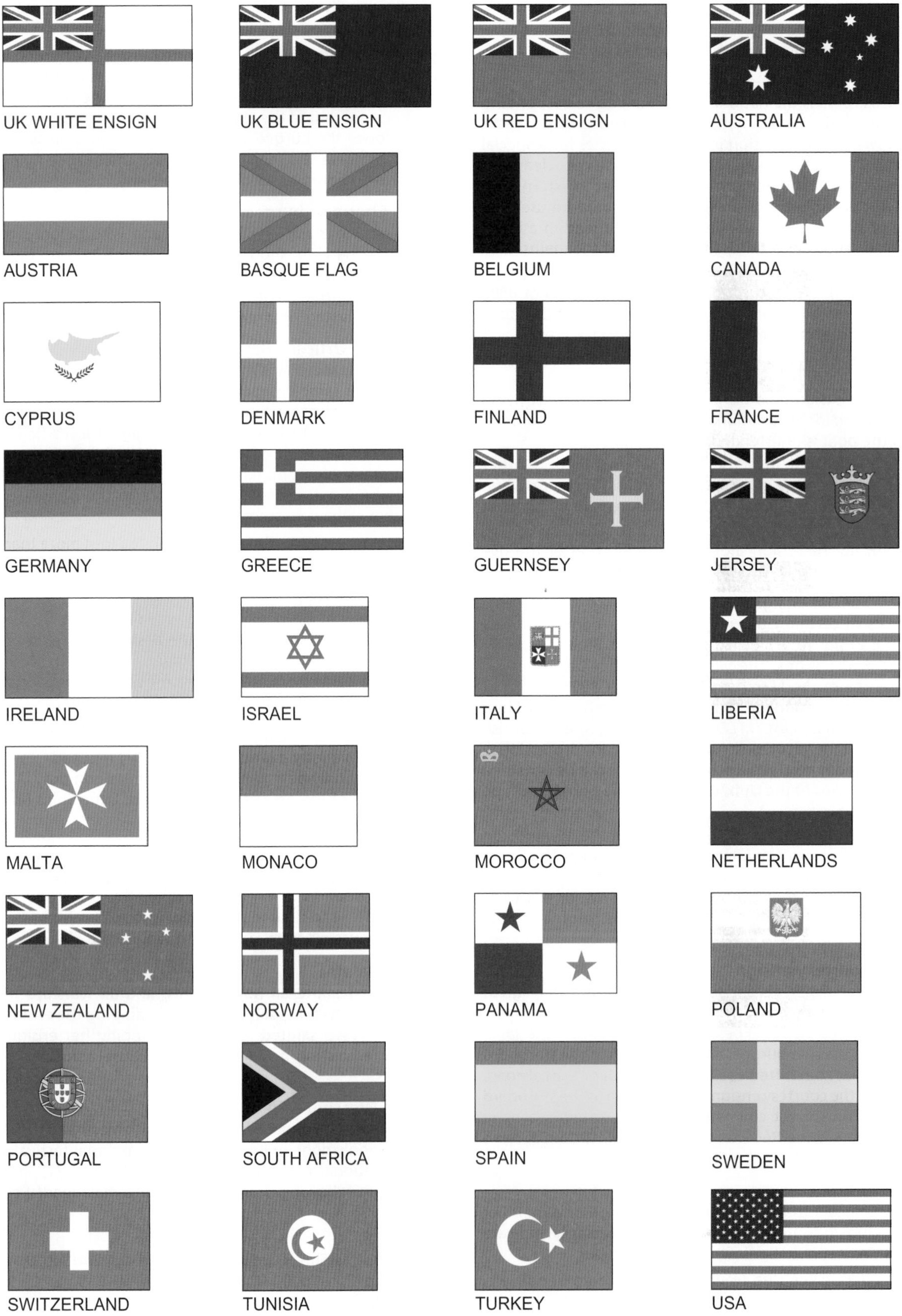
UK WHITE ENSIGN
UK BLUE ENSIGN
UK RED ENSIGN
AUSTRALIA
AUSTRIA
BASQUE FLAG
BELGIUM
CANADA
CYPRUS
DENMARK
FINLAND
FRANCE
GERMANY
GREECE
GUERNSEY
JERSEY
IRELAND
ISRAEL
ITALY
LIBERIA
MALTA
MONACO
MOROCCO
NETHERLANDS
NEW ZEALAND
NORWAY
PANAMA
POLAND
PORTUGAL
SOUTH AFRICA
SPAIN
SWEDEN
SWITZERLAND
TUNISIA
TURKEY
USA

6 Weather

6.1	**Wind/sea state scales and terminology** Beaufort wind scale • Douglas Sea State Scale • Cloud types (pictures) • Terms used in bulletins • Geostrophic scales • Unit conversion	**82**
6.2	**Heavy weather warnings** International storm warning signals	**85**
6.3	**Sources of weather information**	**86**
6.4	**Using weather forecasts**	**86**
6.5	**GMDSS – Maritime Safety Information (MSI)**	**86**
6.6	**NAVTEX** Messages • UK 518 and 490 kHz stations • Coverage abroad	**86**
6.7	**High seas bulletins**	**89**
6.8	**MSI Broadcasts by HM Coastguard** Shipping and Inshore forecasts • Remote CG transmitters	**89**
6.9	**HF radio facsimile broadcasts** GMDSS (Offenbach) • Royal Navy (Northwood)	**91**
6.10	**Met Office/BBC weather forecasts** UK Forecast areas • Shipping Forecast • Frequencies • Schedule	**92**
6.11	**Internet weather resources**	**94**
6.12	**Other weather resources** Newspapers • Television • Volmet	**96**
6.13–6.23	**Weather information abroad** *6.13* Channel Islands – 96 • *6.14* Republic of Ireland – 96 • *6.15* West Denmark – 97 • *6.16* Germany – 98 • *6.17* The Netherlands – 99 • *6.18* Belgium – 100 • *6.19* France – 100 • *6.20* N and NW Spain – 102 • *6.21* Portugal, Azores and Madeira – 103 • *6.22* SW Spain – 103 • *6.23* Gibraltar – 104	**96**

6.1 WIND/SEA STATE SCALES AND TERMINOLOGY

6.1.1 Beaufort wind scale

Force	Wind speed (knots)	(km/h)	(m/sec)	Description	Deep sea criteria	Probable mean (max) wave ht (m)
0	<1	0–2	0–0·5	Calm	Calm, glassy, like a mirror	—
1	1–3	2–6	0·3–1·5	Light air	Calm. Ripples like scales are formed	0·1 (0·1)
2	4–6	7–11	1·6–3·3	Light breeze	Small wavelets, still short but more pronounced, not breaking	0·1 (0·3)
3	7–10	13–19	3·4–5·4	Gentle breeze	Large wavelets, crests begin to break; glassy foam, perhaps a few white horses	0·6 (1)
4	11–16	20–30	5·5–7·9	Moderate breeze	Small waves becoming longer; fairly frequent white horses	1 (1·5)
5	17–21	31–39	8·0–10·7	Fresh breeze	Moderate waves, taking a more pronounced form; many white horses, perhaps some spray	2 (2·5)
6	22–27	41–50	10·8–13·8	Strong breeze	Large waves forming; white foam crests are extensive everywhere; probably some spray	3 (4)
7	28–33	52–61	13·9–17·1	Near gale	Sea heaps up; white foam from breaking waves begins to be blown in streaks	4 (5·5)
8	34–40	63–74	17·2–20·7	Gale	Moderately high waves of greater length; edge of crests break into spindrift; foam blown in well-marked streaks	5·5 (7·5)
9	41–47	76–87	20·8–24·4	Strong gale	High waves with tumbling crests; dense streaks of foam; spray may affect visibility	7 (10)
10	48–55	89–102	24·5–28·4	Storm	Very high waves with long overhanging crests; dense streaks of foam make the surface of sea white. Heavy, shock-like tumbling sea; visibility affected	9 (12·5)
11	56–63	104–117	28·5–32·6	Violent storm	Exceptionally high waves; sea completely covered with long white patches of foam; edges of wave crests blown into froth. Visibility affected	11·5 (16)
12	64 plus	118 plus	32·7 plus	Hurricane	Air filled with foam and spray; sea completely white with driving spray; visibility seriously affected	14 (—)

Notes

- The actual force exerted on a sail is proportional to the square of the windspeed and directly to the density. Thus a wind of Force 6 (say 25 knots) has more than three times the 'weight' of a wind of Force 4 (say 14 knots) – which is why even a small increase in windspeed, or gusts, have a significant effect on a sailing yacht. Temperature has a smaller effect; at 5°C the force of the wind is about 6% higher than at 20°C.
- Wave height depends upon the distance travelled (fetch), the length of time the wind has been blowing and any currents. The probable mean wave heights (max. in brackets) shown in the table above are for open sea, away from land. In enclosed waters, or near to land, with an offshore wind, wave heights will be smaller but often steeper – particularly with wind against tide.

Swell

The length and height in metres of swell waves are described and quantified as follows:

Length of Swell (m)	
Short	0–100
Average	100–200
Long	over 200

Height of Swell (m)	
Low	0–2
Moderate	2–4
Heavy	over 4

6.1.2 Douglas Sea State Scale (wind force/wave height):

Wind force	Wave ht (m)	Douglas	Sea State
0	-	0	Calm
1	0.1	1	Calm
2	0.2	2	Smooth
3	0.6	3	Slight
4	1.0	3-4	Slight-mod
5	2.0	4	Moderate
6	3.0	5	Rough
7	4.0	5-6	Rough-V.Rough
8	5.5	6-7	V.Rough-High
9	7.0	7	High
10	9.0	8	Very High
11	11.5	8	Very High
12	14+	9	Phenomenal

Fig 6(1) Typical sea states associated with various Beaufort wind forces

Photography:
Force 0, 11, 12 © *Crown*; Force 1, 2, 7, © *GJ Simpson*; Force 3, 4, 5, 6, © *IG MacNeil*; Force 8, © *WAE Smith*; Force 9, © *JP Laycock*; Force 10, © *G Allen*

Force 0 0–1kn Calm Wave Ht 0m

Force 1 1–3kn Light Air
Wave Ht 0.1m

Force 2 4–6kn Light Breeze
Wave Ht 0.2m

Force 3 7–10kn Gentle Breeze
Wave Ht 0.6m

Force 4 11–16kn Moderate Breeze
Wave Ht 1m

Force 5 17–21kn Fresh Breeze
Wave Ht 2m

Force 6 22–27kn Strong Breeze
Wave Ht 3m

Force 7 28–33kn Near Gale
Wave Ht 4m

Force 8 34–40kn Gale
Wave Ht 5.5m

Force 9 41–47kn Severe Gale
Wave Ht 7m

Force 10 48–55kn Storm
Wave Ht 9m

Force 11 56–63kn Violent Storm
Wave Ht 11.5m

Force 12 64+kn Hurricane
Wave Ht 14m

6.1.3 Cloud types

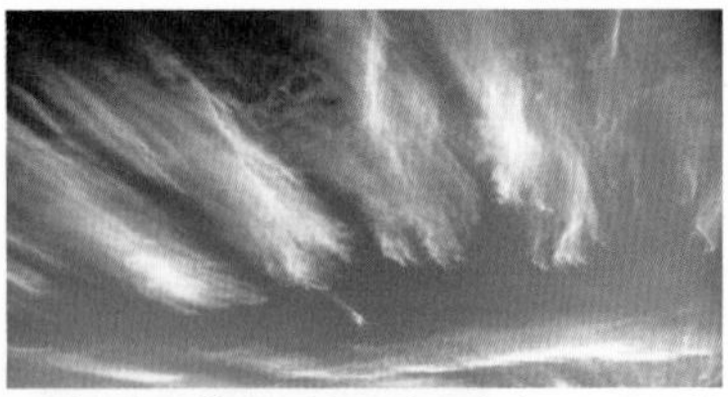

Cirrus (Ci) Very high, silky-white clouds (mare's tails) consisting of ice-particles, associated with strong winds aloft. Often indicates the approach of a frontal system and deteriorating weather conditions. *© RK Pilsbury*

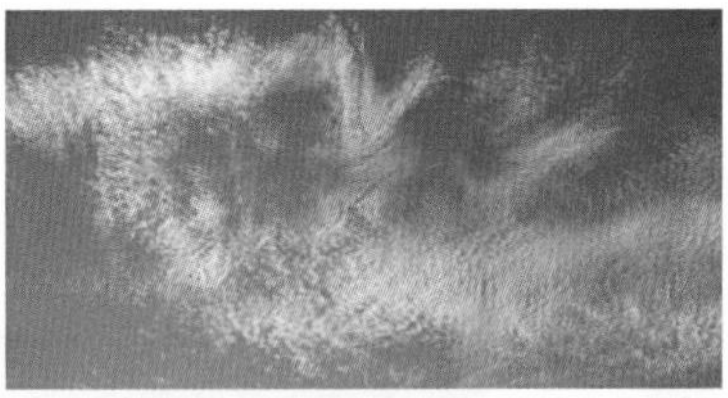

Cirrocumulus (Cc) Very high small white puffs in ripples, sometimes forming banks; the classic Mackerel sky. Thicker than Cirrus and formed by turbulence. Not usually associated with any particular weather. *© RK Pilsbury*

Cirrostratus (Cs) A thin high whitish veil which does not blur the outline of the sun or moon; the only cloud to show a halo. If it thickens, it can indicate an approaching front or depression. *© CS Broomfield*

Altocumulus (Ac) Essentially a greyish-white layer cloud with gaps between rounded globules of cumulus. If forming in bands, it may indicate an approaching front. *© CS Broomfield*

Altostratus (As) A medium level, sheet of blue-grey cloud like a layer of fog. The sun or moon may shine through it, without halo. Usually indicates that frontal rain can be expected in a few hours, turning to Ns. *© S Cornford*

Nimbostratus (Ns) A low, dark grey, rain-bearing cloud mass obscuring the whole sky. Often follows Altostratus and the passing of a front. Steady rain, sleet or snow will set in, the base covering low hills. *© RK Pilsbury*

Stratus (St) Thin, grey, fog-like sheet of cloud as low as 1000 or even 500 feet. Dense Stratus can produce drizzle and poor visibility. It is usually associated with warm sector conditions. *© Crown*

Stratocumulus (Sc) Dense, lumpy grey cloud below 5000 feet; persistent in winter with high pressure. If it thickens to form a solid grey layer across the sky, expect rain at any time. *© GA Watts*

Cumulus (Cu) Fair weather cloud with vertical development due to rising warm air, especially over coasts. Plenty of blue sky but risk of gusty showers due to instability. Disappears by early evening. *© RK Pilsbury*

Cumulonimbus (Cb) Large, dramatic convection cloud rising to great heights with huge tops, some anvil-shaped. Heavy rain and thundery squalls are likely. Down-currents produce sudden strong gusts, hazardous to yachts. *© Crown*

6.1.4 Terms used in weather bulletins

Speed of movement of pressure systems

Slowly	< 15 knots
Steadily	15–25 knots
Rather quickly	25–35 knots
Rapidly	35–45 knots
Very rapidly	> 45 knots

Visibility

Good	> 5 nautical miles
Moderate	2–5 nautical miles
Poor	1000 metres–2 nautical miles
Fog	Less than 1000 metres

Barometric pressure changes (tendency)

Rising or falling slowly:
Pressure change of 0·1 to 1·5 hPa/mb in the preceding 3 hours.

Rising or falling:
Pressure change of 1·6 to 3·5 hPa/mb in the preceding 3 hours.

Rising or falling quickly:
Pressure change of 3·6 to 6 hPa/mb in the preceding 3 hours.

Rising or falling very rapidly:
Pressure change of more than 6 hPa/mb in the preceding 3 hours.

Now rising (or falling):
Pressure has been falling (rising) or steady in the preceding 3 hours, but at the time of observation was definitely rising (falling).

6.1.5 Geostrophic scales

When interpreting a synoptic chart it often helps to be able to estimate the Beaufort wind force; similarly the speed in knots at which warm, cold and occluded fronts are moving – hence when a warm front or a post-cold front clearance may arrive.

On UK charts there is a scale shown. To use, set your dividers between adjacent isobars, then read off from the left (high) end of the scale the gradient windspeed in knots. Be careful to use the scale at the appropriate latitude. Warm fronts move at about 2/3 of this speed and cold or occluded fronts move at about 3/4. Surface winds can be at least 3/4 of the gradient speed in cold, unstable air and between 1/2 and 2/3 in warm, stable air coming from a southerly point.

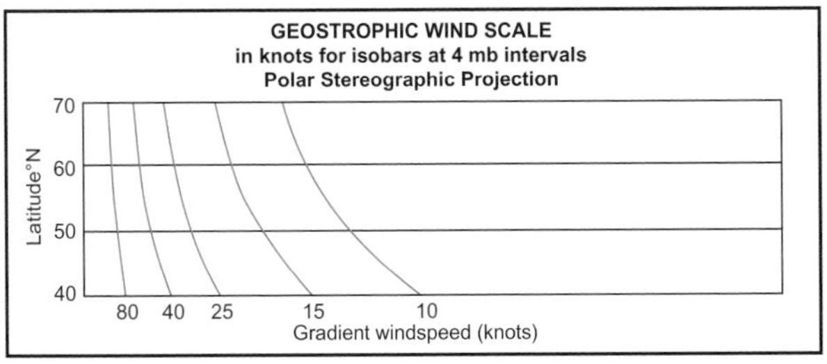

Fig 6(2) Example (not to scale) of geostrophic wind scale found on UK synoptic charts

6.1.6 Unit conversion

Weather administrations may use a variety of units. To convert between them, refer to the following table:

Atmospheric pressure

Hectopascals (hPa) = Millibars (mb).
Hectopascals (hPa) X 0·295 = inches of mercury (InHg).
Hectopascals (hPa) X 0·75 = mm of mercury (mmHg).
Inches of mercury (InHg) X 33·8639 = Hectopascals (hPa).
mm of mercury (mmHg) X 1·33322 = Hectopascals (hPa).

Temperature

Multiply °C by 1·8 then add 32 to obtain °F.
Subtract 32 from °F, then divide by 1·8 to obtain °C.

6.2 HEAVY WEATHER WARNINGS

Gale warnings

A ***Gale*** warning means that average winds of at least F8 (34–40kn) or gusts up to 43–51kn are possible (i.e. may occur) somewhere within the area, but not necessarily over the whole area.

Severe Gale means winds of at least F9 (41–47kn) or gusts reaching 52–60kn.

Storm means winds of F10 (48–55kn) or gusts of 61–68kn.

Violent Storm means winds of F11 (56–63kn) or gusts of 69kn or more.

Hurricane Force means winds of F12 (64kn or more).

Gale warnings remain in force until amended or cancelled ('gales now ceased'). If a gale persists for more than 24 hours the warning is re-issued.

Timing of gale warnings

Imminent:	Within 6hrs from time of issue
Soon:	6–12hrs from time of issue
Later:	More than 12hrs from time of issue

Note: when there is some uncertainty, UK forecasters may say 'Perhaps gale 8 later' but without issuing a gale warning. However within the *Imminent* and *Soon* periods, a warning must be issued even if the forecaster says 'perhaps...'

Strong wind warnings

Strong wind warnings will only be issued if the wind is forecast to reach F6 or more and was not predicted when the last forecast was issued. They will be broadcast on receipt and will be included in the repetition forecasts but will be incorporated into the next new inshore forecast if still in force.

Wind

Wind direction: The direction from which the wind is blowing.

Winds becoming cyclonic: Indicates that there will be considerable changes in wind direction across the path of a depression within the forecast area.

Veering: A clockwise change in the wind direction, eg SW to W.

Backing: An anti-clockwise change in the wind direction, eg W to SW.

6.2.1 International storm warning signals

France and the Netherlands use the international system of visual storm warning signals shown here, shapes by day, lights at night. Portugal and Gibraltar use national variants.

Day	Night	Meaning
	Ⓦ ●	Strong wind (force 6–7)
	● ●	NW gale
	● Ⓦ	NE gale
	Ⓦ Ⓦ	SW gale
	Ⓦ ●	SE gale
	● ● ●	Hurricane force12, any direction
	Rectangular flags of any colour	Wind veering Wind backing

6.3 SOURCES OF WEATHER INFORMATION

There is no shortage of weather information available to today's yachtsman, indeed it could be argued that there is almost too much choice, with 'official' and 'unofficial' forecasts of varying quality provided by both private and government organisations over a variety of media, some entirely free to receive, some not.

For the first 24 to 48 hours, forecasts from national maritime authorities should always be consulted using forecasts from different sources if available. It can then be more useful to compare successive forecasts from the same source.

6.4 USING WEATHER FORECASTS

Weather forecasting has advanced greatly over the past 30 years or so and is still improving, due to increasing computer power, improved measuring equipment and advanced data analysis techniques. This is particularly apparent in the ability to forecast large scale patterns up to five or six days ahead. There are also improvements, but less obvious, in short term detailed prediction of marine weather.

Single observer forecasting, oft-practised in days past, is less relevant in Europe, now there is a well developed meteorological infrastructure. Watching the sky and reading the barometer are still useful but more for verifying the 'official' forecast than for creating your own. Instead, the sailor is better advised to monitor every weather broadcast, paying attention to trends and changes in the forecast. Consistency from one forecast to the next and between forecasts from different sources builds confidence in them; the degree of inconsistency implies the degree of uncertainty. Daily monitoring of forecasts is important over periods of around five days. Monitoring forecasts on a six hourly basis is essential to keep ahead of small but important changes that can occur over such timescales.

It is most productive, and sensible, to use your own observations and experience to interpret forecasts to your local area. Useful observations will include:

- The barometer, logging carefully whether it is steady, rising or falling and at what hourly rate; see 6.1.4.
- Actual wind direction and speed, noting any tendency to back or veer, increase or moderate; see 6.2.
- The appearance of the sky, especially cloud types, their estimated heights and direction of travel; see 6.1.3.
- When precipitation starts and ends may also provide valuable clues to frontal movement.

> The pocket sized *Reeds Weather Handbook*, by Frank Singleton, is a very helpful guide to the use of weather forecasts.

Compare your forecast with what actually happened. Analyse errors, and remember that practice makes perfect.

6.5 GMDSS – MARITIME SAFETY INFORMATION

As well as the better known distress reporting and rescue aspects of the Global Maritime Distress and Safety System (GMDSS) (see 7.3), weather information is grouped with navigational safety information as the second major portion of GMDSS and is collectively termed Maritime Safety Information (MSI).

Member nations of the International Maritime Organization (IMO) are responsible for ensuring that GMDSS MSI is broadcast over communications systems covering inshore, offshore and deep oceanic regions.

GMDSS MSI is the primary source of weather information to yachtsmen worldwide and is disseminated by national maritime administrations (eg MCA) over systems such as SafetyNET, NAVTEX, Marine VHF, MF and HF radio. Its content may also be rebroadcast by national broadcast (eg BBC) and Coast Radio Stations (CRS) and private organisations.

The sources of this information are national Meteorological Offices. Contact details for the UK Met Office are given in 1.2, other nations' are as follows:

> Republic of Ireland 6.14; Denmark 6.15; Germany 6.16; The Netherlands 6.17; Belgium 6.18; France 6.19; Spain 6.20 and 6.22; Portugal 6.21; Gibraltar 6.23.

6.6 NAVTEX

NAVTEX is the prime method of disseminating MSI from the fairway buoy to at least 200 miles offshore. A dedicated aerial and receiver with an LCD screen (or integrated printer) are required. The user selects which stations and message categories are recorded for automatic display or printing. Two frequencies are used: On the international frequency, 518kHz, messages are always available in English with excellent coverage of Europe. Interference between stations is **minimised** by scheduling time slots and by **limiting transmission power**; see Fig 6(3). NAVTEX information applies only to the geographical area for which each station is responsible.

On the national frequency 490 kHz (shown in purple throughout this chapter) the UK issues inshore waters forecasts and coastal station actuals. Elsewhere it is used mainly for transmissions in the national language. 490 khz stations have different identification letters from 518 kHz stations.

NAVTEX is convenient, and particularly useful when preoccupied handling your vessel as you will not miss potentially important information.

6.6.1 NAVTEX Messages

Each message is prefixed by a four-character group: The **first character** is the code letter of the transmitting station (eg E for Niton). The **second character** is the message category, see 6.6.2. The **third and fourth** are message serial numbers, running from 01 to 99 and then re-starting at 01. The serial number 00 denotes urgent messages which are always displayed.

NAVTEX printers reject corrupt or already displayed messages; soft copy sets show all valid messages. Weather messages, and some other message types, are dated/timed. All NAVTEX messages begin with ZCZC, ending with NNNN.

Note: Navareas and Metareas have the same boundaries; in this chapter they are referred to as Metareas, but in Chapter 3 as Navareas. See also Fig 6(5) for Shipping forecast areas and Fig 6(4) for Inshore waters forecast boundaries.

6.6.2 NAVTEX Message categories

A*	Navigational warnings
B*	Meteorological warnings
C*	Ice reports
D*	SAR info and Piracy attack warnings
E	Weather forecasts
F	Pilot service
G	AIS
H	LORAN
I	Spare
J	SATNAV
K	Other electronic Navaids
L	Navwarnings additional to **A**
M-U	Spare
V-Y	Special services – as allocated
Z	No messages on hand

* On SOLAS sets these may not be rejected. Some leisure sets may be set to reject all message types except D.

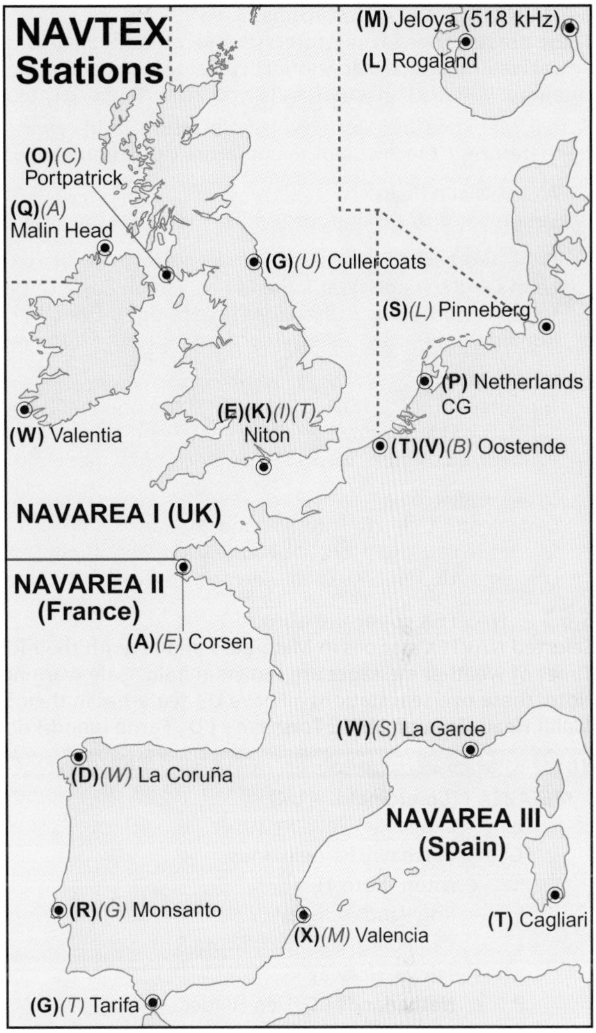

Fig 6(3) NAVTEX stations/areas – UK and W Europe

6.6.3 UK/ROI 518 kHz broadcasts

Below (see next page for overseas), times (UT) of transmissions are in chronological order to facilitate the rapid finding of the next transmission. Weather messages are in **bold**. These are forecasts for 24 hours plus a brief 24 hour outlook. Times of an extended outlook are in italics; this is for 3 to 5 days beyond the shipping forecast 24 hour outlook. The 24 hour outlook and the extended outlook make NAVTEX arguably a more useful source of information than Radio 4. Times of an extended outlook (2 or 3 days beyond the shipping forecast period) are in *italics*.

E	–	**Niton** Thames clockwise to Fastnet, excluding Trafalgar.	***0040***	0440	**0840**	1240	1640	**2040**
G	–	**Cullercoats** Fair Isle clockwise to Thames, excluding N & S Utsire, Fisher and German Bight.	***0100***	0500	**0900**	1300	1700	**2100**
O	–	**Portpatrick** Lundy clockwise to SE Iceland.	***0220***	**0620**	1020	1420	**1820**	2220
Q	–	**Malin Head** Sea areas, Shannon, Rockall, Malin & Bailey		0640			1840	

6.6.4 UK/ROI 490 kHz stations

These provide four 24 hour forecasts and outlooks daily for UK inshore waters (to 12M offshore) at times in bold. Reports of actual weather at the places listed below are broadcast at times in *italics*. To receive these reports select 490 kHz and message category 'V' (6.6.2) on your NAVTEX receiver. Times (UT) of transmissions are listed in chronological order.

Actual Met data includes: Sea level pressure (mb), wind direction and speed (kn), weather, visibility (M), air and sea temperatures (°C), dewpoint temperature (°C) and mean wave height (m).

A – Malin Head	0000	0400	0800	1200	1600	2000
C – Portpatrick	0020	*0420*	0820	1220	*1620*	2020
I – Niton	0120	0520	*0920*	1320	1720	*2120*
U – Cullercoats	*0320*	0720	1120	*1520*	1920	2320

A – Malin Head: Lough Foyle to Carlingford Lough, Mull of Galloway to Cape Wrath, the Minch.

C – Portpatrick: Land's End to Cape Wrath, the Minch, Lough Foyle to Carlingford Lough
N Rona, Stornoway, S Uist, Lusa (Skye bridge), Tiree, Macrihanish, Belfast, Malin Head, Belmullet, St Bees Head, Ronaldsway, Crosby, Valley, Aberporth, Roches Point, Valentia, St Mawgan.

I – Niton: Gibraltar Point to St David's Head and the Channel Islands
Sandettie Lt V, Greenwich Lt V, Solent, Hurn airport, Guernsey airport, Jersey airport, Portland, Channel Lt V, Plymouth, Culdrose, Seven Stones Lt V, St Mawgan and Roches Point (Cork).

U – Cullercoats: Cape Wrath to North Foreland and Shetland
Sandettie Lt V, Manston, Shoeburyness, Weybourne, Donna Nook or Bridlington, Boulmer, Leuchars, Aberdeen, Lossiemouth, Wick, Kirkwall, Lerwick, Foula, K7 Met buoy, Sule Skerry.

6.6.5 NAVTEX coverage abroad

Selected NAVTEX stations in Metareas I and II, with their identity codes, are listed in chronological order of transmissions. Times of weather messages are shown in **bold**. Gale warnings are usually transmitted 4 hourly.
Note: these overseas stations all have UK sea areas in their broadcasts: Rogaland, Hamburg, Oostende, IJmuiden, Valentia, Malin Head. Though MRCC Tórshavn's ('D', Faroe Islands) does not, its forecasts may be useful (www.mrcc.fo)

TABLE 6(1) NAVTEX broadcast schedule for Western Europe

METAREA I (Co-ordinator – UK)	Transmission times (UT)					
B – **Oostende**, Belgium (Note 7)	0010	**0410**	0810	**1210**	1610	**2010**
D – **Tórshavn**, Faroe Islands	0030	0430	0830	1230	1530	2030
K – **Niton** (Note 1)	**0140**	0540	0940	**1340**	1740	2140
L – **Rogaland**, Norway	0150	0550	0950	1350	1750	2150
L – **Pinneberg**, Hamburg (Note 5)	0150	**0550**	0950	**1350**	1750	**2150**
M – **Jeløya**, Norway	**0200**	0600	1000	**1400**	1800	2200
P – **Netherlands CG**, Den Helder	**0230**	0630	1030	**1430**	1830	2230
Q – **Malin Head**, Ireland (Note 3)	0240	**0640**	**1040**	1440	**1840**	**2240**
S – **Pinneberg**, Hamburg (Note 6)	**0300**	**0700**	**1100**	**1500**	**1900**	**2300**
T – **Oostende**, Belgium (Note 4)	0310	**0710**	1110	1510	**1910**	2310
V – **Oostende**, Belgium (Note 2)	0330	0730	1130	1530	1930	2330
W – **Valentia**, Ireland (Note 3)	0340	**0740**	**1140**	1540	**1940**	**2340**

Notes 1 In English, only Nav warnings for coast from Cap Gris Nez to Île de Bréhat. 2 Nav warnings only.
3 See 6.6 and Fig 6(5) for the Atlantic areas covered by 'Q' at 1040, 2240 and by 'W' at 1140, 2340.
4 Forecasts and strong wind warnings for Thames and Dover, plus nav info for the Belgian coast.
5 In German, weather and Nav warnings for German Bight (also W and S Baltic) at times in bold above.
6 Weather broadcasts every 4 hours for the North Sea. 7 Weather & Nav warnings, in Dutch occ English.

METAREA II (Co-ordinator – France)	Transmission times (UT)					
A – **Corsen**, Le Stiff, France	**0000**	0400	0800	**1200**	1600	2000
D – **Coruña**, Spain	0030	0430	**0830**	1230	1630	**2030**
E – **Corsen**, Le Stiff, France (in French)	0040	0440	**0840**	1240	1640	**2040**
F – **São Miguel**, Azores, Portugal	**0050**	**0450**	**0850**	**1250**	**1650**	**2050**
G – **Monsanto**, Portugal (in Portuguese)	**0100**	**0500**	**0900**	**1300**	**1700**	**2100**
M – **Porto Santo**, Madeira, Portugal (in Portuguese)	0100	0500	**0900**	1300	1700	**2100**
G – **Tarifa**, Spain	0100	0500	**0900**	1300	1700	**2100**
I – **Las Palmas**, Islas Canarias, Spain	0120	0520	**0920**	**1320**	**1720**	2120
J – **São Miguel**, Azores, Portugal (in Portuguese)	**0130**	**0530**	**0930**	**1330**	**1730**	**2130**
P – **Porto Santo**, Madeira, Portugal	0230	0630	1030	1430	1830	2230
R – **Monsanto**, Portugal	**0250**	**0650**	**1050**	**1450**	**1850**	**2250**
T – **Tarifa**, Spain (in Spanish)	0310	**0710**	1110	1510	**1910**	2310
W – **Coruña**, Spain (in Spanish)	0340	0740	**1140**	1540	**1940**	2340

6.7 GMDSS HIGH SEAS BULLETINS

In the N Atlantic part of MetArea I, dotted outline in Fig 6(3), weather data is available from:

- SafetyNET which provides MSI to vessels in A3 sea areas. Goonhilly Coast Earth Station (CES) transmits Met data at 0930 & 2130 UT via the **AOR-E** and **AOR-W** satellites.
- NAVTEX. Malin Head (Q) and Valentia (W) cover the E Northern and E Central sections, as well as Sole, Shannon, Rockall and Bailey.

6.8 MSI BROADCASTS BY HM COASTGUARD

MRCC routinely broadcast Maritime Safety Information (MSI) over VHF every 3 hours at the times in Table 6(2) below.

Each broadcast contains one of 3 different Groups of MSI:

Group A
The full broadcast contains the Shipping forecast, Inshore waters forecast (for local Areas as in Table 6(1)), Gale and strong wind warnings.

A Fisherman's 3 day forecast is broadcast (1 Oct–31 Mar) by MRCC which are MF equipped (see 6.8.3), except Tiree.

Times of '**A**' broadcasts in **bold type**.

Group B
Contains a new Inshore waters forecast, new outlook, and Gale warnings.'B' broadcast times in plain type.

Group C
A repeat of the Inshore waters forecast and Gale warnings (as per the previous Group A or B) plus any new Strong wind warnings. 'C' broadcast times are *italicised*.

Notes: Fig 6(4) shows the boundaries of the 18 areas which are covered by Inshore waters forecasts. In the forecast these areas are referred to not by their numbers, but by their defining places/headlands, eg Whitby to Gibraltar Point.

Subfacts & Gunfacts are broadcast by the following CGOCs Falmouth, Aberdeen (occas), Stornoway and Belfast. See 5.5, 5.6, Navigation (WZ) warnings, Subfacts & Gunfacts.

6.8.1 Actual weather

On request MRCC may report the actual weather in their vicinity. HM CG stresses that they are not qualified Met observers and such reports may be no more than a look out of the window or originate from passing ships and yachts.

The National Coastwatch Institution (NCI) operates on VHF Ch 65. There are 50 operational stations (2017) around the English and Welsh coast. Manned by volunteers keeping a visual daylight watch throughout the year, they are able to provide, on request, details of actual weather conditions and sea state at their individual coastal locations (see Safety, 7.12).

TABLE 6(2) VHF broadcasts of shipping and inshore waters forecasts by HM Coastguard

Coastguard	Shipping forecast areas	Inshore waters forecast areas	Broadcast Groups and times LT*							
East Coast			B	C	A	C	B	C	A	C
Aberdeen CGOC	Cromarty, Forties, Forth, Fair Isle Viking, S Utsire, Fisher	1, 2	0130	*0430*	**0730**	*1030*	1330	*1630*	**1930**	*2230*
Humber CGOC	Forties, Forth,Tyne, Dogger, Fisher, Humber, German Bight	3, 4, 5	0150	*0450*	**0750**	*1050*	1350	*1650*	**1950**	*2250*
South Coast			B	C	A	C	B	C	A	C
Dover CGOC	Thames, Dover, Wight	5, 6	0110	*0410*	**0710**	*1010*	1310	*1610*	**1910**	*2210*
Fareham NMOC	Portland, Wight	5, 6, 7	0130	*0430*	**0730**	*1030*	1330	*1630*	**1930**	*2230*
(May be announced as Solent)										
Falmouth CGOC	Portland, Plymouth, Sole, Shannon, Lundy, Fastnet Biscay, Fitzroy	8, 9	0110	*0410*	**0710**	*1010*	1310	*1610*	**1910**	*2210*
West Coast			B	C	A	C	B	C	A	C
Milford Haven CGOC	Lundy, Fastnet, Irish Sea, Shannon	9,10	0150	*0450*	**0750**	*1050*	1350	*1650*	**1950**	*2250*
Holyhead CGOC	Irish Sea	10,11,12	0130	*0450*	**0730**	*1050*	1330	*1650*	**1930**	*2250*
Belfast CGOC	Irish Sea, Rockall, Malin	13,14,15	0210	*0510*	**0810**	*1110*	1410	*1710*	**2010**	*2310*
Stornoway CGOC	Rockall, Malin, Hebrides, Bailey, Fair Is, Faroes, SE Iceland	15,16,17	0110	*0410*	**0710**	*1010*	1310	*1610*	**1910**	*2210*
Shetland CGOC	Viking, Fair Isle, Faroes, N Utsire	18,1	0110	*0410*	**0710**	*1010*	1310	*1610*	**1910**	*2210*

*Although HMCG endeavour to repeat broadcasts at the times shown this can vary and forecasts may be postponed until the next time slot depending on the level of operational activity during emergencies and busy times.

Note: The information on this and the next two pages (Fig 6(4) and 6.8.2) remains subject to possible change and readers are advised to check the MCGA Maritime safety information leaflet (MCA/064) available at www.mcga.gov.uk, but note the publication date; this is not regularly updated. See also the free monthly updates from January 2018 to June 2018 available for download at www.reedsnauticalalmanac.co.uk.

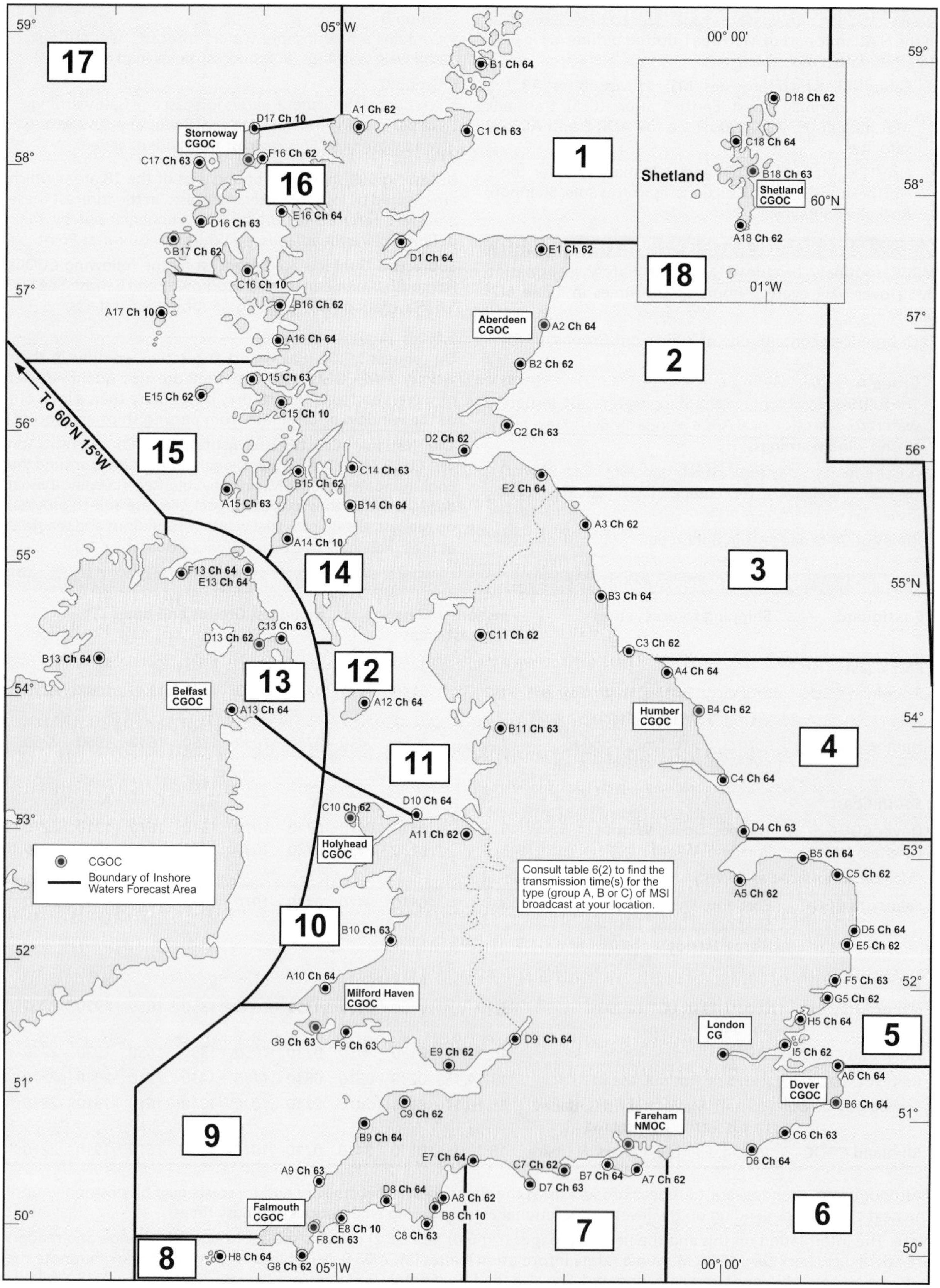
17
16
15
14
13
12
11
10
9
8
7
6
5
4
3
2
1
18
Shetland
Shetland CGOC
D18 Ch 62
C18 Ch 64
B18 Ch 63
A18 Ch 62
60°N
01°W
00° 00'
05°W
59°
58°
57°
56°
55°
55°N
54°
53°
52°
51°
50°
B1 Ch 64
A1 Ch 62
C1 Ch 63
D17 Ch 10
Stornoway CGOC
C17 Ch 63
F16 Ch 62
E16 Ch 64
D16 Ch 63
B17 Ch 62
C16 Ch 10
A17 Ch 10
B16 Ch 62
A16 Ch 64
D1 Ch 64
E1 Ch 62
Aberdeen CGOC
A2 Ch 64
B2 Ch 62
D15 Ch 63
E15 Ch 62
C15 Ch 10
To 60°N 15°W
C2 Ch 63
D2 Ch 62
C14 Ch 63
B15 Ch 62
A15 Ch 63
B14 Ch 64
E2 Ch 64
A3 Ch 62
A14 Ch 10
F13 Ch 64
E13 Ch 64
B3 Ch 64
C11 Ch 62
C13 Ch 63
D13 Ch 62
C3 Ch 62
B13 Ch 64
A4 Ch 64
Belfast CGOC
A12 Ch 64
A13 Ch 64
Humber CGOC
B4 Ch 62
B11 Ch 63
C4 Ch 64
D10 Ch 64
C10 Ch 62
Holyhead CGOC
A11 Ch 62
D4 Ch 63
B5 Ch 64
C5 Ch 62
A5 Ch 62
CGOC
Boundary of Inshore Waters Forecast Area
Consult table 6(2) to find the transmission time(s) for the type (group A, B or C) of MSI broadcast at your location.
D5 Ch 64
E5 Ch 62
B10 Ch 63
A10 Ch 64
Milford Haven CGOC
F5 Ch 63
G5 Ch 62
H5 Ch 64
London CG
G9 Ch 63
F9 Ch 63
D9 Ch 64
E9 Ch 62
I5 Ch 62
A6 Ch 64
Dover CGOC
B6 Ch 64
C9 Ch 62
B9 Ch 64
Fareham NMOC
C6 Ch 63
E7 Ch 64
C7 Ch 62
B7 Ch 64
A7 Ch 62
D6 Ch 64
A9 Ch 63
D7 Ch 63
D8 Ch 64
A8 Ch 62
B8 Ch 10
Falmouth CGOC
E8 Ch 10
F8 Ch 63
C8 Ch 63
H8 Ch 64
G8 Ch 62

Fig 6(4) Remote Coastguard transmitters and Inshore waters forecast areas used by the UK Coastguard network

6.8.2 Remote MSI transmitters

Coastguard MSI broadcasts are transmitted via remote aerial sites giving optimum coverage. Figure 6(4) opposite shows their locations and VHF broadcast channels (either Ch 10, 23, 84 or 86), after a prior announcement on Ch 16. Broadcasts are made every 3 hours from the start times (LT) shown below. **MF frequencies** are also used, see 6.8.3.

INSHORE WATERS FORECAST AREAS/MSI TRANSMITTERS/START TIMES

1 Cape Wrath to Rattray Head inc Orkney, 0130

A1	Durness (Loch Eriboll)
B1	Wideford Hill (Kirkwall, Orkney)
C1	Noss Head (Wick)
D1	Rosemarkie (Cromarty)
E1	Windy Head Hill (2M W Fraserburgh)

2 Rattray Head to Berwick-upon-Tweed, 0130

A2	Greg Ness (MF: see 6.8.3)
B2	Inverbervie
C2	Fife Ness
D2	Craigkelly (Burntisland)
E2	St Abbs Head

3 Berwick-upon-Tweed to Whitby, 0150

A3	Newton
B3	Cullercoats (Blyth) (MF: see 6.8.3)
C3	Boulby (10M N of Whitby)

4 Whitby to Gibraltar Point, 0150

A4	Ravenscar
B4	Flamborough Head
C4	Easington (Spurn Head)
D4	Skegness

5 Gibraltar Point to North Foreland. 0110

A5	Guy's Head (Wisbech)
B5	Langham (Blakeney)
C5	Trimingham (Cromer)
D5	Caister (Great Yarmouth)
E5	Lowestoft
F5	Bawdsey (R Deben)
G5	Walton-on-the-Naze
H5	Bradwell (R Blackwater)
I5	Shoeburyness

6 North Foreland to Selsey Bill, 0110

A6	North Foreland)
B6	Langdon (Dover)
C6	Fairlight (Hastings)
D6	Newhaven

7 Selsey Bill to Lyme Regis, 0130

A7	Boniface Down (Ventnor IoW)
B7	Needles
C7	St Alban's Head
D7	Grove Pt (Portland Bill)
E7	Beer Head (Lyme Bay)

8 Lyme Regis to Land's End inc the Isles of Scilly, 0110

A8	Berry Head (Torbay)
B8	Dartmouth
C8	East Prawle (Salcombe)
D8	Rame Head
E8	Fowey
F8	Falmouth
G8	Lizard
H8	Scillies (MF: see 6.8.3)

9 Land's End to St David's Head, inc the Bristol Channel, 0150

A9	Trevose Head
B9	Hartland Point
C9	Combe Martin (N Devon)
D9	Severn Bridges
E9	St Hilary (Barry)
F9	Monkstone (Tenby)
G9	St Ann's (Milford Haven)

10 St David's Head to Great Orme Head inc St George's Channel, 0150

A10	Dinas Head (Fishguard)
B10	Blaenplwyf (Aberystwyth)
C10	South Stack (Holyhead)
D10	Great Orme

11 Great Orme Head to the Mull of Galloway, 0130

A11	Moel-y-Parc(N Wales)
B11	Langthwaite (Lancaster)
C11	Caldbeck (Carlisle)

12 Isle of Man, 0130

A12	Snaefell (Isle of Man)

13 Lough Foyle to Carlingford Lough, 0210

A13	Slievemartin (Rostrevor)
B13	Orlock Head (Bangor)
C13	Black Mountain (Belfast
D13	West Torr (Fair Head)
E13	Limvady (Lough Foyle)
F13	Navar (Lower Lough Erne)

14 Mull of Galloway to Mull of Kintyre incl the Firth of Clyde and North Channel, 0210

A14	Rhu Staffnish (Kintyre)
B14	Lawhill (Ardrossan)
C14	Clyde (Greenock)

15 Mull of Kintyre to Arnamurchan Point, 0210

A15	Kilchiaran (SW Islay)
B15	South Knapdale (Loch Fyne)
C15	Torosay (E Mull)
D15	Glengorm (N Mull)
E15	Tiree (MF: see 6.8.3)

16 The Minch, 0110

A16	Arisaig (S of Mallaig)
B16	Drumfearn (SE Skye)
C16	Skriag (Portree, Skye)
D16	Rodel (S Harris)
E16	Melvaig (Loch Ewe)
F16	Portnaguran (E Lewis))

17 Arnamurchan Point to Cape Wrath, 0110

A17	Barra
B17	Clettreval (N Uist)
C17	Forsnaval (W Lewis)
D17	Butt of Lewis (MF: see 6.8.3)

18 Shetland Isles and 60 nautical mile radius, 0110

A18	Fitfull Head (Sumburgh)
B18	Lerwick (MF: see 6.8.3)
C18	Collafirth
D18	Saxa Vord (Unst)

6.8.3 MF MSI broadcasts

For the time-being MSI is broadcast via MF from the following Radio Sites (with an initial announcement on 2182 kHz):

MF Radio Site	Group A	Inshore waters gale warnings*
Tiree (1883 kHz)	0810, 2010	0210, 1410
Shetland (1770 kHz)	0710, 1910	0110, 1310
Butt of Lewis (1743 kHz)	0710, 1910	0110, 1310
Scillies (1880 kHz)	0710, 1910	0110, 1310
Gregness (2226 kHz)	0730, 1930	0130, 1330
Cullercoats (1925 kHz)	0750, 1950	0150, 1350

*Only made if there are gale warnings in force.

6.9 HF RADIO FACSIMILE BROADCASTS

Radio-Fax machines (or HF/SSB receiver and a computer) able to receive images, eg weather charts, are useful on board. Isobaric charts, sea and swell charts, satellite cloud images, sea temperature charts and wind charts are all of special interest to the blue water yachtsman. See ALRS, Vol 3.

6.9.1 DWD Offenbach

This reliable GMDSS related broadcast is from the German weather bureau DWD (www.dwd.de). Transmitted from Pinneburg, DDH and DDK on 3855 kHz (10 kW), 7880 and 13881 kHz (both at 20 kW), it includes actual and forecast surface charts and sea state forecast, for up to 108 hours. Broadcast at 1110 UTC daily it can be downloaded from www.dwd.de/sendeplan

6.9.2 RN Northwood

Frequencies for the **RN, Northwood**, North Atlantic schedule are: 2618·5 kHz (2000–0600), 4610 & 8040 (H24), 11086·5 (0600–2000). The full schedule is broadcast at 0100 & 1300 UT; gale warnings: 0348, 0548, 1148, 1548, 1748, 2348.

6.10 SHIPPING FORECAST AREAS

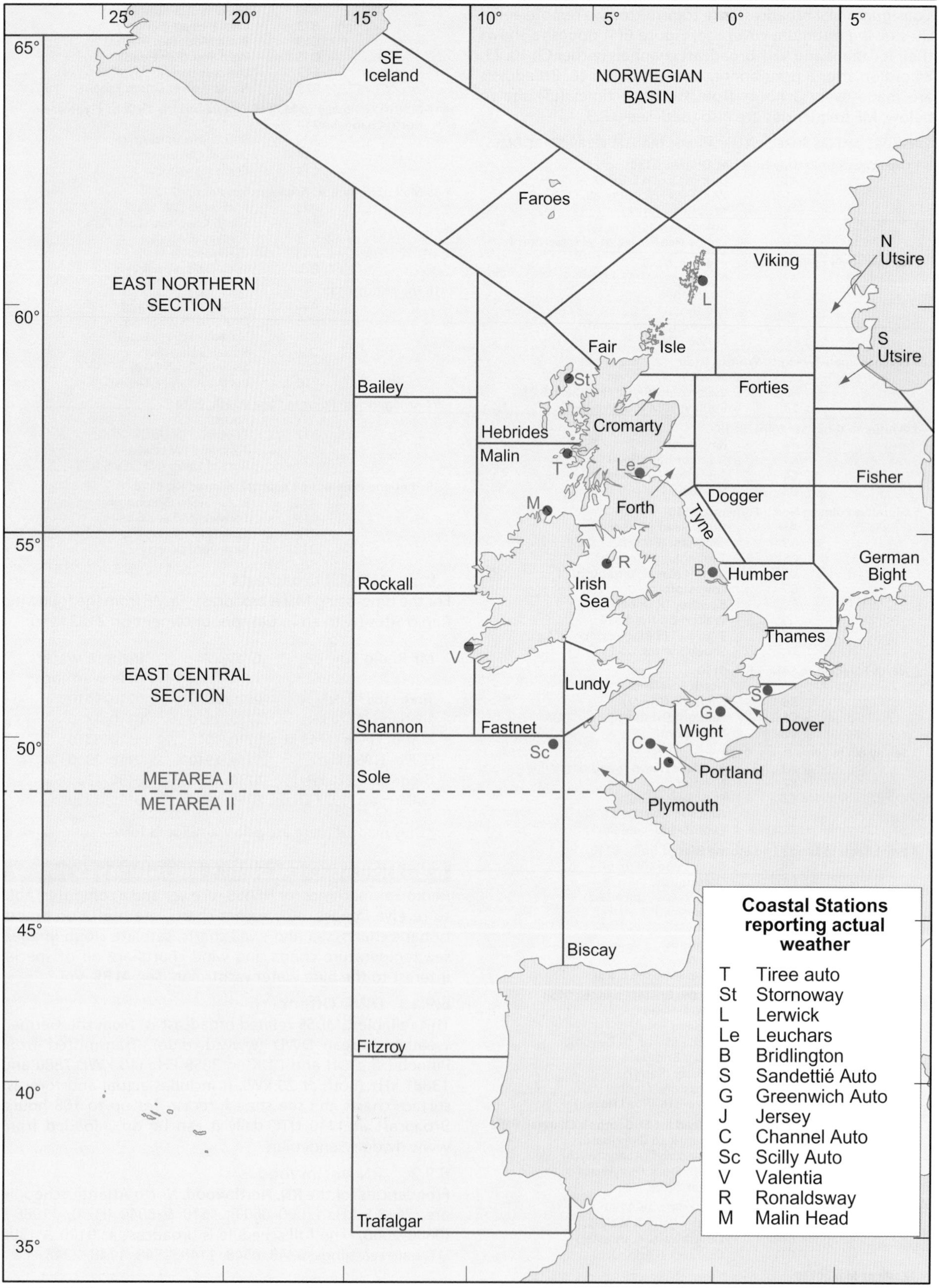

Fig 6(5) UK forecast areas, SafetyNet area I/II boundary

SHIPPING FORECAST RECORD TIME/DAY/DATE ....

GENERAL SYNOPSIS	At 0048, 0520, 1201, 1754 UT/BST			
System	Present position	Movement	Forecast position	At

Gales	**SEA AREA FORECAST**	Wind (At first)	Wind (Later)	Weather	Visibility
	VIKING				
	NORTH UTSIRE				
	SOUTH UTSIRE				
	FORTIES				
	CROMARTY				
	FORTH				
	TYNE				
	DOGGER				
	FISHER				
	GERMAN BIGHT				
	HUMBER				
	THAMES				
	DOVER				
	WIGHT				
	PORTLAND				
	PLYMOUTH				
	BISCAY				
	TRAFALGAR (0048)				
	FITZROY				
	SOLE				
	LUNDY				
	FASTNET				
	IRISH SEA				
	SHANNON				
	ROCKALL				
	MALIN				
	HEBRIDES				
	BAILEY				
	FAIR ISLE				
	FAROES				
	S E ICELAND				

COASTAL REPORTS at .... UT BST	Wind Direction	Wind Force	Weather	Visibility	Pressure	Change
Tiree auto (T)						
Stornoway (St)						
Lerwick (L)						
Leuchars (Le)						
Bridlington (B)						
Sandettié auto (S)						

COASTAL REPORTS	Wind Direction	Wind Force	Weather	Visibility	Pressure	Change
Greenwich auto (G)						
Jersey (J)						
Channel auto (C)						
Scilly auto (Sc)						
Valentia (V)						
Ronaldsway (R)						
Malin Head (M)						

Fig 6(6) UK shipping forecast pro forma

6.10.1 BBC Radio 4 shipping and other forecasts

Although not part of the GMDSS, for many the shipping forecast and its associated reports, as broadcast by BBC Radio 4, remain the principal source of weather data. NAVTEX broadcasts a more complete service, see 6.6. The main benefit of the shipping forecast is that it is updated 6 hourly. HM Coastguard broadcasts repeats as detailed in 6.8.

LT	Bands	Contents summary
0048	LW, MW, FM	Shipping, and 18 inshore waters forecasts. Long list of station reports
0520	LW, MW, FM	Shipping, and 18 inshore waters forecasts. Short list of station reports
1201	LW only	Shipping forecast
1754	LW, FM (Sat/Sun)	Shipping forecast

Sea area Trafalgar is only included in the 0048 forecast.

Frequencies

LW	198 kHz		
MW	Tyneside 603 kHz. London & N Ireland 720 kHz Redruth 756 kHz. Plymouth & Enniskillen 774 kHz Aberdeen 1449 kHz. Carlisle 1485 kHz		
FM	**England**	92·4–94·6 MHz	
	Scotland	91·3–96·1 MHz	103·5–104·9 MHz
	Wales	92·8–96·1 MHz	103·5–104·9 MHz
	N Ireland	93·2–96·0 MHz	103·5–104·6 MHz
	Channel Is	94·8 MHz	

Contents of the shipping forecast

Time of issue; summary of gale warnings in force at that time; a general synopsis of weather systems and their expected development and movement over the next 24 hours; sea area forecasts for the same 24 hours, including wind direction/force, weather and visibility in each; and an outlook for the following 24 hours.

Gale warnings for all affected areas are broadcast at the earliest break in Radio 4 programmes after receipt, as well as after the next news bulletin.

Weather reports from coastal stations follow the 0048 and 0520 shipping forecasts; see Figs 6(5) and 6(6). They include wind direction and force, present weather, visibility, and sea-level pressure and tendency, if available.

Shipping forecasts cover large sea areas. The Inshore waters forecast (below) can provide more specific information to mariners on coastal passages.

6.10.2 BBC Radio 4 Inshore waters forecast

A forecast for inshore waters (up to 12M offshore) in 17 areas around the UK and N Ireland, valid for 24 hours, is broadcast after the 0048 and 0520 coastal station reports. It includes forecasts of wind direction and force, weather, visibility, and sea state. The 17 inshore areas (Fig 6(4)) are defined by the following places and headlands, clockwise around the UK:

Cape Wrath, Orkney, Rattray Hd, Berwick-upon-Tweed, Whitby, Gibraltar Point, N Foreland, Selsey Bill, Lyme Regis, Land's End, St David's Head, Great Ormes Head, Isle of Man, Mull of Galloway, Carlingford Lough, Lough Foyle, Mull of Kintyre, Ardnamurchan Pt and Shetland.

Reports of actual weather. The list of stations changes from time to time. Currently the following station reports are broadcast after the 0048 shipping forecast:

Tiree*, Stornoway, Lerwick, *Wick**, *Aberdeen*, Leuchars, *Boulmer*, Bridlington, Sandettie LV*, Greenwich LV*, *St Catherines Point**, Jersey, Channel LV*, Scilly*, *Milford Haven*, *Aberporth*, *Valley*, *Liverpool Crosby*, Valentia, Ronaldsway, Malin Head, *Macrihanish**.

After the 0520 shipping forecast, stations shown in italics are omitted. Those shown with an asterix are described as automatic weather stations. At these the current weather, such as rain, may not be reported.

Latest observations can also be obtained from the internet. See: www.xcweather.co.uk, www.meteociel.fr (click on temperature and a location) and www.metoffice.gov.uk.

6.10.3 BBC general (land) forecasts

Land area forecasts are broadcast by BBC Radio 4 on the frequencies in 6.10.1. They can often include an outlook up to 48 hours beyond the shipping forecast, and more details of frontal systems and coastal weather.

Land area forecasts – Wind strength

Wind descriptions, with Beaufort scale equivalents, are:

Calm:	0	Fresh:	5
Light:	1–3	Strong:	6–7
Moderate:	4	Gale:	8

Land area forecasts – Visibility

The following definitions apply to land forecasts:

Mist:	Visibility between 2000m and 1000m
Fog:	Visibility less than 1000m
Dense fog:	Less than 50m

6.11 INTERNET WEATHER FORECASTS

The Internet is not an operational system but does provide a useful back-up and an alternative source for GMDSS services as well as information otherwise not available. Website addresses can change without notice; many services are automated and lacking quality control. There are no amendment procedures.

The UK Met Office website www.metoffice.gov.uk/public/weather/marine-shipping-forecast/ has texts of all marine forecasts, warnings and weather actuals from coastal stations, light vessels and data buoys. Text-only versions of forecasts are at www.metoffice.gov.uk/public/weather/marine-printable/. Additionally, the BBC website, http://www.bbc.co.uk/weather/coast_and_sea/coastal/, provides output from the Met Office high resolution weather prediction model. These give objective, 30 hour forecasts, at 6 hour intervals for locations around the UK.

National meteorological services provide the most reliable forecasts for their own waters. Texts of GMDSS forecasts can be downloaded from text-only web pages or by using free email text retrieval services. (See www.weather.mailasail.com/Franks-Weather/Home for details.)

Some private firms offer forecast services, e.g. www.weatheronline.co.uk, or www.metmarine.com, a free Internet service providing a 24 hour marine weather forecast in English, for the UK S Coast, and W and N Coasts of France up to 20M offshore, updated every 6 hours. See also 6.19.4.

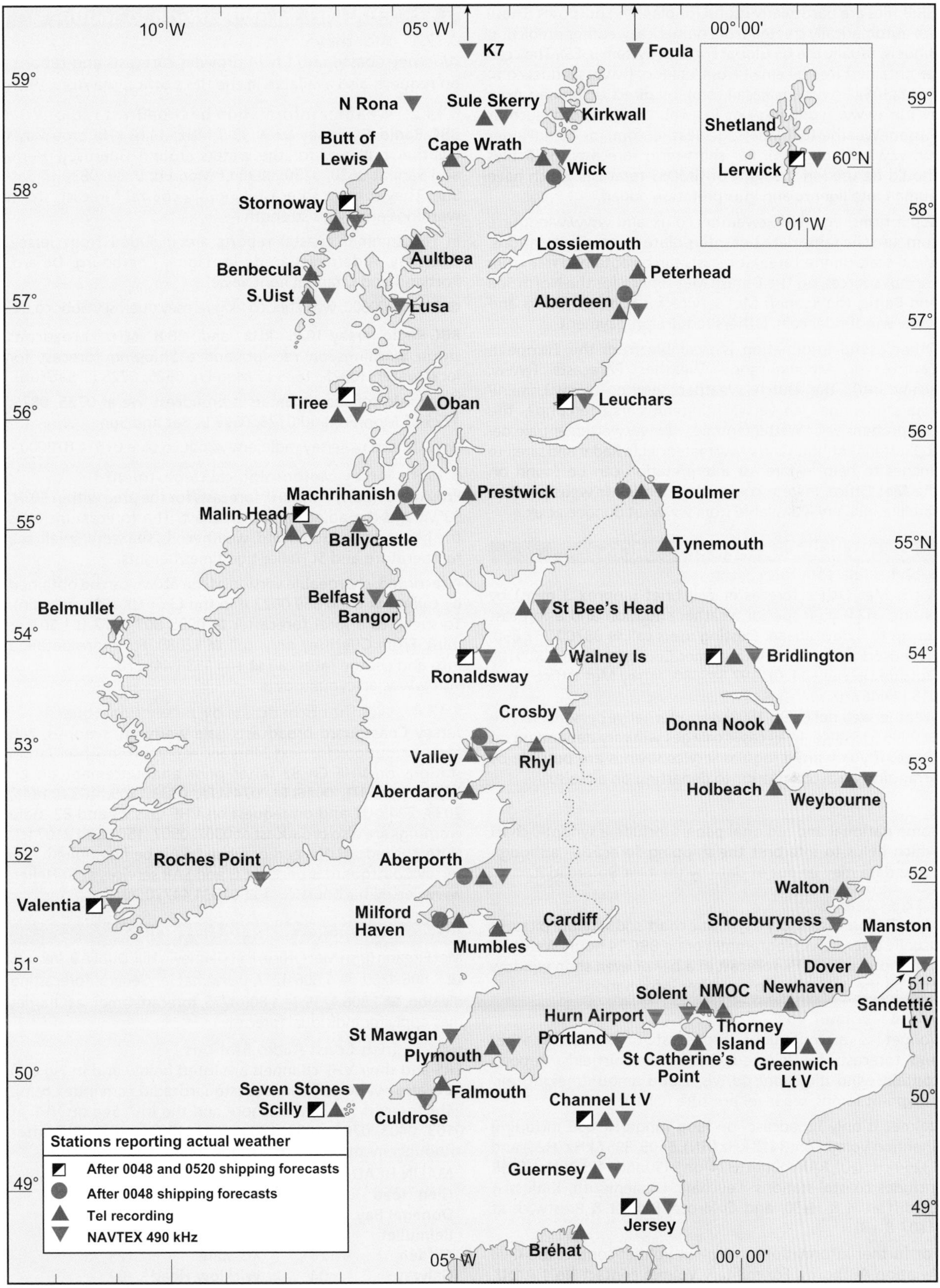

Fig 6(7) Stations reporting actual weather via BBC Radio 4, telephone recordings and NAVTEX

Weather

GRIB files are particularly useful for planning purposes. These are automatically created from numerical weather prediction models, usually the US Global Forecast System (GFS). They can be obtained free by email from Saildocs (www.saildocs.com) or MailASail (www.mailasail.com), by direct download from zyGrib (www.zygrib.org/) or in web browser form such as PassageWeather(www.passageweather.com) or WindFinder (www.windfinder.com). For short-term forecasts, GRIB files should be used in the light of GMDSS forecasts which have human intelligence and interpretation added.

Some firms, eg www.xcweather.co.uk and www.windguru.com, use the same data but interpolate to specific locations. Meso-scale (limited area) forecasts can be obtained free from various sources, eg The Danish Met service for the North Sea and Baltic, the Spanish Met service for Spanish waters and www.windfinder.com. Others require prepayment.

Other useful information is available from the European Centre for Medium-range Weather Forecasts (www.ecmwf.int/), the Dutch weather service, (www.knmi.nl/waarschuwingen_en_verwachtingen/weerkarten.php?, the comprehensive Wetterzentrale (www.wetterzentrale.de/topkarten/tknf.html) and www.meteociel.fr. Radar and satellite images to help in forecast interpretation can be found on the Met Office, meteox.com and meteocielf.fr websites. Free satellite imagery is available from www.sat.dundee.ac.uk.

6.12 OTHER WEATHER RESOURCES

6.12.1 Talk to a forecaster

A UK Met Office forecaster will brief (approx 3 mins) by phone (H24) your special weather situation and a forecast for up to 5 days ahead. Existing users call ☎ 08700 767 890. New users in the UK call Customer Centre ☎ 0370 900 0100 Outside UK call +44 (0)1392 885680. Jersey Met Office (H24) 01534 446770.

Weatherweb.net (0800-1800) is an alternative personal service ☎ 0906 515 0046. In all cases charges will vary depending on usage, if you want a regular service savings are possible by arranging an account prior to departing on a cruise.

6.12.2 Press

Some national and regional papers include a synoptic chart which helps to interpret the shipping forecast – although some data may be out of date by the time you read it.

6.12.3 Television

Most TV forecasts show a synoptic chart and satellite pictures usually after news programmes or on BBC 24 hours Weather. In remote areas a TV forecast in a bar or even shop window may be the only source of weather information.

6.12.4 Volmet

Volmet is a continuous broadcast of actual weather and forecasts for selected civil/military airfields. Reports contain wind direction/spd, vis, cloud amount/height, air/dewpoint temps, sea level pressure (QNH).

Volmet is only broadcast on long range HF SSB including Shannon Volmet on: 3413 kHz (HN), 5505, 8957 kHz (H24) and 13264 kHz (HJ). RAF Volmet (H24) on 5450 and 11253 kHz HF SSB includes coastal stations: Leuchars, Lossiemouth, Kinloss & Cardiff at H & H+30; and Culdrose, Belfast & Prestwick at H+07 & +37.

For further information on civilian Volmet contact the Civil Aviation Authority. For military Volmet contact No 1 AIDU, RAF Northolt, West End Road, Ruislip, Middlesex HA4 6NG.

6.13 CHANNEL ISLANDS (North to South)

6.13.1 Alderney

Alderney Coastguard Ch 74 provides forecasts and reports on request; also available in the HM's office; see Area 19.

6.13.2 Weather information by broadcast radio

BBC Radio Guernsey 93·2, 99·0 MHz; 1116 kHz broadcasts weather bulletins for the waters around Guernsey, Herm and Sark at 0630, 0730, 0830 LT Mon-Fri; 0730, 0830 LT Sat/Sun. They contain forecast, synopsis, coastal forecast, storm warnings and wind strength.

In the summer coastal reports are included from Jersey, Guernsey, Alderney, Cap de la Hague, Cherbourg, Dinard, Portland and Channel light vessel.

☎ 01481 200600. www.bbc.co.uk/guernsey guernsey@bbc.co.uk

BBC Radio Jersey 1026 kHz and 88·8 MHz broadcasts storm warnings on receipt; and a Shipping forecast for local waters (0625, 1625 LT Mon-Fri; 0625, 0725 LT Sat/Sun).

Wind info for Jersey waters is broadcast live at 0725, 0825, 1725 LT Mon-Fri; and 0725, 0825 LT Sat and Sun.

www.bbc.co.uk/jersey radiojersey@bbc.co.uk e 01534 870000.

6.13.3 Jersey Meteorological Department

Provides 6 hourly 24hr VHF forecasts for the area within 50°N, 03°W and the adjacent French coast. The forecast includes the general situation, wind, weather, vis, sea state, swell, sea temperature and St Helier tide times/heights.

A recorded, chargeable version of the above can be obtained by calling ☎ 0900 669 0022 if in the CI or UK (60p per min). To speak to a local forecaster ☎ 0905 807 7777 (£1·50 per min). From Guernsey only, call ☎ 12080. For more detailed info and charge rates call ☎ +44 1534 448770, 📠 448778; or visit www.jerseymet.gov.je

6.13.4 Weather broadcasts by Jersey Coastguard

Jersey Coastguard broadcasts gale warnings, synopsis, 24h forecast, outlook for next 24hrs and reports from observation stations on VHF Ch 82 (after prior announcement on Ch 16) at 0433 UT, 0646LT*, 0745LT*; 0833,1245, 1633, 1845, 2033, 2245 UT and on request on VHF Ch's 25 and 82. Gale warnings are also broadcast at 0307, 0907, 1507 and 2107 UT. Note:*broadcast 1hr earlier when DST is being applied.
Jersey Coastguard is part of CG and SAR services at St Helier. www.jersey-harbours.com ☎ 01534 447705/04.

6.14 REPUBLIC OF IRELAND (ROI)

Met Éireann (Irish Met Office) is at Glasnevin Hill, Dublin 9, Ireland. ☎ 1 806 4200, 📠 1 806 4247, www.met.ie General forecasting division: ☎ 1 806 4255, 📠 1 806 4275, forecasts@met.ie (Charges may apply for individual forecasts.)

6.14.1 Irish Coast Radio Stations

CRS and their VHF channels are listed below and in Fig 6(8) (see also www.malinheadcoastguardradio.com/index.htm). 24hr forecast for 30M offshore and the Irish Sea on VHF at 0103, 0403, 0703, 1003, 1303, 1603, 1903 and 2203LT, after announcement on Ch 16, include gale warnings/synopsis.

MALIN HEAD	23	**Bantry**	23
Glen Head	24	**Mizen Head**	04
Donegal Bay	02	**Cork**	26
Belmullet	83	**Mine Head**	83
Clifden	26	**Rosslare**	23
Galway	04	**Wicklow Head**	02
Shannon	28	**DUBLIN**	83
VALENTIA	24	**Carlingford**	**04**

Gale warnings are broadcast on receipt and at 0033, 0633, 1233 and 1833 UT, after an announcement on Ch 16. **MF** Valentia Radio broadcasts forecasts for Shannon and Fastnet on 1752 kHz at 0833 & 2033 UT, and on request. Gale warnings are broadcast on receipt and at 0303, 0903, 1503 and 2103 (UT) after an announcement on 2182 kHz. Weather is not broadcast on MF by Malin Head or Dublin.

6.14.2 NAVTEX

Malin Head MRCC broadcasts (ID 'A', see Fig 6(3)) an inshore forecast at 0000, 0400, 0800, 1200, 1600 and 2000 for North of Ireland, West of Scotland and North of Scotland.

6.14.3 Weather by telephone

Recorded messages of sea area forecasts and gale warnings are available H24 at Weatherdial (www.weatherdial.ie). Dial ☎ 1550 123 plus suffixes: 850 Munster; 851 Leinster; 852 Connaught; 853 Ulster; 854 Dublin (plus winds in Dublin Bay and HW times); 855 Coastal waters and Irish Sea.

6.14.4 Radio Telefís Éireann (RTE) Radio 1

RTE Radio 1 broadcasts weather bulletins daily at 0602, 1253 and 2355LT on 252 kHz (LW) Summerhill (15M W of Dublin airport) and FM (88·2–90·0 MHz). They contain a situation, forecast and coastal reports for Irish Sea and coastal waters. The forecast includes: wind, weather, vis, swell (if higher than 4m) and a 24hrs outlook. Gale warnings are included in hourly news bulletins on FM and MF.

Coastal reports include wind, weather, visibility, pressure, with pressure tendency over the last 3hrs described as:

Steady	=	0–0·4 hPa change
Rising/falling slowly	=	0·5–1·9
Rising/falling	=	2·0–3·4
Rising/falling rapidly	=	3·5–5·9
Rising/falling very rapidly	=	> 6·0

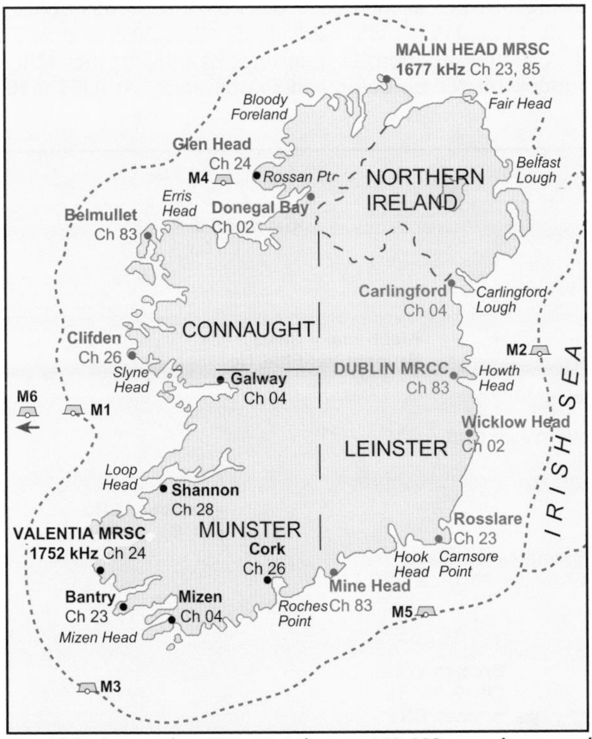

Fig 6(8) shows the CRS, Met buoys M1–M6, provinces and headlands named in forecasts

> ### FOREIGN LANGUAGE WEATHER INFORMATION
>
> It's worth learning some basic meteorological terms in other languages (see 1.6). It is also a good idea to use the Internet before you go, to become familiar with the local forecast structure, terms used and the places they refer to. Do not bank on being able to download an English language forecast in the area!

6.15 WEST DENMARK

6.15.1 Lyngby Radio broadcasts, in Danish and English on MF/SSB1,734 kHz (Blåvand), 2,586 kHz (Rønne) and on VHF Blåvand, Ch 07. Gale warnings for Skagerrak, Fisher and German Bight are issued on receipt after announcement on 2187.5 kHz and Ch 16 with repeats on 2182 kHz and Ch16. Forecasts will be provided on request.

Danish sea area forecasts in English are at: http://www.dmi.dk/en/hav/prognoser/marine-forecasts/

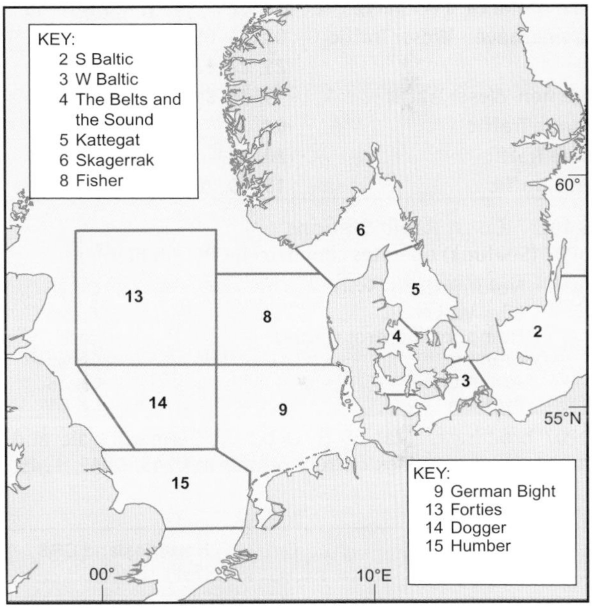

Fig 6(9) Danish forecast areas

6.15.2 Danmarks Radio, Programme 1

Warnings and forecasts for Skagerrak, Fisher and German Bight are broadcast in Danish on 243 kHz at 0545, 0845, 1145, 1745.

6.15.3 Danmarks Meteorologiske Institut (DM)

Provides marine forecasts in **English** on www.dmi.dk/eng/index/forecasts.htm.

> Stockholm Radio offers two PDF downloads showing VHF weather broadcast channels in Denmark: www.stockholmradio.se Click on Kustradio / VHF

6.16 GERMANY

6.16.1 Deutscher Wetterdienst (DWD)

DWD (German weather service) provides Met info which is updated twice daily; more often for weather reports and text forecasts. SEEWIS (Sea Weather Information System) permits data feed by phone/modem into an onboard computer.
DWD ☎ + 49 (0) 69 8062 6201. 📠 + 49 (0) 69 8062 6193. www.dwd.de seeschifffahrt@dwd.de Texts in English of all DWD marine forecasts can be found at: www.dwd.de/EN/specialusers/shipping/weatheratsea_en/northsea/_node.html

6.16.2 Traffic Centres

Traffic Centres, Fig 6(10), broadcast local storm warnings, weather bulletins, visibility in German or English on request.

Traffic Centre	VHF Ch	Every
German Bight Traffic	**79 (West), 80 (East)**	**H+00**
Cuxhaven-Elbe Traffic	**71 (outer Elbe)**	**H+35**
Brunsbüttel-Elbe Traffic	**68 (lower Elbe)**	**H+05**
Kiel Kanal III + IV (E part)	**03, 12**	**H+15 & H+45**
Kiel Kanal I + II (W part)	**13, 02**	**H+20 & H+50**
Bremerhaven-Weser Traffic	**02, 04, 05, 07, 21, 22, 82**	**H+20**
Bremen-Weser Traffic	**19, 78, 81**	**H+30**
Hunte Traffic	**63**	**H+30**
Jade Traffic	**20, 63**	**H+10**
Ems Traffic	**15, 18, 20, 21**	**H+50**

6.16.3 Coast Radio Stations

DP07 (Seefunk) operates commercial CRS, Fig 6(10), at:

Nordfriesland (Sylt)	Ch 26
Elbe-Weser	Ch 24
Hamburg (Control centre)	Ch 83
Bremen	Ch 25
Accumersiel	Ch 28
Borkum	Ch 61

DP07 broadcasts (Mar 25 to Oct 1, in German): gale and strong wind warnings on receipt and at 0745, 0945, 1245, 1645 and 1945 LT for Fisher, German Bight and Humber and a synopsis, 12hr forecast, 24hr outlook, coastal stn reports, and 4–5 day outlook for N Sea/Baltic) at 0945, 1645 and 1945.

6.16.4 NAVTEX

Pinneberg (S) in **English** on 518 kHz and Pinneberg (L) in German on 490 kHz transmit Weather bulletins (and Nav warnings) for German Bight (area N10) at the times listed in Table 6(1).

6.16.5 Public Service Radio

Deutschlandfunk DLF (FM)

Severe weather and gale warnings for the N Sea coast (in **German, LT**) for the general public – not detailed nautical forecasts but still useful, H+00 after news (except 2100), Mon-Fri H+30 0530–1630, Sat H+30 0530–0730: **Eutin** 101·9 MHz; **Flensburg/Eckernförde** 103·3 MHz; **Hamburg/Pinneberg** 88·7 MHz; **Heide** 104·4 MHz; **Helgoland** 107·4 MHz; **Itzehoe** 102·2 MHz; **St Peter-Ording** 102·3 MHz; **Westerland** 90·3 MHz; **Aurich** 101·8 MHz; **Bremen**107·1 MHz; **Bremerhaven** 103·4 MHz; **Cuxhaven** 101·6 MHz.

Digital radio

DRadio Dok Deb (Deutschlandradio Dokumente und Debatten), Shipping forecasts for Eng Chan/N Sea (in **German**) daily via DAB + at 0105, 0640, 1810 LT .

NDR Info Spezial, via DAB+, DVB-S satellite, NDR Radio App and as livestream via the internet, 0005, 0830, 2205 LT, Shipping forecast/synopsis for 12H plus outlook for further 12H for the SW North Sea, German Bight, Fisher, Utsire and Skagerrak. Details of gale and storm warnings, wave heights, station reports and nautical warnings.

6.16.6 HF Radio

Offenbach (Main) Programme 1 broadcasts in **English** (radio teletype F1B and weather maps facsimile F1C) on 4583, 7646 and 10100·8 kHz at 0005, 0020, 0305, 0320, 0535, 0550, 0835, 0850, 1135, 1150, 1435, 1450, 1735, 1750, 2035 and 2050 UT: Weather situation, 12-hour forecast and a further 12hrs outlook for N Sea, Baltic and coastal areas. At 0355,1530

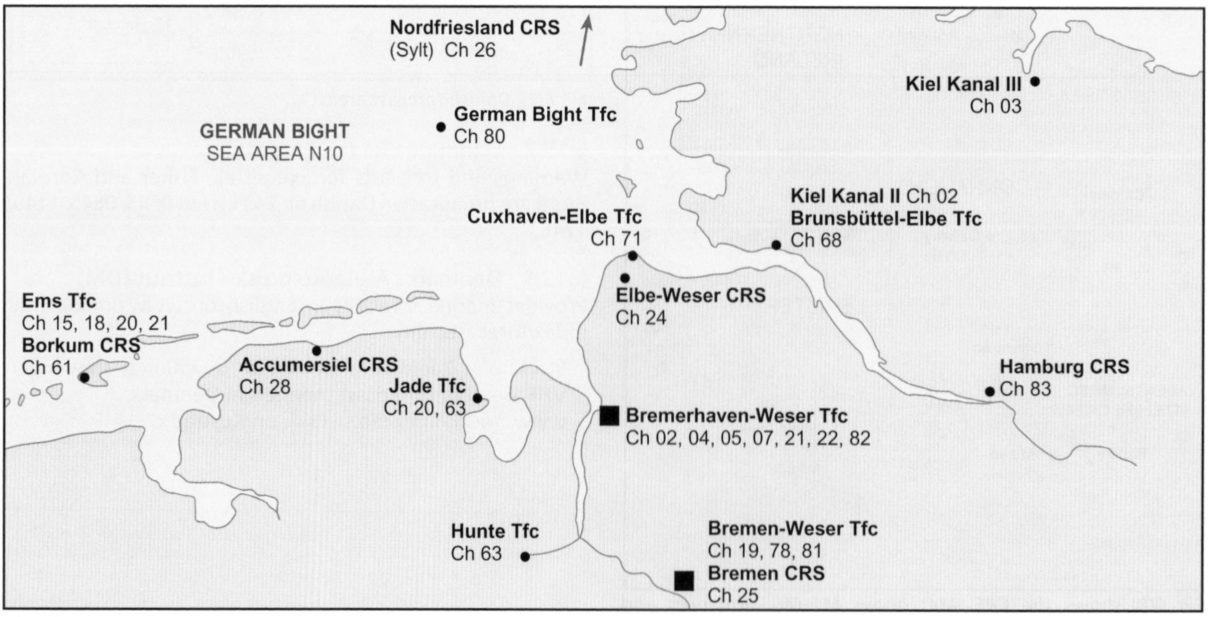

Fig 6(10) German MSI broadcasts

UT: North Sea weather and 5-day forecasts in **English**. Full broadcast schedule: www.dwd.de/sendeplan.

6.16.7 Recorded telephone forecasts for small craft

Call ☎+49(0)69 8062 6101 (H24), updated daily 0630, 1230, 2030, or ☎+49(0) 221 34529918 for wind warnings (> F6) in North Sea areas, updated 0105, 0640, 1800 LT. Alternatively, call ☎+49 (0)69 8062 5799 (H24) then select:

1	for the general situation report.
2	for the SW North Sea, German Bight and Fisher.
3	for the Skagerrak and Kattegat.
4	for the Baltic Sea (South and West).
5	for the German N Sea coast.
6	for the German Baltic coast.

6.16.8 German tidal height differences

Predictions of tidal height differences due to meteorological effects are issued by **Bundesamt für Seeschifffahrt und Hydrographie (BSH)** four times a day at www.bsh.de/aktdat/wvd/wahome.htm. For exceptionally high or low tides, navigational warnings are issued.

6.17 THE NETHERLANDS

6.17.1 Netherlands Coastguard/Traffic Centres

VHF MSI broadcasts – Fig 6(11), NE to SW

For coastal waters 30M out to sea and inland waters, in English and Dutch. Wind warnings (F6+) at 1133, 1543, 1933, 2333 LT. Forecasts at 0805, 1305, 1905, 2305 LT.

VHF Ch 23: Schiermonnikoog, Kornwerderzand, Wezep, Huisduinen (Den Helder), IJmuiden, Renesse, Woensdrecht.

VHF Ch 83: Appingedam, West Terschelling, Hoorn, Schoorl, Scheveningen, Westkapelle.
After prior announcement on Chs 16/70

Weather bulletins specifically for the Westerschelde are also broadcast by **Vlissingen Traffic Centre**, VHF Ch 14, every H+50 LT and **Terneuzen Traffic Centre**, VHF Ch 11, every H+00 LT.

MF/SSB weather broadcasts in English

On 1890 kHz (Appingedam) and 3673 kHz (Scheveningen) after call on 2187·5 kHz. Wind warnings (F7+) for Dogger, Humber, Thames and German Bight at 0333, 7333, 1533, 1933, 2333. Forecasts at 0940, 2140, all UTC.

6.17.2 Radio Noord-Holland (FM)

Coastal forecasts for northern areas, gale warnings and wind strength are broadcast in Dutch, Mon–Fri at 0730, 0838, 1005, 1230 and 1705 LT; Sat/Sun 1005, by:

Wieringermeer 93.9 MHz and **Haarlem** 97.6 MHz.

6.17.3 Omroep Zeeland (FM)

Coastal forecasts for southern areas, synopsis, gale warnings and wind strength are broadcast in Dutch, Mon–Fri at 0715, 0915, 1215 and 1715 LT; Sat/Sun 1015, by:

Philippine 97.8 MHz and **Goes** 101.9 MHz.

Fig 6 (11) Netherlands MSI broadcasts

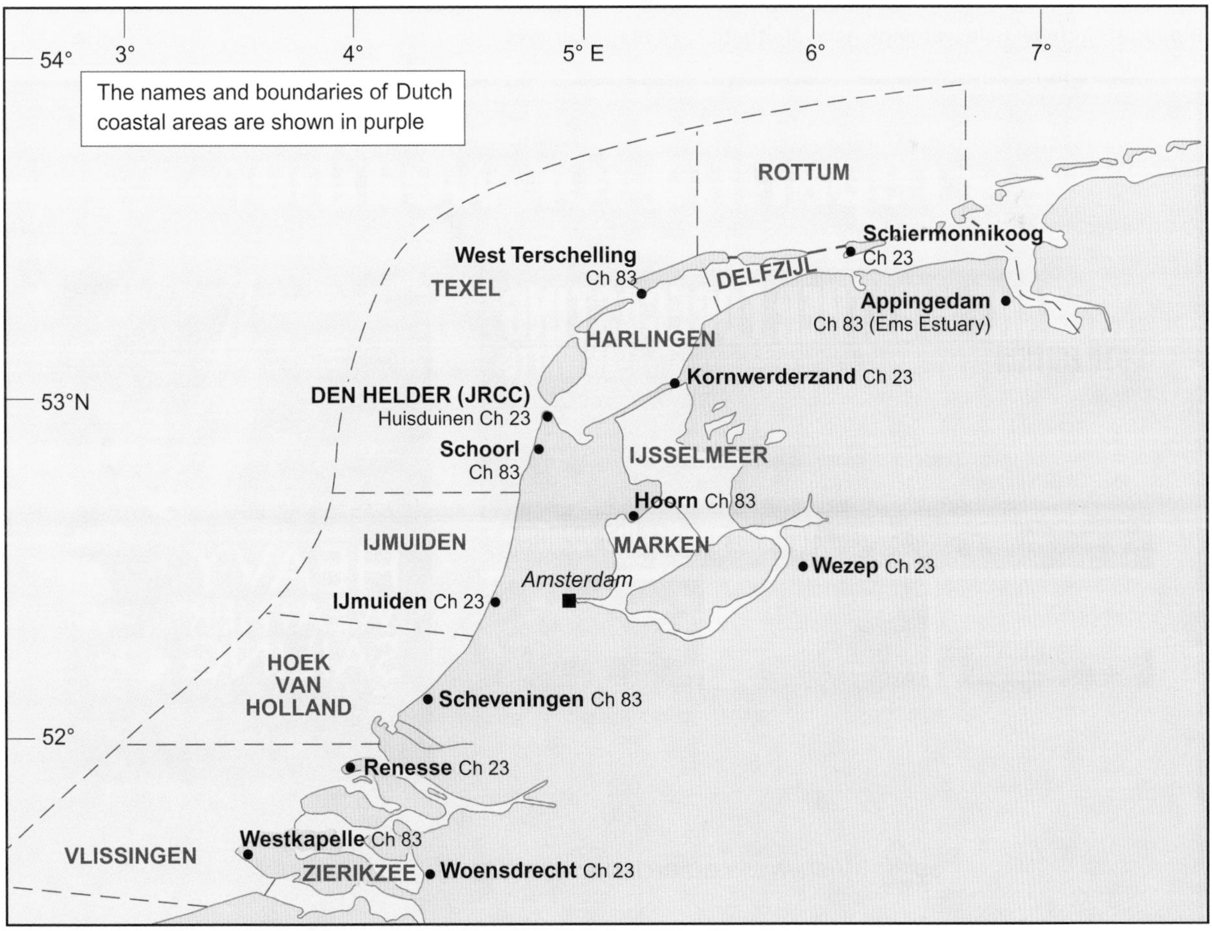

6.18 BELGIUM

Coast Radio Stations

Oostende Radio, after prior notice on VHF 16, DSC 70 and 2182 kHz, broadcasts in **English** and Dutch on VHF 27 and MF 2761 kHz: Strong wind warnings on receipt and after the next 2 silent periods. Forecasts for Thames, Dover and the Belgian coast at 0720 LT and 0820, 1720 UT.

Oostende Radio broadcasts in **English** and Dutch on VHF Ch 24 for the Schelde estuary: Gale warnings and strong wind warnings on receipt and once every H+48.

Zeebrugge Traffic Centre broadcasts weather bulletins for the Westerschelde on VHF Ch 69 every H+10.LT.

6.19 FRANCE

Le Guide Marine, a free annual booklet, summarises how weather forecasts and warnings are issued. It is usually available at marinas or on-line from www.meteofrance.fr/publications/nos-collections/guides-pratiques/guide-marine.

6.19.1 CROSS VHF and MF broadcasts

CROSS broadcasts Met bulletins on VHF in French, after an announcement on Ch 16. In the English Channel broadcasts can be given in **English**, on request Ch 16. Remote stations, VHF channels and local times are shown in Fig 6(12) on page 101. There are continuous broadcasts on VHF Ch 63 from Étel for Pointe de Penmarc'h to L'Anse de L'Aiguillon and from Chassiron for L'Anse de L'Aiguillon to the Spanish border.

A useful source of texts for all Météo France marine forecasts is www.meteo-marine.com/meteo-marine

Broadcasts include: Gale warnings, general situation, 24 hrs forecast (actual weather, wind, sea state and vis) and trends for coastal waters (20M offshore).

Gale warnings (*Bulletins Météorologique Spéciaux* or BMS). are broadcast on VHF at H+03. Warnings and forecasts on MF frequencies are as shown below.

CROSS GRIS-NEZ

Humber, Thames, Dover, Wight. Forecasts at 0833 and 2033. Warnings at HH+03, 1650 kHz after announcement on 2667 kHz.

Thames, Dover, Wight, Portland, Plymouth. 3-day forecast at 1633 on 1650 kHz

CROSS CORSEN

Atlantic and English Channel. Forecasts at 0815 and 2015 repeated every 2 hours at HH+03 on 1650 kHz, repeated on 2667 kHz.

Iroise, Yeu, Rochebonne, Cantabrico, Finisterre. 3-day forecast at 1615, on 1650 kHz.

6.19.2 Commercial radio broadcasting

France Bleu Contentin

Broadcasts 7/7 at 0834 LT: coastal forecast, gale warnings, visibility, wind strength, tidal information, small craft warnings, in French, for the Cherbourg peninsula on the following frequencies:

St Vaast-la-Hougue	95·0 MHz.
Cherbourg	95·0/100·7 MHz.
Cap de la Hague	99·8 MHz.
Carteret	99·9 MHz.

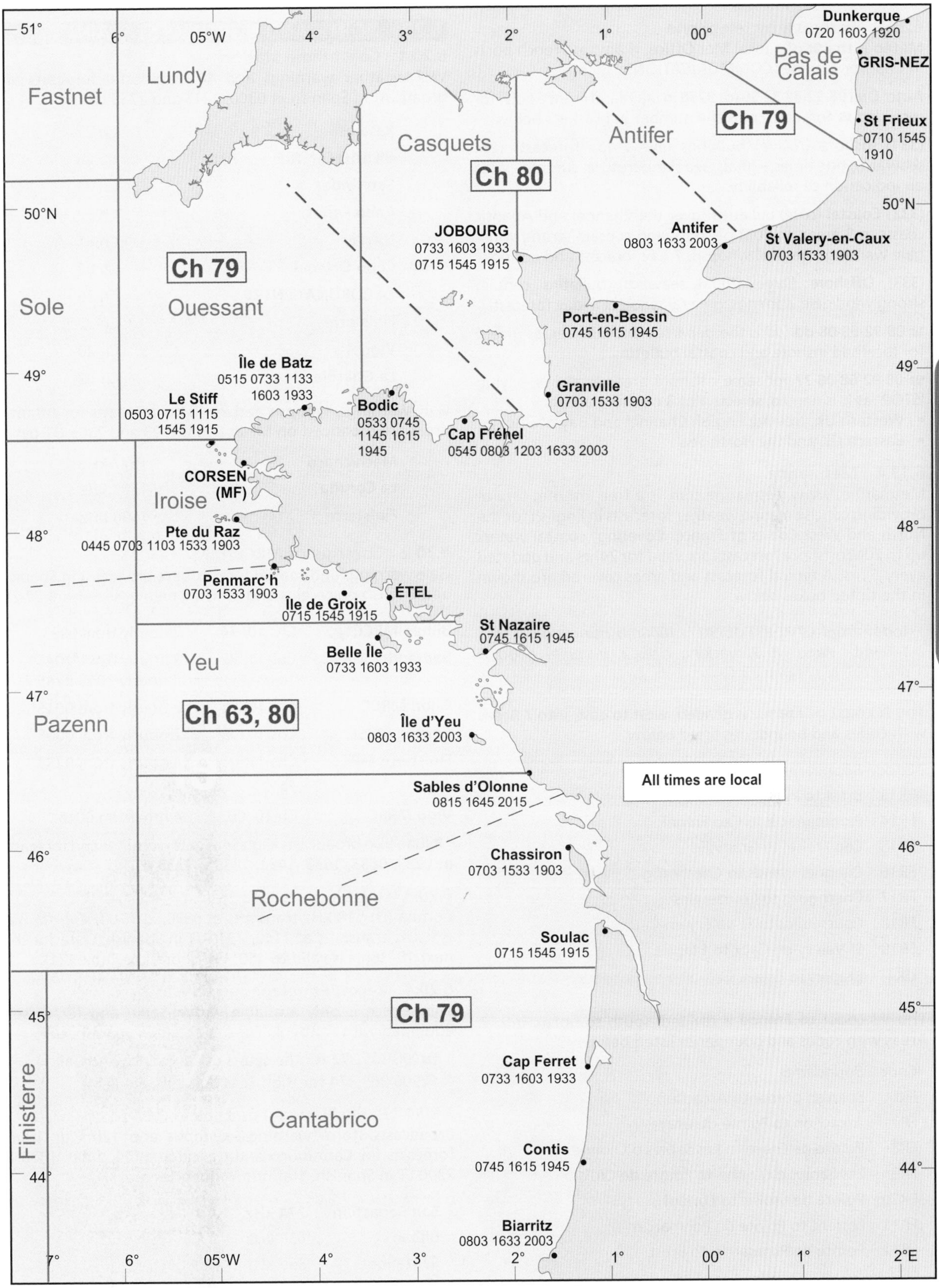
Fastnet
Lundy
Sole
Ouessant
Casquets
Antifer
Pas de Calais
Iroise
Yeu
Pazenn
Rochebonne
Cantabrico
Finisterre
Ch 79
Ch 80
Ch 79
Ch 63, 80
Ch 79
Dunkerque
0720 1603 1920
GRIS-NEZ
St Frieux
0710 1545
1910
Antifer
0803 1633 2003
St Valery-en-Caux
0703 1533 1903
JOBOURG
0733 1603 1933
0715 1545 1915
Port-en-Bessin
0745 1615 1945
Granville
0703 1533 1903
Île de Batz
0515 0733 1133
1603 1933
Le Stiff
0503 0715 1115
1545 1915
Bodic
0533 0745
1145 1615
1945
Cap Fréhel
0545 0803 1203 1633 2003
CORSEN
(MF)
Pte du Raz
0445 0703 1103 1533 1903
Penmarc'h
0703 1533 1903
Île de Groix
0715 1545 1915
ÉTEL
St Nazaire
0745 1615 1945
Belle Île
0733 1603 1933
Île d'Yeu
0803 1633 2003
Sables d'Olonne
0815 1645 2015
All times are local
Chassiron
0703 1533 1903
Soulac
0715 1545 1915
Cap Ferret
0733 1603 1933
Contis
0745 1615 1945
Biarritz
0803 1633 2003
51°
50°N
49°
48°
47°
46°
45°
44°
7°
6°
05°W
4°
3°
2°
1°
00°
1°
2°E

Fig 6(12) Météo France forecast areas and VHF weather broadcasts by CROSS

6.19.3 Forecasts by telephone

Météo is the ☎ of a local Met Office, if any, at French ports in Chapter 9, under COMMUNICATIONS.

Auto: Dial **08·92·68·32·50** (or **3250** in mainland France only) for recorded ☎ forecasts, plus the number in brackets below:

(331) Inshore (*rivage*) bulletins give 7-day forecasts (2M seaward), tide times, signals, sea temperature, surf etc – with an indication of reliability.

(332) Coastal (*côte*) bulletins cover the Channel and Atlantic coasts in 5 areas, to 20M offshore and contain strong wind/gale warnings, general synopsis, 7-day forecast and outlook.

(333) Offshore (*large,* 200M seaward) bulletins contain strong wind/gale warnings, general synopsis, 7-day forecast.

☎ **08·92·68·08·dd** (dd is the *département* number, as given) for localised inshore and coastal bulletins.

☎ **08·92·68·08·77** for same offshore areas as above; saying 'STOP' as it is named, selects 1 of 3 offshore areas:

- Western UK, Ireland, English Channel and Bay of Biscay;
- Eastern UK and the North Sea.

6.19.4 Metmarine

Metmarine, www.metmarine.com, is a free Internet service providing concise marine weather forecasts in English for the North and West Coasts of France. Covering coastal waters up to 20M offshore forecasts are valid for 24hrs and updated every 6 hrs. A typical forecast and areas covered are shown in the tinted boxes below:

Today from 0700 BST 10/9/17. 1008mb rising slowly to 1009mb. Wind NE 2, backing NNE 2. Visibility good, drizzle. Max temp 23°C.

The N coast of France is divided, west to east, into 7 Areas with codes and boundaries listed below:

Code	*Boundaries*
FR13	Brest to Ploumanac'h
FR14	Ploumanac'h to Cap Fréhel
FR15	Cap Fréhel to Granville
FR16	Channel Islands to Cherbourg
FR17	Cherbourg to Courseulles
FR18	Courseulles to St Valéry-en-Caux
FR19	St Valéry-en-Caux to Étaples
UK1	Étaples to Calais

The W coast of France is divided, south to north, into 7 Areas with codes and boundaries listed below:

Code	*Boundaries*
FR6	Spanish border to Arcachon
FR7	Arcachon to Pointe de Grave
FR8	Pointe de Grave to Les Sables d'Olonne
FR9	Les Sables d'Olonne to Pointe de Croisic
FR10	Pointe de Croisic to Lorient
FR11	Lorient to Pointe de Penmarc'h
FR12	Pointe de Penmarc'h to Brest

6.20 NORTH AND NORTH WEST SPAIN

6.20.1 Coast radio stations

VHF weather warnings and 48 hrs coastal forecasts are broadcast in Spanish at 0300, 1215 and 1733 UT by:

Pasajes	Ch 27
BILBAO CENTRE	Ch 26
Santander	Ch 24
Cabo Peñas	Ch 27
Navia	Ch 62
Cabo Ortegal	Ch 02
LA CORUÑA CENTRE	Ch 26
Finisterre	Ch 22
Vigo	Ch 20
La Guardia	Ch 82

Gale warnings, synopsis and 24/48 hrs forecasts for Atlantic areas are broadcast on MF at 0903, 1503 and 2303 UT by:

Machichaco	1677 kHz
La Coruña	1707 kHz
Finisterre	1698 kHz

6.20.2 Coastguard MRCC/MRSC

Gale warnings and coastal forecasts are broadcast in Spanish and **English** on receipt and as listed below (see also 6.22.2):

Bilbao MRCC*	Chs 10, 74	2 hourly from 0033
Santander MRSC	Chs 11, 72	2 hourly 0245 -1045 4 hourly 1045-2245
Gijón MRCC	Chs 10, 06	2 hourly from 0015
Coruña MRSC	Chs 10, 06	2 hourly from 0005
Finisterre MRCC	Chs 11, 06, 74, 72	4 hourly from 0233
Vigo MRSC	Ch 10, 06	4 hrly from 0015

***Bilbao** also broadcasts High Seas gale warnings and forecasts at 0233, 0633, 1033, 1433, 1833 & 2233 UT.

6.20.3 NAVTEX

Coruna (D) 518 kHz transmits at 0830, 2030 UT. Coruna (W) 490 kHz transmits at 1140, 2340 UT in Spanish. Data for the next 18–36hrs is valid to 450M offshore; see Table 6(1).

6.20.4 Recorded telephone forecasts

This service is only available within Spain and for vessels equipped with Autolink. For a bulletin in Spanish, call:

☎906 365 372 for the coasts of Cantábrico and Galicia.
☎906 365 374 for High Seas bulletins; Fig 6(14).

6.20.4 Radio Nacional de España (MW)

Broadcasts storm warnings, synopsis and 12hrs or 18hrs forecasts for Cantábrico and Galicia at 1100, 1400, 1800 & 2200 LT in Spanish. Stations/frequencies are:

San Sebastián	774 kHz
Bilbao	639 kHz
Santander	855 kHz
Oviedo	729 kHz
La Coruña	639 kHz

Fig 6(13) North and North West Spain CRS and Coastguard weather forecasts

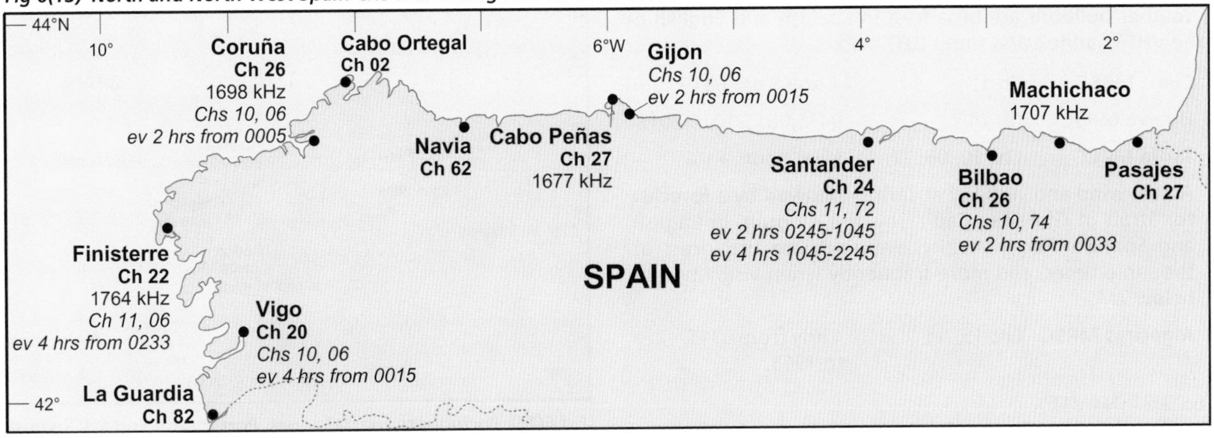

6.21 PORTUGAL, AZORES AND MADEIRA

6.21.1 Radionaval Portugal weather broadcasts

Broadcasts in Portuguese and **English** are on Ch 11 at the times (UT) listed below. They contain: Storm, gale and poor visibility warnings; synopsis and 24 hrs forecasts for three coastal zones out to 20M offshore.

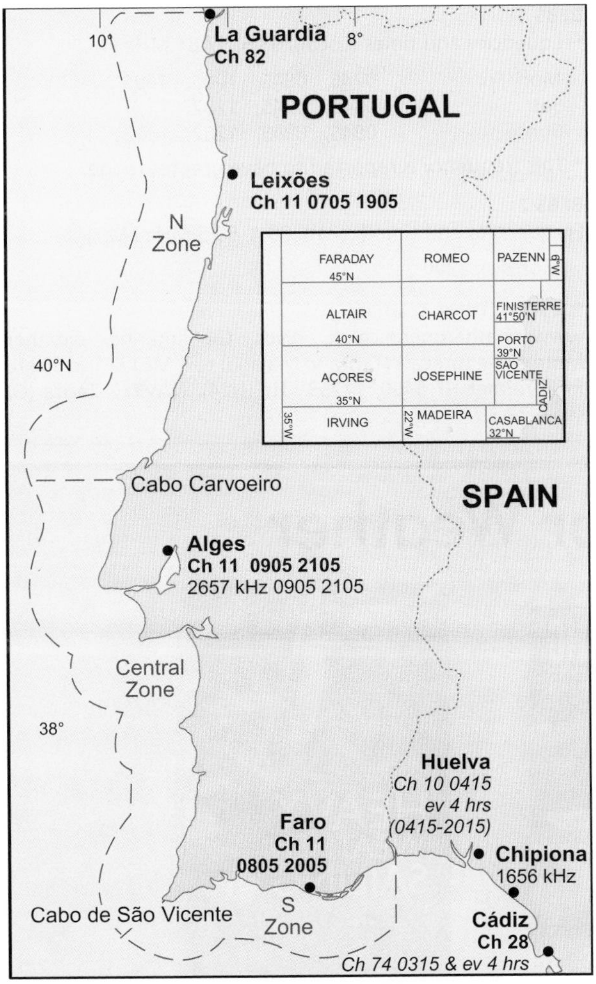

Fig 6(14) Portuguese coastal zones, inset shows forecast areas for MetArea II: High Seas and Coastal/Offshore Areas

Leixões Coastal waters of N and Central zones.	0705, 1905
Cencomar (also on MF 2657 kHz) Coastal waters of all 3 zones.	0905, 2105
Faro Coastal waters of Central and S Zones.	0805, 2005
Horta Azores archipelago (MF 2657 kHz)	0935, 2135 UT
Cencomarmadeira (Madeira) for 20M radius of Madeira and Porto Santo (MF 2657 kHz) VHF Ch 11	 0735, 1935 1030, 1630 LT

6.21.2 Radiofusão Portuguesa

Broadcasts weather bulletins for coastal waters in Portuguese at 1100 UT. Stations and frequencies are:

Porto, Elvas	720 kHz
Viseu, Lisboa 1	666 kHz
Montemer (Coimbra), **Miranda do Douro**	630 kHz
Faro	97·6 MHz, 720 kHz

6.21.3 NAVTEX

Transmitters: Monsanto/Lisbon(R),(G), São Miguel/Azores (F),(J), and Porto Santo/Madeira – (P),(M), broadcast weather forecasts in **English** for the next 24H on 518 kHz, every four hours. (R) starts 0250, (F) 0050, (P) 0230 inc. nav warnings within 20M of the coast. These are repeated in Portuguese on 490 kHz, (G) starts 0100, (J) 0130, (M) 0100.

6.22 SOUTH WEST SPAIN

6.22.1 Coast radio stations

The following CRS broadcast gale warnings, synopsis, 24 hrs and 48 hrs forecasts for Atlantic and Mediterranean areas, in Spanish, at the times (UT) and on the VHF and MF frequencies shown below (gale warnings broadcast on receipt):

Huelva	*Ch 26*	*0340*	*1340*	*1903*
Cádiz	*Ch 28*	*0340*	*1340*	*1903*
Tarifa	*Ch 83*	*0340*	*1340*	*1903*
Area forecast	*1656 kHz*	*0903*	*1503*	*2303*

6.22.2 Coastguard MRCC/MRSC

Weather bulletins are broadcast in Spanish and **English** on the VHF channels and times (UT) below:

Cadiz MRSC	Ch 15	4 hrly from 0315
Huelva MRSC	Ch 74	0415,0815,1215,2015
Tarifa MRCC	Chs 10, 06, 72, 74	Even hours +15.

Actual wind and visibility at Tarifa, followed by a forecast for Strait of Gibraltar, Cádiz Bay and Alborán, in English and Spanish. Fog (visibility) warnings are broadcast at the same times, and more frequently when visibility falls below 2M.

Algeciras MRSC	Chs 15, 06	4 hrly from 0315 to 1915.

6.22.3 NAVTEX

Tarifa (G) 518 kHz transmits weather bulletins in English at 0900 and 2100 UT. These include: Gale warnings, general synopsis and development and a forecast, valid for 18 hrs from 0900 or for 36 hrs from 2100, for the N Atlantic and W Mediterranean within 450M of the coast.

Tarifa (T) 490 kHz transmits at 1110, 2310 UT in Spanish. Data for the next 18–36 hrs is valid to 450M offshore; see 6.6.6.

6.22.4 Recorded telephone forecasts

The service is only available within Spain and for Autolink-equipped vessels. For a coastal waters bulletin in Spanish call:

☎ 906 365 373 for Atlantic Andalucia and the Canaries.
☎ 906 365 374 for High Seas bulletin for Atlantic areas.

6.23 GIBRALTAR

6.23.1 Gibraltar Broadcasting Corporation (GBC)

GBC (Gibraltar Radio) broadcasts in English: General synopsis, situation, wind direction and force, visibility and sea state, radius 5M from Gibraltar. Frequencies are 1458 kHz, 91·3 MHz, 92·6 MHz and 100·5 MHz. Times (UT):

Mon–Fri:	0530, 0630, 0730, 1030, 1230
Sat:	0530, 0630, 0730, 1030
Sun:	0630, 0730, 1030

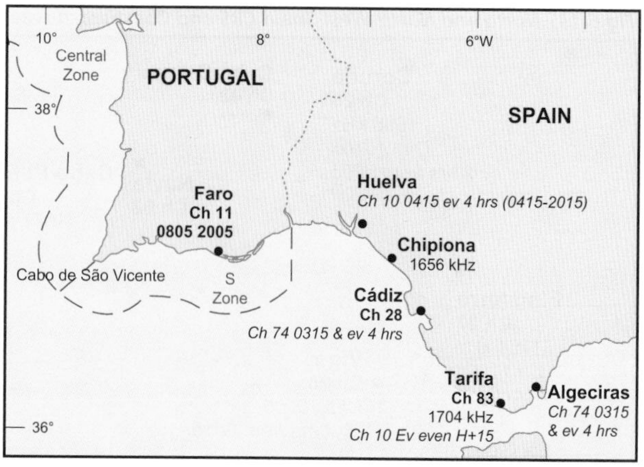

Fig 6(15) Portuguese coastal zones, Portuguese and SW Spanish weather broadcast stations

6.23.2 British Forces Broadcasting Service (BFBS)

Gale warnings for the Gibraltar area are broadcast on receipt by BFBS 1 and 2. All broadcasts are in English for waters within 5M of Gib and contain: Shipping forecast, wind, weather, visibility, sea state, swell, HW and LW times.

BFBS 1

Frequencies and times (Local): 93·5, 97·8* MHz FM.

Mon–Fri:	0745, 0845, 1005, 1605
Sat:	0845, 0945, 1202
Sun:	0845, 0945, 1202, 1602

* This frequency is reported to have greater range.

BFBS 2

Frequencies and time (Local): 89·4, 99·5 MHz FM.

Mon–Fri: 1200

6.23.3 Other sources

www.weatheronline.co.uk gives Gib marine weather. Metmarine forecast (Tarifa to Malaga) text MET SP1 to 80818. RAF Volmet HF 5450, 11253 kHz (H24). NAVTEX Tarifa (G), see 6.22.3.

7
Safety

7.1	**Introduction** Emergency procedures	**107**
7.2	**Safety equipment** Table of recommended safety equipment (Page 106)	**107**
7.3	**GMDSS** Sub-systems • EPIRBs • Sea areas • Functions	**107**
7.4	**Definitions of emergency** Distress – MAYDAY • Urgency – PAN PAN • Safety – SÉCURITÉ	**108**
7.5	**Distress signals by radio** MAYDAY procedures • DSC alerts	**108**
7.6	**Urgency and Safety signals** PAN PAN • SÉCURITÉ • MSI • Medical advice • Mobile telephones	**109**
7.7	**Sound and visual distress signals** Flares • Distress and life-saving signals • SAR aircraft signals	**110**
7.8	**Helicopter rescue** Communications • Preparations • Double lift • Hi-line	**113**
7.9	**Abandon ship**	**113**
7.10	**Search and rescue (SAR) – UK** Raising the alarm • Safety Identification Scheme (CG66)	**114**
7.11	**HM Coastguard** Organisation • Responsibilities	**114**
7.12	**Royal National Lifeboat Institution**	**115**
7.13	**National Coastwatch Institution**	**115**

TABLE 7(1) This is a precis of recommended safety equipment which should be carried, based on the categories in 7.2.1.
A bullet (•) recommends that the item be carried, but the number, method or contents is left to the judgement of the skipper.

	CATEGORY	A	B	C	D
1	**Propulsion**				
1.1	A storm trisail or deep reef to reduce the mainsail area by at least 40% (sailing vessels)	•	•	•	
1.2	For engine starting, a battery isolated from all other electrical systems or hand cranking	•	•	•	
2	**Anchors**, with appropriate lengths/diameter of warp and/or chain	2+	2	2	1
3	**Bailing and pumping**				
3.1	Buckets of 9–14 ltrs capacity with lanyard and strongly secured handle	2	2	2	
3.2	Hand bilge pumps discharging overboard and operable with all hatches closed	2	2	1	
3.3	Softwood bungs attached adjacent to all through-hull fittings	•	•	•	•
4	**Detection**				
4.1	Radar reflector (if practicable) with as large a radar cross-section as is reasonable	1	1	1	1
4.2	Fixed navigation lights complying with IRPCS; motoring cone and anchor ball	•	•	•	
4.3	Foghorn	•	•	•	•
4.4	Powerful torch	•	•	•	
5	**Pyrotechnics (all in date)**				
5.1	Hand-held red flares)	6	4	4	2
5.2	Buoyant orange smoke signals) to SOLAS standards	2	2		
5.3	Red parachute rockets)	12	4	2	
5.4	Hand-held orange smoke signals			2	2
5.5	Hand-held white flares ('ship scarers')	4	4	4	
6	**Fire fighting**				
6.1	Fire blanket (BS EN 1869) for vessels with cooking equipment	•	•	•	•
6.2	Multi-purpose extinguishers (minimum 5A/34B to BS EN 3 (craft with galley *or* with engine fuel)	3	2	1	1
6.3	Additionally, for craft with *both* galley *and* engine fuel, fire extinguishers (as above)	1	1	1	1
6.4	Additionally, for craft with engines over 25hp, a fixed automatic or semi-automatic fire fighting system to discharge into the engine space	•	•	•	•
7	**Personal safety (per crew member)**				
7.1	Warm clothing, oilskins, seaboots and hat	•	•	•	•
7.2	Lifejacket or buoyancy aid (BS EN 395) 100 Newtons				1
7.3	Lifejacket (BS EN 396) 150 Newtons, with crotch straps, spray hood and light	1	1	1	
7.4	Safety harness (may be reduced by 50% for yachts with enclosed wheelhouse)	1	1	1	
7.5	Immersion suit	1			
7.6	Jackstays and cockpit clip-on strong points	•	•	•	
8	**Liferaft**				
8.1	Liferaft, designed solely for saving life, sufficient to carry all on board	1	1	1	
8.2	Emergency grab bag (see text for contents)	1	1	1	
9	**Man overboard recovery**				
9.1	Horseshoe lifebelts fitted with drogue and automatic light	2	2	1	
9.2	Buoyant sling on floating line (may replace 1 horseshoe lifebelt if 2 are carried)	1	1		
9.3	Buoyant heaving line, at least 30m long, with quoit	1	1	1	
9.4	Boarding ladder capable of rapid and secure attachment	1	1	1	
9.5	Dan buoy with a large flag	1	1		
10	**Radio**				
10.1	Radio able to receive shipping forecasts on 198 kHz and local radio station forecasts	1	1	1	1
10.2	VHF (preferably DSC) radio and emergency aerial with prepared deck mounting	1	1	1	
10.3	Waterproof hand-held VHF radio	1	1	1	1
10.4	Navtex receiver	1	1	1	
10.5	Marine band HF/SSB radio and/or global SatCom system	1			
10.6	EPIRB (406 MHz)	1			
10.7	SART	1			
11	**Navigation**				
11.1	Paper charts, tide tables and navigational publications of the cruising area and adjacent areas	•	•	•	
11.2	Steering compass, able to be lit at night.	1	1	1	1
11.3	Hand-bearing compass	•	•	•	
11.4	Navigational drawing instruments	•	•	•	
11.5	Barometer	1	1	1	
11.6	Echosounder and lead line	1	1	1	
11.7	Radio navigation system (eg GPS)	1	1	1	
11.8	Watch or clock	1	1	1	1
11.9	Distance measuring log	1	1	1	
11.10	Binoculars	1	1	1	
11.11	Sextant and associated reduction tables	1			
12	**First aid kit and manual** (see Chapter 8)	1	1	1	1
13	**General equipment**				
13.1	Emergency tiller (for wheel-steered vessels)	1	1	1	1
13.2	Towing warp	1	1	1	
13.3	Bosun's chair (sit harness BS EN 813 1997)	1	1	1	
13.4	Mooring warps and fenders	•	•	•	•
13.5	Waterproof torch	3	2	2	1
13.6	Rigid or inflatable tender	•	•	•	
13.7	Spares and repair tools for engine & electrics, and bosun's bag of shackles, twine etc	•	•	•	•
13.8	Emergency water supply, isolated from main tanks	•	•		
13.9	Emergency repair materials	•	•		

7.1 INTRODUCTION

The safety of the boat and its crew is every skipper's priority. All onboard share the responsibility for their individual safety, but the skipper makes the ultimate decisions. He or she must ensure the boat is sound and properly equipped, the crew well briefed and are capable of undertaking the planned trip. In extremis it is the skipper who decides when to call for help. This chapter includes advice on safety equipment, emergency procedures and the Search and Rescue (SAR) organisations.

7.1.1 Emergency procedures

Knowing when to call for help and the correct procedures to be used may be a matter of life or death. SOLAS requires a table of life-saving signals to be readily available, but an emergency at sea is no time to start reading. The definitions of Distress and Urgency must be thoroughly understood. Unnecessary MAYDAY calls divert scarce resources from more pressing emergencies. A MAYDAY call should only be made if you or your vessel is in ***grave and imminent danger*** and you require ***immediate assistance***; otherwise a PAN PAN or even a routine call may be appropriate.

7.2 SAFETY EQUIPMENT

Table 7(1) is a recommended list of equipment which should be carried onboard depending on Category (see below).

Although non-commercial leisure craft of less than 13·7m LOA are not obliged to carry any specific life saving or fire fighting equipment, SOLAS requires *all* vessels to: plan each passage (see Chapter 3); carry a radar reflector if practicable; have access to a table of life-saving signals (see Figs 7(1) and 7(2)); report serious hazards to navigation (if not already reported); and respond to distress signals.

7.2.1 Recommended safety equipment for seagoing vessels of less than 13·7m LOA

The safety equipment to be carried depends on LOA, cruising area and the risk of being caught out in heavy weather. Based on these parameters yachts are categorised as follows:

A Ocean Ocean passages of any length. LOA is likely to be longer than 10m.

B Offshore Yachts which make offshore passages of 50–500M around the UK and NW Europe. LOA is likely to be 8–13.7m.

C Inshore Coastal cruises by day/night, within 10M of land and 4 hours of a port of refuge. LOA is likely to be less than 8m.

D Sheltered In estuaries, inshore or inland waters, day only. Within 1 hour of a port of refuge. LOA is likely to be less than 6m.

7.3 GMDSS

The Global Maritime Distress and Safety System (GMDSS) came into force in 1999. Seagoing vessels over 300 tons are required by SOLAS to comply with GMDSS. It is not compulsory for yachts, but the principles of the system should be understood, and appropriate equipment fitted. Full details may be found in ALRS Vol 5 (NP 285).

7.3.1 Sub-systems

GMDSS comprises 'sub-systems' co-ordinated through Maritime Rescue Coordination Centres (MRCC) to ensure safety at sea. These are expanding with the recent inclusion of Galileo SAR capabilities. The main sub-systems are:

- **COSPAS/SARSAT** is a network of geostationary and polar orbit satellites which relay digital EPIRB and PLB transmissions to earth stations. Galileo is integrated into the Medium Earth Orbit Search and Rescue (MEOSAR) system, providing coverage between 75°N and 75°S and location down to 10 minutes and 2km across Europe. Galileo/GPS/GLOSNAS SAR systems are interoperable.
- **Satellite Communication System** Inmarsat is currently the only provider of GMDSS communications. Coverage is between 76°N and 76°S. A **Satellite Ship Earth Station (SES)** enables a ship to communicate via satellite.
- **Digital Selective Calling (DSC)** uses terrestrial communications for making initial contact and, in a distress situation, provides the vessel's identity, nature of distress and position (entered manually or automatically if linked with the GPS). Every vessel and relevant shore station has a 9-digit Maritime Mobile Service Identity (MMSI) which is an electronic callsign. Frequencies: VHF Ch 70, MF 2187·5 kHz. See also 7.5.1.
- **Maritime Safety Information (MSI)** includes the broadcast of navigation and meteorological warnings, weather forecasts and other urgent or safety-related messages. See Chapter 6.
- **Emergency Position Indicating Radio Beacons (EPIRB)** Hand-held or float-free, they transmit on 406 MHz. (Note that 121·5 MHz, 243·0 MHz and L-band EPIRBS are no longer used.) Most EPIRBs have a built-in GPS and about 48hrs of battery life. COPAS/SARSAT satellites will relay EPIRB signals to earth with no delay, but the position of a non-GPS EPIRB may take several hours to determine.
- **Personal Locator Beacons (PLB)** operate on the same principle. They must also be registered but they do not have a vessel-specific MMSI. There are also alternative AIS locator beacons, not formally part of GMDSS, which display a red cross on an AIS screen when activated.
- **Search And Rescue Transponders (SART)** are radar transceivers which operate on 9 GHz and respond to 3cm (X-band) radars, like a small portable Racon (see Chapter 3). They are primarily intended for use in liferafts to help searching ships and aircraft find survivors. The transmitted signal shows on a radar screen as 12 dots radiating out from the SART's position.

7.3.2 EPIRB registration

An EPIRB transmits data uniquely coded to each individual beacon and must be registered. This may be done at this link: https://forms.dft.gov.uk/mca-sar-epirb/ The UK centre is:

EPIRB Registry, Maritime and Coastguard Agency, Falmouth CGOC, Pendennis Point, Castle Drive, Falmouth, Cornwall TR11 4WZ; ☎ 01326 211569; email: epirb@mcga.gov.uk.

It is important that any changes are immediately notified.

7.3.3 EPIRB false alerts

False alerts caused by inadvertent or incorrect use of EPIRBs put a significant burden on SAR Centres and may coincide with an actual distress situation. All crew members should be aware of the proper use of the EPIRB onboard. Ensure it is correctly installed and maintained; that testing is supervised; and that it is not activated if assistance is already available. If an EPIRB is activated accidentally, make every effort to advise the nearest MRCC of the false alert as soon as possible.

7.3.4 Sea areas

The type of equipment carried by a vessel depends on her operating area. The four GMDSS Areas are:

A1 An area within R/T coverage of at least one VHF Coastguard or Coast radio station in which continuous VHF alerting is available via DSC. Range: 20–50M from the CG/CRS.

A2 An area, excluding sea area A1, within R/T coverage of at least one MF CG/CRS in which continuous DSC alerting is available. Range: approx 50–250M from the CG/CRS.

A3 An area between 76°N and 76°S, excluding sea areas A1 and A2, within coverage of HF or an Inmarsat satellite in which continuous alerting is available.

A4 An area outside sea areas A1, A2 and A3, ie the polar regions, within coverage of HF.

Vessels must carry radio equipment appropriate to the area: A1, VHF DSC; A2, VHF and MF DSC; A3, VHF, MF and HF or SatCom; A4 VHF, MF and HF. A Navtex receiver must be carried in GMDSS vessels, regardless of their operating area.

Most UK yachts will operate in A1 areas where a DSC VHF radio and a Navtex receiver will meet GMDSS requirements. VHF radios without DSC may still be used for sending distress calls; Coastguard and NCI stations will continue to maintain a loudspeaker watch on Ch 16 for the foreseeable future. DSC is rapidly becoming the preferred method of making initial contact for urgency and, particularly, distress messages.

7.3.5 Functions

Regardless of the sea areas in which they operate, vessels fully complying with GMDSS must be able to:

- Transmit ship-to-shore distress alerts by two independent means;
- Receive shore-to-ship distress alerts;
- Transmit/receive ship-to-ship distress alerts;
- Transmit signals for locating incidents;
- Transmit/receive SAR co-ordination communication;
- Transmit/receive Maritime Safety Information (MSI).

7.4 DEFINITIONS OF EMERGENCY

7.4.1 Distress – MAYDAY

Distress applies to any situation where a ***vessel or person is in grave and imminent danger and requires immediate assistance***. The radio prefix used with a distress message is MAYDAY. A distress call has priority over all other transmissions.

7.4.2 Urgency – PAN PAN

Urgency applies to a ***very urgent message concerning the safety of a vessel or person***. For example, for a vessel disabled but not in immediate danger, or for an urgent medical problem. The radio prefix associated with an urgency message is PAN PAN. An urgency call has priority over all other transmissions except distress.

7.4.3 Safety – SÉCURITÉ

A safety message is usually associated with a notification of a navigational hazard or meteorological warning. The radio prefix used with a safety message is SÉCURITÉ (pronounced SAY-CURE-E-TAY).

7.5 DISTRESS SIGNALS BY RADIO

A distress call may only be made with the skipper's authority, and only if the ***boat or a person*** is in ***grave and imminent danger***. The initial call may be made by DSC or voice. A distress call may also be made on behalf of another vessel which is unable to make her own call. A man overboard will usually justify a distress call.

7.5.1 MAYDAY call by voice

Brief your crew so they are all able to send a distress message; the MAYDAY message format below should be displayed near the radio. A MAYDAY call by voice should usually be sent on VHF Ch 16 or MF 2182 kHz, but any frequency may be used if help would thus be obtained more quickly. A distress call has priority over all other transmissions. If you hear a MAYDAY call, immediately cease all transmissions that may interfere with the call, listen on the frequency concerned and note down the details.

Before making the call check that the main battery switch and the radio are both ON, and that HIGH POWER (25 watts) and Ch 16 (or 2182 kHz for MF) are selected.

Press and hold down the transmit button, and say slowly and distinctly:

- **MAYDAY MAYDAY MAYDAY**
- **THIS IS** ....
  (name of boat, spoken three times)
- **MAYDAY** ....
  (name of boat spoken once)
- **CALLSIGN / MMSI Number** ....
  (Following a DSC alert)
- **MY POSITION IS** ....
  (latitude and longitude, true bearing and distance *from* a known point, or general location)
- **Nature of distress** ....
  (sinking, on fire etc)
- **Help required** ....
  (immediate assistance)
- **Number of persons on board** ....
- **Any other important, helpful information** ....
  (you are taking to the liferaft; distress rockets are being fired etc)
- **OVER**

On completion of the distress message, release the transmit button and listen. The boat's position is of vital importance and should be repeated if time allows. If an acknowledgement is not received, check the set and repeat the distress call.

7.5.2 MAYDAY acknowledgement

In coastal waters an immediate acknowledgement should be expected, as follows:

MAYDAY ....
(name of vessel sending the distress message, spoken three times)

THIS IS ....
(name of station acknowledging, spoken three times)

RECEIVED MAYDAY

If you hear a distress message, write down the details and, if you can help, acknowledge accordingly but only after giving an opportunity for the nearest Coastguard station or more suitable vessel to do so.

7.5.3 MAYDAY relay

If you hear a distress message from a vessel, and it is not acknowledged, you should pass on the message as follows:

MAYDAY RELAY ....
(spoken three times)
THIS IS ....
(name of vessel re-transmitting the distress message, spoken three times), followed by the intercepted message.

7.5.4 Control of MAYDAY traffic

A MAYDAY call imposes general radio silence until the vessel concerned or some other authority (eg the nearest Coastguard station) cancels the distress. If necessary the station controlling distress traffic may impose radio silence as follows:

SEELONCE MAYDAY, followed by its name or other identification, on the distress frequency.

If some other station nearby believes it necessary to do likewise, it may transmit:

SEELONCE DISTRESS, followed by its name or other identification.

7.5.5 Relaxing radio silence

When complete radio silence is no longer necessary on the frequency being used for distress traffic, the controlling station may relax radio silence, indicating that restricted working may be resumed, as follows:

MAYDAY
ALL STATIONS, ALL STATIONS, ALL STATIONS
THIS IS ....
(name or callsign)
Time ....
Name of the vessel in distress ....
PRUDONCE

Normal working on a distress frequency may then be resumed having listened carefully, as always, before transmitting. Subsequent calls from the casualty should be prefixed by the Urgency signal (7.6.1).

If distress working continues on other frequencies these will be identified. For example: PRUDONCE on 2182 kHz, but SEELONCE on VHF Ch 16.

7.5.6 Cancelling radio silence

When the problem is resolved, the distress call must be cancelled by the coordinating station using the prowords SEELONCE FEENEE as follows:

MAYDAY
ALL STATIONS, ALL STATIONS, ALL STATIONS
THIS IS ....
(name or callsign)
The time ....
The name of the vessel in distress ....
SEELONCE FEENEE

7.5.7 Distress alert by DSC

Depending on the layout and switches fitted to your particular VHF DSC radio, a distress alert is typically sent as follows:

- Briefly press the red, guarded Distress button. The set will automatically switch to Ch 70. Press *again* for 5 seconds to transmit a basic distress alert with position and time. The set then reverts to Ch l6.
- If time permits, select the nature of the distress from the menu (eg Collision, Fire, Flooding) then press the Distress button for 5 seconds to send a full distress alert.

A CG/CRS should automatically send a distress acknowledgement on Ch 70 before replying on Ch 16. Ships in range should reply directly on Ch 16.

If a distress acknowledgement is not received from a CG/CRS, the distress alert will automatically be repeated by the radio every four minutes.

When a DSC distress acknowledgement has been received, or after about 15 seconds, the vessel in distress should transmit a MAYDAY message by voice on Ch 16. This follows the format on the next page but should include the **MMSI** and **callsign** after the vessel's name to ensure that the voice and digital messages correlate.

7.5.8 False alerts

If a distress alert is inadvertently transmitted, an All Stations voice message on VHF Ch 16 cancelling the false alert must be sent at once. The message should include the name of the vessel, MMSI number, position, and the words 'Cancel my Distress Alert of (date/time (GMT/UT)'.

7.6 URGENCY AND SAFETY SIGNALS

7.6.1 PAN PAN – Urgency signal

The radio Urgency prefix, consisting of the words PAN PAN spoken three times, indicates that a vessel or station has a very ***urgent message concerning the safety of a ship or person***. It may be used when urgent medical advice is needed.

This is an example of an urgency call:

PAN PAN, PAN PAN, PAN PAN
ALL STATIONS, ALL STATIONS, ALL STATIONS
THIS IS YACHT SEABIRD, SEABIRD, SEABIRD
In position two nine zero degrees Needles lighthouse two miles
Dismasted and propeller fouled
Anchor dragging and drifting east north east towards Shingles Bank
Require urgent tow
OVER

PAN PAN messages take priority over all traffic except distress and are sent on VHF Ch 16 or MF 2182 kHz. They should be cancelled when the urgency is over.

If the message is long (eg a medical call) or communications traffic is heavy, it may be passed on a working frequency after an initial call on Ch 16 or 2182 kHz. At the end of the initial call you should indicate that you are switching to a working frequency.

If you hear an urgency call react in the same way as for a distress call.

7.6.2 SÉCURITÉ – Safety prefix

The word SÉCURITÉ (pronounced SAY-CURE-E-TAY), spoken three times, indicates that the station is about to transmit ***an important navigational or meteorological warning***. Such messages usually originate from a CG Centre or a Coast Radio Station, and are transmitted on a working channel after an announcement on the distress/calling channel (VHF Ch 16 or MF 2182 kHz).

Safety messages are usually addressed to 'All Stations'. An example of a Sécurité message is:

SÉCURITÉ, SÉCURITÉ, SÉCURITÉ ....

THIS IS ....
(CG Centre or Coast Radio Station callsign, spoken three times)

ALL STATIONS ....
(spoken three times) followed by instructions to change channel, then the message.

7.6.3 Maritime Safety Information (MSI)

MSI consists of navigational, weather and safety messages. See also Chapters 5 and 6.

GMDSS transmits MSI in English by two independent but complementary means:

- **Navtex** on MF (518 kHz and 490 kHz) has a range of about 300 miles offshore (see 6.6).
- **SafetyNet** uses Inmarsat satellites to cover beyond MF range.

In coastal areas MSI may be broadcast by CG/CRS on VHF.

7.6.4 Medical advice by R/T

Medical advice and help can be obtained via any UK and most European CG MRCC; such calls are free. The initial call should be by an urgency message (PAN PAN x 3) on VHF Ch 16, by DSC on VHF Ch 70 or MF 2187·5 kHz. The Coastguard is always the first point of contact. See also Chapter 8 for further medical advice.

7.6.5 Survival times

Average sea temperatures around the UK range from +5° to +15°C. If you fall overboard your chances of survival in certain conditions, unless quickly recovered, are not good.

- From 10°–16°C survival is probable up to about 6 hours if wearing a lifejacket.
- At 10°C survival could be 4–8 hours if wearing a survival or wet suit, but otherwise only an hour or so.
- Below 10°C only 50% of people will survive for more than ONE hour; a survival or wet suit might extend this time.

7.6.6 Mobile telephones

Most yachts will have at least one mobile telephone onboard but ***their use in a distress or urgency situation is strongly discouraged*** as the existing dedicated and well-established maritime distress communications system would be by-passed. Mobile telephones have limited coverage (typically no more than about 10M offshore); they do not 'broadcast' so other vessels which might be able to render assistance cannot monitor the situation; and they are extremely vulnerable to getting wet.

However, when all other means of communication have failed, the use of mobile telephones have saved many lives, sometimes in bizarre circumstances.

7.7 SOUND AND VISUAL DISTRESS SIGNALS

Annex IV of the IRPCS lists in full the recognised distress signals. Some are depicted in Fig 7(1); those below, with notes on their use, are most relevant to yachts and small craft.

- Continuous sounding of any fog signalling apparatus.
  To avoid confusion, this is best done by repeatedly sending the letters SOS in Morse (··· ––– ···).
- An SOS signal made by any method.
  For a small craft the most likely methods are by fog horn or by flashing light.
- The International Code signal 'NC'.
  This can be made by hoisting the international code flags 'NC'. See Chapter 5, Fig 5(1).
- A square flag with a ball, or anything resembling a ball, above or below it.
  This is simply made from any square flag and a round fender or anchor ball.
- Slow and repeated raising/lowering of arms out-stretched to each side.
  Raise and lower the arms together, above and below the horizontal; this is usually obvious inside a mile.
- A rocket parachute red flare or a hand-held red flare.
  See 7.7.1 below.
- An orange smoke signal.

By day orange smoke signals are more effective than flares, although the smoke disperses quickly in a strong wind.

If help is needed but the boat is not in immediate danger, the proper signal is 'V', meaning 'I require assistance'. This can be sent by light or sound (···–), or by hoisting flag 'V'.

7.7.1 Use of flares and other pyrotechnics

Fig 7(1) shows how flares are best used to attract attention and to communicate with SAR teams once help has arrived. SOLAS requires this information to be on all sea-going vessels; all crew members should know where to find it.

Flares serve two purposes:

- to raise the alarm, and
- to pinpoint the boat's position.

Within about 3M from land a red hand flare will do both; it is the most effective distress signal at night. At greater distances a red parachute rocket (which projects a suspended flare higher than 1,000ft (300m), burning for more than 40 seconds) is used to raise the alarm, but use red hand flares to pinpoint the boat's position.

If possible wear a protective glove and hold flares firmly, downwind of yourself. Rockets turn into wind: in normal conditions fire them vertically, but in strong winds aim about 15° downwind. Do not aim them into wind, or they will not gain altitude. If there is low cloud, fire rockets at 45° downwind, so that the flare burns under the cloud. Initially, fire two flares in succession – the first to attract attention, the second to confirm.

Note: White flares are not distress signals but are used to indicate your presence to another vessel or acknowledge the sighting of a red flare. On night passages have at least four onboard and have at least one readily to hand from the cockpit. When using them shield your eyes to protect night vision.

Fig 7(1) Distress and life-saving signals

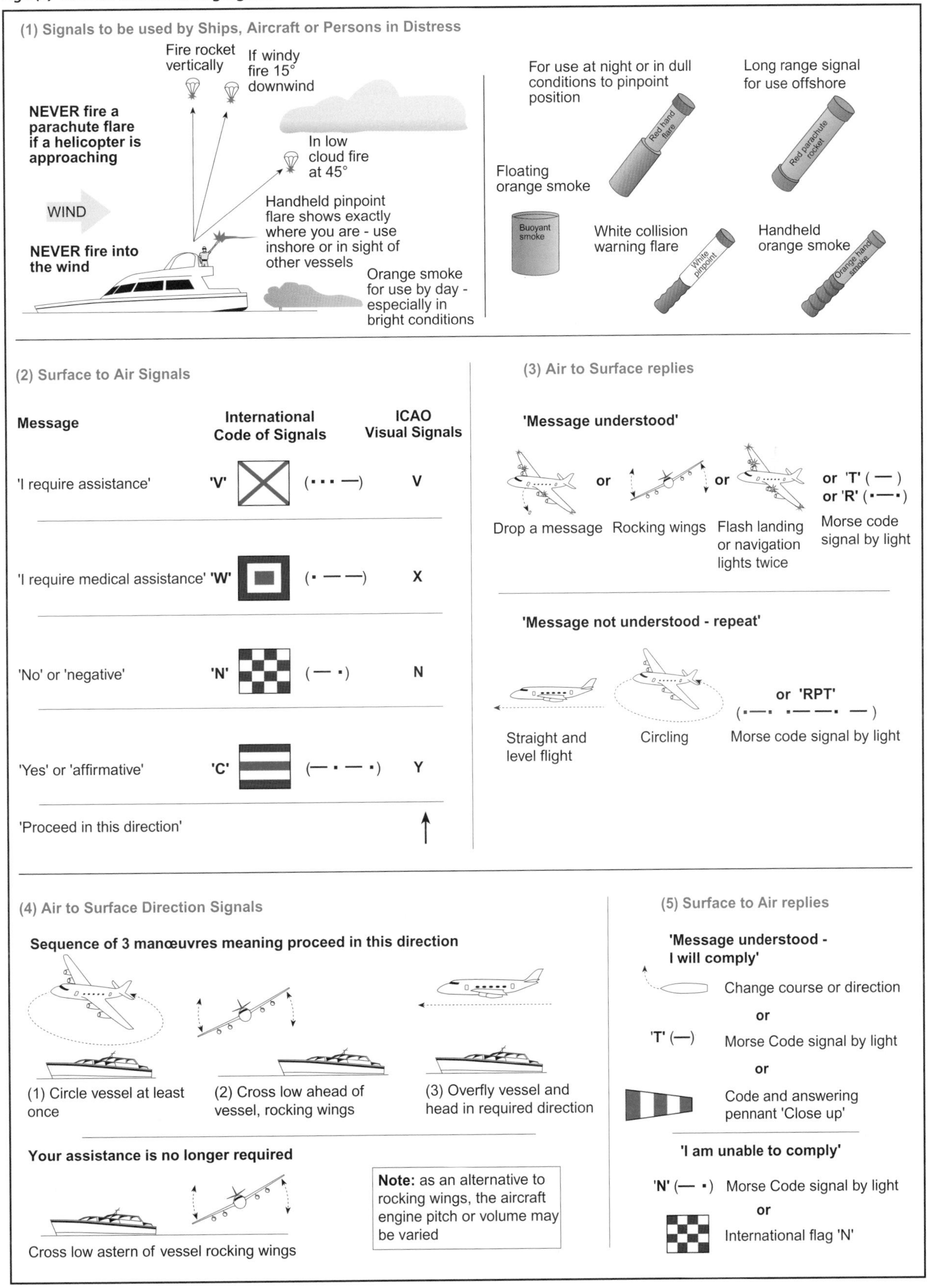
(1) Signals to be used by Ships, Aircraft or Persons in Distress
Fire rocket vertically
If windy fire 15° downwind
NEVER fire a parachute flare if a helicopter is approaching
In low cloud fire at 45°
WIND
Handheld pinpoint flare shows exactly where you are - use inshore or in sight of other vessels
NEVER fire into the wind
Orange smoke for use by day - especially in bright conditions
For use at night or in dull conditions to pinpoint position
Red hand flare
Long range signal for use offshore
Red parachute rocket
Floating orange smoke
Buoyant smoke
White collision warning flare
White pinpoint
Handheld orange smoke
Orange hand smoke
(2) Surface to Air Signals
Message
International Code of Signals
ICAO Visual Signals
'I require assistance' 'V' (• • • —) V
'I require medical assistance' 'W' (• — —) X
'No' or 'negative' 'N' (— •) N
'Yes' or 'affirmative' 'C' (— • — •) Y
'Proceed in this direction'
(3) Air to Surface replies
'Message understood'
Drop a message
or
Rocking wings
or
Flash landing or navigation lights twice
or 'T' (—)
or 'R' (• — •)
Morse code signal by light
'Message not understood - repeat'
Straight and level flight
Circling
or 'RPT'
(• — • • — — • —)
Morse code signal by light
(4) Air to Surface Direction Signals
Sequence of 3 manœuvres meaning proceed in this direction
(1) Circle vessel at least once
(2) Cross low ahead of vessel, rocking wings
(3) Overfly vessel and head in required direction
Your assistance is no longer required
Cross low astern of vessel rocking wings
Note: as an alternative to rocking wings, the aircraft engine pitch or volume may be varied
(5) Surface to Air replies
'Message understood - I will comply'
Change course or direction
or
'T' (—) Morse Code signal by light
or
Code and answering pennant 'Close up'
'I am unable to comply'
'N' (— •) Morse Code signal by light
or
International flag 'N'

Fig 7(2) Life-saving signals (Shore-to-Ship) (see 7.7.4)

Signals (1) to (4) may be indicated by a white flare, a rocket showing white stars on bursting, or an explosive sound signal.

(1) Landing signals for the guidance of small boats with crews or persons in distress

		Other signals	*Meaning*
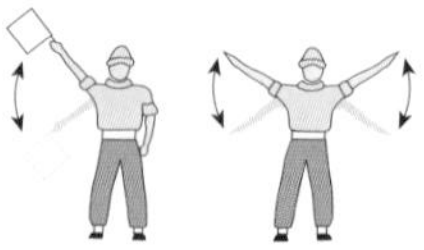	**Vertical** motion of a white flag (or white light or flare by night) or of the arms	International Code letter **'K'** (— • —) by light or sound	**'This is the best place to land'** (An indication of direction may be given by a steady white light or flare at a lower level)
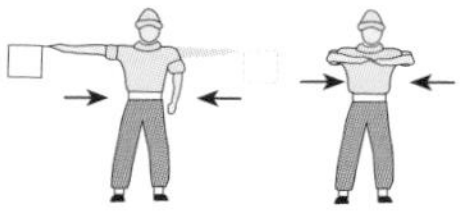	**Horizontal** motion of a white flag (or white light or flare by night) or of the arms extended horizontally	International Code letter **'S'** (• • •) by light or sound	**'Landing here is highly dangerous'**
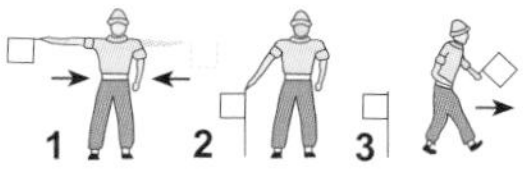	**Horizontal** motion of a white flag followed by 2. placing the white flag in the ground and 3. by carrying another white flag in the direction to be indicated. By night white lights or flares are used instead of white flags	1. Signalling the code letter **'S'** (• • •), followed by the code letter **'R'** (• — •) if the better landing place is more to the right in the direction of the approach, or 2, by the code letter **'L'** (• — • •) if the better landing place is more to the left in the direction of approach	**'Landing here is highly dangerous. A more favourable location for landing is in the direction indicated'**

(2) Signals to be made in connection with the use of shore apparatus for life-saving

Signal	*Meaning*	Signal	*Meaning*
Vertical motion of a white flag (or white light or flare by night) or of the arms 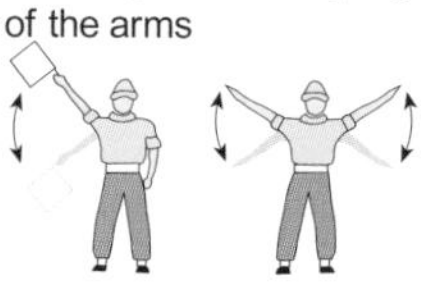	**In general:** 'affirmative' Specifically: 'rocket line is held - tail block is made fast - hawser is made fast - man is in the breeches buoy - haul away'	**Horizontal** motion of a white flag (or white light or flare by night) or of the arms 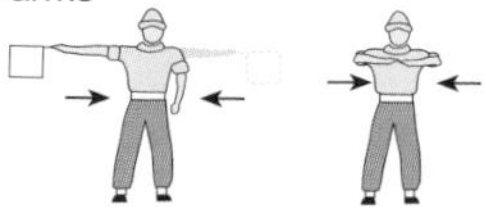	**In general:** 'negative' Specifically: 'slack away - stop hauling'

(3) Replies from life-saving stations etc. to distress signals made by ships or persons

Pyrotechnic signals
Orange smoke signal

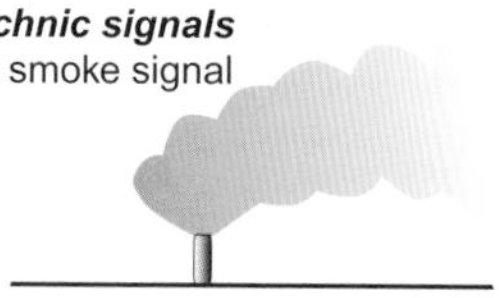

White star rocket - three single signals fired at intervals of about one minute

'You are seen - assistance will be given as soon as possible'

(4) Signals to be used to warn a ship which is standing into danger

International Code signals **'U'**

or **'NF'**

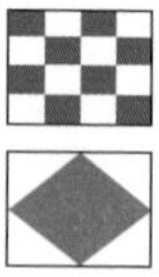

'You are standing into danger'

International Code signals **'U'** by light or sound • • —

(5) Signals used by Sub-Aqua divers

'I am OK'

'I need assistance'

7.7.2 Signals used by SAR aircraft

A searching aircraft normally flies at about 3,000–5,000ft, or below cloud, firing a green Very light every five or ten minutes and at each turning point.

If a green flare is seen, a vessel in distress should take the following action:

- Wait for the green flare to die out.
- Fire one red flare.
- Fire another red flare some 20 seconds later. (The aircraft aligns itself on the transit of both flares.)
- Fire a third red flare when the aircraft is overhead, or if it appears to be going badly off course.

Other signals are shown at Figs 7(1) and 7(2).

7.7.3 Directing signals by aircraft

Fig 7(1) shows how an aircraft directs a vessel towards a ship in distress; how it tells the vessel that its assistance is no longer required; and how the vessel may reply.

7.7.4 Shore-to-ship: visual signals

If no radio contact is possible, some signals shown in Fig 7(2) may be used to a vessel in distress close to the shore.

7.8 HELICOPTER RESCUE

SAR helicopters in the UK are operated by HM Coastguard at Sumburgh, Stornoway, Portland and Lee-on-Solent; the Royal Navy at Prestwick and Culdrose; the RAF at Lossiemouth, Boulmer, Valley, Leconfield, Wattisham and Chivenor.

Sea King SAR helicopters operated by the RN and RAF have a radius of action of 180–240M and can lift up to 18 survivors. The AW139 helicopters operated by HMCG have a radius of action of 180M and can lift 9 survivors or 2 stretchers. Both types are fully night capable.

7.8.1 Communications

SAR helicopters are generally fitted with VHF, FM & AM, UHF and HF SSB radios and can communicate with lifeboats on VHF FM, using callsign *Rescue nn*. Communications between ship and helicopter should normally be on VHF Ch 16 or 67; 2182 kHz SSB may be available. Communication can often be achieved through aircraft, if on scene, a lifeboat or HM CG.

When the helicopter is sighted by a vessel in distress, a flare (fired away from, not at, the helicopter!), an orange smoke signal, dye marker or an signal lamp (not pointed directly at the helicopter) will assist recognition – very important if other vessels are in the vicinity. Spray dodgers with the yacht's name or sail number are useful aids to identification.

7.8.2 On the yacht

The helicopter will pass advice before it gets so close that communications become difficult because of the noise of its rotors. Listen carefully and, if possible, do exactly as requested. You may be asked to keep the sails up in order to stabilise the yacht. If they are lowered, securely lash them and any loose gear. If possible remove items such as danbuoys or long aerials from the cockpit area.

If a crewman descends from the helicopter he will take charge. Obey his instructions promptly. ***Never secure the winch wire to the yacht***, and beware that it may carry a dangerous static charge if it is not dipped (earthed) in the sea before handling.

7.8.3 Double lift

Survivors may be lifted by double lift in a strop, accompanied by the crewman in a canvas seat, or it may be necessary to position yourself in the strop. Put your head and shoulders through the strop so that the padded part is in the small of the back and the toggle is in front of the face. Pull the toggle down, as close to the chest as possible.

When ready, give a thumbs-up sign with an extended arm, then place both arms close down by the side of the body to ensure that the strop does not slide up. Resist the temptation to hang on to the strop. On reaching the helicopter do exactly as instructed by the crew. Injured persons can be lifted in a special stretcher provided by the helicopter.

7.8.4 Hi-line

Often a 'Hi-line' technique using a 'Heaving-in' line is used. This is a rope tail, attached to the helicopter winch wire by a weak link and weighted at its lower end. When it is lowered to the yacht do not make it fast but coil it down carefully. The helicopter pays out the winch wire and then moves to one side of the yacht and descends while the yacht takes in the slack (keeping it outboard and clear of all obstructions) until the winch hook and strop are on board.

A helicopter crewman may be lowered with the strop. When ready to lift, the helicopter ascends and takes in the wire. Pay out the tail, keeping enough weight on it to keep it taut until the end is reached, then cast it off well clear of the yacht. But if a further lift is to be made the tail should be retained on board (again, not made fast) to facilitate recovery of the strop for the next lift.

When leaving a helicopter ashore, beware of the tail rotor which can be difficult to see. Obey all instructions given by the helicopter crew.

7.9 ABANDON SHIP

Do not abandon a vessel unless she is definitely sinking. A vessel is easier to find than a liferaft and provides better shelter. While she is still afloat use her resources (eg the radio for distress communications) and put extra equipment in the liferaft or the dinghy, which should also be taken if possible. Make all preparations.

The aim should be to board the liferaft without getting wet. Before boarding and cutting it adrift:

- Send a MAYDAY call or DSC distress alert, saying that the vessel is being abandoned. Include your position and the number of people on board.
- Dress warmly with sweaters under foul weather gear. Wear life jackets and take extra clothes.
- Fill any available containers with fresh water to about ¾ full so that they will float.
- Collect additional food, tins and tin-opener.
- Collect navigational gear, EPIRB, SART, handheld VHF, torch, extra flares, bucket, length of line, first-aid kit, knife, fenders and any other equipment which might aid your survival.

Some items should already be in a survival bag – essential when a vessel is abandoned in a hurry. See *The Grab Bag Book* (ACN).

Safety

Launch the liferaft on the lee side of the vessel, having first checked the painter is secured to a strongpoint. Pull in the painter, which may be up to 10m long, and give a sharp tug to activate the CO_2 bottle. If the liferaft inflates upside down, try to right it from the vessel. Keep the liferaft close alongside while boarding; release or cut the painter before the vessel sinks. Once in the liferaft, plan for the worst: a long wait for rescue. The priorities, in order, are: protection, location, water, food. Always believe that you will survive.

- Keep the inside of the raft as dry as possible. Huddle together for warmth. Close the openings as necessary, but keep a good lookout for ships and aircraft.
- Stream the drogue if necessary for stability, or so as to stay near the original position.
- Take anti-seasickness pills.
- Don't drink any water in the first 24 hours, then ration fresh water to ½ litre per person per day. Do not drink sea water or urine. Collect rain water.
- Use flares sparingly.

7.10 SEARCH AND RESCUE (SAR) – UK

The Maritime & Coastguard Agency (MCA) is responsible for developing and maintaining a high level of marine safety, minimising loss of life amongst seafarers and protecting the marine environment. Its responsibility for emergency response is met by HM Coastguard, which co-ordinates civil maritime SAR in the UK Search and Rescue Region (SRR).

HM Coastguard (HM CG) manages the UK maritime SAR helicopter service and shore rescues. It co-ordinates the response of ambulance, fire and police services to maritime incidents in and around the UK. HM CG possesses some boats, but lifeboats and their crews are provided by non-governmental charities, primarily the RNLI. HM CG enlists the assistance of merchant vessels and warships in the response to SAR events beyond coastal waters.

7.10.1 Raising the alarm

If you see an incident which merits an emergency response at sea or along the shoreline, dial 999 and ask for the Coastguard. You will be asked for details of the incident and may be asked to remain contactable to provide further information.

If you see a distress signal or receive a distress message at sea and are in the immediate vicinity you are obliged to respond with all speed unless or until you are specifically released. Even if unable to give effective aid, your presence may provide reassurance or act as a beacon for other help.

When alerted, HM CG summons the most appropriate assets: they may direct vessels in the vicinity of the distress, request the launch of a lifeboat or scramble a helicopter and alert other vessels by radio, digital or satellite communications. For shore incidents, including cliff and mud rescue, it will activate its rescue teams and liaise with the other services.

7.11.2 CG66 Voluntary Safety Identification Scheme

Owners/skippers may freely register details of their boat with HM CG. Form CG66 provides accurate information on the vessel including a description to expedite assistance if in difficulty, missing or overdue. It may be completed online (www.gov.uk/register-boat-coastguard-safety-scheme) or it is available from MRCCs, RNLI lifeboat stations and possibly your sailing club or marina. Details are kept for two years then destroyed if not renewed.

7.11 HM COASTGUARD (HM CG)

The EU Integrated Maritime Policy promotes the wellbeing of citizens by ensuring their security and safety as well as responsible economic practice and environmental protection. HM CG contributes to this through dedicated surveillance infrastructure, managed by a resilient command, control and communications network. Vessel monitoring allows greater awareness and understanding of maritime activity in order to to speed response in rescue co-ordination, intervention against illegal acts and pollution prevention.

Nine networked Coastguard Operation Centres CGOC co-ordinated by the Maritime Operations Centre (MOC) at Fareham control nominated areas of responsibility (AOR). Each has the ability to control operations across all AOR, sharing data and access to communcations nationwide.

CG locations and boundaries are shown in Chapter 6, Fig 6(4), and in Chapter 9 on the maps at the start of Areas 1–11.

The Dover CG monitors the TSS in the Dover Strait by radar and AIS, and supports the traffic safety through the Channel Navigation Information Service (CNIS).

The CG manage vessel traffic messages (VTM) for merchant vesels. MSI broadcasts disseminate essential safety information. Details of messages are shown in Chapter 6.

The CG Rescue Service consists of regular officers supported by 3,500 Auxiliary Coastguards who are on call to cover emergencies around the coastline. These rescue teams, respond to, assess and carry out searches and cliff and mud rescues (depending on location). They liaise with the RNLI.

E-mail: CG centre name before coastguard@mcga.gov.uk e.g. Milford Haven is: milfordhavencoastguard@mcga.gov.uk. Radio and phone calls to and from CG Centres are recorded, but HM CG does ***not*** provide or accept telephone link calls.

Appropriate CG (or continental equivalent) telephone numbers are listed for each port entry.

7.11.1 HM CG routine services

HM Coastguard routinely supports maritime activity by:

- Organising and conducting search and rescue operations at sea or on the UK's cliffs or foreshore.
- Keeping an H24 radio watch on VHF and GMDSS.
- Controlling the UK maritime SAR helicopter service.
- Providing medical advice from a doctor via telephone link call; and arranging medical assistance. Call initially on VHF/MF DSC or on Ch 16 or 2182 kHz and expect to be switched to a working Channel/frequency.
- Broadcasting Maritime Safety Information (MSI) messages at 4 hourly intervals on VHF and MF. These include WZ, local Subfacts and Gunfacts in exercise areas as well as local inshore forecasts and warnings related to navigation, weather, tidal surges and the failure of navigation aids.
- Vessel traffic monitoring and surveillance of UK Territorial Waters and Exclusive Economic Zone by AIS and VTM.
- Recording Traffic Reports (TRs) from yachts and other small craft either by VHF or telephone. When passing a TR include your vessel's name, callsign, MMSI number, ETD, ETA and number of persons onboard. The boat's safe arrival should be passed to the nearest CGOC, for relay to the departure CG. Also, be sure to report any change of plan to the nearest CG while on passage. *Overdue action is only taken if concern for the safety of the vessel is reported to HM CG*, by a shore contact, for example.

7.12 ROYAL NATIONAL LIFEBOAT INSTITUTION

The RNLI is a registered charity which provides a 24-hour lifeboat service up to 100M off the UK and Irish coasts. There are more than 230 lifeboat stations. Of these, four are on the River Thames, and another four are inland water stations. The RNLI also operates over 100 lifeguard units. All new lifeboats are capable of at least 25 knots. When launched on service, lifeboats >10m keep watch on VHF and MF DSC as well as VHF Ch 16. They can also use alternative frequencies to contact other vessels, SAR aircraft, HM CG, Coast Radio Stations or other SAR agencies. All lifeboats show a quick-flashing blue light when on operational service.

The RNLI actively promotes safety at sea by providing a free comprehensive safety service (eg the RNLI Sea Safety Check) to members and the general public including advice, publications and demonstrations. The RNLI aims to save lives and prevent accidents by helping people be prepared through water safety awareness. The *RNLI Skippers' Handbook* covers emergencies, seamanship, weather, first aid, navigation and engines. For more details of how the RNLI can help you to be safer at sea, or to support the work of the RNLI, call the RNLI on 0845 122 6999, visit www.rnli.org.uk.

7.13 NATIONAL COASTWATCH INSTITUTION

The National Coastwatch Institution (NCI) – www.nci.org.uk – is a voluntary organisation keeping a visual watch along the UK's coast assisting the preservation and protection of life at sea. The National Office is at 17 Dean St, Liskeard, Cornwall, PL14 4AB, ☎(01579) 347392. There are 50 operational stations (2016) manned by over 2000 volunteers. They are marked on the Area maps by ©. All stations monitor VHF Ch 16 and provide actual weather, sea state, hazards and local information on request on their dedicated channel **VHF Ch 65**. Many are equipped with AIS Ⓐ, DSC Ⓓ and radar Ⓡ. Contact details:

Area 1		
St Mary's	01720	422641
Gwennap Head (Land's End) Ⓐ Ⓓ Ⓡ	01736	871351
Penzance Ⓐ Ⓓ	01736	367063
Bass Point (Lizard) Ⓐ Ⓓ Ⓡ	01326	290212
Nare Point (Helford River) Ⓐ Ⓓ Ⓡ	01326	231113
Portscatho (E of Fal; summer w/e only)	01872	580180
Charlestown Ⓡ	01726	817068
Polruan (Fowey) Ⓐ Ⓡ	01726	870291
Rame Head (Plymouth) Ⓐ Ⓓ Ⓡ	01752	823706
Prawle Point (Salcombe) Ⓐ Ⓓ Ⓡ	01548	511259
Froward Point (Dartmouth) Ⓐ Ⓓ Ⓡ	07976	505649
Torbay Ⓐ Ⓓ Ⓡ	01803	411145
Teignmouth Ⓐ Ⓓ Ⓡ	01626	772377
Exmouth Ⓓ	01395	222492
Lyme Bay Ⓓ	07745	756872
Charmouth Ⓐ Ⓓ Ⓡ	01308	897778
Portland Bill Ⓐ Ⓓ Ⓡ	01305	860178
St Alban's Head Ⓐ Ⓓ Ⓡ	01929	439220
Swanage Ⓐ Ⓓ Ⓡ	01929	422596
Area 2		
Peveril Pt (Swanage) Ⓐ Ⓓ Ⓡ	01929	422596
Needles Ⓐ	01983	754231
Calshot Ⓐ Ⓓ Ⓡ	02380	893562
Lee on Solent Ⓐ Ⓓ	02392	556758
Gosport	02392	765194
Area 3		
Shoreham Ⓐ Ⓓ Ⓡ	01273	463292
Newhaven Ⓐ Ⓡ	01273	516464
Folkestone (Copt Pt) Ⓐ Ⓓ	01303	227132
Area 4		
Herne Bay (w/ends only) Ⓐ Ⓓ Ⓡ	01227	744454
Whitstable (w/ends only) Ⓓ	07864	646209
Holehaven (Canvey Island) Ⓐ Ⓓ	01268	696971
Southend (w/ends only) Ⓐ Ⓓ	07815	945210
Felixstowe Ⓓ	01394	670808
Gorleston (Great Yarmouth) Ⓐ Ⓓ Ⓡ	01493	440384
Caister Ⓐ Ⓓ	07527	977613
Area 5		
Mundesley (Norfolk) Ⓐ Ⓓ Ⓡ	01263	722399
Runton Ⓐ Ⓓ Ⓡ	01263	513725
Wells-next-the-sea (Norfolk) Ⓐ Ⓓ Ⓡ	01328	710587
Mablethorpe Ⓐ Ⓓ	07958	038564
Skegness Ⓐ Ⓓ	07902	076605
Sunderland Ⓐ Ⓡ	01915	672579
Area 10		
Rossall Pt (Fleetwood) Ⓐ Ⓓ Ⓡ	01253	681378
Point Lynas	No landline	
Rhoscolyn Ⓐ	07887	955496
Porth Dinllean Ⓓ	07773	362005
Aberystwyth	07496	012056
Area 11		
Morfa Bychan (Porthmadog) Ⓓ	07521	446050
Wooltack Point (St Brides Bay) Ⓐ Ⓓ	01646	636802
Worms Head (Gower) Ⓓ	01792	390167
Nells Point (Barry) Ⓐ Ⓓ	01446	420746
Boscastle (North Cornwall) Ⓐ Ⓓ Ⓡ	01840	250965
Stepper Point (Padstow) Ⓐ Ⓓ Ⓡ	01841	530039
St Agnes Head (N Cornwall) Ⓐ Ⓡ	01872	552073
St Ives Ⓐ Ⓡ	01736	799398
Cape Cornwall (Land's End) Ⓐ Ⓓ Ⓡ	01736	787890

8 First Aid

8.1–2	First aid objectives – Medical care abroad	118
8.3	Medical advice by R/T	118
8.4	ABC – Emergency resuscitation Airway • Breathing • Circulation • External chest compression	118
8.5–6	Choking – Drowning	120
8.7–8	Hypothermia – Shock	120
8.9	Acute (sudden) illness Abdominal pain • Allergies • Children • Constipation • Convulsions • Diabetes • Diarrhoea • Fever • Heart attack • Heat stroke • Seasickness	121
8.10	Stroke	122
8.11–12	Bites and stings – Fish hook injury	122
8.13–14	Bleeding (open wound) – Bleeding (internal)	122
8.15–16	Burns and scalds – Chest injury	122
8.17–18	Crush injuries – Cuts and wounds	122
8.19–20	Dental problems – Eye injury	123
8.21	Fractures and dislocations Specific fractures • Skull, Nose, Cheek, Jaw, Neck, Spine, Ribs, Upper and Lower limbs • Compound fractures	123
8.22–24	Frostbite – Head problems – Nail injuries	124
8.25–27	Nosebleed – Poisoning – Strains and sprains	125
8.28–30	First aid kit – Drugs – Emergency childbirth	125
8.31–32	Injections – Books on first aid	126
8.33	Normal physiological measurements	126
8.34	Observation form	127

8.1 FIRST AID OBJECTIVES

The objectives of First Aid at sea are to:

- **Preserve life**
- **Prevent further damage**
- **Relieve pain and distress**
- **Deliver a live casualty ashore**

With any casualty be calm, reassuring and methodical. Examine the whole casualty at the earliest opportunity.

Completion of a First Aid Course is strongly recommended. In the UK, RYA approved, one-day, basic training is available through sailing clubs and schools. The St John Ambulance and British Red Cross provide a variety of recognised courses.

8.2 MEDICAL CARE ABROAD

For cruising in European waters it is advisable for each crew member to carry the European Health Insurance Card (EHIC) which entitles you to reduced-cost, sometimes free, medical treatment that becomes necessary while you are in the EU, Iceland, Liechtenstein and Norway. It is available by phone, by post or online; see: *www.dh.gov.uk/en/Policyandguidance/Healthadvicefortravellers/index.htm*.

A useful booklet *Health Advice for Travellers,* which gives details of how to claim in the 28 participating countries, is obtainable from Post Offices. A further 30+ countries have reciprocal health care agreements with the UK, but others, including Turkey, the Americas, Canada, Caribbean, India, Middle East, Africa, Asia, Thailand, Japan, Hong Kong and the Pacific region (except Australia and New Zealand), do not. Private health insurance is strongly advised in these areas.

Skippers should be aware of crew members' medical conditions and any ongoing medication, which may seriously alter the implications of an injury or change treatment. If cruising to distant destinations sufficient medication must be carried and additional sterile needles and syringes may be advisable, if you or a crewman are diabetic, for example. Seek advice from your doctor or local hospital before leaving. Syringes and needles are attractive to intravenous drug abusers so should be securely locked away.

Yachtsmen cruising abroad may naturally be concerned about the risk of being given infected blood. Normally it is not possible to carry blood or plasma in a yacht. If a blood transfusion is essential, try to ensure that the blood used has been screened against HIV and Hepatitis B.

8.3 MEDICAL ADVICE BY R/T

Medical advice can be obtained almost anywhere in European waters (and elsewhere) by making an all-stations 'PAN PAN' call or a DSC Urgency Alert to the Coastguard, or to a Coast Radio Station (CRS) in those countries where CRS still exist. You will be connected to a suitable medical authority – usually a doctor or the nearest hospital.

The Urgency signal 'PAN PAN' is always advised, especially abroad, because it is internationally understood and cuts through most language problems; see also 7.5.

Urgent help needed is shown in bold italic type against the more serious medical problems in the following pages and this implies a PAN PAN call. You should also recognise that as a layman you are not qualified to judge how serious the casualty's condition is – so get the best possible advice and/or help as quickly as possible.

Be ready to give a detailed summary of the patient's symptoms – pulse rate, breathing rate, temperature, skin colour, conscious state (with reference to pupil size, responses to verbal command and to firm pinching); site and description of any pain, site and type of injury, amount of blood lost etc. See the Observation Form at 8.34.

If medical help is needed by way of a doctor coming aboard, or if a serious casualty has to be landed, the arrangements will be made by the Coastguard.

If you are sure that the situation is not urgent, you may wish to forewarn the port authority so that a doctor or paramedic can meet you on arrival. Such a call could be made in adequate time on the harbour's working channel.

8.4 ABC – EMERGENCY RESUSCITATION

Advice at: with www.resus.org.uk/resuscitation-guidelines
The immediate procedure for any collapsed or apparently unconscious person is:

Assess whether or not the casualty is conscious. Carefully shake his shoulders and ask loudly 'What's happened?' or 'Are you all right?' or give a command such as 'Open your eyes'. An unconscious casualty will not respond.

A = Airway

Be aware of the risk of neck or spinal injury following a fall or head injury. If suspected, try to keep the head and neck still and in line, then lift the chin to maintain a clear airway rather than tilting the head. The priority must be to ensure the casualty is indeed breathing. Remove any visible obstruction from the casualty's mouth (leave well-fitting dentures in place). Look, listen at the mouth and feel for ***no more than 10 seconds*** to determine if the casualty is breathing normally. If barley breathing, taking infrequent, slow and noisy gasps or there is any doubt, act as if it is ***not*** normal.

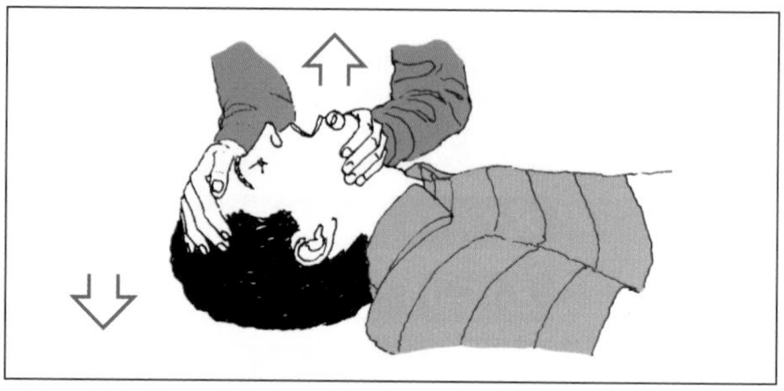

Fig 8(1) Ensuring a clear airway

Tilt the head backwards, using head tilt and chin lift to maintain a clear airway; Fig 8(1). If breathing, place casualty in recovery position; Fig 8(2). Check the area is clear of danger.

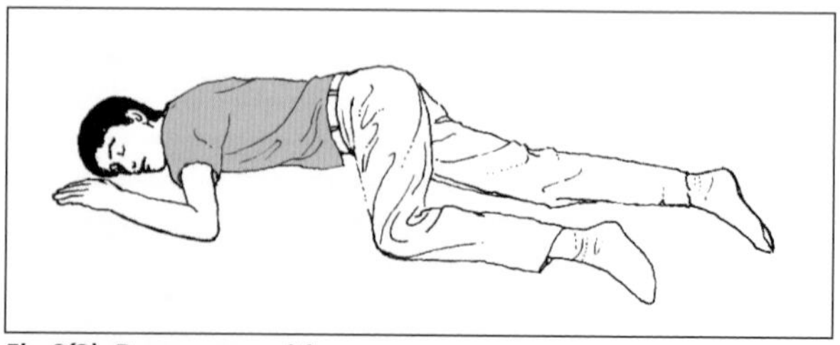

Fig 8(2) Recovery position

B = Breathing and C = Circulation

If not breathing and the airway is clear, start chest compressions; Fig 8(3). This situation is called **cardiac arrest**.

The casualty will be unconscious and may appear very pale, grey or bluish in colour. An artificial circulation will have to be provided by chest compression. If the circulation stops, breathing will also stop. Casualties with cardiac arrest will need a combinatiomn of rescue breaths and chest compression, known as Cardio Pulmonary Resuscitation (**CPR**).

Chest compressions

To start external chest compression, lay the casualty on a hard, flat surface if possible. Kneel beside casualty. The point at which pressure will be applied is the centre of the chest. (It is now considered a waste of valuable time for an amateur first aider to search for the point of pressure by the 'rib margin' method.)

Place the heel of your first hand on top of the other hand and interlock your fingers. Position your shoulders vertically above the victim's chest and keep your arms straight. Depress their breastbone 5–6cm (2–2½in) then release all pressure 100–120 times per minute; Fig 8(3).

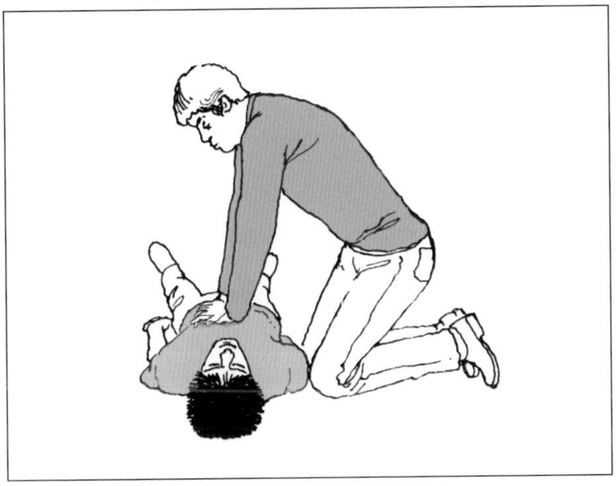

Fig 8(3) Chest compression

With either one or two operators give 30 chest compressions and continue cycles of 2 breaths to 30 compressions; see Fig 8(5) and Fig 8(6). Use a compression rate of 100-120 per minute. If trained, chest compression should be combined with rescue breaths; after 30 compressions, give 2 effective rescue breaths (2 breaths should not take more than 5 secs). ***Do not stop***.

Rescue breaths

Kneel beside the casualty, maintain head tilt and chin lift, and pinch the nostrils. Take a deep breath and blow two full breaths into patient's mouth, each breath should be 1 second in duration. Watch for rise and fall of chest; Fig 8(4).

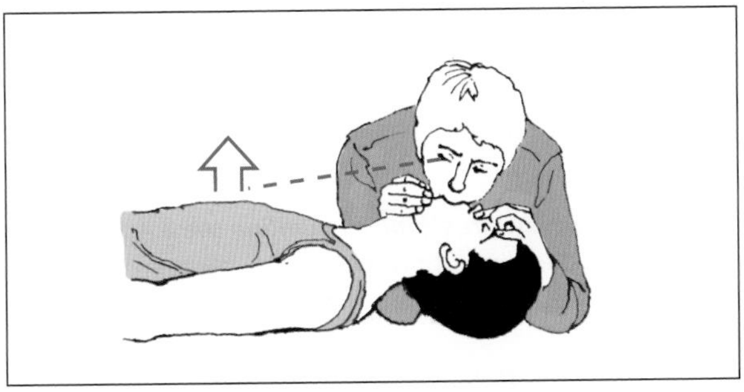

Fig 8(4) Rescue breaths

Action plan for the resuscitation of adults

Casualty is unconscious but is breathing normally:

- ***Urgent help needed***
- Turn casualty into the recovery position
- Check for continued breathing

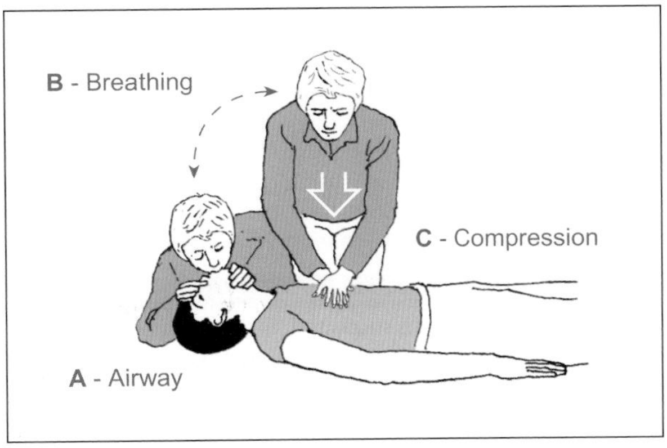

Fig 8(5) One operator

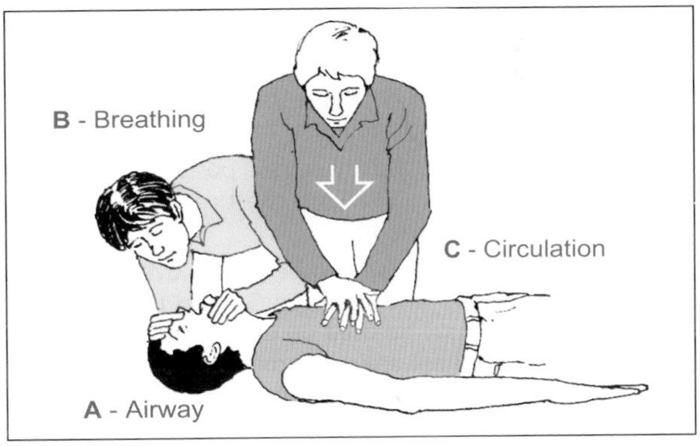

Fig 8(6) Two operators

Casualty is unconscious and not breathing:

- ***Urgent help needed***
- Start chest compressions
- After 30 chest compressions, give 2 rescue breaths

Continue with chest compressions and rescue breaths in a ratio of 30:2. If you are untrained, or are unwilling to give rescue breaths, give chest compressions only. Stop to re-check casualty only if he/she starts to show signs of regaining consciousness; coughing, opening eyes, speaking or moving purposefully ***and*** starts to breathe normally.

If breathing restarts, place casualty in the recovery position.

Otherwise, ***do not interrupt resuscitation***.

Action plan for the resuscitation of children

Resuscitate at 100–120 compressions per min, compressing the chest by at least ⅓ of its depth, approximately 4cm for an infant and 5cm for an older child. Use two fingers for an infant under 1 yr of age and one or two hands for an older child to achieve adequate depth of compression. Give two rescue breaths every 15 compressions.

In case of a baby (younger than 1 year), ensure a neutral position of the head (no head tilt) and apply chin lift. Give up to 5 initial rescue breaths. Blow steadily over 1 second sufficient to make the chest rise visibly.

Problems during resuscitation

It is unlikely that the casualty's pulse will return spontaneously without other more advanced techniques (especially *defibrillation*) so do not waste time by stopping CPR to check the circulation. Only stop and re-check if the casualty shows signs of life (movement or breathing). Otherwise, carry on until either the emergency services arrive, another rescuer can take over, or you are too exhausted to keep going.

Drowning (8.6) and Hypothermia (8.7)

Drowning and hypothermia casualties may exhibit all the signs of apparent death, yet may totally recover. Give 5 initial rescue breaths before starting chest compression and only abandon resuscitation after thorough and repeated attempts have been made to warm the victim.

8.5 CHOKING

If blockage by an object is suspected, tell the casualty to cough. If ineffective stand to the side and slightly behind the victim; support the chest with one hand and lean them well forwards so that any dislodged object comes out of the mouth. Give five sharp blows between the shoulder blades with the heel of the other hand. Check the mouth for any obstruction.

If unsuccessful, wrap both your arms around the victim's waist from behind, and give up to 5 sharp upward thrusts with both fists into the abdomen above the navel but below the ribs so as to initiate coughing. Clear object from mouth.

In an unconscious adult, assist to a safe position attempt to clear the airway and give CPR with chest compressions. Call for assistance. Do not give up.

Infants and small children should be placed over the lap in a head down position and be given 5 sharp blows on the back. Chest thrusts may be used on older childeren but for those less than 1 yr these are performed in the same way as chest compressions but should be sharper and performed at a slower rate, with each thrust trying to relieve the obstruction. Continue if no relief, with the sequence of 5 rescue breaths, 5 back blows and 5 chest thrusts.

8.6 DROWNING

The resuscitation of an apparently drowned person may be complicated by two factors:

- An acute (sudden) illness (8.9 and 8.10) – a stroke, accident or blow to the head, for example – may have precipitated the fall into the water.
- The time spent in the water may have produced marked hypothermia. The water around the UK is rarely warmer than 15°C (60°F).

Medical assistance should always be sought. During rescue and after resuscitation try to keep the head low so that vomit is not inhaled and water is able to drain from the mouth.

Treatment

A = Airway Clear airway: seaweed, dentures etc. See 8.4.

B = Breathing If not breathing start mouth to mouth resucitation as soon as possible and in the water if practicable. See 8.4.

C = Circulation If pulse is absent, start chest compression as soon as aboard. See 8.4.

- If stomach is bulging, turn casualty on to side to empty water, or he may vomit large quantities of water which could be inhaled.
- Prevent cooling. Remove wet clothes; wrap casualty in blankets to warm him/her.
- Continue resuscitation until the casualty revives or death is certain. Hypothermia may mimic death. Do not abandon resuscitation until the casualty has been warmed or signs of death persist despite attempts at warming.
- Once revived, put in the recovery position, Fig 8(2).
- Any person rescued from drowning may collapse in the next 24 hours as the lungs react to inhaled water. ***Urgent help needed***.

8.7 HYPOTHERMIA

Lowered body temperature may follow immersion in the sea or prolonged exposure on deck. In these cases it may be accompanied by a risk of secondary drowning. Hypothermia may lead to collapse, unconsciousness and, ultimately, death. The severity is difficult to determine without core body temperatures. Medical assistance should be sought.

Symptoms include: unreasonable behaviour followed by apathy and confusion; unsteady gait, stumbling; slurring of speech; pale, cold skin; slow, weak pulse; slow breathing; shivering, unconsciousness.

Treatment

A = Airway control; put in recovery position.

B = Breathing If not breathing, start mouth to mouth ventilation.

C = Circulation Be prepared to use chest compressions.

Remove wet clothing. Avoid wind chill. Dry and wrap in blankets or sleeping bag plus warm hat and cover, if available, in foil survival bag. ***Urgent help needed***.

Give hot sweet drinks if conscious.

Do not give alcohol, rub the skin or place very hot objects against skin.

8.8 SHOCK

Shock can result from almost any accident or medical emergency and, depending upon the cause, may range in severity from a simple faint to near death. Shock occurs when the delivery of oxygen to the tissues is impaired because of inadequate or inefficient circulation of the blood. Possible causes include:

- Loss of blood: internal or external bleeding.
- Loss of fluid: diarrhoea, peritonitis, burns.
- Heart failure: heart attack.
- Lung failure: drowning.
- Brain failure: stroke, head injury.
- Illness: diabetes.

Signs and symptoms

Thirst, apathy, nausea, restlessness. Pale, cold, clammy skin, sweating. Rapid, weak pulse. Rapid, shallow breathing. Dull, sunken eyes, bluish lips; it can lead to collapse.

Treatment

- ***ABC – airway, breathing, circulation*** **see 8.4.**
- Control bleeding, if present.
- Lay the casualty flat; elevate legs to 20°.

Exceptions:

i Bleeding from mouth – use recovery position.
ii Unconscious – use recovery position.

iii Chest injury – sitting may be preferred.
- Splint any fractures; avoid movement.
- Keep reasonably warm; don't overheat.
- Relieve pain – give painkillers.

Exceptions:

i Head injury with impaired consciousness.

ii Cases with severe breathing difficulty.

- Reassure the casualty.
- Do not let the casualty eat, drink, smoke or move unnecessarily. If he complains of thirst, moisten the lips with a little water.

Exception

Fluids may be life saving in cases of dehydration (diarrhoea, vomiting, severe burns, for example). Give half a cup of water at 15-minute intervals. Add a pinch of salt and a little sugar. Never give alcohol. Avoid fluids if severe abdominal pain or internal injury. *Never* attempt to give fluids by mouth to an unconscious person.

Collapse and signs of shock after an accident when external blood loss is slight or absent must suggest internal bleeding. Clues may be few. The casualty may cough or vomit blood, or pass blood in urine or from bowel. He/she may complain of worsening pain in abdomen or chest. ***Urgent help needed.***

Medical illnesses, such as diabetes, severe infections or heart disease, may produce shock without giving many clues as to the cause. ***Urgent help needed***.

8.9 ACUTE (SUDDEN) ILLNESS

Before a long passage be aware of any crew medical problems and record medication being taken. Seek medical advice on likely symptoms and treatment. Unless forewarned, diagnosis may be very difficult once at sea.

- ***Abdominal pain (minor)***
  - i Upper abdomen, intermittent, burning, no tenderness, otherwise well. May follow large alcohol intake. Eased by milk or antacid; bland meals; no alcohol.
  - ii More generalised, cramping or colicky pain, no tenderness, may have diarrhoea or vomiting. May be gastroenteritis or food poisoning. Drink fluid with a pinch of salt added. Avoid dehydration. Seek advice.
- ***Abdominal pain (major)*** Severe abdominal pain, usually constant and generalised. Abdomen may be rigid or very tender to touch, possible fever, rapid pulse rate, generally unwell, nausea and vomiting. Make the casualty comfortable, give pain relief (injection if possible). Give nothing to eat or drink. ***Urgent help needed.***
- ***Allergies*** Mild cases may just have a rash which responds to calamine lotion and antihistamine tablets. Severe cases may collapse with breathing difficulty and require emergency ABC resuscitation. Seek advice.
- ***Children*** may become ill with alarming rapidity. Ear and throat infections are especially common. Children are also more susceptible to the effects of dehydration; if ill get them to drink copious fluids. Reduce drug dosage to a proportion of adult dose based on weight (average adult 70kg/155lb). Seek advice.
- ***Constipation*** Common at sea. Prevent by eating fruit, vegetables, bran and, if necessary, anti-constipation medication (eg senna preparations).
- ***Convulsion*** Casualty may be a known epileptic. Prevent injury. **Do not** put anything in the mouth. Place in recovery position; protect airway (he/she may still look very blue). After fit, allow them to sleep. ***Urgent help needed.***
- ***Diabetes*** A diabetic may become unconscious if his/her blood sugar is too high or too low. For **hyper**glycaemia (too much sugar) insulin is needed. **Hypo**glycaemia (too little sugar) may be caused by too much insulin, unusual stress or exercise, or too little food. In either case, if rousable, first give sweets, sugar, soft drinks. If recovery not rapid, ***Urgent help needed***.
- ***Diarrhoea*** Can be serious, especially in young children if much fluid is lost. Stop food, give plenty of fluid. Water is sufficient in most cases or, alternatively, add salt (1 teaspoon/litre) and sugar (4–5 teaspoons/litre) to water. Lomotil or Imodium tablets are very effective in adults.
- ***Fever*** May be associated with anything from common cold, appendicitis, heat stroke to an infected toe. Except for major abdominal problems, prescribe copious fluids, paracetamol or aspirin (not in the case of children) and antibiotics if infection is present. Seek advice.
- ***Heart attack*** Severe central 'crushing' chest pain; may spread to shoulders, neck or arms. Sweating, then bluish lips, then collapse. Breathing and heart may stop. Give one aspirin tablet 300mg, to be chewed not swallowed whole. Some casualties (diabetics, for example) may not experience the chest pains. ***Urgent help needed***.
  - i Early symptoms; rest, reassure.
  - ii If unconscious: recovery position; observe breathing and pulse.
  - iii If breathing stops or pulse is absent, commence mouth to mouth ventilation and chest compression immediately and do not stop. See 8.4.
- ***Heat stroke*** Cool casualty by spraying with cold water or wrap the casualty in a cold wet sheet until their temperature falls to 38°C under the tongue; encourage drinking (one teaspoon of salt/half litre of water). If casualty stops sweating, has a rapid pounding pulse and is becoming unconscious, ***urgent help needed***.
- ***Seasickness*** is basically an inner ear disturbance caused by motion. The condition is aggravated by fear, anxiety, fatigue and boredom. It may manifest itself as lethargy, dizziness or headache as well as nausea and vomiting. Avoid strong food tastes and too much alcohol. Take small amounts of fluid and food frequently if you feel ill. Avoid fatigue; adequate sleep will often relieve the sick feeling. Keep warm. Stay on deck and concentrate on some task if possible – taking the helm can work wonders. Sick crew on deck must be secured by lifeline. Turn in if all else fails. Vomiting may cause serious loss of fluid.

  No one remedy suits everybody. Try the alternatives until you find one that is effective with minimal side effects; most tend to cause a dry mouth and some tiredness. Tablets available over the counter include: Avomine (promethazine) and Stugeron (cinnarizine). Take the first tablet some hours before going to sea, and then regularly for as long as necessary. Take a tablet just before going to sleep if possible. Various preparations can be applied behind the ear or worn as a wrist band. Prolonged seasickness is serious – seek advice.

8.10 STROKE

Stroke presents in different ways. However, if a person develops **sudden** onset weakness on one side of the body, problems with speech &/or visual problems: ***think of stroke***. Recognise a stroke using the FAST test:

- Face – Has one side of face fallen; can they smile?
- Arms – Can both arms be raised and kept up?
- Speech – Is it slurred or muddled?
- Time – To call for help.

If there is difficulty with *any one* of these suspect, a stroke.

Place in recovery position and check airway.

Urgent help needed – specialist treatment within 4½ hours may reverse the effects of a stroke. If you are more than 4½ hours from help, and the casualty is conscious and able to swallow, give 300mg of asprin, even if he/she is improving.

ACCIDENTS AND INJURIES

8.11 BITES AND STINGS

Injected poison from bites and stings usually only causes local swelling and discomfort, but some individuals may react severely. For insect stings, resuscitate if collapse occurs; otherwise give rest, painkillers, antihistamines (eg chlorpheniramine).

In warmer water, sea snakes and various sea stingers can inject deadly poison: prevent drowning, resuscitate if necessary. If sting is caused by jelly fish or Portuguese Man O'War etc, pour vinegar onto sting to reduce further poison release.

If the victim becomes weak and breathless, lightly compress the limb above the wound with a rolled up roller bandage to delay the spread of poison. **Do not** apply a tourniquet; this practice is out of date due to the danger of losing a limb. Start resuscitation. ***Urgent help needed***.

Many large cities maintain a 24-hour poison information centre. Use the radio for advice.

8.12 FISH HOOK INJURY

Push the hook round until the point and barb appear. Cut off the point and barb and withdraw the hook. Dress the holes and give an antibiotic.

8.13 BLEEDING – OPEN WOUND

Bleeding is often dramatic, but is almost always controllable.

Treatment

- Apply firm continuous direct pressure; bandage on a large pad. If bleeding continues, bandage more pads on top of initial pads; then press directly over wound for at least 10 minutes (blood takes this long to clot).
- Elevate if wound is on a limb.
- **Do not** apply a tourniquet. This practice is out of date and risks losing a limb.

8.14 BLEEDING – INTERNAL (CLOSED INJURY)

Follows fractured bones, crush injuries, or rupture of organs such as the liver or spleen. Treat for shock which may appear rapidly. ***Urgent help needed***.

8.15 BURNS AND SCALDS

Treatment

- Move the victim into fresh air to avoid inhaling smoke.
- ***ABC – Airway, Breathing, Circulation;* see 8.4.**
- Stop further injury: dip the whole of the burnt part into cold water for 10–15 minutes. Seawater is excellent but may be very painful.
- Remove loose clothing only; do not pull off clothing stuck to the skin.
- Cover with sterile dressing. If skin is broken or blistered, use sterile paraffin gauze beneath the dressing. Separate burnt fingers with paraffin gauze. Never use adhesive dressings.
- Do not prick blisters or apply ointments.
- Elevate burnt limb and immobilise.
- Give strong painkillers.
- Treat for shock: give frequent and copious drinks of water.
- Start giving antibiotics for major burns.
- If burns are extensive or deep, ***urgent help needed***.

Sunburn can be very severe. Best treated by keeping the skin cool by fanning or careful sponging with chilled water; give painkillers. For prevention keep well covered and only use sunscreen preparations with high protection factor, greater than SPF 20.

8.16 CHEST INJURY

May result in fractured ribs. These are very painful, and breathing may be uncomfortable and shallow. The fractured ribs may puncture the lung or, if a number of ribs are each broken in two places (eg after crush injury), then this part of the chest may move independently of the rest of the chest and seriously impair breathing.

Treatment

- ***ABC – Airway, Breathing, Circulation;* see 8.4.**
- Casualty may be more comfortable sitting up.
- Tape a plastic cover over any hole on 3 sides (top and both sides) if air is sucking in and out.
- Support any unstable chest segment with your hand.
- For fractured ribs prescribe rest and strong pain-killers if necessary. Very painful.

Avoid tight strapping lest it restricts breathing even further. ***Urgent help needed*** for any case with impaired breathing.

8.17 CRUSH INJURIES

These injuries involve skin, underlying muscle and tendon and sometimes bone as well. Common in hands and fingers (from winches and anchor chains) and elsewhere when tissue is sandwiched. Bleeding may be slight, but bruising and swelling considerable and extremely painful. Keep affected part as cold as possible; elevate if a hand or foot and give painkillers. ***Urgent help needed***.

8.18 CUTS AND WOUNDS

Often dramatic but only potentially serious if nerves, tendons or blood vessels are severed.

Treatment

- Clean thoroughly with antiseptic. Remove dirt or other foreign bodies from the wound.
- Small clean cuts can be closed using Steristrips. Skin must be dry. Use as many Steristrips as necessary to keep the skin edges together. Leave for at least 5 days.
- Larger deep cuts may require special suture techniques (stitches); apply a dressing and seek help. Do not try amateur surgery at sea.
- Ragged lacerations or very dirty wounds – do not attempt to close these; dead tissues may have to be trimmed away to prevent infection. Clean as well as possible, sprinkle antibiotic powder in wound and apply a dressing. Seek help.

If in doubt a wound is best left open and lightly covered to keep it clean and dry.

Fingers and toes

Blood may collect under the nail following an injury. Release the blood by piercing the nail with a red hot needle or paper clip. It will not hurt!

8.19 DENTAL PROBLEMS

Dental pain usually seems worse at sea; prevention is better than cure. It is advisable to see a dentist about 4 weeks before departing on a long voyage to allow time for any necessary treatment. If X-Rays are taken, be sure to keep them with you.

Consider carrying a dental mirror, tongue spatula, pen torch, cotton wool rolls, tweezers and a ready-mixed temporary filling. Dentanurse is an emergency treatment pack which enables an amateur to make basic temporary repairs, eg replacing crowns, lost fillings. It contains zinc oxide and Eugenol.

Treatment

- Throbbing toothache, made worse by hot or cold or when bitten on. If a cavity, clean out and apply temporary filling. Take an anti-inflammatory painkiller.
- Dull toothache, tender to bite on; gum swollen or red with possible discharge. Treat as above but also take an antibiotic.
- Broken tooth or filling. Cover exposed surfaces with zinc oxide paste.
- Teeth which have been knocked out should be placed in a clean container with milk or moist gauze and taken to a dentist at the first opportunity for re-implantation. This can be attempted onboard. If the tooth is not re-implanted within 24 hours (preferably within 1 hour), chance of success is poor.
- Bleeding gums. Clean teeth more thoroughly. If accompanied by foul odour and metallic taste, use regular hot salt water rinses and antibiotics.
- Pain around wisdom tooth. Toothbrush to clean area; use hot salt water rinses; take antibiotics and painkillers.

8.20 EYE PROBLEMS

All eye injuries or illnesses are potentially serious. Never put old or previously opened ointment or drops into an eye; serious infection could result.

Treatment

- Foreign object. Flush the eye with clean water, pull the bottom lid out to inspect, remove object with a clean tissue. For objects under upper eyelid, ask casualty to grasp lashes and pull the upper lid over the lower lid. A proper eye-bath is very effective. Blinking under water may also remove the object. After removal of object, insert sterile antibiotic ointment inside pulled out lower lid. Cover with pad.
- Corrosive fluid. Flush continuously with water for 15 minutes. Give painkillers and chloramphenicol ointment; cover with pad. ***Seek help as soon as possible***.
- Conjunctivitis. A sticky, weeping eye with yellow discharge. Chloramphenicol ointment 4 times a day.

8.21 FRACTURES AND DISLOCATIONS

Fracture is a broken bone. Dislocation is a displaced joint. Both result from major trauma and will produce pain (which is worse on attempted movement), localised swelling, abnormal shape, and a grating feeling on movement (when a fracture is present). Blood vessels or nerves around the fracture or dislocation may also be damaged resulting in a cold, pale, or numb limb below the site of the injury.

Fractures of large bones such as the femur (upper leg) will result in major internal bleeding and may cause shock. When complications occur, ***Urgent help needed***.

Early application of a splint and elevation of the injured limb where possible will reduce pain and minimise complications. Treat for shock and pain.

Specific fractures and dislocations

Cheek Caused by a direct blow. Rarely serious but requires specialist care.

Jaw Beware of associated brain or spinal injury. Remove blood and teeth fragments; leave loose teeth in place; protect broken teeth (see 8.19). Ensure airway is clear. Start regular antiseptic mouth washes and antibiotics. Support jaw with bandage over top of the head. Give only fluids by mouth.

Neck May result from a direct blow, a fall or a whiplash type injury. If conscious, casualty may complain of pain, tingling, numbness or weakness in limbs below the injury. ***Mishandling may damage the spinal cord, resulting in paralysis or death***. Avoid movement and support the head. Immobilise by wrapping a folded towel around the neck. If movement is necessary then lift the victim as one rigid piece, never allowing the neck to bend. ***Urgent help needed***.

Nose Control bleeding by pinching (8.25).

Ribs See chest injury (8.16). Often very painful. Strapping is not advised.

Skull See head injury (8.23).

Spine Fracture of the spine may occur below the neck, also resulting in ***paralysis or death***. Mishandling of the victim may greatly worsen the damage. Avoid movement if possible. Lift the casualty without allowing the spine to sag. ***Urgent help needed***.

Upper Limb

Collar bone (clavicle). Support arm in sling, Fig 8(7).

- **Dislocated shoulder**. If this has happened before, the casualty may remedy the dislocation himself; otherwise do not attempt to remedy it in case a fracture exists.
- **Upper arm (humerus)**. Support the arm with a collar and cuff inside the shirt as illustrated in Fig 8(8), ie tie a clove hitch around the wrist and loop the ends behind the neck.
- **Forearm and wrist**. Splint (eg with battens or wood). Do not bandage tightly. Elevate or support in a sling.
- **Fingers**. Elevate hand and, unless badly crushed, leave unbandaged; keep moving. If very wobbly, bandage to adjacent finger.

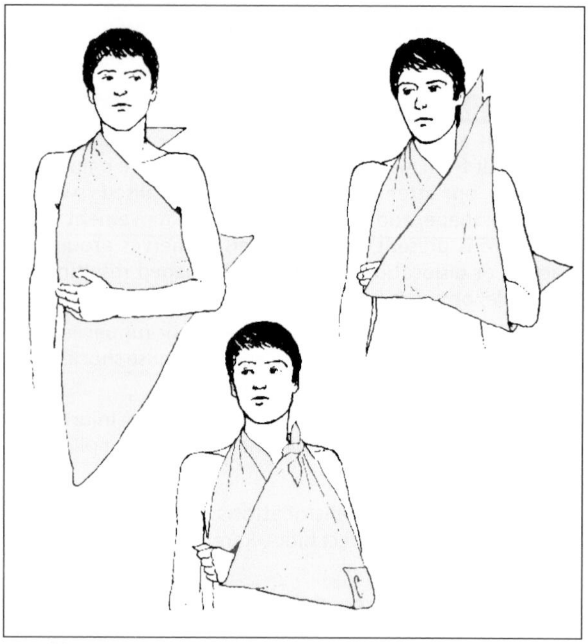

Fig 8(7) Sling

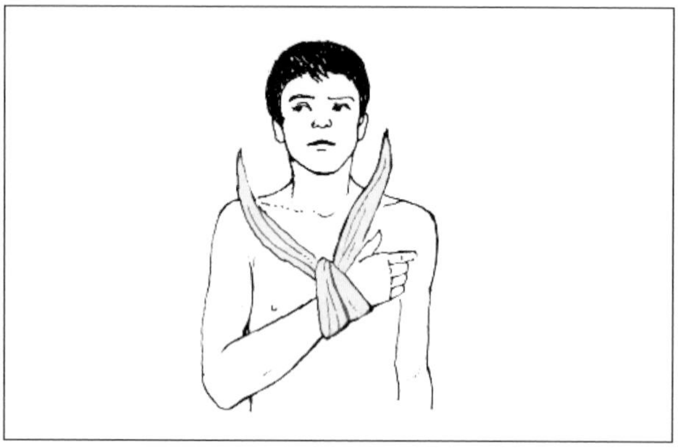

Fig 8(8) Collar and cuff

Lower limb

- **Thigh**. Shock may be considerable. Splint by strapping to other leg with padding between the legs. Gently straighten the casualty's lower leg. If necessary apply traction at the ankle to help straighten the leg. Do not bandage too tightly.
- **Knee**. Twisting injuries or falls damage the ligaments and cartilages of the knee. Very painful and swollen. Treat as for fracture.
- **Lower leg**. Pad very well. Splint using oar, broom handle or similar pieces of wood.
- **Ankle**. Fracture or severe sprain may be indistinguishable. Immobilise in neutral position with foot at right angles. Elevate the limb.

To be really effective a splint must be rigid and extend to the joints above and below the fracture. This is not always possible. The splint must be very well padded.

If the limb beyond the bandage or splint becomes swollen or discoloured, the bandage must be loosened to improve circulation. If you improvise a splint it is essential not to enclose the whole limb and risk cutting off the circulation (see 8.13, reference non-use of tourniquet).

As a general rule, if a fracture is suspected then seek advice.

Compound fractures

If a deep wound overlies the fracture, or the bone ends are visible, do not try to close the wound or replace the bone ends. Clean thoroughly with antiseptic and cover with a sterile dressing. Seek help. Start antibiotics if help is delayed.

8.22 FROSTBITE

Usually affects the extremities: toes, fingers, ears or nose. The affected part may be very painful, numb, stiff and discoloured. Warm gently (on someone else's back, for example).

Immersion in water less than 43°C (110°F); any higher temperature will cause more damage. Do not rub the affected part with anything.

8.23 HEAD INJURY

A blow to the head, with or without fracture, may result in immediate unconsciousness or more delayed effects.

Treatment

- Immediate unconsciousness, but quick recovery with slight drowsiness or headache. Prescribe rest and watch carefully.
- Immediate unconsciousness, no sign of recovery. Put in recovery position (beware of associated spine injury). Check airway. Observe the following and record every 10 minutes: pulse rate, breathing rate, pupil size (both sides), responses to verbal command, response to firm pinching. ***Urgent help needed***.
- Delayed deterioration (either not unconscious immediately, or apparently recovering then worsening). Increasing drowsiness, change in mental state and eventually unconsciousness. Treat as above. ***Urgent help needed***.

Scalp wounds may bleed profusely. Control with very firm pressure; cut away hair, and close using Steristrips if no fracture beneath. ***If in doubt seek help***. Avoid giving drugs after head injury.

8.24 NAIL INJURIES

Nails can be torn or lifted off the underlying flesh and bleeding can be impressive. Do not try to remove the damaged nail which will support the underlying tissue or bone if it is also damaged. Treat as for any bleeding wound with a pad and a bandage wrapped around the finger.

Blood may collect under the nail following a blow. Release the blood by piercing the nail with a red hot needle or paper clip. It will not hurt!

8.25 NOSEBLEED

Lean forwards and pinch the soft part of the nose firmly for at least 10 minutes to allow the blood to clot. Do not blow nose or try to remove clot.

If bleeding continues repeat the pressure for longer than 10 minutes. If still bleeding after 30 minutes insert as much 50mm (2in) gauze bandage (moistened with water) into the nostrils as you can, using forceps to feed the bandage in. *Urgent help needed*.

8.26 POISONING

Poison may reach the body when swallowed, inhaled or injected through the skin (for bites and stings see 8.11).

Treatment

- ***ABC – Airway, Breathing, Circulation;*** see 8.4.
- Recovery position if unconscious.
- *Seek help.*

Swallowed poison

The poison container may give instructions or suggest antidote(s). For corrosive or petroleum products (acids, alkalis, bleach, detergent, petrol) *do not induce vomiting*. Administer copious fluids (eg milk).

For other substances (pills, medicines) *do not induce vomiting* – it is often ineffective and may cause further harm to the casualty. If collapsed or unconscious ***urgent help needed***.

Inhaled poison

Poison may be inhaled from sources such as carbon monoxide or other exhaust fumes, bottled gas which has leaked into the bilge, or fire extinguisher gas. Carbon monoxide inhalation produces cherry red lips and skin. Move into fresh air at once. If breathing is absent, start resuscitation. ***Urgent help needed***.

8.27 STRAINS AND SPRAINS

Torn ligaments, pulled muscles and other injuries. Rest the injured part; elevate if possible; apply ice packs (wrapped in a towel) if possible; administer painkillers. If in doubt, treat as a fracture and immobilise.

8.28 FIRST AID KIT

A made-up Offshore First Aid kit (below) costs about £50; a more comprehensive pre-packed kit might exceed £180. Prescriptions marked * are needed for three of the drugs listed in 8.29. Out of date drugs are potentially dangerous and should be destroyed. Special preparations are available for children. Stow the following suggested items in a readily accessible, clearly marked waterproof container:

Triangular bandage x 2 (doubles as bandage or sling)
Crepe bandage 75mm x 2
Gauze bandage 50mm x 2
Elastoplast 75mm x 1
Band Aids (or similar) various shapes and sizes
Wound dressings, 1 large, 1 medium
Sterile non-adhesive dressing (Melolin) x 5
Steristrips x 5 packs
Cotton wool
Scissors and forceps, good quality stainless steel
Safety pins
Thermometer
Disposable gloves
Antiseptic solution (eg Savlon)
Eye wash
Antifungal powder or cream (athlete's foot)
Insect repellent (DEET, diethyltoluamide)
Individual choice of anti-seasickness tablets
Sunscreen with high protection factor
Moisture cream (for cracked hands and lips)
Medication – see 8.29 for basic suggestions. The list will vary with voyage area, duration and crew embarked

Additional items for extended cruising

Vaccinations (possibly start 6 months before departure)
Syringes 2ml x 2 (if carrying injections)
Dental kit – see 8.19.

8.29 DRUGS AND MEDICATION

Drug	Type/Use	Dose
Paracetamol 500mg tablets	painkiller	1–2 tablets every 4 hours
Aspirin	blood thinner	300mg single dose in case of heart attack or stroke
Ibuprofen	anti-inflammatory	400mg every 8 hours (avoid if history of asthma or stomach ulcer)
*Dihydrocodeine 30mg tablets	strong painkiller	1–2 tablets every 4 hours
Cetirizine	antihistamine	10mg once a day
Aludrox	indigestion	1–2 before meals
Loperamide 2mg capsules	diarrhoea	Take 2 capsules initially followed by 1 after each loose stool, up to a maximum of 8 per day
Senokot tablets	constipation	2–4 tablets daily
*Amoxycillin 250mg	antibiotic	250–500mg every 8 hours (beware penicillin allergy)
*Erythromycin 250mg	antibiotic	For penicillin-allergic adults 4 tablets daily
Cinnarizine 15mg tablets	seasickness	2 before voyage, then 1 every 8 hours
*Scopolamine patches	seasickness	1 patch behind ear 5-6 hrs before voyage; replace after 72 hrs if necessary
Chloramphenicol ointment 1%	eye infection	3-4 times per day

* Only available on prescription.

8.30 EMERGENCY CHILDBIRTH

A yacht is no place to give birth. Unless remaining within about one hour of harbour, a woman who is more than 32 weeks' pregnant should not even consider going to sea in a small boat. Before 30 weeks into the pregnancy, there should be no problem embarking on short offshore passages.

Although giving birth may be an entirely natural process, it is potentially fraught with danger – for both mother and baby – and should ideally be supervised by a midwife or other suitably qualified person. Labour may start with backache, regular pains in the abdomen, a show of blood-stained mucus and a gush of water from the birth canal. Such a situation clearly demands a PAN PAN call followed by rapid assessment and transfer to hospital by lifeboat or helicopter.

Should help not be available, the best advice is to stay calm, unhurried and let nature take its course.

8.31 INJECTIONS

A doctor's prescription is required for injections. Stringent regulations apply to injectable painkiller drugs, which are probably only warranted for long passages. It is safest to inject into the muscle on the outer part of the mid-thigh. Clean the area, then plunge the needle swiftly an inch or so through the skin, pull back on the plunger to ensure that a blood vessel has not been entered, then slowly complete the injection.

8.32 BOOKS ON FIRST AID

The books below give detailed advice. At least one should be on board and the crew should know where it is stowed:

First Aid at Sea by Douglas Justins & Colin Berry (ACN). Recommended by the RORC.

Doctor On Board by Jürgen Hauert (ACN).

Other publications on the internet are:

'The ship captain's medical guide' at https://www.gov.uk/government/publications/the-ship-captains-medical-guide

World Sailing (formerly: ISAF)'s Offshore Special Regulations, http://www.sailing.org/specialregs

8.33 NORMAL PHYSIOLOGICAL MEASUREMENTS

Pulse rate	Adults 60–80/minute Children up to 100/minute
Breathing	12–15/minute
Temperature	36·7°C (98·4°F)

8.34 OBSERVATION FORM

The information recorded by you on this form will be invaluable in helping doctors or paramedics to diagnose the problem and arrange the best possible treatment for your casualty. This is particularly important if there may be a significant time lapse between requesting medical help and the casualty reaching hospital.

- Keep photocopies of this form in your First Aid kit so as to preserve the original.
- Whilst awaiting help, record your observations by ticking or annotating the various boxes at 10-minute intervals; trends can be important and will help doctors detect any improvement or deterioration in the casualty's condition.
- Continue recording observations until help arrives.
- If within radio range of shore attempt to pass the observations via the Coastguard to a medical authority; or ask a ship to relay.
- Before the casualty is taken off the yacht ensure that this form and personal documents are secured to him/her.

DATE .... CASUALTY'S NAME .... AGE .... M/F ....

Times of observations @ 10 minute intervals:		**10**	**20**	**30**	**40**	**50**	**60**
EYES Observe for reactions whilst testing other responses	Open spontaneously						
	Open when spoken to						
	Open to painful stimulus						
	Nil response						
MOVEMENT Apply painful stimulus: Pinch ear lobe or skin on back of hand	Obeys commands						
	Responds						
	Nil response						
SPEECH Speak clearly and directly, close to the casualty's ear	Responds sensibly to queries						
	Seems confused						
	Uses inappropriate words						
	Incomprehensible sounds						
	Nil response						
PULSE (Beats per minute) Take adult's pulse at wrist or neck. Note rate and whether beats are: weak (w); strong (s); regular (reg) or irregular (irreg)	Over 110						
	101-110						
	91-100						
	81-90						
	71-80						
	61-70						
	Below 61						
BREATHING (Breaths per minute) Note rate and whether breathing is: quiet (q); noisy (n); easy (e); or difficult (d)	Over 40						
	31-40						
	21-30						
	11-20						
	Below 11						

9 Harbours, Coasts and Tides

Map of Areas • Area information • Harbour information • Environmental guidance • Distance tables: English Channel, Irish Sea, North Sea, Bay of Biscay

9.1	South West England	137
9.2	Central South England	191
9.3	South East England	247
9.4	East England	271
9.5	North East England	331
9.6	South East Scotland	365
9.7	North East Scotland, Orkney and Shetland	391
9.8	North West Scotland	429
9.9	South West Scotland	469
9.10	NW England, Isle of Man and N Wales	497
9.11	South Wales and Bristol Channel	527
9.12	South Ireland	565
9.13	North Ireland	611
9.14	West Denmark	649
9.15	Germany	665
9.16	Netherlands and Belgium	701
9.17	North France	749
9.18	Central North France	797
9.19	Channel Islands	821
9.20	North Brittany	847
9.21	South Brittany	887
9.22	South Biscay	917
9.23	North and North West Spain	953
9.24	Portugal	987
9.25	South West Spain, Gibraltar and Morocco	1009
9.26	Portuguese Islands, Azores and Madeira	1027

9.0.1 MAP OF AREAS

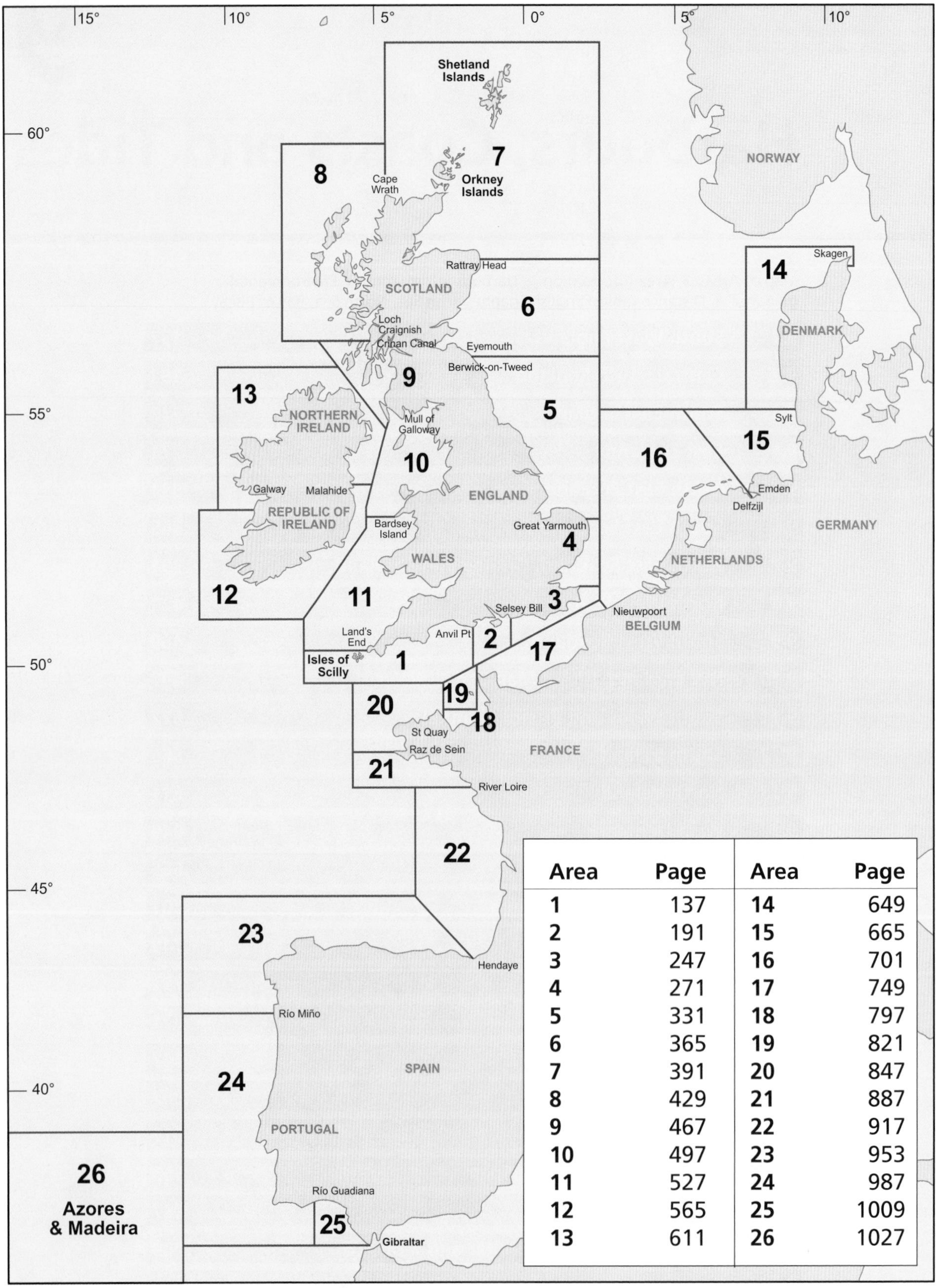
15°
10°
5°
0°
5°
10°
60°
55°
50°
45°
40°
Shetland Islands
7
Orkney Islands
8
Cape Wrath
NORWAY
14
Skagen
DENMARK
Rattray Head
SCOTLAND
6
Loch Craignish
Crinan Canal
Eyemouth
Berwick-on-Tweed
9
13
NORTHERN IRELAND
5
Mull of Galloway
Sylt
16
15
10
Galway
Malahide
ENGLAND
Emden
Delfzijl
REPUBLIC OF IRELAND
Bardsey Island
Great Yarmouth
4
GERMANY
WALES
NETHERLANDS
12
11
3
Selsey Bill
Nieuwpoort
BELGIUM
Land's End
Anvil Pt
2
17
Isles of Scilly
1
19
20
18
St Quay
Raz de Sein
FRANCE
21
River Loire
22
23
Hendaye
Río Miño
24
SPAIN
PORTUGAL
26
Azores & Madeira
Río Guadiana
25
Gibraltar

Area	Page	Area	Page
1	137	14	649
2	191	15	665
3	247	16	701
4	271	17	749
5	331	18	797
6	365	19	821
7	391	20	847
8	429	21	887
9	467	22	917
10	497	23	953
11	527	24	987
12	565	25	1009
13	611	26	1027

9.0.2 AREA INFORMATION

The 26 geographic Areas are arranged as follows:

An Area Map which includes harbours, principal lights, TSS, MRCCs, NCI stations, airports, main ferry routes, magnetic variation and a distance table. Wind farms and other offshore energy installations are not routinely shown.

Tidal stream chartlets showing hourly rates and set.

Lights, buoys and waypoints (LBW) listing positions and characteristics of selected lights and other marks, their daytime appearance, fog signals and Racons. Arcs of visibility and alignment of sector/leading lights are true bearings as seen from seaward. Lights are white unless otherwise stated; any colours are shown between the bearings of the relevant arcs. AIS is fitted to navigational marks and indicated in LBW with MMSI Nos when known. The use of 'Virtual AIS' aids to navigation is slowly increasing and some are indicated with appropriate symbology.

Passage Information (PI) is at Section 5 in most Areas (eg 9.1.5 in Area 1) with further information geographically arranged between the harbour entries, as shown on the Area's Contents page.

Special notes giving data specific to a country or area.

Harbour information (see below).

9.0.3 HARBOUR INFORMATION

Each harbour entry is arranged as follows:

HARBOUR NAME followed by the County or Unitary Council (or foreign equivalent) and the lat/long of the harbour entrance, or equivalent, for use as the final waypoint.

Harbour ratings (❁ ♁ ✿), inevitably subjective, which grade a port based on the following criteria:

Ease of access:

❁❁❁ *Can be entered in almost any weather from most directions and at all states of tide, by day or night.*

❁❁ *Accessible in strong winds from most directions; possible tidal or pilotage constraints.*

❁ *Only accessible in calm, settled conditions by day with little or no swell; possible bar and difficult pilotage.*

Facilities available:

♁♁♁ *Good facilities for vessel and crew.*

♁♁ *Logstic needs met, but limited boatyard facilities.*

♁ *Possibly some domestic facilities, but little else.*

Ambience:

✿✿✿ *An attractive place; well worth visiting.*

✿✿ *Average for this part of the coast.*

✿ *Holds no particular attraction.*

CHARTS show Admiralty (AC), Imray, and foreign charts, smallest scale first. Admiralty Leisure Folios (56XX), which cover most of the UK, Channel Islands and Ireland, and Imray 2000 series folios (2X00) are also shown.

TIDES include a time difference (usually on Dover in the UK), ML, Duration and the harbour's Standard Port. Time and height differences for nearby Secondary Ports are also shown. To support offshore activity Standard Port computer prediction is replacing some Secondary Port differences in ATT. The Almanac continues to replicate these differences, which are shown in italics where alternative information is available.

SHELTER assesses how protected a harbour is from wind, sea, surge and swell. It warns of any access difficulties and advises on safe berths and anchorages.

NAVIGATION gives guidance on the approach and entry, and shows the position of the approach waypoint with its bearing and distance to the harbour entrance or next significant feature. Some waypoints may not be shown on the chartlet. Access times are only stated where a lock, gate, sill or other obstruction restricts entry. Otherwise the minimum charted depth of water in the approaches, where it is less than 2m, is usually shown, but always consult up to date official charts.

Chartlets are based on official charts augmented with local information. Due to their scale, they may not cover the whole area referred to in the text nor do they show every depth, mark, light or feature.

The chartlets are not intended to be used for navigation; *positions taken from them should not be used as waypoints in chart plotters.* The publisher and editors disclaim any responsibility for resultant accidents or damage if they are so used. The largest scale official chart, properly corrected, should always be used.

Drying areas and an indicative 5m depth contour are shown as: Dries <5m >5m

Wrecks around the UK which are of archaeological or historic interest are protected by law. Sites are listed under harbour entries or in Passage Information. Unauthorised interference, including anchoring and diving on these sites, may lead to a substantial fine.

LIGHTS AND MARKS describes, in more detail than is shown on the chartlets, any unusual characteristics of marks, their appearance by day and features not listed elsewhere.

COMMUNICATIONS shows the telephone area code followed by local telephone and VHF contact details for: coastguard, weather, police, doctor/medical, harbourmaster/office, other. Marina contact details are not usually duplicated if they are shown under the marina entry. International telephone calls from/to the UK are described in Special Notes, as are national numbers for emergency services: normally 112 in the EU; 999 in the UK. Radio callsigns, if not obvious, are in *italics*.

FACILITIES symbols describe berthing options and facilities in harbours, marinas and yacht clubs (see the free **Reeds Marina Guide** for detailed marina plans in the UK, Channel Islands and Ireland). Water, electricity, showers and toilets are available in marinas unless otherwise stated. Most yacht clubs welcome visiting crews who belong to a recognised club and arrive by sea. Any rail and air links are also shown.

The overnight cost of a visitor's alongside berth (⊆), *correct with regard to information supplied at the time of going to press (Summer 2017)*, is the average charge per metre LOA (unless otherwise stated) during high season, Jun–Sep. It includes VAT. The cost of pile moorings, 🅥s or ⚓s, where these are the norm, may also be given. Shore electricity is usually free abroad but extra in the UK.

The number of Ⓥ berths is a marina's estimate of how many visitors may be accommodated at any one time. It is always advisable to call the marina beforehand.

TransEurope Marinas (www.transeuropemarinas.com) is a group of independent marinas in the UK and abroad. Many hold Blue Flags and 4/5 Gold Anchor Awards; it is a condition of membership that they are well-equipped and maintain high standards. They operate a discounted reciprocal berthing scheme and are shown by the symbol Ⓐ.

Rover Tickets, offering good discounts, are available for many berthing facilities in Scotland and the offlying islands.

9.0.4 ENVIRONMENTAL GUIDANCE

- You must comply with regulations for navigation and conduct in Marine Nature Reserves, Marine Conservation Zones (MCZ), National Water Parks etc.
- In principle, avoid ditching rubbish at sea; keep it on board then dispose of it in shoreside refuse bins.
- Readily degradable foodstuffs may be ditched at sea when more than 3 miles offshore (more than 12 miles in the English Channel).
- Other foodstuffs and materials which are not readily degradable should never be thrown overboard.
- Only flush the heads overboard when well offshore, and do not discharge holding tanks until at least 3 miles off. Many countries now require holding tanks to be fitted; pump-out facilities (⛽) are shown in the text.
- Avoid discharging 'grey' water into a marina, anchorage or moorings area. Note any harbour/marina regulations.
- Deposit used engine oil and oily waste ashore at a recognised facility. Do not allow an automatic bilge pump to discharge oily bilge water overboard.
- Dispose of toxic waste (some antifoulings, old batteries etc) at an approved disposal facility.
- Minimise noise, wash and disturbance.
- Respect wild birds, plants, fish and marine animals. Avoid protected nesting sites and breeding colonies.
- Do not anchor or dry out on vulnerable seabed species, eg soft corals and eel grass.

9.0.5 DISTANCES (M) ACROSS THE ENGLISH CHANNEL

England / France/CI	Longships	Falmouth	Fowey	Plymouth bkwtr	Salcombe	Dartmouth	Torbay	Exmouth	Weymouth	Poole Hbr Ent	Needles Lt Ho	Nab Tower	Littlehampton	Shoreham	Brighton	Newhaven	Eastbourne	Folkestone	Dover	Ramsgate
Le Conquet	114	118	134	142	139	152	158	168	181	199	203	236	256	260	264	269	281	313	318	342
L'Aberwrac'h	101	103	114	120	122	133	142	151	171	191	197	215	236	246	247	248	258	297	301	327
Roscoff	110	97	101	97	91	100	107	117	130	144	149	165	184	193	197	200	211	246	252	298
Trébeurden	118	105	107	100	95	103	110	122	128	148	148	168	186	197	201	206	218	257	262	288
Tréguier	131	114	112	102	93	99	104	114	118	132	136	153	170	182	187	192	211	252	253	277
Lézardrieux	139	124	119	107	97	102	105	115	117	129	133	150	167	179	184	189	208	249	250	274
St Quay-Portrieux	151	134	128	120	109	114	115	123	128	133	136	151	174	180	185	188	200	238	242	270
St Cast Le Guildo	164	145	139	127	114	117	120	128	124	129	132	147	170	177	181	184	198	234	239	264
St Malo	172	152	145	132	118	121	124	132	125	130	133	148	170	176	182	185	195	235	240	264
St Helier	156	133	124	110	95	97	100	109	103	108	110	125	145	155	160	163	175	211	218	241
St Peter Port	140	115	105	89	75	71	73	81	81	87	90	105	126	135	139	142	155	190	196	227
Braye (Alderney)	149	129	107	90	74	72	71	74	63	68	71	86	108	115	120	123	135	173	178	202
Cherbourg	173	144	130	111	98	94	93	95	67	64	63	72	89	99	102	107	120	153	158	185
St Vaast	194	165	151	134	119	117	119	127	86	78	72	69	84	91	94	97	104	140	147	178
Ouistreham	231	203	190	173	158	155	159	164	121	111	100	88	93	94	94	93	96	132	133	160
Deauville	238	210	198	181	164	163	160	160	127	114	103	89	90	89	87	87	89	124	126	152
Le Havre	239	210	197	180	164	162	165	159	125	112	98	84	84	83	82	82	83	119	120	146
Fécamp	246	218	206	188	173	169	165	164	127	111	98	81	72	69	66	63	63	98	98	122
Dieppe	273	245	231	214	200	194	191	189	151	133	121	97	86	76	72	67	62	78	80	100
Boulogne	294	264	247	231	216	204	202	199	161	143	132	101	86	77	73	65	54	28	28	51
Calais	307	276	261	244	229	218	214	211	174	155	143	114	99	91	86	78	64	29	24	30

NOTES ON DISTANCE TABLES 9.0.5–9.0.8

Approximate distances in nautical miles are by the most direct practicable route, taking into account the requirement to cross Traffic Separation Schemes (or the recommendation to cross main shipping lanes) on a heading at right angles to the general direction of traffic flow. They do not take into account any diversions to avoid exclusion zones around oil or gas installations.

Skippers are reminded of the need to consult up to date official charts, navigational publications and weather forecasts to choose a ground track that avoids dangers (especially lee shores), adding a margin of safety that is appropriate for the conditions likely to be expected during the voyage.

9.0.6 DISTANCES (M) ACROSS THE IRISH SEA

Ireland \ Scotland England Wales	Port Ellen (Islay)	Campbeltown	Troon	Portpatrick	Mull of Galloway	Kirkcudbright	Maryport	Fleetwood	Pt of Ayre (IOM)	Port St Mary (IOM)	Liverpool	Holyhead	Pwllheli	Fishguard	Milford Haven	Swansea	Portishead	Ilfracombe	Padstow	Longships
Tory Island	75	107	132	119	134	170	185	215	156	167	238	207	260	279	307	360	405	372	372	399
Malin Head	45	76	101	88	103	139	154	184	125	136	207	176	229	248	276	329	374	341	341	368
Lough Foyle	33	61	86	73	88	124	139	169	110	121	192	161	214	233	261	314	359	320	326	353
Portrush	31	50	76	64	80	116	131	161	102	113	184	153	206	225	253	306	351	308	318	345
Carnlough	42	35	57	32	45	81	96	126	67	78	149	115	168	187	215	268	313	265	280	307
Larne	51	39	58	24	37	72	88	118	58	70	141	106	159	178	206	259	304	254	271	298
Belfast Lough	64	48	65	26	34	69	85	115	55	66	138	101	154	173	201	254	299	249	266	293
Bangor	63	48	64	22	30	65	81	111	51	62	134	97	150	169	197	250	295	245	262	289
Strangford Loch	89	72	84	36	30	63	76	97	41	37	107	69	121	141	167	219	264	214	231	258
Carlingford Loch	117	100	112	64	60	90	103	112	70	51	118	67	111	124	149	202	247	197	214	241
Dun Laoghaire	153	136	148	100	93	119	126	120	93	69	119	56	82	94	109	162	207	157	174	201
Wicklow	170	153	165	117	108	133	140	127	108	83	123	56	67	71	90	143	188	138	155	182
Arklow	182	165	177	129	120	144	149	133	117	93	131	64	71	65	79	132	178	128	144	167
Rosslare	215	202	208	161	154	179	180	164	152	125	156	90	83	55	58	109	156	110	119	137
Tuskar Rock	216	203	209	162	155	179	182	165	152	126	152	91	82	48	51	105	149	103	112	130
Dunmore East	250	237	243	196	189	213	216	199	186	160	189	127	116	79	76	130	176	124	127	136
Youghal	281	268	274	227	220	244	247	230	217	191	220	158	147	110	103	156	199	148	139	138
Cork Harbour	300	287	293	246	239	263	266	249	236	210	239	177	166	131	118	170	215	163	151	144
Baltimore	346	333	339	292	285	309	312	295	282	256	285	223	212	172	160	209	253	198	178	161
Fastnet Rock	354	341	347	300	293	317	320	303	290	264	293	231	220	181	169	216	259	207	185	170

9.0.7 DISTANCES (M) ACROSS THE NORTH SEA

UK \ Norway to France	Bergen	Stavanger	Lindesnes	Skagen	Esjberg	Sylt (List)	Brunsbüttel	Helgoland	Bremerhaven	Willhelmshaven	Delfzijl	Den Helder	IJmuiden	Scheveningen	Roompotsluis	Vlissingen	Zeebrugge	Oostende	Nieuwpoort	Dunkerque
Lerwick	210	226	288	403	428	442	517	470	510	500	493	486	497	505	551	550	552	555	562	588
Kirkwall	278	275	323	438	439	452	516	467	507	497	481	460	473	481	515	514	516	519	526	545
Wick	292	283	323	437	428	440	498	449	489	479	458	433	444	451	485	484	486	489	496	514
Inverness	356	339	381	485	461	462	529	479	519	509	487	460	471	478	513	512	514	517	524	542
Fraserburgh	288	266	296	410	383	384	451	404	444	434	412	385	396	403	430	429	431	434	441	456
Aberdeen	308	279	298	411	371	378	433	382	432	412	386	353	363	369	401	400	402	405	412	426
Dundee	362	329	339	451	394	401	448	396	436	426	395	352	359	364	390	389	385	388	395	412
Port Edgar	391	355	362	472	409	413	457	405	445	435	401	355	361	366	391	390	386	389	396	413
Berwick	374	325	320	431	356	361	408	355	395	385	355	310	315	320	342	341	337	340	347	364
Hartlepool	409	353	340	440	340	331	367	312	352	342	302	241	243	247	266	265	261	264	271	288
Grimsby	463	395	362	452	324	318	342	291	332	325	288	187	182	185	199	198	190	191	201	198
Kings Lynn	485	416	379	466	330	333	343	292	344	336	283	184	183	183	197	195	187	188	198	195
Lowestoft	508	431	380	453	308	300	295	262	284	271	218	118	104	98	95	99	87	87	89	106
Harwich	540	461	410	483	330	331	320	287	309	296	243	147	126	114	94	100	84	77	80	80
Brightlingsea	558	479	428	501	348	349	338	305	327	314	261	165	144	105	108	106	92	88	86	87
Burnham/Crouch	567	488	437	510	357	358	347	314	336	323	270	174	151	112	109	115	99	92	93	95
London Bridge	620	543	490	560	400	408	395	361	382	374	320	222	199	149	153	149	134	125	126	114
Sheerness	580	503	450	520	360	367	353	319	340	334	280	180	157	109	113	109	94	85	86	74
Ramsgate	575	498	446	516	368	346	339	305	323	315	262	161	144	121	89	85	77	65	58	42
Dover	588	511	459	529	378	359	352	328	336	328	275	174	155	132	101	92	79	65	58	44

NOTES

This Table applies to Areas 3–7 and 14–17, each of which also contains its own internal Distance Table.

9.0.8 DISTANCES (M) ACROSS THE BAY OF BISCAY

West France \ N & NW Spain	Bayona	Vigo	Sanxenxo	Vilagarcia	Muros	Cabo Finisterre	Camariñas	La Coruña	Ria de Cedeira	Cabo Ortegal	Ria de Vivero	Ria de Ribadeo	Cabo Peñas	Gijon	San Vicente de la B	Santander	Bilbao	Cabo Machichaco	Zumaya	Fuenterrabia
Le Conquet	440	435	432	431	409	387	373	348	323	305	308	306	286	297	300	301	315	308	322	330
Lampaul (Ushant)	436	431	428	427	405	383	369	346	321	303	307	306	290	295	306	310	323	317	331	337
Camaret	444	439	436	435	413	391	377	352	327	309	309	306	287	302	300	304	316	308	322	329
Brest (Moulin B)	450	445	442	441	419	397	383	360	335	317	315	314	294	311	307	310	321	315	329	336
Douarnenez	441	436	433	432	410	388	374	350	325	307	309	307	287	295	300	302	316	308	323	329
Audierne	425	420	417	416	394	372	358	331	306	288	291	289	268	272	279	281	290	284	298	304
Port-la-Forêt	439	434	431	430	408	386	372	340	315	297	298	292	270	272	276	271	278	273	285	290
Lorient entrance	443	438	435	434	412	390	376	345	320	302	304	295	266	268	264	261	264	258	270	274
Belle Ile (Le Palais)	439	434	431	430	408	386	372	341	316	298	296	287	255	258	249	244	246	238	250	254
La Trinité	450	445	442	441	419	397	383	352	327	309	311	300	267	270	260	256	258	249	260	247
Piriac	453	448	445	444	422	400	386	353	328	310	311	301	266	265	255	246	246	239	248	252
Pornichet	455	450	447	446	424	402	388	355	330	312	309	298	262	264	249	242	239	229	242	247
L'Herbaudière	461	456	453	452	430	408	394	363	338	320	293	291	253	264	238	245	236	220	228	233
Sables d'Olonne	451	446	443	442	420	398	384	351	326	308	300	284	243	243	217	209	199	187	195	199
La Rochelle	469	464	461	460	438	416	402	363	338	320	311	293	248	249	216	208	193	179	187	192
Royan/Port-Médoc	460	455	452	451	429	407	493	353	328	310	307	287	237	236	198	191	172	158	166	146
Arcachon	470	465	462	461	439	417	403	337	312	294	289	266	214	207	167	150	115	121	112	90
Capbreton	430	425	422	421	399	377	363	323	298	280	272	245	191	186	131	117	78	59	45	23
Anglet/Bayonne	430	425	422	421	399	377	363	324	299	281	267	242	188	186	126	117	77	54	35	16
Hendaye	423	418	415	414	392	370	356	315	290	272	258	232	179	172	115	105	66	44	23	0·6

NOTES

1. This Table can be read in conjunction with those in West France (9.20.2, 9.21.2, 9.22.2) and North Spain (9.23.2).
2. Yachts leaving Ireland for Longships use 9.0.6, if applicable; then use 9.0.5 for distances across the English Channel.
3. **Landes firing range** in SE Biscay (see 9.22.26 and AC 1104) extends 106M S from Pte de la Négade to Capbreton and up to 45M offshore. Distances are based on routes passing west of Landes range, except that from Royan/Port-Médoc* and Arcachon* the distances to Fuenterrabia and Zumaya are by the inshore route E of the range.

If this route is not available, add 25M to the tabulated distance from Royan/Port-Médoc to Fuenterrabia; add nil for Zumaya. From Arcachon add 44M and 16M to Fuenterrabia and Zumaya respectively, using the 8M wide, safe corridor extending 270°/39M from ATT-ARC buoy through the range. This corridor is also used in calculating distances from Arcachon to all headlands and destinations west of Zumaya.

South West England

Isles of Scilly to Anvil Point

9.1.1 Contents 137
9.1.2 Area map 138
9.1.3 Tidal stream charts 140
9.1.4 Lights, buoys and waypoints 142
9.1.5 Passage information 144
Isles of Scilly, Land's End – 144 • Land's End to Falmouth – 148 • Falmouth to Fowey – 152 • Fowey to Plymouth – 156 • Plymouth to Start Point – 158 • Start Point to Teignmouth – 168 • Lyme Bay – 175 • Crossing the English Channel (western part), Portland Race, Portland Bill to Anvil Point – 179
9.1.6 Isles of Scilly 145
9.1.7 St Mary's (Scilly) 147
9.1.8 Newlyn 147
Mousehole
9.1.9 Penzance 148
St Michael's Mount • Porthleven • Mullion Cove • Cadgwith • Coverack
9.1.10 Helford River 149
9.1.11 Falmouth & River Fal, Standard Port, tide tables/curves 150
Portscatho • Gorran Haven • Portmellon • Polkerris
9.1.12 Mevagissey 156
Dodman Pt gunnery range • Charlestown • Par
9.1.13 Fowey 157
9.1.14 Looe 158
Polperro
9.1.15 Plymouth (Devonport), tide tables/curves 159
9.1.16 Naval exercise areas 165
River Lynher • River Tamar
9.1.17 River Yealm 166
River Erme • River Avon • Hope Cove
9.1.18 Salcombe 167
Kingsbridge
9.1.19 Dartmouth, tide tables/curves 168
Dittisham • Totnes
9.1.20 Brixham 173
Paignton
9.1.21 Torquay 174
9.1.22 Teignmouth 174
9.1.23 River Exe 175
Axmouth • Beer
9.1.24 Lyme Regis 178
9.1.25 West Bay (Bridport) 178
9.1.26 Portland tidal stream chartlets 180
9.1.27 Portland Harbour, tide tables/curves 185
9.1.28 Weymouth 187
9.1.29 Lulworth ranges 188
Church Ope Cove • Ringstead Bay • Durdle Door • Lulworth Cove • Worbarrow Bay • Chapman's Pool

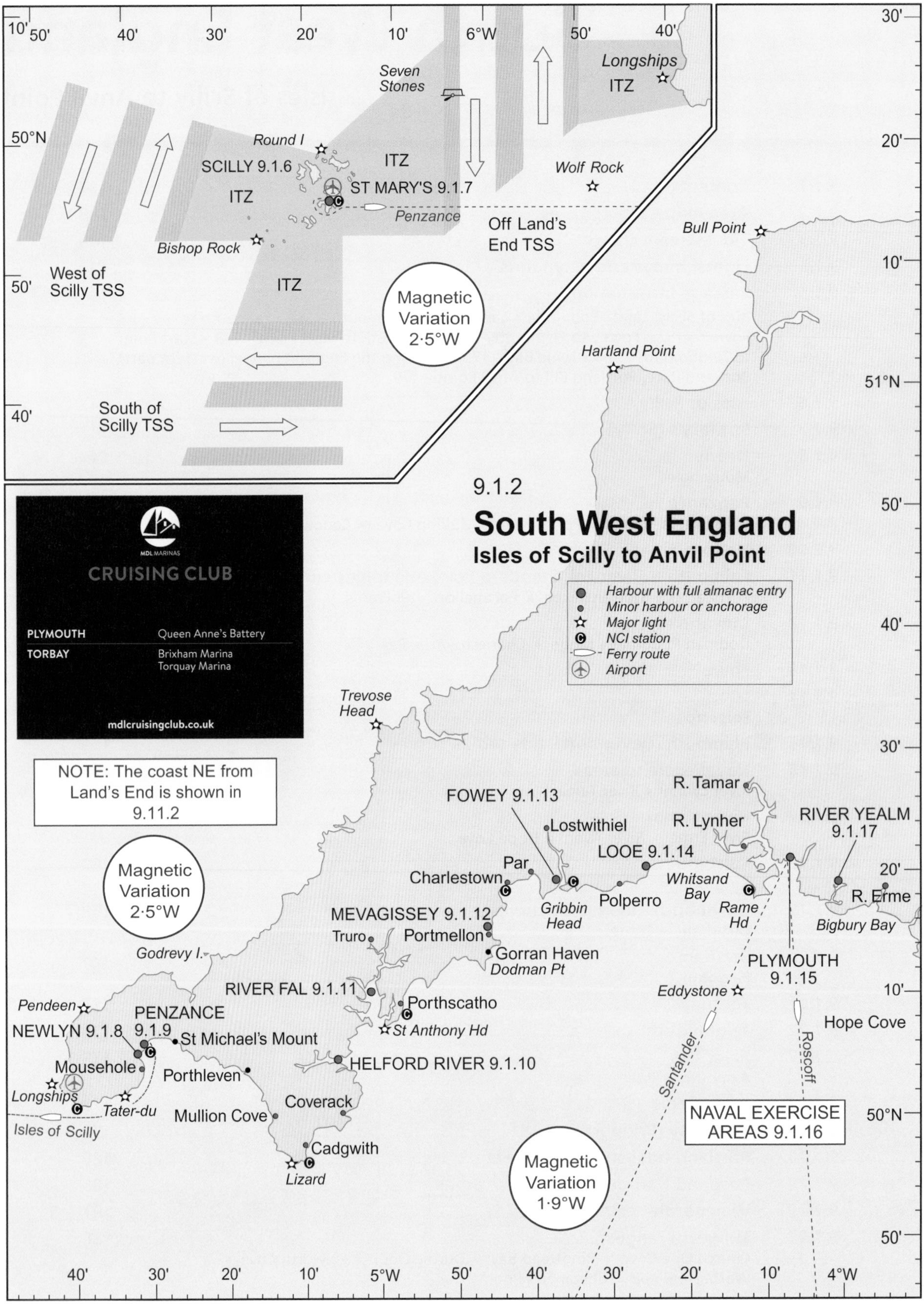
9.1.2
South West England
Isles of Scilly to Anvil Point
Harbour with full almanac entry
Minor harbour or anchorage
Major light
NCI station
Ferry route
Airport
Seven Stones
Longships
ITZ
Round I
SCILLY 9.1.6
ITZ
ST MARY'S 9.1.7
ITZ
Wolf Rock
Penzance
Off Land's End TSS
Bishop Rock
West of Scilly TSS
ITZ
Magnetic Variation 2·5°W
South of Scilly TSS
Bull Point
Hartland Point
MDL MARINAS
CRUISING CLUB
PLYMOUTH Queen Anne's Battery
TORBAY Brixham Marina Torquay Marina
mdlcruisingclub.co.uk
NOTE: The coast NE from Land's End is shown in 9.11.2
Magnetic Variation 2·5°W
Trevose Head
R. Tamar
FOWEY 9.1.13
Lostwithiel
R. Lynher
RIVER YEALM 9.1.17
LOOE 9.1.14
Par
Charlestown
Whitsand Bay
Gribbin Head
Polperro
Rame Hd
R. Erme
Bigbury Bay
MEVAGISSEY 9.1.12
Truro
Portmellon
Gorran Haven
Dodman Pt
PLYMOUTH 9.1.15
Godrevy I.
RIVER FAL 9.1.11
Eddystone
Pendeen
PENZANCE 9.1.9
Porthscatho
St Anthony Hd
Hope Cove
NEWLYN 9.1.8
St Michael's Mount
HELFORD RIVER 9.1.10
Mousehole
Porthleven
Santander
Roscoff
Longships
Tater-du
Coverack
Mullion Cove
NAVAL EXERCISE AREAS 9.1.16
Isles of Scilly
Cadgwith
Lizard
Magnetic Variation 1·9°W
50°N
51°N
6°W
5°W
4°W

DISTANCE TABLE

Approximate distances in nautical miles are by the most direct route while avoiding dangers and allowing for TSS. Places in *italics* are in adjoining areas; places in **bold** are in 9.0.5, Cross-Channel Distances. See also 9.2.2.

1	**Longships**	**1**																						
2	Scilly (Crow Sd)	22	**2**																					
3	**Newlyn**	14	34	**3**																				
4	Penzance	15	35	1	**4**																			
5	Lizard Point	23	42	16	16	**5**																		
6	Helford River	36	57	29	29	13	**6**																	
7	**Falmouth**	39	60	32	32	16	3	**7**																
8	Mevagissey	52	69	46	46	28	19	17	**8**															
9	Fowey	57	76	49	49	34	24	22	7	**9**														
10	Looe	63	80	57	57	39	31	29	16	11	**10**													
11	**Plymouth Bkwtr**	70	92	64	64	49	41	39	25	22	11	**11**												
12	R Yealm (ent)	72	94	66	66	51	43	41	27	24	13	4	**12**											
13	**Salcombe**	81	102	74	74	59	52	50	40	36	29	22	19	**13**										
14	Start Point	86	103	80	80	63	57	55	45	40	33	24	21	7	**14**									
15	Dartmouth	95	116	88	88	72	65	63	54	48	42	35	32	14	9	**15**								
16	Torbay	101	118	96	96	78	72	70	62	55	50	39	36	24	15	11	**16**							
17	Teignmouth	109	126	104	104	86	80	78	70	63	58	47	44	32	23	19	8	**17**						
18	**Exmouth**	113	131	107	107	90	84	82	73	67	61	51	48	33	27	24	12	6	**18**					
19	Lyme Regis	126	144	120	120	104	98	96	86	81	74	63	60	48	41	35	30	25	20	**19**				
20	West Bay	130	148	124	124	108	102	100	90	86	78	67	64	52	45	39	34	30	25	7	**20**			
21	Portland Bill	135	151	128	128	112	106	104	93	89	81	73	70	55	49	45	42	39	36	22	17	**21**		
22	Weymouth	143	159	136	136	120	114	112	111	97	89	81	79	63	57	53	50	47	44	30	25	8	**22**	
23	St Alban's Hd	151	167	144	144	128	122	120	109	105	97	89	86	71	65	61	58	55	52	38	33	16	21	**23**

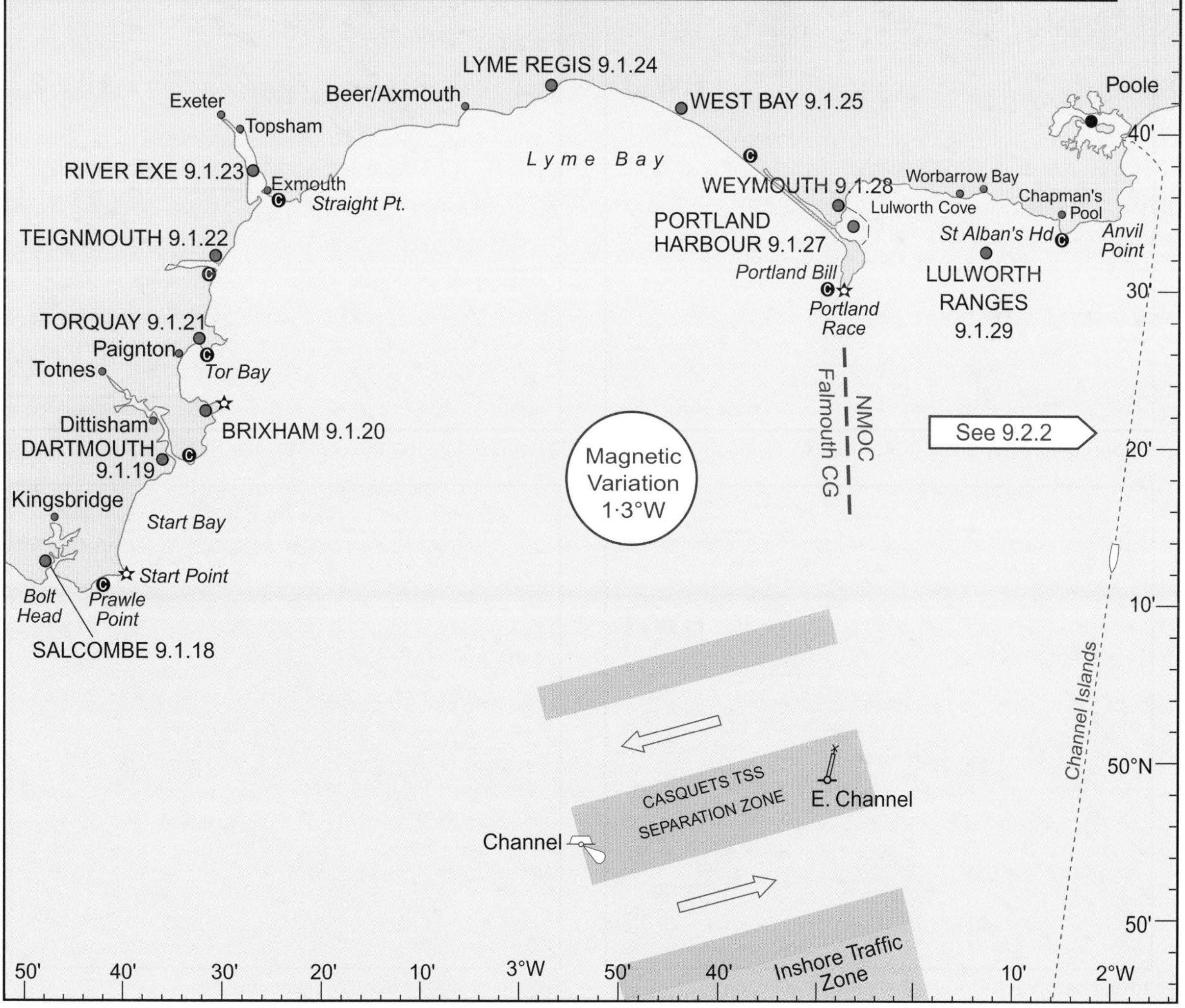
LYME REGIS 9.1.24
Beer/Axmouth
Exeter
Topsham
WEST BAY 9.1.25
Poole
Lyme Bay
RIVER EXE 9.1.23
Exmouth
Straight Pt.
WEYMOUTH 9.1.28
Worbarrow Bay
Lulworth Cove
Chapman's Pool
PORTLAND HARBOUR 9.1.27
St Alban's Hd
Anvil Point
TEIGNMOUTH 9.1.22
Portland Bill
Portland Race
LULWORTH RANGES 9.1.29
TORQUAY 9.1.21
Paignton
Tor Bay
Totnes
Dittisham
BRIXHAM 9.1.20
DARTMOUTH 9.1.19
NMOC Falmouth CG
See 9.2.2
Magnetic Variation 1·3°W
Kingsbridge
Start Bay
Start Point
Bolt Head
Prawle Point
SALCOMBE 9.1.18
Channel Islands
CASQUETS TSS SEPARATION ZONE
E. Channel
Channel
Inshore Traffic Zone
30'
20'
10'
51°N
50'
40'
50°N
50'
40'
30'
20'
10'
3°W
2°W

9.1.3 AREA 1 TIDAL STREAMS

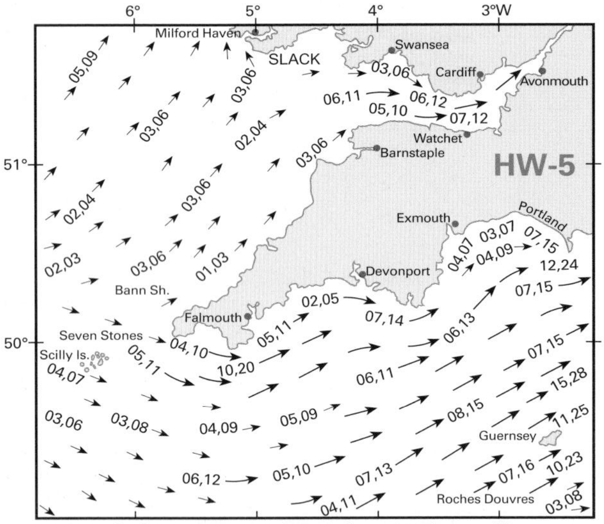

5 Hours before HW Dover (0040 after HW Plymouth)

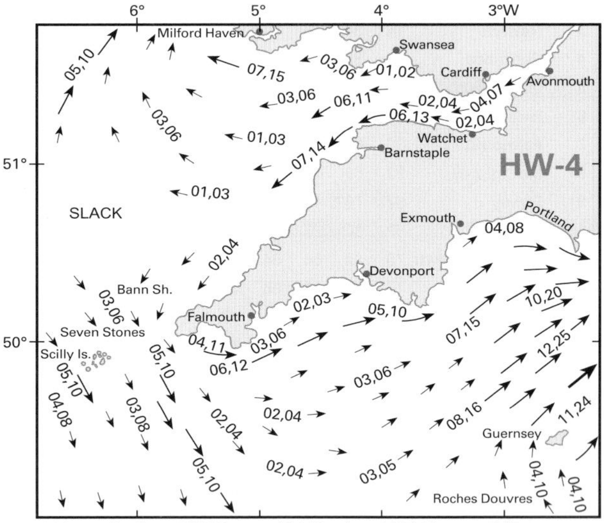

4 Hours before HW Dover (0140 after HW Plymouth)

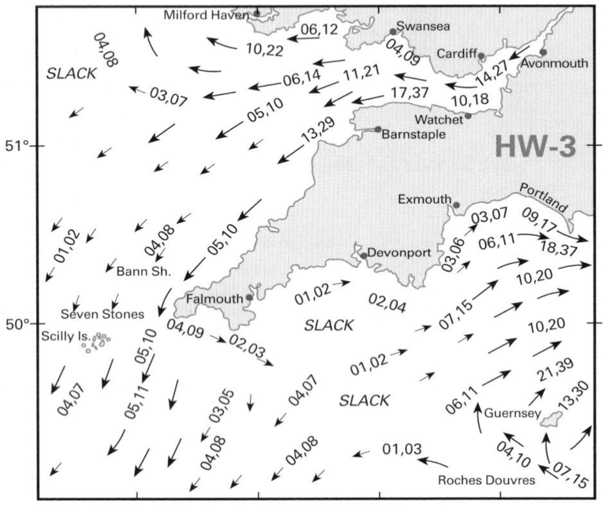

3 Hours before HW Dover (0240 after HW Plymouth)

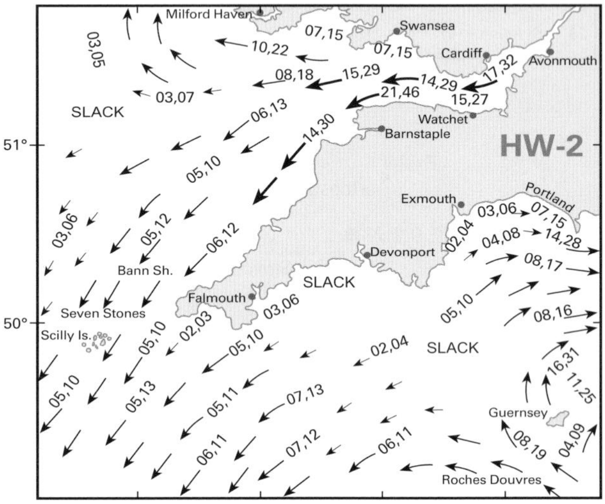

2 Hours before HW Dover (0340 after HW Plymouth)

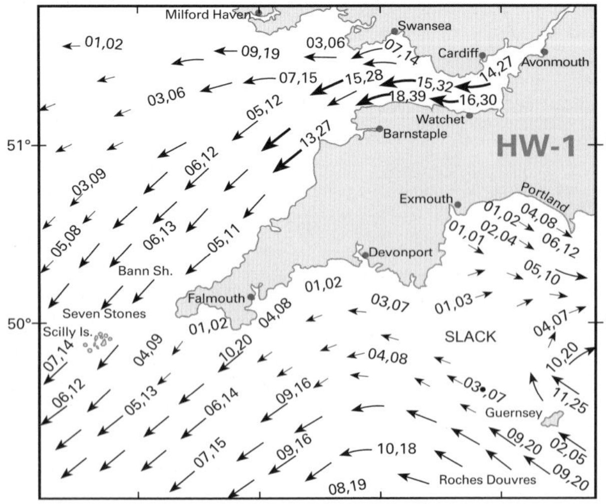

1 Hour before HW Dover (0440 after HW Plymouth)

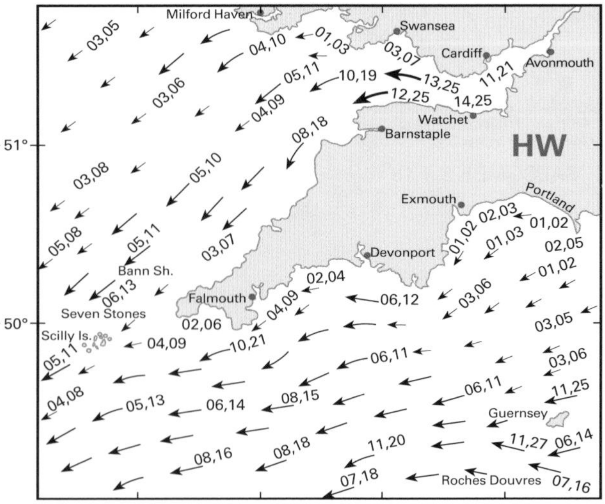

HW Dover (0540 after HW Plymouth)

Eastward 9.2.3 Portland 9.1.26 Isle of Wight 9.2.16 Northward 9.11.3 Southward 9.20.3 Channel Is 9.19.3

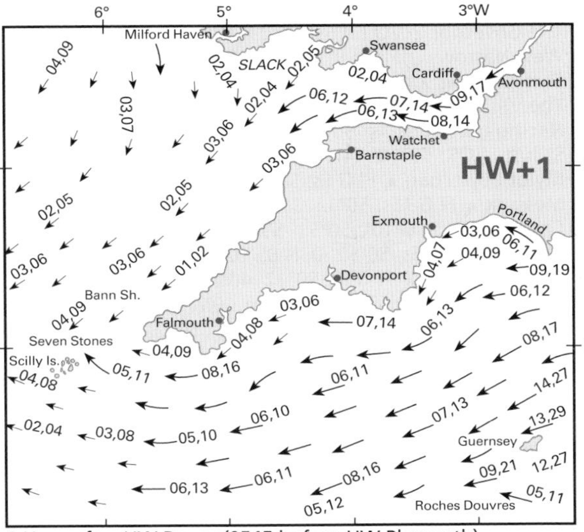

1 Hour after HW Dover (0545 before HW Plymouth)

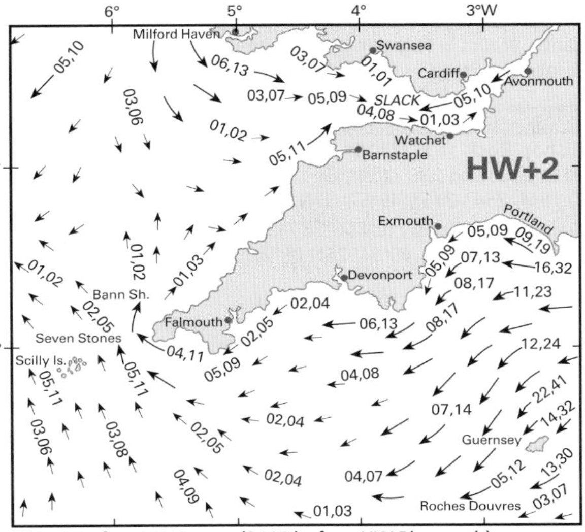

2 Hours after HW Dover (0445 before HW Plymouth)

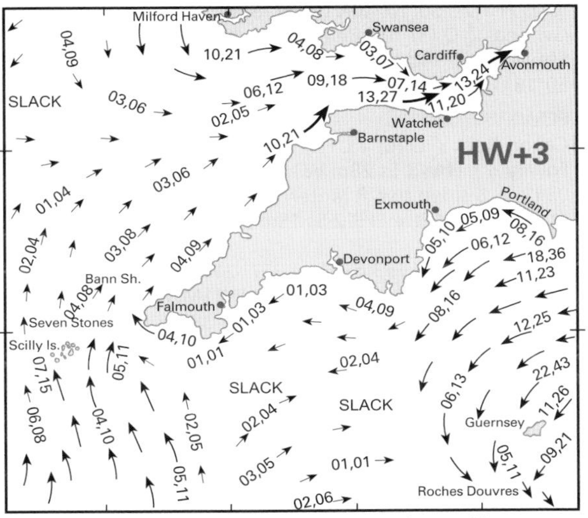

3 Hours after HW Dover (0345 before HW Plymouth)

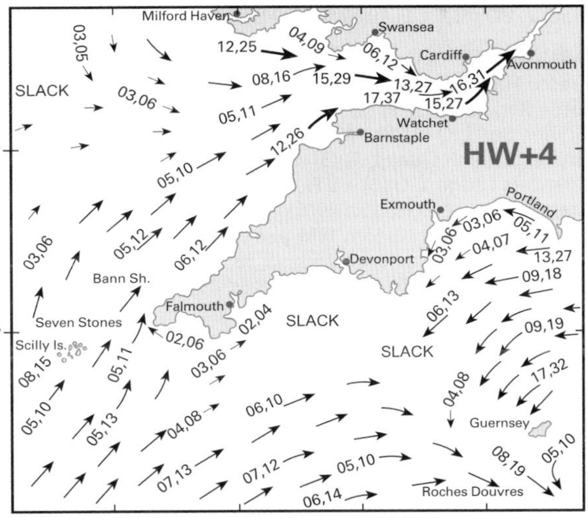

4 Hours after HW Dover (0245 before HW Plymouth)

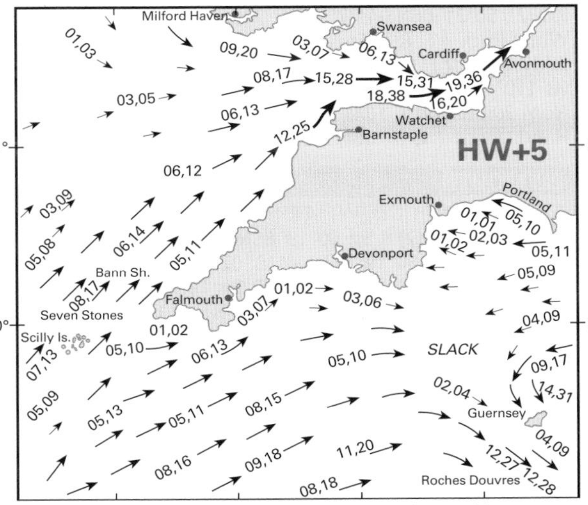

5 Hours after HW Dover (0145 before HW Plymouth)

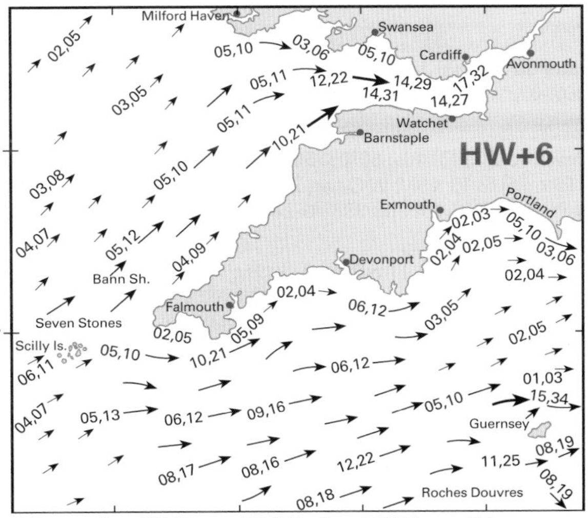

6 Hours after HW Dover (0045 before HW Plymouth)

SW England

9.1.4 LIGHTS, BUOYS AND WAYPOINTS

Bold print = light with a nominal range of 15M or more. CAPITALS = place or feature. *CAPITAL ITALICS* = light-vessel, light float or Lanby. *Italics* = Fog signal. ***Bold italics*** = Racon. Many marks/ buoys are fitted with AIS, MMSI No; see relevant charts.

ISLES OF SCILLY TO LAND'S END

Bishop Rock ☆ Fl (2) 15s 44m **20M**; part obsc 204°-211°, obsc 211°-233° and 236°-259°; Gy ○ twr with helo platform; ***Racon T, 18M, 254°-215°***; 49°52'·37N 06°26'·74W; 992351137.
Round Rk 49°53'·10N 06°25'·19W.
Old Wreck VQ; 49°54'·26N 06°22'·81W.

ST AGNES and ST MARY'S

Peninnis Hd ☆ Fl 20s 36m 9M; 231°-117° but part obsc 048°-083° within 5M; W ○ twr on B frame, B cupola; 49°54'·28N 06°18'·21W.
Gugh Fl (5) Y 20s; 49°53'·52N 06°18'·73W.
Spanish Ledge Q (3) 10s; *Bell;* 49°53'·94N 06°18'·86W.
Woolpack Fl G 5s; 49°54'·40N 06°19'·37W.
Bartholomew Ledges QR 12m; 49°54'·37N 06°19'·89W.
N Bartholomew Fl R 5s; 49°54'·49N 06°19'·99W.
Bacon Ledge Fl (4) R 5s; 49°55'·22N 06°19'·26W.
Ldg lts 097·3°: Front, Iso RW (vert) 2s; W △, 49°55'·12N 06°18'·50W. Rear, Oc WR (vert) 10s; Or X on W bcn.
Crow Rock Fl (2) 10s; 49°56'·26N 06°18'·49W.
Hats VQ (6) + L Fl 10s; 49°56'·21N 06°17'·14W.

AROUND TRESCO, BRYHER and ST MARTIN'S

Tresco Flats, Hulman Fl G 4s, 49°56'·29N 06°20'·30W.
Little Rag Ledge Fl (2) R 5s, 49°56'·44N 06°20'·43W.
Bryher, Bar Q (3) 10s, 49°57'·37N 06°20'·84W.
Bryher, Church Quay Q (3) 10s, 49°57'·18N 06°20'·97W.
Spencers Ledge Q (6) + L Fl 15s; 49°54'·78N 06°22'·06W.
Steeple Rock Q (9) 15s; 49°55'·46N 06°24'·24W.
Round Island ☆ Fl 10s 55m **18M**, also shown in reduced vis; 021°-288°; W ○ twr; *Horn (4) 60s*; 49°58'·74N 06°19'·39W.
St Martin's, Higher Town quay ☆ Fl R 5s, 49°57'·45N 06°16'·84W.

SCILLY to LAND'S END

Seven Stones Lt V Fl (3) 30s 12m **15M**; R hull; *Horn (3) 60s*; ***Racon O, 15M***; 50°03'·63N 06°04'·32W; 992351023.
Wolf Rock ☆ Fl 15s 34m **16M**; H24; *Horn 30s*; ***Racon T, 10M***; 49°56'·72N 05°48'·55W; 992351128.
Longships ☆ Fl (2) WR 10s 35m **W15M**, R11M; 189°-R-327°-W-189°; also shown in reduced vis; Gy ○ twr with helicopter platform; *Horn 10s;* 50°04'·01N 05°44'·81W.
Carn Base Q (9) 15s; 50°01'·48N 05°46'·18W.
Runnel Stone Q (6) + L Fl 15s; *Whis;* 50°01'·18N 05°40'·36W.

LAND'S END TO PLYMOUTH

Tater-du ☆ Fl (3) 15s 34m **20M**; 241°-072°; W ○ twr. FR 31m 13M, 060°-072° over Runnel Stone; 50°03'·14N 05°34'·67W.

NEWLYN

Low Lee Q (3) 10s; 50°05'·56N 05°31'·38W.
S Pier ☆ Fl 5s 10m 9M; W ○ twr; 253°-336°; 50°06'·18N 05°32'·57W.
N Pier ☆ F WG 4m 2M; 238°-G-248°, 50°06'·18N 05°32'·62W.

PENZANCE

S Pier ☆ Fl WR 5s 11m **W17M**, R12M; 159°-R (unintens)-224°-R-268°-W-344·5°-R-shore; 50°07'·06N 05°31'·68W.
Mountamopus Q (6) + L Fl 15s; 50°04'·62N 05°26'·25W.
Lizard ☆ Fl 3s 70m **26M**; 250°-120°, partly visible 235°-250°; W 8-sided twr; *Horn 30s;* 49°57'·61N 05°12'·13W.
Manacle Q (3) 10s; *Bell;* 50°02'·81N 05°01'·91W.

FALMOUTH

St Anthony Head ☆ Iso WR 15s 22m, **W16M**, R14M, H24; 295°-W-004°-R (over Manacles)-022°-W-172°; W 8-sided twr; *Horn 30s;* 50°08'·46N 05°00'·96W.
Black Rock Fl (2) 10s 3M; B IDM bcn twr; 50°08'·72N 05°02'·00W.
Black Rock Fl R 2·5s; 50°08'·68N 05°01'·74W.
Castle Fl G 2·5s; 50°08'·99N 05°01'·62W.
St Mawes Q (6) + L Fl 15s; 50°09'·10N 05°01'·42W.
The Governor VQ (3) 5s; 50°09'·15N 05°02'·40W.
West Narrows Fl (2) R 10s; 50°09'·39N 05°02'·07W.
East Narrows Fl (2) G 10s; 50°09'·43N 05°01'·90W.
The Vilt Fl (4) G 15s; 50°09'·99N 05°02'·28W.
Northbank Fl R 4s; 50°10'·34N 05°02'·26W.
St Just QR; 50°10'·44N 05°01'·72W.
Mylor appr chan Fl G 6s; 50°10'·79N 05°02'·70W. Fl R 5s.
Messack Fl G 15s; 50°11'·31N 05°02'·22W.
Carrick Fl (2) G 10s; 50°11'·59N 05°02'·74W.
Pill Fl (3) G 15s; 50°12'·05N 05°02'·40W.
Turnaware Bar Fl G 5s; 50°12'·40N 05°02'·15W.
Dock Basin Dir ☆ 266°: WRG 2s 15m, 10M; 258°-Iso G-226°-Al WG-264°-Iso W-268°-Al WR-270°-Iso R-274°; 50°09'·38N 05°03'·29W.
N Arm ☆ QR 5m 3M; 50°09'·42N 05°03'·20W.
Inner Hbr Dir ☆ 233°: WRG 3s 5m, 9M; 226°-Iso G-231°-Iso W-236°-Iso R-241°; 50°09'·20N 05°03'·94W.
Falmouth Haven Marina ☆ 2 FR (vert); 50°09'·27N 05°03'·91W.
Falmouth Marina VQ (3) 5s; 50°09'·91N 05°04'·99W.

DODMAN POINT and MEVAGISSEY

Naval gunnery targets SSE of Dodman Point:
'A' Fl Y 10s; 50°08'·53N 04°46'·37W.
'B' Fl Y 5s; 50°10'·30N 04°45'·00W.
'C' Fl Y 2s; 50°10'·40N 04°47'·51W.
Gwineas Q (3) 10s; *Bell;* 50°14'·48N 04°45'·40W.
Mevagissey, Victoria Pier ☆ Fl (2) 10s 9m 12M; *Dia 30s;* 50°16'·15N 04°46'·92W.

FOWEY

Cannis Rock Q (6) + L Fl 15s; *Bell;* 50°18'·45N 04°39'·88W.
Fowey ☆ L Fl WR 5s 28m W11M, R9M; 284°-R-295°-W-028°-R-054°; W 8-sided twr, R lantern; 50°19'·63N 04°38'·83W.
St Catherine's Pt ☆ Fl R 2·5s 15m 2M; vis 150°-295°; 50°19'·69N 04°38'·66W.
Lamp Rock Fl G 5s 3m 2M; vis 357°-214°; 50°19'·70N 04°38'·41W.
Whitehouse Pt ☆ Iso WRG 3s 11m W11M, R/G8M; 017°-G-022°-W-032°-R-037°; R col; 50°19'·98N 04°38'·28W.

POLPERRO, LOOE, EDDYSTONE and WHITSAND BAY

Udder Rock VQ (6) + L Fl 10s; *Bell;* 50°18'·93N 04°33'·85W.
POLPERRO, W pier ☆ FW 4m 4M; FR when hbr closed in bad weather; 50°19'·86N 04°30'·96W.
Spy House Pt ☆ Iso WR 6s 30m 7M; W288°-060°, R060°-288°; 50°19'·81N 04°30'·69W.
LOOE, Ranneys Q (6) + L Fl 15s; 50°19'·85N 04°26'·37W.
Mid Main Q (3) 10s 2M; 50°20'·56N 04°26'·94W.
Banjo Pier ☆ Oc WR 3s 8m **W15M**, R12M; 207°-R267°- W-313°-R-332°; 50°21'·06N 04°27'·06W.
White Rock ☆ Fl R 3s 5m 2M; 50°21'·03N 04°27'·09W.
Eddystone ☆ Fl (2) 10s 41m **17M**. Same twr, Iso R 10s 28m 8M; vis 110°-133° over Hand Deeps; Gy twr, helicopter platform; *Horn 30s;* ***Racon T, 10M***; 50°10'·84N 04°15'·94W; 992351125.
Hand Deeps Q (9) 15s; 50°12'·68N 04°21'·10W.

PLYMOUTH

PLYMOUTH SOUND, WESTERN CHANNEL

Draystone Fl (2) R 5s; 50°18'·85N 04°11'·07W.
Knap Fl G 5s; 50°19'·56N 04°10'·02W.
Plymouth bkwtr W head, ☆ Fl WR 10s 19m W12M, R9M; 262°-W-208°-R-262°; W ○ twr. Same twr, Iso 4s 12m 10M; vis 033°-037°; *Horn 15s;* 50°20'·07N 04°09'·52W.
Maker ☆ Fl (2) WRG 10s 29m, W11M, R/G6M; 270°-G330°-W-004°-R-050°; W twr, R stripe; 50°20'·51N 04°10'·87W.
Queens Ground Fl (2) R 10s; 50°20'·29N 04°10'·08W.
New Ground Fl R 2s; 50°20'·47N 04°09'·43W.
Melampus Fl R 4s; 50°21'·15N 04°08'·72W.

PLYMOUTH SOUND, EASTERN CHANNEL

Wembury Pt ☆ Oc Y 10s 45m; occas; 50°19'·01N 04°06'·63W.

West Tinker VQ (9) 10s; 50°19'·25N 04°08'·64W.
East Tinker Q (3) 10s; 50°19'·20N 04°08'·30W.
Whidbey Oc (2) WRG 10s 29m, W8M, R/G6M, H24; 000°-G-137·5°-W-139·5°-R-159°; Or and W col; 50°19'·53N 04°07'·27W.
The Breakwater, E head L Fl WR 10s 9m W8M, R6M; 190°-R-353°-W-001°-R-018°-W-190°; 50°20'·01N 04°08'·24W.
Staddon Pt Oc WRG 10s 15m W8M, R/G5M; H24. 348°-G-038°-W-050°-R-090°; W structure, R bands; 50°20'·17N 04°07'·54W.
Withyhedge Dir 070° (for W Chan): WRG 13m W13M, R/G5M; H24; 060°-FG-065°-Al WG (W phase increasing with brg) -069°-FW-071°-Al WR (R phase increasing with brg)-075°-F R-080°; W ▽, orange stripe on col. Same col, Fl (2) Bu 5s; vis 120°-160°; 50°20'·75N 04°07'·44W.

SMEATON PASS (W of Mount Batten and S of The Hoe)

Ldg lts 349°. Front, Mallard Shoal Q WRG 5m W10M, R/G3M; W △, Or bands; 233°-G-043°- R-067°- G-087°-W-099°-R-108° (ldg sector); 50°21'·60N 04°08'·33W. Rear, 396m from front, Hoe Oc G 1·3s 11m 3M, 310°-040°; W ▽, Or bands; 50°21'·81N 04°08'·39W.
S Mallard VQ (6) + L Fl 10s; 50°21'·51N 04°08'·30W.
W Mallard QG; 50°21'·57N 04°08'·36W.
S Winter Q (6) + L Fl 15s; 50°21'·40N 04°08'·55W.
NE Winter QR; 50°21'·54N 04°08'·50W.
NW Winter VQ (9) 10s; 50°21'·55N 04°08'·70W.

ENTRANCE TO THE CATTEWATER

QAB (Queen Anne's Battery) ldg lts 048·5°. Front, FR; Or/W bcn; 50°21'·84N 04°07'·84W. Rear, Oc R 8s 14m 3M; 139m NE.
Fishers Nose Fl (3) R 10s 6m 4M; 50°21'·80N 04°08'·01W. Also F Bu ≠ 026·5° with F Bu 50°22'·00N 04°07'·86W, for Cobbler Chan.

DRAKE CHANNEL, THE BRIDGE and THE NARROWS

Ravenness Dir 225°: WRG 11m, W13M, R/G5M; H24. 217°-FG-221°-Al WG-224° (W phase increasing with brg)-FW-226°-Al WR-229° (R phase increasing with bearing)-FR-237°; W ▽, orange stripe on col. In fog, 160°-FW-305°; power failure QY; 50°21'·14N 04°10'·07W.
Asia Fl (2) R 5s; 50°21'·47N 04°08'·85W.
St Nicholas QR; 50°21'·55N 04°09'·20W.
N Drakes Is Fl R 4s; 50°21'·52N 04°09'·38W.
E Vanguard QG; 50°21'·47N 04°09'·70W.
W Vanguard Fl G 3s; 50°21'·49N 04°09'·98W.
Devils Point QG 5m 3M; Fl 5s in fog; 50°21'·59N 04°10'·04W.
Battery Fl R 2s; 50°21'·52N 04°10'·21W.

The Bridge Channel

No 1, QG 4m; 50°21'·03N 04°09'·53W. No 2, QR 4m. No 3, Fl (3) G 10s 4m. No 4, Fl (4) R 10s 4m; 50°21'·09N 04°09'·63W.
Mount Wise, Dir 343°: WRG 7m, W13M, R/G5M; H24. 331°-FG-338°-Al WG-342° (W phase increasing with brg)-FW-344°-Al WR-348° (R phase increasing with bearing)-FR-351°. In fog, 341·5°-FW-344·5°; 50°21'·96N 04°10'·33W.
Ocean Court Dir Q WRG 15m, W11M, R/G3M; 010°-G-080°-W-090°-R-100°; 50°21'·85N 04°10'·11W.

PLYMOUTH TO START POINT

RIVER YEALM Sand bar Fl R 5s; 50°18'·59N 04°04'·12W.

SALCOMBE

Sandhill Pt Dir 000°: Fl WRG 2s 27m W/R/G 8M; 337·5°-G-357·5°-W-002·5°-R-012·5°; R/W on W mast, rear daymark; 50°13'·77N 03°46'·67W. Front daymark, Pound Stone R/W.
Bass Rk Fl R 5s; 50°13'·47N 03°46'·71W.
Wolf Rk Fl G 5s; 50°13'·53N 03°46'·58W.
Blackstone Rk; 50°13'·61N 03°46'·51W.
Ldg lts 042·5°, front Fl 2s 5m 8M, 50°14'·53N 03°45'·31W; rear Fl 5s 45m 8M.
Start Pt ☆ Fl (3) 10s 62m **25M**; 184°-068°. Same twr: FR 55m 9M; 210°-255° over Skerries Bank; *Horn 60s;* 50°13'·34N 03°38'·54W.

START POINT TO PORTLAND BILL

DARTMOUTH

Kingswear Dir 328°: Iso WRG 3s 9m 8M; 318°-G-325°-W-331°-R-340°; W ○ twr; 50°20'·82N 03°34'·09W.
Mewstone VQ (6) + L Fl 10s; 50°19'·92N 03°31'·89W.
West Rock Q (6) + L Fl 15s; 50°19'·86N 03°32'·47W.
Homestone QR; 50°19'·61N 03°33'·55W.
Castle Ledge Fl G 5s; 50°19'·99N 03°33'·11W.
Checkstone Fl (2) R 5s; 50°20'·45N 03°33'·81W.
Dir 104·5°: FW 5m 9M; vis 102°-107°; 50°20'·65N 03°33'·80W.

BRIXHAM

Berry Head ☆ Fl (2) 15s 58m **19M**; vis 100°-023°; W twr; 50°23'·98N 03°29'·01W. R lts on radio mast 5·7M NW, inland of Paignton.
Victoria bkwtr Oc R 15s 9m 6M; W twr; 50°24'·33N 03°30'·78W.
No 1 Fl G; 50°24'·30N 03°30'·89W.
No 2 Fl R; 50°24'·32N 03°30'·83W.

PAIGNTON and TORQUAY

QG (May-Sep); 50°27'·42N 03°31'·80W, 85m off Haldon Pier.
Haldon Pier (E) QG 9m 6M; 50°27'·43N 03°31'·73W.
Princess Pier (W) QR 9m 6M; 50°27'·46N 03°31'·73W.

TEIGNMOUTH

Outfall Fl Y 5s; 50°31'·97N 03°27'·77W, 288°/1·3M to hbr ent.
Bar Fl G 2s; 50°32'·44N 03°29'·25W.
Trng wall, middle Oc R 6s 4m 3M; 50°32'·33N 03°29'·93W.
The Point Oc G 6s 3M & FG (vert); 50°32'·42N 03°30'·05W.

RIVER EXE to SIDMOUTH and AXMOUTH

Exe Mo(A) 10s; 50°35'·86N 03°23'·79W.
No 1 50°36'·05N 03°23'·84W.
No 2 50°36'·02N 03°23'·94W.
Exmouth Dir 305°: WRG 6m, 6M; 299°-Iso G-304°-Iso W-306°-Iso R-311°; W col, 50°36'·99N 03°25'·34W.
No 10 Fl R 3s; 50°36'·73N 03°24'·77W.
No 12 Warren Pt 50°36'·91N 03°25'·41W.
Sidmouth Fl R 5s 5m 2M; 50°40'·48'N 03°14'·43W.
Axmouth jetty Fl G 4s 7m 2M; 50°42'·12N 03°03'·29W.

LYME REGIS

Outfall Q (6) + L Fl 15s; 50°43'·17N 02°55'·66W.
Ldg lts 284°: Front, Victoria Pier Oc WR 8s 6m, W9M, R7M; 284°-R-104°-W-284°; Bu col; 50°43'·19N 02°56'·17W. Rear, FG 8m 9M.

WEST BAY (BRIDPORT)

W pier root, Dir 336°: F WRG 5m 4M; 165°-G-331°-W-341°-R-165°; 50°42'·62N 02°45'·89W.
W pier outer limit Iso R 2s 5m 4M; 50°42'·51N 02°45'·83W.
E pier outer limit Iso G 2s 5m 4M; 50°42'·53N 02°45'·80W.

PORTLAND BILL TO ANVIL POINT

Portland Bill lt ho ☆ Fl (4) 20s 43m **25M**. vis 221°-244° (gradual change from 1 Fl to 4 Fl); 244°-117° (shows 4 Fl); 117°-141° (gradual change from 4 Fl to 1 Fl). W ○ twr; *Dia 30s;* 50°30'·85N 02°27'·39W. Same twr, FR 19m 13M; 265°-291° over Shambles.
W Shambles Q (9) 15s; *Bell;* 50°29'·78N 02°24'·41W.
E Shambles Q (3) 10s; *Bell;* 50°31'·26N 02°20'·08W.

PORTLAND HARBOUR

Outer Bkwtr Fort Head (N end) QR 14m 5M; 013°-268°; 50°35'·11N 02°24'·87W.
NE Bkwtr (A Hd) Fl 2·5s 22m 10M; 50°35'·16N 02°25'·07W.
NE Bkwtr (B Hd) Oc R 15s 11m 5M; 50°35'·65N 02°25'·88W.
N Arm (C Hd) Oc G 10s 11m 5M; 50°35'·78N 02°25'·95W.

WEYMOUTH

Ldg lts 239·6°: both FR 5/7m 7M; Front 50°36'·46N 02°26'·87W, S Pier hd Q 10m 9M; 50°36'·58N 02°26'·49W. IPTS 190m SW.

LULWORTH RANGE TO ANVIL POINT

Targets:	DZ 'A', Fl Y 2s,	50°33'·34N 02°06'·52W.
off	DZ 'B', Fl Y 10s,	50°32'·11N 02°05'·92W.
St Alban's Hd	DZ 'C', Fl Y 5s,	50°32'·76N 02°04'·56W.

Anvil Pt Fl 10s 45m 9M; vis 237°-076° (H24); W ○ twr and dwelling; 50°35'·51N 01°57'·60W. Measured mile close west.

9.1.5 PASSAGE INFORMATION

More passage information is threaded between the harbours in this area. Notes for crossing the western English Channel are after 9.1.25; see 9.0.5 for distances. Admiralty Leisure Folios: 5602 Falmouth to Teignmouth, 5603 Falmouth to Hartland Point, includes the Isles of Scilly. **Bibliography**: *West Country Cruising Companion* (Fernhurst/Fishwick); *Channel Havens* (ACN/Endean); *Shell Channel Pilot* (Imray/Cunliffe); *Channel Pilot* (Admiralty NP27).

ISLES OF SCILLY TO LAND'S END

The 48 islands lie 21-31M WSW of Land's End, with many rocky outcrops and offlying dangers; see AC 34, 883. Care is needed particularly in poor visibility. No one ⚓ gives shelter from all winds and swell, so be ready to move at short notice. Follow the approach transits on AC 34 because the tidal streams are difficult to predict with accuracy. They run harder off Points and over rocks, where overfalls may occur.

The N/S lanes of the Land's End TSS (AC 1148) are roughly defined by Seven Stones rocks to the west and Wolf Rock to the south east. The **Seven Stones** (lt ship, fog sig, Racon, AIS) lie 16M W of Land's End; many of them dry, with ledges in between. **Wolf Rock** (lt ho, fog sig, Racon, AIS) 8M SSW of Land's End, is in contrast steep-to. Beware commercial vessels turning N near Wolf Rock to enter the N-bound lane of the TSS; and those leaving the S-bound lane.

►*Between Scilly and Land's End (AC 1148) streams are rotatory, clockwise, setting W from HW Dover; N from HW + 2; NE from HW + 4; E from HW –6; SSE from HW – 4; and SW from HW – 2. Sp rates are about 1kn. From Mounts Bay to Scilly leave the Runnel Stone at HW Dover –2; a fair W-going tide lasts for only 3 hrs, with cross tides setting SW then NW to N. Consider arriving at dawn. For the return passage streams are a little less critical.*◄

LAND'S END

The peninsula (AC 1148, 1149, 777 and 2345) is always a critical tidal gate and often a dangerous lee shore. There are many inshore and offlying rocks but no ports of refuge. The main features are: Gwennap Head, with Runnel Stone buoy 1M to the S; Land's End and Longships reef 1M to the W; Cape Cornwall and The Brisons; Pendeen and The Wra. Further E see Area 11.

Passage between **Gwennap Head** and the Runnel Stone (0·5m; 7ca S) is not advised even in calm weather at HW, owing to rocks and uncharted wrecks closer inshore. These dangers are in the R sectors of Longships and Tater-du lts. From Gwennap Hd to Land's End, 2M NW, rocks extend up to 1½ca offshore, and depths are irregular causing a rough seas in strong winds against the tide.

4 cables S of Land's End Armed Knight, a jagged 27m high rock, overlooks **Longships**. This is an extensive and very dangerous reef made up of Carn Bras, on which the lt ho stands, and other rky islets. About 5ca to the E and NE are Kettle's Bottom 5m and Shark's Fin 0·9m, both isolated and very dangerous drying rocks. The ½M wide passage between Land's End and Kettle's Bottom is safe in calm, settled weather, but never at night. To clear Kettle's Bottom and Shark's Fin, keep the Brisons High summit just open W of Low summit brg 001°. In adverse weather navigate in the 3M wide ITZ, well W of Longships.

►*Local streams exceed 4kn at Sp and are unpredictable.*◄

1M NNE of Land's End, after rounding Cowloe Rks and Little Bo 3·4m and Bo Cowloe 6m, the transit 150° of two bns on the cliffs E of Sennen Cove leads to an ⚓ in about 2m on the S side of **Whitesand Bay**, only safe in fair weather and offshore winds; avoid all underwater cables. Sennen ✠ twr (110m) is conspic, almost on the 150° transit.

Cape Cornwall (conspic ruined chy) is about 3M further N. It overlooks The Brisons, two rocky islets (27 and 22m, High and Low summits) about 5ca to SW. There is no safe passage inside The Brisons. The Vyneck rock 1·8m is 3 cables to the NW.

3M NNE is **Pendeen Head** (lt ho) with the Wra (Three Stone Oar), drying rocks, close N. Overfalls and a race extend up to 1½M W and SW of Pendeen; avoid except in calm weather and at slack water. A conspic TV mast is 1.5M S of Pendeen.

TIDAL STRATEGY FOR ROUNDING LAND'S END

The tidal stream chartlets and notes below are reproduced by kind permission of the Royal Cruising Club Pilotage Foundation, *Yachting Monthly* magazine in which they were first published and the author Hugh Davies.

►*The chartlets referenced to HW Dover, illustrate tidal streams and inshore currents. Streams run hard around Land's End, setting N/S and E/W past it. It is truly a tidal gate, and one which favours a N-bound passage – with careful timing nearly 9½ hrs of fair tide can be carried, from HWD –3 to HWD +5. Use currents close inshore running counter to the tidal streams.*

Example N-bound: At HWD+1 the N-going flood starts off Gwennap and does not turn NE along the N Cornish coast until HWD+3, but as early as HWD–3 an inshore current is beginning to run N'ly. So, N-bound, use this by arriving off Runnel Stone at HWD–2 and then keep within ¼M of the shore. If abeam Brisons at HWD, the tide and current should serve for the next 6 or 7 hrs to make good St Ives, or even Newquay and Padstow.

Example S-bound: If S-bound from St Ives to Newlyn, aim to reach the Runnel Stone by HWD+5, ie with 2 hrs of E-going tide in hand for the remaining 9M to Newlyn. This would entail leaving St Ives 5 hrs earlier, at HWD, to make the 20M passage; buck a foul tide for the first 3 hrs but use an inshore S-going current, keeping as close inshore as prudent, but having to move offshore to clear the Wra and the Brisons. This timing would suit passages from S Wales and the Bristol Channel, going inshore of Longships if the weather suits.

From Ireland, ie Cork or further W, the inshore passage would not benefit. But plan to be off the Runnel Stone at HWD+5 if bound for Newlyn; or at HWD+3 if bound for Helford/Falmouth, with the W-going stream slackening and 5 hrs of fair tide to cover the remaining 20M past the Lizard.◄

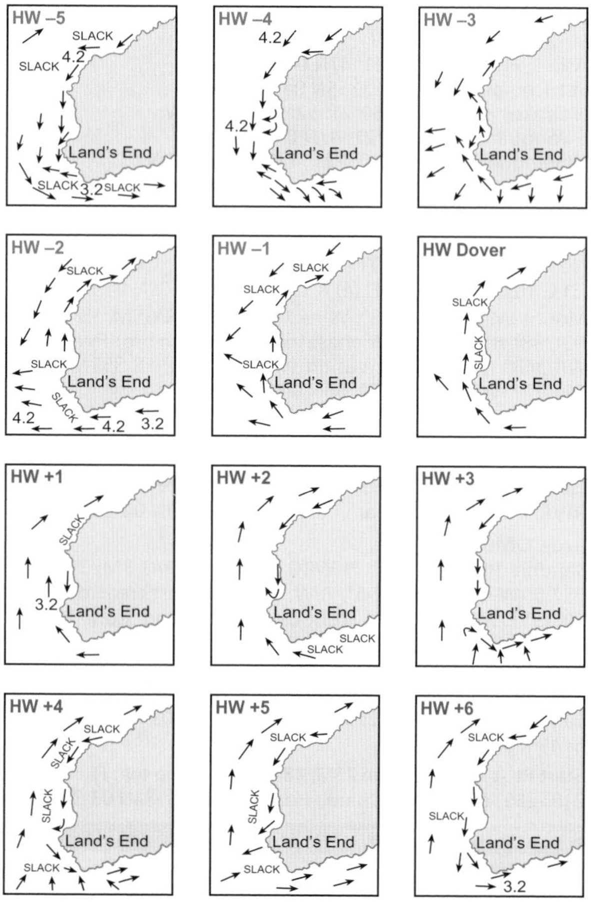

9.1.6 ISLES OF SCILLY

The Isles of Scilly consist of 48 islands and numerous rocky outcrops, covering an area approx 10M by 7M and lying 21–31M WSW of Land's End. Only St Mary's, St Martin's, Tresco, Bryher, St Agnes and Gugh are inhabited. The islands belong to the Duchy of Cornwall. There is a LB and CG Sector Base at St Mary's.

CHARTS AC 1148, 34, 883, 5603; Imray C10, C7, 2400

TIDES Standard Port is Plymouth. Differences for St Mary's are given in 9.1.7.

▶*Tidal heights, times, and streams are irregular. See the 12-hourly tidal stream chartlets below and AC 34 for 5 tidal stream diamonds, all referred to HW Plymouth.*◀

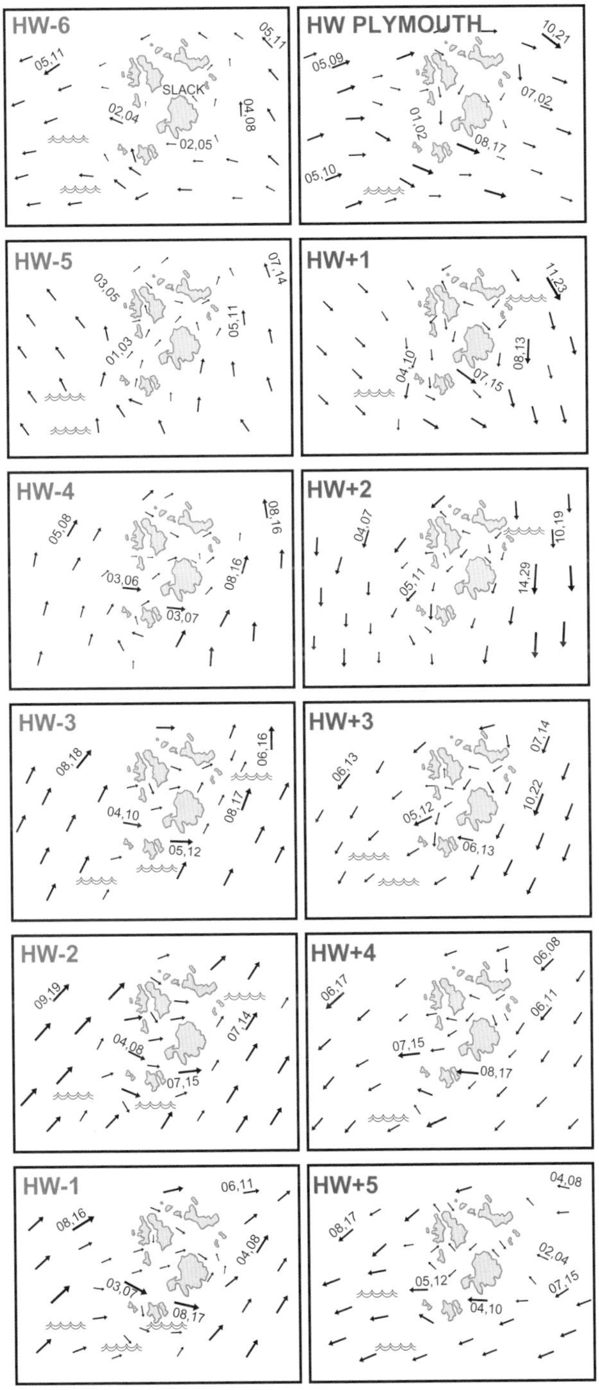

SHELTER The Isles of Scilly are exposed to Atlantic swell and wind. Weather can be unpredictable and fast-changing. Thorough planning and sensible precautions especially with regard to ⚓ and ground tackle are recommended. Boats have been known to drag on fine sand, but holding is mostly good. The islands are most attractive. Listed below are some of the many ⚓s, anti-clockwise:

ST MARY'S Hugh Town Harbour.
Porth Cressa (S of Hugh Town). Beware of dangers on each side of entrance and submarine cables. Good ⚓ (2m) in W/NW'lies, but exposed to swell from SE to SW. 14 🅾s £20/night www.porthcressamoorings.co.uk see 9.1.7 on p. 147.
Watermill Cove (NE corner of St Mary's). Excellent shelter in winds S to NW. ⚓ in approx 5m.

ST MARTIN'S, W end. Tean Sound needs careful pilotage, but attractive ⚓ in settled weather. More suitable for shoal draught boats which can ⚓ or take the ground out of main tidal stream in channel. 4 🅾s £20/night (Star Castle Hotel ☎07730 475559). Hotel re-opened as Karma St Martin's ☎422368.

ST HELEN'S POOL (S of St Helen's Is). Ent via St Helen's Gap to ⚓ in 1·5m–7m. Secure, but may be swell near HW; see chartlet.

OLD GRIMSBY SOUND. Old Grimsby Hbr comprises Green Porth & Raven's Porth, divided by a quay, both dry 2·3m. Beware cable in Green Porth. ⚓s 1½ca NE of quay in 2·5m; access more difficult than New Grimsby. Sheltered in SW'lies but open to swell if wind veers N of W. Facilities: 7 🅾s (R or Y) £20<18m>£30, (quay) hotel.

NEW GRIMSBY SOUND Appr (line G) between Tresco and Bryher, or with adequate rise of tide from the S across Tresco Flats. Good shelter except in NW'lies. Popular ⚓ between Hangman Is and the quay in 1·5-4·5m. Beware cables. 22 🅾s, R or Y, £20<18m>£30; ⚓ £5. Vessels may only beach with Tresco HM permission. ☎423653 mob 07778601237. VHF Ch 08 for ✕ ⛽ ✉. Ferry to St Mary's.

ST AGNES/GUGH The Cove, well sheltered from W and N winds, except when the sandbar between the islands covers near HWS with a strong NW wind. Beware cables.
Porth Conger, N of the sandbar, sheltered in S'lies except when the bar is covered. Facilities: (two quays), ferry to St Mary's; in Middle Town (¾M), ✉ ✕.

NAVIGATION See 9.1.2 for TSS to the E, S and W. If unable to identify approach ldg lines/marks, approach with caution. Many chans between islands have dangerous shallows, often with rky ledges. Some of the most used ldg lines, as on chartlet, include:

Line A. ⊕ 49°53′·55N 06°18′·00W. *North Carn of Mincarlo ≠ W extremity of Great Minalto 307·1°*. This is the usual approach to St Mary's Road, via St Mary's Sound. From the E or SE avoid Gilstone Rk (dries 4m) 3ca E of Peninnis Hd. Spanish Ledges, off Gugh, are marked by an ECM buoy; thence past Woolpack SCM bn, Bartholomew Ledges lt bn and N Bartholomew PHM buoy Fl R 5s to ent St Mary's Road on 040·5° (see Line B).

Line B. ⊕ 49°54′·69N 06°20′·33W. *St Martin's daymark ≠ the top of Creeb 040·5°*. This clears Woodcock Ledge, breaks in bad weather.

Line C. ⊕ 49°52′·06N 06°21′·24W. *Summit of Castle Bryher ≠ gap between the summits of Great Smith 350·5°*. Via Smith Sound, between the drying rocks off St Agnes and Annet.

Line D. ⊕ 49°52′·40N 06°27′·80W. *Summit of Great Ganilly just open north of Bant's Carn 059°*. From the SW enter Broad Sound between Bishop Rk lt ho and Flemming's Ledge, 7ca to the N; pass between Round Rk NCM and Gunner SCM buoys to Old Wreck NCM By; beware Jeffrey Rk, close to port. Ldg marks are more than 7M off and at first not easy to see. See also Line C, Smith Sound.

Line E. ⊕ 49°54′·34N 06°27′·80W. *St Agnes Old lt ho ≠ Carn Irish 099·7°*. From WNW, passing close N of Crim Rocks and Gunners.

Line F. ⊕ 49°56′·34N 06°26′·46W. *St Agnes Old lt ho ≠ Tins Walbert bcn 127°*. The NW Passage is about 7ca wide with good ldg marks, but beware cross tide. A lit WCM marks Steeple Rk (0·1m). Intercept Line D for St Mary's Road.

Line G. ⊕ 49°59′·00N 06°21′·96W. *Star Castle Hotel ≠ W side of Hangman Is 157°*. From the N, leads into New Grimsby Sound between Bryher and Tresco. Crossing Tresco Flats need adequate rise of tide (plan for max drying ht of 1·7m) and moderate vis.

Line H. ⊕ 49°55′·66N 06°14′·38W. *Summit of Samson Hill ≠ the NE extremity of Innisidgen 284·5°*. From the E or NE: Crow Snd can be rough in strong SE'lies, but, with sufficient rise of tide, is not difficult. From the NE pass close to Menawethan and Biggal Rk, avoiding Trinity Rk and the Ridge, which break in bad weather. Hats SCM buoy marks a shoal with an old boiler, ($\underline{0}$·6m) on it. Maintain 284·5° between Bar Pt and Crow Bar ($\underline{0}$·7m), pass N of Crow Rk IDM lt bn (for best water), then turn SSW for St Mary's.

Historic Wrecks are at 49°52'·2N 06°26'·5W Tearing Ledge, 2ca SE of Bishop Rk Lt; and at 49°54'·30N 06°19'·89W, Bartholomew Ledges, 5ca N of Gugh.

LIGHTS AND MARKS See 9.1.4 for lts, including Seven Stones lt float, Wolf Rock lt ho and Longships lt ho. A working knowledge of the following daymarks and conspic features will greatly aid pilotage (from NE to SW):

St Martin's E end: Conical bcn twr (56m) with RW bands.

Round Is: roughly conical shaped, with W lt ho 19/55m high.

Tresco: Abbey & FS, best seen from S. Cromwell's Castle and Hangman Is from the NW.

Bryher: Watch Hill, stone bn (43m); rounded Samson Hill.

St Mary's: TV & radio masts (R lts) at N end, are visible from all over Scilly. Crow Rk IDM bn, 11m on rk drying $\underline{4}$·6m, at N.

St Agnes: Old lt ho, ○ W tr, visible from all directions.

Bishop Rk lt ho: Grey ○ tr, 44m; helo pad above lamp.

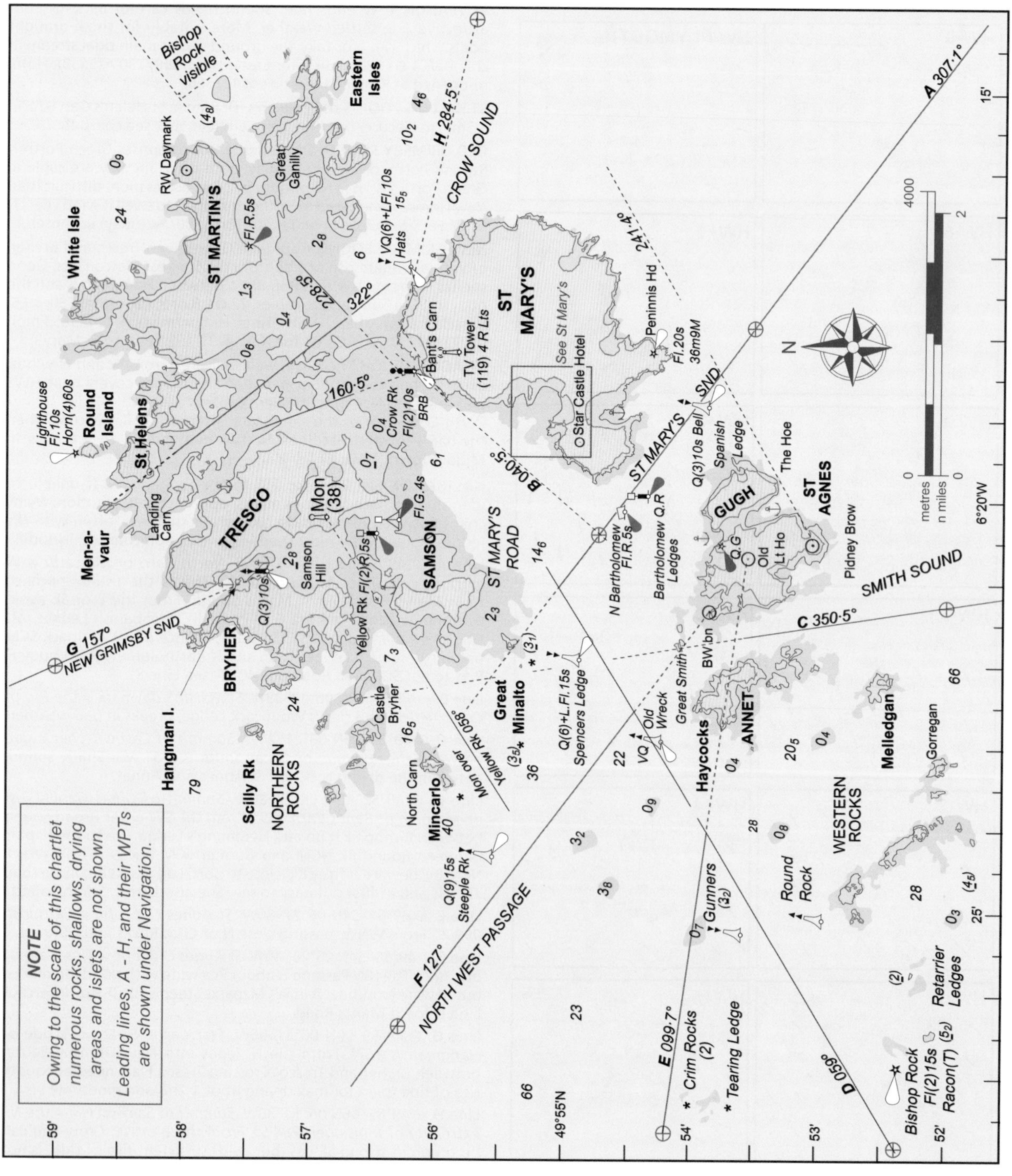

9.1.7 ST MARY'S

Isles of Scilly **49°55'·14N 06°18'·71W** ❁❁❁◊◊◊✿✿✿

CHARTS AC 2665, 34, 883, 5603; Imray C10, C7, 2400

TIDES –0630 Dover; ML 3·2; Duration 0600

Standard Port PLYMOUTH (⟶)

Times				Height (metres)			
High Water		Low Water		MHWS	MHWN	MLWN	MLWS
0000	0600	0000	0600	5·5	4·4	2·2	0·8
1200	1800	1200	1800				
Differences ST MARY'S							
–0052	–0103	–0048	–0045	+0·2	–0·1	–0·2	–0·1

SHELTER Good in St Mary's Hbr, except in W/NW gales when 14 Y ⚓s or ⚓ in Porth Cressa may be more comfortable. Strictly no ⚓ in the approaches and harbour limits (Newman rock to Newford Is).

NAVIGATION WPT 49°53'·96N 06°18'·83W (abeam Spanish Ledge ECM lt buoy) 307°/1·2M via St Mary's Sound to transit line B (040°). The 097·3° transit leads S of Bacon Ledge (0·3m) marked by PHM lt buoy. A charted 151° transit leads into the Pool between Bacon Ledge and the Cow and Calf (drying 0·6m and 1·8m). Pilotage is compulsory for yachts >30m LOA. Hbr speed limit 3kn. NB: Do not impede the ferry *Scillonian III* which arrives about 1200 and sails at 1630 Mon-Fri; Sat times vary with month. Also the blue-hulled cargo ship *Gry Maritha* thrice weekly.

LIGHTS AND MARKS See chartlet and 9.1.4. 097·3° ldg marks: W bcns; front, white △; rear, orange x; lts as chartlet. The pierhead light has been removed and is awaiting replacement. Buzza Hill twr and power stn chy (48m) are conspic.

COMMUNICATIONS (Code 01720) CGOC (01326) 317575; Ⓗ 422392; Dr 422628; Police 101; Tourist Info 422536. Pilot 422078. HM 422768(H24 ansafone); emergency out of hrs 07789 273626.

St Mary's Hbr and Pilot Ch **14**, 16 (0800-1700LT). *Falmouth CG* covers Scilly and the TSS/ITZ off Land's End on Ch 16, 23.

FACILITIES hm@stmarys-harbour.co.uk www.stmarys-harbour.co.uk 38 Y ⚓s lie in 6 trots close E of the ♦ in 1·5-2·7m; 28 ⚓s are for <12m LOA and 10 for <18m. Fees by LOA: £18<8m<£24·00<12m>£36; multihulls +50%. 3 drying ⊆ against hbr wall with tender landing pontoon; ⛽ at inner drying berth H24. (Sibleys ☎422431) at middle berth. @. HM holds mail if addressed c/o HM, St Mary's, Isles of Scilly TR21 0HU.

Hugh Town Essential shops, ACA ✉ Ⓑ ✕.

Porth Cressa 14 Y ⚓ £20<15m Apr-Oct. candpcarss@tiscali.co.uk ☎423758 mob 07825 477695, ⛽ (Sibleys) wi-fi. ⚓ clear of the marked power cable area.

Mainland access: Ferry leaves Penzance 0915 Mon-Fri (not Sun) and 1630 St Mary's (Sat varies); booking ☎0845 710 5555, ✈ to St Just, Newquay, Exeter. Booking www.islesofscilly-travel.co.uk ☎(01736) 334220.

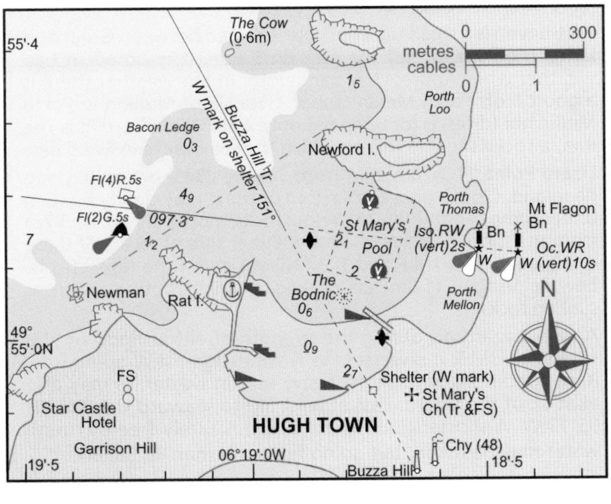

9.1.8 NEWLYN

Cornwall **50°06'·19N 05°32'·58W** ❁❁◊◊◊✿✿

CHARTS AC 777, 2345, 5603; Imray C10, C7, 2400

TIDES –0635 Dover; ML 3·2; Duration 0555

Standard Port PLYMOUTH (⟶)

Times				Height (metres)			
High Water		Low Water		MHWS	MHWN	MLWN	MLWS
0000	0600	0000	0600	5·5	4·4	2·2	0·8
1200	1800	1200	1800				
Differences NEWLYN							
–0053	–0108	–0035	–0036	+0·1	0·0	–0·2	0·0

SHELTER Good, but in strong SE'lies heavy swell enters hbr; access H24. FVs take priority. Good ⚓ in Gwavas Lake in offshore winds.

NAVIGATION WPT 50°06'·19N 05°31'·80W, 270°/0·5M to S pier. From NE, beware The Gear and Dog Rk 3½ca NE of hbr ent; from S, avoid Low Lee (1·1m) ECM buoy Q(3)10s and Carn Base (1·8m).

LIGHTS AND MARKS See chartlet and 9.1.4. Do not confuse S pier hd lt, Fl 5s, with Penzance pierhead lt, Fl WR 5s, 033°/1M. N pierhd lt: G sector (238°-248°) clears The Gear; W sector over hbr.

COMMUNICATIONS (Code 01736) CGOC (01326) 317575, Police 101, Ⓗ, Dr: as Penzance. HM www.newlynharbour.co.uk 362523 non-HO 361017. *Newlyn Hbr* Ch 09 **12** 16 (M-F 0800-1700, Sat 0800-1200LT).

FACILITIES SW of Mary Williams Pier the first 3-4 finger pontoons are offered to visiting yachts if available. Preference is given to FVs and yachtsmen may be asked to move. Dogs are banned from pontoons/harbour property.NE pontoon: 40⊆ <15m (2m on N side, S side shallower); SW pontoon: 40⊆ <10m (0·75m below CD) Charges: £12/night<8m>£18/night<12m>£27.00. at fish market; key from HM or nightwatchman.

Services (6t).

Town ✉ Ⓑ(am only) ✕, bus to Penzance ⇄ ✈.

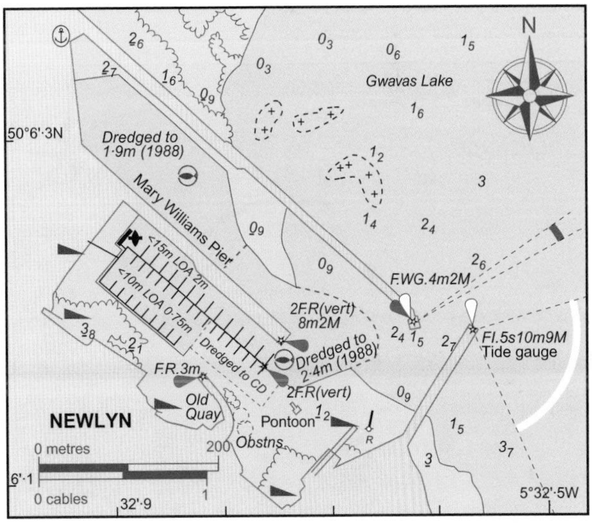

ADJACENT HARBOUR

MOUSEHOLE, Cornwall, **50°04'·97N 05°32'·26W**. ❁❁◊✿✿✿. AC 2345, 5603. HW +0550 on Dover; Tides as Newlyn; ML 3·2m; Duration 0600. Best appr from S, midway between St Clements Is and bkwtr. N pier lt, 2 FG (vert) = hbr open; 3 FR (vert) = hbr closed. Ent 11m wide; hbr dries approx 2·4m. Shelter good except in NE and S or SE winds; protected by St Clements Is from E'lies. Ent closed with timber baulks from Nov-Apr. HM Royden Paynter ☎(01736) 732544 mob 07891 647831. Per night £10, multi hull £12. Facilities limited: . Buses to Penzance.

9.1.9 PENZANCE

Cornwall **50°07′·09N 05°31′·68W**

CHARTS AC 777, 2345, 5603; Imray C10, C7, 2400

TIDES −0635 Dover; ML 3·2; Duration 0550

Standard Port PLYMOUTH (⟶)

Times				Height (metres)			
High Water		Low Water		MHWS	MHWN	MLWN	MLWS
0000	0600	0000	0600	5·5	4·4	2·2	0·8
1200	1800	1200	1800				
Differences PENZANCE are the same as for Newlyn (9.1.8)							
PORTHLEVEN							
−0045	−0105	−0030	−0025	0·0	−0·1	−0·2	0·0
LIZARD POINT							
−0045	−0100	−0030	−0030	−0·2	−0·2	−0·3	−0·2

SHELTER Excellent in the wet dock. ⚓/dry out close N of wet dock or ⚓ E of hbr, but Mounts Bay is unsafe ⚓ in S or SE winds, which, if strong, also render the hbr ent dangerous.

NAVIGATION WPT 50°06′·77N 05°31′·06W, 306°/0·5M to S pier hd. Approach dries. Beware The Gear Rk 4·5ca S. Western Cressar (4ca NE of ent) and Ryeman Rks are marked by unlit SCM bns. Hbr speed limit 5kn. Dock gate opens 2hrs before local HW until 1hr after, 12 waiting buoys are sited S of S pier.

LIGHTS AND MARKS Hbr lts often hard to see against shore lts. No ldg lts/marks. IPTS 2 & 3, shown on N knuckle near dock gate, indicates when it is open/shut, but may not be shown for yachts.

8 unlit Y spar buoy racing marks are laid, Apr-Sep, at: 50°07′·30N 05°31′·48W; 50°07′·11N 05°30′·33W; 50°06′·92N 05°29′·00W; 50°06′·63N 05°32′·03W; 50°06′·55N 05°31′·45W; 50°06′·33N 05°32′·48W; 50°06′·25N 05°30′·30W; 50°05′·70N 05°29′·35W.

COMMUNICATIONS (Code 01736) CGOC (01326) 317575; Police 101; Dr 363866; H 362382. HM 366113, in emergency 07967 240660; VHF Ch 09, **12**, 16 (HW −2 to HW +1, and office hrs).

FACILITIES **Wet dock** 50V<10m £1·80. Registration required. (3t) (dry dock).

Penzance SC ☎364989.

Town @.

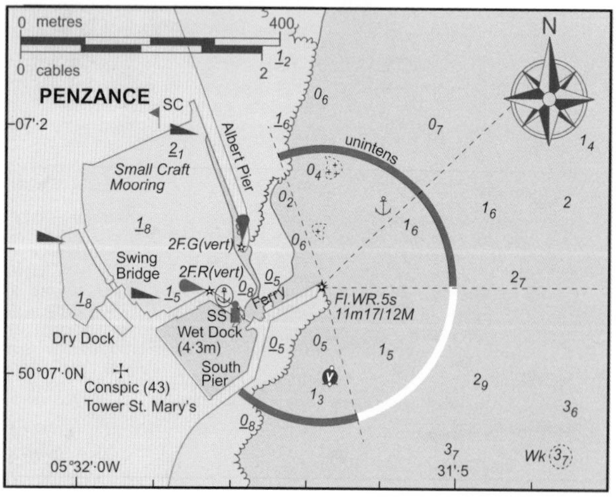

MINOR HARBOURS AROUND MOUNTS BAY

ST MICHAEL'S MOUNT, Cornwall, **50°07′·17N 05°28′·67W**. AC 2345, 777, 5603. HW +0550 on Dover; Tides as Penzance; ML 3·2m; Duration 0550. Beware: Hogus Rks (5·5) 250m NW of hbr; Outer Penzeath Rk (0·4) 5ca W of hbr; and Maltman Rk (0·9) 1ca SSW of the Mount. Shelter good from N to SE, but only in fair wx. Unlit hbr dries 2·1; approx 3·3m at MHWS and 1·4m at MHWN. Dry out against W pier or ⚓ W of the hbr in 2-3m on sand, space for 6 boats. HM mob ☎07870 400282 or 07917 583284. Facilities: café. Marazion, 3ca to N: Mounts Bay SC.

PORTHLEVEN, Cornwall, **50°04′·92N 05°19′·13W**. AC 777, 2345, 5603. HW −0635 on Dover; ML 3·1m; Duration 0545. Hbr dries 2m above the old lifeboat house but has approx 2·3m in centre of ent. It is very exposed to W and SW. Beware rks round pier hd and Deazle Rks to W. Lt on S pier, FG 10m 4M, = hbr open. Inside hbr FG, 033°-067°, shown as required to vessels entering. Visitors berth on the quay 2m, E side of inner hbr. HM ☎(01326) 574270. Facilities: Inner Hbr £8. Village.

MULLION COVE, Cornwall, **50°00′·90N, 05°15′·54W**. AC 777, 2345, 5603. Lizard HW −0630 on Dover, −0050 and −0·2m on HW Plymouth; ML 3·0m; Duration 0545. Porth Mellin hbr dries about 2·4m and is open to SW'lies. Due to lack of space, visiting boats may only stay in hbr briefly to load/unload. No lts. There is a slip on E side of hbr. ⚓ in Mullion Cove where shown on the chart and especially in lee of N end of Mullion Island in approx 4-5m, but best to ask local advice. NT owns the island and the hbr. HM ☎(01326) 240222. Mullion village (1M).

Historic Wrecks are located at:
50°03′·44N 05°17′·16W (*St Anthony*), 2M SE of Porthleven.
50°02′·37N 05°16′·46W (*Schiedam*), 1·5M N of Mullion Is.
49°58′·54N 05°14′·51W, Rill Cove, 1·4M NW of Lizard Pt.
49°57′·49N 05°12′·98W (*Royal Anne*) The Stags, Lizard Pt.

LAND'S END TO FALMOUTH

Close E of Gwennap ⚓ off Porthcurno, owing to cables (AC *777*). Western approach to Mounts Bay is marked by Tater-du Light. The Bucks (3·3m) are 2ca ESE of Tater-du, and Gull Rock (24m) is 9ca NE of close off the E point of Lamorna Cove. Little Heaver (dries) is 100m SW of Gull Rk, and Kemyel Rock (dries) is 1¾ca ENE.

Mousehole is a small drying harbour, sheltered from W and N, but exposed to E or S winds, when entrance may be shut. Approach from SW side of St Clement's Is. In W winds there is good ⚓ off the harbour.

Low Lee, (dangerous rock 1·1m) 4ca NE of Penlee Pt is marked by ECM lit buoy. Carn Base (rk 1·8m) lies 3ca NNW of Low Lee.

Newlyn is the sole harbour in Mount's Bay safe to approach in strong onshore winds, but only near to HW. East towards **Penzance** beware the unmarked Dog Rock (1·1m) and The Gear (1·9m,IDM lt bcn).

From Penzance to St Michael's Mount the head of the bay is shoal, drying 4ca off in places. Dangerous rocks include Cressar, Long, Hogus and Outer Penzeath. Keep south of a limiting line joining Penzance Market Ho Dome (55m) with pierheads of **St Michael's Mount** harbour at 089° to clear these dangers. The tiny hbr dries 2·1m, but is well sheltered, with ⚓ about 1ca W of entrance.

Two dangerous rocks, Guthen and Maltman (0·9m), lie 2ca W and S of St Michael's Mount respectively. 1M SE is The Greeb (7m), with rocks between it and shore. The Bears (dry) lie 1¾ca E of The Greeb. The Stone (dries) is 5ca S of Cudden Pt, while offshore is Mountamopus shoal marked by a SCM lit buoy. Welloe Rk (0·8m) lies 5ca SW of Trewavas Head.

Porthleven is a small tidal harbour, entered between Great and Little Trigg Rocks and the pier on S side. It is closed in bad weather when approach is dangerous. In fair weather there is a good ⚓ off Porth Mellin, about 1½ca NE of Mullion Is; Porth Mellin hbr (dries) is for temp use only. 2·5M W of Lizard Pt is The Boa, a rocky shoal (11m) on which the sea breaks in SW gales.

Lizard Point (Fl 3s70m 26M *Horn 30s*; AC 2345) is a bold, steep headland. Close inshore reflection of the lt may clearly be seen under some conditions. Dangerous rocks, mostly drying, lie 5-7ca from the lt ho in its SW quadrant. Either side of local LW these rocks are visible. 1M E and 1·5M NE of Lizard lt ho respectively, beware Vrogue (1·8m) and Craggan (1·5m) both dangerous sunken rocks.

A race, hazardous during the strength of either flood or ebb extends 2–3M S; it is worst in W'ly winds against W-going tide. Race conditions with short, heavy seas in westerlies may also exist SE of the Lizard. Pass at least 3M to seaward via 49°55′N 05°13′W. A shorter inner route which is rarely free of rough water may be taken, but go no further N than 49°56′·8N.

▶*In the race slack water occurs at about HW Plymouth –4 and the stream sets NE from HWP –3. The next slack water is at HWP +2½ and the stream sets SW from HWP +3; max springs rates reach 2-3kn. Outside the race the NE-going Channel flood starts at approx HWP –3¾ and the SW-going at HWP +3. Study NP 255 tidal stream atlas, Falmouth to Padstow inc Scilly.*◀

To await slack water, ⚓ (W to E) at: Kynance Cove, Housel Bay (3ca ENE of the lt ho and SSE of a conspic hotel), Parn Voose Cove (49°58'·4N 05°11'·1W), Cadgwith or Coverack.

N of Black Head, rocks extend at least 1ca offshore; a rock drying 1·6m lies off Chynhalls Pt (AC 1267). Coverack is a good ⚓ in W'lies. WSW of Lowland Pt drying rocks extend 2½ca offshore.

The Manacles (dry), 7½ca E and SE of Manacle Pt, are marked by ECM lt buoy and are in R sector of St Anthony Hd lt.

▶*Here the stream sets NE from HW Plymouth –0345, and SW from HW+0200, Sp rates 1·25kn.*◀

There are no offshore dangers on courses NNW to Nare Pt and Helford River or N to Falmouth.

MINOR HARBOURS NORTH EAST OF THE LIZARD

CADGWITH, Cornwall, **49°59´·22N 05°10´·68W**. AC 154, 2345, 5603. HW –0625 on Dover; –0030 on Plymouth; –0·2m on Devonport; ML 3·0m. Use Differences Lizard Pt under 9.1.9. Hbr dries; it is divided by The Todden, a rky outcrop. Beware the extension of this, rks called The Mare; also beware Boa Rk to ESE which cover at quarter tide. ⚓ off The Mare in about 2–3m, but not recommended in onshore winds. There are no lts. Many local FVs operate from here and are hauled up on the shingle beach. Facilities: ✉ ✕ shops at Ruan Minor (1M).

COVERACK, Cornwall, **50°01´·44N 05°05´·66W**. AC 154, 147, 5603. HW –0620 on Dover; ML 3·0m; Duration 0550. From the S beware the Guthens, off Chynhalls Pt; from the N, Davas and other rks off Lowland Pt, and to the NE Manacle Rks (ECM lt buoy). There are no lts. The tiny hbr dries and is full of small FVs. It has 3·3m at MHWS and 2·2m at MHWN. In good weather and off-shore winds it is better to ⚓ outside. HM ☎(01326) 280679. Facilities: (hotel) ⛽ from garage (2M uphill) ✉.

9.1.10 HELFORD RIVER

Cornwall **50°05'·79N 05°06'·06W** (Ent)

CHARTS AC 154, 147, 5603; Imray C10, C6, 2400

TIDES –0615 Dover; ML 3·0; Duration 0550

Reference Port PLYMOUTH (⟶)

Times				**Height (metres)**			
High Water		Low Water		MHWS	MHWN	MLWN	MLWS
0000	0600	0000	0600	5·5	4·4	2·2	0·8
1200	1800	1200	1800				
Differences HELFORD RIVER (Entrance)							
–0030	–0035	–0015	–0010	–0·2	–0·2	–0·3	–0·2
COVERACK							
–0030	–0050	–0020	–0015	–0·2	–0·2	–0·3	–0·2

SHELTER Excellent, except in E'lies when an uncomfortable swell reaches Frenchman's Creek. Yachts may ⚓ in Durgan Bay but not inshore of 3 small buoys marking the eelgrass beds (approx 100m from shore). ⚓ /taking the ground is permitted W of Groyne Pt, but not S of Porth Navas Creek owing to oyster beds.

NAVIGATION WPT 50°05´·86N 05°04´·84W, 270°/1·9M to The Pool. From N beware August Rock marked by SHM buoy, Fl G 5s. From SE keep well off Nare Pt and Dennis Hd. At the entrance to Gillan harbour an ECM buoy marks Car Croc, a rock drying 1m. A NCM buoy marks the Voose, a rky reef E of Bosahan Pt.

Beware an extensive drying mud bank N and W of Bar SHM buoy, which is partially obscured by 🅥s. Speed limit 6kn in the river. The channel up to Gweek is buoyed but dries W of 05°10´·35W.

LIGHTS AND MARKS Access by day; no lights. Marks as chartlet; all unlit except seasonal buoys marking August Rk off Rosemullion and Car Croc Q(3) 10s off Dennis Hd.

COMMUNICATIONS (Code 01326) CGOC 317575; Ⓗ 572151; Police 101. Moorings Officer: ian@helford-river.com ☎250749 mob 07808 071485; water taxi ☎250749, Ch M. Ferry also acts as a water taxi, on request HO. Helford River SC Ch **80** M.

FACILITIES Local info at www.helfordrivermoorings.co.uk. In The Pool 25 G 🅥s, marked 'Visitors' with G pick-up buoys, are randomly numbered (see diagram); <10m £15, <11m £17, <12m £18; 7th night free. No prior reservations. Rafting essential in high season.

Ditch rubbish ashore at the Helford River SC or the Ferryboat Inn (N bank).

N bank Helford Passage. **Porth Navas YC**☎340065, limited ✕; www.portnavasyachtclub.co.uk.

S bank: Gillan Creek. **Helford River SC**☎231460 ✕. **Helford village** ✉ bus to Falmouth ⛴.

Gweek Quay ☎221657 221685, info@gweek-quay.com ⛽ (100t) ✉.

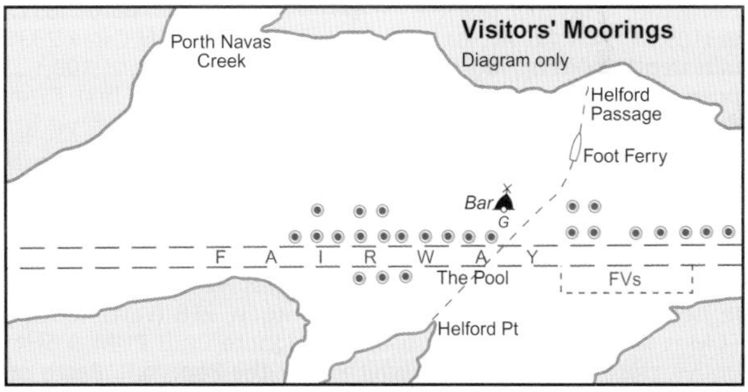

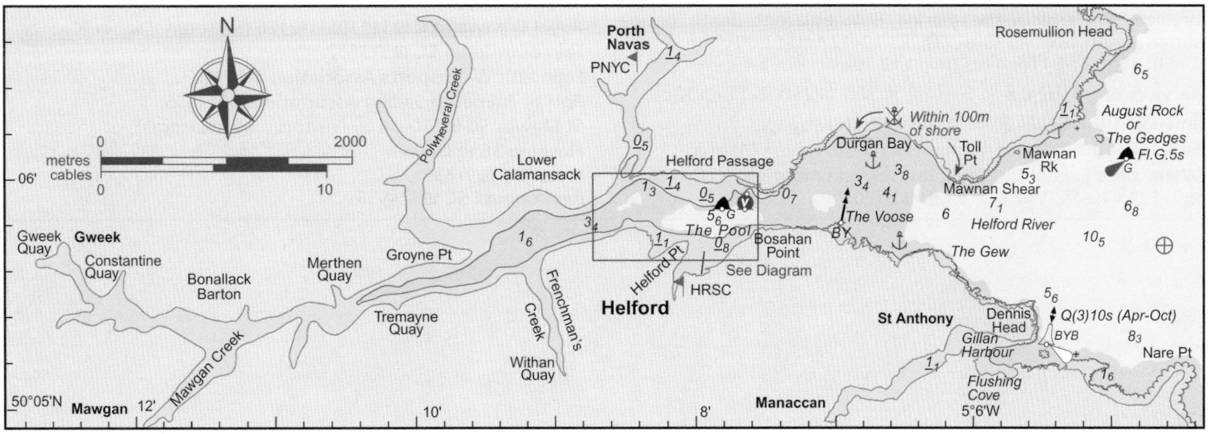

9.1.11 FALMOUTH & RIVER FAL

Cornwall **50°08′·61N 05°01′·48W** (Ent)

CHARTS AC 154, 32, 18, 5602; Imray C6, Y58

TIDES –0610 Dover; ML 3·0; Duration 0550

SHELTER Excellent, depending on wind direction; see Facilities. Access H24 in any weather, although the entrance, 1M wide and deep, is rough in fresh on-shore winds over the ebb.

NAVIGATION WPT 50°08′·00N 05°01′·74W, 000°/7ca to Black Rock PHM lt buoy, which marks the edge of the deep water E channel. At night this is advised, although by day small vessels may pass either side of Black Rk (2·1m), IDM Fl(2) 10s, close W of mid-entrance. A Wave Energy Test Area is situated 155° St Anthony Hd 1.5 NM; a Y SPM Fl(5)Y 20s marks its SW corner.

Falmouth is a deep water port with sizeable commercial docks. Do not impede ships up to 90,000 tons nor ⚓ in prohib areas. Outside the buoyed chans large areas are quite shallow; care is needed below half tide.

Speed limits: 8kn in Falmouth inner hbr (ie W of the docks), the Penryn River and, N of Turnaware Bar, in the R Fal/Truro and offlying creeks.

5kn in St Mawes and the Percuil River, Mylor, Restronguet and St Just Creeks and Portscatho (50°10′·83N 04°58′·32W), 2 pages on.

LIGHTS AND MARKS See chartlet and 9.1.4. R sector of St Anthony Hd lt (H24) covers the Manacles Rocks.

COMMUNICATIONS (Code 01326). CGOC 317575. Police 101. Dr Falmouth 212120, Penryn 372502. Ⓗ Falmouth 434700. Ⓗ Truro (A&E) (01872) 250000.

Falmouth Hbr Radio Ch **12** 14 (M-F 0800-1700). HM Truro and launch Ch 12. Falmouth Haven Marina and St Mawes Hbr: Ch 12. Pendennis & Falmouth marinas, Royal Cornwall YC Ch **80/M**. Mylor Yacht Hbr Ch 80/M, 37/M1, Malpas Marine, St Mawes SC: Ch M (HO).

FACILITIES from seaward, clockwise to St Just:

Port Pendennis Marina 50°09′·15N 05°03′·70W. 45+20Ⓥ in 3-4·5m in outer harbour (access H24) www.portpendennis.com ☎211211 £3·35<25m>£4·75; max LOA 80m, short stay £15. Marina village access HW±3 via ent gate with tfc lts. YC, tennis court.

Falmouth Haven Marina (FHM) 50°09′·22N 05°03′·89W. ☎310990/1; Ch 12. Access H24. Dir bn WRG 3s on N Quay 233°, min depth 1.4m on ldg line leaving 4 Y buoys to port. 100, price standard /Jul-Aug: £2·85/£3·00; short stay (<2 hrs) £1/m. Ⓥ ⚓ up to 200m E of FHM in 2-5m (see FHC below). wi-fi.

Falmouth Harbour Commissioners (FHC) www.falmouthport.co.uk info@falmouthport.co.uk; 21 G s off Prince of Wales pier, prices /⚓: £2·10/£1·40.

Falmouth Marina 50°09′·90N 05°05′·02W up the Penryn River. www.premiermarinas.com ☎316620. Access H24, min depth 2m. In near appr, pass close N of outer pontoon, 2FR (vert), leaving ECM lt bn (hard to see) close to stbd. Ignore unlit PHM & SHM buoys, close NE of ECM bcn, which mark the Penryn R. Berth on J hammerhead/fuel berth, then as directed. A disused pipeline drying 1·8m crosses the marina E/W; adjacent depth gauge shows depth over it. 300+20Ⓥ, £3·10<12.5m>£3·30<16m>£3·80, £4·50>20m; £1·54 for 4 hrs (min £12·30).

Services (H24) (30t) (25t) ©.

Town ACA Ⓑ (Newquay).

Fuel Falmouth & Mylor marinas, Falmouth Haven Marina.

Water taxis Falmouth Water Taxi www.falmouthwatertaxi.co.uk ☎07522 446659, VHF Ch 12 (after 0930).

Penryn HM Penryn River ☎373352. Half tide access via drying buoyed channel to Freeman's Wharf 50°10′·00N 05°05′·75W www.freemanswharf.com ☎377509. 45 ½ tide drying, £2/ft/wk +VAT. (500m), ACA, (20t).

Mylor Yacht Harbour 50°10′·74N 05°03′·14W, NW bank of Carrick Roads. Good shelter in W'lies but exposed to E'lies. PHM and SHM lit buoys mark ent to the fairway to the Yacht Hbr, dredged 2m; access H24. Hbr www.mylor.com enquiries@mylor.com ☎372121. 140 + 40 Ⓥ, £3·50; 15, £2·00. Short stay £3/hr, £2/hr. Ⓔ (35t), (4t).

Mylor Pool has many moorings in 1m to 2·2m. Mylor Creek dries or is shoal, <1m. Mylor Creek Boatyard welcomes visitors who can take the ground www.mylorcreekboatyard.com.

St Mawes Harbour 50°09′·49N 05°00′·84W. Keep S of St Mawes SCM buoy marking Lugo Rk, 0·6m. Beware numerous moorings and oyster beds, esp in Percuil River, upper reaches of which dry above village. HM www.stmaweshabour.co.uk ☎270553. 13 G s to SW of the hbr toward Carricknath Pt. £16<10m>£21<12m>£32<15m. ⚓ above Castle Pt well sheltered from all but SW winds, £0·50. Seasonal water taxi 1 May-30 Sep 1000-1600; VHF Ch 12 *St Mawes Hbr water taxi*; £2/person. Outside hrs above taxi available for hire all yr mob 07971846786.

St Just, good ⚓ off the creek, except in strong W/SW'lies.

FACILITIES UPRIVER TO TRURO See the chartlet overleaf.

Restronguet Creek 50°11′·53N 05°03′·56W, dries completely. Beware Carrick Carlys Rk 0·8m, 3ca E of ent, marked by NCM & SCM posts. Moorings fill the pool (12·4m) so only space to ⚓ is outside. Pandora Inn ☎372678, pontoon dries 0·9m.

River Fal/Truro River At N end of Carrick Roads beware strong tides and rips off Turnaware Point and Bar. *King Harry chain ferry has right of way over all passing vessels* except those with a pilot aboard. She shows restricted in ability to manoeuvre lights/shapes. Fl Y lts indicate her direction of travel. At Tolverne, at www.smugglersmoorings.co.uk, £15<9m>£18<12m>£21 per day. 2 lit PH buoys mark the shallow water on the large bend where the Fal and Truro rivers divide just below midstream Ⓥ pontoon.

HM Truro www.portoftruro.co.uk ☎(01872) 272130 administers 4 Ⓥ pontoons, E of Channals Creek, N of Ruan Creek, off Woodbury Pt and Malpas (max draught 1m): £15/day all LOA; £3 for 2hrs ⚓ £6. 10 visits £120 for pontoon and £50 for anchoring.

A pontoon, W bank just S of King Harry ferry, is for tourist access to Trelissick House (Fl R 5s). Tenders may berth on the inshore side; yachts may berth outboard briefly for only.

Good ⚓s, £6/day, off Tolcarne Creek, Channals Creek, Tolverne, Ruan Creek, Church Creek, Mopus Reach and Malpas.

Upstream, 8ca NW of Malpas a flood barrier gate is usually open, 2 FR/FG (vert). Gate is shut HW ±2¼, and 3 Fl R lts shown, if HW >5·6m is forecast due to storm surge.

Malpas Marine ☎ (01872) 271260. but no Ⓥ facilities. Local pub.

Truro 50°15′·72N 05°02′·85W. HW Truro, Sp & Nps, is approx HW Falmouth –0022 and –2·0m. Drying close SW of HM's office. **City** all facilities.

YACHT CLUBS

Royal Cornwall YC ☎311105/312126 (Secretary).

Falmouth Town SC ☎313662.

Falmouth Watersports Association ☎211223.

Port of Falmouth Sailing Association ☎211555.

St Mawes SC ☎270686 (visitors most welcome).

Flushing SC ☎374043.

Mylor YC ☎374391.

Restronguet SC ☎374536.

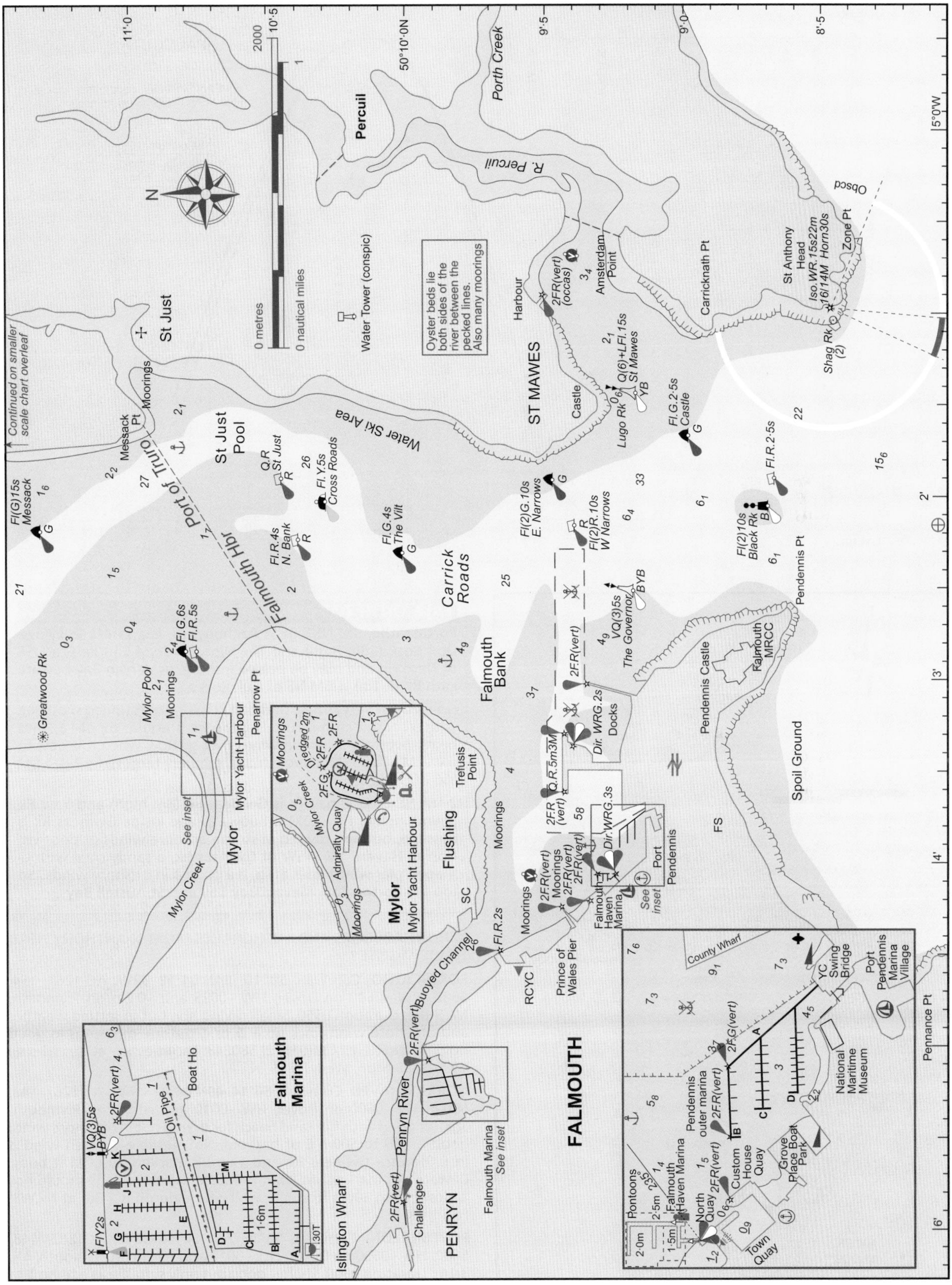
FALMOUTH
PENRYN
Penryn River
Islington Wharf
Challenger
Falmouth Marina
See inset
Buoyed Channel
RCYC
Prince of Wales Pier
Flushing
Trefusis Point
Mylor
Mylor Creek
Mylor Yacht Harbour
Penarrow Pt
Mylor Pool
Moorings
Greatwood Rk
Falmouth Hbr
Port of Truro
Carrick Roads
Falmouth Bank
St Just Pool
St Just
Messack Pt
Continued on smaller scale chart overleaf
Water Ski Area
Water Tower (conspic)
ST MAWES
Castle
Harbour
Amsterdam Point
Percuil
R. Percuil
Porth Creek
Carricknath Pt
St Anthony Head
Iso.WR.15s22m 16/14M Horn30s
Zone Pt
Obscd
Shag Rk (2)
Lugo Rk
Q(6)+LFl.15s St Mawes
Fl.G.2·5s Castle
Fl.R.2·5s
Fl(2)10s Black Rk
Fl(2)G.10s E. Narrows
Fl(2)R.10s W Narrows
VQ(3)5s The Governor
Fl.G.4s The Vilt
Fl.R.4s N. Bank
Q.R St Just
Fl.Y.5s Cross Roads
Fl(G)15s Messack
Fl.G.6s
Fl.R.5s
Oyster beds lie both sides of the river between the pecked lines. Also many moorings
Pendennis Castle
Pendennis Pt
Falmouth MRCC
Spoil Ground
Docks
Dir. WRG.2s
Dir. WRG.3s
Q.R.5m3M
2F.R(vert)
Port Pendennis
Falmouth Haven Marina
Pennance Pt
National Maritime Museum
Port Pendennis Marina Village
Swing Bridge
YC
County Wharf
Pendennis outer marina
Custom House Quay
North Quay
Town Quay
Grove Place Boat Park
Pontoons
Admiralty Quay
Dredged 2m
Falmouth Marina
Boat Ho
Oil Pipe
VQ(3)5s BYB
Fl.Y.2s
0 metres 2000
0 nautical miles 1
50°10'·0N
5°0'W
11'·0
10'·5
9'·5
9'·0
8'·5
6'
4'
3'
2'

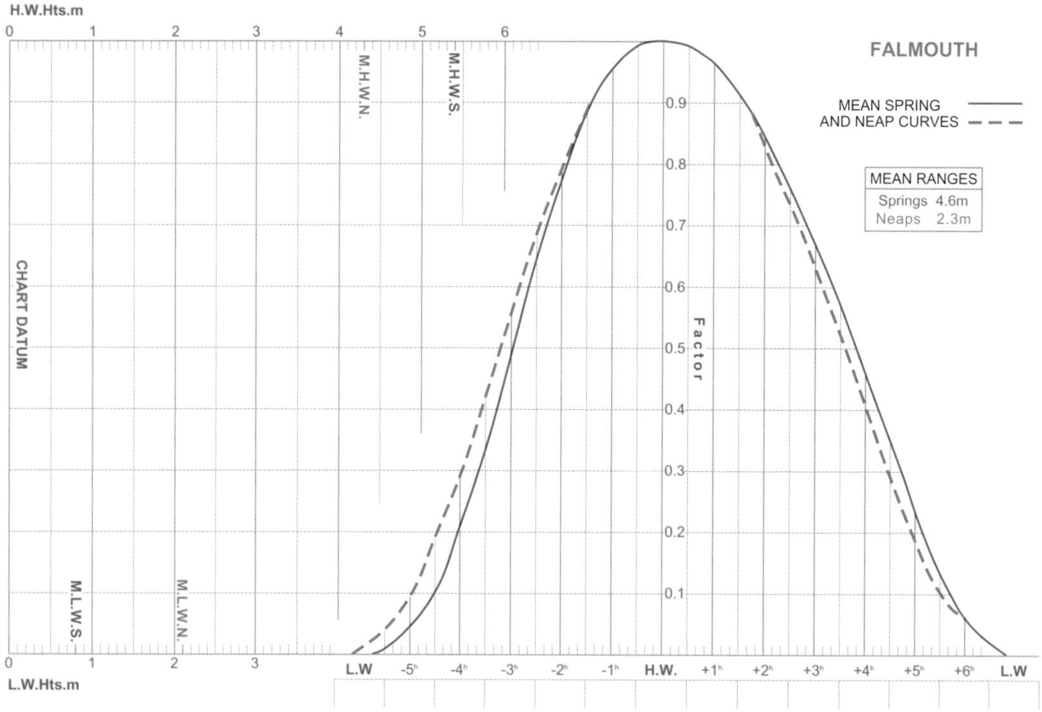

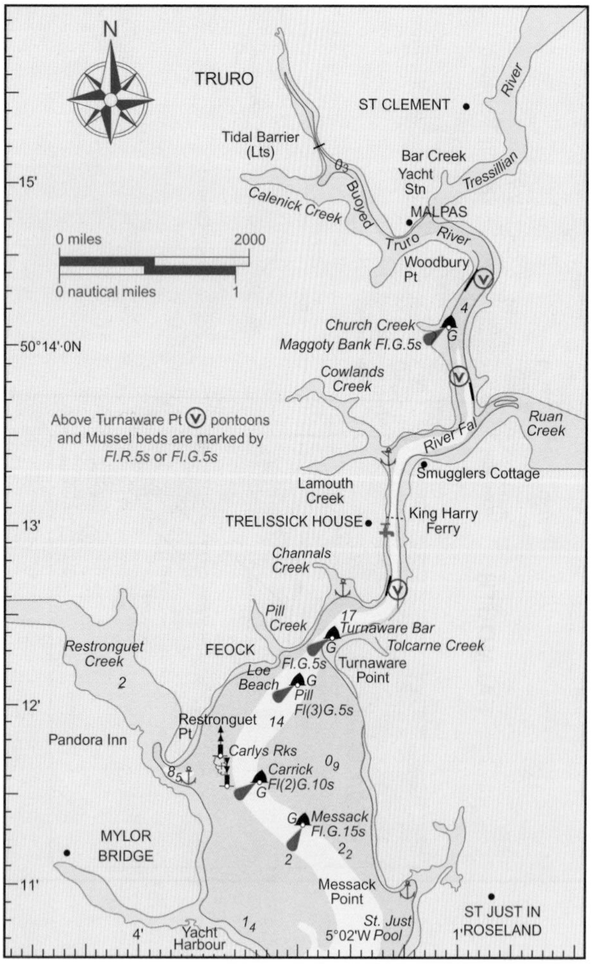

FALMOUTH TO FOWEY

Porthscatho, 3M NNE of St Anthony Hd, is a safe ⚓ in W'lies. Gull Rock (38m high) and The Whelps (dry 4·6m) lie 6ca E/SE of Nare Hd and may be passed inshore. In Veryan Bay beware Lath Rk (2·1m), 1·6M NE of Gull Rock.

On E side of Veryan Bay, Dodman Pt is a 110m rounded shoulder, with a conspic stone cross. Depths are irregular for 1M S, with heavy overfalls in strong winds over sp tide, when it is best to pass 2M off. 3 SPM lt buoys (naval gunnery targets) lie 2·3–4·8M SSE of Dodman Pt.

2·1M NE of Dodman Pt is Gwineas Rk (8m high) and Yaw Rk (0·9m), marked by ECM lt buoy. Passage inside Gwineas Rk is possible, but not advised in strong onshore winds or poor vis. **Gorran Haven**, 1M WSW of Gwineas Rk, a sandy cove with L-shaped pier which dries at sp, is a good ⚓ in offshore winds. So too are **Portmellon, Mevagissey Bay** and **St Austell Bay**.

MINOR HARBOURS AND ANCHORAGES FROM ST ANTHONY HEAD TO MEVAGISSEY

PORTSCATHO, Cornwall, **50°10′·84N 04°58′·32W**. AC 1267, 154, 5602. HW –0600 on Dover, HW –0025 and –0·2m on Plymouth; ML 3·0m; Duration 0550. Small drying hbr, but in settled weather and off-shore winds pick up a 🅐 or ⚓ outside moorings in good holding. No lts. HM ☎(01872) 580243. Facilities: ⛴ 🚰 ⓟ ⓓ ✉ Ⓑ 1000-1230 Mon, Wed, Fri 🛒 ✗ ▭.

GORRAN HAVEN, Cornwall, **50°14′·49N 04°47′·16W**. AC 1267, 148, 5602. HW –0600 on Dover, HW –0010 and –0·1m on Plymouth. Shelter good with flat sand beach for drying out in off-shore wind; good ⚓ 100 to 500m E of harbour. Not suitable ⚓ when wind is in E. Beware Gwineas Rk and Yaw Rk marked by ECM lt buoy. Beware pot markers on appr. Fin keelers without legs should not ⚓ closer than 300m from hbr wall where depth is 1·8m at MLWS. Facilities: ✉ 🛒 ✗ ▭.

PORTMELLON, Cornwall, **50°15′·74N 04°46′·98W**. AC1267, 148, 5602. HW –0600 on Dover, HW –0010 and –0·1m on Plymouth; ML 3·1m; Duration 0600. Shelter good but only suitable as a temp ⚓ in settled weather and offshore winds. Facilities: ✗ ▭ (summer).

POLKERRIS, Cornwall, **50°20′·15N 04°41′·40W**. AC 148. Tides as Charlestown/Par. Very good ⚓ in NE/SE winds. Facilities: ✗ ▭.

STANDARD TIME (UT)
For Summer Time add ONE hour in **non-shaded areas**

FALMOUTH

LAT 50°09'N LONG 5°03'W

TIMES AND HEIGHTS OF HIGH AND LOW WATERS

Dates in red are SPRINGS
Dates in blue are NEAPS

YEAR 2018

JANUARY

Day	Time	m	Time	m	Time	m	Time	m
1 M	0407	5.1	1052	0.6	1633	5.1	2317	0.5
2 TU ○	0500	5.3	1146	0.3	1726	5.2		
3 W	0009	0.3	0550	5.4	1238	0.2	1817	5.2
4 TH	0058	0.2	0639	5.5	1325	0.1	1906	5.1
5 F	0143	0.3	0725	5.4	1410	0.2	1952	5.0
6 SA	0226	0.4	0809	5.3	1454	0.4	2035	4.8
7 SU	0308	0.7	0853	5.0	1537	0.7	2120	4.6
8 M	0352	1.0	0938	4.7	1624	1.1	◑ 2209	4.3
9 TU	0441	1.3	1029	4.4	1716	1.4	2309	4.1
10 W	0537	1.6	1132	4.2	1816	1.6		
11 TH	0023	4.0	0641	1.7	1250	4.1	1923	1.6
12 F	0138	4.1	0752	1.7	1402	4.1	2032	1.5
13 SA	0236	4.2	0859	1.5	1458	4.3	2129	1.3
14 SU	0324	4.5	0954	1.3	1544	4.5	2217	1.1
15 M	0406	4.7	1040	1.1	1626	4.6	2259	1.0
16 TU	0446	4.9	1121	0.9	1706	4.7	2337	0.9
17 W ●	0525	5.0	1159	0.8	1745	4.8		
18 TH	0012	0.8	0601	5.0	1233	0.8	1820	4.8
19 F	0044	0.8	0636	5.0	1303	0.8	1854	4.8
20 SA	0114	0.8	0707	5.0	1333	0.8	1925	4.7
21 SU	0144	0.9	0737	4.9	1405	0.9	1955	4.6
22 M	0217	1.0	0807	4.8	1440	1.0	2024	4.5
23 TU	0254	1.1	0841	4.7	1519	1.1	2059	4.4
24 W	0337	1.3	0927	4.6	1606	1.3	◐ 2158	4.3
25 TH	0431	1.5	1031	4.4	1708	1.5	2312	4.2
26 F	0541	1.6	1144	4.3	1824	1.5		
27 SA	0029	4.2	0703	1.5	1301	4.3	1945	1.4
28 SU	0145	4.4	0825	1.3	1416	4.5	2101	1.2
29 M	0254	4.7	0937	1.0	1523	4.7	2207	0.8
30 TU	0352	5.0	1040	0.6	1621	4.9	2306	0.5
31 W	0446	5.2	1136	0.3	1714	5.1	○ 2359	0.3

FEBRUARY

Day	Time	m	Time	m	Time	m	Time	m
1 TH	0536	5.4	1227	0.1	1804	5.2		
2 F	0047	0.1	0623	5.5	1314	0.0	1849	5.2
3 SA	0131	0.1	0707	5.5	1356	0.0	1931	5.1
4 SU	0211	0.2	0748	5.4	1435	0.2	2009	5.0
5 M	0247	0.5	0826	5.1	1511	0.5	2045	4.7
6 TU	0324	0.8	0902	4.8	1548	0.9	2124	4.5
7 W	0403	1.2	0941	4.5	1629	1.3	◑ 2208	4.2
8 TH	0450	1.5	1028	4.2	1720	1.6	2305	4.0
9 F	0549	1.8	1131	3.9	1825	1.8		
10 SA	0025	3.9	0659	1.9	1310	3.8	1937	1.8
11 SU	0159	4.0	0814	1.8	1430	4.0	2048	1.6
12 M	0259	4.3	0920	1.5	1523	4.3	2145	1.4
13 TU	0345	4.6	1012	1.2	1608	4.5	2232	1.1
14 W	0426	4.8	1057	1.0	1648	4.7	2313	0.9
15 TH	0505	4.9	1136	0.8	1726	4.8	● 2350	0.8
16 F	0542	5.0	1211	0.7	1802	4.9		
17 SA	0024	0.7	0616	5.1	1244	0.6	1835	4.9
18 SU	0056	0.6	0647	5.1	1315	0.6	1906	4.8
19 M	0128	0.6	0717	5.0	1347	0.6	1933	4.8
20 TU	0200	0.7	0744	5.0	1420	0.7	1955	4.7
21 W	0235	0.8	0811	4.8	1456	0.9	2022	4.6
22 TH	0313	1.0	0848	4.7	1537	1.1	2110	4.4
23 F	0401	1.3	0949	4.4	1632	1.4	◐ 2228	4.2
24 SA	0506	1.5	1113	4.2	1746	1.6	2359	4.1
25 SU	0632	1.6	1241	4.1	1917	1.6		
26 M	0125	4.2	0807	1.4	1405	4.3	2047	1.3
27 TU	0240	4.5	0927	1.1	1514	4.6	2158	0.9
28 W	0339	4.9	1030	0.6	1610	4.8	2256	0.6

MARCH

Day	Time	m	Time	m	Time	m	Time	m
1 TH	0431	5.2	1124	0.3	1700	5.0	2347	0.3
2 F ○	0519	5.4	1212	0.0	1746	5.2		
3 SA	0032	0.1	0603	5.5	1256	-0.1	1827	5.2
4 SU	0113	0.0	0645	5.5	1335	0.0	1905	5.2
5 M	0149	0.1	0723	5.3	1410	0.2	1940	5.1
6 TU	0222	0.4	0757	5.1	1441	0.5	2013	4.9
7 W	0253	0.7	0829	4.9	1511	0.9	2047	4.7
8 TH	0326	1.1	0903	4.5	1543	1.3	2124	4.4
9 F	0402	1.5	0943	4.2	1624	1.7	◑ 2213	4.1
10 SA	0455	1.8	1038	3.9	1728	2.0	2318	3.9
11 SU	0611	2.0	1155	3.7	1848	2.0		
12 M	0100	3.9	0730	1.9	1359	3.8	2005	1.9
13 TU	0228	4.1	0843	1.7	1459	4.1	2110	1.5
14 W	0319	4.4	0940	1.3	1544	4.4	2201	1.2
15 TH	0401	4.7	1027	1.0	1624	4.6	2245	0.9
16 F	0439	4.9	1108	0.8	1701	4.8	2325	0.7
17 SA ●	0515	5.0	1145	0.6	1736	4.9		
18 SU	0001	0.6	0549	5.1	1221	0.5	1810	5.0
19 M	0036	0.5	0623	5.1	1254	0.4	1842	5.0
20 TU	0110	0.4	0656	5.1	1328	0.4	1911	5.0
21 W	0143	0.5	0726	5.0	1401	0.5	1937	4.9
22 TH	0218	0.6	0755	4.9	1437	0.7	2007	4.8
23 F	0256	0.8	0833	4.7	1517	1.0	2054	4.5
24 SA	0343	1.2	0933	4.4	1610	1.4	◐ 2208	4.3
25 SU	0447	1.5	1058	4.1	1723	1.6	2341	4.1
26 M	0615	1.6	1232	4.0	1900	1.7		
27 TU	0112	4.2	0759	1.4	1358	4.2	2038	1.4
28 W	0226	4.5	0917	1.0	1504	4.5	2146	1.0
29 TH	0324	4.8	1016	0.6	1556	4.8	2240	0.6
30 F	0413	5.1	1106	0.3	1641	5.0	2328	0.3
31 SA ○	0459	5.3	1152	0.1	1723	5.1		

APRIL

Day	Time	m	Time	m	Time	m	Time	m
1 SU	0011	0.1	0541	5.3	1234	0.0	1802	5.2
2 M	0050	0.1	0620	5.3	1310	0.1	1838	5.2
3 TU	0125	0.2	0657	5.2	1343	0.3	1912	5.1
4 W	0155	0.4	0730	5.0	1411	0.6	1944	5.0
5 TH	0224	0.7	0800	4.8	1437	1.0	2016	4.7
6 F	0252	1.1	0831	4.5	1503	1.3	2050	4.5
7 SA	0320	1.4	0910	4.2	1533	1.7	2134	4.2
8 SU	0401	1.8	1002	3.9	1627	2.0	◑ 2232	4.0
9 M	0519	2.0	1110	3.7	1757	2.1	2347	3.9
10 TU	0645	2.0	1249	3.8	1919	2.0		
11 W	0133	4.0	0758	1.7	1422	4.0	2027	1.7
12 TH	0240	4.3	0859	1.4	1510	4.3	2122	1.3
13 F	0325	4.6	0949	1.1	1550	4.6	2210	1.0
14 SA	0403	4.8	1033	0.8	1626	4.8	2253	0.7
15 SU	0440	5.0	1115	0.5	1702	5.0	2334	0.5
16 M ●	0518	5.1	1154	0.4	1740	5.1		
17 TU	0013	0.4	0557	5.2	1233	0.3	1817	5.1
18 W	0051	0.3	0636	5.2	1309	0.3	1853	5.1
19 TH	0128	0.4	0714	5.1	1346	0.5	1928	5.0
20 F	0205	0.5	0752	4.9	1423	0.7	2007	4.9
21 SA	0246	0.8	0836	4.6	1507	1.0	2057	4.6
22 SU	0336	1.1	0936	4.3	1602	1.3	◐ 2205	4.4
23 M	0442	1.4	1055	4.1	1715	1.6	2331	4.2
24 TU	0608	1.5	1225	4.0	1847	1.6		
25 W	0057	4.3	0744	1.3	1345	4.2	2019	1.3
26 TH	0208	4.5	0857	1.0	1447	4.5	2124	1.0
27 F	0305	4.8	0954	0.6	1536	4.7	2217	0.6
28 SA	0352	5.0	1043	0.4	1619	4.9	2304	0.4
29 SU	0436	5.1	1127	0.3	1658	5.0	2346	0.3
30 M ○	0517	5.1	1207	0.2	1735	5.1		

Chart Datum is 2·91 metres below Ordnance Datum (Newlyn). HAT is 5·7 metres above Chart Datum.

STANDARD TIME (UT)
For Summer Time add ONE hour in **non-shaded areas**

FALMOUTH LAT 50°09′N LONG 5°03′W

TIMES AND HEIGHTS OF HIGH AND LOW WATERS

Dates in red are SPRINGS
Dates in blue are NEAPS

YEAR **2018**

MAY

Day	Time	m	Day	Time	m
1 TU	0024 0555 1244 1811	0.3 5.1 0.3 5.1	16 W	0533 1212 1754	5.2 0.3 5.2
2 W	0059 0631 1315 1845	0.4 5.0 0.5 5.0	17 TH	0034 0619 1254 1838	0.3 5.2 0.3 5.2
3 TH	0130 0705 1343 1918	0.6 4.9 0.8 4.9	18 F	0117 0705 1336 1922	0.3 5.1 0.4 5.1
4 F	0158 0736 1409 1950	0.8 4.7 1.0 4.8	19 SA	0159 0751 1418 2008	0.4 4.9 0.6 5.0
5 SA	0224 0807 1433 2023	1.1 4.5 1.3 4.6	20 SU	0245 0840 1505 2059	0.7 4.7 0.9 4.8
6 SU	0251 0845 1503 2104	1.4 4.3 1.6 4.4	21 M	0337 0937 1601 2201	0.9 4.4 1.2 4.5
7 M	0328 0933 1549 2157	1.6 4.0 1.8 4.1	22 TU	0441 1049 1708 ◐ 2316	1.2 4.2 1.4 4.4
8 TU	0431 1035 1705 ◑ 2302	1.8 3.9 2.0 4.0	23 W	0554 1209 1824	1.3 4.1 1.4
9 W	0553 1146 1827	1.9 3.9 2.0	24 TH	0034 0713 1322 1944	4.3 1.2 4.2 1.3
10 TH	0013 0707 1307 1936	4.1 1.7 4.0 1.7	25 F	0143 0825 1422 2052	4.5 1.0 4.4 1.1
11 F	0128 0810 1413 2036	4.3 1.4 4.3 1.4	26 SA	0240 0924 1511 2148	4.6 0.8 4.6 0.9
12 SA	0228 0905 1502 2129	4.5 1.1 4.5 1.1	27 SU	0328 1014 1553 2236	4.8 0.7 4.8 0.7
13 SU	0317 0955 1544 2219	4.8 0.8 4.8 0.8	28 M	0412 1059 1632 2319	4.8 0.6 4.9 0.6
14 M	0401 1042 1626 2305	5.0 0.6 5.0 0.6	29 TU	0453 1140 1710 ○ 2358	4.9 0.6 5.0 0.6
15 TU	0447 1128 1710 ● 2350	5.1 0.4 5.1 0.4	30 W	0532 1217 1747	4.9 0.6 5.0
			31 TH	0034 0609 1250 1823	0.7 4.8 0.7 5.0

JUNE

Day	Time	m	Day	Time	m
1 F	0107 0644 1320 1857	0.8 4.8 0.9 4.9	16 SA	0110 0657 1331 1915	0.3 5.1 0.4 5.3
2 SA	0137 0717 1347 1930	0.9 4.7 1.1 4.8	17 SU	0157 0746 1417 2004	0.3 5.0 0.5 5.2
3 SU	0204 0749 1413 2003	1.1 4.5 1.3 4.7	18 M	0245 0836 1504 2053	0.5 4.8 0.7 5.0
4 M	0232 0825 1444 2040	1.3 4.4 1.5 4.5	19 TU	0335 0929 1555 2148	0.7 4.6 0.9 4.8
5 TU	0308 0908 1525 2126	1.5 4.2 1.6 4.4	20 W	0429 1029 1650 ◐ 2250	0.9 4.4 1.2 4.5
6 W	0357 1001 1622 ◑ 2223	1.6 4.1 1.8 4.3	21 TH	0528 1138 1751	1.1 4.2 1.3
7 TH	0502 1103 1733 2325	1.7 4.0 1.8 4.2	22 F	0000 0632 1248 1857	4.4 1.2 4.2 1.4
8 F	0613 1207 1844	1.7 4.1 1.7	23 SA	0110 0741 1350 2008	4.3 1.3 4.3 1.3
9 SA	0029 0720 1312 1949	4.3 1.5 4.3 1.5	24 SU	0211 0846 1443 2112	4.4 1.2 4.4 1.2
10 SU	0133 0821 1411 2049	4.5 1.2 4.5 1.2	25 M	0303 0942 1529 2205	4.5 1.0 4.6 1.1
11 M	0233 0918 1505 2145	4.7 1.0 4.7 0.9	26 TU	0349 1030 1610 2252	4.6 0.9 4.7 0.9
12 TU	0328 1013 1556 2239	4.9 0.7 5.0 0.7	27 W	0431 1113 1649 2334	4.7 0.9 4.9 0.9
13 W	0421 1105 1646 ● 2331	5.0 0.5 5.1 0.5	28 TH	0511 1152 1727 ○	4.7 0.9 4.9
14 TH	0514 1155 1737	5.1 0.4 5.3	29 F	0012 0550 1228 1804	0.9 4.7 0.9 4.9
15 F	0021 0606 1244 1826	0.3 5.2 0.3 5.3	30 SA	0047 0627 1259 1840	0.9 4.7 1.0 4.9

JULY

Day	Time	m	Day	Time	m
1 SU	0118 0701 1328 1913	1.0 4.7 1.1 4.9	16 M	0152 0735 1410 1952	0.1 5.1 0.3 5.4
2 M	0146 0734 1356 1944	1.1 4.6 1.2 4.8	17 TU	0237 0822 1454 2037	0.3 5.0 0.5 5.2
3 TU	0215 0807 1426 2017	1.2 4.5 1.3 4.7	18 W	0321 0907 1537 2123	0.5 4.8 0.7 5.0
4 W	0248 0842 1503 2056	1.3 4.4 1.4 4.6	19 TH	0406 0954 1624 ◐ 2212	0.8 4.6 1.0 4.7
5 TH	0329 0925 1548 2144	1.4 4.3 1.5 4.5	20 F	0455 1048 1715 2310	1.1 4.3 1.3 4.4
6 F	0420 1019 1645 ◑ 2242	1.5 4.2 1.6 4.4	21 SA	0549 1154 1813	1.4 4.2 1.6
7 SA	0523 1121 1753 2345	1.5 4.2 1.7 4.4	22 SU	0023 0650 1310 1919	4.2 1.5 4.1 1.6
8 SU	0631 1226 1904	1.5 4.3 1.5	23 M	0139 0759 1415 2031	4.1 1.6 4.2 1.6
9 M	0052 0740 1333 2013	4.5 1.4 4.5 1.3	24 TU	0239 0906 1506 2135	4.2 1.4 4.4 1.4
10 TU	0200 0846 1437 2118	4.6 1.1 4.7 1.1	25 W	0329 1001 1550 2227	4.4 1.3 4.6 1.2
11 W	0304 0948 1535 2219	4.8 0.9 4.9 0.8	26 TH	0412 1048 1630 2311	4.5 1.1 4.8 1.1
12 TH	0404 1047 1630 2318	5.0 0.7 5.2 0.5	27 F	0453 1129 1709 ○ 2351	4.7 1.0 4.9 1.0
13 F	0500 1144 1723 ●	5.1 0.5 5.3	28 SA	0533 1206 1747	4.7 1.0 5.0
14 SA	0013 0554 1236 1814	0.3 5.2 0.3 5.4	29 SU	0026 0610 1239 1822	0.9 4.8 1.0 5.0
15 SU	0104 0646 1325 1904	0.2 5.2 0.3 5.5	30 M	0058 0645 1309 1855	0.9 4.8 1.0 5.0
			31 TU	0126 0717 1337 1924	0.9 4.7 1.0 4.9

AUGUST

Day	Time	m	Day	Time	m
1 W	0155 0747 1407 1953	1.0 4.7 1.1 4.9	16 TH	0258 0836 1512 2051	0.4 5.0 0.7 5.0
2 TH	0227 0815 1440 2024	1.0 4.6 1.2 4.8	17 F	0336 0913 1552 2129	0.8 4.7 1.0 4.7
3 F	0303 0846 1518 2102	1.2 4.5 1.3 4.7	18 SA	0417 0955 1637 ◐ 2214	1.2 4.4 1.4 4.3
4 SA	0345 0931 1606 ◑ 2157	1.3 4.4 1.5 4.5	19 SU	0504 1047 1731 2313	1.6 4.2 1.8 4.0
5 SU	0438 1037 1708 2307	1.5 4.3 1.6 4.4	20 M	0603 1205 1837	1.8 4.0 1.9
6 M	0547 1150 1825	1.6 4.3 1.7	21 TU	0059 0713 1343 1952	3.9 1.9 4.1 1.9
7 TU	0023 0705 1306 1945	4.4 1.6 4.4 1.5	22 W	0217 0829 1443 2107	4.0 1.8 4.3 1.7
8 W	0140 0822 1419 2100	4.5 1.4 4.6 1.2	23 TH	0310 0934 1530 2203	4.3 1.5 4.6 1.4
9 TH	0252 0933 1522 2208	4.7 1.1 4.9 0.9	24 F	0354 1023 1611 2248	4.5 1.3 4.8 1.1
10 F	0353 1037 1617 2308	4.9 0.8 5.2 0.5	25 SA	0434 1105 1649 2327	4.7 1.1 5.0 1.0
11 SA	0449 1134 1710 ●	5.1 0.5 5.4	26 SU	0513 1142 1727 ○	4.8 0.9 5.1
12 SU	0003 0541 1226 1800	0.2 5.2 0.3 5.6	27 M	0002 0549 1216 1801	0.9 4.9 0.9 5.1
13 M	0053 0631 1313 1848	0.1 5.3 0.1 5.6	28 TU	0034 0624 1247 1833	0.8 4.9 0.8 5.1
14 TU	0138 0717 1355 1932	0.0 5.3 0.2 5.5	29 W	0103 0656 1316 1902	0.8 4.9 0.8 5.1
15 W	0219 0758 1434 2013	0.1 5.2 0.4 5.3	30 TH	0133 0724 1346 1930	0.8 4.9 0.9 5.0
			31 F	0204 0748 1418 1956	0.9 4.8 1.0 4.9

Chart Datum is 2·91 metres below Ordnance Datum (Newlyn). HAT is 5·7 metres above Chart Datum.

STANDARD TIME (UT)
For Summer Time add ONE hour in **non-shaded areas**

FALMOUTH LAT 50°09'N LONG 5°03'W

TIMES AND HEIGHTS OF HIGH AND LOW WATERS

Dates in red are SPRINGS
Dates in blue are NEAPS

YEAR **2018**

SEPTEMBER

Date	Day	Time	m	Time	m	Time	m	Time	m
1	SA	0238	1.0	0811	4.7	1453	1.1	2027	4.7
2	SU	0316	1.2	0850	4.6	1536	1.4	2119	4.5
3	M	0403	1.5	0959	4.4	1634	1.6	◑ 2240	4.3
4	TU	0511	1.7	1125	4.3	1756	1.8		
5	W	0006	4.2	0639	1.8	1250	4.3	1930	1.6
6	TH	0132	4.3	0810	1.6	1408	4.6	2053	1.3
7	F	0246	4.6	0926	1.2	1512	4.9	2200	0.9
8	SA	0345	4.9	1028	0.8	1605	5.3	2257	0.5
9	SU	0437	5.1	1122	0.4	1655	5.5	● 2349	0.2
10	M	0525	5.3	1210	0.2	1742	5.6		
11	TU	0035	0.0	0610	5.4	1254	0.1	1826	5.6
12	W	0117	0.0	0651	5.4	1334	0.2	1907	5.5
13	TH	0155	0.2	0728	5.3	1409	0.4	1944	5.3
14	F	0229	0.5	0802	5.1	1443	0.7	2017	5.0
15	SA	0302	0.9	0835	4.8	1517	1.1	2050	4.7
16	SU	0336	1.3	0912	4.5	1556	1.5	◐ 2129	4.3
17	M	0418	1.7	0958	4.3	1648	1.9	2221	4.0
18	TU	0516	2.1	1100	4.0	1757	2.1	2343	3.8
19	W	0630	2.2	1255	4.0	1916	2.1		
20	TH	0151	3.9	0750	2.0	1415	4.2	2034	1.8
21	F	0247	4.2	0900	1.7	1505	4.5	2133	1.5
22	SA	0331	4.5	0952	1.4	1547	4.8	2217	1.2
23	SU	0411	4.7	1035	1.1	1625	5.0	2257	0.9
24	M	0448	4.9	1113	0.9	1700	5.1	2333	0.8
25	TU	0523	5.0	1148	0.8	1735	5.2	○	
26	W	0006	0.7	0557	5.1	1222	0.7	1807	5.2
27	TH	0038	0.6	0629	5.1	1254	0.7	1838	5.2
28	F	0110	0.7	0659	5.0	1326	0.7	1909	5.1
29	SA	0143	0.7	0726	5.0	1358	0.8	1937	5.0
30	SU	0216	0.9	0753	4.8	1434	1.0	2011	4.7

OCTOBER

Date	Day	Time	m	Time	m	Time	m	Time	m
1	M	0253	1.2	0834	4.7	1516	1.3	2106	4.5
2	TU	0341	1.5	0945	4.4	1614	1.6	◑ 2230	4.2
3	W	0449	1.8	1111	4.3	1742	1.8		
4	TH	0000	4.1	0625	1.9	1238	4.3	1924	1.7
5	F	0128	4.3	0803	1.6	1357	4.6	2046	1.3
6	SA	0240	4.6	0916	1.2	1459	4.9	2148	0.8
7	SU	0334	4.9	1013	0.8	1550	5.2	2240	0.4
8	M	0421	5.1	1103	0.4	1637	5.4	2328	0.2
9	TU	0504	5.3	1149	0.2	1720	5.5	●	
10	W	0012	0.1	0545	5.4	1231	0.2	1801	5.5
11	TH	0052	0.1	0622	5.4	1309	0.2	1840	5.4
12	F	0128	0.3	0657	5.3	1342	0.5	1914	5.2
13	SA	0159	0.6	0730	5.1	1414	0.8	1946	4.9
14	SU	0229	1.0	0803	4.9	1445	1.1	2018	4.6
15	M	0258	1.4	0838	4.7	1518	1.5	2055	4.3
16	TU	0332	1.8	0921	4.4	1601	1.9	◐ 2145	4.0
17	W	0423	2.1	1017	4.1	1711	2.2	2254	3.8
18	TH	0544	2.3	1134	4.0	1833	2.2		
19	F	0105	3.8	0705	2.2	1329	4.1	1949	1.9
20	SA	0214	4.1	0817	1.9	1430	4.4	2051	1.6
21	SU	0301	4.4	0913	1.5	1514	4.7	2139	1.2
22	M	0340	4.7	0958	1.2	1553	4.9	2221	0.9
23	TU	0417	4.9	1040	0.9	1628	5.1	2259	0.7
24	W	0451	5.1	1119	0.7	1703	5.2	○ 2337	0.6
25	TH	0526	5.1	1156	0.6	1739	5.2		
26	F	0013	0.5	0602	5.2	1233	0.6	1816	5.2
27	SA	0049	0.6	0637	5.2	1308	0.6	1853	5.1
28	SU	0125	0.7	0712	5.1	1344	0.7	1931	5.0
29	M	0201	0.9	0750	5.0	1422	0.9	2013	4.7
30	TU	0241	1.1	0837	4.8	1508	1.2	2110	4.4
31	W	0331	1.5	0940	4.5	1609	1.5	◑ 2226	4.2

NOVEMBER

Date	Day	Time	m	Time	m	Time	m	Time	m
1	TH	0440	1.7	1058	4.3	1735	1.7	2352	4.1
2	F	0612	1.8	1222	4.4	1910	1.5		
3	SA	0116	4.2	0745	1.6	1339	4.6	2027	1.2
4	SU	0224	4.5	0855	1.2	1440	4.8	2127	0.8
5	M	0316	4.8	0951	0.8	1531	5.1	2218	0.5
6	TU	0401	5.0	1040	0.6	1615	5.2	2304	0.3
7	W	0441	5.2	1125	0.4	1657	5.3	● 2346	0.3
8	TH	0519	5.2	1206	0.4	1737	5.3		
9	F	0025	0.4	0555	5.3	1243	0.4	1814	5.2
10	SA	0100	0.5	0630	5.2	1317	0.6	1849	5.0
11	SU	0131	0.8	0704	5.1	1348	0.9	1921	4.8
12	M	0200	1.1	0737	4.9	1418	1.1	1954	4.6
13	TU	0228	1.4	0812	4.7	1448	1.5	2031	4.4
14	W	0257	1.7	0852	4.5	1522	1.7	2118	4.1
15	TH	0337	1.9	0943	4.3	1617	2.0	◐ 2219	3.9
16	F	0447	2.2	1046	4.1	1737	2.1	2335	3.9
17	SA	0610	2.2	1201	4.1	1854	2.0		
18	SU	0108	4.0	0723	2.0	1322	4.3	2000	1.7
19	M	0213	4.3	0825	1.7	1423	4.5	2054	1.3
20	TU	0259	4.6	0917	1.3	1509	4.8	2141	1.0
21	W	0338	4.8	1004	1.0	1550	5.0	2226	0.8
22	TH	0416	5.0	1048	0.8	1631	5.1	2308	0.6
23	F	0456	5.1	1131	0.6	1714	5.2	○ 2350	0.5
24	SA	0537	5.2	1213	0.5	1758	5.2		
25	SU	0031	0.5	0619	5.3	1255	0.5	1842	5.1
26	M	0112	0.6	0702	5.2	1337	0.6	1927	5.0
27	TU	0153	0.7	0747	5.1	1420	0.8	2014	4.8
28	W	0237	1.0	0836	4.9	1508	1.0	2109	4.5
29	TH	0329	1.2	0933	4.7	1608	1.3	2215	4.3
30	F	0432	1.5	1041	4.5	1720	1.4	◑ 2332	4.2

DECEMBER

Date	Day	Time	m	Time	m	Time	m	Time	m
1	SA	0548	1.6	1156	4.4	1839	1.4		
2	SU	0050	4.2	0708	1.5	1310	4.5	1955	1.2
3	M	0157	4.4	0822	1.3	1414	4.6	2058	1.0
4	TU	0251	4.6	0923	1.0	1507	4.8	2151	0.8
5	W	0337	4.8	1014	0.8	1553	4.9	2238	0.6
6	TH	0417	5.0	1100	0.7	1635	5.0	2321	0.6
7	F	0455	5.1	1141	0.6	1715	5.0	●	
8	SA	0000	0.6	0532	5.1	1220	0.6	1752	4.9
9	SU	0036	0.7	0608	5.1	1255	0.7	1828	4.9
10	M	0108	0.8	0644	5.1	1327	0.9	1902	4.8
11	TU	0138	1.0	0718	5.0	1357	1.1	1936	4.6
12	W	0205	1.2	0753	4.8	1425	1.3	2012	4.5
13	TH	0233	1.4	0829	4.7	1456	1.5	2053	4.3
14	F	0308	1.7	0912	4.5	1536	1.7	2144	4.1
15	SA	0356	1.8	1005	4.3	1634	1.8	◐ 2244	4.0
16	SU	0502	2.0	1106	4.2	1747	1.9	2350	4.0
17	M	0618	1.9	1210	4.2	1859	1.7		
18	TU	0058	4.1	0729	1.8	1316	4.4	2004	1.5
19	W	0200	4.4	0832	1.5	1417	4.6	2101	1.2
20	TH	0254	4.6	0928	1.2	1512	4.8	2153	0.9
21	F	0343	4.9	1020	0.9	1603	5.0	2243	0.7
22	SA	0430	5.1	1110	0.6	1652	5.1	○ 2332	0.5
23	SU	0517	5.2	1159	0.5	1742	5.1		
24	M	0019	0.4	0605	5.3	1247	0.4	1831	5.1
25	TU	0105	0.4	0653	5.3	1333	0.4	1920	5.0
26	W	0150	0.5	0740	5.3	1419	0.5	2008	4.9
27	TH	0235	0.7	0827	5.1	1506	0.7	2057	4.7
28	F	0323	0.9	0918	4.9	1557	0.9	2152	4.4
29	SA	0415	1.1	1014	4.7	1654	1.1	◑ 2256	4.2
30	SU	0515	1.3	1118	4.5	1757	1.3		
31	M	0007	4.1	0621	1.5	1230	4.3	1907	1.4

Chart Datum is 2·91 metres below Ordnance Datum (Newlyn). HAT is 5·7 metres above Chart Datum.

9.1.12 MEVAGISSEY

Cornwall **50°16'·16N 04°46'·93W** ❁❁◊◊✿✿✿

CHARTS AC 1267, 148, 147, 5602; Imray C10, C6, 2400

TIDES –0600 Dover; ML 3·1; Duration 0600

Standard Port PLYMOUTH (⟶)

Times				Height (metres)			
High Water		Low Water		MHWS	MHWN	MLWN	MLWS
0000	0600	0000	0600	5·5	4·4	2·2	0·8
1200	1800	1200	1800				
Differences MEVAGISSEY							
–0015	–0020	–0010	–0005	–0·1	–0·1	–0·2	–0·1

SHELTER Exposed only to E'lies; if >F3 go to Fowey. Appr in strong SE'lies is dangerous. Access all tides.

NAVIGATION WPT 50°16´·16N 04°45´·98W, 270°/6ca to Victoria pier head. Beware rky ledges off N Quay. Speed limit 3kn.

LIGHTS AND MARKS As chartlet and 9.1.4. S Pier lt ho is conspic.

COMMUNICATIONS (Code 01726) CGOC (01326) 317575; Police 101; Dr 843701. HM 843305.

Ch 16 14 (Summer 0900-2100. Winter 0900-1700); call HM for berth.

FACILITIES www.mevagisseyharbour.co.uk meva.harbour@talk21.com **Outer Hbr** Victoria Pier is heavily used by fishing boats Ⓥ may berth only with prior permission in about 2m, £14 all LOAs, short stay free. Keep clear of ⛽ hose & pleasure boats at inner end. Fishing boats use pier as early/late temporary berth to catch tide for entry/exit. Bilge keelers/cats can dry out on sandy beach, SE side of W Quay on request to HM. There are 2 trots of 3 cylindrical Ⓥs off N Pier: moor fore & aft, rafting possible.

No ⚓ inside the hbr due to overcrowding and many FVs. ⚓ off is only advised in settled weather with no E in the wind.

Inner Hbr (dries 1·5m) reserved for FVs, unless taking on ⛽. ⛴ ♿ ⚒ 🚿 ⛵(1t) 🧺. WC 🏴 on W Quay; key held at HM Office.

Village ⛽ ✉ 🏪 Ⓔ Ice ✕ 🛒 @, Ⓑ (Jun-Sep1000-1430, Oct-May1000-1300), ⇌ (bus to St Austell), ✈ Newquay.

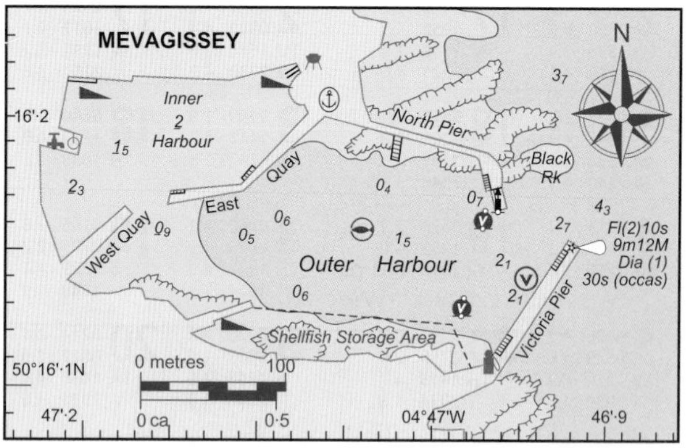

GUNNERY RANGE OFF DODMAN PT AND GRIBBIN HEAD

Naval gunnery practice takes place to seaward of Dodman Point and Gribbin Head, under the control of Flag Officer Sea Training (FOST), HMS Drake, Plymouth PL2 2BG. For info ☎(01752) 557550 (H24) or call *FOST OPS* on VHF Ch 74, which is monitored by all warships in the exercise areas S of Plymouth.

Firing is by day only, approx 1-2 times per week, in a 2hrs block, although actual firing only lasts about 15 mins. Planned firings are broadcast in Gunfacts and Navtex. Advance details are also printed in local newspapers and are available from HMs at Fowey, Looe, Polperro and Mevagissey. Firings are not planned for 2 weeks at Christmas and 4 weeks in August.

Warships, from a position some 2·5 to 9M SSE of Gribbin Hd, fire WSW at 3 target buoys: **A** Fl Y 10s 50°08´·53N 04°46´·37W; **B** Fl Y 5s 50°10´·31N 04°45´·00W; and **C** Fl Y 2s 50°10´·41N 04°47´·51W, about 3·7M SSE of Dodman Pt.

If safety criteria cannot be met, eg owing to vessels in the range area, firing will not take place. A helicopter provides range safety surveillance. A range safety boat will advise other craft of firings and may suggest a course alteration to clear the area. Yachts are legally entitled to transit the range area without undue delay.

MINOR HARBOURS BETWEEN MEVAGISSEY AND FOWEY

CHARLESTOWN, Cornwall, **50°19´·84N 04°45´·35W**. AC 1267, 148, 31. HW –0555 on Dover, –0010 on Plymouth; HW –0·1m on Plymouth; ML 3·1m; Duration 0605. HM ☎01726 70241, VHF Ch 14, 16 (HW –2, only when vessel expected). Still a china clay port, also home to square riggers for filming/publicity.

Enter the inner hbr via entry gate as agreed with HM, but only in W'lies. Ent dries and should only be attempted by day and in off-shore winds with calm weather. Gate fee £35, but free if within Square Sail's schedule. Hbr is shut in SE'lies. Waiting buoy 2ca S of hbr. Bkwtrs 2FG & 2FR(vert) 5m 1M. Ent sig: ● (night) = hbr shut. Facilities: www.square-sail.com; ⛵ £3.12/m, ⛽ Ⓟ Ⓓ (or pre-arranged tanker) ⚒ 🔧 ⛵ ⛵(8t) ✉ ✕ 🛒.

PAR, Cornwall, **50°20´·61N 04°42´·06W**. AC 1267, 148, 31. HW –0555 on Dover. The harbour dries 1·2m and should only be used in an emergency for yachts. There are plans for a marina, but possibly not for several years. Beware Killyvarder Rock (dries 2·4m) 3ca SE of ent, marked by unlit SHM bn. Only enter by day, in calm weather with offshore winds. Facilities in village.

FOWEY TO PLYMOUTH

(AC 1267, 148, 1613) Gribbin Head has a conspic daymark, a 25m high □ twr with R & W bands. In bad weather the sea breaks on rocks around the Head. Cannis Rock (4·3m) is 2½ca SE, marked by a lit SCM.

Fowey is a fine natural harbour, accessible in most conditions although exposed to strong SSW'lies. 3M E of Fowey and 5ca offshore at the East end of Lantivet Bay is Udder Rock (0·6m) marked by a lit SCM. 1M ENE of this buoy Larrick Rock (4·3m) is 1½ca off Nealand Pt.

Polperro harbour dries, but the inlet is a good ⚓ in offshore winds. Beware Polca Rock (1m) roughly in the approach. East of Polperro shoals lie 2½ca off Downend Point. A measured Mile lies between Polperro and **Looe**. The channel between Looe Island and Hannafore Point nearly dries; the charted Boat passage is not advised. The Ranneys (dry, marked by SCM lt buoy) are reefs extending 2½ca E and SE of Looe Island where there are overfalls in bad weather. In Whitsand Bay a buoyed artificial reef (the former *HMS Scylla*) lies 1·4M NW of Rame Head.

Eddystone rocks (AC 1613) lie 8M SSW of Rame Head. NE Rock (0·9m) and shoals are 280m NE. Close NW of the light house is the stump of the old lt ho. The sea can break on Hand Deeps (7m), rocks 3·4M NW of Eddystone, marked by a lit WCM.

9.1.13 FOWEY

Cornwall **50°19'·65N 04°38'·54W** ❀❀❀◊◊◊✿✿✿

CHARTS AC 1267, 148, 31, 5602; Imray C10, C6, 2400

TIDES −0540 Dover; ML 2·9; Duration 0605

Standard Port PLYMOUTH (⟶)

Times				Height (metres)			
High Water		Low Water		MHWS	MHWN	MLWN	MLWS
0000	0600	0000	0600	5·5	4·4	2·2	0·8
1200	1800	1200	1800				
Differences FOWEY							
−0010	−0015	−0010	−0005	−0·1	−0·1	−0·2	−0·2
LOSTWITHIEL							
+0005	−0010	DR	DR	−4·1	−4·1	DR	DR
PAR							
−0010	−0015	−0010	−0005	−0·4	−0·4	−0·4	−0·2

SHELTER Good at Mixtow in all winds. Lower hbr exposed to S-SW, S and SW'ly gales can cause heavy swell and confused seas, especially on the ebb. Entry H24 at any tide in almost any conditions.

NAVIGATION WPT 50°19'·33N 04°38'·80W, 027°/7ca through hbr ent to Whitehouse Pt Dir lt in W sector. Appr in W sector of Fowey lt ho. 3M E of ent beware Udder Rk marked by SCM lt buoy. From SW beware Cannis Rk (4ca SE of Gribbin Hd) marked by SCM lt buoy. Entering hbr, keep well clear of Punch Cross Rks to stbd. Fowey is a busy commercial clay port with ship movements day and night. Speed limit 6kn. Give way to the Bodinnick–Caffa-Mill ferry.

Unmarked, mostly drying chan is navigable up to Golant (1M N of Wiseman's Pt), but moorings restrict ⚓ space. Access on the tide by shoal draught to Lerryn (1·6M) and Lostwithiel (3M) (18m power cables and 5·3m rail bridge).

LIGHTS AND MARKS See chartlet and 9.1.4. A daymark RW twr 33m on Gribbin Hd (1·3M WSW of hbr ent) is conspic from seaward, as is a white house 3ca E of hbr ent. Fowey light house is conspicuous. The W sector (022°-032°) of Whitehouse Pt dir lt leads through the 200m wide harbour entrance. At the entrance, St Catherine's Point is a lamp box; Lamp Rock is on a G bcn. At Whitehouse Pt a conspic radar and CCTV mast monitors traffic in the entrance.

COMMUNICATIONS (Code 01726) CGOC (01326) 317575; NCI Polruan 870291; Police 101; Ⓗ 832241; Dr 829272; HM 832471. *Fowey Hbr Radio* Ch **12** 16 (HO). Hbr Patrol (0900-2000LT) Ch 12. Water taxi (07774 906730) Ch 06. Pilots & Tugs Ch 09, 12.

FACILITIES from seaward:

Polruan Quay (E bank) short stay (2 hrs) pontoon, (3t).
Toms BY ☎870232, (50t).

FOWEY Ⓥs (B) are marked 'FHC VISITORS'. Ⓥ pontoons are in situ May-Oct. Berth/moor as directed by Hbr Patrol. Average overnight fees on Ⓥ/pontoon: £2·00/m, but £2·40/m on Mixtow Pill inc 30 min free wi-fi. Reductions for 3 or 7 days, except Jul/Aug.

Pont Pill, on the E side, offers double-berth fore and aft Ⓥs and in 2m on two 36m floating pontoons; there is also a refuse barge.

Albert Quay HM's Office, . The 'T' shaped landing pontoon is for short stay (2 hrs). Off the E bank is a trot of blue swinging Ⓥs (1-50) and another 36m floating pontoon *(Underhills)*.

Fuel Pontoon W bank 100m N of Caffa Mill H24 only, selfservice card sales only.

Berrills BY short stay (2 hrs 0800-1800 then overnight Ⓥ) landing pontoon, access, 250m N of Albert Quay, oil disposal.

Midway between Bodinnick and Mixtow Pill a sheltered double-sided pontoon *(Gridiron)* is off the E bank with 100m of Ⓥ on its W side.

Mixtow Pill (5ca upriver) 135m walk-ashore pontoon in 2·2m, Ⓥ on S side. (15t) by arrangement. Ⓥ 30m N of Wiseman's Point.

Royal Fowey YC ☎833573, ☎832245 Cafe.
Fowey Gallants SC ☎832335, .
Services M, ACA, Ⓔ (15t).
Town Ⓑ ⇄ (bus to Par), ✈ (Newquay).

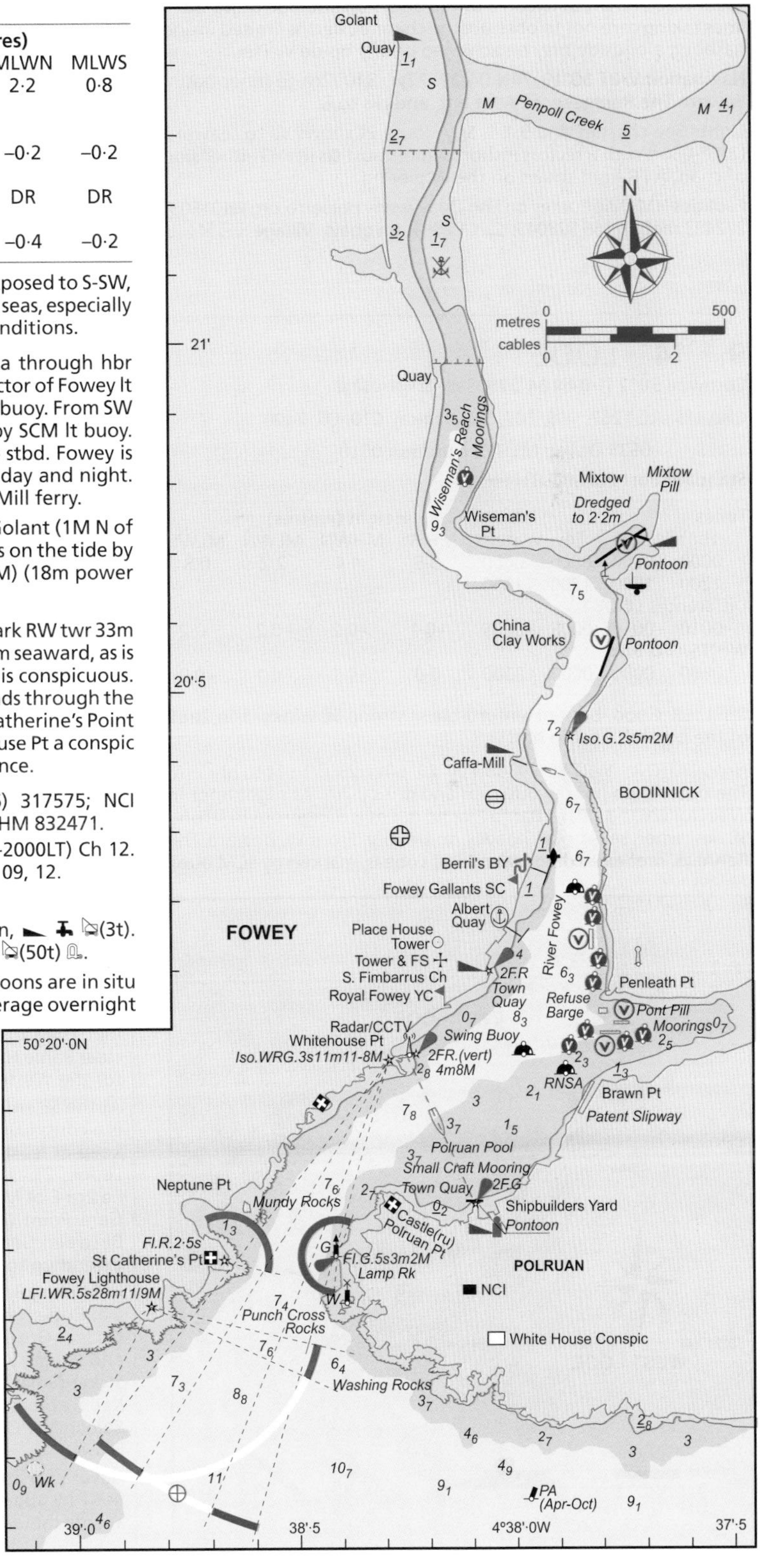

MINOR HARBOUR BETWEEN FOWEY AND LOOE

POLPERRO, Cornwall, **50°19′·78N 04°30′·79W**. AC 1267, 148, 5602. HW –0554 on Dover; HW –0007 and –0·2m on Plymouth; ML 3·1m; Duration 0610. Harbour dries about 2m; depth 2·5m at MHWN.

Shelter Good. Entrance is 9·8m wide (protected by gate in bad weather, but inner basin remains tidal). 6⚓, 3 either side of fairway. Moor fore and aft between 2 of the buoys on one side using short lines taking care not to obstruct the channel. Berths limited inside harbour, alongside may be achieved briefly inside W Pier.

Navigation WPT 50°19′·74N 04°30′·72W, 310°/2ca to inner basin. Beware The Raney, rocks W of ent, and rks to E.

Lights See chartlet and 9.1.4. Spy House Pt shows W to seaward (288°-060°) with R sectors inshore. Outermost ⚓s lit R/G either side of chan. A FR light shows on the W pier hd.

Facilities HM Ollie Puckey on Fish Quay, www.polperro.org ☎(01503) 272423 mob 07966 528045; £1.25. on quays. **Village** ✉ ✕.

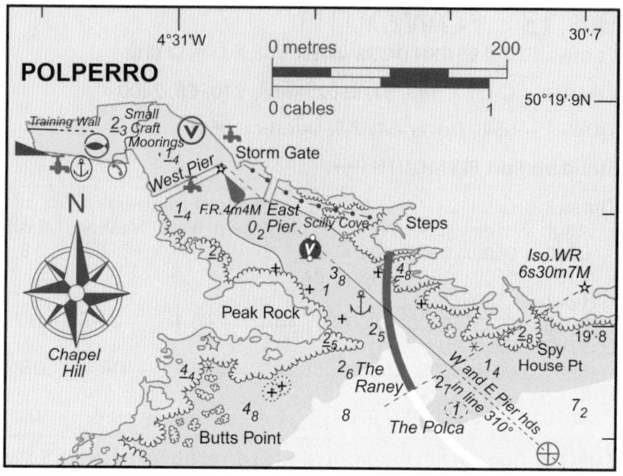

9.1.14 LOOE

Cornwall **50°21′·04N 04°27′·03W**

CHARTS AC 1267, 148, 147, 5602; Imray C10, C6, 2400

TIDES –0538 Dover; ML 3·0; Duration 0610

Standard Port PLYMOUTH (⟶)

Times				**Height (metres)**			
High Water		Low Water		MHWS	MHWN	MLWN	MLWS
0000	0600	0000	0600	5·5	4·4	2·2	0·8
1200	1800	1200	1800				
Differences LOOE							
–0010	–0010	–0005	–0005	–0·1	–0·2	–0·2	–0·2
WHITSAND BAY							
0000	0000	0000	0000	0·0	+0·1	–0·1	+0·2

SHELTER Good, but uncomfortable in strong SE winds. ⚓ in 2m E of the pier hd; no ⚓ in hbr.

NAVIGATION WPT 50°20′·68N 04°25′·60W, 290°/1·0M to hbr ent. The outer chan has rky outcrops and dries 0·7m. At night appr in W sector (267°-313°) of Banjo Pier hd lt. Ent is dangerous in strong SE'lies, when seas break heavily on the bar. From W, beware The Ranneys, reef extending 500m SE of Looe Is, marked by SCM buoy Q (6) + L Fl 15s. 3ca NE of hbr ent, avoid the Limmicks, rks extending 1½ca offshore. Do not attempt the rky passage between Looe Is and the mainland except with local knowledge and at HW. At sp, ebb tide runs up to 5kn. The speed limit within the harbour is 5 mph.

LIGHTS AND MARKS See chartlet and 9.1.4. Looe Island (aka St George's Is) is conspic (45m), 8ca S of the ent. Mid Main ECM lt bcn is off Hannafore Pt, halfway between pier hd and Looe Is. Siren (2) 30s (fishing) at Nailzee Pt. No lts inside hbr.

COMMUNICATIONS (Code 01503) CGOC (01326) 317575; Police 101; Dr 263195. HM: Ch 16 (occas).

FACILITIES Ⓥ berth on W Quay, marked VISITORS, £12.00 all LOA, dries about 3·3m, sloping gently to firm, level sand; rafting is possible and frequently practised.

HM www.looecornwall.com ☎262839, mob 07918 7289550 OH.

W Quay (Wood) Ⓔ.

E Quay For FVs, but access HW ±3 for (3t).

Looe SC www.looesailing club.co.uk ☎262559 ✕.

Town ✉ Ⓑ ✕ @ ⇌.

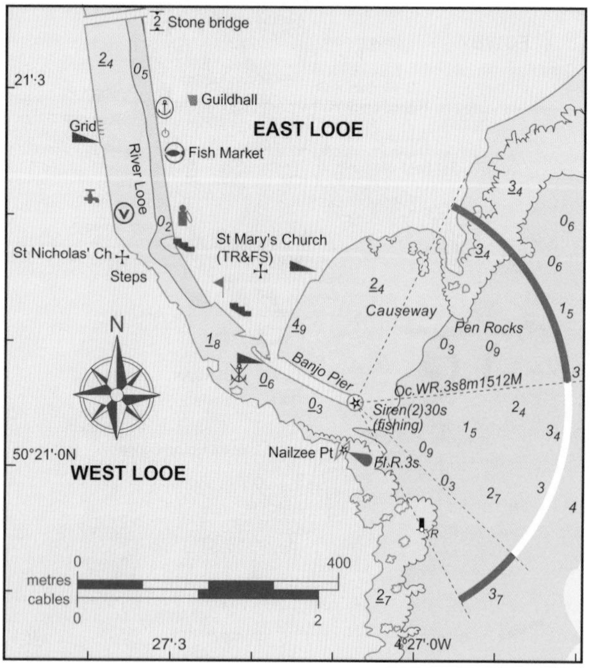

PLYMOUTH TO START POINT

Rame Head, on the W side of the entrance to **Plymouth Sound**, is a conspicuous conical headland, with a small chapel on top; rocks extend about 1ca off and wind-over-tide overfalls may be met 1·5M to seaward. Approaching Plymouth from the West, clear Rame Head and Penlee Point by about 8ca, then steer NNE for the Western end of the Breakwater.

At the SE entrance to Plymouth Sound, Great Mewstone (57m) is a conspicuous rocky islet 4ca off Wembury Pt. From the East keep at least 1M offshore until clear of the drying Mewstone Ledge, 2½ca SW of Great Mewstone. The Slimers, which dry, lie 2ca E of Mewstone. E and W Ebb Rocks (awash) lie 2½ca off Gara Point (AC 30). Wembury Bay leads to the **River Yealm**. Between Gara Point and Stoke Point, 2·5M to the E, dangers extend up to 4ca offshore.

In Bigbury Bay beware Wells Rock (1m) and other dangers 5ca S of Erme Head. From Bolt Tail to Bolt Head keep 5ca offshore to clear Greystone Ledge, sunken rocks near Ham Stone (11m), and Gregory Rocks (2m) 5ca SE of Ham Stone. The Little Mew Stone (3m high) and Mew Stone lie directly below Bolt Head. Keep at least 3ca SE of the Mewstones before turning N for **Salcombe**. Overfalls occur off Prawle Point, 2·6M E of Bolt Head.

Naval exercise areas from the Isles of Scilly to Start Point are used by submarines and warships, especially near Plymouth. Yachts should try to stay clear.

9.1.15 PLYMOUTH

Devon **50°20'·04N 04°10'·07W** (W Chan) ❁❁❁◊◊◊✿✿✿
50°20'·04N 04°08'·07W (E Chan)

CHARTS AC 1267, 1613, 5602, 1900, 30, 1902, 1901, 1967, 871; Imray C10, C14, C6, 2400

TIDES −0540 Dover; ML 3·3; Duration 0610

Standard Port PLYMOUTH (⟶)

Times				Height (metres)			
High Water		Low Water		MHWS	MHWN	MLWN	MLWS
0000	0600	0000	0600	5·5	4·4	2·2	0·8
1200	1800	1200	1800				
Differences BOVISAND PIER							
−0010	−0010	−0008	−0009	−0·1	0·0	+0·2	+0·2
TURNCHAPEL (Cattewater)							
0000	0000	+0010	−0015	0·0	+0·1	+0·2	+0·1
JUPITER POINT (R Lynher)							
+0010	+0005	0000	−0005	0·0	0·0	+0·1	0·0
ST GERMANS (R Lynher)							
0000	0000	+0020	+0020	−0·3	−0·1	0·0	+0·2
SALTASH (R Tamar)							
0000	+0010	0000	−0005	+0·1	+0·1	+0·1	+0·1
LOPWELL (R Tavy)							
ND	ND	DR	DR	−2·6	−2·7	DR	DR
CARGREEN (R Tamar)							
0000	+0010	+0020	+0020	0·0	0·0	−0·1	0·0
COTEHELE QUAY (R Tamar)							
0000	+0020	+0045	+0045	−0·9	−0·9	−0·8	−0·4

NOTE: Winds from SE to W increase the flood and retard the ebb; vice versa in winds from the NW to E.

In Plymouth Sound N all traffic N of the Breakwater conforms to IRPC Rule 9 for 'Narrow channels. There is extensive CCTV coverage of all the enclosed waters.

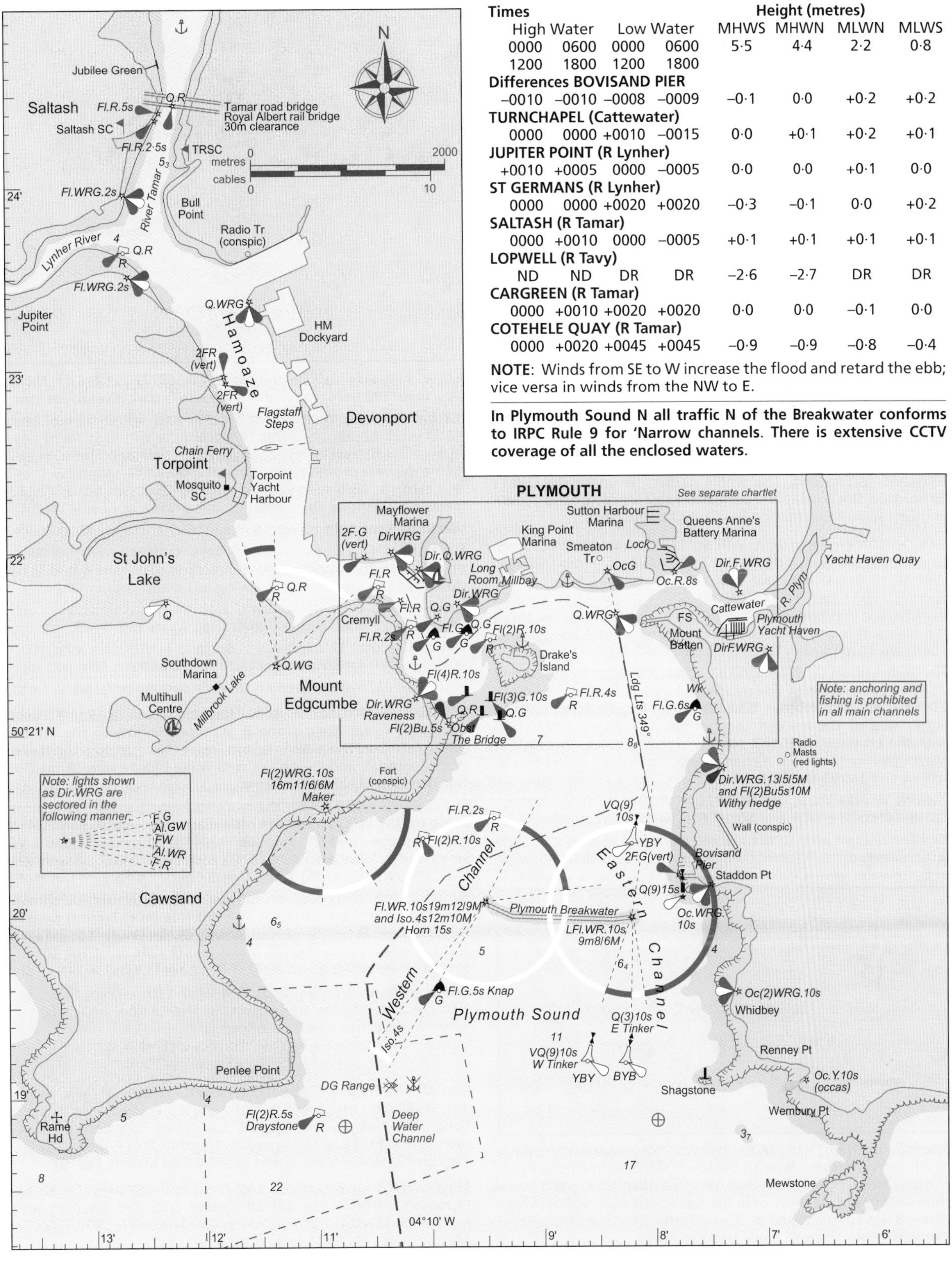

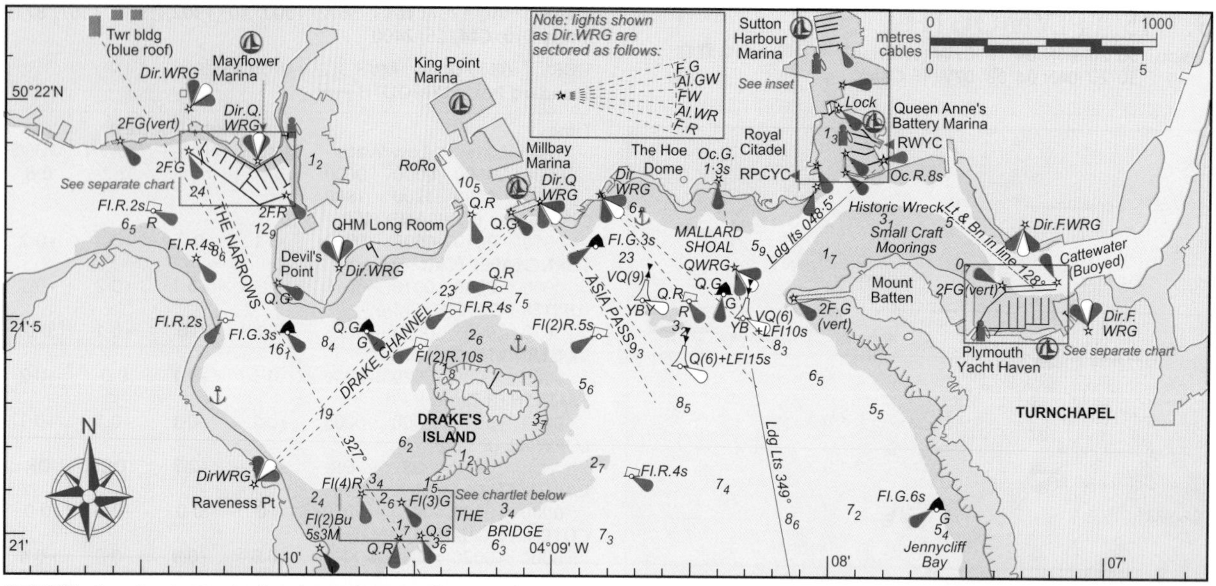

Twr bldg
(blue roof)
Mayflower
Marina
Dir.WRG
50°22'N
Dir.Q.
WRG
2FG(vert)
2F.G
See separate chart
24
2F.R
1₂
12₉
Fl.R.2s
6₅
R
Fl.R.4s
8₆
THE NARROWS
Q.G
Devil's
Point
Dir.WRG
QHM Long Room
King Point
Marina
RoRo
10₅
Q.R
Q.G
Millbay
Marina
Dir.Q
WRG
Note: lights shown
as Dir.WRG are
sectored as follows:
F.G
Al.GW
FW
Al.WR
F.R
The Hoe
Dir
Dome
WRG
Oc.G.
1·3s
Sutton
Harbour
Marina
See inset
Royal
Citadel
RPCYC
metres
cables
0
1000
0
5
Lock
Queen Anne's
Battery Marina
RWYC
Oc.R.8s
Historic Wreck
Small Craft
Moorings
Ldg lts 048·5°
Lt & Bn in line 128°
Dir.F.WRG
Cattewater
(Buoyed)
Mount
Batten
2FG(vert)
Dir.F.
WRG
Plymouth
Yacht Haven
See separate chart
TURNCHAPEL
MALLARD
SHOAL
QWRG
Fl.G.3s
23
VQ(9)
Q.R
YB
Q.G
VQ(6)
YB
LFl10s
Q(6)+LFl15s
2F.G
(vert)
ASIA PASS
21'·5
Fl.R.2s
Fl.G.3s
16₁
Q.G
G
8₄
23
Q.R
Fl.R.4s
7₅
Fl(2)R.5s
Fl(2)R.10s
DRAKE CHANNEL
26
18
DRAKE'S
ISLAND
5₆
3₇
6₂
1₂
19
327°
8₅
6₅
5₅
Ldg Lts 349°
N
DirWRG
Raveness Pt
Fl(4)R
3₄
2₄
Fl(2)Bu
5s3M
2₆
Fl(3)G
1₅
See chartlet below
THE
BRIDGE
3₄
1₇
Q.G
Q.R
3₆
6₃
04°09' W
7₃
2₇
Fl.R.4s
7₄
8₆
7₂
Fl.G.6s
G
5₄
Jennycliff
Bay
21'
10'
08'
07'

SHELTER Good or better in 4 major and some minor marinas; see Facilities. Around the Sound ⚓s, sheltered according to the wind: Cawsand Bay, Barn Pool (below Mt Edgcumbe), N of Drake's Island, below The Hoe and in Jennycliff Bay. Also good shelter W of Cremyll and off the Hamoaze in the R Lynher and R Tamar above Saltash.Plymouth is a Naval Base (Devonport) and a commercial, ferry and fishing port. The whole harbour is under the QHM's jurisdiction, but Millbay and the Cattewater are controlled by ABP and Cattewater Commissioners (Capt Charlesworth).

NAVIGATION From the west: WPT 50°18′·81N 04°10′·90W (abeam Draystone PHM buoy), 035°/1·5M to W Bkwtr lt. From the east: WPT 50°18′·81N 04°08′·00W, 000°/1·2M to abeam E Bkwtr lt. The Sound can be entered via the W (main) or E Chans which are well marked, but in strong W'lies the E Chan has a hazardous lee shore for yachts. It is vital to keep well clear of the unlit Shag Stone. There are 3·2m patches NE of E Tinker ECM lt buoy.

The Bridge (short cut SW of Drake's Island) is marked by 2 PHM and 2 SHM lt bns, both with tide gauges showing height of tide above CD; least charted depth is 1·3m. There are drying rocky patches either side of the marked channel which is aligned 327°/147° with the LH (blue roof) of 3 conspic high-rise blocks (5ca NW of Mayflower marina). In the chan spring tides reach 346°/1·6kn at HW –4 and 150°/2·4kn at HW +4.

Historic Wrecks are at: 50°21′·73N 04°07′·70W (N of Mt Batten), 50°19′·00N 04°11′·64W and 50°18′·61N 04°12′·05W.

Yachts need not keep to the marked chans but must not impede larger vessels or the Torpoint chain ferries at 50°22′·50N 04°11′·30W. In Cattewater vessels <20m LOA keep clear of vessels >20m LOA.

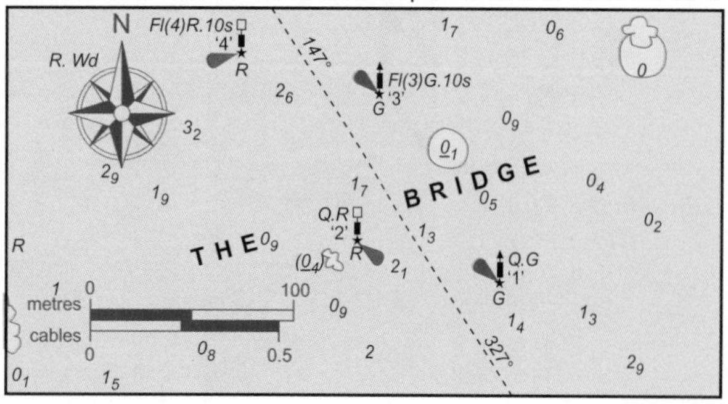

N
Fl(4)R.10s
'4'
R
R. Wd
147°
1₇
0₆
0
Fl(3)G.10s
'3'
G
2₆
3₂
0₉
0₁
2₉
1₉
1₇
BRIDGE
0₅
0₄
Q.R
'2'
R
THE
0₉
1₃
0₂
R
(0₄)
2₁
Q.G
'1'
G
100
metres
cables
0
0₉
1₄
1₃
0
0₈
0.5
2
327°
2₉
0₁
1₅

Speed limits: 10kn* N of Plymouth Bkwtr; 8kn in Cattewater; 4kn N of a line from Fisher's Nose to S side of QAB; 5kn in Sutton Hbr. *Vessels <15m LOA are exempt from the 10kn limit when more than 400m from the shore or in the access lane for water/jet skiers (Fisher's Nose to the W end of Mount Batten Bkwtr and from Royal Plymouth Corinthian YC to W Mallard buoy).

NAVAL ACTIVITY Call Devonport Ops ☎563777 Ext 2182/3. Naval Ops, ☎501182 (H24) www.qhmplymouth.org.uk gives much info.

Exclusion zones: Vessels must not approach within 50m of any MoD establishment, warship or auxiliary or within 100m of any submarine. Buoys (Y) may be deployed to delineate these zones. Some ships are protected by a zone of 250m while underway. They are escorted by armed vessels; listen to **Ch14** (Sound) or Ch13. Failure to respond to warnings will be taken as hostile intent.

Warships have right of way in main/DW chans; obey MoD Police.

Submarines: Do not pass within 200m or cross astern within 800m of any submarine under way. Submarines may secure to a buoy close N of the Breakwater, showing a Fl Y anti-collision light.

Diving: Keep clear of Bovisand Pier, the Breakwater Fort and Ravenness Pt when diving signals (Flag A) are displayed.

Ferries Roscoff: 12/week; 5hrs; Brittany Ferries (www.brittany-ferries.co.uk); Santander: weekly; 19½hrs; Brittany Ferries.

Yachts should avoid impeding the safe passage of larger vessels.

LIGHTS AND MARKS Principal daymarks: conical Rame Head to the W; Great Mew Stone & Staddon Heights to the E; The Breakwater; on The Hoe: Smeaton Tower (R/W bands) & the Naval War Memorial; and Ocean Court (a white bldg) overlooking The Narrows and Mayflower marina.

See chartlets and 9.1.4 for the many lts, some hard to see against shore lts. Dir WRG lts defining the main chans are shown H24** from: Whidbey (138·5°), Staddon Pt (044°), Withyhedge (070°), W Hoe bn (315°), Western King (271°), Millbay** (048·5°), Ravenness (225°), Mount Wise (343°), and Ocean Court** (085°). ** Not H24.

Notes: In fog W lts may, on request to Port Control, be shown from: Mallard (front ldg lt) Fl 5s; West Hoe bn F; Eastern King Fl 5s; Ravenness Fl (2) 15s; Mount Wise F; Ocean Court Fl 5s. Major lts in The Sound show QY if mains power fails. N of The Bkwtr, four large mooring buoys (C, D, E & F) have Fl Y lts.

Wind strength warning flags (R & W vert stripes) are flown at QAB and Mayflower marinas and at The Camber (HO only) to warn of excessive winds as follows:

1 wind flag = Force 5–7 (17–27kn).
2 wind flags = > Force 7 (>27kn).

COMMUNICATIONS (Code 01752) CGOC (01326) 317575; Police 101; 🄷 668080. QHM 836952; DQHM 836485; Port surveyor 836962; Longroom Port Control 836528; *Longroom Port Control* (H24) monitor Ch 13, 14 or 16 underway. Flagstaff Port Control 552413 *Flag* Ch 13, 16. Cattewater HM 665934; ABP Millbay 662191.

Mayflower & QAB marinas and Torpoint Yacht Hbr: Ch **80** M. Plymouth Yacht Haven: Ch **80**. *Sutton Lock,* for opening and marina: Ch **12** (H24). *Cattewater Hbr* Ch 14 (Mon-Fri, 0900-1700LT). *Millbay Docks* Ch 12 14 (only during ferry ops).

FACILITIES Marinas and Rivers from seaward (SE-NW):

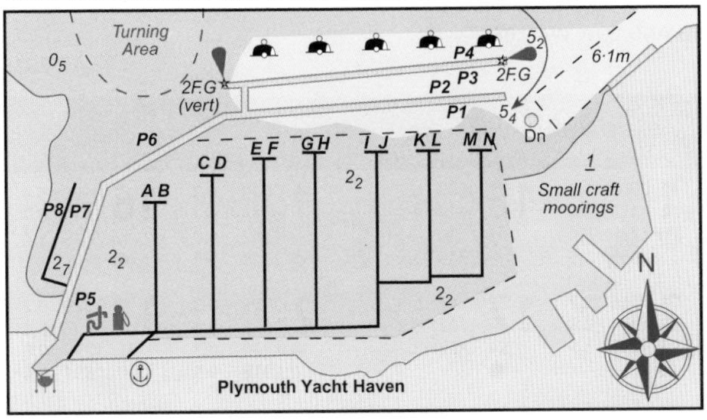

Plymouth Yacht Haven www.yacht havens.com ☎404231, mobile 07721 498422 (o/night); access H24, channel dredged 2·25m. 450 inc Ⓥ £3.25 inc (H24) (75t) mobile (4t) wi-fi.

Turnchapel Wharf ryan@turnchapelwharf.com commercial/large yacht. Max draught 5m max LOA50m, at all states of tide.

Yacht Haven Quay 50°21´·87N 04°06´·61W ☎481190. Access H24 to pontoon in 1·2m, 2 FG (vert); C; dry berths/storage. Ferry: ½hrly from Mount Batten–Barbican, 5 mins: daily 0700-2300, Ch **M** or ☎408590 mob 07930 838614.

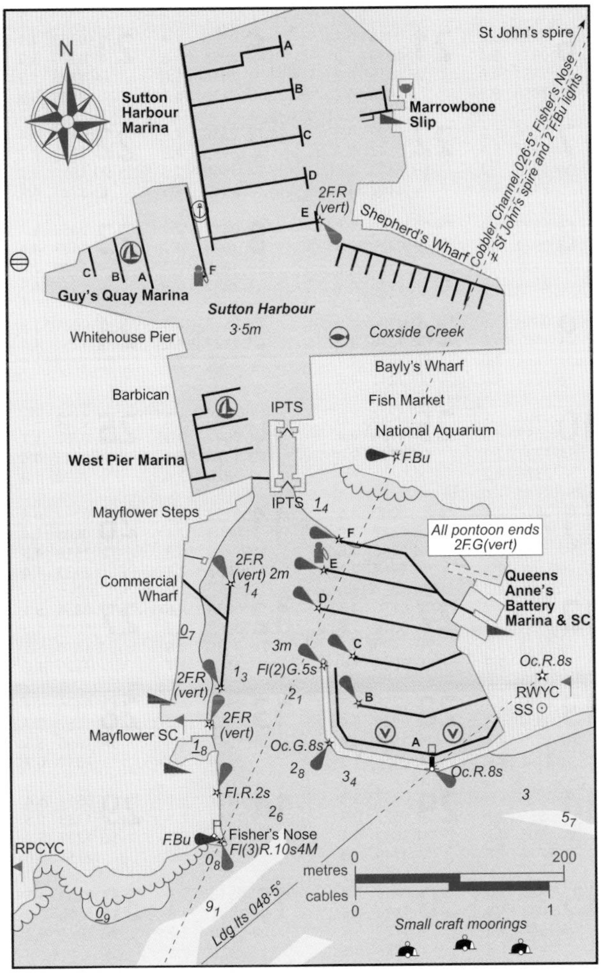

Queen Anne's Battery (QAB) www.queenannesbattery.co.uk ☎671142, mobile 07740 806039. 235+40Ⓥ short stay £8·45, £3·50<12.5m>£4·35<18m>£4·85<18·1m inc (0830-1830, 7/7) (25t) ©. Extensive facilities.

Sutton Harbour 50°21´·98N 04°07´·96W. West Pier and Guy's Quay marinas are mainly for locals (no shwrs).

Lock operates H24, free. IPTS: sigs 1, 2 & 3. Call *Sutton Lock* Ch 12 for entry and allocation of a berth; secure to floating pontoons either side of lock. The lock retains CD +3·5m in the hbr; when rise of tide >3m, approx HW ±3, free-flow is in operation.

Sutton Hbr Marina www.suttonharbourmarina.com ☎204702, 467 inc Ⓥ £3.50 inc (25t) all maintenance/repairs. Nearby.

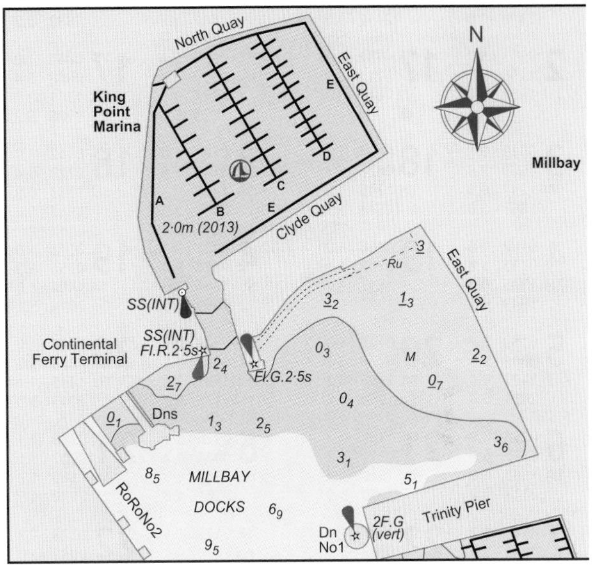

King Point Marina www.kingpointmarina.co.uk ☎424297; 171 inc Ⓥ (development continues), poa approx £3, ice, wi-fi(weak).

Mill Bay Village Marina ☎226785, Ch **M**. No Ⓥ.

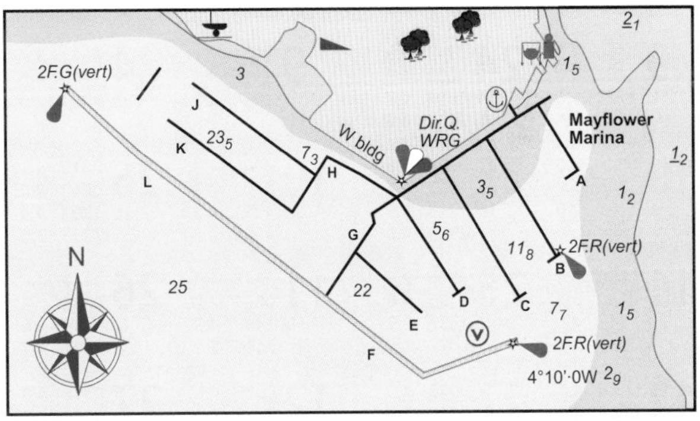

Mayflower Marina www.mayflowermarina.co.uk ☎556633 (HO) mob 07840 116853. 27m max LOA with 3·5m min depth, but 1·5m near and fuel berth. Limit speed to maintain steerage. 396 inc 40Ⓥ £3·20 (inc wi-fi), £5 then £3/hr<4 hrs. (H24) (33t) (1½t) Divers ☎500008.

Southdown Marina www.southdownmarina.co.uk ☎823084. Approach dries 2m. s. 35 in 2m incⓋ £20 all LOA, or at drying quay, (20t).

Torpoint Yacht Hbr www.torpointyachtharbour.co.uk ☎813658. Access H24, 2m. 100 s 70 pre-call for a Ⓥ berth £2.50, free water taxi.

YACHT CLUBS

Royal Western Yacht Club of England ☎660077.

Royal Plymouth Corinthian YC ☎664327, VHF ChM.

Plym YC ☎404991. **RNSA** ☎567854. **Mayflower SC** ☎ 492566.

Torpoint Mosquito SC ☎812508, visitors welcome.

Saltash SC ☎845988. **Tamar River SC** ☎362741.

STANDARD TIME (UT)
For Summer Time add ONE hour in **non-shaded areas**

PLYMOUTH LAT 50°22′N LONG 4°11′W

TIMES AND HEIGHTS OF HIGH AND LOW WATERS

Dates in red are SPRINGS
Dates in blue are NEAPS

YEAR **2018**

JANUARY

Day	Time	m	Day	Time	m
1	0440	5.5	16	0512	5.2
	1104	0.9		1135	1.3
M	1709	5.4	TU	1733	5.1
	2328	0.8		2350	1.3
2	0533	5.7	17	0551	5.3
	1156	0.7		1211	1.2
TU	1802	5.6	W	1811	5.1
○			●		
3	0019	0.7	18	0024	1.2
	0623	5.8		0628	5.4
W	1247	0.5	TH	1245	1.2
	1853	5.6		1848	5.1
4	0107	0.6	19	0056	1.2
	0713	5.8		0705	5.4
TH	1335	0.5	F	1317	1.2
	1943	5.5		1925	5.1
5	0153	0.7	20	0126	1.2
	0801	5.8		0739	5.3
F	1421	0.6	SA	1348	1.2
	2031	5.4		1958	5.0
6	0238	0.8	21	0156	1.3
	0847	5.6		0811	5.2
SA	1505	0.8	SU	1419	1.3
	2117	5.2		2030	5.0
7	0320	1.1	22	0227	1.4
	0932	5.4		0843	5.1
SU	1549	1.1	M	1451	1.4
	2203	5.0		2104	4.9
8	0404	1.4	23	0302	1.5
	1017	5.1		0919	5.0
M	1633	1.5	TU	1529	1.5
◑	2250	4.7		2143	4.8
9	0450	1.7	24	0343	1.6
	1106	4.8		1002	4.9
TU	1723	1.8	W	1614	1.7
	2345	4.5	◐	2231	4.6
10	0544	2.0	25	0434	1.8
	1206	4.6		1057	4.7
W	1821	2.0	TH	1713	1.9
				2333	4.6
11	0050	4.4	26	0544	2.0
	0650	2.2		1205	4.6
TH	1316	4.5	F	1832	2.0
	1932	2.1			
12	0156	4.5	27	0048	4.6
	0806	2.1		0715	2.0
F	1422	4.5	SA	1327	4.7
	2043	2.0		1959	1.8
13	0255	4.6	28	0210	4.7
	0914	2.0		0840	1.8
SA	1519	4.6	SU	1448	4.8
	2142	1.8		2115	1.6
14	0347	4.8	29	0323	5.0
	1009	1.7		0951	1.4
SU	1609	4.8	M	1557	5.0
	2230	1.6		2220	1.2
15	0432	5.1	30	0424	5.3
	1054	1.5		1052	1.0
M	1652	5.0	TU	1656	5.3
	2312	1.4		2317	0.9
			31	0520	5.6
				1146	0.7
			W	1751	5.4
			○		

FEBRUARY

Day	Time	m	Day	Time	m
1	0008	0.6	16	0005	1.1
	0610	5.8		0610	5.3
TH	1237	0.4	F	1228	1.0
	1841	5.5		1832	5.2
2	0056	0.4	17	0040	1.0
	0659	5.8		0648	5.4
F	1323	0.3	SA	1301	0.9
	1929	5.6		1908	5.2
3	0140	0.4	18	0112	1.0
	0746	5.8		0723	5.4
SA	1406	0.3	SU	1333	0.9
	2013	5.5		1942	5.2
4	0221	0.5	19	0143	1.0
	0828	5.7		0756	5.3
SU	1446	0.5	M	1404	1.0
	2053	5.3		2014	5.1
5	0259	0.8	20	0214	1.0
	0907	5.5		0828	5.2
M	1523	0.9	TU	1435	1.1
	2129	5.1		2045	5.0
6	0336	1.1	21	0246	1.1
	0941	5.2		0902	5.1
TU	1559	1.3	W	1509	1.2
	2201	4.8		2120	4.9
7	0413	1.5	22	0323	1.3
	1014	4.8		0941	5.0
W	1638	1.7	TH	1549	1.5
◑	2236	4.6		2203	4.8
8	0456	1.9	23	0409	1.6
	1055	4.5		1032	4.7
TH	1724	2.0	F	1641	1.7
	2325	4.4	◐	2302	4.6
9	0551	2.2	24	0511	1.9
	1155	4.3		1140	4.5
F	1824	2.3	SA	1754	2.0
10	0046	4.3	25	0019	4.5
	0701	2.3		0642	2.0
SA	1331	4.2	SU	1307	4.4
	1939	2.3		1933	2.0
11	0213	4.3	26	0149	4.6
	0824	2.2		0823	1.9
SU	1446	4.3	M	1436	4.6
	2100	2.1		2101	1.7
12	0315	4.6	27	0308	4.9
	0938	1.9		0941	1.4
M	1543	4.6	TU	1548	4.9
	2202	1.8		2210	1.3
13	0406	4.8	28	0412	5.2
	1030	1.6		1042	1.0
TU	1631	4.8	W	1647	5.2
	2249	1.5		2306	0.9
14	0450	5.1			
	1113	1.4			
W	1713	5.0			
	2329	1.3			
15	0531	5.2			
	1152	1.1			
TH	1754	5.1			
●					

MARCH

Day	Time	m	Day	Time	m
1	0506	5.5	16	0505	5.2
	1134	0.6		1124	1.1
TH	1739	5.4	F	1730	5.1
	2355	0.5		2340	1.0
2	0556	5.7	17	0546	5.3
	1221	0.3		1202	0.9
F	1826	5.5	SA	1809	5.2
○			●		
3	0040	0.3	18	0017	0.9
	0642	5.8		0625	5.4
SA	1305	0.2	SU	1238	0.7
	1909	5.6		1846	5.3
4	0122	0.3	19	0052	0.8
	0724	5.8		0702	5.4
SU	1345	0.2	M	1313	0.7
	1948	5.5		1921	5.3
5	0200	0.4	20	0126	0.7
	0802	5.6		0737	5.4
M	1421	0.4	TU	1346	0.7
	2022	5.4		1954	5.3
6	0234	0.6	21	0158	0.8
	0835	5.4		0812	5.3
TU	1454	0.8	W	1419	0.8
	2050	5.2		2026	5.2
7	0306	1.0	22	0232	0.9
	0903	5.1		0847	5.2
W	1525	1.2	TH	1453	1.1
	2115	4.9		2102	5.1
8	0337	1.4	23	0309	1.2
	0931	4.8		0927	5.0
TH	1556	1.6	F	1533	1.4
	2146	4.7		2145	4.9
9	0413	1.8	24	0354	1.5
	1007	4.5		1018	4.7
F	1634	2.0	SA	1623	1.7
◑	2227	4.4	◐	2241	4.6
10	0502	2.1	25	0456	1.8
	1057	4.2		1126	4.4
SA	1731	2.3	SU	1735	2.0
	2328	4.2			
11	0612	2.4	26	0000	4.5
	1217	4.0		0627	2.0
SU	1846	2.4	M	1300	4.3
				1917	2.1
12	0114	4.2	27	0136	4.5
	0731	2.3		0814	1.8
M	1411	4.1	TU	1429	4.5
	2007	2.3		2050	1.8
13	0240	4.4	28	0256	4.8
	0854	2.1		0929	1.4
TU	1515	4.4	W	1538	4.8
	2123	2.0		2156	1.3
14	0336	4.7	29	0357	5.2
	0957	1.7		1027	0.9
W	1605	4.7	TH	1633	5.1
	2217	1.6		2249	0.9
15	0423	5.0	30	0449	5.4
	1043	1.3		1116	0.5
TH	1648	4.9	F	1721	5.4
	2301	1.3		2336	0.5
			31	0536	5.6
				1201	0.3
			SA	1804	5.5
			○		

APRIL

Day	Time	m	Day	Time	m
1	0019	0.3	16	0558	5.4
	0619	5.7		1211	0.7
SU	1242	0.2	M	1819	5.4
	1843	5.5	●		
2	0059	0.3	17	0029	0.7
	0658	5.6		0638	5.4
M	1320	0.3	TU	1250	0.6
	1918	5.5		1857	5.4
3	0134	0.4	18	0107	0.6
	0732	5.5		0717	5.5
TU	1354	0.5	W	1327	0.6
	1947	5.4		1933	5.4
4	0207	0.7	19	0144	0.6
	0801	5.3		0756	5.4
W	1424	0.9	TH	1404	0.8
	2013	5.2		2010	5.4
5	0236	1.0	20	0221	0.8
	0828	5.1		0836	5.2
TH	1451	1.2	F	1442	1.0
	2039	5.0		2049	5.2
6	0305	1.4	21	0302	1.1
	0858	4.8		0920	5.0
F	1518	1.6	SA	1525	1.3
	2110	4.8		2134	5.0
7	0335	1.7	22	0350	1.4
	0933	4.5		1012	4.7
SA	1548	2.0	SU	1617	1.7
	2149	4.5	◐	2231	4.7
8	0417	2.1	23	0453	1.7
	1020	4.2		1123	4.4
SU	1639	2.3	M	1729	2.0
◑	2242	4.3		2349	4.5
9	0528	2.3	24	0621	1.9
	1127	4.0		1254	4.4
M	1802	2.5	TU	1903	2.0
10	0000	4.2	25	0122	4.6
	0647	2.3		0757	1.7
TU	1320	4.1	W	1415	4.6
	1920	2.4		2030	1.8
11	0152	4.3	26	0237	4.8
	0803	2.1		0908	1.4
W	1438	4.3	TH	1518	4.8
	2033	2.1		2133	1.4
12	0258	4.6	27	0336	5.1
	0909	1.7		1004	1.0
TH	1531	4.6	F	1610	5.1
	2134	1.7		2225	1.0
13	0348	4.9	28	0426	5.3
	1002	1.4		1052	0.7
F	1616	4.9	SA	1656	5.3
	2224	1.3		2312	0.7
14	0433	5.1	29	0511	5.4
	1048	1.1		1135	0.5
SA	1659	5.1	SU	1737	5.4
	2308	1.0		2354	0.6
15	0516	5.3	30	0553	5.5
	1131	0.8		1216	0.5
SU	1740	5.2	M	1814	5.4
	2350	0.8	○		

Chart Datum is 3·22 metres below Ordnance Datum (Newlyn). HAT is 5·9 metres above Chart Datum.

STANDARD TIME (UT)
For Summer Time add ONE hour in **non-shaded areas**

PLYMOUTH LAT 50°22′N LONG 4°11′W

TIMES AND HEIGHTS OF HIGH AND LOW WATERS

Dates in red are SPRINGS
Dates in blue are NEAPS

YEAR **2018**

MAY

Date	Day	Time	m	Time	m	Time	m	Time	m	Moon
1	TU	0032	0.5	0630	5.4	1253	0.6	1846	5.4	
2	W	0108	0.6	0702	5.3	1326	0.8	1915	5.3	
3	TH	0140	0.8	0732	5.2	1355	1.0	1942	5.2	
4	F	0209	1.1	0801	5.0	1421	1.3	2012	5.1	
5	SA	0236	1.4	0833	4.8	1447	1.6	2044	4.9	
6	SU	0305	1.7	0909	4.6	1514	1.9	2122	4.7	
7	M	0342	2.0	0954	4.3	1556	2.2	2210	4.5	
8	TU	0444	2.2	1053	4.2	1713	2.4	2312	4.3	◑
9	W	0603	2.2	1212	4.1	1835	2.3			
10	TH	0035	4.3	0715	2.1	1343	4.3	1945	2.1	
11	F	0203	4.5	0820	1.8	1445	4.6	2048	1.8	
12	SA	0303	4.8	0918	1.4	1536	4.8	2143	1.4	
13	SU	0354	5.0	1010	1.1	1623	5.1	2233	1.1	
14	M	0442	5.2	1058	0.9	1707	5.3	2321	0.8	
15	TU	0528	5.4	1144	0.7	1751	5.4			●
16	W	0005	0.7	0613	5.4	1228	0.6	1833	5.5	
17	TH	0049	0.6	0658	5.5	1311	0.6	1915	5.6	
18	F	0132	0.6	0743	5.4	1353	0.7	1958	5.5	
19	SA	0215	0.7	0829	5.3	1436	0.9	2042	5.4	
20	SU	0300	1.0	0917	5.0	1522	1.2	2130	5.2	
21	M	0351	1.3	1012	4.8	1616	1.6	2226	4.9	
22	TU	0451	1.5	1120	4.6	1720	1.8	2338	4.7	◐
23	W	0605	1.7	1237	4.5	1838	1.9			
24	TH	0059	4.7	0726	1.7	1348	4.6	1956	1.8	
25	F	0208	4.8	0836	1.5	1448	4.8	2101	1.5	
26	SA	0307	4.9	0933	1.2	1540	5.0	2156	1.2	
27	SU	0358	5.1	1023	1.0	1626	5.1	2244	1.0	
28	M	0444	5.2	1108	0.9	1707	5.2	2327	0.9	
29	TU	0525	5.2	1149	0.8	1744	5.3			○
30	W	0007	0.9	0602	5.2	1226	0.9	1817	5.3	
31	TH	0043	0.9	0636	5.2	1259	1.0	1849	5.3	

JUNE

Date	Day	Time	m	Time	m	Time	m	Time	m	Moon
1	F	0115	1.0	0708	5.1	1329	1.2	1920	5.2	
2	SA	0145	1.2	0741	5.0	1357	1.4	1952	5.1	
3	SU	0214	1.4	0816	4.8	1424	1.6	2026	5.0	
4	M	0244	1.6	0852	4.6	1453	1.8	2102	4.8	
5	TU	0318	1.8	0934	4.5	1531	2.0	2144	4.7	
6	W	0405	1.9	1024	4.3	1625	2.1	2236	4.5	◑
7	TH	0511	2.0	1124	4.3	1740	2.2	2338	4.5	
8	F	0625	2.0	1235	4.3	1855	2.1			
9	SA	0051	4.6	0733	1.8	1347	4.5	2002	1.9	
10	SU	0207	4.7	0835	1.5	1449	4.8	2104	1.5	
11	M	0311	4.9	0933	1.3	1544	5.0	2201	1.2	
12	TU	0408	5.1	1028	1.0	1635	5.2	2254	0.9	
13	W	0501	5.3	1119	0.8	1725	5.4	2345	0.7	●
14	TH	0552	5.4	1209	0.7	1813	5.6			
15	F	0034	0.6	0642	5.5	1257	0.6	1900	5.6	
16	SA	0122	0.5	0732	5.4	1344	0.7	1948	5.6	
17	SU	0210	0.6	0822	5.3	1431	0.8	2035	5.5	
18	M	0257	0.8	0913	5.2	1518	1.0	2124	5.3	
19	TU	0346	1.0	1006	5.0	1607	1.3	2217	5.1	
20	W	0439	1.3	1103	4.8	1701	1.6	2317	4.9	◐
21	TH	0537	1.5	1206	4.6	1803	1.8			
22	F	0024	4.7	0644	1.7	1311	4.6	1912	1.8	
23	SA	0132	4.7	0754	1.7	1411	4.6	2021	1.8	
24	SU	0233	4.7	0857	1.6	1505	4.8	2122	1.6	
25	M	0327	4.8	0952	1.4	1554	4.9	2215	1.4	
26	TU	0416	4.9	1040	1.3	1638	5.1	2301	1.2	
27	W	0459	5.0	1123	1.2	1718	5.2	2343	1.1	
28	TH	0539	5.0	1202	1.1	1754	5.2			○
29	F	0021	1.1	0615	5.1	1237	1.2	1829	5.3	
30	SA	0055	1.1	0651	5.0	1309	1.2	1903	5.2	

JULY

Date	Day	Time	m	Time	m	Time	m	Time	m	Moon
1	SU	0127	1.2	0727	5.0	1338	1.3	1938	5.2	
2	M	0156	1.3	0802	4.9	1407	1.5	2011	5.1	
3	TU	0226	1.4	0838	4.8	1436	1.6	2045	5.0	
4	W	0258	1.5	0915	4.6	1509	1.7	2121	4.8	
5	TH	0335	1.7	0955	4.5	1550	1.8	2204	4.7	
6	F	0423	1.8	1044	4.5	1645	2.0	2257	4.6	◑
7	SA	0526	1.9	1143	4.4	1757	2.0			
8	SU	0000	4.6	0642	1.8	1252	4.5	1916	1.9	
9	M	0116	4.7	0755	1.7	1404	4.7	2028	1.7	
10	TU	0233	4.8	0902	1.4	1510	4.9	2133	1.4	
11	W	0340	5.0	1003	1.2	1609	5.2	2233	1.1	
12	TH	0440	5.2	1101	0.9	1704	5.4	2330	0.8	
13	F	0536	5.4	1155	0.7	1756	5.6			●
14	SA	0022	0.5	0629	5.4	1246	0.6	1847	5.7	
15	SU	0113	0.4	0721	5.5	1335	0.5	1937	5.7	
16	M	0201	0.4	0812	5.4	1421	0.6	2025	5.7	
17	TU	0247	0.5	0900	5.3	1505	0.8	2111	5.5	
18	W	0331	0.8	0947	5.1	1548	1.0	2156	5.3	
19	TH	0415	1.1	1034	4.9	1633	1.4	2243	5.0	◐
20	F	0502	1.4	1125	4.7	1723	1.7	2337	4.7	
21	SA	0556	1.7	1223	4.5	1822	1.9			
22	SU	0045	4.5	0700	1.9	1328	4.5	1932	2.0	
23	M	0155	4.4	0813	1.9	1429	4.5	2045	1.9	
24	TU	0257	4.5	0920	1.8	1524	4.7	2147	1.7	
25	W	0350	4.6	1014	1.6	1612	4.9	2238	1.5	
26	TH	0437	4.8	1100	1.4	1655	5.1	2322	1.3	
27	F	0518	4.9	1141	1.3	1734	5.2			○
28	SA	0001	1.2	0557	5.0	1218	1.2	1811	5.3	
29	SU	0037	1.1	0635	5.1	1250	1.2	1848	5.3	
30	M	0109	1.1	0712	5.0	1320	1.2	1923	5.3	
31	TU	0138	1.2	0747	5.0	1349	1.3	1956	5.2	

AUGUST

Date	Day	Time	m	Time	m	Time	m	Time	m	Moon
1	W	0207	1.2	0821	4.9	1417	1.4	2027	5.1	
2	TH	0236	1.3	0853	4.8	1447	1.5	2059	5.0	
3	F	0309	1.4	0928	4.7	1523	1.6	2136	4.9	
4	SA	0348	1.6	1010	4.6	1607	1.8	2223	4.7	◑
5	SU	0439	1.8	1104	4.5	1707	1.9	2324	4.6	
6	M	0549	1.9	1212	4.5	1832	2.0			
7	TU	0041	4.5	0718	1.9	1331	4.6	2000	1.9	
8	W	0208	4.6	0838	1.7	1447	4.9	2115	1.5	
9	TH	0324	4.9	0947	1.4	1552	5.2	2220	1.1	
10	F	0427	5.1	1048	1.0	1649	5.5	2318	0.8	
11	SA	0523	5.3	1143	0.7	1742	5.7			●
12	SU	0011	0.5	0616	5.5	1234	0.5	1832	5.8	
13	M	0100	0.3	0706	5.6	1320	0.4	1921	5.8	
14	TU	0145	0.2	0754	5.5	1404	0.4	2006	5.8	
15	W	0227	0.4	0837	5.4	1444	0.6	2048	5.6	
16	TH	0307	0.7	0917	5.2	1522	0.9	2125	5.3	
17	F	0345	1.0	0954	5.0	1600	1.3	2200	5.0	
18	SA	0423	1.5	1030	4.7	1642	1.7	2236	4.6	◐
19	SU	0507	1.9	1115	4.5	1733	2.1	2328	4.3	
20	M	0604	2.2	1229	4.3	1840	2.3			
21	TU	0109	4.2	0719	2.3	1353	4.3	2003	2.3	
22	W	0229	4.3	0845	2.2	1456	4.5	2121	2.0	
23	TH	0328	4.5	0949	1.9	1548	4.8	2216	1.7	
24	F	0415	4.7	1037	1.6	1632	5.0	2300	1.4	
25	SA	0457	4.9	1118	1.3	1712	5.2	2339	1.2	
26	SU	0537	5.1	1155	1.2	1751	5.3			○
27	M	0014	1.1	0615	5.1	1229	1.1	1828	5.4	
28	TU	0046	1.0	0652	5.2	1259	1.1	1904	5.4	
29	W	0116	1.0	0727	5.1	1328	1.1	1937	5.3	
30	TH	0145	1.0	0759	5.1	1357	1.2	2008	5.2	
31	F	0214	1.1	0829	5.0	1426	1.3	2038	5.1	

Chart Datum is 3·22 metres below Ordnance Datum (Newlyn). HAT is 5·9 metres above Chart Datum.

STANDARD TIME (UT)
For Summer Time add ONE hour in **non-shaded areas**

PLYMOUTH LAT 50°22′N LONG 4°11′W

TIMES AND HEIGHTS OF HIGH AND LOW WATERS

Dates in red are SPRINGS
Dates in blue are NEAPS

YEAR **2018**

SEPTEMBER

Date	Day	Time	m	Time	m	Time	m	Time	m
1	SA	0245	1.3	0902	4.9	1459	1.4	2114	5.0
2	SU	0321	1.5	0941	4.8	1540	1.7	2159	4.8
3	M	0407	1.8	1034	4.6	1635	1.9	◑ 2300	4.6
4	TU	0512	2.0	1143	4.5	1800	2.1		
5	W	0020	4.4	0652	2.1	1309	4.6	1944	2.0
6	TH	0156	4.5	0825	1.9	1433	4.8	2106	1.6
7	F	0316	4.8	0937	1.5	1540	5.2	2210	1.2
8	SA	0418	5.1	1037	1.0	1637	5.5	2306	0.7
9	SU	0511	5.4	1129	0.7	1727	5.7	● 2355	0.4
10	M	0600	5.6	1216	0.4	1815	5.9		
11	TU	0041	0.2	0646	5.7	1300	0.3	1900	5.9
12	W	0123	0.2	0729	5.6	1341	0.4	1941	5.8
13	TH	0202	0.4	0807	5.5	1418	0.6	2018	5.6
14	F	0238	0.7	0840	5.3	1452	0.9	2048	5.3
15	SA	0310	1.1	0908	5.1	1526	1.4	2116	4.9
16	SU	0343	1.6	0937	4.8	1602	1.8	◐ 2147	4.6
17	M	0421	2.0	1014	4.5	1649	2.2	2232	4.3
18	TU	0515	2.4	1111	4.3	1755	2.5	2345	4.1
19	W	0630	2.5	1303	4.2	1918	2.5		
20	TH	0159	4.1	0800	2.4	1426	4.4	2048	2.2
21	F	0302	4.4	0918	2.1	1520	4.7	2147	1.8
22	SA	0350	4.7	1008	1.7	1605	5.0	2230	1.5
23	SU	0432	5.0	1049	1.4	1647	5.2	2309	1.2
24	M	0512	5.2	1126	1.2	1726	5.4	2344	1.0
25	TU	0550	5.3	1201	1.0	1804	5.4	○	
26	W	0018	0.9	0627	5.3	1234	1.0	1841	5.4
27	TH	0051	0.9	0702	5.3	1306	1.0	1915	5.4
28	F	0122	0.9	0735	5.3	1336	1.0	1948	5.3
29	SA	0153	1.0	0807	5.2	1408	1.1	2021	5.2
30	SU	0225	1.2	0841	5.1	1442	1.3	2058	5.0

OCTOBER

Date	Day	Time	m	Time	m	Time	m	Time	m
1	M	0301	1.5	0921	4.9	1523	1.6	2144	4.8
2	TU	0347	1.8	1014	4.7	1619	2.0	◑ 2246	4.5
3	W	0453	2.2	1124	4.6	1746	2.2		
4	TH	0011	4.4	0638	2.3	1255	4.6	1936	2.1
5	F	0153	4.5	0816	2.0	1423	4.8	2056	1.6
6	SA	0309	4.9	0925	1.5	1528	5.2	2156	1.1
7	SU	0406	5.2	1021	1.1	1621	5.5	2248	0.7
8	M	0455	5.5	1110	0.7	1709	5.7	2334	0.5
9	TU	0540	5.6	1155	0.5	1754	5.8	●	
10	W	0017	0.3	0621	5.7	1237	0.4	1835	5.8
11	TH	0058	0.4	0700	5.7	1315	0.5	1912	5.7
12	F	0134	0.6	0733	5.5	1350	0.7	1945	5.5
13	SA	0207	0.9	0802	5.4	1422	1.1	2013	5.2
14	SU	0236	1.3	0828	5.2	1453	1.5	2040	4.9
15	M	0305	1.7	0858	4.9	1526	1.9	2114	4.6
16	TU	0336	2.1	0936	4.7	1608	2.2	◐ 2158	4.4
17	W	0424	2.5	1028	4.4	1713	2.5	2300	4.1
18	TH	0544	2.7	1145	4.3	1833	2.6		
19	F	0107	4.1	0708	2.6	1340	4.4	1954	2.3
20	SA	0226	4.4	0827	2.3	1444	4.7	2100	2.0
21	SU	0317	4.7	0924	1.9	1532	5.0	2149	1.6
22	M	0401	5.0	1010	1.5	1615	5.2	2231	1.3
23	TU	0442	5.2	1051	1.3	1657	5.4	2310	1.1
24	W	0522	5.3	1130	1.1	1737	5.5	○ 2348	0.9
25	TH	0600	5.4	1207	0.9	1816	5.5		
26	F	0025	0.9	0636	5.5	1244	0.9	1853	5.5
27	SA	0101	0.9	0712	5.5	1319	0.9	1930	5.4
28	SU	0136	1.0	0748	5.4	1355	1.1	2008	5.3
29	M	0212	1.2	0826	5.3	1433	1.3	2049	5.1
30	TU	0251	1.5	0910	5.1	1518	1.6	2138	4.8
31	W	0340	1.9	1003	4.9	1617	1.9	◑ 2240	4.6

NOVEMBER

Date	Day	Time	m	Time	m	Time	m	Time	m
1	TH	0448	2.2	1112	4.7	1741	2.1		
2	F	0007	4.5	0624	2.3	1242	4.7	1920	2.0
3	SA	0141	4.6	0757	2.0	1405	4.9	2036	1.6
4	SU	0251	4.9	0904	1.6	1508	5.2	2135	1.2
5	M	0346	5.2	0958	1.2	1601	5.4	2225	0.9
6	TU	0433	5.4	1046	0.9	1647	5.6	2310	0.7
7	W	0516	5.6	1131	0.7	1730	5.7	● 2352	0.6
8	TH	0555	5.6	1211	0.7	1810	5.6		
9	F	0031	0.7	0631	5.6	1249	0.8	1845	5.5
10	SA	0106	0.9	0702	5.5	1324	0.9	1916	5.4
11	SU	0138	1.1	0731	5.4	1356	1.2	1945	5.2
12	M	0207	1.4	0800	5.3	1426	1.5	2015	5.0
13	TU	0234	1.7	0832	5.1	1457	1.8	2051	4.7
14	W	0302	2.1	0910	4.8	1533	2.1	2134	4.5
15	TH	0340	2.3	0957	4.6	1629	2.4	◐ 2229	4.3
16	F	0450	2.6	1058	4.4	1744	2.5	2346	4.2
17	SA	0615	2.6	1221	4.4	1859	2.4		
18	SU	0125	4.3	0729	2.4	1348	4.6	2004	2.1
19	M	0231	4.6	0832	2.1	1447	4.8	2101	1.7
20	TU	0321	4.9	0926	1.7	1537	5.1	2150	1.4
21	W	0407	5.1	1014	1.4	1624	5.3	2236	1.2
22	TH	0450	5.3	1059	1.2	1708	5.4	2320	1.0
23	F	0532	5.5	1142	1.0	1751	5.5	○	
24	SA	0002	0.9	0612	5.6	1225	0.9	1834	5.5
25	SU	0043	0.9	0653	5.6	1306	0.9	1916	5.5
26	M	0124	1.0	0735	5.6	1348	1.0	2000	5.4
27	TU	0206	1.1	0818	5.5	1432	1.2	2046	5.2
28	W	0250	1.4	0905	5.3	1521	1.4	2137	4.9
29	TH	0341	1.7	0958	5.1	1618	1.7	2238	4.7
30	F	0443	1.9	1102	4.9	1728	1.9	◑ 2353	4.6

DECEMBER

Date	Day	Time	m	Time	m	Time	m	Time	m
1	SA	0600	2.1	1219	4.8	1850	1.9		
2	SU	0112	4.6	0723	2.0	1335	4.9	2004	1.7
3	M	0220	4.8	0833	1.8	1439	5.0	2106	1.5
4	TU	0317	5.0	0931	1.5	1534	5.2	2158	1.2
5	W	0406	5.2	1021	1.2	1623	5.3	2245	1.1
6	TH	0450	5.4	1107	1.1	1707	5.4	2328	1.0
7	F	0530	5.5	1148	1.0	1747	5.4	●	
8	SA	0007	1.0	0606	5.5	1227	1.0	1822	5.3
9	SU	0043	1.1	0638	5.5	1303	1.1	1855	5.2
10	M	0115	1.2	0710	5.4	1335	1.3	1927	5.1
11	TU	0145	1.4	0741	5.3	1406	1.5	2000	5.0
12	W	0213	1.6	0815	5.2	1436	1.7	2036	4.8
13	TH	0241	1.9	0852	5.0	1509	1.9	2115	4.6
14	F	0313	2.1	0933	4.8	1548	2.1	2202	4.5
15	SA	0358	2.3	1021	4.6	1644	2.2	◐ 2258	4.4
16	SU	0505	2.4	1120	4.5	1757	2.3		
17	M	0006	4.4	0626	2.4	1230	4.6	1908	2.2
18	TU	0122	4.5	0738	2.2	1345	4.7	2012	1.9
19	W	0229	4.7	0841	1.9	1451	4.9	2110	1.6
20	TH	0326	5.0	0938	1.6	1548	5.1	2204	1.3
21	F	0417	5.2	1031	1.3	1640	5.3	2254	1.1
22	SA	0505	5.4	1121	1.0	1730	5.4	○ 2343	0.9
23	SU	0552	5.6	1210	0.8	1819	5.5		
24	M	0030	0.8	0638	5.7	1258	0.8	1906	5.5
25	TU	0117	0.8	0725	5.7	1345	0.8	1954	5.4
26	W	0203	0.9	0812	5.7	1432	0.9	2043	5.3
27	TH	0249	1.1	0900	5.5	1519	1.1	2133	5.1
28	F	0336	1.3	0950	5.3	1609	1.3	2225	4.9
29	SA	0427	1.6	1045	5.1	1703	1.6	◑ 2325	4.7
30	SU	0525	1.8	1147	4.9	1806	1.8		
31	M	0032	4.6	0634	2.0	1257	4.8	1918	1.9

Chart Datum is 3·22 metres below Ordnance Datum (Newlyn). HAT is 5·9 metres above Chart Datum.

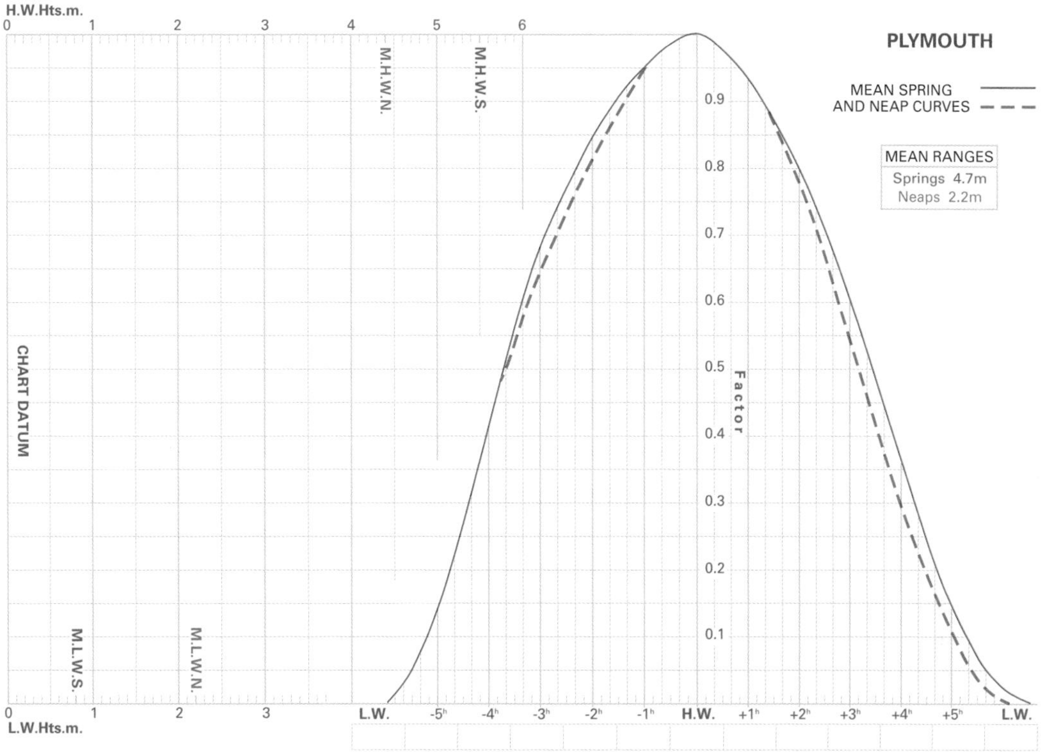

9.1.16 NAVAL EXERCISE AREAS (SUBFACTS AND GUNFACTS)

Submarines and warships frequently exercise south of Plymouth and in the western part of the English Channel. Details of submarine activity and naval gunnery and missile firings are broadcast daily by HM Coastguard. See Chapter 3 for advice when sailing in areas of known submarine activity, and Chapter 6 for timings of daily broadcasts. Although the onus for safety is on the relevant naval vessels, if possible it is best to avoid areas where exercises are taking place.

LYNHER (or ST GERMANS) RIVER AC 871. This river flows into The Hamoaze about 0·8M SSW of the Tamar Bridge. On the tide it is navigable for some 4M inland. The channel, entered at Lynher PHM lt buoy 50°23´·78N 04°12´·83W, is marked by 2 more lt buoys in the first mile to Sandacre Pt and carries 2-5m up to Ince Castle. Caution: underwater cables/gaspipe, as charted. Thereafter it carries less than 1m or dries, except at Dandy Hole, a pool with 3-5m, 50°22´·54N 04°16´·29W. Here the navigable chan bends NW then dries completely; it is marked by small R and G posts.

⚓s, amid local moorings, are: off Sand Acre Bay (N bank, beware foul ground); in 2·5-5m at the ent to Forder Lake (N bank opposite Jupiter Pt, where the pontoons and Y moorings are for naval use only); SE of Ince Pt and Castle in about 3m; and at Dandy Hole. St Germans Quay is private, but temp ⛵, M may be pre-arranged with Quay SC ☎(01503) 250370. Facilities: ✉ 🛒 ⛽(½M).

RIVER TAMAR AC 871. The river is navigable on the tide for 12M via Calstock and Morwellham to Gunnislake weir. **Jubilee Green** (pontoon in 3m, max LOA 10m) is on W bank close N of the Royal Albert (30m) & Tamar (35m) bridges. Pwr cables (21m) cross 0·4M S of Cargreen (50°26´·55N 04°12´·25W) sited on the W bank 0·7M N of the Tavy with a quay and many local moorings/⚓ in 2·5-5m. Overhead cables 1M N have 16m clearance en-route Weir Quay. **Weir Quay BY** ☎(01822) 840474, ⚓s (20t) (12t). **Weir Quay SC** ☎(01822) 840960. Upstream the river S-bends, narrows and partly dries with channel above Halton Quay from 0·1m to >2·5m. N of Cotehele Quay it turns 90° stbd to Calstock, ⚓ in 2m E of viaduct (24m); 🛒 ✉ ⇌. **Calstock BY** ☎(01822) 832502. WC (8t) (10t).

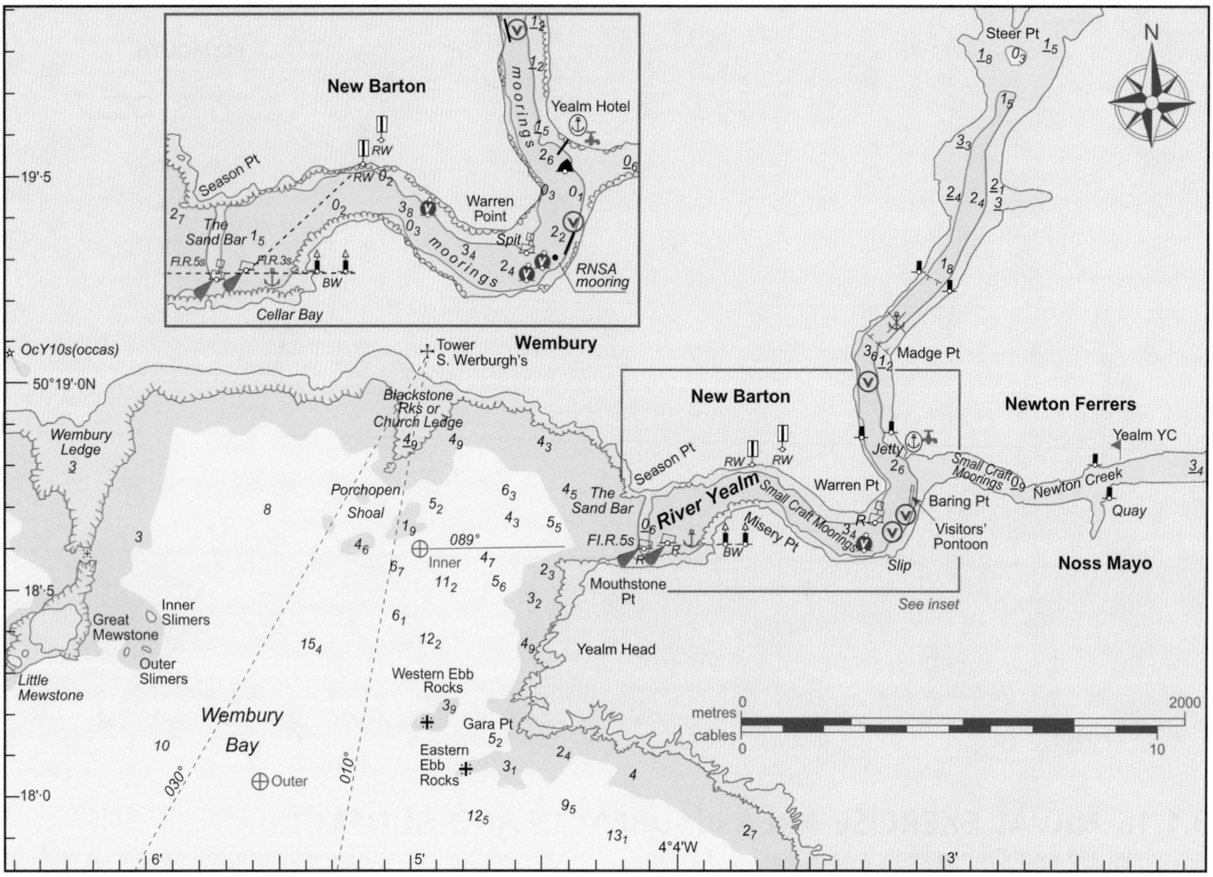

9.1.17 RIVER YEALM

Devon **50°18'·58N 04°04'·13W** (Ent) ❁❁◊◊✿✿✿

CHARTS AC 1613, 1900, 30, 5602; Imray C10, C6, C14, 2400

TIDES –0522 Dover; ML 3·2; Duration 0615

Standard Port PLYMOUTH (⟵)

Times				Height (metres)			
High Water		Low Water		MHWS	MHWN	MLWN	MLWS
0000	0600	0000	0600	5·5	4·4	2·2	0·8
1200	1800	1200	1800				
Differences RIVER YEALM ENTRANCE							
+0006	+0006	+0002	+0002	–0·1	–0·1	–0·1	–0·1

NOTE: Strong SW winds hold up the ebb and raise levels, as does the river if in spate.

SHELTER Very good in river. Entry is easy except in strong SW-W winds; ⚓ in Cellar Bay is open from SW to NW. Space in the hbr is very limited, and in wind-over-tide conditions, when moored yachts lie across the stream, larger vessels may find turning difficult. Vessels >18m LOA may not enter without the HM's permission.

NAVIGATION Outer WPT 50°18'·03N 04°05'·55W, 033°/7ca to the Inner WPT 50°18'·59N 04°04'·98W; then 089°/5½ca to the Sand Bar. Keep St Werburgh's ✠ twr between 010° and 030° to clear the Slimers and the W & E Ebb Rocks, then turn onto 089°; ldg bns (both W △ with B stripe). ≠ clears Mouthstone Ledge, but not the sand bar which extends SW. Two PHM buoys mark the S end of the Sand Bar and must be left to port on entry; the seaward buoy is lit, Fl R 5s. After passing the second (E'ly, unlit) buoy turn onto 047° ldg bns (both W with R stripe), on the N shore, then follow line of the river. There is only 1m at MLWS between the Sand Bar and Misery Point. Leave Spit PHM buoy to port and Office SHM to starboard. No ⚓ in river; speed limit 6kn.

LIGHTS AND MARKS Great Mewstone (57m) is conspic 1·5M to W of river ent; no passage between it and the coast.

COMMUNICATIONS (Code 01752) CGOC (01326) 317575; Dr 880567; Police 101; HM 872533; Water taxi ☎07817 132757.

FACILITIES 1🅥 off Misery Pt, 3🅥 off Warren Pt and Ⓥ pontoons in The Pool and 3ca up-river. Pontoon, ⚓/🅥 £1.70. WC/🚿 at HM. 🔧 ⛽. **Yealm YC** ☎872291, ⛽ Bistro, 🍽.
Newton Ferrers 🔧 ⛵ ⛽ ✉ 🛒 ✕ 🍽.
Noss Mayo ⊆ at Pope's Quay (dries), 🔧 ⛵ ⛽ ✕ 🍽.
Bridgend (Newton Creek) ⊆ (dries), ⛽ 🍺.
🅿 🅳 ⛽ at Yealmpton (3M).

ADJACENT ANCHORAGES IN BIGBURY BAY

RIVER ERME, Devon, **50°18'·15N 03°57'·67W**. AC1613. HW –0525 on Dover; +0015 and –0·6m on HW Plymouth. Temp day ⚓ in 3m at mouth of drying river, open to SW. Enter only in offshore winds and settled weather. Beware Wells Rk (1m) 1M SE of ent. Appr from SW, clear of Edwards Rk. Ent between Battisborough Is and W. Mary's Rk (dries $\underline{1}$·1m) keeping to the W. No facilities. Two Historic Wrecks are at 50°18'·15N 03°57'·41W and 50°18'·41N 03°57'·19W on W side of the ent.

RIVER AVON, Devon, **50°16'·63N 03°53'·33W**. AC1613. Tides as R Erme, above. Appr close E of conspic Burgh Is (⚓) & Murray's Rk, marked by bcn. Enter drying river HW –1, only in offshore winds and settled weather. Narrow chan hugs cliffy NW shore, then S-bends SE and N off Bantham. Local knowledge or a dinghy recce near LW would assist. Streams run hard, but able to dry out in good shelter clear of moorings. HM ☎(01548) 561196. ✉ 🛒 🍽 at Bantham. Aveton Gifford accessible by dinghy, 2·5M.

HOPE COVE, Devon, **50°14'·65N 03°51'·78W**. AC 1613. Tides as R Erme; ML 2·6m; Duration 0615. Popular day ⚓ in centre of cove, but poor holding and only in offshore winds. Appr with old LB ho in SE corner of the cove brg 130° and ⚓ WSW of the pier head, clear of moorings. Basse Rock extends 30m around the pier head. Off the S shore Goody Rock (dries $\underline{2}$·5m) is cleared by brgs of 060° on the pier head and 120° on the old LB ho. No lights. Facilities: very limited in village, good at Salcombe (4M bus).

9.1.18 SALCOMBE

Devon **50°13'·17N 03°46'·67W (The Bar)** ❁❁◊◊◊✿✿✿

CHARTS AC 1613, 1634, 28, 5602; Imray C10, C6, C5, 2300

TIDES –0523 Dover; ML 3·1; Duration 0615

Standard Port PLYMOUTH (⟵)

Times				**Height (metres)**			
High Water		Low Water		MHWS	MHWN	MLWN	MLWS
0100	0600	0100	0600	5·5	4·4	2·2	0·8
1300	1800	1300	1800				
Differences SALCOMBE							
0000	+0010	+0005	–0005	–0·2	–0·3	–0·1	–0·1
START POINT							
+0015	+0015	+0005	+0010	–0·1	–0·2	+0·1	+0·2

SHELTER Good, but fresh S'lies can cause uncomfortable swell off the town. Better shelter in The Bag at Ⓥ pontoon. ⚓s at Sunny Cove; off SE shore from YC start line to fuel barge (where poor holding has been reported); 200m W and 300m SSE of Salt Stone SHM bcn 50°15'·19N 03°45'·55W.

NAVIGATION WPT 50°12'·43N 03°46'·67W, 000°/1·3M to Sandhill Pt lt. In normal conditions The Bar (least depth 1m) is not a problem, *but it should not be crossed on an ebb tide with strong onshore winds or swell when dangerous breakers can occur*; if in doubt, call HM Ch 14 before approaching. The deepest water is close inshore to the west off the leading line. The spring flood reaches 2·5kn. Speed limit 8kn, marked in season by 3 Y SPM between Cadmus and Chapple Rks, but 6kn between Marine Hotel/racing start line and the Saltstone (approx 50°15'·2N 03°45'·5W); minimise wash; radar checks in force. In Jul/Aug within the hbr cruising yachts must motor, not sail. When dinghy racing in progress (Sat/Sun & regatta weeks: Fl Y lt at YC and warning on Ch 14) yachts should use a fairway marked by Y SPM buoys close to the NW bank and straddling the start line. Two Historic Wrecks lie 1M WNW of Prawle Pt at 50°12'·74N 03°44'·40W & 50°12'·73N 03°44'·75W.

LIGHTS AND MARKS Outer 000° ldg marks, both R/W bcns (a conspic gabled house close N is more easily seen): front, Poundstone; rear, Sandhill Pt Dir lt 000°, stay in the W sector (357·5°-002·5°). Close W of ldg line beware Bass Rk (0·8m) marked by PHM lt buoy; and, close E, Wolf Rk (0·6m), marked by SHM lt buoy. When past Wolf Rk, leave Black Stone Rk (5m), G/W bcn, well to stbd and pick up inner ldg lts 042·5°.

COMMUNICATIONS (Code 01548) CGOC (01326) 317575; Police 101; Dr 842284. HM ☎843791: May to mid-Sep: 0900-1645 Mon-Thu; 0900-1615 Fri-Sun; *Salcombe Hbr Launch* (May to mid-Sep: daily 0715 -2300; rest of year: Mon-Fri 0900-1600) Ch 14. *Harbour taxi* Ch 12. *Fuel Barge* Ch 06. ICC HQ, *Egremont* Ch M.

FACILITIES www.salcombeharbour.co.uk www.southhams.gov.uk Numerous Ⓥs either side of the fairway off the town. The Bag (50°14'·58N 03°45'·56W): pontoon for 150Ⓥ. 21 marked Ⓥs (orange <8m LOA, yellow >8m). Pontoon & Ⓥ £1·80 (inc hbr dues). ⚓ £0·90/m. Short stay pontoon (½ hr max, 0700-1900, for ⛽/stores) in 0·9m is E of HM's office for adjacent WC/shower. Public slip, crane(12t) in Batson Creek (Fishermens Quay). Water on pontoon in The Bag. Shower at Whitestrand Quay.

Fuel Barge diesel, petrol ☎07801 798862, summer 7/7 0830-1700; winter Mon-Fri 0830-1700.

Salcombe YC ☎842872 / 842593, slip, ✕, bar.

Island CC ☎531776 in *Egremont*, N of Ox Pt.

Services ACA.

Town ✉ Ⓑ ✕ (bus to Totnes).

ADJACENT HARBOUR, 3M north

KINGSBRIDGE, 50°16'·88N 03°46'·52W. AC 28. HW = HW Salcombe +0005. The 3M chan, which dries approx 2·4m in the upper reaches, is marked beyond Salt Stone SHM perch by R/W PHM poles with R can topmarks. 6ca N of Salt Stone a secondary chan marked by PHM buoys gradually diverges E into Balcombe Creek (dries). Ferry berths at private pontoon at New Quay, 3ca S of drying Kingsbridge basin and on outside of the new mooring pontoon. Max LOA 11m.

Ⓥ boats < 5·5m on pontoon on west wall. Ⓥ 5·5m < < 9m inside middle of pontoon. Ⓥ >9m on the wall N of the pontoon (drying 3·4m to soft mud). Best to pre-check berth availability with Salcombe HM; fees and Hbr dues are payable.

Services slip.

Town ✉ Ⓑ ✕ Ⓗ852349 (A&E).

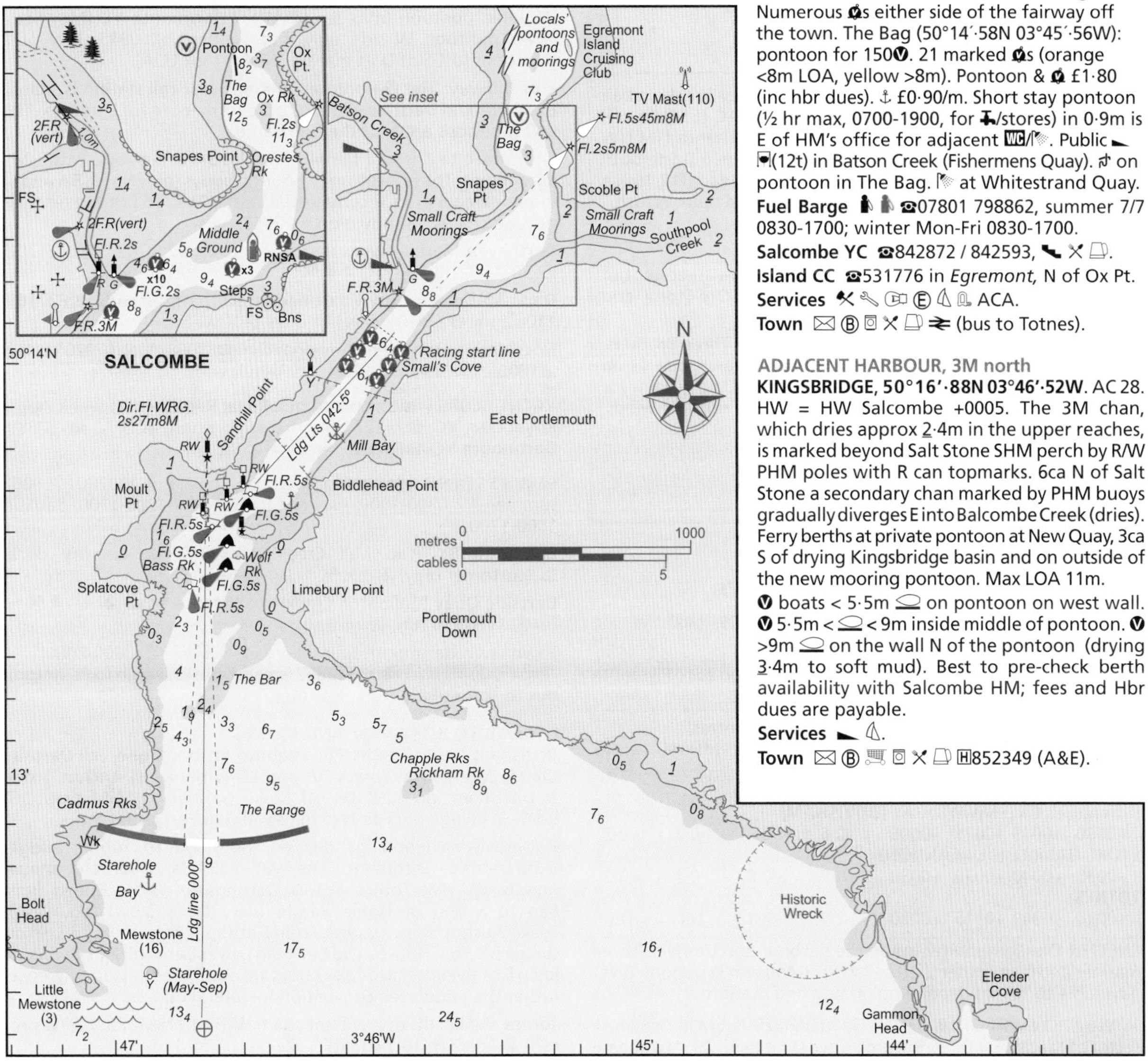

START POINT TO TEIGNMOUTH

(AC 1613, 1634, 3315) Start Point (Fl(3) 10s 62m25M, *Horn 60s*), 3·3M ENE of Prawle Point, is a long headland with a distinctive cock's comb spine, a W lt ho on the Point, and conspicuous radio masts to the WNW. Black Stone rock (6m high) is visible 2½ca SSE of the lt ho, with Cherrick Rocks (1m) 1ca further S; other drying rocks lie closer inshore. A race may extend 1M to the S and 1·6M to the E. In fair weather any overfalls can be avoided by passing close to seaward of rks; there is no clear-cut inshore passage as such. In bad weather keep at least 2M off.

▶*The NE-going flood begins at HW Plymouth –2; max (3·1kn Sp) at HWP –1. The SW-going ebb begins at HWP +5; max (2·2kn Sp) at HWP +6. But at HWP +4 it is possible to round Start Point close inshore using a back eddy. On both the flood and the ebb back eddies form between Start Point and Hallsands, 1M NW. Inshore the tide turns 30 mins earlier.*◀

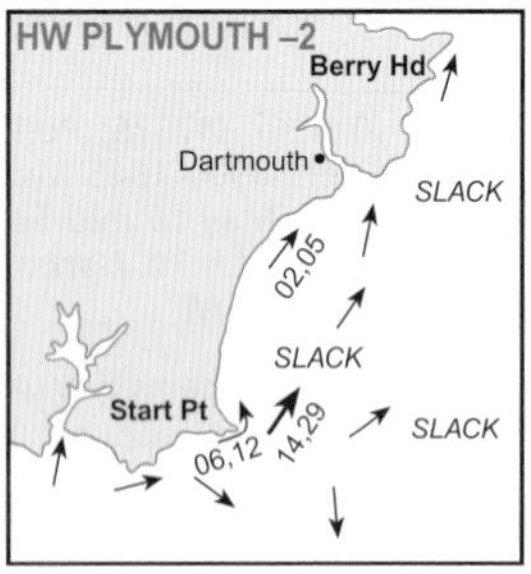

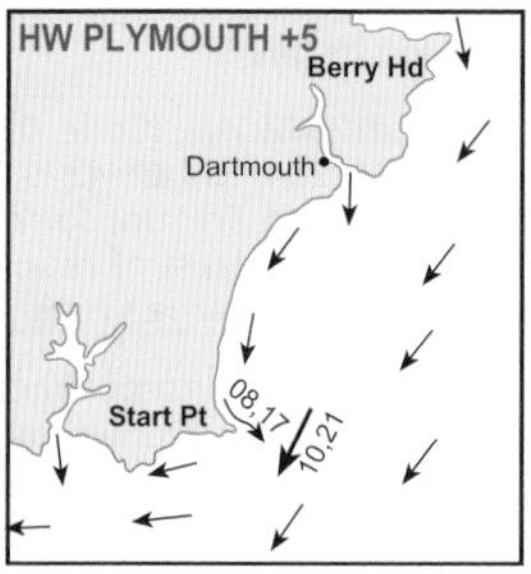

Skerries Bank (least depth 2·1m), on which the sea breaks in bad weather, lies from 9ca to 4·1M NE of Start Pt (AC 1634). In offshore winds there is a good ⚓ in 3m 1ca off Hallsands (1M NW of Start). A fish farm lies about 3½ ca off. Between **Dartmouth** and **Brixham** rocks extend 5ca offshore. Berry Head (Fl 2 15s), a bold, flat-topped headland (55m), gives a good radar return.

▶*Here the stream turns N at HW Plymouth –3, and S at HWP +3; max Sp rates 3kn.*◀

In **Torbay** (AC 26) the more obvious dangers are steep-to, but beware the Sunker (awash at CD) 100m SW of Ore Stone, and Morris Rogue (0·8m) 5ca W of Thatcher Rock.

In W'lies Hope Cove, Anstey's Cove (beware the Three Brothers, rks drying 0·6m, S side) and Babbacombe Bay are good ⚓s on sand. There are no offlying dangers from Long Quarry Point for 4M N to **Teignmouth** whose ent is dangerous in onshore winds.

▶*Off Teignmouth Bar the NNE-going stream begins at HW Plymouth –1½ and the SSW-going at HWP +5¼. In the ent the flood begins at HWP –5½ and the ebb at HWP +¾. The Spr ebb reaches 4–5kn off The Point.*◀

9.1.19 DARTMOUTH

Devon **50°20'·66N 03°33'·96W** ✽✽✽◊◊◊✿✿✿

CHARTS AC 1613, 1634, 2253, 5602; Imray C10, C5, 2300

TIDES –0510 Dover; ML 2·8; Duration 0630

DARTMOUTH (⟶). The differences below are referred to Plymouth as Standard Port, not to Dartmouth.

Times				Height (metres)			
High Water		Low Water		MHWS	MHWN	MLWN	MLWS
0100	0600	0100	0600	5·5	4·4	2·2	0·8
1300	1800	1300	1800				
Differences GREENWAY QUAY (DITTISHAM)							
+0030	+0045	+0025	+0005	–0·6	–0·6	–0·2	–0·2
STOKE GABRIEL (DUNCANNON)							
+0035	+0040	+0020	+0030	–0·9	–0·8	–0·4	–0·3
TOTNES							
+0030	+0040	+0115	+0030	–2·0	–2·1	DR	DR

SHELTER Excellent shelter inside the harbour and up-river. Three marinas and many other ⊆ (for yachts< 14m) and ⚲ options. River navigable to Totnes depending on tide and draught.

NAVIGATION WPT 50°19'·53N 03°32'·83W, 328°/1·5M in the white sector of Kingswear Dir lt. Bayard's Cove Dir lt leads 293° to abeam Royal Dart YC where the main fairway opens. There is no bar and hbr access is H24, but ent can be difficult in strong SE to SW winds. Speed limit 6kn from Castle Ledge buoy up-river to 1M below Totnes. *Caution: The Lower and Higher car ferries S and N of Dartmouth have right of way; give way early.*

LIGHTS AND MARKS as on the chartlet and/or 9.1.4. E of the ent, on Inner Froward Pt (167m) is a conspic daymark, obelisk (24·5m). Lateral and cardinal lt buoys mark all dangers to seaward of conspic Dartmouth Castle. Within hbr, all jetty/ pontoon lts to the W are 2FR (vert); and 2FG (vert) to the E.

COMMUNICATIONS (Code 01803) CGOC (01326) 317575; Police 101; Dr 832212; Ⓗ 832255. HM 832337, 835220 (out of hours emergency); *Dartnav* VHF Ch 11 (summer 0730-2100). Darthaven, Dart and Noss marinas Ch **80**. Fuel barge Ch 06. Water taxis: *Yacht taxi* (DHNA) Ch 69, 07970 346571 (summer 0800-2300, winter 1000-1600). *Greenway ferry* Ch 10 or 844010 (to Dittisham).

FACILITIES **Dart Harbour and Navigation Authority** (DHNA), www.dartharbour.org ☎832337, 450⊆+90Ⓥ.
Town jetty (inside) £2·10/m/day (outside 1700-0840)£1·35/m/nt.
S Embankment £1·60; other pontoons, ⚲s and ⚓ £1·55/m; all inc Hbr dues (£0.85) & VAT. ▬ ⊥ WC/⚐ to N of Boat Float.

DHNA Ⓥ pontoons are marked by blue flags and ⚲s are blue with black '**V**' or 'Visitors' in yellow and black. Check availability with HM or call DHNA. The most likely Ⓥ berths from S to N are:

W bank: pontoon (max 9m LOA) off Dartmouth YC (May-Sep). Town pontoon W side only, but E side 1700-0845. N'ly of 2 pontoons just S of Dart marina (26'/8m max LOA).

E of fairway: The Ⓥ pontoon by Kingswear rail station is shared by DHNA and Darthaven marina; the former are for 2hrs max. The 3 Ⓥ pontoons are N of the fuel barge.

Only space to ⚓ is E of fairway and Nos 3A to 5 buoys, with HM's agreement. These large unlit mooring buoys (plus Nos 3, 5A and 6) in mid-stream are for commercial vessels/FVs; do not ⚓ over their ground chains, as shown on AC 2253.

Darthaven Marina www.darthaven.co.uk ☎752242, 250⊆+20Ⓥ £2·50+VAT+hbr dues. ▢ ⚡ ▲ ✕ 🔧 ⌧ Ⓔ ⚑(35t) ⊡ wi-fi.

Dart Marina ⊕ www.dartmarinayachtharbour.com ☎837161. 110⊆ inc Ⓥ £2·50+VAT+hbr dues. ▢ ✕ wi-fi.

Noss Marina www.premiermarinas.com ☎839087 mob 07920425452. ▲180⊆ £2.98 + dues, ▢ ▲ 🔧 ⌧ ⚑(10t) wi-fi.

YACHT CLUBS (visitors welcome): **Royal Regatta**, last week Aug.
Royal Dart YC ☎752272, short stay pontoon, ⊥ ✕ ▢ ☎752880.
Dartmouth YC ☎832305, ⊥ ⚐ ✕ ▢.

SERVICES **Fuel Barge** next to No 6 buoy, Ch 06, ⛽ ⛽; ☎07801 798861 summer 7/7 0800-1800; winter Mon/Wed/Fri 1200-1700, Sat/Sun 1000-1700.

Creekside BY (Old Mill Creek) ☎832649, ▲ ▬ dry dock, ⊆(customer only) ⊥ ⊐ ✕ 🔧 ⌧ ⚑(14t) ⊡.

Dartside Quay (Galmpton Creek): ☎845445 ▲ ▬ ⊥ ⊐ ▲ ✕ 🔧 ⌧ Ⓔ ⊼ ⚑(65t/16t), ⊡, wi-fi.

Town www.dartmouth-tourism.org.uk, ♿ WC/⚐ ▢ (0800-2000) ☏ ⚠ ✉ Ⓑ ⊞ ✕ ▢ ⇌ ☎555872 (steam train in season to Paignton); bus to Totnes/Paignton, ✈ Exeter.

UPRIVER TO DITTISHAM AND TOTNES
Dittisham ⚓s/⚲s/Berths: For ⚓s above Anchor Stone, call *DartNav* Ch 11. Many W⚲s (black '**V**' and LOA) between Anchor Stone & Dittisham; no ⚓. 4 ⚲s off Stoke Gabriel by SHM bcn, QG. WC/⚐ in village park to N (5 mins walk) of Ferry Boat Inn.

R Dart is navigable by day on the flood to Totnes bridge, 5·5M above Dittisham. Use AC 2253 and DHNA annual handbook. HW Totnes = HW Dartmouth +0015. Speed limit 6kn to S end of Home Reach, then 'Dead Slow' (no wash). Leave Anchor Stone to port. From Dittisham brgs of 020° / 310° on successive Boat Houses lead between Lower Back and Flat Owers; or keep E of the latter. Up-river buoys are numbered 1-11 in sequence, rather than odd/even convention for lateral buoys.

Totnes All berths dry. W bank: Baltic Wharf ☎867922, ⊆ (Ⓥ pre-call) ⊥ ⊐ ⊼ ⚑(16t) ⚑(35t) 🔧 ⊡.

E bank: (Ⓥ call DHNA) for 5 ⚓ at Steamer Quay, keep clear of ferry berths. Limited ⚓ on soft mud in the W Arm N of Steam Packet Inn ☎863880, 🚰 ⛽ ▢ ✕ ▢. **Totnes** All amenities; mainline ⇌.

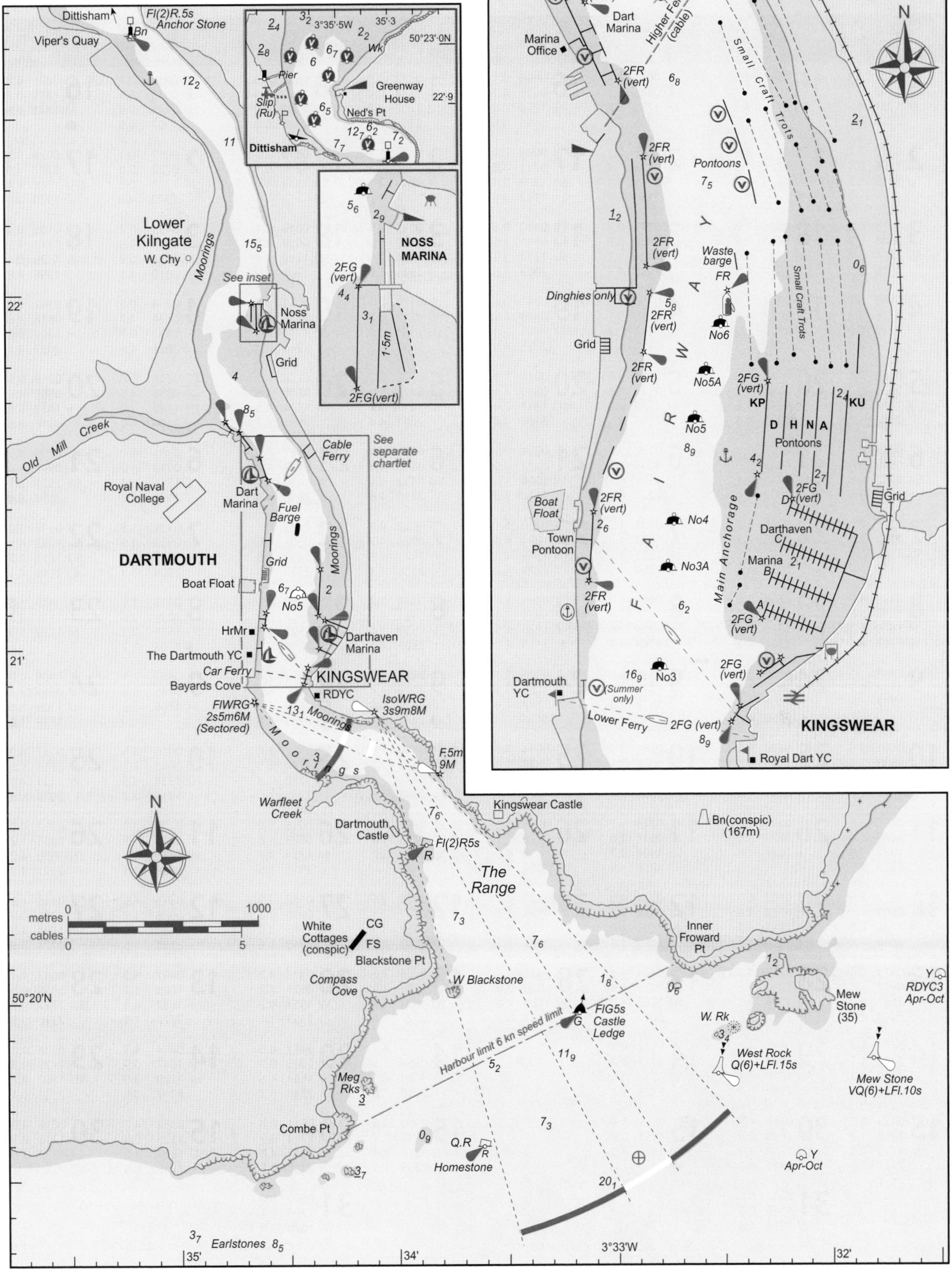

Dittisham
Fl(2)R.5s
Anchor Stone
Viper's Quay
Bn
3°35'·5W
35'·3
50°23'·0N
Pier
Slip (Ru)
Greenway House
22'·9
Ned's Pt
Wk
Dittisham
Lower Kilngate
W. Chy
Moorings
See inset
Noss Marina
Grid
NOSS MARINA
2F.G (vert)
1·5m
Old Mill Creek
Cable Ferry
See separate chartlet
Royal Naval College
Dart Marina
Fuel Barge
DARTMOUTH
Grid
Boat Float
No5
Darthaven Marina
HrMr
The Dartmouth YC
Car Ferry
Bayards Cove
KINGSWEAR
RDYC
FlWRG 2s5m6M (Sectored)
IsoWRG 3s9m8M
Moorings
F.5m 9M
22'
21'
Warfleet Creek
Dartmouth Castle
Kingswear Castle
Fl(2)R5s
The Range
Bn(conspic) (167m)
metres 0 1000
cables 0 5
White Cottages (conspic)
CG
FS
Blackstone Pt
Inner Froward Pt
Compass Cove
W Blackstone
50°20'N
FlG5s Castle Ledge
Harbour limit 6 kn speed limit
W. Rk
West Rock Q(6)+LFl.15s
Mew Stone (35)
RDYC3 Apr-Oct
Mew Stone VQ(6)+LFl.10s
Meg Rks
Combe Pt
Q.R
Homestone
Y Apr-Oct
Earlstones
35'
34'
3°33'W
32'
metres 0 200
cables 0 1
2FR (vert)
Dart Marina
Marina Office
Higher Ferry (cable)
Small Craft Trots
Pontoons
Waste barge
FR
FAIRWAY
No6
No5A
No5
No4
No3A
No3
Dinghies only
Grid
KP
KU
D H N A
Pontoons
Main Anchorage
2FG (vert)
Darthaven Marina
Boat Float
Town Pontoon
Grid
Dartmouth YC
(Summer only)
Lower Ferry
2FG (vert)
KINGSWEAR
Royal Dart YC

STANDARD TIME (UT)
For Summer Time add ONE hour in **non-shaded areas**

DARTMOUTH LAT 50°21′N LONG 3°35′W

TIMES AND HEIGHTS OF HIGH AND LOW WATERS

Dates in red are SPRINGS
Dates in blue are NEAPS

YEAR **2018**

JANUARY

Date	Day	Time	m	Time	m	Time	m	Time	m	Moon
1	M	0502	4.9	1102	0.7	1731	4.8	2326	0.6	
2	TU	0557	5.1	1156	0.5	1825	5.0			○
3	W	0018	0.5	0648	5.2	1246	0.3	1916	5.0	
4	TH	0106	0.4	0736	5.2	1333	0.3	2005	4.9	
5	F	0152	0.5	0823	5.2	1418	0.4	2052	4.8	
6	SA	0235	0.6	0908	5.0	1502	0.6	2138	4.6	
7	SU	0317	0.9	0952	4.8	1545	0.9	2222	4.4	
8	M	0359	1.2	1036	4.5	1629	1.3	2308	4.1	◑
9	TU	0445	1.5	1124	4.2	1717	1.6			
10	W	0001	3.9	0539	1.8	1223	4.0	1816	1.8	
11	TH	0105	3.8	0645	2.0	1331	3.9	1928	1.9	
12	F	0212	3.9	0803	1.9	1438	3.9	2040	1.8	
13	SA	0313	4.0	0912	1.8	1537	4.0	2140	1.6	
14	SU	0406	4.2	1006	1.5	1629	4.2	2229	1.4	
15	M	0453	4.5	1053	1.3	1714	4.4	2311	1.2	
16	TU	0535	4.6	1134	1.1	1756	4.5	2349	1.1	
17	W	0615	4.7	1211	1.0	1835	4.5			●
18	TH	0023	1.0	0653	4.8	1244	1.0	1912	4.5	
19	F	0054	1.0	0728	4.8	1316	1.0	1947	4.5	
20	SA	0125	1.0	0801	4.7	1346	1.0	2021	4.4	
21	SU	0155	1.1	0833	4.6	1416	1.1	2052	4.4	
22	M	0225	1.2	0905	4.5	1449	1.2	2124	4.3	
23	TU	0258	1.3	0940	4.4	1525	1.3	2202	4.2	
24	W	0339	1.5	1022	4.3	1609	1.5	2250	4.0	◐
25	TH	0430	1.6	1115	4.1	1707	1.7	2351	4.0	
26	F	0538	1.8	1222	4.0	1827	1.8			
27	SA	0103	4.0	0710	1.8	1341	4.1	1956	1.6	
28	SU	0227	4.1	0836	1.6	1505	4.2	2112	1.4	
29	M	0341	4.4	0948	1.2	1616	4.4	2218	1.0	
30	TU	0445	4.7	1050	0.8	1718	4.7	2315	0.7	
31	W	0542	5.0	1146	0.5	1814	4.8			○

FEBRUARY

Date	Day	Time	m	Time	m	Time	m	Time	m	Moon
1	TH	0007	0.4	0635	5.2	1235	0.2	1905	4.9	
2	F	0055	0.2	0723	5.2	1321	0.1	1952	5.0	
3	SA	0139	0.2	0808	5.2	1403	0.1	2035	4.9	
4	SU	0219	0.3	0850	5.1	1443	0.3	2114	4.7	
5	M	0257	0.6	0927	4.9	1520	0.7	2149	4.5	
6	TU	0332	0.9	1001	4.6	1556	1.1	2220	4.2	
7	W	0408	1.3	1033	4.2	1633	1.5	2254	4.0	◑
8	TH	0451	1.7	1112	3.9	1718	1.8	2343	3.8	
9	F	0545	2.0	1212	3.7	1819	2.1			
10	SA	0101	3.7	0656	2.1	1346	3.6	1936	2.1	
11	SU	0229	3.7	0821	2.0	1504	3.7	2058	1.9	
12	M	0334	4.0	0935	1.7	1603	4.0	2159	1.6	
13	TU	0426	4.2	1029	1.4	1652	4.2	2247	1.3	
14	W	0512	4.5	1112	1.2	1736	4.4	2328	1.1	
15	TH	0555	4.6	1151	0.9	1817	4.5			●
16	F	0004	0.9	0635	4.7	1226	0.8	1856	4.6	
17	SA	0038	0.8	0711	4.8	1300	0.7	1932	4.6	
18	SU	0110	0.8	0746	4.8	1331	0.7	2005	4.6	
19	M	0141	0.8	0819	4.7	1401	0.8	2035	4.5	
20	TU	0211	0.8	0849	4.6	1433	0.9	2106	4.4	
21	W	0244	0.9	0922	4.5	1506	1.0	2140	4.3	
22	TH	0320	1.1	1001	4.4	1546	1.3	2223	4.2	
23	F	0405	1.4	1051	4.1	1636	1.5	2319	4.0	◐
24	SA	0506	1.7	1156	3.9	1748	1.8			
25	SU	0034	3.9	0637	1.8	1322	3.8	1929	1.8	
26	M	0205	4.0	0820	1.7	1453	4.0	2059	1.5	
27	TU	0327	4.3	0938	1.2	1607	4.3	2207	1.1	
28	W	0432	4.6	1040	0.8	1708	4.6	2304	0.7	

MARCH

Date	Day	Time	m	Time	m	Time	m	Time	m	Moon
1	TH	0529	4.9	1134	0.4	1802	4.8	2355	0.3	
2	F	0619	5.1	1221	0.1	1849	4.9			○
3	SA	0039	0.1	0705	5.2	1304	0.0	1933	5.0	
4	SU	0120	0.1	0747	5.2	1344	0.0	2011	4.9	
5	M	0158	0.2	0825	5.0	1419	0.2	2043	4.8	
6	TU	0231	0.4	0856	4.8	1452	0.6	2110	4.6	
7	W	0302	0.8	0923	4.5	1521	1.0	2136	4.3	
8	TH	0334	1.2	0951	4.2	1553	1.4	2205	4.1	
9	F	0408	1.6	1026	3.9	1630	1.8	2246	3.8	◑
10	SA	0456	1.9	1114	3.6	1725	2.1	2345	3.6	
11	SU	0606	2.2	1233	3.4	1841	2.2			
12	M	0129	3.6	0727	2.1	1427	3.5	2003	2.1	
13	TU	0258	3.8	0851	1.9	1534	3.8	2121	1.8	
14	W	0356	4.1	0954	1.5	1625	4.1	2216	1.4	
15	TH	0443	4.4	1042	1.1	1710	4.3	2259	1.1	
16	F	0528	4.6	1122	0.9	1752	4.5	2340	0.8	
17	SA	0610	4.7	1201	0.7	1833	4.6			●
18	SU	0016	0.7	0649	4.8	1237	0.5	1909	4.7	
19	M	0051	0.6	0726	4.8	1311	0.5	1944	4.7	
20	TU	0124	0.5	0800	4.8	1344	0.5	2016	4.7	
21	W	0157	0.6	0833	4.7	1416	0.6	2048	4.6	
22	TH	0229	0.7	0908	4.6	1451	0.9	2122	4.5	
23	F	0306	1.0	0948	4.4	1529	1.2	2204	4.3	
24	SA	0351	1.3	1036	4.1	1619	1.5	2259	4.0	◐
25	SU	0452	1.6	1144	3.8	1730	1.8			
26	M	0016	3.9	0623	1.8	1314	3.7	1913	1.9	
27	TU	0152	3.9	0810	1.6	1445	3.9	2048	1.6	
28	W	0313	4.2	0927	1.2	1557	4.2	2153	1.1	
29	TH	0417	4.6	1025	0.7	1654	4.5	2248	0.7	
30	F	0511	4.8	1114	0.3	1743	4.8	2335	0.3	
31	SA	0600	5.0	1200	0.1	1828	4.9			○

APRIL

Date	Day	Time	m	Time	m	Time	m	Time	m	Moon
1	SU	0018	0.1	0643	5.1	1241	0.0	1907	4.9	
2	M	0057	0.1	0722	5.0	1318	0.1	1942	4.9	
3	TU	0133	0.2	0755	4.9	1352	0.3	2010	4.8	
4	W	0204	0.5	0824	4.7	1421	0.7	2034	4.6	
5	TH	0234	0.8	0850	4.5	1449	1.0	2101	4.4	
6	F	0301	1.2	0918	4.2	1515	1.4	2131	4.2	
7	SA	0331	1.5	0953	3.9	1545	1.8	2209	3.9	
8	SU	0412	1.9	1039	3.6	1635	2.1	2301	3.7	◑
9	M	0522	2.1	1145	3.4	1756	2.3			
10	TU	0016	3.6	0643	2.1	1334	3.5	1916	2.2	
11	W	0207	3.7	0759	1.9	1455	3.7	2030	1.9	
12	TH	0315	4.0	0906	1.5	1550	4.0	2131	1.5	
13	F	0407	4.3	1000	1.2	1637	4.3	2222	1.1	
14	SA	0454	4.5	1047	0.9	1720	4.5	2307	0.8	
15	SU	0538	4.7	1129	0.6	1803	4.6	2349	0.6	
16	M	0621	4.8	1211	0.5	1843	4.8			●
17	TU	0028	0.5	0702	4.9	1249	0.4	1920	4.8	
18	W	0105	0.4	0740	4.9	1326	0.4	1956	4.8	
19	TH	0142	0.4	0818	4.8	1401	0.6	2032	4.8	
20	F	0219	0.6	0858	4.6	1439	0.8	2110	4.6	
21	SA	0258	0.9	0940	4.4	1521	1.1	2154	4.4	
22	SU	0347	1.2	1031	4.1	1613	1.5	2249	4.1	◐
23	M	0449	1.5	1141	3.8	1723	1.8			
24	TU	0006	4.0	0615	1.7	1309	3.8	1858	1.8	
25	W	0137	4.0	0753	1.5	1431	4.0	2026	1.6	
26	TH	0254	4.2	0905	1.2	1536	4.2	2131	1.2	
27	F	0355	4.5	1001	0.8	1631	4.5	2224	0.8	
28	SA	0447	4.7	1050	0.5	1717	4.7	2310	0.5	
29	SU	0534	4.8	1135	0.3	1800	4.8	2353	0.4	
30	M	0616	4.9	1215	0.3	1838	4.8			○

Chart Datum is 2·62 metres below Ordnance Datum (Newlyn). HAT is 5·3 metres above Chart Datum.

STANDARD TIME (UT)
For Summer Time add ONE hour in **non-shaded areas**

DARTMOUTH LAT 50°21′N LONG 3°35W

TIMES AND HEIGHTS OF HIGH AND LOW WATERS

Dates in red are SPRINGS
Dates in blue are NEAPS

YEAR **2018**

MAY

Date	Day	Time	m	Time	m	Time	m	Time	m	Moon
1	TU	0031	0.3	0654	4.8	1251	0.4	1910	4.8	
2	W	0106	0.4	0726	4.7	1324	0.6	1938	4.7	
3	TH	0138	0.6	0754	4.6	1353	0.8	2005	4.6	
4	F	0206	0.9	0823	4.4	1419	1.1	2033	4.5	
5	SA	0234	1.2	0854	4.2	1444	1.4	2106	4.3	
6	SU	0302	1.5	0930	4.0	1511	1.7	2143	4.1	
7	M	0338	1.8	1014	3.7	1553	2.0	2229	3.9	
8	TU	0439	2.0	1111	3.6	1708	2.2	2330	3.7	◑
9	W	0558	2.0	1229	3.5	1829	2.1			
10	TH	0050	3.7	0711	1.9	1358	3.7	1942	1.9	
11	F	0219	3.9	0817	1.6	1503	4.0	2045	1.6	
12	SA	0322	4.2	0915	1.2	1556	4.2	2141	1.2	
13	SU	0414	4.4	1007	0.9	1643	4.5	2232	0.9	
14	M	0503	4.6	1057	0.7	1730	4.7	2319	0.6	
15	TU	0551	4.8	1143	0.5	1814	4.8			●
16	W	0004	0.5	0638	4.8	1226	0.4	1857	4.9	
17	TH	0048	0.4	0722	4.9	1309	0.4	1939	5.0	
18	F	0130	0.4	0805	4.8	1351	0.5	2020	4.9	
19	SA	0212	0.5	0850	4.7	1433	0.7	2103	4.8	
20	SU	0258	0.8	0937	4.4	1519	1.0	2149	4.6	
21	M	0348	1.1	1031	4.2	1611	1.4	2244	4.3	
22	TU	0447	1.3	1137	4.0	1715	1.6	2355	4.1	◐
23	W	0600	1.5	1252	3.9	1832	1.7			
24	TH	0114	4.1	0723	1.5	1403	4.0	1953	1.6	
25	F	0225	4.2	0833	1.3	1505	4.2	2059	1.3	
26	SA	0325	4.3	0931	1.0	1559	4.4	2153	1.0	
27	SU	0417	4.5	1022	0.8	1646	4.5	2242	0.8	
28	M	0505	4.6	1106	0.7	1730	4.6	2326	0.7	
29	TU	0548	4.6	1148	0.6	1808	4.7			○
30	W	0006	0.7	0627	4.6	1225	0.7	1842	4.7	
31	TH	0041	0.7	0701	4.6	1258	0.8	1912	4.7	

JUNE

Date	Day	Time	m	Time	m	Time	m	Time	m	Moon
1	F	0114	0.8	0732	4.5	1328	1.0	1943	4.6	
2	SA	0144	1.0	0804	4.4	1356	1.2	2015	4.5	
3	SU	0212	1.2	0837	4.2	1422	1.4	2047	4.4	
4	M	0242	1.4	0913	4.0	1451	1.6	2122	4.2	
5	TU	0315	1.6	0953	3.9	1527	1.8	2203	4.1	
6	W	0400	1.7	1042	3.7	1620	1.9	2254	3.9	◑
7	TH	0505	1.8	1141	3.7	1734	2.0	2355	3.9	
8	F	0619	1.8	1250	3.7	1850	1.9			
9	SA	0107	4.0	0729	1.6	1402	3.9	1959	1.7	
10	SU	0224	4.1	0832	1.3	1506	4.2	2101	1.3	
11	M	0330	4.3	0931	1.1	1603	4.4	2158	1.0	
12	TU	0429	4.5	1026	0.8	1657	4.6	2253	0.7	
13	W	0524	4.7	1118	0.6	1747	4.8	2344	0.5	●
14	TH	0616	4.8	1208	0.5	1837	5.0			
15	F	0033	0.4	0706	4.9	1256	0.4	1924	5.0	
16	SA	0121	0.3	0755	4.8	1343	0.5	2010	5.0	
17	SU	0207	0.4	0844	4.7	1428	0.6	2057	4.9	
18	M	0255	0.6	0933	4.6	1514	0.8	2145	4.7	
19	TU	0343	0.8	1025	4.4	1603	1.1	2235	4.5	
20	W	0434	1.1	1121	4.2	1656	1.4	2334	4.3	◐
21	TH	0532	1.3	1223	4.0	1757	1.6			
22	F	0039	4.1	0639	1.5	1325	4.0	1907	1.6	
23	SA	0147	4.1	0750	1.5	1427	4.0	2018	1.6	
24	SU	0250	4.1	0855	1.4	1524	4.2	2120	1.4	
25	M	0346	4.2	0949	1.2	1614	4.3	2213	1.2	
26	TU	0436	4.3	1038	1.1	1700	4.5	2300	1.0	
27	W	0521	4.4	1121	1.0	1740	4.6	2342	0.9	
28	TH	0602	4.4	1201	0.9	1818	4.6			○
29	F	0020	0.9	0640	4.5	1236	1.0	1853	4.7	
30	SA	0054	0.9	0715	4.4	1307	1.0	1927	4.6	

JULY

Date	Day	Time	m	Time	m	Time	m	Time	m	Moon
1	SU	0125	1.0	0749	4.4	1337	1.1	2000	4.6	
2	M	0155	1.1	0825	4.3	1404	1.3	2033	4.5	
3	TU	0224	1.2	0859	4.2	1433	1.4	2106	4.4	
4	W	0255	1.3	0935	4.0	1506	1.5	2141	4.2	
5	TH	0332	1.5	1015	3.9	1547	1.6	2223	4.1	
6	F	0418	1.6	1103	3.9	1640	1.8	2314	4.0	◑
7	SA	0520	1.7	1200	3.8	1751	1.8			
8	SU	0016	4.0	0637	1.6	1307	3.9	1912	1.7	
9	M	0130	4.1	0751	1.5	1421	4.1	2025	1.5	
10	TU	0250	4.2	0859	1.2	1529	4.3	2131	1.2	
11	W	0400	4.4	1001	1.0	1630	4.6	2232	0.9	
12	TH	0502	4.6	1059	0.7	1727	4.8	2328	0.6	
13	F	0559	4.8	1154	0.5	1820	5.0			●
14	SA	0021	0.3	0654	4.9	1245	0.4	1910	5.1	
15	SU	0112	0.2	0745	4.9	1333	0.3	1959	5.1	
16	M	0159	0.2	0833	4.8	1418	0.4	2046	5.1	
17	TU	0244	0.3	0921	4.7	1501	0.6	2132	4.9	
18	W	0327	0.6	1006	4.5	1545	0.8	2216	4.7	
19	TH	0411	0.9	1052	4.3	1629	1.2	2301	4.4	◐
20	F	0456	1.2	1142	4.1	1717	1.5	2354	4.1	
21	SA	0550	1.5	1239	3.9	1816	1.7			
22	SU	0100	3.9	0655	1.7	1343	3.9	1928	1.8	
23	M	0211	3.8	0810	1.7	1446	3.9	2042	1.7	
24	TU	0314	3.9	0917	1.6	1543	4.1	2145	1.5	
25	W	0410	4.0	1012	1.4	1633	4.3	2237	1.3	
26	TH	0458	4.2	1059	1.2	1716	4.5	2321	1.1	
27	F	0541	4.3	1140	1.1	1757	4.6			○
28	SA	0000	1.0	0621	4.4	1216	1.0	1835	4.7	
29	SU	0035	0.9	0659	4.5	1249	1.0	1911	4.7	
30	M	0107	0.9	0735	4.4	1319	1.0	1946	4.7	
31	TU	0137	1.0	0810	4.4	1347	1.1	2019	4.6	

AUGUST

Date	Day	Time	m	Time	m	Time	m	Time	m	Moon
1	W	0204	1.0	0842	4.3	1415	1.2	2049	4.5	
2	TH	0234	1.1	0914	4.2	1445	1.3	2120	4.4	
3	F	0305	1.2	0948	4.1	1519	1.4	2155	4.3	
4	SA	0345	1.4	1029	4.0	1603	1.6	2242	4.1	◑
5	SU	0434	1.6	1121	3.9	1701	1.7	2342	4.0	
6	M	0544	1.7	1228	3.9	1826	1.8			
7	TU	0056	3.9	0714	1.7	1346	4.0	1957	1.7	
8	W	0224	4.0	0835	1.5	1504	4.3	2113	1.3	
9	TH	0342	4.3	0945	1.2	1611	4.6	2219	0.9	
10	F	0447	4.5	1047	0.8	1711	4.9	2317	0.6	
11	SA	0546	4.8	1142	0.5	1806	5.1			●
12	SU	0010	0.3	0640	4.9	1232	0.3	1857	5.2	
13	M	0058	0.1	0730	5.0	1319	0.2	1944	5.2	
14	TU	0144	0.0	0816	4.9	1401	0.2	2028	5.2	
15	W	0225	0.2	0859	4.8	1441	0.4	2108	5.0	
16	TH	0303	0.5	0938	4.6	1519	0.7	2146	4.7	
17	F	0341	0.8	1013	4.4	1557	1.1	2219	4.4	
18	SA	0418	1.3	1049	4.1	1637	1.5	2255	4.0	◐
19	SU	0502	1.7	1133	3.9	1728	1.9	2346	3.7	
20	M	0559	2.0	1245	3.7	1835	2.1			
21	TU	0124	3.6	0714	2.1	1408	3.7	1959	2.1	
22	W	0246	3.7	0842	2.0	1514	3.9	2119	1.8	
23	TH	0346	3.9	0947	1.7	1607	4.2	2215	1.5	
24	F	0436	4.1	1036	1.4	1653	4.4	2259	1.2	
25	SA	0519	4.3	1117	1.1	1735	4.6	2339	1.0	
26	SU	0600	4.5	1155	1.0	1814	4.7			○
27	M	0013	0.9	0639	4.5	1227	0.9	1853	4.8	
28	TU	0045	0.8	0715	4.6	1258	0.9	1927	4.8	
29	W	0115	0.8	0749	4.5	1327	0.9	2000	4.7	
30	TH	0144	0.8	0822	4.5	1355	1.0	2029	4.6	
31	F	0212	0.9	0851	4.4	1424	1.1	2100	4.5	

Chart Datum is 2·62 metres below Ordnance Datum (Newlyn). HAT is 5·3 metres above Chart Datum.

STANDARD TIME (UT)
For Summer Time add ONE hour in **non-shaded areas**

DARTMOUTH

LAT 50°21'N LONG 3°35'W

TIMES AND HEIGHTS OF HIGH AND LOW WATERS

Dates in red are **SPRINGS**
Dates in blue are **NEAPS**

YEAR **2018**

SEPTEMBER

Date	Day	Time	m	Time	m	Time	m	Time	m	Moon
1	SA	0243	1.1	0922	4.3	1457	1.2	2134	4.4	
2	SU	0317	1.3	1001	4.2	1537	1.5	2218	4.2	
3	M	0402	1.6	1052	4.0	1631	1.7	2317	4.0	◑
4	TU	0507	1.8	1159	3.9	1754	1.9			
5	W	0035	3.8	0647	1.9	1323	4.0	1940	1.8	
6	TH	0212	3.9	0822	1.7	1450	4.2	2103	1.4	
7	F	0335	4.2	0935	1.3	1600	4.6	2208	1.0	
8	SA	0439	4.5	1035	0.8	1658	4.9	2304	0.5	
9	SU	0534	4.8	1127	0.5	1750	5.1	2355	0.2	●
10	M	0625	5.0	1216	0.2	1839	5.3			
11	TU	0040	0.0	0709	5.1	1300	0.1	1923	5.3	
12	W	0122	0.0	0751	5.0	1339	0.2	2003	5.2	
13	TH	0200	0.2	0829	4.9	1415	0.4	2039	5.0	
14	F	0235	0.5	0902	4.7	1450	0.7	2109	4.7	
15	SA	0307	0.9	0929	4.5	1522	1.2	2136	4.3	
16	SU	0339	1.4	0956	4.2	1557	1.6	2207	4.0	◐
17	M	0416	1.8	1033	3.9	1644	2.0	2251	3.7	
18	TU	0509	2.2	1129	3.7	1750	2.3			
19	W	0001	3.5	0624	2.3	1319	3.6	1912	2.3	
20	TH	0215	3.5	0756	2.2	1442	3.8	2046	2.0	
21	F	0321	3.8	0916	1.9	1539	4.1	2144	1.6	
22	SA	0410	4.1	1005	1.5	1626	4.4	2229	1.3	
23	SU	0454	4.4	1047	1.2	1708	4.6	2307	1.0	
24	M	0534	4.6	1124	1.0	1749	4.8	2344	0.8	
25	TU	0614	4.7	1200	0.8	1828	4.8			○
26	W	0017	0.7	0652	4.7	1233	0.8	1905	4.8	
27	TH	0050	0.7	0726	4.7	1304	0.8	1939	4.8	
28	F	0121	0.7	0758	4.7	1335	0.8	2010	4.7	
29	SA	0152	0.8	0828	4.6	1405	0.9	2042	4.6	
30	SU	0223	1.0	0902	4.5	1439	1.1	2118	4.4	

OCTOBER

Date	Day	Time	m	Time	m	Time	m	Time	m	Moon
1	M	0258	1.3	0942	4.3	1520	1.4	2204	4.2	
2	TU	0343	1.6	1032	4.1	1614	1.8	2304	3.9	◑
3	W	0449	2.0	1141	4.0	1741	2.0			
4	TH	0027	3.8	0633	2.1	1310	4.0	1932	1.9	
5	F	0209	3.9	0813	1.8	1439	4.2	2053	1.4	
6	SA	0328	4.3	0923	1.3	1547	4.6	2154	0.9	
7	SU	0427	4.6	1019	0.9	1642	4.9	2246	0.5	
8	M	0517	4.9	1108	0.5	1732	5.1	2334	0.3	
9	TU	0603	5.0	1154	0.3	1817	5.2			●
10	W	0016	0.1	0646	5.1	1235	0.2	1859	5.2	
11	TH	0056	0.2	0723	5.1	1313	0.3	1936	5.1	
12	F	0132	0.4	0756	5.0	1348	0.5	2007	4.9	
13	SA	0204	0.7	0825	4.8	1420	0.9	2034	4.6	
14	SU	0234	1.1	0850	4.6	1451	1.3	2102	4.3	
15	M	0301	1.5	0918	4.3	1522	1.7	2134	4.0	
16	TU	0333	1.9	0955	4.1	1603	2.0	2217	3.8	◐
17	W	0420	2.3	1046	3.8	1707	2.3	2318	3.5	
18	TH	0538	2.5	1201	3.7	1828	2.4			
19	F	0122	3.5	0704	2.4	1356	3.8	1950	2.1	
20	SA	0243	3.8	0823	2.1	1501	4.1	2058	1.8	
21	SU	0336	4.1	0922	1.7	1552	4.4	2146	1.4	
22	M	0422	4.4	1007	1.3	1636	4.6	2229	1.1	
23	TU	0503	4.6	1050	1.1	1718	4.8	2309	0.9	
24	W	0544	4.7	1128	0.9	1800	4.9	2348	0.7	○
25	TH	0623	4.8	1207	0.7	1839	4.9			
26	F	0024	0.7	0701	4.9	1242	0.7	1917	4.9	
27	SA	0100	0.7	0736	4.9	1318	0.7	1953	4.8	
28	SU	0134	0.8	0811	4.8	1353	0.9	2029	4.7	
29	M	0209	1.0	0848	4.7	1431	1.1	2110	4.5	
30	TU	0249	1.3	0930	4.5	1514	1.4	2158	4.2	
31	W	0337	1.7	1022	4.3	1612	1.7	2259	4.0	◑

NOVEMBER

Date	Day	Time	m	Time	m	Time	m	Time	m	Moon
1	TH	0443	2.0	1130	4.1	1736	1.9			
2	F	0023	3.9	0620	2.1	1257	4.1	1916	1.8	
3	SA	0157	4.0	0754	1.8	1421	4.3	2033	1.4	
4	SU	0309	4.3	0902	1.4	1527	4.6	2132	1.0	
5	M	0405	4.6	0956	1.0	1621	4.8	2223	0.7	
6	TU	0454	4.8	1045	0.7	1709	5.0	2309	0.5	
7	W	0538	5.0	1129	0.5	1754	5.1	2352	0.4	●
8	TH	0619	5.0	1211	0.5	1833	5.0			
9	F	0030	0.5	0655	5.0	1248	0.6	1908	4.9	
10	SA	0105	0.7	0726	4.9	1322	0.7	1940	4.8	
11	SU	0136	0.9	0753	4.8	1354	1.0	2007	4.6	
12	M	0204	1.2	0822	4.7	1423	1.3	2037	4.4	
13	TU	0231	1.5	0853	4.5	1454	1.6	2111	4.1	
14	W	0259	1.9	0930	4.2	1530	1.9	2153	3.9	
15	TH	0336	2.1	1017	4.0	1624	2.2	2248	3.7	◐
16	F	0445	2.4	1116	3.8	1738	2.3			
17	SA	0003	3.6	0609	2.4	1237	3.8	1853	2.2	
18	SU	0140	3.7	0725	2.2	1403	4.0	2001	1.9	
19	M	0248	4.0	0829	1.9	1505	4.2	2058	1.5	
20	TU	0340	4.3	0924	1.5	1557	4.5	2148	1.2	
21	W	0427	4.5	1013	1.2	1644	4.7	2234	1.0	
22	TH	0511	4.7	1058	1.0	1730	4.8	2318	0.8	
23	F	0555	4.9	1142	0.8	1815	4.9			○
24	SA	0001	0.7	0637	5.0	1223	0.7	1858	4.9	
25	SU	0042	0.7	0717	5.0	1305	0.7	1940	4.9	
26	M	0123	0.8	0757	5.0	1347	0.8	2023	4.8	
27	TU	0203	0.9	0840	4.9	1430	1.0	2108	4.6	
28	W	0248	1.2	0925	4.7	1517	1.2	2157	4.3	
29	TH	0338	1.5	1017	4.5	1613	1.5	2256	4.1	
30	F	0438	1.7	1119	4.3	1722	1.7			◑

DECEMBER

Date	Day	Time	m	Time	m	Time	m	Time	m	Moon
1	SA	0009	4.0	0554	1.9	1235	4.2	1844	1.7	
2	SU	0127	4.0	0718	1.8	1351	4.3	2001	1.5	
3	M	0236	4.2	0829	1.6	1457	4.4	2103	1.3	
4	TU	0335	4.4	0928	1.3	1554	4.6	2156	1.0	
5	W	0426	4.6	1020	1.0	1643	4.7	2243	0.9	
6	TH	0511	4.8	1105	0.9	1729	4.8	2326	0.8	
7	F	0552	4.9	1148	0.8	1810	4.8			●
8	SA	0006	0.8	0630	4.9	1226	0.8	1847	4.7	
9	SU	0041	0.9	0703	4.9	1301	0.9	1918	4.6	
10	M	0114	1.0	0733	4.8	1334	1.1	1949	4.5	
11	TU	0143	1.2	0804	4.7	1403	1.3	2022	4.4	
12	W	0210	1.4	0837	4.6	1434	1.5	2057	4.2	
13	TH	0238	1.7	0912	4.4	1505	1.7	2136	4.0	
14	F	0310	1.9	0952	4.2	1545	1.9	2221	3.9	
15	SA	0354	2.1	1040	4.0	1640	2.0	2315	3.8	◐
16	SU	0500	2.2	1138	3.9	1751	2.1			
17	M	0022	3.8	0621	2.2	1245	4.0	1903	2.0	
18	TU	0136	3.9	0735	2.0	1400	4.1	2009	1.7	
19	W	0246	4.1	0838	1.7	1508	4.3	2108	1.4	
20	TH	0344	4.4	0936	1.4	1607	4.5	2201	1.1	
21	F	0437	4.6	1030	1.1	1702	4.7	2253	0.9	
22	SA	0528	4.8	1120	0.8	1752	4.8	2343	0.7	○
23	SU	0616	5.0	1210	0.6	1842	4.9			
24	M	0029	0.6	0703	5.1	1257	0.6	1930	4.9	
25	TU	0116	0.6	0748	5.1	1344	0.6	2017	4.8	
26	W	0201	0.7	0834	5.1	1429	0.7	2104	4.7	
27	TH	0247	0.9	0921	4.9	1516	0.9	2152	4.5	
28	F	0333	1.1	1010	4.7	1604	1.1	2244	4.3	
29	SA	0423	1.4	1103	4.5	1658	1.4	2342	4.1	◑
30	SU	0520	1.6	1204	4.3	1801	1.6			
31	M	0047	4.0	0630	1.8	1311	4.2	1914	1.7	

Chart Datum is 2·62 metres below Ordnance Datum (Newlyn). HAT is 5·3 metres above Chart Datum.

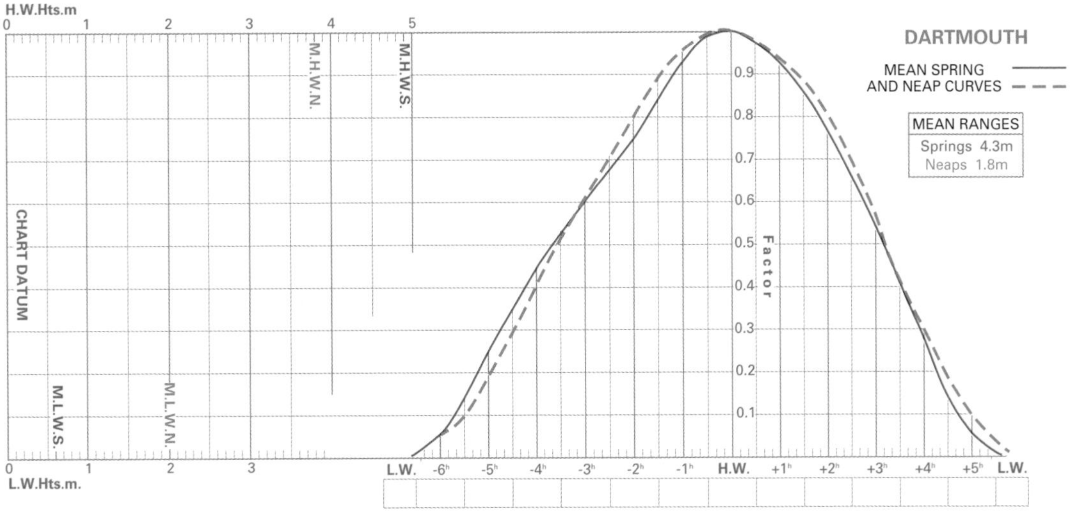
H.W.Hts.m
0 1 2 3 4 5
M.H.W.N.
M.H.W.S.
CHART DATUM
M.L.W.S.
M.L.W.N.
0 1 2 3
L.W.Hts.m.
0.9
0.8
0.7
0.6
0.5
0.4
0.3
0.2
0.1
Factor
L.W. -6h -5h -4h -3h -2h -1h H.W. +1h +2h +3h +4h +5h L.W.
DARTMOUTH
MEAN SPRING AND NEAP CURVES
MEAN RANGES
Springs 4.3m
Neaps 1.8m

9.1.20 BRIXHAM

Devon 50°24′·31N 03°30′·85W

[rating symbols]

CHARTS AC 3315, 1613, 1634, 5602, 26; Imray C10, C5, 2300

TIDES –0505 Dover; ML 2·9; Duration 0635.

Use **TORQUAY** Differences on **PLYMOUTH**.

SHELTER Very good in marina; good at YC pontoon in SW of hbr, but outer hbr is dangerous in strong NW'lies. ⚓ NW of fairway or in Fishcombe and Elberry Coves W of the hbr; beware water skiers.

NAVIGATION WPT 50°24′·70N 03° 31′·09W, (3ca off chartlet), 159°/0·4M to harbour entrance. Beware fish farm 5Ca WNW of harbour; easy access H24. Inshore around Torbay controlled areas (May-Sep, mainly for swimmers) are marked by unlit Y SPM buoys; boats may enter with caution, speed limit 5kn.

LIGHTS AND MARKS Berry Hd, a conspic headland and good radar return, is 1·25M ESE of entrance. The fairway is marked by two pairs of lit lateral buoys. See chartlet and 9.1.4 for lt details.

COMMUNICATIONS (Code 01803) CGOC (01326) 317575; Police 101; Dr 855897; [H] 882153. HM 853321; Pilot 882214; Ch 14 (May-Sep 0800-1800; Oct-Apr 0900-1700, Mon-Fri). Marina Ch 80.

Water Taxi: *Shuttle* Ch M.

FACILITIES Brixham Marina brixham@mdlmarinas.co.uk ☎882929, [slipway] 500[berths] inc [visitors] £3·40<12·5m>£4·20<18m, Short stay<4 hrs £8·00.

Events pontoon (no [electricity]) £2·32 < 12·5m>£2·90.

[fuel](0900-1800, Apr-Oct) [laundry] [hoist](50t).

Brixham YC ☎853332, [visitors] pontoon, [symbols] ✕ [symbol].

Hbr Office [moorings] each side of fairway, [symbols] (4t).

Town pontoon [berths] £1·90, [electricity] no [WC/showers].

Town [symbols] ACA ✕ [symbol] bus to Paignton, [rail] ✈ Exeter.

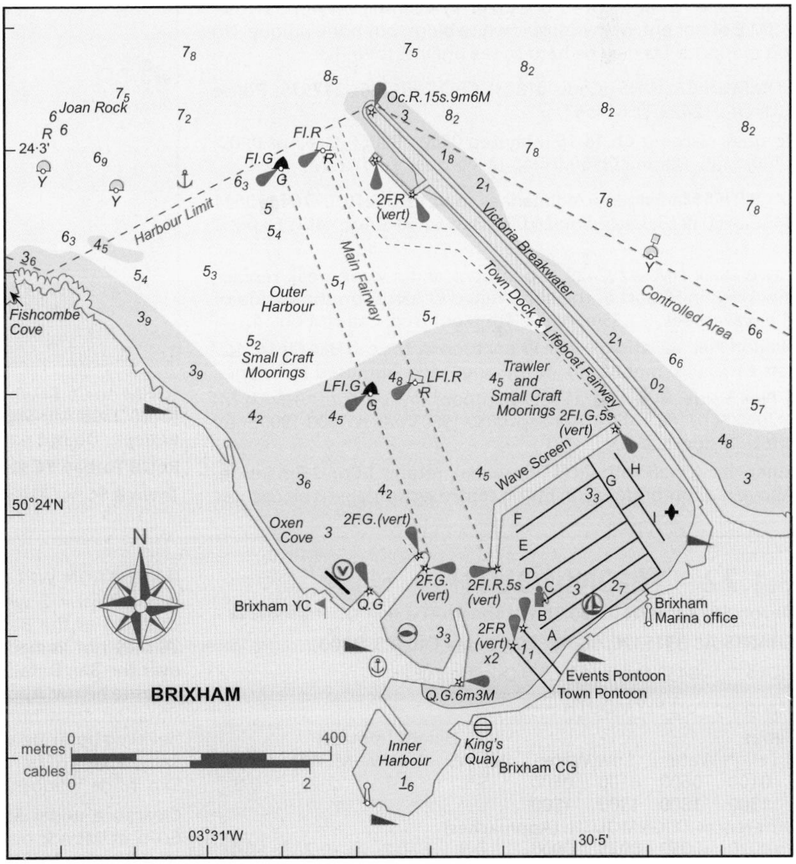
Joan Rock
R 6
24·3'
Y
Harbour Limit
Fl.G
G
Fl.R
R
Oc.R.15s.9m6M
2F.R (vert)
Victoria Breakwater
Town Dock & Lifeboat Fairway
Controlled Area
Main Fairway
Outer Harbour
Small Craft Moorings
Fishcombe Cove
LFl.G
LFl.R
Trawler and Small Craft Moorings
2Fl.G.5s (vert)
Wave Screen
50°24'N
Oxen Cove
2F.G.(vert)
2F.G. (vert)
2Fl.R.5s (vert)
Brixham YC
Q.G
2F.R (vert) x2
Brixham Marina office
Events Pontoon
Town Pontoon
Q.G.6m3M
BRIXHAM
Inner Harbour
King's Quay
Brixham CG
metres 0 400
cables 0 2
03°31'W
30·5'
N

MINOR HARBOUR 2·3M NW OF BRIXHAM

PAIGNTON, Devon, **50°25′·96N 03°33′·36W** 500m S of Paignton pier. AC 1613, 26. HW +0035 and –0·6m on Plymouth; Duration 0640; ML 2·9m. Hbr dries 1·3m, only suitable for max LOA 8·2m. A heavy swell enters in E'lies. Drying rks extend 180m ENE from E pier, ☆ QR, to Black Rk, ECM twr ☆ Q (3) 10s 5m 3M. In the approach chan **keep to port**. HM (summer only) ☎(01803) 557812, VHF Ch 14.

Paignton SC ☎525817. Facilities: [symbols] ACA.

9.1.21 TORQUAY

Devon **50°27'·45N 03°31'·73W** ❁❁❁◊◊◊✿✿

CHARTS AC 3315, 1613, 5602, 26; Imray C5

TIDES –0500 Dover; ML 2·9; Duration 0640

Standard Port PLYMOUTH (⟵)

Times				**Height (metres)**			
High Water		Low Water		MHWS	MHWN	MLWN	MLWS
0100	0600	0100	0600	5·5	4·4	2·2	0·8
1300	1800	1300	1800				
Differences *TORQUAY*							
+0025	*+0045*	*+0010*	*0000*	*–0·6*	*–0·7*	*–0·2*	*–0·1*

NOTE: There is often a stand of about 1hr at HW

SHELTER Good, but some swell in hbr with strong SE'lies. ⚓s NW of Hope's Nose at Hope Cove, Anstey's Cove & Babbacombe Bay are well sheltered in W'lies. No ⚓ in hbr.

NAVIGATION WPT 50°27'·03N 03°31'·57W, 339°/0·40M to round SHM buoy 80m WSW of Haldon pier. Semi-blind ent; keep a good lookout. Access at all tides, but in strong SE winds backwash may make the narrow ent difficult. Hbr speed limit 5kn.

Controlled areas (mainly for swimmers, May-Sep) close inshore around Torbay are marked by unlit Y SPM buoys; boats may enter with caution, speed limit 5kn. Watch out for canoeists.

LIGHTS AND MARKS Ore Stone (32m rk) is conspic off Hope's Nose, 2·3M E of hbr ent. Many conspic white bldgs, but none unique. No ldg marks/lts. Lts may be hard to see against town lts.

COMMUNICATIONS (Code 01803) CGOC (01326) 317575; Police 101; Dr 212429; Ⓗ 614567.

Torquay Harbour Ch **14** 16 (May-Sep 0800-1800LT; Oct-Apr 0900-1700, M-F). Marina Ch **80** (H24), M. *Torquay Fuel* Ch M.

FACILITIES **Marina** www.mdlmarinas.co.uk ☎200210, 07764 175611 440+60 Ⓥ £3.32<12·5m>£4.09<18m>£4.60<24m; <4hrs £8.00;

Town Dock HM ☎292429. 4 pontoons and a wavebreak replace moorings in SE part of the hbr. Limited Ⓥ berths on the W side of the wavebreak, £1.55/m/night, 4th night free. Call HM Ch 14.

Haldon Pier at root, 96m Ⓥ pontoon in 2m, call HM Ch 14: /raft £1.55 (4th night free), (long lead). Also used for events.

S Pier S side: LPG at fuel pontoon, *Riviera Fuel* VHF Ch M; ☎294509, 07786 370324 (Apr-Sept 0830-1900 W/days, 1000-1900 Sun); (6t). N side:

Inner Hbr A wall with sill (11·6m wide), retains 1·0m–2·8m inside. Above it a footbridge with lifting centre section opens on request to HM on *Ch 14* when the flapgate is down, approx HW –3½ to +3 (0700-2300 Apr-Sep, 0900-1700 Oct-Mar). IPTS sigs 2 & 4 control ent/exit. Do not pass under the bridge when it is down.

Royal Torbay YC ☎292006,

Town ACA (Exeter).

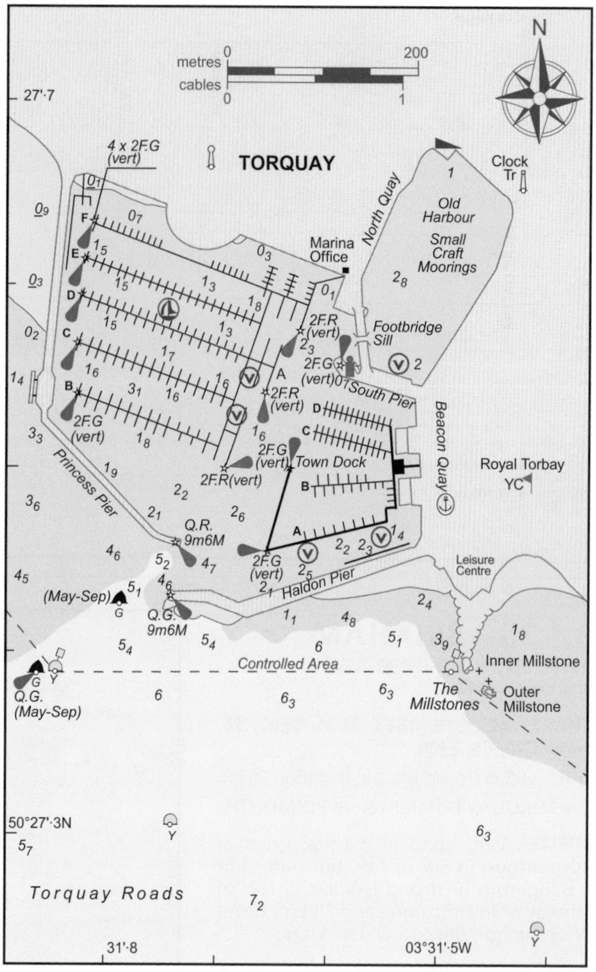

9.1.22 TEIGNMOUTH

Devon **50°32'·37N 03°30'·00W** (Abeam The Point) ❁❁◊◊✿✿

CHARTS AC 3315, 26, 5601, 5602; Imray C10, C5, 2300

TIDES –0450 Dover; ML 2·7; Duration 0625

Standard Port PLYMOUTH (⟵)

Times				**Height (metres)**			
High Water		Low Water		MHWS	MHWN	MLWN	MLWS
0100	0600	0100	0600	5·5	4·4	2·2	0·8
1300	1800	1300	1800				
Differences TEIGNMOUTH (Approaches)							
+0020	+0050	+0025	0000	–0·9	–0·8	–0·2	–0·1
TEIGNMOUTH (New Quay)							
+0025	+0055	+0040	+0005	–0·8	–0·8	–0·2	+0·1

Tidal streams. *At the hbr ent the flood starts HW Plymouth –5½ and the ebb at HWP +¾. Be aware that from about HW –3, as The Salty covers, the flood sets NW across it and a small back eddy flows S past the Ⓥ pontoons. HW slack occurs at approx HWP +½.*

SHELTER Good, but entry hazardous in strong onshore winds (NE-S) when surf forms on the bar.

NAVIGATION WPT 50°32'·37N 03°29'·15W, 265°/5ca to trng wall lt (Oc R 6s) ≠ 2 white □s on seawall beyond. The E-W chan is dredged as the Bar, Pole and Spratt Sands shift frequently; AC 26 may not immediately show such shifts. Depths reduce to CD over the Bar. Detailed pilotage and hbr notes are in the excellent website below. Appr chan is not well buoyed, contact HM for latest situation. Small buoys laid by Pilots near the appr chan, should not be relied upon. Beware rks off The Ness; and variable extent of The Salty, a bank of hard gravel/sand. Max speed 6kn over the ground; 5kn inside Y buoys off The Ness & Teignmouth beaches.

Clearance under Shaldon bridge is 2·9m at MHWS and approx 6·7m at MLWS; near its N end there is a 9m wide drawbridge section. Avoid a Historic wreck site (50°32'·95N 03°29'·24W; just off chartlet), close inshore ENE of Ch twr.

LIGHTS AND MARKS The Ness, a 50m high red sandstone headland, and church tower are both conspic from afar. Close NE of the latter, just off N edge of chartlet, Teign Corinthian YC bldg (cream colour) is also conspic. Ignore two FR (NNE of The Point); they are not ldg lts. N of The Point, two F Bu lts align 023°, but are not ldg lts. A Y can buoy, Fl Y 5s, at 50°31'·97N 03°27'·78W marks the seaward end of outfall, 103° The Ness 1·3M.

COMMUNICATIONS (Code 01626) CGOC (01326) 317575; Police

101; Dr 774355; Ⓗ 772161. HM 773165 (or 07796 178456 in emergency or out of hrs).

Hbr Ch **12** 16 (Mon-Fri 0900-1400).

FACILITIES www.teignmouth-harbour.com; info@teignmouth-harbour.com. In suitable weather up to 10 boats can raft on 2 detached 20m Ⓥ pontoons (Jubilee & Trafalgar) at 50°32′·62N 03°29′·96W in 2·5m; £1.10/m. Third pontoon (Newfoundland) is for local boats only. No ⚓ in hbr due to many moorings and strong tidal streams. In fair weather ⚓ approx 1·5ca SE of The Ness or Teignmouth Pier.

E Quay Polly Steps (up to 10m). **Teign Corinthian YC** ☎772734, £8.

Services (8t).

Town (1M), ✉ Ⓑ ✈(Exeter).

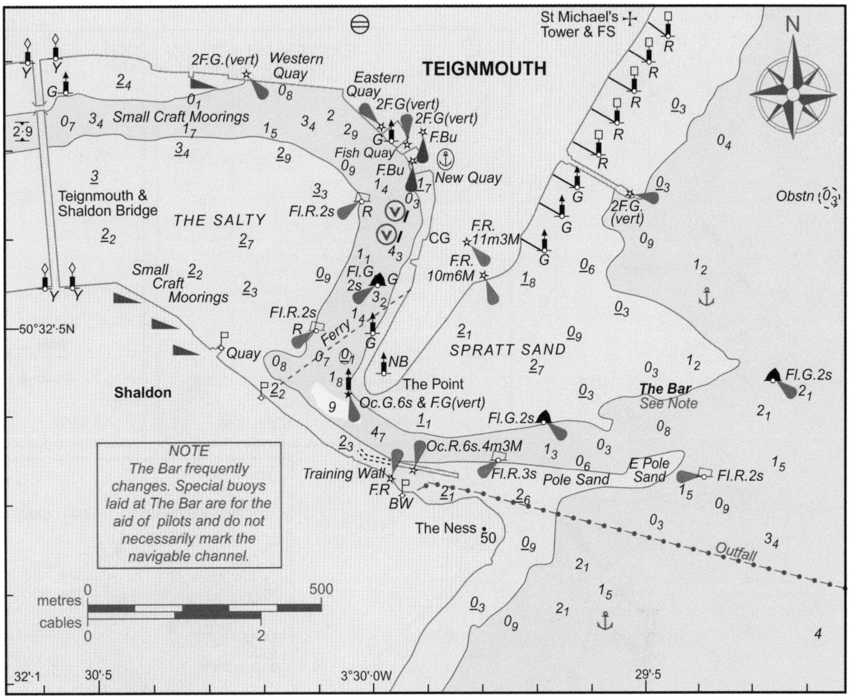

LYME BAY: TEIGNMOUTH TO PORTLAND BILL

Lyme Bay curves 65M in a great arc N, E and SE from Start Pt to Portland Bill (AC 3315).

▶*Tides are weak, rarely more than 0·75kn. From west to east the tidal curve becomes progressively more distorted, especially on the rising tide. The rise is relatively fast for the 1st hr after LW; then slackens noticeably for the next 1½hrs, before resuming the rapid rate of rise. There is often a stand at HW, not very noticeable at Start Pt but lasting about 1½hrs at Lyme Regis.*◀

From Teignmouth to Dawlish rocks extend 1ca offshore. Beware Dawlish Rock (2·1m) about 5ca off North end of town. Pole Sand (dries up to 3·5m) and Warren Sand on the West side of the **River Exe** estuary are liable to shift. A firing range at Straight Point has a danger zone extending 1·5M east marked by 2 Y lit DZ buoys.

3½ M SE of Sidmouth on the 20m contour a mussel farm is marked by 2 pairs of SPM (Fl Y 5s). Another mussel farm, similarly marked, lies 4¾M further S in 25m of water.

Between Torbay and Portland no harbour is accessible in strong onshore winds, and care must be taken not to be caught on a lee shore. Marked by 4 cardinal buoys 2½M E of Hope's Nose is the wk of the *EMSSTROM* (16·5m) . In offshore winds there is a good ⚓ NE of Beer Hd, the western-most chalk cliff in England. Golden Cap (186m and conspic) is 3·5M E of **Lyme Regis**. High Ground (3m) and Pollock (4m) are rocky patches 7ca offshore, respectively 1·5M W and 6ca SW of **West Bay** (Bridport). Numerous wks litter the bay, one dangerous to navigation 222°Hardy's Mt 7.8M.

From 6M SE of Bridport Chesil Beach runs SE for about 9M to the N end of the Isle of Portland. From a distance this peninsula looks like an island, with its distinctive wedge-shaped profile sloping down from 145m at the N to sea level at the Bill. Although mostly steep-to, an 18m high, white obelisk on the tip of the Bill warns of a rocky ledge extending about 50m S of the Bill. If the highest window on the lighthouse is seen above the top of the obelisk, you are clear of the outermost rock, but still very close inshore.

If heading up-Channel from Start Point, Dartmouth or Torbay time your departure to pass Portland Bill with a fair tide at all costs, especially at springs. If late, a temporary ⚓ can be found close inshore at Chesil Cove, abeam the highest part of Portland.

9.1.23 RIVER EXE

Devon **50°36′·94N 03°25′·40W** (Abeam Exmouth)

CHARTS AC 3315, 2290, 5601; Imray C10, C5, 2300

TIDES –0445 Dover; ML 2·1; Duration 0625

Standard Port PLYMOUTH (⟵)

Times				**Height (metres)**			
High Water		Low Water		MHWS	MHWN	MLWN	MLWS
0100	0600	0100	0600	5·5	4·4	2·2	0·8
1300	1800	1300	1800				
Differences EXMOUTH (Approaches)							
+0030	+0050	+0015	+0005	–0·9	–1·0	–0·5	–0·3
EXMOUTH DOCK							
+0035	+0055	+0050	+0020	–1·5	–1·6	–0·9	–0·5
STARCROSS							
+0040	+0100	+0055	+0025	–1·4	–1·5	–0·8	–0·1
TURF LOCK							
+0045	+0100	+0034	ND	–1·6	–1·6	–1·2	–0·4
TOPSHAM							
+0045	+0105	ND	ND	–1·5	–1·6	ND	ND

NOTE: In the appr chan the sp ebb reaches 3·3kn; with wind against tide a confused, breaking sea quickly builds. Off Warren Pt the flood stream runs at 3-4kn and the ebb can exceed 4½kn when the banks uncover.

SHELTER Good upstream of No 13 buoy and in Dock.

NAVIGATION WPT 50°35′·92N 03°23′·75W, Exe SWM buoy, 335°/6ca to No 7 SHM buoy. Up to date AC 2290 is essential. Leave WPT at approx LW+2 (or when there is sufficient rise of the tide) when hazards can be seen and some shelter obtained, or at HW–1 or HW–2 to reach Exmouth or Topsham, respectively, at slack water.

The approach channel, with a least depth of 0·4m, is well marked with PHM/SHM buoys, some of which are lit. Night entry is not advised, the alignment of the ldg lts is questionable. After No 10 PHM buoy do not cut the corner round Warren Point; turn to the SW after passing No 12 PHM buoy. Beware of the flood stream sweeping NW past the marina entrance into moorings and shallow banks.

The estuary bed is sand/mud, free of rocks. Follow the curve of the channel rather than straight lines between the buoys; some bends are marked on the outside only. *Continued overleaf*

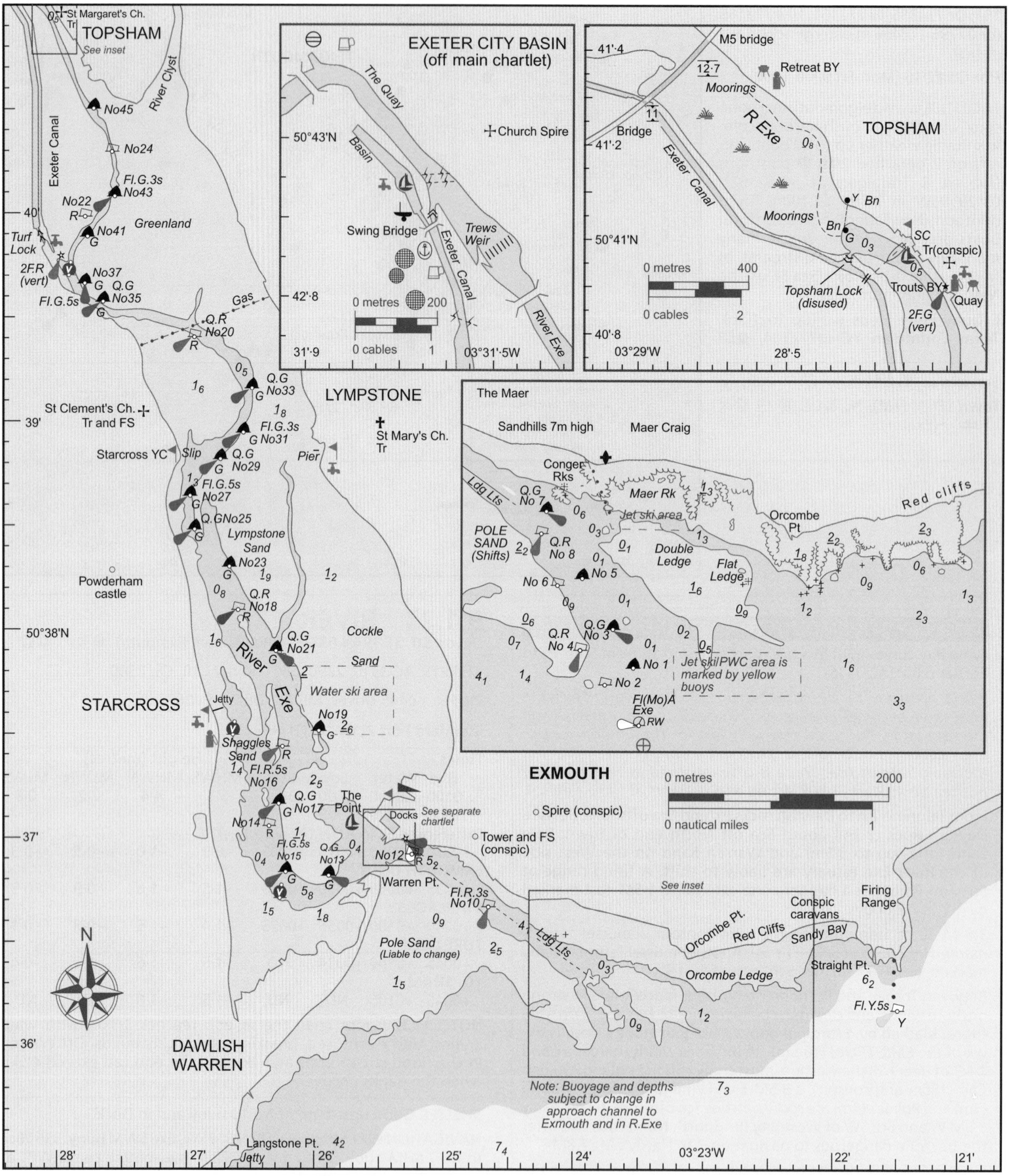
TOPSHAM
See inset
St Margaret's Ch. Tr
River Clyst
Exeter Canal
No45
No24
Fl.G.3s
No43
No22
Greenland
No41
Turf Lock
2F.R (vert)
No37
Q.G
No35
Fl.G.5s
Gas
Q.R
No20
Q.G
No33
LYMPSTONE
St Clement's Ch. Tr and FS
Fl.G.3s
No31
St Mary's Ch. Tr
Starcross YC
Slip
Q.G
No29
Pier
Fl.G.5s
No27
Q.G No25
Lympstone Sand
No23
Powderham castle
Q.R
No18
Cockle Sand
Q.G
No21
River Exe
Water ski area
STARCROSS
Jetty
No19
Shaggles Sand
Fl.R.5s
No16
Q.G
No17
The Point
Docks
See separate chartlet
No14
Fl.G.5s
No15
Q.G
No13
No12
Warren Pt.
Fl.R.3s
No10
Ldg Lts
Pole Sand (Liable to change)
DAWLISH WARREN
Langstone Pt.
Jetty
EXETER CITY BASIN (off main chartlet)
The Quay
Church Spire
Basin
Swing Bridge
Trews Weir
Exeter Canal
River Exe
0 metres 200
0 cables 1
50°43'N
42'·8
31'·9
03°31'·5W
M5 bridge
Retreat BY
Moorings
R Exe
Bridge
Exeter Canal
TOPSHAM
Y Bn
Moorings
Bn
SC
Tr(conspic)
Topsham Lock (disused)
Trouts BY
Quay
2F.G (vert)
0 metres 400
0 cables 2
41'·4
41'·2
50°41'N
40'·8
03°29'W
28'·5
The Maer
Sandhills 7m high
Maer Craig
Conger Rks
Ldg Lts
Q.G No 7
Maer Rk
Jet ski area
Red cliffs
Orcombe Pt
POLE SAND (Shifts)
Q.R No 8
Double Ledge
Flat Ledge
No 5
No 6
Q.G No 3
Q.R No 4
No 1
No 2
Jet ski/PWC area is marked by yellow buoys
Fl(Mo)A Exe RW
EXMOUTH
0 metres 2000
0 nautical miles 1
Spire (conspic)
Tower and FS (conspic)
See inset
Conspic caravans
Firing Range
Orcombe Pt.
Red Cliffs
Sandy Bay
Straight Pt.
Orcombe Ledge
Fl.Y.5s
Note: Buoyage and depths subject to change in approach channel to Exmouth and in R.Exe
N
40'
39'
50°38'N
37'
36'
28'
27'
26'
25'
24'
03°23'W
22'
21'

The estuary is an international conservation area.

LIGHTS AND MARKS See chartlet and 9.1.4. A caravan site is conspic close W of Straight Pt with red cliffs to W and NNE. Exmouth ✠ tr and FS are conspic. At Exmouth follow the 305° directional bn which can be hard to see by day. Following buoys in the upper reaches are lit:

No 22 PHM: Ting Tong	– Fl R 2s.
No 24 PHM: Exe	– Fl R 4s.
No 41 SHM: Turf Green	– Fl G 2s.
No 45 SHM: Topsham reach	– Fl G 4s.

A jetski/PWC area is marked by yellow buoys to NE of SWM.

Caution: Firing range N of Straight Pt has a danger area to ESE, marked by 2 DZ SPM lt buoys (not the sewer outfall SPM buoy, Fl Y 5s, shown on chartlet). R flags are flown when the range is active (likely times 0800-1600, Mon-Fri); call *Straight Pt Range* VHF Ch 08 16. From the E, check also with safety launch.

COMMUNICATIONS (Code 01395) CGOC (01326) 317575; Police 101; Dr 273001; Ⓗ 279684. Council River Team (01392) 274306; Port of Exeter Ch 12 16 (Mon-Fri: 0730-1730LT). Exmouth Marina/ bridge Ch 14. *Water taxi* Ch M.

FACILITIES

EXMOUTH Marina, ☎269314, mostly berth holders, but at least 4 visitors berths in 2.0m depth. Pontoon in ent chan is used by ferries/water taxi and for . Call Ch 14 for berth availability. Strong cross tides at ent. Footbridge lifts on request Ch 14 0800-1700; stays open HN. 172 inc some Ⓥ in 2m £3·80 (15t).

Exe SC ☎264607, ✕ .

Town ✕ Ⓔ ACA ✉ Ⓑ ✕ ⥂. s£12·00, lie near No 15 SHM buoy, off Turf Lock and Topsham SC; call water taxi Ch M ☎07970 918418 for advice.

STARCROSS (01626) **Village** ✉ Ⓑ ⥂. **Starcross Garage** ☎890225, Gas. **Starcross Fishing & Cruising Club** 2 (☎891996 (evenings) for availability). **Starcross YC** ☎890470.

TURF LOCK, 50°39'·88N 03°28'·06W, operates daily in working hours by prior arrangement with the lock keeper ☎274306.

Exeter Ship Canal (3m depth). HM ☎01392 265791 or Ch 12 for non-tidal pontoon Ⓥ berth in Turf Basin, £15·53 min 2 days (and laying up). Canal transit Mon-Fri 1600-1800 £49(extra at w/e).

TOPSHAM (01392) Here the river carries about 0·4m. Options are (pontoon in ¾m at LW) at Trouts BY or ⚓ in appr's, dry out at Town Quay in mud on rough wall (☎07801 203338 – £10·56/day) or find a mooring.

Topsham SC ☎877524, 2s .

Trouts BY www.trouts boatyard.co.uk ☎873044. MLWS max depth 0·75m; £17·50<6m>£23 (+ £20 key deposit); short stay £12.

Retreat BY www.retreatboatyard.co.uk ☎874720, appr channel dries approx $\underline{1}$m, poss (10½t) .

Town ACA ✉ Ⓑ ✕ ⥂.

EXETER www.exeter.gov.uk river.canal@exeter.gov.uk Waterways, Civic Centre, Paris St, Exeter EX1 1JN; 0730-1530 M-F, Sat/Sun as req. The HM ☎01392 265791 is responsible for the whole River Exe and Exeter Canal. www.exe-estuary.org makes interesting reading.

The City Basin accepts visitors and lay-ups by prior arrangement.

City All facilities; ACA @ ⥂ ✈.

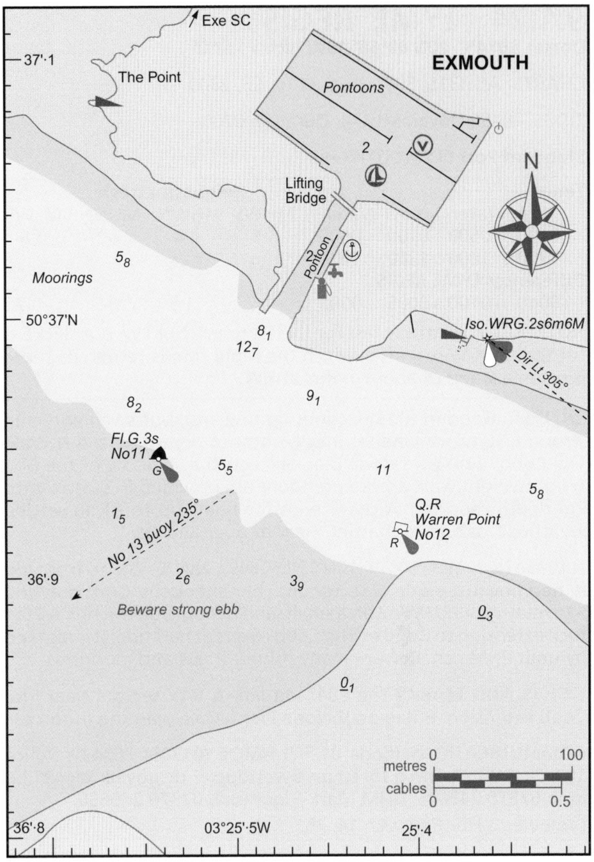

TWO MINOR HARBOURS WEST OF LYME REGIS

BEER, Devon, **50°41'·64N 03°05'·22W. Beer Roads** is an ⚓ in 2-5m on sand, shingle and gravel sheltered by Beer Head from prevailing W'lies, but open to E-SW winds. Beer Head is 142m high, topped by a caravan site. Its chalk cliffs are white, becoming red sandstone to the E towards Seaton. A conspic radio/tel mast is above the centre of the beach. Church tower is conspic. Do not use the historic approach of the beach light ≠ church tower light. All beach lights are purely for illumination, not for navigation. Land on the open beach, as in centuries past; some traditional local boats are still hauled up the beach on skids.

Beer & Seaton are adjacent towns N and NNE of Beer Head.

Beer ✉ ✕ . **Seaton** shops ✕ .

2·5M WSW of Beer Head and 8 cables offshore are the remains of the *MSC Napoli* wreck (50°40'·38N 03°09'·58W), marked by E, S and W cardinal buoys and a No Entry zone, radius 3ca.

AXMOUTH, Devon, **50°42'·13N 03°03'·29W**, 1·85M ENE of Beer Head. AC 3315. HW–0455 on Dover; +0045 and –1·1m on Plymouth; ML 2·3m; Duration 0640. MHWS 4·3m, MHWN 3·2m.

A small drying hbr at the mouth of the R Axe for boats max draught 1·2m, LOA 8·5m (longer by prior arrangement), able to dry out. Appr chan to bar (dries $\underline{0}$·5m) often shifts about a NNE/SSW axis. A dinghy recce (best near LW) to view the access channel and a prior brief by HM/YC are advised. Enter only in settled weather from HW –2½ to +1½ nps; HW –2½ *or* –½ sp. After 7m wide ent and the pierhead SHM beacon, Fl G 4s 7m 2M, turn 90° to port inside; hug the hbr wall to stbd until into the mooring basin; moor as directed. The low bridge (2m clearance) just N of moorings is the head of navigation.

HM ☎(01297) 22180/07939 044109. **Axe YC** ☎20043: pontoon, (6t) . Facilities: . Excellent pilotage notes at www.axeyachtclub.co.uk are essential reading for first time visitors. **Seaton**, as above for victuals etc.

The chartlet is reproduced by kind permission of the Axe Yacht Club whose Commodore and others revised these notes.

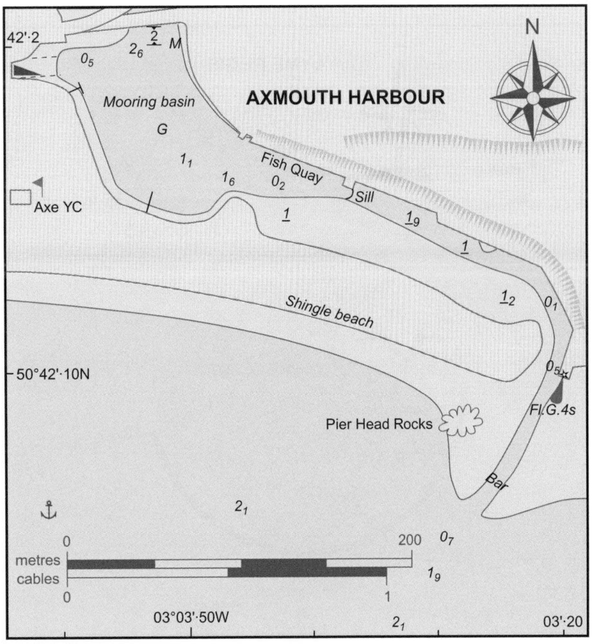

9.1.24 LYME REGIS

Dorset **50°43′·20N 02°56′·19W**

CHARTS AC 3315, 5601; Imray C10, C5, 2300

TIDES –0455 Dover; ML 2·4; Duration 0700

Standard Port PLYMOUTH (⟵)

Times				Height (metres)			
High Water		Low Water		MHWS	MHWN	MLWN	MLWS
0100	0600	0100	0600	5·5	4·4	2·2	0·8
1300	1800	1300	1800				
Differences LYME REGIS							
+0040	+0100	+0005	–0005	–1·2	–1·3	–0·5	–0·2

NOTE: Rise is relatively fast for the 1st hour after LW, but slackens for the next 1½hrs, after which the rapid rate is resumed. There is often a stand of about 1½hrs at HW.

SHELTER Good in the hbr (dries up to 2.1m), but swell enters in strong E/SE winds when it may be best to dry inside the N Wall. The Cobb, a massive stone pier, protects the W and S of the hbr. A lightweight walk ashore pontoons are provided in season with 2m depth reported at outer ends for boats up to 8T. In settled weather ⚓ as on the chartlet, clear of appr and s.

NAVIGATION WPT 50°43′·10N 02°55′·64W, 284°/0·35M to front ldg lt; best line just inside W sector until hbr ent opens. Craft drawing >1m may ground LW ±2 on a small sand bar outside the hbr. A 70m rock extension to E end of The Cobb covers at half tide; it is marked by unlit PHM bcn. Beware many fishing floats and moorings.

LIGHTS AND MARKS The 284° ldg line & R/W sectors clear The Cobb extension. R flag on Victoria Pier = Gale warning in force.

COMMUNICATIONS (Code 01297) NMOC (01305) 760439; Police 101; Dr 445777. HM g.foreshaw@westdorset-dc.gov.uk ☎442137, mob 07870 240645, DHM Mark Higgs mob 07870 240650. *Lyme Regis Hbr Radio* Ch **14**, 16.

FACILITIES www.dorsetforyou/lymeregisharbour.com Dry out against Victoria Pier (0.3–1.3m) on clean, hard sand, max LOA 11m. Pontoon £20 <10m > £25 < 15m > £30 < 20m; 9 Y s lie ENE of hbr ent in 1·5-2m, £10. (mobile)

SC ☎442373,

Power Boat Club ☎07768 725959,

Town bus to Axminster (Exeter).

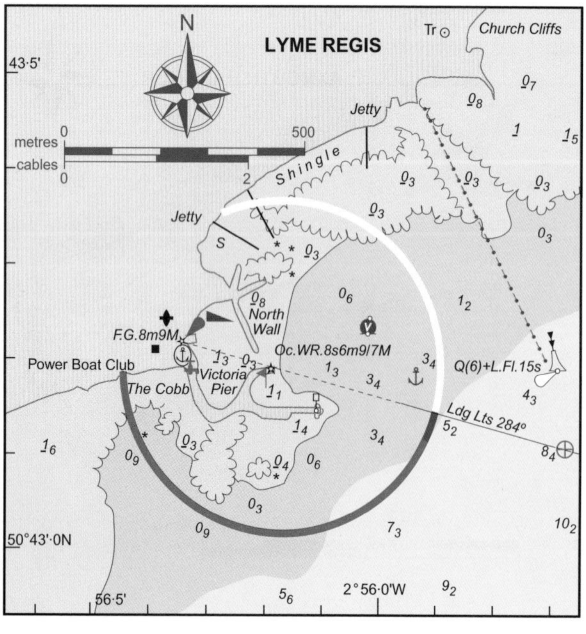

9.1.25 WEST BAY (BRIDPORT)

Dorset **50°42′·51N 02°45′·81W**

CHARTS AC 3315, 5601; Imray C10, C5, 2300

TIDES –0500 Dover; ML 2·3; Duration 0650

Standard Port PLYMOUTH (⟵)

Times				Height (metres)			
High Water		Low Water		MHWS	MHWN	MLWN	MLWS
0100	0600	0100	0600	5·5	4·4	2·2	0·8
1300	1800	1300	1800				
Differences BRIDPORT (West Bay)							
+0025	+0040	0000	0000	–1·4	–1·4	–0·6	–0·1
CHESIL BEACH							
+0040	+0055	–0005	+0010	–1·6	–1·5	–0·5	0·0
CHESIL COVE							
+0035	+0050	–0010	+0005	–1·5	–1·6	–0·5	–0·2

NOTE: Rise is relatively fast for first hr after LW; it then slackens for the next 1½hrs, after which the rapid rise is resumed. There is often a stand of about 1½hrs at HW.

SHELTER Access in W'lies and shelter in the outer hbr are improved by the new W pier, but the ent is exposed to SE'lies and swell/surge may affect the outer hbr in any wind direction.

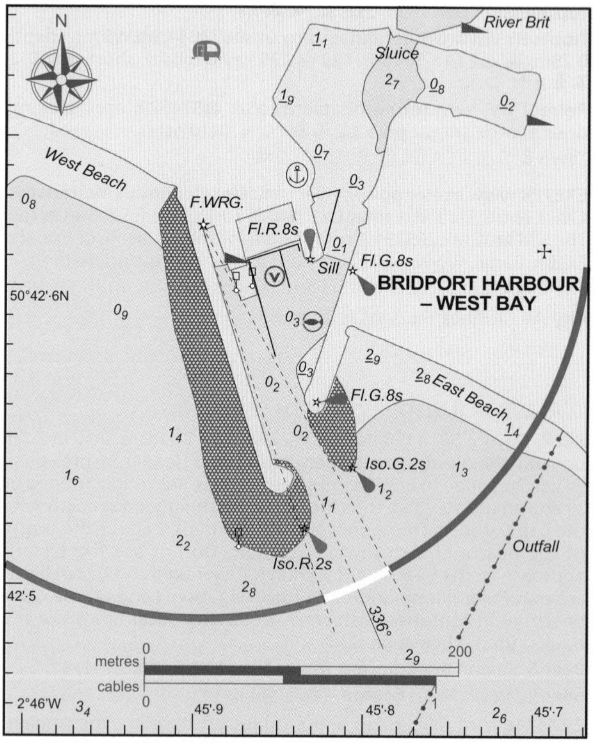

NAVIGATION WPT 50°42′·05N 02°45′·49W, 336°/0·50M to ent in W sector of Dir lt. High Ground shoal 3m is 1·4M W of the ent. 3·7 and 4·6m shoals are SW & SE of hbr. SPM outfall buoy, Fl Y 5s, is 5ca SSW of ent.

LIGHTS AND MARKS See chartlet and 9.1.4 for lts. High cliffs are conspic close ESE of the hbr.

COMMUNICATIONS (Code 01308) NMOC (01305) 760439; Police 101; Dr 421109. *Bridport Radio* Ch **11** 16. HM 423222, mob 07870 240636

FACILITIES, www. dorsetforyou/westbayharbour.com. **Outer hbr** is silted up to 0·5m below CD. pontoon is in front of the slipway, close W of Fl R 8s. £15/night.

Inner hbr dries, except for a pool scoured 2·7m by sluice water, and is full of FVs and local boats. The entry sill dries 0.1m.

Bridport (1½M N of the hbr) (bus to Axminster) (Exeter).

CROSSING THE ENGLISH CHANNEL, WESTERN PART

These notes cover cross-Channel passages from harbours between Scilly and Tor Bay to French harbours between Ouessant and Île de Bréhat. See AC 2655, 2656; 9.2.5 for the Central English Channel; and 9.0.6 for cross-Channel distances. Passage planning advice and SOLAS V requirements are in Chapter 3.

The Western Channel differs from the central and eastern parts; it is wider and its French harbours are less easy to approach.

Distance is a major ingredient in any passage plan. The shortest is 88M (Salcombe to Bréhat or Trébeurden); the longest 108M (Fowey to L'Aberwrac'h). Salcombe and Dartmouth are favourite departure points, for the Channel Islands and points West. Falmouth is often preferred for rounding Ushant. Taking an average distance of 100M:

Time at 5kn is 20hrs, or up to 30hrs if the wind is southerly. Therefore it is important to consider:

- **Crew** stamina and experience. A short-handed crew (husband & wife, for example) may cope quite easily with a 20-hr passage, but 30 hours beating to windward might prove too much.
- **Weather**. A window of at least 24hrs (preferably 48hrs) is needed during which the maximum forecast wind is F5 (depending on direction); wind not N'ly (ie onshore along the Brittany coast); with a low chance of fog on that coast or in mid-Channel.
- **ETD and ETA**. Some night sailing is inevitable, but in Jul/Aug there is only about 6hrs of darkness. To avoid leaving, arriving or crossing shipping lanes in the dark, a departure at about 0900 allows you to cross the lanes in daylight and arrive after dawn.

Shipping lanes. Whilst not having to cross a TSS, lines linking the Casquets TSS and Ushant TSS will indicate where the main W-bound and E-bound traffic is likely to be encountered. Be alert for shipping not using this route, and try to avoid close quarters situations. Do not expect big ships to give way to you; they will probably be travelling fast (24kn is not uncommon, even in poor visibility) and may have difficulty detecting you if it is at all rough.

Contingencies. North Brittany is not the easiest of coasts owing to an abundance of offshore rocks which demand precise landfalls and careful pilotage. Fresh onshore winds complicate the task, as does fog. There is no all-weather, all-tide, port of refuge along this coast, so the forecast weather window is crucial. If things are not going as planned, it is no disgrace to turn back or make for an alternative destination. The Channel Islands are a possible diversion, or consider heaving-to for a rest or to await an improvement in the weather.

PORTLAND RACE

South of the Bill lies Portland Race (AC 2255) in which severe and very dangerous sea states occur. Even in settled weather it should be avoided by small craft, although at neaps it may be barely perceptible.

The Race occurs at the confluence of two strong tidal streams which at springs run S down each side of the Isle of Portland for almost 10hrs out of 12hrs. These streams meet the main E-W stream of the Channel, producing large eddies on either side of Portland Bill and a highly confused sea state with heavy overfalls in the Race. The irregular contours of the seabed, which shoals rapidly from depths of about 100m some 2M S of the Bill to as little as 10m on Portland Ledge 1M further N, greatly contribute to the violence of the Race. Portland Ledge strongly deflects the flow of water upwards, so that on the flood the Race lies SE of the Bill and SW on the ebb. Conditions deteriorate with wind-against-tide, especially at springs. In an E'ly gale against the flood stream the Race may spread eastward to The Shambles bank. The Race normally extends about 2M S of the Bill, but further S in bad weather.

The Race can be avoided by passing to seaward of it, ie 3–5M S of the Bill; or by using the inshore passage if conditions suit.

The **inshore passage** offers relatively smooth water between 1ca and 3ca off the Bill (depending on wind). Do not use it in onshore winds >F4/5, nor at night under power due to lobster pot floats and especially not at springs with wind against tide. From W or E, start close inshore at least 2M N of the Bill to utilise the S-going stream; hug the Bill to avoid being set into the Race.

►*The tidal stream chartlets at 9.1.26 which merit careful study show the approx hourly positions of the Race. They are referred to HW Plymouth, to HW Portland for those bound from/to Weymouth, and to HW Dover if passing S of the Race. See also the smaller scale chartlets at 9.1.3 and 9.2.3 and tidal diamonds 'A' on AC 2610 or 'R' on AC 2255.* ◄

Timing is vital to catch 'slackish' water in the inshore passage and to enjoy a fair tide thereafter. The windows are as follows:

►**Westbound**: *HW Dover –1 to HW +2; HW Plymouth +5 to HW –5; or HW Portland +4 to HW –6. Timing is easier if starting from Portland Harbour, Weymouth or Lulworth Cove.*

Eastbound: *HW Dover +5 to HW –4; HW Plymouth –2 to HW +2; or HW Portland –3 to HW +1.*◄

PORTLAND BILL TO ANVIL POINT

The buoyed Shambles bank lies 2–5M E of Portland Bill and is best avoided, as is the gap between it and the Race (AC 2610). In bad weather the sea breaks heavily on it. E of **Weymouth** rocky ledges extend 3ca offshore as far as Lulworth Cove, which provides a reasonable ⚓ in fine, settled weather and offshore winds; as do Worbarrow Bay and Chapman's Pool further E.

A firing range extends 5M offshore between Lulworth Cove and St Alban's Head. Yachts should avoid the range when it is active or pass through as quickly as possible. Beware Kimmeridge Ledges which extend over 5ca seaward. Three rarely used yellow naval target buoys (DZ A, B and C) lie on St Alban's Ledge.

St Alban's Head (107m) is bold and steep-to.

A sometimes vicious race forms over **St Alban's Ledge**, a rocky dorsal ridge (least depth 8·5m) which extends 4M SW from St Alban's Hd.

►*1M S of St Alban's Head the E-going flood starts at HW Plymouth –1, and the W-going ebb at HWP +0525; inshore max Sp rates 4¾kn; see also diamond 'U' on AC 2610. Slack water lasts barely 30 mins. The race moves E on the flood and W on the ebb, which is more dangerous since overfalls extend 2½M further SW than on the flood. A back eddy sets almost continuously SSE down the W side of the Head.* ◄

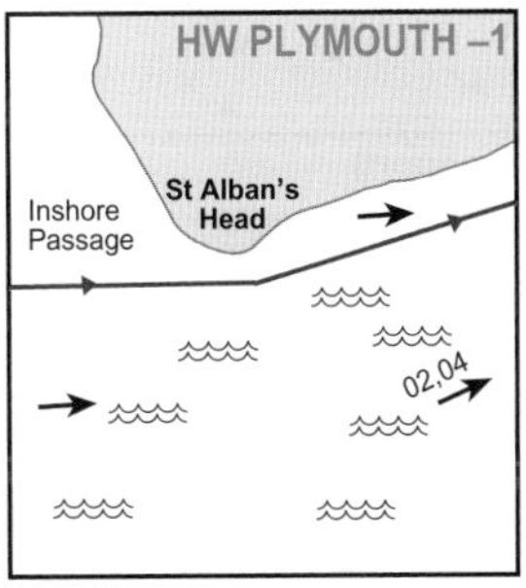

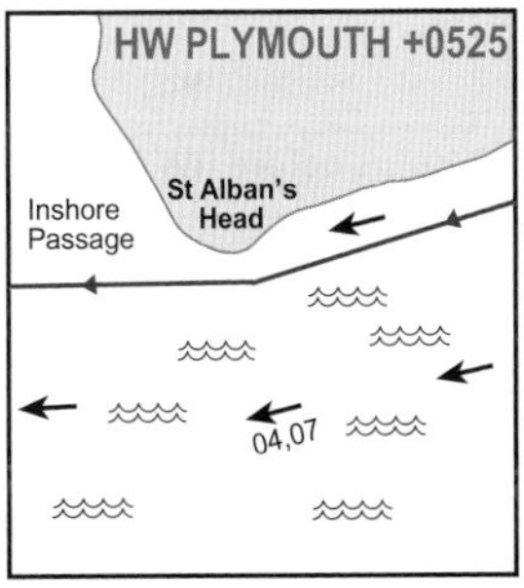

In settled weather and at neaps the race may be barely perceptible and can safely be crossed. Otherwise avoid it by passing to seaward via 50°31'·40N 02°07'·80W (thus clearing Lulworth Range); or by using the inshore passage very close inshore below St Alban's Head. This is at most 5ca wide and avoids the worst of the overfalls, but expect your decks to get wet. In onshore gales stay offshore. The light on St Alban's Hd Iso R 2s is only shown when the ranges are active.

The rugged, cliffy coastline between St Alban's Hd and Anvil Point (Fl 10s 45m 9M) is steep-to quite close inshore. Measured mile beacons stand either side of Anvil Pt lt ho; the track is 083·5°.

9.1.26 PORTLAND TIDAL STREAMS

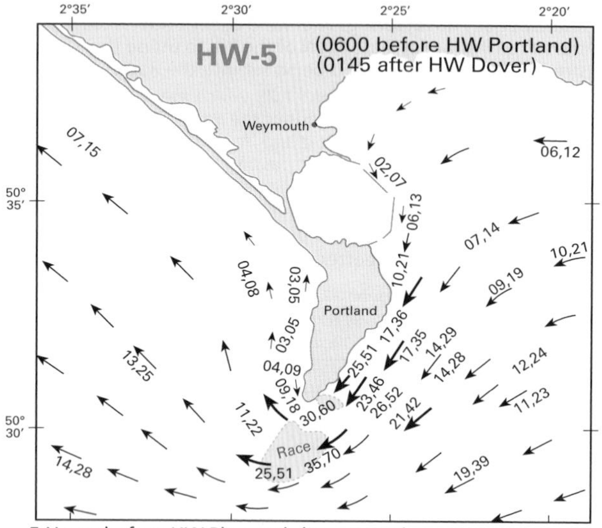

5 Hours before HW Plymouth (Devonport)

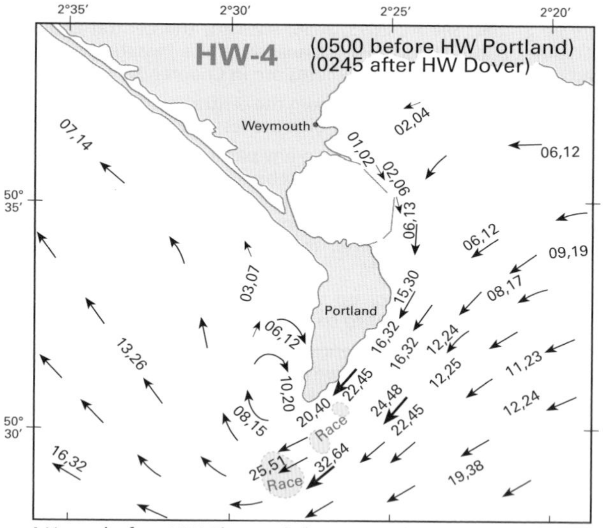

4 Hours before HW Plymouth (Devonport)

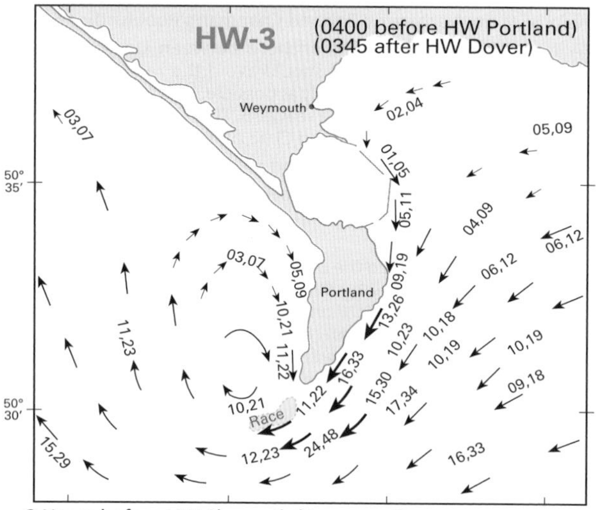

3 Hours before HW Plymouth (Devonport)

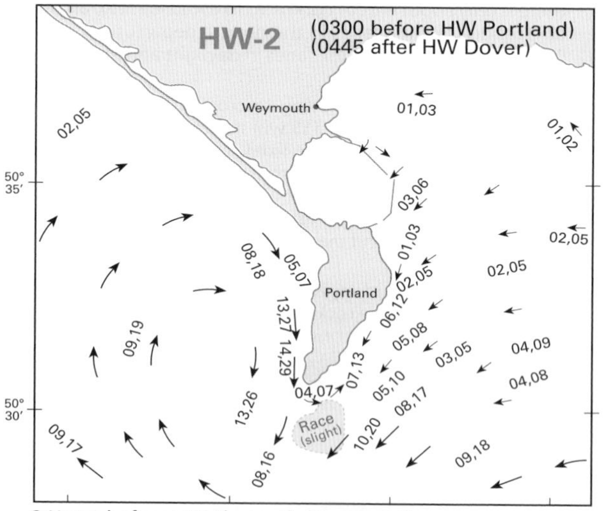

2 Hours before HW Plymouth (Devonport)

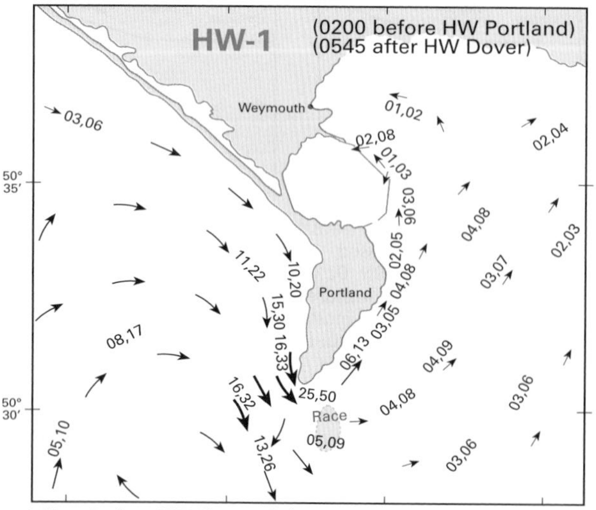

1 Hour before HW Plymouth (Devonport)

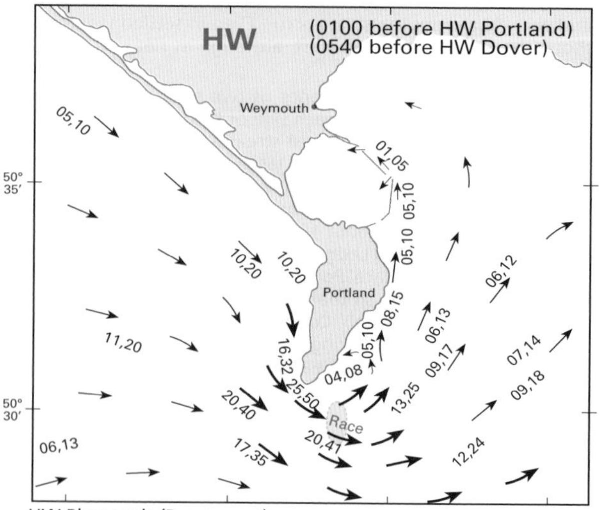

HW Plymouth (Devonport)

General Area 1: 9.1.3 and 9.2.3

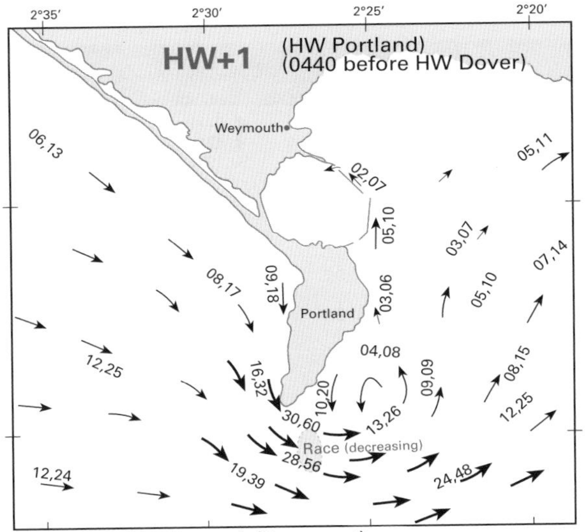

2°35′
2°30′
2°25′
2°20′
HW+1
(HW Portland)
(0440 before HW Dover)
Weymouth
Portland
50° 35′
50° 30′
06,13
02,07
05,11
05,10
03,07
07,14
08,17
09,18
03,06
05,10
12,25
04,08
08,15
16,32
10,20
09,09
12,25
30,60
13,26
Race (decreasing)
28,56
19,39
24,48
12,24

I Hour after HW Plymouth (Devonport)

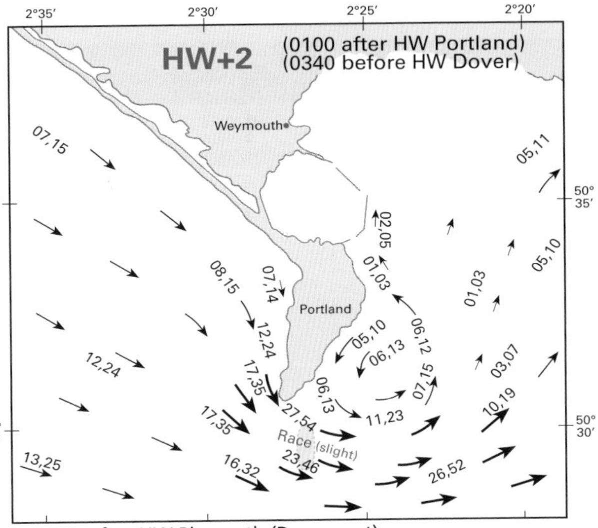

2°35′
2°30′
2°25′
2°20′
HW+2
(0100 after HW Portland)
(0340 before HW Dover)
Weymouth
Portland
50° 35′
50° 30′
07,15
05,11
02,05
05,10
01,03
08,15
07,14
01,03
12,24
12,24
05,10
06,12
06,13
03,07
17,35
07,15
06,13
10,19
17,35
27,54
11,23
Race (slight)
13,25
16,32
23,46
26,52

2 Hours after HW Plymouth (Devonport)

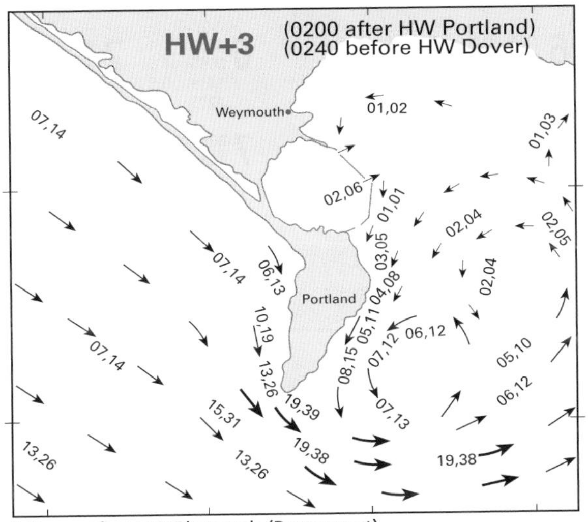

HW+3
(0200 after HW Portland)
(0240 before HW Dover)
Weymouth
Portland
50° 35′
50° 30′
07,14
01,02
01,03
02,06
01,01
02,04
02,05
07,14
06,13
03,05
04,08
02,04
10,19
05,11
06,12
07,14
08,15
07,12
05,10
13,26
06,12
19,39
07,13
15,31
19,38
19,38
13,26
13,26

3 Hours after HW Plymouth (Devonport)

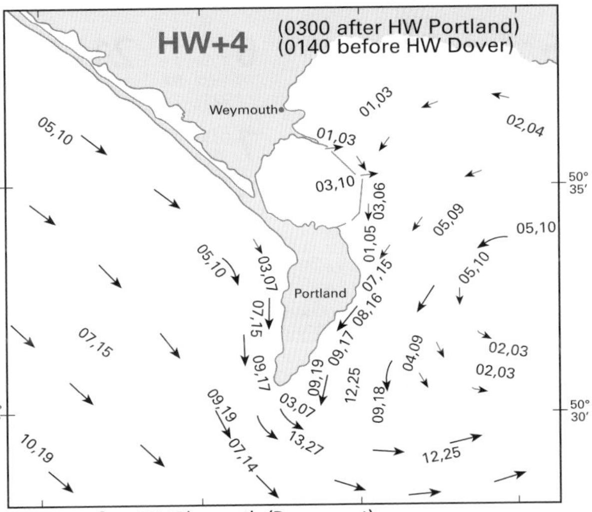

HW+4
(0300 after HW Portland)
(0140 before HW Dover)
Weymouth
Portland
50° 35′
50° 30′
05,10
01,03
01,03
02,04
03,10
03,06
05,09
05,10
05,10
01,05
03,07
07,15
07,15
08,16
07,15
09,17
09,17
04,09
02,03
02,03
09,19
12,25
09,18
09,19
03,07
07,14
13,27
10,19
12,25

4 Hours after HW Plymouth (Devonport)

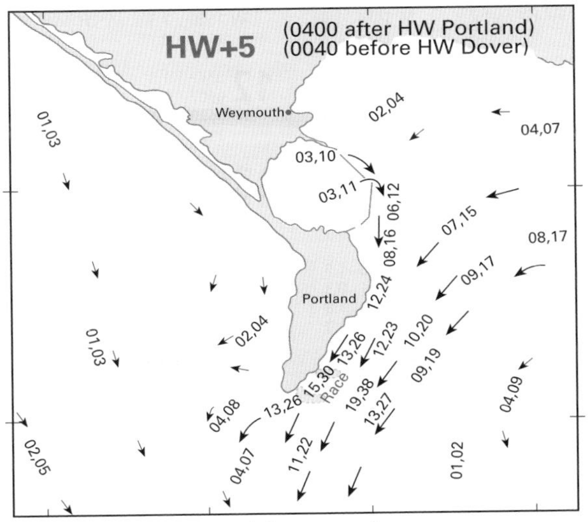

HW+5
(0400 after HW Portland)
(0040 before HW Dover)
Weymouth
Portland
50° 35′
50° 30′
01,03
02,04
04,07
03,10
03,11
06,12
07,15
08,16
08,17
09,17
12,24
02,04
01,03
13,26
12,23
10,20
15,30
Race
09,19
04,09
13,26
19,38
04,08
13,27
02,05
04,07
11,22
01,02

5 Hours after HW Plymouth (Devonport)

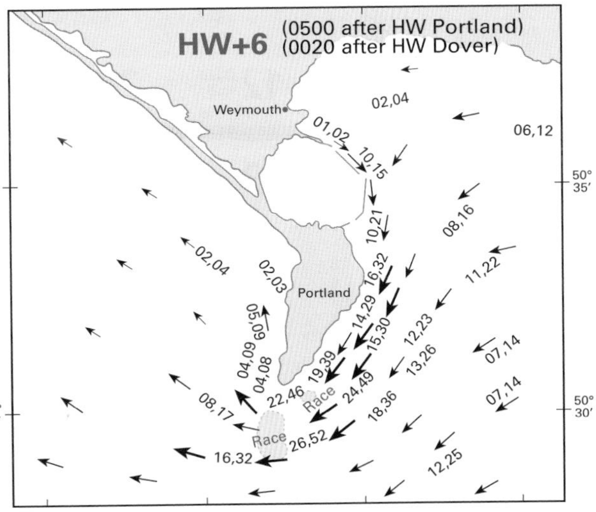

HW+6
(0500 after HW Portland)
(0020 after HW Dover)
Weymouth
Portland
50° 35′
50° 30′
02,04
01,02
06,12
10,15
08,16
10,21
02,04
02,03
16,32
11,22
05,09
14,29
15,30
12,23
04,09
04,08
19,39
13,26
07,14
22,46
Race
24,49
07,14
08,17
18,36
Race
26,52
16,32
12,25

6 Hours after HW Plymouth (Devonport)

STANDARD TIME (UT)
For Summer Time add ONE hour in **non-shaded areas**

PORTLAND LAT 50°34′N LONG 2°26′W

TIMES AND HEIGHTS OF HIGH AND LOW WATERS

Dates in red are SPRINGS
Dates in blue are NEAPS

YEAR **2018**

JANUARY

Date	Day	Time	m	Time	m	Time	m	Time	m
1	M	0532	2.1	1038	0.5	1805	2.0	2304	0.3
2	TU	0622	2.3	1131	0.4	1900	2.1	○ 2353	0.2
3	W	0712	2.4	1219	0.3	1957	2.2		
4	TH	0038	0.2	0802	2.4	1305	0.2	2053	2.2
5	F	0122	0.2	0853	2.4	1350	0.2	2137	2.1
6	SA	0205	0.3	0939	2.2	1435	0.3	2216	2.0
7	SU	0248	0.5	1021	2.1	1521	0.4	2255	1.8
8	M	0333	0.6	1101	1.9	1610	0.5	◑ 2338	1.6
9	TU	0421	0.7	1147	1.7	1703	0.6		
10	W	0036	1.5	0520	0.9	1246	1.5	1804	0.7
11	TH	0155	1.4	0630	0.9	1409	1.4	1907	0.7
12	F	0303	1.5	0738	0.9	1520	1.4	2006	0.7
13	SA	0400	1.6	0836	0.8	1620	1.5	2059	0.6
14	SU	0449	1.8	0929	0.7	1711	1.6	2150	0.6
15	M	0533	1.9	1021	0.6	1756	1.7	2239	0.5
16	TU	0613	2.0	1109	0.5	1837	1.8	2323	0.4
17	W ●	0652	2.1	1152	0.4	1915	1.9		
18	TH	0001	0.4	0729	2.1	1229	0.4	1951	1.9
19	F	0035	0.4	0805	2.1	1301	0.3	2024	1.8
20	SA	0107	0.4	0837	2.0	1333	0.3	2053	1.8
21	SU	0140	0.4	0903	1.9	1406	0.3	2120	1.7
22	M	0213	0.4	0930	1.8	1443	0.3	2149	1.7
23	TU	0248	0.4	1003	1.7	1523	0.4	2228	1.6
24	W	0327	0.5	1046	1.6	1610	0.4	◐ 2317	1.5
25	TH	0419	0.6	1141	1.5	1708	0.5		
26	F	0022	1.4	0529	0.7	1258	1.4	1815	0.6
27	SA	0153	1.5	0645	0.7	1431	1.5	1933	0.6
28	SU	0310	1.6	0812	0.7	1545	1.6	2056	0.5
29	M	0415	1.8	0932	0.6	1653	1.7	2200	0.4
30	TU	0514	2.0	1031	0.4	1755	1.9	2253	0.3
31	W	0609	2.2	1123	0.3	1855	2.0	○ 2342	0.2

FEBRUARY

Date	Day	Time	m	Time	m	Time	m	Time	m
1	TH	0702	2.3	1209	0.2	1957	2.2		
2	F	0026	0.1	0754	2.4	1252	0.1	2046	2.2
3	SA	0107	0.1	0843	2.4	1333	0.1	2122	2.2
4	SU	0147	0.2	0925	2.3	1414	0.1	2154	2.0
5	M	0225	0.3	0959	2.1	1453	0.3	2223	1.9
6	TU	0302	0.4	1030	1.9	1532	0.4	2251	1.7
7	W	0338	0.6	1102	1.7	1610	0.6	◑ 2323	1.5
8	TH	0414	0.7	1140	1.5	1650	0.7		
9	F	0007	1.4	0503	0.9	1233	1.3	1816	0.8
10	SA	0130	1.3	0706	0.9	1419	1.2	1934	0.8
11	SU	0321	1.4	0812	0.8	1548	1.3	2033	0.7
12	M	0420	1.5	0907	0.7	1646	1.4	2126	0.6
13	TU	0507	1.7	1000	0.6	1734	1.6	2217	0.5
14	W	0550	1.9	1049	0.4	1818	1.7	2304	0.4
15	TH	0632	2.0	1134	0.3	1900	1.8	● 2345	0.3
16	F	0714	2.1	1213	0.3	1940	1.9		
17	SA	0020	0.3	0753	2.1	1245	0.2	2016	1.9
18	SU	0053	0.2	0827	2.1	1317	0.2	2043	1.9
19	M	0126	0.2	0851	2.0	1350	0.2	2103	1.8
20	TU	0200	0.2	0913	1.9	1425	0.2	2129	1.8
21	W	0234	0.2	0944	1.8	1502	0.2	2203	1.7
22	TH	0308	0.3	1024	1.7	1543	0.3	2247	1.6
23	F	0349	0.4	1115	1.5	1634	0.5	◐ 2344	1.5
24	SA	0451	0.6	1227	1.4	1742	0.6		
25	SU	0115	1.4	0616	0.7	1418	1.3	1913	0.7
26	M	0252	1.5	1130	0.6	1536	1.5	2055	0.6
27	TU	0401	1.7	0940	0.5	1644	1.6	2152	0.4
28	W	0502	1.9	1026	0.4	1747	1.8	2242	0.3

MARCH

Date	Day	Time	m	Time	m	Time	m	Time	m
1	TH	0557	2.1	1112	0.2	1846	2.0	2328	0.1
2	F ○	0650	2.3	1155	0.1	1939	2.2		
3	SA	0010	0.0	0741	2.4	1234	0.0	2024	2.2
4	SU	0049	0.0	0827	2.4	1312	0.0	2059	2.2
5	M	0125	0.0	0903	2.3	1348	0.1	2128	2.1
6	TU	0159	0.1	0931	2.1	1421	0.2	2149	1.9
7	W	0231	0.3	0957	1.9	1452	0.4	2211	1.7
8	TH	0300	0.5	1025	1.7	1518	0.5	2239	1.5
9	F	0326	0.6	1059	1.4	1540	0.6	◑ 2315	1.4
10	SA	0358	0.7	1142	1.3	1617	0.7		
11	SU	0003	1.3	0643	0.9	1247	1.2	1904	0.8
12	M	0140	1.3	0750	0.8	1500	1.2	2007	0.8
13	TU	0339	1.4	0844	0.6	1616	1.3	2101	0.6
14	W	0435	1.6	0935	0.5	1707	1.5	2152	0.5
15	TH	0522	1.8	1024	0.4	1753	1.7	2239	0.4
16	F	0608	1.9	1109	0.3	1837	1.9	2321	0.3
17	SA	0652	2.0	1148	0.2	1920	2.0	● 2359	0.2
18	SU	0735	2.1	1222	0.1	2000	2.0		
19	M	0033	0.1	0812	2.1	1255	0.1	2030	2.0
20	TU	0108	0.1	0835	2.1	1329	0.1	2045	2.0
21	W	0142	0.1	0855	2.0	1405	0.1	2110	1.9
22	TH	0217	0.2	0928	1.9	1441	0.2	2145	1.8
23	F	0252	0.3	1010	1.7	1521	0.3	2228	1.7
24	SA	0333	0.4	1102	1.5	1610	0.5	◐ 2323	1.5
25	SU	0433	0.6	1218	1.3	1720	0.7		
26	M	0054	1.4	0606	0.7	1414	1.3	1916	0.7
27	TU	0239	1.5	1117	0.5	1528	1.4	2043	0.6
28	W	0348	1.6	0931	0.5	1632	1.6	2136	0.5
29	TH	0448	1.9	1011	0.3	1730	1.9	2224	0.3
30	F	0542	2.1	1055	0.2	1823	2.0	2310	0.2
31	SA	0634	2.2	1135	0.1	1911	2.2	○ 2350	0.1

APRIL

Date	Day	Time	m	Time	m	Time	m	Time	m
1	SU	0721	2.3	1213	0.0	1954	2.2		
2	M	0026	0.0	0803	2.3	1246	0.0	2031	2.2
3	TU	0100	0.1	0835	2.2	1318	0.1	2056	2.1
4	W	0132	0.1	0859	2.0	1349	0.2	2115	1.9
5	TH	0202	0.3	0925	1.8	1417	0.4	2139	1.8
6	F	0230	0.4	0955	1.6	1439	0.5	2208	1.6
7	SA	0254	0.5	1030	1.5	1501	0.6	2242	1.5
8	SU	0326	0.7	1112	1.3	1539	0.7	◑ 2326	1.4
9	M	0422	0.8	1208	1.2	1644	0.8		
10	TU	0031	1.3	0726	0.8	1352	1.2	1938	0.8
11	W	0232	1.3	0819	0.6	1529	1.3	2032	0.7
12	TH	0349	1.5	0907	0.5	1629	1.5	2122	0.6
13	F	0445	1.7	0954	0.4	1719	1.7	2208	0.4
14	SA	0536	1.9	1038	0.3	1807	1.9	2252	0.3
15	SU	0624	2.0	1118	0.2	1853	2.0	2332	0.2
16	M ●	0708	2.1	1155	0.1	1934	2.1		
17	TU	0009	0.1	0748	2.2	1230	0.1	2008	2.1
18	W	0046	0.1	0813	2.1	1307	0.1	2027	2.1
19	TH	0123	0.1	0839	2.1	1345	0.1	2055	2.0
20	F	0201	0.2	0917	1.9	1424	0.2	2134	1.9
21	SA	0241	0.3	1003	1.7	1507	0.4	2221	1.8
22	SU	0328	0.4	1100	1.5	1600	0.6	◐ 2317	1.6
23	M	0433	0.6	1228	1.4	1712	0.7		
24	TU	0047	1.5	0611	0.7	1404	1.4	1849	0.8
25	W	0223	1.5	1059	0.5	1513	1.5	2013	0.7
26	TH	0329	1.7	0903	0.5	1612	1.7	2110	0.5
27	F	0427	1.8	0946	0.3	1705	1.9	2200	0.4
28	SA	0521	2.0	1029	0.2	1755	2.0	2245	0.3
29	SU	0610	2.1	1109	0.1	1841	2.1	2326	0.2
30	M ○	0656	2.2	1145	0.1	1924	2.2		

Chart Datum is 0·93 metres below Ordnance Datum (Newlyn). HAT is 2·5 metres above Chart Datum.

STANDARD TIME (UT)
For Summer Time add ONE hour in **non-shaded areas**

PORTLAND LAT 50°34'N LONG 2°26'W

TIMES AND HEIGHTS OF HIGH AND LOW WATERS

Dates in red are SPRINGS
Dates in blue are NEAPS

YEAR **2018**

MAY

Day	Time	m	Day	Time	m
1	0000	0.2	16	0715	2.1
	0735	2.1		1206	0.1
TU	1217	0.1	W	1938	2.2
	1959	2.2			
2	0034	0.2	17	0025	0.2
	0804	2.1		0751	2.1
W	1250	0.2	TH	1247	0.1
	2024	2.1		2010	2.2
3	0106	0.2	18	0107	0.1
	0830	1.9		0829	2.1
TH	1321	0.3	F	1329	0.2
	2048	1.9		2048	2.2
4	0138	0.3	19	0150	0.2
	0859	1.8		0915	2.0
F	1348	0.4	SA	1412	0.3
	2116	1.8		2132	2.0
5	0206	0.4	20	0235	0.3
	0931	1.6		1006	1.8
SA	1410	0.5	SU	1459	0.4
	2146	1.7		2221	1.9
6	0231	0.5	21	0328	0.4
	1007	1.5		1105	1.6
SU	1435	0.6	M	1554	0.6
	2220	1.5		2316	1.7
7	0306	0.6	22	0431	0.6
	1048	1.4		1222	1.5
M	1514	0.7	TU	1658	0.7
	2301	1.4		◐	
8	0359	0.7	23	0030	1.6
	1140	1.3		0545	0.6
TU	1617	0.8	W	1342	1.5
	◑ 2357	1.4		1810	0.8
9	0658	0.7	24	0156	1.6
	1258	1.2		0707	0.6
W	1733	0.8	TH	1448	1.5
				1925	0.8
10	0124	1.4	25	0302	1.6
	0750	0.6		0819	0.5
TH	1436	1.3	F	1544	1.7
	1952	0.8		2031	0.7
11	0256	1.5	26	0400	1.7
	0836	0.5		0909	0.4
F	1544	1.5	SA	1637	1.8
	2043	0.6		2126	0.6
12	0400	1.6	27	0453	1.8
	0919	0.4		0954	0.4
SA	1639	1.7	SU	1726	2.0
	2130	0.5		2214	0.4
13	0457	1.8	28	0543	1.9
	1001	0.3		1036	0.3
SU	1731	1.9	M	1811	2.1
	2216	0.4		2256	0.4
14	0548	2.0	29	0628	2.0
	1043	0.2		1114	0.2
M	1818	2.0	TU	1853	2.1
	2300	0.3		○ 2335	0.3
15	0634	2.1	30	0706	2.0
	1125	0.1		1150	0.2
TU	1901	2.2	W	1927	2.1
	● 2344	0.2			
			31	0011	0.3
				0737	1.9
			TH	1225	0.3
				1957	2.1

JUNE

Day	Time	m	Day	Time	m
1	0047	0.3	16	0056	0.2
	0807	1.9		0831	2.1
F	1258	0.3	SA	1317	0.2
	2027	2.0		2046	2.3
2	0120	0.4	17	0143	0.2
	0839	1.8		0925	2.0
SA	1327	0.4	SU	1402	0.2
	2058	1.8		2133	2.2
3	0150	0.4	18	0230	0.3
	0913	1.6		1013	1.9
SU	1353	0.5	M	1449	0.4
	2131	1.7		2220	2.1
4	0219	0.5	19	0321	0.3
	0949	1.5		1102	1.7
M	1422	0.5	TU	1540	0.5
	2203	1.6		2308	1.9
5	0254	0.5	20	0415	0.5
	1027	1.4		1158	1.6
TU	1500	0.6	W	1634	0.6
	2240	1.5		◐	
6	0342	0.6	21	0003	1.7
	1113	1.3		0513	0.5
W	1555	0.7	TH	1306	1.5
	◑ 2327	1.5		1734	0.7
7	0442	0.6	22	0113	1.6
	1212	1.3		0615	0.6
TH	1702	0.7	F	1413	1.5
				1838	0.8
8	0028	1.4	23	0224	1.5
	0551	0.6		0720	0.6
F	1335	1.4	SA	1512	1.6
	1813	0.7		1945	0.8
9	0150	1.5	24	0326	1.6
	0711	0.5		0820	0.6
SA	1453	1.5	SU	1606	1.7
	1930	0.7		2045	0.7
10	0305	1.6	25	0423	1.6
	0825	0.4		0912	0.5
SU	1553	1.7	M	1657	1.8
	2041	0.6		2138	0.6
11	0408	1.7	26	0515	1.7
	0918	0.3		1000	0.4
M	1648	1.8	TU	1743	1.9
	2138	0.5		2228	0.5
12	0505	1.9	27	0601	1.8
	1009	0.3		1045	0.4
TU	1739	2.0	W	1825	2.0
	2231	0.4		2314	0.4
13	0558	2.0	28	0642	1.8
	1059	0.2		1128	0.3
W	1826	2.2	TH	1902	2.1
	● 2323	0.3		○ 2356	0.4
14	0648	2.1	29	0717	1.8
	1146	0.1		1207	0.3
TH	1912	2.3	F	1937	2.1
15	0010	0.2	30	0034	0.3
	0738	2.1		0751	1.8
F	1232	0.1	SA	1242	0.3
	1958	2.3		2011	2.0

JULY

Day	Time	m	Day	Time	m
1	0109	0.4	16	0133	0.1
	0825	1.8		0926	2.1
SU	1314	0.4	M	1349	0.2
	2045	1.9		2127	2.3
2	0140	0.4	17	0218	0.2
	0859	1.7		1006	2.0
M	1343	0.4	TU	1433	0.3
	2117	1.8		2209	2.2
3	0210	0.4	18	0303	0.2
	0931	1.6		1044	1.9
TU	1414	0.5	W	1518	0.4
	2147	1.7		2249	2.0
4	0243	0.4	19	0349	0.4
	1004	1.5		1125	1.7
W	1450	0.5	TH	1604	0.5
	2217	1.6		◐ 2331	1.8
5	0324	0.4	20	0438	0.5
	1043	1.5		1216	1.5
TH	1534	0.6	F	1655	0.7
	2257	1.6			
6	0414	0.5	21	0020	1.6
	1132	1.4		0533	0.6
F	1631	0.6	SA	1325	1.4
	◑ 2349	1.5		1758	0.8
7	0512	0.5	22	0133	1.4
	1237	1.4		0636	0.7
SA	1735	0.7	SU	1436	1.4
				1907	0.8
8	0055	1.5	23	0250	1.4
	0617	0.5		0740	0.7
SU	1357	1.5	M	1537	1.5
	1844	0.7		2012	0.8
9	0215	1.5	24	0356	1.4
	0727	0.5		0838	0.6
M	1508	1.6	TU	1630	1.7
	1957	0.6		2110	0.7
10	0328	1.6	25	0451	1.5
	0840	0.4		0931	0.6
TU	1610	1.8	W	1718	1.8
	2109	0.5		2204	0.6
11	0434	1.7	26	0539	1.7
	0943	0.3		1021	0.5
W	1708	2.0	TH	1801	1.9
	2213	0.4		2256	0.5
12	0536	1.9	27	0622	1.7
	1040	0.3		1108	0.4
TH	1802	2.1	F	1841	2.0
	2309	0.3		○ 2342	0.4
13	0633	2.0	28	0702	1.8
	1132	0.2		1151	0.3
F	1853	2.3	SA	1919	2.1
	●				
14	0000	0.2	29	0022	0.3
	0731	2.1		0739	1.8
SA	1219	0.1	SU	1227	0.3
	1946	2.3		1957	2.1
15	0047	0.1	30	0057	0.3
	0836	2.1		0813	1.8
SU	1305	0.1	M	1300	0.3
	2039	2.4		2032	2.0
			31	0126	0.3
				0845	1.8
			TU	1331	0.3
				2103	1.9

AUGUST

Day	Time	m	Day	Time	m
1	0155	0.3	16	0238	0.2
	0913	1.7		1017	2.0
W	1403	0.3	TH	1450	0.3
	2127	1.8		2222	2.0
2	0227	0.3	17	0316	0.3
	0939	1.6		1046	1.8
TH	1436	0.4	F	1529	0.5
	2152	1.7		2253	1.8
3	0302	0.3	18	0355	0.5
	1011	1.6		1116	1.6
F	1512	0.4	SA	1610	0.7
	2227	1.6		◐ 2328	1.5
4	0344	0.4	19	0438	0.7
	1054	1.5		1158	1.4
SA	1557	0.5	SU	1708	0.8
	◑ 2314	1.5			
5	0436	0.4	20	0016	1.3
	1151	1.4		0546	0.8
SU	1659	0.6	M	1334	1.3
				1839	0.9
6	0016	1.5	21	0204	1.2
	0540	0.5		0709	0.8
M	1309	1.4	TU	1511	1.4
	1810	0.7		1949	0.8
7	0142	1.4	22	0334	1.3
	0652	0.6		0812	0.8
TU	1438	1.5	W	1608	1.6
	1930	0.7		2048	0.7
8	0309	1.5	23	0432	1.4
	0819	0.5		0906	0.7
W	1547	1.7	TH	1655	1.7
	2102	0.6		2141	0.6
9	0420	1.6	24	0519	1.6
	0932	0.4		0958	0.5
TH	1649	1.9	F	1738	1.9
	2208	0.5		2233	0.4
10	0524	1.8	25	0602	1.7
	1029	0.3		1047	0.4
F	1746	2.1	SA	1819	2.0
	2302	0.3		2320	0.3
11	0624	2.0	26	0643	1.9
	1120	0.2		1131	0.3
SA	1839	2.3	SU	1859	2.1
	● 2350	0.2		○	
12	0725	2.1	27	0002	0.2
	1206	0.1		0722	1.9
SU	1932	2.4	M	1209	0.3
				1940	2.1
13	0034	0.1	28	0037	0.2
	0828	2.2		0759	2.0
M	1250	0.1	TU	1242	0.2
	2025	2.4		2016	2.1
14	0117	0.0	29	0106	0.2
	0911	2.2		0829	1.9
TU	1331	0.1	W	1313	0.3
	2111	2.4		2046	2.0
15	0158	0.1	30	0134	0.2
	0945	2.1		0851	1.9
W	1411	0.2	TH	1344	0.3
	2149	2.2		2104	1.9
			31	0205	0.2
				0911	1.8
			F	1416	0.3
				2126	1.8

Chart Datum is 0·93 metres below Ordnance Datum (Newlyn). HAT is 2·5 metres above Chart Datum.

STANDARD TIME (UT)
For Summer Time add ONE hour in **non-shaded areas**

PORTLAND LAT 50°34'N LONG 2°26'W

TIMES AND HEIGHTS OF HIGH AND LOW WATERS

Dates in red are SPRINGS
Dates in blue are NEAPS

YEAR **2018**

SEPTEMBER

Date	Day	Time	m	Time	m	Time	m	Time	m
1	SA	0238	0.3	0941	1.7	1449	0.4	2201	1.7
2	SU	0313	0.4	1022	1.6	1526	0.5	2247	1.6
3	M	0359	0.5	1115	1.5	1623	0.6	◑ 2348	1.4
4	TU	0505	0.6	1230	1.4	1743	0.7		
5	W	0132	1.3	0628	0.7	1421	1.5	2233	0.7
6	TH	0305	1.4	0824	0.7	1534	1.7	2117	0.6
7	F	0415	1.6	0925	0.5	1636	1.9	2204	0.4
8	SA	0516	1.8	1017	0.4	1732	2.1	2251	0.3
9	SU	0614	2.0	1105	0.2	1825	2.3	● 2335	0.1
10	M	0708	2.2	1150	0.1	1916	2.4		
11	TU	0017	0.0	0759	2.3	1231	0.1	2005	2.4
12	W	0056	0.0	0841	2.3	1309	0.1	2047	2.4
13	TH	0132	0.1	0915	2.2	1345	0.2	2121	2.2
14	F	0206	0.2	0940	2.0	1419	0.3	2147	2.0
15	SA	0238	0.4	1000	1.8	1452	0.5	2214	1.7
16	SU	0307	0.6	1027	1.6	1524	0.7	◐ 2248	1.5
17	M	0328	0.7	1104	1.5	1559	0.8	2330	1.3
18	TU	0353	0.9	1153	1.3	1822	0.9		
19	W	0034	1.2	0643	1.0	1428	1.3	1928	0.9
20	TH	0320	1.2	0747	0.9	1546	1.5	2024	0.7
21	F	0415	1.4	0841	0.8	1630	1.7	2115	0.6
22	SA	0457	1.6	0932	0.6	1711	1.8	2205	0.4
23	SU	0537	1.8	1020	0.5	1753	2.0	2252	0.3
24	M	0618	1.9	1105	0.4	1835	2.1	2334	0.2
25	TU	0658	2.0	1144	0.3	1916	2.2	○	
26	W	0009	0.2	0737	2.1	1218	0.3	1955	2.2
27	TH	0039	0.2	0807	2.1	1250	0.2	2023	2.1
28	F	0109	0.2	0824	2.0	1323	0.2	2038	2.0
29	SA	0141	0.3	0845	2.0	1356	0.3	2104	1.9
30	SU	0214	0.3	0917	1.9	1429	0.4	2142	1.7

OCTOBER

Date	Day	Time	m	Time	m	Time	m	Time	m
1	M	0248	0.4	0959	1.7	1507	0.5	2231	1.6
2	TU	0330	0.6	1052	1.6	1603	0.7	◑ 2337	1.4
3	W	0440	0.8	1208	1.5	2037	0.8		
4	TH	0139	1.3	0620	0.9	1409	1.5	2221	0.7
5	F	0303	1.5	0820	0.8	1522	1.7	2110	0.6
6	SA	0407	1.7	0912	0.6	1622	1.9	2149	0.4
7	SU	0503	1.9	1000	0.4	1716	2.1	2232	0.3
8	M	0555	2.1	1047	0.3	1808	2.3	2315	0.1
9	TU	0643	2.3	1130	0.2	1855	2.4	● 2355	0.1
10	W	0728	2.3	1209	0.1	1939	2.4		
11	TH	0030	0.1	0808	2.3	1243	0.2	2017	2.3
12	F	0102	0.2	0838	2.2	1317	0.2	2046	2.1
13	SA	0133	0.3	0859	2.1	1349	0.4	2112	1.9
14	SU	0202	0.5	0922	1.9	1420	0.5	2142	1.7
15	M	0226	0.6	0953	1.7	1449	0.7	2217	1.5
16	TU	0241	0.8	1029	1.5	1517	0.8	◐ 2300	1.4
17	W	0305	0.9	1115	1.4	1803	0.9	2357	1.2
18	TH	0404	1.0	1224	1.3	1904	0.9		
19	F	0145	1.2	0720	1.0	1437	1.4	1957	0.7
20	SA	0343	1.4	0814	0.9	1547	1.6	2047	0.6
21	SU	0422	1.6	0903	0.7	1635	1.8	2134	0.5
22	M	0504	1.8	0949	0.6	1720	1.9	2219	0.4
23	TU	0546	2.0	1034	0.5	1805	2.1	2301	0.3
24	W	0628	2.1	1113	0.4	1848	2.1	○ 2336	0.3
25	TH	0707	2.2	1150	0.3	1927	2.2		
26	F	0009	0.2	0737	2.2	1225	0.3	1954	2.2
27	SA	0044	0.2	0756	2.2	1301	0.3	2016	2.1
28	SU	0119	0.3	0824	2.1	1338	0.3	2049	2.0
29	M	0155	0.4	0902	2.0	1416	0.4	2133	1.8
30	TU	0234	0.5	0948	1.9	1502	0.5	2227	1.6
31	W	0322	0.7	1044	1.7	1604	0.7	◑ 2340	1.4

NOVEMBER

Date	Day	Time	m	Time	m	Time	m	Time	m
1	TH	0432	0.9	1200	1.5	2027	0.8		
2	F	0133	1.4	0607	0.9	1352	1.6	2222	0.7
3	SA	0249	1.6	0750	0.9	1504	1.7	2040	0.6
4	SU	0349	1.8	0848	0.7	1602	1.9	2123	0.5
5	M	0441	2.0	0937	0.6	1655	2.0	2207	0.3
6	TU	0530	2.1	1024	0.4	1746	2.2	2249	0.3
7	W	0615	2.3	1106	0.3	1832	2.2	● 2327	0.2
8	TH	0658	2.3	1143	0.3	1913	2.2		
9	F	0000	0.2	0734	2.3	1217	0.3	1947	2.2
10	SA	0032	0.3	0802	2.2	1251	0.3	2015	2.0
11	SU	0104	0.4	0827	2.1	1325	0.4	2045	1.9
12	M	0134	0.5	0856	1.9	1357	0.5	2118	1.7
13	TU	0157	0.6	0929	1.8	1426	0.7	2154	1.6
14	W	0215	0.7	1005	1.6	1455	0.8	2236	1.4
15	TH	0243	0.8	1047	1.5	1542	0.9	◐ 2326	1.3
16	F	0334	1.0	1142	1.4	1837	0.8		
17	SA	0040	1.3	0500	1.0	1310	1.4	1929	0.7
18	SU	0221	1.4	0741	1.0	1443	1.5	2017	0.6
19	M	0330	1.6	0829	0.8	1546	1.7	2101	0.5
20	TU	0421	1.8	0913	0.7	1639	1.8	2142	0.4
21	W	0509	2.0	0955	0.6	1730	2.0	2222	0.4
22	TH	0553	2.1	1038	0.5	1815	2.1	2302	0.3
23	F	0632	2.2	1120	0.4	1855	2.1	○ 2342	0.3
24	SA	0705	2.3	1202	0.3	1928	2.2		
25	SU	0022	0.3	0736	2.3	1243	0.3	2003	2.1
26	M	0103	0.3	0813	2.2	1326	0.3	2044	2.0
27	TU	0145	0.4	0856	2.1	1411	0.4	2134	1.9
28	W	0229	0.5	0946	2.0	1502	0.5	2230	1.7
29	TH	0320	0.7	1042	1.8	1602	0.6	2339	1.6
30	F	0423	0.8	1149	1.7	1712	0.7	◑	

DECEMBER

Date	Day	Time	m	Time	m	Time	m	Time	m
1	SA	0107	1.5	0535	0.9	1320	1.6	1830	0.7
2	SU	0220	1.6	0654	0.9	1433	1.7	1952	0.6
3	M	0319	1.7	0810	0.8	1533	1.8	2047	0.6
4	TU	0412	1.9	0907	0.7	1628	1.9	2134	0.5
5	W	0502	2.0	0955	0.6	1721	1.9	2216	0.4
6	TH	0548	2.1	1039	0.5	1808	2.0	2256	0.4
7	F	0630	2.2	1118	0.5	1849	2.0	● 2333	0.4
8	SA	0706	2.2	1155	0.4	1924	2.0		
9	SU	0009	0.4	0738	2.2	1232	0.4	1955	2.0
10	M	0043	0.4	0808	2.1	1308	0.5	2027	1.9
11	TU	0115	0.5	0840	2.0	1342	0.5	2101	1.7
12	W	0142	0.6	0914	1.8	1414	0.6	2136	1.6
13	TH	0205	0.7	0948	1.7	1443	0.6	2213	1.5
14	F	0235	0.7	1023	1.6	1523	0.7	2254	1.4
15	SA	0318	0.8	1105	1.5	1617	0.7	◐ 2346	1.4
16	SU	0422	0.9	1201	1.4	1722	0.7		
17	M	0101	1.4	0537	0.9	1324	1.4	1839	0.7
18	TU	0226	1.5	0656	0.9	1445	1.5	2005	0.6
19	W	0329	1.7	0814	0.8	1548	1.7	2054	0.5
20	TH	0423	1.8	0912	0.7	1646	1.8	2143	0.4
21	F	0513	2.0	1005	0.6	1740	1.9	2232	0.4
22	SA	0558	2.2	1057	0.5	1828	2.0	○ 2321	0.3
23	SU	0641	2.3	1146	0.4	1914	2.1		
24	M	0008	0.3	0725	2.3	1233	0.3	2002	2.1
25	TU	0053	0.3	0809	2.3	1319	0.3	2051	2.1
26	W	0138	0.3	0857	2.3	1407	0.3	2141	2.0
27	TH	0223	0.4	0947	2.2	1456	0.4	2229	1.9
28	F	0311	0.5	1037	2.0	1547	0.4	2321	1.7
29	SA	0402	0.7	1130	1.8	1642	0.5	◑	
30	SU	0024	1.6	0500	0.8	1236	1.7	1742	0.6
31	M	0136	1.5	0605	0.9	1351	1.6	1849	0.7

Chart Datum is 0·93 metres below Ordnance Datum (Newlyn). HAT is 2·5 metres above Chart Datum.

Visionary
binoculars & telescopes

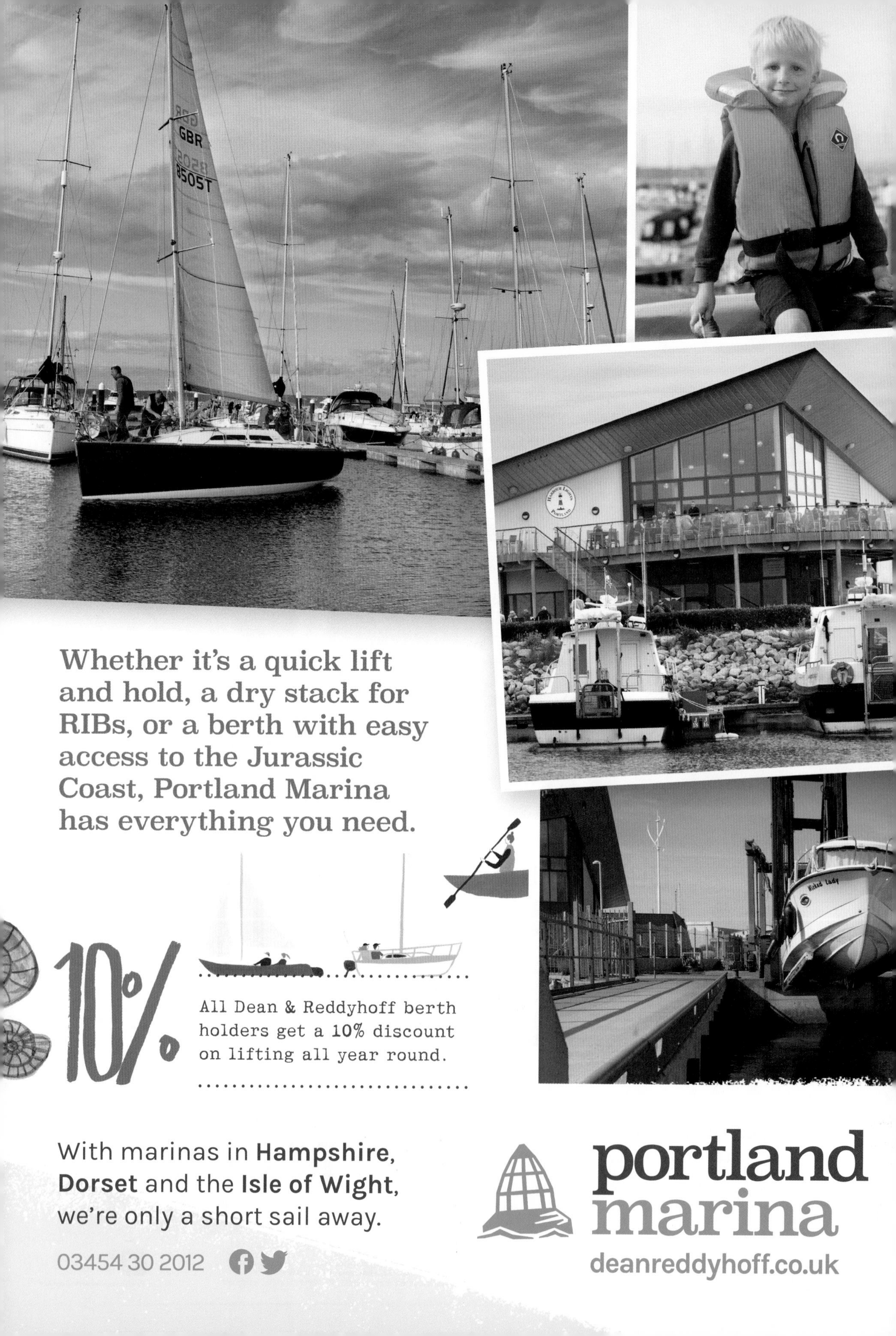
GBR
8505T
Whether it's a quick lift and hold, a dry stack for RIBs, or a berth with easy access to the Jurassic Coast, Portland Marina has everything you need.
10%
All Dean & Reddyhoff berth holders get a 10% discount on lifting all year round.
With marinas in Hampshire, Dorset and the Isle of Wight, we're only a short sail away.
03454 30 2012
portland marina
deanreddyhoff.co.uk

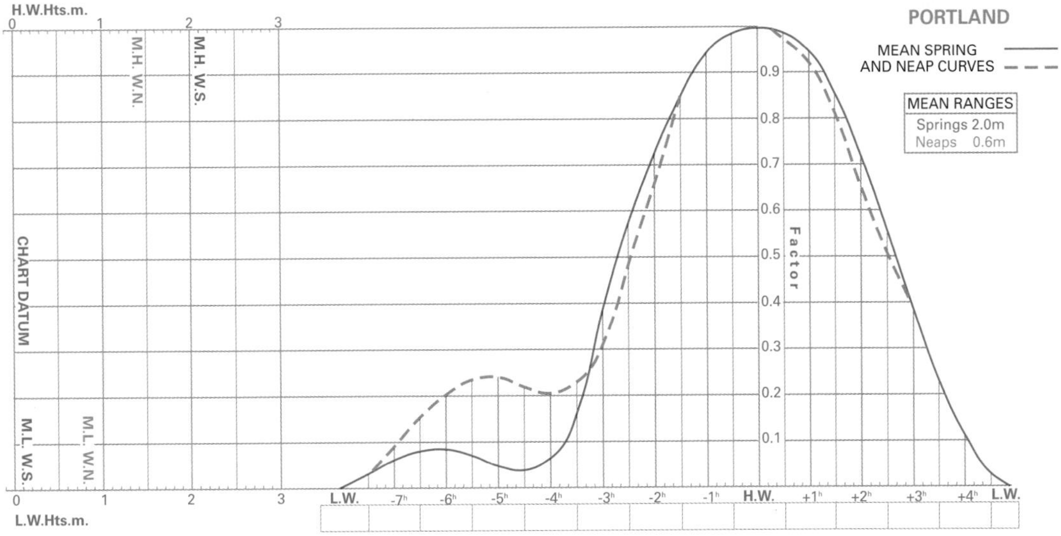

9.1.27 PORTLAND HARBOUR

Dorset **50°35'·72N 02°25'·91W** (N Ship Chan)

CHARTS AC 2610, 2255, 2268, 5601; Imray C10, C12, C5, C4, 2300

TIDES –0430 Dover; ML 1·0

Standard Port PORTLAND (⟶)

Times				**Height (metres)**			
High Water		Low Water		MHWS	MHWN	MLWN	MLWS
0100	0700	0100	0700	2·1	1·4	0·8	0·1
1300	1900	1300	1900				
LULWORTH COVE and MUPE BAY (Worbarrow Bay)							
+0005	+0015	–0005	0000	+0·1	+0·1	+0·2	+0·1

Double LWs occur between Portland and Lulworth Cove. Predictions are for the 1st LW. The 2nd LW occurs 3–4hrs later.

SHELTER The large harbour is exposed to winds from the E and NE, but in westerlies the moorings on the W and S sides are reasonably sheltered by Chesil Beach and the Isle of Portland. The marina is protected by substantial rock breakwaters. ⚓ on W side of hbr in about 3m, as on chartlet, or further N off Castle Cove SC.

NAVIGATION If approaching from the W inshore of Portland Race study the tidal stream diagrams carefully and note the advice in Passage Information.

WPT 50°35'·97N 02°25'·24W, 240°/0·5M to North Ship Channel (NSC). This is the recommended route to the marina via the Marina Access Route, keeping clear of shipping using East Ship Channel (ESC). Small craft (LOA<20m) may use ESC, but must monitor Ch 74 and obey IPTS lights shown on 'C' and Fort Heads. Small craft crossing ESC should remain well clear of the Heads (>0.5M) so that they may be seen by commercial vessels navigating within the channel. Vessels >20m must obtain permission from Portland Harbour Radio before entering or leaving the harbour.

South Ship Channel (SSC) is permanently closed and blocked by overhead wires. 7ca SE of SSC is a noise range, marked by 4 Fl Y buoys. Vessel permanently moored is used for military exercises with an exclusion zone of 50m. There is a rocky reef extending about 1·5ca offshore NE of Castle Cove SC, and shoal water E of Small Mouth.

A 12kn speed limit applies throughout the harbour and in Weymouth Bay, but vessels under 10m LOA are exempt. However, a 6kn speed limit applies to *all* vessels in the areas depicted and within 150m of any breakwater or harbour premises.

Approach to Weymouth & Portland National Sailing Academy (WPNSA) and Portland Marina. The Marina Access Route remains the recommended route for small craft (<20m LOA) transiting the harbour. Engines must be used (if fitted) when proceeding between the marina/WPNSA and NSC. From NSC head SW to the SWM buoy (see chartlet) then S to the marina entrance, leaving the 2 PHM buoys to port. Obey traffic signals on 'C' Head and on the marina breakwater:

- Flashing = Entrance closed; await instructions (Ch 74 for Harbour Control; Ch 80 for Marina)
- Fixed = Commercial vessel/sailing fleet departing; do not impede
- Fixed = Commercial vessel/sailing fleet arriving; do not impede

LIGHTS AND MARKS The precipitous N face of the Verne, near the N end of the Isle of Portland, is conspic from afar. 'A' Hd lt ho is a conspic W twr, Fl 2·5s 22m 10M.

COMMUNICATIONS (Code 01305) NMOC 760439; Police 101; Dorchester Ⓗ 824055; Ⓗ (A&E) 820341. Port Control ☎824044.

Monitor Ch **74** *Portland Hbr Radio* for commercial traffic. *Portland Marina* Ch 80.

FACILITIES **Portland Port**, www.portland-port.co.uk owns the harbour which is a commercial port with an international bunkering station. Port and Harbour Dues (see web site) apply to all vessels in Portland Inner Harbour.

Castle Cove SC ☎783708.

WPNSA The 3 pontoons for keel boats are protected by a rock breakwater. admin@wpnsa.org.uk www.wpnsa.org.uk ☎866000. Temporary pontoon berths may be available for 1 or 2 nights by prior arrangement.

RNSA moorings adjacent to fairway and WPNSA breakwater are private moorings for members occupied Apr-Oct.

Portland Marina The entrance, 50°34'·44N 02°27'·32W, is between the NW end of the marina breakwater and the WPNSA breakwater. www.deanreddyhoff.co.uk ☎03454 302012; 600+Ⓥ berths on pontoons R, S ,T £2.95 inc for <14m LOA, short stay <4hrs £8, (inc bio-diesel) Ⓔ (50t) .

Castletown is SE of the marina. Ⓑ 501 bus to Weymouth (Hurn).

Chartlet overleaf

PORTLAND HARBOUR *continued*

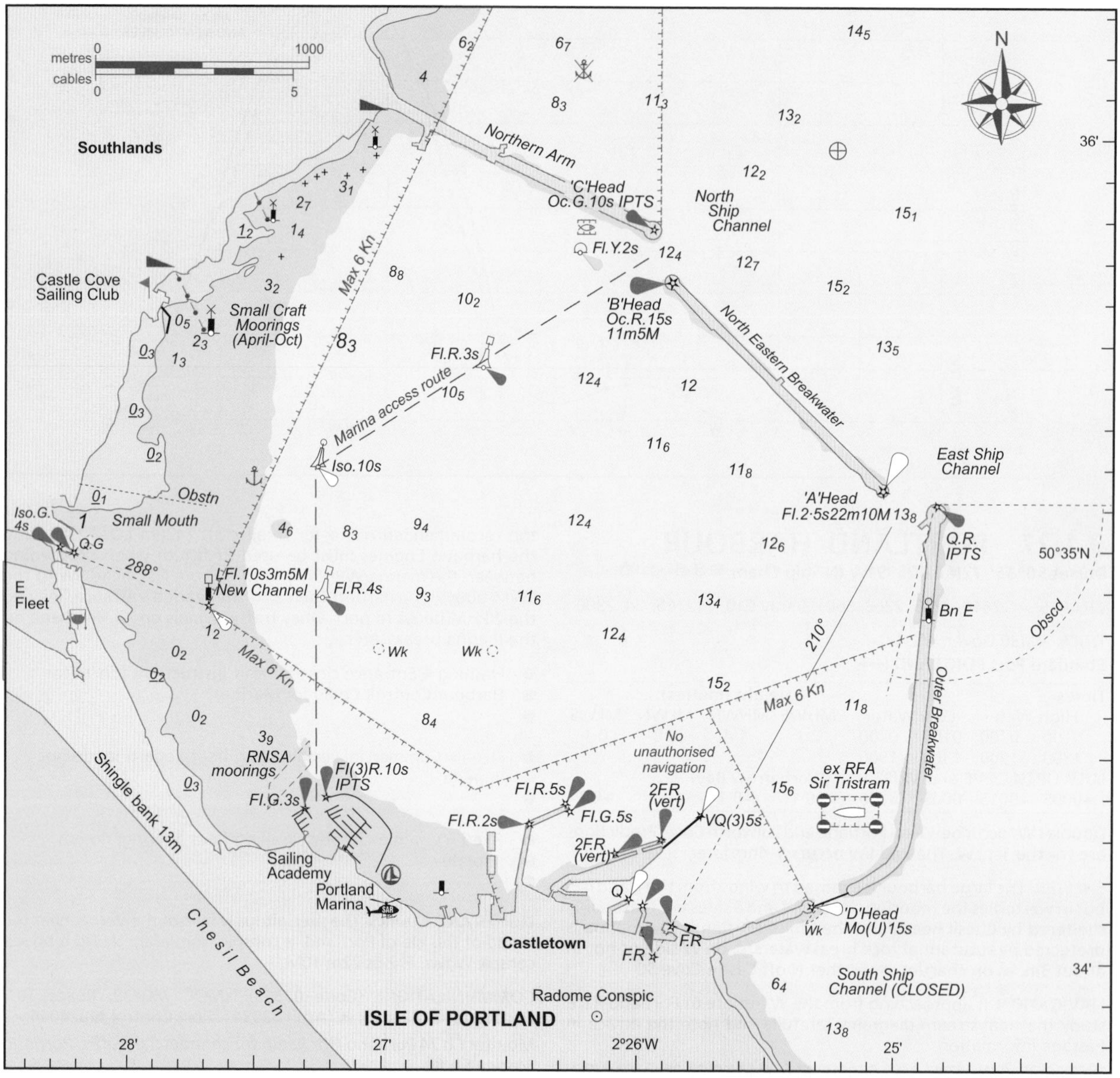

9.1.28 WEYMOUTH

Dorset **50°36′·57N 02°26′·58W** ✿✿✿◊◊◊✿✿✿

CHARTS AC 2610, 2255, 2268, 2172, 5601; Imray C10, C12, C5, C4, 2300

TIDES –0438 Dover; ML 1·1

Standard Port PORTLAND (⟵)

Use Portland predictions and Note. Mean ranges are small: 0·6m at np and 2·0m at sp. NOTE: A LW stand lasts about 4 hrs at sp and 1 hr at nps. Due to an eddy, the tidal stream in Weymouth Roads is W-going at all times except for 2hrs, HW –0510 to HW –0310.

SHELTER Good, but swell enters the outer harbour and The Cove in strong E winds. ⚓ feasible in Weymouth Bay NNE of the ent in about 3·5m, 4ca off the beach to seaward of the buoyed bathing area. Ⓥ berths in The Cove have 1.7m at CD.

NAVIGATION WPT 50°36′·69N 02°26′·23W, 240°/2ca to South Pierhead. The harbour entrance is 1M NW of North Ship Channel into Portland Harbour. Reports indicate a bar may be forming.

When bound to/from the E, check whether Lulworth Firing Ranges are active. See 9.1.29 for further info.

A DG Range, marked by 3 SPM buoys (one Fl Y 2s), lies 2·5ca SE of South Pier; ⚓̸. See ACs 2255 and 2268 for restrictions on ⚓ in Weymouth Bay.

Comply with traffic signals displayed from a RW pole near the root of South Pier (see below). Speed limit is 'Dead Slow'. A ferry (rowed) has right of way across the fairway just E of the LB (see chartlet).

LIGHTS AND MARKS Traffic signals, shown *vertically* on S Pier:

No signals = Proceed with caution;

● ● ● = Large vessel leaving, do not obstruct the pierhead area;

● ● ● = Large vessel is entering, do not leave harbour;

● ● over ● = Harbour closed, do not enter the pierheads area;

● ○ ● = Only proceed on receipt of instructions;

● ● ● (flashing) = All vessels await instructions.

If in any doubt, call *Weymouth Harbour* on Ch 12.

Conspic ✠ spire, 6ca NNW of the harbour ent, is a useful daymark. Pierhead lights may be hard to see against shore lights. Weymouth Eye, a 53m twr on the hard NW of N Pier, is floodlit. Portland 'A' Head lt ho, a conspic W twr 1·7M SE of hbr is readily visible.

Ldg lts 239·6°, 2 FR (H24) and R open ◊s on W poles are 500m inside the pierheads; they are not visible until the S Pier is rounded.

LIFTING BRIDGE allows masted craft access to the marina.

Lifting times (LT):

15 Apr-15 Sep, 0800, 1000, 1200, 1400, 1600, 1800, 2000; **plus Jun, Jul, Aug**, 2100.

16 Sep-14 Apr: 0800, 1000, 1200, 1400, 1600, 1800.

NOTE: Minimum 1hr notice is required for lifts 16 Sep-14 Apr ☎838423 (ansafone), 789357 or Ch 12.

Be visible from bridge 5 mins before lift time; listen on Ch 12 for any broadcasts. Outbound vessels usually have priority. 3FR or 3FG (vert) on both sides of the bridge are traffic lights and must be obeyed at all times, even when the bridge is closed. Clearance when closed is 2·75m above HAT. A 50m pontoon on the S bank immediately outside bridge is for craft waiting for an inwards bridge lift. Craft using this pontoon must take the next available transit. Owing to silting craft of 2m or greater should obtain alternative temporary berth from harbour staff if waiting around LWS – check before remaining o/night. Submerged cable inside bridge has least depth of 1.8m.

COMMUNICATIONS (Code 01305) NMOC 760439; Dr 774411; Ⓗ Dorchester 251150; Police 101. HM ☎838423.

Weymouth Harbour and *Weymouth Town Bridge* (at opening times): Ch 12 (0800-2000 in summer and when vessel due). *Weymouth Marina* Ch 80. Ch 60 for fuel.

FACILITIES (www.weymouth-harbour.co.uk) **Outer Harbour** The Cove (S side) on Ⓥ pontoons <10m LOA> Custom House Quay. Quays from The Cove to lift bridge are for FVs and tourist boats. £2·50 inc showers, £2·50/day discount for >3 nights (not Jul/Aug); <4 hrs £6<6m>£8<12m>£12. (coin operated).

Inner Harbour No Ⓥ berths on council pontoons W of the bridge.

Weymouth Marina www.deanreddyhoff.co.uk ☎767576, dredged 2·5m, 290 inc Ⓥ £2·85 inc showers £8 for <14m short stay <4 hrs: call Ch 80 for berth.

Fuel from jetty W of LB station ☎07747182181 or by bowser (see HM or Harbour Guide for details); no petrol in harbour.

Weymouth SC ☎785481. **Royal Dorset YC** ☎786258.

Town Ⓔ Diver Ⓑ @ (Bournemouth).

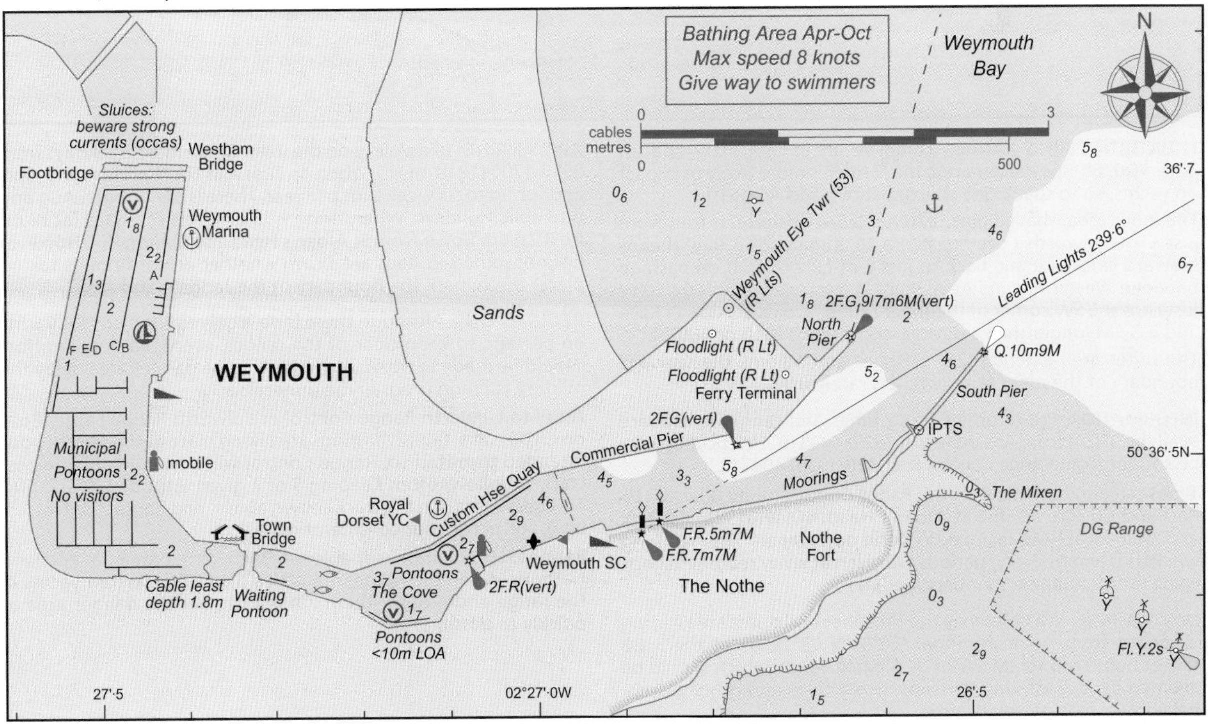

9.1.29 LULWORTH RANGES

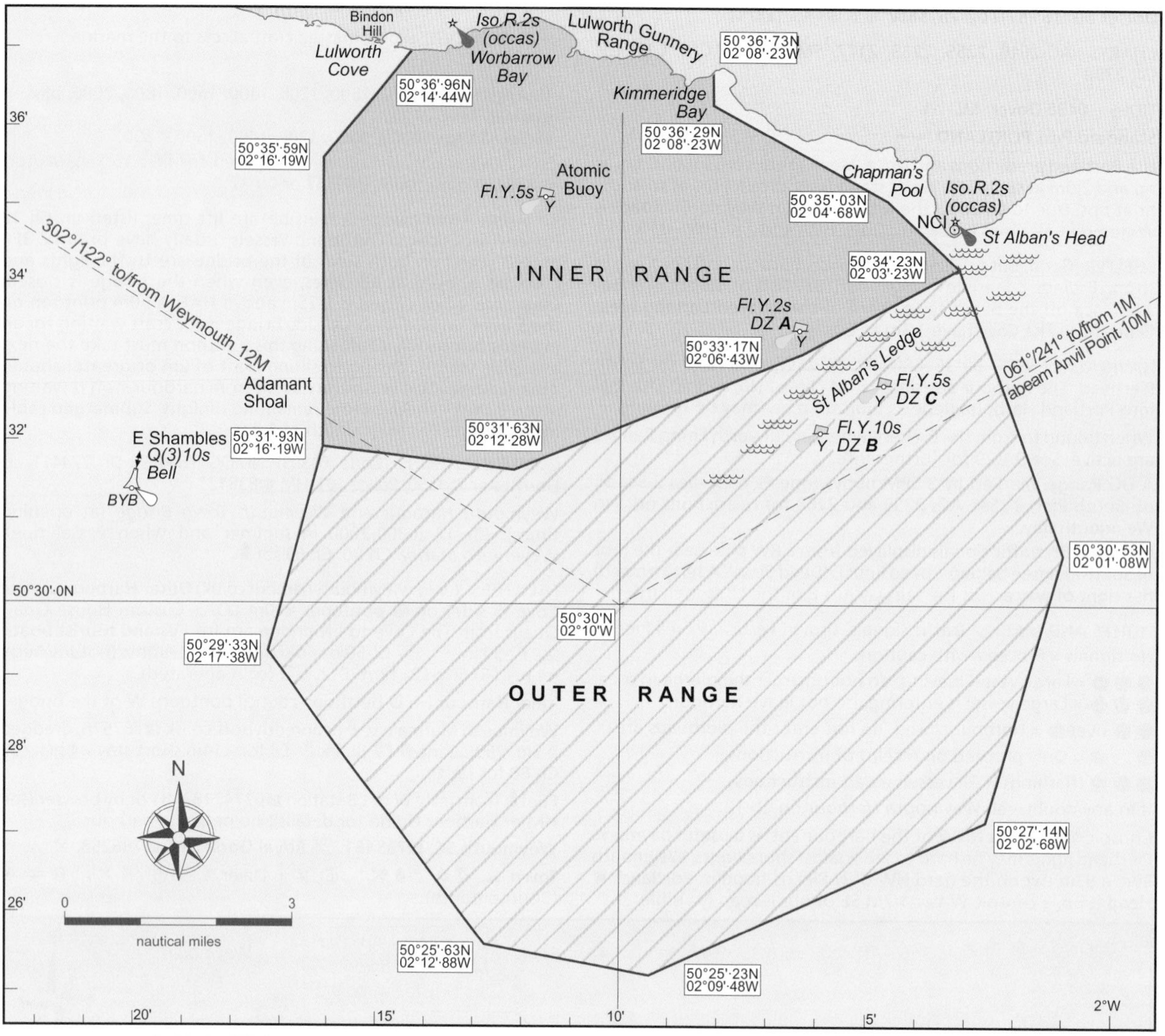

LULWORTH FIRING RANGES comprise an inner (D026) and an outer (D026B) sea danger area; the former is more likely to impact on yachts, so to speak. See chartlet above and AC 2610.

The inner area, shaded pink, extends 5·5M offshore. It runs from just E of Lulworth Cove coastwise to Kimmeridge Bay, thence seaward clockwise and back to just E of Lulworth. If on passage between Weymouth and Anvil Point, a track via 50°30'N 02°10'W just clips the SW corner of the inner range, avoids St Alban's Race and is 3·3M longer than a direct track. See AC 2610 or 5601.4.

The outer area extends 12M offshore and adjoins the seaward boundary of the inner as shown. It is rarely used.

INFORMATION Pre-recorded firing times and range activity are available (H24) from Ansafone ☎(01929) 404819. Clarification may be sought from Range Control (HO) ☎(01929) 404712.

Times can also be obtained from Range Control/Safety Boats Ch 08 Portland CG (Ch 16), the St Alban's Head NCI ☎(01929) 439220; and from local HMs, marinas, YCs and newspapers. Annual firing weekends and No Firing periods are given at www.reedsalmanacs.co.uk in the Almanac's January Update.

NAVAL FIRING Warships may use the inner and outer areas, firing eastward from Adamant Shoal (50°33'N 02°19'W) at the 3 DZ target buoys (up to 3M SW of St Alban's Head), which should be avoided by at least 1M. Warships fly red flags and other vessels/helicopters may patrol the area.

ARMY FIRING takes place on the inner range most weekdays from 0930-1700 (1230 on Fri), often on Tues and Thurs nights for 3–4hrs and for up to six weekends per year. There is NO firing in Aug and on Public Holidays. When firing is in progress red flags (at night Iso R 2s) are flown from St Alban's Head and Bindon Hill. However inshore some red flags are flown whether or not firing is taking place; these mark the boundary of the range's land area.

REGULATIONS Although there is no legal requirement for yachts on passage to keep clear of the ranges, every reasonable effort should be made to do so. Any vessels in the danger area delay the military training programme unnecessarily.

A call to Lulworth Range Control or Lulworth Range Safety Boat on Ch 08 will establish if firings are taking place at the time of your intended transit. If so, Range Control will advise you of the best track to follow, often keeping S of a given latitude (50° 32'.5N). This is shorter than the track shown above, and Range Control will be grateful for your consideration.

Range Safety boats, capable of 30kn, are based in Portland Harbour. When the ranges are active they will intercept yachts in the range and request them (Ch 08) to clear the danger area as quickly as possible.

ANCHORAGES BETWEEN PORTLAND BILL AND ANVIL PT

Helpful to read *Inshore along the Dorset Coast* (Peter Bruce).

CHURCH OPE COVE, Dorset, **50°32′·26N 02°25′·64W**. AC 2255, 2268, 5601.8. Tidal data as for Portland. A small cove on the E side of the Isle of Portland, about midway between the Bill and Portland Hbr. It is used by divers & completely open to the E, but could serve as a temporary ⚓ in about 3m off the shingle beach, to await a fair tide around the Bill.

RINGSTEAD BAY, Dorset, **50°37′·83N 02°20′·48W**. AC 2610, 5601. Tides as for Weymouth, 4M to WSW. Tempy ⚓ in 3-5m toward the E end of the bay. Ringstead Ledges, drying, define the W end of the bay. Rks on the E side restrict the effective width to about 3ca; easiest appr is from SE.

DURDLE DOOR, Dorset, **50°37′·27N 02°16′·58W**. AC 2610, 5601. Tides as for Lulworth Cove, 1M E. Durdle Door is a conspic rock archway. Close E of it Man o' War Cove offers ⚓ for shoal draught in settled weather. To the W, ⚓ may be found – with considerable caution – inside The Bull, Blind Cow, The Cow and The Calf which form part of a rocky reef.

LULWORTH COVE, Dorset, **50°37′·00N 02°14′·82W**. AC 2172, 5601. HW –0449 on Dover. Tides; ML 1·2m. Good shelter in fair weather and offshore winds, but ocasionally a squally katabatic wind may blow down from the surrounding cliffs at night. Heavy swell enters the Cove in S/SW winds; if strong the ⚓ becomes untenable. Enter the Cove slightly E of centre. 8kn speed limit. ⚓ in NE quadrant in 2·5m. Holding is poor. Local village and are on W side. Facilities: taps in car park and at slip, museum.

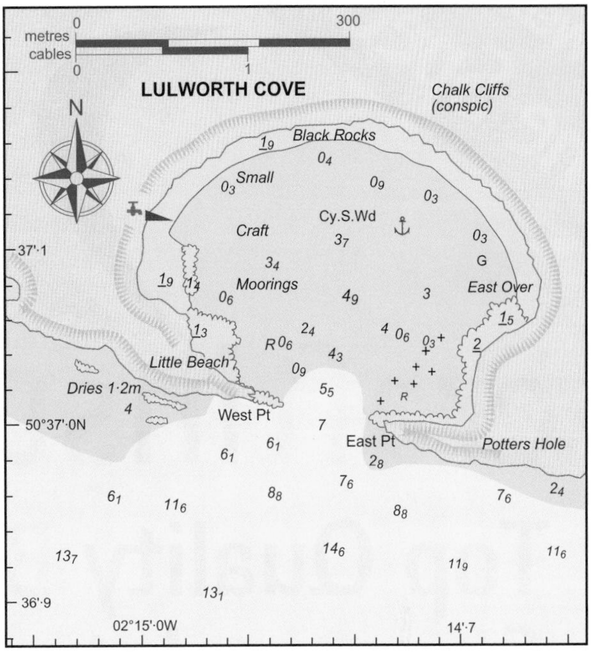

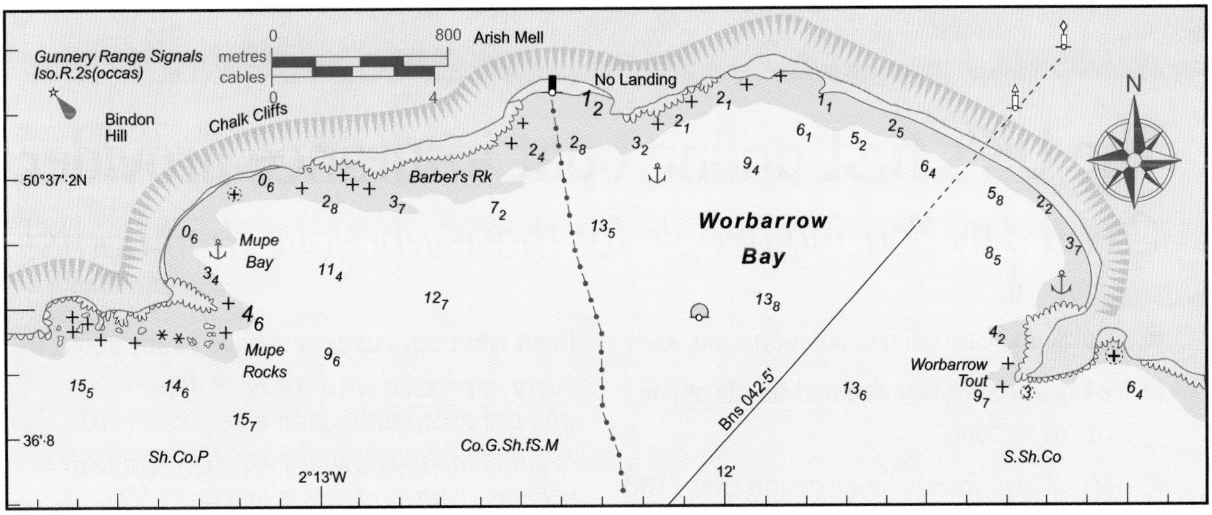

WORBARROW BAY, Dorset, **50°37′·03N 02°12′·08W**. AC 2172, 5601. Tides as Lulworth Cove/Mupe Bay. Worbarrow is a 1½M wide bay, close E of Lulworth Cove. It is easily identified from seaward by the V-shaped gap in the hills at Arish Mell, centre of bay just E of Bindon Hill. Bindon Hill also has a white chalk scar due to cliff falls. Caution: Mupe Rks at W end and other rks 1ca off NW side. ⚓s in about 3m sheltered from W or E winds at appropriate end. The bay lies within Lulworth Ranges; landing prohibited at Arish Mell. No lights/facilities. Tyneham village, deserted since WW2, is close to the E.

CHAPMAN'S POOL, Dorset, **50°35′·53N 02°03′·93W**. AC 2172, 5601. Tidal data: interpolate between Mupe Bay and Swanage. Chapman's Pool, like Brandy Bay and Kimmeridge Bay, is picturesque and comfortable when the wind is offshore. ⚓ in depths of about 3m in centre of bay (to avoid tidal swirl). From here to St Alban's Hd the stream sets SSE almost continuously due to a back eddy. No lts. Facilities: village shop and 'Square & Compass' ☎01929 439229, are at Worth Matravers (1.5M walk).

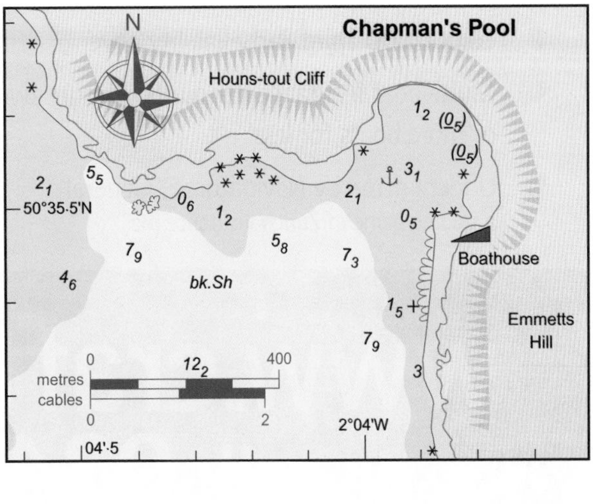

Central South England

Anvil Point to Selsey Bill

9.2.1 **Contents** 191

9.2.2 **Area map, Nab Deep Water Channel and Distance table** 192

9.2.3 **Channel tidal stream charts** 194

9.2.4 **Lights, buoys and waypoints** 196

9.2.5 **Passage information** 198
Crossing the English Channel (central part) – 198 • Swanage to Christchurch, Western approaches to the Solent, the Solent, Isle of Wight south coast – 209 • Eastern approaches to the Solent – 239

9.2.6 **Swanage** 199

9.2.7 **Studland Bay** 200

9.2.8 **Poole Harbour, tide tables/curves** 200
Wareham

9.2.9 **Christchurch** 210

9.2.10 **Keyhaven** 210

9.2.11 **Needles Channel** 211
Alum Bay • Totland Bay • Freshwater Bay

9.2.12 **Yarmouth** 212

9.2.13 **Lymington** 213

9.2.14 **Newtown River** 214

9.2.15 **Beaulieu River** 215

9.2.16 **Isle of Wight and Solent tidal stream charts** 216

9.2.17 **Special tidal curves from Christchurch to Selsey Bill** 218

9.2.18 **The Central Solent** 220

9.2.19 **Cowes/River Medina** 221
Folly Reach • Newport

9.2.20 **Southampton, tide tables/curves** 225

9.2.21 **River Hamble** 230
Ashlett Creek • Hill Head

9.2.22 **Wootton Creek** 232

9.2.23 **Ryde** 232

9.2.24 **Bembridge** 233

9.2.25 **Portsmouth tide tables/curves** 234

9.2.26 **Langstone Harbour** 240

9.2.27 **Chichester Harbour, tide tables/curves** 241

9.2.2

Central Southern England

Anvil Point to Selsey Bill

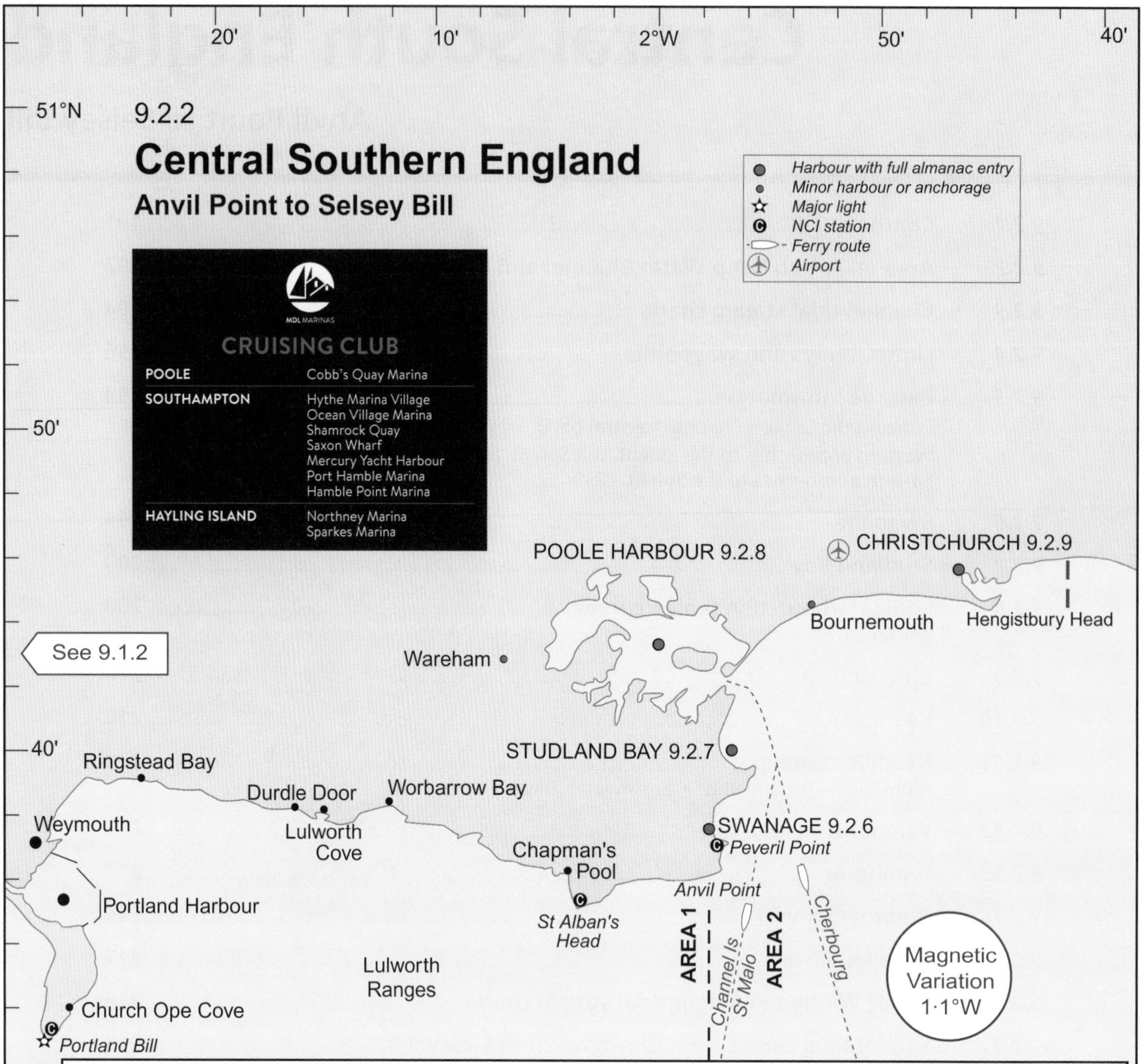
20'
10'
2°W
50'
40'
51°N
50'
40'
30'
20'
MDL MARINAS
CRUISING CLUB
POOLE Cobb's Quay Marina
SOUTHAMPTON Hythe Marina Village
Ocean Village Marina
Shamrock Quay
Saxon Wharf
Mercury Yacht Harbour
Port Hamble Marina
Hamble Point Marina
HAYLING ISLAND Northney Marina
Sparkes Marina
Harbour with full almanac entry
Minor harbour or anchorage
Major light
NCI station
Ferry route
Airport
See 9.1.2
POOLE HARBOUR 9.2.8
CHRISTCHURCH 9.2.9
Bournemouth
Hengistbury Head
Wareham
STUDLAND BAY 9.2.7
Ringstead Bay
Durdle Door
Worbarrow Bay
Weymouth
Lulworth Cove
SWANAGE 9.2.6
Peveril Point
Chapman's Pool
Portland Harbour
Anvil Point
St Alban's Head
AREA 1
AREA 2
Channel Is St Malo
Cherbourg
Magnetic Variation 1·1°W
Lulworth Ranges
Church Ope Cove
Portland Bill

DISTANCE TABLE

Approximate distances in nautical miles are by the most direct route while avoiding dangers and allowing for TSS. Places in *italics* are in adjoining areas; places in **bold** are in 9.0.5, Cross-Channel Distances.

1	Portland Bill	**1**																						
2	*St Alban's Hd*	16	**2**																					
3	Swanage	23	7	**3**																				
4	Poole Hbr (ent)	28	12	6	**4**																			
5	Christchurch	34	18	11	11	**5**																		
6	**Needles (Bridge)**	35	19	13	14	7	**6**																	
7	Keyhaven	40	24	19	19	12	5	**7**																
8	Lymington	42	26	21	21	14	7	3	**8**															
9	Yarmouth (IOW)	40	24	19	19	12	6	2	2	**9**														
10	Newtown R	44	28	23	23	16	10	6	4	4	**10**													
11	Beaulieu R (ent)	46	30	25	25	18	12	9	7	7	4	**11**												
12	Cowes	49	33	28	28	21	15	10	9	9	6	3	**12**											
13	Southampton	55	39	34	34	27	21	16	15	15	12	9	9	**13**										
14	R Hamble (ent)	53	37	32	32	25	19	13	12	12	9	6	6	4	**14**									
15	Wootton Creek	54	38	33	33	26	20	15	13	13	10	6	5	11	8	**15**								
16	Ryde	56	40	35	35	28	22	17	16	16	13	9	7	12	9	2	**16**							
17	Portsmouth	58	42	37	37	30	24	19	18	18	15	11	9	18	15	5	4	**17**						
18	Bembridge	59	43	38	38	31	25	20	19	19	16	12	10	19	16	6	5	6	**18**					
19	Langstone Hbr	61	45	40	40	33	27	23	22	22	19	15	12	16	13	8	7	5	6	**19**				
20	Chichester Bar	63	47	42	42	35	29	25	24	24	21	17	15	20	17	10	9	8	7	5	**20**			
21	**Nab Tower**	60	44	39	39	36	30	26	25	25	22	18	16	21	18	11	10	10	6	7	6	**21**		
22	St Catherine's Pt	45	29	25	25	20	14	19	18	18	26	27	25	30	27	20	19	21	15	20	19	15	**22**	
23	*Owers Lt Buoy*	69	53	49	49	44	38	35	33	33	30	27	25	30	27	20	19	20	16	16	13	11	24	**23**

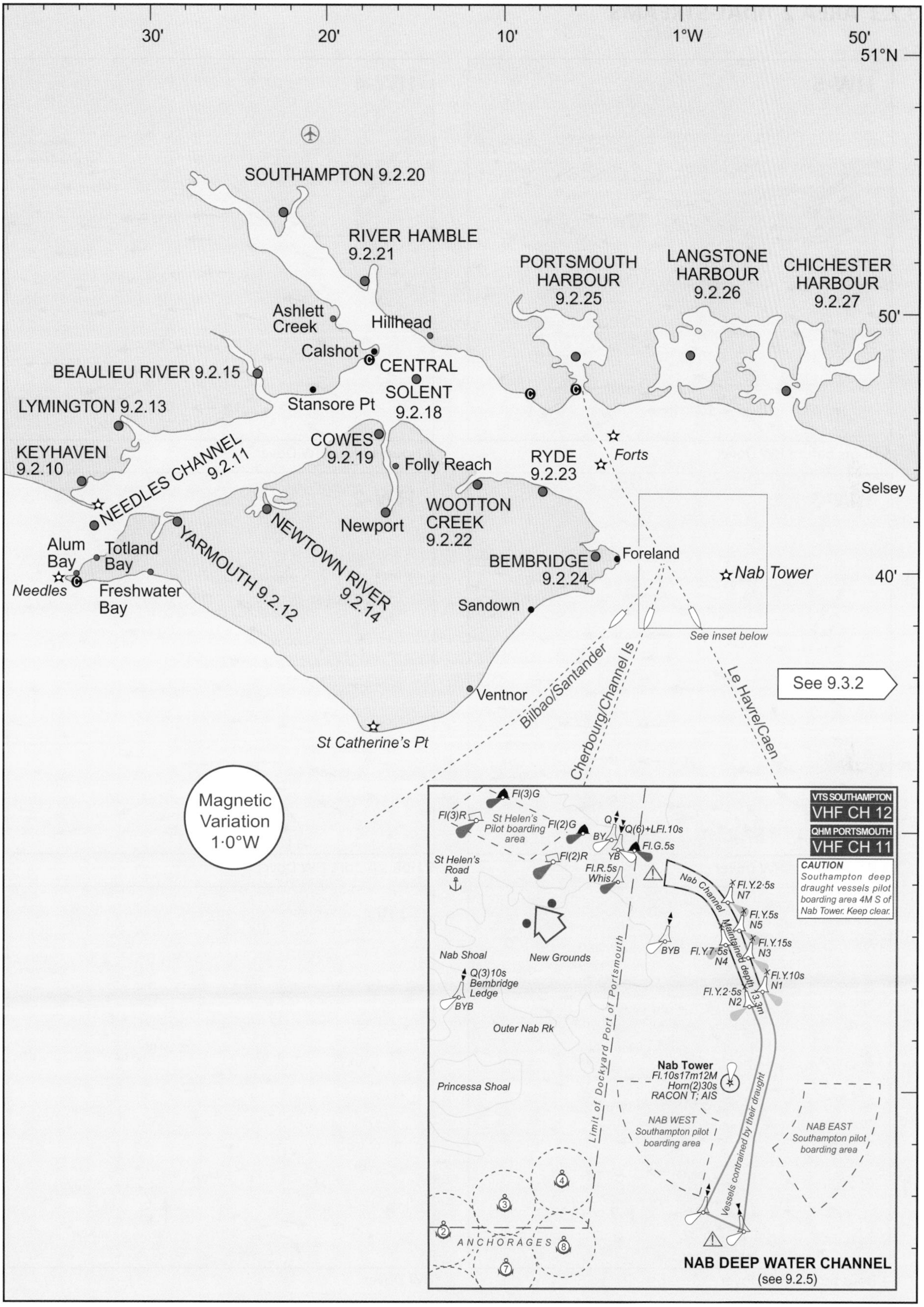
30'
20'
10'
1°W
50'
51°N
50'
40'
SOUTHAMPTON 9.2.20
RIVER HAMBLE 9.2.21
PORTSMOUTH HARBOUR 9.2.25
LANGSTONE HARBOUR 9.2.26
CHICHESTER HARBOUR 9.2.27
Ashlett Creek
Hillhead
Calshot
CENTRAL SOLENT 9.2.18
BEAULIEU RIVER 9.2.15
Stansore Pt
LYMINGTON 9.2.13
COWES 9.2.19
Folly Reach
RYDE 9.2.23
Forts
KEYHAVEN 9.2.10
NEEDLES CHANNEL 9.2.11
Selsey
WOOTTON CREEK 9.2.22
Newport
NEWTOWN RIVER 9.2.14
YARMOUTH 9.2.12
Alum Bay
Totland Bay
Needles
Freshwater Bay
BEMBRIDGE 9.2.24
Foreland
Nab Tower
Sandown
See inset below
See 9.3.2
Bilbao/Santander
Cherbourg/Channel Is
Le Havre/Caen
Ventnor
St Catherine's Pt
Magnetic Variation 1·0°W
Fl(3)G
Fl(3)R
St Helen's Pilot boarding area
Fl(2)G
Q
Q(6)+LFl.10s
BY
YB
Fl.G.5s
Fl(2)R
St Helen's Road
Fl.R.5s Whis
Nab Channel
Fl.Y.2·5s N7
Fl.Y.5s N5
Fl.Y.15s N3
Fl.Y.7·5s N4
Fl.Y.10s N1
Fl.Y.2·5s N2
Maintained depth 13.3m
BYB
Nab Shoal
New Grounds
Q(3)10s Bembridge Ledge
BYB
Outer Nab Rk
Limit of Dockyard Port of Portsmouth
Nab Tower
Fl.10s17m12M
Horn(2)30s
RACON T; AIS
Princessa Shoal
NAB WEST Southampton pilot boarding area
NAB EAST Southampton pilot boarding area
Vessels contrained by their draught
ANCHORAGES
VTS SOUTHAMPTON
VHF CH 12
QHM PORTSMOUTH
VHF CH 11
CAUTION
Southampton deep draught vessels pilot boarding area 4M S of Nab Tower. Keep clear.
NAB DEEP WATER CHANNEL
(see 9.2.5)

9.2.3 AREA 2 TIDAL STREAMS

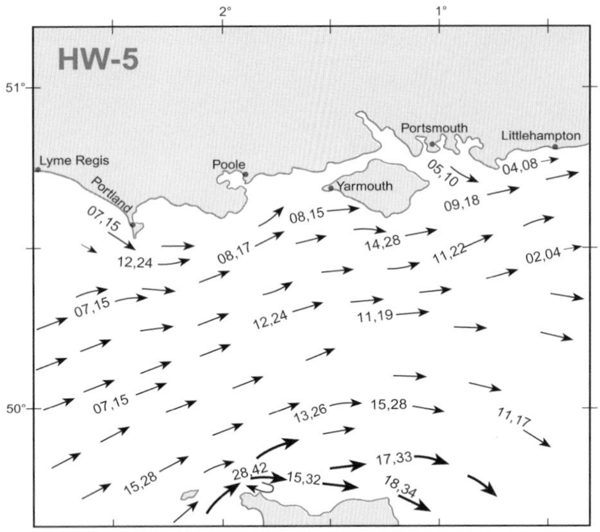

5 Hours before HW Dover

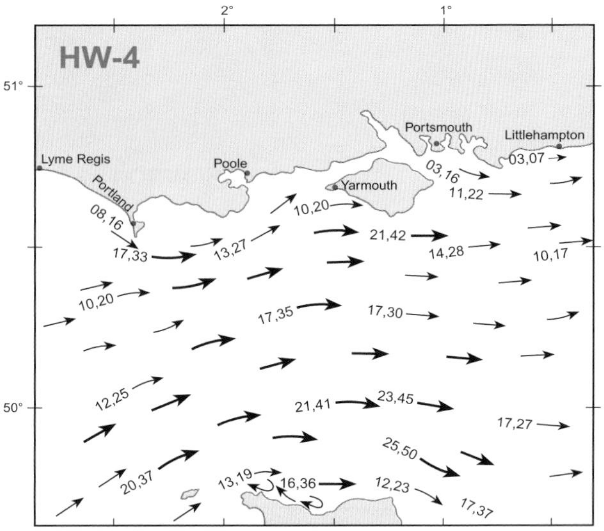

4 Hours before HW Dover

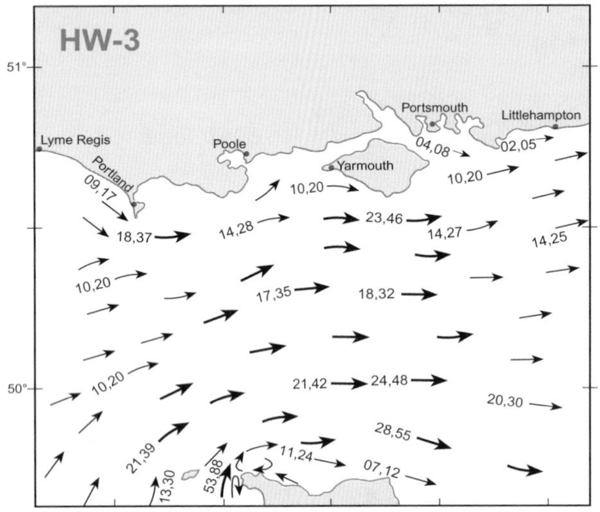

3 Hours before HW Dover

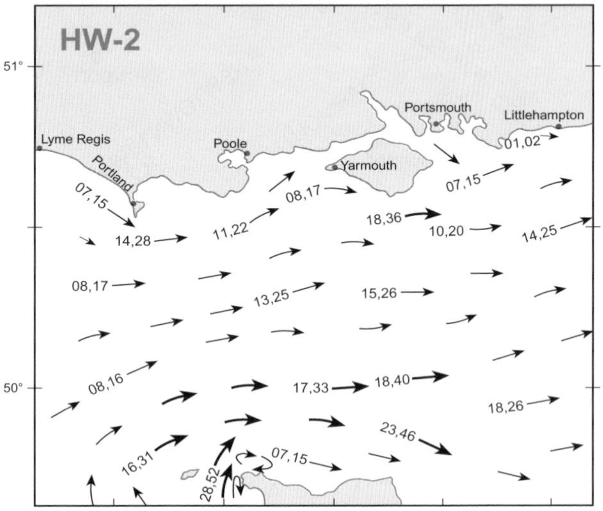

2 Hours before HW Dover

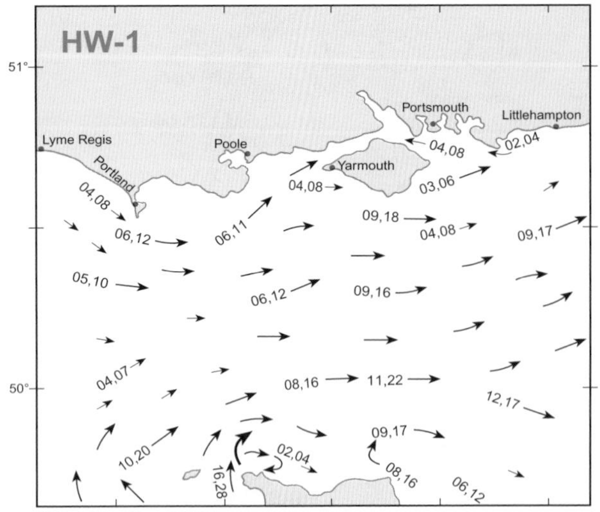

1 Hour before HW Dover

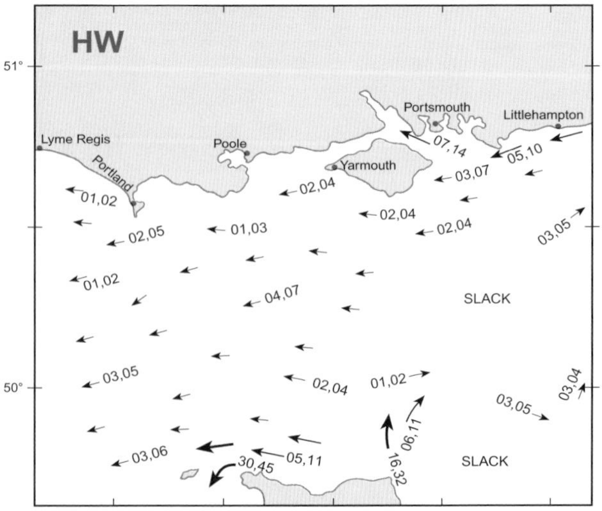

HW Dover

Westward 9.1.3 Portland 9.1.26 Isle of Wight 9.2.16 Eastward 9.3.3 Southward 9.18.3 Channel Is 9.19.3

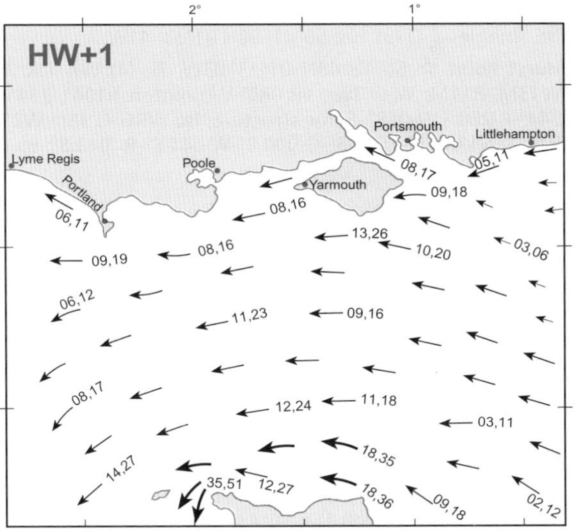
HW+1
2°
1°
51°
50°
Portsmouth
Littlehampton
Lyme Regis
Poole
Yarmouth
Portland
08,17
05,11
09,18
08,16
06,11
13,26
10,20
03,06
09,19
08,16
06,12
11,23
09,16
08,17
12,24
11,18
03,11
18,35
14,27
35,51
12,27
18,36
09,18
02,12
1 Hour after HW Dover

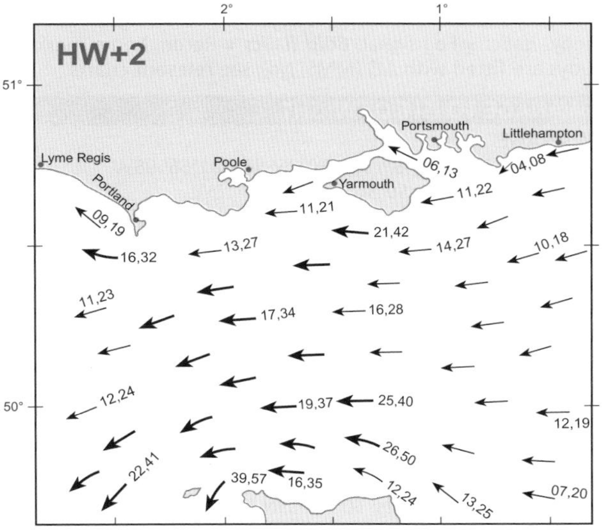
HW+2
2°
1°
51°
50°
Portsmouth
Littlehampton
Lyme Regis
Poole
Yarmouth
Portland
06,13
04,08
11,22
11,21
09,19
21,42
14,27
10,18
16,32
13,27
11,23
17,34
16,28
12,24
19,37
25,40
12,19
26,50
22,41
39,57
16,35
12,24
13,25
07,20
2 Hours after HW Dover

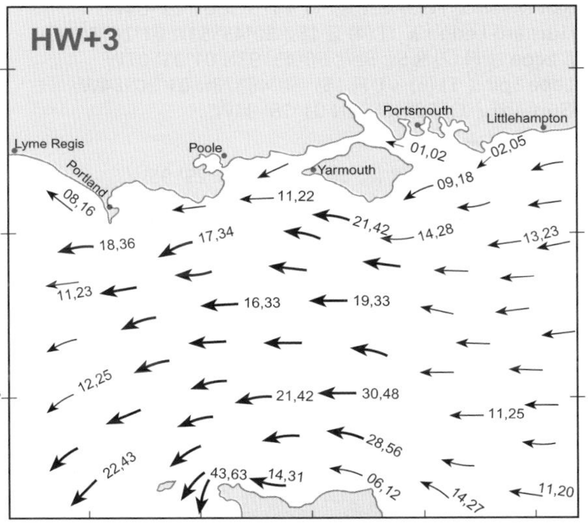
HW+3
51°
50°
Portsmouth
Littlehampton
Lyme Regis
Poole
Yarmouth
Portland
01,02
02,05
09,18
08,16
11,22
21,42
14,28
18,36
17,34
13,23
11,23
16,33
19,33
12,25
21,42
30,48
11,25
28,56
22,43
43,63
14,31
06,12
14,27
11,20
3 Hours after HW Dover

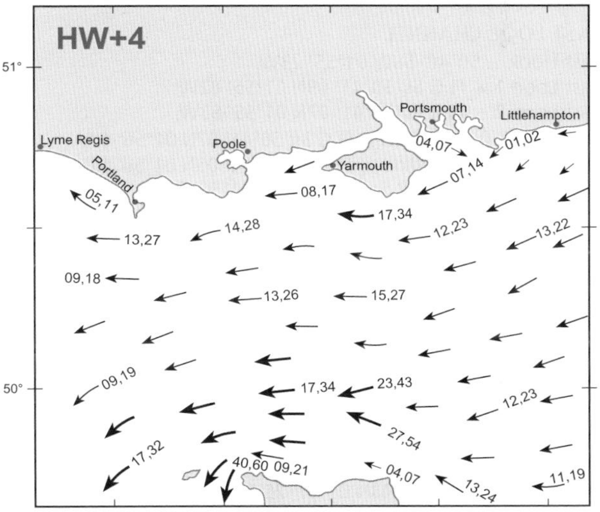
HW+4
51°
50°
Portsmouth
Littlehampton
Lyme Regis
Poole
Yarmouth
Portland
04,07
01,02
07,14
05,11
08,17
17,34
13,27
14,28
12,23
13,22
09,18
13,26
15,27
09,19
17,34
23,43
12,23
27,54
17,32
40,60
09,21
04,07
13,24
11,19
4 Hours after HW Dover

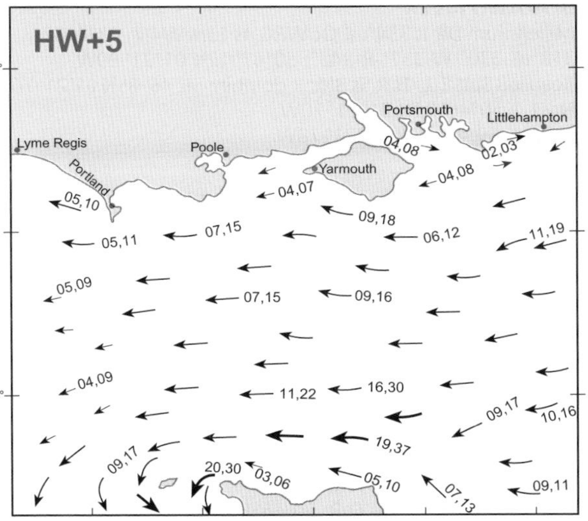
HW+5
51°
50°
Portsmouth
Littlehampton
Lyme Regis
Poole
Yarmouth
Portland
04,08
02,03
04,08
04,07
05,10
09,18
05,11
07,15
06,12
11,19
05,09
07,15
09,16
04,09
11,22
16,30
09,17
10,16
19,37
09,17
20,30
03,06
05,10
07,13
09,11
5 Hours after HW Dover

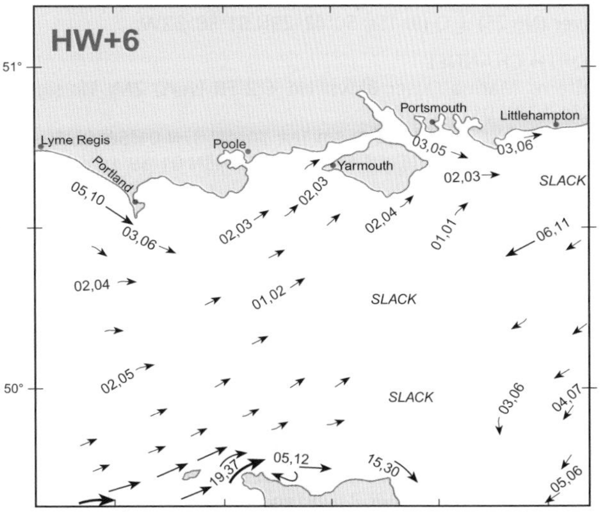
HW+6
51°
50°
Portsmouth
Littlehampton
Lyme Regis
Poole
Yarmouth
Portland
03,05
03,06
02,03
SLACK
05,10
02,03
02,03
02,04
01,01
03,06
06,11
02,04
01,02
SLACK
02,05
SLACK
03,06
04,07
19,37
05,12
15,30
05,06
6 Hours after HW Dover

9.2.4 LIGHTS, BUOYS AND WAYPOINTS

Bold print = light with a nominal range of 15M or more. CAPITALS = place or feature. *CAPITAL ITALICS* = light-vessel, light float or Lanby. *Italics* = Fog signal. ***Bold italics*** = Racon. Some marks/ buoys are fitted with AIS (MMSI No); see relevant charts.

SWANAGE TO ISLE OF WIGHT

SWANAGE

Pier Hd 2 FR (vert) 6m 3M; 50°36'·56N 01°56'·95W.
Peveril Ledge QR; 50°36'·41N 01°56'·10W.

POOLE BAR and SWASH CHANNEL

Poole Bar (No 1) QG; 50°39·29N 01°55'·14W.
(Historic wreck) Fl Y 5s; 50°39'·70N 01°54'·86W.
South Hook 50°39'·70N 01°55'·20W.
No 2 Fl R 2s; 50°39'·23N 01°55'·24W.
No 3 Fl G 3s; 50°39'·76N 01°55'·49W.
No 4 Fl R 2s; 50°39'·72N 01°55'·60W.
Training Bank 2 FR (vert); 50°39'·82N 01°55'·86W.
No 5 Fl G 5s; 50°40'·19N 01°55'·81W.
No 6 Fl R 4s; 50°40'·14N 01°55'·91W.
Hook Sands (No 7) Fl G 3s; 50°40'·50N 01°56'·16W.
Channel (No 8) Fl R 2s; 50°40'·45N 01°56'·27W.
Swash (No 9) Q (9) 15s; 50°40'·88N 01°56'·70W.
No 10 Fl R 4s; 50°40'·84N 01°56'·86W.

EAST LOOE CHANNEL

East Hook 50°40'·58W 01°55'·23W.
East Looe 1 Fl G 5s; 50°41'·09N 01°55'·82W.
East Looe 2 Fl R 4s; 50°41'·07N 01°55'·83W.
East Looe 3 (Limit 10kn) Fl G 3s; 50°41'·07N 01°56'·17W.
East Looe 4 (Limit 10kn) Fl R 2s; 50°41'·05N 01°56'·17W.
North Hook Fl (2) R 5s; 50°40'·97N 01°56'·51W.

BROWNSEA ROADS

No 12 Q R; 50°40'·94N 01°57'·17W.
No14 Fl R 2s; 50°41'·03N 01°57'·32W.
N Haven Q (9) 15s 5m; 50°41'·15N 01°57'·17W.
Brownsea Q (3) 10s; 50°41'·14N 01°57'·39W.
Brownsea Island Dir lt 299°F WRG; 296·5°-G-297·8°-AltWG-298·8°-W-299·2°-AltWR-300·2°-R-301·5°; 50°41'·16N 01°57'·67W (only shown for commercial vessels); 2FR(vert); 301·5°-296·5° (H24).

MIDDLE SHIP CHANNEL

Bell (No 15) Q (6) + L Fl 15s; 50°41'·36N 01°57'·12W.
No 16 VQ R; 50°41'·43N 01°57'·25W.
No 17 Fl G 3s; 50°41'·68N 01°57'·02W.
Aunt Betty (No 22) Q (3)10s; 50°41'·96N 01°57'·39W.
Diver (No 25) Q (9) 15s; 50°42'·29N 01°58'·32W.

NORTH CHANNEL

Salterns Marina Outer Bkwtr Hd 2 FR (vert) 2M; Tfc sigs; 50°42'·23N 01°57'·10W.
Parkstone YC platform Q 8m 1M; 50°42'·37N 01°58'·08W.
Stakes (No 29) Q (6) + L Fl 15s; 50°42'·43N 01°59'·00W.

POOLE BAY

Flag Hd Chine Fl (2); 50°41'·79N 01°55'·10W.
Bournemouth Rocks 50°42'·32N 01°53'·40W.
Christchurch Ledge 50°41'·57N 01°41'·55W (Apr-Oct).
(x2) Fl(5) Y 20s; 50°37'·98N 01°43'·02W; (265°Needles F'wy).

WESTERN APPROACHES TO THE SOLENT

NEEDLES CHANNEL

Needles Fairway L Fl 10s; *Bell*; 50°38'·24N 01°38'·98W.
SW Shingles Fl R 2·5s; 50°39'·29N 01°37'·52W.
Bridge VQ (9) 10s; ***Racon (T) 10M***; 50°39'·63N 01°36'·88W.
NEEDLES ☆ 50°39'·73N 01°35'·50W; Oc (2) WRG 20s 24m **W17M**, R14M, R13M G14M; ○ Twr, R band and lantern; vis: shore-R-300°-W-083°-R (unintens)-212°-W-217°-G-224° (H24). *Horn (2) 30s*.
Shingles Elbow Fl (2) R 5s; 50°40'·37N 01°36'·05W.
Mid Shingles Fl (3) R 10s; 50°41'·21N 01°34'·66W.
Warden Fl G 2·5s; *Bell*; 50°41'·48N 01°33'·55W.
NE Shingles Q (3) 10s; 50°41'·96N 01°33'·41W.

Hurst Point ☆ 50°42'·48N 01°33'·03W; FL (4) WR 15s 23m W13M, R11M; W ○ Twr; vis:080°-W(unintens)-104°, 234°-W-244°-R-250°- W-053°. Same structure, Iso WRG 4s 19m **W21M, R18M, G17M**; vis: 038·8°-G-040·8°-W-041·8°-R- 043·8°; By day W7M, R5M, G5M.

NORTH CHANNEL

North Head Fl (3) G 10s; 50°42'·69N 01°35'·52W.

THE WESTERN SOLENT

Note: Numerous yellow yacht racing buoys are laid throughout the Solent (seasonal, Mar-Dec). Most, but not all, are lit Fl Y 4s.

SOLENT MARKS

Sconce Q; *Bell*; 50°42'·53N 01°31'·43W.
Black Rock Fl G 5s; 50°42'·57N 01°30'·59W.
Lymington Bank Fl (2) R 5s; *Bell*; 50°43'·10N 01°30'·85W.
Solent Bank Fl (3) R 10s; 50°44'·23N 01°27'·37W.
Hamstead Ledge Fl (2) G 5s; 50°43'·87N 01°26'18W.
Newtown River Q (9) 15s; 50°43'·75N 01°24'·96W.
W Lepe Fl R 5s; 50°45'·24N 01°24'·09W.
Salt Mead Fl (3) G 10s; 50°44'·51N 01°23'·04W.
Gurnard Ledge Fl (4) G 15s; 50°45'·51N 01°20'·59W.
E Lepe Fl (2) R 5s; *Bell*; 50°45'·93N 01°21'·07W.
Lepe Spit Q (6) + L Fl 15s; 50°46'·78N 01°20'·64W.
Gurnard Q; 50°46'·22N 01°18'·84W.

YARMOUTH

East Fairway Fl R 2s; 50°42'·62N 01°29'·95W.
Poole Belle Fl Y 5s; 50°42'·54N 01°30'·17W.
Pier Head, centre, 2 FR (vert) 2M; G col. High intensity FW (occas); 50°42'·51N 01°29'·97W.
Ldg Lts 187·6° Front FG 5m 2M; 50°42'·36N 01°30'·06 W. Rear, 63m from front, FG 9m 2M; both W ◊.

LYMINGTON

Ldg Lts 319·5°, Or posts. Front, FR 12m 8M; 50°45'·19N 01°31'·65W. vis: 309·5°-329·5°. Rear, FR 17m 8M.
Jack in the Basket Fl R 2s 9m; 50°44'·27N 01°30'·57W.
No 1 Fl G 2s 2m 3M; G △ on pile; 50°44'·41N 01°30'·48W.
No 2 (Cross Boom) Fl R 2s 4m 3M; 50°44'·36N 01°30'·58W.
Yacht Haven ldg lts 244°. Front FY 4m; R △; 50°45'·09N 01°31'·53W. Rear, 22m from front, FY 6m; R ▽.

BEAULIEU RIVER

Millennium Dir lt 334°. Oc WRG 4s 13m W4M, R3M, G3M; vis: 318°-G-330°-W-337°-R-348°; 50°47'·12N 01°21'·90W.
Beaulieu Spit E Fl R 5s 3M; R dolphin; 50°46'·85N 01°21'·76W.
No 1 50°46'·91N 01°21'·70W.
No 2 50°46'·92N 01°21'·78W.

COWES

Prince Consort VQ; 50°46'·41N 01°17'·56W.
Trinity House Fl Y 5s; 50°46'·31N 01°17'·75W.
No 1 Q G; 50°46'·07N 01°18'·03W.
No 2 Q R; 50°46'·07N 01°17'·87W.
No 2A LFl R 10s; 50°45'·92N 01°17'·70W.
Tide gauge L Fl R 5s; 50°45'·78N 01°17'·66W.
E. Cowes Bkwtr Hd 2F R; 50°45'·88N 01°17'·52W.
Fl G 3s; 50°45'·91N 01°17'·55W.
Fl R 3s; 50°45'·89N 01°17'·53W.
Shrape Mud Fl G 5s; 50°46'·02N 01°17'·38W.
Fl R 5s; 50°46'·00N 01°17'·37W.
Boat Chan Ent Fl G 2s; 50°46'·08N 01°17'·05W.
Q R; 50°46'·06N 01°17'·04W.
Shrape Bn LFl R 10S 3m 3M; 50°46'·09N 01°16'·90W.

CENTRAL SOLENT AND SOUTHAMPTON WATER

Note: Numerous yellow yacht racing buoys are laid throughout the Solent (seasonal, Mar-Dec). Most, but not all, are lit Fl Y 4s.

SOLENT MARKS

Lepe Spit Q (6) + L Fl 15s; 50°46'·78N 01°20'·64W.
NE Gurnard Fl (3) R 10s; 50°47'·06N 01°19'·42W.
South Bramble Fl G 2·5s; 50°46'·98N 01°17'·72W.
W Bramble VQ (9) 10s; *Bell*; ***Racon (T) 3M***; 50°47'·20N 01°18'·65W; AIS.
Thorn Knoll Fl G 5s; 50°47'·50N 01°18'·44W.
Bourne Gap Fl R 3s; 50°47'·83N 01°18'·34W.
West Knoll Fl Y 2·5s; 50°47'·43N 01°17'·84W.
North Thorn QG; 50°47'·92N 01°17'·84W.
East Knoll Fl (2) G 10s; 50°47'·96N 01°16'·86W.
Stanswood Outfall Iso R 10s 6m 5M; 4 FR Lts; 50°48'·26N 01°18'·82W.

CALSHOT REACH

East Knoll 50°47'·96N 01°16'·83W.
CALSHOT SPIT Fl 5s 5m 10M; R hull, Lt Twr amidships; *Horn (2) 60s*; 50°48'·35N 01°17'·64W.
Calshot VQ; *Bell*; 50°48'·44N 01°17'·03W.
Castle Point IQ R 10s; 50°48'·71N 01°17'·67W.
Reach Fl (3) G 10s; 50°49'·05N 01°17'·65W .
Black Jack Fl (2) R 4s; 50°49'·13N 01°18'·09W.
Hook QG; *Horn (1) 15s*; 50°49'·52N 01°18'·30W.
Coronation Fl Y 5s; 50°49'·55N 01°17'·62W.
Bald Head Fl G 2·5s; 50°49'·80N 01°18'·06W.

RIVER HAMBLE

Hamble Pt Q (6) + L Fl 15s; 50°50'·15N 01°18'·66W.
Hamble Common Dir 351·7°, Oc (2) WRG 12s 5m W4M; R4M; G4M; vis: 348·7°-G-350·7°-W-352·7°-R-354·7°; 50°51'·00N 01°18'·84W.
Sailing Club Dir lt 028·9° Iso WRG 6s 5m W4M, R4M, G4M: vis: 025·9°-G-027·9°-W-029·9°-R-031·9°; 50°51'·10N 01°18'·34W.

SOUTHAMPTON WATER

Fawley Terminal SE 2 FR(vert) 9m 10M; 50°50'·06N 01°19'·42W.
Fawley Deep Fl (2) G 4s; 50°50'·42N 01°19'·19W.
Greenland Iso G 2s; 50°51'·11N 01°20'·38W.
Cadland Fl R 3s; 50°51'·02N 01°20'·54W.
After Barn Fl (2) G 4s; 50°51'·53N 01°20'·81W.
Lains Lake Fl (2) R 4s; 50°51'·59N 01°21'·65W.
Hound Fl (3) G 10s; 50°51'·68N 01°21'·52W.
Netley Fl G 3s; 50°52'·03N 01°21'·81W.
Deans Elbow Oc R 4s; 50°52'·20N 01°22'·85W.
NW Netley Q G; 50°52'·31N 01°22'·73W.
Moorhead Q G; 50°52'·55N 01°22'·90W.
Test Fl (2) R 4s; 50°52'·59N 01°23'·45W.
Weston Shelf Fl (2) G 4s; 50°52'·71N 01°23'·26W.

HYTHE

Hythe Pier Hd 2 FR (vert) 12m 5M; 50°52'·49N 01°23'·61W.
Hythe Marina Ent Q (3) 10s; 50°52'·63N 01°23'·88W.
Hythe Knock Fl R 3s; 50°52'·83N 01°23'·81W.

SOUTHAMPTON and RIVER ITCHEN

Swinging Ground No 1 Oc G 4s; 50°53'·00N 01°23'·44W.
E side. No 1 QG; 50°53'·15N 01°23'·40W.
No 2 Fl G 5s 2M; 50°53'·29N 01°23'·38W.
No 3 Fl G 7s; 50°53'·48N 01°23'·28W.
No 4 QG 4m 2M; 50°53'·62N 01°23'·16W.

SOUTHAMPTON and RIVER TEST

Queen Elizabeth II Terminal, S end 4 FG (vert) 16m 3M; 50°53'·00N 01°23'·71W.
Gymp QR; 50°53'·07N 01°24'·16W.
Town Quay Ldg Lts 329°, both F 12/22m 3/2M.
Gymp Elbow Oc R 4s; 50°53'·43N 01°24'·61W.
Dibden Bay Q; 50°53'·70N 01°24'·92W.

THE EASTERN SOLENT

Note: Numerous yellow yacht racing buoys are laid throughout the Solent (seasonal, Mar-Dec). Most, but not all, are lit Fl Y 4s.

SOLENT MARKS

West Ryde Middle Q (9) 15s; 50°46'·48N 01°15'·79W.
Norris Fl (3) R 10s; 50°45'·97N 01°15'·51W.
North Ryde Middle Fl (4) R 20s; 50°46'·61N 01°14'·31W.
South Ryde Middle Fl G 5s; 50°46'·13N 01°14'·16W.
Peel Bank Fl (2) R 5s; 50°45'·49N 01°13'·35W.
SE Ryde Middle VQ (6)+L Fl 10s; 50°45'·93N 01°12'·10W.
NE Ryde Middle Fl (2) R 10s; 50°46'·21N 01°11'·88W.
Mother Bank Fl R 3s; 50°45'·49N 01°11'·21W.
Browndown Fl G 15s; 50°46'·57N 01°10'·95W.
Fort Gilkicker Oc G 10s 7M; 50°46'·43N 01°08'·47W.
N Sturbridge VQ; 50°45'·33N 01°08'·23W.
Ryde Sands Fl R 10s; 50°44'·56N 01°07'·26W.
Ryde Sands L Fl R 12s; 50°44'·16N 01°05'·99W.
No Man's Land Fort Iso R 2s 21m 8M; 50°44'·40N 01°05'·70W.
Horse Sand Fort Iso G 2s 21m 8M; 50°45'·01N 01°04'·34W.
Saddle VQ (3) G 10s; 50°45'·05N 01°04'·94W.

NORTH CHANNEL and HILLHEAD

Calshot VQ; *Bell (1) 30s*; 50°48'·44N 01°17'·03W.
Hillhead Fl R 2·5s; 50°48'·07N 01°16'·00W.
E Bramble VQ (3) 5s; 50°47'·23N 01°13'·64W.

WOOTTON CREEK

Wootton Beacon Q 1M; (NB); 50°44'·53N 01°12'·13W.
Dir lt. Oc WRG 10s vis: 220·8°-G-224·3°-W-225·8°-R-230·8°; 50°44'·03N 01°12'·86W.

RYDE

Ryde Pier , NW corner, N and E corner marked by 2 FR (vert). In fog FY from N corner, vis: 045°-165°, 200°-320°; 50°44'·34N 01°09'·72W.
Leisure Hbr E side 2 FR (vert) 7m 1M. FY 6m shown when depth of water in Hbr greater than 1m; 2 FY 6m when depth exceeds 1·5m; 50°43'·99N 01°09'·29W.

PORTSMOUTH APPROACHES

Horse Sand Fl G 2·5s; 50°45'·53N 01°05'·27W.
Outer Spit (OSB) Q (6) + L Fl 15s; 50°45'·40N 01°05'·54W.
Mary Rose Fl Y 5s; 50°45'·80N 01°06'·20W.
Boyne Fl G 5s; 50°46'·15N 01°05'·26W.
Spit Refuge Fl R 5s; 50°46'·15N 01°05'·46W.
Spit Sand Fort Fl R 5s; 18m 7M. 50°46'·24N 01°05'·94W.
Castle (NB) Fl (2) G 6s; 50°46'·45N 01°05'·38W.
Southsea S Castle Pile Dir 348° WRG 17m 11M day 6M, pile vis: 340°-FG-343°-Al WG (W phase inc with brg)-347°-FW-349°-AlWR(R phase incr with brg)-354°-FR-356°; H24; same structure Fl G 5s; 50°46'·66N 01°05'·65W.
Ridge Fl (2) R 6s; 50°46'·44N 01°05'·65W.
No 1 Bar (NB) Fl (3) G 10s; 50°46'·77N 01°05'·81W.
No 2 Fl (3) R 10s; 50°46'·69N 01°05'·97W.
No 3 QG; 50°47'·08N 01°06'·24W.
No 4 QR; 50°47'·01N 01°06'·36W.
BC Outer Oc R 15s; 50°47'·32N 01°06'·68W.

PORTSMOUTH HARBOUR

Fort Blockhouse Dir 323° WRG 4s 6m WRG 12M; vis: 313°- Oc G-317°-Fl G (phase dec with brg)-321°-Oc W-325°-Fl R (phase inc with brg)-329°-Oc R-333°; 50°47'·37N 01°06'·74W.
Ballast Fl R 2·5s; 50°47'·62N 01°06'·83W.
Hbr Ent Dir 333·75° WRG 2s 2m 12M; vis: 323·75°-Iso G-329·75°-Fl G (phase dec with brg)-332·75°-Iso (main chan)-334·75°-Fl R (phase inc with brg)-337·75°-Iso R-343·75°; H24; same structure
Fuel Jetty 2F R (vert) 8m 4M; 50°47'·85N 01°06'·98W.

EASTERN APPROACHES to THE SOLENT

Outer Nab 1 VQ (9) 10s; 50°38'·18N 00°56'·88W.

Outer Nab 2 VQ (3) 5s; 50°38′·43N 00°57′·70W.
Nab Tower Fl 10s 17m 12M; *Horn (2) 30s; RACON T;* 50°40′·08N 00°57′·15W; 992351136.
N 2 Fl Y 2·5s. 6M; 50°41′·03N 00°56′·74W.
N 1 Fl Y (4)10s; 50°41′·26N 00°56′·52W.
N 4 Fl Y 7·5s; 50°41′·86N 00°57′·24W.
N 3 Fl (3) Y 15s; 50°41′·63N 00°56′·74W.
N 5 Fl Y 5s; 50°41′·99N 00°56′·97W.
N 7 Fl Y 2·5s; 50°42′·35N 00°57′·20W.
New Grounds VQ (3) 5s; 50°41′·84N 00°58′·49W.
Nab End Fl R 5s; *Whis*; 50°42′·63N 00°59′·49W.
Dean Tail Fl G 5s; 50°42′·99N 00°59′·17W.
Dean Tail S VQ (6) + L Fl 10s; 50°43′·04N 00°59′·58W.
Dean Tail N Q; 50°43′·13N 00°59′·57W.
Horse Tail Fl (2) G 10s; 50°43′·23N 01°00′·23W.
Nab East Fl (2) R 10s; 50°42′·86N 01°00′·80W.
Dean Elbow Fl (3) G 15s; 50°43′·69N 01°01′·88W.
St Helens Fl (3) R 15s; 50°43′·36N 01°02′·41W.
Horse Elbow QG; 50°44′·26N 01°03′·88W.
Cambrian Wreck 50°44′·43N 01°03′·43W.
Warner QR; *Whis*; 50°43′·87N 01°03′·99W.

BEMBRIDGE
St Helen's Fort ☆ (IOW) Fl (3) 10s 16m 8M; large ○ stone structure; 50°42′·30N 01°05′·05W.

SOUTH EAST COAST of the ISLE OF WIGHT
St Catherine's Point ☆ 50°34′·54N 01°17′·87W; Fl 5s 41m **25M**; vis: 257°-117°; FR 35m 13M (same Twr) vis: 099°-116°.
Ventnor Haven W Bwtr 2 FR (vert) 3M; 50°35′·50N 01°12′·30W.
Sandown Pier Hd 2 FR (vert) 7m 2M; 50°39′·05N 01°09′·18W.
W Princessa Q (9) 15s; 50°40′·16N 01°03′·65W.
Bembridge Ledge Q (3) 10s; 50°41′·15N 01°02′·81W

LANGSTONE and APPROACHES
Eastney Pt Fraser Trials Range FR, Oc (2) Y 10s, and FY Lts (occas) when firing taking place; 50°47′·19N 01°02′·22W.
Winner ; 50°45′·10N 01°00′·10W.
Roway Wk Fl (2) 5s; 50°46′·11N 01°02′·28W.
Langstone Fairway L Fl 10s; 50°46′·32N 01°01′·36W.
Eastney Pt Outfall QR 2m 2M; 50°47′·23N 01°01′·68W.
East Milton Fl (4) R 10s; 50°48′·16N 01°01′·76W.
NW Sinah Fl G 5s; 50°48′·14N 01°01′·58W.

CHICHESTER ENTRANCE
West Pole (tripod) Fl R 5s 14m 7M; 50°45′·45N 00°56′·59W.
Bar Fl(2) R 10s 10m 4M; 50°45′·92N 00°56′·46W.
Eastoke QR; 50°46′·68N 00°56′·11W.
West Winner QG; Tide gauge. 50°46′·88N 00°55′·98W.

EMSWORTH CHANNEL
Fishery Q (6) + L Fl 15s; 50°47′·38N 00°56′·07W.
NW Pilsey Fl G 5s; 50°47′·50N 00°56′·20W.
Verner Fl R 10s; 50°48′·20N 00°56′·63W.
Marker Pt Fl (2) G 10s 8m; 50°48′·91N 00°56′·72W.
Emsworth Q (6) + L Fl 15s; tide gauge; 50°49′·66N 00°56′·76W.

THORNEY CHANNEL
Camber Q (6) + L Fl 15s; 50°47′·87N 00°54′·06W.
Pilsey Fl (2) R 10s ; 50°47′·98N 00°54′·24W.
Thorney Fl G 5s; 50°48′·20N 00°54′·28W.

CHICHESTER CHANNEL
NW Winner Fl G 10s; 50°47′·19N 00°55′·92W.
N Winner Fl (2) G 10s; 50°47′·31N 00°55′·83W.
Mid Winner Fl (3) G 10s; 50°47′·40N 00°55′·72W.
Stocker Fl (3) R 10s; 50°47′·45N 00°55′·52W.
Copyhold Fl (4) R 10s; 50°47′·50N 00°54′·93W.
East Head Spit Fl (4) G 10s; 50°47′·45N 00°54′·82W.
Snowhill Fl G 5s; 50°47′·52N 00°54′·34W.
Sandhead Fl R 10s; 50°47′·67N 00°54′·25W.
Chalkdock Fl (2) G 10s; 50°48′·49N 00°53′·30W.

9.2.5 PASSAGE INFORMATION
More passage information is threaded between the harbours in this area. See 9.0.5 for distances across the central part of the English Channel. Admiralty Leisure Folio 5601 covers Exmouth to Christchurch, and 5600 covers The Solent & Approaches. **Bibliography:** *Channel Havens* (ACN/Endean); *Shell Channel Pilot* (Imray/Cunliffe); *Channel Pilot* (Admiralty NP27).

CROSSING THE ENGLISH CHANNEL – CENTRAL PART
(AC 2656) These notes cover the crossing (about 13hrs) Weymouth/Poole/Solent to Channel Is/Cherbourg/Le Havre and should help in compiling a cross-Channel passage plan. Distances are tabulated in 9.0.5.

Departure and destination factors to be considered include:

Portland/Weymouth: Good angle on the wind in SW/lies but passage extended by 7/8½M respectively to clear the E end of The Shambles Bank. There is no advantage to closing Portland Bill and Portland Race which should be avoided. Portland Bill Light loom provides a good headmark on night N'ly crossing. Check the tidal streams and monitor course made good.

Poole: Leave on the ebb. At springs with a S/SE wind beware short steep seas in the Swash Channel. Studland Bay or Swanage Roads are useful departure ⚓s. Anvil Pt Light and the Ferries provide useful visual cues on N'ly crossing. Off Handfast, Peveril and Anvil Pts overfalls occur with wind against tide.

Solent ports: Decide whether to leave to the East via Nab Tower, using the tide to gain a lift on the ebb past Bembridge Ledge and across St Catherine's Deep or west via the Needles.

▶*The latter usually requires a fair tide through Hurst Narrows (HW Portsmouth –0100 to +0430) which dictates the ETD.* ◀

The Easterly option has no tidal gate, but is longer if heading to Cherbourg or the Channel Islands and gives a less favourable angle on a SW'ly wind. It can offer better shelter initially in the lee of the IoW, but often has an uncomfortable chop especially on a return passage. Loom of St Catherine's and the Needles are useful guides at night, but can be deceptively far away.

Braye (Alderney) is accessible at all times, but allowance must be made to avoid being swept W to the Casquets at springs. Plan and monitor the track so as to approach from well up-tide. Braye Hbr is unsafe in fresh or strong E/NE'lies. From Braye you may make Guernsey, having negotiated the Alderney Race, or the Swinge. A direct passage is achievable off the Casquets or in benign conditions through Ortac Channel.

Cherbourg is accessible H24. Especially at springs, aim well up-tide and approaching the peninsula allow a large offset angle to maintain track. Harbours on the W side of the Cotentin (**Diélette** to **Granville**) are tidally constrained and exposed to the W but are options in E'lies if conditions in the Alderney Race permit on a W-going ebb tide or at slack water.

To the E, **Barfleur** and **St Vaast** are sheltered from the prevailing W'lies, but are tidally constrained. Barfleur dries and yachts off St Vaast until the marina gates open. Further to the E **Le Havre** is a port of refuge although approach requires care.

Thorough planning is a requirement for a safe and efficient crossing. Refer to panel on next page and 3.1, Passage Planning.

- Study the meteorological situation several days before departure so that advantageous wind and weather windows may be predicted and bad weather avoided.
- High pressure may provide quiescent conditions, but is often accompanied by reduced visibility owing to fog. Even if radar equipped and competent in its use, be wary of crossing if fog or poor visibility is forecast.
- For a yacht, consider the forecast wind direction, likely shifts and sea breezes which may affect the angle on the wind. Prevailing winds are SW/W, except in the spring when NE/E winds are equally likely. Check the tidal stream and the effect that this will have on Course to Steer. It is best to place the tide on the lee bow in order to gain the maximum benefit. It is very advantageous to get well to windward and up-tide of the destination. For example, from the Needles it may be beneficial initially to proceed W'wards, working the tides to advantage.
- For motor boats, windows with the wind in the N provide the best down sea conditions, maximising speed and reducing slamming.
- Choose the route, departure points and landfalls so that passage time out of sight of identifiable marks is minimised. This reduces the risk of navigational errors, anxiety and fatigue. A landfall at night or dawn/dusk is frequently easier due to the visibility of navigational marks on clear nights. The loom of a powerful lighthouse is often visible on the clouds at a distance greater than its nominal range.
- Consider tidal constraints at the points of departure and destination, and any tidal gates en route such as Hurst Narrows or the French coast between Cap Barfleur and Cap de la Hague.

▶ *Calculate the hourly direction/rate of tidal streams expected during the crossing so as to lay off the total drift angle required to make good the desired track. Rarely do 6 hrs of E-going tide cancel out 6 hrs of W-going (or vice versa); streams off the French coast are usually stronger. Note times and areas of races/overfalls and keep well clear.* ◀

- Consider actions to be taken if fog sets in as the risk of collision is much increased. GPS may provide a position, but navigating 'blind' by radar demands intense attention. Other small boats and yachts may not be detected.
- AIS will only display vessels or marks which transmit.
- Cross on a heading as near 90° as practicable to the Traffic Routeing between the Casquets TSS and the Greenwich Meridian. Consider motoring to expedite such a crossing.
- Keep a very sharp lookout particularly when in the Traffic Routeing area in mid-Channel. Ensure the crew is aware of the directions from which to expect approaching traffic. It is commonsense and good seamanship to alter course early in order to keep well clear of large commercial ships. These may not alter for a small craft despite Rule 18 (a) (iv).
- Make use of additional navigational information such as soundings, noting when crossing distinctive seabed contours; the rising or dipping ranges of major lights; if equipped with radar, use clearly identifiable targets.
- Plan a harbour of refuge in case of fog, bad weather, accident or gear failure. For example, if unable to make Cherbourg in a strong SSW'ly and E-going tide, consider bearing away for St Vaast in the lee of the peninsula. Alternatively, in the event of engine failure identify a sheltered ⚓. In extremis heave to and stay at sea notifying the appropriate CG or safety service.

9.2.6 SWANAGE

Dorset **50°36´·70N 01°56´·55W**

CHARTS AC 5601, 2615, 2172; Imray C10, C12, C4, 2300

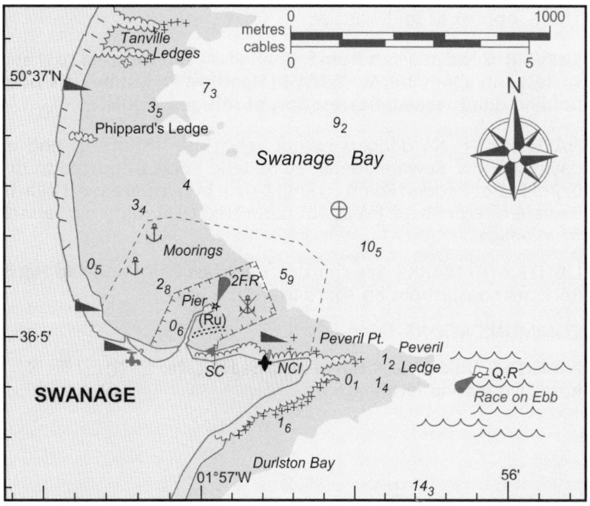

TIDES HW Sp –0235 & +0125, Np –0515 & +0120 on Dover; ML 1·5

Standard Port POOLE HARBOUR (⟶)

Times				**Height (metres)**			
High Water		Low Water		MHWS	MHWN	MLWN	MLWS
—	—	0500	1100	2·2	1·7	1·2	0·6
—	—	1700	2300				
Differences SWANAGE							
—	—	–0045	–0050	–0·1	+0·1	+0·2	+0·2

NOTE: From Swanage to Christchurch double HWs occur except at neaps. HW differences refer to the higher HW and are approximate.

SHELTER Large, well sheltered bay with just 1·6m range at springs. 12 ⓥs, good ⚓ in all winds except from NE to SE; Poole is closest port of refuge. ⊇ may be possible on the pier which is owned by a trust and used extensively in the summer by tourist boats, ferries and other commercial concerns. Seek advice at the gate on arrival. Gate closes at dusk Oct to Apr.

NAVIGATION WPT 50°36´·70N 01°56´·55W, 240°/0.3M to Pier Hd. Tidal races off Peveril Point to the south and Handfast Point to the north can be lively in strong onshore winds and an ebb tide. Do not cut inside Peveril Ledge buoy.

Beware of ruins of old pier south of the main pier; Tanville and Phippard's Ledges in west side of bay both dry. At night, main hazard is other boats which may be difficult to see against background lights.

LIGHTS AND MARKS 2 FR (vert) on the Pier, difficult to see due to back scatter of street lights. Peveril Ledge PHM buoy, Q.R, but can be hard to pick out by day.

COMMUNICATIONS (Code 01929) NMOC (01305) 760439; Police 101; Dr 422231; Ⓗ 422202; Pier 427058. Moorings/water taxi mob 07802 480139. No VHF.

FACILITIES 12 ⓥs £10/boat<40'; Water taxi (May-Oct) £2pp return. **Pier** Possible⊇; **Swanage SC** ☎422987 **Boat Park** (Peveril Pt) **Services:** Diving. **Town** (1½M) Ⓑ ✕ ⇌ (bus to Wareham and Bournemouth), ✈ (Hurn).

9.2.7 STUDLAND BAY

Dorset **50°38'·80N 01°55'·50W**

CHARTS AC 5601, 2175, 2172; Imray C4

TIDES Approx as for Swanage.

SHELTER Good in winds from S, W and NW, but exposed to N and E. Best ⚓ in about 3m, 4ca WNW of Handfast Pt, but beware poor holding due to weed. Nearest port of refuge is Poole.

NAVIGATION No dangers except very close inshore; N end of bay is shallow. Beware unmarked Redend Rocks (reported to dry 0·5m) ESE of Redend Point. Sp limit 5kn in buoyed areas off beach. Beware of swimmers. PWCs not permitted to land on nor launch from beach.

LIGHTS AND MARKS See chartlet. Handfast Point and Old Harry Rock are conspicuous on approach to the bay.

COMMUNICATIONS None.

FACILITIES **Village** at tap behind beach cafe, hotel. No marine facilities.

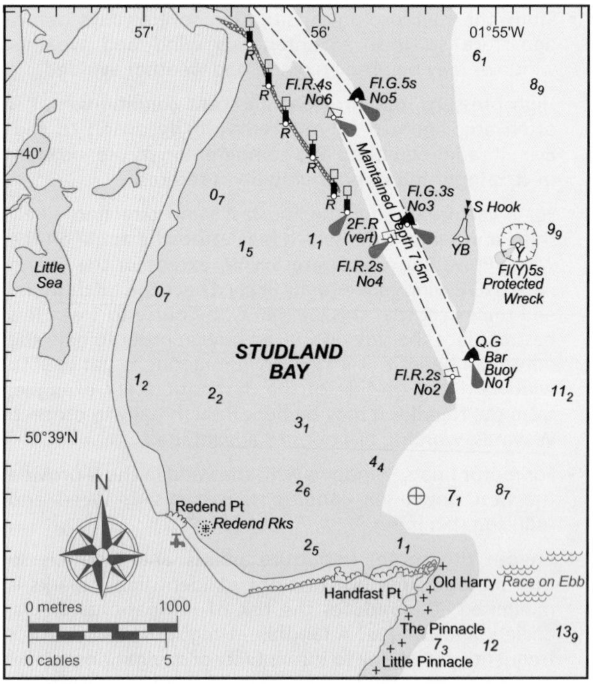

9.2.8 POOLE HARBOUR

Dorset **50°40'·93N 01°56'·96W** (Ent)

CHARTS AC 5601, 2175, 2611; Imray C10, C12, C4, Y23, 2300

TIDES Town Quay ML 1·6. The tide is above ML from about LW+2 to next LW–2.

Standard Port POOLE HARBOUR (⟶)

Times				Height (metres)			
High Water		Low Water		MHWS	MHWN	MLWN	MLWS
—	—	0500	1100	2·2	1·7	1·2	0·6
—	—	1700	2300				
Differences POOLE HARBOUR ENTRANCE							
—	—	–0025	–0010	0·0	0·0	0·0	0·0
POTTERY PIER							
—	—	+0010	+0010	–0·2	0·0	+0·1	+0·2
CLEAVEL POINT							
—	—	–0005	–0005	–0·1	–0·2	0·0	–0·1
WAREHAM (River Frome)							
—	—	+0130	+0045	0·0	0·0	0·0	+0·3

Daily predictions of the times and heights of HW/LW are for the Standard Port of **POOLE HARBOUR** (near the Ro-Ro terminal). Double HWs occur except at neaps. The height of the 2nd HW is always about 1·8m; the height of the 1st HW varies from springs to neaps. The listed time of HW refers to the highest of the two.

Strong and continuous winds from E to SW may raise sea levels by as much as 0·2m; W to NE winds may lower levels by 0·1m. Barometric pressure can affect the tide by as much as 0·3m. At Wareham the height of LW does not usually fall below 0·7m.

SHELTER An excellent natural harbour with a narrow entrance. Accessible in all conditions, the entrance can become very rough, especially on the ebb in E/SE gales. Yachts may berth at the marinas listed under Facilities. The Town Quay, very exposed in strong E/SE winds, is used by yachts >15m and by arrangement with the Boat Haven. At busy periods yachts may be rafted several deep or allocated a berth in the Port of Poole Marina. Good ⚓s may be found wherever sheltered from the wind and clear of channels, moorings and shellfish beds, especially clear of the buoyed fairways in South Deep and off Pottery Pier (W end of Brownsea Island) or off Shipstal Point, about 1·3M west of Pottery Pier. All are within a Quiet Area (see chartlet and speed limits).

NAVIGATION WPT Poole Bar (No 1 SHM) Buoy, QG, 50°39'·29N 01°55'·14W, 328°/1·95M to Haven Hotel. In very strong SE-S winds the Bar is dangerous, especially on the ebb. Beware cross-Channel high speed ferries which operate through the area. Monitor VHF Ch 14 for information about commercial traffic and MOD activity. In Studland Bay and close to training bank beware lobster pots. From Poole Bar to Shell Bay a **Boat Channel**, suitable for craft <3m draught, parallels the W side of the Swash Channel, close E of the Training Bank, and should be used whenever possible.

East Looe Channel The well lit and buoyed channel, least depth 1.3m, is the recommended approach from the E when height of tide allows. It is liable to shift and the buoys moved accordingly. Check LNTMs from www.phc.co.uk; there may be less water than charted. The groynes to the N are marked by SHM beacons, the two most W'ly are lit, 2 FG (vert).

Within the harbour the two principal channels (Middle Ship and North) lead up to Poole Town Quay. Outside of these there are extensive shoal or drying areas.

Middle Ship Chan is dredged to 7·5m depth and 105m width for ferries and commercial shipping to/from the Continental Freight and Ferry Terminal. Vessels designated 'controlled movements' have moving exclusion zones which must be avoided. Small craft should use the **Boat Channel** which runs parallel to the main channel between the PHM buoys and the unlit beacons further S which mark the edge of the bank. Depth is 2·0m in this channel, but 1·5m closer to the stakes. Caution: When large ferries pass, a temporary but significant reduction in depth may be experienced; it is then prudent to keep close to the PHM buoys.

North Channel is no longer routinely dredged but remains usable for leisure craft; the best water is on the outside of channel bends.

Lulworth gunnery range. Prior to proceeding W all craft should check for activity, as shown in the HM's office and in the Updates to this Almanac.

LIGHTS AND MARKS See chartlet and 9.2.4 for main buoys, beacons and lights.

Poole Bridge traffic lights, shown from bridge tower:

- ● (3 vert Fl) = Emergency stop. Do not proceed
- ● (3 vert) = Do not proceed past the signal
- ● + 3 ● vert = Vessels may proceed with caution
- ● (3 vert) = Vessels may proceed

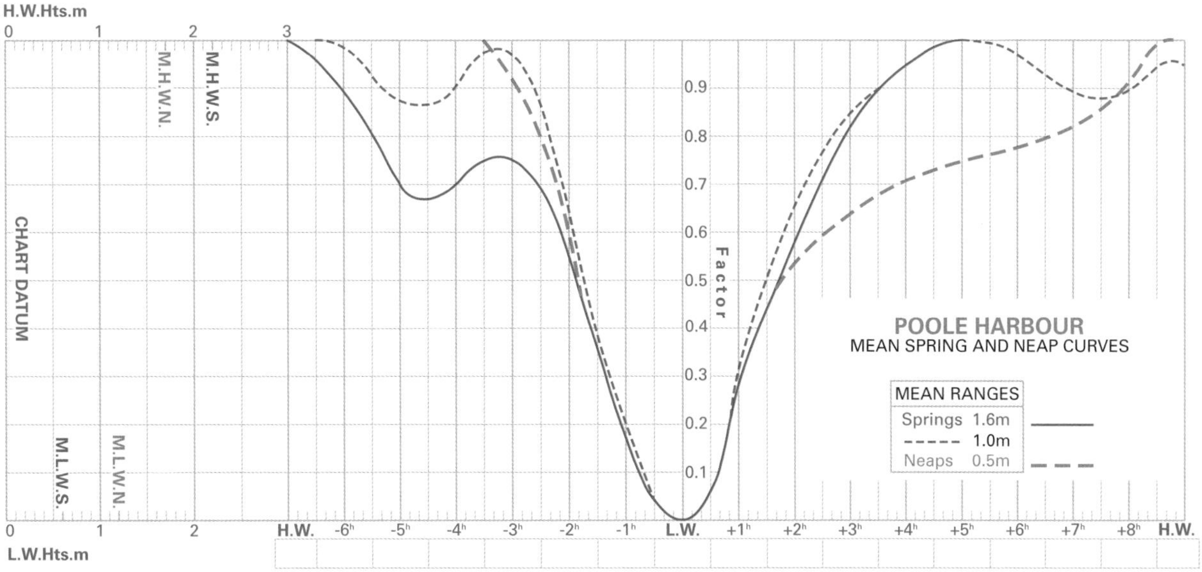

POOLE BRIDGES SUMMER SCHEDULE:

Poole Bridge and the new Twin Sails Bridge co-ordinate openings with *scheduled times* at which vessels are advised to be on station. The timings are biased to outbound traffic am, and inbound pm. The second bridge will open asap after the first, which may open again to release traffic left between the closed bridges. Daily:

Twin Sail: 0530, 0630, 0730, 0930, 1030, 1130, 1230, 1430.

Poole Br: *ASAP thereafter.*

Poole Br: 1530,1630, 1830, 1930, 2130, 2230, 2330.

Twin Sail: *ASAP thereafter*.

+ Sat/Sun: Twin sail: 0830, 1330. Poole Br: 1730, 2030.

Pleasure craft may pass when bridges open for commercial traffic. Timings at www.phc.co.uk. Monitor Ch 12 for more information.

COMMUNICATIONS (Code 01202) NMOC (01305) 760439; Police 101; Ⓗ 665511. HM 440233; *Poole Hbr Control* 440230, Poole Bridge 674115.

VHF Ch **14** 16 (H24), *Poole Bridge* Ch12. Poole Quay Boat Haven, Cobbs Quay (call *CQ Base*) Ch 80; Salterns Marina Ch M 80; Parkstone Haven, Poole YC Haven (*Pike*), Dorset Yacht Co Ch M.

FACILITIES **Marinas** from seaward (harbour dues are usually included, but best to check):

Salterns Marina marina@salterns.co.uk ☎709971, max draught 2·5m, 300 few**Ⓥ**, £3·50/m, short stay £1/m, (H24) Ⓔ (5t) (45t) . Appr from North Channel near NC 7 SHM buoy, Fl G 3s.

Parkstone YC Haven ☎743610 (Parkstone YC). Access from North Channel near NC 11 SHM buoy, Fl G 3s. Approach chan, dredged 2·5m, is marked by PHM and SHM unlit buoys. Ldg daymarks 006°, both Y ◊s. Some **Ⓥ** berths, £4·00; dredged 2m.

Poole Quay Boat Haven poolequayboathaven.co.uk ☎649488. max draught 3·0m, 100**Ⓥ** £4·07 £3/day; short stay <4hrs £6·50<10m, £12·50<20m. . Office hrs 0700-2200 Apr-Sep.

Town Quay (£2·78) **& Port of Poole Marina** ☎660120 by arrangement.

Lake Yard Marina www.lakeyard.com ☎674531. Ent marked by 2FR (vert) and 2FG (vert). £1·30, 56+**Ⓥ** if space £3·20, (5t) (50t) Club: ; Water taxi, weekends Apr-Oct.

Sunseeker International Marina ☎685335, 50 (30t) (36t) .

Cobbs Quay Marina ☎674299, 850 some **Ⓥ** £3·25, LPG Ⓔ (10t) .

Swinging moorings in Poole Harbour £15, contact PHC through the Boat Haven.

Public Landing Places: Steps at Poole Quay. **Public :** Baiter Harbourside Park, car/trailer parking – machine payment.

Services A complete range of marine services is available; consult marina/HM for exact locations. **Fuel**: Corrals (S side of Poole Quay adjacent bridge) .

Town All domestic facilities, ≉ ✈ (Bournemouth 12M and Southampton by direct rail link). **Ferries**:

Cherbourg: 2-3/day; 4½hrs (HSS 2¼hrs); Brittany (www. brittany-ferries.co.uk);

St Malo/Jersey/Guernsey: 2/day HSS; 2¾–4½hrs; Condor (www. condorferries.co.uk).

YACHT CLUBS

Royal Motor YC ☎707227, .
Parkstone YC ☎743610 (Parkstone Haven).
Poole YC ☎672687.

REGULATIONS

The following speed limits are strictly enforced:

- **10kn** speed limit applies to the entire harbour.
- **8kn** speed limit applies within 200m of the beach from S Haven Pt NE'wards through E Looe Channel to Flag Head Chine.
- **6kn** speed limit applies from Stakes SCM past Poole Quay and Poole Bridge up to Cobbs Quay in Holes Bay. It is also an advisory speed limit within the S half of the harbour which is designated as a Quiet Area (see chartlet).
- **4kn** speed limit applies within the Poole Quay Boat Haven.

Exemptions The 10kn speed limit does not apply:

- From 1 Oct to 31 Mar to vessels in the North, Middle Ship and Wareham Channels only.
- To water-skiers within the water-ski area between Gold Pt and No 82 PHM buoy (Wareham Channel; see chartlet). Permits must be obtained from the HM.
- Personal Water Craft (PWC) operating in a designated area N of Brownsea Island must not enter the Quiet Area in the S of the harbour, nor linger in the harbour entrance. Permits must be obtained from the HM.

Sandbanks Chain Ferry has right of way over all vessels not carrying a Pilot. It exhibits a B ● above the control cabin when it is about to leave the slipway. A flashing white strobe light is exhibited in the leading direction when the engines are engaged. In fog it sounds 1 long and 2 short blasts every 2 mins. When stationary at night it shows a FW lt; in fog it rings a bell for 5s every 60s.

POOLE HARBOUR *continued*

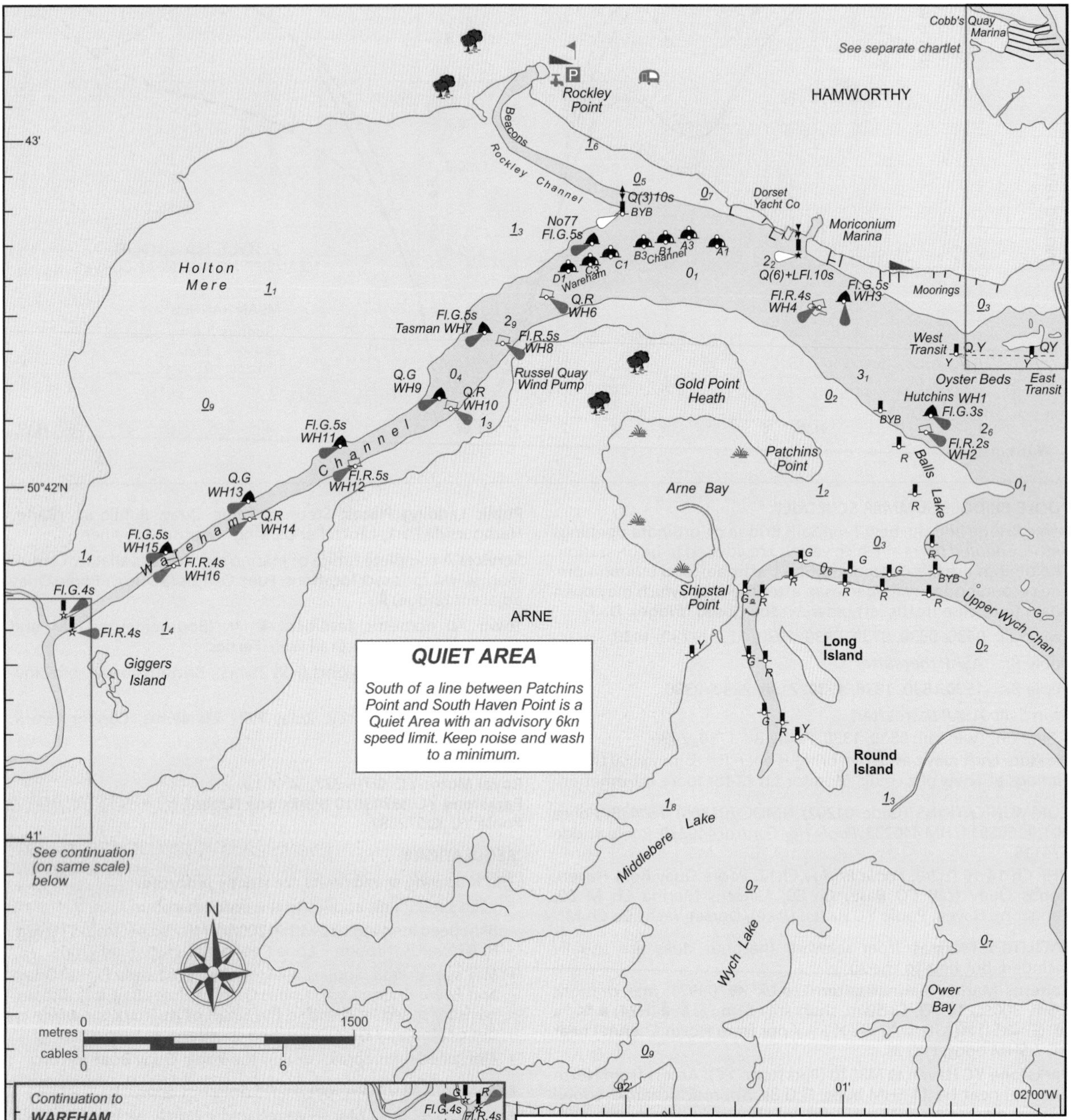
Cobb's Quay Marina
See separate chartlet
Rockley Point
HAMWORTHY
43'
Beacons
Rockley Channel
Q(3)10s
BYB
Dorset Yacht Co
Moriconium Marina
No77
Fl.G.5s
Wareham Channel
Holton Mere
Q(6)+LFl.10s
Fl.G.5s WH3
Fl.R.4s WH4
Moorings
Q.R WH6
Fl.G.5s
Tasman WH7
Fl.R.5s WH8
West Transit
Q.Y
QY
Oyster Beds
East Transit
Russel Quay Wind Pump
Gold Point Heath
Q.G WH9
Q.R WH10
Hutchins WH1
Fl.G.3s
Fl.R.2s WH2
Fl.G.5s WH11
Patchins Point
Balls Lake
Fl.R.5s WH12
50°42'N
Q.G WH13
Arne Bay
Q.R WH14
Fl.G.5s WH15
Fl.R.4s WH16
Shipstal Point
Upper Wych Chan
Fl.G.4s
Fl.R.4s
ARNE
Long Island
Giggers Island
QUIET AREA
South of a line between Patchins Point and South Haven Point is a Quiet Area with an advisory 6kn speed limit. Keep noise and wash to a minimum.
Round Island
Middlebere Lake
41'
See continuation (on same scale) below
Wych Lake
Ower Bay
metres 0 1500
cables 0 6
02'
01'
02°00'W

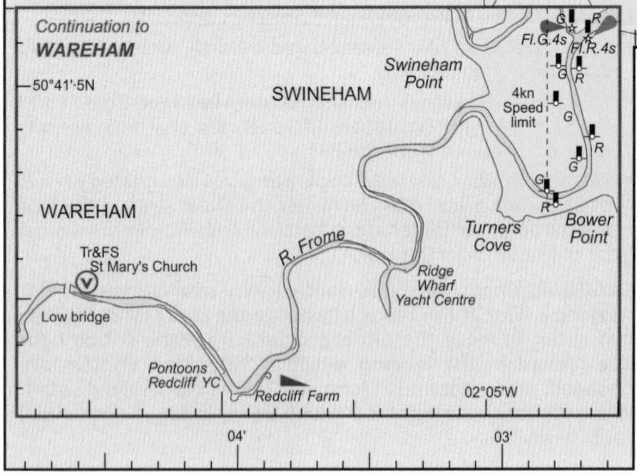
Continuation to WAREHAM
50°41'·5N
SWINEHAM
Swineham Point
Fl.G.4s
Fl.R.4s
4kn Speed limit
WAREHAM
Turners Cove
Bower Point
R. Frome
Tr&FS
St Mary's Church
Ridge Wharf Yacht Centre
Low bridge
Pontoons Redcliff YC
Redcliff Farm
02°05'W
04'
03'

WAREHAM, Dorset, **50°41′·03N 02°06′·56W**. AC 5601, 2611. HW –0030 (Np), +0320 (Sp) on Dover. LWs do not fall below 0·7m except under very low river flow conditions. **Shelter** Very good. Access via narrow and winding chan and R Frome (min depth approx 0·1m), but well marked by buoys and posts, lit to N of Gigger's Island; keep to the outside of all bends. Passage is unlit beyond Gigger's Island. There is a water-ski area between Gold Pt on the N side of the Arne peninsula and WH11/WH12 buoys. Beware prohib ⚓s (salmon holes) marked on the chart. Max draught 1·2m to Wareham Quay. Enforced 4kn speed limit in river.

Facilities: Ridge Wharf Yacht Centre www.ridgewharf.co.uk ☎(01929) 552650. ½M upstream of R Frome ent. 165+Ⓥ £2·70, (18t).

Redcliffe YC ☎551227, Ch 80, Visitors welcome (½M below bridge).

Wareham Quay (free).

Town

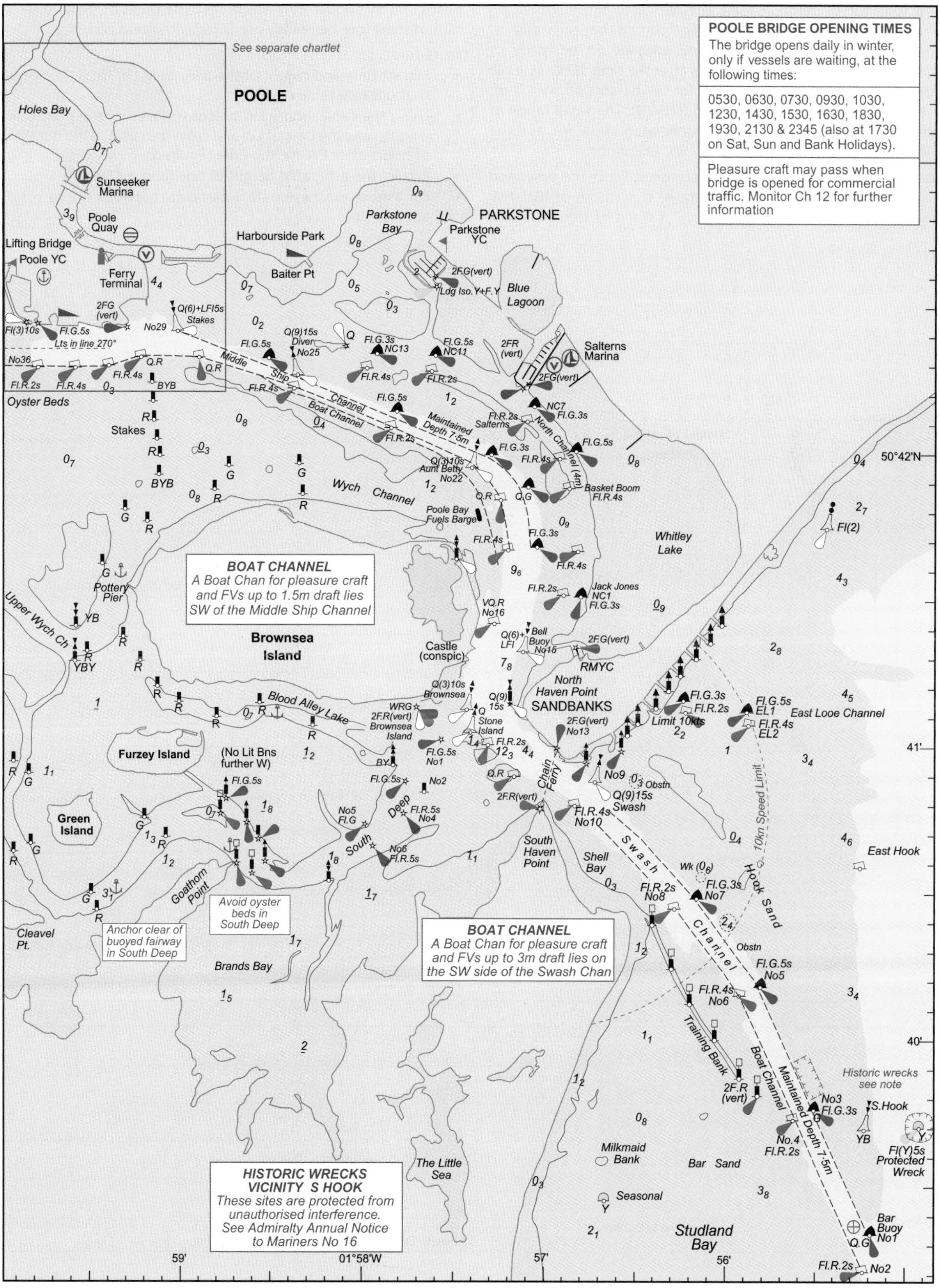
POOLE BRIDGE OPENING TIMES
The bridge opens daily in winter, only if vessels are waiting, at the following times:
0530, 0630, 0730, 0930, 1030, 1230, 1430, 1530, 1630, 1830, 1930, 2130 & 2345 (also at 1730 on Sat, Sun and Bank Holidays).
Pleasure craft may pass when bridge is opened for commercial traffic. Monitor Ch 12 for further information
See separate chartlet
POOLE
Holes Bay
Sunseeker Marina
Poole Quay
Lifting Bridge
Poole YC
Ferry Terminal
Harbourside Park
Baiter Pt
Parkstone Bay
PARKSTONE
Parkstone YC
Blue Lagoon
Salterns Marina
Ldg Iso.Y+F.Y
Lts in line 270°
Oyster Beds
Stakes
Middle Ship Channel
Boat Channel
Maintained Depth 7·5m
North Channel (4m)
Salterns
Aunt Betty No22
Wych Channel
Poole Bay Fuels Barge
Basket Boom
Whitley Lake
Jack Jones NC1
Bell Buoy No15
RMYC
North Haven Point
SANDBANKS
Castle (conspic)
Brownsea Island
BOAT CHANNEL
A Boat Chan for pleasure craft and FVs up to 1.5m draft lies SW of the Middle Ship Channel
Pottery Pier
Upper Wych Ch
Blood Alley Lake
Brownsea Island
Stone Island
Furzey Island
(No Lit Bns further W)
Green Island
Goathorn Point
South Deep
Avoid oyster beds in South Deep
Anchor clear of buoyed fairway in South Deep
Cleavel Pt.
Brands Bay
Chain Ferry
South Haven Point
Shell Bay
Swash Channel
East Looe Channel
Limit 10kts
10kn Speed Limit
Hook Sand
East Hook
Obstn
BOAT CHANNEL
A Boat Chan for pleasure craft and FVs up to 3m draft lies on the SW side of the Swash Chan
Training Bank
Boat Channel
Maintained Depth 7·5m
Historic wrecks see note
S.Hook
Fl(Y)5s Protected Wreck
Milkmaid Bank
Bar Sand
Seasonal
Studland Bay
Bar Buoy No1
The Little Sea
HISTORIC WRECKS VICINITY S HOOK
These sites are protected from unauthorised interference. See Admiralty Annual Notice to Mariners No 16
50°42'N
41'
40'
59'
01°58'W
57'
56'

HEIGHTS OF TIDE AT POOLE (TOWN QUAY)

The four curves below are an alternative to those shown on page 201. Although their accuracy should be regarded as approximate, they enable a speedy estimate to be made of the Height of Tide at hourly intervals after the time of LW at Poole Town Quay. The curves are drawn for LW heights above CD of: 0·3m, 0·6m (MLWS), 0·9m and 1·2m (MLWN). The small range of tide (neaps 0·4m; springs 1·5m) is immediately apparent, as is the HW stand at neaps and the double HWs at springs.

Note: All references to are to LW because at Poole the times and heights of LW are more sharply defined than those of HW. HW times and heights are complicated by a stand of tide at HW at neaps and by double HWs at springs. The times of the two HWs cannot therefore be readily predicted with great accuracy.

Procedure:

- Extract time and height of the preceding LW from the Poole Harbour tide tables (⟶).
- Using the curve whose LW height is closest to the predicted height, note the time of LW and enter the curve at the number of hours after LW for the time required.
- Extract the estimated height of tide (above CD).
- For a more exact estimate, interpolate between the curves if appropriate.

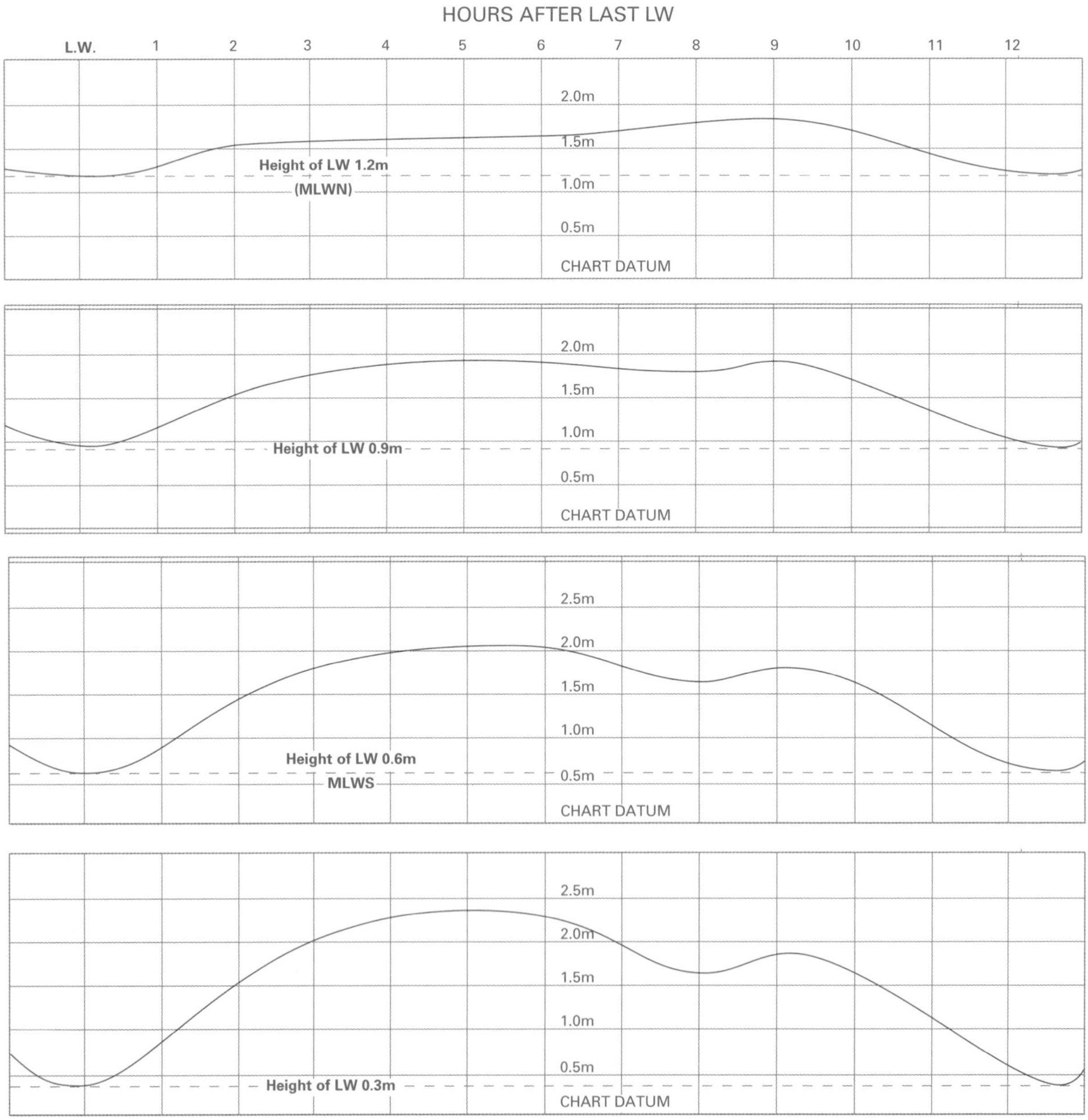

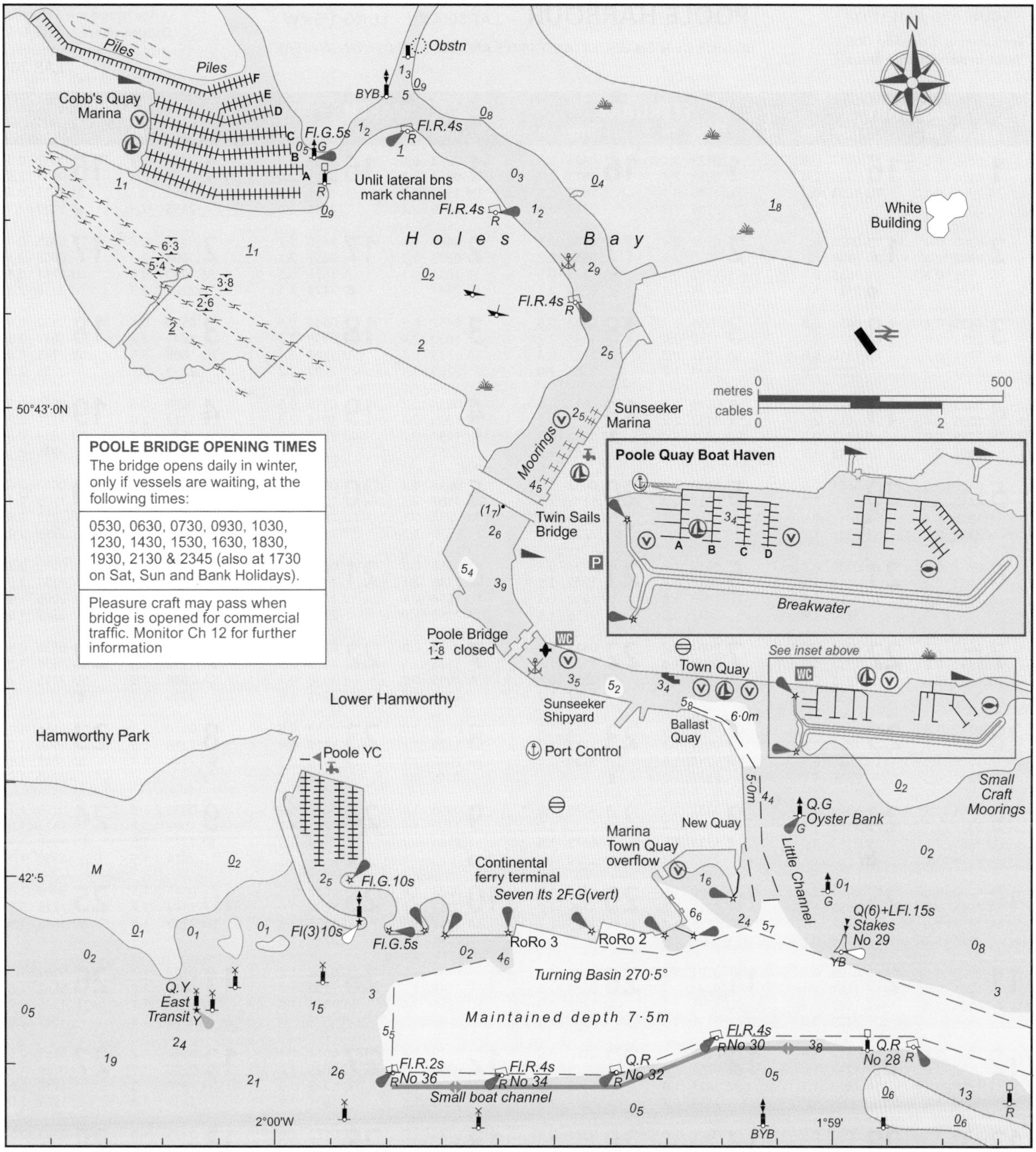

N
Piles
Piles
Cobb's Quay Marina
F
E
D
C
B
A
Fl.G.5s
G
R
Obstn
BYB
Fl.R.4s
R
Unlit lateral bns mark channel
Fl.R.4s
R
H o l e s B a y
Fl.R.4s
R
White Building
metres
cables
0
500
0
2
50°43'·0N
Sunseeker Marina
Moorings
POOLE BRIDGE OPENING TIMES
The bridge opens daily in winter, only if vessels are waiting, at the following times:
0530, 0630, 0730, 0930, 1030, 1230, 1430, 1530, 1630, 1830, 1930, 2130 & 2345 (also at 1730 on Sat, Sun and Bank Holidays).
Pleasure craft may pass when bridge is opened for commercial traffic. Monitor Ch 12 for further information
Twin Sails Bridge
Poole Quay Boat Haven
A
B
C
D
Breakwater
Poole Bridge
1·8 closed
See inset above
Town Quay
Lower Hamworthy
Sunseeker Shipyard
Ballast Quay
6·0m
Hamworthy Park
Poole YC
Port Control
5·0m
Q.G
Oyster Bank
G
Small Craft Moorings
New Quay
Marina Town Quay overflow
Little Channel
Continental ferry terminal
Seven lts 2F.G(vert)
42'·5
M
Fl.G.10s
Fl(3)10s
Fl.G.5s
RoRo 3
RoRo 2
G
Q(6)+LFl.15s
Stakes
No 29
YB
Turning Basin 270·5°
Q.Y
East
Transit
Y
Maintained depth 7·5m
Fl.R.4s
No 30
Q.R
No 28
R
Fl.R.2s
No 36
Fl.R.4s
No 34
Q.R
No 32
Small boat channel
2°00'W
BYB
1°59'
R

SAFETY RECOMMENDATIONS

- Check LNTMs (www.phc.co.uk) to keep abreast of changes.
- Look out for large ferries/commercial ships which are limited in manoeuvrability and speed. **Stay out of exclusion zones.** Keep well clear and make your intentions obvious.
- Use designated small boat channels whenever possible.
- Be alert in the harbour entrance where the stream runs hard; it is a particularly hazardous area with great potential for an accident – **the chain ferry has right of way**.
- Keep to the speed limits and be particularly aware of the wash you are creating. This can cause injury to swimmers and other boaters or damage to other craft and property.
- Proceed slowly in the vicinity of Town Quay, marinas and moorings to minimise wash that can damage moored craft.
- Anticipate sailing craft manoeuvres, give them room to tack.
- Poole Harbour Guide is available from the Harbour Master and at www.phc.co.uk. Areas are designated for personal watercraft, waterskiing, wind & kite surfing. 'Quiet Zones' exclude PWC and have speed limits of 6kn.
- Before sailing check the tidal situation and comply with passage planning requirements.
- Bird sensitive areas exist in most bays and lakes in the harbour. Virtually all intertidal mud areas are nominated Sites of Special Scientific Interest (SSSI).

Note - Sea level is above mean tide level from 2 hrs after LW to 2 hrs before the next LW. HW occurs between 5 hrs after LW and 3 hrs before the next LW, the time shown is approximate and should be checked for suitability.

STANDARD TIME (UT)
For Summer Time add ONE hour in **non-shaded areas**

POOLE HARBOUR

LAT 50°43′N LONG 1°59′W

HEIGHTS OF HIGH WATER AND TIMES AND HEIGHTS OF LOW WATERS

Dates in red are SPRINGS
Dates in blue are NEAPS

YEAR **2018**

JANUARY

Date	Day	Time	m
1	M	0255 0824 1526 2051	0.5 2.2 0.4 2.2
2	TU	0346 0908 1615 ○ 2136	0.4 2.4 0.3 2.3
3	W	0435 0953 1701 2221	0.4 2.4 0.2 2.3
4	TH	0523 1035 1749 2304	0.5 2.4 0.2 2.2
5	F	0612 1116 1836 2347	0.5 2.3 0.3 2.1
6	SA	0701 1153 1925	0.7 2.2 0.5
7	SU	0029 0753 1223 2017	2.0 0.8 2.0 0.6
8	M	0111 0848 1219 ◑ 2112	1.8 1.0 1.9 0.8
9	TU	0151 0948 1253 2216	1.7 1.1 1.7 1.0
10	W	0232 1055 1352 2323	1.6 1.2 1.6 1.1
11	TH	0820 1201 1504	2.0 1.2 1.6
12	F	0026 0652 1300 1614	1.1 1.8 1.1 1.6
13	SA	0123 0724 1354 1717	1.1 1.8 1.0 1.6
14	SU	0214 0555 1441 1817	1.0 1.8 0.9 1.7
15	M	0300 0642 1524 1925	1.0 1.9 0.8 1.8
16	TU	0342 0736 1603 2032	0.9 2.0 0.7 1.9
17	W	0420 0838 1638 ● 2121	0.9 2.1 0.7 1.9
18	TH	0453 0930 1710 2206	0.8 2.1 0.6 2.0
19	F	0527 1013 1743 2248	0.8 2.1 0.6 1.9
20	SA	0601 1049 1817 2328	0.8 2.1 0.6 1.9
21	SU	0638 1112 1855 2359	0.8 2.0 0.6 1.8
22	M	0717 1030 1935 2235	0.9 1.9 0.7 1.7
23	TU	0800 1057 2020 2316	0.9 1.9 0.7 1.7
24	W	0849 1142 2113 ◐	1.0 1.8 0.8
25	TH	0009 0950 1239 2218	1.7 1.1 1.7 0.9
26	F	0122 1101 1527 2329	1.6 1.1 1.7 0.9
27	SA	0612 1212 1819	1.8 1.0 1.7
28	SU	0038 0645 1318 1907	0.9 1.9 0.8 1.8
29	M	0142 0728 1418 1955	0.8 2.0 0.6 2.0
30	TU	0241 0813 1512 2041	0.6 2.1 0.4 2.1
31	W	0334 0857 1602 ○ 2125	0.5 2.3 0.2 2.2

FEBRUARY

Date	Day	Time	m
1	TH	0423 0939 1648 2206	0.4 2.4 0.1 2.3
2	F	0509 1020 1732 2246	0.4 2.4 0.1 2.3
3	SA	0555 1057 1817 2324	0.4 2.4 0.2 2.2
4	SU	0639 1132 1901	0.5 2.2 0.3
5	M	0000 0725 1159 1946	2.0 0.7 2.1 0.6
6	TU	0033 0811 1148 2032	1.8 0.9 1.9 0.8
7	W	0044 0900 1205 ◑ 2123	1.7 1.0 1.7 1.0
8	TH	0038 0959 1243 2232	1.6 1.2 1.6 1.2
9	F	0131 1118 1339 2355	1.5 1.3 1.5 1.2
10	SA	0840 1231 1539	1.8 1.2 1.4
11	SU	0101 0727 1331 2231	1.2 1.7 1.1 1.8
12	M	0155 0753 1421 2037	1.1 1.7 1.0 1.7
13	TU	0242 0621 1504 2038	1.0 1.8 0.8 1.7
14	W	0324 0714 1543 2025	0.9 1.9 0.7 1.8
15	TH	0401 0825 1617 ● 2106	0.8 2.0 0.6 1.9
16	F	0435 0915 1650 2147	0.7 2.1 0.5 2.0
17	SA	0508 0958 1723 2226	0.7 2.2 0.5 2.1
18	SU	0542 1036 1757 2304	0.6 2.2 0.4 2.0
19	M	0617 1113 1833 2341	0.6 2.1 0.5 1.9
20	TU	0653 1148 1910 2222	0.7 2.0 0.5 1.8
21	W	0733 1042 1952 2256	0.7 1.9 0.7 1.8
22	TH	0817 1122 2040 2344	0.8 1.8 0.8 1.7
23	F	0912 1215 2139 ◐	1.0 1.7 1.0
24	SA	0045 1025 1519 2300	1.6 1.0 1.6 1.0
25	SU	0750 1149 1825	1.8 1.0 1.7
26	M	0021 0638 1303 1906	1.0 1.8 0.9 1.8
27	TU	0132 0719 1405 1949	0.9 1.9 0.6 1.9
28	W	0231 0802 1459 2031	0.7 2.1 0.4 2.1

MARCH

Date	Day	Time	m
1	TH	0323 0844 1547 2110	0.5 2.2 0.2 2.2
2	F	0409 0923 1631 ○ 2147	0.4 2.3 0.1 2.3
3	SA	0452 1000 1713 2223	0.3 2.4 0.1 2.3
4	SU	0534 1035 1754 2257	0.3 2.4 0.2 2.2
5	M	0615 1107 1834 2329	0.4 2.2 0.4 2.1
6	TU	0656 1136 1914 2358	0.6 2.1 0.6 1.9
7	W	0736 1126 1955 2327	0.8 1.9 0.8 1.7
8	TH	0816 1129 2036 2345	1.0 1.7 1.1 1.7
9	F	0900 1202 2124 ◑	1.1 1.6 1.2
10	SA	0023 0953 1247 2234	1.6 1.2 1.5 1.4
11	SU	0117 1149 1356	1.5 1.3 1.4
12	M	0039 0715 1304 2200	1.4 1.7 1.2 1.8
13	TU	0135 0742 1355 2257	1.2 1.7 1.0 1.8
14	W	0220 0634 1438 2021	1.1 1.7 0.9 1.7
15	TH	0259 0713 1515 2011	1.0 1.8 0.7 1.9
16	F	0336 0811 1551 2046	0.8 2.0 0.6 2.0
17	SA	0410 0857 1625 ● 2124	0.7 2.1 0.5 2.1
18	SU	0444 0939 1700 2202	0.5 2.2 0.4 2.2
19	M	0519 1018 1735 2240	0.5 2.3 0.4 2.2
20	TU	0554 1056 1810 2317	0.5 2.2 0.4 2.1
21	W	0630 1135 1847 2355	0.5 2.1 0.5 2.0
22	TH	0709 1216 1928 2245	0.6 2.0 0.7 1.9
23	F	0753 1115 2016 2329	0.8 1.8 0.9 1.8
24	SA	0846 1211 2116 ◐	0.9 1.7 1.1
25	SU	0032 1002 1856 2248	1.7 1.0 1.8 1.2
26	M	0335 1134 1948	1.7 1.0 1.8
27	TU	0014 0625 1249 1901	1.1 1.8 0.9 1.9
28	W	0122 0705 1349 1937	1.0 1.9 0.7 1.9
29	TH	0217 0746 1441 2015	0.8 2.0 0.5 2.1
30	F	0306 0825 1527 2050	0.6 2.1 0.3 2.2
31	SA	0351 0901 1610 ○ 2123	0.5 2.2 0.2 2.3

APRIL

Date	Day	Time	m
1	SU	0432 0935 1651 2155	0.4 2.3 0.2 2.3
2	M	0512 1008 1730 2226	0.4 2.3 0.3 2.3
3	TU	0550 1041 1808 2258	0.5 2.2 0.5 2.1
4	W	0628 1112 1846 2326	0.6 2.0 0.7 2.0
5	TH	0704 1121 1922 2252	0.7 1.8 0.9 1.8
6	F	0741 1100 2002 2312	0.9 1.7 1.1 1.7
7	SA	0822 1132 2048 2349	1.0 1.6 1.3 1.7
8	SU	0910 1216 2144 ◑	1.1 1.5 1.4
9	M	0036 1009 1315 2314	1.6 1.2 1.5 1.5
10	TU	0145 1143 2113	1.5 1.2 1.8
11	W	0103 0610 1314 2218	1.3 1.6 1.1 1.8
12	TH	0147 0626 1358 1922	1.2 1.7 1.0 1.8
13	F	0225 0703 1438 1945	1.0 1.8 0.8 1.9
14	SA	0303 0750 1517 2021	0.8 2.0 0.6 2.1
15	SU	0340 0835 1555 2058	0.6 2.1 0.5 2.2
16	M	0418 0917 1633 ● 2137	0.5 2.3 0.4 2.3
17	TU	0455 0958 1711 2216	0.4 2.3 0.4 2.3
18	W	0532 1039 1749 2255	0.4 2.3 0.4 2.3
19	TH	0611 1121 1829 2335	0.5 2.2 0.6 2.1
20	F	0652 1205 1913 2359	0.6 2.1 0.8 2.0
21	SA	0739 1253 2005 2343	0.7 1.9 1.0 1.9
22	SU	0836 1354 2115 ◐	0.9 1.8 1.2
23	M	0156 0956 1847 2244	1.8 1.0 1.9 1.2
24	TU	0259 1117 1950 2358	1.7 1.0 1.9 1.1
25	W	0400 1226 1843	1.7 0.9 1.9
26	TH	0101 0642 1325 1917	1.0 1.8 0.7 2.0
27	F	0155 0724 1416 1953	0.9 1.9 0.6 2.0
28	SA	0243 0803 1503 2026	0.7 2.0 0.5 2.1
29	SU	0328 0837 1547 2055	0.6 2.1 0.4 2.2
30	M	0410 0909 1628 ○ 2122	0.5 2.2 0.5 2.3

Chart Datum: 1·40 metres below Ordnance Datum (Newlyn). HAT is 2·6 metres above Chart Datum.

Note - Sea level is above mean tide level from 2 hrs after LW to 2 hrs before the next LW. HW occurs between 5 hrs after LW and 3 hrs before the next LW, the time shown is approximate and should be checked for suitability.

STANDARD TIME (UT)
For Summer Time add ONE hour in **non-shaded areas**

POOLE HARBOUR

LAT 50°43'N LONG 1°59'W

HEIGHTS OF HIGH WATER AND TIMES AND HEIGHTS OF LOW WATERS

Dates in red are SPRINGS
Dates in blue are NEAPS

YEAR **2018**

MAY

Date	Day	Time	m	Time	m	Time	m	Time	m
1	TU	0449	0.5	0940	2.2	1706	0.6	2153	2.3
2	W	0527	0.6	1014	2.1	1744	0.7	2226	2.2
3	TH	0602	0.7	1049	2.0	1820	0.9	2258	2.0
4	F	0637	0.8	1121	1.9	1855	1.0	2228	1.9
5	SA	0712	0.9	1039	1.7	1935	1.2	2249	1.8
6	SU	0753	1.0	1110	1.7	2021	1.3	2324	1.7
7	M	0840	1.1	1151	1.6	2115	1.4		
8	TU	0008	1.7	0936	1.1	1244	1.5	◑ 2217	1.4
9	W	0107	1.6	1039	1.2	1411	1.5	2331	1.4
10	TH	0234	1.6	1151	1.1	2104	1.9		
11	F	0045	1.2	0605	1.7	1259	1.0	1848	1.8
12	SA	0138	1.1	0642	1.8	1352	0.8	1917	2.0
13	SU	0224	0.9	0727	1.9	1439	0.7	1953	2.1
14	M	0307	0.7	0812	2.1	1524	0.5	2032	2.2
15	TU	0350	0.5	0857	2.2	1606	0.4	● 2114	2.3
16	W	0431	0.4	0941	2.3	1648	0.4	2156	2.4
17	TH	0512	0.4	1024	2.3	1731	0.5	2238	2.3
18	F	0555	0.4	1108	2.3	1816	0.6	2321	2.3
19	SA	0641	0.5	1154	2.1	1905	0.8		
20	SU	0003	2.1	0733	0.7	1242	2.0	2004	1.0
21	M	0046	2.0	0833	0.8	1338	1.9	2113	1.1
22	TU	0132	1.9	0942	0.9	1844	2.1	◐ 2225	1.2
23	W	0220	1.8	1052	0.9	1945	2.1	2331	1.1
24	TH	0311	1.7	1157	0.9	1821	1.9		
25	F	0032	1.0	0404	1.7	1255	0.8	1855	1.9
26	SA	0127	0.9	0459	1.8	1348	0.8	1931	2.0
27	SU	0218	0.8	0743	1.9	1437	0.7	2002	2.0
28	M	0304	0.7	0816	2.0	1523	0.7	2025	2.1
29	TU	0347	0.7	0843	2.0	1606	0.7	○ 2044	2.2
30	W	0428	0.6	0911	2.1	1646	0.8	2118	2.2
31	TH	0505	0.7	0948	2.1	1723	0.9	2158	2.2

JUNE

Date	Day	Time	m	Time	m	Time	m	Time	m
1	F	0540	0.7	1028	2.0	1758	1.0	2235	2.1
2	SA	0614	0.8	1110	1.9	1833	1.1	2218	2.0
3	SU	0648	0.8	1029	1.8	1912	1.2	2234	1.9
4	M	0728	0.9	1053	1.7	1956	1.2	2305	1.8
5	TU	0813	1.0	1129	1.7	2046	1.3	2344	1.8
6	W	0905	1.0	1214	1.6	2142	1.3	◑	
7	TH	0033	1.7	1003	1.1	1316	1.6	2244	1.3
8	F	0141	1.7	1105	1.0	2017	1.9	2348	1.2
9	SA	0321	1.7	1209	1.0	1822	1.8		
10	SU	0049	1.1	0441	1.8	1308	0.9	1852	1.9
11	M	0144	0.9	0704	1.9	1403	0.7	1928	2.1
12	TU	0235	0.7	0753	2.0	1453	0.6	2011	2.2
13	W	0323	0.5	0840	2.2	1542	0.5	● 2056	2.3
14	TH	0410	0.4	0926	2.3	1629	0.5	2141	2.4
15	F	0455	0.3	1012	2.3	1716	0.5	2226	2.4
16	SA	0542	0.3	1057	2.3	1805	0.6	2310	2.4
17	SU	0630	0.4	1142	2.2	1856	0.8	2352	2.2
18	M	0722	0.5	1228	2.1	1952	0.9		
19	TU	0032	2.1	0817	0.7	1315	1.9	2053	1.0
20	W	0106	2.0	0917	0.8	1403	1.8	◐ 2156	1.1
21	TH	0134	1.8	1020	0.9	1924	2.1	2259	1.1
22	F	0221	1.7	1124	0.9	1528	1.7		
23	SA	0000	1.1	0318	1.7	1224	1.0	1839	1.9
24	SU	0058	1.0	0416	1.7	1321	1.0	1705	1.8
25	M	0152	1.0	0515	1.7	1413	0.9	1757	1.9
26	TU	0241	0.9	0616	1.8	1501	0.9	1852	2.0
27	W	0327	0.8	0827	1.9	1546	0.9	1951	2.1
28	TH	0409	0.7	0845	2.0	1627	0.9	○ 2045	2.2
29	F	0447	0.7	0927	2.0	1705	0.9	2134	2.2
30	SA	0522	0.7	1010	2.0	1739	1.0	2218	2.1

JULY

Date	Day	Time	m	Time	m	Time	m	Time	m
1	SU	0554	0.8	1053	2.0	1813	1.0	2255	2.0
2	M	0627	0.8	1137	1.9	1849	1.1	2231	1.9
3	TU	0705	0.8	1048	1.8	1930	1.1	2251	1.9
4	W	0746	0.8	1108	1.7	2016	1.1	2318	1.8
5	TH	0833	0.9	1140	1.7	2107	1.2	2358	1.8
6	F	0926	1.0	1228	1.7	2205	1.2	◑	
7	SA	0054	1.7	1027	1.0	1343	1.7	2307	1.1
8	SU	0218	1.7	1130	1.0	1604	1.8		
9	M	0010	1.1	0407	1.7	1232	0.9	1832	1.9
10	TU	0110	0.9	0648	1.8	1332	0.8	1910	2.0
11	W	0208	0.7	0738	2.0	1429	0.7	1956	2.2
12	TH	0301	0.5	0828	2.1	1522	0.6	2044	2.3
13	F	0352	0.4	0916	2.3	1614	0.5	● 2130	2.4
14	SA	0440	0.3	1001	2.3	1703	0.5	2214	2.5
15	SU	0528	0.2	1045	2.4	1751	0.6	2257	2.5
16	M	0616	0.3	1127	2.3	1840	0.6	2337	2.4
17	TU	0704	0.4	1208	2.2	1931	0.8		
18	W	0013	2.2	0754	0.5	1247	2.0	2024	0.9
19	TH	0039	2.0	0847	0.7	1320	1.9	◐ 2122	1.0
20	F	0050	1.9	0945	0.9	1345	1.7	2224	1.1
21	SA	0132	1.7	1049	1.1	1431	1.7	2329	1.2
22	SU	0232	1.6	1154	1.1	1532	1.7		
23	M	0030	1.1	0340	1.6	1256	1.1	1634	1.8
24	TU	0128	1.1	0445	1.6	1352	1.1	1729	1.8
25	W	0221	1.0	0546	1.7	1443	1.1	1821	2.0
26	TH	0308	0.9	0649	1.8	1529	1.0	1916	2.0
27	F	0351	0.8	0829	1.9	1611	1.0	○ 2019	2.1
28	SA	0429	0.7	0908	2.0	1648	0.9	2113	2.2
29	SU	0503	0.7	0952	2.0	1720	0.9	2200	2.2
30	M	0534	0.7	1033	2.1	1752	0.9	2240	2.2
31	TU	0606	0.7	1112	2.0	1826	0.9	2313	2.1

AUGUST

Date	Day	Time	m	Time	m	Time	m	Time	m
1	W	0640	0.7	1146	1.9	1903	0.9	2304	2.0
2	TH	0718	0.7	1102	1.8	1943	1.0	2252	1.9
3	F	0800	0.8	1107	1.8	2030	1.0	2325	1.9
4	SA	0848	0.9	1149	1.8	2125	1.1	◑	
5	SU	0014	1.8	0947	1.0	1247	1.8	2230	1.1
6	M	0124	1.7	1054	1.0	1534	1.8	2338	1.1
7	TU	0400	1.7	1203	1.0	1818	1.9		
8	W	0045	1.0	0640	1.8	1310	1.0	1858	2.0
9	TH	0148	0.8	0730	2.0	1412	0.8	1945	2.2
10	F	0246	0.6	0820	2.1	1509	0.7	2033	2.3
11	SA	0338	0.4	0905	2.3	1601	0.6	● 2117	2.5
12	SU	0426	0.2	0948	2.4	1648	0.5	2200	2.6
13	M	0511	0.1	1028	2.4	1734	0.5	2239	2.5
14	TU	0556	0.2	1107	2.4	1819	0.5	2317	2.4
15	W	0640	0.3	1144	2.2	1905	0.7	2351	2.3
16	TH	0725	0.5	1218	2.1	1952	0.9		
17	F	0014	2.0	0813	0.8	1241	1.9	2043	1.0
18	SA	0012	1.9	0905	1.0	1248	1.8	◐ 2143	1.2
19	SU	0042	1.7	1009	1.2	1328	1.7	2255	1.3
20	M	0135	1.6	1126	1.3	1456	1.6		
21	TU	0005	1.2	0310	1.5	1236	1.3	1858	1.9
22	W	0107	1.2	1009	1.9	1335	1.3	1928	1.8
23	TH	0201	1.0	0816	1.7	1426	1.2	1811	1.9
24	F	0248	0.9	0840	1.8	1510	1.1	1859	2.0
25	SA	0330	0.8	0831	1.9	1550	1.0	2001	2.1
26	SU	0407	0.7	0850	2.0	1625	0.9	○ 2054	2.2
27	M	0439	0.6	0930	2.1	1657	0.8	2139	2.3
28	TU	0510	0.6	1009	2.2	1728	0.8	2219	2.3
29	W	0542	0.6	1046	2.2	1801	0.8	2256	2.2
30	TH	0615	0.6	1120	2.1	1835	0.8	2330	2.1
31	F	0650	0.6	1152	2.0	1912	0.9	2232	2.0

Chart Datum: 1·40 metres below Ordnance Datum (Newlyn). HAT is 2·6 metres above Chart Datum.

Note - Sea level is above mean tide level from 2 hrs after LW to 2 hrs before the next LW. HW occurs between 5 hrs after LW and 3 hrs before the next LW, the time shown is approximate and should be checked for suitability.

STANDARD TIME (UT)
For Summer Time add ONE hour in **non-shaded areas**

POOLE HARBOUR LAT 50°43'N LONG 1°59'W

HEIGHTS OF HIGH WATER AND TIMES AND HEIGHTS OF LOW WATERS

Dates in red are SPRINGS
Dates in blue are NEAPS

YEAR **2018**

SEPTEMBER

Date	Time	m
1 SA	0728	0.7
	1040	1.9
	1954	0.9
	2257	1.9
2 SU	0812	0.9
	1120	1.9
	2045	1.0
	2345	1.8
3 M	0906	1.0
	1214	1.8
	2153	1.1
	◑	
4 TU	0052	1.7
	1021	1.2
	1925	1.9
	2314	1.1
5 W	0601	1.8
	1144	1.2
	1810	1.9
6 TH	0030	1.0
	0639	1.9
	1259	1.1
	1849	2.0
7 F	0136	0.8
	0725	2.0
	1403	0.9
	1934	2.2
8 SA	0232	0.6
	0809	2.1
	1457	0.7
	2019	2.3
9 SU	0322	0.3
	0850	2.3
	1546	0.5
	● 2100	2.5
10 M	0408	0.2
	0929	2.4
	1630	0.4
	2140	2.6
11 TU	0451	0.1
	1007	2.4
	1713	0.4
	2218	2.6
12 W	0533	0.2
	1042	2.4
	1755	0.5
	2253	2.4
13 TH	0614	0.4
	1116	2.3
	1837	0.6
	2326	2.3
14 F	0656	0.6
	1147	2.1
	1919	0.8
	2351	2.0
15 SA	0739	0.9
	1203	1.9
	2004	1.0
	2336	1.8
16 SU	0824	1.1
	1153	1.8
	2054	1.2
	◐ 2358	1.7
17 M	0919	1.3
	1222	1.7
	2204	1.3
18 TU	0040	1.6
	1057	1.5
	1313	1.6
	2339	1.3
19 W	0207	1.5
	1217	1.4
	1835	1.8
20 TH	0045	1.2
	0943	1.9
	1316	1.3
	1902	1.8
21 F	0137	1.1
	0758	1.8
	1404	1.2
	1837	1.8
22 SA	0222	1.0
	0813	1.8
	1446	1.1
	1857	2.0
23 SU	0302	0.8
	0758	1.9
	1523	0.9
	1946	2.1
24 M	0338	0.7
	0825	2.1
	1558	0.8
	2034	2.2
25 TU	0411	0.6
	0903	2.2
	1630	0.7
	○ 2117	2.3
26 W	0443	0.5
	0941	2.3
	1702	0.7
	2157	2.4
27 TH	0516	0.5
	1018	2.3
	1735	0.6
	2235	2.3
28 F	0550	0.5
	1054	2.2
	1809	0.7
	2314	2.2
29 SA	0624	0.6
	1130	2.1
	1845	0.8
	2354	2.1
30 SU	0702	0.8
	1023	2.0
	1926	0.9
	2241	1.9

OCTOBER

Date	Time	m
1 M	0746	0.9
	1100	1.9
	2014	1.0
	2329	1.8
2 TU	0838	1.1
	1155	1.8
	2124	1.1
	◑	
3 W	0626	1.9
	1003	1.3
	1849	1.9
	2301	1.1
4 TH	0717	1.9
	1139	1.3
	1757	1.9
5 F	0018	1.0
	0634	1.9
	1251	1.1
	1835	2.0
6 SA	0121	0.8
	0712	2.0
	1350	0.9
	1918	2.1
7 SU	0214	0.6
	0752	2.1
	1440	0.7
	2000	2.3
8 M	0302	0.4
	0830	2.3
	1526	0.6
	2040	2.4
9 TU	0346	0.3
	0906	2.4
	1609	0.5
	● 2117	2.5
10 W	0428	0.3
	0941	2.4
	1650	0.4
	2153	2.5
11 TH	0509	0.3
	1013	2.4
	1730	0.5
	2227	2.4
12 F	0549	0.5
	1045	2.3
	1809	0.6
	2301	2.2
13 SA	0628	0.7
	1114	2.2
	1849	0.8
	2331	2.0
14 SU	0708	1.0
	1122	2.0
	1928	1.0
	2301	1.8
15 M	0749	1.2
	1111	1.9
	2011	1.2
	2323	1.7
16 TU	0836	1.4
	1142	1.8
	2101	1.3
	◐	
17 W	0004	1.6
	0940	1.5
	1227	1.7
	2220	1.3
18 TH	0104	1.5
	1152	1.5
	1808	1.8
19 F	0012	1.3
	0704	1.9
	1248	1.4
	1824	1.8
20 SA	0104	1.2
	0735	1.9
	1334	1.3
	1821	1.8
21 SU	0147	1.0
	0722	1.9
	1414	1.1
	1849	1.9
22 M	0226	0.9
	0728	2.0
	1450	1.0
	1929	2.0
23 TU	0302	0.7
	0759	2.1
	1524	0.8
	2012	2.2
24 W	0338	0.6
	0835	2.2
	1600	0.7
	○ 2054	2.3
25 TH	0414	0.5
	0912	2.3
	1636	0.6
	2135	2.4
26 F	0450	0.5
	0951	2.4
	1711	0.5
	2216	2.4
27 SA	0527	0.5
	1030	2.3
	1747	0.6
	2257	2.3
28 SU	0604	0.7
	1109	2.2
	1826	0.7
	2341	2.1
29 M	0645	0.8
	1149	2.1
	1909	0.8
30 TU	0031	2.0
	0732	1.0
	1103	2.0
	2001	0.9
31 W	0133	1.8
	0831	1.2
	1334	1.9
	◑ 2116	1.1

NOVEMBER

Date	Time	m
1 TH	0615	2.0
	1004	1.3
	1444	1.8
	2247	1.1
2 F	0714	2.0
	1127	1.3
	1734	1.9
	2358	0.9
3 SA	0617	2.0
	1233	1.1
	1815	1.9
4 SU	0057	0.8
	0653	2.0
	1328	0.9
	1859	2.0
5 M	0150	0.6
	0731	2.1
	1418	0.8
	1940	2.1
6 TU	0238	0.5
	0808	2.2
	1504	0.6
	2019	2.2
7 W	0323	0.4
	0841	2.3
	1547	0.5
	● 2054	2.3
8 TH	0405	0.5
	0912	2.3
	1628	0.5
	2128	2.3
9 F	0445	0.5
	0942	2.3
	1707	0.6
	2202	2.2
10 SA	0525	0.7
	1013	2.3
	1745	0.7
	2237	2.1
11 SU	0604	0.9
	1044	2.2
	1822	0.8
	2314	2.0
12 M	0641	1.1
	1047	2.0
	1859	0.9
	2238	1.8
13 TU	0721	1.2
	1042	1.9
	1938	1.1
	2257	1.7
14 W	0805	1.4
	1113	1.8
	2024	1.2
	2336	1.6
15 TH	0857	1.4
	1155	1.7
	2118	1.2
	◐	
16 F	0027	1.5
	1002	1.5
	1249	1.6
	2224	1.3
17 SA	0658	1.9
	1154	1.4
	1410	1.6
	2347	1.2
18 SU	0858	1.9
	1247	1.3
	1802	1.7
19 M	0050	1.1
	0648	1.9
	1328	1.2
	1833	1.8
20 TU	0137	0.9
	0705	2.0
	1409	1.0
	1910	1.9
21 W	0221	0.8
	0733	2.1
	1449	0.8
	1951	2.1
22 TH	0304	0.6
	0807	2.2
	1530	0.6
	2033	2.2
23 F	0345	0.5
	0846	2.3
	1610	0.5
	○ 2116	2.3
24 SA	0426	0.5
	0929	2.4
	1650	0.4
	2200	2.3
25 SU	0507	0.6
	1011	2.4
	1731	0.5
	2245	2.3
26 M	0550	0.7
	1054	2.3
	1815	0.5
	2331	2.2
27 TU	0636	0.8
	1138	2.2
	1902	0.7
28 W	0020	2.0
	0728	1.0
	1223	2.1
	1957	0.8
29 TH	0116	1.9
	0831	1.1
	1313	1.9
	2105	0.9
30 F	0612	2.1
	0947	1.2
	1406	1.9
	◑ 2220	0.9

DECEMBER

Date	Time	m
1 SA	0711	2.1
	1100	1.2
	1500	1.8
	2329	0.9
2 SU	0604	1.9
	1204	1.1
	1557	1.8
3 M	0029	0.8
	0635	2.0
	1302	1.0
	1842	1.9
4 TU	0123	0.7
	0712	2.0
	1354	0.9
	1923	1.9
5 W	0213	0.7
	0748	2.1
	1441	0.7
	2002	2.0
6 TH	0300	0.6
	0819	2.1
	1526	0.7
	2035	2.1
7 F	0344	0.7
	0845	2.2
	1608	0.6
	● 2105	2.1
8 SA	0426	0.7
	0909	2.2
	1648	0.6
	2138	2.1
9 SU	0506	0.8
	0943	2.2
	1726	0.7
	2216	2.0
10 M	0544	0.9
	1021	2.2
	1801	0.8
	2257	1.9
11 TU	0620	1.0
	1053	2.0
	1836	0.8
	2346	1.8
12 W	0657	1.1
	1025	1.9
	1912	0.9
	2239	1.7
13 TH	0738	1.2
	1051	1.8
	1954	1.0
	2310	1.6
14 F	0824	1.3
	1126	1.8
	2042	1.0
	2351	1.6
15 SA	0916	1.3
	1210	1.7
	2137	1.1
	◐	
16 SU	0046	1.5
	1017	1.3
	1308	1.6
	2240	1.1
17 M	0742	1.9
	1123	1.3
	1441	1.6
	2345	1.1
18 TU	0852	1.9
	1228	1.2
	1627	1.7
19 W	0046	1.0
	0644	1.9
	1324	1.0
	1851	1.8
20 TH	0141	0.8
	0711	2.0
	1414	0.8
	1932	1.9
21 F	0232	0.7
	0746	2.1
	1502	0.6
	2017	2.1
22 SA	0320	0.6
	0829	2.2
	1548	0.5
	○ 2103	2.2
23 SU	0407	0.5
	0915	2.3
	1634	0.4
	2149	2.3
24 M	0452	0.5
	1001	2.4
	1718	0.3
	2235	2.3
25 TU	0539	0.6
	1046	2.4
	1805	0.4
	2320	2.2
26 W	0628	0.7
	1129	2.3
	1853	0.5
27 TH	0006	2.1
	0720	0.8
	1211	2.2
	1946	0.6
28 F	0054	1.9
	0816	1.0
	1251	2.0
	2043	0.7
29 SA	0144	1.8
	0918	1.1
	1327	1.9
	◑ 2146	0.8
30 SU	0652	2.1
	1025	1.1
	1408	1.8
	2254	0.9
31 M	0748	2.0
	1132	1.1
	1500	1.7
	2358	0.9

Chart Datum: 1·40 metres below Ordnance Datum (Newlyn). HAT is 2·6 metres above Chart Datum.

SWANAGE TO CHRISTCHURCH BAY

Studland Bay (AC 2172) is a good ⚓ especially in winds from the S and W. Poole Bay offers good sailing in waters sheltered from the W and N, with no offlying dangers.

▶*1M NE of Durlston Head, Peveril Ledge runs 2½ca seaward, causing a significant race which extends nearly 1M eastwards, particularly on W-going stream against a SW wind. Proceeding towards the excellent shelter of Poole Harbour, overfalls may be met off Ballard Pt and Old Harry on the W-going stream.*◀

(AC 2615) There is deep water quite close inshore between St Alban's Hd and Anvil Pt.

▶ *Tidal streams are weak North of a line between Handfast Point and Hengistbury Head and within Christchurch Bay. The tide runs hard over the ledge at springs, and there may be overfalls.*◀

Hengistbury Hd is a dark reddish headland S of Christchurch Hbr with a groyne extending 1ca S and Beerpan Rks a further 100m E of groyne. Beware lobster pots in this area. Christchurch Ledge extends 2·75M SE from Hengistbury Hd. There is a passage between Christchurch Ledge and Dolphin Bank, some 1½M further SE. A wreck hazardous to surface navigation (PA) has been reported in this chan (2013).

WESTERN APPROACHES TO THE SOLENT

(AC 2035) The Needles are distinctive rocks at the W end of the Isle of Wight. The adjacent chalk cliffs of High Down are conspic from afar, but the Lt Ho may not be seen by day until relatively close. Goose Rk, which dries, is about 50m WNW of the Lt Ho, 100-150m WSW of which is a drying wreck. When rounding the Needles an offing of 1½ca will clear these. The NW side of Needles Chan is defined by the Shingles bank, parts of which dry and on which the sea breaks violently in the least swell. The SE side of the bank is fairly steep-to; the NW side shelves more gradually.

▶*The ENE-going flood runs from HW Portsmouth +0500 until HW –0130, Sp rates 3.1kn at The Bridge, a reef which runs 8ca W of the Lt ho and is marked by WCM, and 3.9kn at Hurst. The WSW-going ebb runs from HW –0100 until HW +0430, sp rates 4.4kn at Hurst, 3.4kn WSW across the Shingles and at The Bridge. The Needles Chan is well marked and in fair weather presents no significant problems, but in a SW 4 or above over the ebb, breaking seas occur near The Bridge and SW Shingles. In bad weather broken water and overfalls extend along The Bridge. S to W gales against the ebb raise very dangerous breaking seas in the Needles Chan and approaches. The sea state can be at its worst shortly after LW when the flood has just begun. There is then no wind-over-tide situation, but a substantial swell is raised as a result of the recently turned stream.* ◀

In such conditions use the E route to the Solent, S of the IoW and via Nab Tower; or find shelter at Poole or Studland.

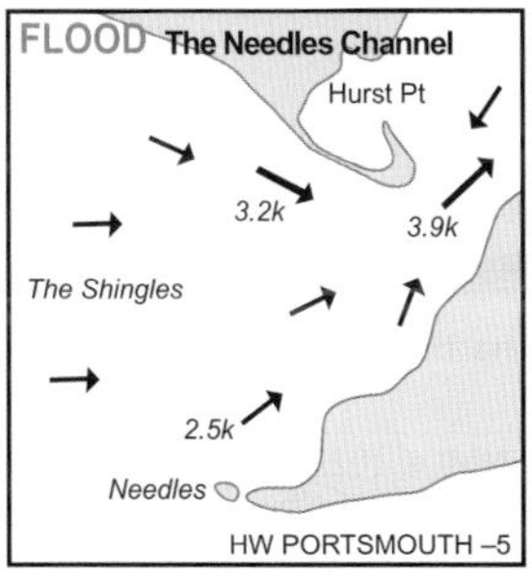
FLOOD The Needles Channel
Hurst Pt
3.2k
3.9k
The Shingles
2.5k
Needles
HW PORTSMOUTH –5

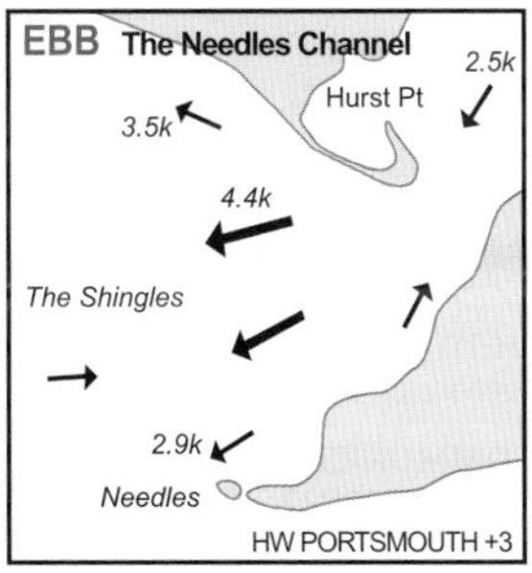
EBB The Needles Channel
2.5k
Hurst Pt
3.5k
4.4k
The Shingles
2.9k
Needles
HW PORTSMOUTH +3

In strong winds the North Channel, N of the Shingles, is preferable to the Needles Channel. The two join S of Hurst Pt, where overfalls and tide rips may be met. Beware The Trap, a very shallow gravel shoal spit, 150m SE of Hurst Castle.

In E winds Alum Bay, with its coloured cliffs close NE of the Needles, is an attractive daytime ⚓ but beware Long Rk (dries) in the middle of the bay, and Five Fingers Rock 1½ca SW of Hatherwood Pt on N side. Totland Bay is good ⚓ in settled weather, but avoid Warden Ledge.

THE SOLENT

(AC 2035, 2036, 2037) There are few dangers in mid-chan. The most significant is Bramble Bank (dries) between Cowes and Calshot. The main fairway (buoyed) passes S and W of the Brambles, but yachts can use the North Chan to the NE of the Brambles at any state of tide.

▶ *Tidal streams are strong at Sp, see 9.2.16.* ◀

A Precautionary Area between Cowes and Calshot provides priority and safety for large commercial shipping. There are many yacht racing buoys *(seasonal, Mar–Dec)* in the Solent and Southampton Water. Most are fitted with a Fl Y 4s light.

Several inshore spits, banks, rocks and ledges include: Pennington and Lymington Spits on the N shore; Black Rk 4ca W of entrance to Yarmouth; Hamstead Ledge 8ca W of entrance to Newtown River and Saltmead Ledge 1·5M to E; Gurnard Ledge 1·5M W of Cowes; Lepe Middle and Beaulieu Spit, S and W of the ent to Beaulieu R; the shoals off Stone Pt, marked by Lepe Spit SCM buoy; Shrape Mud, which extends N from the breakwater of Cowes Hbr and along to Old Castle Pt; the shoals and isolated rks which fringe the island shore from Old Castle Pt to Ryde, including either side of the ent to Wootton Creek; and Calshot Spit which extends almost to the deep water chan into Southampton Water.

Southampton Water is a commercial waterway with large tankers, container ships, frequent Ro-Ro and High Speed ferries. Yachts should monitor VHF Ch 12 (Southampton VTS) for shipping movements. Between the Fawley Marine Terminal and the BP jetty on the E side the fairway is narrow with little room for yachts to take refuge. To the N there is adequate water for yachts close outboard of the main buoyed channel; the banks are of gently shelving soft mud, apart from foul ground between Hythe and Marchwood. At night, unlit marks and large mooring buoys may be hard to see against the many shore lights. Except in strong N'lies, Southampton Water and the R Test and Itchen provide sheltered sailing. The R Hamble is convenient, but crowded.

Depending on the wind direction, there are many good ⚓s: in W winds on E side of Hurst, as close inshore as depth permits, NE of Hurst lt; in S winds, or in good weather, W of Yarmouth Harbour entrance, as near shore as possible; in winds between W and N in Stanswood Bay, about 1M NE of Stansore Pt. Just N of Calshot Spit there is shelter from SW and W, while Osborne Bay, 2M E of Cowes, is sheltered from winds between S and W; in E winds Gurnard Bay, to the W of Cowes, is preferable. Stokes Bay is well sheltered from the N, and at the E end of the IoW there is good ⚓ in Priory Bay off Bembridge in winds from S, SW or W; but clear out if wind goes into E.

Shoal-draught boats can explore the estuaries at the top of the tide: Ashlett Creek between Fawley and Calshot, Eling up the R Test, and the upper reaches of the R Medina.

ISLE OF WIGHT – SOUTH COAST

(AC 2045) From the Needles eastward to Freshwater Bay the cliffs can be approached to within 1ca, but beyond the E end of the chalk cliffs there are ledges off Brook and Atherfield which require at least 5ca offing.

▶ *The E-going stream sets towards these dangers. 4M SSW of the Needles the stream turns NNE at HW Portsmouth +0500, and W at HW –0030, Sp rate 2kn. It is safe to pass 2ca off St Catherine's lt ho (conspic), but a race occurs off the point and can be very dangerous at or near Sp against a strong wind, particularly SE of the point on a W-going stream. St Catherine's should then be rounded at least 2M off. 1·25M SE of the point the stream turns E at HW Portsmouth +0520, and W at HW –0055, sp rate 3·75kn.* ◀

Rocks extend about 2½ca either side of Dunnose where a race occurs. In Sandown Bay ⚓ off Shanklin or Sandown where the tidal streams are weak inshore.

▶*Off the centre of the Bay they turn NE x E at HW Portsmouth +0500, and SW x W at HW –0100, sp rates 2 kn.*◀

The Yarborough Monument is conspicuous above Culver Cliff. Whitecliff Bay provides ⚓ in winds between W and N. From here to Foreland (Bembridge Pt) the coast is fringed by a ledge of drying rocks extending up to 3ca offshore, and it is advisable to keep to seaward of Bembridge Ledge ECM lt buoy.

9.2.9 CHRISTCHURCH

Dorset **50°43'·53N 01°44'·33W** ❁◊◊✿✿✿

CHARTS AC 5601, 2035, 2172; Imray C10, C12, C4, 2300, 2200

TIDES HW Sp –0210, Np, –0140 Dover; ML 1·2

Standard Port PORTSMOUTH (→); Tidal Curve see 9.2.17 (→)

Times				Height (metres)			
High Water		Low Water		MHWS	MHWN	MLWN	MLWS
0000	0600	0500	1100	4·7	3·8	1·9	0·8
1200	1800	1700	2300				
Differences BOURNEMOUTH							
–0240	+0055	–0050	–0030	–2·6	–2·0	–0·6	–0·2
CHRISTCHURCH (Entrance)							
–0230	+0030	–0035	–0035	–2·9	–2·4	–1·2	–0·2
CHRISTCHURCH (Quay)							
–0210	+0100	+0105	+0055	–2·9	–2·4	–1·0	0·0
CHRISTCHURCH (Tuckton bridge)							
–0205	+0110	+0110	+0105	–3·0	–2·5	–1·0	+0·1

NOTE: Double HWs occur, except near neaps; predictions are for the higher HW. Near neaps there is a stand; predictions are for mid-stand. Tidal levels are for inside the bar; outside, the tide is about 0·6m lower at springs. Water flow in Rivers Avon and Stour cause considerable variations from predicted heights. Tuckton LWs do not fall below 0·7m except under very low river flow conditions.

SHELTER Good in lee of Hengistbury Hd; elsewhere exposed to SW winds. R Stour navigable at HW up to Tuckton, and the R Avon up to the first bridge. Both are well sheltered. Most ⚓s in the hbr dry.

NAVIGATION WPT 50°43'·53N 01°43'·58W, 270°/0·5M to NE end of Mudeford Quay. Outer approach is marked with PHM and SHM buoys; the bar and chan are liable to shift will not be as shown on the chart. Beware groynes S of Hengistbury Hd, Beerpan, Yarranton/Clarendon Rks. The ebb stream reaches 4-5kn in The Run; best to enter or leave at HW/stand. Night entry is not recommended without local knowledge. Chan inside hbr is narrow and mostly shallow (approx 0·3m) with sand/mud. No ⚓ in chan. No berthing at ferry jetty by Mudeford sandbank (beware frequent ferries between Mudeford Quay, The Run and Christchurch). Hbr speed limit 4kn. If fishing from any craft, a local licence is obligatory.

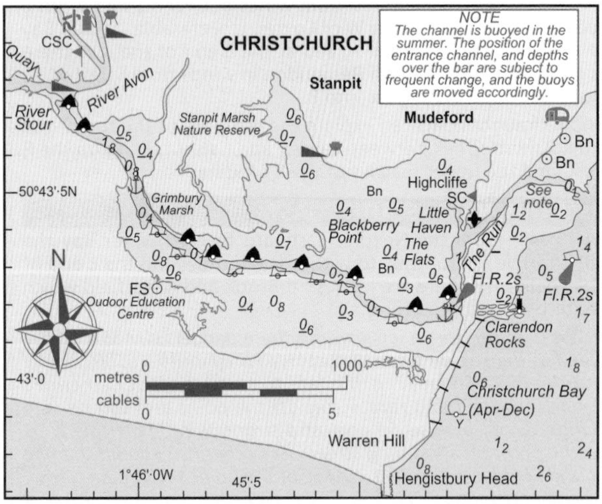

LIGHTS AND MARKS See chartlet and 9.2.4. Unlit chan buoys in hbr and apps are locally laid Apr-Oct inc; info from ☎483250.

COMMUNICATIONS (Code 01202) NMOC (01305) 760439; Police 101; Ⓗ 303626; Casualty 704167.

FACILITIES **Rossiter Yachts** ☎483250, ⊆£30;
Christchurch SC (CSC) ☎483150, ⓥ£10 limited ⊆ £20, please phone in advance to confirm berth availability.
Services ACA.
Town ✉ Ⓑ ⇌ ✈ (Hurn).

9.2.10 KEYHAVEN

Hampshire **50°42'·85N 01°33'·26W** ❁◊✿✿

CHARTS AC 5600, 2035, 2021; Imray C4, C3, 2300, 2200

TIDES –0020, +0105 Dover; ML 2·0

Standard Port PORTSMOUTH (→); Tidal Curve see 9.2.17 (→)

Times				Height (metres)			
High Water		Low Water		MHWS	MHWN	MLWN	MLWS
0000	0600	0500	1100	4·7	3·8	1·9	0·8
1200	1800	1700	2300				
Differences HURST POINT							
–0115	–0005	–0030	–0025	–2·0	–1·5	–0·5	–0·1
TOTLAND BAY							
–0130	–0045	–0035	–0045	–2·2	–1·7	–0·4	–0·1
FRESHWATER BAY							
–0210	+0025	–0040	–0020	–2·1	–1·5	–0·4	0·0

NOTE: Double HWs occur at or near sp; predictions are for the first HW. Off springs there is a stand of about 2hrs; predictions are then for mid-stand.

SHELTER Reasonable, but all moorings and ⚓s are exposed to winds across the marshland. The 'U' bend carries up to 3m but there is only about 0·5m in the entrance. Keyhaven Lake and Mount Lake all but dry. The river gets very congested during the sailing season.

NAVIGATION WPT 50°42'·70N 01°32'·79W is on 308° leading line marked by two B beacons in transit. Follow transit for about 3ca until through the pair of unlit R and G buoys then start turning to port, giving North Point a wide berth. The channel is marked with unlit G buoys. Entry is difficult on the ebb and should not be attempted in strong E winds. Entrance is possible, with local knowledge, via Hawkers Lake (unmarked), approx 0.3m less water than main channel. Beware lobster pots. When approaching from the W beware the Shingles Bank over which seas break and which partly dries. At Hurst Narrows give The Trap a wide berth.

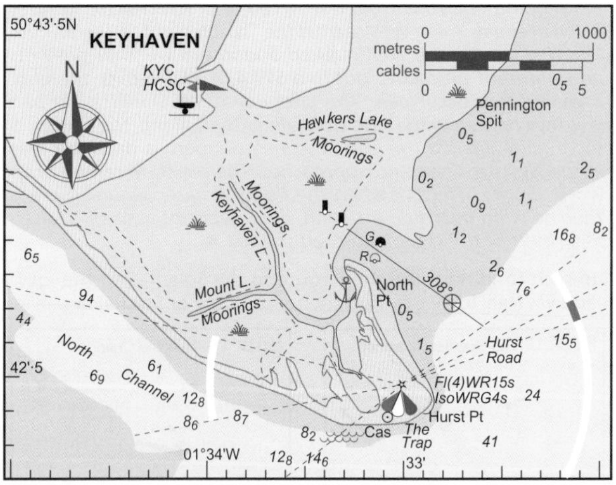

LIGHTS AND MARKS See 9.2.4, chartlet above and 9.2.11 for sectors of Hurst Point light.

COMMUNICATIONS (Code 01590) NMOC (02392) 552100; Police 101; Dr 643022; Ⓗ 677011; *River Warden* VHF Ch 645695.

FACILITIES **Quay**; **Keyhaven YC** ☎642165, ⓥ£12. **Hurst Castle SC** ☎(01590) 645589. **New Forest District Council** (R.Warden).
W Solent Boat Builders ☎642080, (9t).
Village ✕. Milford-on-Sea (1M): ✉ Ⓑ ✕ ⇌ (bus to New Milton), ✈ (Hurn).

9.2.11 NEEDLES CHANNEL

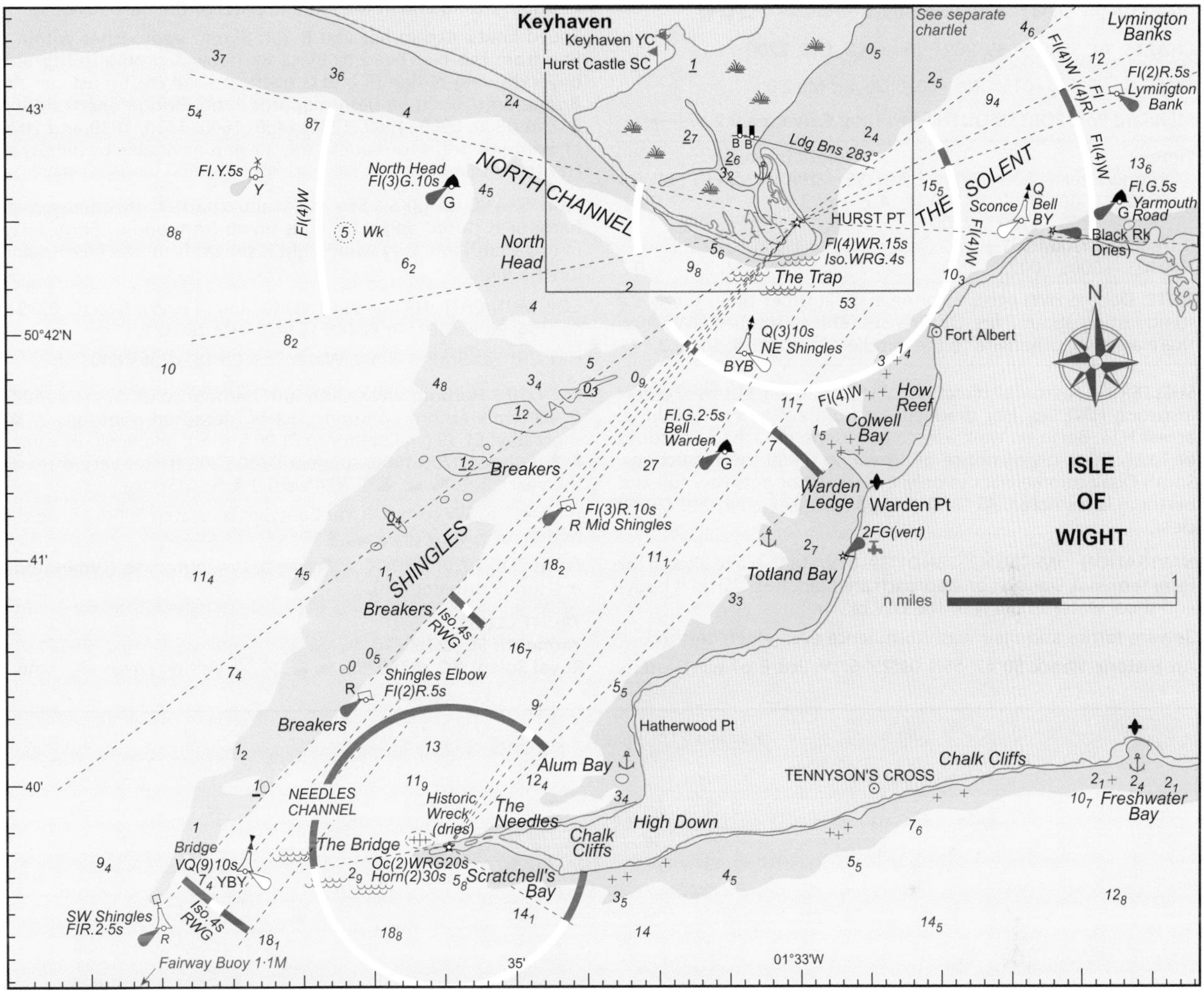

Keyhaven
Keyhaven YC
Hurst Castle SC
See separate chartlet
Lymington Banks
Fl(2)R.5s Lymington Bank
Ldg Bns 283°
NORTH CHANNEL
THE SOLENT
HURST PT
Fl(4)WR.15s
Iso.WRG.4s
The Trap
Fl.Y.5s
Y
North Head
Fl(3)G.10s
G
5 Wk
Fl(4)W
Fl(4)R
Fl
Sconce
Bell
BY
Q
Fl.G.5s Yarmouth Road
Black Rk Dries
Fort Albert
Q(3)10s NE Shingles
BYB
How Reef
Colwell Bay
Fl(4)W
Fl.G.2·5s Bell Warden
Breakers
Warden Ledge
Warden Pt
2FG(vert)
Fl(3)R.10s R Mid Shingles
SHINGLES
Totland Bay
ISLE OF WIGHT
n miles
0
1
Iso.4s RWG
Shingles Elbow Fl(2)R.5s
R
Breakers
Hatherwood Pt
Alum Bay
Chalk Cliffs
TENNYSON'S CROSS
Freshwater Bay
NEEDLES CHANNEL
Historic Wreck (dries)
The Needles
High Down
Chalk Cliffs
The Bridge
Bridge VQ(9)10s YBY
Oc(2)WRG20s
Horn(2)30s
Scratchell's Bay
SW Shingles Fl.R.2·5s
R
Fairway Buoy 1·1M
50°42'N
43'
41'
40'
35'
01°33'W
N

- The NW side of the Needles Channel is defined by the Shingles, a bank parts of which dry, and on which seas breaks in the least swell. The SE side of the bank is fairly steep-to, the NW side is less defined. Dredgers work on the Pot Bank, 4ca S of Bridge WCM.
- On the ebb the stream sets very strongly (3-4kn) WSW across the Shingles. The Needles Channel is well lit and buoyed and in fair weather presents no significant problems. Be aware that even a SW Force 4 against the ebb will raise breaking seas near Bridge and SW Shingles buoys. Contact National Coastwatch Needles on VHF Ch 65 for local conditions.
- In strong winds the North Channel, N of the Shingles, is preferable to the Needles Channel. The two join S off Hurst Point where overfalls and tide rips may be met. Beware The Trap, a shoal spit extending 150m SE of Hurst Castle.
- In bad weather broken water and overfalls extend along The Bridge, a reef which runs 8ca W of the lt ho. Lt's W extremity is marked by Bridge WCM lt buoy, but in calm weather it is feasible to pass E of Bridge buoy to avoid the worst of the ebb stream.
- Gales from S-W raise very dangerous breaking seas against the ebb in the Needles Chan, at points only 250m wide. The sea state can be at its worst shortly after LW when the flood has just begun. Although wind is with tide a substantial swell is raised as a result of turbulence in the recently turned stream. In such conditions consider using North Channel; the E route to the Solent, S of the IoW and via Nab Tower; or find shelter at Poole or Studland.

The Needles are distinctive rocks at the W end of the Isle of Wight (see AC 5600, 2035, 2021). By day the chalk cliffs of High Down are conspic from afar but the lt ho may not be seen by day until relatively close. Goose Rk, dries, is about 50m WNW of the lt ho, 100-150m WSW of which is a drying wreck.

ANCHORAGES BETWEEN THE NEEDLES AND YARMOUTH

ALUM BAY, 50°40'·10N 01°34'·33W. AC 5600, 2021. Tides as for Totland Bay. Very good shelter in E and S winds, but squally in gales. Distinctive white cliffs to S and multi-coloured cliffs and chairlift to E. Appr from due W of chairlift to clear Five Fingers Rk, to the N and Long Rk, a reef drying 0·9m at its E end, to the S. ⚓ in about 4m.

TOTLAND BAY, 50°40'·98N 01°32'·86W. AC 5600, 2035. ML 1·9m. Good shelter in E'lies in wide shelving bay between Warden Ledge (rks 4ca offshore) to the N, and Hatherwood Pt to the SW. Appr W of Warden SHM buoy Fl G 2·5s to ⚓ out of the stream in 2m between pier (2FG vert) and old LB house; good holding. Colwell Bay, to the N between Warden Pt and Fort Albert, is generally rocky and shallow.

ANCHORAGE EAST OF THE NEEDLES, SOUTH IOW

FRESHWATER BAY, 50°40'·07N 01°30'·61W. AC 5600, 2021. ML 1·6m. Good shelter from the N, open to the S. The bay is 3·2M E of Needles Lt ho and 1·2M E of Tennyson's Cross. Conspic marks: Redoubt Fort on W side; a hotel on N side; Stag and Mermaid Rks to the E. The bay is shallow, with rocky drying ledges ¾ca either side and a rock (dries 0·1m) almost in the centre. Best to ⚓ in about 2m just outside the bay. ✉ 🛒 ✕ 🛈.

9.2.12 YARMOUTH

Isle of Wight **50°42'·42N 01°30'·05W**

CHARTS AC 5600, 2035, 2021; Imray C3, C15, 2200

TIDES Sp –0050, +0150, Np +0020 Dover; ML 2·0

Standard Port PORTSMOUTH (⟶); Tidal Curve see 9.2.17 (⟶)

Times				Height (metres)			
High Water		Low Water		MHWS	MHWN	MLWN	MLWS
0000	0600	0500	1100	4·7	3·8	1·9	0·8
1200	1800	1700	2300				
Differences YARMOUTH							
–0105	+0005	–0025	–0030	–1·7	–1·2	–0·3	0·0

NOTE: Double HWs occur at or near sp; at other times there is a stand lasting about 2 hrs. Differences refer to the first HW when there are two; otherwise to the middle of the stand. See 9.2.17.

SHELTER Good from all directions of wind and sea, but swell enters in strong N/NE'lies. Hbr dredged 2m from ent to swing bridge; access H24. Berth on walk ashore pontoons, detached pontoons or Town Quay, giving notice of arrival on Ch 68 for instructions. South Quay commercial use only. In season hbr gets very full and berthing is restricted. 38 Or ⓥs outside hbr (see chartlet). ⚓ well clear.

NAVIGATION WPT 50°42'·58N 01°30'·01W, 188°/2ca to abeam car ferry terminal. Dangers on approach are Black Rock (SHM lt buoy) and shoal water to the N of the E/W bkwtr.

Beware ferries and their wash/turbulence even when berthed.

An **Historic Wreck** 50°42'·55N 01°29'·67W, 2ca E of pierhead, is marked by a Y SPM. Royal Solent moorings lie between the two.

Caution: strong ebb in the ent and parts of the harbour at Sp.

Speed limits: 4kn in hbr and R Yar; 6kn in approaches within a line from the pier head to Black Rk buoy. ⚓ prohib in hbr and beyond swing bridge (R and G traffic lts). All craft must call *Yar Bridge* on VHF Ch 68 before approaching. Bridge opens during BST at 0800, 0900, 1000, 1200, 1400, 1600, 1730, 1830 and 2000 LT; winter months by request only. River is navigable by dinghy at HW to Freshwater.

LIGHTS AND MARKS See 9.2.4 and chartlet. In emergencies harbour is closed and a R flag is flown from end of Ferry Jetty. In fog a high intensity white light is shown from the Pier Hd and inner E pier.

COMMUNICATIONS (Code 01983 (whole of IOW)) NMOC (02392) 552100; Police 101; Dr 08448 151428. HM 760321.

HM and *Yar Bridge* Ch **68**. Water Taxi Ch 15, 07969 840173.

FACILITIES Harbour www.yarmouth-harbour.co.uk Approx 250ⓥ, £3·89 (walk ashore pontoons), £2·44 (detached pontoons or ⓥ) short stay: £1·39 (walk ashore), £1·00 (other); midweek discounts. (winter 0700-1900, summer 0700-2200 (times vary through the year)) (£4/visit) (5t) ice.

Hayles in SW corner; R Yar Boatyard is located 500m above the bridge, or ½M by road.

Town ©(PO). Ferries to Lymington, (Lymington), ✈ (Hurn/Southampton).

YACHT CLUBS

Yarmouth SC ☎760270.

Royal Solent YC ☎760256; visiting crews welcome.

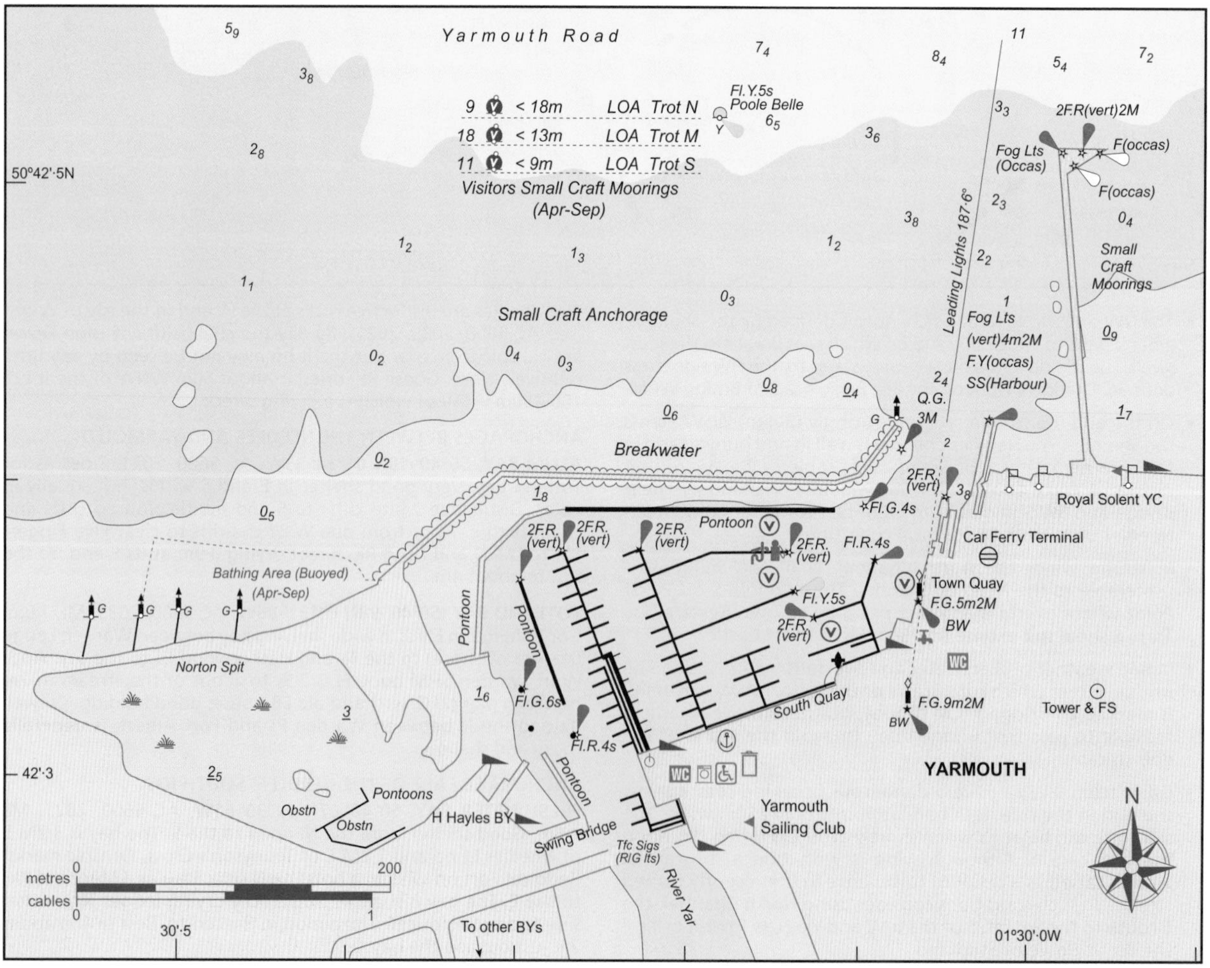

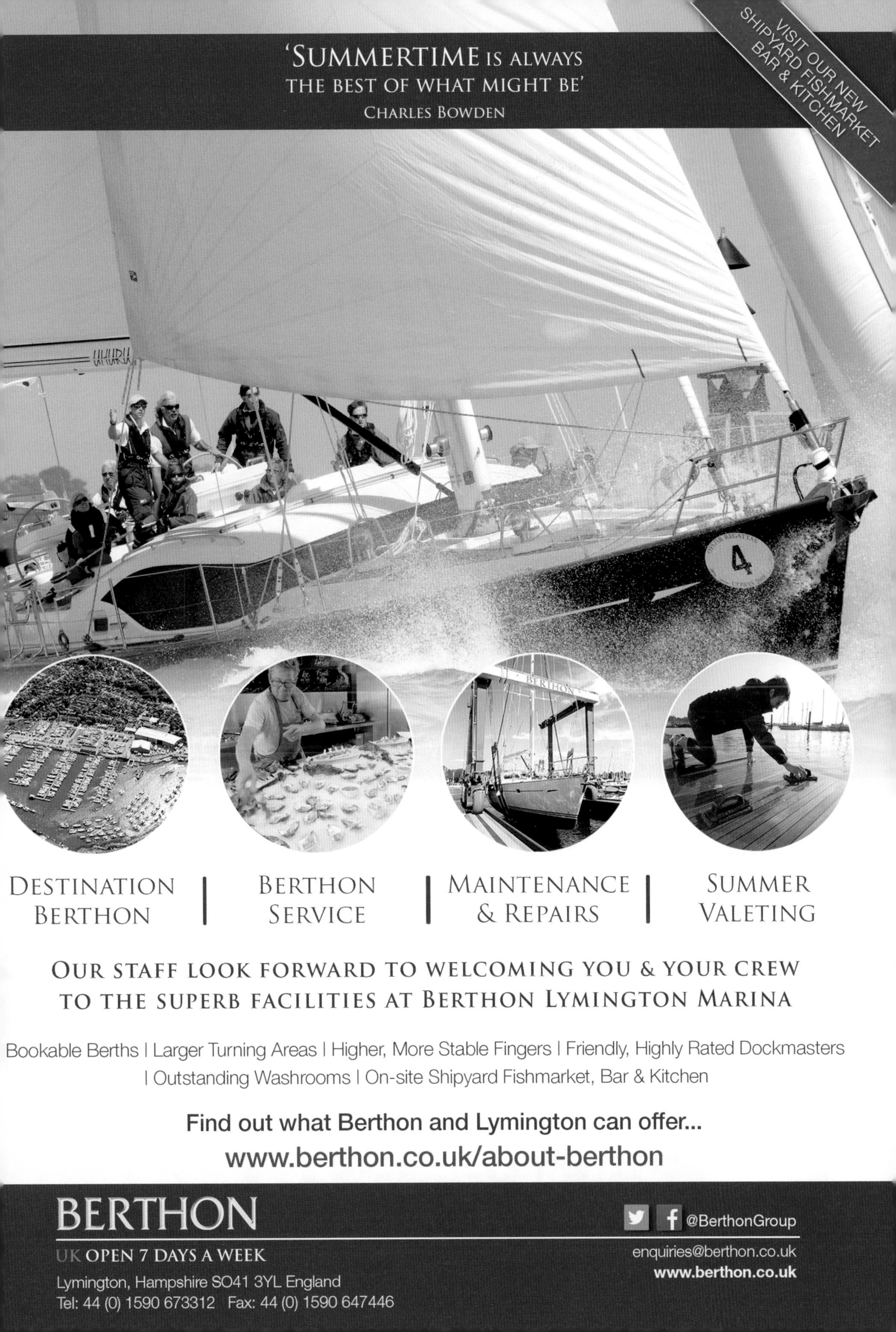
'SUMMERTIME IS ALWAYS
THE BEST OF WHAT MIGHT BE'
CHARLES BOWDEN
VISIT OUR NEW
SHIPYARD FISHMARKET
BAR & KITCHEN
DESTINATION BERTHON
BERTHON SERVICE
MAINTENANCE & REPAIRS
SUMMER VALETING
OUR STAFF LOOK FORWARD TO WELCOMING YOU & YOUR CREW
TO THE SUPERB FACILITIES AT BERTHON LYMINGTON MARINA
Bookable Berths | Larger Turning Areas | Higher, More Stable Fingers | Friendly, Highly Rated Dockmasters
| Outstanding Washrooms | On-site Shipyard Fishmarket, Bar & Kitchen
Find out what Berthon and Lymington can offer...
www.berthon.co.uk/about-berthon
BERTHON
UK OPEN 7 DAYS A WEEK
Lymington, Hampshire SO41 3YL England
Tel: 44 (0) 1590 673312 Fax: 44 (0) 1590 647446
@BerthonGroup
enquiries@berthon.co.uk
www.berthon.co.uk

A TYHA 5 Gold Anchor Marina
Lymington Yacht Haven
The perfect home for your boat
LOOKING FORWARD TO WELCOMING YOU IN 2018
YOUR PERFECT BASE FOR EXPLORING THE SOLENT:
- Berths for yachts up to 25m (80ft)
- 24 hour access, fuel and service
- Luxury facilities and free Wi-Fi at your berth
- Full marina services, boatyard and brokerage
- On-site chandlery and shop
- Fabulous food and stunning views at The Haven Bar & Restaurant
- An easy 10 minute walk to Lymington High Street
- Great savings and benefits for Yacht Havens Berth Holders – visit yachthavens.com
- Special Winter Berthing Rates (Nov-Feb inclusive)
The Yacht Harbour Association Ltd.
UK Coastal Marina of the Year 2016
Over 250 Berths
Lymington Yacht Haven
WINNER
PARTNERED BY
GJW Insurance
Lymington Yacht Haven
CONTACT 01590 677071 OR VHF CH 80 www.yachthavens.com/lymington

9.2.13 LYMINGTON

Hampshire **50°45'·13N 01°31'·40W** ❀❀❀◇◇◇✿✿✿

CHARTS AC 5600, 2035, 2021; Imray C3, C15, 2200

TIDES Sp –0040, +0100, Np +0020 Dover; ML 2·0

Standard Port PORTSMOUTH (⟶); **Tidal Curve see 9.2.17** (⟶)

Times				Height (metres)			
High Water		Low Water		MHWS	MHWN	MLWN	MLWS
0000	0600	0500	1100	4·7	3·8	1·9	0·8
1200	1800	1700	2300				
Differences LYMINGTON							
–0110	+0005	–0020	–0020	–1·6	–1·2	–0·4	–0·1

SEE NOTE under Tides at 9.2.12.

Lymington Harbour Commissioners www.lymington harbour.co.uk ☎672014; HM patrol for berthing advice; wi-fi on river berths.

Dan Bran Pontoon up to 40Ⓥ £15–£35 ⌁+£2 ⛽ and use of LTSC. Long walk ashore pontoon suitable for rallies and other events.

Town Quay public pontoon, many ⚓ ⌓ £18·50-£29/craft (9·5m-10·5m LOA), £8·20 for short stay; >15m LOA by arrangement with HM; ⛵ ▬ (see HM) ⛽ ♿ ♿ WC/🚿.

Scrubbing grids (5) See HM for details.

Berthon Lymington Marina www.berthon.co.uk ☎647405. 250+100Ⓥ £4·05, ⌁ 🚿 🚿 🛢 ♿ 🗑 ✕ 🔧 ⛭ Ⓔ ⛵ ⚑(75t) ⛭ ⛴(20t) 🗎 wi-fi.

Town All facilities, ⇌ Ferries to IoW, ✈ (Hurn or Southampton).

YACHT CLUBS **Royal Lymington YC** ☎672677, ♿ ✕ 🗎.
Lymington Town SC ☎674514, ♿ (Sailability access hoist) ✕ 🗎.

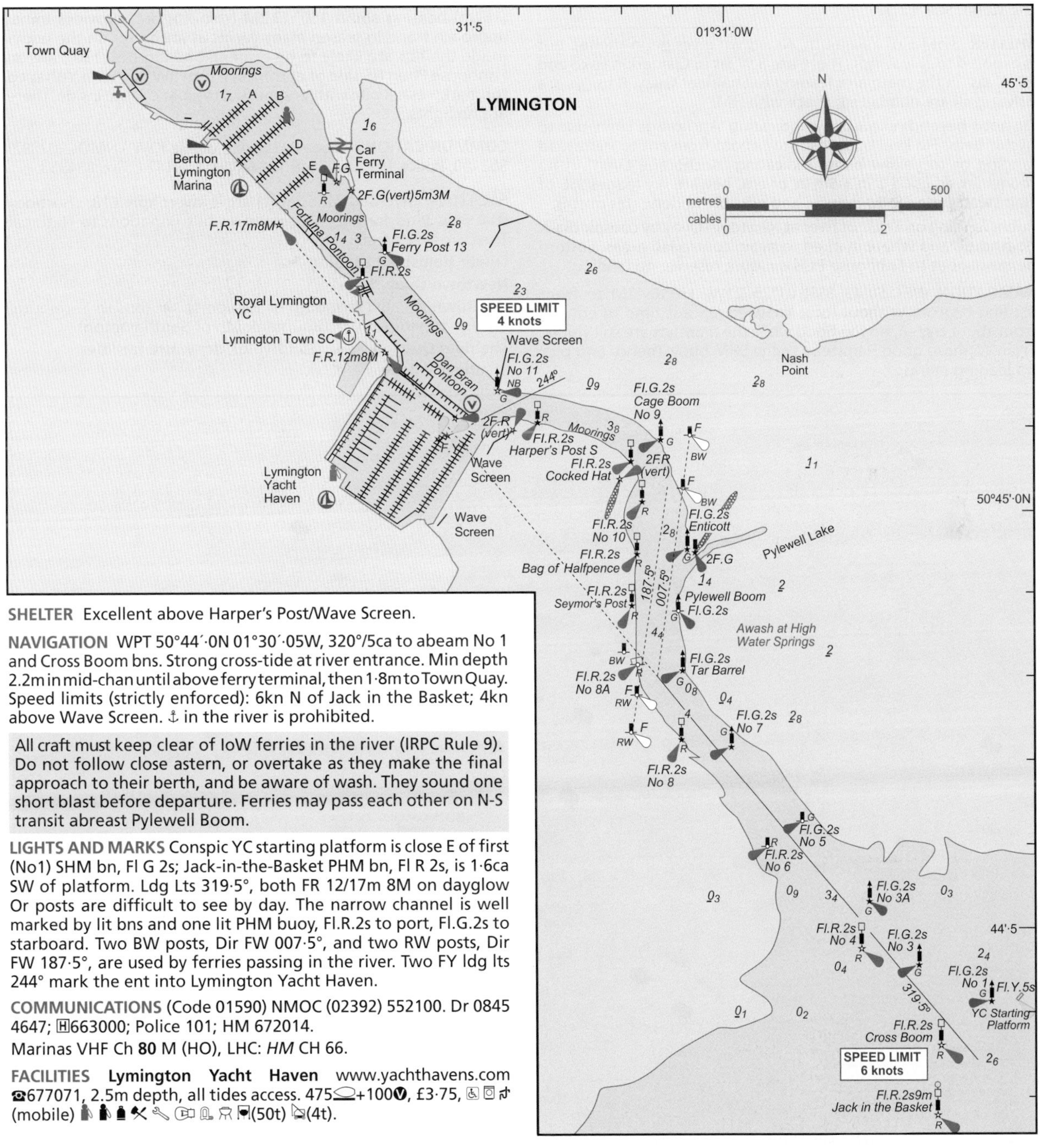

SHELTER Excellent above Harper's Post/Wave Screen.

NAVIGATION WPT 50°44´·0N 01°30´·05W, 320°/5ca to abeam No 1 and Cross Boom bns. Strong cross-tide at river entrance. Min depth 2.2m in mid-chan until above ferry terminal, then 1·8m to Town Quay. Speed limits (strictly enforced): 6kn N of Jack in the Basket; 4kn above Wave Screen. ⚓ in the river is prohibited.

All craft must keep clear of IoW ferries in the river (IRPC Rule 9). Do not follow close astern, or overtake as they make the final approach to their berth, and be aware of wash. They sound one short blast before departure. Ferries may pass each other on N-S transit abreast Pylewell Boom.

LIGHTS AND MARKS Conspic YC starting platform is close E of first (No1) SHM bn, Fl G 2s; Jack-in-the-Basket PHM bn, Fl R 2s, is 1·6ca SW of platform. Ldg Lts 319·5°, both FR 12/17m 8M on dayglow Or posts are difficult to see by day. The narrow channel is well marked by lit bns and one lit PHM buoy, Fl.R.2s to port, Fl.G.2s to starboard. Two BW posts, Dir FW 007·5°, and two RW posts, Dir FW 187·5°, are used by ferries passing in the river. Two FY ldg lts 244° mark the ent into Lymington Yacht Haven.

COMMUNICATIONS (Code 01590) NMOC (02392) 552100. Dr 0845 4647; Ⓗ663000; Police 101; HM 672014.

Marinas VHF Ch **80** M (HO), LHC: *HM* CH 66.

FACILITIES **Lymington Yacht Haven** www.yachthavens.com ☎677071, 2.5m depth, all tides access. 475⌓+100Ⓥ, £3·75, ♿ 🗑 ⚓ (mobile) 🚿 🚿 🛢 ✕ 🔧 ⛭ 🗎 ⛭ ⚑(50t) ⛴(4t).

9.2.14 NEWTOWN RIVER

Isle of Wight **50°43'·45N 01°24'·66W** ❁❁◇✿✿✿

CHARTS AC 5600, 2035, 2036, 2021; Imray C3, C15, 2200

TIDES Sp –0108, Np +0058, Dover; ML 2·3

Standard Port PORTSMOUTH (⟶); Tidal Curve see 9.2.17 (⟶)

Times				Height (metres)			
High Water		Low Water		MHWS	MHWN	MLWN	MLWS
0000	0600	0500	1100	4·7	3·8	1·9	0·8
1200	1800	1700	2300				
Differences YARMOUTH/NEWTOWN ENTRANCE							
–0105	+0005	–0025	–0030	–1·7	–1·2	–0·3	0·0

NOTE: Double HWs occur at or near springs; at other times there is a stand which lasts about 2hrs. Differences refer to the first HW when there are two. At other times they refer to the middle of the stand. See 9.2.17.

SHELTER 3½M E of Yarmouth, Newtown gives good shelter, but is exposed to N'ly winds. There are 5 W Ⓥs in Clamerkin Lake and 20 W Ⓥs in the main arm leading to Shalfleet Quay, R buoys are private; all are numbered; check with HM.

Do not ⚓ beyond yellow buoys indicating 'Anchorage Limit' due to oyster beds. Fin keel boats can stay afloat from ent to Hamstead landing or to yellow buoys indicating 'Anchorage Limit'. If no room in river, good ⚓ in 3-5m W of ent, beware rky ledges SSE of Hamstead Ledge SHM lt buoy, and possible underwater obstns.

Public landing on E side of river at Newtown Quay by conspic black boathouse and where marked to avoid controlled areas. Eastern peninsula out to Fishhouse Pt is a nature reserve; no landing.

NAVIGATION WPT 50°43'·85N 01°25'·21W, 130°/0·42M to front leading beacon. Without local knowledge, best time to enter is from about HW –4, on the flood while the mudflats are still visible. From W, make good Hamstead Ledge SHM buoy, thence E to pick up leading marks.

From E, keep N of Newtown Gravel Banks where fresh W/SW winds over a spring ebb can raise steep breaking seas. Leave WCM buoy, Q(9) 15s, to port.

Min depth to inside the entrance is about 2m. 5kn speed limit in harbour is strictly enforced. Near junction to Causeway Lake depth is only 0·9m and beyond this water quickly shoals.

At ent to Clamerkin Lake (1·2–1·8m) keep to SE to avoid gravel spit off W shore, marked by two SHMs; the rest of chan is marked by occasional buoys. Beware many oyster beds in Western Haven and Clamerkin Lake.

Rifle Range at top of Clamerkin Lake and in Spur Lake; R flags flown during firing. High voltage power line across Clamerkin at 50°42'·81N 01°22'·66W has clearance of only 8·8m and no shore markings.

LIGHTS AND MARKS See 9.2.4 and chartlet. Conspic TV mast (152m) bearing about 150° (3·3M from hbr ent) provides initial approach track. In season many yachts at anchor or on the buoys inside the hbr are likely to be evident. The ldg bns, 130°, are on Fishhouse Pt on NE side of entrance. Front: RW pile with Y-shaped topmark; rear: R pile with W spherical topmark. Once inside, there are no lights.

COMMUNICATIONS (Code 01983 (for whole IOW)) NMOC (02392) 552100; Police 101; Dr 08448 151428; HM 531424; Taxi 884353.

FACILITIES Average mooring charges overnight £18, short/day stay £10. ⚓ no formal charge applies but donations to National Trust are welcomed.

Lower Hamstead Landing ⛕.

Newtown Quay ⛕ ⛵.

Newtown ✉ Ⓑ (Yarmouth or Newport), ⇌ (bus to Yarmouth, ferry to Lymington), ✈ (Bournemouth or Southampton).

Shalfleet Quay ⛵ ⛕ ⛵ (drying), dry waste facilities.

Shalfleet Village 🛒 ✕ ⛵.

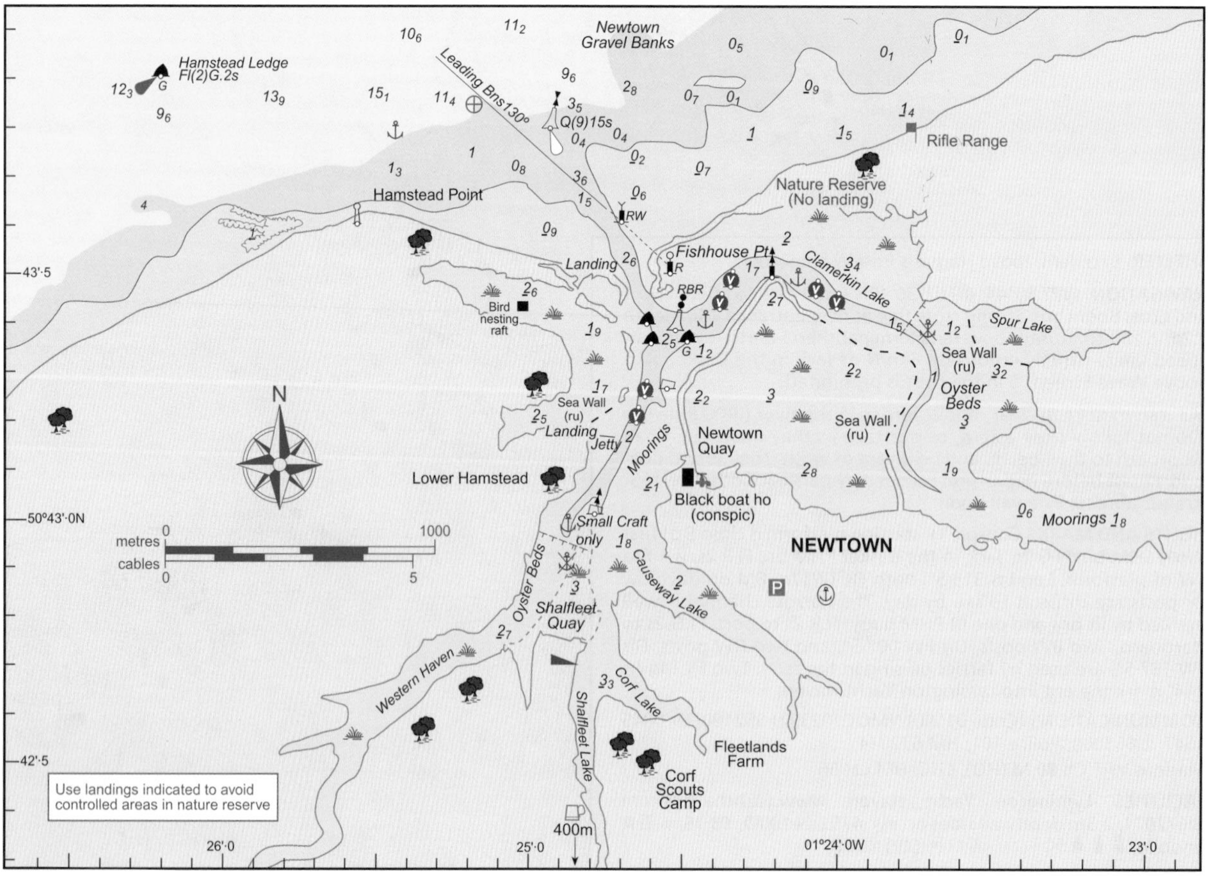

9.2.15 BEAULIEU RIVER

Hampshire **50°46'·89N 01°21'·72W** (Ent) ❀❀👍👍👍✿✿✿

CHARTS AC 5600, 2036, 2021; Imray C3, C15, 2200

TIDES –0100 and +0140 Dover; ML 2·4

Standard Port PORTSMOUTH (⟶); Tidal Curve see 9.2.17 (⟶)

Times				Height (metres)			
High Water		Low Water		MHWS	MHWN	MLWN	MLWS
0000	0600	0500	1100	4·7	3·8	1·9	0·8
1200	1800	1700	2300				
BUCKLERS HARD							
–0040	–0010	+0010	–0010	–1·0	–0·8	–0·2	–0·3
STANSORE POINT							
–0030	–0010	–0005	–0015	–0·7	–0·5	–0·3	–0·3

NOTE: Double HWs occur at or near springs; the 2nd HW is approx 1¾hrs after the 1st. On other occasions there is a stand which lasts about 2hrs. Differences refer to the first HW when there are two, or to the middle of the stand. See 9.2.17.

SHELTER Very good above Needs Ore Pt in all winds. ⚓ possible in reach between Inchmery Ho and Needs Ore Pt, but for facilities proceed to Bucklers Hard Yacht Hbr (3·5M from entrance). No ⚓ E of Inchmery Ho or 1M either side of Bucklers Hard.

NAVIGATION WPT 50°46'·60N 01°21'·40W, close E of seasonal ♁ (*Mar-Oct*) in 4m, 324°/3·3ca to abeam Beaulieu Spit Dn. Least depth between WPT and No 2 beacon approx 0·9m. Speed limit of 5kn applies throughout the river. If possible proceed under power in the river.

Ldg marks 324° at entrance should be carefully aligned due to shoal water either side of ldg line, although there is possibly more water to NE of line. Beaulieu Spit Dn should be left approx 40m to port. At night keep in W sector of Millennium Bn (Lepe) until No 4 PHM Bn abeam.

Many of the landing stages and slips shown on the chartlet and AC 2021 are privately owned and must not be used without permission. The river is navigable for about 2M above Bucklers Hard, but the uppermost reaches are best explored by dinghy. There are limited alongside drying berths at Beaulieu extending from the weir not more than 20m downstream.

LIGHTS AND MARKS See 9.2.4 and chartlet. Front ldg mark is red No 2 Bn, 0·7ca N of Beaulieu Spit Dn; the rear is W edge of Lepe Ho (≠ 324°). The Old CG cottages and Boat House are conspic, approx 320m E of Lepe Ho. The river is clearly marked by R and G bns and withies/perches. SHM bns 5, 9, 19 and 21 are all Fl G 4s; PHM bns 8,12 and 20 are Fl R 4s.

COMMUNICATIONS (Code 01590) NMOC (02392) 552100; Police 101; Dr 612451 or (02380) 845955; Ⓗ 0845 4647.

Beaulieu River Radio Ch 68 (for HM).

FACILITIES Bucklers Hard ⚓ www.beaulieuriver.co.uk ☎616200, 115⌒+40Ⓥ, £3·50/m, short stay £1·50/m. Detached pontoons £2.5/m, Ⓥs £2/m, short stay £1.50/m. Below Needs Ore Pt 8 Ⓥs £10/boat<40', ⚓ £5.50. ♿ ◙ ⛽ ⛽(0800-1800) ⛽ ⚒ 🔧 ⚡ ⚓(35t), scrubbing grid(£25) ⛵ ⊕ 🛒 ✕ ⊡.

Royal Southampton YC (Gins Club) ☎616213, www.rsyc.org.uk; Ch 77(*Sea Echo*); ⌒(temp) ⛽ ⊡ ✕ ⊡.

Village ✉ Ⓑ Ⓒ 🛒 (☎616293), ✕ ⊡(Beaulieu) ⇄ (bus to Brockenhurst), ✈ (Hurn or Southampton).

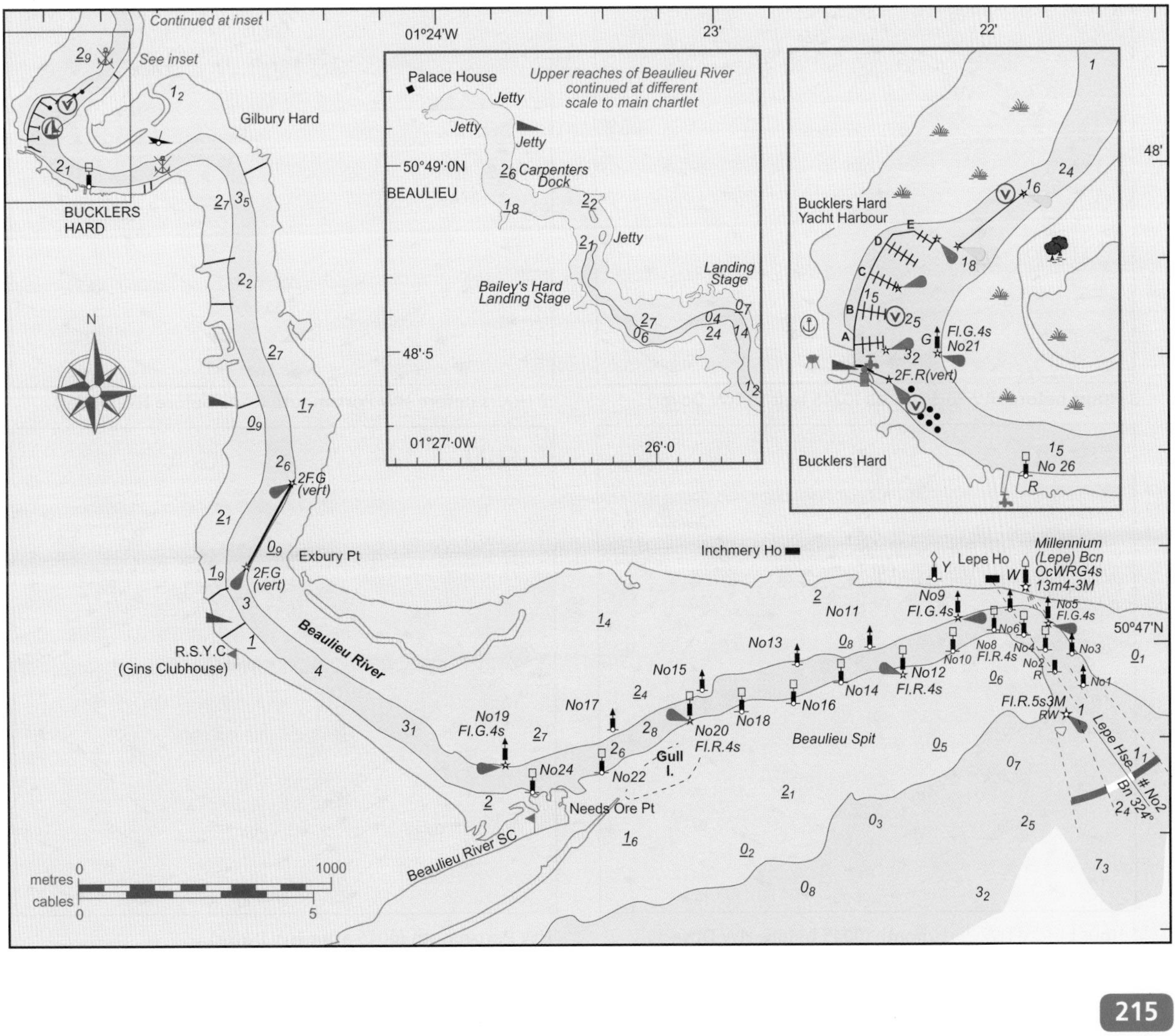

9.2.16 ISLE OF WIGHT AND SOLENT TIDAL STREAMS

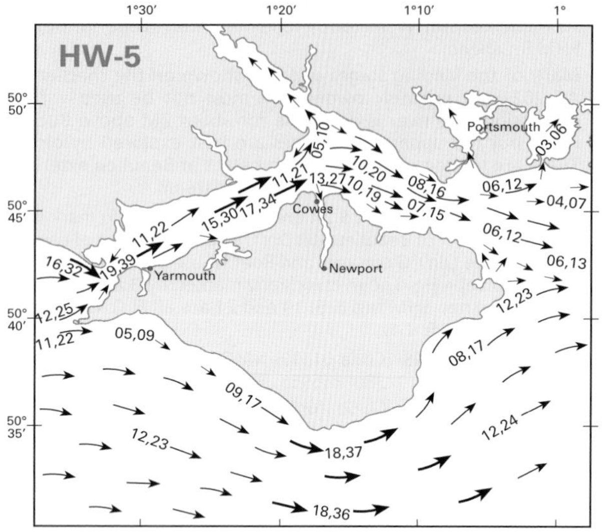

5 Hours before HW Portsmouth (0445 before HW Dover)

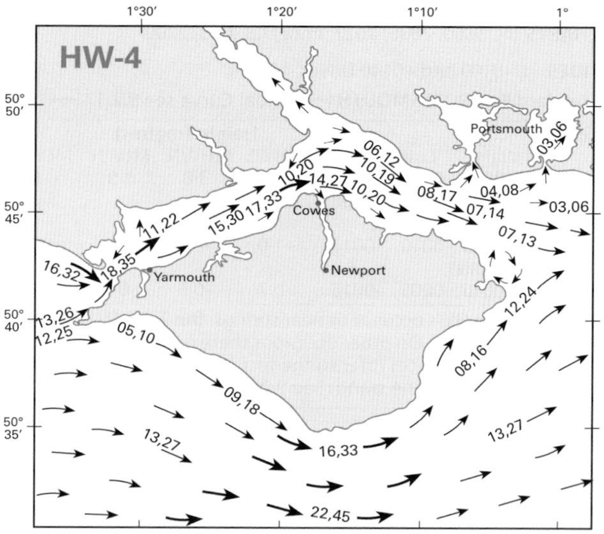

4 Hours before HW Portsmouth (0345 before HW Dover)

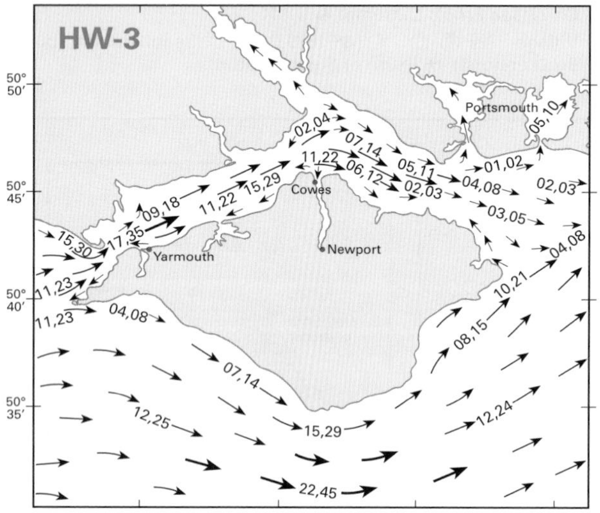

3 Hours before HW Portsmouth (0245 before HW Dover)

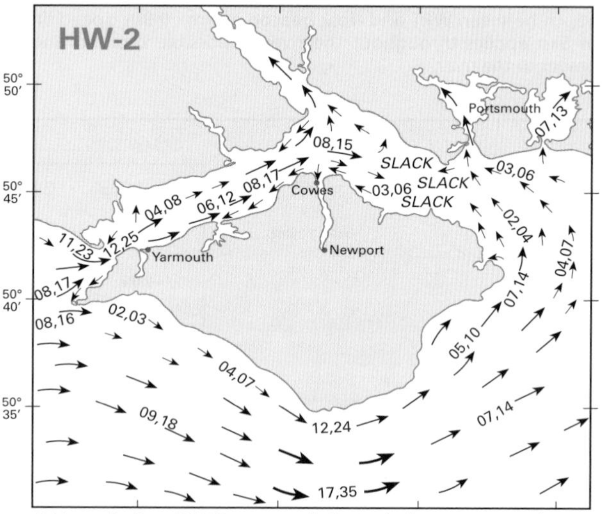

2 Hours before HW Portsmouth (0145 before HW Dover)

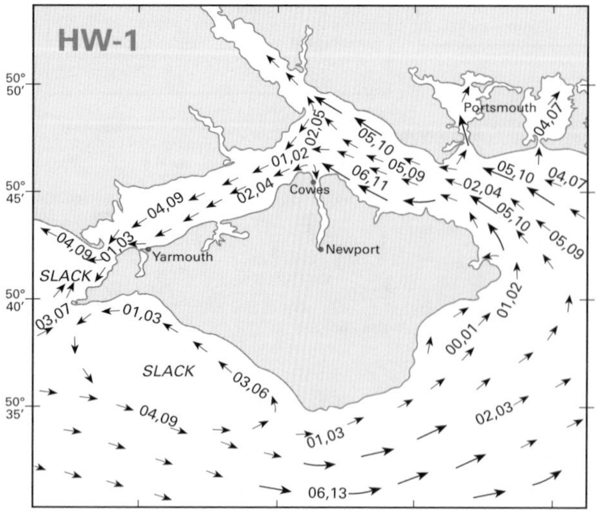

1 Hour before HW Portsmouth (0045 before HW Dover)

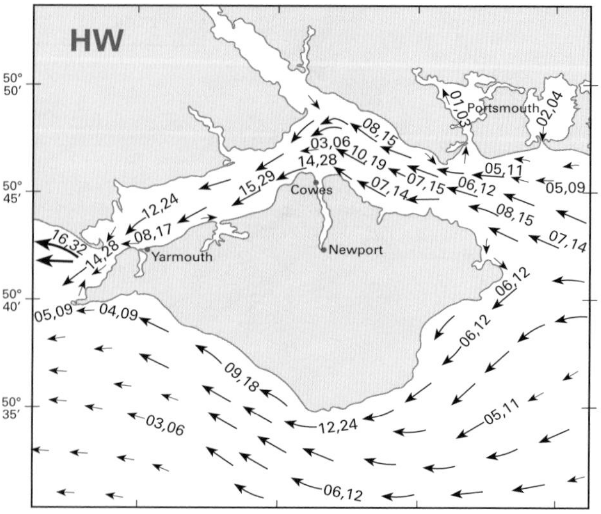

HW Portsmouth (0015 after HW Dover)

General Area 2: 9.2.3

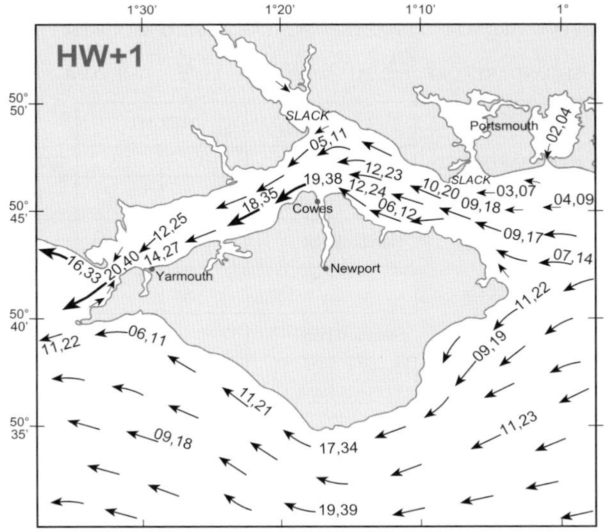

1 Hour after HW Portsmouth (0115 after HW Dover)

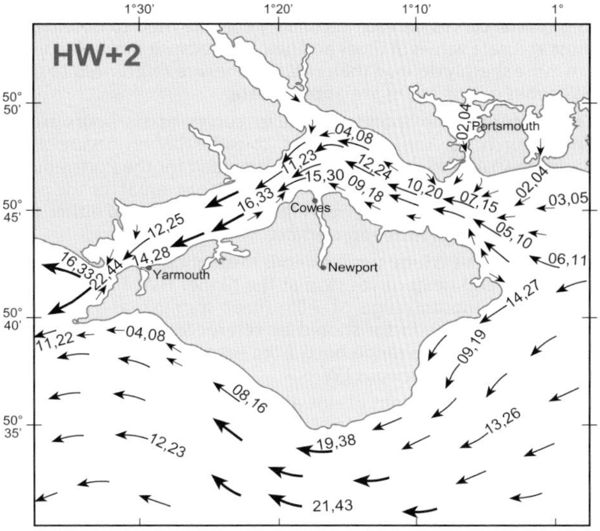

2 Hours after HW Portsmouth (0215 after HW Dover)

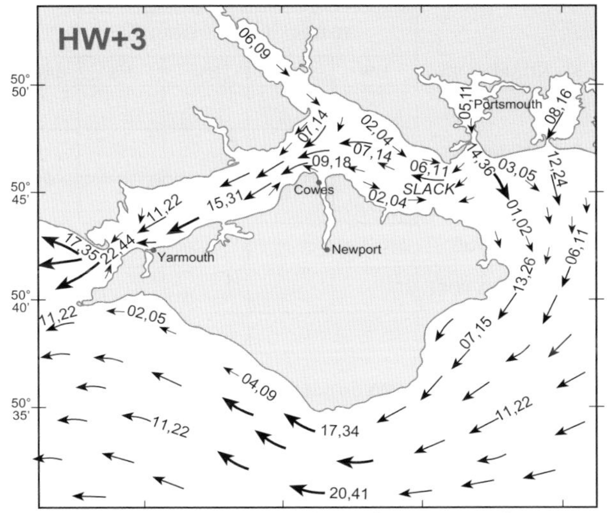

3 Hours after HW Portsmouth (0315 after HW Dover)

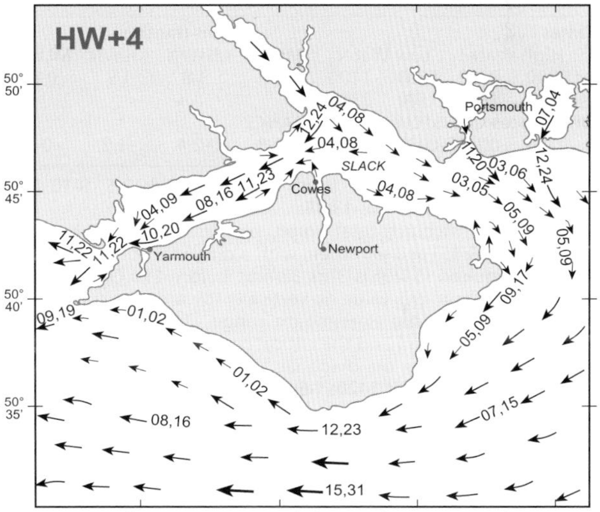

4 Hours after HW Portsmouth (0415 after HW Dover)

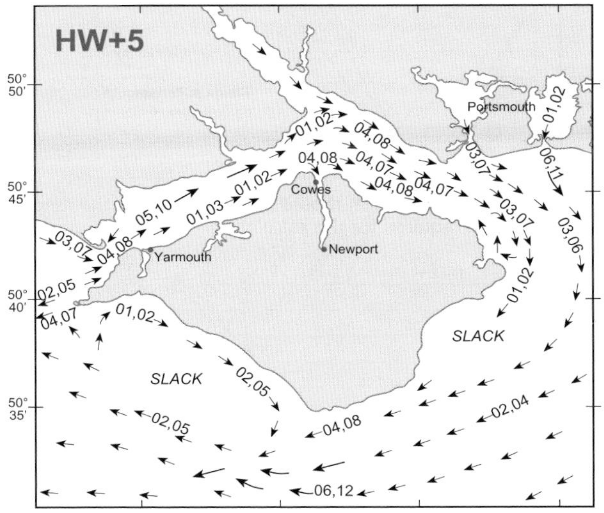

5 Hours after HW Portsmouth (0515 after HW Dover)

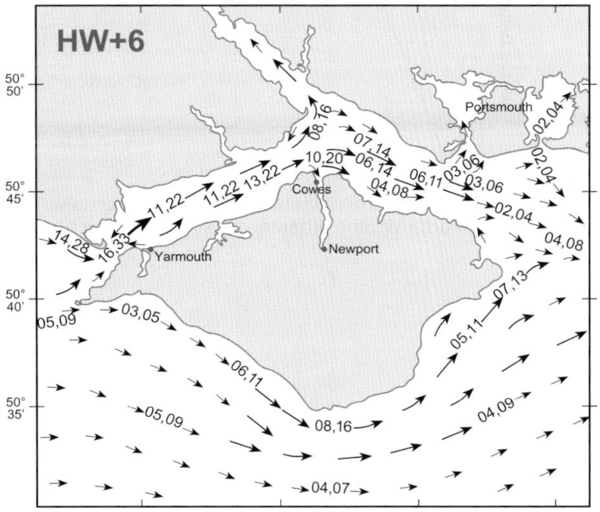

6 Hours after HW Portsmouth (0615 after HW Dover)

9.2.17 SPECIAL TIDAL CURVES FROM CHRISTCHURCH TO SELSEY BILL

Due to the complex tidal patterns between Christchurch and Selsey Bill, **special curves** for each Secondary Port are used to obtain the most accurate values of times and heights. Because their LW points are more sharply defined than HW, *all times are referenced to LW*. HW times on the tables are approximate.

Critical curve. The spring and neap curves at harbours from Christchurch to Yarmouth differ considerably in shape and duration so a third, 'critical', curve is provided for the Portsmouth range at which the heights of the two HWs are equal for the port concerned. Interpolate between this critical curve and either the spring or neap curve as appropriate.

Note: Whilst the critical curve extends throughout the tidal range, the spring and neap curves stop at the higher HW. For example, with a Portsmouth range of 3·8m (near springs), at 7hrs after LW Lymington the factor should be referenced to the *next* LW. Had the Portsmouth range been 2·0m (near neaps), it should be referenced to the *previous* LW.

Example: Find the height of tide at Christchurch at 1420 on a day when the tidal predictions for Portsmouth are:

18	0110	4·6
	0613	1·1
SA	1318	4·6
	1833	1·0

Standard Port PORTSMOUTH

Times				**Height (metres)**			
High Water		Low Water		MHWS	MHWN	MLWN	MLWS
0000	0600	0500	1100	4·7	3·8	1·9	0·8
1200	1800	1700	2300				
Differences CHRISTCHURCH ENTRANCE							
−0230	+0030	−0035	−0035	−2·9	−2·4	−1·2	−0·2

- On the tidal prediction form complete fields 2-5, 8-10 (by interpolation) and thus 13-15.
- On the Christchurch tidal graph, plot the HW & LW heights (fields 14 & 15) and join them with a diagonal line.
- Time required (1420) is 3hrs 38mins before LW Christchurch (field 13); from this value go vertically towards the curves.
- Interpolate for the Portsmouth range (3·6m) between the spring curve (3·9m) and the critical curve (2·6m).
- Go horizontally to the diagonal; thence vertically to read off the height of tide at 1420: 1·6m.

STANDARD PORT Portsmouth TIME/HEIGHT REQUIRED 1420

SECONDARY PORT Christchurch DATE 18 Nov TIME ZONE 0(UT)

	TIME		HEIGHT		
	HW	LW	HW	LW	RANGE
STANDARD PORT	1	2 1833	3 4·6	4 1·0	5 3·6
Seasonal change	Standard Port		6	6	
DIFFERENCES	7	8 −0035	9 −2·8	10 −0·3	
Seasonal change	Standard Port		11	11	
SECONDARY PORT	12	13 1758	14 1·8	15 0·7	
Duration	16				

STANDARD PORT .... TIME/HEIGHT REQUIRED ....

SECONDARY PORT .... DATE .... TIME ZONE ....

	TIME		HEIGHT		
	HW	LW	HW	LW	RANGE
STANDARD PORT	1	2	3	4	5
Seasonal change	Standard Port		6	6	
DIFFERENCES	7	8	9	10	
Seasonal change	Standard Port		11	11	
SECONDARY PORT	12	13	14	15	
	16				

Note*** At Tuckton LWs do not fall below 0·7m except under very low river flow conditions.

H.W.Hts at Secondary Ports

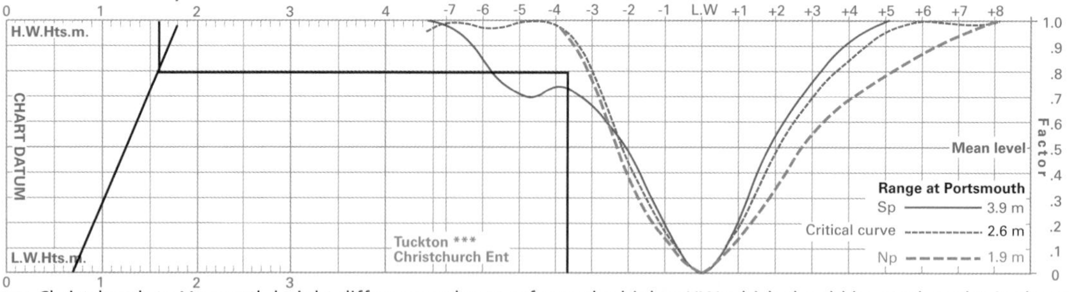

Note: From Christchurch to Yarmouth height differences always refer to the higher HW which should be used to obtain the range at the Secondary Port. HW time differences also refer to the higher HW, but are not required for this calculation.

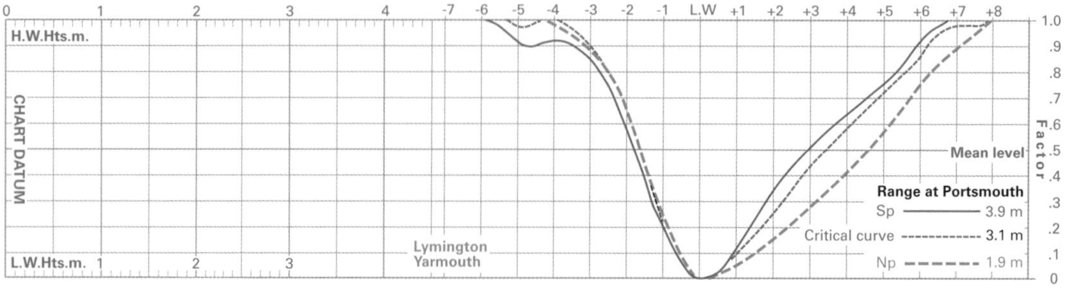

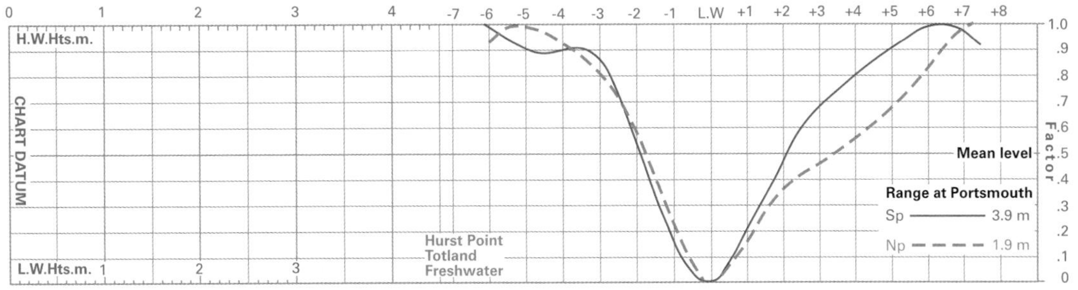

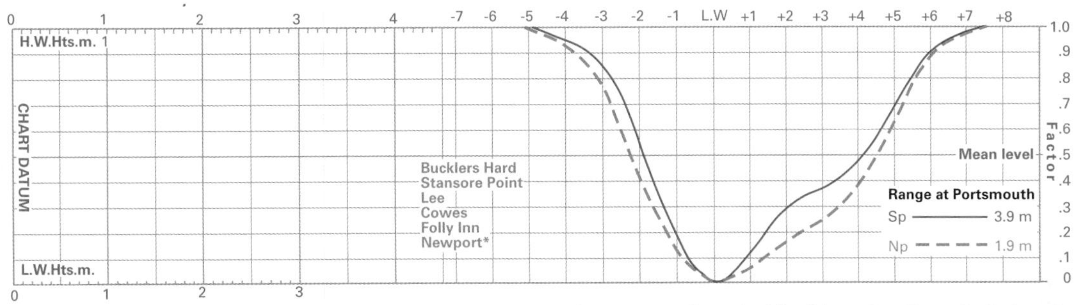

Note* Due to the constriction of the R Medina, Newport requires special treatment since the hbr dries 1·4m. The calculation should be made using the LW time and height differences for Cowes, and the HW height differences for Newport. Any calculated heights which fall below 1·4m should be treated as 1·4m.

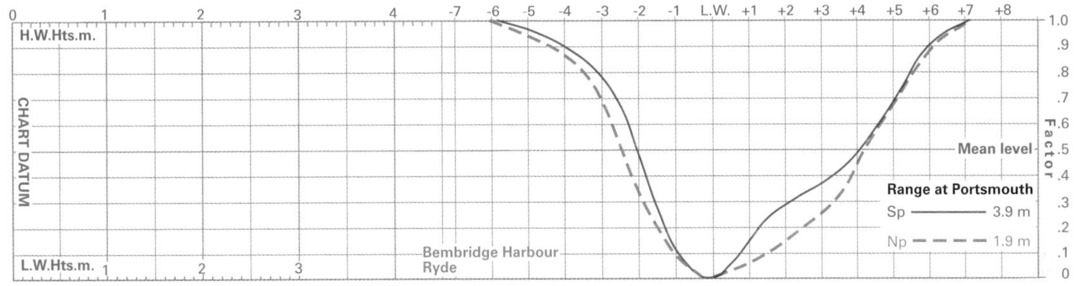

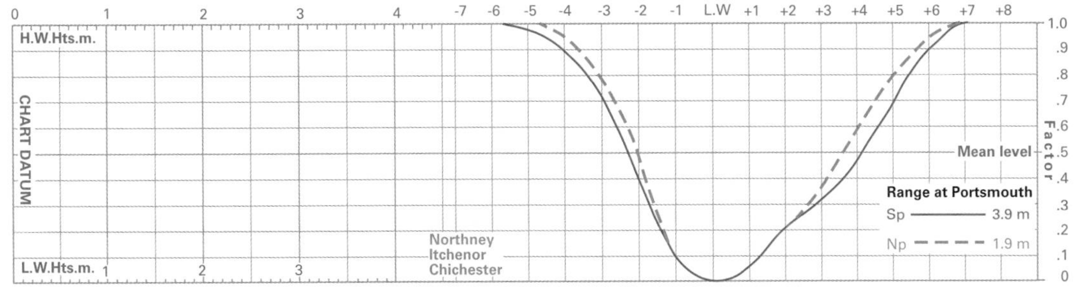

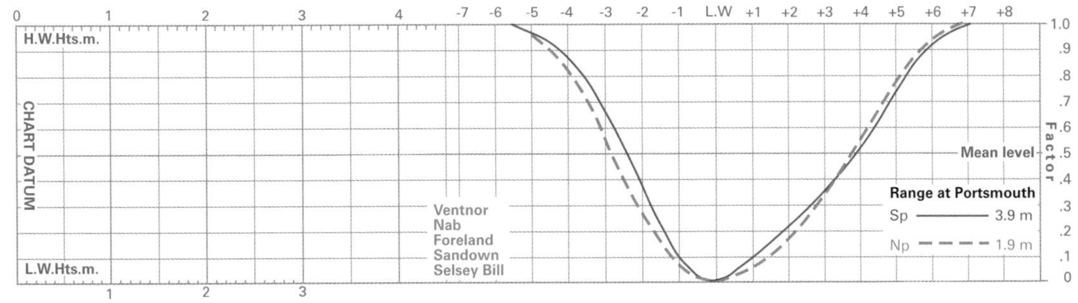

9.2.18 THE CENTRAL SOLENT

CHARTS AC 5600, 2036.

Reference and websites *Solent Cruising Companion,* Fernhurst; *Solent Hazards,* Peter Bruce; *Solent Year Book* SCRA; *Yachtsman's Guide* ABP Southampton www.southampton vts.co.uk for detailed live port info including: shipping movements, VTS radar displays (Southampton to S of Nab Tr), webcams, tide & weather. See www.bramblemet.co.uk for live weather & tidal info at the Bramble Bk.

Vessel Traffic Service (VTS) **Southampton VTS** operates on VHF Ch **12** 14, advising Solent shipping between the Needles and Nab Tower including Southampton Water. VTS monitors and coordinates the safe passage of commercial ships. It includes a radar service on request. **QHM Portsmouth,** VHF Ch **11**, controls Portsmouth Harbour and its approaches N of a line from Gilkicker Pt to Outer Spit Buoy.

All small craft in the Solent are strongly advised to monitor VHF Ch 12 Southampton, and/or Ch 11 QHM Portsmouth.

Small Craft and Commercial Shipping Always consider the restricted field of vision from large ships at close quarters and their limited ability to manoeuvre at slow speeds with minimal under keel clearance in restricted waters. Smaller ships keeping clear of these vessels will be encountered outside the channel. Maintain a proper lookout, especially astern. If crossing the main fairway, try to do so at 90° to it. Southampton Hbr byelaw 2003/10 refers. Be aware of the frequent cross-Solent High Speed and Ro-Ro ferries.

The **Precautionary Area** is the potentially dangerous part of the Solent in which large vessels make tight turns into and out of the Thorn Channel leading to Southampton Water. It extends from just NW of Cowes to the Hook buoy N of Calshot Castle (see chartlet and AC 2036). This can be a very busy area. Be particularly alert when between East Lepe and Ryde Middle. Inbound ships pass Prince Consort NCM turning to ***port*** towards Gurnard NCM, before starting their critical turn to starboard into the Thorn Channel which is, for large ships, very narrow.

Clear Channel Vessels are over 220m LOA and require a clear and unimpeded passage ahead when transiting the Precautionary Area. Vessels may enter the Precautionary Area maintaining a safe distance astern of the 'clear channel vessel'.

Moving Prohibited Zone (MPZ) Any vessel over 150m LOA when in the Precautionary Area is enclosed by an MPZ which extends 1000m ahead of the vessel and 100m on either beam. Small craft under 20m LOA must remain outside the MPZ and use seaman-like anticipation of its route and sea-room required when turning.

Escort Towage for VLCCs From S of the Nab Tr VLCCs over 60,000dwt bound to and from Fawley Marine Terminal will have an escort tug secured to the stern by tow wire. Outwards, the escort tug may leave a tanker at Prince Consort. Use extreme caution when passing round the stern of a large tanker and do not pass between it and the escort tug.

Local Signals Clear Channel & MPZ vessels display a black cylinder by day or 3 all-round ● lts (vert) by night. They are normally preceded by a Harbour Patrol Launch (Ch 12 *Callsign SP*) exhibiting a flashing blue light. Southampton patrol launches have 'HARBOUR MASTER' painted on their superstructure. At night a fixed ● all-round lt is shown above the W masthead light.

Coastguard The National Maritime Operations Centre (NMOC) at Fareham, ☎(02392) 552100, co-ordinates SAR activities from Topsham to mid-channel; E to the Greenwich Lt V; thence N to Beachy Hd. Owing to the concentration of small craft in its area the NMOC keeps watch on VHF Ch 67/16. Uniquely, an initial call to *Solent Coastguard* should be made on Ch 67 for routine traffic and radio checks, although radio checks on a working channel with other stations – marinas, yachts etc – are preferred and encouraged.

Solent Yacht Racing Buoys Numerous yellow yacht racing buoys are laid throughout the Solent (*seasonal, Mar-Dec*). Most, but not all, are lit Fl Y 4s.

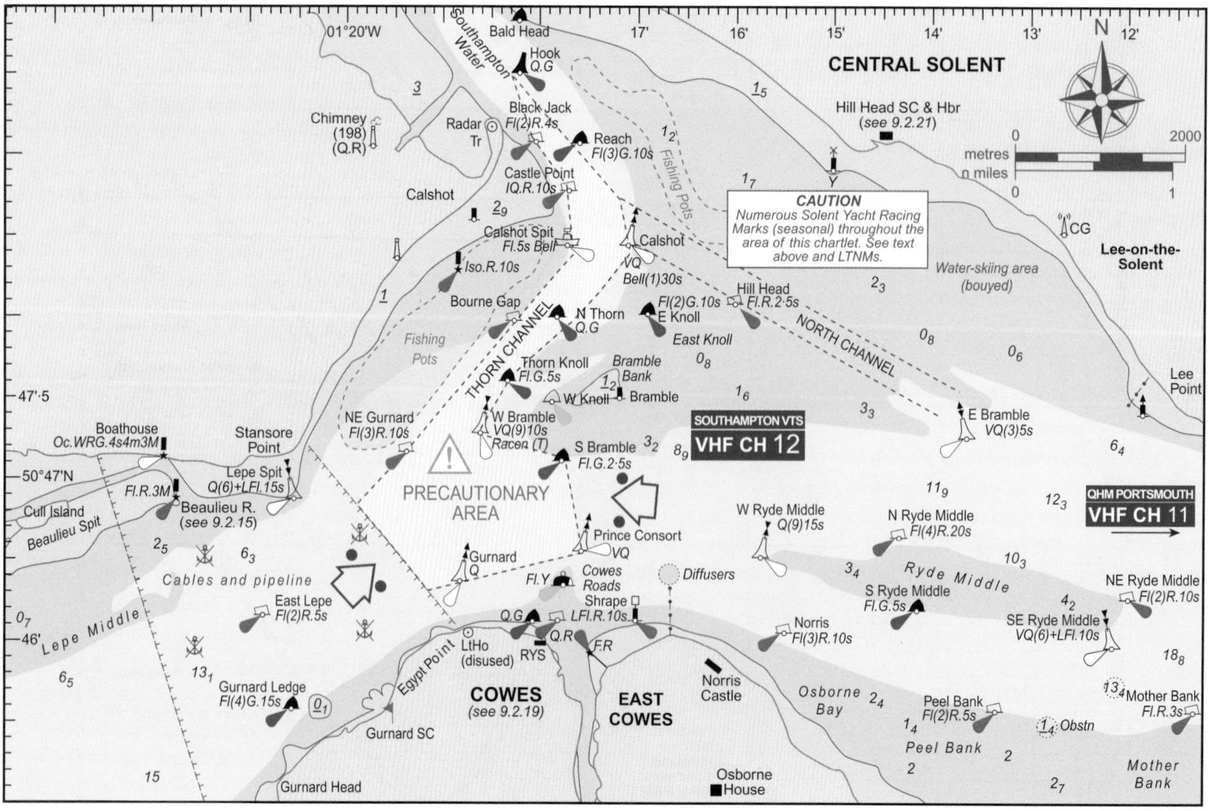

9.2.19 COWES/RIVER MEDINA

Isle of Wight **50°46'·08N 01°17'·95W**

CHARTS AC 5600, 2036, 2793; Imray C3, C15, 2200

TIDES +0029 Dover; ML 2·7

Standard Port PORTSMOUTH (⟶); Tidal Curve see 9.2.17 (⟵)

Times				Height (metres)			
High Water		Low Water		MHWS	MHWN	MLWN	MLWS
0000	0600	0500	1100	4·7	3·8	1·9	0·8
1200	1800	1700	2300				
Differences *COWES*							
–0015	*+0015*	*0000*	*–0020*	*–0·5*	*–0·3*	*–0·1*	*0·0*
FOLLY INN							
–0015	+0015	0000	–0020	–0·6	–0·4	–0·1	+0·2
NEWPORT							
ND	ND	ND	ND	–0·6	–0·4	+0·1	+0·8

NOTE: Double HWs occur at/near Sp. At other times there is a stand of about 2hrs. Times are for the middle of the stand. See 9.2.17.

SHELTER Excellent now that outer hbr is protected from N/NE winds by outer bkwtr. ⚓ prohib in hbr. 10 large Ⓥs off The Green; pontoons S of chain ferry on both sides of river and in Folly Reach and several marinas. Good ⚓ in Osborne Bay, 2M E, sheltered from SE to W but exposed to wash from large ships; no landing.

NAVIGATION WPT 50°46'·35N 01°18'·0W, 173°/2·7ca to mid chan between Nos 1 and 2 buoys. Shrape Mud, on the E side of the hbr, extends to Old Castle Pt. A small craft channel crosses from Shrape Bn to the fairway, passing N of Shrape Bwtr. Depth is 0.2m below CD, but in the approach is close to CD and it should only be used if craft's draught is less than the existing height of tide. R Medina is navigable to Newport, but dries S of Folly Inn.

- Yachts should use engines. Sp limit 6kn enforced in hbr.
- Strong tidal streams run between HW-2½ and HW setting vessels towards W shore in Inner Fairway; see next page
- No sailing through or ⚓ amongst moorings.
- Beware frequent ferry movements, High-Speed to W Cowes, large Ro-Ro ferries to E Cowes, and commercial shipping.
- Ro-Ro ferries use thrust when manoeuvring at E Cowes causing considerable turbulence across the river. Hi-Speed ferries turn short round to stbd when appr Jubilee Pontoon.
- All vessels < 20m must give way to the chain ferry which displays a Y Fl lt when about to depart and under way; daily 0530-0030, Sun 0635-0030. Beware ebb (4·5kn at Sp) in its vicinity.

LIGHTS AND MARKS See 9.2.4 and chartlet. Outer b'water marked along its length by 5 sync lts Fl Y 2.5s. Small craft chan is marked by Shrape Bn LFl R 10s 3m 3M, and paired PHM and SHM: inbound Fl R 2s / Fl G 2s, Fl R 5s / Fl G 5s (Outer Bwtr) Fl R 3s / Fl G 3s (E Bwtr) with 3 lit Y SPM and R Bn, L Fl R 5s where it joins fairway.

COMMUNICATIONS (Code 01983 (for all IOW)) NMOC (02392) 552100; (02380) 228844; Police 101; Ⓗ 524081; Dr 294902; Cowes HM 293952; Folly HM (for ferry and berthing) 07884 400046. Monitor *Cowes Hbr Radio* VHF Ch **69** for hbr launches and HM's Ⓥs. Yachts >20m LOA should advise arr/dep, and call *Chain Ferry* Ch 69 if passing. Marinas Ch 80. Harbour taxi 07855 767918; *Hbr Taxi* Ch 77 or Sally Water Taxi 07831 331717/299033; *Water Taxi* Ch 06. Casualties: (Ch 16/69) for ambulance at S end of Trinity Landing.

FACILITIES www.cowes.co.uk / www.cowesharbourcommission.co.uk from seaward: **RYS Haven** (strictly members only).

Trinity Landing, on The Parade, short stay on inner side only, pick-up/landing on outer side, call HM Ch 69. The concentration of wash W of the b'water impinges on the pontoon which can be lively.

Cowes Yacht Haven www.cowesyachthaven.com ☎299975, 35+ 200 Ⓥ, £3·00, (35t) (12t) ✕.

Shepard's Wharf Marina, www.shepards.co.uk ☎297821, 30+100Ⓥ £2·50, ✕ wi-fi.

UKSA ☎294941, info@uksa.org, 5 Ⓥ, £3.30, ✕.

East Cowes Marina www.eastcowesmarina.co.uk ☎293983, 230 +150Ⓥ £3·00, ✕ wi-fi.

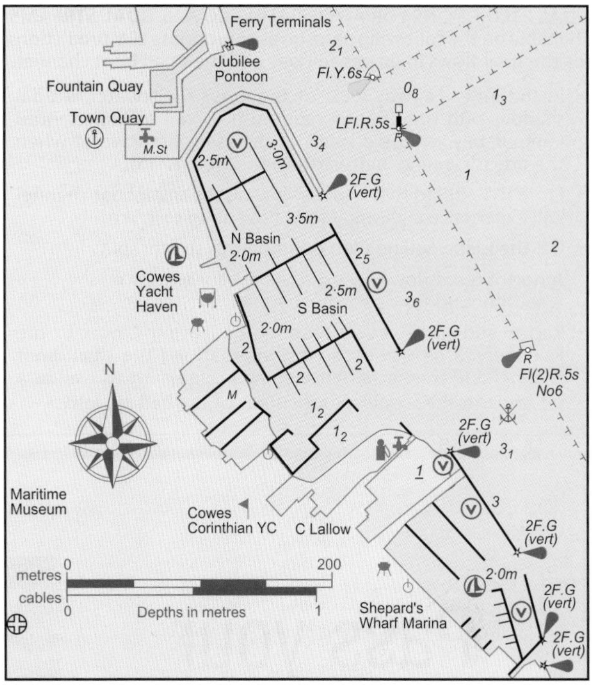

Town All marine services and facilities.

Town Quay, Trinity Landing, and Whitegates public pontoon.

Fuel Lallows, Cowes Hbr Fuels pontoon off Souters.

Scrubbing berths Town Quay, UKSA, Sealift, Folly Inn.

Ferries Red Funnel www.redfunnel.co.uk to/from Southampton: ☎(02380) 334010 Car/pax – E Cowes; foot pax – W Cowes. **Chain Ferry** ☎293041, W/E Cowes.

YACHT CLUBS **Royal Yacht Squadron** ☎292191; **Island SC** ☎296621; **Royal Corinthian YC** ☎293581; **Royal London YC** ☎299727; **Cowes Corinthian YC** ☎296333; **RORC** ☎295144 (Cowes Week); **E Cowes SC** www.eastcowessc.co.uk ☎531687. **Cowes Combined Clubs** ccc@cowesweek.co.uk ☎295744.

RIVER MEDINA, FOLLY REACH TO NEWPORT

FOLLY REACH, 50°44'·03N 01°16'·99W. Above Medham min depth 0·6m to S Folly bn. on Ⓥ pontoons off W bank (£1·25). *Folly Launch* Ch 72/☎07884 400046; Folly Waterbus ☎07974 864627.

Folly Inn ☎297171, scrubbing berth (pontoon) for 9Ⓥ(max LOA 40') £1·80.

Island Harbour Marina (5ca S of Folly Inn) island-harbour.co.uk ☎539994, 96+20Ⓥ £3·00, (50t) ✕. Call *Island Harbour Control* on Ch 80 on entering Folly Reach. Excellent shelter; approach via marked channel (dries approx 0·1m) with waiting pontoon to stbd, withies to port. Access HW±3 (draught 1·5m) via lock (width 7·9m) 0800-1730, or by arrangement.

NEWPORT, 50°42'·21N 01°17'·43W. HM ☎525994/ 07970 009589. VHF Ch 69. Tides: Special treatment is required as the hbr dries 1·4m. Use the LW time and height differences for Cowes, and the HW height differences for Newport. Above Island Hbr Marina the chan to Newport (1·2M) dries, but from HW Portsmouth –1½ to +2 it carries 2m or more. S from Folly Inn, the Hbr Authority is IoW Council. Sp limit 6kn to Seaclose, S of Newport Rowing Club (NRC); thence 4kn to Newport. Buoyed and partially lit chan favours W bank. Power lines have 33m clearance. 192° ldg marks/lts are W ◊ bns (lit) on E bank.

Odessa Boatyard ☎524337, odessaboatyard@hotmail.co.uk 75+5Ⓥs on pontoons downstream on W side £1·50, slipway (35t) (6t).

Newport Yacht Hbr ☎525994, 50Ⓥs pontoons on the E/SE sides of the basin have 1·4m at HW ±2 £1·75. Bilge keelers lie alongside pontoons (soft mud); fin keelers against quay wall (firm level bottom). Fender boards can be supplied. (8t) Classic Boat Centre. **Town**

Chartlets on page 224

TIDAL PREDICTIONS FOR APPRECIATING COWES TIDAL STREAMS

The table on the following page gives appropriate HW predictions for the tidal flows in Cowes Fairway and the small boat channel:

- In the Inner Fairway west of the outer breakwater, a tidal shadow with significantly reduced flow will be experienced immediately west and south of the outer breakwater when the tide is running westwards (HW –2 to HW +5).
- From HW –2·5 to HW, boats following the small boat channel will experience a westerly tidal flow of up to 1.5kn.
- Off the Island Sailing Club pontoon this stream splits into

  A northbound flow towards the harbour entrance
  A southbound flow past the marinas.
- Yachts and small vessels entering or leaving Cowes in the Fairway will be slowed by this approaching the small boat channel and then experience an appreciable lift as well as a set towards the western shore north of the Red Jet jetty.

These HW times mark the start of the stand or 'high water period' as defined by Cowes Commissioners and are useful in appreciating the tidal flows in the Fairway and approaches. The HW times in the table apply throughout the tidal cycle of springs and neaps, simplifying the prediction process.

It should be noted that this table gives the predicted time and height of high water at the beginning of the stand. The normal methodology predicts the first peak high water in ports such as Cowes where there is a double HW or stand. The peak high water will almost invariably be of greater height and later than that shown.

These predictions correlate accurately with those used by Cowes Commissioners and Admiralty Tide Tables. They will deviate from those calculated from the Special Curves (p 219) chart plotters and computer tidal predictions. As with other tables, there will be variations due to meteorological effects.

COWES LAT 50°46'N LONG 1°18'W

2018 TIMES AND HEIGHTS OF HIGH WATER – see note on facing page

JANUARY

Mo	1	0936	4.4	2202	4.3
Tu	2	1029	4.5	2312	4.5
We	3	1116	4.5	--	--
Th	4	0001	4.5	1218	4.5
Fr	5	0051	4.4	1306	4.4
Sa	6	0143	4.3	1355	4.3
Su	7	0238	4.2	1447	4.1
Mo	8	0300	4.0	1517	3.8
Tu	9	0354	3.9	1612	3.6
We	10	0459	3.8	1721	3.5
Th	11	0606	3.7	1834	3.4
Fr	12	0714	3.7	1944	3.5
Sa	13	0808	3.8	2036	3.7
Su	14	0854	3.9	2122	3.8
Mo	15	0941	4.0	2208	4.0
Tu	16	1017	4.1	2245	4.1
We	17	1057	4.1	2322	4.1
Th	18	1126	4.1	2353	4.1
Fr	19	1200	4.1	--	--
Sa	20	0023	4.0	1230	4.1
Su	21	0054	4.0	1301	4.0
Mo	22	0130	4.0	1338	4.0
Tu	23	0209	4.0	1423	3.9
We	24	0257	3.9	1511	3.7
Th	25	0352	3.8	1621	3.7
Fr	26	0502	3.8	1731	3.6
Sa	27	0611	3.8	1845	3.7
Su	28	0722	3.9	1954	3.9
Mo	29	0828	4.1	2059	4.1
Tu	30	0926	4.3	2155	4.2
We	31	1014	4.4	2303	4.4

FEBRUARY

Th	1	1104	4.5	2348	4.4
Fr	2	1203	4.5	--	--
Sa	3	0033	4.4	1246	4.4
Su	4	0118	4.3	1330	4.3
Mo	5	0205	4.2	1417	4.1
Tu	6	0258	4.1	1441	3.8
We	7	0317	3.9	1532	3.6
Th	8	0411	3.7	1630	3.4
Fr	9	0508	3.5	1742	3.3
Sa	10	0622	3.5	1904	3.3
Su	11	0730	3.5	2008	3.5
Mo	12	0827	3.6	2103	3.7
Tu	13	0916	3.8	2145	3.9
We	14	0955	3.9	2222	4.0
Th	15	1033	4.0	2258	4.1
Fr	16	1104	4.1	2327	4.1
Sa	17	1139	4.1	--	--
Su	18	0025	4.1	1209	4.1
Mo	19	0056	4.1	1242	4.1
Tu	20	0130	4.1	1320	4.1
We	21	0144	4.1	1359	4.0
Th	22	0228	4.0	1449	3.8
Fr	23	0323	3.9	1551	3.7
Sa	24	0432	3.7	1709	3.6
Su	25	0546	3.7	1821	3.6
Mo	26	0700	3.7	1943	3.7
Tu	27	0814	3.9	2051	4.0
We	28	0913	4.1	2143	4.2

MARCH

Th	1	1001	4.3	2249	4.3
Fr	2	1103	4.4	2330	4.4
Sa	3	1144	4.4	--	--
Su	4	0011	4.4	1224	4.3
Mo	5	0051	4.3	1305	4.2
Tu	6	0133	4.2	1348	4.1
We	7	0219	4.1	1407	3.9
Th	8	0236	3.9	1453	3.6
Fr	9	0319	3.7	1540	3.4
Sa	10	0405	3.4	1642	3.2
Su	11	0512	3.2	1811	3.2
Mo	12	0642	3.3	1931	3.4
Tu	13	0753	3.4	2031	3.6
We	14	0844	3.6	2114	3.8
Th	15	0928	3.8	2152	4.0
Fr	16	1004	4.0	2254	4.1
Sa	17	1038	4.1	2322	4.2
Su	18	1110	4.2	2353	4.2
Mo	19	1148	4.2	--	--
Tu	20	0027	4.2	1220	4.2
We	21	0104	4.2	1300	4.2
Th	22	0126	4.2	1341	4.0
Fr	23	0206	4.0	1435	3.9
Sa	24	0302	3.9	1536	3.7
Su	25	0408	3.7	1650	3.6
Mo	26	0522	3.6	1808	3.6
Tu	27	0645	3.6	1937	3.7
We	28	0801	3.8	2039	4.0
Th	29	0901	4.0	2129	4.2
Fr	30	0945	4.2	2231	4.3
Sa	31	1043	4.3	2309	4.3

APRIL

Su	1	1123	4.3	2347	4.3
Mo	2	1201	4.3	--	--
Tu	3	0024	4.3	1240	4.2
We	4	0103	4.2	1321	4.1
Th	5	0118	4.1	1338	3.9
Fr	6	0153	3.9	1414	3.7
Sa	7	0231	3.7	1458	3.5
Su	8	0308	3.4	1552	3.3
Mo	9	0405	3.2	1718	3.3
Tu	10	0541	3.2	1841	3.4
We	11	0703	3.3	1947	3.6
Th	12	0802	3.5	2038	3.8
Fr	13	0850	3.7	2118	3.9
Sa	14	0931	3.9	2154	4.1
Su	15	1027	4.1	2248	4.2
Mo	16	1101	4.2	2323	4.3
Tu	17	1139	4.3	--	--
We	18	0001	4.3	1219	4.3
Th	19	0042	4.3	1304	4.2
Fr	20	0108	4.2	1330	4.1
Sa	21	0151	4.0	1425	3.9
Su	22	0249	3.9	1528	3.8
Mo	23	0353	3.7	1639	3.7
Tu	24	0508	3.5	1800	3.7
We	25	0630	3.6	1923	3.8
Th	26	0748	3.7	2024	4.0
Fr	27	0839	3.9	2105	4.1
Sa	28	0925	4.1	2210	4.3
Su	29	1024	4.2	2247	4.3
Mo	30	1102	4.2	2324	4.3

MAY

Tu	1	1141	4.1	--	--
We	2	0000	4.2	1220	4.1
Th	3	0012	4.1	1303	4.0
Fr	4	0051	4.0	1354	3.9
Sa	5	0122	3.9	1346	3.7
Su	6	0158	3.7	1429	3.6
Mo	7	0233	3.5	1518	3.4
Tu	8	0323	3.3	1636	3.4
We	9	0444	3.2	1747	3.4
Th	10	0607	3.3	1858	3.6
Fr	11	0712	3.4	1954	3.8
Sa	12	0810	3.7	2038	3.9
Su	13	0854	3.9	2118	4.1
Mo	14	0935	4.1	2217	4.3
Tu	15	1019	4.2	2256	4.4
We	16	1116	4.3	2339	4.4
Th	17	1202	4.3	--	--
Fr	18	0009	4.3	1252	4.3
Sa	19	0054	4.2	1350	4.2
Su	20	0140	4.1	1418	4.0
Mo	21	0238	3.9	1518	3.9
Tu	22	0340	3.7	1628	3.8
We	23	0448	3.6	1740	3.8
Th	24	0605	3.6	1855	3.8
Fr	25	0719	3.7	1957	4.0
Sa	26	0814	3.8	2043	4.1
Su	27	0901	3.9	2123	4.1
Mo	28	1005	4.0	2206	4.2
Tu	29	1046	4.0	2243	4.1
We	30	1102	4.0	2317	4.1
Th	31	1140	4.0	2354	4.1

JUNE

Fr	1	1219	4.0	--	--
Sa	2	0028	4.0	1253	3.9
Su	3	0101	3.9	1328	3.8
Mo	4	0135	3.8	1409	3.7
Tu	5	0210	3.6	1448	3.6
We	6	0253	3.4	1547	3.6
Th	7	0356	3.3	1655	3.6
Fr	8	0510	3.4	1756	3.6
Sa	9	0616	3.4	1857	3.7
Su	10	0722	3.6	1953	3.9
Mo	11	0817	3.8	2043	4.1
Tu	12	0906	4.0	2130	4.2
We	13	0952	4.2	2220	4.4
Th	14	1059	4.3	2306	4.4
Fr	15	1149	4.3	2350	4.4
Sa	16	1241	4.3	--	--
Su	17	0040	4.3	1339	4.2
Mo	18	0153	4.2	1408	4.1
Tu	19	0225	4.0	1503	4.0
We	20	0318	3.8	1605	3.9
Th	21	0514	3.7	1708	3.8
Fr	22	0528	3.6	1821	3.8
Sa	23	0641	3.6	1919	3.9
Su	24	0746	3.6	2015	3.9
Mo	25	0837	3.7	2059	4.0
Tu	26	0923	3.8	2144	4.0
We	27	1004	3.9	2222	4.1
Th	28	1046	4.0	2300	4.1
Fr	29	1124	4.0	2338	4.1
Sa	30	1204	4.0	--	--

JULY

Su	1	0010	4.0	1239	3.9
Mo	2	0043	3.9	1311	3.9
Tu	3	0111	3.8	1341	3.8
We	4	0146	3.8	1419	3.8
Th	5	0231	3.7	1504	3.7
Fr	6	0318	3.6	1602	3.7
Sa	7	0424	3.5	1709	3.7
Su	8	0533	3.5	1812	3.8
Mo	9	0638	3.6	1917	3.9
Tu	10	0745	3.8	2014	4.0
We	11	0840	4.0	2110	4.2
Th	12	0936	4.2	2159	4.3
Fr	13	1027	4.3	2253	4.4
Sa	14	1137	4.4	2356	4.4
Su	15	1227	4.3	--	--
Mo	16	0043	4.4	1319	4.3
Tu	17	0132	4.3	1414	4.2
We	18	0224	4.1	1439	4.1
Th	19	0321	3.9	1530	3.9
Fr	20	0351	3.7	1632	3.8
Sa	21	0450	3.5	1734	3.7
Su	22	0603	3.5	1842	3.7
Mo	23	0716	3.5	1941	3.7
Tu	24	0814	3.6	2037	3.8
We	25	0905	3.7	2122	3.9
Th	26	0947	3.9	2204	4.0
Fr	27	1029	4.0	2240	4.0
Sa	28	1106	4.0	2316	4.1
Su	29	1144	4.0	2349	4.0
Mo	30	1215	4.0	--	--
Tu	31	0020	4.0	1320	4.0

AUGUST

We	1	0050	4.0	1348	4.0
Th	2	0123	3.9	1351	3.9
Fr	3	0203	3.9	1431	3.9
Sa	4	0248	3.7	1521	3.8
Su	5	0346	3.6	1627	3.8
Mo	6	0456	3.6	1734	3.7
Tu	7	0607	3.6	1842	3.8
We	8	0716	3.7	1952	3.9
Th	9	0825	3.9	2054	4.1
Fr	10	0924	4.1	2148	4.3
Sa	11	1017	4.3	2239	4.4
Su	12	1124	4.4	2339	4.5
Mo	13	1209	4.4	--	--
Tu	14	0023	4.4	1254	4.4
We	15	0108	4.3	1342	4.3
Th	16	0155	4.2	1434	4.2
Fr	17	0248	4.0	1538	4.0
Sa	18	0314	3.7	1550	3.8
Su	19	0412	3.5	1645	3.6
Mo	20	0520	3.4	1757	3.5
Tu	21	0641	3.4	1907	3.5
We	22	0750	3.5	2011	3.6
Th	23	0846	3.7	2057	3.8
Fr	24	0928	3.9	2142	3.9
Sa	25	1005	4.0	2215	4.0
Su	26	1044	4.1	2253	4.1
Mo	27	1116	4.1	2325	4.1
Tu	28	1147	4.1	2354	4.1
We	29	1240	4.1	--	--
Th	30	0025	4.1	1310	4.1
Fr	31	0059	4.1	1345	4.1

SEPTEMBER

Sa	1	0139	4.0	1402	4.0
Su	2	0222	3.9	1449	3.9
Mo	3	0316	3.7	1554	3.8
Tu	4	0429	3.6	1709	3.7
We	5	0548	3.6	1822	3.7
Th	6	0704	3.7	1939	3.9
Fr	7	0817	4.0	2043	4.1
Sa	8	0919	4.2	2137	4.3
Su	9	1025	4.4	2224	4.4
Mo	10	1106	4.5	2321	4.5
Tu	11	1148	4.5	--	--
We	12	0001	4.4	1228	4.4
Th	13	0043	4.3	1310	4.3
Fr	14	0126	4.2	1355	4.2
Sa	15	0215	4.0	1417	4.0
Su	16	0238	3.8	1500	3.8
Mo	17	0329	3.5	1550	3.5
Tu	18	0434	3.4	1655	3.3
We	19	0557	3.4	1820	3.3
Th	20	0716	3.5	1932	3.5
Fr	21	0816	3.7	2027	3.7
Sa	22	0900	3.9	2112	3.9
Su	23	0940	4.1	2149	4.0
Mo	24	1014	4.2	2225	4.1
Tu	25	1108	4.2	2254	4.2
We	26	1137	4.3	2346	4.3
Th	27	1208	4.3	--	--
Fr	28	0004	4.3	1241	4.3
Sa	29	0036	4.2	1318	4.2
Su	30	0117	4.1	1337	4.1

OCTOBER

Mo	1	0203	4.0	1428	4.0
Tu	2	0258	3.8	1528	3.8
We	3	0413	3.7	1644	3.6
Th	4	0534	3.7	1804	3.6
Fr	5	0658	3.8	1931	3.8
Sa	6	0812	4.1	2035	4.1
Su	7	0905	4.3	2122	4.3
Mo	8	0949	4.4	2206	4.4
Tu	9	1047	4.5	2301	4.5
We	10	1125	4.5	2340	4.4
Th	11	1203	4.4	--	--
Fr	12	0019	4.3	1242	4.3
Sa	13	0100	4.2	1322	4.2
Su	14	0146	4.1	1337	4.0
Mo	15	0203	3.8	1417	3.8
Tu	16	0249	3.6	1459	3.5
We	17	0346	3.4	1552	3.3
Th	18	0507	3.4	1722	3.3
Fr	19	0629	3.5	1846	3.4
Sa	20	0735	3.7	1951	3.6
Su	21	0825	3.9	2039	3.8
Mo	22	0902	4.1	2115	4.0
Tu	23	0939	4.2	2150	4.1
We	24	1011	4.3	2226	4.3
Th	25	1106	4.4	2319	4.4
Fr	26	1140	4.4	2357	4.4
Sa	27	1158	4.4	--	--
Su	28	0018	4.3	1239	4.3
Mo	29	0104	4.2	1321	4.2
Tu	30	0152	4.0	1411	4.0
We	31	0248	3.9	1513	3.8

NOVEMBER

Th	1	0402	3.8	1628	3.7
Fr	2	0521	3.8	1750	3.6
Sa	3	0650	3.9	1915	3.8
Su	4	0758	4.1	2013	4.0
Mo	5	0845	4.3	2100	4.2
Tu	6	0925	4.4	2143	4.3
We	7	1027	4.5	2242	4.4
Th	8	1104	4.5	2321	4.3
Fr	9	1142	4.4	--	--
Sa	10	0001	4.3	1158	4.3
Su	11	0043	4.2	1233	4.2
Mo	12	0055	4.0	1309	4.0
Tu	13	0139	3.9	1346	3.8
We	14	0220	3.7	1424	3.6
Th	15	0308	3.6	1509	3.4
Fr	16	0417	3.5	1622	3.3
Sa	17	0528	3.5	1743	3.3
Su	18	0640	3.7	1856	3.5
Mo	19	0739	3.9	1954	3.7
Tu	20	0824	4.0	2038	3.9
We	21	0905	4.2	2118	4.1
Th	22	0939	4.3	2158	4.2
Fr	23	1019	4.4	2242	4.4
Sa	24	1103	4.5	2320	4.4
Su	25	1141	4.4	--	--
Mo	26	0026	4.4	1226	4.4
Tu	27	0053	4.3	1312	4.2
We	28	0222	4.2	1406	4.1
Th	29	0247	4.0	1503	3.9
Fr	30	0351	3.9	1611	3.7

DECEMBER

Sa	1	0502	3.9	1724	3.7
Su	2	0622	3.9	1843	3.8
Mo	3	0726	4.1	1946	3.9
Tu	4	0817	4.2	2040	4.0
We	5	0902	4.3	2124	4.1
Th	6	0944	4.3	2229	4.2
Fr	7	1027	4.3	2245	4.2
Sa	8	1101	4.3	2328	4.2
Su	9	1139	4.2	--	--
Mo	10	0006	4.1	1217	4.2
Tu	11	0045	4.1	1251	4.1
We	12	0122	4.0	1326	3.9
Th	13	0159	3.9	1358	3.7
Fr	14	0239	3.7	1439	3.6
Sa	15	0327	3.6	1531	3.4
Su	16	0427	3.6	1640	3.4
Mo	17	0534	3.6	1751	3.4
Tu	18	0640	3.8	1858	3.6
We	19	0736	3.9	1957	3.8
Th	20	0822	4.0	2048	4.0
Fr	21	0910	4.2	2135	4.2
Sa	22	0956	4.4	2220	4.3
Su	23	1041	4.4	2327	4.4
Mo	24	1131	4.5	--	--
Tu	25	0017	4.4	1215	4.4
We	26	0110	4.4	1305	4.3
Th	27	0208	4.3	1353	4.2
Fr	28	0234	4.1	1447	4.0
Sa	29	0329	4.0	1549	3.8
Su	30	0432	3.9	1651	3.7
Mo	31	0540	3.9	--	--

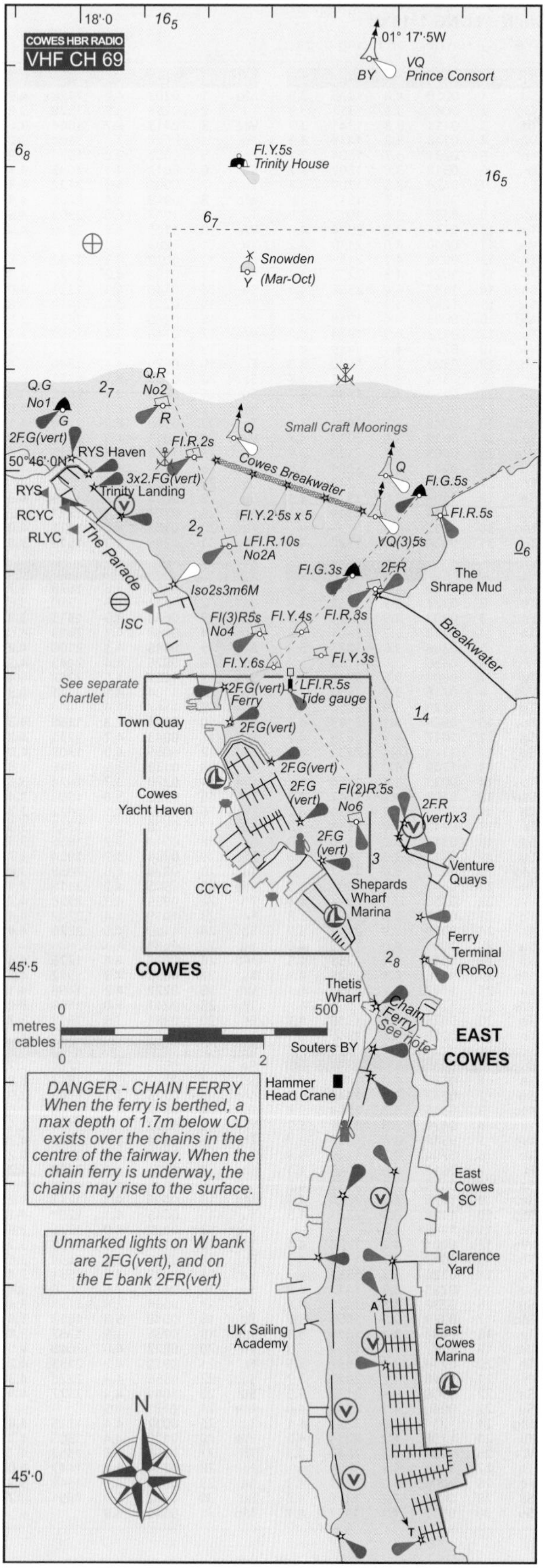
COWES HBR RADIO
VHF CH 69
18'·0
01° 17'·5W
VQ
Prince Consort
BY
Fl.Y.5s
Trinity House
Snowden
(Mar-Oct)
Q.G
No1
Q.R
No2
2F.G(vert)
RYS Haven
50°46'·0N
RYS
RCYC
RLYC
Fl.R.2s
3x2.FG(vert)
Trinity Landing
Small Craft Moorings
Cowes Breakwater
Fl.Y.2·5s x 5
Fl.G.5s
Fl.R.5s
VQ(3)5s
LFl.R.10s
No2A
The Parade
Iso2s3m6M
ISC
Fl.G.3s
2F.R
The Shrape Mud
Fl(3)R5s
No4
Fl.Y.4s
Fl.R.3s
Breakwater
Fl.Y.6s
Fl.Y.3s
See separate chartlet
2F.G(vert)
Ferry
LFl.R.5s
Tide gauge
Town Quay
2F.G(vert)
Cowes Yacht Haven
2F.G(vert)
2F.G (vert)
Fl(2)R.5s
No6
2F.R (vert)x3
2F.G (vert)
Venture Quays
CCYC
Shepards Wharf Marina
Ferry Terminal (RoRo)
COWES
45'·5
Thetis Wharf
Chain Ferry
See note
metres
cables
0
500
0
2
Souters BY
EAST COWES
Hammer Head Crane
DANGER - CHAIN FERRY
When the ferry is berthed, a max depth of 1.7m below CD exists over the chains in the centre of the fairway. When the chain ferry is underway, the chains may rise to the surface.
East Cowes SC
Unmarked lights on W bank are 2FG(vert), and on the E bank 2FR(vert)
Clarence Yard
UK Sailing Academy
East Cowes Marina
N
45'·0

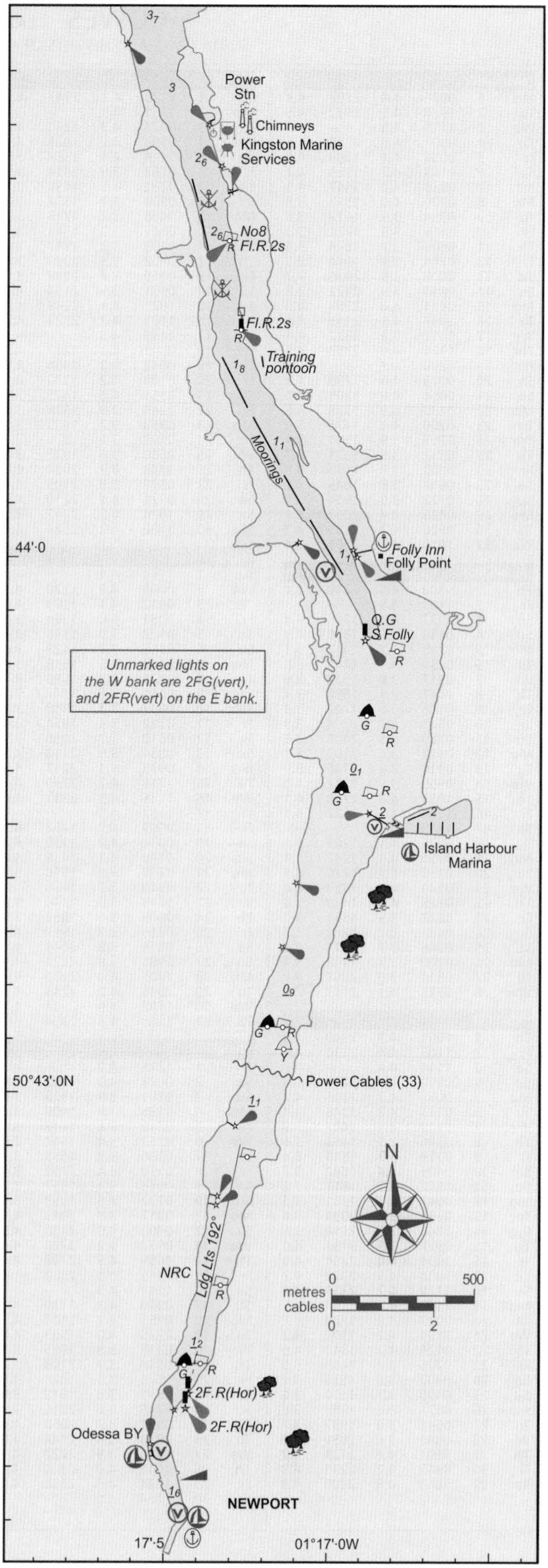
Power Stn
Chimneys
Kingston Marine Services
No8
Fl.R.2s
Fl.R.2s
Training pontoon
Moorings
44'·0
Folly Inn
Folly Point
Q.G
S.Folly
Unmarked lights on the W bank are 2FG(vert), and 2FR(vert) on the E bank.
Island Harbour Marina
50°43'·0N
Power Cables (33)
N
Ldg Lts 192°
NRC
metres
cables
0
500
0
2
2F.R(Hor)
2F.R(Hor)
Odessa BY
NEWPORT
17'·5
01°17'·0W

Note Double HWs occur at Southampton.
The predictions are for the first HW.

STANDARD TIME (UT)
For Summer Time add ONE hour in **non-shaded areas**

SOUTHAMPTON LAT 50°53′N LONG 1°24′W

TIMES AND HEIGHTS OF HIGH AND LOW WATERS

Dates in red are SPRINGS
Dates in blue are NEAPS

YEAR **2018**

JANUARY

Date	Day	Time	m	Time	m	Time	m	Time	m
1	M	0316	0.9	0932	4.7	1544	0.6	2220	4.7
2	TU	0407	0.7	1021	4.8	1633	0.4	○ 2306	4.8
3	W	0454	0.5	1127	4.9	1720	0.3	2353	4.8
4	TH	0541	0.5	1213	4.8	1806	0.3		
5	F	0042	4.7	0628	0.6	1301	4.7	1852	0.5
6	SA	0134	4.6	0714	0.8	1352	4.5	1938	0.7
7	SU	0233	4.5	0802	1.0	1449	4.3	2027	1.0
8	M	0258	4.2	0854	1.3	1558	4.1	◑ 2120	1.3
9	TU	0353	4.1	0951	1.6	1611	3.8	2220	1.6
10	W	0450	4.0	1055	1.8	1713	3.7	2326	1.8
11	TH	0546	3.9	1204	1.9	1813	3.6		
12	F	0033	1.8	0644	3.8	1308	1.8	1910	3.6
13	SA	0133	1.8	0740	3.9	1404	1.6	2011	3.8
14	SU	0226	1.6	0833	4.0	1453	1.4	2105	3.9
15	M	0314	1.4	0926	4.2	1538	1.2	2153	4.1
16	TU	0358	1.3	1010	4.3	1620	1.0	2237	4.2
17	W	0439	1.2	1048	4.3	1659	1.0	● 2314	4.3
18	TH	0516	1.2	1122	4.3	1733	1.0	2345	4.3
19	F	0547	1.2	1155	4.3	1802	1.0		
20	SA	0049	4.4	0615	1.1	1227	4.3	1830	1.0
21	SU	0115	4.4	0646	1.1	1305	4.4	1903	0.9
22	M	0151	4.4	0723	1.1	1405	4.4	1941	1.0
23	TU	0233	4.4	0805	1.2	1430	4.2	2025	1.1
24	W	0321	4.3	0853	1.3	1517	4.1	◐ 2117	1.3
25	TH	0416	4.2	0950	1.5	1611	3.9	2220	1.5
26	F	0450	4.0	1103	1.7	1716	3.8	2338	1.7
27	SA	0555	3.9	1225	1.6	1828	3.8		
28	SU	0059	1.6	0711	4.1	1341	1.4	1947	4.0
29	M	0210	1.4	0824	4.3	1443	1.0	2051	4.3
30	TU	0307	1.0	0918	4.5	1535	0.7	2213	4.5
31	W	0358	0.7	1009	4.7	1624	0.4	○ 2256	4.7

FEBRUARY

Date	Day	Time	m	Time	m	Time	m	Time	m
1	TH	0444	0.5	1113	4.8	1708	0.2	2341	4.7
2	F	0529	0.4	1157	4.7	1752	0.1		
3	SA	0026	4.7	0613	0.4	1241	4.7	1835	0.2
4	SU	0113	4.6	0655	0.5	1328	4.5	1917	0.5
5	M	0205	4.5	0738	0.8	1419	4.3	1959	0.8
6	TU	0221	4.2	0822	1.1	1521	4.1	2044	1.2
7	W	0312	4.0	0910	1.4	1529	3.8	◑ 2136	1.5
8	TH	0406	3.9	1006	1.7	1626	3.6	2238	1.9
9	F	0459	3.7	1115	2.0	1726	3.5	2353	2.0
10	SA	0559	3.6	1233	2.0	1836	3.5		
11	SU	0107	2.0	0707	3.6	1340	1.8	1944	3.6
12	M	0207	1.8	0854	3.9	1433	1.6	2044	3.8
13	TU	0255	1.6	0901	4.0	1518	1.3	2131	4.0
14	W	0339	1.3	0950	4.2	1559	1.0	2214	4.2
15	TH	0418	1.1	1028	4.3	1637	0.9	● 2253	4.3
16	F	0455	1.0	1103	4.3	1712	0.8	2328	4.3
17	SA	0527	0.9	1137	4.4	1743	0.7		
18	SU	0023	4.4	0557	0.8	1211	4.4	1813	0.7
19	M	0051	4.5	0628	0.8	1303	4.5	1845	0.6
20	TU	0126	4.5	0703	0.7	1342	4.5	1921	0.7
21	W	0207	4.5	0742	0.8	1426	4.5	2002	0.8
22	TH	0254	4.4	0826	1.0	1451	4.2	2048	1.1
23	F	0347	4.2	0917	1.3	1545	4.0	◐ 2145	1.5
24	SA	0418	3.9	1026	1.6	1731	3.9	2306	1.8
25	SU	0524	3.8	1206	1.7	1808	3.7		
26	M	0055	1.8	0656	3.9	1338	1.5	1942	3.9
27	TU	0208	1.5	0811	4.1	1436	1.1	2043	4.2
28	W	0300	1.1	0908	4.4	1525	0.7	2205	4.5

MARCH

Date	Day	Time	m	Time	m	Time	m	Time	m
1	TH	0347	0.7	1017	4.6	1610	0.4	2244	4.6
2	F	0431	0.4	1057	4.6	1653	0.1	○ 2325	4.6
3	SA	0513	0.3	1139	4.6	1734	0.1		
4	SU	0008	4.6	0554	0.3	1221	4.6	1814	0.2
5	M	0051	4.5	0634	0.4	1304	4.5	1853	0.4
6	TU	0135	4.4	0712	0.6	1350	4.3	1931	0.7
7	W	0226	4.3	0750	1.0	1442	4.2	2010	1.1
8	TH	0229	4.0	0830	1.3	1442	3.8	2053	1.5
9	F	0310	3.8	0917	1.7	1530	3.6	◑ 2148	1.9
10	SA	0352	3.5	1020	2.0	1619	3.4	2305	2.2
11	SU	0452	3.4	1143	2.1	1750	3.4		
12	M	0042	2.2	0625	3.4	1311	2.0	1910	3.5
13	TU	0146	2.0	0819	3.7	1407	1.7	2017	3.8
14	W	0234	1.7	0837	3.8	1451	1.4	2108	4.0
15	TH	0315	1.4	0923	4.1	1532	1.1	2148	4.2
16	F	0353	1.1	1005	4.3	1610	0.8	2226	4.3
17	SA	0428	0.8	1039	4.4	1645	0.6	● 2301	4.4
18	SU	0502	0.7	1110	4.4	1719	0.5	2355	4.6
19	M	0535	0.6	1206	4.6	1751	0.5		
20	TU	0026	4.6	0608	0.5	1241	4.6	1825	0.5
21	W	0103	4.6	0643	0.5	1321	4.6	1901	0.6
22	TH	0144	4.6	0721	0.6	1405	4.5	1941	0.8
23	F	0230	4.4	0804	0.9	1456	4.3	2026	1.1
24	SA	0326	4.2	0854	1.3	1526	4.0	◐ 2124	1.6
25	SU	0351	3.8	1005	1.7	1633	3.7	2258	1.9
26	M	0510	3.7	1205	1.7	1804	3.7		
27	TU	0056	1.8	0640	3.8	1326	1.5	1930	4.0
28	W	0157	1.5	0756	4.0	1420	1.1	2028	4.2
29	TH	0245	1.1	0849	4.2	1507	0.8	2152	4.5
30	F	0329	0.7	1002	4.4	1550	0.4	2230	4.6
31	SA	0412	0.5	1040	4.5	1632	0.2	○ 2308	4.6

APRIL

Date	Day	Time	m	Time	m	Time	m	Time	m
1	SU	0452	0.3	1121	4.5	1712	0.2	2348	4.5
2	M	0532	0.3	1201	4.5	1751	0.3		
3	TU	0027	4.5	0610	0.4	1242	4.4	1828	0.5
4	W	0105	4.4	0647	0.7	1322	4.3	1904	0.8
5	TH	0144	4.3	0720	0.9	1407	4.2	1938	1.2
6	F	0227	4.1	0753	1.2	1407	3.9	2013	1.5
7	SA	0225	3.8	0830	1.5	1446	3.7	2057	1.9
8	SU	0300	3.6	0925	1.9	1529	3.4	◑ 2212	2.2
9	M	0344	3.3	1047	2.1	1625	3.3	2347	2.3
10	TU	0438	3.1	1214	2.1	1826	3.5		
11	W	0114	2.1	0653	3.5	1326	1.8	2035	3.9
12	TH	0202	1.8	0801	3.7	1415	1.5	2032	4.0
13	F	0242	1.5	0849	4.0	1457	1.2	2116	4.2
14	SA	0320	1.1	0930	4.2	1536	0.8	2153	4.4
15	SU	0357	0.8	1009	4.4	1614	0.6	2229	4.5
16	M	0433	0.6	1046	4.5	1651	0.4	● 2306	4.6
17	TU	0509	0.4	1142	4.7	1727	0.4		
18	W	0001	4.7	0546	0.3	1220	4.7	1805	0.4
19	TH	0041	4.7	0624	0.4	1302	4.7	1844	0.6
20	F	0124	4.6	0705	0.6	1350	4.6	1926	0.8
21	SA	0214	4.4	0750	0.9	1446	4.3	2015	1.2
22	SU	0240	4.1	0844	1.3	1605	4.1	◐ 2119	1.6
23	M	0345	3.8	1002	1.6	1631	3.8	2255	1.9
24	TU	0502	3.7	1141	1.7	1750	3.9		
25	W	0025	1.8	0620	3.8	1255	1.5	1906	4.0
26	TH	0129	1.5	0726	3.9	1352	1.2	2006	4.2
27	F	0219	1.2	0822	4.1	1441	0.9	2137	4.4
28	SA	0304	0.9	0944	4.3	1524	0.7	2212	4.5
29	SU	0347	0.6	1023	4.3	1607	0.5	2249	4.5
30	M	0429	0.5	1103	4.4	1648	0.5	○ 2327	4.5

Chart Datum: 2·74 metres below Ordnance Datum (Newlyn). HAT is 5·0 metres above Chart Datum.

Note Double HWs occur at Southampton. The predictions are for the first HW.

STANDARD TIME (UT)
For Summer Time add ONE hour in **non-shaded areas**

SOUTHAMPTON LAT 50°53′N LONG 1°24′W

TIMES AND HEIGHTS OF HIGH AND LOW WATERS

Dates in red are SPRINGS
Dates in blue are NEAPS

YEAR **2018**

MAY

Date	Day	Time	m	Time	m	Time	m	Time	m
1	TU	0508	0.5	1145	4.3	1727	0.6		
2	W	0004	4.4	0547	0.6	1224	4.3	1805	0.8
3	TH	0038	4.4	0623	0.8	1303	4.3	1839	1.0
4	F	0114	4.3	0654	1.0	1343	4.2	1910	1.3
5	SA	0117	4.1	0722	1.2	1341	4.0	1941	1.5
6	SU	0154	3.9	0757	1.4	1424	3.9	2021	1.8
7	M	0231	3.7	0844	1.7	1505	3.7	2121	2.1
8	TU	0321	3.5	0955	1.9	1601	3.5	◑ 2240	2.2
9	W	0413	3.3	1111	2.0	1708	3.5	2354	2.1
10	TH	0531	3.3	1220	1.9	1841	3.7		
11	F	0101	1.9	0707	3.6	1322	1.6	1951	4.0
12	SA	0154	1.6	0808	3.9	1413	1.3	2038	4.2
13	SU	0239	1.2	0854	4.2	1459	0.9	2120	4.4
14	M	0322	0.8	0938	4.4	1541	0.7	2158	4.6
15	TU	0403	0.5	1019	4.6	1623	0.5	● 2239	4.7
16	W	0445	0.4	1118	4.7	1704	0.4	2339	4.8
17	TH	0526	0.3	1201	4.8	1747	0.4		
18	F	0022	4.8	0609	0.4	1247	4.7	1831	0.6
19	SA	0109	4.7	0653	0.5	1339	4.6	1917	0.9
20	SU	0201	4.5	0742	0.8	1441	4.4	2011	1.2
21	M	0305	4.2	0839	1.1	1511	4.1	2115	1.5
22	TU	0336	3.9	0949	1.4	1619	4.0	◐ 2229	1.7
23	W	0445	3.8	1103	1.5	1726	4.0	2342	1.7
24	TH	0552	3.8	1213	1.5	1832	4.0		
25	F	0049	1.6	0656	3.8	1315	1.4	1930	4.1
26	SA	0146	1.4	0853	4.1	1408	1.2	2124	4.3
27	SU	0235	1.1	0928	4.1	1455	1.0	2153	4.4
28	M	0321	0.9	1009	4.2	1540	0.9	2230	4.4
29	TU	0404	0.8	1053	4.2	1623	0.8	○ 2309	4.4
30	W	0446	0.7	1053	4.2	1705	0.9	2310	4.3
31	TH	0525	0.8	1131	4.2	1744	1.0		

JUNE

Date	Day	Time	m	Time	m	Time	m	Time	m
1	F	0020	4.3	0602	0.9	1207	4.1	1819	1.2
2	SA	0019	4.2	0633	1.1	1244	4.1	1850	1.4
3	SU	0053	4.1	0701	1.2	1320	4.1	1919	1.5
4	M	0131	4.0	0733	1.4	1445	4.1	1956	1.6
5	TU	0213	3.9	0816	1.5	1446	3.9	2045	1.8
6	W	0257	3.7	0910	1.7	1533	3.8	◑ 2147	1.9
7	TH	0350	3.6	1018	1.8	1628	3.8	2255	1.9
8	F	0448	3.5	1125	1.7	1730	3.8		
9	SA	0000	1.8	0557	3.6	1228	1.6	1838	3.9
10	SU	0101	1.6	0711	3.8	1327	1.4	1946	4.1
11	M	0158	1.3	0813	4.1	1421	1.1	2039	4.4
12	TU	0249	0.9	0905	4.3	1511	0.8	2131	4.6
13	W	0337	0.6	0951	4.5	1559	0.6	● 2216	4.7
14	TH	0424	0.4	1100	4.7	1646	0.5	2320	4.8
15	F	0510	0.3	1145	4.7	1733	0.5		
16	SA	0006	4.8	0557	0.3	1234	4.7	1820	0.6
17	SU	0054	4.7	0644	0.5	1327	4.6	1909	0.8
18	M	0147	4.5	0734	0.7	1426	4.5	2001	1.0
19	TU	0245	4.3	0827	0.9	1457	4.3	2057	1.3
20	W	0353	4.1	0925	1.2	1556	4.1	◐ 2158	1.5
21	TH	0418	3.9	1027	1.4	1657	4.1	2302	1.6
22	F	0520	3.8	1131	1.5	1755	4.0		
23	SA	0007	1.6	0619	3.7	1235	1.6	1856	4.0
24	SU	0110	1.6	0721	3.8	1334	1.5	1951	4.0
25	M	0206	1.4	0932	4.0	1428	1.4	2132	4.2
26	TU	0255	1.2	1008	4.1	1516	1.2	2210	4.3
27	W	0341	1.1	1057	4.2	1601	1.1	2209	4.2
28	TH	0425	1.0	1035	4.1	1645	1.1	○ 2248	4.2
29	F	0506	0.9	1117	4.2	1726	1.1	2329	4.2
30	SA	0545	1.0	1153	4.2	1803	1.2		

JULY

Date	Day	Time	m	Time	m	Time	m	Time	m
1	SU	0002	4.2	0618	1.1	1227	4.2	1833	1.3
2	M	0033	4.1	0644	1.2	1341	4.3	1900	1.4
3	TU	0109	4.1	0714	1.2	1410	4.2	1934	1.4
4	W	0151	4.1	0751	1.3	1448	4.2	2015	1.5
5	TH	0235	4.0	0836	1.4	1534	4.1	2105	1.6
6	F	0321	3.9	0930	1.5	1557	4.0	◑ 2205	1.7
7	SA	0417	3.8	1034	1.6	1651	3.9	2312	1.7
8	SU	0517	3.7	1142	1.6	1753	4.0		
9	M	0019	1.6	0625	3.8	1248	1.5	1901	4.1
10	TU	0123	1.4	0732	4.0	1351	1.3	2007	4.3
11	W	0224	1.1	0838	4.2	1449	1.1	2107	4.5
12	TH	0319	0.8	0936	4.5	1543	0.8	2155	4.6
13	F	0410	0.5	1047	4.7	1633	0.6	● 2305	4.8
14	SA	0500	0.3	1133	4.7	1722	0.5	2350	4.8
15	SU	0546	0.3	1220	4.7	1809	0.5		
16	M	0038	4.7	0632	0.3	1311	4.7	1855	0.6
17	TU	0127	4.6	0718	0.5	1405	4.5	1943	0.8
18	W	0221	4.4	0806	0.7	1434	4.3	2032	1.1
19	TH	0323	4.2	0856	1.0	1530	4.2	◐ 2125	1.3
20	F	0444	4.0	0951	1.4	1625	4.1	2224	1.6
21	SA	0444	3.8	1052	1.6	1723	4.0	2328	1.7
22	SU	0547	3.7	1158	1.8	1820	3.9		
23	M	0035	1.8	0648	3.6	1303	1.8	1917	3.9
24	TU	0138	1.7	0746	3.7	1403	1.7	2009	3.9
25	W	0233	1.5	0843	3.8	1455	1.5	2104	4.0
26	TH	0321	1.3	0938	4.0	1543	1.3	2152	4.2
27	F	0406	1.1	1020	4.1	1627	1.2	○ 2231	4.2
28	SA	0448	1.0	1104	4.2	1708	1.1	2313	4.3
29	SU	0526	0.9	1140	4.3	1744	1.2	2346	4.3
30	M	0559	1.0	1211	4.3	1814	1.2		
31	TU	0014	4.2	0626	1.0	1310	4.3	1840	1.2

AUGUST

Date	Day	Time	m	Time	m	Time	m	Time	m
1	W	0048	4.2	0653	1.0	1338	4.4	1910	1.2
2	TH	0128	4.3	0726	1.0	1415	4.4	1947	1.2
3	F	0209	4.2	0806	1.1	1459	4.3	2032	1.3
4	SA	0252	4.1	0853	1.3	1549	4.2	◑ 2123	1.5
5	SU	0346	4.0	0950	1.5	1646	4.1	2228	1.6
6	M	0443	3.8	1100	1.7	1754	4.0	2344	1.7
7	TU	0636	3.9	1217	1.7	1826	3.9		
8	W	0101	1.6	0709	3.9	1334	1.6	1947	4.2
9	TH	0212	1.3	0825	4.2	1439	1.3	2053	4.4
10	F	0310	0.9	0921	4.4	1534	0.9	2143	4.6
11	SA	0401	0.5	1036	4.7	1623	0.6	● 2251	4.8
12	SU	0448	0.3	1120	4.8	1709	0.5	2334	4.8
13	M	0532	0.2	1204	4.8	1753	0.4		
14	TU	0018	4.7	0616	0.2	1250	4.7	1837	0.5
15	W	0105	4.6	0658	0.4	1341	4.6	1920	0.7
16	TH	0154	4.4	0741	0.7	1401	4.4	2004	1.0
17	F	0253	4.2	0826	1.0	1451	4.2	2052	1.3
18	SA	0308	3.9	0916	1.4	1544	4.0	◐ 2146	1.6
19	SU	0408	3.7	1015	1.8	1643	3.9	2250	1.9
20	M	0507	3.6	1123	2.0	1738	3.7		
21	TU	0002	2.0	0615	3.5	1236	2.1	1842	3.7
22	W	0113	1.9	0721	3.6	1342	2.0	2034	3.9
23	TH	0212	1.7	0821	3.8	1437	1.7	2125	4.0
24	F	0301	1.4	0913	4.0	1523	1.5	2128	4.1
25	SA	0344	1.2	0959	4.2	1606	1.2	2210	4.2
26	SU	0424	1.0	1040	4.3	1645	1.1	○ 2252	4.3
27	M	0502	0.9	1113	4.4	1719	1.0	2325	4.4
28	TU	0534	0.9	1147	4.4	1749	1.0	2352	4.4
29	W	0603	0.9	1240	4.5	1816	1.0		
30	TH	0047	4.5	0629	0.9	1310	4.5	1845	1.0
31	F	0121	4.5	0701	0.9	1346	4.5	1921	1.0

Chart Datum: 2·74 metres below Ordnance Datum (Newlyn). HAT is 5·0 metres above Chart Datum.

Note Double HWs occur at Southampton. The predictions are for the first HW.

STANDARD TIME (UT)
For Summer Time add ONE hour in **non-shaded areas**

SOUTHAMPTON LAT 50°53′N LONG 1°24′W

TIMES AND HEIGHTS OF HIGH AND LOW WATERS

Dates in red are SPRINGS
Dates in blue are NEAPS

YEAR **2018**

SEPTEMBER

Date	Day	Time	m	Time	m	Time	m	Time	m
1	SA	0202	4.5	0739	1.0	1429	4.5	2002	1.1
2	SU	0248	4.3	0822	1.2	1519	4.3	2050	1.4
3	M	0313	4.1	0914	1.5	1617	4.1	◑ 2151	1.7
4	TU	0448	3.9	1025	1.8	1733	4.0	2321	1.9
5	W	0523	3.7	1206	2.0	1804	3.8		
6	TH	0059	1.7	0658	3.9	1334	1.7	1934	4.1
7	F	0208	1.4	0818	4.2	1434	1.4	2039	4.4
8	SA	0301	0.9	0909	4.4	1524	1.0	2131	4.6
9	SU	0347	0.6	1025	4.7	1609	0.6	● 2235	4.7
10	M	0431	0.3	1104	4.8	1652	0.4	2316	4.8
11	TU	0513	0.2	1146	4.8	1734	0.4	2358	4.7
12	W	0554	0.2	1229	4.7	1815	0.5		
13	TH	0041	4.6	0635	0.4	1314	4.6	1855	0.7
14	F	0127	4.4	0714	0.7	1407	4.4	1935	1.0
15	SA	0219	4.3	0755	1.1	1409	4.2	2017	1.4
16	SU	0229	3.9	0840	1.5	1454	3.9	◐ 2106	1.7
17	M	0312	3.7	0937	1.9	1544	3.7	2211	2.0
18	TU	0416	3.5	1052	2.2	1651	3.6	2331	2.2
19	W	0537	3.5	1213	2.3	1804	3.6		
20	TH	0046	2.1	0647	3.6	1319	2.1	1954	3.7
21	F	0145	1.9	0754	3.8	1413	1.9	2054	4.0
22	SA	0234	1.6	0849	4.0	1458	1.5	2100	4.1
23	SU	0316	1.3	0932	4.3	1539	1.3	2148	4.3
24	M	0356	1.0	1013	4.4	1616	1.0	2224	4.4
25	TU	0432	0.8	1045	4.5	1650	0.9	○ 2256	4.5
26	W	0505	0.8	1119	4.5	1720	0.9	2330	4.5
27	TH	0535	0.8	1211	4.6	1750	0.8		
28	F	0001	4.6	0605	0.8	1243	4.7	1822	0.8
29	SA	0058	4.7	0638	0.8	1320	4.7	1858	0.9
30	SU	0139	4.6	0716	0.9	1403	4.6	1938	1.1

OCTOBER

Date	Day	Time	m	Time	m	Time	m	Time	m
1	M	0226	4.4	0758	1.2	1453	4.3	2023	1.4
2	TU	0323	4.2	0849	1.6	1558	4.1	◑ 2125	1.8
3	W	0441	4.0	1010	2.0	1628	3.8	2323	2.0
4	TH	0513	3.7	1216	2.0	1758	3.8		
5	F	0056	1.7	0652	4.0	1327	1.8	1919	4.0
6	SA	0154	1.4	0803	4.2	1419	1.4	2021	4.3
7	SU	0242	1.0	0854	4.5	1505	1.0	2110	4.5
8	M	0327	0.7	1010	4.7	1549	0.7	2218	4.7
9	TU	0410	0.4	1046	4.8	1631	0.5	● 2257	4.7
10	W	0450	0.3	1126	4.8	1711	0.4	2338	4.6
11	TH	0530	0.4	1206	4.7	1751	0.5		
12	F	0019	4.6	0610	0.6	1247	4.6	1830	0.8
13	SA	0101	4.4	0648	0.9	1328	4.4	1907	1.1
14	SU	0148	4.3	0725	1.3	1417	4.3	1943	1.4
15	M	0153	4.0	0804	1.7	1408	3.9	2024	1.7
16	TU	0231	3.8	0854	2.0	1447	3.7	◐ 2125	2.1
17	W	0315	3.5	1015	2.3	1526	3.4	2251	2.2
18	TH	0431	3.5	1145	2.4	1708	3.4		
19	F	0010	2.2	0659	3.8	1251	2.2	1916	3.7
20	SA	0110	2.0	0712	3.8	1343	2.0	2018	3.9
21	SU	0159	1.7	0810	4.0	1426	1.7	2031	4.0
22	M	0242	1.4	0858	4.3	1505	1.3	2114	4.3
23	TU	0321	1.1	0941	4.5	1541	1.1	2154	4.4
24	W	0358	0.9	1012	4.6	1616	0.9	○ 2226	4.5
25	TH	0433	0.8	1047	4.7	1650	0.7	2303	4.6
26	F	0507	0.7	1144	4.8	1725	0.7	2358	4.8
27	SA	0542	0.7	1220	4.8	1801	0.7		
28	SU	0038	4.8	0619	0.8	1259	4.7	1839	0.8
29	M	0122	4.7	0659	1.0	1344	4.6	1921	1.0
30	TU	0212	4.5	0744	1.3	1438	4.4	2010	1.4
31	W	0316	4.2	0841	1.7	1501	4.0	◑ 2119	1.8

NOVEMBER

Date	Day	Time	m	Time	m	Time	m	Time	m
1	TH	0348	3.9	1015	2.0	1619	3.8	2311	1.9
2	F	0510	3.9	1155	2.0	1742	3.9		
3	SA	0029	1.7	0628	4.0	1300	1.8	1855	4.0
4	SU	0127	1.5	0735	4.2	1354	1.4	1957	4.2
5	M	0216	1.2	0832	4.5	1441	1.1	2123	4.5
6	TU	0301	0.9	0954	4.7	1524	0.8	2201	4.5
7	W	0345	0.7	1029	4.7	1607	0.7	● 2240	4.6
8	TH	0426	0.6	1107	4.7	1648	0.6	2321	4.5
9	F	0506	0.7	1145	4.6	1728	0.7		
10	SA	0002	4.5	0546	0.9	1222	4.5	1806	0.9
11	SU	0044	4.4	0624	1.1	1300	4.4	1841	1.1
12	M	0128	4.3	0659	1.4	1340	4.3	1915	1.4
13	TU	0125	4.1	0734	1.7	1341	4.0	1948	1.7
14	W	0208	4.0	0812	2.0	1419	3.8	2033	1.9
15	TH	0251	3.8	0913	2.2	1500	3.6	◐ 2147	2.1
16	F	0343	3.6	1039	2.4	1556	3.4	2307	2.2
17	SA	0455	3.6	1159	2.3	1724	3.5		
18	SU	0015	2.1	0619	3.8	1257	2.1	1847	3.7
19	M	0110	1.9	0728	4.0	1342	1.8	1950	3.9
20	TU	0158	1.6	0820	4.2	1423	1.5	2036	4.2
21	W	0241	1.3	0904	4.4	1504	1.1	2120	4.4
22	TH	0322	1.0	0941	4.6	1543	0.9	2159	4.5
23	F	0402	0.8	1018	4.7	1623	0.7	○ 2240	4.7
24	SA	0442	0.7	1059	4.8	1704	0.6	2339	4.8
25	SU	0523	0.7	1159	4.9	1745	0.6		
26	M	0022	4.8	0605	0.8	1243	4.8	1828	0.7
27	TU	0110	4.7	0650	1.0	1332	4.6	1914	0.9
28	W	0204	4.5	0739	1.3	1428	4.4	2006	1.2
29	TH	0310	4.4	0839	1.6	1457	4.1	2113	1.5
30	F	0340	4.1	0954	1.8	1608	3.9	◑ 2233	1.7

DECEMBER

Date	Day	Time	m	Time	m	Time	m	Time	m
1	SA	0450	4.1	1113	1.9	1717	3.9	2348	1.7
2	SU	0601	4.1	1223	1.7	1827	3.9		
3	M	0051	1.5	0701	4.2	1322	1.5	1925	4.0
4	TU	0145	1.4	0915	4.5	1413	1.3	2109	4.3
5	W	0234	1.2	0937	4.5	1500	1.1	2149	4.3
6	TH	0319	1.0	1013	4.5	1544	0.9	2233	4.4
7	F	0403	0.9	1053	4.5	1626	0.8	● 2322	4.4
8	SA	0445	1.0	1051	4.4	1707	0.8	2315	4.3
9	SU	0527	1.0	1127	4.4	1747	1.0	2351	4.2
10	M	0606	1.2	1207	4.3	1823	1.1		
11	TU	0028	4.2	0641	1.4	1243	4.2	1855	1.3
12	W	0109	4.2	0711	1.6	1316	4.1	1924	1.5
13	TH	0146	4.1	0743	1.8	1357	4.0	2000	1.6
14	F	0228	4.0	0825	1.9	1435	3.8	2047	1.8
15	SA	0312	3.9	0921	2.1	1528	3.7	◐ 2151	2.0
16	SU	0404	3.8	1031	2.2	1620	3.5	2302	2.0
17	M	0507	3.8	1139	2.1	1727	3.5		
18	TU	0007	1.9	0611	3.8	1241	1.9	1842	3.7
19	W	0107	1.7	0725	4.1	1337	1.6	1951	4.0
20	TH	0200	1.4	0821	4.3	1428	1.2	2045	4.2
21	F	0250	1.1	0909	4.5	1516	0.9	2131	4.4
22	SA	0337	0.9	0956	4.7	1602	0.6	○ 2241	4.7
23	SU	0424	0.7	1041	4.8	1648	0.5	2325	4.8
24	M	0509	0.6	1144	4.9	1734	0.4		
25	TU	0010	4.8	0556	0.7	1230	4.8	1819	0.5
26	W	0059	4.7	0643	0.8	1319	4.7	1907	0.7
27	TH	0152	4.6	0732	1.0	1412	4.5	1957	0.9
28	F	0252	4.5	0824	1.2	1513	4.3	2052	1.2
29	SA	0324	4.2	0924	1.5	1627	4.1	◑ 2154	1.4
30	SU	0425	4.1	1030	1.7	1647	3.9	2303	1.6
31	M	0527	4.1	1141	1.7	1753	3.8		

Chart Datum: 2·74 metres below Ordnance Datum (Newlyn). HAT is 5·0 metres above Chart Datum.

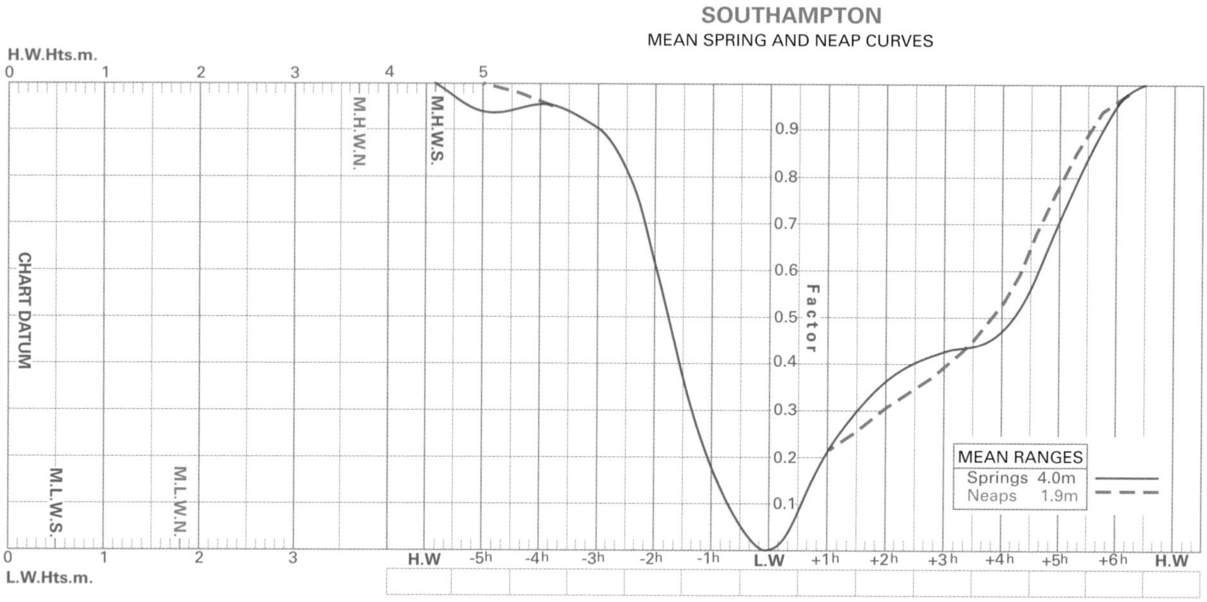

9.2.20 SOUTHAMPTON

Hampshire **50°52′·65N 01°23′·37W**

CHARTS AC 5600, 2036, 2041; Imray C3, C15, 2200

TIDES HW (1st) –0001 Dover; ML 2·9

Standard Port SOUTHAMPTON (⟵)

Times				Height (metres)			
High Water		Low Water		MHWS	MHWN	MLWN	MLWS
0400	1100	0000	0600	4·5	3·7	1·8	0·5
1600	2300	1200	1800				
Differences REDBRIDGE							
–0020	+0005	0000	–0005	–0·1	–0·1	–0·1	–0·1

NOTE: At springs there are two separate HWs about 2hrs apart; at neaps there is a long stand. Predictions are for the first HW when there are two, otherwise for the middle of the stand. NE gales and a high barometer may lower sea level by 0·6m.

SHELTER Good in most winds, although a choppy sea builds in SE winds >F4, when it may be best to shelter in marinas. Ⓥ berths available in Hythe, Town Quay, Ocean Village, Shamrock Quay and Kemp's Marinas. No specific yacht anchorages but temporary ⚓ is permitted (subject to HM) off club moorings at Netley, Hythe, Weston and Marchwood in about 2m. Keep clear of all channels and Hythe Pier. Public moorings for larger yachts opposite Royal Pier near Gymp Elbow PHM buoy in 4m (contact HM); nearest landing is at Town Quay Marina.

NAVIGATION WPT 50°50′·0N 01°18′·6W, just S of Hamble Point SCM, to Weston Shelf SHM buoy 312°/4M. Main channels are well marked.

- For a Yachtsman's Guide see www.southamptonvts.co.uk.
- Yachts should keep just outside the buoyed lit fairway and when crossing it should do so at 90°, abeam Fawley chy, at Cadland and Greenland buoys, abeam Hythe and abeam Town Quay.

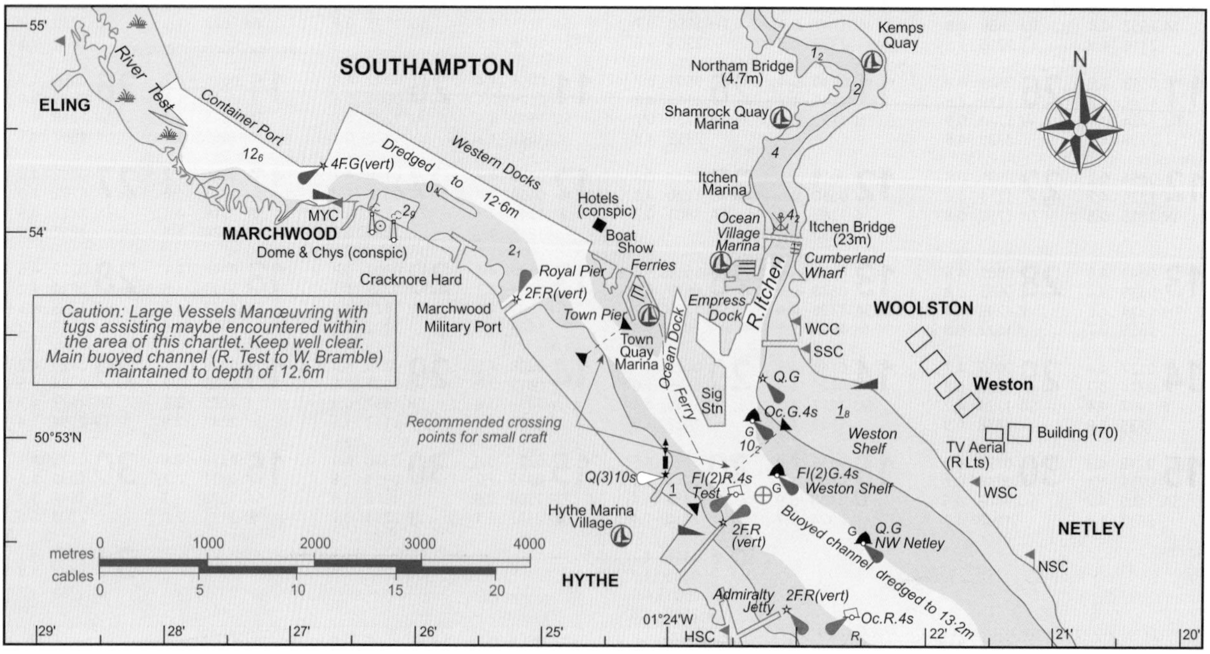

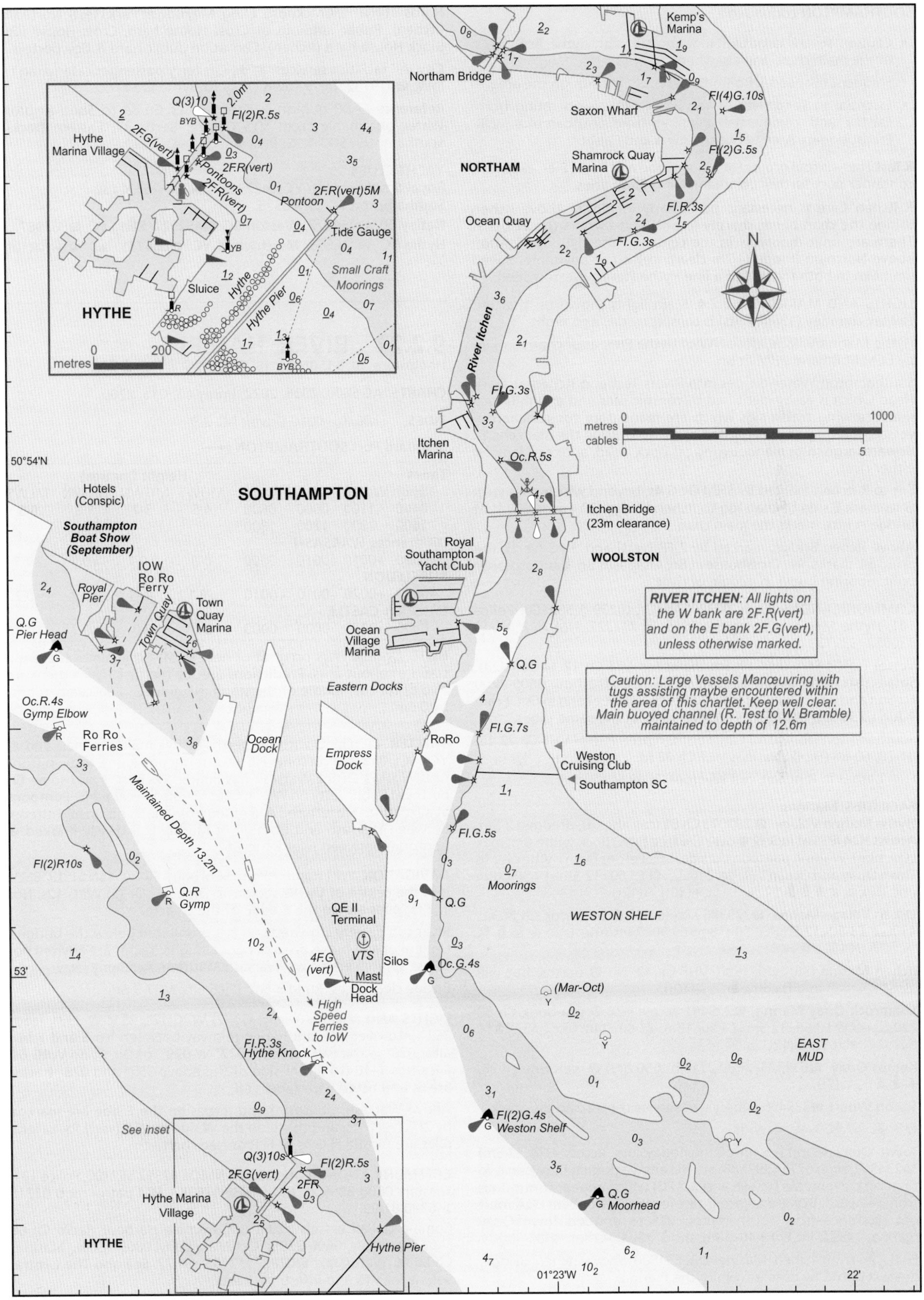

Kemp's Marina
Northam Bridge
Fl(4)G.10s
Saxon Wharf
Shamrock Quay Marina
Fl(2)G.5s
NORTHAM
Fl.R.3s
Ocean Quay
Fl.G.3s
N
River Itchen
Fl.G.3s
metres
cables
0
1000
5
Itchen Marina
Oc.R.5s
50°54'N
SOUTHAMPTON
Hotels (Conspic)
Itchen Bridge (23m clearance)
Southampton Boat Show (September)
Royal Southampton Yacht Club
WOOLSTON
IOW Ro Ro Ferry
Royal Pier
Town Quay
Town Quay Marina
RIVER ITCHEN: All lights on the W bank are 2F.R(vert) and on the E bank 2F.G(vert), unless otherwise marked.
Q.G Pier Head
Ocean Village Marina
Q.G
Eastern Docks
Caution: Large Vessels Manœuvring with tugs assisting maybe encountered within the area of this chartlet. Keep well clear. Main buoyed channel (R. Test to W. Bramble) maintained to depth of 12.6m
Oc.R.4s Gymp Elbow
Ro Ro Ferries
Ocean Dock
Empress Dock
RoRo
Fl.G.7s
Weston Cruising Club
Southampton SC
Maintained Depth 13.2m
Fl.G.5s
Fl(2)R10s
Moorings
Q.R Gymp
Q.G
QE II Terminal
WESTON SHELF
VTS
Silos
4F.G (vert)
Mast Dock Head
Oc.G.4s
53'
(Mar-Oct)
High Speed Ferries to IoW
Fl.R.3s Hythe Knock
EAST MUD
Fl(2)G.4s Weston Shelf
See inset
Q(3)10s
Fl(2)R.5s
2F.G(vert)
2FR
Hythe Marina Village
Q.G Moorhead
HYTHE
Hythe Pier
01°23'W
22'
Q(3)10
BYB
2.0m
Fl(2)R.5s
Hythe Marina Village
2F.G(vert)
2F.R(vert)
Pontoons
2F.R(vert)
2F.R(vert)5M
Pontoon
Tide Gauge
Small Craft Moorings
Sluice
Hythe
Hythe Pier
HYTHE
metres
200

SOUTHAMPTON *continued*

- Caution: several large unlit mooring buoys off Hythe, both sides of the main chan, and elsewhere.
- Frequent hi-speed & Ro-Ro ferries operate through the area.
- Essential to keep clear of very large tankers operating from Fawley and commercial shipping from Southampton. NB Precautionary Area between Cowes and Calshot.

R Test There is foul ground at Marchwood and Royal Pier; extensive container port further upstream. Eling Chan dries.

R Itchen Care is necessary, particularly at night. Above Itchen Bridge the chan bends sharply to port and favours the W bank. There are unlit moorings in the centre of the river. Navigation above Northam Bridge (4·7m clearance) is not advisable. Speed limit 6kn in both rivers N of a line Hythe Pier to Weston Shelf.

LIGHTS AND MARKS See 9.2.4. Main lights shown on chartlet. Fawley chimney (198m, R lts) is conspic by day and night.

Hythe Marina Village, close NW of Hythe Pier: appr chan marked by ECM lit Bn and PHM lit Bn.

Southampton Water divides into Rivers Test and Itchen at Dock Head which is easily identified by conspic silos and a high lattice mast showing traffic sigs which are mandatory for commercial vessels, but may be disregarded by yachts outside the main chans. Beware large ships manoeuvring off Dock Head, and craft leaving either river.

Ent to R Itchen marked by SHM Oc G 4s, beyond which piles with G lts mark E side of chan ldg to Itchen bridge (24·4m); a FW lt at bridge centre marks the main chan.

Above Itchen Bridge, marked by 2 FR (vert) and 2 FG (vert), the principal marks are: Crosshouse lit Bn; Chapel lit Bn. **Caution**: large unlit mooring buoys in middle of river.

COMMUNICATIONS (Code 02380) NMOC (02392) 552100; Police 101; Hythe Medical Centre ☎845955; Ⓗ 777222. HM ABP & VTS 330022 (339733 outside HO).

Vessel Traffic Services Call: *Southampton VTS* Ch **12** 14 16 (H24). Small craft traffic info broadcast on Ch 12 on the hour 0600-2200 Fri-Sun and Bank Holidays from Easter to last weekend in Oct. From 1 Jun to 30 Sep broadcasts are every day at the same times.

Southampton Hbr Patrol Call: *Southampton Patrol* VHF Ch **12** 16, 01-28, 60-88 (H24). Marinas VHF Ch **80** M.

Fuel barges in R Itchen, call *Wyefuel* Ch 08.

FACILITIES **Marinas**:

Hythe Marina Village ☎ 207073 Ch 80 (call ahead), dredged 2·5m. Access H24 IPTS at lock (2 ● over ○ = free flow) (lock width 8m; max LOA 18m). Waiting pontoon outside lock. Ferries from Hythe pier to Town Quay and Ocean Village. 210+Ⓥ £3·60<12·5m>£4·50<18m (inc), (30t) (12t) .

Ocean Village Marina ☎229385 access H24 Ⓥ pre-book Ch 80 450 £3·60<12·5m>£4·50<18m>£5·00<24m (inc), .

Itchen Marina (50) ☎631500, VHF Ch 12. No Ⓥ berths, but will assist a vessel in difficulty, (40t).

Shamrock Quay Marina ☎229461 access H24 Ⓥ pre-book Ch 80 220+40Ⓥ £3·60<12·5m>£4·50<18m>£5·00<24m (inc), (63t) (12t) .

Kemps Quay ☎632323, 260 (all but 50 dry) Ⓥ welcome £4·26, (5t).

Saxon Wharf ☎339490 Superyacht service centre and dry-stack.

Ⓥ wi-fi.

Town Quay Marina @ info@townquay.com access H24 (2·6m) ☎234397, mob 07764 293588; marina ent is a dogleg between two floating wavebreaks (☆ 2 FR and ☆ 2 FG) which appear continuous from seaward. Beware adjacent fast ferries. Craft >20m LOA must get clearance from Southampton VTS to ent/dep Town Quay marina. 133 inc Ⓥ £3·40<13m, short stay £9<13m, .

Fuel from Itchen Marina ☎80631500 above Itchen Bridge, nearest petrol by hose is from Hythe marina.

Hards at Hythe, Cracknore, Eling, Mayflower Park (Test), Northam (Itchen). Public landings at Cross House hard, Cross House slip, Block House hard (Itchen), Carnation public hard & Cowporters.

City All facilities services ⇌ ✈, Car ferry/passenger catamaran to IoW, ☎019192; ferry Town Quay to Hythe ☎840722.

Reference ABP publish a *Yachtsman's Guide to Southampton Water* obtainable from VTS Centre, Berth 37, Eastern Docks, Southampton SO1 1GG. Please send sae.

YACHT CLUBS

Royal Southampton YC ☎223352, .

Southampton SC ☎446575.

Netley SC ☎454272; **Weston SC** ☎452527; **Eling SC** ☎863987.

Hythe SC ☎846563; **Marchwood YC** ☎666141, (10t) .

9.2.21 RIVER HAMBLE

Hampshire **50°51′·0N 01°18′·50W**

CHARTS AC 5600, 2036, 2022; Imray C3, C15, 2200

TIDES +0020, –0010 Dover; ML 2·9

Standard Port SOUTHAMPTON (⟵)

Times				Height (metres)			
High Water		Low Water		MHWS	MHWN	MLWN	MLWS
0400	1100	0000	0600	4·5	3·7	1·8	0·5
1600	2300	1200	1800				
Differences *WARSASH*							
+0020	*+0010*	*+0010*	*0000*	*0·0*	*+0·1*	*+0·1*	*+0·3*
BURSLEDON							
+0020	+0020	+0010	+0010	+0·1	+0·1	+0·2	+0·2
CALSHOT CASTLE							
0000	+0025	0000	0000	0·0	0·0	+0·2	+0·3

NOTE: Double HWs occur at or near sp; at other times there is a stand of about 2hrs. Predictions are for the first HW if there are two or for the middle of the stand. NE gales can decrease depths by 0·6m.

SHELTER Excellent, with Ⓥs berths at five main marinas, and at YCs, SCs, BYs and on some Hbr Authority pontoons. Jetty in front of B/W HM's Office Warsash has limited Ⓥs berths and some Ⓥs berths at Public Jetty on W bank near Bugle Inn car park. Pontoons at all marinas are lettered A, B et seq from the S end. In mid-stream between Warsash and Hamble Pt Marina is a clearly marked Ⓥ pontoon, between piles B1 to B6.

NAVIGATION WPT Hamble Point SCM buoy, 50°50′·15N 01°18′·66W, is in the centre of the W sector of Dir 352°, Oc (2) WRG 12s; Nos 1, 3, 5, piles are on the E edge of the G sector.

River can be very crowded and ⚓ is prohibited below the bridges. Unlit piles and buoys are a danger at night. Yachts are advised not to use spinnakers above Warsash Maritime Academy jetty.

Bridge clearances: Road 3·5m; Rly 5·5m; M27 3·8m.

LIGHTS AND MARKS Dir ☆, Oc (2) WRG 12s, 351°-W-353°, leads 352° into river ent. and when midway between No 5 and 7 bns alter 028° in the white sector, 027°-W-029°, of Dir ☆, Iso WRG 6s. Piles Nos 1–10 (to either side of the above 352° and 028° tracks) are lit and fitted with radar refl.

Above Warsash, pontoons and jetties on the E side are marked by 2FG (vert) lts, and those on the W side by 2FR (vert) lts. Lateral piles are mostly Fl G 4s or Fl R 4s (see chartlet).

COMMUNICATIONS (Code 02380) NMOC 02392 552100; Police 101; Seastart 0800 885500. HM 01489 576387, HM patrol mob 07718 146380/81/99.

Commercial/all vessels >20m call: *Hamble Harbour Radio* Ch **68** (Apr-Sep: daily 0600-2200. Oct-Mar: daily 0800-1800). Marinas Ch **80** M. Water Taxi ☎07827157155, Ch 77. See also The Central Solent for VTS and info broadcasts.

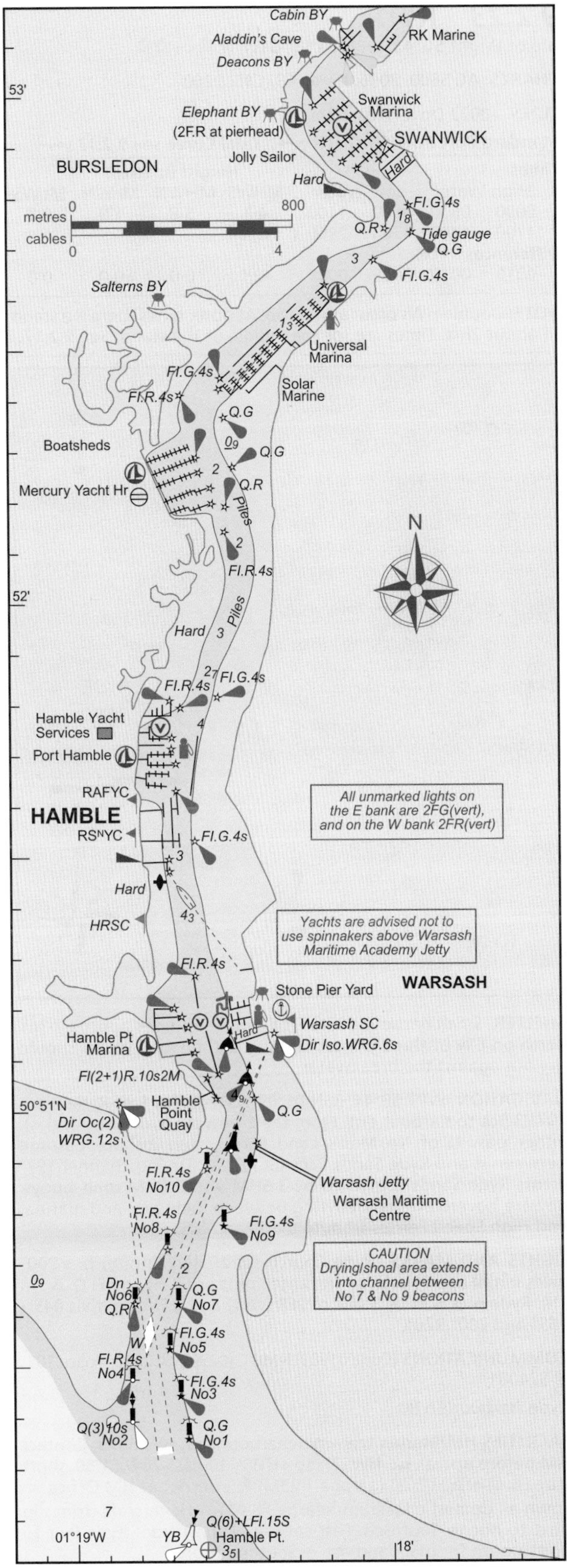

FACILITIES Marinas from seaward:

Hamble Pt Marina ☎452464, access H24, pre-book Ch 80. 220 £3·50, short stay £8·50; Ⓔ (65t) (7t).

Stone Pier Yard ☎01489 579589, access H24, 56 £4·00, <4hrs £8; (10t). Nearby: ✉ Ⓒ.

Port Hamble Marina ☎452741 access H24 pre-book, Ch 80. 310+Ⓥ £3·50; Ⓔ (60t) (7t).

Hamble yacht Services ☎454111 access H24, Ⓥ pre-book, Ch 80. Ⓔ.

Mercury Yacht Hbr ☎455994, access H24, pre-book Ch 80. 346+Ⓥ £3·50, short stay £8·50; Ⓔ (20t).

Universal Marina ☎01489 574272, access H24, pre-book Ch 80. 249+Ⓥ £3·20, short stay £8; (80t) (7t) /café.

Swanwick Marina ☎01489 884081 (H24), 380+Ⓥ £3·55, £1·50 <4hrs (min £5), Ⓔ (60t) (12t) ✉ @.

The Hbr Authority jetty in front of the conspic B/W HM's Office at Warsash has limited (£2), also Ⓥ pontoons in mid-stream (both £1.50), toilets ashore. Public Jetty on W bank near the Bugle Inn car park (£1·75). See www.hants.gov.uk/hamble harbour.

YACHT CLUBS

Hamble River SC ☎452070

RAFYC ☎452208,

Royal Southern YC ☎450300

Warsash SC ☎01489 583575.

SERVICES Wide range of marine services available; consult marina/HM for locations. *Hamble River Guide* available from HM.

Hards At Warsash, Hamble and Swanwick.

Slips at Warsash, Hamble, Bursledon and Lower Swanwick.

Maintenance piles at Warsash by HM's slipway; on W bank upriver of public jetty near Bugle; by slip opposite Swanwick Marina.

✉ (Hamble, Bursledon, Warsash and Lower Swanwick); (Hamble, Bursledon, Sarisbury Green, Swanwick, Warsash).

⇄ (Hamble and Bursledon); ✈ (Southampton).

ADJACENT HARBOURS

ASHLETT CREEK, Hants, **50°50'·01N 01°19'·49W**. AC 5600, 2038, 2022. Tides approx as Calshot Castle (opposite). Small drying (2·1m) inlet across from R Hamble; best for shoal-draught vessels. Appr at HW close to Fawley Marine Terminal. Unlit chan, marked by 3 PHM buoys, then in sequence a pair of PHM and SHM buoys, a PHM beacon and SHM buoy (No 7). Then follow PHM and SHM beacons. The single dog leg is indicated by an arrow on a PHM. A final SHM buoy leads to the drying sailing club pontoon or the drying quay. Ldg bns are hard to find; local knowledge desirable. Berth at drying quay. Facilities: Hard. **Ashlett SC.**

HILL HEAD, Hants, **50°49'·08N 01°14'·54W**. AC 5600, 2036, 2022. HW +0030 on Dover; use LEE-ON-SOLENT differences. Short term ⚓ for small craft at mouth of R Meon. Bar dries ¼M offshore. Ent dries 1·2m at MLWS. Appr on 030° towards Hill Head SC ho (W, conspic); Small hbr to W inside ent (very narrow due to silting) where small yachts can lie in soft mud alongside wall. Facilities: **Hill Head SC** ☎(01329) 664843. **Hill Head village** ✉.

9.2.22 WOOTTON CREEK

Isle of Wight **50°44′·09N 01°12′·77W** ❁❁◊✿✿✿

CHARTS AC 5600, 2036, 2022; Imray C3, C15, 2200

TIDES +0023 Dover; ML 2·8. Use RYDE differences.

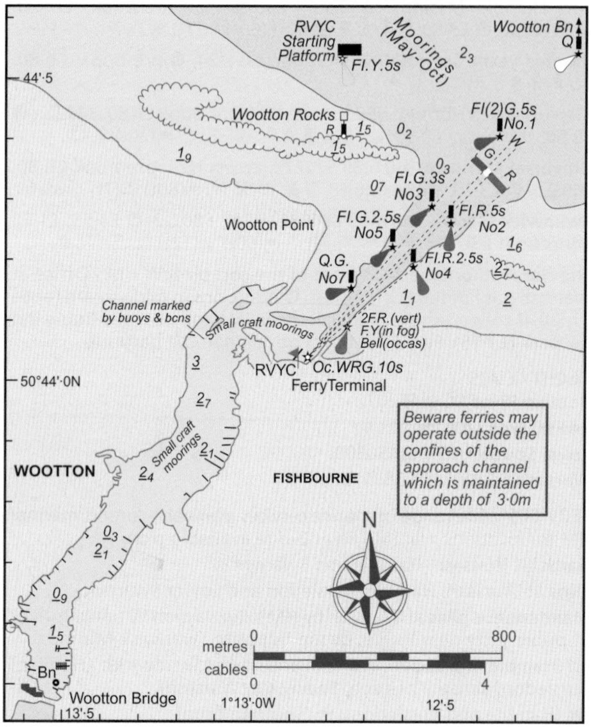

SHELTER Good except in strong N or E winds. Creek dries above the ferry terminal. ABs on RVYC pontoons (dry); No ⚓ in the fairway. Speed limit 5kn.

NAVIGATION WPT Wootton NCM Bn, Q, 50°44′·53N 01°12′·13W, 222°/6·3ca to ferry slip. An obstruction drying 1·4m verges Peel Bank 8 Ca NNE of the Starting Platform. Beware seasonal moorings (May-Oct) laid between the platform & No 1 bn. Large car ferries may operate outside the confines of the approach channel when proceeding to and from Fishbourne Ferry Terminal.

LIGHTS AND MARKS Entrance to approach channel due S of SE Ryde Middle SCM and 1·75M W of Ryde Pier. From the W, pass N of the Starting Platform & No 1 bn. The channel is marked by four SHM bns and two PHMs, all lit. Keep in W sector of Dir lt, Oc WRG 10s, 221°-G-224°-W-225½°-R-230½°. By ferry terminal, turn onto ldg marks on W shore △ ▽, which form a ◇ when in transit 270°.

COMMUNICATIONS (Code 01983) NMOC (02392) 552100; Police 101; Dr 562955.

FACILITIES Fishbourne, **Royal Victoria YC** ☎882325, ⛴ ⛵£1·50/m (shortstay £5·00), ⛽ ♿ ✕ 🍺. **Village** Wootton Bridge 📮 ☎ ✉ Ⓑ 🛒 ✕ 🍺 (Ryde), ⇌ (ferry to Portsmouth), ✈ (Southampton).

9.2.23 RYDE

Isle of Wight **50°43′·98N 01°09′·31W** ❁❁◊◊✿✿

CHARTS AC 5600, 2036; Imray C3, C15, 2200

TIDES +0022 Dover; ML 2·8m

Standard Port PORTSMOUTH (⟶); **Tidal Curve see 9.2.17** (⟵)

Times				**Height (metres)**			
High Water		Low Water		MHWS	MHWN	MLWN	MLWS
0000	0600	0500	1100	4·7	3·8	1·9	0·8
1200	1800	1700	2300				
Differences RYDE							
−0010	−0010	−0005	−0005	−0·1	0·0	0·0	0·0

NOTE: Double HWs occur at/near Sp. At other times there is a stand of about 2hrs. Times are for the middle of the stand. See 9.2.17.

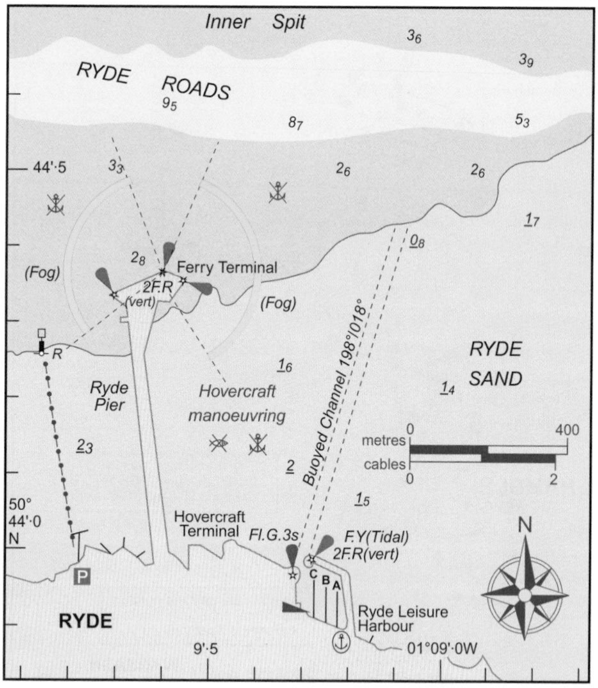

SHELTER Small harbour 300m E of Ryde Pier; dries approx 2·3m. Berth on E'ly of three pontoons; long and fin keel yachts should dry out against the breakwater.

NAVIGATION WPT 50°44′·36N 01°09′·13W (2.7ca E of Ryde Pier), 197°/3·9ca to harbour ent. From the E beware Ryde Sand (dries). Either pass N of No Man's Land Fort or use inshore passage between it and Ryde Sands Bcns (lit PHMs). Drying channel 197° across Ryde Sands is marked by 3 SHM and 3 PHM unlit buoys. Beware hovercraft manoeuvring between Ryde pier and marina, and High Speed Ferries from/to pierhead.

LIGHTS AND MARKS Ryde Church spire (Holy Trinity) brg 200° gives initial appr. Harbour entrance lights are 2 FR and Fl G 3s 7m 1M. Ryde pier is lit by 3 sets of 2FR (vert) and a FY fog lt vis 045°-165° and 200°-320°.

COMMUNICATIONS (Code 01983) NMOC (02392) 552100; Police 101; Ⓗ 524081.

Ryde Harbour Ch 80.

FACILITIES HM/Marina www.rydeharbour.com ☎613879. Contact HM before arrival. ⛴ HW–2½ to +HW2, 100⛵+70Ⓥ £1.50, short stay £6. 🚿 ♿ ✉ 📮 ☎ (garage 1·25M) 🔥. Internet at HM Office.
Town all domestic facilities nearby 🛒 ✕ 🍺. Hovercraft from slip next to hbr to Southsea. Fast cat (passenger) from Ryde Pier to Portsmouth for mainland ⇌; ✈ Southampton.

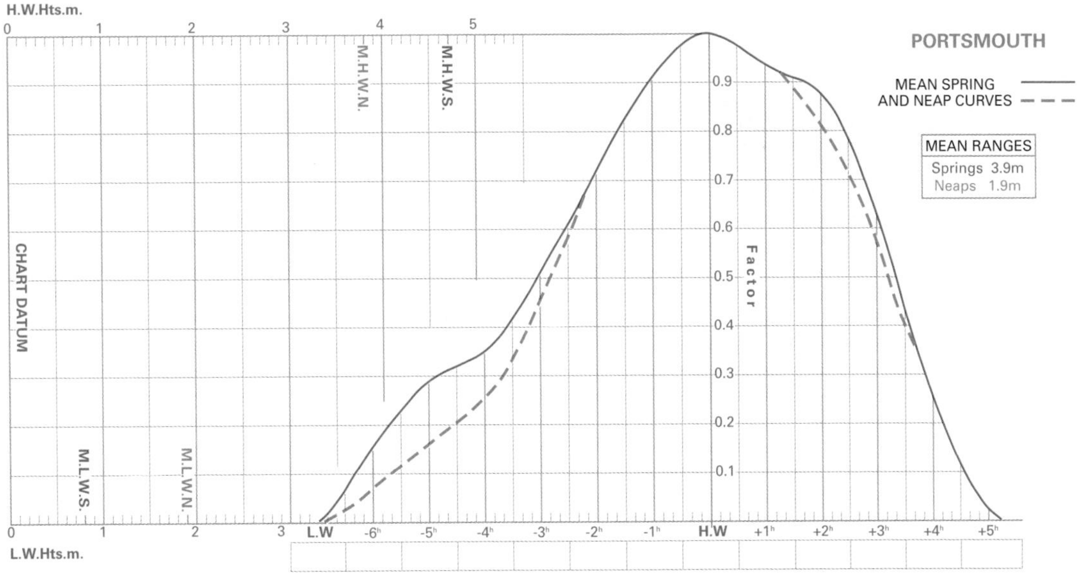

9.2.24 BEMBRIDGE

Isle of Wight **50°41'·62N 01°06'·40W**

CHARTS AC 5600, 2037, 2022; Imray C9, C3, C15, 2200

TIDES +0020 Dover

Standard Port PORTSMOUTH (⟶); Tidal Curve see 9.2.17 (⟵)

Times				Height (metres)			
High Water		Low Water		MHWS	MHWN	MLWN	MLWS
0000	0600	0500	1100	4·7	3·8	1·9	0·8
1200	1800	1700	2300				
Differences BEMBRIDGE APPROACHES							
–0010	–0005	0000	+0005	+0·1	+0·1	0·0	+0·1
BEMBRIDGE HARBOUR							
+0020	0000	+0100	+0020	–1·5	–1·4	–1·3	–1·0
VENTNOR							
–0025	–0030	–0025	–0030	–0·8	–0·6	–0·2	+0·2
SANDOWN							
0000	+0005	+0010	+0025	–0·6	–0·5	–0·2	0·0

NOTE: Double HWs occur at/near Sp. At other times there is a stand of about 2hrs. Times are for the middle of the stand. See 9.2.17.

SHELTER Good, but approach difficult in strong N/NE winds. Ⓥ berths rafting on long pontoons at Duver Marina dredged to 2m, or dry out, with ⚓s fore and aft, on sandy beach to port just inside harbour ent. No ⚓ in chan and hbr, but Priory Bay is sheltered ⚓ in winds from S to WNW (dries inshore but ½M off gives 1·5m).

NAVIGATION Beware the gravel banks between St Helen's Fort, Nodes Pt and N to Seaview. The bar, between Nos 2A and 3 buoys, almost dries. Tide gauge removed. Depths over the bar updated every 60s are online at www.bembridgeharbour.co.uk. Speed limit 6kn.

LIGHTS AND MARKS St Helen's Fort Fl (3) 10s 16m 8M; no ⚓ within 1ca of Fort. Conspic W daymark on shore where chan turns S. Pontoons and fingers lit at Duver and Fishermans Wharf. Beware many unlit Y racing marks off Bembridge and Seaview (Mar-Oct).

COMMUNICATIONS (Code 01983) NMOC (02392) 552100; Police 101; Dr 872614; HM 872828; Hbr staff Ch 80; *Water Taxi* Ch 80.

FACILITIES **Duver Marina** ☎872828, +Ⓥ 140 Ⓥ from £2.65, **Drying out area** £10 flat rate. **St Helen's Quay**. **Bembridge Marina** permanent berthholders. **Brading Haven YC** ☎872289. **Bembridge SC** ☎872686.

Town ⇌ (Ryde), ✈ (So'ton).

HARBOUR ON THE SOUTH COAST OF THE ISLE OF WIGHT

VENTNOR HAVEN, 50°35'·53N 01°12'·50W. AC 2045. Bkwtrs to protect FVs. Very exposed to E to SSE. 8Ⓥ (in <F4; seasonal), ☎07976 009260 or VHF Ch 17 for availability. (quay). **Town** All domestic facilities, some up a steep hill.

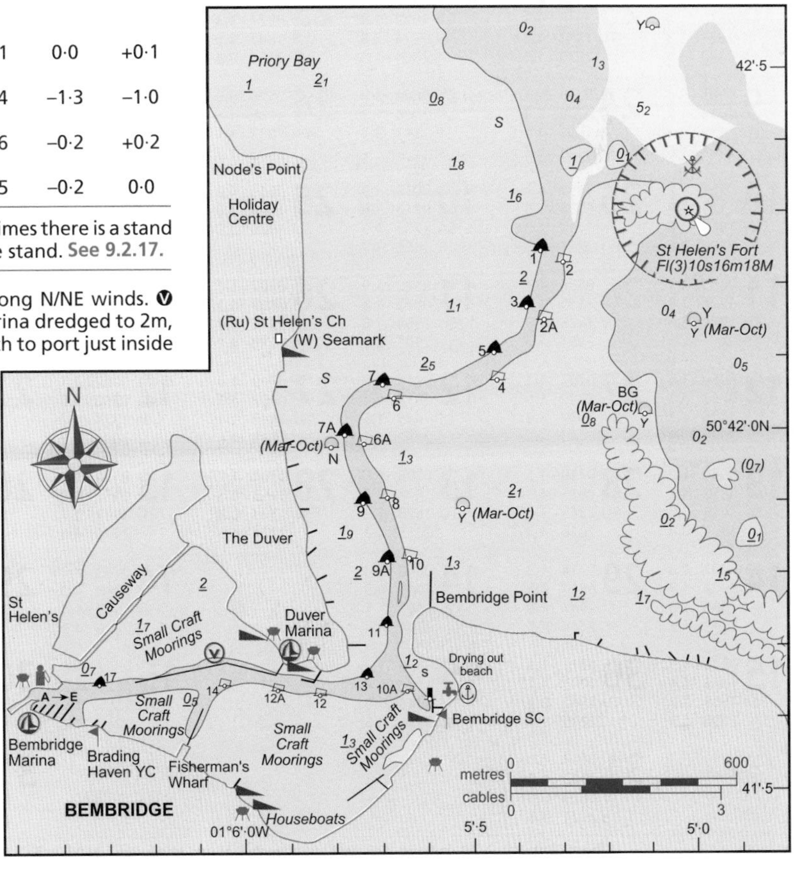

STANDARD TIME (UT)
For Summer Time add ONE hour in **non-shaded areas**

PORTSMOUTH LAT 50°48′N LONG 1°07′W

TIMES AND HEIGHTS OF HIGH AND LOW WATERS

Dates in red are SPRINGS
Dates in blue are NEAPS

YEAR **2018**

JANUARY

Date	Day	Time	m	Date	Day	Time	m
1		0322	0.9	16		0406	1.3
		1018	4.8			1105	4.5
	M	1551	0.7		TU	1628	1.1
		2244	4.8			2336	4.5
2		0412	0.8	17		0446	1.2
		1105	4.9			1144	4.5
	TU	1640	0.5		W	1705	1.0
		○ 2334	4.9			●	
3		0501	0.7	18		0013	4.5
		1152	5.0			0522	1.2
	W	1727	0.4		TH	1218	4.5
						1739	1.0
4		0023	4.9	19		0048	4.5
		0549	0.7			0554	1.1
	TH	1239	4.9		F	1250	4.5
		1814	0.5			1810	1.0
5		0117	4.9	20		0120	4.5
		0636	0.7			0626	1.1
	F	1330	4.8		SA	1321	4.4
		1901	0.6			1842	1.0
6		0217	4.8	21		0152	4.5
		0724	0.9			0657	1.1
	SA	1425	4.7		SU	1353	4.4
		1949	0.8			1914	1.0
7		0321	4.7	22		0227	4.4
		0814	1.2			0732	1.2
	SU	1523	4.5		M	1428	4.3
		2040	1.1			1951	1.0
8		0413	4.6	23		0306	4.4
		0910	1.4			0813	1.2
	M	1621	4.3		TU	1512	4.2
		◑ 2139	1.4			2033	1.1
9		0503	4.4	24		0353	4.3
		1014	1.7			0900	1.4
	TU	1719	4.1		W	1605	4.1
		2245	1.6			◐ 2124	1.3
10		0556	4.2	25		0451	4.2
		1121	1.8			0958	1.5
	W	1819	3.9		TH	1711	4.0
		2350	1.8			2227	1.5
11		0655	4.1	26		0556	4.1
		1226	1.8			1115	1.6
	TH	1924	3.8		F	1826	3.9
						2351	1.6
12		0050	1.8	27		0707	4.1
		0757	4.1			1240	1.6
	F	1325	1.7		SA	1939	4.0
		2028	3.9				
13		0146	1.7	28		0110	1.5
		0853	4.1			0815	4.3
	SA	1418	1.6		SU	1349	1.3
		2125	4.0			2046	4.2
14		0237	1.6	29		0214	1.3
		0942	4.3			0914	4.5
	SU	1505	1.4		M	1447	1.0
		2213	4.2			2144	4.5
15		0324	1.5	30		0311	1.1
		1025	4.4			1005	4.7
	M	1548	1.2		TU	1540	0.7
		2256	4.3			2235	4.7
				31		0403	0.8
						1053	4.8
					W	1629	0.5
						○ 2324	4.8

FEBRUARY

Date	Day	Time	m	Date	Day	Time	m
1		0451	0.6	16		0501	1.0
		1139	4.9			1157	4.5
	TH	1715	0.4		F	1717	0.8
2		0012	4.8	17		0023	4.5
		0537	0.5			0534	0.9
	F	1224	4.9		SA	1228	4.5
		1800	0.3			1750	0.7
3		0102	4.8	18		0055	4.5
		0621	0.6			0606	0.9
	SA	1312	4.8		SU	1259	4.5
		1843	0.4			1823	0.7
4		0156	4.8	19		0127	4.5
		0704	0.7			0638	0.8
	SU	1403	4.7		M	1331	4.5
		1926	0.6			1855	0.7
5		0251	4.7	20		0200	4.5
		0748	0.9			0712	0.8
	M	1455	4.5		TU	1405	4.5
		2010	0.9			1930	0.8
6		0337	4.6	21		0236	4.5
		0833	1.2			0750	0.9
	TU	1547	4.3		W	1446	4.4
		2057	1.2			2010	0.9
7		0420	4.3	22		0320	4.4
		0924	1.5			0834	1.1
	W	1637	4.1		TH	1537	4.2
		◑ 2152	1.6			2056	1.1
8		0506	4.1	23		0417	4.2
		1029	1.8			0927	1.3
	TH	1734	3.8		F	1643	4.0
		2304	1.8			◐ 2154	1.4
9		0604	3.9	24		0526	4.0
		1144	1.9			1038	1.6
	F	1843	3.7		SA	1803	3.9
						2322	1.7
10		0015	2.0	25		0645	4.0
		0715	3.8			1224	1.6
	SA	1253	1.9		SU	1926	3.9
		1956	3.7				
11		0120	1.9	26		0102	1.6
		0822	3.8			0802	4.1
	SU	1354	1.8		M	1340	1.4
		2101	3.8			2038	4.1
12		0218	1.8	27		0209	1.4
		0918	4.0			0902	4.3
	M	1445	1.6		TU	1439	1.1
		2152	4.1			2135	4.4
13		0306	1.6	28		0304	1.1
		1004	4.2			0953	4.5
	TU	1528	1.3		W	1529	0.8
		2235	4.3			2224	4.6
14		0348	1.4				
		1045	4.3				
	W	1607	1.1				
		2314	4.4				
15		0426	1.2				
		1122	4.4				
	TH	1643	0.9				
		● 2350	4.5				

MARCH

Date	Day	Time	m	Date	Day	Time	m
1		0353	0.8	16		0359	1.1
		1039	4.7			1056	4.4
	TH	1616	0.5		F	1615	0.9
		2310	4.7			2321	4.5
2		0438	0.6	17		0434	0.9
		1123	4.8			1130	4.5
	F	1659	0.3		SA	1651	0.7
		○ 2356	4.8			● 2354	4.6
3		0520	0.5	18		0509	0.8
		1207	4.8			1202	4.5
	SA	1741	0.3		SU	1725	0.6
4		0041	4.8	19		0026	4.6
		0602	0.5			0543	0.7
	SU	1252	4.7		M	1234	4.6
		1823	0.4			1800	0.6
5		0128	4.8	20		0059	4.7
		0642	0.6			0617	0.6
	M	1339	4.6		TU	1308	4.6
		1902	0.6			1834	0.6
6		0213	4.7	21		0133	4.6
		0721	0.8			0652	0.6
	TU	1426	4.5		W	1345	4.6
		1940	0.9			1910	0.7
7		0254	4.5	22		0210	4.6
		0758	1.1			0730	0.7
	W	1510	4.3		TH	1429	4.5
		2017	1.2			1950	0.8
8		0332	4.3	23		0256	4.4
		0837	1.4			0813	1.0
	TH	1552	4.1		F	1523	4.3
		2058	1.5			2037	1.2
9		0411	4.1	24		0355	4.2
		0922	1.7			0906	1.3
	F	1638	3.9		SA	1632	4.1
		◑ 2153	1.9			◐ 2136	1.5
10		0458	3.8	25		0507	4.0
		1038	1.9			1021	1.6
	SA	1745	3.6		SU	1754	4.0
		2337	2.1			2324	1.8
11		0611	3.6	26		0630	3.9
		1215	2.0			1218	1.6
	SU	1922	3.6		M	1916	4.0
12		0052	2.1	27		0057	1.7
		0750	3.6			0748	4.0
	M	1324	1.9		TU	1328	1.4
		2033	3.7			2027	4.2
13		0155	1.9	28		0159	1.5
		0852	3.8			0848	4.2
	TU	1417	1.7		W	1424	1.1
		2126	4.0			2123	4.4
14		0243	1.7	29		0251	1.1
		0940	4.0			0937	4.4
	W	1500	1.4		TH	1512	0.8
		2209	4.2			2209	4.6
15		0322	1.4	30		0336	0.9
		1020	4.2			1021	4.6
	TH	1538	1.1		F	1557	0.6
		2247	4.4			2253	4.7
				31		0419	0.6
						1104	4.7
					SA	1639	0.5
						○ 2335	4.8

APRIL

Date	Day	Time	m	Date	Day	Time	m
1		0500	0.5	16		0441	0.7
		1147	4.7			1132	4.6
	SU	1720	0.4		M	1658	0.6
						● 2355	4.7
2		0016	4.7	17		0517	0.6
		0540	0.5			1208	4.7
	M	1231	4.7		TU	1735	0.5
		1759	0.5				
3		0058	4.7	18		0030	4.8
		0618	0.6			0555	0.5
	TU	1315	4.6		W	1246	4.7
		1836	0.7			1813	0.5
4		0137	4.6	19		0108	4.8
		0653	0.8			0633	0.5
	W	1358	4.5		TH	1329	4.7
		1910	1.0			1853	0.7
5		0215	4.5	20		0151	4.7
		0726	1.0			0714	0.7
	TH	1437	4.4		F	1418	4.6
		1944	1.2			1936	0.9
6		0250	4.3	21		0242	4.5
		0800	1.3			0800	1.0
	F	1515	4.2		SA	1519	4.4
		2020	1.5			2026	1.3
7		0327	4.1	22		0344	4.3
		0839	1.6			0857	1.3
	SA	1556	4.0		SU	1630	4.2
		2105	1.8			◐ 2133	1.6
8		0411	3.9	23		0456	4.1
		0931	1.9			1023	1.6
	SU	1647	3.8		M	1746	4.1
		◑ 2222	2.1			2320	1.8
9		0506	3.6	24		0614	4.0
		1118	2.1			1159	1.6
	M	1822	3.6		TU	1902	4.1
10		0013	2.2	25		0036	1.7
		0658	3.5			0728	4.0
	TU	1239	2.0		W	1304	1.4
		1957	3.7			2011	4.3
11		0118	2.0	26		0137	1.5
		0818	3.7			0829	4.2
	W	1336	1.8		TH	1400	1.2
		2054	4.0			2107	4.5
12		0207	1.8	27		0228	1.2
		0909	3.9			0919	4.4
	TH	1421	1.5		F	1448	1.0
		2138	4.2			2152	4.6
13		0248	1.4	28		0314	1.0
		0950	4.2			1002	4.5
	F	1502	1.2		SA	1533	0.8
		2215	4.4			2232	4.7
14		0326	1.2	29		0356	0.8
		1025	4.4			1044	4.5
	SA	1542	0.9		SU	1615	0.7
		2248	4.6			2311	4.7
15		0403	0.9	30		0437	0.7
		1058	4.5			1127	4.6
	SU	1620	0.7		M	1656	0.7
		2321	4.7			○ 2350	4.7

Chart Datum: 2·73 metres below Ordnance Datum (Newlyn). HAT is 5·1 metres above Chart Datum.

STANDARD TIME (UT)
For Summer Time add ONE hour in **non-shaded areas**

PORTSMOUTH LAT 50°48'N LONG 1°07'W

TIMES AND HEIGHTS OF HIGH AND LOW WATERS

Dates in red are SPRINGS
Dates in blue are NEAPS

YEAR 2018

MAY

Day	Time	m
1 TU	0517 1210 1734	0.7 4.6 0.8
2 W	0029 0554 1253 1811	4.6 0.8 4.5 0.9
3 TH	0108 0628 1334 1845	4.6 0.9 4.5 1.1
4 F	0144 0700 1412 1917	4.5 1.1 4.4 1.3
5 SA	0218 0732 1449 1952	4.3 1.3 4.3 1.5
6 SU	0255 0809 1529 2034	4.2 1.5 4.1 1.8
7 M	0339 0857 1617 2131	4.0 1.7 3.9 2.0
8 TU	0431 1002 1716 ◑ 2311	3.8 1.9 3.8 2.1
9 W	0536 1139 1852	3.6 2.0 3.8
10 TH	0025 0720 1244 2010	2.0 3.7 1.8 4.0
11 F	0119 0826 1336 2057	1.8 3.9 1.6 4.2
12 SA	0205 0909 1422 2135	1.5 4.1 1.3 4.4
13 SU	0248 0946 1506 2210	1.2 4.3 1.0 4.6
14 M	0330 1023 1548 2246	0.9 4.5 0.8 4.7
15 TU	0411 1102 1630 ● 2325	0.7 4.7 0.6 4.8
16 W	0452 1144 1712	0.5 4.8 0.6
17 TH	0004 0535 1228 1755	4.9 0.5 4.8 0.6
18 F	0048 0617 1316 1839	4.9 0.5 4.8 0.7
19 SA	0135 0703 1412 1926	4.8 0.7 4.7 1.0
20 SU	0230 0753 1518 2021	4.6 0.9 4.6 1.3
21 M	0334 0852 1625 2130	4.4 1.2 4.4 1.5
22 TU	0442 1010 1732 ◐ 2252	4.2 1.4 4.3 1.7
23 W	0552 1127 1840	4.1 1.5 4.3
24 TH	0002 0702 1231 1947	1.7 4.1 1.5 4.3
25 F	0105 0804 1328 2045	1.6 4.1 1.4 4.4
26 SA	0159 0856 1419 2129	1.4 4.2 1.2 4.5
27 SU	0247 0941 1506 2207	1.2 4.3 1.1 4.6
28 M	0331 1025 1549 2246	1.0 4.4 1.0 4.6
29 TU	0413 1109 1631 ○ 2326	0.9 4.5 1.0 4.6
30 W	0453 1153 1711	0.9 4.5 1.0
31 TH	0006 0532 1236 1749	4.6 0.9 4.5 1.1

JUNE

Day	Time	m
1 F	0044 0607 1317 1824	4.5 1.0 4.5 1.2
2 SA	0120 0639 1354 1857	4.5 1.1 4.4 1.4
3 SU	0154 0711 1429 1931	4.4 1.3 4.3 1.5
4 M	0230 0747 1507 2010	4.2 1.4 4.2 1.6
5 TU	0312 0829 1551 2057	4.1 1.5 4.1 1.8
6 W	0400 0921 1642 ◑ 2156	3.9 1.7 4.0 1.9
7 TH	0457 1026 1741 2311	3.8 1.8 4.0 1.9
8 F	0602 1141 1848	3.8 1.7 4.0
9 SA	0021 0714 1245 1954	1.8 3.9 1.6 4.2
10 SU	0118 0815 1340 2046	1.6 4.1 1.4 4.4
11 M	0209 0905 1430 2131	1.3 4.3 1.1 4.6
12 TU	0257 0952 1518 2216	1.0 4.5 0.9 4.7
13 W	0345 1038 1606 ● 2300	0.8 4.7 0.7 4.8
14 TH	0431 1125 1653 2345	0.6 4.8 0.7 4.9
15 F	0518 1214 1740	0.5 4.8 0.6
16 SA	0031 0605 1306 1828	4.9 0.5 4.8 0.7
17 SU	0121 0653 1405 1917	4.8 0.6 4.8 0.9
18 M	0217 0743 1512 2010	4.7 0.8 4.7 1.1
19 TU	0319 0839 1613 2110	4.5 1.0 4.6 1.4
20 W	0423 0942 1710 ◐ 2217	4.3 1.3 4.5 1.5
21 TH	0525 1050 1808 2324	4.2 1.4 4.4 1.6
22 F	0628 1154 1908	4.1 1.5 4.3
23 SA	0027 0730 1253 2007	1.6 4.1 1.5 4.3
24 SU	0126 0828 1348 2058	1.6 4.1 1.5 4.3
25 M	0218 0922 1439 2142	1.4 4.2 1.4 4.4
26 TU	0306 1010 1526 2224	1.3 4.3 1.3 4.4
27 W	0351 1055 1610 2306	1.2 4.3 1.2 4.5
28 TH	0433 1138 1652 ○ 2346	1.1 4.4 1.2 4.5
29 F	0513 1220 1731	1.0 4.5 1.2
30 SA	0025 0549 1259 1807	4.5 1.1 4.5 1.2

JULY

Day	Time	m
1 SU	0101 0622 1336 1839	4.4 1.1 4.4 1.3
2 M	0134 0653 1410 1911	4.4 1.2 4.4 1.4
3 TU	0207 0726 1445 1946	4.3 1.2 4.3 1.4
4 W	0245 0803 1524 2026	4.2 1.3 4.3 1.5
5 TH	0329 0846 1609 2115	4.1 1.4 4.2 1.6
6 F	0420 0939 1701 ◑ 2213	4.0 1.5 4.1 1.7
7 SA	0519 1042 1759 2322	3.9 1.6 4.1 1.7
8 SU	0624 1154 1902	3.9 1.6 4.2
9 M	0032 0732 1301 2006	1.6 4.0 1.5 4.3
10 TU	0135 0834 1400 2103	1.3 4.2 1.3 4.5
11 W	0232 0931 1456 2154	1.1 4.4 1.1 4.7
12 TH	0325 1023 1549 2243	0.8 4.6 0.9 4.8
13 F	0416 1113 1639 ● 2330	0.6 4.8 0.7 4.9
14 SA	0505 1203 1728	0.5 4.9 0.6
15 SU	0017 0553 1255 1816	4.9 0.4 4.9 0.6
16 M	0106 0640 1352 1903	4.8 0.5 4.9 0.7
17 TU	0200 0727 1457 1952	4.7 0.6 4.8 0.9
18 W	0258 0817 1553 2044	4.6 0.9 4.7 1.2
19 TH	0358 0911 1641 ◐ 2142	4.4 1.2 4.5 1.4
20 F	0455 1013 1731 2246	4.2 1.4 4.4 1.6
21 SA	0553 1117 1826 2350	4.0 1.6 4.2 1.7
22 SU	0655 1220 1927	3.9 1.7 4.1
23 M	0053 0801 1319 2027	1.7 3.9 1.8 4.1
24 TU	0152 0903 1415 2120	1.6 4.0 1.7 4.2
25 W	0245 0956 1506 2205	1.5 4.1 1.5 4.3
26 TH	0332 1039 1553 2247	1.3 4.3 1.4 4.4
27 F	0415 1120 1635 ○ 2327	1.1 4.4 1.3 4.4
28 SA	0454 1159 1713	1.0 4.5 1.2
29 SU	0005 0530 1237 1749	4.5 1.0 4.5 1.2
30 M	0040 0602 1313 1820	4.4 1.0 4.5 1.2
31 TU	0112 0633 1346 1849	4.4 1.0 4.5 1.2

AUGUST

Day	Time	m
1 W	0143 0703 1418 1921	4.4 1.0 4.4 1.2
2 TH	0216 0736 1453 1957	4.3 1.1 4.4 1.2
3 F	0254 0815 1534 2040	4.2 1.2 4.3 1.3
4 SA	0342 0901 1622 ◑ 2132	4.1 1.3 4.2 1.5
5 SU	0440 0957 1720 2237	4.0 1.5 4.1 1.6
6 M	0548 1110 1827 2357	3.9 1.6 4.1 1.6
7 TU	0704 1233 1940	4.0 1.6 4.2
8 W	0113 0818 1344 2047	1.5 4.1 1.5 4.4
9 TH	0217 0921 1444 2141	1.2 4.4 1.2 4.6
10 F	0314 1013 1539 2229	0.9 4.6 1.0 4.8
11 SA	0405 1102 1629 ● 2315	0.6 4.8 0.7 4.9
12 SU	0453 1150 1715	0.4 4.9 0.6
13 M	0001 0539 1238 1801	4.9 0.3 4.9 0.5
14 TU	0048 0623 1331 1845	4.9 0.4 4.9 0.6
15 W	0138 0706 1430 1929	4.8 0.5 4.8 0.8
16 TH	0232 0751 1522 2015	4.6 0.8 4.7 1.1
17 F	0328 0838 1605 2105	4.4 1.1 4.5 1.4
18 SA	0421 0933 1650 ◐ 2206	4.2 1.5 4.3 1.7
19 SU	0516 1041 1742 2316	4.0 1.8 4.1 1.9
20 M	0620 1150 1848	3.8 2.0 3.9
21 TU	0023 0733 1255 1958	1.9 3.8 2.0 3.9
22 W	0128 0843 1356 2058	1.8 3.9 1.9 4.0
23 TH	0225 0938 1449 2146	1.7 4.1 1.7 4.2
24 F	0312 1020 1534 2227	1.4 4.3 1.5 4.3
25 SA	0353 1058 1614 2306	1.2 4.5 1.3 4.4
26 SU	0431 1136 1650 ○ 2342	1.0 4.5 1.1 4.5
27 M	0505 1211 1724	0.9 4.6 1.0
28 TU	0016 0538 1245 1755	4.5 0.9 4.6 1.0
29 W	0047 0609 1316 1825	4.5 0.9 4.6 1.0
30 TH	0116 0639 1347 1856	4.5 0.9 4.5 1.0
31 F	0147 0711 1418 1930	4.5 0.9 4.5 1.0

Chart Datum: 2·73 metres below Ordnance Datum (Newlyn). HAT is 5·1 metres above Chart Datum.

STANDARD TIME (UT)
For Summer Time add ONE hour in **non-shaded areas**

PORTSMOUTH LAT 50°48′N LONG 1°07′W

TIMES AND HEIGHTS OF HIGH AND LOW WATERS

Dates in red are SPRINGS
Dates in blue are NEAPS

YEAR **2018**

SEPTEMBER

Date	Time m	Date	Time m
1 SA	0222 4.4 0747 1.0 1456 4.4 2010 1.2	16 SU	0341 4.3 0848 1.6 1602 4.2 ◐ 2117 1.7
2 SU	0308 4.3 0830 1.2 1544 4.3 2058 1.4	17 M	0432 4.0 0956 2.0 1648 4.0 2238 2.0
3 M	0407 4.1 0923 1.5 1647 4.1 ◑ 2201 1.6	18 TU	0537 3.8 1123 2.2 1756 3.7 2355 2.1
4 TU	0524 4.0 1037 1.8 1803 4.0 2338 1.8	19 W	0701 3.7 1231 2.2 1926 3.7
5 W	0650 3.9 1227 1.8 1927 4.1	20 TH	0101 2.0 0817 3.8 1334 2.1 2033 3.9
6 TH	0107 1.6 0811 4.1 1340 1.6 2036 4.3	21 F	0158 1.8 0915 4.1 1426 1.8 2124 4.1
7 F	0210 1.3 0913 4.4 1438 1.3 2129 4.5	22 SA	0244 1.5 0957 4.3 1508 1.5 2204 4.3
8 SA	0304 1.0 1002 4.7 1529 1.0 2215 4.7	23 SU	0324 1.3 1033 4.5 1546 1.3 2241 4.5
9 SU	0351 0.6 1048 4.9 1615 0.7 ● 2259 4.9	24 M	0400 1.1 1108 4.6 1621 1.1 2316 4.6
10 M	0436 0.4 1132 4.9 1659 0.6 2342 4.9	25 TU	0435 0.9 1142 4.7 1655 1.0 ○ 2348 4.6
11 TU	0519 0.4 1218 5.0 1741 0.5	26 W	0509 0.8 1214 4.7 1728 0.9
12 W	0027 4.9 0602 0.4 1304 4.9 1823 0.6	27 TH	0018 4.6 0542 0.8 1244 4.7 1800 0.9
13 TH	0114 4.8 0642 0.6 1353 4.8 1903 0.8	28 F	0049 4.6 0614 0.8 1314 4.7 1832 0.9
14 F	0203 4.6 0722 0.9 1439 4.7 1944 1.1	29 SA	0121 4.6 0647 0.9 1347 4.6 1907 0.9
15 SA	0253 4.5 0803 1.2 1521 4.5 2026 1.4	30 SU	0159 4.6 0724 1.0 1426 4.5 1947 1.1

OCTOBER

Date	Time m	Date	Time m
1 M	0247 4.4 0807 1.3 1518 4.3 2034 1.4	16 TU	0348 4.1 0858 2.0 1600 4.0 ◐ 2129 2.0
2 TU	0352 4.2 0901 1.7 1627 4.1 ◑ 2139 1.7	17 W	0442 3.9 1052 2.3 1654 3.8 2321 2.2
3 W	0515 4.0 1029 2.0 1750 4.0 2344 1.8	18 TH	0613 3.7 1202 2.3 1835 3.6
4 TH	0643 4.0 1229 1.9 1915 4.1	19 F	0026 2.1 0740 3.8 1302 2.2 1959 3.8
5 F	0059 1.6 0801 4.2 1332 1.7 2022 4.3	20 SA	0121 1.9 0842 4.1 1353 1.9 2054 4.0
6 SA	0157 1.3 0900 4.5 1425 1.4 2113 4.5	21 SU	0207 1.7 0927 4.3 1434 1.6 2137 4.2
7 SU	0247 1.0 0948 4.7 1512 1.0 2158 4.7	22 M	0247 1.4 1004 4.5 1512 1.4 2213 4.4
8 M	0332 0.7 1031 4.9 1556 0.8 2240 4.8	23 TU	0325 1.2 1037 4.7 1548 1.1 2245 4.6
9 TU	0416 0.6 1112 5.0 1638 0.6 ● 2322 4.9	24 W	0402 1.0 1109 4.8 1624 0.9 ○ 2317 4.7
10 W	0457 0.5 1154 5.0 1719 0.6	25 TH	0439 0.8 1140 4.8 1659 0.8 2350 4.7
11 TH	0005 4.8 0538 0.6 1235 4.9 1759 0.7	26 F	0515 0.8 1213 4.8 1734 0.8
12 F	0050 4.8 0617 0.8 1317 4.8 1837 0.9	27 SA	0024 4.8 0551 0.8 1246 4.8 1811 0.8
13 SA	0135 4.7 0654 1.0 1358 4.7 1914 1.1	28 SU	0102 4.8 0628 0.9 1324 4.7 1849 0.9
14 SU	0220 4.5 0731 1.4 1437 4.5 1950 1.4	29 M	0146 4.7 0708 1.1 1408 4.6 1932 1.1
15 M	0303 4.3 0809 1.7 1516 4.2 2030 1.7	30 TU	0240 4.5 0755 1.4 1505 4.4 2023 1.4
		31 W	0351 4.3 0853 1.7 1617 4.2 ◑ 2135 1.7

NOVEMBER

Date	Time m	Date	Time m
1 TH	0510 4.2 1046 2.0 1737 4.1 2331 1.8	16 F	0502 3.9 1120 2.3 1717 3.7 2338 2.1
2 F	0629 4.2 1211 1.9 1856 4.1	17 SA	0638 3.9 1221 2.2 1902 3.7
3 SA	0037 1.6 0744 4.4 1311 1.7 2002 4.3	18 SU	0034 2.0 0756 4.0 1310 2.0 2013 3.9
4 SU	0134 1.4 0845 4.6 1403 1.4 2055 4.5	19 M	0122 1.8 0847 4.2 1353 1.7 2100 4.1
5 M	0223 1.2 0932 4.7 1450 1.1 2139 4.6	20 TU	0206 1.5 0928 4.5 1433 1.5 2137 4.3
6 TU	0309 1.0 1012 4.9 1533 0.9 2221 4.7	21 W	0247 1.3 1001 4.6 1512 1.2 2211 4.5
7 W	0352 0.8 1050 4.9 1615 0.8 ● 2303 4.7	22 TH	0328 1.1 1034 4.8 1552 1.0 2246 4.7
8 TH	0434 0.8 1129 4.9 1656 0.8 2347 4.7	23 F	0409 0.9 1109 4.9 1632 0.8 ○ 2324 4.8
9 F	0514 0.9 1209 4.8 1735 0.8	24 SA	0450 0.8 1146 4.9 1713 0.7
10 SA	0030 4.7 0553 1.0 1248 4.7 1813 1.0	25 SU	0005 4.9 0531 0.8 1225 4.9 1754 0.7
11 SU	0113 4.6 0629 1.2 1327 4.6 1848 1.2	26 M	0049 4.8 0614 0.9 1308 4.8 1837 0.8
12 M	0155 4.5 0705 1.4 1404 4.5 1922 1.4	27 TU	0138 4.8 0659 1.1 1357 4.7 1924 1.0
13 TU	0235 4.4 0741 1.7 1442 4.3 1958 1.6	28 W	0238 4.6 0749 1.3 1456 4.5 2018 1.3
14 W	0316 4.2 0822 2.0 1524 4.1 2044 1.9	29 TH	0349 4.5 0850 1.6 1605 4.3 2128 1.5
15 TH	0403 4.0 0922 2.2 1614 3.9 ◐ 2156 2.1	30 F	0458 4.4 1017 1.8 1717 4.2 ◑ 2257 1.6

DECEMBER

Date	Time m	Date	Time m
1 SA	0606 4.4 1138 1.8 1828 4.1	16 SU	0518 4.0 1050 2.1 1735 3.8 2318 1.9
2 SU	0005 1.6 0716 4.4 1241 1.7 1934 4.2	17 M	0624 4.0 1208 2.0 1848 3.8
3 M	0104 1.5 0818 4.5 1336 1.5 2030 4.3	18 TU	0026 1.8 0738 4.1 1303 1.8 1959 4.0
4 TU	0156 1.3 0910 4.6 1424 1.3 2119 4.4	19 W	0120 1.6 0835 4.3 1352 1.5 2052 4.2
5 W	0243 1.2 0950 4.7 1510 1.1 2204 4.5	20 TH	0210 1.4 0920 4.5 1438 1.3 2137 4.4
6 TH	0328 1.1 1028 4.7 1553 1.0 2249 4.6	21 F	0257 1.2 1001 4.7 1525 1.0 2221 4.6
7 F	0411 1.1 1108 4.7 1635 1.0 ● 2333 4.6	22 SA	0344 1.0 1043 4.8 1611 0.8 ○ 2306 4.7
8 SA	0453 1.1 1148 4.7 1715 1.0	23 SU	0430 0.8 1126 4.9 1656 0.6 2352 4.8
9 SU	0016 4.6 0533 1.2 1227 4.6 1754 1.0	24 M	0516 0.8 1209 4.9 1742 0.6
10 M	0058 4.6 0611 1.3 1305 4.6 1829 1.2	25 TU	0039 4.9 0603 0.8 1255 4.9 1828 0.6
11 TU	0138 4.5 0646 1.4 1341 4.5 1902 1.3	26 W	0131 4.8 0650 0.9 1346 4.8 1916 0.7
12 W	0215 4.4 0719 1.6 1416 4.3 1935 1.5	27 TH	0232 4.8 0740 1.1 1443 4.6 2007 1.0
13 TH	0252 4.3 0755 1.7 1454 4.2 2013 1.6	28 F	0337 4.7 0836 1.3 1547 4.4 2106 1.2
14 F	0333 4.2 0837 1.9 1540 4.0 2059 1.8	29 SA	0437 4.5 0941 1.5 1652 4.3 ◑ 2215 1.4
15 SA	0421 4.1 0932 2.1 1633 3.9 ◐ 2159 1.9	30 SU	0536 4.4 1055 1.7 1755 4.1 2326 1.5
		31 M	0637 4.3 1203 1.7 1858 4.1

Chart Datum: 2·73 metres below Ordnance Datum (Newlyn). HAT is 5·1 metres above Chart Datum.

NEW LOCATION!
NOSS ON DART
GREAT ESCAPES
BUY 5 NIGHTS AND STAY 7
PREMIERMARINAS.COM
THIS SUMMER UPGRADE TO A PREMIER MARINA.
YOU'LL LOVE THE DIFFERENCE.
The best thing about Premier Marinas is its welcoming staff and superb customer service. But we know you want it all, so we continue to invest in making your time with us perfect - from luxury facilities to new locations, new restaurants and more. But don't just take our word for it join us overnight, tour our marinas for a week with Great Escapes, or opt for monthly berthing and enjoy a lazy summer break in a Premier marina. Call now or visit premiermarinas.com
PREMIER
MARINAS
THE BOAT HOUSE CAFE
THE BOAT HOUSE CAFE

Mr John

MARY MOUSE 2

9.2.25 PORTSMOUTH

Hampshire **50°47'·38N 01°06'·67W** (Entrance)

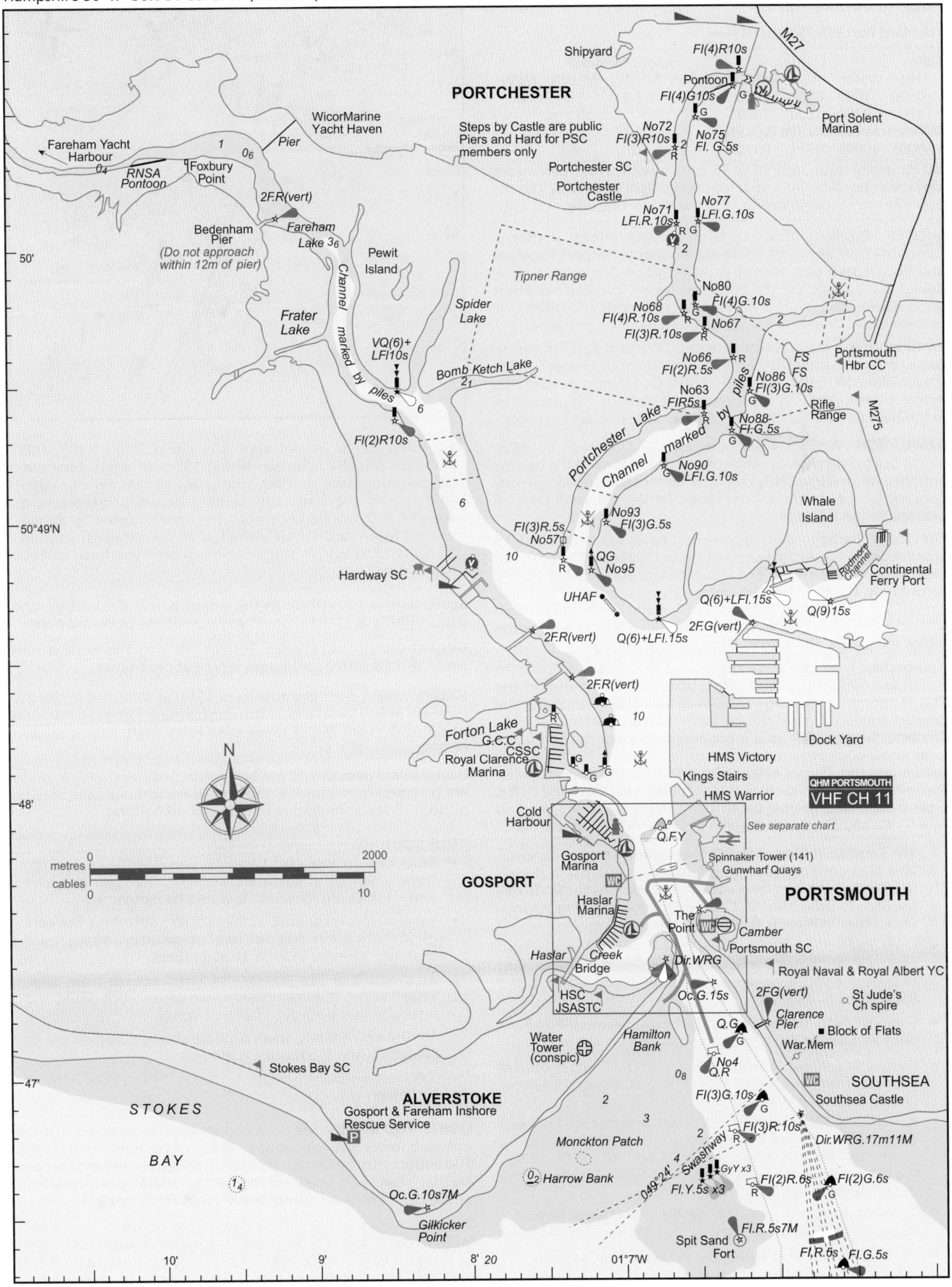
PORTCHESTER
Shipyard
Fl(4)R10s
Pontoon
Fl(4)G10s
M27
Port Solent Marina
WicorMarine Yacht Haven
Steps by Castle are public Piers and Hard for PSC members only
No72
Fl(3)R10s
No75
Fl. G.5s
Portchester SC
Portchester Castle
Fareham Yacht Harbour
RNSA Pontoon
Foxbury Point
Pier
2F.R(vert)
Bedenham Pier
(Do not approach within 12m of pier)
Fareham Lake
Pewit Island
No71
LFl.R.10s
No77
LFl.G.10s
Tipner Range
No80
Fl(4)G.10s
No68
Fl(4)R.10s
No67
Fl(3)R.10s
Frater Lake
Channel marked by piles
Spider Lake
VQ(6)+LFl10s
Bomb Ketch Lake
No66
Fl(2)R.5s
Portsmouth Hbr CC
FS
No86
Fl(3)G.10s
No63
FlR5s
No88
Fl.G.5s
Rifle Range
M275
Fl(2)R10s
Portchester Lake
Channel marked by piles
No90
LFl.G.10s
Whale Island
No93
Fl(3)G.5s
Fl(3)R.5s
No57
QG
No95
Hardway SC
Rudmore Channel
Continental Ferry Port
UHAF
Q(6)+LFl.15s
Q(9)15s
2F.G(vert)
2F.R(vert)
Q(6)+LFl.15s
2F.R(vert)
Forton Lake
G.C.C
CSSC
Royal Clarence Marina
Dock Yard
HMS Victory
Kings Stairs
HMS Warrior
QHM PORTSMOUTH
VHF CH 11
Cold Harbour
Q.F.Y
See separate chart
Spinnaker Tower (141)
Gunwharf Quays
Gosport Marina
GOSPORT
PORTSMOUTH
Haslar Marina
The Point
Camber
Portsmouth SC
Haslar Creek
Bridge
Dir.WRG
Royal Naval & Royal Albert YC
HSC
JSASTC
Oc.G.15s
2FG(vert)
St Jude's Ch spire
Clarence Pier
Q.G
Block of Flats
Water Tower (conspic)
Hamilton Bank
War Mem
No4
Q.R
Stokes Bay SC
SOUTHSEA
Southsea Castle
ALVERSTOKE
Fl(3)G.10s
STOKES
BAY
Gosport & Fareham Inshore Rescue Service
Monckton Patch
Fl(3)R.10s
Dir.WRG.17m11M
Swashway
049°24'
GyY x3
Harrow Bank
Fl.Y.5s x3
Fl(2)R.6s
Fl(2)G.6s
Oc.G.10s7M
Gilkicker Point
Fl.R.5s7M
Spit Sand Fort
Fl.R.6s
Fl.G.5s
metres
cables
0
2000
10
50'
50°49'N
48'
47'
10'
9'
8'
01°7'W

CHARTS AC 5600, 2037, 2625, 2631, 2629, 2628; Imray C9, C3, C15, 2200

TIDES +0020 Dover; ML 2·8

Standard Port PORTSMOUTH (⟵)

Times				Height (metres)			
High Water		Low Water		MHWS	MHWN	MLWN	MLWS
0500	1000	0000	0600	4·7	3·8	1·9	0·8
1700	2200	1200	1800				
Differences LEE-ON-THE-SOLENT							
–0005	+0005	–0015	–0010	–0·2	–0·1	+0·1	+0·2

NOTE: Strong winds from NE to SE, coupled with a high barometer, may lower levels by 1m and delay times of HW and LW by 1hr; the opposite may occur in strong W'lies with low pressure.

SHELTER Excellent. This very large harbour affords shelter in some area from any wind. There are marinas at Gosport, Fareham and Portchester, plus several yacht pontoons/jetties and many swinging moorings. On the Portsmouth side, The Camber offers good shelter, but this is a busy commercial dock and often full; beware Isle of Wight car ferries berthing near the entrance.

Portsmouth is a major Naval Base and Dockyard Port; all vessels come under the authority of the Queen's Harbour Master (QHM). If over 20m LOA, QHM's permission (VHF Ch 11) must be obtained before entering, leaving or moving in the harbour. ⚓ is prohibited in the harbour and fishing only allowed clear of main channels.

NAVIGATION WPT No 4 Bar buoy, QR, 50°47′·01N 01°06′·36W, 330°/4·5ca to entrance. Beware strong tidal streams in the narrow entrance which is invariably very busy. Commercial shipping, cross-Channel ferries, warships, high speed ferries and small craft all operate within this area.

The lower harbour and approaches have been dredged to accommodate the aircraft carrier *Queen Elizabeth*. The chan has been widened, deepened and straightened. Buoyage has moved accordingly, but the effect on small craft movements is minimal. On Spit Sand and upharbour new transit marks consisting of three vertical masts lit Fl Y 5s have been positioned specifically for the use of the carrier owing to its size and offset bridge.

Approaches: From the W, yachts can use the Swashway Chan (to NW of Spit Sand Fort) which carries about 2m. The transit of the War Memorial and RH edge of block of flats (049·4°) indicates the deepest water, but need not be followed exactly except at LWS. The Inner Swashway (Round Tr brg approx 035°) carries only 0·3m; local knowledge required. Approaching inshore from the E, a submerged rock barrier extends from Southsea to Horse Sand Ft. The Inshore Boat Passage (0·9m) 1ca off the beach is marked by R & G piles; Main Passage (min depth 1·2m), lies 7ca further S, marked by a G pile and a concrete dolphin lit Q R andQ G respectively.

- **The Small Boat Channel (SBC)** is *mandatory* for craft under 20m LOA entering or leaving harbour. It runs just outside the W edge of the main dredged channel from abeam No 4 Bar buoy to Ballast Bn PHM. A depth gauge, showing height above chart datum, is on BC4.
- Craft may not enter harbour on the E side of the main chan and must not enter the SBC on its E side; craft may enter or leave the SBC anywhere on its W side (beware Hamilton Bank, some of which dries).
- Engines (if fitted) must be used in the SBC between No 4 Bar buoy and Ballast Bn, *which should always be left to port.*
- If crossing to/from Gunwharf Quays or The Camber obtain approval from QHM (Ch 11) and then do so at 90° to the main channel N of Ballast Bcn.
- At night the SBC is covered by the Oc R sector (324°-330°) of the Dir WRG lt on Fort Blockhouse until close to the hbr ent. Thereafter the Iso R 2s sector (337·5°-345°) of the Dir WRG lt on the dolphin E of Gosport Marina leads 341° through the entrance to Ballast Bcn.
- If joining or leaving the SBC via the Inner Swashway, BC Outer Bn *must* be left to port.
- The SBC may be used even if the main channel is closed.

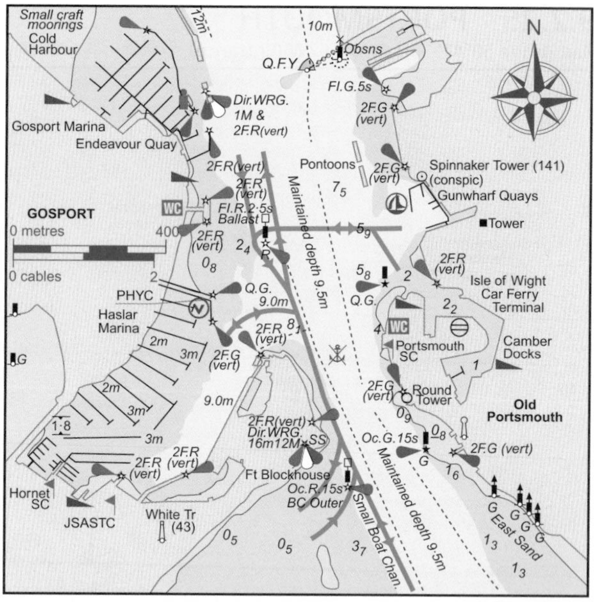

Exclusion zones: Do not approach within 50m of any MoD vessel or establishment, or within 100m of any submarine. Yellow buoys (see chartlet above) are sometimes deployed to delineate the 50m zone. Some ships are protected by a zone of 250m while underway. They are escorted by armed vessels; listen to QHM on VHF 11 or 13 for details. If you fail to respond to warnings it will be assumed you have hostile intentions.

Speed limit is 10kn (through the water) within the harbour and within 1000 yds of the shore in any part of the Dockyard Port.

Gosport Ferry plies between Gosport Pier and The Hard. It runs every 15 mins with a continuous service at peak times.

Historic wrecks are: *Mary Rose* (sank 1545) at 50°45′·8N 01°06′·2W (5ca SSW of Spit Sand Fort), and *Invincible* (sank 1758) *at* 50°44′·36N 01°02′·32W (1·4M ESE of Horse Sand Fort). *Mary Rose* is marked by SPM buoys, Fl Y 5s.

Navigational piles should not be approached too closely as many are on steep-to mudbanks; those lit in Portchester Lake may be difficult to see at night due to background lighting.

FOG ROUTINE

- Broadcast on VHF Ch **11** and **13,** Fog Routine comes into force when QHM considers that visibility is so low that normal shipping movements would be dangerous.
- Small craft may continue at the skipper's discretion, but with great caution, keeping well clear of the main and approach channels. Monitor VHF Ch **11** at all times.
- Be aware that the presence of radar echoes from small vessels within the main channel can cause much doubt and difficulty to the master of a large vessel.
- For their own safety, small craft are strongly advised not to proceed when fog routine is in force.
- 3 W (vert) lights are displayed in fog at the centre of Gosport Ferry pier.

LIGHTS AND MARKS See 9.2.4 and chartlet. From S and E of the IoW Nab Tower is conspic about 9·5M SE of the harbour entrance. The entrance to the Eastern Solent is between Horse Sand Fort and No Man's Land Fort. Spit Sand Fort lies 160°/1·2M from the harbour entrance. All forts are conspic round stone structures.

St Jude's ✠ spire and Southsea Castle light house in transit 003° leads to Outer Spit SCM. At night keep in the W sector (347°-349°) of Southsea Castle Pile Dir WRG 348°. Ft Blockhouse has a Dir lt 323° and traffic sigs, running toward the Harbour Bn Dir lt (fuel jetty).

FIRING RANGE **Tipner Rifle Range,** N of Whale Island, danger area extends 2,500m from firing range. R flag or ● lt on Tipner Range FS indicates firing is in progress; yachts should clear the range danger area or transit it as quickly as possible.

COMMUNICATIONS (Code Portsmouth/Gosport 02392) NMOC 552100; Police 101; Ⓗ 286000; QHM Hbr Control (H24) 723694; Commercial Docks & Camber Berthing Offices ☎297395.

Yachts should monitor Ch **11** (*QHM*) for traffic and navigational information. *Portsmouth Hbr Radio* (Commercial Port) Ch 14 (H24). *Haslar Marina* and *Port Solent* Ch **80** M (H24). *Gosport Marina* call Ch **80** M (HO). Fareham Marine Ch M (summer 0900-1730). Gunwharf Quay Ch 80. **Naval activities** to the S/SE of Portsmouth and IOW may be advised by Solent CG Ch 67 or ☎552100; or Naval Ops ☎722008. Naval vessels use Ch 13. The positions and times of naval firings and underwater explosions are broadcast daily at 0800 and 1400LT Ch 06; preceded by a Securité call on Ch 16. Warnings of underwater explosions will also be broadcast on Ch 16 at 1 hr, at 30 mins and just before the detonation.

FACILITIES

Haslar Marina berths@haslarmarina.co.uk ☎601201. Access H24 580 + 50Ⓥ at L/M pontoons, inboard of green light vessel, £3·20 (max 60m LOA); short stay £9. @ wi-fi. A floating boat lift is at the end of 'F' pontoon. Other Haslar Creek moorings/pontoons are private; Haslar bridge (1·8m clearance).

Gunwharf Quays www.gunwharf-quays.com ☎836732 Ⓥ £3·75 (max 80m LOA), short stay £1·22/m, booking advisable (or try VHF 80 for short notice requirements). £5·50 landing fee/vessel for drop offs to Gunwharf Quays shopping centre. Note Small Boat Channel regulations.

Town Quay (Camber) ☎833166, berth on wall, <12m £17·65, short stay (3hrs) £8·20, pay 'KB Boat Park'; no .

Gosport Marina www.premiermarinas.com ☎524811. 471 inc Ⓥ if berths available, £3·10 with £5 inc, min fee £24·80; short stay £1·48/m, min fee £11·84. (12t) dry stack storage for motor boats, wi-fi.

Endeavour Quay www.endeavourquay.co.uk ☎584200, fully equipped (some Ⓥ berths) (180t) (35t) wi-fi.

Royal Clarence Marina www.royalclarencemarina.org. ☎523523, 150, Ⓥ space varies, up to 50m, <12m £3·00 (winter £27·00). wi-fi.

Port Solent portsolent@premiermarinas.com ☎210765. Lock 9m wide. 900 inc Ⓥ, £3·10 (min fee £24·80) with £5 inc; s/s £1·41/m. (35t) wi-fi.

Portchester Lake is marked by lit and unlit piles. Unusually, PHMs are numbered 57 to 74 (from seaward), and SHMs 95 to 75.

Beware unlit naval buoys at the S end. Do not delay crossing Tipner Range, S limit marked by piles 63/87 and N by 70/78. Portchester Castle is conspic 5ca SSW of marina. Call marina Ch 80 when inbound passing pile 78. Pile B, Fl (4) G 10s, marks the waiting pontoon (see chartlet). Access H24 via chan dredged 1·5m to lock (43m x 9·1m); enter on 3 ● (vert) or on loudspeaker instructions.

WicorMarine Yacht Haven (Portchester) www.wicormarine.co.uk ☎(01329) 237112, some Ⓥ on pontoons, £1·50/m (rallies welcome), (12t) (7t).

Portsmouth Marine Engineering ☎(01329) 232854, (drying) Ⓥ £15/night, £40/week, (18t).

Upper Quay Marina (dries) upperquaymarine1@gmail.com ☎469855 mob 07712189444, 50+Ⓥ by arrangement.

TOWN CENTRES

PORTSMOUTH ACA (Southampton).

Ferries:

Brittany Ferries (www.brittany-ferries.co.uk):-

Bilbao: 2/week; 24hrs or 32hrs; Santander: 2/week; 24hrs;

Caen: 3/day; 6hrs; St Malo: daily; 8½hrs;

Cherbourg HSS: up to 3/day; 3hrs.

Le Havre HSS: up to 2/day (summer only); 3¼hrs.

Condor Ferries (www.condorferries.co.uk):

Guernsey/Jersey: 6/week; 6½–12½hrs.

IoW: frequent car and passenger services to Ryde/Fishbourne.

Water Taxis between Gunwharf Quays, Historic Dockyard and RN Submarine Museum (Haslar Jetty, Gosport).

GOSPORT ACA (Portsmouth) (S'ton).

FAREHAM (01329) (Southampton).

Fareham Lake is well marked, partially lit up to Bedenham Pier and unlit thereafter. Chan dries 0·9m in final 5ca to Town Quay.

YACHT CLUBS

Royal Naval Sailing Association ☎521100.

Royal Naval & Royal Albert YC ☎825924.

Portsmouth SC ☎ 820596.

Portchester SC ☎376375, detached pontoon (close No 71 bn).

Hardway SC secretary@hardwaysailingclub.co.uk

Gosport CC ☎(01329) 47014 or (0860) 966390.

Fareham Sailing & Motor Boat Club ☎(01392) 280738.

EASTERN APPROACHES TO THE SOLENT

(AC 2045, 2036) Nab Tower (Fl 10s, *Horn(2) 30s*), a conspic steel and concrete structure 4·5M E of Foreland, marks Nab Shoal for larger vessels but is of no direct significance to yachts. The Nab Channel (maintained depth 13.3m) runs northwards to the East of the tower. It is indicated by Y SPM as far as New Grounds. Keep well clear of shipping manoeuvring in the Pilot Boarding Areas and using the Nab Deep Water Channel.

NW of Nab Tr the E approach to the Solent via Spithead presents few problems and is far safer in SW/W gales than the Needles Channel. A good lookout should be kept for ferry traffic and vessels anchoring in St Helen's Roads.

The main shipping chan is well buoyed and easy to follow, but there is plenty of water for yachts over New Grounds and Warner Shoal when approaching No Man's Land Fort (Iso R 2s) and Horse Sand Fort (Iso G 2s). A submerged barrier lies N of the latter; the barrier to SW of the former has been demolished and therefore yachts may now pass safely SW of No Man's Land Fort; the Ryde Sand Bcns (both PHM and lit) mark the shallows to the SW. Ryde Sand dries extensively and is a trap for the unwary.

Care should be taken to avoid Hamilton Bank to the South of the small boat channel close East of Portsmouth Harbour entrance.

Langstone and Chichester Harbours have offlying sands which are dangerous in strong S'ly winds. E and W Winner flank the entrance to Langstone Hbr. E and W Pole Sands, drying 1m, lie either side of the appr channel to Chichester Hbr. Bracklesham Bay is shallow, with a distinct inshore set at certain states of the tide. SE along a low-lying coast is Selsey Bill with extensive offshore rocks and shoals. Pass these to seaward via Owers SCM lt buoy or the Looe Chan, which in suitable conditions is much used by yachts on passage to/from points E of the Solent. Although lit, the many lobster pot markers demand caution at night; it is dangerous in onshore gales as searoom is limited by extensive shoals on which the sea breaks.

Looe Channel: ▶ *the E-going flood runs from HW Portsmouth +0430 (HW Dover +0500) until HW Portsmouth –0130 (HW Dover –0100), at sp reaching 2.4kn near the Boulder and Street light buoys which mark its narrow western end; they may be hard to see. Max Neap rate is 1.2kn.*

The W-going ebb runs from HW Portsmouth –0130 (HW Dover –0100) until HW Portsmouth +0430 (HW Dover +0500), at Springs reaching 2.6kn near Boulder and Street. Max Neap rate is 1.3kn.◀

Boulder SHM lt buoy is at the W ent to this chan, about 6M SE of Chichester Bar Bn. Medmery Bank, 3·7m, is 1M WNW of Boulder.

9.2.26 LANGSTONE HARBOUR

Hampshire **50°47'·23N 01°01'·54W** (Ent) ❀❀◊◊◊✿✿

CHARTS AC 5600, 2037, 3418; Imray C3, C9, Y33, 2200

TIDES +0022 Dover; ML 2·9

Standard Port PORTSMOUTH (⟵)

Times				Height (metres)			
High Water		Low Water		MHWS	MHWN	MLWN	MLWS
0500	1000	0000	0600	4·7	3·8	1·9	0·8
1700	2200	1200	1800				
Differences LANGSTONE							
0000	−0015	0000	−0010	+0·1	+0·1	0·0	0·0
NAB TOWER							
+0015	0000	+0015	+0015	−0·2	0·0	+0·2	0·0
SELSEY BILL							
+0010	−0010	+0035	+0020	+0·5	+0·3	−0·1	−0·2

SHELTER Very good in marina (2·4m) to W inside ent, access over tidal flap 1·6m at CD; waiting pontoon. Ent is 7m wide. Buoys on W side of harbour entrance administered by Eastney Cruising Association, max LOA 9m. Or ⚓ out of the fairway in Russell's Lake or Langstone Chan (water ski area); or see HM (E side of ent). Hbr speed limit 10kn; 5kn in Southsea Marina channel.

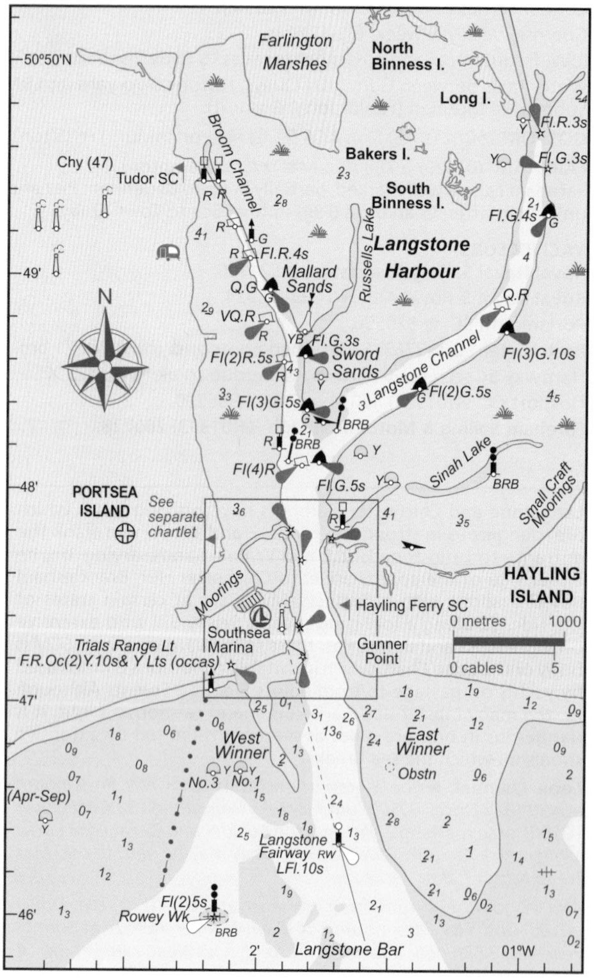

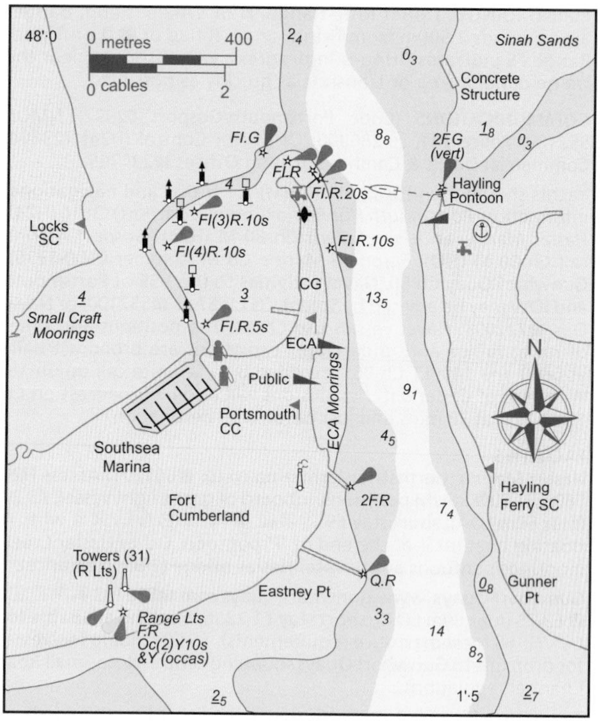

NAVIGATION WPT 50°46'·31N 01°01'·36W, Langstone Fairway SWM Bcn 348°/9·4ca to QR light at ent (Eastney Pt).

Bar has about 1·2m. Entrance channel lies between East and West Winner drying banks, which afford some protection. Appr is straightforward in most conditions, best from HW −3 to +1, but avoid entry against the ebb, esp at sp and in strong onshore winds. In strong S/SE winds do not attempt entry.

LIGHTS AND MARKS Ldg marks (concrete dolphins), or Fairway beacon in line with conspic chy, leads 344° just clear of East Winner. The entrance itself deepens and favours the W side. The narrow approach channel to Southsea Marina is marked by 5 SHM piles, only the first of which is lit, Fl G. There are 9 PHM piles; see chartlet for details.

COMMUNICATIONS (Code 02392) NMOC 552100; Police 101; Ⓗ 286000; HM 463419.

Harbour VHF Ch **12** 16 (0900-1700 daily). Marina Ch **80** M.

FACILITIES **Southsea Marina** www.premiermarinas.com ☎822719. Access channel dredged to 0·5m. Marina entrance, width 7m, has R/G lights indicating if the cill is up or down. 320, £3·10 (min fee £24·80); inc £5 for 2 nights. £1.48/m for <4hrs (min fee £11·84). **Services:** (25t) (18t) wi-fi.

Hayling Pontoon (E side of ent), www.langstoneharbour.org.uk (H24 with pre-payment tag available from HO). Vacant mooring buoys in harbour may be available, £13·60/night.

Langstone SC ☎9248 4577, .

Eastney Cruising Association (ECA) ☎9273 4103, 6 buoys for craft under 9m by prior arrangement, . Visitors welcome – access to ECA by intercom at road barrier or ☎827396 (bar).

Tudor SC (Hilsea) ☎9266 2002, .

Hayling Ferry SC; Locks SC ☎9282 9833.

Towns ✉ (Eastney, Hayling), Ⓑ (Havant, Hayling, Emsworth), ⇄ (bus to Havant), ✈ (Southampton).

9.2.27 CHICHESTER HARBOUR

W. Sussex **50°46'·86N 00°56'·06W** ❀❀♧♧♧✿✿✿

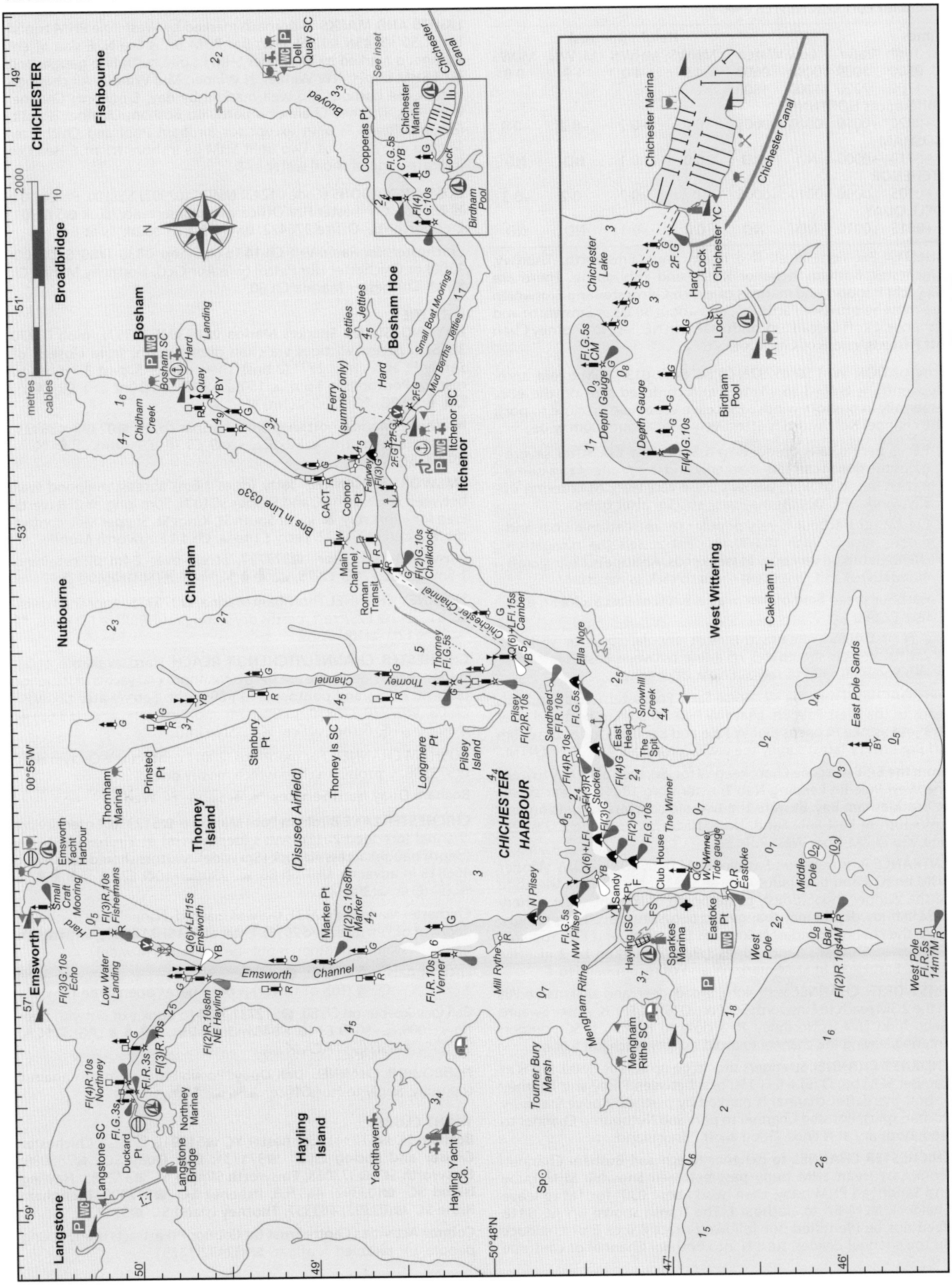

CHICHESTER
Fishbourne
Dell Quay SC
Buoyed
See inset
Chichester Canal
Copperas Pt
Chichester Marina
Fl.G.5s CYB
Lock
Birdham Pool
Fl(4)G.10s
Broadbridge
Bosham
Bosham SC
Hard
Landing
Quay
YBY
Chidham Creek
Jetties
Bosham Hoe
Small Boat Moorings
Mud Berths
Ferry (summer only)
Hard
Itchenor SC
Itchenor
2FG
Fairway
Fl(3)G
CACT
Cobnor Pt
Bns in Line 033°
Chidham
Nutbourne
Main Channel Roman Transit
Fl(2)G.10s Chalkdock
Chichester Channel
Q(6)+LFl.15s Camber
Thorney Fl.G.5s
Thorney Channel
Ella Nore
West Wittering
Cakeham Tr
Pilsey Fl(2)R.10s
Sandhead Fl.R.10s
Fl.G.5s
East Head
Snowhill Creek
The Spit
East Pole Sands
Fl(4)R.10s
Fl(3)R Stocker
Fl(3)G
Fl(4)G
Fl(2)G
Fl.G.10s
The Winner
Pilsey Island
CHICHESTER HARBOUR
Longmere Pt
Thorney Is SC
Stanbury Pt
Prinsted Pt
Thornham Marina
Thorney Island
(Disused Airfield)
Emsworth Yacht Harbour
Q(6)+LFl
Club House
W. Winner Tide gauge
Q.G
Q.R Eastoke
Middle Pole
N Pilsey
Sandy Pt
Hayling ISC
Sparkes Marina
Eastoke Pt
West Pole
Bar
Fl(2)R.10s4M
West Pole Fl.R.5s 14m7M
Fl.G.5s NW Pilsey
Mill Rythe
Mengham Rithe
Mengham Rithe SC
Tourner Bury Marsh
Fl.R.10s Verner
Emsworth Channel
Fl(2)G.10s8m Marker
Marker Pt
Q(6)+LFl15s Emsworth
Fl(3)R.10s Fishermans
Small Craft Mooring
Emsworth
Fl(3)G.10s Echo
Low Water Landing
Fl(2)R.10s8m NE Hayling
Fl(3)R.10s
Fl.R.3s
Fl(4)R.10s Northney
Fl.G.3s
Northney Marina
Duckard Pt
Langstone SC
Langstone
Langstone Bridge
Hayling Island
Yachthaven
Hayling Yacht Co.
Chichester Lake
Chichester YC
Depth Gauge
Fl.G.5s CM
2F.G
Hard
Chichester Marina
Chichester Canal
metres
cables

CHARTS AC 5600, 2045, 3418; Imray C9, C3, Y33, 2200

TIDES +0027 Dover; ML 2·8

Standard Port CHICHESTER (⟶)

Times				Height (metres)			
High Water		Low Water		MHWS	MHWN	MLWN	MLWS
0500	1000	0000	0600	4·9	4·0	1·9	0·9
1700	2200	1200	1800				
Differences NORTHNEY							
+0020	+0010	0000	+0005	0·0	−0·2	−0·2	−0·4
BOSHAM							
+0010	+0005	ND	ND	0·0	−0·1	ND	ND
ITCHENOR							
+0005	0000	−0010	+0005	−0·1	−0·2	−0·2	−0·3
DELL QUAY							
+0015	+0010	ND	ND	0·0	−0·1	ND	ND

SHELTER Excellent in all five main chans: Emsworth, Thorney, Chichester, Bosham, Itchenor Reach and Fishbourne. There are six yacht habours and marinas of which Chichester and Emsworth are most helpful (see Facilities); also about 50 Ⓥs at Emsworth and Itchenor. ⚓s off E Head (uncomfortable in NE'lies); in Thorney Chan off Pilsey Is; and E of Chalkdock Pt.

NAVIGATION WPT 50°45'·32N 00°56'·60W, 013°/1·6M to entrance. Best entry is HW −3 to +1, to avoid confused seas on the ebb, especially in onshore winds >F5. Leave West Pole Bn close to port; the channel Northward is effectively only about 200m wide.

- Bar is periodically dredged to 1.5m below CD. After severe gales the depth can vary markedly and it is prudent to assume a least depth of 0.5m below CD. Be very wary of entering in S'ly winds >F6. Depths may vary ±0·75m after gales.
- Chichester Harbour is very popular for recreational boat and dinghy racing. With 10,000 resident vessels the navigation channels can be very busy at weekends. Anticipate sailing craft manoeuvres and give them room to tack as necessary.
- Harbour speed limit of 8kn in all areas N of East Stoke Pt; max fine £2,500.
- ⚓ N of E Head remains the most popular spot for visiting yachts. Vessels should ⚓ S of a line between East Head Spit and Snowhill SHM to remain clear of channel.

APPROACHES: From the W, Horse Sand Fort astern, bearing 265°, leads to the West Pole Bn. Leave W Pole 30-80m to port and alter 013° as Eastoke Pt opens E of W Pole and Bar bns. Pass approx 50m off Bar Bn. For latest survey see www.conservancy.co.uk or LNTM.

From the E/SE, via Looe Chan, keep W for 2M, then alter NW toward the West Pole Bn keeping Nab Tr astern brg 184° to clear shoals in Bracklesham Bay. Beware the two old concrete targets on and just south of East Pole Sand. Note: Historic Wrecks lie 137°/1·2M and 095°/3·2M from West Pole Bn.

ENTRANCE Pass between Eastoke PHM buoy (QR) and W Winner SHM bn (QG and tide gauge). Three SHM lit buoys mark the edge of the Winner shoal (dries), to starboard of the ent. Near Fishery SCM lit buoy, depths may change and buoys are moved accordingly. Here the channel divides: N towards Emsworth and ENE towards Chichester. Stocker's Sands (dries 1·9m), is marked by 2 lit PHM buoys. East Head lit SHM marks W end of recommended ⚓.

EMSWORTH CHANNEL is straight, broad, deep and well marked/lit in the 2·5M reach to Emsworth SCM bn, Q (6) + L Fl 15s, where Sweare Deep forks NW to Northney. Pass close to Hayling Is SC pontoon entering/leaving this channel to avoid shallow patch just S of bn.

THORNEY CHANNEL Strangers should go up at half-flood. Ent is at Camber SCM bn, Q (6) + L Fl 15s; pass between Pilsey and Thorney Lt bns, thereafter channel is marked by perches. Above Stanbury Pt chan splits, Prinsted Channel to port and Nutbourne Channel to stbd; both dry at N ends. Good ⚓ off Pilsey Island.

CHICHESTER CHANNEL to Itchenor Reach and Bosham Channel. From East Head SHM buoy pass between Snowhill SHM buoy and Sandhead PHM buoy, then head about 030° for 1M to leave Chaldock NCM Bn to starboard. The transit shown on AC 3418 need not be identified nor followed exactly. 6 ca E of Chaldock Bn the channel divides: turn N into Bosham Channel or continue ESE into Itchenor Reach for Birdham Pool and Chichester Marina, beyond which is the drying Fishbourne Channel to Dell Quay. ⚓ in Itchenor Reach and Bosham Channel.

LIGHTS AND MARKS Approach marked by West Pole PHM tripod bn at 50°45'·45N 00°56'·59W; Bar PHM bn is 6ca N. E side of ent channel is marked by W Winner SHM lit pile, with tide gauge; and by 3 SHM buoys: NW Winner, N Winner, Mid Winner. All channels within the harbour are well marked by day. Emsworth Channel is well lit; Thorney Channel is partly lit; Bosham Channel is unlit. Itchenor Reach is unlit except for Birdham Pool and Chichester Marina entrance bns. Two unlit SHM lie inshore NE of E Head to indicate edge of shoal water in ⚓.

COMMUNICATIONS (Code 01243) NMOC (02392) 552100; Police 101; Ⓗ 787970. Chichester Hbr Office www.conservancy.co.uk ☎512301; Emsworth Hbr Office 376422. www.chimet.co.uk ☼ at Bar.

Chichester Hbr Radio VHF Ch **14** 16 (Apr-Sep: 0830-1700; Sat 0900-1300) or Chichester Hbr Patrol (w/e Apr-Oct). Northney Marina Ch **80** M. Chichester Marina Ch 80.

FACILITIES

HAYLING ISLAND Sparkes Marina ☎(02392) 463572, mob 07770 365610. Access all tides via chan dredged 2m; from close N of Sandy Pt appr on ≠ 277° (2 bns); thence alter S, past 3 PH bns to marina. Pontoons in 1·6m. 150+20Ⓥ £3·70 (inc), £9 < 4hrs. LPG, (16t) ✕.

Northney Marina northney@mdlmarinas.co.uk ☎02392 466321, access via chan 1m. 228+20Ⓥ £3·70, £9 <4hrs. (35t).

EMSWORTH CHANNEL Jetty (dries 1·6m) abreast millpond wall between Emsworth SC and Slipper SC to N, 50m long, ☆ 2FR (vert). Free for <2hrs stay, . at South St, Kings St, Slipper Mill; contact the Warden ☎376422. Ferry £1 to Ch 14 *Emsworth Mobile*.

Emsworth Yacht Hbr ☎377727, access over 2·4m sill retaining 1·5m. 200+20Ⓥ £2·75, (50t) (40t).

THORNEY CHANNEL Thornham Marina, ☎375335. Appr chan dries, 81+2Ⓥ £23/craft, berths dry suiting multihull or lift keels. (12t) (10t) ✕.

CHICHESTER CHANNEL/ITCHENOR REACH Hard available at all stages of the tide. There are berths for approx 40 yachts at Itchenor on both buoys and pontoons. £11·80/night. Ferry/water taxi VHF Ch 08, ☎07970 378350, to Bosham and Birdham. (£3·60) Ⓔ (hbr office) ✕ (Ship Inn).

BOSHAM CHANNEL For moorings (200+) contact the Quaymaster ☎573336. ⚓ prohib in chan which mostly dries.

Bosham Quay Hard **Services** . EC Wed.

CHICHESTER LAKE Birdham Pool Marina ☎512310. Enter drying channel (dredged 2015) HW±3 (depth >1m) at Birdham SHM bn (depth gauge) access via lock (5m wide). Visitors should call 07831 466815 in advance. VHF Ch 80. 230+10Ⓥ £2·60, Ⓔ (30t).

Chichester Marina ☎512731, the well marked channel has a minimum depth of of ½m (dredged 2015). Enter at CM SHM lit pile, with depth gauge. A waiting pontoon is outside the lock (7m wide).

Lock signals: ● = Wait; ● = Enter.
Q ● (top of tower) = both gates open (free flow).

Call lock-keeper on Ch 80, ☎512731, H24 to book exit outwith free-flow. 1000+50 Ⓥ £3·10, £1·48/m for <4hrs, LPG, Ⓔ (65t) ACA ✕.

FISHBOURNE CHANNEL Dell Quay: Possible drying berth against the quay, apply to Hbr Office.

YACHT CLUBS

Bosham SC ☎572341; **Chichester YC** ☎512918, ✕; **Chichester Cruiser and Racing Club** ☎371731; **Dell Quay SC** ☎785080; **Emsworth SC** ☎373065; **Emsworth Slipper SC** ☎372523; **Hayling Island SC** ☎(02392) 463768; **Itchenor SC** ☎512400; **Mengham Rithe SC** ☎(02392) 463337; **Thorney Island SC** ☎371731.

Cobnor Activities Centre Trust (at Cobnor Pt) attracts many young people, inc disabled afloat. ☎01243 572791.

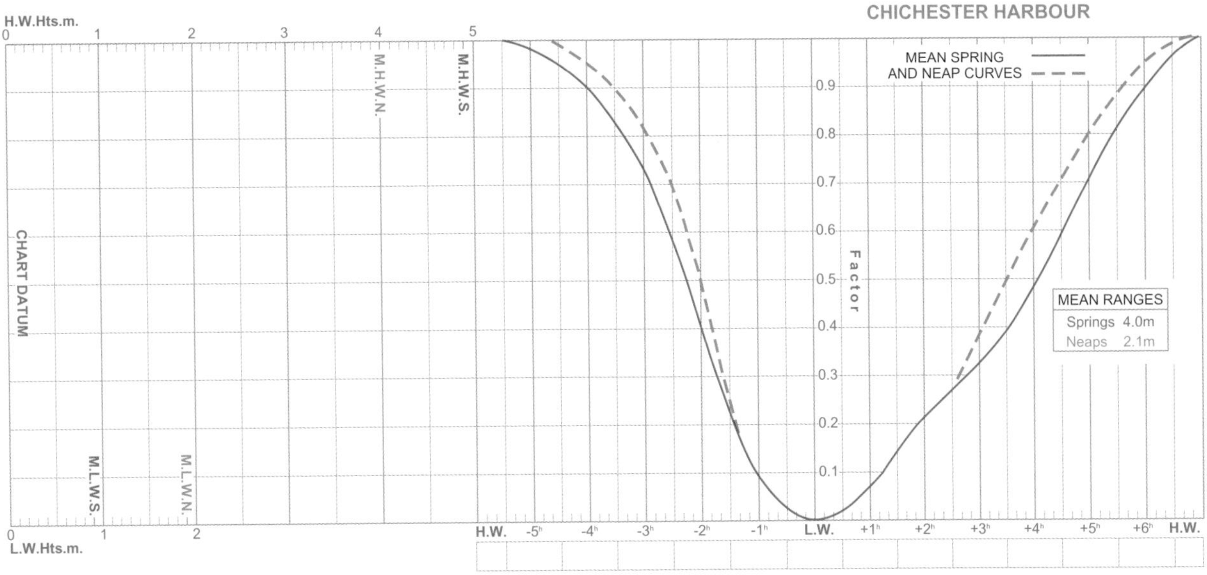
CHICHESTER HARBOUR
H.W.Hts.m.
0
1
2
3
4
5
M.H.W.N.
M.H.W.S.
CHART DATUM
M.L.W.S.
M.L.W.N.
0
1
2
L.W.Hts.m.
MEAN SPRING AND NEAP CURVES
0.9
0.8
0.7
0.6
0.5
0.4
0.3
0.2
0.1
Factor
MEAN RANGES
Springs 4.0m
Neaps 2.1m
H.W.
-5h
-4h
-3h
-2h
-1h
L.W.
+1h
+2h
+3h
+4h
+5h
+6h
H.W.

STANDARD TIME (UT)
For Summer Time add ONE hour in **non-shaded areas**

CHICHESTER HARBOUR LAT 50°47′N LONG 0°56′W

TIMES AND HEIGHTS OF HIGH AND LOW WATERS

Dates in red are SPRINGS
Dates in blue are NEAPS

YEAR **2018**

JANUARY

Date	Day	Time	m	Time	m	Time	m	Time	m
1	M	0326	1.0	1018	5.0	1554	0.8	2249	4.9
2	TU	0415	0.9	1106	5.1	1642	0.7	○ 2342	5.0
3	W	0504	0.8	1155	5.1	1730	0.6		
4	TH	0038	5.0	0552	0.8	1248	5.0	1818	0.7
5	F	0134	5.0	0641	0.9	1341	4.9	1908	0.8
6	SA	0227	4.9	0731	1.0	1434	4.8	1958	0.9
7	SU	0316	4.8	0822	1.2	1527	4.6	2051	1.1
8	M	0404	4.6	0918	1.4	1619	4.4	◑ 2149	1.4
9	TU	0453	4.4	1022	1.7	1713	4.2	2253	1.6
10	W	0546	4.3	1130	1.8	1812	4.0	2359	1.8
11	TH	0646	4.1	1238	1.9	1920	3.9		
12	F	0105	1.8	0753	4.1	1344	1.8	2034	4.0
13	SA	0206	1.8	0857	4.2	1439	1.6	2133	4.2
14	SU	0257	1.7	0946	4.4	1524	1.5	2218	4.3
15	M	0339	1.5	1028	4.5	1602	1.3	2259	4.4
16	TU	0416	1.4	1107	4.6	1637	1.2	2338	4.5
17	W	0450	1.3	1143	4.6	1711	1.1	●	
18	TH	0014	4.6	0523	1.3	1218	4.6	1744	1.1
19	F	0048	4.6	0557	1.2	1250	4.6	1818	1.1
20	SA	0120	4.6	0633	1.2	1323	4.6	1853	1.1
21	SU	0154	4.6	0709	1.2	1358	4.5	1929	1.1
22	M	0230	4.5	0746	1.3	1436	4.4	2007	1.2
23	TU	0311	4.4	0827	1.4	1522	4.3	2050	1.3
24	W	0401	4.3	0917	1.5	1620	4.2	◐ 2145	1.5
25	TH	0500	4.2	1023	1.7	1725	4.1	2255	1.7
26	F	0604	4.2	1140	1.7	1837	4.1		
27	SA	0011	1.7	0714	4.3	1255	1.6	1951	4.2
28	SU	0124	1.6	0821	4.5	1401	1.3	2056	4.5
29	M	0226	1.3	0917	4.7	1456	1.1	2152	4.7
30	TU	0319	1.1	1008	4.9	1545	0.8	2244	4.9
31	W	0407	0.9	1056	5.0	1632	0.6	○ 2336	5.0

FEBRUARY

Date	Day	Time	m	Time	m	Time	m	Time	m
1	TH	0454	0.7	1145	5.0	1719	0.5		
2	F	0028	5.1	0540	0.7	1234	5.0	1804	0.5
3	SA	0116	5.1	0626	0.7	1322	5.0	1850	0.6
4	SU	0200	5.0	0711	0.8	1408	4.9	1935	0.7
5	M	0242	4.9	0756	1.0	1454	4.7	2021	1.0
6	TU	0326	4.7	0842	1.3	1542	4.4	2109	1.3
7	W	0412	4.4	0934	1.6	1633	4.2	◑ 2205	1.6
8	TH	0502	4.2	1042	1.8	1729	3.9	2318	1.9
9	F	0600	4.0	1206	2.0	1835	3.8		
10	SA	0038	2.0	0708	3.9	1322	1.9	1952	3.8
11	SU	0148	1.9	0821	3.9	1421	1.8	2106	3.9
12	M	0240	1.8	0923	4.1	1505	1.5	2200	4.2
13	TU	0321	1.6	1010	4.3	1542	1.3	2243	4.4
14	W	0355	1.4	1050	4.4	1615	1.1	2320	4.5
15	TH	0428	1.2	1124	4.6	1648	1.0	● 2354	4.6
16	F	0502	1.1	1157	4.6	1722	0.9		
17	SA	0025	4.7	0537	1.0	1230	4.7	1757	0.8
18	SU	0057	4.7	0613	0.9	1303	4.7	1832	0.8
19	M	0130	4.7	0649	0.9	1338	4.7	1908	0.8
20	TU	0204	4.7	0724	0.9	1414	4.6	1944	0.9
21	W	0242	4.6	0802	1.0	1455	4.5	2023	1.1
22	TH	0327	4.4	0846	1.2	1548	4.3	2111	1.3
23	F	0425	4.3	0945	1.5	1656	4.1	◐ 2222	1.6
24	SA	0533	4.1	1113	1.6	1811	4.0	2354	1.7
25	SU	0646	4.1	1239	1.6	1931	4.1		
26	M	0114	1.6	0801	4.2	1349	1.4	2046	4.3
27	TU	0217	1.4	0907	4.5	1445	1.1	2148	4.6
28	W	0309	1.1	1001	4.7	1532	0.8	2241	4.8

MARCH

Date	Day	Time	m	Time	m	Time	m	Time	m
1	TH	0355	0.8	1049	4.9	1617	0.5	2330	5.0
2	F	0439	0.6	1135	5.0	1701	0.4	○	
3	SA	0013	5.1	0522	0.5	1219	5.0	1744	0.4
4	SU	0052	5.1	0605	0.5	1301	5.0	1827	0.5
5	M	0130	5.0	0646	0.6	1343	4.9	1908	0.6
6	TU	0209	4.9	0726	0.8	1425	4.7	1947	0.9
7	W	0249	4.7	0804	1.1	1508	4.5	2025	1.2
8	TH	0331	4.4	0842	1.4	1554	4.2	2104	1.6
9	F	0416	4.1	0927	1.7	1645	3.9	◑ 2158	1.9
10	SA	0509	3.8	1052	2.0	1748	3.7	2354	2.1
11	SU	0618	3.7	1246	2.0	1909	3.6		
12	M	0118	2.1	0741	3.7	1349	1.8	2033	3.8
13	TU	0213	1.9	0855	3.9	1434	1.6	2135	4.0
14	W	0253	1.6	0947	4.1	1511	1.4	2218	4.3
15	TH	0328	1.4	1026	4.3	1544	1.1	2253	4.5
16	F	0401	1.1	1059	4.5	1619	0.9	2325	4.6
17	SA	0436	0.9	1131	4.6	1654	0.7	● 2356	4.7
18	SU	0512	0.8	1205	4.7	1731	0.6		
19	M	0029	4.8	0548	0.7	1241	4.8	1807	0.6
20	TU	0104	4.8	0624	0.6	1318	4.8	1843	0.6
21	W	0140	4.8	0701	0.7	1356	4.7	1920	0.7
22	TH	0218	4.7	0740	0.8	1439	4.6	2000	0.9
23	F	0303	4.5	0823	1.0	1532	4.4	2048	1.2
24	SA	0400	4.3	0919	1.3	1638	4.1	◐ 2200	1.6
25	SU	0508	4.1	1051	1.5	1750	4.0	2339	1.7
26	M	0622	4.0	1219	1.5	1912	4.0		
27	TU	0057	1.6	0742	4.0	1328	1.4	2037	4.2
28	W	0200	1.4	0859	4.3	1424	1.1	2144	4.5
29	TH	0251	1.1	0959	4.5	1512	0.8	2235	4.8
30	F	0336	0.8	1046	4.7	1557	0.6	2317	4.9
31	SA	0419	0.6	1125	4.9	1640	0.5	○ 2352	5.0

APRIL

Date	Day	Time	m	Time	m	Time	m	Time	m
1	SU	0501	0.5	1203	4.9	1721	0.5		
2	M	0026	5.0	0541	0.5	1241	4.9	1802	0.5
3	TU	0103	5.0	0620	0.6	1320	4.8	1840	0.7
4	W	0139	4.8	0657	0.8	1400	4.7	1915	0.9
5	TH	0216	4.6	0730	1.0	1439	4.5	1948	1.2
6	F	0253	4.4	0804	1.3	1519	4.3	2024	1.5
7	SA	0332	4.1	0843	1.5	1604	4.0	2109	1.8
8	SU	0418	3.9	0938	1.8	1658	3.8	◑ 2223	2.1
9	M	0516	3.6	1127	2.0	1809	3.6		
10	TU	0028	2.1	0637	3.5	1258	1.9	1942	3.7
11	W	0132	2.0	0810	3.7	1350	1.7	2053	4.0
12	TH	0216	1.7	0910	4.0	1431	1.4	2140	4.2
13	F	0253	1.4	0951	4.2	1508	1.2	2215	4.5
14	SA	0329	1.1	1026	4.4	1545	0.9	2248	4.7
15	SU	0405	0.9	1101	4.6	1622	0.8	2323	4.8
16	M	0442	0.7	1138	4.8	1700	0.6	● 2359	4.9
17	TU	0520	0.6	1218	4.8	1738	0.6		
18	W	0038	4.9	0558	0.5	1259	4.9	1817	0.6
19	TH	0118	4.9	0638	0.6	1342	4.8	1859	0.7
20	F	0200	4.8	0720	0.7	1430	4.7	1944	0.9
21	SA	0248	4.6	0808	0.9	1525	4.5	2036	1.2
22	SU	0346	4.3	0907	1.2	1628	4.3	◐ 2150	1.5
23	M	0451	4.1	1032	1.4	1734	4.2	2319	1.6
24	TU	0600	4.0	1152	1.5	1850	4.1		
25	W	0031	1.6	0720	4.0	1259	1.4	2019	4.2
26	TH	0134	1.4	0849	4.2	1357	1.2	2129	4.5
27	F	0227	1.2	0951	4.4	1448	1.0	2218	4.7
28	SA	0313	0.9	1036	4.6	1533	0.8	2256	4.8
29	SU	0356	0.8	1111	4.7	1616	0.7	2327	4.9
30	M	0438	0.7	1144	4.7	1657	0.7	○	

Chart Datum: 2·74 metres below Ordnance Datum (Newlyn). HAT is 5·3 metres above Chart Datum.

STANDARD TIME (UT)
For Summer Time add ONE hour in **non-shaded areas**

CHICHESTER HARBOUR

LAT 50°47′N LONG 0°56′W

TIMES AND HEIGHTS OF HIGH AND LOW WATERS

Dates in red are SPRINGS
Dates in blue are NEAPS

YEAR **2018**

MAY

Date	Day	Time	m	Time	m	Time	m	Time	m
1	TU	0000	4.9	0517	0.7	1221	4.7	1736	0.8
2	W	0036	4.8	0555	0.8	1259	4.7	1813	0.9
3	TH	0112	4.7	0630	0.9	1337	4.6	1847	1.1
4	F	0148	4.5	0703	1.0	1414	4.5	1920	1.3
5	SA	0221	4.4	0737	1.2	1451	4.3	1957	1.5
6	SU	0257	4.2	0816	1.5	1532	4.1	2041	1.8
7	M	0341	4.0	0906	1.7	1620	4.0	2141	2.0
8	TU	0435	3.8	1018	1.9	1717	3.8	◑ 2310	2.1
9	W	0536	3.7	1142	1.9	1824	3.8		
10	TH	0028	2.0	0650	3.7	1248	1.8	1948	4.0
11	F	0125	1.8	0812	3.9	1339	1.6	2048	4.2
12	SA	0210	1.5	0905	4.2	1424	1.3	2130	4.5
13	SU	0251	1.2	0947	4.4	1506	1.1	2209	4.7
14	M	0330	0.9	1028	4.6	1547	0.9	2248	4.8
15	TU	0410	0.7	1110	4.8	1628	0.8	● 2329	4.9
16	W	0451	0.6	1155	4.8	1711	0.7		
17	TH	0012	4.9	0534	0.6	1242	4.9	1755	0.7
18	F	0058	4.9	0619	0.6	1332	4.8	1842	0.8
19	SA	0146	4.8	0707	0.7	1425	4.8	1932	1.0
20	SU	0239	4.6	0758	0.9	1520	4.6	2029	1.2
21	M	0336	4.4	0859	1.1	1619	4.5	2138	1.4
22	TU	0437	4.3	1013	1.3	1718	4.3	◐ 2253	1.5
23	W	0540	4.1	1123	1.4	1824	4.3		
24	TH	0001	1.6	0651	4.0	1228	1.4	1943	4.3
25	F	0103	1.5	0822	4.1	1327	1.4	2059	4.4
26	SA	0200	1.3	0928	4.3	1422	1.3	2150	4.5
27	SU	0250	1.2	1013	4.4	1510	1.1	2227	4.6
28	M	0335	1.0	1049	4.5	1554	1.1	2258	4.7
29	TU	0417	0.9	1123	4.6	1635	1.1	○ 2333	4.6
30	W	0456	0.9	1200	4.6	1714	1.1		
31	TH	0010	4.6	0533	1.0	1239	4.6	1749	1.2

JUNE

Date	Day	Time	m	Time	m	Time	m	Time	m
1	F	0048	4.5	0608	1.0	1317	4.5	1824	1.3
2	SA	0123	4.5	0642	1.1	1354	4.5	1858	1.4
3	SU	0156	4.4	0717	1.3	1429	4.4	1935	1.5
4	M	0232	4.2	0756	1.4	1508	4.3	2017	1.7
5	TU	0314	4.1	0841	1.6	1552	4.1	2109	1.9
6	W	0404	4.0	0938	1.7	1642	4.1	◑ 2215	2.0
7	TH	0459	3.9	1044	1.8	1737	4.0	2324	1.9
8	F	0559	3.9	1147	1.7	1839	4.1		
9	SA	0025	1.8	0706	4.0	1244	1.6	1946	4.2
10	SU	0120	1.5	0814	4.2	1338	1.4	2044	4.5
11	M	0210	1.3	0909	4.4	1428	1.2	2132	4.7
12	TU	0257	1.0	0957	4.6	1515	1.0	2216	4.8
13	W	0342	0.8	1044	4.7	1602	0.9	● 2301	4.9
14	TH	0428	0.7	1133	4.8	1650	0.8	2349	4.9
15	F	0516	0.6	1227	4.9	1740	0.8		
16	SA	0039	4.9	0605	0.6	1322	4.9	1830	0.9
17	SU	0133	4.8	0656	0.7	1417	4.8	1922	1.0
18	M	0227	4.7	0749	0.8	1511	4.8	2018	1.1
19	TU	0322	4.6	0847	1.0	1604	4.6	2119	1.3
20	W	0418	4.4	0950	1.2	1656	4.5	◐ 2225	1.5
21	TH	0514	4.2	1055	1.4	1751	4.3	2330	1.6
22	F	0615	4.1	1157	1.5	1854	4.2		
23	SA	0032	1.6	0727	4.0	1259	1.5	2007	4.2
24	SU	0134	1.5	0850	4.1	1357	1.5	2110	4.3
25	M	0228	1.4	0943	4.2	1449	1.4	2153	4.4
26	TU	0316	1.3	1023	4.3	1534	1.4	2231	4.4
27	W	0358	1.2	1101	4.4	1615	1.3	2309	4.5
28	TH	0437	1.1	1140	4.4	1653	1.3	○ 2347	4.5
29	F	0514	1.1	1220	4.5	1729	1.3		
30	SA	0025	4.5	0549	1.1	1258	4.5	1804	1.4

JULY

Date	Day	Time	m	Time	m	Time	m	Time	m
1	SU	0100	4.4	0623	1.2	1333	4.5	1839	1.4
2	M	0134	4.4	0659	1.2	1407	4.4	1915	1.5
3	TU	0208	4.3	0735	1.3	1442	4.4	1953	1.5
4	W	0247	4.2	0815	1.4	1523	4.3	2036	1.6
5	TH	0333	4.1	0900	1.5	1609	4.2	2129	1.7
6	F	0425	4.0	0956	1.6	1701	4.2	◑ 2232	1.8
7	SA	0521	4.0	1059	1.7	1757	4.2	2337	1.7
8	SU	0623	4.0	1201	1.6	1900	4.2		
9	M	0038	1.6	0732	4.2	1302	1.5	2005	4.4
10	TU	0138	1.3	0838	4.4	1401	1.3	2102	4.6
11	W	0233	1.1	0933	4.6	1455	1.1	2151	4.8
12	TH	0324	0.9	1024	4.7	1547	1.0	2239	4.9
13	F	0414	0.7	1116	4.8	1637	0.8	● 2329	4.9
14	SA	0503	0.6	1211	4.9	1727	0.8		
15	SU	0021	4.9	0553	0.6	1307	4.9	1817	0.8
16	M	0115	4.9	0643	0.6	1400	4.9	1907	0.9
17	TU	0207	4.8	0734	0.7	1449	4.8	1959	1.0
18	W	0259	4.6	0826	0.9	1537	4.7	2053	1.2
19	TH	0350	4.5	0922	1.1	1625	4.5	◐ 2153	1.4
20	F	0442	4.3	1023	1.4	1715	4.3	2257	1.6
21	SA	0537	4.1	1126	1.6	1810	4.1		
22	SU	0003	1.7	0640	3.9	1231	1.7	1914	4.0
23	M	0109	1.7	0756	3.9	1335	1.7	2025	4.1
24	TU	0209	1.6	0911	4.0	1430	1.6	2124	4.2
25	W	0258	1.5	1002	4.2	1516	1.5	2209	4.3
26	TH	0340	1.3	1043	4.3	1556	1.4	2249	4.4
27	F	0417	1.2	1122	4.4	1632	1.3	○ 2327	4.4
28	SA	0453	1.1	1200	4.5	1707	1.3		
29	SU	0003	4.4	0527	1.0	1236	4.5	1742	1.2
30	M	0038	4.5	0602	1.0	1309	4.5	1817	1.2
31	TU	0110	4.4	0637	1.0	1341	4.5	1852	1.3

AUGUST

Date	Day	Time	m	Time	m	Time	m	Time	m
1	W	0143	4.4	0711	1.1	1414	4.5	1927	1.3
2	TH	0219	4.4	0746	1.2	1451	4.4	2004	1.4
3	F	0259	4.3	0825	1.3	1533	4.3	2048	1.5
4	SA	0347	4.2	0912	1.4	1624	4.2	◑ 2145	1.6
5	SU	0446	4.1	1015	1.6	1722	4.1	2257	1.7
6	M	0551	4.0	1129	1.6	1827	4.2		
7	TU	0012	1.6	0702	4.1	1242	1.6	1937	4.3
8	W	0120	1.4	0817	4.3	1348	1.4	2041	4.5
9	TH	0221	1.1	0919	4.5	1446	1.1	2135	4.7
10	F	0313	0.8	1012	4.7	1537	0.9	2224	4.8
11	SA	0402	0.6	1103	4.9	1625	0.7	● 2313	4.9
12	SU	0450	0.5	1155	5.0	1713	0.6		
13	M	0003	5.0	0537	0.4	1246	5.0	1800	0.6
14	TU	0053	4.9	0624	0.5	1333	5.0	1846	0.7
15	W	0142	4.8	0711	0.6	1418	4.9	1933	0.9
16	TH	0230	4.7	0758	0.8	1503	4.7	2020	1.1
17	F	0318	4.5	0846	1.1	1548	4.5	2111	1.4
18	SA	0408	4.3	0941	1.5	1637	4.3	◐ 2214	1.7
19	SU	0501	4.0	1048	1.7	1730	4.0	2329	1.9
20	M	0601	3.8	1202	1.9	1832	3.9		
21	TU	0043	1.9	0714	3.7	1311	1.9	1946	3.8
22	W	0146	1.8	0840	3.8	1409	1.8	2059	4.0
23	TH	0235	1.6	0944	4.1	1454	1.6	2152	4.1
24	F	0316	1.4	1027	4.3	1532	1.4	2231	4.3
25	SA	0352	1.2	1104	4.4	1607	1.3	2307	4.4
26	SU	0426	1.0	1137	4.5	1642	1.1	○ 2340	4.5
27	M	0501	0.9	1209	4.6	1717	1.0		
28	TU	0011	4.5	0536	0.8	1240	4.6	1752	1.0
29	W	0044	4.6	0610	0.8	1311	4.6	1826	1.0
30	TH	0117	4.6	0644	0.9	1343	4.6	1900	1.0
31	F	0150	4.5	0717	0.9	1417	4.5	1934	1.1

Chart Datum: 2·74 metres below Ordnance Datum (Newlyn). HAT is 5·3 metres above Chart Datum.

STANDARD TIME (UT)
For Summer Time add ONE hour in **non-shaded areas**

CHICHESTER HARBOUR LAT 50°47′N LONG 0°56′W

TIMES AND HEIGHTS OF HIGH AND LOW WATERS

Dates in red are SPRINGS
Dates in blue are NEAPS

YEAR **2018**

SEPTEMBER

Date	Day	Time	m	Time	m	Time	m	Time	m
1	SA	0227	4.4	0753	1.1	1456	4.4	2014	1.2
2	SU	0313	4.3	0837	1.3	1547	4.2	2105	1.4
3	M	0416	4.1	0936	1.6	1652	4.1	◑ 2223	1.6
4	TU	0527	4.0	1108	1.7	1802	4.1	2355	1.6
5	W	0643	4.0	1232	1.7	1916	4.1		
6	TH	0108	1.4	0802	4.2	1339	1.4	2026	4.4
7	F	0208	1.1	0909	4.5	1435	1.1	2124	4.6
8	SA	0300	0.8	1004	4.8	1524	0.9	2213	4.8
9	SU	0347	0.6	1052	5.0	1610	0.6	● 2300	4.9
10	M	0432	0.4	1137	5.1	1654	0.5	2346	5.0
11	TU	0517	0.4	1221	5.1	1738	0.5		
12	W	0031	5.0	0601	0.4	1304	5.0	1821	0.6
13	TH	0117	4.9	0643	0.6	1346	4.9	1903	0.8
14	F	0202	4.7	0725	0.9	1428	4.7	1943	1.1
15	SA	0247	4.5	0804	1.2	1511	4.5	2023	1.4
16	SU	0334	4.3	0846	1.5	1558	4.2	◐ 2109	1.7
17	M	0425	4.0	0942	1.8	1649	3.9	2229	1.9
18	TU	0523	3.8	1120	2.1	1750	3.7		
19	W	0007	2.0	0634	3.7	1240	2.1	1906	3.7
20	TH	0113	1.9	0803	3.8	1340	1.9	2029	3.8
21	F	0204	1.7	0919	4.0	1426	1.7	2129	4.0
22	SA	0245	1.4	1003	4.3	1504	1.5	2209	4.3
23	SU	0321	1.2	1037	4.5	1540	1.2	2241	4.4
24	M	0356	1.0	1107	4.6	1615	1.0	2311	4.6
25	TU	0432	0.8	1136	4.7	1650	0.9	○ 2343	4.6
26	W	0507	0.8	1207	4.8	1724	0.8		
27	TH	0016	4.7	0541	0.7	1240	4.8	1758	0.8
28	F	0051	4.7	0615	0.8	1313	4.7	1833	0.8
29	SA	0126	4.7	0650	0.8	1347	4.7	1909	0.9
30	SU	0205	4.5	0728	1.0	1427	4.5	1950	1.1

OCTOBER

Date	Day	Time	m	Time	m	Time	m	Time	m
1	M	0253	4.4	0813	1.2	1521	4.3	2040	1.3
2	TU	0400	4.2	0913	1.6	1632	4.1	◑ 2159	1.6
3	W	0513	4.1	1055	1.8	1744	4.0	2339	1.6
4	TH	0628	4.1	1218	1.7	1858	4.1		
5	F	0050	1.5	0748	4.2	1324	1.5	2013	4.3
6	SA	0150	1.2	0901	4.5	1418	1.2	2116	4.6
7	SU	0241	0.9	0956	4.8	1506	0.9	2206	4.8
8	M	0327	0.7	1040	5.0	1551	0.7	2248	4.9
9	TU	0411	0.5	1119	5.1	1634	0.6	● 2329	5.0
10	W	0454	0.5	1157	5.1	1715	0.6		
11	TH	0011	4.9	0535	0.6	1237	5.0	1755	0.7
12	F	0054	4.9	0615	0.7	1316	4.9	1834	0.9
13	SA	0136	4.7	0652	1.0	1356	4.7	1910	1.1
14	SU	0219	4.5	0728	1.2	1436	4.5	1945	1.3
15	M	0303	4.3	0806	1.5	1518	4.2	2026	1.6
16	TU	0350	4.1	0852	1.9	1606	4.0	◐ 2122	1.9
17	W	0445	3.9	1009	2.1	1704	3.7	2312	2.1
18	TH	0551	3.7	1158	2.2	1816	3.6		
19	F	0029	2.0	0713	3.8	1303	2.1	1942	3.7
20	SA	0124	1.8	0832	4.0	1352	1.8	2050	4.0
21	SU	0209	1.6	0923	4.3	1433	1.6	2133	4.2
22	M	0247	1.3	0959	4.5	1509	1.3	2207	4.4
23	TU	0324	1.1	1030	4.7	1544	1.1	2239	4.6
24	W	0359	0.9	1100	4.8	1619	0.9	○ 2312	4.7
25	TH	0435	0.8	1134	4.9	1655	0.8	2349	4.8
26	F	0511	0.8	1209	4.9	1731	0.8		
27	SA	0028	4.8	0549	0.8	1247	4.9	1809	0.8
28	SU	0109	4.8	0629	0.9	1326	4.8	1850	0.9
29	M	0154	4.7	0712	1.0	1412	4.6	1935	1.0
30	TU	0249	4.5	0801	1.3	1511	4.4	2030	1.3
31	W	0355	4.3	0905	1.6	1620	4.2	◑ 2149	1.5

NOVEMBER

Date	Day	Time	m	Time	m	Time	m	Time	m
1	TH	0504	4.2	1039	1.7	1729	4.1	2317	1.6
2	F	0614	4.2	1156	1.7	1841	4.1		
3	SA	0025	1.5	0731	4.3	1300	1.5	1959	4.3
4	SU	0125	1.3	0847	4.6	1356	1.3	2108	4.5
5	M	0218	1.1	0942	4.8	1446	1.1	2158	4.7
6	TU	0306	0.9	1024	4.9	1531	0.9	2237	4.8
7	W	0350	0.8	1059	5.0	1613	0.8	● 2314	4.9
8	TH	0432	0.8	1133	5.0	1654	0.8	2353	4.8
9	F	0513	0.8	1211	4.9	1733	0.9		
10	SA	0034	4.8	0551	1.0	1250	4.8	1810	1.0
11	SU	0115	4.7	0627	1.2	1328	4.7	1845	1.2
12	M	0156	4.5	0703	1.4	1405	4.5	1921	1.4
13	TU	0236	4.4	0740	1.6	1443	4.3	2001	1.6
14	W	0320	4.2	0824	1.8	1528	4.1	2051	1.8
15	TH	0410	4.0	0924	2.1	1622	3.9	◐ 2204	2.0
16	F	0507	3.9	1055	2.2	1724	3.8	2331	2.0
17	SA	0613	3.9	1213	2.1	1837	3.8		
18	SU	0034	1.9	0730	4.0	1310	2.0	1953	4.0
19	M	0125	1.8	0831	4.2	1355	1.7	2048	4.2
20	TU	0208	1.5	0914	4.5	1435	1.5	2129	4.4
21	W	0247	1.3	0951	4.7	1512	1.2	2206	4.6
22	TH	0326	1.1	1026	4.9	1549	1.0	2245	4.8
23	F	0405	1.0	1103	4.9	1628	0.9	○ 2326	4.8
24	SA	0446	0.9	1143	5.0	1709	0.8		
25	SU	0010	4.9	0528	0.9	1227	4.9	1752	0.8
26	M	0058	4.8	0614	0.9	1313	4.9	1839	0.9
27	TU	0150	4.8	0703	1.1	1404	4.7	1929	1.0
28	W	0249	4.7	0756	1.2	1504	4.6	2027	1.2
29	TH	0351	4.6	0901	1.5	1609	4.4	2137	1.4
30	F	0453	4.5	1018	1.6	1714	4.3	◑ 2252	1.5

DECEMBER

Date	Day	Time	m	Time	m	Time	m	Time	m
1	SA	0556	4.4	1129	1.7	1820	4.2	2358	1.5
2	SU	0705	4.4	1232	1.6	1935	4.2		
3	M	0058	1.5	0819	4.5	1332	1.5	2050	4.4
4	TU	0156	1.4	0919	4.7	1426	1.3	2144	4.5
5	W	0247	1.2	1003	4.8	1513	1.2	2225	4.6
6	TH	0333	1.1	1037	4.8	1557	1.1	2301	4.7
7	F	0415	1.1	1112	4.8	1638	1.0	● 2338	4.7
8	SA	0455	1.1	1149	4.8	1717	1.1		
9	SU	0018	4.7	0533	1.2	1228	4.7	1754	1.1
10	M	0059	4.6	0609	1.3	1305	4.6	1830	1.2
11	TU	0137	4.5	0646	1.4	1341	4.5	1906	1.3
12	W	0215	4.4	0723	1.6	1417	4.4	1944	1.5
13	TH	0254	4.3	0803	1.7	1458	4.2	2027	1.7
14	F	0338	4.2	0851	1.9	1547	4.1	2120	1.8
15	SA	0428	4.1	0952	2.1	1643	3.9	◐ 2224	2.0
16	SU	0524	4.0	1104	2.1	1744	3.9	2330	2.0
17	M	0626	4.1	1209	2.0	1851	4.0		
18	TU	0028	1.9	0734	4.2	1306	1.9	1959	4.1
19	W	0122	1.7	0831	4.4	1356	1.6	2054	4.4
20	TH	0211	1.5	0917	4.7	1441	1.4	2139	4.6
21	F	0257	1.3	0958	4.8	1525	1.1	2223	4.7
22	SA	0343	1.1	1040	4.9	1609	0.9	○ 2309	4.8
23	SU	0429	1.0	1124	5.0	1655	0.8	2358	4.9
24	M	0517	0.9	1211	5.0	1743	0.7		
25	TU	0050	4.9	0606	0.9	1302	4.9	1833	0.8
26	W	0146	4.9	0657	1.0	1356	4.9	1924	0.8
27	TH	0242	4.8	0750	1.1	1453	4.7	2019	1.0
28	F	0338	4.8	0847	1.3	1552	4.6	2119	1.2
29	SA	0433	4.6	0952	1.4	1651	4.4	◑ 2224	1.4
30	SU	0529	4.5	1059	1.6	1751	4.2	2329	1.5
31	M	0628	4.4	1205	1.7	1857	4.1		

Chart Datum: 2·74 metres below Ordnance Datum (Newlyn). HAT is 5·3 metres above Chart Datum.

South East England

Selsey Bill to North Foreland

9.3.1 Contents 247

9.3.2 Area map and Distance table 248

9.3.3 Tidal stream charts 250

9.3.4 Lights, buoys and waypoints 252

9.3.5 Passage information 253
The Eastern Channel, Selsey Bill and the Owers, Owers to Beachy Head – 253 • Crossing the Eastern English Channel, Beachy Head to Dungeness, Dungeness to North Foreland, Lydd Firing Ranges, Hythe Firing Ranges – 262

9.3.6 Littlehampton 254

9.3.7 Shoreham, tide tables/curves 255

9.3.8 Brighton 259

9.3.9 Newhaven 260

9.3.10 Eastbourne 261
Hastings

9.3.11 Rye 263

9.3.12 Folkestone 264

9.3.13 Dover, tide tables/curves 265

9.3.14 Dover Strait 269

9.3.15 Ramsgate 270
Sandwich

AREA 4
AREA 3

9.3.2
South East England
Selsey Bill to North Foreland

DISTANCE TABLE
Approximate distances in nautical miles are by the most direct route while avoiding dangers and allowing for TSS. Places in *italics* are in adjoining areas; places in **bold** are in 9.0.5, Cross-Channel Distances; places underlined are in 9.0.7, Distances across the North Sea.

1	*Portland Bill*	**1**															
2	Nab Tower	60	**2**														
3	Boulder Lt Buoy	65	5	**3**													
4	Owers Lt Buoy	69	10	6	**4**												
5	**Littlehampton**	78	19	13	12	**5**											
6	**Shoreham**	90	32	24	21	13	**6**										
7	**Brighton**	93	35	28	24	17	5	**7**									
8	**Newhaven**	97	40	34	29	24	12	7	**8**								
9	Beachy Head	104	46	41	36	30	20	14	8	**9**							
10	Eastbourne	111	51	45	40	34	24	19	12	7	**10**						
11	**Rye**	129	72	67	62	56	46	41	34	25	23	**11**					
12	Dungeness	134	76	71	66	60	50	44	38	30	26	9	**12**				
13	**Folkestone**	152	92	84	81	76	65	60	53	43	40	23	13	**13**			
14	Dover	157	97	89	86	81	70	65	58	48	45	28	18	5	**14**		
15	Ramsgate	172	112	104	101	96	85	80	73	63	60	43	33	20	15	**15**	
16	*N Foreland*	175	115	107	104	99	88	83	76	66	63	46	36	23	18	3	**16**

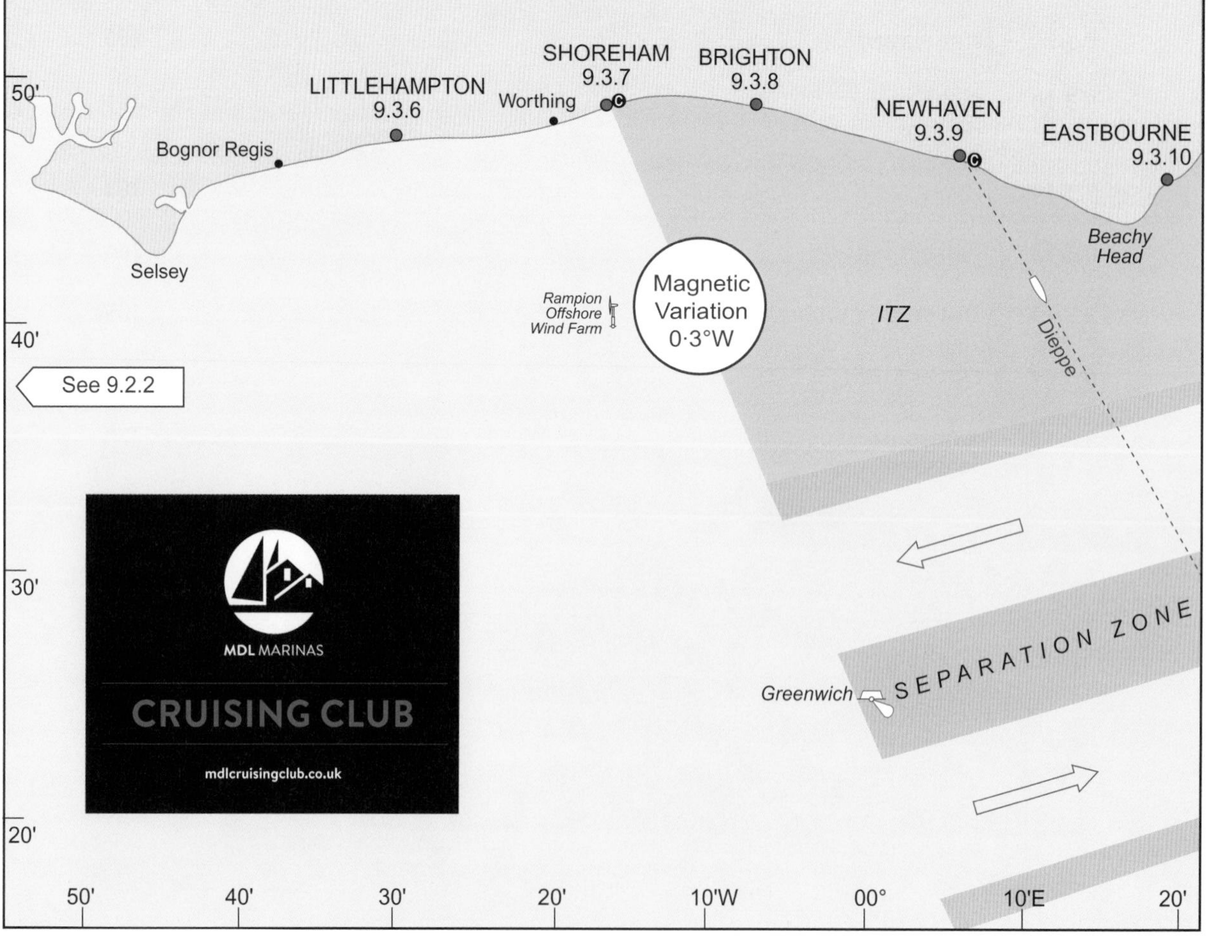

10'
51°N
50'
40'
30'
20'
LITTLEHAMPTON
9.3.6
Bognor Regis
Selsey
Worthing
SHOREHAM
9.3.7
BRIGHTON
9.3.8
NEWHAVEN
9.3.9
EASTBOURNE
9.3.10
Beachy Head
ITZ
Dieppe
Rampion Offshore Wind Farm
Magnetic Variation 0·3°W
See 9.2.2
Greenwich
SEPARATION ZONE
50'
40'
30'
20'
10'W
00°
10'E
20'

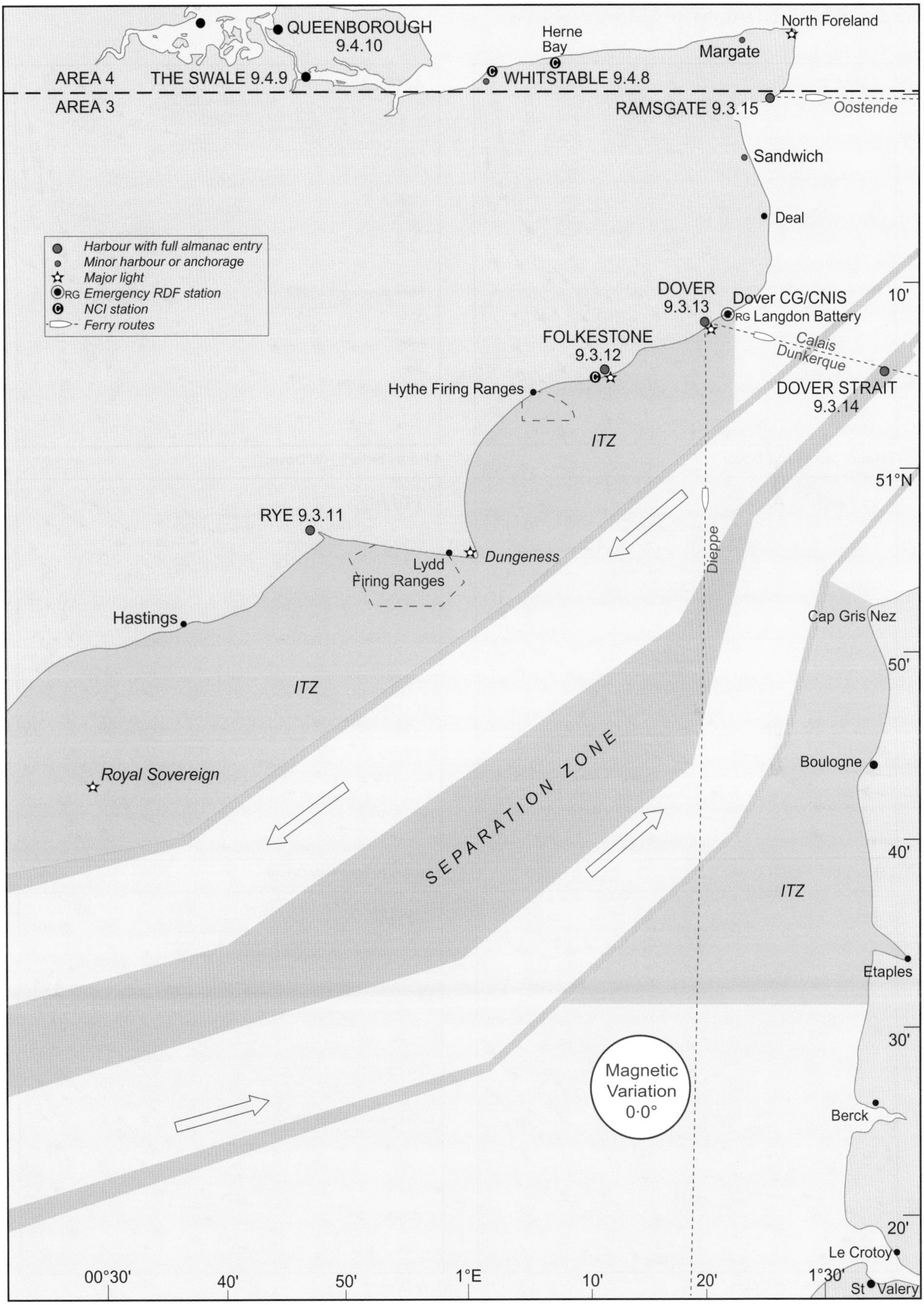
QUEENBOROUGH
9.4.10
Herne
Bay
North Foreland
Margate
AREA 4
THE SWALE 9.4.9
WHITSTABLE 9.4.8
AREA 3
RAMSGATE 9.3.15
Oostende
Sandwich
Deal
Harbour with full almanac entry
Minor harbour or anchorage
Major light
RG Emergency RDF station
NCI station
Ferry routes
DOVER
9.3.13
Dover CG/CNIS
RG Langdon Battery
10'
FOLKESTONE
9.3.12
Calais
Dunkerque
DOVER STRAIT
9.3.14
Hythe Firing Ranges
ITZ
51°N
RYE 9.3.11
Dieppe
Lydd
Firing Ranges
Dungeness
Cap Gris Nez
Hastings
50'
ITZ
SEPARATION ZONE
Boulogne
Royal Sovereign
40'
ITZ
Etaples
30'
Magnetic
Variation
0·0°
Berck
20'
Le Crotoy
00°30'
40'
50'
1°E
10'
20'
1°30'
St Valery

9.3.3 AREA 3 TIDAL STREAMS

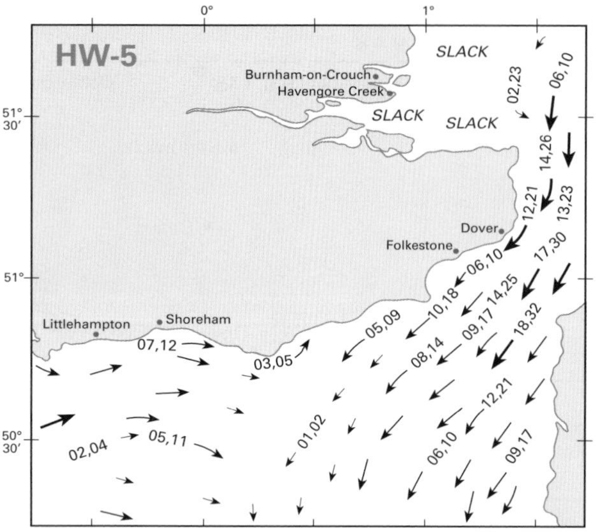

HW-5
0°
1°
51° 30′
51°
50° 30′
SLACK
Burnham-on-Crouch
Havengore Creek
SLACK
SLACK
02,23
06,10
14,26
13,23
12,21
Dover
Folkestone
06,10
17,30
10,18
14,25
05,09
09,17
18,32
08,14
Littlehampton
Shoreham
07,12
03,05
12,21
01,02
06,10
09,17
02,04
05,11

5 Hours before HW Dover

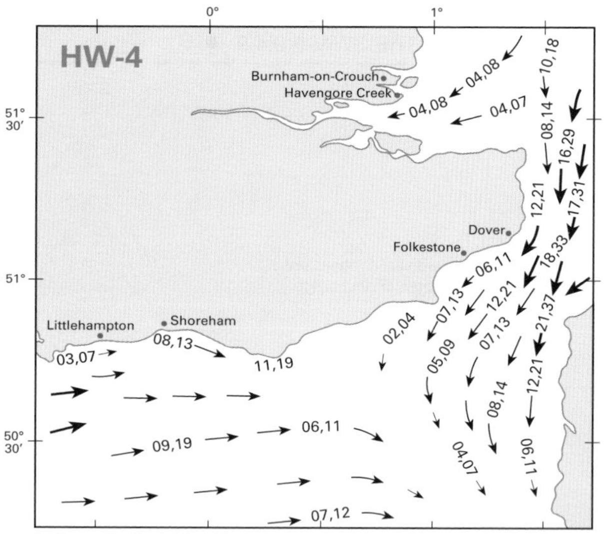

HW-4
0°
1°
51° 30′
51°
50° 30′
Burnham-on-Crouch
Havengore Creek
04,08
04,08
10,18
04,08
04,07
08,14
16,29
12,21
17,31
Dover
Folkestone
06,11
18,33
07,13
12,21
02,04
05,09
07,13
21,37
Littlehampton
Shoreham
08,13
03,07
11,19
08,14
12,21
09,19
06,11
04,07
06,11
07,12

4 Hours before HW Dover

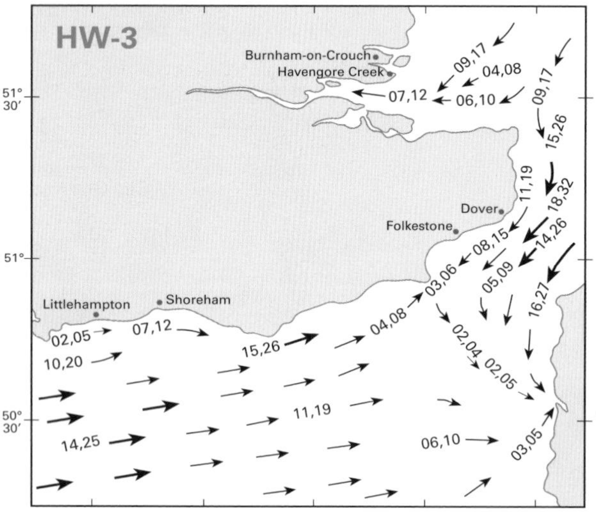

HW-3
0°
1°
51° 30′
51°
50° 30′
Burnham-on-Crouch
Havengore Creek
09,17
04,08
07,12
06,10
09,17
15,26
11,19
18,32
Dover
Folkestone
08,15
14,26
03,06
05,09
16,27
Littlehampton
Shoreham
02,05
07,12
04,08
02,04
10,20
15,26
02,05
11,19
14,25
06,10
03,05

3 Hours before HW Dover

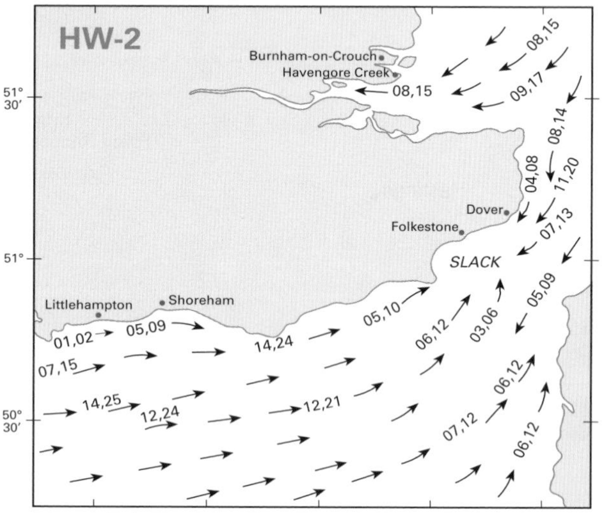

HW-2
0°
1°
51° 30′
51°
50° 30′
Burnham-on-Crouch
Havengore Creek
08,15
08,15
09,17
08,14
04,08
11,20
Dover
Folkestone
07,13
SLACK
05,09
Littlehampton
Shoreham
05,10
01,02
05,09
14,24
06,12
03,06
07,15
14,25
12,24
12,21
06,12
07,12
06,12

2 Hours before HW Dover

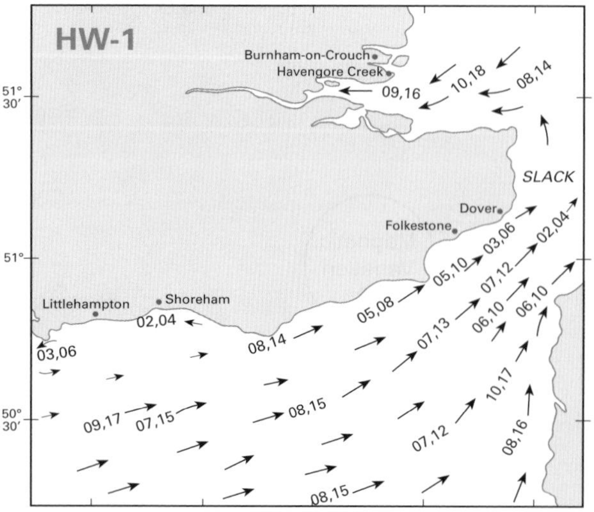

HW-1
0°
1°
51° 30′
51°
50° 30′
Burnham-on-Crouch
Havengore Creek
10,18
08,14
09,16
SLACK
Dover
Folkestone
03,06
02,04
05,10
07,12
05,08
06,10
06,10
Littlehampton
Shoreham
02,04
08,14
07,13
03,06
10,17
09,17
07,15
08,15
07,12
08,16
08,15

1 Hour before HW Dover

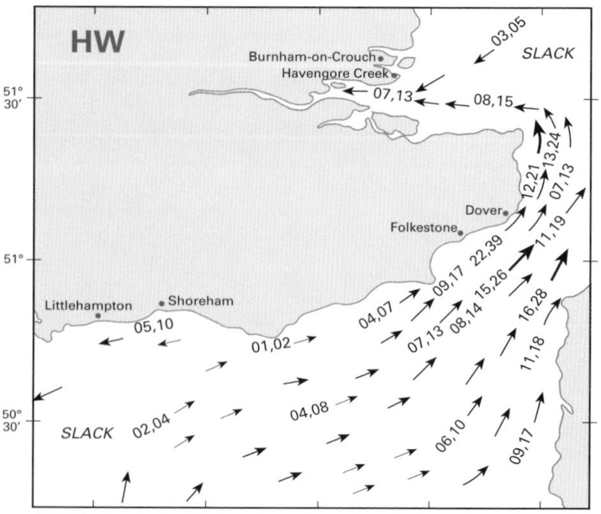

HW
0°
1°
51° 30′
51°
50° 30′
03,05
SLACK
Burnham-on-Crouch
Havengore Creek
07,13
08,15
13,24
12,21
07,13
Dover
Folkestone
11,19
22,39
09,17
15,26
Littlehampton
Shoreham
04,07
08,14
16,28
05,10
07,13
01,02
11,18
SLACK
02,04
04,08
06,10
09,17

HW Dover

Westward 9.2.3 Southward 9.17.3 Northward 9.4.3 Thames Estuary 9.4.6 Eastward 9.16.3

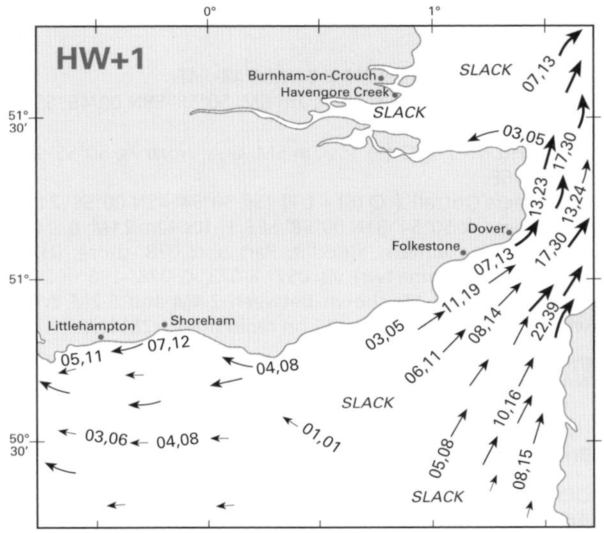
HW+1
0°
1°
51° 30′
51°
50° 30′
Burnham-on-Crouch
Havengore Creek
SLACK
SLACK
07,13
03,05
17,30
13,23
13,24
Dover
Folkestone
07,13
17,30
11,19
08,14
22,39
03,05
06,11
Littlehampton
Shoreham
07,12
05,11
04,08
SLACK
01,01
03,06
04,08
10,16
05,08
08,15
SLACK
1 Hour after HW Dover

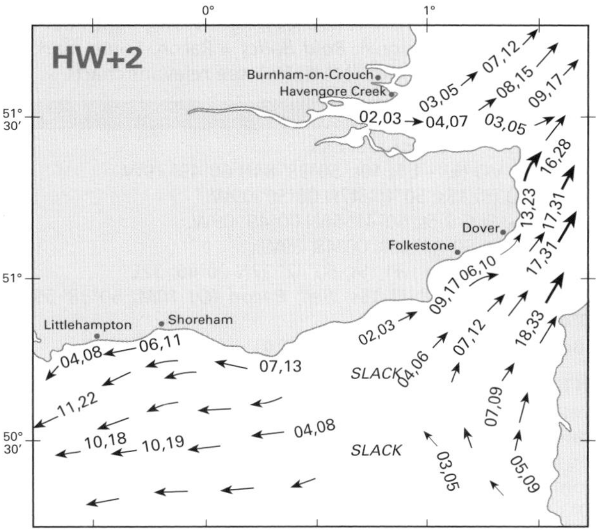
HW+2
0°
1°
51° 30′
51°
50° 30′
Burnham-on-Crouch
Havengore Creek
03,05
07,12
08,15
09,17
02,03
04,07
03,05
16,28
13,23
17,31
Dover
Folkestone
06,10
09,17
17,31
02,03
07,12
18,33
Littlehampton
Shoreham
06,11
04,08
07,13
SLACK
04,06
11,22
07,09
10,18
10,19
04,08
SLACK
03,05
05,09
2 Hours after HW Dover

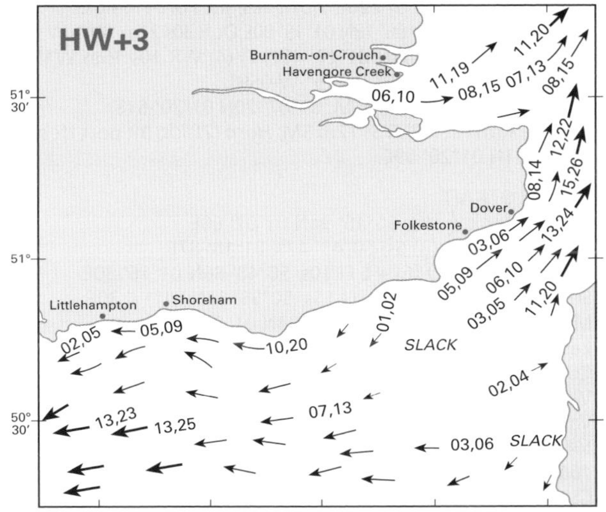
HW+3
51° 30′
51°
50° 30′
Burnham-on-Crouch
Havengore Creek
11,19
11,20
06,10
08,15
07,13
08,15
12,22
08,14
15,26
Dover
Folkestone
03,06
13,24
05,09
06,10
03,05
11,20
Littlehampton
Shoreham
01,02
02,05
05,09
10,20
SLACK
02,04
13,23
13,25
07,13
03,06
SLACK
3 Hours after HW Dover

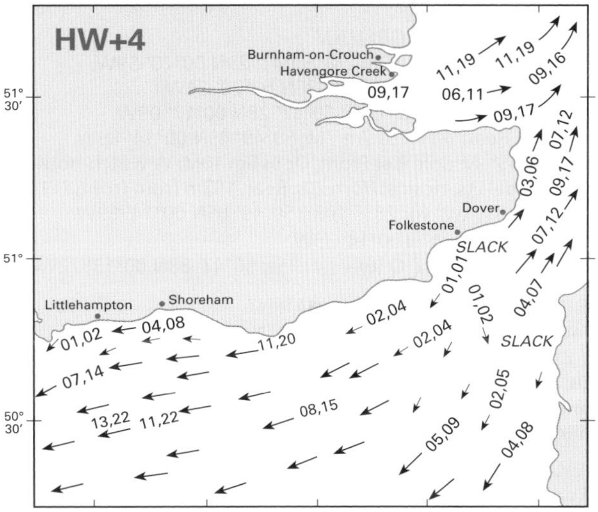
HW+4
51° 30′
51°
50° 30′
Burnham-on-Crouch
Havengore Creek
11,19
11,19
09,16
09,17
06,11
09,17
07,12
03,06
09,17
Dover
Folkestone
SLACK
07,12
01,01
01,02
04,07
Littlehampton
Shoreham
02,04
04,08
01,02
11,20
02,04
SLACK
07,14
02,05
13,22
11,22
08,15
05,09
04,08
4 Hours after HW Dover

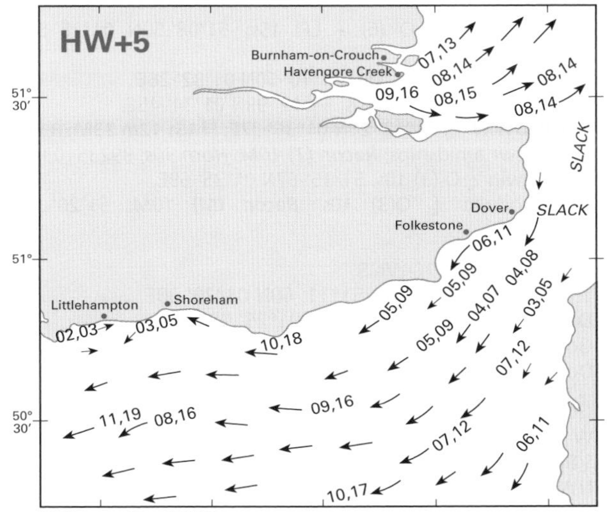
HW+5
51° 30′
51°
50° 30′
Burnham-on-Crouch
Havengore Creek
07,13
08,14
08,14
09,16
08,15
08,14
SLACK
Dover
Folkestone
SLACK
06,11
05,09
04,08
05,09
04,07
03,05
Littlehampton
Shoreham
02,03
03,05
10,18
05,09
07,12
11,19
08,16
09,16
07,12
06,11
10,17
5 Hours after HW Dover

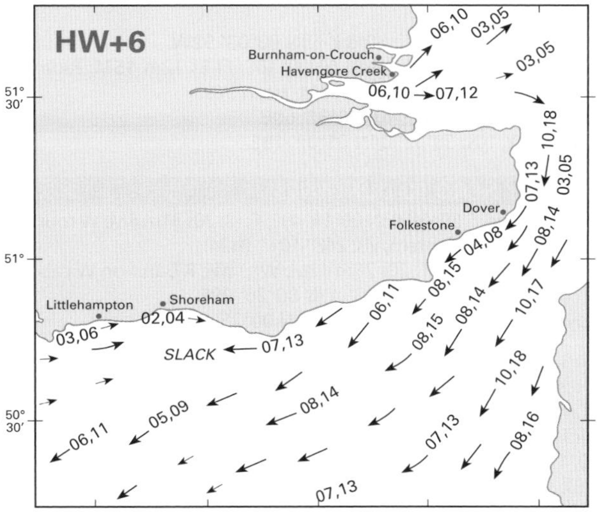
HW+6
51° 30′
51°
50° 30′
Burnham-on-Crouch
Havengore Creek
06,10
03,05
03,05
06,10
07,12
10,18
07,13
03,05
Dover
Folkestone
04,08
08,14
08,15
06,11
08,14
10,17
Littlehampton
Shoreham
02,04
03,06
SLACK
07,13
08,15
10,18
05,09
08,14
06,11
07,13
08,16
07,13
6 Hours after HW Dover

9.3.4 LIGHTS, BUOYS AND WAYPOINTS

Bold print = light with a nominal range of 15M or more. CAPITALS = place or feature. *CAPITAL ITALICS* = light-vessel, light float or Lanby. *Italics* = Fog signal. ***Bold italics*** = Racon. Some marks/ buoys are fitted with AIS (MMSI No); see relevant charts.

OWERS TO BEACHY HEAD

SELSEY BILL and THE OWERS

S Pullar VQ (6) + L Fl 10s; 50°38'·84N 00°49'·29W.
Pullar Q (9) 15s; 50°40'·47N 00°50'·09W.
Boulder Fl G 2·5s; 50°41'·56N 00°49'·09W.
Street QR; 50°41'·69N 00°48'·89W.
Mixon Bn Q(6) + L Fl 15s; 50°42'·37N 00°46'·32E.
Owers Q (6) + L Fl 15s; *Bell*; ***Racon (O) 10M***; 50°38'·59N 00°41'·09W.
E Borough Hd Q (3) 10s *Bell;* 50°41'·54N 00°39'·09W.

LITTLEHAMPTON

West Pier Hd QR 7m 6M; 50°47'·88N 00°32'·46W.
Training Wall Hd QG 10m 2M; 50°47'·87N 00°32'·38W.
Ldg lts 346°. Front, E Pier Hd FG 6m 7M; B col. Rear, 64m from front, Oc W 7·5s 9m10M; W twr; vis: 290°-W- 042°; 50°48'·09N 00°32'·51W.
Outfall Fl Y 5s; 50°46'·27N 00°30'·53W.
Littlehampton Fl (5) Y 20s 9m 5M; 50°46'·19N 00°29'·54W.

WORTHING and SHOREHAM

Met Mast Fl Y 2·5s 12m 2M; 50°41'·29N 00°20'·59W.
Outfall Fl R 2·5s 3m; 50°48'·38N 00°20'·34W.
Express Fl Y 5s; (Apr-Oct); 50°47'·28N 00°17'·09W.
W Bkwtr Head Fl R 5s 7m 7M; 50°49'·49N 00°14'·89W.
Ldg Lts 355°. Middle Pier Front, Oc 5s 8m 10M; W watch-house, R base; tidal Lts, tfc sigs; *Horn 20s*. Rear, 192m from front, Fl 10s 12m 10M; Gy twr vis: 283°-103°; 50°49'·85N 00°14'·89W.
Outfall 50°49'·47N 00°14'·39W.
Shoreham Outfall Q (6) + L Fl 15s; 50°47'·88N 00°13'·72W.

BRIGHTON and BRIGHTON MARINA

Black Rk Ledge Fl Y 4s; 50°48'·07N 00°06'·46W.
W Bkwtr Hd QR 10m 7M; W ○ structure, R bands; *Horn (2) 30s*; 50°48'·50N 00°06'·38W.
E Bkwtr Hd QG 8m 7M.
Saltdean Outfall Fl Y 5s; 50°46'·72N 00°02'·13W.

NEWHAVEN

Bkwtr Head Oc (2) 10s 17m 12M; 50°46'·56N 00°03'·50E.
E Pier Hd Iso G 10s 12m 6M; W twr; 50°46'·81N 00°03'·59E.

OFFSHORE MARKS

CS 1 Fl Y 2·5s; *Whis*; 50°33'·69N 00°03'·92W.
GREENWICH 50°24'·54N 00°00'·10E; Fl 5s 12m **15M**; Riding light FW; R hull; ***Racon (M) 10M***; *Horn 30s*.
CS 2 Fl Y 5s; 50°39'·14N 00°32'·60E.
CS 3 Fl Y 10s; 50°52'·04N 01°02'·18E.

BEACHY HEAD TO DUNGENESS

Beachy Head 50°44'·03N 00°14'·49E; Fl (2) 20s 31m 8M; W round twr, R band and lantern; vis: 248°-101°; (H24).
Royal Sovereign Fl 20s 28m 12M; W ○ twr, R band on W cabin on col; *Horn (2) 30s*; 50°43'·45N 00°26'·09E.
Royal Sovereign QR; 50°44'·23N 00°25'·84E.

EASTBOURNE and SOVEREIGN HARBOUR

SH L Fl 10s; 50°47'·40N 00°20'·71E.
Martello Tower Fl (3) 15s 12m 7M.; 50°47'·24N 00°19'·83E.
Dir lt 260·5° Fl WRG 5s 4m 1M; vis: 255°-G-259°-W-262°-R-265°; 50°47'·28N 00°19'·71E.
S Bkwtr Hd Fl (4) R 12s 3m 6M; 50°47'·30N 00°20'·03E.
St Leonard's Outfall Fl Y 5s; 50°49'·31N 00°31'·95E.

HASTINGS

Ldg Lts 356·3°. Front, FR 14m 4M; 50°51'·29N 00°35'·38E. Rear, West Hill, 357m from front, FR 55m 4M; W twr.

RYE

Rye Fairway, L Fl 10s; 50°54'·04N 00°48'·04E.
W Groyne Hd No 2 LFl R 7s 7m 6M; 50°55'·58N 00°46'·55E; 992351156.
E Arm Hd No 1 Q (9) 15s 7m 5M; G △; *Horn 7s*; 50°55'·73N 00°46'·46E.
Dungeness Outfall Q (6) + L Fl 15s; 50°54'·45N 00°58'·21E.
Dungeness ☆ 50°54'·81N 00°58'·56E; Fl 10s 40m **21M**; B ○ twr, W bands and lantern, floodlit; Part obsc 078°-shore; (H24). F RG 37m 10M (same twr); vis: 057°-R-073°-G-078°-196°-R-216°; *Horn (3) 60s*; FR Lts shown between 2·4M and 5·2M WNW when firing taking place. QR on radio mast 1·2M NW.

DUNGENESS TO NORTH FORELAND

FOLKESTONE

Hythe Flats Outfall Fl Y 5s; 51°02'·52N 01°05'·32E.
Breakwater Head ☆ Fl (2) 10s 14m **22M**; 51°04'·56N 01°11'·69E.

DOVER

Admiralty Pier Extension Head ☆ 51°06'·69N 01°19'·66E; Fl 7·5s 21m **20M**; W twr; vis: 096°-090°, obsc in The Downs by S Foreland inshore of 226°; *Horn 10s;* Int Port Tfc sigs.
S Bkwtr W Hd ☆ 51°06'·78N 01°19'·80E;Oc R 30s 21m **18M**; W twr.
Knuckle ☆ 51°07'·04N 01°20'·49E; Fl (4) WR 10s 15m **W15M**, R13M; W twr; vis: 059°-R-239°-W-059°.
N Head Fl R 2·5s 11m 5M; 51°07'·20N 01°20'·61E.
Eastern Arm Hd Fl G 5s 12m 5M; *Horn (2) 30s*; Int port tfc sigs; 51°07'·31N 01°20'·59E.

DOVER STRAIT

Bullock Bank VQ; 50°46'·94N 01°07'·60E.
Ridens SE VQ (3) 5s; 50°43'·47N 01°18'·87E.
Colbart SW VQ (6) + L Fl 10s; 50°48'·86N 01°16'·30E.
South Varne Q (6) + L Fl 15s; 50°55'·64N 01°17'·30E.
Mid Varne VQ(9)10s; 50°58'·94N 01°19'·88E.
East Varne VQ(3)5s; 50°58'·22N 01°20'·90E.
Colbart N VQ; 50°57'·45N 01°23'·29E.
Varne NW Q; 51°00'·80N 01°22'·70E.
Varne NE Q (3) 10s; 50°59'·80N 01°22'·70E.
VARNE 51°01'·29N 01°23'·90E; Fl R 5s 12m **15M**; ***Racon (T) 10M***; *Horn 30s*; 992351038.
CS 4 Fl (4) Y 15s; 51°08'·62N 01°33'·92E.
MPC Fl Y 2·5s; ***Racon (O) 10M***; 51°06'·12N 01°38'·20E; 992351122.
SW Goodwin Q (6) + LFl 15s; 51°08'·50N 01°28'·88E; 992351036.
S Goodwin Fl (4) R 15s; 51°10'·60N 01°32'·26E.
SE Goodwin Fl (3) R 10s; 51°12'·99N 01°34'·45E.
E GOODWIN 51°13'·26N 01°36'·37E; Fl 15s 12m **23M**; R hull with lt twr amidships; ***Racon (T) 10M***; *Horn 30s*; 992351035.
E Goodwin Q (3) 10s; 51°15'·67N 01°35'·69E.
NE Goodwin Q(3) 10s; ***Racon (M) 10M***. 51°20'·31N 01°34'·16E.

DEAL and THE DOWNS

Trinity Bay VQ (9) 10s; 51°11'·60N 01°29'·00E.
Deal Bank QR; 51°12'·92N 01°25'·57E.
Goodwin Fork Q (6) + L Fl 15s; *Bell;* 51°14'·38N 01°26'·70E.
Downs Fl (2) R 5s; *Bell;* 51°14'·50N 01°26'·22E.

GULL STREAM

W Goodwin Fl G 5s; 51°15'·61N 01°27'·38E.
S Brake Fl (3) R 10s; 51°15'·77N 01°26'·82E.
NW Goodwin Q (9) 15s; 51°16'·74N 01°28'·55E.
Brake Fl (4) R 15s; 51°16'·98N 01°28'·19E.

N Goodwin Fl G 2·5s; 51°18'·12N 01°30'·35E.
Gull Stream QR; 51°18'·26N 01°29'·69E.
Gull VQ (3) 5s; 51°19'·57N 01°31'·30E.
Goodwin Knoll Fl (2) G 5s; 51°19'·57N 01°32'·20E.

RAMSGATE CHANNEL

B2 Fl (2) G 5s; 51°18'·26N 01°23'·93E.
W Quern Q (9) 15s; 51°18'·98N 01°25'·39E.

RAMSGATE

RA Q(6) + L Fl 15s; 51°19'·60N 01°30'·13E.
E Brake Fl R 5s; 51°19'·47N 01°29'·20E.
No 1 QG; 51°19'·56N 01°27'·29E.
No 2 Fl (4) R 10s; 51°19'·46N 01°27'·28E.
No 3 Fl G 2·5s; 51°19'·56N 01°26'·61E.
No 4 QR; 51°19'·46N 01°26'·60E.
N Quern Q; 51°19'·41N 01°26'·11E.
No 5 Q (6) + L Fl 15s; 51°19'·56N 01°25'·91E.
No 6 Fl (2) R 5s; 51°19'·46N 01°25'·91E.
South Bkwtr Hd VQ R 10m 5M; 51°19'·46N 01°25'·41E.
N Bkwtr Hd QG 10m 5M; 51°19'·56N 01°25'·47E.
Western Marine terminal Dir lt 270° , Oc WRG 10s 10m 5M; B △, Or stripe; vis: 259°-G-269°-W- 271°-R-281°; 51°19'·51N 01°24'·85E. Rear 493m from front Oc 5s 17m 5M; B ▽, Or stripe; vis: 263°-278°.

BROADSTAIRS and NORTH FORELAND

Broadstairs Knoll Fl R 2·5s; 51°20'·88N 01°29'·48E.
Pier SE End 2 FR (vert) 7m 4M; 51°21'·50N 01°26'·74E.
Elbow Q; 51°23'·23N 01°31'·59E.

North Foreland ☆ 51°22'·49N 01°26'·70E; Fl (5) WR 20s 57m **W19M, R16M, R15M**; W 8-sided twr; vis: shore-W-150°-R(**16M**)-181°-R(**15M**)-200°-W-011°; H24; 992351020.

OFFSHORE MARKS

SANDETTIE 51°09'·36N 01°47'·12E; Fl 5s 12m **15M**; R hull with lt twr amidships; *Racon*; *Horn 30s;* 992351029.

F1 Fl (4) Y 15s; 51°11'·21N 01°44'·91E.
South Falls Q (6) + L Fl 15s; 51°13'·84N 01°43'·93E.
Sandettie W Fl (3) G 12s; 51°15'·09N 01°54'·47E.
Mid Falls Fl (3) R 10s; 51°18'·63N 01°46'·99E.
Inter Bank Fl Y 5s; *Bell;* ***Racon (M) 10M***; 51°16'·47N 01°52'·23E.
F2 Fl (4) Y 15s; 51°20'·41N 01°56'·19E.

9.3.5 PASSAGE INFORMATION

More passage information is threaded between the harbours in this area. See 9.0.5 for distances across the eastern part of the English Channel. Admiralty Leisure Folio 5605 covers Chichester to Ramsgate including the Dover Strait. **Bibliography:** *Shell Channel Pilot* (Imray/Cunliffe); *Channel Pilot and Dover Strait Pilot* (Admiralty NP27 & 28).

THE EASTERN CHANNEL

One of the greatest densities of commercial shipping occurs in this area. In such waters the greatest danger is a collision with a larger vessel, especially in poor visibility. Even when coastal cruising it is essential to know the limits of the TSS and ITZ. For example, the SW-bound TSS lane from the Dover Strait passes only 3.5M off Dungeness. Radar surveillance of the Dover Strait is maintained at all times by the Channel Navigation Information Service (CNIS). In addition to the many large ships using the traffic lanes, ferries cross between English and continental ports; fishing vessels operate both inshore and offshore; in the summer months many yachts may be encountered; and static dangers such as lobster pots and fishing nets are concentrated in certain places.

▶ *Although the rates of tidal streams vary with locality, they are greatest in the narrower parts of the Channel and off major headlands. In the Dover Strait spring rates can reach 4kn, but elsewhere in open water they seldom exceed 2kn.* ◀

N'ly winds, which may give smooth water and pleasant sailing off the English coast, can cause rough seas on the French coast. In strong S'lies the English coast between the Isle of Wight and Dover is very exposed and shelter is hard to find. The Dover Strait has a funnelling effect, which can increase the wind speed and cause very rough seas.

ON PASSAGE UP CHANNEL

▶ *There are three tidal gates; the Looe, Beachy Head and Dungeness. These form a tidal sequence which can enable a reasonably fast yacht to carry a fair tide from Selsey Bill to Dover. Based on a mean speed over the ground of 7kn, transit the Looe at about slack water, HW Dover +0500 (HW Portsmouth +0430); Beachy Head will be passed at HW D –0100; Dungeness at HW D +0300 and Dover at HW +0530, only stemming the first of the ebb in the last hour. The down-Channel passage is less efficient and a stop at Sovereign Harbour or Brighton may be considered.* ◀

SELSEY BILL AND THE OWERS

(AC 1652) Selsey Bill is a low headland off which lie several drying rocks and shoals. Just W and SW of Selsey, The Streets extend 1·25M seaward. 1·25M SSW of the Bill are The Grounds (or Malt Owers) and The Dries. Inshore1M East of The Dries 1·25M South of the lifeboat house on E side of Selsey Bill is The Mixon, a group of rocks with a red lit bn at the E end. The Owers extend 3M to the S and 5M to the SE of the Bill. Looe Chan is immediately S of these dangers marked by buoys at the W end, where it is narrowest, between Brake (or Cross) Ledge to the N and Boulder Bk to the South. It is navigable in good visibility and suitable weather. Beware of lobster pots.

▶ *The E-going stream begins at HW Portsmouth +0430, and the W-going at HW Portsmouth –0135, spring rate 2·5kn.*◀

In poor visibility, bad weather or at night keep S of the Owers SCM lt buoy, 7M SE of Selsey Bill, marking SE end of the Outer Owers.

▶ *Much of the Outer Owers is less than 3m, and large parts virtually dry. A combination of tidal streams and strong winds produces heavy breaking seas and overfalls over a large area.*◀

OWERS TO BEACHY HEAD

(AC 1652) The coast from Selsey Bill to Brighton is low, faced by a shingle beach and with few off-lying dangers. Bognor Rks (dry in places) extend 1·75M ESE from a point 1M W of the pier, and Bognor Spit extends another 0·5M further E and S. Middleton ledge are rocks running 8ca offshore, about 2M E of Bognor pier, with depths of less than 1m. Shelley Rks lie 5ca S of Middleton ledge, with depths of less than 1m.

Winter Knoll, 2·5M SSW of Littlehampton, has depths of 2·1m. Kingston Rks, depth 2m, lie about 3·25M ESE of Littlehampton. An unlit outfall bn is 3ca off Goring-by-sea (2M W of Worthing). Grass Banks, an extensive shoal with a wreck swept to 1·2m at W end, lie 1M S of Worthing pier with Elbow shoal, depth 2·5m, at their E extremity. A met mast 103m high (Mo(U)W 15s, *Horn Mo(U)*) is 7M S of Worthing and with 8 cardinal buoys, 4 with AIS, marks Rampion Wind Farm (under construction).

Off Shoreham, Church Rks, with depth of 0·3m, lie 1·5M W of the harbour entrance and 2½ca offshore. Jenny Rks, with depth 0·9m, are 1·25M E of the entrance, 3ca offshore. A diffuser is marked by a SCM and a wreck swept to 3.3m by a Y SPM.

High chalk cliffs are conspic from Brighton to Beachy Head. With the exception of outfalls the only danger more than 3ca offshore, is a Wk (10m). From Birling Gap to Head Ledge a shelf extends 4ca S of the cliff, Beachy Hd lt ho (FL(2) 20s 31m 8M) is built between these. Beware of fishing gear markers.

9.3.6 LITTLEHAMPTON

W. Sussex **50°47′·87N 00°32′·43W** ❀◊◊✿✿

CHARTS AC 5605, 1652, 1991; Imray C12, C9, 2100

TIDES +0015 Dover; ML 2·8

Standard Port SHOREHAM (⟶)

Times				Height (metres)			
High Water		Low Water		MHWS	MHWN	MLWN	MLWS
0500	1000	0000	0600	6·3	4·8	1·9	0·6
1700	2200	1200	1800				
Differences LITTLEHAMPTON (ENT)							
+0010	0000	–0005	–0010	–0·4	–0·4	–0·2	–0·2
ARUNDEL							
ND	+0120	ND	ND	–3·1	–2·8	ND	ND
PAGHAM							
+0015	0000	–0015	–0025	–0·7	–0·5	–0·1	–0·1
BOGNOR REGIS							
+0010	–0005	–0005	–0020	–0·6	–0·5	–0·2	–0·1

NOTE: Tidal hts in hbr are affected by flow down R Arun. Tide seldom falls lower than 0·9m above CD.

SHELTER Good, but ent is hazardous in strong SE winds which cause swell up the hbr. The bar is rough in SW'lies. Visitors can berth at Town Quay, where marked, in front of HM's office.

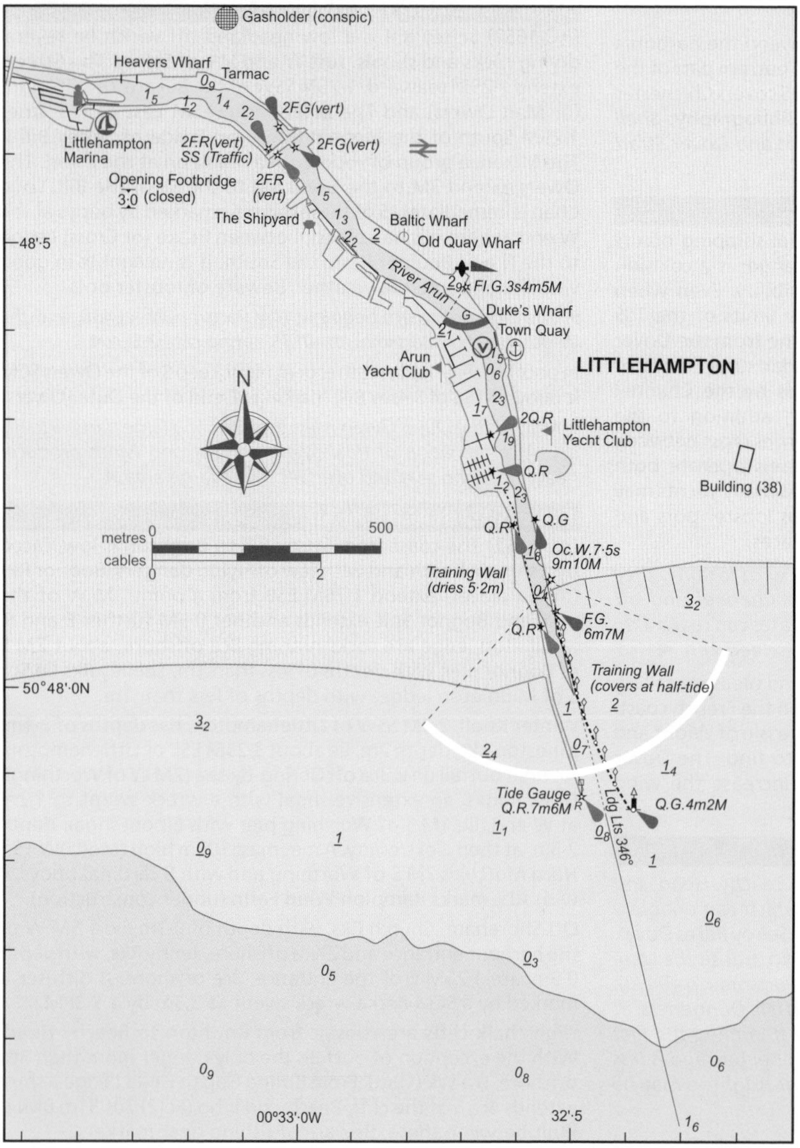

NAVIGATION WPT 50°47′·53N 00°32′·30W, 346°/0·6M to front ldg lt. Bar 5ca offshore.

- Approach and entrance dry up to 0·9m.
- Shoal bank on West side of channel South of East Pier.
- The ebb runs fast (3–5kn) at springs.
- From HW–1 to HW+4 a strong W-going tidal stream sets across the ent; keep to E side. Speed limit 6½kn from 15m S of W Pier – Old Town Bridge in Arundel. NO WASH passing moored craft.

On E side of ent chan a training wall which covers at half-tide is marked by 7 poles and lit bn at S end. The W pier is a long, prominent structure of wood piles; beware shoal ground within its arm. A tide gauge on end shows height of tide above CD. To obtain depth on the bar subtract 0·8m from indicated depth.

River Arun. ⚓. Trawling is prohibited where submarine pipelines run across the channel from a position close N of the Lt ho to the first yacht berths, and SE of a retractable footbridge (3·6m clearance MHWS; 9·4m above CD). Sited 3ca above Town Quay, this gives access for masted craft to Littlehampton Marina. It is opened by request to HM before 1630 previous day. The River Arun is navigable on the tide by small, unmasted craft for 24M.

LIGHTS AND MARKS High-rise bldg (38m) is conspic 0·4M NNE of hbr ent. A pile with small platform and ☆, Fl Y (5) 20s 5M, is 2·5M SE of hbr ent at 50°46′·1N 00°29′·5W.

Ldg lts 346°: Front FG on B column; Rear, lt ho Oc W 7·5s at root of E breakwater, 290°-W-042°. Craft approaching from the W should keep to seaward of the 2m contour until W Pier is positively identified. The Fl G 3s lt at Norfolk Wharf leads craft upstream, once inside hbr ent. The outer ends of some Yacht Club mooring pontoons on the W bank are lit QR.

When Pilot boat with P1 at the bow displays the Pilot flag 'H' or ○ over ● lts, all boats keep clear of entrance; large ship moving.

Footbridge sigs, from high mast to port:
Fl ● = open
Fl ● = bridge moving
○ = closed

Bridge's retractable centre section (22m wide) has 2 FR (vert) to port and 2 FG (vert) to stbd at both upstream and downstream ends.

COMMUNICATIONS (Code 01903) NMOC (02392) 552100; Police 101; Dr 714113. HM www.littlehampton.org.uk 721215, VHF Ch 71 16 (0900-1700LT); Pilots Ch 71 16 when vessel due. Bridge Ch 71. Marinas Ch **80** M (HO).

FACILITIES **Town Quay** pontoon connected to shore £20 <8m>£23<11m>£32, in harbour office. **Services** (pay hbr dues).

Littlehampton Yacht Club ☎713990, www.littlehamptonyachtclub.co.uk.

The Shipyard: www.shipyardlittlehampton.co.uk ☎713327, 6 £1·00, (Wood) (50t).

Arun YC ☎716016, 92+10 £14·00/yacht (dries).

Marina www.littlehamptonmarina.co.uk ☎713553, 120 £2·00, (12t).

Ship and Anchor Marina ☎(01243) 551262, 2M upriver at Ford, 50+.

Town ACA (Gatwick).

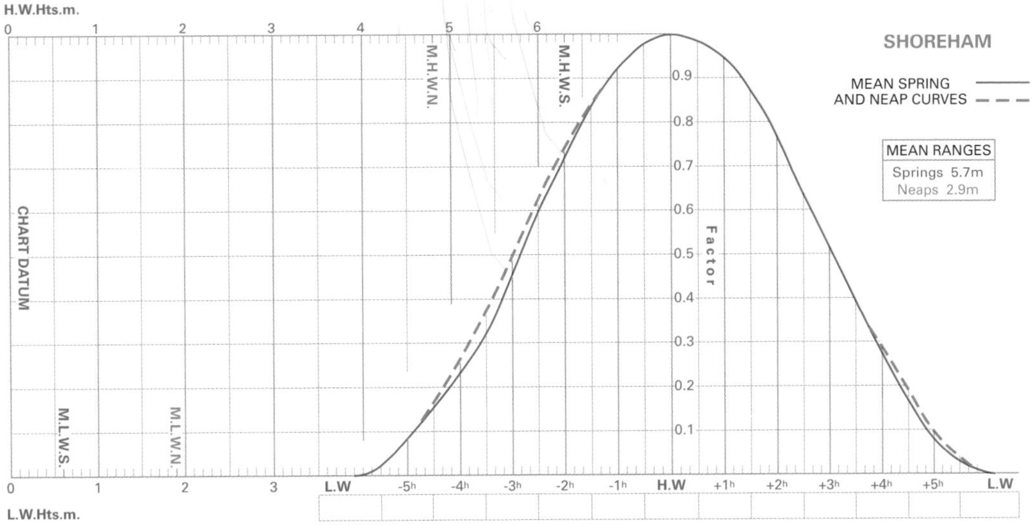

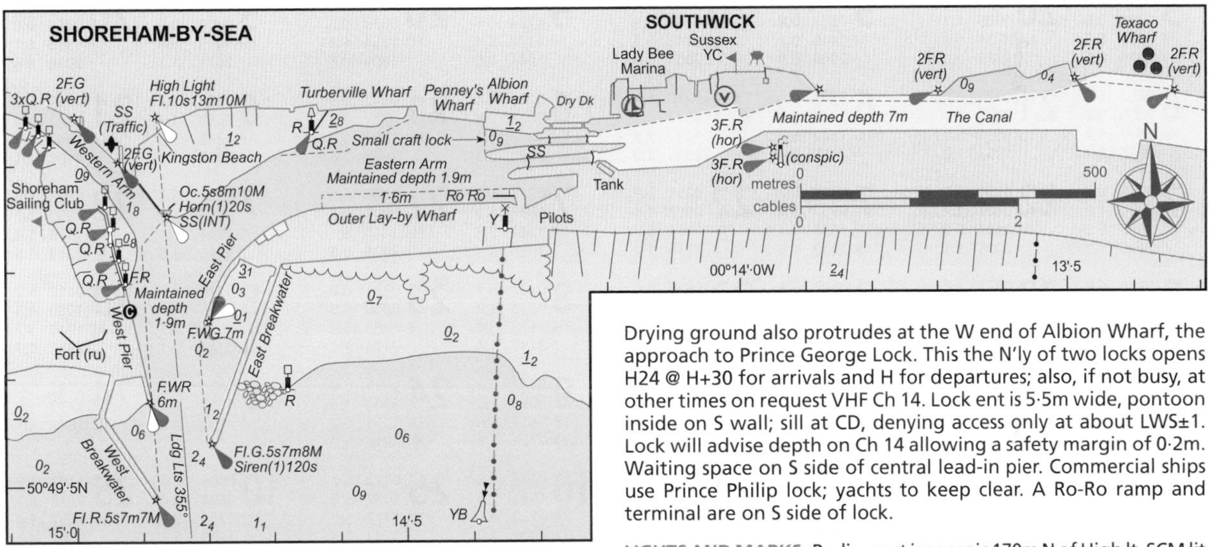

9.3.7 SHOREHAM

W. Sussex **50°49'·53N 00°14'·85W**

CHARTS AC 5605, 1652, 2044; Imray C12, C9, 2100

TIDES +0009 Dover; ML 3·3; Duration 0605

Standard Port SHOREHAM (⟶)

Times				Height (metres)			
High Water		Low Water		MHWS	MHWN	MLWN	MLWS
0500	1000	0000	0600	6·3	4·8	1·9	0·6
1700	2200	1200	1800				
Differences WORTHING							
+0010	0000	–0005	–0010	–0·1	–0·2	0·0	0·0

SHELTER Excellent, once through the lock and into The Canal. The shallow water (dredged 1·9m) at the ent can be very rough in strong onshore winds and dangerous in onshore gales. Lady Bee and Aldrington (E end of The Canal) marinas, least depth 2m, both welcome visitors. They are managed by the Hbr Authority. Visitors are advised not to use the drying Western Arm if possible. Hbr speed limit = 4kn.

NAVIGATION WPT 50°49'·23N 00°14'·81W, 355°/0·52M to front ldg lt. From E beware Jenny Rks (0·9m) and, from the W, Church Rks (0·3m). In the Eastern Arm the North shore off Turberville Wharf has drying patches within magenta dashed line - avoid. Drying ground also protrudes at the W end of Albion Wharf, the approach to Prince George Lock. This the N'ly of two locks opens H24 @ H+30 for arrivals and H for departures; also, if not busy, at other times on request VHF Ch 14. Lock ent is 5·5m wide, pontoon inside on S wall; sill at CD, denying access only at about LWS±1. Lock will advise depth on Ch 14 allowing a safety margin of 0·2m. Waiting space on S side of central lead-in pier. Commercial ships use Prince Philip lock; yachts to keep clear. A Ro-Ro ramp and terminal are on S side of lock.

LIGHTS AND MARKS Radio mast is conspic 170m N of High lt. SCM lit buoy, marks outfall diffusers, 157°/1·8M from hbr ent. Chimney 100m high, silver with blk top. 3F.R(hor) at top and 3F.R(hor) mid height. SYC yacht race signal mast on Shoreham Beach 00°16'·06W.

Ldg lts 355°: front Oc 5s 8m 10M; rear High lt, Fl 10s 13m 10M.

Traffic Sigs IPTS (Sigs 2 and 5, Oc) are shown from Middle Pier. Note: ● Fl lt exempts small craft.
Oc R 3s (from LB ho, directed at E or W Arms) = No exit.

Lock Sigs (Comply strictly to avoid turbulence):
3 ● (vert) = do not approach lock.
● ○ ● (vert) = clear to approach lock.

COMMUNICATIONS (Code 01273) NMOC (02392) 552100; Ⓗ (01903) 205111; Dr (01273) 461101; HM (01273) 598100; Locks (01273) 592366; HM and lock call *Shoreham Hbr Radio* VHF Ch **14** 16 (H24). Lock advises Marina of arrivals, 0830-1800 Mon-Sat; 1000-1400 Sun.

FACILITIES on N side of W Arm HW±3; ACA.

Lady Bee Marina ☎596880 (0900-1700), mob 07802 848915 (best to book), access as lock times, 110 +10 Ⓥ £25/craft<12m inc. FV at Nicholson's Marina ☎598100.

Sussex YC ☎464868, welcomes visitors, on a drying ½ tide pontoon in the Western Arm (limited Ⓥ) but with only 1 in the canal, so prior notice advised; also.

Town Ⓑ ✈ (Gatwick).

STANDARD TIME (UT)
For Summer Time add ONE hour in **non-shaded areas**

SHOREHAM LAT 50°50′N LONG 0°15′W

TIMES AND HEIGHTS OF HIGH AND LOW WATERS

Dates in red are SPRINGS
Dates in blue are NEAPS

YEAR **2018**

JANUARY

Date	Day	Time	m	Time	m	Time	m	Time	m
1	M	0400	0.8	1009	6.4	1627	0.6	2241	6.4
2	TU	0451	0.7	1100	6.6	1717	0.4	○ 2332	6.6
3	W	0541	0.5	1150	6.7	1807	0.4		
4	TH	0023	6.6	0630	0.5	1240	6.6	1857	0.4
5	F	0113	6.6	0720	0.6	1328	6.5	1946	0.5
6	SA	0202	6.5	0809	0.8	1417	6.2	2036	0.7
7	SU	0249	6.2	0900	1.0	1505	5.9	2126	1.0
8	M	0338	5.9	0952	1.2	1556	5.6	◑ 2219	1.3
9	TU	0429	5.6	1050	1.5	1651	5.2	2318	1.6
10	W	0525	5.3	1157	1.7	1753	5.0		
11	TH	0027	1.8	0628	5.1	1307	1.8	1905	4.9
12	F	0135	1.8	0740	5.1	1408	1.7	2020	5.0
13	SA	0233	1.7	0844	5.3	1502	1.5	2117	5.2
14	SU	0324	1.6	0934	5.5	1548	1.3	2203	5.5
15	M	0407	1.4	1016	5.7	1629	1.1	2242	5.7
16	TU	0447	1.2	1052	5.9	1707	1.0	2317	5.9
17	W	0523	1.1	1125	5.9	1742	0.9	● 2349	5.9
18	TH	0558	1.1	1156	6.0	1818	0.9		
19	F	0019	6.0	0632	1.0	1227	6.0	1851	0.9
20	SA	0049	6.0	0705	1.1	1258	5.9	1923	1.0
21	SU	0120	6.0	0735	1.1	1331	5.9	1952	1.0
22	M	0154	5.9	0807	1.2	1407	5.8	2025	1.1
23	TU	0232	5.8	0846	1.3	1448	5.6	2106	1.3
24	W	0315	5.7	0933	1.4	1536	5.4	◐ 2157	1.4
25	TH	0408	5.4	1032	1.6	1636	5.2	2301	1.6
26	F	0516	5.3	1147	1.7	1757	5.1		
27	SA	0022	1.7	0641	5.3	1309	1.6	1925	5.2
28	SU	0143	1.6	0758	5.5	1421	1.3	2036	5.5
29	M	0251	1.3	0903	5.9	1522	1.0	2138	5.9
30	TU	0349	0.9	1000	6.2	1616	0.6	2233	6.3
31	W	0440	0.7	1052	6.5	1706	0.4	○ 2325	6.5

FEBRUARY

Date	Day	Time	m	Time	m	Time	m	Time	m
1	TH	0530	0.5	1143	6.6	1755	0.3		
2	F	0014	6.7	0617	0.4	1231	6.6	1842	0.3
3	SA	0101	6.7	0704	0.4	1316	6.5	1928	0.3
4	SU	0145	6.6	0749	0.6	1359	6.3	2012	0.5
5	M	0226	6.4	0832	0.8	1440	6.1	2054	0.8
6	TU	0307	6.1	0914	1.0	1522	5.7	2135	1.1
7	W	0349	5.7	0957	1.4	1608	5.3	◑ 2220	1.5
8	TH	0437	5.3	1047	1.7	1702	4.9	2314	1.9
9	F	0533	4.9	1156	2.0	1806	4.7		
10	SA	0039	2.1	0640	4.8	1332	2.0	1922	4.6
11	SU	0203	2.0	0758	4.8	1435	1.8	2046	4.9
12	M	0300	1.8	0906	5.1	1525	1.5	2139	5.2
13	TU	0347	1.5	0953	5.4	1608	1.2	2220	5.5
14	W	0426	1.3	1030	5.7	1646	1.0	2255	5.8
15	TH	0503	1.1	1104	5.9	1722	0.9	● 2328	5.9
16	F	0538	1.0	1136	6.0	1757	0.8	2358	6.0
17	SA	0612	0.9	1207	6.0	1831	0.7		
18	SU	0028	6.1	0645	0.9	1240	6.1	1902	0.7
19	M	0100	6.1	0715	0.8	1313	6.1	1931	0.8
20	TU	0133	6.1	0746	0.9	1348	6.1	2003	0.8
21	W	0210	6.1	0823	0.9	1427	5.9	2043	1.0
22	TH	0251	5.9	0907	1.1	1511	5.7	2130	1.2
23	F	0339	5.6	1001	1.4	1607	5.3	◐ 2231	1.5
24	SA	0442	5.2	1113	1.6	1724	5.0	2355	1.8
25	SU	0611	5.1	1245	1.7	1906	5.0		
26	M	0127	1.7	0743	5.2	1408	1.4	2027	5.3
27	TU	0241	1.4	0855	5.6	1512	1.0	2131	5.8
28	W	0339	1.0	0953	6.0	1605	0.6	2226	6.2

MARCH

Date	Day	Time	m	Time	m	Time	m	Time	m
1	TH	0429	0.6	1045	6.3	1653	0.4	2315	6.5
2	F	0516	0.4	1132	6.5	1739	0.2	○	
3	SA	0000	6.7	0600	0.3	1217	6.6	1823	0.2
4	SU	0043	6.7	0643	0.4	1259	6.5	1905	0.3
5	M	0122	6.6	0724	0.5	1337	6.4	1944	0.5
6	TU	0159	6.4	0802	0.6	1413	6.1	2020	0.7
7	W	0233	6.1	0837	0.9	1448	5.8	2055	1.1
8	TH	0307	5.7	0913	1.2	1526	5.4	2133	1.4
9	F	0347	5.2	0956	1.6	1615	5.0	◑ 2221	1.8
10	SA	0442	4.8	1051	2.0	1720	4.6	2326	2.2
11	SU	0553	4.5	1210	2.2	1833	4.5		
12	M	0120	2.2	0707	4.5	1402	2.0	1955	4.7
13	TU	0233	2.0	0825	4.8	1457	1.7	2106	5.1
14	W	0321	1.6	0921	5.2	1540	1.3	2150	5.4
15	TH	0401	1.3	1001	5.5	1618	1.0	2226	5.8
16	F	0437	1.0	1037	5.8	1655	0.8	2259	6.0
17	SA	0512	0.9	1111	6.0	1730	0.7	● 2332	6.1
18	SU	0547	0.7	1145	6.1	1805	0.6		
19	M	0004	6.2	0620	0.7	1220	6.2	1837	0.6
20	TU	0038	6.3	0653	0.6	1254	6.3	1909	0.6
21	W	0112	6.3	0727	0.6	1330	6.2	1945	0.6
22	TH	0150	6.2	0805	0.7	1410	6.1	2026	0.8
23	F	0231	6.0	0850	0.9	1455	5.8	2114	1.1
24	SA	0319	5.6	0944	1.3	1551	5.3	◐ 2216	1.5
25	SU	0422	5.2	1057	1.6	1712	5.0	2343	1.8
26	M	0556	4.9	1231	1.7	1856	5.0		
27	TU	0117	1.7	0733	5.1	1356	1.4	2018	5.3
28	W	0229	1.4	0846	5.5	1458	1.0	2120	5.8
29	TH	0325	1.0	0942	5.9	1549	0.7	2212	6.2
30	F	0413	0.6	1031	6.2	1635	0.4	2257	6.5
31	SA	0457	0.4	1116	6.4	1718	0.3	○ 2340	6.6

APRIL

Date	Day	Time	m	Time	m	Time	m	Time	m
1	SU	0540	0.4	1158	6.5	1800	0.3		
2	M	0019	6.6	0619	0.4	1237	6.4	1838	0.4
3	TU	0056	6.5	0657	0.5	1313	6.3	1914	0.6
4	W	0129	6.3	0731	0.7	1345	6.1	1947	0.8
5	TH	0159	6.0	0804	0.9	1415	5.8	2021	1.1
6	F	0227	5.7	0838	1.2	1449	5.5	2058	1.4
7	SA	0300	5.3	0918	1.5	1531	5.1	2143	1.8
8	SU	0346	4.9	1009	1.8	1636	4.7	◑ 2244	2.1
9	M	0506	4.5	1118	2.1	1753	4.5		
10	TU	0005	2.3	0624	4.4	1254	2.1	1905	4.7
11	W	0150	2.1	0735	4.7	1416	1.8	2013	5.0
12	TH	0245	1.7	0836	5.1	1504	1.4	2105	5.4
13	F	0327	1.3	0922	5.4	1544	1.1	2147	5.8
14	SA	0405	1.0	1003	5.8	1621	0.9	2224	6.0
15	SU	0441	0.8	1041	6.0	1658	0.7	2301	6.2
16	M	0517	0.7	1119	6.2	1735	0.6	● 2338	6.4
17	TU	0554	0.5	1157	6.3	1812	0.5		
18	W	0015	6.4	0631	0.5	1236	6.4	1850	0.5
19	TH	0053	6.4	0711	0.5	1316	6.3	1931	0.6
20	F	0133	6.3	0754	0.6	1358	6.1	2016	0.8
21	SA	0217	6.0	0842	0.9	1447	5.8	2108	1.1
22	SU	0309	5.6	0938	1.2	1548	5.4	◐ 2213	1.5
23	M	0416	5.2	1050	1.5	1710	5.1	2336	1.7
24	TU	0547	5.0	1219	1.6	1842	5.1		
25	W	0102	1.6	0717	5.1	1337	1.4	2000	5.4
26	TH	0211	1.3	0828	5.4	1438	1.1	2100	5.8
27	F	0305	1.0	0923	5.8	1528	0.8	2150	6.1
28	SA	0352	0.7	1011	6.0	1613	0.6	2234	6.3
29	SU	0435	0.6	1055	6.2	1655	0.6	2315	6.4
30	M	0516	0.5	1136	6.2	1734	0.6	○ 2354	6.4

Chart Datum: 3·27 metres below Ordnance Datum (Newlyn). HAT is 6·9 metres above Chart Datum.

STANDARD TIME (UT)
For Summer Time add ONE hour in **non-shaded areas**

SHOREHAM LAT 50°50′N LONG 0°15′W

TIMES AND HEIGHTS OF HIGH AND LOW WATERS

Dates in red are SPRINGS
Dates in blue are NEAPS

YEAR **2018**

MAY

Date	Time	m	Time	m	Time	m	Time	m
1 TU	0555	0.6	1213	6.2	1812	0.6		
2 W	0029	6.3	0630	0.6	1248	6.1	1847	0.8
3 TH	0100	6.1	0704	0.8	1318	6.0	1920	0.9
4 F	0127	5.9	0737	0.9	1348	5.8	1954	1.1
5 SA	0155	5.6	0811	1.1	1421	5.5	2031	1.4
6 SU	0227	5.3	0850	1.4	1459	5.2	2114	1.7
7 M	0309	5.0	0937	1.7	1552	4.9	2209	2.0
8 TU	0412	4.7	1038	1.9	1709	4.7	◑ 2320	2.2
9 W	0541	4.5	1152	2.0	1821	4.8		
10 TH	0039	2.1	0649	4.7	1311	1.9	1923	5.0
11 F	0152	1.8	0749	5.0	1414	1.6	2018	5.4
12 SA	0243	1.4	0841	5.4	1501	1.2	2106	5.7
13 SU	0326	1.1	0927	5.7	1544	1.0	2149	6.0
14 M	0406	0.8	1011	6.0	1624	0.8	2231	6.3
15 TU	0446	0.6	1054	6.2	1706	0.6	● 2312	6.4
16 W	0528	0.5	1137	6.4	1749	0.5	2354	6.5
17 TH	0612	0.4	1220	6.4	1834	0.5		
18 F	0037	6.5	0657	0.4	1306	6.4	1920	0.6
19 SA	0122	6.3	0745	0.6	1354	6.2	2010	0.8
20 SU	0210	6.0	0837	0.8	1447	5.9	2105	1.0
21 M	0306	5.7	0935	1.0	1548	5.6	2208	1.3
22 TU	0412	5.4	1043	1.3	1700	5.4	◐ 2323	1.5
23 W	0529	5.1	1159	1.4	1817	5.3		
24 TH	0039	1.5	0650	5.1	1311	1.3	1930	5.5
25 F	0144	1.3	0800	5.3	1411	1.2	2031	5.7
26 SA	0240	1.1	0857	5.5	1502	1.0	2123	5.9
27 SU	0328	0.9	0947	5.8	1548	0.9	2208	6.1
28 M	0412	0.8	1031	5.9	1631	0.8	2250	6.1
29 TU	0453	0.8	1112	6.0	1711	0.8	○ 2328	6.1
30 W	0532	0.8	1150	6.0	1749	0.9		
31 TH	0002	6.1	0608	0.8	1224	6.0	1824	0.9

JUNE

Date	Time	m	Time	m	Time	m	Time	m
1 F	0034	6.0	0642	0.9	1256	5.9	1858	1.0
2 SA	0102	5.8	0716	1.0	1327	5.8	1933	1.2
3 SU	0132	5.7	0751	1.1	1358	5.6	2009	1.3
4 M	0204	5.4	0828	1.3	1434	5.4	2049	1.6
5 TU	0242	5.2	0909	1.5	1516	5.2	2137	1.8
6 W	0330	5.0	1000	1.7	1612	5.0	◑ 2235	1.9
7 TH	0437	4.8	1101	1.8	1726	5.0	2343	1.9
8 F	0559	4.8	1210	1.8	1834	5.1		
9 SA	0051	1.8	0704	5.0	1317	1.6	1934	5.3
10 SU	0152	1.5	0801	5.3	1415	1.4	2027	5.7
11 M	0245	1.2	0853	5.7	1507	1.1	2116	6.0
12 TU	0333	0.9	0942	6.0	1555	0.8	2204	6.2
13 W	0420	0.7	1031	6.2	1643	0.7	● 2251	6.4
14 TH	0508	0.5	1120	6.4	1731	0.6	2338	6.5
15 F	0557	0.4	1209	6.5	1821	0.5		
16 SA	0026	6.5	0646	0.4	1300	6.5	1910	0.6
17 SU	0116	6.4	0737	0.5	1351	6.4	2002	0.7
18 M	0207	6.2	0829	0.6	1444	6.2	2056	0.9
19 TU	0301	5.9	0925	0.8	1539	5.9	2155	1.1
20 W	0359	5.6	1025	1.1	1637	5.7	◐ 2259	1.3
21 TH	0502	5.3	1130	1.3	1740	5.5		
22 F	0007	1.4	0610	5.2	1237	1.4	1848	5.4
23 SA	0112	1.4	0722	5.1	1339	1.4	1955	5.4
24 SU	0211	1.4	0827	5.3	1435	1.3	2052	5.6
25 M	0303	1.2	0921	5.4	1524	1.2	2141	5.7
26 TU	0349	1.1	1008	5.6	1609	1.1	2225	5.8
27 W	0432	1.0	1051	5.7	1650	1.1	2305	5.9
28 TH	0511	0.9	1129	5.8	1729	1.0	○ 2340	5.9
29 F	0548	0.9	1204	5.9	1805	1.0		
30 SA	0012	5.9	0623	0.9	1236	5.9	1840	1.1

JULY

Date	Time	m	Time	m	Time	m	Time	m
1 SU	0042	5.8	0658	1.0	1307	5.8	1915	1.1
2 M	0112	5.7	0733	1.1	1337	5.8	1950	1.2
3 TU	0144	5.6	0807	1.2	1409	5.7	2025	1.4
4 W	0219	5.5	0842	1.3	1446	5.5	2104	1.5
5 TH	0259	5.3	0922	1.4	1529	5.4	2151	1.6
6 F	0348	5.1	1012	1.6	1623	5.2	◑ 2249	1.7
7 SA	0450	5.0	1113	1.7	1731	5.2	2357	1.7
8 SU	0609	5.0	1224	1.7	1846	5.3		
9 M	0106	1.6	0721	5.2	1335	1.5	1951	5.5
10 TU	0211	1.3	0824	5.5	1438	1.3	2050	5.8
11 W	0309	1.0	0921	5.9	1534	1.0	2144	6.1
12 TH	0402	0.7	1016	6.2	1627	0.7	2236	6.4
13 F	0453	0.5	1109	6.4	1718	0.6	● 2327	6.5
14 SA	0544	0.4	1201	6.5	1809	0.5		
15 SU	0018	6.5	0634	0.3	1253	6.6	1859	0.5
16 M	0109	6.5	0725	0.4	1342	6.6	1949	0.6
17 TU	0158	6.3	0815	0.5	1431	6.4	2040	0.7
18 W	0247	6.1	0906	0.7	1518	6.2	2132	0.9
19 TH	0336	5.8	0957	1.0	1607	5.9	◐ 2227	1.2
20 F	0428	5.5	1052	1.3	1659	5.5	2327	1.5
21 SA	0525	5.1	1155	1.5	1758	5.3		
22 SU	0035	1.6	0631	4.9	1304	1.7	1906	5.1
23 M	0141	1.7	0749	4.9	1407	1.7	2018	5.2
24 TU	0239	1.6	0856	5.1	1502	1.6	2116	5.4
25 W	0329	1.4	0948	5.4	1550	1.4	2204	5.6
26 TH	0413	1.2	1031	5.6	1632	1.2	2244	5.7
27 F	0452	1.0	1109	5.8	1710	1.1	○ 2320	5.8
28 SA	0529	0.9	1144	5.9	1746	1.1	2352	5.9
29 SU	0605	0.9	1215	5.9	1822	1.0		
30 M	0021	5.9	0639	0.9	1245	5.9	1856	1.1
31 TU	0051	5.8	0713	1.0	1313	5.9	1928	1.1

AUGUST

Date	Time	m	Time	m	Time	m	Time	m
1 W	0122	5.8	0744	1.0	1343	5.9	1959	1.2
2 TH	0155	5.7	0813	1.1	1418	5.8	2032	1.3
3 F	0231	5.6	0848	1.2	1457	5.7	2112	1.4
4 SA	0314	5.5	0933	1.4	1544	5.5	◑ 2204	1.6
5 SU	0407	5.2	1029	1.6	1642	5.3	2309	1.7
6 M	0516	5.1	1141	1.7	1800	5.2		
7 TU	0029	1.7	0647	5.1	1305	1.7	1924	5.3
8 W	0147	1.5	0804	5.4	1420	1.4	2033	5.7
9 TH	0254	1.1	0909	5.7	1522	1.1	2133	6.0
10 F	0350	0.8	1007	6.1	1616	0.8	2227	6.3
11 SA	0441	0.5	1100	6.4	1706	0.5	● 2319	6.5
12 SU	0531	0.3	1151	6.6	1755	0.4		
13 M	0008	6.6	0619	0.3	1240	6.7	1842	0.4
14 TU	0056	6.6	0706	0.3	1325	6.7	1930	0.5
15 W	0141	6.5	0753	0.4	1409	6.5	2016	0.6
16 TH	0224	6.2	0837	0.6	1451	6.3	2100	0.9
17 F	0307	5.9	0921	1.0	1533	5.9	2145	1.2
18 SA	0352	5.5	1005	1.4	1619	5.5	◐ 2234	1.6
19 SU	0443	5.1	1058	1.7	1712	5.1	2339	1.9
20 M	0544	4.8	1215	2.0	1817	4.8		
21 TU	0107	2.0	0700	4.7	1340	2.1	1936	4.8
22 W	0215	1.9	0830	4.9	1441	1.9	2053	5.1
23 TH	0308	1.6	0928	5.2	1530	1.6	2143	5.4
24 F	0352	1.3	1011	5.5	1612	1.3	2223	5.7
25 SA	0431	1.1	1047	5.8	1649	1.1	2257	5.8
26 SU	0507	0.9	1120	6.0	1724	1.0	○ 2328	5.9
27 M	0542	0.9	1150	6.0	1759	1.0	2357	6.0
28 TU	0616	0.8	1218	6.1	1833	0.9		
29 W	0027	6.0	0649	0.9	1247	6.1	1903	1.0
30 TH	0058	6.0	0717	0.9	1318	6.1	1932	1.0
31 F	0131	6.0	0745	1.0	1351	6.0	2004	1.1

Chart Datum: 3·27 metres below Ordnance Datum (Newlyn). HAT is 6·9 metres above Chart Datum.

SE England

STANDARD TIME (UT)
For Summer Time add ONE hour in **non-shaded areas**

SHOREHAM

LAT 50°50′N LONG 0°15′W

TIMES AND HEIGHTS OF HIGH AND LOW WATERS

Dates in red are SPRINGS
Dates in blue are NEAPS

YEAR **2018**

SEPTEMBER

Date	Day	Time	m	Time	m	Time	m	Time	m
1	SA	0206	5.9	0821	1.1	1429	5.9	2043	1.2
2	SU	0247	5.7	0904	1.3	1513	5.6	2133	1.5
3	M	0337	5.4	0959	1.6	1609	5.3	◑ 2237	1.7
4	TU	0445	5.0	1113	1.8	1729	5.1		
5	W	0004	1.8	0628	5.0	1249	1.9	1909	5.1
6	TH	0134	1.7	0755	5.3	1411	1.6	2024	5.5
7	F	0244	1.3	0902	5.7	1513	1.1	2126	6.0
8	SA	0340	0.8	0959	6.2	1604	0.8	2218	6.3
9	SU	0428	0.5	1049	6.5	1651	0.5	● 2307	6.6
10	M	0514	0.3	1136	6.7	1737	0.4	2353	6.7
11	TU	0600	0.3	1220	6.8	1822	0.4		
12	W	0037	6.6	0643	0.3	1302	6.7	1905	0.5
13	TH	0118	6.5	0725	0.5	1341	6.5	1946	0.7
14	F	0157	6.3	0804	0.7	1419	6.2	2024	0.9
15	SA	0234	5.9	0841	1.1	1456	5.9	2101	1.3
16	SU	0314	5.5	0920	1.5	1537	5.4	◐ 2143	1.7
17	M	0402	5.1	1006	1.9	1629	5.0	2237	2.0
18	TU	0504	4.7	1109	2.2	1735	4.7		
19	W	0001	2.3	0616	4.6	1305	2.3	1851	4.6
20	TH	0146	2.1	0750	4.7	1416	2.1	2022	4.9
21	F	0242	1.8	0900	5.1	1506	1.7	2117	5.3
22	SA	0327	1.4	0942	5.5	1547	1.4	2155	5.6
23	SU	0405	1.2	1017	5.8	1623	1.1	2228	5.9
24	M	0440	1.0	1048	6.0	1657	1.0	2259	6.0
25	TU	0515	0.9	1118	6.2	1732	0.9	○ 2330	6.1
26	W	0549	0.8	1148	6.2	1805	0.9		
27	TH	0002	6.2	0620	0.8	1220	6.3	1836	0.9
28	F	0035	6.2	0650	0.8	1252	6.3	1907	0.9
29	SA	0108	6.2	0722	0.9	1327	6.2	1942	1.0
30	SU	0145	6.1	0800	1.0	1405	6.0	2023	1.2

OCTOBER

Date	Day	Time	m	Time	m	Time	m	Time	m
1	M	0226	5.8	0845	1.3	1450	5.7	2114	1.5
2	TU	0317	5.4	0943	1.6	1547	5.3	◑ 2220	1.8
3	W	0431	5.1	1101	1.9	1716	5.0	2350	1.9
4	TH	0620	5.0	1239	1.9	1900	5.1		
5	F	0123	1.7	0745	5.3	1400	1.6	2015	5.5
6	SA	0232	1.3	0851	5.8	1459	1.2	2115	5.9
7	SU	0325	0.9	0944	6.3	1548	0.8	2205	6.3
8	M	0411	0.6	1031	6.6	1633	0.5	2250	6.5
9	TU	0455	0.4	1115	6.7	1716	0.4	● 2334	6.6
10	W	0537	0.4	1156	6.8	1758	0.4		
11	TH	0015	6.6	0617	0.5	1235	6.7	1838	0.6
12	F	0053	6.5	0655	0.7	1311	6.4	1915	0.7
13	SA	0128	6.2	0731	0.9	1345	6.2	1950	1.0
14	SU	0202	5.9	0806	1.2	1417	5.8	2025	1.3
15	M	0238	5.6	0843	1.5	1453	5.4	2105	1.7
16	TU	0322	5.2	0928	1.9	1542	5.0	◐ 2155	2.0
17	W	0424	4.8	1027	2.3	1654	4.6	2303	2.3
18	TH	0537	4.6	1149	2.4	1809	4.5		
19	F	0052	2.3	0651	4.7	1338	2.2	1925	4.7
20	SA	0205	2.0	0807	5.1	1433	1.9	2031	5.1
21	SU	0253	1.6	0858	5.5	1515	1.5	2114	5.5
22	M	0332	1.3	0936	5.8	1551	1.2	2151	5.8
23	TU	0408	1.1	1010	6.1	1627	1.0	2226	6.1
24	W	0443	0.9	1044	6.3	1701	0.9	○ 2301	6.2
25	TH	0518	0.8	1118	6.4	1736	0.8	2337	6.3
26	F	0552	0.8	1153	6.4	1811	0.8		
27	SA	0012	6.4	0627	0.8	1229	6.4	1847	0.8
28	SU	0050	6.3	0705	0.9	1307	6.3	1927	0.9
29	M	0130	6.2	0747	1.0	1348	6.1	2012	1.1
30	TU	0215	5.9	0836	1.3	1436	5.7	2105	1.4
31	W	0311	5.5	0937	1.6	1538	5.3	◑ 2213	1.7

NOVEMBER

Date	Day	Time	m	Time	m	Time	m	Time	m
1	TH	0429	5.2	1055	1.9	1709	5.0	2339	1.8
2	F	0607	5.2	1225	1.9	1843	5.1		
3	SA	0105	1.7	0727	5.4	1340	1.6	1957	5.4
4	SU	0211	1.3	0830	5.8	1439	1.2	2055	5.8
5	M	0304	1.0	0922	6.2	1527	0.9	2145	6.2
6	TU	0350	0.8	1008	6.5	1612	0.7	2230	6.4
7	W	0433	0.7	1051	6.6	1654	0.6	● 2312	6.4
8	TH	0514	0.6	1131	6.6	1734	0.6	2352	6.4
9	F	0553	0.7	1208	6.5	1813	0.7		
10	SA	0028	6.3	0629	0.9	1242	6.3	1849	0.8
11	SU	0102	6.2	0704	1.0	1314	6.1	1923	1.0
12	M	0135	6.0	0739	1.3	1344	5.8	1957	1.3
13	TU	0209	5.7	0816	1.5	1418	5.5	2036	1.6
14	W	0248	5.4	0859	1.8	1459	5.1	2123	1.9
15	TH	0341	5.0	0953	2.1	1605	4.8	◐ 2222	2.1
16	F	0453	4.8	1101	2.3	1725	4.6	2335	2.2
17	SA	0603	4.8	1221	2.3	1834	4.7		
18	SU	0057	2.1	0707	5.0	1339	2.0	1935	5.0
19	M	0203	1.8	0804	5.4	1431	1.7	2027	5.4
20	TU	0250	1.5	0850	5.7	1513	1.3	2112	5.7
21	W	0331	1.3	0932	6.0	1552	1.1	2153	6.0
22	TH	0410	1.0	1011	6.3	1630	0.9	2233	6.2
23	F	0448	0.9	1050	6.4	1709	0.8	○ 2314	6.4
24	SA	0527	0.8	1130	6.5	1749	0.7	2355	6.4
25	SU	0609	0.8	1210	6.5	1832	0.7		
26	M	0037	6.4	0653	0.8	1253	6.4	1917	0.8
27	TU	0122	6.3	0740	1.0	1339	6.1	2007	0.9
28	W	0212	6.0	0832	1.2	1431	5.8	2101	1.2
29	TH	0311	5.8	0932	1.4	1534	5.5	2206	1.4
30	F	0422	5.5	1043	1.6	1652	5.3	◑ 2320	1.6

DECEMBER

Date	Day	Time	m	Time	m	Time	m	Time	m
1	SA	0541	5.4	1201	1.7	1814	5.2		
2	SU	0036	1.6	0656	5.5	1312	1.5	1927	5.4
3	M	0142	1.4	0801	5.7	1412	1.3	2029	5.6
4	TU	0238	1.2	0856	6.0	1504	1.1	2121	5.8
5	W	0326	1.1	0943	6.2	1550	0.9	2208	6.0
6	TH	0411	1.0	1027	6.3	1633	0.8	2251	6.1
7	F	0453	0.9	1107	6.3	1714	0.8	● 2331	6.2
8	SA	0532	0.9	1144	6.3	1753	0.8		
9	SU	0008	6.2	0609	1.0	1219	6.2	1828	0.9
10	M	0042	6.1	0644	1.1	1250	6.0	1903	1.0
11	TU	0114	6.0	0718	1.2	1321	5.8	1938	1.2
12	W	0147	5.8	0754	1.4	1353	5.6	2015	1.4
13	TH	0220	5.6	0834	1.6	1429	5.3	2056	1.6
14	F	0259	5.3	0920	1.9	1513	5.0	2144	1.8
15	SA	0350	5.1	1015	2.0	1614	4.8	◐ 2242	2.0
16	SU	0502	5.0	1120	2.1	1736	4.7	2348	2.1
17	M	0613	5.0	1228	2.0	1844	4.9		
18	TU	0056	2.0	0713	5.2	1333	1.8	1942	5.2
19	W	0158	1.7	0808	5.5	1428	1.5	2034	5.5
20	TH	0251	1.5	0857	5.9	1517	1.2	2123	5.8
21	F	0338	1.2	0943	6.1	1602	0.9	2210	6.1
22	SA	0423	1.0	1028	6.4	1647	0.7	○ 2256	6.3
23	SU	0509	0.8	1113	6.5	1733	0.6	2343	6.5
24	M	0555	0.7	1159	6.5	1821	0.5		
25	TU	0030	6.5	0643	0.7	1246	6.5	1909	0.6
26	W	0120	6.4	0732	0.8	1335	6.3	2000	0.7
27	TH	0210	6.3	0824	0.9	1427	6.1	2053	0.8
28	F	0304	6.1	0920	1.1	1523	5.8	2150	1.1
29	SA	0402	5.8	1021	1.3	1625	5.5	◑ 2253	1.3
30	SU	0505	5.6	1128	1.5	1732	5.3		
31	M	0000	1.5	0612	5.5	1238	1.6	1845	5.2

Chart Datum: 3·27 metres below Ordnance Datum (Newlyn). HAT is 6·9 metres above Chart Datum.

9.3.8 BRIGHTON

E. Sussex **50°48'·53N 00°06'·38W** ✿✿✿◊◊◊✿✿✿

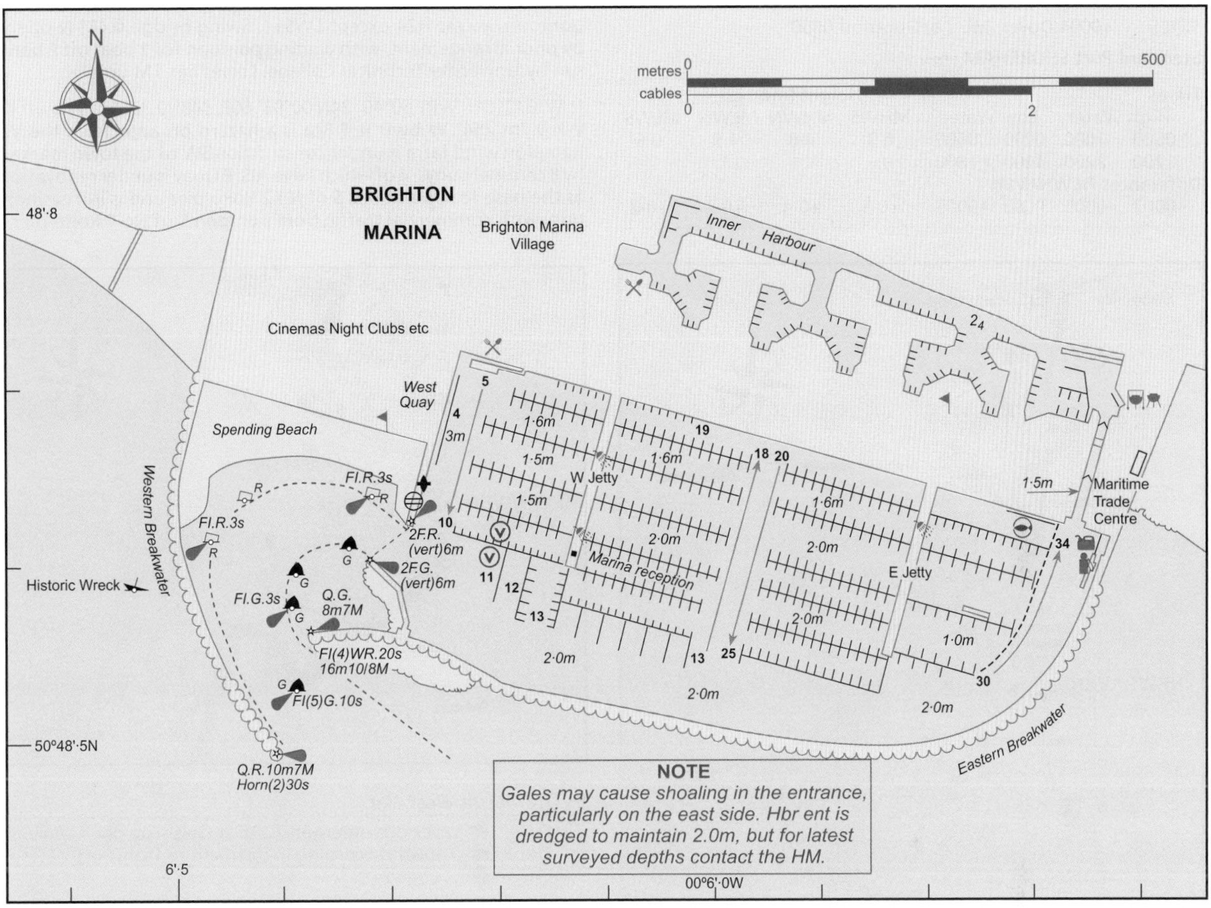

N
metres 0
500
cables 0
2
48'·8
BRIGHTON
MARINA
Brighton Marina Village
Inner Harbour
Cinemas Night Clubs etc
24
West Quay
5
4
3m
1·6m
1·5m
1·5m
19
1·6m
18 20
W Jetty
Spending Beach
Fl.R.3s
R
R
Fl.R.3s
R
2F.R. (vert)6m
10
2F.G. (vert)6m
11
12
13
G
G
G
Fl.G.3s
Q.G. 8m7M
Western Breakwater
Historic Wreck
Marina reception
2·0m
1·6m
2·0m
2·0m
E Jetty
1·5m
Maritime Trade Centre
34
1·0m
Fl(4)WR.20s 16m10/8M
2·0m
13
25
30
2·0m
2·0m
G
Fl(5)G.10s
50°48'·5N
Q.R.10m7M Horn(2)30s
Eastern Breakwater
NOTE
Gales may cause shoaling in the entrance, particularly on the east side. Hbr ent is dredged to maintain 2.0m, but for latest surveyed depths contact the HM.
6'·5
00°6'·0W

CHARTS AC 5605, 1652, 1991; Imray C12, C31, C9, 2100

TIDES +0004 Dover; ML 3·5; Duration 0605

Standard Port SHOREHAM (⟵)

Times				Height (metres)			
High Water		Low Water		MHWS	MHWN	MLWN	MLWS
0500	1000	0000	0600	6·3	4·8	1·9	0·6
1700	2200	1200	1800				
Differences BRIGHTON MARINA							
–0002	–0002	0000	0000	+0·2	+0·2	+0·1	+0·1

SHELTER Good in the marina under all conditions, but in strong S'ly winds confused seas can make the final appr very rough. Speed limit 5kn. Depths reported are less than shown, HM recommends that yachts drawing 2m or more do not to enter hbr at LW ± 2hrs.

NAVIGATION WPT 50°48'·23N 00°06'·39W, 000°/0·26M to W bkwtr lt.

- Ent chan dredged 1·7m, but after gales shoaling occurs especially on E side; craft drawing >1·5m should keep to the W side of chan until past the second SHM buoy.
- In heavy weather, best appr is from SSE to avoid worst of the backlash from bkwtrs; beware shallow water E of ent in R sector of lt Fl (4) WR 20s.

W-going stream starts at Brighton HW–1½ and E-going at HW+4½. Inshore the sp rate reaches approx 1·5kn. A Historic Wreck is at 50°48'·6N 00°06'·49W, immediately W of the marina's W bkwtr.

LIGHTS AND MARKS The marina is at the E end of the town, where white cliffs extend eastward. Daymark: conspic white hospital block, brg 334° leads to ent. Six Y spar lt buoys (up to 2M offshore) used as racing buoys:

1. 50°48'·06N 00°06'·41W	2. 50°47'·61N 00°08'·43W
3. 50°46'·61N 00°07'·00W	4. 50°47'·00N 00°15'·33W
5. 50°48'·40N 00°19'·40W	6. 50°47'·40N 00°05'·00W

A sewer outfall can buoy, Fl Y 5s, is 1·1M off the coast. Navigational lts may be hard to see against shore glare:

E bkwtr hd QG 8m 7M. W bkwtr hd, tr R/W bands, QR 10m 7M; Horn (2) 30s. Inner Hbr lock controlled by normal R/G lts, 0800-1800LT.

COMMUNICATIONS (Code 01273) NMOC (02392) 552100; Police 101; Ⓗ 696955; Dr 686863; HM 819919; Call: *Brighton Control* VHF Ch **M** 80 16 (H24).

FACILITIES **Brighton Marina** www. premiermarinas.com ☎819919; Inner Hbr has least depth of 2·4m. 1600⌓ inc Ⓥ £2·41, £1·00 <4hrs, ♿ ⊡ ⚓ ▲ ⚒ ⚔ ⊡ Ⓔ ⚓ ⚓ ⚓(60t) ⚓(35t) Divers ⚓ ACA ✕ ⊡. Fuel pontoon ⛽ ⛽ ▲ (H24).

Brighton Marina YC ☎818711, ✕ ⊡.

Bus service from marina; timetable info ☎674881. Electric railway runs from marina to Palace Pier, Mar-Oct.

Town ✉ Ⓑ ⊡ ✕ ⊡ ⇌ ✈ (Gatwick).

9.3.9 NEWHAVEN

E. Sussex **50°46′·84N 00°03′·53E** ✽✽✽◊◊◊✿✿

CHARTS AC 5605, 1652, 2154; Imray C12, C31, C9, 2100

TIDES +0004 Dover; ML 3·6; Duration 0550

Standard Port SHOREHAM (⟵)

Times				Height (metres)			
High Water		Low Water		MHWS	MHWN	MLWN	MLWS
0500	1000	0000	0600	6·3	4·8	1·9	0·6
1700	2200	1200	1800				
Differences NEWHAVEN							
–0003	–0005	0000	+0005	+0·5	+0·4	+0·2	+0·2

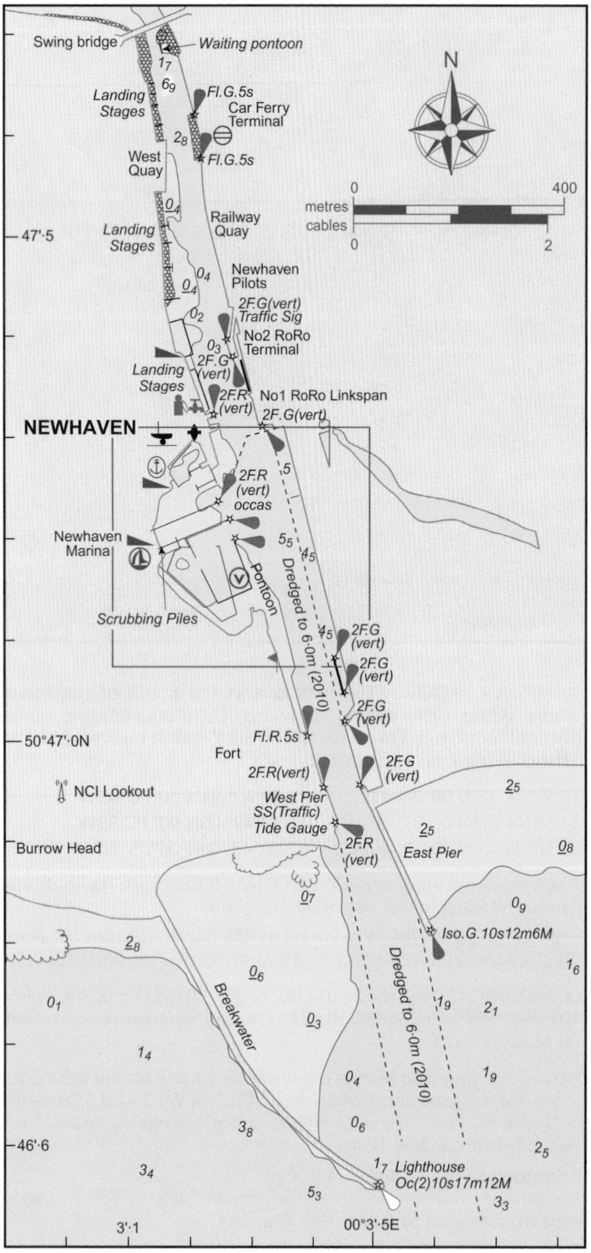

SHELTER Good in all weathers, but in strong onshore winds there is often a dangerous sea at the ent. Appr from the SW, to pass 50m off bkwtr hd to avoid heavy breaking seas on E side of dredged chan. At marina (mostly dredged to 1m), berth on inside of Ⓥ pontoon, access H24 except LWS±1. Swing bridge 0.4M N opens by prior arrangement, with waiting pontoon for 1 boat off E bank run by University Technical College. Lewes lies 7M upriver.

NAVIGATION WPT 50°46′·24N 00°03′·60E, 348°/0·32M to W bwtr lt. Wk 3·7m 254° W bwtr lt 1·8ca is a hazard on appr from the W. Rampion wind farm is under construction SW of the town marked by 8 cardinal buoys, 4 of which have AIS. E Quay is under renovation as the base for operations S of No 2 RoRo pier and is increasingly busy with commercial traffic from pontoon S of No 1 RoRo pier.

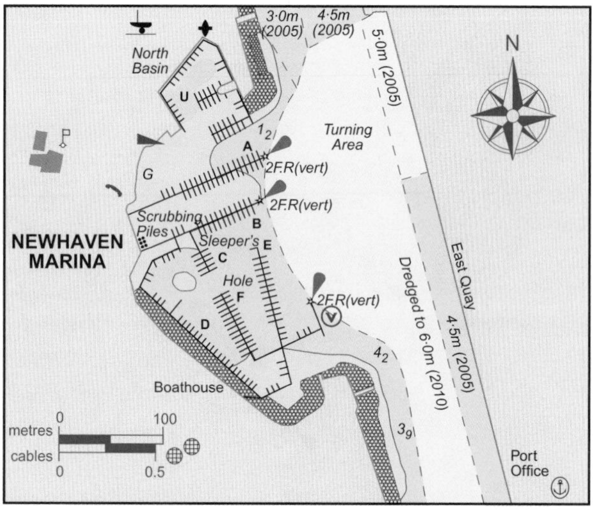

SS (Traffic) on West Pier

Fl Fl Fl	● ● ●	Serious emergency. All vessels stop or divert according to instructions from Port Control
F F F	● ● ●	No vessel to proceed contrary to this signal
F F F	● ● ○	Small vessels may proceed. Two way traffic
F F F	● ○ ●	Proceed only when instructed by Port Control. All other vessels keep clear

Caution: Hbr silts and dredging is continuous. Do not leave marina when 3FR(vert) are lit at NE ent. Do not proceed S of RoRo terminal when 3FR(vert) are lit at NW corner of pontoon. Beware ferries; check on VHF Ch 12. Speed limit 5kn.

LIGHTS AND MARKS Lt ho on west breakwater is conspic.

COMMUNICATIONS (Code 01273) NMOC (02392) 552100; Police 101; Dr 515076; Ⓗ696955; HM / Port Control vts@newhavenport authority.co.uk ☎612926 (H24).

'Newhaven Radio' Ch 12 (H24). Swing bridge opening Ch 12. Marina Ch **80** M (0800-1700).

FACILITIES **Marina** www.newhavenmarina.co.uk ☎513881; 280+20Ⓥ £2·30, (HO,1ca N of marina entrance) (18t) (10t); ☎612612 (£17·50).

Newhaven and Seaford SC ☎(01323) 890077.

Town: Ⓔ ACA Ⓑ (Gatwick); **Ferries:** Dieppe; 2-3/day; 4hrs; Transmanche Ferries (transmancheferries.co.uk).

9.3.10 EASTBOURNE

E. Sussex **50°47′·34N 00°19′·90E**

CHARTS AC 536, 5605; Imray 12, C31, C8, 2100

TIDES –0005 Dover; ML 3·8; Duration 0540

Standard Port SHOREHAM (⟵)

Times				**Height (metres)**			
High Water		Low Water		MHWS	MHWN	MLWN	MLWS
0500	1000	0000	0600	6·3	4·8	1·9	0·6
1700	2200	1200	1800				
Differences EASTBOURNE							
–0010	–0005	+0015	+0020	+1·1	+0·6	+0·2	+0·1

SHELTER Very good, but in strong SE'lies the entrance may be hazardous and should be avoided at HW±1½. Access via buoyed channel (2m) and twin locks into inner basin (4m). The channel is prone to shoaling after gales and is dredged regularly. If uncertain of up-to-date situation, contact HM before entry.

NAVIGATION WPT 50°47′·37N 00°20′·81E, SWM buoy 'SH', L Fl 10s, 259°/0·45M to hbr ent. There are shoals to the NE in Pevensey Bay and from 2·5M SE toward Royal Sovereign lt (tide rips). From Beachy Hd, keep 0·75M offshore to clear Holywell Bank. 3kn speed limit in approach chan and Sovereign Harbour.

LIGHTS AND MARKS See 9.3.4 and chartlet. From E, by day R roofs are conspic. Dir lt, Fl WRG 5s leads 258° through appr channel. Large wreck on N side marked by 2 lit SHM. Eastbourne pier, 2 FR, is 2M S of hbr ent; unlit PHM buoy is approx 5ca S.

COMMUNICATIONS (Code 01323) CGOC (01304) 210008; Police 101; Dr470370; Ⓗ 417400. HM 470099. **VHF Ch 17 call *Sovereign Hbr* at SWM.**

SAFETY RECOMMENDATIONS

- Monitor VHF Ch **17** (H24) for nav info, lock status and berthing.
- Always follow IPTS (Sigs 2, 3 and 5) for locks entry.
- At busy periods obey instructions of Lock Keeper or Assistant on lock-side or directions by VHF.
- Locks close every H and H+30.
- Always approach locks with fenders (set about 1m above the waterline) and mooring lines rigged on both sides of craft. Secure to the pontoons as far to the front of the lock as possible. Set springs to reduce surging, particularly at LW.
- Switch off engines and radar whilst in lock.
- When secured alongside, assist other craft berthing.

FACILITIES **Sovereign Harbour** www.premiermarinas.com ☎470099, 860 £3·10<8m, £3·30<12.5m, (H24) (50t) . **Sovereign Harbour YC** ☎470888, visitors welcome. **Retail Park** with S/market and all domestic facilities. **Town** (2½M) all needs, ✈ (Gatwick).

ADJACENT ANCHORAGE

HASTINGS, E Sussex, **50°50′·88N 00°35′·50E**. AC 536. Tides, see RYE; ML 3·8m; Duration 0530. Strictly a settled weather ⚓ or emergency shelter. The stone breakwater is in disrepair and only protects FVs. Beware dangerous wreck 3ca SE of pier hd. Ldg lts 356°, both FR 14/55m 4M: front on W metal column; rear 357m from front, on 5-sided W tr on West Hill. Pier under refit, now lit Q R 1s. W bkwtr hd Fl R 2·5s 5m 4M; Fl G 5s 2m, 30m from head of No3 Groyne (E bkwtr). A Historic Wreck (*Amsterdam*) is about 2M W of pier, close inshore at 50°50′·7N 00°31′·65E. Facilities: ACA (St Leonards). Few marine services, but domestic facilities at Hastings and St Leonards. YC ☎(01424) 420656.

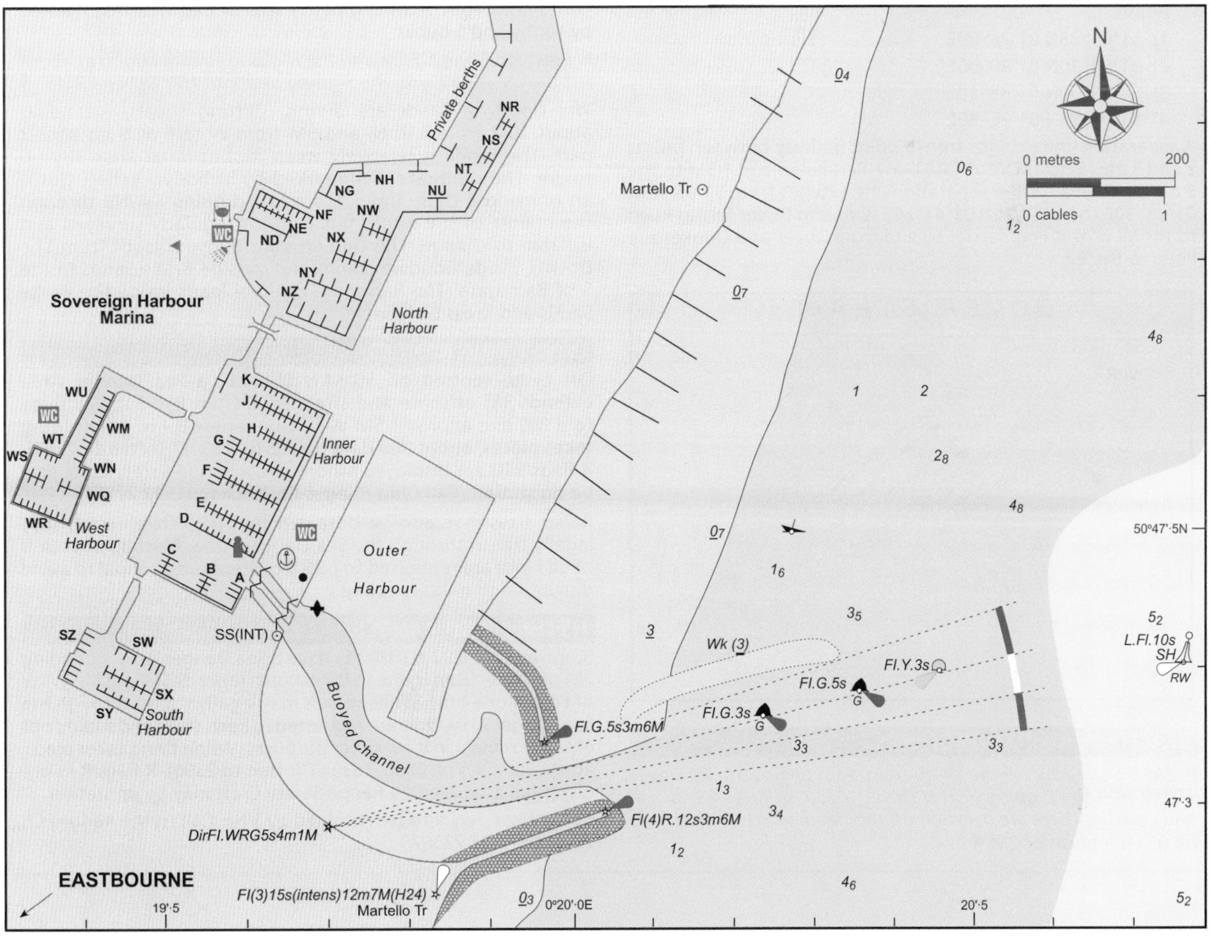

CROSSING THE EASTERN ENGLISH CHANNEL

This section applies to crossings, ranging from the short (4–5hrs) Dover Strait route to Boulogne or Calais to the moderate (10–15hrs) ones from Brighton, Newhaven or Eastbourne to Dieppe and adjacent French ports. Distance tables are at 9.0.5. Routes cross the Dover Strait TSS where the SW-bound lane lies only 7M S of Beachy Head and 4.5M SE of Dover.

- Dover to Calais or Boulogne is only about 25M but crosses the most congested part of Dover Strait TSS.
- Plan to use the tidal streams to minimise crossing time and to be up-tide and to windward of the destination port when clear of the TSS.
- Always cross the TSS on a heading of 90° to the traffic flow, and minimise the time spent in the TSS. Be prepared to motor.
- When crossing the TSS, listen to the VHF broadcasts of navigational and traffic information made by CNIS on Ch 11. These include details of vessels which appear to be contravening Rule 10.
- Keep a very sharp lookout for ships in the traffic lanes and cross-Channel ferries. Ensure that the crew is aware of the directions from which to expect traffic in the TSS.
- Unless equipped with radar, and you are competent in its operation, do not attempt the crossing if fog or poor visibility is forecast. Even with radar, navigate with extreme caution.
- A Voluntary Separation Scheme (VSS) is in use to help ferries safely cross the Dover TSS. It is not a formal separation scheme and is not shown on official charts, but small craft should be aware of its existence. Most cross-Channel ferries can be expected to be using the VSS but high speed ferries are not included in the scheme. The VSS is bounded by the following points:
  1) 51°05′·35N 01°28′·00E
  2) 51°00′·10N 01°40′·00E
  3) 50°59′·30N 01°39′·10E
  4) 51°04′·70N 01°26′·80E

A separation line extends from a point midway between points 2 and 3 above to 1M W of CA6 buoy. Parallel to and 1·5M to the E of this zone a further separation line extends from 51°06′·40N 01°29′·90E to 51°01′·20N 01°41′·60E. Calais to Dover ferries keep to the W of this line; ferries to and from Dover and Dunkerque keep to the E.

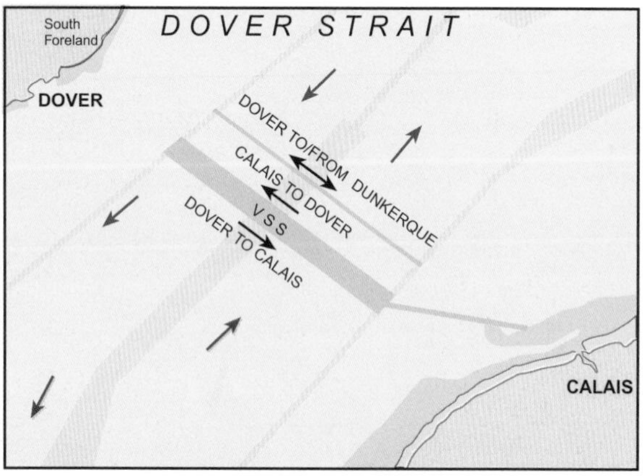

BEACHY HEAD TO DUNGENESS

▶ *2M S of Beachy Hd the W-going stream begins at HW Dover +0030, and the E-going at HW Dover –0520, sp rates 2·25kn. In bad weather there are overfalls off the Head, which should then be given a berth of 2M.*◀

(AC *536*) Royal Sovereign lt tr is 7·4M E of Beachy Head. The extensive Royal Sovereign shoals lie from 3M NW of the tr to 1·5M N of it, and have a minimum depth of 3·5m.

▶ *There are strong eddies over the shoals at Sp, and the sea breaks on them in bad weather.* ◀

On the direct course from the Royal Sovereign to Dungeness there are no dangers. Along the coast in Pevensey and Rye Bays there are drying rocky ledges or shoals extending 5ca offshore in places. These include Boulder Bank near Wish Tr, S of Eastbourne; Oyster Reef off Cooden; Bexhill Reef off Bexhill-on-Sea; Bopeep Rocks off St Leonards; and the shoals at the mouth of R Rother, at the entrance to Rye. There are also banks 2–3M offshore, on which the sea builds in bad weather.

Avoid the firing range danger area between Rye and Dungeness (lt, fog sig, RC). The nuclear power station is conspic at S extremity of the low-lying spit. The point is steep-to on SE side.

▶ *2M SE of Dungeness the NE-going flood starts at HW Dover –0100, max Sp rate 1.9kn. The SW-going ebb starts at HW Dover +0430, max Sp rate 2.1kn.* ◀

DUNGENESS TO NORTH FORELAND

(AC 1892, 1828) From Dungeness to Folkestone the coast forms a bay. Beware Roar bank, depth 2·7m, E of New Romney: otherwise there are no off-lying dangers apart from Hythe firing range. Good ⚓ off Sandgate in offshore winds.

▶ *Off Folkestone the E-going stream starts at HW Dover –0155, Sp rate 2kn; the W-going at HW Dover +0320, sp rate 1·5kn.* ◀

Passing Dover and S Foreland keep 1M offshore. Do not pass too close to Dover as the many ferries leave at speed and there can be considerable backwash. It is advisable to call Dover Port Control (Ch 74) to identify yourself before passing the harbour entrances. 8M S of Dover in the TSS is the Varne, a shoal 7M long, with least depth 3·3m and heavy seas in bad weather, marked by Lanby and 5 buoys.

▶ *Between S and N Foreland the N-going stream begins at about HW Dover –0150, and the S-going at about HW Dover +0415.* ◀

The Goodwin Sands are drying, shifting shoals, extending about 10M from S to N, and 5M from W to E at their widest part. The E side is relatively steep-to, but large areas dry up to 3m. The sands are well marked by lit buoys. Kellett Gut is an unmarked chan about 5ca wide, running SW/NE through the middle of the sands, but it is not regularly surveyed and is liable to change. The Gull Stream (buoyed) leads from The Downs, inside Goodwin Sands and outside Brake Sands to the S of Ramsgate. The Ramsgate channel leads inside the Brake Sands and Cross Ledge.

LYDD FIRING RANGES

Off Lydd, centred on 50°54′N 00°53′E, a Sea Danger Area extends 3M offshore and stretches E from Rye Fairway buoy to a N/S line approx 1·5M W of Dungeness lt ho. When firing takes places, about 300 days p.a. 0830–1630LT (often to 2300), R flags/R lts are displayed ashore and a Range Safety Craft may be on station. Call Lydd Ranges Ch **73** or ☎01303 225518.

Radar fixes may also be obtained by VHF. While vessels may legally transit through the Sea Danger Area, Masters of vessels of all kinds are requested to pass S of Stephenson Shoal to avoid disruption of military firings.

HYTHE FIRING RANGES

(Centred on 51°02′N 01°03′E) have a Sea Danger Area extending 2M offshore, from Hythe to Dymchurch (approx 5M and 8M WSW of Folkestone hbr). While vessels may legally transit through the Sea Danger Area, they are requested to keep clear, and should not enter or remain in it for other purposes. When firing takes place, about 300 days pa 0830–1630 LT (often to 2300), R flags/R lts are displayed ashore and a Range Safety Craft may be on station.

Radar fixes may also be obtained by VHF. Call *Hythe Ranges* Ch **73** or ☎01303 225879.

9.3.11 RYE

E. Sussex **50°55'·60N 00°46'·58E**

CHARTS AC 5605, 536, 1991; Imray C12, C31, C8, 2100

TIDES ML 2·0; Duration 3·25hrs sp, 5hrs nps

Standard Port DOVER (⟶)

Times				**Height (metres)**			
High Water		Low Water		MHWS	MHWN	MLWN	MLWS
0000	0600	0100	0700	6·8	5·3	2·1	0·8
1200	1800	1300	1900				
Differences RYE (approaches)							
+0005	–0010	ND	ND	+1·0	+0·7	ND	ND
RYE HARBOUR							
+0005	–0010	DR	DR	–1·4	–1·7	DR	DR
HASTINGS							
0000	–0010	–0030	–0030	+0·8	+0·5	+0·1	–0·1

SHELTER Very good in R Rother which dries completely to soft mud. Rye Bay is exposed to prevailing SW'lies with little shelter, when there is good ⚓ in lee of Dungeness (6M to E). In N'lies ⚓ 5ca N of the Rye Fairway buoy.

Rye Hbr is a small village, ¾M inside ent on W bank, used by commercial shipping. Berth initially on Admiralty Jetty (E bank) and see HM for pontoon or M. No ⚓. Max speed 6kn.

Rye Town (a Cinque Port) is 2M upriver. Enter via Rock Channel for Ⓥ pontoon along NE side of Strand Quay.

NAVIGATION WPT Rye Fairway SWM lt buoy, 50°54'·04N 00°48'·02E, 329°/1·8M to W Arm tripod lt, 50°55'·55N 00°46'·65E. For details of Lydd and Hythe Firing Ranges see Passage Information (⟵).

- Bar dries 2·75m about 2ca offshore and needs care when wind >F6 from SE to SW. Also shoals E and W of ent with ground swell or surf; narrow ent (42m) and chan (30m).
- Enter HW –2 to HW +2; flood runs 4·5kn (max HW –2 to HW –1).
- Depth of water over the bar can be judged by day from horizontal timbers at base of West Arm tripod structure (approx 2ca N of the bar) these are set at 1·5, 3 and 4·5m above CD.

Note: A Historic Wreck (*Anne*) is about 4M WSW of Rye, close inshore at 50°53'·42N 00°41'·91E.

LIGHTS AND MARKS W Arm lt LFl R 7s 7m 6M, wooden tripod, radar reflector. E Arm hd, Q (9) 15s 7m 5M; Horn 7s, G △. On E Pier a floodlit 'Welcome to Rye' sign may be helpful. Rock Chan entrance marked by a QR and QG lt buoy.

IPTS (Sigs 2 & 5 only) are shown to seaward (3M) from HM's office and upriver (1M) from HM's office.

COMMUNICATIONS (Code 01797) CGOC (01304) 210008; Police 101; Dr 222031; Ⓗ 224499. HM 225225 Ch 14 (0900-1700LT, HW±2 or when vessel due). Call HM and monitor Ch 14 before arrival/departure.

FACILITIES (from seaward) **Admiralty Jetty**

Rye Hbr HW±3 (26t launch £10) Ⓔ (3t/15t) ACA

Rye Hbr SC (Sec'y) ☎223376.

Rye Town, Strand Quay, £14.75<8m>£17.74<10m>£23.57 wood fender posts against steel piled wall with numbered ladders. Ⓥ must stop at timber staging on E bank and report to HM Office.

Town ✉ Ⓑ ⇌ ✈ (Lydd).

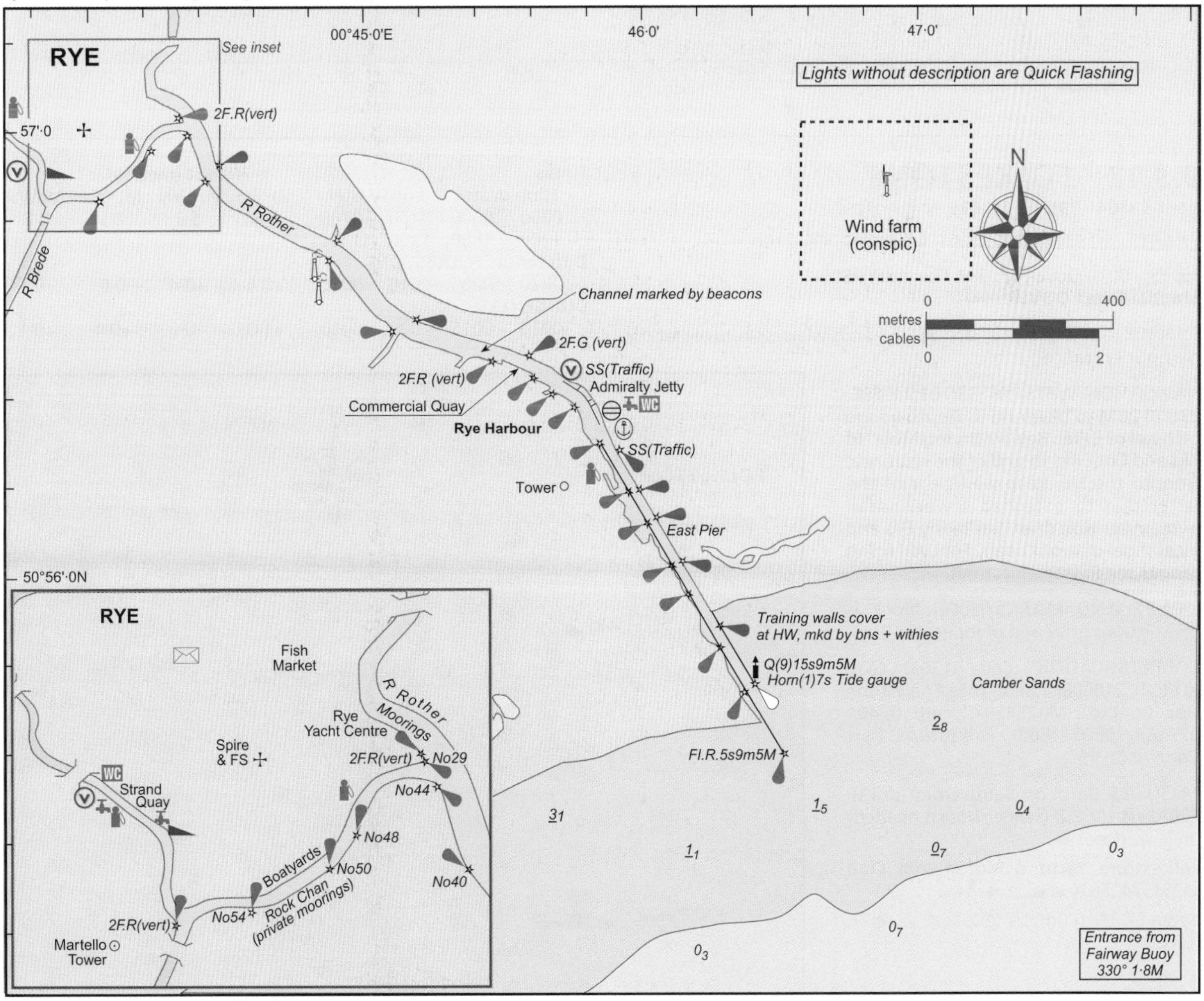
RYE
See inset
00°45·0'E
46·0'
47·0'
Lights without description are Quick Flashing
2F.R(vert)
57'·0
R Rother
R Brede
Wind farm
(conspic)
N
Channel marked by beacons
0
400
metres
cables
0
2
2F.G (vert)
2F.R (vert)
SS(Traffic)
Admiralty Jetty
Commercial Quay
Rye Harbour
SS(Traffic)
Tower
East Pier
50°56'·0N
Training walls cover
at HW, mkd by bns + withies
Q(9)15s9m5M
Horn(1)7s Tide gauge
Camber Sands
Fl.R.5s9m5M
RYE
Fish
Market
R Rother
Moorings
Rye
Yacht Centre
Spire
& FS
2F.R(vert)
No29
Strand
Quay
No44
No48
Boatyards
No50
No40
Rock Chan
(private moorings)
No54
2F.R(vert)
Martello
Tower
Entrance from
Fairway Buoy
330° 1·8M

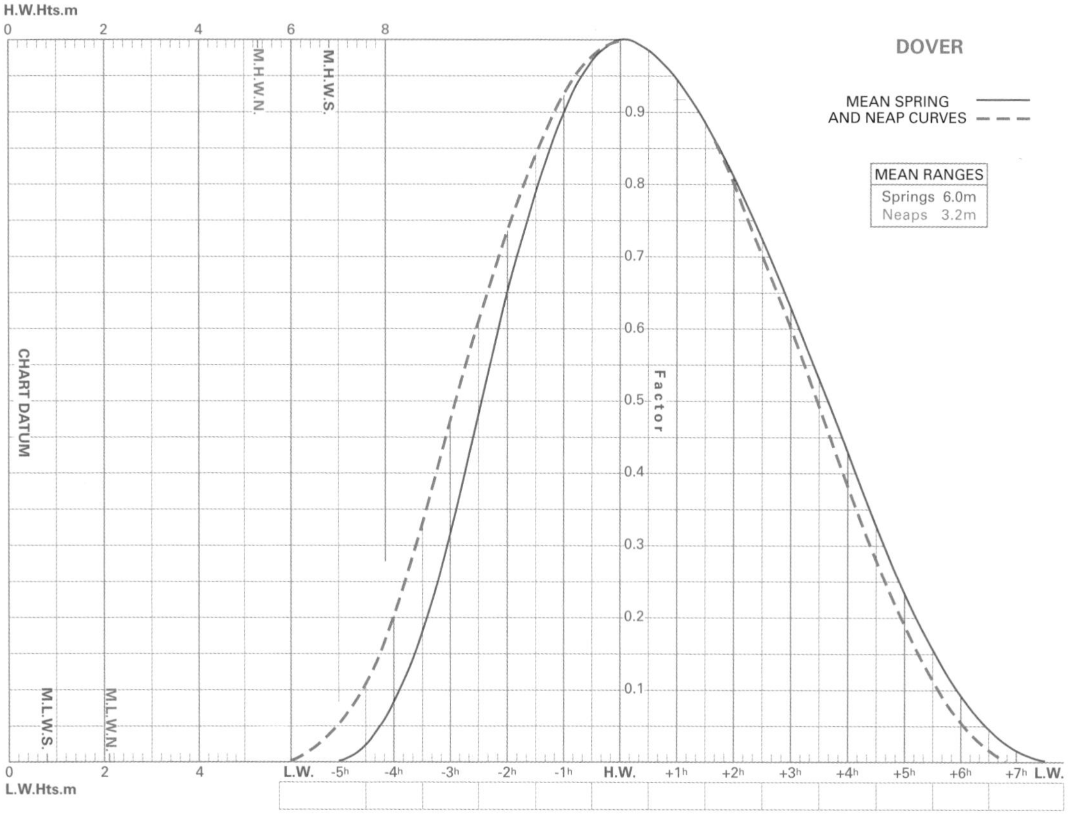

9.3.12 FOLKESTONE

Kent **51°04'·59N 01°11'·67E**

CHARTS AC 5605, 1892, 1991; Imray C12, C8, 2100

TIDES –0010 Dover; ML 3·9; Duration 0500

Standard Port DOVER (⟶)

Times				Height (metres)			
High Water		Low Water		MHWS	MHWN	MLWN	MLWS
0000	0600	0100	0700	6·8	5·3	2·1	0·8
1200	1800	1300	1900				
Differences FOLKESTONE							
–0020	–0005	–0010	–0010	+0·4	+0·4	0·0	–0·1
DUNGENESS							
–0010	–0015	–0020	–0010	+1·0	+0·6	+0·4	+0·1

SHELTER Good except in strong E-S winds when seas break at the harbour entrance.

NAVIGATION WPT 51°04'·33N 01°11'·89E, 330°/0·26M to bkwtr hd lt. Depth gauge on head of E Pier. Beware drying Mole Hd Rks and Copt Rks to stbd of the entrance; from/to the NE, keep well clear of the latter due to extended sewer outfall pipe. Inner Hbr, dries, has many FVs and local shoal draught boats. For Lydd firing ranges see Passage Information.

LIGHTS AND MARKS Hotel block is conspicuous at W end of Inner Hbr.

COMMUNICATIONS (Code 01303) CGOC (01304) 210008; Police 101. Folkestone Hbr Co Ltd/HM 254597, mob 07401 627563 (0600–1800); *Folkestone Port Control* Ch 15.

FACILITIES Berth on **South Quay** (dries); £20/craft for (fender board needed) or ⚓. (free).

Folkestone Yacht & Motor Boat Club ☎251574, F&A.

Town (100m) ✉ Ⓑ ✕ ⇄ ✈ (Lydd).

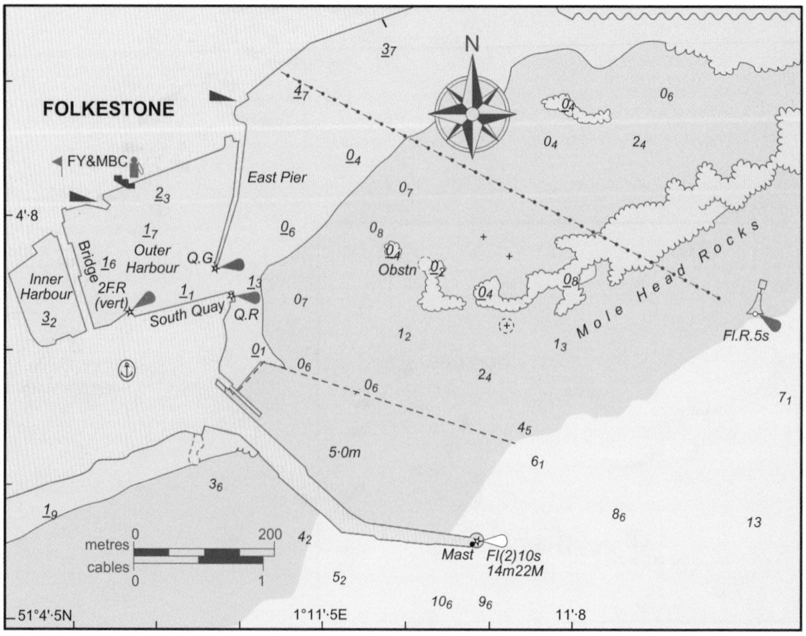

9.3.13 DOVER

Kent **51°06'·74N 01°19'·73E** (W ent) ❀❀❀◊◊◊✿✿
51°07'·25N 01°20'·61E (E ent)

CHARTS AC 5605,1892, 1828, 1698; Imray C30, C12, C8, 2100

TIDES 0000 Dover; ML 3·7; Duration 0505

Standard Port DOVER (⟶)

Times				Height (metres)			
High Water		Low Water		MHWS	MHWN	MLWN	MLWS
0000	0600	0100	0700	6·8	5·3	2·1	0·8
1200	1800	1300	1900				
Differences DEAL							
+0012	+0010	+0004	+0002	−0·5	−0·3	0·0	+0·1

SHELTER Very good in marina. ⚓ in outer harbour only with permission of Port Control clear of extensive seasonal (Apr-Oct) swim zone along N shore. ⚓ Exposed in winds NE'ly through S to SW'ly. Small craft must not be left unattended at ⚓.

NAVIGATION WPT from SW, 51°06'·18N 01°19'·67E, 000°/0·5M to Admiralty Pier lt ho. WPT from NE, 51°07'·30N 01°21'·41E, 270°/0·5M to S end Eastern Arm. Beware overfalls outside the bkwtrs and the frequent ferries and high speed craft using both ents. Strong tides across ents and high walls make ent under sail slow and difficult; use of engine is very strongly recommended.

- **Specific permission** to ent/leave the hbr via E or W ent must first be obtained from Port Control on Ch **74**; Call *Port Control* when 2M off and comply with instructions. Clearance for small/slow craft is not normally given until within 200m of ent. Ⓥ are welcomed by hbr launch and usually escorted to the marina.
- Vessels with a draught >2.5m bound for the marina must inform Port Control, Ch **74**, prior to entry as must yachts without engine.
- **If no VHF**: Stay safe distance clear of either entrance, call Port Control +44(0)1304 241669 or make visual contact (lamp) with Port Control (E Arm) who may direct launch to assist.
- Extensive redevelopment of the W docks and Prince of Wales Pier is underway. Avoid buoyed exclusion zone marking new marina.

Note: A historic wreck is adjacent to the Eastern Arm bkwtr at 51°07'·6N 01°20'·7E (see chartlet). There are 4 more Historic wrecks on the Goodwin Sands.

LIGHTS AND MARKS As per 9.3.4 and chartlet. **IPTS** (for all vessels) are shown for the E ent by Port Control (conspic twr) at S end of E Arm and for W entrance, from the head of Admiralty Pier. Q W lt from Port Control twr or patrol launch = keep clear of ent you are approaching.

COMMUNICATIONS (Code 01304) CGOC 210008; Police 101; Ⓗ (01233) 633331. Port Control 240400 ext 5530 HM 240400 ext 4520. Duty HM mob 07836 262713.

Call *Dover Port Control* (also Hbr launch) Ch **74**, 12, 16 for clearance to enter. Request clearance to leave hbr as soon as clear of the marina. *Dover Marina* Ch 80, only within marina. *Dover Coastguard* Ch 16, maintains TSS surveillance.

Chan Nav Info Service (CNIS) broadcasts tfc/ nav/weather/tidal info Ch 11 at H+40; also, if vis <2M, at H+55.

FACILITIES Dover Harbour Marina ☎241663; on arrival berth at reception pontoon to visit marina office or await gate opening call 241669. 3 berthing options are available in the marina:

- Tidal hbr, E of waiting pontoon (1·5m), access H24. 107 on 3 pontoons (C, B, A) in 2·5m, £2·70. Mostly for single night stop.
- Granville Dock, gate open approx HW–3½ to +4½, 133, £2·40.
- Wellington Dock. Gate and swing bridge open HW ±2 nps and approx HW–1½ to HW+1½ or 2½ sp, depending on range. In the final appr, especially near LW, stay in deep water as defined by the W sector (324°-333°) of the F WR lt, 2 unlit SHM poles and a G conical buoy. IPTS are shown, plus a small Fl ● lt 5 mins before Wellington bridge is swung open. 160 £2·20.

Services www.doverport.co.uk 370 inc Ⓥ (H24) (0500–2100), LPG Ⓔ (50t) ACA, wi-fi.

Royal Cinque Ports YC www.rcpyc.co.uk ☎206262.

White Cliffs M and YC www.wcmyc.co.uk ☎211666.

Town (H24) Ⓑ ≉.

Ferries Services to Calais (passenger/vehicle), Dunkerque (vehicle).

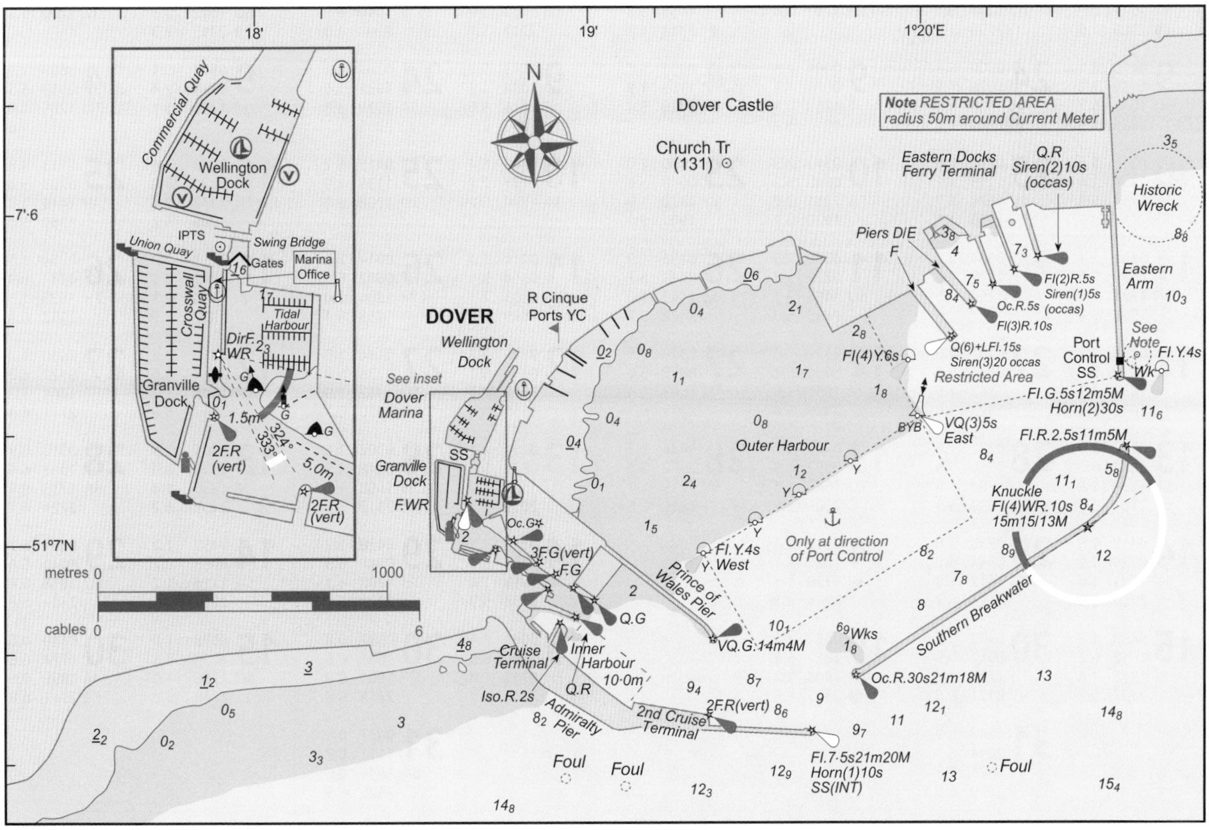

STANDARD TIME (UT)
For Summer Time add ONE hour in **non-shaded areas**

DOVER LAT 51°07′N LONG 1°19′E

TIMES AND HEIGHTS OF HIGH AND LOW WATERS

Dates in red are SPRINGS
Dates in blue are NEAPS

YEAR **2018**

JANUARY

Date	Time	m	Date	Time	m
1	0457	1.1	16	0539	1.4
	0955	6.8		1048	6.2
M	1731	0.9	TU	1753	1.3
	2224	6.8		2307	6.3
2	0555	0.9	17	0614	1.3
	1045	6.9		1120	6.3
TU	1829	0.8	W	1828	1.2
	○ 2312	6.9		● 2339	6.4
3	0650	0.7	18	0648	1.2
	1134	7.0		1152	6.3
W	1922	0.7	TH	1903	1.2
4	0000	7.0	19	0010	6.5
	0743	0.6		0723	1.2
TH	1223	6.9	F	1222	6.3
	2011	0.7		1937	1.2
5	0048	7.0	20	0038	6.5
	0832	0.6		0759	1.2
F	1311	6.8	SA	1250	6.3
	2056	0.8		2012	1.2
6	0136	6.9	21	0106	6.5
	0919	0.7		0834	1.2
SA	1401	6.6	SU	1319	6.3
	2138	1.0		2046	1.3
7	0225	6.7	22	0137	6.5
	1003	0.9		0909	1.3
SU	1453	6.3	M	1353	6.2
	2221	1.3		2120	1.4
8	0316	6.4	23	0215	6.4
	1049	1.2		0945	1.4
M	1547	6.0	TU	1434	6.1
	◑ 2306	1.6		2158	1.5
9	0410	6.1	24	0300	6.3
	1139	1.5		1026	1.5
TU	1646	5.7	W	1524	5.9
	2359	1.9		◐ 2244	1.7
10	0510	5.8	25	0355	6.0
	1234	1.8		1119	1.7
W	1754	5.4	TH	1626	5.7
				2343	1.9
11	0100	2.1	26	0504	5.8
	0618	5.6		1228	1.8
TH	1336	1.9	F	1754	5.5
	1907	5.4			
12	0206	2.1	27	0102	2.0
	0732	5.6		0632	5.8
F	1439	1.9	SA	1348	1.8
	2013	5.5		1923	5.6
13	0312	2.0	28	0222	1.8
	0837	5.7		0750	5.9
SA	1539	1.8	SU	1501	1.6
	2107	5.7		2030	5.9
14	0410	1.8	29	0333	1.5
	0929	5.9		0854	6.2
SU	1631	1.6	M	1612	1.3
	2153	6.0		2128	6.3
15	0459	1.5	30	0442	1.2
	1012	6.1		0952	6.5
M	1715	1.4	TU	1723	1.0
	2231	6.2		2221	6.6
			31	0548	0.9
				1044	6.7
			W	1825	0.8
				○ 2309	6.8

FEBRUARY

Date	Time	m	Date	Time	m
1	0647	0.6	16	0630	1.1
	1132	6.9		1128	6.3
TH	1918	0.6	F	1846	1.1
	2354	7.0		2346	6.5
2	0739	0.4	17	0707	1.0
	1216	6.9		1159	6.4
F	2004	0.6	SA	1922	1.0
3	0037	7.1	18	0015	6.6
	0824	0.4		0744	1.0
SA	1300	6.8	SU	1229	6.5
	2044	0.6		1956	1.0
4	0120	7.0	19	0045	6.6
	0905	0.5		0818	1.0
SU	1343	6.7	M	1259	6.5
	2120	0.8		2030	1.0
5	0203	6.8	20	0117	6.7
	0943	0.7		0852	1.0
M	1426	6.4	TU	1332	6.5
	2154	1.1		2102	1.1
6	0247	6.6	21	0153	6.7
	1019	1.0		0925	1.1
TU	1512	6.1	W	1411	6.4
	2229	1.4		2138	1.2
7	0333	6.2	22	0235	6.5
	1057	1.4		1003	1.3
W	1602	5.8	TH	1458	6.2
	◑ 2308	1.8		2220	1.5
8	0425	5.8	23	0326	6.2
	1143	1.8		1050	1.6
TH	1701	5.4	F	1555	5.8
				◐ 2314	1.8
9	0001	2.1	24	0431	5.8
	0526	5.5		1154	1.9
F	1243	2.1	SA	1719	5.4
	1810	5.2			
10	0113	2.3	25	0030	2.0
	0640	5.3		0608	5.6
SA	1351	2.2	SU	1320	1.9
	1926	5.2		1907	5.5
11	0226	2.3	26	0158	1.9
	0759	5.3		0743	5.7
SU	1456	2.1	M	1443	1.8
	2035	5.4		2022	5.7
12	0332	2.0	27	0316	1.6
	0906	5.6		0853	6.0
M	1555	1.8	TU	1603	1.4
	2129	5.8		2123	6.1
13	0427	1.7	28	0434	1.2
	0952	5.9		0952	6.4
TU	1646	1.5	W	1719	1.1
	2209	6.0		2215	6.5
14	0513	1.4			
	1026	6.1			
W	1729	1.3			
	2244	6.3			
15	0552	1.2			
	1057	6.2			
TH	1808	1.2			
	● 2315	6.4			

MARCH

Date	Time	m	Date	Time	m
1	0543	0.8	16	0526	1.2
	1042	6.6		1028	6.2
TH	1818	0.8	F	1744	1.2
	2301	6.8		2246	6.4
2	0639	0.5	17	0607	1.0
	1126	6.8		1101	6.4
F	1906	0.6	SA	1824	1.0
	○ 2342	7.0		● 2317	6.6
3	0726	0.4	18	0646	0.9
	1205	6.9		1133	6.5
SA	1948	0.5	SU	1901	0.9
				2349	6.7
4	0022	7.1	19	0724	0.8
	0807	0.3		1205	6.6
SU	1243	6.8	M	1937	0.8
	2023	0.6			
5	0101	7.0	20	0021	6.8
	0843	0.4		0759	0.8
M	1321	6.7	TU	1237	6.7
	2055	0.7		2010	0.8
6	0140	6.9	21	0056	6.8
	0915	0.7		0832	0.8
TU	1359	6.5	W	1313	6.7
	2123	1.0		2044	0.9
7	0218	6.6	22	0133	6.8
	0944	1.0		0906	0.9
W	1439	6.2	TH	1353	6.6
	2149	1.3		2121	1.1
8	0258	6.2	23	0216	6.6
	1012	1.4		0944	1.2
TH	1523	5.9	F	1440	6.3
	2217	1.7		2203	1.3
9	0343	5.8	24	0307	6.2
	1044	1.8		1031	1.5
F	1616	5.5	SA	1539	5.8
	◑ 2257	2.1		◐ 2258	1.7
10	0442	5.4	25	0415	5.7
	1137	2.2		1135	1.9
SA	1724	5.2	SU	1708	5.4
11	0010	2.4	26	0014	2.0
	0554	5.1		0602	5.5
SU	1303	2.4	M	1304	2.0
	1839	5.1		1853	5.4
12	0142	2.4	27	0144	1.9
	0714	5.1		0736	5.6
M	1418	2.3	TU	1432	1.9
	1955	5.3		2010	5.7
13	0254	2.1	28	0307	1.6
	0831	5.4		0848	5.9
TU	1521	2.0	W	1558	1.5
	2055	5.6		2112	6.1
14	0353	1.8	29	0428	1.2
	0921	5.7		0944	6.3
W	1615	1.6	TH	1708	1.1
	2138	5.9		2202	6.5
15	0443	1.4	30	0532	0.8
	0956	6.0		1031	6.6
TH	1702	1.4	F	1801	0.8
	2213	6.2		2245	6.8
			31	0623	0.5
				1111	6.7
			SA	1846	0.6
				○ 2325	6.9

APRIL

Date	Time	m	Date	Time	m
1	0706	0.4	16	0620	0.8
	1147	6.8		1105	6.6
SU	1924	0.6	M	1836	0.9
				● 2322	6.8
2	0003	7.0	17	0701	0.7
	0743	0.4		1140	6.8
M	1222	6.8	TU	1915	0.8
	1957	0.6		2358	6.9
3	0040	6.9	18	0738	0.7
	0816	0.6		1216	6.8
TU	1258	6.7	W	1952	0.7
	2026	0.8			
4	0116	6.8	19	0035	6.9
	0844	0.8		0814	0.7
W	1333	6.5	TH	1256	6.8
	2051	1.0		2029	0.8
5	0151	6.5	20	0117	6.8
	0907	1.1		0851	0.9
TH	1409	6.3	F	1341	6.6
	2112	1.3		2109	1.0
6	0225	6.2	21	0204	6.5
	0929	1.4		0932	1.2
F	1447	6.0	SA	1432	6.3
	2139	1.6		2155	1.3
7	0304	5.8	22	0300	6.1
	0958	1.8		1022	1.5
SA	1535	5.6	SU	1537	5.9
	2216	2.0		◐ 2252	1.6
8	0402	5.4	23	0415	5.7
	1041	2.1		1128	1.9
SU	1642	5.3	M	1700	5.6
	◑ 2312	2.3			
9	0516	5.1	24	0009	1.9
	1158	2.4		0553	5.5
M	1756	5.1	TU	1255	2.0
				1831	5.6
10	0053	2.4	25	0133	1.8
	0631	5.0		0723	5.6
TU	1337	2.4	W	1419	1.8
	1908	5.2		1950	5.8
11	0213	2.2	26	0254	1.5
	0742	5.3		0833	5.9
W	1444	2.1	TH	1538	1.5
	2010	5.5		2052	6.1
12	0314	1.9	27	0410	1.2
	0837	5.6		0927	6.2
TH	1540	1.7	F	1644	1.2
	2057	5.9		2141	6.4
13	0406	1.5	28	0510	0.9
	0918	6.0		1011	6.4
F	1629	1.4	SA	1735	0.9
	2135	6.2		2224	6.7
14	0453	1.2	29	0559	0.7
	0955	6.2		1049	6.6
SA	1714	1.2	SU	1818	0.8
	2211	6.5		2303	6.8
15	0538	1.0	30	0640	0.6
	1030	6.5		1124	6.6
SU	1756	1.0	M	1855	0.8
	2246	6.7		○ 2341	6.8

Chart Datum: 3·67 metres below Ordnance Datum (Newlyn). HAT is 7·4 metres above Chart Datum.

STANDARD TIME (UT)
For Summer Time add ONE hour in **non-shaded areas**

DOVER LAT 51°07′N LONG 1°19′E

TIMES AND HEIGHTS OF HIGH AND LOW WATERS

Dates in red are SPRINGS
Dates in blue are NEAPS

YEAR **2018**

MAY

Day	Time	m	Time	m	Time	m	Time	m
1 TU	0716	0.7	1159	6.7	1928	0.8		
2 W	0017	6.7	0746	0.8	1235	6.6	1956	1.0
3 TH	0053	6.6	0811	1.0	1310	6.5	2020	1.1
4 F	0126	6.4	0833	1.2	1344	6.3	2043	1.3
5 SA	0158	6.1	0857	1.4	1418	6.1	2112	1.5
6 SU	0232	5.8	0929	1.7	1456	5.8	2150	1.8
7 M	0322	5.5	1011	2.0	1556	5.5	2240	2.1
8 TU	0437	5.2	1108	2.3	1709	5.3	◑ 2357	2.3
9 W	0549	5.1	1241	2.4	1819	5.3		
10 TH	0125	2.2	0655	5.3	1358	2.2	1920	5.5
11 F	0230	1.9	0751	5.6	1457	1.8	2011	5.8
12 SA	0324	1.5	0838	5.9	1549	1.5	2055	6.2
13 SU	0415	1.2	0919	6.2	1638	1.2	2135	6.5
14 M	0505	1.0	0958	6.5	1725	1.0	2215	6.7
15 TU	0552	0.8	1037	6.7	1810	0.9	● 2255	6.9
16 W	0637	0.7	1117	6.8	1854	0.7	2336	6.9
17 TH	0720	0.7	1159	6.9	1936	0.7		
18 F	0020	6.9	0801	0.7	1245	6.8	2019	0.7
19 SA	0107	6.8	0843	0.9	1334	6.7	2104	0.9
20 SU	0159	6.5	0929	1.1	1430	6.4	2154	1.1
21 M	0300	6.2	1021	1.4	1532	6.1	2253	1.4
22 TU	0411	5.9	1126	1.7	1642	5.9	◐	
23 W	0003	1.6	0533	5.7	1240	1.8	1759	5.8
24 TH	0116	1.6	0658	5.7	1353	1.8	1918	5.8
25 F	0228	1.5	0806	5.8	1503	1.6	2022	6.0
26 SA	0338	1.3	0900	6.0	1608	1.4	2115	6.3
27 SU	0439	1.1	0945	6.2	1702	1.2	2200	6.4
28 M	0529	1.0	1024	6.3	1747	1.1	2241	6.5
29 TU	0610	1.0	1101	6.4	1825	1.0	○ 2319	6.5
30 W	0645	1.0	1137	6.5	1858	1.0	2356	6.5
31 TH	0715	1.1	1214	6.5	1928	1.1		

JUNE

Day	Time	m	Time	m	Time	m	Time	m
1 F	0032	6.4	0741	1.2	1250	6.4	1954	1.2
2 SA	0105	6.3	0807	1.3	1323	6.3	2022	1.3
3 SU	0136	6.1	0835	1.4	1354	6.1	2054	1.5
4 M	0207	5.9	0909	1.6	1426	6.0	2132	1.7
5 TU	0245	5.6	0949	1.8	1508	5.7	2217	1.9
6 W	0341	5.4	1037	2.0	1607	5.6	◑ 2314	2.0
7 TH	0456	5.3	1140	2.1	1718	5.5		
8 F	0029	2.0	0605	5.3	1301	2.1	1825	5.6
9 SA	0140	1.9	0705	5.5	1410	1.9	1923	5.8
10 SU	0241	1.6	0757	5.8	1508	1.6	2014	6.1
11 M	0337	1.3	0844	6.1	1603	1.4	2101	6.4
12 TU	0431	1.1	0929	6.4	1655	1.1	2148	6.6
13 W	0525	0.9	1015	6.6	1747	0.9	● 2234	6.8
14 TH	0617	0.8	1101	6.8	1837	0.7	2321	6.9
15 F	0708	0.7	1148	6.9	1927	0.7		
16 SA	0009	6.9	0756	0.7	1237	6.9	2016	0.7
17 SU	0100	6.8	0844	0.8	1328	6.8	2105	0.7
18 M	0154	6.6	0931	1.0	1422	6.6	2156	0.9
19 TU	0252	6.3	1020	1.2	1518	6.4	2249	1.1
20 W	0353	6.1	1114	1.4	1616	6.2	◐ 2346	1.3
21 TH	0500	5.8	1213	1.7	1721	5.9		
22 F	0047	1.5	0615	5.7	1317	1.8	1833	5.8
23 SA	0151	1.5	0726	5.7	1421	1.7	1945	5.9
24 SU	0255	1.5	0826	5.8	1525	1.6	2045	6.0
25 M	0358	1.4	0916	5.9	1624	1.5	2136	6.1
26 TU	0453	1.3	1000	6.1	1714	1.3	2220	6.2
27 W	0537	1.3	1040	6.3	1755	1.2	2300	6.3
28 TH	0614	1.2	1117	6.4	1831	1.2	○ 2337	6.3
29 F	0647	1.2	1154	6.4	1903	1.2		
30 SA	0012	6.3	0716	1.3	1229	6.4	1934	1.2

JULY

Day	Time	m	Time	m	Time	m	Time	m
1 SU	0045	6.2	0746	1.3	1302	6.3	2006	1.3
2 M	0115	6.1	0819	1.4	1330	6.3	2040	1.3
3 TU	0142	6.0	0853	1.4	1358	6.2	2116	1.5
4 W	0213	5.9	0930	1.6	1433	6.1	2155	1.6
5 TH	0252	5.8	1010	1.7	1517	5.9	2240	1.7
6 F	0343	5.6	1057	1.9	1613	5.8	◑ 2334	1.8
7 SA	0450	5.5	1158	2.0	1721	5.7		
8 SU	0044	1.9	0610	5.5	1316	2.0	1834	5.8
9 M	0157	1.7	0718	5.7	1427	1.8	1939	6.0
10 TU	0301	1.5	0816	6.0	1530	1.5	2036	6.2
11 W	0402	1.3	0910	6.3	1630	1.2	2131	6.5
12 TH	0503	1.0	1002	6.5	1728	1.0	2223	6.7
13 F	0604	0.9	1052	6.7	1826	0.8	● 2314	6.8
14 SA	0701	0.7	1141	6.9	1922	0.6		
15 SU	0004	6.9	0754	0.7	1229	7.0	2014	0.5
16 M	0053	6.8	0841	0.7	1317	7.0	2102	0.5
17 TU	0143	6.7	0925	0.8	1406	6.9	2147	0.6
18 W	0234	6.5	1006	1.0	1456	6.7	2231	0.9
19 TH	0327	6.2	1049	1.3	1547	6.4	◐ 2318	1.2
20 F	0422	5.9	1137	1.6	1643	6.0		
21 SA	0010	1.5	0523	5.6	1234	1.9	1745	5.8
22 SU	0109	1.8	0634	5.5	1337	2.0	1858	5.6
23 M	0211	1.8	0746	5.5	1444	2.0	2013	5.7
24 TU	0315	1.8	0847	5.7	1548	1.8	2114	5.8
25 W	0414	1.7	0938	5.9	1643	1.6	2203	6.0
26 TH	0504	1.5	1020	6.1	1729	1.4	2243	6.1
27 F	0546	1.4	1058	6.3	1807	1.3	○ 2318	6.2
28 SA	0622	1.3	1133	6.4	1842	1.2	2349	6.3
29 SU	0655	1.3	1206	6.5	1915	1.2		
30 M	0020	6.2	0728	1.3	1236	6.4	1949	1.2
31 TU	0049	6.2	0801	1.3	1303	6.4	2023	1.2

AUGUST

Day	Time	m	Time	m	Time	m	Time	m
1 W	0115	6.2	0835	1.3	1330	6.4	2057	1.3
2 TH	0143	6.2	0909	1.4	1402	6.4	2132	1.4
3 F	0218	6.1	0943	1.5	1442	6.3	2208	1.5
4 SA	0302	6.0	1023	1.7	1530	6.1	◑ 2253	1.7
5 SU	0356	5.7	1113	1.9	1630	5.8	2352	1.9
6 M	0511	5.5	1223	2.0	1751	5.7		
7 TU	0113	1.9	0648	5.6	1350	2.0	1916	5.8
8 W	0232	1.8	0801	5.8	1504	1.7	2025	6.1
9 TH	0342	1.5	0901	6.1	1611	1.4	2125	6.4
10 F	0450	1.2	0955	6.5	1717	1.0	2220	6.6
11 SA	0556	0.9	1045	6.8	1819	0.7	● 2310	6.8
12 SU	0654	0.7	1132	7.0	1915	0.5	2357	6.9
13 M	0744	0.6	1217	7.1	2004	0.4		
14 TU	0041	6.9	0827	0.6	1301	7.1	2048	0.4
15 W	0125	6.8	0906	0.7	1345	7.0	2127	0.5
16 TH	0209	6.6	0941	0.9	1430	6.8	2204	0.8
17 F	0255	6.3	1016	1.2	1516	6.5	2242	1.2
18 SA	0344	6.0	1055	1.6	1606	6.1	◐ 2326	1.7
19 SU	0440	5.6	1145	2.0	1704	5.7		
20 M	0023	2.0	0546	5.4	1252	2.3	1813	5.4
21 TU	0130	2.2	0701	5.3	1406	2.3	1937	5.4
22 W	0239	2.2	0817	5.5	1516	2.1	2056	5.6
23 TH	0342	1.9	0915	5.8	1615	1.8	2148	5.9
24 F	0436	1.7	0959	6.1	1703	1.5	2224	6.1
25 SA	0520	1.5	1035	6.3	1743	1.3	2254	6.3
26 SU	0558	1.3	1107	6.5	1819	1.2	○ 2322	6.3
27 M	0632	1.2	1138	6.5	1853	1.1	2351	6.4
28 TU	0706	1.2	1207	6.6	1928	1.1		
29 W	0019	6.4	0740	1.2	1234	6.6	2002	1.1
30 TH	0046	6.4	0813	1.2	1302	6.6	2034	1.1
31 F	0115	6.4	0845	1.2	1334	6.6	2106	1.2

Chart Datum: 3·67 metres below Ordnance Datum (Newlyn). HAT is 7·4 metres above Chart Datum.

STANDARD TIME (UT)
For Summer Time add ONE hour in **non-shaded areas**

DOVER LAT 51°07′N LONG 1°19′E

TIMES AND HEIGHTS OF HIGH AND LOW WATERS

Dates in red are SPRINGS
Dates in blue are NEAPS

YEAR **2018**

SEPTEMBER

Date	Day	Time	m	Time	m	Time	m	Time	m
1	SA	0150	6.4	0918	1.4	1412	6.5	2140	1.4
2	SU	0231	6.2	0956	1.6	1458	6.3	2221	1.7
3	M	0323	5.9	1043	1.8	1556	5.9	◑ 2317	2.0
4	TU	0436	5.5	1149	2.1	1725	5.6		
5	W	0039	2.1	0634	5.4	1323	2.1	1909	5.7
6	TH	0212	2.0	0751	5.7	1447	1.8	2022	6.0
7	F	0331	1.7	0854	6.1	1600	1.4	2123	6.3
8	SA	0444	1.3	0947	6.5	1709	1.0	2215	6.7
9	SU	0547	1.0	1035	6.9	1809	0.7	● 2302	6.9
10	M	0640	0.7	1118	7.1	1901	0.5	2343	7.0
11	TU	0725	0.6	1200	7.2	1946	0.4		
12	W	0022	7.0	0804	0.6	1241	7.2	2024	0.4
13	TH	0101	6.9	0838	0.7	1321	7.0	2059	0.7
14	F	0141	6.7	0910	1.0	1401	6.8	2130	1.0
15	SA	0222	6.4	0939	1.3	1444	6.5	2201	1.4
16	SU	0308	6.1	1010	1.7	1531	6.0	◐ 2235	1.9
17	M	0402	5.7	1047	2.1	1627	5.6	2324	2.3
18	TU	0506	5.3	1155	2.5	1735	5.3		
19	W	0045	2.5	0619	5.2	1328	2.6	1855	5.2
20	TH	0205	2.5	0739	5.4	1444	2.3	2027	5.4
21	F	0311	2.2	0844	5.7	1545	1.9	2121	5.8
22	SA	0406	1.8	0929	6.1	1633	1.6	2154	6.1
23	SU	0451	1.5	1003	6.3	1714	1.3	2221	6.3
24	M	0530	1.3	1035	6.5	1751	1.2	2250	6.5
25	TU	0606	1.2	1105	6.6	1827	1.1	○ 2320	6.6
26	W	0641	1.1	1135	6.7	1903	1.0	2349	6.6
27	TH	0716	1.1	1204	6.8	1937	1.0		
28	F	0018	6.7	0749	1.1	1236	6.8	2010	1.1
29	SA	0050	6.7	0822	1.1	1309	6.8	2042	1.2
30	SU	0126	6.6	0856	1.3	1348	6.6	2117	1.4

OCTOBER

Date	Day	Time	m	Time	m	Time	m	Time	m
1	M	0209	6.4	0935	1.5	1435	6.3	2159	1.7
2	TU	0303	6.0	1024	1.8	1537	5.8	◑ 2255	2.1
3	W	0424	5.5	1131	2.1	1724	5.5		
4	TH	0019	2.3	0620	5.5	1307	2.2	1902	5.6
5	F	0200	2.1	0738	5.7	1435	1.9	2015	6.0
6	SA	0323	1.7	0840	6.2	1551	1.4	2114	6.3
7	SU	0433	1.3	0933	6.6	1657	1.0	2203	6.7
8	M	0530	1.0	1018	6.9	1752	0.7	2246	6.9
9	TU	0618	0.8	1059	7.1	1839	0.5	● 2324	7.0
10	W	0659	0.7	1139	7.2	1920	0.5		
11	TH	0000	7.0	0735	0.7	1218	7.1	1955	0.6
12	F	0036	6.9	0808	0.9	1256	7.0	2026	0.9
13	SA	0113	6.7	0836	1.1	1333	6.7	2054	1.2
14	SU	0152	6.5	0902	1.4	1412	6.4	2118	1.5
15	M	0234	6.1	0928	1.7	1457	6.0	2145	1.9
16	TU	0325	5.8	1001	2.1	1553	5.5	◐ 2223	2.3
17	W	0428	5.4	1053	2.5	1701	5.2	2333	2.6
18	TH	0538	5.2	1236	2.6	1815	5.1		
19	F	0121	2.6	0652	5.3	1402	2.4	1932	5.3
20	SA	0233	2.3	0758	5.6	1504	2.0	2032	5.7
21	SU	0329	2.0	0846	6.0	1554	1.7	2110	6.0
22	M	0416	1.6	0923	6.3	1637	1.4	2143	6.3
23	TU	0457	1.4	0957	6.5	1718	1.2	2215	6.5
24	W	0536	1.2	1030	6.7	1758	1.0	○ 2248	6.7
25	TH	0614	1.1	1102	6.8	1836	1.0	2320	6.8
26	F	0651	1.0	1136	6.9	1913	1.0	2353	6.8
27	SA	0727	1.0	1211	6.9	1948	1.0		
28	SU	0029	6.8	0803	1.1	1250	6.8	2023	1.1
29	M	0111	6.7	0841	1.2	1332	6.6	2101	1.4
30	TU	0158	6.4	0923	1.5	1424	6.3	2146	1.7
31	W	0258	6.0	1015	1.8	1534	5.8	◑ 2244	2.0

NOVEMBER

Date	Day	Time	m	Time	m	Time	m	Time	m
1	TH	0422	5.7	1125	2.0	1718	5.6		
2	F	0010	2.3	0557	5.6	1256	2.0	1847	5.7
3	SA	0144	2.1	0716	5.8	1419	1.8	1959	5.9
4	SU	0304	1.8	0819	6.2	1534	1.4	2057	6.3
5	M	0411	1.4	0911	6.5	1637	1.0	2144	6.5
6	TU	0505	1.1	0956	6.8	1729	0.8	2225	6.7
7	W	0551	0.9	1037	6.9	1814	0.7	● 2301	6.8
8	TH	0631	0.9	1116	7.0	1852	0.8	2337	6.8
9	F	0707	0.9	1154	6.9	1926	0.9		
10	SA	0013	6.8	0738	1.0	1232	6.8	1954	1.1
11	SU	0050	6.7	0806	1.2	1309	6.6	2019	1.3
12	M	0127	6.5	0831	1.4	1345	6.3	2043	1.6
13	TU	0205	6.2	0858	1.7	1425	5.9	2112	1.9
14	W	0249	5.9	0933	2.0	1517	5.6	2151	2.2
15	TH	0345	5.6	1020	2.2	1623	5.3	◐ 2243	2.5
16	F	0452	5.4	1129	2.5	1732	5.2		
17	SA	0009	2.6	0601	5.3	1303	2.4	1840	5.3
18	SU	0139	2.5	0704	5.5	1412	2.1	1938	5.5
19	M	0241	2.1	0757	5.8	1507	1.8	2025	5.9
20	TU	0333	1.8	0839	6.1	1557	1.5	2104	6.2
21	W	0420	1.5	0918	6.4	1643	1.2	2141	6.4
22	TH	0505	1.3	0955	6.7	1728	1.1	2217	6.7
23	F	0547	1.1	1033	6.8	1811	0.9	○ 2255	6.8
24	SA	0629	1.0	1112	6.9	1852	0.9	2334	6.9
25	SU	0710	0.9	1153	6.9	1932	0.9		
26	M	0016	6.9	0750	1.0	1237	6.8	2012	1.1
27	TU	0103	6.8	0834	1.1	1325	6.6	2055	1.3
28	W	0154	6.6	0921	1.3	1422	6.3	2143	1.5
29	TH	0255	6.3	1016	1.5	1531	6.0	2242	1.8
30	F	0405	6.0	1122	1.7	1655	5.7	◑ 2356	2.0

DECEMBER

Date	Day	Time	m	Time	m	Time	m	Time	m
1	SA	0523	5.8	1237	1.8	1820	5.7		
2	SU	0114	2.0	0642	5.9	1351	1.7	1931	5.8
3	M	0227	1.8	0749	6.1	1501	1.5	2030	6.0
4	TU	0336	1.6	0845	6.3	1607	1.2	2119	6.2
5	W	0434	1.3	0933	6.5	1701	1.1	2202	6.4
6	TH	0522	1.2	1016	6.6	1747	1.0	2240	6.5
7	F	0604	1.1	1057	6.7	1825	1.0	● 2317	6.6
8	SA	0641	1.1	1135	6.6	1858	1.1	2354	6.6
9	SU	0714	1.2	1212	6.5	1927	1.2		
10	M	0031	6.6	0743	1.3	1248	6.4	1953	1.4
11	TU	0107	6.5	0810	1.4	1323	6.2	2020	1.5
12	W	0141	6.3	0840	1.5	1357	6.0	2051	1.7
13	TH	0214	6.1	0915	1.7	1435	5.7	2129	1.9
14	F	0252	5.9	0957	1.9	1524	5.5	2213	2.1
15	SA	0343	5.6	1048	2.1	1633	5.3	◐ 2308	2.3
16	SU	0453	5.5	1155	2.2	1744	5.3		
17	M	0024	2.4	0602	5.5	1312	2.1	1846	5.4
18	TU	0143	2.2	0703	5.6	1417	1.9	1940	5.6
19	W	0246	2.0	0755	5.9	1515	1.6	2027	6.0
20	TH	0342	1.7	0842	6.2	1609	1.3	2110	6.3
21	F	0434	1.4	0926	6.5	1700	1.1	2153	6.5
22	SA	0523	1.1	1011	6.7	1749	1.0	○ 2237	6.7
23	SU	0611	1.0	1056	6.9	1837	0.9	2322	6.9
24	M	0659	0.8	1142	6.9	1924	0.9		
25	TU	0009	6.9	0746	0.8	1230	6.8	2011	0.9
26	W	0057	6.9	0835	0.8	1321	6.7	2057	1.0
27	TH	0149	6.8	0924	0.9	1415	6.5	2145	1.2
28	F	0243	6.6	1015	1.1	1515	6.2	2236	1.4
29	SA	0342	6.3	1110	1.3	1621	5.9	◑ 2332	1.7
30	SU	0445	6.1	1209	1.5	1734	5.7		
31	M	0035	1.9	0556	5.9	1313	1.6	1849	5.6

Chart Datum: 3·67 metres below Ordnance Datum (Newlyn). HAT is 7·4 metres above Chart Datum.

9.3.14 DOVER STRAIT

For orientation only – due to scale not all lights and buoys are shown

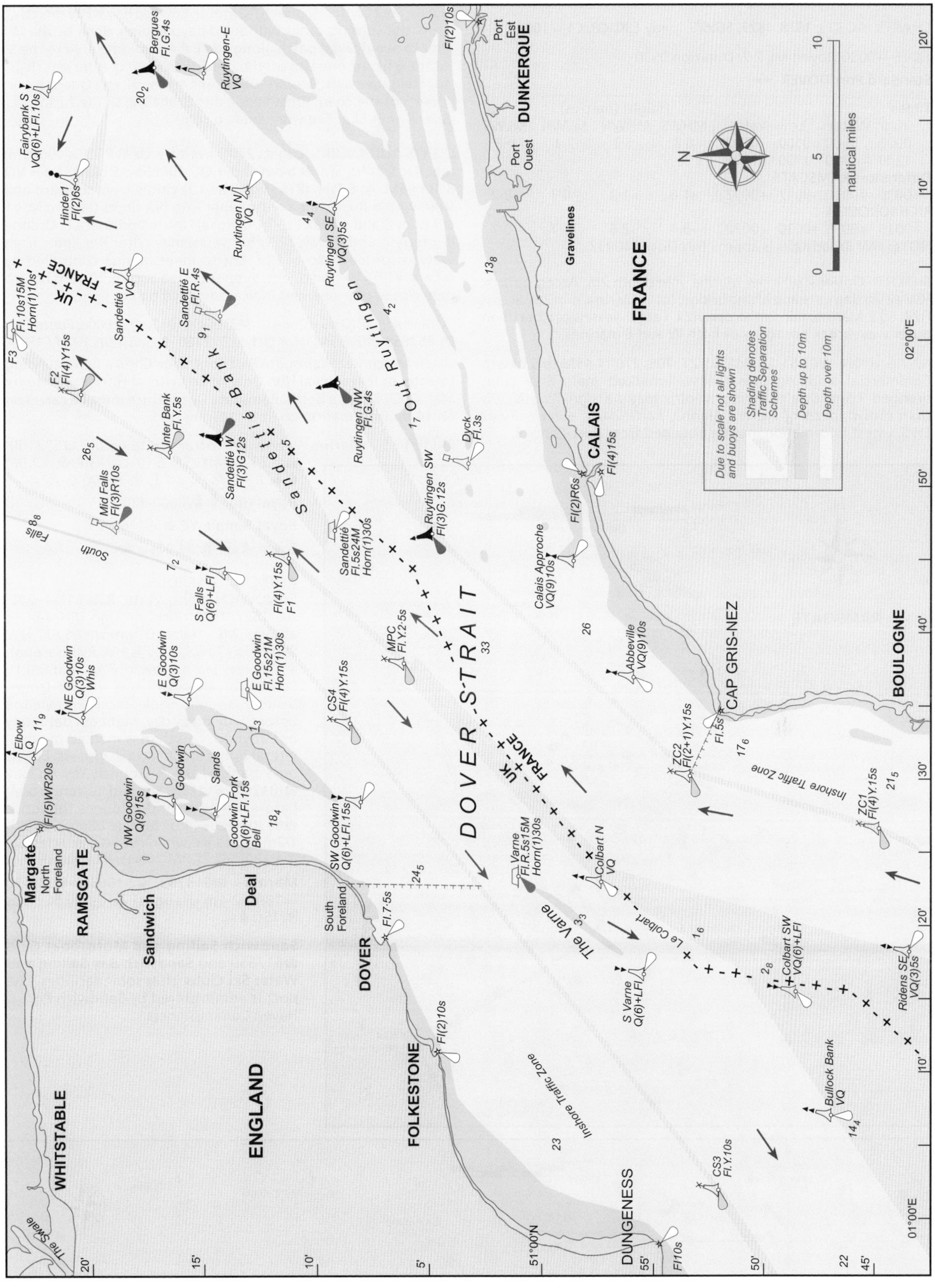

DOVER STRAIT
ENGLAND
FRANCE
WHITSTABLE
The Swale
Margate
North Foreland
RAMSGATE
Sandwich
Deal
South Foreland
DOVER
FOLKESTONE
DUNGENESS
CAP GRIS-NEZ
BOULOGNE
CALAIS
Gravelines
Port Ouest
Port Est
DUNKERQUE
Goodwin Sands
The Varne
Le Colbart
South Falls
Sandettié Bank
Out Ruytingen
Inshore Traffic Zone
UK FRANCE
Fl(5)WR20s
Elbow Q
NE Goodwin Q(3)10s Whis
E Goodwin Q(3)10s
NW Goodwin Q(9)15s
Goodwin Fork Q(6)+LFl.15s Bell
E Goodwin Fl.15s21M Horn(1)30s
SW Goodwin Q(6)+LFl. 15s
CS4 Fl(4)Y.15s
MPC Fl.Y.2·5s
S Falls Q(6)+LFl
Fl(4)Y.15s F1
Mid Falls Fl(3)R10s
Inter Bank Fl.Y.5s
Sandettié W Fl(3)G12s
F2 Fl(4)Y15s
F3 Fl.10s15M Horn(1)10s
Sandettié N VQ
Sandettié E Fl.R.4s
Hinder1 Fl(2)6s
Fairybank S VQ(6)+LFl.10s
Bergues Fl.G.4s
Ruytingen-E VQ
Ruytingen N VQ
Ruytingen SE VQ(3)5s
Ruytingen NW Fl.G.4s
Ruytingen SW Fl(3)G.12s
Sandettié Fl.5s24M Horn(1)30s
Dyck Fl.3s
Fl(2)10s
Fl(4)15s
Fl(2)R6s
Calais Approche VQ(9)10s
Abbeville VQ(9)10s
Fl.5s
ZC2 Fl(2+1)Y.15s
ZC1 Fl(4)Y.15s
Varne Fl.R.5s15M Horn(1)30s
Colbart N VQ
S Varne Q(6)+LFl
Colbart SW VQ(6)+LFl
Ridens SE VQ(3)5s
Bullock Bank VQ
CS3 Fl.Y.10s
Fl.7·5s
Fl(2)10s
Fl10s
N
nautical miles
0 5 10
Due to scale not all lights and buoys are shown
Shading denotes Traffic Separation Schemes
Depth up to 10m
Depth over 10m
01°00'E
10'
20'
30'
40'
50'
02°00'E
51°00'N

9.3.15 RAMSGATE

Kent **51°19'·51N 01°25'·50E**

CHARTS AC 323, 1828, 1827, 5605/6; Imray C30, C8, C1, 2100

TIDES +0030 Dover; ML 2·7; Duration 0530

Standard Port DOVER (⟵)

Times				**Height (metres)**			
High Water		Low Water		MHWS	MHWN	MLWN	MLWS
0000	0600	0100	0700	6·8	5·3	2·1	0·8
1200	1800	1300	1900				
Differences RAMSGATE							
+0030	+0030	+0017	+0007	−1·6	−1·3	−0·7	−0·2
RICHBOROUGH							
+0015	+0015	+0030	+0030	−3·4	−2·6	−1·7	−0·7

NOTE: HW Broadstairs is approx HW Dover +0037.

SHELTER Options: (a) Inner Marina, min depth 2m. Access approx HW±2 via flap gate and lifting bridge; (b) W Marina, min 2m, access H24; (c) E Marina, min 2m, access H24. Larger vessels can berth on outer wavebreak pontoons of both W and E marinas.

NAVIGATION WPT 51°19'·43N 01°27'·70E, 270°/1·45M to S bkwtr. Commercial shipping uses the well-marked main E-W chan dredged 7·5m. *Due to silting, depths may be significantly less than shown; parts of Eastern Marina, particularly, almost dry at LWS.* Latest information may be obtained from Port Control.

For ent/dep yachts must use the Recommended Yacht Track on the S side of the main buoyed chan. Ent/dep under power, or advise Port Control if unable to motor. Ent/dep Royal Hbr directly; cross the turning basin without delay **keeping close to the W Pier to avoid shoal patch alongside E Pier**. Holding area to the S of the S bkwtr must be used by yachts to keep the hbr ent clear for freight vessels. Beware Dike Bank to the N and Quern Bank close S of the chan. Cross Ledge and Brake shoals are further S. Speed limit 5kn. See www.rma.eu.com.

LIGHTS AND MARKS Ldg lts 270°: front Dir Oc WRG 10s 10m 5M; rear, Oc 5s 17m 5M. N bkwtr hd = QG 10m 5M; S bkwtr hd = VQ R 10m 5M. At E Pier, **IPTS** (Sigs 2 and 3) visible from seaward and from within Royal Hbr, control appr into hbr limits (abeam Nos 1 & 2 buoys) and ent/exit to/from Royal Hbr. In addition a Fl Orange lt = ferry is under way; no other vessel may enter Hbr limits from seaward or leave Royal Hbr. Ent to inner marina controlled by separate IPTS to stbd of ent. Siren sounded approx 10 mins before gate closes; non-opening indicated by red ball or light.

COMMUNICATIONS (Code 01843) CGOC (01304) 210008; Police 101; Dr 852853 Ⓗ 225544. Hbr Office 572100; Broadstairs HM 861879. Listen and contact *Ramsgate Port Control* on Ch 14 when intending to enter or leave Royal Hbr. Only when in Royal Hbr call *Ramsgate Marina* Ch 80 for a berth. Ramsgate Dock Office must be called on Ch 14 for information on Inner Marina Lock.

FACILITIES **Marina** www.portoframsgate.co.uk ☎572100, £32/craft<5t; 510 +300 £2.96; (40t) ACA.

Royal Hbr (0600-2200).

Royal Temple YC ☎591766.

Town Ⓑ.

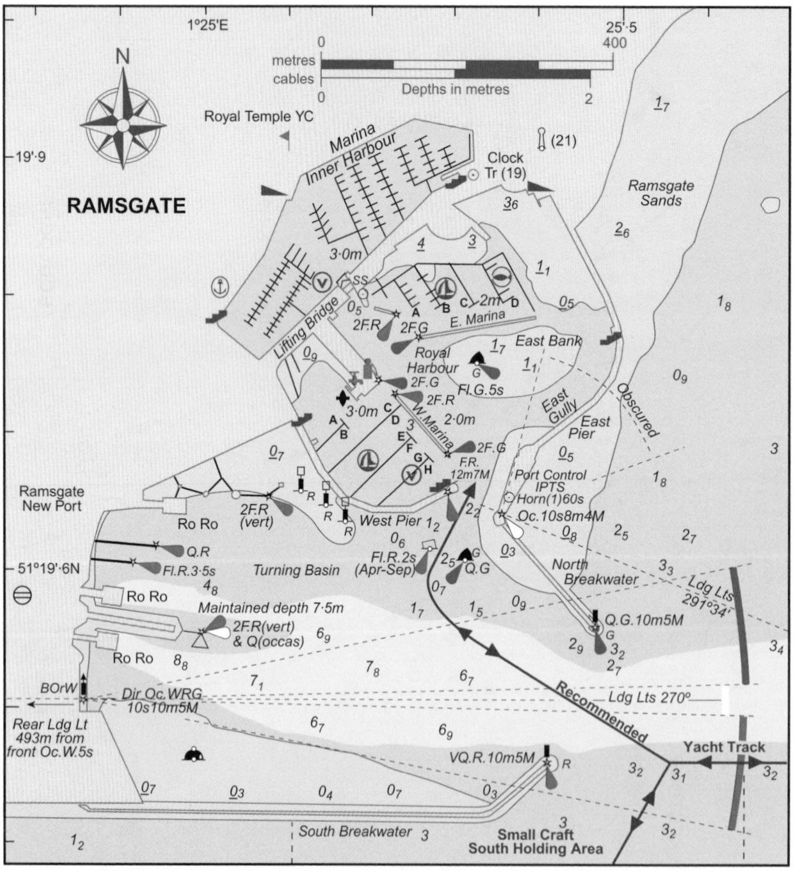

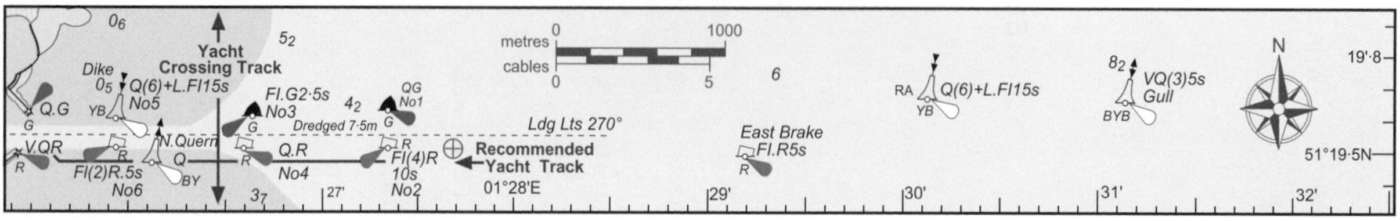

ADJACENT HARBOUR

SANDWICH, Kent, **51°16'·83N 01°21'·20E.** AC 1827 1828. Richborough differences above; ML 1·4m; Duration 0520. HW Sandwich Town quay is HW Richborough +1. Access via narrow drying channel to Sandwich; arrive off ent at HW Dover. Visitors should seek local knowledge before arriving by day; night ent definitely not advised. The chan is marked by small lateral buoys and beacons. Visitors' berths on S bank of the R Stour at Town Quay ☎(01304) 612162. Limited turning room before the swing bridge (opens 1hr notice ☎01304 620644 or Mobile 0860 378792), 1·7m clearance when closed. Facilities: HW±2 Ⓑ (Manston).

Marina ☎613783, 50+ £2.20 (<18m, 2·1m draught) (15t).

Sandwich Sailing and Motorboat Club ☎617650 and **Sandwich Bay Sailing and Water Ski Clubs** offer some facilities. The port is administered by Sandwich Port & Haven Commissioners.

East England

North Foreland to Great Yarmouth

9.4.1	Contents	271
9.4.2	Area map and Distance table	272
9.4.3	Tidal stream charts	274
9.4.4	Lights, buoys and waypoints	276
9.4.5	Passage information Thames Estuary, North Foreland to London Bridge, Thames/Orwell to Belgium or The Netherlands – 279 • Shoeburyness to River Colne – 303 • River Colne to Harwich, Harwich to Orford Ness, Orford Ness to Great Yarmouth – 312	279
9.4.6	Thames Estuary tidal stream charts	280
9.4.7	Thames Estuary (Margate, tide tables/curves)	282
9.4.8	Whitstable Margate • Herne Bay	287
9.4.9	The Swale	288
9.4.10	Queenborough	289
9.4.11	River Medway (Sheerness, tide tables/curves)	290
9.4.12	River Thames (London Bridge, tide tables/curves) Holehaven • Gravesend • Thames tidal barrier • Gallions Point Marina • South Dock Marina • Poplar Dock Marina • Limehouse Basin Marina • St Katharine Haven • Chelsea Harbour • Brentford Dock Marina	295
9.4.13	Southend-on-Sea Leigh-on-Sea	303
9.4.14	River Roach/Havengore	304
9.4.15	Burnham-on-Crouch, tide tables/curves	305
9.4.16	River Blackwater	310
9.4.17	River Colne	311
9.4.18	Walton Backwaters (Walton-on-the-Naze, tide tables/curves)	313
9.4.19	River Stour	318
9.4.20	River Orwell (Harwich, tide tables/curves)	319
9.4.21	River Deben	323
9.4.22	River Ore/Alde	324
9.4.23	Southwold	325
9.4.24	Lowestoft, tide tables/curves	326
9.4.25	Great Yarmouth Norfolk Broads	330

9.4.2

East England

North Foreland to Great Yarmouth

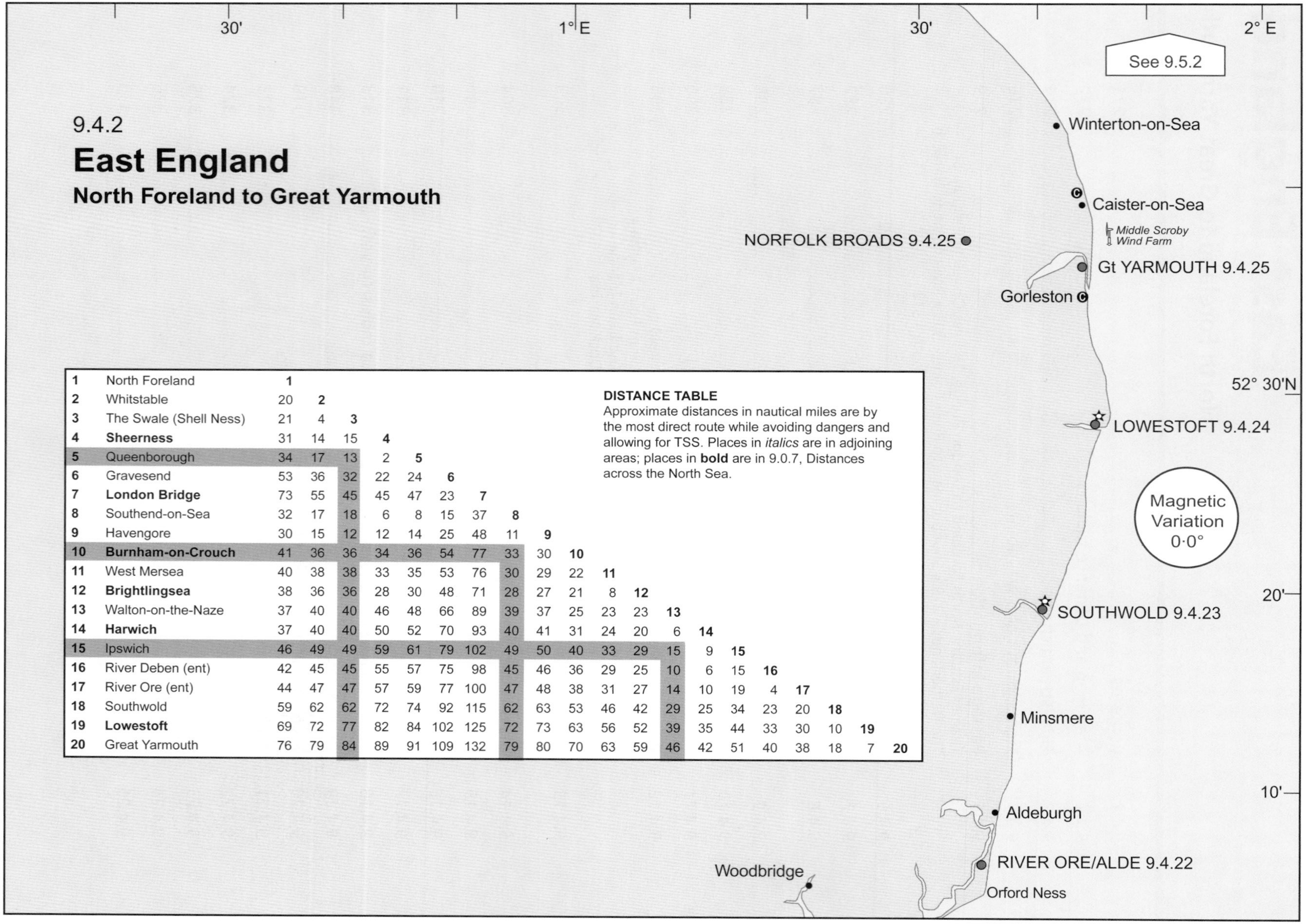
30'
1° E
30'
2° E
See 9.5.2
Winterton-on-Sea
Caister-on-Sea
Middle Scroby Wind Farm
NORFOLK BROADS 9.4.25
Gt YARMOUTH 9.4.25
Gorleston
52° 30'N
LOWESTOFT 9.4.24
Magnetic Variation 0·0°
20'
SOUTHWOLD 9.4.23
Minsmere
10'
Aldeburgh
RIVER ORE/ALDE 9.4.22
Woodbridge
Orford Ness

DISTANCE TABLE

Approximate distances in nautical miles are by the most direct route while avoiding dangers and allowing for TSS. Places in *italics* are in adjoining areas; places in **bold** are in 9.0.7, Distances across the North Sea.

1	North Foreland	**1**																			
2	Whitstable	20	**2**																		
3	The Swale (Shell Ness)	21	4	**3**																	
4	**Sheerness**	31	14	15	**4**																
5	Queenborough	34	17	13	2	**5**															
6	Gravesend	53	36	32	22	24	**6**														
7	**London Bridge**	73	55	45	45	47	23	**7**													
8	Southend-on-Sea	32	17	18	6	8	15	37	**8**												
9	Havengore	30	15	12	12	14	25	48	11	**9**											
10	**Burnham-on-Crouch**	41	36	36	34	36	54	77	33	30	**10**										
11	West Mersea	40	38	38	33	35	53	76	30	29	22	**11**									
12	**Brightlingsea**	38	36	36	28	30	48	71	28	27	21	8	**12**								
13	Walton-on-the-Naze	37	40	40	46	48	66	89	39	37	25	23	23	**13**							
14	**Harwich**	37	40	40	50	52	70	93	40	41	31	24	20	6	**14**						
15	Ipswich	46	49	49	59	61	79	102	49	50	40	33	29	15	9	**15**					
16	River Deben (ent)	42	45	45	55	57	75	98	45	46	36	29	25	10	6	15	**16**				
17	River Ore (ent)	44	47	47	57	59	77	100	47	48	38	31	27	14	10	19	4	**17**			
18	Southwold	59	62	62	72	74	92	115	62	63	53	46	42	29	25	34	23	20	**18**		
19	**Lowestoft**	69	72	77	82	84	102	125	72	73	63	56	52	39	35	44	33	30	10	**19**	
20	Great Yarmouth	76	79	84	89	91	109	132	79	80	70	63	59	46	42	51	40	38	18	7	**20**

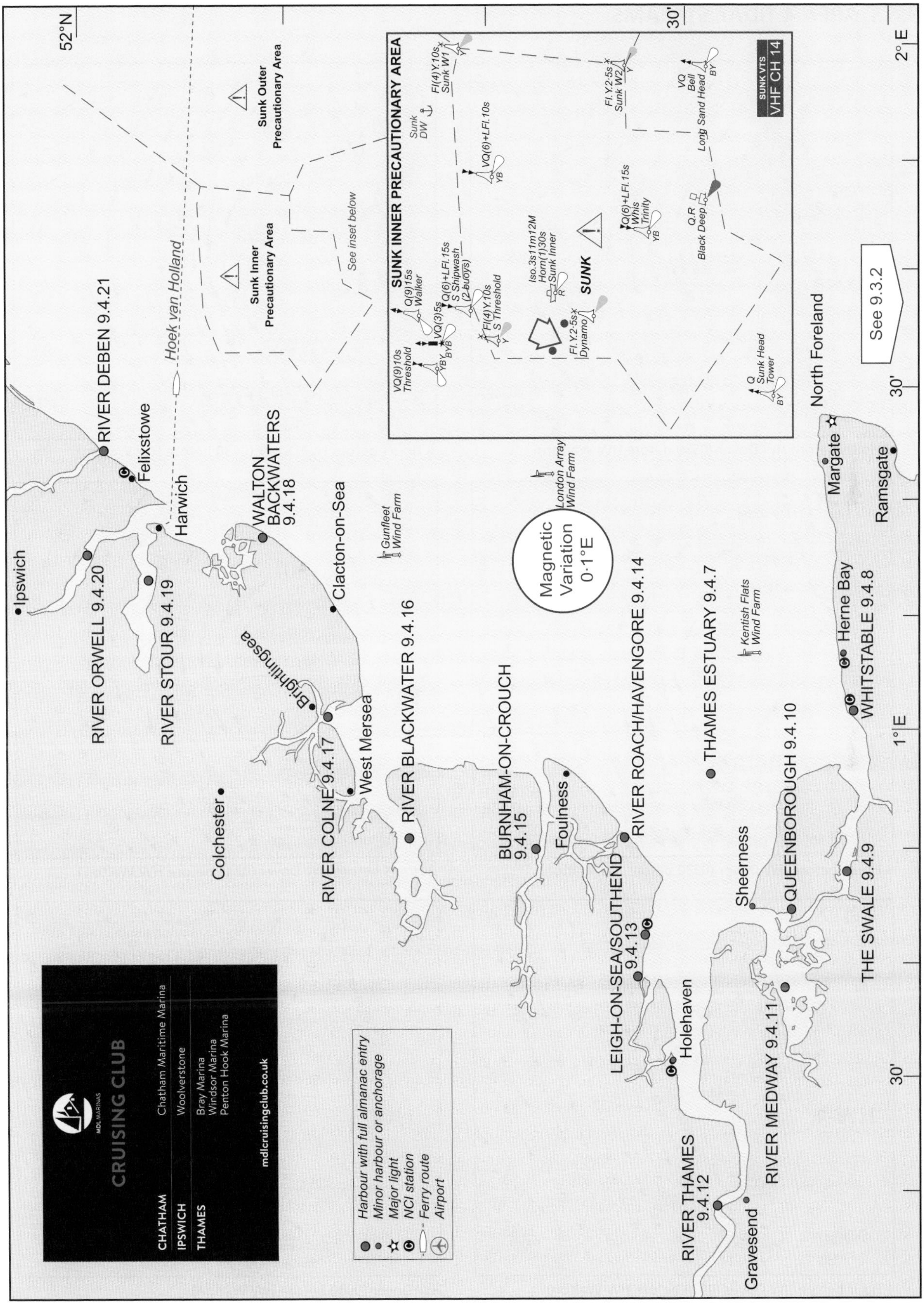
52°N
30'
2° E
1°E
30'
30'
Ipswich
RIVER ORWELL 9.4.20
RIVER DEBEN 9.4.21
Felixstowe
Harwich
RIVER STOUR 9.4.19
Hoek van Holland
WALTON BACKWATERS 9.4.18
Clacton-on-Sea
Brightlingsea
West Mersea
RIVER COLNE 9.4.17
Colchester
RIVER BLACKWATER 9.4.16
BURNHAM-ON-CROUCH 9.4.15
Foulness
RIVER ROACH/HAVENGORE 9.4.14
LEIGH-ON-SEA/SOUTHEND 9.4.13
Holehaven
RIVER THAMES 9.4.12
Gravesend
RIVER MEDWAY 9.4.11
Sheerness
QUEENBOROUGH 9.4.10
THE SWALE 9.4.9
WHITSTABLE 9.4.8
Herne Bay
THAMES ESTUARY 9.4.7
Kentish Flats Wind Farm
Gunfleet Wind Farm
London Array Wind Farm
Magnetic Variation 0·1°E
Margate
Ramsgate
North Foreland
See 9.3.2
Sunk Inner Precautionary Area
Sunk Outer Precautionary Area
See inset below
SUNK INNER PRECAUTIONARY AREA
VQ(9)10s Threshold
Q(9)15s Walker
VQ(3)5s BYB
Q(6)+LFl.15s S Shipwash (2 buoys)
Fl(4)Y.10s S Threshold
Iso.3s11m12M Horn(1)30s Sunk Inner
Fl.Y.2·5s Dynamo
SUNK
VQ(6)+LFl.10s YB
Sunk DW
Fl(4)Y.10s Sunk W1
Q(6)+LFl.15s Whis Trinity YB
Q.R Black Deep
Fl.Y.2·5s Sunk W2
Long Sand Head VQ Bell BY
Q Sunk Head Tower BY
SUNK VTS VHF CH 14
Harbour with full almanac entry
Minor harbour or anchorage
Major light
NCI station
Ferry route
Airport
MDL MARINAS CRUISING CLUB
CHATHAM Chatham Maritime Marina
IPSWICH Woolverstone
THAMES Bray Marina Windsor Marina Penton Hook Marina
mdlcruisingclub.co.uk

E England

9.4.3 AREA 4 TIDAL STREAMS

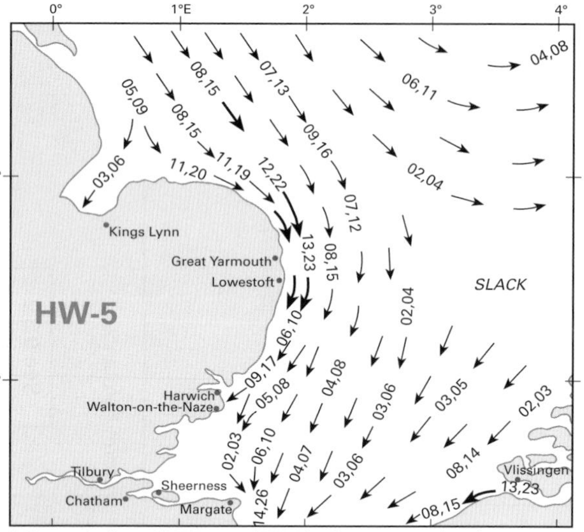

5 Hours before HW Dover (0530 before HW Walton)

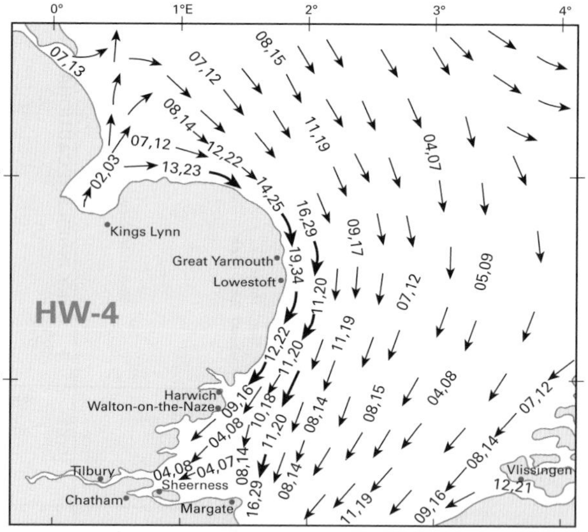

4 Hours before HW Dover (0430 before HW Walton)

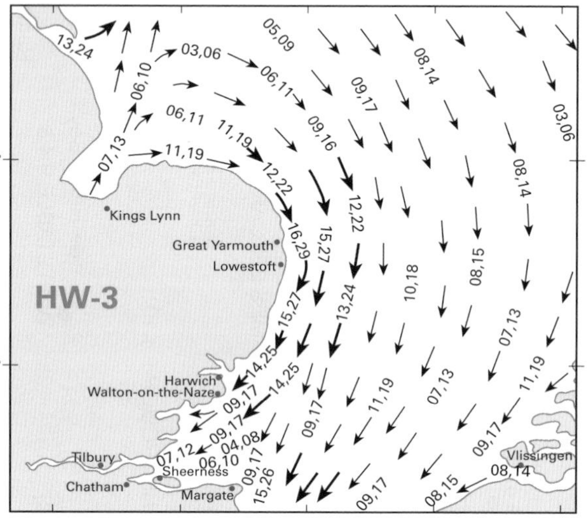

3 Hours before HW Dover (0330 before HW Walton)

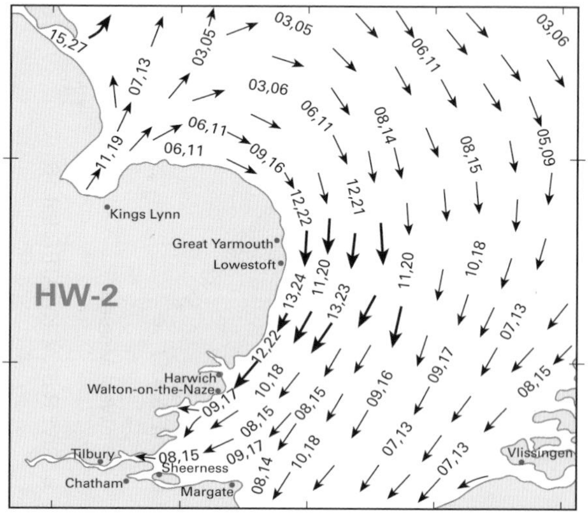

2 Hours before HW Dover (0230 before HW Walton)

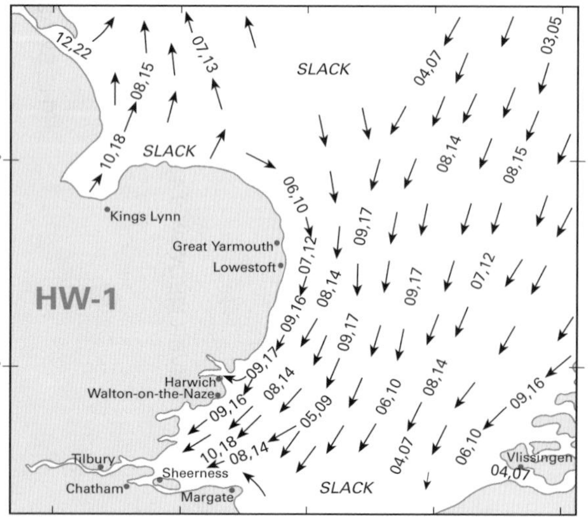

1 Hour before HW Dover (0130 before HW Walton)

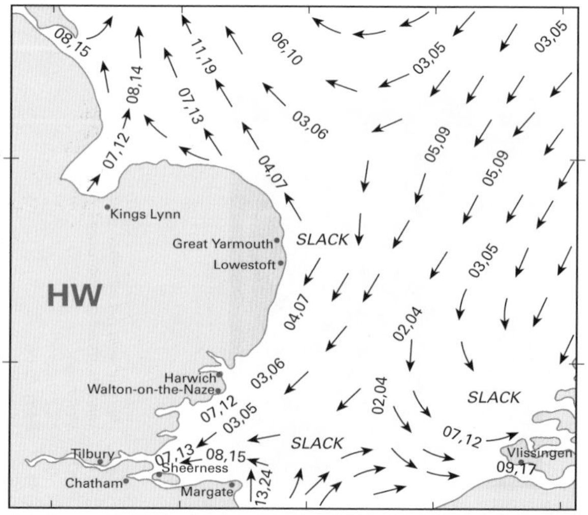

HW Dover (0030 before HW Walton)

Southward 9.3.3 Thames Estuary 9.4.6 Northward 9.5.3 Eastward 9.16.3

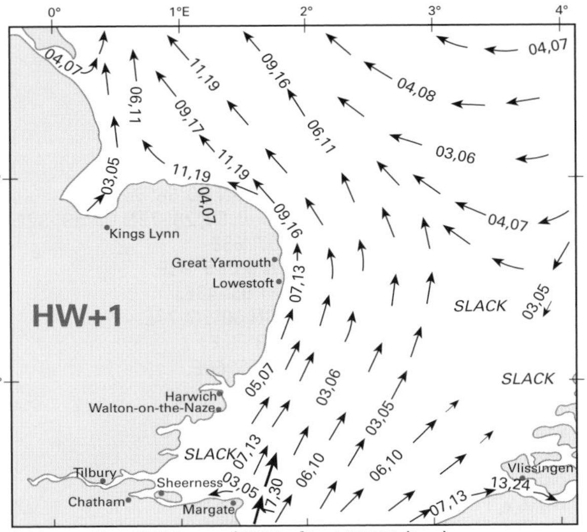

1 Hour after HW Dover (0030 after HW Walton)

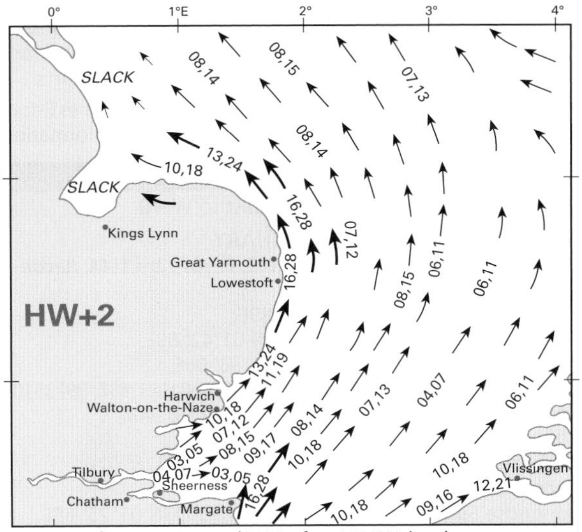

2 Hours after HW Dover (0130 after HW Walton)

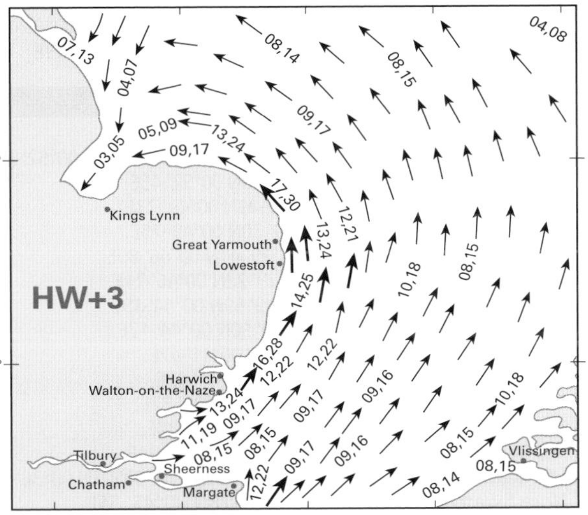

3 Hours after HW Dover (0230 after HW Walton)

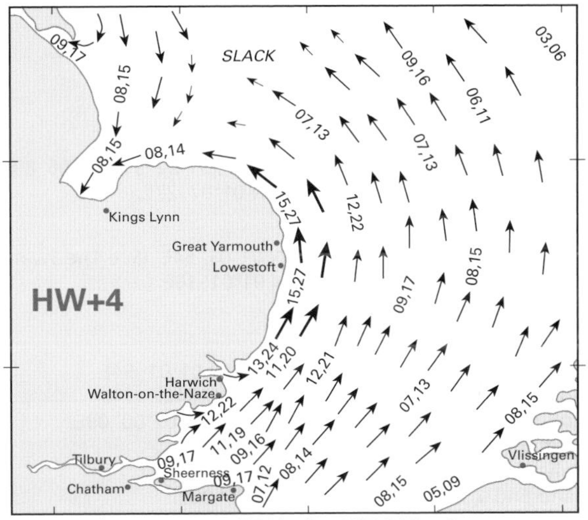

4 Hours after HW Dover (0330 after HW Walton)

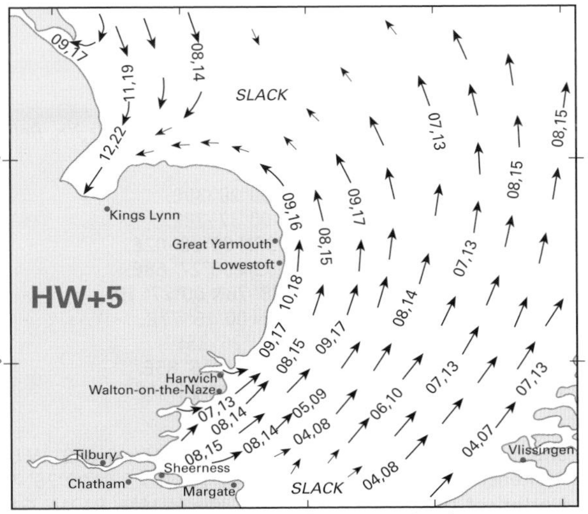

5 Hours after HW Dover (0430 after HW Walton)

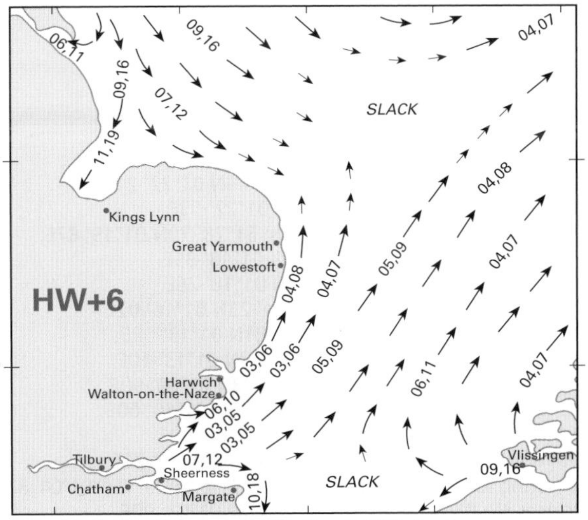

6 Hours after HW Dover (0530 after HW Walton)

9.4.4 LIGHTS, BUOYS AND WAYPOINTS

Bold print = light with a nominal range of 15M or more. CAPITALS = place or feature. *CAPITAL ITALICS* = light-vessel, light float or Lanby. *Italics* = Fog signal. ***Bold italics*** = Racon. Some marks/ buoys are fitted with AIS (MMSI No); see relevant charts.

IMPORTANT NOTE. Regular changes are made to Thames Estuary buoyage. Check Notices to Mariners for the latest information.

THAMES ESTUARY – SOUTHERN

(Direction of buoyage generally East to West)

APPROACHES to THAMES ESTUARY

Foxtrot 3 51°24'·15N 02°00'·38E; Fl 10s 12m **15M**; ***Racon (T) 10M***; *Horn 10s;* 992351033.
Falls Hd Q; 51°28'·23N 01°49'·89E.
Drill Stone Q (3) 10s; 51°25'·88N 01°42'·89E.
Thanet N VQ 15s; 51°28'·28N 01°38'·06E.
NE Spit VQ (3) ***Racon (T) 10M;*** 51°27'·93N 01°29'·89E; 992351037
East Margate Fl R 2·5s; 51°27'·03N 01°26'·40E.
Elbow Q; 51°23'·23N 01°31'·59E.
Foreness Pt Outfall Fl R 5s; 51°24'·61N 01°26'·02E.
Longnose 51°24'·15N 01°26'·08E.
Longnose Spit Fl R 2·5s 5m 2M; 51°23'·93N 01°25'·68E.

MARGATE and GORE CHANNEL

SE Margate Q (3) 10s; 51°24'·05N 01°20'·40E.
S Margate Fl G 2·5s; 51°23'·83N 01°16'·65E.
Copperas QG; 51°23'·81N 01°11'·18E.
Reculver QR; 51°23'·63N 01°12'·56E.

HERNE BAY

Beltinge Bay Bn Fl Y 5s; 51°22'·73N 01°08'·63E.
Landing Stage Q 18m 4M, (isolated); 51°22'·91N 01°06'·89E.
N Pier Hd 2 FR (vert); 51°22'·43N 01°07'·27E.

WHITSTABLE

Whitstable Street ; 51°24'·00N 01°01'·54E. (See The Swale.)
Oyster Fl (2) R 10s; 51°22'·14N 01°01'·16E.
W Quay Dn Fl G 5s 2m.

THE SWALE

Whitstable Street Fl R 2s; 51°24'·00N 01°01'·54E.
Columbine Fl G 2s; 51°24'·26N 01°01'·34E.
Columbine Spit Fl (3) G 10s; 51°23'·86N 01°00'·03E.
Ham Gat Q G; 51°23'·08N 00°58'·32E.
Pollard Spit Q R; 51°22'·98N 00°58'·57E.
Sand End Fl G 5s; 51°21'·43N 00°55'·90E.
Receptive Point Fl G 10s; 51°20'·86N 00°54'·41E.
Queenborough Spit Q (3) 10s; 51°25'·81N 00°43'·93E.
South Oaze Fl R 2s; 51°21'·34N 00°56'·01E.

QUEENS CHANNEL and FOUR FATHOMS CHANNEL

E Margate Fl R 2·5s; 51°27'·03N 01°26'·40E.
Spaniard Q (3) 10s; 51°26'·23N 01°04'·00E.
Spile Fl G 2·5s; 51°26'·43N 00°55'·70E.

PRINCES CHANNEL

Tongue Sand E VQ (3) 5s; 51°29'·48N 01°22'·21E.
Tongue Sand N Q; 51°29'·68N 01°22'·03E.
Princes Outer VQ (6) + L Fl 10s; 51°28'·79N 01°19'·87E.
Princes North Q G; 51°29'·25N 01°18'·35E.
Princes South Q R; 51°28'·74N 01°18'·26E.
Princes No 1 Fl (4) G 15s; 51°29'·23N 01°16'·02E.
Princes No 2 Fl (2) R 5s; 51°28'·81N 01°13'·08E.
Princes No 3 Fl (2) G 5s; 51°29'·33N 01°13'·10E.
Princes No 4 Fl (3) R 10s; 51°28'·83N 01°09'·90E.
Princes No 5 Fl (3) G 10s; 51°29'·39N 01°10'·00E.
Princes Mid Fl Y 5s; 51°29'·19N 01°09'·00E.
Shivering Sand Twr N Q; 51°30'·01N 01°04'·76E.
Shivering Sand Twr S Q (6)+L Fl 15s; *Bell*; 51°29'·75N 01°04'·83E.
Princes No 8 Fl (2) R 5s; 51°29'·14N 01°03'·00E.
Princes Inner Fl Y 2·5s; 51°29'·59N 01°03'·47E.

FOULGER'S GAT and KNOB CHANNEL

N Edinburgh Channel is not buoyed. Foulger's Gat, lies within the boundary of the London Array Wind Farm.
Long Sand Outer Iso 2s; 51°34'·61N 01°28'·34E.
Long Sand Middle Iso 5s; 51°35'·60N 01°26'·45E.
Long Sand Inner Iso 2s; 51°38'·78N 01°25'·44E.
SE Knob Fl G 5s; 51°30'·89N 01°06'·41E.
Knob Iso 5s; *Whis*; 51°30'·69N 01°04'·28E.

OAZE DEEP

Oaze Deep Fl (2) G 5s; 51°29'·18N 00°56'·77E.
Red Sand Trs N Fl (3) R 10s; *Bell*; 51°28'·73N 00°59'·32E.
N Oaze QR; 51°30'·03N 00°57'·65E.
Oaze Fl (4) Y 10s; 51°29'·06N 00°56'·93E.
W Oaze Iso 5s; 51°29'·06N 00°55'·43E.
Oaze Bank Q G 5s; 51°29'·18N 00°56'·77E.
Cant (unlit); 51°27'·77N 00°53'·36E.
East Cant QR; 51°28'·53N 00°55'·60E.

MEDWAY, SHEERNESS

Medway Mo (A) 6s; 51°28'·83N 00°52'·81E.
No 1 Fl G 2·5s; 51°28'·55N 00°50'·50E.
No 2 Q; 51°28'·33N 00°50'·52E.
No 7 Fl G 10s; 51°27'·91N 00°47'·52E.
No 9 Fl G 5s; 51°27'·74N 00°46'·61E.
No 11 Fl (3) G 10s; 51°27'·51N 00°45'·80E.
Grain Hard Fl G 5s; 51°26'·98N 00°44'·17E.
Isle of Grain Q 20m 13M; RW ◊ on R twr; 51°26'·70N 00°43'·38E.
Queenborough Spit Q (3) 10s; 51°25'·81N 00°43'·93E.

RIVER THAMES

SEA REACH, NORE and YANTLET

Sea Reach 1 (N) Fl Y 2·5s; ***Racon (T) 10M***; 51°29'·59N 00°52'·71E.
Sea Reach 1 (S) Fl R 2·5s; 51°29'·39N 00°52'·45E.
Sea Reach 2 (N) Fl R 2·5s; 51°29'·49N 00°49'·73E.
Sea Reach 2 (S) Fl R 2·5s; 51°29'·30N 00°49'·75E.
Sea Reach 3 (N) Q G (sync); 51°29'·41N 00°46'·80E.
Sea Reach 3 (S) Q R (sync); 51°29'·22N 00°46'·71E.
Sea Reach 4 (N) Fl (2) G 5s; 51°29'·69N 00°44'·19E.
Sea Reach 4 (S) Fl (2) R 5s; 51°29'·50N 00°44'·12E.
Sea Reach 5 (N) VQ G; 51°30'·04N 00°41'·47E.
Sea Reach 5 (S) VQ R; 51°29'·85N 00°41'·43E.
Sea Reach 6 (N) Fl G 5s; 51°30'·13N 00°39'·87E.
Sea Reach 6 (S) Fl R 5s; 51°29'·93N 00°39'·84E.
Sea Reach 7 (N) Fl Y 2·5s; 51°30'·21N 00°36'·94E.
Sea Reach 7 (S) Fl R 2·5s; ***Racon (T) 10M***; 51°30'·01N 00°36'·91E.
Nore Swatch Fl (4) R 15s; 51°28'·28N 00°45'·55E.
Mid Swatch Fl G 5s; 51°28'·68N 00°44'·16E.
W Nore Sand Fl (3) R 10s; 51°29'·48N 00°40'·87E.
East Blyth Q; 51°29'·73N 00°37'·81E.
Mid Blyth Q; 51°30'·08N 00°32'·38E.

LEIGH-ON-SEA and SOUTHEND-ON-SEA

Leigh ; 51°31'·07N 00°42'·56E.
Southend Pier E End 2 FG (vert) 7m; *Horn Mo (N) 30s, Bell (1).*

LOWER HOPE REACH

West Blyth Q R; 51°29'·57N 00°28'·39E.
Mucking 1 Q G; 51°29'·70N 00°37'·28E.
Lower Hope Fl R 5s; 51°29'·32N 00°28'·02E.
Mucking 3 Fl G 2·5s; 51°29'·33N 00°27'·68E.
Mucking 5 Fl (3) G 10s; 51°28'·76N 00°27'·19E.
Mucking 7 Fl G 5s; 51°28'·03N 00°26'·77E.
Bell Ovens Q G; 51°27'·50N 00°26'·35E.
Higham Fl (2) R 5s; 51°27'·40N 00°26'·85E.
Tilbury Q(6) + L Fl 15s; 51°27'·16N 00°25'·50E.

GRAVESEND

Shornmead Fl (2) WR 10s 12m, W11/7M, R11M; vis 070°-W-084°-R(Intens)-089°-W(Intens)-094°-W-250°; 51°26'·92N 00°26'·24E.
Northfleet Upper ☆ Oc WRG 10s 30m **W16M**, R12M, G12M; vis:126°-R-149°-W-159°-G-268°-W-279°; 51°26'·93N 00°20'·06E.

THAMES TIDAL BARRIER

Spans B, C, D, E, F, G are navigable. Spans C – F are for large ships. Eastbound small craft/yachts use Span B (51°29′·73N 00°02′·23E) Westbound small craft/yachts use Span G (51°29′·91N 00°02′·21E). **Red X** indicates span closed **Green →** indicates span open. W lights show either side of open spans in poor visibility.

KENTISH KNOCK

Kentish Knock Q (3) 10s; 51°38′·08N 01°40·43E.
S Knock Q (6) + L Fl 15s; *Bell*; 51°34′·13N 01°34′·29E.

KNOCK JOHN CHANNEL

No 7 Fl (4) G 15s; 51°32′·03N 01°06′·40E.
No 5 Fl (3) G 10s; 51°32′·49N 01°07′·75E.
No 4 QR 10s; 51°32′·40 N 01°08′·08E.
No 2 Fl (3) R 10s; 51°33′·03N 01°09′·63E.
No 3 Q (6) + L Fl 15s; 51°33′·29N 01°09′·83E.
No 1 Fl G 5s; 51°33′·75N 01°10′·72E.
Knock John Fl (2) R 5s; 51°33′·61N 01°11′·37E.

BLACK DEEP

No 12 Fl (4) R 15s; 51°33′·83N 01°13′·50E.
No 11 Fl (3) G 10s; 51°34′·33N 01°13′·40E.
No 10 Fl (3) R 10s; 51°34′·74N 01°15′·60E.
No 9 Q (6) + L Fl 15s; 51°35′·13N 01°15′·09E.
No 8 Q (9) 15s; 51°36′·36N 01°20′·43E.
No 7 QG. 51°37′·08N 01°17′·69E.
No 6 Fl R 2·5s; 51°38′·53N 01°24′·41E.
No 5 VQ (3) 5s; 51°39′·53N 01°23′·00E.
No 4 Fl (2) R 5s; 51°41′·42N 01°28′·49E.
Long Sand Bcn ; 51°41′·48N 01°29′·49E.
No 3 Fl (3) G 15s; 51°42′·39N 01°26′·66E.
No 1 Fl G 5s, 51°44′·03N 01°28′·09E.
No 2 Fl (4) R 15s; 51°45′·63N 01°32′·20E.
SHM Fl Y 2·5s; ***Racon (T) 10M***; 51°29′·59N 00°52′·71E.

SUNK

Sunk Head Tower Q; *Whis*; 51°46′·63N 01°30′·51E.
Black Deep QR; 51°48′·26N 01°36′·86E.
Long Sand Head VQ; *Bell*; 51°48′·06N 01°39′·40E.
SUNK CENTRE 51°50′·11N 01°46′·02E; Fl (2) 20s 12m **16M**; ***Racon (C) 10M***; *Horn (2) 60s*; 992351094.
Dynamo Fl Y 2·5s; 51°29′·59N 00°52′·71E.
Trinity Q (6) + L Fl 15s; 51°49′·03N 01°36′·39E.
SUNK INNER 51°51′·17N 01°34′·40E; Fl(5) 15s 11m 12M; ***Racon (C) 10M***; *Horn 30s*; 992351027.

FISHERMANS GAT

Outer Fisherman Q (3) 10s; 51°34′·02N 01°25′·10E.
Fisherman No 1 Fl G 2·5s (sync); 51°34′·50N 01°23′·52E.
Fisherman No 2 Fl R 2·5s (sync); 51°34′·30N 01°23′·50E.
Fisherman No 3 Fl G 5s; 51°34′·78N 01°22′·65E.
Fisherman No 4 Fl (2) R 5s; 51°34′·77N 01°22′·08E.
Fisherman No 5 Fl (2) G 5s; 51°35′·25N 01°21′·84E.
Fisherman No 6 Fl (3) R 10s; 51°35′·08N 01°21′·56E.
Inner Fisherman Q R; 51°36′·15N 01°20′·08E.

BARROW DEEP

SW Barrow Q(6) + L Fl 15s; *Bell*; 51°32′·29N 01°00′·31E.
Alice Wk Fl (2) 5s; 51°32′·33N 01°04′·22E.
Barrow No 14 Fl R 2·5s; 51°31′·83N 01°00′·43E.
Barrow No 13 Fl (2) G 5s; 51°32′·82N 01°03′·07E.
Barrow No 12 Fl (2) R 5s; 51°33′·24N 01°05′·94E.
Barrow No 11 Fl (3) G 10s; 51°34′·08N 01°06′·70E.
Barrow No 9 VQ (3) 5s; 51°35′·34N 01°10′·30E.
Barrow No 8 Fl (2) R 5s; 51°35′·05N 01°11′·37E.
Barrow No 6 Fl (4) R 15s; 51°37′·30N 01°14′·69E.
Barrow No 5 Fl G 10s; 51°40′·03N 01°16′·20E.
Barrow No 4 VQ (9) 10s; 51°39′·88N 01°17′·48E.
Barrow No 3 Q (3) 10s; ***Racon (M)10M***; 51°42′·02N 01°20′·24E.
Barrow No 2 Fl (2) R 5s; 51°41′·98N 01°22′·89E.

WEST SWIN and MIDDLE DEEP

Blacktail Spit Fl (3) G 10s; 51°31′·47N 00°56′·75E.
Maplin Q G (sync with W Swin); *Bell*; 51°33′·66N 01°01′·40E.
W Swin Q R (sync with Maplin); 51°33′·40N 01°01′·97E.
Maplin Edge Fl G 2.5s; 51°35′·33N 01°03′·64E.
Maplin Bank Fl (3) R 10s; 51°35′·50N 01°04′·70E.
Maplin Middle Fl G 5s; *Bell*; 51°36′·78N 01°05′·50E.
E Maplin 51°38′·29N 01°08′·86E.
Maplin Approach Fl (2) G 10s; 51°39′·54N 01°09′·39E.

EAST SWIN and KING'S CHANNEL

N Middle Q; 51°41′·35N 01°12′·61E.
W Sunk Q (9) 15s; 51°44′·33N 01°25′·80E.
Gunfleet Spit Q (6) + L Fl 15s; *Bell*; 51°45′·33N 01°21′·70E.

WHITAKER CHANNEL and RIVER CROUCH

Whitaker Q (3) 10s; *Bell*; 51°41′·43N 01°10′·51E.
Inner Whitaker VQ (6) + L Fl 10s; 51°40′·76N 01°08′·40E.
Swin Spitway Iso 10s; *Bell;* 51°41′·95N 01°08′·35E.
Whitaker 1 FlG 5s (sync Whit 2), 51° 40′·69N 01° 06′·67E.
Whitaker 2 FlR 5s (sync Whit 1), 51° 40′·41N 01° 06′·78E.
Whitaker 3 Fl(2) G 5s (sync Whit 4) 51° 40′·41N 01° 04′·74E.
Whitaker 4 Fl(2) R 5s (sync Whit 4) 51° 40′·16N 01° 04′·91E.
Whitaker 5 Fl(3) G 10s (sync Whit 6) 51° 40′·03N 01° 03′·22E.
Whitaker 6 Fl(3) R 10s(sync Whit 5) 51° 39′·77N 01° 03′·43E.
Whitaker 7 Fl(4) G 10s(sync Whit 8) 51° 39′·54N 01° 02′·00E.
Whitaker 8 Fl(4) R 10s(sync Whit 7), 51° 39′·35N 01° 02′·00E.
Swallowtail 1 Fl Y 5s, 51° 41′·38N 01° 08′·20E.
Swallowtail 2 Fl Y 10s, 51° 41′·19N 01° 06′·28E.
Swallowtail 3 Fl Y 15s, 51° 40.84N 01° 04.39E.
Swallowtail 4 (2) Y 10s, 51° 40′·52N 01° 03′·47E.
Buxey Edge Fl G 10s, 51° 40′·65N 01° 03′·48E.
Swallowtail VQ (9) 10s, 51° 40′·04N 01° 02′·65E.
Sunken Buxey VQ; 51°39′·59N 01°00′·77E.
Buxey No 1 VQ (6) + L Fl 10s; 51°39′·18N 01°01′·13E.
Buxey No 2 Q; 51°39′·08N 01°00′·23E.
Outer Crouch 1 Fl G 5s (sync Cro 2) 51° 38′·71N 00° 59′·00E.
Outer Crouch 2 Fl R 5s (sync Cro 1) 51° 38′·62N 00° 59′·20E.
Outer Crouch 3 Fl G 10s (sync Cro 4) 51° 38′·10N 00° 57′·83E.
Outer Crouch 4 Fl R 10s (sync Cro 3) 51° 37′·95N 00° 58′·00E.
Crouch Q.Fl, 51° 37.650N 00° 56.582E.
Inner Crouch L Fl 10s, 51° 37′·19N 00° 55′·09E.
Branklet (RGR) **Pref Chan to Stbd,** Comp grp Fl (R) 2+1 10s, 51° 36′·99N 00° 52′·10E.

GOLDMER GAT and WALLET

NE Gunfleet Q (3) 10s; 51°49′·93N 01°27′·79E.
Wallet No 2 Fl R 5s; 51°48′·88N 01°22′·99E.
Wallet No 4 Fl (4) R 10s; 51°46′·53N 01°17′·23E.
Wallet Spitway L Fl 10s; *Bell*; 51°42′·86N 01°07′·30E.
Knoll Q; 51°43′·88N 01°05′·07E.
Eagle QG; 51°44′·13N 01°03′·82E.
N Eagle Q; 51°44′·71N 01°04′·32E.
NW Knoll Fl (2) R 5s; 51°44′·35N 01°02′·17E.
Colne Bar Fl (2) G 5s; 51°44′·61N 01°02′·57E.
Bench Head Fl (3) G 10s; 51°44′·69N 01°01′·10E.

RIVER BLACKWATER

The Nass VQ (3) 5s 6m 2M; 51°45′·83N 00°54′·83E.
Thirslet Fl (3) G 10s; 51°43′·73N 00°50′·39E.
No 1 ; 51°43′·44N 00°48′·02E.

RIVER COLNE and BRIGHTLINGSEA

Inner Bench Head No 2 Fl (2) R 5s; 51°45′·96N 01°01′·74E.
Colne Pt No 1 Fl G 3s; 51°46′·01N 01°01′·92E.
No 8 Fl R 3s; 51°46′·90N 01°01′·30E.
No 9 Fl G 3s; 51°47′·36N 01°01′·07E.

Ldg lts 041°. Front, FR 7m 4M; W □, R stripe on post; vis: 020°-080°; 51°48′·39N 01°01′·20E. Rear, 50m from front, FR 10m 4M; W □, R stripe on post. FR lts are shown on 7 masts between 1·5M and 3M NW when firing occurs.

WALTON BACKWATERS
Pye End L Fl 10s; 51°55′·03N 01°17′·90E.
No 2 Fl (2) 5s; 51°54′·62N 01°16′·80E.
Crab Knoll No 3 Fl G 5s; 51°54′·41N 01°16′·41E.
No 16 51°53′·17N 01°15′·52E.

HARWICH APPROACHES
(Direction of buoyage is North to South)

MEDUSA CHANNEL
Medusa Fl G 5s; 51°51′·23N 01°20′·35E.
Stone Banks FlR 5s; 51°53′·19N 01°19′·23E.
Pennyhole ; 51°53′·55N 01°18′·00E (Mar–Sep).

CORK SAND and ROUGH SHOALS
S Cork Q (6) + L Fl 15s; 51°51′·33N 01°24′·09E.
SE Roughs Tower Q (3) 10s; 51°53′·64N 01°28′·94E.
NW Roughs Tower VQ (9) 10s; 51°53′·81N 01°28′·77E.
Cork Sand Fl (3) R 10s; 51°55′·51N 01°25′·42E.

HARWICH CHANNEL
S Threshold Fl (4) Y 10s; 51°52′·20N 01°33′·14E.
S Shipwash 2 By(s) Q (6) + L Fl 15s; 51°52′·71N 01°33′·97E.
Outer Tidal Bn Mo (U) 15s 2m 3M; 51°52′·85N 01°32′·34E.
E Fort Massac VQ (3) 5s; 51°53′·36N 01°32′·79E.
W Fort Massac VQ (9) 10s; 51°53′·36N 01°32′·49E.
Walker Q (9)15s; 51°53′·79N 01°33′·90E.
N Threshold Fl Y 5s; 51°54′·49N 01°33′·47E.
SW Shipwash Fl Y 2·5s; 51°54′·75N 01°34′·21E.
Haven Mo (A) 5s; 51°55′·76N 01°32′·56E.
W Shipwash Fl (2) R 10s; 51°57′·13N 01°35′·89E.
NW Shipwash Fl R 5s; 51°58′·98N 01°37′·01E.
Harwich App (HA) Iso 5s; 51°56′·75N 01°30′·66E.
Cross Fl (3) Y 10s; 51°56′·23N 01°30′·48E.
Harwich Chan No 1 Fl Y 2·5s; ***Racon (T) 10M***; 51°56′·13N 01°27′·06E.
Harwich Chan No 3 Fl (3) Y 10s; 51°56′·04N 01°25′·54E.
Harwich Chan No 5 Fl (5) Y 10s; 51°55′·96N 01°24′·01E.
Harwich Chan No 7 Fl (3) Y 10s; 51°55′·87N 01°22′·49E.
S Bawdsey Q (6) + L Fl 15s; *Whis*; 51°57′·23N 01°30′·19E.
Washington QG; 51°56′·52N 01°26′·59E.
Felixstowe Ledge Fl (3) G 10s; 51°56′·30N 01°23′·72E.
Wadgate Ledge Fl (4) G 15s; 51°56′·16N 01°21′·99E.
Platters Q (6) + L Fl 15s; 51°55′·64N 01°20′·97E.
Rolling Ground QG; 51°55′·55N 01°19′·75E.
Beach End Fl (2) G 5s; 51°55′·62N 01°19′·21E.
Cork Sand Yacht Bn VQ 2M; 51°55′·21N 01°25′·20E.
Rough VQ; 51°55′·19N 01°31′·00E.
Pitching Ground Fl (4) R 15s; 51°55′·43N 01°21′·05E.
Inner Ridge QR; 51°55′·38N 01°20′·20E.
Deane L Fl R 6s; 51°55′·36N 01°19′·28E.
Landguard Q; 51°55′·45N 01°18′·84E.

RIVERS STOUR AND ORWELL

RIVER STOUR and HARWICH
Shotley Spit Q (6) + L Fl 15s; 51°57′·21N 01°17′·69E.
Shotley Marina Lock E side Dir lt 339·5° 3m 1M (uses Moiré pattern); Or structure; 51°57′·46N 01°16′·60E.
Guard Fl R 5s; *Bell*; 51°57′·07N 01°17′·86E.

RIVER ORWELL and IPSWICH
Suffolk Yacht Harbour. Ldg lts Front Iso Y 1M; 51°59′·73N 01°16′·09E. Rear Oc Y 4s 1M.

HARWICH TO ORFORD NESS

FELIXSTOWE, R DEBEN and WOODBRIDGE HAVEN
Woodbridge Haven Mo(A)15s; 51°57′·99N 01°23′·63E.
Deben ; 51°59′·30N 01°23′·53E.

RIVERS ORE and ALDE
Orford Haven L Fl 10s; *Bell*. 52°02′·00N 01°28′·20E.

OFFSHORE MARKS
S Galloper Q (6) L Fl 15s; ***Racon (T) 10M***; 51°43′·98N 01°56′·43E.
N Galloper Q; 51°49′·84N 01°59′·99E.
S Inner Gabbard Q (6) + L Fl 15s. 51°49′·92N 01°51′·89E.
N Inner Gabbard Q; 51°59′·20N 01°56′·00E.
NHR-SE Fl G 5s; 51°45′·39N 02°39′·89E.

SHIPWASH and BAWDSEY BANK
E Shipwash VQ (3) 5s; 51°57′·08N 01°37′·89E.
NW Shipwash Fl R 5s; 51°58′·98N 01°37′·01E.
N Shipwash Q 7M; ***Racon (M) 10M***; *Whis*; 52°01′·73N 01°38′·27E; 992351069.
S Bawdsey Q (6) + L Fl 15s; *Whis*; 51°57′·23N 01°30′·22E.
Mid Bawdsey Fl (3) G 10s; 51°58′·88N 01°33′·59E.
NE Bawdsey Fl G 10s; 52°01′·73N 01°36′·09E.

CUTLER and WHITING BANKS
Cutler QG; 51°58′·51N 01°27′·48E.
SW Whiting Q (6) + L Fl 10s; 52°00′·96N 01°30′·69E.
Whiting Hook Fl R 10s; 52°02′·98N 01°31′·82E.
NE Whiting Q (3) 10s; 52°03′·61N 01°33′·32E.

ORFORD NESS TO WINTERTON
(Direction of buoyage is South to North)
Orford Ness Lt Ho (dis) 52°05′·04N 01°34′·45E; W ○ twr, R bands.
Aldeburgh Ridge QR; 52°06′·49N 01°36′·95E.

SOUTHWOLD
Southwold ☆ 52°19′·63N 01°40′·89E; Fl 10s 37m **W24M**; vis 204°-W-032·5°, 992351019.

LOWESTOFT and APPR VIA STANFORD CHANNEL
E Barnard Q (3) 10s; 52°25′·14N 01°46′·38E.
Newcome Sand QR; 52°26′·28N 01°46′·97E.
S Holm VQ (6) + L Fl 10s; 52°26′·85N 01°47′·15E.
Stanford Fl R 2·5s; 52°27′·35N 01°46′·67E.
SW Holm Fl (2) G 5s; 52°27′·87N 01°46′·99E.
Kirkley ☆ Dir WRG Oc 10s 17m, WRG 10M, vis: 222°-OcG -223°-FlG-224°-Fl W-225°-Oc W-228°-FlW-229°-Fl R-230°-Oc R-232°; 52°27′·71N 01°44′·54E.
Outer Hbr S Pier Hd ☆ Oc R 5s 12m 6M; *Horn (4) 60s*; Tfc sigs; 52°28′·29N 01°45′·36E.
N Newcome Fl (4) R 15s; 52°28′·39N 01°46′·37E.
Lowestoft ☆ 52°29′·22N 01°45′·35; Fl 15s 37m **23M**; W twr; part obscd 347°- shore.

LOWESTOFT NORTH ROAD and CORTON ROAD
Lowestoft Ness SE Q (6) + L Fl 15s; 52°28′·84N 01°46′·25E.
Lowestoft Ness N VQ (3) 5s; *Bell*; 52°28′·89N 01°46′·23E.
W Holm Fl (3) G 10s; 52°29′·80N 01°47′·09E.
NW Holm Fl (4) G 15s; 52°31′·93N 01°46′·70E.

GREAT YARMOUTH APPROACH via HOLM CHANNEL
E Newcome Fl (2) R 5s; 52°28′·51N 01°49′·21E.
Holm Approach Q (3) 10s; 52°30′·88N 01°50′·22E.
Holm Sand Q (9) 15s; 52°33′·18N 01°46′·54E.
S Corton Q (6) + L Fl 15s; *Bell*; 52°32′·90N 01°48′·99E.
NE Holm Fl R 2·5s; 52°32′·69N 01°48′·48E.
Mid Corton Fl G 2·5s; 52°33′·61N 01°47′·98E.
N Holm Q. 52°33′·93N 01°47′·23E.
W Corton Fl (3) G 10s; 52°34′·12N 01°47′·50E.

GREAT YARMOUTH and GORLESTON
Gorleston South Pier Hd ☆ Fl R 3s 11m 11M; vis: 235°-340°; 52°34′·33N 01°44′·28E.
N Pier Hd ☆ QG 8m 6M; vis: 176°-078°; *Horn(3) 60s*; 52°34′·38N 01°44′·38E.
Outer Hbr S Pier ☆ Q R 17m 3M; 52°34′·61N 01°44′·73E.
Outer Hbr N Pier ☆ Q G 17m 3M; 52°34′·70N 01°44′·74E.

9.4.5 PASSAGE INFORMATION

More passage information is threaded between the harbours in this area. See 9.0.7 for distances across the North Sea. Admiralty Leisure Folios: 5606 Thames Estuary from Ramsgate to Tower Bridge, London; 5607 Northern Thames Estuary to Orford Ness; 5614 Orford Ness to Whitby. See also eastcoastsailing.co.uk. **Bibliography:** *East Coast Rivers* (Fernhurst/Harber); *East Coast Pilot* (Imray/Jarman,Holness,Cooper); *Dover Strait Pilot* and *North Sea (West) Pilot* (Admiralty NP28 and 54); *North Sea Passage Pilot* (Imray/Navin).

THE THAMES ESTUARY

(AC 1183, 1975, 1607, 1606, 1609) The sandbanks shift constantly in the Thames Estuary; charted depths cannot be relied upon, and an accurate echo sounder is vital. Up to date charts showing the latest buoyage changes and a detailed tidal stream atlas are essential. The commercial deep water route from the Sunk Inner precautionary area to the Yantlet runs through Black Deep and Knock John Channel. It is well marked, as are Barrow Deep, Princes Channel and Fisherman's Gat. The lesser channels and swatchways, which are convenient for yachtsmen, particularly when crossing the estuary, are mainly unmarked and unlit. They should be used with great caution. Good visibility is needed to pick out buoys and marks, and to avoid shipping. Care should be exercised when plotting electronic waypoints. Many former navigation marks and towers have been removed or allowed to disintegrate. Those that are still standing may be in very shallow water.

Newcomers to the estuary are advised to choose a period of neap tides when minimum depths are greater and tidal streams weaker. If a crossing at springs is unavoidable, keep in deep water even if that involves a longer passage.

Wind strength and direction needs careful consideration for each of the course changes during a typical crossing to avoid becoming trapped between shoals, downwind and downstream of safe water.

▶ *Study the tides carefully so as to work the streams to best advantage and to ensure sufficient depth at the times and places where you expect to be, or might be later. In principle it is best to make most of the crossing on a rising tide. However, a typical passage from N Foreland to the Blackwater will take 7–9hrs, so some adverse stream is almost inevitable. The stream at springs runs at 3kn in places, mostly along the channels but sometimes across the intervening banks. A short, steep sea may be raised with the wind against tide.* ◀

CROSSING THE THAMES ESTUARY

(AC 1183, 1975, 1607, 1606, 1609) *Crossing the Thames Estuary* (Imray) gives 32 suggested routes. Making N from N Foreland to Orford Ness or beyond it may be better to keep to seaward of the main banks, via Kentish Knock and Long Sand Head buoys, thence to N Shipwash lt buoy, 14M further N.

Bound NW from North Foreland it is approximately 35M to the mouths of the Rivers Crouch, Blackwater or Colne. One route is through the Princes Channel, thence N of the Oaze Deep precautionary area and S of the Knob and West Barrow banks to the West Swin, before turning NE into Middle Deep and the East Swin. The Wallet Spitway then leads NW to the Colne and Blackwater. Many routes may be followed, depending on wind direction, tidal conditions and confidence in electronic aids in the absence of marks. Passage over Sunk Sand and Knock John bank is best avoided, particularly in winds >F5.

Southbound from the Colne or Blackwater, leave 1–2hrs before HW and make best speed to skirt or cross the shoals while there is sufficient depth of water. The latter part of the passage will be in generally deeper water of Edinburgh Channel, Fisherman's or Foulger's Gat or (keeping clear of the turbines in the London Array), with a favourable S-going stream just starting off North Foreland.

From the NE follow Goldmer Gat and the Wallet (for Rivers Colne/Blackwater) or King's Channel and Whittaker Channel for the River Crouch.

London VTS has radar coverage from Greenwich to a line between the Naze and Margate. Keep a listening watch on VHF Ch 69 to monitor shipping activity. If really necessary, *London VTS* may be able to give navigational help to yachts.

NORTH FORELAND TO LONDON BRIDGE

North Foreland has a conspic lt ho (AC 1828), with buoys offshore.
▶ *From HW Dover –0120 to +0045 the stream runs N from The Downs and W into Thames Estuary. From HWD +0045 to +0440 the N-going stream from The Downs meets the E-going stream from Thames Estuary, which in strong winds causes a bad sea. From HWD –0450 to –0120 the streams turn W into Thames Estuary and S towards The Downs. If bound for London, round N Foreland against the late ebb in order to carry a fair tide from Sheerness onward.* ◀

The most direct route from North Foreland to the Thames and Medway is via South, Gore and Copperas Channels, then Overland Passage, Four Fathoms Channel and The Cant. Minimum depth is about 2m but may be significantly less off Reculver and leaving Copperas Channel. It is not well marked. Beware of Kentish Flats wind farm (30 turbines) with submarine cables to Herne Bay. An alternative, deeper route is east of Margate Sand and the Tongue, via the Princes Channel to the Oaze Deep. The N & S Edinburgh Channels are unmarked but navigable with caution.

▶ *W-going streams begin at approx HW Sheerness –0600 and E-going at HW Sheerness +0030.* ◀

Margate or Whitstable afford little shelter for yachts. The Swale provides an interesting inside route S of the Isle of Sheppey with access to Sheerness and the R Medway. If sailing from N Foreland to the Thames, Queenborough offers the first easily accessible, all-tide, deep-water shelter. In the east part of The Swale, Harty Ferry provides a sheltered ⚓, but not in strong winds from N or E. The Medway Channel is the main approach to Sheerness from The Warp.

CROSSING FROM THAMES/ORWELL TO BELGIUM OR THE NETHERLANDS

(ACs 1408, 1406, 1610, 1630, 1872, 1183) Up to date charts are *essential*. Thanet Wind Farm is now established 6Nm ENE of N Foreland and bounded by cardinal buoys. The southern North Sea is an extremely busy area with several large and complex Traffic Separation Schemes and associated Precautionary Areas which should be avoided if at all possible. Where practicable, navigate outside the schemes using any available ITZs, and always cross a TSS on a heading at 90° to the traffic flow in accordance with the Collision Regulations. From the Thames to Zeebrugge, the most direct route crosses the Nord Hinder South TSS in the vicinity of F3 light float. This is a focal point for dense crossing traffic. The very busy area around West Hinder must then be negotiated. A longer but much safer route (or if bound for Dunkerque, Nieuwpoort or Oostende) via S Falls, Sandettié and Dyck minimises time spent in the TSS and provides the option of breaking the passage in Ramsgate.

From the Orwell (or adjacent rivers) to the Netherlands, it may be best to pass north of the Sunk Inner and Sunk Outer TSS/Precautionary Areas before setting course for Hoek van Holland. From S Shipwash make for N Inner Gabbard before setting course for NHR-S to cross the North Hinder TSS to NHR-SE, then pass S of the Maas-West TSS leaving MW1, MW3 and MW5 buoys to port before shaping up for MV-N buoy.

▶ *Care must be taken throughout with the tidal streams, which may be setting across the yacht's track.* ◀

The whole area is relatively shallow, and in bad weather seas are steep and short. *(See also Area 16.)*

9.4.6 THAMES ESTUARY TIDAL STREAMS

Due to very strong rates of tidal streams in some areas, eddies may occur. Where possible, some indication of these is shown, but in many areas there is insufficient information or eddies are unstable.

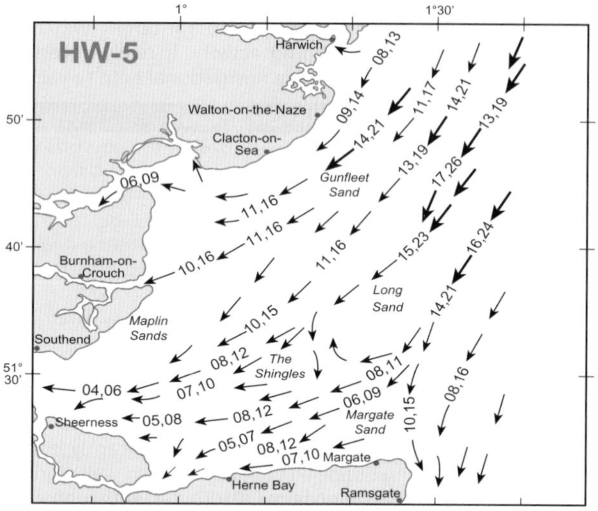

5 Hours before HW Sheerness (0335 before HW Dover)

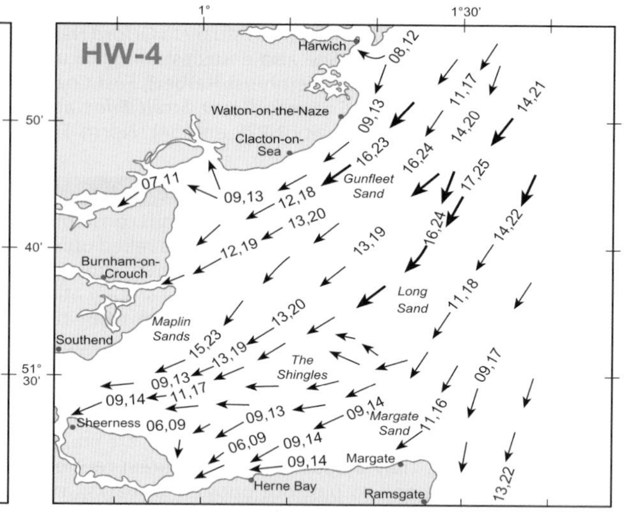

4 Hours before HW Sheerness (0235 before HW Dover)

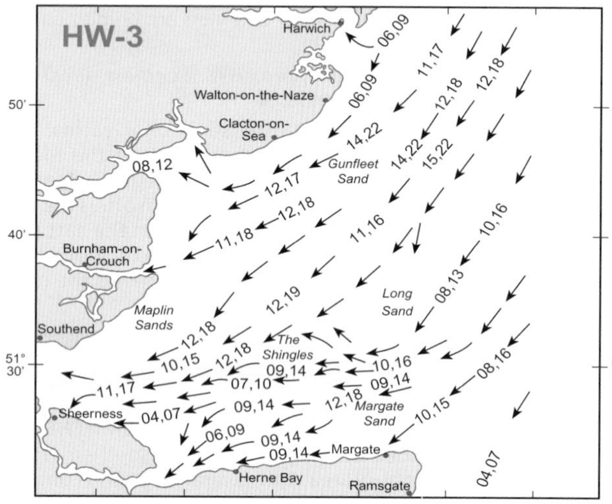

3 Hours before HW Sheerness (0135 before HW Dover)

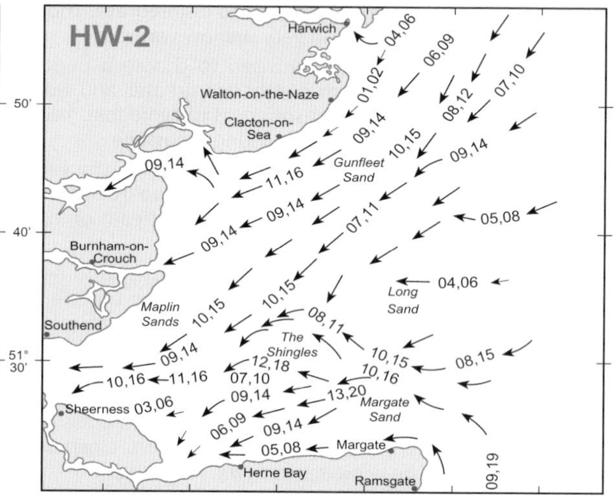

2 Hours before HW Sheerness (0035 before HW Dover)

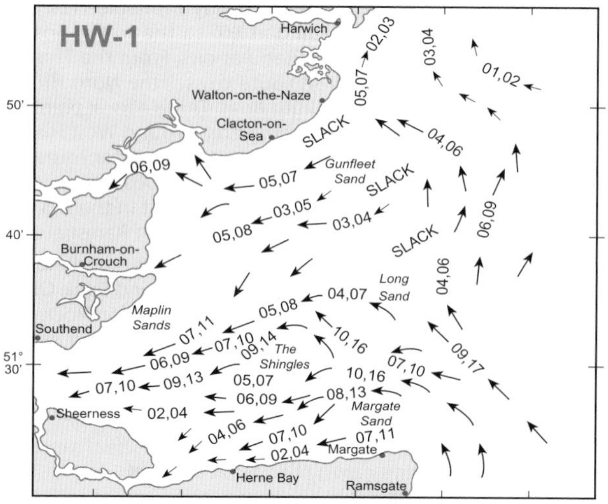

1 Hour before HW Sheerness (0025 after HW Dover)

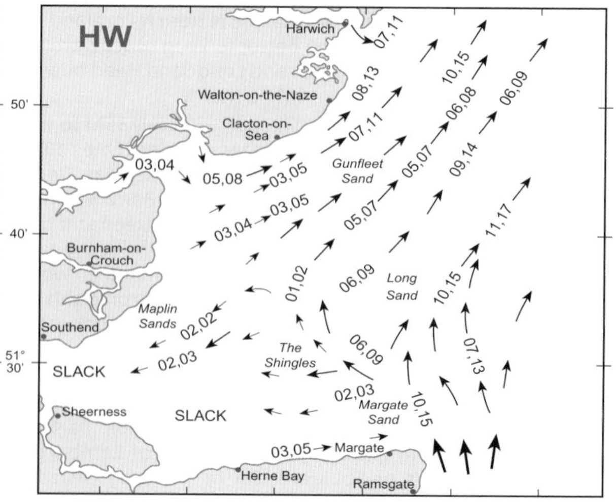

HW Sheerness (0125 after HW Dover)

Due to very strong rates of tidal streams in some areas, eddies may occur. Where possible, some indication of these is shown, but in many areas there is insufficient information or eddies are unstable.

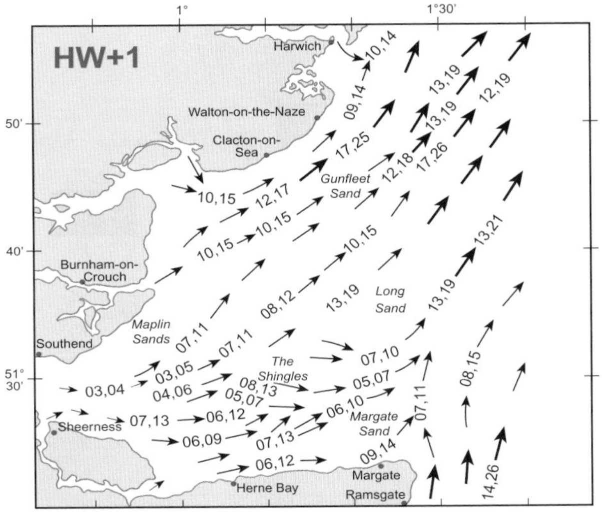
HW+1
Harwich
Walton-on-the-Naze
Clacton-on-Sea
Gunfleet Sand
Burnham-on-Crouch
Maplin Sands
Southend
The Shingles
Long Sand
Sheerness
Margate Sand
Herne Bay
Margate
Ramsgate

1 Hour after HW Sheerness (0225 after HW Dover)

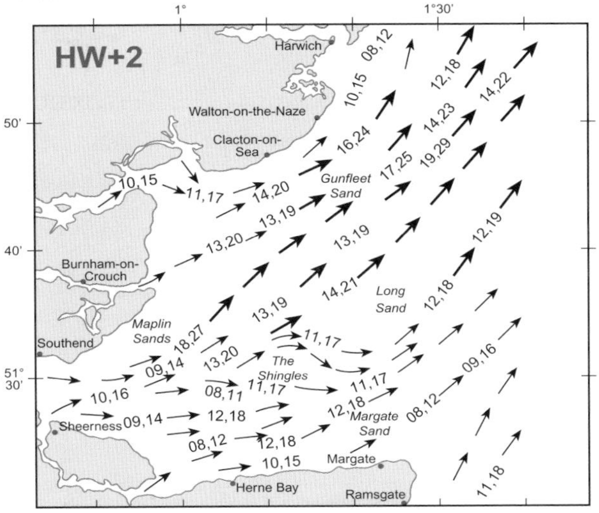
HW+2
Harwich
Walton-on-the-Naze
Clacton-on-Sea
Gunfleet Sand
Burnham-on-Crouch
Maplin Sands
Southend
The Shingles
Long Sand
Sheerness
Margate Sand
Herne Bay
Margate
Ramsgate

2 Hours after HW Sheerness (0325 after HW Dover)

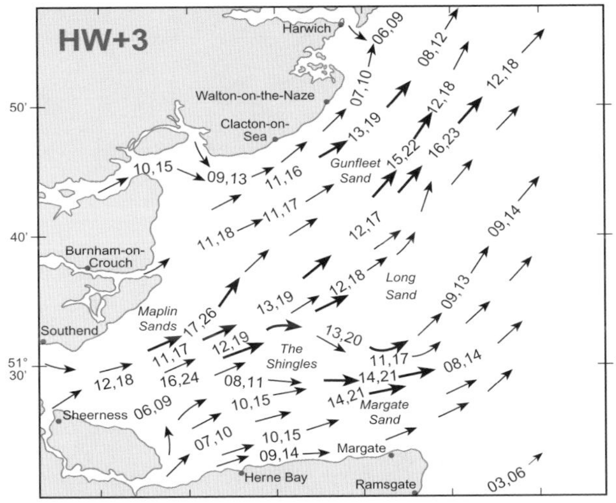
HW+3
Harwich
Walton-on-the-Naze
Clacton-on-Sea
Gunfleet Sand
Burnham-on-Crouch
Maplin Sands
Southend
The Shingles
Long Sand
Sheerness
Margate Sand
Herne Bay
Margate
Ramsgate

3 Hours after HW Sheerness (0425 after HW Dover)

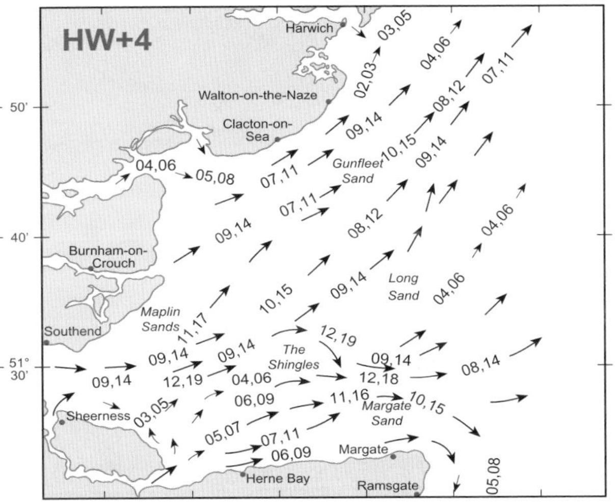
HW+4
Harwich
Walton-on-the-Naze
Clacton-on-Sea
Gunfleet Sand
Burnham-on-Crouch
Maplin Sands
Southend
The Shingles
Long Sand
Sheerness
Margate Sand
Herne Bay
Margate
Ramsgate

4 Hours after HW Sheerness (0525 after HW Dover)

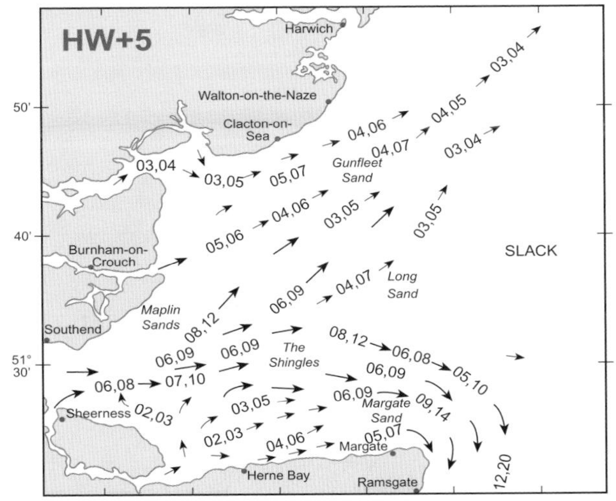
HW+5
Harwich
Walton-on-the-Naze
Clacton-on-Sea
Gunfleet Sand
Burnham-on-Crouch
Maplin Sands
Southend
The Shingles
Long Sand
SLACK
Sheerness
Margate Sand
Herne Bay
Margate
Ramsgate

5 Hours after HW Sheerness (0600 before HW Dover)

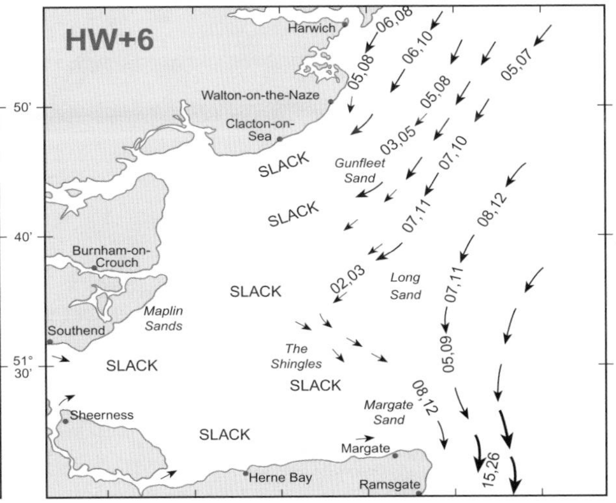
HW+6
Harwich
Walton-on-the-Naze
Clacton-on-Sea
SLACK
Gunfleet Sand
SLACK
Burnham-on-Crouch
SLACK
Long Sand
Maplin Sands
Southend
The Shingles
SLACK
SLACK
Sheerness
Margate Sand
SLACK
Margate
Herne Bay
Ramsgate

6 Hours after HW Sheerness (0500 before HW Dover)

9.4.7 THAMES ESTUARY

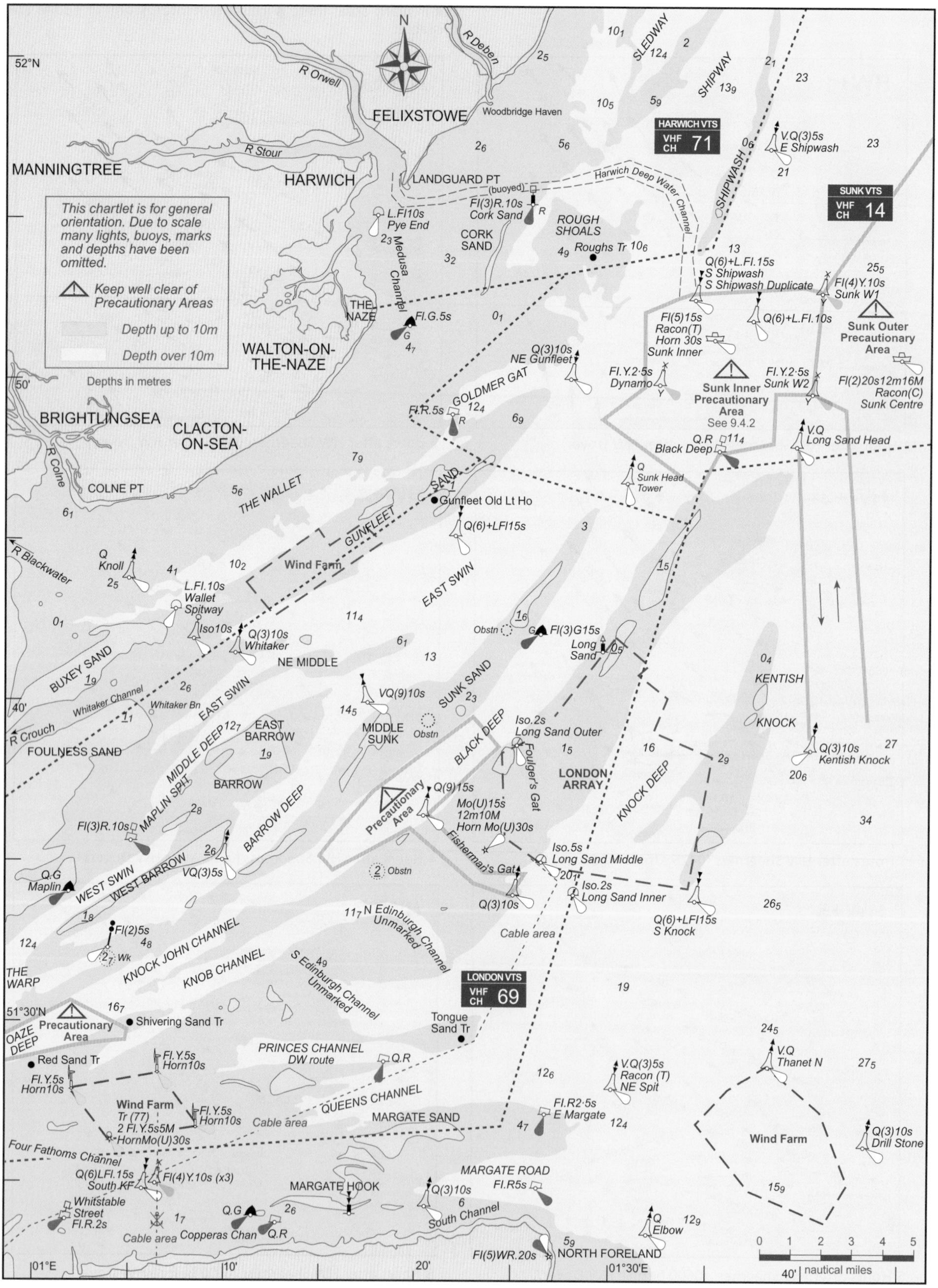
N
52°N
R Orwell
R Deben
FELIXSTOWE
Woodbridge Haven
R Stour
MANNINGTREE
HARWICH
LANDGUARD PT
(buoyed)
Harwich Deep Water Channel
SLEDWAY
SHIPWAY
SHIPWASH
HARWICH VTS
VHF CH 71
SUNK VTS
VHF CH 14
V.Q(3)5s
E Shipwash
This chartlet is for general orientation. Due to scale many lights, buoys, marks and depths have been omitted.
Keep well clear of Precautionary Areas
Depth up to 10m
Depth over 10m
Depths in metres
L.Fl10s
Pye End
Fl(3)R.10s
Cork Sand
CORK SAND
ROUGH SHOALS
Roughs Tr
Medusa Channel
THE NAZE
Fl.G.5s
WALTON-ON-THE-NAZE
Q(6)+L.Fl.15s
S Shipwash
S Shipwash Duplicate
Fl(4)Y.10s
Sunk W1
Q(6)+L.Fl.10s
Sunk Outer Precautionary Area
Fl(5)15s
Racon(T)
Horn 30s
Sunk Inner
Q(3)10s
NE Gunfleet
Fl.Y.2·5s
Dynamo
Sunk Inner Precautionary Area
See 9.4.2
Fl.Y.2·5s
Sunk W2
Fl(2)20s12m16M
Racon(C)
Sunk Centre
50'
BRIGHTLINGSEA
CLACTON-ON-SEA
GOLDMER GAT
Fl.R.5s
V.Q
Long Sand Head
Q.R
Black Deep
R Colne
COLNE PT
THE WALLET
SAND
Gunfleet Old Lt Ho
Q
Sunk Head Tower
Q(6)+LFl15s
R Blackwater
GUNFLEET
Wind Farm
Q
Knoll
L.Fl.10s
Wallet Spitway
EAST SWIN
Iso10s
Q(3)10s
Whitaker
Obstn
Fl(3)G15s
Long Sand
BUXEY SAND
NE MIDDLE
KENTISH
Whitaker Channel
Whitaker Bn
40'
EAST SWIN
VQ(9)10s
SUNK SAND
R Crouch
FOULNESS SAND
MIDDLE DEEP
EAST BARROW
MIDDLE SUNK
Obstn
BLACK DEEP
Iso.2s
Long Sand Outer
KNOCK
Q(3)10s
Kentish Knock
MAPLIN SPIT
BARROW
LONDON ARRAY
Foulger's Gat
KNOCK DEEP
Precautionary Area
Q(9)15s
Mo(U)15s
12m10M
Horn Mo(U)30s
Fl(3)R.10s
BARROW DEEP
Fisherman's Gat
Iso.5s
Long Sand Middle
VQ(3)5s
WEST SWIN
WEST BARROW
Q.G
Maplin
Obstn
Iso.2s
Long Sand Inner
Q(3)10s
Q(6)+LFl15s
S Knock
Fl(2)5s
Wk
N Edinburgh Unmarked
N Edinburgh Channel
Cable area
KNOCK JOHN CHANNEL
THE WARP
KNOB CHANNEL
S Edinburgh Channel
Unmarked
LONDON VTS
VHF CH 69
51°30'N
OAZE DEEP
Precautionary Area
Shivering Sand Tr
Tongue Sand Tr
V.Q
Thanet N
Red Sand Tr
Fl.Y.5s
Horn10s
PRINCES CHANNEL
DW route
Q.R
V.Q(3)5s
Racon (T)
NE Spit
Fl.Y.5s
Horn10s
Wind Farm
Tr (77)
2 Fl.Y.5s5M
HornMo(U)30s
Fl.Y.5s
Horn10s
Cable area
QUEENS CHANNEL
MARGATE SAND
Fl.R2·5s
E Margate
Wind Farm
Q(3)10s
Drill Stone
Four Fathoms Channel
Q(6)LFl.15s
South KF
Fl(4)Y.10s (x3)
MARGATE ROAD
Fl.R5s
MARGATE HOOK
Q(3)10s
Whitstable Street
Fl.R.2s
Q.G
Q.R
South Channel
Q
Elbow
Cable area
Copperas Chan
Fl(5)WR.20s
NORTH FORELAND
01°E
10'
20'
01°30'E
0 1 2 3 4 5
40' nautical miles

STANDARD TIME (UT)
For Summer Time add ONE hour in **non-shaded areas**

MARGATE LAT 51°23′N LONG 1°23′E

TIMES AND HEIGHTS OF HIGH AND LOW WATERS

Dates in red are SPRINGS
Dates in blue are NEAPS

YEAR **2018**

JANUARY

Date	Time	m	Date	Time	m
1 M	0457 1058 1718 2330	0.7 4.8 0.6 4.7	16 TU	0549 1148 1751 2357	0.8 4.4 0.9 4.5
2 TU ○	0552 1152 1808	0.6 4.9 0.6	17 W ●	0625 1223 1825	0.7 4.5 0.9
3 W	0019 0645 1246 1856	4.8 0.4 5.0 0.6	18 TH	0030 0658 1257 1856	4.6 0.7 4.5 0.9
4 TH	0108 0736 1338 1943	4.9 0.4 5.0 0.7	19 F	0106 0729 1333 1928	4.7 0.6 4.6 0.8
5 F	0156 0826 1429 2028	4.9 0.3 4.9 0.8	20 SA	0142 0801 1410 2003	4.7 0.6 4.5 0.8
6 SA	0243 0913 1518 2112	4.8 0.4 4.8 0.9	21 SU	0219 0835 1447 2039	4.6 0.6 4.5 0.9
7 SU	0329 1000 1607 2157	4.7 0.5 4.6 1.1	22 M	0253 0911 1522 2117	4.5 0.7 4.4 1.0
8 M ◑	0417 1049 1700 2248	4.6 0.6 4.4 1.2	23 TU	0326 0949 1558 2158	4.5 0.7 4.3 1.1
9 TU	0512 1143 1800 2351	4.4 0.8 4.2 1.4	24 W ◐	0404 1032 1640 2245	4.4 0.8 4.2 1.2
10 W	0616 1245 1903	4.2 1.0 4.1	25 TH	0453 1124 1733 2346	4.3 0.9 4.1 1.3
11 TH	0108 0721 1348 2005	1.5 4.1 1.1 4.1	26 F	0552 1232 1840	4.2 1.0 4.1
12 F	0219 0825 1447 2105	1.4 4.1 1.1 4.1	27 SA	0106 0706 1352 2007	1.3 4.2 1.0 4.1
13 SA	0323 0928 1541 2200	1.3 4.2 1.1 4.2	28 SU	0230 0831 1504 2122	1.2 4.3 0.9 4.3
14 SU	0420 1023 1630 2246	1.1 4.3 1.0 4.4	29 M	0341 0945 1608 2225	1.0 4.4 0.8 4.5
15 M	0508 1109 1713 2324	1.0 4.4 1.0 4.5	30 TU	0446 1050 1707 2321	0.7 4.6 0.7 4.6
			31 W ○	0545 1147 1800	0.5 4.8 0.7

FEBRUARY

Date	Time	m	Date	Time	m
1 TH	0011 0639 1239 1847	4.8 0.4 4.9 0.7	16 F	0014 0638 1239 1839	4.6 0.6 4.5 0.8
2 F	0059 0728 1329 1932	4.9 0.3 4.9 0.7	17 SA	0048 0709 1313 1911	4.7 0.5 4.6 0.8
3 SA	0145 0813 1416 2014	4.9 0.2 4.9 0.7	18 SU	0124 0740 1350 1946	4.7 0.5 4.6 0.7
4 SU	0228 0855 1500 2053	4.9 0.3 4.8 0.8	19 M	0200 0814 1426 2021	4.7 0.5 4.6 0.8
5 M	0309 0933 1541 2130	4.8 0.4 4.6 1.0	20 TU	0233 0848 1500 2057	4.7 0.5 4.5 0.8
6 TU	0348 1010 1620 2210	4.7 0.6 4.4 1.1	21 W	0304 0923 1532 2135	4.6 0.6 4.4 0.9
7 W ◑	0429 1050 1704 2257	4.5 0.8 4.2 1.3	22 TH	0340 1001 1611 2219	4.5 0.7 4.3 1.0
8 TH	0520 1142 1803	4.2 1.1 4.0	23 F ◐	0426 1048 1702 2315	4.4 0.9 4.2 1.1
9 F	0001 0628 1251 1913	1.5 4.0 1.3 3.9	24 SA	0525 1155 1809	4.3 1.0 4.0
10 SA	0128 0743 1403 2021	1.5 3.9 1.3 3.9	25 SU	0036 0642 1325 1943	1.2 4.1 1.1 4.0
11 SU	0245 0854 1508 2125	1.4 4.0 1.3 4.0	26 M	0209 0817 1448 2106	1.2 4.2 1.1 4.1
12 M	0352 0959 1605 2220	1.2 4.1 1.2 4.2	27 TU	0329 0939 1558 2215	0.9 4.4 1.0 4.4
13 TU	0447 1051 1654 2304	1.0 4.3 1.1 4.4	28 W	0440 1046 1658 2312	0.7 4.6 0.8 4.6
14 W	0530 1132 1733 2341	0.8 4.4 1.0 4.5			
15 TH ●	0606 1207 1807	0.7 4.5 0.9			

MARCH

Date	Time	m	Date	Time	m
1 TH	0538 1141 1748	0.5 4.7 0.7	16 F	0537 1143 1744 2350	0.7 4.4 0.9 4.5
2 F ○	0001 0627 1230 1832	4.8 0.3 4.8 0.7	17 SA ●	0611 1215 1818	0.6 4.5 0.8
3 SA	0045 0711 1314 1914	4.9 0.2 4.9 0.7	18 SU	0024 0643 1249 1851	4.7 0.5 4.6 0.7
4 SU	0127 0751 1356 1953	4.9 0.2 4.8 0.7	19 M	0100 0715 1326 1926	4.8 0.4 4.7 0.7
5 M	0206 0827 1434 2029	4.9 0.3 4.7 0.7	20 TU	0136 0748 1402 2003	4.8 0.4 4.7 0.7
6 TU	0243 0858 1507 2103	4.8 0.5 4.6 0.8	21 W	0211 0822 1437 2039	4.8 0.5 4.6 0.7
7 W	0317 0929 1538 2138	4.7 0.6 4.4 1.0	22 TH	0245 0857 1510 2117	4.7 0.6 4.4 0.8
8 TH	0352 1003 1613 2216	4.5 0.9 4.2 1.1	23 F	0323 0937 1551 2202	4.6 0.7 4.3 0.9
9 F ◑	0434 1045 1657 2306	4.2 1.1 4.0 1.4	24 SA ◐	0411 1026 1643 2300	4.5 0.9 4.1 1.0
10 SA	0528 1144 1802	4.0 1.4 3.8	25 SU	0513 1135 1754	4.3 1.1 4.0
11 SU	0025 0650 1311 1932	1.5 3.7 1.5 3.7	26 M	0024 0637 1309 1929	1.1 4.1 1.3 3.9
12 M	0200 0817 1432 2045	1.5 3.8 1.5 3.8	27 TU	0158 0811 1437 2052	1.1 4.1 1.2 4.1
13 TU	0316 0928 1537 2146	1.3 3.9 1.3 4.1	28 W	0322 0934 1548 2202	0.8 4.3 1.0 4.4
14 W	0415 1023 1628 2236	1.1 4.2 1.1 4.3	29 TH	0430 1038 1645 2258	0.6 4.6 0.9 4.6
15 TH	0500 1107 1709 2316	0.8 4.3 1.0 4.4	30 F	0523 1129 1731 2344	0.4 4.7 0.8 4.7
			31 SA ○	0608 1213 1812	0.3 4.7 0.7

APRIL

Date	Time	m	Date	Time	m
1 SU	0024 0646 1252 1851	4.8 0.3 4.8 0.6	16 M ●	0613 1220 1829	0.5 4.6 0.7
2 M	0103 0720 1328 1929	4.9 0.3 4.7 0.6	17 TU	0032 0647 1259 1906	4.8 0.4 4.7 0.6
3 TU	0139 0753 1401 2006	4.9 0.4 4.7 0.7	18 W	0111 0722 1337 1945	4.8 0.4 4.7 0.6
4 W	0215 0823 1432 2039	4.8 0.5 4.6 0.8	19 TH	0150 0759 1416 2024	4.8 0.4 4.6 0.6
5 TH	0249 0852 1503 2111	4.6 0.7 4.4 0.9	20 F	0231 0838 1456 2107	4.8 0.6 4.5 0.7
6 F	0323 0924 1537 2145	4.4 0.9 4.3 1.0	21 SA	0316 0921 1540 2156	4.6 0.7 4.4 0.8
7 SA	0401 1002 1617 2228	4.2 1.1 4.1 1.2	22 SU ◐	0408 1015 1635 2258	4.5 1.0 4.2 0.9
8 SU ◑	0448 1053 1708 2330	4.0 1.4 3.8 1.4	23 M	0513 1126 1747	4.3 1.2 4.0
9 M	0551 1205 1823	3.7 1.6 3.7	24 TU	0021 0636 1258 1915	1.0 4.1 1.3 4.0
10 TU	0103 0726 1344 1957	1.5 3.7 1.6 3.7	25 W	0149 0803 1422 2032	0.9 4.2 1.2 4.2
11 W	0229 0845 1458 2103	1.3 3.8 1.4 3.9	26 TH	0307 0920 1529 2140	0.7 4.4 1.1 4.4
12 TH	0331 0943 1552 2156	1.1 4.1 1.2 4.2	27 F	0410 1020 1624 2236	0.6 4.5 0.9 4.5
13 F	0420 1030 1636 2240	0.8 4.3 1.0 4.4	28 SA	0500 1109 1708 2321	0.5 4.6 0.8 4.6
14 SA	0501 1109 1715 2318	0.7 4.4 0.9 4.5	29 SU	0541 1150 1748 2359	0.4 4.6 0.7 4.7
15 SU	0538 1144 1752 2355	0.6 4.6 0.8 4.7	30 M ○	0615 1225 1828	0.4 4.6 0.6

Chart Datum: 2·5 metres below Ordnance Datum (Newlyn). HAT is 5·2 metres above Chart Datum.

STANDARD TIME (UT)
For Summer Time add ONE hour in **non-shaded areas**

MARGATE LAT 51°23′N LONG 1°23′E

TIMES AND HEIGHTS OF HIGH AND LOW WATERS

Dates in red are SPRINGS
Dates in blue are NEAPS

YEAR **2018**

MAY

Date	Day	Time	m	Time	m	Time	m	Time	m	Moon
1	TU	0035	4.8	0647	0.4	1257	4.6	1906	0.6	
2	W	0112	4.8	0720	0.5	1328	4.6	1943	0.6	
3	TH	0149	4.7	0752	0.6	1401	4.6	2017	0.7	
4	F	0224	4.6	0822	0.8	1435	4.4	2049	0.8	
5	SA	0259	4.4	0854	0.9	1509	4.3	2121	0.9	
6	SU	0336	4.2	0930	1.1	1548	4.2	2201	1.0	
7	M	0419	4.0	1016	1.3	1634	4.0	2254	1.2	
8	TU	0511	3.8	1116	1.5	1730	3.8			◑
9	W	0005	1.3	0620	3.7	1233	1.6	1848	3.8	
10	TH	0130	1.2	0748	3.8	1402	1.5	2009	3.9	
11	F	0241	1.0	0853	4.0	1507	1.2	2108	4.1	
12	SA	0335	0.8	0945	4.3	1557	1.0	2157	4.3	
13	SU	0421	0.7	1030	4.4	1641	0.9	2241	4.5	
14	M	0503	0.6	1111	4.6	1724	0.7	2322	4.7	
15	TU	0542	0.5	1151	4.6	1806	0.6			●
16	W	0004	4.8	0621	0.4	1233	4.7	1848	0.6	
17	TH	0049	4.9	0701	0.4	1316	4.7	1931	0.5	
18	F	0135	4.9	0742	0.5	1401	4.7	2016	0.5	
19	SA	0224	4.8	0825	0.6	1446	4.6	2103	0.5	
20	SU	0314	4.7	0913	0.8	1534	4.5	2156	0.6	
21	M	0408	4.5	1008	1.0	1629	4.3	2300	0.7	
22	TU	0512	4.4	1116	1.2	1738	4.2			◐
23	W	0014	0.7	0627	4.3	1239	1.2	1854	4.2	
24	TH	0131	0.7	0744	4.3	1357	1.2	2005	4.3	
25	F	0241	0.7	0853	4.4	1502	1.1	2109	4.4	
26	SA	0340	0.6	0953	4.4	1557	1.0	2206	4.5	
27	SU	0429	0.6	1043	4.5	1644	0.9	2253	4.5	
28	M	0509	0.6	1123	4.5	1726	0.8	2333	4.6	
29	TU	0543	0.6	1156	4.5	1807	0.7			○
30	W	0011	4.7	0618	0.6	1228	4.6	1846	0.6	
31	TH	0048	4.7	0653	0.6	1301	4.6	1924	0.6	

JUNE

Date	Day	Time	m	Time	m	Time	m	Time	m	Moon
1	F	0125	4.6	0726	0.7	1336	4.6	1959	0.7	
2	SA	0202	4.5	0758	0.8	1412	4.5	2031	0.7	
3	SU	0239	4.4	0831	0.9	1448	4.4	2103	0.8	
4	M	0317	4.3	0907	1.0	1526	4.3	2141	0.9	
5	TU	0356	4.1	0950	1.2	1607	4.2	2228	1.0	
6	W	0441	4.0	1041	1.3	1654	4.0	2324	1.1	◑
7	TH	0534	3.9	1141	1.4	1751	4.0			
8	F	0031	1.1	0639	3.9	1254	1.4	1900	4.0	
9	SA	0143	1.0	0755	4.0	1411	1.3	2012	4.1	
10	SU	0247	0.9	0858	4.2	1514	1.1	2112	4.3	
11	M	0341	0.7	0952	4.4	1608	0.9	2205	4.5	
12	TU	0430	0.6	1041	4.5	1657	0.8	2254	4.7	
13	W	0516	0.6	1127	4.6	1746	0.6	2342	4.8	●
14	TH	0601	0.5	1213	4.7	1834	0.5			
15	F	0033	4.9	0646	0.5	1301	4.8	1923	0.4	
16	SA	0125	4.9	0732	0.6	1349	4.8	2012	0.4	
17	SU	0217	4.9	0819	0.6	1438	4.7	2103	0.4	
18	M	0309	4.8	0907	0.8	1527	4.7	2155	0.4	
19	TU	0403	4.7	0959	0.9	1619	4.5	2253	0.5	
20	W	0502	4.5	1058	1.1	1719	4.4	2355	0.6	◐
21	TH	0607	4.3	1208	1.2	1826	4.3			
22	F	0101	0.7	0714	4.3	1322	1.3	1931	4.3	
23	SA	0206	0.7	0818	4.3	1428	1.2	2033	4.3	
24	SU	0304	0.8	0918	4.3	1527	1.1	2133	4.4	
25	M	0355	0.8	1011	4.3	1620	1.0	2227	4.4	
26	TU	0439	0.8	1056	4.4	1708	0.9	2312	4.5	
27	W	0518	0.8	1133	4.5	1751	0.8	2352	4.5	
28	TH	0556	0.8	1205	4.5	1831	0.7			○
29	F	0029	4.6	0631	0.8	1239	4.6	1907	0.6	
30	SA	0106	4.6	0706	0.8	1315	4.6	1941	0.7	

JULY

Date	Day	Time	m	Time	m	Time	m	Time	m	Moon
1	SU	0142	4.5	0739	0.8	1352	4.6	2014	0.7	
2	M	0220	4.5	0812	0.9	1430	4.5	2047	0.7	
3	TU	0257	4.4	0848	1.0	1507	4.4	2123	0.8	
4	W	0335	4.3	0927	1.1	1544	4.3	2203	0.8	
5	TH	0414	4.2	1010	1.2	1623	4.3	2249	0.9	
6	F	0457	4.1	1101	1.3	1710	4.2	2344	1.0	◑
7	SA	0549	4.0	1201	1.3	1806	4.2			
8	SU	0049	1.0	0654	4.0	1316	1.3	1914	4.2	
9	M	0200	0.9	0811	4.1	1433	1.2	2028	4.3	
10	TU	0305	0.8	0918	4.3	1538	1.0	2134	4.5	
11	W	0402	0.7	1016	4.5	1636	0.8	2233	4.6	
12	TH	0456	0.7	1109	4.6	1731	0.6	2329	4.8	
13	F	0547	0.6	1159	4.7	1825	0.5			●
14	SA	0023	4.9	0636	0.6	1249	4.8	1917	0.4	
15	SU	0117	5.0	0725	0.6	1338	4.9	2007	0.3	
16	M	0209	5.0	0811	0.7	1427	4.9	2056	0.3	
17	TU	0300	4.9	0857	0.8	1514	4.8	2143	0.4	
18	W	0349	4.7	0942	0.9	1601	4.7	2231	0.5	
19	TH	0440	4.5	1030	1.1	1651	4.6	2322	0.6	◐
20	F	0535	4.4	1126	1.2	1748	4.4			
21	SA	0019	0.8	0635	4.2	1236	1.3	1851	4.3	
22	SU	0122	1.0	0737	4.1	1348	1.4	1956	4.2	
23	M	0223	1.1	0839	4.1	1456	1.3	2101	4.2	
24	TU	0321	1.1	0939	4.2	1558	1.1	2203	4.3	
25	W	0413	1.0	1031	4.3	1653	1.0	2255	4.4	
26	TH	0459	1.0	1113	4.4	1738	0.8	2337	4.5	
27	F	0539	0.9	1148	4.5	1816	0.7			○
28	SA	0014	4.5	0614	0.9	1221	4.6	1850	0.7	
29	SU	0048	4.6	0648	0.9	1256	4.6	1922	0.6	
30	M	0122	4.6	0720	0.8	1332	4.7	1954	0.6	
31	TU	0158	4.6	0754	0.8	1409	4.7	2026	0.6	

AUGUST

Date	Day	Time	m	Time	m	Time	m	Time	m	Moon
1	W	0235	4.5	0829	0.9	1445	4.6	2100	0.7	
2	TH	0311	4.4	0905	1.0	1519	4.5	2136	0.8	
3	F	0346	4.3	0943	1.1	1553	4.4	2214	0.9	
4	SA	0423	4.2	1025	1.2	1634	4.4	2259	1.0	◑
5	SU	0509	4.1	1118	1.3	1727	4.3	2359	1.0	
6	M	0608	4.1	1230	1.3	1832	4.2			
7	TU	0118	1.1	0728	4.1	1358	1.3	1954	4.3	
8	W	0236	1.0	0850	4.2	1514	1.1	2113	4.4	
9	TH	0343	0.9	0957	4.4	1620	0.8	2221	4.6	
10	F	0442	0.8	1055	4.6	1721	0.6	2321	4.8	
11	SA	0536	0.7	1147	4.7	1816	0.4			●
12	SU	0015	4.9	0625	0.7	1237	4.9	1906	0.3	
13	M	0106	5.0	0712	0.7	1324	5.0	1953	0.2	
14	TU	0155	5.0	0756	0.7	1410	5.0	2037	0.3	
15	W	0242	4.9	0838	0.8	1453	4.9	2118	0.4	
16	TH	0325	4.7	0917	0.9	1534	4.8	2157	0.6	
17	F	0406	4.5	0958	1.0	1615	4.7	2237	0.8	
18	SA	0449	4.3	1043	1.2	1703	4.4	2325	1.0	◐
19	SU	0543	4.1	1143	1.4	1804	4.2			
20	M	0029	1.2	0650	4.0	1303	1.5	1917	4.1	
21	TU	0141	1.4	0759	4.0	1422	1.4	2031	4.1	
22	W	0249	1.4	0905	4.1	1534	1.3	2141	4.2	
23	TH	0350	1.3	1004	4.2	1633	1.0	2237	4.3	
24	F	0441	1.1	1051	4.4	1718	0.9	2320	4.5	
25	SA	0521	1.0	1129	4.5	1755	0.8	2356	4.5	
26	SU	0557	1.0	1202	4.6	1828	0.7			○
27	M	0027	4.6	0628	0.9	1234	4.7	1858	0.6	
28	TU	0059	4.6	0700	0.8	1309	4.7	1929	0.6	
29	W	0133	4.7	0733	0.8	1345	4.8	2000	0.6	
30	TH	0209	4.6	0808	0.8	1420	4.7	2032	0.6	
31	F	0244	4.5	0842	0.9	1452	4.6	2105	0.7	

Chart Datum: 2·5 metres below Ordnance Datum (Newlyn). HAT is 5·2 metres above Chart Datum.

STANDARD TIME (UT)
For Summer Time add ONE hour in **non-shaded areas**

MARGATE LAT 51°23'N LONG 1°23'E

TIMES AND HEIGHTS OF HIGH AND LOW WATERS

Dates in red are SPRINGS
Dates in blue are NEAPS

YEAR **2018**

SEPTEMBER

Date	Time	m	Date	Time	m
1 SA	0315 0917 1523 2139	4.4 1.0 4.5 0.9	16 SU	0359 1006 1621 ◐ 2230	4.3 1.2 4.4 1.2
2 SU	0349 0956 1603 2221	4.3 1.1 4.5 1.0	17 M	0442 1055 1714 2328	4.1 1.4 4.1 1.5
3 M	0434 1046 1657 ◑ 2319	4.2 1.2 4.4 1.2	18 TU	0544 1210 1832	3.9 1.5 3.9
4 TU	0534 1158 1805	4.1 1.3 4.2	19 W	0051 0713 1341 1958	1.6 3.8 1.5 3.9
5 W	0045 0659 1334 1936	1.3 4.0 1.3 4.2	20 TH	0215 0827 1500 2111	1.6 3.9 1.4 4.1
6 TH	0216 0830 1458 2103	1.2 4.1 1.1 4.4	21 F	0323 0930 1601 2209	1.5 4.1 1.1 4.3
7 F	0330 0943 1610 2215	1.1 4.4 0.8 4.6	22 SA	0416 1021 1647 2254	1.3 4.3 0.9 4.5
8 SA	0431 1043 1710 2313	0.9 4.6 0.6 4.8	23 SU	0457 1101 1725 2329	1.1 4.5 0.8 4.6
9 SU ●	0523 1134 1801	0.8 4.8 0.4	24 M	0532 1135 1758	1.0 4.6 0.7
10 M	0003 0608 1220 1847	4.9 0.7 4.9 0.3	25 TU	0000 0605 1208 ○ 1829	4.6 0.9 4.7 0.6
11 TU	0050 0652 1304 1929	5.0 0.7 5.0 0.3	26 W	0030 0637 1241 1859	4.7 0.8 4.8 0.6
12 W	0134 0733 1345 2009	5.0 0.7 5.0 0.4	27 TH	0104 0711 1317 1931	4.7 0.8 4.8 0.6
13 TH	0215 0813 1425 2044	4.9 0.8 5.0 0.5	28 F	0139 0745 1352 2002	4.7 0.8 4.8 0.6
14 F	0252 0851 1503 2116	4.7 0.9 4.8 0.7	29 SA	0214 0820 1425 2035	4.6 0.8 4.7 0.7
15 SA	0325 0927 1540 2150	4.5 1.0 4.6 0.9	30 SU	0245 0856 1459 2111	4.5 0.9 4.6 0.9

OCTOBER

Date	Time	m	Date	Time	m
1 M	0321 0937 1543 2155	4.4 1.0 4.5 1.1	16 TU	0359 1017 1635 ◐ 2235	4.2 1.3 4.1 1.5
2 TU	0409 1029 1640 ◑ 2256	4.2 1.1 4.3 1.3	17 W	0450 1117 1737 2346	3.9 1.5 3.9 1.8
3 W	0513 1144 1756	4.0 1.2 4.2	18 TH	0604 1247 1912	3.7 1.5 3.8
4 TH	0026 0643 1321 1929	1.4 3.9 1.2 4.2	19 F	0127 0739 1413 2030	1.8 3.8 1.4 4.0
5 F	0202 0814 1446 2056	1.4 4.1 1.0 4.4	20 SA	0245 0846 1517 2128	1.6 4.0 1.2 4.2
6 SA	0317 0927 1556 2205	1.2 4.3 0.7 4.7	21 SU	0340 0939 1606 2215	1.4 4.2 1.0 4.4
7 SU	0416 1027 1653 2300	1.0 4.6 0.5 4.8	22 M	0424 1023 1647 2253	1.2 4.4 0.8 4.5
8 M	0505 1116 1740 2346	0.9 4.8 0.4 4.9	23 TU	0502 1101 1723 2326	1.0 4.6 0.7 4.6
9 TU ●	0548 1158 1822	0.8 4.9 0.4	24 W	0537 1136 1756 ○ 2358	0.9 4.7 0.7 4.7
10 W	0027 0628 1238 1859	4.9 0.7 5.0 0.4	25 TH	0612 1211 1829	0.8 4.8 0.6
11 TH	0105 0709 1317 1935	4.9 0.7 5.0 0.5	26 F	0033 0648 1248 1901	4.8 0.7 4.8 0.6
12 F	0140 0749 1356 2007	4.8 0.7 4.9 0.6	27 SA	0110 0724 1325 1935	4.8 0.7 4.8 0.7
13 SA	0213 0825 1433 2038	4.7 0.8 4.8 0.8	28 SU	0146 0802 1404 2012	4.7 0.7 4.8 0.8
14 SU	0245 0900 1509 2110	4.5 0.9 4.6 1.0	29 M	0223 0842 1447 2052	4.6 0.8 4.7 0.9
15 M	0319 0935 1548 2147	4.4 1.1 4.4 1.3	30 TU	0305 0927 1536 2141	4.4 0.9 4.5 1.1
			31 W	0357 1024 1637 ◑ 2245	4.3 1.0 4.4 1.3

NOVEMBER

Date	Time	m	Date	Time	m
1 TH	0503 1140 1753	4.1 1.1 4.2	16 F	0507 1144 1802	3.9 1.4 3.8
2 F	0012 0629 1309 1921	1.5 4.0 1.0 4.3	17 SA	0007 0623 1309 1931	1.8 3.8 1.4 3.9
3 SA	0144 0754 1430 2042	1.4 4.1 0.9 4.4	18 SU	0143 0750 1423 2036	1.7 3.9 1.2 4.1
4 SU	0257 0904 1536 2147	1.2 4.4 0.7 4.6	19 M	0252 0850 1518 2128	1.5 4.1 1.0 4.3
5 M	0354 1004 1630 2240	1.1 4.6 0.6 4.7	20 TU	0343 0939 1604 2211	1.3 4.3 0.9 4.5
6 TU	0443 1052 1715 2324	0.9 4.7 0.5 4.8	21 W	0426 1023 1645 2251	1.1 4.5 0.8 4.6
7 W ●	0525 1134 1753	0.8 4.8 0.5	22 TH	0507 1103 1723 2329	0.9 4.6 0.7 4.7
8 TH	0001 0606 1212 1827	4.8 0.7 4.9 0.5	23 F ○	0547 1142 1800	0.8 4.7 0.7
9 F	0034 0646 1251 1902	4.8 0.7 4.9 0.6	24 SA	0006 0627 1223 1836	4.8 0.7 4.8 0.6
10 SA	0107 0726 1330 1936	4.8 0.7 4.8 0.7	25 SU	0046 0708 1307 1915	4.8 0.6 4.9 0.7
11 SU	0141 0803 1408 2008	4.7 0.7 4.7 0.9	26 M	0128 0750 1354 1957	4.8 0.6 4.9 0.8
12 M	0215 0837 1445 2039	4.6 0.9 4.5 1.1	27 TU	0212 0835 1443 2043	4.7 0.6 4.8 0.9
13 TU	0250 0910 1522 2114	4.4 1.0 4.3 1.3	28 W	0259 0925 1536 2134	4.6 0.7 4.6 1.1
14 W	0328 0948 1604 2158	4.2 1.1 4.1 1.5	29 TH	0351 1024 1635 2236	4.4 0.8 4.5 1.3
15 TH	0412 1037 1655 ◐ 2255	4.1 1.3 3.9 1.7	30 F	0453 1134 1746 ◑ 2352	4.3 0.8 4.3 1.4

DECEMBER

Date	Time	m	Date	Time	m
1 SA	0611 1251 1905	4.2 0.8 4.3	16 SU	0522 1200 1810	4.0 1.2 3.9
2 SU	0116 0727 1404 2017	1.4 4.2 0.8 4.4	17 M	0019 0626 1311 1927	1.6 3.9 1.2 3.9
3 M	0228 0834 1507 2120	1.3 4.3 0.7 4.5	18 TU	0139 0745 1420 2035	1.5 4.0 1.1 4.1
4 TU	0328 0935 1601 2215	1.2 4.5 0.7 4.6	19 W	0251 0849 1518 2130	1.4 4.2 0.9 4.3
5 W	0419 1027 1647 2300	1.0 4.6 0.7 4.6	20 TH	0347 0944 1608 2219	1.1 4.4 0.8 4.5
6 TH	0505 1112 1725 2337	0.9 4.7 0.7 4.6	21 F	0437 1033 1654 2304	0.9 4.5 0.8 4.6
7 F ●	0548 1152 1801	0.8 4.7 0.7	22 SA	0525 1120 1738 ○ 2348	0.8 4.7 0.7 4.7
8 SA	0009 0629 1231 1836	4.7 0.7 4.7 0.8	23 SU	0611 1207 1821	0.7 4.8 0.7
9 SU	0042 0709 1309 1911	4.7 0.7 4.7 0.8	24 M	0031 0657 1257 1905	4.8 0.5 4.9 0.7
10 M	0117 0746 1347 1944	4.7 0.7 4.6 0.9	25 TU	0118 0745 1348 1950	4.8 0.5 4.9 0.7
11 TU	0153 0819 1424 2016	4.6 0.8 4.5 1.0	26 W	0205 0834 1440 2037	4.8 0.4 4.9 0.8
12 W	0229 0851 1501 2051	4.5 0.9 4.3 1.2	27 TH	0253 0924 1532 2127	4.7 0.5 4.7 1.0
13 TH	0306 0926 1539 2130	4.4 0.9 4.2 1.3	28 F	0343 1018 1627 2221	4.6 0.5 4.6 1.1
14 F	0345 1008 1622 2218	4.2 1.0 4.1 1.4	29 SA	0439 1117 1728 ◑ 2323	4.5 0.6 4.4 1.3
15 SA	0430 1059 1711 ◐ 2313	4.1 1.1 3.9 1.6	30 SU	0544 1222 1836	4.4 0.7 4.3
			31 M	0037 0653 1329 1943	1.4 4.3 0.8 4.3

Chart Datum: 2·5 metres below Ordnance Datum (Newlyn). HAT is 5·2 metres above Chart Datum.

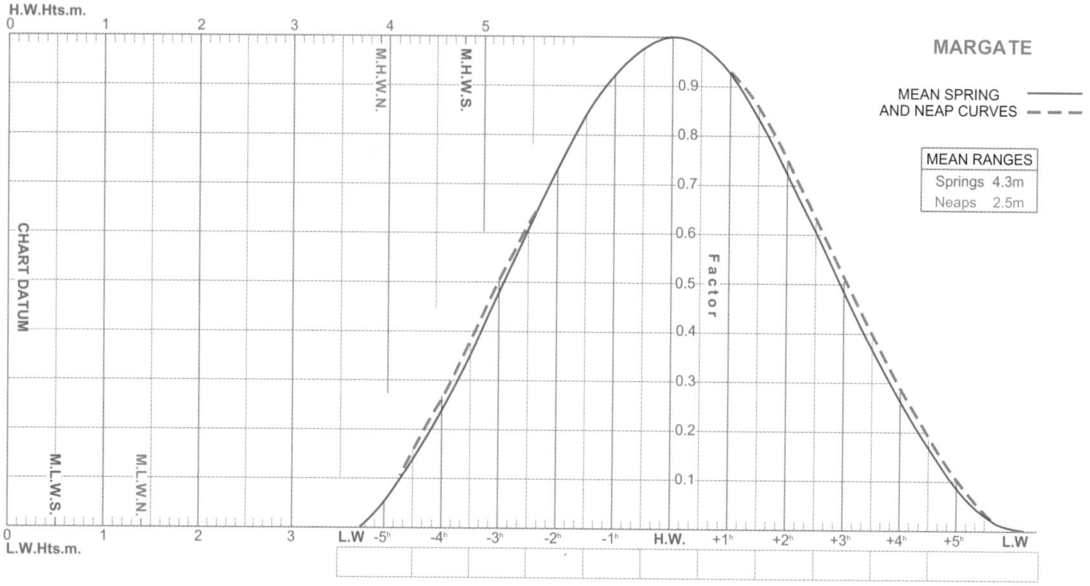
H.W.Hts.m.
0 1 2 3 4 5
M.H.W.N.
M.H.W.S.
MARGATE
MEAN SPRING AND NEAP CURVES
MEAN RANGES
Springs 4.3m
Neaps 2.5m
CHART DATUM
0.9
0.8
0.7
0.6
0.5
0.4
0.3
0.2
0.1
Factor
M.L.W.S.
M.L.W.N.
0 1 2 3
L.W.Hts.m.
L.W -5ʰ -4ʰ -3ʰ -2ʰ -1ʰ H.W. +1ʰ +2ʰ +3ʰ +4ʰ +5ʰ L.W

9.4.8 WHITSTABLE

Kent **51°21′·86N 01°01′·46E**

CHARTS AC 5606, 1607, 2571; Imray C1, 2100

TIDES +0135 Dover; ML 3·0; Duration 0605

Standard Port MARGATE (⟵)

Times				**Height (metres)**			
High Water		Low Water		MHWS	MHWN	MLWN	MLWS
0100	0700	0100	0700	4·8	3·9	1·4	0·5
1300	1900	1300	1900				
Differences HERNE BAY							
+0022	+0020	+0019	+0017	+0·6	+0·3	+0·2	+0·1
WHITSTABLE APPROACHES							
+0042	+0029	+0025	+0050	+0·6	+0·6	+0·1	0·0

SHELTER Good, except in strong winds from NNW to NE. Harbour dries up to 0·4m. Yacht berths are limited since priority is given to commercial shipping. Fender board needed against piled quays or seek a mooring to NW of harbour (controlled by YC).

NAVIGATION WPT 51°22′·65N 01°01′·10E, 345°/0·83M to W Quay dolphin. From E keep well seaward of Whitstable Street, a hard drying sandspit, which extends 1M N from the coast; shoals a further 1M to seaward are marked by Whitstable Street NCM lt buoy. From W avoid Columbine and Pollard Spits.

Approach, not before half flood, via Oyster PHM lt buoy to harbour entrance. Entry best at HW±1.

LIGHTS AND MARKS Off head of W Quay on a dolphin, ☆ Fl G 5s, covers the approaches.

COMMUNICATIONS (Code 01227) NMOC 02392 552100; Police 101; Dr 594400. HM 274086.

Whitstable Harbour Radio VHF Ch **09** 12 16 (Mon–Fri: 0830–1700 LT. Other times: HW –3 to HW+1). Tidal info on request.

FACILITIES www.canterbury.gov.uk HM ☎274086, £10.
Whitstable YC ☎272942, HW ±3.
Services ACA.
Town ⇌ ✈ Lydd/Manston.

MINOR HARBOURS WEST OF NORTH FORELAND

MARGATE, Kent, **51°23′·43N 01°22′·65E.** AC 5606, 1 827, 1828, 323; Imray Y7, C1; Stanfords 5, 8. HW+0045 on Dover; ML 2·6; Duration 0610; Standard Port (⟵). Small hbr drying 3m, inside bkwtr (Stone Pier) FR 17m 4M; exposed to NW'lies. Appr: from E, via Longnose NCM buoy, keeping about 5ca offshore; from N, via Margate PHM lt buoy; from W via Gore Chan and S Chan to SE Margate ECM. Facilities: Margate YC ☎(01843) 292602.

Town 10, HW±2, book at Foreshore Office ☎(01843) 577529, ⇌ ✈ Manston.

HERNE BAY, Kent, **51°22′·40N 01°07′·22E.** AC 5606, 1607. Close E of Pavilion (old pier), 400m long bkwtr 'Neptunes Arm' gives well sheltered drying ⚓ for craft <8m. Exposed to strong NE'lies at HW springs when Thames Barrier closed as seas may then top the bkwtr. 3 (HW±2½ to HW±3). Foreshore Manager ☎(01227) 266719. Herne Bay SC ☎(01227) 375650. Lts: QW 8m 4M is 6ca offshore (former pier hd); bkwtr hd 2FR (vert); pier hd 2FG (vert); R bn on B dolphin, Fl Y 5s, is approx 1M ENE of bkwtr hd. Reculvers twrs are conspic 3M to the E.

Town ⇌ ✈ Lydd/Manston.

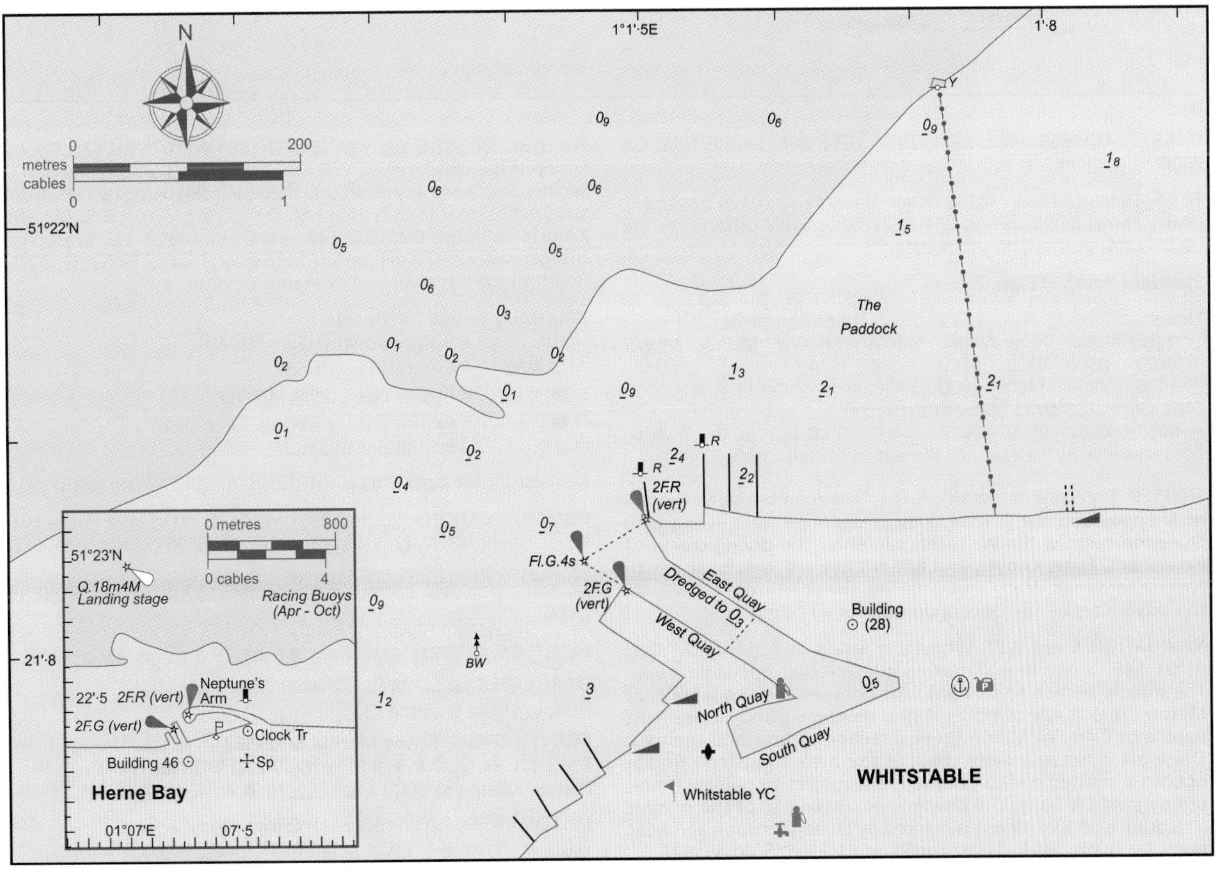

9.4.9 THE SWALE

Kent

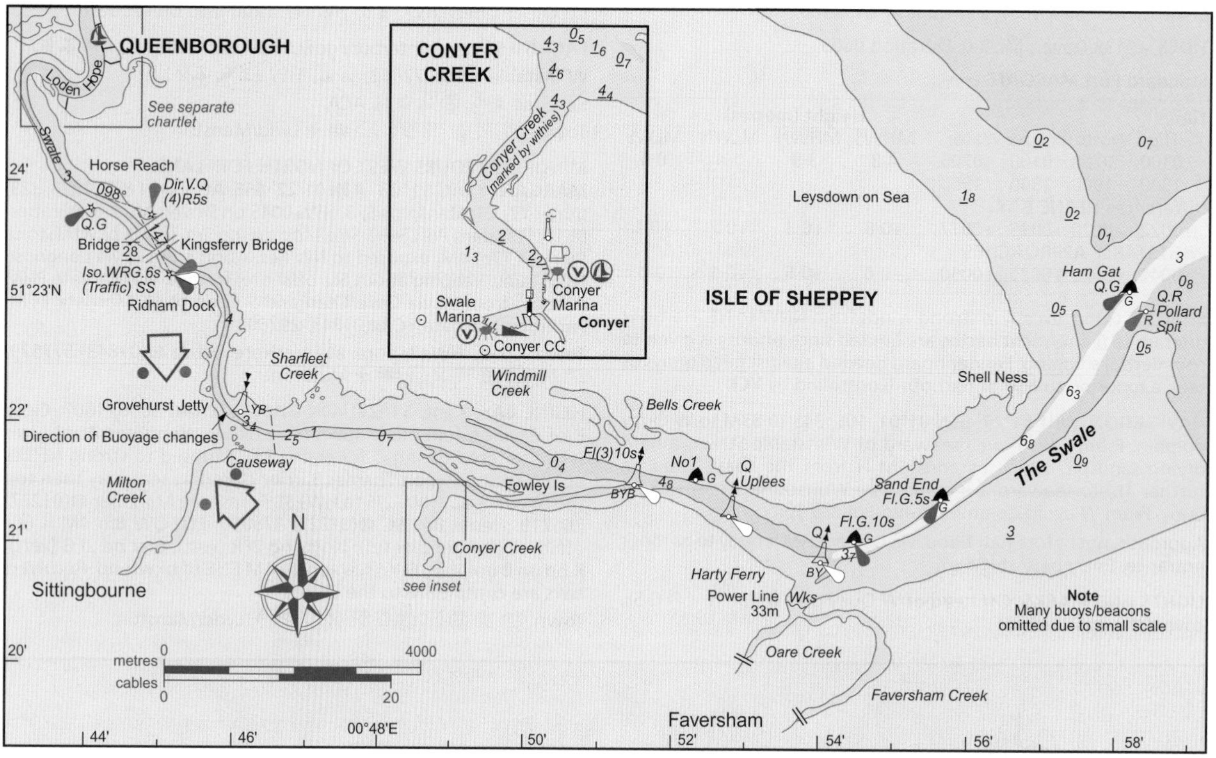

CHARTS AC 5606, 2482, 2571, 2572, 1834, 3683; Imray Y18, C1, 2100

TIDES Queenborough +0130 Dover; Harty Ferry +0120 Dover; ML (Harty Ferry) 3·0; Duration 0610. Faversham HW differences are –0·2m on Sheerness; no other data.

Standard Port SHEERNESS (⟶)

Times				Height (metres)			
High Water		Low Water		MHWS	MHWN	MLWN	MLWS
0200	0800	0200	0700	5·8	4·7	1·5	0·6
1400	2000	1400	1900				
Differences R. SWALE (Grovehurst Jetty)							
–0007	0000	0000	+0016	0·0	0·0	0·0	–0·1

Grovehurst Jetty is close N of the ent to Milton Creek.

SHELTER Excellent in the Swale, the 14M chan between the Isle of Sheppey and the N Kent coast, from Shell Ness in the E to Queenborough in the W. Yachts can enter the drying creeks of Faversham, Oare, Conyer, and Milton. Beware wrecks at ent to Faversham Creek. Many moorings line the chan from Faversham to Conyer Creeks. See Queenborough for all-tide access.

NAVIGATION **E ent** WPT: Whitstable Street lit PHM, 51°24′·00N 01°01′·54E, at ent to well marked buoyed chan. Speed limit 8kn. The middle section from 1·5M E of Conyer Creek to 0·5M E of Milton Creek is narrowed by drying mudbanks and carries least depths of 0·4m. At Milton Creek direction of buoyage changes. There are numerous oyster beds in the area. Kingsferry Bridge opens for masted craft on request, but subject to railway trains; temp ⚓s off SW bank. The power lines crossing SE of the br have a clearance of 30m. **W ent** is marked by Queenborough Spit ECM buoy, Q (3) 10s, 1M S of Garrison Pt, at 51°25′·81N 00°43′·93E.

LIGHTS AND MARKS See chartlet and 9.4.4. In W Swale lights intended for large coasters using the narrow chan are:

No 5 Bn Oc WRG 6s; vis: 161°-G-166°-W-167°-R-172°. Round Loden Hope bend: two Q WG and one Q WRG on bns; keep in G sectors. See Queenborough chartlet. Horse Reach ldg lts 113°: front QG 7m 5M; rear Fl G 3s 10m 6M. Dir lt 098°, VQ (4) R 5s 6m 5M. Kingsferry Bridge: Dir WRG, 142°-G-147°-W-148°-R-153° 9m. Lts on bridge: two x 2 FG (vert) on SW buttresses; two x 2 FR (vert) on NE. Road bridge has a vertical clearance of 28m.

Kingsferry Bridge traffic sigs:

No lts	= Bridge down (3·35m MHWS).
Al Q ●/●	= Centre span lifting.
F ●	= Bridge open (29m MHWS).
Q ●	= Centre span lowering. Keep clear.
Q ●	= Bridge out of action.

Request bridge opening on VHF Ch 10 (or Ch 74 if no response).

COMMUNICATIONS (Code 01795) NMOC 02392 552100; Police 101; Dr or Ⓗ via Medway Navigation Service 663025. HM (Medway Ports Ltd) 596593.

Medway VTS VHF Ch **74** 16 22 (H24); Kingsferry Bridge Ch 10 (H24).

FACILITIES **FAVERSHAM**: **Town** ✉ Ⓑ ✕ ⇌ ✈(Gatwick).

OARE CREEK (8t).

Hollow Shore Cruising Club.

CONYER CREEK: **Swale Marina** ☎521562, (dredged 2m) £14/craft, (30t) (30t); **Conyer CC**.

Conyer Marina ☎521711, £10, Ⓔ.

MILTON CREEK (Sittingbourne): **Crown Quay**.

Town ✉ Ⓑ ✕ ⇌ ✈ (Gatwick); also the Dolphin Yard Sailing Barge Museum.

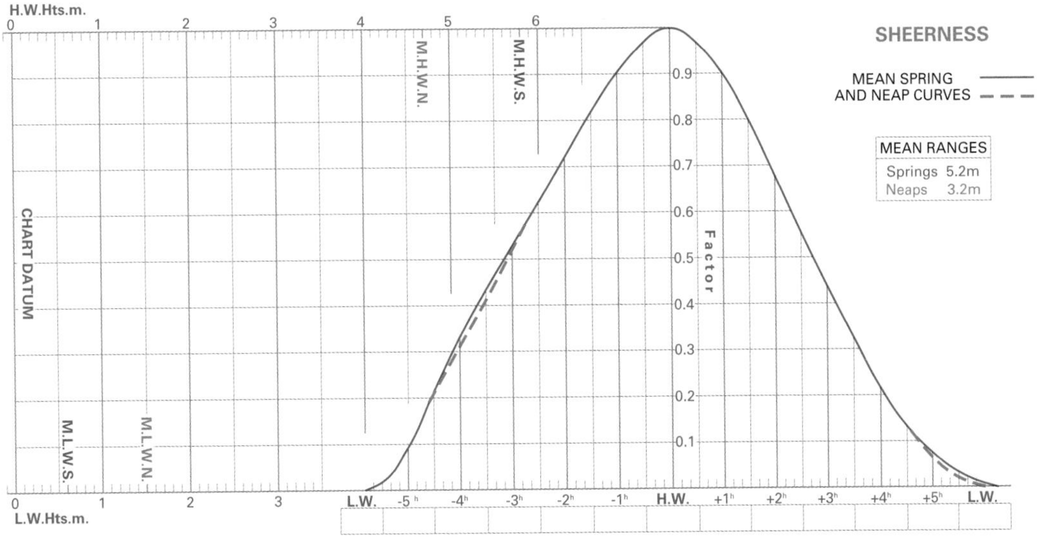

9.4.10 QUEENBOROUGH

Kent (Isle of Sheppey) **51°25'·04N 00°44'·19E** ✵✵✵👍👍✿✿

CHARTS AC 5606, 1834, 2572, 3683; Imray C1, Y18, 2100

TIDES Use 9.4.11 Sheerness, 2M to the N. +0130 Dover; ML 3·0; Duration 0610

SHELTER Good, except near HW in strong N'ly winds. The first deep-water refuge W of N Foreland, accessible at all tides from Garrison Pt (9.4.11); or from the Swale (9.4.9) on the tide.

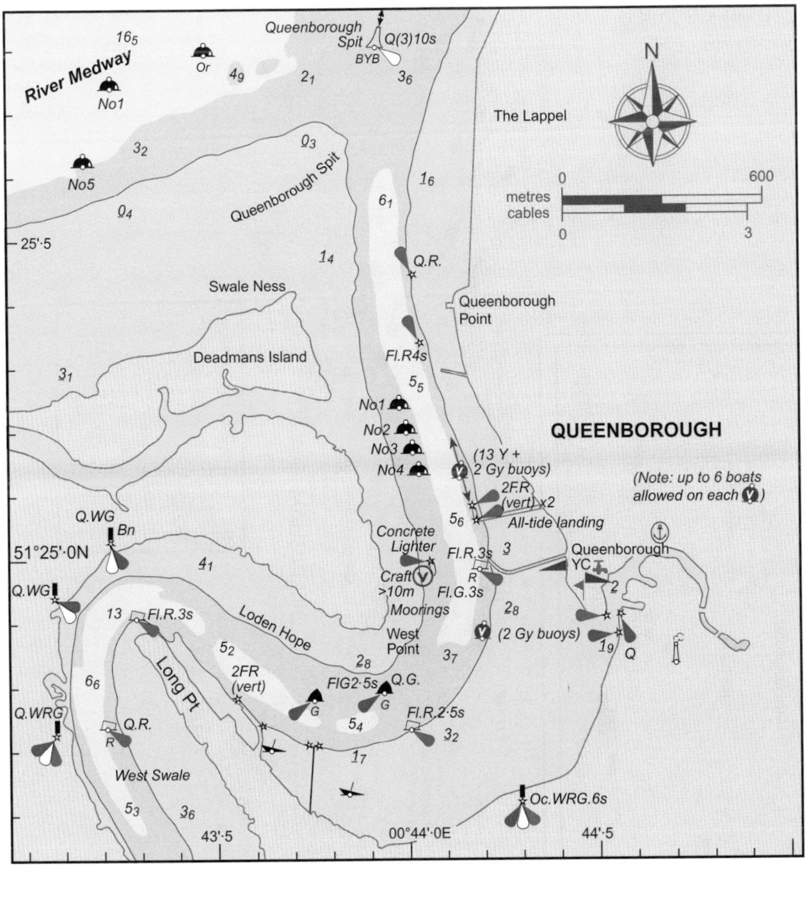

An all-tide walk ashore pontoon (5m depth at end) on E bank is available for overnight/short stay; both sides of the jetty are foul. A pair Gy Ⓥs (raft up to 6 craft <10m each) lie to the S; also single visitors Y Ⓥs Nos 14-24 for craft <10m, with HM's permission craft >10m berth on W side of Concrete Lighter. When Ⓥs are full the hbr controller will offer spare buoys. Smaller R buoys (numbered) are for locals. ⚓ owing to commercial traffic. Speed limit 8kn.

NAVIGATION See River Medway for appr via Garrison Pt. Enter the river at Queenborough Spit ECM, Q (3) 10s, 51°25'·75N 00°43'·93E. The channel narrows between drying banks and moorings. See The Swale if approaching from the E.

LIGHTS AND MARKS Lights as chartlet. Note: No 5 Bn Dir Oc WRG 6s, vis 161°-G-166°-W-167°-R-172°, on river bend covers the appr chan. All-tide landing 2 FR (vert). Concrete lighter Fl G 3s.

COMMUNICATIONS (Code 01795) NMOC 02392 552100; Police 101; Dr 583828; Ⓗ (01634) 830000 (Gillingham). HM 662051 and mob 07456 459754 (trot boat).

Monitor *Medway VTS* VHF Ch **74** for traffic. HM Ch **08**. Call *Sheppey One* for trot boat.

FACILITIES **Queenborough Hbr Trust CIC** (www.queenborough-harbour.co.uk) manages the hbr, walk ashore pontoon, Ⓥ and ⌓ on concrete lighter and town quay. Ⓥ are serviced by a free 'Trot Boat'.

Queenborough Hbr ⌓ (all-tide) <10m £20 (+£2/m), short stay <3hrs £10 (+£2/m), ⛽.
⌓ Quay/concrete ltr/Ⓥ <10m £12, s/s £6.

Queenborough YC Wed, Fri, Sat evenings, Sat, Sun lunchtimes, ⛵ ♿ 🚿 ✕ 🍷.

The Creek ☎07974 349018, ⛴ (HW±1½) Scrubbing grid ⛽ 🚿.

Services ⛽ ⚒ 🔧 🛒 (10t).

Town 🅟 🅓 ✉ 🛒 ✕ 🍷 ⇌ ✈ (Gatwick).

9.4.11 RIVER MEDWAY (SHEERNESS TO ROCHESTER)

Kent **51°27′·03N 00°44′·50E** (Off Garrison Pt)

CHARTS AC 5606, 1835, 1834, 1185, 2482, 3683; IMRAY C1, Y18, 2100

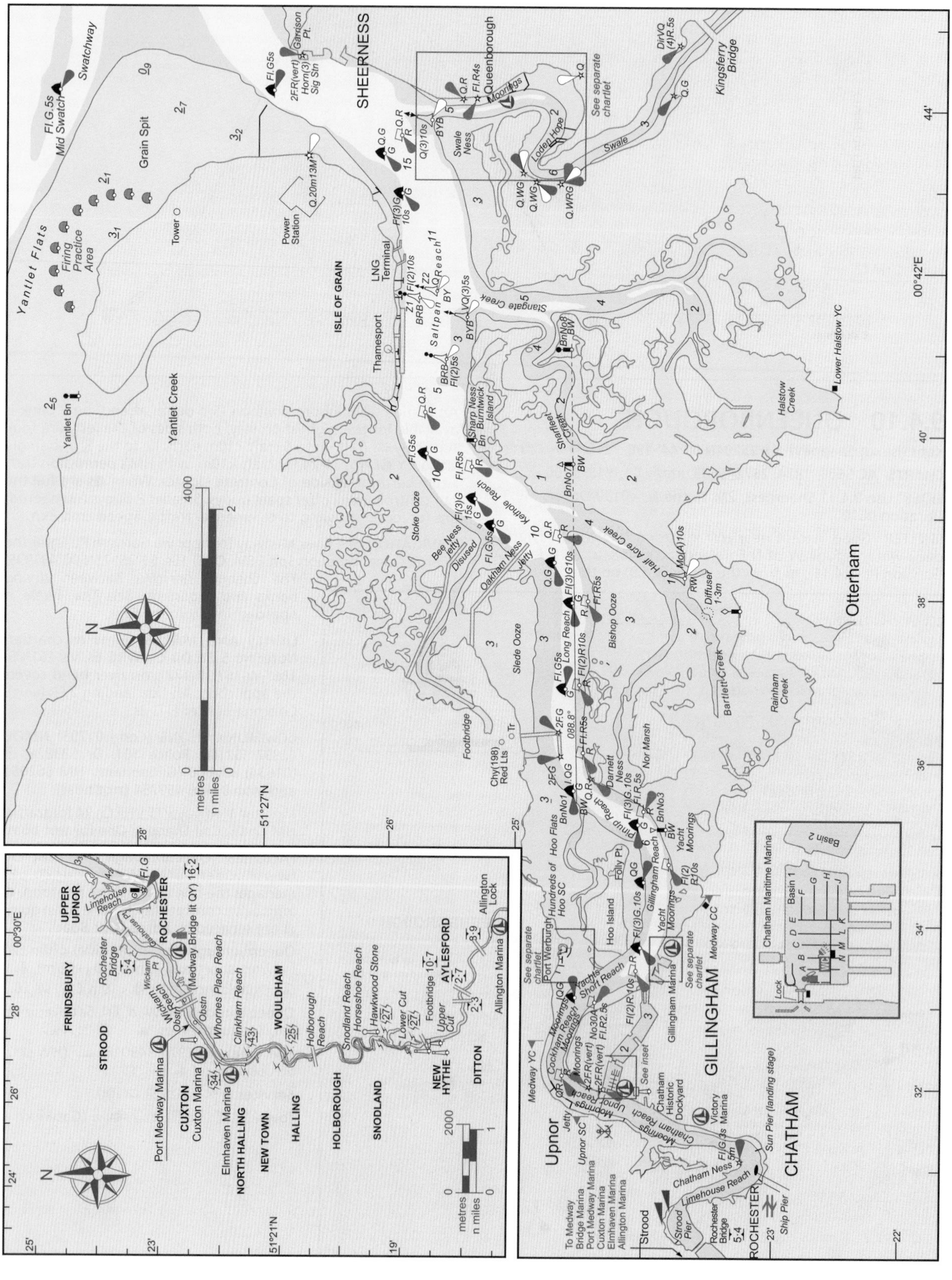

TIDES +0130 Dover; ML 3·1; Duration 0610

Standard Port SHEERNESS (⟶)

Times				Height (metres)			
High Water		Low Water		MHWS	MHWN	MLWN	MLWS
0200	0800	0200	0700	5·8	4·7	1·5	0·6
1400	2000	1400	1900				
Differences BEE NESS							
+0002	+0002	0000	+0005	+0·2	+0·1	0·0	0·0
BARTLETT CREEK							
+0016	+0008	ND	ND	+0·1	0·0	ND	ND
DARNETT NESS							
+0004	*+0004*	*0000*	*+0010*	*+0·2*	*+0·1*	*0·0*	*–0·1*
CHATHAM (Lock Approaches)							
+0010	+0012	+0012	+0018	+0·3	+0·1	–0·1	–0·2
UPNOR							
+0015	+0015	+0015	+0025	+0·2	+0·2	–0·1	–0·1
ROCHESTER (STROOD PIER)							
+0018	+0018	+0018	+0028	+0·2	+0·2	–0·2	–0·3
WOULDHAM							
+0030	+0025	+0035	+0120	–0·2	–0·3	–1·0	–0·3
NEW HYTHE							
+0035	+0035	+0220	+0240	–1·6	–1·7	–1·2	–0·3
ALLINGTON LOCK							
+0050	+0035	ND	ND	–2·1	–2·2	–1·3	–0·4

SHELTER There are 4 marinas downriver of Rochester Bridge and 5 above. Sheerness is solely a commercial hbr. See Queenborough for access to/from The Swale. Lower reaches of the Medway are exposed to strong NE winds, but Stangate and Half Acre Creeks are secure in all winds and give access to lesser creeks. There are good ⚓s in Sharfleet Creek; with sufficient rise of the tide it is possible to go via the 'back-door' into Half Acre Creek. Speed limit is 6kn W of Folly Pt (Hoo Island).

NAVIGATION WPT 51°28´·84N 00°52´·78E, SWM buoy, 253°/4·5M to No 11 SHM buoy, then follow recommended route 240°/1M to Grain Hard SHM buoy. The wreck of the *Richard Montgomery* is visible 2M NE of estuary entrance and a Military Wreck depth 2_2 in Kethole Reach marked by E Bulwark SHM. Observe restrictions off Grain LNG Terminal. There is a huge area to explore, although much of it dries to mud. Some minor creeks are buoyed. The river is well buoyed/marked up to Rochester and tidal up to Allington Lock (21·6M). Above Rochester bridge the river shoals appreciably and in the upper reaches there is only about 1m at LW.

Bridge Clearances (HAT), going upriver:

Rochester	5·4m
Medway (M2)	16·2m
Holborough Reach	5.0m
New Hythe (footbridge)	10·7m
Aylesford (pedestrian)	2·3m
Aylesford (road)	2·7m
Maidstone bypass (M20)	8·9m

LIGHTS AND MARKS See 9.4.4 and chartlet for details of most lts. NB: not all buoys are shown due to small scale. Isle of Grain lt Q 20m 13M. Power stn chy (242m) Oc and FR lts. Tfc Sigs: Powerful lt, Fl 7s, at Garrison Pt means large vessel under way: if shown up river = inbound; if to seaward = outbound.

COMMUNICATIONS (Codes 01634 Medway) NMOC 02392 552100; Police 101; Medway Navigation Service (01795) 663025; Sheerness HM (01795) 596593.

Medway VTS VHF Ch **74** 16 (H24). Monitor Ch 74 underway and Ch 16 at ⚓. Radar assistance is available on request Ch 22. Ch **80** M for marinas: Gillingham, Hoo (H24), Chatham Maritime (H24), Medway Bridge (0900-1700LT) and Port Medway (0800-2000LT).

YACHT CLUBS **Sheppey YC** ☎(01795) 663052.
Lower Halstow YC ☎(01227) 458554.
Medway Cruising Club (Gillingham) ☎856489.
Hoo Ness YC ☎250052.
Hundred of Hoo SC ☎250102.
Medway Motor Cruising Club ☎827194.
Medway Motor YC ☎(01622) 737647.
Medway YC (Upnor) ☎718399; **Upnor SC** ☎718043.
Royal Engineers YC ☎844555; **RNSA Medway** ☎200970.

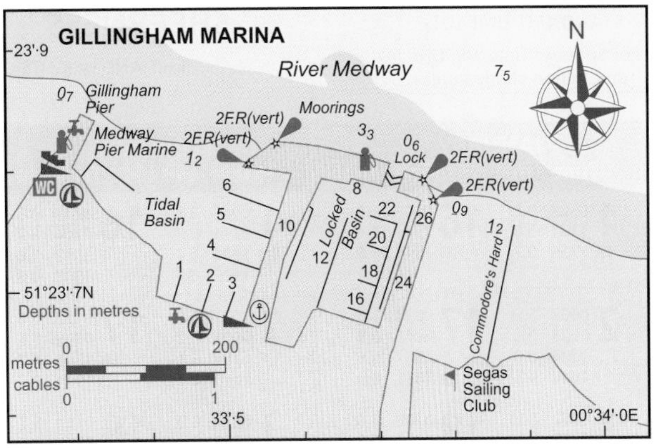

Rochester CC ☎841350.
Strood YC ☎718261, (1½t).

FACILITIES (☎ code 01634 unless otherwise stated). All moorings run by YCs or marinas. Slips at Commodores Hard, and Gillingham.

Marinas (From seaward to Rochester Bridge)

Gillingham Marina cross-tide, esp. the ebb, off the lock ent are reduced by a timber baffle at 90° to the stream (close W of lock). An angled pontoon deflects the stream and is also the fuel berth; the outboard end is lit by 2FR (vert). (252+12🅥s) ☎280022, pre-book. £3·20 locked basin (access via lock (width 6m) HW±4½), £2·10 tidal basin HW±2, (65t) (1t).

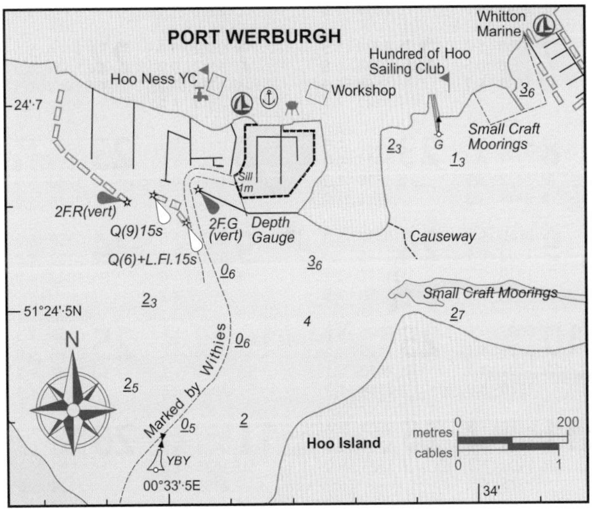

Medway Pier Marine ☎851113, (6t).

Port Werburgh (120+ residential only), ☎252107 access to W basin HW±2½; HW±3 to E basin (via sill 1m above CD); an unlit WCM buoy marks chan ent; 4 waiting buoys in river.

Chatham Maritime Marina – see inset on previous page (⟵) ☎899200 (300), access via lock H24 and sill 1.3m below CD (1.5m at MLWS), £3.20. (15t).

Victory Marina ☎07785 971797.

Marinas (Upriver from Rochester Bridge)

Medway Bridge Marina ☎843576, 160+4🅥 £1.20, (3t) (10t).

Port Medway Marina ☎720033, 50 inc 🅥 (16t).

Cuxton Marina ☎721941, 150+🅥 (12t).

Elmhaven Marina ☎240489, 60.

Allington Lock operates HW–3 to +2, ☎(01622) 752864.

Allington Marina ☎(01622) 752057, above the lock; 120 (10t).

Towns All facilities (Gatwick).

E England

STANDARD TIME (UT)
For Summer Time add ONE hour in **non-shaded areas**

SHEERNESS LAT 51°27′N LONG 0°45′E

TIMES AND HEIGHTS OF HIGH AND LOW WATERS

Dates in red are SPRINGS
Dates in blue are NEAPS

YEAR **2018**

JANUARY

Date	Day	Time	m	Time	m	Time	m	Time	m	Moon
1	M	0523	0.8	1131	5.8	1756	0.7			
2	TU	0003	5.9	0623	0.6	1224	6.0	1849	0.6	○
3	W	0052	5.9	0719	0.5	1315	6.1	1938	0.6	
4	TH	0139	6.0	0810	0.3	1404	6.1	2023	0.6	
5	F	0226	5.9	0858	0.3	1453	6.1	2106	0.8	
6	SA	0312	5.9	0944	0.4	1542	5.9	2147	0.9	
7	SU	0359	5.7	1028	0.5	1631	5.7	2227	1.1	
8	M	0447	5.5	1113	0.7	1723	5.5	2311	1.3	◑
9	TU	0540	5.3	1202	0.9	1819	5.2			
10	W	0003	1.5	0639	5.1	1301	1.1	1920	5.0	
11	TH	0110	1.6	0745	4.9	1406	1.3	2026	4.9	
12	F	0224	1.6	0854	4.9	1509	1.3	2131	5.0	
13	SA	0331	1.5	0959	5.0	1606	1.2	2229	5.1	
14	SU	0432	1.3	1055	5.2	1656	1.1	2317	5.3	
15	M	0523	1.1	1141	5.3	1738	1.1	2358	5.4	
16	TU	0607	1.0	1221	5.4	1816	1.0			
17	W	0034	5.5	0645	0.9	1257	5.5	1851	0.9	●
18	TH	0108	5.6	0720	0.8	1331	5.6	1925	0.9	
19	F	0140	5.6	0755	0.7	1404	5.6	1959	0.8	
20	SA	0213	5.6	0831	0.7	1438	5.6	2035	0.9	
21	SU	0246	5.6	0906	0.7	1513	5.5	2110	1.0	
22	M	0320	5.5	0940	0.8	1550	5.5	2142	1.1	
23	TU	0356	5.4	1011	0.9	1630	5.3	2216	1.2	
24	W	0437	5.3	1045	1.0	1716	5.2	2258	1.3	◐
25	TH	0525	5.2	1129	1.1	1812	5.1	2354	1.3	
26	F	0627	5.1	1231	1.2	1921	5.0			
27	SA	0109	1.4	0743	5.1	1402	1.2	2036	5.1	
28	SU	0241	1.3	0902	5.2	1528	1.1	2148	5.3	
29	M	0359	1.1	1014	5.4	1638	1.0	2252	5.5	
30	TU	0510	0.8	1118	5.7	1742	0.8	2349	5.7	
31	W	0616	0.6	1215	5.9	1838	0.7			○

FEBRUARY

Date	Day	Time	m	Time	m	Time	m	Time	m	Moon
1	TH	0040	5.9	0711	0.4	1306	6.1	1926	0.6	
2	F	0127	6.0	0801	0.2	1353	6.1	2010	0.6	
3	SA	0212	6.0	0846	0.2	1439	6.1	2051	0.7	
4	SU	0255	6.0	0928	0.2	1523	6.0	2127	0.8	
5	M	0337	5.8	1005	0.4	1605	5.8	2201	1.0	
6	TU	0418	5.6	1039	0.7	1648	5.5	2235	1.1	
7	W	0502	5.4	1113	0.9	1734	5.2	2314	1.3	◑
8	TH	0551	5.1	1156	1.2	1825	4.9			
9	F	0006	1.5	0651	4.8	1258	1.4	1927	4.7	
10	SA	0123	1.7	0804	4.6	1416	1.5	2040	4.6	
11	SU	0250	1.6	0923	4.7	1526	1.5	2152	4.8	
12	M	0402	1.4	1029	5.0	1626	1.3	2249	5.0	
13	TU	0501	1.2	1120	5.2	1716	1.2	2335	5.3	
14	W	0549	1.0	1201	5.4	1757	1.0			
15	TH	0014	5.4	0628	0.9	1238	5.5	1833	0.9	●
16	F	0049	5.5	0704	0.7	1312	5.6	1908	0.8	
17	SA	0122	5.6	0739	0.6	1345	5.7	1944	0.7	
18	SU	0154	5.7	0816	0.6	1418	5.7	2020	0.7	
19	M	0227	5.7	0852	0.6	1453	5.7	2055	0.8	
20	TU	0300	5.7	0925	0.6	1528	5.6	2126	0.9	
21	W	0335	5.6	0953	0.8	1606	5.5	2155	1.0	
22	TH	0414	5.5	1020	0.9	1649	5.3	2232	1.1	
23	F	0500	5.4	1059	1.0	1740	5.1	2323	1.2	◐
24	SA	0559	5.2	1159	1.2	1847	4.9			
25	SU	0036	1.3	0716	5.0	1332	1.3	2008	4.9	
26	M	0219	1.3	0843	5.1	1509	1.3	2128	5.0	
27	TU	0346	1.1	1004	5.3	1625	1.1	2239	5.3	
28	W	0504	0.8	1110	5.6	1732	0.9	2337	5.6	

MARCH

Date	Day	Time	m	Time	m	Time	m	Time	m	Moon
1	TH	0609	0.5	1205	5.9	1826	0.7			
2	F	0026	5.8	0700	0.3	1254	6.1	1911	0.6	○
3	SA	0111	5.9	0746	0.2	1338	6.1	1952	0.6	
4	SU	0153	6.0	0827	0.2	1419	6.1	2030	0.6	
5	M	0232	6.0	0903	0.3	1458	6.0	2104	0.7	
6	TU	0310	5.9	0936	0.4	1535	5.8	2134	0.8	
7	W	0347	5.7	1003	0.7	1611	5.5	2202	1.0	
8	TH	0425	5.4	1030	0.9	1648	5.2	2233	1.2	
9	F	0507	5.1	1104	1.2	1731	4.9	2315	1.4	◑
10	SA	0559	4.8	1154	1.5	1826	4.6			
11	SU	0017	1.6	0710	4.5	1315	1.7	1941	4.4	
12	M	0201	1.7	0838	4.5	1446	1.7	2106	4.5	
13	TU	0328	1.5	0955	4.8	1554	1.5	2214	4.8	
14	W	0432	1.2	1050	5.1	1648	1.2	2305	5.2	
15	TH	0522	1.0	1134	5.4	1732	1.1	2346	5.4	
16	F	0603	0.8	1211	5.6	1811	0.9			
17	SA	0022	5.6	0640	0.7	1246	5.7	1847	0.8	●
18	SU	0057	5.7	0718	0.6	1321	5.8	1924	0.7	
19	M	0131	5.8	0755	0.5	1355	5.9	2002	0.6	
20	TU	0205	5.8	0832	0.5	1430	5.9	2039	0.7	
21	W	0239	5.8	0906	0.6	1506	5.8	2111	0.7	
22	TH	0316	5.8	0935	0.7	1544	5.6	2141	0.8	
23	F	0357	5.7	1003	0.9	1626	5.4	2218	1.0	
24	SA	0444	5.5	1044	1.0	1717	5.1	2311	1.1	◐
25	SU	0544	5.2	1146	1.3	1825	4.9			
26	M	0027	1.3	0703	5.0	1321	1.5	1949	4.8	
27	TU	0212	1.2	0834	5.1	1456	1.4	2114	5.0	
28	W	0340	1.0	0955	5.3	1613	1.2	2224	5.3	
29	TH	0456	0.7	1059	5.7	1717	0.9	2321	5.6	
30	F	0555	0.5	1151	5.9	1808	0.8			
31	SA	0008	5.8	0642	0.3	1236	6.0	1851	0.7	○

APRIL

Date	Day	Time	m	Time	m	Time	m	Time	m	Moon
1	SU	0051	5.9	0723	0.3	1317	6.0	1929	0.6	
2	M	0130	6.0	0800	0.3	1354	6.0	2005	0.6	
3	TU	0207	6.0	0833	0.4	1430	5.9	2039	0.7	
4	W	0243	5.9	0903	0.6	1504	5.7	2108	0.8	
5	TH	0318	5.7	0929	0.8	1536	5.5	2134	0.9	
6	F	0353	5.4	0954	1.0	1609	5.3	2201	1.1	
7	SA	0431	5.1	1026	1.2	1646	5.0	2237	1.3	
8	SU	0518	4.8	1110	1.5	1734	4.7	2331	1.5	◑
9	M	0620	4.5	1216	1.8	1842	4.5			
10	TU	0054	1.7	0744	4.4	1355	1.8	2010	4.4	
11	W	0243	1.5	0906	4.7	1513	1.6	2127	4.7	
12	TH	0351	1.3	1009	5.0	1611	1.3	2224	5.1	
13	F	0444	1.0	1056	5.3	1658	1.1	2310	5.3	
14	SA	0529	0.8	1138	5.6	1740	0.9	2350	5.5	
15	SU	0611	0.7	1216	5.8	1821	0.8			
16	M	0027	5.7	0651	0.6	1253	5.9	1902	0.7	●
17	TU	0105	5.8	0731	0.5	1330	6.0	1943	0.6	
18	W	0142	5.9	0810	0.5	1407	6.0	2022	0.6	
19	TH	0220	6.0	0847	0.5	1446	5.9	2100	0.6	
20	F	0301	5.9	0921	0.7	1526	5.7	2136	0.7	
21	SA	0345	5.8	0956	0.9	1611	5.4	2218	0.8	
22	SU	0437	5.5	1041	1.1	1704	5.2	2314	1.0	◐
23	M	0540	5.3	1144	1.4	1813	4.9			
24	TU	0033	1.1	0659	5.1	1313	1.5	1935	4.9	
25	W	0207	1.1	0823	5.2	1439	1.4	2056	5.0	
26	TH	0328	0.9	0939	5.4	1552	1.2	2204	5.3	
27	F	0438	0.6	1041	5.7	1654	1.0	2300	5.5	
28	SA	0533	0.5	1131	5.8	1744	0.9	2346	5.7	
29	SU	0618	0.5	1214	5.9	1826	0.8			
30	M	0027	5.8	0655	0.5	1253	5.9	1903	0.7	○

Chart Datum: 2·90 metres below Ordnance Datum (Newlyn). HAT is 6·3 metres above Chart Datum.

STANDARD TIME (UT)
For Summer Time add ONE hour in **non-shaded areas**

SHEERNESS LAT 51°27′N LONG 0°45′E

TIMES AND HEIGHTS OF HIGH AND LOW WATERS

Dates in red are SPRINGS
Dates in blue are NEAPS

YEAR 2018

MAY

Date	Day	Time	m	Time	m	Time	m	Time	m	Moon
1	TU	0106	5.8	0729	0.5	1329	5.9	1940	0.6	
2	W	0143	5.8	0801	0.6	1402	5.8	2014	0.7	
3	TH	0218	5.8	0831	0.7	1434	5.7	2045	0.8	
4	F	0253	5.6	0859	0.9	1505	5.5	2112	0.9	
5	SA	0328	5.4	0925	1.1	1537	5.3	2138	1.0	
6	SU	0405	5.2	0957	1.3	1613	5.1	2213	1.2	
7	M	0448	4.9	1038	1.5	1656	4.8	2300	1.4	
8	TU	0541	4.7	1134	1.7	1754	4.6			◑
9	W	0005	1.5	0650	4.6	1250	1.8	1912	4.5	
10	TH	0137	1.5	0808	4.7	1416	1.7	2031	4.7	
11	F	0257	1.3	0916	5.0	1522	1.4	2135	5.0	
12	SA	0356	1.0	1012	5.3	1615	1.2	2228	5.3	
13	SU	0448	0.8	1100	5.6	1704	1.0	2314	5.5	
14	M	0536	0.7	1144	5.8	1751	0.8	2357	5.7	
15	TU	0622	0.6	1225	5.9	1838	0.7			●
16	W	0039	5.9	0706	0.5	1307	6.0	1924	0.6	
17	TH	0121	6.0	0749	0.5	1348	6.0	2009	0.5	
18	F	0205	6.0	0830	0.6	1430	5.9	2053	0.5	
19	SA	0250	6.0	0911	0.7	1514	5.7	2137	0.6	
20	SU	0339	5.8	0952	0.9	1602	5.5	2225	0.7	
21	M	0434	5.6	1040	1.1	1657	5.3	2322	0.8	
22	TU	0537	5.4	1140	1.3	1803	5.1			◐
23	W	0033	0.9	0648	5.3	1255	1.4	1917	5.1	
24	TH	0151	0.9	0803	5.3	1411	1.4	2030	5.2	
25	F	0303	0.8	0913	5.4	1520	1.3	2137	5.3	
26	SA	0409	0.7	1014	5.5	1622	1.1	2233	5.4	
27	SU	0503	0.7	1106	5.6	1714	1.0	2322	5.5	
28	M	0547	0.7	1150	5.7	1758	0.9			
29	TU	0005	5.6	0623	0.7	1229	5.7	1838	0.8	○
30	W	0045	5.7	0658	0.7	1305	5.7	1916	0.7	
31	TH	0122	5.7	0731	0.7	1338	5.7	1952	0.7	

JUNE

Date	Day	Time	m	Time	m	Time	m	Time	m	Moon
1	F	0158	5.6	0802	0.8	1410	5.6	2025	0.8	
2	SA	0233	5.6	0833	0.9	1441	5.5	2054	0.9	
3	SU	0308	5.4	0903	1.1	1513	5.4	2124	1.0	
4	M	0344	5.3	0935	1.2	1549	5.2	2158	1.1	
5	TU	0424	5.1	1014	1.4	1629	5.0	2240	1.2	
6	W	0510	4.9	1101	1.5	1718	4.9	2332	1.3	◑
7	TH	0606	4.8	1200	1.6	1820	4.8			
8	F	0038	1.3	0712	4.8	1311	1.6	1932	4.8	
9	SA	0155	1.2	0822	5.0	1426	1.5	2042	5.0	
10	SU	0305	1.1	0925	5.2	1530	1.3	2144	5.2	
11	M	0405	0.9	1022	5.5	1628	1.1	2239	5.5	
12	TU	0501	0.8	1113	5.7	1723	0.9	2329	5.7	
13	W	0554	0.7	1201	5.9	1817	0.7			●
14	TH	0018	5.9	0644	0.6	1247	5.9	1908	0.6	
15	F	0106	6.0	0732	0.6	1332	6.0	1959	0.4	
16	SA	0154	6.1	0818	0.6	1418	5.9	2048	0.4	
17	SU	0243	6.1	0902	0.7	1505	5.8	2137	0.4	
18	M	0333	6.0	0947	0.9	1554	5.7	2226	0.5	
19	TU	0427	5.8	1033	1.0	1647	5.5	2318	0.6	
20	W	0524	5.6	1125	1.2	1745	5.4			◐
21	TH	0017	0.7	0626	5.4	1226	1.3	1849	5.2	
22	F	0122	0.8	0733	5.3	1333	1.4	1957	5.2	
23	SA	0227	0.9	0839	5.3	1441	1.4	2103	5.2	
24	SU	0329	0.9	0942	5.3	1545	1.3	2205	5.3	
25	M	0426	0.9	1038	5.4	1643	1.2	2258	5.4	
26	TU	0513	0.9	1125	5.5	1733	1.0	2345	5.5	
27	W	0553	0.9	1207	5.5	1817	0.9			
28	TH	0027	5.5	0630	0.9	1245	5.6	1857	0.8	○
29	F	0106	5.6	0705	0.9	1319	5.6	1934	0.8	
30	SA	0142	5.6	0738	0.9	1351	5.6	2008	0.8	

JULY

Date	Day	Time	m	Time	m	Time	m	Time	m	Moon
1	SU	0216	5.5	0811	1.0	1423	5.5	2041	0.8	
2	M	0250	5.5	0844	1.0	1455	5.5	2113	0.9	
3	TU	0325	5.4	0918	1.1	1530	5.4	2147	0.9	
4	W	0402	5.3	0954	1.2	1607	5.3	2224	1.0	
5	TH	0443	5.2	1033	1.4	1648	5.1	2304	1.1	
6	F	0529	5.1	1119	1.5	1738	5.0	2352	1.2	◑
7	SA	0625	5.0	1216	1.5	1839	5.0			
8	SU	0055	1.2	0732	5.0	1328	1.5	1951	5.0	
9	M	0213	1.2	0841	5.2	1446	1.4	2103	5.2	
10	TU	0327	1.0	0947	5.4	1555	1.2	2208	5.4	
11	W	0432	0.9	1046	5.6	1659	0.9	2307	5.6	
12	TH	0531	0.8	1141	5.8	1800	0.7			
13	F	0003	5.9	0626	0.7	1232	5.9	1858	0.5	●
14	SA	0055	6.0	0718	0.7	1320	6.0	1951	0.3	
15	SU	0145	6.1	0807	0.6	1407	6.0	2042	0.2	
16	M	0234	6.2	0852	0.7	1453	6.0	2129	0.2	
17	TU	0323	6.1	0935	0.8	1540	5.9	2215	0.3	
18	W	0412	5.9	1017	1.0	1628	5.7	2259	0.5	
19	TH	0502	5.7	1059	1.1	1718	5.5	2346	0.7	◐
20	F	0556	5.5	1147	1.3	1814	5.3			
21	SA	0038	0.9	0654	5.2	1246	1.5	1917	5.1	
22	SU	0139	1.1	0757	5.1	1356	1.5	2025	5.0	
23	M	0244	1.2	0904	5.0	1507	1.5	2134	5.1	
24	TU	0345	1.2	1008	5.1	1614	1.3	2236	5.2	
25	W	0440	1.2	1101	5.3	1713	1.2	2328	5.3	
26	TH	0527	1.1	1147	5.4	1801	1.0			
27	F	0011	5.5	0607	1.1	1226	5.5	1841	0.9	○
28	SA	0050	5.5	0644	1.0	1301	5.6	1917	0.8	
29	SU	0125	5.6	0718	1.0	1334	5.6	1951	0.8	
30	M	0158	5.6	0752	0.9	1405	5.6	2025	0.7	
31	TU	0231	5.6	0827	0.9	1437	5.6	2059	0.8	

AUGUST

Date	Day	Time	m	Time	m	Time	m	Time	m	Moon
1	W	0304	5.6	0901	1.0	1510	5.6	2133	0.8	
2	TH	0338	5.5	0935	1.1	1544	5.5	2205	0.9	
3	F	0415	5.4	1007	1.2	1621	5.4	2236	1.0	
4	SA	0456	5.3	1043	1.3	1704	5.3	2312	1.1	◑
5	SU	0546	5.1	1130	1.4	1758	5.2			
6	M	0004	1.2	0647	5.0	1237	1.5	1908	5.1	
7	TU	0123	1.3	0802	5.0	1407	1.5	2029	5.1	
8	W	0257	1.3	0917	5.2	1531	1.3	2145	5.3	
9	TH	0410	1.1	1025	5.4	1642	1.0	2253	5.6	
10	F	0515	0.9	1125	5.7	1750	0.7	2352	5.9	
11	SA	0614	0.8	1218	5.9	1850	0.5			●
12	SU	0044	6.1	0706	0.7	1306	6.0	1941	0.3	
13	M	0133	6.2	0753	0.7	1352	6.1	2029	0.2	
14	TU	0219	6.2	0836	0.7	1435	6.1	2113	0.2	
15	W	0304	6.1	0916	0.8	1518	6.0	2153	0.3	
16	TH	0348	6.0	0953	0.9	1601	5.9	2230	0.6	
17	F	0432	5.7	1028	1.1	1645	5.6	2305	0.8	
18	SA	0517	5.4	1105	1.3	1733	5.3	2345	1.1	◐
19	SU	0607	5.1	1153	1.5	1831	5.0			
20	M	0039	1.4	0707	4.9	1303	1.7	1942	4.8	
21	TU	0154	1.6	0819	4.8	1430	1.7	2102	4.8	
22	W	0307	1.5	0933	4.9	1547	1.5	2213	5.0	
23	TH	0411	1.4	1035	5.1	1652	1.2	2307	5.3	
24	F	0504	1.3	1124	5.3	1742	1.1	2351	5.5	
25	SA	0547	1.1	1204	5.5	1822	0.9			
26	SU	0029	5.6	0623	1.1	1239	5.6	1856	0.8	○
27	M	0103	5.7	0657	1.0	1312	5.7	1930	0.7	
28	TU	0135	5.7	0731	0.9	1343	5.7	2004	0.7	
29	W	0207	5.8	0807	0.9	1414	5.8	2039	0.7	
30	TH	0239	5.8	0842	0.9	1446	5.7	2112	0.8	
31	F	0313	5.7	0914	1.0	1519	5.7	2142	0.9	

Chart Datum: 2·90 metres below Ordnance Datum (Newlyn). HAT is 6·3 metres above Chart Datum.

STANDARD TIME (UT)
For Summer Time add ONE hour in **non-shaded areas**

SHEERNESS LAT 51°27′N LONG 0°45′E

TIMES AND HEIGHTS OF HIGH AND LOW WATERS

Dates in red are SPRINGS
Dates in blue are NEAPS

YEAR **2018**

SEPTEMBER

Date	Day	Time	m
1	SA	0348	5.6
		0943	1.2
		1555	5.6
		2207	1.0
2	SU	0427	5.4
		1014	1.3
		1637	5.4
		2238	1.2
3	M	0513	5.2
		1058	1.4
		1729	5.2
		◑ 2328	1.3
4	TU	0612	5.0
		1203	1.5
		1839	5.1
5	W	0049	1.5
		0730	4.9
		1341	1.5
		2005	5.0
6	TH	0235	1.5
		0853	5.0
		1515	1.3
		2130	5.3
7	F	0353	1.3
		1008	5.3
		1632	0.9
		2242	5.6
8	SA	0502	1.0
		1110	5.6
		1741	0.6
		2340	5.9
9	SU	0600	0.9
		1202	5.9
		1837	0.4
		●	
10	M	0030	6.1
		0649	0.8
		1248	6.0
		1925	0.3
11	TU	0116	6.2
		0733	0.7
		1331	6.1
		2008	0.2
12	W	0159	6.2
		0814	0.7
		1412	6.1
		2048	0.3
13	TH	0240	6.1
		0851	0.8
		1452	6.1
		2123	0.4
14	F	0319	5.9
		0925	0.9
		1531	5.9
		2154	0.7
15	SA	0357	5.7
		0955	1.1
		1611	5.6
		2223	1.0
16	SU	0435	5.4
		1026	1.3
		1653	5.3
		◐ 2255	1.3
17	M	0518	5.1
		1105	1.5
		1745	5.0
		2340	1.6
18	TU	0611	4.8
		1204	1.7
		1855	4.7
19	W	0054	1.8
		0724	4.6
		1346	1.8
		2021	4.6
20	TH	0228	1.8
		0849	4.6
		1516	1.6
		2141	4.9
21	F	0339	1.6
		1000	4.9
		1622	1.3
		2239	5.2
22	SA	0435	1.4
		1052	5.2
		1712	1.1
		2323	5.5
23	SU	0520	1.2
		1134	5.5
		1753	0.9
24	M	0000	5.6
		0557	1.1
		1210	5.6
		1828	0.8
25	TU	0034	5.7
		0632	1.0
		1243	5.7
		○ 1902	0.7
26	W	0107	5.8
		0707	0.9
		1316	5.8
		1937	0.7
27	TH	0139	5.9
		0744	0.8
		1348	5.9
		2013	0.7
28	F	0213	5.9
		0820	0.9
		1422	5.9
		2047	0.7
29	SA	0247	5.8
		0853	0.9
		1456	5.8
		2117	0.9
30	SU	0323	5.7
		0923	1.1
		1534	5.7
		2143	1.1

OCTOBER

Date	Day	Time	m
1	M	0402	5.5
		0955	1.2
		1618	5.5
		2217	1.2
2	TU	0448	5.2
		1041	1.3
		1712	5.3
		◑ 2311	1.4
3	W	0548	5.0
		1149	1.4
		1824	5.1
4	TH	0035	1.6
		0708	4.8
		1333	1.4
		1953	5.1
5	F	0219	1.6
		0835	5.0
		1505	1.2
		2119	5.3
6	SA	0338	1.3
		0951	5.3
		1622	0.9
		2229	5.7
7	SU	0445	1.1
		1052	5.6
		1727	0.6
		2325	5.9
8	M	0541	0.9
		1142	5.9
		1818	0.4
9	TU	0012	6.1
		0627	0.8
		1227	6.0
		● 1902	0.4
10	W	0055	6.1
		0709	0.7
		1307	6.1
		1941	0.4
11	TH	0134	6.1
		0747	0.7
		1347	6.1
		2017	0.4
12	F	0212	6.0
		0823	0.8
		1425	6.0
		2049	0.6
13	SA	0248	5.9
		0856	0.9
		1502	5.8
		2117	0.9
14	SU	0322	5.6
		0925	1.1
		1540	5.6
		2143	1.1
15	M	0356	5.4
		0952	1.3
		1619	5.3
		2213	1.4
16	TU	0433	5.1
		1026	1.4
		1705	4.9
		◐ 2254	1.6
17	W	0519	4.8
		1116	1.6
		1807	4.6
		2355	1.9
18	TH	0625	4.5
		1237	1.8
		1929	4.5
19	F	0132	2.0
		0752	4.5
		1432	1.7
		2051	4.7
20	SA	0257	1.8
		0911	4.7
		1540	1.4
		2155	5.0
21	SU	0355	1.5
		1009	5.1
		1632	1.1
		2243	5.4
22	M	0443	1.3
		1055	5.4
		1715	0.9
		2324	5.6
23	TU	0524	1.1
		1134	5.6
		1753	0.8
24	W	0000	5.8
		0602	1.0
		1211	5.7
		○ 1830	0.7
25	TH	0036	5.9
		0640	0.9
		1247	5.8
		1908	0.7
26	F	0111	5.9
		0719	0.8
		1322	5.9
		1946	0.7
27	SA	0147	5.9
		0759	0.8
		1359	5.9
		2022	0.7
28	SU	0224	5.9
		0836	0.8
		1438	5.9
		2055	0.9
29	M	0302	5.7
		0912	0.9
		1520	5.8
		2128	1.0
30	TU	0344	5.5
		0951	1.0
		1608	5.6
		2209	1.3
31	W	0432	5.3
		1041	1.2
		1705	5.3
		◑ 2306	1.5

NOVEMBER

Date	Day	Time	m
1	TH	0534	5.0
		1152	1.3
		1818	5.1
2	F	0027	1.6
		0653	4.9
		1328	1.3
		1942	5.1
3	SA	0159	1.6
		0816	5.0
		1451	1.0
		2102	5.4
4	SU	0315	1.4
		0929	5.3
		1604	0.8
		2209	5.6
5	M	0420	1.2
		1029	5.6
		1705	0.6
		2303	5.8
6	TU	0515	1.0
		1119	5.7
		1753	0.6
		2349	5.9
7	W	0601	0.9
		1203	5.9
		1834	0.5
		●	
8	TH	0030	6.0
		0642	0.8
		1244	5.9
		1910	0.6
9	F	0109	5.9
		0720	0.7
		1323	5.9
		1944	0.6
10	SA	0145	5.9
		0757	0.8
		1401	5.9
		2015	0.8
11	SU	0219	5.8
		0831	0.9
		1438	5.7
		2044	1.0
12	M	0252	5.6
		0900	1.0
		1514	5.5
		2110	1.2
13	TU	0324	5.4
		0926	1.2
		1552	5.3
		2140	1.4
14	W	0358	5.2
		0957	1.3
		1634	5.0
		2218	1.6
15	TH	0440	4.9
		1041	1.5
		1726	4.7
		◐ 2310	1.8
16	F	0534	4.7
		1142	1.6
		1832	4.6
17	SA	0020	1.9
		0648	4.5
		1312	1.7
		1948	4.6
18	SU	0151	1.9
		0808	4.6
		1441	1.5
		2056	4.9
19	M	0302	1.6
		0915	4.9
		1540	1.2
		2153	5.2
20	TU	0356	1.4
		1008	5.2
		1629	1.0
		2241	5.5
21	W	0444	1.2
		1055	5.5
		1714	0.9
		2325	5.7
22	TH	0529	1.0
		1138	5.7
		1758	0.8
23	F	0005	5.8
		0613	0.9
		1219	5.8
		○ 1839	0.7
24	SA	0046	5.9
		0657	0.8
		1300	5.9
		1921	0.7
25	SU	0125	5.9
		0741	0.7
		1341	6.0
		2002	0.7
26	M	0206	5.9
		0825	0.7
		1425	6.0
		2041	0.8
27	TU	0248	5.8
		0909	0.7
		1512	5.9
		2121	1.0
28	W	0333	5.6
		0955	0.8
		1603	5.7
		2206	1.2
29	TH	0424	5.4
		1048	0.9
		1701	5.5
		2301	1.4
30	F	0524	5.2
		1153	1.0
		1809	5.3
		◑	

DECEMBER

Date	Day	Time	m
1	SA	0010	1.5
		0635	5.1
		1311	1.0
		1923	5.2
2	SU	0129	1.5
		0750	5.1
		1426	1.0
		2036	5.3
3	M	0241	1.4
		0900	5.2
		1534	0.9
		2141	5.5
4	TU	0347	1.3
		1002	5.4
		1634	0.8
		2238	5.6
5	W	0445	1.1
		1055	5.5
		1723	0.8
		2325	5.7
6	TH	0534	1.0
		1141	5.6
		1804	0.8
7	F	0008	5.7
		0617	0.9
		1224	5.7
		● 1839	0.8
8	SA	0047	5.7
		0657	0.8
		1304	5.7
		1913	0.8
9	SU	0122	5.7
		0735	0.8
		1343	5.7
		1946	0.9
10	M	0156	5.6
		0810	0.8
		1419	5.6
		2016	1.0
11	TU	0228	5.5
		0841	0.9
		1455	5.5
		2045	1.1
12	W	0300	5.4
		0909	1.0
		1531	5.3
		2116	1.2
13	TH	0334	5.3
		0940	1.1
		1609	5.1
		2152	1.4
14	F	0412	5.1
		1018	1.2
		1652	4.9
		2235	1.5
15	SA	0457	4.9
		1106	1.4
		1743	4.8
		◐ 2328	1.7
16	SU	0552	4.8
		1205	1.4
		1845	4.7
17	M	0034	1.8
		0700	4.7
		1319	1.4
		1953	4.8
18	TU	0151	1.7
		0813	4.8
		1437	1.3
		2059	5.0
19	W	0302	1.5
		0918	5.1
		1541	1.1
		2157	5.3
20	TH	0402	1.3
		1015	5.3
		1636	1.0
		2250	5.5
21	F	0457	1.1
		1107	5.5
		1727	0.8
		2338	5.7
22	SA	0549	0.9
		1156	5.7
		1816	0.8
		○	
23	SU	0024	5.8
		0640	0.7
		1243	5.9
		1902	0.7
24	M	0109	5.9
		0730	0.6
		1330	6.0
		1948	0.7
25	TU	0153	5.9
		0820	0.5
		1417	6.0
		2033	0.7
26	W	0238	5.8
		0908	0.5
		1506	6.0
		2117	0.8
27	TH	0325	5.7
		0957	0.5
		1557	5.8
		2201	1.0
28	F	0415	5.6
		1046	0.6
		1651	5.6
		2249	1.2
29	SA	0509	5.4
		1140	0.7
		1750	5.4
		◑ 2344	1.3
30	SU	0610	5.3
		1241	0.9
		1854	5.3
31	M	0048	1.4
		0717	5.2
		1348	1.0
		2001	5.2

Chart Datum: 2·90 metres below Ordnance Datum (Newlyn). HAT is 6·3 metres above Chart Datum.

9.4.12 RIVER THAMES

CHARTS AC 5606, 1185,1186, 2151, 3337, 2484, 3319. Imray C1, C2, Y18, 2100

TIDES The river is tidal up to Teddington. +0252 Dover; ML 3·6; Duration 0555.

Standard Port LONDON BRIDGE (→)

Times				Height (metres)			
High Water		Low Water		MHWS	MHWN	MLWN	MLWS
0300	0900	0400	1100	7·1	5·9	1·3	0·5
1500	2100	1600	2300				
Differences TILBURY							
–0055	–0040	–0050	–0115	–0·7	–0·5	+0·1	0·0
WOOLWICH (GALLIONS POINT)							
–0020	–0020	–0035	–0045	–0·1	0·0	+0·2	0·0
ALBERT BRIDGE							
+0025	+0020	+0105	+0110	–0·9	–0·8	–0·7	–0·4
HAMMERSMITH BRIDGE							
+0040	+0035	+0205	+0155	–1·4	–1·3	–1·0	–0·5
KEW BRIDGE							
+0055	+0050	+0255	+0235	–1·8	–1·8	–1·2	–0·5
TEDDINGTON (RICHMOND) LOCK							
+0105	+0055	+0325	+0305	–2·2	–2·7	–0·9	–0·5

Tide Boards, showing height of tide above CD, are at Lower Pool (Met Police Boatyard), King's Reach (Temple Stairs), Nine Elms Reach (Cringle Wharf) and Battersea Reach (Plantation Wharf). Above Putney the height of LW may be below CD if the water flow over Teddington Weir is low; warnings are broadcast by London VTS. Thames Barrier closure will alter predicted water levels greatly.

SHELTER Very good in marinas. PLA Drawdocks, arrowed, are drying inlets offering emergency refuge, but subject to wash.

NAVIGATION WPT 51°29′·62N 00°44′·17E, Sea Reach No 4 buoy, 276°/6·8M to abm Holehaven Creek and 37·8M to Tower Bridge. Pleasure craft should always keep clear of commercial vessels. To clear tanker berths off Holehaven, Coryton and Thames Haven yachts should navigate following small craft crossing routes:

Inward from north: Keep close to SHM buoys & bns. At W Leigh Middle ensure the fairway is clear, then cross to the S side of Yantlet Channel. Make for E Blyth buoy before turning onto the inward track, so as to clear outward vessels passing close to the PHM buoys. It is safe to pass S of Tanker, Cliffe Fleet, West Blyth and Lower Hope buoys. When safe, cross to the N side in Lower Hope Reach as quickly as possible.

Outward to north: as above in reverse, but cross to the N side between Sea Reach Nos 4 & 5 buoys.

Inward from the south: Keep well south of Yantlet Channel, crossing to the N side in Lower Hope Reach as described above.

Sea Reach, keep well S of the main chan to clear tankers turning off Canvey Is and Coryton. Keep at least 60m clear of oil/gas jetties and give a wide berth to London Gateway container terminal. Warning lights are displayed at Cliffe and Canvey Is when large ships are manoeuvring.

Lower Hope Reach, hold the NW bank until Ovens SHM; long groynes extend from the N bank for the next 2M. Tilbury Landing Stage is used by the Gravesend ferry and cruise liners.

Gravesend Reach, beware 6 groynes off the N bank, WSW of Coalhouse Pt, which project almost into the fairway. Outer ends marked by SHM beacons, Fl G 2·5s. *No inside passage exists.*

Above **Gravesend** keep to stbd side of channel – do not cut corners.

Northfleet Hope, beware ships/tugs turning into Tilbury Docks; container berths and a grain terminal are close upriver. A light, Iso 6s, on Tilbury Cargo Jetty (51°27′·06N 00°20′·95E) is shown when vessels are manoeuvring off Tilbury Dock locks or for a berth in Northfleet Hope. *Proceed with caution.*

Above **Cherry Garden Pier** vessels > 40m LOA and tugs/tows always have priority. Very heavy traffic/frequent River Ferries from/to Greenwich, Tower of London and Westminster. Police and PLA launches are always willing to assist.

Speed limits. Minimise wash. 8kn speed limit applies at Canvey Is, Coryton and Thurrock when gas tankers are berthed, in all creeks and above Wandsworth Bridge. Voluntary 12kn speed limit to Wandsworth Bridge.

Exclusion Zones. These are in place off the Houses of Parliament on the North Embankment and government offices below Vauxhall Br on the S side of the river.

The Port of London Authority (PLA), London River House, Royal Pier Road, Gravesend, Kent DA12 2BG, ☎01474 562200, publish (download free from www.pla.co.uk) *Recreational Users' Guide; General Directions; Permanent Notices to Mariners; Port of London River Byelaws; Tide Tables* and a *Port Handbook.*

LIGHTS AND MARKS See 9.4.4 and chartlets. Glare from shore lts can make navigation by night difficult or even hazardous. Some s show F.Bu lights; High Speed Craft show Fl.Y lights.

COMMUNICATIONS Port of London Authority: www.pla.co.uk HM: lower district 01474 562200, upper district 020 7743 7912; NMOC 02392 552100; Port Controller Gravesend 01474 560311, Police Marine Support Unit 020 7275 4421; Thames Barrier Navigation Centre 020 8855 0315; Tower Bridge 020 7940 3984; Richmond lock 020 8940 0634; Teddington lock 020 8940 8723.

London VTS works from centres at Gravesend and the Thames Barrier, dividing the estuary/river into three sectors. Routine MSI broadcasts are made at the times shown (in brackets) below.

Sector 1: Outer limits – Sea Reach No 4 buoy. Ch **69** (H +15, H +45)

Sector 2: Sea Reach 4 – Crayfordness. Ch **68** (H and H +30)

Sector 3: Crayfordness – Teddington. Ch **14** (H +15 and H +45)

PLA launches *Thames Patrol* Ch 69, 68, 14. Police launches *Thames Police* Ch 14. **Do not** use tug Channels 8, 10, 13, 36, 72, 77. **In emergency** call *London Coastguard* Ch 16, 67, co-located with London VTS at the Thames Barrier Navigation Control and covering from Canvey Island to Teddington. *Thames Coastguard* covers the area to seaward of Canvey Island. The RNLI operates four LB stations at Gravesend, Victoria Embankment (Waterloo Br), Chiswick and Teddington.

HARBOURS IN SEA REACH and GRAVESEND REACH

HOLEHAVEN CREEK, Essex, **51°30′·57N 00°33′·16E**. AC 2484, 1186. HW +0140 on Dover; use differences for Coryton (at 9.4.13); ML 3·0m; Duration 0610. Shelter is good, but beware swell from passing traffic. Keep to Canvey Is side on ent. Temp ⚓ in lee of Chainrock jetty or call PLA ☎01474 562462 for possible mooring. 5ca N of ent an overhead oil pipe (2 FY horiz) crosses chan with 11m clearance, plus. 2 FG (vert) on all jetty heads, plus Chainrock SHM buoy Fl G 5s. from Lobster Smack pub, from Canvey Village (1M); all other facilities on Canvey Is.

GRAVESEND, Kent, **51°26′·61N 00°22′·92E**. AC 1186, 2151. HW +0150 on Dover; ML 3·3m; Duration 0610. Use Tilbury diffs. ⚓ E of Club's Jetty close to S shore, but remote from town.

Gravesend SC www.gravesendsailingclub.co.uk ☎07538 326623.

PLA s are upriver, £25/night. **London River Moorings** ☎01474 535700 All tide s £25/night, half tide. New all tide landing stage available.

Embankment Marina www.theembankmentmarina.co.uk ☎01474 535700; £25/night. Lock into Canal Basin HW –1 to HW Tilbury by arrangement: 1 Apr-31 Oct, 0800-2000; Winter 1000-1600. Lock closes at local HW. Out of hours openings up to HW by arrangement with lock keeper. Facilities: Ⓔ.

Town Tourist info ☎(01474) 337600, Ⓔ (70t) at Denton Wharf, .

Thurrock YC 51°28′·28N 00°19′·47E at Grays, ☎01375 373720. 1 (2M), (occas). M-F 1000-1500; Thu 2000-2300.

E England

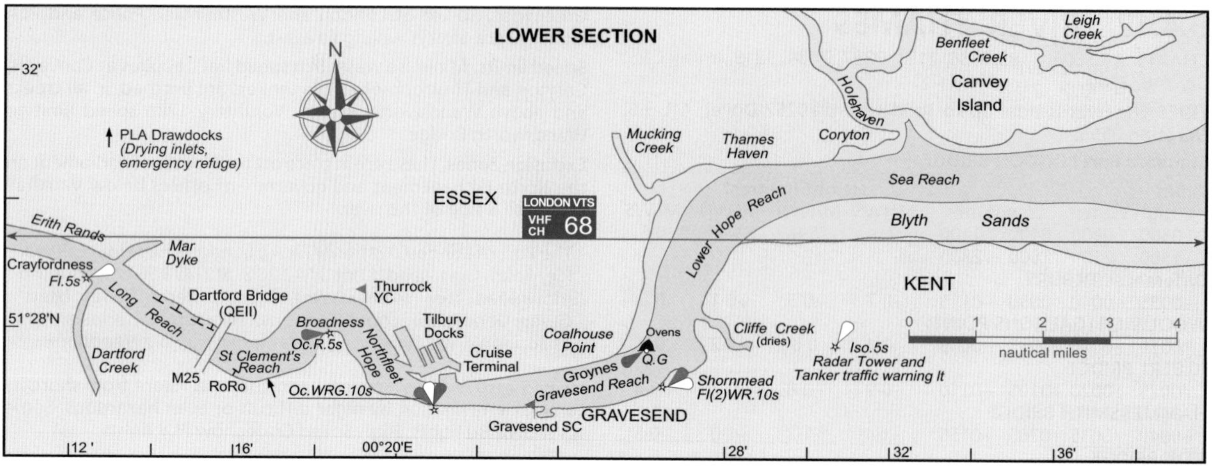
LOWER SECTION
N
PLA Drawdocks
(Drying inlets, emergency refuge)
ESSEX
LONDON VTS
VHF CH 68
Erith Rands
Mar Dyke
Crayfordness
Fl.5s
Long Reach
Dartford Bridge (QEII)
Dartford Creek
M25
RoRo
St Clement's Reach
Broadness
Oc.R.5s
Northfleet Hope
Oc.WRG.10s
Thurrock YC
Tilbury Docks
Cruise Terminal
Coalhouse Point
Groynes
Gravesend Reach
Gravesend SC
GRAVESEND
Ovens
Q.G
Shornmead
Fl(2)WR.10s
Cliffe Creek
(dries)
Iso.5s
Radar Tower and Tanker traffic warning lt
Mucking Creek
Thames Haven
Coryton
Holehaven
Benfleet Creek
Canvey Island
Leigh Creek
Lower Hope Reach
Sea Reach
Blyth Sands
KENT
0 1 2 3 4
nautical miles
32'
51°28'N
12'
16'
00°20'E
28'
32'
36'

CANVEY ISLAND TO CRAYFORDNESS (AC 1185, 1186, 2484, 2151)

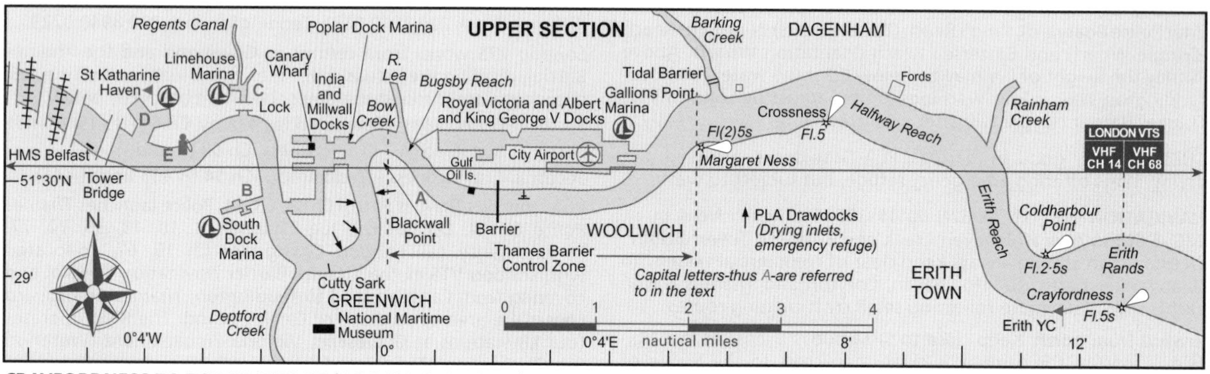
UPPER SECTION
Regents Canal
Poplar Dock Marina
Limehouse Marina
Canary Wharf
St Katharine Haven
C
Lock
D
E
India and Millwall Docks
R. Lea
Bow Creek
Bugsby Reach
Royal Victoria and Albert and King George V Docks
Tidal Barrier
Gallions Point
Marina
Barking Creek
DAGENHAM
Fords
Crossness
Halfway Reach
Fl(2)5s
Fl.5
Margaret Ness
Rainham Creek
LONDON VTS
VHF CH 14
VHF CH 68
HMS Belfast
51°30'N
Tower Bridge
B
South Dock Marina
N
Gulf Oil Is.
City Airport
A
Blackwall Point
Barrier
WOOLWICH
Thames Barrier Control Zone
PLA Drawdocks
(Drying inlets, emergency refuge)
Capital letters-thus A-are referred to in the text
Erith Reach
Coldharbour Point
Fl.2·5s
Erith Rands
Crayfordness
Fl.5s
Erith YC
ERITH TOWN
29'
Cutty Sark
GREENWICH
National Maritime Museum
Deptford Creek
0°4'W
0°
0°4'E
0 1 2 3 4
nautical miles
8'
12'

CRAYFORDNESS TO TOWER BRIDGE (AC 2484, 2151, 3337)

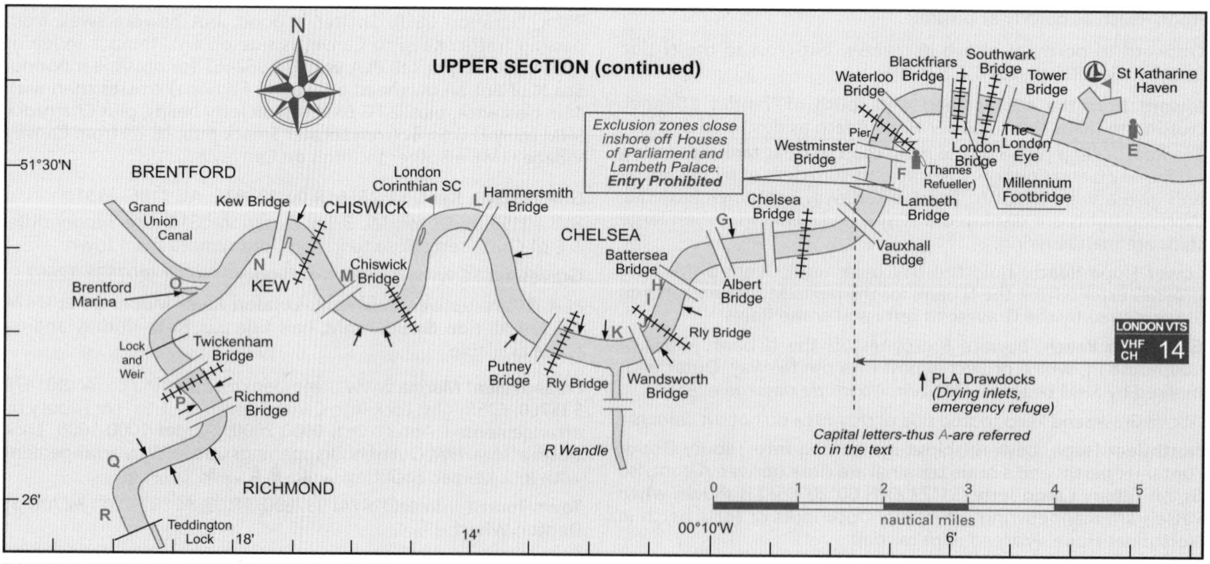
N
UPPER SECTION (continued)
Exclusion zones close inshore off Houses of Parliament and Lambeth Palace.
Entry Prohibited
Waterloo Bridge
Blackfriars Bridge
Southwark Bridge
Tower Bridge
St Katharine Haven
E
Pier
Westminster Bridge
London Bridge
The London Eye
(Thames Refueller)
F
Millennium Footbridge
Lambeth Bridge
51°30'N
BRENTFORD
London Corinthian SC
Hammersmith Bridge
L
Kew Bridge
CHISWICK
Grand Union Canal
CHELSEA
Chelsea Bridge
G
Vauxhall Bridge
N
KEW
O
Brentford Marina
Chiswick Bridge
M
Battersea Bridge
H
I
Albert Bridge
Rly Bridge
K
J
LONDON VTS
VHF CH 14
Lock and Weir
Twickenham Bridge
P
Richmond Bridge
Putney Bridge
Rly Bridge
Wandsworth Bridge
PLA Drawdocks
(Drying inlets, emergency refuge)
R Wandle
Capital letters-thus A-are referred to in the text
Q
RICHMOND
26'
R
Teddington Lock
18'
14'
00°10'W
0 1 2 3 4 5
nautical miles
6'

TOWER BRIDGE TO TEDDINGTON (AC 3319)

OBSTRUCTIONS

THAMES TIDAL BARRIER 51°29′·91N 00°02′·21E (Span G), AC 5606, 2484, 3337. At Woolwich Reach are 9 piers between which gates can be rotated upwards from the river bed to form a barrier. Piers are numbered 1-9 from N to S; Spans are lettered A-K from S to N (see diagram). A, H, J & K are not navigable. C-F, with depth 5·8m and 61m wide, are for larger ships. Spans B and G, with 1·25m, are for small craft: W-bound via G and E-bound via B (51°29′·73N 00°02′·24E). On N side of river (Spans E and F) a cross-tide component is reported.

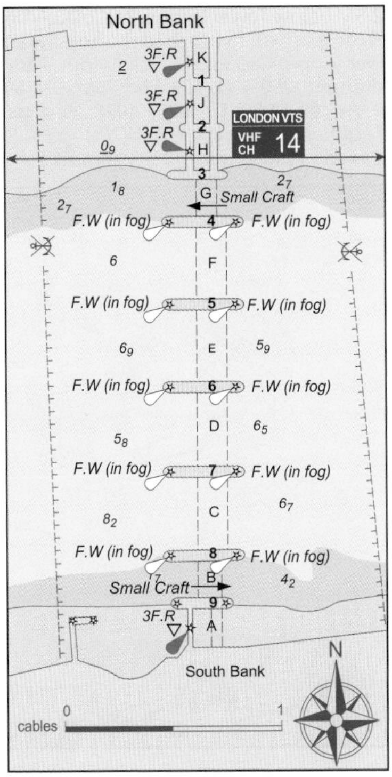

Small craft should not navigate between Thames Refinery Jetty and Gulf Oil Island, unless intending to transit the Barrier. Yachts must transit the barrier under power, not sail. When all spans are closed, keep 200m clear to avoid turbulence. It is dangerous to transit a span closed to navigation as the gate may be semi-raised.

In reduced visibility, open spans are marked by high intensity lts. *London VTS* broadcasts information on Ch **14** at H+15/H+45.

CONTROL AND COMMUNICATIONS The Thames Barrier Navigation Centre controls all traffic in a Zone from Margaret Ness (51°30′·5N 00°05′·56E) to Blackwall Point (51°30′·3N 00°00′·2E), using the callsign *London VTS* on VHF Ch **14**, 22, 16.

Inbound call *London VTS* to obtain clearance to proceed through the Barrier when passing Margaret Ness (51°30′·54N 00°05′·50E).

Outbound call *London VTS* to obtain clearance to proceed through the Barrier when passing Blackwall Point (51°30′·30N 00°00′·18E).

Non-VHF craft should, if possible, pre-notify the Thames Barrier Control ☎020 8855 0315; then observe all visual signals, proceed with caution keeping clear of larger vessels and use spans B or G as appropriate. Call before and after transiting the barrier.

There are fixed warning noticeboards (CEVNI) at: Barking Creek (N bank), Blackwall Stairs (N bank), Blackwall Point (S bank).

TESTING The Barrier is completely closed for testing once a month for about 3hrs, LW ±1½. Visit www.pla.co.uk (navigation safety) or call ☎020 8305 4188 for details. In Sept/Oct an annual closure lasts about 10hrs, LW to LW.

THAMES GATEWAY CABLE CAR Joining the O2 Millennium Dome site at Greenwich with the Excel Centre at Victoria Docks, the Cable Car crosses the river between 2 pylons giving an air draught of 60m.

RICHMOND WEIR & TEDDINGTON LOCK At **Richmond** a half-tide lock and a weir with overhead sluice gates give access upriver; fee payable. 3 R discs (3 ● lts at night) in a ▽ show when the sluice gates are down (closed) and maintaining at least 1·72m between Richmond and Teddington bridges. The half-tide lock, on the Surrey bank, must then be used. At other times (approx HW ±2) two ● lights at each arch = weir open to navigation. Pass freely below the 3 central arches.

Teddington lock marks the end of the tidal Thames (semi-tidal above Richmond). Red/green lights indicate which of the launch or barge locks is in operation.

BRIDGES Craft approaching a bridge against the tide give way to those approaching with the tide. All bridges above Tower Bridge are fixed. A ▽ of R discs (● lts) below a bridge span = this arch closed; a bundle of straw = reduced headroom. Clearances (m) above HAT are as follows:

Tower Bridge fog horn sounds a 10s blast every 20s when bascules are open for shipping; standby signal is a bell 30s. On bridge arches between Tower and Wandsworth bridges high intensity white signal lts are electronically triggered by one or more large vessels approaching a bridge. Iso W 4s means a single large vessel, VQ a second large vessel, nearing the same bridge. Other vessels keep clear of that arch. NB air-draught boards are at Harrods Depository and Chiswick Eyot for Hammersmith Bridge.

Dartford (QEII)	53	Albert	4.5
Tower (closed)	8·0	Battersea road	5·0
Tower (open)	42	Battersea rail	5·5
London	8·2	Wandsworth	5·3
Cannon St	6·7	Fulham	6·3
Southwark	6·8	Putney	4·8
Millennium	8·4	Hammersmith	3·1
Blackfriars rail	6·8	Barnes	4·9
Blackfriars road	6.5	Chiswick	6·1
Waterloo	8·1	Kew rail	5·0
Charing Cross	6·5	Kew road	4·7
Westminster	4·8	Richmond foot	5·0
Lambeth	5·9	Twickenham	8·5*
Vauxhall	5·2	Richmond rail	8·0*
Victoria Railway	5·5	Richmond road	7·9*
Chelsea	6·1	* Above maintained water level	

FACILITIES

Marinas See overleaf for Gallions Point and Poplar Dock. Other marinas and YCs (Bold red letters in brackets appear on River Thames chartlets):

(A) Greenwich YC ☎0844 736 5846, VHF Ch M.

(B) South Dock Marina ☎020 7252 2244 (details overleaf).

(C) Limehouse Marina ☎020 7308 9930 (details overleaf).

(D) St Katharine Haven ☎020 7264 5312 (details overleaf).

West India Dock ☎020 7517 5500; group bookings (min 6) only.

Hermitage Moorings (3·5ca downstream of Tower bridge) ☎020 7481 2122; VHF Ch M/80. 2 on pontoons (max 40m LOA) £30/£40 per night.

(E) Fuel Barge ☎020 7481 1774; VHF Ch 14 *Heiko*. M-F 0630-1430. W/ends Apr-Oct, HW±2, between 0600 & 1800.

(F) Westminster Petroleum Ltd Fuel barge moored off Houses of Parliament. Open Mon-Fri (and Sat from Easter to mid-Oct). Call *Thames Refueller* VHF Ch 14, ☎07831 110681, dry stores.

(G) **Cadogan** 020 8748 2715, give 24hrs notice. Chiswick 020 8742 2713. Dove 020 8748 2715. St Katharine 020 7488 0555. Putney 020 7378 1211. 020 7930 2062 for Kew Pier and Richmond Lndg Stage.

(H) Chelsea Yacht & Boat Co ☎020 7352 1427.

(I) Chelsea Harbour ☎020 7225 9100 (details overleaf).

(J) Imperial Wharf Marina pier@imperialwharfmarina.co.uk. ☎ 07932 603284, 270m pontoon, 2m at MLWS, £4/m/night, visitors welcome.

(K) Hurlingham YC ☎020 8788 5547.

Chiswick Pier ☎020 8742 2713, all tide access, max draught 1·4m £0.95m, long pontoon, 2FG (vert). Visitors welcome.

(L) Chiswick Quay Marina ☎020 8994 8743, Access HW±2 via lock, 50.

(M) Dove Marina.

(N) Kew Marina ☎020 8940 8364.

(O) Brentford Dock ☎020 8232 8941 (details overleaf).

(P) Richmond Slipway

(Q) Eel Pie Island (6t).

(R) Swan Island Hbr (30t).

Piers where landing may be possible, by prior arrangement: Call London River Services ☎020 7941 2400 for: Greenwich, Tower Millennium, Embankment, Bankside, Festival, Westminster, Millbank, Blackfriars and Waterloo.

E England

MARINAS ON THE TIDAL THAMES, from seaward to Brentford AC 2484, 3337, 3319

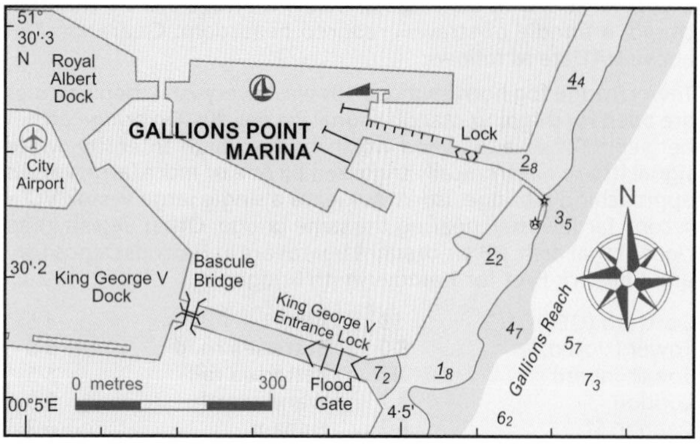

GALLIONS POINT MARINA, 51°30'·30N 00°04'·66E sited in the entry basin for Royal Albert Dock. www.gallionspoint marina.co.uk ☎ 020 7476 7054. Ch M/80, when vessel expected. 2 x ☆s 2FG (vert) on river pier. 8m depth in basin. Access via lock (width 7·6m) HW±5; Locking £5 each way; H24 security, ⊆ from £12/yacht, slip. DLR from N Woolwich to central London, until 0030. Woolwich ferry & foot tunnel 15 mins walk. ✈ (City) is adjacent.

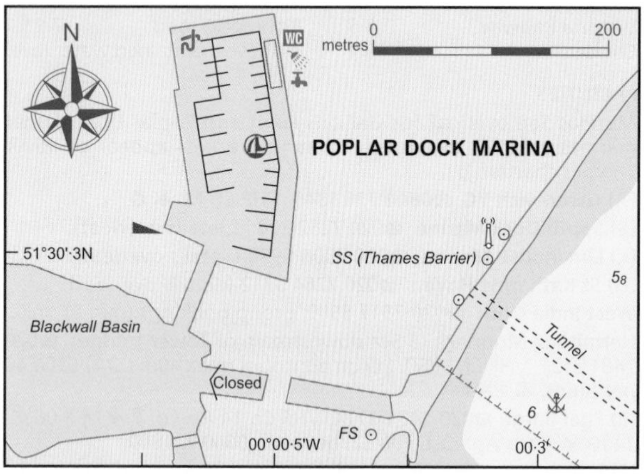

POPLAR DOCK MARINA, 51°30'·07N 00°00'·50W (lock entrance). ☎020 7308 9930, ***but no visitors berths***. Tides: India & Millwall Docks ent. 4·5M below Tower Bridge. Canary Wharf twrs (244m) are conspic 4ca W of marina. Enter via West India Entrance Lock (spanned by Docklands 'Blue Bridge'). Lock (300m x 24m) opens 0700-1700LT at HW for outbound and HW-1 to HW+1 for arrivals, foc, but OT £20. Least width 12·1m into marina. VHF Ch 13 (H24).

Facilities ; Dr ☎020 7237 1078; Ⓗ 020 7955 5000; Police 101. ⇌ Blackwall DLR, Canary Wharf Tube, ✈ City.

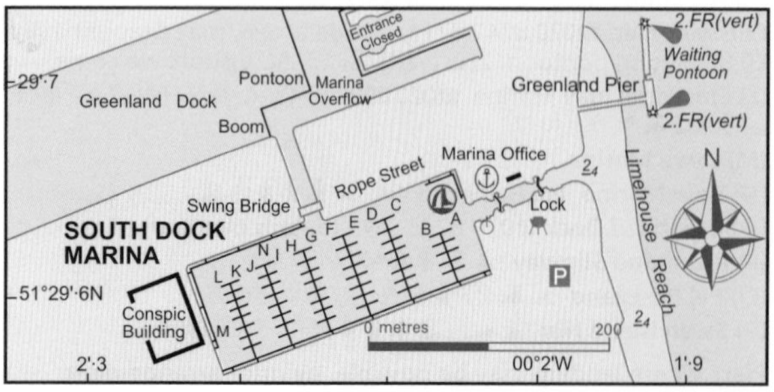

SOUTH DOCK MARINA (B), 51°29'·65N 00°01'·97W. ☎020 7252 2244 Mob 0795 662 10710 (OH 0700-1900 Mon-Fri / 0800-1700 w/e) Tides as for Surrey Dock Greenland Ent. 1·1M above Greenwich, 2·5M below Tower Bridge. Baltic Quay building at SW end of marina is conspic with five arched rooftops. Waiting pontoon at Greenland Pier. Approx access via lock (width 6·4m) HW-2 to HW+1½ for 2m draught. 250 + ♥, £22·62< 9·5m>£24·89<15m>£33·89<20m>£39·6 0.VHF Ch **M** 80; Dr ☎237 1078; Ⓗ; ☎020 7955 5000; Police 101. **Facilities** (20t) ✕ ⇌ Surrey Quays and Canada Water tube, ✈ City Airport.

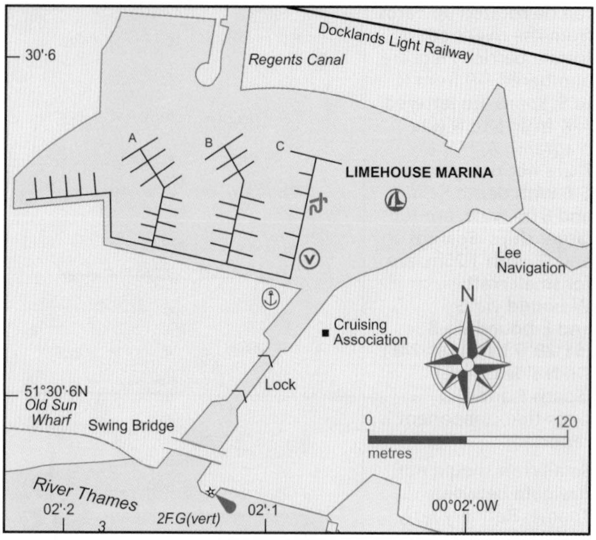

LIMEHOUSE MARINA (C), 51°30'·57N 00°02'·27W www.bwml.co.uk ☎020 7308 9930. Entry HW±3 via swing bridge/lock (width 8m) 0800-1800LT daily Apr-Sep; 0800-1600 Oct-Mar; other times by prior arrangement (24hrs notice) to BWML Lock control ☎020 7308 9930, beware cross-tide at lock cut, mid flood/ebb. Waiting pontoon in lock entrance is accessible outside LW±2. Call VHF Ch 80 *Limehouse Marina*.

Facilities 90⊆ from £28·00/craft ♥ H24 security, ⇌ DLR; also entry to Regents Canal and Lee Navigation. Visitors welcome at CA clubhouse.

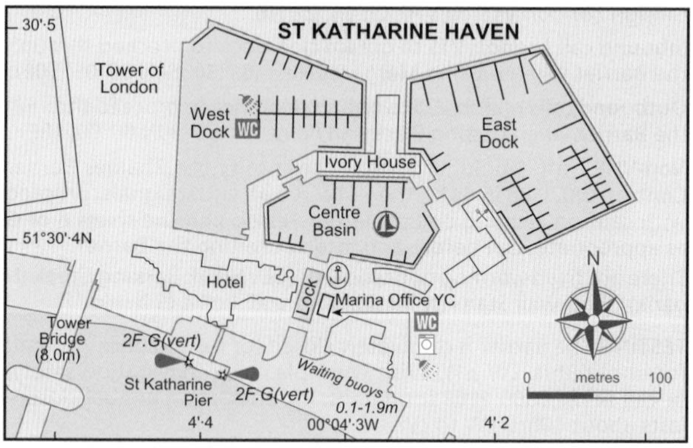

ST KATHARINE HAVEN (D), 51°30'·36N 00°04'·35W www.skdocks.co.uk ☎020 7264 5312 HW +0245 on Dover. Tides as London Bridge. Beware of cross-tide at mid-flood/ebb. Good shelter under all conditions. Tower Bridge and the Tower of London are uniquely conspic, close upriver. Six Y waiting buoys are close downstream of entrance. Berthing on St Katharine Pier, 30m upriver, is strictly by prior arrangement and only for shoal draught vessels with permission. Pleasure launches berth on S side of pier.

St Katharine Haven Ch **80** M. Lock (41m x 12·5m with 2 small lifting bridges), access HW –2 to HW +1½, season 0600-2030, winter 0800-1800LT; other times by prior arrangement. R/G traffic lights at entr.

Facilities 160⊆ inc ♥ in 3 basins £4·50+ – usually Centre Basin or East Dock; ✕ @.

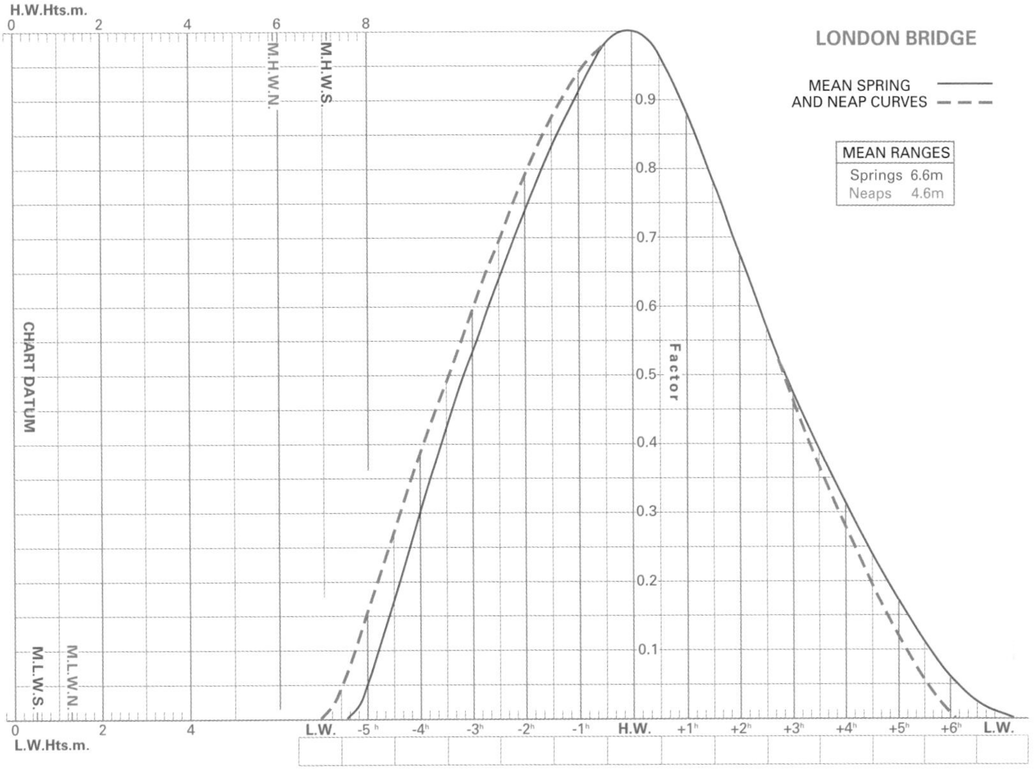

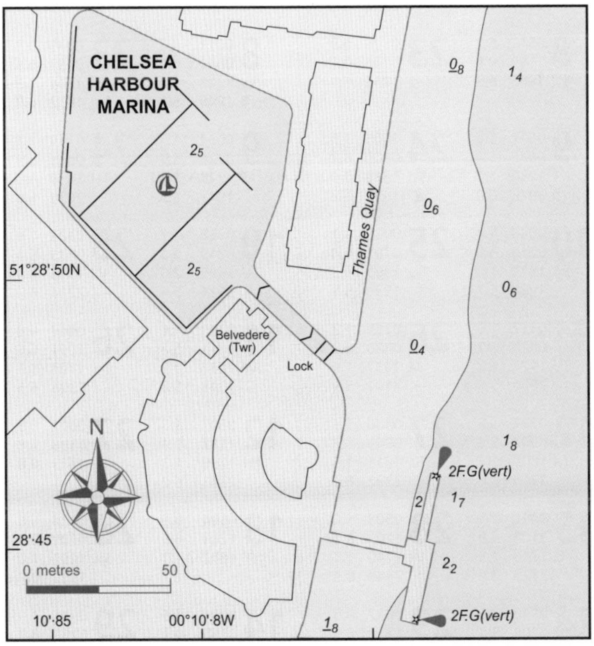

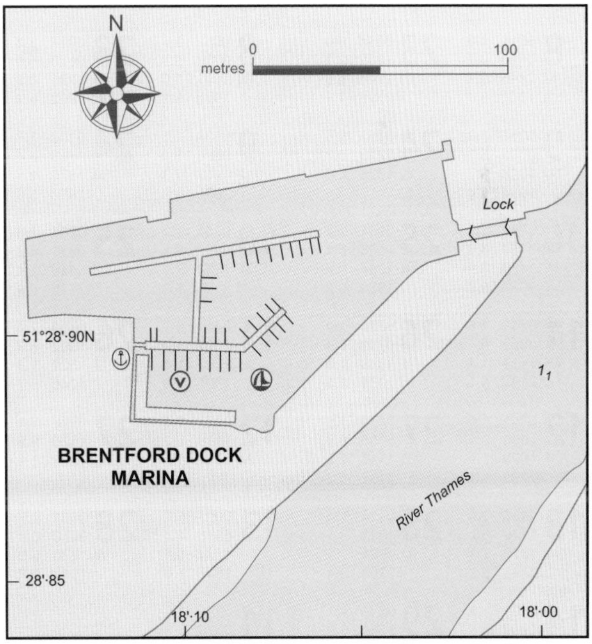

CHELSEA HARBOUR MARINA (I), London, **51°28´·48N 00°10´·82W.** Tides: see Albert Bridge. Good shelter in all conditions, 5M above Tower Bridge, reached via 14 fixed bridges. Battersea railway bridge is 120m upstream. Belvedere Tower (80m high with tide ball) is conspic, next to the lock and bascule bridge. Max sizes for lock: LOA 24m, beam 5·5m, draught 1·8m. Lock opens when there is 2·5m water above sill; tide gauge outside; R/G traffic lights. Limited waiting berths and shore access on Chelsea Hbr Pier (1·7m) close upriver. **Marina** Mobile ☎07770 542783. VHF Ch 80. 50⊆+10Ⓥ £25<12m>£30, ♿ ⛽ 🏁 WC ⊡ Ⓑ ⛟ ✕ ⊐.

BRENTFORD DOCK MARINA (O), 51°28'·92N 00°18'·05W, 1100m beyond Kew bridge. AC 3319. Tides, see Kew Bridge. 60⊆ inc Ⓥ, £20 for all LOA. Mobile ☎07970 143 987. No VHF. Access approx HW±2½ via lock 4·8m x 9·8m (longer LOA during freeflow); 15m waiting pontoon.

Facilities ⊐⊃ ⛽ ⊡ ♟ ✕ 🔧 ⊡ ⛟ ✕ ⊐; Gunnersbury & Ealing tubes. Ent to Grand Union Canal via lock is nearby: ⛺ ⊆.

STANDARD TIME (UT)
For Summer Time add ONE hour in **non-shaded areas**

LONDON BRIDGE LAT 51°30′N LONG 0°05′W

TIMES AND HEIGHTS OF HIGH AND LOW WATERS

Dates in red are SPRINGS
Dates in blue are NEAPS

YEAR **2018**

JANUARY

Date	Time	m	Time	m	Time	m	Time	m
1 M	0029	7.0	0714	0.7	1253	7.3	1939	0.6
2 TU	0124	7.1	0817	0.5	1346	7.5	○ 2039	0.6
3 W	0215	7.2	0913	0.2	1437	7.6	2130	0.6
4 TH	0305	7.2	1003	0.1	1527	7.6	2216	0.6
5 F	0352	7.2	1049	0.0	1615	7.5	2257	0.7
6 SA	0438	7.1	1130	0.1	1703	7.3	2335	0.8
7 SU	0524	6.9	1208	0.2	1751	7.0		
8 M	0011	1.0	0610	6.7	1246	0.5	◑ 1841	6.7
9 TU	0051	1.2	0700	6.5	1328	0.7	1934	6.4
10 W	0139	1.4	0757	6.3	1420	0.9	2031	6.2
11 TH	0241	1.6	0859	6.1	1519	1.1	2132	6.1
12 F	0351	1.6	1004	6.1	1620	1.1	2239	6.1
13 SA	0458	1.4	1110	6.2	1720	1.1	2343	6.3
14 SU	0603	1.2	1209	6.5	1819	1.0		
15 M	0036	6.5	0659	1.0	1258	6.7	1911	0.9
16 TU	0120	6.7	0746	0.8	1340	6.8	1956	0.9
17 W	0158	6.8	0828	0.7	1417	6.9	● 2036	0.9
18 TH	0233	6.8	0906	0.7	1451	6.9	2112	0.9
19 F	0305	6.9	0943	0.6	1522	6.9	2147	0.9
20 SA	0337	6.9	1017	0.6	1555	6.9	2221	0.8
21 SU	0409	6.8	1049	0.6	1629	6.9	2254	0.9
22 M	0443	6.7	1116	0.6	1705	6.7	2324	1.0
23 TU	0518	6.6	1141	0.7	1744	6.6	2356	1.1
24 W	0557	6.5	1213	0.8	1828	6.4	◐	
25 TH	0034	1.2	0643	6.4	1254	0.8	1920	6.2
26 F	0124	1.4	0740	6.3	1349	1.0	2031	6.1
27 SA	0234	1.5	0900	6.3	1517	1.2	2152	6.2
28 SU	0413	1.4	1023	6.5	1648	1.1	2304	6.4
29 M	0537	1.1	1134	6.8	1808	0.9		
30 TU	0012	6.7	0658	0.7	1239	7.1	1927	0.7
31 W	0112	7.0	0807	0.3	1336	7.3	○ 2028	0.6

FEBRUARY

Date	Time	m	Time	m	Time	m	Time	m
1 TH	0205	7.1	0903	0.1	1427	7.5	2120	0.5
2 F	0253	7.3	0953	-0.1	1515	7.6	2206	0.5
3 SA	0337	7.3	1037	-0.2	1600	7.5	2246	0.5
4 SU	0420	7.3	1115	-0.1	1644	7.4	2322	0.7
5 M	0501	7.2	1147	0.1	1726	7.1	2352	0.8
6 TU	0541	6.9	1215	0.4	1808	6.7		
7 W	0020	1.1	0622	6.6	1244	0.7	◑ 1850	6.4
8 TH	0052	1.3	0708	6.3	1321	1.0	1938	6.1
9 F	0134	1.5	0805	6.0	1417	1.3	2036	5.8
10 SA	0243	1.7	0913	5.8	1532	1.5	2145	5.8
11 SU	0411	1.7	1027	5.9	1642	1.4	2302	5.9
12 M	0522	1.4	1138	6.2	1748	1.2		
13 TU	0007	6.2	0626	1.1	1234	6.5	1846	1.0
14 W	0056	6.5	0720	0.8	1319	6.7	1936	0.9
15 TH	0138	6.7	0806	0.7	1358	6.8	● 2020	0.9
16 F	0214	6.8	0848	0.6	1432	6.9	2100	0.9
17 SA	0248	6.9	0927	0.5	1504	6.9	2138	0.8
18 SU	0320	7.0	1004	0.4	1536	7.0	2214	0.7
19 M	0351	7.0	1037	0.4	1609	7.0	2247	0.7
20 TU	0424	7.0	1104	0.5	1645	6.9	2316	0.9
21 W	0459	6.9	1126	0.6	1722	6.7	2344	1.0
22 TH	0537	6.8	1153	0.7	1803	6.4		
23 F	0017	1.1	0620	6.6	1231	0.8	◐ 1852	6.2
24 SA	0102	1.3	0715	6.4	1320	1.1	1958	6.0
25 SU	0207	1.4	0831	6.2	1446	1.4	2125	6.0
26 M	0350	1.4	1002	6.3	1629	1.3	2246	6.2
27 TU	0520	1.1	1120	6.6	1800	1.1		
28 W	0001	6.5	0650	0.7	1230	6.9	1917	0.8

MARCH

Date	Time	m	Time	m	Time	m	Time	m
1 TH	0102	6.9	0756	0.2	1326	7.2	2015	0.6
2 F	0152	7.1	0849	0.0	1415	7.4	○ 2104	0.5
3 SA	0237	7.3	0935	-0.2	1459	7.4	2148	0.4
4 SU	0318	7.4	1016	-0.1	1540	7.4	2227	0.5
5 M	0356	7.4	1050	0.0	1619	7.3	2300	0.6
6 TU	0434	7.3	1118	0.3	1656	7.0	2326	0.8
7 W	0510	7.0	1137	0.5	1731	6.7	2347	1.0
8 TH	0547	6.7	1159	0.8	1807	6.3		
9 F	0012	1.1	0626	6.4	1230	1.1	◑ 1846	6.0
10 SA	0048	1.4	0713	6.0	1312	1.4	1938	5.7
11 SU	0137	1.6	0820	5.7	1424	1.8	2050	5.5
12 M	0311	1.8	0942	5.6	1603	1.7	2215	5.6
13 TU	0442	1.5	1100	5.9	1716	1.5	2329	6.0
14 W	0549	1.2	1202	6.3	1817	1.2		
15 TH	0025	6.4	0647	0.9	1250	6.6	1909	1.0
16 F	0109	6.6	0737	0.7	1330	6.8	1956	0.9
17 SA	0147	6.8	0822	0.6	1405	6.9	● 2039	0.8
18 SU	0222	7.0	0904	0.5	1438	7.0	2120	0.7
19 M	0256	7.1	0942	0.4	1513	7.1	2158	0.6
20 TU	0330	7.2	1017	0.4	1548	7.1	2234	0.6
21 W	0404	7.2	1045	0.4	1624	6.9	2304	0.7
22 TH	0440	7.1	1107	0.6	1702	6.7	2332	0.9
23 F	0520	6.9	1136	0.7	1743	6.4		
24 SA	0005	1.0	0605	6.7	1214	0.9	◐ 1833	6.2
25 SU	0050	1.1	0701	6.4	1305	1.3	1939	5.9
26 M	0155	1.3	0820	6.2	1437	1.6	2107	5.9
27 TU	0336	1.3	0949	6.3	1615	1.5	2232	6.1
28 W	0508	1.0	1109	6.5	1749	1.1	2348	6.5
29 TH	0637	0.5	1218	6.9	1900	0.8		
30 F	0047	6.8	0737	0.2	1312	7.1	1954	0.6
31 SA	0135	7.1	0826	0.0	1357	7.2	○ 2042	0.5

APRIL

Date	Time	m	Time	m	Time	m	Time	m
1 SU	0216	7.2	0909	0.0	1437	7.3	2124	0.5
2 M	0253	7.3	0947	0.1	1515	7.3	2202	0.5
3 TU	0329	7.4	1018	0.3	1550	7.2	2233	0.6
4 W	0405	7.3	1040	0.4	1624	7.0	2255	0.7
5 TH	0440	7.1	1058	0.6	1656	6.7	2315	0.9
6 F	0515	6.7	1122	0.8	1728	6.3	2341	1.0
7 SA	0551	6.4	1152	1.1	1803	6.0		
8 SU	0013	1.2	0631	6.0	1228	1.4	◑ 1846	5.7
9 M	0054	1.5	0724	5.7	1320	1.8	1949	5.5
10 TU	0158	1.7	0849	5.5	1500	2.0	2124	5.4
11 W	0353	1.6	1011	5.7	1632	1.7	2243	5.8
12 TH	0505	1.3	1117	6.1	1736	1.3	2343	6.2
13 F	0604	0.9	1209	6.5	1832	1.1		
14 SA	0031	6.6	0658	0.7	1253	6.7	1923	0.9
15 SU	0113	6.8	0748	0.6	1332	6.9	2011	0.8
16 M	0151	7.0	0834	0.5	1410	7.0	● 2056	0.7
17 TU	0229	7.2	0915	0.4	1448	7.1	2138	0.6
18 W	0307	7.3	0953	0.4	1527	7.1	2217	0.5
19 TH	0345	7.3	1025	0.5	1606	6.9	2252	0.5
20 F	0425	7.2	1052	0.6	1647	6.7	2324	0.6
21 SA	0508	7.0	1124	0.8	1731	6.4	2359	0.8
22 SU	0557	6.8	1206	1.0	1823	6.2	◐	
23 M	0046	0.9	0657	6.5	1304	1.3	1932	6.0
24 TU	0155	1.1	0816	6.3	1430	1.5	2055	6.0
25 W	0323	1.0	0935	6.4	1558	1.4	2214	6.2
26 TH	0448	0.8	1051	6.6	1723	1.1	2326	6.5
27 F	0611	0.5	1158	6.8	1833	0.8		
28 SA	0024	6.8	0709	0.3	1251	7.0	1927	0.7
29 SU	0111	7.0	0757	0.2	1335	7.1	2014	0.6
30 M	0151	7.1	0837	0.3	1413	7.1	○ 2056	0.5

Chart Datum: 3·20 metres below Ordnance Datum (Newlyn). HAT is 7·7 metres above Chart Datum.

STANDARD TIME (UT)
For Summer Time add ONE hour in **non-shaded areas**

LONDON BRIDGE LAT 51°30'N LONG 0°05'W

TIMES AND HEIGHTS OF HIGH AND LOW WATERS

Dates in red are SPRINGS
Dates in blue are NEAPS

YEAR **2018**

MAY

Date	Day	Time	m	Time	m	Time	m	Time	m
1	TU	0227	7.2	0912	0.4	1448	7.1	2133	0.5
2	W	0302	7.3	0940	0.5	1521	7.0	2203	0.6
3	TH	0338	7.2	1000	0.6	1554	6.9	2226	0.7
4	F	0413	7.0	1024	0.7	1626	6.7	2249	0.8
5	SA	0447	6.7	1053	0.9	1657	6.4	2316	0.9
6	SU	0522	6.4	1123	1.1	1730	6.2	2346	1.1
7	M	0600	6.1	1156	1.3	1809	5.9		
8	TU	0021	1.2	0645	5.8	1239	1.6	◑ 1900	5.7
9	W	0112	1.4	0747	5.6	1347	1.9	2017	5.5
10	TH	0238	1.5	0915	5.7	1523	1.8	2149	5.7
11	F	0408	1.3	1023	6.0	1640	1.5	2253	6.1
12	SA	0511	1.0	1121	6.4	1743	1.2	2347	6.5
13	SU	0609	0.7	1212	6.7	1842	1.0		
14	M	0035	6.9	0705	0.6	1259	6.9	1938	0.8
15	TU	0120	7.1	0759	0.5	1343	7.1	● 2030	0.6
16	W	0203	7.3	0848	0.5	1427	7.1	2118	0.5
17	TH	0246	7.4	0931	0.5	1510	7.1	2202	0.4
18	F	0330	7.5	1010	0.5	1554	7.0	2242	0.3
19	SA	0415	7.4	1045	0.6	1639	6.8	2320	0.4
20	SU	0502	7.1	1123	0.8	1726	6.5		
21	M	0000	0.5	0554	6.9	1208	1.0	1820	6.3
22	TU	0049	0.6	0656	6.7	1305	1.2	◐ 1925	6.2
23	W	0153	0.7	0805	6.5	1416	1.3	2037	6.2
24	TH	0304	0.7	0914	6.5	1532	1.3	2147	6.3
25	F	0415	0.7	1023	6.6	1647	1.1	2255	6.5
26	SA	0529	0.6	1129	6.7	1758	1.0	2355	6.7
27	SU	0632	0.5	1225	6.8	1856	0.8		
28	M	0044	6.9	0721	0.5	1310	6.9	1944	0.7
29	TU	0126	7.0	0802	0.6	1349	6.9	○ 2027	0.6
30	W	0204	7.1	0836	0.6	1424	6.9	2104	0.6
31	TH	0240	7.2	0905	0.7	1457	6.9	2136	0.6

JUNE

Date	Day	Time	m	Time	m	Time	m	Time	m
1	F	0315	7.1	0931	0.7	1529	6.8	2203	0.7
2	SA	0350	7.0	1000	0.8	1602	6.7	2230	0.7
3	SU	0425	6.7	1032	0.9	1635	6.5	2259	0.8
4	M	0459	6.5	1105	1.0	1709	6.3	2330	0.9
5	TU	0536	6.3	1138	1.2	1746	6.1		
6	W	0003	1.0	0617	6.1	1217	1.4	◑ 1831	5.9
7	TH	0044	1.1	0707	5.9	1307	1.5	1927	5.8
8	F	0141	1.2	0815	5.9	1416	1.6	2046	5.8
9	SA	0259	1.2	0932	6.0	1537	1.5	2203	6.1
10	SU	0416	1.0	1036	6.4	1653	1.2	2305	6.5
11	M	0521	0.7	1134	6.7	1801	1.0		
12	TU	0000	6.9	0622	0.6	1229	6.9	1906	0.8
13	W	0052	7.2	0727	0.6	1320	7.1	● 2006	0.6
14	TH	0142	7.4	0826	0.5	1409	7.1	2101	0.4
15	F	0230	7.5	0917	0.5	1457	7.1	2151	0.2
16	SA	0319	7.5	1003	0.5	1545	7.1	2237	0.1
17	SU	0407	7.5	1046	0.6	1632	7.0	2320	0.1
18	M	0457	7.3	1126	0.7	1720	6.8		
19	TU	0002	0.2	0548	7.1	1209	0.8	1811	6.6
20	W	0048	0.3	0644	6.9	1258	1.0	◐ 1908	6.5
21	TH	0139	0.4	0744	6.7	1355	1.2	2010	6.4
22	F	0236	0.6	0846	6.6	1500	1.2	2114	6.4
23	SA	0336	0.6	0949	6.5	1607	1.2	2218	6.5
24	SU	0438	0.7	1054	6.5	1715	1.1	2320	6.6
25	M	0541	0.8	1154	6.6	1820	0.9		
26	TU	0016	6.7	0638	0.8	1245	6.7	1914	0.8
27	W	0103	6.8	0726	0.8	1328	6.7	1959	0.7
28	TH	0145	7.0	0806	0.8	1405	6.8	○ 2040	0.6
29	F	0223	7.0	0842	0.8	1440	6.8	2116	0.6
30	SA	0300	7.0	0915	0.8	1513	6.8	2148	0.6

JULY

Date	Day	Time	m	Time	m	Time	m	Time	m
1	SU	0334	6.9	0947	0.8	1546	6.8	2219	0.6
2	M	0407	6.8	1021	0.9	1618	6.7	2251	0.6
3	TU	0440	6.7	1055	0.9	1652	6.5	2322	0.7
4	W	0515	6.5	1128	1.1	1727	6.4	2351	0.8
5	TH	0553	6.4	1202	1.2	1807	6.2		
6	F	0023	0.9	0636	6.2	1241	1.3	◑ 1852	6.1
7	SA	0105	0.9	0729	6.1	1333	1.4	1950	6.0
8	SU	0201	1.0	0841	6.0	1442	1.5	2111	6.1
9	M	0321	1.0	0956	6.2	1609	1.3	2226	6.4
10	TU	0442	0.9	1102	6.5	1727	1.0	2330	6.8
11	W	0551	0.7	1204	6.8	1840	0.7		
12	TH	0029	7.1	0703	0.7	1302	7.0	1949	0.5
13	F	0125	7.4	0812	0.6	1355	7.1	● 2049	0.2
14	SA	0217	7.5	0908	0.5	1445	7.2	2143	0.0
15	SU	0308	7.6	0958	0.5	1533	7.2	2231	-0.2
16	M	0356	7.6	1043	0.5	1620	7.2	2315	-0.2
17	TU	0445	7.5	1123	0.6	1706	7.1	2355	-0.1
18	W	0533	7.3	1201	0.7	1752	6.9		
19	TH	0032	0.1	0622	7.0	1241	0.9	◐ 1841	6.7
20	F	0113	0.4	0714	6.7	1325	1.1	1935	6.5
21	SA	0159	0.6	0810	6.4	1419	1.3	2034	6.4
22	SU	0253	0.8	0908	6.3	1523	1.4	2137	6.3
23	M	0353	1.0	1013	6.2	1631	1.3	2243	6.3
24	TU	0455	1.0	1120	6.3	1740	1.1	2348	6.5
25	W	0558	1.0	1219	6.5	1843	0.9		
26	TH	0042	6.7	0656	0.9	1307	6.6	1935	0.7
27	F	0128	6.9	0744	0.8	1348	6.8	○ 2019	0.6
28	SA	0208	6.9	0826	0.8	1425	6.8	2058	0.5
29	SU	0245	6.9	0904	0.9	1459	6.9	2134	0.5
30	M	0317	6.9	0939	0.8	1530	6.9	2208	0.5
31	TU	0348	6.9	1013	0.8	1601	6.9	2240	0.5

AUGUST

Date	Day	Time	m	Time	m	Time	m	Time	m
1	W	0419	6.8	1047	0.8	1633	6.8	2310	0.6
2	TH	0452	6.7	1118	1.0	1706	6.6	2335	0.7
3	F	0528	6.5	1147	1.1	1742	6.5		
4	SA	0000	0.8	0607	6.3	1219	1.2	◑ 1822	6.4
5	SU	0034	0.9	0653	6.1	1300	1.4	1913	6.3
6	M	0120	1.0	0754	6.0	1359	1.5	2022	6.2
7	TU	0228	1.2	0918	6.0	1532	1.5	2151	6.3
8	W	0411	1.2	1034	6.3	1702	1.1	2305	6.6
9	TH	0530	1.0	1144	6.6	1822	0.8		
10	F	0012	7.0	0652	0.8	1247	6.9	1938	0.4
11	SA	0112	7.3	0802	0.6	1342	7.1	● 2039	0.1
12	SU	0205	7.5	0858	0.5	1431	7.3	2132	-0.2
13	M	0254	7.6	0947	0.4	1517	7.4	2218	-0.3
14	TU	0340	7.6	1031	0.4	1601	7.4	2259	-0.3
15	W	0425	7.5	1109	0.5	1643	7.3	2335	-0.1
16	TH	0509	7.3	1143	0.6	1725	7.1		
17	F	0006	0.2	0552	6.9	1215	0.9	1807	6.8
18	SA	0036	0.5	0636	6.5	1248	1.1	◐ 1853	6.5
19	SU	0111	0.9	0724	6.2	1328	1.4	1947	6.2
20	M	0159	1.2	0819	5.9	1429	1.6	2052	6.0
21	TU	0307	1.4	0925	5.8	1548	1.6	2205	6.0
22	W	0418	1.4	1041	5.9	1701	1.3	2318	6.2
23	TH	0528	1.2	1150	6.2	1811	1.0		
24	F	0018	6.5	0630	1.0	1243	6.5	1907	0.7
25	SA	0107	6.8	0722	0.9	1326	6.7	1954	0.6
26	SU	0147	6.9	0807	0.9	1403	6.8	○ 2035	0.5
27	M	0223	6.9	0847	0.9	1437	6.9	2113	0.5
28	TU	0254	6.9	0924	0.8	1508	7.0	2149	0.5
29	W	0324	7.0	1000	0.8	1538	7.0	2222	0.4
30	TH	0354	6.9	1033	0.8	1609	7.0	2251	0.5
31	F	0427	6.8	1104	0.9	1642	6.8	2313	0.7

Chart Datum: 3·20 metres below Ordnance Datum (Newlyn). HAT is 7·7 metres above Chart Datum.

STANDARD TIME (UT)
For Summer Time add ONE hour in **non-shaded areas**

LONDON BRIDGE

LAT 51°30′N LONG 0°05′W

TIMES AND HEIGHTS OF HIGH AND LOW WATERS

Dates in red are SPRINGS
Dates in blue are NEAPS

YEAR **2018**

SEPTEMBER

Date	Day	Time	m	Time	m	Time	m	Time	m	Moon
1	SA	0502	6.6	1130	1.1	1717	6.7	2335	0.8	
2	SU	0539	6.4	1157	1.2	1758	6.6			
3	M	0005	0.9	0623	6.2	1235	1.3	1846	6.4	◑
4	TU	0048	1.1	0719	5.9	1329	1.5	1952	6.2	
5	W	0151	1.4	0843	5.8	1504	1.6	2125	6.2	
6	TH	0350	1.5	1011	6.0	1643	1.2	2247	6.5	
7	F	0517	1.2	1128	6.4	1812	0.8	2358	6.9	
8	SA	0645	0.9	1233	6.8	1928	0.3			
9	SU	0058	7.2	0749	0.7	1327	7.1	2024	0.0	●
10	M	0150	7.4	0842	0.5	1413	7.3	2113	-0.2	
11	TU	0236	7.5	0929	0.4	1456	7.4	2157	-0.2	
12	W	0319	7.5	1011	0.4	1536	7.5	2235	-0.1	
13	TH	0400	7.4	1048	0.5	1615	7.4	2307	0.2	
14	F	0439	7.2	1119	0.7	1653	7.2	2331	0.5	
15	SA	0517	6.8	1143	0.9	1732	6.9	2352	0.8	
16	SU	0553	6.4	1208	1.2	1812	6.5			◐
17	M	0019	1.1	0632	6.0	1240	1.4	1858	6.1	
18	TU	0059	1.5	0720	5.7	1327	1.6	2001	5.8	
19	W	0206	1.8	0830	5.5	1457	1.8	2122	5.7	
20	TH	0341	1.9	0956	5.5	1624	1.6	2241	5.9	
21	F	0457	1.6	1112	5.9	1733	1.2	2346	6.3	
22	SA	0600	1.3	1210	6.3	1832	0.8			
23	SU	0036	6.6	0653	1.0	1255	6.6	1921	0.7	
24	M	0118	6.8	0740	0.9	1334	6.8	2005	0.6	
25	TU	0153	6.9	0822	0.9	1408	6.9	2045	0.6	○
26	W	0224	6.9	0901	0.9	1440	7.0	2122	0.5	
27	TH	0255	7.0	0939	0.8	1511	7.1	2156	0.5	
28	F	0328	7.0	1015	0.8	1544	7.1	2225	0.6	
29	SA	0402	6.9	1046	0.9	1619	7.0	2247	0.7	
30	SU	0438	6.7	1113	1.0	1656	6.9	2311	0.9	

OCTOBER

Date	Day	Time	m	Time	m	Time	m	Time	m	Moon
1	M	0516	6.4	1141	1.1	1738	6.7	2344	1.1	
2	TU	0600	6.1	1219	1.2	1829	6.4			◑
3	W	0028	1.3	0657	5.9	1313	1.4	1936	6.2	
4	TH	0135	1.7	0820	5.7	1452	1.5	2109	6.2	
5	F	0335	1.7	0952	5.9	1628	1.2	2231	6.5	
6	SA	0504	1.4	1112	6.3	1800	0.7	2343	6.9	
7	SU	0627	1.0	1216	6.7	1909	0.3			
8	M	0042	7.2	0727	0.7	1308	7.0	2002	0.0	
9	TU	0131	7.3	0818	0.6	1351	7.2	2048	0.0	●
10	W	0214	7.4	0904	0.5	1431	7.4	2129	0.1	
11	TH	0254	7.4	0945	0.5	1509	7.5	2204	0.3	
12	F	0331	7.3	1021	0.6	1546	7.4	2231	0.5	
13	SA	0407	7.1	1049	0.8	1623	7.2	2249	0.7	
14	SU	0441	6.7	1110	0.9	1659	6.9	2310	1.0	
15	M	0514	6.4	1132	1.1	1737	6.5	2338	1.2	
16	TU	0547	6.1	1201	1.3	1817	6.1			◐
17	W	0013	1.6	0627	5.7	1240	1.6	1908	5.7	
18	TH	0102	2.0	0724	5.4	1343	1.8	2028	5.5	
19	F	0238	2.2	0859	5.3	1538	1.7	2153	5.6	
20	SA	0415	1.9	1023	5.6	1649	1.4	2300	6.0	
21	SU	0520	1.5	1126	6.1	1747	1.0	2354	6.4	
22	M	0615	1.2	1215	6.5	1839	0.8			
23	TU	0038	6.7	0704	1.1	1257	6.7	1927	0.7	
24	W	0116	6.9	0750	1.0	1333	6.9	2010	0.7	○
25	TH	0151	7.0	0834	0.9	1409	7.1	2051	0.6	
26	F	0227	7.0	0915	0.8	1445	7.2	2127	0.7	
27	SA	0304	7.0	0954	0.7	1522	7.3	2159	0.7	
28	SU	0341	6.9	1030	0.8	1600	7.2	2225	0.8	
29	M	0419	6.7	1101	0.8	1641	7.0	2256	0.9	
30	TU	0500	6.5	1133	0.9	1726	6.8	2334	1.1	
31	W	0546	6.2	1213	1.1	1821	6.5			◑

NOVEMBER

Date	Day	Time	m	Time	m	Time	m	Time	m	Moon
1	TH	0023	1.4	0645	5.9	1312	1.2	1931	6.3	
2	F	0139	1.7	0807	5.8	1444	1.3	2055	6.3	
3	SA	0317	1.7	0933	6.0	1609	1.0	2211	6.5	
4	SU	0441	1.4	1048	6.3	1732	0.7	2321	6.8	
5	M	0559	1.1	1152	6.7	1840	0.4			
6	TU	0020	7.0	0700	0.8	1244	6.9	1932	0.3	
7	W	0109	7.1	0751	0.7	1327	7.1	2017	0.3	●
8	TH	0151	7.1	0836	0.6	1406	7.2	2056	0.4	
9	F	0228	7.1	0917	0.6	1442	7.3	2128	0.6	
10	SA	0303	7.1	0952	0.6	1519	7.3	2152	0.7	
11	SU	0337	7.0	1019	0.8	1556	7.1	2211	0.9	
12	M	0410	6.7	1040	0.9	1632	6.8	2238	1.0	
13	TU	0442	6.4	1104	1.0	1708	6.5	2308	1.3	
14	W	0514	6.2	1134	1.2	1745	6.2	2341	1.5	
15	TH	0549	5.9	1207	1.4	1828	5.9			◐
16	F	0020	1.8	0635	5.7	1253	1.6	1924	5.6	
17	SA	0120	2.1	0739	5.4	1410	1.7	2049	5.6	
18	SU	0254	2.1	0922	5.5	1551	1.5	2202	5.9	
19	M	0422	1.8	1032	5.9	1654	1.2	2301	6.2	
20	TU	0525	1.5	1127	6.3	1749	1.0	2352	6.6	
21	W	0621	1.2	1215	6.7	1841	0.8			
22	TH	0037	6.8	0714	1.0	1259	7.0	1932	0.7	
23	F	0121	7.0	0804	0.9	1341	7.2	2019	0.7	○
24	SA	0203	7.0	0852	0.7	1422	7.3	2103	0.7	
25	SU	0246	7.0	0937	0.6	1505	7.4	2142	0.8	
26	M	0328	7.0	1018	0.6	1548	7.3	2218	0.8	
27	TU	0410	6.8	1057	0.6	1633	7.2	2255	0.9	
28	W	0454	6.6	1135	0.6	1722	7.0	2337	1.1	
29	TH	0543	6.3	1219	0.8	1818	6.7			
30	F	0029	1.3	0641	6.2	1318	0.9	1925	6.5	◑

DECEMBER

Date	Day	Time	m	Time	m	Time	m	Time	m	Moon
1	SA	0137	1.5	0754	6.1	1430	0.9	2036	6.5	
2	SU	0254	1.5	0909	6.2	1541	0.8	2145	6.5	
3	M	0409	1.4	1018	6.4	1652	0.7	2253	6.7	
4	TU	0523	1.2	1122	6.6	1802	0.6	2355	6.8	
5	W	0629	1.0	1217	6.8	1858	0.6			
6	TH	0045	6.9	0722	0.8	1304	6.9	1943	0.6	
7	F	0129	6.9	0809	0.7	1345	7.0	2022	0.7	●
8	SA	0207	6.9	0850	0.7	1422	7.1	2055	0.8	
9	SU	0241	6.9	0927	0.7	1459	7.1	2122	0.9	
10	M	0314	6.9	0956	0.8	1535	7.0	2147	1.0	
11	TU	0347	6.7	1020	0.9	1611	6.8	2217	1.1	
12	W	0420	6.5	1047	0.9	1645	6.6	2250	1.2	
13	TH	0452	6.4	1117	1.0	1720	6.4	2323	1.3	
14	F	0527	6.2	1149	1.1	1759	6.2	2358	1.5	
15	SA	0607	6.0	1224	1.2	1844	6.0			◐
16	SU	0041	1.7	0655	5.8	1311	1.3	1940	5.8	
17	M	0138	1.8	0759	5.7	1415	1.4	2057	5.8	
18	TU	0252	1.8	0929	5.8	1542	1.3	2207	6.1	
19	W	0421	1.6	1037	6.2	1655	1.1	2308	6.4	
20	TH	0534	1.3	1135	6.6	1756	0.9			
21	F	0004	6.7	0637	1.0	1228	6.9	1855	0.8	
22	SA	0056	6.9	0737	0.8	1317	7.2	1954	0.8	○
23	SU	0145	7.0	0833	0.6	1406	7.4	2048	0.7	
24	M	0233	7.1	0925	0.4	1453	7.5	2137	0.7	
25	TU	0319	7.1	1013	0.3	1541	7.5	2222	0.7	
26	W	0405	7.0	1058	0.2	1629	7.4	2303	0.8	
27	TH	0451	6.9	1141	0.2	1718	7.2	2345	0.9	
28	F	0539	6.7	1223	0.3	1811	7.0			
29	SA	0030	1.1	0631	6.5	1310	0.5	1908	6.7	◑
30	SU	0122	1.2	0731	6.4	1405	0.6	2010	6.6	
31	M	0223	1.4	0837	6.4	1505	0.8	2114	6.5	

Chart Datum: 3·20 metres below Ordnance Datum (Newlyn). HAT is 7·7 metres above Chart Datum.

9.4.13 SOUTHEND-ON-SEA/LEIGH-ON-SEA

Essex 51°31'·07N 00°42'·57E

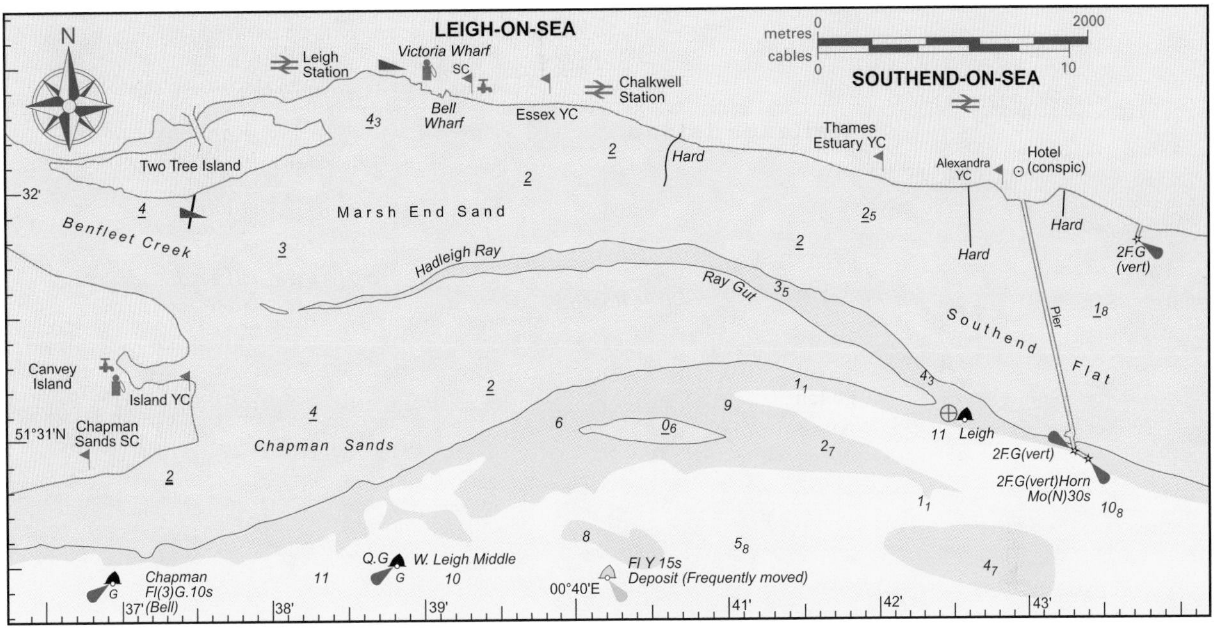

CHARTS AC 5606, 1183, 1185; Imray C1, C2, Y18, 2100

TIDES +0125 Dover; ML 3·0; Duration 0610

Standard Port SHEERNESS (⟵)

Times				Height (metres)			
High Water		Low Water		MHWS	MHWN	MLWN	MLWS
0200	0800	0200	0700	5·8	4·7	1·5	0·6
1400	2000	1400	1900				
Differences SOUTHEND-ON-SEA							
–0005	–0005	–0005	–0005	+0·1	0·0	–0·1	–0·1
CORYTON							
+0005	*+0010*	*+0010*	*+0010*	*+0·4*	*+0·3*	*0·0*	*0·0*

SHELTER The whole area dries soon after half ebb, except Ray Gut (0·4–4·8m) which leads to Leigh Creek and Hadleigh Ray, either side of Two Tree Island, thence to Benfleet Creek where the limit of W navigation is the Tidal Barrier just above Benfleet YC; all are buoyed, but echo-sounder is essential. Craft can take the ground alongside Bell Wharf or Victoria Wharf. It is also possible to secure at the end of Southend Pier to collect stores, water. NOTE: Southend-on-Sea and Leigh-on-Sea are both part of the lower PLA Area and an 8kn speed limit is enforced in inshore areas.

NAVIGATION WPT 51°31'·07N 00°42'·57E, Leigh SHM buoy, at ent to Ray Gut; this SHM buoy can be left close to port on entering Ray Gut, since there is now more water NE of it than to the SW. Appr from Shoeburyness, keep outside the W Shoebury SHM buoy, Fl G 2·5s.

Beware some 3000 small boat moorings 1M either side of Southend Pier. Speed limit in Canvey Island/Hadleigh Ray areas is 8kn.

LIGHTS AND MARKS See chartlet.

COMMUNICATIONS (Code 01702) NMOC 02392 552100; Essex Police Marine Section (01268) 775533; Police 101; Dr 225500; Ⓗ 348911. HM 215620; HM Leigh-on-Sea 710561.

Port Control London: *London VTS* VHF Ch 68 inward from Sea Reach No 4, *London VTS* VHF Ch 69 seaward from Sea Reach No 4.

FACILITIES

SOUTHEND-ON-SEA: Southend Pier ☎215620, (craft to be attended), £20<40'>£40<50'>£50/night (short stay free). **Alexandra YC** ☎340363; **Thorpe Bay YC** ☎587563; **Thames Estuary YC** ☎345967; **Halfway YC** ☎582025, book 1. **Town** Ⓔ ACA ✉ Ⓑ ✕ ⇌ ✈.

LEIGH-ON-SEA: Essex YC ☎478404; **Leigh on Sea SC** ☎476788; **Bell Wharf** 24hrs free then £11/night; **Victoria Wharf** 24hrs free then £11/night (Two Tree Is HW±2½). **Town**.

CANVEY ISLAND: (Code 01268) Access via drying channels. **Island YC** ☎510360, (max 9m), dries; **Benfleet YC** (on S side of Benfleet Creek on Canvey Island) ☎792278, (by day), **Services**.

SHOEBURYNESS TO RIVER COLNE

(Charts 1185, 1975) Maplin and Foulness Sands extend nearly 6M NE from Foulness Pt, the extremity being marked by Whitaker bn. On N side of Whitaker chan leading to R Crouch and R Roach lies Buxey Sand, inshore of which is the Ray Sand chan (dries), a convenient short cut between R Crouch and R Blackwater with sufficient rise of tide.

To seaward of Buxey Sand and the Spitway, Gunfleet Sand extends 10M NE, marked by buoys and dries in places. Gunfleet Sands Wind Farm, lies along the shoal between Swin Spitway and Gunfleet Old Lt Ho. 50 turbines are marked by Fl Y lts and R Aero obstn lts, the northernmost sounds a Horn every 10s in fog.

► *A conspic disused lt tr stands on SE side of Gunfleet Sand, about 6M SSE of the Naze tr, and here the SW-going (flood) stream begins about HW Sheerness +0600, and the NE-going stream at about HW Sheerness –0030, sp rates 2kn.* ◄

The Rivers Blackwater and Colne share a common estuary which is approached from the NE via NE Gunfleet lt buoy; thence along Goldmer Gat and the Wallet towards Knoll and Eagle lt buoys. For the Colne turn NNW via Colne Bar buoy towards Inner Bench Hd buoy keeping in mid-chan. For R Blackwater, head WNW for NW Knoll and Bench Hd buoys. From the S or SE, make for the Whitaker ECM buoy, thence through the Spitway, via Swin Spitway and Wallet Spitway buoys to reach Knoll buoy and deeper water.

9.4.14 RIVER ROACH/HAVENGORE

Essex **51°36′·98N 00°52′·14E** (Branklet SPM buoy), R Roach. **51°33′·62N 00°50′·52E**, Havengore Bridge

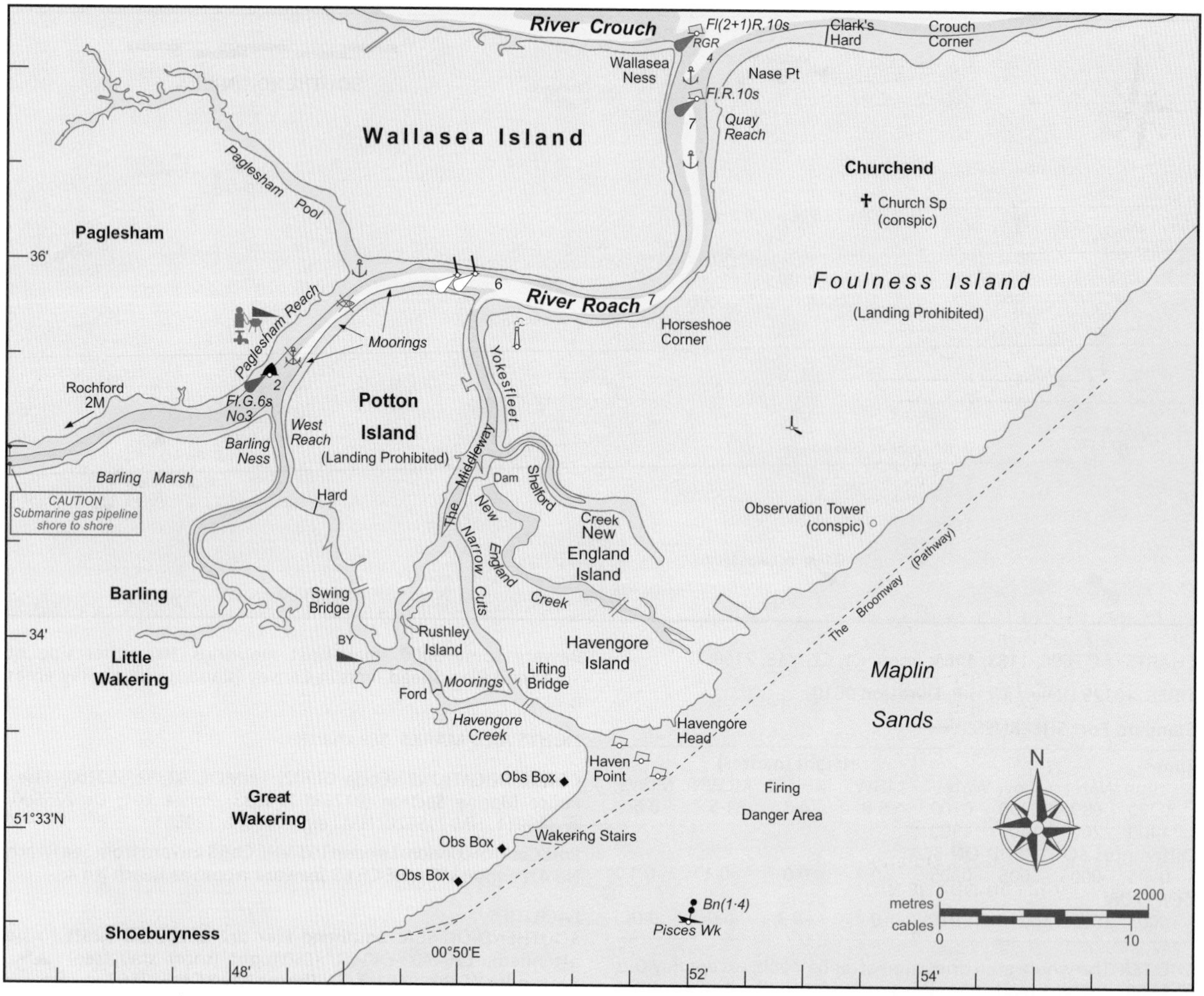

CHARTS AC 5607, 1185, 3750; Imray C1, Y17, 2100, 2000

TIDES +0110 Dover; ML 2·7; Duration 0615

Standard Port WALTON-ON-THE-NAZE (⟶)

Times				Height (metres)			
High Water		Low Water		MHWS	MHWN	MLWN	MLWS
0000	0600	0500	1100	4·2	3·4	1·1	0·4
1200	1800	1700	2300				
Differences ROCHFORD							
+0050	+0040	DR	DR	–0·8	–1·1	DR	DR

SHELTER Good. The Roach gives sheltered sailing and access to a network of secluded creeks, including Havengore (the 'backdoor' from the Crouch to the Thames Estuary). No available in the area. ⚓s behind sea-walls can be found for all winds at: Quay Reach (often more protected than the Crouch), Paglesham Reach, West Reach, Barling Reach and Yokes Fleet. An ⚓ light is essential due to freighters H24. Speed limit 8kn. Crouch Hbr Authority controls R Roach and Crouch, out to Foulness Pt.

NAVIGATION Normal access H24 to the Roach is from R Crouch; the ent between Branklet buoy and Nase Pt is narrowed by mudbanks. Unlit buoys upriver to Barling Ness, above which few boats go. To exit at Havengore Creek, appr via Middleway and Narrow Cuts to reach the bridge before HW.

Entry via **Havengore Creek** is possible in good weather, with great care and adequate rise of tide (max draught 1·5m at HW sp). Shoeburyness Range is usually active Mon-Fri 0600-1700LT; give 24hrs notice to Range Officer by ☎. Subsequent clearance on VHF by Havengore lifting bridge (☎HW±2, HJ); no passage unless bridge raised. Least water is over the shifting bar, just inside creek ent. From the S, cross Maplin Sands at HW –1 from S Shoebury SHM buoy, leaving Pisces wreck (conspic, 1M from ent) to port.

LIGHTS AND MARKS Unlit, but night entry to R Roach may be possible.

COMMUNICATIONS (Code 01702 Southend) NMOC 02392 552100; Dr 218678. Crouch HM (01621) 783602; Range Officer 383211; Havengore Br 383436; Swing Br to Potton Island 219491.

VHF Ch 72 16 is worked by Range Officer (*Shoe Base*) (HO); Radar Control (*Shoe Radar*) (HO); & Bridge keeper (*Shoe Bridge*) (HW±2 by day). Radar guidance may be available.

FACILITIES **Paglesham** (East End) (at). **Gt Wakering** (from at Rochford) **Wakering YC** ☎530926, . **Towns** Gt Wakering & Rochford; (Great Wakering and Barling); most facilities, Ⓑ and ≷ in Rochford and Shoeburyness, ✈ (Southend).

9.4.15 BURNHAM-ON-CROUCH

Essex **51°37′·50N 00°48′·23E** (Yacht Hbr)

CHARTS AC 5607, 1183, 1975, 3750; Imray C1, Y17, 2100, 2000

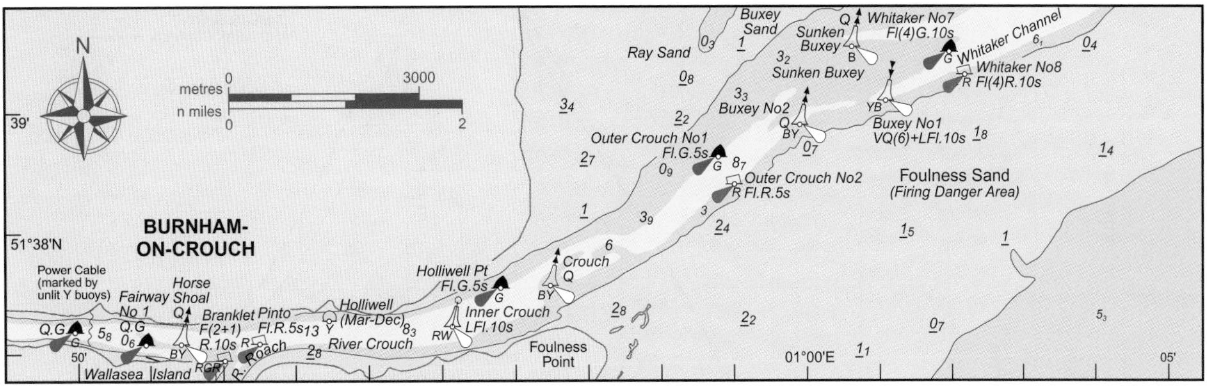

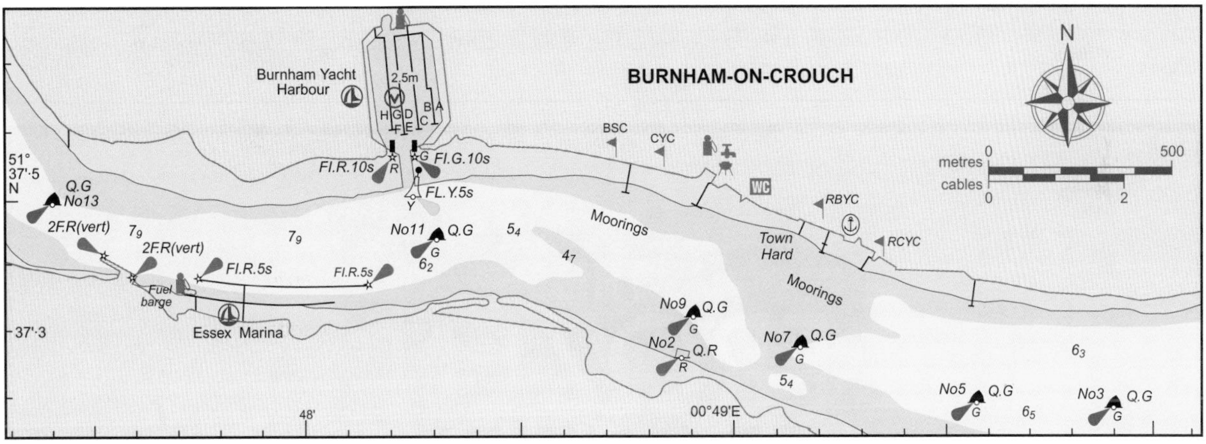

TIDES +0115 Dover; ML 2·5; Duration 0610

Standard Port WALTON-ON-THE-NAZE (⟶)

Times				Height (metres)			
High Water		Low Water		MHWS	MHWN	MLWN	MLWS
0000	0600	0500	1100	4·2	3·4	1·1	0·4
1200	1800	1700	2300				
Differences WHITAKER BEACON							
+0022	+0024	+0033	+0027	+0·6	+0·5	+0·2	+0·1
HOLLIWELL POINT							
+0034	+0037	+0100	+0037	+1·1	+0·9	+0·3	+0.1
NORTH FAMBRIDGE							
+0115	+0050	+0130	+0100	+1·1	+0·8	0·0	–0·1
HULLBRIDGE							
+0115	+0050	+0135	+0105	+1·1	+0·8	0·0	–0·1
BATTLESBRIDGE							
+0120	+0110	DR	DR	–1·8	–2·0	DR	DR

SHELTER River is exposed to most winds. Cliff Reach (off W edge of lower chartlet) is sheltered from SW'lies. ⚓ prohib in fairway but possible just E or W of the moorings.

NAVIGATION Appr from East Swin or the Wallet via Swin Spitway SWM / Whitaker ECM, into the well-marked Whitaker Channel.

Near Sunken Buxey seas can be hazardous with strong wind over tide. Ray Sand Chan (dries 1·7m), usable on the tide by shoal draught boats as a short cut from/to the Blackwater. Shoeburyness Artillery ranges lie E and S of Foulness Pt, clear of fairway. The buoyed chan leads either side of shoal patch 0·7 marked by Sunken Buxey NCM and Buxey No 1 SCM. R Crouch is navigable to Battlesbridge, 10M beyond Burnham. No landing on Foulness or Bridgemarsh Is. Wallasea Wetlands are being developed; keep well clear of ships using unloading pontoon at Ringwood Pt. ⚓ in swinging area between Horse Shoal and No 3 SHM buoy. Work is expected to be complete by 2019.

LIGHTS AND MARKS There are few landmarks to assist entry, but Whitaker Chan, Swallow Tail Bank and the river are well lit/buoyed to 0·5M W of Essex Marina. From Buxey No2 steer 240° in buoyed channel past Foulness Pt, N of Crouch NCM into the river. There is a 1·3M unlit gap between Inner Crouch SWM lit buoy, and the entrance to R Roach, which is marked by Pinto PHM and Branklet PCM en-route Horse Shoal NCM.

COMMUNICATIONS (Code 01621 Maldon) NMOC 02392 552100; Police 101; Dr 782054. HM 783602.

VHF Ch 80 for: Crouch HM Launch (0900-1700LT, w/e); Essex Marina; Burnham Yacht Harbour; W Wick Marina (1000-1700), also Ch M.

FACILITIES There are five marinas or yacht hbrs. Speed limit 8kn.

BURNHAM, Burnham Yacht Hbr ☎782150, access H24, some ⓥs, 350 £2·50 +£2, (30t) .
Royal Corinthian YC ☎782105, .
Royal Burnham YC ☎782044, .
Crouch YC ☎782252, (15t) ACA . **Town** Ⓑ (Southend).

ALTHORNE, Bridgemarsh Marina ☎740414, £20/craft/night .

WALLASEA ISLAND, Essex Marina ☎(01702) 258531, 400 £2·13, LPG (40t) (13t) . Ferry to Burnham Hard at w/ends in season, ☎07704 060482. **Essex YC** ACA.

FAMBRIDGE, Fambridge Yacht Haven www.yachthavens.com ☎740370; Min 1m depth in approach, Stow Cr marked by bn Q(4)Y 8s and ldg bns (F W lts) in line 356°; pontoon Fl(3) G 4s. ⓥs £1·50, (£6-£15) 170+ⓥ £2·50, short stay <3hrs<15m £5, (£6-£15) (40t)(25t)(20t) (30t) YC wi-fi.
Fambridge Yacht Station ⓥ pontoon £2/m, .

Brandy Hole Yacht Stn ☎(01702) 230248, Access via drying channel 120 .

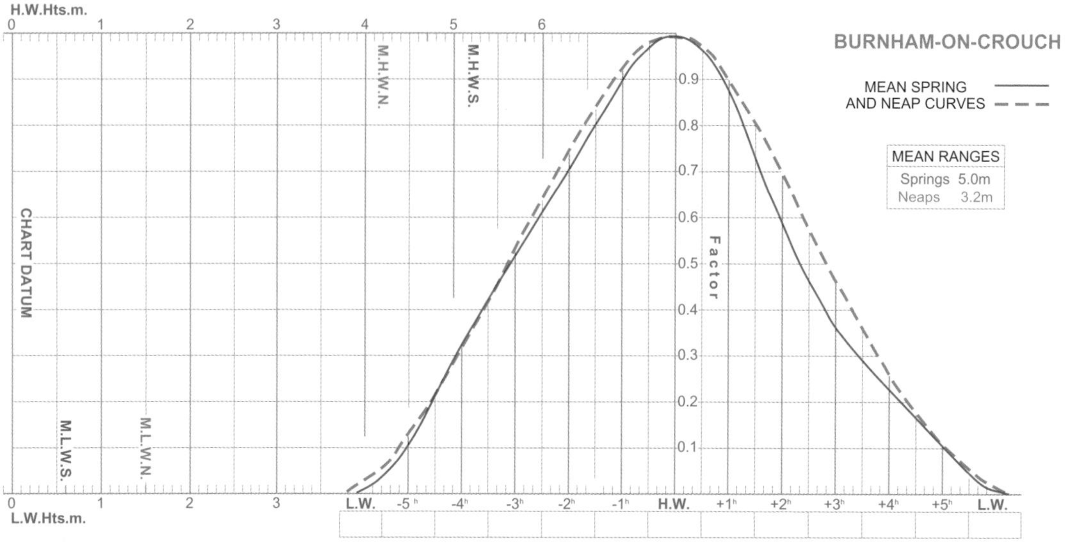

H.W.Hts.m.
0
1
2
3
4
5
6
BURNHAM-ON-CROUCH
MEAN SPRING
AND NEAP CURVES
MEAN RANGES
Springs 5.0m
Neaps 3.2m
M.H.W.N.
M.H.W.S.
CHART DATUM
M.L.W.S.
M.L.W.N.
Factor
0.9
0.8
0.7
0.6
0.5
0.4
0.3
0.2
0.1
L.W.
-5h
-4h
-3h
-2h
-1h
H.W.
+1h
+2h
+3h
+4h
+5h
L.W.
L.W.Hts.m.

STANDARD TIME (UT)
For Summer Time add ONE hour in **non-shaded areas**

BURNHAM-ON-CROUCH LAT 51°37′N LONG 0°48′E

TIMES AND HEIGHTS OF HIGH AND LOW WATERS

Dates in red are SPRINGS
Dates in blue are NEAPS

YEAR **2018**

JANUARY

Date	Day	Moon	Time	m	Time	m	Time	m	Time	m
1	M		0535	0.5	1132	5.2	1800	0.3		
2	TU	○	0002	5.3	0629	0.2	1225	5.4	1849	0.3
3	W		0051	5.4	0719	0.0	1315	5.6	1936	0.2
4	TH		0138	5.5	0808	-0.2	1404	5.6	2022	0.3
5	F		0224	5.4	0856	-0.2	1452	5.5	2107	0.4
6	SA		0309	5.3	0944	-0.2	1541	5.4	2153	0.5
7	SU		0355	5.1	1033	-0.1	1631	5.1	2240	0.7
8	M	◑	0444	4.8	1123	0.1	1723	4.9	2330	0.8
9	TU		0537	4.6	1216	0.3	1820	4.6		
10	W		0025	0.9	0637	4.4	1313	0.4	1920	4.5
11	TH		0125	1.0	0745	4.3	1412	0.6	2023	4.4
12	F		0231	1.0	0852	4.3	1512	0.6	2123	4.5
13	SA		0338	0.9	0952	4.4	1608	0.7	2216	4.6
14	SU		0437	0.8	1046	4.6	1658	0.7	2305	4.7
15	M		0528	0.7	1134	4.7	1741	0.7	2349	4.8
16	TU		0611	0.6	1217	4.7	1819	0.7		
17	W	●	0027	4.8	0649	0.5	1255	4.8	1850	0.7
18	TH		0100	4.9	0721	0.5	1328	4.8	1918	0.7
19	F		0128	4.9	0749	0.5	1357	4.8	1948	0.6
20	SA		0157	5.0	0819	0.5	1429	4.9	2023	0.6
21	SU		0231	5.0	0855	0.4	1506	4.9	2101	0.6
22	M		0311	5.0	0934	0.5	1548	4.9	2143	0.7
23	TU		0354	5.0	1016	0.5	1635	4.9	2228	0.8
24	W	◐	0441	4.8	1103	0.7	1725	4.7	2317	0.9
25	TH		0532	4.7	1155	0.8	1820	4.6		
26	F		0013	1.1	0629	4.5	1300	0.9	1923	4.4
27	SA		0125	1.2	0738	4.3	1422	1.0	2036	4.4
28	SU		0255	1.1	0900	4.4	1546	0.9	2148	4.6
29	M		0419	0.9	1014	4.6	1654	0.6	2250	4.8
30	TU		0524	0.5	1116	5.0	1749	0.4	2345	5.1
31	W	○	0619	0.1	1211	5.3	1839	0.2		

FEBRUARY

Date	Day	Moon	Time	m	Time	m	Time	m	Time	m
1	TH		0035	5.3	0709	-0.2	1302	5.5	1925	0.1
2	F		0123	5.5	0756	-0.4	1349	5.6	2009	0.1
3	SA		0207	5.5	0841	-0.5	1435	5.6	2051	0.1
4	SU		0250	5.4	0925	-0.4	1520	5.4	2132	0.3
5	M		0332	5.2	1008	-0.2	1604	5.1	2212	0.4
6	TU		0414	5.0	1051	0.0	1649	4.8	2254	0.6
7	W	◑	0459	4.7	1135	0.3	1737	4.5	2339	0.8
8	TH		0549	4.4	1222	0.6	1830	4.3		
9	F		0028	1.0	0650	4.1	1315	0.8	1931	4.1
10	SA		0127	1.1	0804	4.0	1416	0.9	2038	4.1
11	SU		0238	1.2	0917	4.0	1523	1.0	2142	4.2
12	M		0357	1.0	1018	4.2	1624	0.9	2236	4.4
13	TU		0458	0.8	1110	4.4	1714	0.8	2324	4.6
14	W		0546	0.6	1155	4.6	1757	0.7		
15	TH	●	0006	4.8	0627	0.5	1236	4.8	1834	0.6
16	F		0044	4.9	0704	0.3	1311	4.9	1908	0.5
17	SA		0116	5.0	0737	0.3	1343	4.9	1941	0.4
18	SU		0146	5.1	0810	0.2	1415	5.0	2014	0.4
19	M		0219	5.1	0843	0.3	1451	5.1	2048	0.4
20	TU		0256	5.1	0918	0.3	1530	5.0	2125	0.5
21	W		0336	5.1	0955	0.4	1612	4.9	2205	0.6
22	TH		0420	5.0	1033	0.6	1659	4.7	2248	0.7
23	F	◐	0507	4.8	1117	0.7	1750	4.5	2337	0.9
24	SA		0601	4.5	1211	0.9	1849	4.2		
25	SU		0039	1.1	0706	4.3	1334	1.1	2004	4.1
26	M		0220	1.1	0835	4.2	1530	1.0	2127	4.2
27	TU		0406	0.8	0959	4.5	1643	0.7	2235	4.6
28	W		0512	0.4	1103	4.9	1737	0.4	2331	4.9

MARCH

Date	Day	Moon	Time	m	Time	m	Time	m	Time	m
1	TH		0605	-0.1	1157	5.2	1825	0.1		
2	F	○	0020	5.3	0653	-0.4	1247	5.5	1909	-0.1
3	SA		0106	5.4	0738	-0.5	1332	5.6	1950	-0.1
4	SU		0148	5.5	0820	-0.5	1414	5.5	2029	0.0
5	M		0228	5.4	0859	-0.4	1455	5.3	2106	0.1
6	TU		0306	5.3	0937	-0.2	1533	5.0	2140	0.3
7	W		0343	5.0	1013	0.1	1611	4.7	2215	0.5
8	TH		0422	4.8	1049	0.4	1650	4.5	2253	0.7
9	F	◑	0503	4.4	1129	0.7	1732	4.2	2335	0.9
10	SA		0552	4.1	1215	0.9	1823	4.0		
11	SU		0025	1.1	0657	3.8	1311	1.1	1931	3.8
12	M		0128	1.2	0830	3.8	1422	1.2	2056	3.9
13	TU		0254	1.1	0944	4.0	1540	1.1	2202	4.1
14	W		0416	0.9	1040	4.3	1641	0.9	2255	4.4
15	TH		0512	0.7	1127	4.6	1730	0.7	2340	4.7
16	F		0557	0.4	1209	4.8	1812	0.5		
17	SA	●	0020	4.9	0637	0.2	1247	5.0	1849	0.3
18	SU		0056	5.0	0714	0.1	1322	5.1	1925	0.3
19	M		0131	5.1	0750	0.1	1357	5.2	2000	0.2
20	TU		0205	5.2	0824	0.2	1433	5.2	2034	0.3
21	W		0241	5.2	0858	0.2	1511	5.1	2110	0.3
22	TH		0321	5.2	0933	0.4	1552	5.0	2148	0.4
23	F		0403	5.0	1010	0.5	1636	4.7	2230	0.5
24	SA	◐	0450	4.8	1053	0.7	1725	4.4	2319	0.7
25	SU		0544	4.5	1146	1.0	1822	4.2		
26	M		0021	0.9	0650	4.3	1303	1.2	1938	4.0
27	TU		0204	1.0	0823	4.2	1514	1.1	2109	4.1
28	W		0350	0.7	0947	4.5	1626	0.7	2218	4.5
29	TH		0453	0.2	1048	4.9	1719	0.4	2313	4.9
30	F		0545	-0.2	1140	5.2	1805	0.1		
31	SA	○	0001	5.2	0631	-0.4	1228	5.4	1848	-0.1

APRIL

Date	Day	Moon	Time	m	Time	m	Time	m	Time	m
1	SU		0046	5.4	0713	-0.5	1311	5.4	1928	-0.1
2	M		0127	5.4	0753	-0.4	1351	5.3	2005	0.0
3	TU		0204	5.3	0829	-0.2	1427	5.1	2038	0.1
4	W		0240	5.2	0901	0.1	1500	4.9	2109	0.3
5	TH		0313	5.0	0931	0.3	1531	4.7	2139	0.4
6	F		0347	4.7	1003	0.6	1605	4.5	2213	0.6
7	SA		0425	4.5	1040	0.8	1642	4.3	2253	0.7
8	SU	◑	0508	4.2	1124	1.0	1726	4.1	2340	0.9
9	M		0601	3.9	1217	1.1	1820	3.9		
10	TU		0039	1.0	0715	3.8	1325	1.2	1938	3.8
11	W		0157	1.0	0854	3.9	1446	1.2	2113	3.9
12	TH		0323	0.9	1000	4.2	1558	1.0	2215	4.3
13	F		0429	0.6	1051	4.5	1654	0.7	2305	4.6
14	SA		0520	0.4	1136	4.9	1741	0.5	2349	4.8
15	SU		0605	0.2	1217	5.1	1824	0.3		
16	M	●	0029	5.1	0646	0.1	1257	5.2	1903	0.2
17	TU		0109	5.2	0725	0.1	1335	5.3	1942	0.2
18	W		0147	5.3	0802	0.2	1414	5.3	2019	0.2
19	TH		0227	5.3	0838	0.3	1453	5.2	2058	0.2
20	F		0308	5.2	0915	0.4	1534	5.0	2138	0.3
21	SA		0352	5.0	0954	0.6	1618	4.7	2224	0.4
22	SU	◐	0441	4.8	1041	0.8	1707	4.5	2317	0.6
23	M		0537	4.6	1138	1.0	1805	4.2		
24	TU		0026	0.7	0647	4.3	1259	1.1	1922	4.0
25	W		0201	0.7	0813	4.3	1446	1.0	2048	4.2
26	TH		0327	0.4	0928	4.6	1558	0.7	2155	4.5
27	F		0428	0.1	1028	4.9	1653	0.4	2250	4.9
28	SA		0519	-0.2	1118	5.2	1740	0.2	2338	5.1
29	SU		0605	-0.3	1204	5.3	1824	0.0		
30	M	○	0022	5.2	0646	-0.2	1247	5.3	1904	0.0

Chart Datum: 2·35 metres below Ordnance Datum (Newlyn). HAT is 5·8 metres above Chart Datum.

STANDARD TIME (UT)
For Summer Time add ONE hour in **non-shaded areas**

BURNHAM-ON-CROUCH

LAT 51°37′N LONG 0°48′E

TIMES AND HEIGHTS OF HIGH AND LOW WATERS

Dates in red are SPRINGS
Dates in blue are NEAPS

YEAR **2018**

MAY

Day	Time	m	Day	Time	m
1	0104	5.2	16	0045	5.2
	0724	-0.1		0701	0.2
TU	1325	5.1	W	1312	5.3
	1941	0.1		1924	0.2
2	0141	5.1	17	0128	5.3
	0757	0.1		0742	0.2
W	1359	5.0	TH	1354	5.3
	2013	0.3		2007	0.2
3	0215	5.0	18	0212	5.3
	0825	0.4		0822	0.3
TH	1427	4.8	F	1436	5.2
	2040	0.4		2051	0.2
4	0246	4.8	19	0257	5.3
	0851	0.5		0904	0.5
F	1455	4.7	SA	1519	5.0
	2107	0.5		2137	0.2
5	0318	4.6	20	0344	5.1
	0922	0.7		0948	0.6
SA	1526	4.6	SU	1605	4.8
	2140	0.6		2227	0.3
6	0354	4.5	21	0435	4.9
	0959	0.8		1038	0.8
SU	1604	4.5	M	1655	4.6
	2220	0.7		2324	0.4
7	0436	4.3	22	0533	4.7
	1043	0.9		1137	0.9
M	1648	4.4	TU	1753	4.4
	2308	0.8	◐		
8	0526	4.1	23	0030	0.4
	1135	1.1		0639	4.5
TU	1739	4.2	W	1249	1.0
◑				1904	4.3
9	0006	0.9	24	0145	0.4
	0625	4.0		0753	4.5
W	1239	1.2	TH	1410	1.0
	1839	4.0		2020	4.3
10	0118	0.9	25	0257	0.2
	0744	4.0		0902	4.7
TH	1354	1.2	F	1522	0.8
	2001	4.0		2127	4.6
11	0235	0.8	26	0358	0.1
	0905	4.2		1000	4.9
F	1509	1.1	SA	1621	0.5
	2122	4.2		2223	4.8
12	0345	0.6	27	0450	0.0
	1006	4.5		1052	5.0
SA	1613	0.9	SU	1713	0.3
	2222	4.5		2313	5.0
13	0442	0.4	28	0537	0.0
	1057	4.8		1139	5.1
SU	1707	0.6	M	1759	0.2
	2313	4.8		2359	5.1
14	0532	0.3	29	0619	0.1
	1144	5.1		1222	5.1
M	1755	0.5	TU	1842	0.3
			○		
15	0000	5.0	30	0042	5.0
	0618	0.2		0657	0.2
TU	1229	5.3	W	1301	5.0
●	1840	0.3		1920	0.3
			31	0121	4.9
				0729	0.4
			TH	1333	4.8
				1952	0.5

JUNE

Day	Time	m	Day	Time	m
1	0154	4.8	16	0158	5.4
	0753	0.6		0813	0.3
F	1359	4.7	SA	1421	5.2
	2016	0.6		2046	0.0
2	0223	4.6	17	0245	5.4
	0817	0.7		0857	0.4
SA	1424	4.7	SU	1506	5.1
	2041	0.6		2135	0.0
3	0252	4.5	18	0334	5.3
	0848	0.7		0944	0.5
SU	1455	4.7	M	1552	5.0
	2114	0.6		2225	0.0
4	0328	4.5	19	0425	5.1
	0927	0.8		1033	0.6
M	1534	4.7	TU	1641	4.8
	2155	0.6		2319	0.1
5	0411	4.4	20	0520	4.9
	1011	0.8		1127	0.7
TU	1619	4.6	W	1736	4.6
	2243	0.7	◐		
6	0459	4.4	21	0017	0.1
	1102	0.9		0619	4.7
W	1709	4.5	TH	1227	0.8
◑	2338	0.7		1839	4.5
7	0553	4.3	22	0119	0.2
	1200	1.0		0724	4.6
TH	1804	4.3	F	1333	0.9
				1948	4.4
8	0043	0.8	23	0223	0.2
	0656	4.2		0829	4.6
F	1307	1.1	SA	1442	0.8
	1908	4.2		2055	4.5
9	0154	0.8	24	0325	0.2
	0809	4.3		0929	4.7
SA	1420	1.1	SU	1547	0.7
	2026	4.2		2155	4.7
10	0303	0.7	25	0420	0.2
	0919	4.5		1024	4.8
SU	1530	1.0	M	1645	0.5
	2138	4.4		2248	4.8
11	0407	0.5	26	0510	0.3
	1019	4.7		1113	4.8
M	1633	0.8	TU	1736	0.4
	2238	4.7		2338	4.9
12	0503	0.4	27	0555	0.3
	1113	5.0		1158	4.8
TU	1729	0.6	W	1822	0.4
	2331	5.0			
13	0554	0.3	28	0022	4.8
	1202	5.2		0634	0.5
W	1821	0.4	TH	1239	4.8
●			○	1902	0.5
14	0021	5.2	29	0103	4.8
	0642	0.2		0707	0.6
TH	1250	5.3	F	1312	4.7
	1910	0.2		1936	0.5
15	0110	5.4	30	0137	4.6
	0728	0.2		0731	0.7
F	1336	5.3	SA	1338	4.7
	1958	0.1		2001	0.6

JULY

Day	Time	m	Day	Time	m
1	0205	4.6	16	0231	5.5
	0754	0.7		0848	0.2
SU	1401	4.7	M	1449	5.3
	2024	0.6		2123	-0.3
2	0233	4.6	17	0319	5.4
	0825	0.7		0932	0.3
M	1433	4.8	TU	1534	5.2
	2055	0.6		2211	-0.3
3	0307	4.6	18	0407	5.2
	0903	0.6		1017	0.4
TU	1511	4.8	W	1621	5.0
	2134	0.6		2259	-0.1
4	0348	4.6	19	0457	5.0
	0946	0.7		1105	0.5
W	1555	4.8	TH	1711	4.8
	2219	0.6	◐	2349	0.0
5	0434	4.6	20	0550	4.7
	1033	0.8		1156	0.7
TH	1643	4.7	F	1806	4.6
	2309	0.6			
6	0525	4.6	21	0044	0.2
	1124	0.9		0648	4.5
F	1734	4.6	SA	1253	0.8
◑				1910	4.4
7	0006	0.7	22	0143	0.4
	0621	4.5		0751	4.4
SA	1223	1.0	SU	1357	0.9
	1831	4.4		2020	4.3
8	0111	0.8	23	0247	0.5
	0725	4.4		0855	4.3
SU	1332	1.1	M	1509	0.9
	1939	4.3		2127	4.4
9	0223	0.8	24	0349	0.6
	0836	4.4		0954	4.4
M	1448	1.1	TU	1616	0.7
	2056	4.3		2225	4.5
10	0335	0.7	25	0444	0.6
	0944	4.5		1047	4.5
TU	1603	0.9	W	1713	0.6
	2207	4.6		2318	4.6
11	0440	0.6	26	0532	0.6
	1045	4.8		1135	4.6
W	1709	0.7	TH	1801	0.5
	2308	4.9			
12	0538	0.4	27	0004	4.7
	1140	5.0		0613	0.6
TH	1806	0.3	F	1218	4.7
			○	1843	0.5
13	0003	5.2	28	0046	4.7
	0629	0.3		0649	0.6
F	1231	5.2	SA	1254	4.7
●	1858	0.1		1918	0.4
14	0054	5.4	29	0121	4.7
	0717	0.2		0717	0.6
SA	1319	5.3	SU	1322	4.7
	1948	-0.1		1946	0.5
15	0143	5.5	30	0150	4.7
	0803	0.2		0741	0.6
SU	1405	5.3	M	1347	4.7
	2036	-0.3		2011	0.4
			31	0217	4.7
				0811	0.5
			TU	1416	4.8
				2040	0.4

AUGUST

Day	Time	m	Day	Time	m
1	0249	4.8	16	0343	5.3
	0846	0.5		0953	0.2
W	1452	4.9	TH	1555	5.1
	2115	0.4		2229	-0.2
2	0327	4.9	17	0428	5.0
	0925	0.5		1035	0.4
TH	1533	4.9	F	1639	4.9
	2154	0.5		2313	0.1
3	0411	4.8	18	0515	4.7
	1006	0.6		1119	0.6
F	1618	4.9	SA	1729	4.6
	2237	0.6	◐		
4	0458	4.7	19	0000	0.4
	1051	0.7		0605	4.4
SA	1706	4.7	SU	1208	0.8
◑	2324	0.7		1827	4.2
5	0550	4.6	20	0053	0.7
	1141	0.9		0705	4.1
SU	1759	4.5	M	1305	1.0
				1940	4.0
6	0019	0.9	21	0155	0.9
	0647	4.4		0814	4.0
M	1241	1.0	TU	1417	1.0
	1901	4.3		2057	4.0
7	0133	1.0	22	0307	1.0
	0757	4.2		0922	4.1
TU	1404	1.1	W	1541	1.0
	2020	4.2		2202	4.2
8	0306	1.0	23	0412	0.9
	0914	4.3		1020	4.3
W	1540	1.0	TH	1645	0.8
	2142	4.4		2256	4.4
9	0425	0.8	24	0505	0.8
	1022	4.5		1111	4.5
TH	1655	0.6	F	1735	0.6
	2250	4.7		2343	4.6
10	0526	0.5	25	0548	0.7
	1121	4.8		1155	4.7
F	1754	0.2	SA	1817	0.4
	2347	5.1			
11	0618	0.3	26	0025	4.7
	1213	5.1		0625	0.6
SA	1846	-0.2	SU	1233	4.8
●			○	1852	0.3
12	0039	5.4	27	0100	4.8
	0704	0.1		0658	0.5
SU	1301	5.3	M	1304	4.8
	1933	-0.4		1923	0.3
13	0128	5.6	28	0131	4.9
	0748	0.0		0727	0.4
M	1346	5.4	TU	1332	4.9
	2019	-0.5		1952	0.3
14	0214	5.6	29	0159	4.9
	0831	0.0		0757	0.4
TU	1430	5.4	W	1401	5.0
	2103	-0.5		2022	0.3
15	0259	5.5	30	0231	5.0
	0912	0.1		0829	0.4
W	1512	5.3	TH	1435	5.0
	2146	-0.4		2054	0.3
			31	0307	5.0
				0905	0.4
			F	1513	5.0
				2129	0.4

Chart Datum: 2·35 metres below Ordnance Datum (Newlyn). HAT is 5·8 metres above Chart Datum.

STANDARD TIME (UT)
For Summer Time add ONE hour in **non-shaded areas**

BURNHAM-ON-CROUCH LAT 51°37'N LONG 0°48'E

TIMES AND HEIGHTS OF HIGH AND LOW WATERS

Dates in red are SPRINGS
Dates in blue are NEAPS

YEAR **2018**

SEPTEMBER

Day	Time	m	Time	m	Time	m	Time	m
1 SA	0348	5.0	0942	0.5	1556	5.0	2205	0.5
2 SU	0432	4.8	1023	0.6	1642	4.8	2246	0.7
3 M	0520	4.6	1110	0.8	1733	4.5	◑ 2334	0.9
4 TU	0615	4.3	1206	1.0	1833	4.3		
5 W	0039	1.1	0721	4.1	1325	1.1	1951	4.1
6 TH	0238	1.2	0847	4.1	1526	1.0	2125	4.3
7 F	0413	0.9	1004	4.4	1643	0.5	2236	4.7
8 SA	0512	0.6	1104	4.8	1739	0.0	2332	5.1
9 SU	0601	0.2	1155	5.1	1828	-0.3	●	
10 M	0022	5.5	0646	0.0	1242	5.4	1913	-0.6
11 TU	0109	5.6	0728	-0.1	1325	5.5	1956	-0.6
12 W	0153	5.6	0808	-0.1	1406	5.5	2036	-0.5
13 TH	0234	5.5	0846	0.0	1446	5.4	2115	-0.3
14 F	0314	5.3	0924	0.2	1526	5.2	2153	0.0
15 SA	0354	4.9	1001	0.4	1606	4.9	2232	0.3
16 SU	0435	4.6	1040	0.6	1650	4.5	◐ 2312	0.6
17 M	0518	4.3	1123	0.8	1740	4.2	2358	0.9
18 TU	0609	4.0	1214	1.0	1847	3.9		
19 W	0055	1.2	0717	3.8	1319	1.1	2018	3.8
20 TH	0207	1.3	0841	3.9	1449	1.1	2132	4.0
21 F	0328	1.2	0948	4.1	1607	0.9	2228	4.3
22 SA	0428	1.0	1041	4.4	1659	0.6	2315	4.6
23 SU	0515	0.7	1126	4.7	1742	0.4	2356	4.8
24 M	0555	0.6	1205	4.9	1820	0.2		
25 TU	0032	5.0	0631	0.4	1240	5.0	○ 1854	0.2
26 W	0106	5.1	0705	0.4	1312	5.1	1927	0.2
27 TH	0138	5.1	0738	0.3	1344	5.1	1959	0.2
28 F	0211	5.2	0811	0.3	1419	5.2	2032	0.3
29 SA	0247	5.1	0846	0.4	1456	5.1	2105	0.4
30 SU	0327	5.0	0922	0.5	1538	5.0	2140	0.6

OCTOBER

Day	Time	m	Time	m	Time	m	Time	m
1 M	0409	4.8	1004	0.6	1624	4.8	2222	0.8
2 TU	0456	4.5	1052	0.8	1715	4.6	◑ 2313	1.0
3 W	0549	4.3	1150	1.0	1816	4.3		
4 TH	0018	1.2	0655	4.0	1315	1.1	1938	4.2
5 F	0217	1.3	0827	4.0	1514	0.8	2111	4.4
6 SA	0354	1.0	0946	4.4	1625	0.4	2219	4.8
7 SU	0451	0.6	1045	4.8	1718	-0.1	2314	5.2
8 M	0539	0.2	1134	5.2	1805	-0.4		
9 TU	0002	5.5	0622	0.0	1220	5.5	● 1848	-0.5
10 W	0047	5.6	0704	-0.1	1302	5.6	1929	-0.5
11 TH	0128	5.5	0743	0.0	1343	5.6	2007	-0.3
12 F	0207	5.4	0819	0.1	1421	5.4	2043	0.0
13 SA	0244	5.1	0854	0.3	1458	5.2	2116	0.3
14 SU	0319	4.8	0928	0.5	1535	4.9	2149	0.5
15 M	0353	4.6	1003	0.7	1615	4.5	2226	0.8
16 TU	0431	4.3	1043	0.9	1659	4.2	◐ 2310	1.1
17 W	0514	4.1	1132	1.0	1753	3.9		
18 TH	0003	1.3	0607	3.9	1233	1.2	1913	3.7
19 F	0111	1.4	0729	3.8	1351	1.1	2046	3.8
20 SA	0229	1.3	0901	4.0	1513	1.0	2148	4.2
21 SU	0340	1.1	1001	4.3	1613	0.7	2237	4.5
22 M	0434	0.8	1049	4.6	1701	0.5	2319	4.8
23 TU	0520	0.6	1131	4.9	1744	0.3	2359	5.1
24 W	0601	0.4	1210	5.1	1824	0.2	○	
25 TH	0036	5.2	0640	0.4	1248	5.2	1900	0.2
26 F	0114	5.3	0717	0.3	1325	5.3	1936	0.3
27 SA	0151	5.3	0754	0.3	1403	5.3	2011	0.4
28 SU	0229	5.2	0831	0.4	1443	5.2	2046	0.5
29 M	0309	5.0	0910	0.5	1526	5.1	2124	0.7
30 TU	0351	4.8	0955	0.6	1614	4.9	2210	0.9
31 W	0439	4.5	1047	0.8	1707	4.6	◑ 2304	1.1

NOVEMBER

Day	Time	m	Time	m	Time	m	Time	m
1 TH	0533	4.3	1152	0.9	1811	4.4		
2 F	0016	1.3	0640	4.1	1321	0.9	1930	4.3
3 SA	0158	1.2	0807	4.2	1454	0.6	2053	4.6
4 SU	0324	0.9	0923	4.5	1559	0.3	2157	4.9
5 M	0423	0.6	1021	4.9	1652	0.0	2250	5.2
6 TU	0513	0.3	1111	5.2	1739	-0.2	2338	5.4
7 W	0558	0.1	1157	5.4	1822	-0.3	●	
8 TH	0022	5.5	0640	0.0	1240	5.5	1902	-0.1
9 F	0103	5.4	0720	0.1	1321	5.4	1939	0.1
10 SA	0141	5.2	0756	0.2	1359	5.3	2011	0.3
11 SU	0214	5.0	0828	0.4	1434	5.0	2040	0.6
12 M	0244	4.7	0858	0.6	1508	4.8	2110	0.8
13 TU	0314	4.6	0930	0.8	1544	4.5	2146	1.0
14 W	0349	4.4	1009	0.9	1625	4.3	2229	1.1
15 TH	0431	4.3	1056	1.0	1713	4.1	◐ 2321	1.3
16 F	0521	4.1	1155	1.1	1812	4.0		
17 SA	0024	1.3	0621	4.0	1306	1.1	1929	4.0
18 SU	0136	1.3	0742	4.0	1419	1.0	2047	4.2
19 M	0247	1.2	0903	4.2	1524	0.8	2147	4.5
20 TU	0349	1.0	1003	4.5	1620	0.6	2237	4.8
21 W	0443	0.7	1053	4.8	1709	0.4	2323	5.1
22 TH	0531	0.5	1139	5.1	1754	0.3		
23 F	0007	5.3	0615	0.4	1223	5.3	○ 1836	0.3
24 SA	0049	5.4	0659	0.3	1306	5.4	1917	0.4
25 SU	0131	5.3	0741	0.3	1349	5.4	1956	0.5
26 M	0212	5.2	0824	0.3	1433	5.3	2036	0.6
27 TU	0254	5.0	0909	0.4	1519	5.2	2119	0.8
28 W	0338	4.8	0958	0.5	1608	5.0	2208	0.9
29 TH	0426	4.6	1054	0.6	1703	4.8	2305	1.1
30 F	0521	4.4	1159	0.6	1805	4.6	◑	

DECEMBER

Day	Time	m	Time	m	Time	m	Time	m
1 SA	0014	1.2	0626	4.3	1311	0.6	1915	4.6
2 SU	0132	1.1	0742	4.3	1425	0.4	2026	4.7
3 M	0248	0.9	0853	4.5	1529	0.2	2129	4.9
4 TU	0352	0.6	0954	4.8	1624	0.1	2224	5.1
5 W	0446	0.4	1046	5.1	1713	0.0	2313	5.3
6 TH	0535	0.2	1135	5.3	1758	0.1	2358	5.3
7 F	0620	0.2	1220	5.3	1839	0.2	●	
8 SA	0040	5.2	0702	0.3	1303	5.2	1915	0.4
9 SU	0118	5.0	0740	0.4	1341	5.0	1946	0.6
10 M	0149	4.8	0811	0.5	1414	4.8	2010	0.8
11 TU	0214	4.7	0836	0.7	1445	4.6	2037	0.9
12 W	0241	4.6	0904	0.8	1517	4.5	2112	1.0
13 TH	0317	4.6	0941	0.8	1556	4.4	2155	1.0
14 F	0359	4.5	1026	0.9	1642	4.4	2244	1.1
15 SA	0447	4.4	1120	0.9	1734	4.3	◐ 2341	1.2
16 SU	0541	4.3	1222	1.0	1834	4.3		
17 M	0046	1.3	0643	4.2	1330	0.9	1943	4.3
18 TU	0155	1.2	0758	4.2	1437	0.8	2053	4.5
19 W	0304	1.1	0912	4.4	1540	0.7	2155	4.7
20 TH	0407	0.9	1015	4.7	1637	0.6	2249	5.0
21 F	0504	0.7	1109	4.9	1730	0.5	2340	5.2
22 SA	0557	0.5	1200	5.2	1818	0.4	○	
23 SU	0027	5.3	0646	0.3	1249	5.4	1904	0.4
24 M	0113	5.3	0734	0.2	1336	5.4	1949	0.5
25 TU	0157	5.3	0822	0.1	1423	5.4	2033	0.6
26 W	0241	5.2	0910	0.1	1510	5.4	2118	0.7
27 TH	0326	5.0	0959	0.1	1559	5.2	2206	0.8
28 F	0414	4.9	1051	0.2	1652	5.0	2258	0.9
29 SA	0505	4.7	1147	0.3	1748	4.8	◑ 2356	0.9
30 SU	0604	4.5	1247	0.3	1850	4.7		
31 M	0059	1.0	0710	4.5	1351	0.4	1955	4.7

Chart Datum: 2·35 metres below Ordnance Datum (Newlyn). HAT is 5·8 metres above Chart Datum.

9.4.16 RIVER BLACKWATER

Essex **51°45'·33N 00°54'·90E**

CHARTS AC 5607, 1183, 1975, 3741; Imray C1, Y17, 2000

TIDES Maldon +0130 Dover; ML 2·8; Duration 0620)

Standard Port WALTON-ON-THE-NAZE (⟶)

Times				Height (metres)			
High Water		Low Water		MHWS	MHWN	MLWN	MLWS
0000	0600	0500	1100	4·2	3·4	1·1	0·4
1200	1800	1700	2300				
Differences SUNK HEAD							
0000	+0002	–0002	+0002	–0·3	–0·3	–0·1	–0·1
WEST MERSEA							
+0035	+0015	+0055	+0010	+0·9	+0·4	+0·1	+0·1
BRADWELL							
+0035	+0023	+0047	+0004	+1·0	+0·8	+0·2	0·0
OSEA ISLAND							
+0057	+0045	+0050	+0007	+1·1	+0·9	+0·1	0·0
MALDON							
+0107	+0055	ND	ND	–1·3	–1·1	ND	ND

SHELTER Good, as appropriate to wind. ⚓ in creeks restricted by oyster beds and many moorings.

NAVIGATION WPT Knoll NCM, Q, 51°43′·88N 01°05′·07E, 287°/6·7M to Nass bn, ECM VQ (3) 5s. Speed limit 8kn W of Osea Is.

WEST MERSEA Min depth 0·6m in approach to Nass Bn. Avoid oyster beds between Cobmarsh and Packing Marsh Is and in Salcott Chan. ⚓ in Mersea Quarters in 5-6m (exposed). Landing pontoon (limited waiting) with pile and pontoon moorings in Ray Channel.

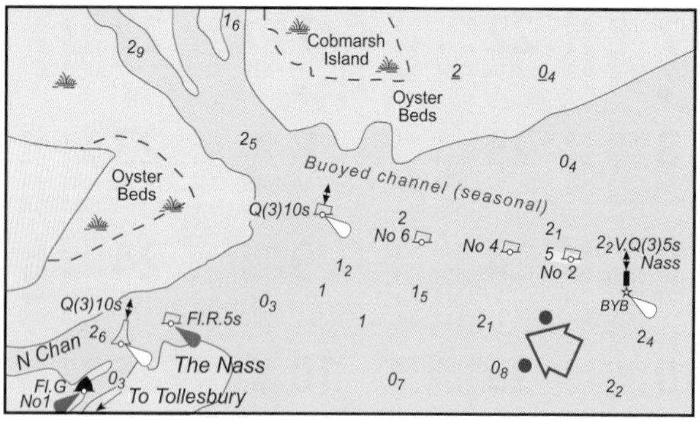

TOLLESBURY FLEET Proceed via S Chan up Woodrolfe Creek. A tide gauge shows depth over marina ent sill (approx 2·4m at MHWS and 1·4m at MHWN). Speed limits: Tollesbury Fleet S Chan 8kn; Woodrolfe Creek upper reaches 4kn.

BRADWELL No dangers. Creek only suitable for small craft and gets very crowded. Ent has SCM bn Q with tide gauge in creek; leave to **STBD** on entry. 4 PHM buoys, 3 SHM withies and 2 B/W △ ldg bns mark the channel which doglegs past a SHM buoy to marina entrance. Min depth 0.2m in approach channel.

MALDON From S of Osea Is, 'The Doctor', No 3 SHM buoy on with Blackwater SC lt, Iso G 5s, lead 300° approx up the chan; or No 3 and No 8 buoys in line at 305°.

LIGHTS AND MARKS See chartlets and 9.4.4. The channel to Maldon has some lit marks.

COMMUNICATIONS (Codes 01621 Maldon; 01206 Colchester/W Mersea) NMOC 02392 552100; Police 101; Dr 854118.

Bradwell and Tollesbury Marinas Ch **80** M (HO); Blackwater Marina Ch M 0900-2300; Heybridge Lock Ch 80 HW –2+1; WMYC launch VHF37/M, c/s *YC1* or Clarke and Carter launch VHF 37/M, c/s *CC1*.

FACILITIES

WEST MERSEA (01206) **W Mersea YC**382947, launch service call *YC1* on Ch 37/M or ☎07752 309435, **Town** (bus to Colchester, Ⓗ01206-853535), ✈ (Southend/Stansted).

TOLLESBURY Marina marina@woodrolfe.com ☎(01621) 869202, Sill to marina dries 1·9m. 220+20Ⓥ: 1 tide £5, <8m £18, <10m £20, <12m £21, >12m £22 LPG (20t) (5t).

Tollesbury Cruising Club ☎869561.

Village Ⓑ (Tues, Thurs 1000-1430), (bus to Witham), ✈ (Southend or Cambridge).

BRADWELL (01621). **Bradwell Marina** ☎776235. Min depth 0·2m in appr chan. 300 some Ⓥ <22' £5.74, <25' £6.11, <28' £6.65, <33' £7.09 (45t). **Bradwell Quay YC** ☎890173. **Town** (bus to Southminster), ✈ (Southend).

MAYLANDSEA (01621). **Blackwater Marina** ☎740264, 150 £5, 230 all dry <10m £15, short stay £5.

MALDON (01621). **Maldon Quay** Beyond No 8 buoy, the chan which shifts and carries 0·2m, is lit and buoyed. Access near HW; pontoons dry to soft mud. HM/River bailiff ☎875837, Mob 07818 013723; £15. **Maldon Little Ship Club** ☎854139.

Services Ⓔ ACA.

Town Ⓑ (bus to Chelmsford, Ⓗ(01245) 440761), ✈ (Southend, Cambridge or Stansted).

HEYBRIDGE BASIN Lock ☎853506 mob 07712079764, opens HW–1 to HW approx (www.essexwaterways.com). SHM opposite the lock marks the deep water ent. Access to Chelmer & Blackwater Canal (small craft only). Ⓥ £2·50 **Blackwater SC** ☎853923 .**Services** at CRS Marine ☎854684, Mobile 07850 543873 (pontoon outside lock). Bus to Heybridge/Maldon.

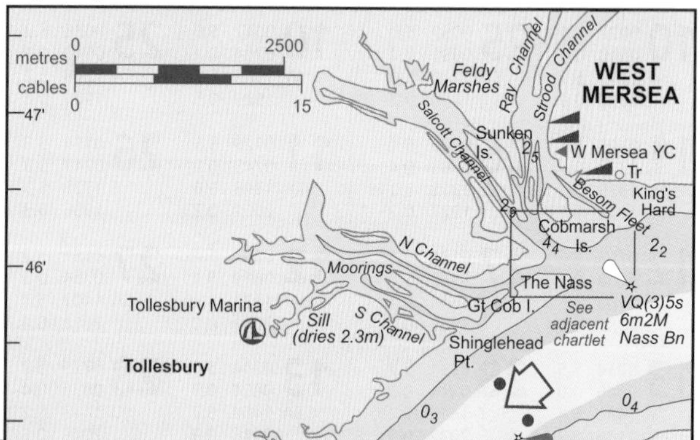
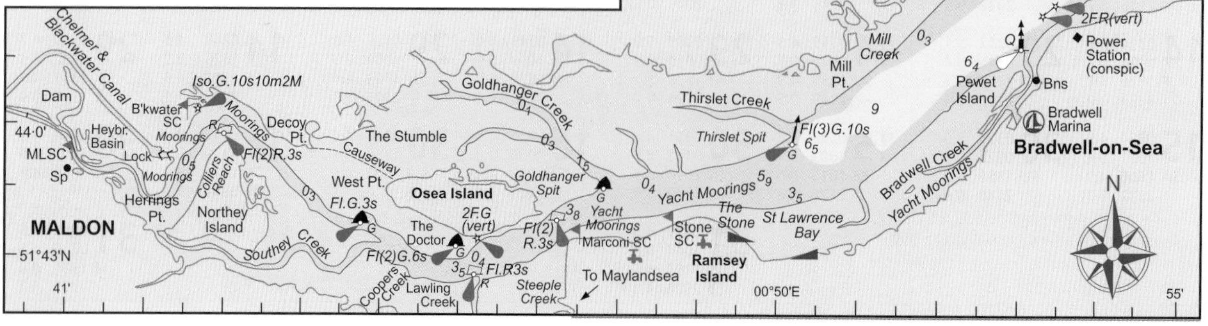

9.4.17 RIVER COLNE

Essex **51°47'·98N 01°00'·60E** (Brightlingsea) ❁❁◊◊◊✿✿

CHARTS AC 5607, 1183, 1975, 3741; Imray C1, Y17, 2000

TIDES +0050 Dover; ML 2·5; Duration 0615

Standard Port WALTON-ON-THE-NAZE (⟶)

Times				Height (metres)			
High Water		Low Water		MHWS	MHWN	MLWN	MLWS
0000	0600	0500	1100	4·2	3·4	1·1	0·4
1200	1800	1700	2300				
Differences BRIGHTLINGSEA							
+0025	+0021	+0046	+0004	+0·8	+0·4	+0·1	0·0
COLCHESTER							
+0035	+0025	DR	DR	0·0	–0·3	DR	DR
CLACTON-ON-SEA							
+0012	+0010	+0025	+0008	+0·3	+0·1	+0·1	+0·1

SHELTER Suitable shelter can be found from most winds. Brightlingsea outer hbr is exposed to W'lies. In the creek S of Cindery Island are moorings and long pontoons in about 1·5m, with possible ⊆ for Ⓥs. ⚓ prohib in Brightlingsea Hbr, but allowed to the NW of Mersea Stone Pt and in Pyefleet Chan, E of Pewit Is. R Colne is navigable for 4·5m draught to Wivenhoe and Rowhedge, where it dries; and to The Hythe, Colchester (3m draught).

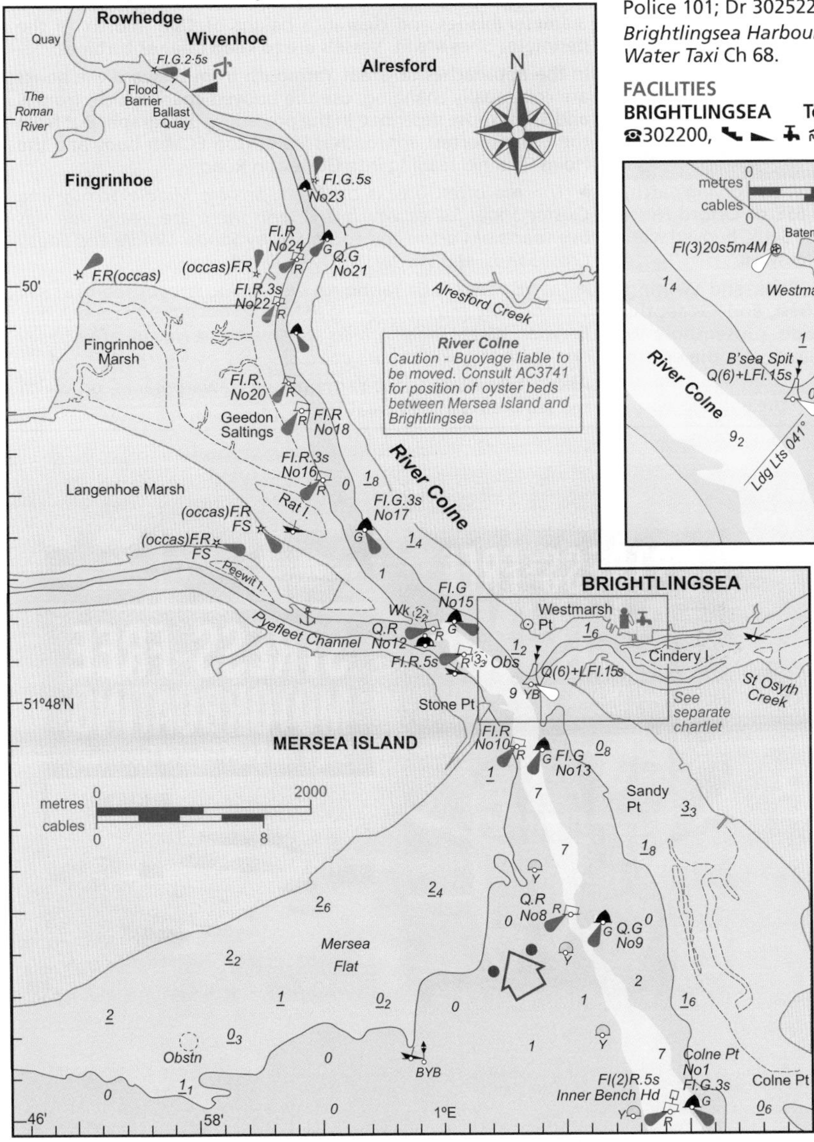

NAVIGATION WPT Colne Bar By, SHM Fl (2) G 5s, 51°44'·61N 01°02'·57E, 340°/3·6M to Mersea Stone. Extensive mud and sand banks flank the entrance channel. Coasters may be encountered in the appr to Brightlingsea and manoeuvring off the quay beyond the hard. At HW sand barges regularly visit Ballast Quay below the tidal barrier at Wivenhoe. The entrance to Brightlingsea Creek is narrow at LW and carries about 1m.

Tidal barrier 2ca below Wivenhoe church is usually open (30m wide) allowing unrestricted passage; keep to stbd, max speed 5kn. 3 F R (vert), shown on N Pier, visible up/downstream indicate barrier gates are shut; see also LIGHTS AND MARKS.

Speed limits in approaches and up-river (by buoy no): No 13–15 = 8kn; No 15–18 = no spd limit; No 18–31 = 8kn; No 31 – Colchester = 5kn; Brightlingsea Harbour = 4kn.

LIGHTS AND MARKS Bateman's Tr (conspic) by Westmarsh Pt Fl(3)20s. Brightlingsea ldg lts/marks 041°; FR 7/10m 4M, W □ on R striped posts; adjusted to suit channel. Pass Spit SCM, and follow lateral marks to NCM (Q) where chan is divided by Cindery Is. Pyefleet Chan and other creeks are unlit.

Lit lateral buoys up to Wivenhoe. Passage through flood barrier marked by 2FR/FG (vert) each side and there are bns, QR/QG, up/downstream on the banks.

COMMUNICATIONS (Brightlingsea 01206) NMOC 02392 552100; Police 101; Dr 302522; HM (B'sea) 302200.

Brightlingsea Harbour Radio VHF Ch 68. *Waterside Marina* Ch 80. *Water Taxi* Ch 68.

FACILITIES

BRIGHTLINGSEA Town Hard www.brightlingseaharbour.org ☎302200, ⚓ ⛴ ⛽ ⚒ ♿. Marina (W) £15 < 23'< £17 < 29' < 42' <£22,

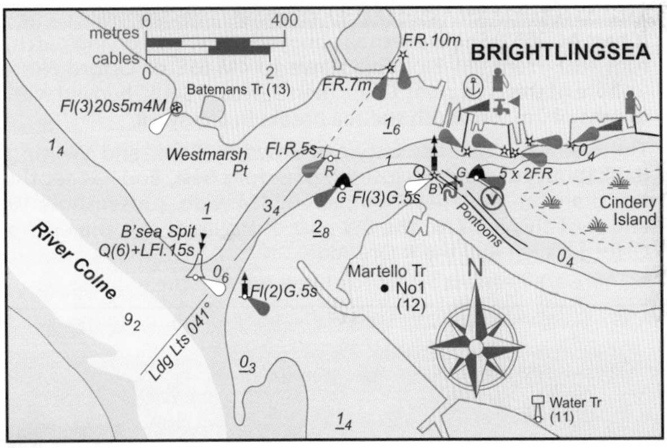

Marina (E) £15 < 23'< £20 < 29' < 42' <£25, (water taxi £1 pp each way) short stay free at fuel jetty.

Waterside Marina ☎308709, sill 1m above CD; ⊆£2·00 inc ⊕.

Colne YC ☎302594, ⚓ ⛽ ✕ ⊐ wi-fi.

Brightlingsea SC ⛴ ⊐.

Services Ⓟ Ⓟ(HO) ⛽ ⚒ 🔧 ⊕ Ⓔ ⛵ ⚓ (mobile) ⛴ ACA.

Town ✉ Ⓑ 🛒 ✕ ⊐ bus (Wivenhoe or Colchester for ⇌), ✈ (Southend or Stansted).

WIVENHOE: Wivenhoe SC ☎822132. ⊆ (drying Ⓥ berths may be available on the inside pontoons – first come first served, no charge). **Village** Ⓟ ✉ 🛒 ⊐ ⇌.

ROWHEDGE: Quay ⊆ for small craft on pontoon above pub (drying) some Ⓥ. Water Bailiff; David Slavinskas 07969605442. EDPC office 01206 729200. Restrictions on Pontoon - 30ft for 3 hr maximum stay, no overnight mooring on pontoon. O/n fees Lion or Pearsons Quay £10; 🛒 ✕ ⊐.

RIVER COLNE TO HARWICH

(Chart AC 1975, 1593) 4M SW of the Naze twr at Hollands Haven a conspic radar twr (67m, unlit) is an excellent daymark. From the S, approach Walton and Harwich via the Medusa chan about 1M E of the twr. Beware pot buoys and drift nets off the Naze. At N end of this chan, 1M off Dovercourt, Pye End buoy marks chan SSW to Walton Backwaters. Harwich and Landguard Pt are close to the N. Making Harwich from the SE beware the drying Cork Sand, which lies N/S.

Sunk Inner SWM buoy, 11M E of The Naze, marks the outer apps to Harwich, an extensive and well sheltered hbr accessible at all times (chart AC 2693).

- Harwich, Felixstowe Docks and Ipswich are referred to collectively as the Haven Ports.
- Small craft should give plenty of sea room to shipping manoeuvring to board/disembark Pilots in the Sunk Inner Precautionary Area, see Thames Estuary chartlet.
- Harwich Deep Water chan runs N from 1·5M NNW of Sunk Inner between Rough and Shipwash shoals, then W past the Cork Sand PHM. Constantly used by commercial shipping, small craft should use the recommended track for yachts.

Approaching from NE and 2M off the ent to R Deben, beware Cutler shoal, with least depth of 1·2m, marked by SHM buoy on E side; Wadgate Ledge and the Platters are about 1·5M ENE of Landguard Point; beware pot buoys off Cobbolds Point.

▶ *S of Landguard Point the W-going (flood) stream begins at HW Harwich +0600, and the E-going stream at HW Harwich, sp rates about 1·5kn. Note: HW Harwich is never more than 7 mins after HW Walton; LW times are about 10 mins earlier.* ◀

HARWICH TO ORFORD NESS

(Chart AC 2052) Shipwash shoal, buoyed and with a drying patch, runs NNE from 9M E of Felixstowe to 4M SSE of Orford Ness. Inshore of this is Shipway Chan, then Bawdsey Bank, buoyed with depths of 2m, on which the sea breaks in E'ly swell.

The Sledway Chan lies between Bawdsey Bank and Whiting Bank (buoyed) which is close SW of Orford Ness, and has depths less than 1m. Hollesley Chan, about 1M wide, runs inshore W and N of this bank. In the SW part of Hollesley B is the ent to Orford Haven and the R Ore/Alde.

▶ *There are overfalls S of Orford Ness on both the ebb and flood streams. 2M E of Orford Ness the SW-going stream begins at HW Harwich +0605, Sp rate 2·5kn; the NE-going stream begins at HW Harwich –0010, Sp rate 3kn.* ◀

Note: The direction of local buoyage becomes S to N off Orford Ness (52°05'N).

ORFORD NESS TO GREAT YARMOUTH

(Chart AC 1543) N of Orford Ness seas break on Aldeburgh Ridge (1·3m), but the coast is clear of offlying dangers past Aldeburgh and Southwold, as far as Benacre Ness, 5M S of Lowestoft. Sizewell power station (conspic) 3 bldg 1·5M N of Thorpe Ness. Keep 1·5M offshore to avoid fishing floats and outfalls marked by lit PHMs.

▶ *Lowestoft is best approached from both S and E by the buoyed/lit Stanford chan, passing E of Newcome Sand and SW of Holm Sand; beware possible strong set across harbour entrance.* ◀

From the N, approach through Cockle Gatway, Caister Road, Yarmouth Road, passing Great Yarmouth (beware of prohibited area N of harbour entrance); then proceed S through Gorleston, Corton and Lowestoft North Roads (buoyed).

▶ *1M E of hbr ent, the S-going stream begins at HW Dover –0600, and the N-going at HW Dover, Sp rates 2·6kn.* ◀

Scroby Sands Wind Farm consists of 30 turbines centred on 52°39'·00N 01°47'·00E. Each turbine is 61m high, with 80m diameter blades and clearance height of 18m and six of the perimeter ones are lit. Vessels are to keep clear of turbines.

In the approaches to Great Yarmouth from seaward the banks are continually changing; use the buoyed chans which, from N and S, are those described in the preceding paragraph. But from the E the shortest approach is via Corton ECM lt buoy and the Holm Channel leading into Gorleston Road.

▶ *The sea often breaks on North Scroby, Middle Scroby and Caister Shoal (all of which dry), and there are heavy tide rips over parts of Corton and South Scroby Sands, Middle and South Cross Sands, and Winterton Overfalls.* ◀

▶ *1M NE of ent to Gt Yarmouth the S-going stream begins at HW Dover –0600, and the N-going at HW Dover –0015, Sp rates 2·3kn. Breydon Water (tidal) affects streams in the Haven; after heavy rain the out-going stream at Brush Quay may exceed 5kn.* ◀

About 12M NE of Great Yarmouth lie Newarp Banks, on which the sea breaks in bad weather.

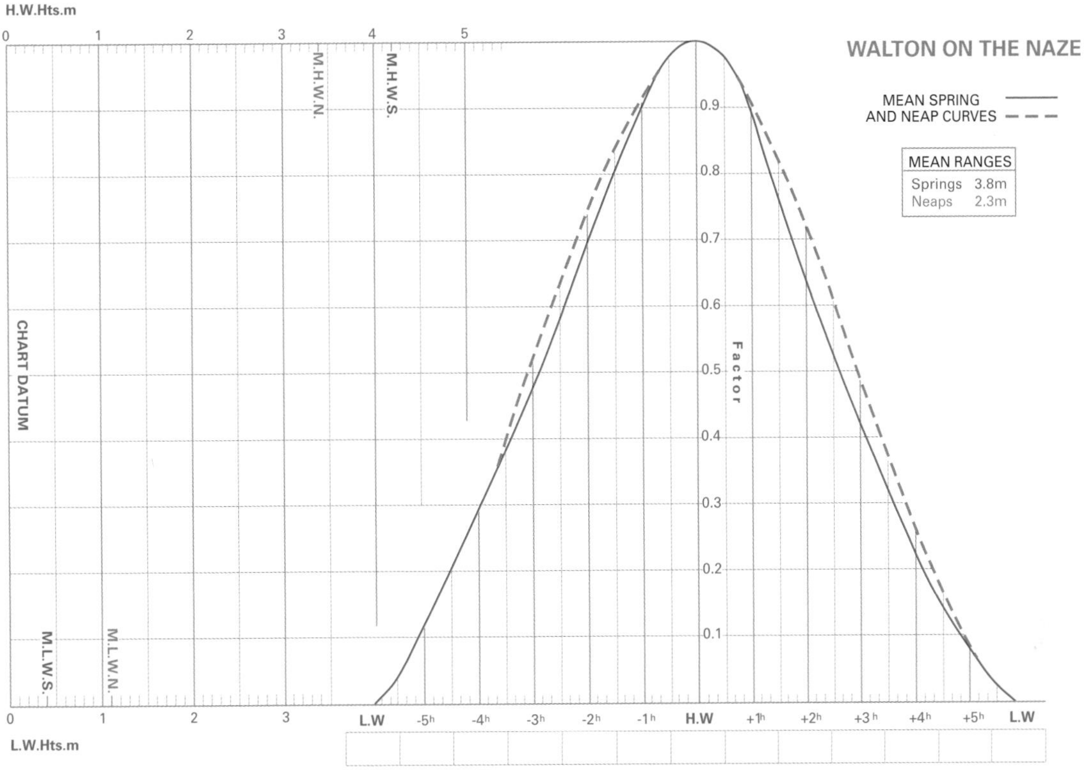

9.4.18 WALTON BACKWATERS

Essex **51°54'·57N 01°16'·79E** (No 2 PHM buoy) ❁❁◊◊◊✿✿

CHARTS AC 5607, 2052, 2695; Imray C1, Y16, 2000

TIDES +0030 Dover; ML 2·2; Duration 0615. Walton is a Standard Port. Predictions are for Walton Pier, ie to seaward. Time differences for Bramble Creek (N of Hamford Water) are +10, –7, –5, +10 mins; height differences are all +0·3m.

SHELTER Good in all weather, but ent not advised if a big sea is running from the NE. Good ⚓s in Hamford Water (clear of Oakley Creek) and in N end of Walton Chan, 2ca S of Stone Pt on E side.

NAVIGATION From S, appr via Medusa Chan; from N and E via the Harwich recomended yacht track (9.4.19). WPT Pye End SWM buoy, L Fl 10s, 51°55'·05N 01°17'·89E, 234°/1·1M to Crab Knoll SHM at chan ent. NB this stretch carries only 0·9m. Beware lobster pots off the Naze and Pye Sands and oyster beds in the Backwaters. Buoys may be moved to suit channel changes.

At narrow ent to Walton Chan leave NCM buoy to stbd, and 3 PHM buoys close to port. Fm No 9 SHM expect significant shoaling, ebb>4kn and strong back eddies around Stone Pt. Best water to E side, with narrowest/shallowest water at No 16 PHM; stay in channel. Beware tidal sheer and vessels with strong tide under them.

LIGHTS AND MARKS Naze Tr (49m) is conspic 3M S of Pye End buoy. 2M NNE at Felixstowe, cranes and Y flood lts are conspic D/N. No 9 SHM Fl G 5s, No 10 PHM Q R.

COMMUNICATIONS (Code 01255) CGOC 020 8312 7380; Police 101; Ⓗ 421145; HM 851899.

Titchmarsh Marina Ch 80, 0800-2000 in season.

FACILITIES

Titchmarsh Marina ☎672185, pontoons on R Twizzle. Access over sill 1·3m (tide gauge at entrance) berths dredged to approx 2m. ◣ 420⛵ inc Ⓥ, £17 <8m, £19 <10m, £20 <12m, £22 <13m, £26m; short stay (<3hrs) £5/hr. ⛽ LPG 🔧 ⛴(10t) (35t) ✕ ☕. **Walton & Frinton YC,** ☎678161, ✕ ☕. **Yacht Basin** ☎675873; appr dries. ◣ 60⛵ (long stay) ♿ 🔧 ⛴(½t) wi-fi.

Town ⛽ ✉ 🛒 ✕ ☕ ⇌ ✈ (Southend/Cambridge/Stansted).

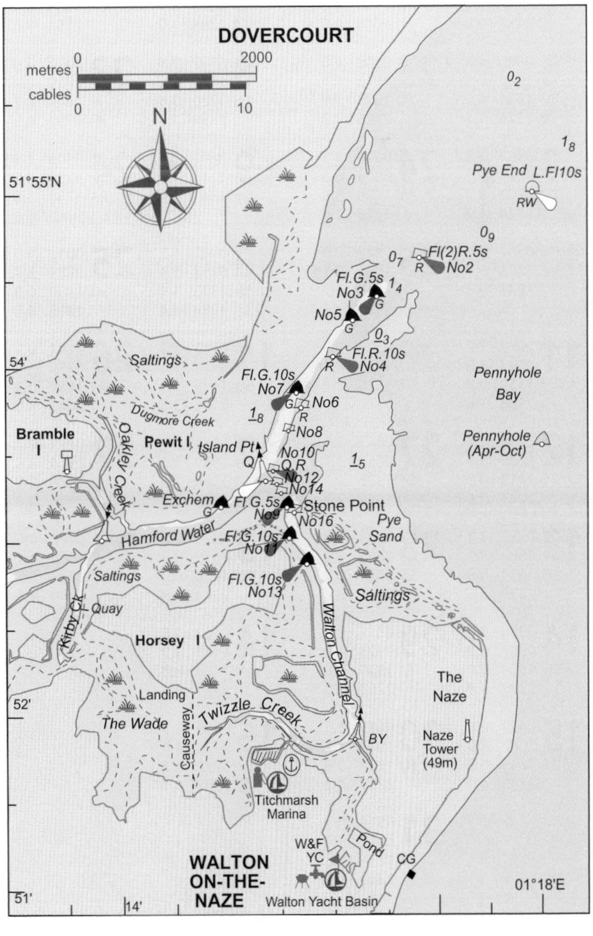

STANDARD TIME (UT)
For Summer Time add ONE hour in **non-shaded areas**

WALTON-ON-THE-NAZE LAT 51°51′N LONG 1°17′E

TIMES AND HEIGHTS OF HIGH AND LOW WATERS

Dates in red are SPRINGS
Dates in blue are NEAPS

YEAR **2018**

JANUARY

Date	Time	m	Date	Time	m
1	0426	0.6	16	0521	0.6
	1036	4.3		1119	4.0
M	1648	0.5	TU	1727	0.8
	2309	4.3		2341	4.0
2	0521	0.4	17	0556	0.5
	1127	4.5		1156	4.0
TU	1740	0.5	W	1801	0.8
○	2359	4.4	●		
3	0615	0.3	18	0016	4.1
	1217	4.6		0629	0.5
W	1830	0.5	TH	1232	4.1
				1832	0.7
4	0048	4.4	19	0050	4.2
	0706	0.2		0701	0.4
TH	1307	4.6	F	1307	4.1
	1917	0.6		1902	0.7
5	0136	4.4	20	0124	4.2
	0756	0.1		0733	0.4
F	1356	4.5	SA	1342	4.1
	2004	0.7		1933	0.7
6	0224	4.4	21	0158	4.1
	0844	0.2		0806	0.4
SA	1446	4.4	SU	1417	4.0
	2049	0.8		2007	0.8
7	0311	4.2	22	0232	4.1
	0931	0.3		0839	0.5
SU	1537	4.2	M	1453	4.0
	2135	0.9		2044	0.8
8	0400	4.1	23	0308	4.0
	1020	0.4		0915	0.5
M	1631	4.0	TU	1533	3.9
◑	2226	1.1		2126	0.9
9	0453	3.9	24	0349	3.9
	1113	0.5		0958	0.6
TU	1729	3.8	W	1620	3.8
	2324	1.2	◐	2216	1.0
10	0551	3.7	25	0438	3.9
	1211	0.7		1053	0.7
W	1831	3.6	TH	1716	3.7
				2321	1.1
11	0032	1.2	26	0538	3.8
	0657	3.6		1205	0.7
TH	1313	0.8	F	1825	3.7
	1938	3.6			
12	0144	1.2	27	0042	1.1
	0806	3.6		0652	3.7
F	1418	0.9	SA	1325	0.7
	2044	3.6		1942	3.7
13	0257	1.1	28	0202	0.9
	0907	3.7		0811	3.8
SA	1520	0.9	SU	1435	0.7
	2139	3.8		2057	3.8
14	0356	0.9	29	0311	0.8
	0957	3.8		0923	4.0
SU	1609	0.9	M	1539	0.6
	2225	3.9		2203	4.0
15	0442	0.8	30	0415	0.5
	1040	3.9		1023	4.2
M	1649	0.8	TU	1637	0.6
	2305	4.0		2259	4.2
			31	0514	0.3
				1117	4.4
			W	1731	0.6
			○	2349	4.3

FEBRUARY

Date	Time	m	Date	Time	m
1	0608	0.2	16	0608	0.4
	1207	4.5		1214	4.1
TH	1820	0.5	F	1813	0.7
2	0036	4.4	17	0031	4.2
	0657	0.1		0640	0.3
F	1255	4.5	SA	1249	4.1
	1906	0.6		1844	0.6
3	0122	4.5	18	0106	4.2
	0743	0.0		0712	0.3
SA	1342	4.5	SU	1323	4.2
	1948	0.6		1916	0.6
4	0205	4.4	19	0140	4.2
	0826	0.1		0744	0.3
SU	1427	4.4	M	1358	4.1
	2029	0.7		1950	0.6
5	0248	4.3	20	0213	4.2
	0905	0.2		0815	0.3
M	1512	4.2	TU	1433	4.0
	2108	0.8		2025	0.7
6	0330	4.2	21	0248	4.1
	0944	0.4		0849	0.4
TU	1558	3.9	W	1512	4.0
	2148	0.9		2104	0.8
7	0413	4.0	22	0326	4.1
	1025	0.6		0928	0.5
W	1646	3.7	TH	1555	3.9
◑	2235	1.0		2151	0.8
8	0502	3.7	23	0412	4.0
	1115	0.8		1019	0.7
TH	1739	3.5	F	1647	3.7
	2334	1.2	◐	2252	0.9
9	0601	3.5	24	0509	3.8
	1215	1.0		1132	0.8
F	1841	3.4	SA	1754	3.6
10	0049	1.2	25	0012	1.0
	0713	3.4		0623	3.7
SA	1325	1.1	SU	1300	0.9
	1956	3.4		1916	3.5
11	0212	1.2	26	0141	0.9
	0829	3.5		0754	3.7
SU	1439	1.1	M	1419	0.9
	2106	3.5		2045	3.6
12	0331	1.0	27	0259	0.7
	0930	3.6		0914	3.9
M	1544	1.0	TU	1528	0.8
	2200	3.7		2154	3.8
13	0423	0.8	28	0408	0.5
	1019	3.8		1016	4.1
TU	1630	0.9	W	1629	0.7
	2243	3.8		2249	4.1
14	0502	0.6			
	1101	3.9			
W	1708	0.8			
	2321	4.0			
15	0536	0.5			
	1138	4.0			
TH	1742	0.7			
●	2357	4.1			

MARCH

Date	Time	m	Date	Time	m
1	0506	0.3	16	0507	0.5
	1109	4.3		1113	4.0
TH	1720	0.6	F	1717	0.7
	2337	4.3		2330	4.0
2	0556	0.1	17	0540	0.4
	1155	4.4		1149	4.1
F	1806	0.6	SA	1749	0.6
○			●		
3	0020	4.4	18	0005	4.2
	0641	0.0		0612	0.3
SA	1239	4.4	SU	1225	4.2
	1848	0.5		1821	0.6
4	0102	4.5	19	0041	4.3
	0722	0.0		0645	0.2
SU	1322	4.4	M	1301	4.2
	1928	0.5		1856	0.5
5	0142	4.5	20	0117	4.3
	0759	0.1		0717	0.2
M	1403	4.3	TU	1337	4.2
	2005	0.6		1931	0.5
6	0220	4.4	21	0152	4.3
	0832	0.3		0749	0.3
TU	1443	4.1	W	1414	4.1
	2040	0.7		2007	0.6
7	0257	4.2	22	0228	4.3
	0904	0.4		0823	0.4
W	1522	3.9	TH	1452	4.0
	2114	0.8		2047	0.6
8	0335	4.0	23	0308	4.2
	0938	0.6		0904	0.5
TH	1602	3.7	F	1535	3.9
	2152	0.9		2134	0.7
9	0418	3.7	24	0354	4.0
	1022	0.8		0957	0.7
F	1648	3.5	SA	1626	3.7
◑	2242	1.1	◐	2236	0.8
10	0512	3.5	25	0452	3.8
	1122	1.1		1113	0.9
SA	1746	3.3	SU	1734	3.5
	2353	1.2		2357	0.9
11	0623	3.3	26	0610	3.6
	1238	1.2		1244	1.0
SU	1858	3.2	M	1903	3.4
12	0121	1.2	27	0128	0.8
	0745	3.3		0746	3.6
M	1359	1.2	TU	1406	1.0
	2019	3.3		2033	3.5
13	0248	1.1	28	0249	0.6
	0857	3.5		0906	3.9
TU	1512	1.1	W	1517	0.9
	2125	3.5		2141	3.8
14	0351	0.8	29	0358	0.4
	0952	3.7		1006	4.1
W	1603	0.9	TH	1615	0.8
	2213	3.7		2234	4.1
15	0432	0.6	30	0452	0.3
	1035	3.8		1055	4.2
TH	1642	0.8	F	1703	0.7
	2254	3.9		2319	4.2
			31	0537	0.1
				1138	4.3
			SA	1745	0.6
			○	2359	4.4

APRIL

Date	Time	m	Date	Time	m
1	0618	0.1	16	0541	0.3
	1218	4.3		1156	4.2
SU	1826	0.5	M	1757	0.5
			●		
2	0037	4.4	17	0012	4.3
	0654	0.1		0616	0.2
M	1258	4.3	TU	1236	4.3
	1904	0.5		1835	0.5
3	0115	4.4	18	0052	4.4
	0727	0.2		0651	0.3
TU	1336	4.2	W	1315	4.3
	1940	0.5		1913	0.4
4	0150	4.3	19	0131	4.4
	0758	0.4		0726	0.3
W	1412	4.1	TH	1356	4.2
	2013	0.6		1953	0.5
5	0225	4.2	20	0211	4.4
	0827	0.5		0804	0.4
TH	1447	3.9	F	1437	4.1
	2044	0.7		2037	0.5
6	0301	4.0	21	0254	4.2
	0857	0.7		0850	0.6
F	1522	3.7	SA	1522	3.9
	2118	0.8		2127	0.6
7	0341	3.8	22	0344	4.1
	0935	0.9		0948	0.8
SA	1602	3.5	SU	1616	3.7
	2201	0.9	◐	2231	0.7
8	0430	3.5	23	0446	3.8
	1028	1.1		1104	1.0
SU	1656	3.3	M	1726	3.5
◑	2302	1.1		2353	0.7
9	0537	3.3	24	0607	3.7
	1147	1.3		1230	1.1
M	1807	3.2	TU	1852	3.5
10	0030	1.1	25	0117	0.7
	0659	3.2		0735	3.7
TU	1317	1.3	W	1348	1.0
	1924	3.2		2013	3.6
11	0156	1.0	26	0234	0.5
	0813	3.4		0850	3.9
W	1431	1.2	TH	1458	0.9
	2035	3.4		2119	3.9
12	0303	0.8	27	0340	0.4
	0912	3.6		0948	4.1
TH	1526	1.0	F	1555	0.8
	2131	3.6		2211	4.1
13	0351	0.6	28	0431	0.3
	1000	3.8		1036	4.2
F	1609	0.8	SA	1641	0.7
	2216	3.8		2255	4.2
14	0430	0.5	29	0513	0.3
	1040	4.0		1117	4.2
SA	1645	0.7	SU	1723	0.6
	2256	4.0		2334	4.3
15	0506	0.4	30	0550	0.3
	1118	4.1		1155	4.2
SU	1721	0.6	M	1802	0.5
	2334	4.2	○		

Chart Datum: 2·16 metres below Ordnance Datum (Newlyn). HAT is 4·7 metres above Chart Datum.

STANDARD TIME (UT)
For Summer Time add ONE hour in **non-shaded areas**

WALTON-ON-THE-NAZE LAT 51°51'N LONG 1°17'E

TIMES AND HEIGHTS OF HIGH AND LOW WATERS

Dates in red are SPRINGS
Dates in blue are NEAPS

YEAR **2018**

MAY

Day	Time	m	Day	Time	m
1 TU	0011 0624 1233 1841	4.3 0.3 4.2 0.5	16 W	0550 1212 1817	0.3 4.3 0.4
2 W	0047 0656 1308 1917	4.3 0.4 4.2 0.5	17 TH	0029 0630 1257 1900	4.5 0.3 4.3 0.4
3 TH	0122 0727 1343 1950	4.3 0.5 4.1 0.6	18 F	0113 0711 1341 1946	4.5 0.4 4.3 0.4
4 F	0157 0755 1416 2021	4.1 0.6 4.0 0.6	19 SA	0158 0756 1427 2034	4.5 0.5 4.1 0.4
5 SA	0233 0825 1449 2052	4.0 0.8 3.8 0.7	20 SU	0246 0846 1516 2128	4.3 0.7 4.0 0.4
6 SU	0311 0900 1527 2131	3.8 0.9 3.7 0.8	21 M	0340 0945 1613 2232	4.1 0.9 3.8 0.5
7 M	0355 0945 1615 2223	3.6 1.1 3.5 0.9	22 TU	0443 1053 1719 ◐ 2345	3.9 1.0 3.7 0.5
8 TU	0452 1049 1718 ◑ 2338	3.4 1.3 3.3 1.0	23 W	0557 1208 1832	3.8 1.1 3.7
9 W	0608 1219 1832	3.3 1.4 3.3	24 TH	0059 0713 1322 1945	0.5 3.8 1.1 3.8
10 TH	0104 0721 1341 1940	1.0 3.4 1.3 3.4	25 F	0210 0823 1430 2050	0.5 3.9 1.0 3.9
11 F	0211 0823 1440 2041	0.8 3.6 1.1 3.6	26 SA	0313 0923 1529 2144	0.5 4.0 0.9 4.0
12 SA	0304 0916 1527 2133	0.7 3.8 0.9 3.8	27 SU	0405 1012 1618 2229	0.5 4.1 0.8 4.1
13 SU	0349 1002 1610 2219	0.5 4.0 0.7 4.0	28 M	0446 1054 1701 2309	0.5 4.1 0.7 4.2
14 M	0430 1046 1651 2302	0.4 4.1 0.6 4.2	29 TU	0522 1133 1742 ○ 2346	0.5 4.1 0.6 4.2
15 TU	0511 1129 1734 ● 2345	0.3 4.2 0.5 4.4	30 W	0556 1209 1821	0.5 4.1 0.5
			31 TH	0022 0630 1245 1858	4.2 0.6 4.1 0.5

JUNE

Day	Time	m	Day	Time	m
1 F	0059 0702 1319 1932	4.2 0.6 4.1 0.5	16 SA	0059 0704 1330 1943	4.6 0.5 4.3 0.3
2 SA	0135 0732 1352 2003	4.1 0.7 4.0 0.6	17 SU	0148 0753 1419 2034	4.5 0.6 4.3 0.3
3 SU	0211 0802 1426 2034	4.0 0.8 3.9 0.6	18 M	0239 0843 1509 2127	4.4 0.7 4.2 0.3
4 M	0248 0836 1503 2111	3.9 0.9 3.8 0.7	19 TU	0333 0936 1602 2224	4.3 0.9 4.1 0.3
5 TU	0328 0918 1545 2156	3.7 1.0 3.7 0.8	20 W	0431 1034 1700 ◐ 2326	4.1 1.0 4.0 0.4
6 W	0415 1008 1637 ◑ 2253	3.6 1.2 3.6 0.9	21 TH	0535 1138 1803	3.9 1.1 3.9
7 TH	0513 1114 1739	3.5 1.3 3.5	22 F	0030 0641 1247 1909	0.5 3.8 1.1 3.8
8 F	0006 0622 1235 1846	0.9 3.5 1.3 3.5	23 SA	0135 0749 1354 2015	0.6 3.8 1.1 3.9
9 SA	0118 0729 1347 1950	0.8 3.6 1.1 3.7	24 SU	0239 0852 1500 2113	0.6 3.9 1.0 3.9
10 SU	0217 0829 1445 2050	0.7 3.8 1.0 3.9	25 M	0335 0946 1556 2203	0.7 3.9 0.9 4.0
11 M	0309 0925 1536 2144	0.6 3.9 0.8 4.1	26 TU	0420 1031 1643 2246	0.7 4.0 0.7 4.1
12 TU	0358 1016 1625 2234	0.5 4.1 0.6 4.3	27 W	0458 1112 1725 2326	0.7 4.0 0.6 4.1
13 W	0445 1105 1714 ● 2322	0.4 4.2 0.5 4.4	28 TH	0534 1150 1805 ○	0.7 4.1 0.6
14 TH	0531 1154 1803	0.4 4.3 0.4	29 F	0003 0610 1226 1841	4.1 0.7 4.1 0.5
15 F	0010 0617 1242 1852	4.5 0.4 4.4 0.3	30 SA	0040 0644 1301 1915	4.2 0.7 4.1 0.5

JULY

Day	Time	m	Day	Time	m
1 SU	0117 0715 1335 1947	4.1 0.8 4.1 0.5	16 M	0137 0745 1406 2026	4.6 0.6 4.4 0.2
2 M	0153 0745 1409 2018	4.1 0.8 4.0 0.6	17 TU	0226 0831 1453 2114	4.5 0.7 4.4 0.2
3 TU	0229 0818 1444 2052	4.0 0.9 4.0 0.6	18 W	0317 0918 1542 2203	4.3 0.8 4.3 0.3
4 W	0305 0856 1521 2130	3.8 0.9 3.9 0.7	19 TH	0409 1007 1632 ◐ 2253	4.1 0.9 4.1 0.4
5 TH	0345 0938 1604 2215	3.8 1.0 3.8 0.7	20 F	0504 1101 1727 2348	4.0 1.0 4.0 0.6
6 F	0432 1029 1654 ◑ 2311	3.7 1.1 3.7 0.8	21 SA	0603 1203 1828	3.8 1.1 3.8
7 SA	0529 1134 1754	3.6 1.2 3.7	22 SU	0048 0708 1312 1936	0.8 3.7 1.2 3.8
8 SU	0021 0637 1253 1902	0.8 3.6 1.2 3.7	23 M	0153 0817 1426 2041	0.9 3.7 1.1 3.8
9 M	0133 0746 1405 2010	0.8 3.7 1.0 3.9	24 TU	0301 0918 1536 2138	0.9 3.8 1.0 3.9
10 TU	0235 0852 1507 2114	0.7 3.9 0.9 4.0	25 W	0356 1009 1630 2226	0.9 3.9 0.8 4.0
11 W	0332 0952 1604 2212	0.6 4.0 0.7 4.2	26 TH	0439 1053 1712 2308	0.9 4.0 0.7 4.0
12 TH	0426 1048 1659 2305	0.6 4.2 0.5 4.4	27 F	0517 1132 1749 ○ 2347	0.8 4.1 0.6 4.1
13 F	0518 1139 1754 ● 2357	0.5 4.3 0.4 4.5	28 SA	0553 1208 1824	0.8 4.1 0.5
14 SA	0609 1229 1847	0.5 4.4 0.2	29 SU	0023 0626 1243 1856	4.1 0.8 4.2 0.5
15 SU	0047 0657 1318 1937	4.6 0.6 4.4 0.2	30 M	0059 0657 1317 1927	4.2 0.8 4.2 0.5
			31 TU	0134 0728 1350 1958	4.1 0.8 4.2 0.5

AUGUST

Day	Time	m	Day	Time	m
1 W	0208 0759 1423 2029	4.1 0.8 4.1 0.5	16 TH	0253 0854 1513 2130	4.4 0.8 4.4 0.4
2 TH	0242 0834 1457 2102	4.0 0.9 4.0 0.6	17 F	0339 0936 1557 2211	4.1 0.9 4.2 0.6
3 F	0318 0911 1534 2138	3.9 1.0 4.0 0.7	18 SA	0427 1022 1645 ◐ 2258	3.9 1.0 4.0 0.8
4 SA	0359 0955 1617 ◑ 2225	3.8 1.1 3.9 0.8	19 SU	0520 1117 1742 2355	3.7 1.1 3.8 1.0
5 SU	0450 1052 1711 2329	3.7 1.1 3.8 0.9	20 M	0621 1225 1852	3.5 1.2 3.6
6 M	0553 1207 1819	3.7 1.2 3.8	21 TU	0103 0734 1346 2008	1.2 3.5 1.2 3.6
7 TU	0052 0708 1332 1937	0.9 3.6 1.1 3.8	22 W	0221 0847 1513 2113	1.2 3.6 1.1 3.7
8 W	0208 0825 1444 2052	0.9 3.7 0.9 4.0	23 TH	0332 0945 1612 2206	1.1 3.8 0.9 3.9
9 TH	0313 0936 1549 2157	0.8 3.9 0.7 4.2	24 F	0420 1031 1654 2249	1.0 3.9 0.7 4.0
10 F	0413 1035 1649 2253	0.7 4.1 0.5 4.4	25 SA	0458 1110 1728 2327	0.9 4.0 0.6 4.1
11 SA	0508 1127 1745 ● 2345	0.7 4.3 0.3 4.5	26 SU	0532 1146 1800 ○	0.8 4.1 0.5
12 SU	0558 1215 1837	0.6 4.4 0.2	27 M	0002 0604 1220 1831	4.2 0.8 4.2 0.5
13 M	0033 0645 1302 1924	4.6 0.6 4.5 0.1	28 TU	0037 0635 1253 1901	4.2 0.8 4.3 0.5
14 TU	0121 0730 1346 2009	4.6 0.6 4.6 0.1	29 W	0111 0706 1326 1931	4.2 0.7 4.3 0.5
15 W	0207 0812 1430 2050	4.5 0.7 4.5 0.2	30 TH	0144 0738 1358 2000	4.2 0.8 4.2 0.5
			31 F	0217 0811 1431 2030	4.1 0.8 4.2 0.6

Chart Datum: 2·16 metres below Ordnance Datum (Newlyn). HAT is 4·7 metres above Chart Datum.

STANDARD TIME (UT)
For Summer Time add ONE hour in **non-shaded areas**

WALTON-ON-THE-NAZE LAT 51°51′N LONG 1°17′E

TIMES AND HEIGHTS OF HIGH AND LOW WATERS

Dates in red are SPRINGS
Dates in blue are NEAPS

YEAR **2018**

SEPTEMBER

Date	Day	Time	m	Time	m	Time	m	Time	m
1	SA	0252	4.0	0847	0.9	1506	4.1	2104	0.7
2	SU	0331	3.9	0928	1.0	1547	4.0	2147	0.8
3	M	0417	3.8	1021	1.1	1639	3.9	◑ 2249	1.0
4	TU	0518	3.6	1135	1.1	1747	3.8		
5	W	0021	1.1	0637	3.5	1308	1.1	1913	3.7
6	TH	0148	1.1	0807	3.6	1428	0.9	2039	3.9
7	F	0259	0.9	0924	3.8	1538	0.6	2147	4.2
8	SA	0401	0.8	1023	4.1	1639	0.4	2242	4.4
9	SU	0455	0.7	1112	4.3	1732	0.2	● 2331	4.5
10	M	0542	0.7	1157	4.5	1819	0.1		
11	TU	0016	4.6	0626	0.6	1240	4.6	1902	0.1
12	W	0100	4.6	0708	0.6	1321	4.6	1942	0.2
13	TH	0143	4.5	0749	0.7	1402	4.5	2019	0.3
14	F	0224	4.3	0827	0.7	1441	4.4	2052	0.5
15	SA	0305	4.1	0904	0.8	1520	4.2	2127	0.7
16	SU	0346	3.9	0944	0.9	1603	3.9	◐ 2208	1.0
17	M	0432	3.6	1032	1.1	1656	3.7	2304	1.2
18	TU	0529	3.4	1137	1.2	1806	3.5		
19	W	0016	1.4	0641	3.3	1300	1.3	1929	3.5
20	TH	0139	1.4	0804	3.4	1432	1.1	2042	3.6
21	F	0258	1.3	0911	3.6	1540	0.9	2138	3.8
22	SA	0352	1.1	1000	3.8	1623	0.7	2222	4.0
23	SU	0431	1.0	1041	4.0	1658	0.6	2300	4.1
24	M	0506	0.9	1116	4.1	1729	0.5	2335	4.2
25	TU	0538	0.8	1150	4.2	1800	0.5		
		○							
26	W	0009	4.3	0609	0.7	1224	4.3	1830	0.5
27	TH	0043	4.3	0642	0.7	1258	4.3	1900	0.5
28	F	0117	4.3	0715	0.7	1332	4.3	1929	0.5
29	SA	0152	4.2	0749	0.7	1406	4.3	2000	0.6
30	SU	0228	4.1	0826	0.8	1443	4.2	2035	0.7

OCTOBER

Date	Day	Time	m	Time	m	Time	m	Time	m
1	M	0307	3.9	0908	0.8	1526	4.1	2121	0.9
2	TU	0353	3.8	1003	0.9	1619	3.9	◑ 2227	1.1
3	W	0453	3.6	1119	1.0	1728	3.8		
4	TH	0003	1.3	0616	3.5	1253	1.0	1902	3.7
5	F	0132	1.2	0753	3.5	1414	0.8	2029	3.9
6	SA	0244	1.1	0908	3.8	1524	0.6	2135	4.2
7	SU	0345	0.9	1005	4.1	1623	0.4	2228	4.4
8	M	0436	0.8	1052	4.3	1712	0.3	2313	4.5
9	TU	0521	0.7	1135	4.5	1755	0.2	● 2355	4.5
10	W	0604	0.6	1215	4.5	1835	0.2		
11	TH	0035	4.5	0644	0.6	1254	4.6	1911	0.3
12	F	0115	4.4	0724	0.6	1331	4.5	1944	0.5
13	SA	0153	4.3	0801	0.7	1408	4.3	2014	0.7
14	SU	0230	4.1	0836	0.8	1445	4.1	2045	0.9
15	M	0306	3.9	0911	0.9	1525	3.9	2121	1.1
16	TU	0345	3.7	0952	1.0	1614	3.6	◐ 2211	1.3
17	W	0436	3.4	1050	1.1	1720	3.4	2325	1.5
18	TH	0547	3.3	1210	1.2	1843	3.4		
19	F	0053	1.5	0706	3.3	1338	1.2	1957	3.5
20	SA	0213	1.4	0819	3.5	1448	1.0	2058	3.7
21	SU	0312	1.2	0916	3.7	1539	0.8	2145	3.9
22	M	0356	1.0	1001	3.9	1618	0.7	2225	4.1
23	TU	0433	0.9	1039	4.1	1652	0.6	2301	4.2
24	W	0507	0.8	1115	4.2	1725	0.5	○ 2337	4.3
25	TH	0542	0.7	1152	4.3	1758	0.5		
26	F	0014	4.3	0617	0.6	1229	4.4	1829	0.5
27	SA	0052	4.3	0654	0.6	1307	4.4	1901	0.5
28	SU	0130	4.3	0731	0.6	1346	4.4	1936	0.6
29	M	0209	4.1	0812	0.6	1427	4.3	2017	0.8
30	TU	0251	4.0	0858	0.7	1513	4.2	2109	1.0
31	W	0339	3.8	0957	0.8	1609	4.0	◑ 2220	1.2

NOVEMBER

Date	Day	Time	m	Time	m	Time	m	Time	m
1	TH	0442	3.6	1114	0.8	1722	3.8	2348	1.3
2	F	0606	3.5	1240	0.8	1852	3.8		
3	SA	0111	1.2	0734	3.6	1356	0.6	2012	3.9
4	SU	0222	1.1	0845	3.8	1504	0.5	2116	4.1
5	M	0323	1.0	0942	4.1	1601	0.4	2208	4.3
6	TU	0414	0.8	1029	4.3	1648	0.4	2252	4.4
7	W	0459	0.7	1111	4.4	1728	0.4	● 2332	4.4
8	TH	0541	0.6	1149	4.4	1805	0.4		
9	F	0011	4.4	0622	0.6	1227	4.4	1840	0.5
10	SA	0048	4.3	0702	0.5	1304	4.4	1912	0.6
11	SU	0124	4.2	0738	0.6	1340	4.3	1943	0.8
12	M	0158	4.1	0812	0.7	1417	4.1	2012	0.9
13	TU	0232	3.9	0844	0.8	1455	3.9	2045	1.1
14	W	0307	3.7	0921	0.9	1539	3.7	2128	1.3
15	TH	0351	3.6	1009	1.0	1634	3.5	◐ 2226	1.4
16	F	0452	3.4	1117	1.1	1749	3.4	2350	1.5
17	SA	0608	3.3	1240	1.1	1902	3.4		
18	SU	0118	1.5	0719	3.4	1351	1.0	2004	3.6
19	M	0223	1.3	0821	3.6	1447	0.8	2057	3.8
20	TU	0313	1.1	0913	3.8	1532	0.7	2144	4.0
21	W	0355	0.9	0959	4.0	1613	0.6	2226	4.1
22	TH	0435	0.8	1041	4.2	1651	0.5	2307	4.3
23	F	0515	0.7	1122	4.3	1728	0.5	○ 2348	4.3
24	SA	0556	0.6	1204	4.4	1806	0.5		
25	SU	0031	4.4	0637	0.5	1248	4.5	1844	0.6
26	M	0114	4.3	0721	0.5	1332	4.5	1925	0.7
27	TU	0158	4.2	0807	0.5	1418	4.4	2012	0.8
28	W	0244	4.1	0858	0.5	1508	4.2	2108	1.0
29	TH	0336	3.9	0958	0.6	1605	4.0	2213	1.1
30	F	0437	3.7	1108	0.6	1715	3.9	◑ 2327	1.2

DECEMBER

Date	Day	Time	m	Time	m	Time	m	Time	m
1	SA	0550	3.7	1222	0.6	1832	3.8		
2	SU	0042	1.2	0706	3.7	1331	0.5	1946	3.9
3	M	0153	1.1	0816	3.8	1436	0.5	2051	4.0
4	TU	0256	1.0	0915	4.0	1534	0.5	2145	4.1
5	W	0351	0.9	1004	4.1	1622	0.5	2231	4.2
6	TH	0439	0.8	1048	4.2	1703	0.6	2312	4.2
7	F	0522	0.6	1127	4.3	1740	0.6	● 2350	4.2
8	SA	0604	0.5	1205	4.3	1815	0.7		
9	SU	0027	4.2	0643	0.5	1242	4.3	1849	0.7
10	M	0102	4.2	0720	0.5	1319	4.2	1920	0.8
11	TU	0135	4.1	0753	0.6	1355	4.1	1950	0.9
12	W	0208	4.0	0824	0.7	1433	3.9	2021	1.0
13	TH	0243	3.9	0858	0.7	1512	3.8	2059	1.1
14	F	0322	3.7	0938	0.8	1555	3.6	2145	1.2
15	SA	0409	3.6	1029	0.9	1648	3.5	◐ 2241	1.4
16	SU	0507	3.5	1133	1.0	1755	3.4	2356	1.4
17	M	0616	3.5	1248	0.9	1903	3.5		
18	TU	0120	1.3	0722	3.5	1353	0.9	2004	3.7
19	W	0224	1.2	0824	3.7	1447	0.7	2100	3.8
20	TH	0316	1.0	0919	3.9	1536	0.6	2153	4.0
21	F	0405	0.8	1010	4.1	1622	0.6	2242	4.2
22	SA	0452	0.6	1059	4.3	1706	0.6	○ 2329	4.3
23	SU	0540	0.5	1146	4.4	1751	0.5		
24	M	0016	4.3	0627	0.4	1234	4.5	1836	0.6
25	TU	0104	4.4	0716	0.3	1322	4.5	1923	0.6
26	W	0151	4.3	0806	0.3	1411	4.5	2011	0.7
27	TH	0239	4.2	0857	0.3	1502	4.3	2102	0.9
28	F	0329	4.1	0951	0.3	1557	4.1	2158	1.0
29	SA	0423	4.0	1050	0.4	1657	4.0	◑ 2259	1.1
30	SU	0524	3.9	1153	0.5	1803	3.8		
31	M	0006	1.2	0631	3.8	1257	0.6	1912	3.8

Chart Datum: 2·16 metres below Ordnance Datum (Newlyn). HAT is 4·7 metres above Chart Datum.

9.4.19 & 20 RIVERS STOUR AND ORWELL

❁❁❁⛵⛵✿✿✿

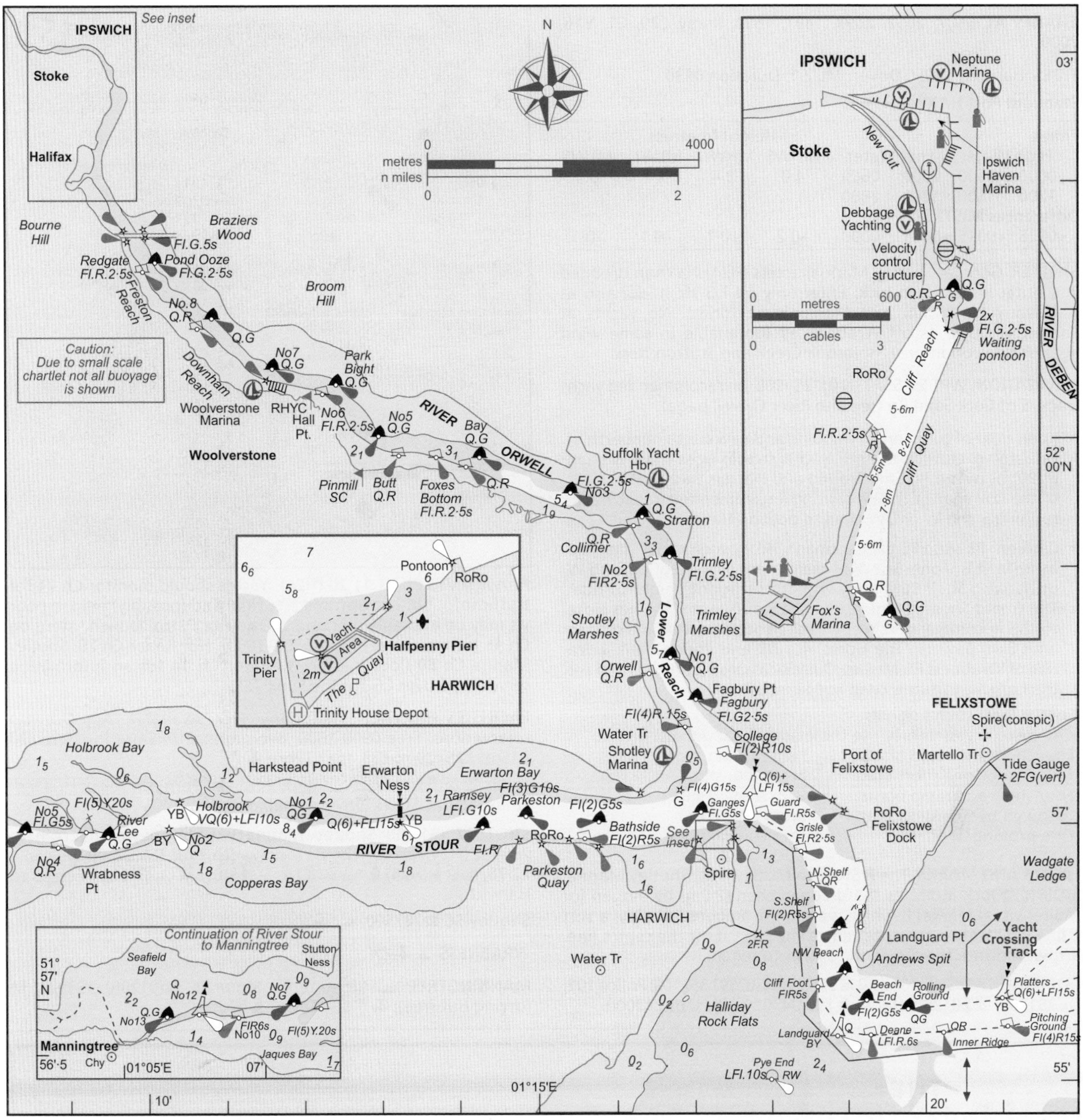

IPSWICH
Stoke
Halifax
See inset
N
metres
n miles
0
4000
2
Bourne Hill
Braziers Wood
Fl.G.5s
Redgate Fl.R.2·5s
Pond Ooze Fl.G.2·5s
Freston Reach
No.8 Q.R
Q.G
Broom Hill
Caution: Due to small scale chartlet not all buoyage is shown
Downham Reach
No7 Q.G
Park Bight Q.G
Woolverstone Marina
RHYC
Hall Pt.
No6 Fl.R.2·5s
No5 Q.G
RIVER ORWELL
Bay Q.G
Woolverstone
Pinmill SC
Butt Q.R
Foxes Bottom Fl.R.2·5s
Q.R
Suffolk Yacht Hbr
Fl.G.2·5s No3
Q.G Stratton
Collimer Q.R
Trimley Fl.G.2·5s
No2 FlR2·5s
Shotley Marshes
Lower Reach
Trimley Marshes
No1 Q.G
Orwell Q.R
Fagbury Pt
Fagbury Fl.G2·5s
Fl(4)R.15s
Water Tr
Shotley Marina
College Fl(2)R10s
Pontoon
RoRo
Halfpenny Pier
Trinity Pier
Yacht Area
The Quay
HARWICH
Trinity House Depot
IPSWICH
Neptune Marina
Stoke
New Cut
Ipswich Haven Marina
Debbage Yachting
Velocity control structure
metres
cables
600
Q.R
Q.G
2x Fl.G.2·5s Waiting pontoon
Cliff Reach
RoRo
Fl.R.2·5s
Cliff Quay
RIVER DEBEN
Fox's Marina
03'
52° 00'N
Holbrook Bay
Harkstead Point
Erwarton Ness
Erwarton Bay
FELIXSTOWE
Spire(conspic)
Martello Tr
Tide Gauge 2FG(vert)
Port of Felixstowe
No5 Fl.G5s
Fl(5)Y.20s
River Lee Q.G
Holbrook VQ(6)+LFl10s
No1 QG
Q(6)+LFl15s YB
Ramsey LFl.G10s
Fl(3)G10s Parkeston
Fl(2)G5s
Fl(4)G15s
G
Ganges Fl.G5s
Q(6)+ LFl 15s
Guard Fl.R5s
Grisle Fl.R2·5s
RoRo Felixstowe Dock
57'
No4 Q.R
BY No2 Q
Wrabness Pt
Copperas Bay
RIVER STOUR
Fl.R
RoRo
Bathside Fl(2)R5s
See inset
Parkeston Quay
Spire
N.Shelf QR
S.Shelf Fl(2)R5s
Wadgate Ledge
HARWICH
Landguard Pt
Yacht Crossing Track
Continuation of River Stour to Manningtree
Seafield Bay
Stutton Ness
No12
No7 Q.G
No13
FlR6s No10
Fl(5)Y.20s
Manningtree
Chy
Jaques Bay
51° 57' N
56'·5
01°05'E
07'
Water Tr
2FR
NW Beach
Andrews Spit
Cliff Foot FlR5s
Beach End Fl(2)G5s
Rolling Ground QG
Platters Q(6)+LFl15s YB
Halliday Rock Flats
Landguard BY
Deane LFl.R.6s
QR Inner Ridge
Pitching Ground Fl(4)R15s
Pye End LFl.10s RW
55'
10'
01°15'E
20'

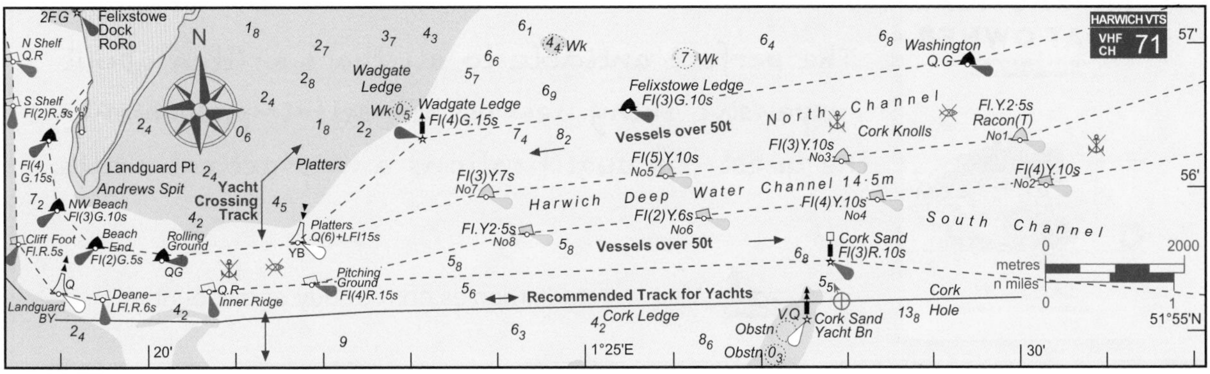

2F.G
Felixstowe Dock RoRo
N Shelf Q.R
S Shelf Fl(2)R.5s
Fl(4) G.15s
N
Wadgate Ledge
Wk
Wadgate Ledge Fl(4)G.15s
Felixstowe Ledge Fl(3)G.10s
Vessels over 50t
Washington Q.G
HARWICH VTS
VHF CH 71
57'
North Channel
Cork Knolls
Fl.Y.2·5s Racon(T) No1
Fl(3)Y.10s No3
Fl(5)Y.10s No5
Landguard Pt
Andrews Spit
Yacht Crossing Track
Platters
NW Beach Fl(3)G.10s
Fl(3)Y.7s No7
Harwich Deep Water Channel 14·5m
Fl(4)Y.10s No4
Fl(4)Y.10s No2
56'
Cliff Foot Fl.R.5s
Beach End Fl(2)G.5s
Rolling Ground QG
Platters Q(6)+LFl15s YB
Fl.Y2·5s No8
Fl(2)Y.6s No6
Vessels over 50t
South Channel
Cork Sand Fl(3)R.10s
metres
n miles
0
2000
1
Landguard BY
Q
Deane LFl.R.6s
Q.R Inner Ridge
Pitching Ground Fl(4)R.15s
Recommended Track for Yachts
Cork Hole
Cork Ledge
V.Q Cork Sand Yacht Bn
Obstn
51°55'N
20'
1°25'E
30'

E England

9.4.19 RIVER STOUR

Essex/Suffolk **51°57'·06N 01°17'·77E** (Guard PHM buoy)

CHARTS AC 5607, 2052, 2693, 1491, 1594; Imray C29, C1, Y16, 2000

TIDES Harwich +0050 Dover; ML 2·1; Duration 0630

Standard Port HARWICH (⟶)

Times				Height (metres)			
High Water		Low Water		MHWS	MHWN	MLWN	MLWS
0000	0600	0000	0600	4·0	3·4	1·1	0·4
1200	1800	1200	1800				
Differences MISTLEY							
+0025	+0015	+0005	0000	+0·2	+0·1	−0·1	−0·1

SHELTER Good at Shotley Marina; access (H24) via chan dredged 2m, outer limits lit, to lock. Enter only on F.G tfc lt. ⊆ also at Halfpenny Pier (H24) and Manningtree (dries). No yachts at Parkeston Quay. ⚓s off Wrabness Pt (untenable in some wind against tide conditions), Holbrook Creek and Stutton Ness.

NAVIGATION WPT 51°55'·33N 01°25'·50E, on recommended yacht track, S of Cork Sand Bn (see also River Orwell page).

- Keep clear of commercial shipping and new container berth at Felixstowe. Outside the hbr, yachts should cross the DW chan at 90° between Rolling Ground and Platters buoys. Stay clear of the DW chan (Y lit SPMs) using Recommended Yacht Track, running S and W of DW chan to beyond Harwich.
- **Caution**: Bkwtr, ESE of Blackman's Hd, covers at HW; marked by PHM lit Bn, only 5ca W of main chan. Beware of passing W of Harwich Shelf ECM buoy without sufficient height of tide. The Guard Shoal (0·8m), about 2ca S of Guard PHM, lies close to the Recommended Yacht Track. R Stour is well marked; sp limit 8kn. Beware 'The Horse' 4ca NE and drying bank 1½ca NW of Wrabness Pt. Mistley Quay local knowledge advised for the narrow, tortuous chan to Manningtree.

Special local sound signals

Commercial vessels may use these additional signals:

Four short and rapid blasts followed by one short blast	=	I am turning short around to stbd.
Four short and rapid blasts followed by two short blasts	=	I am turning short around to port.
One prolonged blast	=	I am leaving dock, quay or ⚓.

LIGHTS AND MARKS The R Stour to Mistley is lit. Shotley Marina: a Dir lt at lock indicates the dredged chan (2·0m) by Inogen (or Moiré) visual marker lt which is a square, ambered display; a vert B line indicates on the appr centre line 339°. If off the centre line, arrows indicate the direction to steer to regain it.

COMMUNICATIONS (Code 01255) NMOC 02392 552100; Police 101; Dr 201299; Ⓗ 201200. Harwich HM 243030; Hbr Ops 243000.

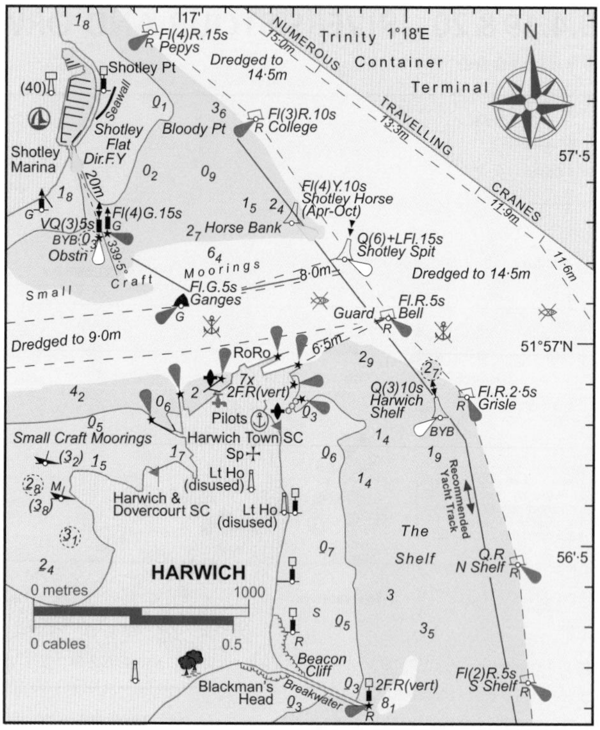

Harwich VTS Ch **71** 11 20 (H24). Yachts should monitor Ch 71 for traffic info, but not transmit. ⛅, tidal and (possibly) help in poor vis may be available on request. The Hbr Patrol launch listens on Ch 11 (summer weekends, 0800–1800). Hbr Radar Ch 20. Shotley Marina Ch **80** (lock master). Monitor Ch 14 for an information service by Dover CG for the Sunk TSS.

FACILITIES HARWICH Halfpenny Pier Available Apr–Oct, no reservations. Free 0900-1600; overnight: £10<5m>£15<10m>£20 <15m>£25<20m>£35, max 72hrs.

Town **Ferries** Hook of Holland: 2/day; 6¼hrs; Stena (www.stenaline.co.uk).

SHOTLEY (01473) **Shotley Marina** www.shotleymarina.com ☎ 788982 (H24), access H24 via lock (width 7m). 350⊆, Ⓥs welcome £2·75, (H24) (40t) Ferries to Harwich.

Shotley SC ☎787500.

WRABNESS

MANNINGTREE ⊆ (drying). **Stour SC** ☎(01206) 393924, M (drying but free). **Town**

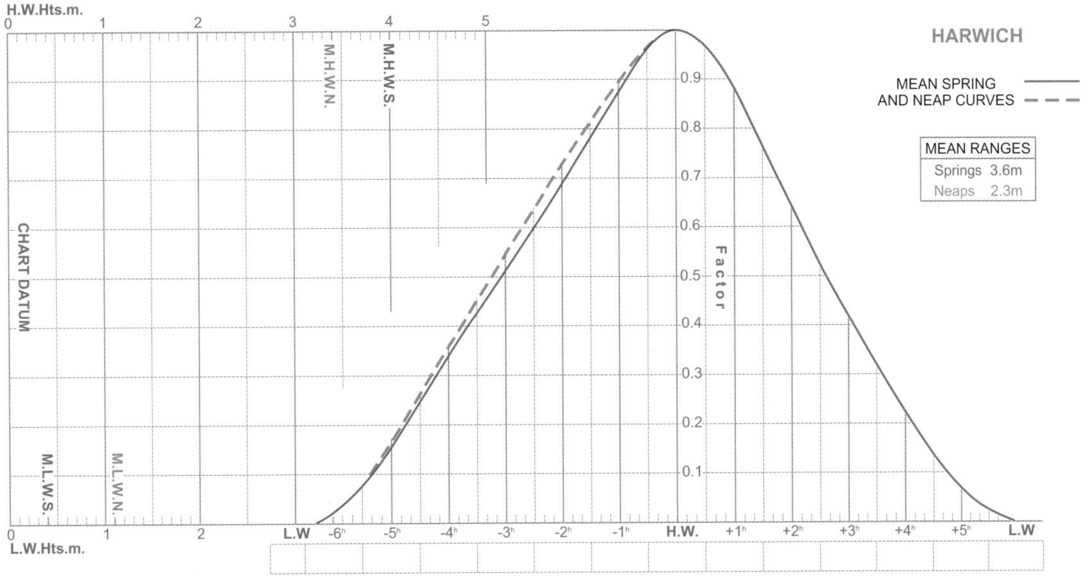

9.4.20 RIVER ORWELL

Suffolk **51°57'·06N 01°17'·77E** (Guard PHM by)

CHARTS AC 5607, 2052, 2693, 1491; Imray C29, C1,Y16, 2000

TIDES Pin Mill +0100 Dover; Ipswich +0115 Dover; ML 2·4; Duration 0555

Standard Port HARWICH (⟶)

Times				Height (metres)			
High Water		Low Water		MHWS	MHWN	MLWN	MLWS
0000	0600	0000	0600	4·0	3·4	1·1	0·4
1200	1800	1200	1800				
Differences IPSWICH							
+0015	+0025	0000	+0010	+0·2	0·0	–0·1	–0·1

SHELTER Good. Ent and river well marked, but many unlit moorings line both banks. ⚓s above Shotley Pt on W side, or off Pinmill. No yacht facilities at Felixstowe. Ⓥ's (pre-book) at Suffolk Yacht Hbr, Woolverstone Marina, Fox's Marina (Ipswich), Neptune Marina, Ipswich Haven Marina, the latter two accessed via Prince Philip Lock; *call Ch 68 at Orwell Bridge*.

NAVIGATION Approach/entry from seaward as for R Stour. WPT Shotley Spit SCM buoy, Q (6)+L Fl 15s, 51°57'·21N 01°17'·68E, at river ent. A *Yachting Guide to Harwich Harbour and its Rivers* has much useful info; it can be obtained free from Harwich Haven Authority, The Quay, Harwich CO12 3HH; ☎(01255) 243030.

- Keep clear of the many large ships, ferries from/to Harwich, Felixstowe and Ipswich, especially container ships turning between Trinity container terminal, Shotley Spit and Guard buoys.
- Ch 71 should be monitored whilst in Harwich Harbour but only used in emergency. Call sign Harwich VTS. Harwich HM 01255 243030. Refer also to 9.4.19 River Stour.
- 6kn speed limit in R Orwell. Ipswich Dock ent closed when tide >4.6m above CD. Ipswich New Cut entrance: ***Velocity Control Structure is raised from seabed when required with the top of it just below sea level***; 3 FR (vert) = no passage.

LIGHTS AND MARKS Suffolk Yacht Hbr appr marked by SWM then four bns and ldg lts: front Iso Y; rear Oc Y 4s.

A14 bridge lts: Centre FY (clearance 38m)
No 9 Pier 2 FR (vert) } shown up- and
No 10 Pier 2 FG (vert) } downstream.
● and ● tfc lts control ent to Ipswich Dock (H24).
Ipswich New Cut: 3 FR (vert) when closed to navigation.

COMMUNICATIONS (Code 01473) NMOC 02392 552100; Police 101; Ⓗ 712233; Orwell Navigation Service 211066, Ipswich HM 211771, Ipswich Lock Control 213526.

Ipswich Port Radio and *Ipswich Lock Control* VHF Ch 68 (H24). Once above Shotley Pt or anywhere in the area, monitor Ch 68 continuously in fog. Suffolk Yacht Hbr, Woolverstone Marina, Fox's Marina: Ch 80 M. Neptune Marina: Ch 80 (0800-1730LT), Ipswich Haven Marina Ch M 80.

FACILITIES

LEVINGTON Suffolk Yacht Hbr (SYH) info@syharbour.co.uk ☎659240, Ch 80. Access H24. (launch £25) 550+Ⓥ £2·76, (0815-1750) LPG ⓔ (10/60/75t) (15t).

Haven Ports YC ☎659658, ✕.

Town (Felixstowe), (bus to Ipswich), (Cambridge).

PIN MILL King's Boatyard ☎780258; M (£10 proceeds to RNLI, 07714 260568), LPG (6t) (1M).

Haven Ports YC ☎659658, ✕.

Pin Mill SC ☎780271.

WOOLVERSTONE Marina ☎780206 (H24), Mob 07803 968209. 235, Ⓥ £3·20 inc, (HO) (20t) ✕.

Royal Harwich YC Marina www.royalharwichyachtclub.co.uk ☎ 780319 mob 07742 145994; £2·11; ✕.

Town Chelmondiston: .

IPSWICH, Fox's Marina www.foxsmarina.com ☎ 689111, Ch 80. 75+Ⓥ £2·20, (0800-1730) € (44/70t) (7t) ACA wi-fi.

Marina YC ☎684111, ✕.

Orwell YC ☎602288.

Prince Philip Lock near city centre gives H24 access to:

Neptune Marina ☎215204, 150+Ⓥ £2·95, (0800-1700).

Ipswich Haven Marina ☎236644, 320+Ⓥ £2·52, (0800-1900) € (70t) ✕ wi-fi.

Town (Cambridge/Norwich).

STANDARD TIME (UT)
For Summer Time add ONE hour in **non-shaded areas**

HARWICH LAT 51°57′N LONG 1°17′E

TIMES AND HEIGHTS OF HIGH AND LOW WATERS

Dates in red are SPRINGS
Dates in blue are NEAPS

YEAR **2018**

JANUARY

Date	Day	Time	m
1	M	0409	0.6
		1038	4.0
		1636	0.5
		2310	4.1
2	TU	0501	0.4
		1130	4.2
		1723	0.4
	○		
3	W	0000	4.2
		0550	0.3
		1222	4.3
		1809	0.4
4	TH	0048	4.2
		0639	0.2
		1311	4.3
		1854	0.5
5	F	0135	4.2
		0727	0.2
		1400	4.3
		1939	0.6
6	SA	0222	4.1
		0816	0.2
		1449	4.1
		2024	0.7
7	SU	0308	4.0
		0906	0.3
		1538	4.0
		2110	0.9
8	M	0357	3.8
		0959	0.5
		1630	3.7
	◑	2202	1.1
9	TU	0449	3.6
		1100	0.6
		1726	3.5
		2306	1.2
10	W	0548	3.5
		1207	0.8
		1828	3.4
11	TH	0026	1.3
		0652	3.4
		1310	0.8
		1932	3.4
12	F	0136	1.2
		0758	3.4
		1406	0.9
		2035	3.4
13	SA	0237	1.1
		0859	3.5
		1459	0.9
		2131	3.6
14	SU	0331	0.9
		0954	3.6
		1546	0.8
		2221	3.7
15	M	0418	0.8
		1043	3.7
		1627	0.8
		2305	3.8
16	TU	0459	0.7
		1127	3.8
		1705	0.8
		2345	3.8
17	W	0533	0.6
		1205	3.8
		1740	0.7
	●		
18	TH	0019	3.8
		0606	0.6
		1240	3.8
		1814	0.7
19	F	0049	3.8
		0641	0.6
		1310	3.8
		1848	0.7
20	SA	0118	3.8
		0716	0.5
		1342	3.8
		1922	0.7
21	SU	0151	3.8
		0751	0.5
		1418	3.8
		1956	0.8
22	M	0226	3.8
		0827	0.5
		1458	3.8
		2033	0.8
23	TU	0306	3.8
		0904	0.6
		1543	3.7
		2115	0.8
24	W	0349	3.7
		0948	0.6
		1634	3.6
	◐	2203	0.9
25	TH	0441	3.6
		1039	0.7
		1732	3.5
		2300	1.0
26	F	0546	3.5
		1144	0.8
		1838	3.4
27	SA	0013	1.1
		0659	3.4
		1309	0.8
		1946	3.4
28	SU	0139	1.0
		0812	3.5
		1425	0.8
		2055	3.5
29	M	0253	0.8
		0922	3.7
		1529	0.7
		2159	3.7
30	TU	0357	0.6
		1024	3.9
		1624	0.6
		2256	3.9
31	W	0452	0.4
		1120	4.1
		1712	0.5
	○	2347	4.1

FEBRUARY

Date	Day	Time	m
1	TH	0542	0.2
		1211	4.2
		1757	0.4
2	F	0035	4.2
		0629	0.1
		1259	4.3
		1840	0.4
3	SA	0120	4.2
		0714	0.1
		1345	4.3
		1923	0.5
4	SU	0204	4.2
		0759	0.1
		1429	4.1
		2004	0.6
5	M	0245	4.1
		0842	0.2
		1512	4.0
		2044	0.7
6	TU	0327	3.9
		0925	0.4
		1554	3.8
		2124	0.9
7	W	0409	3.7
		1012	0.6
		1638	3.5
	◑	2210	1.0
8	TH	0457	3.5
		1110	0.8
		1727	3.3
		2312	1.2
9	F	0555	3.3
		1220	1.0
		1826	3.2
10	SA	0044	1.2
		0707	3.2
		1326	1.0
		1944	3.2
11	SU	0204	1.2
		0826	3.3
		1425	1.0
		2058	3.3
12	M	0307	1.0
		0930	3.4
		1518	0.9
		2155	3.5
13	TU	0358	0.8
		1022	3.6
		1604	0.8
		2243	3.7
14	W	0438	0.7
		1108	3.7
		1643	0.8
		2324	3.8
15	TH	0513	0.6
		1147	3.8
		1720	0.7
	●		
16	F	0001	3.8
		0546	0.5
		1223	3.8
		1755	0.7
17	SA	0034	3.8
		0621	0.5
		1255	3.8
		1830	0.6
18	SU	0104	3.8
		0656	0.4
		1325	3.8
		1904	0.6
19	M	0134	3.8
		0730	0.4
		1359	3.8
		1937	0.6
20	TU	0206	3.9
		0803	0.4
		1436	3.8
		2013	0.6
21	W	0243	3.9
		0839	0.4
		1517	3.8
		2053	0.6
22	TH	0324	3.8
		0920	0.5
		1603	3.6
		2139	0.7
23	F	0411	3.7
		1008	0.6
		1657	3.4
	◐	2232	0.9
24	SA	0511	3.5
		1108	0.8
		1803	3.3
		2341	1.0
25	SU	0629	3.3
		1239	1.0
		1918	3.2
26	M	0116	1.0
		0753	3.4
		1412	0.9
		2037	3.3
27	TU	0243	0.8
		0912	3.6
		1519	0.8
		2146	3.6
28	W	0350	0.6
		1016	3.8
		1614	0.6
		2243	3.9

MARCH

Date	Day	Time	m
1	TH	0444	0.3
		1109	4.1
		1700	0.5
		2332	4.1
2	F	0531	0.1
		1158	4.2
		1743	0.4
	○		
3	SA	0018	4.2
		0615	0.0
		1243	4.3
		1824	0.4
4	SU	0101	4.2
		0656	0.0
		1325	4.2
		1903	0.4
5	M	0141	4.2
		0736	0.1
		1405	4.1
		1940	0.5
6	TU	0219	4.1
		0813	0.3
		1442	3.9
		2015	0.6
7	W	0256	4.0
		0848	0.4
		1518	3.8
		2049	0.7
8	TH	0334	3.8
		0924	0.6
		1555	3.6
		2128	0.9
9	F	0417	3.6
		1008	0.9
		1638	3.4
	◑	2218	1.0
10	SA	0508	3.3
		1116	1.1
		1729	3.2
		2334	1.2
11	SU	0611	3.1
		1240	1.2
		1832	3.1
12	M	0114	1.2
		0742	3.1
		1349	1.2
		2008	3.1
13	TU	0231	1.0
		0903	3.3
		1447	1.0
		2123	3.3
14	W	0326	0.9
		0958	3.5
		1536	0.9
		2214	3.5
15	TH	0407	0.7
		1043	3.7
		1618	0.8
		2257	3.7
16	F	0444	0.5
		1123	3.8
		1656	0.7
		2335	3.8
17	SA	0520	0.4
		1158	3.9
		1732	0.6
	●		
18	SU	0010	3.8
		0556	0.4
		1232	3.9
		1807	0.5
19	M	0042	3.8
		0631	0.3
		1304	3.9
		1842	0.5
20	TU	0114	3.9
		0705	0.3
		1338	3.9
		1917	0.4
21	W	0147	3.9
		0739	0.3
		1414	3.9
		1954	0.4
22	TH	0224	4.0
		0816	0.3
		1454	3.8
		2035	0.5
23	F	0305	3.9
		0857	0.5
		1538	3.7
		2121	0.6
24	SA	0354	3.7
		0945	0.7
		1630	3.4
	◐	2215	0.8
25	SU	0454	3.5
		1045	1.0
		1737	3.2
		2327	0.9
26	M	0616	3.3
		1230	1.1
		1901	3.1
27	TU	0111	0.9
		0747	3.3
		1402	1.0
		2024	3.3
28	W	0236	0.7
		0903	3.6
		1506	0.9
		2130	3.6
29	TH	0339	0.4
		1003	3.9
		1558	0.7
		2225	3.8
30	F	0430	0.2
		1054	4.1
		1643	0.5
		2313	4.0
31	SA	0514	0.1
		1140	4.2
		1725	0.4
	○	2357	4.1

APRIL

Date	Day	Time	m
1	SU	0555	0.1
		1222	4.2
		1805	0.4
2	M	0038	4.1
		0633	0.1
		1302	4.1
		1842	0.4
3	TU	0117	4.1
		0709	0.2
		1338	4.0
		1917	0.5
4	W	0152	4.0
		0741	0.4
		1411	3.9
		1948	0.6
5	TH	0227	3.9
		0810	0.5
		1444	3.8
		2019	0.6
6	F	0304	3.8
		0843	0.7
		1519	3.6
		2057	0.7
7	SA	0345	3.6
		0922	0.9
		1601	3.5
		2144	0.9
8	SU	0433	3.4
		1017	1.1
		1651	3.3
	◑	2249	1.1
9	M	0531	3.2
		1148	1.3
		1751	3.1
10	TU	0020	1.1
		0642	3.1
		1308	1.3
		1902	3.1
11	W	0137	1.0
		0819	3.2
		1409	1.1
		2031	3.2
12	TH	0237	0.9
		0922	3.4
		1501	1.0
		2133	3.4
13	F	0326	0.7
		1009	3.7
		1546	0.8
		2220	3.6
14	SA	0409	0.5
		1050	3.8
		1626	0.7
		2301	3.7
15	SU	0449	0.4
		1127	3.9
		1705	0.5
		2339	3.8
16	M	0528	0.3
		1203	4.0
		1743	0.4
	●		
17	TU	0015	3.9
		0604	0.3
		1240	4.0
		1820	0.4
18	W	0052	4.0
		0641	0.3
		1317	4.0
		1858	0.3
19	TH	0129	4.0
		0718	0.3
		1355	4.0
		1939	0.3
20	F	0210	4.0
		0758	0.4
		1437	3.9
		2022	0.4
21	SA	0255	3.9
		0841	0.6
		1522	3.7
		2111	0.5
22	SU	0347	3.7
		0931	0.8
		1615	3.4
	◐	2208	0.7
23	M	0451	3.5
		1035	1.1
		1726	3.3
		2329	0.8
24	TU	0614	3.4
		1223	1.2
		1850	3.2
25	W	0105	0.7
		0736	3.5
		1343	1.1
		2004	3.4
26	TH	0218	0.6
		0845	3.7
		1444	0.9
		2107	3.6
27	F	0317	0.4
		0942	3.9
		1536	0.7
		2201	3.8
28	SA	0407	0.3
		1032	4.1
		1622	0.6
		2249	4.0
29	SU	0450	0.2
		1117	4.1
		1704	0.5
		2333	4.0
30	M	0530	0.2
		1159	4.1
		1744	0.5
	○		

Chart Datum: 2·02 metres below Ordnance Datum (Newlyn). HAT is 4·4 metres above Chart Datum.

STANDARD TIME (UT)
For Summer Time add ONE hour in **non-shaded areas**

HARWICH LAT 51°57′N LONG 1°17′E

TIMES AND HEIGHTS OF HIGH AND LOW WATERS

Dates in red are SPRINGS
Dates in blue are NEAPS

YEAR **2018**

MAY

Date	Time	m	Date	Time	m
1 TU	0014	4.0	16 W	0540	0.3
	0607	0.3		1215	4.1
	1238	4.0		1800	0.3
	1821	0.5			
2 W	0052	4.0	17 TH	0031	4.1
	0641	0.4		0620	0.3
	1312	3.9		1258	4.1
	1854	0.5		1842	0.3
3 TH	0127	3.9	18 F	0115	4.2
	0710	0.5		0701	0.3
	1342	3.8		1341	4.0
	1924	0.6		1927	0.2
4 F	0201	3.9	19 SA	0201	4.1
	0739	0.6		0744	0.5
	1413	3.8		1426	3.9
	1956	0.6		2014	0.3
5 SA	0237	3.8	20 SU	0250	4.0
	0811	0.8		0831	0.6
	1448	3.7		1514	3.8
	2034	0.7		2106	0.4
6 SU	0318	3.6	21 M	0345	3.8
	0850	0.9		0923	0.8
	1530	3.6		1610	3.6
	2119	0.8		2207	0.5
7 M	0404	3.4	22 TU	0450	3.7
	0937	1.1		1029	1.1
	1619	3.4		1718	3.4
	2218	0.9		◐ 2326	0.6
8 TU	0458	3.3	23 W	0603	3.6
	1049	1.3		1159	1.2
	1718	3.2		1831	3.4
	◑ 2336	1.0			
9 W	0601	3.2	24 TH	0045	0.6
	1219	1.3		0713	3.6
	1823	3.2		1314	1.1
				1937	3.5
10 TH	0049	1.0	25 F	0152	0.5
	0710	3.2		0817	3.7
	1325	1.2		1415	1.0
	1931	3.2		2038	3.6
11 F	0149	0.8	26 SA	0249	0.4
	0822	3.4		0914	3.8
	1420	1.0		1509	0.8
	2038	3.4		2133	3.8
12 SA	0243	0.7	27 SU	0339	0.4
	0920	3.6		1006	4.0
	1509	0.9		1558	0.7
	2134	3.6		2223	3.9
13 SU	0332	0.5	28 M	0423	0.4
	1008	3.8		1053	4.0
	1554	0.7		1643	0.6
	2222	3.7		2310	3.9
14 M	0417	0.4	29 TU	0504	0.4
	1052	4.0		1135	4.0
	1637	0.5		1724	0.6
	2306	3.9		○ 2352	3.9
15 TU	0459	0.3	30 W	0541	0.5
	1134	4.1		1214	3.9
	1718	0.4		1803	0.6
	● 2349	4.0			
			31 TH	0031	3.9
				0615	0.6
				1249	3.9
				1836	0.6

JUNE

Date	Time	m	Date	Time	m
1 F	0106	3.8	16 SA	0103	4.2
	0645	0.7		0648	0.4
	1318	3.8		1329	4.1
	1907	0.6		1918	0.2
2 SA	0140	3.8	17 SU	0153	4.2
	0715	0.7		0734	0.5
	1348	3.8		1417	4.0
	1939	0.6		2008	0.2
3 SU	0215	3.7	18 M	0244	4.1
	0749	0.8		0821	0.6
	1423	3.7		1507	3.9
	2017	0.6		2101	0.3
4 M	0254	3.6	19 TU	0338	4.0
	0827	0.9		0912	0.8
	1503	3.7		1600	3.8
	2100	0.7		2159	0.4
5 TU	0338	3.5	20 W	0436	3.8
	0910	1.0		1011	1.0
	1550	3.5		1659	3.6
	2151	0.8		◐ 2306	0.5
6 W	0428	3.4	21 TH	0538	3.7
	1002	1.2		1123	1.1
	1645	3.4		1802	3.6
	◑ 2254	0.9			
7 TH	0524	3.4	22 F	0015	0.5
	1115	1.2		0642	3.6
	1745	3.3		1238	1.1
				1904	3.5
8 F	0003	0.9	23 SA	0119	0.6
	0625	3.4		0744	3.6
	1232	1.2		1343	1.1
	1848	3.3		2006	3.6
9 SA	0106	0.8	24 SU	0216	0.6
	0728	3.4		0843	3.7
	1334	1.1		1441	0.9
	1950	3.4		2104	3.7
10 SU	0203	0.7	25 M	0308	0.6
	0830	3.6		0938	3.8
	1429	0.9		1534	0.8
	2049	3.6		2158	3.8
11 M	0256	0.6	26 TU	0355	0.6
	0927	3.8		1028	3.8
	1521	0.8		1622	0.7
	2145	3.7		2247	3.8
12 TU	0347	0.5	27 W	0438	0.6
	1019	3.9		1113	3.9
	1610	0.6		1707	0.6
	2237	3.9		2333	3.9
13 W	0434	0.4	28 TH	0517	0.7
	1108	4.1		1154	3.9
	1657	0.4		1747	0.6
	● 2326	4.1		○	
14 TH	0519	0.3	29 F	0014	3.8
	1155	4.1		0552	0.7
	1744	0.3		1230	3.8
				1821	0.6
15 F	0014	4.2	30 SA	0051	3.8
	0603	0.3		0625	0.8
	1242	4.2		1301	3.8
	1830	0.2		1853	0.6

JULY

Date	Time	m	Date	Time	m
1 SU	0124	3.7	16 M	0142	4.3
	0658	0.8		0721	0.5
	1329	3.8		1404	4.2
	1926	0.6		1958	0.1
2 M	0156	3.7	17 TU	0231	4.2
	0732	0.8		0807	0.6
	1402	3.8		1451	4.1
	2003	0.6		2047	0.1
3 TU	0232	3.7	18 W	0321	4.1
	0807	0.9		0854	0.7
	1440	3.7		1539	4.0
	2042	0.6		2138	0.3
4 W	0313	3.7	19 TH	0411	3.9
	0846	0.9		0944	0.9
	1522	3.7		1629	3.8
	2124	0.7		◐ 2235	0.4
5 TH	0358	3.6	20 F	0505	3.7
	0929	1.0		1042	1.1
	1610	3.6		1725	3.7
	2211	0.7		2338	0.6
6 F	0450	3.5	21 SA	0604	3.6
	1020	1.1		1154	1.2
	1705	3.5		1826	3.5
	◑ 2309	0.8			
7 SA	0547	3.5	22 SU	0041	0.7
	1124	1.2		0706	3.5
	1806	3.4		1307	1.2
				1931	3.5
8 SU	0016	0.8	23 M	0141	0.8
	0648	3.5		0809	3.5
	1240	1.1		1412	1.1
	1909	3.4		2035	3.5
9 M	0122	0.8	24 TU	0237	0.9
	0750	3.5		0909	3.6
	1347	1.0		1511	1.0
	2012	3.5		2135	3.6
10 TU	0223	0.7	25 W	0328	0.8
	0852	3.7		1003	3.7
	1449	0.9		1604	0.8
	2115	3.7		2228	3.7
11 W	0321	0.6	26 TH	0414	0.8
	0952	3.8		1051	3.8
	1547	0.7		1651	0.7
	2214	3.9		2315	3.8
12 TH	0414	0.5	27 F	0455	0.8
	1047	4.0		1134	3.9
	1641	0.5		1731	0.6
	2309	4.1		○ 2357	3.8
13 F	0504	0.4	28 SA	0532	0.8
	1139	4.1		1212	3.9
	1732	0.3		1805	0.6
	●				
14 SA	0002	4.2	29 SU	0035	3.8
	0550	0.4		0606	0.8
	1229	4.2		1246	3.8
	1821	0.2		1836	0.6
15 SU	0053	4.3	30 M	0108	3.8
	0636	0.4		0640	0.8
	1317	4.2		1314	3.8
	1909	0.1		1909	0.5
			31 TU	0138	3.7
				0713	0.8
				1343	3.8
				1943	0.5

AUGUST

Date	Time	m	Date	Time	m
1 W	0210	3.8	16 TH	0256	4.1
	0747	0.8		0830	0.7
	1416	3.8		1511	4.1
	2018	0.5		2109	0.3
2 TH	0246	3.8	17 F	0340	3.9
	0822	0.8		0913	0.8
	1452	3.8		1554	3.9
	2053	0.6		2156	0.5
3 F	0328	3.7	18 SA	0425	3.7
	0900	0.9		0959	1.0
	1533	3.7		1642	3.7
	2132	0.6		◐ 2252	0.8
4 SA	0415	3.6	19 SU	0515	3.5
	0945	1.0		1100	1.2
	1621	3.6		1738	3.5
	◑ 2219	0.7		2359	1.0
5 SU	0509	3.5	20 M	0614	3.3
	1038	1.1		1226	1.3
	1720	3.5		1849	3.3
	2318	0.8			
6 M	0611	3.4	21 TU	0105	1.1
	1145	1.1		0728	3.3
	1830	3.4		1343	1.2
				2007	3.3
7 TU	0038	0.9	22 W	0205	1.1
	0716	3.4		0839	3.4
	1308	1.1		1448	1.1
	1941	3.5		2112	3.5
8 W	0156	0.9	23 TH	0301	1.0
	0824	3.5		0938	3.6
	1425	1.0		1545	0.9
	2052	3.6		2207	3.7
9 TH	0303	0.8	24 F	0350	0.9
	0931	3.7		1027	3.8
	1532	0.7		1631	0.7
	2159	3.8		2254	3.8
10 F	0401	0.7	25 SA	0432	0.9
	1031	3.9		1111	3.9
	1631	0.5		1708	0.6
	2257	4.1		2337	3.9
11 SA	0451	0.5	26 SU	0509	0.8
	1124	4.1		1151	3.9
	1723	0.3		1740	0.6
	● 2350	4.3		○	
12 SU	0538	0.5	27 M	0014	3.9
	1213	4.2		0543	0.8
	1811	0.1		1225	3.9
				1811	0.5
13 M	0039	4.4	28 TU	0047	3.9
	0621	0.5		0617	0.8
	1300	4.3		1254	3.9
	1856	0.0		1844	0.5
14 TU	0126	4.4	29 W	0116	3.8
	0705	0.5		0651	0.8
	1345	4.3		1321	3.9
	1941	0.0		1917	0.5
15 W	0212	4.3	30 TH	0145	3.8
	0747	0.6		0724	0.7
	1428	4.2		1350	3.9
	2025	0.1		1950	0.5
			31 F	0219	3.8
				0757	0.7
				1423	3.9
				2022	0.5

Chart Datum: 2·02 metres below Ordnance Datum (Newlyn). HAT is 4·4 metres above Chart Datum.

STANDARD TIME (UT)
For Summer Time add ONE hour in **non-shaded areas**

HARWICH LAT 51°57′N LONG 1°17′E

TIMES AND HEIGHTS OF HIGH AND LOW WATERS

Dates in red are SPRINGS
Dates in blue are NEAPS

YEAR **2018**

SEPTEMBER

Date	Day	Time	m	Time	m	Time	m	Time	m
1	SA	0257	3.8	0835	0.8	1501	3.9	2059	0.6
2	SU	0340	3.7	0918	0.8	1545	3.8	2143	0.7
3	M	0431	3.5	1008	1.0	1641	3.6	◑ 2237	0.9
4	TU	0534	3.4	1111	1.1	1755	3.4	2355	1.1
5	W	0647	3.3	1240	1.1	1919	3.4		
6	TH	0139	1.1	0803	3.4	1412	1.0	2039	3.5
7	F	0251	1.0	0916	3.6	1524	0.7	2149	3.8
8	SA	0349	0.8	1016	3.9	1622	0.4	2245	4.1
9	SU	0438	0.6	1108	4.1	1710	0.2	● 2335	4.3
10	M	0522	0.5	1154	4.3	1755	0.1		
11	TU	0021	4.4	0603	0.5	1239	4.3	1836	0.1
12	W	0105	4.4	0644	0.5	1321	4.3	1917	0.1
13	TH	0147	4.2	0724	0.6	1401	4.2	1956	0.3
14	F	0226	4.1	0802	0.7	1439	4.1	2034	0.4
15	SA	0304	3.9	0839	0.8	1518	3.9	2113	0.7
16	SU	0343	3.7	0918	1.0	1600	3.7	◐ 2156	0.9
17	M	0424	3.5	1007	1.1	1651	3.5	2302	1.2
18	TU	0514	3.3	1127	1.3	1756	3.2		
19	W	0024	1.3	0620	3.2	1309	1.3	1933	3.2
20	TH	0133	1.3	0801	3.2	1418	1.1	2047	3.4
21	F	0231	1.2	0907	3.5	1515	0.9	2142	3.6
22	SA	0322	1.1	0958	3.7	1600	0.8	2229	3.8
23	SU	0404	0.9	1042	3.8	1635	0.6	2310	4.0
24	M	0441	0.8	1121	3.9	1707	0.5	2346	4.0
25	TU	0517	0.7	1156	3.9	1741	0.5	○	
26	W	0018	4.0	0551	0.7	1226	3.9	1815	0.5
27	TH	0048	3.9	0626	0.7	1255	3.9	1849	0.5
28	F	0119	4.0	0700	0.7	1324	4.0	1921	0.5
29	SA	0152	3.9	0735	0.6	1358	4.0	1955	0.5
30	SU	0229	3.9	0813	0.7	1438	4.0	2033	0.6

OCTOBER

Date	Day	Time	m	Time	m	Time	m	Time	m
1	M	0311	3.8	0857	0.8	1523	3.8	2117	0.8
2	TU	0359	3.6	0948	0.9	1619	3.6	◑ 2211	1.1
3	W	0501	3.3	1052	1.1	1735	3.4	2330	1.3
4	TH	0624	3.2	1232	1.1	1908	3.4		
5	F	0129	1.2	0749	3.3	1404	0.9	2030	3.6
6	SA	0237	1.1	0859	3.6	1511	0.6	2135	3.9
7	SU	0332	0.9	0956	3.9	1605	0.4	2228	4.2
8	M	0419	0.7	1046	4.1	1651	0.2	2315	4.3
9	TU	0502	0.6	1132	4.2	1733	0.2	● 2359	4.3
10	W	0543	0.5	1214	4.3	1812	0.2		
11	TH	0040	4.3	0622	0.5	1255	4.3	1850	0.3
12	F	0119	4.2	0700	0.6	1332	4.2	1925	0.4
13	SA	0155	4.0	0735	0.7	1409	4.1	1958	0.6
14	SU	0229	3.9	0808	0.8	1446	3.9	2030	0.8
15	M	0303	3.7	0844	0.9	1526	3.7	2106	1.0
16	TU	0342	3.6	0928	1.0	1614	3.5	◐ 2156	1.3
17	W	0430	3.4	1032	1.2	1712	3.3	2327	1.5
18	TH	0531	3.2	1213	1.2	1830	3.2		
19	F	0051	1.5	0648	3.2	1331	1.1	2009	3.3
20	SA	0154	1.3	0821	3.3	1428	1.0	2107	3.5
21	SU	0245	1.2	0918	3.5	1513	0.8	2154	3.8
22	M	0329	1.0	1004	3.7	1553	0.6	2235	3.9
23	TU	0409	0.8	1044	3.8	1631	0.5	2311	4.0
24	W	0447	0.7	1121	3.9	1709	0.5	○ 2346	4.1
25	TH	0525	0.7	1155	4.0	1746	0.4		
26	F	0019	4.1	0601	0.6	1229	4.0	1821	0.5
27	SA	0054	4.1	0638	0.6	1304	4.1	1856	0.5
28	SU	0130	4.0	0716	0.5	1342	4.1	1933	0.6
29	M	0208	3.9	0758	0.6	1425	4.0	2014	0.7
30	TU	0251	3.8	0843	0.7	1513	3.9	2100	0.9
31	W	0339	3.6	0936	0.8	1612	3.6	◑ 2155	1.1

NOVEMBER

Date	Day	Time	m	Time	m	Time	m	Time	m
1	TH	0442	3.4	1045	0.9	1730	3.5	2319	1.3
2	F	0611	3.3	1226	0.9	1859	3.5		
3	SA	0108	1.3	0730	3.4	1346	0.8	2012	3.7
4	SU	0214	1.1	0835	3.6	1448	0.6	2112	3.9
5	M	0308	0.9	0931	3.9	1541	0.4	2205	4.1
6	TU	0356	0.8	1022	4.0	1626	0.3	2252	4.2
7	W	0440	0.6	1107	4.1	1707	0.3	● 2335	4.2
8	TH	0522	0.6	1150	4.2	1746	0.4		
9	F	0015	4.2	0601	0.6	1231	4.1	1822	0.5
10	SA	0053	4.1	0638	0.6	1308	4.1	1856	0.6
11	SU	0126	4.0	0712	0.7	1343	4.0	1925	0.8
12	M	0157	3.9	0743	0.7	1419	3.9	1956	0.9
13	TU	0229	3.8	0818	0.8	1458	3.7	2032	1.0
14	W	0308	3.7	0901	0.9	1543	3.5	2116	1.2
15	TH	0355	3.5	0956	1.0	1635	3.4	◐ 2217	1.4
16	F	0452	3.3	1113	1.1	1738	3.2	2352	1.5
17	SA	0559	3.2	1229	1.1	1850	3.2		
18	SU	0103	1.4	0711	3.3	1331	1.0	2005	3.4
19	M	0200	1.2	0818	3.4	1423	0.8	2103	3.6
20	TU	0249	1.1	0914	3.6	1511	0.7	2150	3.8
21	W	0334	0.9	1002	3.8	1556	0.6	2232	4.0
22	TH	0417	0.7	1045	3.9	1639	0.5	2313	4.1
23	F	0458	0.6	1126	4.0	1719	0.5	○ 2353	4.1
24	SA	0539	0.5	1206	4.1	1758	0.5		
25	SU	0033	4.1	0620	0.5	1248	4.2	1837	0.5
26	M	0114	4.1	0702	0.4	1332	4.2	1918	0.6
27	TU	0156	4.0	0747	0.5	1419	4.1	2002	0.7
28	W	0241	3.8	0836	0.5	1510	3.9	2050	0.9
29	TH	0332	3.6	0931	0.6	1610	3.7	2145	1.1
30	F	0436	3.5	1040	0.7	1721	3.6	◑ 2301	1.3

DECEMBER

Date	Day	Time	m	Time	m	Time	m	Time	m
1	SA	0552	3.4	1206	0.7	1836	3.6		
2	SU	0034	1.3	0703	3.5	1319	0.7	1944	3.7
3	M	0143	1.2	0806	3.6	1419	0.6	2044	3.8
4	TU	0240	1.0	0904	3.8	1512	0.5	2138	3.9
5	W	0332	0.9	0956	3.9	1559	0.5	2227	4.0
6	TH	0419	0.7	1045	4.0	1642	0.5	2312	4.0
7	F	0503	0.7	1129	4.0	1722	0.6	● 2353	4.0
8	SA	0544	0.6	1211	4.0	1759	0.7		
9	SU	0030	4.0	0622	0.6	1249	3.9	1831	0.7
10	M	0103	3.9	0655	0.6	1324	3.9	1901	0.8
11	TU	0133	3.8	0726	0.7	1358	3.8	1933	0.9
12	W	0205	3.8	0800	0.7	1435	3.7	2008	1.0
13	TH	0242	3.7	0841	0.8	1516	3.6	2049	1.1
14	F	0326	3.6	0928	0.9	1603	3.5	2136	1.2
15	SA	0417	3.5	1025	0.9	1657	3.4	◐ 2238	1.3
16	SU	0516	3.3	1133	1.0	1757	3.3	2357	1.4
17	M	0620	3.3	1238	0.9	1900	3.4		
18	TU	0105	1.3	0723	3.4	1338	0.9	2002	3.5
19	W	0204	1.1	0824	3.5	1432	0.7	2102	3.7
20	TH	0257	1.0	0921	3.7	1524	0.6	2155	3.8
21	F	0347	0.8	1013	3.8	1612	0.6	2244	4.0
22	SA	0434	0.6	1102	4.0	1657	0.5	○ 2331	4.1
23	SU	0520	0.5	1149	4.1	1741	0.5		
24	M	0017	4.1	0606	0.4	1237	4.2	1823	0.5
25	TU	0103	4.1	0652	0.3	1325	4.2	1907	0.6
26	W	0149	4.0	0740	0.3	1414	4.2	1952	0.7
27	TH	0236	3.9	0829	0.3	1505	4.0	2040	0.8
28	F	0326	3.8	0922	0.4	1600	3.9	2131	1.0
29	SA	0421	3.7	1022	0.5	1700	3.7	◑ 2231	1.1
30	SU	0523	3.6	1133	0.6	1804	3.6	2349	1.2
31	M	0629	3.5	1244	0.7	1910	3.5		

Chart Datum: 2·02 metres below Ordnance Datum (Newlyn). HAT is 4·4 metres above Chart Datum.

9.4.21 RIVER DEBEN

Suffolk **51°59'·38N 01°23'·58E** (Felixstowe Ferry)

CHARTS AC 5607, 2052, 2693; Imray C29, C1, C28, Y16, 2000

TIDES Woodbridge Haven +0025 Dover; Woodbridge +0105 Dover; ML 1·9; Duration 0635

Standard Port WALTON-ON-THE-NAZE (⟵)

Times				Height (metres)			
High Water		Low Water		MHWS	MHWN	MLWN	MLWS
0100	0700	0100	0700	4·2	3·4	1·1	0·4
1300	1900	1300	1900				
Differences *FELIXSTOWE PIER* (51° 57'N 1° 21'E)							
–0005	*–0007*	*–0018*	*–0020*	*–0·5*	*–0·4*	*0·0*	*0·0*
BAWDSEY							
–0016	–0020	–0030	–0032	–0·8	–0·6	–0·1	–0·1
WOODBRIDGE HAVEN (Entrance)							
0000	–0005	–0020	–0025	–0·5	–0·5	–0·1	+0·1
WOODBRIDGE (Town)							
+0045	+0025	+0025	–0020	–0·2	–0·3	–0·2	0·0

SHELTER Good in Tide Mill Yacht Hbr (TMYH) Woodbridge. ⚓s upriver, clear of moorings: N of Horse Sand; off Ramsholt, The Rocks, Waldringfield, The Tips, Methersgate, Kyson Pt and Woodbridge.

NAVIGATION WPT 51°58'·20N 01°23'·85E Woodbridge Haven SWM buoy, thence NNW'ly past W Knoll PHM to Mid Knoll SHM and then head north upriver to the entrance hugging the sea wall/W bank until close to Deben PHM. Chartlet shows the ent at latest survey (2017), showing west'ly movement of the Knolls. Depths can change significantly and buoyage is often adjusted. Visitors may obtain updates at www.debenestuarypilot.co.uk.

Cross the shifting shingle bar HW–3 to HW+2 depending on draught. When Horse Sand is covered there is approx 2m at the bar. Best to enter after half-flood, and leave on the flood. The ent is only 1ca wide and in strong onshore winds gets dangerously choppy; channel is well buoyed/marked. Keep to the W shore until PHM opposite the SC, then move E of Horse Sand. No commercial traffic. 8kn max speed N of Green Reach.

LIGHTS AND MARKS See 9.4.4 and chartlets.

COMMUNICATIONS (Code 01473) NMOC 02392 552100; Police 101.

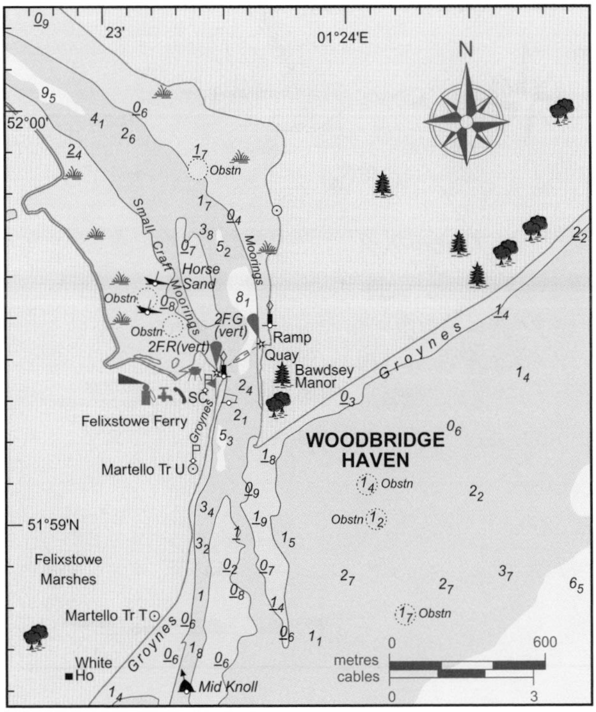

HM mob 07803 476621, Asst HM mob 07860 191768.

Pilotage for river entr, call *Odd Times* Ch 08 or HM on mobile.

FACILITIES

FELIXSTOWE FERRY (01394); Felixstowe Ferry SC ☎283785, 200 (£10) ☎282173.

RAMSHOLT HM ☎07930 304061.

WALDRINGFIELD AC 2693. Craft >11m should ⚓ at the Rocks (NW of Prettyman's Pt) or upriver at The Tips. Possibly for <11m by arrangement with HM waldringfieldhm @ btinternet.com ☎736291 mob 07925 081062; may have, ☎736260 VHF 80;. Sailing Club www.waldringfieldsc.com (Wed and Sat evenings only).

WOODBRIDGE (01394) **Tide Mill Yacht Hbr**, 200+Ⓥ (max 24m) £2. info@tidemillyachtharbour.co.uk; ☎385745. Ent by No 26 PHM. Depth over sill, dries 1·5m, is 1·6m at MHWN and 2·5m MHWS, with very accurate tide gauge and 6 waiting buoys. Ⓔ (18t) ACA.

Woodbridge Cruising Club ☎386737.

Deben YC www.debenyachtclub.co.uk.

Town Ⓑ ✈ (Cambridge, Norwich).

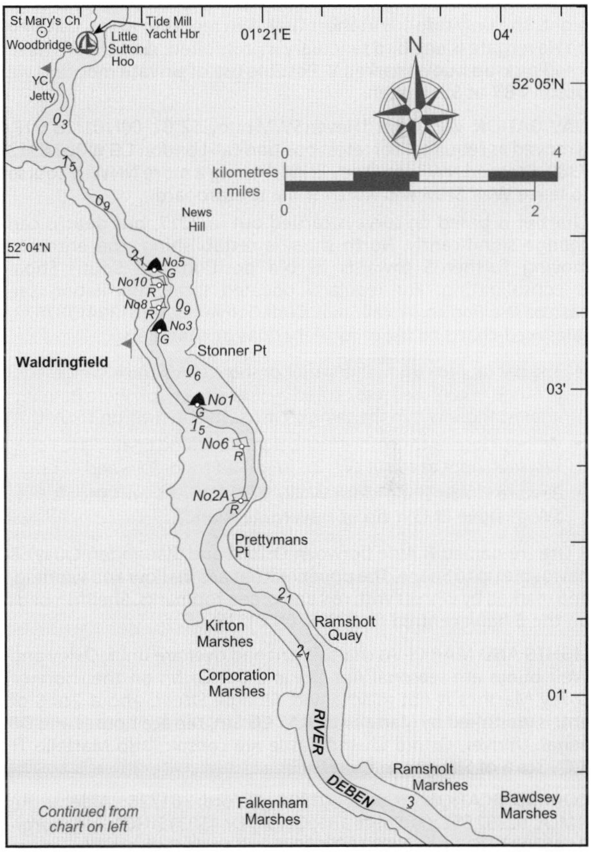

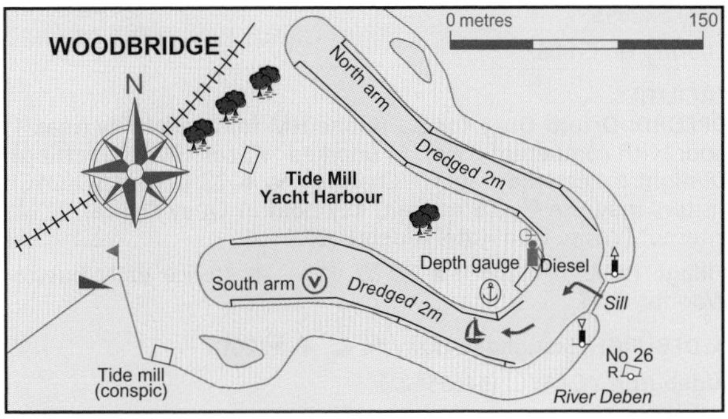

9.4.22 RIVER ORE/ALDE

Suffolk **52°02'·13N 01°27'·49E** (Ent) ❀◊◊◊✿✿✿

CHARTS AC 5607, 1543, 2052, 2693, 2695; Imray C29, C28, 2000

TIDES Ent. +0015 Dover Slaughden Quay +0155 Dover; ML1·6; Duration 0620

Standard Port WALTON-ON-THE-NAZE (⟵)

Times				Height (metres)			
High Water		Low Water		MHWS	MHWN	MLWN	MLWS
0100	0700	0100	0700	4·2	3·4	1·1	0·4
1300	1900	1300	1900				
Differences ORFORD HAVEN BAR							
–0026	–0030	–0036	–0038	–1·0	–0·8	–0·1	0·0
ORFORD QUAY							
+0040	+0040	+0055	+0055	–1·4	–1·1	0·0	+0·2
SLAUGHDEN QUAY							
+0105	+0105	+0125	+0125	–1·3	–0·8	–0·1	+0·2
IKEN CLIFF							
+0130	+0130	+0155	+0155	–1·3	–1·0	0·0	+0·2

SHELTER Good shelter within the river, but the entrance should not be attempted in strong E/ESE onshore winds and rough seas or at night. The only safe ⚓ is in Short Gull; ⚓ in mooring areas. Landing on Havergate Island bird sanctuary is prohibited. Ⓜ at Orford have small pick-up buoys marked V. Possible use of private mooring via Upson's BY at Slaughden.

NAVIGATION WPT Orford Haven SWM buoy, 52°02'·00N 01°28'·21E, is moved as required. For latest position call London CG ☎020 8312 7380. Proceed NW'ly to Oxley PHM shaping a more NNW'ly course to leave Weir SHM and North Shoal to starboard.

Chartlet is based on surveys carried out in 2017, but depths can change significantly. North shoal is restablishing, the entrance moving further S towards its old position and South Shoal is consolidating. For regularly updated local information see *eastcoastsailing.co.uk*, call Small Craft Deliveries: ☎(01394) 387672, sales@scd-charts.co.uk; or local marinas or chandlers.

- The bar (approx 0·5m) shifts after onshore gales and is dangerous in rough or confused seas caused by tidal streams offshore running against those within the shingle banks. Sp ebb runs up to 6kn.
- Without local info do not enter before half flood or at night. For a first visit, appr at about LW+2½ in settled conditions and at nps.
- Beware Horse Shoal close WNW of N Weir Pt and shoals S & SW of Dove Pt (SW tip of Havergate Island).

R Ore (re-named R Alde between Orford and Slaughden Quay) is navigable up to Snape. The upper reaches are shallow and winding, and marked by withies with red and green topmarks. Shellfish beds on the E bank centred on 52°08'·0N 01°35'·6E.

LIGHTS AND MARKS As chartlet. Ent and river are unlit. Oxley and Weir buoys are seasonal Apr-Oct and the Or bn on the shore of Oxley Marshes is not maintained. Shingle Street, about 2ca S of ent, is identified by Martello tr 'AA', CG Stn, terrace houses and DF aerial. Upriver, Orford Ch and Castle are conspic; also Martello Tr 'CC', 3ca S of Slaughden Quay.

COMMUNICATIONS (Codes 01394 Orford; 01728 Aldeburgh) NMOC 02392 552100; Police 101; Orford Dr 450315(HO); Aldeburgh Dr 452027(HO). HM 07528 092635; Small Craft Deliveries (pilotage info) 382655.

Chantry on Ch 08.

FACILITIES

ORFORD: Orford Quay for ⛵ phone HM for availability (max 1 hour with competent crew); M (marked 'V'; call HM. No rafting) £8/night collected by launch 'Chantry'; ⛵ ⛽ ☏ Orford SC (OSC) visitors may use 🚿 (£6 deposit, key held in Quay Office), ✕ ☐ Internet (White Lion Hotel Aldeburgh).

Village (¼M) ☏ ☏(HO) ⚗ ✉ 🛒 ✕ ☐ ⇄ (twice daily bus to Woodbridge).

ALDEBURGH: Slaughden Quay ⛵ ⛵ ⛽ ⚑(20t).

Aldeburgh YC (AYC) ☎452562 ♿.

Slaughden SC (SSC). **Services** ⛵ (via Upson's BY if any vacant) £5, ⚒ ⛵ ⚗ ⚗ 🔧 ⚓ ⚗.

Town (¾M) ☏ 🛒 ✕ ☐ ✉ Ⓑ ⇄ (bus to Wickham Market), ✈ (Norwich).

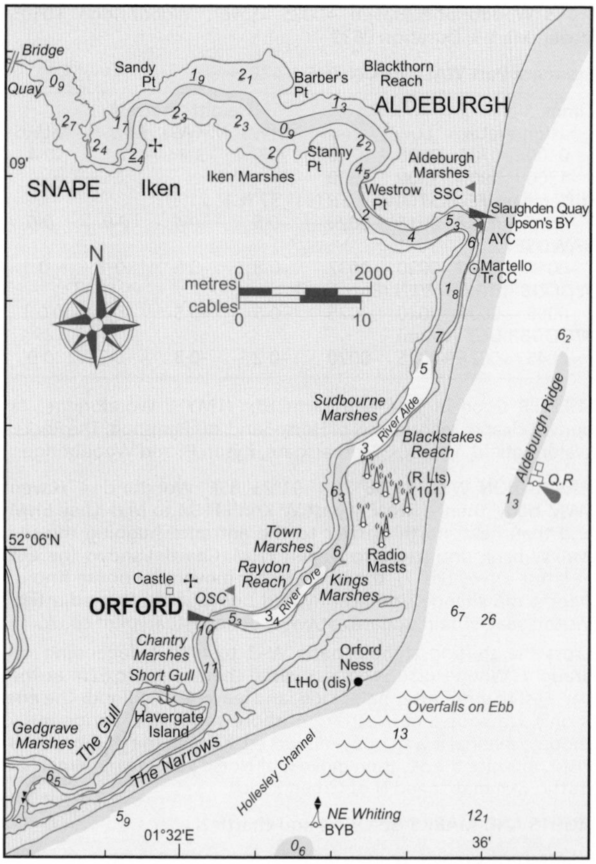

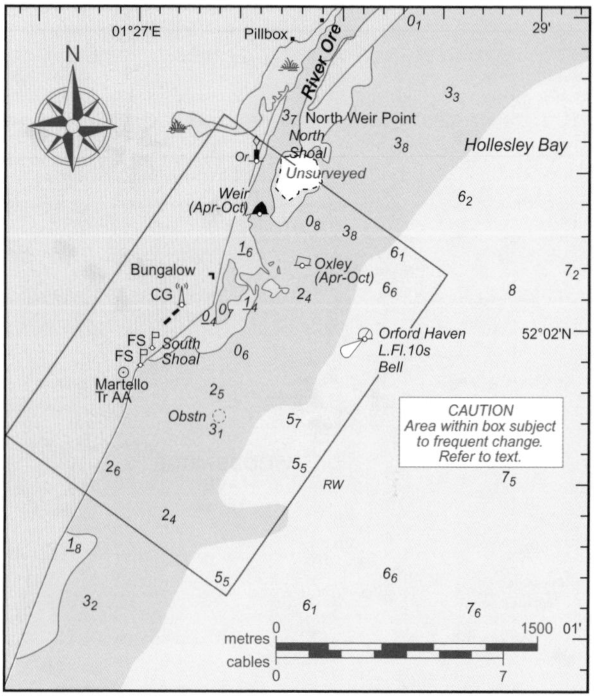

9.4.23 SOUTHWOLD

Suffolk **52°18'·78N 01°40'·54E**

CHARTS AC 5614, 1543, 2695; Imray C29, C28

TIDES –0105 Dover; ML 1·5; Duration 0620

Standard Port LOWESTOFT (⟶)

Times				Height (metres)			
High Water		Low Water		MHWS	MHWN	MLWN	MLWS
0300	0900	0200	0800	2·4	2·1	1·0	0·5
1500	2100	1400	2000				
Differences SOUTHWOLD							
+0105	+0105	+0055	+0055	0·0	0·0	–0·1	0·0
MINSMERE SLUICE							
+0110	+0110	+0110	+0110	0·0	–0·1	–0·2	–0·2
ALDEBURGH (seaward)							
+0130	+0130	+0115	+0120	+0·3	+0·2	–0·1	–0·2
ORFORD NESS							
+0135	+0135	+0135	+0125	+0·4	+0·6	–0·1	0·0

NOTE: HW time differences (above) for Southwold apply up the hbr. At the ent mean HW is HW Lowestoft +0035.

SHELTER Good, but the ent is dangerous in strong winds from N through E to S. Visitors berth (must book ahead) on pontoon by HM office or a staging 6ca from the ent, on N bank near to the Harbour Inn. If rafted, shore lines are essential due to current. Some larger vessels moor on N wall of Dock and may encroach channel.

NAVIGATION WPT 52°18'·09N 01°41'·69E, 315°/1M to N Pier lt.

- Enter on the flood as the ebb runs up to 6kn. Shoals are unpredictable up to ¼M offshore; a sand and shingle bar, extent/depth variable, lies off the ent and a shoal builds inside N Pier. Obtain details of appr chans from HM before entering.
- Enter between piers in midstream. When chan widens keep close to The Knuckle (2 FG vert), turn stbd towards LB House; keep within 3m of quay wall until it ends, then resume midstream.
- **Caution** Rowing ferry (which has right of way at all times) 3ca and unlit low footbridge 7.5ca upstream of ent.

LIGHTS AND MARKS See 9.4.4 and chartlet. Walberswick ✠ in line with N Pier lt ≠ 268°. Hbr ent opens on 300°. 3 FR (vert) at N pier ≠ port closed. Lt ho, W ○ tr, Fl 10s 24M, in Southwold town, 0·86M NNE of hbr ent.

COMMUNICATIONS (Code 01502) CGOC (01262) 672317; Police 101; Dr 722326; H 723333. HM 724712.

Southwold Port Radio Ch **12** 16 (as reqd). HM for fuel 12.

FACILITIES **Hbr** southwoldharbour@waveney.gov.uk HW±3 (Hbr due £8·00) £17·50<20ft, £20·50<30ft, £25<40ft, £31<50ft (+£4·30) also by bowser 100 l/min, (20t) .

Southwold SC; Town (¾M) Ⓑ (bus to Brampton/ Darsham), ✈ (Norwich).

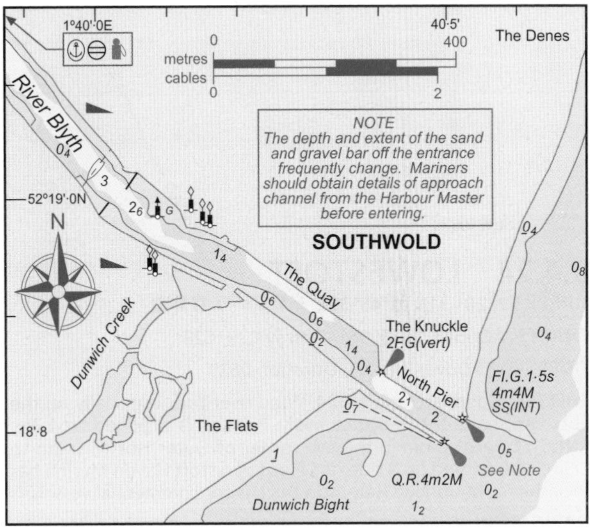

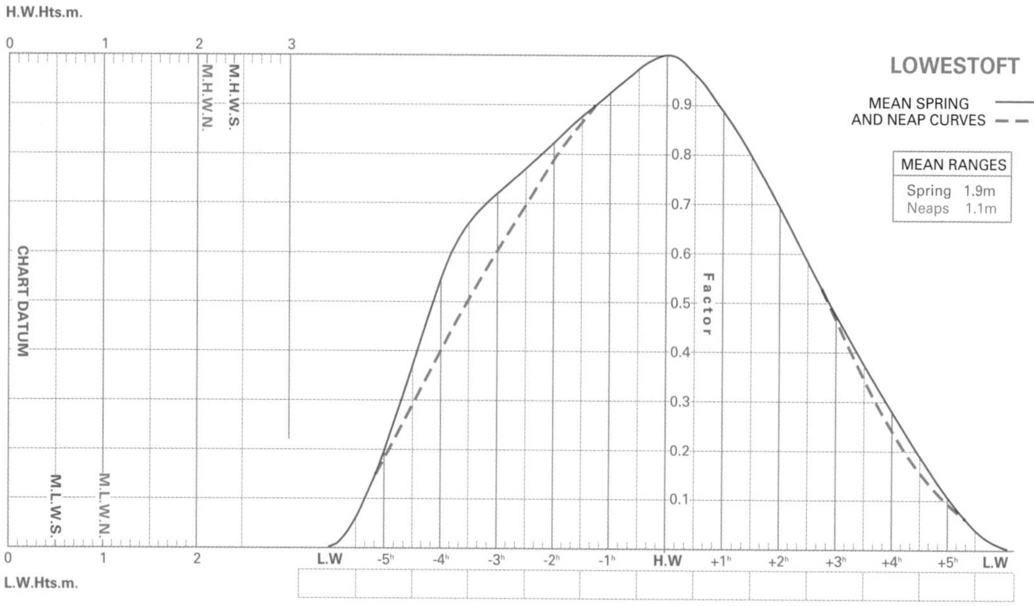

9.4.24 LOWESTOFT

Suffolk **52°28'·31N 01°45'·39E**

CHARTS AC 1543, 1535, 5614; Imray C29, C28

TIDES –0133 Dover; ML 1·6; Duration 0620

SHELTER Good; accessible H24. Wind over tide, especially on the ebb, can make the entrance lively. Fairway is dredged to 4·7m. RN&S YC yacht basin in the SW corner of Outer Hbr with 2m to 2·5m; no berthing on N side of S Pier. Lowestoft Haven Marina has facilities 1.5M upriver. Hamilton Dock is for commercial vessels.

NAVIGATION Keep watch on Ch 14; req permission from *Harbour Control* to enter/leave harbour and pass (either way) between Outer Harbour and Waveney/Hamilton Docks to deconflict with helicopter movements. Sands continually shift and buoys are moved to suit. Beware shoals and drying areas esp S of hbr ent; do not cross banks in bad weather, nor at mid flood/ebb. Speed limit in harbour is 4 kn.

From S, WPT is E Barnard ECM buoy, Q (3) 10s, 52°25'·15N 01°46'·36E; thence via Stanford Chan E of Newcome Sand QR, Stanford Fl R 2.5s and N Newcome Fl (4) R 15s, all PHM buoys. S Holm SCM, VQ (6)+L Fl 10s, and SW Holm SHM, Fl (2) G 5s, buoys mark the seaward side of this channel.

From E, WPT is Holm Approach ECM buoy, Q (3) 10s, 52°30'·88N 01°50'·22E, then via Holm Chan (buoyed) into Corton Road. Or approach direct to S Holm SCM buoy for Stanford Channel.

From N, appr via Yarmouth, Gorleston and Corton Roads.

Bridge to Inner Hbr (Lake Lothing and Lowestoft CC) lifts at the following times (20 mins notice required): daily 0300, 0500, 0700, 0945, 1115, 1430, 1600, (1800 W/Es + BHs only) 1900, 2100 and 2400. Small craft may pass under the bridge (clearance 2·2m) at any time but call on Ch 14. Craft are to await bridge opening on pontoon at E end of Trawl Dock. **Vessels may only transit bridge chan when G lights shown on N side of appr** (showing Br locked in position).

LIGHTS AND MARKS Lowestoft lt ho, W twr, is 1M N of entrance.

Traffic Signals shown on E arm of RN&SYC Yacht Basin to exit, and tip of S Pier for entry/exit:

3 FR (vert) = Do not proceed
GWG (vert) = proceed only as/when instructed

Bridge Sigs (on N bank each side of bridge):
● = bridge operating, keep 100m clear.
● = vessels may pass through bridge channel.

Oulton Rwy Br centre span lit Iso 10s, S side Fl R 2.5s, N side Fl G 2.5s.

COMMUNICATIONS (Code 01502) CGOC (01262) 672317; Police 101; H 01493 452452. HM & Bridge Control 572286; Mutford Bridge and Lock 531778 (+Ansafone, checked daily at 0830, 1300 & 1730); Oulton Broad Yacht Stn 574946.

Lowestoft Hbr Control (ABP) VHF Ch **14** 16 11 (H24). *Lowestoft Haven Marina* Ch **80**, 37. *Oulton Broad YS and Mutford Lock Control* Ch 73. Pilot Ch 14. RN & SYC Ch 14, 80.

FACILITIES

Royal Norfolk & Suffolk YC (www.rnsyc.net) admin@rnsyc.org.uk, ☎566726, £2·75 inc YC facilities.

Lowestoft Cruising Club www.lowestoftcruisingclub.co.uk, ☎07810 522515, (max 13m) £2·00, (emergency).

Lowestoft Haven Marina www. lowestofthavenmarina.co.uk ☎580300, 140 £2·30 @ (70t) ACA.

Town (Norwich).

Entry to the Broads: See Gt Yarmouth & www.norfolkbroads.com. Passage to Oulton Broad from Lake Lothing is via two bridges and Mutford Lock (width 5·9m). The lock is available 0800-1200 and 1300-1730 daily; 0800-1200 and 1300-1930 at weekends/Bank Holidays; 0900-1200 only 1 Nov to 31 Mar. Charge is £13/day. Booking 24hrs in advance is recommended, ☎(01502) 531778 or Ch 73. Oulton Broad Yacht Station ☎(01502) 574946. From Oulton Broad, access into the R Waveney is via Oulton Dyke.

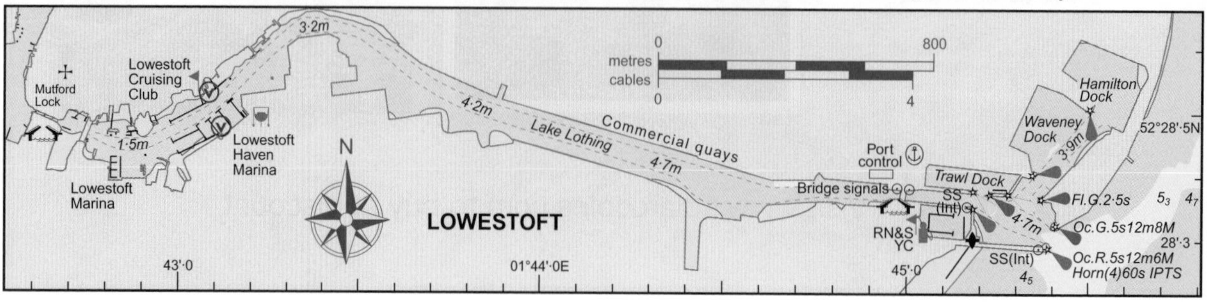

STANDARD TIME (UT)
For Summer Time add ONE hour in **non-shaded areas**

LOWESTOFT LAT 52°28′N LONG 1°45′E

TIMES AND HEIGHTS OF HIGH AND LOW WATERS

Dates in red are SPRINGS
Dates in blue are NEAPS

YEAR **2018**

JANUARY

Date	Day	Time	m	Time	m	Time	m	Time	m
1	M	0211	0.8	0813	2.6	1438	0.6	2047	2.6
2	TU	0307	0.6	0908	2.6	1529	0.6	○ 2133	2.6
3	W	0401	0.5	1002	2.6	1618	0.6	2220	2.7
4	TH	0452	0.4	1055	2.6	1704	0.7	2306	2.7
5	F	0541	0.3	1146	2.6	1749	0.8	2352	2.7
6	SA	0629	0.3	1237	2.5	1832	0.9		
7	SU	0039	2.7	0718	0.4	1333	2.3	1915	1.0
8	M	0128	2.6	0810	0.5	1440	2.2	◑ 2003	1.1
9	TU	0221	2.5	0908	0.7	1556	2.2	2100	1.3
10	W	0325	2.4	1013	0.8	1700	2.2	2224	1.3
11	TH	0439	2.3	1117	0.9	1759	2.2	2342	1.3
12	F	0547	2.2	1214	0.9	1854	2.2		
13	SA	0046	1.2	0653	2.2	1307	1.0	1941	2.3
14	SU	0141	1.1	0754	2.3	1352	1.0	2020	2.4
15	M	0226	0.9	0842	2.3	1432	1.0	2052	2.4
16	TU	0306	0.8	0922	2.3	1506	0.9	2122	2.5
17	W	0343	0.8	0956	2.3	1538	0.9	● 2153	2.5
18	TH	0418	0.7	1028	2.3	1610	0.9	2226	2.5
19	F	0452	0.7	1101	2.3	1643	0.8	2301	2.6
20	SA	0527	0.7	1134	2.3	1719	0.9	2338	2.5
21	SU	0603	0.7	1209	2.3	1756	0.9		
22	M	0015	2.5	0639	0.7	1247	2.2	1834	1.0
23	TU	0054	2.5	0719	0.7	1329	2.2	1917	1.0
24	W	0136	2.4	0803	0.8	1418	2.2	◐ 2007	1.1
25	TH	0224	2.4	0857	0.8	1522	2.1	2105	1.1
26	F	0324	2.3	1009	0.9	1652	2.2	2224	1.1
27	SA	0446	2.3	1127	0.9	1755	2.2	2349	1.1
28	SU	0600	2.4	1230	0.8	1849	2.3		
29	M	0055	0.9	0704	2.4	1328	0.8	1940	2.4
30	TU	0158	0.7	0806	2.5	1424	0.7	2030	2.5
31	W	0257	0.5	0903	2.5	1518	0.7	○ 2117	2.6

FEBRUARY

Date	Day	Time	m	Time	m	Time	m	Time	m
1	TH	0351	0.4	0955	2.6	1606	0.7	2204	2.7
2	F	0440	0.3	1043	2.6	1650	0.7	2249	2.7
3	SA	0526	0.2	1129	2.5	1731	0.7	2333	2.7
4	SU	0610	0.3	1214	2.4	1810	0.8		
5	M	0017	2.7	0652	0.4	1301	2.3	1848	0.9
6	TU	0102	2.6	0736	0.5	1350	2.2	1928	1.0
7	W	0149	2.5	0823	0.7	1451	2.1	◑ 2014	1.1
8	TH	0244	2.3	0920	0.9	1606	2.1	2116	1.2
9	F	0402	2.2	1035	1.0	1709	2.1	2302	1.3
10	SA	0520	2.2	1143	1.1	1809	2.1		
11	SU	0017	1.2	0636	2.1	1241	1.1	1907	2.2
12	M	0117	1.0	0746	2.2	1331	1.1	1953	2.3
13	TU	0206	0.9	0832	2.2	1413	1.0	2028	2.3
14	W	0246	0.8	0908	2.3	1447	1.0	2059	2.4
15	TH	0322	0.7	0938	2.3	1519	0.9	● 2131	2.5
16	F	0357	0.6	1007	2.3	1552	0.8	2205	2.5
17	SA	0432	0.6	1038	2.4	1627	0.7	2240	2.6
18	SU	0507	0.5	1110	2.4	1703	0.7	2316	2.6
19	M	0542	0.5	1144	2.3	1738	0.8	2352	2.6
20	TU	0617	0.6	1221	2.3	1815	0.8		
21	W	0029	2.5	0653	0.6	1301	2.3	1854	0.9
22	TH	0111	2.5	0733	0.7	1346	2.2	1940	0.9
23	F	0158	2.4	0822	0.8	1441	2.2	◐ 2036	1.0
24	SA	0259	2.3	0928	0.9	1600	2.1	2153	1.0
25	SU	0427	2.3	1102	1.0	1721	2.2	2331	1.0
26	M	0551	2.3	1215	1.0	1823	2.2		
27	TU	0043	0.8	0702	2.3	1317	0.9	1920	2.3
28	W	0148	0.6	0806	2.4	1416	0.8	2012	2.4

MARCH

Date	Day	Time	m	Time	m	Time	m	Time	m
1	TH	0247	0.5	0858	2.5	1507	0.7	2100	2.6
2	F	0338	0.3	0943	2.5	1552	0.7	○ 2145	2.7
3	SA	0424	0.2	1026	2.5	1633	0.6	2229	2.7
4	SU	0506	0.2	1107	2.5	1711	0.6	2312	2.7
5	M	0545	0.3	1147	2.4	1747	0.7	2354	2.6
6	TU	0623	0.4	1227	2.3	1822	0.8		
7	W	0035	2.5	0700	0.6	1306	2.2	1859	0.9
8	TH	0120	2.4	0738	0.8	1347	2.1	1940	1.0
9	F	0211	2.3	0821	1.0	1438	2.1	◑ 2031	1.1
10	SA	0325	2.1	0923	1.2	1555	2.0	2204	1.2
11	SU	0453	2.1	1108	1.3	1708	2.1	2346	1.1
12	M	0612	2.1	1215	1.2	1811	2.1		
13	TU	0046	1.0	0725	2.2	1308	1.2	1908	2.2
14	W	0136	0.9	0811	2.2	1349	1.1	1952	2.2
15	TH	0217	0.8	0844	2.3	1424	1.0	2028	2.3
16	F	0253	0.7	0912	2.3	1456	0.9	2103	2.4
17	SA	0329	0.6	0940	2.4	1531	0.7	● 2138	2.5
18	SU	0405	0.5	1011	2.4	1607	0.7	2215	2.6
19	M	0442	0.4	1044	2.4	1644	0.6	2252	2.6
20	TU	0518	0.4	1119	2.4	1721	0.7	2329	2.6
21	W	0553	0.5	1156	2.4	1758	0.7		
22	TH	0008	2.5	0629	0.6	1236	2.3	1838	0.7
23	F	0052	2.5	0709	0.7	1321	2.3	1924	0.8
24	SA	0143	2.4	0757	0.9	1414	2.2	◐ 2021	0.9
25	SU	0249	2.3	0901	1.0	1524	2.1	2145	0.9
26	M	0429	2.2	1045	1.1	1649	2.1	2321	0.8
27	TU	0553	2.3	1203	1.1	1758	2.2		
28	W	0031	0.7	0704	2.3	1307	1.0	1858	2.3
29	TH	0135	0.5	0802	2.4	1405	0.9	1952	2.4
30	F	0232	0.4	0846	2.4	1452	0.8	2039	2.5
31	SA	0319	0.3	0926	2.5	1534	0.7	○ 2124	2.6

APRIL

Date	Day	Time	m	Time	m	Time	m	Time	m
1	SU	0401	0.3	1004	2.5	1612	0.6	2208	2.6
2	M	0440	0.3	1042	2.4	1649	0.6	2250	2.6
3	TU	0517	0.4	1119	2.4	1724	0.6	2331	2.5
4	W	0552	0.5	1155	2.3	1758	0.7		
5	TH	0012	2.4	0624	0.7	1230	2.3	1833	0.8
6	F	0055	2.3	0657	0.9	1306	2.2	1912	0.9
7	SA	0143	2.2	0734	1.0	1348	2.2	1958	1.0
8	SU	0251	2.1	0819	1.2	1442	2.1	◑ 2103	1.1
9	M	0424	2.0	0928	1.4	1557	2.1	2306	1.1
10	TU	0537	2.1	1138	1.3	1715	2.1		
11	W	0007	1.0	0644	2.1	1232	1.2	1815	2.1
12	TH	0055	0.9	0734	2.2	1313	1.1	1906	2.2
13	F	0137	0.8	0809	2.3	1350	1.0	1950	2.3
14	SA	0216	0.6	0840	2.3	1426	0.9	2029	2.4
15	SU	0255	0.5	0910	2.4	1505	0.7	2108	2.5
16	M	0334	0.4	0943	2.4	1545	0.6	● 2148	2.5
17	TU	0414	0.4	1018	2.5	1625	0.6	2227	2.6
18	W	0452	0.4	1055	2.5	1705	0.6	2308	2.6
19	TH	0531	0.5	1134	2.4	1746	0.6	2352	2.5
20	F	0610	0.6	1216	2.4	1829	0.6		
21	SA	0040	2.5	0652	0.8	1302	2.3	1918	0.7
22	SU	0137	2.4	0742	0.9	1356	2.3	◐ 2020	0.7
23	M	0253	2.3	0847	1.1	1502	2.2	2146	0.7
24	TU	0434	2.2	1027	1.2	1621	2.2	2308	0.7
25	W	0550	2.3	1144	1.2	1733	2.2		
26	TH	0014	0.6	0656	2.3	1249	1.1	1834	2.3
27	F	0115	0.5	0748	2.4	1345	1.0	1929	2.4
28	SA	0209	0.4	0829	2.4	1431	0.8	2018	2.5
29	SU	0255	0.4	0906	2.4	1512	0.7	2103	2.5
30	M	0336	0.4	0942	2.4	1551	0.6	○ 2147	2.5

Chart Datum: 1·50 metres below Ordnance Datum (Newlyn). HAT is 2·9 metres above Chart Datum.

STANDARD TIME (UT)
For Summer Time add ONE hour in **non-shaded areas**

LOWESTOFT LAT 52°28′N LONG 1°45′E

TIMES AND HEIGHTS OF HIGH AND LOW WATERS

Dates in red are SPRINGS
Dates in blue are NEAPS

YEAR **2018**

MAY

Day	Time	m	Day	Time	m
1	0413	0.4	16	0346	0.4
	1018	2.4		0954	2.5
TU	1628	0.6	W	1606	0.6
	2230	2.5		2206	2.6
2	0448	0.5	17	0429	0.4
	1053	2.4		1034	2.5
W	1703	0.6	TH	1651	0.5
	2311	2.4		2253	2.6
3	0520	0.7	18	0512	0.5
	1126	2.4		1116	2.5
TH	1738	0.7	F	1737	0.5
	2352	2.3		2342	2.5
4	0551	0.8	19	0555	0.7
	1159	2.3		1200	2.5
F	1812	0.7	SA	1826	0.5
5	0033	2.2	20	0035	2.4
	0621	0.9		0640	0.8
SA	1234	2.3	SU	1249	2.4
	1849	0.8		1918	0.5
6	0119	2.2	21	0136	2.4
	0656	1.1		0731	1.0
SU	1315	2.3	M	1342	2.4
	1933	0.9		2021	0.6
7	0216	2.1	22	0256	2.3
	0738	1.2		0832	1.1
M	1404	2.2	TU	1443	2.3
	2027	1.0	◐	2135	0.6
8	0344	2.0	23	0425	2.3
	0831	1.3		0957	1.2
TU	1501	2.1	W	1554	2.3
◑	2157	1.0		2247	0.6
9	0456	2.1	24	0534	2.3
	0948	1.4		1115	1.2
W	1614	2.1	TH	1706	2.3
	2317	0.9		2350	0.6
10	0555	2.1	25	0635	2.3
	1132	1.3		1219	1.1
TH	1726	2.1	F	1809	2.3
11	0008	0.8	26	0048	0.6
	0646	2.2		0727	2.3
F	1224	1.2	SA	1318	1.0
	1821	2.2		1906	2.3
12	0053	0.7	27	0142	0.6
	0727	2.3		0808	2.4
SA	1309	1.0	SU	1408	0.9
	1910	2.3		1958	2.4
13	0137	0.6	28	0228	0.6
	0804	2.3		0845	2.4
SU	1353	0.9	M	1451	0.8
	1954	2.4		2046	2.4
14	0220	0.5	29	0309	0.6
	0839	2.4		0921	2.4
M	1437	0.8	TU	1531	0.7
	2038	2.4	○	2131	2.4
15	0303	0.5	30	0346	0.6
	0916	2.5		0955	2.5
TU	1521	0.6	W	1609	0.7
●	2122	2.5		2215	2.4
			31	0420	0.7
				1029	2.5
			TH	1645	0.7
				2256	2.3

JUNE

Day	Time	m	Day	Time	m
1	0451	0.8	16	0457	0.6
	1101	2.4		1101	2.6
F	1720	0.7	SA	1730	0.4
	2335	2.3		2335	2.5
2	0521	0.9	17	0543	0.7
	1134	2.4		1147	2.6
SA	1755	0.7	SU	1821	0.3
3	0014	2.2	18	0029	2.5
	0551	1.0		0629	0.8
SU	1209	2.4	M	1236	2.6
	1831	0.8		1912	0.4
4	0055	2.2	19	0128	2.4
	0626	1.0		0717	1.0
M	1249	2.4	TU	1326	2.5
	1911	0.8		2009	0.4
5	0141	2.1	20	0239	2.3
	0707	1.1		0810	1.1
TU	1334	2.3	W	1421	2.5
	1958	0.9	◐	2112	0.5
6	0238	2.1	21	0401	2.3
	0755	1.2		0916	1.2
W	1423	2.2	TH	1525	2.4
◑	2056	0.9		2218	0.6
7	0404	2.1	22	0507	2.3
	0852	1.3		1034	1.2
TH	1519	2.2	F	1638	2.3
	2211	0.9		2321	0.6
8	0508	2.1	23	0606	2.3
	1007	1.3		1145	1.2
F	1629	2.2	SA	1744	2.3
	2317	0.8			
9	0600	2.2	24	0019	0.7
	1128	1.2		0700	2.3
SA	1737	2.2	SU	1249	1.1
				1845	2.3
10	0010	0.7	25	0113	0.8
	0646	2.3		0746	2.3
SU	1228	1.1	M	1345	1.0
	1831	2.3		1944	2.3
11	0100	0.7	26	0201	0.8
	0729	2.3		0825	2.4
M	1320	1.0	TU	1432	0.9
	1922	2.4		2036	2.3
12	0148	0.6	27	0243	0.8
	0810	2.4		0901	2.4
TU	1410	0.8	W	1514	0.8
	2011	2.4		2123	2.3
13	0235	0.5	28	0321	0.8
	0851	2.5		0935	2.5
W	1500	0.7	TH	1554	0.7
●	2100	2.5	○	2204	2.3
14	0323	0.5	29	0355	0.9
	0932	2.5		1008	2.5
TH	1551	0.5	F	1630	0.7
	2151	2.6		2243	2.3
15	0410	0.5	30	0426	0.9
	1016	2.6		1040	2.5
F	1641	0.4	SA	1705	0.7
	2243	2.6		2319	2.3

JULY

Day	Time	m	Day	Time	m
1	0456	0.9	16	0530	0.7
	1113	2.5		1131	2.7
SU	1739	0.7	M	1809	0.2
	2353	2.3			
2	0528	0.9	17	0015	2.5
	1148	2.5		0613	0.8
M	1814	0.7	TU	1218	2.7
				1857	0.3
3	0029	2.2	18	0107	2.4
	0603	1.0		0656	0.9
TU	1226	2.5	W	1305	2.7
	1850	0.7		1946	0.4
4	0107	2.2	19	0206	2.3
	0642	1.0		0742	1.0
W	1307	2.4	TH	1356	2.6
	1931	0.8	◐	2040	0.5
5	0150	2.1	20	0321	2.2
	0726	1.1		0834	1.2
TH	1350	2.4	F	1454	2.5
	2017	0.8		2141	0.7
6	0242	2.1	21	0430	2.2
	0816	1.2		0943	1.2
F	1438	2.3	SA	1608	2.4
◑	2113	0.9		2247	0.8
7	0402	2.1	22	0529	2.2
	0915	1.2		1109	1.2
SA	1535	2.3	SU	1720	2.3
	2222	0.8		2349	0.9
8	0513	2.2	23	0627	2.3
	1032	1.2		1221	1.2
SU	1650	2.3	M	1830	2.2
	2330	0.8			
9	0607	2.3	24	0046	1.0
	1149	1.1		0720	2.3
M	1758	2.3	TU	1324	1.1
				1939	2.3
10	0027	0.8	25	0138	1.0
	0655	2.3		0805	2.4
TU	1251	1.0	W	1416	0.9
	1855	2.4		2032	2.3
11	0121	0.7	26	0223	1.0
	0742	2.4		0842	2.4
W	1348	0.8	TH	1459	0.8
	1951	2.4		2115	2.3
12	0213	0.7	27	0301	1.0
	0828	2.5		0915	2.5
TH	1444	0.7	F	1538	0.8
	2047	2.5	○	2152	2.3
13	0305	0.6	28	0334	1.0
	0913	2.6		0946	2.5
F	1539	0.5	SA	1613	0.7
●	2142	2.6		2225	2.3
14	0356	0.6	29	0404	0.9
	0959	2.7		1018	2.6
SA	1631	0.4	SU	1647	0.7
	2234	2.6		2256	2.3
15	0444	0.7	30	0435	0.9
	1045	2.7		1051	2.6
SU	1721	0.3	M	1720	0.6
	2325	2.6		2328	2.3
			31	0508	0.9
				1126	2.6
			TU	1753	0.7

AUGUST

Day	Time	m	Day	Time	m
1	0000	2.3	16	0038	2.4
	0542	0.9		0632	0.9
W	1202	2.6	TH	1241	2.7
	1827	0.7		1916	0.5
2	0036	2.3	17	0127	2.3
	0619	1.0		0713	1.0
TH	1240	2.5	F	1328	2.6
	1903	0.7		2002	0.7
3	0114	2.2	18	0223	2.2
	0700	1.0		0758	1.1
F	1319	2.5	SA	1423	2.5
	1942	0.8	◐	2054	0.9
4	0158	2.2	19	0336	2.2
	0745	1.1		0855	1.2
SA	1403	2.4	SU	1538	2.3
◑	2029	0.8		2204	1.0
5	0252	2.2	20	0443	2.2
	0839	1.2		1031	1.3
SU	1456	2.4	M	1658	2.2
	2130	0.9		2318	1.1
6	0414	2.2	21	0543	2.2
	0947	1.2		1156	1.2
M	1609	2.3	TU	1816	2.2
	2250	0.9			
7	0527	2.3	22	0021	1.2
	1117	1.1		0644	2.3
TU	1732	2.3	W	1302	1.1
				1930	2.3
8	0001	0.9	23	0117	1.2
	0624	2.3		0736	2.3
W	1229	1.0	TH	1355	1.0
	1838	2.4		2021	2.3
9	0100	0.9	24	0204	1.1
	0716	2.4		0816	2.4
TH	1331	0.8	F	1438	0.9
	1941	2.4		2100	2.3
10	0157	0.8	25	0241	1.1
	0806	2.5		0848	2.5
F	1431	0.6	SA	1515	0.8
	2041	2.5		2132	2.4
11	0252	0.8	26	0312	1.0
	0854	2.6		0919	2.5
SA	1527	0.4	SU	1549	0.7
●	2134	2.6	○	2201	2.4
12	0343	0.7	27	0342	0.9
	0941	2.7		0951	2.6
SU	1619	0.3	M	1621	0.6
	2222	2.6		2229	2.4
13	0429	0.7	28	0414	0.9
	1026	2.8		1025	2.6
M	1706	0.2	TU	1654	0.6
	2308	2.6		2259	2.4
14	0512	0.7	29	0448	0.8
	1111	2.8		1101	2.6
TU	1750	0.2	W	1727	0.6
	2353	2.5		2331	2.4
15	0553	0.8	30	0522	0.9
	1156	2.8		1136	2.6
W	1833	0.3	TH	1800	0.6
			31	0005	2.4
				0558	0.9
			F	1213	2.6
				1834	0.7

Chart Datum: 1·50 metres below Ordnance Datum (Newlyn). HAT is 2·9 metres above Chart Datum.

STANDARD TIME (UT)
For Summer Time add ONE hour in **non-shaded areas**

LOWESTOFT LAT 52°28′N LONG 1°45′E

TIMES AND HEIGHTS OF HIGH AND LOW WATERS

Dates in red are SPRINGS
Dates in blue are NEAPS

YEAR **2018**

SEPTEMBER

Date	Time	m	Date	Time	m
1 SA	0043 0636 1251 1910	2.4 1.0 2.5 0.8	16 SU	0132 0728 1354 ◐ 2005	2.3 1.0 2.4 1.0
2 SU	0125 0719 1335 1954	2.3 1.0 2.5 0.9	17 M	0223 0819 1508 2100	2.2 1.1 2.3 1.2
3 M	0215 0811 1430 ◑ 2050	2.3 1.1 2.4 1.0	18 TU	0335 0944 1636 2241	2.2 1.2 2.2 1.3
4 TU	0320 0917 1546 2214	2.2 1.1 2.3 1.1	19 W	0447 1128 1754 2356	2.2 1.2 2.2 1.3
5 W	0446 1056 1720 2341	2.3 1.1 2.3 1.1	20 TH	0550 1231 1909	2.2 1.1 2.3
6 TH	0553 1213 1833	2.3 0.9 2.4	21 F	0052 0649 1323 1959	1.3 2.3 1.0 2.3
7 F	0045 0650 1317 1939	1.0 2.4 0.8 2.5	22 SA	0138 0735 1406 2035	1.2 2.4 0.9 2.4
8 SA	0144 0743 1418 2034	1.0 2.5 0.6 2.6	23 SU	0214 0812 1442 2104	1.1 2.5 0.8 2.4
9 SU	0239 0833 1513 ● 2120	0.9 2.7 0.4 2.6	24 M	0244 0846 1516 2130	1.0 2.5 0.7 2.5
10 M	0327 0919 1600 2203	0.8 2.8 0.3 2.6	25 TU	0316 0921 1550 ○ 2158	0.9 2.6 0.6 2.5
11 TU	0411 1004 1644 2245	0.7 2.8 0.2 2.6	26 W	0350 0957 1624 2229	0.8 2.7 0.6 2.5
12 W	0451 1049 1725 2327	0.7 2.9 0.3 2.5	27 TH	0426 1033 1658 2302	0.8 2.7 0.6 2.5
13 TH	0529 1132 1805	0.8 2.8 0.4	28 F	0502 1110 1732 2338	0.8 2.7 0.6 2.5
14 F	0008 0607 1216 1843	2.5 0.8 2.7 0.6	29 SA	0539 1148 1807	0.8 2.6 0.7
15 SA	0049 0645 1302 1922	2.4 0.9 2.6 0.8	30 SU	0015 0617 1229 1843	2.5 0.9 2.6 0.8

OCTOBER

Date	Time	m	Date	Time	m
1 M	0058 0700 1316 1927	2.4 0.9 2.5 1.0	16 TU	0135 0749 1438 ◐ 2004	2.3 1.1 2.2 1.3
2 TU	0147 0754 1415 ◑ 2023	2.3 1.0 2.4 1.1	17 W	0227 0856 1608 2106	2.3 1.2 2.2 1.5
3 W	0248 0905 1541 2147	2.3 1.0 2.3 1.2	18 TH	0337 1050 1721 2318	2.2 1.1 2.2 1.5
4 TH	0407 1045 1719 2324	2.3 1.0 2.4 1.2	19 F	0452 1152 1830	2.2 1.0 2.3
5 F	0523 1159 1832	2.3 0.8 2.4	20 SA	0016 0553 1242 1922	1.4 2.3 1.0 2.3
6 SA	0030 0624 1302 1932	1.2 2.4 0.7 2.5	21 SU	0100 0645 1324 1959	1.3 2.3 0.9 2.4
7 SU	0129 0719 1401 2020	1.1 2.5 0.5 2.6	22 M	0136 0729 1402 2028	1.2 2.4 0.8 2.4
8 M	0222 0809 1452 2102	1.0 2.7 0.4 2.6	23 TU	0210 0809 1438 2056	1.1 2.5 0.7 2.5
9 TU	0307 0856 1537 ● 2141	0.8 2.8 0.3 2.6	24 W	0245 0848 1514 ○ 2127	0.9 2.6 0.6 2.5
10 W	0349 0941 1619 2220	0.8 2.8 0.3 2.6	25 TH	0324 0927 1552 2200	0.8 2.6 0.6 2.6
11 TH	0428 1026 1657 2259	0.7 2.8 0.4 2.6	26 F	0403 1006 1629 2235	0.8 2.7 0.6 2.6
12 F	0506 1110 1734 2337	0.7 2.7 0.6 2.5	27 SA	0443 1046 1706 2313	0.7 2.7 0.6 2.6
13 SA	0544 1153 1809	0.8 2.6 0.8	28 SU	0523 1128 1744 2353	0.8 2.6 0.7 2.5
14 SU	0014 0621 1239 1843	2.4 0.9 2.5 0.9	29 M	0605 1213 1824	0.8 2.6 0.9
15 M	0053 0702 1329 1920	2.4 1.0 2.3 1.1	30 TU	0036 0652 1306 1910	2.5 0.8 2.5 1.0
			31 W	0127 0749 1411 ◑ 2006	2.4 0.9 2.4 1.2

NOVEMBER

Date	Time	m	Date	Time	m
1 TH	0226 0904 1547 2127	2.4 0.9 2.3 1.3	16 F	0241 0943 1639 2114	2.3 1.1 2.2 1.5
2 F	0338 1032 1715 2302	2.3 0.8 2.4 1.3	17 SA	0348 1103 1739 2310	2.3 1.0 2.2 1.5
3 SA	0454 1140 1822	2.4 0.7 2.4	18 SU	0501 1155 1831	2.3 1.0 2.3
4 SU	0009 0558 1241 1917	1.2 2.4 0.6 2.5	19 M	0006 0558 1239 1913	1.4 2.3 0.9 2.3
5 M	0107 0654 1338 2002	1.1 2.5 0.5 2.5	20 TU	0050 0648 1319 1949	1.2 2.4 0.8 2.4
6 TU	0159 0745 1428 2041	1.0 2.6 0.5 2.5	21 W	0132 0733 1359 2022	1.1 2.4 0.7 2.5
7 W	0245 0834 1511 ● 2119	0.9 2.7 0.5 2.6	22 TH	0214 0816 1440 2057	0.9 2.5 0.6 2.5
8 TH	0327 0921 1552 2156	0.8 2.7 0.5 2.6	23 F	0258 0859 1522 ○ 2133	0.8 2.6 0.6 2.6
9 F	0407 1006 1629 2233	0.7 2.7 0.6 2.6	24 SA	0342 0942 1604 2212	0.7 2.6 0.6 2.6
10 SA	0446 1051 1704 2310	0.7 2.6 0.7 2.5	25 SU	0427 1027 1645 2252	0.7 2.6 0.6 2.6
11 SU	0524 1135 1736 2344	0.8 2.5 0.9 2.5	26 M	0512 1115 1728 2335	0.6 2.6 0.8 2.6
12 M	0601 1218 1808	0.8 2.4 1.0	27 TU	0600 1205 1812	0.6 2.5 0.9
13 TU	0019 0640 1306 1841	2.5 0.9 2.3 1.2	28 W	0021 0650 1302 1859	2.5 0.7 2.4 1.0
14 W	0059 0723 1403 1921	2.4 1.0 2.2 1.3	29 TH	0112 0748 1408 1953	2.5 0.7 2.4 1.2
15 TH	0146 0817 1526 ◐ 2010	2.3 1.1 2.1 1.4	30 F	0208 0857 1540 ◑ 2102	2.4 0.7 2.3 1.3

DECEMBER

Date	Time	m	Date	Time	m
1 SA	0312 1011 1659 2228	2.4 0.7 2.3 1.3	16 SU	0255 0944 1646 2129	2.3 1.0 2.1 1.4
2 SU	0425 1117 1801 2339	2.4 0.7 2.4 1.3	17 M	0359 1056 1740 2254	2.3 1.0 2.2 1.4
3 M	0533 1216 1856	2.4 0.6 2.4	18 TU	0511 1151 1827	2.3 0.9 2.3
4 TU	0040 0631 1312 1941	1.2 2.5 0.6 2.4	19 W	0002 0609 1239 1910	1.2 2.3 0.8 2.3
5 W	0136 0726 1402 2021	1.1 2.5 0.7 2.5	20 TH	0056 0700 1325 1950	1.1 2.4 0.7 2.4
6 TH	0225 0817 1446 2058	0.9 2.5 0.7 2.5	21 F	0146 0748 1411 2030	1.0 2.4 0.7 2.5
7 F	0309 0906 1526 ● 2135	0.8 2.5 0.7 2.5	22 SA	0235 0837 1457 ○ 2110	0.8 2.5 0.6 2.6
8 SA	0351 0953 1603 2211	0.7 2.5 0.8 2.6	23 SU	0325 0926 1544 2152	0.7 2.6 0.6 2.6
9 SU	0430 1038 1637 2246	0.7 2.5 0.9 2.5	24 M	0415 1016 1630 2236	0.6 2.6 0.7 2.6
10 M	0508 1120 1708 2319	0.7 2.4 0.9 2.5	25 TU	0505 1107 1716 2321	0.5 2.6 0.7 2.6
11 TU	0544 1200 1738 2353	0.8 2.3 1.0 2.5	26 W	0555 1159 1801	0.4 2.5 0.8
12 W	0621 1241 1810	0.8 2.2 1.1	27 TH	0008 0645 1253 1847	2.6 0.4 2.4 1.0
13 TH	0031 0659 1325 1848	2.5 0.9 2.2 1.2	28 F	0056 0738 1352 1936	2.6 0.5 2.3 1.1
14 F	0115 0743 1416 1933	2.4 0.9 2.1 1.3	29 SA	0148 0837 1512 ◑ 2031	2.5 0.6 2.3 1.2
15 SA	0202 0836 1534 ◐ 2025	2.4 1.0 2.1 1.4	30 SU	0245 0942 1631 2142	2.5 0.6 2.2 1.3
			31 M	0356 1047 1732 2302	2.4 0.7 2.3 1.3

Chart Datum: 1·50 metres below Ordnance Datum (Newlyn). HAT is 2·9 metres above Chart Datum.

9.4.25 GREAT YARMOUTH

Norfolk **52°34'·36N 01°44'·39E**

CHARTS AC 5614, 1543, 1535, 1534; Imray C29, C28

TIDES –0210 Dover; ML 1·5; Duration 0620

Standard Port LOWESTOFT (⟵)

Times				Height (metres)			
High Water		Low Water		MHWS	MHWN	MLWN	MLWS
0300	0900	0200	0800	2·4	2·1	1·0	0·5
1500	2100	1400	2000				
Differences GORLESTON (To be used for Great Yarmouth)							
–0035	–0035	–0030	–0030	0·0	0·0	0·0	0·0
CAISTER-ON-SEA							
–0120	–0120	–0100	–0100	0·0	–0·1	0·0	0·0
WINTERTON-ON-SEA							
–0225	–0215	–0135	–0135	+0·8	+0·5	+0·2	+0·1

- Rise of tide occurs mainly during 3½hrs after LW. From HW Lowestoft –3 until HW the level is usually within 0·3m of predicted HW. Flood tide runs until about HW+15 and ebb until about LW+25.

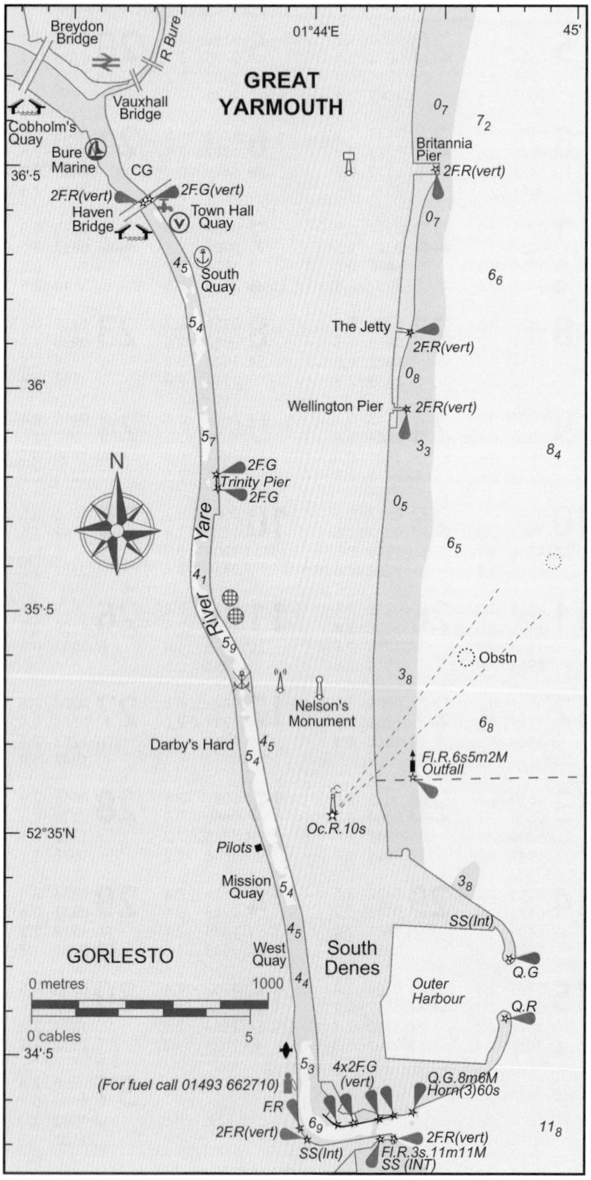

SHELTER Excellent on Town Hall Quay, close S of Haven Bridge; yachts and small craft are not allowed in the outer harbour and ⚓ prohibited in the commercial hbrs, R Yar and its approaches.

NAVIGATION WPT 52°34'·43N 01°45'·56E, 264°/1M to front ldg lt.

- Access is H24, subject to clearance, but small craft must not attempt ent in strong SE winds which cause dangerous seas, especially on the ebb. Except at local slack water, which occurs at HW+1½ and LW+1¾, tidal streams at the ent are strong.
- On the flood, the stream eddies NW past S pier, thence upriver; a QY tidal lt on S pier warns of this D/N. Beware being set onto the N pier.
- Temporary shoaling may occur in the ent during strong E'lies, with depths 1m less than those charted.
- Beware strong tidal streams that sweep through the Haven Bridge. Proceed slowly past Bure Marine.
- Outer Harbour is for commercial vessels only.

LIGHTS AND MARKS See 9.4.4 and Chartlet. Gorleston Pier lt, Fl R 3s, is on R brick building (W lower half floodlit). Entrance and bend marked by five 2FG(vert) and seven 2FR(vert).

TRAFFIC SIGNALS Port operations advise on Ch 12, this should always be heeded. **Inbound**: now IALA sigs on S pier: 3 Fl ● = hbr closed; 3F ● = do not proceed; 3 F ● = vessels may proceed, oneway; ● ○ ● = proceed only when told to; **Outbound**: 3 ● (vert) = no vessel to go downriver south of LB shed. Haven and Breydon bridges: 3 ● (vert) = passage prohib.

COMMUNICATIONS (Code 01493) CGOC (01262) 672317; Police 101; HM 335511; Breydon Bridge 651275.

Yarmouth Radio Ch **12** (H24). *Breydon Bridge* Ch **12** (HO).

FACILITIES **Town Hall Quay** (50m stretch) £15/yacht, then £7 for successive days.

Burgh Castle Marina (top of Breydon Water 5M) ☎780331, access HW ±4 for 1m draught 90+10 £16, diving ACA .

Goodchild Marine Services (top of Breydon Water 5M) ☎782301, access 6ft at LW. (27+6 £12.50), (32t, including mast stepping).

Town ACA (Norwich).

NORFOLK BROADS: The Broads comprise about 120 miles of navigable rivers and lakes in Norfolk and Suffolk. The main rivers (Bure, Yare and Waveney) are tidal, flowing into the sea at Great Yarmouth. The N Broads have a 2·3m headroom limit. Br clearances restrict cruising to R Yare (Great Yarmouth to Norwich, but note that 3M E of Norwich, Postwick viaduct on S bypass has 10.7m HW clearance) and River Waveney (Lowestoft to Beccles). The Broads may be entered also at Lowestoft (9.4.24). Broads Navigation Authority ☎(01603) 610734.

Entry to the Broads: Pass up R Yare at slack LW, under Haven Bridge (1·8m HAT) thence to Breydon Water via Breydon Bridge (4·0m) or to R Bure. Both bridges lift in co-ordination to pass small craft in groups. All br lifts on request to Hbr Office (01493) 335503 during office hrs. Weekend and bank holiday lifts to be requested working afternoon before. Call the Bridge Officer on VHF Ch 12. R Bure has two fixed bridges (2·3m MHWS).

Tidal data on the rivers and Broads is based on the time of LW at Yarmouth Yacht Stn (mouth of R Bure), which is LW Gorleston +0100 (see TIDES). Add the differences below to time of LW Yarmouth Yacht Stn to get local LW times:

R Bure		**R Waveney**		**R Yare**	
Acle Bridge	+0230	Berney Arms	+0100	Reedham	+0130
Horning	+0300	St Olaves	+0130	Cantley	+0200
Potter Heigham	+0300	Oulton Broad	+0300	Norwich	+0300

LW at Breydon (mouth of R Yare) is LW Yarmouth Yacht Stn +0100. Tide starts to flood on Breydon Water whilst still ebbing from R Bure. Max draught is 1·8m; 2m with care. Tidal range 0·6m to 1·8m.

Licences (compulsory) are obtainable from: The Broads Authority, 18 Colegate, Norwich NR3 1BQ, ☎01603 610734; the Info Centre, Yarmouth Yacht Stn or the River Inspectors. *Hamilton's Guide to the Broads* is recommended. www.hamilton publications.com.

North East England

Winterton to Berwick-upon-Tweed

9.5.1 Contents 331

9.5.2 Area map and Distance table 332

9.5.3 Tidal stream charts 334

9.5.4 Lights, buoys and waypoints 336

9.5.5 Passage information 338
North Sea passages, Offshore Energy Installations, North Norfolk Coast – 338
The Wash – 339 • The Wash to the River Humber, River Humber – 342 •
River Humber to Hartlepool, Hartlepool to Coquet Island – 348 • Hartlepool to
Southern Netherlands, Hartlepool to the German Bight – 355 • Coquet Island to
Farne Islands, Farne Islands, Holy Island to Berwick – 363

9.5.6 Blakeney 338

9.5.7 Wells-next-the-Sea 339
Burnham Overy Staithe • Brancaster Staithe

9.5.8 King's Lynn 340

9.5.9 Wisbech 340

9.5.10 Boston 341
River Welland • Wainfleet

9.5.11 River Humber (Immingham, tide tables/curves) 346
Grimsby • Hull • Goole • South Ferriby • Brough Haven • Naburn

9.5.12 Bridlington 349
Filey

9.5.13 Scarborough 349

9.5.14 Whitby (River Tees, tide tables/curves) 350
Runswick Bay • River Tees, Middlesbrough

9.5.15 Hartlepool 355

9.5.16 Seaham 356

9.5.17 Sunderland 356

9.5.18 River Tyne/North Shields, tide tables/curves 357
Cullercoats

9.5.19 Blyth 361
Newbiggin

9.5.20 Amble 362
Boulmer • Craster • Newton Haven and Beadnell Bay •
Seahouses (North Sunderland) • Farne Islands

9.5.21 Holy Island 363

9.5.22 Berwick-upon-Tweed 364

9.5.2

North East England

Blakeney to Berwick-upon-Tweed

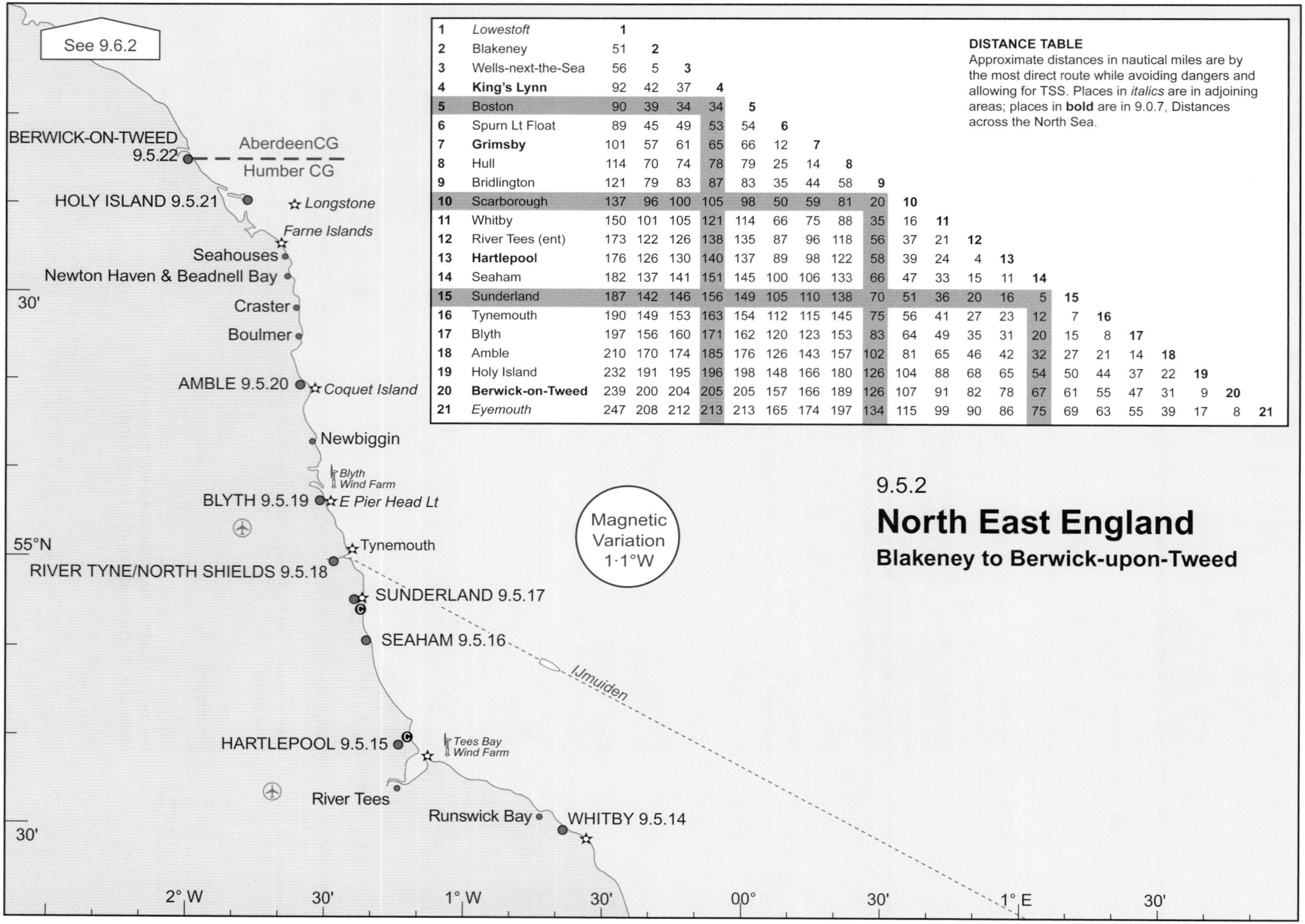

See 9.6.2
BERWICK-ON-TWEED 9.5.22
AberdeenCG
Humber CG
HOLY ISLAND 9.5.21
Longstone
Farne Islands
Seahouses
Newton Haven & Beadnell Bay
Craster
Boulmer
AMBLE 9.5.20
Coquet Island
Newbiggin
Blyth Wind Farm
BLYTH 9.5.19
E Pier Head Lt
Tynemouth
RIVER TYNE/NORTH SHIELDS 9.5.18
SUNDERLAND 9.5.17
SEAHAM 9.5.16
IJmuiden
HARTLEPOOL 9.5.15
Tees Bay Wind Farm
River Tees
Runswick Bay
WHITBY 9.5.14
Magnetic Variation 1·1°W
55°N
30'
2° W
1° W
00°
1° E

DISTANCE TABLE

Approximate distances in nautical miles are by the most direct route while avoiding dangers and allowing for TSS. Places in *italics* are in adjoining areas; places in **bold** are in 9.0.7, Distances across the North Sea.

1	*Lowestoft*	**1**																				
2	Blakeney	51	**2**																			
3	Wells-next-the-Sea	56	5	**3**																		
4	**King's Lynn**	92	42	37	**4**																	
5	Boston	90	39	34	34	**5**																
6	Spurn Lt Float	89	45	49	53	54	**6**															
7	**Grimsby**	101	57	61	65	66	12	**7**														
8	Hull	114	70	74	78	79	25	14	**8**													
9	Bridlington	121	79	83	87	83	35	44	58	**9**												
10	Scarborough	137	96	100	105	98	50	59	81	20	**10**											
11	Whitby	150	101	105	121	114	66	75	88	35	16	**11**										
12	River Tees (ent)	173	122	126	138	135	87	96	118	56	37	21	**12**									
13	**Hartlepool**	176	126	130	140	137	89	98	122	58	39	24	4	**13**								
14	Seaham	182	137	141	151	145	100	106	133	66	47	33	15	11	**14**							
15	Sunderland	187	142	146	156	149	105	110	138	70	51	36	20	16	5	**15**						
16	Tynemouth	190	149	153	163	154	112	115	145	75	56	41	27	23	12	7	**16**					
17	Blyth	197	156	160	171	162	120	123	153	83	64	49	35	31	20	15	8	**17**				
18	Amble	210	170	174	185	176	126	143	157	102	81	65	46	42	32	27	21	14	**18**			
19	Holy Island	232	191	195	196	198	148	166	180	126	104	88	68	65	54	50	44	37	22	**19**		
20	**Berwick-on-Tweed**	239	200	204	205	205	157	166	189	126	107	91	82	78	67	61	55	47	31	9	**20**	
21	*Eyemouth*	247	208	212	213	213	165	174	197	134	115	99	90	86	75	69	63	55	39	17	8	**21**

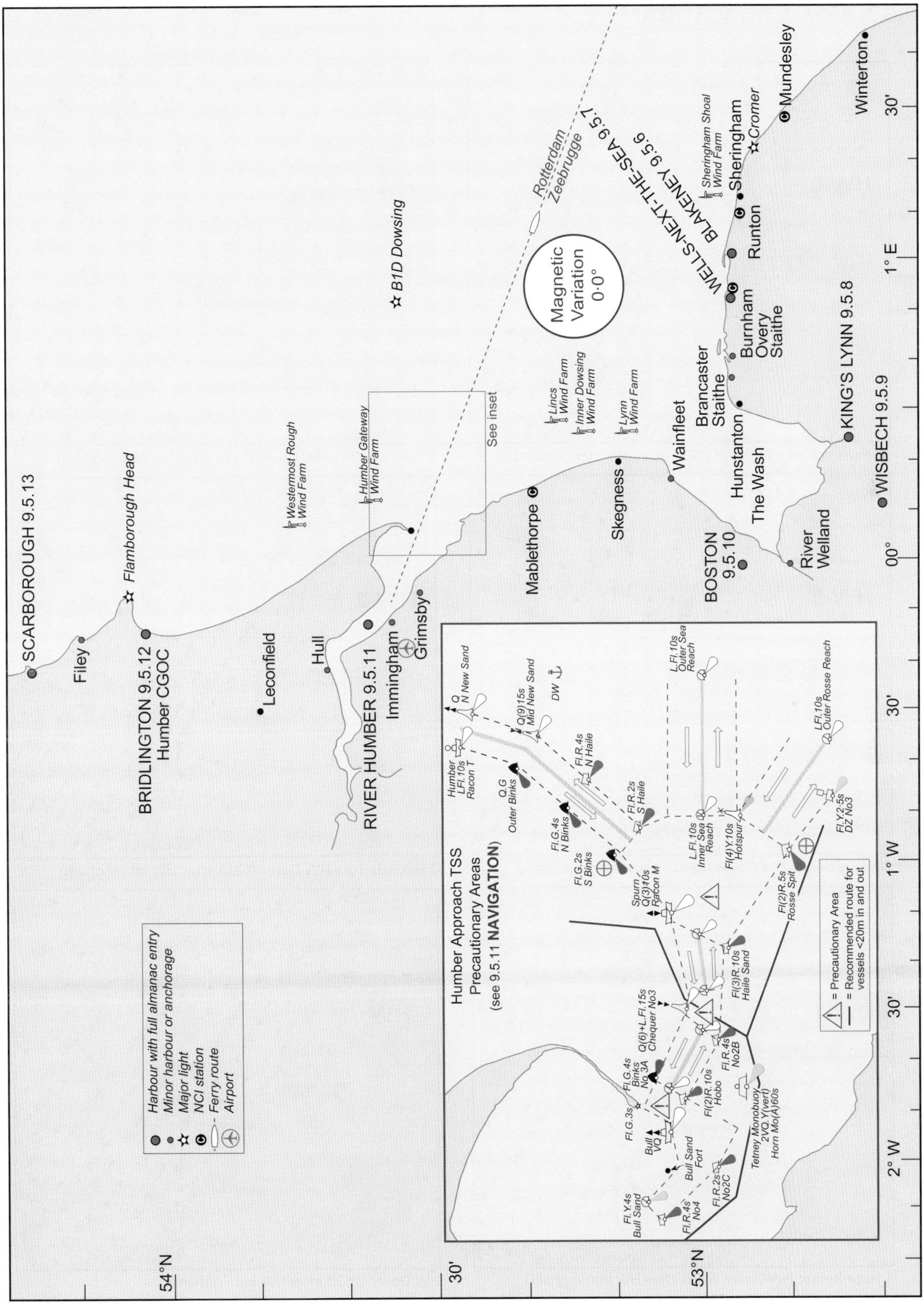
SCARBOROUGH 9.5.13
Filey
Flamborough Head
BRIDLINGTON 9.5.12
Humber CGOC
Leconfield
Hull
RIVER HUMBER 9.5.11
Immingham
Grimsby
Westermost Rough Wind Farm
Humber Gateway Wind Farm
See inset
B1D Dowsing
Mablethorpe
Skegness
Lincs Wind Farm
Inner Dowsing Wind Farm
Lynn Wind Farm
Wainfleet
BOSTON 9.5.10
River Welland
The Wash
Hunstanton
Brancaster Staithe
Burnham Overy Staithe
WELLS-NEXT-THE-SEA 9.5.7
BLAKENEY 9.5.6
Runton
Sheringham
Sheringham Shoal Wind Farm
Cromer
Mundesley
Winterton
KING'S LYNN 9.5.8
WISBECH 9.5.9
Rotterdam
Zeebrugge
Magnetic Variation 0·0°
54°N
30'
53°N
2° W
30'
1° W
30'
00°
30'
1° E
30'
Harbour with full almanac entry
Minor harbour or anchorage
Major light
NCI station
Ferry route
Airport
Humber Approach TSS Precautionary Areas (see 9.5.11 NAVIGATION)
Humber LFl.10s Racon T
Q N New Sand
Q(9)15s Mid New Sand
DW
Q.G Outer Binks
Fl.R.4s N Haile
Fl.R.2s S Haile
Fl.G.4s N Binks
Fl.G.2s S Binks
Spurn Q(3)10s Racon M
L.Fl.10s Inner Sea Reach
L.Fl.10s Outer Sea Reach
Fl(4)Y.10s Hotspur
Fl(2)R.5s Rosse Spit
L.Fl.10s Outer Rosse Reach
Fl.Y.2.5s DZ No3
Fl(3)R.10s Haile Sand
Q(6)+L.Fl.15s Chequer No3
Fl.G.4s Binks No 3A
Fl.R.4s No2B
Fl(2)R.10s Hobo
Fl.G.3s
Bull VQ
Bull Sand Fort
Tetney Monobuoy 2VQ.Y(vert) Horn Mo(A)60s
Fl.Y.4s Bull Sand
Fl.R.4s No4
Fl.R.2s No2C
= Precautionary Area
= Recommended route for vessels <20m in and out

9.5.3 AREA 5 TIDAL STREAMS

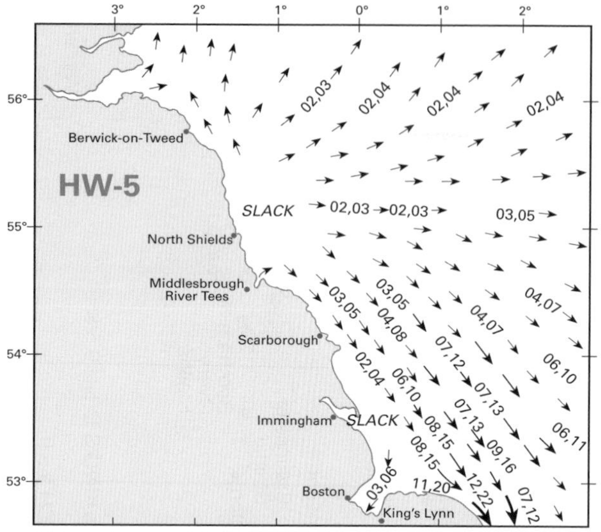

5 Hours before HW Dover (0030 after HW Immingham)

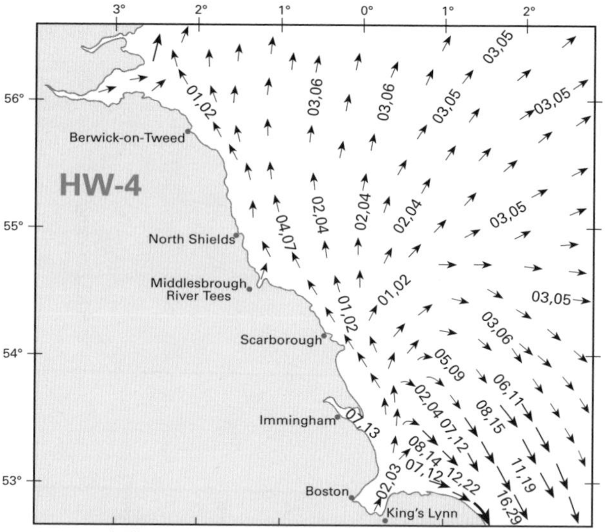

4 Hours before HW Dover (0130 after HW Immingham)

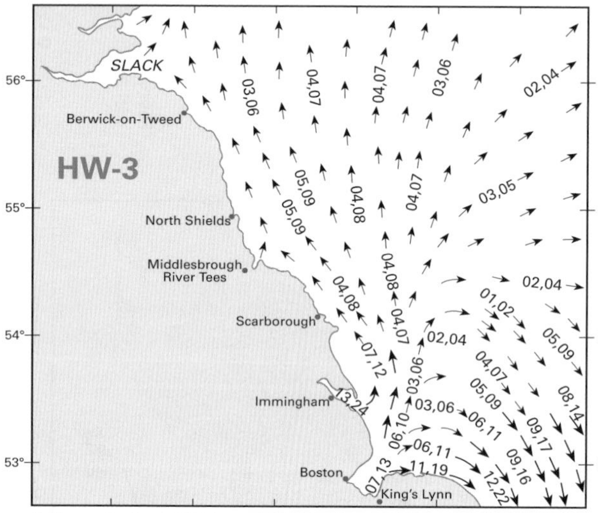

3 Hours before HW Dover (0230 after HW Immingham)

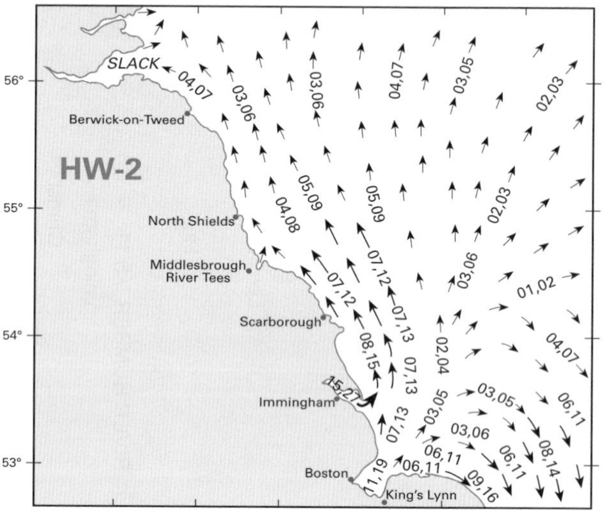

2 Hours before HW Dover (0330 after HW Immingham)

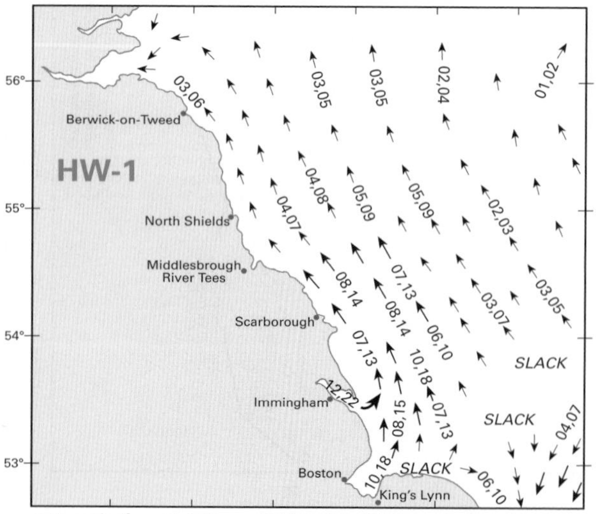

1 Hour before HW Dover (0430 after HW Immingham)

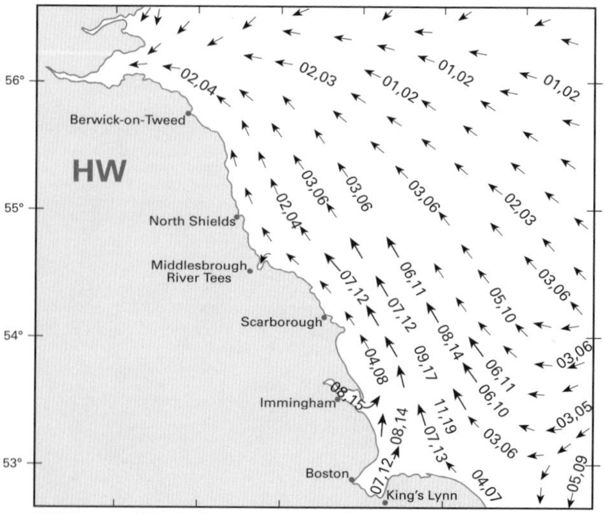

HW Dover (0530 after HW Immingham)

Northward 9.6.3   Southward 9.4.3

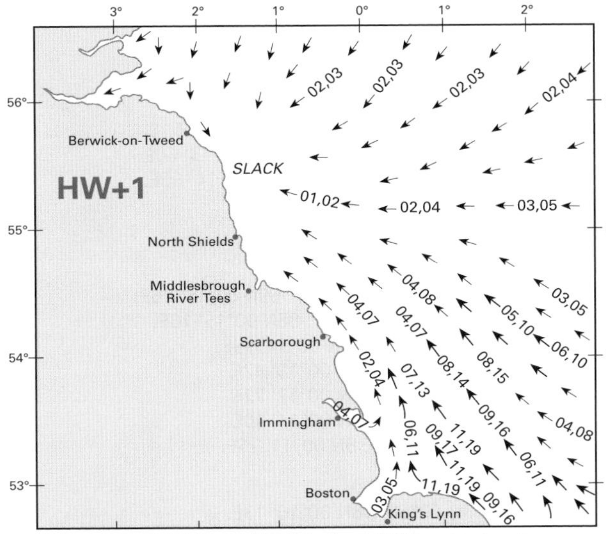

1 Hour after HW Dover (0555 before HW Immingham)

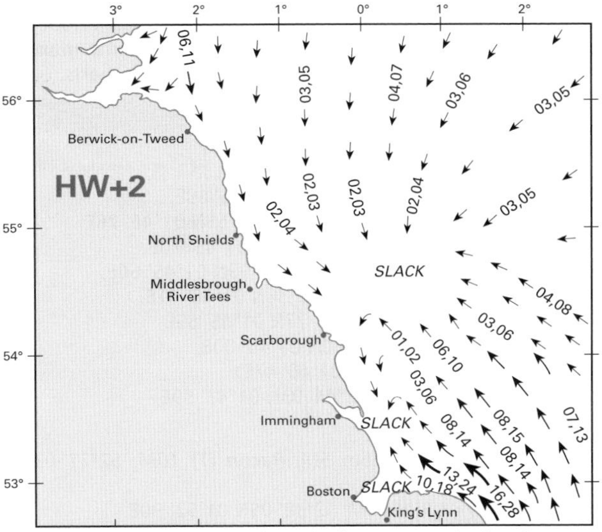

2 Hours after HW Dover (0455 before HW Immingham)

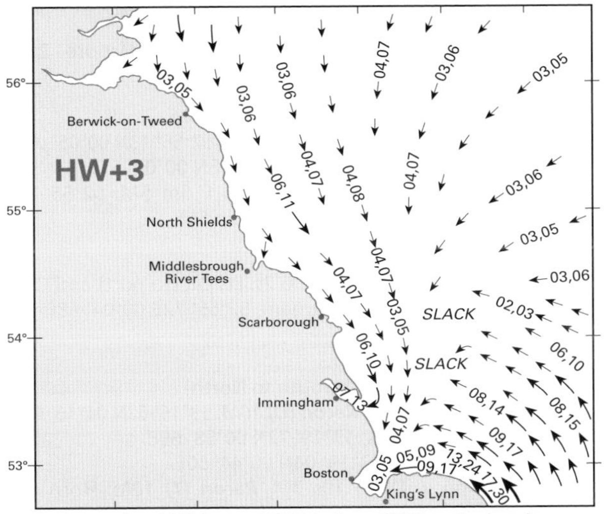

3 Hours after HW Dover (0355 before HW Immingham)

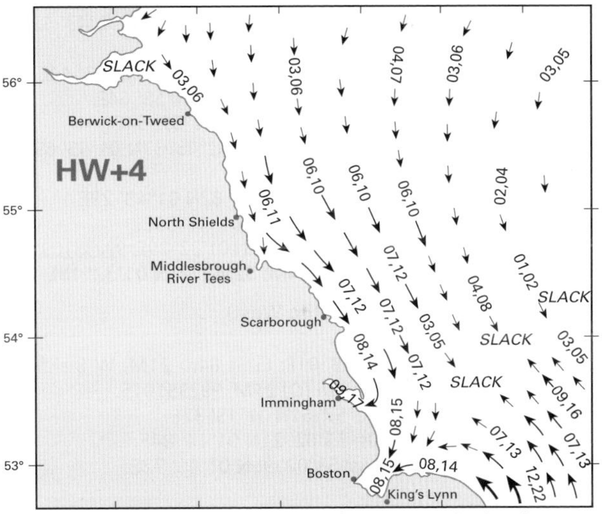

4 Hours after HW Dover (0255 before HW Immingham)

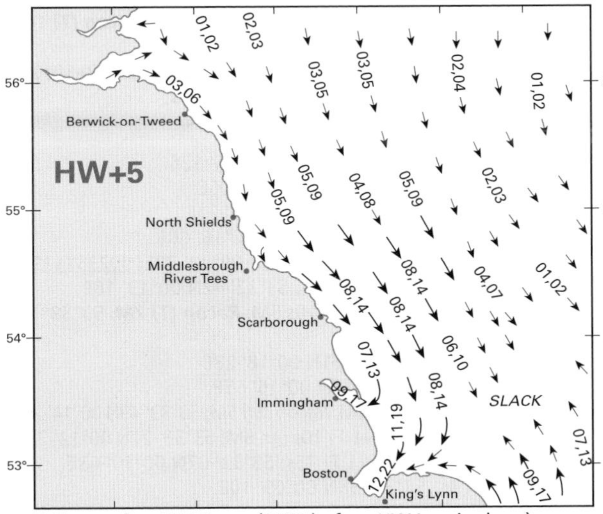

5 Hours after HW Dover (0155 before HW Immingham)

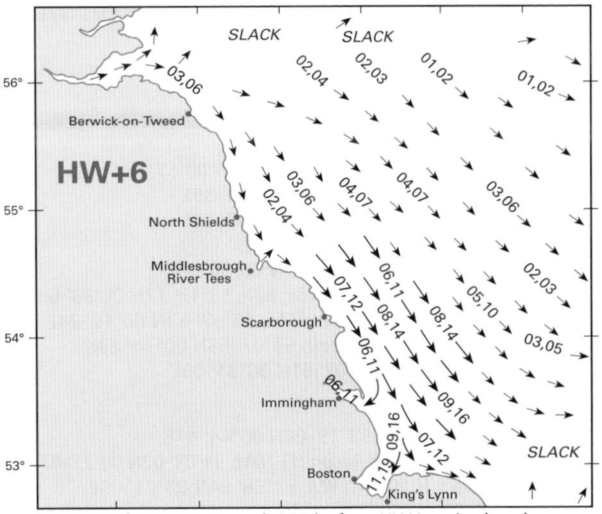

6 Hours after HW Dover (0055 before HW Immingham)

9.5.4 LIGHTS, BUOYS AND WAYPOINTS

Bold print = light with a nominal range of 15M or more. CAPITALS = place or feature. *CAPITAL ITALICS* = light-vessel, light float or Lanby. *Italics* = Fog signal. ***Bold italics*** = Racon. Some marks/ buoys are fitted with AIS (MMSI No); see relevant charts.

GREAT YARMOUTH TO THE WASH

(Direction of buoyage South to North)

YARMOUTH and CAISTER ROADS/COCKLE GATEWAY

SW Scroby Fl G 2·5s; 52°35′·13N 01°46′·69E.
Scroby Elbow Fl (2) G 5s; *Bell*; 52°36′·55N 01°46′·26E.
Yarmouth Outfall Q R; 52°37′·58N 01°45′·70E.
Mid Caister Fl (2) R 5s; *Bell*; 52°38′·99N 01°45′·66E.
NW Scroby Fl (3) G 10s; 52°40′·36N 01°46′·31E.
N Caister Fl (3) R 10s; 52°40′·77N 01°45′·65E.
Hemsby Fl R 2·5s; 52°41′·80N 01°46′·00E.
N Scroby VQ; 52°41′·39N 01°46′·47E.
Cockle VQ (3) 5s; *Bell*; 52°44′·03N 01°43′·59E.

OFFSHORE ROUTE

Cross Sand L Fl 10s 6m 5M; ***Racon (T) 10M***; 52°37′·03N 01°59′·14E.
Barley Q (6) + L Fl 15s 6M; 52°38′·05N 01°52′·90E.
E Cross Sand Fl (4) R 15s; 52°38′·55N 01°53′·55E.
NE Cross Sand VQ (3) 5s; 52°44′·22N 01° 53′·80E.
Smith's Knoll Q (6) + L Fl 15s 7M; ***Racon (T) 10M***; 52°43′·52N 02°17′·89E.
S Winterton Ridge Q (6) + L Fl 15s; 52°47′·21N 02°03′·44E.
E Hammond Knoll Q (3) 10s; 52°52′·32N 01°58′·64E.
Hammond Knoll Q (9) 15s; 52°49′·68N 01°57′·54E.
Newarp L Fl 10s 7M; ***Racon (O) 10M***; 52°48′·37N 01°55′·69E; 992351118.
S Haisbro Q (6) + L Fl 15s; *Bell*; 52°50′·82N 01°48′·29E.
Mid Haisbro Fl (2) G 5s; 52°54′·22N 01°41′·59E.
N Haisbro Q; ***Racon (T) 10M***; 53°00′·22N 01°32′·29E; 992351031.
Happisburgh ☆ Fl (3) 30s 41m 14M; 52°49′·21N 01°32′·18E.

(Direction of buoyage East to West)

CROMER

Cromer ☆ 52°55′·45N 01°19′·01E; Fl 5s 84m **21M**; W 8-sided twr; vis: 102°-307° H24; ***Racon (O) 25M***; 992351015.
Tayjack Wk Fl R 2·5s; 52°57′·61N 01°15′·37E.
E Sheringham Q (3) 10s; 53°02′·21N 01°14′·84E.
W Sheringham Q (9) 15s; 53°02′·95N 01°06′·72E.

BLAKENEY

Blakeney Fairway (SWM) ; 52°59′·31N 00°57′·83E (approx).
Blakeney Overfalls Fl (2) R 5s; *Bell*; 53°03′·01N 01°01′·37E.

WELLS-NEXT-THE-SEA/BRANCASTER STAITHE

Wells WCM Q(9) 15s; 52°59′·69N 00°50′·33E.
Bridgirdle Fl R 2·5s; 53°01′·73N 00°43′·95E.

APPROACHES TO THE WASH

S Race Q (6) + L Fl 15s; *Bell*; 53°07′·81N 00°57′·34E.
E Docking Fl R 2·5s; 53°09′·82N 00°50′·39E.
N Race Fl G 5s; *Bell*; 53°14′·98N 00°43′·87E.
N Docking Q; 53°14′·82N 00°41′·49E.
Scott Patch VQ (3) 5s; 53°11′·12N 00°36′·39E.
S Inner Dowsing Q (6) + L Fl 15s; *Bell*; 53°12′·12N 00°33′·69E.
Boygrift Tower Fl (2) 10s 12m 5M; 53°17′·63N 00°19′·24E.
Burnham Flats Q (9) 15s; *Bell*; 53°07′·53N 00°34′·89E.
Lincs WF E Q (3) 10s; 53°07′·61N 00°31′·06E.

THE WASH

West Ridge Q (9) 15s; 53°19′·06N 00°44′·47E.
N Well L Fl 10s; *Whistle*; ***Racon (T) 10M***; 53°03′·02N 00°27′·87E.
Roaring Middle L Fl 10s 7m 8M; 52°58′·64N 00°21′·08E.

KING'S LYNN

Sunk Q (9) 15s; 52°56′·29N 00°23′·40E.
Seal Sand Q; *Bell*; 52°56′·00N 00°20′·00E.
No 1 Fl G 3s; 52°56′·00N 00°21′·50E.
No 2 Fl (2)R 6s; 52°55′·00N 00°21′·90E.

WISBECH CHANNEL/RIVER NENE

Nene Roads *Mo(A) 6s*; 52°53′·85N 01°15′·51E
Wisbech No 1 Fl G 3s; 52°53′·33N 00°13′·60E.
East Knock VQ (3) 5s; 52°52′·06N 00°14′·66E.
Tide Guage ; 52°52′·53N 00°13′·03E.
Beacons are moved as required.

FREEMAN CHANNEL

Boston Roads L Fl 10s; 52°57′·69N 00°16′·96E.
Boston No 1 Fl G 3s; 52°57′·88N 00°15′·16E.
Alpha Fl R 3s; 52°57′·65N 00°14′·99E.
No 3 Fl G 6s; 52°57′·93N 00°15′·42E.
No 5 Fl G 3s; 52°58′·51N 00°12′·72E.
No 7 Fl G 6s; 52°58′·63N 00°11′·40E.
Delta Fl R 6s; 52°58′·38N 00°11′·25E.

BOSTON LOWER ROAD

Echo Fl R 3s; 52°58′·38N 00°10′·13E.
Foxtrot Fl R 3s; 52°57′·60N 00°08′·94E.
Boston No 9 Fl G 3s; 52°57′·58N 00°08′·36E.
Black Buoy Fl (2) R 6s; 52°56′·82N 00°07′·74E.
Tabs Head Q WG 4m 1M; R □ on W mast; vis: W shore - 251°- G - shore; 52°56'·00N 00°04'·91E.

BOSTON, NEW CUT AND RIVER WITHAM

Ent N side, Dollypeg QG 4m 1M; B △; 52°56′·13N 00°05′·03E.
New Cut Fl G 3s; △ on pile; 52°55′·98N 00°04′·67E.
New Cut Ldg Lts 240°. Front, No 1, F 5m 5M; 52°55′·85N 00°04′·40E. Rear, 90m from front, F 8m 5M.

WELLAND CUT/RIVER WELLAND

SE side Iso R 2s; NW side Iso G 2s. Lts QR (to port) and QG (to stbd) mark the chan upstream; 52°55′·72E 00°04′·68E.

THE WASH TO THE RIVER HUMBER

(Direction of buoyage South to North)

Dudgeon Q (9) 15s 7M; ***Racon (O) 10M***; 53°16′·62N 01°16′·90E.
E Dudgeon Q (3) 10s; 53°19′·72N 00°58′·69E.
W Ridge Q (9) 15s; 53°19′·04N 00°44′·50E.
Inner Dowsing Q (3) 10s 7M, ***Racon (T) 10M***; Horn 60s; 53°19′·10N 00°34′·80E.
Mid Outer Dowsing Fl (3) G 10s; 53°24′·82N 01°07′·79E.
N Outer Dowsing Q; 53°33′·52N 00°59′·59E; ***Racon (T) 10M***; 992351031.
B.1D Platform Dowsing 53°33′·68N 00°52′·63E; Fl (2) 10s 28m **22M**; Morse (U) R 15s 28m 3M; *Horn (2) 60s*.

RIVER HUMBER APPROACHES

Protector Fl R 2·5s; 53°24′·84N 00°25′·12E.
DZ No 4 Fl Y 5s; 53°27′·15N 00°19′·06E.
DZ No 3 Fl Y 2·5s 53°29′·30N 00°19′·21E.
Rosse Spit Fl (2) R 5s 53°30′·56N 00°16′·60E.
Outer Sand Q (3) 10s; 53°36′·41N 00°29′·39E; 992351119.
Haile Sand No 2 Fl (3) R 10s; 53°32′·42N 00°13′·18E.
HUMBER LT FLOAT L Fl G 10s 5M; ***Racon (T) 7M***; 53°38′·70N 00°21′·24E; AIS.
N Binks Fl G 4s; 53°36′·01N 00°18′·28E.
S Binks Fl G 2s 53°34′·74N 00°16′·55E.
SPURN Q (3) 10s 10m 8M; ***Racon (M) 5M***; 53°33′·49N 00°14′·20E.
SE CHEQUER VQ (6)+L Fl 10s 6m 6M; 53°33′·27N 00°12′·33E.
Chequer No 3 Q (6) + L Fl 15s; 53°33′·07N 00°10′·63E.
No 2B Fl R 4s; 53°32′·33N 00°09′·10E.

TETNEY 2 VQ Y (vert); *Horn Mo (A)60s*; QY on 290m floating hose; 53°32'·35N 00°06'·76E.

RIVER HUMBER/GRIMSBY/HULL

Binks No 3A Fl G 4s; 53°33'·92N 00°07'·43E.
Spurn Pt Fl G 3s 11m 5M; 53°34'·37N 00°06'·47E.
BULL VQ 8m 6M; 53°33'·54N 00°05'·70E.
Bull Sand Q R ; 53°34'·45N 00°03'·69E.
North Fort Q; 53°33'·80N 00°04'·19E.
South Fort Q (6) + L Fl 15s; 53°33'·65N 00°03'·96E.
Haile Sand Fort Fl R 5s 21m 3M; 53°32'·07N 00°01'·99E.
Haile Chan No 4 Fl R 4s; 53°33'·64N 00°02'·84E.
Middle No 7 VQ (6) + L Fl 10s; 53°35'·80N 00°01'·50E.
Grimsby Royal Dock ent E side Fl (2) R 6s 10m 8M; Dn; 53°35'·08N 00°04'·04W.
Immingham Bulk Terminal Dir Lt 291° Dir WRG 1s 17m 3M; vis: 288·5°-FG-289·5°-IsoG-290·5-FW-291·5-IsoR-292·5°-FR-295·5; on bldg; 53°38'·41N 00°11'·97W.

RIVER HUMBER TO WHITBY

Canada & Giorgios Wreck VQ (3) 5s; 53°42'·37N 00°07'·16E.
Albrough intake Q R 17m 2M; 53°49'·01N 00°03'·38W.

BRIDLINGTON

SW Smithic Q (9) 15s; 54°02'·41N 00°09'·21W.
N Pier Hd Fl 2s 12m 9M; *Horn 60s*; (Tidal Lts) Fl R or Fl G; 54°04'·77N 00°11'·19W.
N Smithic VQ; *Bell*; 54°06'·22N 00°03'·90W.
Flamborough Hd ☆ 54°06'·98N 00°04'·96W; Fl (4) 15s 65m **24M**; W ○ twr; *Horn (2) 90s*.

FILEY/SCARBOROUGH/WHITBY

Filey Brigg Q (3) 10s; *Bell*; 54°12'·74N 00°14'·60W.
Scarborough E Pier Hd QG 8m 3M; 54°16'·88N 00°23'·36W.
Scarborough Pier Iso 5s 17m 9M; W ○ twr; vis: 219°- 039° (tide sigs); *Dia 60s*; 54°16'·91N 00°23'·40W.
Whitby Q; *Bell*; 54°30'·33N 00°36'·58W.
Whitby High ☆ 54°28'·67N 00°34'·10W; Fl WR 5s 73m **18M**,R16M; W 8-sided twr & dwellings; vis:128°-R-143°-W-319°.
Whitby E Pier Fl(2) R 4s 16m 5M; 54°29'·57N 00°36'·71W; Twr.
Whitby E Pier Ext Hd Q R 12m 5M; 54°29'·65N 00°36'·74W.
Whitby W Pier Fl(2) G 4s 24m 5M; 54°29'·57N 00°36'·78W; Twr.
Whitby W Pier Ext Hd Q G 12m 5M; 54°29'·65N 00°36'·80W.

WHITBY TO THE RIVER TYNE

RUNSWICK/REDCAR

Salt Scar 54°38'·12N 01°00'·12W VQ; *Bell*.
Luff Way Ldg Lts 197°. Front, on Esplanade, FR 8m 7M; vis: 182°-212°; 54°37'·10N 01°03'·71W. Rear, 115m from front, FR 12m 7M; vis: 182°-212°.
High Stone. Lade Way Ldg Lts 247°. Front, Oc R 2·5s 9m 7M; 54°37'·15N 01°03'·92W. Rear, 43m from front, Oc R 2·5s 11m 7M; vis: 232°-262°.

TEES APPROACHES/HARTLEPOOL

Tees Approach Mo(A) 5s 8M; ***Racon (B)***; *Horn*; 54°40'·60N 01°04'·00W; AIS.
Bkwtr Hd S Gare ☆ 54°38'·85N 01°08'·25W; Fl WR 12s 16m **W20M, R17M**; W ○ twr; vis: 020°-W-240°-R-357°; Sig Stn.
Ldg Lts 210·1° Front, FR 18m 13M; 54°37'·22N 01°10'·20W. **Rear**, 560m from front, FR 20m **16M**.
Longscar Q (3) 10s; *Bell*; 54°40'·86N 01°09'·89W.
The Heugh ☆ 54°41'·79N 01°10'·56W; Fl (2) 10s 19m **19M**; W twr.

Hartlepool Marina Lock Dir Lt 308° Dir Fl WRG2s 6m 3M; vis: 305·5°-G-307°-W-309°-R-310·5°; 54°41'·45N 01°11'·92W.

SEAHAM/SUNDERLAND

Seaham N Pier Hd Fl G 10s 12m 5M; W col, B bands; 54°50'·26N 01°19'·26W.
Sunderland Roker Pier Hd ☆ 54°55'·28N 01°21'·15W; Fl 5s 25m **18M**; W □ twr, 3 R bands and cupola: vis: 211°- 357°; *Siren 20s*.
Old N Pier Hd QG 12m 8M; metal column; 54°55'·13N 01°21'·61W.
DZ 54°57'·04N 01°18'·90W and 54°58'·61N 01°19'·90W; both Fl Y 2·5s.

TYNE ENTRANCE/NORTH SHIELDS

Ent North Pier Hd ☆ 55°00'·88N 01°24'·18W; Fl (3) 10s 26m **26M**; Gy □ twr, W lantern; *Horn 10s*.
Herd Groyne Hd Dir Ldg Lt 249°, Oc 10s 14m **19M**; vis: 246·5°-W-251·5°; R pile structure, R&W lantern. Same structure Oc RG 10s 13m, 11M; vis: 224°-G-246·5°, 251·5°-R-277°; sync with Dir lt FR (unintens) 080°-224°. *Bell (1) 5s*; 55°00'·49N 01°25'·44W.

RIVER TYNE TO BERWICK-UPON-TWEED

CULLERCOATS and BLYTH

Cullercoats Ldg Lts 256°. Front, FR 27m 3M; 55°02'·06N 01°25'·91W. Rear, 38m from front, FR 35m 3M.
Blyth Ldg Lts 324°. Front , F Bu 11m 10M; 55°07'·42N 01°29'·82W. Rear , 180m from front, F Bu 17m 10M. Both Or on twr.
Blyth E Pier Hd ☆ 55°06'·98N 01°29'·21W; Fl (4) 10s 19m **21M**, W twr; same structure FR 13m 13M, vis:152°-249°; Horn (3) 30s.
Met Mast ; Mo(U)15s 17m 10M; 55°08'·78N 01°25'·25W; Aero 3 FR (107m), *Horn 30s*.

COQUET ISLAND, AMBLE and WARKWORTH

Coquet ☆ 55°20'·03N 01°32'·39W; Fl (3) WR 20s 25m **W19M, R15M**; W □ twr, turreted parapet, lower half Gy; vis: 330°-R-140°-W-163°-R-180°-W-330°; sector boundaries are indeterminate and may appear as Alt WR; *Horn 30s*.
Amble N Pier Head Fl G 6s 12m 6M; 55°20'·39N 01°34'·25W.

SEAHOUSES, BAMBURGH and FARNE ISLANDS

N Sunderland Fl R 2·5s; 55°34'·62N 01°37'·12W.
Bamburgh Black Rocks Point ☆ 55°36'·99N 01°43'·45W; Oc(2) WRG 8s 12m **W14M**, R11M, G11M; W bldg; vis: 122°-G-165°-W-175°-R-191°-W- 238°-R- 275°-W- 289°-G-300°.
Inner Farne Fl (2) WR 15s 27m W10M, R7M; W ○ twr; vis: 119°- R - 280° - W -119°; 55°36'·92N 01°39'·35W.
Longstone ☆ **W side** 55°38'·62N 01°36'·65W; Fl 20s 23m **18M**; R twr, W band; 992351127.
Swedman Fl G 2·5s; 55°37'·65N 01°41'·63W.

HOLY ISLAND

Ridge Q (3) 10s; 55°39'·70N 01°45'·97W.
Plough Rock Q (9) 15s; 55°40'·24N 01°46'·00W.
Old Law E Bn (Guile Pt) Oc WRG 6s 9m 4M; vis: 180·5°-G-258·5°-W-261·5°-R-300°, 55°39'·49N 01°47'·59W; stone obelisk.
Heugh Oc WRG 6s 24m 5M; vis: 135°-G-308°-W-311-R- shore; 55°40'·09N 01°47'·99W.
Plough Seat QR; 55°40'·37N 01°44'·97W.
Goldstone QG; 55°40'·25N 01°43'·64W.

BERWICK-UPON-TWEED

Bkwtr Hd Fl 5s 15m 6M; vis: 201°-009°, (obscured 155°-201°); W ○ twr, R cupola and base; FG (same twr) 8m 1M; vis 009°-G-155°; 55°45'·88N 01°59'·06W.

9.5.5 PASSAGE INFORMATION

More passage information is threaded between the harbours in this area. Admiralty Leisure Folios: 5614 Orford Ness to Whitby, 5615 Whitby to Berwick-upon-Tweed. **Bibliography:** *Forth, Tyne, Dogger, Humber* – Blakeney to St Abbs – (Imray/Irving) covers the southern part of this less frequented cruising ground. Northwards, use Royal Northumberland *YC's Sailing Directions Humber to Rattray Head.* The *North Sea (West) Pilot* (Admiralty NP54) covers the whole area.

NORTH SEA PASSAGES

See 9.0.7 for distances across the North Sea. There is further Passage Information in Area 4 for the southern North Sea, in Area 6 for crossing to Norway and the Baltic, and in Area 16 for crossings from the Frisian Islands, German Bight, Belgium and the Netherlands.

OFFSHORE ENERGY INSTALLATIONS

See 3.14. Any craft going offshore in the N Sea is likely to encounter oil or gas installations and wind farms. These are shown on Admiralty charts, where scale permits; the position of mobile rigs is updated in weekly NMs. Safety zones of radius 500m are established round all permanent platforms, mobile exploration rigs, and tanker loading moorings, as described in the Annual Summary of Admiralty Notices to Mariners No 20. Some of these platforms are close together or inter-linked. Unauthorised vessels, including yachts, must not enter these zones except in emergency or due to stress of weather. Platforms show a main lt, Fl Mo (U) 15s 15M. In addition secondary lts, Fl Mo (U) R 15s 2M, synchronised with the main lt, may mark projections at each corner of the platform if not marked by a W lt. Fog signal is Horn Mo (U) 30s. See the Admiralty List of Lights and Fog Signals, Vol A.

Increasing numbers of wind farms both under construction and complete are serviced by numerous fast work boats operating from Lowestoft, Gt Yarmouth, Wells, Wash and the Humber.

NORTH NORFOLK COAST

(AC 1503, 108) The coast of N Norfolk is unfriendly in bad weather, with no harbour accessible when there is any N in the wind. The hbrs all dry, and seas soon build up in the entrances or over the bars, some of which are dangerous even in a moderate breeze and an ebb tide. But in settled weather and moderate offshore winds it is a peaceful area to explore, particularly for boats which can take the ground. At Blakeney and Wells chans shift almost every year, so local knowledge is essential and may best be acquired in advance from the HM.

Haisborough Sand (buoyed) lies parallel to and 8M off the Norfolk coast at Happisburgh lt ho, with depths of less than 1m in many places, and drying 0·4m near the mid-point. The shoal is steep-to, on its NE side in particular, and there are tidal eddies. Even a moderate sea or swell breaks on the shallower parts. There are dangerous wks near the S end. Haisborough Tail and Hammond Knoll (with wk depth 1.6m) lie to the E of S end of Haisborough Sand. Newarp lt F is 5M SE. Similar banks lie parallel to and up to 60M off the coast.

▶ *The streams follow the generally NW/SE direction of the coast and offshore chans. But in the outer chans the stream is somewhat rotatory: when changing from SE-going to NW-going it sets SW, and when changing from NW-going to SE-going it sets NE, across the shoals. Close S of Haisborough Sand the SE-going stream begins at HW Immingham –0030; the NW-going at HW Immingham +0515, sp rates up to 2·5kn. It is possible to carry a fair tide from Gt Yarmouth to the Wash.* ◀

If proceeding directly from Cromer to the Humber, pass S of Sheringham Shoal (buoyed) and the windfarm close North. Head to the NE of Blakeney Overfalls (min depth 1m) and Docking Shoal, and then SW of Race Bank, where a wind farm is under construction so as to fetch Inner Dowsing lt (lt, fog sig). Thence pass E of Protector Overfalls, and steer for Rosse Spit buoy at SE ent to R Humber.

▶ *At Sheringham Shoal the ESE-going stream begins at HW Immingham –0225, and the WNW-going at +0430.* ◀

9.5.6 BLAKENEY

Norfolk **52°59'·19N 00°57'·90E** (ent shifts)

CHARTS AC 1190, 108; Imray C29, C28, Y9

TIDES –0445 Dover; ML Cromer 2·8; Duration 0530; Zone 0 (UT)

Standard Port IMMINGHAM (⟶)

Times				**Height (metres)**			
High Water		Low Water		MHWS	MHWN	MLWN	MLWS
0100	0700	0100	0700	7·3	5·8	2·6	0·9
1300	1900	1300	1900				
Differences BLAKENEY BAR (approx 52°59'N 00°59'E)							
+0035	+0025	+0030	+0040	–1·6	–1·3	ND	ND
BLAKENEY (approx 52°57'N 01°01'E)							
+0115	+0055	ND	ND	–3·9	–3·8	ND	ND
CROMER							
+0044	+0032	+0108	+0059	–2·3	–1·8	–0·7	0·0

SHELTER Very good but limited access over bar to shallow harbour. In fresh onshore winds conditions at the entrance deteriorate quickly, especially on the ebb. Moorings in The Pit dry out.

NAVIGATION WPT 53°00'·00N 00°58'·20E, approx 225°/1M to RW SWM 52°59'·37N 00°57'·85E (2015) which is moved as required.

- Hjordis lit IDM bn Fl(2) 5s marks large dangerous wreck, close E of entrance.
- The bar is shallow, shifts often and the channel is marked by SHM Nos 1, 2, 4, 5 and PHM buoys 3, 6 which are lit and relaid each spring. Other marks are unlit. Speed limit 8kn.
- Strangers are best advised to follow local boats in. Pilotage is available from Blakeney Harbour Boatman's Association.

LIGHTS AND MARKS Blakeney and Langham churches (conspic) a chimney on the house on Blakeney Point neck, TV mast (R lts) approx 2M S of entrance.

COMMUNICATIONS (Code 01263) CGOC (01262) 672317; Police 101 Blakeney Harbour Boatman's Association – Charlie Ward ☎740377 or 07771597985; Dr 712461.

FACILITIES (drying) may be rented, contact Charlie Ward.
Services Blakeney Marine Services ☎0776944361; Neil Thompson Boats Ltd ☎741172.
Village (garage ☎741456) (Sheringham) ✈(Norwich).

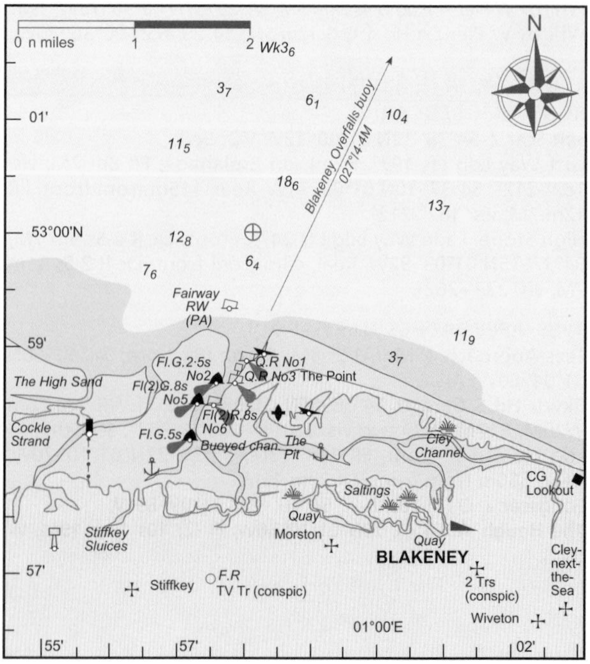

9.5.7 WELLS-NEXT-THE-SEA

Norfolk **52°59'·30N 00°49'·75E** (ent shifts)

CHARTS AC 1190, 108; Imray C29, C28, Y9

TIDES –0445 Dover; ML 1·2 Duration 0540

Standard Port IMMINGHAM (⟶)

Times				**Height (metres)**			
High Water		Low Water		MHWS	MHWN	MLWN	MLWS
0100	0700	0100	0700	7·3	5·8	2·6	0·9
1300	1900	1300	1900				
Differences WELLS BAR (approx 52°59'N 00°49'E)							
+0020	+0020	+0020	+0020	–1·3	–1·0	ND	ND
WELLS-NEXT-THE-SEA (approx 52°58'N 00°51'E)							
+0035	+0045	+0340	+0310	–3·8	–3·8	CD+	CD+
BURNHAM OVERY STAITHE							
+0045	+0055	ND	ND	–5·0	–4·9	ND	ND
HUNSTANTON							
+0010	+0020	+0105	+0025	+0·1	–0·2	–0·1	0·0

NOTE: LW time differences at Wells are for the end of a LW stand which lasts about 4hrs at sp and about 5hrs at nps.

SHELTER Good, but entrance difficult in strong onshore winds. Outer Harbour is mainly for commercial wind farm tenders and survey vessels, but with HM prior permission, vessels >2m draught may shelter in adverse conditions. Limited access (max draught 3m at springs); best attempted on the flood. Quay berths/pontoons at W end of Town Quay with 2m+ at LW.

NAVIGATION WPT WCM 52°59'·69N 00°50'·33E. Entry varies in depth and position; buoys are altered to suit. Initially keep to W side of chan to counter E-going tide; and to E side of chan from No 12 PHM lt buoy to Quay.

Obtain HM's advice, Hbr Launch often available to escort visitors into hbr & up to Quay. Spd limits: No 6 buoy to Quay 8kn; above this 5kn. See www.wellsharbour.co.uk for latest harbour chart.

LIGHTS AND MARKS From WCM Q (9) 15s the channel is well marked by lateral buoys, all Fl.3s, R to port, G to stbd. The lifeboat house (W with R roof) at N end of harbour is conspicuous.

COMMUNICATIONS (Code 01328) CGOC (01262) 672317; Police 101; Dr 710741. HM 711646, mob 07775 507284.

Call '*Wells Harbour*' Ch 12 16 before entering, listens HW–2 to HW+2 and when vessels expected.

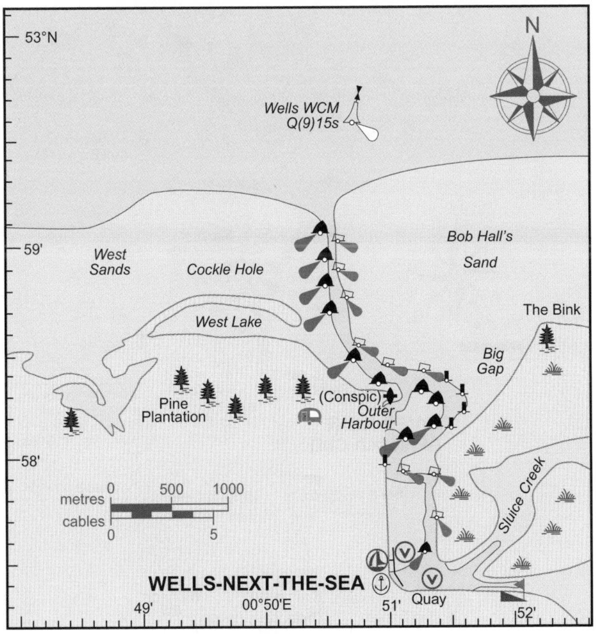

FACILITIES **Main Quay** on pontoons or quay, £21-£27/night; (9t) (25t mobile).

E Quay (£12/craft/day).

Wells SC ☎710622.

Services Ⓔ ACA LB.

Town (Hbr fuelling stn HW-2 to HW+3; up to 14,000 ltrs), Ⓑ (bus to Norwich/King's Lynn), ✈ (Norwich).

ADJACENT HARBOURS

BURNHAM OVERY STAITHE, Norfolk, **52°58'·95N 00°46'·55E**. AC 1190, 108. HW –0420 on Dover. See 9.5.8. Small drying hbr; ent chan has 0·3m MLWS. ⚓ off the Staithe only suitable in good weather. No lts. Scolt Hd is conspic to W and Gun Hill to E; Scolt Hd Island is conspic 3M long sandbank which affords some shelter. Chan varies constantly and buoys are moved to suit. Local knowledge advisable. Facilities: **Burnham Overy Staithe SC** ☎(01328) 738348. Services: **Burnham Market** EC Wed.

BRANCASTER STAITHE, Norfolk, **52°59'·02N 00°37'·65E**. AC 1190, 108. HW –0425 on Dover; as Burnham. Small drying hbr, dangerous to enter except by day in settled weather. Spd limit 6kn. Appr from due N. Conspic golf club house with lt, Fl 5s 8m 3M, is 0·5M S of chan ent and Fairway buoy. Beware wk shown on chart. Sandbanks shift; buoys changed to suit. Scolt Hd conspic to E. Local knowledge or Pilot advised. Possible in The Hole. HM ☎(01485) 210638. Facilities: **Brancaster Staithe SC** ☎210249; **Hunstanton SC** ☎(01485) 534705. Services:

THE WASH

(AC 108,1200) The Wash is formed by the estuaries of the rivers Great Ouse, Nene, Welland and Witham; it is an area of shifting sands, most of which dry. Important features are the strong tidal streams, the low-lying shore, and the often poor vis. Watch the echo sounder carefully, buoys are often moved to accommodate changes in the channel.

▶*Near North Well, the in-going stream begins at HW Immingham –0430, and the out-going at HW Immingham +0130, sp rates about 2kn. The in-going stream is usually stronger than the out-going, but its duration is less. Prolonged NE winds cause an in-going current, which can increase the rate and duration of the in-going stream and raise the water level at the head of the estuary. Do not attempt entry to the rivers too early on the flood, which runs hard in the rivers.* ◀

North Well SWM lt buoy and Roaring Middle lt float are the keys to entering the Wash from N or E. But from the E it is also possible to appr via a shallow route N of Stiffkey Overfalls and Bridgirdle PHM buoy; thence via Sledway and Woolpack PHM lt buoy to North Well and into Lynn Deeps. Near N end of Lynn Deeps there are overfalls over Lynn Knock at sp tides. Approach King's Lynn from No 1 light buoy, Fl G 3s, via Daseley Sled and well buoyed/lit channel. For R Nene (Wisbech) follow Old Lynn Channel and Wisbech Eye Channel to E Knock ECM which marks entrance to buoyed approach.

Boston and R Welland are reached via Freeman Channel, westward from Roaring Middle; or via Boston Deep, all lit. King's Lynn ⚓ is marked by Roaring Middle, Sunk and Seal Outer. ⚓ for Boston and Wisbech each have AIS enhanced marks.

The NW shore of The Wash is fronted by mudflats extending 2–3M offshore and drying more than 4m; a bombing range is marked by Y bns and buoys. Wainfleet Swatchway should only be used in good vis; the buoyed chan shifts constantly, and several shoals (charted depths unreliable) off Gibraltar Pt obstruct access to Boston Deep. In an emergency Wainfleet offers good shelter (dries).

Wisbech Cut provides access inland to the Fens Middle Levels, navigable by narrow boat and river cruisers. Dog in a Doublet Lock above Wisbech is the practical limit of sea-going vessels.

The Gt Ouse is navigable as far as Ely 24M upstream. There is a lock half-way at Denver Sluice ☎(01366) 382340/VHF Ch 73, and low bridges beyond.

9.5.8 KING'S LYNN

Norfolk **52°49′·72N 00°21′·14E** (W Stones Bn)

CHARTS AC 1190, 108, 1200, 5614. Imray C29, Y9

TIDES –0443 Dover, +0030 Immingham; ML 3·6; Duration 0340

Standard Port IMMINGHAM (⟶)

Times				Height (metres)			
High Water		Low Water		MHWS	MHWN	MLWN	MLWS
0100	0700	0100	0700	7·3	5·8	2·6	0·9
1300	1900	1300	1900				
Differences KING'S LYNN							
+0030	+0030	+0305	+0140	–0·5	–0·8	–0·8	+0·1
WEST STONES							
+0025	+0025	+0115	+0040	–0·3	–0·4	–0·3	+0·2

SHELTER Port is well sheltered; entry only recommended HW–3½. A busy commercial and fishing port. 3 Ⓥ pontoons on S quay. River moorings available from local clubs; keep clear of FV moorings.

NAVIGATION WPT No 1 SHM, Fl G 3s, 52° 56′.00N 00° 21′.25E follow Daseley Sled and well buoyed/lit chan to King's Lynn. Upstream to Denver Sluice (ent to inland routes) 6 bridges span river, min clearance 9·15m less ht of tide above dock sill at King's Lynn. Allow 1½hrs for passage. Sandbanks regularly shift and extend several miles into the Wash; buoyage is altered accordingly. Contact HM (www.kingslynnport.co.uk) in advance or www.sailthewash.com.

LIGHTS AND MARKS See 9.5.4 and chartlet.

COMMUNICATIONS Code (01553) CGOC (01262) 672317; Police 101; HM 0773411; Docks 691555.

Kings Lynn Hbr Radio Ch **14** 11 (M-F: 0800-1730 LT. Other times: HW –4 to HW+1) (ABP) Ch **14** 16 11 (HW–2½ to HW).

FACILITIES 6 £42 (<9m/48hrs), (32t) .
Town ⇌ ✈(Norwich).

Ely Marina 24M up the Great Ouse River, ☎(01353) 664622, (10t) .

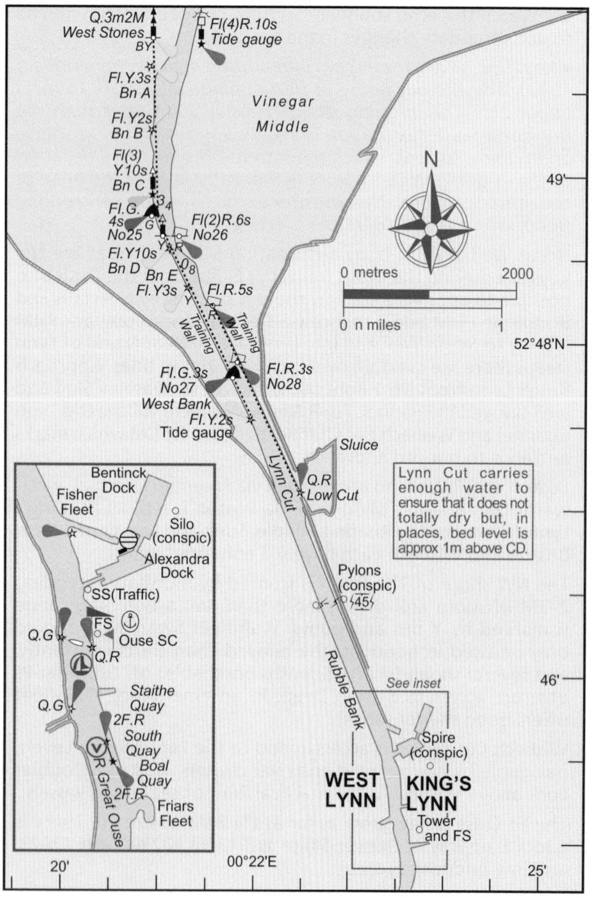

9.5.9 WISBECH

Cambridgeshire **52°40′·02N 00°09′·55E**

CHARTS AC 1190, 108, 1200, 5614. Imray C29, Y9

TIDES –0443 Dover, +0030 Immingham; ML 3·6; Duration 0340

Standard Port IMMINGHAM (⟶)

Times				Height (metres)			
High Water		Low Water		MHWS	MHWN	MLWN	MLWS
0100	0700	0100	0700	7·3	5·8	2·6	0·9
1300	1900	1300	1900				
OUTER WESTMARK KNOCK							
+0010	+0015	+0040	+0020	–0·2	–0·5	–0·6	–0·4
WISBECH CUT							
+0020	+0010	+0120	+0055	–0·3	–0·7	–0·4	ND
WISBECH							
+0055	+0040	DR	DR	–0·2	–0·6	DR	DR

SHELTER Excellent in river with Wisbech Yacht Harbour pontoon berths and facilities immediately below Freedom Br in Wisbech. Vessels of 4·8m draught can reach Wisbech at sp (3·4m at nps).

NAVIGATION WPT Roaring Middle Lt Flt 52° 58′.64N 00° 21′.08E 220°/7M to Wisbech No 1 SHM Fl G 5s. Call HM at RAF No 4 ECM (s for waiting) to check commercial traffic and Cross Keys Sw Br. Red flags and lights shown when Holbeach Firing Range in use. Chan to R Nene well marked with lit buoys/bns. Best ent HW–3. Cross Keys Sw Br manned HW±4 if booked at least 24H in advance. Waiting pontoon 0.5M below bridge thence 6M to Wisbech. Departure best at HW; if draught >3m, clear Kerr NCM by HW+3. For pilotage notes ☎ Hbr Office or visit www.fenland.gov.uk.

LIGHTS AND MARKS See 9.5.4 and chartlet.

COMMUNICATIONS Code (01945) CGOC (01262) 672317; Police 101; Dr 582133; Ⓗ 585781; HM 588059 (24H); Cross Keys Swing Bridge ☎01406 350364.

HM *Wisbech Harbour* Ch **09** call HM and Cross Keys Sw Br HW±3.

FACILITIES **Yacht Hbr** (102+15Ⓥ) £1, min charge £5, (barge). **Town** .

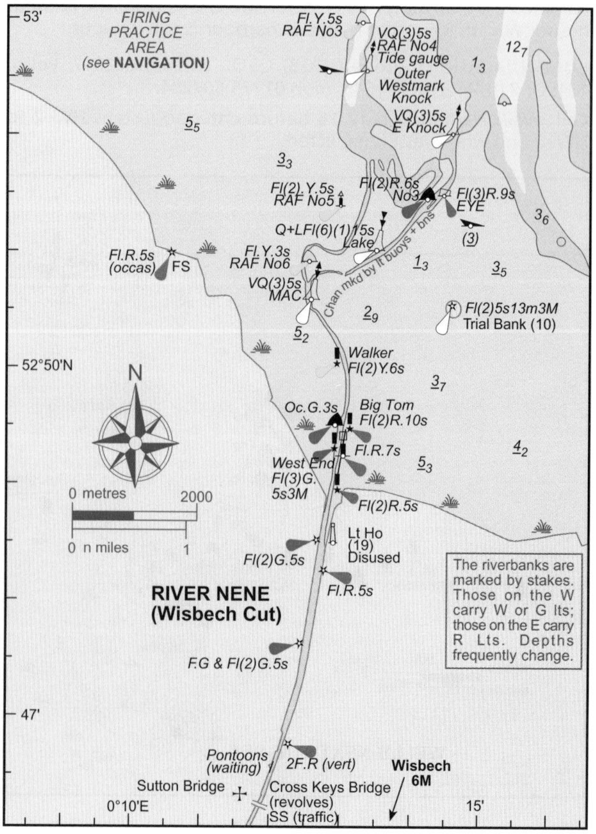

9.5.10 BOSTON

Lincs **52°56'·00N 00°04'·92E** (Tabs Head bn)

CHARTS AC 108, 1200, 5614; Imray C29, Y9

TIDES –0415 Dover; ML 3·3; Duration Flood 0500, Ebb 0700

Standard Port IMMINGHAM (⟶)

Times				Height (metres)			
High Water		Low Water		MHWS	MHWN	MLWN	MLWS
0100	0700	0100	0700	7·3	5·8	2·6	0·9
1300	1900	1300	1900				
Differences BOSTON							
0000	+0010	+0140	+0050	–0·5	–1·0	–0·9	–0·5
TABS HEAD (WELLAND RIVER)							
0000	+0005	+0125	+0020	+0·2	–0·2	–0·2	–0·2
SKEGNESS							
+0010	+0015	+0030	+0020	–0·4	–0·5	–0·1	0·0
INNER DOWSING LIGHT TOWER							
0000	0000	+0010	+0010	–0·9	–0·7	–0·1	+0·3

SHELTER Very good. Except in emergency, berthing in the Dock is prohib without HM permission. Yachts secure just above Dock ent and see HM. The port is administered by Port of Boston Ltd.

Yachts capable of lowering masts can pass through the Grand Sluice (***24hrs notice required***) into fresh water. Sluice 16m x 9m and opens twice a tide at approx HW±2. It leads into the R Witham Navigation which goes 31M to Lincoln. Marina is to stbd immediately beyond the sluice. British Waterways have 50 berths, with water and fuel, beyond Grand Sluice.

NAVIGATION WPT Boston Rds SWM lt buoy, 52°57'·61N 00°16'·29E, 282°/0·75M to Freeman Chan ent. Thence Bar Chan is well marked, but liable to change. SW of Clay Hole a new chan has formed which dries 0.6m at entr; it is marked by SHM lt buoys Nos 11N, 13N, and 15. Tabs Head marks the ent to the river; it should be passed not earlier than HW–3 to enable the Grand Sluice to be reached before the start of the ebb. Beware rocky bottom within 100m of the Sluice. On reaching Boston Dock, masts should be lowered to negotiate swing bridge (cannot always be opened) and three fixed bridges. Chan through town is unnavigable at LW.

LIGHTS AND MARKS St Boltoph's ch tr (the Boston Stump) is conspic from afar. New Cut and R Witham are marked by bns with topmarks. FW lts mark ldg lines: three pairs going upstream and six pairs going downstream.

COMMUNICATIONS (Code 01205) CGOC (01262) 672317; Police 101; Ⓗ 364801. Dock office 365571 (H24 & emergency); HM 362328; Grand Sluice Control 364864 (not always manned but has answerphone) mob 07712 010920.

All vessels between No 9 buoy and Grand Sluice must listen Ch 12 (also advisable to maintain watch while in local tidal waters). Call: *Boston Port Control* VHF Ch 12 (HW –2½ to HW +1½ when commercial shipping is moving). Ch 11 used by dock staff as required. *Grand Sluice* Ch 74.

FACILITIES **Boston Gateway Marina** ☎07480525230, (48+Ⓥ) £10/night any size inc in dock (see HM).

Grand Sluice WC; **BWB** moorings: 1st night free, then £5·00.

Services

Town Thurs; ✉ Ⓑ ✕ ⇌ ✈(Humberside).

ADJACENT HARBOURS

RIVER WELLAND, Lincolnshire, **52°56'·00N 00°04'·92E** (Tabs Head bn). AC 1190, 1200. At Welland Cut HW –0440 on Dover; ML 0·3m; Duration 0520. See 9.5.10. At Tabs Head bn HW ±3, ent Welland Cut which is defined by training walls and lt bns. Beware sp flood of up to 5kn. Berth 6M up at **Fosdyke Yacht Haven** ☎01205 260240. (50 + 6Ⓥ 2m depth); WC by prior arrangement, (50t) – only one between R Humber & Lowestoft ✕.

WAINFLEET, Lincolnshire, **53°04'·79N 00°19'·89E** (chan ent). AC 108. Skegness HW +0500 on Dover. See 9.5.10 (Skegness). ML 4·0m; Duration 0600. Shelter good. Recommended max boat length 10m, draught 1·5m. Lit PHM indicates entrance to drying channel close S of Gibraltar Point. Chan through saltings marked by buoys and bns with lateral topmarks but no lts. Enter HW ±1½. Facilities: (larger boats at fishing jetties, smaller at YC), at YC.
Town All facilities at Skegness (3½ miles).

Skegness YC skegnessyachtclub.co.uk ☎0779 941856 (Commodore) on the R Steeping inside Gibraltar Pt has a membership of about 65 with a small clubhouse. at WC.

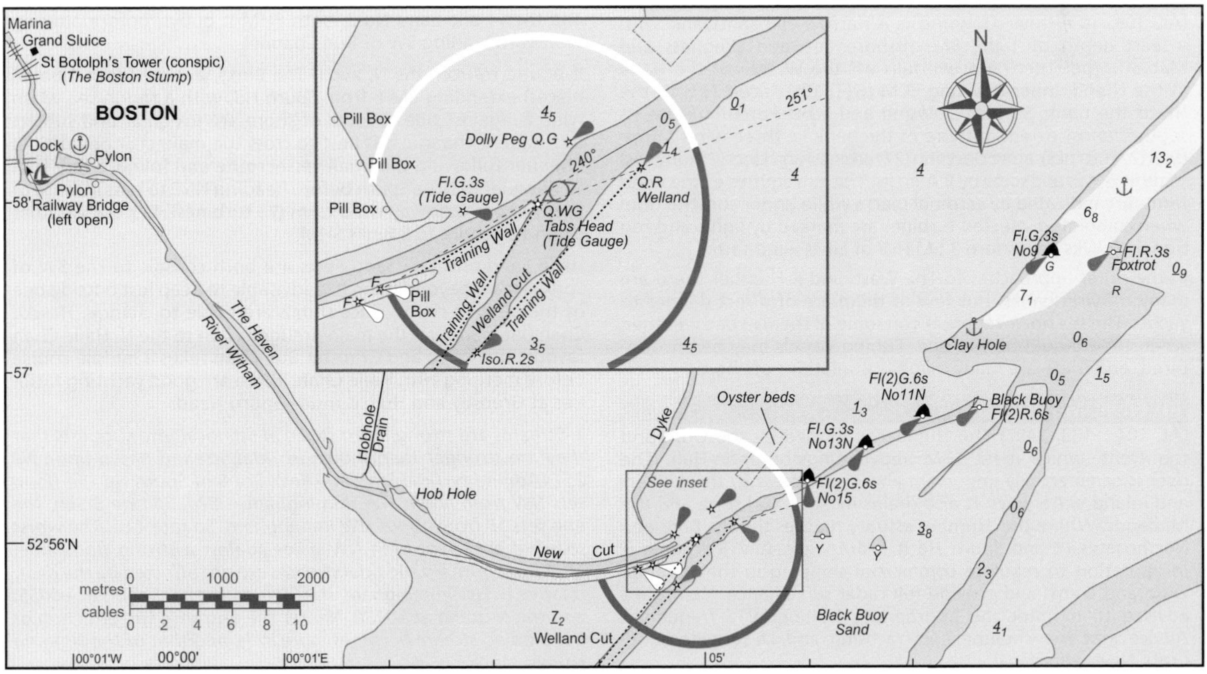

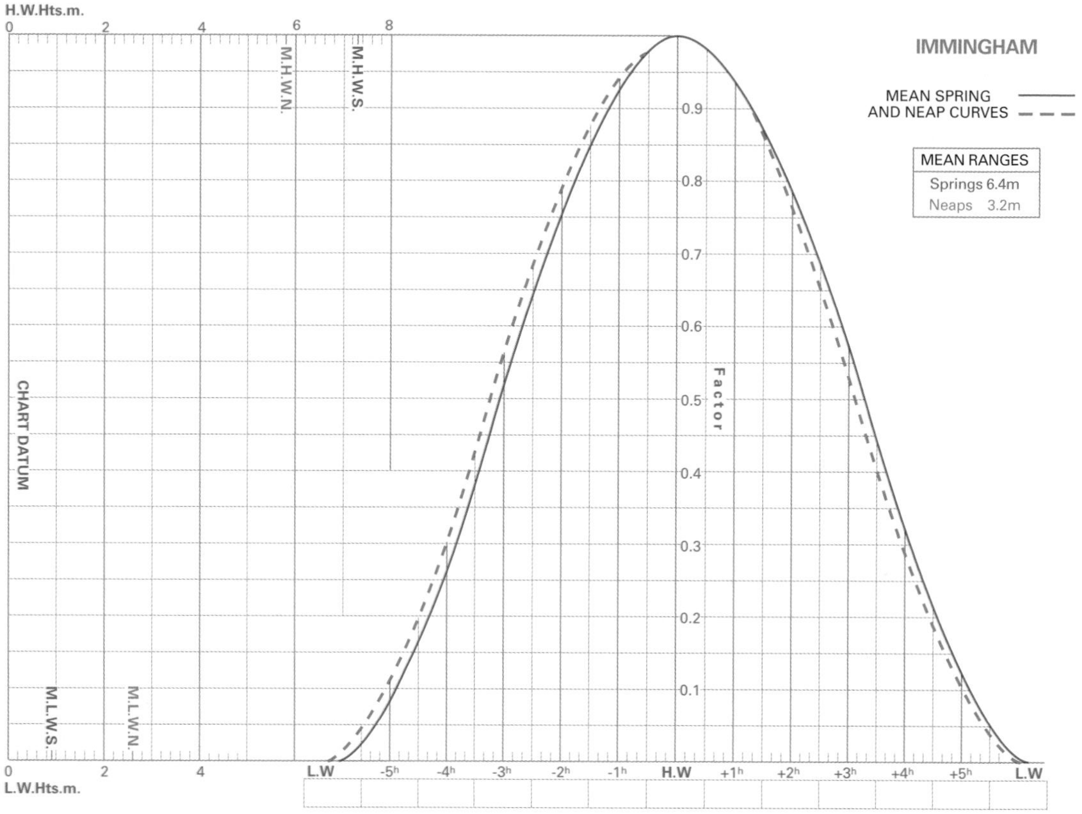
H.W.Hts.m.
0 2 4 6 8
M.H.W.N.
M.H.W.S.
IMMINGHAM
MEAN SPRING AND NEAP CURVES
MEAN RANGES
Springs 6.4m
Neaps 3.2m
0.9
0.8
0.7
0.6
0.5
0.4
0.3
0.2
0.1
Factor
CHART DATUM
M.L.W.S.
M.L.W.N.
0 2 4
L.W.Hts.m.
L.W -5h -4h -3h -2h -1h H.W +1h +2h +3h +4h +5h L.W

THE WASH TO THE RIVER HUMBER

(AC 108, 107) Inner Dowsing is a narrow N/S sandbank with a least depth of 1·2m, 8M offshore between Skegness and Mablethorpe. There are overfalls off the W side of the bank at the N end. Inner Dowsing ECM (Q(3) 10s, Racon T) is to the NE of the bank, S Inner Dowsing and Scott Patch indicate its southernmost extent. Inshore of the bank lie three wind farms: Lynn (27 turbines), Inner Dowsing (27 turbines) and Lincs (75 turbines) some lit Fl Y 5s and some by R Aero lts. The extremities of the wind farms are indicated by cardinal marks while under construction; when completed selected turbines are marked by lights and fog signals. 2 Wks lie inshore 3.5M NW of Lincs wind farm.

In the outer approaches to The Wash and R Humber there are many offlying banks, but few of them are of direct danger to yachts. The sea however breaks on some of them in bad weather, when they should be avoided. Fishing vessels may be encountered, and there are many oil/gas installations offshore.

RIVER HUMBER

(AC 104, 1188, 3497) The Humber is formed by the Ouse and the Trent, which meet 13M above Kingston-upon-Hull. The river is commercially important and gives access to these rivers and inland waterways; it also drains most of Yorkshire and the Midlands. Where the Humber estuary reaches the sea between Northcoates Pt and Spurn Hd it is 4M wide. A VTS scheme is in operation to regulate commercial shipping in the Humber, Ouse and Trent and provide full radar surveillance. Yachts are advised to monitor the appropriate Humber VTS frequency. Advice is at www.humber.com/Yachting_and_Leisure/Pleasure_Craft_Navigation/

Approaching from the S, a yacht should make good Rosse Spit and then Haile Sand No 2, both PHM lt buoys, before altering westward leading SW of Bull Channel.

If bound to/from the N, avoid The Binks, a shoal (dries 1·6m in places) extending 3M E from Spurn Hd, with a rough sea when wind is against tide. Depths offshore are irregular and subject to frequent change; it is best to cross the main channel at No 3 Chequer following the small vessel route and follow a line N of SE Chequer to close Spurn before heading NNE to pass inshore of the Humber Gateway wind farm (73 turbines). In poor weather extend offshore to S Binks SHM.

Haile Sand and Bull Sand Forts are both conspic to the SW of Spurn Head; beyond them it is advisable to keep just outside one of the buoyed chans, since shoals are liable to change. Hawke Chan (later Sunk) is the main dredged chan to the N. Haile Chan favours the S side and Grimsby. Bull Chan takes a middle course before merging with Haile Chan. There are good yachting facilities at Grimsby and Hull. ⚓ inside Spurn Head.

▶ *Streams are strong, even fierce at Sp; local info suggests that they are stronger than shown in Tidal Streams based upon NP 251 (Admiralty Tidal Stream Atlas). 5ca S of Spurn Hd the flood sets NW from about HW Immingham –0520, Sp rate 3·5kn; the ebb sets SE from about HW Immingham, Sp rate 4kn. The worst seas are experienced in NW gales against a strong flood tide. 10M E of Spurn Hd the tidal streams are not affected by the river; relative to HW Immingham, the S-going stream begins at –0455, and the N-going at +0130. Nearer the entrance the direction of the S-going stream becomes more W'ly, and that of the N-going stream more E'ly.* ◀

STANDARD TIME (UT)
For Summer Time add ONE hour in **non-shaded areas**

IMMINGHAM LAT 53°38′N LONG 0°11′W

TIMES AND HEIGHTS OF HIGH AND LOW WATERS

Dates in red are SPRINGS
Dates in blue are NEAPS

YEAR **2018**

JANUARY

Date	Time	m	Date	Time	m
1 M	0442 1109 1715 2339	7.1 1.2 7.2 1.0	16 TU	0531 1140 1741	6.5 1.7 6.9
2 TU ○	0537 1201 1802	7.4 1.0 7.4	17 W	0009 0607 1219 ● 1816	1.5 6.6 1.6 7.0
3 W	0032 0629 1251 1847	0.8 7.5 0.9 7.6	18 TH	0048 0642 1255 1850	1.4 6.7 1.5 7.0
4 TH	0123 0720 1338 1932	0.6 7.5 0.9 7.6	19 F	0123 0716 1327 1924	1.4 6.7 1.5 7.0
5 F	0212 0809 1422 2016	0.6 7.4 1.1 7.5	20 SA	0155 0751 1358 1956	1.4 6.7 1.6 7.0
6 SA	0259 0857 1505 2101	0.7 7.1 1.4 7.3	21 SU	0225 0824 1429 2027	1.5 6.6 1.7 6.9
7 SU	0345 0947 1547 2150	1.0 6.8 1.7 6.9	22 M	0256 0858 1503 2100	1.5 6.5 1.8 6.8
8 M	0433 1042 1633 ◑ 2245	1.4 6.4 2.1 6.6	23 TU	0331 0936 1542 2141	1.6 6.3 1.9 6.7
9 TU	0525 1140 1724 2349	1.8 6.1 2.5 6.2	24 W	0413 1021 1630 ◐ 2231	1.8 6.2 2.2 6.5
10 W	0623 1242 1828	2.1 5.9 2.7	25 TH	0507 1119 1731 2333	2.0 6.0 2.4 6.3
11 TH	0057 0727 1343 1946	6.0 2.3 5.9 2.8	26 F	0615 1234 1847	2.1 5.9 2.4
12 F	0205 0831 1443 2100	6.0 2.3 6.0 2.6	27 SA	0051 0731 1358 2006	6.2 2.1 6.0 2.3
13 SA	0308 0927 1537 2157	6.1 2.2 6.2 2.3	28 SU	0218 0847 1508 2122	6.3 2.0 6.3 2.0
14 SU	0404 1015 1623 2245	6.2 2.0 6.5 2.0	29 M	0332 0954 1608 2229	6.6 1.7 6.7 1.5
15 M	0450 1059 1704 2329	6.4 1.8 6.7 1.7	30 TU	0436 1054 1701 2329	6.9 1.4 7.1 1.0
			31 W ○	0533 1148 1750	7.2 1.1 7.4

FEBRUARY

Date	Time	m	Date	Time	m
1 TH	0023 0625 1239 1836	0.7 7.4 0.9 7.6	16 F	0030 0622 1238 1830	1.3 6.7 1.4 7.1
2 F	0113 0713 1324 1920	0.4 7.5 0.9 7.7	17 SA	0107 0657 1312 1904	1.2 6.8 1.4 7.1
3 SA	0159 0757 1407 2002	0.4 7.4 0.9 7.6	18 SU	0140 0730 1343 1937	1.2 6.9 1.4 7.2
4 SU	0242 0838 1446 2043	0.5 7.2 1.1 7.4	19 M	0210 0803 1413 2008	1.2 6.8 1.4 7.1
5 M	0322 0919 1522 2124	0.8 6.9 1.5 7.1	20 TU	0239 0834 1446 2041	1.2 6.8 1.4 7.1
6 TU	0400 1001 1557 2207	1.3 6.5 1.8 6.7	21 W	0310 0909 1521 2120	1.3 6.6 1.6 6.9
7 W	0438 1047 1637 ◑ 2259	1.7 6.1 2.2 6.2	22 TH	0346 0950 1604 2206	1.5 6.4 1.8 6.6
8 TH	0522 1143 1726	2.2 5.8 2.6	23 F	0433 1042 1700 ◐ 2306	1.9 6.1 2.1 6.3
9 F	0005 0618 1249 1830	5.8 2.5 5.6 2.8	24 SA	0539 1152 1817	2.2 5.8 2.4
10 SA	0123 0731 1358 2001	5.6 2.7 5.6 2.8	25 SU	0026 0704 1326 1945	6.0 2.4 5.8 2.3
11 SU	0238 0849 1501 2130	5.7 2.6 5.9 2.5	26 M	0208 0829 1449 2110	6.0 2.2 6.1 2.0
12 M	0341 0949 1555 2224	5.9 2.3 6.2 2.1	27 TU	0330 0942 1554 2220	6.4 1.9 6.5 1.5
13 TU	0432 1037 1640 2309	6.2 2.0 6.5 1.8	28 W	0434 1043 1648 2318	6.8 1.5 7.0 1.0
14 W	0513 1120 1719 2351	6.4 1.7 6.7 1.5			
15 TH ●	0549 1201 1755	6.6 1.6 6.9			

MARCH

Date	Time	m	Date	Time	m
1 TH	0528 1136 1737	7.1 1.2 7.3	16 F	0524 1137 1728	6.6 1.6 6.9
2 F	0010 0615 1224 ○ 1821	0.6 7.3 0.9 7.5	17 SA	0005 0558 1216 ● 1804	1.2 6.8 1.4 7.1
3 SA	0057 0658 1308 1903	0.4 7.4 0.8 7.7	18 SU	0043 0632 1251 1840	1.1 6.9 1.2 7.2
4 SU	0140 0736 1347 1942	0.3 7.4 0.8 7.6	19 M	0118 0706 1324 1915	1.0 7.0 1.1 7.3
5 M	0219 0813 1423 2020	0.5 7.2 1.0 7.4	20 TU	0149 0739 1357 1949	0.9 7.1 1.1 7.3
6 TU	0253 0846 1455 2056	0.8 7.0 1.3 7.1	21 W	0220 0811 1431 2024	1.0 7.0 1.2 7.3
7 W	0324 0919 1525 2132	1.3 6.6 1.6 6.7	22 TH	0251 0847 1507 2104	1.2 6.8 1.3 7.0
8 TH	0355 0952 1559 2212	1.7 6.3 2.0 6.2	23 F	0327 0927 1549 2152	1.5 6.6 1.6 6.6
9 F	0432 1035 1642 ◑ 2308	2.2 5.9 2.4 5.7	24 SA	0413 1018 1646 ◐ 2254	1.9 6.2 2.0 6.2
10 SA	0523 1140 1740	2.6 5.5 2.7	25 SU	0518 1128 1805	2.3 5.9 2.2
11 SU	0035 0630 1309 1856	5.4 2.9 5.4 2.9	26 M	0022 0648 1306 1936	5.9 2.5 5.8 2.2
12 M	0204 0758 1424 2051	5.4 2.9 5.6 2.7	27 TU	0209 0817 1433 2101	5.9 2.4 6.0 1.8
13 TU	0314 0919 1523 2156	5.7 2.6 6.0 2.2	28 W	0326 0930 1538 2207	6.3 2.0 6.5 1.3
14 W	0407 1012 1611 2243	6.0 2.2 6.3 1.8	29 TH	0426 1028 1631 2302	6.7 1.6 6.9 0.9
15 TH	0449 1056 1651 2325	6.3 1.8 6.6 1.5	30 F	0515 1118 1717 2350	7.1 1.2 7.2 0.6
			31 SA ○	0558 1204 1801	7.2 1.0 7.4

APRIL

Date	Time	m	Date	Time	m
1 SU	0034 0635 1246 1841	0.5 7.3 0.9 7.5	16 M	0012 0605 1225 ● 1813	1.0 7.0 1.1 7.3
2 M	0115 0710 1325 1920	0.5 7.3 0.9 7.4	17 TU	0050 0640 1303 1852	0.9 7.2 1.0 7.4
3 TU	0151 0743 1359 1956	0.7 7.2 1.0 7.3	18 W	0126 0715 1341 1931	0.8 7.2 0.9 7.4
4 W	0222 0813 1429 2030	1.0 7.0 1.2 7.0	19 TH	0201 0751 1419 2011	0.9 7.2 1.0 7.3
5 TH	0251 0841 1458 2102	1.4 6.7 1.5 6.6	20 F	0237 0829 1500 2056	1.1 7.0 1.1 7.0
6 F	0320 0910 1529 2138	1.8 6.4 1.8 6.2	21 SA	0317 0912 1546 2147	1.4 6.7 1.4 6.6
7 SA	0353 0947 1609 2225	2.2 6.0 2.2 5.7	22 SU	0405 1005 1646 ◐ 2253	1.9 6.3 1.8 6.2
8 SU	0439 1040 1704 ◑ 2341	2.6 5.7 2.6 5.4	23 M	0510 1116 1803	2.3 6.0 2.0
9 M	0544 1209 1817	2.9 5.4 2.7	24 TU	0028 0635 1250 1927	5.9 2.6 5.9 1.9
10 TU	0122 0705 1339 1942	5.3 3.0 5.5 2.6	25 W	0200 0759 1412 2044	6.0 2.4 6.1 1.6
11 W	0237 0832 1444 2111	5.5 2.7 5.8 2.3	26 TH	0311 0909 1515 2145	6.3 2.1 6.5 1.3
12 TH	0332 0936 1534 2205	5.9 2.3 6.2 1.8	27 F	0408 1005 1608 2237	6.7 1.7 6.8 1.0
13 F	0416 1023 1616 2250	6.3 1.9 6.5 1.5	28 SA	0454 1055 1655 2324	6.9 1.4 7.1 0.8
14 SA	0453 1106 1656 2332	6.6 1.6 6.8 1.2	29 SU	0533 1140 1738	7.1 1.1 7.2
15 SU	0529 1146 1735	6.8 1.3 7.1	30 M	0007 0608 1223 ○ 1818	0.8 7.1 1.0 7.2

Chart Datum: 3·90 metres below Ordnance Datum (Newlyn). HAT is 8·0 metres above Chart Datum.

STANDARD TIME (UT)
For Summer Time add ONE hour in **non-shaded areas**

IMMINGHAM LAT 53°38′N LONG 0°11′W

TIMES AND HEIGHTS OF HIGH AND LOW WATERS

Dates in red are SPRINGS
Dates in blue are NEAPS

YEAR **2018**

MAY

Date	Day	Time	m	Time	m	Time	m	Time	m	Moon
1	TU	0047	0.8	0643	7.1	1301	1.0	1857	7.2	
2	W	0122	1.0	0715	7.1	1335	1.1	1933	7.0	
3	TH	0153	1.2	0744	6.9	1406	1.3	2007	6.8	
4	F	0222	1.5	0812	6.8	1435	1.5	2039	6.5	
5	SA	0251	1.8	0842	6.5	1507	1.8	2114	6.2	
6	SU	0324	2.1	0917	6.2	1545	2.1	2157	5.8	
7	M	0405	2.5	1003	5.9	1637	2.3	2259	5.5	
8	TU	0503	2.8	1111	5.6	1742	2.5			◑
9	W	0026	5.4	0615	2.9	1242	5.5	1855	2.5	
10	TH	0145	5.5	0732	2.8	1353	5.7	2009	2.2	
11	F	0246	5.9	0842	2.5	1448	6.1	2113	1.9	
12	SA	0335	6.2	0938	2.1	1536	6.4	2206	1.5	
13	SU	0417	6.6	1027	1.7	1621	6.8	2254	1.2	
14	M	0458	6.8	1113	1.4	1704	7.0	2339	1.0	
15	TU	0537	7.1	1158	1.1	1748	7.3			●
16	W	0022	0.9	0616	7.2	1242	0.9	1832	7.4	
17	TH	0104	0.8	0655	7.3	1326	0.8	1917	7.4	
18	F	0145	0.9	0735	7.3	1410	0.8	2003	7.3	
19	SA	0227	1.1	0817	7.1	1457	0.9	2051	7.1	
20	SU	0311	1.4	0904	6.9	1548	1.2	2147	6.7	
21	M	0401	1.8	0958	6.5	1647	1.5	2256	6.3	
22	TU	0503	2.2	1107	6.2	1756	1.7			◐
23	W	0020	6.1	0616	2.4	1229	6.1	1908	1.7	
24	TH	0136	6.1	0732	2.4	1343	6.2	2017	1.6	
25	F	0243	6.3	0840	2.2	1447	6.4	2116	1.4	
26	SA	0339	6.5	0938	1.9	1542	6.6	2208	1.2	
27	SU	0425	6.7	1029	1.6	1631	6.8	2255	1.2	
28	M	0504	6.8	1115	1.4	1715	6.9	2338	1.2	
29	TU	0541	6.9	1158	1.3	1758	6.9			○
30	W	0018	1.2	0616	7.0	1239	1.2	1837	6.9	
31	TH	0055	1.3	0649	7.0	1315	1.3	1913	6.8	

JUNE

Date	Day	Time	m	Time	m	Time	m	Time	m	Moon
1	F	0128	1.4	0720	6.9	1348	1.4	1948	6.6	
2	SA	0159	1.6	0751	6.8	1419	1.5	2021	6.4	
3	SU	0229	1.8	0822	6.6	1451	1.7	2056	6.2	
4	M	0301	2.0	0857	6.4	1528	1.9	2137	6.0	
5	TU	0340	2.3	0938	6.1	1613	2.1	2227	5.8	
6	W	0428	2.5	1030	5.9	1709	2.2	2331	5.6	◑
7	TH	0529	2.7	1139	5.8	1812	2.2			
8	F	0045	5.6	0637	2.7	1253	5.8	1916	2.1	
9	SA	0152	5.8	0745	2.5	1358	6.1	2021	1.9	
10	SU	0250	6.1	0849	2.2	1455	6.4	2122	1.6	
11	M	0341	6.4	0948	1.8	1547	6.7	2217	1.4	
12	TU	0427	6.8	1042	1.5	1638	7.0	2309	1.1	
13	W	0512	7.0	1134	1.1	1728	7.2	2358	1.0	●
14	TH	0557	7.2	1225	0.9	1819	7.4			
15	F	0046	0.9	0640	7.4	1315	0.7	1908	7.4	
16	SA	0132	0.9	0724	7.4	1404	0.6	1958	7.3	
17	SU	0218	1.0	0809	7.3	1453	0.7	2049	7.1	
18	M	0304	1.3	0856	7.1	1544	0.9	2144	6.8	
19	TU	0352	1.6	0949	6.9	1638	1.1	2247	6.5	
20	W	0446	2.0	1050	6.6	1737	1.4	2354	6.3	◐
21	TH	0547	2.3	1159	6.3	1840	1.6			
22	F	0100	6.1	0655	2.4	1309	6.2	1943	1.7	
23	SA	0203	6.1	0804	2.4	1414	6.3	2043	1.7	
24	SU	0301	6.2	0908	2.2	1514	6.3	2138	1.7	
25	M	0351	6.4	1003	1.9	1608	6.5	2226	1.6	
26	TU	0435	6.6	1052	1.7	1656	6.5	2311	1.6	
27	W	0515	6.7	1137	1.5	1740	6.6	2352	1.5	
28	TH	0552	6.8	1219	1.4	1820	6.6			○
29	F	0031	1.5	0627	6.9	1258	1.4	1856	6.6	
30	SA	0107	1.5	0701	6.9	1334	1.4	1931	6.6	

JULY

Date	Day	Time	m	Time	m	Time	m	Time	m	Moon
1	SU	0141	1.6	0734	6.9	1408	1.5	2004	6.5	
2	M	0212	1.7	0807	6.8	1439	1.6	2039	6.4	
3	TU	0243	1.9	0840	6.6	1512	1.7	2116	6.2	
4	W	0317	2.0	0916	6.5	1550	1.8	2157	6.1	
5	TH	0358	2.2	0957	6.3	1634	2.0	2245	5.9	
6	F	0448	2.4	1049	6.1	1728	2.0	2346	5.8	◑
7	SA	0548	2.5	1152	6.1	1830	2.1			
8	SU	0057	5.8	0656	2.5	1305	6.1	1936	2.0	
9	M	0206	6.0	0807	2.3	1416	6.3	2043	1.8	
10	TU	0307	6.3	0914	2.0	1521	6.6	2147	1.6	
11	W	0402	6.6	1018	1.6	1620	6.8	2245	1.3	
12	TH	0453	6.9	1117	1.2	1717	7.1	2340	1.1	
13	F	0541	7.2	1212	0.8	1812	7.3			●
14	SA	0032	1.0	0628	7.4	1305	0.6	1903	7.4	
15	SU	0121	0.9	0714	7.6	1355	0.4	1953	7.4	
16	M	0207	0.9	0759	7.6	1444	0.4	2042	7.3	
17	TU	0251	1.1	0845	7.4	1531	0.6	2131	7.0	
18	W	0336	1.4	0933	7.2	1619	0.9	2222	6.7	
19	TH	0421	1.8	1025	6.8	1708	1.3	2317	6.4	◐
20	F	0510	2.1	1125	6.5	1802	1.7			
21	SA	0016	6.1	0607	2.4	1230	6.2	1902	2.1	
22	SU	0117	5.9	0719	2.6	1338	6.0	2006	2.2	
23	M	0218	5.9	0836	2.5	1445	6.0	2107	2.2	
24	TU	0315	6.1	0940	2.3	1547	6.1	2200	2.1	
25	W	0406	6.3	1032	2.0	1639	6.3	2247	1.9	
26	TH	0450	6.6	1119	1.7	1724	6.4	2331	1.7	
27	F	0529	6.8	1202	1.5	1803	6.6			○
28	SA	0011	1.6	0606	6.9	1242	1.4	1838	6.6	
29	SU	0050	1.6	0641	7.0	1320	1.3	1912	6.7	
30	M	0124	1.6	0715	7.0	1354	1.4	1945	6.7	
31	TU	0155	1.6	0749	7.0	1425	1.4	2018	6.6	

AUGUST

Date	Day	Time	m	Time	m	Time	m	Time	m	Moon
1	W	0225	1.7	0821	6.9	1454	1.5	2052	6.5	
2	TH	0255	1.8	0853	6.8	1524	1.6	2126	6.4	
3	F	0330	1.9	0928	6.6	1600	1.8	2206	6.2	
4	SA	0412	2.1	1012	6.4	1646	1.9	2255	6.0	◑
5	SU	0507	2.3	1108	6.2	1746	2.1			
6	M	0001	5.9	0615	2.5	1221	6.1	1857	2.2	
7	TU	0124	5.9	0733	2.4	1347	6.1	2014	2.1	
8	W	0240	6.1	0851	2.1	1506	6.4	2126	1.9	
9	TH	0343	6.5	1003	1.7	1613	6.7	2230	1.6	
10	F	0438	6.9	1106	1.2	1712	7.1	2327	1.3	
11	SA	0528	7.3	1202	0.8	1806	7.3			●
12	SU	0019	1.0	0615	7.5	1254	0.4	1856	7.5	
13	M	0107	0.9	0700	7.7	1342	0.3	1941	7.5	
14	TU	0151	0.9	0744	7.7	1427	0.3	2024	7.4	
15	W	0233	1.0	0826	7.6	1509	0.5	2105	7.2	
16	TH	0312	1.3	0909	7.3	1550	1.0	2148	6.8	
17	F	0349	1.6	0954	6.9	1630	1.5	2233	6.4	
18	SA	0428	2.1	1046	6.5	1712	2.0	2325	6.0	◐
19	SU	0514	2.5	1148	6.0	1805	2.4			
20	M	0028	5.8	0615	2.8	1302	5.7	1916	2.7	
21	TU	0135	5.7	0755	2.8	1417	5.7	2035	2.7	
22	W	0240	5.9	0919	2.5	1526	5.9	2136	2.4	
23	TH	0338	6.2	1013	2.1	1621	6.2	2226	2.1	
24	F	0425	6.5	1059	1.8	1706	6.4	2310	1.9	
25	SA	0506	6.8	1141	1.5	1743	6.6	2351	1.7	
26	SU	0542	7.0	1221	1.3	1816	6.7			○
27	M	0029	1.5	0617	7.1	1259	1.2	1848	6.8	
28	TU	0104	1.5	0652	7.1	1333	1.2	1921	6.9	
29	W	0136	1.5	0726	7.1	1403	1.2	1953	6.9	
30	TH	0204	1.5	0758	7.1	1430	1.3	2024	6.8	
31	F	0233	1.6	0829	7.0	1457	1.5	2055	6.7	

Chart Datum: 3·90 metres below Ordnance Datum (Newlyn). HAT is 8·0 metres above Chart Datum.

STANDARD TIME (UT)
For Summer Time add ONE hour in **non-shaded areas**

IMMINGHAM LAT 53°38'N LONG 0°11'W

TIMES AND HEIGHTS OF HIGH AND LOW WATERS

Dates in red are SPRINGS
Dates in blue are NEAPS

YEAR **2018**

SEPTEMBER

Date	Time	m	Date	Time	m
1 SA	0305 0903 1528 2131	1.7 6.9 1.6 6.4	16 SU	0349 1005 1621 ◐ 2227	2.0 6.4 2.2 6.1
2 SU	0344 0945 1609 2217	1.9 6.6 1.9 6.2	17 M	0429 1103 1707 2330	2.4 5.9 2.7 5.7
3 M	0434 1039 1707 ◑ 2319	2.2 6.3 2.2 5.9	18 TU	0525 1224 1813	2.8 5.5 3.0
4 TU	0545 1154 1827	2.5 6.0 2.5	19 W	0051 0645 1348 1950	5.6 3.0 5.5 3.0
5 W	0049 0711 1335 1955	5.8 2.5 6.0 2.5	20 TH	0205 0853 1459 2110	5.7 2.7 5.7 2.7
6 TH	0220 0838 1502 2114	6.0 2.2 6.3 2.2	21 F	0307 0948 1556 2201	6.1 2.3 6.1 2.3
7 F	0328 0954 1609 2218	6.5 1.6 6.7 1.7	22 SA	0357 1032 1640 2245	6.4 1.8 6.4 1.9
8 SA	0423 1055 1705 2313	6.9 1.1 7.1 1.4	23 SU	0437 1113 1716 2325	6.8 1.5 6.7 1.7
9 SU	0512 1148 1755 ●	7.3 0.7 7.4	24 M	0514 1152 1748	7.0 1.3 6.9
10 M	0002 0557 1237 1839	1.1 7.6 0.4 7.5	25 TU	0003 0549 1230 ○ 1820	1.5 7.1 1.2 7.0
11 TU	0048 0641 1321 1920	0.9 7.8 0.3 7.5	26 W	0039 0624 1305 1853	1.4 7.2 1.1 7.1
12 W	0130 0722 1403 1957	0.9 7.8 0.4 7.4	27 TH	0111 0659 1336 1925	1.4 7.3 1.1 7.1
13 TH	0209 0803 1440 2033	1.0 7.7 0.7 7.2	28 F	0141 0733 1404 1956	1.4 7.3 1.2 7.0
14 F	0244 0842 1514 2109	1.2 7.4 1.1 6.9	29 SA	0212 0806 1432 2028	1.4 7.2 1.4 6.9
15 SA	0316 0922 1546 2145	1.6 6.9 1.7 6.5	30 SU	0246 0843 1504 2104	1.6 7.0 1.6 6.6

OCTOBER

Date	Time	m	Date	Time	m
1 M	0324 0927 1544 2150	1.8 6.7 2.0 6.3	16 TU	0354 1019 1621 ◐ 2227	2.3 5.9 2.7 5.8
2 TU	0416 1024 1641 ◑ 2252	2.1 6.3 2.4 6.0	17 W	0447 1137 1722 2355	2.7 5.5 3.1 5.6
3 W	0530 1145 1807	2.4 5.9 2.7	18 TH	0600 1309 1847	2.9 5.4 3.2
4 TH	0025 0700 1334 1941	5.8 2.4 5.9 2.7	19 F	0123 0744 1422 2025	5.6 2.8 5.6 3.0
5 F	0201 0830 1455 2101	6.0 2.1 6.3 2.3	20 SA	0229 0908 1520 2126	5.9 2.4 6.0 2.5
6 SA	0309 0941 1558 2202	6.5 1.5 6.8 1.8	21 SU	0320 0955 1605 2212	6.3 2.0 6.4 2.1
7 SU	0404 1037 1650 2254	7.0 1.0 7.1 1.4	22 M	0402 1037 1642 2252	6.6 1.6 6.7 1.8
8 M	0451 1126 1735 2341	7.3 0.7 7.4 1.1	23 TU	0440 1117 1716 2331	6.9 1.3 6.9 1.6
9 TU	0535 1212 1815 ●	7.6 0.5 7.5	24 W	0518 1155 1750 ○	7.1 1.2 7.1
10 W	0025 0617 1255 1852	1.0 7.7 0.5 7.5	25 TH	0008 0555 1232 1824	1.4 7.3 1.1 7.2
11 TH	0106 0658 1334 1927	0.9 7.7 0.7 7.4	26 F	0044 0632 1306 1858	1.3 7.4 1.1 7.2
12 F	0143 0738 1408 2000	1.1 7.5 1.0 7.2	27 SA	0119 0710 1339 1931	1.2 7.4 1.1 7.2
13 SA	0216 0815 1438 2031	1.3 7.2 1.4 6.9	28 SU	0155 0748 1412 2006	1.2 7.3 1.3 7.1
14 SU	0245 0851 1507 2101	1.6 6.8 1.8 6.6	29 M	0233 0830 1448 2045	1.4 7.1 1.6 6.8
15 M	0316 0930 1539 2136	1.9 6.4 2.3 6.2	30 TU	0316 0918 1531 2133	1.6 6.7 2.0 6.5
			31 W	0411 1019 1630 ◑ 2236	1.9 6.3 2.4 6.1

NOVEMBER

Date	Time	m	Date	Time	m
1 TH	0525 1145 1752	2.2 6.0 2.7	16 F	0521 1212 1750	2.7 5.5 3.1
2 F	0006 0650 1323 1921	6.0 2.2 6.0 2.7	17 SA	0022 0636 1329 1911	5.7 2.7 5.6 3.1
3 SA	0136 0811 1437 2037	6.1 1.9 6.3 2.4	18 SU	0135 0755 1430 2026	5.8 2.5 5.9 2.8
4 SU	0244 0917 1538 2138	6.5 1.5 6.7 2.0	19 M	0232 0859 1520 2123	6.1 2.1 6.2 2.4
5 M	0339 1012 1627 2229	6.9 1.1 7.0 1.6	20 TU	0320 0950 1602 2210	6.4 1.8 6.5 2.0
6 TU	0428 1100 1709 2316	7.2 0.9 7.2 1.3	21 W	0403 1035 1641 2254	6.7 1.5 6.8 1.7
7 W	0512 1144 1748 ●	7.4 0.8 7.3	22 TH	0445 1117 1719 2336	7.0 1.3 7.1 1.4
8 TH	0000 0555 1226 1823	1.1 7.4 0.9 7.3	23 F	0527 1159 1757 ○	7.2 1.1 7.2
9 F	0041 0636 1303 1858	1.1 7.4 1.0 7.3	24 SA	0018 0609 1239 1834	1.2 7.4 1.1 7.3
10 SA	0118 0715 1337 1930	1.2 7.3 1.2 7.2	25 SU	0101 0652 1319 1912	1.1 7.4 1.1 7.3
11 SU	0151 0752 1407 2000	1.3 7.0 1.5 7.0	26 M	0143 0736 1358 1952	1.1 7.3 1.3 7.2
12 M	0221 0827 1436 2029	1.6 6.7 1.8 6.7	27 TU	0227 0823 1440 2034	1.1 7.1 1.5 7.0
13 TU	0251 0903 1507 2103	1.8 6.3 2.2 6.4	28 W	0315 0915 1526 2123	1.3 6.8 1.9 6.7
14 W	0328 0946 1546 2146	2.2 5.9 2.6 6.1	29 TH	0411 1017 1622 2224	1.6 6.4 2.3 6.4
15 TH	0416 1046 1639 ◐ 2251	2.5 5.6 2.9 5.8	30 F	0517 1136 1732 ◑ 2343	1.8 6.2 2.6 6.2

DECEMBER

Date	Time	m	Date	Time	m
1 SA	0631 1257 1851	1.9 6.1 2.6	16 SU	0544 1218 1805	2.5 5.6 2.9
2 SU	0103 0743 1406 2004	6.3 1.8 6.3 2.4	17 M	0025 0650 1328 1916	5.8 2.4 5.7 2.8
3 M	0212 0847 1507 2108	6.4 1.6 6.5 2.1	18 TU	0134 0756 1428 2023	6.0 2.2 6.0 2.6
4 TU	0312 0942 1558 2203	6.7 1.4 6.7 1.8	19 W	0233 0857 1520 2123	6.2 2.0 6.3 2.2
5 W	0404 1031 1641 2252	6.9 1.3 6.9 1.6	20 TH	0326 0952 1607 2217	6.5 1.7 6.6 1.8
6 TH	0451 1116 1720 2337	7.0 1.2 7.0 1.4	21 F	0416 1042 1652 2308	6.8 1.4 6.9 1.5
7 F	0536 1158 1758 ●	7.1 1.3 7.1	22 SA	0504 1131 1735 ○ 2358	7.1 1.2 7.1 1.2
8 SA	0019 0617 1236 1833	1.3 7.0 1.3 7.1	23 SU	0553 1218 1817	7.3 1.1 7.3
9 SU	0058 0657 1311 1907	1.3 7.0 1.5 7.1	24 M	0047 0641 1304 1859	0.9 7.4 1.1 7.4
10 M	0133 0733 1342 1938	1.4 6.8 1.6 7.0	25 TU	0135 0729 1349 1942	0.8 7.4 1.1 7.4
11 TU	0204 0808 1412 2009	1.6 6.6 1.8 6.9	26 W	0223 0818 1433 2027	0.8 7.3 1.3 7.3
12 W	0235 0842 1444 2041	1.7 6.4 2.0 6.6	27 TH	0312 0910 1519 2115	0.9 7.0 1.6 7.1
13 TH	0309 0920 1519 2119	1.9 6.1 2.3 6.4	28 F	0403 1007 1609 2210	1.2 6.7 1.9 6.8
14 F	0350 1006 1602 2206	2.2 5.9 2.6 6.1	29 SA	0500 1111 1705 ◑ 2315	1.4 6.4 2.2 6.5
15 SA	0442 1106 1658 ◐ 2309	2.4 5.7 2.8 5.9	30 SU	0602 1219 1811	1.7 6.2 2.5
			31 M	0026 0707 1325 1923	6.3 1.9 6.1 2.5

Chart Datum: 3·90 metres below Ordnance Datum (Newlyn). HAT is 8·0 metres above Chart Datum.

9.5.11 RIVER HUMBER

S bank: NE and N Lincolnshire. N bank: E Riding of Yorks and City of Kingston-upon-Hull.
Hull marina: **53°44′·24N 00°20′·15W**

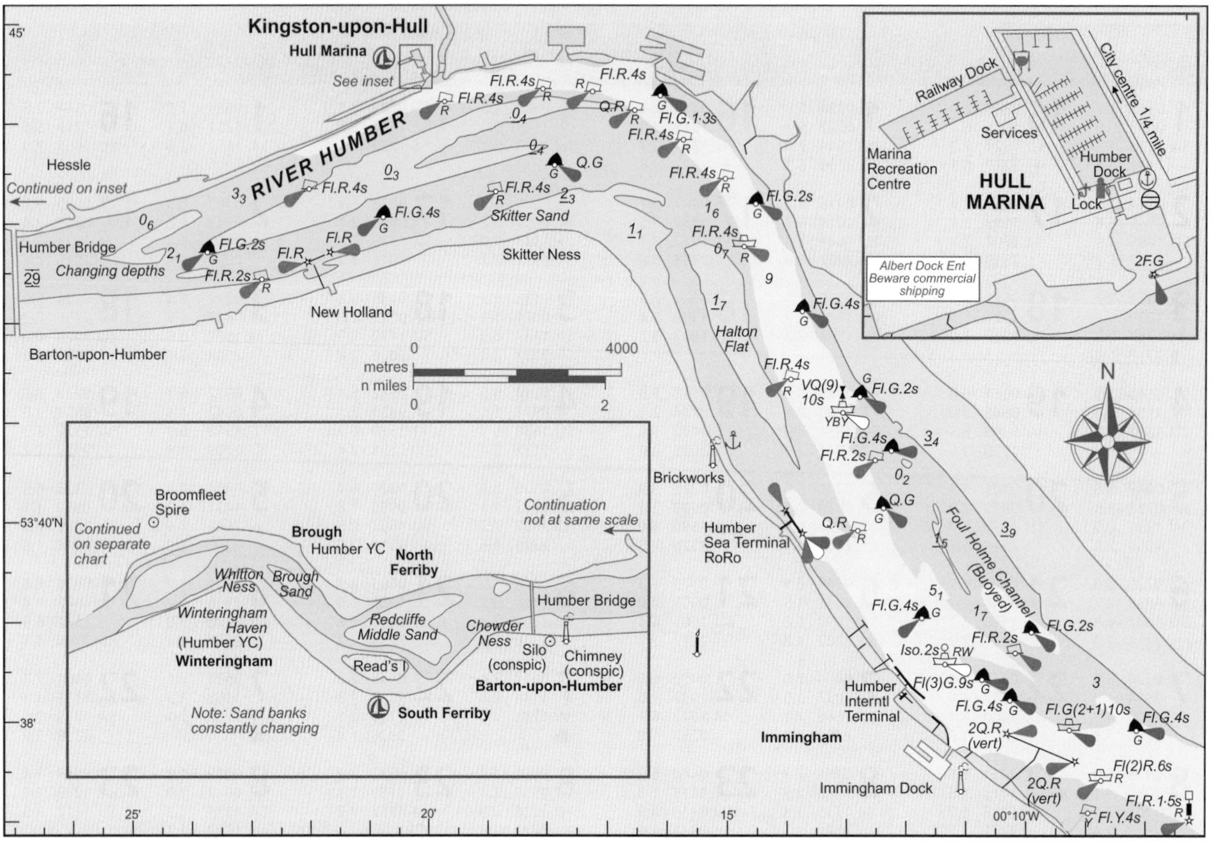

CHARTS AC 1190, 107, 104, 1188, 3496, 3497, 5614; Imray C29; ABP

TIDES –0510 Immingham, –0452 Hull, Dover; ML 4·1; Duration 0555

Standard Port IMMINGHAM (⟵)

Times				Height (metres)			
High Water		Low Water		MHWS	MHWN	MLWN	MLWS
0100	0700	0100	0700	7·3	5·8	2·6	0·9
1300	1900	1300	1900				
Differences BULL SAND FORT							
–0020	–0030	–0035	–0015	–0·4	–0·3	+0·1	+0·2
GRIMSBY							
–0012	–0014	–0015	–0013	–0·3	–0·2	+0·1	+0·4
HULL (ALBERT DOCK)							
+0019	*+0019*	*+0033*	*+0027*	*+0·3*	*+0·1*	*–0·1*	*–0·2*
HUMBER BRIDGE							
+0027	+0022	+0049	+0039	–0·1	–0·4	–0·7	–0·6
BURTON STATHER (R Trent)*							
+0105	+0050	+0240	+0205	–2·0	–2·7	–2·2	–1·1
KEADBY (R Trent)*							
+0135	+0120	+0425	+0410	–2·8	–3·3	–2·3	–0·9
BLACKTOFT (R Ouse)†							
+0100	+0055	+0325	+0255	–1·6	–1·8	–2·2	–1·1
GOOLE (R Ouse)†							
+0130	+0115	+0355	+0350	–1·6	–2·1	–1·9	–0·6

* Normal river level at Burton Stather is about 0·1m below CD, and at Keadby 0·1m to 0·2m below CD.

† Heights of LW can increase by up to 0·3m at Blacktoft and 0·6m at Goole when river in spate. HW hts are little affected.

SHELTER R Humber is the estuary of the rivers Ouse and Trent. The estuary has strong tidal streams: a strong NW'ly against a spring flood of 3-4kn causes a short steep sea, as does a SE'ly over the ebb stream. Off Hull Marina it can be very choppy with fresh winds over spring tidal streams.

Anchorages Inside Spurn Hd only with winds from NE to ESE, or close off Haile Sand Fort in fair weather. In S to W winds there is a good ⚓ off the SW bank 8ca above N Killingholme Oil jetty, well out of main chan. In N'lies ⚓ off Hawkin's Pt, N of S9 buoy.

Marinas at Hull, S Ferriby and the docks at Goole are all entered by lock access HW±3. At Grimsby lock best to await levels at HW±2. Otherwise £10 lock fee. Gates may shut at extreme HW Sp. Immingham should only be used in emergency. S Ferriby should not be attempted without up-to-date ABP charts for the ever-changing buoyed chan above Hull. Waiting pontoon at S Ferriby.

Do not attempt entry to Winteringham or Brough Havens without contacting Humber Yawl Club for details of approach channel and mooring availability. Both dry to soft mud. Winteringham is prone to heavy silting, but is dredged.

NAVIGATION Note TSS on chartlet 9.5.2 and on AC 109, guidance at www.humber.com/Yachting_and_Leisure/Pleasure_Craft_Navigation

From S, WPT 53°30′·50N 00°16′·50E, 1ca SW of Rosse Spit PHM buoy, Fl (2) R 5s. Thence pass S of Haile Sand No 2, then via No 2B, Tetney monobuoy and No 2C into Haile Channel.

From N, WPT 53°34′·74N 00°16′·55E, S Binks SHM buoy, Fl G 2s. Thence passing N of Spurn Lt Float, SE Chequer to Chequer No 3 crossing to S of Bull Channel at this point. This avoids strong tidal streams off Spurn Hd. Best arrival at LW. Sp tides are fierce: 4·4kn ebb off Spurn Head and Immingham. There is a big ship ⚓ S of Spurn Hd. Keep clear of large commercial vessels using Hawke (8·4m) and Sunk (8·8m) Chans; these are marked by S1-S9 SHM buoys, all Fl G 1·5s (S8 is a SHM bn, Fl G 1·5s with tide gauge); and by P2-P9 PHM buoys, all Fl R 1·5s. Foul Holme Chan (SHM buoys FH1 to FH9) off Immingham is recommended for small craft.

For **Grimsby,** the lock into Fish Docks is 255°/1·35M from Lower Burcom No 6 Lt Float, Fl R 4s. The jetty off the W entrance to Royal Dock has been extended further into Grimsby Road. Many offshore energy service cats use the port travelling at up to 28kn.

Off **Kingston-upon-Hull** a tidal eddy and streams can be rotatory: the flood makes W up Hull Roads for ¾hr whilst the ebb is already running downriver over Skitter Sand on the opposite bank (reaches 2½kn at sp). Humber Bridge (conspic) has 29m clearance.

LIGHTS AND MARKS The Humber is well marked. At Grimsby a conspic tr (94m with 'minaret' on top) is 300m W of Fish Dock lock. IPTS at Grimsby, Killingholme, Hull and Goole. A number of jetties with F lts have additional FL lts shown in fog.

COMMUNICATIONS (Codes: Grimsby 01472; Hull 01482) Police 101; Humber HM 01482 327171; see also: www.humber.com

Advise *VTS Humber* on Ch 14 (or ☎01482 212191) position and intentions on appr from seaward of Clee Ness lt float; listen on Ch 14 / 12 when W of the float and Ch 15 upstream fm the Humber Bridge to Gainsborough (R Trent) and Goole (R Ouse). ⛅, nav & tidal information is broadcast on Ch 12/14 every odd H+03; more detailed info, including height of tide, is available on request.

GRIMSBY Port Director 327171; CGOC (01262) 672317.

HULL Lock ☎330508; CGOC (01262) 672317; ⊜ 782107.

Other VHF stns: *Grimsby Docks Radio* Ch **74** (H24) 18 79 call Humber *Fishdock Island* for lock keeper or Meridian Quay. Immingham *Docks Radio* Ch 19 68 (H24). R Hull Port Ops Service call *Drypool Radio* Ch 22 (Mon-Fri HW–2 to HW+1; Sat 0900-1100 LT). *Hull Marina* Ch M **80** (H24); *Albert Dock Radio* Ch 09. *Ferriby Sluice* (R Ancholme Lock) Ch 74. Humber YC, Ch M (if racing). *Goole Docks Radio* Ch 14 (H24) 09 19. Boothferry Bridge Ch 09 (H24). Selby Railway and Toll Bridges Ch 09. Br Waterways locks Ch 74. *Brough and Winteringham Havens, Humber Yawl Club* Ch M.

FACILITIES

Humber Mouth YC ☎(01472) 812063, M drying at Tetney Haven. Humber Cruising Association.

GRIMSBY NE Lincs (01472) **Fish Docks** Lock access (R/G tfc lts) HW±3 £10 locking fee for Ⓥ, both gates open for free flow HW±2, enter free of charge with authorisation by *Fish Dock Island*, Ch **74**. Gates may close at extreme HW springs to prevent flooding.

Meridian Quay Marina www.hcagrimsby.co.uk ☎(01472) 268424, 200 ⛵+30 Ⓥ, £2·00 inc ⊐D, ⊡, ♠ ✕ ⚒ ⊡ ⊡ ⊡(35t) ⊡ wi-fi.

Grimsby and Cleethorpes YC ☎(01482) 356678; enter via ABP Royal Dock, avoiding the extended piers enclosing tidal basin to N and W, limited ⛵; ⊡ ⊡ ⊡ ✕ ⊡. **Town** All facilities.

Hull Marina ⊛ www.bwml.co.uk/hull_marina ☎(01482) 609960; (312+20Ⓥ £2·85), access HW±3 via lock (width 8·5m) 150m to the E. 1 Apr-31 Oct H24, 1 Nov-31 Mar 0700-2100 – otherwise 24hrs notice. **No** shelter from W through S to E when waiting outside lock in river especially in strong W winds or if marina shut. The pontoon in basin for craft awaiting lock in dries, *do not settle into the mud*. Marina office open 0900-1700 daily; ⊡ ⊡ ♠ ⊡ ⊡ ✕ ⚒ ⊡ ⊡ ⊡(50t) ⊡(2t) ⊡ ACA. **City** All facilities.

Ferries: Rotterdam/Zeebrugge daily; 10hrs; www.poferries.com.

South Ferriby Marina N Lincs. southferribymarina.com ☎(01652) 635620; access HW±3, 100+20Ⓥ £10/craft<10m<+£1/m max LOA 12m. Lock fee £7. VHF 80; ⊡ ⊐D ♠ ⊡ ⊡ ⊡(20t). **Village** ⊡ ⊡.

S Ferriby Lock ☎01652 635219. River Authority Ⓥ berths £8/48hrs. Lock Fee £7 (70ft LOA, 18ft beam, 6ft draught); ⊡. VHF 74: 0730-1600.

Humber Yawl Club has two facilities: **Brough Haven** E Riding, ☎(01482) 667224, entry HW±1½; Ch 37/M1 limited ⛵; ⊡ ⊡ ⊡. **Winteringham Haven** N Lincs ☎(01724) 734452. Limited access, dredging in progress; Ch 37/M1. ⊡(10t) ⊠.

GOOLE Take the flood up the R Humber, follow the buoyed channel past Hull, Brough and when approaching Trent Falls Apex alter course to stbd and follow the R Ouse to Goole. Situated off the Aire and Calder Navigation and accessed via the commercial lock for Goole Docks (Ch 14) are two havens, limited Ⓥ.

Goole Boathouse ☎(01405) 763985 ⛵£5<64ft, max draught 1·5m.

Viking Marina www.vikingmarine.com ☎(01405) 765737, ⛵ £8·00/boat/nt, <80' LOA, 20' beam, 9' draught; ⊡ ⊡ ♠ ⊡ ✕ ⚒ ⊡(18t) ⊡.

NABURN follow R Ouse, 4M S of York and 80M above Spurn Pt; **Naburn Marina** ☎(01904) 621021; 300+50Ⓥ max draught 1m £3·15 (min £21) ⊡ ⊐D (£2·00) WC/⊡ ♠ ♠ ⊡ ✕ ⚒ ⊡(16t) ⊡ ✕.

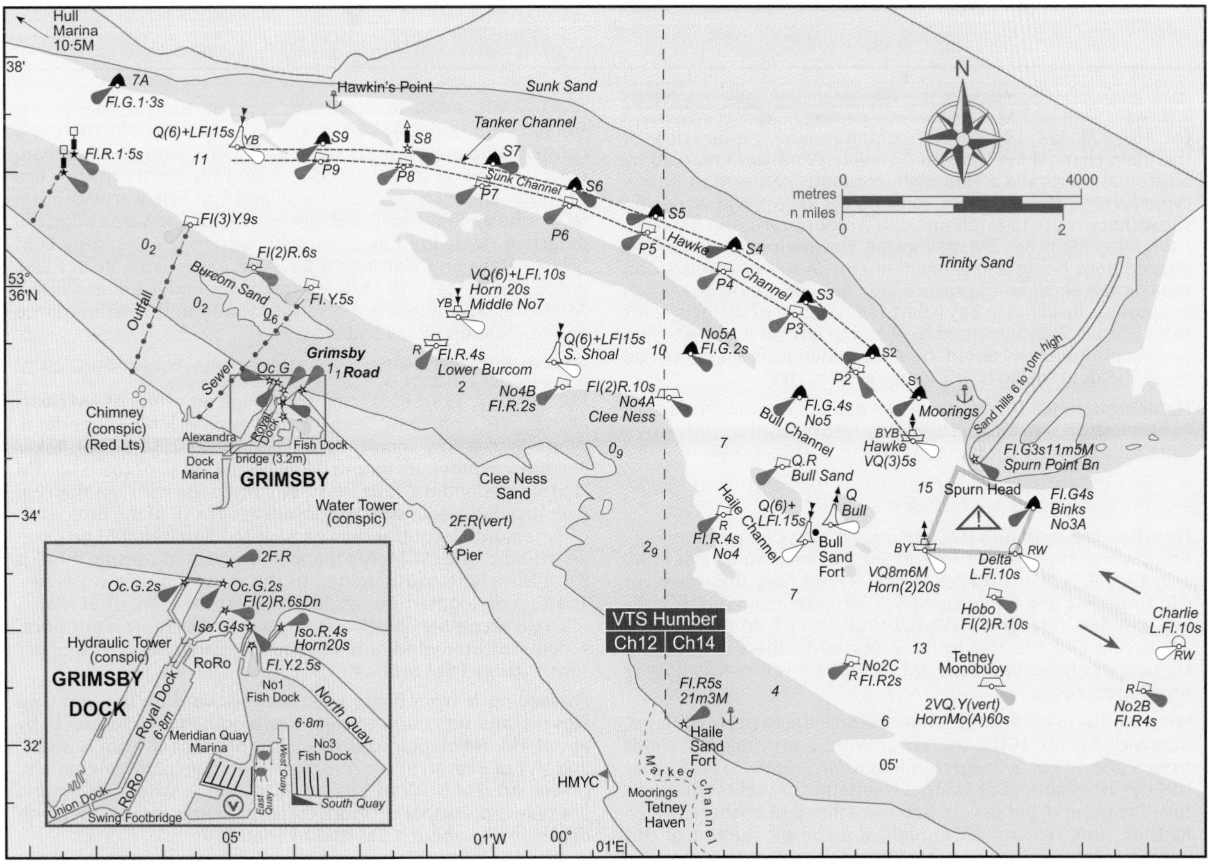

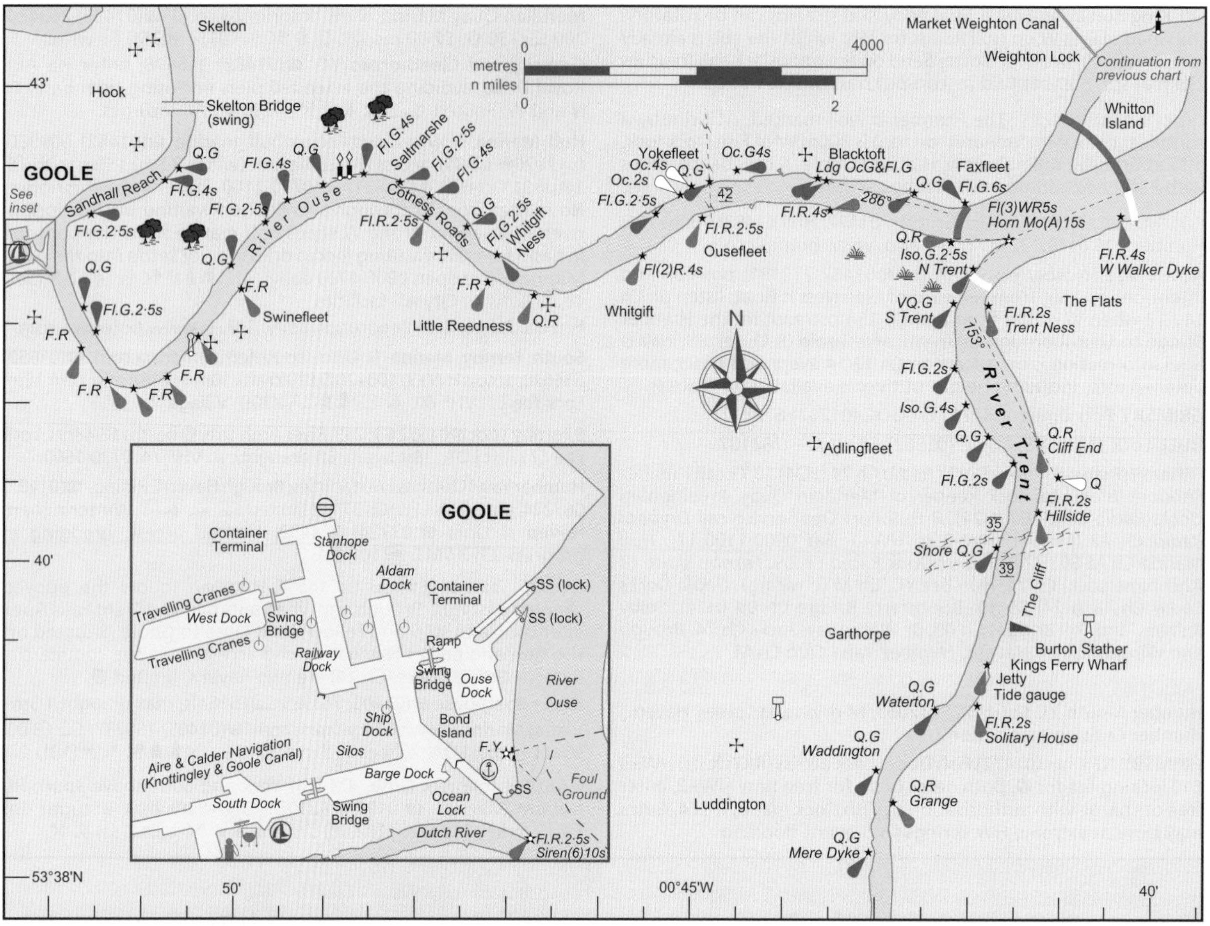
Skelton
Hook
Skelton Bridge (swing)
GOOLE
See inset
Sandhall Reach
River Ouse
Saltmarshe
Cotness Roads
Whitgift Ness
Swinefleet
Little Reedness
Whitgift
Yokefleet
Blacktoft
Faxfleet
Ousefleet
Market Weighton Canal
Weighton Lock
Continuation from previous chart
Whitton Island
Horn Mo(A)15s
W Walker Dyke
The Flats
Trent Ness
N Trent
S Trent
River Trent
Adlingfleet
Cliff End
Hillside
The Cliff
Garthorpe
Burton Stather
Kings Ferry Wharf
Jetty
Tide gauge
Waterton
Solitary House
Waddington
Grange
Luddington
Mere Dyke
metres
n miles
GOOLE
Container Terminal
Stanhope Dock
Aldam Dock
Travelling Cranes
West Dock
Swing Bridge
Railway Dock
Ramp
Ouse Dock
River Ouse
Ship Dock
Bond Island
Aire & Calder Navigation (Knottingley & Goole Canal)
Silos
Barge Dock
South Dock
Ocean Lock
Foul Ground
Dutch River
Siren(6)10s
53°38'N
00°45'W

RIVER HUMBER TO HARTLEPOOL

(AC 107, 121, 129, 134, 5615) NE of the Humber Estuary clear of the main channel lies Humber Gateway Wind Farm marked by 5 cardinal buoys and a 79m high met mast. Westermost Rough Wind Farm, with 35 turbines, some lit, lies 3M off Withernsea on the inshore route to Bridlington. A wreck hazardous to surface navigation lies in 8m, 2M off Tunstall. Navigation is aided by the disused light house and prominent church spires/towers along the coast. A small firing practice area lies inshore off the beach at Royston. Bridlington Bay (chart 1882) is clear of dangers apart from Smithic Shoals (marked by N and S cardinal lt buoys), lying S of Flamborough Hd about 2½M off Bridlington; seas break on these shoals in strong N or E winds even at HW.

Flamborough Head (lt, fog sig, RG) is a steep, W cliff with conspic light house on summit. The light may be obscured by cliffs when close inshore. An old lt ho, also conspic, is 2½ca WNW.

▶ *Tides run hard around the Head which, in strong winds against a sp tide, is best avoided by 2M.* ◀

From here the coast runs NW, with no offshore dangers until Filey Brigg where rocky ledges extend 5ca ESE, marked by a lit ECM. ⚓ in Filey B in N or offshore winds. NW of Filey Brigg beware Old Horse Rks and foul ground 5ca offshore; maintain this offing past Scarborough to Whitby High Lt. Off Whitby beware Whitby Rk and The Scar (dries in places) to the E of hbr, and Upgang Rks (dries in places) 1M to WNW; swell breaks heavily on all these rocks.

From Whitby to Hartlepool dangers lie no more than 1M offshore. Runswick Bay (AC 1612), 5M NW of Whitby, provides ⚓ in winds from S and W but is dangerous in onshore winds. 2½M further NW the little harbour of Staithes is suitable for yachts which can take the ground, but only in good weather and offshore winds. Redcliff, dark red and 205m high, is a conspic feature of this coast which, along to Hunt Cliff, is prone to landslides and is fringed with rky ledges which dry for about 3ca off. There is a conspic radio mast 4ca SSE of Redcliff. Off Redcar and Coatham beware Salt Scar and West Scar, drying rky ledges lying 1–8ca offshore. Other ledges lie close SE and S of Salt Scar which has NCM lt buoy. Between R Tees and Hartlepool beware Long Scar, detached rky ledge (dries $\underline{2}$m) with extremity marked by ECM lt buoy. Tees and Hartlepool Bays are exposed to strong E/SE winds. The R Tees and Middlesbrough are highly industrialised. At Hartlepool there is a centre specialising in the maintenance and restoration of Tall Ships.

HARTLEPOOL TO COQUET ISLAND

(AC 134, 152, 156, 5615) From The Heugh an offing of 1M clears all dangers until past Seaham and approaching Sunderland. White Stones, rky shoals (depth 1·8m) lie 1·75M SSE of Roker Pier lt ho; Hendon Rk (depth 0·9m) lies 1·25M SE of the lt ho. 1M N of Sunderland is Whitburn Steel, a rky ledge with less than 2m over it; a dangerous wreck (buoyed) lies 1ca SE of it. The coast N of Tynemouth is foul, and on passage to Blyth it should be given an offing of 1M. St Mary's Island (with disused conspic lt ho) is 3·5M N of Tynemouth, joined to the mainland by a causeway. The tiny drying harbour of Seaton Sluice, 1M NW of St Mary's Island, is accessible only in offshore winds via a narrow entrance. A demonstrator wind farm marked by 6 cardinal buoys is under construction 3·5M off Blyth.

Proceeding N from Blyth, keep well seaward of The Sow and Pigs rks, and set course to clear Newbiggin Pt and Beacon Pt by about 1M. Newbiggin church spire is prominent from N and S, and NW of Beacon Pt are conspic chys of aluminium smelter and power stn. 2M NNW of Beacon Pt is Snab Pt where rks extend 3ca seaward. Further offshore Cresswell Skeres, rky patches with depth 3m, lie about 1·5M NNE of Snab Pt.

9.5.12 BRIDLINGTON

E Riding of Yorkshire **54°04′·78N 00°11′·21W**

CHARTS AC 1191, 1190, 129, 121, 1882, 5614; Imray C29

TIDES +0553 Dover; ML 3·6; Duration 0610

Standard Port RIVER TEES (→)

Times				Height (metres)			
High Water		Low Water		MHWS	MHWN	MLWN	MLWS
0000	0600	0000	0600	5·5	4·3	2·0	0·9
1200	1800	1200	1800				
Differences BRIDLINGTON							
+0100	+0050	+0055	+0050	+0·6	+0·4	+0·3	+0·2
FILEY BAY							
+0042	+0042	+0047	+0034	+0·3	+0·6	+0·4	+0·1

SHELTER Good, except in E, SE and S winds. Hbr dries completely to soft black mud. Berth on S pier or near HM's Office as directed. A marina is planned but agreement not yet reached.

NAVIGATION WPT SW Smithic WCM, Q (9) 15s, 54°02′·41N 00°09′·21W, 333°/2·6M to ent. Close-in appr is with N pier hd lt on brg 002° to keep W of drying patch (The Canch). Beware bar, 1m at MLWN, could dry out at MLWS.

LIGHTS AND MARKS Hbr is 4M WSW of Flamborough Hd lt, Fl (4) 15s 65m 24M. Y racing marks are laid in the Bay, Apr-Oct. Tidal sigs, by day from S pier: R flag = >2·7m in hbr; No flag = < 2·7m. At night from N pier: Fl ● = >2·7m in hbr; Fl ● = < 2·7m.

COMMUNICATIONS (Code 01262) CGOC 672317; Police 101; Ⓗ 606666. HM 670148/9, mob 0860 275150.

Call on VHF Ch 16, then Ch **12** for working.

FACILITIES **S Pier** £2.80/m²/week or £20/yacht <3 days, see HM, (☎500227), (3t) (75t); **Royal Yorks YC** ☎672041.

Town Ⓑ ✕ ⇌ ✈(Humberside).

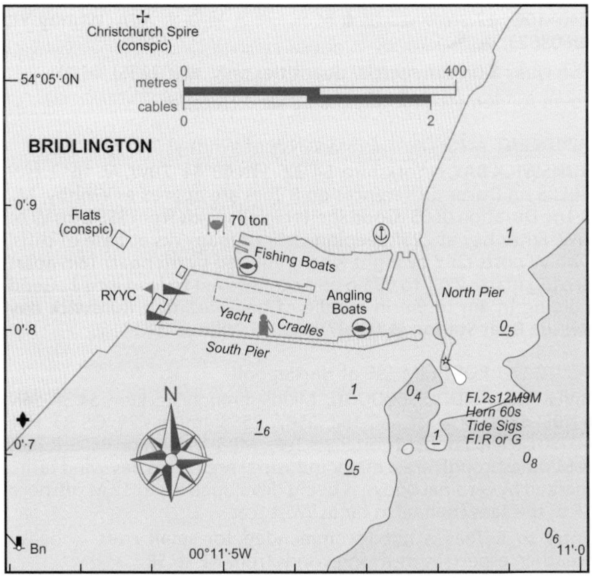

ADJACENT ANCHORAGE (7M SE of Scarborough)

FILEY, N Yorkshire, 54°12′·80N 00°16′·20W, AC 1882, 129. HW +0532 on Dover; ML 3·5m; Duration 0605. See 9.5.12. Good ⚓ in winds from S to NNE in 4–5m on hard sand. Lt on cliff above CG Stn, G metal column, FR 31m 1M vis 272°-308°. Filey Brigg, a natural bkwtr, is marked by ECM buoy, Q(3)10s, Bell. Beware Old Horse Rks, 2M WNW of Filey Brigg, foul ground extending ½M offshore. An unmarked Historic Wreck (see 9.0.3) lies at 54°11′·51N 00°13′·48W. Facilities: Ⓑ ✕ Ⓗ ☎(01723) 68111 ⇌.

9.5.13 SCARBOROUGH

N. Yorkshire **54°16′·88N 00°23′·36W**

CHARTS AC 1191, 129, 1612, 5614; Imray C29

TIDES +0527 Dover; ML 3·5; Duration 0615

Standard Port RIVER TEES (→)

Times				Height (metres)			
High Water		Low Water		MHWS	MHWN	MLWN	MLWS
0000	0600	0000	0600	5·5	4·3	2·0	0·9
1200	1800	1200	1800				
Differences SCARBOROUGH							
+0040	+0040	+0030	+0030	+0·2	+0·3	+0·3	0·0

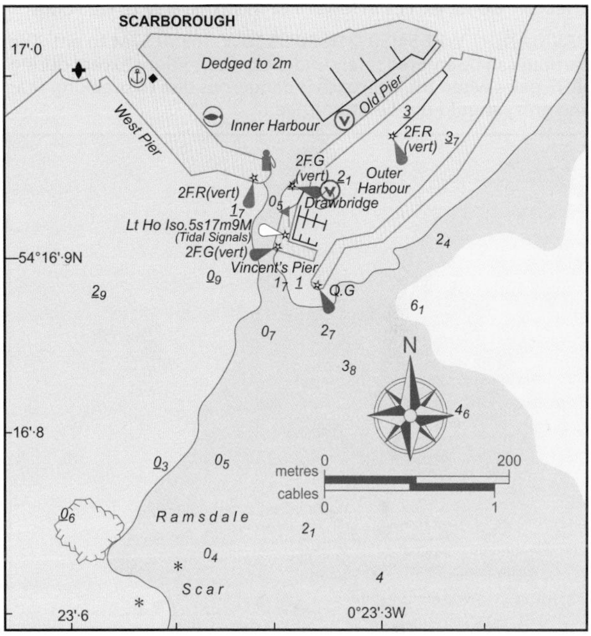

SHELTER Good in Outer Harbour (dries) for local residents, access via narrow (10m) entrance by East pier, but not in strong E/SE'lies. In winter months. Outer Harbour access is via the drawbridge.

Ⓥ on SE side of pontoons in Inner Harbour. Berths have 2m alongside pontoon, but bottom shelves rapidly just beyond one boat's breadth from pontoons limiting access to approx HW ±2hrs.

NAVIGATION WPT 54°16′·50N 00°22′·00W, 302°/0·83M to E pier lt. Appr from the E to avoid Ramsdale Scar, rky shoal 0·9m. Keep careful watch for salmon nets E & SE of ent. Beware rks extending approx 20m SW of E pier head. Give Castle Headland close N of hbr a wide berth due to coastal defences. Min depths in approach and entrance to Inner Harbour approx 0·1m.

LIGHTS AND MARKS Lt ho (conspic), Iso 5s, Dia 60s, on Vincent Pier is shown by night or B ● by day when there is more than 3·7m over bar in entrance. A Y SPM Fl Y 4s, 110° E pier 1·8M marks the end of an outfall; another, N of the harbour 0·7NM NE of Scalby Ness, is marked by a PHM Fl R 5s. Scarborough YC sets lit Y SPM. Other lts as shown on chartlet.

COMMUNICATIONS (Code 01723) CGOC (01262) 672317; Police 101; Ⓗ 368111. Port Control 373877. Call *Scarborough Port Control* VHF Ch **12** 16 (H24). Watchkeeper will offer guidance to approaching visitors.

FACILITIES HM www.scarboroughbc.gov.uk ☎373530 (HO); £14/night, inner harbour pontoon berth £28/night <10m LOA, (4t) (£11·50).

Scarborough YC www.syc.org.uk ☎373821.

Services Ⓔ.

Town Ⓑ ✕ ⇌ ✈(Humberside).

9.5.14 WHITBY

N. Yorkshire **54°29'·65N 00°36'·78W** ✵✵✪✪✪✿✿✿

CHARTS AC 129, 134, 1612, 5614, 5615; Imray C29, C24

TIDES +0500 Dover; ML 3·3; Duration 0605

Standard Port RIVER TEES (⟶)

Times				Height (metres)			
High Water		Low Water		MHWS	MHWN	MLWN	MLWS
0000	0600	0000	0600	5·5	4·3	2·0	0·9
1200	1800	1200	1800				
Differences WHITBY							
+0020	+0020	+0018	+0017	+0·1	+0·1	+0·2	+0·1

SHELTER Good, except in lower hbr in strong NW to NE winds.

NAVIGATION WPT 54°30'·21N 00°36'96W, 169°/0·57M to ent. The harbour can be entered safely under most conditions except during N-NE gales when the approach is dangerous due to breaking seas and entry should not be attempted.

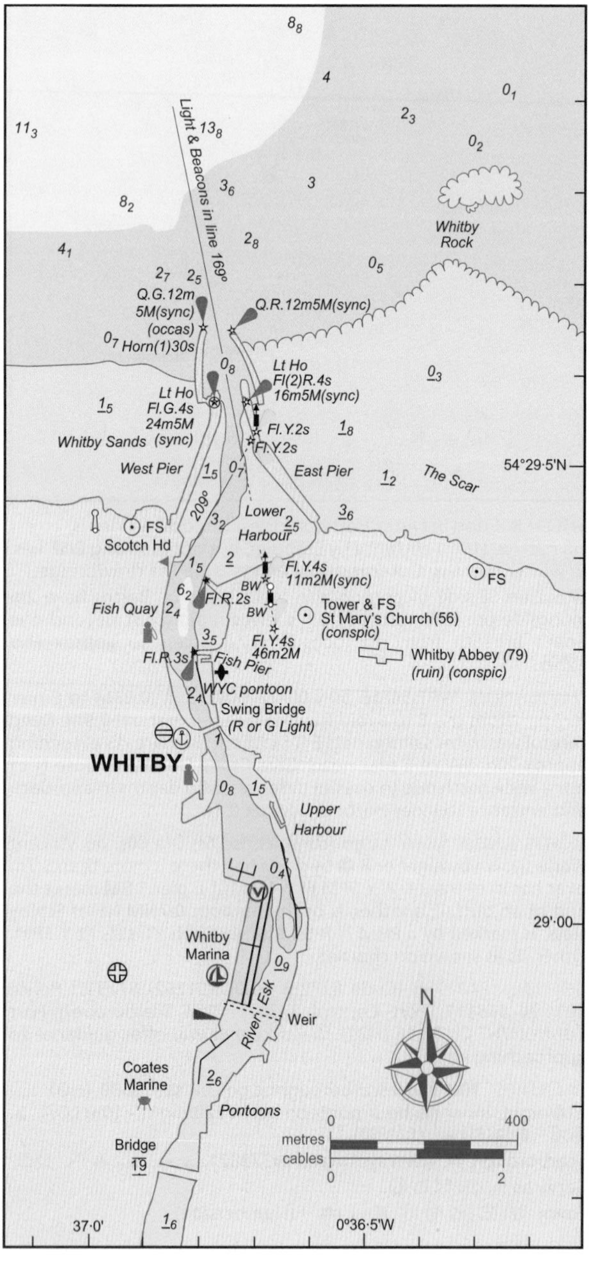

- From the SE beware Whitby Rk; leave Whitby NCM lit buoy to port.
- Beware strong set to E from HW –2 to HW, when nearing piers.

Vessels >37m LOA must embark pilot; via HM. All vessels must proceed at a safe speed within the Harbour and sailing vessels are to use auxiliary power if so equipped.

Min depth in entrance approx 1·0m. Bridge opens on request HW±2 every H and H+30. Additional openings at w/e and BH: May-Sep 0930 and1730; Aug 1300 (irrespective of tides). FG lts = open; FR lts = shut. Wait on pontoon at Fish Pier if necessary. If alongside Fish Quay or FVs, craft must not be left unattended.

Priority for Swing Bridge passage:
1. Commercial vessels with pilot embarked (keep well clear);
2. Large vessels; 3. Vessels inbound fm seaward; 4. When both bridge sections open 2-way traffic in single file keeping to stbd. Establish comms with Whitby Bridge Ch **11** prior to transit.

LIGHTS AND MARKS See Lights, buoys & waypoints and chartlet. Ruins of Whitby Abbey are to the E of the entrance. Whitby High Lt ho (white 8-sided tower) is 2M ESE of harbour entrance, which is marked on either side by 5m high R and G wooden towers respectively lit with QR and QG lts. The E Pier Lt Ho Fl (2)R 4s on a 16m masonry tower has been recommissioned. This together with The W Pier Lt Ho Fl(2)G 4s 24m, are synchronised with lts on the pier extensions. Leading lines for entering hbr:

2 bns (W △, and W ○ with B stripe) seen between the outer pierheads (Q Fl R and Q Fl G), lead 169° into hbr. At night the Fwd bn sync Fl Y 4s, aligns with a lt sync Fl Y 4s (46m) on a lamp post. Maintain this line until bns on E pier (2 sync Fl Y 2s) are abeam. Thence keep these same bns in transit astern bearing 029°.

COMMUNICATIONS (Code 01947) CGOC (01262) 672317; Police 101; Dr 820888. HM www.yorkshireports.co.uk 602354/602272.

Hbr and Marina VHF Ch **11** 16 12 (H24). Whitby Bridge Ch **11** 16 06 (listens on Ch 16 HW–2 to HW+2).

FACILITIES **Whitby Marina** (dredged 1.5m) is 2ca beyond swing bridge; visitor berths at seaward end of long pontoon. ☎600165. 240+10Ⓥ, £2.20; ♿ ⛴ ⓓ ⛽ ⚒ 🔧 ⓔ ⛵ ⛟ ⛃ ACA. **Whitby YC** ☎603623, ⛺ ⛴ 🗋.

Fish Quay ⛽(in commercial quantities only, ☎602255) ⛃(1t).

Town All domestic facilities, ✕ 🗋 ⇌ ✈(Teesside).

ADJACENT ANCHORAGE (5M WNW of Whitby)

RUNSWICK BAY, N Yorkshire, **54°32'·11N 00°44'·20W**. AC 1612. HW +0505 on Dover: Differences on R Tees are approx as Whitby; ML 3·1m; Duration 0605. Good shelter in all winds from SSE thru W to NW. Enter bay at 225° keeping clear of many rks at base of cliffs. Two W posts (2FY by night when required by lifeboat) 18m apart are ldg marks 270° to LB ho and can be used to lead into ⚓. Good holding in 6m to 9m in middle of bay. Facilities: **Runswick Bay Rescue Boat Station** ☎(01947) 840965. **Village** 🛒 ✕ 🗋.

ADJACENT PORT (3M SSE of Hartlepool)

RIVER TEES/MIDDLESBROUGH, Middlesbrough/Stockton, **54°38'·94N 01°08'·48W**. ✵✵✪✿. AC 152, 2567, 2566; Imray C29; OS 93. HW +0450 Dover; Standard Port River Tees. ML 3·1; duration 0605. R Tees & Middlesbrough are a major industrial area. Tees Bay wind farm, marked by cardinal buoys, is being developed up to 1½M offshore SE of the Tees channel as far as West Scar.

Entry to R Tees is not recommended for small craft in heavy weather, especially in strong winds from NE to SE.

Tees Approach SWM, Mo(A) 5s 8M, Horn 5s, Racon, is at 54°40'·60N 01°04'·00W, 055°/3·0M from S Gare bkwtr. The channel is well buoyed from the Fairway buoy to beyond Middlesbrough. Ldg lts 210°, both FR on framework trs. At Old CG stn a Q lt, or 3 ● (vert), = no entry without HM's consent. Call: *Tees Port Control* VHF Ch **14** 22 16 12 (H24). Monitor Ch 14; also info Ch 14 22. *Tees Barrage Radio* Ch M (37). HM ☎(01642) 277201.

South Gare Marine Club ☎491039(occas) ⛺ ⛴ ⚓; **Castlegate Marine Club** ☎583299, ⛺ ⛴ ⚓ ⚒ 🔧; **Tees Motor Boat Club** ⛺; Services: ⓔ 🔧 Ⓔ ⛃ ACA. **City** All domestic facilities, ⇌ ✈. Hartlepool Marina (9.5.14) lies 3M to NNW with all yacht facilities.

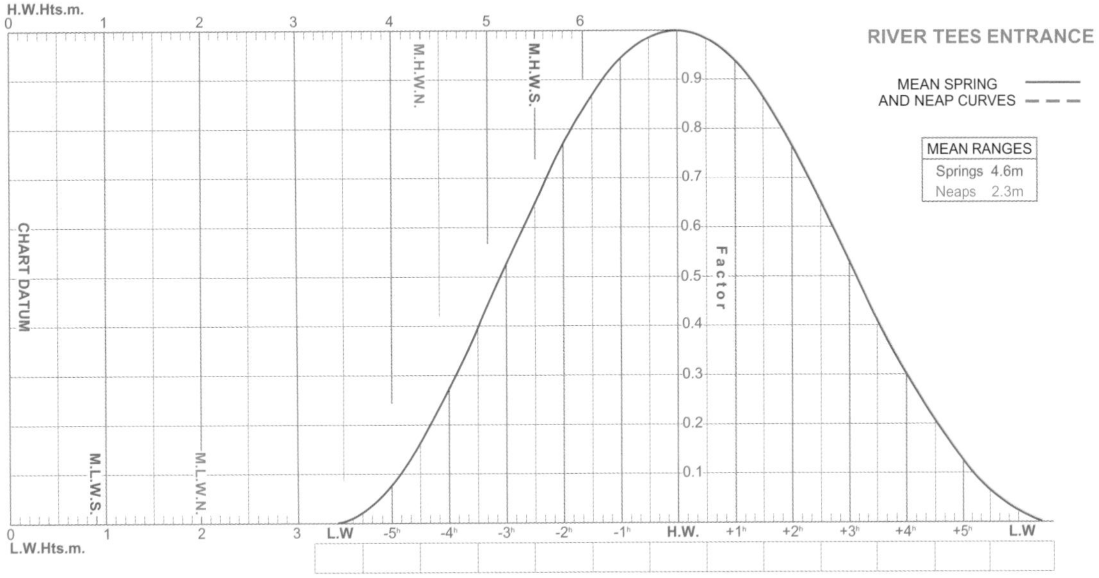

RIVER TEES ENTRANCE
MEAN SPRING AND NEAP CURVES
MEAN RANGES
Springs 4.6m
Neaps 2.3m
H.W.Hts.m.
L.W.Hts.m.
CHART DATUM
M.H.W.N.
M.H.W.S.
M.L.W.S.
M.L.W.N.
Factor
L.W -5h -4h -3h -2h -1h H.W. +1h +2h +3h +4h +5h L.W

STANDARD TIME (UT)
For Summer Time add ONE hour in **non-shaded areas**

RIVER TEES LAT 54°38'N LONG 1°09'W

TIMES AND HEIGHTS OF HIGH AND LOW WATERS

Dates in red are SPRINGS
Dates in blue are NEAPS

YEAR **2018**

JANUARY

Date	Day	Time	m	Time	m	Time	m	Time	m
1	M	0219	5.4	0849	0.9	1451	5.4	2116	0.8
2	TU	0313	5.5	0940	0.8	1539	5.6	○ 2208	0.5
3	W	0406	5.6	1029	0.7	1627	5.7	2258	0.4
4	TH	0457	5.6	1116	0.8	1714	5.7	2346	0.4
5	F	0548	5.5	1202	1.0	1802	5.6		
6	SA	0034	0.5	0638	5.4	1249	1.2	1849	5.5
7	SU	0123	0.7	0730	5.1	1336	1.5	1940	5.2
8	M	0213	1.0	0823	4.8	1428	1.8	◑ 2035	4.9
9	TU	0308	1.3	0921	4.6	1527	2.0	2135	4.7
10	W	0411	1.6	1023	4.4	1637	2.2	2242	4.5
11	TH	0520	1.8	1129	4.4	1751	2.2	2352	4.4
12	F	0626	1.8	1233	4.4	1857	2.0		
13	SA	0057	4.5	0721	1.8	1328	4.6	1949	1.8
14	SU	0152	4.6	0806	1.6	1413	4.8	2032	1.6
15	M	0237	4.8	0846	1.5	1452	5.0	2112	1.4
16	TU	0317	4.9	0923	1.4	1527	5.1	2148	1.2
17	W	0354	5.0	0957	1.3	1559	5.2	● 2222	1.1
18	TH	0428	5.0	1029	1.3	1630	5.2	2256	1.1
19	F	0501	5.0	1102	1.3	1703	5.3	2328	1.1
20	SA	0535	5.0	1136	1.3	1737	5.2		
21	SU	0002	1.1	0610	5.0	1212	1.4	1813	5.2
22	M	0039	1.1	0650	4.9	1250	1.5	1853	5.1
23	TU	0119	1.2	0734	4.7	1331	1.7	1938	4.9
24	W	0204	1.4	0824	4.6	1420	1.8	◐ 2030	4.8
25	TH	0258	1.5	0922	4.5	1522	1.9	2133	4.7
26	F	0405	1.7	1027	4.4	1638	2.0	2244	4.6
27	SA	0519	1.7	1135	4.5	1755	1.8	2356	4.7
28	SU	0633	1.5	1241	4.7	1906	1.5		
29	M	0106	4.9	0740	1.3	1343	5.0	2010	1.1
30	TU	0209	5.2	0838	1.1	1438	5.3	2108	0.8
31	W	0306	5.4	0931	0.9	1528	5.6	○ 2200	0.5

FEBRUARY

Date	Day	Time	m	Time	m	Time	m	Time	m
1	TH	0358	5.6	1019	0.8	1615	5.7	2248	0.3
2	F	0446	5.6	1104	0.7	1700	5.8	2333	0.2
3	SA	0532	5.6	1146	0.8	1744	5.7		
4	SU	0016	0.3	0616	5.4	1227	1.0	1826	5.6
5	M	0058	0.6	0701	5.2	1307	1.2	1911	5.3
6	TU	0140	0.9	0746	4.9	1348	1.5	1958	5.0
7	W	0225	1.3	0835	4.6	1436	1.9	◑ 2051	4.7
8	TH	0316	1.7	0929	4.3	1537	2.1	2154	4.4
9	F	0422	2.0	1033	4.2	1657	2.2	2307	4.2
10	SA	0539	2.1	1144	4.2	1819	2.2		
11	SU	0023	4.2	0648	2.1	1253	4.3	1922	1.9
12	M	0128	4.4	0741	1.9	1347	4.6	2011	1.7
13	TU	0217	4.6	0825	1.7	1431	4.8	2053	1.4
14	W	0259	4.8	0904	1.5	1507	5.0	2130	1.2
15	TH	0336	4.9	0939	1.3	1540	5.1	● 2204	1.0
16	F	0409	5.1	1013	1.2	1611	5.3	2237	0.9
17	SA	0441	5.1	1045	1.1	1642	5.3	2308	0.8
18	SU	0512	5.1	1118	1.1	1714	5.4	2341	0.8
19	M	0546	5.1	1152	1.1	1748	5.3		
20	TU	0016	0.8	0622	5.0	1228	1.2	1825	5.3
21	W	0054	1.0	0703	4.9	1306	1.3	1908	5.1
22	TH	0135	1.2	0749	4.7	1351	1.5	2000	4.9
23	F	0225	1.5	0846	4.5	1448	1.7	◐ 2103	4.7
24	SA	0330	1.7	0953	4.4	1606	1.9	2220	4.5
25	SU	0452	1.8	1108	4.4	1733	1.8	2341	4.5
26	M	0618	1.7	1223	4.6	1856	1.5		
27	TU	0058	4.7	0731	1.5	1331	4.9	2003	1.1
28	W	0204	5.0	0829	1.2	1427	5.2	2059	0.7

MARCH

Date	Day	Time	m	Time	m	Time	m	Time	m
1	TH	0258	5.3	0919	0.9	1516	5.5	2148	0.4
2	F	0345	5.5	1004	0.8	1600	5.7	○ 2232	0.2
3	SA	0429	5.6	1046	0.7	1641	5.7	2313	0.2
4	SU	0510	5.5	1124	0.7	1721	5.7	2351	0.3
5	M	0550	5.4	1200	0.9	1800	5.6		
6	TU	0027	0.6	0628	5.2	1236	1.1	1840	5.3
7	W	0104	1.0	0707	4.9	1311	1.3	1923	5.0
8	TH	0140	1.4	0749	4.6	1350	1.7	2011	4.6
9	F	0222	1.8	0837	4.3	1440	2.0	◑ 2110	4.3
10	SA	0319	2.1	0936	4.1	1558	2.2	2222	4.1
11	SU	0444	2.3	1051	4.0	1735	2.2	2345	4.0
12	M	0611	2.3	1210	4.1	1850	2.0		
13	TU	0058	4.2	0712	2.0	1314	4.4	1943	1.7
14	W	0152	4.5	0759	1.8	1401	4.7	2026	1.4
15	TH	0234	4.7	0839	1.5	1440	4.9	2104	1.1
16	F	0310	4.9	0915	1.3	1513	5.1	2139	0.9
17	SA	0343	5.1	0949	1.1	1545	5.3	● 2212	0.7
18	SU	0414	5.2	1023	0.9	1616	5.4	2244	0.6
19	M	0446	5.3	1056	0.8	1649	5.5	2317	0.6
20	TU	0520	5.3	1131	0.8	1724	5.5	2352	0.6
21	W	0556	5.2	1207	0.9	1804	5.4		
22	TH	0030	0.8	0636	5.0	1246	1.1	1848	5.2
23	F	0112	1.1	0722	4.8	1332	1.3	1942	4.9
24	SA	0201	1.4	0819	4.6	1430	1.6	◐ 2048	4.6
25	SU	0307	1.8	0928	4.4	1551	1.7	2208	4.4
26	M	0436	2.0	1049	4.3	1723	1.7	2334	4.4
27	TU	0608	1.9	1210	4.5	1848	1.4		
28	W	0054	4.7	0720	1.6	1319	4.8	1952	1.0
29	TH	0156	5.0	0815	1.3	1413	5.2	2044	0.6
30	F	0245	5.2	0902	1.0	1459	5.4	2129	0.4
31	SA	0328	5.4	0944	0.8	1541	5.6	○ 2210	0.3

APRIL

Date	Day	Time	m	Time	m	Time	m	Time	m
1	SU	0407	5.4	1022	0.7	1619	5.6	2247	0.4
2	M	0444	5.4	1058	0.7	1656	5.6	2322	0.5
3	TU	0520	5.3	1132	0.8	1734	5.4	2355	0.7
4	W	0554	5.2	1206	1.0	1812	5.2		
5	TH	0028	1.1	0629	5.0	1240	1.2	1852	4.9
6	F	0101	1.4	0708	4.7	1316	1.5	1937	4.6
7	SA	0138	1.8	0752	4.4	1400	1.8	2031	4.3
8	SU	0226	2.1	0846	4.2	1506	2.1	◑ 2139	4.0
9	M	0345	2.3	0956	4.0	1642	2.1	2301	4.0
10	TU	0521	2.3	1116	4.1	1806	2.0		
11	W	0017	4.1	0632	2.1	1228	4.3	1905	1.7
12	TH	0115	4.4	0724	1.8	1320	4.5	1951	1.4
13	F	0159	4.7	0806	1.5	1402	4.8	2030	1.1
14	SA	0236	4.9	0844	1.3	1438	5.1	2107	0.8
15	SU	0310	5.1	0921	1.0	1513	5.3	2142	0.6
16	M	0344	5.3	0957	0.8	1548	5.4	● 2217	0.5
17	TU	0418	5.4	1033	0.7	1625	5.5	2253	0.5
18	W	0455	5.4	1111	0.7	1705	5.5	2331	0.6
19	TH	0534	5.3	1150	0.7	1749	5.4		
20	F	0011	0.8	0616	5.2	1234	0.9	1838	5.2
21	SA	0056	1.1	0704	4.9	1323	1.1	1935	4.9
22	SU	0148	1.5	0802	4.7	1426	1.4	◐ 2043	4.6
23	M	0257	1.8	0912	4.5	1546	1.5	2202	4.4
24	TU	0425	2.0	1033	4.4	1713	1.5	2326	4.4
25	W	0551	1.9	1153	4.6	1831	1.2		
26	TH	0042	4.7	0659	1.6	1300	4.8	1932	0.9
27	F	0139	4.9	0753	1.4	1353	5.1	2022	0.7
28	SA	0225	5.1	0839	1.1	1438	5.3	2105	0.6
29	SU	0306	5.2	0920	1.0	1519	5.4	2144	0.6
30	M	0343	5.3	0958	0.9	1556	5.4	○ 2219	0.6

Chart Datum: 2·85 metres below Ordnance Datum (Newlyn). HAT is 6·1 metres above Chart Datum.

STANDARD TIME (UT)
For Summer Time add ONE hour in **non-shaded areas**

RIVER TEES LAT 54°38′N LONG 1°09′W

TIMES AND HEIGHTS OF HIGH AND LOW WATERS

Dates in red are SPRINGS
Dates in blue are NEAPS

YEAR **2018**

MAY

Date	Day	Time	m	Time	m	Time	m	Time	m
1	TU	0417	5.3	1033	0.8	1633	5.3	2253	0.8
2	W	0450	5.2	1107	0.9	1710	5.2	2325	1.0
3	TH	0523	5.1	1140	1.0	1747	5.1	2356	1.2
4	F	0557	5.0	1215	1.2	1827	4.8		
5	SA	0029	1.4	0635	4.8	1252	1.4	1910	4.6
6	SU	0106	1.7	0718	4.6	1334	1.7	2000	4.3
7	M	0151	2.0	0809	4.4	1430	1.9	2059	4.1
8	TU	0255	2.2	0909	4.2	1547	2.0	◑ 2209	4.0
9	W	0422	2.3	1020	4.1	1707	1.9	2322	4.1
10	TH	0538	2.2	1129	4.3	1812	1.7		
11	F	0024	4.3	0636	1.9	1228	4.5	1904	1.4
12	SA	0113	4.6	0724	1.6	1317	4.8	1949	1.1
13	SU	0155	4.9	0807	1.3	1400	5.0	2030	0.9
14	M	0234	5.1	0849	1.0	1441	5.3	2111	0.7
15	TU	0313	5.3	0930	0.8	1523	5.5	● 2151	0.5
16	W	0353	5.4	1012	0.6	1606	5.6	2233	0.5
17	TH	0434	5.5	1054	0.6	1652	5.6	2315	0.6
18	F	0517	5.4	1139	0.6	1741	5.4	2359	0.8
19	SA	0603	5.3	1227	0.7	1834	5.2		
20	SU	0047	1.1	0653	5.1	1322	0.9	1933	5.0
21	M	0142	1.5	0751	4.9	1424	1.1	2038	4.7
22	TU	0249	1.8	0858	4.7	1535	1.3	◐ 2150	4.5
23	W	0406	1.9	1012	4.6	1651	1.3	2305	4.5
24	TH	0523	1.9	1127	4.6	1804	1.2		
25	F	0016	4.6	0630	1.7	1234	4.8	1905	1.1
26	SA	0114	4.8	0726	1.5	1329	5.0	1955	1.0
27	SU	0201	4.9	0814	1.3	1416	5.1	2039	0.9
28	M	0242	5.1	0856	1.2	1458	5.1	2118	0.9
29	TU	0319	5.1	0934	1.1	1536	5.2	○ 2153	1.0
30	W	0353	5.1	1010	1.0	1614	5.1	2227	1.0
31	TH	0425	5.1	1045	1.0	1650	5.1	2259	1.2

JUNE

Date	Day	Time	m	Time	m	Time	m	Time	m
1	F	0457	5.1	1120	1.1	1727	5.0	2331	1.3
2	SA	0532	5.0	1155	1.2	1806	4.8		
3	SU	0005	1.5	0609	4.9	1233	1.3	1847	4.7
4	M	0043	1.7	0651	4.8	1313	1.5	1932	4.5
5	TU	0126	1.9	0738	4.6	1401	1.7	2023	4.3
6	W	0218	2.1	0831	4.4	1459	1.8	◑ 2122	4.2
7	TH	0326	2.2	0931	4.3	1606	1.8	2225	4.2
8	F	0438	2.1	1034	4.4	1712	1.7	2327	4.4
9	SA	0543	2.0	1136	4.5	1812	1.5		
10	SU	0023	4.6	0638	1.7	1232	4.8	1905	1.2
11	M	0114	4.8	0730	1.4	1324	5.0	1955	1.0
12	TU	0201	5.1	0819	1.1	1414	5.2	2043	0.8
13	W	0247	5.3	0907	0.8	1503	5.4	● 2130	0.7
14	TH	0332	5.4	0955	0.6	1553	5.6	2217	0.6
15	F	0417	5.5	1043	0.5	1643	5.6	2304	0.7
16	SA	0504	5.5	1132	0.4	1735	5.5	2352	0.8
17	SU	0552	5.5	1223	0.5	1829	5.3		
18	M	0041	1.1	0643	5.3	1317	0.7	1924	5.1
19	TU	0134	1.3	0738	5.1	1413	0.9	2023	4.9
20	W	0233	1.6	0839	4.9	1514	1.1	◐ 2126	4.7
21	TH	0337	1.8	0944	4.8	1620	1.3	2232	4.5
22	F	0447	1.9	1053	4.7	1728	1.4	2340	4.5
23	SA	0556	1.9	1201	4.7	1832	1.4		
24	SU	0041	4.6	0657	1.7	1302	4.8	1927	1.3
25	M	0134	4.7	0750	1.6	1354	4.8	2013	1.3
26	TU	0219	4.9	0835	1.4	1439	4.9	2054	1.3
27	W	0258	5.0	0915	1.3	1520	5.0	2131	1.3
28	TH	0333	5.1	0952	1.2	1558	5.0	○ 2206	1.3
29	F	0406	5.1	1028	1.1	1635	5.0	2239	1.3
30	SA	0438	5.1	1103	1.1	1711	5.0	2312	1.3

JULY

Date	Day	Time	m	Time	m	Time	m	Time	m
1	SU	0511	5.1	1138	1.2	1747	4.9	2346	1.4
2	M	0547	5.0	1213	1.2	1824	4.8		
3	TU	0022	1.5	0626	4.9	1251	1.3	1905	4.7
4	W	0102	1.7	0708	4.8	1333	1.5	1950	4.6
5	TH	0147	1.8	0755	4.7	1421	1.6	2041	4.4
6	F	0239	2.0	0848	4.6	1516	1.6	◑ 2137	4.4
7	SA	0343	2.0	0947	4.5	1619	1.7	2238	4.4
8	SU	0451	2.0	1051	4.6	1724	1.6	2340	4.5
9	M	0556	1.8	1155	4.7	1828	1.4		
10	TU	0039	4.7	0657	1.5	1256	4.9	1927	1.2
11	W	0134	5.0	0755	1.2	1354	5.2	2023	1.0
12	TH	0226	5.2	0850	0.9	1449	5.4	2116	0.9
13	F	0316	5.4	0943	0.6	1543	5.6	● 2207	0.8
14	SA	0404	5.6	1035	0.4	1635	5.6	2256	0.7
15	SU	0452	5.7	1125	0.3	1726	5.6	2343	0.8
16	M	0540	5.7	1214	0.3	1816	5.5		
17	TU	0030	0.9	0628	5.6	1303	0.5	1907	5.3
18	W	0117	1.2	0718	5.4	1352	0.7	1959	5.0
19	TH	0207	1.4	0811	5.1	1445	1.0	◐ 2053	4.8
20	F	0302	1.7	0910	4.9	1542	1.4	2152	4.5
21	SA	0405	1.9	1015	4.6	1647	1.6	2257	4.4
22	SU	0517	2.0	1125	4.5	1756	1.8		
23	M	0003	4.4	0627	1.9	1235	4.5	1858	1.8
24	TU	0105	4.5	0727	1.8	1334	4.6	1949	1.7
25	W	0156	4.7	0816	1.6	1423	4.8	2033	1.6
26	TH	0238	4.9	0858	1.4	1505	4.9	2112	1.5
27	F	0315	5.0	0936	1.2	1543	5.0	○ 2147	1.4
28	SA	0349	5.1	1012	1.1	1619	5.0	2221	1.3
29	SU	0420	5.2	1046	1.1	1652	5.0	2254	1.3
30	M	0452	5.2	1119	1.1	1725	5.0	2327	1.3
31	TU	0525	5.2	1152	1.1	1759	5.0		

AUGUST

Date	Day	Time	m	Time	m	Time	m	Time	m
1	W	0001	1.4	0600	5.1	1227	1.1	1836	4.9
2	TH	0038	1.5	0637	5.1	1304	1.2	1917	4.8
3	F	0116	1.6	0719	4.9	1346	1.4	2003	4.6
4	SA	0201	1.8	0808	4.8	1436	1.5	◑ 2056	4.5
5	SU	0256	1.9	0906	4.7	1536	1.7	2157	4.4
6	M	0406	2.0	1014	4.6	1646	1.7	2304	4.4
7	TU	0522	1.9	1127	4.7	1800	1.7		
8	W	0011	4.6	0634	1.6	1238	4.8	1909	1.5
9	TH	0114	4.9	0740	1.3	1343	5.1	2011	1.2
10	F	0211	5.2	0840	0.9	1440	5.4	2106	1.0
11	SA	0303	5.5	0934	0.5	1533	5.6	● 2156	0.8
12	SU	0351	5.7	1024	0.3	1623	5.7	2243	0.7
13	M	0437	5.8	1111	0.2	1710	5.7	2327	0.7
14	TU	0522	5.8	1156	0.2	1756	5.6		
15	W	0009	0.8	0606	5.7	1240	0.4	1841	5.4
16	TH	0051	1.0	0651	5.5	1323	0.7	1927	5.1
17	F	0134	1.3	0739	5.2	1409	1.1	2015	4.8
18	SA	0221	1.7	0833	4.9	1500	1.6	◐ 2108	4.5
19	SU	0319	2.0	0935	4.5	1602	1.9	2210	4.3
20	M	0434	2.1	1048	4.3	1716	2.1	2321	4.2
21	TU	0557	2.1	1207	4.3	1829	2.1		
22	W	0033	4.4	0704	1.9	1314	4.5	1926	2.0
23	TH	0131	4.6	0756	1.7	1404	4.7	2011	1.8
24	F	0217	4.8	0838	1.4	1446	4.9	2051	1.6
25	SA	0255	5.0	0916	1.2	1523	5.0	2127	1.4
26	SU	0328	5.2	0951	1.1	1557	5.1	○ 2201	1.3
27	M	0359	5.3	1023	1.0	1629	5.2	2233	1.2
28	TU	0429	5.3	1055	0.9	1700	5.2	2305	1.1
29	W	0459	5.4	1126	0.9	1731	5.2	2338	1.2
30	TH	0532	5.3	1159	1.0	1806	5.1		
31	F	0012	1.3	0606	5.3	1235	1.1	1844	5.0

Chart Datum: 2·85 metres below Ordnance Datum (Newlyn). HAT is 6·1 metres above Chart Datum.

STANDARD TIME (UT)
For Summer Time add ONE hour in **non-shaded areas**

RIVER TEES LAT 54°38′N LONG 1°09′W

TIMES AND HEIGHTS OF HIGH AND LOW WATERS

Dates in red are SPRINGS
Dates in blue are NEAPS

YEAR **2018**

SEPTEMBER

Date	Day	Time	m	Time	m	Time	m	Time	m
1	SA	0048	1.4	0646	5.1	1315	1.3	1927	4.8
2	SU	0129	1.6	0734	4.9	1401	1.5	2019	4.6
3	M	0221	1.8	0834	4.7	1500	1.8	◑ 2122	4.4
4	TU	0333	1.9	0948	4.5	1618	1.9	2235	4.4
5	W	0501	1.9	1110	4.5	1743	1.9	2350	4.5
6	TH	0623	1.6	1228	4.8	1859	1.7		
7	F	0100	4.8	0732	1.2	1336	5.1	2001	1.4
8	SA	0159	5.2	0830	0.8	1432	5.4	2053	1.1
9	SU	0249	5.5	0921	0.5	1520	5.6	● 2140	0.8
10	M	0334	5.8	1007	0.3	1605	5.7	2224	0.7
11	TU	0417	5.9	1050	0.2	1648	5.7	2304	0.7
12	W	0459	5.9	1131	0.3	1730	5.6	2343	0.8
13	TH	0540	5.7	1210	0.5	1810	5.4		
14	F	0021	1.0	0621	5.5	1249	0.9	1851	5.1
15	SA	0059	1.3	0706	5.2	1328	1.3	1933	4.8
16	SU	0141	1.6	0756	4.8	1413	1.8	◐ 2022	4.5
17	M	0233	1.9	0856	4.4	1510	2.2	2120	4.3
18	TU	0349	2.2	1010	4.2	1631	2.4	2233	4.2
19	W	0522	2.2	1134	4.2	1755	2.4	2353	4.2
20	TH	0636	2.0	1247	4.3	1858	2.1		
21	F	0059	4.5	0729	1.7	1340	4.6	1945	1.9
22	SA	0148	4.8	0812	1.4	1421	4.9	2025	1.6
23	SU	0227	5.0	0850	1.2	1457	5.1	2101	1.4
24	M	0301	5.2	0924	1.0	1530	5.2	2135	1.2
25	TU	0332	5.3	0956	0.9	1600	5.3	○ 2208	1.1
26	W	0402	5.4	1027	0.8	1631	5.4	2240	1.0
27	TH	0432	5.5	1058	0.8	1702	5.3	2313	1.0
28	F	0505	5.5	1132	0.8	1737	5.3	2348	1.1
29	SA	0541	5.4	1208	1.0	1814	5.1		
30	SU	0024	1.2	0623	5.2	1248	1.3	1857	4.9

OCTOBER

Date	Day	Time	m	Time	m	Time	m	Time	m
1	M	0107	1.4	0713	5.0	1334	1.6	1949	4.7
2	TU	0201	1.7	0816	4.7	1434	1.9	◑ 2055	4.5
3	W	0316	1.9	0935	4.5	1559	2.1	2213	4.4
4	TH	0449	1.8	1101	4.5	1732	2.1	2334	4.5
5	F	0615	1.5	1223	4.7	1848	1.8		
6	SA	0046	4.9	0721	1.1	1328	5.1	1946	1.4
7	SU	0143	5.2	0815	0.8	1418	5.4	2035	1.2
8	M	0231	5.5	0902	0.5	1503	5.6	2119	0.9
9	TU	0315	5.7	0945	0.4	1544	5.7	● 2201	0.8
10	W	0355	5.8	1025	0.4	1623	5.6	2239	0.8
11	TH	0434	5.8	1103	0.5	1701	5.6	2316	0.8
12	F	0514	5.6	1139	0.8	1737	5.4	2352	1.0
13	SA	0554	5.4	1214	1.1	1815	5.2		
14	SU	0028	1.3	0636	5.1	1249	1.5	1853	4.9
15	M	0107	1.6	0723	4.7	1327	1.9	1937	4.6
16	TU	0153	1.9	0818	4.4	1416	2.2	◐ 2031	4.4
17	W	0301	2.1	0929	4.1	1535	2.5	2140	4.2
18	TH	0435	2.2	1052	4.1	1709	2.5	2302	4.2
19	F	0556	2.1	1208	4.3	1820	2.3		
20	SA	0014	4.4	0652	1.8	1305	4.5	1911	2.0
21	SU	0108	4.6	0737	1.5	1348	4.8	1953	1.7
22	M	0150	4.9	0816	1.2	1424	5.0	2030	1.5
23	TU	0226	5.1	0851	1.0	1457	5.2	2105	1.2
24	W	0259	5.3	0924	0.9	1529	5.4	○ 2140	1.1
25	TH	0332	5.4	0957	0.8	1601	5.4	2215	0.9
26	F	0406	5.5	1032	0.7	1635	5.5	2251	0.9
27	SA	0443	5.5	1108	0.8	1712	5.4	2328	0.9
28	SU	0524	5.5	1146	1.0	1752	5.3		
29	M	0009	1.0	0610	5.3	1228	1.3	1837	5.1
30	TU	0056	1.2	0704	5.0	1317	1.6	1930	4.8
31	W	0153	1.5	0810	4.7	1419	2.0	◑ 2036	4.6

NOVEMBER

Date	Day	Time	m	Time	m	Time	m	Time	m
1	TH	0309	1.7	0927	4.5	1545	2.2	2154	4.5
2	F	0437	1.6	1051	4.5	1714	2.1	2314	4.6
3	SA	0557	1.4	1210	4.7	1828	1.9		
4	SU	0025	4.9	0701	1.1	1311	5.0	1925	1.6
5	M	0123	5.2	0754	0.8	1400	5.3	2013	1.3
6	TU	0211	5.4	0840	0.7	1443	5.4	2057	1.1
7	W	0254	5.5	0921	0.6	1522	5.5	● 2137	1.0
8	TH	0334	5.6	0959	0.7	1558	5.5	2215	0.9
9	F	0413	5.5	1035	0.8	1633	5.4	2252	1.0
10	SA	0452	5.4	1109	1.0	1707	5.3	2327	1.1
11	SU	0531	5.2	1142	1.3	1743	5.2		
12	M	0003	1.2	0611	5.0	1216	1.6	1820	5.0
13	TU	0041	1.5	0656	4.7	1252	1.9	1902	4.8
14	W	0124	1.7	0746	4.4	1335	2.2	1951	4.5
15	TH	0218	2.0	0845	4.2	1436	2.4	◐ 2050	4.4
16	F	0334	2.1	0958	4.1	1604	2.5	2200	4.3
17	SA	0455	2.1	1112	4.2	1723	2.4	2313	4.3
18	SU	0602	1.9	1214	4.4	1823	2.2		
19	M	0014	4.5	0653	1.6	1303	4.7	1911	1.9
20	TU	0104	4.8	0736	1.4	1344	4.9	1953	1.6
21	W	0146	5.0	0815	1.1	1421	5.1	2033	1.3
22	TH	0226	5.2	0852	0.9	1457	5.3	2112	1.1
23	F	0305	5.4	0930	0.8	1534	5.5	○ 2152	0.9
24	SA	0346	5.5	1009	0.8	1613	5.5	2233	0.8
25	SU	0429	5.5	1049	0.8	1653	5.5	2316	0.8
26	M	0515	5.5	1132	1.0	1737	5.4		
27	TU	0001	0.8	0605	5.3	1218	1.2	1824	5.3
28	W	0052	1.0	0701	5.1	1309	1.6	1918	5.1
29	TH	0150	1.2	0804	4.8	1411	1.9	2021	4.9
30	F	0259	1.4	0914	4.6	1526	2.1	◑ 2132	4.7

DECEMBER

Date	Day	Time	m	Time	m	Time	m	Time	m
1	SA	0414	1.4	1029	4.6	1644	2.1	2246	4.7
2	SU	0529	1.4	1142	4.7	1757	1.9	2357	4.8
3	M	0635	1.2	1245	4.9	1859	1.7		
4	TU	0058	5.0	0729	1.1	1337	5.0	1951	1.5
5	W	0151	5.1	0816	1.0	1421	5.2	2036	1.3
6	TH	0236	5.2	0858	1.0	1501	5.3	2118	1.2
7	F	0318	5.3	0936	1.0	1537	5.3	● 2156	1.1
8	SA	0357	5.2	1012	1.1	1611	5.3	2233	1.1
9	SU	0436	5.2	1046	1.2	1644	5.3	2309	1.1
10	M	0514	5.1	1118	1.4	1718	5.2	2345	1.2
11	TU	0552	4.9	1151	1.6	1755	5.1		
12	W	0021	1.4	0632	4.8	1226	1.7	1834	4.9
13	TH	0100	1.5	0716	4.6	1306	2.0	1919	4.8
14	F	0143	1.7	0805	4.4	1355	2.2	2010	4.6
15	SA	0236	1.9	0902	4.3	1456	2.3	◐ 2107	4.4
16	SU	0341	2.0	1005	4.2	1611	2.4	2209	4.4
17	M	0450	1.9	1108	4.3	1720	2.3	2313	4.5
18	TU	0553	1.8	1206	4.5	1820	2.0		
19	W	0012	4.6	0648	1.5	1258	4.7	1912	1.7
20	TH	0106	4.9	0737	1.3	1344	5.0	2001	1.4
21	F	0155	5.1	0823	1.1	1428	5.2	2048	1.1
22	SA	0243	5.3	0908	0.9	1512	5.4	○ 2134	0.9
23	SU	0331	5.5	0953	0.9	1555	5.5	2221	0.7
24	M	0420	5.5	1039	0.9	1640	5.6	2308	0.6
25	TU	0509	5.5	1125	0.9	1726	5.6	2357	0.6
26	W	0601	5.4	1212	1.1	1815	5.5		
27	TH	0047	0.7	0654	5.2	1302	1.3	1906	5.3
28	F	0141	0.8	0751	5.0	1356	1.6	2002	5.1
29	SA	0238	1.1	0851	4.8	1457	1.8	◑ 2104	4.9
30	SU	0342	1.3	0956	4.6	1606	2.0	2211	4.8
31	M	0451	1.4	1104	4.6	1719	2.0	2322	4.7

Chart Datum: 2·85 metres below Ordnance Datum (Newlyn). HAT is 6·1metres above Chart Datum.

9.5.15 HARTLEPOOL

Hartlepool **54°41'·26N 01°11'·90W** (West Hbr ent)

CHARTS AC 152, 2567, 2566, 5615; Imray C24

TIDES +0437 Dover; ML 3·0; Duration 0600

Standard Port RIVER TEES (⟵)

Times				**Height (metres)**			
High Water		Low Water		MHWS	MHWN	MLWN	MLWS
0000	0600	0000	0600	5·5	4·3	2·0	0·9
1200	1800	1200	1800				
Differences HARTLEPOOL							
–0004	–0004	–0006	–0006	–0·1	–0·1	–0·2	–0·1
MIDDLESBROUGH							
0000	+0002	0000	–0003	+0·1	+0·2	+0·1	–0·1

SHELTER Excellent in marina (5m) 4Ca SW of port. Strong E/SE winds raise broken water and swell in the bay, making ent channel hazardous, but possible. In such conditions, ask marina's advice.

NAVIGATION WPT 54°40'·86N 01°09'·90W, Longscar ECM buoy, 295°/1·06M to W Hbr ent. (For Victoria Hbr, 308°/0·65M to Nos 1/2 buoys.) From S, beware Longscar Rks, 4ca WSW of WPT. Tees Fairway SWM buoy (54°40'·60N 01°04'·00W) is 2M E of Longscar ECM buoy and may assist the landfall. Tees Bay Wind Farm consists of 27 turbines (extremities Fl Y 5s 13m 5M) up to 1½M offshore SE of the Tees channel as far as West Scar. Speed limit 4kn in W Hbr.

LIGHTS AND MARKS Tees Fairway Iso 4s 8m 8M, Horn(1) 5s. Longscar ECM buoy Q(3), bell, lies off the entrance. Steetly Works chimney, 1·4M NW of marina ent, and St Hilda's Church tower on The Heugh, are both prominent. Entry to commercial port on ldg lt Dir Iso WRG 324° following clearly buoyed channel. Dir lt Fl WRG leads 308° to marina lock, between W Hbr outer piers, Oc R and Oc G, and inner piers, FR and FG; bright street lts on S pier.

Lock sigs: ● = Proceed; ● = Wait; ● ● = Lock closed.

Dir lt, Iso WRG, leads 325° via lit buoyed chan to Victoria Hbr.

COMMUNICATIONS (Code 01429) CGOC (01262) 672317; Police 101; Dr 272679; Tees Port Authority (01642) 277205;

Marina Lock Ch 80. Marina Ch **M**, 80. *Tees Port Control* info Ch 14, 22 (H24). *Hartlepool Dock Radio* Ch 12, only for ship docking.

FACILITIES

Hartlepool Marina www.hartlepool-marina.com ☎865744 Access via channel dredged to CD and lock(max beam 8.5m), over tidal sill 0.8m below CD (HW± 5), (H24). 500+100 £2.16, (H24) LPG (40/300t) (13t).

Victoria Hbr (commercial dock, not normally for yachts), access H24. Call *Tees Port Control* Ch 14 for short-stay.

Tees & Hartlepool YC ☎233423.

Town (H24) (Teesside).

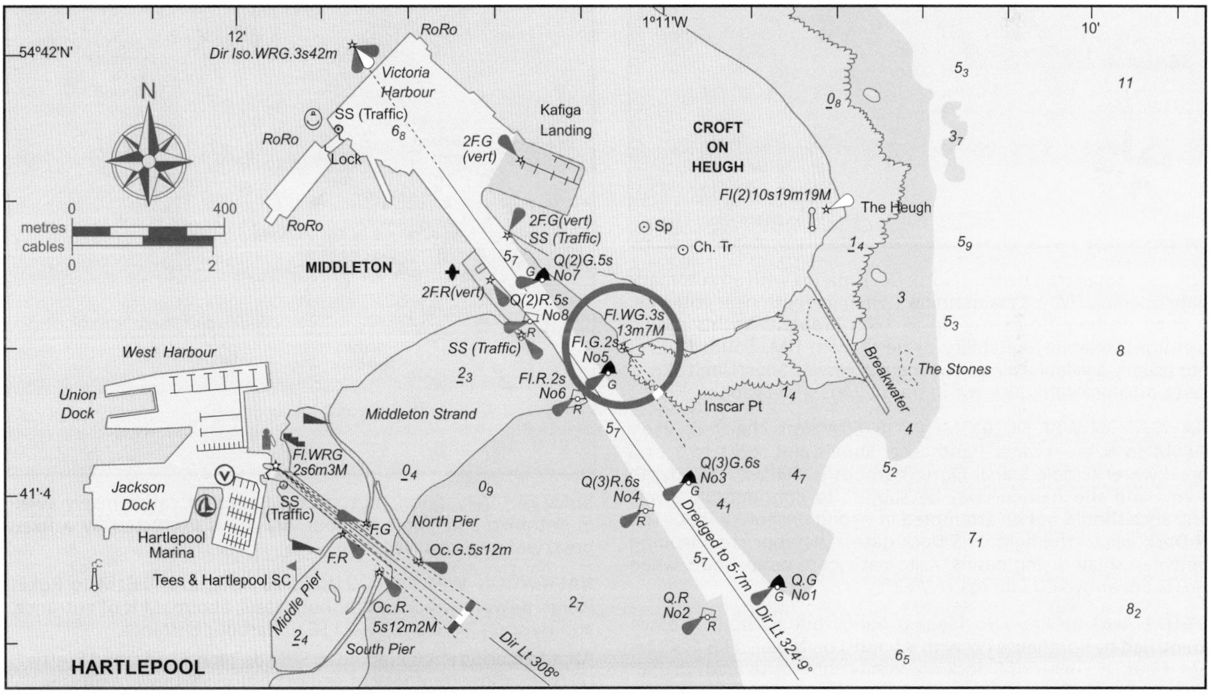

HARTLEPOOL TO SOUTHERN NETHERLANDS

(AC 2182A, 1191, 1190, 1503, 1408, 1610, 3371, 110) From abeam Whitby the passage can, theoretically, be made on one direct course, but this would conflict with oil/gas activities and platforms including Rough and Amethyst fields off Humber, Hewett off Cromer and very extensive fields further offshore.

Commercial, offshore support and fishing vessels may be met S of Flamborough Hd and particularly off NE Norfolk where it is advisable to follow an inshore track avoiding wind farms. After passing Flamborough Hd, N Outer Dowsing and Dudgeon cardinals leave Dudgeon Wind Farm (under construction with cardinal marks) and Haisborough Shoal to the E, and either:

Proceed SSE inshore of Cross Sand to Outer Gabbard departing SE to cross Nord Hinder TSS at right angles before heading for Roompotsluis via Middelbank and subsequent buoyed channel.

Or, set course ESE from the vicinity of Smith's Knoll, so as to cross the N/S deep-water traffic routes to the E altering SE towards Hoek van Holland, keeping N of Maas Approaches TSS.

HARTLEPOOL TO THE GERMAN BIGHT

(AC 2182A, 1191, 266, 1405) Taking departure eastward from abeam Whitby High lt, skirt the SW Patch off Dogger Bank, clearing S of Katy Gas Field passing E Friesland wind farm and then N of German Bight W Approach TSS. Thence head for the Elbe or Helgoland. The latter may also serve as a convenient haven in order to adjust the passage for Elbe tides and streams, without greatly increasing passage distance.

▶ *Tidal streams are less than 1kn away from the coast and run E/W along much of the route.* ◀

9.5.16 SEAHAM

Durham **54°50'·24N 01°19'·28W** ✿✿✿

CHARTS AC 152, 1627, 5615; Imray C24

TIDES +0435 Dover; ML 3·0; Duration 0600

Standard Port RIVER TEES (←)

Times				**Height (metres)**			
High Water		Low Water		MHWS	MHWN	MLWN	MLWS
0000	0600	0000	0600	5·5	4·3	2·0	0·9
1200	1800	1200	1800				
Differences SEAHAM							
−0015	−0015	−0015	−0015	−0·3	−0·2	0·0	−0·2

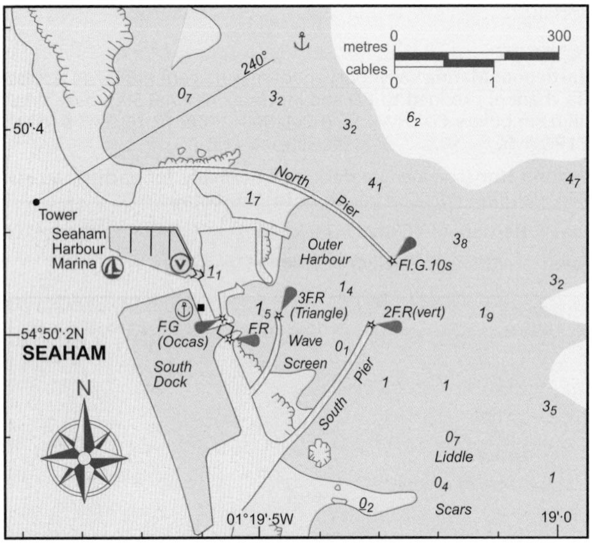

SHELTER Small craft berth in North Dock marina with an automatic gate opening HW ± 3 maintaining 1.5m min depth near entrance. 4 Ⓥ to starboard on entry up to 1·9m draught. Yachts should confirm availability/suitability of berth with HM. South Dock is not usually available to non-commercial vessels. Speed limit 5kn. ⚓ 2½ca offshore with clock twr in transit 240° with St John's ✠ twr.

NAVIGATION WPT 54°50'·36N 01°18'·60W (off chartlet), 256°/0·40M to N breakwater lighthouse. Shoals and rocks to S of S breakwater (Liddle Scars). Outer harbour is shallow, min depth 1.2m, and the harbour can be subject to considerable swell; entrance should not be attempted in strong onshore winds. The N Dock lies to the right of S Dock gates, the appr chan leading between small drying basins. Automatic gate opens/shuts when HoT 2.5m above CD (approx HW ±3½).

LIGHTS AND MARKS No leading lights, but harbour is easily identified by lighthouse (W with B bands) on N pier, Fl G 10s 12m 5M. FS at NE corner of S dock on with N lighthouse leads in 256° clear of Tangle Rocks. 3FR lts on wave screen are in form of a △.

Traffic sigs at S Dock: ● = Vessels enter: ● = Vessels leave.

Traffic sigs at N Dock gate: 3 ● (vert) = shut : 3 ● (vert) = open.

COMMUNICATIONS (Code 0191) CGOC (01262) 672317; Police 101; Dr 5812332. HM 07801 215236.

VHF Ch **12** 16 06 0800–1700 (Mon-Fri), *Seaham Marina* Ch 80.

FACILITIES **N Dock** Marina ☎581 8998; 78 ⊆ inc 4Ⓥ up to 10m. **S Dock** (Seaham Hbr Dock Co) ☎516 1700, ⛽ (40t).

Town (½M) and available out of town (about 5M). ✉ Ⓑ ✕ ⇌ ✈(Teesside or Newcastle).

9.5.17 SUNDERLAND

Tyne and Wear **54°55'·23N 01°21'·15W** ✿✿✿✿✿✿✿

CHARTS AC 152, 1627, 5615; Imray C24

TIDES +0430 Dover; ML 2·9; Duration 0600; Zone 0 (UT)

Standard Port RIVER TEES (←)

Times				**Height (metres)**			
High Water		Low Water		MHWS	MHWN	MLWN	MLWS
0000	0600	0000	0600	5·5	4·3	2·0	0·9
1200	1800	1200	1800				
Differences *SUNDERLAND*							
−0017	*−0017*	*−0016*	*−0016*	*−0·2*	*−0·1*	*0·0*	*0·0*

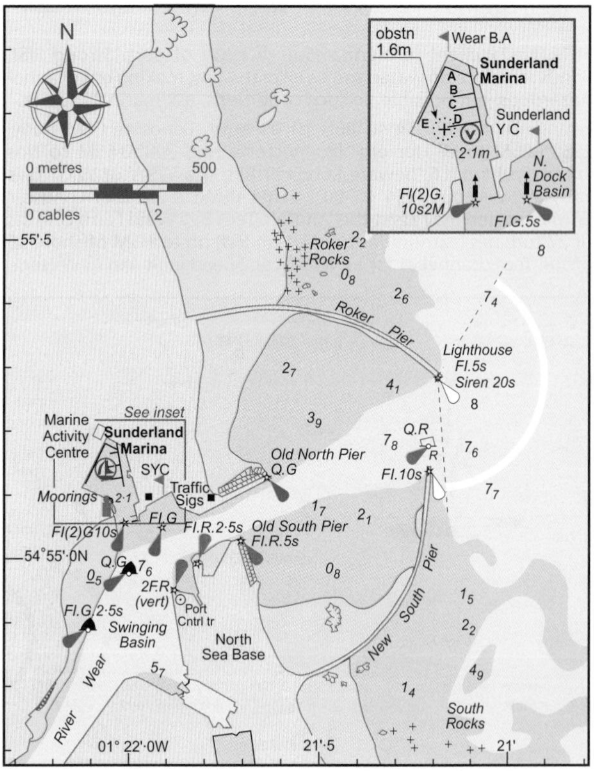

SHELTER Very good, but strong Easterlies cause heavy swell in entrance and outer harbour. Marina is protected by a fixed breakwater; access H24.

NAVIGATION WPT 54°55'·21N 01°20'·10W, 278°/0·61M to Roker Pier lt. Beware wreck at Whitburn Steel, about 1M N of entrance, and Hendon Rk (0·9m), 1·2M SE of harbour entrance.

Appr to marina ent is marked by SHM dolphin, Fl G 5s, and E jetty, Fl (2) G 10s. Close (4m) SSW of end of pontoon beware substantial obst'n (1·6m) in surrounding depth 2·1m, see chartlet.

LIGHTS AND MARKS 3 Fl ● at Pilot Stn (Old N Pier) = danger in harbour; no entry/departure.

COMMUNICATIONS (Code 0191) CGOC (01262) 672317; ⊖(0191) 257 9441; Police 101; Ⓗ 565 6256. HM 567 2626 (HO), 567 0161 (OT).

Sunderland Marina Ch 80. Port VHF Ch **14** (H24); tide and visibility reports on request.

FACILITIES **Sunderland Marina** 120 pontoon berths in 2·1m, max LOA 13m; and 110. ☎ 5144721. Ⓥ (if available) £2·40/m; half-tide shelf £12/day, ⛽ (H24).

Sunderland YC ☎ 5675133, (dinghy) ⊆ ⛽.

Wear Boating Association ☎5675313, ⊆.

Services

Town ✉ Ⓑ ✕ ⇌ ✈(Newcastle).

9.5.18 R TYNE/NORTH SHIELDS

Tyne and Wear **55°00'·89N 01°24'·10W** ❀❀◊◊◊✿✿

CHARTS AC 152, 1191, 1934, 5615; Imray C24

TIDES +0430 Dover; ML 3·0; Duration 0604

Standard Port NORTH SHIELDS (⟶)

Times				Height (metres)			
High Water		Low Water		MHWS	MHWN	MLWN	MLWS
0200	0800	0100	0800	5·0	3·9	1·8	0·7
1400	2000	1300	2000				
Differences NEWCASTLE-UPON-TYNE							
+0003	+0003	+0008	+0008	+0·3	+0·2	+0·1	+0·1

SHELTER Good in all weather. Access H24, but in strong E and NE winds appr may be difficult for smaller craft due to much backwash off the piers. Confused seas can build at the ent in severe weather, and a large steep swell can break dangerously when meeting an ebb tide up to half a mile inside the harbour. In emergency or as a refuge yachts may berth on Fish Quay; contact HM.

NAVIGATION WPT 55°01´·00N 01°23´·00W, 250°/0·7M to hbr ent, recommended route in Ldg lt Oc W sector. Outbound keep S of hbr ent centreline. From S, no dangers. From N, beware Bellhues Rk (approx 1M N of hbr and ¾M offshore); give N pier a wide berth. Dredged chan in Lower Hbr is buoyed. 6kn speed limit in the river west of Herd Groyne Lt Ho. In river proceed under power keeping to the starboard side; if <20m or under sail conform to Colreg Rule 9 – do not impede large vessels. Millennium Br air draft is 4.5m when closed, the clearance for all bridges is 25m when it is open.

LIGHTS AND MARKS See 9.5.4 and chartlet. W Lt LFl 10s shows from centre span of the Millennium Bridge when fully open.

COMMUNICATIONS (Code 0191) CGOC (01262) 672317; ☁ 2326453; Police 101; Ⓗ (Tynemouth) 2596660; Ⓗ (Newcastle) 2325131. HM 2570407; Tyne VTS 2572080.

Tyne VTS Ch **12**, 11 (H24) call on arrival and prior to departure. Marinas: Royal Quays Ch 80. St Peter's Ch 80 M.

FACILITIES A conservancy fee (£10) may be levied by the Port Authority on all visiting craft. Craft waiting to enter the marinas should do so outside the fairway.

Royal Quays Marina ⚓ 54°59'·79N 01°26'·84W ☎2728282 2M upriver from pierheads in former Albert Edward Dock; 302 ⊆ inc Ⓥ, £2·30 7·9m depth. Lock (42.5m x 7·5m) departures H and H+30; arrivals H+15 and H+45, or on request at quiet times. Waiting pontoon outside lock. ⛽ ▣ ⛽ ⛽(H24) ⛽ ⛟ ⛟ ⛟(30t) ⛟ ⛟.

St Peter's Marina 54°57´·94N 01°34´·35W, 8M upriver, and 1M E of city. ☎2654472; 140+20Ⓥ, £2.27. Access approx HW±3½ over sill, dries 0·8m, which retains 2·5m within. Traffic lights at ent. ⛽ on pontoon outside ent in 2m. ⛟ ▣ ⛟ ⛟ ACA, Ⓔ.

Millennium Bridge in city centre, limited pontoon berthing below the bridge; pre-book ☎2211363.

Newcastle City Marina enquiries@newcastlecitymarina.co.uk ☎2211348, mob 07435 788426; Boats <26m: price on sliding scale 5m £10 → £30 >14m, short stay (< 5hrs) free. ⛟ ⛽.

City All amenities, ⇌ (Newcastle/S Shields), ✈ (Newcastle). **Ferries:** IJmuiden; daily; 16hrs; DFDS (www.dfdsseaways.co.uk).

ADJACENT HARBOUR

CULLERCOATS, 55°02'·08N 01°25'·81W. AC 1191. +0430 Dover. Tides as 9.5.17. Small drying hbr 1·6M N of R Tyne ent. Appr on ldg line 256°, two bns (FR lts), between drying rks. An occasional fair weather ⚓ or dry against S pier. Facilities at Tynemouth.

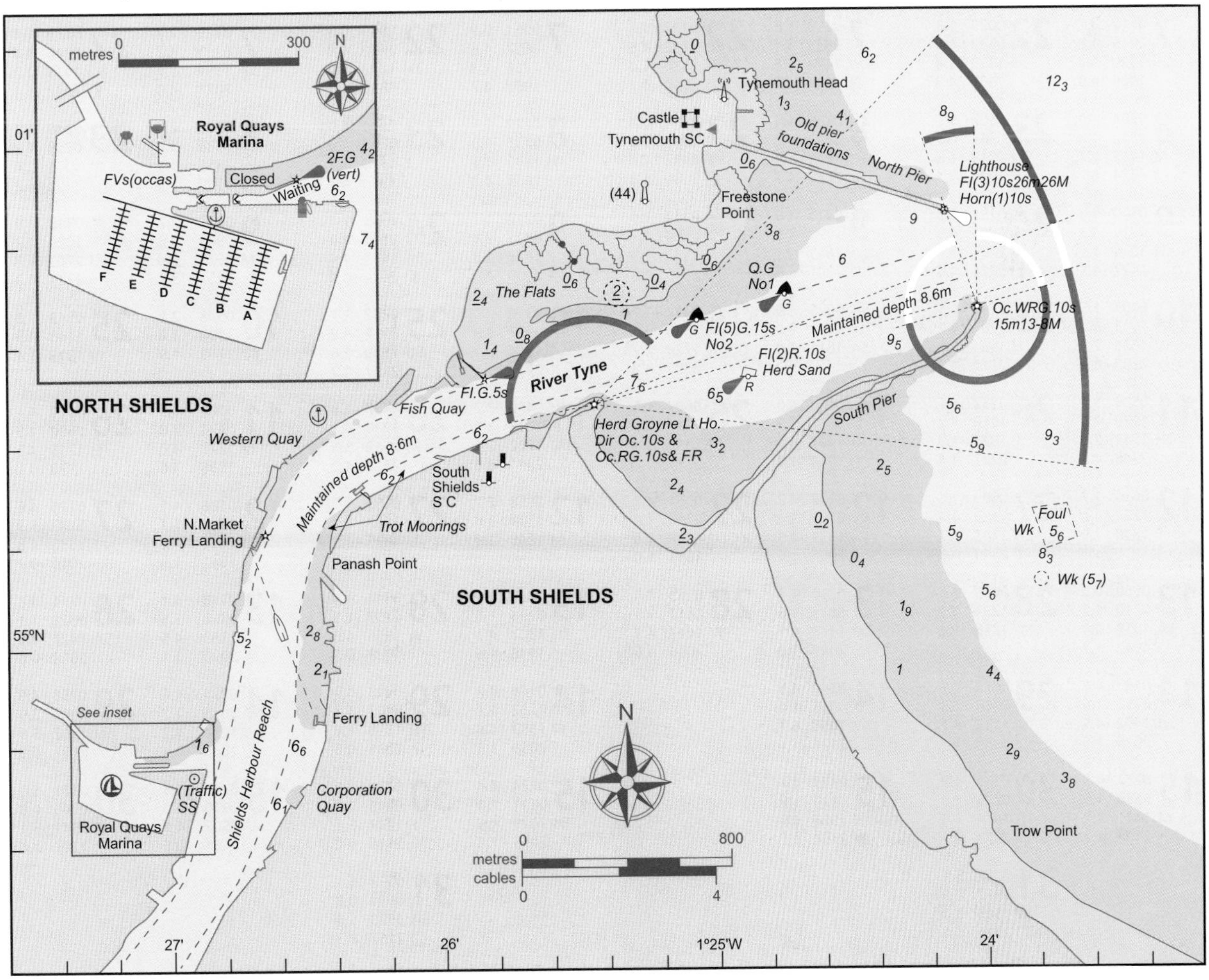

STANDARD TIME (UT)
For Summer Time add ONE hour in **non-shaded areas**

RIVER TYNE/NORTH SHIELDS

LAT 55°00′N LONG 1°26′W

TIMES AND HEIGHTS OF HIGH AND LOW WATERS

Dates in red are SPRINGS
Dates in blue are NEAPS

YEAR **2018**

JANUARY

Date	Time	m	Date	Time	m
1 M	0207 0837 1437 2104	5.1 0.9 5.2 0.8	16 TU	0306 0912 1515 2139	4.6 1.3 4.8 1.2
2 TU	0259 0927 1523 ○ 2155	5.3 0.8 5.3 0.5	17 W	0341 0946 1548 ● 2212	4.7 1.3 4.9 1.1
3 W	0350 1015 1609 2244	5.4 0.7 5.4 0.4	18 TH	0415 1019 1619 2245	4.8 1.2 5.0 1.0
4 TH	0440 1102 1655 2333	5.4 0.8 5.4 0.4	19 F	0448 1051 1651 2318	4.8 1.2 5.0 1.0
5 F	0531 1147 1743	5.3 1.0 5.3	20 SA	0521 1124 1724 2353	4.7 1.2 5.0 1.0
6 SA	0022 0623 1233 1833	0.5 5.0 1.2 5.2	21 SU	0556 1157 1759	4.7 1.3 4.9
7 SU	0112 0716 1320 1926	0.7 4.8 1.4 4.9	22 M	0029 0633 1233 1836	1.1 4.6 1.4 4.8
8 M	0204 0812 1412 ◑ 2024	1.0 4.5 1.7 4.7	23 TU	0108 0714 1313 1920	1.2 4.5 1.6 4.7
9 TU	0300 0910 1514 2127	1.3 4.3 1.9 4.5	24 W	0151 0803 1401 ◐ 2011	1.3 4.3 1.7 4.6
10 W	0403 1013 1626 2235	1.5 4.2 2.1 4.3	25 TH	0245 0901 1504 2114	1.5 4.2 1.8 4.4
11 TH	0509 1120 1741 2346	1.7 4.1 2.0 4.2	26 F	0352 1010 1623 2227	1.6 4.2 1.9 4.4
12 F	0614 1224 1848	1.7 4.2 1.9	27 SA	0509 1123 1743 2345	1.6 4.3 1.7 4.5
13 SA	0050 0710 1318 1942	4.3 1.7 4.4 1.7	28 SU	0622 1233 1856	1.5 4.5 1.4
14 SU	0143 0756 1402 2025	4.4 1.6 4.5 1.5	29 M	0057 0728 1333 1959	4.7 1.3 4.7 1.1
15 M	0227 0836 1441 2104	4.5 1.5 4.7 1.3	30 TU	0159 0826 1424 2055	4.9 1.0 5.0 0.7
			31 W	0252 0917 1511 ○ 2146	5.1 0.9 5.2 0.4

FEBRUARY

Date	Time	m	Date	Time	m
1 TH	0342 1004 1556 2234	5.3 0.8 5.4 0.3	16 F	0355 1001 1559 2226	4.8 1.1 5.0 0.8
2 F	0429 1048 1641 2320	5.3 0.7 5.5 0.2	17 SA	0427 1033 1630 2259	4.8 1.0 5.0 0.7
3 SA	0515 1130 1725	5.2 0.8 5.4	18 SU	0458 1105 1702 2332	4.9 1.0 5.1 0.7
4 SU	0004 0600 1211 1810	0.4 5.1 1.0 5.2	19 M	0531 1137 1735	4.8 1.0 5.1
5 M	0046 0646 1250 1856	0.6 4.8 1.2 5.0	20 TU	0006 0606 1212 1812	0.8 4.7 1.1 5.0
6 TU	0129 0733 1332 1946	0.9 4.6 1.5 4.7	21 W	0042 0645 1249 1854	0.9 4.6 1.3 4.8
7 W	0213 0823 1419 ◑ 2041	1.3 4.3 1.8 4.4	22 TH	0122 0730 1334 1944	1.1 4.5 1.4 4.7
8 TH	0306 0919 1522 2145	1.6 4.1 2.0 4.1	23 F	0211 0825 1432 ◐ 2046	1.4 4.3 1.6 4.4
9 F	0410 1025 1645 2301	1.9 3.9 2.1 4.0	24 SA	0317 0934 1552 2205	1.6 4.2 1.8 4.3
10 SA	0525 1139 1811	2.0 4.0 2.0	25 SU	0442 1055 1723 2332	1.7 4.1 1.7 4.3
11 SU	0020 0637 1247 1918	4.0 1.9 4.1 1.8	26 M	0607 1214 1844	1.6 4.3 1.4
12 M	0122 0733 1339 2006	4.2 1.8 4.3 1.6	27 TU	0051 0719 1320 1951	4.5 1.4 4.6 1.0
13 TU	0210 0817 1421 2046	4.4 1.6 4.5 1.3	28 W	0153 0817 1413 2046	4.8 1.1 4.9 0.6
14 W	0249 0855 1456 2121	4.5 1.4 4.7 1.1			
15 TH	0323 0929 1528 ● 2154	4.7 1.2 4.9 1.0			

MARCH

Date	Time	m	Date	Time	m
1 TH	0244 0906 1459 2134	5.0 0.9 5.2 0.4	16 F	0257 0905 1502 2128	4.6 1.2 4.8 0.8
2 F	0330 0950 1541 ○ 2219	5.2 0.7 5.3 0.2	17 SA	0329 0938 1533 ● 2201	4.8 1.0 5.0 0.7
3 SA	0413 1030 1623 2300	5.2 0.7 5.4 0.2	18 SU	0400 1010 1604 2234	4.9 0.9 5.1 0.6
4 SU	0454 1109 1704 2339	5.2 0.7 5.4 0.3	19 M	0432 1043 1637 2308	5.0 0.8 5.2 0.5
5 M	0533 1145 1744	5.0 0.8 5.2	20 TU	0506 1117 1713 2343	5.0 0.8 5.2 0.6
6 TU	0015 0612 1220 1826	0.6 4.8 1.0 5.0	21 W	0541 1153 1752	4.9 0.9 5.1
7 W	0051 0652 1256 1909	0.9 4.6 1.3 4.7	22 TH	0019 0620 1232 1836	0.8 4.8 1.0 4.9
8 TH	0129 0735 1336 1959	1.3 4.3 1.6 4.3	23 F	0100 0705 1318 1928	1.0 4.6 1.2 4.7
9 F	0212 0825 1428 ◑ 2059	1.7 4.1 1.9 4.0	24 SA	0149 0801 1417 ◐ 2034	1.4 4.4 1.4 4.4
10 SA	0310 0927 1544 2214	2.0 3.9 2.1 3.8	25 SU	0257 0912 1539 2157	1.7 4.2 1.6 4.2
11 SU	0430 1043 1722 2341	2.2 3.8 2.1 3.8	26 M	0428 1036 1713 2327	1.8 4.1 1.5 4.2
12 M	0558 1204 1845	2.1 3.9 1.9	27 TU	0558 1159 1835	1.7 4.3 1.3
13 TU	0053 0705 1307 1938	4.0 1.9 4.1 1.6	28 W	0044 0709 1306 1939	4.5 1.5 4.6 0.9
14 W	0144 0752 1352 2019	4.2 1.7 4.4 1.3	29 TH	0143 0803 1358 2031	4.7 1.2 4.8 0.6
15 TH	0224 0831 1429 2055	4.4 1.4 4.6 1.1	30 F	0231 0849 1442 2116	4.9 1.0 5.1 0.4
			31 SA	0313 0931 1523 ○ 2157	5.1 0.8 5.2 0.3

APRIL

Date	Time	m	Date	Time	m
1 SU	0351 1009 1602 2235	5.1 0.7 5.3 0.3	16 M	0331 0945 1537 ● 2207	5.0 0.8 5.1 0.5
2 M	0428 1045 1640 2310	5.1 0.7 5.2 0.5	17 TU	0405 1021 1613 2243	5.1 0.7 5.2 0.5
3 TU	0504 1119 1719 2343	5.0 0.8 5.1 0.7	18 W	0441 1058 1653 2321	5.1 0.6 5.2 0.6
4 W	0540 1152 1758	4.8 0.9 4.9	19 TH	0519 1138 1737	5.0 0.7 5.1
5 TH	0016 0615 1227 1839	1.0 4.6 1.2 4.6	20 F	0001 0601 1222 1825	0.8 4.9 0.8 4.9
6 F	0050 0654 1304 1925	1.3 4.4 1.4 4.3	21 SA	0045 0649 1312 1922	1.1 4.7 1.0 4.6
7 SA	0129 0739 1351 2021	1.7 4.2 1.7 4.0	22 SU	0139 0746 1415 ◐ 2032	1.4 4.4 1.2 4.4
8 SU	0220 0836 1455 ◑ 2130	2.0 4.0 1.9 3.8	23 M	0248 0858 1535 2154	1.7 4.2 1.4 4.2
9 M	0335 0947 1625 2251	2.2 3.8 2.0 3.7	24 TU	0418 1020 1703 2317	1.9 4.2 1.3 4.3
10 TU	0508 1108 1753	2.2 3.8 1.9	25 W	0543 1140 1819	1.8 4.3 1.1
11 W	0009 0624 1220 1856	3.9 2.0 4.0 1.6	26 TH	0029 0650 1246 1920	4.4 1.5 4.5 0.9
12 TH	0106 0717 1312 1941	4.1 1.7 4.2 1.3	27 F	0126 0743 1338 2010	4.6 1.3 4.8 0.7
13 F	0148 0758 1353 2020	4.4 1.5 4.5 1.1	28 SA	0211 0828 1422 2053	4.8 1.1 4.9 0.6
14 SA	0224 0835 1428 2055	4.6 1.2 4.7 0.8	29 SU	0251 0908 1502 2131	4.9 0.9 5.0 0.5
15 SU	0258 0910 1502 2131	4.8 1.0 4.9 0.6	30 M	0327 0946 1541 ○ 2207	5.0 0.8 5.1 0.6

Chart Datum: 2·60 metres below Ordnance Datum (Newlyn). HAT is 5·7 metres above Chart Datum.

STANDARD TIME (UT)
For Summer Time add ONE hour in **non-shaded areas**

RIVER TYNE/NORTH SHIELDS LAT 55°00′N LONG 1°26′W

TIMES AND HEIGHTS OF HIGH AND LOW WATERS

Dates in red are SPRINGS
Dates in blue are NEAPS

YEAR **2018**

MAY

Date	Time	m	Date	Time	m
1 TU	0402	5.0	16 W	0339	5.1
	1021	0.8		1000	0.6
	1619	5.0		1553	5.2
	2241	0.7		2222	0.5
2 W	0436	4.9	17 TH	0419	5.2
	1056	0.8		1043	0.5
	1657	4.9		1638	5.2
	2313	0.9		2304	0.6
3 TH	0511	4.8	18 F	0501	5.1
	1129	0.9		1128	0.5
	1735	4.7		1727	5.1
	2345	1.1		2349	0.8
4 F	0546	4.7	19 SA	0547	5.0
	1203	1.1		1216	0.6
	1815	4.5		1820	4.9
5 SA	0018	1.4	20 SU	0037	1.1
	0623	4.5		0638	4.8
	1241	1.3		1310	0.8
	1859	4.3		1920	4.7
6 SU	0057	1.6	21 M	0132	1.4
	0705	4.3		0737	4.6
	1325	1.5		1413	1.0
	1950	4.1		2028	4.5
7 M	0143	1.9	22 TU	0239	1.7
	0756	4.1		0845	4.4
	1420	1.7		1526	1.1
	2050	3.9	◐	2141	4.3
8 TU	0245	2.1	23 W	0359	1.8
	0858	3.9		1000	4.4
	1531	1.8		1643	1.2
◑	2159	3.8		2255	4.3
9 W	0408	2.2	24 TH	0515	1.8
	1009	3.9		1114	4.4
	1651	1.8		1753	1.1
	2311	3.9			
10 TH	0527	2.1	25 F	0003	4.4
	1119	4.0		0621	1.6
	1759	1.6		1220	4.5
				1853	1.0
11 F	0014	4.1	26 SA	0100	4.5
	0627	1.8		0717	1.4
	1220	4.2		1314	4.6
	1852	1.4		1944	0.9
12 SA	0104	4.3	27 SU	0147	4.7
	0716	1.5		0804	1.2
	1308	4.4		1401	4.8
	1938	1.1		2027	0.9
13 SU	0146	4.6	28 M	0227	4.8
	0758	1.3		0846	1.1
	1350	4.7		1443	4.8
	2019	0.8		2105	0.9
14 M	0224	4.8	29 TU	0304	4.8
	0838	1.0		0924	1.0
	1430	4.9		1522	4.8
	2059	0.6	○	2141	0.9
15 TU	0301	5.0	30 W	0339	4.9
	0918	0.8		1001	0.9
	1511	5.1		1601	4.8
●	2140	0.5		2214	1.0
			31 TH	0413	4.9
				1036	0.9
				1639	4.8
				2247	1.1

JUNE

Date	Time	m	Date	Time	m
1 F	0447	4.8	16 SA	0447	5.2
	1110	1.0		1120	0.4
	1716	4.6		1719	5.2
	2320	1.2		2339	0.8
2 SA	0522	4.7	17 SU	0535	5.2
	1145	1.1		1211	0.4
	1755	4.5		1814	5.0
	2354	1.4			
3 SU	0558	4.6	18 M	0028	1.0
	1221	1.2		0626	5.0
	1836	4.4		1305	0.6
				1911	4.8
4 M	0031	1.6	19 TU	0121	1.3
	0638	4.5		0723	4.9
	1303	1.4		1402	0.8
	1921	4.2		2013	4.6
5 TU	0114	1.7	20 W	0220	1.5
	0723	4.3		0826	4.7
	1350	1.5		1506	1.0
	2012	4.0	◐	2117	4.4
6 W	0205	1.9	21 TH	0327	1.7
	0816	4.2		0932	4.5
	1447	1.6		1612	1.1
◑	2111	4.0		2223	4.3
7 TH	0308	2.0	22 F	0438	1.8
	0916	4.1		1041	4.4
	1552	1.7		1719	1.2
	2214	4.0		2329	4.3
8 F	0422	2.0	23 SA	0546	1.7
	1020	4.1		1148	4.4
	1700	1.6		1821	1.3
	2317	4.1			
9 SA	0530	1.9	24 SU	0029	4.4
	1123	4.2		0648	1.6
	1800	1.4		1249	4.5
				1915	1.3
10 SU	0015	4.3	25 M	0120	4.5
	0628	1.6		0741	1.4
	1221	4.4		1341	4.5
	1854	1.2		2001	1.2
11 M	0106	4.5	26 TU	0204	4.6
	0720	1.4		0827	1.3
	1314	4.7		1427	4.6
	1944	1.0		2041	1.2
12 TU	0151	4.8	27 W	0244	4.7
	0808	1.1		0907	1.1
	1403	4.9		1508	4.7
	2031	0.8		2118	1.2
13 W	0235	5.0	28 TH	0320	4.8
	0856	0.8		0944	1.0
	1450	5.1		1546	4.7
●	2118	0.6	○	2153	1.2
14 TH	0318	5.1	29 F	0354	4.8
	0943	0.6		1019	1.0
	1538	5.2		1623	4.7
	2205	0.6		2227	1.2
15 F	0402	5.2	30 SA	0427	4.8
	1031	0.4		1054	1.0
	1628	5.3		1658	4.7
	2252	0.7		2300	1.2

JULY

Date	Time	m	Date	Time	m
1 SU	0501	4.8	16 M	0521	5.3
	1128	1.0		1201	0.3
	1734	4.6		1801	5.1
	2333	1.3			
2 M	0536	4.8	17 TU	0013	0.9
	1203	1.1		0610	5.2
	1812	4.5		1250	0.4
				1853	4.9
3 TU	0008	1.4	18 W	0101	1.1
	0613	4.7		0702	5.1
	1241	1.2		1341	0.7
	1851	4.4		1947	4.7
4 W	0047	1.5	19 TH	0150	1.4
	0653	4.6		0758	4.8
	1322	1.3		1434	1.0
	1935	4.3	◐	2043	4.5
5 TH	0129	1.7	20 F	0247	1.6
	0737	4.4		0858	4.6
	1408	1.4		1533	1.2
	2024	4.2		2143	4.3
6 F	0220	1.8	21 SA	0353	1.8
	0829	4.3		1004	4.4
	1502	1.5		1637	1.5
◑	2121	4.1		2247	4.2
7 SA	0322	1.9	22 SU	0506	1.9
	0928	4.3		1114	4.3
	1605	1.5		1743	1.6
	2223	4.1		2354	4.2
8 SU	0434	1.9	23 M	0619	1.8
	1033	4.3		1224	4.3
	1712	1.5		1846	1.6
	2328	4.2			
9 M	0543	1.7	24 TU	0053	4.3
	1140	4.4		0721	1.6
	1816	1.3		1323	4.3
				1938	1.6
10 TU	0029	4.4	25 W	0143	4.5
	0646	1.5		0810	1.5
	1244	4.6		1412	4.5
	1915	1.1		2022	1.5
11 W	0124	4.7	26 TH	0225	4.6
	0744	1.2		0851	1.3
	1343	4.8		1454	4.6
	2010	1.0		2100	1.3
12 TH	0214	4.9	27 F	0302	4.7
	0839	0.8		0928	1.1
	1437	5.1		1531	4.7
	2102	0.8	○	2135	1.3
13 F	0301	5.1	28 SA	0336	4.8
	0931	0.5		1003	1.0
	1528	5.2		1605	4.7
●	2152	0.7		2208	1.2
14 SA	0347	5.3	29 SU	0408	4.9
	1022	0.3		1035	0.9
	1618	5.3		1638	4.7
	2240	0.7		2240	1.2
15 SU	0434	5.4	30 M	0440	4.9
	1112	0.2		1108	0.9
	1709	5.3		1711	4.7
	2327	0.8		2313	1.2
			31 TU	0513	4.9
				1141	0.9
				1745	4.7
				2346	1.2

AUGUST

Date	Time	m	Date	Time	m
1 W	0547	4.9	16 TH	0033	1.0
	1216	1.0		0635	5.2
	1821	4.6		1310	0.7
				1913	4.7
2 TH	0020	1.3	17 F	0116	1.3
	0622	4.8		0725	4.9
	1252	1.1		1355	1.1
	1859	4.5		2003	4.5
3 F	0058	1.5	18 SA	0204	1.6
	0702	4.7		0821	4.6
	1332	1.2		1446	1.4
	1942	4.4	◐	2058	4.2
4 SA	0141	1.6	19 SU	0304	1.8
	0749	4.5		0924	4.3
	1419	1.4		1548	1.8
◑	2035	4.3		2201	4.1
5 SU	0236	1.8	20 M	0421	2.0
	0846	4.4		1038	4.1
	1519	1.5		1701	1.9
	2137	4.2		2313	4.0
6 M	0347	1.8	21 TU	0548	2.0
	0954	4.3		1157	4.1
	1632	1.6		1816	1.9
	2248	4.2			
7 TU	0508	1.8	22 W	0024	4.2
	1110	4.3		0700	1.8
	1747	1.5		1305	4.2
				1916	1.8
8 W	0000	4.4	23 TH	0120	4.3
	0623	1.5		0752	1.6
	1227	4.5		1355	4.4
	1856	1.4		2002	1.6
9 TH	0104	4.6	24 F	0205	4.6
	0729	1.2		0833	1.3
	1332	4.8		1436	4.5
	1957	1.1		2041	1.5
10 F	0158	4.9	25 SA	0242	4.7
	0828	0.8		0908	1.1
	1428	5.1		1511	4.7
	2051	0.9		2115	1.3
11 SA	0247	5.2	26 SU	0314	4.9
	0921	0.5		0941	1.0
	1518	5.3		1543	4.8
●	2140	0.8	○	2147	1.2
12 SU	0333	5.4	27 M	0345	5.0
	1010	0.2		1012	0.8
	1606	5.4		1614	4.9
	2226	0.7		2218	1.1
13 M	0417	5.5	28 TU	0415	5.1
	1057	0.1		1044	0.8
	1653	5.3		1645	4.9
	2310	0.7		2250	1.0
14 TU	0502	5.5	29 W	0447	5.1
	1142	0.2		1116	0.8
	1739	5.2		1716	4.8
	2352	0.8		2322	1.1
15 W	0548	5.4	30 TH	0519	5.1
	1226	0.4		1149	0.8
	1826	5.0		1750	4.8
				2355	1.2
			31 F	0554	5.0
				1222	1.0
				1826	4.7

Chart Datum: 2·60 metres below Ordnance Datum (Newlyn). HAT is 5·7 metres above Chart Datum.

STANDARD TIME (UT)
For Summer Time add ONE hour in **non-shaded areas**

RIVER TYNE/NORTH SHIELDS

LAT 55°00′N LONG 1°26′W

TIMES AND HEIGHTS OF HIGH AND LOW WATERS

Dates in red are SPRINGS
Dates in blue are NEAPS

YEAR **2018**

SEPTEMBER

Date	Day	Time	m	Time	m	Time	m	Time	m
1	SA	0030	1.3	0633	4.9	1300	1.1	1907	4.5
2	SU	0112	1.5	0719	4.7	1344	1.4	1957	4.4
3	M	0204	1.6	0816	4.5	1443	1.6	◑ 2101	4.2
4	TU	0317	1.8	0930	4.3	1603	1.8	2218	4.2
5	W	0446	1.8	1056	4.3	1730	1.8	2339	4.3
6	TH	0610	1.5	1219	4.5	1846	1.6		
7	F	0049	4.6	0720	1.1	1325	4.8	1947	1.3
8	SA	0145	4.9	0817	0.7	1418	5.1	2039	1.0
9	SU	0232	5.2	0907	0.4	1505	5.3	● 2124	0.8
10	M	0316	5.4	0953	0.2	1549	5.4	2207	0.7
11	TU	0358	5.6	1037	0.1	1631	5.4	2247	0.7
12	W	0440	5.5	1118	0.2	1712	5.2	2326	0.8
13	TH	0522	5.4	1157	0.5	1753	5.0		
14	F	0004	1.0	0606	5.2	1235	0.8	1834	4.8
15	SA	0043	1.2	0652	4.9	1314	1.2	1919	4.5
16	SU	0125	1.5	0743	4.5	1357	1.6	◐ 2010	4.3
17	M	0217	1.8	0845	4.2	1454	2.0	2111	4.1
18	TU	0332	2.1	0959	3.9	1612	2.2	2225	4.0
19	W	0509	2.1	1124	3.9	1741	2.2	2346	4.0
20	TH	0632	1.9	1238	4.1	1850	2.0		
21	F	0050	4.3	0725	1.6	1331	4.3	1937	1.8
22	SA	0137	4.5	0806	1.4	1411	4.5	2016	1.5
23	SU	0214	4.7	0841	1.1	1444	4.7	2050	1.3
24	M	0247	4.9	0913	0.9	1515	4.9	2122	1.1
25	TU	0317	5.0	0944	0.8	1545	5.0	○ 2153	1.0
26	W	0348	5.2	1016	0.7	1616	5.0	2225	0.9
27	TH	0419	5.2	1048	0.7	1647	5.0	2258	0.9
28	F	0453	5.2	1121	0.8	1721	5.0	2332	1.0
29	SA	0529	5.1	1155	0.9	1757	4.9		
30	SU	0009	1.2	0610	5.0	1234	1.2	1839	4.7

OCTOBER

Date	Day	Time	m	Time	m	Time	m	Time	m
1	M	0052	1.3	0700	4.7	1319	1.4	1930	4.5
2	TU	0147	1.5	0801	4.5	1420	1.8	◑ 2036	4.3
3	W	0303	1.7	0920	4.3	1546	2.0	2158	4.2
4	TH	0436	1.7	1050	4.3	1720	1.9	2323	4.3
5	F	0601	1.4	1212	4.5	1836	1.7		
6	SA	0033	4.6	0708	1.1	1315	4.8	1934	1.4
7	SU	0129	5.0	0802	0.7	1405	5.1	2022	1.1
8	M	0215	5.2	0849	0.5	1448	5.2	2105	0.9
9	TU	0257	5.4	0932	0.3	1527	5.3	● 2145	0.8
10	W	0337	5.5	1012	0.3	1605	5.3	2223	0.7
11	TH	0417	5.5	1050	0.5	1643	5.2	2300	0.8
12	F	0457	5.3	1125	0.7	1721	5.1	2337	1.0
13	SA	0539	5.1	1200	1.0	1759	4.8		
14	SU	0013	1.2	0622	4.8	1235	1.4	1838	4.6
15	M	0053	1.5	0710	4.5	1314	1.8	1924	4.4
16	TU	0140	1.8	0808	4.1	1404	2.1	◐ 2021	4.1
17	W	0244	2.0	0917	3.9	1517	2.4	2132	4.0
18	TH	0415	2.1	1038	3.9	1652	2.4	2252	4.0
19	F	0543	2.0	1157	4.0	1809	2.2		
20	SA	0005	4.2	0644	1.7	1254	4.3	1902	1.9
21	SU	0058	4.4	0728	1.5	1336	4.5	1943	1.6
22	M	0139	4.6	0806	1.2	1411	4.7	2019	1.4
23	TU	0214	4.9	0840	1.0	1444	4.9	2053	1.2
24	W	0246	5.0	0913	0.8	1515	5.1	○ 2126	1.0
25	TH	0319	5.2	0947	0.7	1547	5.1	2201	0.9
26	F	0353	5.3	1021	0.7	1620	5.2	2236	0.9
27	SA	0431	5.3	1057	0.8	1656	5.1	2314	0.9
28	SU	0511	5.2	1134	1.0	1735	5.0	2355	1.0
29	M	0557	5.0	1215	1.2	1820	4.8		
30	TU	0043	1.2	0650	4.8	1305	1.5	1913	4.6
31	W	0142	1.4	0756	4.5	1408	1.8	◑ 2020	4.4

NOVEMBER

Date	Day	Time	m	Time	m	Time	m	Time	m
1	TH	0257	1.5	0915	4.3	1534	2.0	2141	4.3
2	F	0425	1.5	1040	4.3	1704	2.0	2303	4.4
3	SA	0545	1.3	1156	4.5	1817	1.8		
4	SU	0013	4.7	0649	1.0	1257	4.8	1913	1.5
5	M	0109	4.9	0742	0.8	1346	5.0	2001	1.2
6	TU	0156	5.1	0828	0.7	1427	5.1	2044	1.0
7	W	0238	5.3	0909	0.6	1505	5.2	● 2124	0.9
8	TH	0317	5.3	0946	0.7	1541	5.2	2202	0.9
9	F	0357	5.3	1022	0.8	1617	5.2	2238	0.9
10	SA	0437	5.1	1056	1.0	1653	5.0	2314	1.0
11	SU	0517	4.9	1129	1.2	1729	4.9	2350	1.2
12	M	0559	4.7	1203	1.5	1806	4.7		
13	TU	0028	1.4	0643	4.5	1240	1.8	1848	4.5
14	W	0111	1.7	0734	4.2	1324	2.1	1938	4.3
15	TH	0205	1.9	0835	4.0	1424	2.3	◐ 2040	4.1
16	F	0315	2.0	0944	3.9	1546	2.4	2151	4.0
17	SA	0436	2.0	1056	4.0	1709	2.3	2303	4.1
18	SU	0546	1.8	1201	4.1	1812	2.1		
19	M	0005	4.3	0639	1.6	1252	4.4	1901	1.8
20	TU	0054	4.5	0723	1.3	1333	4.6	1943	1.5
21	W	0136	4.7	0803	1.1	1410	4.9	2021	1.3
22	TH	0214	5.0	0841	0.9	1445	5.0	2100	1.1
23	F	0253	5.1	0919	0.8	1521	5.2	○ 2139	0.9
24	SA	0332	5.2	0958	0.8	1558	5.2	2220	0.8
25	SU	0415	5.3	1039	0.8	1637	5.2	2303	0.8
26	M	0500	5.2	1121	1.0	1720	5.1	2349	0.8
27	TU	0550	5.1	1206	1.2	1807	5.0		
28	W	0040	1.0	0646	4.9	1258	1.5	1901	4.8
29	TH	0139	1.1	0751	4.6	1359	1.8	2006	4.6
30	F	0248	1.3	0903	4.4	1515	2.0	◑ 2120	4.5

DECEMBER

Date	Day	Time	m	Time	m	Time	m	Time	m
1	SA	0405	1.3	1018	4.4	1636	2.0	2235	4.5
2	SU	0518	1.3	1130	4.5	1747	1.8	2345	4.6
3	M	0623	1.2	1231	4.6	1848	1.6		
4	TU	0045	4.8	0718	1.1	1323	4.8	1939	1.4
5	W	0137	4.9	0805	1.0	1406	4.9	2025	1.3
6	TH	0221	5.0	0846	1.0	1445	5.0	2106	1.1
7	F	0303	5.0	0924	1.0	1521	5.0	● 2145	1.0
8	SA	0343	5.0	0959	1.1	1557	5.1	2222	1.0
9	SU	0422	4.9	1033	1.2	1631	5.0	2257	1.1
10	M	0501	4.8	1106	1.3	1706	4.9	2332	1.2
11	TU	0539	4.7	1139	1.5	1742	4.8		
12	W	0008	1.3	0619	4.5	1214	1.7	1820	4.7
13	TH	0048	1.5	0703	4.3	1254	1.9	1904	4.5
14	F	0132	1.6	0753	4.2	1341	2.1	1954	4.3
15	SA	0225	1.8	0849	4.0	1440	2.2	◐ 2052	4.2
16	SU	0329	1.9	0952	4.0	1554	2.3	2156	4.2
17	M	0438	1.8	1056	4.1	1707	2.2	2301	4.2
18	TU	0541	1.7	1157	4.2	1809	2.0		
19	W	0002	4.4	0636	1.5	1250	4.5	1902	1.7
20	TH	0056	4.6	0726	1.3	1336	4.7	1950	1.4
21	F	0145	4.8	0812	1.1	1418	4.9	2036	1.1
22	SA	0231	5.0	0857	0.9	1459	5.1	○ 2122	0.9
23	SU	0317	5.2	0942	0.9	1540	5.2	2208	0.7
24	M	0404	5.3	1027	0.9	1623	5.3	2256	0.6
25	TU	0453	5.3	1112	0.9	1708	5.3	2344	0.6
26	W	0544	5.2	1159	1.1	1757	5.2		
27	TH	0035	0.7	0638	5.0	1248	1.3	1849	5.0
28	F	0130	0.8	0737	4.8	1342	1.6	1947	4.9
29	SA	0229	1.0	0840	4.5	1444	1.8	◑ 2052	4.7
30	SU	0335	1.2	0945	4.4	1556	1.9	2201	4.6
31	M	0443	1.4	1053	4.3	1709	1.9	2313	4.5

Chart Datum: 2·60 metres below Ordnance Datum (Newlyn). HAT is 5·7 metres above Chart Datum.

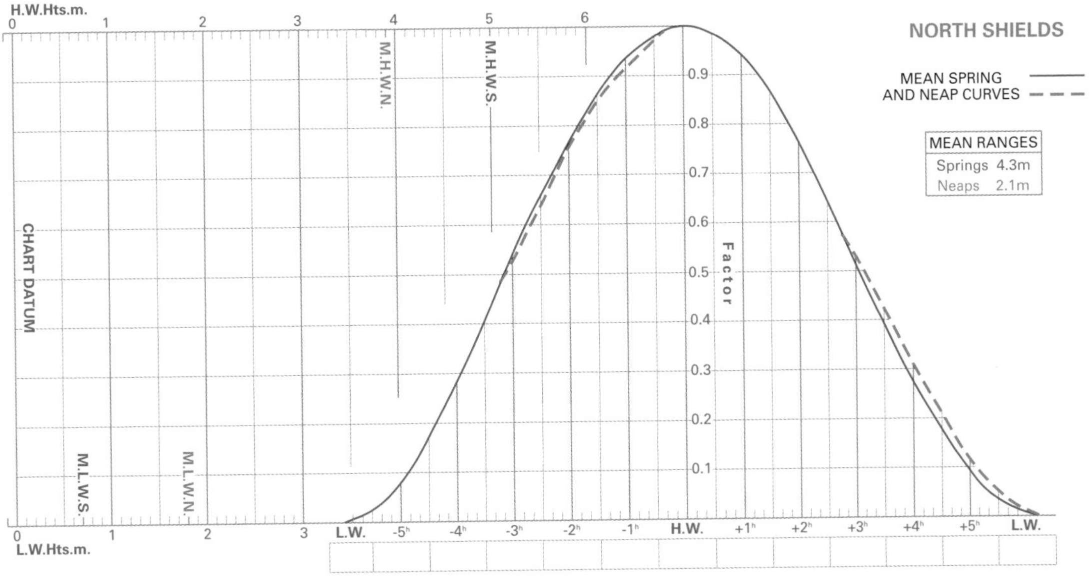

9.5.19 BLYTH

Northumberland **55°06'·98N 01° 29'·27W**

CHARTS AC 152, 156, 1626, 5615; Imray C24

TIDES +0430 Dover; ML 2·8; Duration 0558

Standard Port NORTH SHIELDS (⟵)

Times				Height (metres)			
High Water		Low Water		MHWS	MHWN	MLWN	MLWS
0200	0800	0100	0800	5·0	3·9	1·8	0·7
1400	2000	1300	2000				
Differences BLYTH							
+0005	–0007	–0001	+0009	0·0	0·0	–0·1	+0·1

SHELTER Very good. Access H24 but at LW in strong SE winds, seas break across entrance.

NAVIGATION WPT 55°06'·57N 01°28'·74W, 324°/0·5M to harbour entrance. From N, beware The Pigs, The Sow and Seaton Sea Rks. A wind farm is under construction marked by 6 cardinal buoys with a met mast 3M offshore and 2 wind turbines on North Spit (1·2M N of hbr ent) centred on 55°08'·16N 01°29'·41W. No dangers from S. See RNYC Sailing Directions, from RNYC, House Yacht Tyne, S Hbr, Blyth NE24 3PB (website below).

LIGHTS AND MARKS Blyth E Pier Hd, W twr on S end. Outer ldg lts 324°, Or ◊ on framework trs. Inner ldg lts 338°, front W 6-sided tr; rear W △ on mast. See chartlet and 9.5.4 for lt details.

COMMUNICATIONS (Code 01670) CGOC (01262) 672317; Police 101. HM 352678, Call *Blyth Hbr Control* Ch **12** 11 (H24) for clearance to enter/ leave.

FACILITIES **R Northumberland YC** www.rnyc.org.uk ☎353636. In SE part of South Hbr, E side of Middle Jetty, Ⓥ berth on N side of RNYC pontoons in 4·4m least depth. 123 £1·50, (20t) (1½t for trailer sailers) @ (www.millermarine.co.uk).

South Hbr ☎352678, (50t).

Town ✉ Ⓑ ✕ bus to Newcastle ⇄ ✈.

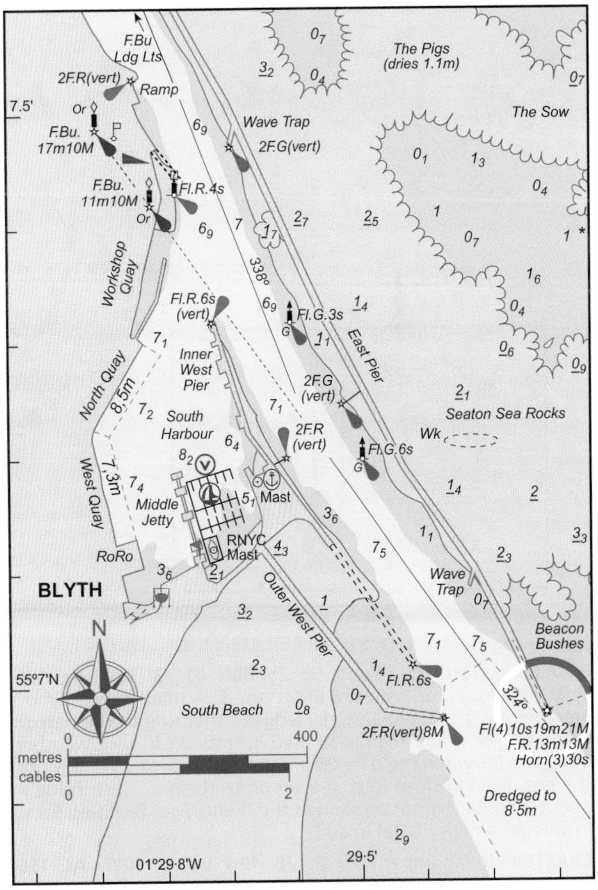

ADJACENT ANCHORAGE

NEWBIGGIN, Northumberland, **55°10'·75N 01°30'·10W**. AC 156. Tides approx as for Blyth, 3·5M to the S. Temp, fair weather ⚓ in about 4m in centre of the bay, off the conspic sculptures on the breakwater; sheltered from SW to N winds. Caution: offlying rky ledges to N and S. Conspic church on N side of bay; bkwtr lt Fl G 10s 4M. Facilities: **SC** (dinghies). **Town** ✕.

9.5.20 AMBLE

Northumberland **55°20'·37N 01°34'·25W** ✲✲⛵⛵⛵✿✿

CHARTS AC 156, 1627, 5615; Imray C24

TIDES +0412 Dover; ML 3·1; Duration 0606

Standard Port NORTH SHIELDS (⟵)

Times				Height (metres)			
High Water		Low Water		MHWS	MHWN	MLWN	MLWS
0200	0800	0100	0800	5·0	3·9	1·8	0·7
1400	2000	1300	2000				
Differences AMBLE							
–0013	–0013	–0016	–0020	0·0	0·0	+0·1	+0·1
COQUET ISLAND							
–0010	–0010	–0020	–0020	+0·1	+0·1	0·0	+0·1

SHELTER The Hbr (alias Warkworth Hbr) is safe in all winds. But ent is dangerous in strong N to E winds or in swell, when heavy seas break on Pan Bush shoal and on the bar at hbr ent, where least depth is 0·8m. ⚓ in Coquet Road or NNE of North Pier.

NAVIGATION WPT 55°21'·00N 01°33'·10W, 225° to hbr ent, 0·9M. Ent recommended from NE, passing N and W of Pan Bush. The S-going stream sets strongly across ent. Once inside the N bkwtr, beware drying banks to stbd, ie on N side of channel; keep close (15m) to S quays. 4kn speed limit in hbr.

- In NE'ly gales broken water can extend to Coquet Island, keep E of island and go to Blyth where appr/ent may be safer.
- Coquet Chan (min depth 0·3m) is not buoyed and is only advised with caution, by day, in good vis/weather, slight sea state and with adequate rise of tide, ie HW–2.

LIGHTS AND MARKS Coquet Island lt ho, (conspic) W □ tr, turreted parapet, lower half grey; horn 30s. See chartlet and 9.5.4.

COMMUNICATIONS (Code 01665) HM 710306; CGOC (01262) 672317; local CG 710575; Police 101; Ⓗ (01670) 521212.

Amble Marina Ch **80** (7/7, 0900-1700). HM Ch 16, works Ch 14 (Mon-Fri 0900-1700 LT). Coquet YC Ch M (occas).

FACILITIES **Amble Marina** marina@ amble.co.uk ☎712168, is about 5ca from hbr ent. Tidal gauge shows depth over sill, 0·8m above CD; access between PHM buoy and old jetty, both unlit. Pontoons are 'A' to 'F' from sill; Ⓥ berth on 'B' initially. 200 +40 Ⓥ, £2·50. (50t) **Hbr**

Coquet YC ☎711179,

Town ✉ ✕ (Alnmouth), ✈ (Newcastle).

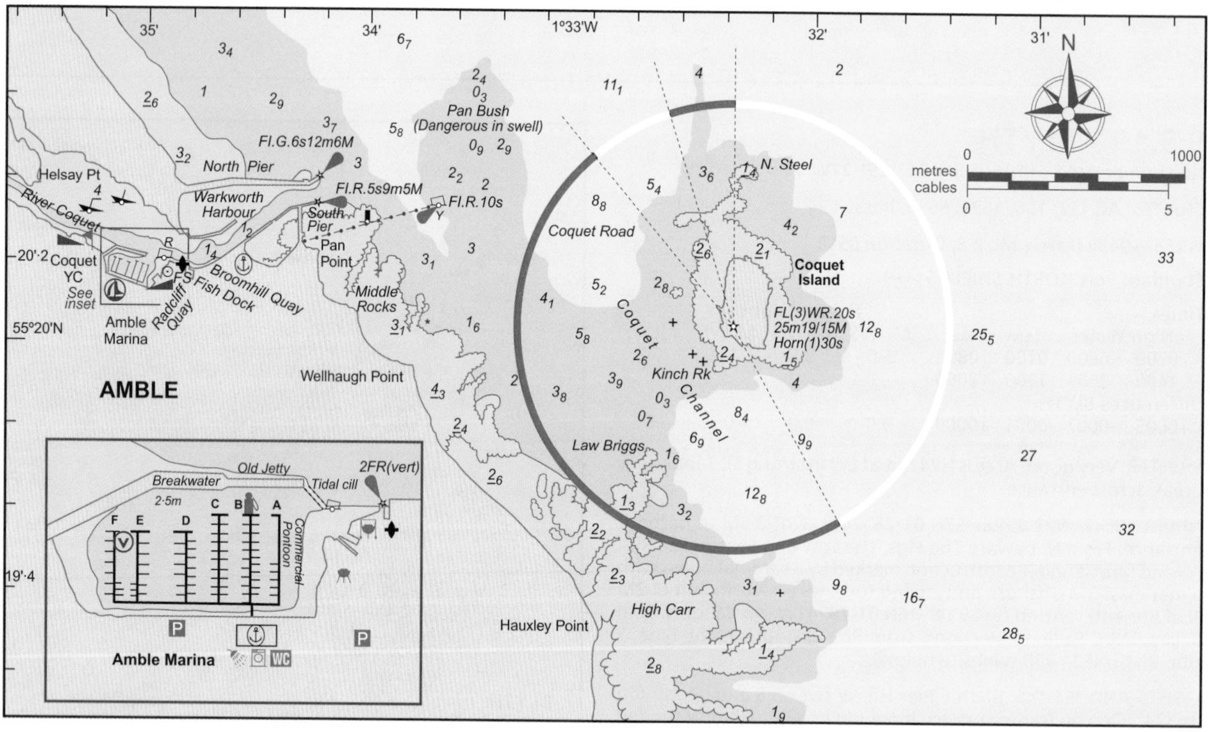

HBRS AND ANCHORAGES BETWEEN AMBLE AND HOLY ISLAND

BOULMER, Northumberland, **55°25'·00N 01°33'·90W**. AC 156. Tides approx as for Amble, 4·6M to the S. A small haven almost enclosed by N and S Rheins, rky ledges either side of the narrow (30m) ent, Marmouth; only advised in settled offshore weather. 2 FW bns (lit when req'd by LB or FVs) lead approx 257° through the ent, leaving close to stbd a bn on N Rheins. ⚓ just inside in about 1·5m or dry out on sand at the N end. Few facilities: ✉ in village. Alnwick is 4M inland.

CRASTER, Northumberland, **55°28'·40N 01°35'·30W**. AC 156. Tidal differences: interpolate between Amble (9.5.20) and N Sunderland (9.5.21). Strictly a fair weather ⚓ in offshore winds, 1M S of the conspic Dunstanburgh Castle (ru). The ent, 40m wide, is N of Muckle Carr and S of Little Carr which partly covers and has a bn on its S end. ⚓ in about 3·5m just inshore of these 2 rocky outcrops; or berth at the E pier on rk/sand inside the tiny drying hbr. Facilities: ✕.

NEWTON HAVEN and BEADNELL BAY, Northumberland, **55°30'·90N 01° 36'·70W**. AC 156. HW +0342 on Dover; Tidal differences: interpolate between Amble (9.5.20) and N Sunderland (9.5.21). ML 2·6m; Duration 0625. A safe ⚓ in winds from NNW to SE via S but susceptible to swell. Ent to S of Newton PHM buoy and Newton Pt. Beware Fills Rks. ⚓ between Fills Rks and Low Newton by the Sea in 4/5m. A very attractive ⚓ with no lts, marks or facilities except a pub. Further ⚓ S of Beadnell Pt (1M N of Newton Pt) in 4–6m; small, fishing hbr whose wall is newly rebuilt; Beadnell SC. Village 0·5M.

SEAHOUSES (N Sunderland), Northumberland, **55°35'·04N 01°38'·91W**. AC 1612. HW +0340 on Dover; Duration 0618. See 9.5.21. Good shelter except in onshore winds when swell makes outer hbr berths (0·7m) very uncomfortable and dangerous. Inner hbr has excellent berths but usually full of FVs. Beware The Tumblers (rks) to the W of ent and rks protruding NE from bkwtr hd Fl R 2·5s 6m NW pier hd FG 11m 3M; vis 159°-294°, W tr; traffic sigs; Siren 90s when vessels expected. Good facilities. If dangerous to enter, ● is shown over the FG lt (or R flag over a Bu flag) on NW pier hd.

FARNE ISLANDS, Northumberland, **55°37′·15N 01°39′·37W**. AC 160, 156, 111. HW +0345 on Dover; ML 2·6m; Duration 0630. See 9.5.21. The islands are a NT nature reserve in a beautiful area; they should only be attempted in good weather. Landing is only allowed on Farne Is, Staple Is and Longstone. In the inner group, ⚓ in The Kettle on the NE side of Inner Farne; near the Bridges (connecting Knocks Reef to West Wideopen); or to the S of West Wideopen. In the outer group, ⚓ in Pinnacle Haven (between Staple Is/Brownsman). Beware turbulence over Knivestone and Whirl Rks and eddy S of Longstone during NW tidal streams. Lts and marks: Black Rocks Pt, Oc (2) WRG 8s 12m 14/11M;122°-G-165°-W-175°-R-191°-W-238°-R-275°-W-289°-G-300°. Bamburgh Castle is conspic 6ca to the SE. Farne Is lt ho at SW Pt, Fl (2) WR 15s 27m 8/6M; W ○ tr; 119°-R-280°-W-119°. Longstone Fl 20s 23m 24M, R tr with W band (conspic), temp'ly replaced by Light vessel Fl(2) 20s15M (2015). Caution: reefs extend about 7ca seaward. No facilities.

NATIONAL NATURE RESERVE (Holy Island) A National Nature Reserve (NNR) extends from Budle Bay (**55°37′N 01°45′W**, close to Black Rocks Point lt ho) along the coast to Cheswick Black Rocks, 3M SE of Berwick-upon-Tweed. The NNR extends seaward from the HW shoreline to the drying line; it includes Holy Island and the adjacent islets.

Visiting craft are asked to respect two constraints:

- Landing is prohibited on the small island of Black Law (55°39′·68N 01°47′·50W) from April to August inclusive.
- Boats should not be landed or recovered anywhere in the NNR except at the designated and buoyed watersports zone on the SE side of Budle Bay.

COQUET ISLAND TO FARNE ISLANDS

(AC 156) Coquet Is (lt, fog sig) lies about 5ca offshore at SE end of Alnmouth B, and nearly 1M NNE of Hauxley Pt, off which dangerous rks extend 6ca offshore, drying 1·9m. On passage, normally pass 1M E of Coquet Is in the W sector of the lt. Coquet chan may be used in good vis by day; but it is only 2ca wide, not buoyed, has least depth of 0·9m near the centre. A Wk lies 3ca SE of the Is S tip in Coquet Channel on the boundary of the R/W sectors. In S or W winds, there are good ⚓s in Coquet Road, W and NW of the Island.

▶*The stream runs strongly: S-going from HW Tyne −0515 and N-going from HW Tyne +0045.* ◀

Amble (Warkworth) Hbr ent is about 1M W of Coquet Is, and 1·5M SE of Warkworth Castle (conspic). 4ca NE and ENE of ent is Pan Bush, rky shoal with least depth of 0·9m on which dangerous seas can build in any swell. The bar has varying depths, down to less than 1m. The entrance is dangerous in strong winds from N/E when broken water may extend to Coquet Is. Once inside, the hbr is safe.

Between Coquet Is and the Farne Is, 19M to N, keep at least 1M offshore to avoid various dangers. To seaward, Craster Skeres lie 5M E of Castle Pt, and Dicky Shad and Newton Skere lie 1·75M and 4·5M E of Beadnell Pt; these are three rky banks on which the sea breaks heavily in bad weather.

FARNE ISLANDS

(AC 111, 160) The coast between N Sunderland Pt (Snook) and Holy Island, 8M NW, has fine hill (Cheviots) scenery fronted by dunes and sandy beaches. The Farne Is and offlying shoals extend 4·5M offshore, and are a mini-cruising ground well worth visiting in good weather. The islands are a bird sanctuary, owned and operated by the National Trust, with large colonies of sea birds and grey seals. The R Northumberland YC's Sailing Directions (see 9.5.19) are useful; AC 111 is essential.

Inner Sound separates the islands from the mainland. In good conditions it is a better N/S route than keeping outside the whole group; but the stream runs at 3kn at sp, and with strong wind against tide there is rough water. If course is set outside the Farne Islands, pass 1M E of Longstone (lit) to clear Crumstone Rk 1M to S, and Knivestone (dries 3·6m) and Whirl Rks (depth 0·6m) respectively 5 and 6ca NE of Longstone lt ho. The sea breaks on these rocks.

The islands, rks and shoals are divided by Staple Sound, running NW/SE, into an inner and outer group. The former comprises Inner Farne, W and E Wideopens and Knock's Reef. Inner Farne (lt) is the innermost Is; close NE there is ⚓ called The Kettle, sheltered except from NW, but ⚓ out of stream close to The Bridges connecting Knock's Reef and W Wideopen. 1M NW of Inner Farne Is and separated by Farne Sound, which runs NE/SW, lies the Megstone, a rk 5m high. Beware Swedman reef (dries 0·5m), marked by SHM buoy 4ca WSW of Megstone.

The outer group of Islands comprises Staple and Brownsman Islands, N and S Wamses, the Harcars and Longstone. There is occas ⚓ between Staple and Brownsman Is.

▶ *Piper Gut and Crafords Gut may be negotiated in calm weather and near HW, stemming the S-going stream.* ◀

HOLY ISLAND TO BERWICK

(AC 1612, 111, 160)

▶ *Near the Farne Is and Holy Is the SE-going stream begins at HW Tyne −0430, and the NW-going at HW Tyne +0130. Sp rates are about 2.5kn in Inner Sound, 4kn in Staple Sound and about 3·5kn 1M NE of Longstone, decreasing to seaward. There is an eddy S of Longstone on NW-going stream.* ◀

Holy Is (or Lindisfarne) lies 6M WNW of Longstone, and is linked to mainland by a causeway covered at HW. There is a good ⚓ on S side (AC 1612) with conspic daymarks and dir lts. The castle and a W obelisk at Emmanuel Head are also conspic.

▶ *The stream runs strongly in and out of hbr, W-going from HW Tyne +0510, and E-going from HW Tyne −0045. E of Holy Is, Goldstone chan runs N/S between Goldstone Rk (dries) SHM buoy on E side and Plough Seat Reef and Plough Rk (both dry) on W side, with PHM buoy.* ◀

Berwick Bay has some offlying shoals. Berwick-upon-Tweed is easily visible against the low shoreline, which rises again to high cliffs further north. The hbr entrance is restricted by a shallow bar, dangerous in onshore winds.

9.5.21 HOLY ISLAND

Northumberland **55°39′·57N 01°46′·81W** ❁❁◊✿✿✿

TIDES +0344 Dover; ML No data; Duration 0630

Standard Port NORTH SHIELDS (⟵)

Times				Height (metres)			
High Water		Low Water		MHWS	MHWN	MLWN	MLWS
0200	0800	0100	0800	5·0	3·9	1·8	0·7
1400	2000	1300	2000				
Differences HOLY ISLAND							
−0043	−0039	−0105	−0110	−0·2	−0·2	−0·3	−0·1
NORTH SUNDERLAND (Seahouses)							
−0048	−0044	−0058	−0102	−0·2	−0·2	−0·2	0·0

CHARTS AC 111, 1612, 5615; Imray C24

SHELTER Good S of The Heugh in 3-6m, but ⚓ is uncomfortable in fresh W/SW winds esp at sp flood, and foul in places; trip-line advised. Better shelter in The Ouse on sand/mud if able to dry out; but not in S/SE winds. For detailed information for trailer sailers see www.dca.uk.com.

NAVIGATION WPT 55°39′·76N 01°44′·88W, 260°/1·55M to Old Law E bn. From N identify Emmanuel Hd, conspic W △ bn, then appr via Goldstone Chan leaving Plough Seat PHM buoy to stbd. From S, clear Farne Is thence to WPT. Outer ldg bns lead 260° close past Ridge ECM and Triton SHM buoys. Possible overfalls in chan across bar (1·6m) with sp ebb up to 4kn. Inner ldg marks lead 310° to ⚓. Inshore route, round Castle Pt via Hole Mouth and The Yares, may be more sheltered, but is not for strangers.

Continued overleaf

HOLY ISLAND *continued*

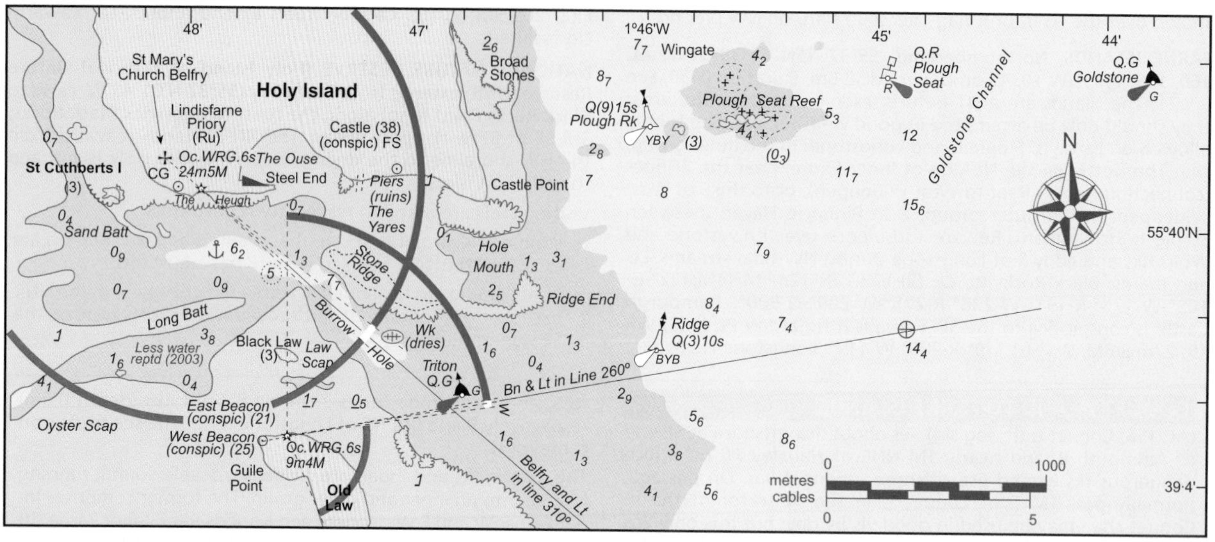

LIGHTS AND MARKS See 9.5.4 and chartlet. Outer leading marks/lts are Old Law beacons (conspic), 2 reddish obelisks 21/25m on 260°; E beacon has directional light, Oc WRG 6s. Inner leading marks/lights are The Heugh tower, B △, on with St Mary's church belfry 310°. The Heugh has directional light, Oc WRG 6s. Directional lights Oc WRG are aligned on 260° and 309·5° respectively.

COMMUNICATIONS (Code 01289) CGOC (01262) 672317; HM 389248.

FACILITIES Limited. Slipway (contact HM prior to launching) £5.00, on village green, limited from Beal (5M); bus (occas) to Berwick. Note Lindisfarne is ancient name; Benedictine Abbey (ruins) and Castle (NT) are worth visiting. Causeway to mainland, covers at HW, is usable approx HW+3½ to HW-2.

9.5.22 BERWICK-UPON-TWEED

Northumberland **55°45'·87N 01°59'·05W**

CHARTS AC 111, 160, 1612, 5615; Imray C24

TIDES +0348 Dover; ML 2·5; Duration 0620

Standard Port NORTH SHIELDS (⟵)

Times				**Height (metres)**			
High Water		Low Water		MHWS	MHWN	MLWN	MLWS
0200	0800	0100	0800	5·0	3·9	1·8	0·7
1400	2000	1300	2000				
Differences BERWICK-UPON-TWEED							
–0053	–0053	–0109	–0109	–0·3	–0·1	–0·5	–0·1

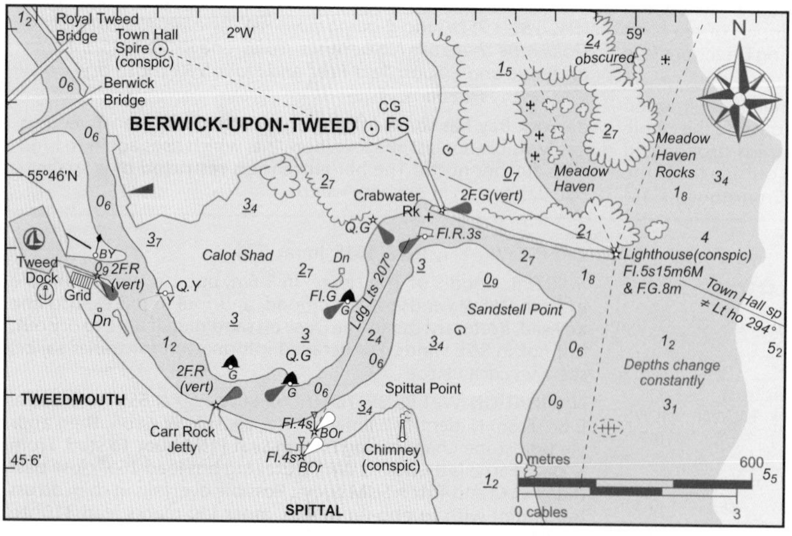

SHELTER Good shelter or ⚓ except in strong E/SE winds. Berth may be available in Tweed Dock (no dock gates) which is primarily used by commercial shipping. If possible contact HM beforehand to avoid disappointment. Alternative temporary berth possible at W end of Fish Jetty (1·2m).

NAVIGATION WPT 55°45'·62N 01°58'·0W, 294°/0·65M to breakwater lighthouse.

- Onshore winds and ebb tides cause very confused seas over the bar, minimum depth 0·6m. From HW–2 to HW+1 strong flood tide sets S across the entrance; keep well up to breakwater.
- The sands at the mouth of the Tweed shift so frequently that local knowledge is essential to enter the harbour.

Town Hall Spire and Lt ho in line at 294°. Keep close to breakwater to avoid Sandstell Point. When past PHM buoy and S of Crabwater Rk, keep Spittal Bns (Or ▽ on B Or Bn) in line brg 207°; best water may be further W. Berwick Bridge (first/lowest) has about 3m clearance.

LIGHTS AND MARKS See 9.5.4 and chartlet.

COMMUNICATIONS (Code 01289) CGOC (01262) 672317; Police 101; Dr 307484. HM 307404.

VHF Ch 12 16 (0800-1700).

FACILITIES **Tweed Dock** ☎307404, £8.00 (3t) Mobile.

Town and ✈ (Newcastle or Edinburgh).

South East Scotland

Eyemouth to Buchan Ness

9.6.1	**Contents**	365
9.6.2	**Area map and Distance table**	366
9.6.3	**Tidal stream charts**	368
9.6.4	**Lights, buoys and waypoints**	370
9.6.5	**Passage information** Berwick-upon-Tweed to Bass Rock – 372 • Firth of Forth south shore, River Forth to Kincardine, Firth of Forth north shore, Forth to Norway and Baltic – 374 • Fife Ness to Montrose – 382 • Montrose to Buchan Ness – 385	372
9.6.6	**Eyemouth** Burnmouth • St Abbs	372
9.6.7	**Dunbar** North Berwick	373
9.6.8	**Firth of Forth** Port Edgar • Granton • Inchcolm • Aberdour • Burntisland • Kirkcaldy • Methil• Elie • St Monans • Fisherrow • Cramond	375
9.6.9	**Forth and Clyde Canal (Leith, tide tables/curves)**	377
9.6.10	**Anstruther** Pittenweem • Crail • Isle of May	381
9.6.11	**River Tay** Perth • St Andrews	383
9.6.12	**Arbroath**	384
9.6.13	**Montrose** Johnshaven • Gourdon	384
9.6.14	**Stonehaven**	385
9.6.15	**Aberdeen, tide tables/curves**	386

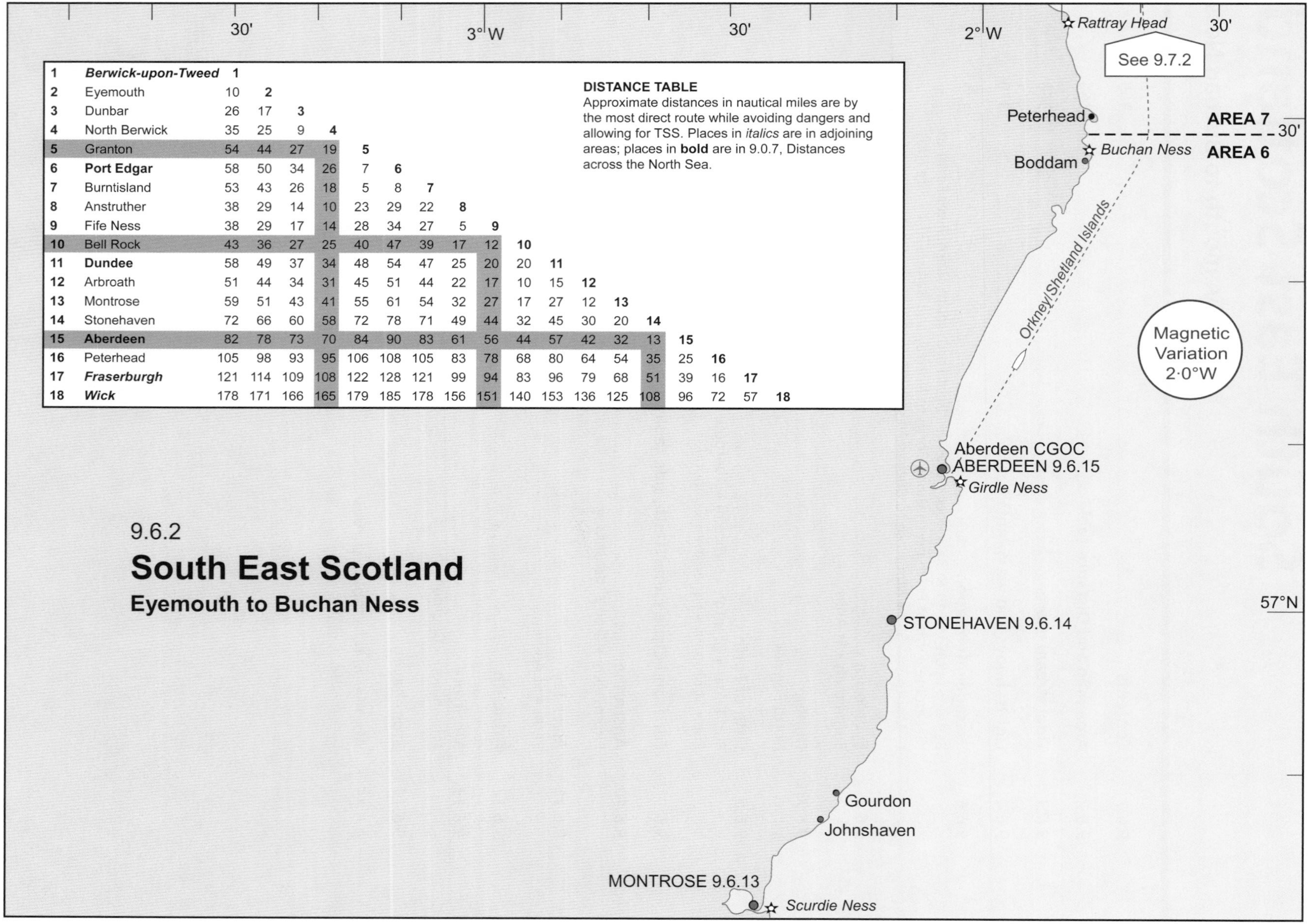
30'
3° W
30'
2° W
30'
Rattray Head
See 9.7.2
Peterhead
AREA 7
30'
Buchan Ness
AREA 6
Boddam
Orkney/Shetland Islands
Magnetic Variation 2·0°W
Aberdeen CGOC
ABERDEEN 9.6.15
Girdle Ness
57°N
STONEHAVEN 9.6.14
Gourdon
Johnshaven
MONTROSE 9.6.13
Scurdie Ness

9.6.2

South East Scotland

Eyemouth to Buchan Ness

DISTANCE TABLE
Approximate distances in nautical miles are by the most direct route while avoiding dangers and allowing for TSS. Places in *italics* are in adjoining areas; places in **bold** are in 9.0.7, Distances across the North Sea.

1	***Berwick-upon-Tweed***	**1**																	
2	Eyemouth	10	**2**																
3	Dunbar	26	17	**3**															
4	North Berwick	35	25	9	**4**														
5	Granton	54	44	27	19	**5**													
6	**Port Edgar**	58	50	34	26	7	**6**												
7	Burntisland	53	43	26	18	5	8	**7**											
8	Anstruther	38	29	14	10	23	29	22	**8**										
9	Fife Ness	38	29	17	14	28	34	27	5	**9**									
10	Bell Rock	43	36	27	25	40	47	39	17	12	**10**								
11	**Dundee**	58	49	37	34	48	54	47	25	20	20	**11**							
12	Arbroath	51	44	34	31	45	51	44	22	17	10	15	**12**						
13	Montrose	59	51	43	41	55	61	54	32	27	17	27	12	**13**					
14	Stonehaven	72	66	60	58	72	78	71	49	44	32	45	30	20	**14**				
15	**Aberdeen**	82	78	73	70	84	90	83	61	56	44	57	42	32	13	**15**			
16	Peterhead	105	98	93	95	106	108	105	83	78	68	80	64	54	35	25	**16**		
17	***Fraserburgh***	121	114	109	108	122	128	121	99	94	83	96	79	68	51	39	16	**17**	
18	***Wick***	178	171	166	165	179	185	178	156	151	140	153	136	125	108	96	72	57	**18**

Harbour with full almanac entry
Minor harbour or anchorage
Major light
Ferry route
Airport
Magnetic Variation 2·0°W
See 9.5.2
56°N
30'
3°W
2°W
ARBROATH 9.6.12
RIVER TAY 9.6.11
Tayport
Perth
St Andrews
Bell Rock
Fife Ness
Forth CGOC
Crail
Pittenweem
St Monans
Elie Ness
Elie
ANSTRUTHER 9.6.10
Isle of May
Methil
Kirkcaldy
Aberdour
Inchkeith
Inchcolm
Rosyth
Port Edgar
Cramond
Granton
Leith
FIRTH OF FORTH 9.6.8
FORTH & CLYDE CANAL 9.6.9
Fisherrow
Cockenzie
Fidra
North Berwick
Bass Rock
DUNBAR 9.6.7
EYEMOUTH 9.6.6
Burnmouth
St Abb's
St Abb's Head

9.6.3 AREA 6 TIDAL STREAMS

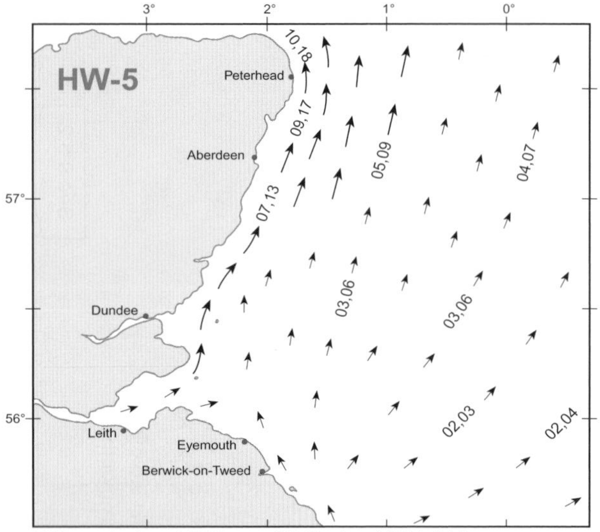

5 Hours before HW Dover (0340 after HW Leith)

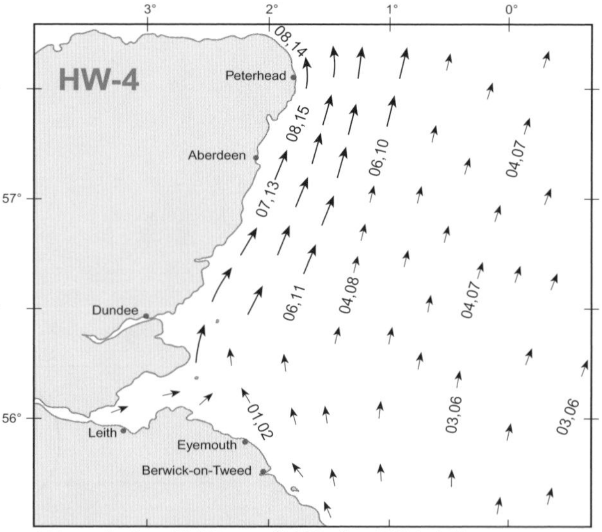

4 Hours before HW Dover (0440 after HW Leith)

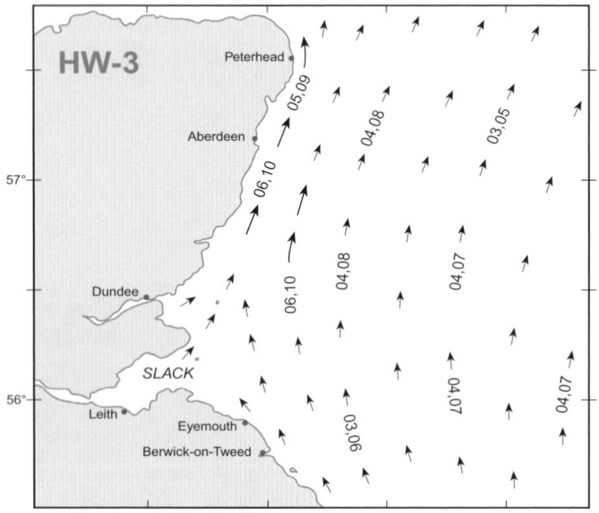

3 Hours before HW Dover (0540 after HW Leith)

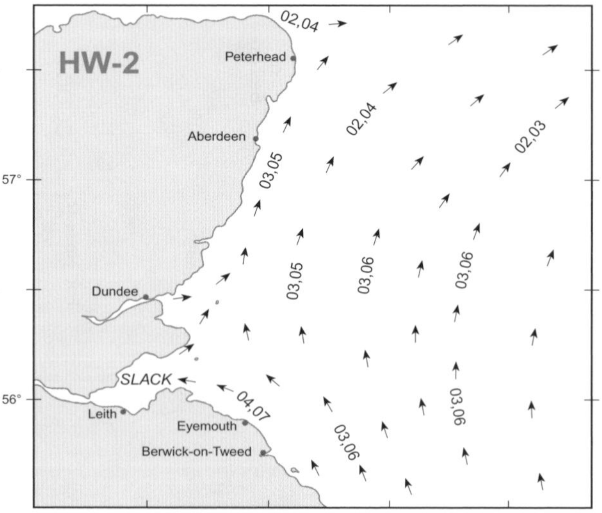

2 Hours before HW Dover (0545 before HW Leith)

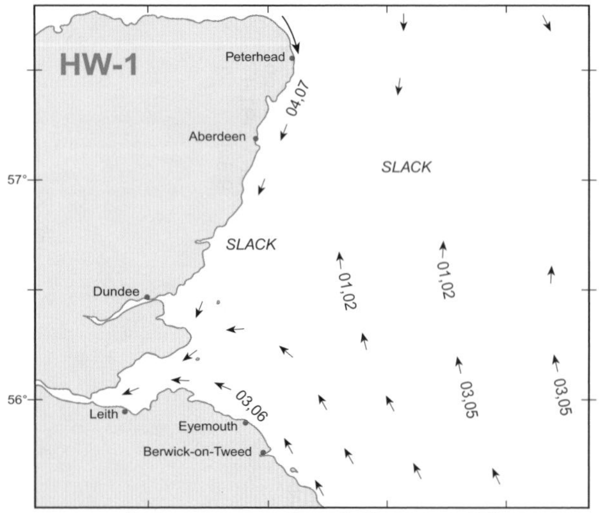

1 Hour before HW Dover (0445 before HW Leith)

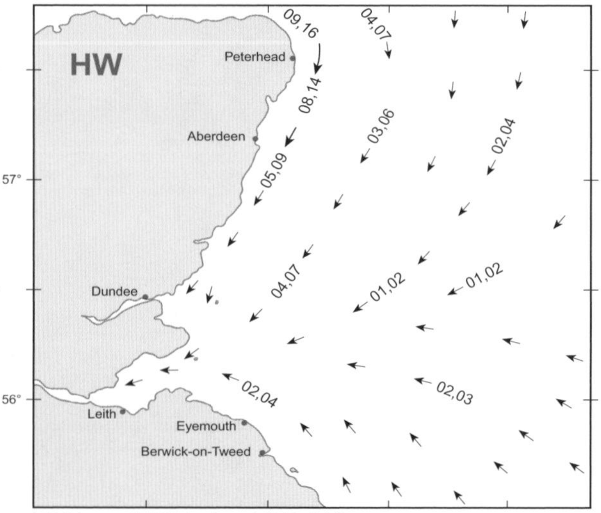

HW Dover (0345 before HW Leith)

Northward 9.7.3 Southward 9.5.3

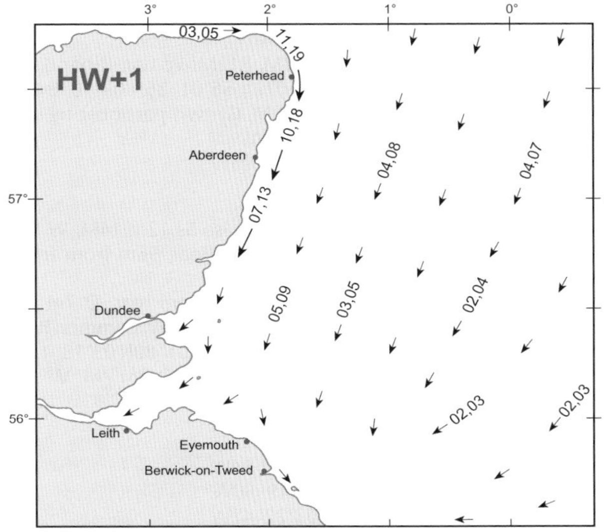

1 Hour after HW Dover (0245 before HW Leith)

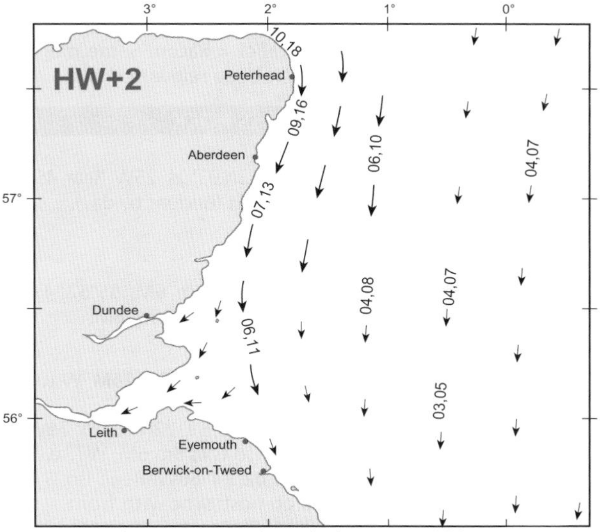

2 Hours after HW Dover (0145 before HW Leith)

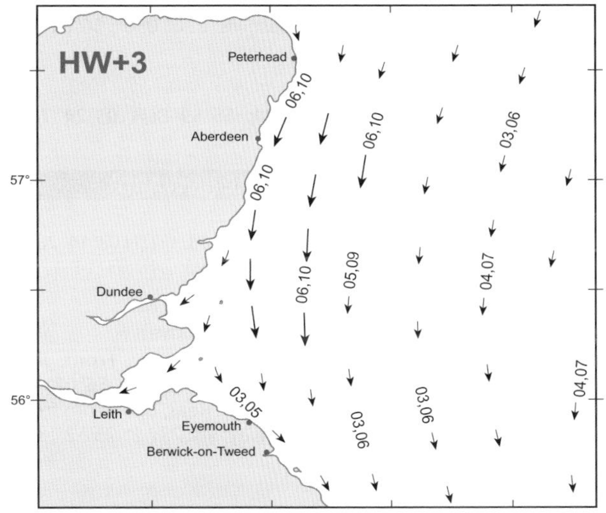

3 Hours after HW Dover (0045 before HW Leith)

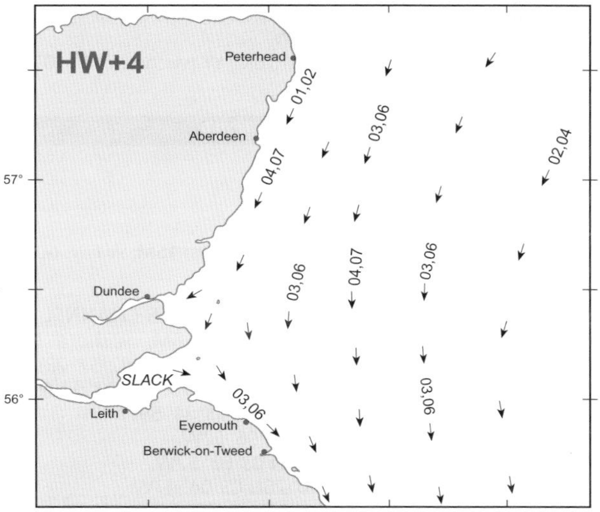

4 Hours after HW Dover (0015 after HW Leith)

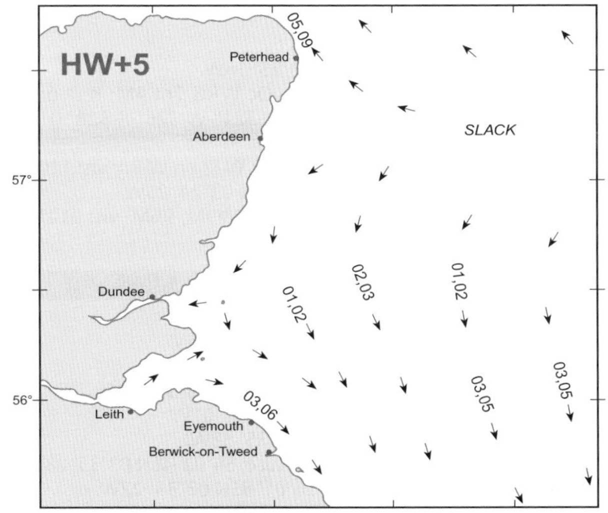

5 Hours after HW Dover (0115 after HW Leith)

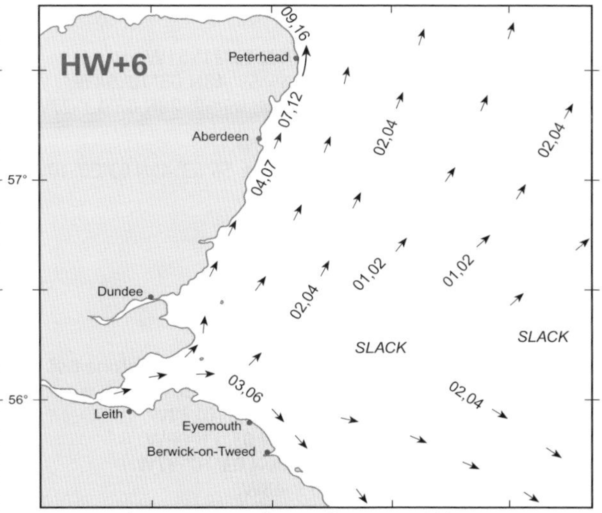

6 Hours after HW Dover (0215 after HW Leith)

9.6.4 LIGHTS, BUOYS AND WAYPOINTS

Bold print = light with a nominal range of 15M or more. CAPITALS = place or feature. *CAPITAL ITALICS* = light-vessel, light float or Lanby. *Italics* = Fog signal. ***Bold italics*** = Racon. Some marks/ buoys are fitted with AIS (MMSI No); see relevant charts.

BERWICK-UPON-TWEED TO BASS ROCK

BURNMOUTH

Ldg lts 241°. Front, FR 29m 4M; 55°50'·53N 02°04'·25W. Rear, 45m from front, FR 35m 4M. Both on W posts (unclear by day).

EYEMOUTH

Blind Buss Q; 55°52'·80N 02°05'·25E.
Ldg Lts 174°. Front, W Bkwtr Hd, FG 9m 6M; 55°52'·47N 02°05'·29W. Rear, elbow 55m from front, FG 10m 6M.

ST ABBS to DUNBAR and BASS ROCK

St Abbs Hd ☆ 55°54'·96N 02°08'·29W; Fl 10s 68m **26M**; W twr; ***Racon (T) 18M***.
Barns Ness Tower (Lt ho disused 36m); 55°59'·22N 02°26'·76W.
Torness Pwr Stn Ldg Lts 215°. Front, Iso G 4s 6m 6M; W □ with B vert stripe on plinth; 55°58'·27N 02°24'·86W. Rear, Iso G 4s 22m 3M; W □ with B vert stripe on post; sync with front.
Dunbar Hbr Ldg Lts (Bayswell Hill) 198°. Front, Oc G 6s 15m 3M; 3 Or △ on col; 56°00'·26N 02°31'·21W. Rear, Oc G 6s 22m 3M; 3 Or ▽; sync with front; both lts 188°-G(intens)-208°.
S Carr Q; 56°03'·60N 02°37'·65W.
Bass Rock, S side, Fl (3) 20s 46m 10M; W twr; vis: 241°-107°; 56°04'·61N 02°38'·48W.

FIRTH OF FORTH AND SOUTH SHORE

(Direction of buoyage East to West)

NORTH BERWICK

Outfall Fl Y; 56°04'·29N 02°40'·89W.

Fidra ☆ 56°04'·39N 02°47'·13W; Fl(4) 30s 34m **15M**; W twr; obsc by Bass Rock, Craig Leith and Lamb Island.

PORT SETON, COCKENZIE, FISHERROW and S CHANNEL

Port Seton, E Pier Hd Iso WR 4s 10m W9M, R6M; vis: shore - R - 105°- W - 225°- R - shore; *Bell (occas)*; 55°58'·40N 02°57'·23W.
Fisherrow E Pier Hd Oc 6s 5m 6M; 55°56'·79N 03°04'·11W.
Narrow Deep Fl(2) R 10s; 56°01'·46N 03°04'·59W.
Herwit Fl(3) G 10s; 56°01'·05N 03°06'·52W.
North Craig Q(3) 10s; 56°01'·02N 03°03'·52W.
Craigh Waugh Fl(2) 10s; 56°00'·26N 03°04'·47W.
Diffuser Hds (Outer) Q; 55°59'·81N 03°07'·84W.
Diffuser Hds (Inner) Q(6) + LFl 15s; 55°59'·38N 03°08'·02W.

LEITH and GRANTON

Leith Approach Fl R 3s; 55°59'·95N 03°11'·51W.
East Bkwtr Hd Iso R 4s 7m 9M; 55°59'·48N 03°10'·94W.
GrantonE Pier Head Fl R 2s 5m 6M; 55°59'·28N 03°13'·27W.

NORTH CHANNEL and MIDDLE BANK

Inchkeith Fairway Iso 2s; ***Racon (T) 5M***; 56°03'·49N 03°00'·10W.
No 1 Fl G 9s; 56°03'·22N 03°03'·71W.
No 2 Fl R 9s; 56°02'·90N 03°03'·72W.
No 3 Fl G 6s; 56°03'·22N 03°06'·10W.
No 4 Fl R 6s; 56°02'·89N 03°06'·11W.
No 5 Fl G 3s; 56°03'·18N 03°07'·88W.
No 6 Fl R 3s; 56°03'·05N 03°08'·44W.
No 8 Fl R 9s 56°02'·95N 03°09'·62W.
Inchkeith 56°02'·01N 03°08'·17W; Fl 15s 67m 14M; stone twr.
Pallas Rock VQ (9) 10s 56°01'·50N 03°09'·30W.
East Gunnet Q (3) 10s; 56°01'·41N 03°10'·38W.
West Gunnet Q (9) 15s 56°01'·34N 03°11'·06W.
No 7 QG; ***Racon (T) 5M***; 56°02'·80N 03°10'·97W.
No 9 Fl G 6s; 56°02'·32N 03°13'·48W.
No 10 Fl R 6s; 56°02'·07N 03°13'·32W.
No 11 Fl G 3s 56°02'·08N 03°15'·26W.
No 12 Fl R 3s; 56°01'·78N 03°15'·15W.
No 13 Fl G 9s; 56°01'·77N 03°16'·94W.
No 14 Q R; 56°01'·51N 03°16'·90W.
Oxcars Fl (2) WR 7s 16m W13M, R12M; W twr, R band; vis: 072°-W-087°- R-196°-W-313°-R-072°; 56°01'·36N 03°16'·84W.
Inchcolm E Pt Fl (3) 15s 20m 10M; Gy twr; part obsc by land 075°-145·5°; 56°01'·72N 03°17'·83W.
No 15 Fl G 6s; 56°01'·39N 03°18'·95W.

MORTIMER'S DEEP

Hawkcraig Point Ldg Lts 292°. Front, Iso 5s 12m 14M; W twr; vis: 282°-302°; 56°03'·03N 03°17'·07W. Rear, 96m from front, Iso 5s 16m 14M; W twr; vis: 282°-302°.
Inchcolm S Lts in line 066°. Front, 84m from rear, Q 7m 7M; W twr; vis: 062·5°-082·5°; 56°01'·78N 03°18'·28W. Common Rear, Iso 5s 11m 7M; W twr; vis: 062·5°-082·5°; 56°01'·80N 03°18'·13W. N Lts in line 076·7°. Front, 80m from rear, Q 7m 7M; W twr; vis: 062·5°-082·5°.

APPROACHES TO FORTH BRIDGES

No 17 Fl G 3s; 56°01'·23N 03°19'·84W.
No 16 Fl R 3s; 56°00'·87N 03°19'·60W.
No 19 Fl G 9s; 56°00'·71N 03°22'·47W.
Beamer Rk W Fl 3s 5m 9M; W post; vis: 050°-230°; 56°00'·30N 03°24'·79W.
Beamer Rk E Fl 3s 5m 9M; W post; vis: 230°-050°; 56°00'·27N 03°24'·72W.

PORT EDGAR

W Bkwtr Hd Fl R 4s 4m 8M; 55°59'·86N 03°24'·78W. W blockhouse.

FIRTH OF FORTH – NORTH SHORE (INWARD)

BURNTISLAND

W Pier Outer Hd Fl (2) R 6s 7m; W twr; 56°03'·22N 03°14'·26W.
E Pier Outer Hd Fl (2) G 6s 7m 5M; 56°03'·24N 03°14'·17W.

ABERDOUR, BRAEFOOT BAY and INCHCOLM

Hawkcraig Pt (see **MORTIMER'S DEEP** above).

Braefoot Bay Terminal, W Jetty. Ldg Lts 247·3°. **Front**, Fl 3s 6m **15M**; W △ on E dolphin; vis: 237·2°-257·2°; 56°02'·16N 03°18'·71W; 4 dolphins with 2 FG (vert). **Rear**, 88m from front, Fl 3s 12m **15M**; W ▽ on appr gangway; vis: 237·2°-257·2°; sync with front.

INVERKEITHING BAY

St David's Fl G 5s 3m 7M; Or □, on pile; 56°01'·37N 03°22'·29W.
Channel QG; 56°01'·43N 03°23'·02W.

ROSYTH

No 2 Q (3) 10s; 56°00'·69N 03°25'·18W.
Main Chan Dir lt 323·5°. Bn 'A' Oc WRG 7m 4M; R □ on W post with R bands; vis: 318°-G-321°-321°-W-326°-R-328° (H24); 56°01'·19N 03°25'·61W.
Dir lt 115°, Bn 'C' Oc WRG 6s 7m 4M; W ▽ on W Bn; vis: 110°- R -113° W -116·5° - G -120°; 56°00'·61N 03°24'·25W.
S Arm Jetty Hd L Fl (2) WR 12s 5m W9M; R6M; vis: 010°-W-280°-R-010°; 56°01'·09N 03°26'·58W.

RIVER FORTH

ROSYTH to GRANGEMOUTH

Dhu Craig Fl G 5s; 56°00'·74N 03°27'·23W.
Blackness QR; 56°01'·06N 03°30'·30W.
Tancred Bank Fl (2) R 10s; 56°01'·58N 03°31'·91W.
Dods Bank Fl R 3s; 56°02'·03N 03°34'·07W.
Bo'ness Fl R 10s; 56°02'·23N 03°35'·38W.
Torry Fl G 10s 5m 7M; G ○ structure; 56°02'·46N 03°35'·28W.
Bo'ness Bcns 2 QR 3m 2M; 56°01'·85N 03°36'·22W.
Bo'ness Hbr ; 56°01'·26N 03°36'·46W.

GRANGEMOUTH
Grangemouth App No 1 Fl (3) 10s 4m 6M;56°02'·12N 03°38'·10W.
Hen & Chickens Fl (3) G 10s; 56°02'·35N 03°38'·08W.

FIRTH OF FORTH – NORTH SHORE (OUTWARD)

KIRKCALDY and METHIL
Kirkcaldy W Pier Hd ☆ Fl R 5s 7m 3M; 56°06'·80N 03°08'·97W.
Kirkcaldy E Pier Hd ☆ Fl G 5s 12m 3M; 56°06'·78N 03°08'·90W.
Methil Outer Pier Hd ☆ Oc G 6s 8m 5M; W twr; vis: 280°-100°; 56°10'·76N 03°00'·48W.

ELIE and ST MONANS
Elie Ness ☆ 56°11'·04N 02°48'·77W; Fl 6s 15m **17M**; W twr.
St Monans Bkwtr Hd ☆ Oc WRG 6s 5m W7M, R4M, G4M; vis: 282°-G-355°-W-026°-R-038°; 56°12'·20N 02°45'·94W.

PITTENWEEM and ANSTRUTHER EASTER
Pittenweem, Ldg Lts 037° Middle Pier Hd. Front, FR 4m 5M. Rear, FR 8m 5M. Both Gy Cols, Or stripes; 56°12'·69N 02°43'·69W.
Pittenweem, E Bkwtr Hd ☆ Fl (2) RG 5s 9m R9M, G6M; vis: 265°-R-345°-G-055°; 56°12'·63N 02°43'·74W.
Anstruther, Ldg Lts 019°. Front FG 7m 4M; 56°13'·28N 02°41'·76W. Rear, 38m from front, FG 11m 4M (both W masts).

MAY I, CRAIL, ST ANDREWS and FIFE NESS to MONTROSE
Isle of May ☆ 56°11'·12N 02°33'·46W(Summit); Fl (2) 15s 73m **22M**; □ twr on stone dwelling.
Crail, Ldg Lts 295°. Front, FR 24m 6M (not lit when hbr closed); 56°15'·46N 02°37'·84W. Rear, 30m from front, FR 30m 6M.
Fife Ness ☆ 56°16'·74N 02°35'·19W; Iso WR 10s 12m **W15M**, R12M; W bldg; vis: 143°-W-197°-R-217°-W-023°; 002320798.
N Carr Q (3) 10s 3m 5M; 56°18'·05N 02°32'·94W.
St Andrews ☆ 56°20'·38N 02°47'·07W; Dir lt 277·7; Iso WRG 2s 17m 9M; vis: 272°-G-276°-AlWG-277°-W-278°-AlWR-279°-R-283°.
St Andrews N Bkwtr Bn ☆ Fl G 3M 56°20'·36N 02°46'·77W.
Bell Rk ☆ 56°26'·08N 02°23'·21W; Fl 5s 28m **18M**; ***Racon (M) 18M***.
Met Mast ☆ Mo(U) 15s 22m 10M; Aero FR (116m), *Horn Mo(U) 30s;* 56°26'·40N 02°14'·49W; 992351153.

RIVER TAY, TAYPORT, DUNDEE and PERTH
Tay Fairway L Fl 10s; *Bell;* 56°28'·30N 02°36'·60W.
Middle Fl G 3s; 56°28'·08N 02°38'·24W.
Middle Fl (2) R 6s 56°27'·82N 02°37'·97W.
Abertay N Q (3) 10s; 56°27'·40N 02°40'·34W.
Abertay S (Elbow) Fl R 6s 56°27'·13N 02°39'·83W.
Tayport High Lt ☆ 56°27'·17N 02°53'·95W; Dir lt 269°; Iso WRG 3s 24m W14M, R14M, G14M; W twr vis: 267°-G-268°-W-270°-R-271°.

ARBROATH
Ldg lts 299·2°. Front , FR 7m 5M; W col; 56°33'·29N 02°35'·16W. Rear, 50m from front, FR 13m 5M; W col.

MONTROSE
Scurdie Ness ☆ 56°42'·10N 02°26'·24W; Fl (3) 20s 38m **23M**; W twr; ***Racon (T) 14-16M***.
Outer Ldg Lts 271·5°; Front, FR 11m 5M; W twin pillars, R bands; 56°42'·21N 02°27'·41W; Rear, 272m from front, FR 18m 5M; W twr, R cupola.
Inner Ldg Lts 265°; Front FG 21m 5M; Rear FG 33m 5M.

MONTROSE TO RATTRAY HEAD

JOHNSHAVEN and GOURDON HARBOUR
Johnshaven, Ldg Lts 316°. Front, FR 5m; 56°47'·62N 02°20'·26W. Rear, 85m from front, FG 20m; shows R when unsafe to ent hbr.
Gourdon Hbr, Ldg Lts 358°. Front, FR 5m 5M; W twr; shows G when unsafe to enter; *Siren (2) 60s* (occas); 56°49'·69N 02°17'·24W. Rear, 120m from front, FR 30m 5M; W twr.
Gourdon E B'water ☆ Q 3m 3M; 49°57'·60N 02°17'·19W.
Todhead Lighthouse (disused), white tower, 13m.

STONEHAVEN to GIRDLE NESS
Outer Pier Hd ☆ Iso WRG 4s 7m 5M; vis: 214°-G-246°-W-268°-R-280°; 56°57'·59N 02°12'·00W.
Girdle Ness ☆ Fl (2) 20s 56m **22M**; obsc by Greg Ness when brg more than about 020°; ***Racon (G) 25M***; 57°08'·34N 02°02'·91W.

ABERDEEN
Fairway Mo (A) 5s; ***Racon (T) 7M***; 57°09'·31N 02°01'·95W.
Torry Ldg lts 237·2°, Front FR or G 14m 5M; R when ent safe, FG when dangerous to navigate; W twr; 57°08'·38N 02°04'·50W. Rear, 220m from front, FR or G 19m 5M; R when ent safe, FG when dangerous to navigate; W twr; 57°08'·31N 02°04'·68W.
Aberdeen Harbour Ent ☆ 57°08'·38N 02°04'·48W; Dir lt 237·2° Fl WRG 1s 7m 9M; metal post; vis: 235·2°-QG-236·2°-AlQGW-236·7°-QW-237·7°-AlQRW-238·2°-QR-239·2°.
S Bkwtr Hd ☆ Fl (3) R 8s 23m 7M; 57°08'·69N 02°03'·34W.
N Pier Hd ☆ Iso G 4s 11m 10M; W twr; 57°08'·74N 02°03'·69W. In fog FY 10m (same twr) vis: 136°-336°; *Bell (3) 12s.*
S Skates Nose Jetty Hd ☆ Q R 4m 4M; 57°08'·49N 02°04'·06W.
Abercrombie Jetty Hd ☆ Oc G 4s 5m 4M; 57°08'·53N 02°04'·15W.

9.6.5 PASSAGE INFORMATION

More passage information is threaded between the harbours in this area. Admiralty Leisure Folios 5615 and 5617 cover the area from Eyemouth to Peterhead. **Bibliography:** *North and East Scotland* – Farne Islands to Cape Wrath – (Lawrence/Imray), the Royal Northumberland *YC's Sailing Directions Humber to Rattray Head* and *Forth Yacht Clubs Association Pilot Handbook* for the the Firth of Forth. The *North Sea (West) Pilot* (Admiralty NP54) covers the entire area.

A *'Rover Ticket'*, £75 from Aberdeenshire and Moray Councils, allows berthing for one week from the date of arrival at the first harbour. It includes, Johnshaven, Gourdon, Stonehaven, Rosehearty, Banff, Portsoy, Cullen, Portknockie, Findochty, Hopeman and Burghead.

BERWICK-UPON-TWEED TO BASS ROCK

(AC 160,175) From Berwick-upon-Tweed to the Firth of Forth there is no good harbour which can be approached with safety in strong onshore winds. So, if on passage with strong winds from N or E, plan accordingly and keep well to seaward. In late spring and early summer fog (haar) is likely in onshore winds.

The coast North from Berwick is rocky with cliffs rising in height to Burnmouth, then diminishing gradually to Eyemouth. Keep 5ca offshore to clear outlying rocks. Burnmouth, although small, has more alongside space than Eyemouth, which is a crowded fishing hbr. 2·1M NW is St Abb's Harbour, with temp ⚓ in offshore winds in Coldingham Bay close to the South. St Abb's Hd (Fl 10s 68m 26M) is a bold, steep headland, 92m high, with no offlying dangers.

▶ *The stream runs strongly round the Hd, causing turbulence with wind against tide; this can be largely avoided by keeping close inshore. The ESE-going stream begins at HW Leith –0345, and the WNW-going at HW Leith +0240.* ◀

There is a good ⚓ in Pettico Wick, on NW side of St Abb's Hd, in S winds, but dangerous if the wind shifts onshore. There are no offlying dangers between St Abb's Hd and Fast Castle Hd, 3M WNW. Between Fast Castle Hd and Barns Ness, about 8M NW, is the attractive little harbour of Cove; but it dries and should only be approached in ideal conditions.

Torness Power Station (conspic, lt on bkwtr) and 2 SPM Fl(5) Y 20s 5ca off Chapel Pt is 1·75M SE of Barns Ness (lt ho disused); this lies 2·5M ESE of Dunbar and is fringed with rocks. Tidal streams as for St Abb's Hd. Conspic chys (119m) are 7½ca WSW inland of Barns Ness. Between here and Dunbar keep at least 2½ca offshore to clear rocky patches. Sicar Rk (7·9m) lies about 1·25M ENE of Dunbar, and seas break on it in onshore gales.

The direct course from Dunbar to Bass Rk (Fl(3) 20s 46m 10M) is clear of all dangers; inshore of this line beware Wildfire Rks (dry) on NW side of Bellhaven Bay. In offshore winds there is ⚓ in Scoughall Road. 1M ESE of Gin Hd Carr bn (stone tr surmounted by cross) marks the N end of Great Carr, a ledge of rocks, nearly covering at HW. Drying ledges of rks extend 1M SE of Great Carr, up to 3ca offshore. Keep at least 5ca off Carr bn in strong onshore winds. Tantallon Castle (ruins) is on cliff edge 1M W of Great Car. Bass Rk (lt) lies 1·25M NNE of Gin Hd, and is a sheer, conspic rk (115m) with no offlying dangers; landing difficult due to swell.

9.6.6 EYEMOUTH

Borders **55°52'·52N 02°05'·29W**

CHARTS AC 160, 1612, 5615; Imray C24

TIDES +0330 Dover; ML No data; Duration 0610

Standard Port LEITH (⟶)

Times				**Height (metres)**			
High Water		Low Water		MHWS	MHWN	MLWN	MLWS
0300	0900	0300	0900	5·6	4·4	2·0	0·8
1500	2100	1500	2100				
Differences EYEMOUTH							
–0005	+0007	+0012	+0008	–0·4	–0·3	0·0	+0·1

SHELTER Good in all weathers except uncomfortable surge in N over F5. Busy FV hbr which encourages yachtsmen to visit. Berth as directed by HM. The options are:

- Middle Quay (100m pontoon), depth 0.9m bottom soft mud.
- On the W wall of the N-pointing jetty by the LB.
- On W wall of the centre jetty W of Gunsgreen House (conspic).
- ⚓ in bay only in offshore winds.

NAVIGATION WPT 55°52'·80N 02°05'·34W, 174°/3ca to E bkwtr lt.

- Appr can be made N or S of Hurkars:
  From the N, beware Blind Buss 1·2m.
  From the S, approach on 250° midway between Hurkars and Hettle Scar (no ldg marks).
- Approaching vessels are advised to contact HM Ch 12 (mob 07885 742505) for latest information.
- Entry should not be attempted in strong N to E winds. F.R ● (occas) or R flag indicates unsafe to enter bay or hbr.

Caution, the entrance is 17m wide and is maintained to 2m depth with soundings taken monthly due to frequent sand movement and silting. E of E pier inwards CD reduces to 1m. Depth as charted 0.9m on Ⓥ pontoon but river inflow in front of RNLI office very shallow. Inbound keep to W side of channel until past lift bridge.

LIGHTS AND MARKS St Abbs Hd lt ho Fl 10s 68m 26M is 3M NW. Ldg lts 174° both FG 9/10m 6M, orange columns on W pier.

COMMUNICATIONS (Code 01890) CGOC (01224) 592334; Police 101; Dr 750599, Ⓗ (0131) 536 1000. HM 750223, Mobile 07885 742505.

VHF Ch 16 **12** (HO). Advisable to listen to VHF Ch 6 for FVs entering/leaving port.

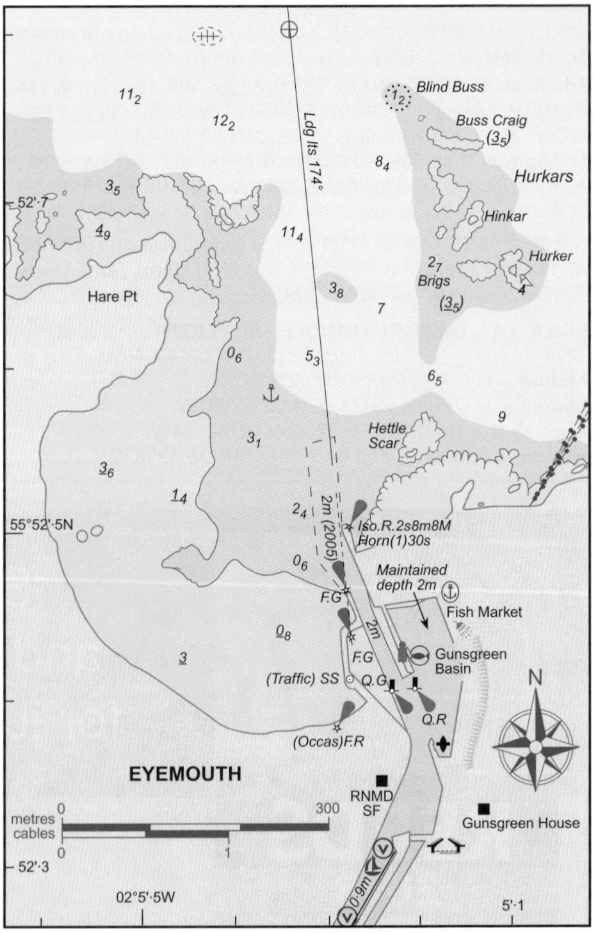

FACILITIES **Hbr** www.eyemouth-harbour.co.uk. For 10m LOA £14.80 (quay), £18.90 (pontoon) discount >3 nts. (at harbour bldg). Ⓔ (12t mob) wi-fi.

Town LB, Ⓑ. (bus to Berwick-on-Tweed and Edinburgh), ✈ (Edinburgh).

ADJACENT HARBOURS

BURNMOUTH, Borders, **55°50′·61N 02°04′·10W**. AC 160. HW +0315 on Dover, –0025 on Leith; Duration 0615. Use Eyemouth tides 9.6.6. From S beware Quarry Shoal Rks; and E & W Carrs from N. 2 W posts (unclear by day, FR 29/35m 4M) 45m apart, lead 253° to close N of the hbr; as hbr mouth opens, enter on about 185° with outer hbr ent in line with 2FG (vert). Min depth at ent at LWS is 0·6m. Shelter is good especially in inner hbr (dries). With onshore winds, swell makes outer hbr uncomfortable. HM (018907) 81283 (home). Facilities: £10 (all LOA), limited.

ST ABB'S, Borders, **55°54′·10N 02°07′·74W**. AC 175. HW +0330 on Dover, –0017 on Leith; HW –0·6m on Leith; Duration 0605. Ldg line (about 228°) S face of Maw Carr on village hall (conspic R roof) leads SW until the hbr ent opens to port and the 2nd ldg line (about 176°) can be seen 2FR 2/4m 1M, or Y LB ho visible through ent. On E side of ent chan, beware Hog's Nose and on W side the Maw Carr. Shelter good. In strong onshore winds outer hbr suffers from waves breaking over E pier. Inner hbr (dries) is best but often full of FVs. HM (0775 1136758) directs visitors. Facilities: £15 (all LOA) (launching £15), at quay, more facilities & at Coldingham.

9.6.7 DUNBAR

East Lothian **56°00′·39N 02°31′·09W**

CHARTS AC 175, 734, 5615; Imray C24, C23, C27

TIDES +0330 Dover; ML 3·0; Duration 0600

Standard Port LEITH (⟶)

Times				Height (metres)			
High Water		Low Water		MHWS	MHWN	MLWN	MLWS
0300	0900	0300	0900	5·6	4·4	2·0	0·8
1500	2100	1500	2100				
Differences DUNBAR							
–0005	+0003	+0003	–0003	–0·3	–0·3	0·0	+0·1
FIDRA							
–0001	0000	–0002	+0001	–0·2	–0·2	0·0	0·0

SHELTER Outer (Victoria) Hbr is subject to surge in strong NW to NE winds. N side dries; berth signed by rubber ladder on W wall beneath castle, dries approx HW±2. Contact HM. Keep steps clear. Inner (Old or Cromwell) Hbr dries and is safe in strong onshore conditions; enter under bridge, lifted by HM on request.

NAVIGATION WPT 56°00′·60N 02°31′·49W, 132°/3ca to hbr ent, preferable entry in marginal conditions.

- Entry is dangerous in heavy onshore swell with no access in strong winds from NW to E.
- Beware Wallace's Head Rock, Half Ebb Rock (2_1m), 1½ca from ent. and Outer Buss 4ca E of ent.
- Min depth at ent 0·5m, but may be much less in abnormal circumstances.
- Keep to port on entry to avoid rockfall off castle.

LIGHTS AND MARKS Church and Castle ruin both conspic. From NE, ldg lts, Oc G 6s 15/22m 3M, synch, intens 188°-208°, 2 W △ on Or cols, lead 198° through the outer rks to the Roads; thence narrow ent opens with QR brg 132°. From NW, appr on brg 132° between bns on Wallaces Head and Half Ebb Rk.

COMMUNICATIONS (01368) CGOC (01224) 592334; Police 101; Dr 863704; Ⓗ (0131) 536 1000. HM mob 07958 754858, Dep HM 07583 463991, harbourmaster@dunbarharbourtrust.co.uk.

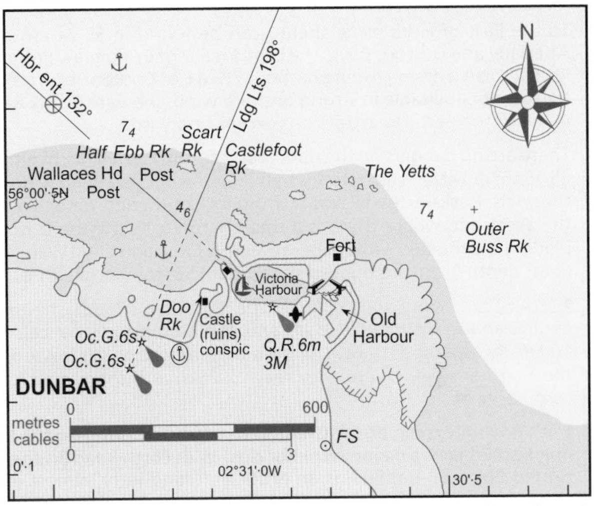

FACILITIES www.dunbarharbourtrust.co.uk **Quay** (launch £10) £16 (£20 >12m LOA).

N Wall ; **Inner Hbr** .

Town Edinburgh.

ADJACENT HARBOUR

NORTH BERWICK, East Lothian, **56°03′·74N 02°43′·04W**. AC 734. Fidra HW +0344 on Dover; ML 3·0m; Duration 0625. See 9.6.7 Fidra. Shelter good with winds from S to W but dangerous with onshore winds. Very small drying harbour with entrance 8m wide. Max LOA normally 30′; LOA >40′ only in emergency. From E or W, from position 0·25M S of Craigleith, steer S for Plattock Rks, thence SSW 40m off harbour wall (beware Maiden Rocks to the W) before turning 180° to port into hbr. Galloway Pier extends N from hbr wall.

Bkwtr light F R 7m 3M and FG 6m 3M (about 1ca S) in transit 188° (2 F R (vert) when harbour closed). Facilities: on pier, £15, HM www.nbharbour.org.uk ☎(01620) 893333, mob 0777 6467373.

East Lothian YC ☎(01620) 892698, s.

Town and bus Edinburgh.

FIRTH OF FORTH – SOUTH SHORE

(AC 734, 735) Westward of Bass Rk, Craigleith (51m), Lamb Is (24m) and Fidra (31m) lie 5ca or more offshore, while the coast is generally foul. Craigleith is steep-to, and temporary ⚓ can be found on SE and SW sides; if passing inshore of it keep well to N side of chan. N Berwick hbr (dries) lies S of Craigleith, but is unsafe in onshore winds. Between Craigleith and Lamb Is, beware drying rocks up to 3ca from land. Lamb Is is 1·5M WNW of N Berwick and has a rocky ledge extending 2½ca SW. Fidra Is (Fl(4) 30s 34m 15M) is a bird reserve, nearly connected to the shore by rocky ledges, and should be passed to the N; passage and ⚓ on S side are tricky. ⚓ on E or W sides, depending on wind, in good weather.

To the East of Fidra some shelter can be found in SE winds in Aberlady and Gosford Bays. The best ⚓ is SW of Craigielaw Point. Port Seton is a drying fishing harbour 7½ca E of Cockenzie (dries); entry is not advisable in strong onshore winds; beware Corsik Rk 400m to the East. No attractions except boatyard.

There are no dangers on the direct course from Fidra to Inchkeith (Fl 15s 67m 14M), which stands between the buoyed deep water channels. Rocks extend 7½ca SE from Inchkeith, and for 5ca off the West side where there is a small harbour below the lt ho; landing is forbidden without permission. N Craig and Craig Waugh (least depth 0·2m) are buoyed shoals 2·5M SE from Inchkeith lt.

►*In N Chan, close to Inchkeith the W-going (flood) stream begins about HW Leith –0530, and the E-going at HW Leith +0030, Sp rates about 1kn. The streams gather strength towards the Forth Bridges, where they reach 2·25kn and there may be turbulence.*◄

Leith is wholly commercial; Granton has yacht moorings in the E hbr; Port Edgar is a major yacht hbr close W of Forth Road Bridge. Hound Point oil terminal is an artificial 'island-jetty' almost in mid-stream, connected to the shore by underwater pipeline (⚓). Yachts may pass the terminal on either side at least 30m off keeping well clear of manoeuvring ships.

CROSSING THE FIRTH OF FORTH

►*Tidal streams are quite weak in the outer part of the Firth, apart from the stream in the Tay, which attains 5kn in most places. Coastwise tidal streams between Fife Ness and Arbroath are weak.*

Northbound. *Leave before HW (Dover +0400) to be at N Carr at Dover +0600. Bound from Forth to Tay aim to arrive at Abertay By at LW slack (Dover –0200).*

Southbound. *Leave before LW (Dover -0200) to be at Bass Rk at HW Dover. If bound from Tay to Forth, leave late in ebb to pick up early flood off St Andrews to N Carr and into Forth.*◄

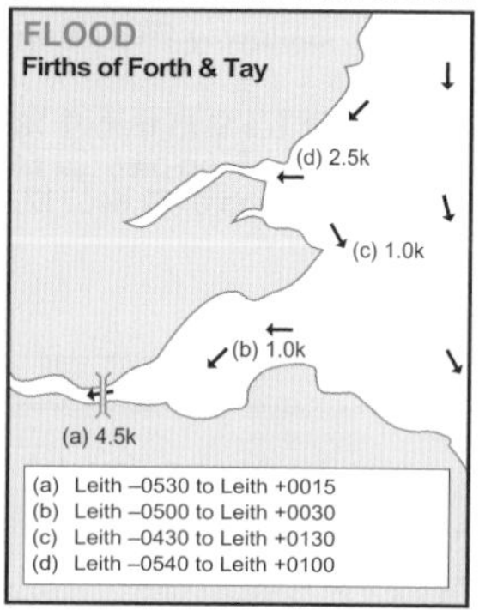
FLOOD
Firths of Forth & Tay
(d) 2.5k
(c) 1.0k
(b) 1.0k
(a) 4.5k
(a) Leith –0530 to Leith +0015
(b) Leith –0500 to Leith +0030
(c) Leith –0430 to Leith +0130
(d) Leith –0540 to Leith +0100

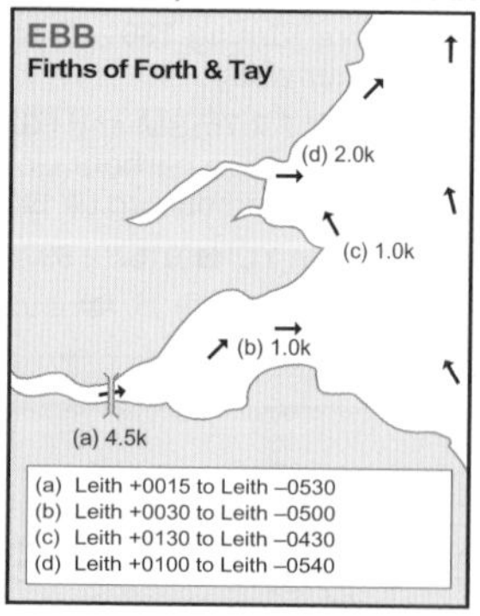
EBB
Firths of Forth & Tay
(d) 2.0k
(c) 1.0k
(b) 1.0k
(a) 4.5k
(a) Leith +0015 to Leith –0530
(b) Leith +0030 to Leith –0500
(c) Leith +0130 to Leith –0430
(d) Leith +0100 to Leith –0540

RIVER FORTH TO KINCARDINE

(AC 736, 737, 738) The main shipping channel under the N span of the rail bridge N of Inchgarvie is busy with commercial traffic for Grangemouth and Rosyth. W of Beamer Rk, which supports the Queensferry Crossing the Firth widens as far as Bo'ness (small drying hbr) on the S shore where the channel narrows between drying mudbanks.

The Queensferry Crossing is W of the Forth Road Bridge between 56° 00′·76N, 3° 24′·44W (shore) and 55° 59′·61N, 3° 25′·16W (shore). There are 3 pillars, one on Beamer Rk and two clear of the main navigable routes. The North span gives access to Rosyth while the South span allows traffic to pass upstream to Grangemouth. Forth and Tay Navigation Service broadcast information and vessels should maintain a listening watch on VHF Ch 71.

Charlestown (N bank) dries, but is a secure harbour. Grangemouth is industrially conspicuous. Beware of gas carriers, tankers and other cargo vessels; there are no facilities for yachts. Few yachts go beyond Kincardine swing bridge, clearance 6·5m, which is no longer opened. Clackmannanshire Bridge, clearance 6·5m, is about 4ca further upriver.

FIRTH OF FORTH – NORTH SHORE

(AC 734, 190) From Burntisland the N shore of Firth of Forth leads E to Kinghorn Ness. 1M SSW of Kinghorn Ness Blae Rk (SHM I) has least depth of 4·1m, and seas break on it in E gales.

► *Rost Bank lies halfway between Kinghorn Ness and Inchkeith, with tide rips at Sp tides or in strong winds.* ◄

From Kinghorn Ness to Kirkcaldy, drying rocks lie up to 3ca offshore. Kirkcaldy Hbr is effectively closed, but yachts can enter inner dock near HW by arrangement; entry is dangerous in strong E'lies, when seas break a long way out.

Between Kirkcaldy and Methil the only dangers more than 2ca offshore are The Rockheads, extending 4ca SE of Dysart, and marked by 2 SHM. Largo Bay is ⚓, well sheltered from N and E, but avoid gaspipes near the E side. Close SW of Elie, beware W Vows (dries) and E Vows (dries, bn). There is ⚓ close W of Elie Ness (9.6.8). Ox Rock (dries 2m) lies 5ca ENE of Elie Ness, and 2½ca offshore; otherwise there are no dangers more than 2ca offshore past St Monance, Pittenweem and Anstruther, but in bad weather the sea breaks on Shield Rk 4ca off Pittenweem. From Anstruther to Crail and on to Fife Ness keep 3ca offshore to clear Caiplie Rk and other dangers.

May Island (Fl(2) 15s 73m 22M) lies about 5M S of Fife Ness; its shores are bold except at NW end where rks extend 1ca off. ⚓ near N end at E or W Tarbert, on lee side according to winds; in good weather it is possible to land. Lt ho boats use Kirkhaven, close SE of lt ho.

FORTH TO NORWAY AND THE BALTIC

(AC 2182B, 2182C) Heading ENE'ly from the Firth of Forth the main hazards result from offshore industrial activities and their associated traffic. Particularly in summer months oil/gas exploration, movement of drilling rigs and pipe laying create potentially hazardous situations for small craft. Rig movements and many of the more intense activities are published in Notices to Mariners, but even so it is wise to avoid the gas and oil fields where possible and never to approach within 500m of installations.

There are TSS to be avoided off the S and SW coast of Norway. Strong currents and steep seas may be experienced in the approaches to the Skagerrak.

9.6.8 FIRTH OF FORTH

E and W Lothian/City of Edinburgh/Fife

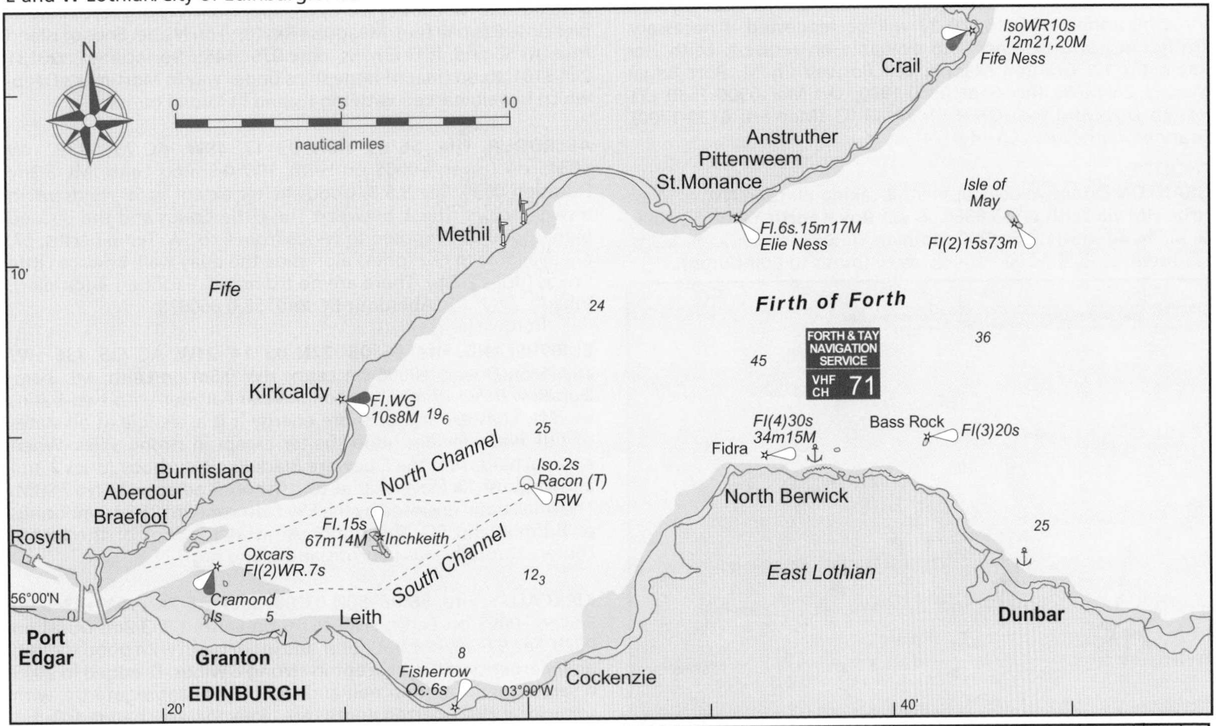

CHARTS AC 734, 735, 736, 737, 741, 5615; Imray C23, C27

TIDES +0350 (Granton) Dover; ML 3·3; Duration 0620

Standard Port LEITH (⟶)

Times				Height (metres)			
High Water		Low Water		MHWS	MHWN	MLWN	MLWS
0300	0900	0300	0900	5·6	4·4	2·0	0·8
1500	2100	1500	2100				
Differences COCKENZIE							
−0007	−0015	−0013	−0005	−0·2	0·0	ND	ND
GRANTON: Same as LEITH							

SHELTER Port Edgar offers good shelter, but surge at LW esp in E winds. Silting in centre of entrance and close to wavebreak. Granton mostly dries but is open to violent swell in N'lies. Pontoons on E side of Middle Pier in about 2m and RFYC welcomes visitors. Pilot launches berth at seaward end. Leith is purely commercial. Rosyth should only be used in emergency. Forth Navigation Service controls Firth of Forth, Granton Hbr and all commercial docks.

NAVIGATION Port Edgar 56°N 03°24'·3W, 244°/3ca to W bkwtr. Do not enter E of wavebreak, beware of shallows at W end; 3kn sp limit. Granton WPT 56°00'·00N 03°13'·31W, 180°/0·72M to entry.

- Beware Hound Pt terminal; Forth Railway and Road Bridges; vessels bound to/from Rosyth and Grangemouth especially in local fog (haar). 12kn speed limit W of Forth Rly Bridge.
- On N shore, no vessel may enter Mortimer's Deep (Braefoot gas terminal) without approval from Forth Navigation Service.
- Protected chan runs from Nos 13 & 14 buoys (NNW of Oxcars) under the bridges (N of Inch Garvie and Beamer Rk), to Rosyth. When activated (occas) via Forth Ports plc, other vessels must clear the chan for Rosyth traffic.
- Caution: strong tidal streams.

LIGHTS AND MARKS See 9.6.4 and chartlets. Granton: R flag with W diagonal cross (or ● lt) on signal mast at middle pier hd = Entry prohibited.

COMMUNICATIONS (Code 0131) CGOC (01224) 592334; Police 101; 🄷 Edinburgh Royal Infirmary 2292477; Forth and Tay Navigation Service (01324) 498584; QHM Rosyth (01383) 425050.

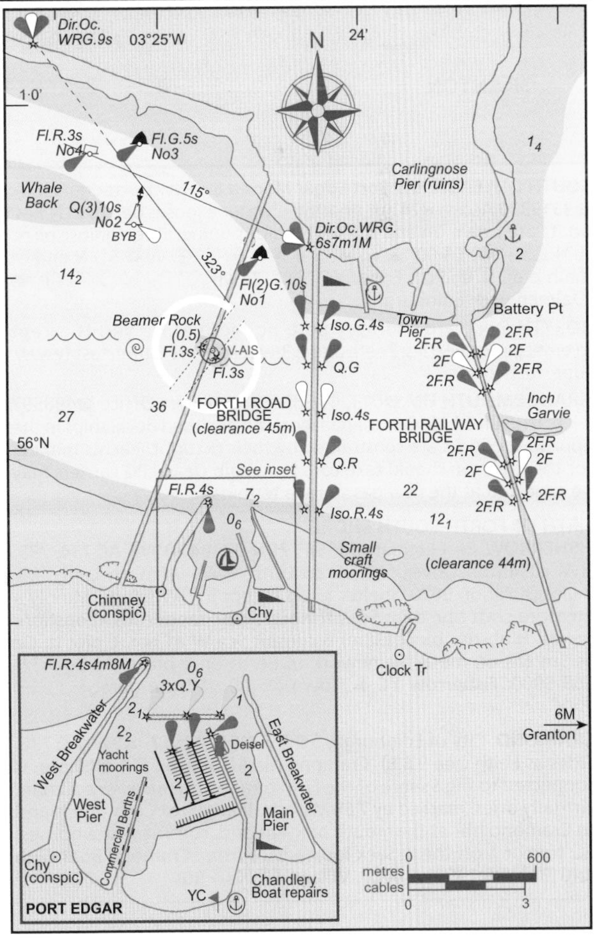

HMNB CLYDE (01436) 674321 ext 3206, for naval activity off Scotland; Forth Yacht Clubs Ass'n 5523452.

Call *Forth Navigation* (at Grangemouth) Ch **71** (calling and short messages, H24) 16; **20** 12 will be requested if necessary. Traffic, nav and weather info available on request. Leith Hbr Radio Ch 12. Granton Marina, call *Boswell* Ch M. Port Edgar Marina Ch M **80** (Apr-Sept 0900-1930; Oct-Mar 0900-1630 LT). Rosyth Dockyard, call *QHM* Ch 74 13 73 (Mon-Fri: 0730-1700). Grangemouth Docks Ch 14 (H24).

FACILITIES

GRANTON Extensive development is taking place in NW of West Hrbr. HM via Leith ☎555 8866; **Royal Forth YC** ☎552 3006, (5t); **Forth Corinthian YC** ☎552 5939. **Town** (buses to Edinburgh).

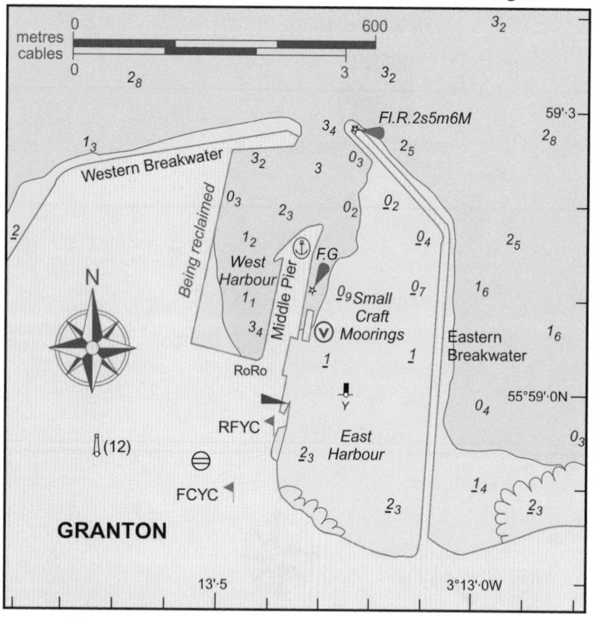

SOUTH QUEENSFERRY Port Edgar Marina www.portedgar.co.uk ☎3313330 Access H24 but floating b'water exposes berths in N'lies; boats are beam on and roll with pulpits vulnerable against piles. (301 +8) £3·00, (5t) N end of main pier, @; Port Edgar YC. **Town** (Dalmeny), Edinburgh.

ROSYTH Dockyard and ferry port; no facilities for yachts except in emergency. Ferries: Zeebrugge; 3/week; 17hrs; Superfast (www.superfast.com).

GRANGEMOUTH HM ☎01324 498566 (H24); Port Office ☎498597 (HO). VHF Ch 14 16. Commercial port. An enclosed dock, ships in the appr to the locks are constrained by their draught. Yachts making for the R Carron should take care to remain clear. LPG carriers may be expected at the new gas storage terminal.

FIRTH OF FORTH SOUTH SHORE

FISHERROW, East Lothian, **55°56′·79N 03°04′·09W**. AC 734, 735. HW +0345 on Dover, –0005 on Leith; HW –0·1m on Leith; ML 3·0m; Duration 0620. Shelter good except in NW winds. Mainly a pleasure craft hbr, dries 5ca offshore. Appr dangerous in onshore winds. High-rise block (38m) is conspic 9ca W of hbr. E pier lt, Oc 6s 5m 6M on metal framework tr. Berth on E pier. HM ☎(0131) 665 5900; **Fisherrow YC**. **Town** from garage.

CRAMOND, City of Edinburgh, **55°59′·80N 03°17′·49W**. AC 736. Tides as Leith (see 9.6.8). Cramond Island, approx 1M offshore, is connected to the S shore of the Firth by a drying causeway. A chan, virtually dries, marked by 7 SHM posts, leads W of Cramond Island to Cramond hbr at the mouth of R Almond, conspic white houses. free or ⚓ off the Is. Seek local advice from: **Cramond Boat Club** ☎(0131) 336 1356. **Village** Bus.

FIRTH OF FORTH NORTH SHORE

INCHCOLM, Fife, **56°01′·85N 03°17′·89W**. AC 736. Tides see 9.6.8. Best ⚓ in 4m, N of abbey (conspic); appr from NW or ESE, to land at pier close E (small fee). Meadulse Rks (dry) on N side. Ends of island foul. At SE end, lt Fl (3) 15s, obsc 075°-145°. No facilities. ☎0131 244 3101. Keep clear of large ships under way in Mortimer's Deep, which is well marked with ldg lts and lit lateral buoys.

ABERDOUR, Fife, **56°03′·00N 03°17′·49W**. AC 735, 736. HW +0345 on Dover; +0005 on Leith; HW 0·5m on Leith; ML 3·3m; Duration 0630. See 9.6.8. Good shelter except in SE winds when a swell occurs. The ⚓ between The Little Craigs and the disused pier is good but exposed to winds from E to SW. Temp berths, £7, are available in hbr (dries) alongside the quay wall. Beware Little Craigs (dries 2·2m). There are no lts/ marks. Facilities: (on pier). **Village**. **Aberdour BC** ☎(01383) 860029.

BURNTISLAND, Fife, **56°03′·22N 03°14′·21W**. AC 735, 736. HW +0345 on Dover; +0005 on Leith; HW 0·5m on Leith; ML 3·3m; Duration 0630. Primarily a commercial harbour with two basins used by coasters and offshore energy it is accessible at all states of tide and provides good shelter except in strong S'lies. When approaching from the E beware Black Rks, Heuchboy (dries 2·3m) and Kirkbush Rk (covers). Blae Rk offshore is adjacent to No 7 SHM. The small basin enclosed by the E'ly bwtr contains 25 F&A moorings of Burnt Island SC. The clubhouse is at the root of the bkwtr, contact through www.burntislandsailing.org.

KIRKCALDY, Fife, **56°06′·80N 03°08′·96W**. AC 741. HW +0340 on Dover, –0005 on Leith; HW –0·1m on Leith; ML 3·2m; Duration 0620. See 9.6.10. Hbr has outer and inner basin with good shelter; an emergency refuge except in strong E winds. Dredged in 2015 it serves the local flour mill and commercial aggregate tfc, with some local FVs. Charted depths are likely to have changed. Outer piers lit Fl G 5s /Fl R 5s respectively. W pier is high concrete wall and care needed when coming to the. Small craft should contact Forth Ports Authority ☎01383 421800, Forth Navigation (H24) Ch 71.

METHIL, Fife, **56°10′·75N 03°00′·55W.** AC 734,741. HW +0330 Dover; –0020 and –0·1 on Leith; ML 3m; Duration 0615. Commercial activity greatly reduced; infrastructure limited. Access at all states of the tide and provides shelter from E'lies. Ent is difficult in strong E and SE winds until within lee of bwtr. In bad weather seas can pile up in the shallow appr esp on a shallow bar which forms to seaward of the bwtr lt. The Fife Energy Park has a buoyed area and wind turbine on the foreshore W of the dock entrance. This is lit on each side by 2 F R (vert) and 2 F G (vert). Dock ☎(01333) 426725. Berthing by prior arrangement at Methil Boat Club ☎(01333) 421110. In emergency call Forth Navigation Ch 71 (H24) or Forth CG.

ELIE, Fife, **56°11′·20N 02°49′·29W**. AC 734. HW +0325 on Dover, –0015 on Leith; HW –0·1m on Leith; ML 3·0m; Duration 0620; Elie B provides good shelter from N winds for small craft but local knowledge is needed. Hbr dries; 3 short term waiting buoys available. Beware ledge off end of pier which dries. From E beware Ox Rk (dries 1m) 5M ENE of Elie Ness; from W beware rks off Chapel Ness, W Vows, E Vows (surmounted by cage bn) and Thill Rk, marked by PHM buoy. Lt: Elie Ness Fl 6s 15m 17M, W tr. HM (01333) 330219; (3) drying £10/night, SC. Police 08456 005702. Dr ☎330302. Services: (tanker). Elie & Earlsferry.

ST MONANS, Fife, **56°12′·25 N 02°45′·94W**. AC 734. HW +0335 on Dover, –0020 on Leith; HW –0·1m on Leith; ML 3·0m; Duration 0620. Shelter good except in strong SE to SW winds when scend occurs in the hbr (dries). Berth alongside E pier until contact with HM. From NE keep at least 2½ca from coast. Bkwtr hd Oc WRG 6s 5m 7/4M; E pier hd 2 FG (vert) 6m 4M. W pier hd 2 FR (vert)6m4M. Facilities: HM ☎07930 869538 (part time) if no reply, 01333 310836 (Anstruther HM assists); (example for 10m LOA) £17.20 then £8.60/day thereafter; Services: (tanker ☎730622). Police ☎08456 005702. **Village**.

9.6.9 FORTH AND CLYDE CANAL

Lowland Carron River Ent. **51°02′·30N 03°41′·46W**

These notes are for the convenience of those entering the canal at Grangemouth. Refer to 9.9.21 for the W entrance at Bowling Sea Lock, R Clyde. The eastern extension, by-passes low bridges and gives access to the Forth via R Carron through either Carron or Helix locks, which handle boats of different sizes in daylight 0800–2000. Legs join at Kepples lock 1a.

CHARTS AC 737, 741, 5615; Imray C27; *The Skipper's Guide* Forth & Clyde and Union Canal essential. Obtain from, Lowland Canals Office, Canal House, Applecross Street, Glasgow, G4 9SP. ☎(0141) 332 6936, www.scottishcanals.co.uk or www.waterscape.com.

TIDES Carron River +0325 Dover, 0030 Leith.
Helix 1 lock - HW-4 - HW+2½; Carron lock - HW-4 - HW+1½.

SHELTER Temporary berthing at Grangemouth YC or at nearby Refuge Posts. Pontoon outside Helix and Carron sea locks. Temp'y ⚓s close WNW of Carron PHM and close SSW of Carron Bn SHM.

NAVIGATION R Carron entrance approached from Grangemouth Roads via Small Craft Recommended Track. River dries at LW.

- Canal passage has to be booked in advance, ☎07810 0794468. Masts must be unstepped before proceeding above sea lock 1.
- Helix 1 lock - 20m long, 5m beam, 1.8m depth, 3m air draught. Carron lock - 6m beam. Kerse Rd Bridge is 5m above river bed, which at is highest pt is 2.3m above CD; it is equipped with air draught gauges calibrated for the canal dimensions. Add 0.1m/4in to draught for freshwater.
- Mast craneage at Bowling, Helix Lock (500kg), Grangemouth YC and Port Edgar for larger yachts.
- The canal is about 30M long with 39 locks. Allow a minimum of 21 hours underway for a passage to Bowling Sea Lock. Transit of the canal can be achieved in 2 days by reaching the Summit Pound at Lock 20, Wyndford, on the first day.
- Vessels should have a reliable engine and be capable of a minimum speed through the water of 4kn against adverse conditions. Ebb tide attains rates of up to 6kn in R Carron after heavy rainfall. 4mph speed limit throughout the canal.
- Access via Falkirk Wheel to Union Canal and Edinburgh, refer to *Scottish Canals Skipper's Guide*.
- The canal is occasionally closed at short notice for safety works check www.scottishcanals.co.uk for notices.

LOCKS Carron Sea Lock and 9.9.21 Bowling Sea Lock are operated by canal staff. Locks operate over long 4-day weekends with 10-day passage licence bridging 2 adjacent operating periods, including access to the Falkirk Wheel, Union Canal and Edinburgh.

LIGHTS AND MARKS Carron River channel is marked by lighted By PHM & Bn SHM and unlit By(s) PHM & SHM. Bkwtr/Training Bank to W & N of channel marked with Bn(s) & Bol(s).

BOAT SAFETY SCHEME *The Skipper's Guide* refers. At Carron Sea Lock transient/visiting craft staying no more than 28 days will be subject to a Boat Safety Check of gas and fuel systems. Also required to complete a boat condition declaration and provide evidence of insurance for £1 million third party liability.

COMMUNICATIONS Carron Sea Lock (01324) 483034/07810794468. *Carron Sea Lock* VHF Ch **74**.

FACILITIES **Carron Sea Lock** P WC. **Falkirk Wheel (on Forth & Clyde)** WC. For details refer to *The Skipper's Guide*.

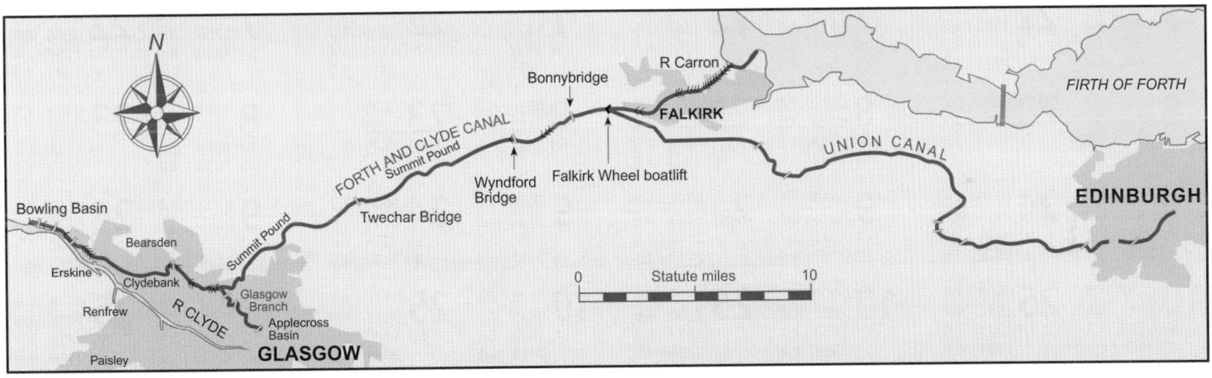

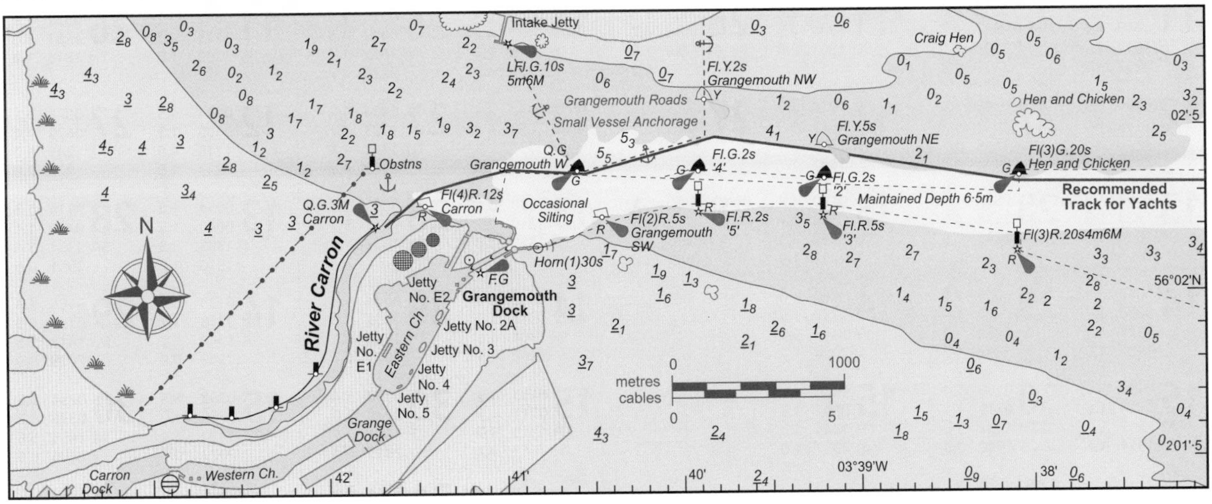

STANDARD TIME (UT)
For Summer Time add ONE hour in **non-shaded areas**

LEITH LAT 55°59′N LONG 3°11′W

TIMES AND HEIGHTS OF HIGH AND LOW WATERS

Dates in red are SPRINGS
Dates in blue are NEAPS

YEAR **2018**

JANUARY

Date	Day	Time	m	Time	m	Time	m	Time	m
1	M	0118	5.6	0728	1.0	1347	5.7	1954	0.8
2	TU	0209	5.8	0822	0.8	1433	5.8	○ 2050	0.5
3	W	0258	5.9	0913	0.7	1520	5.9	2143	0.4
4	TH	0347	6.0	1001	0.8	1608	5.9	2233	0.4
5	F	0437	5.8	1047	0.9	1657	5.8	2320	0.5
6	SA	0528	5.6	1130	1.2	1749	5.6		
7	SU	0007	0.8	0621	5.4	1211	1.5	1845	5.4
8	M	0053	1.1	0718	5.1	1252	1.8	◑ 1945	5.1
9	TU	0144	1.5	0817	4.8	1347	2.1	2047	4.9
10	W	0247	1.8	0917	4.6	1502	2.2	2149	4.7
11	TH	0359	1.9	1019	4.6	1619	2.2	2253	4.7
12	F	0505	1.9	1122	4.6	1725	2.1	2356	4.7
13	SA	0557	1.9	1223	4.8	1821	1.9		
14	SU	0053	4.8	0638	1.7	1313	4.9	1905	1.6
15	M	0139	5.0	0714	1.6	1353	5.1	1944	1.4
16	TU	0219	5.1	0749	1.4	1429	5.2	2019	1.3
17	W	0253	5.2	0823	1.3	1502	5.3	● 2052	1.1
18	TH	0326	5.2	0858	1.2	1534	5.4	2126	1.0
19	F	0359	5.3	0933	1.2	1607	5.4	2200	1.0
20	SA	0433	5.2	1007	1.3	1640	5.3	2233	1.1
21	SU	0509	5.2	1039	1.4	1715	5.3	2305	1.2
22	M	0547	5.1	1105	1.5	1752	5.2	2335	1.3
23	TU	0629	5.0	1135	1.7	1834	5.1		
24	W	0010	1.4	0715	4.8	1219	1.8	◐ 1922	4.9
25	TH	0100	1.6	0810	4.7	1327	2.0	2021	4.8
26	F	0210	1.8	0917	4.7	1504	2.0	2137	4.8
27	SA	0349	1.8	1029	4.7	1634	1.9	2255	4.9
28	SU	0514	1.7	1138	4.9	1745	1.6		
29	M	0005	5.1	0620	1.4	1239	5.2	1849	1.2
30	TU	0106	5.4	0719	1.1	1332	5.5	1949	0.8
31	W	0158	5.7	0812	0.9	1421	5.8	○ 2044	0.4

FEBRUARY

Date	Day	Time	m	Time	m	Time	m	Time	m
1	TH	0247	5.9	0901	0.7	1507	5.9	2133	0.2
2	F	0334	5.9	0947	0.7	1553	6.0	2219	0.2
3	SA	0421	5.8	1029	0.7	1640	5.9	2302	0.3
4	SU	0507	5.6	1107	0.9	1728	5.7	2341	0.6
5	M	0554	5.4	1137	1.2	1816	5.4		
6	TU	0014	1.0	0642	5.1	1203	1.5	1908	5.1
7	W	0043	1.4	0733	4.8	1241	1.9	◑ 2004	4.8
8	TH	0125	1.8	0828	4.5	1343	2.2	2103	4.6
9	F	0233	2.1	0926	4.4	1521	2.3	2207	4.4
10	SA	0409	2.2	1031	4.3	1653	2.2	2319	4.4
11	SU	0521	2.1	1144	4.5	1801	2.0		
12	M	0028	4.6	0613	1.9	1248	4.7	1851	1.7
13	TU	0120	4.8	0655	1.7	1333	4.9	1930	1.5
14	W	0200	5.0	0732	1.5	1410	5.1	2004	1.2
15	TH	0234	5.1	0807	1.3	1444	5.3	● 2037	1.0
16	F	0306	5.3	0843	1.1	1516	5.4	2111	0.9
17	SA	0338	5.3	0919	1.0	1547	5.4	2146	0.8
18	SU	0411	5.4	0954	1.0	1619	5.5	2219	0.8
19	M	0445	5.3	1025	1.1	1653	5.4	2249	0.9
20	TU	0522	5.3	1047	1.2	1729	5.4	2311	1.0
21	W	0601	5.1	1109	1.3	1810	5.3	2338	1.2
22	TH	0645	5.0	1147	1.5	1857	5.1		
23	F	0021	1.5	0736	4.8	1246	1.8	◐ 1954	4.8
24	SA	0129	1.8	0841	4.6	1422	1.9	2110	4.7
25	SU	0323	2.0	1000	4.6	1617	1.9	2236	4.7
26	M	0503	1.8	1118	4.7	1738	1.5	2353	5.0
27	TU	0613	1.6	1225	5.1	1845	1.1		
28	W	0056	5.3	0710	1.2	1320	5.4	1943	0.7

MARCH

Date	Day	Time	m	Time	m	Time	m	Time	m
1	TH	0147	5.6	0800	0.9	1407	5.7	2033	0.4
2	F	0233	5.8	0845	0.7	1451	5.9	○ 2118	0.2
3	SA	0317	5.8	0927	0.6	1535	5.9	2159	0.1
4	SU	0400	5.8	1006	0.6	1619	5.9	2237	0.3
5	M	0442	5.6	1040	0.8	1703	5.7	2310	0.6
6	TU	0524	5.4	1105	1.1	1747	5.4	2333	1.0
7	W	0606	5.1	1123	1.3	1832	5.1	2353	1.4
8	TH	0650	4.8	1155	1.7	1921	4.8		
9	F	0030	1.8	0739	4.5	1246	2.0	◑ 2017	4.5
10	SA	0128	2.2	0835	4.3	1407	2.3	2119	4.2
11	SU	0304	2.4	0939	4.2	1618	2.3	2229	4.2
12	M	0447	2.3	1051	4.2	1737	2.1	2352	4.3
13	TU	0548	2.1	1210	4.5	1829	1.8		
14	W	0052	4.6	0633	1.8	1304	4.8	1908	1.5
15	TH	0133	4.9	0711	1.5	1343	5.0	1943	1.2
16	F	0208	5.1	0747	1.2	1418	5.2	2016	0.9
17	SA	0240	5.3	0823	1.0	1450	5.4	● 2050	0.7
18	SU	0312	5.4	0859	0.8	1522	5.5	2125	0.6
19	M	0345	5.5	0935	0.8	1555	5.6	2200	0.6
20	TU	0420	5.5	1008	0.8	1630	5.6	2231	0.7
21	W	0457	5.4	1033	0.9	1709	5.5	2253	0.9
22	TH	0537	5.3	1055	1.1	1752	5.4	2317	1.2
23	F	0621	5.1	1133	1.3	1841	5.1		
24	SA	0001	1.5	0711	4.8	1236	1.6	◐ 1940	4.9
25	SU	0116	1.9	0817	4.6	1420	1.8	2058	4.6
26	M	0320	2.1	0942	4.5	1612	1.7	2226	4.7
27	TU	0454	1.9	1103	4.7	1733	1.4	2343	4.9
28	W	0600	1.6	1211	5.0	1837	1.0		
29	TH	0044	5.2	0654	1.3	1305	5.3	1929	0.7
30	F	0133	5.4	0740	1.0	1351	5.6	2015	0.4
31	SA	0215	5.6	0823	0.7	1433	5.7	○ 2056	0.3

APRIL

Date	Day	Time	m	Time	m	Time	m	Time	m
1	SU	0256	5.7	0904	0.6	1515	5.8	2134	0.3
2	M	0336	5.6	0941	0.6	1557	5.7	2209	0.5
3	TU	0416	5.5	1014	0.8	1638	5.5	2237	0.8
4	W	0454	5.3	1037	1.0	1719	5.3	2255	1.1
5	TH	0533	5.1	1053	1.2	1800	5.0	2315	1.4
6	F	0612	4.8	1122	1.5	1845	4.7	2349	1.8
7	SA	0657	4.6	1206	1.8	1936	4.4		
8	SU	0041	2.1	0749	4.3	1314	2.1	◑ 2034	4.2
9	M	0202	2.4	0851	4.2	1511	2.3	2139	4.2
10	TU	0402	2.4	1000	4.2	1658	2.1	2252	4.2
11	W	0512	2.2	1113	4.3	1752	1.8		
12	TH	0004	4.5	0600	1.9	1218	4.6	1833	1.5
13	F	0054	4.8	0640	1.5	1305	4.9	1910	1.2
14	SA	0133	5.1	0718	1.2	1344	5.2	1945	0.9
15	SU	0208	5.3	0756	1.0	1420	5.4	2022	0.7
16	M	0243	5.5	0834	0.8	1455	5.6	● 2059	0.5
17	TU	0319	5.6	0913	0.6	1531	5.7	2137	0.5
18	W	0355	5.6	0951	0.6	1610	5.7	2213	0.6
19	TH	0434	5.5	1028	0.7	1652	5.6	2247	0.9
20	F	0516	5.4	1104	0.9	1738	5.4	2320	1.2
21	SA	0603	5.2	1150	1.2	1831	5.2		
22	SU	0011	1.6	0656	4.9	1257	1.4	◐ 1933	4.9
23	M	0133	1.9	0805	4.7	1428	1.6	2052	4.7
24	TU	0312	2.0	0929	4.6	1603	1.5	2213	4.7
25	W	0434	1.9	1045	4.8	1718	1.3	2326	4.9
26	TH	0537	1.6	1151	5.0	1818	1.0		
27	F	0026	5.1	0629	1.4	1245	5.2	1908	0.8
28	SA	0114	5.3	0715	1.1	1331	5.4	1951	0.6
29	SU	0155	5.4	0758	0.9	1413	5.5	2029	0.5
30	M	0234	5.5	0838	0.7	1455	5.6	○ 2105	0.6

Chart Datum: 2·90 metres below Ordnance Datum (Newlyn). HAT is 6·3 metres above Chart Datum.

STANDARD TIME (UT)
For Summer Time add ONE hour in **non-shaded areas**

LEITH LAT 55°59′N LONG 3°11′W

TIMES AND HEIGHTS OF HIGH AND LOW WATERS

Dates in red are SPRINGS
Dates in blue are NEAPS

YEAR **2018**

MAY

Date	Day	Time	m	Time	m	Time	m	Time	m
1	TU	0312	5.5	0915	0.7	1535	5.5	2137	0.7
2	W	0350	5.4	0948	0.8	1615	5.4	2203	0.9
3	TH	0427	5.2	1013	1.0	1654	5.2	2223	1.2
4	F	0503	5.1	1034	1.2	1733	5.0	2247	1.5
5	SA	0540	4.9	1102	1.4	1815	4.8	2321	1.7
6	SU	0622	4.7	1143	1.7	1901	4.5		
7	M	0008	2.0	0710	4.5	1240	1.9	1953	4.4
8	TU	0117	2.3	0807	4.3	1356	2.1	◑ 2053	4.3
9	W	0251	2.4	0912	4.3	1548	2.0	2158	4.3
10	TH	0420	2.2	1019	4.4	1658	1.8	2304	4.5
11	F	0516	1.9	1123	4.6	1746	1.5		
12	SA	0003	4.8	0601	1.6	1219	4.8	1827	1.2
13	SU	0052	5.0	0642	1.3	1305	5.1	1908	1.0
14	M	0134	5.3	0724	1.0	1347	5.4	1949	0.7
15	TU	0214	5.5	0806	0.8	1427	5.6	● 2032	0.6
16	W	0253	5.6	0851	0.6	1509	5.7	2116	0.6
17	TH	0333	5.7	0937	0.5	1553	5.8	2200	0.7
18	F	0415	5.6	1024	0.6	1639	5.7	2245	0.9
19	SA	0501	5.5	1112	0.7	1729	5.5	2332	1.2
20	SU	0550	5.3	1205	0.9	1824	5.3		
21	M	0025	1.5	0647	5.1	1306	1.2	1927	5.0
22	TU	0131	1.8	0756	4.9	1421	1.3	◐ 2040	4.8
23	W	0249	1.9	0912	4.8	1541	1.3	2153	4.8
24	TH	0402	1.9	1022	4.9	1651	1.3	2300	4.9
25	F	0504	1.7	1126	5.0	1751	1.2		
26	SA	0000	5.0	0558	1.5	1222	5.1	1840	1.1
27	SU	0051	5.1	0647	1.3	1311	5.2	1922	1.0
28	M	0134	5.2	0731	1.1	1355	5.3	1959	0.9
29	TU	0213	5.3	0812	1.0	1437	5.3	○ 2033	0.9
30	W	0251	5.3	0850	0.9	1516	5.3	2104	1.0
31	TH	0328	5.3	0924	1.0	1555	5.2	2132	1.1

JUNE

Date	Day	Time	m	Time	m	Time	m	Time	m
1	F	0403	5.2	0953	1.1	1632	5.1	2159	1.3
2	SA	0438	5.1	1020	1.2	1709	5.0	2228	1.4
3	SU	0514	5.0	1051	1.3	1748	4.9	2303	1.6
4	M	0554	4.8	1128	1.5	1831	4.7	2345	1.9
5	TU	0638	4.7	1215	1.7	1918	4.5		
6	W	0040	2.1	0727	4.5	1313	1.8	◑ 2011	4.4
7	TH	0151	2.2	0824	4.5	1424	1.9	2110	4.4
8	F	0312	2.2	0928	4.5	1545	1.8	2213	4.5
9	SA	0422	2.0	1033	4.6	1651	1.6	2315	4.7
10	SU	0517	1.7	1133	4.8	1743	1.3		
11	M	0011	5.0	0605	1.4	1228	5.1	1830	1.1
12	TU	0101	5.3	0653	1.1	1318	5.4	1919	0.9
13	W	0147	5.5	0742	0.8	1405	5.6	● 2009	0.7
14	TH	0230	5.6	0834	0.6	1451	5.8	2100	0.7
15	F	0314	5.7	0927	0.4	1539	5.8	2150	0.7
16	SA	0400	5.7	1019	0.4	1628	5.8	2239	0.9
17	SU	0448	5.7	1110	0.5	1719	5.6	2327	1.1
18	M	0539	5.5	1201	0.6	1814	5.4		
19	TU	0017	1.4	0636	5.3	1256	0.9	1914	5.2
20	W	0111	1.6	0741	5.1	1357	1.1	◐ 2019	5.0
21	TH	0214	1.8	0849	5.0	1505	1.3	2124	4.8
22	F	0322	1.9	0954	4.9	1613	1.4	2227	4.8
23	SA	0427	1.9	1056	4.9	1715	1.4	2328	4.8
24	SU	0527	1.7	1156	4.9	1808	1.4		
25	M	0024	4.9	0620	1.6	1251	5.0	1851	1.4
26	TU	0113	5.0	0708	1.4	1338	5.1	1928	1.3
27	W	0155	5.1	0750	1.2	1421	5.1	2002	1.2
28	TH	0233	5.2	0828	1.1	1500	5.2	○ 2035	1.2
29	F	0309	5.2	0902	1.1	1536	5.2	2107	1.2
30	SA	0343	5.2	0934	1.0	1611	5.1	2139	1.3

JULY

Date	Day	Time	m	Time	m	Time	m	Time	m
1	SU	0417	5.2	1005	1.1	1646	5.1	2213	1.3
2	M	0452	5.1	1038	1.2	1723	5.0	2247	1.5
3	TU	0529	5.0	1113	1.3	1802	4.9	2323	1.6
4	W	0608	4.9	1152	1.4	1845	4.8		
5	TH	0004	1.8	0651	4.8	1236	1.6	1932	4.7
6	F	0058	2.0	0740	4.7	1330	1.7	◑ 2026	4.6
7	SA	0207	2.1	0837	4.6	1437	1.7	2128	4.6
8	SU	0325	2.0	0945	4.7	1554	1.7	2232	4.7
9	M	0435	1.8	1053	4.8	1704	1.5	2335	4.9
10	TU	0535	1.6	1157	5.0	1804	1.3		
11	W	0032	5.2	0630	1.2	1255	5.3	1859	1.1
12	TH	0124	5.4	0727	0.9	1347	5.6	1955	0.9
13	F	0212	5.6	0824	0.6	1437	5.8	● 2049	0.7
14	SA	0259	5.8	0919	0.3	1526	5.9	2139	0.7
15	SU	0346	5.9	1011	0.2	1615	5.9	2227	0.7
16	M	0434	5.8	1059	0.2	1705	5.8	2313	0.9
17	TU	0525	5.7	1147	0.4	1757	5.5	2356	1.2
18	W	0618	5.5	1233	0.7	1851	5.3		
19	TH	0039	1.4	0716	5.3	1322	1.1	◐ 1949	5.0
20	F	0128	1.7	0818	5.0	1416	1.4	2048	4.8
21	SA	0231	2.0	0920	4.8	1524	1.7	2149	4.6
22	SU	0347	2.0	1023	4.7	1634	1.8	2251	4.6
23	M	0458	2.0	1128	4.7	1734	1.8	2355	4.7
24	TU	0601	1.8	1230	4.8	1822	1.7		
25	W	0051	4.9	0652	1.6	1323	4.9	1901	1.6
26	TH	0138	5.0	0734	1.4	1406	5.0	1936	1.4
27	F	0217	5.1	0810	1.2	1443	5.1	○ 2011	1.3
28	SA	0251	5.2	0843	1.1	1517	5.2	2046	1.2
29	SU	0324	5.3	0916	1.0	1549	5.2	2121	1.2
30	M	0356	5.3	0949	0.9	1622	5.2	2156	1.2
31	TU	0430	5.3	1023	1.0	1657	5.2	2229	1.3

AUGUST

Date	Day	Time	m	Time	m	Time	m	Time	m
1	W	0504	5.2	1055	1.0	1734	5.1	2300	1.4
2	TH	0540	5.2	1126	1.2	1813	5.0	2327	1.6
3	F	0619	5.0	1157	1.3	1857	4.9		
4	SA	0002	1.7	0703	4.9	1238	1.5	◑ 1946	4.7
5	SU	0100	1.9	0756	4.8	1338	1.7	2045	4.7
6	M	0226	2.0	0903	4.7	1504	1.8	2155	4.7
7	TU	0400	1.9	1021	4.7	1639	1.7	2306	4.8
8	W	0515	1.7	1134	5.0	1750	1.5		
9	TH	0010	5.1	0619	1.3	1239	5.3	1849	1.3
10	F	0107	5.4	0720	0.9	1334	5.6	1944	1.0
11	SA	0157	5.7	0817	0.5	1424	5.8	● 2036	0.8
12	SU	0243	5.9	0909	0.2	1511	6.0	2124	0.6
13	M	0329	6.0	0957	0.0	1558	6.0	2209	0.6
14	TU	0416	6.0	1042	0.1	1645	5.8	2251	0.7
15	W	0503	5.9	1124	0.3	1732	5.6	2329	1.0
16	TH	0553	5.6	1202	0.7	1821	5.3		
17	F	0002	1.3	0645	5.3	1238	1.2	1912	5.0
18	SA	0036	1.7	0742	5.0	1315	1.6	◐ 2007	4.7
19	SU	0130	2.0	0842	4.7	1414	2.0	2106	4.5
20	M	0259	2.2	0946	4.5	1545	2.2	2209	4.4
21	TU	0435	2.2	1056	4.5	1702	2.1	2319	4.5
22	W	0548	2.0	1208	4.6	1758	2.0		
23	TH	0027	4.7	0641	1.7	1305	4.8	1839	1.8
24	F	0117	4.9	0720	1.5	1347	5.0	1916	1.6
25	SA	0156	5.1	0753	1.2	1422	5.1	1951	1.3
26	SU	0230	5.3	0824	1.0	1454	5.3	○ 2026	1.2
27	M	0301	5.4	0856	0.9	1525	5.3	2102	1.0
28	TU	0333	5.4	0929	0.8	1557	5.4	2137	1.0
29	W	0405	5.5	1002	0.8	1630	5.4	2209	1.1
30	TH	0438	5.4	1032	0.9	1706	5.3	2234	1.2
31	F	0512	5.4	1055	1.0	1743	5.2	2254	1.4

Chart Datum: 2·90 metres below Ordnance Datum (Newlyn). HAT is 6·3 metres above Chart Datum.

STANDARD TIME (UT)
For Summer Time add ONE hour in **non-shaded areas**

LEITH LAT 55°59′N LONG 3°11′W

TIMES AND HEIGHTS OF HIGH AND LOW WATERS

Dates in red are SPRINGS
Dates in blue are NEAPS

YEAR **2018**

SEPTEMBER

Date	Day	Time	m	Time	m	Time	m	Time	m
1	SA	0551	5.2	1117	1.2	1825	5.0	2325	1.5
2	SU	0635	5.1	1153	1.5	1912	4.9		
3	M	0015	1.8	0728	4.9	1252	1.8	◑ 2010	4.7
4	TU	0144	2.0	0836	4.7	1434	2.0	2124	4.6
5	W	0341	2.0	1001	4.7	1628	2.0	2244	4.7
6	TH	0508	1.7	1121	4.9	1742	1.7	2354	5.0
7	F	0615	1.2	1227	5.2	1840	1.4		
8	SA	0051	5.4	0713	0.8	1322	5.6	1931	1.0
9	SU	0140	5.7	0805	0.4	1408	5.8	● 2018	0.8
10	M	0225	5.9	0852	0.1	1452	5.9	2103	0.6
11	TU	0309	6.1	0936	0.0	1536	5.9	2146	0.6
12	W	0354	6.0	1017	0.2	1620	5.8	2225	0.7
13	TH	0439	5.9	1055	0.5	1704	5.6	2258	1.0
14	F	0525	5.6	1126	0.9	1748	5.3	2322	1.3
15	SA	0613	5.3	1148	1.3	1834	5.0	2347	1.6
16	SU	0705	4.9	1217	1.8	1925	4.7	◐	
17	M	0034	2.0	0803	4.6	1310	2.2	2022	4.5
18	TU	0155	2.3	0905	4.4	1442	2.5	2125	4.3
19	W	0411	2.3	1015	4.3	1631	2.4	2235	4.4
20	TH	0529	2.1	1136	4.4	1733	2.2	2351	4.6
21	F	0620	1.8	1238	4.7	1817	1.9		
22	SA	0047	4.9	0657	1.5	1321	5.0	1854	1.6
23	SU	0128	5.1	0729	1.2	1355	5.2	1929	1.4
24	M	0202	5.3	0759	1.0	1426	5.3	2004	1.1
25	TU	0234	5.4	0831	0.8	1457	5.5	○ 2039	1.0
26	W	0305	5.5	0904	0.7	1529	5.5	2114	0.9
27	TH	0338	5.6	0936	0.7	1603	5.5	2146	0.9
28	F	0412	5.6	1005	0.8	1638	5.5	2212	1.0
29	SA	0448	5.5	1026	1.0	1716	5.3	2233	1.2
30	SU	0529	5.4	1048	1.2	1757	5.2	2305	1.4

OCTOBER

Date	Day	Time	m	Time	m	Time	m	Time	m
1	M	0616	5.2	1126	1.6	1845	4.9	2359	1.7
2	TU	0711	4.9	1229	1.9	1945	4.7	◑	
3	W	0140	1.9	0822	4.7	1434	2.2	2104	4.6
4	TH	0336	1.9	0949	4.7	1619	2.1	2227	4.8
5	F	0502	1.6	1109	4.9	1729	1.8	2338	5.1
6	SA	0606	1.2	1214	5.3	1824	1.5		
7	SU	0034	5.4	0700	0.8	1306	5.6	1911	1.1
8	M	0122	5.7	0747	0.5	1350	5.8	1956	0.9
9	TU	0205	5.9	0831	0.3	1431	5.9	● 2039	0.7
10	W	0248	6.0	0912	0.3	1512	5.8	2120	0.6
11	TH	0331	5.9	0949	0.4	1553	5.7	2158	0.8
12	F	0415	5.8	1023	0.7	1635	5.5	2228	1.0
13	SA	0459	5.5	1046	1.1	1715	5.3	2247	1.3
14	SU	0544	5.2	1102	1.5	1757	5.0	2311	1.6
15	M	0631	4.9	1132	1.9	1843	4.7	2353	1.9
16	TU	0724	4.6	1221	2.2	1937	4.5	◐	
17	W	0059	2.2	0823	4.3	1339	2.6	2039	4.4
18	TH	0318	2.4	0928	4.3	1546	2.6	2146	4.3
19	F	0451	2.2	1041	4.3	1657	2.4	2258	4.5
20	SA	0542	1.9	1153	4.6	1745	2.0		
21	SU	0002	4.7	0621	1.6	1241	4.9	1824	1.7
22	M	0049	5.0	0655	1.3	1318	5.2	1900	1.4
23	TU	0127	5.3	0727	1.1	1353	5.4	1936	1.2
24	W	0202	5.4	0800	0.9	1427	5.5	○ 2012	1.0
25	TH	0236	5.6	0834	0.7	1501	5.6	2048	0.9
26	F	0311	5.7	0908	0.7	1536	5.7	2124	0.9
27	SA	0348	5.7	0941	0.8	1613	5.6	2159	0.9
28	SU	0429	5.6	1009	1.0	1652	5.5	2232	1.1
29	M	0513	5.5	1038	1.3	1736	5.3	2314	1.3
30	TU	0603	5.3	1123	1.7	1827	5.1		
31	W	0021	1.6	0701	5.0	1246	2.0	◑ 1928	4.8

NOVEMBER

Date	Day	Time	m	Time	m	Time	m	Time	m
1	TH	0148	1.7	0814	4.8	1429	2.2	2049	4.7
2	F	0326	1.7	0937	4.8	1559	2.1	2210	4.8
3	SA	0445	1.4	1052	5.0	1706	1.9	2318	5.1
4	SU	0547	1.2	1155	5.2	1800	1.6		
5	M	0014	5.4	0639	0.9	1247	5.4	1847	1.3
6	TU	0103	5.6	0725	0.7	1330	5.6	1932	1.0
7	W	0146	5.7	0806	0.6	1410	5.7	● 2015	0.9
8	TH	0229	5.8	0844	0.6	1450	5.7	2056	0.8
9	F	0311	5.7	0919	0.8	1529	5.6	2133	0.9
10	SA	0354	5.6	0949	1.0	1608	5.5	2202	1.1
11	SU	0436	5.4	1009	1.3	1646	5.3	2224	1.3
12	M	0517	5.1	1030	1.6	1725	5.1	2249	1.5
13	TU	0601	4.9	1101	1.9	1807	4.8	2327	1.8
14	W	0648	4.6	1145	2.2	1855	4.6		
15	TH	0021	2.0	0740	4.4	1249	2.5	◐ 1952	4.5
16	F	0135	2.2	0839	4.3	1421	2.6	2056	4.4
17	SA	0340	2.2	0942	4.4	1602	2.5	2202	4.5
18	SU	0449	2.0	1047	4.5	1700	2.2	2305	4.6
19	M	0534	1.7	1147	4.8	1746	1.9		
20	TU	0000	4.9	0613	1.5	1235	5.1	1826	1.6
21	W	0048	5.1	0650	1.2	1317	5.3	1905	1.3
22	TH	0129	5.4	0727	1.0	1356	5.5	1945	1.1
23	F	0209	5.6	0805	0.9	1434	5.7	○ 2025	0.9
24	SA	0249	5.7	0845	0.8	1512	5.7	2109	0.8
25	SU	0330	5.8	0927	0.9	1552	5.7	2154	0.8
26	M	0414	5.7	1010	1.1	1635	5.6	2242	0.9
27	TU	0502	5.6	1056	1.3	1721	5.4	2334	1.1
28	W	0554	5.4	1148	1.6	1814	5.2		
29	TH	0032	1.3	0652	5.1	1252	1.9	1916	5.0
30	F	0141	1.4	0802	4.9	1407	2.1	◑ 2032	4.9

DECEMBER

Date	Day	Time	m	Time	m	Time	m	Time	m
1	SA	0301	1.5	0917	4.9	1525	2.1	2147	4.9
2	SU	0416	1.4	1027	4.9	1633	2.0	2253	5.1
3	M	0520	1.3	1129	5.1	1731	1.7	2352	5.2
4	TU	0615	1.2	1223	5.2	1823	1.5		
5	W	0043	5.3	0700	1.1	1310	5.4	1910	1.3
6	TH	0131	5.4	0740	1.0	1352	5.4	1954	1.1
7	F	0214	5.5	0817	1.0	1432	5.5	● 2035	1.0
8	SA	0257	5.5	0850	1.1	1510	5.5	2112	1.1
9	SU	0337	5.4	0918	1.2	1547	5.4	2142	1.1
10	M	0416	5.3	0944	1.4	1623	5.3	2208	1.3
11	TU	0454	5.1	1010	1.5	1658	5.1	2236	1.4
12	W	0533	5.0	1042	1.7	1737	5.0	2310	1.6
13	TH	0615	4.8	1121	1.9	1819	4.8	2353	1.8
14	F	0701	4.6	1209	2.2	1908	4.7		
15	SA	0046	1.9	0752	4.5	1315	2.4	◐ 2003	4.5
16	SU	0153	2.1	0849	4.4	1438	2.4	2105	4.5
17	M	0317	2.0	0951	4.5	1559	2.3	2210	4.6
18	TU	0432	1.9	1053	4.7	1659	2.1	2312	4.7
19	W	0526	1.7	1151	4.9	1749	1.8		
20	TH	0008	5.0	0613	1.4	1243	5.2	1835	1.5
21	F	0059	5.2	0658	1.2	1329	5.4	1920	1.2
22	SA	0146	5.5	0743	1.0	1411	5.6	○ 2009	0.9
23	SU	0231	5.7	0831	0.9	1453	5.7	2059	0.7
24	M	0316	5.8	0920	0.9	1536	5.8	2151	0.6
25	TU	0403	5.8	1009	1.0	1622	5.8	2242	0.6
26	W	0451	5.7	1057	1.1	1710	5.7	2332	0.7
27	TH	0543	5.6	1145	1.4	1802	5.5		
28	F	0024	0.9	0638	5.3	1235	1.6	1900	5.3
29	SA	0120	1.2	0741	5.1	1333	1.9	◑ 2009	5.1
30	SU	0224	1.4	0848	4.9	1441	2.0	2118	5.0
31	M	0336	1.5	0954	4.8	1552	2.0	2224	4.9

Chart Datum: 2·90 metres below Ordnance Datum (Newlyn). HAT is 6·3 metres above Chart Datum.

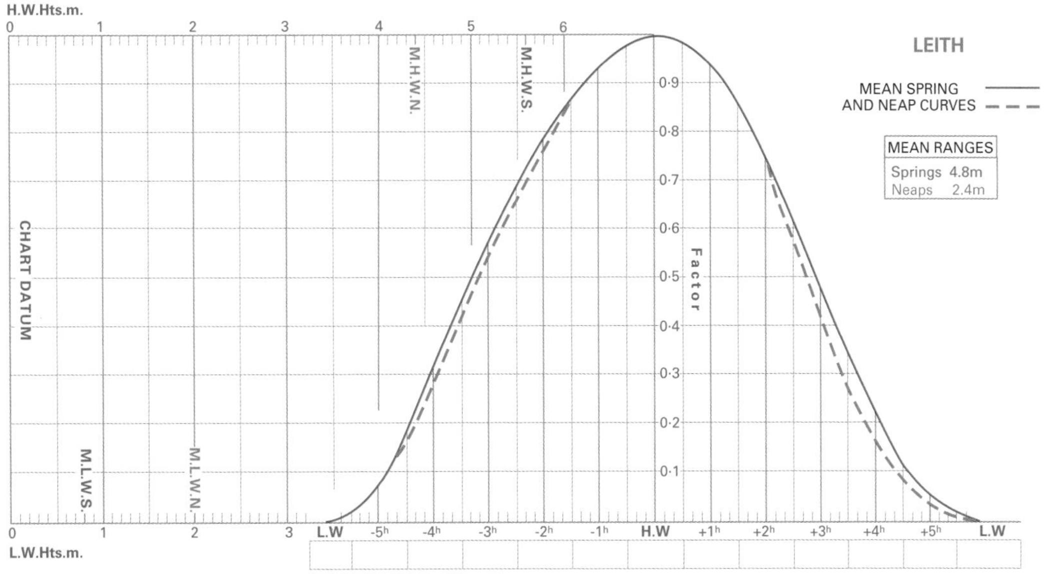

9.6.10 ANSTRUTHER

Fife **56°13′·15N 02°41′·82W**

CHARTS AC 175, 734, 5615; Imray C24, C23, C27

TIDES +0315 Dover; ML 3·1; Duration 0620

Standard Port LEITH (⟵)

Times				Height (metres)			
High Water		Low Water		MHWS	MHWN	MLWN	MLWS
0300	0900	0300	0900	5·6	4·4	2·0	0·8
1500	2100	1500	2100				
Differences ANSTRUTHER EASTER							
–0018	–0012	–0006	–0008	–0·3	–0·2	0·0	0·0

SHELTER Good, but dangerous to enter in strong E to S winds. Hbr dries, soft mud. Pontoon berths for bilge keel craft only.

NAVIGATION WPT 56°12′·59N 02°42′·20W, 019° to ent, 0·60M. Beware FVs and creels in the area. Do not go N of W Pier Lt due to rks extending N & W across the mouth of Dreel Burn.

LIGHTS AND MARKS Conspic tr on W pier. Ldg lts 019°, both FG 7/11m 4M. Pier lts as chartlet. Horn (3) 60s in conspic tr.

COMMUNICATIONS (Code 01333) CGOC 450666; Police: 101, Dr 310352; Ⓗ St Andrews 01334 472327, Kirkaldy 01592 643355; ⊖ 0800 595000. HM 310836 (HO).

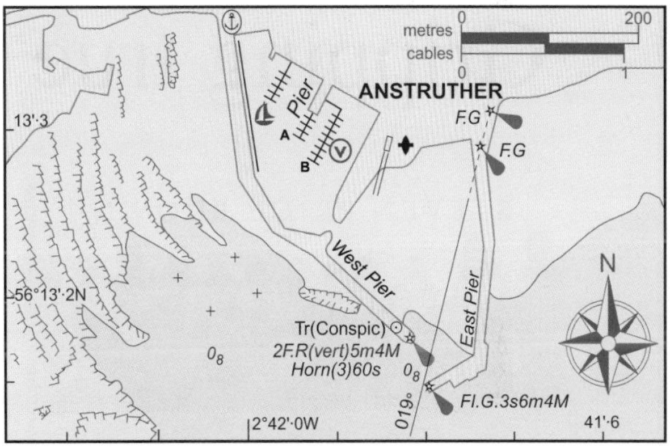

Anstruther Hbr VHF Ch 11 16 (HO) or Forth CG 16 (OT).

FACILITIES Harbour: wall 22+8Ⓥ <10m LOA: entry £16·00 then £8/day; pontoons (no fin keels, 100+8Ⓥ check availability with HM) 1st night £23·90, then £13·70 per day; 0800-2100; **Services** (tanker ☎730622) Ⓔ (☎311459) ACA.

Town (☎01383 622444), SC (08456 0057023492) Ⓑ (bus Cupar or Leuchars) ✈(Edinburgh/Dundee).

ADJACENT HARBOURS AND ANCHORAGE

PITTENWEEM, Fife, **56°12′·60N 02°43′·79W**. AC 734. HW +0325 Dover; –0015 and –0·1m on Leith; ML 3m; Duration 0620. Busy fishing hbr, dredged 1-2m, access all tides, but seek advice before entering at LW springs. Yachts not encouraged; contact HM for berth at W end of inner hbr, but only for emergency use. Outer hbr dries to rock; is only suitable for temp stop in calm weather. Appr 037° on ldg marks/lts, W cols, both FR 3/8m 5M. Rks to port marked by bn, Fl R 4s 3m 2M, and 3 unlit bns. VHF Ch 11 (0700-2100 Mon-Fri) or Forth CG Ch 16 (other times). HM ☎(01333) 312591. Facilities: (tanker: ☎730622).

CRAIL, Fife, **56°15′·35N 02°37′·29W**. AC 175. HW +0320 on Dover, –0020 on Leith; HW–0·2m on Leith; ML 3·0m; Duration 0615. Good shelter for boats able to take the ground, but limited manoeuvring area. Appr between S pier and bn on rks to S following ldg line 295°, two W concrete pillars with FR lts, 24/30m 6M. Turn 150° to stbd for ent. Call Forth CG before entering. Beware FVs and creel ends. HM ☎07540 672809 (part-time, Mon-Fri). Facilities: , entry £16·00/craft then £8/day, . **Village** Ⓑ.

ISLE OF MAY, Fife, 56°11′·40N 02°33′·69W. AC 734. HW +0325 on Dover, –0025 on Leith. In settled weather only, and depending on the wind, ⚓ at E or W Tarbert in 4m; landing at Altarstanes. Near the SE tip there is a tiny hbr at Kirkhaven, with narrow, rky ent; yachts can moor fore-and-aft to rings in rks, in about 1-1·5m. SDs are needed. Beware Norman Rk to N of Island, and Maiden Hair Rk to S. At the summit, a 3 tr on stone ho, Fl (2) 15s 73m 22M. The island is a National Nature Reserve managed by Scottish National Heritage (☎01334 654038). It is a bird/seal colony sanctuary. **Sensitive seasons**: (a) breeding birds Apr to Sep; (b) breeding seals Oct to Jan; (c) moulting seals Jan to Mar. Land only at Alterstanes or (where restrictions may apply) Kirkhaven. Warden in residence Easter to end October when visitor centre open 1000-1730 BST. Contact on VHF Ch 16 or 6, or on first landing. No overnight accommodation or camping. Avoid marked out areas to minimise disturbance to wildlife and ongoing conservation experiments.

FIFE NESS TO MONTROSE

(AC 190) Fife Ness is fringed by rocky ledges, and a reef extends 1M NE to N Carr Rk (dries 1·4m, marked by bn). In strong onshore winds keep to seaward of N Carr ECM lit buoy. From here keep 5ca offshore to clear dangers entering St Andrews Bay ⚓; the little harbour dries, and should not be approached in onshore winds.

Northward from Firth of Forth to Rattray Head the coast is mostly rocky and steep-to, and there are no out-lying dangers within 2M of the coast except those off the River Tay and Bell Rock. In an onshore blow there are few safe havens; both yachts and crews need to be prepared for offshore cruising rather than coast-crawling.

The **River Tay** (AC 1481) is approached from the NE via Fairway buoy; it is dangerous to cut corners from the S. The Bar, NE of Abertay lt buoy, is dangerous in heavy weather, particularly in strong onshore wind or swell. Abertay Sands extend nearly 4M East of Tentsmuir Point on the South side of the buoyed chan. Elbow is a shoal extension eastward. Gaa Sands, running 1¾M East from Buddon Ness, are marked by Abertay lit buoy (Racon) on the North side of the channel. Passage across Abertay and Gaa Sands is very dangerous. The estuary is shallow, with many shifting sandbanks.

Tayport is a good passage stop and although it dries, is the best yacht harbour in the Tay.

▶ *2M E of Bell Rk the S-going stream begins HW Aberdeen –0220, and the N-going at HW Aberdeen +0405, Sp rates 1kn. W of Bell Rock the streams begin earlier.* ◀

Bell Rock (Fl 5s 28m 18M, Racon(M)) lies 11½M E of Buddon Ness.

▶ *S of Buddon Ness the W-going (flood) stream begins about HW Aberdeen –0400, and the E-going at about HW Aberdeen +0230, Sp rates 2kn.* ◀

N from Buddon Ness the coast is sandy. 1·25M SW of Arbroath beware Elliot Horses, rocky patches, which extend about 5ca offshore with with min depth 1·9m. Between Whiting Ness and Scurdie Ness, 9·5M NNE, the coast is clear of out-lying dangers, but is mostly fringed with drying rocks up to 1ca off. In offshore winds there is temp ⚓ in SW of Lunan B, off Ethie Haven.

Scurdie Ness (Fl(3) 20s 38m 23M, Racon T) is conspicuous on S side of entrance to Montrose. Scurdie Rks (dry) extend 2ca E of the Ness. On N side of the channel Annat Bank dries up to about 5ca East of the shore, opposite Scurdie Ness (AC 1438).

▶ *The in-going stream begins at HW Aberdeen –0500, and the out-going at HW Aberdeen +0115;* ***both streams are very strong, up to 7kn at sp,*** *and there is turbulence off the ent on the ebb. The ent is dangerous in strong onshore winds, with breaking seas extending to Scurdie Ness on the ebb. In marginal conditions the last quarter of the flood is best time to enter.* ◀

9.6.11 RIVER TAY

Fife/Angus Tayport **(56°27'·10N 02°52'·87W)**

CHARTS AC 190, 1481, 5617; Imray C23

TIDES +0401 (Dundee) Dover; ML 3·1; Duration 0610

Standard Port ABERDEEN (⟶)

Times				Height (metres)			
High Water		Low Water		MHWS	MHWN	MLWN	MLWS
0000	0600	0100	0700	4·3	3·4	1·6	0·6
1200	1800	1300	1900				
Differences BAR							
+0100	+0100	+0050	+0110	+0·9	+0·8	+0·3	+0·1
DUNDEE							
+0140	+0120	+0055	+0145	+1·2	+1·0	+0·5	+0·4
NEWBURGH							
+0215	+0200	+0250	+0335	–0·2	–0·4	–1·1	–0·5
PERTH							
+0220	+0225	+0510	+0530	–0·9	–1·4	–1·2	–0·3

NOTE: At Perth LW time differences give the start of the rise, following a LW stand of about 4 hours.

SHELTER Good in Tay Estuary, but entrance is dangerous in strong E/SE winds or onshore swell. **Tayport** dredged to 0.6m below CD, best for yachts on passage; keels sink into soft mud; ⚓ on S side. **Dundee** – commercial port. Possible ⚓ at Royal Tay YC or ⚓ off. The city is exposed/landing difficult. Good shelter at Woodhaven and Ⓜs from Wormit BC. There are other ⚓s up-river at Balmerino, Newburgh and Inchyra. Upriver 4M below Perth ⚓ in scenic mouth of R Earn crossing bar at half/full tide.

NAVIGATION WPT Tay Fairway SWM buoy, 56°28'·30N 02°36'·60W, 239°/1M to Middle Bar buoys. Chan is well buoyed, least depth 5·2m. Keep N of Larick, a conspic disused lt bn.

> Beware strong tidal streams. No passage across Abertay or Gaa Sands; charted depths are unreliable.

LIGHTS AND MARKS See 9.6.4 and chartlet. 'Abertay' ECM buoy (Racon), at E end of Gaa Sands is a clear visual mark.

COMMUNICATIONS (Code 01382) CGOC (01224) 592334; Forth and Tay Navigation Service (01324) 498584; HM (Dundee) 224121; HM (Perth) (01738) 624056. Police 101; Dr 221976; ⊕ 660111.

Forth & Tay Navigation Service VHF Ch **71**; *Dundee Hbr Radio* VHF Ch **12** 16 (H24); nav warnings, weather, vis and tides on request. Royal Tay YC, Ch M.

FACILITIES

N BANK: Royal Tay YC (Broughty Ferry) ☎477516, Ⓜs free, ✕ 🍺.
Services (2t) ACA.
Dundee City ⓟ ⓓ ✉ Ⓑ ✕ 🍺 ⇌ ✈.

Tayport Hbr Tayport Hbr Trust, (phil.tayportharbour@gmail.com) Berthing Master 553799; Access HW±4, ent chan dredged 0.8m below CD. SWM at edge of chan 100m from hbr; ldg marks (185°) R △ on slipway and post. R/W post, lit FL R 5s on East wall. W Inner wall G/W post, lit Fl G 5s. Ent walls painted W for better visibility. (88 + 7Ⓥ on walls) £18/day; ✉ Ⓑ ✕(hbr cafe) 🍺(Bell Rock Tavern) bus to St Andrews/Dundee for ⇌.

Wormit Boating Club ☎541400 Ⓜs free.

ADJACENT HARBOURS

PERTH, Perth & Kinross, **56°22'·89N 03°25'·74W**. AC 1481; OS 53, 58. Tides, see 9.6.12. FYCA Pilot Handbook needed. Leave Tay Rly bridge about HW Dundee –2 to carry the tide for 16·5M to Perth. Keep clear of coasters which travel at speed and are constrained by their draught. Lit chan favours S bank for 9M to Newburgh. ⚓ to N of chan at W of town in 2m, use piers with caution. Care is required due to mudbanks mid-stream; keep S of Mugdrum Is. Upriver, power cables clearance 33m and Friarton Bridge 26m. Keep S of Willow Is, past gasworks to Hbr on W bank. Hbr has approx 1·5m. See HM, ☎(01738) 624056, for berth. VHF Ch 09 16. ⓟ ⓓ all city amenities, ⇌ ✈.

ST ANDREWS, Fife, **56°20'·32N 02°46'·79W**. AC 190. HW –0015 Leith. Small drying hbr 7M S of Tay Estuary /8M NW of Fife Ness. In strong onshore winds breaking seas render appr/ent impossible. Appr near HW on 270°, N bkwtr bn in transit with cathedral twr; Dir Iso WRG 2s (277·5°) on lookout bldg. Recce by dinghy is useful. Best water is about 10m S of the bkwtr; 8m wide ent to inner hbr (drying 2·5m) has lock gates, usually open, and sliding footbridge, which opens on req to HM (07506 409792 – call in advance) or berth temp'ly on W side. Gates shut on some HW Sp to hold back water. Facilities: SC; all amenities of university town, inc golf course.

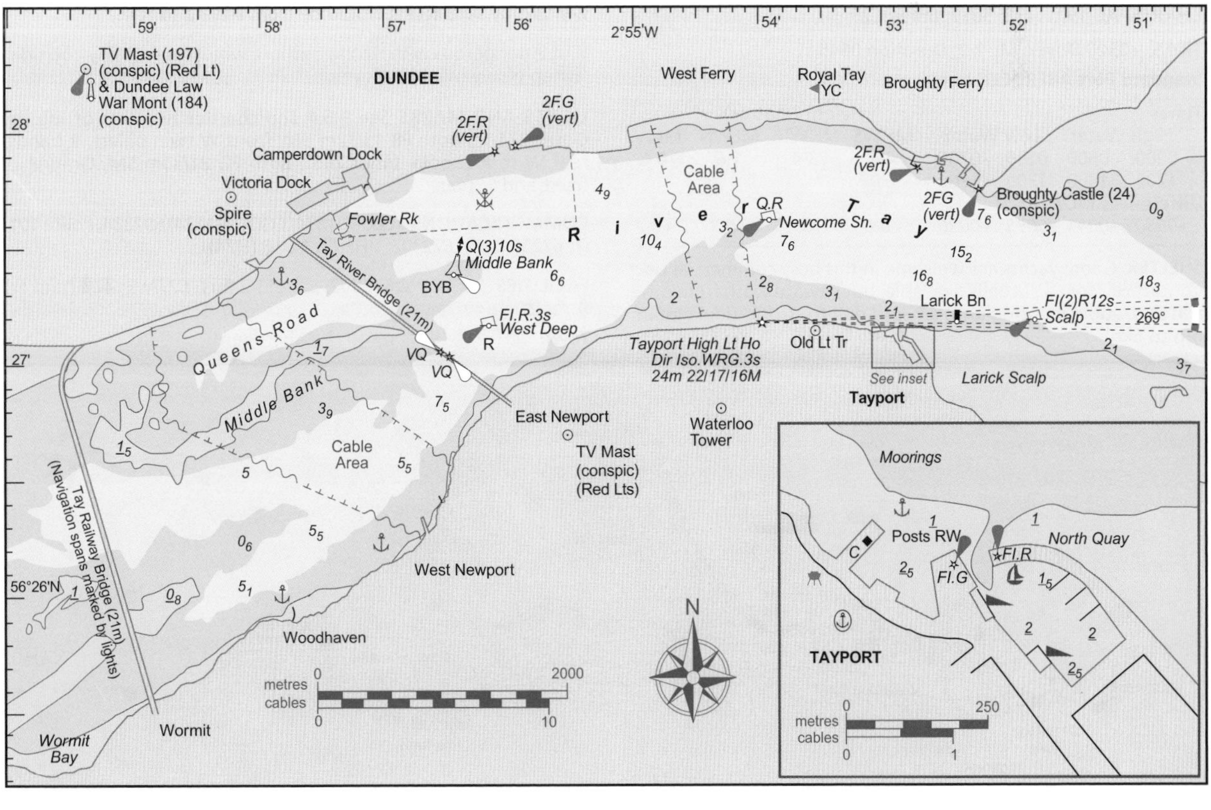

9.6.12 ARBROATH

Angus **56°33'·22N 02°34'·99W**

CHARTS AC 190, 1438, 5617; Imray C23

TIDES +0317 Dover; ML 2·9; Duration 0620

Standard Port ABERDEEN (⟶)

Times				**Height (metres)**			
High Water		Low Water		MHWS	MHWN	MLWN	MLWS
0000	0600	0100	0700	4·3	3·4	1·6	0·6
1200	1800	1300	1900				
Differences ARBROATH							
+0056	+0037	+0034	+0055	+1·0	+0·8	+0·4	+0·2

SHELTER Good, especially in Inner Basin with lock gates, afloat pontoon berths with 2.5m depth maintained. Ent can be dangerous in moderate SE swell. Inside the entrance, turn to starboard and then to starboard again. HM manned 0700 - 2000 (2200 on selected weekends), during which time lock opens approx HW±3.

NAVIGATION WPT 56°32´·98N 02°34´·21W, 299°/0·5M to ent.

Entry should not be attempted LW±2½. Beware Knuckle rks to stbd and Cheek Bush rks to port on entering.

LIGHTS AND MARKS Ldg lts 299°, both FR 7/13m 5M, or twin trs of St Thomas' ✠ visible between N pier lt ho and W bkwtr bn. Hbr entry sigs: Fl G 3s on E pier = Entry safe. Same lt shows FR when hbr closed, entry dangerous. Siren (3) 60s at E pier lt is occas, for FVs. Inner Basin Lock Gates, FR = closed, FG = open >2.5m over sill.

COMMUNICATIONS (Code 01241) CGOC (01224) 592334; Police 101; Dr 876836. HM 872166; harbourmaster@angus,gov.uk.

Arbroath Harbour VHF Ch **11** 16.

FACILITIES Inner Basin 59 inc Ⓥ £14·50/craft, Ⓔ. **Pier** £13/craft, (Oil Pier) (8t).
Town Ⓑ ✕ ⇌ ✈ (Dundee).

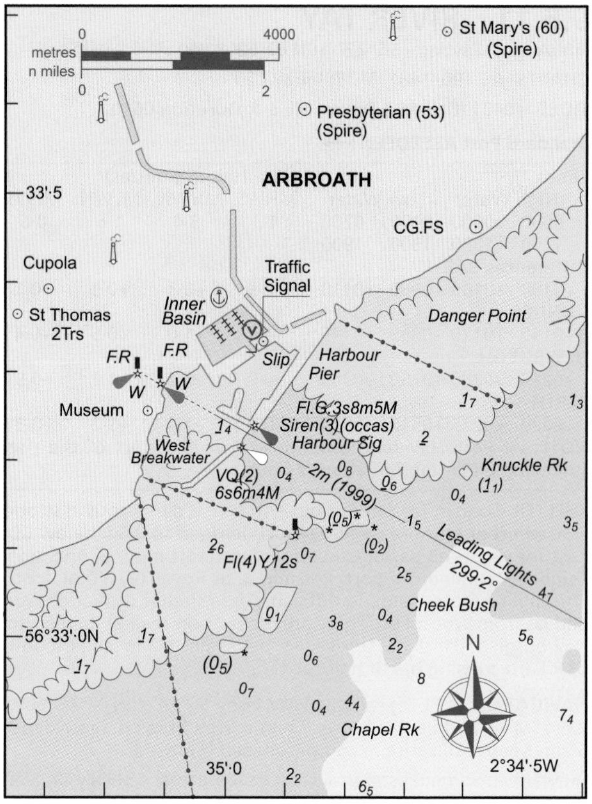

9.6.13 MONTROSE

Angus **56°42'·19N 02°26'·60W**

CHARTS AC 190, 1438, 5617; Imray C23

TIDES +0320 Dover; ML 2·9; Duration 0645

Standard Port ABERDEEN (⟶)

Times				**Height (metres)**			
High Water		Low Water		MHWS	MHWN	MLWN	MLWS
0000	0600	0100	0700	4·3	3·4	1·6	0·6
1200	1800	1300	1900				
Differences *MONTROSE*							
+0050	*+0045*	*+0035*	*+0030*	*+0·6*	*+0·4*	*+0·3*	*+0·2*

SHELTER Good; yachts are welcome in this busy commercial port. Contact HM for , usually available, but beware wash from other traffic. Double mooring lines advised due to strong tidal streams (up to 6kn).

NAVIGATION WPT 56°42´·18N 02°25´·11W, 271°/1·25M to front ldg lt. Beware Annat Bank to N and Scurdie Rks to S of ent chan. In quiet weather best access is LW to LW+1, but in strong onshore winds only safe access would be from HW –2 to HW.

Ent is dangerous with strong onshore winds against any ebb tide when heavy overfalls develop.

LIGHTS AND MARKS See 9.6.4 and chartlet two sets of ldg lts: Outer 271·5°, both FR 11/18m 5M, front W twin pillars, R bands; rear W tr, R cupola. Inner 265°, both FG 21/33m 5M, Orange △ front and ▽ rear.

COMMUNICATIONS (Code 01674) CGOC (01224) 592334; Police 101; Dr 672554. HM 672302. VHF Ch **12** 16 (H24).

FACILITIES N Quay ☎672302, £11/24hrs, £27/wk; (tanker) (40t).

Town Ⓑ ✕ ⇌ ✈ (Aberdeen).

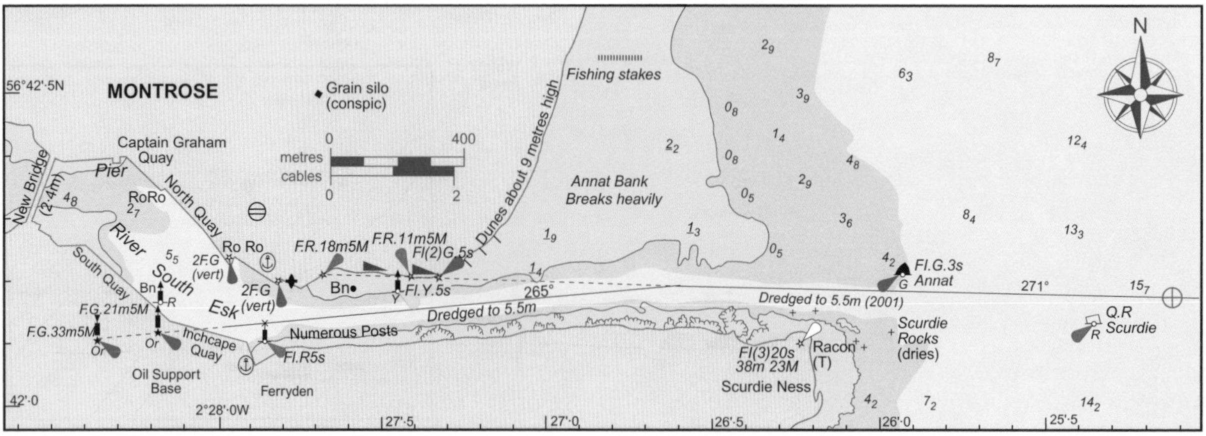

MONTROSE TO BUCHAN NESS

(AC 210) North from Montrose the coast is sandy for 5M to Milton Ness, where there is an ⚓ on the S side in N winds. Johnshaven, 2M NE, is a small harbour (dries) with a tight entrance, which should not be approached with onshore wind or swell. 5ca NE, off Brotherton Castle, drying rks extend 4ca offshore. Gourdon has a small harbour (mostly dries) approached on leading line between rocky ledges; with storm gates to inner basin. Outside the harbour rocks extend both sides of the entrance, and the sea breaks heavily in strong E winds. Keep a sharp lookout for lobster pot dan buoys between Montrose and Stonehaven.

North to Inverbervie the coast is fringed with rocky ledges up to 2ca offshore. Just N of Todhead Pt is Catterline, a small bay which forms a natural ⚓ in W winds, but open to E. Downie Pt, SE of Stonehaven, should be rounded 1ca off. The Bay is encumbered by rocky ledges up to 2ca from shore and exposed to the E; ⚓ 6ca E of Bay Hotel or berth afloat in outer harbour.

From Garron Pt to Girdle Ness (Fl(2) 20s 56m 22M, Racon G) the coast is mostly steep-to. Fishing nets may be met off headlands during fishing season. Craigmaroinn and Seal Craig (dry) are reefs 3ca offshore SE of Portlethen, a fishing village with landing sheltered by rocks. Cove Bay has a very small fishing harbour, off which there is ⚓ in good weather; Mutton Rk (dries 2·1m) lie 1½ca offshore. From Cove to Girdle Ness keep 5ca offshore, avoiding Hasman Rks (dries 3·4m) 1ca off Altens. Greg Ness and Girdle Ness, at SE corner of Aberdeen Bay, are fringed by rocks. Girdlestone is a rocky patch, depth less than 2m, 2ca ENE of the lt ho. A drying patch extends 2ca SE of lt ho.

▶ *Off Girdle Ness the S-going stream begins at HW Aberdeen –0430, and the N-going at HW Aberdeen +0130, sp rates 2·5kn. A race forms on S-going stream.* ◀

(AC 213) Few dangers lie between Aberdeen and Buchan Ness. Black Dog firing range lies 4½M N of Aberdeen marked by SPM, seaward buoy Fl(5)Y 20s is fitted with AIS. Drums Links is 8¾M N of Aberdeen, but not buoyed; red flags and lights are shown when firing.

R Ythan, 1·75M SSW of Hackley Hd, is navigable by small craft, but channel shifts constantly. 3M North is the very small harbour of Collieston (mostly dries), only accessible in fine weather. 4¾M NNE of Hackley Head The Skares, rocks (marked by lit PHM) extend 3½ca from South arm of Cruden Bay, where there is ⚓ in offshore winds. On N side of Cruden B is Port Erroll (dries 2·5m).

HARBOURS SOUTH OF STONEHAVEN

JOHNSHAVEN, Aberdeenshire, 56°47'·60N 02°20'·07W. AC 210. HW +0245 on Dover; +0045 and +0·4m on Aberdeen; ML 2·7m; Duration 0626. Very small, attractive drying hbr 6·5M N of Montrose.

Entry impossible in strong onshore winds; strictly a fair weather visit with great caution. Even in calm weather swell is a problem inside the hbr.

Appr from 5ca SE at near HW. Conspic W shed at N end of hbr. Ldg marks/lts on 316°: front, R structure with FR 5m; rear is G structure, 20m up the hill and 85m from front, with FG (FR when entry unsafe). Transit leads between rky ledges to very narrow (20m) ent. Turn 90° port into Inner Basin (dries 2·5m) and berth on outer wall or secure to mooring chains, rigged NE/SW. Stonehaven HM ☎(01569) 762741 (part-time). Facilities: £20/night, (5t). Bus to Montrose/Aberdeen.

GOURDON, Aberdeenshire, 56°49'·49N 02°17'·21W. AC 210. HW +0240 on Dover; +0035 on Aberdeen; HW +0·4m on Aberdeen; ML 2·7m; Duration 0620. Shelter good in inner W hbr (dries about 2m; protected by storm gates); access from about mid-flood. E (or Gutty) hbr is rky, with difficult access. Beware rky ledges marked by bn and extending 200m S from W pier end. **A dangerous rk dries on the ldg line** about 1½ca S of pier heads. Ldg marks/lts 358°, both FR 5/30m 5M, 2 W trs; front lt shows G when not safe to enter. W pier hd Fl WRG 3s 5m 9/7M, vis 180°-G-344°-W-354°-R-180°. Essential to keep in W sector until R Ldg Lts are aligned. E bkwtr hd Q 3m 7M. HM ☎(01569) 762741 (part-time, same as 9.6.14). Facilities: from standpipe.

For details of 'Rover Ticket' see 9.6.5.

9.6.14 STONEHAVEN

Aberdeenshire **56°57'·57N 02°12'·02W**

CHARTS AC 210, 1438, 5617; Imray C23

TIDES +0235 Dover; ML 2·6; Duration 0620

Standard Port ABERDEEN (⟶)

Times				Height (metres)			
High Water		Low Water		MHWS	MHWN	MLWN	MLWS
0000	0600	0100	0700	4·3	3·4	1·6	0·6
1200	1800	1300	1900				
Differences STONEHAVEN							
+0013	+0008	+0013	+0009	+0·2	+0·2	+0·1	0·0

SHELTER Good, especially from offshore winds. Berth in Outer harbour on W side of breakwater (3m to 2m) or N wall; sandbank forms with varying depths (not <0.6m to date) in middle to W side. Or ⚓ outside in fair weather. Hbr speed limit 3kn. Inner hbr dries 3·4m and in bad weather is closed, indicated by FG(occas) lt as shown. Do not go S of leading line, to clear rocks close E of inner harbour wall.

NAVIGATION WPT 56°57'·69N 02°11'·11W, 258°/0·5M to bkwtr lt. Give Downie Pt a wide berth. ***Do not enter in strong onshore winds.***

LIGHTS AND MARKS N pier Iso WRG 4s 7m 5M; appr in W sector, 246°-268°. Inner hbr ldg lts 273° only apply to inner hbr: front FW 6m 5M; rear FR 8m 5M. FG on SE pier is shown when inner hbr is closed by boom in bad weather. Conspic monument on hill top to S of hbr. Wave Buoy (temp'y) 5ca NE of B'water lt in G sector.

COMMUNICATIONS (Code 01569) CGOC (01224) 592334; Police 101; Dr 762945; Maritime Rescue Institute 765768.

HM (part-time) 762741, Mobile 07741050210; VHF Ch 11.

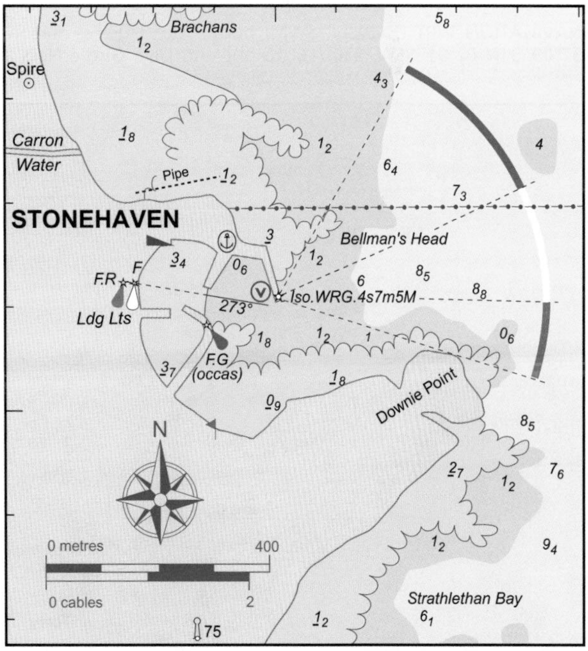

FACILITIES (£15) £20/night (1½t) (tanker, Fri early am). **Aberdeen & Stonehaven SC**. **Town** (Aberdeen).

Berthing Fees: *For details of a 'Rover Ticket' see 9.6.5.*

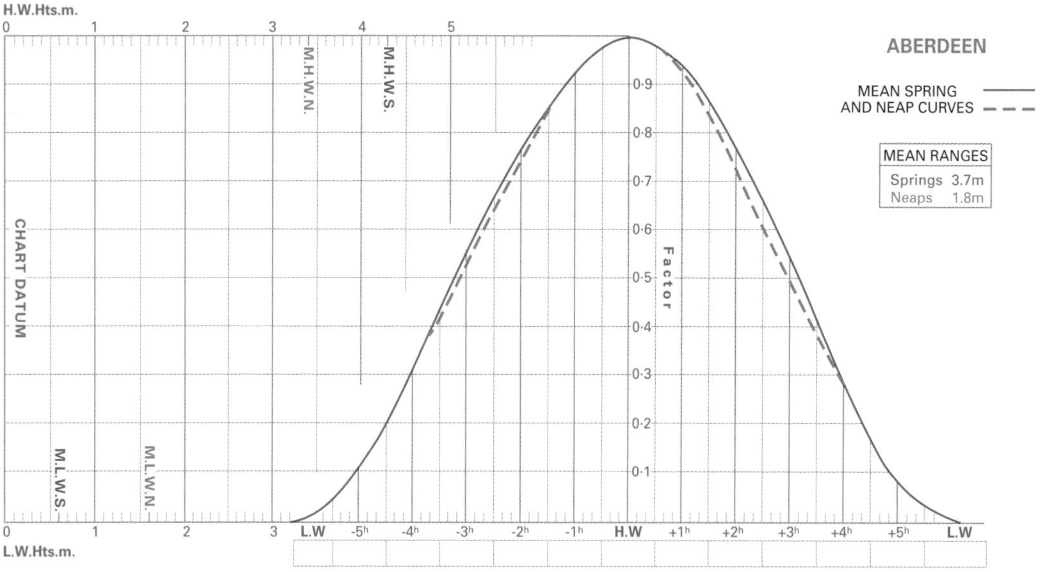

9.6.15 ABERDEEN

Aberdeenshire **57°08'·70N 02°03'·59W** ❁❁❁⛵✿✿

CHARTS AC 210, 1446, 5617; Imray C23

TIDES +0231 Dover; ML 2·5; Duration 0620

SHELTER Good in hbr; open at all tides, but do not enter in strong NE/ESE winds. Call Aberdeen VTS when 3M off for permission to enter VTS area and berthing availability.

Yachts are not encouraged in this busy commercial port, but usually lie on N side of Albert Basin alongside floating linkspan.

⚓ in Aberdeen Bay gives some shelter from S and W winds. Peterhead is 25M to N; Stonehaven is 13M S.

NAVIGATION WPT Fairway SWM buoy, Mo (A) 5s, Racon, 57°09'·31N 02°01'·96W, 236°/1M to hbr ent. Give Girdle Ness a berth of at least ¼M (more in bad weather). Do not pass close round pier hds. Strong tidal streams and, with river in spate, overfalls. Chan dredged to 6m on ldg line.

LIGHTS AND MARKS Dir lt 237·2° Fl WRG 1s 7m 9M. Ldg lts FR 237·2° 5M (FG when unsafe). Traffic sigs at root of N pier:

● ●	=	Entry prohib
●	=	Dep prohib
● & ●	=	Port closed

COMMUNICATIONS (Code 01224) CGOC 592334; ☼ 722334; Police 101.

Aberdeen VTS 597000; VHF Ch **12** 16 (H24).

FACILITIES Services ⛵ £18/craft for up to 5 days, 🔧 ⚙ Ⓔ ACA. **City** all amenities, ⇌ ✈. **Ferries** Kirkwall and Lerwick (www.northlinkferries.co.uk).

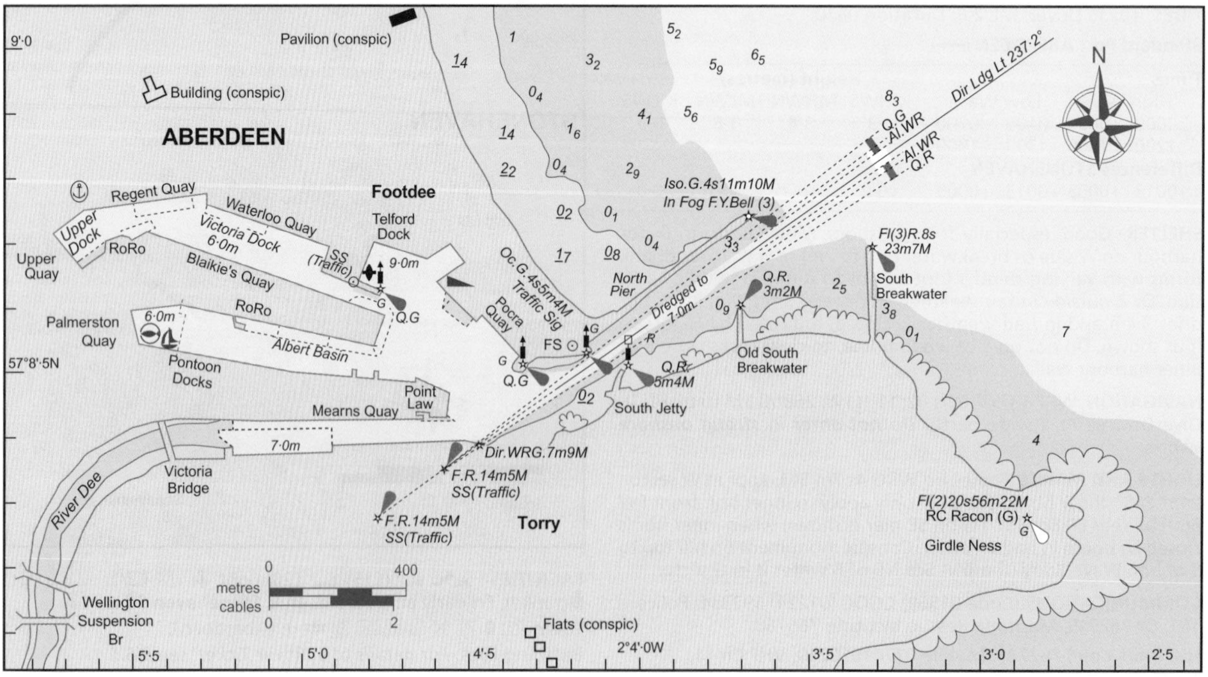

STANDARD TIME (UT)
For Summer Time add ONE hour in **non-shaded areas**

ABERDEEN LAT 57°09'N LONG 2°04'W

TIMES AND HEIGHTS OF HIGH AND LOW WATERS

Dates in red are SPRINGS
Dates in blue are NEAPS

YEAR **2018**

JANUARY

Date	Day	Time	m	Time	m	Time	m	Time	m
1	M	0002	4.3	0612	0.9	1231	4.4	1839	0.8
2	TU ○	0054	4.5	0701	0.8	1317	4.5	1929	0.6
3	W	0144	4.6	0748	0.7	1402	4.6	2018	0.4
4	TH	0234	4.6	0835	0.8	1449	4.6	2107	0.4
5	F	0326	4.5	0921	0.9	1537	4.5	2157	0.5
6	SA	0418	4.3	1008	1.1	1628	4.4	2248	0.7
7	SU	0512	4.1	1057	1.3	1722	4.2	2341	0.9
8	M ◑	0607	3.8	1151	1.6	1820	4.0		
9	TU	0037	1.2	0705	3.7	1252	1.7	1921	3.8
10	W	0138	1.4	0809	3.5	1401	1.9	2030	3.6
11	TH	0247	1.6	0918	3.5	1521	1.9	2142	3.6
12	F	0358	1.6	1021	3.6	1630	1.7	2245	3.7
13	SA	0452	1.5	1112	3.7	1721	1.6	2336	3.7
14	SU	0536	1.4	1155	3.9	1803	1.4		
15	M	0020	3.8	0614	1.3	1234	4.0	1840	1.2
16	TU	0059	3.9	0649	1.3	1308	4.1	1915	1.1
17	W ●	0135	4.0	0723	1.2	1340	4.2	1948	1.0
18	TH	0209	4.0	0755	1.1	1412	4.2	2021	1.0
19	F	0242	4.0	0828	1.1	1443	4.2	2054	0.9
20	SA	0316	4.0	0900	1.2	1516	4.2	2128	1.0
21	SU	0351	3.9	0934	1.2	1551	4.1	2203	1.0
22	M	0428	3.9	1010	1.3	1629	4.1	2242	1.1
23	TU	0511	3.8	1051	1.4	1713	4.0	2327	1.2
24	W ◐	0601	3.7	1141	1.5	1807	3.8		
25	TH	0022	1.3	0700	3.6	1247	1.7	1911	3.8
26	F	0130	1.4	0807	3.6	1403	1.7	2023	3.7
27	SA	0243	1.4	0917	3.7	1521	1.6	2138	3.8
28	SU	0359	1.3	1026	3.8	1635	1.3	2251	4.0
29	M	0507	1.2	1126	4.0	1737	1.0	2352	4.2
30	TU	0602	1.0	1217	4.3	1831	0.7		
31	W ○	0046	4.4	0651	0.8	1305	4.5	1920	0.5

FEBRUARY

Date	Day	Time	m	Time	m	Time	m	Time	m
1	TH	0136	4.5	0737	0.7	1350	4.6	2007	0.3
2	F	0223	4.5	0821	0.7	1434	4.6	2053	0.3
3	SA	0309	4.4	0903	0.8	1519	4.6	2137	0.4
4	SU	0355	4.3	0945	0.9	1604	4.5	2221	0.6
5	M	0441	4.1	1026	1.1	1652	4.2	2305	0.9
6	TU	0529	3.8	1111	1.3	1742	4.0	2352	1.2
7	W ◑	0619	3.6	1201	1.6	1838	3.7		
8	TH	0044	1.5	0715	3.4	1304	1.8	1941	3.5
9	F	0148	1.7	0821	3.4	1423	1.9	2057	3.4
10	SA	0307	1.8	0935	3.4	1559	1.8	2215	3.4
11	SU	0424	1.7	1041	3.5	1700	1.6	2316	3.5
12	M	0515	1.6	1132	3.7	1745	1.4		
13	TU	0003	3.7	0555	1.4	1213	3.8	1822	1.2
14	W	0042	3.8	0631	1.3	1249	4.0	1856	1.1
15	TH ●	0117	3.9	0704	1.1	1321	4.1	1929	0.9
16	F	0149	4.0	0736	1.0	1352	4.2	2001	0.8
17	SA	0221	4.1	0808	0.9	1423	4.3	2033	0.7
18	SU	0253	4.1	0840	0.9	1455	4.3	2106	0.7
19	M	0326	4.1	0913	0.9	1529	4.3	2139	0.8
20	TU	0401	4.0	0947	1.0	1606	4.2	2215	0.9
21	W	0440	3.9	1025	1.1	1648	4.1	2256	1.0
22	TH	0526	3.8	1111	1.3	1739	3.9	2348	1.2
23	F ◐	0623	3.6	1212	1.5	1844	3.7		
24	SA	0055	1.4	0732	3.5	1332	1.6	2000	3.6
25	SU	0217	1.5	0849	3.5	1501	1.5	2124	3.7
26	M	0346	1.5	1007	3.7	1625	1.3	2244	3.8
27	TU	0459	1.3	1112	3.9	1729	0.9	2347	4.1
28	W	0554	1.1	1205	4.2	1821	0.6		

MARCH

Date	Day	Time	m	Time	m	Time	m	Time	m
1	TH	0038	4.3	0640	0.9	1252	4.4	1907	0.4
2	F ○	0124	4.4	0723	0.7	1335	4.5	1951	0.2
3	SA	0206	4.4	0803	0.6	1416	4.6	2033	0.2
4	SU	0247	4.4	0842	0.7	1457	4.5	2112	0.4
5	M	0327	4.2	0919	0.8	1538	4.4	2150	0.6
6	TU	0407	4.1	0955	0.9	1621	4.2	2227	0.9
7	W	0448	3.8	1034	1.2	1705	3.9	2307	1.2
8	TH	0531	3.6	1117	1.4	1756	3.6	2353	1.5
9	F ◑	0622	3.4	1212	1.7	1857	3.4		
10	SA	0052	1.8	0723	3.3	1328	1.8	2010	3.2
11	SU	0210	1.9	0837	3.2	1510	1.8	2137	3.2
12	M	0348	1.9	0958	3.3	1632	1.7	2248	3.4
13	TU	0450	1.7	1100	3.5	1719	1.4	2338	3.6
14	W	0532	1.5	1145	3.7	1757	1.2		
15	TH	0017	3.7	0608	1.3	1223	3.9	1830	1.0
16	F	0052	3.9	0641	1.1	1256	4.0	1902	0.8
17	SA ●	0123	4.0	0713	0.9	1327	4.2	1935	0.6
18	SU	0155	4.1	0745	0.8	1359	4.3	2007	0.5
19	M	0227	4.2	0818	0.7	1432	4.3	2041	0.5
20	TU	0300	4.2	0852	0.7	1508	4.3	2115	0.6
21	W	0335	4.1	0927	0.8	1547	4.3	2152	0.7
22	TH	0415	4.0	1006	0.9	1631	4.1	2233	1.0
23	F	0500	3.8	1054	1.1	1724	3.9	2326	1.2
24	SA ◐	0557	3.6	1157	1.3	1832	3.7		
25	SU	0036	1.5	0708	3.5	1319	1.4	1951	3.6
26	M	0205	1.6	0828	3.5	1452	1.4	2119	3.6
27	TU	0339	1.6	0951	3.6	1616	1.1	2239	3.8
28	W	0448	1.4	1058	3.8	1717	0.8	2338	4.0
29	TH	0540	1.1	1150	4.1	1807	0.6		
30	F	0025	4.1	0624	0.9	1235	4.3	1850	0.4
31	SA ○	0106	4.3	0704	0.7	1316	4.4	1930	0.3

APRIL

Date	Day	Time	m	Time	m	Time	m	Time	m
1	SU	0144	4.3	0742	0.6	1355	4.4	2008	0.3
2	M	0221	4.3	0818	0.6	1434	4.4	2044	0.5
3	TU	0257	4.2	0853	0.7	1513	4.3	2118	0.7
4	W	0333	4.0	0928	0.9	1553	4.1	2152	0.9
5	TH	0409	3.9	1003	1.0	1635	3.8	2227	1.2
6	F	0448	3.7	1043	1.3	1722	3.6	2308	1.5
7	SA	0534	3.5	1132	1.5	1820	3.4		
8	SU ◑	0002	1.8	0632	3.3	1239	1.7	1927	3.2
9	M	0118	1.9	0741	3.2	1407	1.8	2046	3.2
10	TU	0251	2.0	0900	3.2	1544	1.6	2206	3.3
11	W	0411	1.8	1014	3.4	1641	1.4	2302	3.5
12	TH	0459	1.6	1107	3.6	1722	1.2	2343	3.7
13	F	0537	1.3	1147	3.8	1757	1.0		
14	SA	0019	3.9	0611	1.1	1223	4.0	1830	0.7
15	SU	0053	4.0	0645	0.9	1257	4.1	1905	0.6
16	M ●	0126	4.2	0719	0.7	1332	4.3	1940	0.5
17	TU	0200	4.2	0755	0.6	1409	4.4	2016	0.5
18	W	0235	4.3	0832	0.6	1449	4.4	2054	0.5
19	TH	0313	4.2	0912	0.6	1532	4.3	2134	0.7
20	F	0355	4.1	0956	0.8	1620	4.1	2220	1.0
21	SA	0443	3.9	1048	0.9	1718	3.9	2316	1.3
22	SU ◐	0542	3.7	1154	1.1	1829	3.7		
23	M	0028	1.5	0654	3.6	1315	1.2	1947	3.6
24	TU	0156	1.7	0812	3.5	1442	1.2	2111	3.6
25	W	0323	1.6	0932	3.6	1600	1.0	2225	3.7
26	TH	0430	1.4	1039	3.8	1658	0.8	2321	3.9
27	F	0521	1.2	1131	4.0	1746	0.6		
28	SA	0005	4.0	0604	1.0	1216	4.1	1828	0.5
29	SU	0045	4.1	0643	0.8	1256	4.2	1906	0.5
30	M ○	0120	4.2	0721	0.7	1334	4.3	1942	0.6

Chart Datum: 2·25 metres below Ordnance Datum (Newlyn). HAT is 4·8 metres above Chart Datum.

STANDARD TIME (UT)
For Summer Time add ONE hour in **non-shaded areas**

ABERDEEN LAT 57°09'N LONG 2°04'W

TIMES AND HEIGHTS OF HIGH AND LOW WATERS

Dates in red are SPRINGS
Dates in blue are NEAPS

YEAR **2018**

MAY

Date	Time	m	Date	Time	m
1	0155	4.2	16	0134	4.3
	0756	0.7		0735	0.6
TU	1413	4.2	W	1349	4.4
	2016	0.7		1955	0.5
2	0229	4.1	17	0213	4.3
	0831	0.8		0817	0.5
W	1451	4.1	TH	1434	4.4
	2049	0.8		2037	0.6
3	0303	4.0	18	0255	4.3
	0905	0.9		0902	0.5
TH	1529	3.9	F	1522	4.3
	2122	1.0		2122	0.8
4	0338	3.9	19	0340	4.2
	0940	1.0		0951	0.6
F	1610	3.8	SA	1615	4.1
	2156	1.3		2212	1.0
5	0415	3.8	20	0431	4.0
	1018	1.2		1047	0.7
SA	1655	3.6	SU	1716	3.9
	2235	1.5		2310	1.3
6	0458	3.6	21	0532	3.9
	1103	1.3		1152	0.9
SU	1748	3.4	M	1824	3.8
	2324	1.7			
7	0551	3.4	22	0019	1.5
	1200	1.5		0640	3.7
M	1848	3.3	TU	1305	1.0
			◐	1934	3.6
8	0029	1.9	23	0136	1.6
	0654	3.3		0752	3.7
TU	1314	1.6	W	1421	1.0
◑	1954	3.2		2050	3.6
9	0150	1.9	24	0253	1.6
	0802	3.3		0906	3.7
W	1433	1.6	TH	1533	1.0
	2106	3.3		2200	3.7
10	0309	1.8	25	0402	1.4
	0912	3.3		1014	3.8
TH	1543	1.4	F	1633	0.9
	2211	3.4		2256	3.8
11	0410	1.6	26	0456	1.3
	1015	3.5		1108	3.9
F	1634	1.2	SA	1722	0.8
	2300	3.6		2341	3.9
12	0456	1.4	27	0542	1.1
	1104	3.7		1155	4.0
SA	1716	1.0	SU	1804	0.8
	2341	3.8			
13	0536	1.1	28	0021	4.0
	1146	3.9		0623	1.0
SU	1755	0.8	M	1237	4.0
				1842	0.8
14	0019	4.0	29	0058	4.0
	0615	0.9		0701	0.9
M	1227	4.1	TU	1316	4.1
	1834	0.6	○	1917	0.8
15	0056	4.2	30	0132	4.1
	0654	0.7		0737	0.8
TU	1307	4.3	W	1355	4.0
●	1914	0.5		1951	0.9
			31	0206	4.1
				0812	0.8
			TH	1433	4.0
				2025	1.0

JUNE

Date	Time	m	Date	Time	m
1	0240	4.0	16	0241	4.4
	0847	0.9		0855	0.4
F	1511	3.9	SA	1514	4.4
	2058	1.1		2114	0.8
2	0314	4.0	17	0329	4.3
	0922	1.0		0946	0.4
SA	1550	3.8	SU	1609	4.2
	2132	1.3		2204	1.0
3	0350	3.9	18	0421	4.2
	0959	1.1		1041	0.5
SU	1632	3.6	M	1707	4.0
	2210	1.4		2259	1.2
4	0430	3.7	19	0519	4.1
	1040	1.2		1141	0.7
M	1719	3.5	TU	1808	3.9
	2253	1.6		2359	1.4
5	0517	3.6	20	0621	3.9
	1129	1.3		1243	0.9
TU	1811	3.4	W	1911	3.7
	2346	1.7	◐		
6	0612	3.5	21	0104	1.5
	1227	1.4		0725	3.8
W	1908	3.3	TH	1349	1.0
◑				2017	3.6
7	0052	1.8	22	0214	1.6
	0712	3.4		0834	3.7
TH	1333	1.5	F	1458	1.1
	2009	3.3		2126	3.6
8	0204	1.8	23	0326	1.5
	0814	3.4		0943	3.7
F	1438	1.4	SA	1602	1.1
	2112	3.4		2226	3.7
9	0310	1.7	24	0429	1.4
	0917	3.5		1044	3.7
SA	1539	1.2	SU	1656	1.1
	2211	3.6		2316	3.8
10	0409	1.5	25	0521	1.3
	1017	3.7		1136	3.8
SU	1633	1.1	M	1741	1.1
	2302	3.8		2359	3.9
11	0459	1.2	26	0605	1.1
	1110	3.9		1221	3.9
M	1721	0.9	TU	1820	1.1
	2347	4.0			
12	0547	1.0	27	0037	4.0
	1159	4.1		0644	1.0
TU	1808	0.7	W	1302	3.9
				1856	1.1
13	0030	4.2	28	0113	4.0
	0632	0.7		0721	1.0
W	1246	4.3	TH	1341	3.9
●	1853	0.6	○	1931	1.1
14	0113	4.3	29	0147	4.1
	0718	0.5		0756	0.9
TH	1334	4.4	F	1417	3.9
	1939	0.6		2005	1.1
15	0156	4.4	30	0221	4.1
	0806	0.4		0830	0.9
F	1423	4.4	SA	1454	3.9
	2026	0.7		2038	1.1

JULY

Date	Time	m	Date	Time	m
1	0254	4.0	16	0315	4.5
	0904	0.9		0935	0.3
SU	1530	3.8	M	1556	4.3
	2112	1.2		2149	0.9
2	0328	4.0	17	0405	4.4
	0940	1.0		1026	0.4
M	1608	3.7	TU	1648	4.1
	2147	1.3		2237	1.0
3	0405	3.9	18	0458	4.3
	1017	1.1		1118	0.6
TU	1648	3.7	W	1742	3.9
	2226	1.4		2329	1.3
4	0446	3.8	19	0554	4.1
	1058	1.1		1212	0.9
W	1733	3.6	TH	1839	3.7
	2309	1.5	◐		
5	0532	3.7	20	0026	1.5
	1146	1.2		0653	3.9
TH	1824	3.5	F	1310	1.1
				1938	3.6
6	0002	1.6	21	0131	1.6
	0625	3.6		0758	3.7
F	1242	1.3	SA	1413	1.3
◑	1919	3.5		2044	3.5
7	0106	1.7	22	0245	1.7
	0725	3.6		0910	3.6
SA	1344	1.3	SU	1525	1.4
	2020	3.5		2150	3.5
8	0215	1.7	23	0403	1.6
	0829	3.6		1020	3.6
SU	1449	1.3	M	1629	1.5
	2123	3.6		2249	3.6
9	0323	1.5	24	0502	1.5
	0935	3.7		1118	3.6
M	1553	1.2	TU	1719	1.4
	2225	3.7		2337	3.8
10	0427	1.3	25	0549	1.3
	1040	3.8		1206	3.7
TU	1653	1.0	W	1801	1.3
	2319	3.9			
11	0524	1.0	26	0019	3.9
	1138	4.0		0628	1.1
W	1748	0.9	TH	1248	3.8
				1838	1.2
12	0008	4.1	27	0056	4.0
	0616	0.8		0705	1.0
TH	1232	4.2	F	1326	3.9
	1838	0.8	○	1913	1.2
13	0055	4.3	28	0130	4.1
	0707	0.5		0739	0.9
F	1323	4.4	SA	1400	3.9
●	1927	0.7		1946	1.1
14	0141	4.5	29	0202	4.1
	0756	0.3		0812	0.8
SA	1414	4.5	SU	1434	4.0
	2014	0.7		2018	1.1
15	0228	4.5	30	0234	4.1
	0846	0.2		0844	0.8
SU	1504	4.4	M	1507	3.9
	2101	0.7		2050	1.1
			31	0306	4.1
				0917	0.8
			TU	1541	3.9
				2123	1.1

AUGUST

Date	Time	m	Date	Time	m
1	0340	4.1	16	0430	4.4
	0951	0.9		1047	0.6
W	1617	3.8	TH	1709	4.0
	2158	1.2		2254	1.2
2	0416	4.0	17	0522	4.1
	1028	1.0		1133	1.0
TH	1656	3.7	F	1759	3.8
	2236	1.3		2345	1.4
3	0457	3.9	18	0618	3.8
	1108	1.1		1225	1.3
F	1741	3.7	SA	1855	3.6
	2321	1.4	◐		
4	0545	3.8	19	0045	1.6
	1157	1.2		0721	3.6
SA	1835	3.6	SU	1325	1.6
◑				1957	3.4
5	0018	1.6	20	0200	1.8
	0644	3.7		0834	3.4
SU	1258	1.4	M	1441	1.7
	1936	3.5		2109	3.4
6	0130	1.6	21	0335	1.8
	0752	3.6		0954	3.4
M	1409	1.4	TU	1603	1.7
	2044	3.6		2219	3.5
7	0247	1.6	22	0444	1.6
	0906	3.7		1100	3.5
TU	1524	1.4	W	1659	1.6
	2154	3.7		2314	3.7
8	0404	1.4	23	0531	1.4
	1021	3.8		1150	3.7
W	1636	1.2	TH	1742	1.5
	2258	3.9		2357	3.8
9	0510	1.1	24	0610	1.2
	1126	4.0		1230	3.8
TH	1736	1.1	F	1819	1.3
	2352	4.1			
10	0606	0.8	25	0034	4.0
	1222	4.2		0645	1.0
F	1828	0.9	SA	1306	3.9
				1852	1.2
11	0040	4.4	26	0108	4.1
	0656	0.5		0717	0.9
SA	1313	4.4	SU	1338	4.0
●	1915	0.7	○	1924	1.1
12	0127	4.5	27	0139	4.2
	0744	0.2		0748	0.8
SU	1401	4.5	M	1409	4.1
	2000	0.7		1955	1.0
13	0212	4.6	28	0210	4.3
	0831	0.2		0819	0.7
M	1448	4.5	TU	1440	4.1
	2043	0.7		2026	1.0
14	0257	4.6	29	0241	4.3
	0917	0.2		0851	0.7
TU	1534	4.4	W	1512	4.1
	2126	0.8		2058	1.0
15	0343	4.5	30	0314	4.3
	1001	0.4		0923	0.8
W	1621	4.2	TH	1545	4.0
	2209	0.9		2131	1.1
			31	0349	4.2
				0957	0.9
			F	1622	3.9
				2207	1.2

Chart Datum: 2·25 metres below Ordnance Datum (Newlyn). HAT is 4·8 metres above Chart Datum.

STANDARD TIME (UT)
For Summer Time add ONE hour in **non-shaded areas**

ABERDEEN LAT 57°09'N LONG 2°04'W

TIMES AND HEIGHTS OF HIGH AND LOW WATERS

Dates in red are SPRINGS
Dates in blue are NEAPS

YEAR **2018**

SEPTEMBER

Day	Time	m	Day	Time	m
1	0429	4.1	16	0542	3.8
	1035	1.0		1138	1.5
SA	1704	3.8	SU	1808	3.6
	2249	1.3		◐	
2	0515	3.9	17	0001	1.6
	1120	1.2		0643	3.5
SU	1756	3.7	M	1236	1.8
	2344	1.5		1909	3.4
3	0615	3.8	18	0115	1.8
	1221	1.4		0756	3.4
M	1901	3.6	TU	1351	2.0
	◑			2021	3.4
4	0059	1.6	19	0257	1.9
	0729	3.6		0921	3.3
TU	1341	1.6	W	1529	2.0
	2015	3.6		2139	3.4
5	0226	1.6	20	0419	1.7
	0850	3.6		1034	3.5
W	1508	1.6	TH	1634	1.8
	2132	3.7		2243	3.6
6	0352	1.4	21	0507	1.5
	1012	3.8		1125	3.6
TH	1627	1.4	F	1718	1.6
	2242	3.9		2329	3.8
7	0501	1.0	22	0545	1.2
	1119	4.0		1205	3.8
F	1726	1.2	SA	1754	1.4
	2338	4.2			
8	0555	0.7	23	0007	4.0
	1213	4.3		0618	1.0
SA	1815	1.0	SU	1239	4.0
				1827	1.2
9	0025	4.4	24	0040	4.1
	0642	0.4		0649	0.9
SU	1300	4.4	M	1310	4.1
	● 1859	0.8		1858	1.1
10	0110	4.6	25	0111	4.3
	0727	0.2		0720	0.7
M	1343	4.5	TU	1340	4.2
	1941	0.7		○ 1929	0.9
11	0152	4.7	26	0142	4.3
	0810	0.2		0751	0.7
TU	1425	4.5	W	1411	4.2
	2021	0.7		2001	0.9
12	0234	4.7	27	0214	4.4
	0851	0.3		0823	0.7
W	1506	4.4	TH	1443	4.2
	2100	0.7		2033	0.9
13	0317	4.6	28	0249	4.4
	0931	0.5		0855	0.7
TH	1548	4.2	F	1516	4.2
	2139	0.9		2107	0.9
14	0401	4.4	29	0326	4.3
	1011	0.8		0929	0.9
F	1630	4.0	SA	1553	4.1
	2220	1.1		2144	1.1
15	0449	4.1	30	0407	4.2
	1052	1.1		1007	1.1
SA	1716	3.8	SU	1635	4.0
	2305	1.4		2228	1.2

OCTOBER

Day	Time	m	Day	Time	m
1	0456	4.0	16	0608	3.5
	1055	1.3		1147	1.9
M	1727	3.8	TU	1819	3.5
	2326	1.4		◐	
2	0559	3.8	17	0029	1.8
	1159	1.6		0715	3.3
TU	1835	3.6	W	1300	2.1
	◑			1928	3.4
3	0044	1.5	18	0157	1.9
	0718	3.6		0834	3.3
W	1325	1.8	TH	1433	2.1
	1953	3.6		2045	3.4
4	0216	1.5	19	0334	1.8
	0842	3.7		0953	3.4
TH	1459	1.7	F	1556	2.0
	2114	3.7		2158	3.5
5	0343	1.3	20	0430	1.5
	1006	3.8		1049	3.6
F	1617	1.5	SA	1645	1.8
	2226	3.9		2251	3.7
6	0448	1.0	21	0510	1.3
	1109	4.1		1131	3.8
SA	1713	1.3	SU	1723	1.5
	2321	4.2		2332	3.9
7	0540	0.7	22	0545	1.1
	1159	4.3		1206	4.0
SU	1759	1.0	M	1757	1.3
8	0008	4.4	23	0007	4.1
	0625	0.5		0616	0.9
M	1242	4.4	TU	1238	4.1
	1840	0.9		1829	1.1
9	0050	4.6	24	0041	4.3
	0707	0.4		0648	0.8
TU	1322	4.5	W	1310	4.3
	● 1920	0.7		○ 1902	1.0
10	0131	4.7	25	0114	4.4
	0746	0.4		0721	0.7
W	1400	4.5	TH	1342	4.4
	1958	0.7		1936	0.9
11	0211	4.6	26	0149	4.4
	0824	0.5		0755	0.7
TH	1437	4.4	F	1415	4.4
	2035	0.8		2011	0.8
12	0252	4.5	27	0227	4.4
	0900	0.7		0830	0.8
F	1515	4.3	SA	1451	4.3
	2112	0.9		2049	0.9
13	0334	4.3	28	0307	4.4
	0936	1.0		0908	0.9
SA	1553	4.1	SU	1530	4.2
	2150	1.1		2130	1.0
14	0419	4.0	29	0353	4.2
	1012	1.3		0950	1.1
SU	1634	3.9	M	1614	4.1
	2231	1.4		2219	1.1
15	0509	3.8	30	0446	4.0
	1054	1.6		1041	1.4
M	1721	3.7	TU	1708	3.9
	2322	1.6		2320	1.3
			31	0554	3.8
				1148	1.7
			W	1817	3.8
				◑	

NOVEMBER

Day	Time	m	Day	Time	m
1	0038	1.4	16	0058	1.8
	0711	3.7		0739	3.4
TH	1314	1.8	F	1328	2.1
	1935	3.7		1944	3.5
2	0204	1.4	17	0218	1.8
	0832	3.7		0851	3.4
F	1443	1.8	SA	1449	2.1
	2053	3.8		2054	3.5
3	0325	1.2	18	0330	1.6
	0952	3.9		0957	3.5
SA	1557	1.6	SU	1555	1.9
	2205	4.0		2159	3.6
4	0429	1.0	19	0422	1.5
	1052	4.0		1047	3.7
SU	1653	1.4	M	1642	1.7
	2302	4.2		2249	3.8
5	0520	0.8	20	0503	1.2
	1140	4.2		1128	3.9
M	1739	1.2	TU	1721	1.4
	2349	4.3		2330	4.0
6	0604	0.7	21	0540	1.1
	1221	4.3		1204	4.1
TU	1821	1.0	W	1758	1.2
7	0031	4.5	22	0009	4.2
	0644	0.6		0616	0.9
W	1259	4.4	TH	1240	4.3
	● 1859	0.9		1835	1.0
8	0112	4.5	23	0048	4.3
	0721	0.7		0653	0.8
TH	1335	4.4	F	1315	4.4
	1937	0.8		○ 1914	0.9
9	0151	4.5	24	0128	4.5
	0757	0.8		0732	0.8
F	1411	4.4	SA	1352	4.5
	2014	0.9		1954	0.8
10	0231	4.3	25	0210	4.5
	0832	0.9		0812	0.8
SA	1446	4.3	SU	1431	4.4
	2050	1.0		2037	0.8
11	0312	4.2	26	0255	4.4
	0906	1.2		0855	1.0
SU	1522	4.1	M	1514	4.4
	2127	1.1		2124	0.8
12	0354	4.0	27	0345	4.3
	0941	1.4		0941	1.2
M	1559	4.0	TU	1601	4.2
	2206	1.3		2216	0.9
13	0441	3.8	28	0442	4.1
	1019	1.6		1034	1.4
TU	1641	3.8	W	1656	4.1
	2250	1.5		2317	1.1
14	0534	3.6	29	0548	3.9
	1106	1.9		1138	1.6
W	1733	3.6	TH	1802	3.9
	2346	1.7			
15	0634	3.4	30	0027	1.2
	1207	2.1		0657	3.8
TH	1837	3.5	F	1254	1.8
	◐			◑ 1913	3.9

DECEMBER

Day	Time	m	Day	Time	m
1	0143	1.2	16	0109	1.7
	0811	3.8		0747	3.4
SA	1412	1.8	SU	1335	2.0
	2026	3.9		1950	3.5
2	0257	1.2	17	0216	1.7
	0925	3.8		0851	3.5
SU	1526	1.7	M	1446	2.0
	2138	3.9		2054	3.6
3	0403	1.1	18	0319	1.6
	1027	3.9		0953	3.6
M	1627	1.5	TU	1548	1.8
	2239	4.1		2156	3.7
4	0457	1.0	19	0414	1.4
	1117	4.0		1045	3.8
TU	1718	1.3	W	1641	1.6
	2330	4.2		2251	3.9
5	0543	1.0	20	0503	1.2
	1200	4.2		1130	4.0
W	1802	1.2	TH	1728	1.3
				2340	4.1
6	0015	4.2	21	0548	1.0
	0623	0.9		1212	4.2
TH	1239	4.2	F	1813	1.1
	1842	1.1			
7	0057	4.3	22	0026	4.3
	0700	1.0		0632	0.9
F	1315	4.3	SA	1253	4.4
	● 1921	1.0		○ 1857	0.9
8	0137	4.2	23	0112	4.4
	0735	1.0		0716	0.8
SA	1350	4.3	SU	1334	4.5
	1958	1.0		1943	0.7
9	0216	4.2	24	0159	4.5
	0810	1.1		0800	0.8
SU	1424	4.3	M	1417	4.5
	2034	1.0		2030	0.6
10	0255	4.1	25	0247	4.5
	0843	1.3		0846	0.9
M	1459	4.2	TU	1501	4.5
	2109	1.1		2118	0.6
11	0335	4.0	26	0339	4.4
	0917	1.4		0934	1.1
TU	1534	4.1	W	1550	4.4
	2145	1.2		2210	0.7
12	0416	3.8	27	0434	4.2
	0953	1.5		1024	1.2
W	1612	4.0	TH	1643	4.3
	2225	1.3		2306	0.8
13	0501	3.7	28	0533	4.0
	1034	1.7		1120	1.4
TH	1656	3.8	F	1742	4.1
	2311	1.5			
14	0551	3.5	29	0007	1.0
	1121	1.9		0634	3.9
F	1749	3.7	SA	1224	1.6
				◑ 1846	4.0
15	0005	1.6	30	0112	1.1
	0647	3.4		0739	3.7
SA	1223	2.0	SU	1332	1.7
	◐ 1848	3.6		1954	3.9
			31	0219	1.3
				0849	3.7
			M	1446	1.7
				2106	3.8

Chart Datum: 2·25 metres below Ordnance Datum (Newlyn). HAT is 4·8 metres above Chart Datum.

North East Scotland

Buchan Ness to Cape Wrath including Orkney and Shetland Islands

9.7.1	Contents	391
9.7.2	Area map and Distance table	392
9.7.3	Tidal stream charts	394
9.7.4	Lights, buoys and waypoints	396
9.7.5	Passage information Buchan Ness to Rattray Head – 398 • Moray Firth: south coast – 399 • Moray Firth: north west coast – 409 • Pentland Firth – 413 • Pentland Firth to Cape Wrath, Orkney Islands – 418 • Shetland Islands – 421	398
9.7.6	Peterhead Boddam	399
9.7.7	Fraserburgh Rosehearty	400
9.7.8	Macduff/Banff Portsoy	401
9.7.9	Whitehills Cullen • Portknockie • Findochty	401
9.7.10	Buckie	402
9.7.11	Lossiemouth	402
9.7.12	Hopeman	403
9.7.13	Burghead	403
9.7.14	Findhorn	404
9.7.15	Nairn	404
	Invergordon, tide tables/curves	405
9.7.16	Inverness Caledonian Canal • Fortrose, Avoch • Cromarty, Cromarty Firth, Dornoch Firth, Golspie, Lybster	409
9.7.17	Portmahomack	411
9.7.18	Helmsdale	412
9.7.19	Wick, tide tables/curves	412
9.7.20	Scrabster Kyle of Tongue • Loch Eriboll	417
9.7.21	Orkney Islands Houton Bay • Shapinsay • Auskerry • Pierowall • Rapness	418
9.7.22	Stromness	420
9.7.23	Kirkwall	420
9.7.24	Stronsay	421
9.7.25	Shetland Islands Scalloway • Foula • Out Skellies • Yell • Unst • Fair Isle	422
9.7.26	Lerwick, tide tables/curves	424

DISTANCE TABLE
Approximate distances in nautical miles are by the most direct route while avoiding dangers and allowing for TSS. Places in *italics* are in adjoining areas; places in **bold** are in 9.0.7, Distances across the North Sea.

		1	2	3	4	5	6	7	8	9	10	11	12	13	14	15	16	17	18	19	20
1	*Peterhead*																				
2	**Fraserburgh**	16																			
3	Banff/Macduff	33	18																		
4	Whitehills	36	21	3																	
5	Buckie	46	31	15	12																
6	Lossiemouth	56	41	25	22	11															
7	Hopeman/Burghead	64	49	33	30	19	8														
8	Findhorn	69	54	38	35	24	14	6													
9	Nairn	79	64	48	45	34	23	15	10												
10	**Inverness**	90	75	59	56	45	34	26	23	13											
11	Tarbat Ness	72	57	41	38	27	18	13	14	17	27										
12	Helmsdale	74	59	44	42	33	26	25	28	32	43	16									
13	**Wick**	72	57	50	49	46	44	44	51	58	69	42	29								
14	Duncansby Head	82	67	62	61	58	57	57	64	71	81	54	41	13							
15	Scrabster	100	85	80	79	76	75	75	82	89	99	72	59	31	18						
16	**Kirkwall**	115	100	95	94	91	90	90	97	104	114	87	74	46	34	50					
17	Stromness	104	89	84	83	80	79	79	85	92	103	76	63	35	22	25	32				
18	Fair Isle	122	111	116	115	118	120	120	130	137	148	121	108	79	68	85	55	77			
19	**Lerwick**	160	150	156	155	160	162	162	172	170	190	162	148	120	109	124	95	110	42		
20	*Cape Wrath*	145	130	125	124	121	120	120	127	126	144	117	104	76	63	47	79	58	120	155	

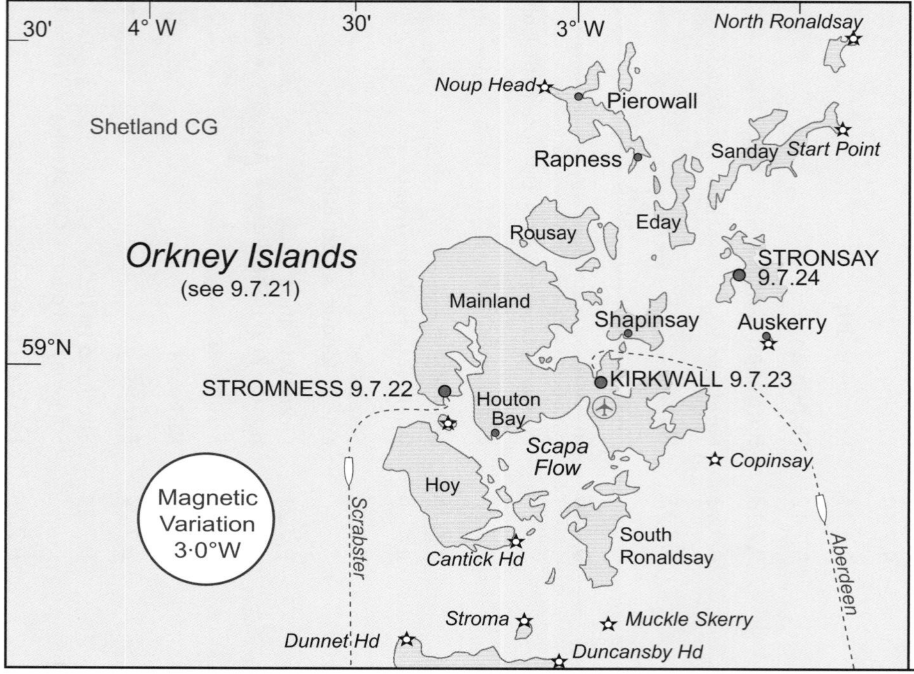
Orkney Islands
(see 9.7.21)
30'
4° W
30'
3° W
59°N
Shetland CG
North Ronaldsay
Noup Head
Pierowall
Rapness
Sanday
Start Point
Eday
Rousay
STRONSAY 9.7.24
Mainland
Shapinsay
Auskerry
STROMNESS 9.7.22
KIRKWALL 9.7.23
Houton Bay
Scapa Flow
Copinsay
Hoy
South Ronaldsay
Cantick Hd
Scrabster
Aberdeen
Stroma
Muckle Skerry
Dunnet Hd
Duncansby Hd
Magnetic Variation 3·0°W

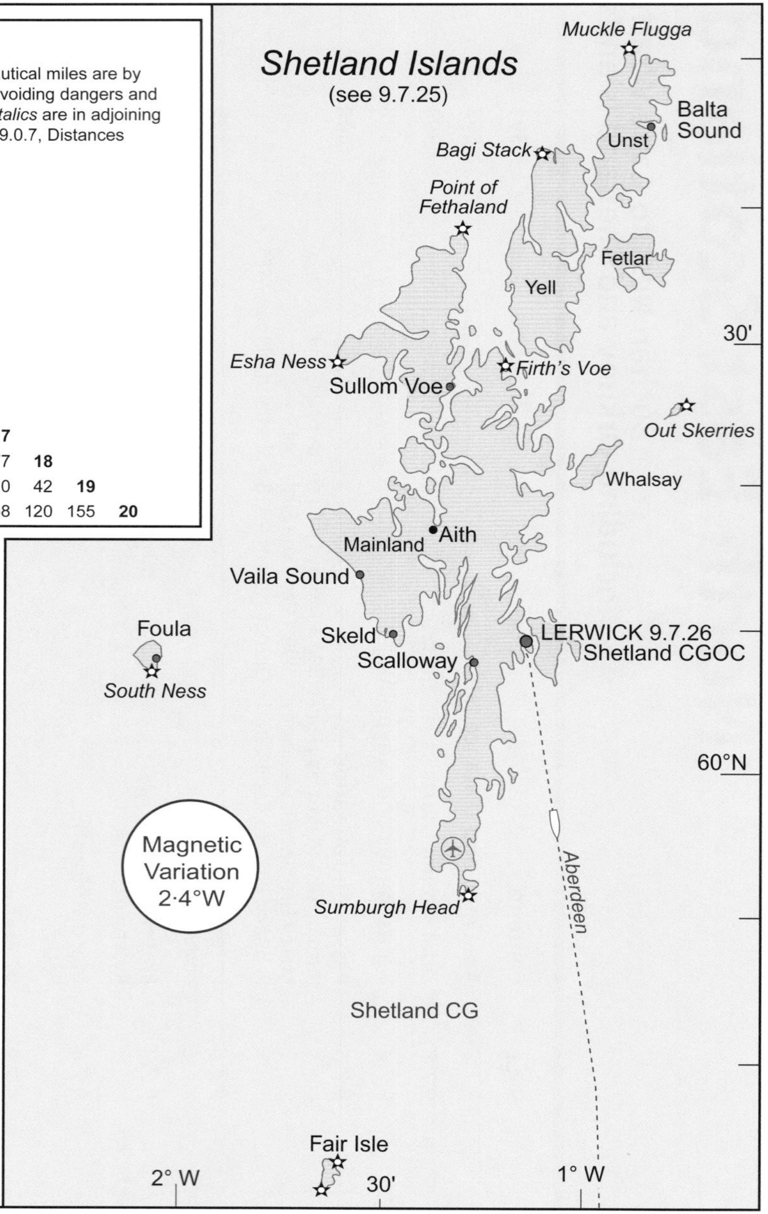
Shetland Islands
(see 9.7.25)
Muckle Flugga
Balta Sound
Unst
Bagi Stack
Point of Fethaland
Fetlar
Yell
30'
Esha Ness
Firth's Voe
Sullom Voe
Out Skerries
Whalsay
Mainland
Aith
Vaila Sound
Foula
South Ness
Skeld
Scalloway
LERWICK 9.7.26
Shetland CGOC
60°N
Magnetic Variation 2·4°W
Aberdeen
Sumburgh Head
Shetland CG
Fair Isle
2° W
30'
1° W

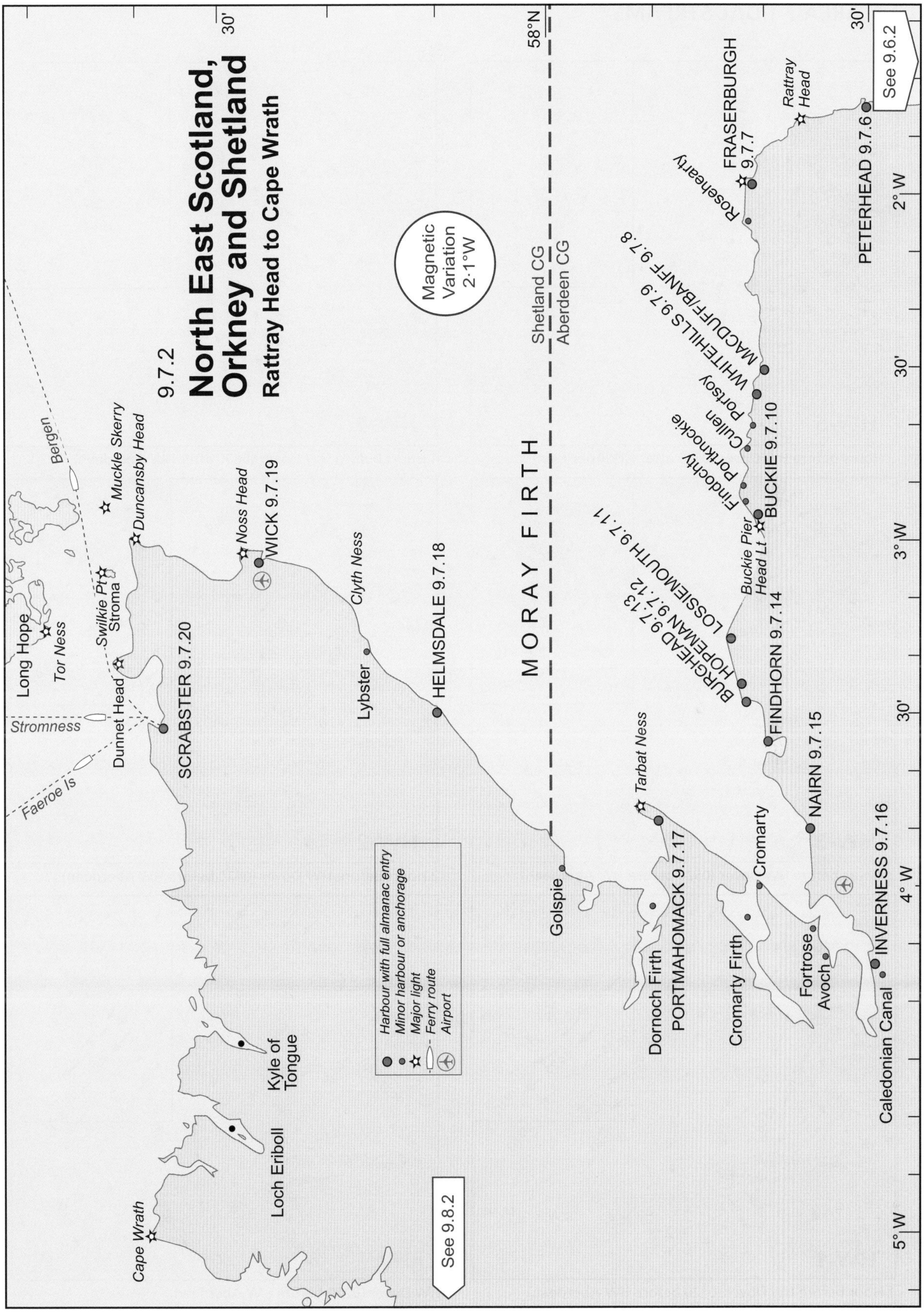
9.7.2
North East Scotland, Orkney and Shetland
Rattray Head to Cape Wrath
Magnetic Variation 2·1°W
MORAY FIRTH
Shetland CG
Aberdeen CG
58°N
30'
2° W
3° W
4° W
5° W
See 9.6.2
See 9.8.2
Harbour with full almanac entry
Minor harbour or anchorage
Major light
Ferry route
Airport
Bergen
Faeroe Is
Stromness
Muckle Skerry
Duncansby Head
Long Hope
Tor Ness
Swilkie Pt
Stroma
Dunnet Head
SCRABSTER 9.7.20
Noss Head
WICK 9.7.19
Clyth Ness
Lybster
HELMSDALE 9.7.18
Golspie
Tarbat Ness
PORTMAHOMACK 9.7.17
Dornoch Firth
Cromarty
Cromarty Firth
Fortrose
Avoch
INVERNESS 9.7.16
Caledonian Canal
NAIRN 9.7.15
FINDHORN 9.7.14
BURGHEAD 9.7.13
HOPEMAN 9.7.12
LOSSIEMOUTH 9.7.11
Buckie Pier Head Lt
BUCKIE 9.7.10
Findochty
Portknockie
Cullen
Portsoy
WHITEHILLS 9.7.9
MACDUFF/BANFF 9.7.8
Rosehearty
FRASERBURGH 9.7.7
Rattray Head
PETERHEAD 9.7.6
Cape Wrath
Loch Eriboll
Kyle of Tongue

9.7.3 AREA 7 TIDAL STREAMS

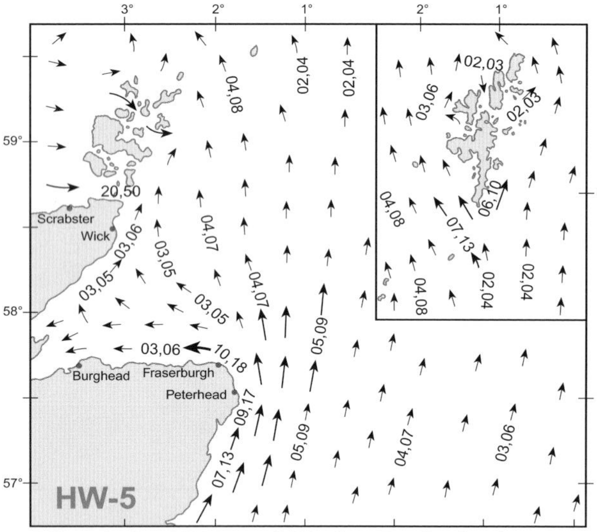

5 Hours before HW Dover (0500 after HW Aberdeen)

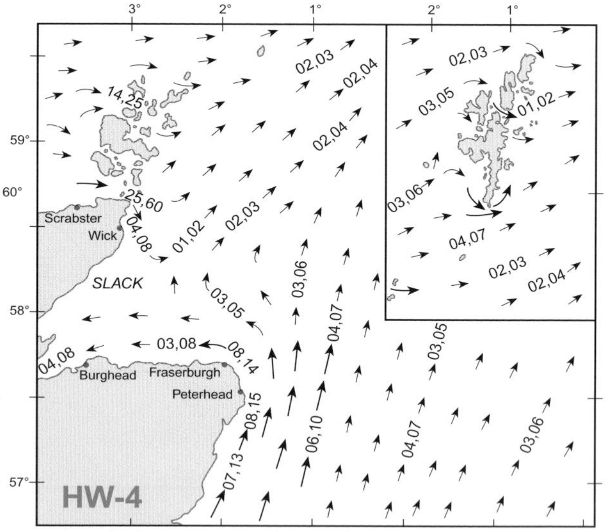

4 Hours before HW Dover (0600 after HW Aberdeen)

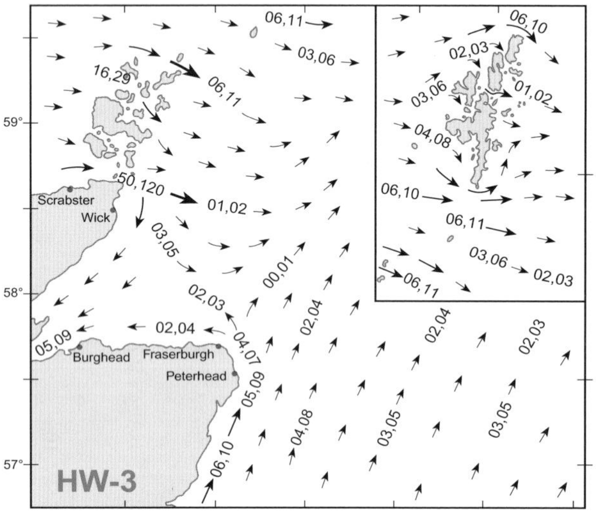

3 Hours before HW Dover (0520 before HW Aberdeen)

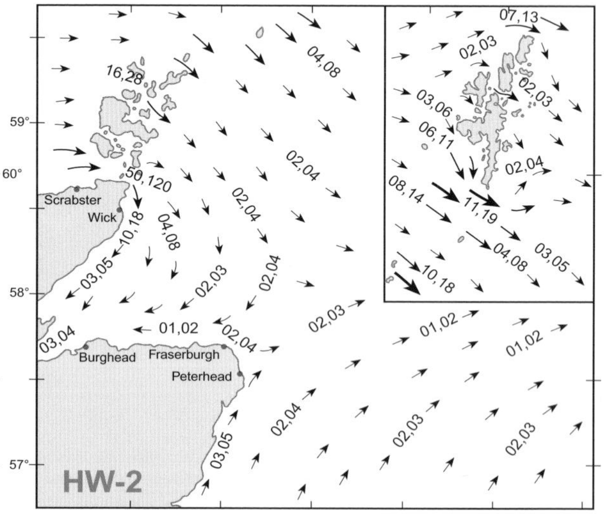

2 Hours before HW Dover (0420 before HW Aberdeen)

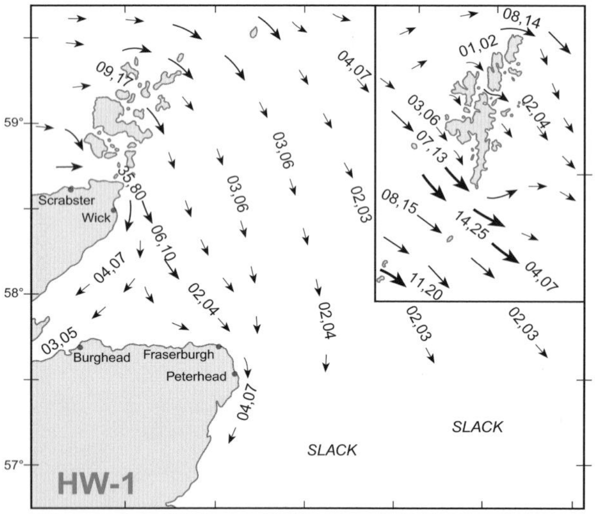

1 Hour before HW Dover (0320 before HW Aberdeen)

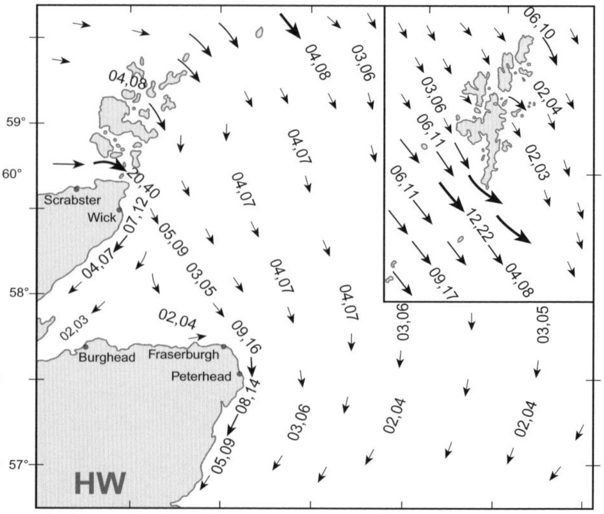

HW Dover (0220 before HW Aberdeen)

Southward 9.6.3 Westward 9.8.3

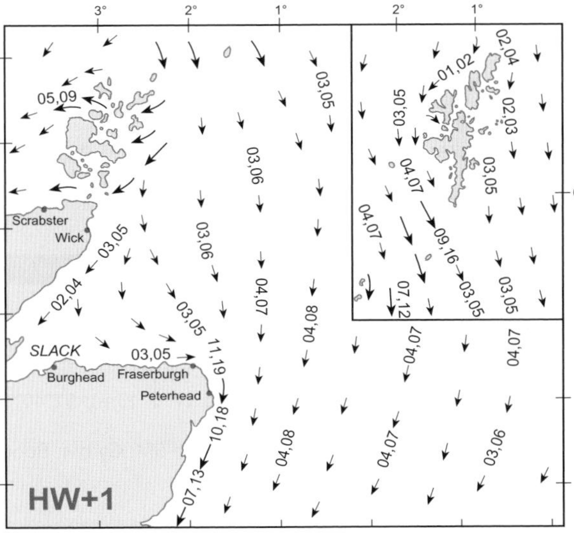

1 Hour after HW Dover (0120 before HW Aberdeen)

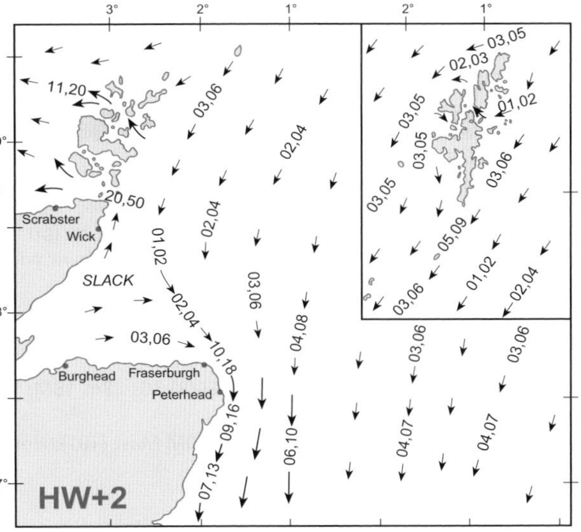

2 Hours after HW Dover (0020 before HW Aberdeen)

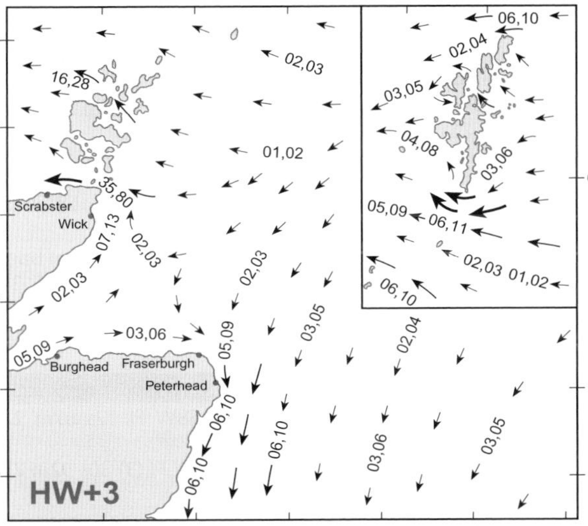

3 Hours after HW Dover (0040 after HW Aberdeen)

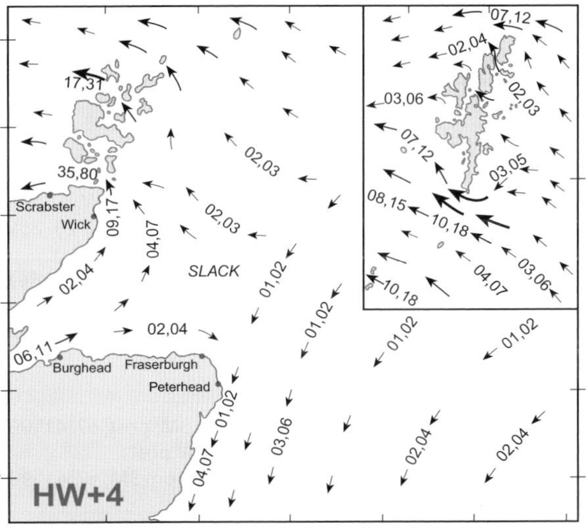

4 Hours after HW Dover (0140 after HW Aberdeen)

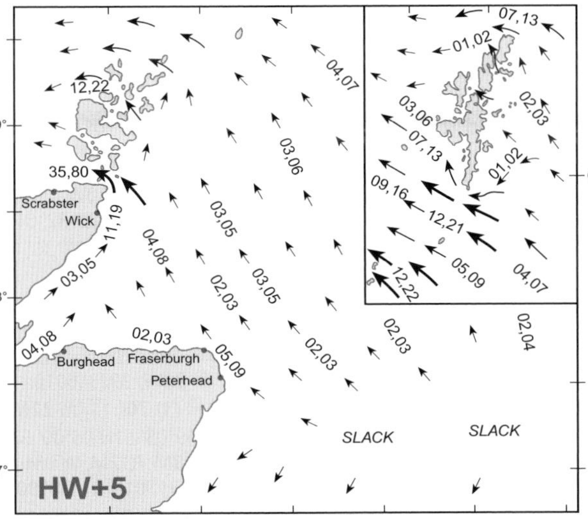

5 Hours after HW Dover (0240 after HW Aberdeen)

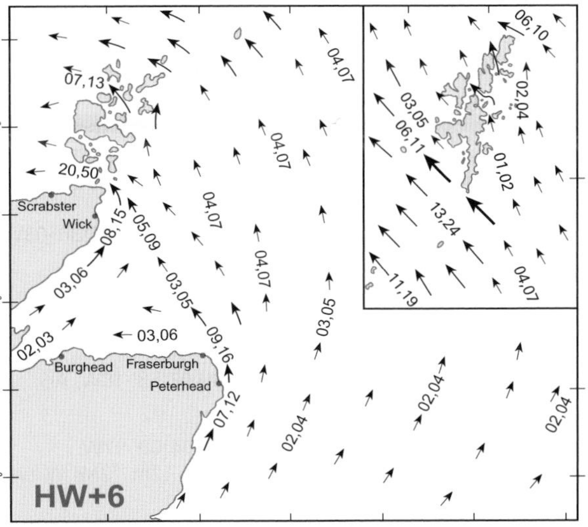

6 Hours after HW Dover (0340 after HW Aberdeen)

9.7.4 LIGHTS, BUOYS AND WAYPOINTS

Bold print = light with a nominal range of 15M or more. CAPITALS = place or feature. *CAPITAL ITALICS* = light-vessel, light float or Lanby. *Italics* = Fog signal. ***Bold italics*** = Racon. Some marks/ buoys are fitted with AIS (MMSI No); see relevant charts.

BUCHAN NESS TO INVERNESS

PETERHEAD and RATTRAY HEAD

Buchan Ness ☆ Fl 5s 40m **18M**; W twr, R bands; ***Racon (O) 14-16M***; 57°28′·23N 01°46′·51W.

Kirktown Ldg lts 314°. Front, Oc R 6s 14m 10M; Or △ on lattice mast; 57°30′·22N 01°47′·21W. Rear, Oc R 6s 21m 10M (sync with front); Or ▽ on lattice mast.

S Bkwtr Hd ☆ Fl (2) R 12s 24m 7M; 57°29′·79N 01°46′·54W.

N Bkwtr Hd ☆ Iso RG 6s 19m 11M; W tripod; vis: 171°-R-236°-G-171°; *Horn 30s;* 57°29′·84N 01°46′·32W.

Rattray Hd ☆ 57°36′·61N 01°49′·03W Fl (3) 30s 28m **18M**; W twr; ***Racon (M) 15M***; *Horn (2) 45s*.

Smith Bank Met Mast Mo(U) 15s 17m 10M Mast (101); Horn Mo(U) 30s; 58°10′·93N 02°49′·22W.

FRASERBURGH

Balaclava Bkwtr Head ☆ Fl (2) G 8s 26m 6M; dome on W twr; vis: 178°-326°; 57°41′·51N 01°59′·70W.

N Pier ☆ WRG 2s 7m 8M; metal post; 285°-G-287°-WG-289°-W-293°-WR-295°-R-297°; 57°41′·54N 01°59′·99W.

Kinnaird Hd ☆ 57°41′·87N 02°00′·26W Fl 5s 25m **22M**; vis: 092°-297°.

MACDUFF, BANFF and WHITEHILLS

Macduff Pier Hd ☆ Fl (2) WRG 6s 12m W9M, R7M; W twr; vis: shore-G-115°-W-174°-R-210°; 57°40′·26N 02°30′·01W.

Macduff Ldg Lts 130°, Front FR 28m 3M; 57°40′·18N 02°29′·85W. Rear, 220m from front, FR 55m 3M; both Or △ on mast.

Banff Ldg Lts 295°, Front Fl R 4s; 57°40·30N 02°31·36W. Rear, QR; both vis: 210°-345°.

Whitehills Pier Hd ☆ 57°40′·80N 02°34′·88W Fl WR 3s 7m W9M, R6M; W twr; vis: 132°-R-212°-W-245°.

PORTSOY and FINDOCHTY

Portsoy Pier Ldg Lts 173°, Front Fl G 4s 20m 3M; post; 57°41′·09N 02°41′·40W; Rear Q G 22m 3M; R △ on BW post.

Findochty Middle Pier Ldg Lts 166°, Front FR 6m 3M; 57°41′·90N 02°54′·20W. Rear FR 10m 3M.

BUCKIE

West Muck ☆ QR 5m 7M; tripod; 57°41′·06N 02°58′·01W.

N Pier Ldg Lts 096°, Front, FR 6m 9M; 57°40′·83N 02°57′·71W.

Rear ☆, 60m from front, Oc R 10s 15m 15M; W twr.

LOSSIEMOUTH, HOPEMAN and BURGHEAD

Lossiemouth S Pier Hd ☆ Fl R 6s 11m 5M; 57°43′·42N 03°16′·69W.

Halliman Skerries Q; ***Racon M***, 57°44′·33N 03°18′·57W.

Hopeman Ldg Lts 081°, Front, FR 3m; 57°42′·71N 03°26′·18W. Rear, 10m from front, FR, 4m.

Burghead N Bkwtr Hd ☆ Oc 8s 7m 5M; 57°42′·09N 03°30′·03W.

FINDHORN, NAIRN and INVERNESS FIRTH

Findhorn Landfall LF 10s 57°40′·34N 03°38′·77W.

Nairn E Pier Hd ☆ Oc WRG 4s 6m 5M; 8-sided twr; vis: shore-G-100°-W-207°-R-shore; 57°35′·62N 03°51′·65W.

Riff Bank E Fl Y 10s 3m 5M 57°38′·38N 03°58′·18W; AIS.

SOUTH CHANNEL

Riff Bank S Q (6) + L Fl 15s; 57°36′·73N 04°00′·97W.

Chanonry ☆ 57°34′·45N 04°05′·56W Oc 6s 12m 12M; W twr; vis: 148°-073°.

Munlochy L Fl 10s; 57°32′·91N 04°07′·65W.

Petty Bank Fl R 5s 57°31′·58N 04°08′·98W.

Meikle Mee Fl G 3s 57°30′·26N 04°12′·02W.

Longman Pt Fl WR 2s 7m W5M, R4M; vis: 078°-W-258°-R-078°; 57°29′·99N 04°13′·31W.

Craigton Point ☆ Fl WRG 4s 6m W11M, R7M, G7M; vis: 312° - W - 048° - R - 064° - W - 085°- G - shore; 57°30′·05N 04°14′·09W.

Bridge Centre , Or △; ***Racon (K) 6M***; 57°29′·97N 04°13′·79W.

INVERNESS and CALEDONIAN CANAL

R. Ness Outer QR 3m 4M; 57°29′·83N 04°13′·93W.

Carnarc Pt ☆ Fl G 2s 8m 4M; G lattice twr; 57°29′·72N 04°14′·25W.

Clachnaharry, S Tr'ng Wall Hd Iso G 4s 5m 2M; tfc sigs; 57°29′·43N 04°15′·86W.

INVERNESS TO DUNCANSBY HEAD

CROMARTY FIRTH and INVERGORDON

Fairway L Fl 10s; ***Racon (M) 5M***; 57°39′·96N 03°54′·19W.

Cromarty Bank Fl (2) G 10s; 57°40′·66N 03°56′·78W.

Buss Bank Fl R 3s 57°40′·97N 03°59′·54W.

Cromarty – The Ness (Lt ho disused W tr 13m); 57°40′·98N 04°02′·20W

Nigg Oil Terminal Pier Hd ☆ Oc G 5s 31m 5M; Gy twr, floodlit; 57°41′·54N 04°02′·60W.

DORNOCH FIRTH to LYBSTER

Tarbat Ness ☆ 57°51′·88N 03°46′·76W Fl (4) 30s 53m **24M**; W twr, R bands; ***Racon (T) 14-16M***.

Met Mast ☆ Mo(U) 15s 17m 10M; FR (101m), *Horn Mo(U) 30s;* 58°10′·94N 00°49′·20W.

Lybster, S Pier Hd ☆ Oc R 6s 10m 3M; 58°17′·79N 03°17′·41W.

Clyth Ness Lt Ho (unlit); W twr, R band; 58°18′·64N 03°12′·74W.

WICK

S Pier Hd ☆ Fl WRG 3s 12m W12M, R9M, G9M; W 8-sided twr; vis: 253°-G-270°-W-286°-R-329°; *Bell (2) 10s* (occas); 58°26′·34N 03°04′·73W.

Dir lt 288·5° F WRG 9m W10M, R7M, G7M; col, N end of bridge; vis: 283·5°-G-287·2°-W-289·7°-R-293·5°; 58°26′·54N 03°05′·34W

Noss Hd ☆ 58°28′·71N 03°03′·09W Fl WR 20s 53m **W25M, R21M**; W twr; vis: shore-R-191°-W-shore.

DUNCANSBY HEAD TO CAPE WRATH

Duncansby Hd ☆ 58°38′·65N 03°01′·58W Fl 12s 67m **22M**; W twr; **Racon (T)**.

Muckle Skerry ☆ 58°41′·41N 02°55′·49W Fl (3) 30s 52m **23M**; W twr; 992351086.

Lother Rock ☆ Fl 2s 13m 6M; ***Racon (M) 10M***; 58°43′·79N 02°58′·69W.

Swona ☆ Fl 8s 17m 9M; vis: 261°-210°; 58°44′·25N 03°04′·24W.

Swona N Hd ☆ Fl (3) 10s 16m 10M; 58°45′·11N 03°03′·10W.

Stroma ☆, Swilkie Point 58°41′·75N 03°07′·01W Fl (2) 20s 32m **20M**; W twr; 992351092.

Dunnet Hd ☆ 58°40′·28N 03°22′·60W Fl (4) 30s 105m **23M**.

THURSO, SCRABSTER and CAPE WRATH

Thurso ☆ FG 5m 4M; Gy post; 58°35′·91N 03°30′·80W.

Scrabster Q. E. Pier Hd ☆ Fl (2) 4s 8m 8M 58°36′·66N 03°32′·31W.

Strathy Pt Lt Ho (disused) W twr on W dwelling; 58°36′·04N 04°01′·12W.

Sule Skerry ☆ 59°05′·09N 04°24′·38W Fl (2) 15s 34m **21M**; W twr; ***Racon (T)***.

Sule Stack ⊙; V-AIS; ; 59°01′·45N 04°30′·40W; 992356017.

Nun Rock ⊙; V-AIS; ; 58°52′·65N 04°58′·30W; 992356016.

North Rona ☆ 59°07′·27N 05°48′·91W Fl (3) 20s 114m **22M**.

Sula Sgeir ☆ Fl 15s 74m 11M; ☐ structure; 59°05′·61N 06°09′·57W.

Loch Eriboll, White Hd ☆ Fl WR10s 18m W13M, R12M; W twr and bldg; vis: 030°-W-172°-R-191°-W-212°; 58°31′·01N 04°38′·90W.

Cape Wrath ☆ 58°37′·54N 04°59′·99W Fl (4) 30s 122m **22M**; W twr.

ORKNEY ISLANDS

Tor Ness ☆ 58°46'·78N 03°17'·86W Fl 5s 21m **17M**; W twr.
Cantick Hd (S Walls, SE end) ✩ 58°47'·23N 03°07'·88W Fl 20s 35m 13M; W twr.

SCAPA FLOW and APPROACHES

Long Hope, S Ness Pier Hd ✩ Fl WRG 3s 6m W7M, R5M, G5M; vis: 082°-G- 242°-W- 252°-R-082°; 58°48'·05N 03°12'·35W.

Hoxa Head ✩ Fl WR 3s 15m W9M, R6M; W twr; vis: 026°-W-163°-R-201°-W-215°; 58°49'·31N 03°02'·09W.
Nevi Skerry Fl (2) 6s 7m 6M; 58°50'·67N 03°02'·70W.
Flotta Grinds Fl (2) R; 58°50'·97N 03°00'·77W; 992351083.
Rose Ness ✩ 58°52'·33N 02°49'·97W Fl 6s 24m 8M; W twr.
Barrel of Butter ✩ Fl (2) 10s 6m 7M; 58 53'·40N 03°07'·62W.
Cava ✩ Fl WR 3s 11m W10M, R8M; W ○ twr; vis: 351°-W-143°-196°-W-251°-R-271°-R-298°; 58°53'·21N 03°10'·70W .
Holm of Houton ✩ 58°54'·62N 03°10'·97W; Fl R 3s 7m 5M.
Houton Bay Ldg Lts 316°. Front Fl G 3s 8m. Rear , 200m from front, FG 16m; vis: 312°- 320°; 58°54'·97N 03°11'·56W.

CLESTRAN SOUND and HOY SOUND

Graemsay Is Hoy Sound ☆ Ldg Lts 104°. Front Low, Iso 3s 17m 12M; W twr; vis: 070°-255°, 58°56'·42N 03°18'·60W. **High Rear**, 1·2M from front, Oc WR 8s 35m **W19M,** R14M; W twr; vis: 097°-R-112°-W-163°-R-178°-W-332°; obsc on Ldg line within 0·5M.
Skerry of Ness ✩ Fl WG 4s 7m W7M, G4M; vis: shore -W-090°-G-shore; 58°56'·95N 03°17'·83W.

STROMNESS

Ldg Lts 317°. Front FR 29m 11M; W twr; 58°57'·61N 03°18'·15W. Rear, 55m from front, FR 39m 11M; vis: 307°-327°; H24.

AUSKERRY

Copinsay ✩ Fl (5) 30s 79m 14M; W twr; 58°53'·77N 02°40'·35W.
Auskerry ☆ 59°01'·51N 02°34'·34W Fl 20s 34m **20M**; W twr.
Helliar Holm, S end ✩ Fl WRG 10s 18m W14M, R11M, G11M; W twr; vis: 256°-G-276°-W-292°-R-098°-W-116°-G-154°; 59°01'·13N 02°54'·09W.
Balfour Pier Shapinsay ✩ Fl (2) WRG 5s 5m W3M, R2M, G2M; vis: 270°-G-010°-W-020°-R-090°; 59°01'·86N 02°54'·49W.

KIRKWALL

Thieves Holm, ✩ Q R 8M; 59°01'·09N 02°56'·21W.
Pier N end ☆ 58°59'·29N 02°57'·72W Iso WRG 5s 8m **W15M**, R13M, G13M; W twr; vis: 153°-G-183°-W-192°-R-210°.

WIDE FIRTH

Linga Skerry Q (3) 10s; 59°02'·39N 02°57'·56W.
Boray Skerries Q (6) + L Fl 15s; 59°03'·65N 02°57'·66W.
Skertours Q; 59°04'·11N 02°56'·72W.
Galt Skerry Q; 59°05'·21N 02°54'·20W.
Seal Skerry ✩ Fl R 3s 5m 3M; platform; 59°05'·21N 02°54'·20W.
Brough of Birsay ☆ 59°08'·19N 03°20'·41W Fl (3) 25s 52m **18M**.
Papa Stronsay NE end, The Ness ✩ Fl(4)20s 8m 9M; W twr; 59°09'·34N 02°34'·93W.

SANDAY ISLAND and NORTH RONALDSAY

Quiabow Fl (2) G 12s; 59°09'·82N 02°36'·30W.
Start Pt ☆ 59°16'·69N 02°22'·71W Fl (2) 20s 24m **18M**.
Kettletoft Pier Hd ✩ Fl WRG 3s 7m W7M, R5M, G5M; vis: 351°-W- 011°-R-180°-G-351°; 59°13'·80N 02°35'·86W.
N Ronaldsay ☆ NE end, 59°23'·34N 02°22'·91W Fl 10s 43m **24M**; R twr, W bands; ***Racon (T) 14-17M***.

EDAY and EGILSAY

Calf Sound ✩ Fl (3) WRG 10s 6m W8M, R6M, G6M; W twr; vis: shore-R-215°-W-222°-G-301°-W-305°; 59°14'·21N 02°45'·82W.
Backaland Pier ✩ 59°09'·43N 02°44'·88W Fl R 3s 5m 4M; vis: 192°-250°.
Egilsay Graand Q (6) + L Fl 15s; 59°06'·86N 02°54'·42W.

WESTRAY and PIEROWALL

Noup Head ☆ 59°19'·86N 03°04'·23W Fl 30s 79m **20M**; W twr; vis: about 335°-282° but partially obsc 240°-275°.
Pierowall E Pier Head ✩ Fl WRG 3s 7m W11M, R7M, G7M; vis: 254°-G-276°-W-291°-R-308°-G-215°; 59°19'·35N 02°58'·53W.
Papa Westray, Moclett Bay Pier Head ✩ Fl WRG 5s 7m W5M, R3M, G3M; vis: 306°-G-341°-W-040°-R-074°; 59°19'·60N 02°53'·52W.

SHETLAND ISLES

FAIR ISLE

Skadan South ☆, 59°30'·84N 01°39'·16W Fl (4) 30s 32m **22M**; W twr; vis: 260°-146°, obsc inshore 260°-282°.
Skroo ☆ N end 59°33'·13N 01°36'·58W Fl (2) 30s 80m **22M**; W twr; vis: 086·7°-358°.

MAINLAND, SOUTH

Sumburgh Head ☆ 59°51'·21N 01°16'·58W Fl (3) 30s 91m **23M**.
Lt Ho disused 59°51'·48N 01°16'·28W; W twr.
Mousa, Perie Bard ✩ Fl 3s 20m 10M; 59°59'·84N 01°09'·51W.

BRESSAY and LERWICK

Bressay, Kirkabister Ness ✩ 60°07'·20N 01°07'·31W; Fl (2) 10s 18m 10M. Adjacent Lt Ho disused.
Maryfield Ferry Terminal ✩ Oc WRG 6s 5m 5M; vis: W008°-R013°-G-111°-008°; 60°09'·43N 01°07'·45W.
North Ness ✩ Iso WG 4s 4m 5M; vis: shore-W-158°-G-216°-W-301°; 60°09'·57N 01°08'·77W
Loofa Baa Q (6) + L Fl 15s 4m 5M; 60°09'·72N 01°08'·79W.
Soldian Rock Q (6) + L Fl 15s 60°12'·51N 01°04'·73W.
N ent Dir lt 215°, Oc WRG 6s 27m 8M; Y △, Or stripe; vis: 211°-R-214°-W-216°-G-221°; 60°10'·47N 01°09'·53W.
Rova Hd ✩ 60°11'·46N 01°08'·60W; Fl WRG 4s (sync) 12m W12M, R/G9M; W twr; vis: 090°-R-182°-W-191°-G-213°-R-241°-W-261·5°-G-009°-R-040°; same structure: **Dir** ☆ 186·5° Fl WRG 4s (sync) 14m **W16M**, R/G13M; (sync) vis: 176·5°-R-182°-W-191°-G-196·5°.
Dales Voe ✩ Fl (2) WRG 8s 5m W4M, R3M, G3M; vis: 220°-G-227°-W-233°-R-240°; 60°11'·79N 01°11'·23W.
Hoo Stack ✩ Fl (4) WRG 12s 40m W7M, R5M, G5M; W pylon; vis: 169°-R-180°-W-184°-G-193°-W-169°. Same structure, Dir lt 182°. Fl (4) WRG 12s 33m W9M, R6M, G6M; vis: 177°- R-180°-W-184°-W-187°; synch with upper lt; 60°14'·96N 01°05'·38W.
Mull (Moul) of Eswick ✩ Fl WRG 3s 50m W9M, R6M, G6M; W twr; vis: 028°-R-200°-W-207°-G-018°-W-028°; 60°15'·74N 01°05'·90W.
Inner Voder Q (9) 15s; 60°16'·44N 01°05'·18W; AIS.

WHALSAY and SKERRIES

Symbister Ness ✩ Fl (2) WG 12s 11m W8M, G6M; W twr; vis: shore-W-203°-G-shore; 60°20'·43N 01°02'·29W.
Suther Ness ✩ Fl WRG 3s 10m W10M, R8M, G7M; vis: shore -W-038°-R-173°-W-206°-G-shore; 60°22'·12N 01°00'·20W.
Bound Skerry ☆ 60°25'·47N 00°43'·72W Fl 20s 44m **20M**; W twr.
South Mouth. Ldg Lts 014°. Front, FY3m 2M; 60°25'·33N 00°45'·01W. Rear, FY 12m 2M.
Muckle Skerry ✩ Fl (2) WRG 10s 15m W7M, R5M, G5M; W twr; vis: 046°-W-192°-R-272°-G-348°-W-353°-R-046°; 60°26'·41N 00°51'·84W.

YELL SOUND

S ent, Lunna Holm ✩ Fl (3) WRG 15s 19m W10M,R7M,G7M; W ○ twr; vis: shore-R-090°-W-094°-G-209°-W-275°-R-shore; 60°27'·34N 01°02'·52W.
Firths Voe ☆, N shore 60°27'·21N 01°10'·63W Oc WRG 8s 9m **W15M**, R10M, G10M; W twr; vis: 189°-W-194°-G-257°-W-261°-R-339°-W-066°.
Linga Is. Dir lt 150° ✩ Q (4) WRG 8s 10m W9M, R9M, G9M; vis: 145°-R-148°-W-152°-G-155°. Q (4) WRG 8s 10m W7M, R4M, G4M; same structure; vis: 052°-R-146°, 154°-G-196°-W-312°; synch; 60°26'·80N 01°09'·13W.
The Rumble Bn ✩ R Bn; Fl 10s 8m 4M; ***Racon (O)***; 60°28'·16N 01°07'·26W.

Yell, Ulsta Ferry Term. Bkwtr Hd ☆ Oc RG 4s 7m R5M, G5M; vis: shore-G-354°, 044°-R-shore. Same structure; Oc WRG 4s 5m W8M, R5M, G5M; vis: shore-G-008°-W-036°-R-shore; 60°29'·74N 01°09'·52W.

Toft Ferry Terminal ☆,Dir lt 241° (H24); Dir Oc WRG 10s 8m **W16M**, R10M, G10M; vis: 236° -G-240°-W-242°-R-246°; by day W2M, R1M, G1M. 60°27'·96N 01°12'·34W.

Ness of Sound, W side ☆ Fl (3) WRG 12s 18m W9M, R6M, G6M; vis: shore-G-345°-W-350°-R-160°-W-165°-G-shore; 60°31'·34N 01°11'·28W.

Brother Is. Dir lt 329°, Fl (4) WRG 8s 16m W10M, R7M, G7M; vis: 323·5°-G-328°-W-330°-R-333·5°; 60°30'·95N 01°14'·11W.

Mio Ness ☆ Q (2) WR 10s 12m W7M, R4M; W ○ twr; vis: 282° - W - 238° - R - 282°; 60°29'·66N 01°13'·68W.

Tinga Skerry ☆ Q(2)G 10s 9m 5M. W ○ twr; 60°30'·48N 01°14'·86W.

YELL SOUND, NORTH ENTRANCE

Bagi Stack ☆ Fl (4) 20s 45m 10M; 60°43'·53N 01°07'·54W.

Gruney Is ☆ Fl WR 5s 53m W8M, R6M; W twr; vis: 064°-R-180°-W-012°; ***Racon (T) 14M***; 60°39'·15N 01°18'·17W.

Pt of Fethaland ☆ 60°38'·05N 01°18'·70W Fl (3) WR 15s 65m **W19M, R15M**; vis 080°-R-103°-W-160°-R-206°-W-340°.

Muckle Holm ☆ Fl (4) 10s 32m 10M 60°34'·83N 01°16'·01W.

Little Holm ☆ Iso 4s 12m 6M; W twr; 60°33'·42N 01°15'·88W.

Outer Skerry ☆ Fl 6s 12m 8M; 60°33'·04N 01°18'·32W.

Quey Firth ☆ Oc WRG 6s 22m W12M, R8M, G8M; W twr; vis: shore (through S & W)-W-290°-G-327°-W-334°-W-shore; 60°31'·43N 01°19'·58W.

Lamba, S side ☆Fl WRG 3s 30m W8M, R5M, G5M; W twr; vis: shore-G-288°-W-293°-R-327°-W-044°-R-140°-W-shore. Dir lt 290·5° Fl WRG 3s 24m W10M, R7M, G7M; vis: 285·5°-G-288°-W-293°-W-295·5°; 60°30'·73N 01°17'·84W.

SULLOM VOE

Gluss Is ☆ Ldg Lts 194·7° (H24). **Front**, 60°29'·77N 01°19'·44W F 39m **19M**; □ on Gy twr; **Rear**, 0·75M from front, F 69m **19M**; □ on Gy twr; both Lts 9M by day.

Little Roe ☆ Fl (3) WR 10s 16m W5M, R4M; W structure, Or band; vis: 036°-R-095·5°-W-036°; 60°29'·99N 01°16'·46W.

Skaw Taing ☆ Ldg Lts 150·5°. Front, Oc WRG 5s 21m W8M, R5M, G5M; Or and W structure; vis: 049°-W-078°-G-147°-W-154°-R-169°-W-288°; 60°29'·10N 01°16'·86W. Rear, 195m from front, Oc 5s 35m 8M; vis: W145°-156°.

Ness of Bardister ☆ Oc WRG 8s 20m W9M, R6M, G6M; Or &W structure; vis: 180·5°- W-240°- R-310·5°- W-314·5°- G-030·5°; 60°28'·19N 01°19'·63W.

Fugla Ness. Lts in line 212·3°. Rear, 60°27'·25N 01°19'·74W Iso 4s 45m 14M. Common front 60°27'·45N 01°19'·57W Iso 4s 27m 14M; synch with rear Lts. Lts in line 203°. Rear, 60°27'·26N 01°19'·81W Iso 4s 45m 14M.

Sella Ness ☆ Dir lt 133·5°; 60°26'·76N 01°16'·66W Oc WRG 10s 19m **W16M**, R3M, G3M; vis: 123·5° -G- 130·5°-Al WG (white phase increasing with brg)-132·5°-W-134·5°-Al WR(R phase inc with brg)-136·5°-R-143·5°; H24. By day Oc WRG 10s 19m W2M, R1M,G1M as above.

EAST YELL, UNST and BALTA SOUND

Whitehill ☆ Fl WR 3s 24m W9M, R6M; W clad metal frame twr; vis: 147°-W-163°-R-211°-W-352°-R-003°; 60°34'·80N 01°00'·22W.

Fetlar. Hamars Ness ☆ Iso G 6s 5m 3M; 60°37'·78N 00°55'·73W.

Balta Sound ☆Fl WR 10s 17m 10M, R7M; vis: 249°-W-008°-R-058°-W-154°; 60°44'·43N 00°47'·68W.

Holme of Skaw ☆ Fl 5s 8m 8M; white metal framework twr; 60°49'·87N 00°46'·30W.

Muckle Flugga ☆ 60°51'·32N 00°53'·13W Fl (2) 20s 66m **22M**.

Yell. Cullivoe Bkwtr Hd ☆ Fl (2) WRG 10s 3m 4M; vis: 080°-G-294°-W-355°-R-080°; 60°41'·86N 00°59'·70W.

Unst. Head of Mula ☆ Fl WRG 5s 48m W10M, G7M, R7M; metal framework twr; vis: 292°-G-357°-W-002°-R-157°-W-161·5; 60°40'·76N 00°57'·58W.

MAINLAND, WEST

Esha Ness ☆ 60°29'·34N 01°37'·65W Fl 12s 61m **25M**.

Ness of Hillswick ☆ Fl (4) WR 15s 34m W9M, R6M; vis: 217°-W-093°-R-114°; 60°27'·21N 01°29'·80W.

Muckle Roe, Swarbacks Minn ☆ Fl WR 3s 30m W9M, R6M; vis: 314°-W-041°-R-075°-W-137°; 60°20'·98N 01°27'·07W.

W Burra Firth Outer ☆ Oc WRG 8s 27m W9M, R7M, G7M; vis: 136°-G-142°-W-150°-R-156°. H24; 60°17'·79N 01°33'·56W.

W Burra Firth Inner ☆ 60°17'·78N 01°32'·17W F WRG 9m **W15M**, R9M, G9M; vis: 095°-G-098°-W-102°-105°; H24.

Ve Skerries ☆ Fl (2) 20s 17m 11M; W twr; ***Racon (T) 15M***; 60°22'·36N 01°48'·78W.

Papa Stour Housa Voe Dir lt 228° ☆ F WRG 2m W9M, R7M, G7M; vis: 219°- G-226°- W-230°-R-239°; 60°19'·58N 01°40'·47W.

Rams Head ☆ Fl WRG 8s 16m W9M, R6M; G6M; W house; vis: 265°-G-355°-W-012°-R-090°-W-136°, obsc by Vaila I when brg more than 030°; 60°11'·96N 01°33'·47W.

North Havra ☆ Fl(3) WRG 12s 24m W11M, R8M, G8M; W twr; vis: 001°-G-053·5°-W-060·5°-R-144°, 274°- G-334°-W-337·5°-R -001°; 60°09'·85N 01°20'·29W.

SCALLOWAY

Bullia Skerry ☆ Fl 5s 5m 5M; stainless steel pillar & platform 60°06'·55N 01°21'·57W.

Point of the Pund ☆ Fl WRG 5s 20m W7M, R5M, G5M; W GRP twr; vis: 267°-W-350°-R-090°-G-111°-R-135°-W-140°-G-177°; 60°07'·99N 01°18'·31W.

Whaleback Skerry ⥿ Q; 60°07'·95N 01°18'·90W.

Blacks Ness Pier SW corner ☆ Oc WRG 10s 10m W11M, G8M, R8M; vis: 052°-G-063·5°-W-065·5°-R-077°; 60°08'·02N 01°16'·59W.

Fugla Ness ☆ Fl (2) WRG 10s 20m W10M, R7M, G7M; W twr; vis: 014°-G-032°-W-082°-R-134°-W-shore; 60°06'·38N 01°20'·85W.

FOULA

South Ness ☆ 60°06'·75N 02°03'·86W Fl WR (3) 15s 36m **W18M** R14M; W twr; vis: 221°-W-255°-R-277°-W-123°-obscured-221°.

9.7.5 PASSAGE INFORMATION

More passage information is threaded between the harbours in this area. Admiralty Leisure Folio: 5617 Fraserburgh to Inverness and the Caledonian Canal. **Bibliography:** *North and East Scotland* Farne Islands to Cape Wrath(Imray/Lawrence). *N&NE Scotland and Orkney Islands. Shetland Islands* (Both Clyde Cruising Club sailing directions and anchorages). *Shetland Islands Pilot* (Imray/Buchanan). The *N Coast of Scotland Pilot* (Admiralty NP52).

A £75 *'Rover ticket'* (Aberdeenshire and Moray Councils) allows berthing for one week from arrival at the first harbour at other ports in the scheme. Orkney Marinas 'Weekly Rover' costs £11/m, to berth in their 3 marinas or on Port Authority Harbours, piers and moorings except St Margaret's Hope (9.7.21) which is independent.

BUCHAN NESS TO RATTRAY HEAD

Buchan Ness (lt, fog sig, Racon) is a rky peninsula. 2ca N is Meikle Mackie islet, close W of which is the small hbr of Boddam (dries). 3ca NE of Meikle Mackie is The Skerry, a rk 6m high on S side of Sandford B; rks on which the sea breaks extend 2ca NNE. The chan between The Skerry and the coast is foul with rks and not advised. Peterhead is easy to enter in almost all conditions and is an excellent passage port with marina at SW corner of the Bay.

Numerous submarine pipelines lead ashore to St Fergus Terminal in Rattray Bay. **Notes on offshore installations, see 3.14 and 9.5.5.** Rattray Hd (light on The Ron, rk 2ca E of Hd) has rocky foreshore, drying to 2ca off. Rattray Briggs is a detached reef, depth 0·2m, 2ca E of lt ho. Rattray Hard is a rky patch, depth 10·7m, 1·5M ENE of the lt ho, which raises a dangerous sea during onshore gales.

▶ *Off Rattray Hd the S-going stream begins at HW Aberdeen –0420, and the N-going at HW Aberdeen +0110, sp rates 3kn. In normal conditions keep about 1M E of Rattray Hd, but pass 5M off in bad weather, preferably at slack water.* ◀

Conspic radio masts with red aero lights lie 2·5M WNW and 2·2M W of lighthouse.

MORAY FIRTH: SOUTH COAST

(AC 115, 222, 223) Crossing the Moray Firth from Rattray Hd (lt, fog sig) to Duncansby Hd (lt, Racon) heavy seas may be met in strong W winds. Most hbrs in the Firth are exposed to NE-E winds. For oil installations, see 9.5.5; the Beatrice Field is 20M S of Wick.

▶ *Tidal streams attain 3kn at Sp close off Rattray Hd. 5M NE of the Head the NE-going stream begins at HW Aberdeen +0140, and the SE-going stream at HW Aberdeen –0440, Sp rates 2kn. Except in the inner part of the Moray Firth streams are weak.* ◀

In late spring/early summer fog (haar) is likely in onshore winds. In strong winds the sea breaks over Steratan Rk and Colonel Rk, respectively 3M E and 1M ENE of Fraserburgh. Banff B is shallow; N of Macduff beware Collie Rks. Banff hbr dries, and should not be approached in fresh NE-E winds, when seas break well offshore; Macduff is a possible alternative.

From Meavie Pt to Scar Nose dangers extend up to 3ca from shore in places. Beware Caple Rk (depth 0·2m) 7½ca W of Logie Hd.

Spey B is clear of dangers more than 7½ca from shore; ⚓ here, but only in offshore winds. Beware E Muck (dries) 5ca SW of Craigenroan, an above-water rky patch 5ca SW of Craig Hd, and Middle Muck and W Muck in approach to Buckie; Findochty & Portknockie are 2 and 3.5M ENE. Halliman Skerries (dry; bn) lie 1·5M WNW of Lossiemouth. Covesea Skerries (dry) lie 5ca NW of their lt ho (disused).

To the SW of a line between Helmsdale and Lossiemouth is a EU Special Area of Conservation to protect a vulnerable population of bottlenose dolphins. Mariners are advised to proceed at a safe, constant speed through the area and avoid disturbing them.

Inverness Firth is approached between Nairn and S Sutor. In heavy weather there is a confused sea with overfalls on Guillam Bank, 9M S of Tarbat Ness. The sea also breaks on Riff Bank (S of S Sutor) which dries in places. Chans run both N and S of Riff Bank.

▶ *Off Fort George, on E side of ent to Inverness Firth (AC1078), the SW-going stream begins HW Aberdeen +0605, sp rate 2·5kn; the NE-going stream begins at HW Aberdeen –0105, sp rate 3·5kn. There are eddies and turbulence between Fort George and Chanonry Pt when stream is running hard. Tidal streams in the Inverness Firth and approaches are not strong, except in the Cromarty Firth Narrows, the Fort George Narrows and the Kessock Road, including off the entrance to the Caledonian Canal.* ◀

There is a firing range between Nairn and Inverness marked, when in operation, by flags at Fort George. Much of Inverness Firth is shallow, but a direct course from Chanonry Pt to Kessock Bridge, via Munlochy SWM and Meikle Mee SHM lt buoys, carries a least depth of 2·1m. Meikle Mee bank dries 0·2m.

9.7.6 PETERHEAD

Aberdeenshire **57°29'·81N 01°46'·42W**

CHARTS AC 213, 1438, 5617; Imray C23

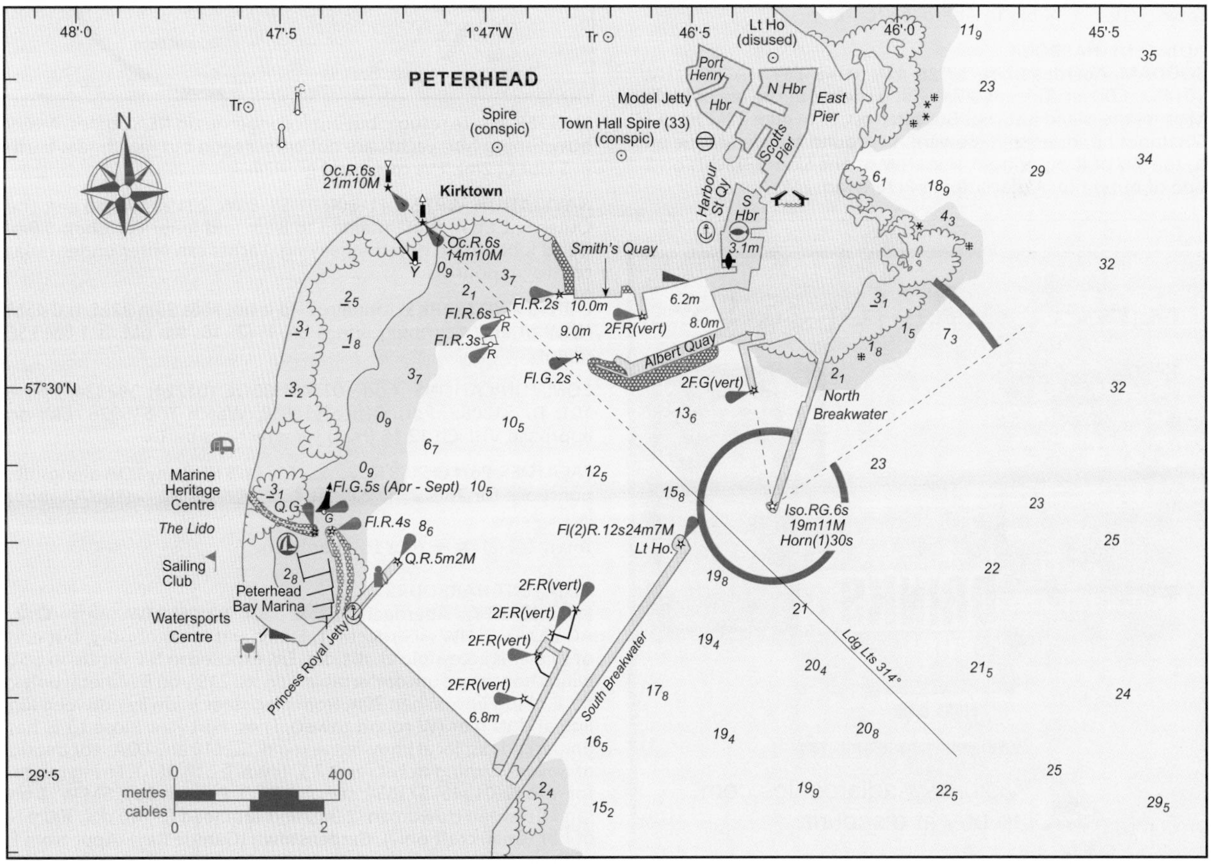

Continued overleaf

PETERHEAD *continued*

TIDES +0140 Dover; ML 2·3; Duration 0620

Standard Port ABERDEEN (⟵)

Times				Height (metres)			
High Water		Low Water		MHWS	MHWN	MLWN	MLWS
0000	0600	0100	0700	4·3	3·4	1·6	0·6
1200	1800	1300	1900				
Differences *PETERHEAD*							
–0035	*–0045*	*–0035*	*–0040*	*–0·3*	*–0·2*	*0·0*	*+0·1*

SHELTER Good in marina (2·8m). A useful passage hbr, also a major fishing and oil/gas industry port. Access any weather/tide.

NAVIGATION WPT 57°29′·44N 01°45′·75W, 314°/0·5M to ent. No dangers. 5kn speed limit in Bay; 4kn in marina. Chan between marina bkwtr and SHM lt buoy is <30m wide.

LIGHTS AND MARKS Power stn chy (183m) is conspic 1·25M S of entrance. Ldg marks 314°, front Or △, rear Or ▽, on lattice masts; lights as chartlet. Marina E bkwtr ☆ Fl R 4s 6m 2M; W bkwtr hd, QG 5m 2M, vis 185°-300°. Buchan Ness ☆ Fl 5s 40m 28M is 1·6M S of entrance.

COMMUNICATIONS (Code 01779) CGOC (01224) 592334; Police 101; Dr 474841; Ⓗ 472316. Marina Manager (Port Authority: www.peterheadport.co.uk) 477868; Hr Control (H24) 483630.

All vessels, including yachts, **must** call *Peterhead Harbour Radio* VHF Ch **14** for clearance to enter/depart the Bay.

FACILITIES **Peterhead Bay Marina** marina@peterheadport.co.uk ☎477868, access all tides, 2·3m at ent, max LOA 20m. Pontoons are 'E' to 'A' from entrance.150, £13 up to 6m LOA + £1/m (7 days for price of 5); ; from bowser at end of Princess Royal jetty (☆ Q R); ✕ at caravan site.

Peterhead SC ☎(01358) 751340 (Sec); **Services** ⓔ .

Town ✉ ✕ bus to Aberdeen for ⇄ ✈.

ADJACENT HARBOUR

BODDAM, Aberdeenshire, **57°28′·47N 01°46′·56W**. AC 213. HW +0145 on Dover; Tides as 9.7.6. Good shelter in the lee of Meikle Mackie, the island just N of Buchan Ness, Fl 5s 40m 28M Horn (3) 60s. Inner hbr dries/unlit. Beware rks around Meikle Mackie and to the SW of it. Appr from 1½ca NW of The Skerry. Yachts on S side of outer hbr. All facilities at Peterhead, 2M N.

9.7.7 FRASERBURGH

Aberdeenshire **57°41′·50N 01°59′·79W**

CHARTS AC 115, 222, 1462, 5617; Imray C23

TIDES +0120 Dover; ML 2·3; Duration 0615

Standard Port ABERDEEN (⟵)

Times				Height (metres)			
High Water		Low Water		MHWS	MHWN	MLWN	MLWS
0000	0600	0100	0700	4·3	3·4	1·6	0·6
1200	1800	1300	1900				
Differences *FRASERBURGH*							
–0122	*–0118*	*–0115*	*–0115*	*–0·5*	*–0·4*	*–0·1*	*+0·2*

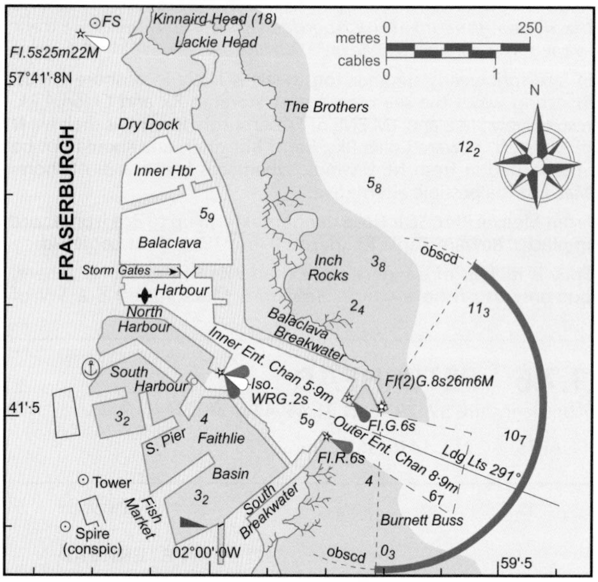

SHELTER A safe refuge, but ent is dangerous in NE/SE gales. A very busy fishing hbr; yachts are not encouraged but may find a berth in S Hbr (3.2m). FVs come and go H24.

NAVIGATION WPT 57°41′·30N 01°58′·80W, 291°/0·57M to ent. The Outer Ent Chan is maintained to 8·9m and Inner Ent Chan 5.9m. Good lookout on entering/leaving. Yachts can enter under radar control in poor vis.

LIGHTS AND MARKS Kinnairds Hd lt ho, Fl 5s 25m 22M, is 0·45M NNW of ent. Cairnbulg Briggs bn, Fl (2) 10s 9m 6M, is 1·8M ESE of ent.

COMMUNICATIONS (Code 01346) CGOC (01224) 592334; Police 101; Dr 518088. Port Office 515858; Watch Tr 515926. Call on approach VHF Ch **12** 16 (H24) for directions/berth.

FACILITIES **Port** ☎515858, £10 (in S Hbr) any LOA alongside; pontoons for 26 inc 2 ; (30t/70t mob) ✕ .

Town ✉ Ⓑ ⇄ ✈ (bus to Aberdeen).

ADJACENT HARBOURS

ROSEHEARTY, Aberdeen, **57°42′·08N 02°06′·87W.** AC 222, 213. HW Aberdeen –1. E pier and inner hbr dry, but end of W pier is accessible at all tides. Ent exposed in N/E winds; in E/SE winds hbr can be uncomfortable. Ldg lts, 219°, on BW metal poles; rks E of ldg line. When 30m from pier, steer midway between ldg line and W pier (W round tower), Fl 4s. Port Rae, close to E, has unmarked rks; local knowledge req'd. £10 any LOA. *For details of Rover berthing ticket see 9.7.5.* **Town** ✉ ✕ . Firing range: for info ☎(01346) 571634; see also 9.7.5. **Pennan Bay**, 5M W: ⚓ on sand between Howdman (2·9m) and Tamhead (2·1m) rks, 300m N of hbr (small craft only). **Gardenstown** (Gamrie Bay). Appr from E of Craig Dagerty rk (4m, conspic). Harbour dries, or ⚓ off.

9.7.8 MACDUFF/BANFF

Aberdeenshire Macduff **57°40'·25N 02°30'·03W**
Banff **57°40'·22N 02°31'·27W**

CHARTS AC 115, 222, 1462, 5617; Imray C23

TIDES + 0055 Dover; ML 2·0; Duration 0615

Standard Port ABERDEEN (←)

Times				Height (metres)			
High Water		Low Water		MHWS	MHWN	MLWN	MLWS
0200	0900	0400	0900	4·3	3·4	1·6	0·6
1400	2100	1600	2100				
Differences BANFF							
–0100	–0150	–0150	–0050	–0·4	–0·2	–0·1	+0·2

SHELTER **Macduff**: Reasonably good, but ent not advised in strong NW winds. Slight/moderate surge in outer hbr with N/NE gales. Hbr ent is 17m wide with 3 basins; approx 2·6m in outer hbr and 2m inner hbr. A busy cargo/fishing port with limited space for yachts. **Banff**: Popular hbr which dries. When Macduff ent is very rough in strong NW/N winds, Banff can be a safe refuge; pontoon berths in both basins. Best to contact HM beforehand. In strong E/ENE winds Banff is unusable.

NAVIGATION WPT 57°40'·48N 02°30'·59W, 127°/0·4M to **Macduff** ent. WPT 57°40'·11N 02°30'·85W, 115°/0·25M to **Banff** ent. Beware Feachie Craig, Collie Rks and rky coast N and S of hbr ent.

LIGHTS AND MARKS **Macduff**: Ldg lts/marks 127° both FR 28/55m 3M, orange △s. Pier hd lt, Fl (2) WRG 6s 12m 9/7M, W tr; shore-G-115°-W-174°-R-210°. **Banff**: Fl 4s end of New Quay and ldg lts 295° rear Fl R 2s, front Fl R 4s.

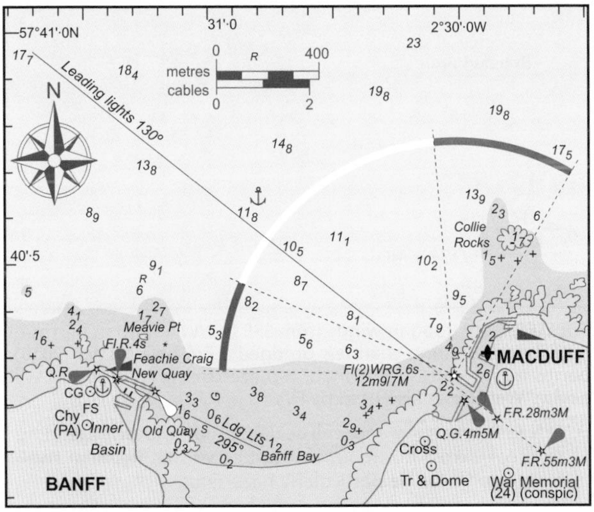

COMMUNICATIONS (Code 01261) CGOC (01224) 592334; Police 101; Dr (**Banff**) 812027. HM (**Macduff**) 832236, Watch tr 833962; HM (**Banff**) 815544.

Macduff Ch 12 16 (H24); **Banff** Ch 12.

FACILITIES **Macduff**: **Hbr** £10 any LOA;
Town (bus to Keith).

Banff: **Hbr** www.banffmarina.com in Inner Hbr marina, £10 any LOA, *Rover berthing ticket see 9.7.5*; **Banff SC**:
Town (Aberdeen).

ADJACENT HARBOURS

PORTSOY, Aberdeenshire, **57°41'·34N 02°41'·59W**. AC 222. HW +0047 on Dover; –0132 and Ht –0·3m on Aberdeen. Small drying hbr; ent exposed to NW/NE'lies. New Hbr to port of ent partially dries; Inner Hbr dries to clean sand. Ldg lts 173°, front Fl G 4s 20m 3M, metal post; rear Q G 22m 3M, R △ on BW post. HM ☎(01261) 815544. Facilities: few but hosts Scottish Traditional Boat Festival late June/early July. £10, *for details of a 'Rover Ticket' see 9.7.5*,

Sandend Bay, 1·7M W (57°41'N 02°44'·5W). ⚓ on sand E of hbr.

9.7.9 WHITEHILLS

Aberdeenshire **57°40'·80N 02°34'·87W**

CHARTS AC 115, 222, 5617; Imray C23

TIDES +0050 Dover; ML 2·4; Duration 0610

Standard Port ABERDEEN (←)

Times				Height (metres)			
High Water		Low Water		MHWS	MHWN	MLWN	MLWS
0200	0900	0400	0900	4·3	3·4	1·6	0·6
1400	2100	1600	2100				
Differences WHITEHILLS							
–0122	–0137	–0117	–0127	–0·4	–0·3	+0·1	+0·1

SHELTER Safe. In strong NW/N winds beware surge in the narrow ent and outer hbr, when ent is best not attempted. See HM for vacant pontoon berth.

NAVIGATION WPT 57°41'·98N 02°34'·89W, 180°/1·2M to bkwtr lt. Reefs on S side of chan marked by 2 rusty/white SHM bns. Beware fishing floats. Narrow entrance 1·7m below CD, Outer Hbr pontoon berths 2m and Inner Hbr 1.5m–1·8m.

LIGHTS AND MARKS Fl WR 3s on pier hd, vis 132°-R-212°-W-245°; approach in R sector.

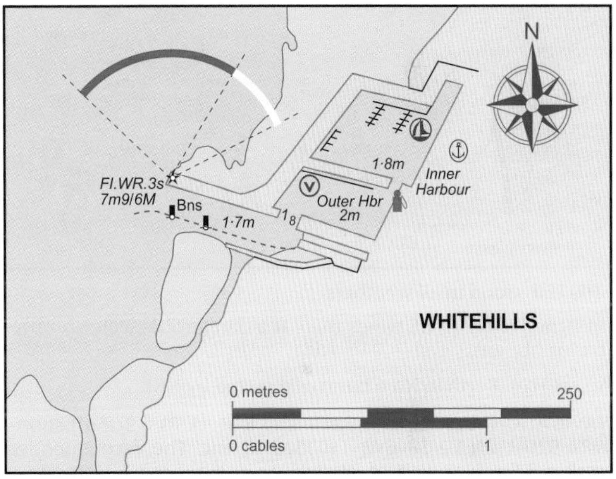

COMMUNICATIONS (Code 01261) CGOC (01224) 592334; Police 101; Dr 812027. HM www.whitehillsharbour.co.uk 861291, mobile 07906 135786.

Whitehills Hbr Radio VHF Ch **14** 16.

FACILITIES **Marina** (47+12), £18 (+£2) Quayside £12 @; **Town** (bus to Keith), (Aberdeen).

ADJACENT HARBOURS

CULLEN, Moray, **57°41'·63N 02°49'·29W**. AC 222. HW +0045 on Dover, HW –0135 & –0·3m on Aberdeen; Duration 0555; ML 2·4m. Shelter good, but ent hazardous in strong W/N winds. Appr on 180° toward conspic viaduct and W bn on N pier. Caple Rk, 0·2m, is 5ca NE of hbr. Small drying hbr, best for shoal draught. Moor S of Inner jetty if < 1m draught with F G bn close S of the root of N pier. Beware moorings across inner basin ent. Pontoons in inner hbr (1·8m at HW Np). *For details of a 'Rover Ticket' see 9.7.5.* HM ☎(01542) 831700. **Town** (hardware store),

PORTKNOCKIE, Moray, **57°42'·28N 02°51'·79W**. AC 222. HW +0045 on Dover; –0135 and ht –0·3m Aberdeen; ML 2·3m; Duration 0555; access H24. Good shelter in one of the safest hbrs on S side of Moray Firth, but scend is often experienced; care needed in strong NW/N winds. FW ldg lts, on white-topped poles, lead approx 151°, to ent. Orange street lts surround the hbr. Limited ABs on N Quay; most of inner hbr dries. HM ☎(01542) 840833 (home, p/time); Facilities: ; *for details of a 'Rover Ticket' see 9.7.5*, ; Dr ☎ 840272. **Town**

9.7.10 BUCKIE

Moray **57°40'·84N 02°57'·63W**

CHARTS AC 223, 1462, 5617; Imray C23

TIDES +0040 Dover; ML 2·4; Duration 0550

Standard Port ABERDEEN (⟵)

Times				Height (metres)			
High Water		Low Water		MHWS	MHWN	MLWN	MLWS
0200	0900	0400	0900	4·3	3·4	1·6	0·6
1400	2100	1600	2100				
Differences BUCKIE							
–0130	–0145	–0125	–0140	–0·2	–0·2	0·0	+0·1

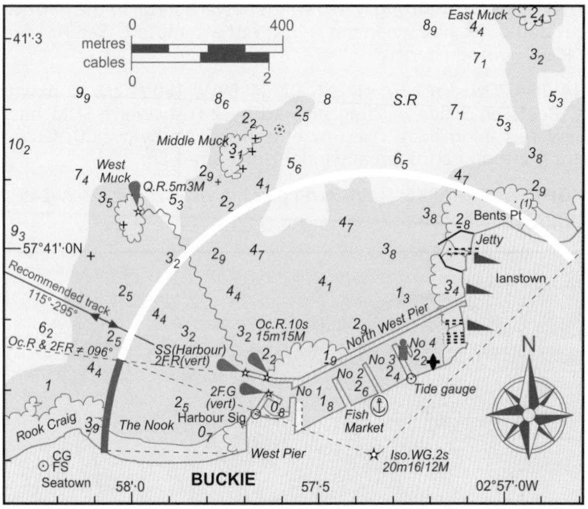

SHELTER Good in all weathers.

In strong NNW to NE winds there is a dangerous swell over the bar at hbr ent, which is 24m wide.

Access H24. Berth in No 4 basin as directed by HM.

NAVIGATION Beware W, Middle and E Muck Rks, 3ca off shore. WPT 57°41'·0N 02°58'·6W, 110°/5ca to ent. The recommended track is 3.5 cables west of West Muck and approach Harbour at 115°. Approx 2 cables from entrance alter to 100° just as the 2FR (vert) and the Oc R 10s on the N breakwater come into line (096°). Traffic is controlled by VHF.

LIGHTS AND MARKS W Muck QR 5m 2M (tripod); N bkwtr, Oc R 10s 15m 15M (W twr), N bwtr hd 2FR(vert), S bwtr hd 2FG(vert). Harbour Lt Iso WG 2s 20m 16/12M, (W tr, R top inshore of hbr).

COMMUNICATIONS (Code 01542) CGOC (01224) 592334; Police 101; Dr 831555. HM 831700(H24), fax 834742 mob 07779888599. VHF Ch 12 16 (H24).

FACILITIES £18 or £9 <12hrs (delivery) (50t) (15t). **Town** at Strathlene caravan site 1½M E, (bus to Elgin), (Aberdeen or Inverness).

ADJACENT HARBOURS

Findochty, Cullen and Portknockie are managed from Buckie.

FINDOCHTY (2M ENE Buckie), Moray, **57°41'·94N 02°54'·29W**. AC 222. HW +0045 on Dover, HW –0135 & ht –0·2m on Aberdeen; ML 2·3m; Duration 0550. Ent is about 2ca W of conspic church belfry. 1ca N of ent, leave Beacon Rock (3m high) to stbd. Ldg lts, FR, lead 166° into Outer Basin which dries 0·2m and has many rky outcrops. Ent faces N and is 20m wide; unlit white bn at hd of W pier. Good shelter in inner basin for 100 small craft/yachts on 3 pontoons (the 2 W'ly pontoons dry); possible on Sterlochy Pier in 2m £18 or £9 <12hrs; (£10) *for details of a 'Rover Ticket' see 9.7.5.* HM Buckie mob 07779888599. **Town** Ⓑ.

9.7.11 LOSSIEMOUTH

Moray **57°43'·41N 03°16'·63W**

CHARTS AC 223, 1462, 5617; Imray C23

TIDES +0040 Dover; ML 2·3; Duration 0605

Standard Port ABERDEEN (⟵)

Times				Height (metres)			
High Water		Low Water		MHWS	MHWN	MLWN	MLWS
0200	0900	0400	0900	4·3	3·4	1·6	0·6
1400	2100	1600	2100				
Differences LOSSIEMOUTH							
–0125	–0200	–0130	–0130	–0·2	–0·2	0·0	0·0

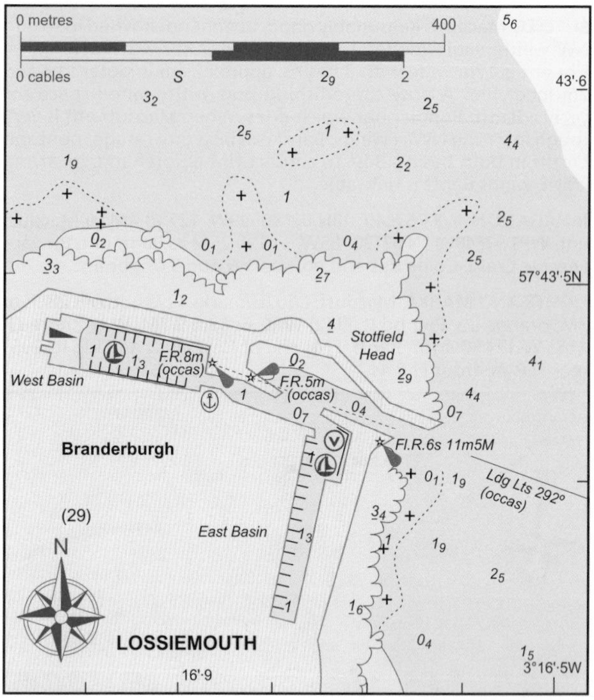

SHELTER Very good in winds from SSE to NW. Pontoon berths in both basins; marina channels dredged 1·8m below LWS (2016), berths may be less in soft mud, esp at extreme springs. HM will advise. West Basin also used by FVs.

- In N to SE winds >F6 appr can be dangerous, with swell tending to break across hbr mouth and in outer hbr. Residual swell from E to SE can be particularly hazardous.
- Near ent, beware current from R Lossie setting in N'ly direction, causing confused water in N to SE winds at sp.
- Vessels drawing >2m would have little clearance at LWS ±2.

NAVIGATION WPT 57°43'·38N 03°16'·09W, 277°/0·3M to ent. Rks to N and S of hbr ent; appr from E. Approx 1·5m in entrance at LWS.

LIGHTS AND MARKS Halliman Skerries (drying) 1M W of harbour entrance are marked by NCM, Q; ***Racon M***. SPM marks outfall ½M NE of hbr. Unlit bn and disused Lt Ho on adjacent mainland shore. Ldg lts 292°, both FR 5/8m; S pier hd Fl R 6s 11m 5M.

COMMUNICATIONS (Code 01343) CGOC (01224) 592334; Police 101; Dr 0345 337 1190.

VHF Ch 12 16 HO.

FACILITIES **Lossiemouth Marina** ☎813066 (95 inc Ⓥ) £20 for first 24hrs and £15 thereafter/craft wi-fi.

Hbr (£50 pa) (25t) (1t).

Hbr Service Stn ☎813001 Mon-Fri 0800-2030, Sat 0800-1930, Sun 0930-1900.

Town Ⓑ Ⓒ (bus to Elgin) (Inverness).

9.7.12 HOPEMAN

Moray **57°42'·70N 03°26'·31W** ✿✿✿✿✿

CHARTS AC 223, 1462, 5617; Imray C23

TIDES +0050 Dover; ML 2·4; Duration 0610

Standard Port ABERDEEN (⟵)

Times				Height (metres)			
High Water		Low Water		MHWS	MHWN	MLWN	MLWS
0200	0900	0400	0900	4·3	3·4	1·6	0·6
1400	2100	1600	2100				
Differences HOPEMAN							
−0120	−0150	−0135	−0120	−0·2	−0·2	0·0	0·0

SHELTER Once in Inner Basin, shelter good from all winds; but hbr dries. Ent is difficult in winds from NE to SE. A popular yachting hbr with ⛵.

NAVIGATION WPT 57°42'·66N, 03°26'·59W, 083° to ent, 0·17M.

Dangerous rks lie off hbr ent. Do not attempt entry in heavy weather. Beware lobster pot floats E and W of hbr (Mar-Aug).

LIGHTS AND MARKS See 9.7.4 and chartlet.

COMMUNICATIONS (Code 01343) CGOC (01224) 592334; Police 101; Dr 543141. HM 835337 (part-time).

Burghead Radio Ch 14 (HX).

FACILITIES **Hbr** ⛵£9, *for details of a 'Rover Ticket' see 9.7.5*, ⛴ ⛽ ✕ 🔧 🛠.

Town ✉ Ⓑ 🛒 ✕ 🍴 ⇌(bus to Elgin), ✈ (Inverness).

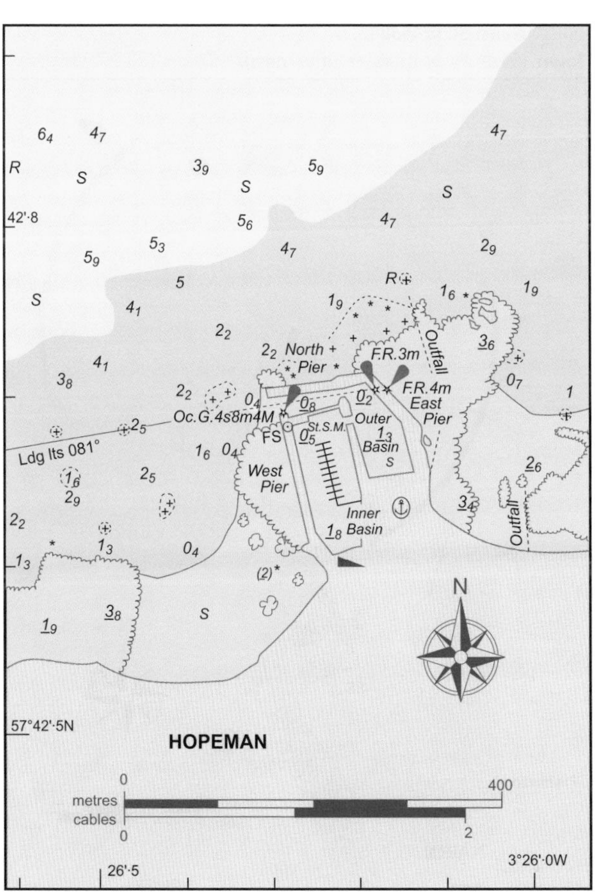

9.7.13 BURGHEAD

Moray **57°42'·06N 03°30'·02W** ✿✿✿✿✿

CHARTS AC 223, 1462, 5617; Imray C23

TIDES +0035 Dover; ML 2·4; Duration 0610

Standard Port ABERDEEN (⟵)

Times				Height (metres)			
High Water		Low Water		MHWS	MHWN	MLWN	MLWS
0200	0900	0400	0900	4·3	3·4	1·6	0·6
1400	2100	1600	2100				
Differences BURGHEAD							
−0120	−0150	−0135	−0120	−0·2	−0·2	0·0	0·0

SHELTER One of the few Moray Firth hbrs accessible in strong E winds. Go alongside where available and contact HM. Can be very busy with FVs.

NAVIGATION WPT 57°42'·28N 03°30'·39W, 137°/0·28M to N pier lt QR. 0·6m in ent chan and 1·4m in hbr, but depths variable due to sand movement. Advisable to contact HM if entering near LW. 3kn speed limit.

LIGHTS AND MARKS No ldg lts but night ent is safe after identifying the N pier lts: QR 3m 5M and Oc 8s 7m 5M.

COMMUNICATIONS (Code 01343) CGOC (01224) 592334; Police 101; Dr 812277. HM 835337.

Burghead Radio VHF Ch **14** 12 (HO and when vessel due).

FACILITIES **Hbr** ⛵£9, *for details of a 'Rover Ticket' see 9.7.5*, ⛴ ⛽ ✕ 🔧 (50t) mobile.

Town ✉ Ⓑ 🛒 🍴 ⇌(bus to Elgin), ✈(Inverness).

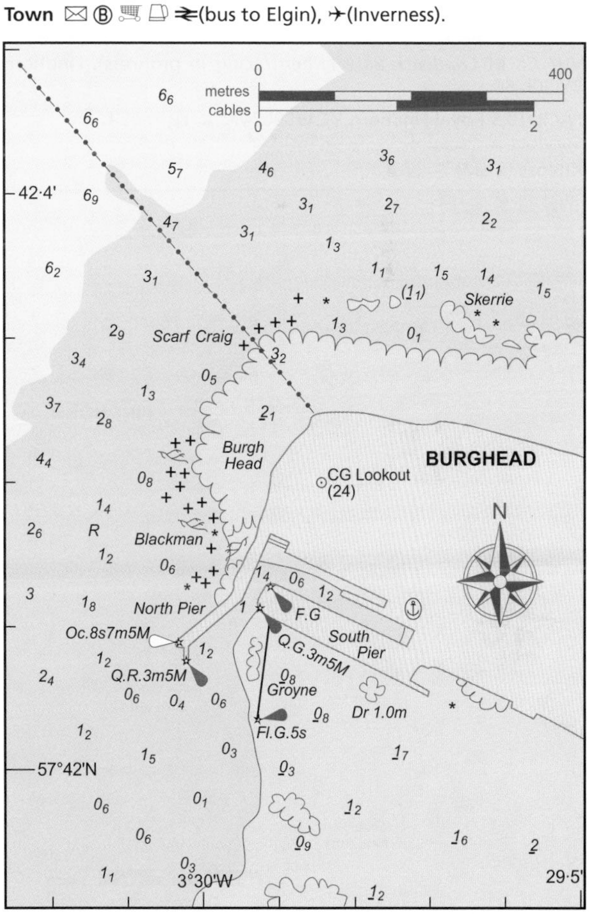

9.7.14 FINDHORN

Moray **57°39'·64N 03°37'·47W**

CHARTS AC 223, 5617; Imray C23

TIDES +0110 Dover; ML 2·5; Duration 0615

Standard Port ABERDEEN (⟵)

Times				Height (metres)			
High Water		Low Water		MHWS	MHWN	MLWN	MLWS
0200	0900	0400	0900	4·3	3·4	1·6	0·6
1400	2100	1600	2100				
Differences FINDHORN							
–0120	–0150	–0135	–0130	0·0	–0·1	0·0	+0·1

SHELTER ⚓ in pool off boatyard or off N pier or dry out alongside, inside piers and ask at YC; or pick up Y 🅥 off N pier.

Do not attempt entry in strong NW/NE winds or with big swell running; expect breakers/surf either side of entrance.

NAVIGATION From the SWM Landfall Buoy the bar, which dries, is marked (Fl R marker); thence follow marked chan to entrance.

- Bar and sands shift frequently esp following bad weather.
- Buoys (inc SWM) often move to follow channel into the bay.
- Marks may be lifted Nov to early Apr.

Once past The Ee, turn port inside G buoys. The S part of Findhorn Bay dries extensively.

LIGHTS AND MARKS Unlit. There is a windsock on FS by The Ee. Boatyard building is conspic.

COMMUNICATIONS (Code 01309) CGOC (01224) 592334; Police 101; Dr 678866/678888; Findhorn Pilot (Derek Munro) 690802, mob 07747 840916; Findhorn BY 690099. Fairways Committee (via BY) 690099.

VHF Ch M *Chadwick Base* (when racing in progress). Findhorn BY: Ch 80.

FACILITIES **Royal Findhorn YC ☎690247,** 🅥(free). **Services** (16t) ACA.

Kinloss (2½M).

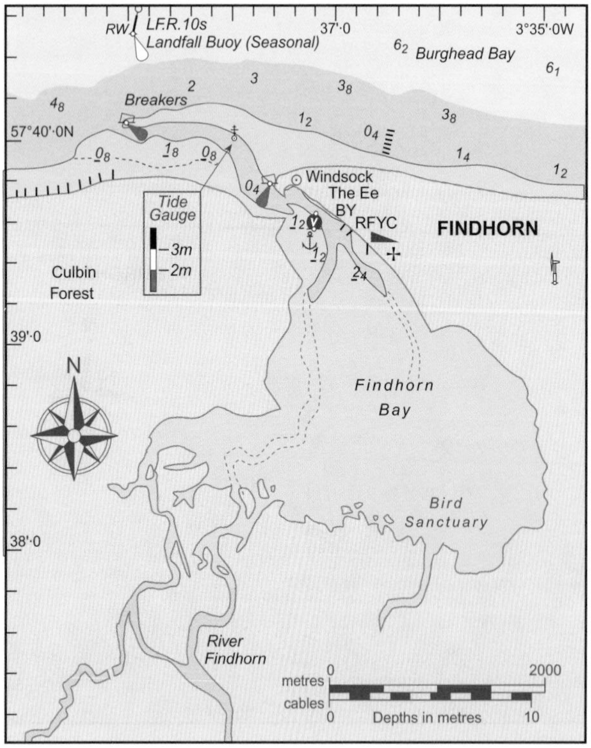

9.7.15 NAIRN

Highland **57°35'·61N 03°51'·65W**

CHARTS AC 223, 1462, 5617; Imray C23

TIDES +0110 Dover; ML 2·2; Duration 0615

Standard Port INVERGORDON (⟶)

Times				Height (metres)			
High Water		Low Water		MHWS	MHWN	MLWN	MLWS
0100	0700	0000	0700	4·3	3·3	1·6	0·7
1300	1900	1200	1900				
Differences NAIRN							
+0005	–0015	0000	–0015	0·0	0·0	0·0	0·0
McDERMOTT BASE							
+0015	–0005	+0015	0000	–0·1	0·0	+0·1	+0·2

SHELTER Good, but entry difficult in fresh NNE'ly. Pontoons in hbr with 🅥 berths. Best entry HW ± 1½. No commercial shipping.

NAVIGATION The beach dries to 100m off the pierheads. A mark is laid in the deepest water off the entrance to indicate line of approach. A gravel bar shows 200m NNW of ent at LAT. Inside, the best water is to the E side of the river chan which dries approx 1·9m.

- Buoy and sands shift frequently esp following bad weather.
- Mark may be lifted Nov to early Apr.

LIGHTS AND MARKS Lt ho on E pier hd, Oc WRG 4s 6m 5M, vis shore-G-100°-W-207°-R-shore. Keep in W sector.

COMMUNICATIONS (Code 01667) CGOC (01224) 592334; Police 101; Clinic 452096; Dr 453421. Hbr Office 456008, HM mob 07821 302944.

VHF Ch M (weekends only).

FACILITIES **Nairn Basin** £15.28/48hrs (launch £6) (110 V); **Nairn SC ☎453897**.

Town (Inverness).

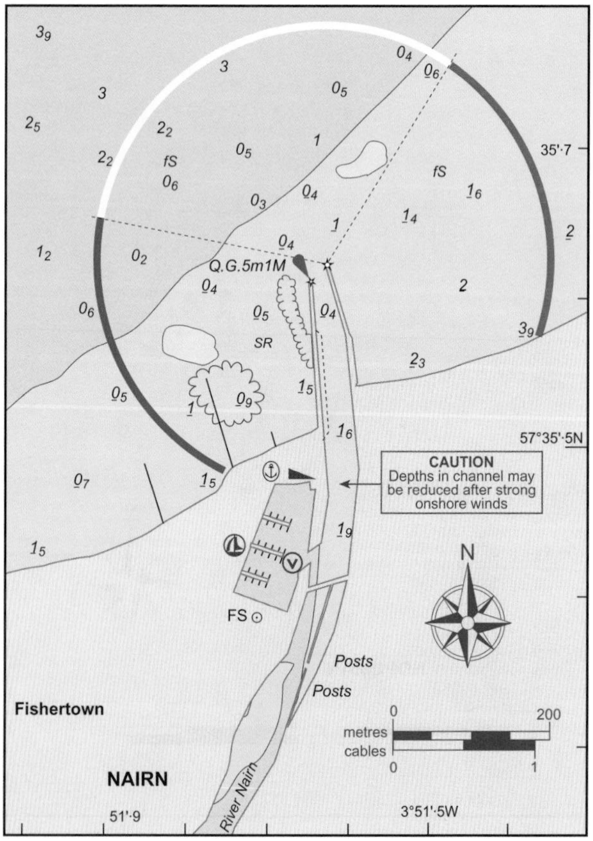

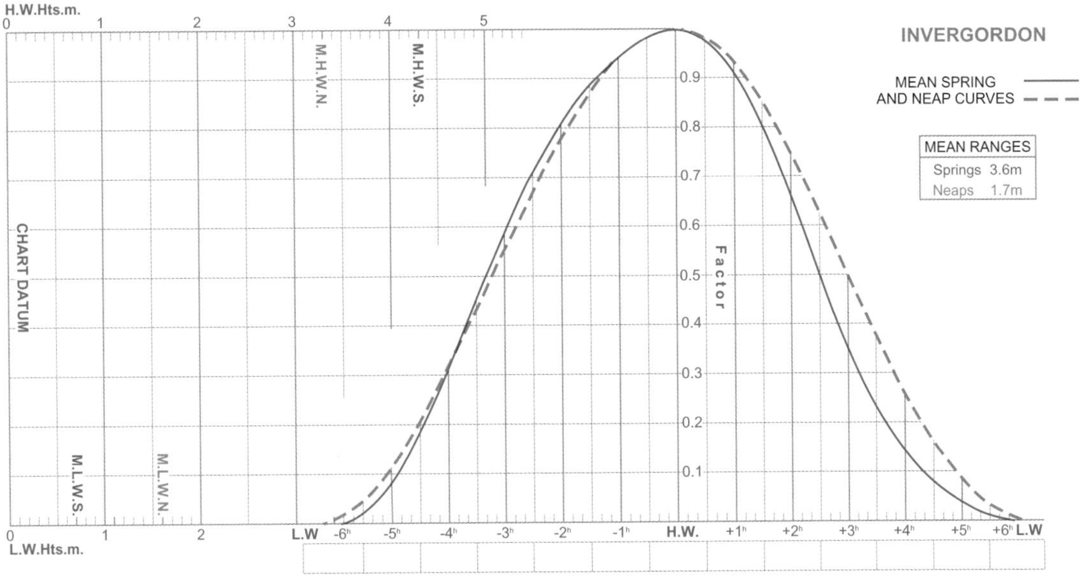
INVERGORDON
MEAN SPRING AND NEAP CURVES
MEAN RANGES
Springs 3.6m
Neaps 1.7m
H.W.Hts.m.
L.W.Hts.m.
CHART DATUM
M.H.W.N.
M.H.W.S.
M.L.W.S.
M.L.W.N.
Factor
L.W
H.W.

STANDARD TIME (UT)
For Summer Time add ONE hour in **non-shaded areas**

INVERGORDON LAT 57°41′N LONG 4°10′W

TIMES AND HEIGHTS OF HIGH AND LOW WATERS

Dates in red are **SPRINGS**
Dates in blue are **NEAPS**

YEAR **2018**

JANUARY

Date	Day	Time	m
1	M	0512 1115 1744 2335	0.9 4.4 0.7 4.5
2	TU ○	0603 1207 1833	0.8 4.6 0.5
3	W	0029 0648 1256 1920	4.6 0.8 4.7 0.4
4	TH	0121 0733 1343 2007	4.6 0.8 4.7 0.4
5	F	0211 0815 1431 2055	4.5 0.9 4.6 0.5
6	SA	0300 0855 1518 2143	4.4 1.1 4.5 0.7
7	SU	0348 0930 1605 2233	4.2 1.4 4.3 1.0
8	M	0435 1001 1654 ◑ 2330	3.9 1.6 4.1 1.2
9	TU	0523 1042 1746	3.7 1.8 3.8
10	W	0049 0614 1142 1846	1.5 3.6 1.9 3.7
11	TH	0205 0713 1445 1951	1.6 3.5 1.9 3.6
12	F	0306 0816 1544 2059	1.6 3.5 1.7 3.6
13	SA	0356 0919 1633 2202	1.6 3.7 1.6 3.7
14	SU	0433 1014 1712 2251	1.5 3.8 1.4 3.8
15	M	0443 1059 1738 2331	1.4 4.0 1.3 3.9
16	TU	0504 1138 1802	1.3 4.1 1.1
17	W	0007 0546 1215 ● 1833	4.0 1.2 4.2 1.0
18	TH	0042 0627 1250 1908	4.0 1.1 4.2 1.0
19	F	0116 0705 1324 1944	4.0 1.1 4.2 1.0
20	SA	0149 0738 1357 2017	3.9 1.2 4.1 1.0
21	SU	0224 0800 1431 2045	3.9 1.2 4.1 1.1
22	M	0301 0759 1506 2106	3.8 1.3 4.0 1.2
23	TU	0341 0826 1546 2102	3.7 1.4 3.9 1.3
24	W	0425 0910 1633 ◐ 2242	3.6 1.5 3.8 1.4
25	TH	0517 1038 1729	3.5 1.7 3.7
26	F	0008 0618 1227 1837	1.5 3.5 1.7 3.6
27	SA	0133 0728 1419 1953	1.4 3.6 1.5 3.7
28	SU	0249 0841 1534 2109	1.3 3.8 1.3 3.9
29	M	0359 0952 1638 2223	1.2 4.0 0.9 4.1
30	TU	0500 1056 1733 2327	1.0 4.3 0.6 4.3
31	W ○	0551 1152 1822	0.8 4.5 0.4

FEBRUARY

Date	Day	Time	m
1	TH	0021 0635 1242 1907	4.5 0.7 4.7 0.2
2	F	0111 0717 1329 1951	4.6 0.7 4.8 0.2
3	SA	0157 0755 1414 2034	4.5 0.8 4.7 0.3
4	SU	0240 0831 1458 2115	4.4 0.9 4.6 0.6
5	M	0323 0901 1541 2155	4.2 1.1 4.4 0.9
6	TU	0403 0926 1625 2233	4.0 1.4 4.1 1.2
7	W	0445 0955 1712 ◑ 2315	3.7 1.6 3.8 1.5
8	TH	0531 1046 1807	3.5 1.8 3.5
9	F	0032 0625 1222 1911	1.8 3.4 2.0 3.4
10	SA	0223 0725 1512 2017	1.8 3.4 1.8 3.4
11	SU	0320 0825 1608 2123	1.7 3.5 1.6 3.5
12	M	0401 0924 1652 2223	1.6 3.6 1.4 3.6
13	TU	0417 1021 1722 2309	1.5 3.8 1.3 3.8
14	W	0449 1110 1746 2348	1.3 4.0 1.1 3.9
15	TH ●	0532 1152 1816	1.2 4.2 0.9
16	F	0023 0614 1230 1850	4.0 1.0 4.2 0.8
17	SA	0058 0653 1306 1926	4.1 0.9 4.3 0.7
18	SU	0131 0729 1340 2001	4.1 0.9 4.3 0.7
19	M	0206 0802 1415 2034	4.0 1.0 4.2 0.8
20	TU	0242 0822 1451 2103	4.0 1.1 4.1 1.0
21	W	0320 0805 1529 2026	3.9 1.1 4.0 1.1
22	TH	0402 0843 1613 2108	3.7 1.3 3.9 1.3
23	F	0449 0939 1707 ◐ 2335	3.6 1.5 3.7 1.5
24	SA	0548 1208 1815	3.5 1.6 3.6
25	SU	0108 0657 1400 1935	1.6 3.5 1.5 3.6
26	M	0238 0811 1519 2100	1.5 3.6 1.2 3.7
27	TU	0351 0928 1626 2221	1.3 3.9 0.9 4.0
28	W	0451 1040 1721 2322	1.1 4.2 0.5 4.3

MARCH

Date	Day	Time	m
1	TH	0538 1138 1807	0.9 4.5 0.3
2	F	0012 0619 1227 ○ 1849	4.5 0.7 4.7 0.1
3	SA	0056 0656 1311 1928	4.5 0.6 4.8 0.1
4	SU	0137 0731 1353 2006	4.5 0.7 4.7 0.3
5	M	0216 0804 1434 2042	4.4 0.8 4.6 0.6
6	TU	0253 0834 1514 2115	4.2 1.0 4.3 0.9
7	W	0330 0856 1555 2142	3.9 1.2 4.0 1.3
8	TH	0407 0907 1639 2146	3.7 1.4 3.7 1.6
9	F	0450 0942 1731 ◑ 2241	3.5 1.7 3.4 1.8
10	SA	0542 1121 1835	3.3 1.9 3.2
11	SU	0113 0644 1428 1941	2.0 3.3 1.8 3.2
12	M	0237 0747 1531 2046	1.9 3.3 1.6 3.3
13	TU	0324 0846 1617 2150	1.7 3.5 1.4 3.5
14	W	0359 0942 1650 2242	1.5 3.7 1.2 3.7
15	TH	0435 1035 1718 2323	1.3 3.9 1.0 3.9
16	F	0516 1122 1751	1.1 4.1 0.8
17	SA	0000 0555 1204 ● 1826	4.1 0.9 4.2 0.6
18	SU	0035 0634 1242 1903	4.2 0.8 4.3 0.5
19	M	0110 0711 1320 1939	4.2 0.7 4.4 0.5
20	TU	0146 0747 1358 2015	4.2 0.7 4.4 0.6
21	W	0223 0820 1436 2048	4.1 0.8 4.3 0.8
22	TH	0302 0844 1517 2012	4.0 1.0 4.1 1.1
23	F	0343 0835 1602 2051	3.9 1.1 3.9 1.3
24	SA	0431 1033 1657 ◐ 2316	3.7 1.3 3.7 1.6
25	SU	0529 1204 1805	3.5 1.4 3.5
26	M	0053 0636 1351 1927	1.7 3.5 1.3 3.5
27	TU	0238 0750 1509 2100	1.6 3.6 1.1 3.7
28	W	0346 0909 1613 2218	1.3 3.8 0.8 3.9
29	TH	0440 1025 1705 2312	1.1 4.1 0.5 4.2
30	F	0524 1122 1749 2357	0.9 4.4 0.3 4.4
31	SA ○	0601 1209 1828	0.7 4.6 0.2

APRIL

Date	Day	Time	m
1	SU	0037 0634 1251 1903	4.5 0.7 4.6 0.3
2	M	0114 0706 1330 1936	4.4 0.6 4.6 0.4
3	TU	0149 0737 1408 2008	4.3 0.7 4.4 0.7
4	W	0222 0807 1446 2036	4.1 0.9 4.2 1.0
5	TH	0256 0827 1526 2038	3.9 1.1 3.9 1.3
6	F	0331 0827 1607 2052	3.7 1.3 3.6 1.5
7	SA	0409 0901 1656 2138	3.5 1.5 3.3 1.8
8	SU	0457 1004 1757 ◑ 2315	3.4 1.7 3.2 2.0
9	M	0601 1331 1904	3.3 1.8 3.1
10	TU	0155 0708 1437 2009	1.9 3.3 1.6 3.2
11	W	0250 0808 1524 2109	1.8 3.4 1.4 3.4
12	TH	0332 0903 1603 2204	1.6 3.6 1.2 3.7
13	F	0412 0956 1641 2250	1.3 3.8 1.0 3.9
14	SA	0452 1047 1720 2331	1.1 4.0 0.8 4.1
15	SU	0533 1133 1800	0.9 4.2 0.6
16	M	0009 0613 1217 ● 1838	4.3 0.7 4.4 0.5
17	TU	0047 0652 1258 1917	4.3 0.6 4.5 0.5
18	W	0126 0730 1340 1955	4.4 0.6 4.5 0.6
19	TH	0205 0809 1422 2032	4.3 0.7 4.4 0.8
20	F	0246 0848 1507 2108	4.2 0.8 4.2 1.1
21	SA	0330 0936 1556 2152	4.0 1.0 3.9 1.4
22	SU	0419 1039 1653 ◐ 2301	3.8 1.2 3.7 1.6
23	M	0516 1206 1800	3.6 1.3 3.5
24	TU	0052 0621 1343 1921	1.7 3.6 1.2 3.5
25	W	0230 0733 1456 2053	1.6 3.6 1.0 3.7
26	TH	0333 0851 1556 2202	1.4 3.8 0.7 3.9
27	F	0425 1005 1647 2254	1.2 4.0 0.6 4.1
28	SA	0507 1102 1729 2337	1.0 4.2 0.5 4.3
29	SU	0542 1149 1805	0.9 4.4 0.5
30	M	0015 0613 1230 ○ 1836	4.3 0.8 4.4 0.5

Chart Datum: 2·10 metres below Ordnance Datum (Local). HAT is 5·0 metres above Chart Datum.

STANDARD TIME (UT)
For Summer Time add ONE hour in **non-shaded areas**

INVERGORDON

LAT 57°41'N LONG 4°10'W

TIMES AND HEIGHTS OF HIGH AND LOW WATERS

Dates in red are SPRINGS
Dates in blue are NEAPS

YEAR **2018**

MAY

Date	Day	Time	m	Time	m	Time	m	Time	m	Moon
1	TU	0049	4.3	0642	0.7	1307	4.4	1906	0.7	
2	W	0121	4.2	0713	0.8	1344	4.2	1934	0.9	
3	TH	0152	4.1	0743	0.9	1421	4.0	1956	1.1	
4	F	0225	4.0	0803	1.1	1458	3.8	2000	1.3	
5	SA	0257	3.8	0804	1.2	1537	3.6	2024	1.5	
6	SU	0332	3.6	0837	1.4	1619	3.4	2107	1.7	
7	M	0414	3.4	0933	1.6	1714	3.2	2212	1.9	
8	TU	0511	3.3	1234	1.7	1821	3.2			◑
9	W	0106	1.9	0621	3.3	1342	1.6	1926	3.2	
10	TH	0209	1.8	0726	3.4	1431	1.4	2025	3.4	
11	F	0256	1.6	0823	3.5	1515	1.2	2121	3.6	
12	SA	0339	1.4	0916	3.8	1601	1.0	2212	3.9	
13	SU	0423	1.2	1010	4.0	1648	0.8	2258	4.1	
14	M	0508	0.9	1102	4.2	1733	0.6	2342	4.3	
15	TU	0551	0.7	1151	4.4	1816	0.5			●
16	W	0024	4.4	0634	0.6	1238	4.5	1857	0.5	
17	TH	0106	4.4	0716	0.5	1324	4.5	1938	0.7	
18	F	0149	4.4	0800	0.5	1411	4.4	2019	0.9	
19	SA	0233	4.3	0847	0.7	1500	4.2	2100	1.1	
20	SU	0320	4.1	0940	0.8	1552	4.0	2147	1.4	
21	M	0411	4.0	1042	1.0	1649	3.8	2244	1.6	
22	TU	0506	3.8	1202	1.1	1752	3.7			◐
23	W	0030	1.7	0607	3.7	1326	1.0	1904	3.6	
24	TH	0208	1.6	0714	3.7	1435	1.0	2026	3.6	
25	F	0310	1.5	0826	3.8	1534	0.9	2134	3.8	
26	SA	0404	1.3	0939	3.9	1625	0.8	2228	4.0	
27	SU	0449	1.2	1039	4.0	1708	0.8	2312	4.1	
28	M	0526	1.0	1127	4.1	1743	0.8	2350	4.2	
29	TU	0556	1.0	1208	4.2	1810	0.9			○
30	W	0023	4.2	0623	0.9	1246	4.1	1835	0.9	
31	TH	0055	4.2	0653	0.9	1322	4.1	1901	1.0	

JUNE

Date	Day	Time	m	Time	m	Time	m	Time	m	Moon
1	F	0127	4.1	0725	0.9	1357	3.9	1924	1.1	
2	SA	0159	4.0	0752	1.1	1434	3.8	1939	1.3	
3	SU	0232	3.9	0757	1.2	1509	3.6	2005	1.4	
4	M	0305	3.7	0823	1.3	1545	3.5	2043	1.6	
5	TU	0342	3.6	0910	1.4	1626	3.3	2135	1.7	
6	W	0428	3.5	1018	1.5	1721	3.3	2247	1.8	◑
7	TH	0524	3.4	1232	1.5	1829	3.3			
8	F	0018	1.8	0629	3.4	1339	1.4	1935	3.4	
9	SA	0209	1.7	0735	3.5	1430	1.3	2035	3.6	
10	SU	0300	1.5	0835	3.7	1521	1.1	2131	3.8	
11	M	0351	1.2	0934	3.9	1615	0.9	2225	4.0	
12	TU	0442	1.0	1033	4.1	1708	0.8	2315	4.2	
13	W	0532	0.7	1129	4.3	1756	0.7			●
14	TH	0002	4.4	0619	0.6	1221	4.5	1841	0.7	
15	F	0049	4.5	0706	0.4	1312	4.5	1925	0.7	
16	SA	0135	4.5	0754	0.4	1402	4.5	2009	0.8	
17	SU	0222	4.5	0844	0.5	1454	4.3	2053	1.0	
18	M	0311	4.4	0937	0.6	1546	4.2	2137	1.2	
19	TU	0401	4.2	1034	0.8	1638	4.0	2221	1.4	
20	W	0453	4.0	1140	0.9	1733	3.8	2312	1.6	◐
21	TH	0548	3.9	1256	1.1	1834	3.6			
22	F	0130	1.7	0649	3.8	1407	1.1	1942	3.6	
23	SA	0242	1.6	0756	3.7	1508	1.1	2053	3.6	
24	SU	0340	1.5	0907	3.8	1601	1.1	2153	3.8	
25	M	0431	1.3	1011	3.8	1647	1.1	2242	3.9	
26	TU	0513	1.2	1104	3.9	1722	1.2	2323	4.0	
27	W	0545	1.1	1147	4.0	1744	1.2	2358	4.1	
28	TH	0610	1.0	1225	4.0	1805	1.1			○
29	F	0031	4.1	0638	1.0	1302	4.0	1834	1.1	
30	SA	0105	4.1	0712	1.0	1337	3.9	1905	1.1	

JULY

Date	Day	Time	m	Time	m	Time	m	Time	m	Moon
1	SU	0138	4.1	0746	1.0	1412	3.8	1932	1.2	
2	M	0211	4.0	0814	1.1	1444	3.7	1955	1.3	
3	TU	0243	3.9	0826	1.1	1516	3.6	2023	1.4	
4	W	0317	3.8	0852	1.2	1551	3.5	2100	1.5	
5	TH	0356	3.7	0936	1.3	1634	3.4	2153	1.7	
6	F	0442	3.6	1045	1.4	1727	3.4	2309	1.7	◑
7	SA	0536	3.5	1215	1.4	1831	3.4			
8	SU	0030	1.7	0641	3.6	1343	1.4	1943	3.5	
9	M	0211	1.6	0752	3.7	1446	1.2	2049	3.7	
10	TU	0319	1.3	0901	3.9	1546	1.1	2151	3.9	
11	W	0419	1.0	1008	4.1	1646	0.9	2249	4.2	
12	TH	0516	0.8	1111	4.3	1740	0.8	2342	4.4	
13	F	0608	0.5	1209	4.5	1828	0.7			●
14	SA	0032	4.6	0657	0.3	1302	4.5	1913	0.7	
15	SU	0121	4.7	0745	0.2	1352	4.6	1956	0.8	
16	M	0209	4.7	0833	0.2	1442	4.5	2038	0.9	
17	TU	0257	4.6	0921	0.4	1530	4.3	2117	1.1	
18	W	0345	4.4	1010	0.6	1618	4.1	2152	1.3	
19	TH	0433	4.2	1102	0.9	1705	3.9	2231	1.5	◐
20	F	0523	4.0	1208	1.2	1756	3.6	2323	1.7	
21	SA	0619	3.7	1330	1.4	1853	3.5			
22	SU	0208	1.8	0723	3.6	1438	1.4	1958	3.5	
23	M	0315	1.6	0832	3.6	1535	1.5	2105	3.6	
24	TU	0411	1.5	0942	3.6	1624	1.4	2204	3.7	
25	W	0458	1.3	1041	3.8	1700	1.4	2251	3.9	
26	TH	0534	1.2	1127	3.9	1716	1.3	2331	4.1	
27	F	0558	1.1	1206	3.9	1737	1.2			○
28	SA	0007	4.1	0622	1.0	1242	4.0	1813	1.1	
29	SU	0042	4.2	0655	0.9	1316	4.0	1851	1.1	
30	M	0116	4.2	0730	0.9	1348	3.9	1926	1.1	
31	TU	0149	4.1	0804	0.9	1419	3.9	1955	1.2	

AUGUST

Date	Day	Time	m	Time	m	Time	m	Time	m	Moon
1	W	0221	4.0	0833	1.0	1449	3.8	2013	1.3	
2	TH	0253	4.0	0851	1.1	1523	3.7	2027	1.4	
3	F	0329	3.9	0842	1.2	1602	3.6	2059	1.5	
4	SA	0411	3.8	0916	1.3	1648	3.5	2158	1.6	◑
5	SU	0500	3.7	1113	1.5	1744	3.5	2351	1.7	
6	M	0603	3.6	1300	1.5	1855	3.5			
7	TU	0135	1.6	0719	3.6	1420	1.4	2010	3.6	
8	W	0255	1.3	0838	3.8	1526	1.2	2120	3.9	
9	TH	0402	1.0	0952	4.0	1630	1.1	2225	4.2	
10	F	0502	0.7	1101	4.3	1726	0.9	2324	4.5	
11	SA	0555	0.4	1159	4.5	1814	0.8			●
12	SU	0016	4.7	0643	0.2	1250	4.6	1856	0.7	
13	M	0105	4.8	0728	0.1	1338	4.6	1937	0.7	
14	TU	0151	4.8	0812	0.1	1423	4.6	2015	0.8	
15	W	0237	4.7	0855	0.3	1507	4.4	2050	1.0	
16	TH	0321	4.5	0937	0.6	1549	4.2	2123	1.2	
17	F	0406	4.3	1019	1.0	1632	3.9	2157	1.5	
18	SA	0454	4.0	1105	1.4	1717	3.6	2244	1.7	◐
19	SU	0547	3.7	1224	1.7	1809	3.5			
20	M	0005	1.9	0650	3.5	1403	1.8	1911	3.4	
21	TU	0249	1.8	0759	3.4	1506	1.7	2014	3.5	
22	W	0349	1.6	0911	3.5	1557	1.7	2115	3.7	
23	TH	0438	1.4	1017	3.7	1634	1.6	2212	3.9	
24	F	0515	1.3	1105	3.8	1648	1.4	2258	4.0	
25	SA	0536	1.1	1143	4.0	1715	1.3	2338	4.2	
26	SU	0558	1.0	1218	4.0	1755	1.1			○
27	M	0015	4.3	0630	0.8	1251	4.1	1834	1.0	
28	TU	0050	4.3	0706	0.7	1322	4.1	1911	1.0	
29	W	0124	4.3	0741	0.7	1352	4.1	1944	1.0	
30	TH	0157	4.2	0815	0.8	1424	4.0	2011	1.1	
31	F	0231	4.2	0843	1.0	1458	3.9	2004	1.2	

Chart Datum: 2·10 metres below Ordnance Datum (Local). HAT is 5·0 metres above Chart Datum.

STANDARD TIME (UT)
For Summer Time add ONE hour in **non-shaded areas**

INVERGORDON LAT 57°41′N LONG 4°10′W

TIMES AND HEIGHTS OF HIGH AND LOW WATERS

Dates in red are SPRINGS
Dates in blue are NEAPS

YEAR **2018**

SEPTEMBER

Date	Time	m	Date	Time	m
1 SA	0308 0805 1536 2028	4.1 1.1 3.8 1.4	16 SU	0422 1003 1636 ◐ 2201	3.9 1.6 3.7 1.7
2 SU	0349 0839 1620 2117	3.9 1.3 3.7 1.5	17 M	0514 1051 1728 2334	3.6 1.9 3.5 1.9
3 M	0438 0930 1715 ◑ 2336	3.8 1.5 3.6 1.7	18 TU	0617 1318 1830	3.4 2.0 3.4
4 TU	0541 1233 1824	3.6 1.7 3.5	19 W	0218 0726 1433 1935	1.8 3.3 2.0 3.4
5 W	0120 0700 1406 1941	1.6 3.6 1.6 3.6	20 TH	0319 0837 1525 2035	1.7 3.4 1.8 3.6
6 TH	0241 0826 1518 2056	1.3 3.7 1.4 3.9	21 F	0407 0945 1602 2130	1.5 3.6 1.7 3.8
7 F	0348 0946 1620 2206	1.0 4.0 1.2 4.2	22 SA	0441 1035 1626 2220	1.3 3.8 1.5 4.0
8 SA	0448 1054 1712 2307	0.6 4.3 1.0 4.5	23 SU	0500 1114 1656 2304	1.1 4.0 1.3 4.2
9 SU	0539 1148 1757 ● 2359	0.3 4.5 0.8 4.7	24 M	0527 1149 1735 2344	0.9 4.2 1.1 4.3
10 M	0624 1234 1836	0.1 4.7 0.7	25 TU	0602 1222 1813 ○	0.8 4.2 1.0
11 TU	0045 0705 1318 1913	4.9 0.1 4.7 0.7	26 W	0021 0639 1254 1850	4.4 0.7 4.3 0.9
12 W	0130 0745 1359 1948	4.9 0.2 4.6 0.7	27 TH	0057 0716 1326 1926	4.4 0.7 4.3 0.9
13 TH	0212 0824 1438 2022	4.7 0.4 4.4 0.9	28 F	0134 0751 1400 1959	4.4 0.8 4.2 1.0
14 F	0254 0901 1516 2053	4.5 0.8 4.2 1.2	29 SA	0211 0824 1436 2026	4.3 0.9 4.1 1.1
15 SA	0337 0935 1554 2122	4.2 1.2 3.9 1.5	30 SU	0251 0743 1515 2020	4.2 1.1 4.0 1.3

OCTOBER

Date	Time	m	Date	Time	m
1 M	0335 0818 1600 2205	4.0 1.4 3.8 1.5	16 TU	0440 0919 1643 ◐ 2215	3.5 1.9 3.5 1.9
2 TU	0426 0912 1656 ◑ 2331	3.8 1.7 3.6 1.6	17 W	0540 1034 1747	3.3 2.1 3.4
3 W	0530 1212 1803	3.6 1.8 3.6	18 TH	0132 0647 1350 1855	1.9 3.3 2.1 3.4
4 TH	0111 0650 1402 1920	1.5 3.6 1.7 3.7	19 F	0235 0755 1446 1957	1.7 3.4 1.9 3.6
5 F	0231 0821 1513 2037	1.2 3.7 1.5 3.9	20 SA	0319 0858 1527 2051	1.5 3.6 1.7 3.7
6 SA	0337 0942 1610 2150	0.9 4.0 1.3 4.2	21 SU	0348 0952 1600 2140	1.4 3.8 1.5 4.0
7 SU	0433 1043 1658 2250	0.6 4.3 1.0 4.5	22 M	0416 1036 1635 2227	1.2 4.0 1.3 4.2
8 M	0521 1132 1739 2340	0.4 4.5 0.9 4.7	23 TU	0452 1115 1713 2311	1.0 4.2 1.1 4.3
9 TU	0603 1215 1815 ●	0.3 4.7 0.7	24 W	0533 1151 1752 ○ 2352	0.8 4.4 1.0 4.5
10 W	0025 0641 1255 1849	4.8 0.3 4.7 0.7	25 TH	0613 1226 1830	0.7 4.4 0.9
11 TH	0106 0717 1332 1923	4.8 0.4 4.6 0.8	26 F	0032 0651 1303 1908	4.5 0.7 4.4 0.8
12 F	0146 0751 1407 1955	4.6 0.7 4.4 1.0	27 SA	0112 0729 1339 1945	4.5 0.8 4.4 0.9
13 SA	0226 0823 1441 2024	4.4 1.0 4.2 1.2	28 SU	0154 0805 1418 2023	4.4 1.0 4.3 1.0
14 SU	0306 0843 1515 2041	4.1 1.3 3.9 1.4	29 M	0237 0838 1500 2109	4.3 1.2 4.1 1.2
15 M	0350 0840 1554 2106	3.8 1.6 3.7 1.7	30 TU	0325 0817 1547 2209	4.1 1.5 3.9 1.3
			31 W	0420 1022 1643 ◑ 2326	3.8 1.7 3.8 1.4

NOVEMBER

Date	Time	m	Date	Time	m
1 TH	0524 1148 1748	3.7 1.9 3.7	16 F	0009 0601 1121 1805	1.8 3.3 2.2 3.4
2 F	0101 0640 1352 1901	1.4 3.6 1.8 3.7	17 SA	0127 0706 1356 1912	1.8 3.3 2.0 3.5
3 SA	0219 0811 1500 2019	1.2 3.7 1.6 3.9	18 SU	0216 0807 1446 2009	1.6 3.5 1.8 3.6
4 SU	0322 0928 1555 2132	0.9 4.0 1.4 4.2	19 M	0254 0903 1528 2100	1.4 3.7 1.6 3.8
5 M	0416 1024 1642 2232	0.7 4.2 1.2 4.4	20 TU	0333 0953 1608 2149	1.2 3.9 1.4 4.1
6 TU	0502 1111 1722 2321	0.6 4.4 1.0 4.5	21 W	0417 1038 1650 2238	1.1 4.2 1.2 4.3
7 W	0541 1153 1757 ●	0.6 4.5 0.9	22 TH	0504 1120 1731 2324	0.9 4.3 1.0 4.4
8 TH	0004 0616 1230 1829	4.6 0.6 4.5 0.9	23 F	0548 1201 1813 ○	0.8 4.5 0.9
9 F	0044 0649 1304 1901	4.5 0.7 4.5 0.9	24 SA	0010 0630 1241 1854	4.5 0.8 4.5 0.8
10 SA	0122 0719 1336 1932	4.4 0.9 4.3 1.0	25 SU	0055 0711 1322 1936	4.5 0.9 4.5 0.8
11 SU	0159 0744 1407 1959	4.2 1.2 4.2 1.2	26 M	0140 0752 1404 2021	4.5 1.0 4.4 0.9
12 M	0238 0749 1439 2007	4.0 1.4 4.0 1.4	27 TU	0228 0832 1449 2111	4.3 1.2 4.3 1.0
13 TU	0319 0807 1513 2034	3.7 1.6 3.8 1.6	28 W	0319 0915 1539 2209	4.2 1.5 4.1 1.1
14 W	0404 0846 1555 2128	3.5 1.8 3.6 1.7	29 TH	0414 1008 1633 2317	4.0 1.7 4.0 1.2
15 TH	0458 0945 1652 ◐	3.4 2.0 3.5	30 F	0515 1113 1733 ◑	3.8 1.8 3.8

DECEMBER

Date	Time	m	Date	Time	m
1 SA	0040 0621 1321 1840	1.2 3.7 1.8 3.8	16 SU	0602 1130 1802	3.3 2.0 3.5
2 SU	0157 0741 1437 1955	1.2 3.7 1.7 3.9	17 M	0109 0709 1353 1913	1.6 3.4 1.9 3.5
3 M	0301 0858 1535 2108	1.1 3.9 1.5 4.0	18 TU	0204 0810 1448 2015	1.5 3.6 1.7 3.7
4 TU	0356 0958 1625 2210	1.0 4.0 1.3 4.2	19 W	0252 0906 1536 2111	1.4 3.8 1.5 3.9
5 W	0443 1047 1708 2302	0.9 4.2 1.2 4.3	20 TH	0343 0959 1625 2206	1.2 4.0 1.3 4.1
6 TH	0522 1129 1745 2346	0.9 4.3 1.1 4.3	21 F	0436 1049 1713 2300	1.0 4.2 1.0 4.3
7 F	0554 1206 1816 ●	1.0 4.4 1.0	22 SA	0527 1137 1759 ○ 2351	0.9 4.4 0.8 4.4
8 SA	0025 0621 1239 1846	4.3 1.1 4.3 1.0	23 SU	0615 1222 1845	0.9 4.5 0.7
9 SU	0101 0647 1310 1917	4.2 1.1 4.3 1.1	24 M	0041 0659 1308 1931	4.5 0.9 4.6 0.6
10 M	0137 0710 1341 1947	4.1 1.2 4.2 1.2	25 TU	0131 0743 1354 2019	4.5 1.0 4.6 0.6
11 TU	0213 0725 1413 2004	3.9 1.4 4.1 1.3	26 W	0221 0826 1441 2108	4.4 1.1 4.5 0.7
12 W	0250 0747 1445 2019	3.8 1.5 3.9 1.4	27 TH	0313 0908 1530 2200	4.3 1.3 4.3 0.8
13 TH	0329 0822 1521 2101	3.6 1.7 3.8 1.5	28 F	0404 0950 1621 2256	4.1 1.4 4.2 1.0
14 F	0410 0909 1604 2201	3.5 1.8 3.6 1.6	29 SA	0457 1036 1714 ◑	3.9 1.6 4.0
15 SA	0500 1011 1657 ◐ 2324	3.4 2.0 3.5 1.7	30 SU	0004 0552 1131 1813	1.2 3.7 1.8 3.9
			31 M	0125 0655 1402 1922	1.3 3.6 1.8 3.8

Chart Datum: 2·10 metres below Ordnance Datum (Local). HAT is 5·0 metres above Chart Datum.

MORAY FIRTH: NORTH WEST COAST

(AC 115) Cromarty Firth (AC 1889, 1890) is entered between North and South Sutor Hds, fringed by rks, some of which dry.

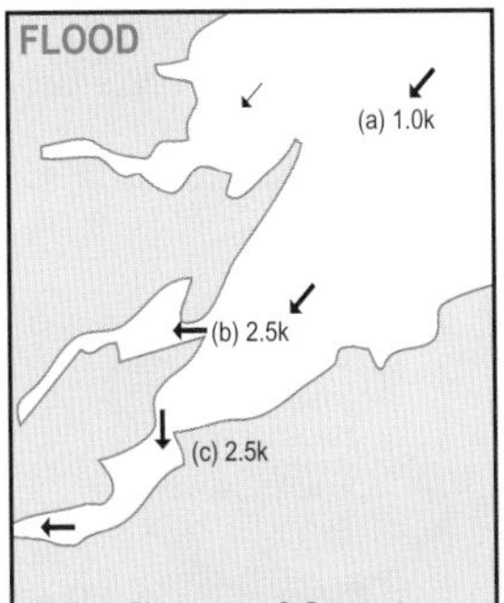
FLOOD
(a) 1.0k
(b) 2.5k
(c) 2.5k

Firths of Inverness & Cromarty
(a) Aberdeen +0430 to Aberdeen –0030
(b) Aberdeen +0600 to Aberdeen –0130
(c) Aberdeen +0430 to Aberdeen –0030

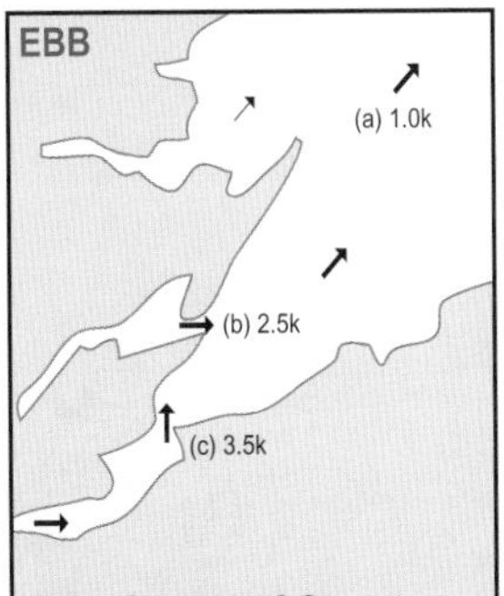
EBB
(a) 1.0k
(b) 2.5k
(c) 3.5k

Firths of Inverness & Cromarty
(a) Aberdeen –0030 to Aberdeen +0430
(b) Aberdeen –0130 to Aberdeen +0600
(c) Aberdeen –0030 to Aberdeen +0430

▶ *Off the entrance the in-going stream starts at HW Aberdeen +0600, and the out-going at HW Aberdeen –0130, sp rates 1·5 kn, stronger in the narrows between Nigg and Cromarty* ◀

Buss Bank buoy, Fl R 3s, marks the entrance, and there are good sheltered ⚓s within the firth. Keep 100m clear of the Nigg Oil Terminal on the north side. A buoyed deep-water channel runs to Invergordon; outside the channel there are shallows and drying banks. Beware large ships and tugs using Invergordon, Nigg Oil Terminal and Nigg Energy park jetties.

The coast NE to Tarbat Ness (lt) is fringed with rocks. Beware Three Kings (dries) about 3M NE of N Sutor.

▶ *Culloden Rk, a shoal with depth of 1·8m, extends 2½ca NE of Tarbat Ness, where stream is weak.* ◀

Beware salmon nets between Tarbat Ness and Portmahomack. Dornoch Firth is shallow, with shifting banks, and in strong E'lies the sea breaks heavily on the bar E of Dornoch Pt.

At Lothbeg Pt, 5M SW of Helmsdale, a rocky ledge extends 5ca offshore. Near Berriedale, 7M NE of Helmsdale, The Pinnacle,a detached rk 61m high, stands close offshore. Beatrice oil field lies on Smith Bank, 28M NE of Tarbat Ness, and 11M off Caithness coast. A wind farm with 84 turbines is under development seviced from Buckie and Wick. Between Dunbeath and Lybster there are no dangers more than 2ca offshore. Clyth Ness is fringed by detached and drying rks. From here to Wick the only dangers are close inshore. There is ⚓ in Sinclair's B in good weather, but Freswick B further N is better to await the tide in Pentland Firth (beware wreck in centre of bay). Stacks of Duncansby and Baxter Rk (depth 2·7m) lie 1M and 4ca S of Duncansby Hd.

9.7.16 INVERNESS

Highland **57°29'·73N 04°14'·17W** ❁❁◊◊◊✿✿

CHARTS AC 223, 1077, 1078, 5617; Imray C23

TIDES +0100 Dover; ML 2·7; Duration 0620

Standard Port INVERGORDON (⟵)

Times				Height (metres)			
High Water		Low Water		MHWS	MHWN	MLWN	MLWS
0100	0700	0000	0700	4·3	3·3	1·6	0·7
1300	1900	1200	1900				
Differences INVERNESS							
+0010	+0015	+0015	+0010	+0·3	+0·2	+0·1	+0·1
FORTROSE							
0000	+0010	+0010	–0010	0·0	+0·1	ND	ND
CROMARTY							
–0005	0000	0000	–0005	0·0	0·0	0·0	0·0
DINGWALL							
+0020	+0015	ND	ND	0·0	+0·1	ND	ND

SHELTER Good in all weathers. Berth at Inverness Marina (2.5m at CD) or at one of the 2 marinas in the Caledonian Canal, entr to which can be difficult in strong tidal streams. The sea lock is normally available HW±4 in canal hours; the gates cannot be opened LW±2 during Spring tides.

NAVIGATION WPT Meikle Mee SHM By Fl G 3s, 57°30'·25N 04°12'·03W, 250°/0·74M to Longman Pt bn. Inverness Firth is deep from Chanonry Pt to Munlochy SWM buoy, but shoal (2·1m) to Meikle Mee buoy. Meikle Mee partly dries. Beware bird rafts S of Avoch (off chartlet). Tidal streams are strong S of Craigton Pt (E-going stream at sp exceeds 5kn). Ent to R Ness is narrow, dredged to 3m CD. Take care to avoid Carnarc Pt W of R mouth and its associated shoal which is marked by a lit N Cardinal buoy. For the entrance to the Caledonian Canal, keep to N Kessock bank until clear of unmarked shoals on S bank.

LIGHTS AND MARKS Longman Pt bn Fl WR 2s 7m 5/4M, vis 078°-W-258°-R-078°. Craigton Pt lt, Fl WRG 4s 6m 11/7M vis 312°-W-048°-R-064°-W-085°-G-shore. Caledonian Canal ent marked by QR and Iso G 4s on ends of training walls.

COMMUNICATIONS (Code 01463) CGOC (01224) 592334; Police 101; Dr 234151. HM 715715; Clachnaharry Sea Lock 725512; Canal Office 725500.

Inverness Hbr Office VHF Ch 12 (Mon-Fri: 0800 -1700 LT). *Inverness Marina* Ch 12. Caledonian Canal: Ch 74 is used by all stations. Call: *Clachnaharry Sea Lock*; or for office: *Caledonian Canal*.

FACILITIES **Inverness Marina** www.invernessmarina.com ☎220501, Dredged to 3m 150⛵ inc 20Ⓥ £2.50, £16/m wkly, short stay (4hr) £16; ♿ 🗑 ⛽ 🚻 ⚓(45t) 🔧 ⛽ 🔧 ✕ 📖. **City** All domestic facilities, ⇄ ✈.

MINOR HARBOURS IN INVERNESS FIRTH

FORTROSE, Highland, **57°34'·71N 04°08'·04W**. AC 1078. Tides 9.7.16. HW +0055 on Dover; ML 2·5m; Duration 0620. Small drying unlit hbr, soft silt bottom, well protected by Chanonry Ness to E, limited space. Follow ldg line 296°, Broomhill Ho (conspic on hill to NW) in line with school spire until abeam SPM buoy; then turn W to avoid Craig an Roan rks (1·8m) ESE of ent. Chanonry Pt lt, Oc 6s 12m 15M, obscd 073°-shore. HM ☎(01381)620504 mob 078 08933775; Dr ☎622000. Facilities: ⛵ £10, 4Ⓥ ⛺ 🔧 ⛴ scrubbing grid ⛽ ⛽ ⛽ ✉ Ⓑ 🛒 ✕. **Chanonry SC** (near pier) ☎01381 621973.

AVOCH, Highland, **57°34'·03N 04°09'·94W**. AC 1078. Tides as Fortrose (1·25M to the ENE). Hbr dries, mostly on the N side, but is bigger than Fortrose. Small craft may stay afloat at neaps against the S pier (2FR (vert)). ⛵ may be available on drying pontoons £10 /H24; one Ⓥ (max 35ft LOA) off harbour entrance. Appr from the East via safe channel between two pairs of lateral buoys. A rock armour groyne extends approx 30m SSE on the South side of the harbour entrance and approx 3M high. It covers at HW Springs and is marked by a small, unlit south cardinal buoy. HM ☎(01381) 622383 mob 07825667281.
Facilities: ⛵£7 🚰 ⛽. **Village** ⛽ ⛽ 🔧 ✉ 🛒 ✕ 📖.

NORTH KESSOCK PIER, Highlands, **57°30'·06N 4°14'·87W.** AC 1078. Tides as Inverness (1 M to the ESE). Unlit tidal slipway, suitable for leisure craft up to 20m. 2m depth at MLWS. Mud and rounded stones bottom, sheltered from SW by Bkwtr. Ideal if awaiting sea lock at Caledonian Canal. Approach on N shore to avoid shallows at Inverness Harbour and South Kessock. Facilities: ⛴ ⛵ (tidal) donations in honesty box, 🚰 (by arrangement). **Village** LB(inshore), Ⓑ 🛒 ✕ 📖 Dolphin & Seal Centre, Bus. Jim Prentice ☎07802 915741.

INVERNESS *continued*

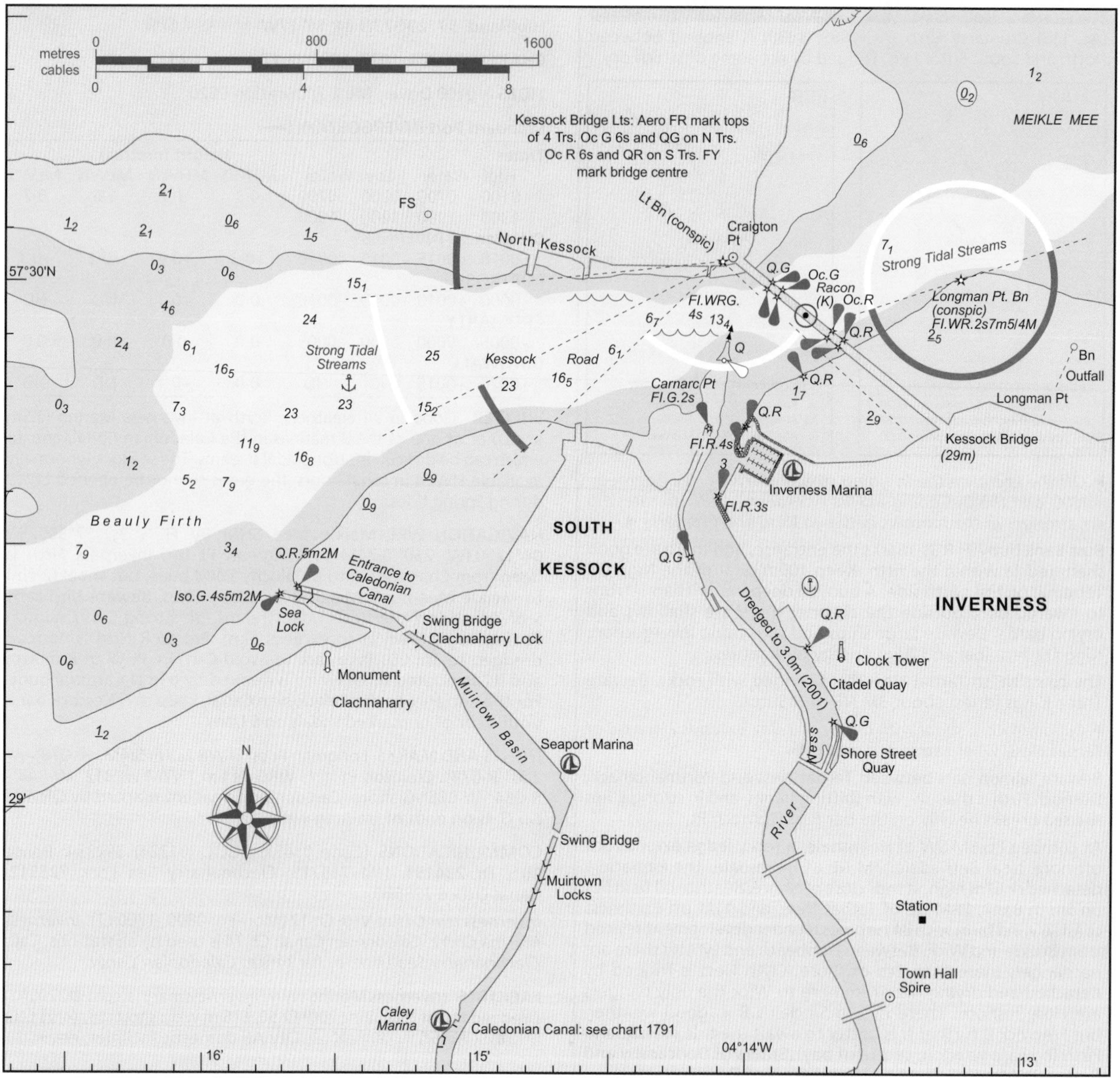

metres
cables
0
800
1600
0
4
8
Kessock Bridge Lts: Aero FR mark tops of 4 Trs. Oc G 6s and QG on N Trs. Oc R 6s and QR on S Trs. FY mark bridge centre
MEIKLE MEE
FS
Lt Bn (conspic)
Craigton Pt
North Kessock
57°30'N
Q.G
Oc.G
Racon (K)
Oc.R
Q.R
Strong Tidal Streams
Longman Pt. Bn (conspic) Fl.WR.2s7m5/4M
Fl.WRG. 4s
Q
Strong Tidal Streams
Kessock Road
Carnarc Pt Fl.G.2s
Bn
Outfall
Longman Pt
Kessock Bridge (29m)
Fl.R.4s
Inverness Marina
Fl.R.3s
Beauly Firth
SOUTH KESSOCK
Q.R.5m2M
Entrance to Caledonian Canal
Iso.G.4s5m2M
Sea Lock
Swing Bridge
Clachnaharry Lock
Monument
Clachnaharry
Muirtown Basin
Dredged to 3.0m (2001)
INVERNESS
Clock Tower
Citadel Quay
Shore Street Quay
Ness
River
N
Seaport Marina
Swing Bridge
Muirtown Locks
Station
Town Hall Spire
Caley Marina
Caledonian Canal: see chart 1791
29'
16'
15'
04°14'W
13'

CALEDONIAN CANAL

Clachnaharry Sea Lock 57°29'·44N 04°15'·84W. These notes are for the convenience of those entering the Canal at Inverness. They should be used with the main information/chartlet in 9.8.17.

CHARTS AC 1791, 1078, 5617. *Scottish Canals Skipper's Guide*.

TIDES Differences: Clachnaharry +0116 on Dover.

SHELTER Clachnaharry sea lock operates HW±4 (sp) within canal hours. The road and rail swing bridges may cause delays up to 25 mins. Seaport and Caley marinas: see Facilities.

NAVIGATION The 60M Caledonian Canal consists of 38M through three lochs (Lochs Ness, Oich and Lochy), connected by 22M through canals. It can take vessels 45m LOA, 10m beam, 4m draught and max mast ht 27·4m. The passage normally takes two full days, possibly longer in the summer; 13hrs is absolute minimum.

Speed limit is 5kn in canal sections. There are 10 swing bridges; road tfc has priority at peak hrs. Do not pass bridges without the keeper's instructions. From Clachnaharry sea lock to Loch Ness (Bona Ferry lt ho) is approx 7M, via Muirtown and Dochgarroch locks.

LOCKS All 29 locks are manned and operate early May to early Oct, 0800-1800LT daily. Dues: see 9.8.17. For regulations and *Scottish Canals Skipper's Guide* apply: Canal Manager, Muirtown Wharf, Inverness IV3 5LS, www. scottishcanals.co.uk ☎01463 725500.

BOAT SAFETY SCHEME Visiting vessels will be checked for apparent dangerous defects eg leaking gas or fuel, damaged electrical cables, taking in water, risk of capsize. £1 million 3rd party insurance is required. For details see 9.8.17.

LIGHTS AND MARKS Chans are marked by posts, cairns and unlit buoys, PHM on the NW side of the chan and SHM on the SE side.

COMMUNICATIONS Clachnaharry sea lock ☎(01463) 713896; Canal Office, Inverness ☎(01463) 233140.

Sea locks and main lock flights operate VHF Ch **74** (HO).

FACILITIES **Seaport Marina** www.scottishcanals.co.uk ☎(01463) 725500, 80⊆+20❿, (40t).

Caley Marina www.caleymarina.com ☎(01463) 236539, 25⊆+25❿ £1.50, (20t) ACA.

MINOR HARBOURS FROM CROMARTY FIRTH TO WICK

CROMARTY FIRTH, Highland, **57°41′·18N 04°02′·09W**. AC 1889, 1890. HW +0100 on Dover –0135 on Aberdeen; HW height 0.0m on Aberdeen; ML 2·5m; Duration 0625. See 9.7.16. Excellent hbr extending 7·5M W, past Invergordon, then 9M SW. Good shelter always available, depending on wind direction. Beware rks and reefs round N and S Sutor at the ent; many unlit oil rig mooring buoys and numerous lit rigs. *Cromarty Firth Port Control* VHF Ch 11 16 13 (H24) ☎(01349) 852308.

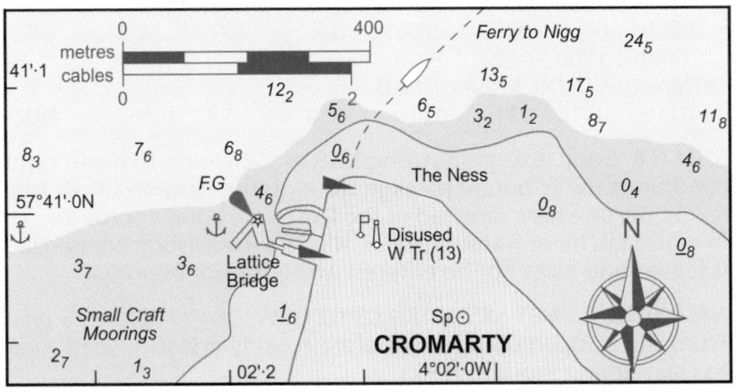

CROMARTY HARBOUR, Highland. **57°41′·00N 04°02′·35W**. From WPT 57°41′·10N 04°02′·50W, 142°/1.3ca to entrance. When inside harbour beware of set towards lattice bridge, tide runs at up to 4kn. Sheltered from N through E to S. Approx 20 Ⓥ on 50m central pontoon, £20 o/n, short stay £10 depths range from 1·6m to 1m at inner end. 3 ⚓ 2ca W of S pier hd, or ⚓ in approx 6m with good holding but exposed to the West. HM mob 07751244065 available. **Cromarty Boat Club** www.cromartyboatclub.org 3⚓ in 0·5m–1·5m (free) ; WC (owned by Boat Club; coin operated, key held by HM). ✉. Local seasonal ferry to Nigg on N shore where the energy park dominates the foreshore.

INVERGORDON WEST HARBOUR, Highland. **57°41′·12N 04°10′·05W.** on pontoons, (3t) ✉ ✗. Dinghy landing at Invergordon Boat Club (1·5M W), ☎(01349) 893772 mob 07762904041.

DORNOCH FIRTH, Highland. **57°51′·28N 03°59′·39W**. AC 115, 223. HW +0115 on Dover; ML 2·5m; Duration 0605; see 9.7.17. Excellent shelter but difficult entry. There are many shifting sandbanks, especially near the ent, from N edge of Whiteness Sands to S edge of Gizzen Briggs. ⚓s in 7m ¾M ESE of Dornoch Pt (sheltered from NE swell by Gizzen Briggs); in 7m 2ca SSE of Ard na Cailc; in 3·3m 1M below Bonar Bridge. Firth extends 15M inland, but AC coverage ceases ¼M E of Ferry Pt. The A9 road bridge, 3·3M W of Dornoch Pt, with 11m clearance, has 3 spans lit on both sides; span centres show Iso 4s, N bank pier Iso G 4s, S bank pier Iso R 4s and 2 midstream piers QY. Tarbat Ness lt ho Fl (4) 30s 53m 24M. Fl R 5s lt shown when Tain firing range active. Very limited facilities at Ferrytown and Bonar Bridge. CGOC ☎01224 592334. **Dornoch**: Dr ✉ Ⓑ ✗.

GOLSPIE, Highland, **57°58′·71N 03°56′·79W**. AC 223. HW +0045 on Dover; ML 2·3m; Duration 068. See 9.7.17. Golspie pier projects 60m SE across foreshore with arm projecting SW at the head, giving shelter during NE winds. Beware The Bridge, a bank (0·3m to 1·8m) running parallel to the shore ¼M to seaward of pier hd. Seas break heavily over The Bridge in NE winds. There are no lts. To enter, keep Duke of Sutherland's Memorial in line 316° with boathouse SW of pier, until church spire in village is in line 006° with hd of pier, then keep on those marks. Harbour gets very congested; good ⚓ off pier. HM ☎01431 821692, £22 <10m (single visit - 2nd nt free) short stay £7.
Town Ⓗ Dr ✉ Ⓑ ✗ ⇌.

LYBSTER, Highland, **58°17′·72N 03°17′·39W**. AC 115. HW +0020 on Dover; HW -0150 sp, -0215 np; HW ht -0·6m on Aberdeen; ML 2·1m; Duration 0620. Excellent shelter in SW corner of inner hbr; on W side of pier in about 1·2m, £7.00/wk. Most of hbr dries to sand/mud and is much used by FVs; no bollards on N wall. Appr on about 350°. Beware rks close on E side of ent; narrow (10m) ent is difficult in strong E to S winds. Min depth 2·5m in ent. S pier hd, Oc R 6s 10m 3M, occas in fishing season. on W quay. at Waterlines Visitor Centre, 01593 721520. **Town** ✗.

9.7.17 PORTMAHOMACK

Highland **57°50′·25N 03°50′·00W**

CHARTS AC 115, 223; Imray C23

TIDES +0035 Dover; ML 2·5; Duration 0600

Standard Port ABERDEEN (⟵)

Times				**Height (metres)**			
High Water		Low Water		MHWS	MHWN	MLWN	MLWS
0300	0800	0200	0800	4·3	3·4	1·6	0·6
1500	2000	1400	2000				
Differences PORTMAHOMACK							
–0120	–0210	–0140	–0110	–0·2	–0·1	+0·1	+0·1
MEIKLE FERRY (Dornoch Firth)							
–0100	–0140	–0120	–0055	+0·1	0·0	–0·1	0·0
GOLSPIE							
–0130	–0215	–0155	–0130	–0·3	–0·3	–0·1	0·0

SHELTER Good, but uncomfortable in SW/NW winds. Hbr dries, access only at HW, but good ⚓ close SW of pier.

NAVIGATION WPT 57°53′·00N 03°50′·00W, 180°/2.7M to 1ca W of hbr ent. Beware Curach Rks which lie from 2ca SW of pier to the shore. Rks extend N and W of the pier. Beware lobster pot floats and salmon nets N of hbr. Tain firing & bombing range is about 3M to the W, S of mouth of Dornoch Firth; R flags, R lts, shown when active.

LIGHTS AND MARKS Tarbert Ness lt ho Fl (4) 30s 53m 24M, W twr R bands, is 2·6M to NE of hbr. Pier hd 2 FR (vert) 7m 5M.

COMMUNICATIONS (Code 01862) CGOC (01224) 592334; Dr 892759. No HM; enquiries: harbours@highland.gov.uk (01571) 844807.

FACILITIES **Harbour,** £22 <10m (single visit - 2nd nt free) short stay £7; pontoon in harbour but dries out for half its length and heavily used by local boats, WC.
Town ✉ ✗ ⇌ (bus to Tain), ✈ (Inverness).

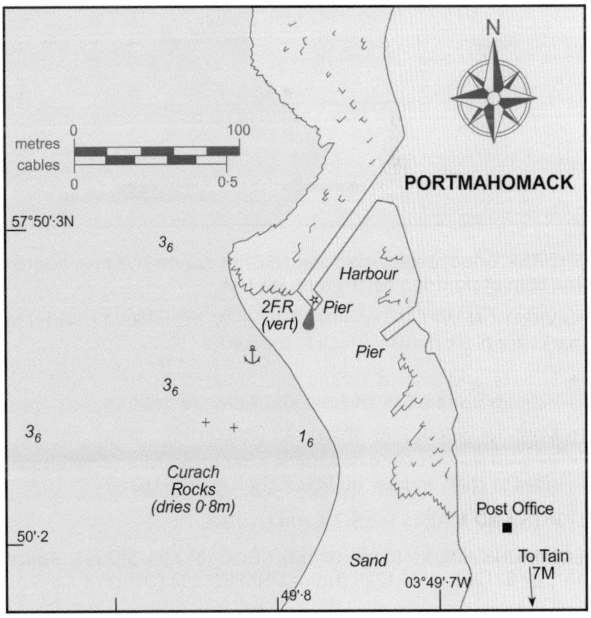

9.7.18 HELMSDALE

Highland **58°06'·83N 03°38'·89W**

CHARTS AC 115, 1462; Imray C23

TIDES +0035 Dover; ML 2·2; Duration 0615

Standard Port WICK (⟶)

Times				Height (metres)			
High Water		Low Water		MHWS	MHWN	MLWN	MLWS
0000	0700	0200	0700	3·5	2·8	1·4	0·7
1200	1900	1400	1900				
Differences HELMSDALE							
+0025	+0015	+0035	+0030	+0·5	+0·3	+0·1	–0·1

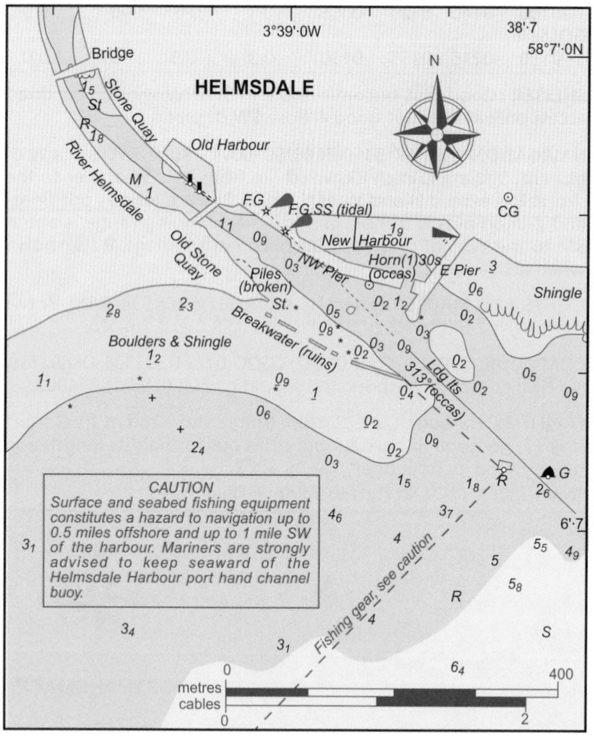

SHELTER Good, except in strong E/SE'lies. on NW pier, approx 1m. 80m of pontoon berths through HM.

NAVIGATION WPT 58°06'·59N 03°38'·39W, 313°/0·35M to ent; ldg marks are black masts with Or □ topmarks.

- Surface and seabed fishing gear, hazardous to navigation, extends up to 0.5M offshore and 1.0M SW of hbr.
- Essential to pass seaward of Hbr Chan PHM.
- Beware spate coming downriver after heavy rain. Shoals both sides of chan and bar build up when river in spate.

LIGHTS AND MARKS See 9.7.4 and chartlet.

COMMUNICATIONS (Code 01431) CGOC (01224) 592334; Police 101; Dr 821221, or 821225 (Home). HM 821692 (Office).

VHF Ch 13 16.

FACILITIES £22 <10m (single visit – 2nd nt free) short stay £7 (see HM); (access code from HM).

Town (hardware store), Ⓑ(Brora) ⇄.

9.7.19 WICK

Highland **58°26'·38N 03°04'·72W**

CHARTS AC 115, 1462; Imray C23, C68

TIDES +0010 Dover; ML 2·0; Duration 0625. Wick is a Standard Port. Daily tidal predictions are given below.

Standard Port WICK (⟶)

Times				Height (metres)			
High Water		Low Water		MHWS	MHWN	MLWN	MLWS
0000	0700	0200	0700	3·5	2·8	1·4	0·7
1200	1900	1400	1900				
Differences DUNCANSBY HEAD							
–0115	–0115	–0110	–0110	–0·4	–0·4	ND	ND

SHELTER Good, except in strong NNE to SSE winds, to await right conditions for W-bound passage through the Pentland Firth (see 9.7.5). Berth where directed in the Outer Harbour, approx 2m, or in marina in Inner Harbour, 2·0m. NB: The River Hbr (commercial) is leased and must not be entered without prior approval.

NAVIGATION WPT 58°26'·18N 03°03'·39W, 284°/0·72M to S pier. From the N, open up hbr ent before rounding North Head so as to clear drying Proudfoot Rks.

Hbr ent is dangerous in strong E'lies as craft have to turn 90° to port at the end of S pier.

On S side of bay, unlit NCM, 300m ENE of LB slip, marks end of ruined bkwtr.

LIGHTS AND MARKS S pier lt, Fl WRG 3s 12m 12/9M, 253°-G-270°-W-286°-R-329°, Bell (2) 10s (fishing). Ldg lts, both FR 5/8m, lead 234° into outer hbr. Traffic signals:

B ● (●) at CG stn on S Head = hbr closed by weather.
B ● (●) at S pier head = caution; hbr temp obstructed.

COMMUNICATIONS (Code 01955) HM 602030; CGOC (01224) 592334; Police 101; Ⓗ 602434, 602261.

VHF Ch 14 16 (Mon-Fri 0800-1700).

FACILITIES Poss temporary on pontoons in Outer Harbour. **Wick Marina** (Inner Harbour) dredged to 2·0m 70 inc 15 ♥; £20 <10m< +£2/m + ; max 25m LOA. 50m from marina .

Fish Jetty . **Services** (15/100t).

Town (at Heat Centre) Ⓑ ⇄ ✈.

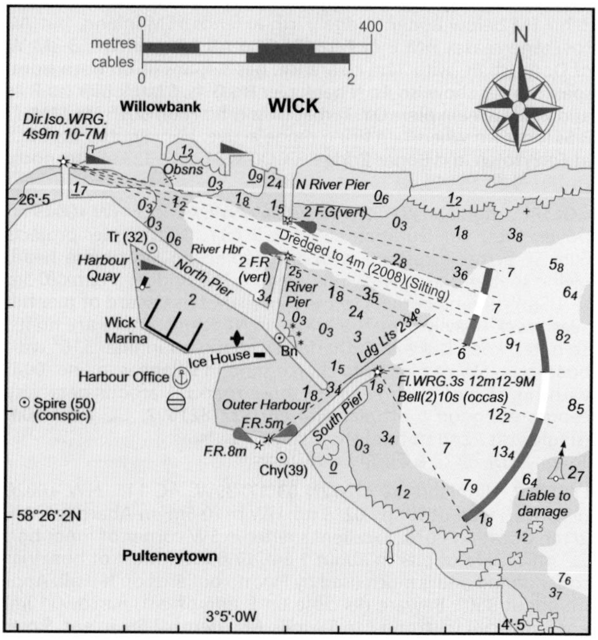

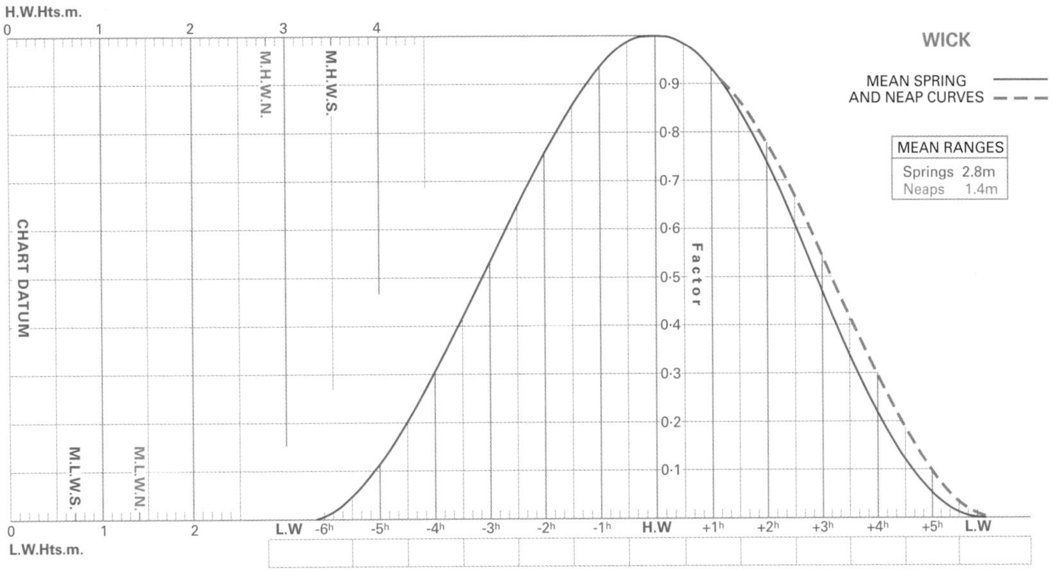
H.W.Hts.m.
0 1 2 3 4
M.H.W.N.
M.H.W.S.
WICK
MEAN SPRING AND NEAP CURVES
MEAN RANGES
Springs 2.8m
Neaps 1.4m
CHART DATUM
Factor
0·9 0·8 0·7 0·6 0·5 0·4 0·3 0·2 0·1
M.L.W.S.
M.L.W.N.
0 1 2
L.W.Hts.m.
L.W -6h -5h -4h -3h -2h -1h H.W +1h +2h +3h +4h +5h L.W

PENTLAND FIRTH

(AC 2162, 2581) **This potentially dangerous chan should only be attempted with moderate winds (less than F4), good vis, no swell and a fair np tide.** In such conditions it presents few problems. A safe passage depends on a clear understanding of tidal streams and correct timing.

▶ *The Admiralty Tidal Stream Atlas for Orkney and Shetland (NP 209) gives large scale vectors and is essential. Even in ideal conditions the races off Duncansby Hd, Swilkie Pt (N end of Stroma), and Rks of Mey (Merry Men of Mey) must be avoided as they are always dangerous to small craft. Also avoid the Pentland Skerries, Muckle Skerry, Old Head, Lother Rock (S Ronaldsay), and Dunnet Hd on E-going flood. For passages across the Firth see CCC SDs for Orkney.* ◀

At E end the Firth is entered between Duncansby Hd and Old Hd (S Ronaldsay), between which lie Muckle Skerry and the Pentland Skerries. Near the centre of Firth are the Islands of Swona (N side) and Stroma (S side). Outer Sound (main chan, 2·5M wide) runs between Swona and Stroma; Inner Sound (1·5M wide) between Stroma and the mainland. Rks of Mey extend about 2ca N of St John's Pt. The W end of the Firth is between Dunnet Hd and Tor Ness (Hoy).

Tide flows strongly around and through the Orkney Islands. **The Pentland Firth is a dangerous area for all craft, tidal flows reach 12kn between Duncansby Head and S Ronaldsay.** W of Dunnet Hd and Hoy is less violent. There is little tide within Scapa Flow. **Tidal streams reach 8-9kn at Sp in the Outer Sound, and 9-12kn between Pentland Skerries and Duncansby Hd. The resultant dangerous seas, very strong eddies and violent races should be avoided by yachts at all costs.** ◀

▶ *The E-going stream begins at HW Aberdeen +0500, and the W-going at HW Aberdeen –0105.* ***Duncansby Race*** *extends ENE towards Muckle Skerry on the SE-going stream, but by HW Aberdeen –0440 it extends NW from Duncansby Hd. Note: HW at Muckle Skerry is the same time as HW Dover. A persistent race off* ***Swilkie Pt****, at N end of Stroma,* ***is very dangerous with a strong W'ly wind over a W-going stream. The most dangerous and extensive race in the Firth is Merry Men of Mey****. It forms off St John's Pt on W-going stream at HW Aberdeen –0150 and for a while extends right across to Tor Ness with heavy breaking seas even in fine weather.* ◀

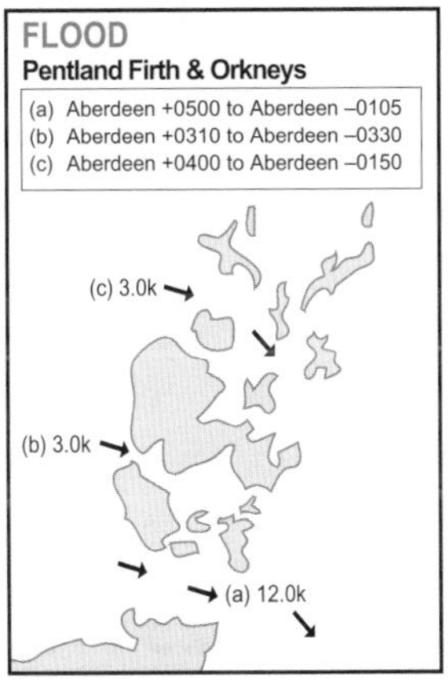
FLOOD
Pentland Firth & Orkneys
(a) Aberdeen +0500 to Aberdeen –0105
(b) Aberdeen +0310 to Aberdeen –0330
(c) Aberdeen +0400 to Aberdeen –0150
(c) 3.0k
(b) 3.0k
(a) 12.0k

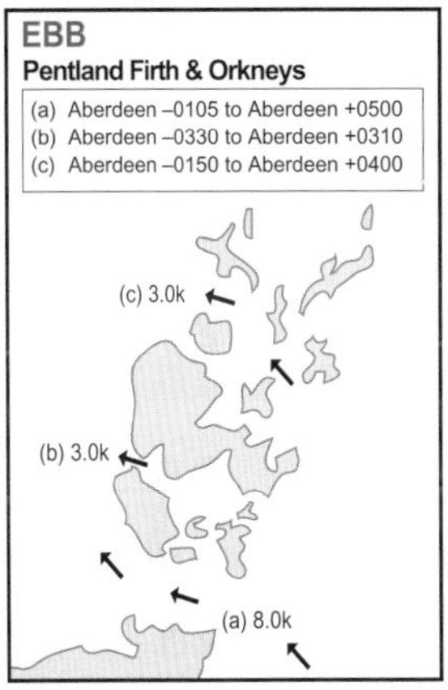
EBB
Pentland Firth & Orkneys
(a) Aberdeen –0105 to Aberdeen +0500
(b) Aberdeen –0330 to Aberdeen +0310
(c) Aberdeen –0150 to Aberdeen +0400
(c) 3.0k
(b) 3.0k
(a) 8.0k

Passage Westward: This is the more difficult direction due to prevailing W winds. Freswick B, 3·5M S of Duncansby Hd, is a good waiting ⚓.

▶ *Here an eddy runs N for 9hrs. Round Duncansby Hd close in at HW Aberdeen –0220, as the ebb starts to run W.* ◀

Take a mid-course through the Inner Sound to appr the Rks of Mey from close inshore. Gills Bay is a temp anch if early; do not pass Rks of Mey until ebb has run for at least 2hrs. Pass 100m N of the Rks (awash).

Passage Eastward: With a fair wind and tide, no race forms and the passage is easier.

▶ *Leave Scrabster at local LW+1 so as to be close off Dunnet Hd not before HW Aberdeen +0340 when the E-going flood starts to make. If late, give the Hd a wide berth.* ◀

Having rounded the Rks of Mey, steer S initially to avoid being set onto the rky S tip of Stroma, marked by unlit SCM bn. Then keep mid-chan through the Inner Sound and maintain this offing to give Duncansby Hd a wide berth. Tide turbines sit in the centre of the Sound S of Stroma with 9.9m over them

STANDARD TIME (UT)
For Summer Time add ONE hour in **non-shaded areas**

WICK LAT 58°26′N LONG 3°05′W

TIMES AND HEIGHTS OF HIGH AND LOW WATERS

Dates in red are SPRINGS
Dates in blue are NEAPS

YEAR **2018**

JANUARY

Date	Time	m	Date	Time	m
1 M	0358 1024 1626 2248	0.8 3.6 0.7 3.7	16 TU	0434 1059 1702 2325	1.1 3.4 1.0 3.2
2 TU	0446 1113 1715 ○ 2340	0.7 3.8 0.6 3.7	17 W	0507 1133 1735 ●	1.1 3.4 0.9
3 W	0532 1200 1804	0.7 3.8 0.5	18 TH	0000 0539 1206 1807	3.3 1.0 3.5 0.9
4 TH	0030 0618 1247 1853	3.7 0.8 3.8 0.4	19 F	0034 0611 1239 1840	3.3 1.0 3.5 0.8
5 F	0120 0703 1334 1943	3.6 0.9 3.8 0.5	20 SA	0108 0643 1312 1913	3.2 1.0 3.5 0.9
6 SA	0210 0748 1421 2035	3.5 1.0 3.7 0.7	21 SU	0142 0717 1347 1948	3.2 1.1 3.4 0.9
7 SU	0301 0835 1512 2129	3.3 1.2 3.5 0.9	22 M	0219 0753 1424 2026	3.1 1.1 3.3 1.0
8 M	0354 0927 1607 ◑ 2228	3.1 1.4 3.3 1.1	23 TU	0300 0832 1506 2110	3.0 1.2 3.3 1.1
9 TU	0451 1030 1707 2333	2.9 1.5 3.1 1.2	24 W	0347 0920 1555 ◐ 2207	3.0 1.4 3.2 1.2
10 W	0551 1146 1811	2.9 1.6 3.0	25 TH	0444 1027 1656 2322	2.9 1.5 3.1 1.2
11 TH	0044 0656 1313 1920	1.3 2.8 1.6 3.0	26 F	0551 1153 1808	2.9 1.5 3.0
12 F	0149 0802 1420 2028	1.3 2.9 1.5 3.0	27 SA	0038 0702 1314 1923	1.2 3.0 1.4 3.1
13 SA	0240 0858 1510 2124	1.3 3.0 1.4 3.0	28 SU	0152 0811 1427 2037	1.2 3.1 1.2 3.2
14 SU	0322 0944 1551 2209	1.2 3.2 1.2 3.1	29 M	0256 0915 1527 2143	1.0 3.3 0.9 3.4
15 M	0359 1023 1628 2249	1.2 3.3 1.1 3.2	30 TU	0349 1010 1619 2240	0.9 3.5 0.7 3.5
			31 W	0436 1100 1707 ○ 2331	0.8 3.7 0.5 3.6

FEBRUARY

Date	Time	m	Date	Time	m
1 TH	0521 1147 1753	0.7 3.8 0.3	16 F	0521 1146 1747	0.9 3.5 0.7
2 F	0019 0603 1233 1838	3.7 0.7 3.9 0.3	17 SA	0013 0551 1219 1818	3.3 0.9 3.5 0.6
3 SA	0105 0645 1317 1922	3.6 0.8 3.8 0.4	18 SU	0047 0623 1252 1851	3.3 0.8 3.5 0.6
4 SU	0148 0725 1400 2006	3.5 0.9 3.7 0.6	19 M	0120 0657 1326 1924	3.3 0.8 3.5 0.7
5 M	0232 0804 1444 2049	3.3 1.0 3.5 0.8	20 TU	0155 0731 1402 2000	3.2 0.9 3.4 0.8
6 TU	0316 0845 1531 2136	3.1 1.2 3.3 1.0	21 W	0233 0809 1443 2040	3.1 1.0 3.3 0.9
7 W	0404 0933 1624 ◑ 2231	2.9 1.4 3.1 1.3	22 TH	0316 0852 1530 2129	3.0 1.1 3.2 1.1
8 TH	0459 1040 1726 2339	2.8 1.5 2.9 1.4	23 F	0408 0950 1629 ◐ 2241	2.9 1.3 3.0 1.2
9 F	0602 1213 1838	2.7 1.6 2.7	24 SA	0515 1122 1745	2.8 1.3 2.9
10 SA	0102 0713 1352 1957	1.5 2.7 1.5 2.8	25 SU	0011 0632 1257 1909	1.3 2.8 1.3 2.9
11 SU	0213 0824 1451 2102	1.4 2.8 1.4 2.8	26 M	0140 0750 1419 2031	1.3 3.0 1.1 3.1
12 M	0302 0918 1535 2150	1.4 3.0 1.2 3.0	27 TU	0249 0900 1520 2138	1.1 3.2 0.8 3.2
13 TU	0342 1001 1612 2231	1.2 3.1 1.1 3.1	28 W	0341 0957 1609 2231	1.0 3.4 0.6 3.4
14 W	0417 1038 1645 2306	1.1 3.3 0.9 3.2			
15 TH	0449 1112 1716 ● 2340	1.0 3.4 0.8 3.2			

MARCH

Date	Time	m	Date	Time	m
1 TH	0425 1046 1654 2318	0.8 3.6 0.4 3.5	16 F	0426 1046 1650 2315	1.0 3.3 0.7 3.2
2 F	0506 1131 1737 ○	0.7 3.7 0.3	17 SA	0457 1120 1721 ● 2348	0.8 3.4 0.6 3.3
3 SA	0002 0545 1215 1817	3.6 0.6 3.8 0.2	18 SU	0529 1155 1753	0.7 3.5 0.5
4 SU	0043 0622 1256 1856	3.5 0.6 3.7 0.3	19 M	0022 0601 1230 1825	3.4 0.6 3.5 0.5
5 M	0122 0659 1336 1933	3.4 0.7 3.6 0.5	20 TU	0056 0636 1306 1900	3.3 0.6 3.5 0.5
6 TU	0159 0734 1415 2009	3.3 0.8 3.4 0.8	21 W	0131 0712 1344 1937	3.3 0.7 3.4 0.6
7 W	0237 0810 1456 2047	3.1 1.0 3.2 1.0	22 TH	0209 0751 1426 2017	3.2 0.8 3.3 0.8
8 TH	0317 0849 1542 2131	2.9 1.2 2.9 1.3	23 F	0252 0835 1515 2106	3.1 0.9 3.1 1.0
9 F	0404 0943 1640 ◑ 2235	2.8 1.4 2.7 1.5	24 SA	0343 0936 1616 ◐ 2219	2.9 1.1 3.0 1.3
10 SA	0505 1114 1755	2.7 1.5 2.6	25 SU	0450 1112 1737 2358	2.8 1.2 2.8 1.4
11 SU	0000 0619 1309 1919	1.6 2.6 1.5 2.6	26 M	0612 1251 1905	2.8 1.1 2.8
12 M	0137 0737 1423 2035	1.5 2.7 1.3 2.7	27 TU	0132 0733 1411 2027	1.3 2.9 0.9 3.0
13 TU	0237 0843 1509 2126	1.4 2.8 1.2 2.8	28 W	0239 0845 1508 2128	1.2 3.1 0.7 3.2
14 W	0319 0931 1546 2206	1.3 3.0 1.0 3.0	29 TH	0328 0941 1555 2217	1.0 3.3 0.5 3.3
15 TH	0354 1010 1619 2241	1.1 3.1 0.8 3.1	30 F	0409 1029 1636 2300	0.8 3.5 0.3 3.4
			31 SA	0447 1112 1714 ○ 2340	0.7 3.6 0.3 3.5

APRIL

Date	Time	m	Date	Time	m
1 SU	0523 1153 1751	0.6 3.6 0.3	16 M	0503 1127 1725 ● 2355	0.6 3.5 0.4 3.4
2 M	0017 0559 1233 1826	3.4 0.6 3.6 0.4	17 TU	0539 1206 1801	0.5 3.5 0.4
3 TU	0053 0634 1310 1900	3.4 0.6 3.5 0.6	18 W	0032 0616 1247 1838	3.4 0.5 3.5 0.5
4 W	0127 0708 1347 1933	3.3 0.7 3.3 0.8	19 TH	0110 0656 1329 1918	3.4 0.5 3.4 0.6
5 TH	0201 0742 1425 2006	3.1 0.9 3.1 1.0	20 F	0151 0739 1415 2002	3.3 0.6 3.3 0.8
6 F	0237 0819 1508 2044	3.0 1.1 2.9 1.2	21 SA	0236 0830 1508 2055	3.1 0.8 3.1 1.1
7 SA	0319 0906 1600 2138	2.8 1.2 2.7 1.5	22 SU	0329 0940 1613 ◐ 2213	3.0 0.9 2.9 1.3
8 SU	0412 1025 1711 ◑ 2304	2.7 1.4 2.5 1.6	23 M	0436 1112 1734 2347	2.9 1.0 2.8 1.4
9 M	0523 1206 1833	2.6 1.4 2.5	24 TU	0556 1240 1857	2.8 0.9 2.8
10 TU	0040 0641 1337 1952	1.6 2.6 1.3 2.6	25 W	0115 0713 1354 2012	1.3 2.9 0.8 2.9
11 W	0157 0752 1431 2049	1.5 2.7 1.1 2.7	26 TH	0220 0823 1449 2110	1.2 3.0 0.6 3.1
12 TH	0245 0848 1511 2132	1.3 2.8 1.0 2.9	27 F	0308 0920 1534 2157	1.0 3.2 0.5 3.2
13 F	0323 0932 1545 2209	1.1 3.0 0.8 3.1	28 SA	0348 1008 1613 2238	0.8 3.3 0.5 3.3
14 SA	0356 1012 1618 2244	0.9 3.2 0.6 3.2	29 SU	0425 1051 1649 2316	0.7 3.4 0.4 3.3
15 SU	0429 1050 1650 2319	0.8 3.3 0.5 3.3	30 M	0501 1131 1724 ○ 2351	0.6 3.4 0.5 3.4

Chart Datum: 1·71 metres below Ordnance Datum (Newlyn). HAT is 4·0 metres above Chart Datum.

STANDARD TIME (UT)
For Summer Time add ONE hour in **non-shaded areas**

WICK LAT 58°26'N LONG 3°05'W

TIMES AND HEIGHTS OF HIGH AND LOW WATERS

Dates in red are SPRINGS
Dates in blue are NEAPS

YEAR **2018**

MAY

Date	Day	Time	m	Time	m	Time	m	Time	m
1	TU	0537	0.6	1209	3.4	1758	0.6		
2	W	0025	3.3	0612	0.6	1246	3.3	1831	0.7
3	TH	0058	3.3	0647	0.7	1323	3.2	1903	0.9
4	F	0131	3.2	0721	0.8	1400	3.0	1936	1.1
5	SA	0206	3.0	0759	1.0	1440	2.8	2012	1.2
6	SU	0245	2.9	0843	1.1	1528	2.7	2059	1.4
7	M	0332	2.8	0947	1.2	1628	2.5	2211	1.5
8	TU	0432	2.7	1110	1.3	1742	2.5	◑ 2338	1.6
9	W	0545	2.6	1229	1.2	1853	2.5		
10	TH	0055	1.5	0653	2.7	1336	1.1	1955	2.7
11	F	0157	1.3	0753	2.8	1424	1.0	2046	2.8
12	SA	0242	1.2	0846	2.9	1505	0.8	2129	3.0
13	SU	0322	1.0	0933	3.1	1543	0.6	2210	3.2
14	M	0400	0.8	1017	3.3	1620	0.5	2250	3.3
15	TU	0438	0.6	1101	3.4	1659	0.4	● 2329	3.5
16	W	0519	0.5	1145	3.5	1739	0.4		
17	TH	0010	3.5	0601	0.4	1231	3.5	1821	0.5
18	F	0053	3.5	0646	0.4	1318	3.4	1905	0.7
19	SA	0137	3.4	0735	0.5	1408	3.3	1953	0.9
20	SU	0225	3.3	0832	0.6	1504	3.1	2050	1.1
21	M	0319	3.1	0943	0.8	1610	2.9	2203	1.3
22	TU	0424	3.0	1101	0.8	1722	2.8	◐ 2324	1.4
23	W	0537	2.9	1218	0.8	1835	2.8		
24	TH	0045	1.3	0647	3.0	1329	0.8	1944	2.9
25	F	0152	1.2	0756	3.0	1424	0.7	2043	3.0
26	SA	0244	1.1	0855	3.1	1510	0.7	2131	3.1
27	SU	0327	1.0	0946	3.2	1548	0.7	2213	3.2
28	M	0405	0.8	1030	3.2	1624	0.7	2251	3.3
29	TU	0443	0.8	1111	3.2	1659	0.7	○ 2327	3.3
30	W	0519	0.7	1149	3.2	1733	0.8		
31	TH	0001	3.3	0555	0.7	1226	3.2	1806	0.8

JUNE

Date	Day	Time	m	Time	m	Time	m	Time	m
1	F	0034	3.3	0630	0.8	1302	3.1	1840	0.9
2	SA	0108	3.2	0706	0.8	1339	3.0	1913	1.1
3	SU	0142	3.1	0742	0.9	1418	2.9	1949	1.2
4	M	0220	3.0	0824	1.0	1501	2.8	2031	1.3
5	TU	0303	2.9	0914	1.1	1550	2.7	2125	1.4
6	W	0352	2.8	1019	1.2	1650	2.6	◑ 2238	1.5
7	TH	0451	2.7	1128	1.2	1755	2.6	2353	1.5
8	F	0557	2.7	1233	1.1	1857	2.7		
9	SA	0058	1.4	0700	2.8	1332	1.0	1955	2.8
10	SU	0156	1.2	0759	2.9	1423	0.9	2047	3.0
11	M	0246	1.0	0855	3.1	1509	0.7	2136	3.2
12	TU	0332	0.8	0948	3.3	1553	0.6	2222	3.3
13	W	0418	0.7	1039	3.4	1638	0.5	● 2307	3.5
14	TH	0504	0.5	1129	3.5	1723	0.5	2352	3.6
15	F	0551	0.4	1219	3.5	1809	0.6		
16	SA	0038	3.6	0640	0.4	1310	3.5	1856	0.7
17	SU	0126	3.5	0732	0.4	1402	3.4	1945	0.9
18	M	0215	3.4	0829	0.5	1456	3.2	2039	1.0
19	TU	0308	3.3	0931	0.6	1555	3.0	2140	1.2
20	W	0407	3.2	1037	0.7	1658	2.9	◐ 2249	1.3
21	TH	0511	3.1	1145	0.8	1802	2.8		
22	F	0003	1.3	0616	3.0	1254	0.9	1907	2.8
23	SA	0117	1.3	0723	3.0	1354	0.9	2009	2.9
24	SU	0219	1.2	0828	3.0	1444	0.9	2103	3.0
25	M	0308	1.1	0924	3.0	1526	0.9	2149	3.1
26	TU	0350	1.0	1011	3.1	1603	0.9	2229	3.2
27	W	0429	0.9	1053	3.1	1639	0.9	2306	3.3
28	TH	0506	0.8	1132	3.1	1713	0.9	○ 2341	3.3
29	F	0541	0.8	1209	3.1	1748	0.9		
30	SA	0014	3.3	0616	0.8	1245	3.1	1821	1.0

JULY

Date	Day	Time	m	Time	m	Time	m	Time	m
1	SU	0048	3.3	0650	0.8	1320	3.0	1854	1.0
2	M	0122	3.2	0725	0.8	1356	3.0	1928	1.1
3	TU	0158	3.2	0802	0.9	1434	2.9	2006	1.2
4	W	0236	3.1	0842	1.0	1516	2.8	2048	1.3
5	TH	0319	3.0	0930	1.0	1605	2.7	2140	1.4
6	F	0408	2.9	1031	1.1	1701	2.7	◑ 2251	1.4
7	SA	0507	2.9	1137	1.1	1805	2.7		
8	SU	0005	1.4	0612	2.9	1242	1.1	1907	2.8
9	M	0113	1.3	0719	2.9	1345	1.0	2008	3.0
10	TU	0216	1.1	0824	3.1	1442	0.9	2106	3.2
11	W	0312	0.9	0926	3.2	1534	0.8	2159	3.3
12	TH	0404	0.7	1024	3.4	1623	0.7	2249	3.5
13	F	0453	0.5	1118	3.5	1711	0.6	● 2338	3.6
14	SA	0543	0.3	1209	3.6	1758	0.6		
15	SU	0025	3.7	0632	0.2	1300	3.6	1844	0.7
16	M	0113	3.7	0722	0.3	1349	3.5	1930	0.8
17	TU	0200	3.6	0813	0.4	1439	3.3	2017	0.9
18	W	0250	3.5	0906	0.5	1530	3.1	2107	1.1
19	TH	0342	3.3	1002	0.8	1624	2.9	◐ 2205	1.3
20	F	0439	3.1	1102	1.0	1722	2.8	2314	1.4
21	SA	0542	3.0	1209	1.1	1824	2.8		
22	SU	0036	1.4	0649	2.9	1319	1.2	1930	2.8
23	M	0155	1.3	0802	2.8	1418	1.2	2033	2.9
24	TU	0253	1.2	0905	2.9	1506	1.2	2125	3.0
25	W	0338	1.1	0955	3.0	1545	1.1	2208	3.1
26	TH	0417	1.0	1038	3.0	1622	1.1	2246	3.2
27	F	0452	0.9	1116	3.1	1656	1.0	○ 2322	3.3
28	SA	0526	0.8	1151	3.1	1729	1.0	2355	3.4
29	SU	0559	0.7	1225	3.2	1802	0.9		
30	M	0028	3.4	0630	0.7	1259	3.1	1833	0.9
31	TU	0102	3.4	0703	0.7	1332	3.1	1906	1.0

AUGUST

Date	Day	Time	m	Time	m	Time	m	Time	m
1	W	0135	3.3	0736	0.8	1407	3.0	1940	1.0
2	TH	0210	3.2	0811	0.8	1444	3.0	2017	1.1
3	F	0249	3.2	0850	0.9	1526	2.9	2100	1.2
4	SA	0334	3.1	0938	1.0	1617	2.8	◑ 2156	1.3
5	SU	0428	3.0	1044	1.1	1718	2.8	2318	1.4
6	M	0535	2.9	1201	1.2	1828	2.8		
7	TU	0040	1.3	0650	2.9	1317	1.2	1937	2.9
8	W	0157	1.2	0805	3.0	1426	1.1	2043	3.1
9	TH	0301	0.9	0915	3.2	1524	0.9	2142	3.3
10	F	0355	0.7	1015	3.4	1613	0.8	2234	3.5
11	SA	0444	0.4	1108	3.5	1659	0.7	● 2323	3.7
12	SU	0531	0.2	1157	3.6	1743	0.6		
13	M	0010	3.8	0617	0.2	1244	3.6	1825	0.6
14	TU	0055	3.8	0702	0.2	1329	3.5	1907	0.7
15	W	0140	3.7	0746	0.4	1413	3.4	1948	0.8
16	TH	0225	3.6	0831	0.6	1457	3.2	2030	1.0
17	F	0312	3.4	0918	0.9	1544	3.0	2118	1.2
18	SA	0404	3.1	1011	1.1	1637	2.8	◐ 2223	1.4
19	SU	0505	2.9	1116	1.3	1738	2.8	2351	1.5
20	M	0615	2.7	1235	1.4	1847	2.7		
21	TU	0131	1.5	0735	2.7	1352	1.4	1959	2.8
22	W	0236	1.3	0846	2.8	1446	1.4	2059	3.0
23	TH	0322	1.2	0937	2.9	1528	1.3	2145	3.1
24	F	0359	1.0	1019	3.0	1603	1.2	2224	3.2
25	SA	0433	0.9	1055	3.1	1636	1.0	2259	3.3
26	SU	0504	0.8	1129	3.2	1708	0.9	○ 2332	3.4
27	M	0535	0.7	1201	3.3	1739	0.9		
28	TU	0005	3.5	0605	0.6	1234	3.3	1810	0.8
29	W	0038	3.5	0636	0.6	1306	3.3	1842	0.9
30	TH	0111	3.5	0708	0.7	1339	3.2	1915	0.9
31	F	0145	3.4	0741	0.8	1414	3.1	1950	1.0

Chart Datum: 1·71 metres below Ordnance Datum (Newlyn). HAT is 4·0 metres above Chart Datum.

STANDARD TIME (UT)
For Summer Time add ONE hour in **non-shaded areas**

WICK LAT 58°26′N LONG 3°05′W

TIMES AND HEIGHTS OF HIGH AND LOW WATERS

Dates in red are SPRINGS
Dates in blue are NEAPS

YEAR **2018**

SEPTEMBER

Date	Day	Time	m	Time	m	Time	m	Time	m
1	SA	0223	3.3	0818	0.9	1454	3.1	2030	1.1
2	SU	0307	3.2	0901	1.1	1542	3.0	2122	1.3
3	M	0401	3.0	1001	1.2	1642	2.9	◑ 2244	1.4
4	TU	0511	2.9	1132	1.3	1757	2.9		
5	W	0023	1.3	0634	2.9	1302	1.3	1914	2.9
6	TH	0149	1.1	0757	3.0	1418	1.2	2026	3.1
7	F	0253	0.9	0909	3.2	1515	1.1	2127	3.4
8	SA	0345	0.6	1005	3.4	1601	0.9	2219	3.6
9	SU	0430	0.4	1054	3.6	1643	0.7	● 2306	3.8
10	M	0514	0.2	1139	3.7	1724	0.6	2350	3.9
11	TU	0555	0.2	1222	3.6	1803	0.6		
12	W	0033	3.9	0635	0.3	1303	3.6	1841	0.7
13	TH	0116	3.8	0715	0.5	1342	3.4	1919	0.8
14	F	0157	3.6	0753	0.7	1421	3.2	1957	1.0
15	SA	0240	3.3	0832	1.0	1502	3.1	2038	1.2
16	SU	0327	3.1	0916	1.3	1549	2.9	◐ 2133	1.4
17	M	0426	2.8	1017	1.5	1648	2.8	2304	1.5
18	TU	0539	2.7	1141	1.7	1801	2.7		
19	W	0057	1.5	0703	2.7	1319	1.6	1917	2.8
20	TH	0211	1.4	0821	2.8	1421	1.5	2025	2.9
21	F	0257	1.2	0913	2.9	1504	1.4	2115	3.1
22	SA	0334	1.0	0953	3.1	1540	1.2	2155	3.2
23	SU	0406	0.9	1029	3.2	1612	1.1	2230	3.4
24	M	0436	0.8	1101	3.3	1642	0.9	2304	3.5
25	TU	0506	0.7	1133	3.4	1713	0.8	○ 2338	3.5
26	W	0536	0.6	1205	3.4	1745	0.8		
27	TH	0011	3.6	0607	0.6	1238	3.4	1817	0.8
28	F	0046	3.6	0640	0.6	1312	3.4	1852	0.8
29	SA	0122	3.5	0714	0.8	1348	3.3	1929	0.9
30	SU	0202	3.4	0752	0.9	1428	3.2	2011	1.1

OCTOBER

Date	Day	Time	m	Time	m	Time	m	Time	m
1	M	0248	3.2	0836	1.1	1516	3.1	2105	1.2
2	TU	0345	3.1	0936	1.4	1617	3.0	◑ 2234	1.3
3	W	0500	2.9	1117	1.5	1735	2.9		
4	TH	0016	1.3	0628	2.9	1254	1.5	1856	3.0
5	F	0140	1.1	0752	3.0	1408	1.3	2010	3.2
6	SA	0241	0.8	0859	3.2	1501	1.1	2110	3.4
7	SU	0329	0.6	0951	3.4	1544	1.0	2201	3.6
8	M	0412	0.4	1036	3.6	1624	0.8	2246	3.8
9	TU	0452	0.3	1117	3.6	1702	0.7	● 2329	3.8
10	W	0530	0.4	1156	3.6	1739	0.7		
11	TH	0010	3.8	0607	0.5	1234	3.6	1816	0.7
12	F	0051	3.7	0642	0.6	1310	3.5	1853	0.8
13	SA	0130	3.5	0717	0.9	1346	3.3	1929	1.0
14	SU	0210	3.3	0752	1.1	1423	3.2	2008	1.2
15	M	0254	3.0	0829	1.4	1505	3.0	2056	1.4
16	TU	0348	2.8	0920	1.6	1558	2.9	◐ 2216	1.5
17	W	0459	2.7	1044	1.8	1709	2.8	2358	1.6
18	TH	0621	2.6	1221	1.8	1826	2.8		
19	F	0127	1.4	0739	2.7	1342	1.7	1936	2.9
20	SA	0220	1.3	0837	2.9	1431	1.5	2033	3.0
21	SU	0259	1.1	0919	3.1	1508	1.3	2117	3.2
22	M	0332	1.0	0955	3.2	1542	1.1	2156	3.3
23	TU	0404	0.8	1029	3.3	1614	1.0	2232	3.5
24	W	0435	0.7	1103	3.5	1646	0.9	○ 2308	3.6
25	TH	0506	0.6	1137	3.5	1720	0.8	2345	3.6
26	F	0540	0.6	1211	3.6	1756	0.7		
27	SA	0024	3.6	0615	0.7	1248	3.5	1834	0.8
28	SU	0105	3.6	0653	0.8	1327	3.5	1915	0.9
29	M	0149	3.4	0734	1.0	1409	3.4	2002	1.0
30	TU	0239	3.3	0821	1.2	1459	3.2	2103	1.1
31	W	0339	3.1	0927	1.5	1601	3.1	◑ 2234	1.2

NOVEMBER

Date	Day	Time	m	Time	m	Time	m	Time	m
1	TH	0456	3.0	1105	1.6	1718	3.0		
2	F	0004	1.2	0619	3.0	1236	1.6	1837	3.1
3	SA	0122	1.0	0737	3.1	1348	1.4	1948	3.2
4	SU	0222	0.8	0841	3.2	1441	1.2	2049	3.4
5	M	0310	0.7	0931	3.4	1524	1.1	2140	3.6
6	TU	0350	0.6	1014	3.5	1603	0.9	2226	3.7
7	W	0428	0.6	1054	3.6	1641	0.8	● 2308	3.7
8	TH	0504	0.6	1131	3.6	1718	0.8	2349	3.6
9	F	0540	0.7	1207	3.6	1756	0.8		
10	SA	0028	3.5	0614	0.9	1242	3.5	1832	0.9
11	SU	0107	3.4	0648	1.0	1316	3.4	1908	1.0
12	M	0145	3.2	0721	1.2	1352	3.3	1946	1.2
13	TU	0227	3.0	0757	1.4	1431	3.2	2031	1.3
14	W	0315	2.9	0840	1.6	1518	3.0	2133	1.4
15	TH	0415	2.7	0946	1.8	1617	2.9	◐ 2255	1.5
16	F	0528	2.7	1114	1.8	1729	2.8		
17	SA	0016	1.5	0639	2.7	1236	1.8	1837	2.9
18	SU	0124	1.4	0743	2.8	1341	1.6	1938	3.0
19	M	0213	1.2	0833	3.0	1428	1.4	2030	3.1
20	TU	0253	1.1	0915	3.2	1507	1.3	2116	3.3
21	W	0328	0.9	0954	3.3	1544	1.1	2158	3.4
22	TH	0403	0.8	1031	3.5	1621	0.9	2240	3.6
23	F	0439	0.7	1109	3.6	1659	0.8	○ 2323	3.6
24	SA	0517	0.7	1148	3.7	1739	0.7		
25	SU	0007	3.7	0556	0.8	1229	3.7	1822	0.7
26	M	0052	3.6	0638	0.9	1311	3.6	1908	0.8
27	TU	0141	3.5	0724	1.1	1357	3.5	2001	0.9
28	W	0234	3.3	0815	1.3	1448	3.4	2105	1.0
29	TH	0334	3.2	0918	1.5	1548	3.3	2223	1.0
30	F	0445	3.0	1040	1.6	1659	3.2	◑ 2341	1.1

DECEMBER

Date	Day	Time	m	Time	m	Time	m	Time	m
1	SA	0558	3.0	1202	1.6	1811	3.2		
2	SU	0054	1.0	0709	3.1	1317	1.5	1920	3.2
3	M	0157	0.9	0813	3.2	1416	1.4	2024	3.3
4	TU	0247	0.9	0906	3.3	1504	1.2	2119	3.4
5	W	0329	0.9	0951	3.4	1546	1.1	2207	3.5
6	TH	0407	0.9	1032	3.5	1625	1.0	2251	3.5
7	F	0442	0.9	1109	3.5	1703	0.9	● 2332	3.5
8	SA	0517	0.9	1145	3.5	1741	0.9		
9	SU	0010	3.4	0551	1.0	1220	3.5	1817	0.9
10	M	0048	3.3	0625	1.1	1254	3.5	1853	1.0
11	TU	0125	3.2	0659	1.2	1329	3.4	1930	1.1
12	W	0203	3.1	0734	1.4	1405	3.3	2010	1.2
13	TH	0245	3.0	0812	1.5	1446	3.2	2056	1.3
14	F	0333	2.8	0859	1.6	1533	3.0	2156	1.4
15	SA	0430	2.8	1004	1.7	1630	2.9	◐ 2305	1.4
16	SU	0534	2.7	1124	1.7	1734	2.9		
17	M	0013	1.4	0637	2.8	1235	1.7	1838	2.9
18	TU	0114	1.3	0736	2.9	1338	1.5	1938	3.0
19	W	0207	1.2	0830	3.1	1430	1.4	2034	3.2
20	TH	0253	1.0	0918	3.3	1515	1.2	2127	3.3
21	F	0335	0.9	1002	3.4	1559	1.0	2217	3.5
22	SA	0417	0.8	1046	3.6	1643	0.8	○ 2306	3.6
23	SU	0500	0.8	1130	3.7	1728	0.7	2354	3.7
24	M	0544	0.8	1214	3.7	1815	0.6		
25	TU	0043	3.7	0629	0.9	1300	3.7	1904	0.6
26	W	0134	3.6	0716	1.0	1347	3.7	1957	0.6
27	TH	0226	3.4	0805	1.1	1437	3.6	2055	0.7
28	F	0321	3.3	0859	1.3	1532	3.4	2159	0.9
29	SA	0422	3.1	1004	1.4	1634	3.3	◑ 2307	1.0
30	SU	0526	3.0	1117	1.5	1740	3.2		
31	M	0017	1.1	0631	3.0	1236	1.5	1848	3.1

Chart Datum: 1·71 metres below Ordnance Datum (Newlyn). HAT is 4·0 metres above Chart Datum.

9.7.20 SCRABSTER

Highland **58°36'·61N 03°32'·61W**

CHARTS AC 1954, 2162, 1462; Imray C68

TIDES -0240 Dover; ML 3·2; Duration 0615

Standard Port WICK (⟵)

Times				Height (metres)			
High Water		Low Water		MHWS	MHWN	MLWN	MLWS
0200	0700	0100	0700	3·5	2·8	1·4	0·7
1400	1900	1300	1900				
Differences SCRABSTER							
–0255	–0225	–0240	–0230	+1·5	+1·2	+0·8	+0·3
GILLS BAY							
–0150	–0150	–0202	–0202	+0·7	+0·7	+0·6	+0·3
STROMA							
–0115	–0115	–0110	–0110	–0·4	–0·5	–0·1	–0·2
LOCH ERIBOLL (Portnancon)							
–0340	–0255	–0315	–0255	+1·6	+1·3	+0·8	+0·4
KYLE OF DURNESS							
–0350	–0350	–0315	–0315	+1·1	+0·7	+0·4	–0·1
SULE SKERRY (59°05'N 04°24'W)							
–0320	–0255	–0315	–0250	+0·4	+0·3	+0·2	+0·1
RONA (59°08'N 05°49'W)							
–0350	–0350	–0350	–0340	–0·3	–0·4	–0·2	–0·4

SHELTER Very good except for swell in NW and N winds. Yachts usually lie in the Inner (0·9–1·2m) or Centre Basins (0·9–2·7m). Pontoons in inner hbr. ⚓ is not advised.

- A good hbr to await the right conditions for E-bound passage through Pentland Firth (see 9.7.5).
- Beware floating creel lines in E of hbr.

NAVIGATION WPT 58°36'·58N 03°32'·09W, 278°/0·25M to E pier lt. Can be entered H24 in all weathers. Beware FVs and the Orkney ferries.

LIGHTS AND MARKS No ldg marks/lts but entry is simple once the conspic ice plant tr and/or pier lts have been located. Do not confuse hbr lts with the shore lts of Thurso.

COMMUNICATIONS (Code 01847) CGOC (01224) 592334; Police 101; Dr 893154. HM 892779 mobile 07803 290366.

Call HM VHF Ch 12 16 (H24) for berthing directions, before entering hbr. From the W reception is very poor due to masking by Holborn Head.

FACILITIES www.scrabster.co.uk £13·00/night on quay, pontoon by request (15/30/99t). **Pentland Firth YC** (keys held by Duty HM). **Thurso** (Wick). **Ferries** Stromness 3/day 1½hrs; Northlink (www.northlinkferries.co.uk). Faroe Islands (Torshavn) weekly (seasonal) 12hrs; Bergen weekly (seasonal) 16hrs; Smyril (www.smyril.co.uk).

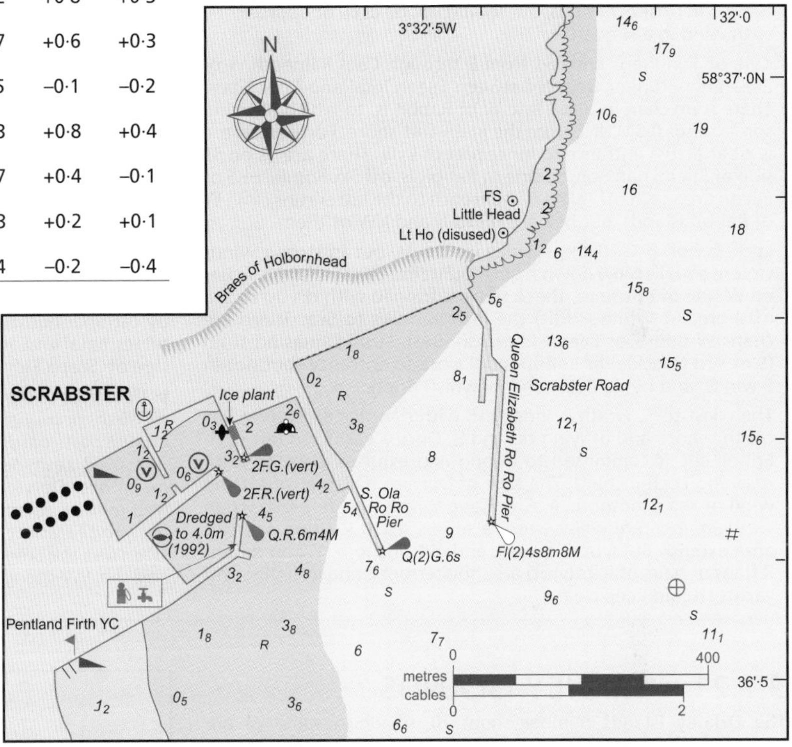

ANCHORAGES BETWEEN SCRABSTER AND CAPE WRATH

KYLE OF TONGUE, Highland, **58°31'·97N 04°22'·67W** (ent). AC 2720, 1954. HW +0050 on Ullapool; HW ht –0·4m; see 9.7.20. The Kyle runs about 7M inland.

Entry (see 9.7.5) should not be attempted in strong N winds.

⚓ at Talmine (W of Rabbit Is) protected from all but NE winds; at Skullomie Hr, protected from E'lies; off Mol na Coinnle, a small bay on SE side of Eilean nan Ron, protected from W and N winds; off S of Rabbit Is, protected from W to N winds. No ldg lts/marks. Facilities: Limited at Talmine (½M from slip) or at Coldbachie (1½M from Skullomie).

LOCH ERIBOLL, Highland, **58°32'·58N 04°37'·48W**. AC 2076. HW –0345 on Dover; ML 2·7m. See 9.7.20. Enter between Whiten Hd and Klourig Is in W sector of White Hd lt. See 9.7.4.

In SW winds fierce squalls funnel down the loch.

Yachts can enter drying Rispond Hbr and dry out alongside; no lts/marks and very limited facilities. Good ⚓s at: Rispond Bay on W side of loch, ent good in all but E winds, in approx 5m; off Portnancon in 5·5m; at the head of the loch; Camus an Duin and in bays to N and S of peninsula at Heilam on E side of loch. Beware numerous marine farms in the S half of the loch.

PENTLAND FIRTH TO CAPE WRATH

(AC 1954) Dunnet B, S of Dunnet Hd (lt) gives temp ⚓ in E or S winds, but dangerous seas enter in NW'lies. On W side of Thurso B is Scrabster sheltered from S and W. ▶ *Between Holborn Hd and Strathy Pt the E-going stream begins at HW Ullapool –0150, and the W-going at HW Ullapool +0420, sp rates 1·8kn. Close to Brims Ness off Ushat Hd the sp rate is 3kn, and there is often turbulence.* ◀

SW of Ushat Hd the Dounreay power stn is conspic, near shore. Dangers extend 2½ca seaward off this coast.▶ *Along E side of Strathy Pt (lt) an eddy gives almost continuous N-going stream, but there is usually turbulence off the Pt where this eddy meets the main E or W stream.*◀ Several small bays along this coast give temp ⚓ in offshore winds, but should not be used or approached with wind in a N quarter.

Kyle of Tongue is entered from E through Caol Raineach, S of Eilean nan Ron, or from N between Eilean Iosal and Cnoc Glass. There is no chan into the kyle W of Rabbit Is, to which a drying spit extends 0·5M NNE from the mainland shore. Further S there is a bar across entrance to inner part of kyle. There are ⚓s on SE side of Eilean nan Ron, SE side of Rabbit Is, off Skullomie, or S of Eilean Creagach off Talmine. Approach to the latter runs close W of Rabbit Islands, but beware rks to N and NW of them.

Loch Eriboll (AC 2076) provides secure ⚓s, but in strong winds violent squalls blow down from mountains. Eilean Cluimhrig lies on W side of entrance; the E shore is fringed with rks up to 2ca offshore. At White Hd (lt) the loch narrows to 6ca. There are chans W and E of Eilean Choraidh. Best ⚓s in Camas an Duin (S of Ard Neackie) or in Rispond B close to entrance (but not in E winds, and beware Rispond Rk which dries).

The coast to C Wrath is indented, with dangers extending 3ca off the shore and offlying rks and Is. Once a yacht has left Loch Eriboll she is committed to a long and exposed passage until reaching Loch Inchard. The Kyle of Durness is dangerous if the wind or sea is onshore. ▶ *Give Cape Wrath a wide berth when wind-against-tide which raises a severe sea.*◀ A firing exercise area extends 8M E of C. Wrath, and 4M offshore. When in use, R flags or pairs of R lts (vert) are shown from E and W limits, and yachts should keep clear.

ORKNEY ISLANDS

(AC 2249, 2250) The Islands are mostly indented and rocky, but with sandy beaches especially on NE sides.

▶*Pilotage is easy in good vis, but in other conditions great care is needed since tides run strongly. For details refer to* **Clyde Cruising Club's Orkney Sailing Directions** *and the* **Admiralty Tidal Atlas NP 209**. *When cruising in Orkney it is essential to understand and use the tidal streams to the best advantage, avoiding the various tide races and overfalls, particularly near sp.*◀

A good engine is needed since, there are many places where it is dangerous to get becalmed. Swell from the Atlantic or North Sea can contribute to dangerous sea conditions, or penetrate to some of the ⚓s. During summer months winds are not normally unduly strong, and can be expected to be Force 7 or more on about two days a month. In winter the wind reaches this strength for 10-15 days per month, and gales can be very severe in late winter and early spring. Cruising conditions are best near midsummer, when of course the hours of daylight are much extended.

Stronsay Firth and Westray Firth run SE/NW through the group. The many good ⚓s include: Deer Sound (W of Deer Ness); Bays of Firth, Isbister, and off Balfour in Elwick B (all leading fm Wide Firth); Rysa Snd, B of Houton, Hunda Snd (Scapa Flow); Rousay Sound; and Pierowall Road (Westray). Plans for some of these are on AC 2622. The European Marine Energy test site with underwater turbines and large static vessels lies between Eday and Muckle Green Holm, and an offshore wave test site marked by cardinal buoys NNW of Hoy Mouth (emec.org.uk). A major oil terminal and associated prohibited area is at Flotta, on the S side of Scapa Flow.

▶ *Tide races or dangerous seas occur at the entrances to most of the firths or sounds when the stream is against strong winds. This applies particularly to Hoy Sound, Eynhallow Sound, Papa Sound (Westray), Lashy Sound, and North Ronaldsay Firth. Also off Mull Head, over Dowie Sand, between Muckle Green Holm and War Ness (where violent turbulence may extend right across the firth), between Faraclett Head and Wart Holm, and off Sacquoy Hd. Off War Ness the SE-going stream begins at HW Aberdeen +0435, and the NW-going at HW Aberdeen –0200, sp rates 7kn.* ◀

9.7.21 ORKNEY ISLANDS

The Orkney Islands number about 70, of which some 24 are inhabited. They extend 5 to 50M NNE from Duncansby Hd, are mostly low-lying, but Hoy in the SW of the group reaches 475m (1560ft). Coasts are rocky and much indented, but there are many sandy beaches. A passage with least width of about 3M runs NW/SE through the group. The islands are separated from Scotland by the Pentland Firth, a very dangerous stretch of water. The principal island is Mainland (or Pomona) on which stands Kirkwall, the capital. For inter island ferries see www.orkneyferries.co.uk.

Severe gales blow in winter and early spring. The climate is mild but windy, and very few trees grow. There are LBs at Longhope, Stromness and Kirkwall.

CHARTS AC 2162, 2250 and 2249, at medium scale. For larger scale charts, see under individual hbrs; Imray C68

TIDES Wick (9.7.19) is the Standard Port. Tidal streams are strong, particularly in Pentland Firth and in the islands' firths and sounds.

SHELTER/MARINA CHARGES There are piers (fender board advised) at all main islands www.sailnorthscotland.com. For details of charges at marinas or piers throughout the Orkney Islands, except St Margaret's Hope, www.orkneymarinas.co.uk. Some of the many ⚓s are listed:

MAINLAND **Scapa Bay**: good except in S winds. No yacht berths alongside pier due to heavy hbr traffic. Only ents to Scapa Flow are via Hoy Snd, Hoxa Snd or W of Flotta.

St Marys (Holm/Ham): 58°53'·80N 02°54'·50W; N side of Kirk Sound; ⚓ in B of Ayre or berth E side of Pier, HW±4.
Bus to Kirkwall/Burwick Ferry.

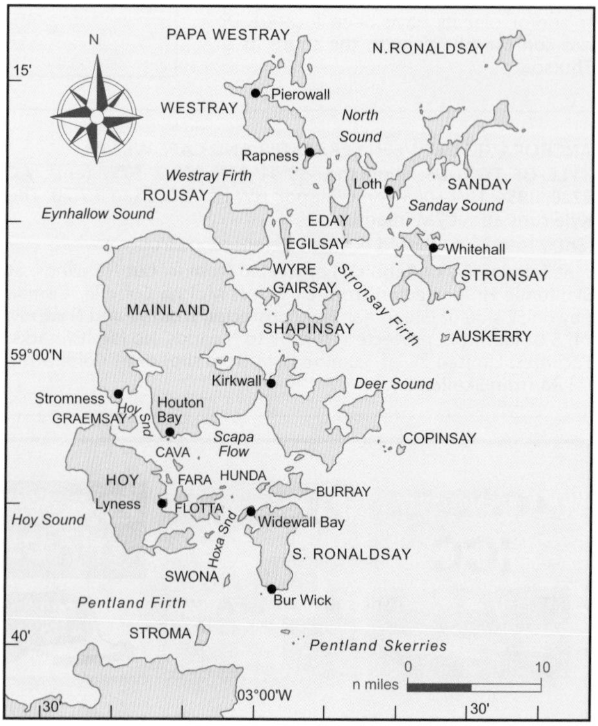

Kirk Sound (E ent): ⚓ N of Lamb Holm; beware fish cages.

Deer Sound: ⚓ in Pool of Mirkady or off pier on NW side of sound; very good shelter, no facilities.

Hunda Sound: good ⚓ in all winds.

SOUTH RONALDSAY/BURRAY **St Margaret's Hope/Water Sound**: . Ldg Lts, F.G, 174°. ⚓ in centre of bay; or £7/day at pier (but limited space and keep clear of ferry berth on S side of pier), beware salmon farm. HM ☎01856 831440, mob 07879 688040; Dr 831206. Bus to Kirkwall, vehicle ferry to Gill's Bay/Caithness.

Widewall Bay: ⚓ sheltered except SW'lies.

FLOTTA **58°50'·20N 03°07'·90W**; berth on Sutherland Pier, SW of oil terminal. HM ☎01856 701411.

HOY **Long Hope: 58°48'·07N 03°12'·25W**; ⚓ E of Pier, used by ferry, or berth on pier (safest at slack water). 2 's < 18 tonnes close to Pier. ☎01856 701263; Dr 701209. Facilities: .

Lyness: 58°50'·20N 03°11'·40W; berth on Pier; not piles (disused); ⚓ in Ore Bay. HM ☎01856 791387. Avoid fish cages.

Pegal Bay: good ⚓ except in strong W winds.

ROUSAY **Wyre Sound: 59°09'·40N 02°44'·70W**; ⚓ E of Rousay Pier or berth on it. Piermaster ☎01856 821261.

EDAY **Fersness Bay**: good holding, sheltered from S winds. Dr ☎ 01857 622243.

Backaland Bay: 59°09'·40N 02°44'·70W: berth on Pier clear of ferry; Piermaster ☎01856 622282; or ⚓ to NW. Beware cross-tides.

Calf Sound: ⚓ in Carrick B; good shelter from SW-NW'lies.

PAPA WESTRAY **Bay of Moclett 58°21'·40N 02°26'·30W**: Good ⚓ but open to S. Pier. Piermaster ☎01857 644259.

South Wick: ⚓ off the old pier or ESE of pier off Holm of Papa. Backaskaill: .

SANDAY **Loth Bay: 59°11'·50N 02°41'·80W**; berth on Pier clear of ferry. Piermaster ☎01857 600227; beware strong tides.

Kettletoft Bay: 59°13'·90N 02°35'·80W; ⚓ in bay or berth on Pier, very exposed to SE'lies. HM ☎01857 600227, Dr 600221; hotel.

North Bay: on NW side of island, exposed to NW.

Otterswick: good ⚓ except in N or E winds.

NORTH RONALDSAY **South Bay: 58°21'·40N 02°26'·30W**; ⚓ in middle of bay or berth on Pier. Piermaster ☎01857 633239; open to S & W and swell.

Linklet Bay: ⚓ off jetty at N of bay, open to E.

NAVIGATION From the mainland, appr from Scrabster to Stromness and Scapa Flow via Hoy Mouth and Hoy Sd. From the Moray Firth keep well E of the Pentland Skerries if going N to Kirkwall. If bound for Scapa Flow via Hoxa Sd, keep close to Duncansby Hd, passing W of the Pentland Skerries and between Swona and S Ronaldsay. Keep clear of Lother Rk (dries 1·8m) off SW tip of S Ronaldsay. Time this entry for slack water in the Pentland Firth (about HW Aberdeen –1¾ and +4). Beware of tankers off Flotta oil terminal and in S part of Scapa Flow, where are the remains of the German WW1 Battle Fleet; classified as Historic Wrecks (see 9.0.3) protected, but authorised diving allowed.

Elsewhere in Orkney navigation is easy in clear weather, apart from the strong tidal streams in all the firths and sounds. Beware races and overfalls off Brough of Birsay (Mainland), Noup Head (Westray) and Dennis Head (N Ronaldsay). Keep a good lookout for the many lobster pots (creels).

LIGHTS AND MARKS The main hbrs and sounds are well lit; for details see 9.7.4. Powerful lts are shown offshore from Cantick Hd, Graemsay Island, Copinsay, Auskerry, Kirkwall, Brough of Birsay, Sanday Island, N Ronaldsay and Noup Hd.

Orkney Hbrs Navigation Service (call: *Orkney Hbr Radio*, Ch 09 11 20 16 (H24)) covers Scapa Flow and apprs, Wide Firth, Shapinsay Sound and Kirkwall Bay.

COMMUNICATIONS Area Code for islands SW of Stronsay and Westray Firths is 01856; islands to the NE are 01857.

MEDICAL SERVICES Doctors are available at Kirkwall, Stromness, Rousay, Hoy, Shapinsay, Eday, S and N Ronaldsay, Stronsay, Sanday and Westray (Pierowall); Papa Westray is looked after by Westray. The only hospital (and dentist) are at Kirkwall. Serious cases are flown to Aberdeen (1 hour).

MARINE FARMS Fish cages/farms approx 30m x 50m may be found anywhere in sheltered waters within anchoring depths. Some are well buoyed, others are marked only by poles. Too many to list but the following will show the scale of the operations:

Beware **salmon cages** (may be marked by Y buoys/lts) at:

Kirkwall Bay	Toy Ness (Scapa Flow)
Rysa Sound	St Margaret's Hope
Bring Deeps	Backaland Bay (Eday)
Pegal Bay (Hoy)	Hunda Sound
Lyrawa Bay	Kirk Sound
Ore Bay (Hoy)	Carness Bay
Widewall Bay (S Ronaldsay)	Bay of Ham
	Bay of London (Eday)

Beware **oysters and longlines** at:

Widewall Bay	Bay of Firth
Swanbister Bay	Damsay Sound
Water Sound	Millburn Bay (Gairsay)
Hunda Sound	Pierowall
Deer Sound	Bay of Skaill (Westray)
Inganess Bay	Longhope

MINOR HARBOURS IN THE ORKNEY ISLANDS

HOUTON BAY, Mainland, **58°54'·85N 03°11'·33W**. AC 35, 2568. HW –0140 on Dover, –0400 on Aberdeen; HW ht +0·3m on Kirkwall; ML 1·8m; Duration 0615. ⚓ in the bay in approx 5·5m at centre, sheltered from all winds. Ent is to the E of Holm of Houton marked by bn Fl R 3s 7m 5M; chan dredged 3·5m for 15m each side of ldg line. Keep clear of shipping/ferries plying to Flotta. Ldg lts 316°: front Fl G 3s 8m, rear FG 16m; both R △ on W pole, B bands. Ro Ro terminal in NE corner marked by Iso R 4s with SHM Fl G on edge of ldg line. Bus to Kirkwall; close E of piers. Yachtsmen may contact **M.Grainger** ☎01856 811397 for help.

SHAPINSAY, Orkney Islands, **59°01'·97N 02°54'·10W**. AC 2249, 2584. HW –0015 on Dover, –0330 on Aberdeen; HW ht –1·0m on Aberdeen. Good shelter in Elwick Bay off Balfour on SW end of island in 2·5-3m. Enter bay passing W of Helliar Holm which has lt Fl WRG 10s on S end. Keep mid-chan. Balfour Pier lt Q WRG 5m 3/2M; vis 270°-G-010°-W-020°-R-090°. Piermaster ☎01856 711358; Tides in The String reach 5kn at sp. Facilities: shop.

AUSKERRY, Orkney Islands, **59°02'·02N 02°34'·65W**. AC 2250. HW –0010 on Dover, -0315 on Aberdeen, HW ht -1m on Aberdeen. Small island at ent to Stronsay Firth with small hbr on W side. Safe ent and good shelter except in SW winds. Ent has 3·5m; 1·2m alongside pier. Yachts can lie secured between ringbolts at ent and the pier. Auskerry Sound and Stronsay Firth are dangerous with wind over tide. Auskerry lt at S end, Fl 20s 34m 18M, W tr. No facilities.

PIEROWALL, Westray, **59°19'·32N 02°58'·51W**. AC 2250, 2622. HW –0135 on Dover; ML 2·2m; Duration 0620. See 9.7.24. The bay is a good ⚓ in 2-7m and well protected. Marina pontoons in deep water alongside pier at Gill Pt. From S, beware Skelwick Skerry rks, and from the N the rks extending approx 1ca off Vest Ness. The N ent via Papa Sound should be approached with caution; tide race on the ebb. A dangerous tide race, The Bore Röst, runs off Mull Hd at the N of Papa Westray. Lights: E Pier Hd Fl WRG 3s 7m 11/7M. W Pier Hd 2 FR (vert) 4/6m 3M. VHF Ch 16. HM ☎01857 677216. **Marina** ☎07787364934 www.orkneymarinas.co.uk, £2.00m (see 9.7.5). Services: . Dr 01857 677209.

RAPNESS: **58°14'·90N 02°51'·50W**, berth on Pier clear of Ro-Ro. Piermaster ☎01857 677212; Open to SSW.

NE Scotland

9.7.22 STROMNESS

Orkney Islands, Mainland **58°57'·78N 03°17'·72W**

CHARTS AC 2249, 2568; Imray C68

TIDES –0145 Dover; ML 2·0; Duration 0620

Standard Port WICK (⟵)

Times				Height (metres)			
High Water		Low Water		MHWS	MHWN	MLWN	MLWS
0000	0700	0200	0700	3·5	2·8	1·4	0·7
1200	1900	1400	1900				
Differences STROMNESS							
–0225	–0135	–0205	–0205	+0·1	–0·1	0·0	0·0
ST MARY'S (Scapa Flow)							
–0140	–0140	–0140	–0140	–0·2	–0·2	0·0	–0·1
BURRAY NESS (Burray)							
+0005	+0005	+0015	+0015	–0·2	–0·3	–0·1	–0·1
WIDEWALL BAY (S Ronaldsay)							
–0155	–0155	–0150	–0150	+0·1	–0·1	–0·1	–0·3
BUR WICK (S Ronaldsay)							
–0100	–0100	–0150	–0150	–0·1	–0·1	+0·2	+0·1
MUCKLE SKERRY (Pentland Firth)							
–0025	–0025	–0020	–0020	–0·9	–0·8	–0·4	–0·3

SHELTER Very good. Northern Lights Board have sole use of pier near to ldg lts. Marina in N of hbr; or ⚓ where shown.

NAVIGATION WPT 58°56'·93N 03°17'·00W, 317°/0·9M to front ldg lt. Turn N to pass between N Pier and Coplands Pier to marina.

- Entry from the W should not be attempted with strong wind against tide due to heavy overfalls.
- If entering against the ebb, stand on to avoid being swept onto Skerry of Ness.
- Tides in Hoy Sound are >7kn at springs. No tidal stream in hbr.

LIGHTS AND MARKS For Hoy Sound, ldg lts 104° on Graemsay Is: front Iso 3s 17m 15M, W tr; rear Oc WR 8s 35m 20/16M, ldg sector is 097°-R-112°. Skerry of Ness, Fl WG 4s 7m 7/4M; shore-W-090°-G-shore. Hbr ldg lts 317°, both FR 29/39m 11M (H24), W trs, vis 307°-327°. Coplands Pier 2 F G. Stromness Marina ent. Fl(2)R 5s.

COMMUNICATIONS (Code 01856) CGOC 01595 692976; Police 850222; Dr 850205; Dentist 850658. HM 07810 465825; Fuel 851286. For advice Yachtsmen may contact: **Orkney Marinas** ✆871313.

VHF Ch 14 16 (0900-1700 LT). (See also 9.7.23.)

FACILITIES **Stromness Marina:** ✆07810 465825, 10 £2.00m (see 9.7.5), (0800-2100 ✆8851286) (mob 30t). **Town** (Ferries to Scrabster, bus to Thurso), (Kirkwall).

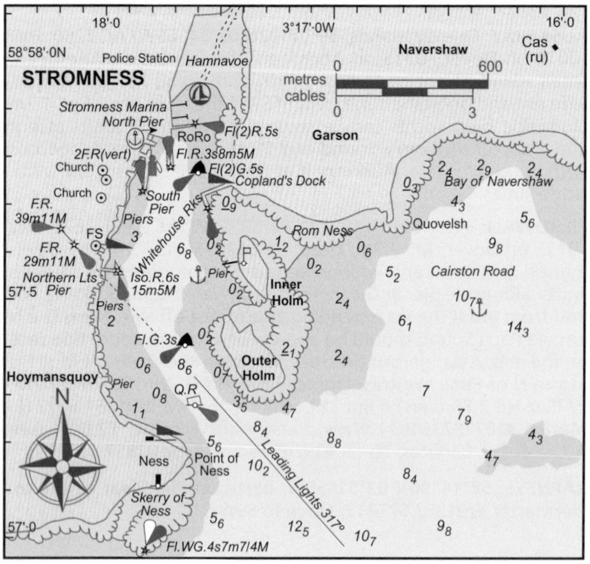

9.7.23 KIRKWALL

Orkney Islands, Mainland **58°59'·30N 02°57'·70W**

CHARTS AC 2250, 2249, 2584, 1553; Imray C68

TIDES –0045 Dover; ML 1·8; Duration 0620

Standard Port WICK (⟵)

Times				Height (metres)			
High Water		Low Water		MHWS	MHWN	MLWN	MLWS
0000	0700	0200	0700	3·5	2·8	1·4	0·7
1200	1900	1400	1900				
Differences *KIRKWALL*							
–0042	*–0042*	*–0041*	*–0041*	*–0·5*	*–0·4*	*–0·1*	*–0·1*
DEER SOUND							
–0040	–0040	–0035	–0035	–0·3	–0·3	–0·1	–0·1
TINGWALL							
–0200	–0125	–0145	–0125	–0·4	–0·4	–0·1	–0·1

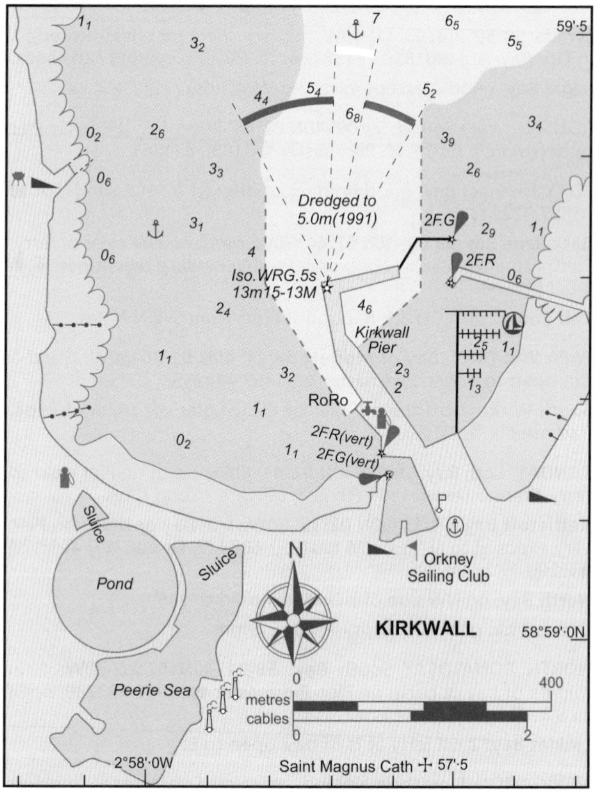

SHELTER Good except in N winds or W gales when there is a surge at the ent. Berth in marina on E of main pier, or SW end of main pier in inner hbr (very full in Jun/Jul). Safe ⚓ between pier and Crow Ness Pt. Hatston RoRo terminal in NW of bay (2 FG (vert)).

NAVIGATION WPT 59°01'·37N 02°57'·10W, 188°/2·2M to pier hd lt. Appr in W sector of pier hd lt, leaving newly extended Hatston Pier (2FG) / commercial terminal to W. Bay is shoal to SW beyond hbr.

LIGHTS AND MARKS See 9.7.4 and chartlet. Appr with St Magnus Cathedral (conspic) brg about 185°.

COMMUNICATIONS (Code 01856) CGOC (01595) 692976; 873802; Police 872241; Dr 888000 (Ⓗ). HM 872292; Port Office 873636; Fuel 873105.

Kirkwall Hbr Radio VHF Ch 14 16 (0800-1700 LT). Orkney Hbrs Navigation Service, call: *VTS Orkney* Ch 09 11 20 16 (0915–1715).

FACILITIES **Kirkwall Marina** ✆871313 (berths 07810 465835), 71 inc £2.00m (see 9.7.5). **Pier** (HO ✆873105) (mob 25t); **N and E Quays** M; **Orkney SC** ✆872331, (£15/4days). **Town** @ Library(HO). Ferries to Scrabster, Aberdeen and Shetland.

9.7.24 STRONSAY

Orkney Islands, Stronsay **59°08'·57N 02°36'·01W** ❀❀◊◊✿✿

CHARTS AC 2250, 2622; Imray C68

TIDES As Dover; ML 1·7; Duration 0620

Standard Port WICK (⟵)

Times				Height (metres)			
High Water		Low Water		MHWS	MHWN	MLWN	MLWS
0000	0700	0200	0700	3·5	2·8	1·4	0·7
1200	1900	1400	1900				
Differences WHITEHALL (Stronsay)							
–0030	–0030	–0025	–0030	–0·1	0·0	+0·2	+0·2
LOTH (Sanday)							
–0045	–0045	–0055	–0105	–0·4	–0·3	+0·1	+0·2
EGILSAY (Rousay Sound)							
–0125	–0125	–0125	–0125	–0·1	0·0	+0·2	+0·1
KETTLETOFT PIER (Sanday)							
–0030	–0025	–0025	–0025	0·0	0·0	+0·2	+0·2
RAPNESS (Westray)							
–0205	–0205	–0205	–0200	+0·1	+0·1	+0·2	0·0
PIEROWALL (Westray)							
–0150	–0150	–0145	–0145	+0·2	0·0	0·0	–0·1

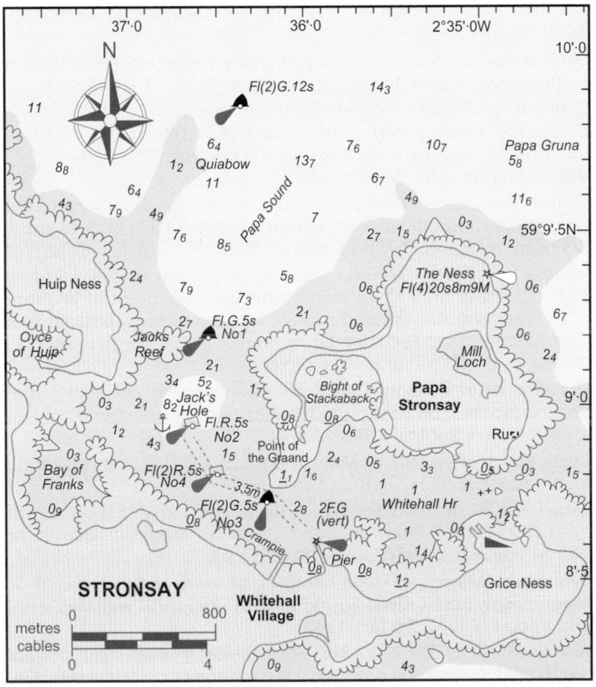

SHELTER Good from all winds. Good ⚓ between seaward end of piers, or berth on outer end of W pier and contact HM. The extended E pier head is berth for Ro-Ro ferry. There are many other sheltered ⚓s around the bay.

NAVIGATION WPT 59°09'·82N 02°36'·31W, Quiabow SHM lt buoy, 189°/6·5ca to No 1 lt buoy. 800m NE of Huip Ness is Quiabow, a submerged rk. Jack's Reef extends 400m E from Huip Ness, and is marked by No 1 SHM lt buoy. A bank extends 350m SW from Papa Stronsay. Crampie Shoal is in mid-chan, marked by No 3 buoy. The buoyed chan to Whitehall pier is dredged 3·5m. Spit to E of Whitehall pier extends 400m N. The E ent is narrow and shallow and should not be attempted.

LIGHTS AND MARKS See chartlet.

COMMUNICATIONS (Code 01857) CGOC (01595) 692976; Police (01856) 872241; Dr 616321. Piermaster 07901 984328. See Kirkwall for VHF comms.

FACILITIES W Pier ⛵ ⚒ ⛭; **Main (E) Pier** ⛵ ⚒ ⛽ ⛭ clear of ferry. **Village (Whitehall)** Ⓟ Ⓓ ✉ Ⓑ 🛒 ⊡ ⇄ (Ferry to Scrabster, bus to Thurso) ✈.

SHETLAND ISLANDS

(AC 3281, 3282, 3283) ▶ *These Islands mostly have bold cliffs and are relatively high, separated by narrow sounds through which the tide runs strongly, so that in poor vis great care is needed. Avoid sp tides, swell and wind against tide conditions. The tidal flow around the Shetland Islands rotates as the cycle progresses. When the flood begins, at –0400 HW Dover, the tidal flow is to the E, at HW Dover it is S, at Dover +0300 it is W, and at –0600 Dover it is N.* ◀

Between Mainland and Whalsay passage can be made E or W of W Linga with spring rates of about 2kn with weaker streams to be found to the W in Lunning Sound.

▶ *Slack water at Lunning Sound occurs simultaneously at Lerwick, either 4hrs before or 2hrs after HW Lerwick.* ◀

Passage further Northward can be made through Yell Sound or Colgrave/Bluemell Sounds with shelter at Cullivoe.

▶ *Tides in Yell Sound are slack at the same time as high and low water in Lerwick. The stream normally runs at about 4 kts between the islands at the narrowest part between Yell and the Mainland but may reach 8kn at springs. Colgrave Sound to the W of Yell experiences somewhat less tidal stream.* ◀

Bluemull Sound between Yell and Unst is a longer narrower passage. Well marked, passage is best attempted in daylight keeping to the middle of the channel clear of the fishing vesssels en-route to Cullivoe.

▶ The stream runs at up to 6kn at springs for longer duration and may be carried throughout a transit. ◀

Although there are many secluded and attractive ⚓s, remember that the weather can change very quickly, with sudden shifts of wind. Also beware salmon fisheries and mussel rafts (unlit) in many Voes, Sounds and hbrs. Lerwick is the busy main port and capital; other hbrs are Scalloway, Walls (Vaila Sound), Uyesound (S Unst), Mid Yell (E Yell), Cullivoe (N Yell), Burravoe (S Yell), Symbister (Whalsay, Out Skerries (Skerries Isle) and Balta Sound. Refer to the CCC's *Shetland Sailing Directions.*

▶ *Coming from the S, beware a most violent and dangerous race (roost) off Sumburgh Hd (at S end of Mainland) on both streams. Other dangerous areas include between Ve Skerries and Papa Stour; the mouth of Yell Sound with strong wind against N-going stream; and off Holm of Skaw (N end of Unst). Tidal streams run mainly NW/SE and are not strong except off headlands and in the major sounds; the Admiralty Tidal Atlas NP 209 gives detail. The sp range is about 2m.*◀

The 50M passage from Orkney can conveniently be broken by a stop at Fair Isle (North Haven). ▶ *Note that races form off both ends of the Is, especially S (Roost of Keels).*◀

Recommended Traffic Routes: NW-bound ships pass to the NE (no closer than 10M to Sumburgh Hd) or SW of Fair Isle; SE-bound ships pass no closer than 5M off N Ronaldsay (Orkney). Lerwick to Bergen, Norway, is about 210M.

FLOOD
Shetland Islands

(a) Dover –0410 to Dover +0020
(b) Dover –0400 to Dover +0030
(c) Dover –0530 to Dover +01 00
(d) Dover –0400 to Dover –0200

EBB
Shetland Islands

(a) Dover +0050 to Dover –0410
(b) Dover +0130 to Dover –0500
(c) Dover +01 00 to Dover –0530
(d) Dover +0200 to Dover +0500

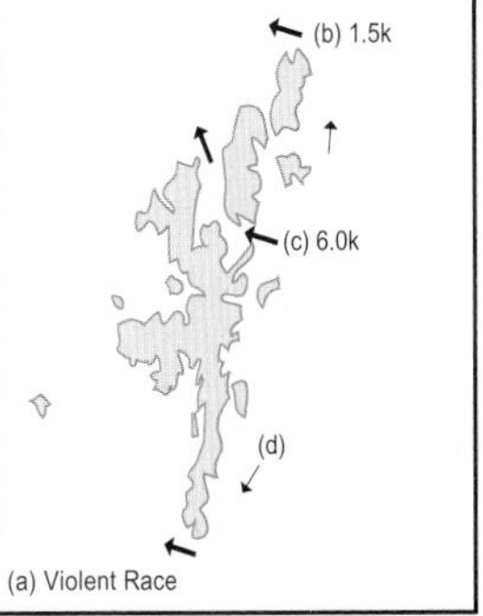

9.7.25 SHETLAND ISLANDS

The Shetland Islands number about 100 islands, holms and rks with fewer than 20 inhabited. Lying 90 to 150M NNE of the Scottish mainland, the biggest island is Mainland with Lerwick (9.7.26), the capital, on the E side. Scalloway, the only other town and old capital, is on the W side. At the very S is Sumburgh airport, with other airstrips at Baltasound, Scalsta and Tingwall. Two offlying islands of the Shetland group are Fair Isle, 20M SSW of Sumburgh Hd and owned by the NT for Scotland, and Foula, 12M WSW of Mainland. Mariners in the vicinity of inter-island ferry ports should check carefully for ferries entering or leaving the following ports and allow them free passage. (Fair Isle North Haven, Grutness, Dury Voe, Vidlin Voe, Symbister Out Skerries, Mossbank, Ulsta, Gutcher, Belmont , NW Fetlar and West Burrafirth.)

There are LBs at Lerwick and Aith. The CGOC Lerwick ☎(01595) 692976, with an Auxilliary Stn at Fair Is.

CHARTS AC: medium scale 3281, 3282, 3283; larger scale 3271, 3272, 3292, 3293, 3294, 3295, 3297, 3298.

TIDES Standard Port Lerwick. Tidal streams run mostly N-S or NW-SE; in open waters to the E and W they are mostly weak. Rates >6kn can cause dangerous disturbances at the N and S extremities of the islands and in the two main sounds (Yell Sound and BlueMull/Colgrave Sounds). Keep 3M off Sumburgh Head to clear a dangerous race (Röst) or pass close inshore.

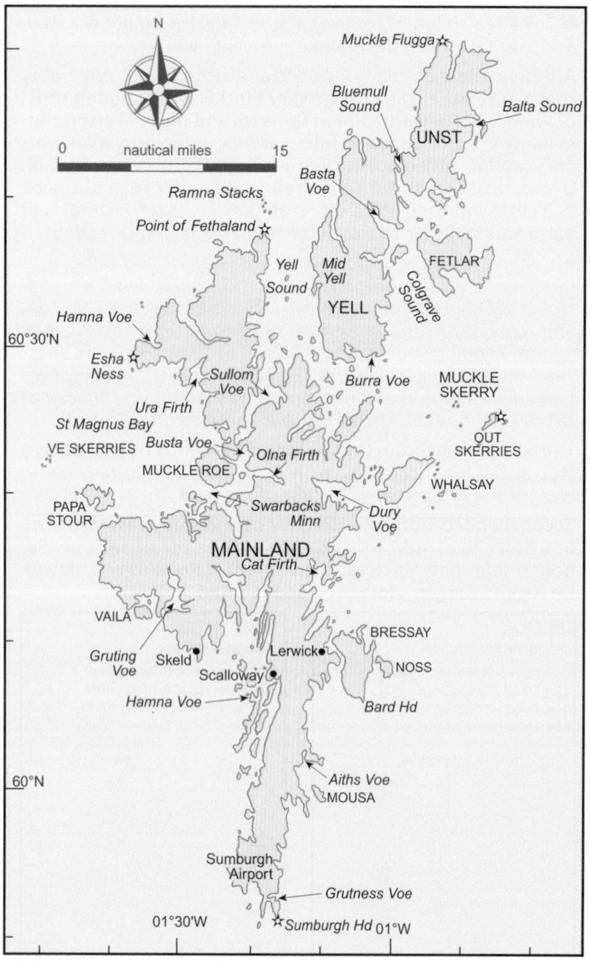

SHELTER Weather conditions are bad in winter; yachts should only visit Apr-Sept. Around mid-summer it is daylight H24. Some small marinas are asterisked* in the column on the right (see www.visitshetland.com); they may have room for visitors. Of the many ⚓s, the following are safe to enter in most conditions.

NAVIGATION A careful lookout must be kept for marine farms, mostly marked by Y buoys and combinations of Y lts. Clyde CC's *Shetland Sailing Directions and Anchorages* are essential for visitors. Local magnetic anomalies may be experienced.

LIGHTS AND MARKS See 9.7.4. Powerful lighthouses at Fair I, Sumburgh Hd, Kirkabister Ness, Bound Skerry, Muckle Flugga, Pt of Fethaland, Esha Ness and Foula. All inter-island ferry ports have leading sectored lights.

COMMUNICATIONS (Code 01595; 01806 for Sullom Voe) CGOC 692976; Sullom Voe Port Control (01806) 242551, ⚓ 242237; ⛅ 692239; Forecaster (01806) 242069; Sumburgh Airport (01950) 460654. Port Radio services see 9.7.26. No Coast Radio Station.

FACILITIES All stores obtainable in Lerwick and Scalloway. Elsewhere yachts should be prepared for extended offshore cruising and obtain water and diesel as and when they can:

MAINLAND (anti-clockwise from Sumburgh Head)

Grutness Voe: 1·5M N of Sumburgh Hd, a convenient passage ⚓, open to NE. Beware 2 rocks awash in mid-ent.

Pool of Virkie*: **59°53'N 01°17W**; Close N of Grutness Voe. Ness Boating Club Marina ☎01950 477260, (pontoon 1🅥< 1m £10/craft/week), . Shallow and narrow/entrance.

Cat Firth: excellent shelter, ⚓ in approx 6m. Facilities: ✉ (Skellister), ✉ (Lax Firth).

Grunna Voe: Off S side of Dury Voe, good shelter and holding, ⚓ in 5-10m; beware prohib ⚓ areas. Facilities: ✉ (Lax Firth).

South of Yell Sound*: Tides –0025 on Lerwick. W of Lunna Ness, well protected ⚓s with good holding include: Boatsroom Voe, W Lunna Voe (small hotel,), Colla Firth* and Dales Voe. No facilities.

Vidlin: marina shop, bus service.

Sullom Voe: Tides –0130 on Lerwick. 6·5M long deep water voe, Commercial harbour. Contact Sullom Voe VTS (Ch14) prior to entry. ⚓ S of the narrows. Facilities at Brae: ✉ .

Hamna Voe: Tides –0200 on Lerwick; very good shelter. Ldg line 153° old house on S shore with prominent rock on pt of W shore 3ca within ent. Almost land-locked; ⚓ in 6m approx, bottom foul with old moorings. Facilities: s, (at pier lit Fl R 3s), (1·5M), ✉ (0·5M), cafe, WC/ at nearby campsite.

Ura Firth: NE of St Magnus Bay, ⚓ off Hills Wick on W side or in Hamar Voe (no facilities) on E side, which has excellent shelter/good holding in all weathers. Facilities: **Hills Wick** ✉ ✕ .

Busta Voe: N of Swarbacks Minn. 4 🅥 (<12m LOA) at Delting Marina in 2m (☎01806 522479); Brae (½M): ✉ ✕.

Olna Firth: NE of Swarbacks Minn, beware rk 1ca off S shore which dries. ⚓ in firth, 4-8m or in Gon Firth or go alongside marina or pier at Voe. Facilities: (Voe) ✉ .

Swarbacks Minn*: A large complex of voes and isles SE of St Magnus Bay. Best ⚓ Uyea Sound or Aith Voe, both well sheltered and good holding. No facilities.

Aith Voe*: **60°17·3'N 01°22·3W**; Good shelter from all directions depth LW 1.2m (marina pontoon 2 🅥s) otherwise on pier access H24, WC/ (leisure centre) ✉ ✕ .

Vaila Sound (Walls), 60°13'·65N 01°33'·87W. AC 3295. Tides approx as Scalloway (above); see 9.7.26. Very good shelter. Appr to E of Vaila island (do not attempt Wester Sound) in the W sector (355°-012°) of Rams Head lt, Fl WRG 8s 16m 9/6M. Gruting Voe lies to the NE. Enter Easter Sound and go N for 1·5M, passing E of Linga islet, to Walls at the head of Vaila Voe. Navigate by echo sounder. Beware fish farms. ⚓ N of Salt Ness in 4-5m in mud. Temporary on Bayhaa pier (covers). Close E, £1 Peter Georgeson's pontoon. **Marina**: Sec ☎(01595) 809273, . **Walls Regatta Club** welcomes visitors; . **Village** ✉ .

Gruting Voe*: HW –0150 on Lerwick, ⚓ in main voe or in Seli, Scutta or Browland* voes. Facilities: ✉ at Bridge of Walls (head of Browland Voe).

Skeld, 60°09'·65N 01°27'W. AC 3283, 3294. Tides approx as Scalloway. Appr from Skelda Voe which is subject to heavy seas and swell in strong S'lies. Beware Braga Rk (dries 2m) and drying rk 1ca S of it. At E of ent also Snap Rk (dries 3.5m) with isolated rks inshore. **Marina** offers good shelter as virtually landlocked, welcomes visitors; 8🅥 £10/craft/week; James Scott ☎(01595) 860287 WC/ bus to Lerwick 2/daily.

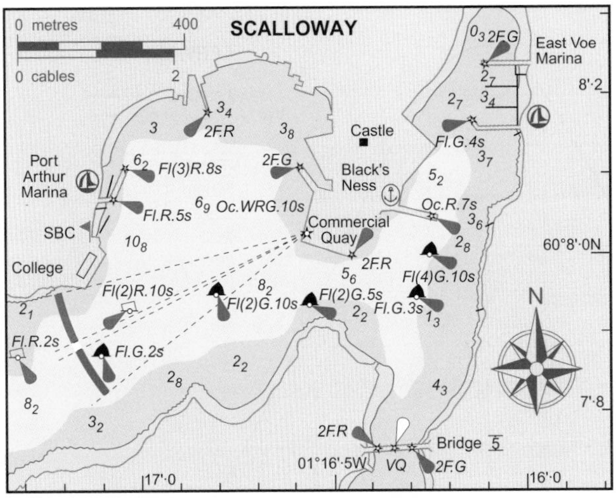
SCALLOWAY
0 metres 400
0 cables 2
East Voe Marina
Port Arthur Marina
SBC
College
Castle
Black's Ness
Commercial Quay
Fl(3)R.8s
2F.R
2F.G
Fl.R.5s
Oc.WRG.10s
Fl.G.4s
Oc.R.7s
Fl(4)G.10s
Fl(2)R.10s
Fl(2)G.10s
Fl(2)G.5s
Fl.G.3s
Fl.R.2s
Fl.G.2s
2F.R
Bridge 5
VQ
2F.G
01°16'·5W
17'·0
16'·0
60°8'·0N
8'·2
7'·8
N

Scalloway, 60°08'·02N 01°16'·59W. AC 3294. HW –0200 on Dover; ML 0·9m; Duration 0620. See 9.7.26. A busy fishing port; good shelter and ⚓ in all weathers. Care is needed negotiating the islands in strong SW'lies. The N Chan is easier and safer than the S Chan, both are well lit and marked. Castle and warehouse (both conspic) lead 054° through S Chan. Dir Oc WRG 10s on hbr quay leads 064·5° into hbr (dredged 8.5m). Lts as chartlet. Ⓥ pontoon in 3m off SBC is best option; marina close N or new marina in E Voe (though mostly full of local boats). ⚓s in hbr 6–10m or in Hamna Voe (W Burra). Info at www.shetland.gov.uk/ports/scalloway or e-mail scalloway.harbour@shetland.gov.uk (cc to sullomvoevts@shetland.gov.uk). Call *Scalloway Hbr Radio* VHF Ch **12** 16 (Mon-Fri 0600-1800; Sat 0600-1230LT). Piermaster ☎(01595) 744221. Facilities: **Scalloway Boat Club** (SBC) ☎880409, ⊆ ⊡.
Town ⊑ ⊥ ⊡ ⊡ ✕ ⊡ ⊡ ⊡ ⊡ ⊡ ⊡ ⊠ ⊡ ✕ ⊡ bus to Lerwick.

Hamna Voe*: 60°06·3'N 01°20·3W (West Burra) Entered between Fugla Ness and Alta Ness. Open to the NW; good shelter in small marina. Small village, bus to Lerwick and all other routes.

WHALSAY* 60°20'·60N 01°01'·60W; Fishing hbr with small marina at Symbister welcomes visitors. ⊥ ⊡ ⊆ (pontoon or pier 20Ⓥs) £7.17/craft/4 days; ⊡ ⊡ ⊥ ⊡ ⊡ WC ⊡ ⊡ ⊡ ⊠.

FOULA 60°08'·02N 02°02'·92W. AC 3283. HW -0150 on Dover; ML 1·3m. See 9.7.26. Highest ground is 416m. S Ness sectored Lt ho, Fl WR(3) 15s, is at the S tip. Beware both Foula Shoal (7·6m) 4·3M E of the island and Hœvdi Grund (1·4m), 2M to the SE of Ham Voe. **Ham Voe:** is a narrow inlet on the E coast with a quay; rks on both sides. Two R ▲ ldg marks, approx 270°, are hard to see. ☆ 2 FG (vert) on pierhead. Berthing or landing is only possible in settled weather with no swell. Take advice from mail boat skipper out of Walls and call Foula, ☎(01595) 753222. Small ✈. No other facilities.

OUT SKERRIES 60°25'·3N 00°45'·1W AC 3282. Good shelter at pier. The NE entrance is buoyed and is the easier and has a leading light (Local ferry port). There are two Historic Wrecks (*Kennemerland* and *Wrangels Palais*) on Out Skerries at 60°25'·2N 00°45'·0W and 60°25'·5N 00°43'·3W (see 9.0.3). Shops, WC ⊡ at pier. Beware strong tidal conditions off the NE entrance ferries approaching or leaving. Pier (£2/craft/night); ⊥ ⊡ ⊡ (by arrangement), toilet/⊡ wi-fi; **Village** ⊠ shop. Good ⚓ at Bruray.

YELL Mid Yell Voe*: 60°36'N 01°03·4W; tides –0040 on Lerwick, enter via S Sd or Hascosay Sd, good ⚓ in wide part of voe 2·5-10m. Berth at marina £5/week or Pier £7.17/4 days/craft. Facilities: ⊠ ⊥ at pier on S side, ⊡ ✕ ⊡ ⊡ ⊡.
Basta Voe: good ⚓ above shingle bank in 5-15m; good holding in places. Facilities: ⊥ ⊡ Hotel, ⊠.
Blue Mull Sound/Cullivoe*: 60°42'N 00°59'·7W; Hbr with small craft marina depth 1.2m ⊆£5/craft/day, ⊑ ⊥ ⊡. Pier ⊆ 20Ⓥs £7.17/craft/4 days; ⊥ ⊡ ⊡ ⊡ WC ⊡ ⊡. **Town** ⊠ ⊡ ✕ ⊡. ⚓ off pier.
Burra Voe*: 60°29'·8N 01°02'·4W; Entrance to voe has 2.5m bar. Good ⚓ at head of voe, but buoy ⚓ as precaution against fouling old moorings. ⊆ at small marina £5/visit or on Pier £12/visit, ⊥ ⊡ WC ⊡ ⊠ ⊡ ⊡.

FETLAR Hamars Ness 60°37'·78N 00°55'·76W; small hbr with new b'water (Iso G 6s 5m 3M) at W end of rocky bay. Appr W of WCM.

UNST Balta Sound: 60°44'·32N 00°48'·12W. AC 3293. HW –0105 on Dover; ML 1·3; Duration 0640. See 9.7.25. Balta Sound is a large almost landlocked inlet with good shelter from all winds. Beware fish farms and bad holding on kelp. Safest and main entry is via S Chan between Huney Is and Balta Is; inner chan marked by two PHM lt buoys. N Chan is deep but narrow; keep to Unst shore. ⚓ off Sandisons Wharf (2FG vert) in approx 6m pontoon on W side of pier is derelict and reported unsafe (Oc WRG 10s 5m 2M, 272°-G-282°-W-287°-R-297°). Small boat marina has single shallow Ⓥ berth. VHF Ch 16; 20 (HO or as required). Facilities: ⊥ ⊡ ✕ ⊡ ⊡ ⊡ hotel. **Baltasound village**, ⊠ ⊡ ✕ ⊡.

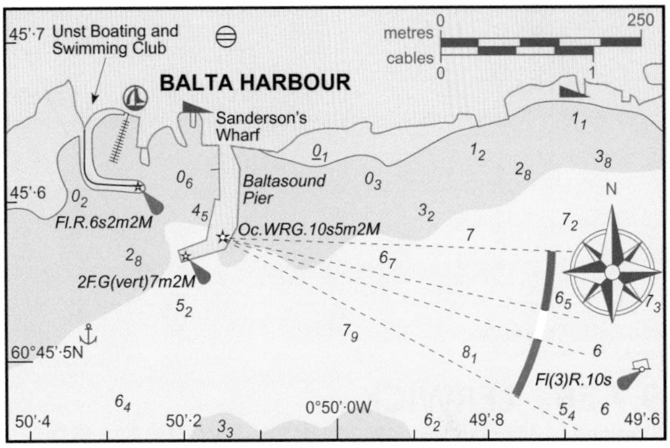
BALTA HARBOUR
Unst Boating and Swimming Club
0 metres 250
cables 0 1
Sanderson's Wharf
Baltasound Pier
Fl.R.6s2m2M
Oc.WRG.10s5m2M
2F.G(vert)7m2M
Fl(3)R.10s
45'·7
45'·6
60°45'·5N
50'·4
50'·2
0°50'·0W
49'·8
49'·6
N

FAIR ISLE 59°32'·37N 01°36'·21W. AC 3299. HW -0030 on Dover; ML 1·4m; Duration 0620. See 9.7.26. Good shelter in North Haven, except in NE winds. ⊆ on pier or ⚓ in approx 2m. Beware strong cross-tides in the apprs; rocks all round Fair Isle, esp in S Haven and S Harbour which are hazardous. Ldg marks 199° into N Haven: front, Stack of N Haven (a dark 'tooth' sticking up from the jumble of blocks which form the bkwtr) in transit with conspic summit of Sheep Craig (rear). Dir lt into N Haven, Oc WRG 8s 10m 6M; vis 204°-G-208°-W-211°-R-221°. Lights: N tip, Skroo Fl(2) 30s 80m **22**M, S tip, Skadan Fl(4) 30s 31m **22**M. Facilities: ⊠ ⊡ at N Shriva, ✈, bi-weekly mail boat to Grutness. No fuel or water. Bird observatory offers WC ⊡/meals. Use large fenders supplied against pier to protect from scend/swell.

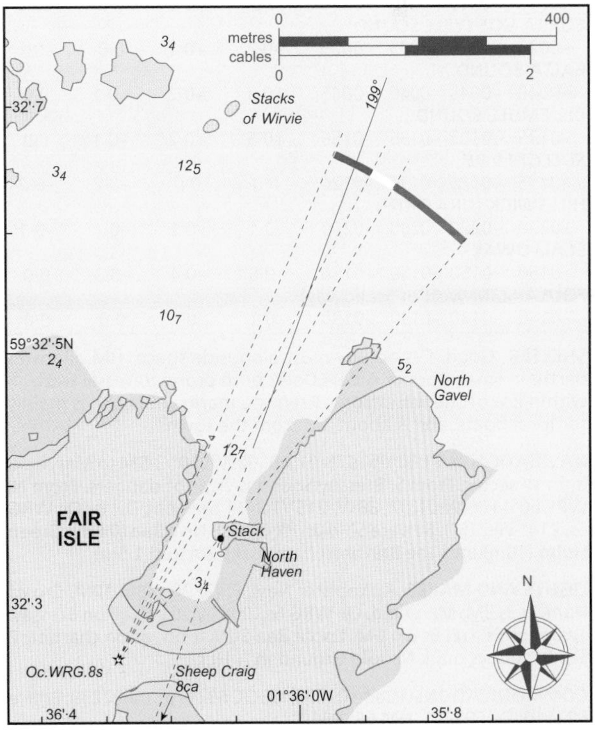
0 metres 400
cables 0 2
Stacks of Wirvie
199°
-32'·7
59°32'·5N
North Gavel
FAIR ISLE
Stack
North Haven
32'·3
Oc.WRG.8s
Sheep Craig 8ca
01°36'·0W
36'·4
35'·8
N

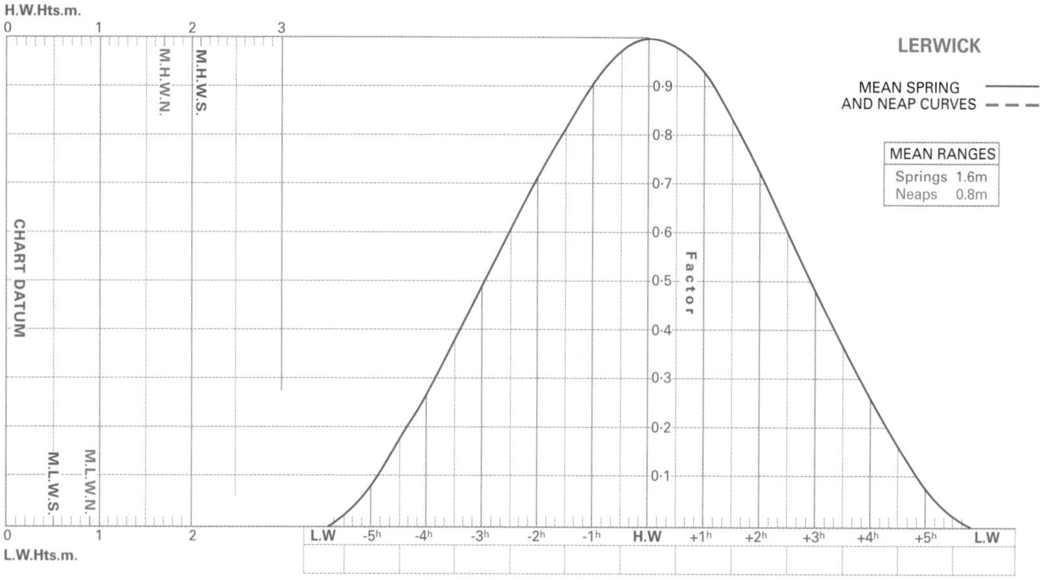

9.7.26 LERWICK

Shetland Is, Mainland **60°09'·26N 01°08'·42W** ❁❁❁◊◊✿✿

CHARTS AC 3283, 3272, 3271

TIDES –0001 Dover; ML 1·4; Duration 0620

Standard Port LERWICK (⟵)

Times				Height (metres)			
High Water		Low Water		MHWS	MHWN	MLWN	MLWS
0000	0600	0100	0800	2·1	1·7	0·9	0·5
1200	1800	1300	2000				
Differences FAIR ISLE							
–0006	–0015	–0031	–0037	+0·1	0·0	+0·1	+0·1
SUMBURGH (Grutness Voe)							
+0006	+0008	+0004	–0002	–0·3	–0·3	–0·2	–0·1
DURY VOE							
–0015	–0015	–0010	–0010	0·0	–0·1	0·0	–0·2
BURRA VOE (YELL SOUND)							
–0025	–0025	–0025	–0025	+0·2	+0·1	0·0	–0·1
BALTA SOUND							
–0040	–0045	–0040	–0045	+0·3	+0·2	+0·1	0·0
BLUEMULL SOUND							
–0135	–0135	–0155	–0155	+0·5	+0·2	+0·1	0·0
SULLOM VOE							
–0135	*–0125*	*–0135*	*–0120*	*0·0*	*0·0*	*–0·2*	*–0·2*
HILLSWICK (URA FIRTH)							
–0220	–0220	–0200	–0200	–0·1	–0·1	–0·1	–0·1
SCALLOWAY							
–0150	–0150	–0150	–0150	–0·5	–0·4	–0·3	0·0
FOULA (23M West of Scalloway)							
–0140	–0140	–0130	–0130	–0·1	–0·1	0·0	0·0

SHELTER Good. FVs occupy most alongside space. HM allocates berths in Small Dock or Albert Dock, both prone to vessel wash. ⚓ within 2ca of the waterfront. Gremista marina in N hbr, is mainly for local boats, and is about 1M from the town.

NAVIGATION WPT 60°05'·97N 01°08'·62W, 010°/3·5M to Maryfield lt, in W sector. From S, Bressay Sound is clear of dangers. From N, WPT 60°11'·60N 01°07'·88W, 215°/1·34M to N ent Dir lt (Oc WRG 6s, 214°-W-216°). Beware Soldian Rk (dries), Nive Baa (0·6m), Green Holm (10m) and The Brethren (two rocks 2m and 1·5m).

LIGHTS AND MARKS Kirkabister Ness, Fl (2) 20s 18m 10M; Cro of Ham, Fl 3s 3M; Maryfield, Oc WRG 6s, 008°-W-013°; all on Bressay. Twageos Pt, L Fl 6s 8m 6M. Loofa Baa SCM lt bn, as on chartlet. 2 SHM lt buoys mark Middle Ground in N Hbr.

COMMUNICATIONS (Code 01595) CGOC 692976; 692239; Police 692110; Dr 693201; HM 692991.

Lerwick Harbour VHF Ch **12** 16 (H24) for Vessel Information Service. Other stns: *Sullom Voe Hbr Radio* broadcasts traffic info and local forecasts on request Ch **14** 12 20 16 (H24).

FACILITIES Hbr .

Lerwick Port Authority ☎692991, Ⓥpontoons £0.60, ramps/WC.

Lerwick Boating Club ☎692407, .

Services Ⓔ ACA.

Town ✉ Ⓑ ✕ @ **Ferries** Aberdeen via Kirkwall; daily; overnight; North Link (www.northlinkferries.co.uk), ✈. See www.shetlandtimes.co.uk and www.lerwickboating.co.uk.

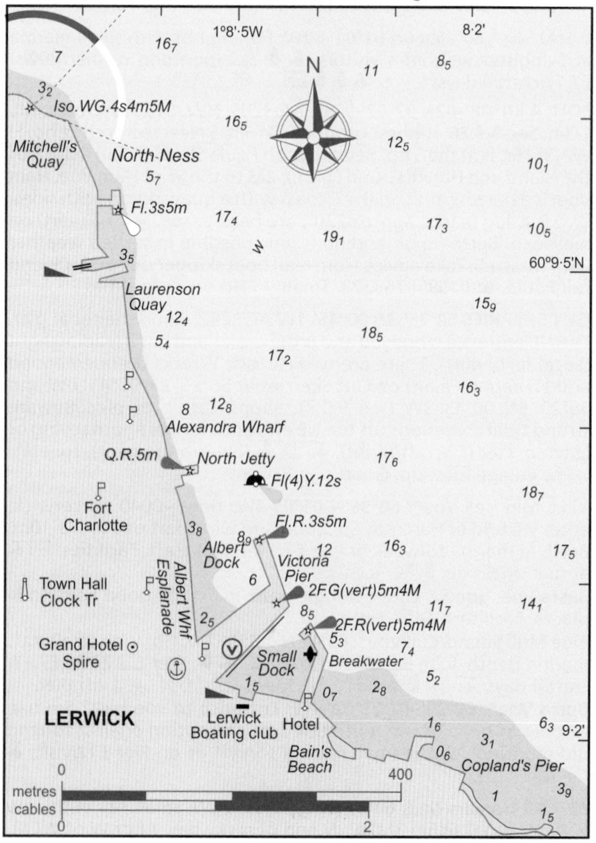

STANDARD TIME (UT)
For Summer Time add ONE hour in **non-shaded areas**

LERWICK LAT 60°09'N LONG 1°08'W

TIMES AND HEIGHTS OF HIGH AND LOW WATERS

Dates in red are SPRINGS
Dates in blue are NEAPS

YEAR **2018**

JANUARY

Date	Time	m	Date	Time	m
1	0342 0958 M 1610 2225	0.6 2.3 0.5 2.3	16	0420 1033 TU 1649 2303	0.8 2.1 0.7 2.0
2	0431 1047 TU 1659 ○ 2319	0.6 2.4 0.4 2.3	17	0453 1108 W 1721 ● 2339	0.8 2.2 0.7 2.0
3	0518 1136 W 1747	0.6 2.4 0.3	18	0525 1141 TH 1754	0.8 2.2 0.6
4	0013 0603 TH 1225 1835	2.3 0.6 2.4 0.3	19	0013 0557 F 1214 1827	2.0 0.8 2.2 0.6
5	0104 0650 F 1314 1924	2.3 0.7 2.4 0.4	20	0047 0631 SA 1246 1901	2.0 0.8 2.2 0.6
6	0154 0736 SA 1402 2014	2.2 0.8 2.3 0.5	21	0121 0705 SU 1320 1938	2.0 0.8 2.1 0.6
7	0242 0824 SU 1452 2107	2.0 0.9 2.2 0.6	22	0158 0743 M 1358 2018	1.9 0.8 2.1 0.7
8	0332 0917 M 1543 ◑ 2207	1.9 1.0 2.1 0.8	23	0240 0826 TU 1442 2104	1.9 0.9 2.0 0.7
9	0426 1021 TU 1642 2317	1.8 1.0 1.9 0.9	24	0329 0916 W 1534 ◐ 2157	1.8 0.9 1.9 0.8
10	0529 1145 W 1753	1.8 1.1 1.8	25	0426 1017 TH 1636 2304	1.8 1.0 1.9 0.8
11	0029 0637 TH 1306 1904	0.9 1.8 1.1 1.8	26	0532 1139 F 1749	1.8 1.0 1.9
12	0132 0739 F 1409 2007	0.9 1.8 1.0 1.8	27	0025 0645 SA 1304 1909	0.9 1.8 0.9 1.9
13	0224 0832 SA 1459 2100	0.9 1.9 0.9 1.9	28	0137 0753 SU 1411 2020	0.8 1.9 0.8 2.0
14	0308 0917 SU 1540 2145	0.9 2.0 0.8 1.9	29	0238 0852 M 1509 2122	0.7 2.1 0.6 2.1
15	0345 0957 M 1616 2226	0.9 2.1 0.8 2.0	30	0332 0945 TU 1601 2219	0.7 2.2 0.5 2.2
			31	0420 1036 W 1649 ○ 2312	0.6 2.3 0.3 2.3

FEBRUARY

Date	Time	m	Date	Time	m
1	0505 1125 TH 1735	0.5 2.4 0.2	16	0507 1122 F 1732 2352	0.7 2.2 0.5 2.0
2	0001 0549 F 1212 1819	2.3 0.5 2.4 0.2	17	0538 1154 SA 1805	0.6 2.2 0.4
3	0048 0631 SA 1257 1903	2.2 0.5 2.4 0.3	18	0024 0611 SU 1226 1838	2.0 0.6 2.2 0.4
4	0131 0713 SU 1340 1947	2.1 0.6 2.3 0.4	19	0057 0645 M 1300 1913	2.0 0.6 2.2 0.5
5	0213 0756 M 1424 2032	2.0 0.7 2.2 0.6	20	0132 0722 TU 1336 1951	2.0 0.6 2.1 0.5
6	0255 0840 TU 1508 2120	1.9 0.8 2.0 0.7	21	0210 0803 W 1417 2034	1.9 0.7 2.0 0.6
7	0339 0931 W 1558 ◑ 2216	1.8 0.9 1.9 0.9	22	0255 0850 TH 1507 2124	1.9 0.8 1.9 0.7
8	0430 1042 TH 1659 2329	1.7 1.0 1.7 1.0	23	0349 0948 F 1609 ◐ 2227	1.8 0.9 1.8 0.8
9	0537 1222 F 1823	1.7 1.1 1.7	24	0455 1107 SA 1725 2357	1.7 0.9 1.8 0.9
10	0050 0657 SA 1343 1939	1.0 1.7 1.0 1.7	25	0614 1245 SU 1856	1.7 0.8 1.8
11	0157 0802 SU 1440 2039	1.0 1.8 0.9 1.7	26	0124 0735 M 1401 2014	0.9 1.8 0.7 1.9
12	0247 0853 M 1524 2126	1.0 1.9 0.8 1.8	27	0230 0839 TU 1500 2117	0.8 2.0 0.5 2.0
13	0328 0935 TU 1559 2207	0.9 2.0 0.7 1.9	28	0322 0935 W 1550 2211	0.7 2.1 0.4 2.1
14	0402 1013 W 1630 2244	0.8 2.0 0.6 2.0			
15	0435 1048 TH 1701 ● 2318	0.7 2.1 0.6 2.0			

MARCH

Date	Time	m	Date	Time	m
1	0408 1024 TH 1635 2259	0.6 2.2 0.2 2.2	16	0410 1022 F 1633 2251	0.6 2.0 0.4 2.0
2	0450 1111 F 1717 ○ 2343	0.5 2.3 0.2 2.2	17	0442 1056 SA 1705 ● 2324	0.6 2.1 0.4 2.0
3	0530 1154 SA 1758	0.4 2.4 0.2	18	0515 1129 SU 1738 2357	0.5 2.1 0.3 2.0
4	0024 0609 SU 1235 1838	2.2 0.4 2.3 0.2	19	0549 1203 M 1812	0.4 2.2 0.3
5	0102 0648 M 1315 1917	2.1 0.5 2.2 0.4	20	0031 0624 TU 1239 1848	2.0 0.4 2.2 0.3
6	0139 0727 TU 1354 1956	2.0 0.6 2.1 0.5	21	0106 0702 W 1317 1927	2.0 0.5 2.1 0.4
7	0215 0807 W 1434 2036	1.9 0.7 1.9 0.7	22	0144 0744 TH 1359 2010	2.0 0.5 2.0 0.6
8	0253 0850 TH 1518 2121	1.8 0.8 1.8 0.9	23	0227 0833 F 1451 2100	1.9 0.6 1.9 0.7
9	0337 0948 F 1611 ◑ 2223	1.7 0.9 1.6 1.0	24	0321 0932 SA 1557 ◐ 2204	1.8 0.7 1.8 0.8
10	0430 1124 SA 1727 2355	1.6 1.0 1.5 1.1	25	0428 1054 SU 1717 2344	1.7 0.8 1.7 0.9
11	0553 1303 SU 1910	1.6 1.0 1.5	26	0552 1236 M 1853	1.7 0.7 1.7
12	0120 0725 M 1410 2014	1.0 1.6 0.9 1.6	27	0116 0719 TU 1350 2009	0.9 1.7 0.6 1.8
13	0220 0823 TU 1455 2101	1.0 1.7 0.8 1.7	28	0219 0825 W 1447 2107	0.8 1.9 0.4 1.9
14	0303 0907 W 1530 2141	0.9 1.8 0.7 1.8	29	0309 0920 TH 1534 2156	0.6 2.0 0.3 2.0
15	0338 0946 TH 1602 2217	0.8 1.9 0.5 1.9	30	0351 1008 F 1616 2240	0.5 2.1 0.2 2.1
			31	0431 1052 SA 1656 ○ 2319	0.4 2.2 0.2 2.1

APRIL

Date	Time	m	Date	Time	m
1	0509 1132 SU 1734 2356	0.4 2.2 0.2 2.1	16	0449 1102 M 1710 ● 2329	0.4 2.1 0.2 2.1
2	0547 1211 M 1810	0.3 2.2 0.3	17	0526 1140 TU 1747	0.3 2.1 0.3
3	0030 0623 TU 1248 1846	2.0 0.4 2.1 0.4	18	0005 0604 W 1220 1826	2.1 0.3 2.1 0.3
4	0104 0700 W 1325 1922	2.0 0.5 2.0 0.5	19	0043 0646 TH 1303 1907	2.1 0.3 2.1 0.4
5	0137 0738 TH 1404 1957	1.9 0.6 1.9 0.7	20	0123 0731 F 1351 1953	2.0 0.4 2.0 0.6
6	0212 0818 F 1446 2036	1.8 0.7 1.7 0.9	21	0209 0823 SA 1448 2046	1.9 0.5 1.8 0.7
7	0252 0908 SA 1535 2128	1.7 0.8 1.6 1.0	22	0305 0925 SU 1555 ◐ 2153	1.8 0.6 1.7 0.9
8	0340 1027 SU 1636 ◑ 2259	1.6 0.9 1.5 1.0	23	0412 1050 M 1714 2334	1.7 0.6 1.6 0.9
9	0440 1202 M 1824	1.5 0.9 1.5	24	0535 1221 TU 1843	1.7 0.6 1.6
10	0029 0622 TU 1316 1938	1.0 1.5 0.8 1.5	25	0058 0659 W 1331 1952	0.9 1.7 0.5 1.7
11	0137 0741 W 1409 2026	1.0 1.6 0.7 1.6	26	0200 0805 TH 1427 2047	0.8 1.8 0.4 1.8
12	0225 0830 TH 1449 2106	0.8 1.7 0.6 1.7	27	0249 0859 F 1513 2133	0.6 1.9 0.3 1.9
13	0304 0910 F 1525 2142	0.7 1.8 0.5 1.8	28	0331 0946 SA 1554 2215	0.5 2.0 0.3 2.0
14	0339 0948 SA 1600 2218	0.6 1.9 0.4 1.9	29	0410 1030 SU 1631 2252	0.4 2.1 0.3 2.0
15	0414 1025 SU 1635 2253	0.5 2.0 0.3 2.0	30	0448 1110 M 1708 ○ 2327	0.4 2.1 0.3 2.0

Chart Datum: 1·22 metres below Ordnance Datum (Local). HAT is 2·5 metres above Chart Datum.

NE Scotland

STANDARD TIME (UT)
For Summer Time add ONE hour in **non-shaded areas**

LERWICK LAT 60°09′N LONG 1°08′W

TIMES AND HEIGHTS OF HIGH AND LOW WATERS

Dates in red are SPRINGS
Dates in blue are NEAPS

YEAR **2018**

MAY

Date	Time	m	Date	Time	m
1	0525 1147 TU 1743 2359	0.4 2.0 0.4 2.0	16	0505 1119 W 1725 2342	0.3 2.1 0.3 2.1
2	0601 1224 W 1817	0.4 2.0 0.5	17	0548 1205 TH 1808	0.2 2.1 0.3
3	0032 0637 TH 1301 1851	2.0 0.5 1.9 0.6	18	0024 0633 F 1255 1853	2.1 0.2 2.1 0.5
4	0105 0714 F 1339 1925	1.9 0.5 1.8 0.7	19	0110 0722 SA 1349 1941	2.1 0.3 2.0 0.6
5	0140 0754 SA 1420 2003	1.8 0.6 1.7 0.8	20	0200 0817 SU 1448 2036	2.0 0.4 1.8 0.7
6	0218 0840 SU 1506 2049	1.7 0.7 1.6 0.9	21	0258 0920 M 1551 2142	1.9 0.5 1.7 0.8
7	0304 0941 M 1600 2200	1.7 0.8 1.5 1.0	22	0401 1037 TU 1701 ◐ 2308	1.8 0.5 1.6 0.9
8	0358 1103 TU 1707 ◑ 2333	1.6 0.8 1.5 1.0	23	0514 1158 W 1817	1.7 0.5 1.6
9	0504 1214 W 1841	1.5 0.8 1.5	24	0029 0631 TH 1306 1923	0.8 1.7 0.5 1.7
10	0042 0631 TH 1313 1939	0.9 1.5 0.7 1.6	25	0133 0737 F 1402 2018	0.8 1.8 0.5 1.8
11	0138 0739 F 1401 2023	0.8 1.6 0.6 1.7	26	0225 0833 SA 1449 2105	0.7 1.9 0.5 1.8
12	0223 0827 SA 1444 2103	0.7 1.7 0.5 1.8	27	0310 0923 SU 1530 2147	0.6 1.9 0.4 1.9
13	0305 0911 SU 1525 2142	0.6 1.9 0.4 1.9	28	0351 1007 M 1608 2225	0.5 1.9 0.4 2.0
14	0344 0953 M 1604 2222	0.5 2.0 0.3 2.0	29	0430 1048 TU 1644 ○ 2300	0.5 1.9 0.5 2.0
15	0424 1036 TU 1644 ● 2301	0.4 2.1 0.3 2.1	30	0507 1127 W 1718 2334	0.4 1.9 0.5 2.0
			31	0543 1204 TH 1753	0.5 1.9 0.6

JUNE

Date	Time	m	Date	Time	m
1	0007 0618 F 1241 1826	2.0 0.5 1.8 0.7	16	0012 0623 SA 1250 1841	2.2 0.2 2.1 0.5
2	0041 0655 SA 1318 1901	1.9 0.5 1.8 0.7	17	0101 0714 SU 1345 1931	2.1 0.2 2.0 0.6
3	0115 0733 SU 1358 1938	1.9 0.6 1.7 0.8	18	0153 0807 M 1439 2023	2.1 0.3 1.9 0.7
4	0153 0816 M 1440 2021	1.8 0.6 1.6 0.9	19	0247 0905 TU 1535 2121	2.0 0.4 1.8 0.8
5	0235 0905 TU 1527 2114	1.7 0.7 1.6 0.9	20	0345 1011 W 1634 ◐ 2230	1.9 0.5 1.7 0.8
6	0325 1004 W 1621 ◑ 2223	1.7 0.7 1.5 1.0	21	0447 1124 TH 1740 2350	1.8 0.6 1.7 0.9
7	0422 1114 TH 1724 2343	1.6 0.7 1.5 0.9	22	0558 1233 F 1846	1.8 0.6 1.7
8	0526 1218 F 1835	1.6 0.7 1.6	23	0101 0706 SA 1333 1944	0.8 1.8 0.6 1.7
9	0047 0637 SA 1314 1934	0.9 1.6 0.6 1.7	24	0202 0806 SU 1424 2035	0.8 1.8 0.6 1.8
10	0142 0742 SU 1405 2023	0.8 1.7 0.6 1.8	25	0252 0900 M 1508 2120	0.7 1.8 0.6 1.9
11	0230 0835 M 1452 2109	0.7 1.9 0.5 1.9	26	0336 0948 TU 1548 2201	0.6 1.8 0.6 1.9
12	0316 0925 TU 1537 2154	0.5 2.0 0.4 2.0	27	0416 1030 W 1624 2238	0.6 1.9 0.6 2.0
13	0402 1014 W 1622 ● 2239	0.4 2.1 0.4 2.1	28	0452 1110 TH 1659 ○ 2314	0.5 1.9 0.6 2.0
14	0448 1104 TH 1708 2324	0.3 2.1 0.4 2.2	29	0528 1147 F 1733 2348	0.5 1.9 0.7 2.0
15	0535 1156 F 1754	0.2 2.1 0.4	30	0602 1223 SA 1807	0.5 1.9 0.7

JULY

Date	Time	m	Date	Time	m
1	0022 0637 SU 1259 1841	2.0 0.5 1.8 0.7	16	0051 0700 M 1331 1914	2.3 0.2 2.1 0.5
2	0056 0712 M 1335 1916	2.0 0.5 1.8 0.8	17	0140 0750 TU 1420 2002	2.2 0.2 2.0 0.6
3	0131 0750 TU 1413 1955	1.9 0.6 1.7 0.8	18	0229 0841 W 1509 2052	2.1 0.4 1.9 0.7
4	0210 0832 W 1455 2038	1.9 0.6 1.7 0.8	19	0320 0936 TH 1600 ◐ 2149	2.0 0.5 1.8 0.8
5	0254 0919 TH 1543 2130	1.8 0.7 1.6 0.9	20	0415 1040 F 1656 2303	1.9 0.7 1.7 0.9
6	0346 1014 F 1637 ◑ 2233	1.7 0.7 1.6 0.9	21	0519 1152 SA 1802	1.8 0.8 1.7
7	0444 1120 SA 1739 2352	1.7 0.7 1.6 0.9	22	0029 0632 SU 1301 1908	0.9 1.7 0.8 1.7
8	0549 1228 SU 1846	1.7 0.7 1.7	23	0140 0741 M 1400 2006	0.9 1.7 0.8 1.8
9	0101 0700 M 1329 1947	0.8 1.8 0.7 1.8	24	0237 0840 TU 1449 2056	0.8 1.7 0.8 1.8
10	0200 0806 TU 1425 2041	0.7 1.9 0.6 1.9	25	0323 0931 W 1531 2140	0.7 1.8 0.8 1.9
11	0254 0904 W 1517 2132	0.6 2.0 0.5 2.0	26	0403 1014 TH 1608 2219	0.7 1.9 0.8 2.0
12	0345 0959 TH 1607 2221	0.4 2.1 0.5 2.2	27	0438 1053 F 1643 ○ 2256	0.6 1.9 0.7 2.0
13	0435 1054 F 1655 ● 2311	0.3 2.1 0.5 2.2	28	0511 1129 SA 1715 2330	0.5 1.9 0.7 2.1
14	0524 1148 SA 1742	0.2 2.2 0.5	29	0543 1204 SU 1748	0.5 1.9 0.7
15	0001 0612 SU 1241 1828	2.3 0.1 2.2 0.5	30	0003 0615 M 1238 1820	2.1 0.5 1.9 0.7
			31	0035 0648 TU 1310 1853	2.1 0.5 1.9 0.7

AUGUST

Date	Time	m	Date	Time	m
1	0108 0723 W 1344 1928	2.0 0.5 1.8 0.7	16	0204 0810 TH 1436 2021	2.2 0.4 1.9 0.7
2	0143 0800 TH 1422 2008	2.0 0.6 1.8 0.8	17	0250 0858 F 1520 2111	2.1 0.6 1.8 0.8
3	0224 0842 F 1506 2054	1.9 0.6 1.8 0.8	18	0340 0952 SA 1609 ◐ 2217	1.9 0.8 1.7 0.9
4	0311 0930 SA 1557 ◑ 2149	1.9 0.7 1.7 0.9	19	0438 1102 SU 1710 2355	1.7 0.9 1.7 1.0
5	0408 1029 SU 1657 2301	1.8 0.8 1.7 0.9	20	0556 1224 M 1828	1.7 1.0 1.7
6	0514 1144 M 1805	1.8 0.8 1.7	21	0118 0718 TU 1335 1938	0.9 1.7 1.0 1.7
7	0028 0630 TU 1302 1918	0.9 1.8 0.8 1.8	22	0221 0823 W 1430 2033	0.9 1.7 1.0 1.8
8	0140 0747 W 1407 2021	0.8 1.8 0.7 1.9	23	0307 0912 TH 1513 2118	0.8 1.8 0.9 1.9
9	0240 0852 TH 1504 2116	0.6 2.0 0.7 2.1	24	0345 0954 F 1549 2158	0.7 1.9 0.8 2.0
10	0334 0951 F 1555 2208	0.4 2.1 0.6 2.2	25	0418 1031 SA 1622 2234	0.6 1.9 0.7 2.1
11	0424 1045 SA 1642 ● 2258	0.3 2.2 0.5 2.3	26	0448 1106 SU 1654 ○ 2308	0.5 2.0 0.7 2.1
12	0511 1136 SU 1727 2347	0.2 2.2 0.5 2.4	27	0519 1139 M 1725 2340	0.5 2.0 0.6 2.2
13	0556 1224 M 1810	0.1 2.2 0.5	28	0550 1210 TU 1756	0.5 2.0 0.6
14	0033 0641 TU 1310 1852	2.4 0.1 2.1 0.5	29	0011 0621 W 1242 1828	2.2 0.5 2.0 0.6
15	0119 0725 W 1353 1936	2.3 0.3 2.1 0.6	30	0043 0655 TH 1314 1903	2.1 0.5 2.0 0.6
			31	0117 0731 F 1349 1942	2.1 0.5 1.9 0.7

Chart Datum: 1·22 metres below Ordnance Datum (Local). HAT is 2·5 metres above Chart Datum.

STANDARD TIME (UT)
For Summer Time add ONE hour in **non-shaded areas**

LERWICK LAT 60°09′N LONG 1°08′W

TIMES AND HEIGHTS OF HIGH AND LOW WATERS

Dates in red are SPRINGS
Dates in blue are NEAPS

YEAR **2018**

SEPTEMBER

Date	Day	Time	m	Time	m	Time	m	Time	m
1	SA	0156	2.0	0811	0.6	1431	1.9	2026	0.8
2	SU	0242	1.9	0857	0.7	1521	1.8	2120	0.9
3	M	0340	1.8	0953	0.9	1622	1.8	◑ 2231	0.9
4	TU	0450	1.8	1112	0.9	1734	1.7		
5	W	0009	0.9	0615	1.8	1248	0.9	1857	1.8
6	TH	0129	0.8	0741	1.8	1359	0.9	2007	1.9
7	F	0231	0.6	0847	2.0	1455	0.7	2104	2.1
8	SA	0323	0.4	0942	2.1	1543	0.6	2155	2.2
9	SU	0410	0.3	1032	2.2	1626	0.5	● 2243	2.4
10	M	0454	0.2	1118	2.2	1707	0.5	2328	2.4
11	TU	0535	0.1	1201	2.2	1748	0.4		
12	W	0011	2.4	0616	0.2	1242	2.2	1828	0.5
13	TH	0054	2.3	0657	0.3	1321	2.1	1908	0.6
14	F	0136	2.2	0737	0.5	1359	2.0	1950	0.7
15	SA	0218	2.1	0819	0.7	1439	1.9	2036	0.8
16	SU	0305	1.9	0905	0.9	1523	1.8	◐ 2135	1.0
17	M	0359	1.7	1007	1.1	1616	1.7	2313	1.0
18	TU	0514	1.6	1139	1.1	1734	1.7		
19	W	0049	1.0	0652	1.6	1304	1.1	1906	1.7
20	TH	0155	0.9	0800	1.7	1404	1.1	2006	1.8
21	F	0242	0.8	0848	1.8	1448	1.0	2051	1.9
22	SA	0318	0.7	0927	1.9	1524	0.9	2131	2.0
23	SU	0349	0.6	1002	2.0	1556	0.8	2206	2.1
24	M	0419	0.5	1036	2.0	1627	0.7	2240	2.2
25	TU	0449	0.5	1109	2.1	1658	0.6	○ 2312	2.2
26	W	0521	0.4	1140	2.1	1731	0.6	2345	2.2
27	TH	0553	0.4	1212	2.1	1805	0.6		
28	F	0018	2.2	0627	0.5	1245	2.1	1841	0.6
29	SA	0054	2.2	0704	0.6	1321	2.1	1921	0.7
30	SU	0135	2.1	0745	0.7	1401	2.0	2007	0.7

OCTOBER

Date	Day	Time	m	Time	m	Time	m	Time	m
1	M	0223	2.0	0831	0.8	1451	1.9	2103	0.8
2	TU	0325	1.9	0930	1.0	1555	1.8	◑ 2217	0.9
3	W	0440	1.8	1056	1.0	1712	1.8		
4	TH	0001	0.9	0612	1.8	1241	1.0	1841	1.8
5	F	0119	0.7	0736	1.9	1349	0.9	1953	2.0
6	SA	0219	0.6	0837	2.0	1441	0.8	2049	2.1
7	SU	0308	0.4	0928	2.1	1526	0.7	2138	2.3
8	M	0352	0.3	1013	2.2	1607	0.6	2224	2.4
9	TU	0433	0.3	1055	2.2	1646	0.5	● 2307	2.4
10	W	0512	0.3	1134	2.3	1725	0.5	2348	2.4
11	TH	0550	0.4	1211	2.2	1804	0.5		
12	F	0028	2.3	0628	0.5	1246	2.2	1843	0.6
13	SA	0108	2.2	0705	0.7	1322	2.1	1923	0.7
14	SU	0149	2.0	0743	0.8	1359	2.0	2007	0.8
15	M	0234	1.9	0823	1.0	1440	1.9	2100	1.0
16	TU	0324	1.7	0916	1.1	1529	1.8	◐ 2222	1.0
17	W	0428	1.6	1045	1.2	1631	1.7	2357	1.0
18	TH	0611	1.6	1216	1.2	1813	1.7		
19	F	0110	1.0	0725	1.7	1325	1.1	1928	1.8
20	SA	0202	0.9	0814	1.8	1413	1.0	2016	1.9
21	SU	0240	0.8	0853	1.9	1450	0.9	2056	2.0
22	M	0313	0.7	0928	2.0	1524	0.8	2133	2.1
23	TU	0345	0.6	1002	2.1	1557	0.7	2208	2.2
24	W	0418	0.5	1036	2.2	1631	0.6	○ 2243	2.2
25	TH	0452	0.5	1109	2.2	1707	0.6	2319	2.3
26	F	0527	0.5	1144	2.2	1744	0.5	2357	2.3
27	SA	0603	0.5	1220	2.2	1823	0.6		
28	SU	0037	2.2	0642	0.6	1258	2.2	1906	0.6
29	M	0123	2.1	0726	0.7	1341	2.1	1956	0.7
30	TU	0217	2.0	0815	0.9	1433	2.0	2054	0.8
31	W	0322	1.9	0916	1.0	1539	1.9	◑ 2210	0.8

NOVEMBER

Date	Day	Time	m	Time	m	Time	m	Time	m
1	TH	0437	1.8	1045	1.1	1656	1.9	2347	0.8
2	F	0604	1.8	1223	1.1	1823	1.9		
3	SA	0101	0.7	0721	1.9	1330	1.0	1933	2.0
4	SU	0200	0.6	0818	2.0	1422	0.9	2029	2.1
5	M	0248	0.5	0907	2.1	1507	0.7	2119	2.2
6	TU	0331	0.5	0950	2.2	1547	0.6	2204	2.3
7	W	0410	0.4	1030	2.2	1627	0.6	● 2247	2.3
8	TH	0448	0.5	1107	2.3	1706	0.5	2327	2.3
9	F	0525	0.5	1142	2.2	1744	0.6		
10	SA	0006	2.2	0601	0.6	1216	2.2	1822	0.6
11	SU	0045	2.1	0636	0.8	1251	2.2	1901	0.7
12	M	0125	2.0	0712	0.9	1327	2.1	1943	0.8
13	TU	0208	1.9	0750	1.0	1406	2.0	2030	0.9
14	W	0255	1.8	0835	1.1	1452	1.9	2132	1.0
15	TH	0348	1.7	0943	1.2	1546	1.8	◐ 2252	1.0
16	F	0456	1.7	1115	1.2	1650	1.8		
17	SA	0004	1.0	0630	1.7	1228	1.2	1820	1.8
18	SU	0103	0.9	0728	1.8	1324	1.1	1928	1.8
19	M	0151	0.8	0812	1.9	1410	1.0	2015	1.9
20	TU	0231	0.7	0850	2.0	1449	0.9	2056	2.0
21	W	0309	0.7	0927	2.1	1528	0.8	2136	2.2
22	TH	0347	0.6	1004	2.2	1606	0.7	2216	2.2
23	F	0425	0.5	1042	2.3	1645	0.6	○ 2258	2.3
24	SA	0504	0.5	1120	2.3	1726	0.5	2341	2.3
25	SU	0544	0.6	1201	2.3	1810	0.5		
26	M	0028	2.3	0627	0.7	1244	2.3	1857	0.5
27	TU	0120	2.2	0714	0.8	1331	2.2	1949	0.6
28	W	0217	2.1	0805	0.9	1426	2.1	2047	0.7
29	TH	0318	2.0	0905	1.0	1528	2.0	2158	0.7
30	F	0425	1.9	1020	1.1	1638	2.0	◑ 2321	0.7

DECEMBER

Date	Day	Time	m	Time	m	Time	m	Time	m
1	SA	0540	1.8	1150	1.1	1754	2.0		
2	SU	0035	0.7	0652	1.9	1302	1.0	1906	2.0
3	M	0136	0.7	0751	1.9	1359	0.9	2005	2.1
4	TU	0226	0.7	0842	2.0	1448	0.8	2058	2.1
5	W	0310	0.6	0926	2.1	1531	0.7	2146	2.2
6	TH	0350	0.6	1007	2.2	1612	0.7	2230	2.2
7	F	0428	0.7	1044	2.2	1651	0.6	● 2311	2.2
8	SA	0504	0.7	1120	2.2	1729	0.6	2350	2.1
9	SU	0540	0.8	1154	2.2	1807	0.7		
10	M	0028	2.1	0614	0.8	1229	2.2	1844	0.7
11	TU	0106	2.0	0649	0.9	1304	2.1	1923	0.8
12	W	0145	1.9	0725	1.0	1341	2.1	2004	0.8
13	TH	0227	1.8	0804	1.1	1421	2.0	2050	0.9
14	F	0312	1.8	0852	1.1	1508	1.9	2146	1.0
15	SA	0403	1.7	0955	1.2	1602	1.8	◐ 2254	1.0
16	SU	0503	1.7	1118	1.2	1703	1.8		
17	M	0001	0.9	0616	1.7	1228	1.1	1814	1.8
18	TU	0059	0.9	0720	1.8	1325	1.0	1923	1.9
19	W	0149	0.8	0809	1.9	1414	0.9	2017	2.0
20	TH	0235	0.8	0853	2.1	1500	0.8	2106	2.1
21	F	0319	0.7	0936	2.2	1544	0.7	2154	2.2
22	SA	0402	0.6	1019	2.3	1628	0.6	○ 2242	2.3
23	SU	0446	0.6	1103	2.3	1714	0.5	2332	2.3
24	M	0531	0.6	1148	2.4	1801	0.4		
25	TU	0023	2.3	0616	0.7	1235	2.4	1849	0.4
26	W	0116	2.2	0704	0.7	1325	2.3	1940	0.4
27	TH	0210	2.1	0753	0.8	1417	2.2	2034	0.5
28	F	0304	2.0	0846	0.9	1513	2.2	2134	0.6
29	SA	0401	1.9	0946	1.0	1612	2.1	◑ 2244	0.7
30	SU	0504	1.8	1103	1.0	1720	2.0	2359	0.8
31	M	0613	1.8	1227	1.0	1833	1.9		

Chart Datum: 1·22 metres below Ordnance Datum (Local). HAT is 2·5 metres above Chart Datum.

HOME OF SCOTLAND'S BOAT SHOW
scotlandsboatshow.co.uk
kip marina
CRAOBH marina
SAIL SCOTLAND from Scotland's Premier Marinas
Fairlie QUAY marina
HOLIDAY COTTAGE RENTALS
THE CHARTROOM
RESTAURANT · BAR · VENUE

North West Scotland

Cape Wrath to Crinan Canal

9.8.1 Contents 429

9.8.2 Area map and Distance table 430

9.8.3 Tidal stream charts 432

9.8.4 Lights, buoys and waypoints 434

9.8.5 Passage information 437
Outer Hebrides, Cape Wrath to Ullapool, Ullapool to Loch Torridon – 437 • Skye and the Inner Sound – 449 • Kyle Akin to Mallaig, Ardnamurchan to Crinan, Firth of Lorne and Sound of Luing – 453 • The Small Isles – 454

9.8.6 Stornoway, tide tables/curves 438
Loch Shell (Lewis) • Shiant Islands • E Loch Tarbert (Harris) • Sound of Harris • **N Uist**: Loch Maddy, Loch Eport • **S Uist**: Loch Carnan, Loch Skipport, Loch Eynort, Loch Boisdale • Acairseid Mhór (Eriskay) • North Bay, Castle Bay (Barra) • Loch Rodel • Kallin • Flannan, St Kilda, Rockall and Monach Islands

9.8.7 Kinlochbervie 444
Loch Laxford • Loch Inver

9.8.8 Ullapool, tide tables/curves 445
Loch Kanaird • Summer Isles • Little Loch Broom • Loch Ewe • Loch Gairloch

9.8.9 Portree 450
Loch Torridon • Loch A'Bhraige (Rona) • Acairseid Mhór • **Around Skye**: Loch Dunvegan • Loch Harport • Soay • Armadale Bay • Crowlin Islands

Submarine exercise areas 451

9.8.10 Plockton 451
Loch Carron

9.8.11 Loch Alsh 452
⚓s in The Sound of Sleat • Loch Hourn • Loch Nevis

9.8.12 Mallaig 454
⚓s in The Small Islands: Canna, Rum, Eigg, Muck

9.8.13 Loch Sunart 455
Arinagour (Coll) • Gott Bay (Tiree)

9.8.14 Tobermory 456
Sound of Mull • Craignure • **Around Mull**: Treshnish Isles • Staffa • Gometra • Loch na Keal • Loch Lathaich • Sound of Iona • Tinker's Hole • Carsaig Bay • Loch Spelve • Lynn of Lorn • Loch Creran • Loch Leven • Corran Narrows

9.8.15 Loch Aline 457

9.8.16 Fort William/Corpach 457

9.8.17 Caledonian Canal (Oban, tide tables/curves) 458

9.8.18 Oban 462
Dunstaffnage • Loch Etive • Loch Feochan • Puilladobhrain • Cuan Sound • Ardinamar

9.8.19 Loch Melfort 464

9.8.20 Craobh Marina (Loch Shuna) 465

9.8.21 Loch Craignish 465
Ardfern

9.8.22 Ferries on the west coast of Scotland 466

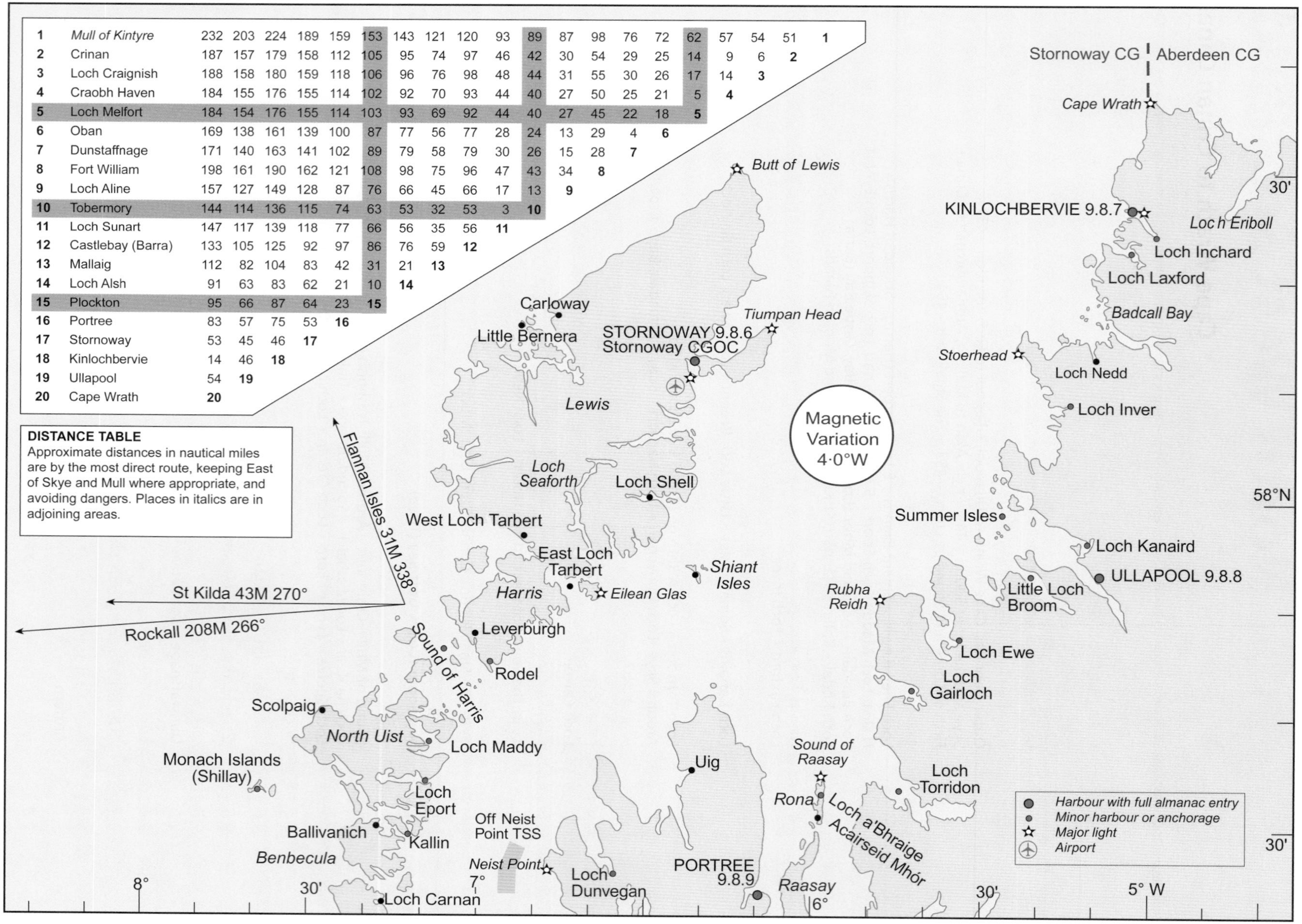
Stornoway CG
Aberdeen CG
Cape Wrath
Butt of Lewis
KINLOCHBERVIE 9.8.7
Loch Eriboll
Loch Inchard
Loch Laxford
Badcall Bay
Tiumpan Head
Carloway
Little Bernera
STORNOWAY 9.8.6
Stornoway CGOC
Stoerhead
Loch Nedd
Loch Inver
Lewis
Magnetic Variation 4·0°W
Loch Seaforth
Loch Shell
Summer Isles
Flannan Isles 31M 338°
West Loch Tarbert
East Loch Tarbert
Loch Kanaird
ULLAPOOL 9.8.8
Shiant Isles
Harris
Eilean Glas
Rubha Reidh
Little Loch Broom
St Kilda 43M 270°
Rockall 208M 266°
Leverburgh
Sound of Harris
Rodel
Loch Ewe
Loch Gairloch
Scolpaig
North Uist
Loch Maddy
Monach Islands (Shillay)
Uig
Sound of Raasay
Loch Torridon
Loch Eport
Rona
Loch a'Bhraige
Acairseid Mhór
Off Neist Point TSS
Ballivanich
Kallin
Benbecula
Neist Point
Loch Dunvegan
PORTREE 9.8.9
Raasay
Loch Carnan
Harbour with full almanac entry
Minor harbour or anchorage
Major light
Airport
8°
30'
7°
6°
5° W
58°N

1	*Mull of Kintyre*	232	203	224	189	159	153	143	121	120	93	89	87	98	76	72	62	57	54	51	**1**
2	Crinan	187	157	179	158	112	105	95	74	97	46	42	30	54	29	25	14	9	6	**2**	
3	Loch Craignish	188	158	180	159	118	106	96	76	98	48	44	31	55	30	26	17	14	**3**		
4	Craobh Haven	184	155	176	155	114	102	92	70	93	44	40	27	50	25	21	5	**4**			
5	Loch Melfort	184	154	176	155	114	103	93	69	92	44	40	27	45	22	18	**5**				
6	Oban	169	138	161	139	100	87	77	56	77	28	24	13	29	4	**6**					
7	Dunstaffnage	171	140	163	141	102	89	79	58	79	30	26	15	28	**7**						
8	Fort William	198	161	190	162	121	108	98	75	96	47	43	34	**8**							
9	Loch Aline	157	127	149	128	87	76	66	45	66	17	13	**9**								
10	Tobermory	144	114	136	115	74	63	53	32	53	3	**10**									
11	Loch Sunart	147	117	139	118	77	66	56	35	56	**11**										
12	Castlebay (Barra)	133	105	125	92	97	86	76	59	**12**											
13	Mallaig	112	82	104	83	42	31	21	**13**												
14	Loch Alsh	91	63	83	62	21	10	**14**													
15	Plockton	95	66	87	64	23	**15**														
16	Portree	83	57	75	53	**16**															
17	Stornoway	53	45	46	**17**																
18	Kinlochbervie	14	46	**18**																	
19	Ullapool	54	**19**																		
20	Cape Wrath	**20**																			

DISTANCE TABLE
Approximate distances in nautical miles are by the most direct route, keeping East of Skye and Mull where appropriate, and avoiding dangers. Places in italics are in adjoining areas.

9.8.2
North West Scotland
Cape Wrath to Crinan Canal

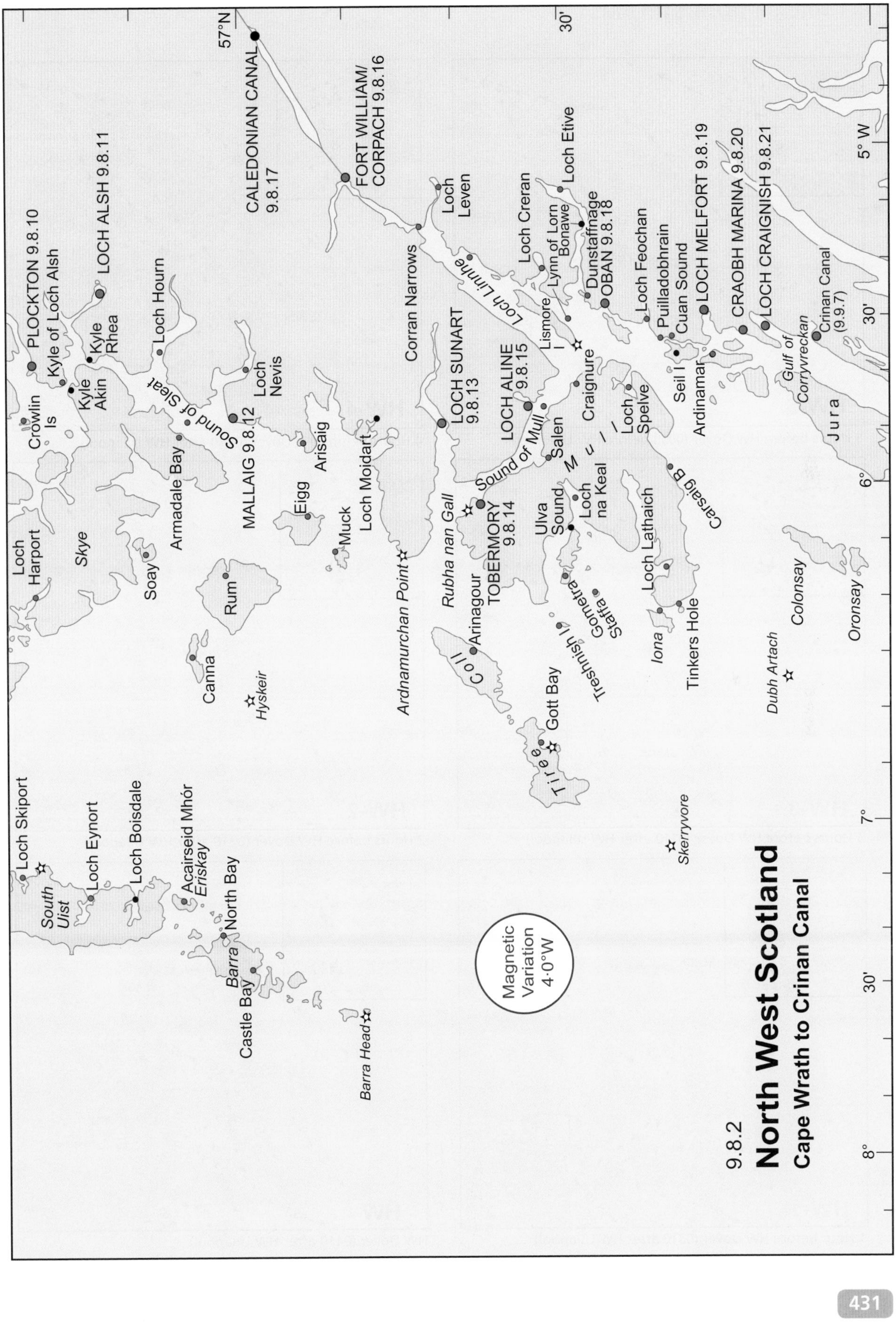
57°N
30'
5° W
30'
6°
7°
30'
8°
CALEDONIAN CANAL
9.8.17
FORT WILLIAM/
CORPACH 9.8.16
PLOCKTON 9.8.10
Kyle of Loch Alsh
LOCH ALSH 9.8.11
Kyle
Rhea
Kyle
Akin
Crowlin
Is
Loch Hourn
Sound of Sleat
Loch
Nevis
MALLAIG 9.8.12
Armadale Bay
Loch
Harport
Skye
Soay
Rum
Canna
Hyskeir
Eigg
Muck
Arisaig
Loch Moidart
Ardnamurchan Point
Corran Narrows
Loch
Leven
Loch Linnhe
LOCH SUNART
9.8.13
Rubha nan Gall
TOBERMORY
9.8.14
Arinagour
Coll
Gott Bay
Tiree
LOCH ALINE
9.8.15
Sound of Mull
Salen
Mull
Ulva
Sound
Loch
na Keal
Treshnish I
Gometra
Staffa
Iona
Tinkers Hole
Loch Lathaich
Carsaig B
Loch
Spelve
Craignure
Lismore
I
Lynn of Lorn
Bonawe
Loch Creran
Loch Etive
Dunstaffnage
OBAN 9.8.18
Loch Feochan
Puilladobhrain
Cuan Sound
Seil I
LOCH MELFORT 9.8.19
Ardinamar
CRAOBH MARINA 9.8.20
LOCH CRAIGNISH 9.8.21
Gulf of
Corryvreckan
Crinan Canal
(9.9.7)
Jura
Colonsay
Oronsay
Dubh Artach
Skerryvore
Loch Skiport
South
Uist
Loch Eynort
Loch Boisdale
Acairseid Mhór
Eriskay
North Bay
Barra
Castle Bay
Barra Head
Magnetic
Variation
4·0°W

9.8.3 AREA 8 TIDAL STREAMS

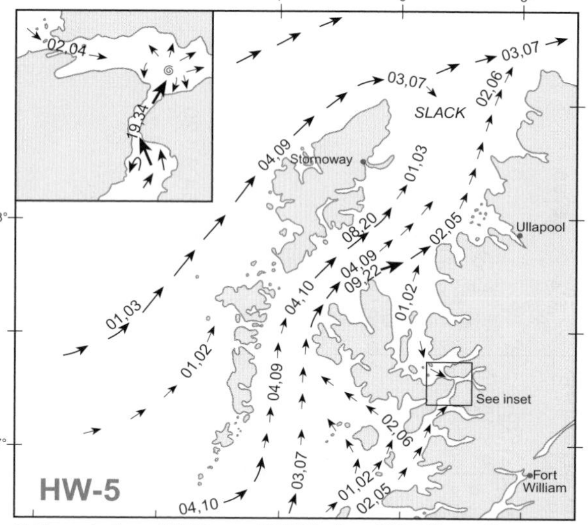

5 Hours before HW Dover (0050 before HW Ullapool)

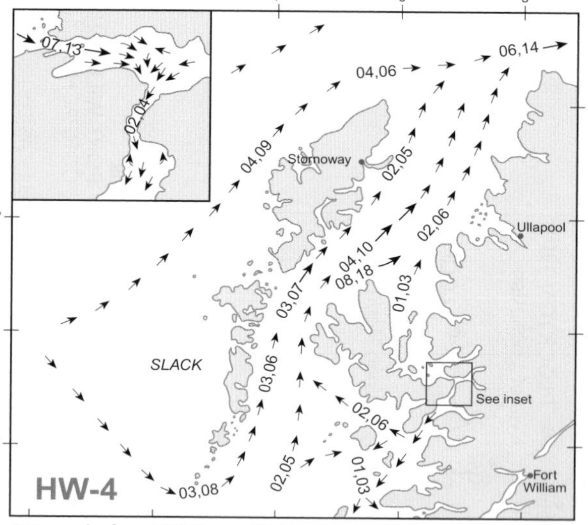

4 Hours before HW Dover (0010 after HW Ullapool)

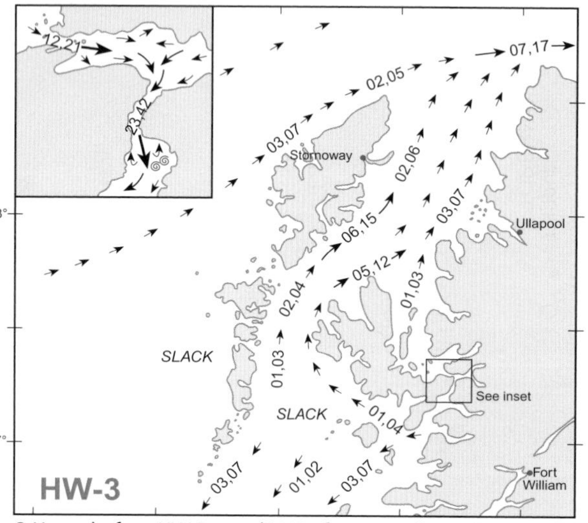

3 Hours before HW Dover (0110 after HW Ullapool)

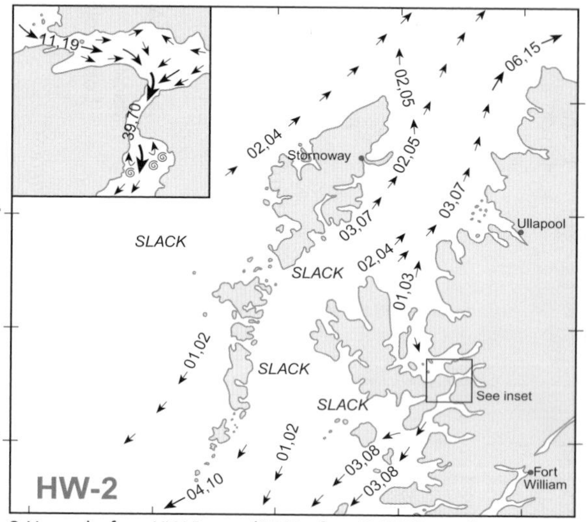

2 Hours before HW Dover (0210 after HW Ullapool)

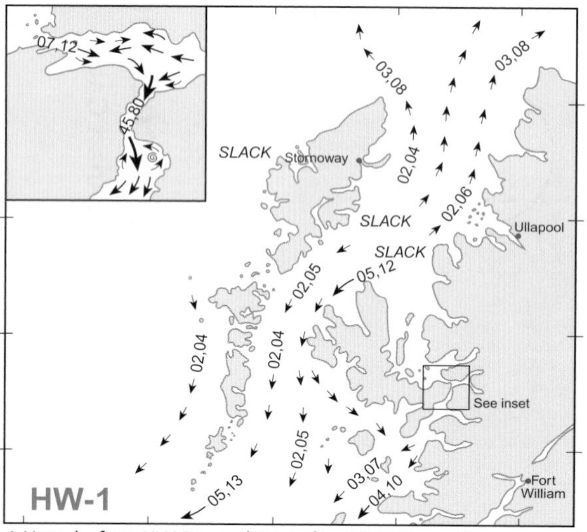

1 Hour before HW Dover (0310 after HW Ullapool)

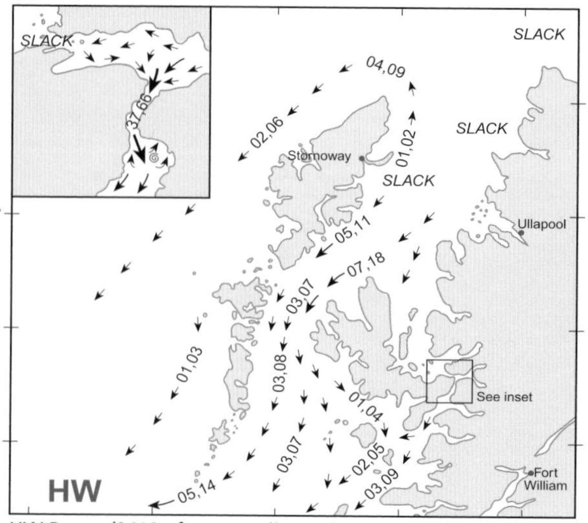

HW Dover (0410 after HW Ullapool)

Eastward 9.7.3 Southward 9.9.3 Mull of Kintyre 9.9.11

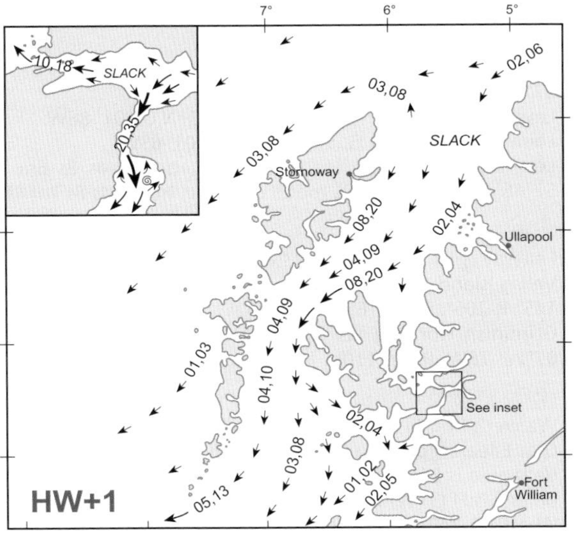

1 Hour after HW Dover (0510 after HW Ullapool)

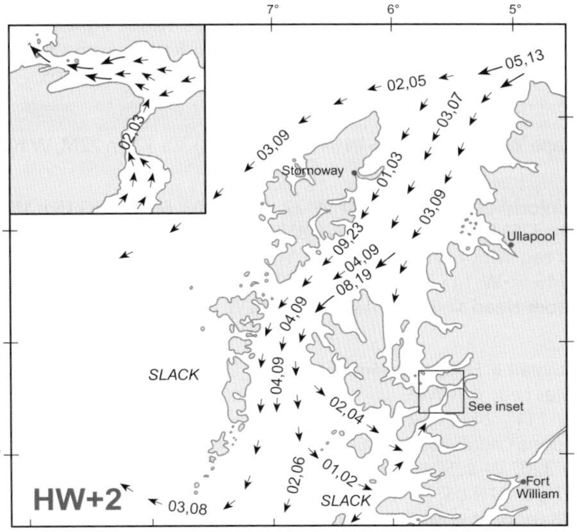

2 Hours after HW Dover (0615 before HW Ullapool)

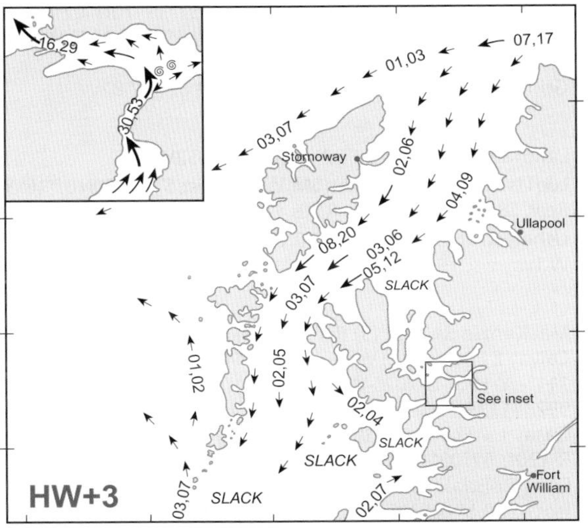

3 Hours after HW Dover (0515 before HW Ullapool)

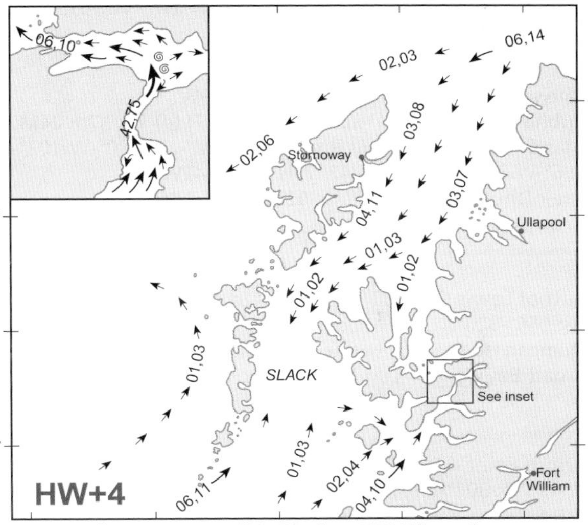

4 Hours after HW Dover (0415 before HW Ullapool)

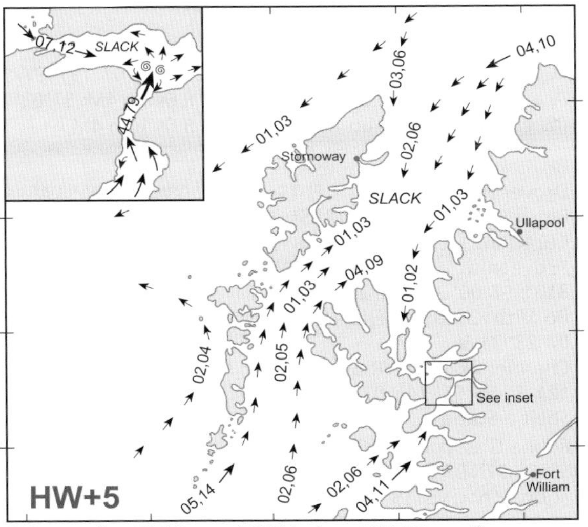

5 Hours after HW Dover (0315 before HW Ullapool)

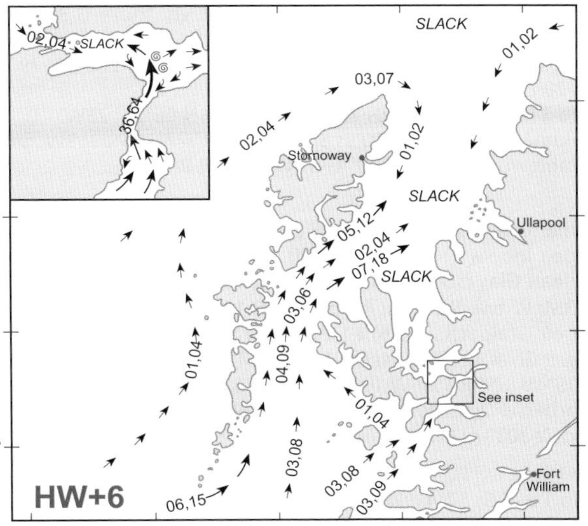

6 Hours after HW Dover (0215 before HW Ullapool)

9.8.4 LIGHTS, BUOYS AND WAYPOINTS

Bold print = light with a nominal range of 15M or more. CAPITALS = place or feature. *CAPITAL ITALICS* = light-vessel, light float or Lanby. *Italics* = Fog signal. ***Bold italics*** = Racon. Some marks/buoys are fitted with AIS (MMSI No); see relevant charts.

CAPE WRATH TO LOCH TORRIDON

Cape Wrath ☆ 58°37′·54N 04°59′·99W Fl (4) 30s 122m **22M**; W twr.

LOCH INCHARD and LOCH LAXFORD

Kinlochbervie Dir lt 327° ☆ 58°27′·49N 05°03′·08W WRG 15m **16M** vis: 326°-FG-326·5°-AlGW-326·8°-FW-327·3°-AlRW-327·5°-FR-328°.
Creag Mhòr Dir lt 147°; Iso WRG 2s 16m 4M; vis: 136·5°-R -146·5°-W-147·5°-G-157·5°; 58°26′·99N 05°02′·45W.
Stoer Head ☆ 58°14′·43N 05°24′·07W Fl 15s 59m **24M**; W twr.

LOCH INVER, SUMMER ISLES and ULLAPOOL

Soyea I ☆ Fl (2) 10s 34m 6M; 58°08′·56N 05°19′·67W.
Glas Leac ☆ Fl WRG 3s 7m 5M; vis: 071°- W-078°-R-090°-G-103°-W-111°, 243°-W-247°-G-071°; 58°08′·68N 05°16′·36W.
Rubha Cadail ☆ Fl WRG 6s 11m W9M, R6M, G6M; W twr; vis: 311°-G-320°-W-325°-R-103°-W-111°-G-118°-W-127°-R-157°-W-199°; 57°55′·51N 05°13′·40W.
Ullapool Pt ☆ Iso R 4s 8m 6M; W twr; vis: 258°-108°; 57°53′·59N 05°09′·93W.
Cailleach Head ☆ Fl (2) 12s 60m 9M; W twr; vis: 015°-236°; 57°55′·81N 05°24′·23W.

LOCH EWE and LOCH GAIRLOCH

Fairway L Fl 10s; 57°51′·98N 05°40′·09W.
Rubha Reidh ☆ 57°51′·52N 05°48′·72W Fl (4) 15s 37m **24M**.
Glas Eilean ☆ Fl WRG 6s 9m W6M, R4M; vis: 080°-W-102°-R-296°-W-333°-G-080°; 57°42′·79N 05°42′·42W.
Sgeir Dhubh Mhór; 57°42′·02N 05°42′·72W.

OUTER HEBRIDES – EAST SIDE

LEWIS

Butt of Lewis ☆ 58°30′·89N 06°15′·84W Fl 5s 52m **25M**; R twr; vis: 056°-320°.
Tiumpan Hd ☆ 58°15′·66N 06°08′·29W Fl (2)15s 55m **25M**; W twr.
Broad Bay Tong ⚓ Ldg Lts 320°, Oc R 8s 8m 4M; 58°14′·48N 06°19′·98W. Rear, 70m from front, Oc R 8s 9m 4M.

STORNOWAY

Arnish Point ☆ Fl WR 10s 17m W9M, R7M; W ○ twr; vis: 088°-W-198°-R-302°-W-013°; 58°11′·50N 06°22′·16W.
Sandwick Bay, NW side ☆ Oc WRG 6s 10m 9M; vis: 334°-G-341°-W-347°-R-354°; 58°12′·20N 06°22′·11W.
No 1 Pier SW corner ☆ Q WRG 5m 11M; vis: shore-G-335°-W-352°-R-shore; 58°12′·36N 06°23′·43W.
Creed Estuary ☆ Iso WRG 10s 24m 5M; vis: 277°-G-282°-W-290°-R-295°; 58°12′·03N 06°23′·47W.
No 3 Pier ☆ Q (2) G 10s 7m 2M 58°12′·31N 06°23′·28W.
Glumaig Hbr ☆ Iso WRG 3s 8m 3M; 58°11′·27N 06°22′·9W; grey framework twr; vis: 150°-G-174°-W-180°-R-205°.

LOCH ERISORT, LOCH SHELL and EAST LOCH TARBERT

Shiants QG; 57°54′·57N 06°25′·70W.
Sgeir Inoe Fl G 6s; ***Racon (M) 5M***; 57°50′·93N 06°33′·93W.
Eilean Glas (Scalpay) ☆ 57°51′·41N 06°38′·55W Fl (3) 20s 43m **23M**; W twr, R bands; ***Racon (T) 16-18M***; 992356014.
Sgeir Graidach Q (6) + L Fl 15s; 57°50′·36N 06°41′·37W.
Sgeir Ghlas ☆ Iso WRG 4s 9m W9M, R6M, G6M; W ○ twr; vis: 282°-G-319°-W-329°-R-153°-W-164°-G-171°; 57°52′·36N 06°45′·24W.
Tarbert ☆ Dir Iso WRG 4s 9m 4M; vis : 290°-Iso G-297°-Al WG-300°-Iso W-303°-Al WR-306°-Iso R306°-313°; 57°53′·82N 06°47′·93W.

SOUND OF HARRIS, LEVERBURGH and BERNERAY

No 1 QG; 57°41′·20N 07°02′·67W.
No 3 Fl G 5s; 57°41′·86N 07°03′·44W.
No 4 Fl R 5s; 57°41′·76N 07°03′·63W.
Suilven Fl (3)R 10s; 57°41′·68N 07°04′·36W.
Cabbage Fl (2) R 6s; ***Racon (T) 5M (3cm)***; 57°42′·13N 07°03′·96W.
Leverburgh Ldg Lts 014·7°. Front, Q 10m 4M 57°46′·23N 07°02′·04W. Rear, Oc 3s 12m 4M.
Jane's Tower Q (2) G 5s 6m 4M; vis: obscured 273°-318°; 57°45′·76N 07°02′·11W.
Leverburgh Reef Fl R 2s 4m 57°45′·97N 07°01′·86W.
Laimhrig Mhor ☆ Q G; 57°45′·92N 07°01′·65W.
Leverburgh Pier Ldg Lts 063°. Front, Iso Bu 4s 8s 6m 4M; 57°46′·00N 07°01′·61W, metal col. Rear, Iso Bu 4s 8s 7m 4M.

NORTH UIST

Fairway L Fl 10s; 57°40′·23N 07°01′·39W.
Vallay Island ☆ Fl WRG 3s 4m 8M; vis: 206°-W-085°-G-140°-W-145°-R-206°; 57°39′·69N 07°26′·42W.
Griminish Hbr Ldg Lts 183°. Front, QG 6m 4M; 57°39′·38N 07°26′·75W. Rear, 110m from front, QG 7m 4M.

LOCH MADDY and GRIMSAY

Weaver's Pt ☆ Fl 3s 24m 7M; W hut; 57°36′·49N 07°06′·00W.
Glas Eilean Mòr ☆ Fl (2) G 4s 8m 5M; 57°35′·95N 07°06′·70W.
Vallaquie Is Dir lt 207·5°/ 255·5° ☆ 57°35′·50N 07°09′·40W; W pillar; vis:Fl (3) WRG 8s 11m W5M, R5M, G5M; shore - G -205°-W-210°-R-240°; Fl (3) WRG 8s 11m W8M, R8M, G8M; 249°-G-254°-W-257°-R-262°.
Lochmaddy Ro-Ro Pier, Dir lt 300° ☆ 57°35′·79N 07°09′·46W; post; Iso WRG 2s W6M, R4M, G4M; vis: 288°-G-295°-WG-298°-W-302°-WR-305°-R-311°.
Grimsay No 1 Fl (2) R 8s; 57°28′·26N 07°11′·82W.

SOUTH UIST and LOCH CARNAN

Landfall L Fl 10s; 57°22′·27N 07°11′·52W.
Ldg Lts 222°. Front Fl R 2s 7m 5M; W ◇ on post; 57°22′·00N 07°16′·34W. Rear, 58m from front, Iso R 10s 11m 5M; W ◇ on post.
Ushenish ☆ (S Uist) 57°17′·90N 07°11′·57W Fl W 20s 54m **W19M**; W twr; vis: 193°- 018°.

LOCH BOISDALE

MacKenzie Rk Fl (3) R 15s 3m 4M; 57°08′·24N 07°13′·71W.
Calvay E End ☆ Fl (2) WRG 10s 16m W7M, R7M, G7M; W twr; vis: 111°-W-190°-G-202°-W-286°-R-111°; 57°08′·53N 07°15′·38W; 992351139.
Gasay I ☆ Fl WR 5s 10m W7M, R7M; W twr; vis: 120°-W-284°-R-120°; 57°08′·93N 07°17′·39W.
Loch Boisdale Dir lt ☆, 292·5°; WRG 4s 4m 5M; vis: 287·5°-IsoG-290·5°-AlWG-292°-IsoW-293°-AlW-294·5°-IsoR-298·5°; 57°09′·19N 07°18′·24W.
2 FG 8m 3M on dn; 57°09′·13N 07°18′·18W.

LUDAIG and ERISKAY

Ludaig Bwtr ☆ 2 FR (vert) 6m 3M; 57°06′·17N 07°19′·49W.
Acairseid Mhor Ldg Lts 285°. Front, Oc R 6s 9m 4M; 57°03′·89N 07°17′·25W. Rear, 24m from front, Oc R 6s 10m 4M.

BARRA, CASTLEBAY and VATERSAY SOUND

Drover Rocks Q (6) + L Fl 15s; 57°04′·08N 07°23′·54W.
Binch Rock Q (6) + L Fl 15s; 57°01′·60N 07°17′·12W.
Curachan Q (3) 10s; 56°58′·56N 07°20′·51W.
Ardveenish ☆ Oc WRG 6m 9/6M; vis: 300°-G-304°-W-306°-R-310°; 57°00′·21N 07°24′·43W.
Bo Vich Chuan Q(6)+L Fl 15s; ***Racon (M) 5M***; 56°56′·15N 07°23′·31W.
Channel Rk ☆ Fl WR 6s 4m W6M, R4M; vis: 121·5°-W-277°-R-121·5°; 56°56′·24N 07°28′·94W.
Sgeir a Scape Fl (2) G 8s; 56°56′·25N 07°27′·21W.
Rubha Glas. Ldg Lts 295°. Front FBu 9m 6M; Or △ on W twr; 56°56′·77N 07°30′·64W. Rear, 457m from front, FBu 15m 6M; Or ▽ on W twr; vis: 15° and 8° respectively either side of ldg line.
Barra Hd ☆ 56°47′·12N 07°39′·21W Fl 15s 208m **18M**; W twr; obsc by islands to NE; 992351095.

OUTER HEBRIDES – WEST SIDE

Flannan I ☆, Eilean Mór Fl (2) 30s 101m **20M**; W twr; 58°17'·29N 07°35'·29W, obsc in places by Is to W of Eilean Mór.
Rockall ☆ Fl 15s 19m 8M (unreliable); 57°35'·76N 13°41'·27W.
Gasker Lt ☆ Fl (3) 10s 38m 10M; 57°59'·05N 07°17'·20W.
Whale Rock Q (3) 10s 5m 5M; ***Racon (T)***; 57°54'·40N 07°59·91W.
Haskeir I ☆ 57°41'·96N 07°41·31W Fl 20s 44m **24M**; W twr; ***Racon (M) 17–15M***; 992351140.
Monach Is ☆ Fl (2)15s 47m **18M**; red brick twr; 57°31'·55N 07°41'·68W.

EAST LOCH ROAG

Aird Laimishader Carloway ☆ Fl 6s 63m 8M; W hut; obsc on some brgs; 58°17'·06N 06°49'·50W.
Ardvanich Pt ☆ Fl G 3s 4m 2M; 58°13'·48N 06°47'·68W.
Tidal Rk ☆ Fl R 3s 2m 2M (sync with Ardvanich Pt above); 58°13'·45N 06°47'·57W.
Grèinam ☆ Fl WR 6s 8m W8M, R7M; W bn; vis: R143°-169°, W169°-143°; 58°13'·30N 06°46'·16W.

LOCH ROAG

Rubha Domhain ☆ Fl G 5s 9m 1M; post; 58°12'·96N 06°45'·40W.
Bogha na Muilne Fl (2) 10s; 58°12'·70N 06°54'·23W.
Mia Vaig Bay Fl G 2s 2m 1M; bn; 58°11'·83N 06°56'·60W.

NORTH UIST and SOUTH UIST

Vallay I ☆ Fl WRG 3s 8M; vis: 206°-W-085°-G-140°-W-145°-R-206°; 57°39'·70N 07°26'·34W.
Falconet twr ☆ FR 25m 8M (3M by day); shown 1hr before firing, changes to Iso R 2s 15 min before firing until completion; 57°22'·04N 07°23'·58W.

ST KILDA

Ldg Lts 270°. Front, Oc 5s 26m 3M; 57°48'·32N 08°34'·31W. Rear, 100m from front, Oc 5s 38m 3M; sync.

LOCH TORRIDON TO MALLAIG

LITTLE MINCH and W SKYE

Eugenie Rock Q 6 + LF 15s; 57°46'·47N 06°27'·28W.
Eilean Trodday ☆ Fl (2) WRG 10s 52m W12M, R9M, G9M; W Bn; vis: W062°-R088°-130°-W-322°-G-062°; 57°43'·63N 06°17'·93W; 992351084.
Uig, Edward Pier Hd ☆ 57°35'·09N 06°22'·29W Iso WRG 4s 9m W7M, R4M, G4M; vis: 180-W-006°-G-050°-W-073°-R-180°.
Waternish Pt ☆ Fl 20s 21m 8M; W twr; 57°36'·48N 06°37'·99W.
Loch Dunvegan, Uiginish Pt ☆ Fl WRG 3s 16m W7M,R5M,G5M; W lattice twr; vis: 041°-G-132°-W-145°-R-148°-W-253°-R-263°-W-273°-G-306°, (>148° obsc by Fiadhairt Pt); 57°26'·84N 06°36'·53W.
Neist Point ☆ 57°25'·41N 06°47'·30W Fl 5s 43m **16M**; W twr.
Loch Harport, Ardtreck Pt ☆ 57°20'·38N 06°25'·80W Fl 6s 18m 9M; small W twr.

RONA, LOCH A'BHRAIGE and INNER SOUND

Na Gamhnachain Q; 57°35'·89N 05°57'·71W.
Rona NE Point ☆ 57°34'·69N 05°57'·54W Fl 12s 69m **19M**; W twr; vis: 050°-358°; 992351045.
Loch A'Bhraige, Sgeir Shuas ☆ Fl R 2s 6m 3M; vis: 070°-199°; 57°35'·02N 05°58'·61W.
Ldg Lts 136·5°. Front, Q WRG 3m W4M, R3M; vis: 135°-W- 138°-R-318°-G-135°; 57°34'·41N 05°58'·09W. Rear, Iso 6s 28m 5M.
Rubha Ard Ghlaisen Fl R 3s; 57°29'·67N 05°58'·71W.
Screapadal Fl R (2) 5s; 57°25'·54N 06°01'·90W.

SOUND OF RAASAY, PORTREE and CROWLIN ISLANDS

Sgeir Mhór Fl G 5s; 57°24'·57N 06°10'·53W.
Eilean Beag ☆ Fl 6s 32m 6M; W Bn; 57°21'·21N 05°51'·42W.
Eyre Pt ☆ Fl WR 3s 6m W9M R6M; W clad framework twr; vis: 215°-W-267°-R-288°-W-063°; 57°20'·01N 06°01'·28W.
Sgeir Thraid ☆ Q 12m 3M; metal twr; 57°19'·82N 05°56'·50W.
Sgeir Ghobhlach ☆ Fl(3)10s 10m 3M; metal twr; 57°15'·69N 05°52'·25W.

LOCH CARRON

Sgeir Golach ☆ Fl 10s 5m 3M; 57°21'·20N 05°39'·01W.
Eilean a Chait Lt ho (dis) 13M; 57°20'·96N 05°38'·87W.
Bogha Dubh Sgeir Fl (2)R 6s 4m 2M; 57°20'·92N 05°37'·85W.

RAASAY and LOCH SLIGACHAN

Suisnish ☆ 2 FG (vert) 8m 2M; 57°19'·87N 06°03'·91W.
Eyre Point ☆ Fl WR 3s 6m W9M, R6M; W twr; vis: 215°-W-266°-R- 288°-W-063°; 57°20'·01N 06°01'·29W.

KYLEAKIN and KYLE OF LOCH ALSH

Carragh Rk Fl (2) G 12s; ***Racon (T) 5M***; 57°17'·18N 05°45'·36W.
Bow Rk Fl (2) R 12s; 57°16'·71N 05°45'·85W.
Fork Rks Fl G 6s; 57°16'·85N 05°44'·93W.
Black Eye Rk Fl R 6s; 57°16'·72N 05°45'·31W.
Eileanan Dubha East ☆ Fl (2) 10s 9m 8M; vis: obscured 104°-146°; 57°16'·56N 05°42'·32W.
8 Metre Rock ☆ Fl G 6s 5m 4M; 57°16'·60N 05°42'·69W.
String Rock Fl R 6s; 57°16'·50N 05°42'·89W.
Sgeir-na-Caillich ☆ Fl (2) R 6s 3m 4M; 57°15'·59N 05°38'·90W.

SOUND OF SLEAT

Kyle Rhea ☆ Fl WRG 3s 7m W8M, R5M, G5M; W Bn; vis: shore-R-219°-W-228°-G-338°-W-346°-R-shore; 57°14'·22N 05°39'·93W.
Sandaig I, NW point ☆ Fl 6s 13m 8M; W twr; 57°10'·05N 05°42'·29W.
Ornsay ☆ Oc 8s 18m 12M; vis: 157°-030°; 57°08'·60N 05°46'·85W.
Pt. of Sleat ☆ Fl 3s 20m9M; W twr; 57°01'·08N 06°01'·08W.

MALLAIG and LOCH NEVIS ENTRANCE

Sgeir Dhearg QG; 57°00'·74N 05°49'·50W.
Northern Pier E end ☆ Iso WRG 4s 6m W9M, R6M, G6M; Gy twr; vis: 181°-G-185°-W-197°-R-201°. Fl G 3s 14m 6M; same structure; 57°00'·47N 05°49'·50W.
Sgeir Dhearg ☆ 57°00'·63N 05°49'·61W Fl (2) WG 8s 6m 5M; Gy Bn; vis: 190°-G-055°-W-190°.

SMALL ISLES AND WEST OF MULL

CANNA and RUM

Sanday ☆ Fl 10s 32m 9M; vis: 152°-061°; 57°02'·82N 06°28'·02W.
Loch Scresort Q; 57°00'·79N 06°14'·61W.

HYSKEIR, EIGG, MUCK and ARISAIG

Humla Fl G 6s 3m 4M 57°00'·46N 06°37'·39W.
Hyskeir ☆ 56°58'·16N 06°40'·83W Fl (3) 30s 41m **24M**; W twr. ***Racon (T) 14-17M***; 992351094.
SE point Eigg (Eilean Chathastail) ☆ Fl 6s 24m 8M; W twr; vis: 181°-shore; 56°52'·25N 06°07'·28W.
Eigg, Sgeir nam Bagh (Ferry Terminal) ☆ Dir 245°; Fl WRG 3s 9m W14, R11, G11; H24; steel pole; vis: 242·5°-G-244°-W-246°-R-247·5°. 2FR(vert) on same structure; 56°52'·79N 06°07'·56W.
Isle of Muck ☆ Dir 322° Fl WRG 3s 7m W14 RG11, by day WRG1; twr; vis: 319·5°-G-321°-W-323°-R-324·5°; 56°49'·96N 06°13'·64W.
Bogha Ruadh☆ Fl G 5s 4m 3M; 56°49'·56N 06°13'·05W.
Bo Faskadale Fl (3) G 18s; 56°48'·18N 06°06'·37W.
Ardnamurchan ☆ 56°43'·63N 06°13'·58W Fl (2) 20s 55m **22M**; Gy twr; vis: 002°-217°.
Suil Ghorm ☆ Fl 12s 23m 10M; W twr; 56°42'·26N 06°26'·75W.

TIREE, COLL and ARINAGOUR

Loch Eatharna, Pier Head ☆ Dir 325°; Oc WRG 7s 6m 2M; vis: 316°-G-322°-W-328°-R-334°; 56°36'·86N 06°31'·29W.
Loch Eatharna, Bogha Mór Fl G 6s; 56°36'·65N 06°30'·90W.
Roan Bogha Q (6) + L Fl 15s 3m 5M; 56°32'·23N 06°40'·18W.
Placaid Bogha Fl G 4s; 56°33'·22N 06°44'·06W.
Scarinish ☆ Fl 3s 11m 12M; W □ twr; vis: 210°-030°; S side of ent, 56°30'·02N 06°48'·26W.
Cairn na Burgh More (Treshnish Is), Fl (3) 15s 36m 8M; solar panels on framework tr; 56°31'·05N 06°22'·95W.
Gott Bay Ldg Lts 286·5°. Front FR 8m; 56°30'·61N 06°47'·82W. Rear 30m from front FR 11m.
Skerryvore ☆ Fl 10s 46m **23M**; Gy twr; ***Racon (M) 18M***. 56°19'·36N 07°06'·88W; 992351091.

LOCH NA KEAL, LOCH NA LÀTHAICH and IONA

Sgeir a Charraigein Q(6) + LFl 15s; 56°28'·29N 06°07'·71W.
Eileanan na Liathanaich, SE end Fl WR 6s 12m W8M, R6M; vis: R088°- W108°-088°; 56°20'·56N 06°16'·38W.
Bo na Sliganach Q(6) + LFl 15s; 56°19'·45N 06°23'·12W.
Bogha hun a Chuhoil Q(6) + LFl 15s; 56°16'·57N 06°24'·86W.

DUBH ARTACH

Dubh Artach ☆ 56°07'·94N 06°38'·08W Fl (2) 30s 44m **20M**; Gy twr, R band; 992351088.

SOUND OF MULL

LOCH SUNART, TOBERMORY and LOCH ALINE

Ardmore Pt Fl (2) 10s 18m 13M; 56°39'·37N 06°07'·70W.
New Rks Q (9) 15s; 56°39'·07N 06°03'·55W; AIS.
Rubha nan Gall ☆ 56°38'·33N 06°04'·00W Fl 3s 17m **15M**; W twr.
Tobermory Slip Iso WRG 3s 5m 4M; vis: 220°-G-232°-W-244°-R-256°; metal column; 56°37'·41N 06°03'·77W.
Dearg Sgeir Fl 6s 7m 8M; W ○ twr; 56°32'·25N 05°54'·80W.
Fiunary Spit Fl G 6s; 56°32'·66N 05°53'·17W.
Fishnish Ferry Slip Iso WRG 3s 5m 4M; vis: 158°-G-170°-W-195°-R-230°; metal column; 56°30'·89N 05°48'·61W.
Loch Aline, Dir 357°; Oc WRG 6s 2m 4M; vis: 353°-G-356°-W-358°-R-002°; Or concrete plinth; 56°32'·38N 05°46'·47W.
Ardtornish Pt Fl (2) WRG 10s 8m W8M, R6M, G6M; W twr; vis: G shore- 301°-W-308°-R-342°-W-057°-R-095°-W-108°-G-shore; 56°31'·09N 05°45'·21W.
Craignure Ldg Lts 240·9°. Front, FR 10m; 56°28'·26N 05°42'·28W. Rear, 150m from front, FR 12m; vis: 225·8°-255·8°.

MULL TO CALEDONIAN CANAL AND OBAN

Lismore ☆, SW end 56°27'·34N 05°36'·45W Fl 10s 31m **17M**; W twr; vis: 237°-208°.
Lady's Rk Fl 6s 12m 5M; Red clad lattice tower on W base 56°26'·92N 05°37'·05W; 992351093.
Duart Pt Fl (3) WR 18s 14m W5M, R3M; vis: 162°-W-261°-R-275°-W-353°-R-shore; 56°26'·84N 05°38'·77W.

LOCH LINNHE

Corran Shoal QR 56°43'·69N 05°14'·39W.
Corran Pt Iso WRG 4s 12m W10M, R7M, G7M; W twr; vis: shore-R-195°-W-215°-G-020-W-030°-R-shore; 56°43'·25N 05°14'·54W.
Corran Narrows NE Fl 5s 4m 4M; W twr; vis: S shore-214°; Dir lt 033° Iso WRG 2s 4m 4M (1M day), vis: 029·5°-Iso G-031·5°-Alt W/G-032·5°-W-033·5°-Alt W/R-034·5°-Iso R-036·5°; co-located 56°43'·62N 05°13'·90W.
Clovullin Spit Fl (2) R 15s; 56°42'·29N 05°15'·56W.
Cuil-cheanna Spit Fl G 6s; 56°41'·17N 05°15'·72W.
Mc Lean Rk QR 56°49'·80N 05°07'·04W.
Eilean na Creiche Fl (2) 5s; 56°50'·25N 05°07'·02W.
Eilean na Craobh Fl (2) R 6s 4m 2M; 56°50'·43N 05°07'·95W.

FORT WILLIAM and CALEDONIAN CANAL

Corpach, Caledonian Canal Lock ent Iso WRG 4s 6m 5M; W twr; vis: G287°- W310°- R335°-030°; 56°50'·52N 05°07'·44W.

LYNN OF LORN

Sgeir Bhuidhe Appin Fl (2) WR 7s 8m W9M R6M; W Bn; vis: W013·5°- R184°-220°; 56°33'·63N 05°24'·65W.
Appin Point Fl G 6s; 56°32'·69N 05°25'·97W.
Dearg Sgeir, off Aird's Point Fl WRG 2s 2m W3M, R1M, G1M; vis: 196°-R-246°-W-258°-G-041°-W-058°-R-093°-W-139°; 56°32'·20N 05°25'·22W.
Rubha nam Faoileann (Eriska) QG 2m 2M; G col; vis 128°-329°; 56°32'·20N 05°24'·11W.
Branra Rk Fl(2) 10s 4m 5M; metal frame on W twr; 56°32'·02N 05°26'·60W.

OBAN

N spit of Kerrera Fl R 3s 9m 5M; W col; 56°25'·49N 05°29'·56W.
Dunollie Fl (2) WRG 6s 6m W8M, R6M, G6M; vis: 351°-G- 020°-W-047°-R-120°-W-138°-G-143°; twr; 56°25'·37N 05°29'·05W.
Rubh'a'Chruidh Q R 3m 2M; W post; 56°25'·32N 05°29'·29W.
Corran Ledge VQ (9) 10s; 56°25'·19N 05°29'·11W.
Oban Bay Q; 56°24'·92N 05°29'·23W.
Sgeir Rathaid Q(6)+L Fl 15s; 56°24'·75N 05°29'·37W.
North Pier 2 F G (vert); metal post; 56°24'·89N 05°28'·49W.
Ro-Ro Jetty 2 F G (vert); post on dn; 56°24'·69N 05°28'·65W.
Northern Lt Pier 2 F G (vert); metal post; 56°24'·71N 05°28'·91W.

OBAN TO LOCH CRAIGNISH

Heather Is Fl R 2·5s 11m 2M; 56°24'·41N 05°30'·24W.
Ferry Rks NW Q G; 56°24'·11N 05°30'·69W.
Kerrera Q R; 56°24'·15N 05°30'·81W.
Ferry Rks SE Q (3) 10s; 56°23'·99N 05°30'·53W.
Ferry Pier 2 FL (vert); 56 23'.92N 005 31'.02W.
Little Horseshoe Fl R 12 s; 56 23'.22N 005 31'.83W.
Sgeirean Dubha Fl (2) 12s 7m 5M; W ○ twr; 56°22'·81N 05°32'·27W.
Sgeir an Fheuran Fl G 3s; 56°22'·80N 05°31'·94W.
Bogha Nuadh Q (6) + LFl 15s; 56°21'·69N 05°37'·87W; 992351090.
Bogha Ghair Q (3) 10s; 56°16'·50N 05°40'·44W.
Bono Rock Q (9) 15s; 56°16'·21N 05°41'·22W.
Fladda Fl (2) WRG 9s 13m W11M, R9M, G9M; W twr; vis: 169°-R-186°-W-337°-G-344°-W-356°-R-026°; 56°14'·89N 05°40'·83W.
Dubh Sgeir (Luing) Fl WRG 6s 9m W6M, R4M. G4M; W twr; vis: W000°- R010°- W025°- G199°-000°; ***Racon (M) 5M***; 56°14'·76N 05°40'·20W.
The Garvellachs, Eileach an Naoimh, SW end Fl 6s 21m 9M; W Bn; vis: 240°-215°; 56°13'·04N 05°49'·06W.

LOCH MELFORT and CRAOBH HAVEN

Melfort Pier Dir FR 6m 3M; (Apr -Nov); 56°16'·14N 05°30'·19W.
56°12'·88N 05°33'·59W.
Craobh Marina Bkwtr Hd Iso WRG 5s 10m, W5M, R3M, G3M; vis:114°-G-162°-W-183°-R-200°; 56°12'·78N 05°33'·52W.

9.8.5 PASSAGE INFORMATION

More passage information is threaded between the harbours in this area. It is essential to carry large scale charts and current pilot books for this area which is only partially covered between Ardnamurchan Point and the Shiant Isles by Admiralty Leisure Folio 5616. **Bibliography:** *Clyde Cruising Club Sailing Directions-Kintyre to Arnamurchan, CCC Sailing Directions-Ardnamurchan to Cape Wrath, CCC Sailing Directions-Outer Hebrides*(all Imray/ Clyde Cruising Club, Lawrence). *The Yachtsman's Pilot to Skye and Northwest Scotland* (Imray/Lawrence). The *North West Coast of Scotland Pilot* (Admiralty NP66B) covers the whole area.

Scotland's west coast provides splendid, if boisterous, sailing and matchless scenery. In summer the long daylight hours and warmth of the Gulf Stream compensate for the lower air temperatures and higher wind speeds experienced when depressions run typically north of Scotland. Inshore winds are often unpredictable, due to geographical effects of lochs, mountains and islands offshore; calms and squalls can alternate rapidly.

Good anchors, especially on kelp/weed, are essential. 🅥s are listed but do not be assume that these will be available. Particularly in N of area, facilities are very dispersed; key for fuel pumps in the W Isles is available from Comhairlenan Eilean Siar (Hbr Authority) ☎01870 604992 harbourmaster@cne-siar.gov.uk. A *'Rover Ticket'* from Highland Council allows berthing for 15 days; the scheme includes: Kinlochbervie, Lochinver, Gairloch, Kyle of Lochalsh, Kyleakin, Portree and Uig. VHF communications with shore stations may be limited by high ground. Beware ever more fish farms in many inlets. Local magnetic anomalies occur in Kilbrannan Sound, Passage of Tiree, Sound of Mull, Canna, and East Loch Roag. Submarines exercise throughout these waters.

OUTER HEBRIDES

(AC 1785, 1794, 1795) The E sides of these Is have many good, sheltered ⚓s, but W coasts give little shelter. The CCC's *Outer Hebrides SDs* or *The Western Isles* (Imray) are advised.

▶ *The Minches and Sea of the Hebrides can be very rough, particularly in the Little Minch between Skye and Harris, and around Shiant Is where tide runs 4kn at sp, and heavy overfalls occur. The NE-going stream on both shores begins at HW Ullapool -0340 (HW Dover +0430), with the strongest flow from mid-channel to the Skye coast. A W-going counter tide runs E of Vaternish Pt.*

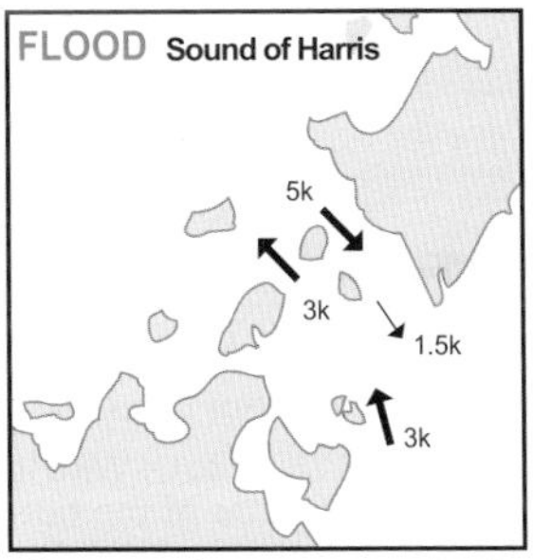

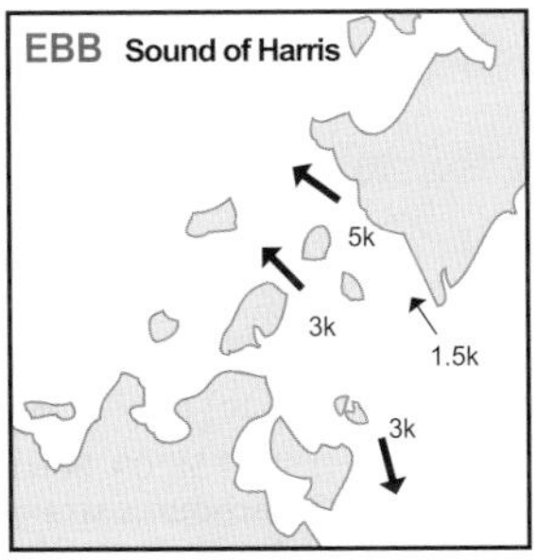

The SW-going stream on both shores begins at HW Ullapool +0240 (HW Dover –0130), with the strongest flow from mid-channel to the Skye coast, sp rates 2·5kn. The E-going stream in Sound of Scalpay runs at up to 2kn.The E going flood and W going ebb in Sound of Scalpay run at up to 2kn.◀

▶ **Sound of Harris.** *The behaviour of tidal streams is complicated and varies from day to night, springs to neaps, and winter to summer. In the NE part of the Sound, at springs, the stream sets SE from Ullapool +0535 to –0035. At neaps, in the summer, the stream sets SE during the day and NW during the night. To the SW of the Sound, the NW stream starts at Ullapool –0545; the SE stream starts at Ullapool +0025. The approximate maximum rates are as shown. For more detailed information refer to the Admiralty West Coast of Scotland Pilot.*◀

From N to S, the better harbours in the Outer Hebrides include:

Lewis. Stornoway; Loch Grimshader (beware Sgeir a'Chaolais, dries in entrance); Loch Erisort; Loch Odhairn; Loch Shell. Proceeding S from here, or to E Loch Tarbert beware Sgeir Inoe (dries 2·3m) 3M ESE of Eilean Glas lt ho at SE end of Scalpay.

Harris. E Loch Tarbert; Loch Scadaby; Loch Stockinish; Loch Finsby; W Loch Tarbert; Loch Rodel (🅥). A well-marked ferry channel connects Leverburgh (South Harris) to Berneray.

N Uist. Loch Maddy (🅥); Loch Eport, Kallin Hbr (🅥).

S Uist. Loch Carnan (🅥); Loch Skiport; Loch Eynort; Loch Boisdale (🅥).

Barra. Castlebay (🅥), and Berneray, on N side, E of Shelter Rk.

There are numerous ⚓s. Bratanish Mor in Loch Roag is very sheltered and provides respite on W coast. Yachts should register in advance at www.cne-siar.gov.uk.

Activity at the Hebrides Range, S Uist ☎(01870) 604441, is broadcast daily at 0950LT and Mon-Fri 1100-1700LT on VHF Ch **12** (Ch 73 in emergency) and on MF 2660 kHz.

CAPE WRATH TO ULLAPOOL

(AC 1785, 1794) C Wrath (lt fog sig) is a steep headland (110m).

▶ *To N of it the E-going stream begins at HW Ullapool – 0350, and W-going at HW Ullapool + 0235, sp rates 3kn. Eddies close inshore cause almost continuous W-going stream E of Cape, and N-going stream SW of it. Where they meet is turbulence, with dangerous seas in bad weather.* ◀

Duslic Rk, 7ca NE of lt ho, dries 3·4m. 6M SW of C Wrath, islet of Am Balg (45m) is foul for 2ca around.

There are ⚓ in Loch Inchard (AC 2503), the best shelter being in Kinlochbervie on N shore; also good ⚓s among Is along S shore of Loch Laxford, entered between Ardmore Pt and Rubha Ruadh. Handa Is to WSW is a bird sanctuary. Handa Sound is navigable with care, but beware Bogha Morair in mid-chan and associated overfalls.

▶ *Tide turns 2hrs earlier in the Sound than offshore. Strong winds against tide raise a bad sea off Pt of Stoer.*◀

The best shelter is 8M S at Loch Inver (AC 2504), with good ⚓ off hotel near head of loch. ⚓s to the N of Loch Inver may be found at Kylesku, Culkein Drumbeg, Drumbeg, Loch Nedd and Loch Roe. To the S lies Enard Bay.

ULLAPOOL TO LOCH TORRIDON

(AC 1794, 2210, 5616) The Summer Isles (AC 2501), 12M NW of the major fishing port of Ullapool, offer some sheltered ⚓s and tight approaches. The best include the bay on E side of Tanera Mor; off NE of Tanera Beg (W of Eilean Fada Mor); and in Caolas Eilean Ristol, between the island and mainland.

Loch Ewe (AC 3146) provides good shelter and easy access. Best ⚓s are in Poolewe Bay (beware Boor Rks off W shore) and in SW corner of Loch Thuirnaig (entering, keep close to S shore to avoid rocks extending from N side). Off Rubha Reidh (lt) seas can be dangerous.

▶ *The NE-going stream begins at HW Ullapool –0335; the SW-going at HW Ullapool +0305. Sp rates 3kn, but slacker to SW of point.* ◀

Longa Is lies N of ent to Loch Gairloch (AC 2528). The channel N of it is navigable but narrow at E end. Outer loch is free of dangers, but exposed to swell. Best ⚓ is on S side of loch in Caolas Bad a' Chrotha, W of Eilean Horrisdale.

Entering L Torridon (AC 2210) from S or W beware Murchadh Breac (dries 1·5m) 3ca NNW of Rubha na Fearna. Best ⚓s are SW of Eilean Mor (to W of Ardheslaig); in Loch a' Chracaich, 7ca further SE; E of Shieldaig Is; and near head of Upper L Torridon.

▶ *Streams are weak except where they run 2-3kn in narrows between L Shieldaig and Upper L Torridon.*◀

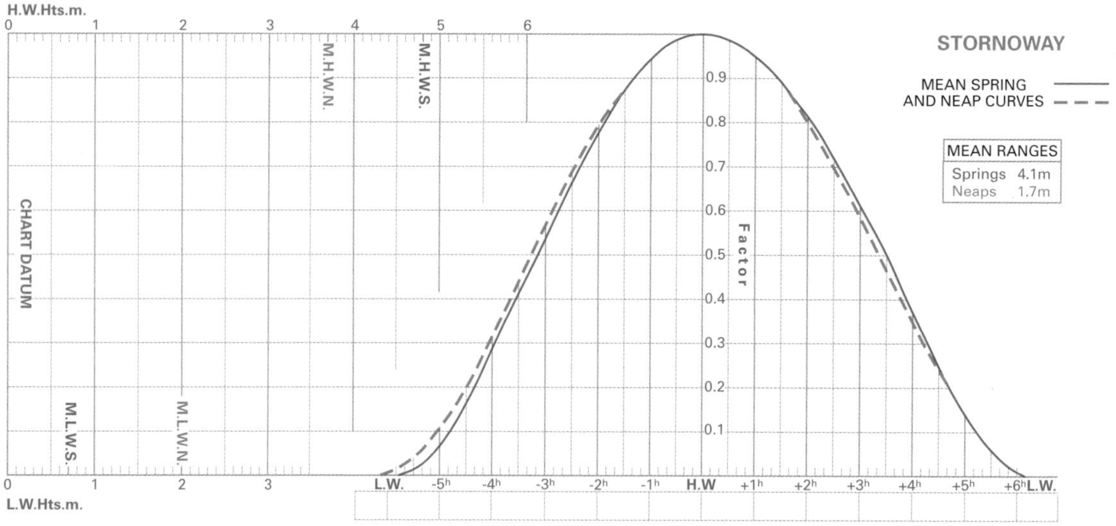

9.8.6 STORNOWAY

Lewis (Western Isles) **58°11'·58N 06°21'·82W** ❁❁❁

CHARTS AC 1785, 1794, 2529; Imray C67

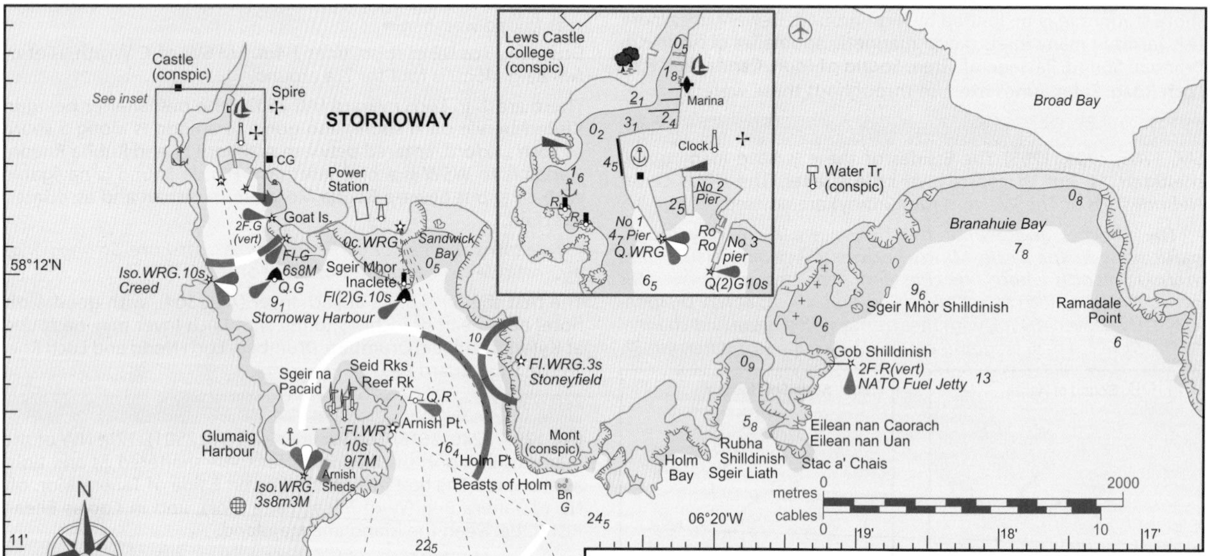

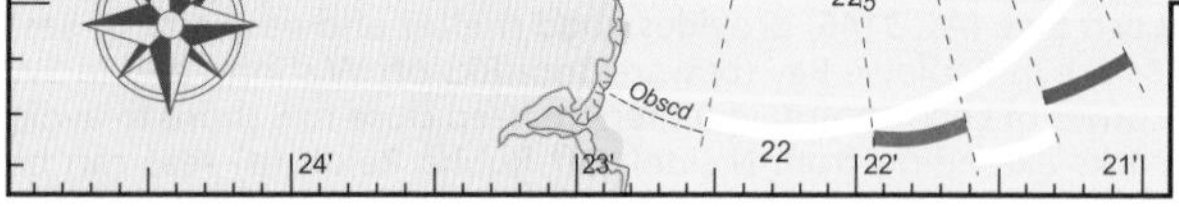

TIDES

Standard Port STORNOWAY (⟶)

Times				**Height (metres)**			
High Water		Low Water		MHWS	MHWN	MLWN	MLWS
0100	0700	0300	0900	4·8	3·7	2·0	0·7
1300	1900	1500	2100				
Differences CARLOWAY (W Lewis)							
−0040	+0020	−0035	−0015	−0·7	−0·5	−0·3	0·0
LITTLE BERNERA (W Lewis)							
−0021	−0011	−0017	−0027	−0·5	−0·6	−0·4	−0·2
WEST LOCH TARBERT (W Harris)							
−0015	−0015	−0046	−0046	−1·1	−0·9	−0·5	0·0

SHELTER Good. New marina (2014), max LOA 24m, in Inner Hbr, has depths to 3m. Visitors should report to Stornoway Port Authority; large boats may request berth on 80m pontoon on Esplanade Quay. Ferries use W side No 3 pier, and commercial vessels on Nos 1 and 2 Piers. South'ly swells can make anchoring uncomfortable. ⚓ on chartlet at: Poll nam Portan to W of inner chan in bay NW of Goat Is (Eilean na Gobhair) clear of foul ground. Glumaig Hbr is best ⚓.

NAVIGATION WPT 58°09'·98N 06°20'·87W, 343°/2·3M to Oc WRG lt. Access to the harbour is straightforward at all states of the tide. Reef Rk, N of Arnish Pt to W of entrance, indicated by PHM, QR. To E side of entrance an unlit G bn marks the Beasts of Holm, a rky patch. This lies off Holm Pt, on which is a conspic memorial. A local magnetic anomaly exists over a small area in mid-hbr, 1·75ca N of Seid Rks PHM bn.

LIGHTS AND MARKS Arnish sheds are conspic 3ca SW of Arnish Pt lt, W sector 302°-013° covers ent. Then in turn follow W sectors of: Sandwick Bay lt (close E of water tr, 3 power stn chys; all conspic), then Creed Estuary, Iso WRG 10s, across the harbour, and No 1 Pier, Q WRG. Lit bns in inner hbr mark appr chan to marina.

COMMUNICATIONS (Code 01851) CGOC 702013; Police 101; Dr 703145; ⊖ 703626. HM 702688.
HM VHF Ch 12 16 (H24).

FACILITIES **Marina** 80 inc 8Ⓥ, £2/m/day, £10/m/wk; wi-fi.
Piers 1 & 2 (10t). **Pier 3** (mob) (road tanker).
Services ACA.
Town Ⓑ ⇌ (Ferry to Ullapool, bus to Garve), ✈.

STANDARD TIME (UT)
For Summer Time add ONE hour in **non-shaded areas**

STORNOWAY LAT 58°12′N LONG 6°23′W

TIMES AND HEIGHTS OF HIGH AND LOW WATERS

Dates in red are SPRINGS
Dates in blue are NEAPS

YEAR **2018**

JANUARY

Date	Day	Time	m	Time	m	Time	m	Time	m	Moon
1	M	0554	4.9	1219	0.9	1816	5.0			
2	TU	0036	0.8	0638	5.2	1309	0.7	1905	5.1	○
3	W	0123	0.7	0723	5.3	1357	0.6	1954	5.1	
4	TH	0209	0.7	0809	5.3	1445	0.5	2043	4.9	
5	F	0254	0.8	0857	5.2	1533	0.7	2134	4.7	
6	SA	0339	1.0	0947	4.9	1622	0.9	2228	4.4	
7	SU	0426	1.3	1043	4.7	1712	1.2	2327	4.1	
8	M	0517	1.6	1147	4.4	1807	1.5			◑
9	TU	0033	3.9	0613	1.9	1259	4.1	1909	1.8	
10	W	0145	3.8	0720	2.1	1413	4.0	2020	1.9	
11	TH	0255	3.8	0839	2.2	1523	3.9	2133	1.9	
12	F	0356	3.9	0955	2.1	1621	4.0	2233	1.8	
13	SA	0446	4.1	1054	1.9	1708	4.1	2320	1.7	
14	SU	0526	4.3	1141	1.7	1748	4.2			
15	M	0000	1.5	0601	4.5	1221	1.6	1822	4.3	
16	TU	0036	1.4	0633	4.6	1257	1.4	1853	4.4	
17	W	0110	1.3	0704	4.7	1331	1.3	1923	4.4	●
18	TH	0143	1.2	0734	4.8	1404	1.2	1953	4.4	
19	F	0214	1.2	0804	4.8	1437	1.1	2024	4.4	
20	SA	0246	1.2	0837	4.8	1510	1.1	2057	4.3	
21	SU	0319	1.3	0912	4.7	1545	1.2	2134	4.2	
22	M	0354	1.4	0952	4.5	1623	1.3	2217	4.1	
23	TU	0434	1.6	1038	4.4	1706	1.4	2309	3.9	
24	W	0521	1.8	1135	4.2	1756	1.6			◐
25	TH	0018	3.8	0619	1.9	1245	4.1	1859	1.7	
26	F	0138	3.8	0736	2.0	1401	4.1	2016	1.8	
27	SA	0253	3.9	0900	2.0	1515	4.1	2134	1.7	
28	SU	0359	4.2	1016	1.7	1621	4.3	2241	1.4	
29	M	0456	4.5	1118	1.3	1719	4.6	2337	1.1	
30	TU	0545	4.8	1212	1.0	1810	4.8			
31	W	0026	0.9	0629	5.1	1301	0.6	1856	5.0	○

FEBRUARY

Date	Day	Time	m	Time	m	Time	m	Time	m	Moon
1	TH	0113	0.7	0712	5.3	1348	0.4	1941	5.1	
2	F	0156	0.6	0755	5.3	1432	0.4	2024	5.0	
3	SA	0239	0.6	0837	5.2	1515	0.5	2107	4.8	
4	SU	0320	0.8	0920	5.0	1557	0.7	2151	4.5	
5	M	0401	1.0	1005	4.7	1639	1.0	2239	4.2	
6	TU	0444	1.3	1054	4.3	1724	1.4	2335	3.9	
7	W	0531	1.7	1158	4.0	1814	1.8			◑
8	TH	0046	3.7	0626	2.0	1321	3.7	1917	2.0	
9	F	0204	3.6	0741	2.3	1443	3.6	2042	2.2	
10	SA	0318	3.7	0918	2.3	1555	3.7	2203	2.1	
11	SU	0418	3.9	1034	2.1	1651	3.8	2258	1.9	
12	M	0505	4.1	1124	1.8	1733	4.0	2341	1.6	
13	TU	0542	4.3	1204	1.6	1808	4.1			
14	W	0018	1.4	0615	4.5	1240	1.3	1837	4.3	
15	TH	0052	1.2	0644	4.7	1313	1.1	1905	4.4	●
16	F	0124	1.1	0713	4.8	1345	1.0	1933	4.5	
17	SA	0156	1.0	0743	4.9	1416	0.9	2001	4.5	
18	SU	0227	0.9	0814	4.9	1448	0.8	2032	4.5	
19	M	0259	0.9	0847	4.8	1521	0.8	2107	4.4	
20	TU	0333	1.0	0925	4.7	1557	1.0	2146	4.3	
21	W	0410	1.2	1008	4.5	1636	1.1	2232	4.1	
22	TH	0453	1.4	1101	4.3	1722	1.4	2334	3.9	
23	F	0547	1.7	1212	4.0	1820	1.7			◐
24	SA	0059	3.8	0700	1.9	1339	3.9	1939	1.9	
25	SU	0227	3.8	0838	1.9	1503	3.9	2114	1.8	
26	M	0344	4.0	1007	1.7	1616	4.1	2231	1.6	
27	TU	0445	4.3	1111	1.3	1714	4.4	2328	1.2	
28	W	0534	4.7	1203	0.9	1801	4.7			

MARCH

Date	Day	Time	m	Time	m	Time	m	Time	m	Moon
1	TH	0015	0.9	0616	5.0	1250	0.5	1843	4.9	
2	F	0059	0.7	0656	5.2	1332	0.3	1922	5.0	○
3	SA	0140	0.5	0734	5.3	1412	0.3	2000	4.9	
4	SU	0219	0.5	0812	5.2	1450	0.4	2038	4.8	
5	M	0257	0.6	0850	4.9	1528	0.6	2115	4.6	
6	TU	0335	0.8	0928	4.6	1605	0.9	2154	4.3	
7	W	0413	1.2	1008	4.2	1643	1.3	2239	4.0	
8	TH	0454	1.5	1057	3.9	1725	1.7	2340	3.7	
9	F	0541	1.9	1219	3.6	1816	2.0			◑
10	SA	0106	3.5	0644	2.2	1357	3.4	1936	2.3	
11	SU	0229	3.5	0828	2.3	1521	3.4	2124	2.2	
12	M	0340	3.7	1006	2.1	1625	3.6	2232	2.0	
13	TU	0433	3.9	1100	1.8	1710	3.8	2317	1.7	
14	W	0514	4.1	1140	1.5	1745	4.0	2354	1.5	
15	TH	0548	4.4	1214	1.2	1814	4.2			
16	F	0028	1.2	0617	4.6	1247	1.0	1840	4.4	
17	SA	0100	1.0	0646	4.8	1319	0.8	1907	4.6	●
18	SU	0132	0.8	0716	4.9	1350	0.6	1936	4.7	
19	M	0204	0.7	0748	4.9	1422	0.5	2007	4.7	
20	TU	0237	0.7	0823	4.9	1456	0.6	2042	4.6	
21	W	0312	0.8	0902	4.7	1532	0.7	2121	4.4	
22	TH	0350	1.0	0948	4.5	1611	1.0	2208	4.2	
23	F	0434	1.2	1044	4.2	1656	1.3	2310	4.0	
24	SA	0528	1.5	1202	3.9	1753	1.7			◐
25	SU	0038	3.8	0644	1.8	1332	3.8	1917	1.9	
26	M	0210	3.8	0830	1.8	1456	3.8	2101	1.9	
27	TU	0328	4.0	0959	1.5	1608	4.0	2219	1.6	
28	W	0430	4.3	1100	1.1	1703	4.3	2314	1.3	
29	TH	0518	4.6	1149	0.8	1747	4.6	2359	0.9	
30	F	0559	4.8	1232	0.5	1825	4.8			
31	SA	0041	0.7	0636	5.0	1311	0.3	1900	4.9	○

APRIL

Date	Day	Time	m	Time	m	Time	m	Time	m	Moon
1	SU	0120	0.5	0712	5.0	1348	0.3	1935	4.9	
2	M	0157	0.5	0747	4.9	1423	0.4	2008	4.8	
3	TU	0233	0.6	0822	4.7	1458	0.6	2042	4.6	
4	W	0309	0.8	0857	4.4	1532	0.9	2117	4.3	
5	TH	0345	1.1	0934	4.1	1607	1.3	2157	4.1	
6	F	0423	1.4	1018	3.8	1644	1.6	2247	3.8	
7	SA	0506	1.7	1125	3.5	1729	2.0			
8	SU	0004	3.6	0601	2.0	1306	3.3	1833	2.2	◑
9	M	0133	3.5	0728	2.2	1433	3.3	2024	2.3	
10	TU	0248	3.6	0917	2.1	1545	3.5	2151	2.1	
11	W	0349	3.7	1021	1.8	1635	3.7	2241	1.8	
12	TH	0435	4.0	1103	1.5	1712	3.9	2321	1.5	
13	F	0512	4.2	1140	1.2	1742	4.2	2356	1.2	
14	SA	0544	4.5	1213	0.9	1810	4.4			
15	SU	0030	0.9	0615	4.7	1247	0.6	1838	4.6	
16	M	0105	0.7	0648	4.9	1321	0.5	1910	4.8	●
17	TU	0139	0.6	0724	4.9	1356	0.4	1944	4.8	
18	W	0216	0.5	0803	4.9	1432	0.4	2022	4.7	
19	TH	0254	0.6	0847	4.7	1511	0.6	2104	4.6	
20	F	0336	0.8	0938	4.4	1552	0.9	2155	4.3	
21	SA	0424	1.1	1042	4.1	1640	1.3	2302	4.1	
22	SU	0522	1.4	1202	3.9	1740	1.7			◐
23	M	0028	3.9	0642	1.6	1325	3.7	1905	1.9	
24	TU	0153	3.9	0820	1.6	1444	3.8	2043	1.9	
25	W	0308	4.0	0942	1.4	1552	4.0	2157	1.6	
26	TH	0410	4.2	1040	1.1	1645	4.2	2252	1.3	
27	F	0458	4.4	1127	0.8	1727	4.4	2338	1.1	
28	SA	0539	4.6	1209	0.6	1804	4.6			
29	SU	0019	0.9	0615	4.7	1247	0.5	1838	4.7	
30	M	0058	0.7	0650	4.7	1323	0.5	1911	4.7	○

Chart Datum: 2·71 metres below Ordnance Datum (Newlyn). HAT is 5·5 metres above Chart Datum.

STANDARD TIME (UT)
For Summer Time add ONE hour in **non-shaded areas**

STORNOWAY **LAT 58°12′N LONG 6°23′W**

TIMES AND HEIGHTS OF HIGH AND LOW WATERS

Dates in red are SPRINGS
Dates in blue are NEAPS

YEAR **2018**

MAY

Date	Day	Time	m	Time	m	Time	m	Time	m
1	TU	0135	0.7	0724	4.6	1357	0.6	1943	4.7
2	W	0211	0.8	0758	4.5	1430	0.8	2016	4.5
3	TH	0246	0.9	0833	4.3	1503	1.0	2050	4.4
4	F	0322	1.1	0911	4.0	1537	1.3	2128	4.2
5	SA	0359	1.4	0955	3.8	1614	1.6	2214	3.9
6	SU	0441	1.6	1053	3.5	1655	1.9	2316	3.7
7	M	0531	1.8	1213	3.4	1750	2.1		
8	TU ◑	0035	3.6	0638	2.0	1335	3.3	1914	2.3
9	W	0150	3.6	0807	2.0	1447	3.4	2047	2.2
10	TH	0253	3.7	0922	1.8	1545	3.6	2151	1.9
11	F	0346	3.9	1015	1.5	1629	3.8	2238	1.6
12	SA	0429	4.1	1057	1.2	1704	4.1	2319	1.3
13	SU	0508	4.4	1136	0.9	1737	4.4	2358	1.0
14	M	0545	4.6	1215	0.7	1811	4.6		
15	TU ●	0037	0.8	0623	4.8	1253	0.5	1846	4.8
16	W	0117	0.6	0704	4.9	1332	0.4	1925	4.9
17	TH	0158	0.5	0749	4.9	1413	0.5	2007	4.8
18	F	0241	0.6	0838	4.7	1455	0.7	2055	4.7
19	SA	0328	0.7	0935	4.4	1540	0.9	2150	4.5
20	SU	0420	0.9	1042	4.2	1631	1.3	2257	4.2
21	M	0521	1.2	1155	3.9	1732	1.6		
22	TU ◐	0015	4.1	0634	1.4	1309	3.8	1848	1.8
23	W	0132	4.0	0756	1.4	1422	3.8	2012	1.8
24	TH	0243	4.0	0911	1.4	1528	3.9	2126	1.7
25	F	0345	4.1	1012	1.2	1622	4.1	2225	1.5
26	SA	0437	4.2	1101	1.1	1706	4.3	2314	1.3
27	SU	0520	4.4	1144	0.9	1743	4.4	2358	1.1
28	M	0558	4.4	1223	0.9	1818	4.5		
29	TU ○	0038	1.0	0633	4.4	1300	0.9	1851	4.6
30	W	0116	1.0	0708	4.4	1334	0.9	1923	4.6
31	TH	0152	1.0	0742	4.3	1407	1.0	1956	4.5

JUNE

Date	Day	Time	m	Time	m	Time	m	Time	m
1	F	0227	1.0	0817	4.2	1441	1.1	2030	4.4
2	SA	0303	1.1	0854	4.0	1515	1.3	2107	4.3
3	SU	0340	1.3	0936	3.8	1551	1.5	2150	4.1
4	M	0420	1.5	1024	3.7	1630	1.7	2240	4.0
5	TU	0505	1.6	1124	3.5	1717	1.9	2342	3.8
6	W ◑	0558	1.8	1234	3.4	1819	2.1		
7	TH	0050	3.7	0703	1.8	1344	3.5	1936	2.1
8	F	0156	3.8	0814	1.8	1447	3.6	2050	2.0
9	SA	0254	3.9	0918	1.6	1540	3.8	2150	1.8
10	SU	0346	4.1	1012	1.3	1626	4.1	2241	1.5
11	M	0433	4.3	1100	1.1	1707	4.3	2327	1.2
12	TU	0519	4.5	1145	0.8	1747	4.6		
13	W ●	0013	0.9	0604	4.7	1230	0.6	1828	4.8
14	TH	0059	0.7	0651	4.8	1314	0.5	1911	4.9
15	F	0145	0.5	0740	4.8	1358	0.6	1957	5.0
16	SA	0232	0.5	0833	4.7	1444	0.7	2047	4.9
17	SU	0322	0.6	0929	4.5	1532	0.9	2142	4.7
18	M	0414	0.7	1029	4.3	1622	1.2	2243	4.5
19	TU	0511	1.0	1134	4.1	1718	1.4	2352	4.3
20	W ◐	0613	1.2	1242	3.9	1822	1.7		
21	TH	0103	4.1	0720	1.4	1350	3.8	1933	1.8
22	F	0213	4.0	0831	1.5	1457	3.8	2047	1.8
23	SA	0319	4.0	0937	1.5	1555	3.9	2155	1.7
24	SU	0416	4.0	1033	1.4	1644	4.1	2252	1.6
25	M	0504	4.1	1120	1.3	1725	4.3	2340	1.4
26	TU	0545	4.1	1202	1.2	1802	4.4		
27	W	0022	1.3	0622	4.2	1240	1.2	1835	4.5
28	TH ○	0101	1.2	0657	4.2	1316	1.1	1908	4.6
29	F	0137	1.1	0730	4.2	1349	1.1	1940	4.6
30	SA	0212	1.1	0803	4.2	1423	1.2	2013	4.5

JULY

Date	Day	Time	m	Time	m	Time	m	Time	m
1	SU	0246	1.1	0837	4.1	1456	1.3	2047	4.4
2	M	0321	1.2	0913	4.0	1530	1.4	2125	4.3
3	TU	0358	1.3	0953	3.9	1607	1.5	2207	4.2
4	W	0438	1.4	1039	3.7	1648	1.7	2257	4.0
5	TH	0522	1.5	1136	3.6	1736	1.8	2355	3.9
6	F ◑	0614	1.6	1243	3.6	1837	2.0		
7	SA	0100	3.9	0715	1.7	1352	3.6	1949	2.0
8	SU	0206	3.9	0823	1.6	1455	3.8	2102	1.9
9	M	0308	4.0	0929	1.5	1552	4.0	2206	1.6
10	TU	0407	4.2	1029	1.3	1643	4.3	2303	1.3
11	W	0501	4.4	1123	1.0	1730	4.6	2356	1.0
12	TH	0553	4.6	1212	0.8	1816	4.8		
13	F ●	0046	0.7	0643	4.8	1301	0.7	1901	5.0
14	SA	0135	0.5	0732	4.9	1347	0.6	1947	5.1
15	SU	0224	0.4	0821	4.8	1433	0.6	2034	5.1
16	M	0312	0.4	0912	4.7	1519	0.8	2124	4.9
17	TU	0400	0.5	1005	4.5	1606	1.0	2217	4.7
18	W	0449	0.8	1102	4.2	1655	1.2	2318	4.4
19	TH ◐	0541	1.1	1205	4.0	1749	1.5		
20	F	0027	4.1	0637	1.4	1312	3.8	1850	1.8
21	SA	0139	3.9	0743	1.7	1421	3.7	2004	2.0
22	SU	0251	3.8	0857	1.8	1527	3.8	2124	2.0
23	M	0357	3.8	1005	1.7	1622	3.9	2233	1.8
24	TU	0451	3.9	1059	1.6	1708	4.1	2325	1.7
25	W	0535	4.0	1144	1.5	1746	4.3		
26	TH	0009	1.5	0612	4.1	1223	1.4	1820	4.5
27	F ○	0047	1.3	0645	4.2	1259	1.3	1852	4.6
28	SA	0122	1.2	0715	4.3	1332	1.2	1922	4.6
29	SU	0155	1.1	0745	4.3	1405	1.1	1952	4.7
30	M	0228	1.0	0814	4.3	1437	1.2	2024	4.6
31	TU	0300	1.0	0846	4.2	1509	1.2	2057	4.6

AUGUST

Date	Day	Time	m	Time	m	Time	m	Time	m
1	W	0333	1.1	0920	4.1	1543	1.3	2134	4.4
2	TH	0408	1.2	0959	4.0	1619	1.4	2217	4.3
3	F	0447	1.3	1047	3.9	1702	1.6	2308	4.1
4	SA ◑	0532	1.5	1148	3.8	1753	1.8		
5	SU	0013	4.0	0626	1.6	1304	3.7	1900	2.0
6	M	0128	3.9	0735	1.7	1419	3.8	2023	2.0
7	TU	0243	3.9	0855	1.7	1527	4.0	2143	1.8
8	W	0352	4.1	1008	1.5	1627	4.2	2250	1.4
9	TH	0453	4.3	1109	1.3	1719	4.6	2346	1.0
10	F	0546	4.6	1201	1.0	1805	4.9		
11	SA ●	0037	0.7	0634	4.8	1249	0.7	1848	5.1
12	SU	0125	0.4	0719	5.0	1334	0.6	1931	5.3
13	M	0210	0.2	0803	5.0	1418	0.5	2014	5.3
14	TU	0254	0.3	0847	4.8	1500	0.6	2058	5.1
15	W	0336	0.4	0932	4.6	1543	0.8	2144	4.8
16	TH	0419	0.7	1021	4.3	1627	1.1	2236	4.4
17	F	0504	1.1	1118	4.0	1713	1.5	2341	4.1
18	SA ◐	0553	1.5	1227	3.8	1808	1.8		
19	SU	0102	3.8	0651	1.9	1342	3.7	1918	2.1
20	M	0223	3.6	0810	2.1	1455	3.7	2054	2.2
21	TU	0337	3.6	0938	2.1	1558	3.9	2217	2.0
22	W	0436	3.7	1040	1.9	1647	4.0	2311	1.8
23	TH	0521	3.9	1125	1.7	1726	4.3	2352	1.5
24	F	0556	4.1	1204	1.5	1800	4.5		
25	SA	0028	1.3	0626	4.2	1239	1.3	1830	4.6
26	SU ○	0101	1.1	0654	4.4	1312	1.2	1859	4.7
27	M	0133	1.0	0721	4.4	1343	1.1	1927	4.8
28	TU	0203	0.9	0748	4.5	1414	1.0	1957	4.8
29	W	0234	0.8	0817	4.5	1445	1.0	2029	4.8
30	TH	0305	0.9	0849	4.4	1517	1.1	2104	4.6
31	F	0339	1.0	0925	4.3	1552	1.2	2144	4.4

Chart Datum: 2·71 metres below Ordnance Datum (Newlyn). HAT is 5·5 metres above Chart Datum.

STANDARD TIME (UT)
For Summer Time add ONE hour in **non-shaded areas**

STORNOWAY

LAT 58°12'N LONG 6°23'W

TIMES AND HEIGHTS OF HIGH AND LOW WATERS

Dates in red are SPRINGS
Dates in blue are NEAPS

YEAR **2018**

SEPTEMBER

Date	Day	Time	m	Time	m	Time	m	Time	m	Moon
1	SA	0415	1.1	1007	4.1	1633	1.5	2233	4.2	
2	SU	0457	1.4	1104	3.9	1721	1.7	2340	4.0	
3	M	0548	1.6	1224	3.8	1826	1.9			◑
4	TU	0106	3.8	0658	1.9	1354	3.8	1959	2.0	
5	W	0231	3.9	0832	1.9	1512	4.0	2134	1.8	
6	TH	0346	4.0	0957	1.7	1616	4.3	2244	1.4	
7	F	0448	4.3	1059	1.4	1707	4.6	2338	1.0	
8	SA	0537	4.6	1150	1.1	1751	5.0			
9	SU	0025	0.6	0620	4.9	1235	0.8	1831	5.2	●
10	M	0109	0.3	0700	5.0	1317	0.6	1911	5.3	
11	TU	0150	0.2	0739	5.1	1358	0.5	1950	5.3	
12	W	0230	0.3	0818	4.9	1437	0.6	2029	5.1	
13	TH	0308	0.5	0857	4.7	1517	0.8	2110	4.8	
14	F	0347	0.8	0938	4.4	1557	1.1	2153	4.4	
15	SA	0426	1.2	1026	4.1	1640	1.5	2248	4.0	
16	SU	0509	1.6	1131	3.8	1728	1.9			◐
17	M	0018	3.7	0600	2.0	1257	3.7	1833	2.2	
18	TU	0150	3.5	0716	2.3	1416	3.7	2015	2.3	
19	W	0310	3.5	0903	2.3	1525	3.8	2154	2.1	
20	TH	0413	3.7	1015	2.1	1618	4.0	2248	1.9	
21	F	0459	3.9	1101	1.8	1659	4.2	2327	1.6	
22	SA	0533	4.1	1139	1.6	1733	4.4			
23	SU	0001	1.3	0601	4.3	1214	1.3	1803	4.6	
24	M	0033	1.1	0627	4.5	1246	1.1	1831	4.8	
25	TU	0104	0.9	0653	4.6	1317	1.0	1859	4.9	○
26	W	0134	0.8	0720	4.7	1348	0.9	1929	5.0	
27	TH	0205	0.7	0748	4.7	1419	0.9	2002	4.9	
28	F	0237	0.7	0820	4.7	1453	1.0	2038	4.8	
29	SA	0311	0.9	0856	4.5	1529	1.1	2120	4.6	
30	SU	0348	1.1	0939	4.3	1611	1.4	2212	4.3	

OCTOBER

Date	Day	Time	m	Time	m	Time	m	Time	m	Moon
1	M	0430	1.4	1035	4.1	1700	1.7	2326	4.0	
2	TU	0522	1.7	1201	3.9	1809	1.9			◑
3	W	0059	3.8	0635	2.0	1338	3.9	1951	2.0	
4	TH	0225	3.9	0820	2.1	1457	4.0	2128	1.7	
5	F	0339	4.1	0947	1.8	1601	4.3	2233	1.3	
6	SA	0437	4.4	1046	1.5	1652	4.7	2323	0.9	
7	SU	0523	4.7	1133	1.1	1734	5.0			
8	M	0007	0.6	0602	4.9	1216	0.8	1812	5.2	
9	TU	0048	0.4	0639	5.0	1257	0.7	1849	5.3	●
10	W	0126	0.4	0714	5.1	1336	0.6	1926	5.2	
11	TH	0203	0.5	0750	5.0	1414	0.7	2002	5.0	
12	F	0239	0.7	0825	4.8	1451	0.9	2040	4.7	
13	SA	0315	1.0	0902	4.5	1530	1.2	2119	4.3	
14	SU	0351	1.4	0942	4.3	1610	1.5	2206	3.9	
15	M	0430	1.7	1035	4.0	1655	1.9	2322	3.6	
16	TU	0516	2.1	1157	3.8	1753	2.2			◐
17	W	0103	3.5	0620	2.4	1325	3.7	1922	2.3	
18	TH	0227	3.5	0808	2.5	1438	3.8	2109	2.2	
19	F	0336	3.6	0936	2.3	1537	3.9	2210	2.0	
20	SA	0426	3.8	1027	2.0	1623	4.2	2252	1.7	
21	SU	0502	4.1	1107	1.7	1700	4.4	2327	1.4	
22	M	0531	4.3	1142	1.5	1731	4.6	2359	1.1	
23	TU	0558	4.5	1215	1.2	1801	4.8			
24	W	0031	0.9	0624	4.7	1248	1.0	1831	5.0	○
25	TH	0104	0.7	0652	4.9	1321	0.9	1904	5.0	
26	F	0137	0.7	0724	4.9	1356	0.8	1940	5.0	
27	SA	0211	0.7	0758	4.9	1433	0.9	2020	4.9	
28	SU	0248	0.9	0837	4.7	1512	1.0	2107	4.6	
29	M	0327	1.1	0923	4.5	1557	1.3	2206	4.3	
30	TU	0412	1.4	1024	4.3	1652	1.6	2324	4.0	
31	W	0507	1.8	1149	4.1	1805	1.8			◑

NOVEMBER

Date	Day	Time	m	Time	m	Time	m	Time	m	Moon
1	TH	0051	3.9	0623	2.1	1320	4.0	1942	1.8	
2	F	0212	3.9	0803	2.1	1437	4.2	2109	1.6	
3	SA	0323	4.1	0925	1.9	1541	4.4	2212	1.3	
4	SU	0420	4.4	1024	1.6	1633	4.6	2302	1.0	
5	M	0505	4.6	1112	1.3	1716	4.9	2345	0.8	
6	TU	0543	4.8	1156	1.1	1754	5.0			
7	W	0025	0.7	0618	5.0	1237	0.9	1830	5.0	●
8	TH	0103	0.7	0652	5.0	1315	0.9	1906	5.0	
9	F	0138	0.8	0726	5.0	1353	0.9	1942	4.8	
10	SA	0213	0.9	0800	4.8	1430	1.1	2018	4.5	
11	SU	0248	1.2	0835	4.7	1507	1.3	2056	4.3	
12	M	0323	1.5	0913	4.4	1546	1.5	2140	4.0	
13	TU	0400	1.8	0958	4.2	1629	1.8	2236	3.7	
14	W	0442	2.1	1058	4.0	1719	2.0	2358	3.6	
15	TH	0535	2.3	1219	3.8	1826	2.2			◐
16	F	0123	3.5	0655	2.5	1337	3.8	1953	2.2	
17	SA	0238	3.6	0830	2.4	1442	3.9	2110	2.0	
18	SU	0337	3.8	0937	2.2	1536	4.1	2203	1.8	
19	M	0421	4.0	1025	1.9	1619	4.3	2245	1.5	
20	TU	0455	4.2	1105	1.7	1656	4.5	2322	1.3	
21	W	0526	4.5	1142	1.4	1731	4.7	2358	1.0	
22	TH	0557	4.7	1219	1.1	1807	4.9			
23	F	0035	0.8	0629	4.9	1258	1.0	1844	5.0	○
24	SA	0112	0.7	0704	5.0	1337	0.8	1925	5.0	
25	SU	0151	0.7	0744	5.0	1418	0.8	2011	4.9	
26	M	0231	0.9	0827	4.9	1503	1.0	2103	4.7	
27	TU	0314	1.1	0918	4.8	1552	1.1	2204	4.4	
28	W	0402	1.4	1018	4.5	1649	1.4	2315	4.2	
29	TH	0458	1.7	1133	4.3	1757	1.6			
30	F	0031	4.0	0608	2.0	1254	4.2	1917	1.7	◑

DECEMBER

Date	Day	Time	m	Time	m	Time	m	Time	m	Moon
1	SA	0146	4.0	0731	2.1	1409	4.3	2036	1.6	
2	SU	0257	4.1	0850	2.0	1516	4.3	2143	1.4	
3	M	0356	4.2	0956	1.8	1612	4.5	2237	1.3	
4	TU	0445	4.4	1049	1.5	1659	4.6	2323	1.1	
5	W	0525	4.6	1137	1.4	1740	4.7			
6	TH	0004	1.1	0602	4.8	1220	1.2	1818	4.7	
7	F	0043	1.0	0636	4.9	1300	1.2	1854	4.7	●
8	SA	0118	1.1	0710	4.9	1337	1.1	1929	4.6	
9	SU	0153	1.1	0744	4.8	1414	1.2	2005	4.5	
10	M	0227	1.3	0818	4.7	1450	1.3	2041	4.3	
11	TU	0302	1.5	0853	4.6	1527	1.5	2119	4.1	
12	W	0337	1.7	0933	4.4	1607	1.6	2203	3.9	
13	TH	0416	1.9	1019	4.2	1650	1.8	2256	3.7	
14	F	0500	2.1	1116	4.1	1740	2.0			
15	SA	0005	3.6	0555	2.3	1226	3.9	1841	2.1	◐
16	SU	0122	3.6	0708	2.4	1336	3.9	1952	2.1	
17	M	0231	3.7	0826	2.3	1438	4.0	2100	1.9	
18	TU	0329	3.8	0931	2.1	1532	4.1	2156	1.7	
19	W	0415	4.1	1024	1.9	1620	4.3	2244	1.5	
20	TH	0455	4.4	1111	1.6	1704	4.6	2328	1.2	
21	F	0533	4.6	1155	1.3	1747	4.8			
22	SA	0011	1.0	0611	4.9	1239	1.0	1831	4.9	○
23	SU	0054	0.8	0652	5.1	1324	0.8	1917	5.0	
24	M	0137	0.8	0735	5.2	1409	0.7	2006	5.0	
25	TU	0220	0.8	0821	5.1	1457	0.7	2057	4.8	
26	W	0306	1.0	0911	5.0	1546	0.9	2153	4.6	
27	TH	0354	1.2	1006	4.8	1639	1.1	2254	4.4	
28	F	0446	1.5	1108	4.6	1738	1.3			
29	SA	0000	4.1	0544	1.7	1220	4.4	1842	1.5	◑
30	SU	0111	4.0	0651	1.9	1334	4.2	1953	1.6	
31	M	0222	4.0	0807	2.0	1446	4.2	2105	1.7	

Chart Datum: 2·71 metres below Ordnance Datum (Newlyn). HAT is 5·5 metres above Chart Datum.

HARBOURS/ANCHORAGES ON THE EAST OF THE OUTER HEBRIDES

Visitor moorings mentioned in this section are inspected annually, have pick up buoys, can take yachts <15tons, and there is no charge <7 days. Refer to www.w-isles.gov.uk/harbour master.

TIDES

Standard Port STORNOWAY (⟵)

Times				Height (metres)			
High Water		Low Water		MHWS	MHWN	MLWN	MLWS
0100	0700	0300	0900	4·8	3·7	2·0	0·7
1300	1900	1500	2100				
Differences East side of Outer Hebrides, N to S							
LOCH SHELL (Harris)							
–0013	0000	0000	–0017	0·0	–0·1	–0·1	0·0
EAST LOCH TARBERT (Harris)							
–0025	–0010	–0010	–0020	+0·2	0·0	+0·1	+0·1
LOCH MADDY (N Uist)							
–0044	–0014	–0016	–0030	0·0	–0·1	–0·1	0·0
LOCH CARNAN (S Uist)							
–0050	–0010	–0020	–0040	–0·3	–0·5	–0·1	–0·1
LOCH SKIPORT (S Uist)							
–0100	–0025	–0024	–0024	–0·2	–0·4	–0·3	–0·2
LOCH BOISDALE (S Uist)							
–0055	–0030	–0020	–0040	–0·7	–0·7	–0·3	–0·2
BARRA (North Bay)							
–0103	–0031	–0034	–0048	–0·6	–0·5	–0·2	–0·1
CASTLE BAY (Barra)							
–0115	–0040	–0045	–0100	–0·5	–0·6	–0·3	–0·1
BARRA HEAD (Berneray)							
–0115	–0040	–0045	–0055	–0·8	–0·7	–0·2	+0·1

SHELTER

LOCH SHELL, Lewis, **57°59′·00N 06°25′·50W**. AC 1794. HW –0437 on Dover; ML 2·7m. See 9.8.6. Pass S of Eilean Iuvard; beware rks to W of Is. ⚓ in Tob Eishken, 2½M up loch on N shore (beware rk awash on E side of ent), or at head of loch (exposed to E winds; dries some distance). Facilities: ✉/Stores at Lemreway.

SHIANT ISLANDS, Lewis, **57°53′·68N 06°21′·37W**. AC 1794, 1795. Tides as Loch Shell 9.8.6. Beware strong tidal streams and overfalls in Sound of Shiant. Strictly a fair weather ⚓; in W winds ⚓ E of Mol Mor, isthmus between Garbh Eileen (159m) and Eileen an Tighe. In E winds ⚓ W of Mol Mor. No lights or facilities.

EAST LOCH TARBERT, Harris, **57°49′·98N 06°41′·07W**. AC 2905. HW –0446 on Dover; ML 3·0m; Duration 0605. See 9.8.6. Appr via Sound of Scalpay; beware Elliot Rk (2m) 2½ca SSW of Rubha Crago. A bridge (57°52′·80N 06°41′·73W) joins Scalpay to Harris (20m ht). Bridge lts: Centre Oc 6s; N side Iso G 4s 35m; S side Iso R 4s 35m. Eilean Glas lt ho at E end of Scalpay, Fl (3) 20s 43m 23M; W tr, R bands. In Sound of Scalpay, stream sets W from HW +3, and E from HW –3. ⚓ off Tarbert WSW of Steamer pier in 2·5m. ☎(01589) 502444. Facilities: ⛽ Ⓟ Ⓓ Dr, ✉ 🛒 ✕ ▢ ferry to Uig. Alternatively Scalpay N Hbr gives good shelter. Beware rk 5ca off Aird an Aiseig, E side of ent. SHM buoy marks wk off Coddem; 5ca E of the buoy is a rk, depth 1·1m. Ldg Lt Dir Iso WRG 4s 9m 4M. Both piers have 2FG (vert) lts; ⚓ 7ca N, in 3m. Facilities: ⛽ ✉ 🛒 Ferry to Harris.

LOCH STOCKINISH, Harris. AC 1757. Entr via Loch Chlual marked by metal Bn Fl R 2s at 57°48′·49N 06°48′·79W and SCM Q(6)+L Fl 15s atop B/Y perch at 57°48′·56N 06°48′·81W; pier landing and fish farms in loch.

LOCH RODEL, Harris. AC 2802. 3🅐s at **57°44′·2N 06°57′·4W** in Poll an Tigh-mhàil; enter from SW past jetties. No lts.

SOUND OF HARRIS, 57°43′N 06°58′W. Passages through this difficult Sound are detailed in the *W Coast of Scotland Pilot*. The Stanton and Outer Stromay Chans off the Harris shore are the most feasible for yachts. AC 2802 shows the ferry routes from Leverburgh to Berneray.

LOCH MADDY, North Uist, **57°35′·98N 07°06′·07W**. AC 2825. HW –0500 on Dover. See 9.8.6. With strong wind against tide there can be bad seas off ent. Appr clear, but from S beware submerged rk ½ca N of Leacnam Madadh. Lts: Weaver's Pt Fl 3s 21m 7M; Glas Eilean Mor Fl (2) G 4s 8m 5M; Rubna Nam Pleac Fl R 4s 7m 5M. Inside loch: Ruigh Liath QG 6m 5M; Vallaquie Is Dir Fl (3) WRG 8s. Ro-Ro pier Iso WRG 2s 6M dir sector light. Pontoon lit Fl R 3s. 2🅐s Bagh Aird nam Madadh; 2 🅐s W of and 4 🅐s SW of ferry pier ☎(01870) 602425; 2🅐s E of Oronsay. ⚓s: clear S of ferry pier; NE of Vallaquie Is; Charles Hbr; Oronsay (⚓ not advised due to moorings), tidal berth on private pier; Sponish Hbr; Loch Portain. VHF Ch **12** 16. Port Manager ☎(01876) 5003337(day), 5003226(night). Facilities: Lochmaddy, 26⛵ 2🅥 on lit pontoon (Fl R 3s 2M) £2/night inc ⚡, ⛽ Ⓟ Ⓓ ⛽ ✉ Ⓑ 🛒; WC 🚿 at hotel. Loch Portain ✉ Shop, Bus to Benbecula.

LOCH EPORT, North Uist, **57°33′·45N 07°08′·12W**. AC 2825, but not the head of loch. Tides, approx as L Maddy; 3kn sp stream. On the S side of ent are rks, some drying. The ent proper is clean but very narrow (about 100m) for 5ca, then widens. Follow the charted clearing line 082°. Best ⚓s are: Bàgh a' Bhiorain (S of chan; line up cairn and Bu boulder on 129°); and Acairseid Lee (N bank) E or W of Deer Is. ✉ 🛒 ✕ ▢ at Clachan, head of loch.

KALLIN, Grimsay. **57°28′·9N 07°12′·2W**. AC 2904. 1🅐 in NE of hbr. 3 chan lt buoys and 2 FR (vert) on hbr bkwtr. ☎(01870) 602425.

LOCH CARNAN, South Uist, **57°22′·03N 07°16′·39W**. AC 2825. Tides, see 9.8.6. SWM buoy, L Fl 10s, at 57°22′·30N 07°11′·57W is almost 2M E of app chan proper, marked by Nos 1 and 2 buoys, Fl G 2·5s and Fl R 2s, at 57°22′·45N 07°14′·90W. Round No 3 PHM buoy, Fl R 5s, between Gasay and Taigh Iamain, then pick up ldg lts 222° to Sandwick Quay; front Fl R 2s, rear Iso R 10s, both 5M, W ◇s on posts. Power stn and 2 chys are conspic close to SE of quay. ☎(01870) 602425 for permission to berth on the quay (MoD property). ⚓ or 2🅐s about 2ca WNW of the quay in deep water. ☎(01870) 610238. The passage S of Gasay is unmarked and needs careful pilotage.

LOCH SKIPPORT, South Uist, **57°19′·98N 07°13′·67W**. AC 2904, 2825. HW –0602 on Dover; see 9.8.6. Easy ent 3M NNE of Hecla (604m). No lights, but 2¼M SSE is Usinish lt ho Fl WR 20s 54m 19/15M. ⚓s at: Wizard Pool in 7m; beware Float Rk, dries 2·3m; on N side of Caolas Mor in 7m; Bagh Charmaig in 5m. Linne Arm has narrow ent, many fish farms and poor holding. No facilities.

LOCH EYNORT, South Uist, **57°13′·13N 07°16′·87W**. AC 2825. Tides: interpolate between Lochs Skipport and Boisdale, see 9.8.6. ⚓s in the outer loch at Cearcdal Bay and on the N side just before the narrows are exposed to the E. The passage to Upper L Eynort is very narrow and streams reach 5-7kn; best not attempted unless local fishermen offer guidance. Good ⚓ inside at Bàgh Lathach.

LOCH BOISDALE, South Uist, **57°08′·78N 07°16′·07W**. AC 2770. HW –0455 on Dover; ML 2·4m; Duration 0600. See 9.8.6. Good shelter except in SE gales when swell runs right up the 2M loch. From N, approach between Rubha na Cruibe and Calvay Is leading line 245°: Hollisgeir (0·3m) on with pier (ru). From S beware Clan Ewan Rk, which dries 1·2m, and McKenzie Rk (2·4m), marked by PHM lt buoy Fl (3) R 15s. A new harbour with marina is formed by a causeway from Rubha Bhuailt to Gasay, with two b'waters (G 6s & Fl R 6s with traffic sigs) and an entrance to the N with access from the channel to Boisdale Hbr which lies N of Gasay Is. Off E end beware rock and further development. ⚓ off pier in approx 4m, or SW of Gasay Is in approx 9m. 4🅐s NE of pier; ☎(01870) 602425. There are fish cages W of Rubha Bhuailt. Lts: Dir Lt 292·5° WRG 4s 4m 5M, Ro-Ro jetty hd Iso RG 4s 8m 2M; close SE, Eilean Dubh Fl (2) R 5s. E Calvay Is Fl (2) WRG 10s 16m 7M. Gasay Is Fl WR 5s 10m 7M, opposite shore, Fl G 6s 3m 3M; See 9.8.4. ☎(0187) 700288. Facilities: ⛽ (on pier), Ⓟ ✉ ✕ ▢. Ferry to mainland.

ACAIRSEID MHÓR, Eriskay, ⊕ **57°03′·78N 07°16′·35W**. AC 2770. Tides approx as for North Bay (Barra), see 9.8.6. Ben Scrien (183m) is a conspicuous, pointed peak N of the harbour. Leading lts 285°, both Oc R 6s 9/10m 4M, W △ ▽ on orange posts, lead for 0·5M from the waypoint between two drying rocks into the outer loch. A SHM buoy, Fl G 6s, marks a rock drying 3m. Possible ⛵ on pontoon; 2🅐s (perhaps submerged at HW) are at 57°03′·95N 07°17′·40W on S side of inner loch, opp pier, 2 FG (vert). ☎(01870) 602425, ✉ 🛒 ✕ ▢ at Haun, 1·5M at N end of island.

NORTH BAY, Barra, **57°00′·11N 07°24′·67W**. AC 2770. Tides see 9.8.6. Well-marked approach to inlet sheltered from both S and W winds. There are 🅐s in N part of Bay Hirivagh, ⚓ 1ca WNW of Black Island or temporarily ⛵ on the quay in 4·5m. WPT 56°58′·68N 07°20′·31W is about 200m NE of Curachan ECM buoy, Q (3) 10s, and in the white sector (304°-306°) of Ardveenish Dir ☆ 305°, Oc WRG 3s, 2·5M to the WNW. ⛽ 🛒 ▢ bus to Castlebay.

CASTLE BAY, Barra, **56°56´·78N 07°29´·67W**. AC 2769. HW –0525 on Dover; ML 2·3m; Duration 0600. See 9.8.6. Very good shelter & holding. Best ⚓ is in approx 8m NW of Kiessimul Castle; NE of castle are rocks. About 20 ⚓s lie to W of the pier; they may be encroaching on the recommended ⚓ ☎(01870) 602425. Alternatively ⚓ in Vatersay Bay in approx 9m. W end of Vatersay Sound is closed by a causeway. Beware rocks NNW of Sgeir Dubh a conspic W/G tower, Q(3)G 6s 6m 5M, which leads 283° in transit with Sgeir Liath bn. Channel Rock, 2ca to the South, is marked by Fl WR 6s 4m 6/4M. Close-in leading lts 295°, both FBu 6M on W framework towers: front 9m Or △ on Rubha Glas; rear 457m from front, 15m Or ▽, vis: 15° and 8° respectively either side of ldg line. ☎(01871) 810306.
Facilities: ✉ ✕. Ferry to mainland.

ISLANDS WEST OF THE OUTER HEBRIDES (N TO S)

TIDES

Standard Port STORNOWAY (⟵)

Times				**Height (metres)**			
High Water		Low Water		MHWS	MHWN	MLWN	MLWS
0100	0700	0300	0900	4·8	3·7	2·0	0·7
1300	1900	1500	2100				
Differences West side of Outer Hebrides, N to S							
SCOLPAIG (W North Uist)							
–0033	–0033	–0040	–0040	–1·0	–0·9	–0·5	0·0
BALIVANICH (W Benbecula)							
–0103	–0017	–0031	–0045	–0·7	–0·6	–0·5	–0·2
FLANNAN ISLES							
–0026	–0016	–0016	–0026	–0·9	–0·7	–0·6	–0·2
VILLAGE BAY (St Kilda)							
–0040	–0040	–0045	–0045	–1·4	–1·1	–0·8	–0·3
ROCKALL							
–0055	–0055	–0105	–0105	–1·8	–1·5	–0·9	–0·2
SHILLAY (Monach Islands)							
–0103	–0043	–0047	–0107	–0·6	–0·7	–0·7	–0·3

SHELTER

FLANNAN ISLES, Western Isles, centred on **58°17´·28N 07°35´·27W** (Eilean Mór). AC 2524, 2721. Tides, as above. Uninhabited group of several rky islets, 18M WNW of Gallan Head (Lewis). The main islet is Eilean Mór where landing can be made on SW side in suitable conditions. Lt ho, Fl (2) 30s 101m 20M, is a 23m high W tr on NE tip of Eilean Mór; the lt is obscured by islets to the W which are up to 57m high. No recommended ⚓s and the few charted depths are by lead-line surveys.

ST KILDA, Western Isles, **57°48´·28N 08°33´·07W**. AC 2721, 2524. Tides at Village Bay, Hirta: HW –0510 on Dover; ML 1·9m; Duration 0615; see above. A group of four isles and three stacks, the main island is Hirta. The facility is now manned by a civilian company, Qinetiq ☎(01870) 604443, based at South Uist. Hirta is owned by National Trust for Scotland, who employ a Seasonal Warden, ☎01870 604628. ⚓ in Village Bay, SE-facing, in approx 5m about 1·5ca off the pier. Ldg lts 270°, both Oc 5s 26/38m 3M. If wind is between NE and SSW big swells enter the bay; good holding, but untenable if winds strong. Levenish Is (55m) is 1·5M E of Hirta with offlying rks. Courtesy call to *Kilda Radio* VHF Ch 16 **12** 73 (HJ) before landing; or Qinetic ☎(01870) 604406 (HO), 604612 (OT). Alternative ⚓ at Glen Bay on N side is only safe in S & E winds. Facilities: from wells near landings.

ROCKALL, 57°35´·7N 13°41´·2W. AC 1128, 2524. Tides, as above. A 19m high granite rock, 200M W of N Uist. Best access by helicopter. Lt, Fl 15s 13M, is often extinguished for long periods due to weather damage. Helen's Reef, 1·4m, on which the sea breaks is 2M ENE.

MONACH ISLANDS (Heisker Is), centred on **57°31´·28N 07°38´·07W**. AC 2721, 2722. Tides, see 9.8.6 Shillay. The group lies 5M SW of N Uist and 8M WNW of Benbecula. The 5 main islands (W-E) are Shillay, Ceann Iar, Shivinish, Ceann Ear and Stockay; all uninhabited. Many rky offliers from NW through N to SE of the group. On Shillay there is a conspic red brick lt ho, Fl (2) 15s. ⚓s at: E of lt ho; Croic Hbr, bay N of Shivinish; and S Hbr on W side of Shivinish.

9.8.7 KINLOCHBERVIE

Highland **58°27'·26N 05°02'·78W** ❀❀❀◊◊✿✿

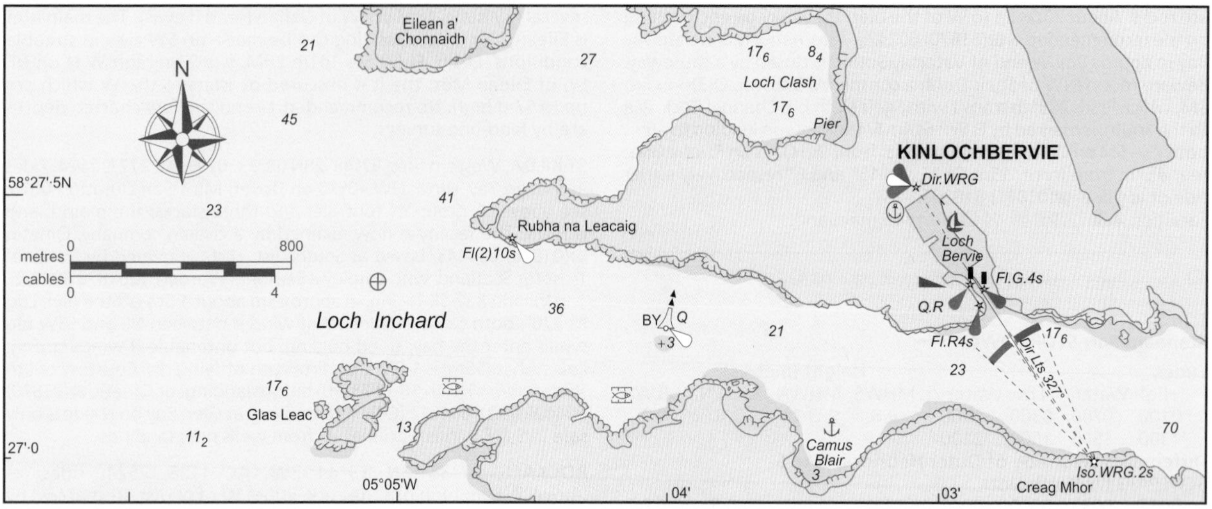

CHARTS AC 1954, 1785, 2503; Imray C67

TIDES –0400 Dover; ML 2·7; Duration 0610

Standard Port ULLAPOOL (⟶)

Times				**Height (metres)**			
High Water		Low Water		MHWS	MHWN	MLWN	MLWS
0000	0600	0300	0900	5·2	3·9	2·1	0·7
1200	1800	1500	2100				
Differences LOCH BERVIE							
+0017	+0020	+0015	+0015	–0·4	–0·2	–0·1	+0·1

SHELTER Very good in Kinlochbervie Hbr off the N shore of Loch Inchard. A useful passage port, only 14.5 track miles S of Cape Wrath. It is an active FV port, but yachts ⊆ on pontoon (contact HM for details); NE side is shoal/foul. If full, ⚓ at Loch Clash, open to W, but sheltered in winds n through SE; landing jetty in 2·7m. Other ⚓s at: Camus Blair on S shore, 5ca SW of hbr ent, and up the loch at L Sheigra, Achriesgill Bay and 5ca short of the head of the loch.

NAVIGATION WPT 58°27'·34N 05°05'·08W (at mouth of Loch Inchard), 100°/1·3M to hbr ent. The sides of the loch are clean, but keep to N side of Loch Inchard to clear Bodha Ceann na Saile NCM and rk (3m depth) almost in mid-chan.

LIGHTS AND MARKS From offshore in good vis Ceann Garbh, a conspic mountain 900m (6M inland), leads 110° toward ent of Loch Inchard. Rubha na Leacaig, Fl (2) 10s 30m 8M, marks N side of loch ent. Dir ☆ WRG (H24) 15m 16M, Y framework tr (floodlit) leads 327° into hbr; see 9.8.4 for vis sectors. The 25m wide ent chan (and hbr) is dredged 4m and marked by 2 PHM poles, Fl R 4s and QR, and by a SHM pole, Fl G 4s. On S shore of loch Creag Mhòr, Dir Oc lt WRG 2.8s 16m 9M, is aligned 147°/327° with hbr ent chan; see 9.8.4.

COMMUNICATIONS (Code 01971) CGOC (01851) 702013; ⊖ (0141) 887 9369 (H24); Police 101; Dr 502002. HM 521235, mob 07901 514350.

VHF Ch **14** 16 HX. Ch 06 is used by FVs in the Minches.

FACILITIES harbours@highland.gov.uk ⊆ (pontoon) £1.50<10m for 48hrs to E side of hbr; 8 ❶ in new development with ⊕ and ⛽ to W side. ⛽ ♦ at FV quay, ℗ ♦ ⌂ ✎ ✉ ⌂ ⌂ ✕ ⚑ (Mission & Hbr Office), ♿. In summer, bus to Inverness.

ANCHORAGES & HBRS BETWEEN KINLOCHBERVIE & ULLAPOOL

LOCH LAXFORD Highland, **58°24'·78N 05°07'·18W**. AC 2503. HW –0410 on Dover. ML 2·7m. See 9.8.7. Ent between Rubha Ruadh and Ardmore Pt, 1M ENE, clearly identified by 3 isolated mountains (N-S) Ceann Garbh, Ben Arkle and Ben Stack. The many ⚓s in the loch include: Loch a'Chadh-fi, on N/NE sides of islet (John Ridgeway's Adventure School on Pt on W side of narrows has moorings); Bagh nah-Airde Beag, next bay to E, (beware rk 5ca off SE shore which covers at MHWS); Weaver's Bay on SW shore, 3M from ent (beware drying rk off NW Pt of ent); Bagh na Fionndalach Mor on SW shore (4-6m); Fanagmore Bay on SW shore (beware head of bay foul with old moorings). Beware many fish farming cages. Facilities: None, nearest stores at Scourie (5M).

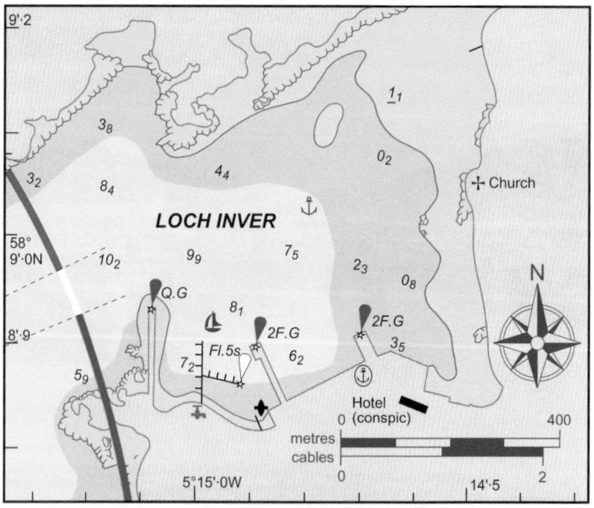

LOCH INVER Highland, **58°08'·98N 05°15'·08W**. AC 2504. HW –0433 on Dover; ML 3·0m. See 9.8.7. Good shelter in all weathers at head of loch in busy fishing hbr on S side. Appr N or S of Soyea Is, Fl (2) 10s 34m 6M; beware rock drying 1·7m about 50m off Kirkaig Point (S side of ent). Glas Leac, a small islet 7ca WSW of hbr, may be passed on either side. ☆, Fl WRG 3s, has 3 different approaches (see 9.8.4) covering the chans N and S of Soyea Is and into the hbr. The church, hotel (S side) and white ho (N side) are all conspic. A 22-berth marina is between the breakwater (QG) and the first FV pier. Or, in W'ly gales, ⚓ in the lee of bkwtr in about 8m; or where HM directs. Other ⚓s on S shore of Loch Inver. VHF Ch 12 16. HM ☎(01571) 844247; mob 07958 734610. Health Centre 01571 844452. Facilities: ⛽ ℗ ♦ ⌂ ⚑ (Leisure Centre), ⌂ ⌂ ✉ ♦.

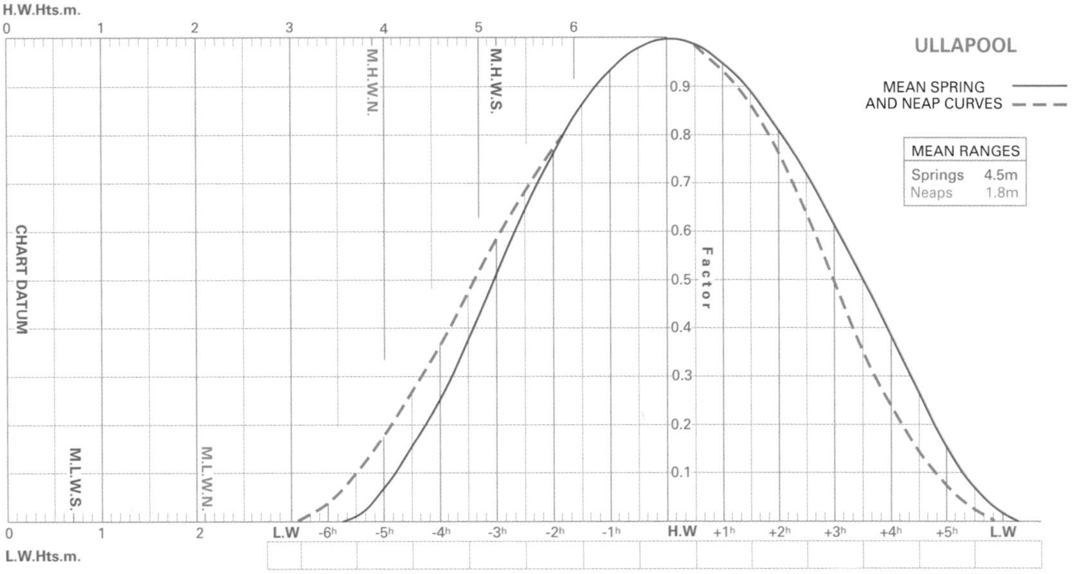

9.8.8 ULLAPOOL

Highland **57°53′·70N 05°09′·38W**

CHARTS AC 1794, 2500, 2501, 2509; Imray C67

TIDES –0415 Dover; ML 3·0; Duration 0610

Standard Port ULLAPOOL (⟶)

Times				**Height (metres)**			
High Water		Low Water		MHWS	MHWN	MLWN	MLWS
0000	0600	0300	0900	5·2	3·9	2·1	0·7
1200	1800	1500	2100				
Differences LOCH LAXFORD							
+0015	+0015	+0005	+0005	–0·3	–0·4	–0·2	0·0
BADCALL BAY							
+0005	+0005	+0005	+0005	–0·7	–0·5	–0·5	+0·2
LOCH NEDD							
0000	0000	0000	0000	–0·3	–0·2	–0·2	0·0
LOCH INVER							
–0005	–0005	–0005	–0005	–0·2	0·0	0·0	+0·1
SUMMER ISLES (Tanera Mor)							
–0005	–0005	–0010	–0010	–0·1	+0·1	0·0	+0·1
LOCH EWE (Mellon Charles, 57°51′N 05°38′W)							
–0005	–0010	–0005	–0005	–0·1	–0·1	–0·1	+0·1
LOCH GAIRLOCH							
–0012	–0011	–0011	–0011	–0·2	+0·1	–0·2	+0·2

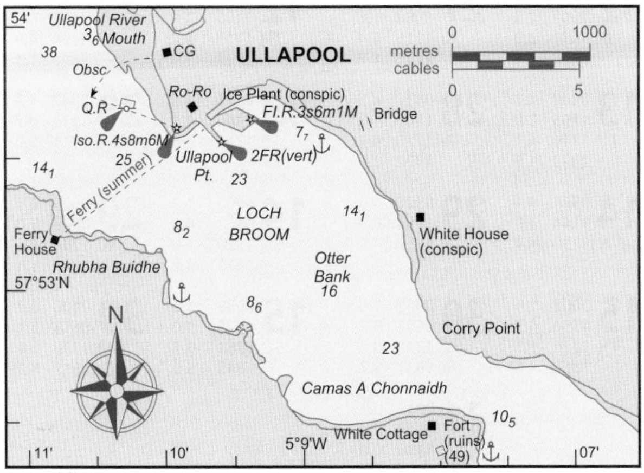

SHELTER A commercial port but yachts welcome. Good ⚓ E of pier, 8 visitor buoys or possible ⊆ on pier (consult HM). Convenient landing inside pier, which may be busy with tourist vessels. Loch Kanaird (N of ent to Loch Broom) has good ⚓ E of Isle Martin. Possible ⚓s 6ca S of Ullapool Pt, and beyond the narrows 3ca ESE of W cottage. The upper loch is squally in strong winds.

NAVIGATION WPT L Broom ent 57°55′·78N 05°15′·08W, 129°/3.5M to Ullapool Pt lt. N of Ullapool Pt extensive drying flats off the mouth of Ullapool R are marked by QR buoy. Beware fish pens and unlit buoys SE of narrows off W shore. A wreck which may be hazardous lies in 21m of water 1·5ca SE of the tip of the E ferry wharf.

LIGHTS AND MARKS Rhubha Cadail, N of L. Broom ent, Fl WRG 6s 11m 9/6M. Cailleach Hd, W of ent, Fl (2) 12s 60m 9M. Ullapool Pt Iso R 4s 8m 6M; grey mast, vis 258°-108°.

COMMUNICATIONS (Code 01854) CG (non-emergency) 613076; Police 101; Dr Dr 08454 242424; Dentist 613289 or 612660; ⊜ (0141) 887 9369. HM 612724, mob 07734 004843.

Ullapool Harbour Ch 14 16 (H24).

FACILITIES **Pier** ⛽ ⛽ ⬚; **Loch Broom SC Services** ⛽ 🔧 & GRP repairs Mobile Marine Services ☎633719, mob 07866 516067, ⬚ Ⓔ ⚒ A.Morgan ☎666383; **Town** ⬚ ⬚ (0700-2100), @ at Captains Cabin, Library and Ceilidh Place Hotel, all domestic facilities, ⚑ at swimming pool, ⬚ ✕ ⬚ ⇄ (bus to Garve). Daily buses to Inverness (✈)(no Sunday bus service. **Ferries** Stornoway; 2-3/day; 2¾hrs; Calmac (www.calmac.co.uk).

ADJACENT ANCHORAGES

LOCH KANAIRD, 57°56′·60N 05°12′·20W. AC 2500. HW –0425 Dover; See 9.8.8; streams are weak and irreg. Situated E of the entrance to Loch Broom, S of the Summer Is and protected by Isle Martin. Good ⚓ (tripping line recommended) ENE of Sgeir Mhor or E of Isle Martin, N of Rubha Beag (also ⊆ on pontoon). Beware cables and marine farms. Ent from S (1ca wide) between two rocky spits, leading line E extremity of Isle Martin in transit with dark streak on cliff behind brg 000°. Ent from N, deep and clear of dangers. Facilities: Ardmair Boat Centre P. Fraser ☎(01854) 612054, ⛺ ⛽ ⚑ some repairs. Isle Martin, Landing permitted (voluntary donation to Trust ☎(01854) 612531).

STANDARD TIME (UT)
For Summer Time add ONE hour in **non-shaded areas**

ULLAPOOL

LAT 57°54′N LONG 5°09′W

TIMES AND HEIGHTS OF HIGH AND LOW WATERS

Dates in red are SPRINGS
Dates in blue are NEAPS

YEAR **2018**

JANUARY

Date	Time	m	Time	m	Time	m	Time	m
1 M	0558	5.3	1226	1.0	1823	5.4		
2 TU	0043	0.8	0644	5.5	1315	0.7	○ 1911	5.5
3 W	0131	0.7	0729	5.6	1403	0.6	2001	5.5
4 TH	0217	0.7	0816	5.6	1451	0.6	2050	5.4
5 F	0302	0.9	0904	5.5	1539	0.7	2141	5.1
6 SA	0348	1.1	0954	5.3	1627	1.0	2234	4.8
7 SU	0436	1.4	1049	4.9	1718	1.3	2333	4.5
8 M	0527	1.7	1151	4.6	1812	1.6	◑	
9 TU	0037	4.3	0624	2.0	1303	4.4	1914	1.9
10 W	0149	4.1	0732	2.2	1419	4.2	2026	2.1
11 TH	0301	4.1	0850	2.3	1531	4.2	2138	2.1
12 F	0402	4.3	1003	2.2	1629	4.3	2238	2.0
13 SA	0451	4.4	1101	2.0	1715	4.4	2326	1.8
14 SU	0532	4.6	1147	1.8	1755	4.5		
15 M	0006	1.6	0607	4.8	1227	1.6	1829	4.6
16 TU	0043	1.5	0639	5.0	1303	1.5	1901	4.7
17 W	0118	1.4	0710	5.1	1337	1.3	● 1931	4.8
18 TH	0150	1.3	0740	5.1	1410	1.2	2000	4.8
19 F	0222	1.3	0810	5.1	1443	1.2	2031	4.8
20 SA	0254	1.3	0842	5.1	1516	1.2	2104	4.7
21 SU	0327	1.4	0917	5.0	1550	1.3	2140	4.6
22 M	0402	1.5	0956	4.9	1628	1.4	2222	4.5
23 TU	0442	1.7	1042	4.7	1711	1.5	2314	4.3
24 W	0529	1.9	1139	4.5	1802	1.7	◐	
25 TH	0022	4.2	0628	2.1	1251	4.4	1904	1.9
26 F	0140	4.1	0744	2.2	1407	4.3	2021	1.9
27 SA	0254	4.2	0907	2.1	1520	4.4	2139	1.8
28 SU	0402	4.5	1022	1.8	1627	4.7	2247	1.5
29 M	0500	4.8	1123	1.4	1726	4.9	2343	1.2
30 TU	0550	5.1	1217	1.0	1817	5.2		
31 W	0034	0.9	0635	5.4	1307	0.7	○ 1903	5.4

FEBRUARY

Date	Time	m	Time	m	Time	m	Time	m
1 TH	0121	0.7	0719	5.6	1354	0.5	1948	5.5
2 F	0205	0.6	0801	5.7	1438	0.4	2031	5.4
3 SA	0247	0.7	0843	5.6	1520	0.5	2114	5.2
4 SU	0329	0.8	0926	5.3	1602	0.8	2158	4.9
5 M	0410	1.1	1011	5.0	1645	1.1	2246	4.6
6 TU	0453	1.4	1100	4.6	1729	1.5	2341	4.3
7 W	0540	1.8	1203	4.3	1820	1.9	◑	
8 TH	0049	4.0	0636	2.2	1323	4.0	1923	2.2
9 F	0207	3.9	0751	2.4	1449	3.9	2047	2.3
10 SA	0324	4.0	0924	2.4	1603	4.0	2208	2.2
11 SU	0424	4.2	1038	2.2	1657	4.1	2304	2.0
12 M	0510	4.4	1128	1.9	1739	4.3	2348	1.8
13 TU	0548	4.6	1209	1.7	1814	4.5		
14 W	0025	1.5	0621	4.8	1245	1.4	1844	4.7
15 TH	0100	1.3	0651	5.0	1319	1.2	● 1912	4.8
16 F	0132	1.2	0720	5.1	1351	1.0	1940	4.9
17 SA	0203	1.1	0749	5.2	1422	0.9	2008	4.9
18 SU	0234	1.0	0820	5.2	1454	0.9	2039	4.9
19 M	0306	1.0	0853	5.2	1527	0.9	2113	4.8
20 TU	0340	1.1	0930	5.0	1602	1.0	2152	4.7
21 W	0418	1.3	1013	4.8	1642	1.2	2238	4.5
22 TH	0501	1.5	1107	4.6	1729	1.5	2339	4.2
23 F	0555	1.8	1219	4.3	1827	1.8	◐	
24 SA	0103	4.1	0708	2.1	1344	4.2	1946	2.0
25 SU	0229	4.1	0844	2.1	1507	4.2	2120	2.0
26 M	0347	4.3	1011	1.8	1622	4.5	2237	1.7
27 TU	0450	4.6	1117	1.4	1720	4.8	2335	1.3
28 W	0540	5.0	1209	0.9	1808	5.1		

MARCH

Date	Time	m	Time	m	Time	m	Time	m
1 TH	0023	1.0	0623	5.3	1256	0.6	1850	5.3
2 F	0107	0.7	0703	5.5	1338	0.4	○ 1929	5.4
3 SA	0148	0.5	0741	5.6	1418	0.3	2007	5.4
4 SU	0227	0.5	0819	5.5	1456	0.4	2045	5.2
5 M	0305	0.7	0856	5.3	1533	0.6	2122	5.0
6 TU	0343	0.9	0934	4.9	1611	1.0	2202	4.6
7 W	0421	1.2	1015	4.6	1649	1.4	2246	4.3
8 TH	0502	1.6	1104	4.2	1731	1.8	2346	4.0
9 F	0549	2.0	1221	3.9	1824	2.2	◑	
10 SA	0107	3.8	0653	2.3	1358	3.7	1945	2.4
11 SU	0233	3.8	0833	2.4	1527	3.7	2130	2.4
12 M	0347	3.9	1007	2.3	1631	3.9	2238	2.1
13 TU	0440	4.2	1103	2.0	1716	4.1	2323	1.9
14 W	0521	4.4	1144	1.6	1750	4.4		
15 TH	0001	1.6	0554	4.7	1220	1.3	1819	4.6
16 F	0035	1.3	0624	4.9	1253	1.0	1846	4.8
17 SA	0108	1.0	0653	5.1	1325	0.8	● 1914	5.0
18 SU	0139	0.9	0723	5.2	1356	0.6	1942	5.1
19 M	0211	0.7	0755	5.3	1428	0.6	2014	5.1
20 TU	0244	0.7	0830	5.2	1502	0.6	2048	5.0
21 W	0319	0.8	0908	5.1	1538	0.8	2127	4.8
22 TH	0358	1.0	0954	4.8	1618	1.0	2214	4.6
23 F	0442	1.3	1051	4.5	1704	1.4	2315	4.3
24 SA	0536	1.6	1208	4.2	1803	1.8	◐	
25 SU	0043	4.1	0652	1.9	1336	4.1	1926	2.0
26 M	0213	4.1	0835	1.9	1501	4.1	2109	2.0
27 TU	0334	4.2	1003	1.6	1615	4.4	2226	1.7
28 W	0437	4.5	1105	1.2	1710	4.7	2322	1.3
29 TH	0526	4.9	1155	0.9	1753	4.9		
30 F	0008	1.0	0606	5.2	1238	0.6	1831	5.2
31 SA	0049	0.7	0643	5.3	1318	0.4	○ 1907	5.3

APRIL

Date	Time	m	Time	m	Time	m	Time	m
1 SU	0128	0.6	0719	5.4	1355	0.4	1942	5.3
2 M	0205	0.5	0754	5.3	1430	0.5	2016	5.1
3 TU	0241	0.7	0828	5.1	1504	0.7	2050	4.9
4 W	0316	0.9	0904	4.8	1538	1.0	2125	4.7
5 TH	0352	1.2	0941	4.4	1614	1.4	2204	4.4
6 F	0431	1.5	1025	4.1	1652	1.7	2254	4.1
7 SA	0514	1.8	1131	3.8	1738	2.1		
8 SU	0008	3.9	0608	2.1	1304	3.6	◑ 1844	2.4
9 M	0135	3.7	0734	2.3	1436	3.6	2034	2.4
10 TU	0254	3.8	0918	2.2	1550	3.7	2158	2.2
11 W	0357	4.0	1023	1.9	1640	4.0	2248	1.9
12 TH	0443	4.2	1108	1.6	1717	4.2	2328	1.6
13 F	0520	4.5	1145	1.3	1747	4.5		
14 SA	0003	1.3	0551	4.8	1220	1.0	1815	4.8
15 SU	0038	1.0	0623	5.0	1254	0.7	1845	5.0
16 M	0112	0.8	0656	5.2	1328	0.5	● 1916	5.1
17 TU	0146	0.6	0731	5.3	1403	0.4	1950	5.2
18 W	0223	0.6	0810	5.2	1439	0.5	2028	5.1
19 TH	0301	0.7	0853	5.1	1518	0.7	2111	4.9
20 F	0343	0.9	0945	4.8	1601	1.0	2201	4.6
21 SA	0431	1.2	1049	4.5	1649	1.4	2309	4.4
22 SU	0530	1.5	1208	4.2	1751	1.8	◐	
23 M	0034	4.2	0648	1.7	1329	4.1	1916	2.0
24 TU	0158	4.1	0825	1.7	1449	4.1	2053	2.0
25 W	0316	4.2	0946	1.5	1559	4.3	2206	1.7
26 TH	0419	4.5	1045	1.2	1652	4.5	2301	1.4
27 F	0507	4.7	1133	0.9	1734	4.8	2347	1.1
28 SA	0547	4.9	1215	0.7	1811	5.0		
29 SU	0028	0.9	0623	5.0	1254	0.6	1844	5.1
30 M	0106	0.7	0658	5.1	1330	0.6	○ 1917	5.1

Chart Datum: 2·75 metres below Ordnance Datum (Newlyn). HAT is 5·9 metres above Chart Datum.

STANDARD TIME (UT)
For Summer Time add ONE hour in **non-shaded areas**

ULLAPOOL LAT 57°54'N LONG 5°09'W

TIMES AND HEIGHTS OF HIGH AND LOW WATERS

Dates in red are SPRINGS
Dates in blue are NEAPS

YEAR **2018**

MAY

Date	Time	m	Time	m	Time	m	Time	m
1 TU	0143	0.7	0732	5.0	1404	0.7	1950	5.0
2 W	0218	0.8	0806	4.8	1437	0.9	2023	4.9
3 TH	0253	1.0	0841	4.6	1511	1.1	2057	4.7
4 F	0328	1.2	0918	4.3	1545	1.4	2135	4.4
5 SA	0406	1.4	1002	4.1	1623	1.7	2221	4.2
6 SU	0447	1.7	1058	3.8	1705	2.0	2321	4.0
7 M	0537	1.9	1214	3.7	1801	2.2		
8 TU ◑	0039	3.8	0643	2.1	1335	3.6	1925	2.4
9 W	0155	3.8	0811	2.1	1450	3.7	2058	2.3
10 TH	0301	3.9	0927	1.9	1549	3.9	2200	2.0
11 F	0354	4.1	1020	1.6	1633	4.2	2246	1.7
12 SA	0437	4.4	1103	1.3	1709	4.4	2327	1.4
13 SU	0515	4.7	1143	1.0	1743	4.7		
14 M	0005	1.1	0552	4.9	1222	0.7	1816	5.0
15 TU ●	0044	0.8	0630	5.1	1300	0.5	1852	5.2
16 W	0124	0.6	0711	5.2	1340	0.5	1931	5.2
17 TH	0205	0.5	0756	5.2	1420	0.5	2014	5.2
18 F	0248	0.6	0846	5.0	1503	0.7	2101	5.0
19 SA	0335	0.7	0943	4.8	1550	1.0	2157	4.8
20 SU	0427	1.0	1049	4.5	1642	1.3	2305	4.5
21 M	0527	1.3	1200	4.3	1744	1.7		
22 TU ◐	0021	4.3	0640	1.5	1313	4.1	1900	1.9
23 W	0138	4.2	0801	1.6	1427	4.1	2023	1.9
24 TH	0251	4.3	0916	1.5	1534	4.2	2136	1.7
25 F	0355	4.4	1017	1.3	1628	4.4	2234	1.5
26 SA	0445	4.5	1107	1.1	1712	4.6	2323	1.3
27 SU	0528	4.6	1151	1.0	1750	4.8		
28 M	0006	1.1	0605	4.7	1230	0.9	1824	4.9
29 TU ○	0046	1.0	0641	4.7	1307	0.9	1857	4.9
30 W	0123	1.0	0716	4.7	1341	1.0	1930	4.9
31 TH	0159	1.0	0750	4.6	1415	1.1	2003	4.8

JUNE

Date	Time	m	Time	m	Time	m	Time	m
1 F	0234	1.1	0825	4.5	1449	1.2	2037	4.7
2 SA	0309	1.2	0902	4.3	1523	1.4	2114	4.5
3 SU	0346	1.4	0943	4.2	1600	1.6	2156	4.4
4 M	0425	1.5	1030	4.0	1640	1.8	2246	4.2
5 TU	0510	1.7	1128	3.8	1727	2.0	2347	4.0
6 W ◑	0603	1.9	1236	3.7	1829	2.2		
7 TH	0056	4.0	0707	1.9	1346	3.8	1946	2.2
8 F	0203	4.0	0819	1.9	1449	3.9	2059	2.1
9 SA	0301	4.1	0924	1.7	1543	4.1	2158	1.8
10 SU	0353	4.3	1018	1.4	1629	4.4	2248	1.5
11 M	0441	4.6	1106	1.2	1711	4.7	2334	1.2
12 TU	0526	4.8	1152	0.9	1752	4.9		
13 W ●	0019	0.9	0611	5.1	1237	0.7	1833	5.2
14 TH	0105	0.7	0658	5.2	1322	0.6	1917	5.3
15 F	0152	0.5	0748	5.2	1407	0.6	2004	5.3
16 SA	0239	0.5	0840	5.1	1453	0.7	2054	5.2
17 SU	0329	0.6	0937	4.9	1541	0.9	2150	5.0
18 M	0421	0.8	1037	4.7	1633	1.2	2251	4.7
19 TU	0517	1.0	1140	4.4	1729	1.5	2358	4.5
20 W ◐	0619	1.3	1246	4.2	1833	1.7		
21 TH	0109	4.3	0725	1.5	1355	4.1	1944	1.9
22 F	0220	4.2	0836	1.6	1502	4.2	2057	1.9
23 SA	0328	4.2	0942	1.6	1601	4.3	2203	1.8
24 SU	0424	4.3	1039	1.5	1650	4.4	2259	1.6
25 M	0512	4.4	1127	1.4	1731	4.6	2347	1.5
26 TU	0553	4.4	1209	1.3	1808	4.7		
27 W	0029	1.3	0630	4.5	1248	1.2	1842	4.8
28 TH ○	0107	1.2	0705	4.5	1323	1.2	1915	4.8
29 F	0143	1.2	0738	4.5	1358	1.2	1947	4.8
30 SA	0218	1.1	0811	4.5	1431	1.3	2020	4.8

JULY

Date	Time	m	Time	m	Time	m	Time	m
1 SU	0252	1.2	0845	4.4	1505	1.3	2054	4.7
2 M	0327	1.2	0920	4.3	1539	1.5	2131	4.6
3 TU	0403	1.3	0959	4.2	1616	1.6	2212	4.4
4 W	0443	1.5	1045	4.1	1657	1.8	2301	4.3
5 TH	0527	1.6	1140	4.0	1746	1.9		
6 F ◑	0001	4.2	0618	1.7	1247	3.9	1846	2.1
7 SA	0108	4.1	0719	1.8	1354	3.9	1958	2.1
8 SU	0213	4.1	0828	1.8	1457	4.1	2110	1.9
9 M	0315	4.3	0935	1.6	1554	4.3	2213	1.7
10 TU	0413	4.5	1035	1.4	1646	4.6	2310	1.4
11 W	0508	4.7	1130	1.1	1735	4.9		
12 TH	0002	1.0	0600	5.0	1220	0.9	1821	5.2
13 F ●	0053	0.7	0650	5.2	1309	0.7	1907	5.3
14 SA	0142	0.5	0739	5.3	1356	0.6	1953	5.4
15 SU	0230	0.4	0829	5.2	1442	0.6	2041	5.4
16 M	0318	0.4	0919	5.1	1529	0.8	2131	5.2
17 TU	0406	0.6	1012	4.8	1616	1.0	2225	5.0
18 W	0455	0.9	1108	4.6	1705	1.3	2325	4.7
19 TH ◐	0547	1.2	1209	4.3	1759	1.6		
20 F	0032	4.4	0643	1.5	1316	4.1	1901	1.9
21 SA	0145	4.1	0749	1.8	1426	4.1	2014	2.0
22 SU	0259	4.0	0902	1.9	1532	4.1	2132	2.0
23 M	0405	4.1	1011	1.9	1628	4.2	2238	1.9
24 TU	0458	4.1	1106	1.7	1713	4.4	2330	1.7
25 W	0542	4.3	1151	1.6	1752	4.6		
26 TH	0014	1.5	0618	4.4	1231	1.5	1826	4.7
27 F ○	0052	1.4	0652	4.5	1307	1.3	1858	4.8
28 SA	0127	1.2	0723	4.6	1341	1.2	1929	4.9
29 SU	0201	1.1	0752	4.6	1413	1.2	1959	4.9
30 M	0233	1.1	0822	4.6	1445	1.2	2030	4.9
31 TU	0305	1.1	0853	4.6	1517	1.3	2103	4.8

AUGUST

Date	Time	m	Time	m	Time	m	Time	m
1 W	0338	1.1	0926	4.5	1550	1.4	2140	4.7
2 TH	0413	1.2	1005	4.4	1627	1.5	2222	4.5
3 F	0452	1.4	1052	4.2	1710	1.7	2314	4.4
4 SA ◑	0538	1.6	1152	4.1	1802	1.9		
5 SU	0019	4.2	0632	1.7	1307	4.0	1908	2.0
6 M	0135	4.1	0741	1.8	1420	4.1	2030	2.0
7 TU	0248	4.2	0901	1.8	1529	4.2	2149	1.8
8 W	0358	4.4	1015	1.6	1630	4.5	2255	1.5
9 TH	0500	4.6	1116	1.3	1723	4.9	2352	1.1
10 F	0553	5.0	1209	1.0	1810	5.2		
11 SA ●	0043	0.7	0640	5.2	1257	0.8	1854	5.5
12 SU	0131	0.4	0726	5.4	1343	0.6	1938	5.6
13 M	0216	0.3	0810	5.4	1426	0.5	2021	5.6
14 TU	0259	0.3	0854	5.2	1509	0.6	2105	5.4
15 W	0342	0.5	0939	5.0	1552	0.9	2151	5.1
16 TH	0425	0.8	1028	4.7	1636	1.2	2243	4.7
17 F	0510	1.2	1123	4.4	1723	1.6	2346	4.3
18 SA ◐	0559	1.6	1230	4.1	1818	1.9		
19 SU	0104	4.0	0658	2.0	1345	4.0	1928	2.2
20 M	0229	3.9	0817	2.2	1500	4.0	2059	2.3
21 TU	0344	3.9	0943	2.2	1604	4.1	2219	2.1
22 W	0442	4.0	1046	2.0	1653	4.3	2314	1.9
23 TH	0526	4.2	1132	1.8	1732	4.5	2356	1.6
24 F	0602	4.4	1211	1.6	1806	4.7		
25 SA	0032	1.4	0632	4.6	1247	1.4	1837	4.9
26 SU ○	0106	1.2	0701	4.7	1319	1.2	1906	5.0
27 M	0138	1.0	0728	4.8	1351	1.1	1934	5.1
28 TU	0209	0.9	0755	4.8	1421	1.1	2003	5.1
29 W	0239	0.9	0823	4.8	1452	1.1	2035	5.1
30 TH	0311	0.9	0855	4.8	1524	1.2	2110	4.9
31 F	0344	1.0	0930	4.6	1559	1.3	2149	4.7

Chart Datum: 2·75 metres below Ordnance Datum (Newlyn). HAT is 5·9 metres above Chart Datum.

STANDARD TIME (UT)
For Summer Time add ONE hour in **non-shaded areas**

ULLAPOOL LAT 57°54′N LONG 5°09′W

TIMES AND HEIGHTS OF HIGH AND LOW WATERS

Dates in red are SPRINGS
Dates in blue are NEAPS

YEAR **2018**

SEPTEMBER

Date	Day	Time	m	Time	m	Time	m	Time	m	Moon
1	SA	0421	1.2	1013	4.5	1640	1.5	2239	4.5	
2	SU	0504	1.5	1108	4.2	1729	1.8	2346	4.3	
3	M	0556	1.8	1228	4.1	1835	2.0			◑
4	TU	0112	4.1	0706	2.0	1355	4.1	2005	2.1	
5	W	0236	4.1	0839	2.0	1514	4.2	2138	1.9	
6	TH	0352	4.3	1004	1.8	1620	4.5	2248	1.5	
7	F	0454	4.7	1107	1.5	1713	4.9	2343	1.0	
8	SA	0544	5.0	1157	1.1	1757	5.3			
9	SU	0030	0.6	0626	5.3	1243	0.8	1838	5.5	●
10	M	0114	0.4	0707	5.4	1325	0.6	1917	5.7	
11	TU	0156	0.2	0746	5.5	1406	0.5	1956	5.6	
12	W	0235	0.3	0824	5.3	1445	0.6	2036	5.4	
13	TH	0314	0.5	0904	5.1	1525	0.8	2116	5.1	
14	F	0353	0.9	0945	4.8	1605	1.2	2200	4.7	
15	SA	0432	1.3	1032	4.4	1648	1.6	2255	4.3	
16	SU	0516	1.7	1135	4.1	1737	2.0			◐
17	M	0017	3.9	0608	2.2	1257	3.9	1841	2.3	
18	TU	0151	3.7	0725	2.4	1420	3.9	2019	2.4	
19	W	0316	3.8	0910	2.4	1532	4.0	2154	2.3	
20	TH	0418	3.9	1021	2.2	1625	4.2	2250	2.0	
21	F	0503	4.2	1108	1.9	1706	4.5	2331	1.7	
22	SA	0538	4.4	1146	1.7	1740	4.7			
23	SU	0006	1.4	0607	4.6	1221	1.4	1810	4.9	
24	M	0039	1.1	0633	4.8	1253	1.2	1838	5.1	
25	TU	0110	0.9	0659	5.0	1324	1.0	1906	5.2	○
26	W	0140	0.8	0726	5.1	1355	0.9	1936	5.3	
27	TH	0211	0.7	0755	5.1	1426	0.9	2008	5.2	
28	F	0243	0.8	0826	5.0	1459	1.0	2044	5.1	
29	SA	0317	0.9	0902	4.9	1536	1.2	2126	4.9	
30	SU	0354	1.2	0944	4.7	1617	1.4	2218	4.6	

OCTOBER

Date	Day	Time	m	Time	m	Time	m	Time	m	Moon
1	M	0438	1.5	1040	4.4	1708	1.7	2332	4.3	
2	TU	0531	1.8	1205	4.2	1816	2.0			◑
3	W	0103	4.1	0645	2.1	1340	4.1	1955	2.1	
4	TH	0229	4.2	0829	2.2	1501	4.3	2131	1.8	
5	F	0345	4.4	0954	1.9	1608	4.6	2237	1.4	
6	SA	0443	4.7	1053	1.5	1659	5.0	2328	1.0	
7	SU	0529	5.0	1141	1.2	1741	5.3			
8	M	0012	0.7	0608	5.3	1224	0.9	1819	5.5	
9	TU	0054	0.5	0645	5.4	1305	0.7	1856	5.6	●
10	W	0132	0.4	0721	5.5	1343	0.6	1932	5.5	
11	TH	0209	0.5	0756	5.4	1421	0.7	2009	5.3	
12	F	0245	0.7	0832	5.2	1459	0.9	2046	5.0	
13	SA	0321	1.0	0908	4.9	1537	1.2	2126	4.6	
14	SU	0358	1.4	0949	4.6	1617	1.6	2213	4.3	
15	M	0438	1.8	1041	4.3	1702	2.0	2324	3.9	
16	TU	0525	2.2	1159	4.0	1759	2.3			◐
17	W	0100	3.7	0631	2.5	1326	3.9	1925	2.5	
18	TH	0230	3.7	0818	2.6	1445	4.0	2108	2.4	
19	F	0341	3.9	0943	2.4	1546	4.2	2212	2.1	
20	SA	0430	4.1	1034	2.1	1631	4.4	2255	1.8	
21	SU	0506	4.4	1114	1.8	1707	4.7	2331	1.5	
22	M	0536	4.6	1149	1.5	1739	4.9			
23	TU	0005	1.2	0603	4.9	1222	1.3	1808	5.1	
24	W	0038	1.0	0630	5.1	1255	1.1	1838	5.3	○
25	TH	0110	0.8	0658	5.2	1328	0.9	1911	5.4	
26	F	0143	0.7	0729	5.3	1402	0.9	1947	5.3	
27	SA	0218	0.8	0804	5.2	1439	0.9	2027	5.2	
28	SU	0255	0.9	0843	5.1	1519	1.1	2113	5.0	
29	M	0335	1.2	0929	4.8	1604	1.4	2212	4.6	
30	TU	0421	1.5	1029	4.6	1658	1.7	2330	4.4	
31	W	0517	1.9	1154	4.3	1810	1.9			◑

NOVEMBER

Date	Day	Time	m	Time	m	Time	m	Time	m	Moon
1	TH	0054	4.2	0634	2.2	1323	4.3	1945	2.0	
2	F	0215	4.2	0812	2.2	1443	4.4	2113	1.8	
3	SA	0328	4.4	0933	2.0	1549	4.6	2217	1.4	
4	SU	0425	4.7	1032	1.6	1640	4.9	2307	1.1	
5	M	0510	5.0	1120	1.3	1723	5.2	2351	0.9	
6	TU	0549	5.2	1204	1.1	1801	5.3			
7	W	0031	0.8	0624	5.3	1244	0.9	1837	5.4	●
8	TH	0109	0.7	0659	5.4	1323	0.9	1913	5.3	
9	F	0145	0.8	0733	5.3	1400	0.9	1949	5.1	
10	SA	0220	1.0	0807	5.2	1437	1.1	2025	4.9	
11	SU	0255	1.2	0842	5.0	1514	1.3	2103	4.6	
12	M	0331	1.5	0920	4.7	1553	1.6	2146	4.3	
13	TU	0409	1.9	1004	4.5	1635	1.9	2241	4.1	
14	W	0452	2.2	1103	4.2	1725	2.2	2358	3.9	
15	TH	0546	2.4	1222	4.1	1830	2.3			◐
16	F	0122	3.8	0707	2.6	1341	4.0	1957	2.4	
17	SA	0241	3.9	0840	2.5	1450	4.1	2114	2.2	
18	SU	0341	4.1	0945	2.3	1544	4.3	2208	1.9	
19	M	0425	4.3	1032	2.0	1627	4.5	2250	1.6	
20	TU	0500	4.6	1112	1.7	1703	4.8	2328	1.4	
21	W	0531	4.8	1149	1.4	1738	5.0			
22	TH	0004	1.1	0601	5.1	1227	1.2	1813	5.2	
23	F	0041	0.9	0634	5.3	1304	1.0	1851	5.4	○
24	SA	0119	0.8	0710	5.4	1343	0.9	1932	5.4	
25	SU	0158	0.8	0749	5.4	1425	0.9	2018	5.3	
26	M	0239	0.9	0833	5.3	1509	1.0	2110	5.1	
27	TU	0323	1.2	0923	5.1	1558	1.2	2211	4.8	
28	W	0411	1.5	1024	4.8	1655	1.5	2321	4.5	
29	TH	0508	1.8	1139	4.6	1802	1.7			
30	F	0035	4.4	0619	2.1	1259	4.5	1921	1.8	◑

DECEMBER

Date	Day	Time	m	Time	m	Time	m	Time	m	Moon
1	SA	0150	4.3	0742	2.1	1415	4.5	2040	1.7	
2	SU	0302	4.4	0900	2.0	1524	4.6	2147	1.6	
3	M	0402	4.6	1004	1.8	1620	4.8	2242	1.4	
4	TU	0450	4.8	1058	1.6	1707	4.9	2329	1.2	
5	W	0531	5.0	1144	1.4	1748	5.0			
6	TH	0010	1.1	0608	5.1	1227	1.3	1825	5.0	
7	F	0049	1.1	0643	5.2	1306	1.2	1901	5.0	●
8	SA	0126	1.1	0717	5.2	1344	1.2	1937	4.9	
9	SU	0201	1.2	0750	5.2	1420	1.3	2012	4.8	
10	M	0235	1.4	0824	5.0	1456	1.4	2048	4.6	
11	TU	0310	1.5	0900	4.9	1533	1.5	2126	4.5	
12	W	0346	1.8	0938	4.7	1612	1.7	2209	4.3	
13	TH	0425	2.0	1023	4.5	1655	1.9	2301	4.1	
14	F	0509	2.2	1120	4.3	1744	2.1			
15	SA	0007	3.9	0604	2.4	1230	4.2	1845	2.2	◐
16	SU	0123	3.9	0717	2.5	1341	4.1	1956	2.2	
17	M	0233	4.0	0836	2.4	1445	4.2	2105	2.1	
18	TU	0331	4.2	0940	2.2	1539	4.4	2202	1.8	
19	W	0418	4.4	1031	2.0	1627	4.6	2250	1.6	
20	TH	0459	4.7	1117	1.7	1711	4.9	2334	1.3	
21	F	0538	5.0	1201	1.3	1754	5.1			
22	SA	0017	1.1	0616	5.2	1246	1.1	1838	5.3	○
23	SU	0101	0.9	0657	5.4	1330	0.9	1924	5.4	
24	M	0144	0.8	0741	5.5	1416	0.8	2013	5.4	
25	TU	0229	0.9	0827	5.5	1503	0.8	2104	5.2	
26	W	0315	1.0	0917	5.3	1552	0.9	2200	5.0	
27	TH	0403	1.3	1012	5.1	1645	1.1	2300	4.7	
28	F	0455	1.5	1115	4.9	1743	1.4			
29	SA	0005	4.5	0554	1.8	1226	4.7	1847	1.6	◑
30	SU	0115	4.3	0702	2.0	1339	4.5	1957	1.8	
31	M	0227	4.3	0817	2.1	1453	4.4	2110	1.8	

Chart Datum: 2·75 metres below Ordnance Datum (Newlyn). HAT is 5·9 metres above Chart Datum.

ADJACENT ISLANDS

SUMMER ISLES, 58°01'N 05°25'W. AC 2509, 2501. HW –0425 Dover; See 9.8.8; streams are weak and irregular. In the N apps to Loch Broom some 30 islands and rks, the main ones being Eilean Mullagrach, Isle Ristol, Glas-leac Mor, Tanera Beg, Eilean a' Char, Eilean Fada Mor. Beware rocks at S end of Horse Sound. ⚓s:

Isle Ristol, ⚓ to S of drying causeway and clear of moorings; beware landings frequented by local FVs. Close to slip is lt Fl G 3s. Facilities: (at Polbain 2M).

Tanera Beg, ⚓ in the chan to the E inside Eilean Fada Mor.

Tanera Mor, on E side, ⚓ in bay to N off pier or in W corner off stone jetty; beware many moorings and fish pens. Also poss ⚓ close NW of Is and close E of Eilean na Saille, but N of drying rock. Facilities: ☎(01854) 622272 B Wilder for tea room.

Badentarbat Bay, Temp'y ⚓ NW part of bay ESE of pier which is busy with marina farm activity. Beware N part of bay is shoal. Suitable for Achiltibuie or Polbain on mainland. Facilities: (emerg) ☎(01854) 622261, ✕.

LITTLE LOCH BROOM, 57°54'·98N 05°24'·68W. AC 2500. HW –0415 Dover as per Ullapool, see 9.8.8; streams are weak (approx 1kn). Between Loch Broom and Gruinard Bay, entered S of Cailleach Hd it is deep (115m in centre) and shoreline steep to. In approaches beware of Ardross Rk (depth 0.6m) 0.38M ENE of Stattic Pt.

Camusnagaul, on S side of loch 1.6M from head and Dundonnel Hotel, ⚓ to E of hamlet.

Scoraig, inside narrows on N shore in N'lies, ⚓ off jetty clear of submarine cables and marine farm. C.Dawson ☎01845 613380.

ANCHORAGES BETWEEN LITTLE LOCH BROOM & LOCH GAIRLOCH

LOCH EWE, 57°52'·0N 05°40'·0W (SWM buoy, L Fl 10s). AC 2509, 3146. Tides: See 9.8.8; HW–0415 on Dover; ML 2·6m; Duration 0610. Shelter in all winds. Easy ent with no dangers in loch. Rhubha Reidh lt, Fl (4) 15s 37m 24M, W tr, is 4·5M W of ent. No 1 buoy Fl (3) G 10s. Loch approx 7M long with Isle Ewe and 2 small islets about 2M from ent in centre; can be passed on either side. Temp ⚓ in bay of Isle of Ewe. Beware unlit buoy A2 between E side Isle Ewe & Aultbea Pier, 2 FG (vert); NATO fuelling jetty 2 FG (vert) and dolphins Fl G 4s.

Loch Thurnaig, 1.7M SSE of Isle of Ewe, sheltered ⚓ off Ob na Bà Rùaidhe, SE of pier to W of drying reef. Beware of numerous marine farms in approaches.

Aultbea, ⚓ off Aultbea Hotel on E shore or in NW'lies close E of pier. N part of bay is shoal. Facilities: Dr, ✕.

Poolewe Bay, ⚓ in SW part of bay in 3·5m, at head of loch: Boor Rks(3m) with drying rocks extending 1ca NW lie off W shore about 9ca NW of Poolewe. Head of Loch dries for a considerable distance. Facilities: on pier, (at garage) ✕. Landing difficult at E side of bay.

Inverewe Gdns on NE side of bay, ⚓ to SW of Jetty at Port na Cloiche Gile.

LOCH GAIRLOCH, 57°43'N 05°45'W. AC 228, 2528. HW –0440 on Dover. See 9.8.8. A wide loch facing W. Ent clear of dangers but Submarine Exercise Area (see 9.8.22) to S of Longa Is. Quite heavy seas enter in bad weather. Lts: Glas Eilean Fl WRG 6s 9m 6/4M, Gairloch Pier Hd, QR 9m. HM ☎(01445) 712140.

Badachro, good shelter SW of Eilean Horrisdale on SW side of loch but busy with FVs and local craft. Unlit PHM/SHM mark rock ledges in approach. Passage to S of of Eilean Horrisdale is possible with caution. ⚓ on E side NNW of Sgeir Dhubh Bhea. ✕ (Bad Inn). HM ☎(01445) 741255 for availability.

Loch Shieldaig, At SE end of the loch many moorings for local craft. in Ob Na Acarseid from Torridon Yacht Charter when vacant £10/night. If unavailable ⚓ to SSW of Eilean an t-Sabhail. Beware marine farms.

Flowerdale Bay, ⚓ in approx 6m near Gairloch pier or berth on pontoons (2m depth N side, 3m S side) at pier. HM ☎(01445) 712140. VHF Ch 16 (occas). Gairloch Pier: fees charged. SC, Hotel.

SKYE AND THE INNER SOUND

(AC 1795, 2210, 2209, 2208, 2207, 5616) Skye and the islands around it provide many good and attractive anchorages, of which the most secure are: Acairseid Mhor on the W side of Rona; Portree (9.8.9); Oronsay, Portnalong, near the entrance to Loch Harport, and Carbost at the head; Loch Dunvegan; and Uig Bay in Loch Snizort. s at Stein (Loch Dunvegan), Portree, Acairseid Mhor (Rona), Churchton Bay (Raasay) and Armadale Bay (S tip).

►*Tides are strong off Rubha Hunish at N end of Skye, and heavy overfalls occur with tide against fresh or strong winds.*◄

⚓ behind Fladday Is near the N end of Raasay can be squally and uncomfortable; and Loch Scavaig (S. Skye, beneath the Cuillins) more so, though the latter is so spectacular as to warrant a visit in fair weather. Soay Is has a small, safe harbour on its N side, but the bar at entrance almost dries at LW springs.

Between N Skye and the mainland there is the choice of Sound of Raasay or Inner Sound. **The direction of buoyage in both Sounds is Northward.** In the former, coming S from Portree, beware Sgeir Chnapach (3m) and Ebbing Rk (dries 2·9m), both NNW of Oskaig Pt. Beware McMillan's Rk (0·4m depth) in mid-channel, marked by SHM lt buoy.

► *At the Narrows (chart 2534) the SE-going stream begins at HW Ullapool –0605, and the NW-going at HW Ullapool +0040; sp rate 1·4kn in mid-chan, but more near shoals each side.* ◄

The channel between Scalpay and Skye narrows to 2.5ca with drying reefs each side and least depth 0·1m. ► *Here the E-going stream begins at HW Ullapool +0550, and W-going at HW Ullapool –0010, sp rate 1kn.* ◄

Inner Sound, which is a Submarine exercise area, is wider and easier than Sound of Raasay; the two are connected by Caol Rona and Caol Mor, respectively N and S of Raasay. Dangers extend about 1M N of Rona, and Cow Is lies off the mainland 8M to S; otherwise approach from N is clear to Crowlin Is, which should be passed to W. There is a good ⚓ between Eilean Mor and Eilean Meadhonach.

A military torpedo range in the Inner Sound does not normally restrict passage, but vessels may be requested to keep to the E side of the Sound if it is active. Range activity is broadcast at 0800 and 1800LT first on VHF Ch 16 and then on Ch 8, and is indicated by Red Flags flown on the range building at Applecross, by range vessels and at the naval pier at Kyle of Lochalsh, ☎(01599) 534262.

9.8.9 PORTREE

Skye (Highland) 57°24'·73N 06°11'·07W

CHARTS AC 2209, 2534, 5616; Imray C66

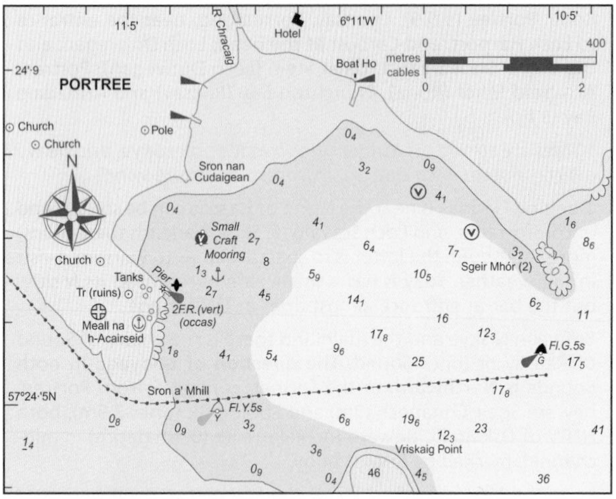

TIDES –0445 Dover; ML no data; Duration 0610

Standard Port ULLAPOOL (⟶)

Times				Height (metres)			
High Water		Low Water		MHWS	MHWN	MLWN	MLWS
0000	0600	0300	0900	5·2	3·9	2·1	0·7
1200	1800	1500	2100				
Differences PORTREE (Skye)							
–0025	–0025	–0025	–0025	+0·1	–0·2	–0·2	0·0
SHIELDAIG (Loch Torridon)							
–0020	–0020	–0015	–0015	+0·4	+0·3	+0·1	0·0
LOCH A'BHRAIGE (Rona)							
–0020	0000	–0010	0000	–0·1	–0·1	–0·1	–0·2
LOCH SNIZORT (Uig Bay, Skye)							
–0045	–0020	–0005	–0025	+0·1	–0·4	–0·2	0·0
LOCH DUNVEGAN (Skye)							
–0105	–0030	–0020	–0040	0·0	–0·1	0·0	0·0
LOCH HARPORT (Skye)							
–0115	–0035	–0020	–0100	–0·1	–0·1	0·0	+0·1
SOAY (Camus nan Gall)							
–0055	–0025	–0025	–0045	–0·4	–0·2	ND	ND

SHELTER Secure in all but strong S to SW'lies, when Camas Bàn is more sheltered. In the NW of the bay there are 8 ⓥs for <15t. Short stay pontoon on pier.

NAVIGATION WPT 57°24'·58N 06°10'·07W, 275°/0·72M to pier. From the S, avoid rks off An Tom Pt (1·5M to E, off chartlet).

LIGHTS AND MARKS Only lts are a SHM buoy Fl G 5s marking Sgeir Mhór, 2 FR (vert) 6m 4M (occas) on the pier and a SPM buoy Fl Y 5s.

COMMUNICATIONS (Code 01478) CGOC (01851) 702013; ⊜ (0141) 887 9369; Police 101; Dr 612013; Ⓗ 612704. HM 612926; Moorings 612341.

VHF Ch 16 12 (occas).

FACILITIES **Pier** £14 (Mon-Fri).
Town Ⓑ bus to Kyle of Lochalsh, ⇌.

ANCHORAGES AROUND OR NEAR SKYE

LOCH TORRIDON Highland, **57°36'N 05°49'W**. AC 2210. Tides, see 9.8.9. Three large lochs: ent to outer loch (Torridon) is 3M wide, with isolated Sgeir na Trian (2m) almost in mid-chan; ⚓s on SW side behind Eilean Mór and in L Beag. L Sheildaig is middle loch with good ⚓ and 2 ⓥs (up to 10t) between the Is and village. 1M to the N, a 2ca wide chan leads into Upper L Torridon; many fish cages and prone to squalls. Few facilities, except Shieldaig: Garage; Diabeg: ✕.

LOCH A'BHRAIGE Rona (Highland), **57°34'·6N 05°57'·9W**. AC 2479, 2534. HW –0438 on Dover; ML 2·8m; Duration 0605. See 9.8.9. A good ⚓ in NW of the island, safe except in NNW winds. Beware rks on NE side up to 1ca offshore. Hbr in NE corner of loch head. Ldg lts 137°, see 9.8.4. Facilities: jetty, and a helipad, all owned by MOD (DRA). Before ent, call *Rona* Range Control VHF Ch 13.

Acarseid Mhór is ⚓ on W of Rona. One ⓥ £12, ☎07831 293963. App S of Eilean Garbh marked by W arrow. SD sketch of rks at ent is necessary. At **Churchton Bay**, SW tip of Raasay, there are 4 HIE ⓥs; ☎(01478) 612341, ✕.

LOCH DUNVEGAN 4 ⓥs off Stein, **57°30'·9N 06°34'·5W**. 2 ⓥs off Dunvegan, 57°26'·3N 06°35'·2W. Fuel, ✕. ☎(01478) 612341.

LOCH HARPORT Skye (Highland), **57°20'·6N 06°25'·8W**. AC 1795. HW –0447 (sp), –0527 (np) on Dover. See 9.8.9. On E side of Loch Bracadale, entered between Oronsay Is and Ardtreck Pt (W lt ho, Fl 6s 18m 9M). SW end of Oronsay has conspic rk pillar, called The Castle; keep ¼M offshore here and off E coast of Oronsay which is joined to Ullinish Pt by drying reef. ⚓ Oronsay Is, N side of drying reef (4m), or on E side, but beware rk (dries) 0·5ca off N shore of Oronsay. Fiskavaig Bay 1M S of Ardtreck (7m); Loch Beag on N side of loch, exposed to W winds; Port na Long E of Ardtreck, sheltered except from E winds (beware fish farm); 1 ⓥ off the distillery and 2 ⓥ off *The Old Inn* at Carbost on SW shore. Facilities: Carbost ✕ (garage). Port na Long.

LOCH SLIGACHAN Skye (Highland), **57°19'·0N 06°06'·0W**. AC 2534. Tides see 9.8.9. Differences as for Portree. Steep sided sheltered Loch S of Narrows of Raasay. In sheltered weather ⚓ outside in Balmeanach Bay. Entr marked by ECM and SHM. Sconser harbour with pier and pontoon (lit Fl R 3s 2m 3M) inside narrows used to service fish farms and shellfish beds, which should be avoided.

SOAY HARBOUR Skye (Highland), **57°09'·5N 06°13'·4W**. AC 2208. Tides see 9.8.9. Narrow inlet on NW side of Soay; enter from Soay Sound above half flood to clear bar, dries 1·0m. Appr on 135° from 5ca out to avoid reefs close each side of ent. Cross bar slightly E of mid-chan, altering 20° stbd for best water; ent is 15m wide between boulder spits marked by W poles with Or tops. ⚓ in 3m mid-pool or shoal draught boats can enter inner pool. Good shelter and holding. Camas nan Gall (poor holding); no other facilities.

ARMADALE BAY Skye (Highland), 4M NW of Mallaig. AC 2208. 6 ⓥs £12 at **57°04'·0N 05°53'·6W**, ☎(01471) 844216. Bay is sheltered from SE to N winds but subject to swell in winds from N to SE. From S, beware the Eilean Maol & Sgorach rocks. Ferry pier, Oc R 6s 6m 6M, with conspic W shed. Facilities: Skye Yachts ☎01471 844216, M (£12·50), at pontoon (not Sat pm or Sun), free pontoon for tenders, ferry to Mallaig for ⇌. Ardvasar ¾ mile: HW±3 at (launching/parking £5), (not Sun) ✕.

CROWLIN ISLANDS Highland, **57°21'·1N 05°50'·6W**. AC 2209, 2498. HW –0435 on Dover, –0020 on Ullapool; HW +0·3m on Ullapool. See 9.8.8. ⚓ between Eilean Meadhonach and Eilean Mor, appr from N, keep E of Eilean Beg. Excellent shelter except in strong N winds. There is an inner ⚓ with 3½m but ent chan dries. Eilean Beg lt ho Fl 6s 32m 6M, W tr. No facilities.

SUBMARINE EXERCISE INFORMATION

Details of submarine activity in the Exercise Areas north of Mull are broadcast at 0710 and1910 UT by Stornoway CG on a specified VHF Ch after an initial announcement on Ch 16. Areas are referred to by the names given below, rather than by the numbers indicated on the chartlet. For Areas 22–85 (South of Mull), see page 484.

SUBFACTS

General information on SUBFACTS is also broadcast twice daily at 0620 & 1820 UT on Navtex. Stornoway CGOC will provide SUBFACTS on request; call on Ch 16.

A 'Fisherman's hotline' (☎(01436) 677201) is available on a 24 hour basis and may be used for any queries relating to SUBFACTS from any mariner.

Submarines on the surface and at periscope depth always listen on Ch 16.

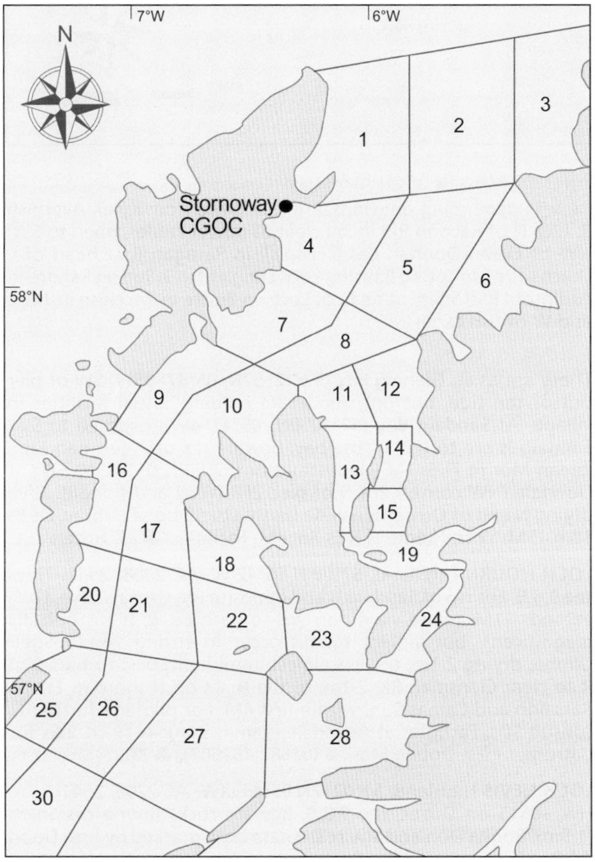

1	Tolsta	**16**	Wiay
2	Pulteney	**17**	Pooltiel
3	Eddrachillis	**18**	Bracadale
4	Erisort	**19**	Crowlin
5	Clynelish	**20**	Boisdale
6	Broom	**21**	Dalwhinnie
7	Shiant	**22**	Canna
8	Balbair	**23**	Rum
9	Hermitray	**24**	Sleat
10	Waternish	**25**	Hellisayl
11	Flodigarry	**26**	Edradour
12	Longa	**27**	Hawes
13	Portree	**28**	Eigg
14	Rona	**29**	Sandray
15	Raasay	**30**	Glenturret

9.8.10 PLOCKTON

Highland **57°20′·52N 05°38′·47W**

CHARTS AC 2209, 2528, 5616; Imray C66

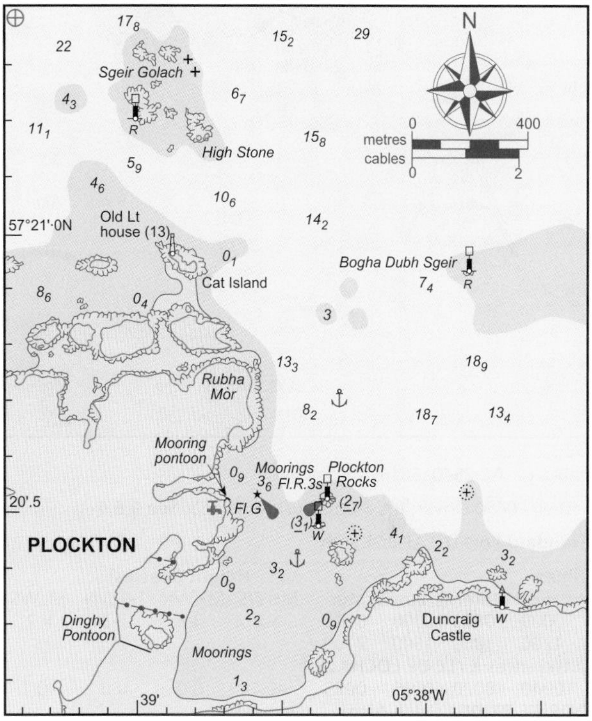

TIDES −0435 Dover; ML 3·5m; Duration 0600; See 9.8.9

Standard Port ULLAPOOL (⟶)

Times				**Height (metres)**			
High Water		Low Water		MHWS	MHWN	MLWN	MLWS
0000	0600	0300	0900	5·2	3·9	2·1	0·7
1200	1800	1500	2100				
Differences PLOCKTON							
+0005	−0025	−0005	−0010	+0·5	+0·5	+0·5	+0·2

SHELTER Good, exposed only to N/NE'lies. 9 Y ⚓s or ⚓ in centre of bay in approx 3·5m. Inner part of bay shoals and dries to the SW.

NAVIGATION WPT 57°21′·16N 05°39′·44W; thence towards Bogha Dubh Sgeir Bn, between Eilean a Chait disused Lt ho and Sgeir Golach Bn / High Stone (1m) to the North. Hawk Rock (0.1m) will be cleared when Duncraig Castle bears 158°. Alter S to the ⚓. Beware Plockton Rks ($\underline{3}$·1m) on E side of bay.

LIGHTS AND MARKS See 9.8.4 and chartlet. Old lt ho (13m) on Eilean a Chait is conspic, as is Duncraig Castle. Sgeir Golach Bn a twr with W panels Fl W 10s, Dubh Sgeir Bn a tower with R panels Fl(2) R 6s and Plockton Rks a PHM Bn Fl R 3s.

COMMUNICATIONS HM (01599) 534589, 534167, Mobile 07802 367253 (at Kyle of Lochalsh); CGOC (01851) 702013; ⊖ (0141) 887 9369; Police101; Dr via HM.

FACILITIES **Village** £5, at 50m dinghy pontoon (H24 except MLWS), Ⓔ ✕ ⇌ airstrip (bus to Kyle of Lochalsh).

ADJACENT MOORINGS

LOCH CARRON Strome Narrows are not buoyed or lit. Appr on 328° between Sgeir Chreagach and Sgeir Fhada. Fish farms on W shore of Loch Kishorn.

9.8.11 LOCH ALSH

Highland **57°16´·68N 05°42´·87W** ❀❀❀◊◊✿✿✿

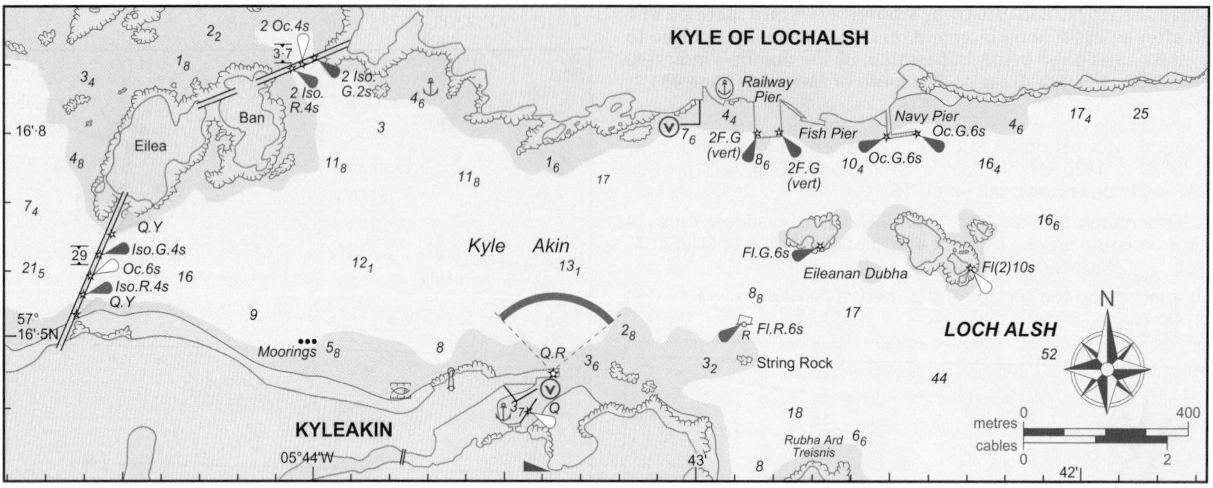

CHARTS AC 2540, 5616; Imray C66

TIDES −0450 Dover; ML 3·0m; Duration 0555; See 9.8.9

Standard Port ULLAPOOL (⟶)

Times				Height (metres)			
High Water		Low Water		MHWS	MHWN	MLWN	MLWS
0000	0600	0300	0900	5·2	3·9	2·1	0·7
1200	1800	1500	2100				
Differences KYLE OF LOCHALSH							
−0040	−0020	−0005	−0025	+0·1	0·0	0·0	−0·1
DORNIE BRIDGE (Loch Alsh)							
−0040	−0010	−0005	−0020	+0·1	−0·1	0·0	0·0
GLENELG BAY (Kyle Rhea)							
−0105	−0035	−0035	−0055	−0·4	−0·4	−0·9	−0·1
LOCH HOURN							
−0125	−0050	−0040	−0110	−0·2	−0·1	−0·1	+0·1

SHELTER **Kyle of Lochalsh:** ⊆ on Railway Pier, with FVs, or on 40m L-shaped pontoon (seasonal), close W of Railway Pier; or ⚓ off the hotel in 11m. **Kyle Akin:** 3 free ⚓s are subject to tidal stream. Lit Ⓥ pontoon on NW side of hbr for yachts, shoal on N side.

NAVIGATION WPT (from Inner Sound) 57°16´·98N 05°45´·77W, 123°/0·75M to bridge. Chan to bridge is marked by 2 PHM and 2 SHM lt buoys. Bridge to Skye, 29m clearance, is lit Oc 6s in centre of main span, Iso R 4s on S pier and Iso G4s on N pier. The secondary NE span is lit, but has only 3.7m clearance.

LIGHTS AND MARKS See chartlet. Direction of buoyage is N in Kyle Rhea, thence E up Loch Alsh; but W through Kyle Akin and the bridge, ie SHMs are on N side of channel. Iso G.4s shown on SW corrner of Ⓥ pontoon at Kyle of Localsh Mar-Oct.

COMMUNICATIONS (Code 01599) CGOC (01851) 702013; ⊜ (0141) 887 9369; Police 101; Dr, Ⓗ: via HM. Skye bridge 534844. HM 534306, Mobile 07990 971161, Deputy 07771 816900.

VHF Ch **11** 16.

FACILITIES **Kyle of Lochalsh**: www.kyleandlochalsh.org.uk/index.asp ⊆ pontoon, £15 1st night then £10, ⛽ (Fish pier via HM, Mon-Fri) Ⓔ ✉ Ⓑ ✕ £2 (honesty box). ⇌ (useful railhead), Bus to Glasgow & Inverness; buses every ½hr to/from Kyleakin.

Kyleakin: ☎534167 or VHF Ch 11, 120m ⊆ (£14/craft) depth varies from 3m to drying. ✕.

ANCHORAGES IN LOCH ALSH (see also 9.8.9)

⚓s, safe depending on winds, are (clockwise from Kyle): Avernish B, (2ca N of Racoon Rk) in 3m clear of power cables, open to SW; NW of Eilean Donnan Cas (conspic); in Ratagan B at head of L Duich in 7m; in Totaig B facing Loch Long ent in 3·5m; on S shore in Ardintoul B in 5·5m; at head of Loch na Béiste in 7m close inshore and W of fish cages.

SOUND OF SLEAT

There are ⚓s at: **Glenelg Bay (57°12'·57N 05°37'·95W)** SW of pier out of the tide, but only moderate holding. Usual facilities in village. At **Sandaig Bay** (57°10'·0N 05°41'·4W), exposed to SW. Sandaig Is are to NW of the bay; beware rks off Sgeir nan Eun. Eilean Mór lit Fl 6s. At **Isleornsay Hbr** (57°09'N 05°48'W) 5⚓s at Duisdale (NW corner) 2ca N of pier, 2FR (vert) and floodlit. Give drying N end of Ornsay Is a wide berth. Lts: SE tip of Ornsay, Oc 8s 18m 15M, W tr; N end, Fl R 6s 8m 4M. Facilities: ✉ Hotels.

LOCH HOURN Highland, **57°08'N 05°42'W**. AC 2208, 2541. Tides see 9.8.9. Ent is S of Sandaig Is and opposite Isle Ornsay, Skye. Loch extends 11M inland via 4 narrows to Loch Beag; it is scenically magnificent, but violent squalls occur in strong winds. Sgeir Ulibhe, drying 2·1m, bn, lies almost in mid-ent; best to pass S of it to clear Clansman Rk, 2·1m, to the N. ⚓s on N shore at Eilean Ràrsaidh and Camas Bàn, within first 4M. For pilotage further E, consult SDs. Facilities at Arnisdale (Camas Bàn): ✕ 2⚓s for patrons, ✉. Doune Marine (01687 462667).

LOCH NEVIS Highland, **57°02´·2N 05°43´·3W**. AC 2208, 2541.
HW −0515 on Dover. See 9.8.9. Beware rocks Bogha cas Sruth (1·8m), Bogha Don and Sgeirean Glasa both marked by bns. Good ⚓ NE of Eilean na Glaschoille, except in S winds; 9 Or ⚓s off Inverie, £5 (free if dining), 10m max LOA. Call *Old Forge* VHF Ch 16, 12. ✕. In strong winds expect violent unpredictable squalls. Enter the inner loch with caution, and ⚓ N or SE of Eilean Maol.

ARISAIG (Loch nan Ceall), Highland, **56°53´·64N 05°55´·77W** (ent). AC 2207. HW −0515 on Dover; +0030 and +0·9m on Oban. Exposed to strong winds, especially from SE to NW. SDs essential. W mark on Rubh' Arisaig on S side of ent. S Chan is winding, marked by 8 perches. Appr HW±4 to avoid strongest streams LW±1½. Caution: many unmarked rks; no lts. Sheltered ⚓ at head of loch, clear of moorings. Call **Arisaig Marine** ☎(01687) 450224, VHF Ch 16, M; few ⚓s, pontoon (loading, & fuel) (10t). **Village** at hotel, ✉ ✕ ⇌.

KYLE AKIN TO MALLAIG

Approaching Kyle Akin (AC 2540) from W, beware dangerous rks to N, off Bleat Is (at S side of entrance to Loch Carron); on S side of chan, Bogha Beag (dries 1·2m) and Black Eye Rk (depth 3·2m), respectively 6ca and 4ca W of bridge. Pass at least 100m N or S of Eileanan Dubha in Kyle Akin. On S side of chan String Rk (dries) is marked by PHM lt buoy. Kyle Rhea connects Loch Alsh with NE end of Sound of Sleat.

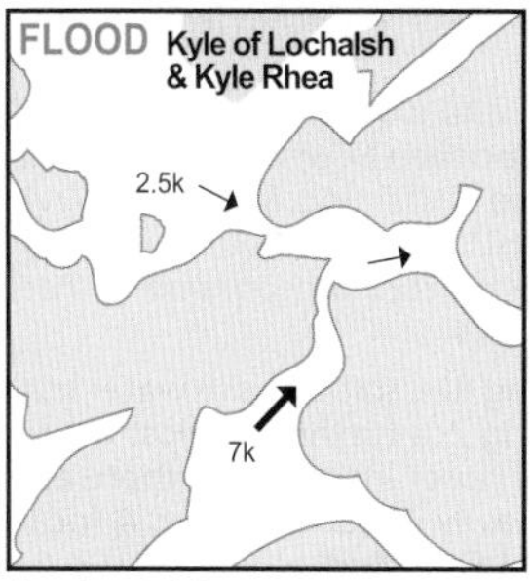
FLOOD
Kyle of Lochalsh & Kyle Rhea
2.5k
7k

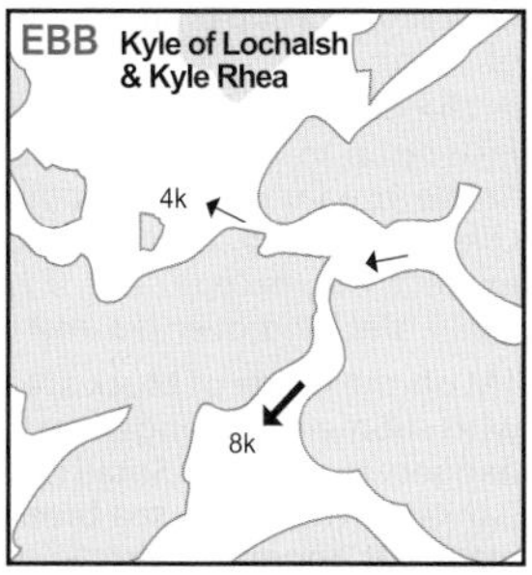
EBB
Kyle of Lochalsh & Kyle Rhea
4k
8k

▶ *The tidal streams are very strong: N-going stream begins HW Ullapool + 0600, sp rate 6-7kn; S-going stream begins at HW Ullapool, sp rate 8kn. N-going stream in Kyle Rhea begins HW Dover +0140 (HW Ullapool +0555) and runs for 6hrs. The E-going stream in Kyle Akin begins (Sp) HW Dover +0350 (HW Ullapool –0415). (Nps) HW Dover –0415 (HW Ullapool).*
S-going stream in Kyle Rhea begins HW Dover –0415 (HW Ullapool) and runs for 6hrs. The W-going stream in Kyle Akin begins (Sp) HW Dover –0015 (HW Ullapool +0400). (Nps) HW Dover +0140 (HW Ullapool +0555). Eddies form both sides of the Kyle with dangerous overfalls off S end in fresh S'ly winds on S-going stream. ◀
Temp ⚓ in Sandaig Bay, 3M to SW.

The Sound of Sleat widens to 4M off Point of Sleat and is exposed to SW winds unless Eigg and Muck give a lee. Mallaig is a busy fishing and ferry harbour, convenient for supplies. Further S the lochs require intricate pilotage. 6M NE of Ardnamurchan Pt (lt, fog sig) are Bo Faskadale rks, drying 0·5m and marked by SHM lt buoy, and Elizabeth Rock with depth of 0·7m.

▶ *Ardnamurchan Pt is an exposed headland onto which the ebb sets. With onshore winds, very heavy seas extend 2M offshore and it should be given a wide berth. Here the N-going stream begins at HW Oban – 0525, and the S-going at HW Oban + 0100, sp rates 1·5kn.* ◀

ARDNAMURCHAN TO CRINAN

(AC 2171, 2169, 5616) S of Ardnamurchan the route lies either W of Mull via Passage of Tiree (where headlands need to be treated with respect in bad weather); or via the more sheltered Sound of Mull and Firth of Lorne. The former permits a visit to Coll and Tiree, where best ⚓s are at Arinagour (Ⓥs) and Gott Bay respectively. Beware Cairns of Coll, off the N tip.

The W coast of Mull is rewarding in settled weather, but careful pilotage is needed. Beware tide rip off Caliach Pt (NW corner) and Torran Rks off SW end of Mull (large-scale AC 2617 required). Apart from the attractions of Iona and of Staffa (Fingal's Cave), the remote Treshnish Is are worth visiting. The best ⚓s in this area are at Ulva, Gometra, Bull Hole and Tinker's Hole in Iona Sound. The usual passage through Iona Sound avoids overfalls W of Iona, but heed shoal patches. Loch Lathaich on the N side of Ross of Mull is 5M to the E; a good base with ⚓ at Bunessan.

The Sound of Mull gives access to Tobermory, Dunstaffnage Bay, Oban, and up Loch Linnhe through Corran Narrows (where tide runs strongly) to Fort William and to Corpach for the Caledonian Canal. Apart from these places, there are dozens of ⚓s in the sheltered lochs inside Mull, as for example in Loch Sunart with Ⓥs at Kilchoan.

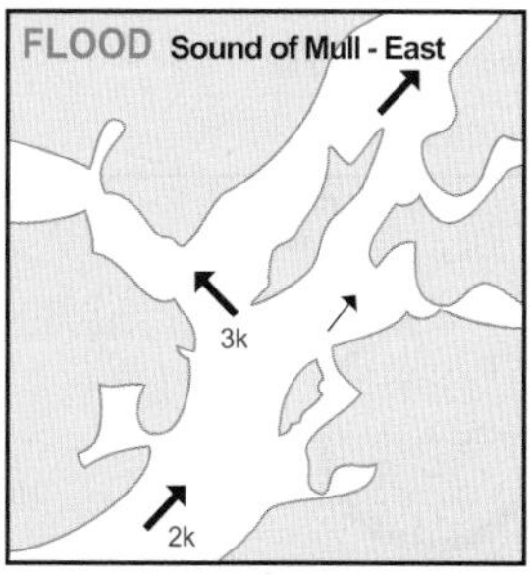
FLOOD
Sound of Mull - East
3k
2k

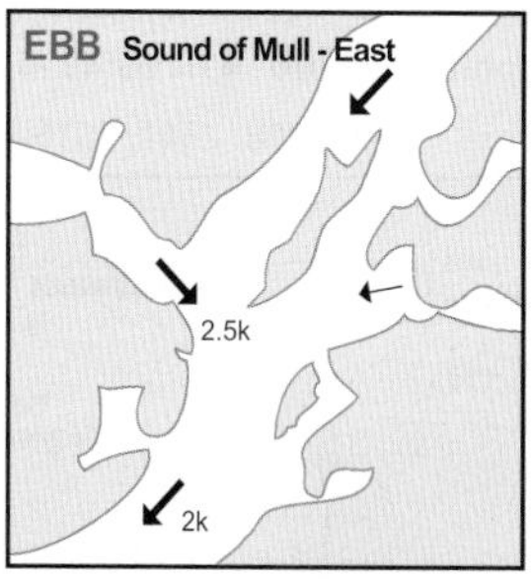
EBB
Sound of Mull - East
2.5k
2k

FIRTH OF LORNE AND SOUND OF LUING

▶ **Firth of Lorne:** *the N-going stream begins at HW Oban +0430 (HW Dover –0100). The W-going stream in the Sound of Mull begins at HW Oban –0550 (HW Dover +0105). The ingoing tides at Lochs Feochan, Etive and Creran begin at HW Oban –0350, +0430 and +0600. The S-going stream in the Firth of Lorne begins at HW Oban –0155 (HW Dover +0500). The E-going stream in the Sound of Mull begins at HW Oban –0025 (HW Dover +0555).* ◀

On the mainland shore Puilladobhrain is a sheltered ⚓. Cuan Sound is a useful short cut to Loch Melfort, and Craobh Marina. Good shelter, draught permitting, in Ardinamar B, SW of Torsa.

Sound of Luing (AC 2326) between Fladda (lt), Lunga and Scarba on the W side, and Luing and Dubh Sgeir (lt) on the E side, is the normal chan to or from Sound of Jura, despite dangers at the N end and strong tidal streams.

▶ *The N- and W-going flood begins at HW Oban + 0430; the S- and E-going ebb at HW Oban –0155. Sp rates are 2·5kn at S end of Sound, increasing to 6kn or more in Islands off N entrance, where there are eddies, races and overfalls. The N- or W-going stream begins in the following sequence:* ◀

Dorus Mor:	*HW Oban +0330. Sp: 8kn.*
Corryvreckan:	*HW Oban +0410. Sp: 8.5kn.*
Cuan Sound:	*HW Oban +0420. Sp: 6kn.*
Sound of Jura:	*HW Oban +0400. Sp: 4kn.*
Sound of Luing:	*HW Oban +0430. Sp: 7kn.*

The S- or E-going stream begins as follows:

Dorus Mor:	*HW Oban –0215. Sp: 8kn.*
Corryvreckan:	*HW Oban –0210. Sp: 8.5kn.*
Cuan Sound:	*HW Oban –0200. Sp: 6kn.*
Sound of Jura:	*HW Oban –0205. Sp: 4kn.*
Sound of Luing:	*HW Oban –0155. Sp: 7kn.*

▶ *From the N, beware very strong streams, eddies and whirlpools in Dorus Mór, off Craignish Pt. Streams begin to set W and N away from Dorus Mór at HW Oban +0345, and E and S towards Dorus Mór at HW Oban –0215, sp rates 7kn.* ◀

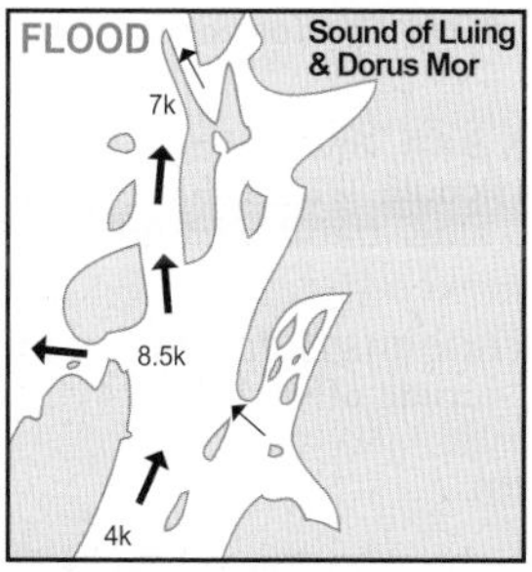
FLOOD
Sound of Luing & Dorus Mor
7k
8.5k
4k

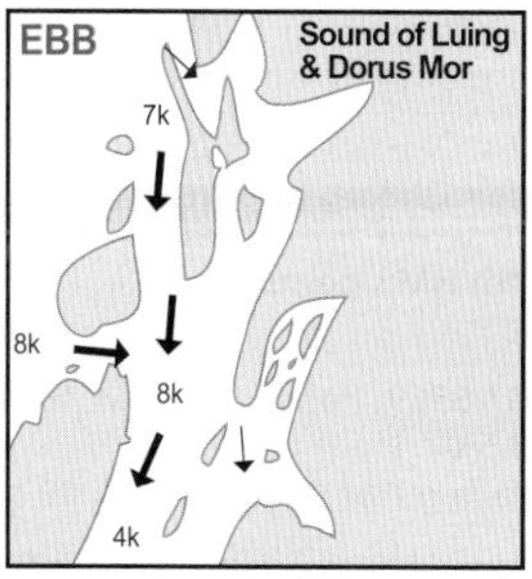
EBB
Sound of Luing & Dorus Mor
7k
8k
8k
4k

At N end of Sound of Jura (AC 2326) is Loch Craignish. For Gulf of Corryvreckan, Colonsay, Islay, Loch Crinan and passage south through the Sound of Jura, see 9.9.5.

NW Scotland

9.8.12 MALLAIG

Highland **57°00'·47N 05°49'·47W**

CHARTS AC 2208, 2541, 5616; Imray C65, C66

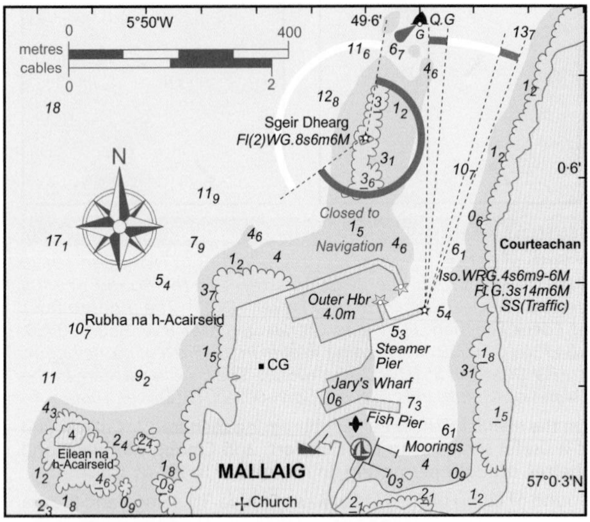

TIDES −0515 Dover; ML 2·9; Duration 0605

Standard Port OBAN (⟶)

Times				Height (metres)			
High Water		Low Water		MHWS	MHWN	MLWN	MLWS
0000	0600	0100	0700	4·0	2·9	1·8	0·7
1200	1800	1300	1900				
Differences MALLAIG							
+0017	+0017	+0030	+0024	+1·0	+0·7	+0·3	+0·1
INVERIE BAY (Loch Nevis)							
+0030	+0020	+0035	+0020	+1·0	+0·9	+0·2	0·0
BAY OF LAIG (Eigg)							
+0015	+0030	+0040	+0005	+0·7	+0·6	−0·2	−0·2
LOCH MOIDART							
+0015	+0015	+0040	+0020	+0·8	+0·6	−0·2	−0·2
LOCH EATHARNA (Coll)							
+0025	+0010	+0015	+0025	+0·4	+0·3	ND	ND
GOTT BAY (Tiree)							
0000	+0010	+0005	+0010	0·0	+0·1	0·0	0·0

SHELTER Good in SW'lies but open to N. Access H24. Small marina or 9 🟊s in SE part of hbr. Mallaig is a reasonably busy FV harbour. It is also a hub for Skye, Small Isles and S Uist ferries.

NAVIGATION WPT 57°00'·75N 05°49'·40W, 191°/0·3m to Steamer Pier lt, passing E of Sgeir Dhearg lt bn. The former W chan is permanently closed to navigation.

LIGHTS AND MARKS As chartlet & 9.8.4. Town lts may obscure Sgeir Dhearg lt. Outer Hbr Pier Hds floodlit. IPTS (3 FR vert at pier hd) when ferries manoeuvring, no other traffic allowed except with HM's permission.

COMMUNICATIONS (Code 01687) CGOC (01851) 702013; ⊖ (0141) 887 9369; Police 101. HM 462154, outside office hrs 462411; Dr 462202.

Mallaig Hbr Radio VHF Ch 09 16 (HO).

FACILITIES in marina, £2.40/m/night, short stay <4hrs £12. £3.60 /night. If marina full berth on Fish Pier with HM permission. 🟊 £15/night. Ⓔ (mob 10t) ACA, wi-fi.

Town Ⓑ.

THE SMALL ISLES

(AC 2207, 2208, 5616) These consist of Canna, Rum, Eigg and Muck. The hbrs at Eigg (SE end), Rhum (Loch Scresort) and Canna (between Canna and Sanday) are all exposed to E'lies; Canna has best shelter and is useful for the Outer Hebrides. Dangers extend SSW from Canna: at 1M Jemina Rk (depth 1·5m) and Belle Rk (depth 3·6m); at 2M Humla Rk (5m high), marked by buoy and with offlying shoals close W of it; at 5M Hyskeir (lt, fog sig), the largest of a group of small islands; and at 7M Mill Rks (with depths of 1·8m).

▶ *The tide runs hard here, and in bad weather the sea breaks heavily up to 15M SW of Canna. Between Skerryvore and Neist Pt the stream runs generally N and S, starting N-going at HW Ullapool + 0550, and S-going at HW Ullapool −0010. It rarely exceeds 1kn, except near Skerryvore, around headlands of The Small Isles, and over rks and shoals.* ◀

1M off the N side of Muck are Godag Rks, some above water but with submerged dangers extending 2ca further N. Most other dangers around the Small Isles are closer inshore, but there are banks on which the sea breaks heavily in bad weather. A local magnetic anomaly exists about 2M E of Muck.

ANCHORAGES IN THE SMALL ISLES

CANNA The Small Isles, **57°03'·3N 06°29'·4W**. AC 1796, 2208. HW −0457 (Sp), −0550 (Np) on Dover; HW −0035 and −0·4m on Ullapool; Duration 0605. Good shelter, except in strong E'lies, in hbr between Canna and Sanday Is. 10🟊s (£10) around edge of the bay and middle is clear to ⚓ but holding is poor due to kelp. Appr along Sanday shore, keeping N of Sgeir a' Phuirt, dries 4·6m. Ldg marks as in SDs. ⚓ in 3–4m W of Canna pier, off which beware drying rky patch. ⚓ Lt advised due to FVs. Conspic bn, Fl W10s 32m 9M, vis 152°-061°, at E end of Sanday Is. Magnetic anomaly off NE Canna. Facilities: shower at farm (01687 462963), limited ✉ (H24-honesty) free wi-fi, ✕ (☎01687 460164). Note: NTS manage island.

RUM The Small Isles, **57°00'·1N 06°15'·7W**. AC 2207, 2208. HW −0500 on Dover; −0035 and −0·3m on Ullapool; ML 2·4m; Duration 0600. SNH owns Is. The mountains (809m) are unmistakable. Landing is only allowed at L Scresort on E side; no dogs beyond village limit. Beware drying rks 1ca off N point of ent and almost 3ca off S point. The head of the loch dries 2ca out; ⚓ off slip on S side or further in, to NE of jetty. Hbr is open to E winds/swell. Facilities: (eco) by landing pier, ✉ (limited) ✕ ferry to Mallaig.

EIGG HARBOUR The Small Isles, **56°52'·6N 06°07'·6W**. AC 2207. HW −0523 on Dover. See 9.8.12. Entering from N or E use Sgeir nam Bagh (Ferry Terminal) Dir lt 245° Fl WRG 3s, leads between Garbh Sgeir Bn Fl (2) G 10s & Flod Sgeir Bn Fl R 5s. An Sgùrr is a conspic 391m high peak/ridge brg 281°/1·3M from Sgeir nam Bagh. Most of hbr dries, but good ⚓ 1ca NE of Galmisdale Pt pier, except in NE winds when yachts should go through the narrows and ⚓ in South Bay in 6–8m; tide runs hard in the narrows. Also ⚓ in 2·5m at Poll nam Partan, about 2ca N of Flod Sgeir. SE point of Eilean Chathastail Fl 6s 24m 8M, vis 181°-shore, W tr. VHF Ch 08 *Eigg Hbr*. HM ☎ via (01687) 482428. repairs. **Pierhead** ✉ ✕ ☎01687 482487. **Cleadale village** (2M to N).

MUCK The Small Isles, **56°49'·8N 06°13'·3W**. AC 2207. Tides approx as Eigg, 9.8.12. Port Mór at SE end is the main hbr, with a deep pool inside offlying rks, but open to S'lies. Approach: Dir lt Fl WRG 3s 7m 11M (vis 1M by day) leads between Dubh Sgeir (Fl(2) R 10s) and Bogha Ruadh (Fl(2) G 10s) rks; see 9.8.4. ⚓ towards the NW side of inlet; NE side has drying rks. To N of Is, Bagh a' Ghallanaich is ⚓ protected from S. Few facilities.

9.8.13 LOCH SUNART

Highland **56°39'·49N 06°00'·07W** ❁❁✪✪✿✿

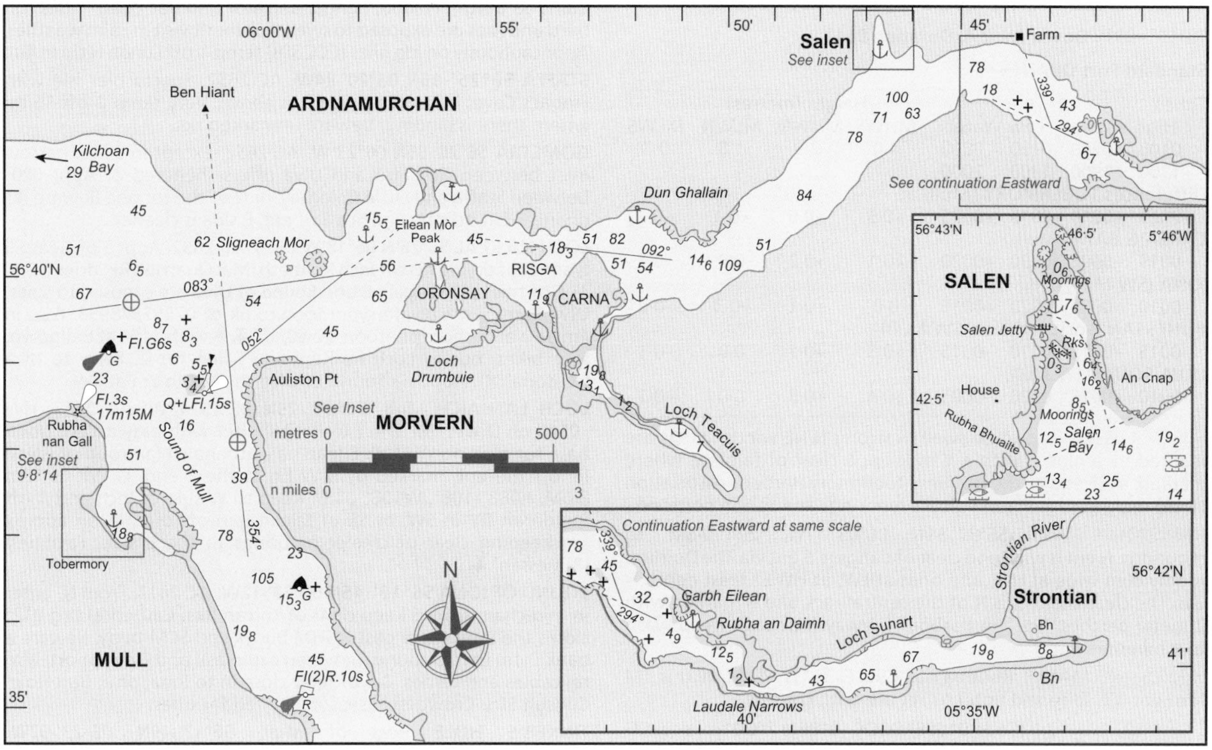

CHARTS AC 5611, 2171, 2392, 2394; Imray C65, 2800

TIDES Salen –0500 Dover; ML 2·0

Standard Port OBAN (⟶)

Times				Height (metres)			
High Water		Low Water		MHWS	MHWN	MLWN	MLWS
0100	0700	0100	0800	4·0	2·9	1·8	0·7
1300	1900	1300	2000				
Differences SALEN (Loch Sunart)							
–0015	+0015	+0010	+0005	+0·6	+0·5	–0·1	–0·1

SHELTER 🅐s at Kilchoan Bay (2M N of Ardmore Pt). ⚓s in Loch Drumbuie (S of Oronsay) sheltered in all winds; in Sailean Mór (N of Oronsay) convenient and easy ent; between Oronsay and Carna; in Loch Teacuis (very tricky ent); E of Carna; Salen Bay, with 🅐s and pontoon, open only to SSE (see facilities); Garbh Eilean (NW of Rubha an Daimh), and E of sand spit by Strontian R.

NAVIGATION **West WPT**, 56°39´·69N 06°03´·07W, 083°/3·7M to Creag nan Sgarbh (NW tip of Orinsay). **South WPT**, 56°38´·00N 06°00´·65W, 1M S of Auliston Pt; there are extensive rky reefs, The Stirks W of this pt. AC 2394 and detailed directions are needed to navigate the 17M long loch, particularly in its upper reaches. Beware Ross Rk, S of Risga; Broad Rk, E of Risga; Dun Ghallain Rk; shoals extending 3ca NNW from Eilean mo Shlinneag off S shore; drying rock 1ca W of Garbh Eilean and strong streams at sp in Laudale Narrows. Fish farms on both sides of the loch.

LIGHTS AND MARKS Unlit. Transits as on the chart: from W WPT, Risga on with N tip of Oronsay at 083°; N pt of Carna on with top of Risga 092°. From S WPT, Ben Hiant bearing 354°, thence Eilean Mor Peak at 052°. Further up the loch, 339° and 294°, as on chartlet, are useful. Other transits are shown on AC 2394.

COMMUNICATIONS (Code 01967) CGOC (01851) 702013; ⊜ (0141) 887 9369; Dr 431231. No VHF, except at Salen Bay (below).

FACILITIES

Kilchoan Bay (56°41'·5N 06°07'·3W); ☎(01972) 510305, 4 🅐s £13/night, WC, showers, Ⓟ Ⓓ, shop, hotel (1M).

Salen Bay (56°42´·39N 05°46´·17W); www.salenjetty.co.uk ☎(01967) 431510, mob 07909944494. VHF Ch 80 (occas). Keep on E side of entrance to avoid a drying reef on W side. Pontoon 8 Ⓥ, O/night £10< 6m <£2·40 /m, £5 <4hrs; 4 R 🅐s(15t) (other moorings private); buoy advised, as bottom is generally foul. slip, water, fuel, gas, shop, ✕, launderette.

Acharacle (2½M), ✉, shop, ⇌ (bus to L. Ailort/Ft William), ✈ Oban.

Strontian water, Ⓟ, ✉, shop, gas, launderette, hotel, bus to Ft William.

ANCHORAGES IN COLL AND TIREE (Argyll and Bute)

ARINAGOUR, Loch Eatharna, Coll, **56°37´·0N 06°31´·2W**. AC 5611, 2171, 2474. HW –0530 on Dover; ML 1·4m; Duration 0600; see 9.8.12. Good shelter except with SE swell or strong winds from ENE to SSW. Enter at SHM buoy, Fl G 6s, marking Bogha Mòr. Thence NW to Arinagour ferry pier, 2 FR(vert) 10m and Dir Oc WRG 7s. Beware McQuarrie's Rk (dries 2·9m) 1ca E of pier hd and unmarked drying rks further N on E side of fairway. ✠ and hotel are conspic ahead. Continue N towards old stone pier; ⚓ S of it or use 12🅐s S of Dgeir Dubh for boats <10t at £10/night, pay at ferry terminal. Also ⚓ E of Eilean Eatharna. Piermaster ☎(01879) 230347; VHF Ch 31. Facilities: HIE Trading Post ☎230349, slip, water, fuel, gas, launderette, shop, ✕. **Village** Ⓟ, water, Ⓟ, ✉ Ferry to Oban (⇌).

GOTT BAY, Tiree, **56°30'·74N 06°48'·07W**. AC 5611, 2474. Tides as 9.8.12; HW –0540 on Dover. HM ☎(01879) 230337, VHF Ch 31. Adequate shelter in calm weather, but exposed in winds ENE to S. (in which case use Wilson hbr in Balephetrish Bay IM W, Ldg lts F.G/Oc.G). The bay, at NE end of island, can be identified by conspic latticed tr at Scarinish about 8ca SW of ent, with lt Fl 3s 11m 16M close by (obscd over hbr). Appr on NW track, keeping to SW side of bay which is obstructed on NE side by Soa Is and drying rks. The ferry pier at S side of ent has FR ldg lts 286½°. ⚓ 1ca NW of pier head in 3m on sand; slip at pier. Facilities: Ⓟ Ⓓ, gas, shop, ✕, launderette, ✉ at Scarinish (½M), Ferry to Oban (⇌).

9.8.14 TOBERMORY

Mull (Argyll and Bute) **56°37′·19N 06°03′·87W** ❀❀❀◊◊✿✿✿

CHARTS AC 5611, 2171, 2390, 2474; Imray C65, 2800

TIDES –0519 Dover; ML 2·4; Duration 0610

Standard Port OBAN (⟶)

Times				Height (metres)			
High Water		Low Water		MHWS	MHWN	MLWN	MLWS
0100	0700	0100	0800	4·0	2·9	1·8	0·7
1300	1900	1300	2000				
Differences TOBERMORY (Mull)							
+0025	+0010	+0015	+0025	+0·5	+0·6	+0·1	+0·2
CARSAIG BAY (S Mull)							
–0015	–0005	–0030	+0020	+0·1	+0·2	0·0	–0·1
IONA (SW Mull)							
–0010	–0005	–0020	+0015	0·0	+0·1	–0·3	–0·2
BUNESSAN (Loch Lathaich, SW Mull)							
–0015	–0015	–0010	–0015	+0·3	+0·1	0·0	–0·1
ULVA SOUND (W Mull)							
–0010	–0015	0000	–0005	+0·4	+0·3	0·0	–0·1

SHELTER Good, but some swell in strong N/NE winds. 26 ⚲s are marked by a blue ◯ with a Y pick-up. ⚓ clear of fairway, where marked; at SE end of The Doirlinn. Tobermory Harbour Association (THA) manages local and visitor's moorings and ⊆ on pontoon.

NAVIGATION WPT 56°37′·59N 06°03′·17W, 224°/0·5M to moorings. N ent is wide and clear of dangers. S ent via The Doirlinn is only 80m wide at HW, and dries at LW; at HW±2 least depth is 2m. The clear channel is N of the central rock and is marked with 2 metal perches. No ⚓ in harbour fairway (buoyed). Keep wash to a minimum.

LIGHTS AND MARKS Rhubha nan Gall, Fl 3s 17m 15M, W tr is 1M N of ent. Ch spire and hotel turret are both conspic.

COMMUNICATIONS (Code 01688) CGOC (01851) 702013; Local CG 302200; Police 101; Dr 302013. Cal-Mac Piermaster 302017; THA Moorings Officer ☎302876, mob 07917 832497.

VHF Ch 16 12 (HO), M.

FACILITIES www.tobermoryharbour.co.uk 25⚲s £15/nt ⌞ <25′; pontoon 50⊆ £2.25 inc ⚡ ⛽ ⛽; **Taigh Solais** (THA Harbour Building) WC ⚑ ▣ wi-fi, Ⓟ in car park.

Western Isles YC ☎302371. **Town** ⛽ ✎ Ⓔ ⛽ ACA ✉ Ⓑ Ⓒ 🛒 ✕ ⛴ ⇄ (ferry to Oban), ✈ (helipad on golf course).

SOUND OF MULL Dearg Sgeir Fl 6s 7m 8M marks Eileann Glasa, 2·3M to SE Rubha na Leitrach, 2 F R (vert), marks N ent to Fishnish Bay.

SALEN BAY (Mull, **56°31′·44N 05°56′·82W**). Beware Bogha, drying rks 6ca E of the bay; ⚲s £10; ⌞ at Salen Jetty, fee £1/person. **Facilities** ⛽ ⛽. **Village** Dr, ✎ Ⓔ ⛽ ✉ 🛒 ✕.

CRAIGNURE, (Mull, **56°28′·37N 05°42′·25W**) ldg lts 241°, both FR 10/12m. Facilities: ⛽ ✉ 🛒 ⛴ Ferry to Oban. Tides, see 9.8.15.

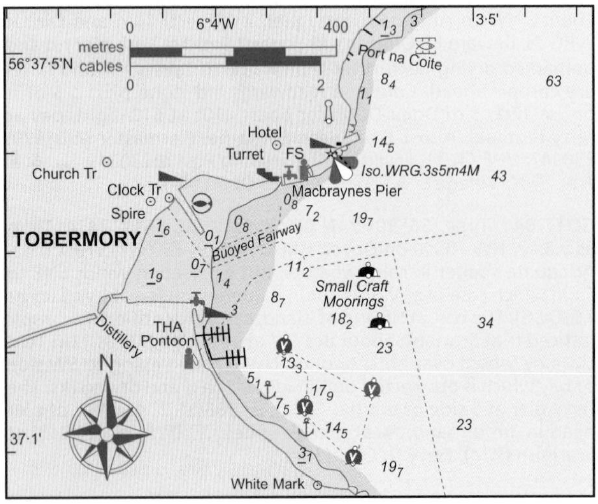

ANCHORAGES on WEST and SOUTH COASTS OF MULL **(Anti-clockwise from the north) SDs essential** Tides as 9.8.14.

TRESHNISH ISLES 56°29′N 06°31′W. AC 2652. Main Is (N to S) are: Cairn na Burgh, Fladda, Lunga, Bac Mòr and Bac Beag. Tides run hard and isles are exposed to swell, but merit visit in calm weather. Appr cautiously on ldg lines (CCC SDs) temp ⚓ off Lunga N tip in 4m.

STAFFA 56°25′·96N 06°20′·34W. AC 2652. Spectacular isle with Fingal's Cave, but same caveats as above. Very temp ⚓ off SE tip where there is landing; beware unmarked rks.

GOMETRA 56°28′·85N 06°23′W. AC 2652. Except in S'lies, narrow inlet between Gometra and Ulva offers sheltered ⚓. Appr 020° between Staffa and Little Colonsay, or N of the former. Beware rks drying 3·2m, to stbd and 5ca S of ent. E side is cleaner.

LOCH NA KEAL 56°26′N 06°18′W (ent). AC 2652. Appr S of Geasgill Is and N of drying rks off **Inch Kenneth**, MacQuarrie's Rk, dries 0·8m. ⚓s E of this Is, in Cragaig B and **Sound of Ulva** are exposed to S'lies. **Ulva Ferry** www.ulvaferrypontoon.co.uk ☎ 07557378953; 8⊆ in 4m on walk-ashore pontoon, £2·50; ⚡ ⛽ ⛽ wi-fi, ✕ ⚑ at Ballgown. Hire bikes, bus to Loch na Keal and Salen for ▣. Ferry to Ulva (seasonal ✕). Appr via Sound of Ulva shelves to 2m at LW.

LOCH LATHAICH Mull, **56°19′·29N 06°15′·47W**. AC 2617. HW –0545 on Dover; ML 2·4. Excellent shelter with easy access; good base for cruising W Mull. Eilean na Liathanaich (a group of islets) lie off the ent, marked by a W bn at the E end, Fl WR 6s 12m 8/6M, R088°-108°, W108°-088°. Keep to W side of loch and ⚓ off Bendoran BY in SW, or SE of Eilean Ban off the pier in approx 5m keeping clear of creeler moorings to the E side. Facilities: (Bunessan) ⛽ ✉ 🛒 ✕ ⛴.

SOUND OF IONA 56°19′·45N 06°23′·12W. AC 2617. From N, enter in mid-chan; from S keep clear of Torran Rks. Cathedral brg 012° closes the Iona shore past 2 SHM buoys and SCM buoy. Beware a bank 0·1m in mid-sound, between cathedral and Fionnphort; also tel cables and ferries. ⚓ S of ferry close in to Iona, or in Bull Hole. Consult SDs. Crowded in season; limited facilities.

TINKER'S HOLE Ross of Mull, **56°17′·49N 06°23′·07W**. AC 2617. Beware Torran Rks, reefs extending 5M S and SW of Erraid. Usual app from S, avoiding Rankin's Rks, drying 0·8m, and rk, dries 2·3m, between Eilean nam Muc and Erraid. Popular ⚓ in mid-pool between Eilean Dubh and Erraid.

CARSAIG BAY Ross of Mull, **56°19′·19N 05°59′·07W**. AC 2386. Temp, fair weather ⚓s to N of Gamhnach Mhòr, reef 2m high, or close into NW corner of bay. ⌞ at stone quay on NE side.

LOCH SPELVE Mull, **56°23′N 05°41′W**. AC 2387. Tides as Oban. Landlocked water, prone to squalls off surrounding hills. Ent narrows to ½ca due to shoal S side and drying rk N side marked by G pole, Fl G 5s 3m 2M, 56°23′·24N 05°42′·04W. CCC SDs give local ldg lines. ⚓s in SW and NW arms, clear of fish farms. Pier at Croggan; no facilities.

ANCHORAGES ALONG LOCH LINNHE (AC 5611, 2378, 2379, 2380) **LYNN OF LORN 56°33′N 05°25′·2W**. At NE end are ⚓s off **Port Appin**, clear of ferry and cables (beware Appin Rks); and in Airds Bay, open to SW. At NW tip of Lismore, Port Ramsey offers good ⚓s between the 3 main islets.

Linnhe Marina ☎(01631) 730401 offers pontoon and moorings.

LOCH CRERAN 56°32′·14N 05°25′·22W. Tides 9.8.16. Enter at Airds Pt, Dir lt 050°, Fl WRG 2s, W vis 041-058°. Chan turns 90° stbd with streams of 4kn. Sgeir Callich, rky ridge extends NE to SHM By, Fl G 3s; ⚓ W of it. ⚲s (max LOA 7m) off Barcaldine; also 3⚲s (max LOA 9m) off Creagan Inn, ☎(01631) 573250. Bridge has 12m clearance. Beware of extensive marine farms in loch.

LOCH A'CHOIRE 56°22′.2N 05°18′.6W on west side of Loch Linnhe. Entrance offers no difficulties, fish farm on north side and restaurant moorings (condition unknown) 6⚲s E of boathouse, ⚲ in SW corner or anchor as depths permit. Sheltered from west but beware downdrafts in strong winds.

LOCH LEVEN 56°42′N 05°12′W. Tides 9.8.16. Ballachulish Bay ⚓s: N shore Onich and off St Brides, S shore Kentallen Bay (deep). Approach Ballachullish Bridge (16m clnce) on 114°. Moorings are 4ca to ENE with sheltered ⚓ at Poll an Dùnan, ent W of perch. Loch navigable 7M to Kinlochleven. **Ballachulish**: Hotels, ✉ Ⓑ 🛒 ✕.

CORRAN NARROWS 56°43′·27N 05°14′·34W. AC 2372. Sp rate 6kn. Well buoyed; Corran Pt lt ho, Iso WRG 4s, and lt bn 5ca NE. ⚓ 5ca NW of Pt, off Camas Aiseig pier/slip.

9.8.15 LOCH ALINE

Highland **56°32'·09N 05°46'·47W** ⚙⚙⚙◊✿✿✿

CHARTS AC 5611, 2390; Imray C65, 2800

TIDES –0523 Dover; Duration 0610

Standard Port OBAN (⟶)

Times				**Height (metres)**			
High Water		Low Water		MHWS	MHWN	MLWN	MLWS
0100	0700	0100	0800	4·0	2·9	1·8	0·7
1300	1900	1300	2000				
Differences LOCH ALINE							
+0012	+0012	ND	ND	+0·5	+0·3	ND	ND
SALEN (Sound of Mull)							
+0045	+0015	+0020	+0030	+0·2	+0·2	–0·1	0·0
CRAIGNURE (Sound of Mull)							
+0030	+0005	+0010	+0015	0·0	+0·1	–0·1	–0·1

SHELTER Very good. ⚓s in SE end of loch and in N and E part of loch. Temp berth on old stone slip on W side of ent, depth and ferries permitting. Walk ashore pontoons N of sand mine pier with 10 Y ⚓ for boats <12m and 4 Crown Estate ⚓ on E side of loch.

NAVIGATION WPT 56°31'·49N 05°46'·37W, 176°/0·9M toldg bn. Bn (bright orange) leads 357°, 100m W of Bogha Lurcain, drying rk off Bolorkle Pt on E side of ent. Buoyed ent is easy, but narrow with a bar (min depth 2·1m); stream runs 2½kn at springs. Beware coasters (which completely fill the ent) from the sand mine going to/from the jetty and ferries to/from Mull. Last 5ca of loch dries.

LIGHTS AND MARKS Ardtornish Pt lt ho, 1M SSE of ent, Fl (2) WRG 10s 8m 8/6M. Lts and buoys as chartlet. War memorial, 9m high (inconspic), stands on W side of ent. Dir Ldg lt, Oc WRG 6s 4M, 357°, co-located with front ldg bn (Or). 1M up the loch on E side a bn with rusty ● topmark marks a reef; ½M further up a similar bn marks a larger reef on W side. Clock tr is very conspic at head of loch.

COMMUNICATIONS (Code 01967) CGOC (01851) 702013; ⊖ (0141) 887 9369; Ⓗ (01631) 563727; Dr 421252. No VHF.

FACILITIES Pontoons, www.lochalineharbour.co.uk ☎ 07583 800500, 26 ⛵ inc Ⓥ £2·50, ⚓ £15/night, WC ⛽ ⊡. **Village:** ⛽ at pier, ⛽ Ⓟ ⛽ ✉ 🛒 ✕ ◻ (Ⓑ ⇌ ✈ at Oban), Ferry to Fishnish Bay (Mull).

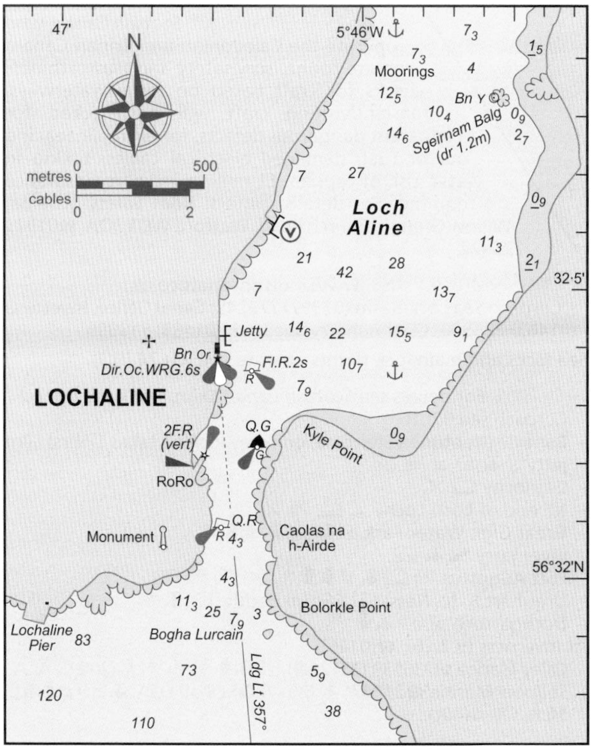

9.8.16 FORT WILLIAM/CORPACH

Highland 56°48'·99N 05°07'·07W (off Fort William)

CHARTS AC 5611, 2372, 2380, 5617; Imray C65, C63, 2800

TIDES –0535 Dover; ML 2·3; Duration 0610

Standard Port OBAN (⟶)

Times				**Height (metres)**			
High Water		Low Water		MHWS	MHWN	MLWN	MLWS
0100	0700	0100	0800	4·0	2·9	1·8	0·7
1300	1900	1300	2000				
Differences CORPACH							
0000	+0020	+0040	0000	0·0	0·0	–0·2	–0·2
LOCH EIL (Head)							
+0025	+0045	+0105	+0025	ND	ND	ND	ND
CORRAN NARROWS							
+0007	+0007	+0004	+0004	+0·4	+0·4	–0·1	0·0
LOCH LEVEN (Head)							
+0045	+0045	+0045	+0045	ND	ND	ND	ND
LOCH LINNHE (Port Appin)							
–0005	–0005	–0030	0000	+0·2	+0·2	+0·1	+0·1
LOCH CRERAN (Barcaldine Pier)							
+0010	+0020	+0040	+0015	+0·1	+0·1	0·0	+0·1
LOCH CRERAN (Head)							
+0015	+0025	+0120	+0020	–0·3	–0·3	–0·4	–0·3

SHELTER ⚓ off Fort William pier exposed to winds SW thro' N to NE. Other ⚓ in Camus na Gall; SSW of Eilean A Bhealaidh; and off Corpach Basin, where there is a waiting pontoon. Sea lock usually available HW±4 during canal hrs. Caledonian Canal see 9.8.17.

NAVIGATION Corpach WPT 56°50'·29N 05°07'·07W, 315°/0·32M to lock ent.

Beware McLean Rk, dries 0·3m, buoyed, 8ca N of Fort William. Lochy Flats dry 3ca off the E bank. In Annat Narrows at ent to Loch Eil streams reach 5kn.

LIGHTS AND MARKS Iso WRG 4s lt is at N jetty of sea lock ent, W310°-335°. Jetty NE of Eileann nan Craobh lit Fl (2) R 6s 4m 2M. A long pier/viaduct off Ft William is unlit.

COMMUNICATIONS (Code 01397) CGOC (01851) 702013; ⊖ 702948; Police 101; Dr 703136. HM 772249.

Corpach Lock VHF Ch **74** 16 (during canal hours).

FACILITIES **Fort William Pier** ☎703881, ⛴ ⛴ ⛵. **Town** Ⓟ ✕ ⚒ ⊡ ⛽ ACA ✉ Ⓑ 🛒 ✕ ◻ YC Ⓗ ⇌.

Corpach Corpach Basin ☎772249, ⛴ ⛵ ⛽ ⛽.

Lochaber YC ☎703576, ⛵ ⛴ ⛴ ⛽. **Services** ✕ ⚒ ⊡ ⛽ Divers. **Village** Ⓟ Ⓓ ✉ Ⓑ 🛒 ✕ ◻ ⇌.

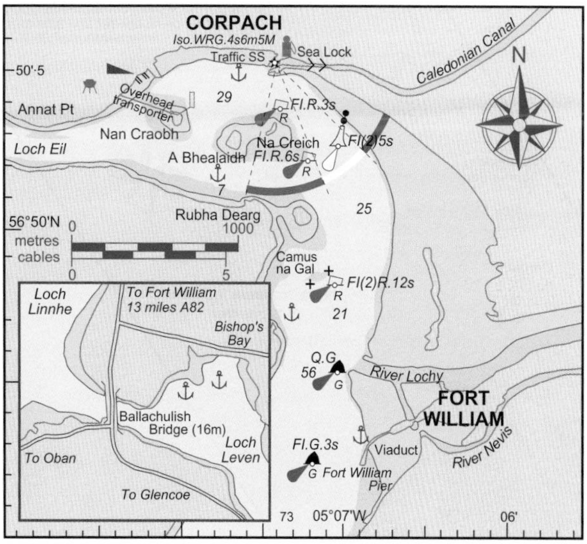

9.8.17 CALEDONIAN CANAL

Highland

CHARTS AC 1791, 5617; Imray C63; *Scottish Canals Skippers Guide*

TIDES Tidal differences: Corpach –0455 on Dover; See 9.8.16. Clachnaharry: +0116 on Dover; See 9.7.16.

SHELTER Corpach is at the SW ent of the Caledonian Canal, see 9.8.16; the sea locks at both ends do not open LW±2 at springs. For best shelter transit the sea lock and lie above the double lock. Numerous pontoons along the canal; cost is included in the canal dues. For Inverness see 9.7.16.

NAVIGATION The 60M canal consists of 38M through Lochs Lochy, Oich and Ness, connected by 22M of canal.

Loch Oich is part of a hydro-electric scheme which varies the water level. The passage normally takes two full days, possibly longer in summer; absolute minimum is 14hrs. Speed limit is 5kn in the canal sections. There are 10 swing bridges; road traffic has priority at peak hrs. Do not pass bridges without the keeper's instructions.

LOCKS There are 29 locks: 14 between Loch Linnhe (Corpach), via Lochs Lochy and Oich to the summit (106ft above sea level) and 15 from the summit down via Loch Ness to Inverness. **The Canal has endured winter closures in the recent past check www.scottishcanals.co.uk for works in progress**

Hours: Winter Mon-Fri 0900-1600
Spring Mon-Sun 0830-1730
Summer Mon-Sun 0800-1730
Autumn Mon-Sun 0830-1730

Dues payable at Corpach: transit/lock fee outward £16/m for 8-day passage or less; return £12/m. £20/m is charged for a 2-week sojourn. For regulations and useful booklet *Scottish Canals Skipper's Guide* apply: Canal Manager, Canal Office, Seaport Marina, Muirtown Wharf, Inverness IV3 5LE, ☎(01463) 233140, or download from: www.waterscape.com

LIGHTS AND MARKS See 9.8.16 and 9.7.16 for ent lts. Channel is marked by posts, cairns and unlit buoys, PHM on the NW side of the chan and SHM on the SE side.

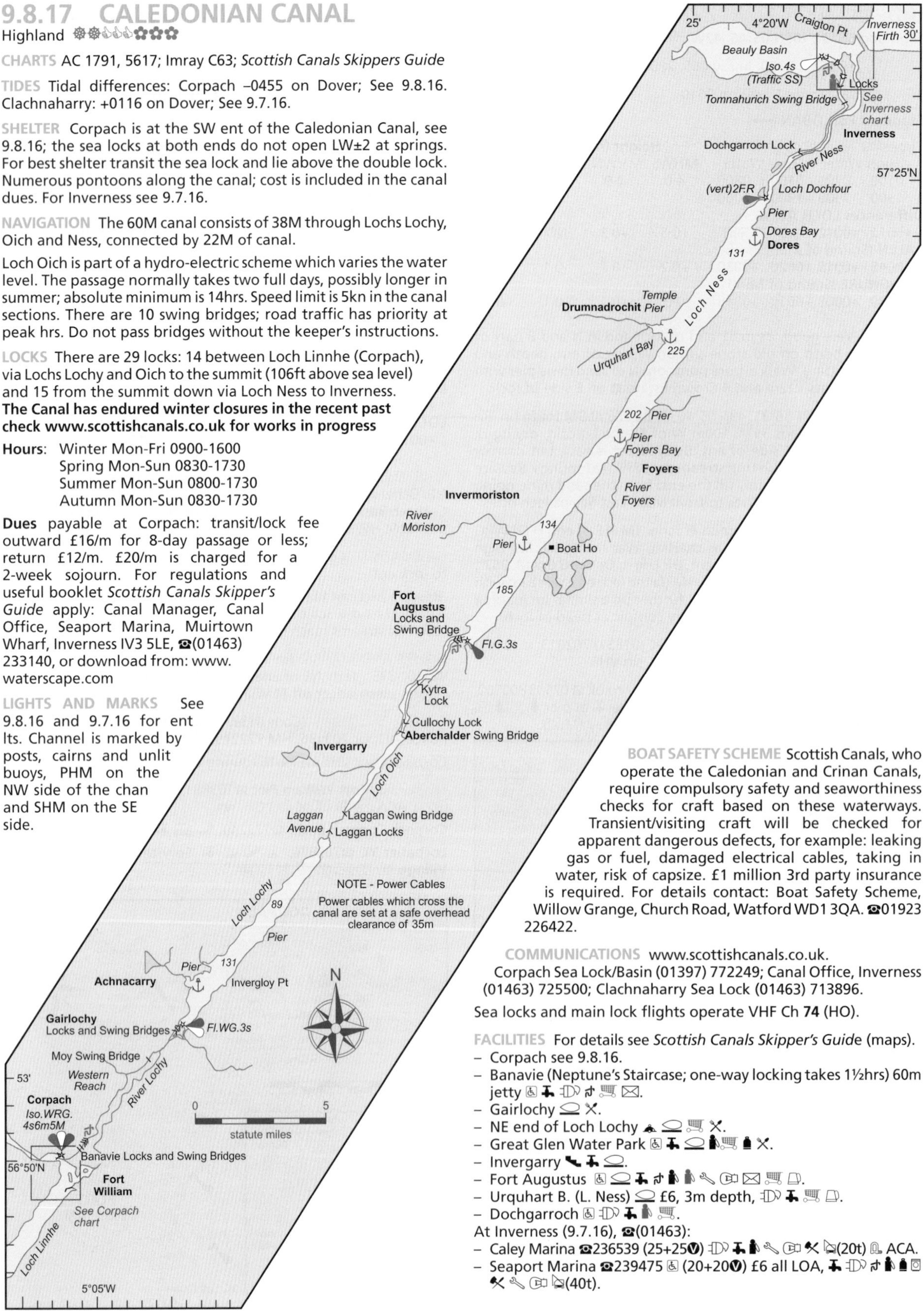

BOAT SAFETY SCHEME Scottish Canals, who operate the Caledonian and Crinan Canals, require compulsory safety and seaworthiness checks for craft based on these waterways. Transient/visiting craft will be checked for apparent dangerous defects, for example: leaking gas or fuel, damaged electrical cables, taking in water, risk of capsize. £1 million 3rd party insurance is required. For details contact: Boat Safety Scheme, Willow Grange, Church Road, Watford WD1 3QA. ☎01923 226422.

COMMUNICATIONS www.scottishcanals.co.uk. Corpach Sea Lock/Basin (01397) 772249; Canal Office, Inverness (01463) 725500; Clachnaharry Sea Lock (01463) 713896.

Sea locks and main lock flights operate VHF Ch **74** (HO).

FACILITIES For details see *Scottish Canals Skipper's Guide* (maps).

- Corpach see 9.8.16.
- Banavie (Neptune's Staircase; one-way locking takes 1½hrs) 60m jetty.
- Gairlochy.
- NE end of Loch Lochy.
- Great Glen Water Park.
- Invergarry.
- Fort Augustus.
- Urquhart B. (L. Ness) £6, 3m depth.
- Dochgarroch.

At Inverness (9.7.16), ☎(01463):

- Caley Marina ☎236539 (25+25Ⓥ) (20t) ACA.
- Seaport Marina ☎239475 (20+20Ⓥ) £6 all LOA, (40t).

STANDARD TIME (UT)
For Summer Time add ONE hour in **non-shaded areas**

OBAN LAT 56°25'N LONG 5°29'W

TIMES AND HEIGHTS OF HIGH AND LOW WATERS

Dates in red are SPRINGS
Dates in blue are NEAPS

YEAR **2018**

JANUARY

Date	Time	m	Date	Time	m
1	0440	3.9	16	0519	3.8
	1108	0.9		1140	1.4
M	1714	4.1	TU	1733	3.7
	2321	0.7		2359	1.2
2	0526	4.1	17	0556	3.9
	1159	0.7		1216	1.3
TU	1758	4.1	W	1809	3.8
○			●		
3	0008	0.5	18	0034	1.1
	0610	4.2		0632	4.0
W	1249	0.6	TH	1252	1.3
	1841	4.1		1843	3.8
4	0055	0.5	19	0108	1.1
	0655	4.2		0706	4.0
TH	1337	0.7	F	1327	1.3
	1925	4.0		1914	3.8
5	0142	0.5	20	0138	1.2
	0739	4.1		0738	3.9
F	1425	0.8	SA	1400	1.3
	2009	3.8		1943	3.7
6	0229	0.6	21	0206	1.2
	0824	3.9		0809	3.8
SA	1514	1.0	SU	1430	1.4
	2054	3.6		2013	3.6
7	0317	0.8	22	0234	1.3
	0910	3.7		0841	3.7
SU	1605	1.3	M	1502	1.5
	2142	3.3		2047	3.5
8	0407	1.1	23	0309	1.4
	0959	3.4		0919	3.6
M	1659	1.5	TU	1543	1.6
◑	2239	3.1		2128	3.3
9	0500	1.3	24	0354	1.5
	1058	3.2		1007	3.4
TU	1800	1.7	W	1638	1.7
	2356	3.0	◐	2218	3.2
10	0558	1.5	25	0452	1.6
	1220	3.0		1109	3.3
W	1913	1.8	TH	1747	1.7
				2324	3.1
11	0120	2.9	26	0608	1.7
	0704	1.7		1240	3.2
TH	1354	3.0	F	1903	1.7
	2030	1.8			
12	0226	3.0	27	0058	3.1
	0817	1.7		0732	1.6
F	1458	3.1	SA	1426	3.3
	2129	1.7		2016	1.5
13	0316	3.2	28	0237	3.2
	0927	1.7		0855	1.4
SA	1541	3.3	SU	1534	3.5
	2213	1.6		2122	1.3
14	0400	3.4	29	0343	3.5
	1020	1.6		1007	1.2
SU	1618	3.4	M	1627	3.7
	2251	1.4		2219	1.0
15	0440	3.6	30	0435	3.8
	1102	1.5		1105	0.9
M	1655	3.6	TU	1712	3.9
	2325	1.3		2311	0.7
			31	0521	4.0
				1155	0.7
			W	1754	4.0
			○	2358	0.5

FEBRUARY

Date	Time	m	Date	Time	m
1	0604	4.2	16	0016	1.0
	1242	0.6		0616	3.9
TH	1834	4.1	F	1234	1.0
				1828	3.8
2	0044	0.4	17	0047	0.9
	0645	4.2		0649	4.0
F	1326	0.6	SA	1306	1.0
	1913	4.0		1855	3.8
3	0128	0.3	18	0115	0.9
	0726	4.2		0718	4.0
SA	1409	0.7	SU	1337	1.0
	1952	3.9		1921	3.8
4	0211	0.5	19	0142	0.9
	0805	4.0		0746	3.9
SU	1451	0.9	M	1404	1.0
	2029	3.7		1949	3.7
5	0253	0.7	20	0210	0.9
	0843	3.8		0817	3.8
M	1532	1.1	TU	1435	1.1
	2107	3.5		2023	3.6
6	0336	0.9	21	0245	1.1
	0921	3.5		0853	3.6
TU	1615	1.4	W	1514	1.2
	2147	3.2		2101	3.5
7	0421	1.2	22	0328	1.2
	1003	3.2		0937	3.4
W	1703	1.7	TH	1605	1.4
◑	2235	3.0		2148	3.3
8	0511	1.5	23	0424	1.4
	1055	3.0		1035	3.2
TH	1801	1.8	F	1711	1.5
	2351	2.9	◐	2249	3.1
9	0609	1.7	24	0544	1.6
	1221	2.8		1205	3.0
F	1914	1.9	SA	1832	1.6
10	0137	2.9	25	0027	3.0
	0719	1.9		0717	1.6
SA	1437	2.8	SU	1421	3.1
	2050	1.9		1953	1.5
11	0251	3.0	26	0231	3.1
	0856	1.8		0851	1.4
SU	1540	3.0	M	1535	3.3
	2153	1.7		2106	1.3
12	0343	3.2	27	0342	3.4
	1009	1.7		1006	1.1
M	1611	3.2	TU	1626	3.5
	2236	1.5		2208	1.0
13	0425	3.4	28	0431	3.7
	1053	1.5		1101	0.9
TU	1645	3.4	W	1708	3.8
	2312	1.3		2259	0.7
14	0504	3.7			
	1128	1.3			
W	1721	3.6			
	2344	1.1			
15	0541	3.8			
	1201	1.2			
TH	1756	3.8			
●					

MARCH

Date	Time	m	Date	Time	m
1	0513	4.0	16	0519	3.8
	1146	0.6		1137	1.0
TH	1745	3.9	F	1734	3.7
	2346	0.4		2350	0.9
2	0552	4.2	17	0554	3.9
	1228	0.5		1208	0.8
F	1820	4.0	SA	1805	3.8
○			●		
3	0029	0.3	18	0019	0.7
	0629	4.2		0625	4.0
SA	1308	0.5	SU	1240	0.7
	1855	4.0		1830	3.9
4	0111	0.3	19	0048	0.6
	0706	4.2		0653	4.0
SU	1346	0.6	M	1309	0.7
	1929	4.0		1856	3.9
5	0150	0.4	20	0118	0.6
	0740	4.0		0722	4.0
M	1422	0.8	TU	1340	0.7
	2001	3.8		1926	3.8
6	0228	0.6	21	0151	0.7
	0813	3.8		0755	3.8
TU	1458	1.0	W	1414	0.8
	2033	3.6		2001	3.7
7	0306	0.9	22	0229	0.8
	0846	3.5		0833	3.6
W	1535	1.3	TH	1455	1.0
	2107	3.4		2041	3.5
8	0346	1.2	23	0315	1.0
	0920	3.2		0918	3.4
TH	1619	1.6	F	1546	1.2
	2146	3.1		2128	3.3
9	0433	1.5	24	0415	1.3
	1001	3.0		1017	3.1
F	1713	1.8	SA	1652	1.4
◑	2240	2.9	◐	2232	3.1
10	0529	1.8	25	0539	1.5
	1100	2.7		1155	2.8
SA	1819	1.9	SU	1812	1.5
11	0034	2.8	26	0017	2.9
	0637	1.9		0713	1.5
SU	1408	2.6	M	1415	2.9
	1947	1.9		1934	1.4
12	0227	2.9	27	0226	3.1
	0814	1.9		0852	1.4
M	1531	2.8	TU	1524	3.1
	2123	1.7		2050	1.2
13	0325	3.1	28	0331	3.4
	0952	1.7		1000	1.1
TU	1557	3.0	W	1614	3.4
	2212	1.5		2152	0.9
14	0406	3.3	29	0417	3.7
	1033	1.5		1049	0.8
W	1627	3.3	TH	1653	3.6
	2248	1.3		2243	0.7
15	0444	3.6	30	0456	3.9
	1106	1.2		1130	0.7
TH	1701	3.5	F	1727	3.8
	2320	1.0		2327	0.5
			31	0533	4.1
				1208	0.6
			SA	1759	4.0
			○		

APRIL

Date	Time	m	Date	Time	m
1	0009	0.4	16	0557	4.0
	0607	4.1		1208	0.6
SU	1244	0.6	M	1802	3.9
	1831	4.0	●		
2	0049	0.4	17	0021	0.5
	0641	4.1		0628	4.0
M	1319	0.6	TU	1242	0.5
	1903	4.0		1831	3.9
3	0127	0.5	18	0058	0.5
	0713	4.0		0700	4.0
TU	1352	0.8	W	1318	0.5
	1933	3.9		1906	3.9
4	0202	0.7	19	0138	0.6
	0744	3.8		0737	3.8
W	1426	1.0	TH	1358	0.6
	2004	3.7		1945	3.8
5	0238	1.0	20	0222	0.7
	0815	3.5		0819	3.6
TH	1502	1.3	F	1443	0.8
	2037	3.5		2029	3.6
6	0316	1.3	21	0314	1.0
	0848	3.3		0908	3.3
F	1544	1.5	SA	1536	1.0
	2115	3.3		2120	3.3
7	0402	1.6	22	0419	1.2
	0924	3.0		1011	3.0
SA	1635	1.7	SU	1640	1.2
	2203	3.0	◐	2227	3.1
8	0457	1.8	23	0538	1.4
	1013	2.8		1201	2.8
SU	1738	1.9	M	1755	1.3
◑	2323	2.8			
9	0605	2.0	24	0012	3.0
	1224	2.6		0709	1.5
M	1853	1.9	TU	1356	2.9
				1913	1.3
10	0150	2.8	25	0205	3.1
	0730	2.0		0841	1.3
TU	1446	2.7	W	1503	3.1
	2025	1.8		2028	1.2
11	0255	3.0	26	0308	3.3
	0908	1.8		0943	1.1
W	1525	2.9	TH	1552	3.3
	2129	1.6		2130	1.0
12	0337	3.3	27	0355	3.6
	0955	1.5		1029	0.9
TH	1558	3.2	F	1629	3.5
	2210	1.3		2220	0.8
13	0414	3.5	28	0433	3.8
	1031	1.2		1108	0.8
F	1632	3.4	SA	1701	3.7
	2244	1.1		2305	0.6
14	0450	3.7	29	0509	3.9
	1104	0.9		1143	0.7
SA	1704	3.6	SU	1733	3.9
	2316	0.8		2346	0.6
15	0525	3.9	30	0543	3.9
	1136	0.7		1217	0.7
SU	1734	3.8	M	1805	3.9
	2347	0.6	○		

Chart Datum: 2·10 metres below Ordnance Datum (Newlyn). HAT is 4·5 metres above Chart Datum.

STANDARD TIME (UT)
For Summer Time add ONE hour in **non-shaded areas**

OBAN LAT 56°25′N LONG 5°29′W

TIMES AND HEIGHTS OF HIGH AND LOW WATERS

Dates in red are SPRINGS
Dates in blue are NEAPS

YEAR **2018**

MAY

Date	Time	m	Date	Time	m
1	0025	0.6	16	0606	4.0
	0615	3.9		1218	0.5
TU	1251	0.8	W	1812	3.9
	1837	3.9			
2	0102	0.7	17	0042	0.5
	0647	3.8		0644	4.0
W	1324	0.9	TH	1300	0.4
	1908	3.9		1852	3.9
3	0138	0.9	18	0128	0.5
	0719	3.7		0726	3.8
TH	1358	1.1	F	1345	0.5
	1940	3.8		1935	3.8
4	0213	1.1	19	0218	0.7
	0752	3.5		0812	3.6
F	1434	1.3	SA	1433	0.7
	2015	3.6		2022	3.7
5	0252	1.4	20	0314	0.9
	0825	3.3		0904	3.3
SA	1515	1.5	SU	1527	0.9
	2054	3.4		2116	3.4
6	0336	1.6	21	0416	1.1
	0903	3.1		1008	3.0
SU	1601	1.7	M	1627	1.1
	2140	3.2		2221	3.2
7	0429	1.8	22	0529	1.3
	0949	2.9		1147	2.9
M	1657	1.8	TU	1734	1.2
	2241	3.0		◐ 2353	3.1
8	0533	2.0	23	0653	1.4
	1107	2.7		1323	2.9
TU	1802	1.9	W	1846	1.3
◑					
9	0025	2.9	24	0132	3.1
	0647	1.9		0814	1.3
W	1333	2.7	TH	1432	3.0
	1912	1.9		1957	1.2
10	0204	3.0	25	0238	3.2
	0803	1.8		0916	1.2
TH	1436	2.9	F	1522	3.2
	2021	1.7		2101	1.1
11	0256	3.2	26	0327	3.4
	0902	1.5		1004	1.1
F	1518	3.1	SA	1559	3.4
	2115	1.4		2155	1.0
12	0338	3.5	27	0407	3.5
	0947	1.3		1043	1.0
SA	1555	3.3	SU	1633	3.6
	2158	1.2		2241	0.9
13	0416	3.7	28	0443	3.6
	1025	1.0		1118	1.0
SU	1629	3.5	M	1707	3.7
	2237	0.9		2323	0.9
14	0453	3.9	29	0518	3.7
	1102	0.7		1151	1.0
M	1702	3.7	TU	1741	3.8
	2317	0.7	○		
15	0529	4.0	30	0002	0.9
	1139	0.6		0551	3.7
TU	1735	3.9	W	1225	1.0
	● 2358	0.5		1814	3.9
			31	0039	1.0
				0625	3.7
			TH	1300	1.0
				1848	3.9

JUNE

Date	Time	m	Date	Time	m
1	0116	1.1	16	0122	0.5
	0700	3.6		0719	3.8
F	1335	1.1	SA	1333	0.4
	1923	3.8		1929	3.9
2	0153	1.3	17	0213	0.6
	0735	3.5		0806	3.6
SA	1412	1.3	SU	1422	0.5
	1959	3.7		2018	3.8
3	0232	1.4	18	0307	0.8
	0811	3.4		0858	3.4
SU	1450	1.4	M	1514	0.7
	2038	3.5		2109	3.6
4	0314	1.6	19	0405	1.0
	0848	3.2		0956	3.2
M	1530	1.6	TU	1608	0.9
	2119	3.3		2207	3.4
5	0401	1.8	20	0508	1.2
	0930	3.0		1110	3.0
TU	1614	1.7	W	1707	1.1
	2208	3.2		◐ 2317	3.2
6	0456	1.9	21	0619	1.4
	1023	2.9		1236	2.9
W	1707	1.8	TH	1811	1.2
	◑ 2310	3.1			
7	0559	1.9	22	0044	3.1
	1137	2.8		0735	1.4
TH	1807	1.8	F	1347	2.9
				1918	1.3
8	0036	3.1	23	0200	3.1
	0705	1.8		0843	1.4
F	1317	2.9	SA	1444	3.1
	1909	1.7		2026	1.3
9	0157	3.2	24	0258	3.2
	0806	1.6		0936	1.4
SA	1424	3.0	SU	1528	3.2
	2011	1.5		2126	1.3
10	0254	3.4	25	0343	3.3
	0900	1.4		1019	1.3
SU	1511	3.2	M	1607	3.4
	2109	1.3		2217	1.3
11	0341	3.6	26	0422	3.4
	0947	1.1		1056	1.2
M	1554	3.5	TU	1644	3.6
	2202	1.0		2301	1.2
12	0425	3.8	27	0459	3.5
	1031	0.8		1130	1.2
TU	1635	3.7	W	1722	3.7
	2252	0.8		2342	1.2
13	0508	3.9	28	0535	3.6
	1115	0.6		1205	1.1
W	1717	3.9	TH	1758	3.8
	● 2342	0.6	○		
14	0551	4.0	29	0020	1.2
	1200	0.5		0611	3.6
TH	1800	4.0	F	1241	1.1
				1834	3.9
15	0031	0.5	30	0058	1.2
	0634	4.0		0647	3.6
F	1246	0.4	SA	1317	1.1
	1844	4.0		1910	3.8

JULY

Date	Time	m	Date	Time	m
1	0136	1.3	16	0205	0.6
	0723	3.6		0756	3.8
SU	1352	1.2	M	1409	0.4
	1945	3.8		2008	3.9
2	0214	1.4	17	0254	0.7
	0757	3.5		0842	3.6
M	1425	1.3	TU	1456	0.5
	2021	3.7		2053	3.7
3	0251	1.5	18	0344	0.9
	0830	3.4		0930	3.3
TU	1458	1.4	W	1545	0.8
	2057	3.5		2141	3.5
4	0329	1.6	19	0437	1.2
	0906	3.2		1025	3.1
W	1532	1.5	TH	1636	1.0
	2136	3.4		◐ 2233	3.2
5	0412	1.7	20	0535	1.4
	0947	3.1		1134	2.9
TH	1615	1.6	F	1732	1.3
	2222	3.3		2339	3.0
6	0505	1.7	21	0641	1.6
	1038	3.0		1254	2.9
F	1709	1.7	SA	1833	1.5
	◑ 2321	3.2			
7	0608	1.7	22	0108	2.9
	1144	2.9		0757	1.6
SA	1813	1.7	SU	1404	2.9
				1942	1.6
8	0041	3.2	23	0230	2.9
	0713	1.6		0907	1.6
SU	1310	3.0	M	1501	3.1
	1922	1.6		2056	1.6
9	0209	3.3	24	0328	3.0
	0817	1.5		0959	1.5
M	1431	3.2	TU	1547	3.2
	2033	1.4		2200	1.5
10	0314	3.5	25	0409	3.2
	0916	1.2		1040	1.4
TU	1530	3.4	W	1628	3.4
	2139	1.2		2248	1.4
11	0408	3.7	26	0446	3.3
	1009	0.9		1116	1.2
W	1620	3.6	TH	1706	3.6
	2240	0.9		2328	1.3
12	0457	3.8	27	0523	3.5
	1059	0.7		1150	1.1
TH	1708	3.9	F	1744	3.8
	2334	0.7	○		
13	0543	3.9	28	0005	1.2
	1147	0.5		0559	3.6
F	1753	4.0	SA	1225	1.0
●				1820	3.9
14	0026	0.6	29	0042	1.2
	0627	4.0		0635	3.7
SA	1235	0.3	SU	1259	1.0
	1838	4.1		1855	3.9
15	0116	0.5	30	0118	1.2
	0712	3.9		0708	3.7
SU	1322	0.3	M	1331	1.1
	1923	4.1		1929	3.9
			31	0153	1.2
				0738	3.6
			TU	1400	1.1
				2000	3.8

AUGUST

Date	Time	m	Date	Time	m
1	0225	1.3	16	0314	0.9
	0806	3.5		0857	3.5
W	1426	1.2	TH	1518	0.7
	2031	3.7		2107	3.6
2	0255	1.4	17	0359	1.2
	0836	3.4		0939	3.3
TH	1456	1.3	F	1603	1.0
	2104	3.6		2148	3.3
3	0329	1.5	18	0447	1.4
	0913	3.3		1029	3.0
F	1534	1.4	SA	1653	1.4
	2144	3.4		◐ 2236	3.0
4	0415	1.6	19	0544	1.7
	0958	3.2		1148	2.9
SA	1624	1.6	SU	1749	1.6
	◑ 2235	3.3		2351	2.8
5	0517	1.6	20	0656	1.8
	1055	3.0		1327	2.9
SU	1731	1.7	M	1858	1.8
	2347	3.1			
6	0632	1.6	21	0211	2.7
	1217	3.0		0831	1.8
M	1852	1.7	TU	1442	3.0
				2030	1.8
7	0139	3.1	22	0353	2.9
	0746	1.5		0938	1.6
TU	1409	3.1	W	1533	3.2
	2015	1.5		2152	1.7
8	0306	3.3	23	0406	3.1
	0855	1.3		1024	1.4
W	1523	3.4	TH	1613	3.4
	2133	1.3		2239	1.5
9	0406	3.5	24	0434	3.3
	0955	1.0		1101	1.2
TH	1617	3.7	F	1651	3.6
	2238	1.0		2315	1.4
10	0454	3.7	25	0508	3.5
	1048	0.7		1134	1.1
F	1703	3.9	SA	1727	3.8
	2331	0.7		2348	1.2
11	0538	3.9	26	0543	3.7
	1137	0.5		1206	1.0
SA	1746	4.1	SU	1802	4.0
●			○		
12	0019	0.5	27	0021	1.1
	0618	4.0		0616	3.8
SU	1223	0.3	M	1237	0.9
	1828	4.2		1835	4.0
13	0105	0.5	28	0054	1.0
	0658	4.0		0647	3.8
M	1308	0.2	TU	1306	0.9
	1909	4.2		1906	4.0
14	0149	0.5	29	0126	1.0
	0738	3.9		0712	3.8
TU	1351	0.3	W	1332	0.9
	1949	4.1		1934	3.9
15	0232	0.7	30	0155	1.0
	0817	3.7		0737	3.7
W	1435	0.5	TH	1357	1.0
	2028	3.9		2002	3.8
			31	0222	1.1
				0807	3.6
			F	1427	1.1
				2034	3.7

Chart Datum: 2·10 metres below Ordnance Datum (Newlyn). HAT is 4·5 metres above Chart Datum.

STANDARD TIME (UT)
For Summer Time add ONE hour in **non-shaded areas**

OBAN LAT 56°25′N LONG 5°29′W

TIMES AND HEIGHTS OF HIGH AND LOW WATERS

Dates in red are SPRINGS
Dates in blue are NEAPS

YEAR **2018**

SEPTEMBER

Day	Time m	Day	Time m
1	0256 1.2 0842 3.5 SA 1505 1.3 2112 3.5	16	0404 1.5 0937 3.2 SU 1618 1.5 ◐ 2144 3.0
2	0340 1.4 0925 3.3 SU 1555 1.5 2201 3.3	17	0458 1.7 1035 3.0 M 1713 1.8 2240 2.8
3	0441 1.6 1021 3.1 M 1706 1.7 ◑ 2315 3.0	18	0605 1.9 1251 2.9 TU 1822 2.0
4	0602 1.6 1148 3.0 TU 1840 1.7	19	0211 2.7 0739 1.9 W 1425 3.0 2008 2.0
5	0142 3.0 0724 1.6 W 1414 3.1 2014 1.6	20	0332 2.8 0910 1.7 TH 1518 3.2 2139 1.8
6	0309 3.2 0839 1.4 TH 1524 3.4 2136 1.3	21	0352 3.0 0959 1.5 F 1555 3.4 2221 1.6
7	0404 3.5 0943 1.0 F 1613 3.7 2235 1.0	22	0415 3.3 1037 1.3 SA 1629 3.7 2253 1.3
8	0449 3.7 1036 0.7 SA 1654 4.0 2322 0.7	23	0446 3.5 1110 1.1 SU 1703 3.9 2323 1.1
9	0527 3.9 1123 0.5 SU 1733 4.2 ●	24	0519 3.7 1140 0.9 M 1737 4.0 2354 1.0
10	0005 0.5 0602 4.0 M 1208 0.3 1810 4.3	25	0551 3.8 1208 0.9 TU 1810 4.1 ○
11	0046 0.5 0638 4.1 TU 1250 0.2 1847 4.3	26	0025 0.8 0618 3.9 W 1236 0.8 1838 4.1
12	0125 0.5 0713 4.0 W 1331 0.3 1922 4.2	27	0056 0.8 0642 3.9 TH 1304 0.8 1905 4.1
13	0203 0.7 0747 3.9 TH 1410 0.5 1957 3.9	28	0125 0.8 0709 3.9 F 1333 0.9 1935 3.9
14	0241 0.9 0821 3.7 F 1450 0.8 2030 3.6	29	0155 0.9 0741 3.8 SA 1406 1.1 2009 3.7
15	0320 1.2 0856 3.4 SA 1531 1.2 2105 3.3	30	0232 1.1 0818 3.6 SU 1447 1.3 2049 3.5

OCTOBER

Day	Time m	Day	Time m
1	0318 1.3 0902 3.4 M 1541 1.5 2141 3.2	16	0420 1.8 0954 3.2 TU 1644 2.0 ◐ 2155 2.9
2	0420 1.5 1000 3.2 TU 1702 1.7 ◑ 2301 2.9	17	0524 2.0 1131 3.0 W 1752 2.1 2356 2.7
3	0541 1.6 1138 3.0 W 1839 1.8	18	0644 2.0 1355 3.1 TH 1926 2.1
4	0145 2.9 0704 1.6 TH 1410 3.2 2018 1.6	19	0242 2.8 0821 1.9 F 1450 3.2 2104 1.9
5	0259 3.2 0822 1.4 F 1512 3.5 2132 1.3	20	0318 3.0 0922 1.7 SA 1528 3.5 2146 1.7
6	0351 3.4 0926 1.1 SA 1557 3.8 2223 1.0	21	0346 3.3 1002 1.4 SU 1601 3.7 2219 1.4
7	0432 3.7 1018 0.8 SU 1636 4.1 2305 0.8	22	0417 3.5 1036 1.2 M 1635 3.9 2250 1.2
8	0507 3.9 1104 0.5 M 1712 4.2 2344 0.6	23	0450 3.7 1106 1.1 TU 1708 4.1 2321 1.0
9	0540 4.1 1147 0.4 TU 1747 4.3 ●	24	0520 3.9 1135 0.9 W 1740 4.2 ○ 2352 0.8
10	0021 0.6 0612 4.1 W 1228 0.4 1820 4.3	25	0547 4.0 1206 0.8 TH 1810 4.2
11	0057 0.6 0645 4.1 TH 1307 0.5 1853 4.2	26	0024 0.7 0614 4.0 F 1239 0.8 1839 4.1
12	0133 0.8 0717 4.0 F 1345 0.8 1925 3.9	27	0058 0.7 0645 4.0 SA 1315 0.9 1913 4.0
13	0208 1.0 0750 3.8 SA 1422 1.0 1957 3.7	28	0135 0.8 0721 3.9 SU 1355 1.0 1952 3.8
14	0245 1.3 0823 3.6 SU 1502 1.4 2031 3.4	29	0217 1.0 0802 3.7 M 1443 1.2 2036 3.5
15	0328 1.5 0903 3.4 M 1548 1.7 2107 3.1	30	0306 1.2 0851 3.5 TU 1544 1.5 2132 3.2
		31	0407 1.4 0953 3.3 W 1703 1.7 ◑ 2255 2.9

NOVEMBER

Day	Time m	Day	Time m
1	0522 1.5 1130 3.2 TH 1833 1.7	16	0549 2.0 1245 3.1 F 1834 2.2
2	0124 3.0 0641 1.5 F 1346 3.3 2007 1.6	17	0124 2.8 0704 2.0 SA 1407 3.2 1954 2.0
3	0237 3.2 0758 1.4 SA 1449 3.5 2114 1.3	18	0228 3.0 0819 1.9 SU 1451 3.4 2052 1.8
4	0329 3.4 0903 1.2 SU 1535 3.8 2202 1.1	19	0307 3.2 0912 1.7 M 1527 3.6 2134 1.5
5	0409 3.6 0956 0.9 M 1613 4.0 2243 1.0	20	0342 3.4 0952 1.5 TU 1603 3.8 2211 1.3
6	0442 3.8 1042 0.8 TU 1648 4.1 2320 0.9	21	0416 3.6 1027 1.2 W 1637 4.0 2246 1.1
7	0514 4.0 1125 0.7 W 1722 4.2 ● 2355 0.8	22	0448 3.8 1102 1.0 TH 1712 4.1 2321 0.9
8	0546 4.1 1206 0.7 TH 1755 4.2	23	0519 4.0 1139 0.9 F 1746 4.2 ○ 2358 0.7
9	0029 0.9 0619 4.1 F 1245 0.8 1827 4.1	24	0552 4.0 1219 0.8 SA 1821 4.1
10	0104 1.0 0652 4.1 SA 1322 1.0 1900 3.9	25	0037 0.7 0629 4.1 SU 1303 0.9 1859 4.0
11	0140 1.1 0725 4.0 SU 1359 1.3 1933 3.7	26	0120 0.7 0710 4.0 M 1350 1.0 1942 3.8
12	0218 1.3 0801 3.8 M 1438 1.5 2007 3.5	27	0206 0.8 0755 3.9 TU 1442 1.1 2030 3.6
13	0259 1.5 0840 3.6 TU 1523 1.8 2045 3.3	28	0256 1.0 0846 3.7 W 1542 1.3 2126 3.3
14	0347 1.8 0928 3.4 W 1616 2.0 2130 3.0	29	0354 1.2 0947 3.5 TH 1652 1.5 2239 3.1
15	0444 1.9 1032 3.2 TH 1719 2.2 ◐ 2241 2.9	30	0459 1.3 1108 3.3 F 1811 1.6 ◑

DECEMBER

Day	Time m	Day	Time m
1	0039 3.0 0611 1.4 SA 1305 3.3 1936 1.6	16	0550 2.0 1221 3.2 SU 1844 2.1
2	0201 3.1 0725 1.4 SU 1417 3.4 2045 1.5	17	0042 3.0 0652 2.0 M 1350 3.3 1947 1.9
3	0258 3.3 0833 1.3 M 1509 3.6 2137 1.3	18	0205 3.1 0756 1.8 TU 1445 3.5 2042 1.7
4	0340 3.5 0930 1.2 TU 1550 3.7 2219 1.2	19	0257 3.3 0855 1.6 W 1529 3.6 2129 1.5
5	0415 3.7 1020 1.1 W 1626 3.8 2256 1.1	20	0339 3.5 0947 1.4 TH 1610 3.8 2212 1.2
6	0449 3.8 1104 1.0 TH 1700 3.9 2331 1.1	21	0419 3.7 1034 1.2 F 1650 4.0 2254 0.9
7	0524 4.0 1145 1.0 F 1734 3.9 ●	22	0459 3.9 1121 1.0 SA 1730 4.1 ○ 2337 0.7
8	0006 1.1 0558 4.1 SA 1225 1.1 1807 3.9	23	0539 4.0 1208 0.8 SU 1810 4.1
9	0042 1.1 0633 4.1 SU 1302 1.2 1842 3.9	24	0021 0.6 0621 4.1 M 1256 0.8 1852 4.0
10	0119 1.2 0709 4.0 M 1340 1.4 1917 3.8	25	0107 0.6 0705 4.1 TU 1345 0.8 1936 3.9
11	0157 1.3 0745 3.9 TU 1418 1.6 1953 3.6	26	0155 0.6 0750 4.0 W 1436 0.9 2022 3.7
12	0236 1.5 0824 3.7 W 1500 1.8 2030 3.4	27	0244 0.7 0839 3.8 TH 1531 1.1 2113 3.4
13	0317 1.7 0905 3.6 TH 1546 1.9 2110 3.3	28	0337 0.9 0933 3.6 F 1630 1.3 2212 3.2
14	0402 1.8 0953 3.4 F 1639 2.1 2158 3.1	29	0434 1.1 1036 3.4 SA 1735 1.5 ◑ 2330 3.0
15	0452 2.0 1053 3.2 SA 1739 2.1 ◐ 2301 3.0	30	0537 1.3 1200 3.3 SU 1849 1.6
		31	0102 3.0 0644 1.4 M 1332 3.2 2004 1.6

Chart Datum: 2·10 metres below Ordnance Datum (Newlyn). HAT is 4·5 metres above Chart Datum.

9.8.18 OBAN

Argyll and Bute **56°24'·99N 05°29'·07W**

CHARTS AC 2171, 2387, 2388, 1790; Imray C65, 2800

TIDES –0530 Dover; ML 2·4; Duration 0610

Standard Port OBAN (⟵)

Times				Height (metres)			
High Water		Low Water		MHWS	MHWN	MLWN	MLWS
0100	0700	0100	0800	4·0	2·9	1·8	0·7
1300	1900	1300	2000				
Differences DUNSTAFFNAGE BAY							
+0005	0000	0000	+0005	+0·1	+0·1	+0·1	+0·1
CONNEL							
+0020	+0005	+0010	+0015	–0·3	–0·2	–0·1	+0·1
ARDCHATTAN PT							
+0150	+01505	+0215	+0200	–2·0	–1·3	–1·0	–0·3
BONAWE							
+0150	+0205	+0240	+0210	–2·0	–1·7	–1·3	–0·5
RUBHA Na CREIGE							
+0200	+0200	+0230	+0215	–1·9	–1·3	–1·0	–0·3

SHELTER Good shelter in bay except in strong SW/NW winds, but Oban Marina in Ardantrive Bay (Kerrera) is well sheltered from all directions, but as yet has no water on pontoons. ⚓s convenient for town are in deep water off the Esplanade and NW of Sailing Club, beware of moorings. Alternatively ⚓ at N end of Kerrera to S of Rubh'a Chruidh Is or Horseshoe and Little Horseshoe Bay, Kerrera Sound. Beware fish farms S of Ardantrive Bay.

NAVIGATION **WPT (N)** 56°25′·85N 05°30′·0W, 132°/0·7M to Dunollie lt; **WPT (S)** 56°22′N 05°33′W, 035°/1M to 1·5ca E of Sgeirean Dubha, thence through Kerrera Sound to Oban Bay. Ferry Rks can be passed on either side. Direction of the buoyage is **NE**, thus pass to the East of ECM Q (3) 10s, or to West of the SH QG buoy. The N'ly SHM must be passed to the West. In Oban Bay beware Sgeir Rathaid (buoyed) in middle of the bay and ferries running to/from Railway Pier.

LIGHTS AND MARKS See 9.8.4 and chartlet.

COMMUNICATIONS (Code 01631) CGOC (01851) 702013; ⊖ 08457 231110; Police 101; Dr 563175; N Pier ☎562892.

North Pier Ch **12** 16 (0900-1700); Railway Pier, *CalMac* Ch 06 12 16; *Oban Marina* Ch 80.

FACILITIES **North Pier** (15t mob) via Piermaster.

Railway Pier (H24, ☎562849) ACA divers.

Oban Sailing Club 16 s £15/night, pay at Y honesty box £5 until 1600; short stay (with), £2/half hour; free for 30 mins.

Oban Marina (Ardantrive Bay) www.obanmarina.com ☎565333; 30 s £18/nt (20t), £30/nt (50t); 100 £2.35+ (limited) (50t). Water taxi to/from Oban (0900-1700), free for boat crews.

A new pontoon is under construction off N Pier (info welcome).

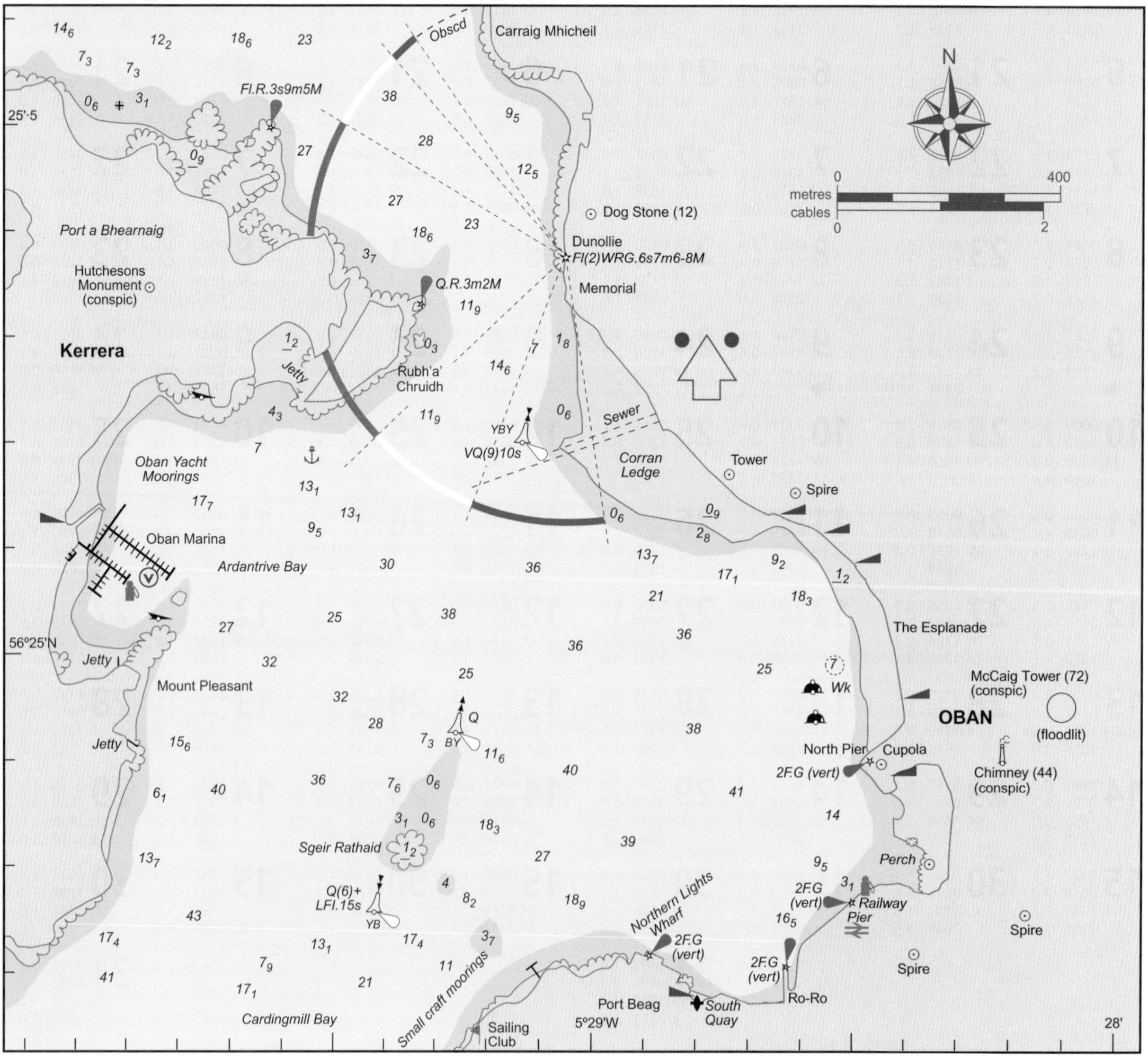

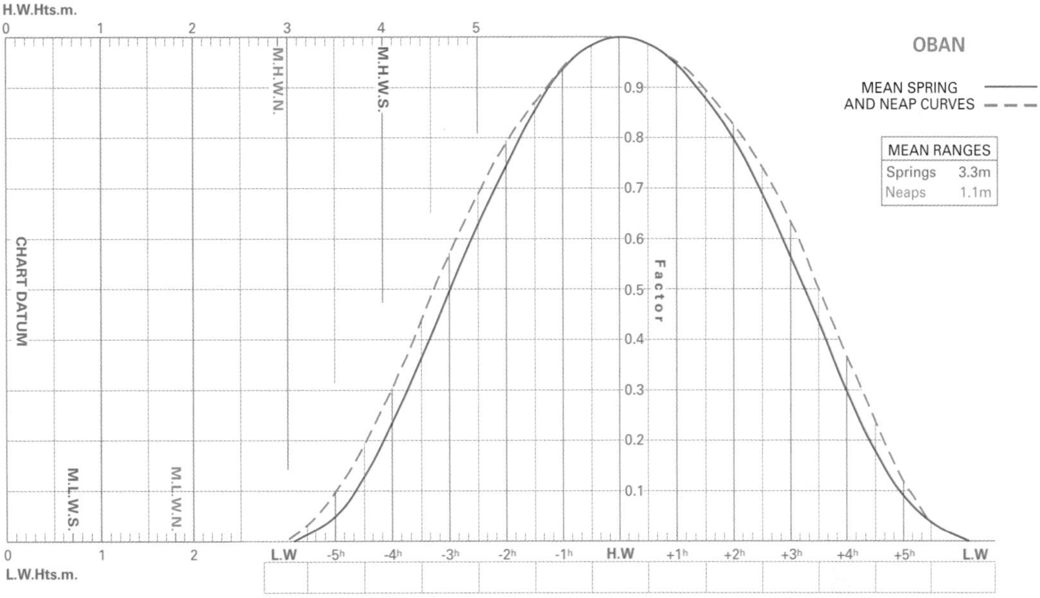

Town Ⓟ (½M), all facilities, Ⓗ, ⇌ Connel (airstrip) 3M, Glasgow (✈) 3hrs, ferries to Inner & Outer Hebrides.

Heather Is Ⓥs 3Y 15t, 1 Gy 20t, 1 Or 50t; £10/nt (pay Ardantrive Fm).

ADJACENT HARBOUR ON MAINLAND TO N OF OBAN

DUNSTAFFNAGE Marina, Argyll and Bute, **56°27'·04N 05°25'·97W**. AC 2388, 5611. Within the bay the rotary tidal stream sets mainly E through the marina and running strongly through the moorings. Enter between Rubha Garbh and Eilean Mór – subject to swell in NW winds. No navigational hazards; W and SW sides of bay dry. Use buoyed fairway, keeping clear of moorings, spd limit 4kn.

☎(01631) 566555, VHF Ch37/M1 (launch H24 except LWS ±2hrs) 200 inc Ⓥ £2·45+£3 (0830-2000 summer) (40t) (masting) ✕ (½M) Ⓟ (¾M), bus, ⇌ Oban (3M).

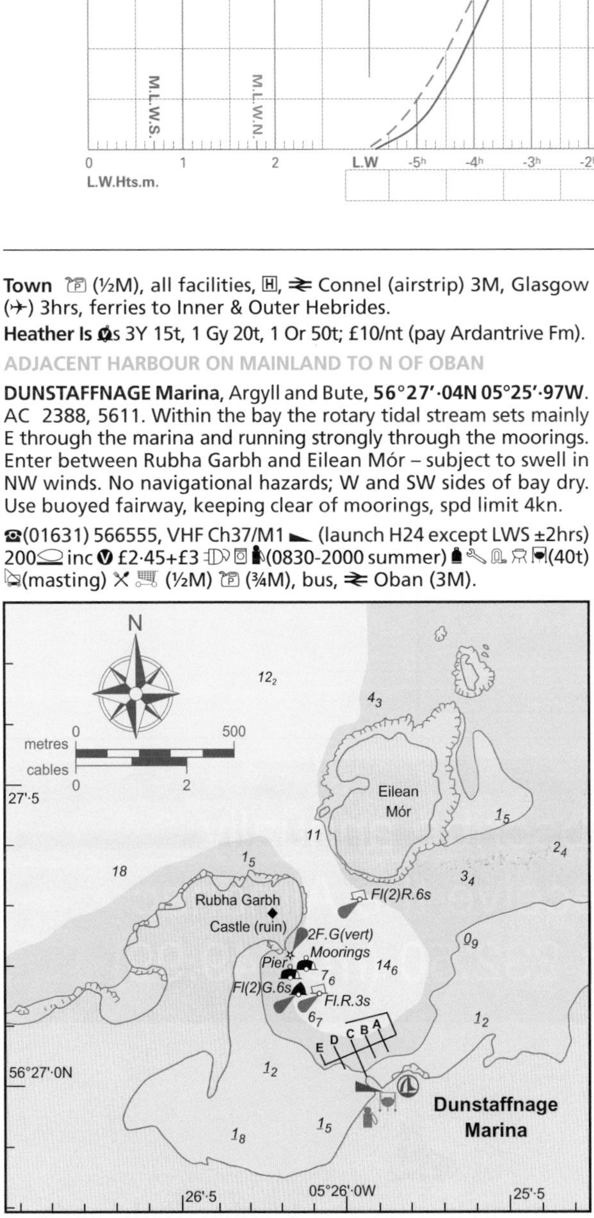

ANCHORAGES ON MAINLAND SHORE OF FIRTH OF LORN

LOCH FEOCHAN, Argyll and Bute, **56°21'·39N 05°29'·77W**. AC 5611, 2387. HW = HW Oban; flood runs 4 hrs, ebb for 8hrs. Caution: strong streams off Ardentallan Pt. Good shelter, 5M S of Oban and 1·5M SE of Kerrera. Best appr at local slack LW = LW Oban +0200; beware strong cross currents in narrow buoyed channel, which is in parts shallower than charted. ⚓ off pier, or moor off.

Ardoran Marine ☎(01631) 566123, 566611; 4 Ⓥs £16·00 <11m.

PUILLADOBHRAIN, Argyll and Bute, **56°19'·47N 05°35'·22W**. AC 5611, 2386/2387. Tides as Oban. Popular ⚓ on the SE shore of the Firth of Lorne, approx 7M S of Oban, sheltered by the islets to the W of it. At N end of Ardencaple Bay identify Eilean Dùin (18m) and steer SE keeping 1½ca off to clear a rk awash at its NE tip. Continue for 4ca between Eilean nam Beathach, with Orange drum on N tip, and Dun Horses rks drying 2·7m. Two W cairns on E side of Eilean nam Freumha lead approx 215° into the inner ⚓ in about 4m. Landing at head of inlet. Nearest facilities: ☎ at Clachan Br (½M); ☎ ✉ at Clachan Seil.

CUAN SOUND, Argyll and Bute, **56°15'·84N 05°37'·47W**. AC 2386, 2326. Tides see 9.8.18 SEIL SOUND. Streams reach 6kn at sp; N-going makes at HW Oban +0420, S-going at HW Oban –2. The Sound is a useful doglegged short cut from Firth of Lorne to Lochs Melfort and Shuna, but needs care due to rks fish farms and tides. There are ⚓s at either end to await the tide. At the 90° dogleg, pass close N of Cleit Rk onto which the tide sets; it is marked by a Y △ perch. The chan is only ¾ca wide here due to rks off Seil. Overhead cables (35m) cross from Seil to Luing. There are ⚓s out of the tide to the S of Cleit Rk. No lts/facilities. See CCC SDs.

ARDINAMAR, Luing/Torsa, **56°14'·92N 05°37'·04W.** AC 2326. HW –0555 on Dover; ML 1·7m; see 9.8.18 SEIL SOUND. A small cove and popular ⚓ between Luing and Torsa, close W of ent to L. Melfort. Appr on brg 290°. Narrow, shallow (about 1m CD) ent has drying rks either side, those to N marked by 2 SHM perches. Keep about 15m S of perches to ⚓ in 2m in centre of cove; S part dries. Few facilities: ✉ ☎ at Cullipool 1·5M WNW. at Cuan Sound ferry 2M NNW.

9.8.19 LOCH MELFORT ❁❁❁◊◊◊✿✿✿

Argyll and Bute **56°14'·59N 05°34'·07W**

CHARTS AC 5611, 2169, 2326; Imray C65, 2800

TIDES Loch Shuna –0615 Dover; ML Loch Melfort 1·7; Duration Seil Sound 0615

Standard Port OBAN (⟵)

Times				Height (metres)			
High Water		Low Water		MHWS	MHWN	MLWN	MLWS
0100	0700	0100	0800	4·0	2·9	1·8	0·7
1300	1900	1300	2000				
Differences LOCH MELFORT							
–0055	–0025	–0040	–0035	–1·2	–0·8	–0·5	–0·1
SEIL SOUND							
–0035	–0015	–0040	–0015	–1·3	–0·9	–0·7	–0·3

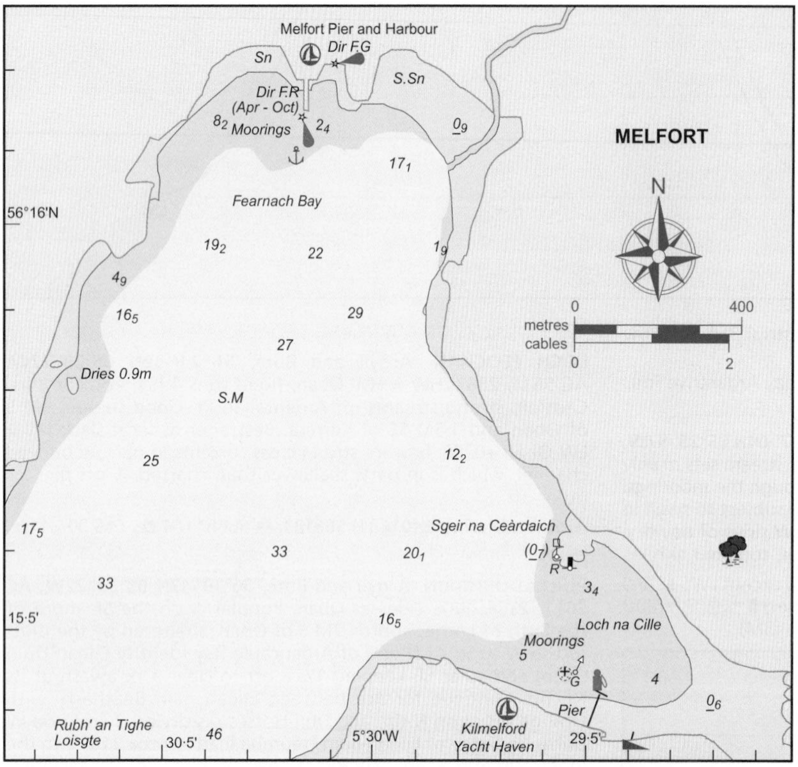

SHELTER Good at Kilmelford Yacht Haven in Loch na Cille; access at all tides for 3m draught, W lts at end of pier and along its length. Or lt at Melfort Pier (Fearnach Bay at N end of loch): pier/pontoon in 2m, but chan to inner hbr dries; good ⚓ in N winds. ⚓'ge sheltered from S to W at Kames Bay clear of moorings and rocks. Beware extensive marine farm activity inshore NE of Arduaine Point.

NAVIGATION WPT 56°13'·90N 05°34'·80W, 000°/3·5ca to Eilean Gamhna. Pass either side of Eilean Gamhna. 8ca NE lies Campbell Rk (1·8m). A rk drying 1m lies 1½ca ESE of the FS on Eilean Coltair. The S side of L Melfort is mostly steep-to, except in Kames Bay. At Loch na Cille, beware drying reef ¾ca off NE shore (PHM perch), and rk near S shore (SHM perch); boats may obscure perches.

LIGHTS AND MARKS A Dir FR ☆ 6m 3M on Melfort pier (also depth gauge) and a Dir FG ☆ close NE on the shore are not ldg lts, nor do they form a safe transit. Approach on a N'ly track keeping them an equal angle off each bow.

COMMUNICATIONS (Code 01852) Police 101; 🄷 (01631) 567500; CGOC (01851) 702013; ⊖ (0141) 887 9369.

Kilmelford VHF Ch **80** M (HO).

FACILITIES

Melfort Pier melharbour@aol.com ☎200333, ⊂⊃ < 6m or 🅐 £15/day, ▬ ⊡ @ wi-fi, hotel accommodation.

Kilmelford Yacht Haven ☎ 200248, 📠 200343, ▬ HW±4; ⊂⊃£16/craft (any LOA) ⛽(Mon-Sat 0800-2000) ⛽ ⊡ ⚒(20t) ⚒ 🔧 ⊡.

Kilmelford Village (1¼M): ✉ 🛒 ✕ ⊡.

9.8.20 CRAOBH MARINA (L SHUNA)

Argyll & Bute **56°12'·80N 05°33'·54W**

CHARTS AC 5611, 2169, 2326; Imray C65, 2800

TIDES HW Loch Shuna –0100 Oban; –0615 Dover; Seil Sound Duration 0615, ML 1·4. For tidal figures see 9.8.19.

SHELTER Very good. Craobh (pronounced Croove) Marina (access H24) on SE shore of Loch Shuna is enclosed by N and S causeways between islets. The ent is between 2 bkwtrs on the N side. In the marina, a shoal area S of the E bkwtr is marked by 9 PHM and 2 SHM buoys. A Y perch in W corner of hbr marks a spit; elsewhere ample depth. There are ⚓s in Asknish Bay 1M to the N, and in the bays E of Eilean Arsa and at Bàgh an Tigh-Stòir, S of Craobh.

NAVIGATION WPT 56°13'·01N 05°33'·57W, 173°/2ca to ent. Tidal streams in Loch Shuna are weak. Beware fish farm 2ca N of Shuna, lobster pots in appr's and unmarked rks (dr 1·5m) 4ca NNE of ent. An unlit SHM buoy marks a rk (1m) 150m NNW of the W bkwtr. 1M N of marina, Eich Donna, an unmarked reef (1·5m), lies between Eilean Creagach and Arduaine Pt.

LIGHTS AND MARKS The W sector, 162°-183°, of Dir Lt, Iso WRG 5s 10m 5/3M, on E bkwtr hd leads 172° between the close-in rks above. Multi-coloured marina buildings are conspic.

COMMUNICATIONS (Code 01852) CGOC (01851) 702013; ⊖ (0141) 887 9369; Police 101; Ⓗ (01546) 602323.
VHF Ch M 80 (summer 0830-2000; winter 0830-1800).

FACILITIES **Craobh Marina** www.craobhmarina.co.uk ☎500222, mob 07917 805386; (launch/recover £3.70/m); (200+50Ⓥ) £2·30; (30t) (12t) Ⓔ free wi-fi, sailing club.
Village ✉(Kilmelford) Ⓑ(Fri) ≷ (Oban by bus) ✈ (Glasgow).

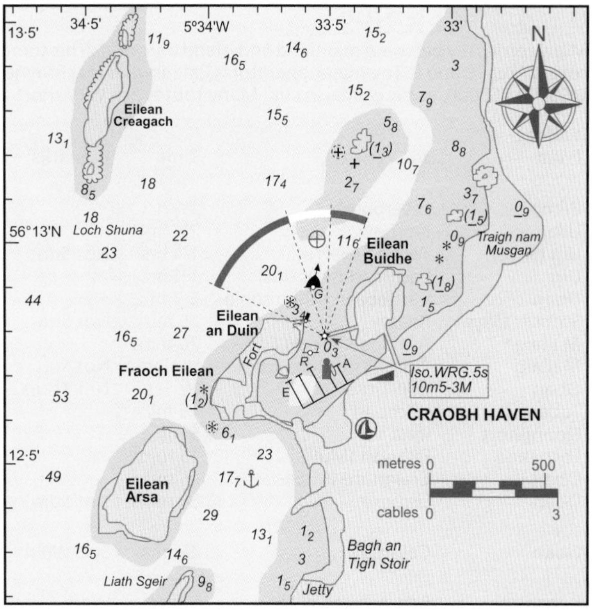

9.8.21 LOCH CRAIGNISH

Argyll and Bute **56°07'·99N 05°35'·07W**

CHARTS AC 5611, 2169, 2326; Imray C65, C63, 2800

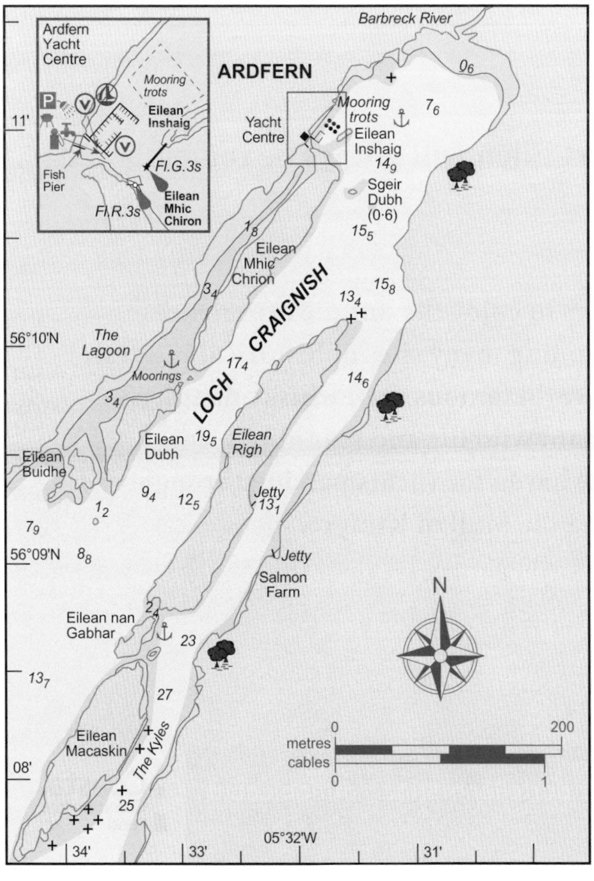

TIDES +0600 Dover; ML (Loch Beag)1·2; Duration (Seil Sound) 0615

Standard Port OBAN (⟵)

Times				Height (metres)			
High Water		Low Water		MHWS	MHWN	MLWN	MLWS
0100	0700	0100	0800	4·0	2·9	1·8	0·7
1300	1900	1300	2000				
Differences LOCH BEAG (3M SSW of Ardfern)							
–0110	–0045	–0035	–0045	–1·6	–1·2	–0·8	–0·4

NOTE: HW Ardfern is approx HW Oban –0045; times/heights much affected by local winds and barometric pressure.

SHELTER Beware squalls in E'lies, especially on E side of loch. Good at Ardfern, 56°11'·0N 05°31'·8W, access H24 appr chan unlit; ⚓s at:

- Eilean nan Gabhar; appr from E chan and ⚓ E of island.
- Eilean Righ; midway up the E side of the island.
- Eilean Dubh in the 'lagoon' between the island and mainland bounded by moorings to the NE and SW of the entrance.

NAVIGATION WPT 56°07'·59N 05°35'·37W (off chartlet) between Dorus Mór and Liath-sgier Mhòr.

Beware: strong tidal streams (up to 8kn) in Dorus Mór; a reef extending 1ca SSW of Eilean Macaskin; rk 1½ca SSW of Eilean Dubh; fish cages especially on E side of loch; a drying rock at N end of Ardfern ⚓ with a rock awash ¼ca E of it. (These 2 rks are ½ca S of the more S'ly of little islets close to mainland.) The main fairway is free from hazards, except for Sgeir Dhubh (0·6m), an unmarked rk 3½ca SSE of Ardfern, with a reef extending about ½ca all round. Ardfern is 1ca W of Eilean Inshaig.

LIGHTS AND MARKS Ent to Ardfern Yacht Centre marked by PHM buoy, Fl R 3s, and end of floating bkwtr, Fl G 3s, which extends 90m SW from Eilean Inshaig.

COMMUNICATIONS CGOC (01851) 702013; ⊖ (0141) 887 9369; Dr (01546) 602921; Ⓗ (01546) 602449.

Ardfern Yacht Centre VHF Ch 80 M (office hrs).

FACILITIES **Ardfern Yacht Centre** www.ardfernyacht.co.uk ☎ 01852 500247; 12 £1·40) 87+20 Ⓥ £2.20; (HW±3, £1.75/m) (HO) (40t) (25t) ACA.
Village ✉ Ⓑ(Fri) ≷(Oban) ✈(Glasgow).

9.8.22 FERRIES

Many ferries ply between mainland and island harbours. This summary may prove useful when plans or crews change in remote places. It covers Areas 8 and 9. The major operator is Caledonian MacBrayne: Head Office, The Ferry Terminal, Gourock PA19 1QP. For reservations: ☎08000 665000; www.calmac.co.uk. Many routes are very short and may not be pre-bookable; seasonal routes are marked *.

CalMac From	To	Time	Remarks
Areas 8			
Berneray	Leverburgh	1¼ hrs	
Ullapool	Stornoway	2¾ hrs	
Uig (Skye)	Tarbert (Harris)	1¾ hrs	Not Sun
Uig	Lochmaddy (N Uist)	1¾ hrs	
Oban	Castlebay/Lochboisdale	5-7 hrs	
Sconser (Skye)	Raasay	15 mins	Not Sun
Mallaig*	Armadale (Skye)	20 mins	
Mallaig	Eigg-Muck-Rum-Canna	Varies	Not Sun
Oban	Coll-Tiree	Varies	Not Thurs
Tobermory	Kilchoan	35 mins	
Fionnphort	Iona	5 mins	
Lochaline	Fishnish (Mull)	15 mins	
Oban	Craignure (Mull)	45 mins	
Oban	Lismore	50 mins	Not Sun
Areas 8/9			
Oban	Colonsay	2¼ hrs	Sun/W/Fri
Area 9			
Kennacraig	Port Askaig/Colonsay	Varies	Wed
Kennacraig	Port Ellen	2 hrs 10m	
Kennacraig	Port Askaig	2 hrs	
Tayinloan	Gigha	20 mins	
Ardrossan	Brodick	55 mins	
Claonaig	Lochranza (Arran)	30 mins	
Largs	Cumbrae Slip	10 mins	
Tarbert (L Fyne)	Portavadie*	25 mins	
Colintraive	Rhubodach (Bute)	5 mins	
Wemyss Bay	Rothesay (Bute)	35 mins	
Gourock	Dunoon	20 mins	

Other Island Ferry Operators From	To	Operator	Telephone
Areas 8			
Corran - V	Ardgour	Highland Council	01855 841243
Easdale - P	Seil	Area Manager	01631 562125
Firth of Lorn - P	Colonsay Uisken (Ross of Mull) Scalasaig (Colonsay) Tarbert (Jura) Port Askaig (Islay)	K & C Byrne	01951 200320
Jura - V	Port Askaig (Islay)	Serco Denholm	01496 840681
Kerrara - P	Oban	Oban Yachts	01631 565333
Kilgregan - P	Gourock	Clyde Marine Motoring	01475 721281
Lismore - P	Port Appin	Area Manager	01631 562125
Loch Nevis - P	Mallaig	Bruce Watt	01687 462233
Luing - P/V	Seil	Area Manager	01631 562125
Morvern	Sunart	Pre-book via	01688 302851
Mull	Drimnin	Sound of Mull	or mobile
Ardnamurchan	Tobermory Kilchoan	Transport	07799 608199
Skye - V	Glenelg	IOSFCIC	01599 522236
Staffa - P	Iona	D Kirkpatrick	01681 700373
Staffa - P	Mull	Gordon Grant	01681 700338
Staffa - P	Mull	Turus Mara	01688 400242

P = Passenger only V = Cars and Passengers

South West Scotland

Crinan Canal to Mull of Galloway

9.9.1 **Contents** ... 467

9.9.2 **Area map and Distance table** ... 468

9.9.3 **Tidal stream charts** ... 470

9.9.4 **Lights, buoys and waypoints** ... 472

9.9.5 **Passage information** ... 474
Corryvreckan to Crinan, West of Jura to Islay, Sound of Jura to Gigha – 474 • Mull of Kintyre to Upper Loch Fyne – 477 • Arran, Bute and Firth of Clyde – 483 • Firth of Clyde to Mull of Galloway, Scotland SW coast – 488

9.9.6 **Port Ellen** ... 475
Scalasaig (Colonsay) • Loch Tarbert (Jura) • Port Askaig (Islay) • Craighouse (Jura)• Loch Sween • West Loch Tarbert (Kintyre) • Gigha Island

9.9.7 **Crinan Canal** ... 476

9.9.8 **Ardrishaig** ... 477

9.9.9 **Tarbert** ... 478

9.9.10 **Portavadie** ... 478

9.9.11 **Tidal stream charts for Mull of Kintyre** ... 479

9.9.12 **Campbeltown** ... 480
Carradale Bay

9.9.13 **Lamlash** ... 481
Brodick (Arran) • Loch Ranza (Arran) • St Ninian's Bay (Bute) • West Kyle • Caladh Harbour • Loch Riddon • Burnt Islands • Kilchattan Bay (Bute)

9.9.14 **Rothesay** ... 482
Millport (Cumbraes)

9.9.15 **Port Bannatyne** ... 482

9.9.16 **Fairlie Quay** ... 483

9.9.17 **Largs** ... 483

9.9.18 **Submarine Exercise Areas** ... 484

9.9.19 **Inverkip (Kip Marina)** ... 485
Dunoon • Gourock

9.9.20 **Holy Loch** ... 485

9.9.21 **Gareloch/Rhu** ... 486
Loch Long/Loch Goil

9.9.22 **River Clyde, Greenock tide tables/curves** ... 487
Greenock • Dumbarton (Sandpoint) • Bowling Harbour

9.9.23 **Ardrossan** ... 492
Irvine • Ayr

9.9.24 **Troon** ... 493
Girvan

9.9.25 **Loch Ryan/Stranraer** ... 494
Drummore • Isle of Whithorn • Garlieston • Pt William

9.9.26 **Portpatrick** ... 495

9.9.27 **Kirkcudbright** ... 496
Kippford

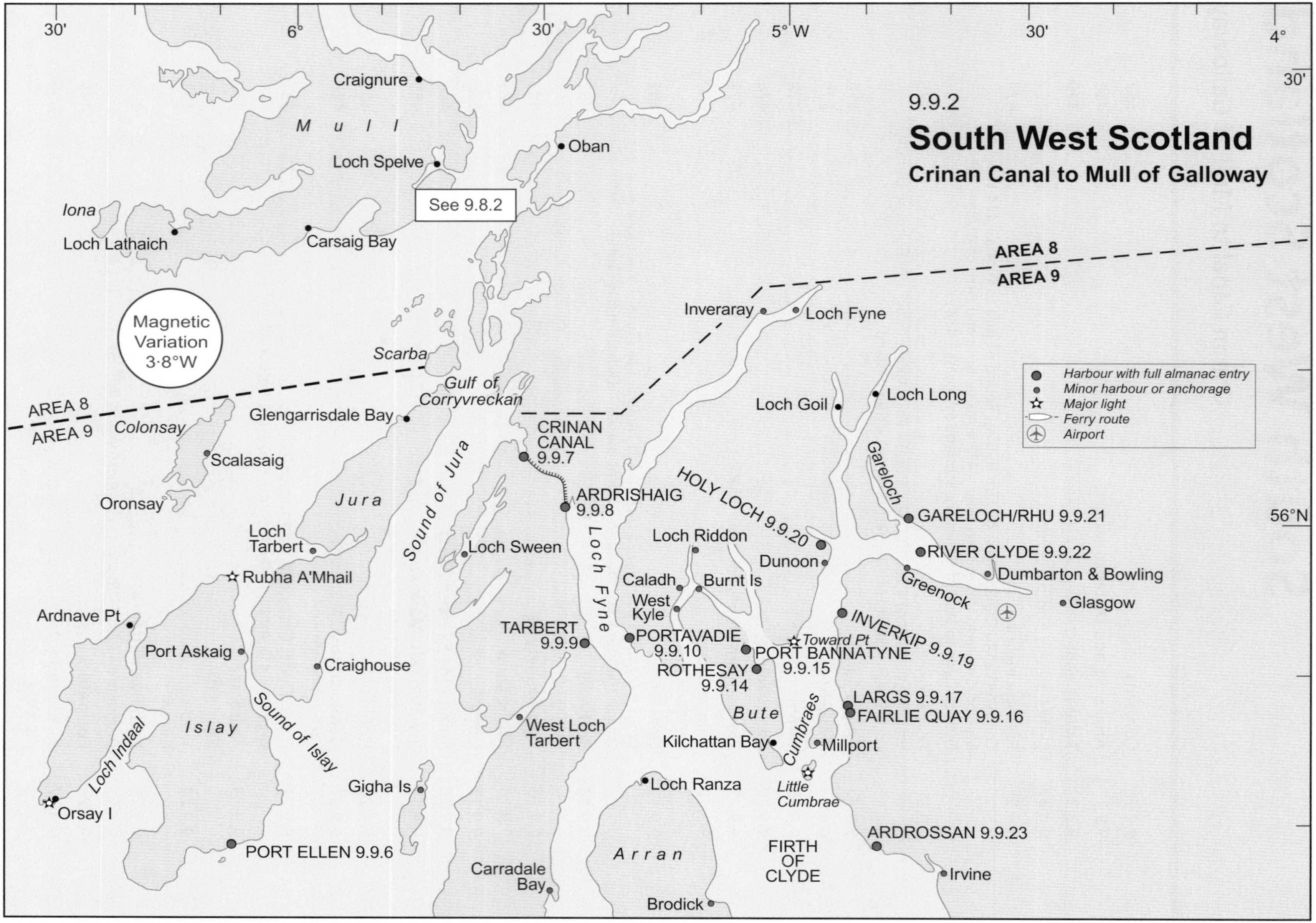
9.9.2
South West Scotland
Crinan Canal to Mull of Galloway
30'
6°
30'
5° W
30'
4°
30'
56°N
Craignure
Mull
Loch Spelve
Oban
See 9.8.2
Iona
Loch Lathaich
Carsaig Bay
Magnetic Variation 3·8°W
Scarba
Gulf of Corryvreckan
AREA 8
AREA 9
Colonsay
Glengarrisdale Bay
Scalasaig
Oronsay
Jura
Sound of Jura
Loch Tarbert
Rubha A'Mhail
Ardnave Pt
Port Askaig
Craighouse
Islay
Sound of Islay
Loch Indaal
Orsay I
Gigha Is
PORT ELLEN 9.9.6
CRINAN CANAL 9.9.7
ARDRISHAIG 9.9.8
Loch Sween
Loch Fyne
TARBERT 9.9.9
West Loch Tarbert
Carradale Bay
Inveraray
Loch Fyne
Loch Goil
Loch Long
Gareloch
HOLY LOCH 9.9.20
Loch Riddon
Dunoon
Caladh
Burnt Is
West Kyle
PORTAVADIE 9.9.10
PORT BANNATYNE 9.9.15
ROTHESAY 9.9.14
Toward Pt
Bute
Kilchattan Bay
Cumbraes
Millport
Little Cumbrae
Loch Ranza
Arran
Brodick
FIRTH OF CLYDE
GARELOCH/RHU 9.9.21
RIVER CLYDE 9.9.22
Dumbarton & Bowling
Greenock
Glasgow
INVERKIP 9.9.19
LARGS 9.9.17
FAIRLIE QUAY 9.9.16
ARDROSSAN 9.9.23
Irvine
Harbour with full almanac entry
Minor harbour or anchorage
Major light
Ferry route
Airport

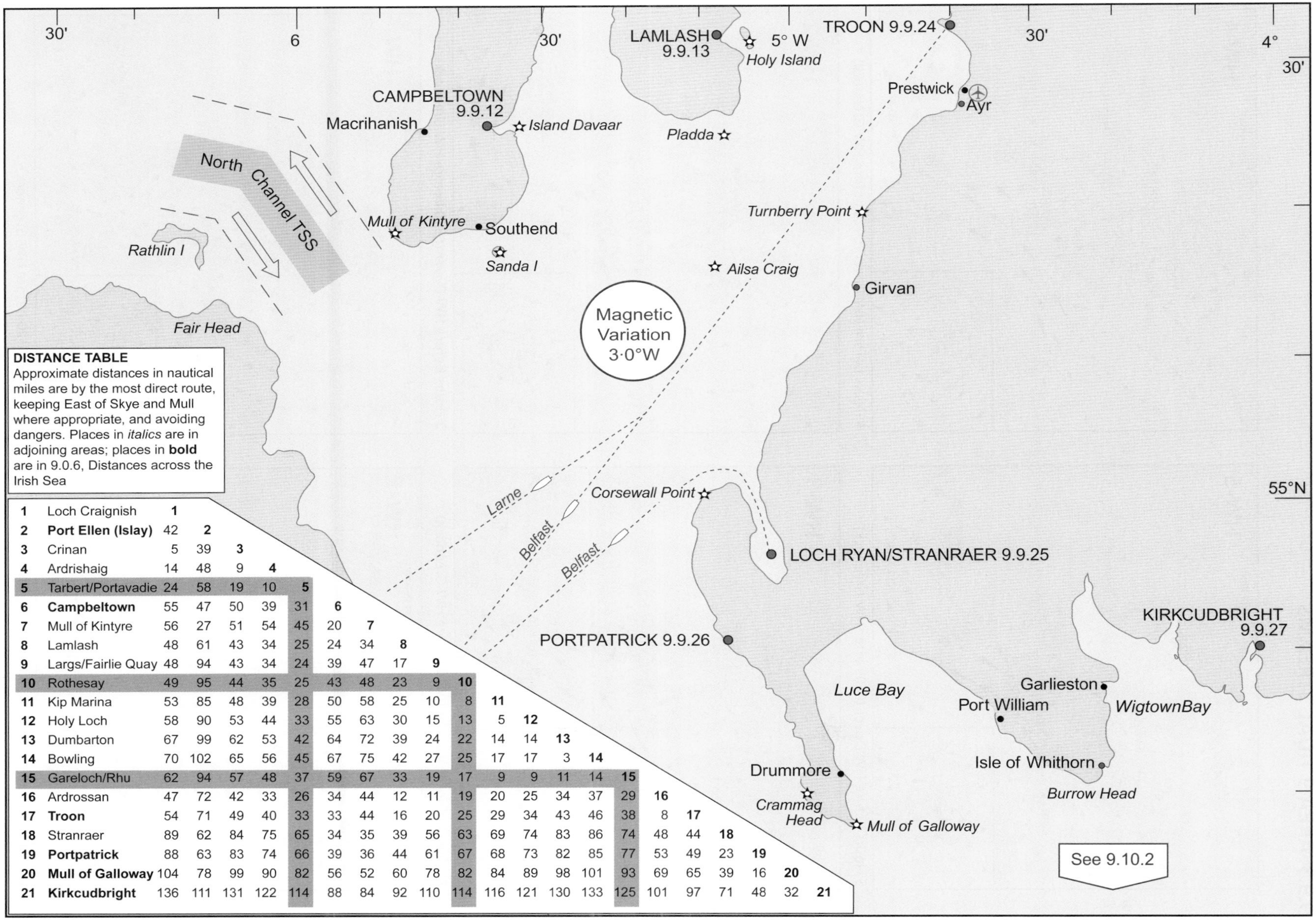

30'
6
30'
5° W
30'
4°
30'
55°N
CAMPBELTOWN 9.9.12
Macrihanish
Island Davaar
LAMLASH 9.9.13
Holy Island
Pladda
TROON 9.9.24
Prestwick
Ayr
North Channel TSS
Rathlin I
Mull of Kintyre
Southend
Sanda I
Fair Head
Turnberry Point
Ailsa Craig
Girvan
Magnetic Variation 3·0°W
Larne
Belfast
Belfast
Corsewall Point
LOCH RYAN/STRANRAER 9.9.25
PORTPATRICK 9.9.26
Luce Bay
Drummore
Crammag Head
Mull of Galloway
Port William
Garlieston
WigtownBay
Isle of Whithorn
Burrow Head
KIRKCUDBRIGHT 9.9.27
See 9.10.2

DISTANCE TABLE
Approximate distances in nautical miles are by the most direct route, keeping East of Skye and Mull where appropriate, and avoiding dangers. Places in *italics* are in adjoining areas; places in **bold** are in 9.0.6, Distances across the Irish Sea

1	Loch Craignish	**1**																				
2	**Port Ellen (Islay)**	42	**2**																			
3	Crinan	5	39	**3**																		
4	Ardrishaig	14	48	9	**4**																	
5	Tarbert/Portavadie	24	58	19	10	**5**																
6	**Campbeltown**	55	47	50	39	31	**6**															
7	Mull of Kintyre	56	27	51	54	45	20	**7**														
8	Lamlash	48	61	43	34	25	24	34	**8**													
9	Largs/Fairlie Quay	48	94	43	34	24	39	47	17	**9**												
10	Rothesay	49	95	44	35	25	43	48	23	9	**10**											
11	Kip Marina	53	85	48	39	28	50	58	25	10	8	**11**										
12	Holy Loch	58	90	53	44	33	55	63	30	15	13	5	**12**									
13	Dumbarton	67	99	62	53	42	64	72	39	24	22	14	14	**13**								
14	Bowling	70	102	65	56	45	67	75	42	27	25	17	17	3	**14**							
15	Gareloch/Rhu	62	94	57	48	37	59	67	33	19	17	9	9	11	14	**15**						
16	Ardrossan	47	72	42	33	26	34	44	12	11	19	20	25	34	37	29	**16**					
17	**Troon**	54	71	49	40	33	33	44	16	20	25	29	34	43	46	38	8	**17**				
18	Stranraer	89	62	84	75	65	34	35	39	56	63	69	74	83	86	74	48	44	**18**			
19	**Portpatrick**	88	63	83	74	66	39	36	44	61	67	68	73	82	85	77	53	49	23	**19**		
20	**Mull of Galloway**	104	78	99	90	82	56	52	60	78	82	84	89	98	101	93	69	65	39	16	**20**	
21	**Kirkcudbright**	136	111	131	122	114	88	84	92	110	114	116	121	130	133	125	101	97	71	48	32	**21**

9.9.3 AREA 9 TIDAL STREAMS

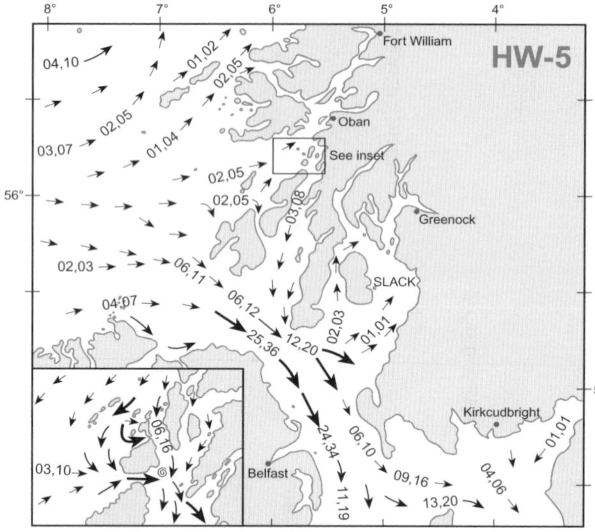

5 Hours before HW Dover (0605 after HW Greenock)

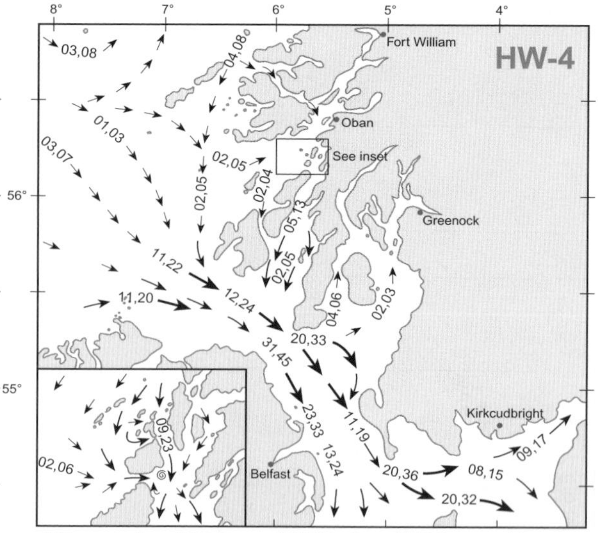

4 Hours before HW Dover (0520 before HW Greenock)

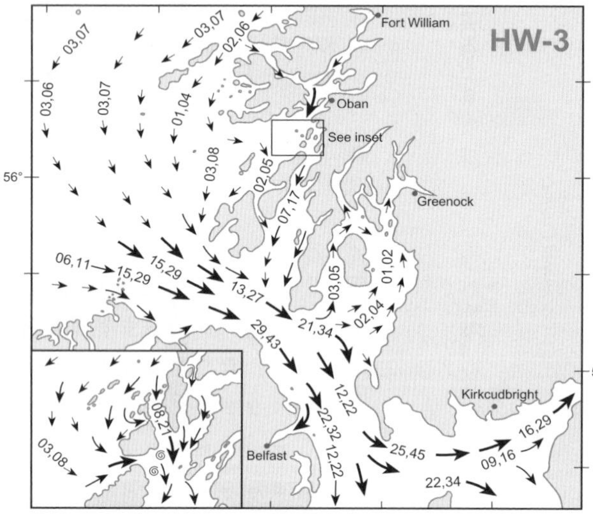

3 Hours before HW Dover (0420 before HW Greenock)

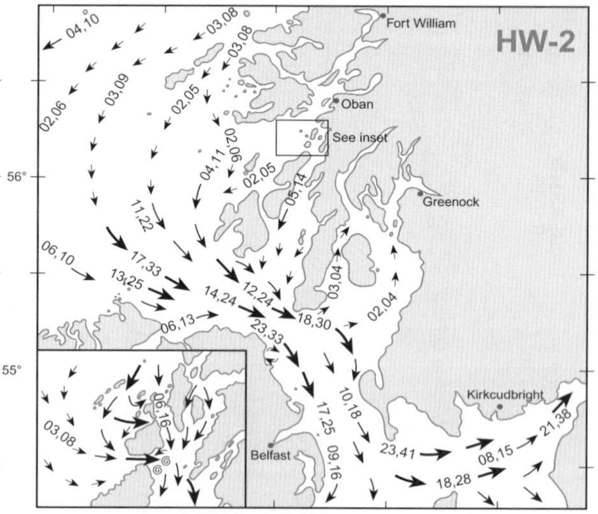

2 Hours before HW Dover (0320 before HW Greenock)

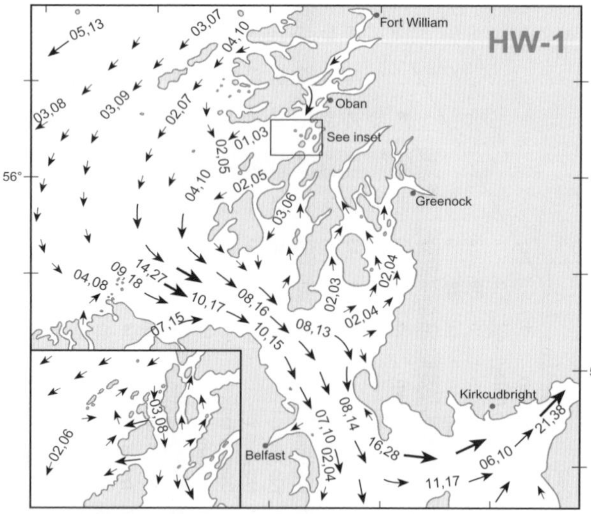

1 Hour before HW Dover (0220 before HW Greenock)

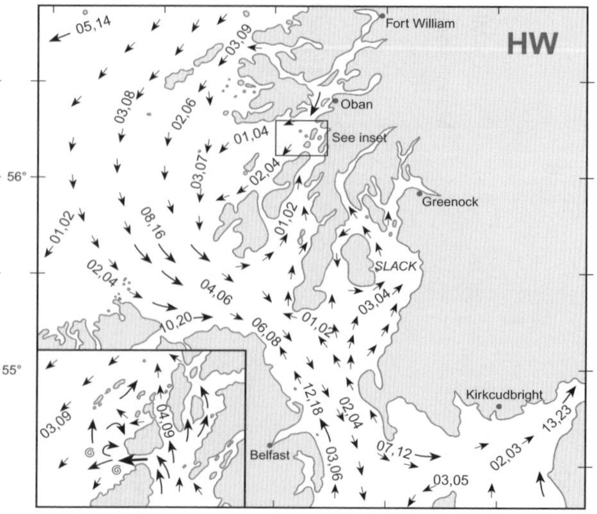

HW Dover (0120 before HW Greenock)

Northward 9.8.3 Mull of Kintyre 9.9.11 Irish Sea 9.10.3 North Ireland 9.13.3

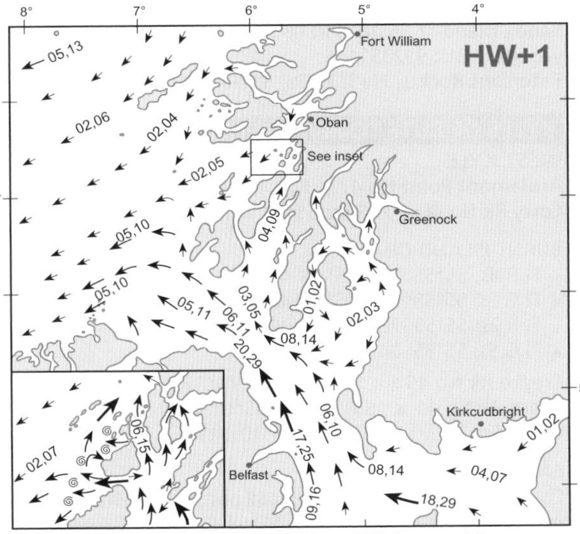

1 Hour after HW Dover (0020 before HW Greenock)

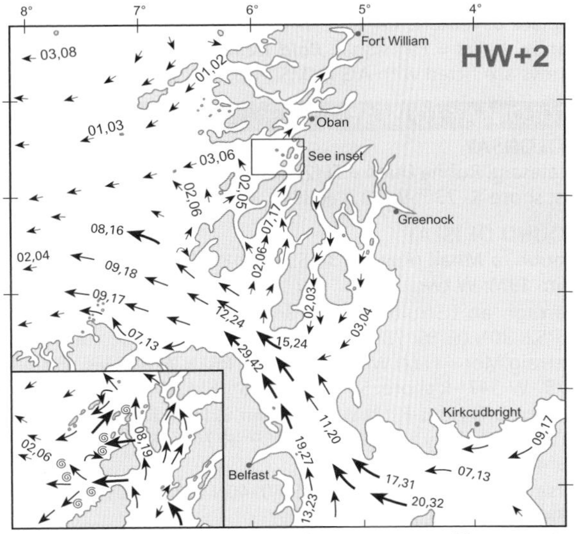

2 Hours after HW Dover (0040 after HW Greenock)

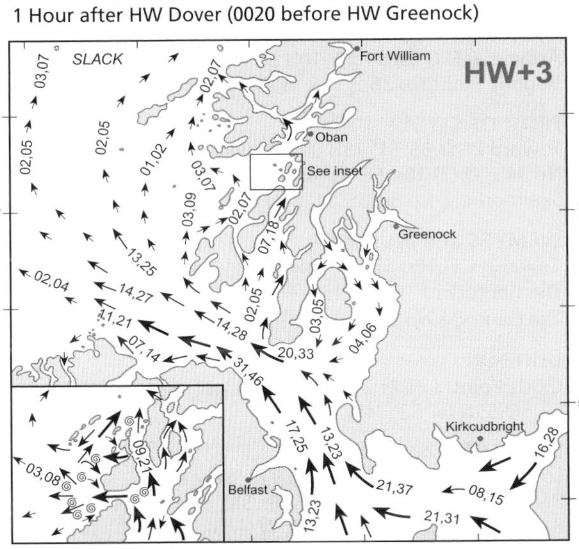

3 Hours after HW Dover (0140 after HW Greenock)

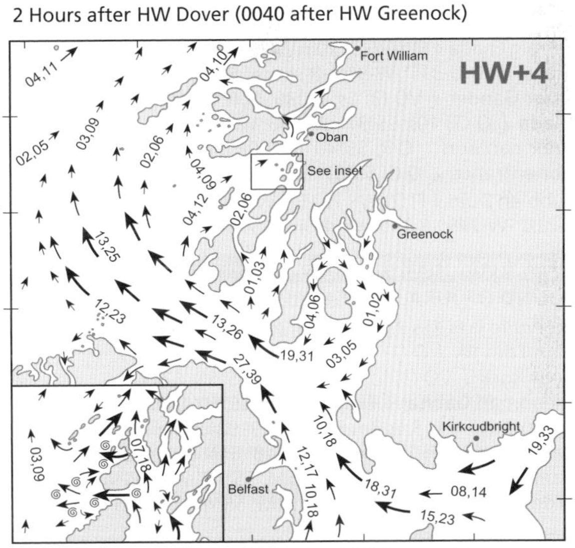

4 Hours after HW Dover (0240 after HW Greenock)

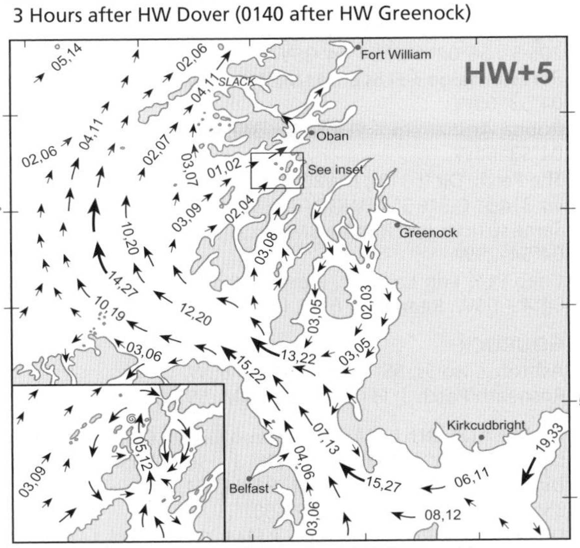

5 Hours after HW Dover (0340 after HW Greenock)

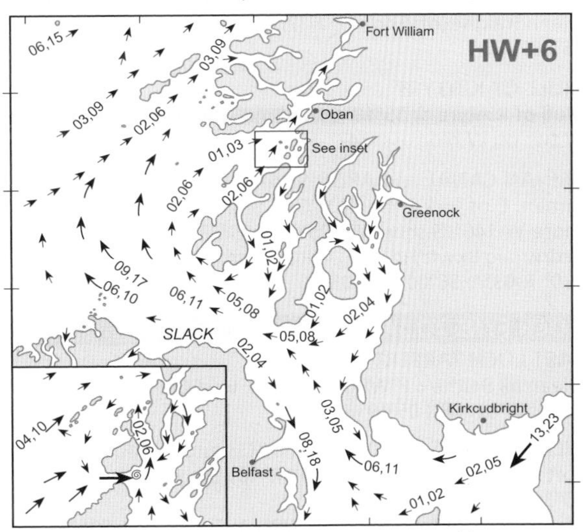

6 Hours after HW Dover (0440 after HW Greenock)

9.9.4 LIGHTS, BUOYS AND WAYPOINTS

Bold print = light with a nominal range of 15M or more. CAPITALS = place or feature. *CAPITAL ITALICS* = light-vessel, light float or Lanby. *Italics* = Fog signal. ***Bold italics*** = Racon. Some marks/ buoys are fitted with AIS (MMSI No); see relevant charts.

COLONSAY TO ISLAY

COLONSAY

Scalasaig, Rubha Dubh ☆ Fl (2) WR 10s 8m W8M, R6M; W bldg; vis: shore-R- 230°-W-337°-R-354°; 56°04′·01N 06°10′·90W.

SOUND OF ISLAY

Rhubh' a Mháil (Ruvaal) ☆ 55°56′·18N 06°07′·46W Fl (3) 15s 45m **19M**; W twr.

Carragh an t'Struith ☆ Fl 3s 8m 9M; W twr; vis: 354°-180°; 55°52′·30N 06°05′·78W.

Carraig Mòr ☆ Fl (2) WR 6s 7m W8M, R6M; W twr; vis: shore-R-175°-W-347°-R-shore; 55°50′·42N 06°06′·13W.

McArthur's Hd ☆ Fl (2) WR 10s 39m W13M, R10M; W twr; W in Sound of Islay from NE coast,159°-R-244°-W-E coast of Islay; 55°45′·84N 06°02′·90W.

Orsay Is, **Rhinns of Islay** ☆ 55°40′·40N 06°30′·80W Fl 5s 46m **18M**; W twr; vis: 256°-184°.

PORT ELLEN and LOCH INDAAL

Carraig Fhada ☆ Fl WRG 3s 20m W8M, R6M, G6M; W □ twr; vis: W shore- 248°-G-311°-W-340°-R-shore; 55°37′·22N 06°12′·71W.

Otter Gander VQ (3) 5s; 55°36′·60N 06°12′·34W.

Fhada Q (3) 10s; 55°37′·21N 06°12′·41W.

Sgeir nan Ron Q R; 55°45′·53N 06°17′·32W.

Hbr entrance Q G; 55°37′·55N 06°11′·45W.

Rubh'an Dùin ☆ Fl (2) WR 7s 15m W11M, R8M; W twr; vis: shore-R-218°-W-249°-R-350°-W-shore; 55°44′·70N 06°22′·28 W.

JURA TO MULL OF KINTYRE

SOUND OF JURA, CRAIGHOUSE, L SWEEN and GIGHA

Skervuile ☆ Fl 15s 22m 9M; 55°36′·60N 06°12′·34W; W twr.

Nine Foot Rk Q (3) 10s; 55°52′·44N 05°52′·91W.

Goat Rock VQ (3) 5s; 55°50′·12N 05°55′·67W.

Eilean nan Gabhar ☆ Fl 5s 9m 8M; 55°50′·01N 05°56′·25W.

Craighouse ☆ Fl R 6s 3m 5M; 55°49′·98N 05°56′·43W.

Na Cùiltean ☆ Fl 10s 9m 9M; 55°48′·64N 05°54′·90W.

Gamhna Gigha ☆ Fl (2) 6s 7m 5M; 55°43′·78N 05°41′·08W.

Ardminish Bay, ☆ Q (3) 10s 3m 2M; 55°40′·56N 05°43′·99W.

WEST LOCH TARBERT

Dunskeig Bay ☆ Q (2) 10s 11m 8M; 55°45′·22N 05°35′·00W.

Eileen Tráighe (off S side) Fl (2) R 5s 5m 3M; R post; 55°45′·37N 05°35′·75W.

MULL OF KINTYRE

Mull of Kintyre ☆ 55°18′·64N 05°48′·25W Fl (2) 20s 91m **24M**; W twr on W bldg; vis: 347°-178°.

CRINAN CANAL and ARDRISHAIG

Crinan, E of lock ent ☆ Fl WG 3s 8m 4M; W twr, R band; vis: shore-W-146°-G-shore; 56°05′·48N 05°33′·37W.

Ardrishaig Bkwtr Hd ☆ L Fl WRG 6s 9m 4M; vis: 287°-G-339°-W-350°-R-035°; 56°00′·76N 05°26′·59W.

LOCH FYNE TO SANDA ISLAND

EAST LOCH TARBERT

Eilean na Beithe ☆ Fl WRG 3s 7m 5M; vis: G036°- W065°- R078°-106°; 55°52′·68N 05°19′·62W.

KILBRANNAN SOUND, CRANNAICH and CARRADALE BAY

Port Crannaich Bkwtr Hd ☆ Fl R 10s 5m 6M; vis: 099°-279°; 55°35′·60N 05°27′·84W.

Claonaig Ferry Terminal ☆ Iso WRG 3s 5m 4M; vis: 305°-G-350° -W-020°-R-040°; metal column; 55°35′·60N 05°27′·84W.

CAMPBELTOWN LOCH to SANDA ISLAND

Davaar N Pt ☆ 55°25′·69N 05°32′·42W Fl (2) 10s 37m **15M**; W twr; vis: 073°-330°.

Sanda Island ☆ 55°16′·50N 05°35′·01W Fl 10s 50m **15M**; W twr; vis: 242°-121°; 992351116.

Patersons Rock Fl (3) R 18s; 55°16′·90N 05°32′·48W.

KYLES OF BUTE TO RIVER CLYDE

WEST KYLE

Ardlamont Point No 47 Fl R 4s; 55°49′·59N 05°11′·76.

Carry Rk No 46 Fl R 4s; 55°51′·40N 05°12′·14W.

BURNT ISLAND CHANNEL

Fl R 4s; 55°55′·80N 05°10′·46W.

Fl G 3s; 55°55′·79N 05°10′·48W.

Fl R 2s; 55°55′·76N 05°10′·39W.

Fl G 5s; 55°55′·74N 05°10′·38W.

Creyke Rk No 45 ; 55°55′·68N 05°10′·89W.

Beere Rk No 44 ; 55°55′·10N 05°10′·63W.

Wood Fm Rk ; 55°55′·42N 05°10′·31W.

EAST KYLE

Colintrave Pt ☆ Fl R 3s 7m 2M; metal post; 55°55′·39N 05°09′·22W.

Ardmaleish Point No 41 Q; 55°53′·02N 05°04′·70W.

ROTHESAY SOUND

Ardyne Fl G 3s; 55°52′·10N 05°03′·20W.

Bogany Point No 36 Fl R 4s; 55°50′·78N 05°01′·41W.

FIRTH OF CLYDE

Toward Pt ☆ 55°51′·73N 04°58′·79W Fl 10s 21m **22M**; W twr.

No 34 Q (3) 10s; 55°51′·44N 04°59′·11W.

Skelmorlie Iso 5s; 55°51′·65N 04°56′·34W.

WEMYSS and INVERKIP

Cowal L Fl 10s; 55°56′·00N 04°54′·83W.

The Gantocks Fl R 6s 12m 6M; ○ twr; 55°56′·45N 04°55′·08W.

The Gantocks No 31 Q; 55°56′·56N 04°55′·13W.

DUNOON

Cloch Point ☆ Fl 3s 24m 8M; W ○ twr, B band, W dwellings; 55°56′·55N 04°52′·74W.

LOCH LONG and LOCH GOIL

Loch Long Oc 6s; 55°59′·15N 04°52′·42W.

Baron's Pt No 3 ☆ Oc (2) Y 10s 5m 3M; 55°59′·18N 04°51′·12W.

Ravenrock Pt ☆ Fl 4s 12m 10M; W twr on W col. Dir lt 204°, WRG 9m (same twr); vis: 201·5°-F R-203°-Al WR(W phase incr with brg)-203·5°-FW-204·5°-Al WG(G phase incr with brg)-205°-FG-206·5°; 56°02′·14N 04°54′·39W.

Port Dornaige ☆ Fl 6s 8m 11M; W col; vis: 026°-206°; 56°03·75N 04°53′·65W.

Rubha Ardnahein ☆ Fl R 5s 3m 3M; vis: 132°-312°; 56°06′·15N 04°53′·60W.

The Perch, Dir lt 318°; F WRG 3m W8M RG 6M, by day WRG 3M; vis: 314·5°-G-316·5°-Al WG-317·5°-W-318·5°-Al RG-319·5°-R-324·5°. Same structure, Fl R 3s 3m 3M (occas); vis: 187°-322°; 56°06′·91N 04°54′·29W.

Cnap Pt ☆ Ldg Lts 031°. Front, Q 8m 10M; W col; 56°07′·40N 04°49′·96W. Rear, 87m from front F 13m; R line on W twr.

GOUROCK

Ashton Iso 5s; 55°58′·10N 04°50′·65W.

Rosneath Patch Fl (2) 10s 5m 10M; 55°58′·52N 04°47′·45W.

ROSNEATH, RHU NARROWS and GARELOCH

Ldg Lts 356°. **Front, No 7N** 56°00′·05N 04°45′·36W Dir lt 356°. WRG 5m **W16M**, R13M, G13M; vis: 353°-Al WG-355°- FW-357°-Al WR-000°-FR-002°.

Dir lt 115° WRG 5m **W16M**, R13M, G13M; vis: 111°-Al WG-114°-FW- 116°-Al WR-119°-FR-121°. Passing lt Oc G 6s 6m 3M;

G △ on G pile. Rear, Ardencaple Castle Centre ☆ 56°00'·54N 04°45'·43W 2 FG (vert) 26m 12M; twr on Castle NW corner; vis: 335°-020°.

No 8N Lt Bn 55°59'·09N 04°44'·21W Dir lt 080° WRG 4m; **W16M**, R13M,G13M;vis: 075°-FG-077·5°-Al WG-079·5°-FW-080·5°-AltWR-082·5°-FR-085°. **Dir lt 138°** WRG 4m **W16M**, R13M, G13M; vis: 132°-FG-134°-Al WG- FW137°-139°-Al WR-142°. Passing lt Fl Y 3s 6m 3M.

Gareloch No 1 Lt Bn ☆ VQ (4) Y 5s 9m; Y 'X' on Y structure; 55°59'·12N 04°43'·89W.

No 3N Lt Bn 56°00'·07N 04°46'·72W Dir lt 149° WRG 9m **W16M**, R13M, G13M F & Al; vis: 144°-FG-145°-Al WG-148°-FW-150°-Al WR-153°-FR-154°. Passing lt Oc R 8s 9m 3M.

Rosneath DG Jetty ☆ 2 FR (vert) 5M; W col; vis: 150°-330°; 56°00'·39N 04°47'·51W.

Rhu Pt Dir lt 318° WRG **W16M**, R13M, G13M; vis: 315°-Al WG-317°-F-319°-Al WR-321°-FR-325°; Dir W; vis: 325°-QW-340°-FW-345°-OcW-350°; 56°00'·95N 04°47'·20W.

Limekiln No 2N Lt Bn 56°00'·67N 04°47'·64W Dir lt 295° WRG 5m **W16M**, R13M, G13M F & Al; R □ on R Bn; vis: 291°-Al WG-294°-FW- 296°-Al WR-299°-FR-301°.

Carraig an Roin ☆ Fl Y 5s 2m 2M; Y post with 'x' topmark; 56°00'·99N 04°48'·40W.
Mambeg Dir lt 331°, Q (4) WRG 8s 10m 14M; vis: 328·5°-G-330°-W- 332°-R-333°; H24; 56°03'·74N 04°50'·47W.

GREENOCK and PORT GLASGOW

Anchorage Lts in line 196°. Front, FG 7m 12M; Y col; 55°57'·62N 04°46'·58W. Rear, 32m from front, FG 9m 12M. Y col.

Lts in line 194·5°. Front, FG 18m; 55°57'·45N 04°45'·91W. Rear, 360m from front, FG 33m.
Steamboat Quay, W end ☆ FG 12m 12M; B&W chequered col; vis 210°-290°; 55°56'·25N 04°41'·44W. From here to Glasgow Lts on S bank are Fl G and Lts on N bank are Fl R.

CLYDE TO MULL OF GALLOWAY

HUNTERSTON CHANNEL

'C' Fl G 5s; 55°48'·10N 05°55'·30W.
Hun 1 (Y) Fl (4) Y 15s; 55°48'·10N 04°54'·21W.
Hun 3 Fl R 2s; 55°47'·60N 04°53'·52W.

LARGS and FAIRLIE

Approach L Fl 10s; 55°46'·40N 04°51'·85W.
Fairlie Patch Fl G 1·5s; 55°45'·38N 04°52'·34W.

MILLPORT and GREAT CUMBRAE

Tomont End Daymark 55°47'·56N 04°54'·10W.
Tattie Pier ☆ WRG 3s 5m 4M; vis: 222°-G-234°-W-246°-R-258°; metal column; 55°47'·20N 04°53'·89W.
Ldg Lts 333°. Pier Head front, 55°45'·04N 04°55'·85W FR 7m 5M. Rear, 137m from front, FR 9m 5M.
Mountstuart L Fl 10s; 55°48'·00N 04°57'·57W.
Runnaneun Pt (Rubha'n Eun) ☆ Fl R 6s 8m 12M; W twr; 55°43'·79N 05°00'·23W.
Little Cumbrae Is, Cumbrae Elbow ☆ Fl 6s 28m 14M; W twr; vis: 334°-193°; 55°43'·22N 04°58'·06W.

ARDROSSAN

Approach Dir lt 055°, WRG 15m W14M, R11M, G11M; vis: 050°-F G-051·2°-Alt WG(W phase inc with Brg)- 053·8°-FW-056·2°-Alt WR(R phase inc with brg)-058·8°-FR-060°; 55°38'·66N 04°49'·22W. Same structure FR 13m 6M; vis: 325°-145°.
Lt ho Pier Hd ☆ Iso WG 4s 11m 9M; W twr; vis: 035°-W-317°-G-035°; 55°38'·47N 04°49'·57W.

IRVINE

Ldg Lts 051°. Front, FG 10m 5M; 55°36'·40N 04°41'·57W. Rear, 101m from front, FR 15m 5M; G masts, both vis: 019°-120°.

TROON

Troon Approach Fl G 4s; 55°33'·08N 04°41'·42W.
W Pier Hd ☆ Fl (2) WG 5s 11m 9M; W twr; vis: 036°-G-090°-W-036°; 55°33'·07N 04°41'·02W.
Lady I ☆ Fl 2s 19m 11M; W Tr R vert stripes; ***Racon (T) 13-11M***; 55°31'·63N 04°44'·05W.

ARRAN, RANZA, LAMLASH and BRODICK

Pillar Rk Pt ☆ (Holy Island), 55°31'·04N 05°03'·65W Fl (2) 20s 38m **18M**; W □ twr.
Holy Is SW end ☆ Fl G 3s 14m 6M; W twr; vis: 282°-147°; 55°30'·73N 05°04'·21W.

Pladda ☆ 55°25'·50N 05°07'·12W Fl (3) 30s 40m **17M**; W twr.

AYR and AILSA CRAIG

S Pier Hd ☆ Q 7m 7M; R twr; vis: 012°-161°. Also FG 5m 5M; vis: 012°-082°; 55°28'·17N 04°38'·74W.
Ldg Lts 098°. Front, FR 10m 5M; Tfc sigs; 55°28'·15N 04°38'·38W. Rear, 130m from front Oc R 10s 18m 9M.
Maidens Hbr, E side ☆ Fl G 5s 4m 3M; 55°20'·24N 04°49'·20W.
Maidens Hbr, W side ☆ Fl R 3s 4m 2M; 55°20'·23N 04°49'·19W.

Turnberry Point ☆, near castle ruins 55°19'·57N 04°50'·69W Fl 15s 29m 12M; W twr.

Ailsa Craig ☆ 55°15'·12N 05°06'·52W Fl 4s 18m **17M**; W twr; vis: 145°-028°.

GIRVAN

S Pier Hd ☆2 FG (vert) 8m 4M; W twr; 55°14'·72N 04°51'·90W.

LOCH RYAN and STRANRAER

Milleur Point Q; 55°01'·28N 05°05'·66W.
Fairway Iso 4s; 54°59'·77N 05°03'·82W.
Forbes Shoal QR; 54°59'·47N 05°02'·96W.
Loch Ryan W QG;54°59'·23N 05°03'·24W .
Cairn Pt ☆ Fl (2) R 10s 14m 12M; W twr; 54°58'·46N 05°01'·85W.
Cairnryan ☆ Fl R 5s 5m 5M; 54°57'·77N 05°00'·99W.
Stranraer No 1 Oc G 6s; 54°56'·67N 05°01'·32W.
No 3 QG; 54°55'·87N 05°01'·60W.
No 5 Fl G 3s; 54°55'·08N 05°01'·86W.
E Pier Hd ☆ 2 FR (vert) 9m; 54°54'·61N 05°01'·60W.

Corsewall Point ☆ 55°00'·41N 05°09'·58W Fl (5) 30s 34m **22M**; W twr; vis: 027°-257°.
Black Head Old Lighthouse (disused); W tower, 22m; 54°51'·70N 05°08'·80W.

PORTPATRICK

Ldg Lts 050·5°. Front, FG (occas); 54°50'·50N 05°07'·02W. Rear, 68m from front, FG 8m (occas).

Crammag Hd ☆ 54°39'·90N 04°57'·92W Fl 10s 35m **18M**; W twr.

Mull of Galloway ☆, SE end 54°38'·08N 04°51'·45W Fl 20s 99m **28M**; W twr; vis: 182°-105°.

MULL OF GALLOWAY and WIGTOWN BAY

Port William Ldg Lts 105°. Front, Pier Hd Fl G 3s 7m 3M; 54°45'·66N 04°35'·28W. Rear, 130m from front, FG 10m 2M.
Isle of Whithorn ☆ Fl WR 3s 20m 6/4M; vis: 310°-W-005°- R-040°; 54°41'·79N 04°21'·54W.
Whithorn Ldg Lts 335°. Front, Oc R 8s 7m 7M; Or ♦; 54°42'·01N 04°22'·05W. Rear, 35m from front, Oc R 8s 9m 7M; Or ♦, synch.

Little Ross ☆ Fl 5s 50m 12M; W twr; obsc in Wigtown B when brg more than 103°; 54°45'·93N 04°05'·10W.

KIRKCUDBRIGHT BAY and KIPPFORD

Little Ross NNE end of Is ☆ Fl (2) 5s 21m 5M; Stone bcn; 54°46'·06N 04°05'·02W.
Hestan I, E end ☆ Fl (2) 10s 42m 9M; 54°49'·95N 03°48'·53W.

9.9.5 PASSAGE INFORMATION

More passage information is threaded between the harbours in this area. Conditions in the SW of Scotland are generally less rugged south of Mull but good charts and up to date Pilots are still essential. Admiralty Leisure Folios 5611 covers the Mull of Kintyre to Point of Ardnamurchan, 5610, the Firth of Clyde. 5613, Irish Sea eastern part including Isle of Man, covers the Scottish coast south of the Clyde to Kirkcudbright. **Bibliography:** *The Yachtsman's Pilot, Clyde to Colonsay* (Imray/Lawrence). *Clyde Cruising Club Sailing Directions-Firth of Clyde including Solway Firth and North Channel* (Imray/Clyde Cruising Club, Lawrence). The *South West Coast of Scotland Pilot* (Admiralty NP66A) covers the whole area.

Submarines regularly exercise in this area, see **9.9.18, SUBMARINE EXERCISE AREAS** and SUBFACTS for information on this activity.

Some of the following more common *Gaelic* terms may help with navigation: *Acairseid*: anchorage. *Ailean*: meadow. *Aird, ard*: promontory. *Aisir, aisridh*: passage between rocks. *Beag*: little. *Beinn*: mountain. *Bo, boghar, bodha*: rock. *Cala*: harbour. *Camas*: channel, bay. *Caol*: strait. *Cladach*: shore, beach. *Creag*: cliff. *Cumhamn*: narrows. *Dubh, dhubh*: black. *Dun*: castle. *Eilean, eileanan*: island. *Garbh*: rough. *Geal, gheal*: white. *Glas, ghlas*: grey, green. *Inis*: island. *Kyle*: narrow strait. *Linn, Linne*: pool. *Mor, mhor:* large. *Mull*: promontory. *Rinn, roinn*: point. *Ruadh*: red, brown. *Rubha, rhu*: cape. *Sgeir*: rock. *Sruth*: current. *Strath*: river valley. *Tarbert*: isthmus. *Traigh*: beach. *Uig*: bay.

CORRYVRECKAN TO CRINAN

(AC 2326, 2343) Between Scarba and Jura is the Gulf of Corryvreckan (AC 2343) which is best avoided, and should never be attempted by small craft except at slack water and in calm conditions. (In any event the Sound of Luing is always a safer and not much longer alternative.) The Gulf has a least width of 6ca and is free of dangers apart from its very strong tides which, in conjunction with a very uneven bottom, cause extreme turbulence. This is particularly dangerous with strong W winds over a W-going (flood) tide which spews out several miles to seaward of the gulf, with overfalls extending 5M from the W of ent (The Great Race). Keep to the S side of the gulf to avoid the worst turbulence and the whirlpool known as The Hag, in depths of only 29m, as opposed to more than 100m in the fairway.

▶ *The W-going stream in the gulf begins at HW Oban + 0410, and the E-going at HW Oban – 0210. Sp rate W-going is 8·5kn, and E-going about 6kn. The range of tide at sp can vary nearly 2m between the E end of the gulf (1·5m) and the W end (3·4m), with HW 30 mins earlier at the E end. Slack water occurs at HW Oban +0400 and –0230 and lasts almost 1hr at Nps, but only 15 mins at sps. On the W-going (flood) stream eddies form both sides of the gulf, but the one on the N (Scarba) shore is more important. Where this eddy meets the main stream off Camas nam Bairneach there is violent turbulence, with heavy overfalls extending W at the division of the eddy and the main stream.* ◀

There are temp ⚓s with the wind in the right quarter in Bàgh Gleann a' Mhaoil in the SE corner of Scarba, and in Bàgh Gleann nam Muc at N end of Jura but the latter has rks in approaches E and SW of Eilean Beag.

SE of Corryvreckan is Loch Crinan, which leads to the Crinan Canal. Beware Black Rk, 2m high and 2ca N of the canal sea lock, and dangers extending 100m from the rock.

WEST OF JURA TO ISLAY

(AC 2481, 2168) The W coasts of Colonsay and Oronsay (AC 2169) are fringed with dangers up to 2M offshore. A narrow drying channel crossed by an overhead cable (10m) separates them.

The Sound of Islay presents no difficulty; hold to the Islay shore, where all dangers are close in. There are ⚓s in the Sound, but holding is mostly poor. The best places are alongside at Port Askaig, or at ⚓ off the distillery in Bunnahabhain B, 2·5M to the N.

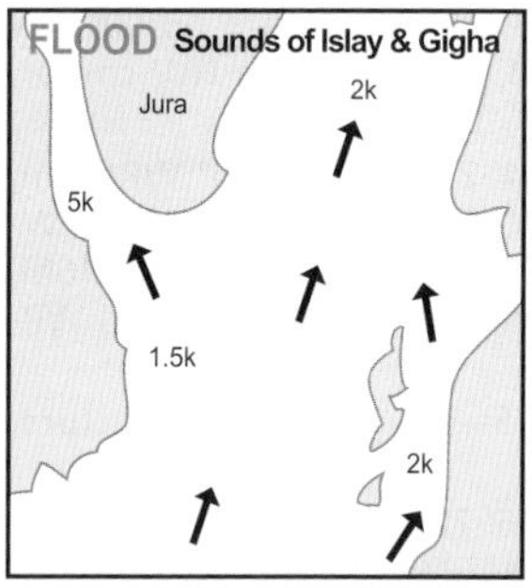

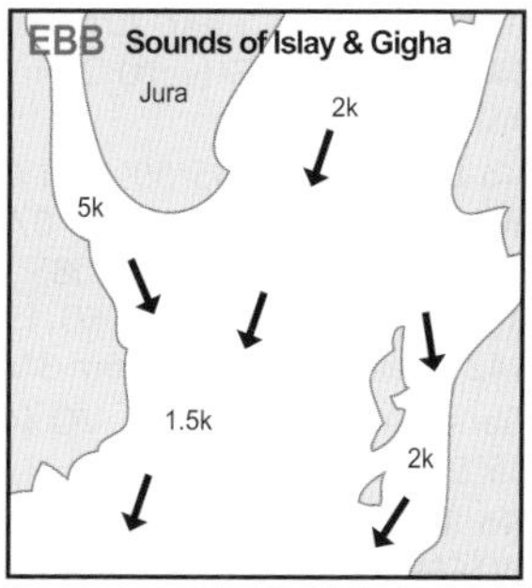

▶ *The N-going stream begins at HW Oban + 0440, and the S-going at HW Oban – 0140. Main flood begins HW Oban +0545. Streams turn approx 1hr earlier in Gigha Sd and at Kintyre and Jura shores. S going stream for 9hrs close inshore between Gigha and Machrihanish starting HW Oban –0530.*

Main ebb begins HW Oban –0015. Streams turn 1hr earlier in Gigha Sd, Kintyre and Jura shores. Overfalls off McArthur's Hd. The Sp rates are 2·5kn at N entrance and 1·5kn at S entrance, ***but reaching 5kn in the narrows off Port Askaig.*** *There are overfalls off McArthur's Hd (Islay side of S entrance) during the S-going stream.* ◀

The N coast of Islay and Rhinns of Islay are very exposed. In the N there is an ⚓ SE of Nave Island at entrance to Loch Gruinart; beware Balach Rks which dry, just to N.

▶ *To the SW off Orsay (lt), Frenchman's Rks and W Bank there is a race and overfalls which should be cleared by 3M. Here the NW-going stream begins at HW Oban + 0530, and the SE-going at HW Oban – 0040;* ***Sp rates are 6-8kn inshore,*** *but decrease to 3kn 5M offshore.* ◀

Loch Indaal gives some shelter; beware rks extending from Laggan Pt on E side of ent. Off the Mull of Oa there are further overfalls. Port Ellen, the main hbr on Islay, has HIE Øs; there are some dangers in approach, and it is exposed to S; see AC 2474.

SOUND OF JURA TO GIGHA

(AC 2397, 2396, 2168) From Crinan to Gigha the Sound of Jura is safe if a mid-chan course is held. Ruadh Sgeir (lt) are rocky ledges in mid-fairway, about 3M W of Crinan. Loch Sween (AC 2397) can be approached N or SE of MacCormaig Islands, where there is an attractive ⚓ on NE side of Eilean Mor, but exposed to NE. Coming from N beware Keills Rk and Danna Rk. Sgeirean a Mhain is a rk in fairway 1·5M NE of Castle Sween (conspic on SE shore). ⚓ at Tayvallich, near head of loch on W side.

W Loch Tarbert (AC 2477) is long and narrow, with good ⚓s and lts near ent, but unmarked shoals. On entry give a berth of at least 2½ca to Eilean Traighe off N shore, E of Ardpatrick Pt. Dun Skeig, an isolated hill, is conspic on S shore. Good ⚓ near head of loch, 1M by road from E Loch Tarbert, Loch Fyne.

On W side of Sound, near S end of Jura, are The Small Is (AC 2396) across the mouth of Loch na Mile. Beware Goat Rk (dries 0·3m) 1.5ca off S'most Is, Eilean nan Gabhar, behind which is good ⚓. Also possible to go alongside Craighouse Pier (HIE Ø). Another ⚓ is in Lowlandman's B, about 3M to N, but exposed to S winds; Ninefoot Rks with depth of 2·4m and ECM lt buoy lie off ent. Skervuile (lt) is a reef to the E, in middle of the Sound.

S of W Loch Tarbert, and about 2M off the Kintyre shore, is Gigha Is (AC 2475). Good ⚓s on E side in Druimyeon B and Ardminish B (HIE Øs), respectively N and S of Ardminish Pt. Outer and Inner Red Rks (least depth 2m) lie 2M SW of N end of Gigha Is. Dangers extend 1M W off S end of Gigha Is. Gigalum Is and Cara Is are off the S end. Gigha Sound needs very careful pilotage, since there are several dangerous rks, some buoyed/lit, others not.

▶ *The N-going stream begins at HW Oban + 0430, and S-going at HW Oban – 0155, sp rates 1·3kn.* ◀

HARBOURS AND ANCHORAGES IN COLONSAY, JURA, ISLAY AND THE SOUND OF JURA

SCALASAIG, Colonsay, **56°04′·14N 06°10′·86W**. AC 2169. HW +0542 on Dover; ML 2·2m. See 9.9.6. Conspic monument ½M SW of hbr. Beware group of rks N of pier hd marked by bn. 2Ⓥ berths run by CMAL on N side of pier, inner end approx 2·5m. Inner hbr to SW of pier is safe, but dries. Ldg lts 262°, both FR 8/10m on pier. Also ⚓ clear of cable in **Loch Staosnaig**; SW of Rubha Dubh lt, Fl (2) WR 10s 8m 8/6M; shore-R-230°-W-337°-R-354°. Facilities: Ⓟ Ⓓ 🛒 (all at ✉), 🚰 Hotel ☎(01951) 200316, Dr (0951) 200328.

LOCH TARBERT, W Jura, **55°57′·69N 06°00′·06W**. AC 2169, 2481. Tides as Rubha A'Mhàil (N tip of Islay). See 9.9.6. HW –0540 on Dover; ML 2·1m; Duration 0600. Excellent shelter inside the loch, but subject to squalls in strong winds; ⚓ outside in Glenbatrick Bay in approx 6m in S winds, or at Bagh Gleann Righ Mor in approx 2m in N winds. To enter inner loch via Cumhann Beag, there are four pairs of ldg marks (W stones) at approx 120°, 150°, 077°, and 188°, the latter astern, to be used in sequence; pilot book required. There are no facilities.

PORT ASKAIG, Islay, **55°50′·87N 06°06′·26W**. AC 2168, 2481. HW +0610 on Dover; ML 1·2m. See 9.9.6. Hbr on W side of Sound of Islay. ⚓ close inshore in 4m or secure to ferry pier. Beware strong tide/eddies. ☆ FR at LB. Facilities: 🚰(on pier) Ⓟ Ⓓ ⛽ ✉ 🛒 ✕ Hotel ferries to Jura and Kintyre. Other ⚓s in the Sound at: Bunnahabhainn (2M N); Whitefarland Bay, Jura, opp Caol Ila distillery; NW of Am Fraoch Eilean (S tip of Jura); Aros Bay, N of Ardmore Pt.

CRAIGHOUSE, SE Jura, **55°49′·99N 05°56′·31W**. AC 2168, 2481, 2396. HW +0600 on Dover; ML 0·5m; Duration 0640 np, 0530 sp. See 9.9.6. Good shelter, but squally in strong W winds with uncomfortable swell in ⚓ in winds from E–S. Enter between lit bn on SW end of Eilean nan Gabhar, Fl 5s 7m 8M vis 225°-010°, and unlit bn close SW. There are 16 Jura Dev Trust 🅥s (£10/night) N of pier (☎(01496) 810332), where yachts may berth alongside; or ⚓ in 5m at the N end of Loch na Mile (poor holding in heavy weed). Facilities: very limited, short stay pontoon 🚰 Ⓟ Ⓓ ⛽ ✉ 🛒 ✕ 🗎. **Lowlandman's Bay** is 1M further N, with ECM buoy, Q (3) 10s, marking Nine Foot Rk (2·4m) off the ent. ⚓ to SW of conspic houses, off stone jetty.

LOCH SWEEN, Argyll and Bute, **55°55′·69N 05°41′·26W**. AC 2397. HW +0550 on Dover; ML 1·5m; Duration = 0610. See 9.9.7 Carsaig Bay. Off the ent to loch, **Eilean Mòr** (most SW'ly of MacCormaig Isles) has tiny ⚓ on N side in 3m; local transit marks keep clear of two rks, 0·6m and 0·9m. Inside the loch, beware Sgeirean a'Mhain, a rk in mid-chan to S of Taynish Is, 3M from ent. Good shelter in Loch a Bhealaich (⚓ outside **Tayvallich** in approx 7m on boulders) or enter inner hbr to ⚓ W of central reef. There are no lights. Facilities: ⛽ 🗎 ✉ with 🚰 🛒 ✕. Close to NE are ⚓s at **Caol Scotnish** and **Fairy Is**, the former obstructed by rks 3ca from ent.

WEST LOCH TARBERT, Argyll and Bute, (Kintyre), **55°45′N 05°36′W**. AC 2476. Tides as Gigha Sound, 9.9.6. Good shelter. Ent S of Eilean Traighe, Fl (2) R 5s, and NW of Dun Skeig, Q (2) 10s, where there is conspic conical hill (142m). Avoid shallows inshore to each side. Loch is lit for 5M by 3 bns, QG, QR and QG in sequence, up to Kennacraig ferry pier, 2FG (vert). PHM buoy, QR, is 2½ca NW of pier. Caution: many drying rks and fish farms outside the fairway and near head of loch. ⚓s are NE of Eilean Traighe (beware weed and ferry wash); near Rhu Pt, possible 🅥s; NE of Eilean dà Gallagain, and at loch hd by pier (ru). Tarbert (9.9.9) is 1·5M walk/bus.

GIGHA ISLAND, Argyll and Bute, **55°40′·6N 05°44′·0W**. AC 2168, 2475. HW +0600 on Dover; ML 0·9m; Duration 0530. See 9.9.6. **Ardminish Bay**: 23 Gigha Heritage Trust 🅥s in the centre (£10) 17 rated at 15t and 6 at 25t or ⚓ NE of Ferry Jetty. Refurbished pontoon and walkway for landing marked by seasonal lts Fl R 3s. Reefs extend off both points, the S'ly reef is marked by a NCM. Sgeir na h-Atho (Kiln Rk) NE of pontoon marked by ECM dries 1·5m. **Druimyeon Bay** is more sheltered in E'lies, but care needed entering from S. ⚓s sheltered from winds in Kilnaughton Bay, Port Mór (S-W), Bàgh na Dòirlinne (SE-S), W Tarbert Bay (NE). Caolas Gigalum (⚓ 50m SE of pier) is safe in all but NE-E winds. Beware many rks in Gigha Sound. Lts: Fl (2) 6s, on Gamhna Gigha (off NE tip); WCM buoy Fl (9) 15s marks Gigalum Rks, at S end of Gigha. **Ardminish** ☎(01583) 505254, 🚰 Ⓟ Ⓓ ⛽ 🗎 ✉ 🛒 ✕ 🗎.

9.9.6 PORT ELLEN

Islay (Argyll and Bute) **55°37′·29N 06°12′·26W**

CHARTS AC 2168, 2476; Imray C64

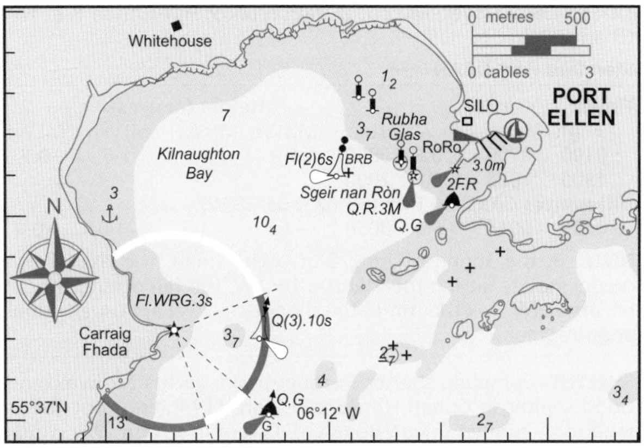

TIDES HW +0620 np, +0130 sp on Dover; ML 0·6. Sea level is much affected by the weather, rising by 1m in S/E gales; at nps the tide is sometimes diurnal and range negligible.

Standard Port OBAN (⟵)

Times				Height (metres)			
High Water		Low Water		MHWS	MHWN	MLWN	MLWS
0100	0700	0100	0800	4·0	2·9	1·8	0·7
1300	1900	1300	2000				
Differences PORT ELLEN (S Islay)							
–0530	–0050	–0045	–0530	–3·1	–2·1	–1·3	–0·4
SCALASAIG (E Colonsay)							
–0020	–0005	–0015	+0005	–0·3	–0·2	–0·3	0·0
GLENGARRISDALE BAY (N Jura)							
–0020	0000	–0010	0000	–0·4	–0·2	0·0	–0·2
CRAIGHOUSE (SE Jura)							
–0230	–0250	–0150	–0230	–3·0	–2·4	–1·3	–0·6
RUBHA A'MHÀIL (N Islay)							
–0020	0000	+0005	–0015	–0·3	–0·1	–0·3	–0·1
ARDNAVE POINT (NW Islay)							
–0035	+0010	0000	–0025	–0·4	–0·2	–0·3	–0·1
ORSAY ISLAND (SW Islay)							
–0110	–0110	–0040	–0040	–1·4	–0·6	–0·5	–0·2
BRUICHLADDICH (Islay, Loch Indaal)							
–0105	–0035	–0110	–0110	–1·8	–1·3	–0·4	+0·3
PORT ASKAIG (Sound of Islay)							
–0030	–0035	–0015	–0025	–1·8	–1·3	–0·7	–0·2
GIGHA SOUND (Sound of Jura)							
–0450	–0210	–0130	–0410	–2·5	–1·6	–1·0	–0·1
MACHRIHANISH							
–0520	–0350	–0340	–0540	Mean range 0·5 metres.			

SHELTER Good shelter on 2 of 3 pontoons (3m at MLWS), most NE'ly for shallow local boats. In S winds swell sets into the bay. In W'lies ⚓ in Kilnaughton Bay, N of Carraig Fhada lt ho; or 4M ENE at Loch-an-t-Sàilein.

NAVIGATION WPT 55°36′·69N 06°12′·06W, 326°/0·63M to Carraig Fhada lt ho. Beware Otter Rk 4M SE of hbr marked by ECM, rks on both sides of ent and in NE corner of bay. W of Rubha Glas rocks marked by 3 bns with reflective topmarks. Keep close to pier.

LIGHTS AND MARKS On W side 10 radio masts (103m) and Carraig Fhada lt ho (conspic), Fl WRG 3s 20m 8/6M; keep in W sector until past the SHM lt buoy. Inbound, Sgeir nan Ròn Bn Q R, dolphin off Ro-Ro Pier 2 FG (vert), SHM Iso G 2s and marina pontoon Fl G 4s. Dredged area around pier and pontoons area marked by buoys.

COMMUNICATIONS CGOC (02891) 463933. Moorings are run by local community – Marina ☎07464151200 portellenmarina.co.uk

FACILITIES Marina 🅥 in bay, slip, 75 inc 38Ⓥ, dredged to 3m, many on 10m fingers, £18>10m>£20; WC/shower, launderette, ⛽ wi-fi (☎300301).
Village 🚰 ⛽ ✉ 🛒 ✕ 🗎.

9.9.7 CRINAN CANAL

Argyll and Bute **56°05'·50N 05°33'·38W** Crinan ❁❁◊◊✿✿✿

CHARTS AC 2326, 2476; Imray C65, C63.

TIDES –0608 Dover; ML 2·1; Duration 0605; HW Crinan is at HW Oban –0045

Standard Port OBAN (⟵)

Times				Height (metres)			
High Water		Low Water		MHWS	MHWN	MLWN	MLWS
0100	0700	0100	0800	4·0	2·9	1·8	0·7
1300	1900	1300	2000				
Differences CARSAIG BAY (56°02'N 05°38'W)							
–0105	–0040	–0050	–0050	–2·1	–1·6	–1·0	–0·4

NOTE: In the Sound of Jura, S of Loch Crinan, the rise of tide occurs mainly during the 3½hrs after LW; the fall during the 3½ hrs after HW. At other times the changes in level are usually small and irregular.

SHELTER Complete shelter in canal basin; yachts are welcome. Good shelter in Crinan Hbr (E of Eilean da Mheinn) but full of moorings, contact Crinan Boatyard. Except in strong W/N winds, ⚓ E of the canal ent, clear of fairway or SW of Eilean da Mheinn. Good holding in Gallanach Bay on N side of L Crinan in about 3m.

NAVIGATION WPT 56°05'·70N 05°33'·64W, 146°/0·27M to Fl WG 3s lt. Beware Black Rock (2m high) in appr NE of ldg line 146° to dir Fl WG 3s lt. Off NW corner of chartlet, no ⚓ in a nearly rectangular shellfish bed, 6ca by 6ca. SPM lt buoys mark each corner: Fl (4) Y 12s at the NE and NW corners, Fl Y 6s at the SW and SE corners; the latter being about 100m NE of Black Rock.

CANAL Canal is 9M (14.5km) long with 15 locks and 7 opening bridges. Transit time is at least 6hrs, observing the 4kn speed limit. Entry at all tides. Max LOA: 26·82m, 6.09m beam, 2·7m draught (add 0.10m to salt water draught. If >2.2m contact Canal Office or Sea Locks 24hrs in advance to confirm canal level will allow passage – there may be some delay to raise water levels) mast 28.95m. The canal operates Mon-Fri in winter months increasing to 6/7 days in peak season. Contact Crinan Canal Office for timings or consult www.scottishcanals.co.uk. Periods of closure may be expected during winter months. It is closed between Christmas and New Year. Long warps and fenders are essential; sea locks can be turbulent at low tide and care is to be taken handling warps – always take a turn round a suitable cleat. Do not pump out bilges or heads in the canal. Water points are supplied but not hoses. Bellanoch pontoons / moorings are reserved for long term berth holders and should not be used by those in transit.

BOAT SAFETY SCHEME Transit craft may be subject to random safety checks on gas systems. £1M 3rd party insurance is required. See also 9.8.17.

LIGHTS AND MARKS Crinan Hotel is conspic W bldg. A conspic chy, 3ca SW of hotel, leads 187° into Crinan Hbr. E of sea-lock: Dir Fl WG 3s 8m 4M, vis 114°-W-146°-G-280°. Ent: 2 FG (vert) and 2FR (vert).

COMMUNICATIONS (Code 01546) CGOC (02891) 463933; Police 101; Dr 462001. Canal Office 603210 (HO). Sea lock 830285 (for advice at w/e and if no response to VHF – staff carry phone). VHF Ch **74** 16 only at sea locks, ⛱ Ch 12.

FACILITIES **Canal Office** (Mon-Fri), www.scottishcanals.co.uk. All fees are under review; contact office for details. *Skippers Guide* is essential reading; **Sea Basin** (overnight rate available). Use shore toilets, not yacht heads, whilst in canal.

Services Crinan Boatyard www.crinanboatyard.co.uk ☎830232, (5t) ✕.

Village ✉ Ⓑ ✕ (Ardrishaig), ⇌ (Oban), ✈ (Glasgow).

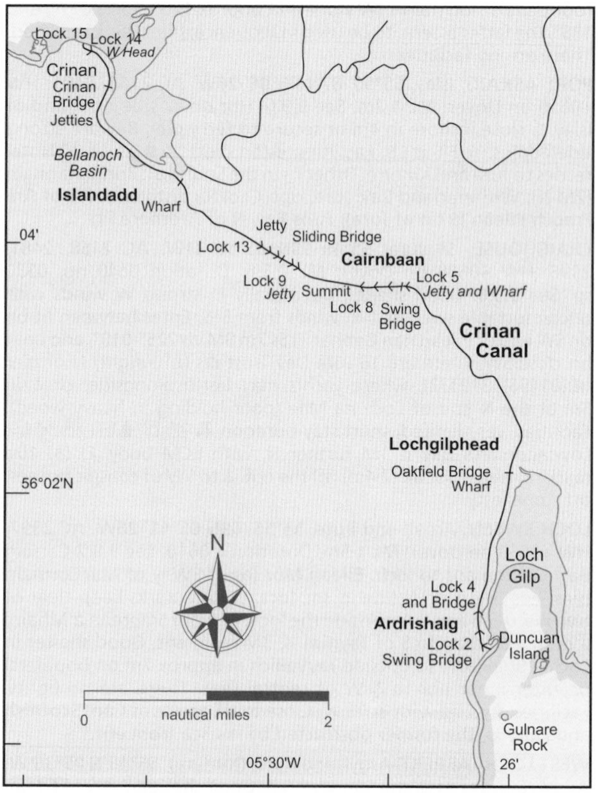

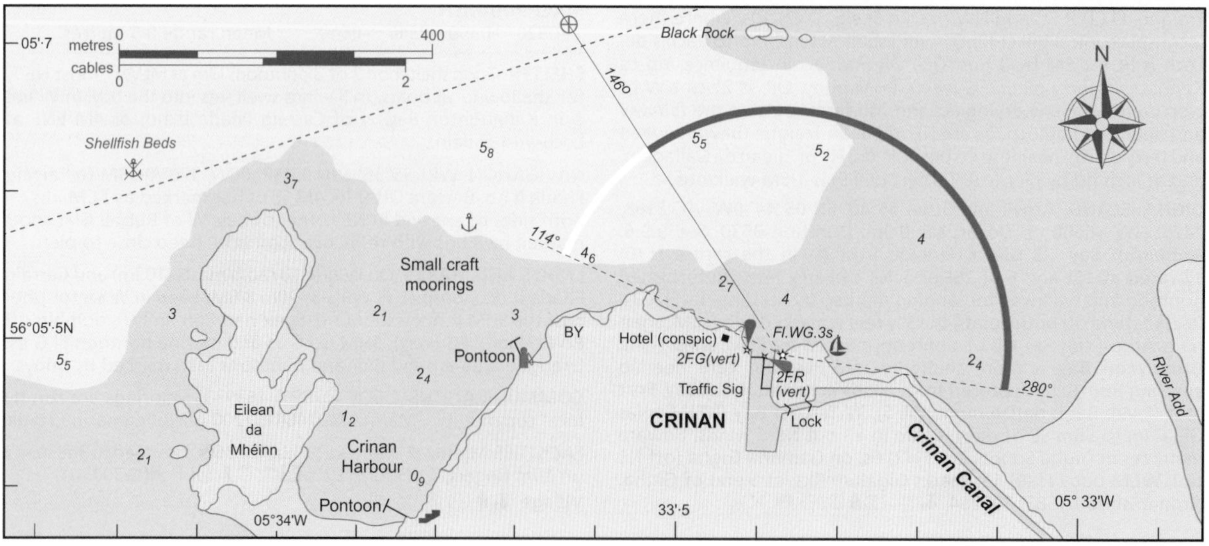

MULL OF KINTYRE

(AC 2126, 2199, 2798) From Crinan to Mull of Kintyre is about 50M. Passage round the Mull of Kintyre within 2M or 3M of the coast requires great care. Races exist S and SW of the Mull, and fresh to strong S winds cause dangerous breaking seas especially during E-going (flood) tidal streams. Best to keep at least 3M offshore and S of Sanda Island.

▶*In Sanda Sound the W-going stream starts HW Dover –0110, and the E-going stream starts HW Dover +0500. Sp rates 5kn. Close W of the Mull the N-going stream starts at HW Dover –0130, and the S-going stream at HW Dover +0430. Sp rates 5kn. Careful timing is needed, especially W-bound.*◀

The Traffic Separation Scheme in the North Channel, is only 2M W of the Mull and limits sea-room in the ITZ.

Sanda Sound separates Sanda Island and its rocks and islets from Kintyre. On the mainland shore beware Macosh Rks (dry, PHM lt buoy), forming part of Barley Ridges, 2ca offshore; and Arranman's Barrels, drying and submerged, marked by PHM lt buoy. Sanda Is provides useful stopping point while waiting for the tide. Beware Paterson's Rk (9ca E, dries). There is good ⚓ on N side in Sanda Roads. Approach with Boat Ho bearing 155°; beware strong tidal stream across entrance, and drying rocks in middle of bay. See Plan on AC 2126.

▶ *Once E of Mull of Kintyre, tidal conditions and pilotage much improve.*◀

MULL OF KINTYRE TO UPPER LOCH FYNE

(AC 2126, 2383, 2381, 2382). Campbeltown is entered N of Island Davaar (lt). 1·5M N off lt ho is Otterard Rk (depth 3·8m), with Long Rk (dries 1·1m) 5ca W of it; only Otterard Rock is buoyed.

▶*E of Island Davaar tide runs 3kn at Sp, and there are overfalls.*◀

Kilbrannan Sound runs 21M from Island Davaar to Skipness Pt, where it joins Inchmarnock Water, Lower Loch Fyne and Bute Sound.

▶*There are few dangers apart from overfalls off Carradale Pt and on Erins Bank, 10M S of Skipness, on S-going stream.*◀

Good ⚓ in Carradale Bay, off Torrisdale Castle.

Lower L Fyne (AC 2381) is mainly clear of dangers to East L Tarbert. On E shore beware rks off Ardlamont Pt; 4M to NW is Skate Is which is best passed to W. 3M S of Ardrishaig beware Big Rk (depth 2·1m). Further N, at entrance to Loch Gilp (mostly dries), note shoals (least depth 1·5m) round Gulnare Rk, PHM lt buoy; also Duncuan Is with dangers extending SW to Sgeir Sgalag (depth 0·6m), buoyed.

Where Upper L Fyne turns NE (The Narrows) it is partly obstructed by Otter Spit (dries 0·9m), extending 8ca WNW from E shore and marked by lt bn. The stream runs up to 2kn here. A buoyed/lit rk, depth less than 2m, lies about 7ca SW of Otter Spit bn. In Upper L Fyne (AC 2382) off Minard Pt, the chan between rks and islands in the fairway is buoyed/lit.

9.9.8 ARDRISHAIG

Argyll and Bute **56°00'·78N 05°26'·62W** ✽✽◊◊✿✿

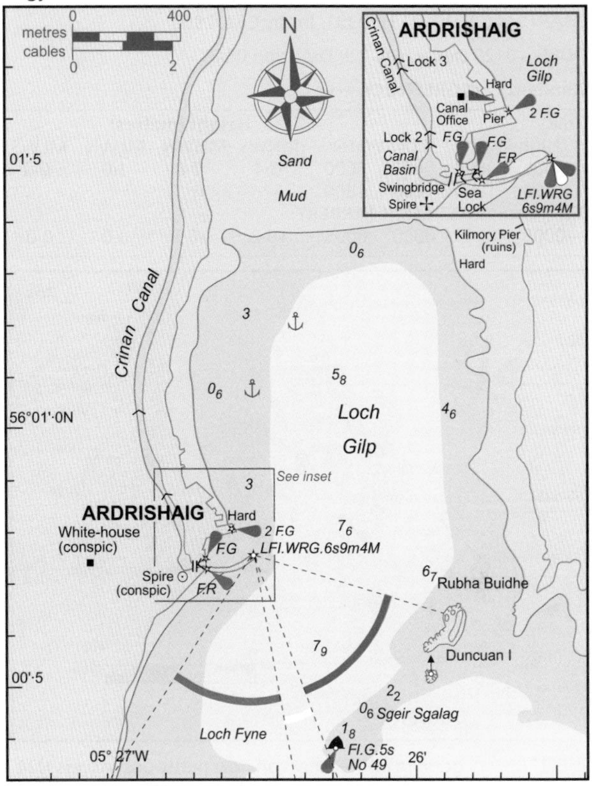

CHARTS AC 5610, 2131, 2381; Imray C63, 2900

TIDES +0120 Dover; ML 1·9; Duration 0640

Standard Port GREENOCK (⟶)

Times				Height (metres)			
High Water		Low Water		MHWS	MHWN	MLWN	MLWS
0000	0600	0000	0600	3·4	2·8	1·0	0·3
1200	1800	1200	1800				
Differences ARDRISHAIG							
+0006	+0006	-0015	+0020	0·0	0·0	+0·1	–0·1
INVERARAY							
+0011	+0011	+0034	+0034	–0·1	+0·1	–0·5	–0·2

SHELTER Hbr is sheltered except from strong E'lies; do not berth on pier or ⚓ due to commercial vessels H24. Sea lock into the Crinan Canal is usually left open, however, a waiting pontoon has been installed outside the lock, with restricted depth, for use in fair weather only. Access at all tides. Complete shelter in the canal basin, or beyond lock No 2. Also ⚓ 2ca N of hbr, off the W shore of L Gilp. Head of Loch dries for nearly 1M.

NAVIGATION WPT No 48 PHM buoy, Fl R 4s, 56°00'·18N 05°26'·31W, 345°/0·6M to bkwtr lt. Dangerous drying rocks to E of appr chan are marked by No 49 Fl.G.5s SHM buoy.

LIGHTS AND MARKS Conspic W Ho on with block of flats leads 315° between Nos 48 and 49 buoys. Bkwtr lt, L Fl WRG 6s, W339°-350°. Pier is floodlit. Other lights as plan.

COMMUNICATIONS (Code 01546) CGOC (02891) 463933; Police 101; Dr 462001. Canal Office 603210 (Mon-Fri); Sea lock 602458.

VHF Ch **74** 16.

FACILITIES **Pier/Hbr** ☎603210, ⌓ (fees under review) ▬ ⊥.

Crinan Canal www.scottishcanals.co.uk

Sea Lock ☎602458, ⌓ ⛺ ⊥ ✕ ⊡; dues, see 9.9.7.

Services ⛽ ✕ 🔧 ⊡ ⛬ ⊡.

Village ✉ Ⓑ 🛒 ✕ ⊡ ⇌ (Oban), ✈ (Glasgow or Campbeltown).

9.9.9 TARBERT

Entrance **55°52'·05N 05°24'·22W**

CHARTS AC 5610, 2131, 2381; Imray C63, 2900

TIDES +0120 Dover; ML 1·9; Duration 0640

Standard Port GREENOCK (⟶)

Times				Height (metres)			
High Water		Low Water		MHWS	MHWN	MLWN	MLWS
0000	0600	0000	0600	3·4	2·8	1·0	0·3
1200	1800	1200	1800				
Differences EAST LOCH TARBERT							
–0005	–0005	0000	–0005	+0·2	+0·1	0·0	0·0

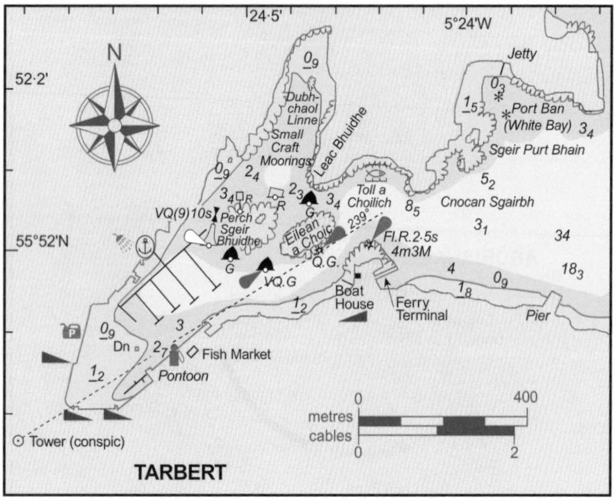

SHELTER Very good in all weathers on new pontoons. Access H24. 100 Ⓥ on pontoons (call on VHF Ch 14 for berth); only use Fish Quay if directed by HM.

NAVIGATION WPT 55°52´·02N 05°23´·03W, 270°/0·7M to Fl R 2·5s lt. Ent is 60m wide and well marked. Cock Isle divides the ent in half: Main hbr to the S, Buteman's Hole to the N, where ⚓s are fouled by heavy moorings and lost chains. Speed limit 3kn.

LIGHTS AND MARKS Outer ldg lts 252° to S ent: Fl R 2·5s on with Cock Is lt QG. Inner ldg line 239°: same QG, G column, on with conspic ✠ tr. Note: The W sector, 065°-078°, of Eilean na Beithe ☆, Fl WRG 3s 7m 5M (on E shore of Lower Loch Fyne), could be used to position for the initial appr to Tarbert.

COMMUNICATIONS (Code 01880) CGOC (02891) 463933; Police 101; Ⓗ (01546) 602323. HM 820344, www.tarbertharbour.co.uk.

VHF Ch **14** (0900-1700LT).

FACILITIES **Yacht Berthing Facility**, www.tarbertharbour.co.uk, £2.54.

Fish Quay (Mon-Fri 0800-1800); **Tarbert YC**.

Town (0800-1800) ACA, (bus to Glasgow), ✈ (Glasgow/Campbeltown).

ANCHORAGES IN LOCH FYNE

• ***Beware discarded wires on seabed throughout the area.***

In Lower L Fyne there is a Ⓜ at Kilfinan Bay, ☎(01700) 821201. In Upper Loch Fyne: 10 Ⓜ for patrons of the Oyster Bar at Cairndow 6M N of Inverary; ⚓ SSW of pier in 4m or dry out NW of the pier; (on pier), bus to Glasgow. On NW bank at Port Ann, Loch Gair and Minard Bay; and on SE bank at Otter Ferry, Sailors' Bothy run by Otter Ferry Pier Association with dinghy pontoon, and toilets (15Ⓜs at Oyster Catcher Inn), Strachur Bay (pontoon and 5Ⓜs off Creggans Inn, ☎(01369) 860279) and St Catherine's.

9.9.10 PORTAVADIE

55°52'·23N 05°18'·98W

CHARTS AC 5610, 2131, 2381; Imray C63, 2900

TIDES +0120 Dover; ML 1·9; Duration 0640

Standard Port GREENOCK (⟶)

Times				Height (metres)			
High Water		Low Water		MHWS	MHWN	MLWN	MLWS
0000	0600	0000	0600	3·4	2·8	1·0	0·3
1200	1800	1200	1800				
Differences PORTAVADIE							
–0005	–0005	0000	–0005	+0·2	+0·1	0·0	0·0

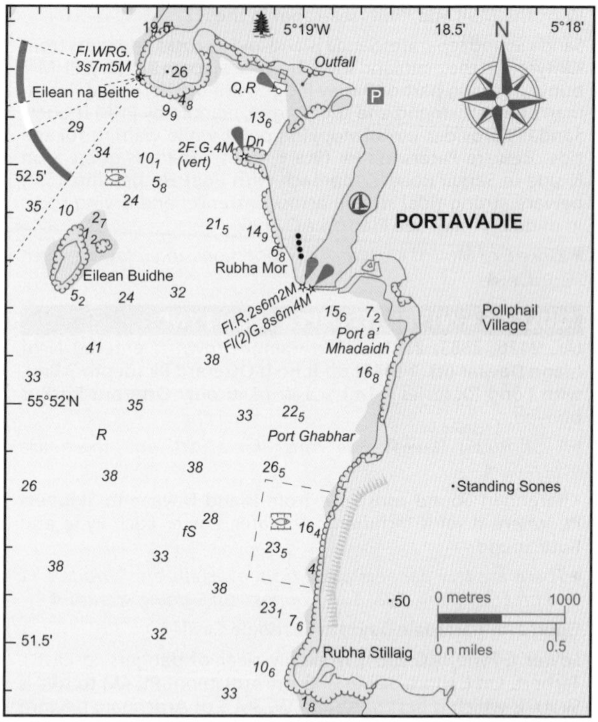

SHELTER Very good in a well protected deep water facility. Access H24. 230 Ⓥ on pontoons with assistance available (call on VHF Ch 80 for berth). If arriving after hours use S, A, B or pontoons.

NAVIGATION WPT 55°52´·00N 05°19´·20W, 027°/0·27M to entrance. When approaching from north pass SW of Eilean Buidhe which has fish farm to the NE. Inshore passage may be used with local knowledge. From the S Clear Sgat Mor and round Rubha Stillaig avoiding fish farm inshore. Harbour has a narrow entrance between lit bwaters off which is a 4m deep bar. Speed limit 3kn.

LIGHTS AND MARKS Eilean na Beithe to North Fl WRG 3s 7m 5M 036°-G-065°-W-078°-R-106° marks access to Glenan Bay and inshore passage NE of Eilean Buidhe. Sgat Mor Fl 3s 9m 12M. Entrance marked by beacons PH Fl R 2s 6m 2M; SH Fl (2) G 8s 6m 4M.

COMMUNICATIONS (Code 01880) CGOC (02891) 463933; Police 101.

VHF Ch **80** (0900-1700LT).

FACILITIES **Marina**, www.portavadiemarina.com ☎811075, 206 inc Ⓥ £2.15, (12t) wi-fi, small shop, ✈ (Glasgow). Other local shops at Kames (2.5M).

ADJACENT ANCHORAGES

Glenan Bay to NW ⚓ in 15m steep to bay open to SW.

Asgog B 1.5M to S entered between Sgat Mor and Sgat Beag. ⚓ in 15M to E of Eilean Aoidhe.

9.9.11 TIDAL STREAMS AROUND THE MULL OF KINTYRE

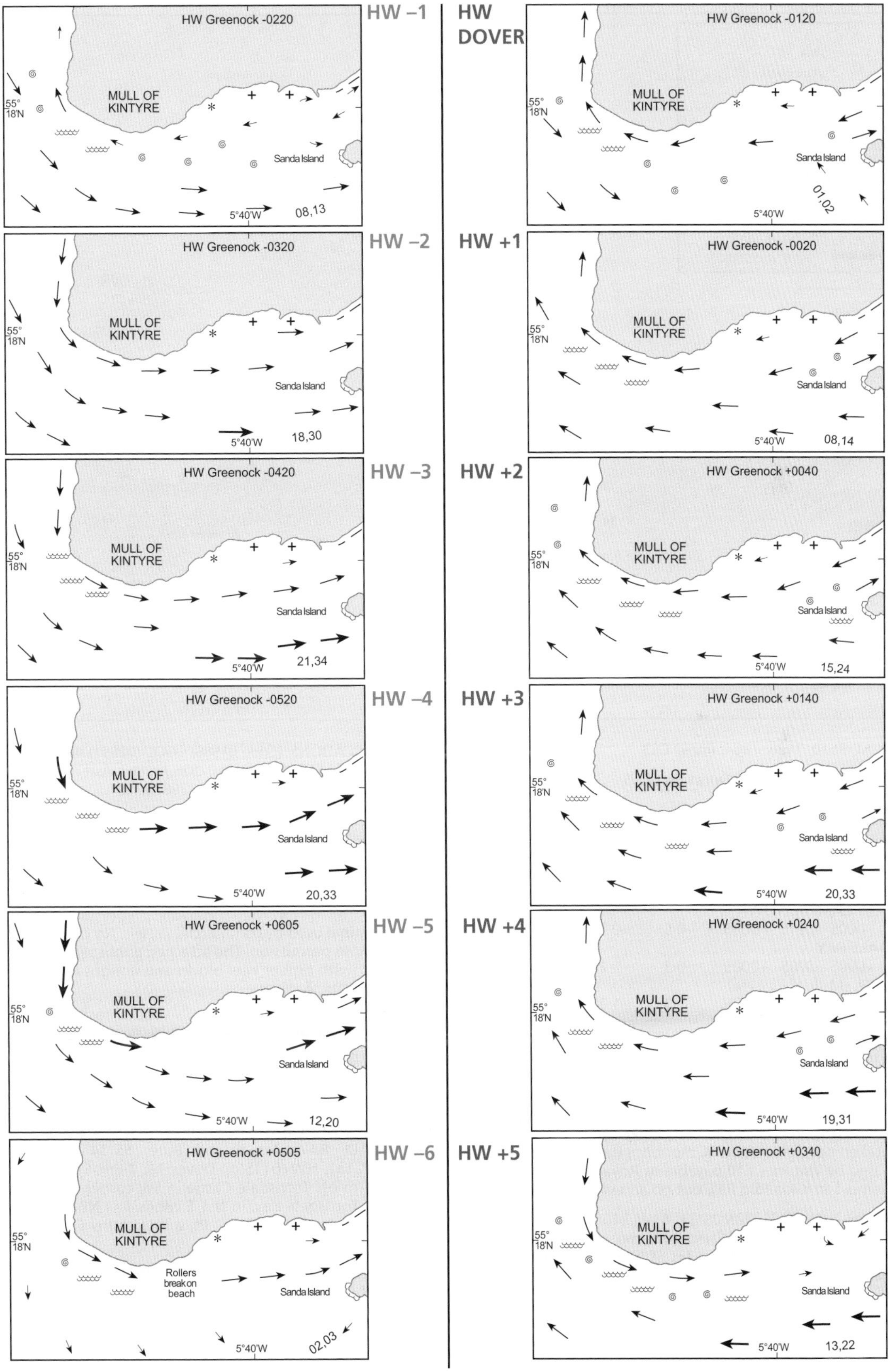
HW –1
HW Greenock -0220
MULL OF KINTYRE
55° 18'N
Sanda Island
5°40'W
08,13
HW DOVER
HW Greenock -0120
MULL OF KINTYRE
55° 18'N
Sanda Island
5°40'W
01,02
HW –2
HW Greenock -0320
MULL OF KINTYRE
55° 18'N
Sanda Island
5°40'W
18,30
HW +1
HW Greenock -0020
MULL OF KINTYRE
55° 18'N
Sanda Island
5°40'W
08,14
HW –3
HW Greenock -0420
MULL OF KINTYRE
55° 18'N
Sanda Island
5°40'W
21,34
HW +2
HW Greenock +0040
MULL OF KINTYRE
55° 18'N
Sanda Island
5°40'W
15,24
HW –4
HW Greenock -0520
MULL OF KINTYRE
55° 18'N
Sanda Island
5°40'W
20,33
HW +3
HW Greenock +0140
MULL OF KINTYRE
55° 18'N
Sanda Island
5°40'W
20,33
HW –5
HW Greenock +0605
MULL OF KINTYRE
55° 18'N
Sanda Island
5°40'W
12,20
HW +4
HW Greenock +0240
MULL OF KINTYRE
55° 18'N
Sanda Island
5°40'W
19,31
HW –6
HW Greenock +0505
MULL OF KINTYRE
55° 18'N
Rollers break on beach
Sanda Island
5°40'W
02,03
HW +5
HW Greenock +0340
MULL OF KINTYRE
55° 18'N
Sanda Island
5°40'W
13,22

9.9.12 CAMPBELTOWN

Argyll & Bute **55°25'·90N 05°32'·56W** Hbr ent ❁❁❁◊◊✿✿✿

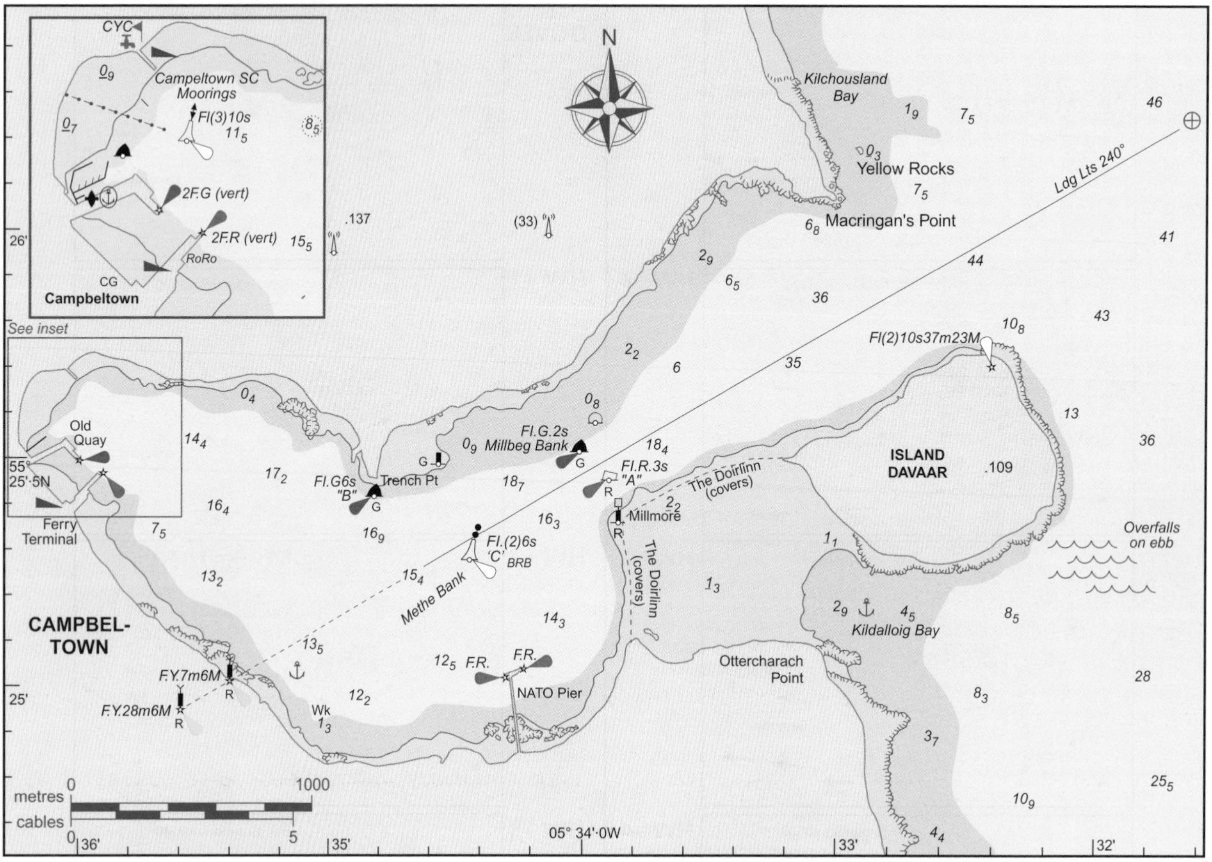

CHARTS AC 5610, 2126, 1864; Imray C63

TIDES +0125 Dover; ML 1·8; Duration 0630

Standard Port GREENOCK (⟶)

Times				Height (metres)			
High Water		Low Water		MHWS	MHWN	MLWN	MLWS
0000	0600	0000	0600	3·4	2·8	1·0	0·3
1200	1800	1200	1800				
Differences CAMPBELTOWN							
−0025	−0005	−0015	+0005	−0·5	−0·3	+0·1	+0·2
CARRADALE BAY							
−0015	−0005	−0005	+0005	−0·3	−0·2	+0·1	+0·1
SOUTHEND, (Mull of Kintyre)							
−0030	−0010	+0005	+0035	−1·3	−1·2	−0·5	−0·2

SHELTER Good, but gusts off the hills in strong SW'lies. Main harbour dredged to 9m for commercial vessels. Yacht pontoon dredged 3·0m is close NW of Old Quay and gives excellent sheltered berthing. Yachts >12m LOA should notify ETA to the berthing master by ☎. Good ⚓ on S side of loch, E of front leading light. ⚓ possible in N of harbour, but is exposed to SE winds. Holding is poor and great care must be taken not to foul local SC moorings (large Y buoys). Some may be used by visitors – £10 payable at Royal Hotel. S of Island Davaar temp ⚓ in Kildalloig Bay, but no access to the loch.

NAVIGATION WPT 55°26'·24N 05°31'·61W, 240°/1·4M to first chan buoys. The ent is easily identified by radio masts N and NE of Trench Pt and conspic lt ho on N tip of Island Davaar off which streams are strong (4kn sp). Caution: The Doirlinn, a bank drying 2·5m which covers at HW, is close S of the ldg line.

LIGHTS AND MARKS See 9.9.5 and chartlet. Otterard Rk (3·8m depth, off chartlet, 1·5M NNE of Island Davaar), is marked by ECM lt buoy. Small, unlit SHM guards shallows on marina approach.

COMMUNICATIONS (Code 01586) CGOC (02891) 463933; Police 101; Dr 552105. HM 552552 mobile 07825 732862, Asst HM 551242 mobile 07876 580950. Berthing mobile 07798 524821.

VHF Ch 13 16 (Mon-Fri 0900-1700).

FACILITIES Yacht pontoon ☎07798 524821, ⛵ (20+30Ⓥ) £2·30, 🚰 ⚡ WC/🚿 on pier, keypad entry, payment to berthing master.

Old Quay D (and by cans from across road, opposite pontoon), 🚰 LB.

Ferry Terminal used by commercial vessels. No berthing alongside without HM's permission. The attached public slipway has a drying out berth (with timber keel blocks and upright leaning posts) for FVs and yachts, 🚰 ⚡.

Campbeltown SC ⛵ (dinghies), regular racing.

Town P D ⛽ 🔧 Ⓔ (10t) ACA, 🛒(2) ✕ ✉ Ⓑ; ♿ WC about 100m from yacht pontoon (keypad, number displayed on pontoon). Bus 3/day to Glasgow, ✈ twice daily to Glasgow, (nearest ⇌ Arrochar, 90 miles N by road). Car hire/taxi.

ADJACENT ANCHORAGE IN KILBRANNAN SOUND

CARRADALE BAY, Argyll and Bute, **55°34'·40N 05°28'·66W**. AC 5610, 2131, HW+0115 on Dover. ML 1·8m. See 9.9.12. Good ⚓ 1 M S in 7m off Torrisdale Castle in SW corner. Beware shoal on S edge of Torrisdale Bay. In N & E winds ⚓ in NE corner of bay, W of Carradale Pt. 3ca E of this Pt, a PHM buoy Fl (2) R 12s marks Crubon Rk.

In S and E winds a swell sets into bay, when good shelter can be found 1M N in **Carradale Harbour** (Port Crannaich); use 4Ⓥ immediately to N or ⚓ 100m N of Hbr. Bkwtr lt, Fl R 10s 5m 6M. Call HM Campbeltown for overnight berth, £10 pay in honesty box. Facilities: ⛵ to SW of hbr, 🚰 on pier, ✉ 🛒 ✕.

9.9.13 LAMLASH

Isle of Arran, N Ayrshire **55°32'·00N 05°07'·06W** ❁❁❁◊◊✿✿✿

CHARTS AC 5610, 2131, 2220, 1864; Imray C63

TIDES +0115 Dover; ML no data; Duration 0635

Standard Port GREENOCK (⟶)

Times				Height (metres)			
High Water		Low Water		MHWS	MHWN	MLWN	MLWS
0000	0600	0000	0600	3·4	2·8	1·0	0·3
1200	1800	1200	1800				
Differences LAMLASH							
–0016	–0036	–0024	–0004	–0·2	–0·2	ND	ND
BRODICK BAY							
–0013	–0013	–0008	–0008	–0·2	–0·1	0·0	+0·1
LOCH RANZA							
–0015	–0005	–0010	–0005	–0·4	–0·3	–0·1	0·0

SHELTER Very good in all weathers. Lamlash is a natural hbr with sheltered ⚓s as follows: off Lamlash except in E'lies – depth may be 20m but shoals rapidly to the W; off Kingscross Point, good except in strong N/NW winds; off the NW of Holy Island in E'lies. Ø off Lamlash Pier. Dry out against pier if in need of repairs. See also Brodick 5M N, and Loch Ranza 14M N (RH col).

NAVIGATION WPT 55°32'·63N 05°03'·06W, 270°/1M to N Chan buoy (Fl R 6s).

> Beware: submarines exercise frequently in this area (see 9.9.18), and also wreck of landing craft (charted) off farmhouse on Holy Is.

LIGHTS AND MARKS See 9.9.5 and chartlet.

COMMUNICATIONS (Code 01770) CGOC (02891) 463933; Police 101; Ⓗ 600777. No VHF.

FACILITIES Lamlash Old Pier (£3–£5), **Arran YC** ☎01770 600333 25Ø £10. **Village** (Lamlash/Brodick) ⇌ (bus to Brodick, Ferry to Ardrossan), ✈ (Glasgow or Prestwick).

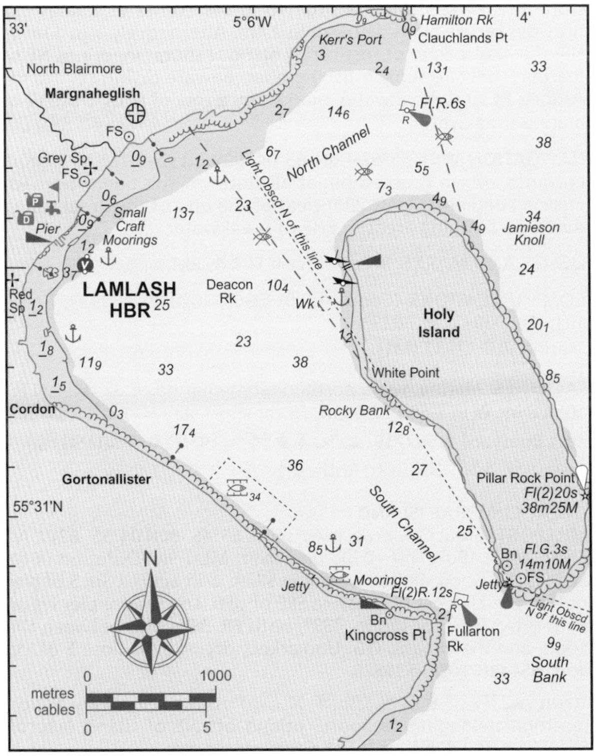

OTHER HARBOURS ON ARRAN (AC 2724, 2131, 2126)

BRODICK, Arran, **55°35'·50N 05°08'·66W**. AC 2131, 2220, 1864. HW +0115 on Dover; ML 1·8m; Duration 0635. See 9.9.13. Shelter good except in E winds. ⚓ W of ferry pier in 3m; on NW side just below Castle in 4·5m, or further N off Merkland Pt in 3-4m. Also 10Øs. There are no navigational dangers but the bay is in a submarine exercise area; see 9.9.18. Lts: RoRo pier dolphin 2 F R (vert) 9m 4M and 2 F G (vert) 9m 4M on pier hd. Facilities: (at pier hd) Ⓑ. Ferry to Ardrossan.

LOCH RANZA, Arran, **55°42'·60N 05°17'·96W**. AC 2131, 2383, 2221. HW +0120 on Dover; ML 1·7m; Duration 0635. See 9.9.13. Good shelter, but swell enters loch in N'lies. The 850m mountain 4M to S causes fierce squalls in the loch in S winds. Beware Screda Reef extending SW off Newton Pt. 12Øs. ⚓ in 5m off castle (conspic); holding is suspect in soft mud. Dinghy landing and temp on pontoon at Lochranza. 2F G lts on RoRo pier at Coillemore. S shore dries. Facilities: at ferry slip, ✕. Ferry to Claonaig.

HARBOURS AND ANCHORAGES AROUND BUTE

(Clockwise from Garroch Head, S tip of Bute) (AC 2131, 1906/7)

ST NINIAN'S BAY, Bute, **55°48'·15N 05°07'·86W**. AC 2221, 2383. Inchmarnock Is gives some shelter from the W, but Sound is exposed to S'lies. At S end, beware Shearwater Rk, 0·9m, almost in mid-sound. ⚓ in about 7m, 2ca E of St Ninian's Pt; beware drying spit to S of this Pt. Or ⚓ off E side of Inchmarnock, close abeam Midpark Farm.

WEST KYLE, Bute, **55°54'N 05°12'·7W**. AC1906. Tides, see 9.9.14 (Tighnabruaich). On W bank PHM buoys, each Fl R 4s, mark Ardlamont Pt, Carry Pt and Rubha Ban; N of which are two Fl Y buoys (fish farms). ⚓ close off Kames or Tighnabruaich, where space allows; or in Black Farland Bay (N of Rubha Dubh). Some Øs off Kames and Royal Hotels, maintained by them on a 'use at own risk basis': Kames Hotel ☎(01700) 811489; Kyles of Bute Hotel 811350; Royal Hotel 811239; and Tighnabruaich Hotel 811615. Facilities:

CALADH HARBOUR, Argyll and Bute, **55°56'·00N, 05°11'·73W**. AC 1906. HW (Tighnabruaich) +0015 on Dover; ML 2·1m. See 9.9.14. Perfectly sheltered natural hbr on W side of ent to Loch Riddon. Enter Caladh Hbr to N or S of Eilean Dubh; keep to the middle of the S passage. When using the N ent, keep between R and G bns to clear a drying rk marked by perch. ⚓ in the middle of hbr clear of moorings. No facilities/stores; see West Kyle above.

LOCH RIDDON, Argyll and Bute, **55°57'N 05°11'·6W**. AC 1906. Tides, see 9.9.14. Water is deep for 1·3M N of Caladh and shore is steep-to; upper 1·5M of loch dries. ⚓ on W side close N of Ormidale pier; on E side at Salthouse; off Eilean Dearg (One Tree Is); and at NW corner of Fearnoch Bay.

BURNT ISLANDS, Bute, **55°55'·76N 05°10'·39W**. AC 1906. Tides, see 9.9.17. The three islands (Eilean Mor, Fraoich and Buidhe) straddle the East Kyle. There are 2 channels: North, between Buidhe and the other 2 islets, is narrow, short and marked by 2 SHM buoys (the NW'ly one is Fl G 3s), and one PHM buoy, Fl R 2s. South chan lies between Bute and Fraoich/Mor; it is unlit, but marked by 2 lateral buoys and a NCM (bn). Depths may be less than charted. A SHM buoy, Fl G 3s, is off Rubha a' Bhodaich, 4ca ESE. Direction of buoyage is to SE. Sp streams reach 5kn in N Chan and 3kn in S Chan. ⚓ in Wreck Bay, Balnakailly Bay or in the lee of Buidhe and Mor in W'lies; also W of Colintraive Pt, clear of ferry and cables. There are 6Øs off the hotel, ☎(01700) 841207.

KILCHATTAN BAY, Bute, **55°45'N 05°01'·1W**. AC 1907. Bay is deep, but dries 3ca off the W shore. Temp ⚓s only in offshore winds: off the village on SW side, or on N side near Kerrytonlia Pt. Rubh' an Eun Lt, Fl R 6s, is 1·1M to SSE. Facilities: bus to Rothesay.

9.9.14 ROTHESAY

Isle of Bute, Argyll and Bute **55°50′·32N 05°03′·08W**

CHARTS AC 5610, 2131, 1907, 1906, 1867; Imray C63, 2900

TIDES +0100 Dover; ML 1·9; Duration 0640

Standard Port GREENOCK (⟶)

Times				Height (metres)			
High Water		Low Water		MHWS	MHWN	MLWN	MLWS
0000	0600	0000	0600	3·4	2·8	1·0	0·3
1200	1800	1200	1800				
Differences ROTHESAY BAY							
–0020	–0015	–0010	–0002	+0·2	+0·2	+0·2	+0·2
RUBHA A'BHODAICH (Burnt Is)							
–0020	–0010	–0007	–0007	–0·2	–0·1	+0·2	+0·2
TIGHNABRUAICH							
+0007	–0010	–0002	–0015	0·0	+0·2	+0·4	+0·5

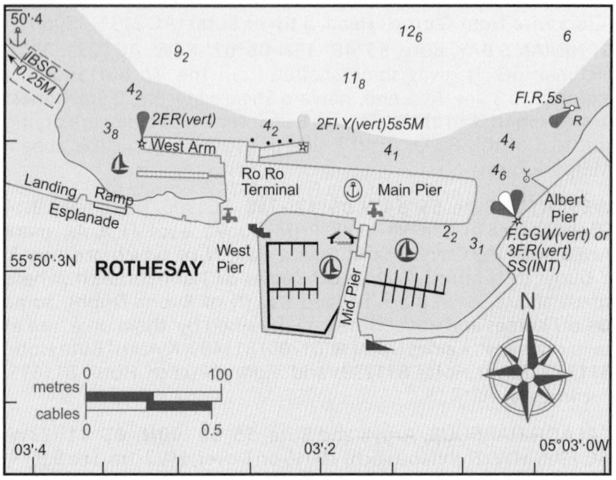

SHELTER Good in Outer and Inner Harbours (max 2m draught and very limited space for LOA > 40ft), and on pontoons S of West Arm, but beware of very strong easterly flow towards the rocks on the E side of the harbour due to wash during ferry manoeuvres (and whilst berthed). No berthing on north and east faces of Main Pier. Good ⚓ off Isle of Bute SC in west side of bay. Exposed to N/NE; **Port Bannatyne Marina** (Kames Bay) offers better shelter.

NAVIGATION WPT 55°51′·00N 05°02′·76W, 194°/0·69M to Outer hbr ent. From E keep 1ca off Bogany Pt PHM buoy, Fl R 4s. Call HM for bridge openings to Inner Harbour. Entry/exit to/from hbr controlled by traffic lights. Extreme care needed; very limited room to manoeuvre.

LIGHTS AND MARKS Lts as chartlet, hard to see against shore lts. Conspicuous church spire leads 190° to outer harbour. Port Sigs:

● (3 vert) = Harbour closed to all traffic movements.

● (2 vert) + ○ = Harbour open.

COMMUNICATIONS (Code 01700) CGOC (02891) 463933; Police 101; Dr 503985; Ⓗ 503938. HM 503842; Bute Berthing Co mob 07799 724225. *Bute Berthing* **M**; *Rothesay Harbour* Ch **12** 16.

FACILITIES 68 ⊆ Ⓥ (Bute Berthing Co) call ahead for availability. £16 for 8m LOA, £21 for 11m LOA, short stay £6, on Pier; by arrangement weekdays (min 200 galls).

Town (Wed – early closing) (closes 1800) @(0900-1700) Ⓑ (ferry to Wemyss Bay) ✈(Glasgow). Ferries to Wemyss Bay and Skelmorlie N.

9.9.15 PORT BANNATYNE

Isle of Bute, Argyll and Bute **55°51′·75N 05°05′·17W**

CHARTS AC 5610, 2131, 1907, 1906, 1867; Imray C63, 2900

TIDES As for Rothesay

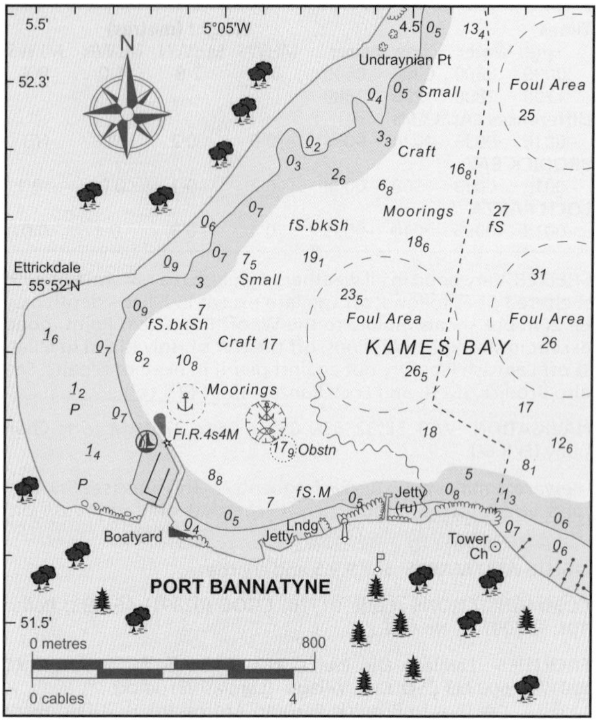

SHELTER Well sheltered from westerly winds and protected by stone breakwater. Marina situated in SW corner of Kames Bay provides secure alonside berth in 2.4m. Alternatively ⚓ in 11m to NE of b'water clear of small craft along N shore. moorings NE of marina – beware sunken fishing boat. Beware drying rks 1ca off Ardbeg Pt, and shoal water, marked by a row of piles, close W of marina breakwater.

NAVIGATION WPT 55°52′·00N 05°04′·00W, 252°/0·7M to marina entrance, which is accessible at all states of the tide. Approach marina keeping at least 20m clear of the end of the breakwater. Avoid no ⚓/fishing areas to ENE of breakwater.

LIGHTS AND MARKS Breakwater lt Fl R 4s 2M.

COMMUNICATIONS (Code 01700) CGOC (02891) 463933; Police 101; Dr 503985; Ⓗ 503938.
Marina VHF Ch 37 (M1).

FACILITIES **Marina**, www.portbannatynemarina.co.uk, ☎503116, 105⊆ inc Ⓥ in 2·5m, £2·00/m, £6 for short stay (4 hrs) wi-fi.

Port Boatyard ☎502719, Ⓔ (15t).

Town ✕ bus to Rothesay.

GREAT CUMBRAE ISLAND

MILLPORT, Great Cumbrae, N Ayrshire, **55°45′·00N 04°55′·82W**. AC 5610, 1867, 1907. HW +0100 on Dover; ML 1·9m; Duration 0640. See 9.9.17. Good shelter, except in S'lies. ⚓ in approx 3m S of pier or E of the Eileans. 12 Ⓥs 1½ca SSE of pier. Ldg marks: pier hd on with ✠ twr 333°; or ldg lts 333°, both FR 7/9m 5M, between the Spoig and the Eileans, QG. Unmarked, drying rk is close E of ldg line. HM ☎(01475) 530826.

Town ✕. Possible temporary ⊆ on pontoon belonging to SportScotland off NE of island (approx 55°47′·1N 04°53′·8W) in 3.5m–4.5m; no services.

9.9.16 FAIRLIE QUAY

N Ayrshire **55°46'·07N 04°51'·78W**

CHARTS AC 5610, 2131, 1907, 1867; Imray C63, 2900

TIDES +0105 Dover; ML 1·9; Duration 0640

Standard Port GREENOCK (→)

Times				Height (metres)			
High Water		Low Water		MHWS	MHWN	MLWN	MLWS
0000	0600	0000	0600	3·4	2·8	1·0	0·3
1200	1800	1200	1800				
Differences *MILLPORT*							
–0005	*–0025*	*–0025*	*–0005*	*0·0*	*-0·1*	*0·0*	*+0·1*

SHELTER Access H24. Poor shelter; pontoon subject to swell in fresh conditions and wash from passing vessels. Craft should not be left unsupervised unless calm settled weather is forecast. Cumbrae Island gives shelter from westerlies; Largs Channel is open to S or N winds.

NAVIGATION WPT 55°46'·08N 04°51'·84W. From S beware Hunterston Sands, Southannan Sands and outfalls from Hunterston Power Stn (conspic).

LIGHTS AND MARKS Lts as on chartlet. Fairlie Quay, 2 FG (vert) N & S ends of Pier.

COMMUNICATIONS (Code 01475) CGOC (02891) 463933; Dr 673380; Ⓗ 733777; Police 101. Fairlie Quay 568267.

Fairlie Quay Marina Ch **80** M (H24).

FACILITIES **Fairlie Quay** Fuel H24: (80t). **Fairlie YC; Town** ✉ Ⓑ ✕ ⇌ (Fairlie & Largs; 50 mins to Glasgow), ✈.

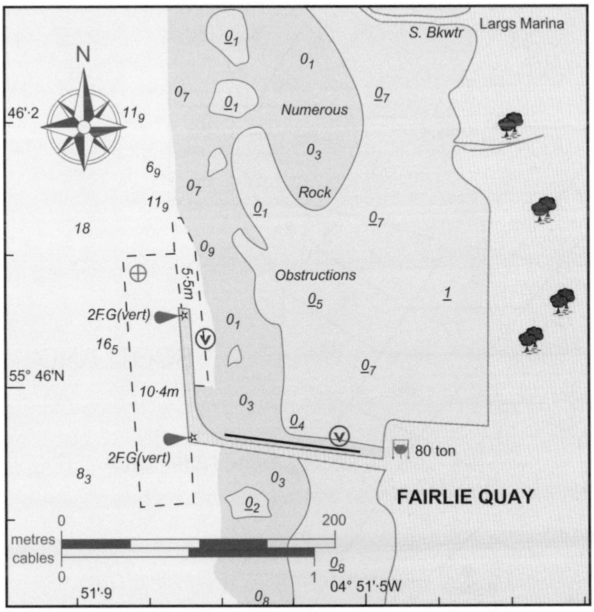

9.9.17 LARGS

N Ayrshire **55°46'·40N 04°51'·84W**

CHARTS AC 5610, 2131, 1907, 1867; Imray C63, 2900

TIDES +0105 Dover; ML 1·9; Duration 0640

Standard Port GREENOCK (→)

Times				Heights (metres)			
High Water		Low Water		MHWS	MHWN	MLWN	MLWS
0000	0600	0000	0600	3·4	2·8	1·0	0·3
1200	1800	1200	1800				
Differences *MILLPORT*							
–0005	*–0025*	*–0025*	*–0005*	*0·0*	*-0·1*	*0·0*	*+0·1*

SHELTER Excellent in Largs Yacht Haven, access all tides (2·5m in ent; 3m deep berths). 7 pontoons; Ⓥ on 'C/D'. Cumbrae Is gives shelter from W'lies; Largs Chan is open to S or N winds.

NAVIGATION WPT 55°46'·40N 04°51'·84W, SWM lt buoy, off ent. From S beware Hunterston Sands, Southannan Sands and outfalls from Hunterston Power Stn (conspic). From the S bkwtr to Fairlie Quay is a restricted, no ⚓ area.

LIGHTS AND MARKS 'Pencil' monument (12m) conspic 4ca N of ent. Lts as on chartlet. Largs Pier, 2 FG (vert) when vessel expected.

COMMUNICATIONS (Code 01475) CGOC (02891) 463933; Dr 673380; Ⓗ 733777; Police 101; Largs SC 670000.

Largs Yacht Haven Ch **80** M (H24).

FACILITIES **Largs Yacht Haven** www.yachthavens.com ☎ 675333, (730 inc Ⓥ), £3·35; (H24) (H24) Ⓔ (70t)(45t) (17t) ✕ wi-fi.
Town (1M) ✉ Ⓑ ✕ ⇌ (50 mins to Glasgow), ✈.

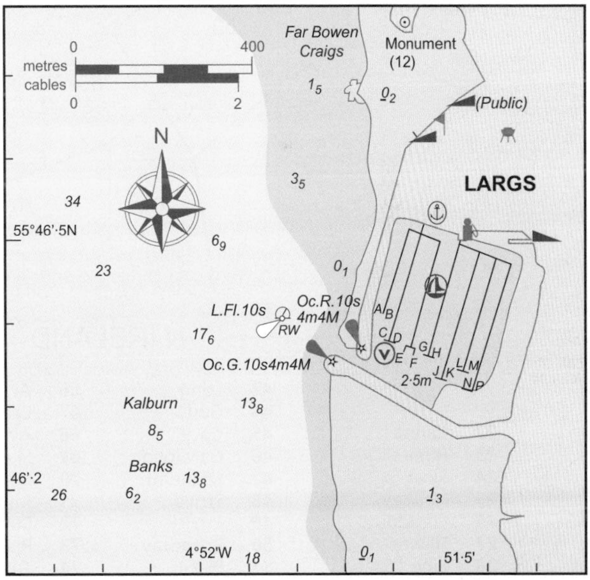

ARRAN, BUTE AND FIRTH OF CLYDE

(AC1906, 1907) Arran's mountains tend to cause squalls or calms, but there are good ⚓s at Lamlash, Brodick and Loch Ranza. Sannox Rock (depth 1·5m) is 2½ca off Arran coast 8M N of Lamlash. 1ca off W side of Inchmarnock is Tra na-h-uil, a rock drying 1·5m. In Inchmarnock Sound, Shearwater Rk (depth 0·9m) lies in centre of S entrance.

The Kyles of Bute are attractive channels N of Bute, and straightforward apart from the Burnt Islands where it is best to take the north channel, narrow but well buoyed, passing between Eilean Buidhe and Eilean Fraoich/Eilean Mor. ►*Spring stream may reach 5kn.*◄ Caladh Hbr is a beautiful ⚓ 7ca NW of Burnt Is.

The N lochs in Firth of Clyde are less attractive. Loch Goil is worth a visit; Loch Long is squally with few ⚓s but no hidden dangers; Gareloch has Rhu Marina, Faslane submarine base and small craft moorings at the northern end. ► *Navigation in Firth of Clyde is straightforward since tidal streams are weak, seldom exceeding 1kn. It is however a busy area with many large commercial vessel movements and extensive naval training which takes place involving submarines, ships and aircraft. All users are recommended to read The Clydeport CLYDE LEISURE NAVIGATION GUIDE – www.clydeport.co.uk.* ◄ Channels are well marked; but beware unlit moorings. There are marinas on the mainland at Largs, Holy Loch, Portavadie and Inverkip. Rothesay Hbr on E Bute, and Kilchattan B (⚓ 6M to S) are both sheltered from SSE to WNW.

9.9.18 SUBMARINE EXERCISE AREAS

Submarines keep a constant listening watch on Ch 16. Submarines on the surface comply strictly with IRPCS; submarines at periscope depth will not close to within 1500 yds of a FV without her express agreement. See 3.13.1 for more guidance.

A 'Fisherman's hotline' (☎(01436) 677201) is available on a 24hr basis and may be used for any queries relating to SUBFACTS – from any mariner.

SUBFACTS broadcasts detail submarine activity in the exercise areas between Barra and the Isle of Man. They are transmitted by CGOC Belfast at 0710 and 1910 on a specified VHF Ch after an initial announcement on Ch 16.

The areas are referred to by the names given in the table for Areas 1–25 (North of Mull), see 9.8.9.

General information on SUBFACTS is also broadcast twice daily at 0620 & 1820 UT on Navtex.

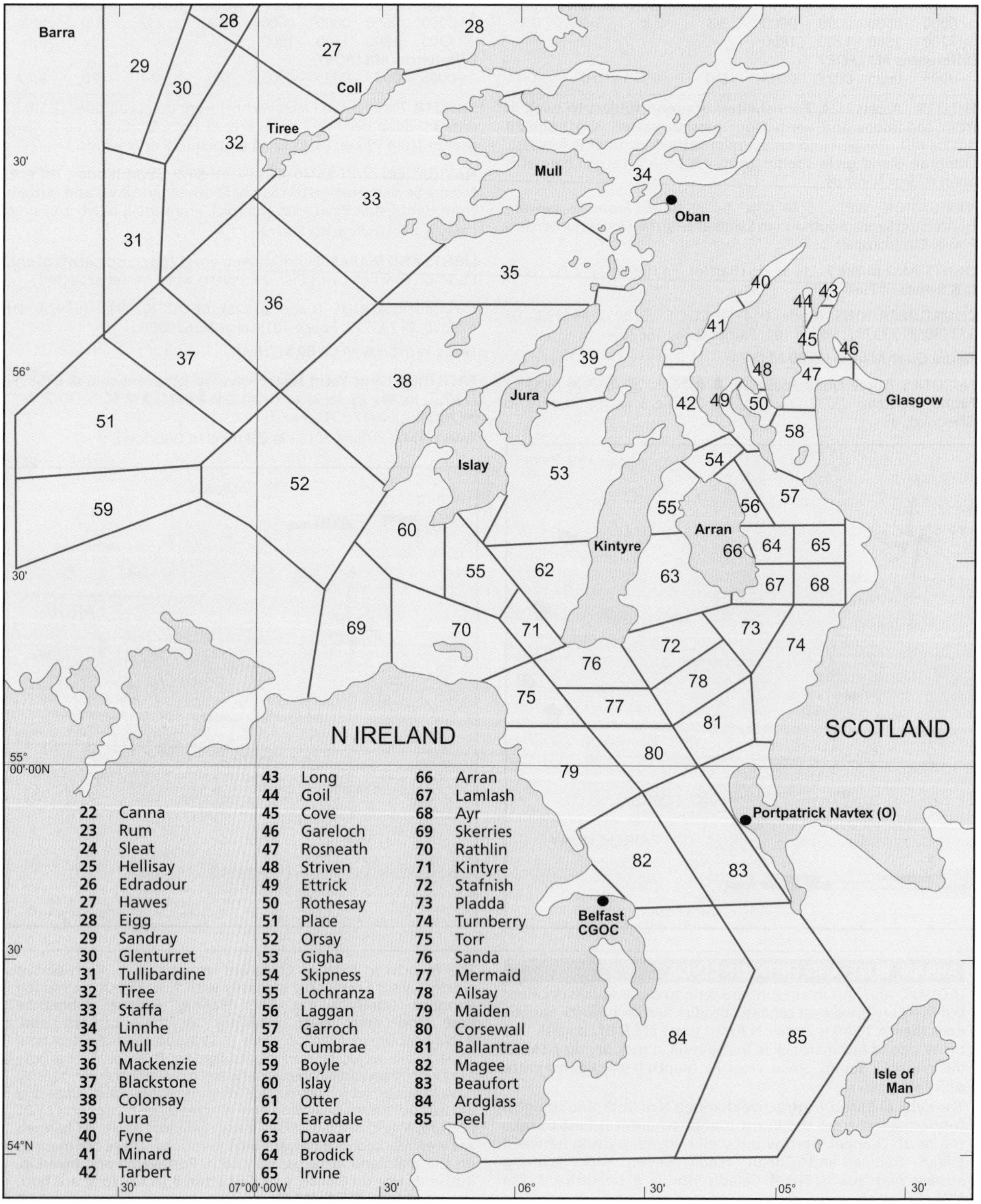

Barra
Coll
Tiree
Mull
Oban
Jura
Islay
Kintyre
Arran
Glasgow
N IRELAND
SCOTLAND
Portpatrick Navtex (O)
Belfast CGOC
Isle of Man
30'
56°
55° 00'·00N
54°N
07°00'·00W
06°
05°
22 Canna
23 Rum
24 Sleat
25 Hellisay
26 Edradour
27 Hawes
28 Eigg
29 Sandray
30 Glenturret
31 Tullibardine
32 Tiree
33 Staffa
34 Linnhe
35 Mull
36 Mackenzie
37 Blackstone
38 Colonsay
39 Jura
40 Fyne
41 Minard
42 Tarbert
43 Long
44 Goil
45 Cove
46 Gareloch
47 Rosneath
48 Striven
49 Ettrick
50 Rothesay
51 Place
52 Orsay
53 Gigha
54 Skipness
55 Lochranza
56 Laggan
57 Garroch
58 Cumbrae
59 Boyle
60 Islay
61 Otter
62 Earadale
63 Davaar
64 Brodick
65 Irvine
66 Arran
67 Lamlash
68 Ayr
69 Skerries
70 Rathlin
71 Kintyre
72 Stafnish
73 Pladda
74 Turnberry
75 Torr
76 Sanda
77 Mermaid
78 Ailsay
79 Maiden
80 Corsewall
81 Ballantrae
82 Magee
83 Beaufort
84 Ardglass
85 Peel

9.9.19 INVERKIP (KIP MARINA)

Inverclyde **55°54'·50N 04°53'·00W**

CHARTS AC 5610, 2131, 1907; Imray C63, 2900

TIDES +0110 Dover; ML 1·8; Duration 0640

Standard Port GREENOCK (⟶)

Times				Height (metres)			
High Water		Low Water		MHWS	MHWN	MLWN	MLWS
0000	0600	0000	0600	3·4	2·8	1·0	0·3
1200	1800	1200	1800				
Differences WEMYSS BAY							
–0005	–0005	–0005	–0005	0·0	0·0	+0·1	+0·1

SHELTER Excellent inside marina. Chan and marina are dredged 3·5m; accessible H24. Inverkip Bay is exposed to SW/NW winds.

NAVIGATION WPT 55°54′·49N 04°52′·95W, Kip SHM buoy, Fl G 5s, at ent to buoyed chan; beware shifting bank to the N.

LIGHTS AND MARKS SHM 55°54′·55N 04°54′·47W Fl G 1·06M 093° to entr which is ½M N of conspic chmy (238m). SPM buoy marks sewer outfall off Ardgowan Pt. From Kip SHM buoy, 3 SHM and 3 PHM buoys mark 365m long appr chan.

COMMUNICATIONS (Code 01475) CGOC (02891) 463933; Police 101; Dr 520248; Ⓗ 33777.

Kip Marina Ch **80** M (H24). *Clydeport Estuary Radio* VHF Ch **12** 16 (H24). Info on weather and traffic available on request.

FACILITIES Kip Marina www.scottishmarinas.co.uk ☎521485; 625 inc Ⓥ, £2.25, £12 <5hrs, Ⓔ (50t) Diver, YC. **Town** Ⓑ (Gourock), (Glasgow).

ADJACENT ANCHORAGE

DUNOON, Argyll and Bute, **55°56'·70N 04°55'·20W**. AC 5610, 2131, 1907, 1994. Use Greenock tides. Temp ⚓ in West or East Bays (S and N of Dunoon Pt). The former is open to the S; the latter more shoal. The Gantocks, drying rks 3ca SE of Dunoon Pt, have W ○ bn tr, Fl R 6s 12m 6M. 2FR (vert) on ferry pier. Facilities: ferry to Gourock. 3Ⓥs off Innellan, 3·7M S of Dunoon, ☎(01369) 830445.

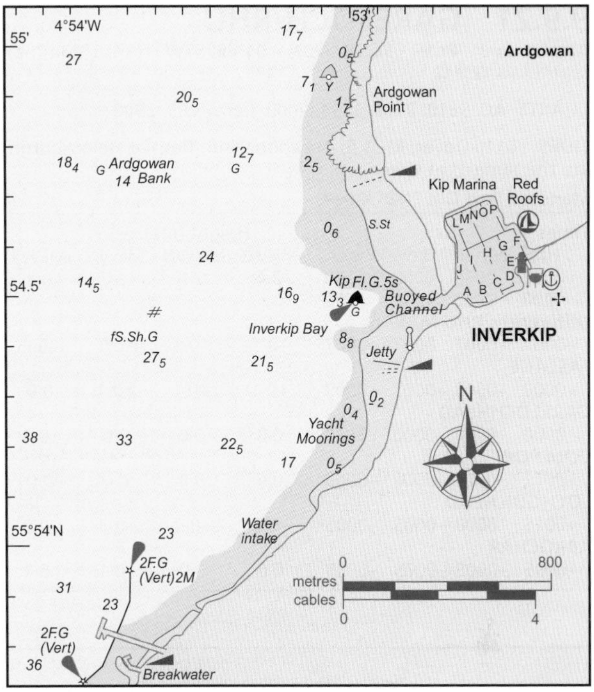

ANCHORAGE IN THE UPPER FIRTH OF CLYDE

GOUROCK, Inverclyde, **55°58'·00N 04°49'·00W**. AC 5610, 2131, 1994, Imray C63, 2900 Series; OS 63. Use Greenock tides. ⚓ in W of Gourock Bay, beware of moorings and foul ground. It is exposed in NW/NE'lies. No navigational dangers, but much shipping and ferries in the Clyde. The S edge of the Firth of Clyde recommended channel lies 2ca N of Kempock Pt. The pier at the S end of Gourock Bay is disused and unsafe. Facilities: Royal Gourock YC ☎632983. **Town** Ⓑ Ferry (to Dunoon) (Glasgow).

9.9.20 HOLY LOCH

Argyll **55°59'·03N 04°56'·82W**

CHARTS AC 5610, 2131, 1994; Imray C63, 2900

TIDES +0122 Dover; ML 2·0; Duration 0640

Standard Port GREENOCK (⟶)

SHELTER Good, but exposed to to E/NE.

NAVIGATION WPT 55°59′·03N 04°55′·75W 270° to marina ent 0.60M. No offshore dangers. Holy Loch is controlled by QHM Clyde but navigation is not restricted; keep well clear of ferries when entering or leaving the loch.

LIGHTS AND MARKS No 30 SCM 55°58′·75N 04°53′·82W off Strone Pt. 2FR at SE end of pier. Marina floodlit.

COMMUNICATIONS (Code 01369) CGOC (02891) 463933; Police 101; Dr 703279; Ⓗ 704341.

Holy Loch Marina Ch 80 M.

FACILITIES Marina www.holylochmarina.co.uk ☎701800, 270+ Ⓥ in 3m £2.20, 2nd night ½ price; short stay £5.50. (25t) . Possible on bkwtr pontoon for larger yachts in depth >5m, but open to the E. Commercial timber yard operating alongside marina facilities. **Holy Loch SC** ☎702707.

Sandbank (town) PO, Ferries from Hunter's Quay to McInroy's Pt, Gourock, connecting with trains and coaches to Glasgow Airport. Good local area bus service.

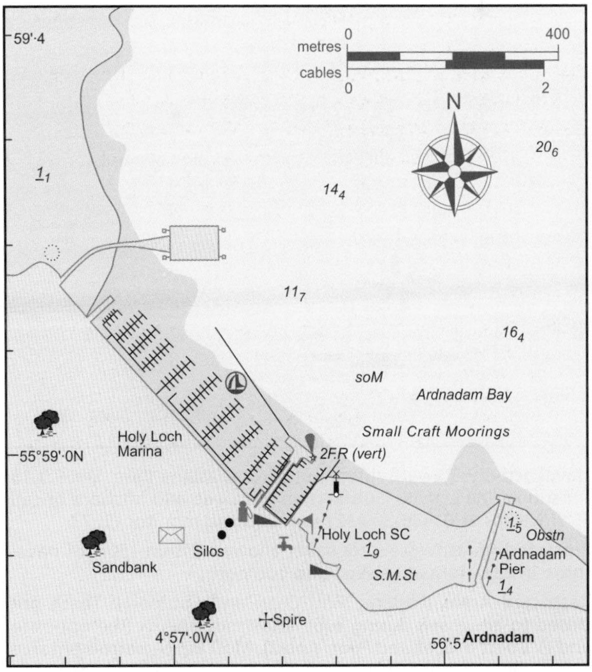

9.9.21 GARELOCH/RHU

Argyll and Bute **56°00'·70N 04°46'·57W** (Rhu Marina)

CHARTS AC 5610, 2131, 1994, 2000; Imray C63, 2900

TIDES +0110 Dover; ML 1·9; Duration 0640. Tides at Helensburgh are the same as at Greenock.

Standard Port GREENOCK (⟶)

Times				Height (metres)			
High Water		Low Water		MHWS	MHWN	MLWN	MLWS
0000	0600	0000	0600	3·4	2·8	1·0	0·3
1200	1800	1200	1800				
Differences RHU MARINA							
−0007	−0007	−0007	−0007	−0·1	−0·1	−0·1	−0·2
FASLANE							
+0003	+0003	+0003	+0003	+0·1	+0·1	+0·1	0·0
GARELOCHHEAD							
0000	0000	0000	0000	0·0	0·0	0·0	−0·1
COULPORT							
−0011	*−0011*	*−0008*	*−0008*	*0·0*	*0·0*	*0·0*	*0·0*
LOCHGOILHEAD							
+0015	0000	−0005	−0005	−0·2	−0·3	−0·3	−0·3
ARROCHAR							
−0005	−0005	−0005	−0005	0·0	0·0	−0·1	−0·1

BYELAWS Loch Long and Gareloch are Dockyard Ports under the jurisdiction of the Queen's Harbour Master. All submarines and other warships at anchor or underway have an Exclusion Zone around them enforced by MOD Police.

SHELTER Rhu Marina rock bkwtr 1m above MHWS, now extended with submerged section (end marked by SHM Fl G 5s) replacing floating wavebreak, protects the berths from strong winds from E to S. Helensburgh Pier is a temp'y drying berth, rather exposed, used by occas steamers. ⚓ E of marina or in Rosneath Bay. Moorings N of the narrows at Stroul B & Clynder; and at the head of the loch. Clyde Naval Base at Faslane must be avoided by yachts.

NAVIGATION WPT 55°59'·29N 04°45'·26W, 356°/1·3M to bn No 7. Beaches between Cairndhu Pt and Helensburgh Pier are strewn with large boulders above/below MLWS. Gareloch ent is via Rhu Narrows. Marina entrance not easy to find at night between pontoon breakwater and Fl G Bn of marina entrance; beware cross-tides. There are large unlit MoD buoys and barges off W shore of Gareloch; for Garelochhead keep to W shore until well clear of Faslane Naval Base.

LIGHTS AND MARKS Ldg/dir lts into Gareloch 356°, 318°, 295°, 329° and 331°. Conspic ✠ tr at Rhu Point.

COMMUNICATIONS (Code 01436) CGOC (02891) 463933; Police 101; H (01389) 754121; Dr 672277. QHM 674321.

MoD Police/QHM Ch 16/73. Rhu Marina Ch **80** M (H24 in season).

FACILITIES Rhu Marina, sbell@quaymarinas.com ☎820238; (235) £2·70 (min £20·50, short stay £10·50) pontoons A-J, (35t) wi-fi.

Royal Northern and Clyde YC ☎820322; club Øs; **Helensburgh SC** ☎672778 (dinghies). **Town** All services, (Glasgow). **DRB Marine** (Rosneath) ☎831231, use jetty only to load, some Øs, (40t). **Silvers Yard** private moorings.

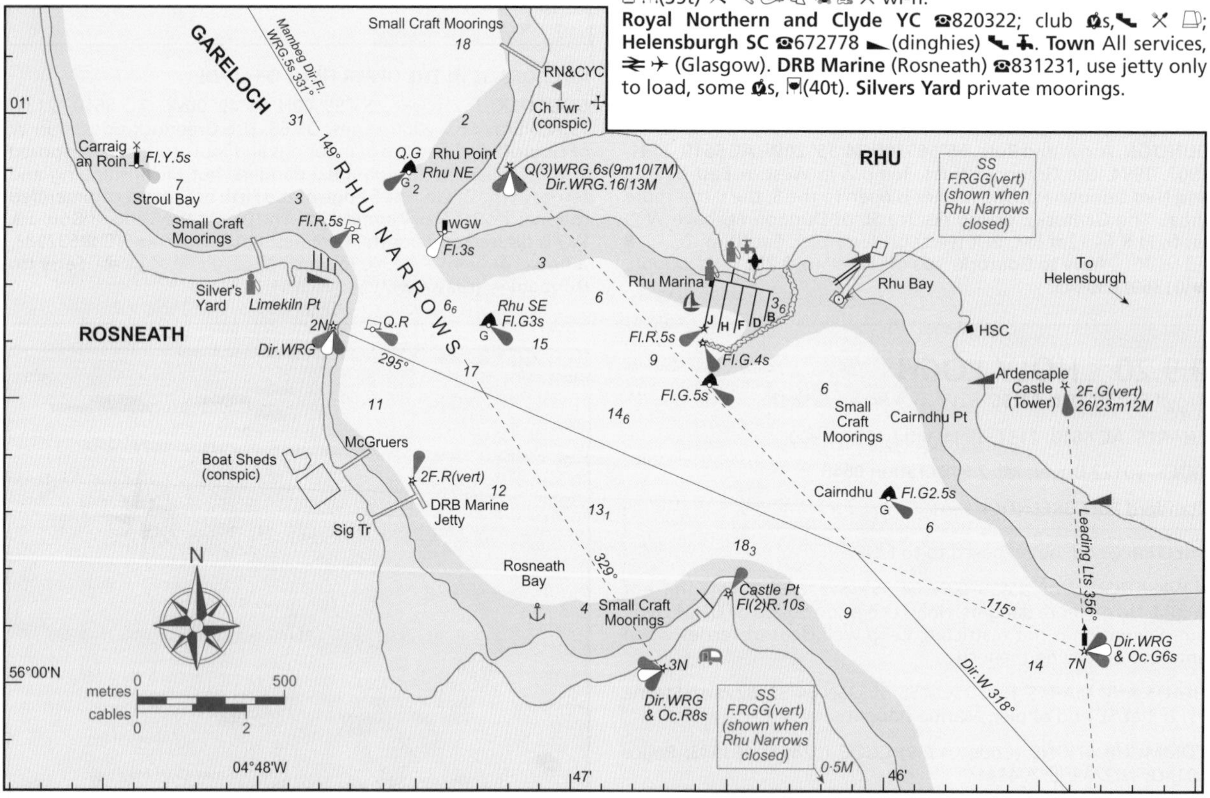

Naval activity: Beware submarines from Faslane Base. See 9.9.18 for submarine activity (Subfacts) in the Clyde and offshore or call FOSNNI Ops ☎(01436) 674321 Ext 3206 and monitor Ch 73.

Protected Areas: Vessels are never allowed within 150m of naval shore installations at Faslane and Coulport.

Restricted Areas (Faslane, Rhu Chan and Coulport): These are closed to all vessels during submarine movements (see opposite and *W Coast of Scotland Pilot*, App 2). MoD Police patrols enforce areas which are shown on charts. The S limit of Faslane Restricted area is marked by two Or posts with X topmarks on Shandon foreshore. The W limit is marked by Iso WRG 4s, vis W356°-006°, at Gareloch Oil fuel depot N jetty. The following signals are shown when restrictions are in force:

Entrance to Gareloch

Day & Night: ● ● ● (vert), supplemented by R flag with W diagonal bar.

Faslane and Coulport

Day & Night: ● ● ● (vert), supplemented by International Code pendant over pendant Nine.

LOCH LONG and LOCH GOIL, Argyll and Bute, approx 56°00′N 04°52′·5W to 56°12′·00N 04°45′·00W. AC *5610,* 3746. Tides: See 9.9.21 for differences. ML 1·7m; Duration 0645.

SHELTER Loch Long is about 15M long. Temp ⚓s (south to north) at: Cove, Blairmore (not in S'lies), Ardentinny, Portincaple, Coilessan (about 1M S of Ardgartan Pt), and near head of loch (Arrochar) on either shore. In Loch Goil ⚓ at Swines Hole and off Carrick Castle (S of the pier, in N'lies a swell builds). Avoid ⚓ near Douglas Pier. The head of the loch is crowded with private/dinghy moorings, and is either too steep-to or too shallow to ⚓. The loch is frequently closed to navigation due to the trial range half way down.

LIGHTS Coulport Jetty, 2FG (vert) each end; Covered Berth L Fl G (SW corner) with 3F G(vert) and F G to NE; Port Dornaige Fl 6s 8m 11M, vis 026°-206°; Dog Rock (Carraig nan Ron) Fl 2s 11M; Finnart Oil Terminal has FG lts and ldg lts 031° QW/FW on Cnap Pt. Upper Loch Long is unlit. Loch Goil ent is marked by 2 PHM buoys (Fl R 3s and QR), a SHM buoy (QG) and ldg lts 318°: front (The Perch) Dir FWRG and Fl R 3s; rear FW. Rubha Ardnahein Fl R5s.

FACILITIES Loch Long (Cove), Cove SC, ⛽ 🛒 ⛵; ⛽(pier); (Portincaple) ✉ 🛒 hotel, ⛽; (Ardentinny) shop, 🛒 ✕ hotel, ⛺; (Blairmore) ⛴ ⛽ ✉ 🛒; (Arrochar) shops, hotel, ⛽ 🔥 ✉. Loch Goil (Carrick Castle) has 2 blue ⚓s (£10/night, max 15t, free wi-fi), WC. Lochgoilhead: ⛽ 🔥 ✉ 🛒.

9.9.22 RIVER CLYDE

Dunbartonshire **55°57′·50N 04°45′·70W** (Tail of the Bank)

❁❁❁◇◇✿✿

CHARTS AC 5610, 2131, 1994, 2007: *BW Skipper's Guide for Forth and Clyde Canal, BW Skipper's Handbook for Lowland Canals*; Imray C63, 2900

TIDES +0122 Dover; ML 2·0; Duration 0640

Standard Port GREENOCK (⟶)

Times				Height (metres)			
High Water		Low Water		MHWS	MHWN	MLWN	MLWS
0000	0600	0000	0600	3·4	2·8	1·0	0·3
1200	1800	1200	1800				
Differences PORT GLASGOW (55°56′·10N 04°40′·50W)							
+0010	+0005	+0010	+0020	+0·2	+0·1	0·0	0·0
DUMBARTON							
+0015	+0010	+0020	+0040	+0·4	+0·3	+0·1	0·0
BOWLING							
+0020	+0010	+0030	+0055	+0·6	+0·5	+0·3	+0·1
RENFREW							
+0025	+0015	+0035	+0100	+0·9	+0·8	+0·5	+0·2
GLASGOW							
+0025	*+0015*	*+0035*	*+0105*	*+1·4*	*+1·1*	*+0·8*	*+0·4*

SHELTER Good at Greenock (James Watt Dock Marina), Dumbarton (Sandpoint Marina) Bowling Harbour and city centre pontoons.

NAVIGATION WPT 55°57′·50N 04°45′·70W, 1·2M to James Watt Dock (JWD), which experiences strong tidal streams flowing in the dredged channel across the entrance. Sandpoint Marina and Bowling Harbour are, respectively, about 6M and 9M up-river. The density of shipping and numerous ferries in the Clyde warrant particular attention. Large vessels manoeuvre at the Greenock Container/Ocean Terminal and masters are to maintain communication with Harbour Control.

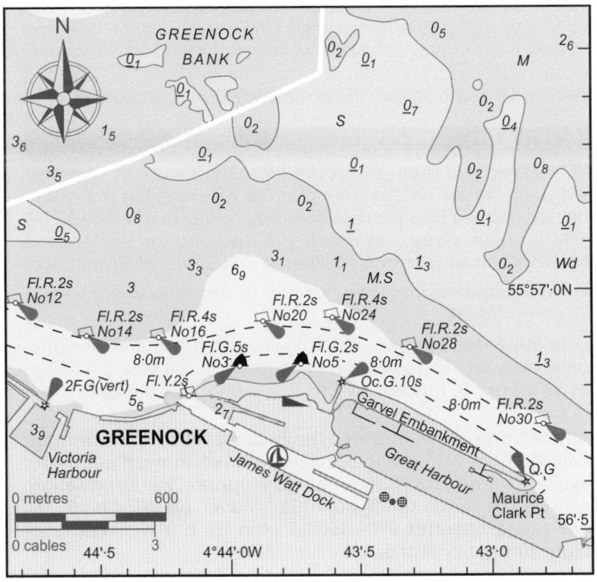

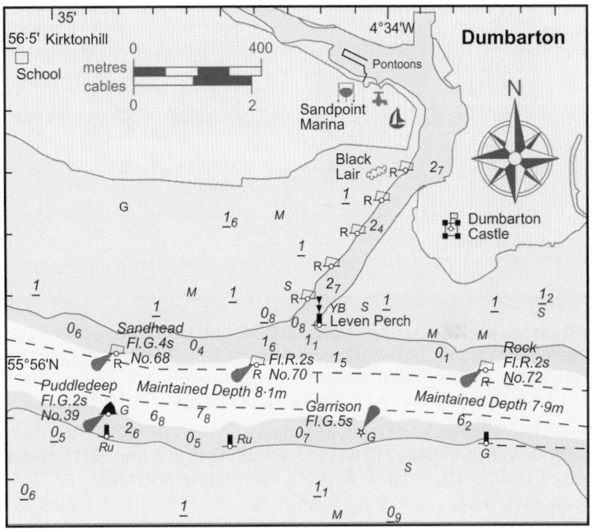

Speed limit above Cloch Pt is 12kn but 5kn where boards mark Dead Slow. Sailing vessels must conform to Rules for Narrow Channels and E of Bowling may proceed under power alone. All vessels planning an upriver passage are to contact their berth or destination before proceeding. Keep just inboard of chan lateral marks as depths shoal rapidly outboard. For Dumbarton cross the river at 90° at No 39 SHM buoy. Depths in R Leven may be less than charted. For Bowling Hbr cross at No 45 SHM buoy.

LIGHTS AND MARKS The River Clyde is well buoyed/lit.

COMMUNICATIONS (Codes: Greenock 01475; Glasgow 0141). CGOC (02891) 463933; Police 101; Dr 634617; H 01389 754121. HM 725775; Estuary Control 726221; Scottish Canals 332 6936.

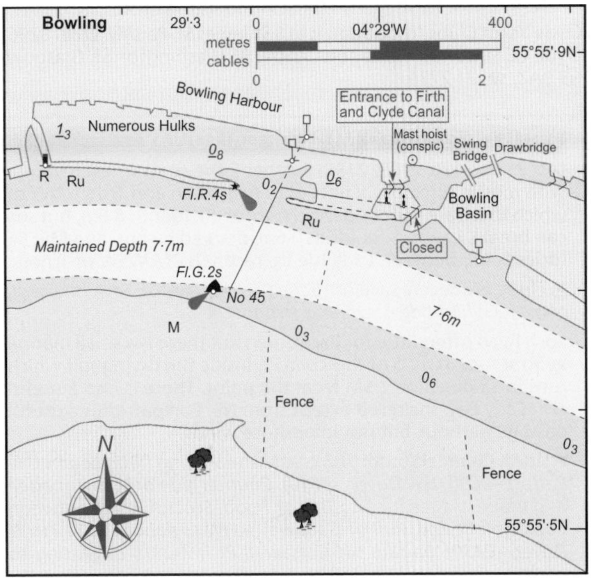

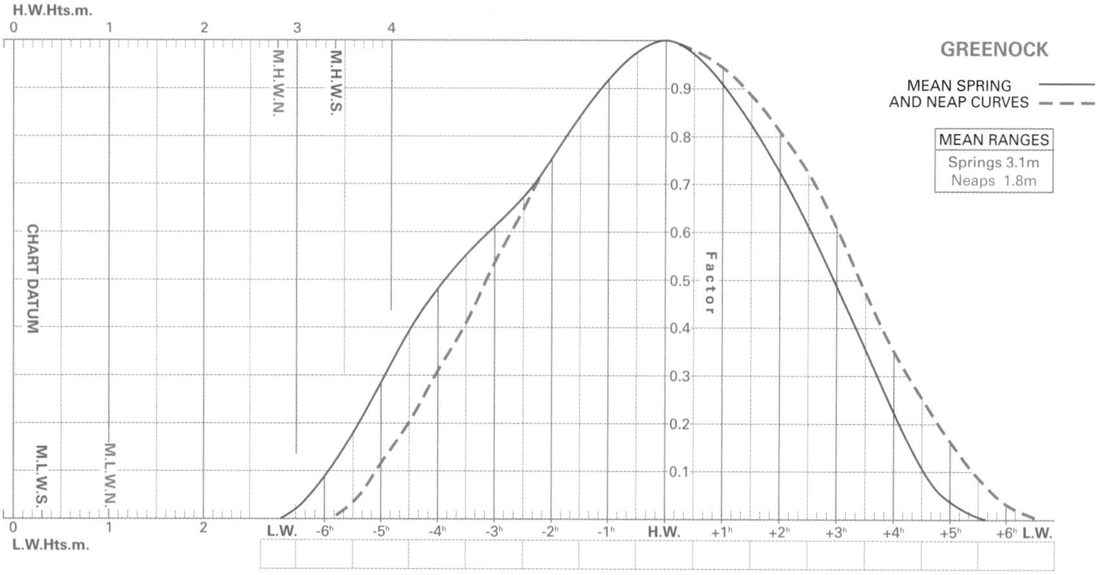

All vessels seeking passage upstream beyond No 1 buoy are to seek permission from *Clyde Harbour Control* Ch **12** 16 (H24) at charted reporting points. Weather/traffic info on request. James Watt Dock Ch 80; Marinas Ch M. Bowling lockkeeper Ch 74, HW±2.

FACILITIES James Watt Dock Marina 55°56'·72N 04°44'·01W. info@jwdmarina.co.uk ☎07710 611117; 65 inc ⊗ in 4.5m, £2.15, short stay £11.50/craft. at marina entrance.

Greenock

Sandpoint Marina 55°56'·48N 04°34'·07W www.sandpoint-marina.co.uk ☎01389 762396/731500. Limited ⊗, £10 per night. VHF Ch **M.** (40t) ☎01389 742438. **Town** ⇌.

Bowling Basin 55°55'·8N 04°29'·0W, W end of Forth & Clyde Canal, see 9.6.9. ☎01389 877969. Basin Lock access dries 0·7m. Call VHF Ch 74 for t lock schedule. *Skipper's Brief* www.scottishcanals.co.uk. Facilities: £3.75, by prior notice, (mast). **Town** ⇌.

GLASGOW 55°55'·94N 04°34'·25W www.glasgow.gov.uk ☎2879650. Pontoons are at Govan (Water Row), Yorkhill Quay, Broomielaw Quay and Plantation Quay for stays of up to 3 nts. Millennium Br (3.2m) opens ☎4205030 as does Bells Br (3.5m) ☎01436 831222. Boats may also berth at Braehead Shopping Centre.

Clyde Yacht Clubs Association is at 8 St James St, Paisley. ☎8878296. Clyde CC Suite 408, Pentagon Centre, 36 Washington St, Glasgow, G3 8AZ, ☎221 2774.

FIRTH OF CLYDE TO MULL OF GALLOWAY

(AC 2131, 2126, 2199, 2198) Further S the coast is less inviting, with mostly commercial hbrs until Ardrossan and Troon, NW of which there are various dangers: Troon Rk (depth 5·6m, but sea can break), Lappock Rk (dries 0·6m, marked by bn), and Mill Rk (dries 0·4m, buoyed). Lady Isle (lt, racon) is 2M WSW of Troon.

▶ *There is a severe race off Bennane Hd (8M SSE of Ailsa Craig, conspic) when tide is running strongly.*◀

Loch Ryan offers little for yachtsmen but there is a small marina at Stranraer and ⚓ S of Kirkcolm Pt, inside the drying spit which runs in SE direction 1·5M from the point. There is also a useful ⚓ in Lady Bay, sheltered except from NE. Portpatrick is a useful passage harbour, but not in onshore winds.

▶ **North Channel South:** *Irish coast – the S-going flood begins HW Belfast –0600 (HW Dover +0610). Counter tide off Donaghadee and Island Magee for last 3hrs of flood. Scottish coast between Corsewall Pt and Mull of Galloway – HW Greenock +0310 (HW Dover +0430). Sp rate off Corsewall Pt is 2–3kn, increasing* ***to 5kn off and S of Black Hd.*** *Races occur off Copeland Is. Morroch B, Money Hd Mull of Logan and Mull of Galloway.*

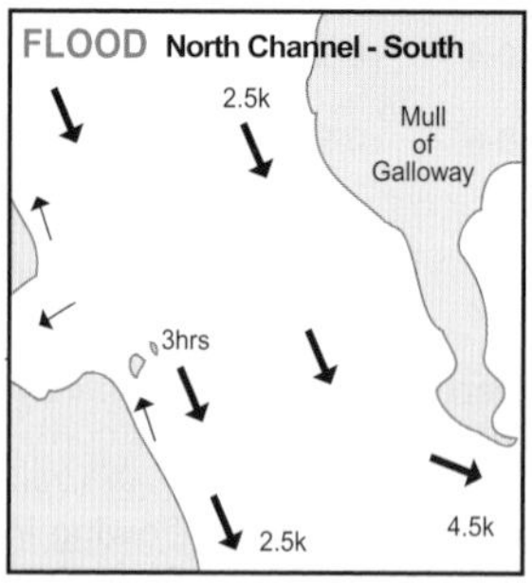

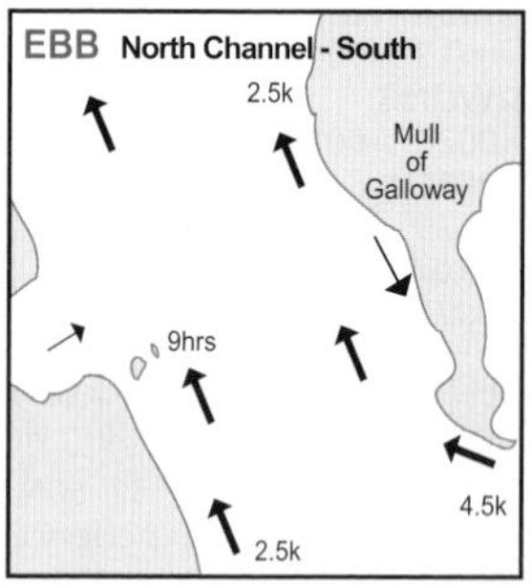

Irish coast – N-going ebb begins at HW Belfast (HW Dover –0015). Scottish coast – HW Greenock –0250 (HW Dover –0130). Races off Copeland Is and Mull of Galloway. Flood begins 2 hrs early close inshore N of Mull of Galloway. A race SSE of Crammag Hd is bad if wind against tide. Mull of Galloway (lt) is a high (82m), steep-to headland with ***a dangerous race extending nearly 3M to S.*** *On E-going stream it extends NNE into Luce B; on W-going stream it extends SW and W. Give the race a wide berth, or pass close inshore at slack water nps and calm weather. SW wind >F4 against W-going stream, do not attempt inshore route.*◀

SCOTLAND – SW COAST

The Scares, two groups of rocks, lie at the mouth of Luce Bay which elsewhere is clear more than 3ca offshore; but the whole bay is occupied by a practice bombing range, marked by 12 DZ SPM lt buoys. Good ⚓ at E Tarbert B awaiting the tide around Mull of Galloway, or good shelter in drying hbr of Drummore.

▶ *Off Burrow Hd there is a bad race in strong W winds with a W-going tide.*◀

Luce Bay Firing Range (D402/403) lies at the NW end. For info on activity ☎(01776) 888792. In Wigtown B the best ⚓ is in Isle of Whithorn B, but exposed to S. It is also possible to dry out in Garlieston.

A tank firing range, between the E side of ent to Kirkcudbright Bay and Abbey Hd, 4M to E, extends 14M offshore. If unable to avoid the area, cross it at N end close inshore. For information contact the Range safety boat 'Gallovidian' on VHF Ch 16, 73. The range operates 0900-1600LT Mon-Fri, but weekend and night firing may also occur.

STANDARD TIME (UT)
For Summer Time add ONE hour in **non-shaded areas**

GREENOCK LAT 55°57′N LONG 4°46′W

TIMES AND HEIGHTS OF HIGH AND LOW WATERS

Dates in red are SPRINGS
Dates in blue are NEAPS

YEAR **2018**

JANUARY

Date	Day	Time	m	Time	m	Time	m	Time	m
1	M	0435	0.3	1128	3.6	1658	0.3		
2	TU	0002	3.6	0524	0.2	1217	3.7	○ 1746	0.2
3	W	0055	3.6	0613	0.2	1303	3.8	1834	0.1
4	TH	0147	3.6	0701	0.2	1349	3.9	1922	0.1
5	F	0237	3.6	0751	0.3	1434	3.9	2011	0.1
6	SA	0325	3.5	0841	0.4	1519	3.9	2102	0.3
7	SU	0413	3.4	0933	0.5	1605	3.7	2155	0.4
8	M	0501	3.2	1027	0.7	1652	3.6	◑ 2254	0.6
9	TU	0552	3.1	1128	0.8	1742	3.4		
10	W	0000	0.7	0648	3.0	1236	0.9	1839	3.2
11	TH	0111	0.8	0754	2.9	1346	1.0	1947	3.1
12	F	0215	0.9	0906	3.0	1448	0.9	2105	3.0
13	SA	0310	0.8	1007	3.1	1541	0.8	2213	3.1
14	SU	0359	0.8	1056	3.3	1628	0.6	2305	3.1
15	M	0441	0.7	1139	3.4	1709	0.5	2349	3.2
16	TU	0520	0.7	1217	3.5	1746	0.5		
17	W	0026	3.2	0554	0.7	1251	3.6	● 1819	0.5
18	TH	0102	3.3	0625	0.7	1323	3.6	1851	0.5
19	F	0136	3.3	0657	0.7	1354	3.6	1922	0.5
20	SA	0211	3.3	0730	0.6	1427	3.6	1956	0.5
21	SU	0247	3.3	0807	0.6	1501	3.6	2034	0.5
22	M	0325	3.3	0848	0.6	1539	3.6	2117	0.5
23	TU	0404	3.3	0933	0.7	1618	3.5	2205	0.6
24	W	0445	3.2	1023	0.8	1702	3.3	◐ 2259	0.6
25	TH	0530	3.1	1118	0.9	1753	3.2		
26	F	0001	0.7	0623	3.0	1223	1.0	1901	3.1
27	SA	0109	0.7	0735	3.0	1335	0.9	2029	3.0
28	SU	0220	0.7	0905	3.0	1448	0.8	2152	3.1
29	M	0326	0.5	1018	3.2	1552	0.5	2258	3.3
30	TU	0422	0.4	1115	3.4	1646	0.3	2355	3.4
31	W	0513	0.2	1205	3.6	1735	0.1	○	

FEBRUARY

Date	Day	Time	m	Time	m	Time	m	Time	m
1	TH	0048	3.5	0601	0.2	1253	3.7	1821	0.0
2	F	0138	3.5	0647	0.1	1338	3.8	1906	0.0
3	SA	0224	3.5	0733	0.2	1422	3.8	1951	0.0
4	SU	0308	3.4	0818	0.2	1504	3.8	2035	0.1
5	M	0349	3.4	0903	0.3	1545	3.7	2121	0.3
6	TU	0428	3.3	0950	0.5	1626	3.6	2209	0.5
7	W	0508	3.1	1041	0.6	1708	3.4	◑ 2303	0.7
8	TH	0552	3.0	1141	0.8	1753	3.1		
9	F	0009	0.9	0644	2.9	1259	1.0	1845	2.9
10	SA	0131	1.0	0755	2.8	1415	0.9	1955	2.8
11	SU	0241	1.0	0927	2.9	1516	0.8	2141	2.8
12	M	0336	0.9	1031	3.1	1606	0.7	2248	2.9
13	TU	0422	0.8	1118	3.3	1648	0.5	2333	3.1
14	W	0501	0.7	1158	3.4	1726	0.4		
15	TH	0012	3.1	0536	0.6	1234	3.5	● 1759	0.4
16	F	0047	3.2	0606	0.6	1305	3.5	1830	0.4
17	SA	0120	3.2	0635	0.5	1335	3.5	1859	0.4
18	SU	0152	3.3	0706	0.5	1407	3.5	1931	0.3
19	M	0225	3.3	0742	0.4	1441	3.6	2007	0.3
20	TU	0300	3.4	0823	0.4	1518	3.6	2049	0.3
21	W	0337	3.4	0907	0.4	1557	3.5	2136	0.4
22	TH	0415	3.3	0955	0.5	1638	3.4	2229	0.5
23	F	0455	3.2	1049	0.6	1724	3.2	◐ 2329	0.7
24	SA	0543	3.1	1152	0.8	1824	3.0		
25	SU	0040	0.8	0645	2.9	1309	0.8	2003	2.8
26	M	0201	0.8	0834	2.9	1433	0.7	2148	3.0
27	TU	0315	0.6	1004	3.1	1542	0.5	2255	3.2
28	W	0414	0.4	1103	3.3	1637	0.2	2349	3.3

MARCH

Date	Day	Time	m	Time	m	Time	m	Time	m
1	TH	0503	0.2	1153	3.5	1723	0.0		
2	F	0038	3.4	0548	0.1	1239	3.6	○ 1806	-0.1
3	SA	0123	3.4	0631	0.1	1323	3.7	1846	-0.1
4	SU	0205	3.4	0712	0.1	1405	3.7	1926	0.0
5	M	0243	3.4	0752	0.1	1444	3.7	2005	0.1
6	TU	0318	3.4	0832	0.2	1521	3.6	2045	0.3
7	W	0352	3.3	0913	0.3	1559	3.5	2127	0.5
8	TH	0429	3.2	0958	0.5	1637	3.3	2214	0.7
9	F	0508	3.0	1050	0.7	1718	3.1	◑ 2309	0.9
10	SA	0554	2.9	1159	0.9	1806	2.8		
11	SU	0025	1.2	0653	2.7	1334	1.0	1905	2.6
12	M	0202	1.2	0825	2.7	1445	0.8	2045	2.6
13	TU	0307	1.0	0958	2.9	1537	0.7	2223	2.8
14	W	0356	0.9	1049	3.1	1621	0.5	2310	3.0
15	TH	0436	0.7	1131	3.3	1659	0.3	2349	3.1
16	F	0511	0.6	1207	3.3	1732	0.3		
17	SA	0024	3.2	0540	0.5	1240	3.4	● 1802	0.2
18	SU	0057	3.2	0609	0.4	1312	3.4	1831	0.2
19	M	0128	3.3	0641	0.3	1345	3.5	1904	0.1
20	TU	0200	3.4	0718	0.2	1421	3.5	1943	0.1
21	W	0235	3.5	0759	0.2	1459	3.5	2026	0.2
22	TH	0311	3.5	0844	0.2	1539	3.5	2114	0.3
23	F	0349	3.4	0933	0.3	1620	3.3	2207	0.4
24	SA	0430	3.3	1028	0.5	1707	3.1	◐ 2309	0.7
25	SU	0517	3.1	1134	0.7	1808	2.9		
26	M	0023	0.8	0617	2.9	1257	0.7	2001	2.7
27	TU	0150	0.9	0815	2.8	1424	0.6	2146	2.9
28	W	0304	0.7	0949	3.0	1531	0.4	2246	3.1
29	TH	0401	0.4	1047	3.3	1623	0.1	2335	3.3
30	F	0449	0.2	1135	3.5	1707	0.0		
31	SA	0020	3.4	0532	0.1	1221	3.6	○ 1746	0.0

APRIL

Date	Day	Time	m	Time	m	Time	m	Time	m
1	SU	0103	3.4	0611	0.1	1303	3.6	1824	0.0
2	M	0140	3.4	0649	0.1	1343	3.6	1859	0.1
3	TU	0214	3.4	0724	0.1	1420	3.6	1935	0.2
4	W	0246	3.4	0800	0.2	1455	3.5	2012	0.3
5	TH	0319	3.4	0839	0.3	1531	3.4	2052	0.5
6	F	0354	3.3	0921	0.4	1609	3.2	2136	0.7
7	SA	0432	3.1	1009	0.6	1650	3.0	2225	0.9
8	SU	0515	2.9	1112	0.8	1737	2.8	◑ 2328	1.1
9	M	0609	2.8	1238	0.9	1834	2.6		
10	TU	0058	1.3	0723	2.7	1402	0.8	1953	2.6
11	W	0223	1.2	0907	2.8	1459	0.7	2138	2.7
12	TH	0319	1.0	1009	3.0	1545	0.5	2233	2.9
13	F	0402	0.8	1054	3.1	1624	0.3	2316	3.1
14	SA	0437	0.6	1132	3.2	1658	0.2	2353	3.2
15	SU	0509	0.4	1207	3.3	1730	0.1		
16	M	0027	3.3	0541	0.3	1243	3.4	● 1802	0.1
17	TU	0100	3.3	0616	0.2	1322	3.4	1840	0.0
18	W	0135	3.5	0656	0.1	1402	3.5	1922	0.1
19	TH	0212	3.5	0739	0.1	1443	3.5	2008	0.1
20	F	0250	3.6	0826	0.1	1525	3.4	2058	0.3
21	SA	0330	3.5	0918	0.2	1611	3.3	2154	0.5
22	SU	0412	3.4	1017	0.4	1702	3.1	◐ 2258	0.7
23	M	0501	3.2	1128	0.5	1812	2.8		
24	TU	0014	0.8	0604	3.0	1252	0.6	2005	2.8
25	W	0134	0.8	0759	2.9	1409	0.5	2130	2.9
26	TH	0245	0.7	0926	3.1	1512	0.3	2226	3.1
27	F	0342	0.5	1024	3.3	1602	0.2	2314	3.3
28	SA	0430	0.3	1112	3.4	1646	0.1	2357	3.3
29	SU	0512	0.2	1157	3.4	1725	0.1		
30	M	0036	3.4	0551	0.1	1239	3.4	○ 1800	0.2

Chart Datum: 1·62 metres below Ordnance Datum (Newlyn). HAT is 3·9 metres above Chart Datum.

STANDARD TIME (UT)
For Summer Time add ONE hour in **non-shaded areas**

GREENOCK LAT 55°57′N LONG 4°46′W

TIMES AND HEIGHTS OF HIGH AND LOW WATERS

Dates in red are SPRINGS
Dates in blue are NEAPS

YEAR **2018**

MAY

Date	Time	m	Date	Time	m
1 TU	0112	3.4	16 W	0032	3.4
	0626	0.1		0555	0.1
	1317	3.4		1259	3.4
	1833	0.3		1819	0.0
2 W	0144	3.4	17 TH	0113	3.5
	0659	0.2		0638	0.0
	1353	3.4		1345	3.5
	1908	0.3		1905	0.1
3 TH	0216	3.4	18 F	0153	3.6
	0733	0.2		0725	0.0
	1429	3.3		1431	3.5
	1945	0.4		1955	0.2
4 F	0249	3.4	19 SA	0234	3.7
	0810	0.3		0814	0.1
	1505	3.3		1518	3.4
	2024	0.5		2048	0.3
5 SA	0324	3.4	20 SU	0316	3.6
	0852	0.4		0909	0.2
	1543	3.2		1609	3.2
	2107	0.7		2146	0.4
6 SU	0400	3.2	21 M	0402	3.5
	0939	0.6		1010	0.3
	1625	3.0		1707	3.1
	2154	0.9		2249	0.6
7 M	0441	3.1	22 TU	0453	3.3
	1036	0.7		1120	0.4
	1712	2.9		1819	2.9
	2249	1.0		◐ 2357	0.7
8 TU	0530	2.9	23 W	0600	3.1
	1147	0.8		1235	0.4
	1807	2.7		1945	2.9
	◑ 2357	1.2			
9 W	0634	2.7	24 TH	0108	0.8
	1304	0.8		0733	3.0
	1913	2.7		1345	0.4
				2059	3.0
10 TH	0114	1.2	25 F	0216	0.7
	0755	2.7		0854	3.1
	1409	0.7		1445	0.3
	2035	2.8		2156	3.1
11 F	0223	1.0	26 SA	0315	0.5
	0913	2.9		0955	3.2
	1459	0.5		1536	0.3
	2144	2.9		2245	3.2
12 SA	0315	0.8	27 SU	0406	0.4
	1006	3.0		1046	3.3
	1542	0.3		1621	0.3
	2233	3.1		2329	3.3
13 SU	0358	0.6	28 M	0451	0.3
	1050	3.2		1132	3.3
	1620	0.2		1702	0.3
	2315	3.2			
14 M	0436	0.4	29 TU	0009	3.3
	1131	3.3		0530	0.2
	1657	0.1		1214	3.3
	2354	3.3		○ 1737	0.4
15 TU	0515	0.2	30 W	0045	3.4
	1214	3.4		0606	0.2
	1737	0.0		1252	3.3
	●			1811	0.4
			31 TH	0118	3.4
				0639	0.3
				1328	3.2
				1846	0.5

JUNE

Date	Time	m	Date	Time	m
1 F	0150	3.5	16 SA	0138	3.7
	0713	0.3		0713	0.0
	1403	3.2		1423	3.4
	1923	0.5		1943	0.2
2 SA	0223	3.5	17 SU	0222	3.7
	0749	0.3		0804	0.0
	1440	3.2		1514	3.3
	2002	0.6		2037	0.2
3 SU	0257	3.4	18 M	0307	3.7
	0829	0.4		0858	0.1
	1519	3.1		1608	3.3
	2044	0.7		2132	0.4
4 M	0333	3.3	19 TU	0354	3.6
	0913	0.5		0956	0.2
	1601	3.1		1704	3.1
	2129	0.8		2230	0.5
5 TU	0411	3.2	20 W	0445	3.4
	1004	0.6		1100	0.3
	1646	3.0		1804	3.0
	2218	0.9		◐ 2332	0.6
6 W	0455	3.0	21 TH	0544	3.2
	1102	0.7		1208	0.4
	1737	2.9		1909	3.0
	◑ 2313	1.0			
7 TH	0549	2.9	22 F	0037	0.7
	1207	0.7		0655	3.1
	1833	2.8		1314	0.4
				2016	2.9
8 F	0014	1.0	23 SA	0144	0.7
	0654	2.8		0812	3.0
	1310	0.6		1414	0.5
	1936	2.8		2118	3.0
9 SA	0119	1.0	24 SU	0246	0.6
	0807	2.9		0921	3.1
	1407	0.5		1509	0.5
	2043	2.9		2213	3.1
10 SU	0222	0.9	25 M	0341	0.5
	0913	3.0		1018	3.1
	1458	0.3		1557	0.5
	2144	3.0		2301	3.2
11 M	0317	0.7	26 TU	0429	0.4
	1009	3.1		1108	3.1
	1544	0.2		1640	0.5
	2236	3.2		2344	3.3
12 TU	0406	0.4	27 W	0512	0.3
	1100	3.3		1151	3.1
	1629	0.1		1720	0.5
	2323	3.3			
13 W	0452	0.2	28 TH	0022	3.4
	1150	3.3		0550	0.3
	1715	0.1		1230	3.1
	●			○ 1755	0.5
14 TH	0009	3.5	29 F	0057	3.4
	0538	0.1		0624	0.3
	1241	3.4		1306	3.1
	1802	0.1		1830	0.6
15 F	0054	3.6	30 SA	0129	3.5
	0624	0.0		0658	0.3
	1332	3.4		1341	3.1
	1852	0.1		1905	0.6

JULY

Date	Time	m	Date	Time	m
1 SU	0201	3.5	16 M	0212	3.8
	0732	0.4		0749	-0.1
	1417	3.1		1506	3.3
	1942	0.6		2019	0.2
2 M	0234	3.5	17 TU	0257	3.8
	0808	0.4		0839	0.0
	1455	3.1		1556	3.3
	2021	0.6		2111	0.3
3 TU	0308	3.4	18 W	0343	3.7
	0847	0.4		0932	0.1
	1536	3.1		1645	3.2
	2103	0.7		2204	0.4
4 W	0344	3.3	19 TH	0429	3.5
	0931	0.5		1028	0.3
	1618	3.1		1733	3.1
	2147	0.7		◐ 2259	0.5
5 TH	0424	3.2	20 F	0518	3.3
	1020	0.6		1130	0.4
	1703	3.0		1824	3.0
	2236	0.8			
6 F	0510	3.1	21 SA	0001	0.7
	1116	0.6		0611	3.1
	1752	3.0		1238	0.6
	◑ 2329	0.9		1920	2.9
7 SA	0606	3.0	22 SU	0108	0.8
	1216	0.6		0715	3.0
	1846	2.9		1343	0.7
				2028	2.9
8 SU	0029	0.9	23 M	0216	0.8
	0713	2.9		0835	2.9
	1318	0.5		1442	0.7
	1948	2.9		2137	2.9
9 M	0135	0.9	24 TU	0317	0.7
	0828	3.0		0952	2.9
	1418	0.4		1535	0.7
	2057	3.0		2235	3.1
10 TU	0241	0.7	25 W	0409	0.5
	0937	3.1		1050	3.0
	1514	0.3		1622	0.6
	2202	3.1		2322	3.2
11 W	0341	0.5	26 TH	0454	0.4
	1038	3.2		1136	3.0
	1607	0.2		1703	0.6
	2259	3.3			
12 TH	0434	0.3	27 F	0003	3.4
	1134	3.3		0533	0.3
	1658	0.1		1215	3.0
	2350	3.5		○ 1740	0.6
13 F	0524	0.1	28 SA	0040	3.4
	1228	3.4		0609	0.3
	1748	0.1		1249	3.1
	●			1814	0.6
14 SA	0039	3.6	29 SU	0111	3.5
	0612	-0.1		0641	0.3
	1322	3.4		1322	3.1
	1838	0.1		1846	0.6
15 SU	0126	3.7	30 M	0141	3.5
	0700	-0.1		0712	0.4
	1415	3.4		1355	3.1
	1928	0.1		1919	0.6
			31 TU	0212	3.5
				0744	0.4
				1431	3.2
				1954	0.6

AUGUST

Date	Time	m	Date	Time	m
1 W	0245	3.5	16 TH	0324	3.7
	0818	0.4		0900	0.1
	1508	3.2		1612	3.2
	2033	0.5		2131	0.3
2 TH	0320	3.5	17 F	0405	3.6
	0857	0.4		0948	0.3
	1547	3.2		1652	3.2
	2115	0.6		2221	0.5
3 F	0357	3.4	18 SA	0446	3.4
	0942	0.4		1043	0.6
	1627	3.2		1734	3.0
	2201	0.6		◐ 2318	0.7
4 SA	0438	3.3	19 SU	0531	3.2
	1034	0.5		1149	0.8
	1711	3.1		1821	2.9
	◑ 2253	0.7			
5 SU	0525	3.1	20 M	0029	0.8
	1133	0.6		0621	2.9
	1800	3.0		1307	0.9
	2351	0.8		1921	2.8
6 M	0626	3.0	21 TU	0147	0.9
	1238	0.6		0728	2.7
	1859	3.0		1416	1.0
				2051	2.8
7 TU	0058	0.9	22 W	0253	0.8
	0748	2.9		0925	2.7
	1346	0.6		1514	0.9
	2015	3.0		2208	3.0
8 W	0212	0.8	23 TH	0347	0.6
	0915	3.0		1036	2.8
	1453	0.5		1602	0.8
	2136	3.1		2300	3.2
9 TH	0322	0.6	24 F	0433	0.5
	1027	3.1		1121	3.0
	1553	0.4		1645	0.7
	2242	3.3		2342	3.4
10 F	0421	0.3	25 SA	0513	0.4
	1126	3.3		1158	3.1
	1646	0.2		1721	0.6
	2336	3.5			
11 SA	0512	0.1	26 SU	0019	3.5
	1220	3.3		0547	0.3
	1736	0.1		1232	3.1
	●			○ 1753	0.6
12 SU	0026	3.6	27 M	0051	3.5
	0559	-0.1		0619	0.3
	1312	3.4		1302	3.2
	1823	0.1		1822	0.6
13 M	0113	3.7	28 TU	0120	3.5
	0644	-0.1		0648	0.3
	1402	3.4		1332	3.2
	1910	0.1		1851	0.6
14 TU	0159	3.8	29 W	0149	3.5
	0729	-0.1		0716	0.3
	1448	3.3		1404	3.3
	1956	0.2		1925	0.5
15 W	0242	3.8	30 TH	0221	3.5
	0814	0.0		0748	0.3
	1532	3.3		1439	3.3
	2043	0.2		2003	0.5
			31 F	0257	3.5
				0826	0.3
				1516	3.4
				2044	0.5

Chart Datum: 1·62 metres below Ordnance Datum (Newlyn). HAT is 3·9 metres above Chart Datum.

STANDARD TIME (UT)
For Summer Time add ONE hour in **non-shaded areas**

GREENOCK LAT 55°57′N LONG 4°46′W

TIMES AND HEIGHTS OF HIGH AND LOW WATERS

Dates in red are SPRINGS
Dates in blue are NEAPS

YEAR **2018**

SEPTEMBER

Date	Day	Time	m	Time	m	Time	m	Time	m	Phase
1	SA	0334	3.5	0910	0.4	1554	3.3	2130	0.5	
2	SU	0412	3.4	1000	0.5	1635	3.3	2222	0.7	
3	M	0455	3.2	1058	0.7	1721	3.1	2321	0.8	◑
4	TU	0551	3.0	1207	0.8	1818	3.0			
5	W	0031	0.9	0717	2.8	1326	0.9	1938	3.0	
6	TH	0154	0.9	0908	2.9	1442	0.7	2119	3.1	
7	F	0312	0.6	1025	3.1	1544	0.5	2229	3.3	
8	SA	0411	0.3	1121	3.3	1635	0.3	2322	3.5	
9	SU	0459	0.1	1210	3.4	1722	0.2			●
10	M	0011	3.7	0543	-0.1	1257	3.4	1805	0.1	
11	TU	0057	3.8	0624	-0.1	1341	3.4	1848	0.1	
12	W	0140	3.8	0705	0.0	1422	3.4	1930	0.2	
13	TH	0221	3.8	0745	0.1	1459	3.4	2012	0.3	
14	F	0300	3.7	0825	0.3	1534	3.3	2055	0.4	
15	SA	0338	3.6	0908	0.5	1611	3.3	2140	0.5	
16	SU	0416	3.4	0954	0.7	1650	3.2	2232	0.7	◐
17	M	0458	3.2	1051	1.0	1735	3.0	2341	0.9	
18	TU	0545	2.9	1215	1.2	1830	2.9			
19	W	0114	1.0	0645	2.7	1347	1.2	1950	2.8	
20	TH	0226	0.9	0832	2.6	1449	1.1	2134	3.0	
21	F	0321	0.7	1013	2.8	1539	0.9	2230	3.2	
22	SA	0406	0.5	1056	3.0	1620	0.8	2313	3.4	
23	SU	0446	0.4	1133	3.2	1656	0.7	2350	3.5	
24	M	0520	0.3	1206	3.2	1727	0.6			
25	TU	0023	3.5	0551	0.3	1237	3.3	1754	0.6	○
26	W	0053	3.5	0619	0.3	1306	3.3	1823	0.5	
27	TH	0124	3.5	0647	0.3	1337	3.4	1857	0.5	
28	F	0159	3.6	0720	0.3	1411	3.5	1936	0.4	
29	SA	0236	3.6	0800	0.3	1448	3.5	2018	0.4	
30	SU	0314	3.6	0844	0.4	1526	3.5	2105	0.5	

OCTOBER

Date	Day	Time	m	Time	m	Time	m	Time	m	Phase
1	M	0354	3.4	0935	0.6	1607	3.4	2158	0.7	
2	TU	0437	3.2	1035	0.8	1653	3.3	2300	0.8	◑
3	W	0533	3.0	1148	1.0	1749	3.1			
4	TH	0016	0.9	0707	2.8	1315	1.0	1914	3.0	
5	F	0147	0.9	0912	2.9	1433	0.9	2105	3.1	
6	SA	0302	0.6	1018	3.2	1532	0.6	2213	3.4	
7	SU	0357	0.3	1108	3.4	1622	0.4	2305	3.6	
8	M	0443	0.1	1153	3.5	1706	0.3	2351	3.7	
9	TU	0524	0.1	1236	3.5	1747	0.2			●
10	W	0036	3.8	0603	0.1	1316	3.5	1826	0.2	
11	TH	0118	3.8	0639	0.2	1352	3.5	1904	0.3	
12	F	0157	3.7	0716	0.3	1425	3.5	1942	0.3	
13	SA	0235	3.7	0753	0.4	1459	3.5	2021	0.4	
14	SU	0311	3.6	0833	0.6	1535	3.4	2104	0.6	
15	M	0349	3.4	0916	0.9	1614	3.3	2153	0.8	
16	TU	0430	3.2	1006	1.1	1658	3.2	2256	1.0	◐
17	W	0517	2.9	1114	1.4	1751	3.0			
18	TH	0027	1.1	0616	2.7	1257	1.4	1900	2.9	
19	F	0149	1.0	0740	2.7	1413	1.3	2039	3.0	
20	SA	0246	0.8	0927	2.9	1506	1.1	2149	3.2	
21	SU	0332	0.6	1019	3.1	1548	0.9	2235	3.3	
22	M	0412	0.5	1059	3.3	1624	0.8	2314	3.4	
23	TU	0448	0.4	1135	3.4	1656	0.7	2349	3.5	
24	W	0519	0.3	1207	3.4	1726	0.6			○
25	TH	0023	3.5	0548	0.3	1238	3.5	1757	0.5	
26	F	0100	3.6	0620	0.3	1312	3.6	1834	0.4	
27	SA	0138	3.6	0658	0.3	1348	3.7	1915	0.4	
28	SU	0218	3.6	0741	0.4	1426	3.7	1959	0.4	
29	M	0259	3.6	0828	0.5	1506	3.7	2049	0.5	
30	TU	0343	3.5	0921	0.7	1548	3.6	2144	0.7	
31	W	0430	3.3	1022	0.9	1635	3.4	2250	0.8	◑

NOVEMBER

Date	Day	Time	m	Time	m	Time	m	Time	m	Phase
1	TH	0532	3.0	1137	1.1	1734	3.3			
2	F	0010	0.9	0714	2.9	1301	1.1	1901	3.1	
3	SA	0136	0.8	0858	3.0	1414	1.0	2043	3.2	
4	SU	0244	0.6	0959	3.3	1514	0.7	2150	3.4	
5	M	0337	0.4	1047	3.4	1604	0.5	2242	3.6	
6	TU	0423	0.3	1131	3.5	1648	0.4	2329	3.7	
7	W	0504	0.2	1211	3.6	1728	0.3			●
8	TH	0013	3.7	0541	0.3	1249	3.6	1806	0.3	
9	F	0055	3.7	0616	0.4	1323	3.6	1842	0.4	
10	SA	0133	3.6	0651	0.5	1356	3.6	1917	0.4	
11	SU	0210	3.6	0727	0.6	1431	3.6	1955	0.5	
12	M	0247	3.5	0806	0.7	1507	3.6	2036	0.6	
13	TU	0326	3.4	0848	0.9	1545	3.5	2123	0.8	
14	W	0407	3.2	0935	1.1	1627	3.3	2219	1.0	
15	TH	0454	3.0	1030	1.3	1715	3.2	2331	1.1	◐
16	F	0549	2.9	1143	1.5	1815	3.0			
17	SA	0052	1.1	0658	2.8	1307	1.5	1930	3.0	
18	SU	0158	1.0	0823	2.9	1415	1.3	2049	3.1	
19	M	0250	0.8	0930	3.1	1505	1.1	2146	3.2	
20	TU	0333	0.6	1019	3.3	1546	0.9	2232	3.4	
21	W	0411	0.5	1100	3.4	1623	0.8	2313	3.5	
22	TH	0446	0.4	1137	3.5	1658	0.6	2354	3.5	
23	F	0522	0.4	1212	3.6	1736	0.5			○
24	SA	0037	3.6	0559	0.3	1250	3.7	1816	0.4	
25	SU	0121	3.6	0641	0.4	1330	3.8	1900	0.4	
26	M	0206	3.6	0727	0.4	1411	3.8	1947	0.4	
27	TU	0251	3.6	0817	0.5	1453	3.8	2039	0.5	
28	W	0338	3.4	0912	0.7	1537	3.7	2135	0.6	
29	TH	0431	3.3	1012	0.9	1626	3.6	2241	0.7	
30	F	0536	3.1	1121	1.0	1725	3.4	2355	0.7	◑

DECEMBER

Date	Day	Time	m	Time	m	Time	m	Time	m	Phase
1	SA	0701	3.0	1235	1.1	1843	3.3			
2	SU	0111	0.7	0825	3.1	1347	1.0	2010	3.3	
3	M	0217	0.6	0929	3.2	1449	0.8	2120	3.4	
4	TU	0313	0.5	1020	3.4	1542	0.6	2217	3.5	
5	W	0401	0.5	1106	3.5	1629	0.5	2307	3.5	
6	TH	0444	0.5	1147	3.6	1711	0.4	2352	3.5	
7	F	0523	0.5	1225	3.6	1750	0.4			●
8	SA	0034	3.5	0559	0.6	1301	3.6	1825	0.4	
9	SU	0113	3.5	0633	0.6	1334	3.7	1900	0.5	
10	M	0149	3.4	0709	0.7	1408	3.7	1936	0.5	
11	TU	0226	3.4	0747	0.8	1444	3.7	2015	0.6	
12	W	0305	3.3	0827	0.9	1521	3.6	2058	0.7	
13	TH	0346	3.2	0910	1.0	1600	3.5	2147	0.8	
14	F	0430	3.1	0956	1.1	1642	3.3	2242	0.9	
15	SA	0519	3.0	1050	1.3	1732	3.2	2346	1.0	◐
16	SU	0614	3.0	1152	1.3	1832	3.1			
17	M	0052	1.0	0718	2.9	1301	1.3	1939	3.0	
18	TU	0154	0.9	0828	3.0	1405	1.2	2048	3.1	
19	W	0247	0.7	0931	3.1	1501	1.0	2148	3.2	
20	TH	0333	0.6	1023	3.3	1549	0.8	2241	3.4	
21	F	0416	0.5	1108	3.4	1634	0.6	2331	3.5	
22	SA	0459	0.4	1150	3.6	1718	0.4			○
23	SU	0020	3.5	0542	0.3	1233	3.7	1802	0.3	
24	M	0109	3.6	0628	0.3	1316	3.8	1848	0.2	
25	TU	0158	3.6	0717	0.4	1400	3.9	1937	0.2	
26	W	0246	3.5	0807	0.4	1444	3.9	2028	0.3	
27	TH	0336	3.4	0900	0.5	1530	3.8	2123	0.4	
28	F	0428	3.3	0956	0.7	1619	3.7	2222	0.5	
29	SA	0525	3.2	1056	0.8	1713	3.6	2328	0.6	◑
30	SU	0628	3.1	1203	0.9	1814	3.4			
31	M	0038	0.7	0738	3.0	1313	0.9	1927	3.3	

Chart Datum: 1·62 metres below Ordnance Datum (Newlyn). HAT is 3·9 metres above Chart Datum.

9.9.23 ARDROSSAN

N Ayrshire **55°38'·50N 04°49'·61W**

CHARTS AC 5610, 2126, 2221, 2491, 1866; Imray C63

TIDES +0055 Dover; ML 1·9; Duration 0630

Standard Port GREENOCK (⟵)

Times				Height (metres)			
High Water		Low Water		MHWS	MHWN	MLWN	MLWS
0000	0600	0000	0600	3·4	2·8	1·0	0·3
1200	1800	1200	1800				
Differences ARDROSSAN							
–0020	–0010	–0010	–0010	–0·2	–0·2	+0·1	+0·1
IRVINE							
–0020	–0020	–0030	–0010	–0·3	–0·3	–0·1	0·0

SHELTER Good in marina (formerly Eglinton Dock), access at all tides over sill, 5·2m least depth. A storm gate is fitted; max acceptable beam is 8·6m (28ft). Strong SW/NW winds cause heavy seas in the apprs and the hbr may be closed in SW gales. Ferries berth on both sides of Winton Pier.

NAVIGATION WPT 55°38´·13N 04°50´·55W, 055°/0·65M to hbr ent. From the W/NW keep clear of low-lying Horse Isle (conspic W tower on its S end) ringed by drying ledges. The passage between Horse Isle and the mainland is obstructed by unmarked drying rks and should not be attempted. Be aware of following dangers: From the S/SE, Eagle Rk 3ca S of hbr ent, marked by SHM buoy, Fl G 5s. 3ca SE of Eagle Rk lies unmarked Campbell Rk (0·2m). W Crinan Rk (1·1m) is 300m W of hbr ent, marked by PHM buoy, Fl R 4s.

LIGHTS AND MARKS Dir lt WRG 15m W14M, R/G11M (see 9.9.4); W sector leads 055° to hbr ent between lt ho and detached bkwtr. Lt ho Iso WG 4s 11m 9M, 317°-G-035°, W elsewhere. On S end of detached bkwtr, Fl R 5s 7m 5M.

Traffic Signals, shown H24 from control twr at ent to marina:

3 F ● lts (vert) = hbr and marina closed; no entry/exit for commercial and pleasure vessels.

3 F ● lts (vert) = marina open, hbr closed; pleasure craft may enter/exit the marina, no commercial movements.

2 F ● lts over 1 F ● = hbr open, marina closed; in severe weather marina storm gate is closed. Commercial vessels may enter/exit hbr, subject to approval by Hbr Control on VHF. Pleasure craft must clear the approach channel, ferry turning area (between the detached bkwtr and Winton Pier) and the outer basin. Yachts may not manoeuvre under sail alone until seaward of the outer breakwater.

COMMUNICATIONS (Code 01294) CGOC (02891) 463933; Police 101; Dr 463011.
Clyde Marina VHF Ch **80** M. *Hbr Control* Ch 12 14 16 (H24).

FACILITIES **Clyde Marina** www. clyde marina.com ☎607077 252 inc 50Ⓥ £2·77, £10·50 < 4hrs, access H24, office hrs 0900-1800 (50t) ✕.

Town ✉ Ⓑ ✕. ⇌ ✈ (Prestwick/Glasgow). Ferry to Brodick (Arran).

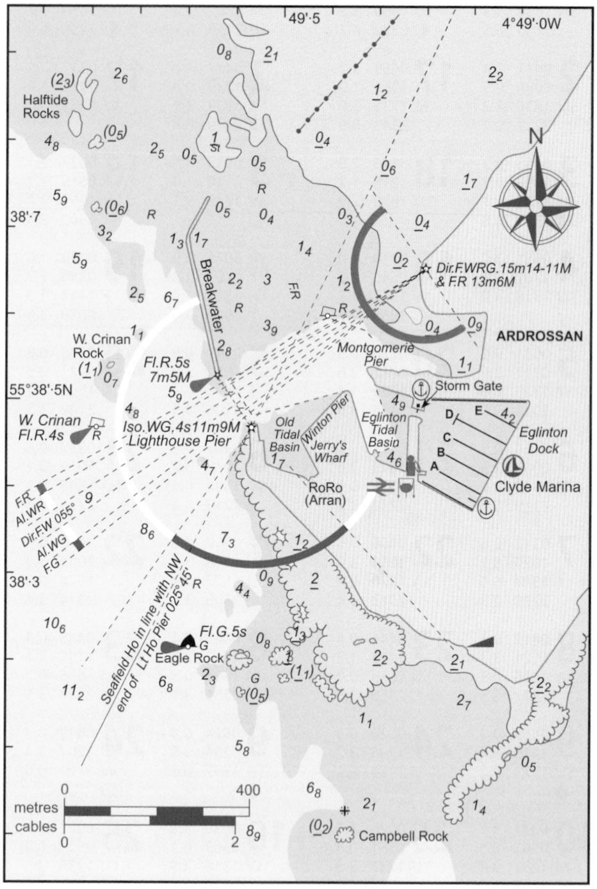

ADJACENT HARBOURS

IRVINE, N Ayrshire, **55°36'·17N 04°42'·07W**. AC 2126, 2220, 1866. HW +0055 on Dover. Tides: see 9.9.23.

Do not attempt entrance in heavy onshore weather. Goodshelter once across the bar which carries approx 0·5m. The IB-B SPM buoy, Fl Y 3s, is 1·15M from hbr ent, close NW of ldg line. 5 blocks of flats and chimneys are conspic ENE of entrance. Ldg lts 051°: front, FG 10m 5M; rear, FR 15m 5M. The S ent groyne is lit, Fl G 3s; groynes inside the ent have unlit perches. White Pilot tower with mast is conspic 3ca inside entrance.

HM ☎(01294) 487286, 487111, VHF Ch 12 (0800-1600 Tues and Thurs; 0800-1300 Wed).

⚓ prohib. Visitors' pontoons on N side or on S side at visitors' quay (2·2m). Berths available above opening footbridge which opens at 5 mins notice ☎08708 403123 or VHF Ch 12 (call *Irvine Bridge*). **Quay**, 5m<£4<10m<£6<15m £9, (3t).

Town (1·5km), ✕ ⇌ ✈ (Prestwick).

AYR, S Ayrshire, **55°28´·22N 04°38´·78W**. AC 5610, 2126, 2220, 1866. HW +0050 on Dover; ML 1·8m. Duration 0630. See 9.9.24.

Good shelter in S dock although berth space limited. Heavy rains may wash large amounts of debris down the R Ayr. From the W, harbour ent lies between conspic gasholder to the N and townhall spire to the S.

St Nicholas SHM, Fl G 2s, guards shoals and a drying rk (0·8m) 150m S of ent. PHM, Fl R 2s marks rk awash at LW 120m NW of N B'water. Ldg lts 098°: front, by Pilot Stn, FR 10m 5M R tower, rear (130m from front), Oc R 10s 18m 9M. Traffic signals (near front ldg lt):

2 ● (vert) = hbr closed to incoming traffic.

N Bkwtr Hd, QR 9m 5M. S Pier Hd, Q 7m 7M, vis 012°-161°, and FG 5m 5M, same structure, vis 012°-082°, over St Nicholas Rk.

HM ☎(01292) 281687; VHF Ch 14 16.

Ayr Y & CC at S dock, limited on pontoon on N side of harbour (access key, £10 deposit, from Ship Inn).

Services.

Town ✉ Ⓑ ✕ ⇌.

9.9.24 TROON

S Ayrshire **55°33'·10N 04°40'·97W** ❁❁◇◇✿✿

CHARTS AC 5610, 2126, 2220, 1866; Imray C63

TIDES +0050 Dover; ML 1·9; Duration 0630

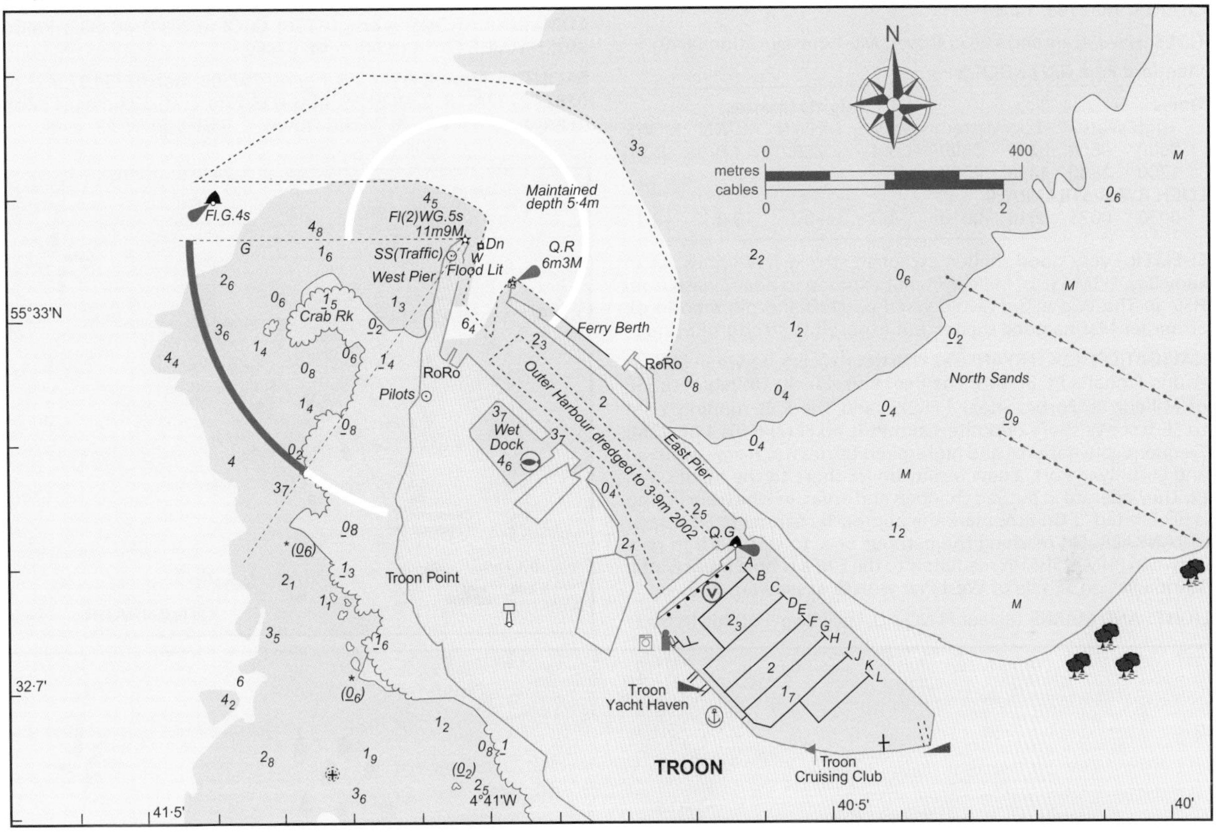

Standard Port GREENOCK (⟵)

Times				Height (metres)			
High Water		Low Water		MHWS	MHWN	MLWN	MLWS
0000	0600	0000	0600	3·4	2·8	1·0	0·3
1200	1800	1200	1800				
Differences TROON							
−0025	−0025	−0020	−0020	−0·2	−0·2	0·0	0·0
AYR							
−0025	−0025	−0030	−0015	−0·4	−0·3	+0·1	+0·1
GIRVAN							
−0025	−0040	−0035	−0010	−0·3	−0·3	−0·1	0·0

SHELTER Complete in marina (2·4m at ent, 1·6m at SE end); speed limit 5kn. *Strong W winds cause heavy seas in the hbr approach.*

NAVIGATION WPT 55°33'·20N 04°42'·00W, 103°/0·6M to W pier lt. Appr in sector SW to NW. Beware Lady Isle, Fl (4) 30s 19m 8M, W bn, 2·2M SW; Troon Rock (5·6m, occas breaks) 1·1M W; Lappock Rock (0·6m, bn with G barrel topmark) 1·6M NNW; Mill Rock (0·4m) ½M NNE of hbr ent, marked by unlit PHM buoy.

LIGHTS AND MARKS No ldg lts. Floodlit dolphin 14m SE of W pier hd lt, Fl (2) WG 5s. A SHM, FG, marks the chan in the ent to marina. Traffic signals (H24) on W Pier: 3 F●(vert) + ●(strobe) = hbr closed to fishing/pleasure vessels during commercial/fast ferry moves.

COMMUNICATIONS (Code 01292) CGOC (02891) 463933; Police 101; Dr 313593; ⊞ 610555 (Ayr). HM 281687; Troon CC 311865; Troon YC 316770. HM Ch 14. Marina Ch **80** M.

FACILITIES Troon Yacht Haven ⊛ www.yachthavens.com ☎315553 all tide access 300⊆+50Ⓥ, £2·87 (short stay £10). Ⓥ berth on pontoon **A**, first to stbd. 36m x 3m draught ⊆ at hammerheads. ◣ ⊡ ♞(H24) ▮ ✕ ⚒ ⊡ Ⓔ ⊡ ⚓(daily pick-up) ⊡ (50t) ⊡(25t) ⊡ ⊡ ✕ ☎311523.

Town ✉ Ⓑ ⇌ ✈ (Prestwick/Glasgow).

HARBOUR ON THE FIRTH OF CLYDE SOUTH OF TROON

GIRVAN, S Ayrshire, **55°14'·77N 04°51'·87W**. AC 2199, 1866. HW +0043 on Dover; ML 1·8m; Duration 0630. See 9.9.24.

Good shelter. Brest Rks, 3·5M N of the harbour extend 6ca offshore. Bar carries approx 1·5m. Beware Girvan Patch, 1·7m, 4ca SW of ent. Ch spire (conspic) brg 104° leads between N Bkwtr, Fl R 4s 5m 2M, and S pier, 2 FG (vert) 8m 4M. Inner N groyne, Iso 4s 3m 4M. Traffic sig at root of S pier: 2 B discs (hor)/ 2 ● (hor) = hbr shut.

HM ☎(01465) 713648; VHF Ch 12 16 (HO)

35 ⊆ (£2·00) on fingers around perimeter of inner hbr (1·7m). Coasters and FVs berth on adjacent quay: ⚓ ◣.

Town ⊡ ⊡ Ⓑ ✉ ⊡ ✕ ⇌.

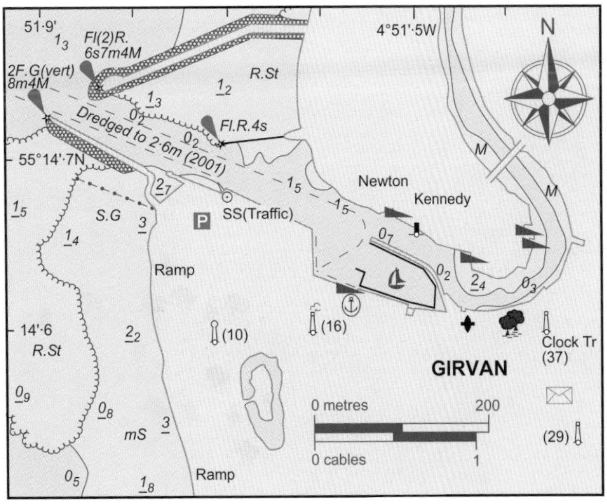

9.9.25 LOCH RYAN/STRANRAER

Dumfries and Galloway **55°01'N 05°05'W**

CHARTS AC 2198, 1403

TIDES HW (Stranraer) +0055 Dover; ML 1.6m; Duration 0640

Standard Port GREENOCK (⟵)

Times				Heights (metres)			
High Water		Low Water		MHWS	MHWN	MLWN	MLWS
0000	0600	0200	0800	3.4	2.8	1.0	0·3
1200	1800	1400	2000				
LOCH RYAN/STRANRAER							
−0030	−0025	−0010	−0010	−0·2	−0·1	0·0	+0·1

SHELTER Very good shelter except in strong NW winds. ⚓s in Lady Bay, 1·3M SSE of Milleur Pt, but exposed to heavy wash from HSS; in The Wig in 3m (avoid weed patches and old moorings); Stranraer Marina good shelter, but exposed to strong NE winds.

NAVIGATION LOCH RYAN: (see chartlet rhs). Ent between Milleur Pt and Finnarts Pt. Beware The Beef Barrel rock, 1m high 6ca SSE of Milleur Pt, Forbes Shoal Fl(2)5s and The Spit running 1·5M to SE from W shore opposite Cairn Pt lt ho Fl (2) R10s 14m 12M. Frequent conventional and high-speed ferries run from Cairnryan and Loch Ryan Port, a new facility on NE shore to the NE of Cairn Pt. They operate in buoyed channels and areas, in which anchoring is prohibited. 3 Gn Bcns mark the approach channel to Stranraer. STRANRAER: On reaching the harbour bear to starboard to pass between PHM & SHM immediately to the E of a rubble breakwater. Marina lies on SE side of West Pier with Ⓥ at seaward end.

LIGHTS AND MARKS Milleur Pt NCM Q; Loch Ryan Port ldg lts Iso 2s 9M; Cairn Pt Fl(2) R 10s 14m; Cairnryan ferry terminal Fl R 5s 5m 5M. Stranraer, centre pier hd 2FBu (vert), E pier hd 2FR (vert); PHM Fl R 5s, SHM Fl G 5s.

COMMUNICATIONS (Code 01776) CGOC (02891) 463933; Police 101; HM VHF Ch **14** (H24) or ☎702460.

FACILITIES Marina ☎706565, hbr off 707500; mob 07734 073421 or 07827 277247. 8 Ⓥ £1.55. Max LOA 27m; craft >23m must book in advance (30t). **Town**

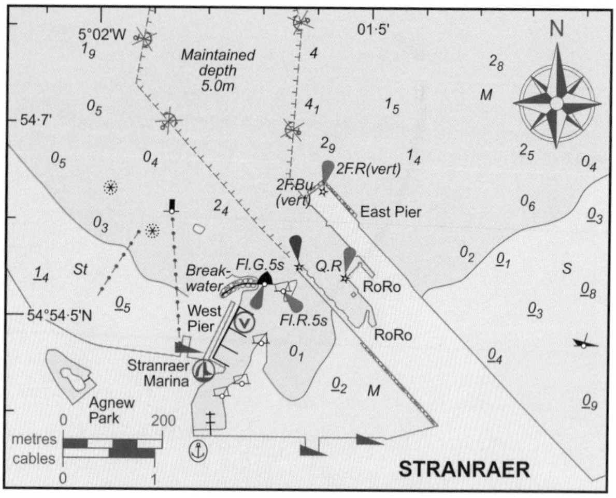

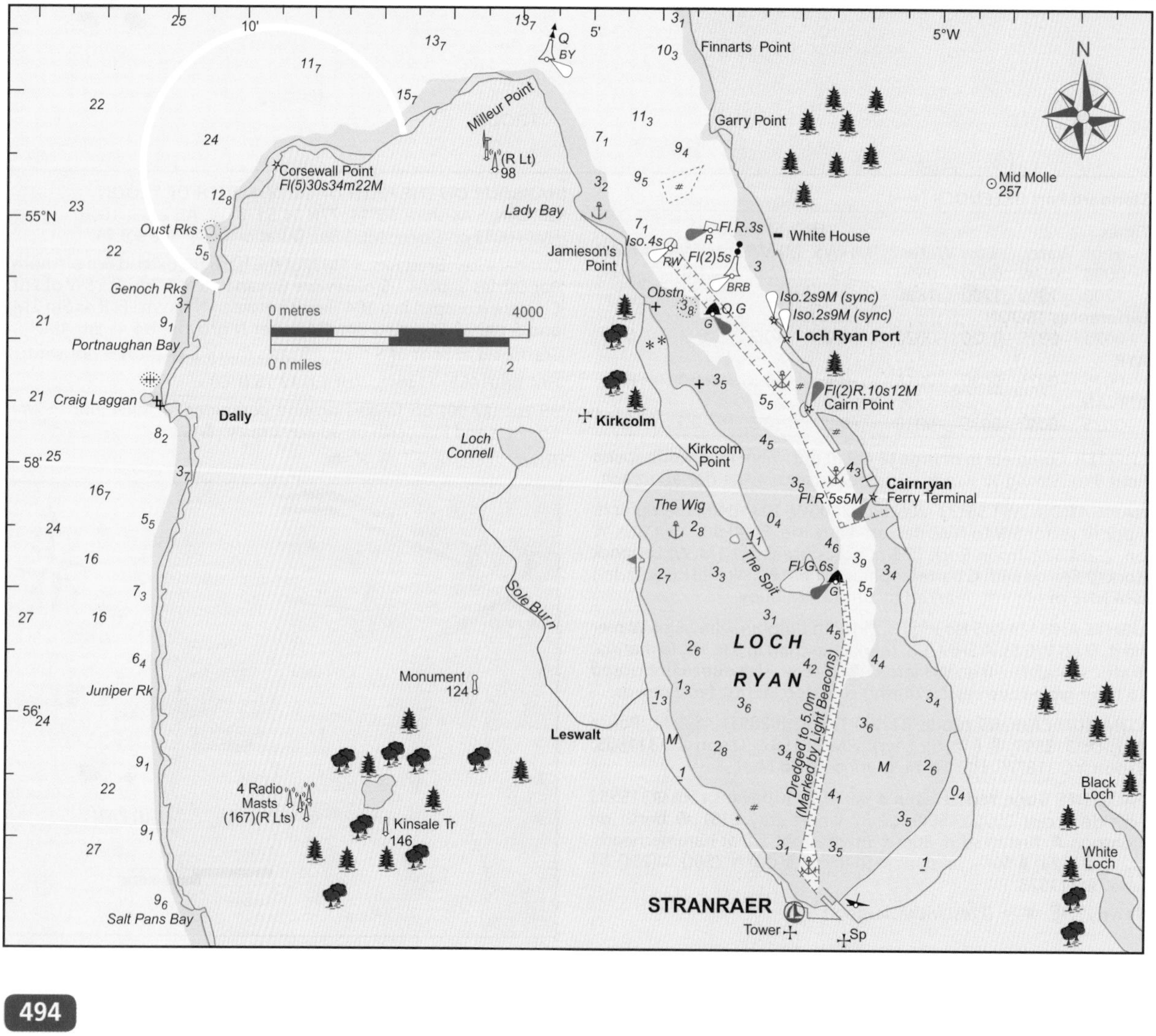

HARBOURS FROM MULL OF GALLOWAY TO WIGTOWN BAY

DRUMMORE, Dumfries and Galloway, **54°41′·57N 04°53′·49W.** AC 2094, 5613. HW +0040m on Dover; ML 3.3m; Duration 0610. Owned by Drummore Hbr Trust the small drying harbour has now silted almost entirely rendering of little interest to passing mariners. Temp'y ⚓ 5.5ca NNE of hbr ent in 4m. Facilities in village: ⚓ ⚓ ⚓ ✉ ⚓ ✕ ⚓ ⇌ (bus to Stranraer), ✈ (Carlisle).

PORT WILLIAM, Dumfries and Galloway, **54°45′·70N 04°35′·10W.** AC 1826, 2094, 5613. HW +0035 on Dover; ML 3·7m; Duration 0545. See 9.9.27. Sheltered harbour dries having approx 1m at HW±2. ⚓ in 3m approx 0.4M off hbr ent. Ldg lts F G 2M on shore Front lt on pier Fl G 3s 3M. HM ☎07734 073419.

ISLE OF WHITHORN, Dumfries and Galloway, **54°41′·91N 04°21′·88W.** AC 1826, 2094, 5613. HW +0035 on Dover; ML 3·7m; Duration 0545. See 9.9.27. Shelter good but hbr dries, having approx 2·5m at HW±3. On W side of ent beware the Skerries ledge. St Ninian's Tr (Fl WR 3s 20m 6/4M viz: 310°-W-005°-R-040°; W □ tr) is conspic at E side of ent. E pier hd has QG 4m 5M; ldg lts 335°, both Oc R 8s 7/9m 7M, synch, Or masts and ◊. HM ☎07734 073420, www.isleofwhithorn.com; Facilities: on quay £4.83/yacht, 2 (launching £1.00), (by arrangement with HM), VHF Ch 08 (occas).

GARLIESTON, Dumfries and Galloway, **54°47′·36N 04°21′·83W.** AC 1826, 2094, 5613. HW +0035 on Dover; ML no data; Duration 0545. See 9.9.27. Hbr affords complete shelter but dries. Pier hd lt 2FR (vert) 5m 3M. Beware rky outcrops in W side of bay marked by a perch. HM ☎(01988) 600295, Mobile 07734 073422. Facilities: £3, on quay, . **Town:** .

9.9.26 PORTPATRICK

Dumfries and Galloway **54°50′·42N 05°07′·18W**

CHARTS AC 2724, 2198; Imray C62

TIDES +0032 Dover; ML 2·1; Duration 0615

Standard Port LIVERPOOL (⟶)

Times				Heights (metres)			
High Water		Low Water		MHWS	MHWN	MLWN	MLWS
0000	0600	0200	0800	9·4	7·5	3·2	1·1
1200	1800	1400	2000				
Differences PORTPATRICK							
+0038	+0032	0009	–0008	–5·5	–4·4	–2·0	–0·6

SHELTER Good in tiny Inner harbour (on rough stone wall), but entrance is difficult in strong SW/NW winds.

NAVIGATION WPT 54°50′·00N 05°08′·07W, 050°/0·7M to ent. Ent to outer hbr by short narrow chan with hazards either side, including rky shelf covered at HW. Beware cross tides off ent, up to 3kn springs. Barrel buoy (a mooring buoy) marks end of Half Tide Rk; do not cut inside.

LIGHTS AND MARKS Old Lt Ho (W tower, 22m) on Black Head is conspic 1·6M north of entrance. Ldg lts 050·5°, FG (H24) 6/8m: Front on sea wall; rear on bldg; 2 vert orange stripes by day. Conspic features include: TV mast 1M NE, almost on ldg line; large hotel on cliffs about 1½ca NNW of hbr ent; Dunskey Castle (ru) 4ca SE of hbr.

COMMUNICATIONS (Code 01776) CGOC (02891) 463933; Police 101; Ⓗ 702323; RNLI Coxswain (for local advice) 07771 741717. HM 810355.

FACILITIES Hbr (small craft), £16, . **Village** (bulk tanker) ⇌ (bus to Stranraer Ⓑ), ✈ (Prestwick).

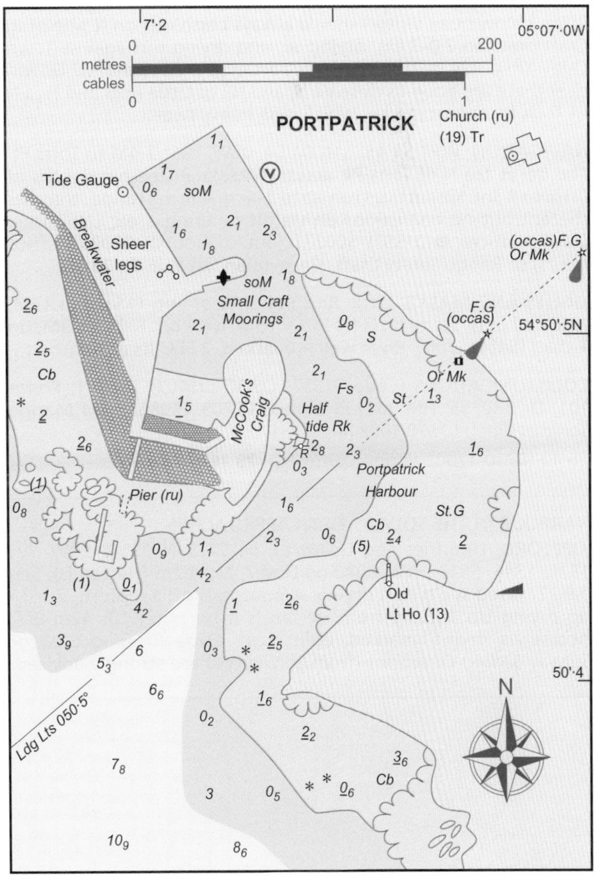

9.9.27 KIRKCUDBRIGHT

Dumfries and Galloway **54°50′·33N 04°03′·47W**

CHARTS AC 1826, 2094, 1346, 1344, 5613; Imray C62

TIDES +0030 Dover; ML 4·1; Duration 0545

Standard Port LIVERPOOL (9.10.17) (⟶)

Times				Height (metres)			
High Water		Low Water		MHWS	MHWN	MLWN	MLWS
0000	0600	0200	0800	9·4	7·5	3·2	1·1
1200	1800	1400	2000				
Differences KIRKCUDBRIGHT BAY							
+0020	+0020	+0005	–0005	–1·9	–1·6	–0·8	–0·3
DRUMMORE							
+0035	+0045	+0010	+0015	–3·5	–2·6	–1·2	–0·5
PORT WILLIAM							
+0035	+0035	+0020	–0005	–3·0	–2·3	–1.1	ND
GARLIESTON							
+0030	+0040	+0025	0000	–2·4	–1·8	–0·8	ND
ISLE OF WHITHORN							
+0025	+0030	+0020	0000	–2·5	–2·1	–1.1	–0.4
HESTAN ISLET (Kippford)							
+0030	+0030	+0015	+0020	–1·1	–1·2	–0.8	–0.2
SOUTHERNESS POINT							
+0035	+0035	+0025	+0005	–0·8	–0·8	ND	ND
ANNAN WATERFOOT							
+0055	+0110	+0215	+0305	–2·3	–2·7	–3·0	CD+
TORDUFF POINT							
+0110	+0145	+0515	+0405	–4·2	–5·0	CD+	CD+
REDKIRK							
+0115	+0220	+0710	+0440	–5·6	–6·3	CD+	CD+

NOTES: At Annan Waterfoot, Torduff Pt and Redkirk the LW time differences are for the start of the rise, which at sp is very sudden. CD+ = At LW the tide does not usually fall below CD; ND = No Data.

SHELTER Very good. Depths at LW: 1·0–2·0m at the floating pontoon 300m below quay, visitors should always berth/raft on N side of it. Craft drawing 2·0–3·0m, drying, and drying out against Town Quay (used H24 by FVs) by advance arrangement with HM. Downriver there are good ⚓s close W, N, and NE of Little Ross and ½ca N of Torrs Pt, except in S'lies which raise heavy swell.

NAVIGATION WPT 54°45′·51N 04°04′·08W, 005°/1·4M to Torrs Pt. The Bar is 1ca N of Torrs Pt; access HW±2½. R Dee has depths of 0·1m to 4·3m. Spring tides run up to 3–4kn. A firing range straddles the ent but no restrictions on transit of firing area; call Range Safety Officer ☎(01557) 500271 (out of hours), 830236 office hours) or Range Safety Craft, Gallavidian, on VHF Ch **73** 16.

LIGHTS AND MARKS Little Ross Lt ho, W of ent, Fl 5s 50m 12M, NNE end of Is, Stone bn Fl (2) 5s 21m 5M. No 1 bn, Fl 3s 7m 3M, on ♦ shed (54°47′·70N). River well lit/marked, 2 Fl G lts at pontoon.

COMMUNICATIONS (Code 01557) CGOC (01407) 762051; Police 101; Dr 330755; HM 331135 Mobile 07709 479663; GM Marine Services (Fuel) 07970 109814.

Ch 12 (0730-1700). *Range Control* Ch **73** 16.

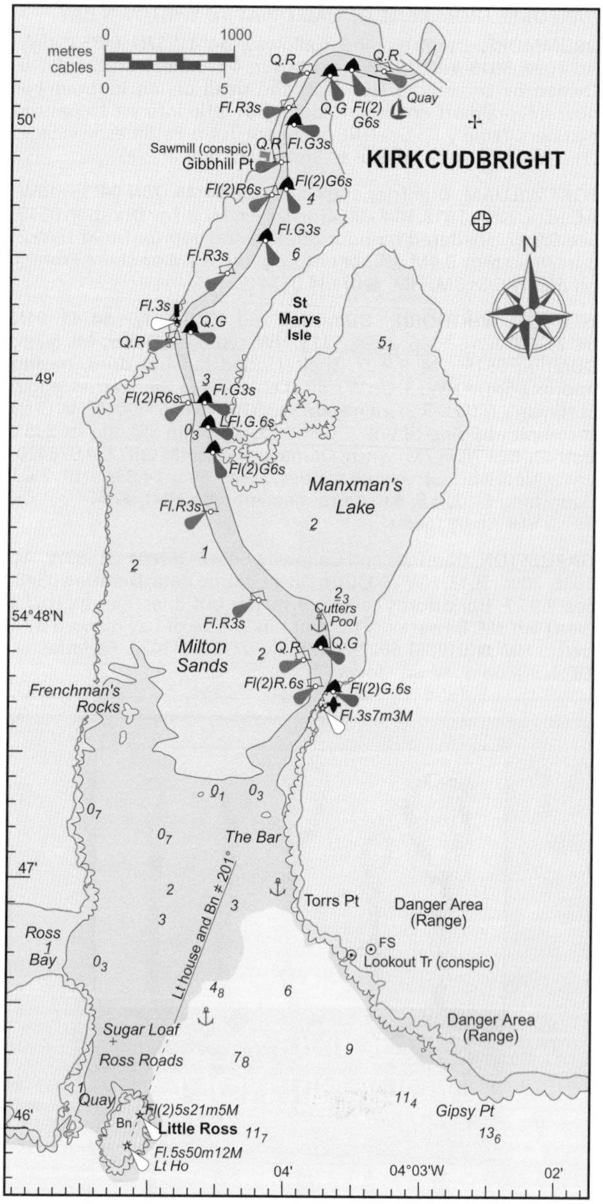

FACILITIES Pontoon/jetty max LOA 20m £1.40 inc
Town Quay (by arrangement with HM) (15t).
KYC ☎330963; **SC** ☎330032
Town (Dumfries 30M), ✈ (Glasgow 100M).

HARBOUR IN THE SOLWAY FIRTH APPROACHES

KIPPFORD, Dumfries and Galloway, **54°52′·36N 03°48′·93W**. AC 1826, 1346, 5613. HW +0040 on Dover; ML 4·2m (Hestan Is). See 9.9.27. Good shelter on drying /pontoons off Kippford, 2·75M up drying Urr Estuary from Hestan Is lt ho Fl (2) 10s 42m 9M. Access via drying, marked, unlit chan. *Clyde Cruising Club* or *Solway Sailing Directions* (from Solway YC) are strongly advised.

Beware Craig Roan on E side of ent. Temp ⚓s NE or W of Hestan Is to await tide. VHF: Ch M call *Kippford Startline* (YC) HW±2 in season. Ch 16 *Kippford Slipway* (Pilotage). Facilities: **Solway YC** www.thesyc.com ☎(01556) 600221; M; **Services:** £6, *Kippford Slipway Ltd* (01556) 620249. **Town**

NW England, IoM & N Wales

Mull of Galloway to Bardsey Island

9.10.1	**Contents**	497
9.10.2	**Area map and Distance table**	498
9.10.3	**Tidal stream charts**	500
9.10.4	**Lights, buoys and waypoints**	502
9.10.5	**Passage information** Solway Firth – 503 • Isle of Man, Barrow to Conwy – 506 • Menai Strait, Anglesey to Bardsey Island – 518	503
9.10.6	**Maryport**	504
9.10.7	**Workington** Silloth • Harrington	504
9.10.8	**Whitehaven** Ravenglass	505
9.10.9	**Isle of Man** Port Erin • Castletown • Laxey	505
9.10.10	**Peel**	507
9.10.11	**Port St Mary** Derby Haven	507
9.10.12	**Douglas**	508
9.10.13	**Ramsey**	508
9.10.14	**Glasson Dock** Barrow-in-Furness • Heysham	509
9.10.15	**Fleetwood**	510
9.10.16	**River Ribble/Preston**	511
9.10.17	**Liverpool, tide tables/curves** River Alt • Rhyl	512
9.10.18	**Conwy and Deganwy**	517
9.10.19	**Menai Strait** Beaumaris • Bangor • The Swellies • Port Dinorwic • Caernarfon	520
9.10.20	**Holyhead, tide tables/curves** Porth Dinllaen • Aberdaron • Bardsey Island	522

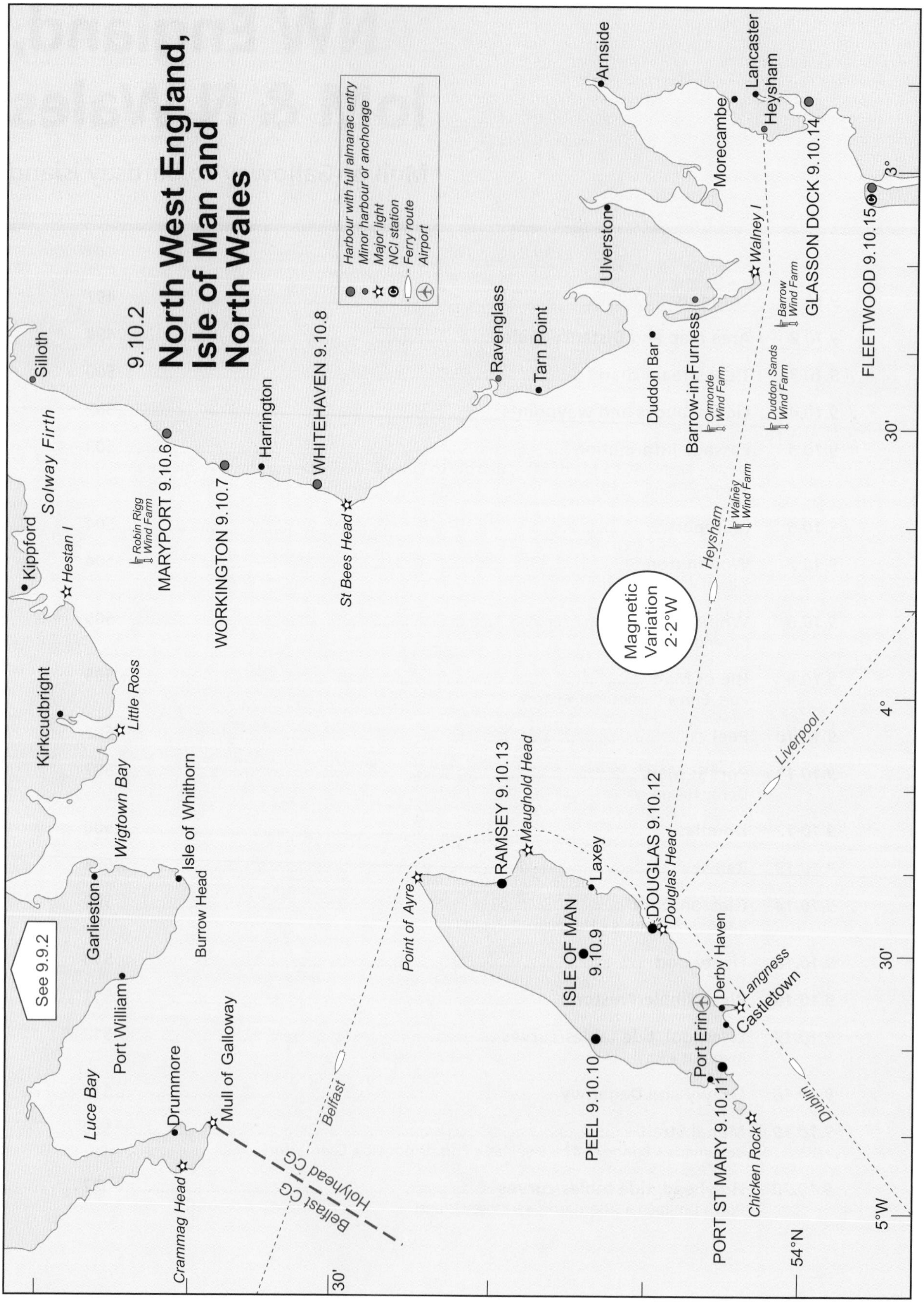
9.10.2
North West England, Isle of Man and North Wales
Harbour with full almanac entry
Minor harbour or anchorage
Major light
NCI station
Ferry route
Airport
See 9.9.2
Magnetic Variation 2·2°W
Silloth
Solway Firth
Kippford
Hestan I
Kirkcudbright
Little Ross
Wigtown Bay
Garlieston
Isle of Whithorn
Burrow Head
Port William
Luce Bay
Drummore
Mull of Galloway
Crammag Head
Holyhead CG
Belfast CG
Belfast
MARYPORT 9.10.6
Robin Rigg Wind Farm
WORKINGTON 9.10.7
Harrington
WHITEHAVEN 9.10.8
St Bees Head
Ravenglass
Tarn Point
Arnside
Ulverston
Morecambe
Lancaster
Heysham
Walney I
Duddon Bar
Barrow-in-Furness
Ormonde Wind Farm
Duddon Sands Wind Farm
Barrow Wind Farm
Walney Wind Farm
GLASSON DOCK 9.10.14
FLEETWOOD 9.10.15
Heysham
Liverpool
Dublin
Point of Ayre
RAMSEY 9.10.13
Maughold Head
Laxey
DOUGLAS 9.10.12
Douglas Head
ISLE OF MAN 9.10.9
PEEL 9.10.10
Derby Haven
Langness
Castletown
Port Erin
PORT ST MARY 9.10.11
Chicken Rock
54°N
30'
5°W
30'
4°
30'
3°

DISTANCE TABLE
Approximate distances in nautical miles are by the most direct route, whilst avoiding dangers and allowing for Traffic Separation Schemes. Places in *italics* are in adjoining areas; places in **bold** are in 9.0.6, Distances across the Irish Sea.

1	***Fishguard***	158	175	175	169	163	153	140	126	134	144	153	147	142	136	100	88	78	89	45	**1**
2	*Bardsey Island*	113	129	129	123	117	107	94	80	88	98	107	101	96	90	53	41	31	43	**2**	
3	**Holyhead**	81	94	96	90	84	68	62	46	50	65	79	73	74	68	36	32	26	**3**		
4	Menai (Caernarfon)	103	104	105	99	93	81	73	68	68	80	76	70	68	59	22	10	**4**			
5	Menai (Beaumaris)	93	94	95	89	83	71	73	58	58	70	66	60	58	49	12	**5**				
6	**Conwy/Deganwy**	95	95	92	86	80	72	72	57	59	68	62	56	55	46	**6**					
7	**Liverpool**	102	97	89	83	77	80	86	76	70	77	52	46	30	**7**						
8	River Ribble Ent	86	76	68	62	56	65	89	69	61	62	32	27	**8**							
9	**Fleetwood**	79	68	59	53	47	58	80	63	57	55	10	**9**								
10	Glasson Dock	85	74	66	60	54	64	85	69	63	61	**10**									
11	Ramsey	28	34	41	35	32	6	24	27	15	**11**										
12	Douglas	42	46	50	44	39	19	30	13	**12**											
13	**Port St Mary**	41	61	63	57	51	35	18	**13**												
14	Peel	26	46	55	49	49	18	**14**													
15	**Point of Ayre**	22	28	37	31	31	**15**														
16	Whitehaven	44	23	12	7	**16**															
17	Workington	47	25	6	**17**																
18	**Maryport**	49	26	**18**																	
19	**Kirkcudbright**	32	**19**																		
20	***Mull of Galloway***	**20**																			

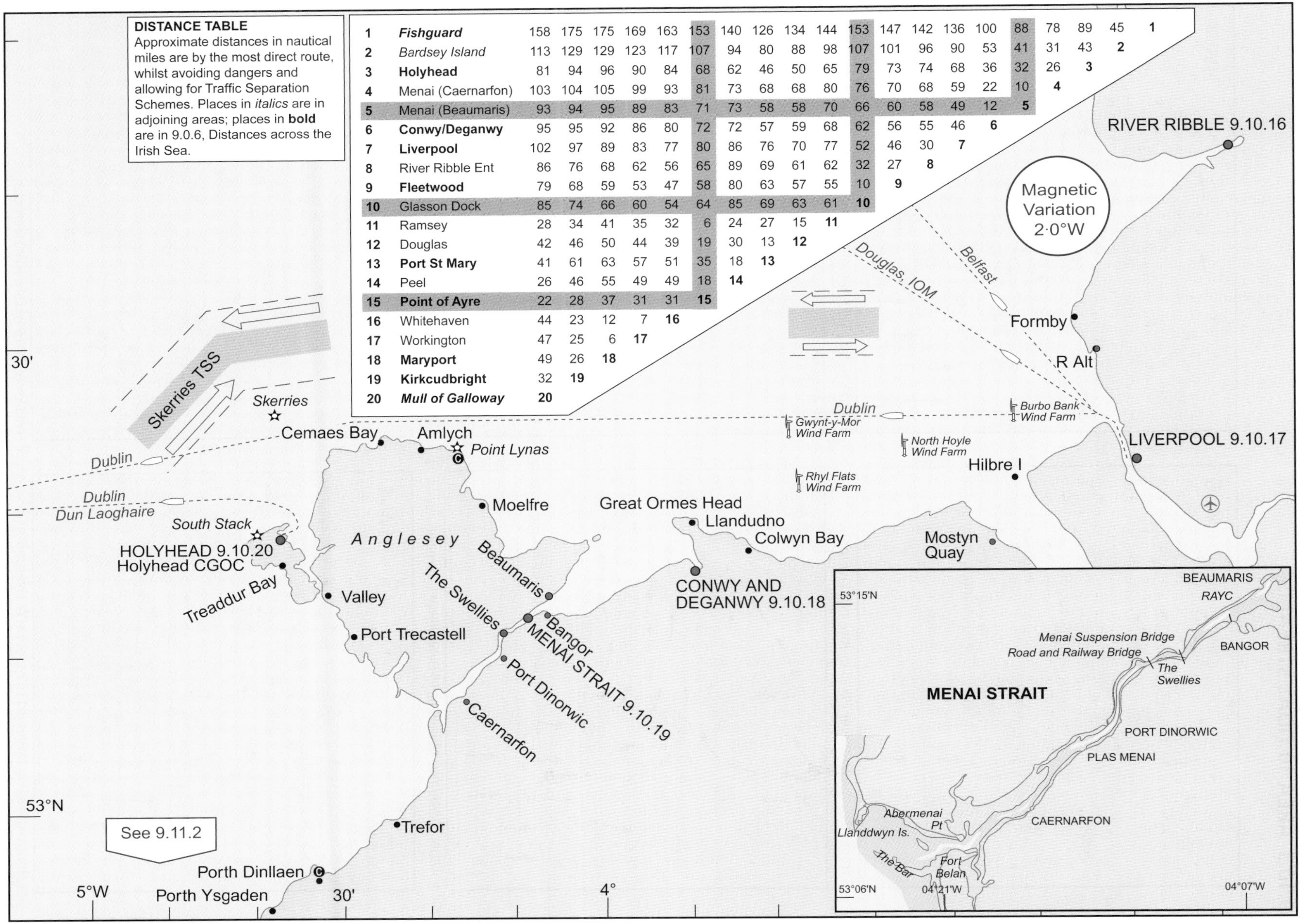
RIVER RIBBLE 9.10.16
Magnetic Variation 2·0°W
Belfast
Douglas, IOM
Formby
R Alt
Dublin
Burbo Bank Wind Farm
Gwynt-y-Mor Wind Farm
North Hoyle Wind Farm
Rhyl Flats Wind Farm
LIVERPOOL 9.10.17
Hilbre I
30'
Skerries TSS
Skerries
Cemaes Bay
Amlych
Point Lynas
Dublin
Dublin
Dun Laoghaire
Moelfre
Great Ormes Head
Llandudno
Colwyn Bay
Mostyn Quay
South Stack
HOLYHEAD 9.10.20
Holyhead CGOC
Anglesey
Treaddur Bay
Valley
Beaumaris
The Swellies
Bangor
MENAI STRAIT 9.10.19
CONWY AND DEGANWY 9.10.18
Port Trecastell
Port Dinorwic
Caernarfon
53°N
See 9.11.2
Trefor
Porth Dinllaen
Porth Ysgaden
5°W
30'
4°
MENAI STRAIT
53°15'N
BEAUMARIS
RAYC
BANGOR
Menai Suspension Bridge
Road and Railway Bridge
The Swellies
PORT DINORWIC
PLAS MENAI
CAERNARFON
Abermenai Pt
Llanddwyn Is.
The Bar
Fort Belan
53°06'N
04°21'W
04°07'W

9.10.3 AREA 10 TIDAL STREAMS

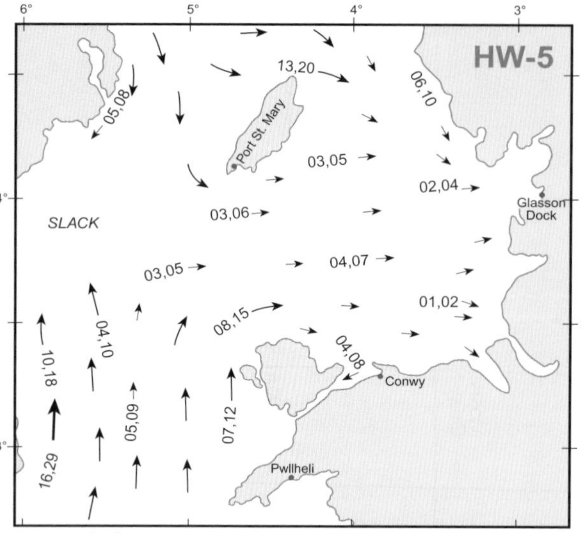

5 Hours before HW Dover (0515 before HW Liverpool)

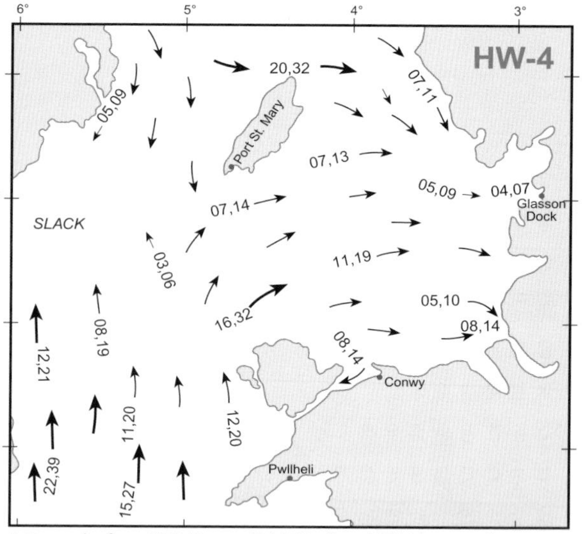

4 Hours before HW Dover (0415 before HW Liverpool)

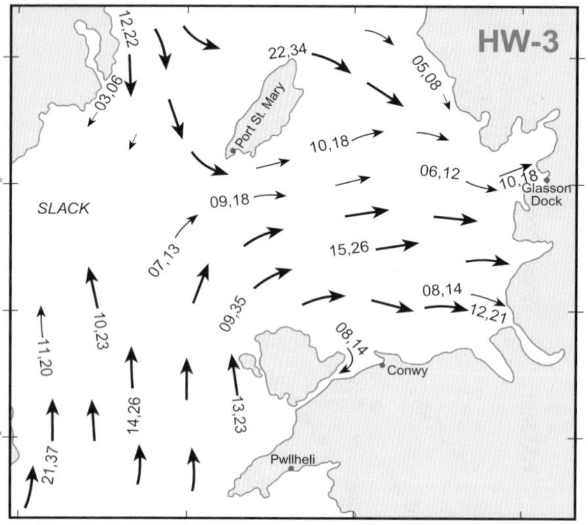

3 Hours before HW Dover (0315 before HW Liverpool)

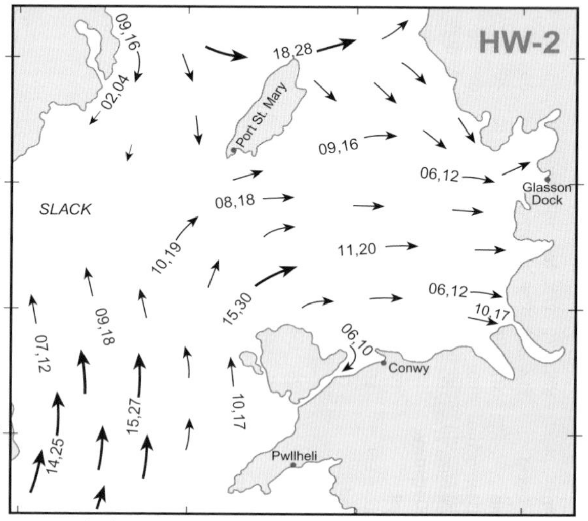

2 Hours before HW Dover (0215 before HW Liverpool)

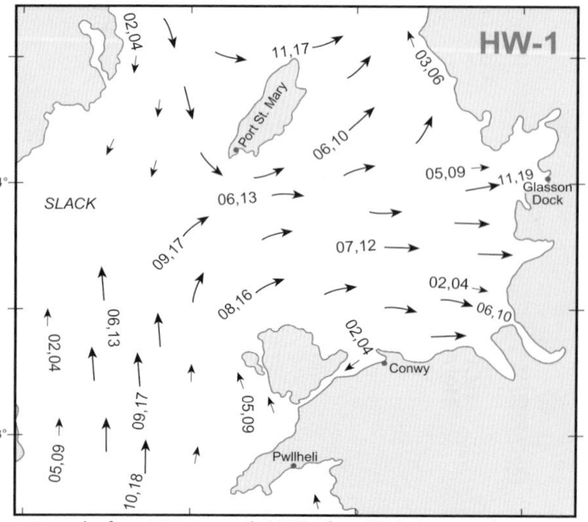

1 Hour before HW Dover (0115 before HW Liverpool)

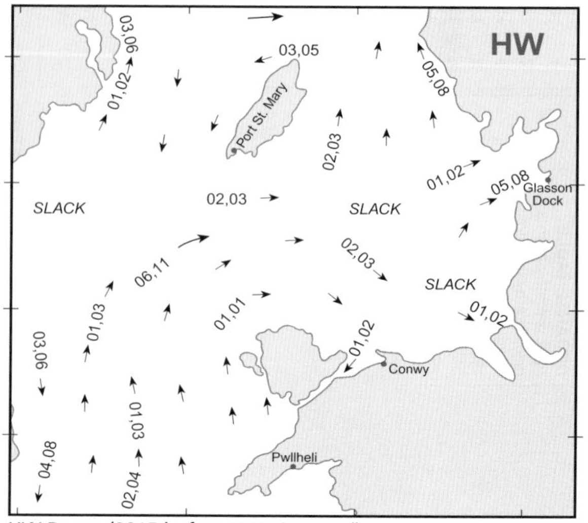

HW Dover (0015 before HW Liverpool)

Northward 9.9.3 Southward 9.11.3 North Ireland 9.13.3 Mull of Kintyre 9.9.11 South Ireland 9.12.3

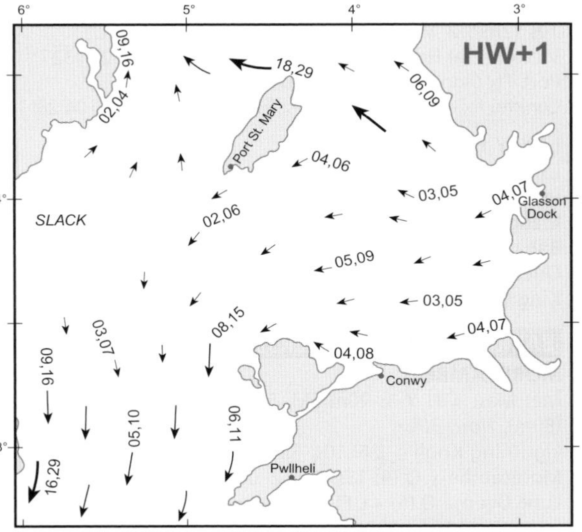

1 Hour after HW Dover (0045 after HW Liverpool)

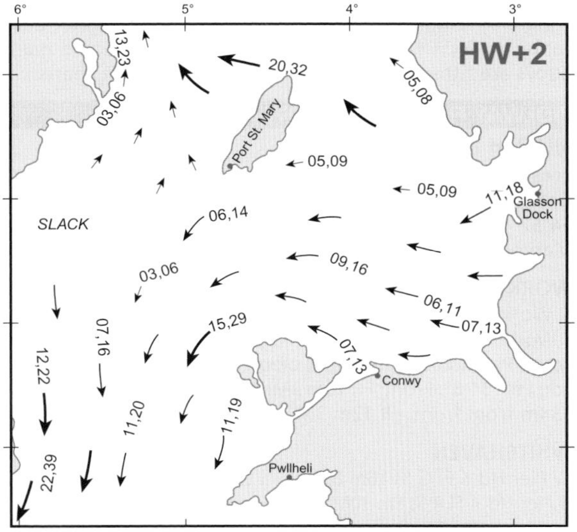

2 Hours after HW Dover (0145 after HW Liverpool)

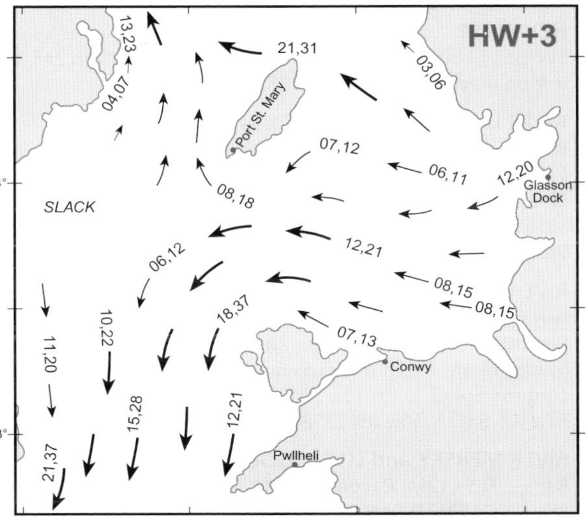

3 Hours after HW Dover (0245 after HW Liverpool)

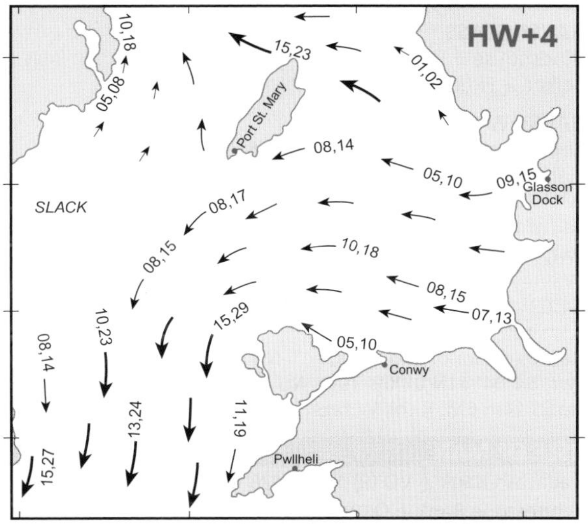

4 Hours after HW Dover (0345 after HW Liverpool)

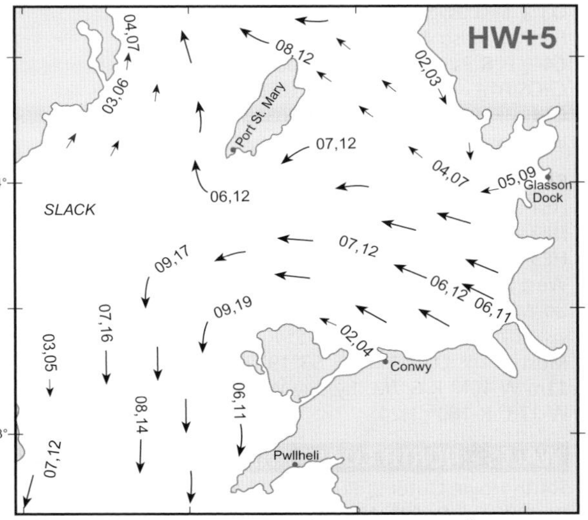

5 Hours after HW Dover (0445 after HW Liverpool)

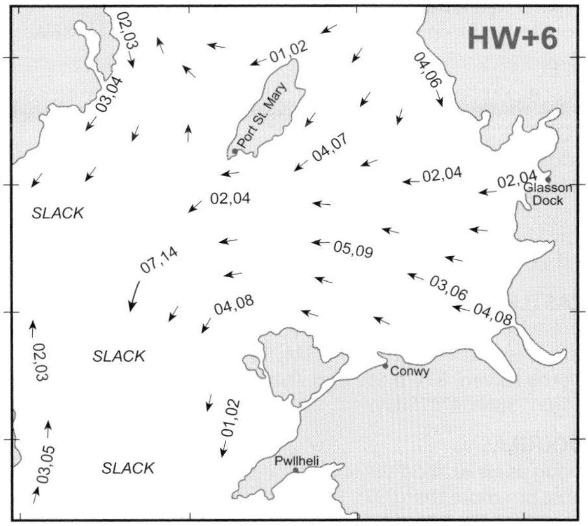

6 Hours after HW Dover (0545 after HW Liverpool)

9.10.4 LIGHTS, BUOYS AND WAYPOINTS

Bold print = light with a nominal range of 15M or more. CAPITALS = place or feature. *CAPITAL ITALICS* = light-vessel, light float or Lanby. *Italics* = Fog signal. ***Bold italics*** = Racon. Some marks/buoys are fitted with AIS (MMSI No); see relevant charts.

SOLWAY FIRTH TO BARROW-IN-FURNESS

SILLOTH and MARYPORT

Lees Scar Fl G 5s 11m 4M; W piles; 54°51′·78N 03°24′·79W.
Groyne Hd 2 FG (vert) 4m 4M; Fl Bu tfc signals close by; 54°52′·14N 03°23′·93W.
Maryport S Pier Hd .Fl 1·5s 10m 6M; 54°43′·07N 03°30′·64W.

WORKINGTON and HARRINGTON

N Workington Q; 54°40′·10N 03°38′·18W.
S Workington VQ (6) + L Fl 10s; 54°37′·01N 03°38′·58W.
South Pier Fl 5s 11m 5M; R bldg; 54°39′·12N 03°34′·67W.
Ldg Lts 131·8°. Front, FR 10m 3M; 54°38′·92N 03°34′·19W. Rear, 134m from front, FR 12m 3M.

WHITEHAVEN

W Pier Hd Fl G 5s 16m 8M; W ○ twr; 54°33′·17N 03°35′·92W.
N Pier Hd Fl R 5s 8m 10M; W ○ twr; 54°33′·17N 03°35′·75W.
Saint Bees Hd ☆ 54°30′·81N 03°38′·23W Fl (2) 20s 102m **18M**; W○ twr; obsc shore-340°.

RAVENGLASS

Blockhouse FG; (Eskdale Range); 54°20′·16N 03°25′·34W.
Selker Fl (3) G 10s; *Bell;* 54°16′·14N 03°29′·58W.

BARROW-IN-FURNESS

Lightning Knoll L Fl 10s; 53°59′·83N 03°14′·28W.
Halfway Shoal QR 19m 10s; R&W chequer Bn; 54°01′·46N 03°11′·88W.
Isle of Walney ☆ 54°02′·92N 03°10′·64W Fl 15s 21m **23M**; stone twr; obsc 122°-127° within 3M of shore.
Walney Chan Ldg Lts 040·7°. No 1 Front, Q 7m 10M; B Pile; 54°03′·19N 03°09′·22W. No 2 Rear, 0·61M from front, Iso 2s 13m 10M; Pile.
Rampside Sands Ldg Lts 005·1°. No 3 Front, Q 9m10M; W ○ twr; 54°04′·41N 03°09′·79W. No 4 Rear, 0·77M from front, Iso 2s 14m 6M; R col, W face.

ISLE OF MAN

Ballacash Bank VQ (9) 10s; 54°26′·50N 04°16′·70W.
Whitestone Bank Q (9) 15s; 54°24′·58N 04°20′·41W.
Point of Ayre ☆ 54°24′·94N 04°22′·13W Fl (4) 20s 32m **19M**; W twr, two R bands, ***Racon (M) 13-15M***.
Low Lt Ho (unlit), RW twr, B base, 54°25′·03N 04°21′·86W.

PEEL

Peel Bkwtr Hd Oc 7s 11m 6M; W twr; 54°13′·67N 04°41′·69W.

PORT ERIN and PORT ST MARY

Ldg Lts 099·1°. Front, 54°05′·23N 04°45′·57W FR 10m 5M; W twr, R band. Rear, 39m from front, FR 19m 5M; W col, R band.
Calf of Man Lighthouse (disused), white 8-sided tower.
Chicken Rk ☆ Fl 5s 38m **20M**; ***Racon (C)*** 54°02′·27N 04°50′·32W
Alfred Pier Hd Oc R 10s 8m 6M; 54°04′·33N 04°43′·82W.

CASTLETOWN and DERBY HAVEN

Dreswick Pt Fl (2) 30s 23m 12M; W twr; 54°03′·29N 04°37′·45W.
New Pier Hd Oc R 15s 8m 5M; 54°04′·33N 04°38′·97W.
Derby Haven, Bkwtr SW end Iso G 2s 5m 5M; W twr, G band; 54°04′·58N 04°37′·06W.

DOUGLAS

Douglas Head ☆ 54°08′·60N 04°27′·95W Fl 10s 32m **24M**; W twr; obsc brg more than 037°. FR Lts on radio masts 1 and 3M West.
No 1 Q (3) G 5s; 54°09′·04N 04°27′·68W.
Princess Alexandra Pier Hd Fl R 5s 16m 8M; R mast; *Whis (2) 40s;* 54°08′·84N 04°27′·85W.
Ldg Lts 229·3°, Front, Oc Bu 10s 9m 5M; W △ R border on mast; 54°08′·72N 04°28′·25W. Rear, 62m from front, Oc Bu 10s 12m 5M; W ▽ on R border; synch with front.
Victoria Pier Hd Iso G 10s 10m 3M; W col; vis: 225°-327°; Intnl Port Tfc Signals; 54°08′·84N 04°28′·08W.
Conister Rk Refuge Q 3M; vis: 234°-312°; 54°09′·03N 04°28′·12W.

LAXEY to RAMSEY

Laxey Pier Hd Oc R 3s 7m 5M; W twr, R band; obsc when brg less than 318°; 54°13′·50N 04°23′·43W.
Maughold Head ☆ 54°17′·72N 04°18′·58W Fl (3) 30s 65m **21M**.
Bahama VQ (6) + L Fl 10s; 54°20′·01N 04°08′·57W.
Queens Pier Dn Fl R 5s; 54°19′·28N 04°21′·95W.
King William Bank Q (3) 10s; 54°26′·01N 04°00′·08W.

BARROW TO RIVERS MERSEY AND DEE

MORECAMBE

Met Mast Fl Y 5s 20m 5M*;* 54°00′·13N 03°33′·38W; Aero FR (80m), *Horn 30s.*
Lightning Knoll L Fl 10s; 53°59′·84N 03°14′·28W.
Morecambe Q (9) 15s; 53°52′·00N 03°22′·00W.
Lune Deep Q (6) + L Fl 15s; ***Racon (T)***; 53°56′·07N 03°12·90W.
Lts in line about 090°. Front, FR 10m 2M; G mast; 54°04′·41N 02°52′·63W. Rear, 140m from front, FR 14m 2M; G mast.

HEYSHAM

SW Quay Ldg Lts 102·2°. Front, both F Bu 11/14m 2M; Or & B ♦ on masts; 54°01′·91N 02°55′·22W.

RIVER LUNE, GLASSON DOCK and FLEETWOOD

R Lune Q (9) 15s; 53°58′·63N 03°00′·03W.
Fairway No 1(Fleetwood) 53°57′·67N 03°02′·03W Q; *Bell.*
Fleetwood Esplanade Ldg Lts 156°. Front, Iso G 2s 14m 9M; 53°55′·71N 03°00′·56W. Rear, 320m from front, Iso G 4s 28m 9M. Both vis on Ldg line only. (H24) (chan liable to change).

RIVER RIBBLE

Gut L Fl 10s; 53°41′·74N 03°08′·98W.
Perches show Fl R on N side, and Fl G on S side of chan.
S side, 14¼M Perch Fl G 5s 6m 3M; 53°42′·75N 03°04′·90W.
Jordan's Spit Q (9) 15s; 53°35′·76N 03°19′·28W.
FT Q; 53°34′·56N 03°13′·20W.

RIVER MERSEY and LIVERPOOL

Bar Fl.5s 12M; ***Racon (T) 10M***; 53°32′·02N 03°20′·98W.
Q1 VQ; 53°31′·01N 03°16′·70W.
Q2 VQ R; 53°31′·48N 03°14′·94W.
Q3 Fl G 3s; 53°30′·97N 03°15′·08W.
Formby Iso 4s; 53°31′·14N 03°13′·48W.
C4 Fl R 3s; 53°31′·83N 03°08′·50W.
CROSBY Oc 5s; 53°30′·74N 03°06′·30W.
C14 Fl R 3s; 53°29′·93N 03°05′·35W.
Brazil QG; G hull,53°26′·85N 03°02′·23W.

RIVER DEE, MOSTYN and CONNAH'S QUAY

HE1 Q (9) 15s; 53°26′·33N 03°18′·08W.
HE2 Fl G 2·5s; 53°24′·90N 03°12′·88W.
HE3 Q G; 53°24′·55N 03°12′·74W.
West Hoyle Spit (Earwig) Dir Lt 090. 53°21′·21N 03°24′·07W; Iso WRG 2s W10M, R7M, G7M (day W3M, R2M, G2M). vis: 087·5°-G-089·5°-W-090·5°-R-092·5°; occasional.
Mostyn Dir Lt 177·5°. 53°19′·23N 03°16′·38W Iso WRG 2s 11m W 10M R,G 7M, by day W 3M R,G 2M; vis: 175°-G-177°-W-178°-R-180°; H24.

WALES – NORTH COAST AND INNER PASSAGE

South Hoyle Outer Fl R 2·5s; 53°21′·47N 03°24′·70W.
Prestatyn Q; 53°21′·37N 03°29′·00W.
Inner Passage Fl R 5s; 53°21′·91N 03°31′·95W.

Mid Patch Spit QR; 53°22'·25N 03°32'·67W.
Mast Fl Y 5s 18m 5M; Mast (80); 53°28'·84N 03°30'·50W.
W Constable Q (9) 15s; ***Racon (M) 10M***; 53°23'·14N 03°49'·26W.

RHYL, LLANDUDNO and CONWY
River Clwyd Outfall Q R 7m 2M; 53°19'·45N 03°30'·34W.
Rhyll SWM Mo(A) 10s; 53°19'·60N 03°32'·00W.
Llandudno Pier Hd 2 FG (vert) 8m 4M; 53°19'·90N 03°49'·51W.
Great Ormes Hd Lt Ho, (unlit); 53°20'·56N 03°52'·17W.
Conwy Fairway L Fl 10s; 53°17'·95N 03°55'·58W.
C1 Fl G 10s; 53°17'·83N 03°54'·58W.
C2 Fl (2) R 10s; 53°17'·94N 03°54'·52W.
River Conwy ent, L Fl G 15s 5m 2M; 53°18'·03N 03°50'·86W.

ANGLESEY
Point Lynas ☆ 53°24'·98N 04°17'·35W Oc 10s 39m **18M**; W castellated twr; vis: 109°-315°; H24.

AMLWCH to HOLYHEAD BAY
Main Bkwtr Fl G 15s 11m 3M; W mast; vis: 141°-271°; 53°25'·02N 04°19'·91W.
Furlong Fl G 2·5s; 53°25'·41N 04°30'·47W.
Archdeacon Rock Q; 53°26'·71N 04°30'·87W.
Victoria Bank VQ; 53°25'·61N 04°31'·37W.
Coal Rk Q (6) + L Fl 15s; 53°25'·91N 04°32'·79W.
Ethel Rk VQ; 53°26'·64N 04°33'·67W.
The Skerries ☆ 53°25'·27N 04°36'·50W Fl (2) 15s 36m **20M**; W ○ twr, R band; ***Racon (T) 25M***. Iso R 4s 26m 10M; same twr; vis: 233°-252°, sector unreliable > 4M; *Horn (2) 60s*. H24 in periods of reduced visibility; 992351084.
Langdon Q (9) 15s; 53°22'·74N 04°38'·74W.
Bolivar FL G 2·5s; 53°21'·51N 04°35'·33W.
Wk Fl (2) R 10s; 53°20'·43N 04°36'·60W.

HOLYHEAD to SOUTH STACK
Bkwtr Head Fl (3) G 10s 21m 14M; W □ twr, B band; Fl Y vis: 174°-226°; *Siren 20s;* 53°19'·86N 04°37'·16W.
Spit Fl G 3s; 53°19'·79N 04°37'·15W.
South Stack ☆ 53°18'·41N 04°41'·98W Fl 10s 60m **24M**; (H24); W ○ twr; obsc to N by N Stack and part obsc in Penrhos bay; *Horn 30s*. Fog Det lt vis: 145°-325°.

MENAI STRAIT TO BARDSEY ISLAND

Ten Feet Bank QR; 53°19'·47N 04°02'·82W.
Dinmor QG; 53°19'·34N 04°03'·32W.
Trwyn-Du Fl 5s 19m 12M; W ○ castellated twr, B bands; vis: 101°-023°; *Bell (1) 30s*, sounded continuously; 53°18'·77N 04°02'·44W. FR on radio mast 2M SW.

APPROACHES to BEAUMARIS and BANGOR
(Direction of buoyage NE to SW)
Perch Rock Fl R 5s; 53°18'·73N 04°02'·09W.

PORT DINORWIC and CAERNARFON
Port Dinorwic Pier Hd 53°11'·21N 04°12'·60W F WR 5m 2M; vis: 225°-R- 357°-W-225°.

(Direction of buoyage SW to NE)
Caernarfon N Pier Hd 2 FG (vert) 5m 2M; 53°08'·72N 04°16'·56W.
Abermenai Point Fl WR 3·5s 6m 3M; W mast; vis: 065°-R-245°-W-065°; 53°07'·62N 04°19'·72W.
C1 Fl G 5s; 53°06'·79N 04°24'·63W.
C2 Fl R 10s; 53°07'·01N 04°24'·25W.
Caernarfon Bar L Fl 10s; 53°06'·45N 04°25'·00W.
Llanddwyn I Fl WR 2·5s 12m W7M, R4M; W twr; vis: 280°-R-015°-W-120°; 53°08'·05N 04°24'·79W.

PORTH DINLLÄEN
CG Stn FR when firing 10M N; 52°56'·82N 04°33'·89W.
Careg y Chwislen Fl(2) 10s 2M 52°56'·99N 04°33'·51W.
Bardsey I ☆ 52°44'·97N 04°48'·02W Fl R 10s 39m **18M**; W □ twr, R bands; obsc by Bardsey Is 198°-250° and in Tremadoc B when brg < 260°.

9.10.5 PASSAGE INFORMATION

More passage information is threaded between the harbours in this area. Admiralty Leisure Folio 5613, Irish Sea eastern part including Isle of Man, covers the Mull of Galloway to Great Ormes Head including the Isle of Man. Folio 5609, North West Wales including Menai Strait, covers Colwyn Bay to Aberystwyth, including Anglesey. **Bibliography:** *Irish Sea Pilot* (Imray/Rainsbury). *Cruising Anglesey and Adjoining Waters* (Imray/Morris).The *West Coasts of England and Wales Pilot* (Admiralty NP37) covers the whole area.

SOLWAY FIRTH

(AC 1346) Between Abbey Hd and St Bees Hd lies the Solway Firth, most of which is encumbered by shifting sandbanks. *Solway SDs* are essential. Off the entrances to the Firth, and in the approaches to Workington, beware shoals over which strong W winds raise a heavy sea. The area N of Silloth is unsurveyed but buoyed channels are navigable as far as Dumfries and Annan on the N shore. Buoys are laid primarily for the aid of pilots.

► *Local knowledge is required, particularly in the upper Firth, where streams run very strongly in the channels when the banks are dry, and less strongly over the banks when covered. In Powfoot Channel the flood stream begins at HW L'pool –0300, and the ebb at HW L'pool + 0100,* ***Sp rates up to 6kn.*** ◄

The River Nith, approached between Borron Point and Blackshaw Spit, leads to Carsethorn, Glencaple, Kingholm Quay and Dumfries. There are 2 ⚓s at Caresthorn; Kingholm Quay offers drying berths, and on pontoons. Local knowledge is essential, but pilotage for visiting yachts is available. Contact cargo@nith-navigation.co.uk ☎07801 321457 / 07860 522598.

On the south side of the Solway Firth are Maryport, Workington, Harrington and Whitehaven. South of St Bees Head lies the Nuclear processing plant at Sellafield. The large shallow drying harbour at Ravenglass lies south again with Eskmeals Firing Range. Selker rocks and Black Leg Rk are notable shoals between Ravenglass and the Duddon Estuary. This dries at LW and is only navigable by small shoal draught craft. The Isle of Walney has an airfield and shelters Barrow-in-Furness which is reached by Walney Chan on rounding South East Point.

Morecambe Bay is shallow and mostly dries. Heysham harbour is exclusively for commercial traffic. The R Lune gives access to Port Glasson and the R Wyre to Fleetwood. The Channels which traverse the extensive offshore sandbanks are buoyed and shift frequently. Shell Flat extends 11M off the beach at Blackpool.

WIND FARMS

Robin Rigg wind farm is approximately 7M WNW of Maryport. Be aware of Walney, Ormonde Barrow and West of Duddon Sands wind farms between 6M and 12M off Walney Island. Burbo Bank wind farm is directly S of the approaches to Liverpool with an extension under construction to the W. North Hoyle, Gwynt y Mor (160 Turbines) and Rhyl Flats wind farms WSW lie between 6M and 12M off the coast of N Wales.

An extensive area has been earmarked for development between Anglesey and the Isle of Man. Known collectively as the Celtic Array this will consist of 3 large wind farms. the first of these, Rhiannon, is undergoing public consultation.

9.10.6 MARYPORT

Cumbria **54°43'·03N 03°30'·38W**

CHARTS AC 1826, 1346, 2013, 5613; Imray C62

TIDES +0038 Dover; ML no data; Duration 0550

Standard Port LIVERPOOL (⟶)

Times				Height (metres)			
High Water		Low Water		MHWS	MHWN	MLWN	MLWS
0000	0600	0200	0800	9·4	7·5	3·2	1·1
1200	1800	1400	2000				
Differences MARYPORT							
+0021	+0036	+0017	+0002	–0·8	–0·9	–0·7	–0·2
SILLOTH							
+0035	+0045	+0040	+0050	–0·2	–0·4	–0·9	–0·3

SHELTER Good in marina, sill 3·1m above CD, 2.5m above sill for entry; at other times Workington is a refuge. Elizabeth Dock gates u/s. Elizabeth Basin dries 2m; commercial, not used by yachts.

NAVIGATION WPT 54°43´·09N 03°32´·47W, 090°/1M to S pier. Overfalls at ent in W/SW winds over ebb. At HW–3 1·8m over bar at ent and in river chan; mudbanks cover HW –2. Max speed 4kn.

LIGHTS AND MARKS SHM bn Fl G 5s marks outfall 6ca SW of S pier. SSS displays IPTS signals 2 and 5 (see IPTS 5.20)

COMMUNICATIONS (Code 01900) CGOC (01407) 762051; Police 101; Dr 815544; Ⓗ 812634. HM 817440; Hbr Authority 604351.

Port VHF Ch **12** 16. Marina (H24) Ch **12** 16.

FACILITIES Maryport Marina www.maryportmarina.com ☎814431, 190 inc Ⓥ £20.80/craft inc (±3HW) (25t) **Maryport Yachting Association** www.maryportyachting.co.uk. **Town** Ⓑ ✕ ⇄ ✈ (Manchester/Newcastle).

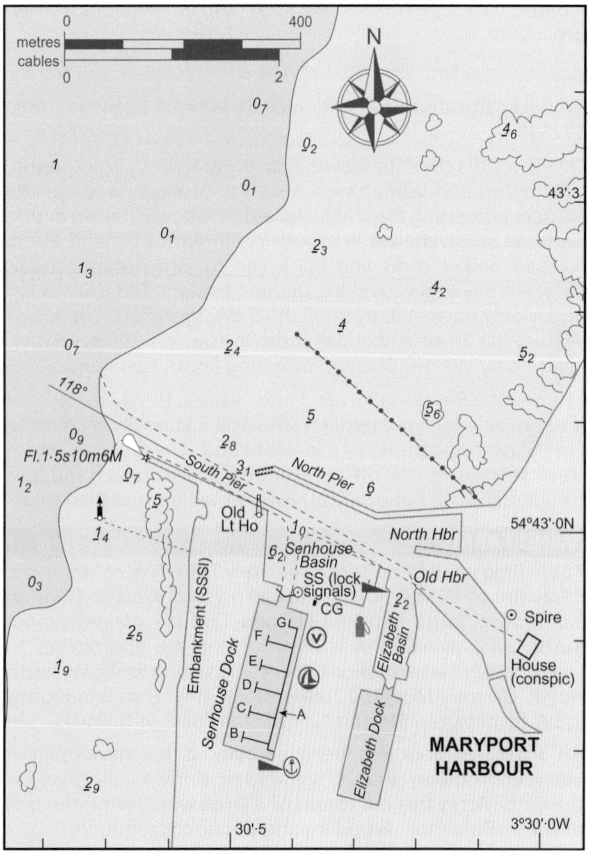

9.10.7 WORKINGTON

Cumbria 54°39'·03N 03°34'·38W

CHARTS AC 1826, 1346, 2013, 5613; Imray C62

TIDES +0025 Dover; ML 4·5; Duration 0545

Standard Port LIVERPOOL (⟶)

Times				Height (metres)			
High Water		Low Water		MHWS	MHWN	MLWN	MLWS
0000	0600	0200	0800	9·4	7·5	3·2	1·1
1200	1800	1400	2000				
Differences WORKINGTON							
+0029	+0027	+0014	+0004	–1·1	–1·1	–0·5	–0·1

SHELTER Good. Ent and chan to Prince of Wales Dock are maintained at 1·2m. Berth/moor by prior arrangement with Vanguard SC (☎07707 785328) in drying Tidal Dock; no ⚓ in Turning Basin. Prince of Wales Dock for commercial vessels only.

NAVIGATION WPT 54°39´·59N 03°35´·38W, 131°/1M to front ldg lt.

- Tide sets strongly across ent. In periods of heavy rain a strong freshet from R Derwent may be encountered in the hbr ent.

LIGHTS AND MARKS Workington Bank, least depth 5·5m, is 2M W of hbr ent; and is marked by NCM and SCM lt buoys (see 9.10.4). Ldg lts 132°, both FR 10/12m 3M, on W pyramidal trs with R bands. Two sets of F Bu lts in line mark NE and SW edges of chan. There are 16 wind-turbines on shore between ¾M and 2M NE of hbr ent.

COMMUNICATIONS (Code 01900) CGOC (01407) 762051; Police 101; Dr 64866; Ⓗ 602244. HM 602301.

VHF Ch 14 16 (HW–2½ to HW+2 approx).

FACILITIES Dock .

Vanguard SC www.vanguard-workington.co.uk ☎01228 674238, .

Town Ⓑ ✕ ⇄ ✈ (Carlisle).

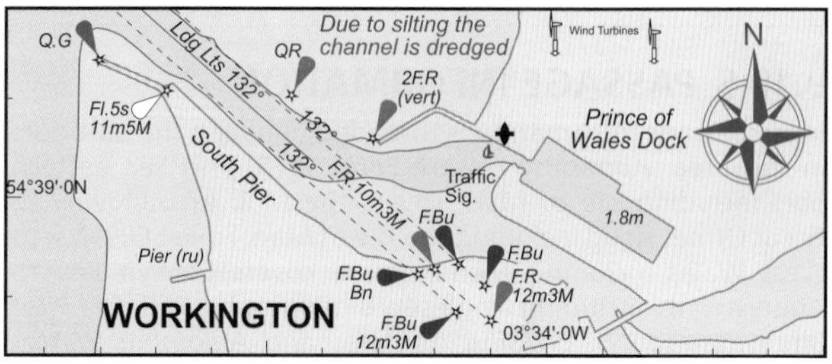

MINOR HARBOUR 10M NNE OF MARYPORT

SILLOTH, Cumbria, **54°52´·16N 03°23´·86W**. AC 1826, 1346, 2013, 5613. HW –0050 on Dover; ML no data; Duration 0520. See 9.10.6. Commercial harbour which welcomes occasional visiting yachts. Appr via English or Middle Chans; requires local knowledge, Beware constantly shifting chans and banks, and unsurveyed areas. East Cote Dir lt 052° FG 15m 12M; vis 046°-058°, intens 052°. Ldg lts, both F, 115°. Middle dn 2 FG (vert). Outer hbr dries 2·8m; lock into New Dock (4m) HW-1½ to HW+½. Ent marked by Oc R/G lts. Subtract 1m from height of tide to calculate draught over sill. £24 covers entry/exit and 1 week stay. Traffic sigs on mast at New Dock; must receive permission before proceeding. VHF Ch 16 12. HM ☎(01697) 331358. ⚓ WSW of ent in about 4m off Lees Scar, Fl G 5s 11m 4M; exposed to SW winds. Facilities: Ⓑ ✕ .

MINOR HARBOUR 2M S OF WORKINGTON

HARRINGTON, Cumbria, **54°36´·77N 03°34´·29W**. AC 1826, 1346, 2013, 5613. HW +0025 on Dover; Duration 0540; Use Diff's Workington 9.10.7. Good shelter in small hbr only used by local FVs and yachts; dries 3ca offshore. Ent, marked by PHM perches on N side, difficult in strong W winds. Berth on N wall of inner hbr (free). Call ☎(01946) 823741 Ext 148 for moorings. Limited facilities. **SC** ☎(01946) 830600.

9.10.8 WHITEHAVEN

Cumbria **54°33′·18N 03°35′·82W** ❁❁❁◊◊✿✿

CHARTS AC 1826, 1346, 2013, 5613; Imray C62

TIDES +0015 Dover; ML 4·5; Duration 0550

Standard Port LIVERPOOL (⟶)

Times				Height (metres)			
High Water		Low Water		MHWS	MHWN	MLWN	MLWS
0000	0600	0200	0800	9·4	7·5	3·2	1·1
1200	1800	1400	2000				
Differences WHITEHAVEN							
+0010	+0020	+0005	0000	–1·4	–1·2	–0·8	–0·1
TARN POINT (54°17′N 03°25′W)							
+0010	+0010	+0005	–0005	–1·1	–1·1	–0·7	–0·2
DUDDON BAR (54°09′N 03°20′W)							
+0007	+0007	+0005	–0001	–0·9	–0·9	–0·6	–0·2

SHELTER Very good, entry safe in most weathers. One of the more accessible ports of refuge in NW England, with a marina in the Inner Hbr. Appr chan across the outer hbr is dredged to 1·0m above CD. Sea lock (30m x 13.7m), with sill at CD, maintains 7m within inner hbr. N Hbr is for commercial and FV use.

NAVIGATION WPT 54°33′·34N 03°36′·21W, 133°/4½ca to W pier hd. There are no hazards in the offing. Hold closer to the North Pier, and beware bar at end of W Pier.

LIGHTS AND MARKS Several tall chimneys are charted within 1·5M S of hbr. St Bees Head Lt ho is 2·7M SSW of hbr ent. SHM bn, Fl G 2·5s, 4½ca S of W pierhead marks sewer outfall. IPTS sigs 1-3 shown from N side of lock ent to seaward only at present: priority to inward-bound vessels.

COMMUNICATIONS (Code 01946) CGOC (01407) 762051; Police 101; HM 692435; Sealock 694672.

HM VHF Ch 12 16.

FACILITIES Marina www.whitehavenmarina.co.uk ☎692435 285 inc Ⓥ in Inner Harbour (Lowther Marina) and Queen's Dock (Queen's Marina) £2.20, Ⓔ (45t) SC.
Town Market days Thurs, Sat; Ⓑ.

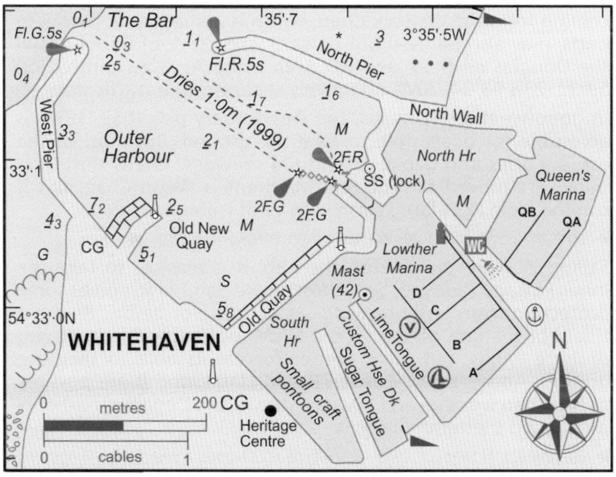

MINOR HARBOUR BETWEEN ST BEES HD AND MORECAMBE BAY

RAVENGLASS, Cumbria, **54°20′·00N 03°26′·80W** (drying line). AC 1346, 1826, 5613. HW +0020 on Dover; ML no data; Duration 0545. See 9.10.8 (Tarn Pt). Large drying hbr, into which R's Mite, Irt and Esk flow; approx 2·5m in ent at HW–2. Sellafield power stn with WCM lt buoy and outfall buoys are 5M NNW. FG ☆ (occas) on blockhouse at S side of ent. *Solway Sailing Directions* with pilotage notes by Ravenglass Boating Ass'n, local knowledge advisable. From N beware Drigg Rk and from S Selker Rks, SHM lt buoy, 5M SSW of ent. Firing range D406 close S at Eskmeals; Mon-Thur 0800-1600LT (1500 Fri). When in use R flags flown, R lts at night; *Eskmeals Gun Range* VHF Ch 16 11, ☎(01229) 712245/5.
Village.

9.10.9 ISLE OF MAN

Charts AC Irish Sea 1826, 1411; 2094 (small scale); 2696 (ports), 5613; Imray C62, Y70

The Isle of Man a British Island, set in the Irish Sea roughly equidistant from England, Scotland, Wales and Ireland but is not part of the UK. It has a large degree of self-government. Lights are maintained by the Northern Lighthouse Board. Manx harbours are administered by the IoM Government, see www.gov.im/harbours/

Distances See 9.10.2 for distances between ports in Area 10 and 9.0.6 for distances across the Irish Sea, North Channel and St George's Channel.

Harbours and anchorages Most of the harbours are on the E and S sides, but a visit to the W coast with its characteristic cliffs is worth while. The four main harbours are described in an anti-clockwise direction from Peel on the W coast to Ramsey in the NE. There are good ⚓s at: Port Erin in the SW, Castletown and Derby Haven in the SE, and Laxey Bay in the E. All IOM harbours charge the same overnight berthing rate, depending on your berth location.
All outer harbour Berths – £1.47 a metre per day.
All inner harbour Berths – £2.21 a metre per day.
Pontoon Berths – £2.55 a metre per day.
All Marina Berths when available – £3.00 a metre per day.
Multihulls are charged at 1.5 times the usual monohull rate.

R/T If contact with local Harbour Offices cannot be established on VHF, vessels should call *Douglas Hbr Control* Ch **12** 16 for urgent messages or other info.

Coastguard Call Holyhead CGOC Ch 16 67 86; the Snaefell (IoM) aerial is linked to the CG network.

Customs The IOM is under the same customs umbrella as the rest of the UK, and there are no formalities on arriving from or returning to the UK.

Weather Forecasts can be obtained direct from the forecaster at Ronaldsway Met Office ☎0900 6243 3200, H24. **Douglas Hbr Control** (9.10.12) can supply visibility and wind info on request.

MINOR HARBOURS ON THE ISLE OF MAN

PORT ERIN, Isle of Man, **54°05′·31N 04°46′·34W**. AC 2094, 2696, 5613. HW –0020 on Dover; ML 2·9m; Duration 0555. See 9.10.11. From S and W, Milner's Twr on Bradda Hd is conspic. Ldg lts, both FR 10/19m 5M, lead 099° into the bay. Beware the ruined bkwtr (dries 2·9m) extending N from the SW corner, marked by an unlit SHM buoy. A small hbr on the S side dries 0·8m. Raglan Pier (E arm of hbr), Oc G 5s 8m 5M. 2Ⓥs W of Raglan Pier. Good ⚓ in 3-8m N of Raglan Pier, but exposed to W'lies. Call Port St. Mary Harbour (VHF Ch 12) ☎833205.

CASTLETOWN BAY, Isle of Man, **54°03′·51N 04°38′·57W**. AC 2094, 2696, 5613. HW +0025 on Dover; ML 3·4m; Duration 0555. The bay gives good shelter except in SE to SW winds. From the E, keep inside the race off Dreswick Pt, or give it a wide berth. Beware Lheeah-rio Rks in W of bay, marked by PHM buoy, Fl R 3s, Bell. Hbr dries 3·1m to level sand. Berth in outer hbr or go via swing footbridge (manually opened) into inner hbr below fixed bridge. ⚓ between Lheeah-rio Rks and pier in 3m; or NW of Langness Pt. Lts: Langness lt, on Dreswick Pt, Fl (2) 30s 23m 12M. Hbr S (New) Pier, Oc R 15s 8m 5M; Inner S pier (Irish Quay), Oc R 4s 5m 5M, vis 142°-322°. 150m NW is swing bridge marked by 2 FR (hor). N pier, Oc G 4s 3m (W metal post on concrete column). VHF Ch 12 16 (when vessel due). HM ☎823549; Dr 823597. Facilities: **Outer hbr** (mob); **Irish Quay**; **Inner hbr**; **Town**.

LAXEY, Isle of Man, **54°13′·46N 04°23′·32W**. AC 2094, 5613. HW +0025 on Dover; +0010 and –2·0m on Liverpool; ML 4m; Duration 0550. The bay gives good shelter in SW to N winds. 2 yellow Ⓥs (seasonal) are close E of hbr ent; 2 more are 1M S in Garwick Bay. ⚓ about 2ca S of pier hds or in Garwick Bay. The hbr dries 3·0m to rk and is only suitable for small yachts. Beware rks on N side of the narrow ent. Keep close to pier after entering to avoid training wall on NE side. on inside of pier; inner basin is full of local boats. Pier hd lt Oc R 3s 7m 5M, obsc when brg <318°. Bkwtr hd lt Oc G 3s 7m. Harbour Office ☎861663. Facilities: Ⓑ.

ISLE OF MAN

(Charts 2094, 2696, 5613) For pilotage information and harbours of IoM, see *IOM Sailing Directions, Tidal Streams and Anchorages*, published by Hunter Publications. For notes on crossing the Irish Sea, see 9.13.5. There are four choices rounding S of IoM:

- In bad weather, or at night, keep S of Chicken Rk.
- In good conditions, pass between Chicken Rk and Calf of Man.
- By day, with winds <F 3 and a reliable engine giving >5kn, Calf Snd between Calf of Man and IoM is navigable. Pass between Kitterland Is and Thousla Rk, marked by bn Fl R 3s 9m 4M.
- Little Sound, a minor unmarked channel, runs E of Kitterland Is.

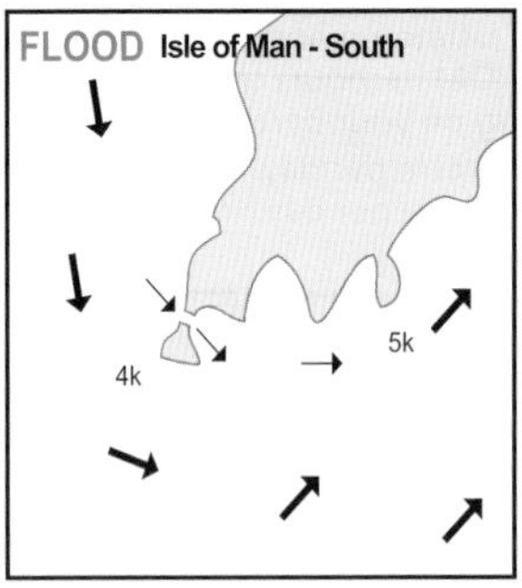
FLOOD Isle of Man - South
4k
5k

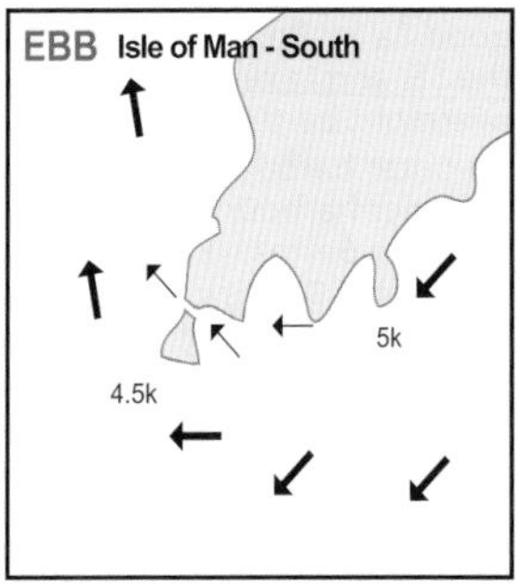
EBB Isle of Man - South
4.5k
5k

▶ *The stream runs strongly through Calf Sound, N-going at HW Liverpool –0145, and S-going at HW Liverpool +0345, Sp rate 3·5kn. W of Calf of Man the stream runs N and S, but changes direction off Chicken Rk running E/W between Calf of Man and Langness Pt. Overfalls extend E from Chicken Rk on E-going stream, beginning at HW L'pool + 0610, and N from the rock on W-going stream, which begins at HW L'pool. The Skerranes (drying) extend 1ca SW Of Langness Pt (lt). Tidal stream run strongly, with eddies and a race. A dangerous sea builds to the E of Langness peninsula in strong winds. Here the NE-going stream begins at HW L'pool +0545, and the SW-going at HW L'pool –0415, sp rates 2·25kn.* ◀

⚓ (exposed to the E) in Derby Haven, N of St Michael's Is. From here to Douglas and on to Maughold Hd (lt), there are no dangers more than 4ca offshore.

▶ *Inshore the SW-going stream runs for 9 hrs and the NE-going for 3 hrs, since an eddy forms during the second half of the main NE-going stream. Off Maughold Hd the NE-going stream begins at HW L'pool +0500, and the SW-going at HW L'pool –0415.* ◀

SE, E and NW of Pt of Ayre are dangerous banks, on which seas break in bad weather. These are Whitestone Bank (least depth 2·0m), Bahama Bank (1·5m), Ballacash Bank (2·7 m), King William Banks (3·3m), and Strunakill Bank (6·7m).

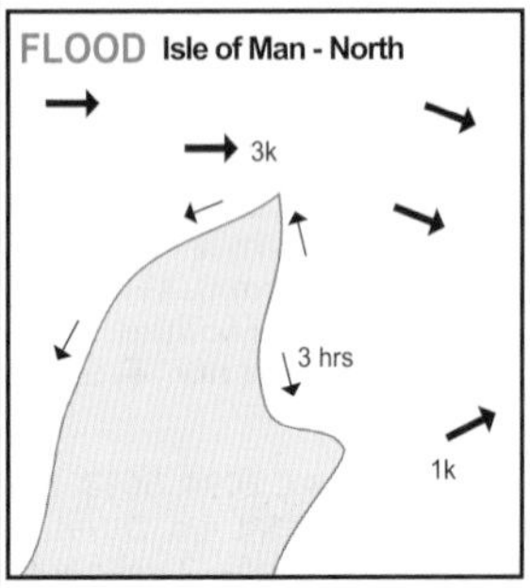
FLOOD Isle of Man - North
3k
3 hrs
1k

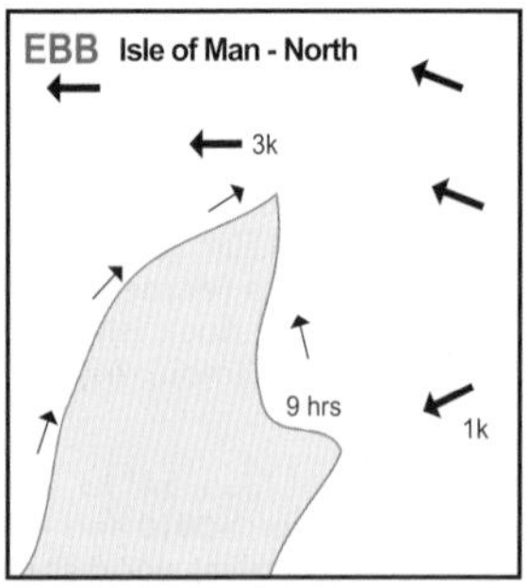
EBB Isle of Man - North
3k
9 hrs
1k

▶ *At Point of Ayre E-going stream begins HW Liverpool –0600 (HW Dover –0545). W-going stream at Point of Ayre begins HW L'pool (HW Dover +0015). A counter tide runs inside the banks to the East. In Ramsey Bay the S-going tide runs for 3hrs from L'pool +0515 (Dover +0530). In Ramsey Bay the N-going tide runs for 9 hours from L'pool –0345 (Dover –0330).*◀

The W coast of IOM has few pilotage hazards. A spit with depth of 1·4m runs 2ca offshore from Rue Pt. Jurby Rk (depth 2·7m) lies 3ca off Jurby Hd. Craig Rk (depth 4m) and shoals lie 2·5M NNE of Peel.

BARROW TO CONWY

(AC 2010, 1981, 1978, 5613) Ent to Barrow-in-Furness (AC 3164) is about 1M S of Hilpsford Pt at S end of Walney Island where the lt ho is prominent. W winds cause rough sea in the entrance. Moorings and ⚓ off Piel and Roa Islands, but space is limited.

▶ *The stream sets across the narrow channel, which is well marked, but shallow in patches. Stream runs hard on ebb. Coming from the S it is possible with sufficient rise of tide to cross the sands between Fleetwood and Barrow.* ◀

Barrow Wind Farm (30 turbines) marked by FR and Fl Y lights and fog signals on some structures is centred approx 7·6M SSW of Barrow-in-Furness. Further W lies the W Duddon Sands Wind Farm (108 turbines). Its W extremity is marked by a Met Mast. To the N Walney (102 turbines) and Ormonde (30 turbines) straddle the northern approaches to Barrow and the Lune.

Lune Deep, 2M NW of Rossall Pt, is the entrance to Morecambe Bay (chart 2010), and gives access to the ferry/commercial port of Heysham, Glasson Dock, and Fleetwood; it is well buoyed.

▶ *Streams run 3·5kn at sp.* ◀

Most of the Bay is encumbered with drying sands, intersected by chans which are subject to change. S of Morecambe B, beware shoals and drying outfall (2·0m) extending 3M W of Rossall Pt. Further S, R. Ribble gives access via a long drying chan to the marina at Preston.

Queen's Channnel and Crosby Chan (AC 1951 & 1978) are entered E of the Bar light float. They are well buoyed, dredged and preserved by training banks, and give main access to R Mersey and Liverpool. Keep clear of commercial shipping. From the N the old Formby chan is abandoned, but possible near HW. Towards HW in moderate winds a yacht can cross the training bank (level varies between 2m and 3m above CD) E of Great Burbo Bank, if coming from the W; Rock Chan, which is unmarked and dries in parts, may also be used but beware wrecks. W of Bar Lt Vessel the Douglas oil field, an IMO Area to be Avoided centred on 53°32´·23N 03°34´·70W, effectively separates the traffic flow.

In good weather at neaps, the Dee Estuary (AC 1953, 1978) is accessible for boats able to take the ground. But most of the estuary dries and banks extend 6M seaward. Chans shift, and buoys are moved as required. Main ent is Welsh Chan, but if coming from N, Hilbre Swash runs W of Hilbre Is.

▶ *Stream runs hard in chans when banks are dry.* ◀

Sailing W from the Dee on the ebb, it is feasible to take the Inner Passage (buoyed) S of West Hoyle Spit, which gives some protection from onshore winds at half tide or below. Rhyl is a tidal hbr marked offshore by a SWM, not accessible in strong onshore winds, but gives shelter for yachts able to take the ground. Abergele Rd, Colwyn B and Llandudno B are possible ⚓s in settled weather and S winds. Conwy and Deganwy harbours offer good shelter in marinas.

▶ *Between Point of Ayr and Great Ormes Head the E-going stream begins at HW Liverpool +0600, and the W-going at HW Liverpool –0015, sp rates 3kn.* ◀

North Hoyle Wind Farm consists of 30 turbines and is centred on 53°25'·00N 03°27'·00W. Each turbine is 58m high, with 40m diameter blades and clearance of 18m. Many of them are lit. Gwynt-y-Mor Wind Farm centred on 53°28'·20N 03°37'·70W. The area is delineated by cardinal and yellow buoys. Underwater obstructions will exist throughout. Vessels are advised to keep well clear and not enter the area.

9.10.10 PEEL

Isle of Man 54°13'·61N 04°41'·68W

CHARTS AC 2094, 2696, 5613; Imray C62; Y70

TIDES +0005 Dover; ML 2·9; Duration 0545

Standard Port LIVERPOOL (⟶)

Times				Height (metres)			
High Water		Low Water		MHWS	MHWN	MLWN	MLWS
0000	0600	0200	0700	9·4	7·5	3·2	1·1
1200	1800	1400	1900				
Differences PEEL							
+0010	+0010	-0020	–0030	–4·2	–3·2	–1·7	–0·7

SHELTER Good, except in strong NW to NE winds when ent should not be attempted. 4 Y 🝔s (seasonal) off S groyne in about 2m. Fin keelers may be able to berth on N bkwtr in 5m. Marina is in the Inner Harbour with berthing on pontoons and alongside harbour wall for boats up to 15m LOA. Pass dimensions on Ch 12. Approach dries 1·4m; access approx HW±2 when flapgate lowered and through swing bridge. Depth generally 2m, around pontoons.

NAVIGATION WPT 54°14'·00N 04°41'·78W, 207°/5ca to groyne lt. Beware groyne on S side of harbour ent, submerged at half tide.

LIGHTS AND MARKS Power stn chy (83m, grey with B top) at S end of inner hbr is conspic from W and N; chy brg 203° leads to hbr ent. Groyne lt and Clock Tr (conspic) in transit 200° are almost on same line. Peel Castle and 2 twrs are conspic on St Patrick's Isle to NW of hbr. 207° ldg lts, Fl R 5s. The E and W abutments to the Inner Hbr ent are marked by lts Fl R 3s and Fl G 3s respectively. Traffic signals at marina entrance. Swing bridge has FR lts at centre span. Fl Y lts = flap gate being raised lowered; bridge opening/closing.

COMMUNICATIONS (Code 01624) CGOC (01407) 762051; 0900 6243 322; Police 697327; Dr 843636. Harbour Office 842338, Mobile 07624 495036.

Peel Hbr VHF Ch **12** 16 (HW±2), HO for Swing Bridge – other times call *Douglas Hbr Control* Ch 12 for remote bridge opening.

FACILITIES Outer Hbr, see 9.10.9; **Marina** 120 inc Ⓥ, £1.72; access via flapgate; (mob); **Peel Sailing & Cruising Club** ☎842390, (key from Harbour Office). **Town** ACA Ⓑ (bus to Douglas & ferry), ✈ Ronaldsway.

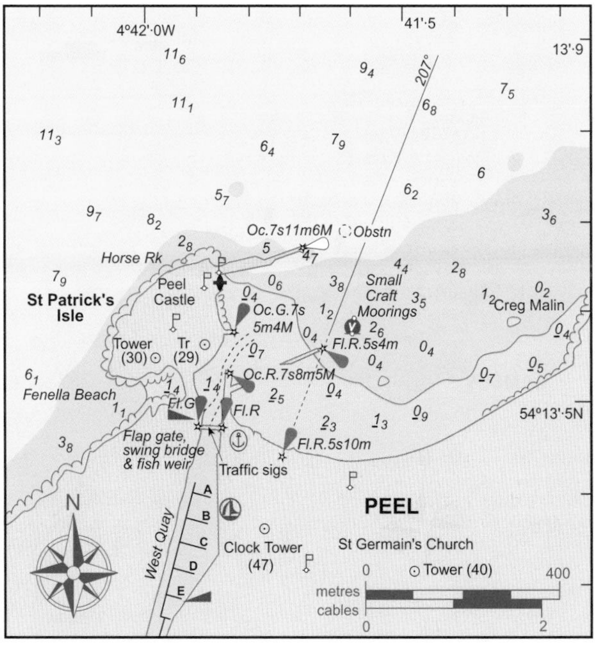

9.10.11 PORT ST MARY

Isle of Man **54°04'·43N 04°43'·73W**

CHARTS AC 2094, 2696, 5613; Imray C62; Y70

TIDES +0020 Dover; ML 3·2; Duration 0605

Standard Port LIVERPOOL (⟶)

Times				Height (metres)			
High Water		Low Water		MHWS	MHWN	MLWN	MLWS
0000	0600	0200	0700	9·4	7·5	3·2	1·1
1200	1800	1400	1900				
Differences PORT ST MARY							
+0010	+0020	–0015	–0035	–3·5	–2·7	–1·6	–0·6
CALF SOUND							
+0010	+0010	–0020	–0030	–3·3	–2·7	–1·2	–0·5
PORT ERIN							
+0018	+0010	–0013	–0028	–4·1	–3·3	–1·6	–0·6

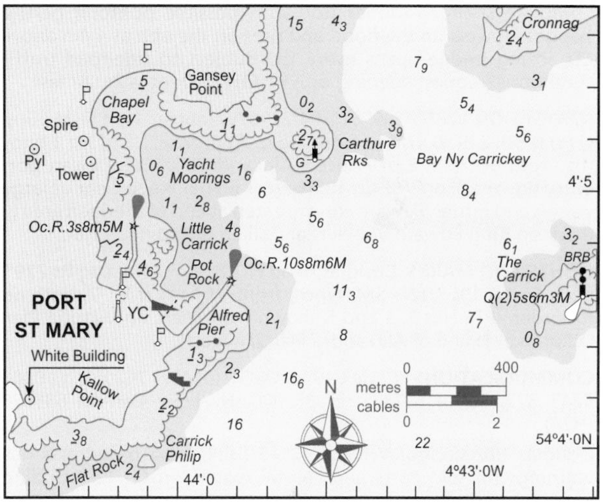

SHELTER Very good except in E or SE winds. ⚓ S of Gansey Pt, but poor holding. 5 yellow 🝔s (seasonal) between Alfred Pier and Little Carrick.

NAVIGATION WPT 54°04'·21N 04°43'·37W, 295°/0·3M to Alfred Pier lt. Rocky outcrops to SE of pier to 2ca offshore. Beware lobster/crab pots, especially between Calf of Man and Langness Pt.

LIGHTS AND MARKS Alfred Pier, Oc R 10s, in transit 295° with Inner Pier, Oc R 3s, W twr + R band, leads clear S of The Carrick Rk, in centre of bay, which is marked by IDM bn, Q (2) 5s 6m 3M. A conspic TV mast (133m), 5ca WNW of hbr, in transit with Alfred Pier lt leads 290° towards the hbr and also clears The Carrick rock.

COMMUNICATIONS (Code 01624) CGOC (01407) 762051; 0900 6243 322, Police 697327; Dr 832226. HM 833205.

Port St Mary Hbr VHF Ch 12 16 (when vessel due or through Douglas Hbr Control Ch 12).

FACILITIES Alfred Pier see 9.10.9, (mob); **Inner Hbr** dries 2·4m on sand; ; **Isle of Man YC** ☎832088, . **Town** Ⓑ (bus to Douglas, qv for ferries), ✈ Ronaldsway.

MINOR HARBOUR EAST OF CASTLETOWN

DERBY HAVEN, Isle of Man, **54°04'·65N 04°36'·45W.** Tides & charts as above. Rather remote bay exposed only to NE/E winds. ⚓ in centre of bay, NW of St Michael's Island, in 3-5m. A detached bkwtr on NW side of the bay gives shelter to craft able to dry out behind it. Lts: Iso G 2s on S end of bkwtr. Aero FR (occas) at Ronaldsway airport, NW of bay. Facilities: at Castletown (1½M) or Port St Mary.

9.10.12 DOUGLAS

Isle of Man **54°08′·87N 04°27′·96W**

CHARTS AC 2094, 2696, 5613; Imray C62; Y70

TIDES +0009 Dover; ML 3·8; Duration 0600

Standard Port LIVERPOOL (⟶)

Times				Height (metres)			
High Water		Low Water		MHWS	MHWN	MLWN	MLWS
0000	0600	0200	0700	9·4	7·5	3·2	1·1
1200	1800	1400	1900				
Differences DOUGLAS							
+0010	+0020	−0020	−0030	−2·5	−2·1	−0·8	−0·3

SHELTER Good except in NE winds. Very heavy seas run in during NE gales. Outer hbr: Victoria and King Edward VIII piers are for commercial vessels/ferries. At inner end of Battery Pier in summer about 18 boats can raft up on pontoon; untenable in NE/E winds. Complete shelter in inner hbr, with possible pontoon berths, flapgate lowers on the flood and rises on the ebb at 4·4m above CD, lifting bridge opens every ½hr subject to tide/road traffic conditions (request opening on VHF Ch12). Depths 2m or less.

NAVIGATION WPT 54°09′·01N 04°27′·67W (abeam No 1 SHM buoy, Q (3) G 5s), 229°/0·47M to front ldg lt. Appr from NE of No 1 buoy (to avoid overfalls E of Princess Alexandra Pier) and await port entry sig, or call on VHF Ch 12. There is no bar. Keep clear of large vessels and ferries. Beware concrete step at end of dredged area (◊ mark on King Edward VIII Pier) and sill at ent to inner hbr.

LIGHTS AND MARKS Douglas Head Fl 10s 32m 24M. Ldg lts 229°, both Oc Bu 10s 9/12m 5M, synch; front W △; rear W ▽, both on R border. IPTS Nos 2, 3 and 5 shown from mast on Victoria Pier. Dolphin at N end of Alexandra Pier 2FR (vert).

COMMUNICATIONS (Code 01624) CGOC (01407) 762051; 0900 6243 322, Police 697327; Ⓗ 650000. Harbour Control 686628 (H24).

Douglas Hbr Control VHF Ch **12** 16 (H24); also broadcasts nav warnings for IoM ports and coastal waters on Ch 12 including weather and tidal info on request.

FACILITIES Outer Hbr see 9.10.9, at pontoon, (mob); **Inner Hbr** (Pontoons, N and S Quays) 110; according to space, ; **Douglas Bay YC** ☎673965, 0930-2300. **Services** ACA, Kos. **Town** www.gov.im ✈ Ronaldsway. **Ferries** Liverpool; 16/week; 2½ hrs; IoM. Heysham; 16/week; 3½hrs; Steam Packet (www.steam-packet.com). Also to Dublin and Belfast.

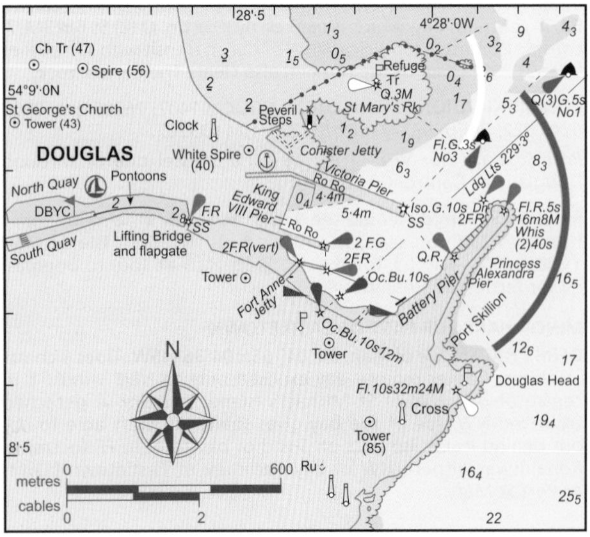

9.10.13 RAMSEY

Isle of Man **54°19′·44N 04°22′·49W**

CHARTS AC 2094, 2696, 5613; Imray C62; Y70

TIDES +0020 Dover; ML 4·2; Duration 0545

Standard Port LIVERPOOL (⟶)

Times				Height (metres)			
High Water		Low Water		MHWS	MHWN	MLWN	MLWS
0000	0600	0200	0700	9·4	7·5	3·2	1·1
1200	1800	1400	1900				
Differences RAMSEY							
+0010	+0020	−0010	−0020	−2·0	−1·6	−0·9	−0·2

SHELTER Very good in inner harbour but entrance difficult in strong NE-E winds. Hbr dries 1·8m–6m. Access approx HW −2½ to HW +2. Berth on Town quay (S side) or as directed by HM on entry. 5 yellow 🅥s are close to Queen's Pier hd (seasonal). Note: Landing on Queen's Pier is prohibited.

NAVIGATION WPT 54°19′·44N 04°21′·89W, 270°/0·37M to ent. The foreshore dries out 1ca to seaward of the pier hds.

LIGHTS AND MARKS No ldg lts/marks. Relative to hbr ent, Pt of Ayre, Fl (4) 20s 32m 19M, is 5·5M N; Maughold Hd, Fl (3) 30s 65m 21M, is 3M SE; Albert Tr (□ stone tr 14m, on hill 130m) is conspic 7ca S; and Snaefell (617m) bears 220°/5M. Inside the hbr an Iso G 4s, G SHM post, marks the S tip of Mooragh Bank; it is not visible from seaward. 2FR (hor) on each side mark the centre of swing bridge.

COMMUNICATIONS (Code 01624) CGOC (01407) 762051; 0900 6243 322, Police 812234; Dr 813881; Ⓗ 811811. Harbour Office 812245, mob 07624 460304.

Ramsey Hbr VHF Ch **12** 16 (0800-1600LT and when a vessel is due); Other times call *Douglas Hbr Control* Ch **12**.

FACILITIES Outer Hbr: E Quay ☎812245, only for commercial vessels (frequent movements H24); **Town Quay** (S side) see 9.10.9. **Inner Hbr, W Quay** (Grid); **N Quay** ; **Shipyard Quay** ; **Old Hbr** ; **Manx S&CC** ☎813494, ; **Services** Ⓔ. **Town** Kos, Ⓑ @ in Library, (bus to Douglas for ferries), ✈ Ronaldsway.

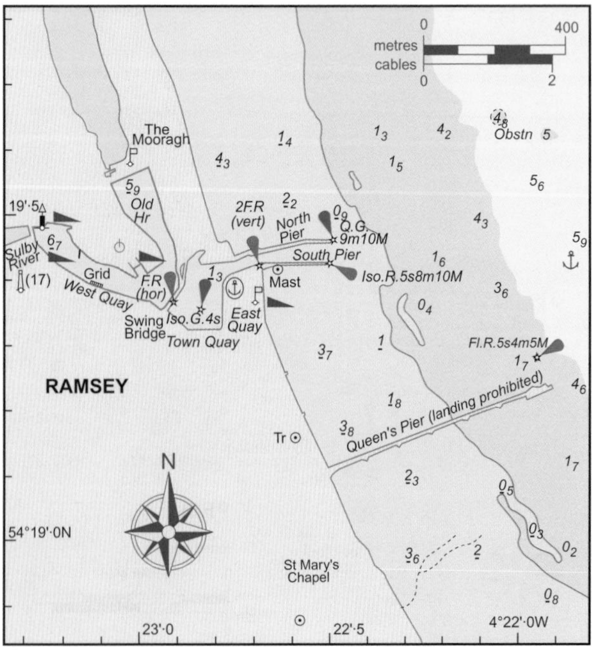

9.10.14 GLASSON DOCK

Lancashire **53°59'·98N 02°50'·93W** ❀❀◊◊◊✿✿

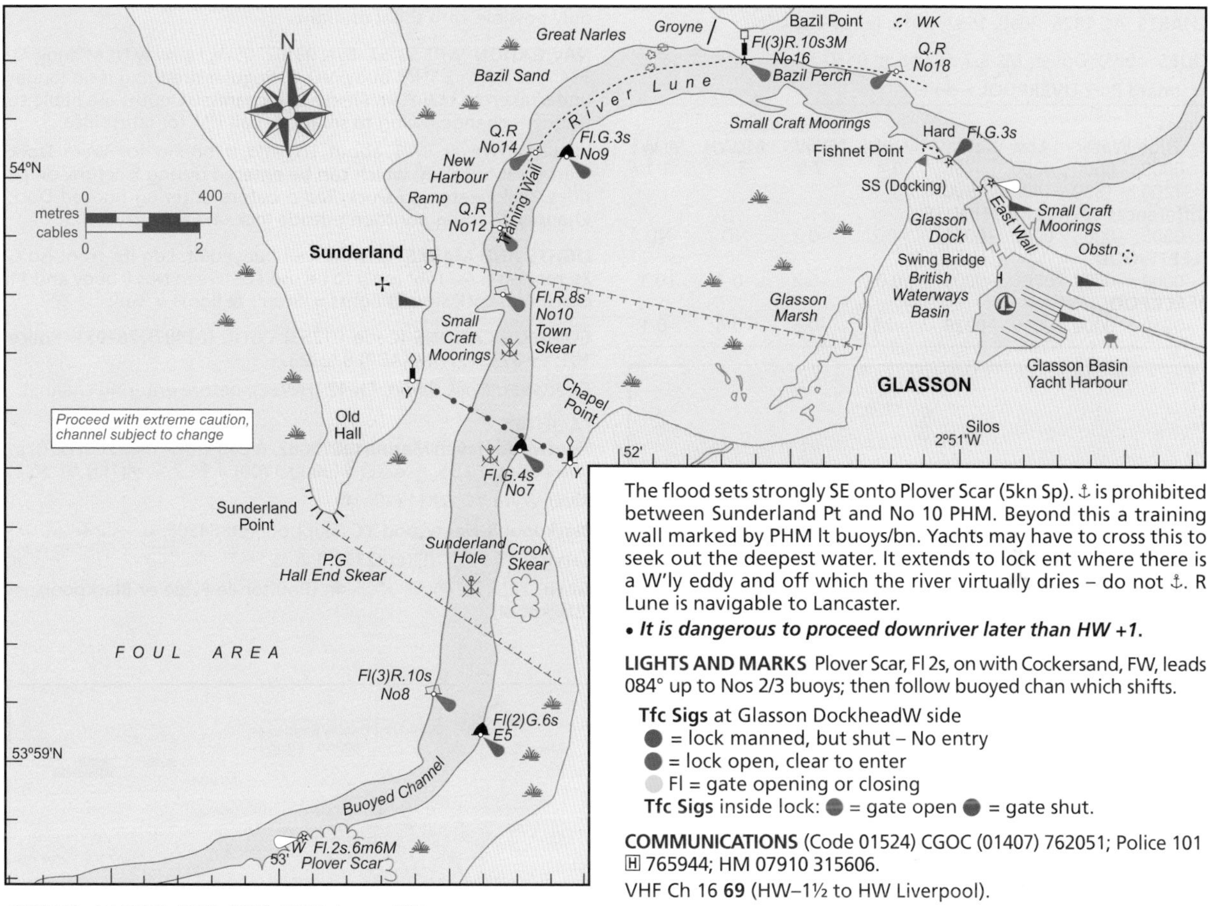

CHARTS AC 1826, 1552, 2010, 5613; Imray C62

TIDES +0020 Dover; ML No data; Duration 0535

Standard Port LIVERPOOL (⟶)

Times				Height (metres)			
High Water		Low Water		MHWS	MHWN	MLWN	MLWS
0000	0600	0200	0700	9·4	7·5	3·2	1·1
1200	1800	1400	1900				
Differences BARROW-IN-FURNESS (Ramsden Dock)							
+0020	+0020	+0010	+0010	–0·1	–0·4	0·0	+0·1
ULVERSTON							
+0025	+0045	ND	ND	–0·1	–0·2	ND	ND
ARNSIDE							
+0105	+0140	ND	ND	+0·4	+0·1	ND	ND
MORECAMBE							
+0010	+0015	+0025	+0010	+0·1	–0·1	–0·3	0·0
HEYSHAM							
+0014	+0012	+0002	–0003	+0·2	–0·1	–0·1	+0·1
GLASSON DOCK							
+0025	+0035	+0215	+0235	–2·8	–3·1	ND	ND
LANCASTER							
+0115	+0035	DR	DR	–5·1	–5·0	DR	DR

NOTE: At Glasson Dock LW time differences give the end of a LW stand which lasts up to 2 hrs at sp.

SHELTER Very good in marina, sea lock (9m wide) opens into Glasson Dock HW–¾ to HW (Liverpool) (daylight hrs only Nov-Mar) Inner lock/swing bridge lead into BWML basin. There are no safe LW berths on the outer quay walls.

NAVIGATION WPT 53°58'·63N 03°00'·03W (Lune WCM), 4·2M to Plover Scar. Enter buoyed chan at HW–1½ (-1¼ Nps). It changes frequently. For latest info call Port Commission (☎01524 751724). The flood sets strongly SE onto Plover Scar (5kn Sp). ⚓ is prohibited between Sunderland Pt and No 10 PHM. Beyond this a training wall marked by PHM lt buoys/bn. Yachts may have to cross this to seek out the deepest water. It extends to lock ent where there is a W'ly eddy and off which the river virtually dries – do not ⚓. R Lune is navigable to Lancaster.

- ***It is dangerous to proceed downriver later than HW +1.***

LIGHTS AND MARKS Plover Scar, Fl 2s, on with Cockersand, FW, leads 084° up to Nos 2/3 buoys; then follow buoyed chan which shifts.

Tfc Sigs at Glasson DockheadW side
● = lock manned, but shut – No entry
● = lock open, clear to enter
● Fl = gate opening or closing
Tfc Sigs inside lock: ● = gate open ● = gate shut.

COMMUNICATIONS (Code 01524) CGOC (01407) 762051; Police 101 Ⓗ 765944; HM 07910 315606.
VHF Ch 16 **69** (HW–1½ to HW Liverpool).

FACILITIES Glasson Basin Marina www.bwml.co.uk ☎751491; 240 +20Ⓥ (£12·50/craft); ♿ ⛵ 🚿 🔧 (50t) 🧺.
Glasson SC ☎751089, ⚓ ⛵ ✉; **Lune CC** Access only near HW.
Town 🅟 ✉ 🛒 ✕ 🍺 ⇌ (bus to Lancaster 4M), ✈ (Blackpool).

ADJACENT HARBOURS IN MORECAMBE BAY

BARROW-IN-FURNESS, Cumbria, **54°05'·64N 03°13'·44W**. AC 1826, 2010, 3164, 5613. HW +0030 on Dover; ML 5·0m; Duration 0530 (⟵). Good shelter but open to SE winds. Drying moorings off Piel and Roa Islands or ⚓ clear of fairway. Marks/lts: Walney Island Lt ho (conspic stone tr), Fl 15s 21m 23M (obsc 122°-127° within 3M of shore). Directions: From Lightning Knoll SWM lt buoy, ldg lts, front Q 7m 14M; rear (6ca from front), Iso 2s 13m 14M (lattice structures) lead 041°/3·7M past Halfway Shoal bn, QR 16m 10M (RY chequers), to Bar lt buoy abeam Walney Is lt ho in dredged chan (call HM for latest depth). Inner Chan ldg lts, front Q 9m 14M, rear Iso 2s 14m 14M, lead 005° past Piel Is. 3M NW at Barrow, commercial docks reached via buoyed/lit Walney Chan, dredged to 2·5m, which must be kept clear. HM ☎(01229) 822911; VHF *Barrow Port Radio* Ch 12 16 (H24).

Piel Is, ruined castle, jetty and moorings on E side. Facilities: Inn.

Roa Is, 5ca N, has jetty at S end and moorings on E & W sides. ⛵ (Roa Is Boat Club ☎(01229) 825291). Causeway joins to mainland. Facilities: Hotel at Rampside, 🛒.

HEYSHAM, Lancashire, **54°02'·01N 02°55'·96W**. AC 1826, 2010, 1552, 5613. HW +0015 on Dover; ML 5·1m; Duration 0545. See 9.10.14. Good shelter, but yachts not normally accepted without special reason. Beware high speed ferries and oil rig supply ships. Ldg lts 102°, both F Bu 11/14m 2M, Y+B ◊ on masts. S jetty lt 2 FG (vert), Siren 30s. S pier hd ,Oc G 7·5s 9m 6M. N pier hd, 2FR (vert) 11m, obsc from seaward. Ent sigs: R flag or ● = no entry; no sig = no dep; 2 R flags or 2 ● = no ent or dep. VHF Ch 14 74 16 (H24). HM ☎(01524) 852373. Facilities: ⛽ 🛒 ✕ 🍺 at Morecambe (2M).

9.10.15 FLEETWOOD

Lancashire **53°55′·49N 03°00′·15W** ❀❀❀◊◊◊✿✿

CHARTS AC 1826, 2010, 1552, 5613; Imray C62

TIDES +0015 Dover; ML 5.2; Duration 0530

Standard Port LIVERPOOL (⟶)

Times				**Height (metres)**			
High Water		Low Water		MHWS	MHWN	MLWN	MLWS
0000	0600	0200	0700	9·4	7·5	3·2	1·1
1200	1800	1400	1900				
Differences WYRE LIGHTHOUSE							
–0005	–0005	0000	–0005	–0·2	–0·2	ND	ND
FLEETWOOD							
–0004	–0004	–0006	–0006	0·0	–0·2	–0·1	+0·1
BLACKPOOL							
–0010	0000	–0010	–0020	–0·5	–0·5	–0·4	–0·1

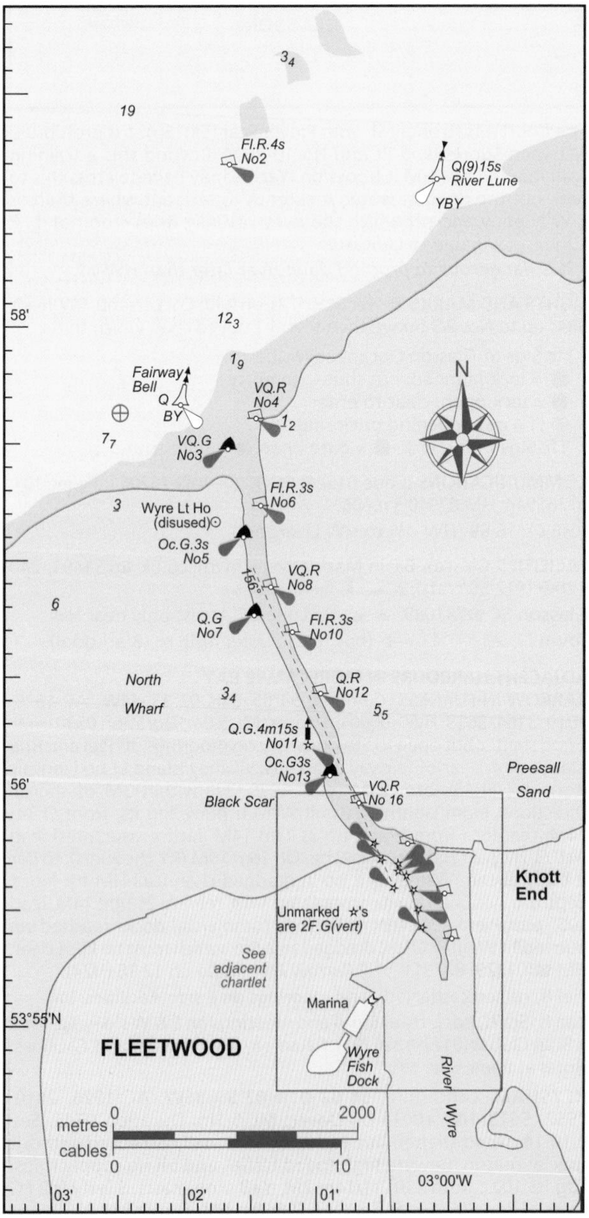

SHELTER Excellent in Fleetwood Haven Marina. Sheltered ⚓, clear of turning circle, off Knott End pier on E bank to await tide. Passage upriver to Skippool (5M) needs local knowledge and is only possible with shoal draught.

NAVIGATION WPT 53°57′·67N 03°02′·05W, Fairway NCM buoy, Q, 134°/3ca to No 3 SHM buoy, VQ.G. Regular dredging is no longer undertaken to maintain Fleetwood channel. Depths are liable to frequent change owing to siltation. Call HM for latest info.

Ideally arrive at WPT about HW–1½ if bound for Wyre Dock marina, 3M upriver, which can be entered during freeflow on all tides. Call *Fleetwood Dock Radio* before entering buoyed Dock Channel. Waiting pontoon outside lock on East Jetty.

LIGHTS AND MARKS Chan is well buoyed/lit. Ldg lts, front Iso G 2s; rear Iso G 4s, 156° (only to be used between Nos 8 buoy and 11 perch bn). Lock sigs: ● lights = 'Stop'; ● lights = 'Go'.

COMMUNICATIONS (Code 01253) CGOC (01407) 762051; Police 101; Dr 873312. HM (ABP) 872323.

Fleetwood Dock Radio, Ch 12 (HW±2), before entering channel.

FACILITIES

Fleetwood Haven Marina ☎879062, 340 inc ⓥ (max 20m LOA) in two basins, £2.35, (0800-1700) (75t).

River Wyre YC ☎811948, 1ⓥ.

Blackpool & Fleetwood YC (Skippool) ☎884205.

Services Ⓔ(☎823535).

Town Ⓑ (Poulton-le-Fylde or Blackpool), ✈ (Blackpool).

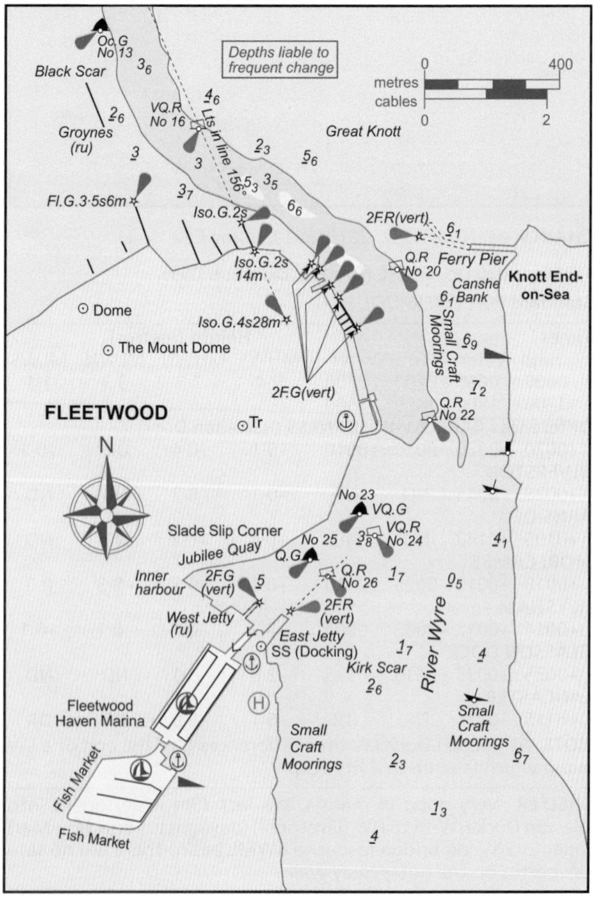

9.10.16 RIVER RIBBLE/PRESTON

Lancashire **53°43′·51N 03°00′·08W**

CHARTS AC 1826, 1981, 5613; Imray C62

TIDES +0013 Dover; ML No data; Duration 0520

Standard Port LIVERPOOL (⟶)

Times				Height (metres)			
High Water		Low Water		MHWS	MHWN	MLWN	MLWS
0000	0600	0200	0700	9·4	7·5	3·2	1·1
1200	1800	1400	1900				
Differences PRESTON							
+0015	+0015	+0330	+0305	–4·1	–4·2	–3·1	–1·0
LW time differences give the end of a LW stand lasting 3½ hrs.							
SOUTHPORT							
–0015	–0005	ND	ND	–0·4	–0·4	ND	ND
FORMBY							
–0010	–0005	–0025	–0025	–0·4	–0·2	–0·3	–0·1

SHELTER Good in Preston Marina (5m depth) 15M upriver. Possible drying berths on the N bank at Lytham or Freckleton, or 2M up R Douglas access only near HW.

NAVIGATION WPT **A** 53°41′·75N 03°08′·90W, Gut SWM lt buoy. The chartlet shows only the outer 6M of the estuary. Due to changes to the Gut Channel and South Gut, best water is now in the Gut Channel which almost dries but not to the extent shown on AC 1981. It is navigable approx HW±2. South Gut is no longer discernible and should not be used without local knowledge.

Leave WPT **A** at HW Liverpool –2 then track 070°/2·6M to WPT **B** (53°42′·90N 03°05′·00W). Continue up Gut Channel leaving the first 3 perches about 100m to starboard. Leave 11½M perch 100m to port. The river trends 080° between training walls (dry 3m), marked by lit perches. The remaining channel is straightforward but night entry is not advised.

LIGHTS AND MARKS 14½M perch is the most seaward channel mark. Upriver of 11½M perch there is a PHM buoy and perch (off chartlet), both Fl R 5s. 4 SHM perches, Fl G 5s, lead to 5M perch, Fl (2) G 10s, marking mouth of unlit R Douglas. 3M and 2M perches are Fl G 5s; 1M perch is Fl G 10s. Warton airfield beacon, Mo (WQ) G 9s occas, is N abeam 6M perch, Fl G 5s.

COMMUNICATIONS (Code 01772) CGOC (01407) 762051; Police 101; H 710408. Preston locks 726871. At Preston, for locks call *Riversway* Ch **16** 14 (HW –1½ to +2); Marina Ch 80 (HO); Douglas BY Ch 16 when vessel due.

FACILITIES Waiting berth (2m draught) outside storm gates (usually open). Traffic lts at marina lock; plan below. Lockmaster on duty HW±2, on daylight tides (0700-2000 Apr-Sep by Lavers Liverpool Tide Tables). This and tidal height should permit locking from –1 HW +2 on demand. Swing bridge opens in unison with locks. From 1 Oct-31 Mar contact marina to book locking 24hrs in advance.

Preston Marina www.prestonmarina. co.uk ☎733595, mob 07770 505094, £1·60, (25t, 45t by arrangement) ACA

Douglas BY, ☎812462 mob 07967 184528, £0·70 (20t)

Freckleton BY ☎632439 mob 07957 820881, £5/yacht

Ribble Cruising Club ☎(01253) 739983.

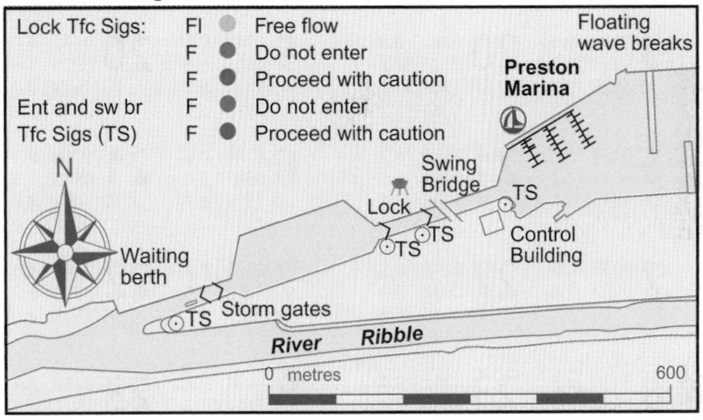
Lock Tfc Sigs: Fl Free flow
F Do not enter
F Proceed with caution
Ent and sw br Tfc Sigs (TS) F Do not enter
F Proceed with caution
Floating wave breaks
Preston Marina
N
Swing Bridge
Lock
TS
Control Building
Waiting berth
Storm gates
River Ribble
0 metres 600

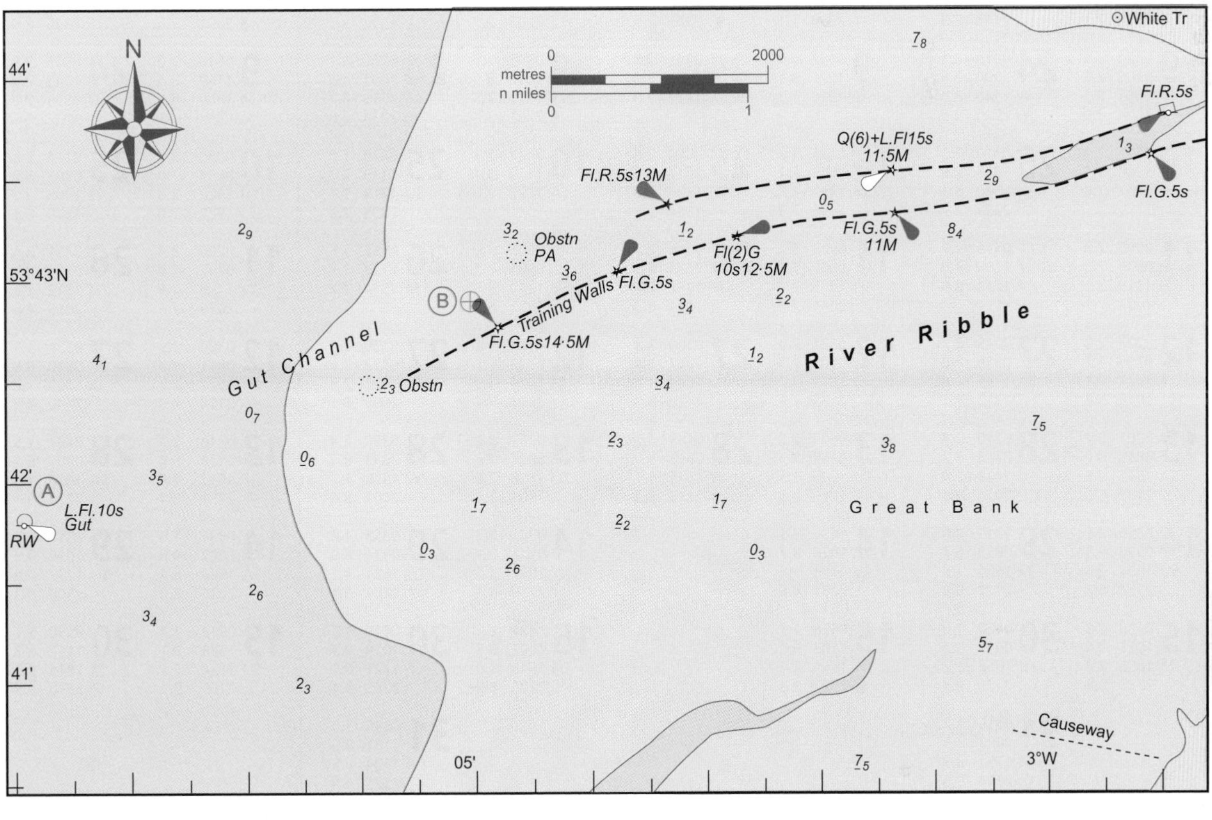
White Tr
N
44'
0 2000
metres
n miles
0 1
Fl.R.5s
Q(6)+L.Fl15s 11·5M
Fl.R.5s13M
Fl.G.5s
Fl.G.5s 11M
Fl(2)G 10s12·5M
Obstn PA
Training Walls Fl.G.5s
Fl.G.5s14·5M
53°43'N
Gut Channel
Obstn
River Ribble
42'
L.Fl.10s Gut
RW
Great Bank
41'
05'
Causeway
3°W

STANDARD TIME (UT)
For Summer Time add ONE hour in **non-shaded areas**

LIVERPOOL (GLADSTONE DOCK) LAT 53°27′N LONG 3°01′W

TIMES AND HEIGHTS OF HIGH AND LOW WATERS

Dates in red are SPRINGS
Dates in blue are NEAPS

YEAR **2018**

JANUARY

Date	Day	Time	m	Time	m	Time	m	Time	m
1	M	0436	1.3	1007	9.4	1708	1.2	2231	9.6
2	TU	0529	1.0	1057	9.7	1800	0.8	○ 2322	9.8
3	W	0618	0.9	1145	9.9	1851	0.6		
4	TH	0012	9.8	0705	0.9	1234	9.9	1940	0.6
5	F	0102	9.6	0752	1.1	1323	9.7	2028	0.8
6	SA	0151	9.3	0837	1.4	1411	9.5	2115	1.2
7	SU	0239	8.9	0923	1.8	1501	9.1	2204	1.6
8	M	0330	8.5	1012	2.3	1553	8.6	◑ 2256	2.1
9	TU	0424	8.0	1106	2.8	1651	8.2	2354	2.6
10	W	0527	7.7	1209	3.1	1757	7.8		
11	TH	0058	2.8	0636	7.6	1319	3.2	1907	7.7
12	F	0203	2.8	0745	7.7	1427	3.1	2013	7.8
13	SA	0301	2.7	0843	8.0	1525	2.8	2108	8.0
14	SU	0350	2.5	0930	8.3	1614	2.5	2154	8.3
15	M	0433	2.2	1011	8.6	1655	2.2	2233	8.5
16	TU	0510	2.1	1047	8.8	1732	2.0	2309	8.7
17	W	0544	1.9	1122	9.0	1807	1.8	● 2342	8.8
18	TH	0617	1.8	1155	9.1	1841	1.7		
19	F	0014	8.8	0651	1.7	1228	9.1	1915	1.6
20	SA	0047	8.8	0726	1.8	1302	9.1	1951	1.7
21	SU	0120	8.7	0801	1.9	1336	8.9	2026	1.8
22	M	0155	8.5	0838	2.1	1412	8.8	2103	2.0
23	TU	0232	8.4	0916	2.4	1452	8.6	2142	2.3
24	W	0316	8.1	1000	2.6	1540	8.4	◐ 2230	2.5
25	TH	0410	7.9	1055	2.9	1640	8.1	2331	2.7
26	F	0519	7.7	1206	3.0	1754	8.0		
27	SA	0049	2.7	0638	7.8	1331	2.8	1912	8.1
28	SU	0210	2.4	0753	8.2	1448	2.4	2024	8.5
29	M	0319	2.0	0858	8.7	1555	1.8	2127	8.9
30	TU	0420	1.6	0955	9.2	1656	1.2	2223	9.3
31	W	0516	1.2	1047	9.6	1751	0.7	○ 2314	9.6

FEBRUARY

Date	Day	Time	m	Time	m	Time	m	Time	m
1	TH	0607	0.9	1135	9.9	1841	0.4		
2	F	0002	9.8	0654	0.7	1222	10.0	1927	0.3
3	SA	0048	9.7	0737	0.8	1306	9.9	2010	0.5
4	SU	0131	9.5	0818	1.1	1349	9.6	2052	0.9
5	M	0212	9.1	0858	1.5	1431	9.2	2132	1.5
6	TU	0254	8.6	0937	2.0	1514	8.7	2213	2.1
7	W	0338	8.2	1019	2.6	1602	8.1	◑ 2259	2.7
8	TH	0431	7.7	1111	3.1	1702	7.6	2358	3.1
9	F	0537	7.3	1221	3.4	1816	7.3		
10	SA	0111	3.3	0655	7.2	1342	3.4	1936	7.3
11	SU	0223	3.2	0808	7.5	1453	3.1	2044	7.6
12	M	0321	2.9	0905	7.9	1549	2.7	2135	7.9
13	TU	0409	2.5	0950	8.3	1635	2.3	2216	8.3
14	W	0450	2.1	1028	8.7	1714	1.9	2251	8.6
15	TH	0526	1.9	1103	9.0	1750	1.6	● 2323	8.8
16	F	0601	1.6	1135	9.1	1825	1.4	2355	8.9
17	SA	0636	1.4	1208	9.3	1900	1.3		
18	SU	0026	9.0	0710	1.4	1241	9.3	1934	1.2
19	M	0059	9.0	0745	1.4	1314	9.2	2007	1.4
20	TU	0132	8.9	0820	1.6	1349	9.1	2041	1.6
21	W	0208	8.7	0855	1.9	1427	8.9	2116	1.9
22	TH	0249	8.5	0934	2.2	1513	8.6	2158	2.2
23	F	0339	8.1	1024	2.6	1610	8.2	◐ 2255	2.6
24	SA	0445	7.8	1133	2.8	1727	7.9		
25	SU	0014	2.8	0611	7.6	1306	2.8	1854	7.8
26	M	0146	2.7	0736	7.9	1432	2.4	2014	8.2
27	TU	0304	2.3	0847	8.4	1544	1.8	2120	8.7
28	W	0409	1.7	0945	9.0	1646	1.1	2215	9.2

MARCH

Date	Day	Time	m	Time	m	Time	m	Time	m
1	TH	0505	1.2	1035	9.5	1739	0.6	2302	9.5
2	F	0554	0.8	1121	9.8	1825	0.3	○ 2346	9.7
3	SA	0637	0.7	1204	9.9	1908	0.3		
4	SU	0027	9.7	0717	0.7	1244	9.8	1946	0.5
5	M	0105	9.5	0754	0.9	1322	9.6	2022	0.9
6	TU	0142	9.2	0829	1.3	1359	9.2	2056	1.4
7	W	0217	8.8	0902	1.8	1436	8.7	2128	2.1
8	TH	0256	8.3	0936	2.4	1518	8.1	2203	2.7
9	F	0342	7.8	1018	3.0	1610	7.5	◑ 2251	3.3
10	SA	0442	7.3	1119	3.4	1722	7.0		
11	SU	0006	3.6	0601	7.0	1249	3.6	1852	6.9
12	M	0137	3.6	0725	7.2	1414	3.3	2013	7.2
13	TU	0247	3.2	0832	7.6	1518	2.8	2109	7.7
14	W	0341	2.7	0921	8.1	1607	2.3	2150	8.1
15	TH	0424	2.2	1001	8.5	1648	1.9	2226	8.5
16	F	0503	1.8	1036	8.9	1726	1.5	2258	8.8
17	SA	0540	1.5	1109	9.2	1802	1.2	● 2329	9.1
18	SU	0616	1.2	1142	9.4	1838	1.0		
19	M	0001	9.2	0652	1.0	1217	9.5	1913	0.9
20	TU	0035	9.3	0727	1.0	1252	9.5	1947	1.0
21	W	0110	9.2	0802	1.2	1329	9.3	2020	1.3
22	TH	0147	9.0	0837	1.5	1409	9.1	2055	1.6
23	F	0229	8.7	0917	1.9	1456	8.6	2137	2.1
24	SA	0320	8.2	1007	2.3	1555	8.1	◐ 2234	2.6
25	SU	0429	7.8	1119	2.7	1715	7.7	2355	2.9
26	M	0557	7.6	1253	2.7	1844	7.7		
27	TU	0130	2.8	0722	7.9	1421	2.3	2005	8.1
28	W	0250	2.4	0833	8.4	1532	1.7	2109	8.6
29	TH	0355	1.8	0931	8.9	1631	1.1	2201	9.1
30	F	0449	1.3	1019	9.3	1721	0.7	2245	9.4
31	SA	0535	1.0	1101	9.6	1804	0.5	○ 2325	9.5

APRIL

Date	Day	Time	m	Time	m	Time	m	Time	m
1	SU	0616	0.8	1141	9.7	1842	0.5		
2	M	0002	9.5	0652	0.8	1219	9.6	1917	0.7
3	TU	0038	9.4	0727	0.9	1254	9.4	1950	1.0
4	W	0111	9.2	0759	1.3	1329	9.0	2020	1.5
5	TH	0145	8.8	0830	1.7	1403	8.6	2048	2.1
6	F	0221	8.4	0901	2.2	1442	8.1	2118	2.6
7	SA	0303	7.9	0938	2.8	1529	7.5	2159	3.2
8	SU	0356	7.4	1030	3.2	1633	7.0	◑ 2301	3.6
9	M	0510	7.0	1149	3.5	1800	6.8		
10	TU	0035	3.7	0634	7.0	1322	3.3	1927	7.0
11	W	0200	3.4	0747	7.4	1433	2.9	2029	7.5
12	TH	0300	2.9	0841	7.9	1527	2.3	2114	8.0
13	F	0348	2.3	0924	8.4	1613	1.8	2151	8.4
14	SA	0431	1.8	1002	8.8	1654	1.4	2225	8.8
15	SU	0512	1.4	1038	9.2	1734	1.1	2259	9.1
16	M	0551	1.1	1114	9.4	1813	0.9	● 2334	9.4
17	TU	0630	0.9	1151	9.6	1850	0.8		
18	W	0011	9.4	0708	0.9	1230	9.6	1926	0.9
19	TH	0050	9.4	0746	1.0	1311	9.4	2003	1.1
20	F	0131	9.2	0825	1.3	1356	9.1	2041	1.6
21	SA	0217	8.8	0909	1.7	1447	8.7	2126	2.1
22	SU	0312	8.4	1003	2.1	1550	8.1	◐ 2225	2.6
23	M	0423	8.0	1117	2.4	1709	7.8	2345	2.9
24	TU	0546	7.8	1245	2.4	1833	7.8		
25	W	0114	2.8	0705	8.0	1405	2.1	1949	8.1
26	TH	0231	2.4	0814	8.4	1512	1.6	2050	8.5
27	F	0334	1.9	0910	8.8	1609	1.2	2140	8.9
28	SA	0427	1.5	0957	9.1	1656	1.0	2222	9.1
29	SU	0511	1.2	1038	9.3	1737	0.9	2300	9.3
30	M	0550	1.1	1117	9.3	1814	0.9	○ 2336	9.3

Chart Datum: 4·93 metres below Ordnance Datum (Newlyn). HAT is 10·3 metres above Chart Datum.

STANDARD TIME (UT)
For Summer Time add ONE hour in **non-shaded areas**

LIVERPOOL (GLADSTONE DOCK) LAT 53°27′N LONG 3°01′W

TIMES AND HEIGHTS OF HIGH AND LOW WATERS

Dates in red are SPRINGS
Dates in blue are NEAPS

YEAR **2018**

MAY

Date	Day	Time	m	Time	m	Time	m	Time	m
1	TU	0626	1.1	1153	9.2	1847	1.1		
2	W	0010	9.2	0700	1.2	1228	9.1	1918	1.3
3	TH	0043	9.1	0732	1.4	1302	8.8	1947	1.7
4	F	0117	8.8	0802	1.8	1337	8.5	2015	2.1
5	SA	0152	8.5	0834	2.1	1414	8.1	2047	2.5
6	SU	0232	8.1	0910	2.5	1457	7.6	2126	3.0
7	M	0320	7.7	0957	2.9	1551	7.2	2219	3.4
8	TU	0422	7.3	1100	3.2	1703	6.9	◑ 2333	3.6
9	W	0538	7.2	1220	3.2	1824	7.0		
10	TH	0057	3.5	0650	7.4	1337	2.9	1933	7.3
11	F	0208	3.0	0750	7.8	1438	2.4	2025	7.8
12	SA	0304	2.5	0839	8.3	1531	1.9	2109	8.3
13	SU	0354	2.0	0922	8.7	1618	1.5	2149	8.8
14	M	0440	1.5	1004	9.1	1703	1.1	2228	9.2
15	TU	0525	1.1	1045	9.4	1746	0.9	● 2308	9.4
16	W	0609	0.9	1128	9.6	1828	0.8	2350	9.5
17	TH	0652	0.8	1212	9.6	1909	0.9		
18	F	0033	9.5	0734	0.8	1259	9.5	1950	1.1
19	SA	0120	9.3	0819	1.1	1348	9.2	2033	1.5
20	SU	0210	9.0	0908	1.4	1443	8.7	2122	1.9
21	M	0308	8.6	1005	1.8	1546	8.3	2221	2.4
22	TU	0415	8.3	1113	2.0	1656	8.0	◐ 2333	2.6
23	W	0528	8.1	1227	2.1	1811	7.9		
24	TH	0050	2.6	0639	8.1	1339	2.0	1922	8.1
25	F	0202	2.4	0746	8.3	1444	1.8	2023	8.3
26	SA	0305	2.1	0843	8.6	1540	1.6	2114	8.6
27	SU	0359	1.9	0932	8.7	1628	1.5	2157	8.8
28	M	0444	1.7	1015	8.9	1708	1.4	2235	9.0
29	TU	0524	1.5	1054	8.9	1745	1.4	○ 2311	9.0
30	W	0601	1.5	1130	8.9	1818	1.5	2346	9.0
31	TH	0635	1.5	1206	8.8	1850	1.6		

JUNE

Date	Day	Time	m	Time	m	Time	m	Time	m
1	F	0019	9.0	0708	1.6	1240	8.6	1919	1.8
2	SA	0054	8.8	0739	1.8	1315	8.4	1950	2.1
3	SU	0130	8.6	0813	2.0	1351	8.2	2024	2.4
4	M	0208	8.3	0849	2.3	1431	7.8	2103	2.7
5	TU	0250	8.0	0932	2.6	1516	7.5	2149	3.0
6	W	0341	7.7	1043	2.8	1612	7.3	◑ 2247	3.2
7	TH	0443	7.5	1127	2.9	1719	7.2	2357	3.3
8	F	0550	7.6	1237	2.8	1828	7.4		
9	SA	0109	3.0	0654	7.8	1346	2.5	1931	7.8
10	SU	0216	2.6	0752	8.2	1447	2.1	2025	8.2
11	M	0315	2.2	0844	8.6	1542	1.7	2114	8.7
12	TU	0409	1.7	0933	9.0	1633	1.3	2200	9.1
13	W	0500	1.3	1022	9.3	1722	1.0	● 2246	9.4
14	TH	0549	0.9	1110	9.5	1809	0.9	2333	9.6
15	F	0638	0.7	1159	9.6	1855	0.9		
16	SA	0021	9.6	0726	0.7	1250	9.5	1940	1.0
17	SU	0111	9.5	0815	0.8	1341	9.3	2027	1.3
18	M	0203	9.3	0905	1.0	1435	8.9	2116	1.7
19	TU	0258	9.0	0959	1.4	1532	8.6	2211	2.1
20	W	0357	8.6	1057	1.7	1633	8.2	◐ 2311	2.4
21	TH	0500	8.3	1159	2.0	1738	8.0		
22	F	0017	2.6	0606	8.2	1305	2.1	1846	7.9
23	SA	0126	2.6	0713	8.1	1409	2.2	1950	8.0
24	SU	0231	2.5	0814	8.2	1507	2.1	2045	8.2
25	M	0329	2.3	0907	8.3	1557	2.0	2132	8.5
26	TU	0418	2.1	0954	8.4	1640	1.9	2213	8.7
27	W	0501	2.0	1035	8.5	1718	1.8	2251	8.8
28	TH	0540	1.8	1112	8.6	1753	1.8	○ 2326	8.9
29	F	0615	1.8	1148	8.6	1826	1.8		
30	SA	0000	8.9	0648	1.7	1222	8.6	1857	1.9

JULY

Date	Day	Time	m	Time	m	Time	m	Time	m
1	SU	0035	8.9	0721	1.8	1256	8.5	1930	2.0
2	M	0110	8.7	0755	1.9	1331	8.3	2005	2.1
3	TU	0146	8.6	0831	2.0	1407	8.2	2043	2.4
4	W	0224	8.4	0910	2.2	1446	7.9	2124	2.6
5	TH	0305	8.1	0953	2.4	1531	7.7	2211	2.8
6	F	0355	7.9	1043	2.6	1625	7.6	◑ 2308	3.0
7	SA	0454	7.8	1144	2.7	1730	7.6		
8	SU	0015	3.0	0601	7.9	1254	2.6	1840	7.7
9	M	0130	2.8	0708	8.1	1405	2.3	1946	8.1
10	TU	0239	2.4	0812	8.4	1510	1.9	2045	8.6
11	W	0342	1.9	0910	8.8	1608	1.6	2139	9.0
12	TH	0440	1.4	1005	9.2	1702	1.2	2231	9.4
13	F	0535	1.0	1058	9.5	1754	1.0	● 2321	9.6
14	SA	0628	0.6	1149	9.6	1843	0.8		
15	SU	0010	9.8	0718	0.5	1240	9.6	1931	0.9
16	M	0100	9.8	0806	0.5	1329	9.5	2017	1.1
17	TU	0149	9.6	0853	0.7	1418	9.2	2103	1.4
18	W	0238	9.3	0941	1.1	1507	8.8	2150	1.8
19	TH	0329	8.9	1030	1.6	1559	8.3	◐ 2240	2.3
20	F	0424	8.4	1123	2.1	1657	7.9	2337	2.7
21	SA	0526	8.0	1223	2.5	1802	7.7		
22	SU	0044	2.9	0634	7.7	1330	2.7	1912	7.7
23	M	0155	2.9	0744	7.7	1433	2.7	2016	7.8
24	TU	0300	2.7	0845	7.9	1529	2.5	2109	8.1
25	W	0356	2.5	0936	8.1	1616	2.3	2154	8.4
26	TH	0442	2.2	1019	8.3	1657	2.1	2233	8.7
27	F	0522	2.0	1057	8.5	1733	2.0	○ 2308	8.9
28	SA	0558	1.8	1131	8.6	1807	1.9	2342	9.0
29	SU	0631	1.7	1203	8.7	1839	1.8		
30	M	0016	9.0	0704	1.6	1236	8.7	1913	1.8
31	TU	0049	9.0	0737	1.6	1308	8.6	1947	1.8

AUGUST

Date	Day	Time	m	Time	m	Time	m	Time	m
1	W	0122	8.9	0812	1.7	1341	8.5	2023	2.0
2	TH	0156	8.7	0847	1.9	1416	8.3	2100	2.2
3	F	0233	8.5	0924	2.1	1456	8.1	2140	2.5
4	SA	0316	8.3	1006	2.4	1543	7.9	◑ 2228	2.8
5	SU	0409	8.1	1059	2.6	1643	7.7	2331	2.9
6	M	0517	7.9	1208	2.7	1759	7.7		
7	TU	0051	2.9	0635	7.9	1330	2.6	1917	7.9
8	W	0212	2.5	0750	8.2	1444	2.2	2026	8.4
9	TH	0323	2.0	0857	8.6	1549	1.8	2126	8.9
10	F	0426	1.4	0955	9.1	1647	1.4	2219	9.4
11	SA	0524	0.9	1048	9.5	1741	1.0	● 2309	9.8
12	SU	0616	0.5	1137	9.7	1831	0.8	2356	9.9
13	M	0705	0.3	1224	9.7	1917	0.7		
14	TU	0042	10.0	0749	0.3	1310	9.6	1959	0.9
15	W	0128	9.8	0832	0.6	1353	9.3	2041	1.2
16	TH	0211	9.4	0913	1.1	1436	8.9	2121	1.7
17	F	0255	8.9	0955	1.7	1520	8.4	2204	2.3
18	SA	0343	8.3	1040	2.4	1611	7.9	◐ 2254	2.8
19	SU	0439	7.8	1135	2.9	1713	7.5	2358	3.2
20	M	0551	7.4	1245	3.2	1829	7.3		
21	TU	0118	3.3	0712	7.3	1359	3.2	1945	7.5
22	W	0234	3.1	0824	7.5	1503	2.9	2046	7.9
23	TH	0334	2.7	0919	7.9	1554	2.6	2134	8.3
24	F	0423	2.3	1002	8.2	1636	2.3	2213	8.7
25	SA	0503	2.0	1038	8.5	1713	2.0	2248	8.9
26	SU	0538	1.7	1110	8.7	1747	1.8	○ 2321	9.1
27	M	0611	1.5	1141	8.9	1820	1.6	2353	9.2
28	TU	0644	1.4	1212	8.9	1854	1.5		
29	W	0024	9.2	0716	1.4	1243	8.9	1928	1.6
30	TH	0057	9.2	0750	1.4	1315	8.8	2002	1.7
31	F	0129	9.0	0823	1.6	1348	8.7	2037	2.0

Chart Datum: 4·93 metres below Ordnance Datum (Newlyn). HAT is 10·3 metres above Chart Datum.

STANDARD TIME (UT)
For Summer Time add ONE hour in **non-shaded areas**

LIVERPOOL (GLADSTONE DOCK) LAT 53°27'N LONG 3°01'W

TIMES AND HEIGHTS OF HIGH AND LOW WATERS

Dates in red are SPRINGS
Dates in blue are NEAPS

YEAR **2018**

SEPTEMBER

Day	Time	m	Day	Time	m
1	0205	8.8	16	0301	8.2
	0857	1.9		0953	2.6
SA	1426	8.5	SU	1526	7.9
	2114	2.3		◐ 2210	2.9
2	0246	8.5	17	0353	7.6
	0935	2.3		1040	3.2
SU	1511	8.2	M	1624	7.5
	2159	2.6		2310	3.4
3	0338	8.2	18	0504	7.1
	1024	2.6		1151	3.6
M	1610	7.8	TU	1742	7.2
	◑ 2300	2.9			
4	0448	7.8	19	0036	3.6
	1135	2.9		0635	6.9
TU	1732	7.6	W	1320	3.7
				1907	7.3
5	0026	3.0	20	0202	3.4
	0615	7.7		0758	7.2
W	1306	2.9	TH	1433	3.3
	1859	7.8		2016	7.7
6	0156	2.6	21	0305	2.9
	0739	8.0		0856	7.7
TH	1427	2.5	F	1527	2.9
	2014	8.3		2106	8.2
7	0310	2.0	22	0354	2.4
	0849	8.6		0938	8.2
F	1535	2.0	SA	1610	2.4
	2115	8.9		2146	8.6
8	0415	1.3	23	0434	2.0
	0947	9.1		1013	8.6
SA	1634	1.4	SU	1647	2.0
	2207	9.5		2221	9.0
9	0511	0.8	24	0510	1.6
	1036	9.5		1044	8.8
SU	1727	1.0	M	1722	1.7
	● 2254	9.8		2253	9.2
10	0600	0.4	25	0545	1.4
	1121	9.8		1114	9.0
M	1813	0.8	TU	1757	1.5
	2338	10.0		○ 2325	9.4
11	0645	0.3	26	0619	1.2
	1204	9.8		1144	9.2
TU	1856	0.7	W	1832	1.4
				2357	9.4
12	0020	10.0	27	0653	1.2
	0726	0.4		1216	9.2
W	1245	9.7	TH	1907	1.4
	1936	0.9			
13	0101	9.8	28	0030	9.4
	0804	0.7		0726	1.3
TH	1323	9.4	F	1249	9.1
	2013	1.2		1942	1.5
14	0140	9.4	29	0105	9.2
	0841	1.3		0759	1.5
F	1401	8.9	SA	1324	9.0
	2050	1.7		2016	1.8
15	0219	8.8	30	0143	9.0
	0916	1.9		0833	1.8
SA	1440	8.5	SU	1403	8.7
	2127	2.3		2054	2.1

OCTOBER

Day	Time	m	Day	Time	m
1	0227	8.6	16	0313	7.6
	0912	2.3		0948	3.3
M	1449	8.3	TU	1540	7.6
	2140	2.5		◐ 2223	3.4
2	0321	8.2	17	0417	7.1
	1003	2.7		1049	3.8
TU	1552	7.9	W	1654	7.2
	◑ 2245	2.9		2343	3.7
3	0435	7.7	18	0546	6.8
	1116	3.1		1224	3.9
W	1718	7.7	TH	1819	7.2
4	0016	2.9	19	0115	3.5
	0606	7.7		0715	7.0
TH	1251	3.1	F	1349	3.6
	1847	7.9		1933	7.5
5	0146	2.5	20	0223	3.1
	0731	8.0		0818	7.5
F	1414	2.6	SA	1447	3.1
	2001	8.4		2028	8.0
6	0259	1.9	21	0314	2.5
	0839	8.6		0903	8.0
SA	1522	2.1	SU	1534	2.6
	2101	9.0		2111	8.5
7	0400	1.3	22	0357	2.1
	0933	9.1		0939	8.5
SU	1619	1.5	M	1614	2.1
	2151	9.5		2147	8.9
8	0453	0.8	23	0436	1.7
	1019	9.5		1012	8.9
M	1708	1.1	TU	1653	1.8
	2235	9.8		2222	9.2
9	0539	0.6	24	0514	1.4
	1101	9.7		1043	9.1
TU	1752	0.9	W	1731	1.5
	● 2317	9.9		○ 2256	9.4
10	0620	0.5	25	0551	1.2
	1140	9.7		1116	9.3
W	1832	0.9	TH	1809	1.3
	2356	9.8		2330	9.5
11	0658	0.7	26	0628	1.1
	1217	9.6		1150	9.4
TH	1910	1.0	F	1847	1.3
12	0034	9.6	27	0007	9.5
	0733	1.0		0704	1.2
F	1253	9.4	SA	1226	9.4
	1945	1.4		1924	1.4
13	0111	9.2	28	0046	9.4
	0806	1.6		0739	1.4
SA	1328	9.0	SU	1305	9.2
	2019	1.8		2002	1.6
14	0147	8.7	29	0129	9.1
	0838	2.2		0816	1.8
SU	1405	8.6	M	1348	8.9
	2053	2.4		2044	2.0
15	0226	8.2	30	0217	8.7
	0909	2.8		0859	2.3
M	1447	8.1	TU	1439	8.5
	2131	2.9		2134	2.4
			31	0315	8.2
				0953	2.7
			W	1545	8.1
				◑ 2243	2.7

NOVEMBER

Day	Time	m	Day	Time	m
1	0430	7.8	16	0447	7.0
	1107	3.1		1115	3.9
TH	1708	7.9	F	1722	7.3
2	0009	2.7	17	0009	3.5
	0555	7.8		0609	7.0
F	1236	3.1	SA	1242	3.8
	1830	8.0		1835	7.4
3	0130	2.4	18	0125	3.2
	0715	8.1		0721	7.3
SA	1355	2.7	SU	1353	3.4
	1942	8.5		1937	7.8
4	0240	1.9	19	0224	2.7
	0821	8.5		0815	7.8
SU	1501	2.2	M	1448	2.9
	2041	8.9		2026	8.3
5	0339	1.4	20	0314	2.3
	0914	9.0		0857	8.3
M	1557	1.8	TU	1536	2.4
	2131	9.3		2109	8.7
6	0430	1.1	21	0359	1.8
	0959	9.3		0935	8.7
TU	1645	1.4	W	1620	1.9
	2214	9.5		2148	9.0
7	0514	1.0	22	0442	1.5
	1039	9.5		1012	9.1
W	1728	1.3	TH	1704	1.6
	● 2255	9.6		2227	9.3
8	0553	1.0	23	0524	1.3
	1116	9.5		1049	9.4
TH	1807	1.2	F	1746	1.3
	2333	9.5		○ 2307	9.5
9	0630	1.1	24	0605	1.2
	1152	9.5		1128	9.5
F	1844	1.3	SA	1829	1.2
				2348	9.6
10	0010	9.3	25	0645	1.2
	0703	1.4		1209	9.5
SA	1227	9.3	SU	1911	1.2
	1919	1.6			
11	0046	9.0	26	0033	9.5
	0735	1.8		0725	1.4
SU	1301	9.0	M	1253	9.4
	1952	2.0		1954	1.4
12	0121	8.6	27	0120	9.2
	0805	2.3		0807	1.7
M	1337	8.7	TU	1341	9.2
	2025	2.4		2041	1.7
13	0159	8.2	28	0212	8.9
	0835	2.7		0853	2.1
TU	1416	8.3	W	1435	8.8
	2100	2.8		2135	2.0
14	0241	7.7	29	0311	8.5
	0912	3.2		0948	2.5
W	1504	7.9	TH	1539	8.5
	2145	3.2		2240	2.3
15	0335	7.3	30	0419	8.1
	1002	3.6		1056	2.8
TH	1606	7.5	F	1651	8.3
	◐ 2248	3.5		◑ 2352	2.3

DECEMBER

Day	Time	m	Day	Time	m
1	0534	8.0	16	0456	7.2
	1212	2.9		1131	3.6
SA	1805	8.2	SU	1728	7.5
2	0105	2.2	17	0015	3.2
	0648	8.1		0607	7.2
SU	1327	2.7	M	1246	3.5
	1914	8.4		1834	7.7
3	0212	2.0	18	0125	2.9
	0754	8.3		0713	7.5
M	1434	2.4	TU	1355	3.1
	2016	8.7		1934	8.0
4	0312	1.8	19	0227	2.6
	0850	8.7		0809	8.0
TU	1532	2.1	W	1455	2.7
	2108	8.9		2027	8.4
5	0404	1.6	20	0322	2.1
	0936	8.9		0858	8.5
W	1622	1.9	TH	1548	2.2
	2154	9.0		2116	8.8
6	0448	1.5	21	0412	1.7
	1018	9.1		0943	8.9
TH	1706	1.7	F	1639	1.7
	2236	9.1		2203	9.2
7	0528	1.5	22	0500	1.4
	1056	9.2		1028	9.3
F	1746	1.6	SA	1727	1.4
	● 2315	9.1		○ 2249	9.4
8	0604	1.6	23	0546	1.2
	1132	9.2		1112	9.6
SA	1823	1.6	SU	1815	1.1
	2352	9.0		2336	9.6
9	0637	1.7	24	0631	1.1
	1206	9.2		1158	9.7
SU	1858	1.8	M	1903	1.0
10	0027	8.8	25	0024	9.6
	0709	1.9		0716	1.2
M	1241	9.0	TU	1245	9.7
	1931	2.0		1950	1.0
11	0102	8.6	26	0114	9.5
	0739	2.2		0801	1.4
TU	1316	8.8	W	1335	9.5
	2003	2.2		2039	1.1
12	0137	8.3	27	0205	9.2
	0811	2.5		0849	1.7
W	1353	8.5	TH	1427	9.3
	2038	2.5		2130	1.4
13	0216	8.0	28	0300	8.8
	0846	2.9		0939	2.0
TH	1434	8.2	F	1524	8.9
	2117	2.8		2225	1.8
14	0300	7.7	29	0358	8.4
	0930	3.2		1036	2.4
F	1523	7.9	SA	1624	8.6
	2205	3.0		◑ 2325	2.1
15	0352	7.4	30	0501	8.1
	1024	3.5		1139	2.7
SA	1621	7.6	SU	1730	8.3
	◐ 2305	3.2			
			31	0031	2.3
				0610	7.9
			M	1249	2.8
				1839	8.2

Chart Datum: 4·93 metres below Ordnance Datum (Newlyn). HAT is 10·3 metres above Chart Datum.

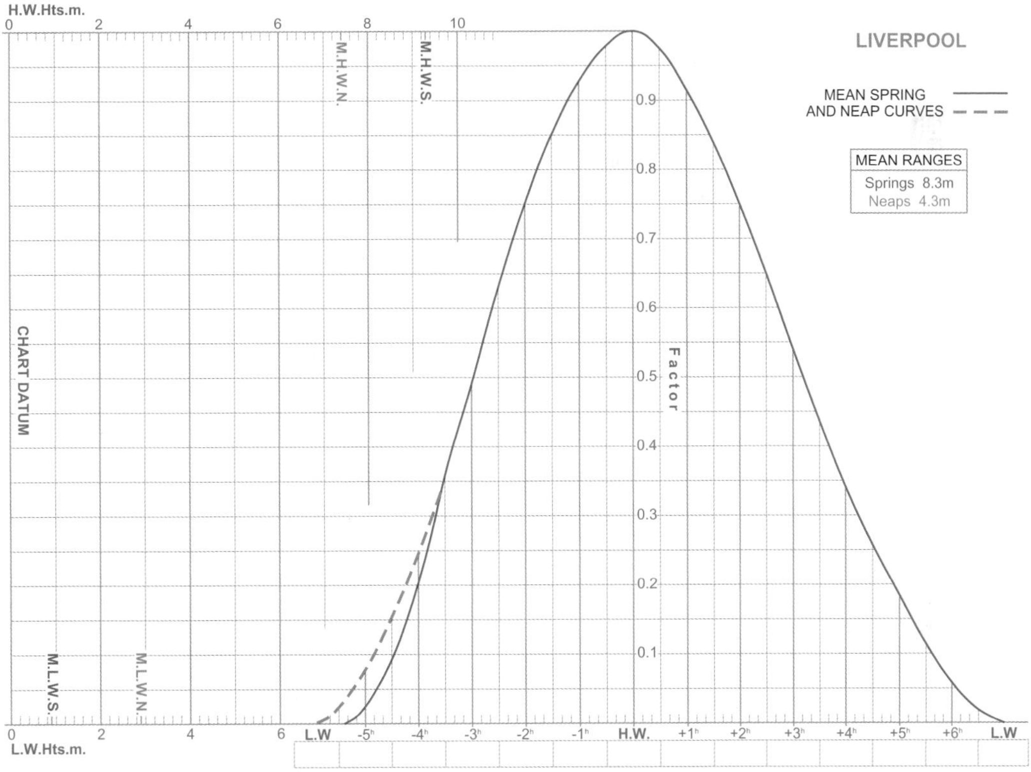

9.10.17 LIVERPOOL

Merseyside **53°24'·22N 03°00'·28W** (Liver Bldg)

CHARTS AC 1826, 1978, 1951, 3490, 5613; Imray C62, C52

TIDES +0015 Dover; ML 5·2; Duration 0535

Standard Port LIVERPOOL (GLADSTONE DOCK) (⟵)

Times				Height (metres)			
High Water		Low Water		MHWS	MHWN	MLWN	MLWS
0000	0600	0200	0700	9·4	7·5	3·2	1·1
1200	1800	1400	1900				
Differences SEACOMBE (ALFRED DK)							
+0007	+0007	+0000	+0000	–0·1	–0·1	–0·3	–0·2
GARSTON							
+0026	+0022	+0017	+0020	+0·3	+0·1	–0·4	–0·5
EASTHAM (River Mersey)							
+0014	+0014	+0006	+0006	+0·2	0·0	0·0	+0·2
HALE HEAD (River Mersey)							
+0035	+0030	ND	ND	–2·5	–2·6	ND	ND
WIDNES (River Mersey)							
+0045	*+0050*	*+0355*	*+0340*	*–4·3*	*–4·5*	*–2·8*	*–0·6*
FIDDLER'S FERRY (River Mersey)							
+0105	+0120	+0535	+0445	–6·0	–6·4	–2·7	–0·6
HILBRE ISLAND (River Dee)							
–0011	–0008	–0013	–0018	–0·4	–0·3	+0·1	+0·2
MOSTYN DOCKS (River Dee)							
–0015	–0010	–0025	–0025	–0·9	–0·8	ND	ND
CONNAH'S QUAY (River Dee)							
+0005	+0020	+0350	+0335	–4·7	–4·5	DR	DR
CHESTER (River Dee)							
+0110	+0110	+0455	+0455	–5·4	–5·5	DR	DR
COLWYN BAY							
–0015	–0015	ND	ND	–1·6	–1·4	ND	ND
LLANDUDNO							
–0009	–0021	–0031	–0038	–1·7	–1·6	–0·9	–0·6

NOTE: LW time differences at Connah's Quay give the end of a LW stand lasting about 3¾hrs at sp and 5hrs at nps. A bore occurs in the R Dee at Chester.

SHELTER Good at marinas in Brunswick/Coburg docks and in Canning/Albert Docks. Fair weather ⚓ on the SW side of river. Strong winds from any direction raise a swell on the bar. Wind against tide causes steep, breaking seas in outer reaches of R Mersey with disturbed waters into the Crosby Channel.

NAVIGATION WPT 53°32'·02N 03°20'·98W, Bar light float, 111°/2·8M to Q1 NCM lt F. From Q1 to marina is 15·5M via Queens and Crosby Channels. Both have training banks which cover and it is unsafe to navigate between these and the floats/buoys. Sp tidal streams exceed 5kn within the river. Elsewhere great caution is needed as the whole area (R Dee, R Mersey to R Alt and N to Morecambe Bay) is littered with sandbanks and damaged training walls. Local knowledge is advisable inshore outside marked passages.

Leeds and Liverpool Canal (BWB) gives access to E Coast, ent at Stanley Dock. Max draught 1·0m, air draught 2·2m, beam 4·3m, LOA 18·3m. Liverpool to Goole 161M, 103 locks.

Manchester Ship Canal, ent at Eastham Locks (outer wall bn Iso YR 4s), leads 31M to Salford Quays or R Weaver for boatyards at Northwich. Obtain info pack from Peel Ports https://www.peelports.com/media/2259/mpf3-pleasure-craft-induction-pack-2017-2018.pdf.

R Dee: WPT 53°25'·13N 03°13'·17W, Hilbre Swash HE2 ECM buoy, Q (3) 10s, (chan shifts). From the W use Welsh Chan. The Dee estuary mostly dries.

LIGHTS AND MARKS Bar SWM lt float, Fl 5s Racon. Keep 5ca clear of SPM, 5ca W of Bar lt float. Formby SWM buoy, Iso 4s, is at the ent to Queen's Chan which is marked by light floats and buoys, and 3 NCM buoys, numbered Q1-Q12. Crosby Chan is similarly marked, C1-C23. From Crosby SWM buoy, Oc 5s, the track upriver is approx 145°. The Liver Bldg (twin spires) and Port of Liverpool Bldg (dome) are conspic on the E bank opposite Birkenhead Docks.

COMMUNICATIONS (Code 0151) CGOC (01407) 762051; Police 101; Ⓗ 709 0141. Port Ops 949 6134/5; ⛅949 6095.

Contact *Mersey VTS* Ch **12** 16 (H24) before Bar lighted Buoy. Nav /gale warnings are broadcast on receipt on Ch 12. Movements, nav warnings and weather are b/cast on Ch 09 at HW–3 and –2. *Canning Dock/Liverpool Marina* Ch **M**. Eastham Locks Ch 07 (H24). Manchester Ship Canal Ch 14. Liverpool NTM for further detail.

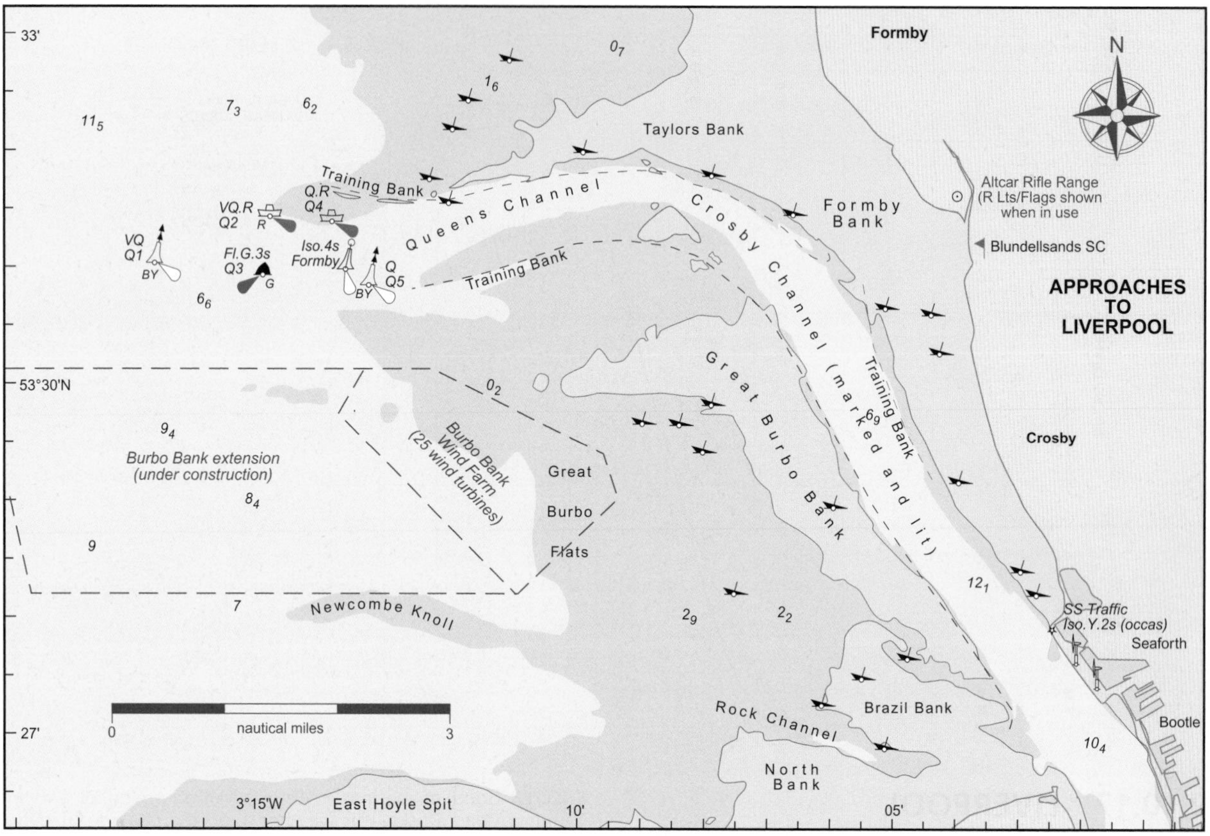
APPROACHES TO LIVERPOOL
Formby
Taylors Bank
Formby Bank
Altcar Rifle Range (R Lts/Flags shown when in use
Blundellsands SC
Training Bank
Queens Channel
Crosby Channel (marked and lit)
Training Bank
Q.R Q4
VQ.R Q2
VQ Q1
Fl.G.3s Q3
Iso.4s Formby
Q Q5
Great Burbo Bank
Burbo Bank Wind Farm (25 wind turbines)
Burbo Bank extension (under construction)
Great Burbo Flats
Crosby
Newcombe Knoll
SS Traffic Iso.Y.2s (occas)
Seaforth
Brazil Bank
Rock Channel
Bootle
North Bank
East Hoyle Spit
nautical miles
53°30'N
3°15'W
10'
05'
33'
27'

FACILITIES Liverpool Marina entrance is 1M S of the Liver Bldg, abeam Pluckington Bank WCM buoy. **IPTS** (sigs 2, 3 & 5) from conspic black control bldg at lock ent. 2m depth over sill at Brunswick Dock lock (width 8m) approx HW ±2¼ sp, ±1½ nps, 0600-2200 Mar-Oct. Pontoons inside, min depth 3·5m; night locking by arrangement. www.liverpoolmarina.co.uk ☎7076777 (0600-2200 Mar–Oct). 350, £2·20; (½M) (60t), (☎7076888) wi-fi.

Albert Dock ☎7096558; access HW–2 to HW via Canning Dock, but not on every tide. VHF Ch M when manned.

Royal Mersey YC ☎6453204.

W Kirby SC ☎6255579, M (in Dee Est) (at HW), (30t).

Hoylake SC ☎6322616.

City all facilities.

ADJACENT ANCHORAGE

RIVER ALT, Merseyside, **53°31′·42N 03°03′·80W**. AC 1978, 1951, 5613. HW –0008 on Dover. Good shelter but only for LOA <8·5m x 1·2m draught on a HW of at least 8m. Mersey E training wall can be crossed HW±2. Entrance to channel (shifts frequently) is E of C14 PHM lt float. The channel runs NW of, and parallel to the large fixed marks on the training wall (outer is a R basket; inner a Y cross), then between R and G perches. Inadvisable to ⚓ in R Alt without local knowledge; pick up a free mooring off the SC and contact club. Facilities are very limited. **Blundell Sands SC** ☎(0151) 9292101 (occas), (at HW).

ADJACENT HARBOUR

RHYL, Denbigh, **53°19′·0N 03°30′·4W**. AC 1978, 1951, 5613. Good shelter for vessels able to take the ground on pontoons in outer hbr. Inner hbr dries. Strong tides rip across ent between SWM and Hope's Nose, but training and harbour walls make entry achievable with care. Training wall marked by 4 lit bns Fl(2) R 4s with outer PHM Q R 7m 2M. Lifting bridge divides hbr opening on req Ch 14. Contact HM prior to visit: ☎01745 360625.

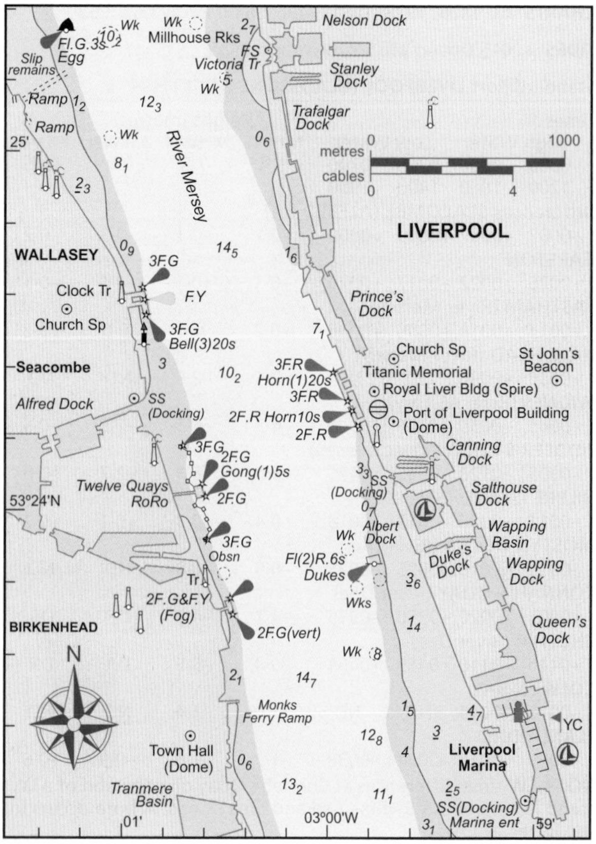
LIVERPOOL
Nelson Dock
Millhouse Rks
Victoria Tr
Stanley Dock
Trafalgar Dock
Fl.G.3s Egg
Slip remains
Ramp
River Mersey
metres
cables
WALLASEY
Clock Tr
Church Sp
Seacombe
Alfred Dock
Prince's Dock
Church Sp
St John's Beacon
Titanic Memorial
Royal Liver Bldg (Spire)
Port of Liverpool Building (Dome)
Canning Dock
Salthouse Dock
Twelve Quays RoRo
Albert Dock
Wapping Basin
Duke's Dock
Wapping Dock
Queen's Dock
BIRKENHEAD
Monks Ferry Ramp
Town Hall (Dome)
Tranmere Basin
Liverpool Marina
SS(Docking) Marina ent
YC
53°24'N
03°00'W

9.10.18 CONWY AND DEGANWY

Conwy **53°17'·48N 03°50'·23W** (marina) ❁❁◊◊◊✿✿✿
Deganwy **53°17'·41N 03°49'·66W** (marina) ❁❁◊◊◊✿✿✿

CHARTS AC 5609, 1826, 1977, 1978, 1463; Imray C52

TIDES –0015 Dover; ML 4·3; Duration 0545

Standard Port HOLYHEAD (→)

Times				Height (metres)			
High Water		Low Water		MHWS	MHWN	MLWN	MLWS
0000	0600	0500	1100	5·6	4·4	2·0	0·7
1200	1800	1700	2300				
Differences CONWY							
+0025	+0035	+0120	+0105	+2·3	+1·8	+0·6	+0·4

NOTE: HW Conwy is approx HW Liverpool –0040 sp and –0020 nps.

SHELTER Good in river, except in NW gales. Good in marinas.

NAVIGATION Hbr guide www.conwy.gov.uk/harbourandseaboard WPT 53°17'·95N 03°55'·58W, Fairway buoy LFl 10s; 095°/6·2ca to channel between C1/C2 buoys.

After C1/C2 buoys the channel up to Deganwy is marked by lit lateral marks in sequence: C2A, C4, then paired SHM/PHM: C3/C6, C5/C8, C7/C10, C9/C12, C11/C14. C16 (Fl R 6s) at narrows into R Conwy. A bar, dries $\underline{1}$·0m, forms at The Scabs adjacent to No 6 PHM. Perch Lt bcn Fl G 15s 5M marks turn to river ent. 10kn speed limit above.

Beware unlit moorings throughout the harbour, Beacons Jetty in the narrows and unlit pontoons upstream from Bodlondeb Pt. Spring ebb runs at 5kn and vacant moorings may be submerged.

North Deep, a buoyed inshore passage (close SW of Gt Orme's Hd to Deganwy Point), is only advised with local knowledge.

LIGHTS AND MARKS Penmaenmawr SPM outfall buoy (SW of C1 buoy) is not a channel mark. The 4 towers of Conwy castle and the 2 adjacent bridge towers are conspic once in the river.

COMMUNICATIONS (Code 01492) CGOC (01407) 762051; Police 101; Dr 592424; HM 596253.

HM Ch **14**. Summer 0900-1700LT daily; winter, same times Mon-Fri). Marinas, pre-call Ch 80 (H24) for a berth. N Wales CC launch Ch **M** water taxi.

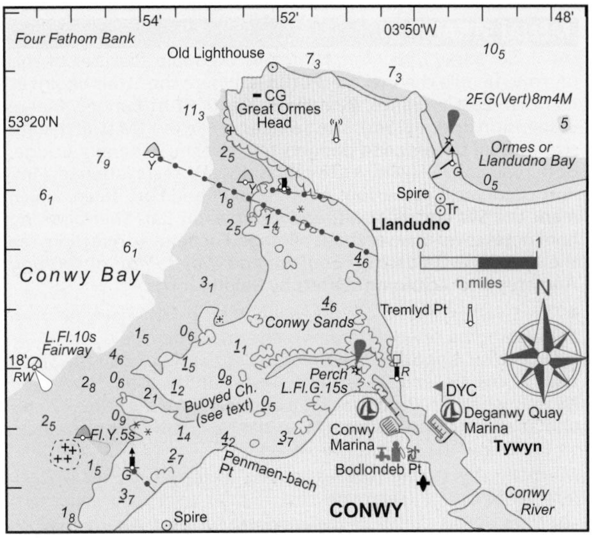

FACILITIES Beacons Jetty HW±3.

Conwy Marina www.quaymarinas.com ☎593000. Access when height of tide above CD exceeds 3·5m; waiting pontoon outside. Gate times are on an electronic noticeboard. Obey R/G entry lts. 505 inc ♥, £2·60m (short stay £10·95) (0700-2200) (30t) wi-fi.

Deganwy Quay Marina www.quaymarinas.com ☎576888. Access when height of tide above CD exceeds 4m, approx HW ±3¼. Keep close to 3 lit PHM lt marking the appr channel (see below). Min depth in chan is 2·5m when gate open. Obey R/G entry lights. 150 inc ♥, £2·60 (short stay £10·95) (0700-2200) (20t) wi-fi.

Harbour Above Bodlondeb Pt contact HM for: ♥'s, pontoon £13; **Town Quay** 3 drying £11<8m>£12·50<12·3m; (Town Quay HW±2, call Ch 14 to confirm).

N Wales Cruising Club (Conwy) ☎593481.

Conwy YC (Deganwy) ☎583690.

Town (Liverpool).

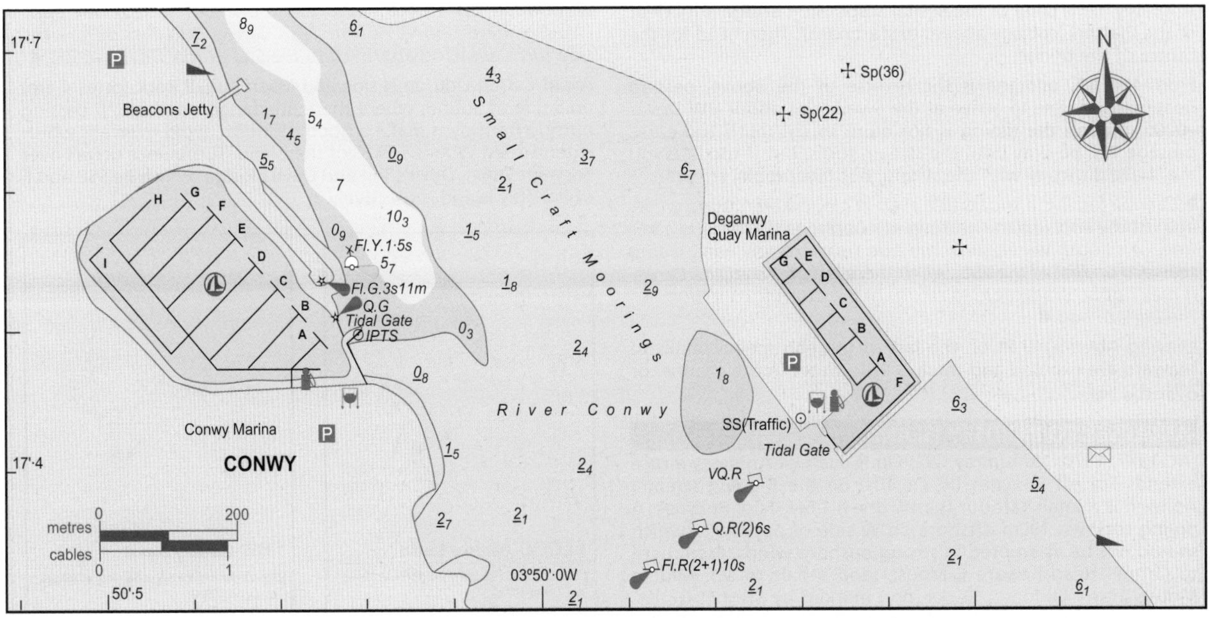

MENAI STRAIT

(AC 1464, Imray C52) From NE to SW the main features of this narrow, 16 mile channel are: Puffin Is, where the Strait begins at its North-East entrance; Beaumaris; Garth Pt at Bangor; Menai Suspension Bridge (29m); The Swellies, a narrow 1M stretch with strong tidal streams and dangers mid-stream; Britannia Bridge, both road and rail (26m), with cables close W at elevation of 21m; Port Dinorwic; Caernarfon; Abermenai Pt and Fort Belan, which mark the SW end of Strait; and Caernarfon Bar. The following brief notes cover only very basic pilotage. For detailed directions see the UKHO *West Coasts of England and Wales Pilot*, or *Cruising Anglesey and Adjoining Waters* by Ralph Morris.

►*The Swellies should be taken near local HW slack, and an understanding of tidal streams is essential. The tide is about 1hr later, and sp range about 2·7m more, at the NE end of the Strait than at the SW end. Levels differ most at 1hr after HW at the NE end where sea level is > 1·8m above the level at the SW end and at about 4¾hrs before HW at the NE end where sea level is >1·8m below the level at the SW end.*

Normally the stream runs as follows (referred to HW Dover).

Interval fm HW	*Direction*
–0110 to +0340	*SW between Garth Pt and Abermenai Pt.*
+0340 to +0510	*Outwards from The Swellies, (NE towards Garth Pt / SW towards Abermenai Pt)*
+0510 to -0110	*NE between Abermenai Pt and Garth Pt.*

See diagram on adjacent page.

Sp rates are generally about 3kn, ***but more in narrows, eg 5kn off Abermenai Pt, 6kn between the bridges, and 8kn through The Swellies.*** *Timings and rates of streams may be affected by strong winds in either direction and storm surges in the Irish Sea.*◄

Note: Direction of buoyage becomes NE off Caernarfon.

From SW to NE, aim to arrive at the Swellies early HW Dover –0300 to take the last of the E-going tidal stream to pass Menai bridge between HW Dover –0230 to –0200. Better to arrive too early, and wait, than too late and risk not making it through the narrows before the stream turns to the W. Approach the S arch of Britannia Bridge keeping the white pyramid in line with the centre of the arch. Once through the bridge run parallel to the shore until abeam the pyramid. At this point, look astern and keep the white leading marks (beneath the S arch of the bridge) in line. When Price's Point is abeam, turn to starboard to pass 20-30m S of Swelly Perch rock, then head just S of the Anglesey (ie N) pillar of the Menai Suspension Bridge until clear of the Platters (cottage abeam to starboard). Then head for the centre of the bridge.

From the NE, pilotage is the reverse of the above, passing Beaumaris in time to arrive at the Swellies at about HW Dover –0200, though the timing is not quite so critical. If too early, passage will be slow until the stream turns, but if too late you may have difficulty with the strong, but favourable, stream.

► *Caernarfon Bar is impassable even in moderately strong winds against the ebb, and the narrows at Abermenai Pt demand a fair tide, or slackish water, since the tide runs strongly here. Going seaward on first of the ebb, when there is water over the banks, it may not be practicable to return to the Strait if conditions on the bar are bad.*◄

Leaving Abermenai Pt on the last of the ebb means banks to seaward are exposed and there is little water in the channel or over the bar.

ANGLESEY TO BARDSEY ISLAND

(AC 1977, 1970, 1971 Imray C52) On N coast of Anglesey a race extends 5ca off Pt Lynas (lt, Oc 10s) on the E-going stream. Amlwch is a small harbour (partly dries) 1·5M W of Pt Lynas. A drying rock lies 100m offshore on W side of approach, which should not be attempted in strong onshore winds. From here to Carmel Head beware E Mouse (and shoals to SE), Middle Mouse, Harry Furlong's Rocks (dry) marked by SHM Fl G 2½s, Victoria Bank (least depth 1·8m) and W Mouse (with dangers to W & SW). Further offshore are the shoals of Archdeacon Rk, Coal Rk and Ethel Rk which lie in the red sector of Skerries Lt Ho. Cardinal buoys mark their position. The outermost of these dangers is 2M offshore. Overfalls and races occur at headlands and over the many rocks and shoals along this coast.

In good conditions by day and at slack water, Carmel Hd can be rounded close inshore following a track outside East Mouse, inshore of Middle & West Mouse, staying N of Furlong SHM and passing S of Victoria Bank. Short, steep seas break here in even moderate winds against tide and can be dangerous. The best passage at night or in bad weather, is to pass 1M off Skerries, in the TSS ITZ. Holyhead (port of refuge), is accessible H24 in all weathers. The marina is within New Harbour; beware fast ferries across the entrance and note the TSS.

►*Between Carmel Hd and The Skerries the NE-going stream begins at HW Dover +0530 (HW Holyhead +0615), and the SW-going at HW Dover –0045 (HW Holyhead +0005),* ***Sp rates 5kn.*** *1M NW of Skerries the stream turns 0130 later, running less strongly.* ***Flood and Ebb tides close to the coast runs at over 5k springs,*** *and at about 2.5kn 7M offshore. The brief period of slack water offshore is HW Dover –0100 and +0500. There is no significant counter tide in Holyhead Bay, where slack water lasts longer.*◄

►*Races occur off N Stack and S Stack. There is a severe and dangerous race off South Stack starting at HW-0600 on the flood* ***(Sp rate 5kn)*** *extending 8M to the Skerries and another dangerous race off Carmel Hd (Sp rate 6kn). Races are less extensive on SSW-going stream, which begins at HW Holyhead +0020,* ***(Sp rate 5kn).***◄

The W coast of Anglesey is rugged with rks, some drying, up to 1·5M offshore. Races run off Penrhyn Mawr and Rhoscolyn Hd, between which is Maen Piscar a dangerous, drying rock (1·2m).

►*A W-going eddy occurs E of Penrhyn Mawr during the SE-going stream and eddies form in Abraham's Bosom and Gogarth Bay.*◄

E of Llanddwyn Is, Pilot's Cove is a good ⚓ to await suitable conditions.

On the Lleyn Peninsula Porth Dinllaen is a good ⚓, but exposed to NW through N to SE. Braich y Pwll is the steep, rky point at end of Lleyn Peninsula (AC 1971). About 1M N of it and up to 1M offshore lie The Tripods, a bank on which there are overfalls and steep seas with wind against tide.

►*Bardsey Sound, 1·5M wide, can be used by day in moderate winds.* ***Stream reaches 8kn at Sp, and passage should be made at slack water,*** *which occurs about 2¼hrs after local high and low water: HW Dover –0100 (HW Holyhead –0010) going E, or westbound LW Dover –0100 (LW Holyhead +0030). An eddy ('Young flood') flows W from N of Carreg Ddu 2hrs before the tide turns allowing approach to the Snd at HW Dover +0500.*◄

Avoid Carreg Ddu on N side and Maen Bugail Rock (dries 4·1m) on S side of Sound, where there are dangerous races. If passing outside Bardsey Is make a good offing to avoid overfalls which extend 1·5M W and 2·5M S of the island. Turbulence occurs over Bastram Shoal, Devil's Tail and Devil's Ridge, which lie SSE and E of Bardsey Island respectively.

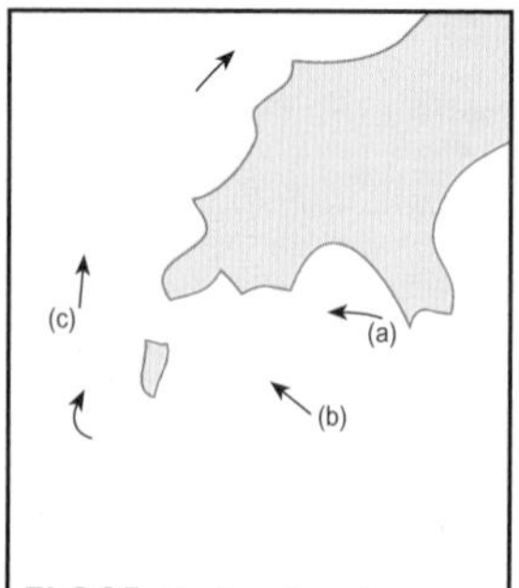

FLOOD Bardsey Sound

The tide turns to the NW or NE (flood) as follows:
(a): Dover +0300;
(b): Dover +0500;
(c): Dover +0600.
These times are approximate.

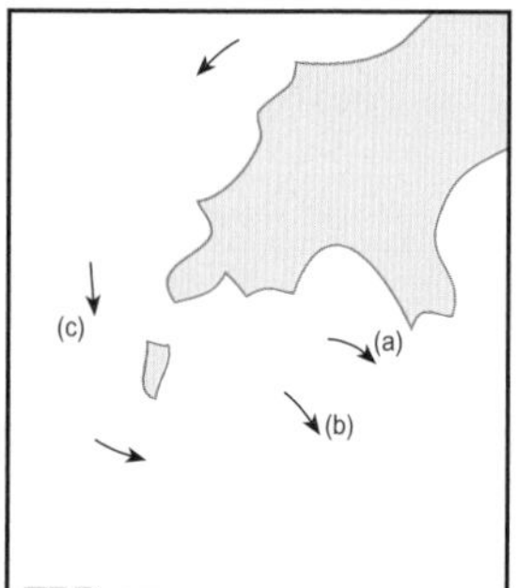

EBB Bardsey Sound

The tide turns to the SW or SE (ebb) as follows:
(a): Dover –0300;
(b): Dover –0100;
(c): Dover +0030.
These times are approximate.

NOTE: There is a strong eddy down tide off Bardsey Island and overfalls throughout the area.

FLOOD

(T): turning → : < 2k ➡ : 2-4k ➡ : 4k +

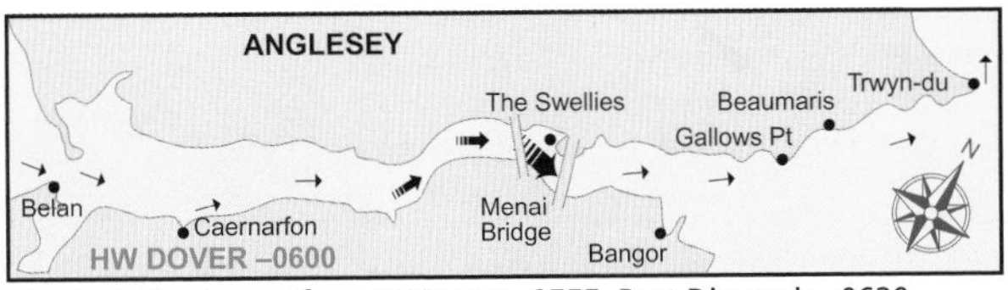

LOCAL LW: Caernarfon HW Dover –0555. Port Dinorwic –0620. Menai –0540. Beaumaris –0605.

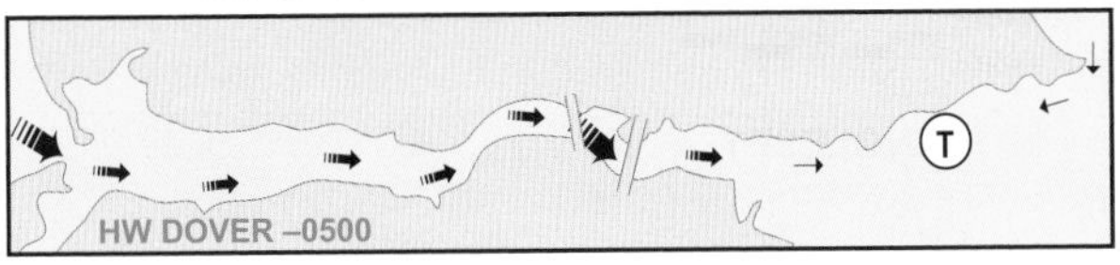

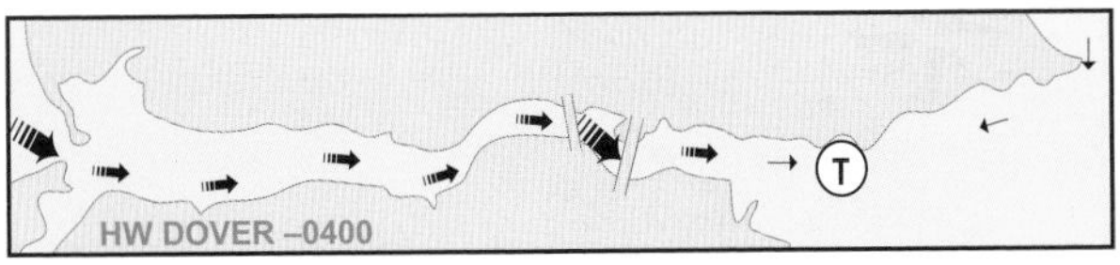

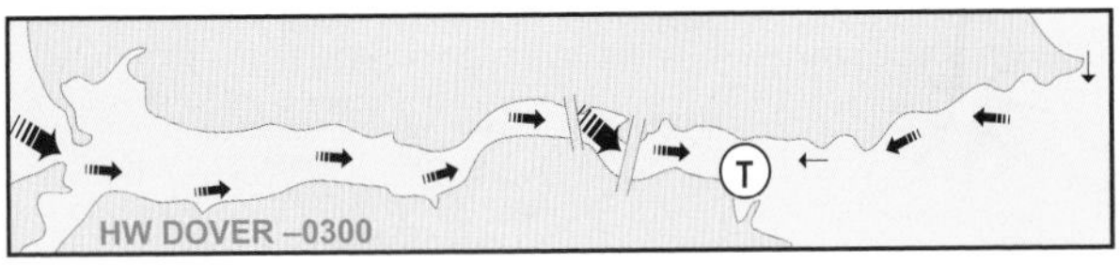

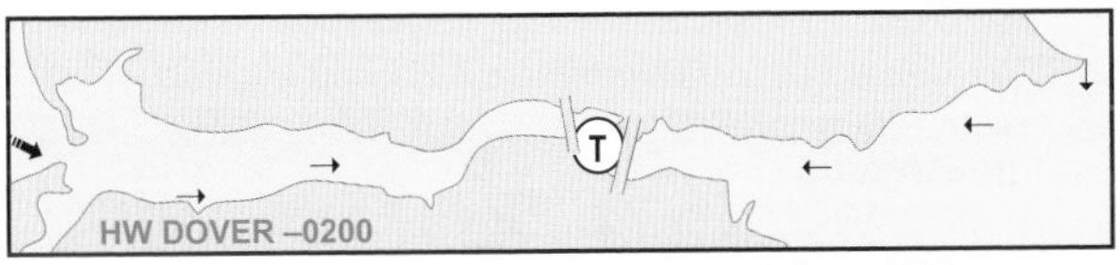

SLACK WATER IN THE SWELLIES: HW Dover –0200 to –0230.

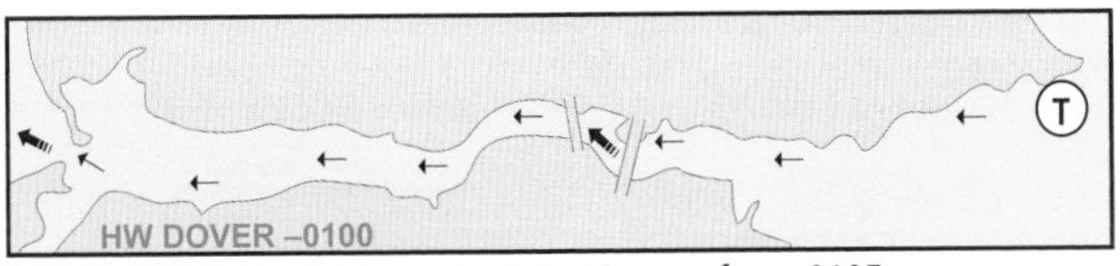

LOCAL HW: Belan: HW Dover –0115. Caernarfon: –0105. Port Dinorwic: –0050.

EBB

(T): turning → : < 2k ➡ : 2-4k ➡ : 4k +

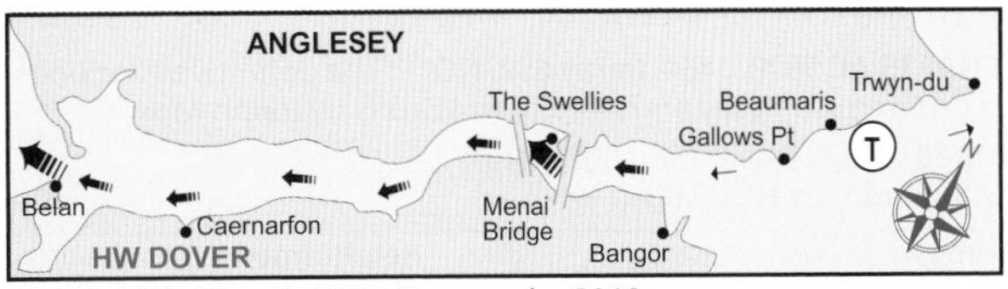

LOCAL HW: Menai –0005. Beaumaris –0010.

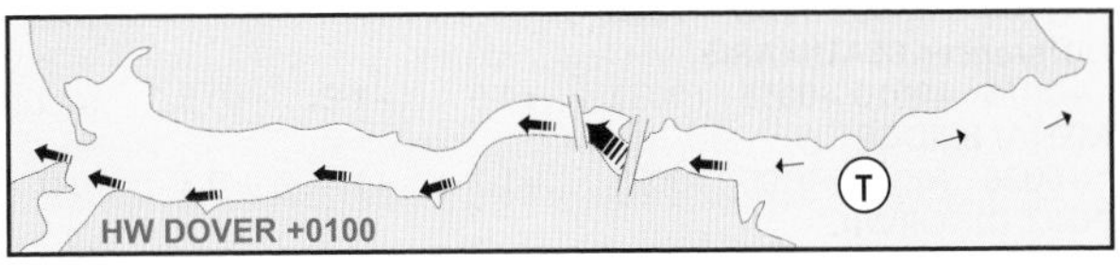

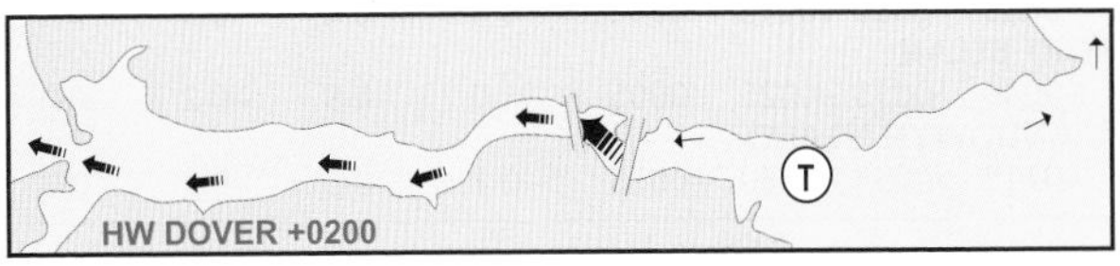

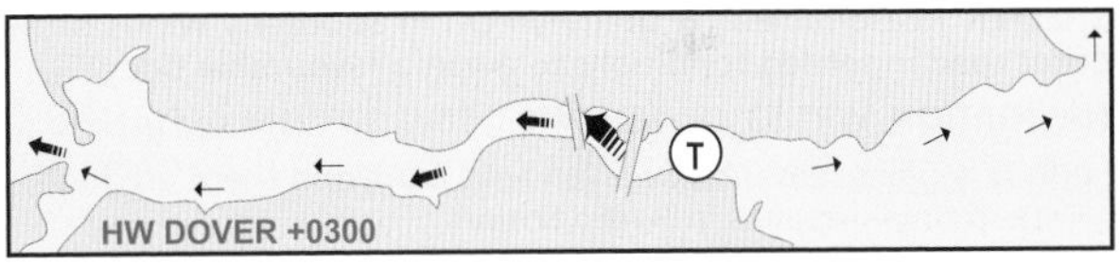

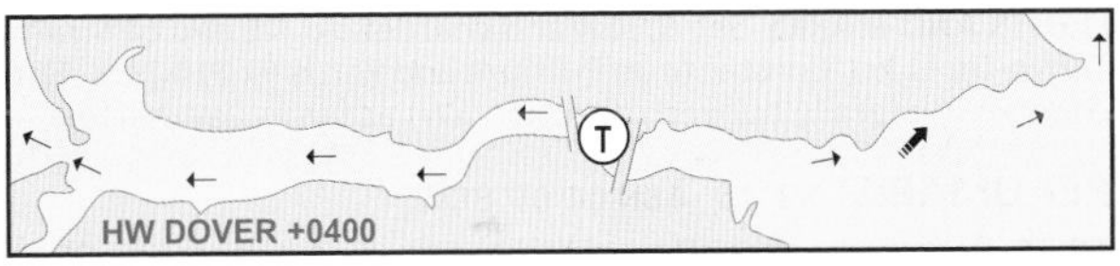

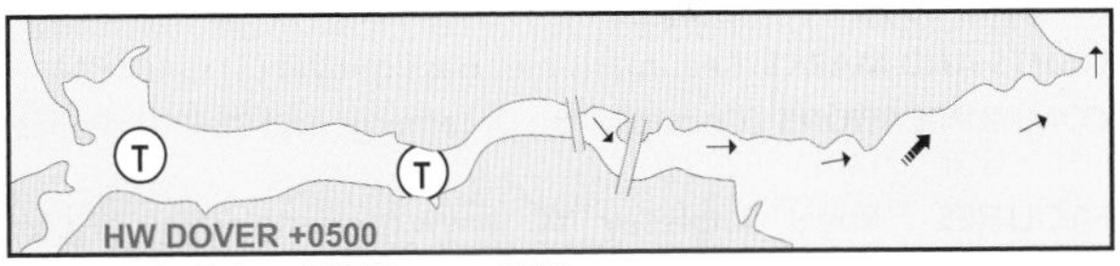

LOCAL LW: Belan: HW Dover +0520.

9.10.19 MENAI STRAIT

Gwynedd/Isle of Anglesey

CHARTS AC 5609, 1464, Imray C52. NOTE: The definitive Pilot book is *Cruising Anglesey and Adjoining Waters* by Ralph Morris.

TIDES −0035 Dover (Sp), 0020 (Np)

Standard Port HOLYHEAD (⟶)

Times				Height (metres)			
High Water		Low Water		MHWS	MHWN	MLWN	MLWS
0000	0600	0500	1100	5·6	4·4	2·0	0·7
1200	1800	1700	2300				
Differences BEAUMARIS							
+0025	+0010	+0055	+0035	+2·0	+1·6	+0·5	+0·1
MENAI BRIDGE							
+0030	+0010	+0100	+0035	+1·7	+1·4	+0·3	0·0
PORT DINORWIC							
−0015	−0025	+0030	0000	0·0	0·0	0·0	+0·1
CAERNARFON							
−0030	−0030	+0015	−0005	−0·4	−0·4	−0·1	−0·1
FORT BELAN							
−0040	−0015	−0025	−0005	−1·0	−0·9	−0·2	−0·1
LLANDDWYN ISLAND							
−0115	−0055	−0030	−0020	−0·7	−0·5	−0·1	0·0

NORTH EAST ENTRANCE

SHELTER Reasonable ⚓ N of Trwyn Du in Southerly winds or in outer road in settled conditions to await a favourable tide.

NAVIGATION WPT 53°19′·48N 04°03′·28W, 137°/1M to Perch Rk.

- In N'ly gales seas break on Ten Feet Bank and there are high, steep breaking seas in Puffin Sound.
- In N Strait keep to buoyed chan, nearer Anglesey taking care to avoid the SHM marking a wreck W of B1 SHM.

LIGHTS AND MARKS See 9.10.4 and chartlet. At NE end of Strait, Trwyn-Du Lt ho, Conspic tr on Puffin Is and Perch Rk PHM bn. The channel is laterally buoyed (direction SW) as far as Caernarfon.

BEAUMARIS 53°15′·66N 04°05′·38W

TIDES Beaumaris −0025 Dover; ML Beaumaris 4·2; Duration 0540

SHELTER Reasonable off Beaumaris except from NE winds. ⚓ S of B10 PHM buoy.

LIGHTS AND MARKS Beaumaris pier has light 2Fl (3) G 10s 6M.

COMMUNICATIONS (Code 01248); Dr (emergency) 384001; Police 101; CGOC (01407) 762051.

FACILITIES Royal Anglesey YC www.royalangleseyyc.org.uk ☎810295.

North West Venturers' YC, at Gallows Pt www.nwyc.org.uk.

Power Marine (20t) (2t).

Town (bus to Bangor), ✈ (Anglesey/Liverpool).

BANGOR 53°14′·46N 04°07′·58W

SHELTER Good, but open to winds from N to NE, at Dickies BY or Port Penrhyn dock. Dock and approaches dry approx 3m.

COMMUNICATIONS (Code 01248) Penrhyn HM ☎352525.

FACILITIES Dickies, Port Penrhyn, www.dickies.co.uk ☎363400, 5 £15/night, (30t).

Town (1M) ✈ (Anglesey/Liverpool).

MENAI BRIDGE 53°13′·20N 04°09′·79W

COMMUNICATIONS (Code 01248) Piermaster Menai Bridge 712312, mobile 07990 531595. At Menai Bridge, all moorings are private. Pier is owned and managed by Bangor University.

FACILITIES St George's Pier (Fl G 10s) at all tides.

The Marine Club, Porth Daniel, ☎717484.

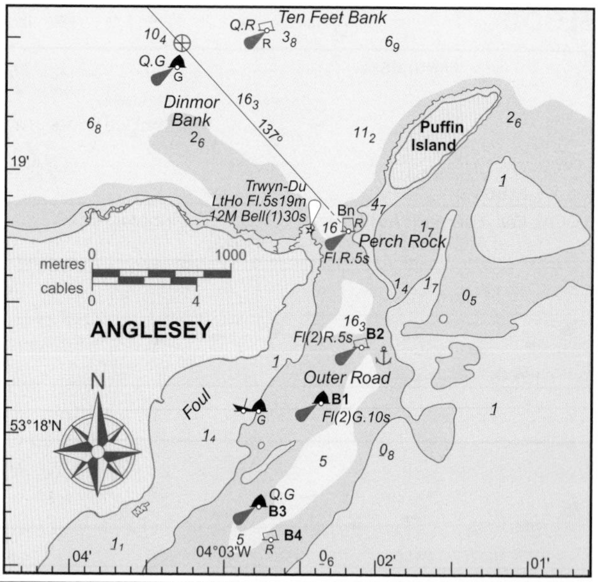

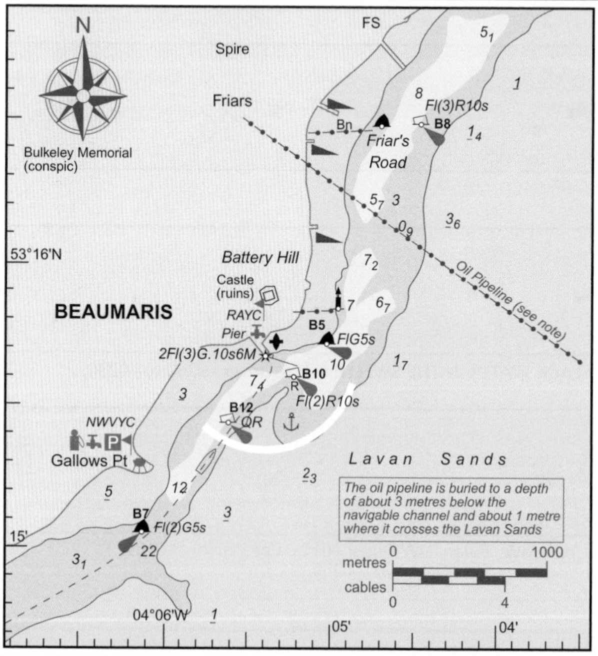

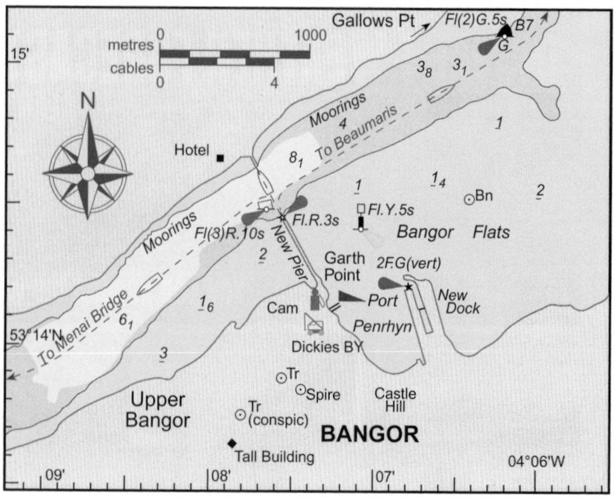

THE SWELLIES

NAVIGATION

- The passage should only be attempted at slack HW, which is –0145 HW Dover.
- The shallow rky narrows between the bridges may be dangerous for yachts at other times, when the stream can reach 8kn.
- At slack HW Sp there is 3m over The Platters and the outcrop off Price Pt, which can be ignored.
- For shoal-draught boats passage is also possible at slack LW Nps, when there are depths of 0·5m close E of Britannia Bridge.
- Bridges and power cables have a least clearance of 21m at MHWS.
- Night passage is not recommended.

LIGHTS AND MARKS See 9.10.4. and chartlet.
Britannia Bridge, E side ldg lts 231°, both FW. Br lts, both sides: Centre span Iso 5s 27m 3M; S end, FR 21m 3M; N end, FG 21m 3M.

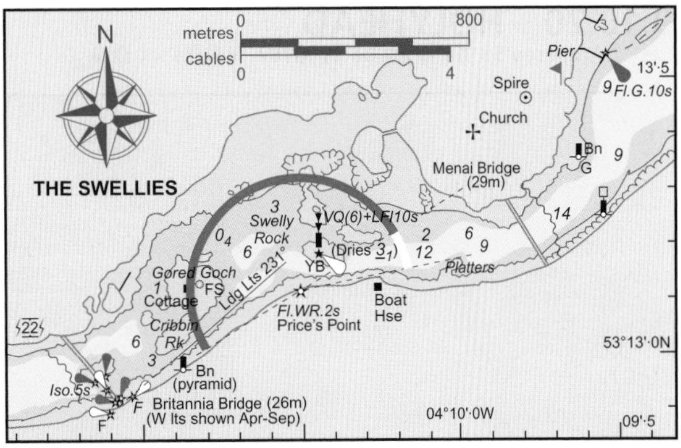

PORT DINORWIC/Y Felinheli 53°11'·20N 04°13'·70W

LIGHTS AND MARKS Pier Hd F WR 5m 2M, vis R225°- W357°-225°.

COMMUNICATIONS(Code 01248); Dr 670423. Marina 671500. *Dinorwic Marina* VHF Ch, Plas Menai Centre *Menai Base* Ch **80** M.

FACILITIES Port Dinorwic Marina portdinorwic.co.uk ☎671500; **Tidal basin** dries at Sp; lock (width 9·7m) opens HW±2. 180 (15t).

Dinas Boatyard ☎671642, all facilities.
Town (Bangor or Caernarfon), (Bangor), ✈ (Liverpool).
Plas Menai (between Port Dinorwic and Caernarfon), Sailing and Sports Centre ☎670964, day moorings only.

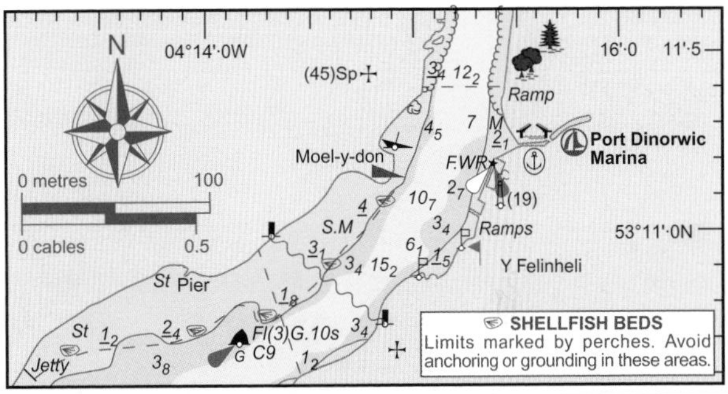

CAERNARFON 53°08'·51N 04°16'·83W

SHELTER Good in Victoria Dock Marina, access HW±2 via lifting sill, traffic lts (HO); pontoons at SW end in 2m, Ⓥ to starboard of ent. In river hbr (S of conspic castle) berth against wall, dries to mud/ gravel, access HW±3 via swing bridge; for opening sound B (–•••). ⚓ off Foel Ferry only with local knowledge; temp ⚓ off Abermenai Pt, sheltered from W, but strong streams. waiting 1½ca SW of C9.

COMMUNICATIONS (Code 01286) Police 101; Ⓗ 01248 384384; Dr (emergency) 01248 384001. HM 672118, Mobile 07786 730865. *Victoria Dock Marina* Ch **80**. *Caernarfon Hbr* Ch **14** 16 (HJ).

FACILITIES River £9·60<20'<£13·20<30'<£18 /craft.
Victoria Dock ☎672346, 46 £2·35.
Caernarfon SC ☎(01248) 672861.
Royal Welsh YC ☎(01248) 672599.

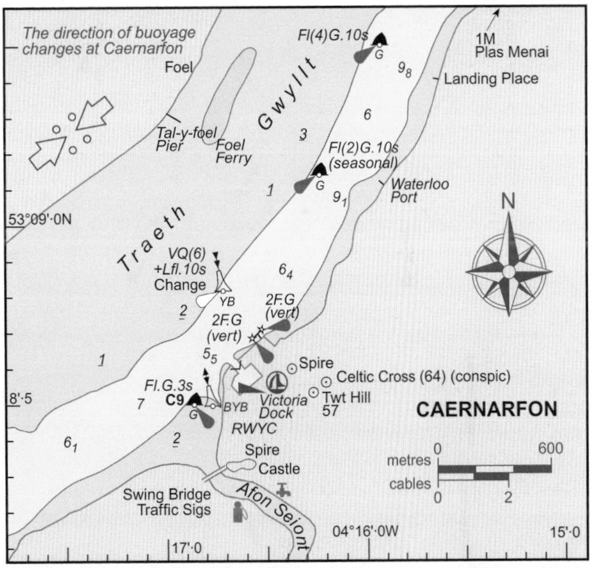

SOUTH WEST ENTRANCE – CAERNARFON BAR

NAVIGATION A dangerous sea can build in even a moderate breeze against tide, especially if a swell is running. Bar Chan should not be used at any time other than local HW-3 to HW+3. Caernarfon Bar shifts often and unpredictably see website at www.caernarfonharbour.org.uk.

Direction of buoyage changes to NE at Caernarfon.

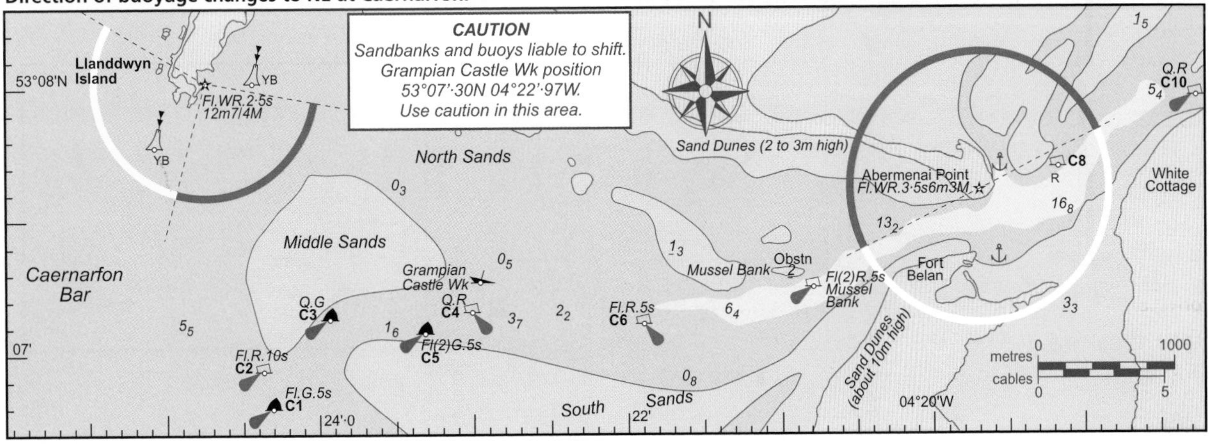

9.10.20 HOLYHEAD

Isle of Anglesey **53°19'·72N 04°37'·07W** ❁❁❁◊◊◊✿✿

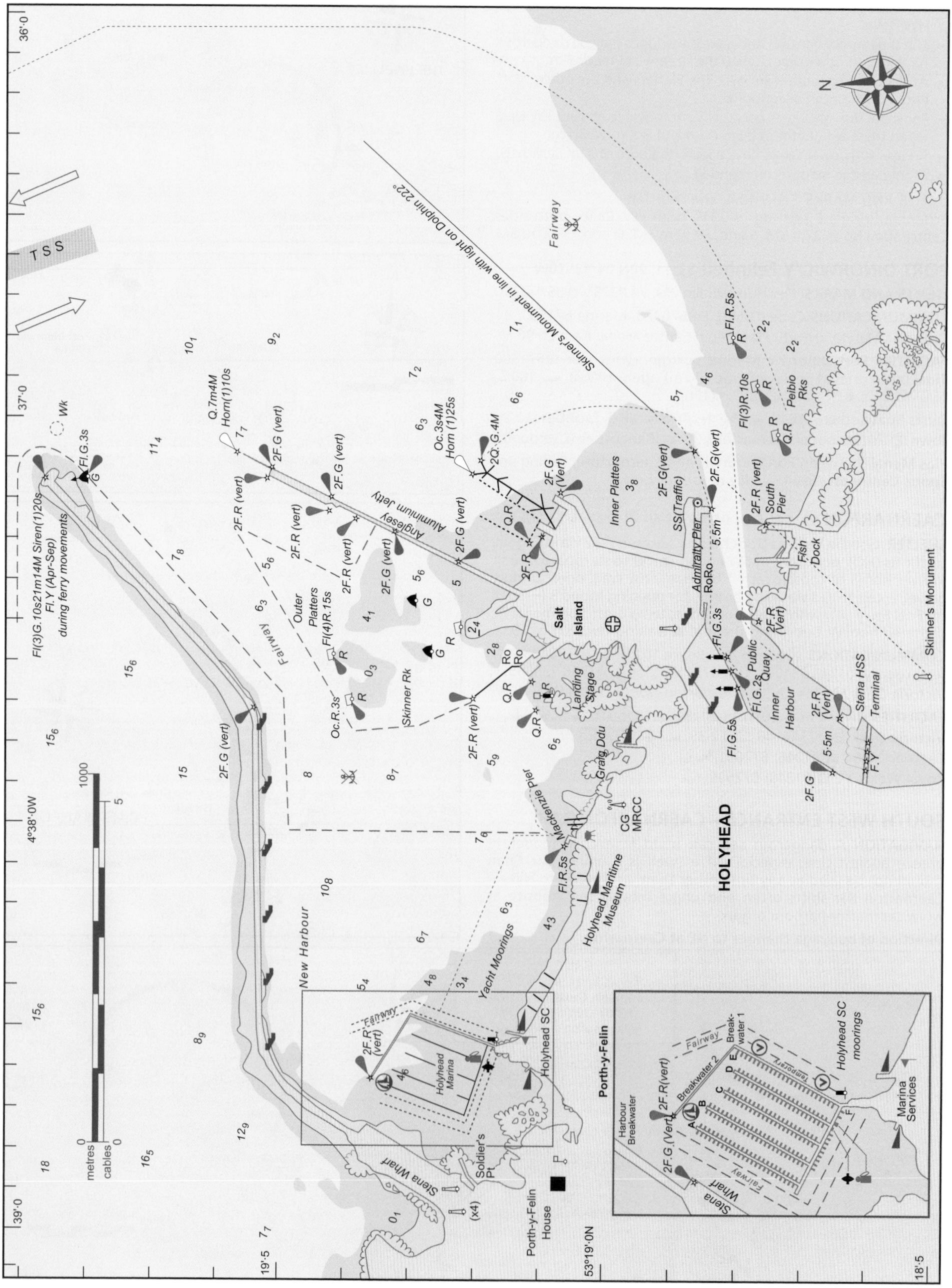

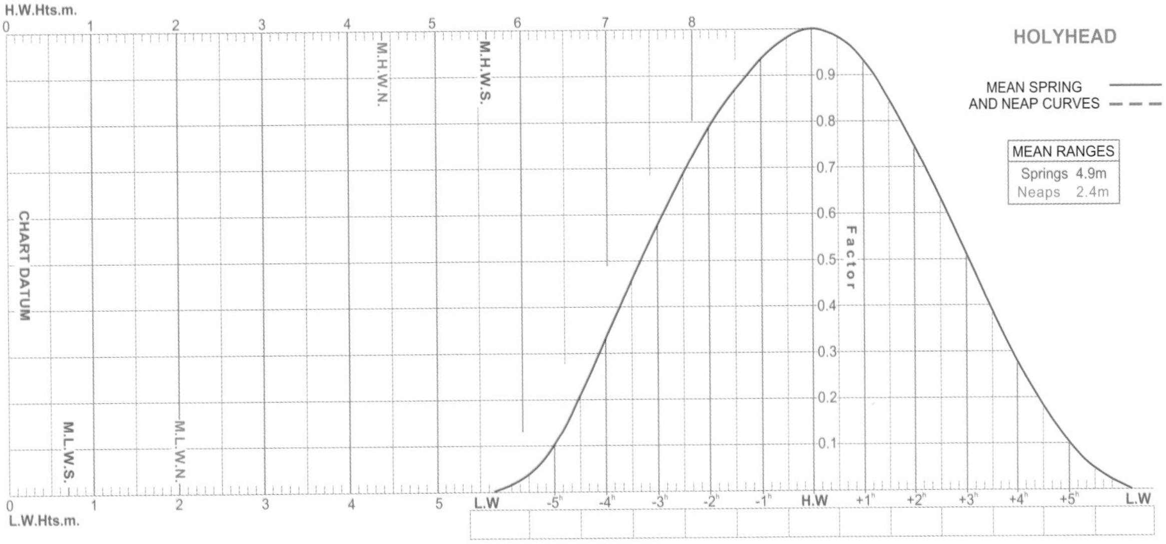

H.W.Hts.m.
L.W.Hts.m.
CHART DATUM
M.H.W.N.
M.H.W.S.
M.L.W.S.
M.L.W.N.
Factor
L.W -5h -4h -3h -2h -1h H.W +1h +2h +3h +4h +5h L.W
HOLYHEAD
MEAN SPRING AND NEAP CURVES
MEAN RANGES
Springs 4.9m
Neaps 2.4m

CHARTS AC 5609, 1826, 1970, 1977, 1413, 2011; Imray C61, C52

TIDES –0050 Dover; ML 3·2; Duration 0615

Standard Port HOLYHEAD (⟶)

Times				Height (metres)			
High Water		Low Water		MHWS	MHWN	MLWN	MLWS
0000	0600	0500	1100	5·6	4·4	2·0	0·7
1200	1800	1700	2300				
Differences TRWYN DINMOR (W of Puffin Is)							
+0025	+0015	+0050	+0035	+1·9	+1·5	+0·5	+0·2
MOELFRE (NE Anglesey)							
+0025	+0020	+0050	+0035	+1·9	+1·4	+0·5	+0·2
AMLWCH (N Anglesey)							
+0020	+0010	+0035	+0025	+1·6	+1·3	+0·5	+0·2
CEMAES BAY (N Anglesey)							
+0020	+0025	+0040	+0035	+1·0	+0·7	+0·3	+0·1
TREARDDUR BAY (W Anglesey)							
–0045	–0025	–0015	–0015	–0·4	–0·4	0·0	+0·1
PORTH TRECASTELL (SW Anglesey)							
–0045	–0025	–0005	–0015	–0·6	–0·6	0·0	0·0
TREFOR (Lleyn peninsula)							
–0115	–0100	–0030	–0020	–0·8	–0·9	–0·2	–0·1
PORTH DINLLAEN (Lleyn peninsula)							
–0120	–0105	–0035	–0025	–1·0	–1·0	–0·2	–0·2
PORTH YSGADEN (Lleyn peninsula)							
–0125	–0110	–0040	–0035	–1·1	–1·0	–0·1	–0·1
BARDSEY ISLAND							
–0220	–0240	–0145	–0140	–1·2	–1·2	–0·5	–0·1

SHELTER Accessible at all times. Good in marina, least depth 2m, and on YC moorings which are uncomfortable in strong NE-E winds. Temporary visitors' berths on E side of marina floating breakwater are exposed to the east. ⚓ not recommended – foul ground. Strong NW-NE winds raise an uncomfortable sea.

NAVIGATION WPT 53°20´·12N 04°37´·27W, 165°/0·28M to Bkwtr Lt ho. Small craft should leave Spit SHM buoy to starboard and maintain a safe distance from bkwtr to allow for obstns before heading for marina/moorings. Yachts should keep well clear of commercial shipping and the Outer Platters. Beware numerous fishing markers close to the breakwater. No ⚓ in the fairways.

Frequent HSS and Ro-Ro ferries to and from Ireland use inner hbr south of aluminium jetty and comply with a mini-TSS 100-500m off bkwtr hd.

LIGHTS AND MARKS Ldg marks 165°: bkwtr lt ho on with chy (127m, grey + B top; R lts); chy and Holyhead Mountain (218m) are conspic from afar. Cranes on aluminium jetty conspic closer to.

COMMUNICATIONS (Code 01407) CGOC 762051; Police 101; Dr via CGOC. Marina 764242; Port Control 763071.

Holyhead Marina and *Holyhead SC*: Ch **M**. Monitor *Holyhead* Ch 14 16 (H24) for ferry traffic. Broadcast of local nav info/warnings 1200 (UT) daily on Ch 14.

FACILITIES Marina www.holyheadmarina.co.uk, ☎764242; 500 + Ⓥ, £2·73, short stay £10/craft, (0800-1800) Ⓔ (15t) ✕ wi-fi.

Inner Hbr ☎762304, used by Stena HSS; not advised for yachts.

Holyhead SC (HSC) ☎762526; M £8.00, launch (call Ch M: 0900-2100, Fri/Sat to 2330) ✕.

Town Ⓑ ✕ ✈ (Anglesey/Liverpool). Ferry/HSS to Dun Laoghaire and Dublin.

MINOR HARBOURS (HW –0240 on Dover, see table (⟵)).
May be useful, in settled conditions only, on passage N, see Pl.

Trearddur Bay (3M south) **53°16´·66N 04°37´·50W.** AC 1970, 5609, Imray C52. (private, small craft only) or poss ⚓; open to prevailing SW'lies.

PORTH DINLLAEN, Gwynedd, **52°56´·68N 04°33´·66W**. AC 1971, 1512. Shelter good in S to W winds but strong NNW to NNE winds cause heavy seas in the bay. Beware Carreg-y-Chad (1·8m) 0·75M SW of the point, and Carreg-y-Chwislen (dries, with unlit IDM Bn) 2ca ENE of the point. From N, Garn Fadryn (369m) brg 182° leads into the bay. Best ⚓ 1ca S of LB ho in approx 2m.
HM ☎(01758) 720276. Facilities: by landing stage.
Morfa Nefyn (1M) ✕.

ABERDARON BAY, Gwynedd, **52°47´·75N 04°42´·82W**. AC 5609, 1410, 1411, 1971, 5609. In SE appr to bay are 2 islets Ynys Gwylan-fawr and Ynys Gwylan-bâch with a deep water passage between them, also passage between Ynys Gwylan-fawr and Trwyn Gwningaer (shore). ⚓ 4ca SSW of church in 5-10m, limited protection and subject to swell at times but sheltered in winds from W through N to NE. **Do not leave craft unattended due to poor holding ground.** Dinghy landing with care on shingle beach at Porth Simddy or Meudwy, W side of bay.
Village Limited facilities: ✕ ⇌ (Pwllheli).

BARDSEY ISLAND – YNYS ENNLI, Gwynedd, **52°45´·00N 04°47´·40W.** AC 5609, 1410, 1411, 1971. Island of historical interest with ruined abbey and religious settlement since 6th century (now a managed farm and nature reserve, see 9.0.3). ⚓ W of Pen Cristin in appr to Henllwyn Cove in 4m is sheltered in winds from WSW through N to NE but is subject to swell at times. Small craft may ⚓ in the cove with caution, but beware isolated rocks and shoals. Landing at jetty in rocks marked by small boathouse at top of slip.

STANDARD TIME (UT)
For Summer Time add ONE hour in **non-shaded areas**

HOLYHEAD LAT 53°19'N LONG 4°37'W

TIMES AND HEIGHTS OF HIGH AND LOW WATERS

Dates in red are SPRINGS
Dates in blue are NEAPS

YEAR **2018**

JANUARY

Date	Day	Time	m
1	M	0301	0.8
		0921	5.7
		1530	0.8
		2144	5.8
2	TU	0351	0.7
		1008	5.9
		1620	0.5
		○ 2234	5.9
3	W	0439	0.6
		1056	6.1
		1710	0.4
		2324	5.9
4	TH	0527	0.6
		1144	6.1
		1800	0.4
5	F	0014	5.8
		0615	0.7
		1233	6.0
		1850	0.5
6	SA	0104	5.6
		0704	1.0
		1322	5.8
		1942	0.8
7	SU	0156	5.3
		0755	1.2
		1414	5.6
		2037	1.1
8	M	0251	5.0
		0850	1.6
		1510	5.3
		◑ 2135	1.4
9	TU	0351	4.8
		0951	1.8
		1612	5.0
		2240	1.7
10	W	0459	4.6
		1100	2.0
		1722	4.8
		2346	1.8
11	TH	0610	4.6
		1211	2.1
		1834	4.7
12	F	0051	1.9
		0714	4.7
		1318	2.0
		1938	4.7
13	SA	0149	1.8
		0807	4.9
		1414	1.8
		2030	4.9
14	SU	0236	1.6
		0851	5.1
		1500	1.6
		2113	5.0
15	M	0317	1.5
		0928	5.2
		1538	1.5
		2150	5.1
16	TU	0352	1.4
		1002	5.4
		1613	1.3
		2223	5.2
17	W	0424	1.3
		1035	5.5
		1646	1.2
		● 2255	5.3
18	TH	0456	1.2
		1107	5.6
		1718	1.1
		2327	5.3
19	F	0529	1.2
		1140	5.6
		1752	1.1
20	SA	0001	5.3
		0602	1.2
		1215	5.6
		1826	1.1
21	SU	0036	5.2
		0637	1.3
		1251	5.5
		1902	1.2
22	M	0113	5.1
		0714	1.4
		1329	5.4
		1941	1.3
23	TU	0153	5.0
		0756	1.5
		1411	5.2
		2026	1.4
24	W	0239	4.8
		0845	1.7
		1500	5.1
		◐ 2119	1.5
25	TH	0336	4.7
		0946	1.8
		1601	4.9
		2224	1.7
26	F	0448	4.6
		1059	1.9
		1716	4.9
		2338	1.7
27	SA	0607	4.7
		1216	1.8
		1834	4.9
28	SU	0050	1.5
		0718	4.9
		1326	1.5
		1943	5.1
29	M	0154	1.3
		0817	5.3
		1427	1.1
		2043	5.4
30	TU	0250	1.0
		0909	5.6
		1521	0.8
		2136	5.6
31	W	0341	0.7
		0957	5.9
		1612	0.5
		○ 2225	5.8

FEBRUARY

Date	Day	Time	m
1	TH	0428	0.6
		1044	6.0
		1659	0.3
		2312	5.9
2	F	0513	0.5
		1129	6.1
		1746	0.3
		2357	5.8
3	SA	0558	0.5
		1214	6.1
		1831	0.4
4	SU	0042	5.6
		0641	0.7
		1259	5.9
		1916	0.6
5	M	0127	5.4
		0726	1.0
		1344	5.6
		2002	1.0
6	TU	0212	5.1
		0812	1.3
		1431	5.3
		2051	1.4
7	W	0300	4.8
		0904	1.7
		1522	4.9
		◑ 2146	1.7
8	TH	0357	4.5
		1005	2.0
		1625	4.6
		2253	2.0
9	F	0507	4.4
		1121	2.2
		1744	4.4
10	SA	0006	2.1
		0627	4.4
		1240	2.2
		1906	4.4
11	SU	0116	2.1
		0737	4.6
		1348	2.0
		2010	4.6
12	M	0213	1.9
		0828	4.8
		1440	1.7
		2056	4.8
13	TU	0257	1.6
		0909	5.1
		1520	1.5
		2134	5.0
14	W	0333	1.4
		0943	5.3
		1554	1.2
		2206	5.1
15	TH	0406	1.2
		1015	5.4
		1626	1.1
		● 2236	5.3
16	F	0437	1.1
		1047	5.6
		1657	0.9
		2307	5.3
17	SA	0508	0.9
		1119	5.7
		1729	0.8
		2339	5.4
18	SU	0541	0.9
		1153	5.7
		1802	0.8
19	M	0012	5.4
		0614	0.9
		1228	5.6
		1836	0.9
20	TU	0048	5.3
		0650	1.0
		1305	5.5
		1913	1.0
21	W	0126	5.2
		0730	1.2
		1345	5.4
		1955	1.1
22	TH	0208	5.0
		0816	1.4
		1431	5.2
		2045	1.4
23	F	0300	4.8
		0914	1.6
		1530	4.9
		◐ 2149	1.6
24	SA	0409	4.6
		1029	1.8
		1648	4.7
		2309	1.8
25	SU	0537	4.6
		1155	1.8
		1818	4.7
26	M	0032	1.7
		0659	4.8
		1313	1.5
		1936	5.0
27	TU	0143	1.4
		0805	5.1
		1418	1.1
		2037	5.2
28	W	0241	1.1
		0858	5.5
		1512	0.7
		2127	5.5

MARCH

Date	Day	Time	m
1	TH	0330	0.8
		0945	5.8
		1600	0.4
		2212	5.7
2	F	0414	0.5
		1028	6.0
		1643	0.2
		○ 2255	5.8
3	SA	0456	0.4
		1111	6.1
		1725	0.2
		2336	5.8
4	SU	0536	0.4
		1152	6.0
		1806	0.4
5	M	0016	5.6
		0616	0.6
		1234	5.8
		1846	0.6
6	TU	0055	5.4
		0656	0.8
		1314	5.5
		1926	1.0
7	W	0134	5.2
		0737	1.2
		1354	5.2
		2007	1.3
8	TH	0214	4.9
		0822	1.5
		1438	4.8
		2054	1.7
9	F	0302	4.6
		0915	1.9
		1532	4.5
		◑ 2153	2.1
10	SA	0404	4.4
		1025	2.2
		1649	4.2
		2312	2.3
11	SU	0526	4.2
		1153	2.3
		1826	4.2
12	M	0035	2.3
		0653	4.4
		1312	2.1
		1942	4.4
13	TU	0142	2.1
		0756	4.6
		1410	1.8
		2032	4.6
14	W	0230	1.8
		0840	4.9
		1452	1.5
		2110	4.9
15	TH	0308	1.5
		0916	5.2
		1527	1.2
		2142	5.1
16	F	0340	1.2
		0949	5.4
		1559	0.9
		2211	5.3
17	SA	0411	0.9
		1021	5.6
		1630	0.7
		● 2241	5.4
18	SU	0443	0.8
		1054	5.7
		1702	0.6
		2313	5.5
19	M	0516	0.7
		1128	5.7
		1735	0.6
		2347	5.5
20	TU	0551	0.7
		1204	5.7
		1811	0.6
21	W	0023	5.5
		0628	0.7
		1243	5.6
		1848	0.8
22	TH	0102	5.4
		0709	0.9
		1324	5.4
		1931	1.0
23	F	0146	5.2
		0757	1.1
		1413	5.2
		2022	1.3
24	SA	0238	4.9
		0856	1.4
		1514	4.9
		◐ 2128	1.7
25	SU	0347	4.7
		1014	1.7
		1637	4.6
		2253	1.9
26	M	0519	4.6
		1143	1.6
		1812	4.6
27	TU	0019	1.8
		0644	4.8
		1303	1.4
		1929	4.9
28	W	0132	1.5
		0751	5.1
		1407	1.0
		2027	5.2
29	TH	0228	1.2
		0843	5.4
		1459	0.7
		2114	5.4
30	F	0315	0.9
		0928	5.7
		1543	0.5
		2155	5.6
31	SA	0356	0.6
		1009	5.8
		1623	0.3
		○ 2234	5.7

APRIL

Date	Day	Time	m
1	SU	0435	0.5
		1049	5.9
		1702	0.4
		2311	5.7
2	M	0514	0.5
		1129	5.8
		1739	0.5
		2348	5.6
3	TU	0551	0.6
		1207	5.6
		1816	0.7
4	W	0024	5.4
		0628	0.8
		1245	5.4
		1852	1.0
5	TH	0101	5.2
		0707	1.1
		1322	5.1
		1930	1.4
6	F	0138	5.0
		0748	1.4
		1402	4.8
		2012	1.7
7	SA	0220	4.7
		0836	1.8
		1450	4.4
		2103	2.1
8	SU	0313	4.5
		0937	2.1
		1559	4.2
		◑ 2213	2.4
9	M	0427	4.3
		1059	2.2
		1732	4.1
		2342	2.4
10	TU	0554	4.3
		1223	2.1
		1859	4.3
11	W	0057	2.2
		0707	4.5
		1326	1.8
		1955	4.5
12	TH	0151	1.9
		0759	4.8
		1413	1.5
		2035	4.8
13	F	0232	1.5
		0840	5.1
		1451	1.2
		2109	5.1
14	SA	0307	1.2
		0915	5.3
		1525	0.9
		2140	5.3
15	SU	0341	0.9
		0950	5.5
		1558	0.7
		2213	5.5
16	M	0415	0.7
		1025	5.7
		1633	0.5
		● 2247	5.6
17	TU	0451	0.6
		1103	5.8
		1709	0.5
		2323	5.7
18	W	0529	0.5
		1142	5.8
		1748	0.5
19	TH	0002	5.6
		0610	0.6
		1225	5.7
		1829	0.7
20	F	0045	5.5
		0655	0.8
		1311	5.4
		1916	1.0
21	SA	0132	5.3
		0747	1.0
		1404	5.1
		2010	1.3
22	SU	0227	5.0
		0850	1.3
		1509	4.8
		◐ 2118	1.7
23	M	0338	4.8
		1009	1.5
		1634	4.6
		2241	1.9
24	TU	0505	4.7
		1132	1.5
		1803	4.7
25	W	0004	1.8
		0626	4.8
		1247	1.3
		1915	4.9
26	TH	0113	1.5
		0731	5.1
		1349	1.0
		2010	5.1
27	F	0209	1.3
		0823	5.3
		1439	0.8
		2055	5.3
28	SA	0255	1.0
		0908	5.5
		1522	0.6
		2134	5.4
29	SU	0336	0.8
		0948	5.6
		1601	0.6
		2211	5.5
30	M	0414	0.7
		1027	5.6
		1637	0.6
		○ 2247	5.6

Chart Datum: 3·05 metres below Ordnance Datum (Newlyn). HAT is 6·3 metres above Chart Datum.

STANDARD TIME (UT)
For Summer Time add ONE hour in **non-shaded areas**

HOLYHEAD LAT 53°19′N LONG 4°37′W

TIMES AND HEIGHTS OF HIGH AND LOW WATERS

Dates in red are SPRINGS
Dates in blue are NEAPS

YEAR **2018**

MAY

Date	Day	Time	m	Time	m	Time	m	Time	m
1	TU	0452	0.7	1105	5.5	1713	0.7	2323	5.5
2	W	0528	0.8	1143	5.4	1748	0.9	2358	5.4
3	TH	0605	0.9	1219	5.2	1823	1.1		
4	F	0032	5.3	0642	1.1	1255	5.0	1859	1.4
5	SA	0109	5.1	0722	1.4	1334	4.8	1939	1.7
6	SU	0149	4.9	0806	1.6	1419	4.5	2026	2.0
7	M	0236	4.6	0900	1.9	1517	4.3	2125	2.2
8	TU	0338	4.5	1007	2.0	1636	4.2	◑ 2239	2.3
9	W	0455	4.4	1123	2.0	1758	4.2	2357	2.2
10	TH	0609	4.5	1231	1.8	1903	4.5		
11	F	0059	2.0	0708	4.7	1324	1.5	1950	4.7
12	SA	0148	1.6	0756	5.0	1408	1.2	2030	5.0
13	SU	0229	1.3	0838	5.2	1448	0.9	2107	5.3
14	M	0308	1.0	0918	5.5	1526	0.7	2143	5.5
15	TU	0347	0.7	0958	5.6	1605	0.5	● 2222	5.6
16	W	0428	0.5	1040	5.8	1646	0.5	2302	5.7
17	TH	0511	0.5	1124	5.8	1729	0.5	2346	5.7
18	F	0557	0.5	1212	5.7	1816	0.7		
19	SA	0032	5.6	0647	0.6	1303	5.4	1906	1.0
20	SU	0124	5.4	0743	0.8	1400	5.2	2003	1.3
21	M	0221	5.2	0846	1.1	1506	4.9	2109	1.6
22	TU	0329	5.0	0958	1.3	1623	4.7	◐ 2224	1.7
23	W	0446	4.9	1113	1.3	1741	4.7	2339	1.7
24	TH	0600	4.9	1223	1.2	1850	4.8		
25	F	0047	1.6	0706	5.0	1324	1.1	1946	5.0
26	SA	0145	1.4	0800	5.1	1415	1.0	2032	5.1
27	SU	0234	1.2	0847	5.2	1459	0.9	2112	5.3
28	M	0316	1.1	0928	5.3	1539	0.9	2149	5.4
29	TU	0355	1.0	1007	5.3	1615	0.9	○ 2225	5.4
30	W	0433	0.9	1045	5.3	1650	1.0	2300	5.4
31	TH	0509	1.0	1122	5.2	1724	1.1	2335	5.4

JUNE

Date	Day	Time	m	Time	m	Time	m	Time	m
1	F	0545	1.1	1157	5.1	1759	1.2		
2	SA	0009	5.3	0621	1.2	1233	5.0	1834	1.4
3	SU	0046	5.2	0659	1.3	1311	4.8	1913	1.6
4	M	0124	5.0	0741	1.5	1353	4.6	1956	1.8
5	TU	0208	4.9	0828	1.7	1442	4.5	2046	2.0
6	W	0259	4.7	0923	1.8	1542	4.3	◑ 2146	2.1
7	TH	0401	4.6	1025	1.8	1654	4.3	2255	2.1
8	F	0510	4.6	1131	1.7	1802	4.4		
9	SA	0002	2.0	0614	4.7	1232	1.6	1900	4.7
10	SU	0100	1.7	0711	4.9	1325	1.3	1950	4.9
11	M	0151	1.4	0801	5.1	1413	1.0	2034	5.2
12	TU	0238	1.1	0849	5.4	1458	0.8	2117	5.4
13	W	0324	0.8	0935	5.6	1543	0.6	● 2201	5.6
14	TH	0410	0.6	1023	5.7	1629	0.5	2246	5.8
15	F	0458	0.4	1112	5.7	1716	0.5	2333	5.8
16	SA	0548	0.4	1202	5.7	1805	0.7		
17	SU	0022	5.8	0640	0.5	1255	5.5	1856	0.9
18	M	0115	5.6	0735	0.6	1351	5.3	1951	1.1
19	TU	0210	5.4	0834	0.9	1452	5.0	2051	1.4
20	W	0311	5.2	0938	1.1	1558	4.8	◐ 2157	1.6
21	TH	0418	5.0	1045	1.3	1708	4.7	2307	1.7
22	F	0528	4.9	1151	1.4	1816	4.7		
23	SA	0014	1.7	0635	4.9	1254	1.4	1916	4.8
24	SU	0117	1.6	0735	4.9	1349	1.4	2008	4.9
25	M	0212	1.5	0827	5.0	1437	1.3	2051	5.1
26	TU	0259	1.4	0911	5.0	1519	1.2	2130	5.2
27	W	0340	1.2	0952	5.1	1556	1.2	2207	5.3
28	TH	0417	1.2	1029	5.1	1631	1.2	○ 2241	5.4
29	F	0453	1.1	1104	5.1	1705	1.2	2315	5.4
30	SA	0527	1.1	1138	5.1	1738	1.2	2349	5.4

JULY

Date	Day	Time	m	Time	m	Time	m	Time	m
1	SU	0602	1.1	1212	5.0	1813	1.3		
2	M	0024	5.3	0638	1.2	1249	4.9	1849	1.4
3	TU	0102	5.2	0716	1.3	1327	4.8	1928	1.6
4	W	0142	5.1	0757	1.4	1409	4.7	2012	1.7
5	TH	0226	4.9	0843	1.5	1457	4.6	2102	1.9
6	F	0316	4.8	0936	1.6	1555	4.5	◑ 2202	2.0
7	SA	0415	4.7	1037	1.7	1703	4.5	2309	1.9
8	SU	0523	4.7	1142	1.6	1812	4.6		
9	M	0016	1.8	0630	4.8	1246	1.4	1913	4.8
10	TU	0118	1.5	0731	5.0	1343	1.2	2007	5.1
11	W	0214	1.2	0828	5.3	1436	1.0	2057	5.4
12	TH	0306	0.9	0920	5.5	1527	0.8	2145	5.6
13	F	0357	0.6	1011	5.7	1615	0.6	● 2232	5.8
14	SA	0447	0.4	1101	5.7	1704	0.5	2320	5.9
15	SU	0537	0.3	1151	5.7	1752	0.6		
16	M	0009	6.0	0627	0.3	1242	5.6	1841	0.7
17	TU	0059	5.8	0718	0.5	1333	5.4	1931	0.9
18	W	0150	5.6	0811	0.7	1425	5.1	2025	1.2
19	TH	0244	5.4	0907	1.1	1522	4.9	◐ 2123	1.5
20	F	0343	5.1	1008	1.4	1625	4.7	2228	1.7
21	SA	0449	4.8	1113	1.6	1734	4.6	2338	1.9
22	SU	0601	4.7	1219	1.7	1843	4.6		
23	M	0048	1.9	0711	4.6	1322	1.7	1943	4.7
24	TU	0151	1.8	0810	4.7	1416	1.6	2032	4.9
25	W	0243	1.6	0858	4.8	1501	1.5	2113	5.1
26	TH	0326	1.4	0938	4.9	1540	1.4	2150	5.2
27	F	0403	1.3	1014	5.0	1614	1.3	○ 2223	5.4
28	SA	0436	1.1	1046	5.1	1646	1.2	2256	5.4
29	SU	0508	1.1	1118	5.1	1718	1.2	2328	5.5
30	M	0541	1.0	1150	5.1	1751	1.2		
31	TU	0002	5.5	0614	1.1	1224	5.1	1824	1.2

AUGUST

Date	Day	Time	m	Time	m	Time	m	Time	m
1	W	0038	5.4	0649	1.1	1300	5.0	1900	1.3
2	TH	0114	5.3	0725	1.2	1337	4.9	1939	1.5
3	F	0153	5.2	0806	1.3	1419	4.8	2024	1.6
4	SA	0238	5.0	0853	1.5	1509	4.7	◑ 2118	1.8
5	SU	0332	4.9	0951	1.6	1612	4.6	2225	1.9
6	M	0440	4.7	1101	1.7	1729	4.6	2341	1.8
7	TU	0558	4.8	1215	1.6	1845	4.8		
8	W	0054	1.6	0712	4.9	1323	1.4	1948	5.0
9	TH	0159	1.3	0815	5.2	1422	1.1	2043	5.4
10	F	0255	0.9	0910	5.4	1515	0.9	2132	5.7
11	SA	0346	0.5	1000	5.7	1603	0.6	● 2219	5.9
12	SU	0435	0.3	1048	5.8	1649	0.5	2305	6.1
13	M	0522	0.2	1134	5.8	1735	0.5	2351	6.1
14	TU	0608	0.2	1220	5.7	1820	0.6		
15	W	0037	6.0	0654	0.4	1306	5.5	1905	0.8
16	TH	0123	5.7	0741	0.8	1352	5.2	1953	1.1
17	F	0211	5.4	0830	1.1	1441	5.0	2044	1.5
18	SA	0303	5.0	0924	1.5	1537	4.7	◐ 2145	1.8
19	SU	0405	4.7	1028	1.9	1644	4.5	2258	2.1
20	M	0521	4.4	1141	2.1	1802	4.5		
21	TU	0017	2.1	0645	4.4	1253	2.1	1915	4.6
22	W	0129	2.0	0753	4.5	1354	1.9	2011	4.8
23	TH	0225	1.7	0843	4.7	1442	1.7	2054	5.0
24	F	0308	1.5	0922	4.9	1520	1.5	2129	5.2
25	SA	0343	1.3	0955	5.1	1553	1.3	2201	5.4
26	SU	0414	1.1	1025	5.2	1623	1.2	○ 2232	5.5
27	M	0444	1.0	1054	5.3	1654	1.1	2304	5.6
28	TU	0515	0.9	1125	5.3	1725	1.0	2336	5.6
29	W	0547	0.9	1157	5.3	1758	1.0		
30	TH	0010	5.6	0619	0.9	1231	5.3	1832	1.1
31	F	0046	5.5	0653	1.1	1307	5.2	1909	1.3

Chart Datum: 3·05 metres below Ordnance Datum (Newlyn). HAT is 6·3 metres above Chart Datum.

STANDARD TIME (UT)
For Summer Time add ONE hour in **non-shaded areas**

HOLYHEAD LAT 53°19′N LONG 4°37′W

TIMES AND HEIGHTS OF HIGH AND LOW WATERS

Dates in red are SPRINGS
Dates in blue are NEAPS

YEAR **2018**

SEPTEMBER

Date	Day	Time	m	Time	m	Time	m	Time	m
1	SA	0124	5.3	0732	1.2	1346	5.0	1952	1.5
2	SU	0207	5.1	0818	1.4	1434	4.9	2045	1.7
3	M	0300	4.9	0915	1.7	1535	4.7	◑ 2154	1.9
4	TU	0411	4.7	1030	1.8	1658	4.6	2319	1.9
5	W	0541	4.7	1155	1.8	1825	4.8		
6	TH	0040	1.7	0703	4.9	1310	1.6	1934	5.1
7	F	0149	1.3	0808	5.2	1411	1.3	2029	5.4
8	SA	0245	0.8	0901	5.5	1502	0.9	2117	5.8
9	SU	0333	0.5	0947	5.7	1548	0.7	● 2202	6.0
10	M	0418	0.3	1030	5.8	1631	0.5	2245	6.1
11	TU	0501	0.2	1113	5.9	1713	0.5	2328	6.1
12	W	0543	0.3	1154	5.8	1755	0.6		
13	TH	0011	6.0	0625	0.5	1236	5.6	1837	0.8
14	F	0054	5.7	0707	0.9	1317	5.3	1920	1.1
15	SA	0138	5.3	0751	1.3	1400	5.0	2007	1.5
16	SU	0224	4.9	0839	1.7	1449	4.8	◐ 2102	1.9
17	M	0320	4.6	0938	2.1	1551	4.5	2213	2.2
18	TU	0437	4.3	1055	2.3	1712	4.4	2340	2.3
19	W	0613	4.3	1217	2.4	1837	4.5		
20	TH	0058	2.1	0729	4.4	1325	2.2	1940	4.7
21	F	0157	1.9	0820	4.7	1415	1.9	2025	5.0
22	SA	0240	1.6	0858	4.9	1454	1.6	2102	5.2
23	SU	0315	1.3	0929	5.1	1526	1.4	2133	5.4
24	M	0345	1.1	0958	5.3	1556	1.2	2204	5.6
25	TU	0415	0.9	1026	5.4	1627	1.0	○ 2236	5.7
26	W	0445	0.8	1057	5.5	1658	0.9	2309	5.7
27	TH	0517	0.8	1129	5.5	1731	0.9	2343	5.7
28	F	0550	0.8	1203	5.5	1807	1.0		
29	SA	0020	5.6	0625	1.0	1240	5.4	1845	1.1
30	SU	0100	5.4	0705	1.2	1321	5.2	1930	1.4

OCTOBER

Date	Day	Time	m	Time	m	Time	m	Time	m
1	M	0145	5.2	0753	1.5	1410	5.0	2025	1.6
2	TU	0241	4.9	0853	1.8	1514	4.8	◑ 2139	1.8
3	W	0358	4.7	1013	2.0	1640	4.7	2308	1.8
4	TH	0535	4.7	1142	2.0	1810	4.8		
5	F	0030	1.6	0657	4.9	1258	1.7	1919	5.2
6	SA	0137	1.2	0759	5.2	1358	1.4	2014	5.5
7	SU	0231	0.8	0848	5.5	1447	1.0	2100	5.8
8	M	0317	0.6	0930	5.7	1530	0.8	2143	6.0
9	TU	0358	0.4	1010	5.8	1610	0.6	● 2224	6.1
10	W	0438	0.4	1049	5.9	1650	0.6	2305	6.0
11	TH	0517	0.5	1128	5.8	1730	0.7	2346	5.8
12	F	0556	0.7	1206	5.6	1810	0.9		
13	SA	0026	5.6	0634	1.1	1245	5.4	1851	1.2
14	SU	0107	5.2	0714	1.4	1324	5.2	1934	1.6
15	M	0149	4.9	0758	1.8	1408	4.9	2025	1.9
16	TU	0239	4.6	0850	2.2	1502	4.6	◐ 2128	2.2
17	W	0349	4.3	1000	2.5	1616	4.5	2251	2.3
18	TH	0524	4.2	1128	2.6	1742	4.5		
19	F	0013	2.2	0648	4.4	1243	2.4	1854	4.7
20	SA	0116	2.0	0744	4.6	1337	2.1	1946	4.9
21	SU	0202	1.7	0824	4.9	1418	1.8	2025	5.2
22	M	0239	1.4	0857	5.1	1453	1.5	2100	5.4
23	TU	0311	1.1	0927	5.4	1525	1.2	2133	5.6
24	W	0343	0.9	0957	5.5	1558	1.0	○ 2207	5.8
25	TH	0415	0.8	1028	5.6	1631	0.9	2242	5.8
26	F	0448	0.7	1103	5.7	1707	0.8	2319	5.8
27	SA	0525	0.8	1140	5.7	1746	0.9	2359	5.7
28	SU	0604	0.9	1220	5.6	1829	1.0		
29	M	0043	5.5	0647	1.2	1305	5.4	1918	1.3
30	TU	0134	5.3	0738	1.5	1357	5.2	2017	1.5
31	W	0235	5.0	0841	1.8	1503	5.0	◑ 2132	1.7

NOVEMBER

Date	Day	Time	m	Time	m	Time	m	Time	m
1	TH	0355	4.7	1001	2.0	1626	4.9	2257	1.7
2	F	0526	4.7	1126	2.0	1751	5.0		
3	SA	0014	1.5	0642	4.9	1240	1.8	1859	5.2
4	SU	0119	1.2	0742	5.2	1339	1.5	1954	5.5
5	M	0212	0.9	0829	5.4	1428	1.2	2041	5.7
6	TU	0257	0.8	0910	5.6	1511	1.0	2123	5.8
7	W	0338	0.7	0949	5.7	1551	0.8	● 2204	5.9
8	TH	0416	0.7	1026	5.8	1631	0.8	2244	5.8
9	F	0453	0.8	1104	5.7	1709	0.9	2324	5.6
10	SA	0530	1.0	1141	5.6	1748	1.1		
11	SU	0002	5.4	0606	1.2	1218	5.5	1827	1.3
12	M	0041	5.2	0644	1.5	1255	5.3	1908	1.6
13	TU	0120	4.9	0724	1.8	1335	5.1	1953	1.8
14	W	0205	4.6	0811	2.2	1422	4.8	2047	2.1
15	TH	0303	4.4	0908	2.4	1523	4.6	◐ 2154	2.2
16	F	0421	4.3	1022	2.6	1638	4.6	2311	2.2
17	SA	0544	4.3	1142	2.5	1753	4.6		
18	SU	0019	2.0	0650	4.5	1245	2.3	1853	4.8
19	M	0112	1.8	0739	4.8	1334	2.0	1942	5.1
20	TU	0156	1.5	0818	5.1	1415	1.6	2023	5.3
21	W	0234	1.2	0853	5.3	1453	1.3	2101	5.5
22	TH	0310	1.0	0927	5.5	1530	1.1	2139	5.7
23	F	0347	0.9	1003	5.7	1608	0.9	○ 2219	5.8
24	SA	0425	0.8	1041	5.8	1649	0.8	2301	5.8
25	SU	0506	0.8	1122	5.8	1732	0.8	2345	5.8
26	M	0549	0.9	1206	5.8	1820	0.9		
27	TU	0034	5.6	0637	1.1	1255	5.6	1912	1.1
28	W	0128	5.3	0730	1.4	1349	5.4	2013	1.3
29	TH	0229	5.1	0832	1.7	1452	5.2	2122	1.4
30	F	0343	4.9	0944	1.9	1607	5.1	◑ 2237	1.5

DECEMBER

Date	Day	Time	m	Time	m	Time	m	Time	m
1	SA	0503	4.8	1101	1.9	1723	5.1	2349	1.5
2	SU	0617	4.9	1212	1.8	1833	5.2		
3	M	0053	1.3	0717	5.1	1315	1.6	1932	5.3
4	TU	0149	1.2	0808	5.3	1408	1.4	2022	5.4
5	W	0237	1.1	0851	5.4	1454	1.2	2107	5.5
6	TH	0319	1.0	0930	5.6	1536	1.1	2148	5.6
7	F	0357	1.0	1008	5.6	1616	1.1	● 2228	5.5
8	SA	0434	1.1	1045	5.7	1654	1.1	2306	5.4
9	SU	0510	1.2	1121	5.6	1731	1.2	2343	5.3
10	M	0545	1.3	1156	5.5	1808	1.3		
11	TU	0019	5.2	0620	1.5	1232	5.4	1846	1.5
12	W	0057	5.0	0658	1.7	1309	5.2	1926	1.6
13	TH	0136	4.8	0739	1.9	1351	5.1	2012	1.8
14	F	0223	4.6	0826	2.2	1439	4.9	2104	2.0
15	SA	0319	4.5	0923	2.3	1538	4.7	◐ 2204	2.1
16	SU	0429	4.4	1030	2.4	1646	4.7	2310	2.0
17	M	0542	4.5	1140	2.3	1753	4.8		
18	TU	0013	1.9	0643	4.6	1242	2.1	1853	4.9
19	W	0108	1.7	0735	4.9	1334	1.8	1945	5.1
20	TH	0156	1.4	0820	5.2	1421	1.5	2032	5.4
21	F	0241	1.2	0901	5.4	1506	1.2	2117	5.6
22	SA	0324	0.9	0943	5.7	1550	0.9	○ 2202	5.7
23	SU	0408	0.8	1025	5.8	1636	0.7	2248	5.8
24	M	0452	0.7	1110	5.9	1723	0.6	2336	5.8
25	TU	0539	0.8	1156	5.9	1813	0.6		
26	W	0026	5.7	0628	0.9	1246	5.9	1905	0.7
27	TH	0119	5.5	0719	1.1	1338	5.7	2001	0.9
28	F	0216	5.3	0816	1.4	1435	5.5	2101	1.1
29	SA	0318	5.0	0918	1.6	1539	5.3	◑ 2207	1.4
30	SU	0428	4.8	1027	1.8	1649	5.1	2316	1.5
31	M	0540	4.8	1138	1.9	1801	5.0		

Chart Datum: 3·05 metres below Ordnance Datum (Newlyn). HAT is 6·3 metres above Chart Datum.

South Wales & Bristol Channel

Abersoch to Land's End

9.11.1 Contents 527

9.11.2 Area map and Distance table 528

9.11.3 Tidal stream charts 530

9.11.4 Lights, buoys and waypoints 532

9.11.5 Passage information 534
Cardigan Bay, Ramsey Sound, The Bishops, The Smalls to Milford Haven – 534 • Milford Haven to Mumbles Head, Firing Ranges – Linney Head to Burry Inlet – Mumbles Head to Cardiff – Severn Estuary – 546 • Avonmouth to Hartland Point – 558 • Hartland Point to Land's End – 561

9.11.6 Abersoch 535

9.11.7 Pwllheli 536
Llanbedrog • Mochras

9.11.8 Porthmadog 537

9.11.9 Barmouth 537

9.11.10 Aberdovey 538
Aberaeron • New Quay

9.11.11 Aberystwyth 538
Port Cardigan

9.11.12 Fishguard 539
Solva • St Brides Bay • Skomer Island

9.11.13 Milford Haven, tide tables/curves 540

9.11.14 Tenby 547
Saundersfoot • Carmarthen

9.11.15 Burry Port 548

9.11.16 Swansea 549
Mumbles • River Neath • Porthcawl

9.11.17 Barry 550

9.11.18 Cardiff/Penarth 550
Newport

9.11.19 Sharpness 552
The Severn Bridges

9.11.20 Bristol (City Docks) (Avonmouth, tide tables/curves) 556

9.11.21 Portishead 558
Weston-super-Mare

9.11.22 Burnham-on-Sea 559

9.11.23 Watchet 559

9.11.24 Ilfracombe 560
Minehead • Porlock Weir • Lynmouth • Watermouth

9.11.25 Rivers Taw and Torridge 561
Clovelly • Lundy Island • Bude • Boscastle

9.11.26 Padstow 563
Port Isaac • Newquay • Portreath • Hayle • St Ives

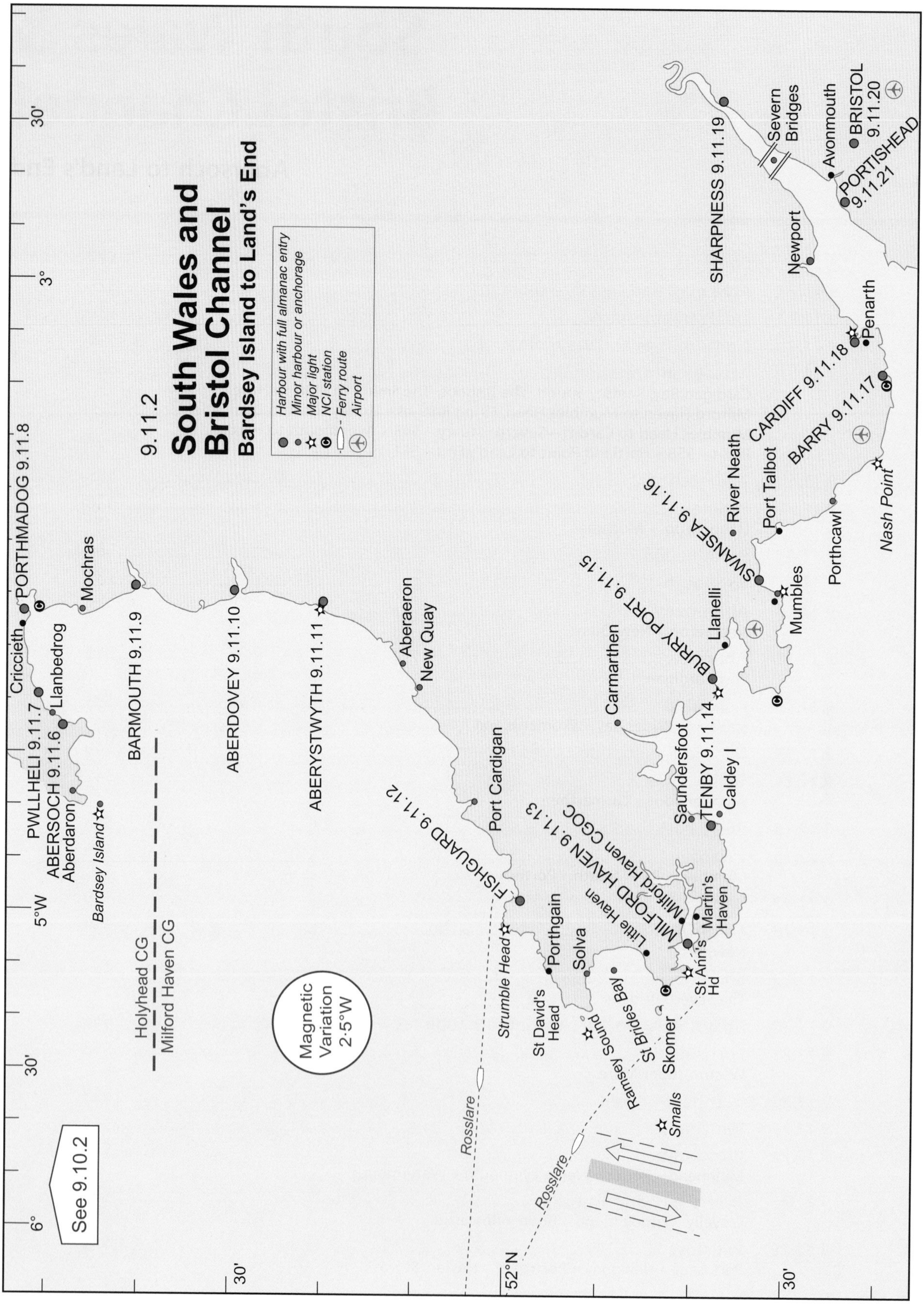
9.11.2
South Wales and Bristol Channel
Bardsey Island to Land's End
Harbour with full almanac entry
Minor harbour or anchorage
Major light
NCI station
Ferry route
Airport
See 9.10.2
Magnetic Variation 2·5°W
Holyhead CG
Milford Haven CG
PORTHMADOG 9.11.8
Criccieth
PWLLHELI 9.11.7
Llanbedrog
ABERSOCH 9.11.6
Aberdaron
Bardsey Island
Mochras
BARMOUTH 9.11.9
ABERDOVEY 9.11.10
ABERYSTWYTH 9.11.11
Aberaeron
New Quay
Port Cardigan
FISHGUARD 9.11.12
Strumble Head
Porthgain
St David's Head
Solva
Ramsey Sound
St Brides Bay
Skomer
Smalls
Little Haven
MILFORD HAVEN 9.11.13
Milford Haven CGOC
Martin's Haven
St Ann's Hd
TENBY 9.11.14
Caldey I
Saundersfoot
Carmarthen
BURRY PORT 9.11.15
Llanelli
Mumbles
SWANSEA 9.11.16
River Neath
Port Talbot
Porthcawl
Nash Point
BARRY 9.11.17
CARDIFF 9.11.18
Penarth
Newport
SHARPNESS 9.11.19
Severn Bridges
Avonmouth
PORTISHEAD 9.11.21
BRISTOL 9.11.20
Rosslare
Rosslare
6°
30'
5°W
30'
4°
30'
3°
30'
52°N
30'
30'

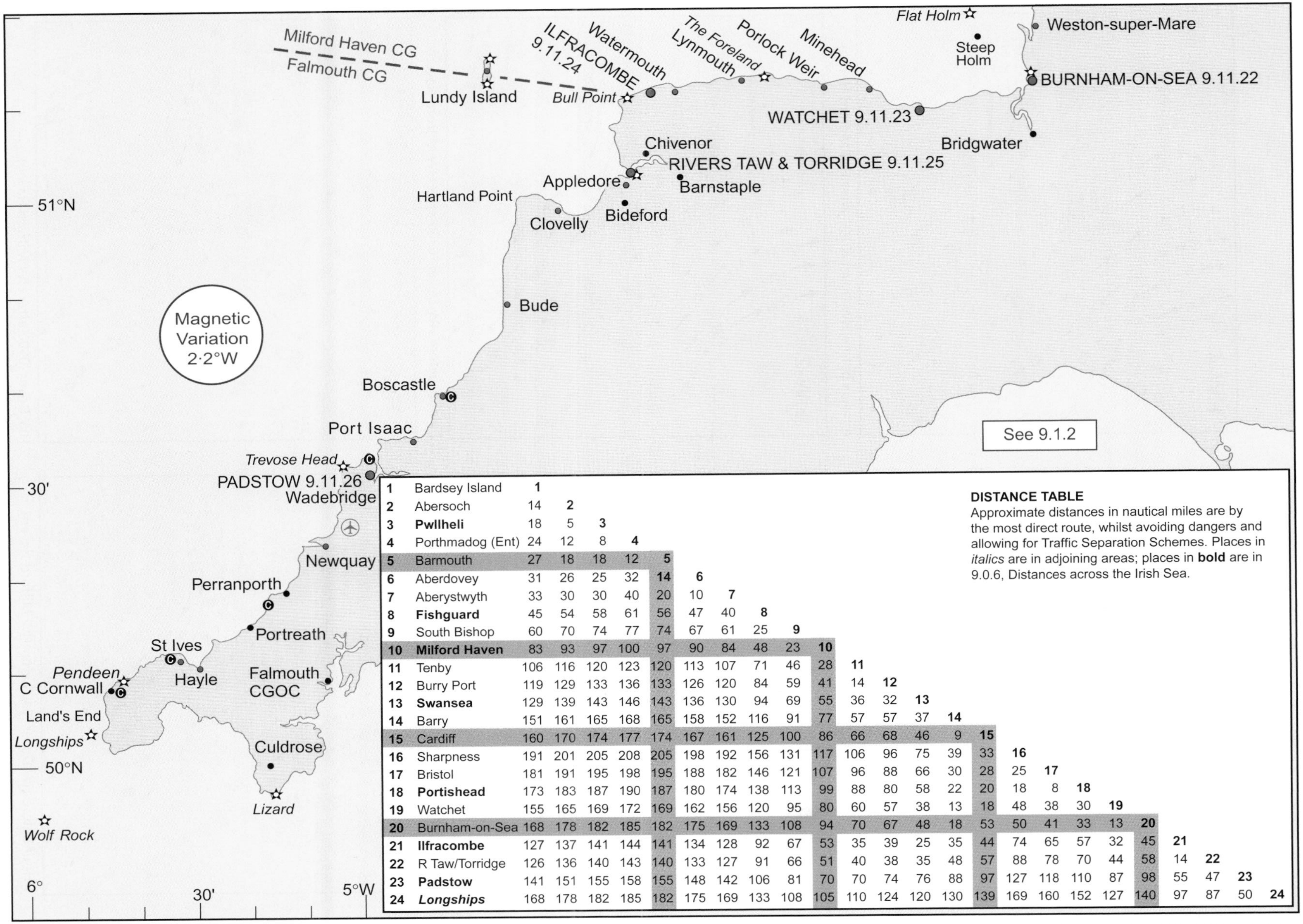
Milford Haven CG
Falmouth CG
Lundy Island
ILFRACOMBE 9.11.24
Bull Point
Watermouth
Lynmouth
The Foreland
Porlock Weir
Minehead
Flat Holm
Steep Holm
Weston-super-Mare
BURNHAM-ON-SEA 9.11.22
WATCHET 9.11.23
Bridgwater
Chivenor
RIVERS TAW & TORRIDGE 9.11.25
Appledore
Barnstaple
Hartland Point
Clovelly
Bideford
51°N
Bude
Magnetic Variation 2·2°W
Boscastle
Port Isaac
See 9.1.2
Trevose Head
PADSTOW 9.11.26
Wadebridge
30'
Newquay
Perranporth
Portreath
St Ives
Pendeen
C Cornwall
Hayle
Falmouth CGOC
Land's End
Longships
Culdrose
50°N
Lizard
Wolf Rock
6°
30'
5°W

DISTANCE TABLE

Approximate distances in nautical miles are by the most direct route, whilst avoiding dangers and allowing for Traffic Separation Schemes. Places in *italics* are in adjoining areas; places in **bold** are in 9.0.6, Distances across the Irish Sea.

1	Bardsey Island	**1**																							
2	Abersoch	14	**2**																						
3	**Pwllheli**	18	5	**3**																					
4	Porthmadog (Ent)	24	12	8	**4**																				
5	Barmouth	27	18	18	12	**5**																			
6	Aberdovey	31	26	25	32	14	**6**																		
7	Aberystwyth	33	30	30	40	20	10	**7**																	
8	**Fishguard**	45	54	58	61	56	47	40	**8**																
9	South Bishop	60	70	74	77	74	67	61	25	**9**															
10	**Milford Haven**	83	93	97	100	97	90	84	48	23	**10**														
11	Tenby	106	116	120	123	120	113	107	71	46	28	**11**													
12	Burry Port	119	129	133	136	133	126	120	84	59	41	14	**12**												
13	**Swansea**	129	139	143	146	143	136	130	94	69	55	36	32	**13**											
14	Barry	151	161	165	168	165	158	152	116	91	77	57	57	37	**14**										
15	Cardiff	160	170	174	177	174	167	161	125	100	86	66	68	46	9	**15**									
16	Sharpness	191	201	205	208	205	198	192	156	131	117	106	96	75	39	33	**16**								
17	Bristol	181	191	195	198	195	188	182	146	121	107	96	88	66	30	28	25	**17**							
18	**Portishead**	173	183	187	190	187	180	174	138	113	99	88	80	58	22	20	18	8	**18**						
19	Watchet	155	165	169	172	169	162	156	120	95	80	60	57	38	13	18	48	38	30	**19**					
20	Burnham-on-Sea	168	178	182	185	182	175	169	133	108	94	70	67	48	18	53	50	41	33	13	**20**				
21	**Ilfracombe**	127	137	141	144	141	134	128	92	67	53	35	39	25	35	44	74	65	57	32	45	**21**			
22	R Taw/Torridge	126	136	140	143	140	133	127	91	66	51	40	38	35	48	57	88	78	70	44	58	14	**22**		
23	**Padstow**	141	151	155	158	155	148	142	106	81	70	70	74	76	88	97	127	118	110	87	98	55	47	**23**	
24	***Longships***	168	178	182	185	182	175	169	133	108	105	110	124	120	130	139	169	160	152	127	140	97	87	50	**24**

9.11.3 AREA 11 TIDAL STREAMS

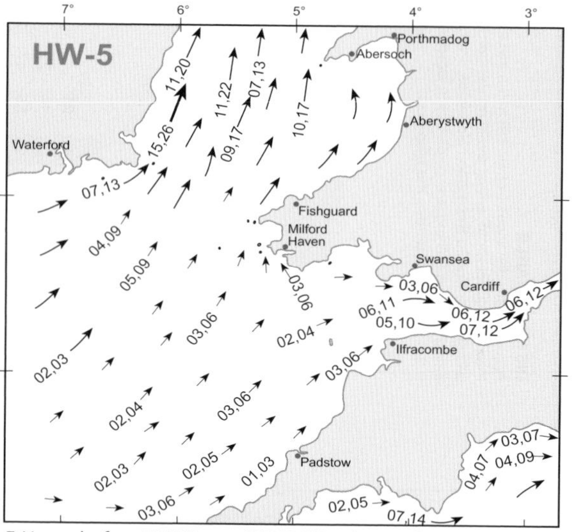

5 Hours before HW Dover (HW Milford Haven)

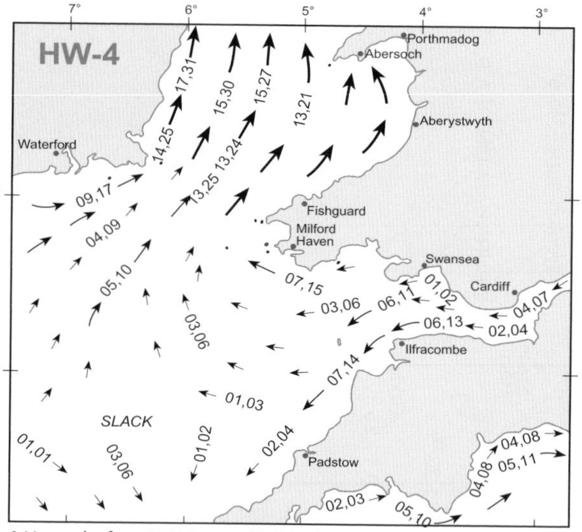

4 Hours before HW Dover (0100 after HW Milford Haven)

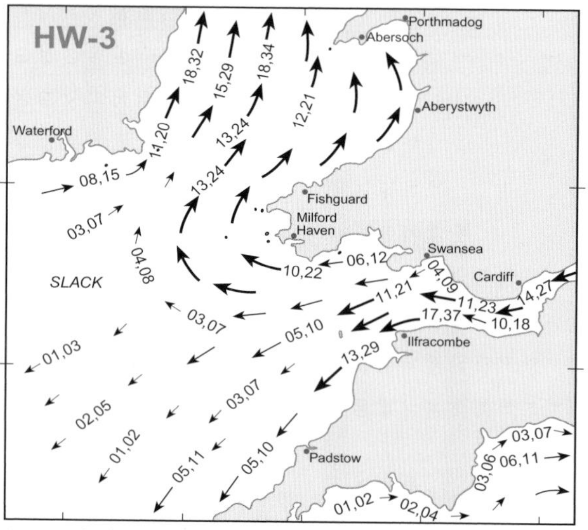

3 Hours before HW Dover (0200 after HW Milford Haven)

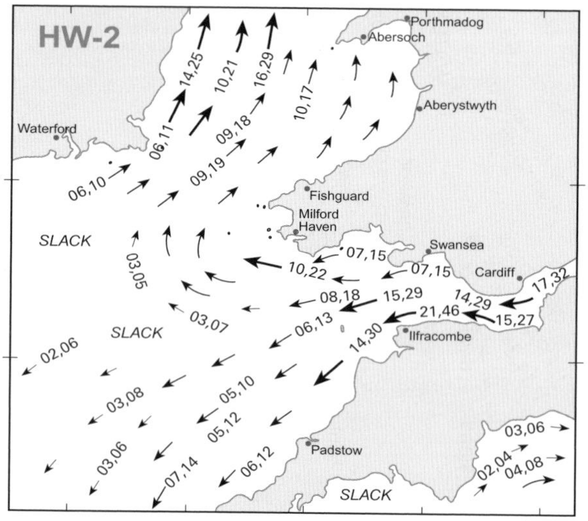

2 Hours before HW Dover (0300 after HW Milford Haven)

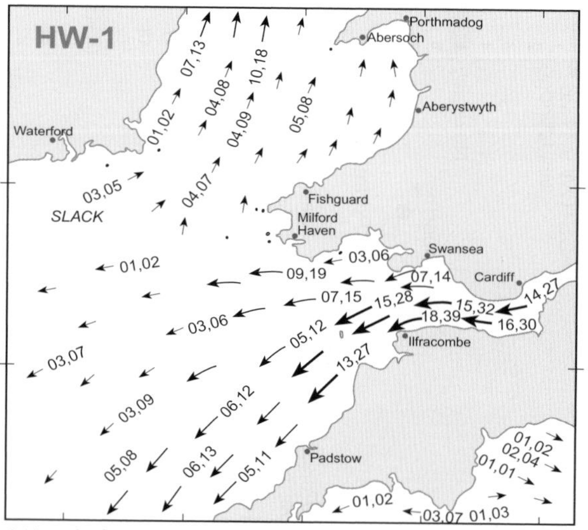

1 Hour before HW Dover (0400 after HW Milford Haven)

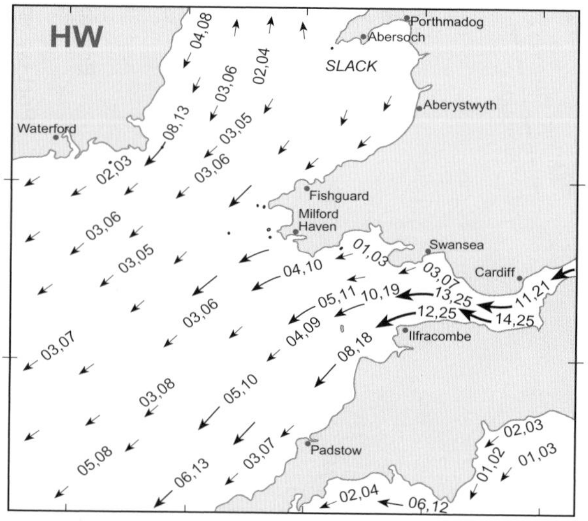

HW Dover (0500 after HW Milford Haven)

Southward 9.1.3 Northward 9.10.3 South Ireland 9.12.3

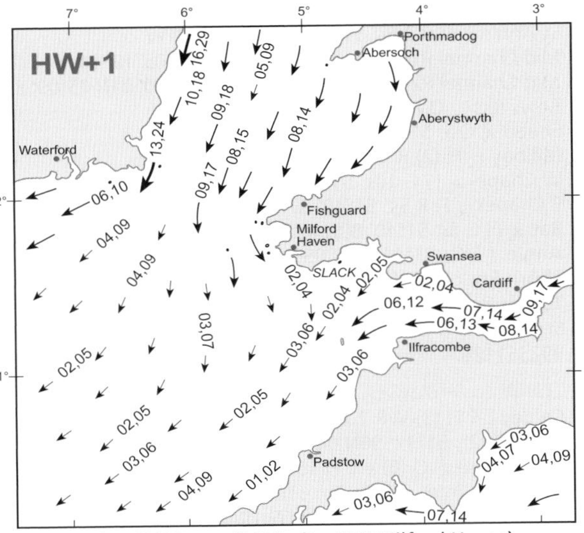
HW+1
Porthmadog
Abersoch
Aberystwyth
Waterford
Fishguard
Milford Haven
Swansea
Cardiff
Ilfracombe
Padstow
SLACK

1 Hour after HW Dover (0600 after HW Milford Haven)

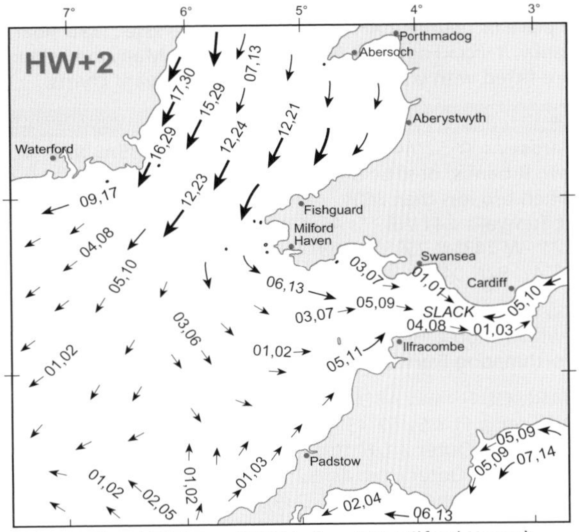
HW+2
Porthmadog
Abersoch
Aberystwyth
Waterford
Fishguard
Milford Haven
Swansea
Cardiff
Ilfracombe
Padstow
SLACK

2 Hours after HW Dover (0525 before HW Milford Haven)

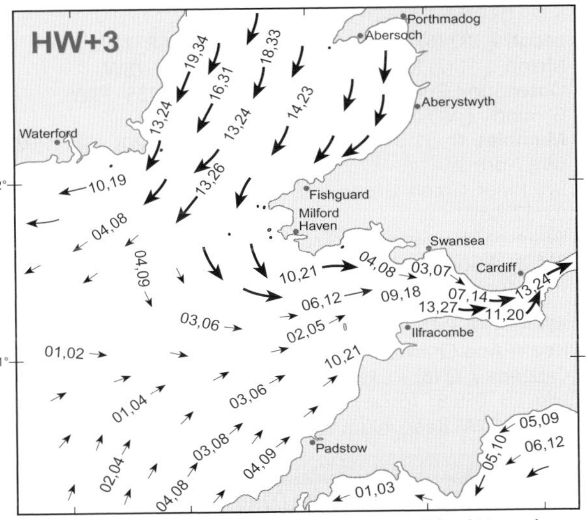
HW+3
Porthmadog
Abersoch
Aberystwyth
Waterford
Fishguard
Milford Haven
Swansea
Cardiff
Ilfracombe
Padstow

3 Hours after HW Dover (0425 before HW Milford Haven)

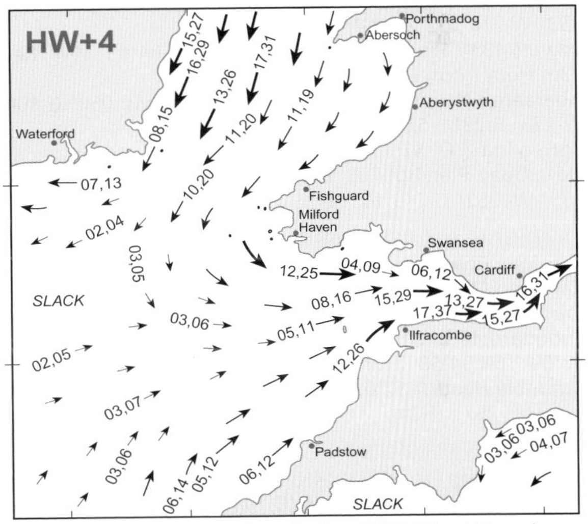
HW+4
Porthmadog
Abersoch
Aberystwyth
Waterford
Fishguard
Milford Haven
Swansea
Cardiff
Ilfracombe
Padstow
SLACK

4 Hours after HW Dover (0325 before HW Milford Haven)

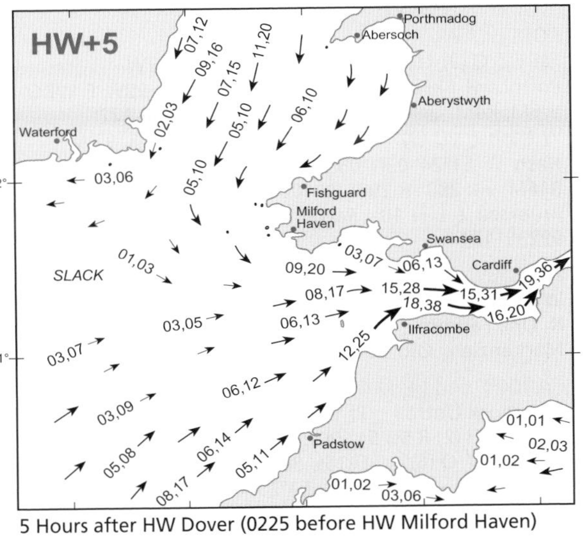
HW+5
Porthmadog
Abersoch
Aberystwyth
Waterford
Fishguard
Milford Haven
Swansea
Cardiff
Ilfracombe
Padstow
SLACK

5 Hours after HW Dover (0225 before HW Milford Haven)

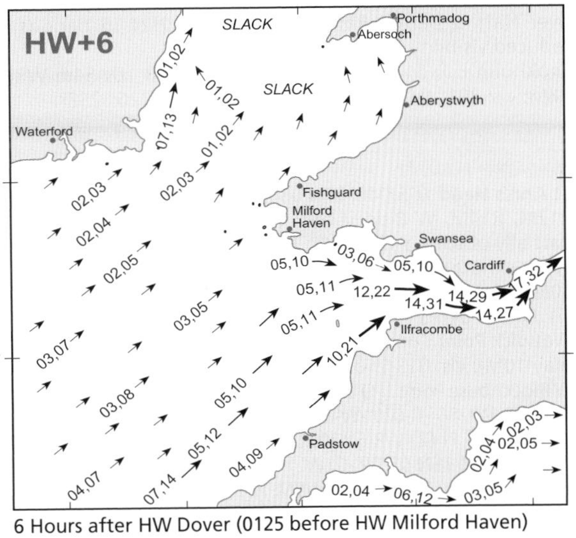
HW+6
Porthmadog
Abersoch
Aberystwyth
Waterford
Fishguard
Milford Haven
Swansea
Cardiff
Ilfracombe
Padstow
SLACK

6 Hours after HW Dover (0125 before HW Milford Haven)

9.11.4 LIGHTS, BUOYS AND WAYPOINTS

Bold print = light with a nominal range of 15M or more. CAPITALS = place or feature. *CAPITAL ITALICS* = light-vessel, light float or Lanby. *Italics* = Fog signal. ***Bold italics*** = Racon. Many marks/buoys are fitted with with AIS (MMSI No); see relevant charts.

CARDIGAN BAY (SEE ALSO 9.10.4)

Bardsey I ☆ 52°44′·98N 04°48′·01W Fl R 10s 39m **18M**; W □ twr, R bands; obsc by Bardsey I 198°-250° and in Tremadoc B when brg less than 260°.
St Tudwal's Fl WR 15s 46m W14, R10M; vis: 349°-W-169°-R-221°-W-243°-R-259°-W-293°-R-349°; obsc by East I 211°-231°; 52°47′·92N 04°28′·30W.

PWLLHELI and PORTHMADOG

Pwllheli App Iso 2s; 52°53′·03N 04°22′·90W.
Porthmadog Fairway L Fl 10s; 52°52′·96N 04°11′·18W.

BARMOUTH and ABERDOVEY

Diffuser Fl Y 5s; 52°43′·19N 04°05′·38W.
Barmouth Outer L Fl 10s; 52°42′·73N 04°04′·92W.
Aberdovey Outer Iso 4s; 52°32′·00N 04°05′·55W.
Cynfelyn Patches, Patches Q (9) 15s; 52°25′·83N 04°16′·41W.

ABERYSTWYTH, ABERAERON and NEW QUAY

Aberystwyth S Bkwtr Hd Fl (2) WG 10s 12m 10M; vis: 030°-G-053°-W-210°; 52°24′·40N 04°05′·52W.
Ldg Lts 133°. Front, FR 4m 5M; 52°24′·37N 04°05′·39W. Rear, 52m from front, FR 7m 6M.
Aberaeron N Pier Fl (4) WRG 15s 10m 6M; vis: 050°-G-104°-W-178°-R-232°; 52°14′·61N 04°15′·87W.
Carreg Ina Q; 52°13′·25N 04°20′·75W.
New Quay Pier Hd Fl WG 3s 12m W8M, G5M; G △; vis: 135°-W- 252°-G-295; 52°12′·95N 04°21′·35W.

CARDIGAN and FISHGUARD

Cardigan Channel Fl (2) 5s; 52°06′·44N 04°41′·43W.
Cardigan Cliff Base Bn 1 Fl R 4s 3M; 52°07′·05N 04°41′·39W.
Cardigan Cliff Base Bn 2 Fl R 2s 3M; 52°06′·91N 04°41′·34W.
Fishguard N Bkwtr Hd Fl G 4·5s 18m 13M; *Bell (1) 8s;* 52°00′·76N 04°58′·23W.
Strumble Head ☆ 52°01′·79N 05°04′·43W Fl (4) 15s 45m **26M**; vis: 038°-257°; (H24).

BISHOPS and SMALLS

South Bishop ☆ 51°51′·14N 05°24′·74W Fl 5s 44m **16M**; W ○ twr; *Horn (3) 45s;* ***Racon (O)10M***; (H24).
The Smalls ☆ 51°43′·27N 05°40′·19W Fl (3) 15s 36m **18M**; ***Racon (T)***; *Horn (2) 60s*. Same twr, Iso R 4s 33m 13M; vis: 253°-285° over Hats & Barrels Rk; both Lts shown H24 in periods of reduced visibility; 992351123.
Skokholm I , 51°41′·64N 05°17′·22W Fl WR 10s 54m W8M, R8M; vis: 301°-W-154°-R-301°; partially obsc 226°-258°.

WALES – SOUTH COAST – BRISTOL CHANNEL

MILFORD HAVEN

St Ann's Head ☆ 51°40′·87N 05°10′·42W Fl WR 5s 48m **W18M, R17M**, R14M; W 8-sided twr; vis: 233°-W-247°-R-332°-W131°, partially obscured 124°-129°; *Horn (2) 60s*.
W Blockhouse Point Ldg Lts 022·5°. Front, F 54m 13M (day 10M); B stripe on W twr; vis: 004·5°-040·5°; intens on lead line. vis: 004·5°-040·5°; ***Racon (Q)***; 51°41′·31N 05°09′·56W.
Watwick Point Common Rear ☆, 0·5M from front, F 80m **15M** (day 10M); vis: 013·5°-031·5°; ***Racon (Y)***.
W Blockhouse Point Q WR 21m W9M, R7M; R lantern on W base: vis: 220°-W-250°-R-020°-W-036°-R-049°; 51°41′·31N 05°09′·56W.
Dale Fort Fl (2) WR 5s 20m W5M, R3M; vis: 222°-R-276°-W-019°; 51°42′·16N 05°09′·01W.
Gt Castle Hd F WRG 27m W5M, R3M, G3M; vis: 243°-R-281°-G-299°-W-029°; 51°42′·68N 05°07′·06W. Co-located Dir WRG (040°); vis: 038·25°-G-039°-AlWG-039·5°-W-040·5°-AlWR-041°-R-041·75° (**not** used in conjunction with the front ldg light below)
Ldg Lts ≠ 039·7° **Front,** Oc 4s 27m **15M**; vis: 031·2°-048·2°. **Rear,** 890m from front. Oc 8s 53m **15M** (day 10M); vis: 031·2°-048·2°.
St Ann's Fl R 2·5s; 51°40′·25N 05°10′·51W.
Mid Channel Rks Q (9) 15s; 51°40′·18N 05°10′·14W.
Mid Channel Rk Fl (3) G 7s 18m 8M; 51°40′·31N 05°09′·83W.
Rows Rks Q R; 51°40′·22N 05°09′·02W.
Sheep QG; 51°40′·06N 05°08′·31W.
Millbay Fl (2) R 5s; 51°41′·05N 05°09′·45W.
W Chapel Fl G 10s; 51°40′·98N 05°08′·67W.
E Chapel Fl R 5s; 51°40′·87N 05°08′·15W.
Rat Fl G 5s; 51°40′·80N 05°07′·86W.
Angle VQ; 51°41′·63N 05°08′·27W.
Thorn Rock Q (9) 15s; 51°41′·53N 05°07′·76W.
Turbot Bank VQ (9) 10s; 51°37′·41N 05°10′·08W.
St Gowan Q (6) + L Fl 15s; ***Racon (T) 10M***; 51°31′·93N 04°59′·77W; 992351126.

TENBY to SWANSEA BAY

Caldey I Fl (3) WR 20s 65m W13M, R9M; vis: R173°- W212°-R088°-102°; 51°37′·90N 04°41′·08W.
Woolhouse Q (6) + L Fl 15s; 51°39′·35N 04°39′·69W.
Burry Port Inlet Fl 5s 7m 6½M; 51°40′·62N 04°15′·06W.
W. Helwick (9) 15s; ***Racon (T) 10M***; 51°31′·40N 04°23′·65W.
E. Helwick VQ (3) 5s; *Bell;* 51°31′·80N 04°12′·68W.

SWANSEA BAY and SWANSEA

Ledge VQ (6) + L Fl 10s; 51°29′·93N 03°58′·77W.
Mixon Fl (2) R 5s; *Bell;* 51°33′·12N 03°58′·78W.
Outer Spoil Gnd Fl Y 2·5s; 51°32′·11N 03°55′·73W.
Grounds VQ (3) 5s; 51°32′·81N 03°53′·47W.
Mumbles ☆ 51°34′·01N 03°58′·27W Fl (4) 20s 35m **15M**; W twr; *Horn 3s*.
SW Inner Green Grounds Q(6)+L Fl 15s; *Bell;* 51°34′·06N 03°57′·03W.
Swansea Lts in line 020°. Front: E Breakwater head, Oc G 4s 5m 2M & 2FG(vert) 10m 6M; 51°36′·38N 03°55′·62W. Rear, 3·1ca from front: FG 6M.

SWANSEA BAY, RIVER NEATH and PORT TALBOT

Neath App Chan Fl G 5s; 51°35′·71N 03°52′·83W.
Cabenda Q (6) + L Fl 15s; ***Racon (Q)***; 51°33′·36N 03°52′·23W.
Ldg Lts 059·8° (occas). Front, Oc R 3s 12m 6M; 51°34′·92N 03°48′·10W. Rear, 400m from front, Oc R 6s 32m 6M.

BRISTOL CHANNEL – NORTH SHORE (EASTERN PART)

W Scar Q (9) 15s, *Bell*, ***Racon (T) 10M***; 51°28′·31N 03°55′·57W.
South Scar (S SCAR) Q (6) + L Fl 15s; 51°27′·61N 03°51′·58W.
E. Scarweather Q (3) 10s; *Bell;* 51°27′·98N 03°46′·76W.

PORTHCAWL

Fairy Q (9) 15s; *Bell;* 51°27′·86N 03°42′·07W.
Porthcawl Bkwtr Hd 51°28′·39N 03°41′·98W F WRG 10m W6M, R4M, G4M; vis: 302°-G-036°-W-082°-R-122°.
W Nash VQ (9) 10s ; *Bell;* 51°25′·99N 03°45′·95W.
Nash ☆ 51°24′·03N 03°33′·06W Fl (2) WR 15s 56m **W21M, R16M**; vis: 280°-R-290°-W-100°-R-120°-W-128°.
Breaksea L Fl 10s; ***Racon (T) 10M***; 51°19′·88N 03°19′·08W; 992351124.

BARRY

W Bkwtr Hd Fl 2·5s 12m 10M; 51°23′·46N 03°15′·52W.
N. One Fathom Q; 51°20′·94N 03°12′·17W.
Mackenzie QR; 51°21′·75N 03°08′·24W.

CARDIFF and PENARTH ROADS

Lavernock Outfall Fl Y 5s; 51°23′·95N 03°09′·50W.
Ranie Fl (2) R 5s; 51°24′·23N 03°09′·39W.
S Cardiff Q (6) + L Fl 15s; *Bell;* 51°24′·18N 03°08′·57W.
Mid Cardiff Fl (3) G 10s; 51°25′·60N 03°08′·09W.
Cardiff Spit QR; 51°24′·57N 03°07′·12W.
N Cardiff QG; 51°26′·52N 03°07′·19W.

Wrach Chan Dir lt 348·5°. Oc WRG 10s 5m; W3M, R3M, G3M; vis: 344·5°-G-347°-W-350°-R-352°; H24; 51°27'·16N 03°09'·75W.
Outer Wrach Q (9) 15s; 51°26'·20N 03°09'·46W.

FLATHOLM to THE BRIDGE

Flat Holm ☆, SE Pt 51°22'·54N 03°07'·14W Fl (3) WR 10s 50m **W15M**, R12M; W ○ twr; vis: 106°-R-140°-W-151°-R-203°-W-106°; (H24).
Monkstone ☆ Fl 5s 13m 12M; R column on W ○ twr; 51°24'·89N 03°06'·01W.
Tail Patch QG; 51°23'·53N 03°03'·65W.
Hope Q (3) 10s; 51°24'·84N 03°02'·68W.
NW Elbow VQ (9) 10s; *Bell;* 51°26'·28N 02°59'·93W.
EW Grounds L Fl 10s 7M; *Whis;* ***Racon (T) 7M***; 51°27'·12N 02°59'·95W.

NEWPORT DEEP, RIVER USK and NEWPORT

Newport Deep Fl (3) G 10s; *Bell;*51°29'·36N 02°59'·12W.
East Usk ☆ 51°32'·40N 02°58'·01W; Fl (2) WRG 10s 11m W11M,R10M, G10M; vis: 284°-W-290° -obscured shore-324°-R-017°-W-037°-G-115°-W-120°. Also Oc WRG 10s 10m W11M, R9M, G9M; vis: 013°-G-017°-W- 019°-R-023°.
Julians Pill Ldg Lts 062°. Front, F Bu 5m 5M; 51°33'·32N 02°57'·94W. Rear, `44m from front, F Bu 8m 5M.

BRISTOL CHANNEL – SOUTH SHORE (EASTERN PART)

BRISTOL DEEP

N Elbow QG; *Bell;* 51°26'·97N 02°58'·65W.
S Mid Grounds VQ(6) + L Fl 10s; 51°27'·62N 02°58'·68W.
E Mid Grounds Fl R 5s; 51°27'·75N 02°54'·98W.
Clevedon VQ; 51°27'·39N 02°54'·93W.
Welsh Hook Q(6) + L Fl 15s; 51°28'·53N 02°51'·86W.
Avon Fl G 2·5s; 51°27'·92N 02°51'·73W.
Black Nore Pt Lt Ho; W ○ twr on frame; 51°29'·09N 02°48'·05W.
Newcome 51°30'·01N 02°46'·71W Fl (3) R 10s.
Denny Shoal VQ(6) + L Fl 10s; 51°30'·15N 02°45'·45W.
Cockburn 51°30'·45N 02°44'·10W Fl R 2·5s.
W Dock Middle 51°29.95'·01N 02°44'·20W Q G.
W Dock Outer 51°30'·00N 02°44'·85W Fl G 5s.
Firefly Fl(2) G 5s; 51°29'·96N 02°45'·35W.
Portishead Point ☆ 51°29'·68N 02°46'·42W Q (3) 10s 9m **16M**; B twr, W base; vis: 060°-262°; *Horn 20s.*

PORTISHEAD

Pier Hd ☆ Iso G 2s 5m 3M; 51°29'·69N 02°45'·27W.
Seabank. Dir WG 6m 5M; vis: 085·8°-FG-086·7°-AltWG-086·9°-FW-089·7°. 5M; vis: 070·3°-103·3°; by day 1M, vis: 076·8°-096·8°.
Lts in line 086·8°. Q(8) 5M 10/16m; vis: 070·3°-103·3°; day 1M vis: 076·8°-096·8° Front 51°30'·07N 02°43'·80W; Rear, 500m behind.
Knuckle Lts in line 099·6°, Oc G 5s 6m 6M; 51°29'·94N 02°43'·67W. Rear, 165m from front, FG 13m 6M; vis: 044°-134°.

AVONMOUTH

Royal Edward Dock N Pier Hd ☆ Fl 4s 15m 10M; vis: 060°-228·5°; 51°30'·49N 02°43'·09W.
King Road Ldg Lts 072·4°. N Pier Hd ☆ Front, Oc R 5s 5m 9M; W obelisk, R bands; vis: 062°-082°; 51°30'·49N 02°43'·09W. Rear ☆, 546m from front, QR 15m 10M; vis: 066°- 078°.

RIVER AVON, CUMBERLAND BASIN and AVON BRIDGE

S Pier Hd ☆ Oc RG 30s 9m 10M and FBu 4m 1M; vis: 294°-R-036°-G-194°; 51°30'·37N 02°43'·10W. *Bell(1) 10s.*
Ldg Lts 127·2°. Front, Iso R 2s 6m 3M, vis: 010°-160°; 51°30'·10N 02°42'·59W. Rear, Iso R 2s10m 3M, vis: 048°-138°.

BRISTOL CHANNEL (SOUTH SHORE)

WESTON-SUPER-MARE

Pier Hd ☆ 2 FG (vert) 6m; 51°20'·88N 02°59'·26W.
E Culver Q (3) 10s; 51°18'·00N 03°15'·44W.
W Culver VQ (9) 10s; 51°17'·47N 03°19'·00W.
Gore Iso 5s; *Bell;* 51°13'·94N 03°09'·79W.

BURNHAM-ON-SEA and RIVER PARRETT

Ent ☆ Fl 7·5s 7m 12M; vis: 074°-164°; 51°14'·89N 03°00'·36W; Dir lt 076°. F WRG 4m W12M, R10M, G10M; vis: 071°-G- 075°-W-077°- R-081°.
DZ No 1 Fl Y 2·5s; 51°15'·28N 03°09'·49W.
DZ No 2 Fl Y 10s; 51°13'·77N 03°19'·86W.
DZ No 3 Fl Y 5s; 51°16'·34N 03°14'·98W.

WATCHET, MINEHEAD and PORLOCK WEIR

Watchet W Bkwtr Hd ☆ Oc G 3s 9m 9M; 51°11'·03N 03°19'·74W.
Watchet E Pier ☆ 2 FR (vert) 3M; 51°11'·01N 03°19'·72W.
Minehead Bkwtr Hd ☆ Fl(2) G 5s 4M; vis: 127°-262°; 51°12'·81N 03°28'·36W.
Lynmouth Foreland ☆ 51°14'·73N 03°47'·21W Fl (4) 15s 67m **18M**; W ○ twr; vis: 083°-275°; (H24).

LYNMOUTH and WATERMOUTH

River Training Arm ☆ 2 FR (vert) 6m 5M; 51°13'·90N 03°49'·83W.
Harbour Arm ☆ 2 FG (vert) 6m 5M; 51°13'·92N 03°49'·84W.
Sand Ridge Q G; 51°15'·01N 03°49'·77W.
Copperas Rock Fl G 2·5s; 51°13'·78N 04°00'·60W.
Watermouth ☆ Oc WRG 5s 1m 3M; W △; vis: 149·5°-G-151·5°-W-154·5°-R-156·5°; 51°12'·93N 04°04'·60W.

ILFRACOMBE to BAGGY POINT

Ldg Lts 188°. Front, Oc 10s 8m 3M; 51°12'·53N 04°06'·65W. Rear, Oc 10s 6m 3M.
Horseshoe Q; 51°15'·02N 04°12'·96W.
Bull Point ☆ 51°11'·94N 04°12'·09W Fl (3) 10s 54m **20M**; W ○ twr, obscd shore-056°. Same twr; FR 48m 12M; vis: 058°-096°.
Morte Stone Fl G 5s; 51°11'·30N 04°14'·95W.
Baggy Leap Fl(2) G 10s; 51°08'·92N 04°16'·97W.

BIDEFORD, RIVERS TAW and TORRIDGE

Bideford Fairway L Fl 10s; *Bell;* 51°05'·25N 04°16'·25W.
Bideford Bar Q G; 51°04'·89N 04°14'·62W.
Instow ☆ Ldg Lts 118°. **Front**, 51°03'·62N 04°10'·66W Oc 6s 22m **15M**; vis: 103·5°-132°. **Rear**, 427m from front, Oc 10s 38m **15M**; vis: 103°-132·5°; (H24).
Crow Pt ☆ Fl WR 2. 5s 8m W6M R5M; vis: 225°-R-232°-W-237°-R-358°-W- 015°-R-045°; 51°03'·96N 04°11'·39W.

LUNDY

North Pt ☆ 51°12'·10N 04°40'·65W Fl 15s 48m **17M**; vis: 009°-285°.
South East Pt ☆ 51°09'·72N 04°39'·37W Fl 5s 53m **15M**; vis: 170°-073°.
Hartland Point ☆ 51°01'·3N 04°31'·6W Fl (6) 15s 30m 8M; adjacent to Hartland Point Light House (disused).

NORTH CORNWALL

BUDE, PADSTOW and NEWQUAY

Compass Pt twr 50°49'·71N 04°33'·42W.
Stepper Pt (Padstow) ☆ LFl 10s 12m 4M; 50°34'·12N 04°56'·72W.
Middle Gnd (Padstow) Fl(2+1)R 10s; 50°32'·84N 04°55'·96W.
Trevose Head ☆ 50°32'·94N 05°02'·13W Fl 7·5s 62m **21M**.
North Pier Hd (Newquay) ☆ 2 FG (vert) 5m 2M; 50°25'·07N 05°05'·19W.

HAYLE and ST IVES

The Stones Q; 50°15'·64N 05°25'·51W.
Godrevy I ☆ Fl WR 10s 28m 8M; metal post; vis: 022°-W-101°-R-145°-W-272°; 50°14'·56N 05°24'·01W; adjacent to Godrevy Light House (disused).
Hayle App QR; 50°12'·26N 05°26'·30W.
St Ives App 50°12'·85N 05°28'·42W.
Bann Shoal Fl G 2.5s; ***Racon (B) 10M***; 50°20'·03N 05°51'·11W; 992351053.
Pendeen ☆ 50°09'·90N 05°40'·30W Fl (4) 15s 59m **16M**; vis: 042°-240°; between Gurnard Hd and Pendeen it shows to coast.

9.11.5 PASSAGE INFORMATION

More passage information is threaded between the harbours in this area. Admiralty Leisure Folio 5620 covers South West Wales, 5608 the Bristol Channel and 5603 the approach to Bristol Channel from Land's End. For additional tidal information east of Ilfracombe/Swansea see *Arrowsmith's Bristol Channel Tide Tables* from J.W. Arrowsmith Ltd ☎(0117) 9667545. **Bibliography:** *Bristol Channel and River Severn Cruising Guide,* Milford Haven to St Ives (Imray/Cumberlidge). The *West Coasts of England and Wales Pilot* (Admiralty NP37) covers the whole area.

It is useful to know some Welsh words with navigational significance.

Aber: estuary	*Afon:* river
Bach, bychan, fach: little	*Borth:* cove
Bryn: hill	*Careg, craig:* rock
Coch, goch: red	*Dinas:* fort
Ddu: black	*Fawr, Mawr:* big
Ffrydiau: tide rip	*Llwyd:* grey
Moel: bare conical hill	*Mor:* sea
Morfa: sandy shore	*Mynydd:* mountain
Penrhyn: headland	*Porth:* cove.
Ynys, Ynysoedd: island(s)	

CARDIGAN BAY

(AC 1971, 1972, 1973) Harbours are mostly on a lee shore, and/or have bars which make them dangerous to approach in bad weather. Abersoch and Pwllheli offer best shelter from the prevailing westerlies. There may be overfalls off Trwyn Cilan, SW of St Tudwal's Is (lit). In N part of the bay there are three major dangers to coasting yachts: St Patrick's Causeway (Sarn Badrig) runs 12M SW from Mochras Pt. It is mostly large loose stones, and dries (up to 1·5m) for much of its length. In strong winds the sea breaks heavily at all states of tide. The outer end is marked by a WCM light buoy. At the inner end there is a channel about 5ca offshore, which can be taken with care at half tide.

Sarn-y-Bwch runs 4M WSW from Pen Bwch Pt. It is consists of rocky boulders, drying in places close inshore and with least depth 0·3m over 1M offshore. There is a WCM buoy off the W end. NW of Aberystwyth, Sarn Cynfelyn and Cynfelyn Patches extend 6·5M offshore, with depths of 1·5m in places. A WCM buoy is at the outer end. Almost halfway along the bank is Main Channel, 3ca wide, running roughly N/S but not marked.

Aberporth MOD Range occupies much of Cardigan Bay. It is usually active Mon-Fri 0900-1630LT, and some weekends, but times are subject to change. Active danger areas vary in size and location and may include the area off the Range head to the west of Aberporth. Beware of targets and buoys within the danger area, some unlit. Range activity is broadcast on VHF Ch 16 one hour before live firings. Flags are flown either side of the Range head to signify activity in the inner (yellow flags) or outer (red flags) danger areas. If passing through the area during operational hours contact *Aberporth Marine Control* on Ch 16 or Ch 13. Further information may be obtained from Aberporth Marine Control, ☎ (01239) 813760, or Aberporth Range Control ☎(01239) 813480.

If on passage N/S through St George's Chan (ie not bound for Cardigan B or Milford Haven) the easiest route, and always by night, is W of the Bishops and the Smalls, noting the TSS. If bound to/from Milford Haven or Cardigan Bay, passage inside both the Smalls and Grassholm is possible.

RAMSEY SOUND, THE BISHOPS, THE SMALLS TO MILFORD HAVEN

(AC 1478, 1482) The Bishops and the Clerks are islets and rocks 2·5M W and NW of Ramsey Island, a bird sanctuary SSW of St David's Head. N Bishop is the N'ly of the group, 3ca ENE of which is Bell Rock (depth 1·9m). S Bishop (Lt, fog sig) is 3M to the SSW.

Between S Bishop and Ramsey Is the dangers include Daufraich with offlying dangers to the E and heavy overfalls; Llech Isaf and Llech Uchaf drying rocks are further ENE. Carreg Rhoson and other dangers are between Daufraich and N Bishop. The navigable routes between most of these islets and rocks trend NE/SW. Use only by day, in good visibility and with local knowledge. The N/S route close W of Ramsey Is is considered easier than Ramsey Sound.

▶ *2M W of The Bishops the S-going stream begins at Milford Haven +0400, and the N-going at Milford Haven –0230, sp rates 2kn. Between The Bishops and Ramsey Is the SW-going stream begins at Milford Haven +0330, and the NE-going at Milford Haven –0300,* ***sp rates 5kn.*** *Ramsey Sound should be taken at slack water. S-going stream begins at Milford Haven +0300, and the N-going at Milford Haven –0330,* ***sp rates 6kn at The Bitches,*** *where the channel is narrow (2ca), decreasing N & S.* ◀

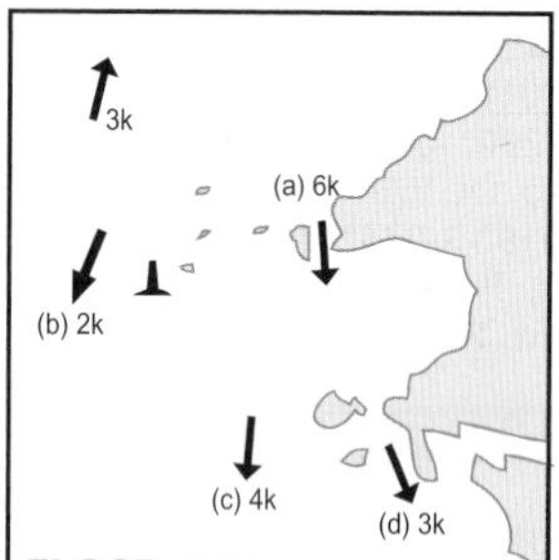

FLOOD SW Wales

The tide turns to the S or SE (Bristol Channel flood) as follows:
(a): Milford Haven +0330;
(b) & (c): Milford Haven +0400;
(d): Milford Haven +0200.

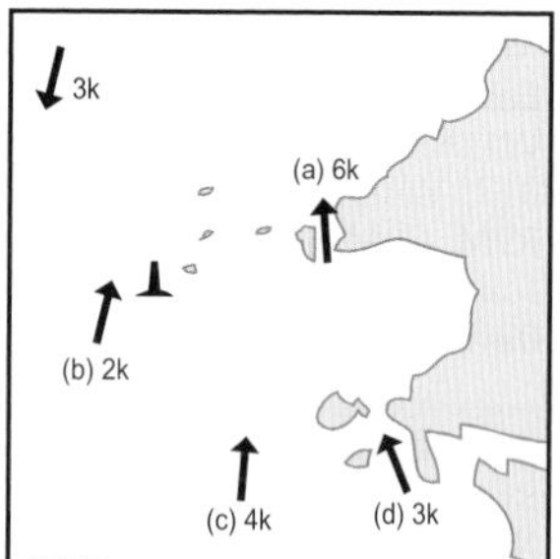

EBB SW Wales

The tide turns to the N or NW (Bristol Channel ebb) as follows:
(a): Milford Haven –0300;
(b) & (c): Milford Haven –0230 ;
(d): Milford Haven –0430.

At the N end of Ramsey Snd 2ca E of Trwyn Ogof Hen on the 30m contour is a submerged tidal turbine with a least depth of 13m. The Bitches are rocks up to 4m high extending 2ca from E side of Ramsey Island. Other dangers are: Gwahan and Carreg-gafeiliog, both 3m high at N end of Sound, to W and E; Horse Rock (dries 0·9m) almost in mid-channel about 5ca NNE of The Bitches, with associated overfalls; Shoe Rock (dries 3m) at SE end of channel; and rocks extending 5ca SSE from S end of Ramsey Island.

St Brides Bay is a regular anchorage for tankers, but ⚓ only in settled weather/offshore winds as it is a trap in westerlies. Solva is a little hbr with shelter for boats able to take the ground, or ⚓ behind Black Rk (dries 3·6m) in the middle of the entrance.

The Smalls Lt, where there is a Historic Wreck (see 9.0.3) is 13M W of the Welsh mainland (Wooltack Pt). 2M and 4M E of The Smalls are the Hats and Barrels, rocky patches on which the sea breaks.

▶ *7M E of The Smalls is Grassholm Island with a race either end and strong tidal eddies so that it is advisable to pass about 1M off. The chan between Barrels and Grassholm is 2·5M wide, and here the S-going stream begins at Milford Haven +0440, and the N-going at Milford Haven –0135,* ***sp rates 5kn.***◀

Five miles of clear water lie between Grassholm and Skomer Is/Skokholm Is to the E. Wildgoose Race, which forms W of Skomer and Skokholm is very dangerous, so keep 2M W of these two Is. To E of Skomer Island Midland Island, and between here and Wooltack Point is Jack Sound, least width about 1ca. Do not attempt it without AC 1482, detailed pilotage directions, and only at slack water neaps.

▶ *Correct timing is important. The S-going stream begins at Milford Haven +0200, and the N-going at Milford Haven –0430,* ***sp rates 6-7kn.*** ◀

Rocks which must be identified include, from N to S: On E side of chan off Wooltack Pt, Tusker Rock (2m), steep-to on its W side; and off Anvil Point, The Cable (2·4m), The Anvil and Limpet Rocks (3·7m). On the W side lie the Crabstones (3·7m) and the Blackstones (1·5m).

9.11.6 ABERSOCH

Gwynedd **52°49'·29N 04°29'·20W** (⚓)

CHARTS AC 5609, 1410, 1411, 1971, 1512; Imray C61, C52, C51

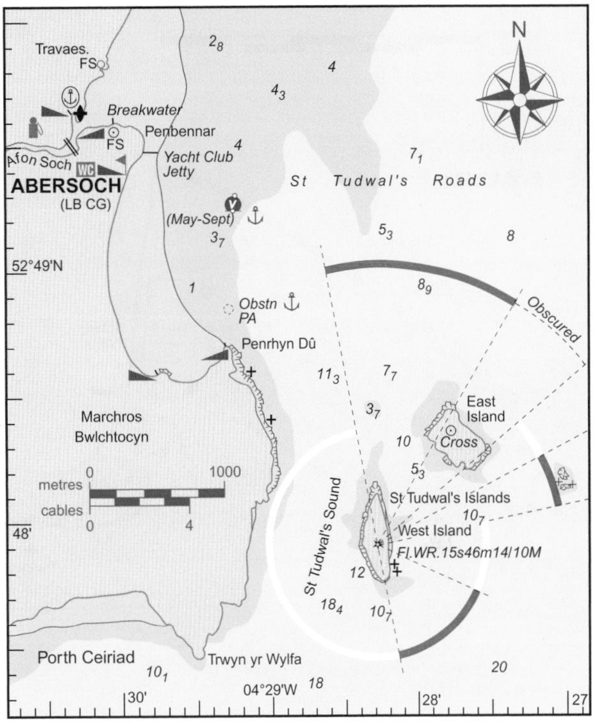

TIDES –0315 Dover; ML 2·5; Duration 0520; Zone 0 (UT)

Standard Port MILFORD HAVEN (⟶)

Times				Height (metres)			
High Water		Low Water		MHWS	MHWN	MLWN	MLWS
0100	0800	0100	0700	7·0	5·2	2·5	0·7
1300	2000	1300	1900				
Differences ST TUDWAL'S ROADS							
+0155	+0145	+0240	+0310	–2·2	–1·9	–0·7	–0·2
ABERDARON							
+0210	+0200	+0240	+0310	–2·4	–1·9	–0·6	–0·2

SHELTER There are few moorings for visitors. Apply to HM or SC. ⚓ in St Tudwal's Roads clear of moored yachts; sheltered from SSE through S to NE.

NAVIGATION WPT 52°48´·52N 04°26´·13W, 293°/2·4M to YC jetty. There are no navigational dangers, but steer well clear of the drying rks to the E of East Island; Carred y Trai buoy FlR 2·5s is 2ca E of these rks (just off chartlet). St Tudwal's islands themselves are fairly steep-to, except at N ends. St Tudwal's Sound is clear of dangers.

LIGHTS AND MARKS The only lt is on St Tudwal's West Island, Fl WR 15s 46m 14/10M (see chartlet and 9.11.4).

COMMUNICATIONS (Code 01758) CGOC (01407) 762051; Police 101; Dr 612535. HM 712203.

S Caernarfon YC Ch **80** M.

FACILITIES **South Caernarvonshire YC** ☎712338, ✕ (May-Sept).

Abersoch Power Boat Club ☎812027.

Services (12t).

Town ACA, ✉ Ⓑ ✕ ⇌ (Pwllheli), ✈ (Chester).

9.11.7 PWLLHELI

Gwynedd **52°53′·23N 04°23′·75W**

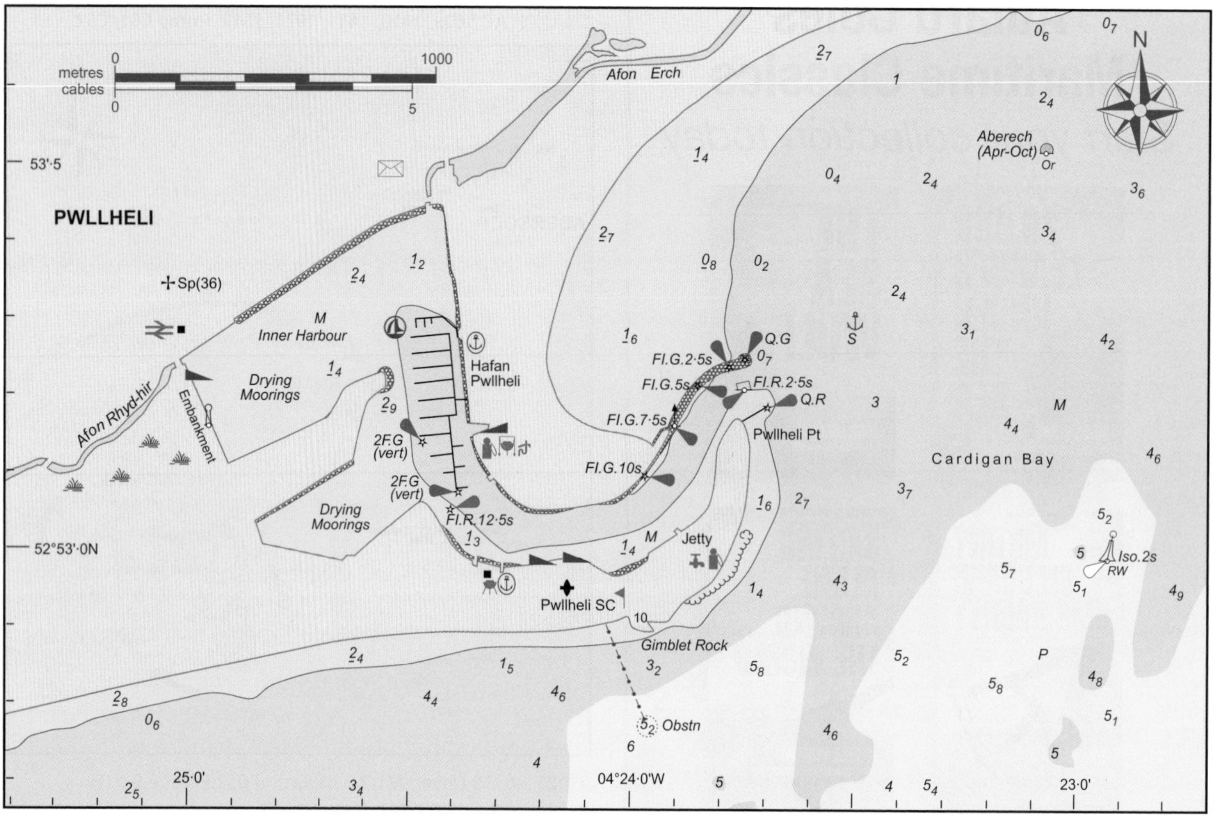

CHARTS AC 1410, 1971, 1512; Imray C61, C52, C51

TIDES –0315 Dover; ML 2·6; Duration 0510

Standard Port MILFORD HAVEN (⟶)

Times				Height (metres)			
High Water		Low Water		MHWS	MHWN	MLWN	MLWS
0100	0800	0100	0700	7·0	5·2	2·5	0·7
1300	2000	1300	1900				
Differences PWLLHELI							
+0210	+0150	+0245	+0320	–1·9	–1·6	–0·6	–0·1
CRICCIETH							
+0210	+0155	+0255	+0320	–2·0	–1·8	–0·7	–0·3

SHELTER Good in hbr and marina. Drying moorings in inner hbr (SW and NW bights).

NAVIGATION WPT 52°53′·02N 04°23′·07W, SWM lt buoy 299°/0·47M to QG lt at head of Training Arm.

- Ent is safe in most winds, but in strong E to SW winds sea breaks on offshore shoals.
- Ent subject to silting; 3 tide gauges. Average tidal stream 2kn.
- No ⚓ in hbr; 4kn speed limit.

LIGHTS AND MARKS See 9.11.4 and chartlet. Gimblet Rock (30m) is conspic conical rock 3ca SW of ent.

COMMUNICATIONS (Code 01758) CGOC (01407) 762051; Ⓗ Bangor (A&E) 01248 384384; Police 101; Dr 701457. HM ☎704081.

Marina: Ch **80** M H24. HM: VHF Ch **16** (0900-1715).

FACILITIES **Marina** www.hafanpwllheli.co.uk ☎701219; 420, £2·63+ £3·22, £13·30 <4hrs. Pontoons are numbered 4–12 from S–N; Pile berths on S side of appr channel.

Services Ⓔ (50t) (14t) wi-fi.

Marina Boat Club ☎612271, .

Harbour 6 , £8/craft/day, .

Town Ⓑ ✕ ✈ (Chester).

YACHT CLUBS

South Caernarvonshire YC ☎712338.

Pwllheli SC pwllhelisailingclub@btinternet.com ☎614442.

Marina Boat Club ☎612271, .

ADJACENT HARBOURS AND ANCHORAGES

LLANBEDROG, Gwynedd, **52°51′·14N 04°28′·09W**. AC 5609, 1410, 1411, 1971, 1512. HW –0245 on Dover, see 9.11.6 (St Tudwal's Roads). Good ⚓ N of Trwyn Llanbedrog (steep sided headland 131m) 1.0ca ENE of Bcn PHM in 2-3m. Beach has numerous conspicuous bathing huts. Sheltered in winds from N through W to SW. ⚓ well clear of local craft moorings as they have a long scope. Dinghy landing near boathouse.

Village limited facilities: (½M) ✕ (Pwllheli).

MOCHRAS, Gwynedd, **52°49′·57N 04°07′·77W**. AC 1971, 1512. HW –0310 on Dover. Small yacht hbr in drying Mochras lagoon on SE side of Shell Is. Bar, about 2ca seaward. Appr advised HW±2, but HW±1 at Sp. 3 grey posts, R topmarks, mark NE side of chan. Ebb tide runs strongly in the narrow ent between the sea wall and Shell Is (lt Fl WRG 4s, 079°-G-124°-W-134°-R-179°; Mar-Nov); at sp beware severe eddies inside. Inside ent, buoyed chan runs WSW to Shell Island Yacht Hbr ☎01341 241453.

Facilities: ✕ . Shifting chan, marked by posts and buoys, runs NE to Pensarn, where permanent moorings limit space. Drying .

9.11.8 PORTHMADOG

Gwynedd **52°55'·32N 04°07'·77W**

CHARTS AC 1410, 1971, 1512; Imray C61, C51, C52

TIDES –0247 Dover; ML no data; Duration 0455

Standard Port MILFORD HAVEN (⟶)

Times				Height (metres)			
High Water		Low Water		MHWS	MHWN	MLWN	MLWS
0100	0800	0100	0700	7·0	5·2	2·5	0·7
1300	2000	1300	1900				
Differences PORTHMADOG							
+0235	+0210	ND	ND	–1·9	–1·8	ND	ND

SHELTER Inner hbr (N of Cei Ballast): Good all year round; visitors' drying berths adjacent Madoc YC or afloat rafted on moored yachts. Outer hbr: Summer only, exposed to S winds. Speed limit 6kn in hbr upstream of No 8 buoy.

NAVIGATION WPT, 52°52'·96N 04°11'·18W, (SWM) Head ESE to enter laterally buoyed chan, which turns N at No 4 buoy to the E of N bank before turning NE off Ynys Gyngar (W Ho conspic).

- Channel shifts frequently and may divide but is well marked.
- Channel varies from that charted.
- In SW'lies, short steep-sided seas, especially on the ebb.
- Latest info from HM on request. Advise entering HW±1½.

LIGHTS AND MARKS Fairway buoy RW, L Fl 10s. SPM Fl Y 5s marks outfall 6ca to NW. Chan marker buoys Nos 1–9, 12,14, 15, 17 lit (May-Oct), have R/G reflective top marks and reflective numbers. Moel-y-Gest is conspic hill (259m) approx 1M WNW of harbour. Harlech Castle (ru) is about 3M SE of approach channel.

COMMUNICATIONS (Code 01766) CGOC (01407) 762051; Police 101; Dr 512284. HM 512927, mobile (07879) 433147; Pilot 530684. HM Ch 16 **12** (HO and when vessel due). Madoc YC Ch M.

FACILITIES **Harbour** £8·00 all craft, pilot, slip access HW±4 (£10), (quay), (8t) ACA.

Porthmadog SC ☎513546, .

Madoc YC ☎512976, .

Town (Chester).

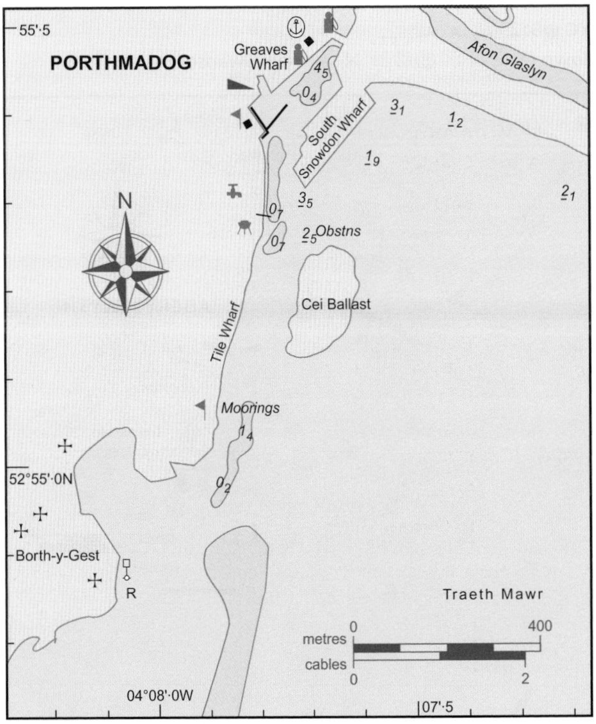

9.11.9 BARMOUTH

Gwynedd **52°42'·97N 04°03'·07W**

CHARTS AC 5609, 1410, 1971, 1484; Imray C61, C51

TIDES –0255 Dover; ML 2·6; Duration 0515

Standard Port MILFORD HAVEN (⟶)

Times				Height (metres)			
High Water		Low Water		MHWS	MHWN	MLWN	MLWS
0100	0800	0100	0700	7·0	5·2	2·5	0·7
1300	2000	1300	1900				
Differences BARMOUTH							
+0207	+0200	+0300	+0233	–2·0	–1·5	–0·6	0·0

SHELTER Good. Entry safe HW±2½, but impossible in strong SW'lies. Exposed ⚓ W of Barmouth Outer buoy in 6 to 10m. In hbr there are 5 buoys, a pontoon for up to 10 boats <10m able to take the ground to the N of the quay, at the W end of which is a visitors' berth that dries at half-tide. Secure as directed by HM because of submarine cables and strong tidal streams. Drying ⚓ inside Penrhyn Pt.

NAVIGATION WPT, Barmouth Outer SWM buoy, 52°42'·72N 04°05'·02W, 082°/0·8M to Y Perch lt, QR. Appr from SW between St Patrick's Causeway (Sarn Badrig) and Sarn-y-Bwch. Barmouth can be identified by Cader Idris, a mountain 890m high, 5M ESE. Fegla Fawr, a rounded hill, lies on S side of hbr.

- The Bar, 0·75M W of Penrhyn Pt, min depth 0·3m, is constantly changing. Chan is marked by buoys fitted with radar reflectors and reflective tape and moved as required.
- Spring ebb runs 3–5kn.
- The estuary and river (Afon Mawddach) are tidal and can be navigated for about 7M above railway br (clearance approx 5·5m); but chan is not buoyed, and sandbanks move constantly – local knowledge essential.

LIGHTS AND MARKS Outer SWM L Fl 10s; Bar SHM Fl G; No2 PHM Fl R. Y Perch Sth Cardinal bn Q6 +LFl 15s marks S end of stony ledge extending 3ca SW from Ynys y Brawd across N Bank, 50m to SE PHM, Q R, marks channel. Ynys y Brawd groyne, with bn, Fl R 5s 5M at SE end. NW end of railway bridge is lit, 2 FR (hor).

COMMUNICATIONS (Code 01341) CGOC (01407) 762051; Police 101; Dr 280521. HM 280671 mob 07795 012747; Local information www.barmouthwebcam.co.uk

Call *Barmouth Hbr* VHF Ch **12** 16 (Apr-Sep 0900-1700 later for HW; Oct-Mar 0900-1600); wind and sea state are available.

FACILITIES 3 drying buoys M (call HM in advance for deep water buoys), 8 berths inc 6 visitors' on pontoon/quay £10/£6 yacht (inc), 2 slips (HW±3, £10/day). (E) at . **Merioneth YC** ☎280000.

Town (Manchester/ L'pool); Ferry to Penrhyn Pt for **Fairbourne** .

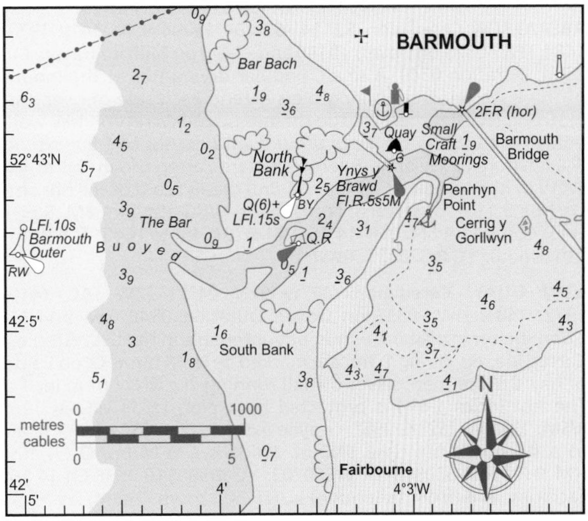

9.11.10 ABERDOVEY

Gwynedd **52°32'·57N 04°02'·72W** (Jetty)

CHARTS AC 5609, 1410, 1972, 1484; Imray C61, C51

TIDES –0257 Dover; ML 2·6; Duration 0535. For differences see 9.11.11.

SHELTER Good except in strong W/SW winds. Berth on jetty in 3m; to the E there is heavy silting.

NAVIGATION WPT Aberdovey Outer SWM buoy, 52°32´·00N 04°05´·56W, 093°/0.43M to Bar buoy.

- Bar and channel constantly shift and are hazardous below half-tide; buoys moved accordingly.
- Enter channel at gateway between Bar SHM and PHM Fl R 5s. Visitors should call HM on VHF before entering.

LIGHTS AND MARKS See 9.11.4 and chartlet. No daymarks. Lts may be unreliable. Submarine cables (prohib ⚓s) marked by bns with R ◊ topmarks.

COMMUNICATIONS (Code 01654) CGOC (01646) 690909; Police 101; Dr 710414; H 710411. HM 767626, mob 07879 433148.

Call *Aberdovey Hbr* VHF Ch **12** 16.

FACILITIES **Jetty/Wharf** 5 £8·00.
Dovey YC ☎767607, (£4.50 if engine <10hp).
Ynyslas BY (S shore) (16t).
Town ≈ ✈ (Birmingham).

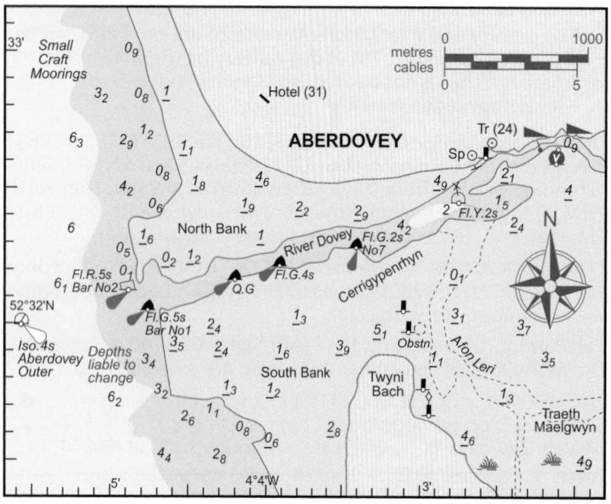

OTHER HARBOURS IN SOUTH PART OF CARDIGAN BAY

ABERAERON, Ceredigion, **52°14´·62N 04°15´·94W.** AC 1410, 1972, 1484. HW –0325 on Dover; +0140 and –1·9m on Milford Haven; ML 2·7m; Duration 0540. A small, popular drying hbr at the mouth of the R Aeron. Short drying piers extend each side of river ent. In strong NW'lies there is little shelter. £8·50/craft on NW wall, only in calm conditions. Foul ground with depths of 1·5m extend 3ca offshore to SW of Aberaeron. Beware Carreg Gloyn (0·3m) 4ca WSW of hbr, and Sarn Cadwgan (1·8m) shoals 5ca N of the hbr ent. Lts (see 9.11.4 for sectors): N pier Fl (4) WRG 15s 10m 6M. S pier Fl (3) G 10s 11m 6M. VHF **14** 16. HM ☎(01545) 571645, (from fishermen). **YC** ☎570077. **Town**.

NEW QUAY, Ceredigion, **52°12´·92N 04°21´·22W.** AC 1410, 1972, 1484. HW –0335 on Dover; Duration 0540; see 9.11.11. Good shelter in offshore winds, but untenable in North Westerlies. Carreg Ina, rks drying 1·3m, are marked by NCM buoy, Q, on E side of bay. 2 Y bns mark sewer outfall running 7ca NNW from Ina Pt. The hbr (dries 1·6m) is protected by a pier; Lt, Fl WG 3s 12m 8/5M; 135°-W-252°-G-295°. Groyne extends 80m SSE of pier head to a starboard bn; close ENE of which is a ECM bn, Q (3) 10s. HM ☎(01545) 560368; Dr ☎560203; YC ☎560516. VHF Ch **14** 16. Facilities: (from fishermen) (£8·50). **Town** (3M).

9.11.11 ABERYSTWYTH

Ceredigion **52°24'·42N 04°05'·47W**

CHARTS AC 5609, 5620, 1410, 1972, 1484; Imray C61, C51

TIDES – 0330 Dover; ML 2·7; Duration 0540

Standard Port MILFORD HAVEN (⟶)

Times				Height (metres)			
High Water		Low Water		MHWS	MHWN	MLWN	MLWS
0100	0800	0100	0700	7·0	5·2	2·5	0·7
1300	2000	1300	1900				
Differences ABERDOVEY							
+0215	+0200	+0230	+0305	–2·0	–1·7	–0·5	0·0
ABERYSTWYTH							
+0145	+0130	+0210	+0245	–2·0	–1·7	–0·7	0·0
NEW QUAY							
+0150	+0125	+0155	+0230	–2·1	–1·8	–0·6	–0·1
ABERPORTH							
+0135	+0120	+0150	+0220	–2·1	–1·8	–0·6	–0·1

SHELTER Good, in marina (1·7m) on E side of chan; or dry against Town Quay.

NAVIGATION WPT 52°24´·83N 04°06´·22W, 133/0·6M° to ent. Appr dangerous in strong on-shore winds. The Bar, close off S pier hd, has 0·7m least depth. From N, beware Castle Rks, in R sector of N bkwtr lt; also rks drying 0·5m W of N bkwtr and boulders below S pier hd. Turn 90° port inside narrow ent. E edge of inner hbr chan 0·3m is defined by WCM bn which in line with Y daymark gives a daytime lead into the harbour.

LIGHTS AND MARKS N Bkwtr Hd ≠ 140° Wellington Mon't (on top Pendinas, conspic hill 120m high) clears to S of Castle Rks. Ldg lts 133°, both FR on Ystwyth Bridge, white daymarks. WCM bn on with Y daymark leads 100° across bar into harbour entrance.

COMMUNICATIONS (Code 01970) CGOC (01646) 690909; Police 101; Dr 624855. HM 611433, Mobile 07974 023965; Marina 611422.

HM Ch **14** 16. Marina Ch 80.

FACILITIES **Marina (Y Lanfa),** ☎611422 (launch £10), 88+15 £3+£3 (10t) (15t by arrangement) wi-fi.
Town Quay £8.50/craft, Ⓔ (25t).
YC ☎612907.
Town ≈ ✈ (Swansea).

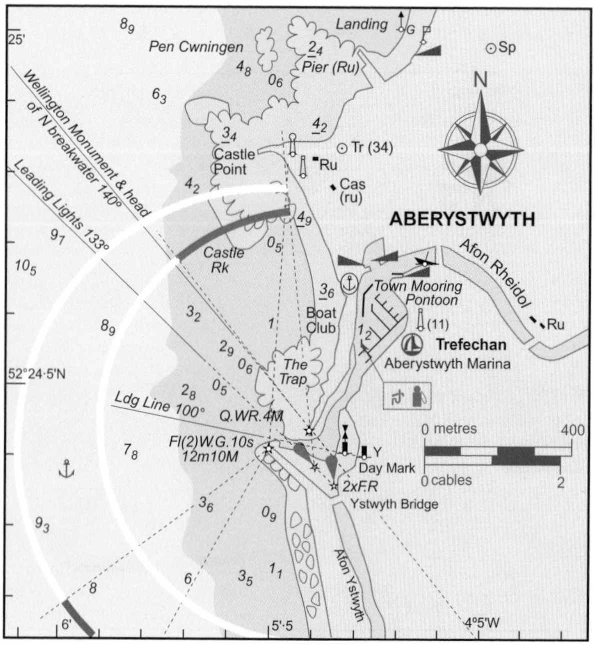

MINOR HARBOUR, 12M NE of Fishguard

PORT CARDIGAN, Ceredigion, **52°07′·02N 04°42′·07W**. AC 1973, 1484. HW –0405 on Dover; ML 2·4m; Duration 0550. Good shelter, but ent dangerous in strong N/NW winds. **Large scale charts are essential**; contact Afon Teifi Fairways Ltd, www.afonteififairways.com or Mooring Master (see below) in advance. The bar has 0·5m or less. ⚓ near Hotel (conspic) on E side of ent (2 bns Fl.R.4s, Fl.R.2s). Chan is usually close to E side marked by W posts; IDM (Fl (2) 5s) should be left to stbd when clear of the bar. ⚓ off Pen-yr-Ergyd. Inside spit pontoon or 🅐s off Teifi Boating Club, Mooring Master ☎(01239) 613966, mob 07799 284206. Upstream to Bryn-Du chan is marked by SWM but shifts constantly. St Dogmaels chan lies between 🅐s and pontoon, Mooring Master ☎07909 830752. Above the Ferry Inn chan runs up to the old bridge (3m clearance)through Netpool with deeper water moorings, Mooring Master ☎07814 035438.

Teifi Boating Club ☎613846; Services.

Town Ⓑ.

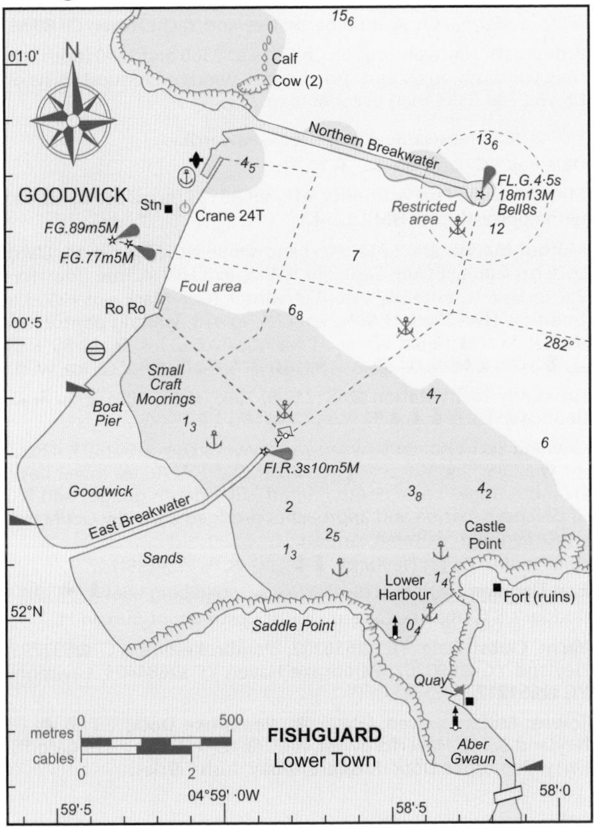

9.11.12 FISHGUARD

Pembrokeshire **52°00′·12N 04°58′·40W**

Commercial Hbr; Lower Hbr

CHARTS AC 5620, 1178, 1410, 1973, 1484; Imray C61, C51, C60

TIDES –0400 Dover; ML 2·6; Duration 0550

Standard Port MILFORD HAVEN (⟶)

Times				Height (metres)			
High Water		Low Water		MHWS	MHWN	MLWN	MLWS
0100	0800	0100	0700	7·0	5·2	2·5	0·7
1300	2000	1300	1900				
Differences FISHGUARD							
+0115	+0100	+0110	+0135	–2·2	–1·8	–0·5	+0·1
PORT CARDIGAN							
+0140	+0120	+0220	+0130	–2·3	–1·8	–0·5	0·0
CARDIGAN (Town)							
+0220	+0150	ND	ND	–2·2	–1·6	ND	ND
PORTHGAIN							
+0055	+0045	+0045	+0100	–2·5	–1·8	–0·6	0·0
RAMSEY SOUND							
+0030	+0030	+0030	+0030	–1·9	–1·3	–0·3	0·0
SOLVA							
+0015	+0010	+0035	+0015	–1·5	–1·0	–0·2	0·0
LITTLE HAVEN							
+0010	+0010	+0025	+0015	–1·1	–0·8	–0·2	0·0
MARTIN'S HAVEN							
+0010	+0010	+0015	+0015	–0·8	–0·5	+0·1	+0·1
SKOMER IS							
–0005	–0005	+0005	+0005	–0·4	–0·1	0·0	0·0

SHELTER Good, except in strong NW/NE winds. Beware large swell, especially in N winds. No ⚓, except SW of ferry quay. Good holding in most of the bay. At Lower town ⚓ off Saddle or Castle Points in 1·4m. Strong S'lies funnel down the hbr.

NAVIGATION WPT 52°01′·02N 04°57′·57W, 237°/0·48M to N bkwtr lt. *Keep at least 1ca clear of N bkwtr head; beware of ferries and High-Speed SeaCats manoeuvring.*

LIGHTS AND MARKS See 9.11.4 and chartlet. Strumble Hd Lt ho, Fl (4) 15s 45m 26M, is approx 4M WNW of hbr. The SHM (bn) at Aber Gwaun is very small.

COMMUNICATIONS (Code 01348) CGOC (01646) 690909; Police 101; Dr 872802. Commercial Hbr Supervisor 404425.

HM Ch **14** 16. Goodwick Marine Ch M (occas).

FACILITIES **Fishguard** (Lower town) dries 3·2m; limited, £5/night, 15🅐 (drying, max 5t), (from Goodwick Marine) ACA.

Fishguard Bay YC.

Town @ (Cardiff), Ferry to Rosslare; 2/day; 1¾hrs; Stena Line (www.stenaline.ie).

HARBOURS IN ST BRIDES BAY (See AC 5620)

SOLVA, Pembrokeshire, **51°52′·02N 05°11′·67W**. AC 1478. HW –0450 on Dover; ML 3·2m; Duration 0555. See 9.11.12. Good shelter for small boats that can take the ground. Avoid in strong S winds. Black Scar, Green Scar and The Mare are rks 5ca S. Ent via SSE side; best water near Black Rk in centre of ent. Beware stone spit at Trwyn Caws on W just inside ent. There are 9 Or 🅐s drying on hard sand (£6.00), drying/rafting ABs for <9·5m LOA; or ⚓ behind the rk in approx 3m. Yachts can go up to the quay (£7.50) Facilities: in village. on quay, (launching £5). HM (01437) 721703 mob 07974 020139, VHF Ch 16 8. **Solva Boat Owners Assn** ☎721489 mob 07974 020139.

ST BRIDES BAY, Pembrokeshire, **51°49′02N 05°10′·07W**. AC 1478. HW (Little Haven) –0450 on Dover; ML 3·2m; Duration 0555. See 9.11.12. A SPM buoy, Fl (5) Y 20s, is midway between Ramsey and Skomer islands at 51°48′·2N 05°20′·0W. Keep at least 100m offshore 1/9-28/2 to avoid disturbing seals, and ditto nesting sea birds 1/3-31/7. Many good ⚓s, especially between Little Haven and Borough Head in S or E winds or between Solva and Dinas Fawr in N or E winds. In W'lies boats should shelter in Solva (above), Skomer (below) or Pendinas Bach. Tankers ⚓ in mouth of bay. For apprs from the N or S see 9.11.5. Facilities: (Little Haven) (cans).

SKOMER, Pembrokeshire, **51°44′·42N 05°16′·77W**. AC 1478, 2878. HW –0455 Dover. See 9.11.12. The island is a National Nature Reserve (fee payable to Warden on landing) and also a Marine Nature Reserve, extending to Marloes Peninsula. Keep at least 100m offshore 1/9-28/2 to avoid disturbing seals and ditto nesting sea birds 1/3-31/7. There is a 5kn speed limit within 100m of the island. ⚓ in S Haven (N Haven no ⚓ due to eel grass). Enter N Haven close to W shore, and land on W side of bay on beach or at steps. In N Haven pick up 🅐s provided. No access to the island from S Haven. For Jack Sound see 9.11.5. There are no lts, marks or facilities. For info, Marine Conservation Officer ☎(01646) 636736.

9.11.13 MILFORD HAVEN

Pembrokeshire **51°40'·13N 05°08'·16W**

CHARTS AC 5620, 1410, 1178, 1478, 2878, 3273/4/5; Imray C60, C13, 2600

TIDES –0500 Dover; ML 3·8; Duration 0605

Standard Port MILFORD HAVEN (⟶)

Times				Height (metres)			
High Water		Low Water		MHWS	MHWN	MLWN	MLWS
0100	0800	0100	0700	7·0	5·2	2·5	0·7
1300	2000	1300	1900				
Differences DALE ROADS							
–0005	–0005	–0008	–0008	0·0	0·0	0·0	–0·1
NEYLAND							
+0002	*+0010*	*0000*	*0000*	*0·0*	*0·0*	*0·0*	*0·0*
HAVERFORDWEST							
+0010	+0025	DR	DR	–4·8	–4·9	DR	DR
LLANGWM (Black Tar)							
+0010	+0020	+0005	0000	+0·1	+0·1	0·0	–0·1

SHELTER Very good in various places round the hbr, especially in Milford Marina and Neyland Yacht Haven. ⚓s in Dale Bay; off Chapel Bay and Angle Pt on S shore; off Scotch Bay, E of Milford marina; and others beyond Pembroke Dock. Free pontoons (May-Oct) include: Dale Bay, Gelliswick Bay; waiting pontoons off Milford Dock and Hobbs Pt (for Pembroke Dock); and drying pontoons at Dale Beach, Hazelbeach, Neyland and Burton; mainly intended for tenders. It is possible to dry out safely at inshore areas of Dale, Sandy Haven and Angle Bay, depending on weather.

NAVIGATION WPT (W) 51°40′·25N 05°10′·65W. WPT (E) 51°40′·05N 05°08′·06W.

- The tide sets strongly across the ent to the Haven particularly at sp. In bad weather avoid passing over Mid Chan Rks and St Ann's Hd shoal, where a confused sea and swell will be found. Give St Ann's Head a wide berth especially on the ebb, when East Chan by Sheep Island is better.
- Beware large tankers entering/departing the Haven and ferries moving at high speed in the lower Haven. **Keep outside the main shipping channels if possible.**
- Milford Haven Port Authority has a jetty, Port Control and offices near Hubberston Pt. Their launches have G hulls and W upperworks with 'PILOT' in black letters and fly a Pilot flag while on patrol; Fl Bu lt at night. Their instructions must be obeyed. No vessel may pass within 100m of any terminal or any tanker, whether at ⚓ or under way.

River Cleddau is navigable 6M to Picton Pt, at junction of West and East arms, at all tides for boats of moderate draught. Clearance under Cleddau Bridge above Neyland is 36m; and 25m under power cable 1M upstream. Chan to Haverfordwest has 2m at HW and clearances of only 6m below cables and bridge; only feasible for shoal draught/lifting keel and unmasted craft.

Firing Ranges to the S and SE, see 9.11.14 and AC 1076.

LIGHTS AND MARKS See 9.11.4 and chartlets. Y SPM have been established in W Angle, Gelliswick, Dale Bays and off Jenkins Pt to prohibit high speed craft and water skiing.

Milford Haven leading lights are specifically for VLCCs entering/leaving hbr and proceeding to/from the oil refineries. The Haven is very well buoyed and lit as far as Cleddau bridge.

Milford Dock ldg lts 348°, both F.Bu, with W ○ daymarks. Dock entry sigs on E side of lock: 2 FG (vert) = gates open, vessels may enter. VHF Ch 18 is normally used for ent/exit by day and night.

COMMUNICATIONS (Code 01646) Lock 696310; CGOC 690909; Police 101; Ⓗ Haverfordwest (01437) 764545; Dr 690674. Port Control 696136/7.

Monitor *Milford Haven Port Control* Ch 12 (H24) while underway in the Haven. *Milford Haven Patrol* launches Ch11/12 (H24). To lock in to Milford Dock marina call *Pierhead,* Ch 14, for clearance, then call *Milford Marina,* Ch for a berth. Neyland Yacht Haven Ch 80/M.

Broadcasts: Nav warnings on Ch 12 14 at 0300 and 1500 (both UT). Gale warnings on receipt. Tide hts and winds on request. Bcsts on Ch 16 67 at 0335 then every 4hrs to 2335.

FACILITIES **Marinas/Berthing** (from seaward):

Dale Bay YC Pontoon.

Milford Haven Port Authority jetty ☎696133 (occas use by visitors with approval from HM).

Milford Marina ☎696312, Pierhead ☎696310. VHF Ch 14, 80/M. Lock hrs summer (Apr–Sep): ent HW–5, exit HW–4, free flow HW–2¼ to HW–¼, ent+3½, exit+4½; winter (Oct–Mar): ent HW–3¼, free flow HW–2¼ to HW–¼, ent+2½, exit+3; waiting pontoon or shelter in lock, 3·5m water at MLWS. 280 inc Ⓥ, £2·85 (H24) Ⓔ (14t) Ⓑ ice, wi-fi.

Lawrenny Yacht Station ☎651212/651065, £5, 100; (launch £5) (15t).

Neyland Yacht Haven, www.yachthavens.com ☎601601, 420 inc Ⓥ £2.95, Ⓔ (20t); Access lower basin H24, but upper basin depth limited (sill + depth gauges and R/G lit perches); marina and approaches dredged annually Oct/March – proceed with extreme caution.

Dale Sailing Co (at Neyland) LPG (35t).

East Llannion Marine: access HW±3, scrubbing piles (30t).

Rudder's BY, small but useful, is just upstream of Burton Pt.

Yacht Clubs: Dale YC ☎636362; Pembrokeshire YC ☎692799; Neyland YC ☎600267; Pembroke Haven YC ☎684403; Lawrenny YC ☎651212.

Towns: Milford Haven, Ⓑ. Pembroke Dock; Ⓑ Ⓗ. Neyland, Ⓑ. Haverfordwest, Ⓗ Ⓑ ✈ (Swansea or Cardiff). Ferry: Pembroke Dock–Rosslare; 2/day; Irish Ferries.

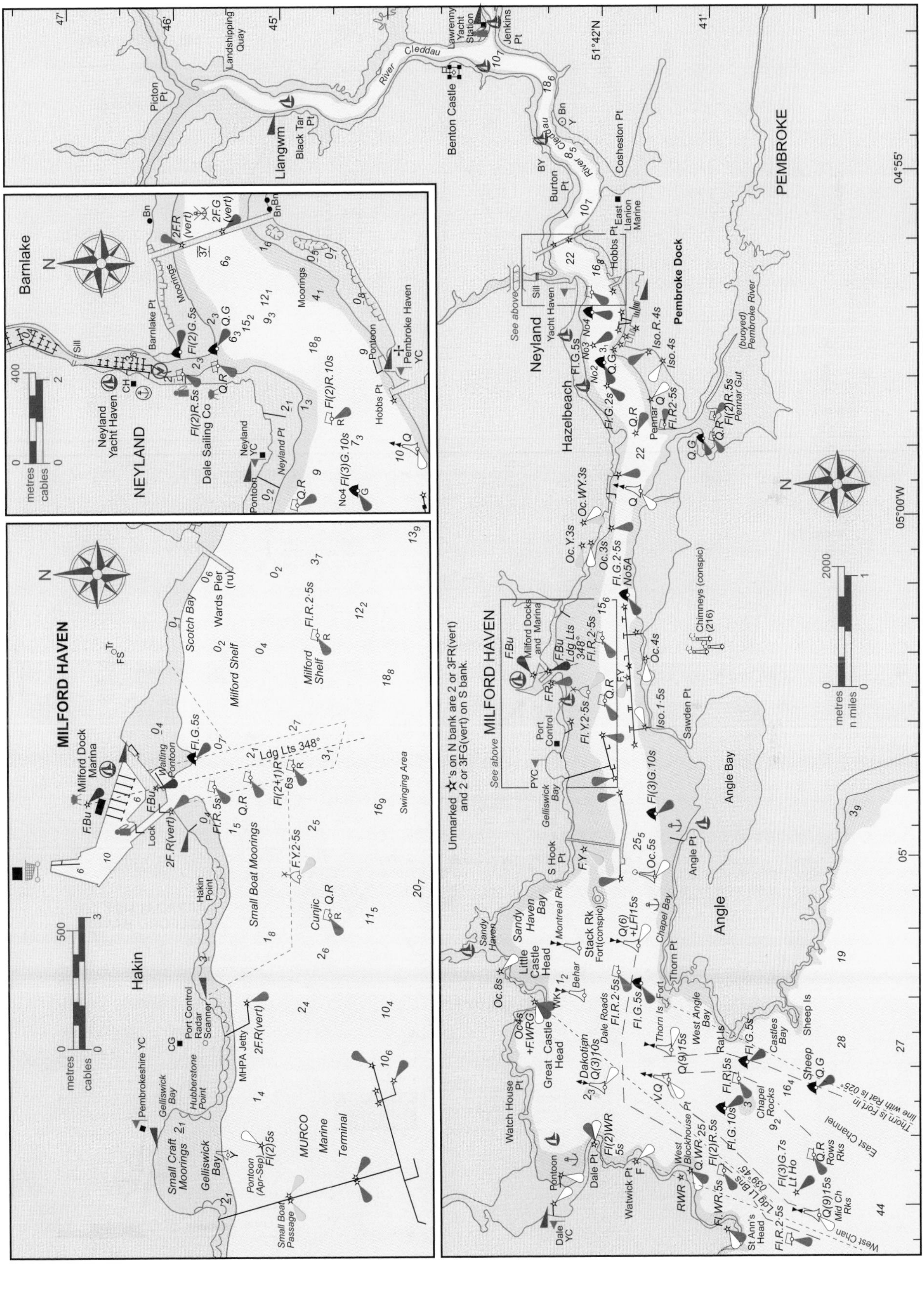
MILFORD HAVEN
Milford Dock Marina
Hakin
Hakin Point
Scotch Bay
Wards Pier (ru)
Milford Shelf
Small Boat Moorings
Swinging Area
Ldg Lts 348°
Cunjic
MURCO Marine Terminal
MHPA Jetty
Port Control Radar Scanner
Pembrokeshire YC
Gelliswick Bay
Hubberstone Point
Small Craft Moorings
Small Boat Passage
Pontoon (Apr-Sep)
Waiting Pontoon
Lock
NEYLAND
Neyland Yacht Haven
Dale Sailing Co
Neyland YC
Neyland Pt
Barnlake
Barnlake Pt
Hobbs Pt
Pembroke Haven YC
Moorings
Sill
metres
cables
Picton Pt
Landshipping Quay
Llangwm
Black Tar Pt
River Cleddau
Benton Castle
Lawrenny Yacht Station
Jenkins Pt
51°42'N
Burton Pt
Cosheston Pt
East Llanion Marine
PEMBROKE
Pembroke Dock
Pembroke River
Pennar Gut
Hazelbeach
Neyland
Yacht Haven
See above
Milford Docks and Marina
Port Control
PYC
S Hook Pt
Sandy Haven
Sandy Haven Bay
Little Castle Head
Montreal Rk
Stack Rk Fort(conspic)
Chapel Bay
Thorn Pt
Angle
Angle Bay
Angle Pt
Sawden Pt
Chimneys (conspic) (216)
Great Castle Head
Dale Roads
Thorn Is Fort
West Angle Bay
Rat Is
Castles Bay
Sheep Is
Chapel Rocks
Watch House Pt
Dale Pt
Dale YC
Watwick Pt
West Blockhouse Pt
St Ann's Head
Mid Ch Rks
Rows Rks
East Channel
West Chan
Ldg Lt Bns 039·45°
Thorn Is Fort in line with Rat Is 025°
Unmarked ☆'s on N bank are 2 or 3FR(vert) and 2 or 3FG(vert) on S bank.
05°00'W
04°55'
05'
n miles

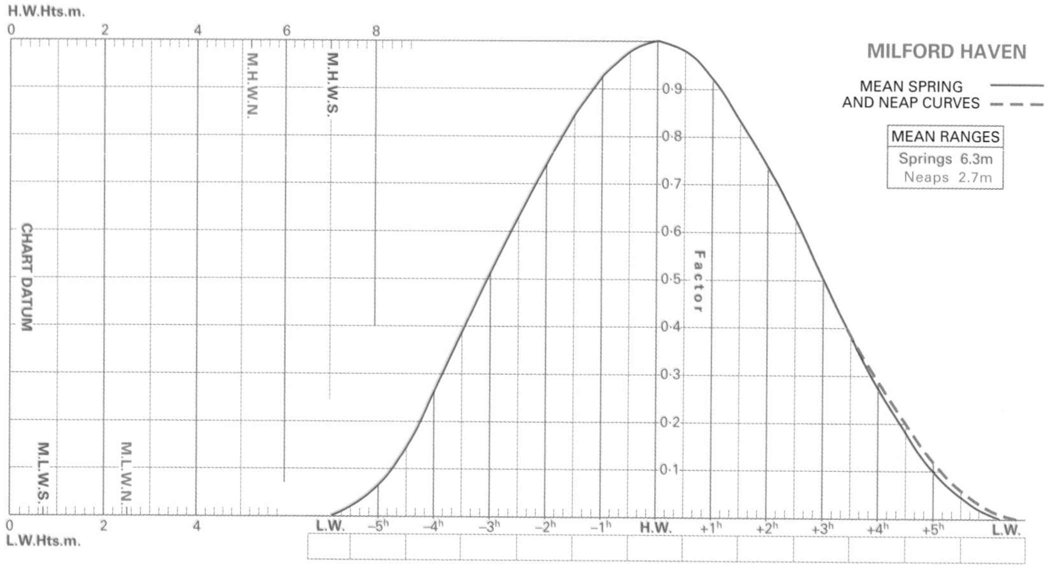
H.W.Hts.m.
0
2
4
6
8
M.H.W.N.
M.H.W.S.
CHART DATUM
M.L.W.S.
M.L.W.N.
0·9
0·8
0·7
0·6
0·5
0·4
0·3
0·2
0·1
Factor
0
2
4
L.W.Hts.m.
L.W.
−5h
−4h
−3h
−2h
−1h
H.W.
+1h
+2h
+3h
+4h
+5h
L.W.
MILFORD HAVEN
MEAN SPRING
AND NEAP CURVES
MEAN RANGES
Springs 6.3m
Neaps 2.7m

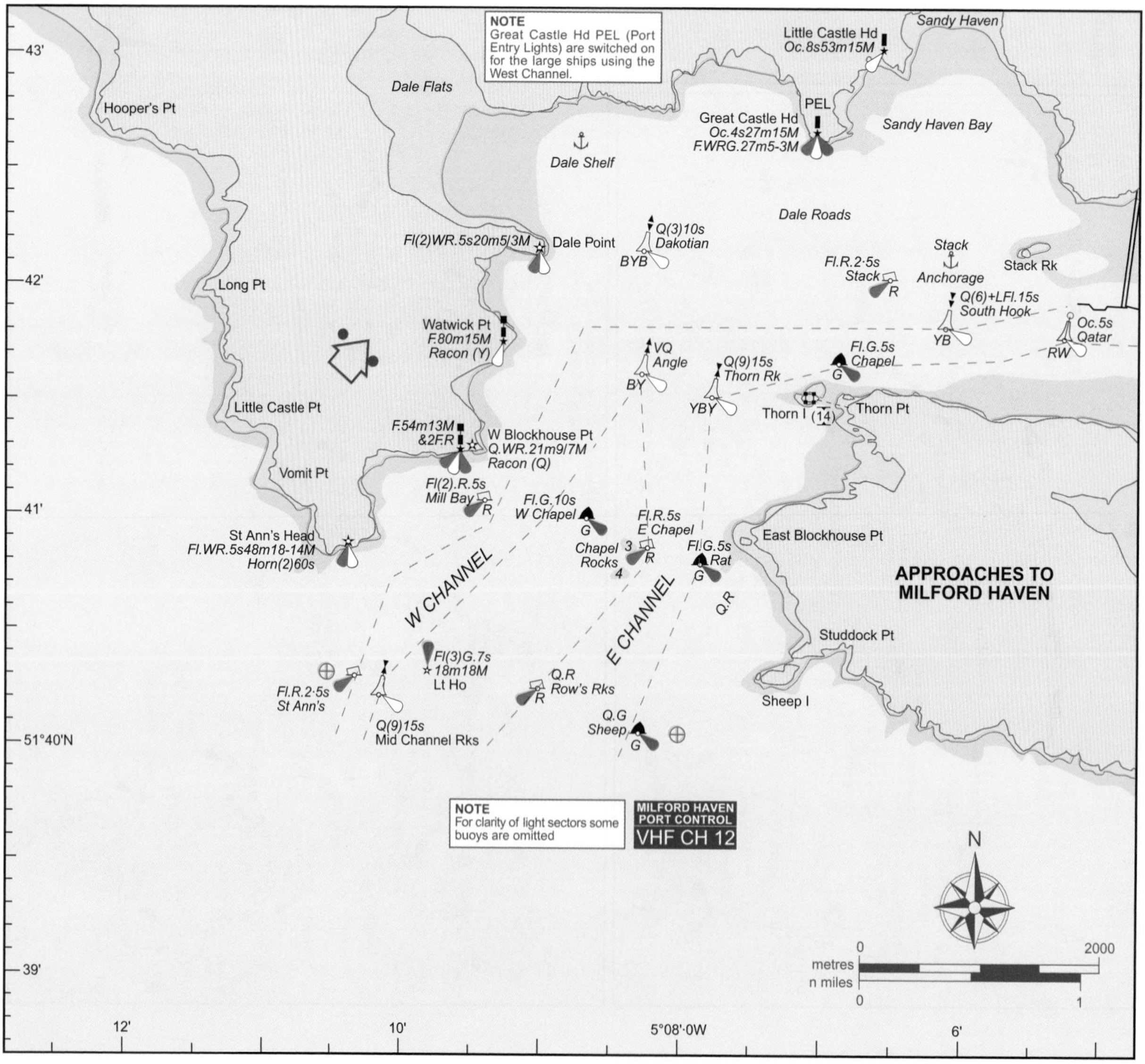
NOTE
Great Castle Hd PEL (Port Entry Lights) are switched on for the large ships using the West Channel.
Little Castle Hd
Oc.8s53m15M
Sandy Haven
Hooper's Pt
Dale Flats
PEL
Great Castle Hd
Oc.4s27m15M
F.WRG.27m5-3M
Sandy Haven Bay
Dale Shelf
Dale Roads
Q(3)10s
Dakotian
BYB
Fl(2)WR.5s20m5/3M
Dale Point
Fl.R.2·5s
Stack
R
Stack
Anchorage
Stack Rk
Long Pt
Q(6)+LFl.15s
South Hook
YB
Oc.5s
Qatar
RW
Watwick Pt
F.80m15M
Racon (Y)
VQ
Angle
BY
Q(9)15s
Thorn Rk
YBY
Fl.G.5s
Chapel
G
Thorn I
14
Thorn Pt
Little Castle Pt
F.54m13M
&2F.R
W Blockhouse Pt
Q.WR.21m9/7M
Racon (Q)
Vomit Pt
Fl(2).R.5s
Mill Bay
R
Fl.G.10s
W Chapel
G
Fl.R.5s
E Chapel
3
R
Chapel
Rocks
4
Fl.G.5s
Rat
G
East Blockhouse Pt
St Ann's Head
Fl.WR.5s48m18-14M
Horn(2)60s
W CHANNEL
E CHANNEL
Q.R
APPROACHES TO
MILFORD HAVEN
Studdock Pt
Fl(3)G.7s
18m18M
Lt Ho
Fl.R.2·5s
St Ann's
Q(9)15s
Mid Channel Rks
Q.R
Row's Rks
R
Q.G
Sheep
G
Sheep I
NOTE
For clarity of light sectors some buoys are omitted
MILFORD HAVEN
PORT CONTROL
VHF CH 12
N
0
2000
metres
n miles
0
1
43'
42'
41'
51°40'N
39'
12'
10'
5°08'·0W
6'

STANDARD TIME (UT)
For Summer Time add ONE hour in **non-shaded areas**

MILFORD HAVEN LAT 51°42′N LONG 5°03′W

TIMES AND HEIGHTS OF HIGH AND LOW WATERS

Dates in red are SPRINGS
Dates in blue are NEAPS

YEAR **2018**

JANUARY

Date	Day	Time	m	Time	m	Time	m	Time	m
1	M	0507	7.0	1133	0.9	1735	7.1	2356	0.7
2	TU ○	0559	7.3	1225	0.6	1827	7.3		
3	W	0046	0.6	0649	7.5	1315	0.5	1916	7.4
4	TH	0134	0.5	0738	7.5	1403	0.5	2004	7.3
5	F	0221	0.6	0825	7.4	1451	0.7	2051	7.0
6	SA	0307	0.9	0912	7.1	1538	1.0	2138	6.7
7	SU	0353	1.2	0959	6.8	1625	1.4	2226	6.3
8	M ◑	0441	1.6	1048	6.3	1716	1.8	2317	5.9
9	TU	0534	2.0	1143	5.9	1814	2.1		
10	W	0017	5.6	0637	2.3	1247	5.6	1921	2.3
11	TH	0126	5.4	0750	2.4	1357	5.5	2033	2.3
12	F	0236	5.5	0900	2.3	1505	5.6	2135	2.2
13	SA	0339	5.7	0959	2.1	1604	5.8	2226	2.0
14	SU	0431	6.0	1047	1.9	1652	6.0	2309	1.7
15	M	0514	6.3	1129	1.6	1733	6.2	2347	1.5
16	TU	0552	6.5	1207	1.5	1810	6.4		
17	W ●	0023	1.4	0627	6.6	1242	1.3	1843	6.5
18	TH	0056	1.3	0700	6.7	1316	1.2	1916	6.6
19	F	0128	1.2	0733	6.8	1349	1.2	1948	6.6
20	SA	0201	1.2	0806	6.7	1422	1.2	2021	6.5
21	SU	0234	1.3	0840	6.6	1457	1.3	2055	6.4
22	M	0309	1.5	0915	6.5	1533	1.5	2132	6.2
23	TU	0346	1.7	0955	6.3	1613	1.7	2214	6.0
24	W ◐	0428	1.9	1041	6.0	1659	1.9	2305	5.7
25	TH	0521	2.1	1138	5.8	1759	2.1		
26	F	0010	5.6	0630	2.3	1250	5.7	1916	2.2
27	SA	0128	5.6	0757	2.2	1409	5.8	2039	2.0
28	SU	0246	5.8	0917	1.9	1522	6.1	2150	1.6
29	M	0355	6.3	1024	1.4	1628	6.5	2251	1.2
30	TU	0456	6.7	1123	1.0	1726	6.9	2345	0.8
31	W ○	0550	7.2	1215	0.6	1818	7.2		

FEBRUARY

Date	Day	Time	m	Time	m	Time	m	Time	m
1	TH	0035	0.5	0639	7.4	1305	0.3	1905	7.4
2	F	0122	0.4	0725	7.6	1351	0.3	1950	7.3
3	SA	0206	0.4	0809	7.5	1434	0.4	2032	7.2
4	SU	0248	0.6	0851	7.3	1515	0.7	2113	6.9
5	M	0328	0.9	0932	6.9	1554	1.1	2154	6.4
6	TU	0407	1.4	1013	6.4	1633	1.6	2235	6.0
7	W ◑	0448	1.8	1057	5.9	1717	2.1	2323	5.6
8	TH	0538	2.2	1149	5.5	1813	2.4		
9	F	0025	5.2	0644	2.6	1259	5.2	1930	2.6
10	SA	0145	5.1	0811	2.6	1422	5.1	2055	2.6
11	SU	0304	5.3	0928	2.4	1536	5.4	2159	2.3
12	M	0406	5.6	1024	2.1	1631	5.7	2248	1.9
13	TU	0453	6.0	1110	1.7	1714	6.0	2328	1.6
14	W	0532	6.3	1148	1.4	1751	6.3		
15	TH ●	0004	1.3	0607	6.6	1224	1.2	1824	6.5
16	F	0038	1.1	0641	6.8	1257	1.0	1857	6.7
17	SA	0110	1.0	0713	6.9	1330	0.9	1929	6.8
18	SU	0143	0.9	0746	6.9	1403	0.9	2001	6.8
19	M	0216	0.9	0819	6.9	1436	0.9	2034	6.7
20	TU	0250	1.0	0854	6.8	1511	1.1	2109	6.5
21	W	0325	1.3	0931	6.6	1548	1.3	2148	6.3
22	TH	0404	1.5	1014	6.2	1630	1.6	2234	5.9
23	F ◐	0452	1.9	1107	5.9	1724	2.0	2335	5.6
24	SA	0556	2.2	1218	5.6	1841	2.2		
25	SU	0057	5.4	0730	2.3	1345	5.5	2016	2.2
26	M	0226	5.6	0903	2.0	1509	5.8	2137	1.8
27	TU	0344	6.1	1015	1.5	1619	6.3	2240	1.3
28	W	0446	6.6	1113	1.0	1716	6.7	2333	0.8

MARCH

Date	Day	Time	m	Time	m	Time	m	Time	m
1	TH	0539	7.1	1204	0.5	1805	7.1		
2	F ○	0021	0.5	0625	7.4	1250	0.3	1848	7.3
3	SA	0105	0.3	0708	7.5	1332	0.2	1929	7.4
4	SU	0145	0.3	0748	7.5	1410	0.3	2008	7.2
5	M	0223	0.5	0826	7.2	1446	0.6	2045	6.9
6	TU	0259	0.8	0902	6.9	1520	1.0	2120	6.6
7	W	0333	1.2	0937	6.4	1553	1.5	2155	6.1
8	TH	0408	1.7	1014	6.0	1627	2.0	2235	5.7
9	F ◑	0447	2.1	1056	5.5	1710	2.4	2325	5.2
10	SA	0543	2.6	1155	5.0	1820	2.8		
11	SU	0042	5.0	0711	2.8	1330	4.8	2003	2.8
12	M	0221	5.0	0848	2.6	1501	5.0	2125	2.5
13	TU	0333	5.4	0954	2.2	1603	5.4	2219	2.1
14	W	0424	5.8	1042	1.8	1647	5.9	2302	1.7
15	TH	0505	6.2	1122	1.4	1724	6.2	2338	1.3
16	F	0541	6.6	1157	1.1	1759	6.6		
17	SA ●	0013	1.0	0614	6.8	1232	0.9	1831	6.8
18	SU	0047	0.8	0648	7.0	1306	0.7	1904	7.0
19	M	0121	0.7	0722	7.1	1340	0.6	1938	7.0
20	TU	0155	0.7	0757	7.1	1415	0.7	2013	7.0
21	W	0230	0.8	0833	7.0	1450	0.8	2049	6.8
22	TH	0307	1.0	0911	6.7	1527	1.1	2128	6.5
23	F	0347	1.3	0955	6.3	1610	1.5	2215	6.1
24	SA ◐	0435	1.7	1049	5.9	1704	2.0	2316	5.7
25	SU	0541	2.1	1201	5.5	1822	2.3		
26	M	0040	5.4	0719	2.2	1333	5.4	2003	2.2
27	TU	0214	5.6	0853	1.9	1500	5.7	2124	1.8
28	W	0332	6.0	1003	1.4	1608	6.2	2226	1.3
29	TH	0432	6.5	1059	1.0	1701	6.7	2318	0.9
30	F	0522	7.0	1146	0.6	1746	7.0		
31	SA ○	0002	0.6	0605	7.2	1229	0.4	1827	7.2

APRIL

Date	Day	Time	m	Time	m	Time	m	Time	m
1	SU	0043	0.4	0645	7.3	1307	0.4	1905	7.2
2	M	0121	0.4	0723	7.3	1342	0.5	1941	7.1
3	TU	0156	0.6	0758	7.1	1416	0.7	2015	6.9
4	W	0230	0.8	0831	6.8	1447	1.1	2047	6.6
5	TH	0302	1.2	0904	6.4	1517	1.5	2121	6.2
6	F	0334	1.6	0938	6.0	1548	1.9	2157	5.8
7	SA	0410	2.0	1016	5.5	1625	2.3	2241	5.4
8	SU ◑	0458	2.5	1108	5.1	1722	2.7	2345	5.0
9	M	0616	2.7	1226	4.8	1900	2.9		
10	TU	0122	4.9	0754	2.7	1412	4.9	2035	2.7
11	W	0247	5.2	0910	2.3	1521	5.3	2138	2.3
12	TH	0344	5.7	1003	1.9	1609	5.7	2225	1.8
13	F	0427	6.1	1046	1.5	1649	6.2	2304	1.4
14	SA	0506	6.5	1124	1.1	1726	6.6	2342	1.1
15	SU	0543	6.8	1201	0.8	1801	6.9		
16	M ●	0019	0.8	0619	7.1	1239	0.6	1837	7.1
17	TU	0056	0.6	0657	7.2	1316	0.5	1914	7.2
18	W	0134	0.6	0735	7.2	1354	0.6	1952	7.1
19	TH	0213	0.6	0815	7.1	1432	0.8	2032	6.9
20	F	0253	0.9	0857	6.8	1513	1.1	2115	6.6
21	SA	0337	1.2	0944	6.4	1559	1.5	2206	6.2
22	SU ◐	0429	1.6	1042	5.9	1656	1.9	2309	5.8
23	M	0539	2.0	1154	5.5	1815	2.2		
24	TU	0030	5.6	0711	2.1	1320	5.5	1948	2.2
25	W	0157	5.7	0837	1.8	1442	5.7	2105	1.8
26	TH	0312	6.1	0943	1.5	1547	6.1	2205	1.4
27	F	0410	6.5	1037	1.1	1639	6.5	2255	1.1
28	SA	0459	6.8	1122	0.8	1723	6.8	2338	0.8
29	SU	0542	7.0	1202	0.7	1803	7.0		
30	M ○	0018	0.7	0620	7.0	1239	0.7	1839	7.0

Chart Datum: 3·71 metres below Ordnance Datum (Newlyn). HAT is 7·9 metres above Chart Datum.

STANDARD TIME (UT)
For Summer Time add ONE hour in **non-shaded areas**

MILFORD HAVEN **LAT 51°42'N LONG 5°03'W**

TIMES AND HEIGHTS OF HIGH AND LOW WATERS

Dates in red are SPRINGS
Dates in blue are NEAPS

YEAR **2018**

MAY

Date	Day	Time	m	Time	m	Time	m	Time	m	Moon
1	TU	0055	0.7	0656	7.0	1314	0.8	1913	6.9	
2	W	0129	0.8	0730	6.8	1347	1.0	1947	6.8	
3	TH	0203	1.0	0803	6.6	1418	1.2	2019	6.6	
4	F	0235	1.3	0836	6.3	1448	1.5	2052	6.3	
5	SA	0308	1.6	0909	6.0	1520	1.9	2128	5.9	
6	SU	0343	1.9	0947	5.6	1556	2.2	2210	5.6	
7	M	0428	2.3	1034	5.2	1644	2.5	2305	5.3	
8	TU	0530	2.5	1137	5.0	1759	2.8			◑
9	W	0018	5.1	0654	2.6	1302	4.9	1931	2.7	
10	TH	0144	5.2	0811	2.4	1423	5.2	2042	2.4	
11	F	0250	5.6	0912	2.0	1520	5.6	2137	2.0	
12	SA	0341	6.0	1002	1.6	1606	6.1	2224	1.5	
13	SU	0426	6.4	1046	1.2	1648	6.5	2307	1.2	
14	M	0508	6.8	1128	0.9	1729	6.9	2349	0.8	
15	TU	0550	7.1	1210	0.6	1811	7.1			●
16	W	0032	0.6	0633	7.2	1253	0.5	1852	7.2	
17	TH	0115	0.6	0716	7.2	1336	0.6	1935	7.2	
18	F	0159	0.6	0801	7.1	1419	0.7	2020	7.1	
19	SA	0244	0.8	0848	6.8	1504	1.0	2108	6.8	
20	SU	0333	1.1	0939	6.4	1553	1.4	2202	6.4	
21	M	0428	1.5	1037	6.0	1651	1.8	2304	6.1	
22	TU	0536	1.8	1143	5.7	1804	2.0			◐
23	W	0015	5.9	0654	1.9	1259	5.6	1923	2.0	
24	TH	0131	5.9	0809	1.8	1413	5.7	2036	1.9	
25	F	0241	6.0	0914	1.6	1517	6.0	2137	1.6	
26	SA	0341	6.3	1009	1.4	1610	6.3	2228	1.4	
27	SU	0432	6.5	1055	1.2	1656	6.5	2312	1.2	
28	M	0516	6.6	1135	1.1	1737	6.6	2352	1.1	
29	TU	0556	6.6	1212	1.1	1815	6.7			○
30	W	0029	1.1	0632	6.6	1248	1.1	1849	6.7	
31	TH	0105	1.1	0707	6.6	1321	1.2	1923	6.7	

JUNE

Date	Day	Time	m	Time	m	Time	m	Time	m	Moon
1	F	0140	1.2	0740	6.4	1354	1.3	1957	6.5	
2	SA	0213	1.4	0814	6.3	1426	1.5	2031	6.3	
3	SU	0247	1.6	0848	6.0	1458	1.8	2107	6.1	
4	M	0323	1.8	0925	5.8	1535	2.0	2146	5.9	
5	TU	0405	2.0	1007	5.5	1618	2.3	2233	5.6	
6	W	0455	2.2	1059	5.3	1713	2.5	2331	5.4	◑
7	TH	0558	2.4	1202	5.2	1826	2.5			
8	F	0039	5.4	0710	2.3	1315	5.2	1941	2.4	
9	SA	0149	5.6	0816	2.1	1423	5.5	2045	2.1	
10	SU	0251	5.9	0915	1.7	1520	5.9	2142	1.7	
11	M	0345	6.3	1008	1.4	1612	6.4	2233	1.3	
12	TU	0436	6.6	1058	1.0	1700	6.8	2323	1.0	
13	W	0525	6.9	1146	0.8	1748	7.1			●
14	TH	0012	0.7	0613	7.1	1234	0.6	1835	7.2	
15	F	0100	0.6	0702	7.2	1321	0.6	1923	7.3	
16	SA	0149	0.5	0751	7.1	1408	0.7	2012	7.2	
17	SU	0238	0.7	0841	6.9	1456	0.9	2102	7.0	
18	M	0328	0.9	0932	6.6	1546	1.2	2154	6.7	
19	TU	0421	1.2	1025	6.3	1640	1.5	2249	6.4	
20	W	0520	1.5	1123	6.0	1741	1.8	2350	6.1	◐
21	TH	0624	1.8	1226	5.7	1849	2.0			
22	F	0056	5.9	0732	1.9	1335	5.7	1958	2.0	
23	SA	0204	5.8	0838	1.9	1440	5.8	2103	1.9	
24	SU	0308	5.9	0936	1.8	1539	5.9	2159	1.7	
25	M	0403	6.0	1026	1.6	1630	6.2	2247	1.6	
26	TU	0452	6.2	1110	1.5	1714	6.3	2330	1.5	
27	W	0534	6.3	1149	1.4	1754	6.5			
28	TH	0009	1.4	0612	6.4	1226	1.3	1830	6.6	○
29	F	0046	1.3	0648	6.4	1301	1.3	1905	6.6	
30	SA	0121	1.3	0722	6.4	1334	1.4	1939	6.5	

JULY

Date	Day	Time	m	Time	m	Time	m	Time	m	Moon
1	SU	0155	1.3	0756	6.3	1407	1.4	2013	6.5	
2	M	0229	1.4	0829	6.2	1440	1.6	2047	6.3	
3	TU	0304	1.6	0904	6.0	1515	1.7	2124	6.1	
4	W	0341	1.7	0942	5.8	1554	1.9	2204	5.9	
5	TH	0423	1.9	1025	5.6	1638	2.1	2252	5.8	
6	F	0512	2.1	1116	5.5	1732	2.3	2348	5.6	◑
7	SA	0612	2.2	1219	5.4	1840	2.3			
8	SU	0054	5.6	0722	2.1	1330	5.5	1955	2.2	
9	M	0205	5.8	0832	1.9	1439	5.8	2104	1.9	
10	TU	0310	6.1	0935	1.6	1541	6.2	2206	1.5	
11	W	0410	6.4	1034	1.2	1637	6.6	2303	1.1	
12	TH	0506	6.8	1128	0.9	1731	7.0	2357	0.8	
13	F	0600	7.0	1219	0.7	1823	7.2			●
14	SA	0049	0.5	0651	7.2	1309	0.5	1913	7.4	
15	SU	0139	0.4	0741	7.2	1357	0.5	2002	7.4	
16	M	0228	0.5	0829	7.1	1445	0.7	2049	7.2	
17	TU	0316	0.7	0916	6.8	1531	0.9	2137	7.0	
18	W	0403	1.0	1003	6.5	1619	1.3	2225	6.6	
19	TH	0451	1.4	1053	6.1	1709	1.6	2317	6.2	◐
20	F	0544	1.8	1148	5.8	1806	2.0			
21	SA	0015	5.8	0645	2.1	1251	5.5	1913	2.2	
22	SU	0122	5.6	0755	2.2	1401	5.5	2026	2.3	
23	M	0232	5.5	0903	2.2	1508	5.6	2131	2.1	
24	TU	0337	5.6	1001	2.0	1607	5.8	2226	1.9	
25	W	0432	5.9	1049	1.8	1655	6.1	2311	1.7	
26	TH	0517	6.1	1130	1.6	1736	6.3	2352	1.5	
27	F	0556	6.2	1208	1.4	1813	6.5			○
28	SA	0028	1.3	0631	6.4	1243	1.3	1847	6.6	
29	SU	0103	1.3	0704	6.4	1315	1.3	1920	6.7	
30	M	0136	1.2	0736	6.4	1347	1.3	1953	6.7	
31	TU	0209	1.2	0808	6.4	1420	1.3	2026	6.6	

AUGUST

Date	Day	Time	m	Time	m	Time	m	Time	m	Moon
1	W	0242	1.3	0841	6.3	1453	1.4	2059	6.5	
2	TH	0316	1.4	0915	6.2	1529	1.6	2136	6.3	
3	F	0353	1.6	0953	6.0	1607	1.8	2217	6.0	
4	SA	0435	1.8	1038	5.8	1653	2.1	2307	5.8	◑
5	SU	0526	2.1	1134	5.6	1752	2.2			
6	M	0011	5.6	0633	2.2	1247	5.5	1912	2.3	
7	TU	0128	5.6	0756	2.1	1407	5.6	2037	2.1	
8	W	0245	5.8	0913	1.8	1520	6.0	2150	1.7	
9	TH	0354	6.2	1018	1.4	1623	6.5	2251	1.2	
10	F	0455	6.7	1115	1.0	1720	7.0	2346	0.7	
11	SA	0550	7.0	1207	0.7	1812	7.3			●
12	SU	0037	0.4	0639	7.3	1256	0.4	1900	7.5	
13	M	0126	0.3	0726	7.4	1342	0.4	1946	7.6	
14	TU	0211	0.3	0810	7.3	1426	0.5	2030	7.4	
15	W	0254	0.5	0853	7.0	1508	0.7	2112	7.1	
16	TH	0335	0.9	0935	6.7	1549	1.1	2154	6.7	
17	F	0416	1.4	1017	6.2	1632	1.6	2238	6.2	
18	SA	0459	1.9	1104	5.8	1719	2.1	2328	5.7	◐
19	SU	0551	2.3	1201	5.4	1822	2.5			
20	M	0033	5.3	0703	2.6	1317	5.2	1944	2.6	
21	TU	0155	5.1	0829	2.6	1438	5.3	2105	2.5	
22	W	0313	5.3	0938	2.3	1545	5.6	2206	2.2	
23	TH	0413	5.6	1029	2.0	1636	6.0	2253	1.8	
24	F	0458	6.0	1111	1.7	1717	6.3	2333	1.5	
25	SA	0536	6.2	1148	1.5	1753	6.6			
26	SU	0008	1.3	0610	6.5	1222	1.3	1826	6.7	○
27	M	0042	1.1	0642	6.6	1254	1.1	1858	6.8	
28	TU	0113	1.0	0713	6.7	1325	1.1	1929	6.9	
29	W	0145	1.0	0744	6.7	1357	1.1	2001	6.9	
30	TH	0218	1.1	0816	6.6	1430	1.2	2034	6.7	
31	F	0251	1.2	0848	6.5	1504	1.4	2108	6.5	

Chart Datum: 3·71 metres below Ordnance Datum (Newlyn). HAT is 7·9 metres above Chart Datum.

STANDARD TIME (UT)
For Summer Time add ONE hour in **non-shaded areas**

MILFORD HAVEN LAT 51°42′N LONG 5°03′W

TIMES AND HEIGHTS OF HIGH AND LOW WATERS

Dates in red are SPRINGS
Dates in blue are NEAPS

YEAR **2018**

SEPTEMBER

Date	Day	Time	m	Time	m	Time	m	Time	m	Moon
1	SA	0325	1.4	0924	6.3	1540	1.6	2147	6.3	
2	SU	0404	1.7	1006	6.0	1623	1.9	2235	5.9	
3	M	0452	2.0	1100	5.7	1721	2.2	2339	5.6	◑
4	TU	0559	2.3	1215	5.5	1846	2.4			
5	W	0103	5.5	0734	2.3	1347	5.5	2025	2.2	
6	TH	0232	5.7	0900	2.0	1508	5.9	2141	1.7	
7	F	0346	6.1	1008	1.5	1614	6.5	2243	1.2	
8	SA	0446	6.6	1103	1.0	1709	7.0	2335	0.7	
9	SU	0537	7.1	1153	0.6	1758	7.4			●
10	M	0023	0.4	0623	7.4	1239	0.4	1842	7.6	
11	TU	0107	0.2	0706	7.4	1322	0.3	1925	7.6	
12	W	0148	0.3	0746	7.4	1402	0.5	2005	7.4	
13	TH	0227	0.6	0825	7.1	1440	0.8	2043	7.1	
14	F	0303	1.0	0903	6.7	1517	1.2	2121	6.6	
15	SA	0338	1.5	0940	6.3	1554	1.7	2159	6.1	
16	SU	0414	2.0	1021	5.8	1635	2.2	2242	5.6	◐
17	M	0458	2.5	1111	5.4	1730	2.6	2340	5.1	
18	TU	0604	2.8	1225	5.1	1857	2.9			
19	W	0111	4.9	0747	2.9	1403	5.1	2035	2.7	
20	TH	0245	5.1	0910	2.6	1518	5.5	2141	2.4	
21	F	0348	5.5	1004	2.2	1609	5.9	2228	1.9	
22	SA	0433	5.9	1046	1.8	1650	6.3	2307	1.6	
23	SU	0510	6.3	1122	1.5	1726	6.6	2342	1.3	
24	M	0544	6.6	1156	1.2	1759	6.9			
25	TU	0015	1.1	0615	6.8	1228	1.0	1831	7.0	○
26	W	0047	0.9	0646	6.9	1301	0.9	1903	7.1	
27	TH	0120	0.9	0718	7.0	1334	0.9	1936	7.1	
28	F	0153	0.9	0751	6.9	1407	1.0	2010	7.0	
29	SA	0227	1.1	0825	6.8	1442	1.2	2046	6.7	
30	SU	0302	1.3	0902	6.5	1520	1.5	2126	6.4	

OCTOBER

Date	Day	Time	m	Time	m	Time	m	Time	m	Moon
1	M	0342	1.7	0945	6.2	1606	1.9	2215	6.0	
2	TU	0432	2.1	1041	5.8	1706	2.3	2323	5.6	◑
3	W	0542	2.4	1200	5.5	1839	2.5			
4	TH	0052	5.4	0724	2.5	1336	5.6	2019	2.2	
5	F	0224	5.6	0851	2.1	1459	6.0	2132	1.7	
6	SA	0337	6.2	0956	1.6	1602	6.6	2230	1.2	
7	SU	0433	6.7	1049	1.1	1654	7.1	2319	0.8	
8	M	0520	7.1	1136	0.7	1740	7.4			
9	TU	0003	0.5	0603	7.3	1219	0.5	1821	7.5	●
10	W	0044	0.4	0643	7.4	1258	0.5	1901	7.5	
11	TH	0122	0.5	0720	7.3	1336	0.6	1938	7.3	
12	F	0157	0.8	0756	7.1	1412	0.9	2014	7.0	
13	SA	0231	1.1	0831	6.8	1447	1.3	2048	6.6	
14	SU	0304	1.6	0906	6.4	1521	1.8	2124	6.1	
15	M	0336	2.0	0944	5.9	1558	2.2	2203	5.6	
16	TU	0414	2.5	1029	5.5	1647	2.6	2255	5.2	◐
17	W	0510	2.9	1133	5.2	1806	2.9			
18	TH	0014	4.9	0648	3.1	1312	5.1	1946	2.9	
19	F	0201	4.9	0826	2.9	1436	5.4	2101	2.5	
20	SA	0311	5.3	0927	2.5	1532	5.8	2152	2.1	
21	SU	0358	5.8	1012	2.0	1615	6.2	2233	1.7	
22	M	0436	6.2	1050	1.6	1652	6.6	2309	1.3	
23	TU	0511	6.6	1125	1.3	1727	6.9	2344	1.1	
24	W	0545	6.9	1200	1.1	1802	7.1			○
25	TH	0019	0.9	0618	7.1	1236	0.9	1836	7.2	
26	F	0055	0.8	0653	7.2	1311	0.9	1912	7.2	
27	SA	0131	0.8	0729	7.1	1349	1.0	1950	7.1	
28	SU	0208	1.0	0807	7.0	1427	1.2	2030	6.8	
29	M	0247	1.3	0848	6.7	1510	1.5	2115	6.5	
30	TU	0331	1.7	0935	6.3	1559	1.8	2209	6.0	
31	W	0424	2.1	1035	6.0	1704	2.2	2318	5.7	◑

NOVEMBER

Date	Day	Time	m	Time	m	Time	m	Time	m	Moon
1	TH	0537	2.4	1153	5.7	1835	2.3			
2	F	0043	5.5	0712	2.4	1322	5.8	2005	2.1	
3	SA	0209	5.7	0833	2.1	1440	6.1	2115	1.7	
4	SU	0318	6.2	0937	1.7	1542	6.6	2211	1.3	
5	M	0412	6.6	1029	1.3	1633	6.9	2259	1.0	
6	TU	0459	6.9	1115	1.0	1718	7.2	2341	0.8	
7	W	0541	7.1	1156	0.8	1759	7.2			●
8	TH	0019	0.8	0619	7.2	1235	0.8	1837	7.2	
9	F	0056	0.9	0656	7.2	1312	0.9	1913	7.0	
10	SA	0131	1.0	0731	7.0	1347	1.1	1948	6.8	
11	SU	0204	1.3	0805	6.8	1422	1.4	2022	6.5	
12	M	0236	1.7	0840	6.4	1456	1.8	2057	6.1	
13	TU	0308	2.0	0916	6.1	1532	2.1	2135	5.7	
14	W	0343	2.4	0958	5.7	1616	2.5	2221	5.3	
15	TH	0430	2.7	1052	5.4	1717	2.8	2322	5.0	◐
16	F	0544	3.0	1205	5.2	1842	2.8			
17	SA	0048	5.0	0717	2.9	1333	5.3	2001	2.6	
18	SU	0213	5.2	0831	2.7	1440	5.6	2102	2.3	
19	M	0310	5.6	0926	2.3	1530	6.0	2150	1.9	
20	TU	0355	6.0	1011	1.8	1613	6.4	2232	1.5	
21	W	0434	6.5	1052	1.5	1653	6.7	2312	1.2	
22	TH	0513	6.8	1132	1.2	1732	7.0	2352	1.0	
23	F	0552	7.1	1212	1.0	1813	7.2			○
24	SA	0032	0.8	0631	7.2	1253	0.9	1854	7.2	
25	SU	0113	0.8	0712	7.3	1335	0.9	1937	7.2	
26	M	0155	0.9	0756	7.1	1419	1.0	2022	6.9	
27	TU	0238	1.2	0842	6.9	1506	1.3	2111	6.6	
28	W	0326	1.5	0933	6.6	1559	1.6	2206	6.2	
29	TH	0420	1.8	1032	6.3	1702	1.9	2310	5.9	
30	F	0528	2.1	1140	6.0	1819	2.0			◑

DECEMBER

Date	Day	Time	m	Time	m	Time	m	Time	m	Moon
1	SA	0023	5.7	0648	2.2	1257	6.0	1937	2.0	
2	SU	0140	5.8	0804	2.1	1410	6.1	2046	1.8	
3	M	0248	6.0	0910	1.8	1514	6.3	2145	1.6	
4	TU	0346	6.3	1005	1.6	1609	6.6	2235	1.3	
5	W	0436	6.6	1053	1.3	1657	6.7	2318	1.2	
6	TH	0519	6.8	1136	1.2	1739	6.8	2357	1.2	
7	F	0559	6.9	1215	1.2	1818	6.8			●
8	SA	0034	1.2	0636	6.9	1252	1.2	1854	6.8	
9	SU	0109	1.2	0712	6.9	1328	1.3	1929	6.6	
10	M	0143	1.4	0746	6.7	1403	1.4	2003	6.4	
11	TU	0215	1.6	0821	6.5	1437	1.7	2037	6.2	
12	W	0248	1.8	0856	6.3	1512	1.9	2113	5.9	
13	TH	0322	2.1	0934	6.0	1551	2.1	2153	5.6	
14	F	0402	2.4	1018	5.7	1637	2.4	2241	5.4	
15	SA	0453	2.6	1112	5.5	1737	2.6	2340	5.2	◐
16	SU	0601	2.8	1216	5.4	1850	2.6			
17	M	0052	5.2	0720	2.7	1329	5.5	1959	2.4	
18	TU	0205	5.4	0828	2.5	1434	5.7	2100	2.1	
19	W	0305	5.8	0927	2.1	1529	6.1	2153	1.8	
20	TH	0356	6.2	1018	1.7	1619	6.5	2241	1.4	
21	F	0443	6.6	1106	1.3	1707	6.8	2328	1.1	
22	SA	0529	7.0	1153	1.0	1754	7.1			○
23	SU	0014	0.9	0615	7.2	1240	0.8	1841	7.2	
24	M	0100	0.7	0701	7.3	1327	0.7	1928	7.2	
25	TU	0146	0.7	0749	7.3	1414	0.7	2016	7.1	
26	W	0232	0.9	0837	7.2	1502	0.9	2106	6.9	
27	TH	0320	1.1	0927	7.0	1553	1.1	2157	6.5	
28	F	0411	1.4	1020	6.6	1648	1.5	2251	6.2	
29	SA	0508	1.7	1118	6.3	1749	1.8	2352	5.9	◑
30	SU	0613	2.0	1222	6.0	1858	2.0			
31	M	0100	5.7	0724	2.1	1332	5.9	2008	2.0	

Chart Datum: 3·71 metres below Ordnance Datum (Newlyn). HAT is 7·9 metres above Chart Datum.

MILFORD HAVEN TO MUMBLES HEAD

(AC 1179, 1076) Milford Haven is a long natural, all-weather harbour with marinas beyond the oil terminals. Beware Turbot Bank (WCM lt buoy) 3M S of the entrance. Crow Rk (dries 5·5m) is 5ca SSE of Linney Hd, and The Toes are dangerous submerged rocks close W and SE of Crow Rock. There is a passage inshore of these dangers. There are overfalls on St Gowan Shoals which extend 4M SW of St Govan's Hd, and the sea breaks on the shallow patches in bad weather. There are firing areas from Linney Hd to Carmarthen Bay.

Caldey Is (lit) lies S of Tenby. Off its NW pt is St Margaret's Is connected by a rocky reef. Caldey Sound, between St Margaret's Is and Giltar Pt (AC 1482), is buoyed, but beware Eel Spit near W end of Caldey Is where there can be a nasty sea with wind against tide, and Woolhouse Rocks (dry 3·6m) 1ca NE of Caldey Is. Saundersfoot harbour (dries) is 2M N of Tenby, with an ⚓ well sheltered from N and W but subject to swell. Streams are weak here. Carmarthen Bay has no offshore dangers for yachts, other than the extensive drying sands at head of the bay and on its E side off Burry Inlet.

S of Worms Head, Helwick Sands (buoyed at each end) extend 7M W from Port Eynon Pt; least depth of 1·3m is near their W end. Stream sets NE/SW across the sands. There is a narrow channel inshore, close to Port Eynon Pt.

▶ *Between here and Mumbles Hd the stream runs roughly along coast, sp rates 3kn off headlands, but there are eddies in Port Eynon Bay and Oxwich Bay (both yacht anchorages), and overfalls SSE of Oxwich Pt.* ◀

FIRING RANGES – LINNEY HEAD TO BURRY INLET

For daily info on all range firing times call *Milford Haven CG* Ch 16/67 or ☎01646 690909.

Castlemartin Range Danger Area extends 12M WNW from Linney Hd, thence in an anti-clockwise arc to a point 12M S of St Govan's Hd. The exact Danger Area operative on any one day depends on the ranges/ammunition used; it is primarily a tank range. When firing is in progress R flags are flown (Fl R lts at night) along the coast from Freshwater West to Linney Head to St Govan's Head. Yachts are requested to keep clear of ranges when active.

Firing takes place on weekdays 0900–1630, exceptionally to 1700. Night firing takes place on Mon to Thurs, up to 2359, depending on the hours of darkness. In Jan only small arms are usually fired and the danger area is reduced.

Days/times of firing are published locally and can be obtained by VHF from *Castlemartin Range* Ch 16 or ☎01646 662367 (H24 answering service); Range safety launches Ch 16 or 12; and Milford Haven CG Ch 16. Also from the Range Office ☎(01646) 662287 or Warren Tower 01646 662336.

Manorbier Range (further E) covers a sector arc radius 12M centred on Old Castle Head; E/W extent is approximately between St Govan's Hd and Caldey Is (see AC Q6402). It is usually active Mon-Fri 0900-1700LT, occasionally Sat and Sun, and is primarily a surface to air missile range, but active areas depend on the weapons in use on any given day. On firing days warnings are broadcast on Ch 16, 73 at 0830, 1430 and on completion; red flags are flown either side of Old Castle Hd. Yachts on passage should either keep 12M offshore or transit close inshore via Stackpole Hd, Trewent Pt, Priest's Nose and Old Castle Hd. Firing days/times are available from local HMs and YCs. For further info call: *Manorbier Range Control* Ch 16, 73 (also manned by Range safety launches); *Milford Haven CG* Ch 16; or Range Control ☎(01834) 871282 ext 209, 📠 871283.

Penally Range (further E at Giltar Pt) is for small arms only and seldom interferes with passage through Caldey Sound. Info ☎(01834) 843522.

Pendine Range (between Tenby and Burry Inlet) is a MOD range for testing explosive devices. It is usually possible to steer the rhumb line course from Tenby to Worms Hd without interference. Info ☎(01994) 453243. Broadcasts on VHF Ch 16, 73 at 0900 and 1400LT. Range active 0800-1615.

Pembrey Range (approx 5M NW of Burry Inlet) is used for bombing practice by the RAF. Info ☎(01554) 891224.

MUMBLES HEAD TO CARDIFF

(AC 1165, 1182) Off Mumbles Hd (Lt, fog sig) beware Mixon Shoal (dries 0·3m), marked by PHM buoy. In good conditions pass N of shoal, 1ca off Mumbles Hd. ⚓ N of Mumbles Hd, good holding but exposed to swell. At W side of Swansea Bay, Green Grounds, rky shoals, lie in appr's to Swansea.

Scarweather Sands, much of which dry (up to 3·3m) with seas breaking heavily, extend 7M W from Porthcawl (9.11.16) and are well buoyed (AC 1161). There is a chan between the sands and coast to E, but beware Hugo Bank (dries 2·6m) and Kenfig Patches (0·5m) with o'falls up to 7ca offshore between Sker Pt and Porthcawl.

Nash Sands extend 7·5M WNW from Nash Pt. Depths vary and are least at inshore end (dries 3m), but Nash Passage, 1ca wide, runs close inshore between E Nash ECM buoy and ledge off Nash Pt. ▶ *On E-going stream there are heavy overfalls off Nash Pt and at W end of Nash Sands. Between Nash Pt and Breaksea Pt the E-going stream begins at HW Avonmouth +0535, and the W-going at HW Avonmouth –0035, sp rates 3kn. Off Breaksea Pt there may be overfalls.* ◀

From Rhoose Pt to Lavernock Pt the coast is fringed with foul ground. Lavernock Spit extends 1·75M S of Lavernock Pt, and E of the spit is main chan to Cardiff; the other side of the chan being Cardiff Grounds, a bank drying 5·4m which lies parallel with the shore and about 1·5M from it.

SEVERN ESTUARY

(AC 1176, 1166) Near the centre of the Bristol Channel, either side of the buoyed fairway, are the islands of Flat Holm (Lt, fog sig) and Steep Holm. 7M SW of Flat Holm lies Culver Sand (0·9m), 3M in length, buoyed with W and ECM. Monkstone Rk (Lt, dries) is 2M NW of the buoyed channel to Avonmouth and Bristol. Extensive drying banks cover the North shore of the estuary, beyond Newport and the Severn bridges (AC 1176). Call Bristol VTS VHF Ch 12 when passing reporting points inwards/outwards.

▶ *The tidal range in the Bristol Channel is exceptional, 12·2m at sp and 6·0m np. Care must be taken to understand the changes in chart datum in the upper reaches of the estuary. Tidal streams are very powerful, particularly above Avonmouth. Between Flat and Steep Holm the E-going stream begins at HW Avonmouth –0610, sp 3kn, and the W-going at HW Avonmouth +0015, sp 4kn.* ◀

The entrance to the R Avon is just to the S of Avonmouth S Pier Hd. Bristol City Docks lie some 6M upriver. Approach the entrance via King Road and the Newcombe and Cockburn lt buoys and thence via the Swash channel into the Avon. The entrance dries at LW but the river is navigable at about half tide.

▶ *Tidal streams are strong in the approaches to Avonmouth, up to **5kn at sp**. The tide is also strong in the R. Avon which is best entered no earlier than HW Avonmouth – 0200.* ◀

From Avonmouth it is 16M to Sharpness, which you should aim to reach at about HW Avonmouth. The passage between Avonmouth and Sharpness requires considerable attention to timing and tidal conditions if it is to be undertaken safely. Plan your passage to arrive off Sharpness no earlier than HW Sharpness –1 and no later than HW Sharpness. Information to assist in passage planning is available from Gloucester Harbour Trustees (see entry for Sharpness). Pilots are available (see entry for Sharpness). To ensure the safety of navigation of all vessels, the fairway between Avonmouth approaches and Sharpness old Dock entrance must be recognised as a 'narrow channel' and attention is drawn to the provisions of rule 9 of the 'collision regulations'.

▶ ***Spring streams can run 8kn at the Shoots, and 6kn at the Severn bridges**. At the Shoots the flood begins at HW Avonmouth –0430 and the ebb at HW Avonmouth +0045. The Severn Bore can usually be seen if Avonmouth range is 13·5m or more. For tidal streams 'Arrowsmiths' is recommended, from Arrowsmiths, Winterstoke Rd, Bristol, BS3 2NT.* ◀

9.11.14 TENBY

Pembrokeshire **51°40'·42N 04°41'·93W**

CHARTS AC 5620, 1179, 1076, 1482; Imray C60, 2600

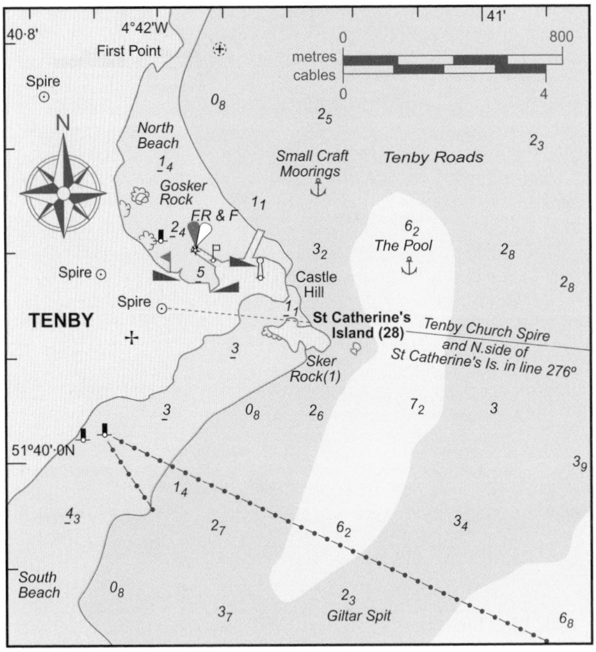

TIDES –0510 Dover; ML 4·5; Duration 0610

Standard Port MILFORD HAVEN (⟵)

Times				Height (metres)			
High Water		Low Water		MHWS	MHWN	MLWN	MLWS
0100	0800	0100	0700	7·0	5·2	2·5	0·7
1300	2000	1300	1900				
Differences TENBY							
–0015	–0010	–0015	–0020	+1·4	+1·1	+0·5	+0·2
STACKPOLE QUAY (7M W of Caldey Island)							
–0005	+0025	–0010	–0010	+0·9	+0·7	+0·2	+0·3

SHELTER Good, but hbr dries up to 5m. 12 cylindrical GRP 🅐 fitted with mooring eyes, but not strops in deep water off North Beach. Sheltered ⚓s, depending on wind direction, to NE in Tenby Roads, in Lydstep Haven (2·5M SW), and around Caldey Is as follows: Priory Bay to the N but shallow, Jones Bay (NE), Drinkim Bay (E) or Sandtop Bay (W).

NAVIGATION WPT 51°40'·02N 04°38'·08W, 279°/2·2M to monument on Castle Hill. The ⊕ WPT (off chartlet) is 2ca W of DZ2 SPM lit buoy. Beware Woolhouse Rks (3·6m) 1·5M SExE of the Hbr, marked by lit SCM buoy; and Sker Rk (1m high) closer in off St Catherine's Island (28m). From the W, Caldey Sound is navigable with care between Eel Pt SHM and Giltar Spit PHM lit buoys. Approaching Tenby Roads, keep outside the line of mooring buoys and look out for swimmers. Tenby is a popular triathlon training destination. For adjacent Firing ranges, see overleaf. Caldey Island is private and no landing without permission from the Abbot.

LIGHTS AND MARKS See 9.11.4 and chartlet. Church spire transit N side of St Catherine's Is 276°. FR 7m 7M on pier hd. Inside hbr, FW 6m 1M marks landing steps PHM beacon (unlit) marks outcrop from Gosker Rk on beach close N of hbr ent. Hbr is floodlit.

COMMUNICATIONS (Code 01834) CGOC (01646) 690909; Police 101; Dr 844161; Ⓗ 842040. HM 842717 (end May-end Sept), Mobile 07977 609947.

Ch 16, 80 (listening during HO).

FACILITIES **Hbr** (<4·2m). **Town** ⇌ ✈ (Swansea; and a small airfield at Haverfordwest).

OTHER ADJACENT HARBOURS (See AC 5620)

SAUNDERSFOOT, Pembrokeshire, **51°42'·60N 04°41'·76W**. AC 1179, 1076, 1482. HW –0510 on Dover; ML 4·4m; Duration 0605. See 9.11.14. A half-tide hbr with good shelter, but there may be a surge in prolonged E winds. On appr, beware buoys marking restricted area (power boats, etc) between Coppett Hall Pt and Perry's Pt. Keep a lookout for swimmers especially those triathlon training. may be available (see HM), or moorings in the middle. Pier hd lt Fl R 5s 6m 7M on stone cupola. VHF: HM 11 16. HM ☎(01834) 812094/(Home 831389). Facilities: 6 (on SW wall). **Town** Ⓑ ✕ ⇌ (Tenby/Saundersfoot).

CARMARTHEN, Carmarthenshire, **51°46'·27N 04°22'·53W**. AC 1179, 1076. HW –0455 on Dover. See 9.11.15. R Towy & Taf dry. Beware Carmarthen Bar in S winds F4 and over with strong sp streams. Nav info is available from Carmarthen Bar Navigation Committee ☎ (01267) 231250 or YC's. Appr on N'ly hdg toward Wharley Pt, leaving DZ8 & 9 buoys 5ca to stbd. Chan shifts frequently and is unmarked so local knowledge reqd unless conditions ideal. ⚓ in mid-stream or 🅐s at R Towy YC off Ferryside (7M below Carmarthen) or R Towey Boat Club 1M N on W bank. 4 power lines cross in last 2·5M before Carmarthen, clearance 7·4m. **R Towy YC** ☎(01267) 238356. **R Towy BC** ☎(01267) 238316. **Town** Ⓑ ⇌ ✈ (Cardiff).

9.11.15 BURRY PORT

Carmarthenshire **51°40'·52N 04°14'·93W** (Burry Port)

CHARTS AC 5620, 5608 1179, 1076; Imray C59, C60, 2600

TIDES –0500 Dover; ML 4·7; Duration 0555

Standard Port MILFORD HAVEN (⟵)

Times				Height (metres)			
High Water		Low Water		MHWS	MHWN	MLWN	MLWS
0100	0800	0100	0700	7·0	5·2	2·5	0·7
1300	2000	1300	1900				
Differences BURRY PORT							
+0003	+0003	+0007	+0007	+1·6	+1·4	+0·5	+0·4
LLANELLI							
–0003	–0003	+0150	+0020	+0·8	+0·6	ND	ND
FERRYSIDE							
0000	–0010	+0220	0000	–0·3	–0·7	–1·7	–0·6
CARMARTHEN							
+0010	0000	DR	DR	–4·4	–4·8	DR	DR

SHELTER Good in Burry Port Marina via lock with flapgate controlled by R/G lts. Access HW±2 (max) over sill depth 2·5m. Sp tides run hard. Note: If bad weather precludes access, especially in W'lies, see 9.11.14 for ⚓s around Caldey Island.

NAVIGATION WPT 51°36'·50N 04°23'·00W, 090°/2·5M to Burry Holms, then about 5M to Burry Port over Lynch Sands which dry approx 1·5m. Carmarthen Bar and the approaches to Burry Port should not be attempted in W winds >F5, nor at night. Depths are changeable. Pendine Range may be active (look for red flags) but clear range procedures are in force and there are no restrictions on navigation.

From close NW of Burry Holms, with sufficient rise of tide, track 015° for 2·5M with the W edge of Burry Holms in transit astern with Worms Head. When Whiteford lighthouse (disused) bears 086° alter to approx 065° until Barrel Post bears 015°.

Near approaches to the harbour are marked by a buoyed channel, dries 3.2m. Barrel Post should not be rounded too close.

LIGHTS AND MARKS Whiteford lt ho is conspic, but no longer lit. On head of W bkwtr is Barrel post; 1½ca N is conspic old lt ho (W tr, R top) Fl 5s 7m 6½M, and flagstaff.

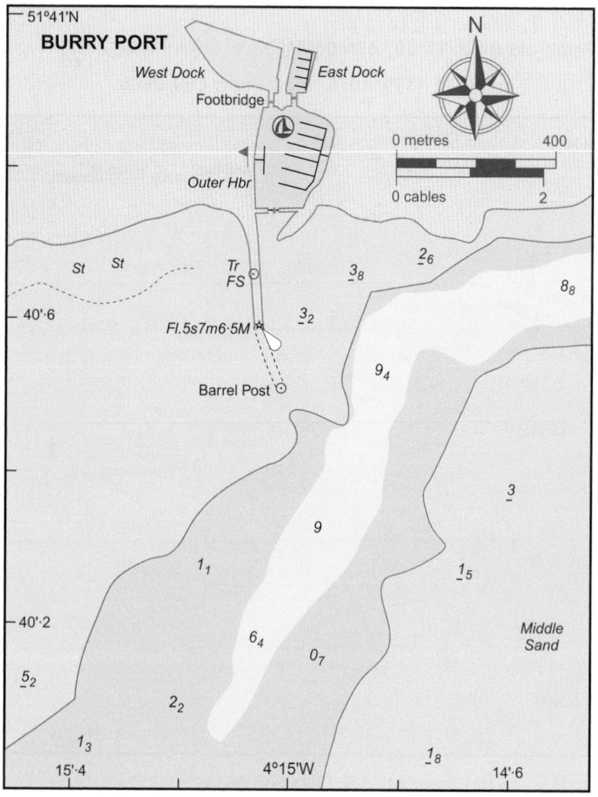

COMMUNICATIONS (Code 01554); CGOC (01646) 690909; Pendine Range (01994) 453243 Ext 240; Police 101; Dr 832240. HM 835691, mob (emergencies only) 07817 395710. Marina Ch M (HO).

FACILITIES **Burry Port Marina** 450 inc Ⓥ, £1.65, max LOA 11m, max draught 1·5m; **Burry Port YC**; **Services**. **Town** (approx 1M), (Cardiff).

9.11.16 SWANSEA

Swansea 51°36′·43N 03°55′·67W

CHARTS AC 5608, 1179, 1165, 1161; Imray C59, 2600

TIDES –0500 Dover; ML 5·2; Duration 0620

Standard Port MILFORD HAVEN (⟵)

Times				Height (metres)			
High Water		Low Water		MHWS	MHWN	MLWN	MLWS
0100	0800	0100	0700	7·0	5·2	2·5	0·7
1300	2000	1300	1900				
Differences SWANSEA							
+0004	+0006	–0006	–0003	+2·6	+2·1	+0·7	+0·3
MUMBLES							
+0001	+0003	–0012	–0005	+2·5	+2·0	+0·8	+0·4
PORT TALBOT							
0000	*+0005*	*–0010*	*–0005*	*+2·7*	*+2·1*	*+1·0*	*+0·4*
PORTHCAWL							
+0005	+0010	–0010	–0005	+2·9	+2·3	+0·8	+0·3

SHELTER Very good in marina.

NAVIGATION WPT 51°35′·53N 03°56′·08W (SHM buoy) 020°/0·92M to E bkwtr lt. Keep seaward of Mixon Shoal. When N of SW Inner Green Grounds (SWIGG) SCM lt buoy keep to W of dredged chan and clear of commercial ships. *Yachts must motor in approaches and in harbour*, max speed 4kn. In Swansea Bay tidal streams flow anti-clockwise for 9½hrs (Swansea HW–3½ to +6), with at times a race off Mumbles Hd. From HW–6 to –3 the stream reverses, setting N past Mumbles Hd towards Swansea.

LOCKS Enter via R Tawe barrage locks, which operate on request HW±4½ (co-ordinated with the marina lock), 0700-2200BST; out of season, 0700-1900UT, but to 2200 at w/ends. There are pontoons in both locks.

Vessels usually exit Tawe barrage locks at H+00, and enter at H+30. Locks are closed when ht of tide falls to 1·5m above CD, usually at MLWS. At sp, do not enter river until LW+1½. Two large Or holding buoys below barrage in mid-stream; also, at W side of barrage lock, a landing pontoon (dries, foul ground).

LIGHTS AND MARKS See 9.11.4 and chartlet. Mumbles Hd, Fl (4) 20s 35m 16M, is 3M SSW of hbr ent. A conspic TV mast (R lts) NNE of hbr is almost aligned with the fairway. Ldg lts 020° mark E side of chan dredged 3m. When N of Swansea Middle West (QR) and Swansea Middle East (QG) chan buoys stay inside dredged chan. Barrage lock lit by 2FR/FG (vert) to seaward.

Port Traffic sigs are conspic at W side of ent to King's Dock; there are 9 lts, ● or ●, arranged in a 3 x 3 frame. Yachts arriving must obey the middle lt in left column:

● = Do not enter the river; hold SW of W Pier.

● = Yachts may enter the river, keeping to mid-chan, then to W of holding buoys.

Lock Master will advise on tfc movements Ch 18.

Lock sigs for barrage and marina locks alike are:

●● = Lock closed. Do not proceed

● = Wait

● = Enter with caution

●● = Free flow operating; proceed with caution

COMMUNICATIONS (Code 01792) CGOC 366534; Police 101; Ⓗ 205666; Dr 653452; DVLA (for SSR) 783355. HM 653787; Barrage 456014.

Barrage, *Tawe Lock* Ch 18. *Swansea Marina* Ch **80**. For commercial docks call *Swansea Docks Radio* VHF Ch14 (H24).

FACILITIES **Swansea Marina** (340+50Ⓥ) ☎470310, £1·85, lock 9m wide Ⓔ (25t) (1t) ACA, ice, wi-fi.

Swansea Yacht & Sub Aqua Club (SY & SAC) ☎654863, No visitors, (5t static).

City Ⓑ.

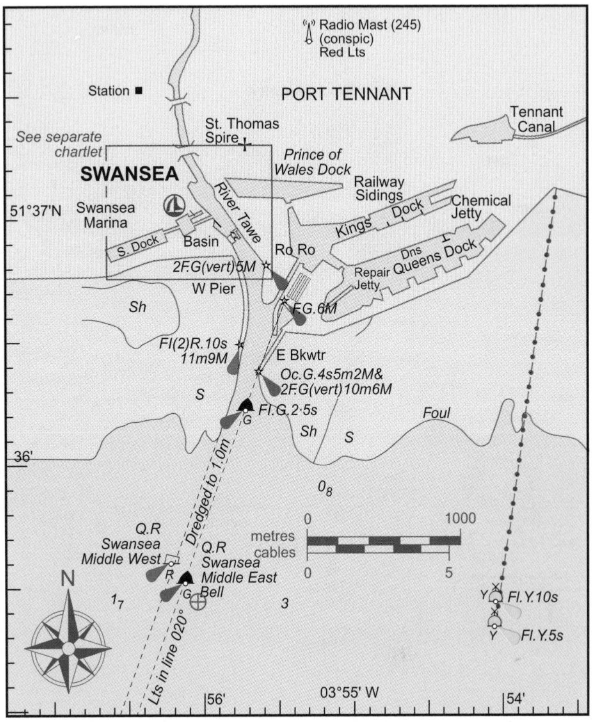

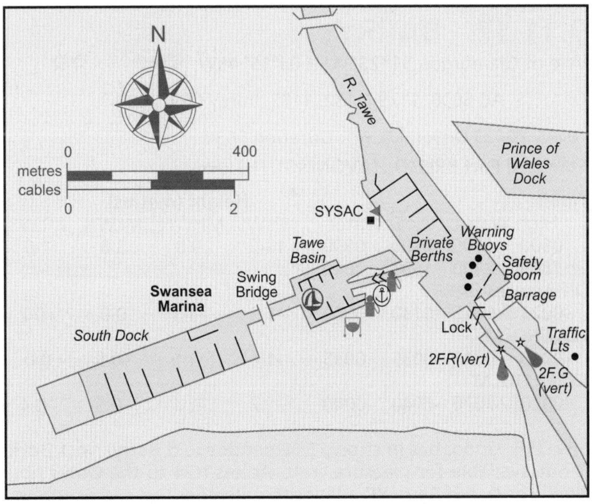

ADJACENT HARBOURS AND ANCHORAGES

Mumbles, 51°34′·2N 03°58′·2W. Good ⚓ in W'lies 5ca N of Mumbles **Bristol Chan YC** ☎(01792) 366000; **Mumbles YC** ☎369321, (hire).

R Neath, 51°37′·88N 03°49′·97W. Ent over bar HW±2½ via 1·5M chan, marked/lit training wall to stbd. Tfc info from *Neath Pilot* VHF Ch 77, if on stn. **Monkstone Marina**, W bank just S of bridge, dries 4m: 2 Y Ⓥs, (15t). Visitors welcome. **Monkstone C & SC,** ☎(01792) 812229; VHF Ch **M** (occas).

PORTHCAWL, Bridgend, **51°28′·48N 03°42′·02W.** AC 1165, 1169. HW–0500 on Dover; ML 5·3m. See 9.11.16. Hbr protected by bkwtr running SE from Porthcawl Pt. Beware rk ledges and appr drying 5m above CD. Porthcawl lt ho, F WRG (see 9.11.4). Tidal streams off bkwtr can reach 6kn at Sp. 3 Ⓥs or ⚓ approx 3ca SSE of lt ho. Look out for swimmers. Marina access gate opens HW±3, R/G tfc lts, sill 3.5m above CD; Ⓥ by arrangement, HM ☎(01656) 815715 VHF Ch 80. Facilities: 70. **Porthcawl Hbr B C** ☎782342. **Town** Ⓑ ⇌(Bridgend) ✈(Cardiff).

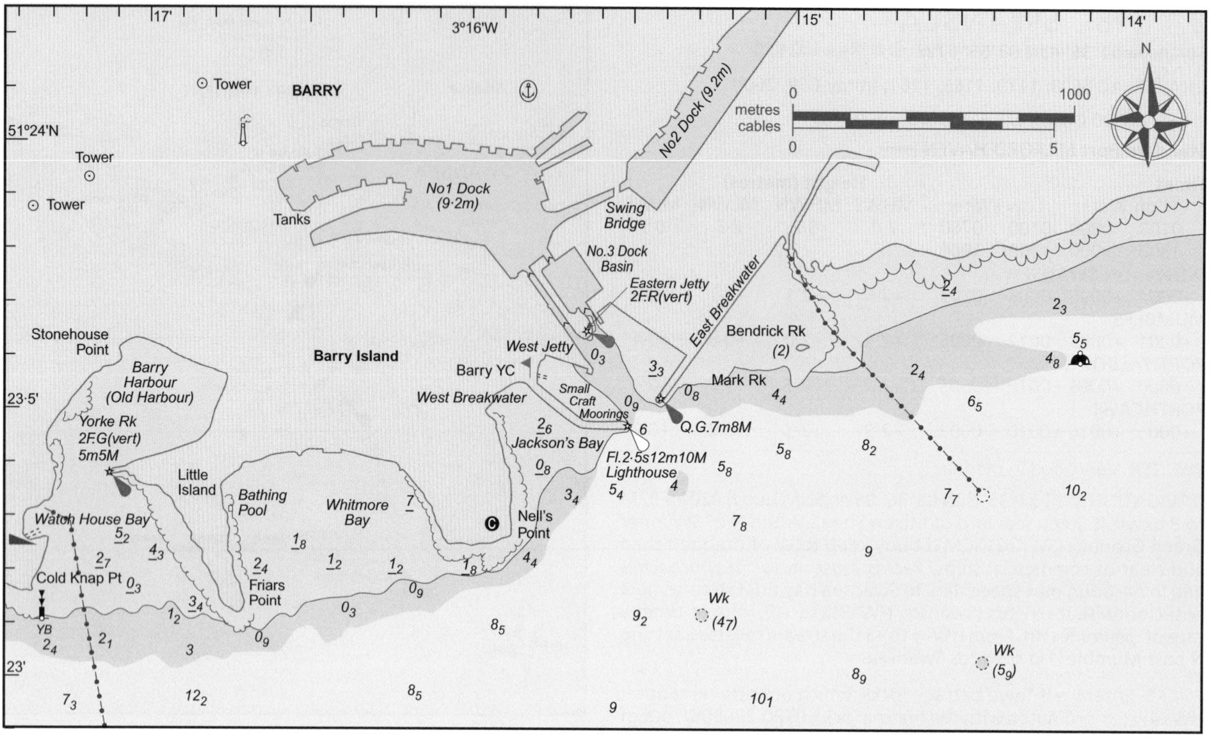

9.11.17 BARRY

Vale of Glamorgan **51°23'·48N 03°15'·45W**

CHARTS AC 5608, 1179, 1152, 1182; Imray C59, 2600

TIDES –0423 Dover; ML 6·1; Duration 0630

Standard Port BRISTOL (AVONMOUTH) (⟶)

Times				**Height (metres)**			
High Water		Low Water		MHWS	MHWN	MLWN	MLWS
0600	1100	0300	0800	13·2	9·8	3·8	1·0
1800	2300	1500	2000				
Differences BARRY							
–0025	–0025	–0130	–0045	–1·5	–1·1	0·0	+0·2
FLAT HOLM							
–0015	–0015	–0035	–0035	–1·4	–1·0	–0·5	0·0
STEEP HOLM							
–0020	–0020	–0040	–0040	–1·7	–1·1	–0·5	–0·4

SHELTER Good, but in strong E/SE winds avoid Barry; No 1 Dock is not available for pleasure craft. Access H24 to the Outer hbr. No ⌓ or ⚓, but Barry YC administers all moorings and welcomes visitors. Temporary mooring may be available from Bristol Pilots on request.

NAVIGATION WPT 51°23'·03N 03°15'·08W, 332°/0·53M to entrance. Beware heavy commercial traffic. Approaching from E keep well out from the shore. Strong tidal stream across entrance.

LIGHTS AND MARKS Welsh Water Barry West PHM buoy, Fl R 5s, and Merkur PHM buoy, Fl R 2·5s, lie respectively 217°/1·5M and 191°/1·65M from harbour entrance. W bkwtr Fl 2·5s 10M. E bkwtr QG 8M.

COMMUNICATIONS (Code 01446) CGOC (01646) 690909; Police 101; Dr 733355. HM 0870 609 6699. BY 678186.

Barry Radio VHF Ch **11** 10 16 (HW–4 to HW+3); tidal info on request. *Bristol Pilot* via Ch 16 may advise on vacant moorings.

FACILITIES **Barry YC** (130) ☎735511, approaches dry approx 2m; (50t). **Town** (2M) (2M) Ⓑ ✕ ⇌ ✈ (Cardiff).

9.11.18 CARDIFF/PENARTH

Vale of Glamorgan **51°26'·74N 03°09'·92W** (marina)

CHARTS AC 5608, 1179, 1176, 1182; Imray C59, 2600

TIDES –0425 Dover; ML 6·4; Duration 0610

Standard Port BRISTOL (AVONMOUTH) (⟶)

Times				**Height (metres)**			
High Water		Low Water		MHWS	MHWN	MLWN	MLWS
0600	1100	0300	0800	13·2	9·8	3·8	1·0
1800	2300	1500	2000				
Differences CARDIFF							
–0015	–0015	–0035	–0030	–0·9	–0·7	+0·2	+0·2
NEWPORT							
–0005	–0010	–0015	–0015	–0·9	–0·9	–0·2	–0·2
CHEPSTOW (River Wye)							
+0020	+0020	ND	ND	ND	ND	ND	ND

NOTE: At Newport the ht of LW does not normally fall below MLWS. Tidal hts are based on a minimum river flow; max flow may raise ht of LW by as much as 0·3m.

SHELTER Very good in marinas. See above for barrage locks. Waiting trot berths in outer hbr; or ⚓ off Penarth seafront in W'lies; in E'lies cramped ⚓ off Alexandra Dock ent in 2m.

NAVIGATION WPT 51°24'·03N 03°08'·81W (2½ca SW of S Cardiff SCM lt buoy), 349°/2·9M to barrage locks.

The outer approaches from W or SW are via Breaksea lt float and N of One Fathom Bk. Keep S of Lavernock Spit SCM lt buoy and NW of Flat Holm and Wolves NCM lt buoy drying rk. From NE, drying ledges and shoals extend >1M offshore. From E, appr via Monkstone Lt ho and S Cardiff SCM buoy. Ranny Spit (dries 0·4m) is 3½ca to the W, and Cardiff Grounds (dries 5·4m) 3½ca to the E.

The Wrach Chan is buoyed/lit and dredged 1·2m; it passes 1½ca E of Penarth Hd. The locks appr chan, is dredged 0·7m below CD. Pont Y Werin Br opens on request to Barrage Control. Closed air draught 4.5m. IPTS control traffic.

Do not impede merchant ships, especially those entering/leaving Alexandra Dock.

Cardiff Bay Barrage and Marina lock

- Call *Barrage Control* VHF Ch 18 or ☎02920 700234 to request lock-in or lock-out. Waiting berth on a barge in outer hbr.
- If entering near LW ask Barrage Control for up-to-date depths.
- Subject to VHF instructions, enter the outer hbr (Wpt 51°26′·71N 03°09′·84W) and lock in.
- IPTS (sigs 1, 2, 3, 5) are shown at lock ent.
- Departures on H and H +30. Arrivals at H +15 and H +45.
- Lock into marina operates H24 on free-flow from the bay.

LIGHTS AND MARKS Directional light, Oc WRG 10s 5m3M, on a W metal post marks Wrach Channel. SPM Fl Y 3s mark the 5kn limit.

COMMUNICATIONS (Code 02920) CGOC (01646) 690909; ⛅397020; Police101; Dr 415258; HM 400500; Barrage control 700234; Cardiff Bay Authority 877900.

Port VHF Ch **14** 16 (HW–4 to HW+3). *Barrage Control* Ch 18 H24. Penarth Quays Marina Ch 80 H24. Cardiff Marina Ch M.

FACILITIES **Penarth Quays Marina** www.quaymarinas.com ☎705021, H24, 350+Ⓥ welcome, £1.80 (short stay £11), max draught 3m, lock width 7·3m; (0930-1630, E pontoon) Ⓔ (20t) (20t) ACA ✕.

Penarth YC ☎ 708196.

Mermaid Quay Ⓥ on pontons (£1/craft/hr) near city centre; many Rs and Bars.

Cardiff Marina www.themarinegroup.co.uk ☎396078, mob 07784 928592; 320 inc 50Ⓥ £2·50, (4½t) (short walk).

Cardiff YC ☎463697, (floating pontoon).

Cardiff Bay YC ☎226575.

City Ⓑ ✕ ≥ ✈ (15 mins).

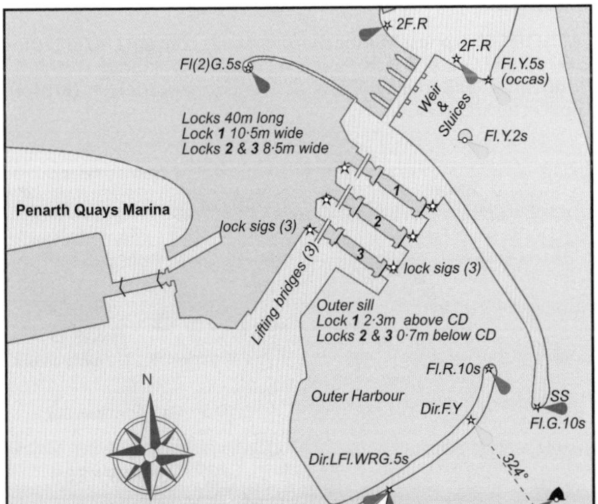

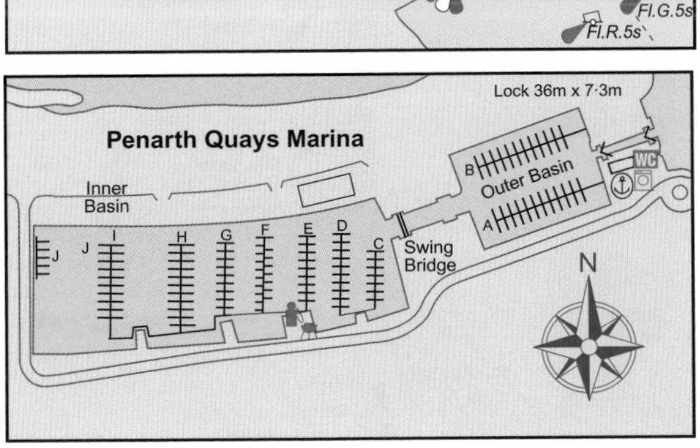

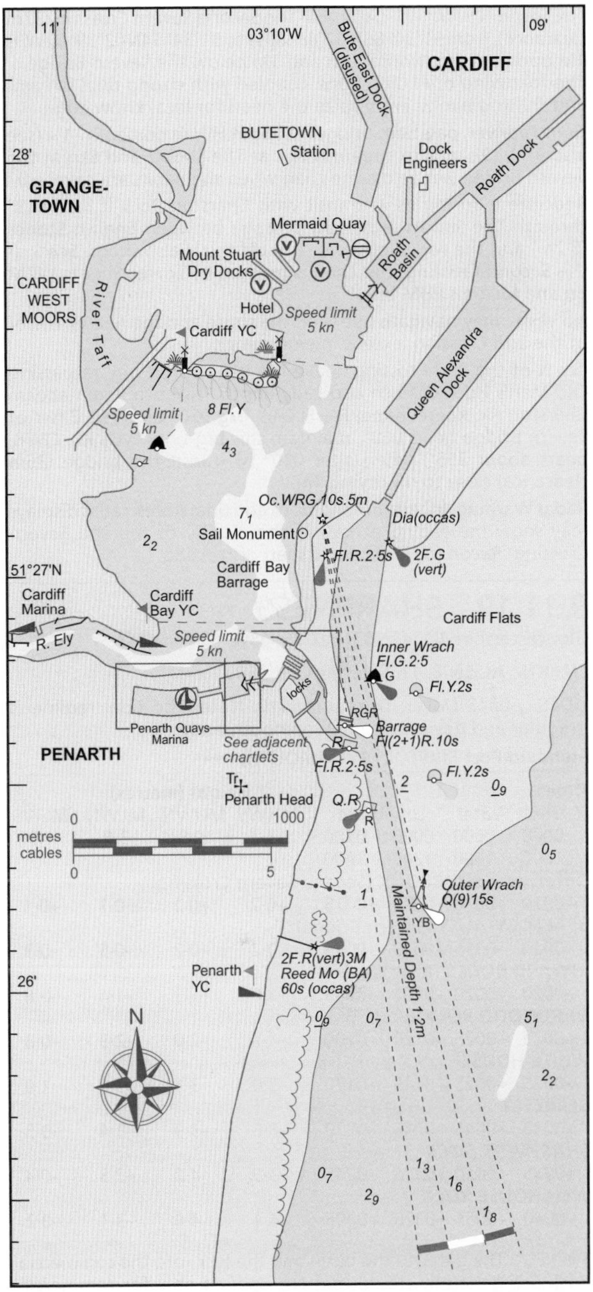

ADJACENT HARBOUR

NEWPORT, Newport, **51°32′·95N 02°59′·13W**. AC 5608, 1179, 1152, 1176. HW –0425 on Dover; ML 6·0m; Duration 0620. See 9.11.18. A commercial port controlled by ABP, but a safe shelter for yachts. Enter R Usk over bar (approx 0·5m) E of West Usk buoy, QR, and follow buoyed and lit chan to S Lock ent; turn NE (ldg lts 062°) for yacht moorings on S side between power stn pier and YC. Beware overhead cables in Julian's Pill, clearance 3·8m.

Lights, see 9.11.4. East Usk lt ho Fl (2) WRG 10s. Ldg lts 062°, both FG. Alexandra Dock, S lock W pier head 2 FR (vert) 9/7m 6M. E pier head 2 FG (vert) 9/7m 6M.

Port VHF, *Newport Radio,* and VTS: Ch 09, **71**, 74 (HW ±4). HM (ABP) ☎0870 609 6699. Facilities: Ⓔ. **Newport and Uskmouth SC** M. **Town** All facilities.

THE SEVERN BRIDGES (AC 1166) The Second Severn Crossing (37m clearance), from 51°34'·88N 02°43'·80W to 51°34'·14N 02°39'·82W, is 4M upriver from Avonmouth and 3M below the Severn Bridge. The following brief directions, coupled with strong tidal streams and shifting banks, emphasize the need for local knowledge.

Going upriver, pass both bridges at about HW Avonmouth –1¼ (see also 9.11.19); max sp stream is 8kn at The Shoots and 6kn at the Severn Bridge (set across the chan when the banks are covered).

Redcliffe F Bu ldg lts in transit with Charston Rock lt lead 013° through The Shoots, a narrow passage between English Stones (6·2m) and the rocky ledges (5·1m) off the Welsh shore. 5ca S of the Second Crossing, the chan is marked by Lower Shoots WCM bn and Mixoms PHM bn.

No vessel may navigate between the shore and the nearer Tower of the 2nd Crossing, except in emergency.

4ca N of the 2nd Crossing, leave the 013° transit before passing Old Man's Hd WCM bcn and Lady Bench PHM bcn. From abeam Charston Rk, keep Chapel Rk, Fl 2·6s, brg 050° until the E twr of Severn Bridge bears 068°; maintain this brg until Lyde Rk, QWR, bears about 355°, when alter 010° to transit the bridge (36m clearance) close to rks drying 1m.

Radar Warning. In certain conditions and tidal states, radar displays may show misleading echoes in the vicinity of the 2nd Severn Crossing. ***Racon (O)*** is at centre span of crossing.

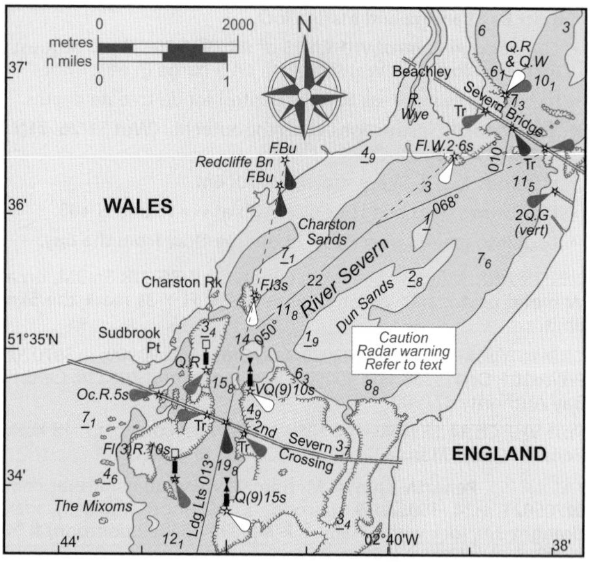

9.11.19 SHARPNESS

Gloucestershire **51°43'·03N 02°29'·08W**

CHARTS AC 5608, 1166, Imray C59, 2600

TIDES –0315 Dover; Duration 0415. Note: The tidal regime is irregular and deviates from Avonmouth curve.

Standard Port BRISTOL (AVONMOUTH) (⟶)

Times				Height (metres)			
High Water		Low Water		MHWS	MHWN	MLWN	MLWS
0000	0600	0000	0700	13·2	9·8	3·8	1·0
1200	1800	1200	1900				
Differences SUDBROOK (Second Severn Crossing)							
+0010	+0010	+0025	+0015	+0·2	+0·1	–0·1	+0·1
BEACHLEY/AUST (Severn Bridge)							
+0010	+0015	+0040	+0025	–0·2	–0·2	–0·5	–0·3
INWARD ROCKS (River Severn)							
+0020	+0020	+0105	+0045	–1·0	–1·1	–1·4	–0·6
NARLWOOD ROCKS							
+0025	+0025	+0120	+0100	–1·9	–2·0	–2·3	–0·8
WHITE HOUSE							
+0025	+0025	+0145	+0120	–3·0	–3·1	–3·6	–1·0
BERKELEY							
+0030	+0045	+0245	+0220	–3·8	–3·9	–3·4	–0·5
SHARPNESS DOCK							
+0035	*+0050*	*+0305*	*+0245*	*–3·9*	*–4·2*	*–3·3*	*–0·4*
WELLHOUSE ROCK							
+0040	+0055	+0320	+0305	–4·1	–4·4	–3·1	–0·2

SHELTER The gates to the basin and the lock into the commercial dock are generally closed and are opened only for commercial shipping movements and other craft which have made the required booking and given appropriate notice (min. 24hrs). It is essential for arrangements to be made by contacting the Pierhead office which is generally manned during daylight tides, HW-4 to HW+1 (if unmanned leave a message). Plan your passage to arrive no sooner than HW-1 and no later than HW. Detailed information on lock fees and canal licences is available from the Pierhead office. Comprehensive information on the passage from Avonmouth is available from Gloucester Harbour Trustees. Fog signals are available from Sharpness Radio on VHF Ch 13 or Pierhead office.

NAVIGATION Use transits shown on AC 1166. Study guidance notes from Gloucester Harbour Trustees in good time.

- Leave King Road, Avonmouth (17M downriver) not before HW Sharpness –3, to be off Hbr ent about HW –½. Stem strong flood S of F Bu lt; beware tidal eddy.
- Do not proceed above the Severn Bridge except HW–1¼ /+2. There is a 5hr flood and a 7hr ebb.

LIGHTS AND MARKS Lights as chartlet, but night passage not advised without local knowledge/pilot (07774 226143).

COMMUNICATIONS (Code 01453) Police 101; Ⓗ 810777. Pierhead 511968 (HW–4 to HW+1). Gloucester Harbour Trustees www.gloucesterharbourtrustees.org ☎811913 (HO).

Call Gloucester and Sharpness Canal Ch 74 for bridges (no locks). Call *Bristol VTS* VHF Ch 12 when passing reporting points inwards/outwards E/W Grounds PHM, Welsh Hook SCM and at Lower Shoots Bcn.

FACILITIES **Sharpness Marina** sharpness@f2s.com ☎811476. 170 inc 2 Ⓥ, £8 all LOA. **Town** (above Fretherne Bridge), ✉ Ⓑ(Berkeley) ✕, ⇌ (Stonehouse), ✈ (Bristol). Gloucester: ACA.

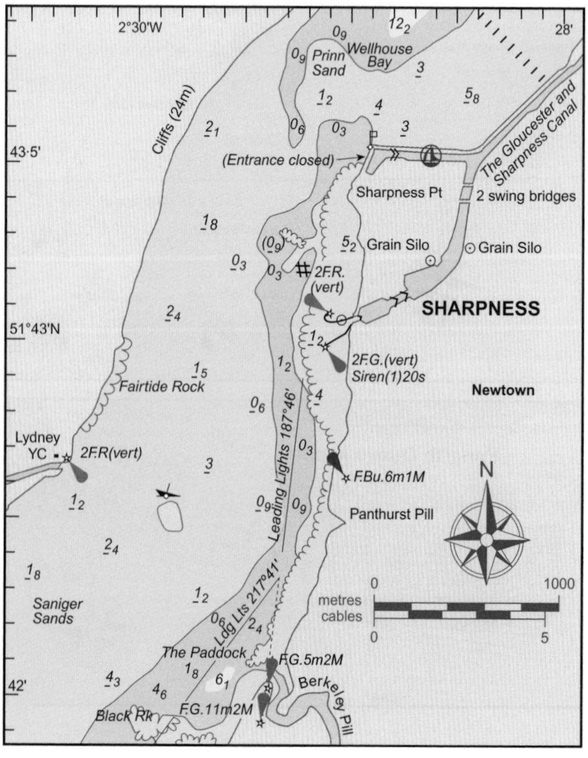

STANDARD TIME (UT)
For Summer Time add ONE hour in **non-shaded areas**

BRISTOL (AVONMOUTH) LAT 51°30'N LONG 2°44'W

TIMES AND HEIGHTS OF HIGH AND LOW WATERS

Dates in red are SPRINGS
Dates in blue are NEAPS

YEAR **2018**

JANUARY

Date	Day	Time	m	Time	m	Time	m	Time	m
1	M	0030	1.6	0610	13.1	1259	1.5	1838	13.4
2	TU	0125	1.1	0700	13.8	1354	1.1	○ 1929	13.8
3	W	0218	0.8	0749	14.1	1446	0.8	2018	14.0
4	TH	0306	0.7	0837	14.1	1534	0.8	2106	13.9
5	F	0351	0.8	0924	13.9	1616	1.0	2151	13.5
6	SA	0430	1.1	1008	13.5	1654	1.4	2235	12.9
7	SU	0505	1.6	1052	12.8	1728	1.9	2318	12.1
8	M	0539	2.2	1137	12.0	1803	2.5	◑	
9	TU	0004	11.3	0617	2.8	1230	11.2	1844	3.0
10	W	0101	10.6	0705	3.3	1336	10.6	1936	3.5
11	TH	0212	10.2	0807	3.6	1446	10.4	2043	3.7
12	F	0319	10.3	0923	3.6	1549	10.5	2206	3.5
13	SA	0419	10.7	1040	3.2	1645	11.0	2314	2.9
14	SU	0511	11.3	1139	2.5	1735	11.5		
15	M	0007	2.3	0557	11.9	1230	2.0	1819	12.0
16	TU	0056	1.8	0640	12.4	1317	1.7	1901	12.3
17	W	0141	1.7	0720	12.6	1402	1.6	● 1940	12.4
18	TH	0223	1.7	0758	12.6	1444	1.7	2017	12.4
19	F	0300	1.9	0834	12.5	1519	1.9	2052	12.3
20	SA	0329	2.1	0907	12.4	1547	2.1	2124	12.1
21	SU	0351	2.1	0938	12.2	1611	2.1	2156	12.0
22	M	0417	2.1	1011	12.1	1640	2.1	2230	11.9
23	TU	0450	2.2	1049	11.9	1716	2.2	2310	11.6
24	W	0529	2.4	1133	11.5	1758	2.5	◐ 2357	11.2
25	TH	0614	2.8	1227	11.1	1849	2.9		
26	F	0055	10.8	0711	3.3	1334	10.7	1954	3.3
27	SA	0209	10.5	0832	3.6	1458	10.7	2137	3.3
28	SU	0339	10.8	1026	3.2	1622	11.3	2306	2.7
29	M	0455	11.7	1142	2.4	1729	12.2		
30	TU	0012	1.9	0555	12.7	1245	1.6	1826	13.0
31	W	0111	1.2	0648	13.5	1342	1.0	○ 1918	13.7

FEBRUARY

Date	Day	Time	m	Time	m	Time	m	Time	m
1	TH	0206	0.7	0738	14.1	1436	0.6	2007	14.0
2	F	0256	0.4	0825	14.3	1524	0.4	2052	14.1
3	SA	0340	0.4	0909	14.2	1605	0.5	2135	13.8
4	SU	0418	0.7	0950	13.8	1640	1.0	2214	13.3
5	M	0448	1.2	1028	13.2	1706	1.6	2249	12.5
6	TU	0513	1.7	1103	12.3	1729	2.1	2323	11.7
7	W	0541	2.3	1140	11.4	1759	2.7	◑	
8	TH	0000	10.8	0617	2.9	1225	10.5	1840	3.3
9	F	0053	10.0	0708	3.6	1331	9.8	1938	3.8
10	SA	0215	9.6	0817	3.9	1500	9.7	2055	4.0
11	SU	0337	9.8	0940	3.8	1610	10.1	2224	3.5
12	M	0440	10.5	1100	3.1	1707	10.8	2334	2.7
13	TU	0532	11.4	1200	2.3	1756	11.5		
14	W	0028	2.1	0617	12.1	1252	1.8	1839	12.1
15	TH	0119	1.7	0659	12.5	1341	1.5	● 1920	12.4
16	F	0205	1.5	0738	12.7	1427	1.5	1958	12.6
17	SA	0248	1.6	0815	12.8	1507	1.5	2034	12.6
18	SU	0323	1.7	0850	12.8	1540	1.7	2107	12.6
19	M	0347	1.8	0922	12.7	1603	1.8	2138	12.6
20	TU	0407	1.8	0954	12.6	1625	1.7	2211	12.4
21	W	0434	1.8	1030	12.4	1655	1.8	2248	12.1
22	TH	0508	1.9	1111	11.9	1732	2.1	2331	11.6
23	F	0548	2.4	1159	11.3	1817	2.7	◐	
24	SA	0024	10.9	0638	3.0	1303	10.6	1916	3.4
25	SU	0136	10.3	0751	3.7	1432	10.2	2103	3.7
26	M	0316	10.4	1011	3.5	1608	10.8	2251	3.0
27	TU	0440	11.2	1130	2.5	1718	11.8	2358	2.0
28	W	0543	12.4	1232	1.5	1815	12.8		

MARCH

Date	Day	Time	m	Time	m	Time	m	Time	m
1	TH	0057	1.1	0636	13.4	1328	0.8	1905	13.6
2	F	0151	0.5	0724	14.0	1420	0.3	○ 1951	14.1
3	SA	0240	0.1	0809	14.3	1507	0.1	2034	14.2
4	SU	0323	0.1	0850	14.3	1546	0.3	2113	13.9
5	M	0359	0.4	0928	13.9	1618	0.8	2148	13.4
6	TU	0426	1.0	1001	13.2	1638	1.5	2217	12.7
7	W	0444	1.6	1030	12.4	1654	2.0	2245	11.9
8	TH	0505	2.0	1059	11.5	1718	2.5	2315	11.0
9	F	0536	2.6	1134	10.6	1751	3.1	◑ 2355	10.1
10	SA	0618	3.4	1223	9.7	1841	3.8		
11	SU	0059	9.4	0725	4.0	1352	9.1	2002	4.3
12	M	0249	9.3	0852	4.1	1531	9.4	2135	4.0
13	TU	0406	10.0	1019	3.4	1637	10.3	2259	3.1
14	W	0503	10.9	1130	2.5	1728	11.2		
15	TH	0001	2.3	0550	11.8	1226	1.8	1813	12.0
16	F	0053	1.7	0633	12.4	1317	1.4	1855	12.5
17	SA	0142	1.5	0713	12.8	1404	1.3	● 1934	12.8
18	SU	0226	1.4	0752	13.0	1447	1.2	2011	13.0
19	M	0305	1.4	0827	13.1	1522	1.3	2045	13.0
20	TU	0334	1.5	0902	13.1	1548	1.4	2118	13.0
21	W	0356	1.5	0936	13.0	1610	1.5	2152	12.8
22	TH	0420	1.5	1012	12.7	1637	1.6	2229	12.4
23	F	0451	1.7	1053	12.1	1711	2.0	2311	11.8
24	SA	0529	2.2	1140	11.3	1754	2.7	◐	
25	SU	0003	10.9	0617	3.0	1244	10.4	1852	3.5
26	M	0118	10.2	0732	3.7	1422	10.0	2057	3.8
27	TU	0306	10.2	1001	3.4	1557	10.6	2236	3.0
28	W	0427	11.1	1115	2.4	1704	11.7	2340	1.9
29	TH	0528	12.3	1213	1.4	1759	12.7		
30	F	0036	1.0	0618	13.2	1307	0.7	1846	13.5
31	SA	0128	0.4	0704	13.8	1356	0.2	○ 1929	13.9

APRIL

Date	Day	Time	m	Time	m	Time	m	Time	m
1	SU	0216	0.1	0747	14.1	1441	0.2	2010	14.0
2	M	0259	0.2	0826	14.0	1520	0.4	2047	13.7
3	TU	0334	0.6	0902	13.6	1551	1.0	2119	13.2
4	W	0400	1.1	0932	13.0	1609	1.6	2146	12.6
5	TH	0416	1.6	0959	12.3	1621	2.0	2212	11.9
6	F	0434	2.0	1026	11.5	1642	2.3	2239	11.1
7	SA	0502	2.4	1056	10.7	1712	2.8	2313	10.3
8	SU	0539	3.1	1136	9.9	1753	3.6	◑	
9	M	0002	9.5	0636	3.8	1244	9.1	1905	4.3
10	TU	0144	9.1	0808	4.1	1439	9.2	2048	4.2
11	W	0323	9.6	0934	3.6	1557	9.9	2215	3.5
12	TH	0425	10.6	1050	2.8	1653	10.9	2324	2.6
13	F	0516	11.5	1151	2.0	1741	11.8		
14	SA	0020	2.0	0601	12.3	1245	1.5	1824	12.5
15	SU	0110	1.6	0643	12.8	1334	1.2	1904	13.0
16	M	0157	1.3	0724	13.2	1418	1.1	● 1943	13.3
17	TU	0238	1.2	0802	13.4	1457	1.1	2021	13.4
18	W	0314	1.2	0841	13.4	1529	1.1	2058	13.3
19	TH	0343	1.2	0919	13.3	1557	1.3	2136	13.1
20	F	0411	1.4	0959	12.9	1625	1.5	2216	12.6
21	SA	0442	1.7	1042	12.2	1700	2.0	2300	11.9
22	SU	0521	2.2	1131	11.3	1744	2.7	◐ 2354	11.0
23	M	0613	3.0	1237	10.4	1847	3.5		
24	TU	0113	10.3	0741	3.6	1415	10.2	2047	3.6
25	W	0253	10.5	0939	3.2	1537	10.7	2212	2.9
26	TH	0405	11.2	1048	2.3	1641	11.6	2313	1.9
27	F	0504	12.1	1145	1.5	1734	12.5		
28	SA	0008	1.2	0554	12.9	1238	0.9	1821	13.2
29	SU	0059	0.7	0639	13.4	1326	0.6	1903	13.5
30	M	0146	0.5	0721	13.5	1411	0.6	○ 1942	13.5

Chart Datum: 6·50 metres below Ordnance Datum (Newlyn). HAT is 14·7 metres above Chart Datum.

STANDARD TIME (UT)
For Summer Time add ONE hour in **non-shaded areas**

BRISTOL (AVONMOUTH) LAT 51°30′N LONG 2°44′W

TIMES AND HEIGHTS OF HIGH AND LOW WATERS

Dates in red are SPRINGS
Dates in blue are NEAPS

YEAR **2018**

MAY

Date	Day	Time	m	Time	m	Time	m	Time	m	Moon
1	TU	0229	0.6	0800	13.4	1450	0.8	2018	13.3	
2	W	0306	0.9	0835	13.0	1522	1.3	2050	12.9	
3	TH	0334	1.4	0905	12.6	1542	1.8	2119	12.4	
4	F	0352	1.8	0933	12.0	1555	2.1	2145	11.8	
5	SA	0410	2.1	1000	11.5	1616	2.3	2213	11.2	
6	SU	0438	2.4	1030	10.9	1646	2.7	2245	10.6	
7	M	0513	2.8	1109	10.2	1724	3.2	2330	10.0	
8	TU	0603	3.4	1204	9.6	1821	3.9			◑
9	W	0040	9.5	0719	3.8	1328	9.4	1952	4.1	
10	TH	0221	9.6	0844	3.6	1500	9.8	2121	3.7	
11	F	0336	10.3	0959	3.0	1607	10.7	2235	3.0	
12	SA	0434	11.2	1106	2.3	1701	11.6	2337	2.3	
13	SU	0524	12.0	1205	1.8	1749	12.4			
14	M	0032	1.7	0610	12.7	1258	1.4	1833	13.0	
15	TU	0122	1.4	0655	13.2	1346	1.1	1916	13.4	●
16	W	0209	1.1	0739	13.5	1431	1.0	1958	13.6	
17	TH	0252	1.0	0822	13.5	1511	0.9	2041	13.6	
18	F	0331	1.0	0906	13.4	1547	1.1	2124	13.3	
19	SA	0407	1.2	0950	13.0	1622	1.4	2208	12.8	
20	SU	0444	1.6	1036	12.4	1700	1.9	2255	12.1	
21	M	0526	2.1	1128	11.6	1746	2.5	2351	11.3	
22	TU	0620	2.7	1232	10.9	1849	3.1			◐
23	W	0106	10.8	0736	3.1	1354	10.6	2016	3.2	
24	TH	0228	10.8	0903	2.9	1507	10.8	2136	2.8	
25	F	0335	11.2	1012	2.5	1609	11.4	2239	2.2	
26	SA	0433	11.8	1111	1.9	1703	12.0	2335	1.7	
27	SU	0524	12.3	1204	1.5	1751	12.5			
28	M	0025	1.3	0610	12.7	1253	1.2	1834	12.9	
29	TU	0113	1.1	0653	12.8	1338	1.2	1914	12.9	○
30	W	0158	1.1	0733	12.7	1420	1.3	1951	12.8	
31	TH	0237	1.3	0809	12.5	1455	1.6	2025	12.6	

JUNE

Date	Day	Time	m	Time	m	Time	m	Time	m	Moon
1	F	0310	1.7	0843	12.2	1520	1.9	2057	12.2	
2	SA	0334	2.0	0914	11.8	1539	2.2	2127	11.8	
3	SU	0355	2.2	0944	11.5	1600	2.3	2156	11.4	
4	M	0423	2.3	1015	11.1	1630	2.5	2229	11.0	
5	TU	0457	2.6	1051	10.7	1707	2.8	2310	10.6	
6	W	0542	2.9	1138	10.3	1755	3.3			◑
7	TH	0005	10.2	0638	3.2	1239	10.1	1859	3.6	
8	F	0115	10.1	0750	3.3	1352	10.1	2020	3.6	
9	SA	0232	10.4	0905	3.1	1509	10.6	2141	3.2	
10	SU	0343	11.0	1018	2.6	1616	11.3	2253	2.6	
11	M	0444	11.8	1125	2.1	1714	12.1	2355	2.0	
12	TU	0539	12.5	1224	1.6	1805	12.8			
13	W	0051	1.5	0629	13.1	1318	1.2	1853	13.4	●
14	TH	0144	1.2	0718	13.4	1408	0.9	1940	13.7	
15	F	0234	0.9	0807	13.6	1456	0.8	2027	13.8	
16	SA	0321	0.9	0855	13.5	1540	0.9	2114	13.6	
17	SU	0405	1.0	0943	13.3	1621	1.1	2201	13.2	
18	M	0447	1.3	1030	12.8	1701	1.5	2249	12.6	
19	TU	0529	1.7	1120	12.1	1744	2.0	2341	12.0	
20	W	0615	2.2	1215	11.4	1834	2.6			◐
21	TH	0043	11.3	0708	2.6	1320	10.9	1934	2.9	
22	F	0153	11.0	0812	2.9	1428	10.8	2046	3.0	
23	SA	0258	11.0	0923	2.9	1531	10.9	2157	2.8	
24	SU	0357	11.2	1030	2.7	1628	11.3	2258	2.4	
25	M	0452	11.5	1127	2.3	1719	11.8	2352	2.0	
26	TU	0541	11.9	1219	1.9	1806	12.2			
27	W	0041	1.7	0626	12.1	1307	1.7	1847	12.4	
28	TH	0128	1.5	0708	12.2	1351	1.6	1927	12.5	○
29	F	0211	1.6	0747	12.2	1431	1.7	2004	12.4	
30	SA	0250	1.8	0824	12.1	1505	2.0	2039	12.2	

JULY

Date	Day	Time	m	Time	m	Time	m	Time	m	Moon
1	SU	0322	2.0	0858	11.9	1531	2.2	2113	11.9	
2	M	0348	2.2	0931	11.7	1552	2.3	2144	11.7	
3	TU	0413	2.3	1002	11.5	1619	2.4	2215	11.4	
4	W	0444	2.3	1035	11.3	1653	2.5	2251	11.2	
5	TH	0522	2.5	1115	11.0	1734	2.7	2336	10.9	
6	F	0607	2.7	1204	10.7	1823	3.1			◑
7	SA	0032	10.7	0702	3.0	1303	10.5	1925	3.4	
8	SU	0139	10.6	0809	3.1	1414	10.6	2045	3.4	
9	M	0254	10.8	0931	3.0	1532	11.0	2213	3.0	
10	TU	0408	11.4	1050	2.5	1642	11.7	2326	2.4	
11	W	0513	12.1	1157	1.9	1742	12.5			
12	TH	0028	1.7	0610	12.8	1256	1.4	1835	13.2	
13	F	0127	1.2	0703	13.3	1352	1.0	1926	13.7	●
14	SA	0222	0.9	0755	13.6	1445	0.7	2015	14.0	
15	SU	0314	0.7	0845	13.7	1533	0.6	2103	14.0	
16	M	0400	0.7	0932	13.6	1616	0.8	2150	13.7	
17	TU	0442	0.9	1018	13.2	1655	1.1	2234	13.2	
18	W	0519	1.3	1102	12.6	1730	1.6	2319	12.5	
19	TH	0554	1.9	1147	11.9	1806	2.2			◐
20	F	0008	11.7	0631	2.4	1238	11.1	1849	2.8	
21	SA	0107	10.9	0716	3.0	1341	10.5	1943	3.3	
22	SU	0215	10.5	0814	3.4	1449	10.3	2054	3.5	
23	M	0320	10.4	0931	3.5	1552	10.5	2215	3.3	
24	TU	0420	10.7	1048	3.1	1649	11.0	2319	2.7	
25	W	0514	11.2	1146	2.5	1739	11.6			
26	TH	0012	2.2	0602	11.6	1238	2.1	1824	12.1	
27	F	0102	1.8	0645	12.0	1326	1.8	1906	12.4	○
28	SA	0149	1.6	0726	12.1	1411	1.7	1945	12.5	
29	SU	0233	1.7	0805	12.2	1452	1.8	2022	12.4	
30	M	0312	1.8	0841	12.1	1525	2.1	2057	12.3	
31	TU	0343	2.0	0914	12.0	1548	2.2	2128	12.1	

AUGUST

Date	Day	Time	m	Time	m	Time	m	Time	m	Moon
1	W	0406	2.2	0945	11.8	1608	2.3	2157	11.9	
2	TH	0429	2.2	1015	11.7	1636	2.3	2230	11.7	
3	F	0500	2.2	1051	11.6	1711	2.4	2310	11.5	
4	SA	0538	2.4	1133	11.2	1752	2.7	2358	11.1	◑
5	SU	0623	2.7	1226	10.8	1843	3.2			
6	M	0059	10.7	0721	3.2	1332	10.5	1952	3.6	
7	TU	0216	10.5	0844	3.4	1456	10.6	2141	3.5	
8	W	0342	10.9	1026	3.0	1619	11.3	2309	2.7	
9	TH	0456	11.7	1140	2.3	1726	12.2			
10	F	0016	1.9	0557	12.5	1243	1.5	1822	13.1	
11	SA	0116	1.2	0652	13.3	1341	1.0	1913	13.8	●
12	SU	0212	0.7	0743	13.8	1434	0.5	2002	14.2	
13	M	0304	0.3	0831	14.0	1522	0.3	2049	14.3	
14	TU	0349	0.3	0916	13.9	1604	0.5	2132	14.1	
15	W	0428	0.6	0957	13.5	1639	0.9	2213	13.5	
16	TH	0500	1.2	1036	12.9	1707	1.5	2250	12.7	
17	F	0524	1.9	1112	12.0	1733	2.2	2328	11.7	
18	SA	0550	2.5	1150	11.1	1805	2.8			◐
19	SU	0010	10.7	0625	3.2	1239	10.3	1849	3.5	
20	M	0113	9.9	0717	3.8	1357	9.7	1954	4.0	
21	TU	0240	9.6	0829	4.1	1517	9.8	2121	4.0	
22	W	0350	9.9	1003	3.8	1621	10.4	2248	3.3	
23	TH	0449	10.6	1118	3.0	1715	11.2	2347	2.5	
24	F	0539	11.3	1213	2.3	1802	12.0			
25	SA	0038	1.8	0623	11.9	1303	1.8	1844	12.5	
26	SU	0127	1.5	0704	12.3	1351	1.6	1923	12.7	○
27	M	0213	1.5	0743	12.4	1434	1.6	2001	12.7	
28	TU	0255	1.6	0820	12.4	1512	1.8	2036	12.6	
29	W	0330	1.8	0853	12.3	1540	2.1	2107	12.5	
30	TH	0355	2.0	0923	12.2	1556	2.2	2136	12.3	
31	F	0412	2.1	0953	12.1	1617	2.2	2208	12.2	

Chart Datum: 6·50 metres below Ordnance Datum (Newlyn). HAT is 14·7 metres above Chart Datum.

STANDARD TIME (UT)
For Summer Time add ONE hour in **non-shaded areas**

BRISTOL (AVONMOUTH) LAT 51°30′N LONG 2°44′W

TIMES AND HEIGHTS OF HIGH AND LOW WATERS

Dates in red are SPRINGS
Dates in blue are NEAPS

YEAR **2018**

SEPTEMBER

Day	Time	m	Time	m	Time	m	Time	m
1 SA	0437	2.1	1026	11.9	1648	2.2	2246	11.8
2 SU	0510	2.3	1106	11.5	1724	2.6	2331	11.2
3 M ◑	0550	2.7	1155	10.9	1809	3.2		
4 TU	0028	10.5	0643	3.4	1301	10.3	1913	3.8
5 W	0149	10.1	0805	3.9	1434	10.2	2129	3.9
6 TH	0330	10.4	1015	3.4	1607	11.0	2302	2.9
7 F	0447	11.4	1129	2.4	1714	12.1		
8 SA	0006	1.9	0547	12.5	1230	1.5	1809	13.2
9 SU	0103	1.0	0639	13.4	1326	0.8	● 1859	14.0
10 M	0156	0.4	0726	14.0	1417	0.3	1945	14.4
11 TU	0246	0.1	0811	14.2	1504	0.2	2029	14.5
12 W	0329	0.2	0853	14.1	1544	0.4	2109	14.1
13 TH	0406	0.6	0931	13.6	1616	0.9	2146	13.5
14 F	0432	1.4	1005	12.9	1639	1.6	2218	12.7
15 SA	0449	2.1	1035	12.1	1658	2.3	2248	11.7
16 SU	0509	2.6	1105	11.1	1724	2.9	◐ 2321	10.7
17 M	0538	3.3	1143	10.2	1802	3.6		
18 TU	0007	9.7	0622	4.0	1247	9.4	1903	4.3
19 W	0143	9.0	0738	4.5	1441	9.3	2034	4.5
20 TH	0320	9.4	0916	4.3	1552	10.0	2213	3.8
21 F	0422	10.2	1049	3.4	1648	10.9	2321	2.7
22 SA	0513	11.2	1147	2.5	1735	11.8		
23 SU	0012	1.9	0557	12.0	1237	1.9	1817	12.5
24 M	0101	1.5	0638	12.5	1325	1.6	1857	12.9
25 TU	0148	1.3	0716	12.7	1410	1.5	○ 1935	13.0
26 W	0230	1.4	0753	12.8	1449	1.7	2010	13.0
27 TH	0307	1.6	0827	12.8	1521	1.9	2043	12.9
28 F	0335	1.8	0858	12.7	1541	2.0	2115	12.7
29 SA	0354	2.0	0930	12.5	1601	2.1	2148	12.5
30 SU	0416	2.0	1005	12.2	1629	2.2	2227	12.0

OCTOBER

Day	Time	m	Time	m	Time	m	Time	m
1 M	0447	2.3	1046	11.7	1704	2.6	2311	11.3
2 TU ◑	0526	2.8	1134	11.0	1748	3.2		
3 W	0009	10.4	0618	3.6	1241	10.2	1852	4.0
4 TH	0136	9.9	0747	4.2	1427	10.1	2129	4.0
5 F	0324	10.3	1006	3.5	1556	11.0	2249	2.8
6 SA	0435	11.4	1113	2.4	1700	12.1	2348	1.7
7 SU	0532	12.6	1210	1.4	1753	13.2		
8 M	0042	0.9	0620	13.5	1304	0.7	1840	14.0
9 TU	0133	0.4	0705	14.0	1353	0.3	● 1924	14.3
10 W	0220	0.2	0747	14.1	1438	0.3	2005	14.3
11 TH	0302	0.4	0827	13.9	1518	0.6	2044	13.9
12 F	0337	0.9	0903	13.5	1549	1.2	2118	13.3
13 SA	0402	1.6	0934	12.8	1610	1.9	2147	12.5
14 SU	0416	2.2	1001	12.0	1626	2.4	2214	11.6
15 M	0433	2.7	1029	11.2	1650	2.9	2243	10.7
16 TU	0459	3.2	1102	10.4	1724	3.5	◐ 2321	9.8
17 W	0535	3.9	1150	9.5	1816	4.2		
18 TH	0027	9.0	0639	4.6	1345	9.1	1948	4.6
19 F	0236	9.1	0827	4.7	1515	9.7	2121	4.1
20 SA	0346	9.9	1003	3.9	1613	10.6	2241	3.1
21 SU	0439	10.9	1111	2.9	1702	11.6	2338	2.2
22 M	0525	11.8	1203	2.2	1746	12.3		
23 TU	0028	1.7	0607	12.5	1252	1.8	1827	12.8
24 W	0115	1.4	0646	12.9	1337	1.6	○ 1906	13.1
25 TH	0159	1.3	0724	13.1	1419	1.6	1943	13.2
26 F	0238	1.4	0800	13.2	1454	1.7	2019	13.2
27 SA	0311	1.6	0836	13.1	1524	1.8	2056	13.1
28 SU	0338	1.7	0912	12.9	1550	1.9	2134	12.7
29 M	0404	1.9	0951	12.5	1619	2.1	2215	12.2
30 TU	0436	2.3	1033	11.9	1655	2.6	2302	11.4
31 W ◑	0516	2.9	1124	11.1	1742	3.3		

NOVEMBER

Day	Time	m	Time	m	Time	m	Time	m
1 TH	0001	10.5	0610	3.6	1234	10.4	1853	3.9
2 F	0131	10.1	0753	4.0	1417	10.4	2109	3.7
3 SA	0306	10.5	0942	3.4	1536	11.1	2223	2.8
4 SU	0413	11.4	1048	2.4	1637	12.1	2322	1.8
5 M	0508	12.4	1143	1.6	1729	13.0		
6 TU	0014	1.1	0556	13.2	1235	1.0	1816	13.6
7 W	0104	0.7	0640	13.7	1324	0.7	● 1859	13.8
8 TH	0150	0.6	0721	13.8	1409	0.7	1940	13.8
9 F	0232	0.8	0800	13.6	1449	1.0	2018	13.4
10 SA	0308	1.3	0835	13.2	1522	1.5	2052	12.9
11 SU	0334	1.8	0907	12.7	1545	2.0	2122	12.3
12 M	0349	2.3	0935	12.0	1602	2.4	2150	11.6
13 TU	0407	2.6	1003	11.4	1627	2.8	2219	10.9
14 W	0433	3.0	1035	10.7	1659	3.2	2254	10.2
15 TH	0508	3.5	1117	10.0	1745	3.8	◐ 2345	9.6
16 F	0558	4.1	1225	9.5	1856	4.2		
17 SA	0109	9.2	0724	4.5	1413	9.5	2023	4.2
18 SU	0248	9.6	0858	4.2	1524	10.2	2141	3.5
19 M	0353	10.4	1015	3.5	1620	11.1	2249	2.8
20 TU	0445	11.3	1118	2.7	1708	11.9	2346	2.1
21 W	0532	12.2	1211	2.1	1753	12.6		
22 TH	0037	1.7	0614	12.8	1300	1.8	1836	13.0
23 F	0125	1.4	0656	13.2	1346	1.5	○ 1918	13.3
24 SA	0208	1.3	0737	13.4	1429	1.5	2000	13.4
25 SU	0249	1.3	0818	13.5	1508	1.5	2042	13.3
26 M	0325	1.4	0900	13.3	1545	1.6	2126	13.0
27 TU	0400	1.7	0943	12.9	1621	1.9	2210	12.5
28 W	0437	2.1	1029	12.4	1701	2.4	2259	11.8
29 TH	0519	2.6	1120	11.7	1750	2.9	2356	11.1
30 F ◑	0613	3.2	1226	11.0	1856	3.3		

DECEMBER

Day	Time	m	Time	m	Time	m	Time	m
1 SA	0112	10.6	0732	3.5	1351	10.8	2028	3.4
2 SU	0234	10.7	0903	3.3	1505	11.2	2145	2.9
3 M	0341	11.2	1012	2.7	1606	11.7	2247	2.3
4 TU	0438	11.9	1111	2.1	1701	12.3	2342	1.8
5 W	0529	12.5	1203	1.6	1750	12.8		
6 TH	0032	1.4	0614	13.0	1253	1.3	1835	13.1
7 F	0119	1.2	0656	13.2	1339	1.2	● 1916	13.1
8 SA	0202	1.3	0735	13.1	1421	1.4	1955	12.9
9 SU	0241	1.5	0812	12.9	1458	1.7	2031	12.6
10 M	0312	1.9	0846	12.6	1527	2.1	2104	12.2
11 TU	0333	2.3	0917	12.1	1548	2.4	2134	11.7
12 W	0352	2.5	0948	11.7	1613	2.6	2204	11.3
13 TH	0418	2.7	1019	11.2	1644	2.8	2238	10.8
14 F	0451	3.0	1056	10.7	1723	3.1	2319	10.4
15 SA ◐	0534	3.4	1143	10.2	1814	3.5		
16 SU	0012	10.0	0629	3.8	1248	10.0	1920	3.8
17 M	0122	9.8	0745	4.0	1407	10.1	2037	3.7
18 TU	0242	10.1	0909	3.8	1522	10.6	2153	3.3
19 W	0354	10.8	1025	3.2	1624	11.3	2301	2.6
20 TH	0453	11.6	1130	2.6	1719	12.1		
21 F	0000	2.0	0544	12.4	1227	2.0	1809	12.7
22 SA	0054	1.6	0631	13.1	1319	1.6	○ 1857	13.2
23 SU	0144	1.2	0718	13.5	1409	1.3	1945	13.5
24 M	0232	1.1	0804	13.7	1457	1.2	2032	13.6
25 TU	0317	1.1	0850	13.7	1543	1.2	2119	13.4
26 W	0359	1.2	0936	13.5	1625	1.4	2205	13.1
27 TH	0440	1.5	1023	13.1	1706	1.7	2252	12.5
28 F	0520	1.9	1111	12.5	1748	2.1	2342	11.9
29 SA ◑	0605	2.4	1206	11.8	1836	2.6		
30 SU	0040	11.2	0658	2.9	1313	11.2	1934	3.0
31 M	0151	10.8	0805	3.2	1425	11.0	2049	3.3

Chart Datum: 6·50 metres below Ordnance Datum (Newlyn). HAT is 14·7 metres above Chart Datum.

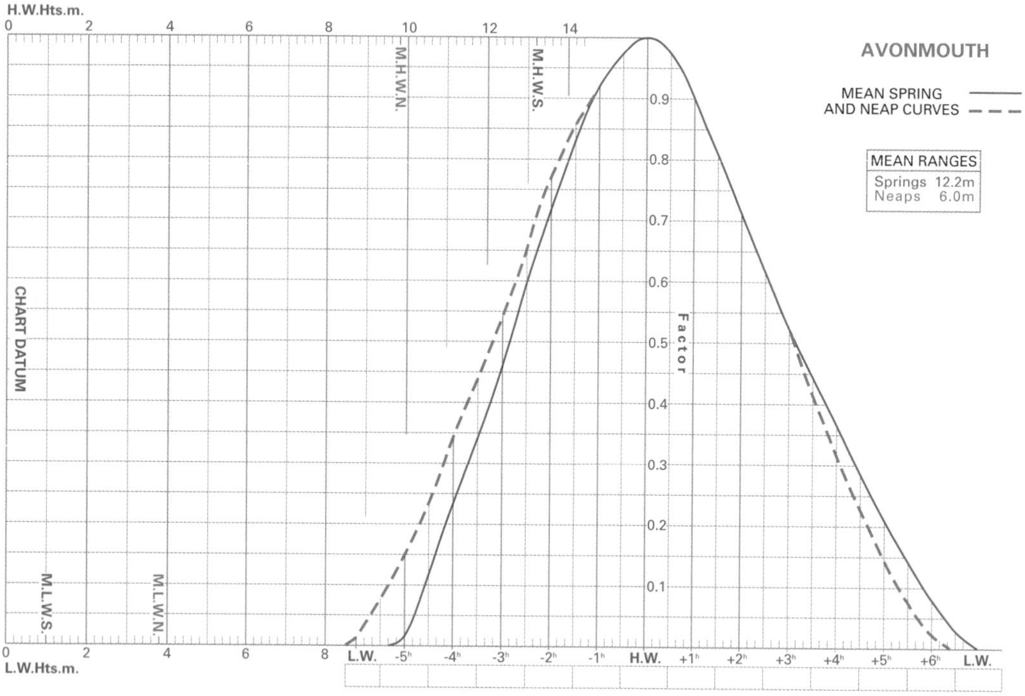

9.11.20 BRISTOL (CITY DOCKS)

Ent to R Avon **51°30'·44N 02°43'·31W** ⚙⚙👍👍✿✿✿

CHARTS AC 5608, 1179, 1176, 1859; Imray C59, 2600

TIDES −0410 on Dover; ML 7·0; Duration 0620. NB very large range

Standard Port BRISTOL (AVONMOUTH) (⟵)

Times				Height (metres)			
High Water		Low Water		MHWS	MHWN	MLWN	MLWS
0200	0800	0300	0800	13·2	9·8	3·8	1·0
1400	2000	1500	2000				
Differences SHIREHAMPTON (R Avon, 51°29'N 02°41'W)							
0000	0000	+0035	+0010	−0·7	−0·7	−0·8	0·0
SEA MILLS (R Avon, 51°29'N 02°39'W)							
+0005	+0005	+0105	+0030	−1·4	−1·5	−1·7	−0·1
CUMBERLAND BASIN (Ent)							
+0010	*+0010*	*DR*	*DR*	*−2·9*	*−3·0*	*DR*	*DR*

SHELTER Excellent in Bristol Floating Harbour. Avonmouth and Royal Portbury Docks are prohib to yachts, except in emergency. If early/late on the tide, ⚓ as close inshore as depth allows in Portishead Pool between Portishead Dock and Royal Portbury Dock, but avoid in onshore winds.

NAVIGATION **From the south and west**: from Avon SHM buoy (51°27'·92N 02°51'·73W) either follow the Bristol Deep shipping channel taking care not to impede the safe passage of commercial traffic or stay well clear to the S passing close to Portishead Pt. If to the north, cross the shipping channel by the most direct route keeping clear of inbound/outbound traffic.

From the north: Conform to the channel taking care not to impede the safe passage of commercial traffic.

- Beware large ships transiting/turning in the main channel.
- Beware ships and tugs leaving the docks at any time.
- When on passage up/down the Severn estuary without stopping at Bristol or Portishead, use the *Offshore Route*.

Entering R Avon keep N of shallows (Swash Bank) between Royal Portbury Dock and Avonmouth Docks. Speed limit in river: 6kn if draught >2m; 9kn if draught <2m.

LIGHTS AND MARKS Ldg lts 127°, both Iso R 2s, to R Avon ent abeam S pier lt, Oc RG 30s. St George ldg lts 173°, both Oc G 5s, front/rear W/Or posts, clear Swash Bank (dries). Upriver, G or R ☆s mark the outside of bends.

Entry signals to Bristol Hbr may be shown from E bank, 1½ and 2½ca S of Clifton Suspension Bridge: ● = continue with caution; ● = stop and await orders.

LOCKS Floating Harbour (approx 7M upriver) is accessed via Entrance Lock into Cumberland Basin and Junction Lock into Floating Hbr. Aim to reach the Ent lock no later than HW−0015. Ent lock opens approx HW−2½, −1½ and −¼hr for arrivals; departures approx 15 mins after these times. Plimsoll swing bridge opens in unison with lock, except weekday rush hours 0800–0900 and 1700–1800.

Junction lock is always open, unless ht of HW is >9·6m ('stopgate' tide) when it closes; read special instructions. If you miss the last lock-in, call Ch 12 for advice.

BRIDGES Prince St Bridge opens (by arrangement only) summer 0915–2130, winter 0915–1830. Call Duty Office ☎9031484 or VHF Ch 73. Same for Redcliffe Bridge, but only opened in exceptional circumstances. Clearances above HAT: St Augustine's Reach 1·8m & 0·7m; Prince St 0·7m; Redcliffe 2·1m; Bristol 2·6m. The R Avon leads to Netham lock ☎9776590, Keynsham, Bath and the Kennett & Avon canal.

COMMUNICATIONS (Code 0117) CGOC (01646) 690909; Police 101; Cumberland Basin Dock Master 9273633 Ⓗ 923 0000.

Bristol VTS, Ch 12, ☎0117 980 2638.

- All vessels are to maintain a listening watch on Ch 12 in Bristol VTS area and monitor commercial ship movements.
- At Black Rks (1M to run) call City Docks Radio Ch 14, 11 low power, (HW−3 to HW+1) for locking instructions.
- For berth: Bristol Floating Hbr Ch 73; Bristol Marina Ch 80.

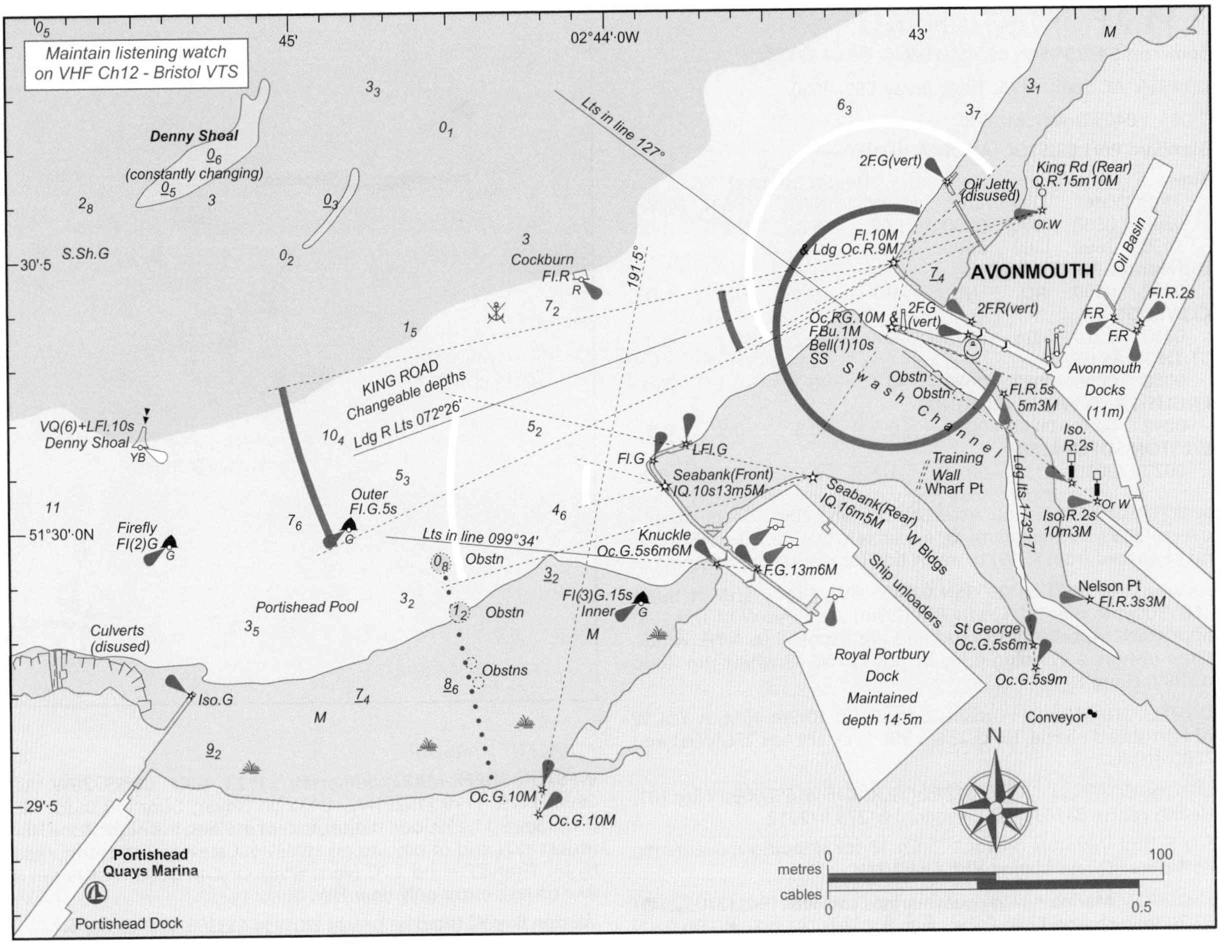

Maintain listening watch on VHF Ch12 - Bristol VTS
45'
02°44'·0W
43'
Denny Shoal
(constantly changing)
S.Sh.G
30'·5
Cockburn
Fl.R
Lts in line 127°
2F.G(vert)
Oil Jetty (disused)
King Rd (Rear) Q.R.15m10M
Or.W
Fl.10M & Ldg Oc.R.9M
AVONMOUTH
Oil Basin
Fl.R.2s
2F.G (vert)
2F.R(vert)
Oc.RG.10M & F.Bu.1M Bell(1)10s SS
Swash Channel
Obstn
Fl.R.5s 5m3M
Avonmouth Docks (11m)
KING ROAD Changeable depths
Ldg R Lts 072°26'
VQ(6)+LFl.10s Denny Shoal
YB
Fl.G
LFl.G
Seabank(Front) IQ.10s13m5M
Seabank(Rear) IQ.16m5M
Training Wall
Wharf Pt
Iso. R.2s
Or W
Iso.R.2s 10m3M
Ldg lts 173°17'
Outer Fl.G.5s
Firefly Fl(2)G
51°30'·0N
Lts in line 099°34'
Obstn
Knuckle Oc.G.5s6m6M
F.G.13m6M
W Bldgs
Ship unloaders
Nelson Pt Fl.R.3s3M
Portishead Pool
Fl(3)G.15s Inner
Obstn
Obstns
Culverts (disused)
Iso.G
St George Oc.G.5s6m
Oc.G.5s9m
Royal Portbury Dock
Maintained depth 14·5m
Conveyor
Oc.G.10M
Oc.G.10M
29'·5
Portishead Quays Marina
Portishead Dock
metres
cables
0
100
0.5

FACILITIES (from seaward) **Portishead Cruising Club** at Crockerne Pill, S bank, 5ca above M5 bridge; www.portisheadcruisingclub.org.uk ☎01275 373988, Drying ⚓ (soft mud) ▬ grid (£5/day).

Bristol Hbr HM, Underfall Yard, Cumberland Rd, Bristol BS1 6XG. www.bristol-city.gov.uk ☎9031484; approx 40 Ⓥ consult website and HM in advance for detailed info on lock and bridge opening times ⌒ near ent to St Augustine's Reach, £2.67 inc licence fee. ▬ (launching £9.22) ; ferries ply between various landing stages around the hbr.

Baltic Wharf Leisure Centre contact HM ☎9031484, ▬.

Bristol Marina Access–3HW+1. www.bristolmarina.co.uk ☎9213198, 170⌒, inc about 5Ⓥ (21m max LOA) £2.00. ▬ (£2.25/m) Ⓔ (6/12t) (50t).

Bathurst Basin. **Cabot CC** ☎9268318.

City All domestic facilities, ACA, ⇄ ✈.

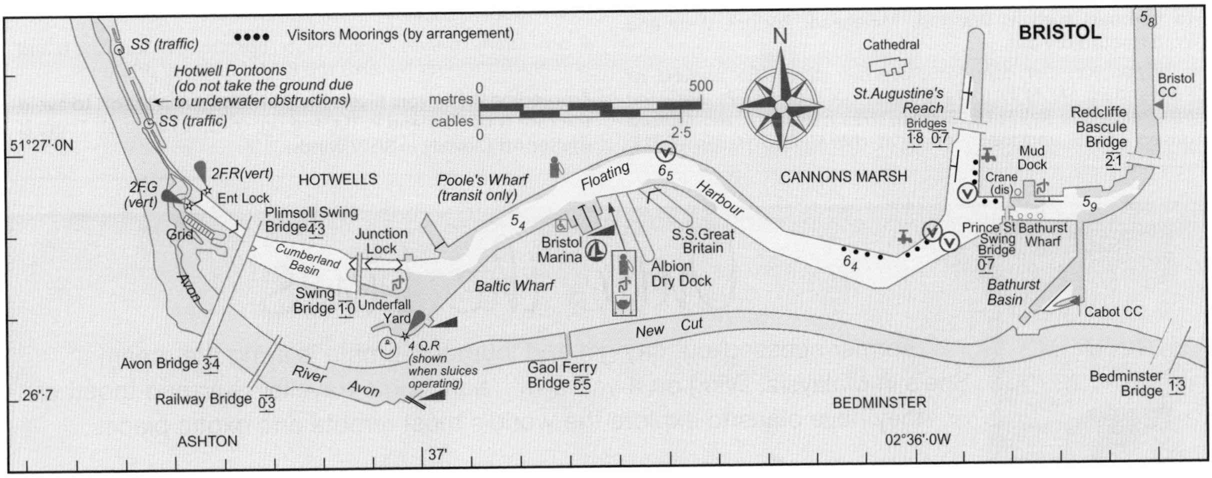

SS (traffic)
Visitors Moorings (by arrangement)
BRISTOL
Hotwell Pontoons (do not take the ground due to underwater obstructions)
SS (traffic)
metres
cables
0
500
2·5
Cathedral
St.Augustine's Reach
Bridges 1·8 0·7
Bristol CC
Redcliffe Bascule Bridge 2·1
51°27'·0N
2F.R(vert)
2F.G (vert)
Ent Lock
HOTWELLS
Poole's Wharf (transit only)
Floating Harbour
CANNONS MARSH
Mud Dock
Crane (dis)
Plimsoll Swing Bridge 4·3
Junction Lock
Grid
Cumberland Basin
Bristol Marina
S.S.Great Britain
Prince St Bridge 0·7
Bathurst Wharf
Swing Bridge 1·0
Underfall Yard
Baltic Wharf
Albion Dry Dock
Bathurst Basin
Cabot CC
Avon
4 Q.R (shown when sluices operating)
New Cut
Avon Bridge 3·4
River Avon
Gaol Ferry Bridge 5·5
Bedminster Bridge 1·3
26'·7
Railway Bridge 0·3
BEDMINSTER
ASHTON
37'
02°36'·0W

9.11.21 PORTISHEAD

Somerset **51°29'·56N 02°45'·41W** ❀❀◊◊◊✿✿✿

CHARTS AC 5608, 1176, 1859; Imray C59, 2600

TIDES –0405 Dover; ML 6·8

Standard Port BRISTOL (AVONMOUTH) (⟵)

Times				Height (metres)			
High Water		Low Water		MHWS	MHWN	MLWN	MLWS
0200	0800	0300	0800	13·2	9·8	3·8	1·0
1400	2000	1500	2000				
Differences PORTISHEAD							
–0002	0000	ND	ND	–0·1	–0·1	ND	ND
CLEVEDON							
–0010	–0020	–0025	–0015	–0·4	–0·2	+0·2	0·0
ST THOMAS HEAD							
0000	0000	–0030	–0030	–0·4	–0·2	+0·1	+0·1
ENGLISH AND WELSH GROUNDS							
–0008	–0008	–0030	–0030	–0·5	–0·8	–0·3	0·0
WESTON-SUPER-MARE							
–0020	–0030	–0130	–0030	–1·2	–1·0	–0·8	–0·2

SHELTER Good in marina. Access by lock 9m x 40m x 5m min depth over cill HW ±3½ (minimum). ⓋS available in marina. ⚓ 1ca NE of pier hd (sheltered from SE-W) to await tide for marina or Sharpness.

NAVIGATION WPT 51°29'·96N 02°45'·35W, Firefly SHM lt buoy, 168°/500m to pier hd. Firefly Rks (0·9m) are close W of the 168° appr track. Appr's dry to mud and are exposed to N/NE winds. Close inshore a W-going eddy begins at HW –3 whilst the flood is still making E.

LIGHTS AND MARKS Portishead Pt, Q (3) 10s9m 16M, is 7ca W of Portishead pierhd, Iso G 2s 5m 3M. Lock ent has 2FG(vert) and 2FR(vert) lts.

COMMUNICATIONS (Code 01275) CGOC (01646) 690909; Police 101; Health centre 841630; Ⓗ (Clevedon) 01275 872212.

See Bristol. Monitor *Bristol VTS* Ch **12** for shipping movements. Portishead Quays Marina VHF Ch 80 24H.

FACILITIES **Marina** www.quaymarinas.com ☎841941 (270+Ⓥ) £2·70 (min charge £23); (35t) wi-fi.

Portishead Cruising Club ☎373988.

Town ✉ Ⓑ ⇌ ✈ (Bristol). 3M to Junction 19 of M5.

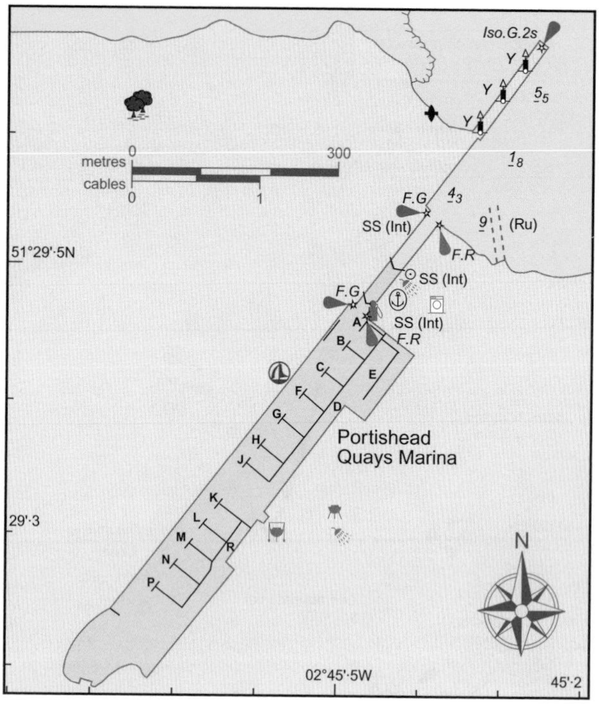

ADJACENT HARBOUR

WESTON-SUPER-MARE, Somerset, **51°21'·03N 02°59'·28W**. AC 5608, 1179, 1176,1152. HW –0435 on Dover; Duration 0655; ML 6·1m. See 9.11.21. Good shelter, except in S'lies, in Knightstone Hbr (dries) at N end of bay; access HW±1½. Causeway at ent marked by bn. Grand Pier hd 2 FG (vert) 6/5m. Or ⚓ in good weather in R Axe (dries), enter only near HW.

Weston Bay YC (sited on beach) ☎01934 413366, VHF Ch 80.

Uphill Boat Centre ☎01934 418617. (lower R Axe-drying) (10t).

Town ✉ Ⓑ ✕ ⇌.

AVONMOUTH TO HARTLAND POINT

(AC 1152, 1165) From Avonmouth to Sand Pt, the part-drying English Grounds extend 3M off the S shore. Portishead Quays Marina offers good shelter. Extensive mudflats fill the bays S to Burnham-on-Sea. Westward, the S shore of Bristol Chan is cleaner than N shore. But there is less shelter since the approaches to harbours such as Watchet, Minehead, Porlock Weir and Watermouth dry out.

▶ *In bad weather dangerous overfalls occur NW and NE of Foreland Pt. 5M to W there is a race off Highveer Pt. Between Ilfracombe and Bull Pt the E-going stream begins at HW Milford Haven +0540, and the W-going at HW Milford Haven –0025, sp rates 3kn. Overfalls occur up to 1·5M N of Bull Pt and over Horseshoe Rks, which lie 3M N. There is a dangerous race off Morte Pt, 1·5M to W of Bull Pt.* ◀

Shelter is available under the lee of Lundy Island; but avoid bad races to NE (White Horses), NW (Hen and Chickens), and SE; also overfalls over NW Bank.

▶ *W of Lundy streams are moderate, but strong around the island and much stronger towards the Bristol Channel proper.* ◀

Proceeding WSW from Rivers Taw/Torridge, keep 3M off to avoid the race N of Hartland Pt (Lt, fog sig, conspic radome). There is shelter off Clovelly in S/SW winds.

9.11.22 BURNHAM-ON-SEA

Somerset **51°14'·23N 03°00'·33W**

CHARTS AC 5608, 1179, 1152; Imray C59, 2600

TIDES –0435 Dover; ML 5·4; Duration 0620

Standard Port BRISTOL (AVONMOUTH) (⟵)

Times				Height (metres)			
High Water		Low Water		MHWS	MHWN	MLWN	MLWS
0200	0800	0300	0800	13·2	9·8	3·8	1·0
1400	2000	1500	2000				
Differences BURNHAM-ON-SEA							
–0020	–0025	–0030	0000	–2·3	–1·9	–1·4	–1·1
BRIDGWATER							
–0015	–0030	+0305	+0455	–8·6	–8·1	DR	DR

SHELTER Ent is very choppy in strong winds, especially from SW to W and from N to NE. ⚓ S of town jetty or, for best shelter, Ⓥ/🏵 in R Brue (dries). Contact HM by ☎ in advance.

NAVIGATION WPT 51°13'·46N 03°09'·80W, 0·5M S of Gore SWM buoy. Enter HW–2 to HW; not advised at night. From WPT track 090°/1.35M, then 070°/2.20M, then 079°/1.00M, then 112° on ldg lts, 180° into river channel when clear of No 3 buoy. Deepest water on E (shore) side of channel. Banks and depths change frequently.

Beware unmarked fishing stakes outside approach channels.

No access to Stert Marshes Nature Reserve from R Parrett.

LIGHTS AND MARKS *Sectors of low light under revision (2017)* Ldg lts/marks 112° (moved as chan shifts) *within RH edge of sandbank*: front FR 6m 3M, R stripe on □ W background on sea wall; rear FR 12m 3M, RH edge of church tr. New No 2 PHM buoy will be laid between No 1 PHM and existing No 2 SHM, which will be re-numbered 3. Existing No 3 & 4 will become No 4 & 5.

COMMUNICATIONS (Code 01278) Police 101; Ⓗ 773100. HM 01934 822666 H24; harbour.master@sedgemoor.gov.uk.

FACILITIES **Burnham-on-Sea MB&SC** ☎792911 (Wed eve and Sun am) ⛵ two drying pontoon berths in R Brue (free).
Town ⛽ ✕ 🔧 📪 ✉ Ⓑ 🛒 ≈ (Highbridge), ✈(Bristol).

ADJACENT FACILITY

Combwich A cargo wharf has been constructed to facilitate the inload of large indivisible loads to Hinkley Pt C Power Station. The approaches can be busy on appropriate tides.

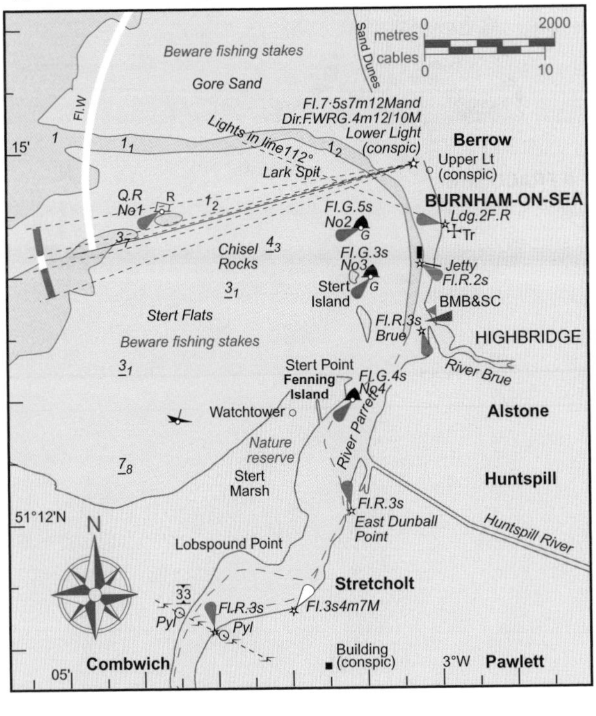

9.11.23 WATCHET

Somerset **51°11'·03N 03°19'·72W**

CHARTS AC 5608, 1179, 1152, 1160; Imray C59, 2600

TIDES –0450 Dover; ML 5·9; Duration 0655

Standard Port BRISTOL (AVONMOUTH) (⟵)

Times				Height (metres)			
High Water		Low Water		MHWS	MHWN	MLWN	MLWS
0200	0800	0300	0800	13·2	9·8	3·8	1·0
1400	2000	1500	2000				
Differences HINKLEY POINT							
–0032	–0028	–0055	–0049	–1·4	–1·1	–0·1	0·0
WATCHET							
–0035	–0050	–0145	–0040	–1·9	–1·5	+0·1	+0·1
MINEHEAD							
–0037	–0052	–0155	–0045	–2·6	–1·9	–0·2	0·0
PORLOCK BAY							
–0045	–0055	–0205	–0050	–3·0	–2·2	–0·1	–0·1
LYNMOUTH							
–0055	–0115	ND	ND	–3·6	–2·7	ND	ND

SHELTER Good, but open to N and E winds. Outer hbr (controlled by HM on VHF) dries 6·5m, but has about 6m depth at MHWS. Marina subject to silting, some berths allow boats to settle in soft mud; some berths have limited accessibility. Approx gate opening times HW ±2½H Sp, HW ±1½H Np. **Outer harbour** 6 drying ⛵ on W wall, also used by commercial shipping.

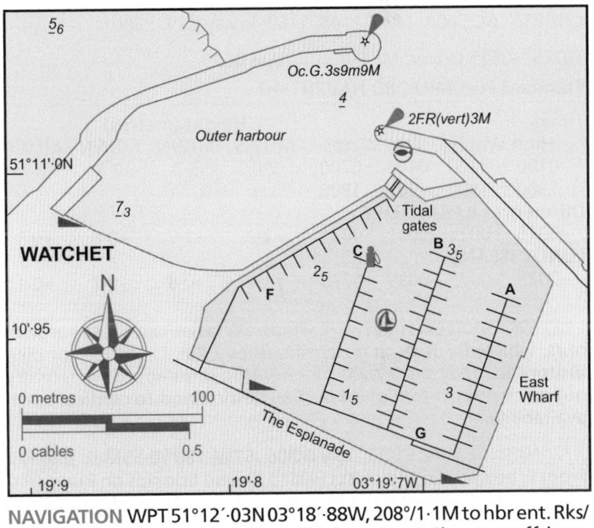

NAVIGATION WPT 51°12'·03N 03°18'·88W, 208°/1·1M to hbr ent. Rks/mud dry 5ca to seaward. Beware tidal streams 4-5kn at sp offshore and around W pier hd. Marina entered through a dropping sill gate (width 7m) which opens when tide level is at least CD +6.92m (retained water level). Entrance is controlled by automatic stop/go R/G lts. Min clearance over the gate is 2.5m. Min retained water depths vary 1.5–3.0m. 3kn speed limit in marina.

LIGHTS AND MARKS Two lit (FR) radio masts (206m) bearing 208° Station is conspic 7·5M to the E. W pier hd Oc G 3s 9m 9M on Red (R) tr. E pier hd 2 FR (vert) 3M.

COMMUNICATIONS (Code 01984) CGOC (01646) 690909; Police 101. **Marina** ☎631264 mob below; Watchet Boat Owners Association (01643) 702569.

Harbour/Marina Ch 80.

FACILITIES **Watchet Harbour Marina** www.watchetharbour.co.uk ☎631264 mob 07957208980 (H24) contact prior to arrival for berth. 250⛵ inc Ⓥ £2·60 inc, (20t) ACA.

Town ✉ 🛒 ✕. At Williton (2M): ⛽; Ⓗ (Minehead 8M), ≈ (Taunton 18M), ✈ (Bristol).

ADJACENT JETTY

Hinkley Pt C Power Station. The redevelopment includes the construction of a jetty and dolphins on Hinkley Pt. Limits marked by lit SPM. Craft are not allowed within 100m except in emergency.

HARBOURS ON THE SOUTH SHORE OF THE BRISTOL CHANNEL

MINEHEAD, Somerset, **51°12′·79N 03°28′·37W.** AC 1179, 1165, 1160. HW –0450 on Dover. ML 5·7m. See 9.11.23. Small hbr, dries 7·5m. Good shelter within pier curving E and then SE, over which seas may break in gales at MHWS; exposed to E'lies. Best appr from N or NW; beware The Gables, shingle bank (dries 3·7m) about 5ca ENE of pier. Keep E of a sewer outfall which passes ½ca E of pier hd and extends 1¾ca NNE of it; outfall is protected by rk covering, drying 2·8m and N end marked by SHM Bn QG 6m 7M. Shingle bank extends 20m all round pierhead, lit Fl (2) G 5s 4M, vis 127°-262°. There are 2 R s at hbr ent just seaward of 3 posts or Med moor on quay at inner end of pier; £3·00/m/day, £10/m/wk. Hbr has live webcam. Holiday camp conspic 6ca SE.

HM (01984) 634594, mob 07528 208758.

Facilities: **Hbr** (launching £14·50/day £31/wk), at . **Town** (Taunton).

PORLOCK WEIR, Somerset, **51°13′·17N 03°37′·64W.** AC 1179, 1165, 1160. HW –0500 on Dover; ML 5·6m. See 9.11.23. Access only near HW. Ent chan (250°), about 15m wide marked by withies (3 PHM and 1 SHM), between shingle bank/wood pilings to stbd and sunken wooden wall to port is difficult in any seas. A small pool (1m) just inside ent is for shoal draught boats; others dry out on pebble banks. Or turn 90° stbd, via gates (but opening bridge usually closed), into inner drying dock with good shelter. No lts. HM 01643 863187 (not local). **Porlock Weir SC.** Facilities: and limited .

LYNMOUTH, Devon, **51°14′·16N 03°49′·79W.** AC 1160, 1165. HW–0515 on Dover. See 9.11.23. Tiny hbr, dries approx 5m, only suitable in settled offshore weather. Appr from Sand Ridge SHM lt buoy, 1·6M W of Foreland Pt and 9ca N of hbr ent. The narrow appr channel between drying boulder ledges is marked by 7 unlit posts. After first 2 posts keep 10m away from next SH post then next 2PH posts keep to middle of ent. Hbr ent is between piers, 2FR/FG lts, on W side of river course. Berth on E pier, which covers (beware) at MHWS. Resort facilities. Admin by Council 01598 752384.

WATERMOUTH, Devon, **51°13′·03N 04°04′·6W.** AC 1179, 1165. HW –0525 on Dover; ML 4·9m; Duration 0625. Use 9.11.24. Good shelter in drying hbr, but heavy surge runs in strong NW winds. Dir lt 153° Oc WRG 5s 1m, W sector 151·5°-154·5°, W△ on structure, 1½ca inside ent on S shore. Bkwtr, covered at high tide, has Y poles along its length and a G pole with conical topmark at the end. 9 Y s with B handles £6.50. HM (01271) 865422. Facilities: Hbr (cans) (12t) ; **YC,** . **Combe Martin** 1½M all facilities.

9.11.24 ILFRACOMBE

Devon **51°12′·65N 04°06′·65W**

CHARTS AC 5608, *1179, 1165,* 1160; Imray C59, 2600

TIDES –0525 Dover; ML 5·0; Duration 0625

Standard Port MILFORD HAVEN (←)

Times				Height (metres)			
High Water		Low Water		MHWS	MHWN	MLWN	MLWS
0100	0700	0100	0700	7·0	5·2	2·5	0·7
1300	1900	1300	1900				
Differences ILFRACOMBE							
–0016	–0016	–0041	–0031	+2·2	+1·7	+0·6	+0·3
LUNDY ISLAND							
–0025	–0025	–0035	–0030	+1·0	+0·8	+0·2	+0·1

SHELTER Good except in NE/E winds. SW gales can cause surge in hbrs, which dry. 8 s in outer hbr, dries 2·7m. Or clear of pier. Visitors on N snd S walls of Inner Hbr, dries approx 4m, or dry out on chains off foot of N Pier. Call beforehand to confirm berth availability.

NAVIGATION WPT 51°13′·23N 04°06′·67W, 180°/0·55M to pier hd. From E, beware Copperas Rks (4M to E), and tide rips on Buggy Pit, 7ca NE of ent. On entry keep toward Pier to clear drying ledges and lobster keep-pots obstructing Hbr ent on SE side.

LIGHTS AND MARKS See 9.11.4 and chartlet.

COMMUNICATIONS (Code 01271) CGOC (01646) 690909; Police 101; Dr 863119. HM 862108 mob 07775 532606.

Ilfracombe Hbr VHF Ch 12 16 (not H24).

FACILITIES **Hbr** (launching £5.84/day, £1·45/week) and s £1·32 (inc use of) (S Quay) . **Ilfracombe YC** 863969, (35t as arranged) .
Town bus to Barnstaple (), (Exeter).

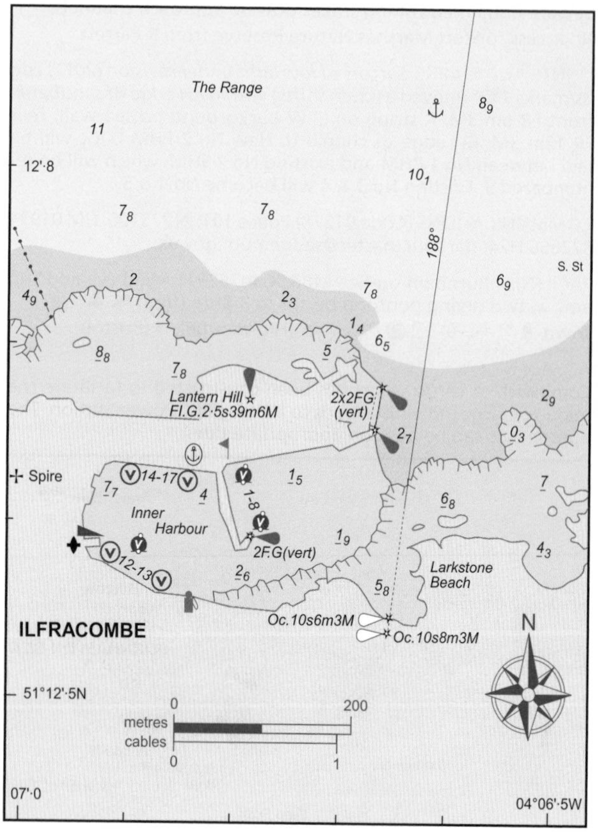

HARTLAND POINT TO LAND'S END

(AC 1156, 1149) The N coast of Cornwall and SW approaches to Bristol Chan are very exposed. Yachts need to be sturdy and well equipped since, if bad weather develops, no shelter may be at hand.

Bude dries, and is not approachable in W winds; only accessible in calm weather or offshore winds. Boscastle is a tiny hbr (dries) 3M NE of Tintagel Hd. Only approach in good weather or offshore winds; ⚓ off or dry out alongside.

Padstow can be a refuge, but in strong NW winds the sea breaks on bar and prevents entry. Off Trevose Hd beware Quies Rks which extend 1M to W. From here S the coast is relatively clear to Godrevy Is, apart from Bawden Rks 1M N of St Agnes Hd. Newquay Bay is good ⚓ in offshore winds, and the hbr (dries) is sheltered but uncomfortable in N winds. Off Godrevy Is are The Stones, drying rky shoals extending 1·5M offshore, marked by NCM lt buoy.

In St Ives Bay (AC 1168), Hayle is a commercial port (dries); seas break heavily on bar at times, especially with a ground swell. ► *Stream is strong, so enter just before HW.* ◄ The bottom is mostly sand. St Ives (dries) gives shelter from winds E to SW, but is very exposed to N; there is sometimes a heavy breaking sea if there is ground swell. Keep clear of the renewable energy development area centred approx 325°/10M from St Ives Bay (see AC 2565).

From St Ives to Land's End coast is rugged and exposed. There are o'falls SW of Pendeen Pt. Vyneck Rks lie awash about 3ca NW of C Cornwall. The Brisons are two high rky islets 5ca SW of C Cornwall, with rky ledges inshore and to the S. The Longships group of rks is about 1M W of Land's End. The inshore passage (001° on Brisons) is about 4ca wide with unmarked drying rks on the W side; only to be considered in calm weather and beware of fishing gear marker buoys.

For Isles of Scilly, South Cornwall and Tides, see 9.1.5.

9.11.25 RIVERS TAW AND TORRIDGE

Devon **51°04'·37N 04°12'·88W** ❁❁⚓⚓✿✿✿

CHARTS AC 5608, 1179, 1164, 1160; Imray C58, 2600

TIDES –0525 (Appledore) Dover; ML 3·6; Duration 0600

Standard Port MILFORD HAVEN (⟵)

Times				Height (metres)			
High Water		Low Water		MHWS	MHWN	MLWN	MLWS
0100	0700	0100	0700	7·0	5·2	2·5	0·7
1300	1900	1300	1900				
Differences APPLEDORE							
–0020	–0025	+0015	–0045	+0·5	0·0	–0·9	–0·5
YELLAND MARSH (R Taw)							
–0010	–0015	+0100	–0015	+0·1	–0·4	–1·2	–0·6
FREMINGTON (R Taw)							
–0010	–0015	+0030	–0030	–1·1	–1·8	–2·2	–0·5
BARNSTAPLE (R Taw)							
0000	–0015	–0155	–0245	–2·9	–3·8	–2·2	–0·4
BIDEFORD (R Torridge)							
–0020	–0025	0000	0000	–1·1	–1·6	–2·5	–0·7
CLOVELLY							
–0030	–0030	–0020	–0040	+1·3	+1·1	+0·2	+0·2

SHELTER Very well protected, but ent is dangerous in strong on-shore winds and/or swell. Yachts can ⚓ or pick up RNLI buoy (please donate to RNLI, Boathouse ☎473969) in Appledore Pool N of Skern Pt where spring stream can reach 5kn. Yachts that can take the ground may dry out on Instow beach in calm, settled weather. Bideford quay dries to hard sand; used by commercial shipping.

NAVIGATION WPT 51°05'·43N 04°16'·11W, 118°/0·9M to Bar.

Bar and sands constantly shift; buoys are moved occasionally to comply. For advice on bar contact Bideford HM. Least depths over bar vary from 0·1m and 0·4m. Following 2014 storms a bank has formed which just dries at LW on the leading line. Estuary dries and access is only feasible from HW–2 to HW. Night entry not advised for strangers. Once tide is ebbing, breakers quickly form between Bideford Bar SHM lt buoy and Middle Ridge SHM lt buoy. Hold the ldg line 118° only up to Outer Pulley where chan deviates stbd toward Pulley buoy and Grey Sand Hill, thence to Appledore Pool. 2M passage to Bideford is not difficult. Barnstaple (7M): seek local advice or take pilot.

LIGHTS AND MARKS See 9.11.4 and chartlet. Ldg marks are W trs, lit H24. R Torridge: Lt QY at E end of Bideford bridge, 2FR vert & 2FG vert indicate preferred chan; then SHM bn, QG, on W bank.

COMMUNICATIONS (Appledore/Bideford: Code 01237) CGOC (01326) 317575; Police 101; Dr 474994. (Instow/Barnstaple: Code 01271) Dr 372672. Appledore HM 428700; Bideford HM/Pilot 475834, mob 07967 333725.

2 Rivers Port/Pilots VHF Ch 12 16 (From HW–2 occasional).

FACILITIES

APPLEDORE: no ⌓; slips at town quay. **Services** ⛴ ⛽ ⚒ 🔧 ⓔ Ⓔ ⛭ ⛓(70t) ⛵.

BIDEFORD: some ⌓(contact HM) 🚰 ⛽ 🛒 ✕ 🍺. Ferry to Lundy Is.

INSTOW: North Devon YC, ☎861390, ⛴ 🚰 ✕ 🍺; **Services** ⚓ ⌓ via Instow Marine ☎861081, 🚰 ⛽ 🔧 Ⓔ ⛓(4t) ⛵. **Town** 🚰 ✕ 🍺.

BARNSTAPLE: Access above Fremlington Quay advisable only with local knowledge or after recce in dinghy. ⌓ (free for short stay): limited facilities; 🚰 ☏ ☏ ⛽ 🛒 🍺.

Towns ✉ (all four), Ⓑ (Barnstaple, Bideford) ⇌ (Barnstaple) ✈ (Exeter).

CLOVELLY, Devon, **51°00'·18N 04°23'·77W** ❁⚓⚓✿✿✿. AC 1164. Tides see above. HW –0524 on Dover. Tiny drying hbr, 5M E of Hartland Pt, is sheltered from S/SW winds; useful to await the tide into Bideford or around Hartland Pt. Some ⌓ (max LOA 12m) £7 on pier, access only near HW; or ⚓ off in 5m. Lt Fl G 5s 5m 5M on hbr wall. HM mob: 07975 501830. Facilities: ⛴ 🚰 ✉ limited 🛒 ☏ ☏.

RIVERS TAW & TORRIDGE *continued*

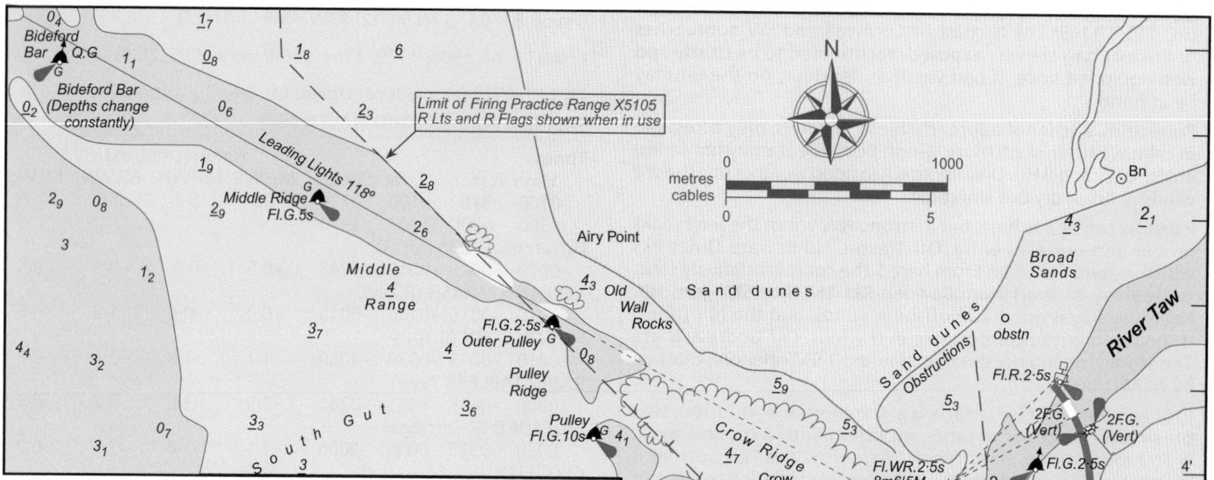
Bideford Bar
Q.G
Bideford Bar (Depths change constantly)
Limit of Firing Practice Range X5105 R Lts and R Flags shown when in use
Leading Lights 118°
Middle Ridge Fl.G.5s
Middle Range
Fl.G.2·5s Outer Pulley
Pulley Ridge
Pulley Fl.G.10s
South Gut
Airy Point
Old Wall Rocks
Sand dunes
metres
cables
0
1000
5
Bn
Broad Sands
River Taw
obstn
Sand dunes
Obstructions
Fl.R.2·5s
2F.G. (Vert)
2F.G. (Vert)
Fl.G.2·5s
Crow Ridge
Crow Rock
Fl.WR.2·5s 8m6/5M
Crow Point
Cool Stone
Sprat Ridge
Q.R
Fl(3)R.10s
Oc.6s 22m15M
Oc.10s 38m15M
Instow Sands
FS
Skern Point
Obstn
APPLEDORE
Tr
Yacht Moorings
Dry Dock
Instow
51°3'N
FS
NDYC
Crane (41)
Covered Shipyard (27)
Obstns
Zeta Berth
Northam
Bideford Quay 1M
4°12'W
R Torridge
Obstructions
11'
Westeigh Tr
4'

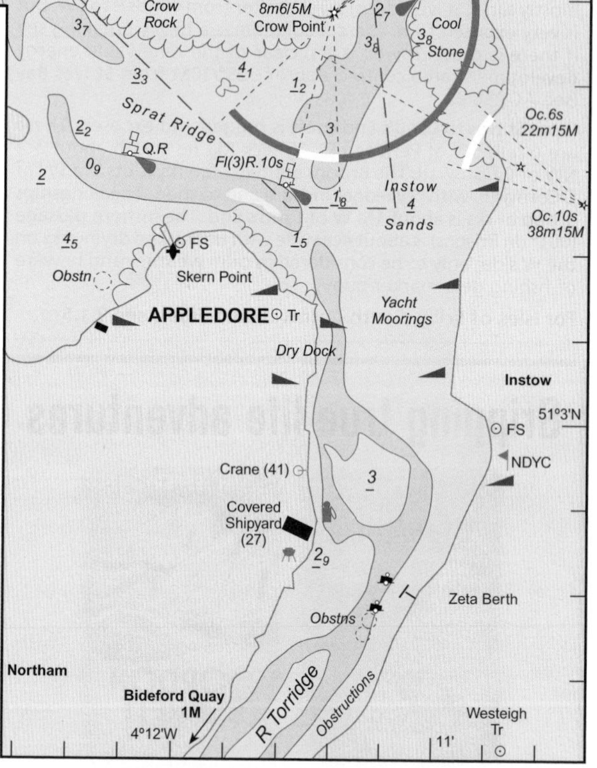

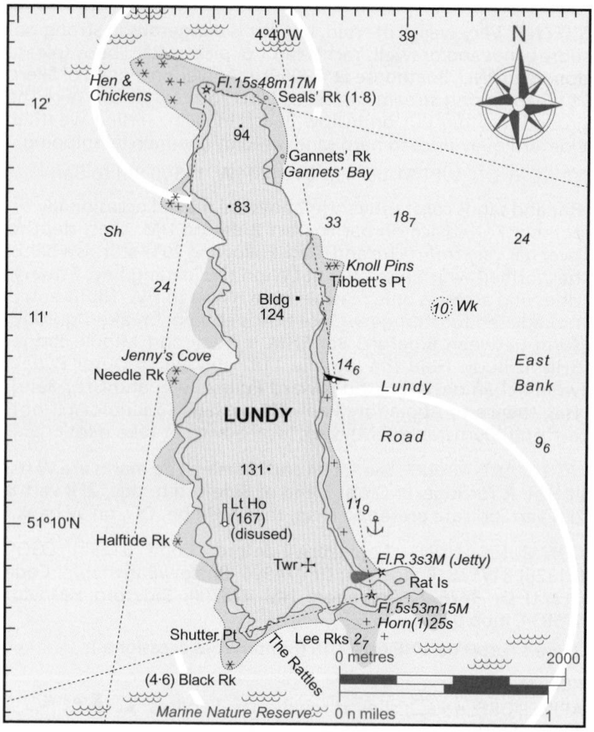
4°40'W
39'
N
12'
Hen & Chickens
Fl.15s48m17M
Seals' Rk (1·8)
Gannets' Rk
Gannets' Bay
Sh
Knoll Pins
Tibbett's Pt
Bldg 124
Wk
11'
Jenny's Cove
Needle Rk
East Bank
Lundy Road
LUNDY
Lt Ho (167) (disused)
51°10'N
Halftide Rk
Twr
Fl.R.3s3M (Jetty)
Rat Is
Fl.5s53m15M
Horn(1)25s
Shutter Pt
Lee Rks
The Rattles
0 metres
2000
(4·6) Black Rk
Marine Nature Reserve
0 n miles
1

ISLAND IN BRISTOL CHANNEL, 10M NNW of Hartland Pt

LUNDY ISLAND, Devon, **51°09′·83N 04°39′·27W**. AC 5608, *1179, 1164*. HW –0530 on Dover; ML 4·3m; Duration 0605. See 9.11.24. Shore Office ☎01237 470074, Island ☎01237 431831. Beware bad tide races, esp on E-going flood, off the N and SE tips of the island; and to the SW on the W-going ebb. A violent race forms over Stanley Bank 3M NE of the N tip. Shelter good in lee of island's high ground (145m). In SSW to NW winds, usual ⚓ is close inshore to NW of SE Pt and Rat Island, clear of ferry. In N'lies ⚓ in The Rattles, small bay on S side. In E'lies Jenny's Cove is safe if no W'ly swell. Lts: NW Pt, Fl 15s 48m 17M, vis 009°-285°, W ○ tr. On SE Pt, Fl 5s 53m 15M, vis 170°-073°, W ○ tr. Two Historic Wrecks (see 9.0.3) lie on the E side of island, at 51°11′N 04°39′·4W, and 4ca further E. Facilities: Landing by the ⚓ off SE end of island or using N side of jetty to disembark passengers only, boats may not remain alongside; £5.00/person landing fee. The waters around Lundy are a Marine Nature Reserve. **Lundy Co**: ♜ ✉ 🛒 limited stores.

MINOR HARBOURS ON THE NW COAST OF CORNWALL

BUDE, Cornwall, **50°49′·93N 04°33′·37W**. AC 5608, 1156. HW –0540 on Dover. Duration 0605. See 9.11.26. Limited shelter in drying hbr, access near HW in daylight, quiet weather, no swell conditions but sea lock gives access to canal basin with 2m. Conspic W radar dish aerials 3·3M N of hbr. Outer ldg marks 075°, front W spar with Y ◇ topmark, rear W flagstaff; hold this line until inner ldg marks in line at 131°, front W pile, rear W spar, both with Y △ topmarks. There are no lts. VHF Ch 16 12 (when vessel expected). Advise HM of ETA with 24H notice ☎(01288) 353111; 🚰 on quay; **Town** (½M); ♜ ✉ Ⓑ 🛒 ✕ 🛒.

BOSCASTLE, Cornwall, **50°41′·48N 04°42·17W**. AC 5608, 1156. HW –0543 on Dover; see 9.11.26. A tiny, picturesque hbr, almost a land-locked cleft in the cliffs. Access near HW, but not in onshore winds when swell causes surge inside. An E'ly appr, S of Meachard Rk (37m high, 2ca NW of hbr), is best. 2 short bkwtrs at ent; moor as directed on drying S quay. HM ☎01840 250200.

9.11.26 PADSTOW

Cornwall **50°32′·51N 04°56′·17W**

CHARTS AC 5608, 1156, 1168; Imray C58, 2400

TIDES –0550 Dover; ML 4·0; Duration 0600

Standard Port MILFORD HAVEN (⟵)

Times				Height (metres)			
High Water		Low Water		MHWS	MHWN	MLWN	MLWS
0100	0700	0100	0700	7·0	5·2	2·5	0·7
1300	1900	1300	1900				
Differences BUDE							
–0040	–0040	–0035	–0045	+0·7	+0·6	ND	ND
BOSCASTLE							
–0045	–0010	–0110	–0100	+0·3	+0·4	+0·2	+0·2
PADSTOW							
–0055	–0050	–0040	–0050	+0·3	+0·4	+0·1	+0·1
WADEBRIDGE (R Camel)							
–0052	–0052	+0235	+0245	–3·8	–3·8	–2·5	–0·4
NEWQUAY							
–0100	–0110	–0105	–0050	0·0	+0·1	0·0	–0·1
PERRANPORTH							
–0100	–0110	–0110	–0050	–0·1	0·0	0·0	+0·1
ST IVES							
–0050	–0115	–0105	–0040	–0·4	–0·3	–0·1	+0·1
CAPE CORNWALL							
–0130	–0145	–0120	–0120	–1·0	–0·9	–0·5	–0·1

NOTE: At Wadebridge LW time differences give the start of the rise, following a LW stand of about 5hrs.

SHELTER Good in inner hbr 3m+, access approx HW±2 sp, ±1½ nps via tidal gate. If too late for gate, moor in the Pool or ⚓ close N in 1·5m LWS. Drying moorings available for smaller craft. Good ⚓ at Wadebridge 4.5M up R Camel.

NAVIGATION WPT 50°34′·56N 04°56′·07W, 044° Stepper Pt 6ca. From SW, beware Quies Rks, Gulland Rk, The Hen, Gurley Rk, Chimney Rks and a wreck 5ca W of Stepper Pt (all off the chartlet). From N, keep well off Newland Island and its offlying reef.

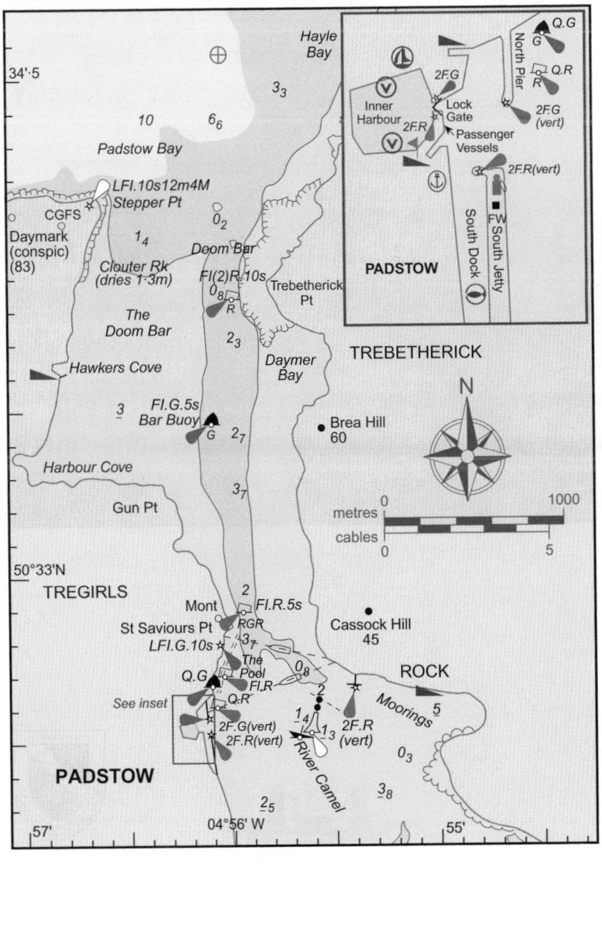

34′·5
Hayle Bay
10
6₆
3₃
Padstow Bay
LFl.10s12m4M
Stepper Pt
CGFS
Daymark (conspic) (83)
1₄
0₂
Doom Bar
Clouter Rk (dries 1·3m)
Fl(2)R.10s
0₈
Trebetherick Pt
The Doom Bar
2₃
Daymer Bay
TREBETHERICK
Hawkers Cove
3
Fl.G.5s Bar Buoy
2₇
Brea Hill 60
N
Harbour Cove
3₇
Gun Pt
metres 0 1000
cables 0 5
50°33′N
TREGIRLS
2
Mont
Fl.R.5s
St Saviours Pt
LFl.G.10s
Cassock Hill 45
The Pool
Fl.R
0₈
ROCK
Q.G
Q.R
Moorings
See inset
2F.G(vert)
2F.R(vert)
1₄
1₃
2F.R (vert)
5
0₃
River Camel
PADSTOW
3₈
2₅
57′
04°56′ W
55′
Q.G
North Pier
Q.R
2F.G
Inner Harbour
2F.R
Lock Gate
2F.G (vert)
Passenger Vessels
2F.R(vert)
FW
South Dock
South Jetty
PADSTOW

- Best appr HW–2½, do not try LW±1½; least depth on the bar is 0·5m at MLWS. Waiting ⚓s in Port Quin Bay in lee of Rumps Pt and Mother Ivey's Bay 3M WSW Stepper Pt.
- Shifting banks in estuary require care and a rising tide (ditto the drying R Camel to Wadebridge, 4M). In doubt, consult HM.
- Identify the first 2 chan buoys before entry. In strong onshore winds or heavy ground swell, seas can break on Doom Bar and in the adjacent chan.
- S of St Saviour's Pt the chan lies very close to W shore.

LIGHTS AND MARKS See 9.11.4 and chartlet.

COMMUNICATIONS (Codes 01841) CGOC (01326) 317575; Police 101; Dr 532346. HM padstowharbour@btconnect.com , ☎532239; **Ferry** to Rock, (01326) 317575 it also acts as water taxi.

HM VHF Ch **12** 16 (Mon-Fri 0800–1700 and HW±2). Ferry Ch 12.

FACILITIES **Hbr** £2·00, M £1·01, (£4·00 <10 hp engine<£6·00) (extra). **Services** (60t).

Town Bus (to Bodmin ⇌/✈ Newquay).

Rock SC ☎(01208) 862431.

Wadebridge HM as Padstow; only; **Town**

MINOR HBRS BETWEEN BOSCASTLE AND LAND'S END

PORT ISAAC, Cornwall, **50°35′·75N 04°49′·57W**. AC 1156, 1168. HW –0548 on Dover; ML 4·0m. Small drying hbr. Conspic tr bears 171°/1·3M. Rks close E of 50m wide ent between short bkwtrs. HM ☎01208 880321, mob 07855 429422; LB.

NEWQUAY, Cornwall, **50°25′·06N 05°05′·19W**. AC 1149, 1168. HW –0604 on Dover; ML 3·7m; see 9.11.26. Ent to drying hbr ('The Gap') between two walls, is 23m wide. Beware Old Dane Rk and Listrey Rk outside hbr towards Towan Hd. Swell causes a surge in the hbr. Enter HW±2 but not in strong onshore winds. Lts: N pier 2 FG (vert) 2M; S pier 2 FR (vert) 2M. VHF Ch 08 16 14. Facilities: **Town** . Note: Shoal draught boats can dry out in Gannel Creek, close S of Newquay, but only in settled weather. Beware causeway bridge halfway up creek.

PORTREATH, Cornwall, **50°15′·88N 05°17′·57W**. AC 1149. HW –0600 on Dover. Conspic W daymark (38m) at E side of ent to small drying hbr. Gull Rk (23m) is 3ca W of ent and Horse Rk is close N. Keep close to pier on W side of chan. in either of 2 basins, both dry.

HAYLE, Cornwall, **50°12′·14N 05°26′·13W** (NCM). AC 1149, 1168. HW –0605 on Dover; ML 3·6m; Duration 0555. See 9.11.26. Drying hbr gives very good shelter, but is not advised for yachts. In ground swell dangerous seas break on the bar, drying 2·7m; approx 4m at ent @ MHWS. Cross in good weather HW±1. Marks do not necessarily indicate best water. Ldg marks/lts 180°: both W □ R horiz band, ☆ FW 17/23m 4M. NCM buoy, Q is about 7ca N of the front ldg lt. Training wall on W side of ent chan is marked by 5 lit perches, all Oc G 4s. The hbr is divided by long central island (about 700m long, with lt bn QG at NW end) which should be left to stbd. Follow the SE arm of hbr to Hayle; the S arm leads to Lelant Quay. Visitors must contact HM ☎(01736) 754043, Mob 07500993867, VHF Ch 16 prior to arrival. £5. Facilities: (can) ⇌.

ST IVES, Cornwall, **50°12′·79N 05°28′·67W**. AC 1149, 1168. HW –0610 on Dover; ML 3·6m; Duration 0555. See 9.11.26. Drying hbr with about 4·5m @ MHWS. Good shelter except in onshore winds when heavy swell works in. ⚓ in 3m between the hbr and Porthminster Pt to S and drying Or s in hbr. From the NW beware Hoe Rk off St Ives Hd, and obstn drying 0·9m at collapsed b'water E of Smeaton pier inshore of unlit SHM. From SE off Porthminster Pt avoid The Carracks and obstn drying 1·0m in Carbis Bay. Keep E of SHM buoy about 1½ ca ENE of E pier. Lts: E pier hd 2 FG (vert) 8m 5M. W pier hd 2 FR (vert) 5m 3M. VHF Ch 12 16 (occas). HM ☎(01736) 795018. Facilities: s £12.13; **E Pier** . **Town** ⇌.

South Ireland

Malahide clockwise to Liscannor Bay

9.12.1 **Contents** 565
9.12.2 **Area map** 566
9.12.3 **Tidal stream charts** 568
9.12.4 **Lights, buoys and waypoints** 570
9.12.5 **Passage information including Area 12 Distance table** 572
Malahide to Dun Laoghaire – 575 • Dun Laoghaire to Tuskar Rk – 582 • Tuskar Rk to Cobh – 584 • Cobh to Mizen Hd – 594 • West Coast – 598 • Mizen Hd to Dingle Bay, Dingle Bay to Liscannor Bay – 604
9.12.6 **Special notes for Ireland (including useful Gaelic words)** 572
9.12.7 **Malahide** 574
9.12.8 **Howth** 575
9.12.9 **Dublin (tide tables/curves)** 576
9.12.10 **Dun Laoghaire** 580
9.12.11 **Greystones** 581
9.12.12 **Wicklow** 581
9.12.13 **Arklow** 582
Courtown • Polduff Pier
9.12.14 **Wexford** 583
9.12.15 **Rosslare** 584
9.12.16 **Kilmore Quay** 585
9.12.17 **Waterford** 586
9.12.18 **Dunmore East** 587
9.12.19 **Youghal** 587
Dungarvan Bay • Ballycotton
9.12.20 **Cork Harbour (Cobh, tide tables/curves)** 589
9.12.21 **Kinsale** 594
Oysterhaven
9.12.22 **Courtmacsherry** 595
9.12.23 **Glandore/Unionhall** 595
9.12.24 **Castletownshend** 596
Barloge Creek
9.12.25 **Baltimore** 597
Horseshoe Harbour • Clear Island, North Harbour • Roaringwater Bay
9.12.26 **Schull** 598
9.12.27 **Crookhaven** 598
Goleen • Dunmanus Bay
9.12.28 **Dunmanus/Bantry Bay** 599
Castletown • Lawrence Cove • Lonehort Harbour • Adrigole • Glengarriff • Bantry
9.12.29 **Castletown Bearhaven** 600
9.12.30 **Kenmare River** 601
Garnish Bay • Ballycrovane • Cleanderry • Ardgroom • Kilmakilloge • Ormond's Harbour • Kenmare • Dunkerron Harbour • Sneem • Darrynane
9.12.31 **Dingle Bay** 602
9.12.32 **Valentia Harbour** 602
9.12.33 **Dingle** 603
Portmagee • Ventry • Smerwick Harbour • Brandon Bay • Tralee Bay
9.12.34 **Fenit Harbour** 604
9.12.35 **Shannon Estuary** 605
9.12.36 **Kilrush (Tarbert Island, tide tables/curves)** 606

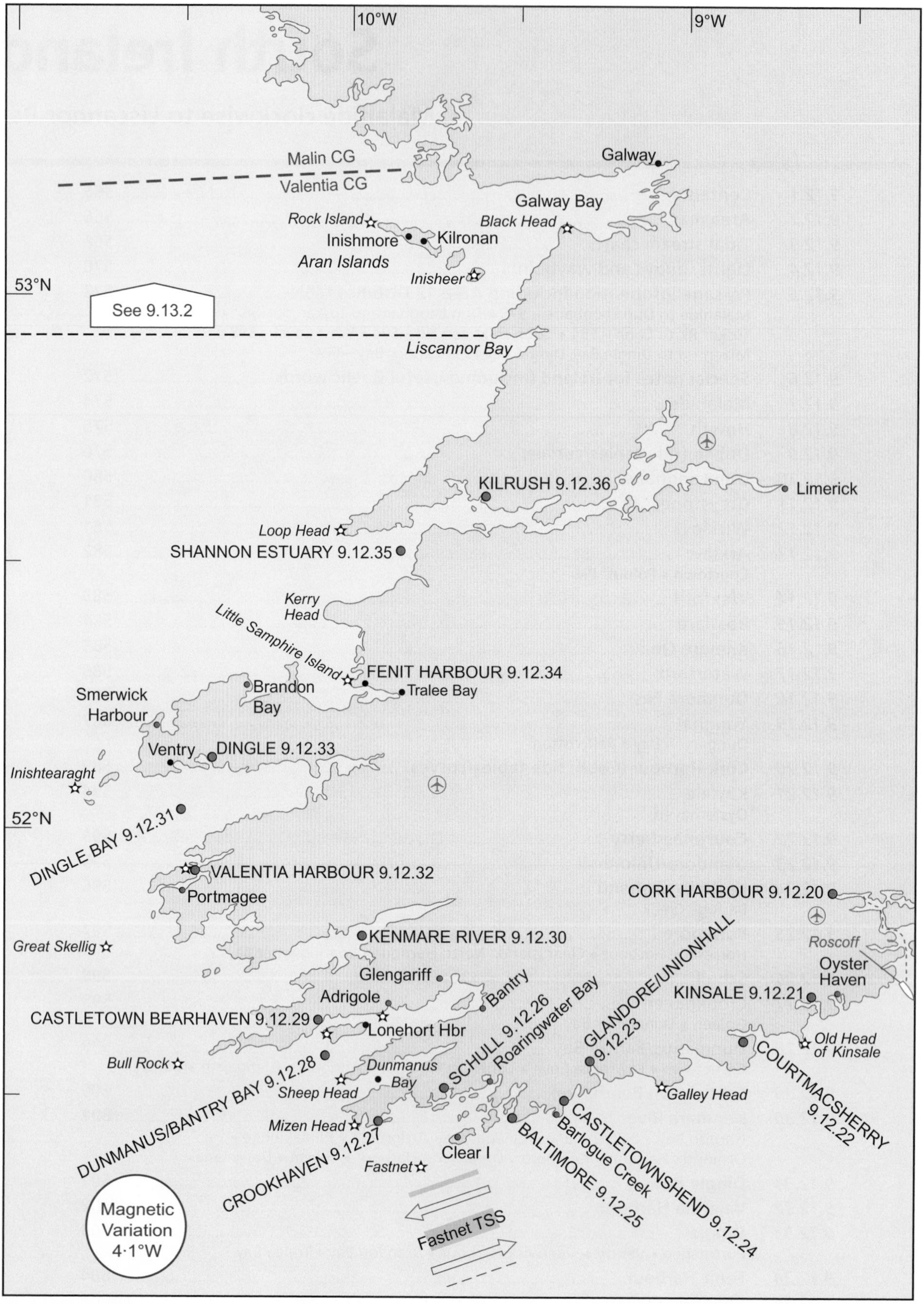
10°W
9°W
53°N
52°N
Malin CG
Valentia CG
Galway
Galway Bay
Black Head
Rock Island
Inishmore
Kilronan
Aran Islands
Inisheer
See 9.13.2
Liscannor Bay
KILRUSH 9.12.36
Limerick
Loop Head
SHANNON ESTUARY 9.12.35
Kerry Head
Little Samphire Island
FENIT HARBOUR 9.12.34
Tralee Bay
Brandon Bay
Smerwick Harbour
Ventry
DINGLE 9.12.33
Inishtearaght
DINGLE BAY 9.12.31
VALENTIA HARBOUR 9.12.32
Portmagee
CORK HARBOUR 9.12.20
Great Skellig
KENMARE RIVER 9.12.30
Roscoff
Oyster Haven
Glengariff
GLANDORE/UNIONHALL 9.12.23
KINSALE 9.12.21
Adrigole
Bantry
CASTLETOWN BEARHAVEN 9.12.29
Lonehort Hbr
SCHULL 9.12.26
Roaringwater Bay
Old Head of Kinsale
COURTMACSHERRY 9.12.22
Bull Rock
Dunmanus Bay
DUNMANUS/BANTRY BAY 9.12.28
Sheep Head
Galley Head
CASTLETOWNSHEND 9.12.24
Mizen Head
Barlogue Creek
Clear I
BALTIMORE 9.12.25
CROOKHAVEN 9.12.27
Fastnet
Fastnet TSS
Magnetic Variation 4·1°W

9.12.2

South Ireland

Malahide clockwise to Liscannor Bay

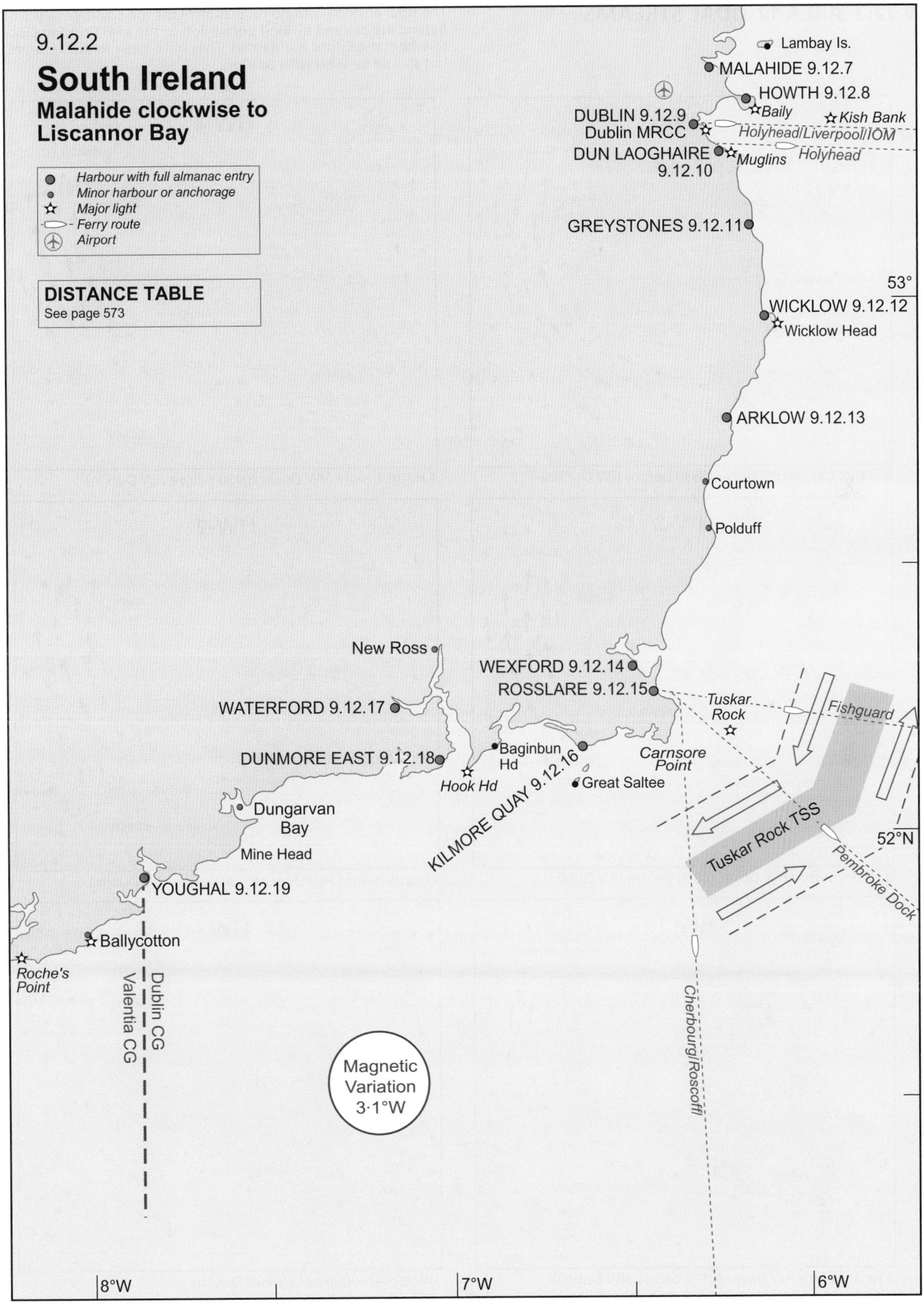
Harbour with full almanac entry
Minor harbour or anchorage
Major light
Ferry route
Airport
DISTANCE TABLE
See page 573
Lambay Is.
MALAHIDE 9.12.7
HOWTH 9.12.8
Baily
DUBLIN 9.12.9
Dublin MRCC
Kish Bank
Holyhead/Liverpool/IOM
DUN LAOGHAIRE 9.12.10
Muglins
Holyhead
GREYSTONES 9.12.11
53°
WICKLOW 9.12.12
Wicklow Head
ARKLOW 9.12.13
Courtown
Polduff
New Ross
WEXFORD 9.12.14
ROSSLARE 9.12.15
Tuskar Rock
Fishguard
WATERFORD 9.12.17
Baginbun Hd
DUNMORE EAST 9.12.18
Carnsore Point
Hook Hd
KILMORE QUAY 9.12.16
Great Saltee
Tuskar Rock TSS
Dungarvan Bay
52°N
Mine Head
Pembroke Dock
YOUGHAL 9.12.19
Ballycotton
Roche's Point
Dublin CG
Valentia CG
Cherbourg/Roscoff
Magnetic Variation 3·1°W
8°W
7°W
6°W

9.12.3 AREA 12 TIDAL STREAMS

The tidal arrows (with no rates shown) off the S and W coasts of Ireland are printed by kind permission of the Irish Cruising Club, to whom the Editor is indebted. They have been found accurate, but should be used with caution.

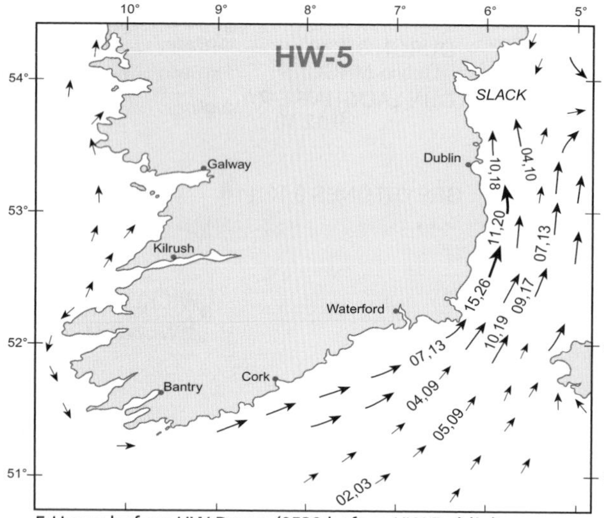
HW-5
SLACK
Galway
Dublin
Kilrush
Waterford
Cork
Bantry
10,18
04,10
11,20
15,26
09,17
07,13
10,19
07,13
04,09
05,09
02,03
5 Hours before HW Dover (0530 before HW Dublin)

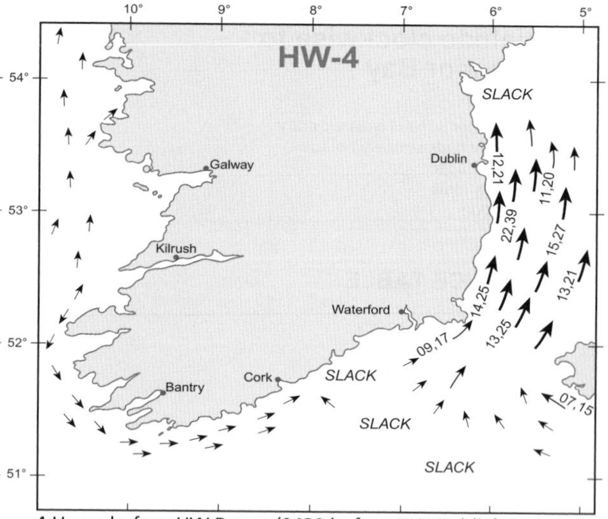
HW-4
SLACK
Galway
Dublin
Kilrush
Waterford
Cork
Bantry
12,21
11,20
22,39
15,27
14,25
13,21
13,25
09,17
SLACK
SLACK
07,15
SLACK
4 Hours before HW Dover (0430 before HW Dublin)

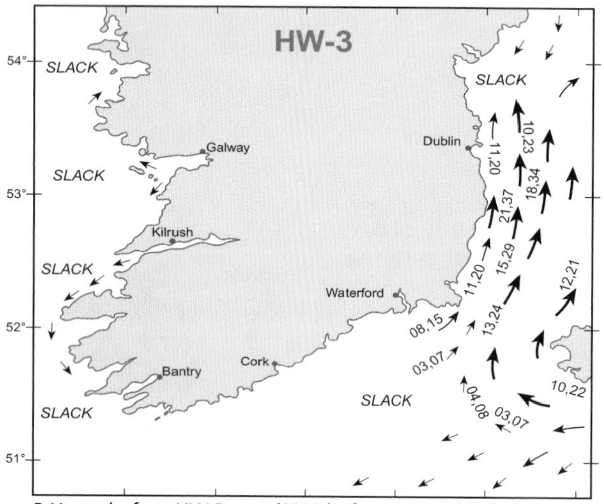
HW-3
SLACK
SLACK
Galway
Dublin
SLACK
Kilrush
SLACK
Waterford
Cork
Bantry
SLACK
11,20
10,23
18,34
21,37
15,29
11,20
12,21
13,24
08,15
03,07
SLACK
04,08
03,07
10,22
3 Hours before HW Dover (0330 before HW Dublin)

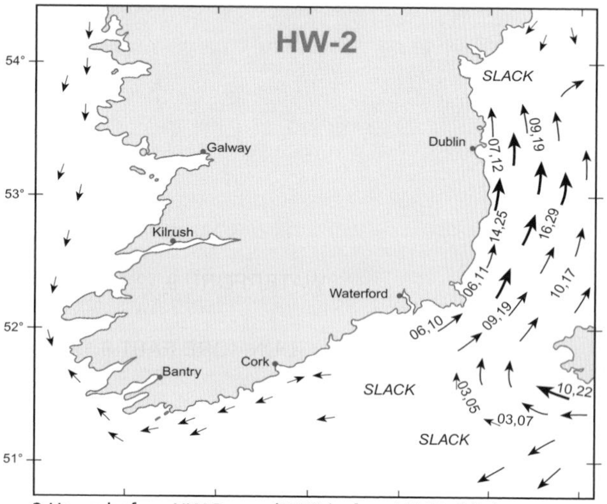
HW-2
SLACK
Galway
Dublin
Kilrush
Waterford
Cork
Bantry
07,12
09,19
14,25
16,29
06,11
10,17
09,19
06,10
SLACK
03,05
10,22
03,07
SLACK
2 Hours before HW Dover (0230 before HW Dublin)

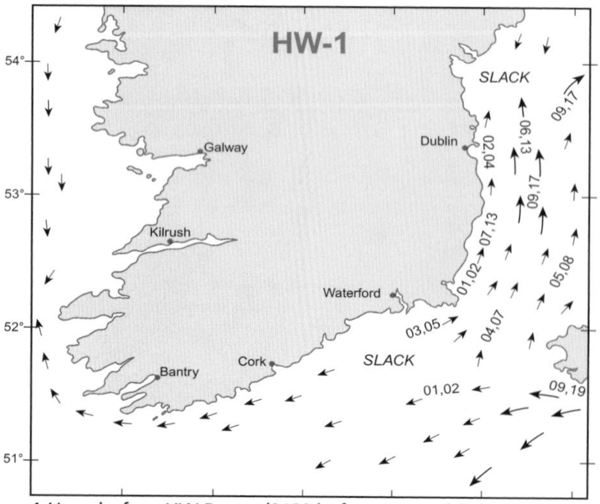
HW-1
SLACK
Galway
Dublin
Kilrush
Waterford
Cork
Bantry
02,04
06,13
09,17
09,17
07,13
05,08
01,02
04,07
03,05
SLACK
01,02
09,19
1 Hour before HW Dover (0130 before HW Dublin)

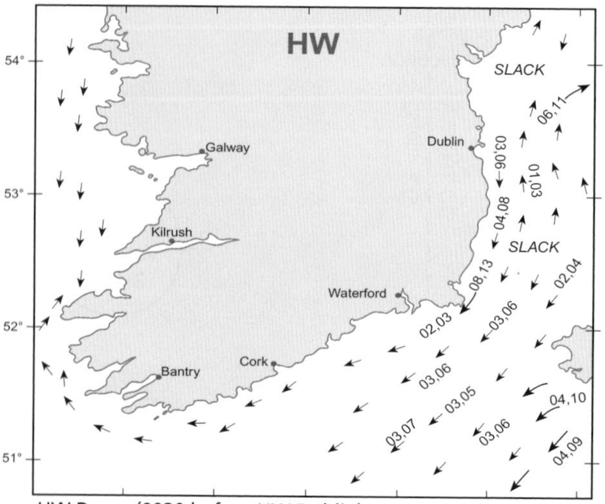
HW
SLACK
Galway
Dublin
Kilrush
Waterford
Cork
Bantry
06,11
03,06
01,03
04,08
SLACK
08,13
02,04
02,03
03,06
03,06
03,05
04,10
03,07
03,06
04,09
HW Dover (0030 before HW Dublin)

Northward 9.13.3 South Irish Sea 9.11.3

The tidal arrows (with no rates shown) off the S and W coasts of Ireland are printed by kind permission of the Irish Cruising Club, to whom the Editor is indebted. They have been found accurate, but should be used with caution.

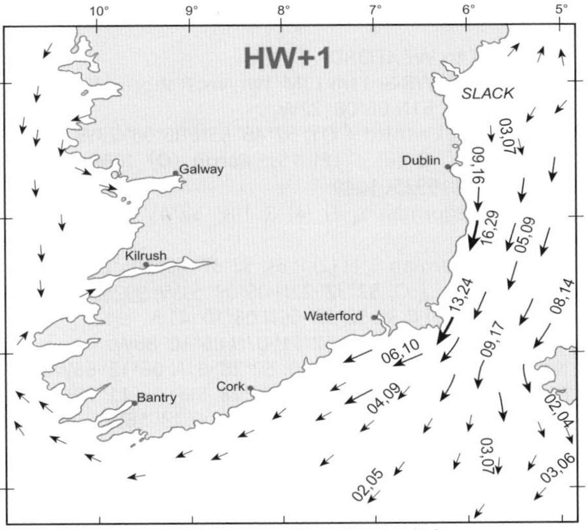
HW+1
SLACK
Dublin
Galway
Kilrush
Waterford
Cork
Bantry
03,07
09,16
16,29
05,09
13,24
08,14
06,10
09,17
04,09
02,04
03,07
03,06
02,05

1 Hour after HW Dover (0030 after HW Dublin)

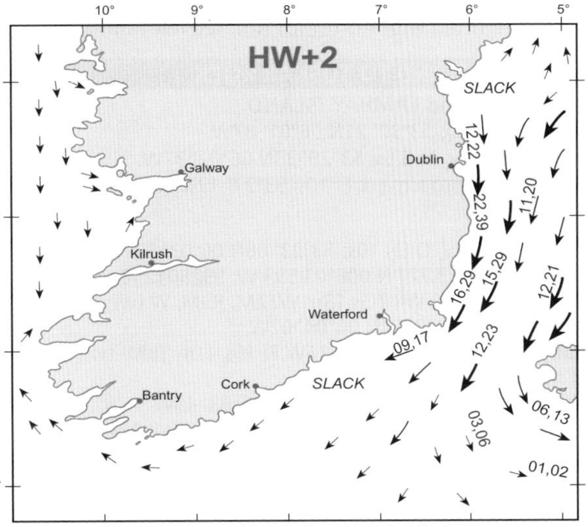
HW+2
SLACK
Dublin
Galway
Kilrush
Waterford
Cork
Bantry
12,22
22,39
11,20
16,29
15,29
12,21
09,17
12,23
SLACK
03,06
06,13
01,02

2 Hours after HW Dover (0130 after HW Dublin)

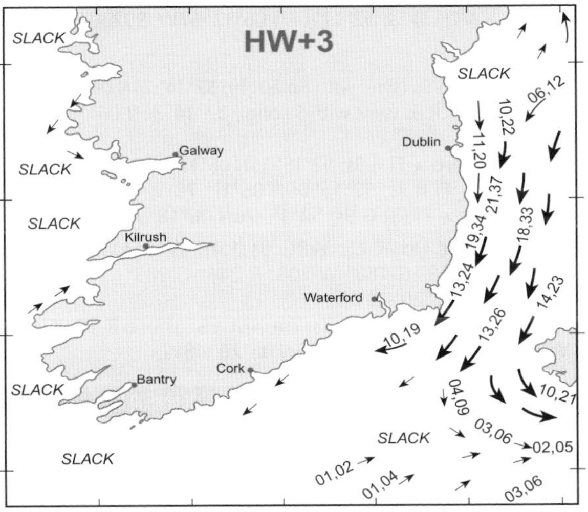
HW+3
SLACK
SLACK
SLACK
SLACK
SLACK
SLACK
Dublin
Galway
Kilrush
Waterford
Cork
Bantry
06,12
10,22
11,20
21,37
19,34
18,33
13,24
14,23
10,19
13,26
04,09
10,21
03,06
02,05
SLACK
01,02
01,04
03,06

3 Hours after HW Dover (0230 after HW Dublin)

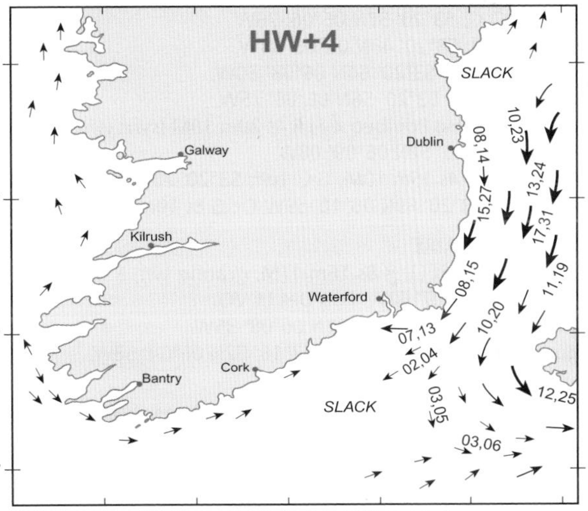
HW+4
SLACK
Dublin
Galway
Kilrush
Waterford
Cork
Bantry
10,23
08,14
13,24
15,27
17,31
11,19
08,15
10,20
07,13
02,04
03,05
12,25
SLACK
03,06

4 Hours after HW Dover (0330 after HW Dublin)

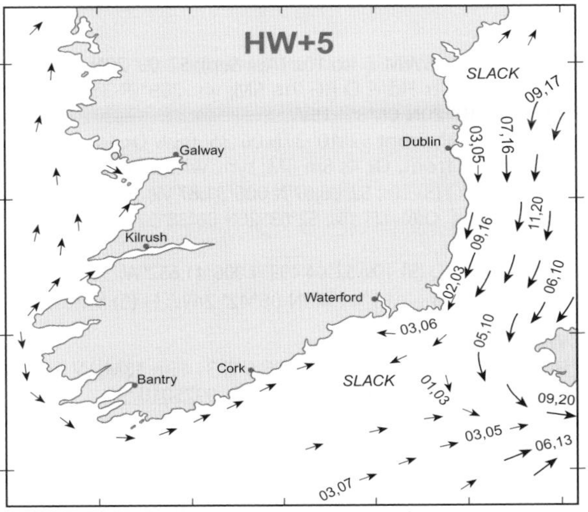
HW+5
SLACK
Dublin
Galway
Kilrush
Waterford
Cork
Bantry
09,17
03,05
07,16
11,20
09,16
02,03
06,10
03,06
05,10
SLACK
01,03
09,20
03,05
06,13
03,07

5 Hours after HW Dover (0430 after HW Dublin)

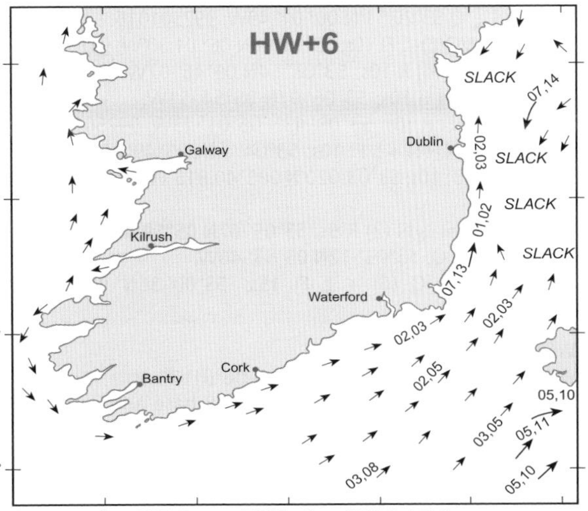
HW+6
SLACK
Dublin
Galway
Kilrush
Waterford
Cork
Bantry
07,14
02,03
SLACK
SLACK
01,02
SLACK
07,13
02,03
02,03
02,05
05,10
03,05
05,11
03,08
05,10

6 Hours after HW Dover (0530 after HW Dublin)

9.12.4 LIGHTS, BUOYS AND WAYPOINTS

Bold print = light with a nominal range of 15M or more. CAPITALS = place or feature. *CAPITAL ITALICS* = light-vessel, light float or Lanby. *Italics* = Fog signal. ***Bold italics*** = Racon. Many marks/buoys are fitted with AIS (MMSI No); see relevant charts.

LAMBAY ISLAND TO TUSKAR ROCK

MALAHIDE and LAMBAY ISLAND

Taylor Rks Q; 53°30'·21N 06°01'·87W.
Burren Rocks Fl G 5s; 53°29'·33N 06°02'·37W.
Malahide approach L Fl 10s; 53°27'·12N 06°06'·87W.

HOWTH

Rowan Rocks Q (3) 10s; 53°23'·88N 06°03'·27W.
Howth 53°23.727'N 006°03.593'W; 992501250.
E Pier Hd Fl (2) WR 7·5s 13m W12M, R9M; W twr; vis: W256°-R295°-256°; 53°23'·64N 06°04'·02W.
Baily ☆ 53°21'·69N 06°03'·16W Fl 15s 41m **18M**; twr. Fog Det Lt VQ; 992501010.
Rosbeg E Q (3) 10s; 53°21'·02N 06°03'·45W.
Rosbeg S Q (6) + L Fl 15s; 53°20'·22N 06°04'·17W.

PORT OF DUBLIN

Dublin Bay Mo (A) 10s; ***Racon (M)***; 53°19'·92N 06°04'·65W; 992351301.
No 1 Fl (3) G 5s; 53°20'·30N 06°05'·56W.
No 3 IQ G; 53°20'·57N 06°06'·76W.
No 4 IQ R; 53°20'·48N 06°06'·93W.
No 5 Fl G 2s; 53°20'·64N 06°08'·60W.
No 6 Fl R 2s; 53°20'·56N 06°08'·75W.
Great S Wall Hd Poolbeg Fl R 4s 20m 10M *(sync with N.Bull)*; R ○ twr; 53°20'·52N 06°09'·08W.
N Bull Fl G 4s 15m 10M; G ○ twr; 53°20'·70N 06°08'·98W.
N Bank ☆ 53°20'·69N 06°10'·59W Oc G 8s 10m **16M**; G □ twr.

DUN LAOGHAIRE

E Bkwtr Hd Fl (2) R 8s 16m **17M**; granite twr, R lantern 7M; 53°18'·14N 06°07'·62W. Fog Det Lt VQ.
Outfall Fl Y 5s; 53°18'·41N 06°08'·35W.
Muglins Fl R 5s 14m 11M; 53°16'·52N 06°04'·58W.

OFFSHORE MARKS

Bennett Bank Q(6)+ L Fl 15s; 53°20'·17N 05°55'·11W; 992501012.
Kish Bank ☆ 53°18'·65N 05°55'·54W Fl (2) 20s 29m **21M** (H24); W twr, R band; ***Racon (T) 15M***; 992501017.
N Kish VQ; 53°18'·56N 05°56'·44W.
E Kish Fl (2) R 10s; 53°14'·35N 05°53'·56W; 992501020.
N Burford Q 53°20.51'N 06° 01'.49W; 992501016.
S Burford VQ(6)+L Fl 10s; 53°18'.06N 06° 01.30'W; 992501018.
E Codling Fl (4) R 10s; 53°08'·54N 05°46'·07W; 992501024.
W Codling Fl G 10s; 53°06'·97N 05°54'·51W.
Moulditch Fl R 10s; 53°08'·43N 06°01'·23W; 992501022.
S Codling VQ (6) + L Fl 10s; 53°04'·54N 05°49'·13W.
Codling Q(3) 10s; 53°03.020'N 005°40.815'W, ***Racon (G) 10M***, 992501028.
Breaches Shoal Fl (2) R 6s; 53°05'·67N 05°59'·81W.
North India Q; 53°03'·12N 05°53'·46W.
South India Q (6) + L Fl 15s; 53°00'·36N 05°53'·31W; 992501030.

WICKLOW to ARKLOW

Wicklow Fl (4) Y 10s; 52°59'·54N 06°01'·29W.
E Pier Hd Fl WR 5s 11m 6M; W twr, R base and cupola; vis: 136°-R-293°-W-136°; 52°58'·99N 06°02'·07W.
W Packet Quay Hd Fl WG 10s 5m 6M; vis: 076°-G-256°-W-076°; 52°58'·88N 06°02'·08W.
Wicklow Hd ☆ 52°57'·95N 05°59'·89W Fl (3) 15s 37m **23M**; W twr; 992501031.
Horseshoe Fl R 3s; 52°56'·84N 05°58'·47W; 992501032.
N Arklow Q; 52°53'·86N 05°55'·21W; 992501034.
Arklow Bank Wind Farm from 52°48'·47N 05°56'·57W to 52°46'·47N 05°57'·11W, N and S Turbines Fl Y 5s14m 10M. No 7 Turbine 992501302. Other turbines Fl Y 5s. See 9.12.5.

ARKLOW to WEXFORD

S Pier Hd Fl WR 6s 11m 13M; twr; vis: R shore- W223°- R350°-shore; 52°47'·61N 06°08'·22W.
Roadstone Bkwtr Hd QY; 52°46'·65N 06°08'·23W.
S Arklow Q (6) + LFl 15s; ***Racon (O) 10M***; 52°40'·20N 05°58'·89W; 992501040.
No 2 Glassgorman Fl (4) R 10s; 52°45'·35N 06°05'·34W; 992501038.
No 1 Glassgorman Fl (2) R 6s; 52°37'·69N 06°07'·46W.
N Blackwater Q; 52°32'·22N 06°09'·51W; 992501046.
No 6 Rusk Fl R 3s; 52°32'·65N 06°10'·41W.
No 4 Rusk Fl (2) R 5s; 52°31'·07N 06°10'·86W.
No 2 Rusk Fl (2) R 5s (sync); 52°28'·61N 06°12'·66W.
No 1 Rusk Fl (2) G 5s (sync); 52°28'·56N 06°11'·78W.
W Blackwater Fl G 6s; 52°25'·87N 06°13'·56W.
SE Blackwater Q (3) 10s, 52°25'·64N 06°08'·42W; ***Racon (M) 6M***; 992501050.
S Blackwater Q (6) + L Fl 15s; 52°22'·76N 06°12'·87W.
North Long Q; 52°21'·44N 06°17'·04W.
West Long QG; 52°18'·18N 06°17'·96W.
Lucifer VQ (3) 5s; 52°17'·02N 06°12'·67W; 992501054.

ROSSLARE

S Long Fl G 6s (sync with Splaugh); 52°14'·74N 06°15'·80W.
Splaugh Fl R 6s (sync with S Long); 52°14'·36N 06°16'·78W; 992501062.
South Holdens Fl G 3s; 52°15'·15N 06°17'·25W. (sync Calmines).
Calmines Fl R 3s; 52°15'·00N 06°17'·78W. (sync S Holdens).
W Holdens Fl (3) G 9s; 52°15'·76N 06°18'·75W.
Rosslare Pier Hd Oc WRG 5s 15m W13M, R10M, G10M; R twr; vis:098°-G-188°-W-208°-R-246°-G-283°-W-286°-R-320°; 52°15'·43N 06°20'·29W.
Ballygeary Oc WR 1·7s 7m 4M vis: shore-R-152°-W-200°-W(unintens)-205°; 52°15'·25N 06°20'·48W.

TUSKAR ROCK TO OLD HEAD OF KINSALE

Tuskar ☆ 52°12'·17N 06°12'·44W Q (2) 7·5s 33m **24M**; W twr; ***Racon (T) 18M***; 992501065.
S Rock Q (6)+L Fl 15s; 52°10'·80N 06°12'·84W; 992501068.
Fundale Fl (2) R 10s; 52°11'·04N 06°19'·78W.
Barrels Q (3) 10s; 52°08'·32N 06°22'·05W; 992501070.

KILMORE

Kilmore Quay SWM Iso 10s; (Apr-Sep); 52°09'·20N 06°35'·30W.
Kilmore Bkwtr Hd Q RG 7m 5M; vis: 269°-R-354°-G-003°-R-077°; 52°10'·20N 06°35'·15W.
Ldg lts 007·9°, Front 52°10'·37N 06°35'·08W Oc 4s 3m 6M. Rear, 100m from front, Oc 4s 6m 6M; sync with front.
Bore Rks Q (3) 10s; 52°06.07'N 006°31.87'W; 992501072.
Coningbeg Q(6)+LFl 15s; 52°03'·20N 06°38'·57W; ***Racon (G) 9M***; 992501074.
Red Bank VQ (9) 10s; 52°04.499'N 006°41.652'W; 992501076.
'M5' ODAS 35 51°41'·40N 06°42'·24W; Fl (5) Y 20s.

WATERFORD

Hook Hd ☆ 52°07'·42N 06°55'·76W Fl 3s 46m **18M**; W twr, two B bands; ***Racon (K) 10M***. Fog Det Lt VQ. 992501079.
Waterford Fl R 3s. Fl (3) R 10s; 52°08'·95N 06°57'·00W.
Duncannon Dir lt F WRG 13m 10M, white tower on fort, 359·5°-FG-001·2°-Alt GW-001·7°-FW-002·4°-Alt WR-002·9°-FR-004·5°; 52°13'·23N 06°56'·25W; Oc WR 4s 13m W 9M R 7M on same tower, 119°-R-149°-W-172°.

Passage Pt ☆ Fl WR 5s 7m W6M, R5M; R pile structure; vis: 114°-W-127°-R-180°-W-302°-R-021° (shore); 52°14′·26N 06°57′·77W.
Cheek Pt ☆ Q WR 6m 5M; W mast; vis: W007°-R289°-007°; 52°16′·12N 06°59′·38W.
Sheagh ☆ Fl R 3s 29m 3M; Gy twr; vis: 090°-318°; 52°16′·29N 06°59′·34W.
Snowhill Point Ldg lts 255°. Front, Fl WR 2·5s 5m 3M; vis: W222°- R020°- W057°-107°; 52°16′·39N 07°00′·91W. Rear, Flour Mill, 750m from front, Q 12m 5M.
Queen's Chan Ldg lts 098°. Front, QR 8m 5M; B twr, W band; vis: 030°-210°;52°15′·32N 07°02′·38W. Rear, 550m from front, Q 15m 5M; W mast.
Beacon Quay ☆ Fl G 3s 9m; vis: 255°-086°; 52°15′·50N 07°04′·21W.
Cove ☆ Fl WRG 6s 6m 2M; W twr; vis: R111°- G161°- W234°-111°; 52°15′·05N 07°05′·16W.
Smelting Ho Pt ☆ Q 8m 3M; W mast; 52°15′·15N 07°05′·27W.
Ballycar ☆ Fl RG 3s 5m; vis: G127°- R212°-284°; 52°15′·06N 07°05′·51W.

DUNMORE EAST

East Pier Head ☆ 52°08′·93N 06°59′·34W Fl WR 8s 13m **W17M**, R13M; Gy twr, vis: W225°- R310°-004°.
Dunmore East 1 ▲ Q G; 52°09′·06N 06°59′·38W.
Dunmore East 2 ▲ Fl G 2s; 52°09′·00N 06°59′·47W.
W Wharf ☆ Fl G 2s 6m 4M; vis: 165°-246°; 52°08′·97N 06°59′·45W.

DUNGARVAN

Ballinacourty Pt ☆ Fl (2) WRG 10s 16m W10M, R8M, G8M; W twr; vis: G245°- W274°- R302°- W325°-117°; 52°04′·69N 07°33′·18W.
Helvick ⅈ Q (3) 10s; 52°03′·61N 07°32′·25W.

Mine Head ☆ 51°59′·56N 07°35′·23W Fl (4) 30s 87m 12M; W twr, B band; vis: 228°-052°; 992501085.

YOUGHAL

Bar Rocks ⅈ Q (6) + L Fl 15s; 51°54′·85N 07°50′·05W.
Blackball Ledge ⅈ 51°55′·34N 07°48′·53W Q (3) 10s.
W side of ent ☆ 51°56′·57N 07°50′·53W Fl WR 2·5s 24m **W17M**, R13M; W twr; vis: W183°- R273°- W295°- R307°- W351°-003°.

BALLYCOTTON

Ballycotton ☆ 51°49′·50N 07° 59′·13W; Fl WR 10s 59m **W18M, R14M**; B twr, within W walls, B lantern; vis: 238°-W-048°-R-238°; 992501093.
The Smiths ◺ Fl (3) R 10s; 51°48′·62N 08°00′·71W.
Power ⅈ Q (6) + L Fl 15s; 51°45′·59N 08°06′·67W; 992501098.

CORK

Cork ⅈ L Fl 10s; 51°42′·92N 08°15′·60W; ***Racon (T) 7M***; 992501100.
Daunt Rock ◺ Fl (2) R 6s; 51°43′·53N 08°17′·50W; 992501102.
Fort Davis Ldg lts 354·1°. Front, 51°48′·82N 08°15′·80W Dir WRG 29m **17M**; vis: FG351·5°-AlWG352·25°-FW353°-AlWR355°-FR355·75°-356·5°. Rear, Dognose Quay, 203m from front, Oc 5s 37m 10M; Or 3, synch with front.
Roche's Pt ☆ 51°47′·59N 08°15′·29W Fl WR 3s 30m **W20M, R16M**; vis: shore-R-292°-W-016°-R-033°, 033°- W (unintens)-159°-R-shore; 992501099.
Outer Hbr Rk E2 ◺ Fl R 2·5s; 51°47′·52N 08°15′·67W.
Chicago Knoll E1 ▲ Fl G 5s; 51°47′·66N 08°15′·54W.
W1 ▲ Fl G 10s; 51°47′·69N 08°16′·05W.
W2 ◺ Fl R 10s; 51°47′·69N 08°16′·34W.
White Bay Ldg lts 034·6°. Front, Oc R 5s 11m 5M; W hut; 51°48′·53N 08°15′·22W. Rear, 113m from front, Oc R 5s 21m 5M; W hut; synch with front.
Spit Bank Pile ☆ Iso WR 4s 10m W10M, R7M; W house on R piles; vis: R087°- W196°- R221°- 358°; 51°50′·72N 08°16′·45W.

KINSALE and OYSTER HAVEN

Bulman ⅈ Q (6) + L Fl 15s; 51°40′·14N 08°29′·74W; 992501104.
Charlesfort ☆ Fl WRG 5s 18m W9M, R6M, G7M; vis: G348°-W358°- R004°-168°; H24; 51°41′·75N 08°29′·84W.

OLD HEAD OF KINSALE TO MIZEN HEAD

Old Head of Kinsale ☆, S point 51°36′·29N 08°32′·02W Fl (2) 10s 72m **20M**; B twr, two W bands; 992501107.

COURTMACSHERRY

Barrel Rock ⅈ 51°37′·01N 08°37′·30W.
Black Tom ▲ Fl G 5s; 51°36′·41N 08°37′·95W; 992501110.
Wood Pt (Land Pt) ☆ Fl (2) WR 5s 15m 5M; vis: W315°- R332°-315°; 51°38′·16N 08°41′·00W.

Galley Head ☆ summit 51°31′·80N 08°57′·21W Fl (5) 20s 53m **23M**; W twr; vis: 256°-065°.

GLANDORE and CASTLETOWNSHEND

Glandore Dir lt ☆ Oc WRG 37m 7M, metal tower, vis: 294°-G-304°-W-312°-R-342°; 51°33′·33N 09°07′·08W.
Reen Point ☆ Fl WRG 10s 9m W5M, R3M, G3M; W twr; vis: shore-G-338°-W-001°-R-shore; 51°30′·98N 09°10′·50W.
Kowloon Bridge ⅈ Q (6) + L Fl 15s; 51°27′·58N 09°13′·75W; 992501118.

BALTIMORE and FASTNET

Barrack Pt ☆ Fl (2) WR 6s 40m W6M, R3M; vis: R168°- W294°-038°; 51°28′·33N 09°23′·65W.
Loo Rock ▲ Fl G 3s; 51°28′·44N 09°23′·46W; 992501119.
Lousy Rks ⅈ Q (6) + L Fl 15s; 51°28′·93N 09°23′·39W.
Wallis Rk ◺ Fl (3) R 10s; 51°28′·93N 09°22′·99W.
Lettuce Pt ⅈ VQ (3) 5s; 51°29′·32N 09°23′·81W.
Mealbeg ⅈ Q (6) + L Fl 15s; 51°29′·68N 09°24′·69W.
Inane Pt ⅈ Q (6) + L Fl 15s; 51°30′·02N 09°23′·66W.
Hare Is ⅈ Q; 51°30′·17N 09°25′·38W.

Fastnet ☆, W end 51°23′·35N 09°36′·19W Fl 5s 49m **27M**; Gy twr, ***Racon (G) 18M***. Fog Det Lt VQ; 992501123.

SCHULL and LONG ISLAND CHANNEL

Amelia ▲; 51°29.979′N 009°31.461′W; 992501120.
Copper Point ☆ 51°30′·25N 09°32′·06W Q (3) 10s 16m 8M.
Ldg lts 346° Front, Oc 5s 5m 11M, W mast; 51°31′·68N 09°32′·43W. Rear, 91m from front, Oc 5s 8m11M; W mast.

CROOKHAVEN

Rock Is Pt ☆ L Fl WR 8s 20m W13M, R11M; W twr; vis: W over Long Is B to 281°-R-340°; inside harbour 281°-R-348°- towards N shore; 51°28′·59N 09°42′·27W; 992501124.

MIZEN HEAD TO DINGLE BAY

Mizen Head ☆ Iso 4s 55m 12M; vis: 313°-133°; 51°26′·99N 09°49′·23W; 992501127.
Sheep's Hd ☆ 51°32′·59N 09°50′·92W Fl (3) WR 15s 83m **W15M** R9M; W bldg; vis: 011·3°-R-016·6°-W-212·5°-(partially obs) 233° (shore); 992501129.

BANTRY BAY, CASTLETOWN BEARHAVEN, WHIDDY ISLE, BANTRY and GLENGARIFF

Roancarrigmore ☆ Fl WR 5s 13m W11M, R9M, R(unintens)5M; s/steel twr; vis: 312°-W-050°-R-122°-R(unintens)-207°-obsc-246°-R-312°; 51°39′·18N 09°44′·82W. Old Lt ho W twr, B band; 992501130.
Ardnakinna Pt ☆ 51°37′·10N 09°55′·09W Fl (2) WR 10s 62m W14M, R9M; W ○ twr; vis: 319°-R- 348°-W- 066°-R-shore; 992501131.
Walter Scott Rk ⅈ Q (6) + L Fl 15s; 51°38′·52N 09°54′·20W; 992501128.
Castletown (Dinish Is) Dir lt 023·25° ☆ Oc WRG 5s 7m W15M, R12M, G12M; W hut, R stripe; vis: 019·5°-G-023°-W-023·5°-R-027°; 51°38′·78N 09°54′·32W; 992501125.
Castletown Ldg lts 008°. Front, Oc Bu 6s 4m 6M; W col, R stripe; vis: 005°-013°; 51°39′·16N 09°54′·40W. Rear, 80m from front, Oc Bu 6s 7m 6M; W with R stripe; vis: 005°-013°.

Bull Rock ☆ 51°35′·52N 10°18′·07W Fl 15s 91m **18M**; W twr; 992501131.

KENMARE RIVER, DARRYNANE and BALLYCROVANE

Illaunnameanla (Ballycrovane) ☆ Fl R 3s; 51°42′·60N 09°57′·50W.
Book Rks Fl(2) R 10s; 51°46′·54N 09°49′·74W.
Cuskeal Fl R 5s; 51°46′·45N 09°48′·85W.
Bunaw Ldg Lts 041°. Front, Oc R 3s 9m 2M; B col, Y bands; 51°46′·80N 09°48′·40W. Rear, 200m from front Iso R 2s 11m 2M.
Maiden Rk Fl G 5s; 51°49′·00N 09°47′·99W; 992501134.
Bat Rk Fl G 5s; 51°50′·89N 09°40′·89W.
Carrignaronebeg Fl R 5s; 51°50′·99N 09°41′·39W.
No1 Fl G 5s; 51°52′·09N 09°36′·35W.
Carrignarone (Seal Rk) Fl 5s 2m 2M; 51°48′·58N 09°52′·65W.
Castlecove Ldg Lts 045°. Front, Oc 2s 5m 6M; concrete post W front; 51°46′·29N 10°02′·04W. Rear, 400m from front Oc 2s 18m 6M.
West Cove Hbr ☆ Fl R 3s; post W front; 51°46′·00N 10°02′·93W.
West Cove Hbr Ldg Lts 312°. Front, Fl 2s 2m 6M; concrete post; 51°46′·11N 10°03′·08W. Rear, 200m from front Fl 2s 4m 6M.
Darrynane Ldg lts 034°. Front, Oc 3s 10m 4M; 51°45′·90N 10°09′·20W. Rear, Oc 3s 16m 4M.

SKELLIG ISLANDS

Skelligs Rock ☆ Fl (3) 15s 53m 12M; W twr; vis: 262°-115°; part obsc within 6M 110°-115°; 51°46′·11N 10°32′·52W; 992501137.

VALENTIA and PORTMAGEE

Fort (Cromwell) Point ☆ 51°56′·02N 10°19′·27W Fl WR 2s 16m **W17M, R10M**; W twr; vis: 304°-R-351°,104°-W-304°; obsc from seaward by Doulus Head when brg more than 180°; 992501141.
Dir lt 141° ☆ Oc WRG 4s 25m W11M, R8M, G8M (by day: W3M, R2M, G2M); W twr, R stripe; vis:136°-G-140°-W-142°-R-146°; 51°55′·51N 10°18′·42W.
The Foot VQ (3) 5s; 51°55′·72N 10°17′·07W; 992501140.

DINGLE BAY TO LOOP HEAD

DINGLE BAY, VENTRY and DINGLE

Ldg lts 182° Oc 3s. Front 52°07′·41N 10°16′·59W, rear 100m behind.
Inishtearaght ☆, W end Blasket Islands 52°04′·54N 10°39′·67W Fl (2) 20s 84m **18M**; W twr; vis: 318°-221°; ***Racon (O)***; 992501143.

BRANDON BAY, TRALEE BAY and FENIT HARBOUR

Little Samphire Is ☆ 52°16′·26N 09°52′·91W Fl WRG 5s 17m W14M, R11M; G11M; Bu ◯ twr; vis: 262°-R-275°, 280-R-090°-G-140°-W-152°-R-172°.
Great Samphire I ☆ QR 15m 3M; vis: 242°-097°; 52°16′·15N 09°51′·81W.
Fenit Hbr Pier Hd ☆ 2 FR (vert) 12m 3M; vis: 148°-058°; 52°16′·24N 09°51′·55W.

SHANNON ESTUARY

Ballybunnion VQ; ***Racon (M) 6M***; 52°32′·52N 09°46′·93W; 992501146.
Kilstiffin Fl R 3s; 52°33′·80N 09°43′·83W; 992501148.
Kilcredaun Q R (sync); 52°34′·42N 09°41′·16W.
Tail of Beal Q G (sync); 52°34′·37N 09°40′·71W; 992501150.
Kilcredaun Head, W twr; 52°34′·78N 09°42′·58W.
Carrigaholt Fl (2) R 6s (sync); 52°34′·90N 09°40′·47W.
Beal Spit Fl (2) G 6s (sync); 52°34′·80N 09°39′·94W.
Beal Bar Fl G 3s (sync); 52°35′·18N 09°39′·05W.
Doonaha Fl R 3s (sync); 52°35′·54N 09°39′·01W; 992501154.
Letter Point Fl R 7s; 52°35′·44N 09°35′·89W.
Asdee Fl R 5s; 52°35′·09N 09°34′·55W.
Rineanna QR; 52°35′·59N 09°31′·24W.
North Carraig Q; 52°35′·60N 09°29′·76W.
Scattery Is, Rineanna Pt ☆ Fl (2) 8s 15m 10M; W twr; vis: 208°-092°; 52°36′·35N 09°31′·07W.

KILRUSH

Marina Ent Chan Ldg lts 355°. Front, Oc 3s; 52°37′·99N 09°30′·27W. Rear, 75m from front, Oc 3s.
Tarbert Is N Point ☆ Q WR 4s 18m W14M, R10M; W ◯ twr; vis: W069°- R277°- W287°-339°; 52°35′·52N 09°21′·83W.
Tarbert (Ballyhoolahan Pt) Ldg lts 128·2°. Front, Iso 3s 13m 3M; △ on W twr; vis: 123·2°-133·2°; 52°34′·35N 09°18′·80W. Rear, 400m from front, Iso 5s 18m 3M; G stripe on W Bn.
Garraunbaun Pt ☆ Fl (3) WR 10s 16m W8M, R5M; W □ col, vis: R shore - W072°- R242°- shore; 52°35′·62N 09°13′·94W.
Rinealon Pt ☆ Fl 2·5s 4m 7M; B col, W bands; vis: 234°-088°; 52°37′·12N 09°09′·82W.

FOYNES

W Chan Ldg lts 107·9° (may be moved for changes in chan). Front, Oc 4s 34m 12M; 52°36′·91N 09°06′·59W . Rear, Oc 4s 39m 12M.

RIVER SHANNON

Beeves Rock ☆ Fl WR 5s 12m W12M, R9M; vis: 064·5°-W-091°-R-238°-W-265°-W(unintens)-064·5°; 52°39′·01N 09°01′·35W .
North Channel Ldg lts 093°. Front, Tradree Rock Fl R 2s 6m 5M; W Trs; vis: 246°-110°; 52°41′·00N 08°49′·87W. Rear 0·65M from front, Iso 6s 14m 5M; W twr, R bands; vis: 327°-190°.
N side, Ldg lts 061°. Front, 52°40′·72N 08°45′·27W, Crawford Rock 490m from rear, Fl R 3s 6m 5M. Crawford No 2, Common Rear, Iso 6s 10m 5M; 52°40′·85N 08°44′·88W.
Ldg lts 302·1°, Flagstaff Rock, 670m from rear, Fl R 7s 7m 5M; 52°40′·66N 08°44′·40W.
Ldg lts 106·5°. Meelick Rk, Front Iso R 4s 6m 5M; 52°40′·24N 08°42′·32W. Meelick No 2, rear 275m from front Iso R 4s 9m 5M; both W beacons.

LOOP HEAD

Loop Head ☆ 52°33′·67N 09°55′·94W Fl (4) 20s 84m **23M**; vis: 280°-218°; 992501161.
Mal Bay Fl(5) Y 20s 52°46.42′N 009°35.15′W; *AIS*.

9.12.5 PASSAGE INFORMATION

More passage information is threaded between the harbours in this area.The latest editions of the Irish Cruising Club Sailing Directions are strongly recommended for all Irish waters (www.irishcruisingclub.com). Particularly useful on the N and W coast where other information is scarce they are published in two volumes, *E and N coasts of Ireland* and *S and W coasts of Ireland*. (Both available from Imray in UK or Todd Chart Services, Bangor, Co Down, ☎028 9146 6640 (www.toddchart.com).) See also *Cruising Cork and Kerry* (Imray/Swanson).

For notes on crossing the Irish Sea, see 9.13.5; and for Distances across it see 9.0.6. More Passage Information is threaded between the harbours of this Area.

9.12.6 SPECIAL NOTES FOR IRELAND

Céad Míle Fáilte! One hundred thousand Welcomes!

Lifejackets: It is compulsory to wear lifejackets in Irish waters on all craft of <7m LOA. Children under 16 years must wear a lifejacket or personal flotation device at all times on deck when underway. Every vessel, irrespective of size, must carry a lifejacket or personal flotation device for each person on board. These regulations are mandatory.

Irish Customs: First port of call should preferably be at Customs posts in one of the following hbrs: Dublin, Dun Laoghaire, Waterford, New Ross, Cork, Ringaskiddy, Bantry, Foynes, Limerick, Galway, Sligo and Killybegs. Yachts may, in fact, make their first call anywhere and if no Customs officer arrives within a reasonable time, the skipper should inform the nearest Garda (Police) station of the yacht's arrival. Only yachts from non-EU member states should fly flag Q or show ● over ○ lts on arrival. Passports are not required by UK citizens. All current Northern Ireland 5 and 6 digit telephone numbers have become 8 digits **028 90**12 3456.

Telephone: To call the **Republic of Ireland (RoI)** from the UK, dial **+353**, then the area code minus the initial 0, followed by the number. To call UK from the RoI: dial +44, followed by the area code minus the initial 0, then the number.

Salmon drift nets are now illegal and should not be encountered. Draft netting (across a river or estuary) is still permitted, but is rare.

Liquefied petroleum gas: In RoI LPG is supplied by Kosan, a sister company of Calorgas Ltd, but the smallest bottle is taller than the Calor equivalent fitted in most yachts with different connections. Calor bottles can be filled in larger towns. Camping Gaz is widely available.

Useful Irish websites:

Commissioners of Irish Lights	www.cil.ie
Irish Sailing Association	www.sailing.ie
Irish Tourist Board	www.discoverireland.com
Sea Area Forecast	www.met.ie/forecasts/sea-area.asp

Currency is the Euro (€), readily available from ATMs. VAT is 23%.

Access by air: Intl airports in RoI are at Dublin, Cork & Shannon. Regional airports in Waterford, Farranfore (Kerry), Knock (Mayo) and Carrickfinn (Donegal) provide some scheduled flights between Ireland and Britain. For details, see http://www.irishairports.com/.

Northern Ireland: Belfast CG (MRCC) is at Bangor, Co Down, ☎(091) 463933. HM Customs (⊜) should be contacted H24 on ☎(090) 358250 at the following ports, if a local Customs Officer is not available: Belfast, Warrenpoint, Kilkeel, Ardglass, Portavogie, Larne, Londonderry, Coleraine. Northern Ireland's main airport is Belfast (Aldergrove).

AIS stations: 73 AIS stations have been established on navigational marks around the coast of Ireland under the control of the Commissioners of Irish Lights. These are located at lighthouses, and in more remote areas fitted to dedicated lit Y buoys offshore.

GAELIC: It helps to understand some of the more common words for navigational features (courtesy of the Irish Cruising Club):

Ail, alt	cliff, height
Aird, ard	height, high
Anna, annagh	marsh
Ath	ford
Bal, Bally	town
Barra	sandbank
Bel, beal	mouth, strait
Beg	little
Ben, binna	hill
Bo	sunken rock
Boy, bwee	yellow
Bullig	shoal, round rock, breaker
Bun	end, river mouth
Caher	fort
Camus	bay, river bend
Carrick	rock
Cladach	shore
Cuan, coon	harbour
Derg, dearg	red
Drum	hill, ridge
Duff, dubh	black
Dun, doon	fort
Ennis	island
Fad, fadda	long
Fan	slope
Fin	white
Freagh, free	heather
Gall	stranger
Glas, glass	green
Glinsk	clear water
Gorm	blue
Gub	point of land
Hassans	swift current
Inish, illaun	island
Inver	river mouth
Keal, keel	narrow place, sound
Kill	church, cell
Kin, ken	promontory, head
Knock	hill
Lag	hollow
Lahan	broad
Lea	grey
Lenan	weed-covered rock
Lis	ancient fort
Long, luing	ship
Maan	middle
Maol, mwee	bare
Mara	of the sea
More, mor	big
Rannagh	point
Ron, roan	seal
Roe, ruadh	red
Scolt	split, rky gut
Scrow	boggy, grassy sward
Slieve	mountain
Slig	shells
Stag, stac	high rock
Tawney	low hill
Tigh, ti	house
Togher	causeway
Tra, traw	strand
Turlin	boulder, beach
Vad, bad	boat

DISTANCE TABLE

Approximate distances in nautical miles are by the most direct route, whilst avoiding dangers and allowing for Traffic Separation Schemes. Places in *italics* are in adjoining areas; places in **bold** are in 9.0.6, Distances across the Irish Sea.

1	***Carlingford Lough***	**1**																											
2	Malahide	36	**2**																										
3	Howth	39	4	**3**																									
4	**Dublin/Dun Laoghaire**	48	12	8	**4**																								
5	**Wicklow**	63	29	25	21	**5**																							
6	**Arklow**	75	43	37	36	15	**6**																						
7	Wexford (Bar Buoy)	104	71	66	62	43	30	**7**																					
8	**Rosslare**	108	75	70	66	47	34	4	**8**																				
9	Kilmore Quay	128	95	90	86	67	54	25	21	**9**																			
10	Waterford	154	127	116	117	99	84	51	47	32	**10**																		
11	**Dunmore East**	139	112	101	102	84	69	36	32	17	15	**11**																	
12	**Youghal**	172	143	134	133	115	100	69	65	51	52	37	**12**																
13	**Crosshaven**	192	165	154	155	137	122	89	85	69	74	59	25	**13**															
14	Kinsale	202	178	164	168	150	135	99	95	79	84	69	35	17	**14**														
15	Courtmacsherry	201	177	163	167	149	136	109	105	85	90	75	44	26	13	**15**													
16	Glandore	213	189	175	179	161	148	121	117	97	102	87	56	38	25	23	**16**												
17	Castletownshend	224	200	186	190	172	159	132	128	108	113	98	67	49	36	26	6	**17**											
18	**Baltimore**	239	205	201	196	177	164	136	132	112	117	102	70	54	42	34	16	12	**18**										
19	**Fastnet Rock**	250	216	212	207	189	174	148	144	122	127	112	78	60	49	42	24	20	10	**19**									
20	Schull	256	222	218	213	195	180	154	150	128	133	118	84	66	55	48	30	26	14	9	**20**								
21	Crookhaven	256	222	218	213	195	180	154	150	128	133	118	84	66	55	47	29	25	16	8	10	**21**							
22	Bantry	286	252	237	243	225	210	184	180	158	163	148	114	96	85	78	60	56	45	36	41	35	**22**						
23	Kenmare R (Scariff Is)	285	251	236	242	224	209	183	179	157	162	147	113	95	84	77	59	55	44	35	40	34	42	**23**					
24	Valentia Hbr	295	261	257	252	242	227	192	188	175	180	165	131	113	102	96	78	74	56	54	60	53	55	20	**24**				
25	Dingle	308	274	270	265	246	233	205	201	181	186	171	139	123	111	104	86	82	69	62	67	61	63	28	13	**25**			
26	Fenit Hbr	344	310	306	301	283	268	242	238	216	221	206	172	154	143	136	118	114	105	95	99	93	100	60	47	45	**26**		
27	Kilrush	361	333	323	318	299	286	258	254	234	239	224	192	176	164	155	137	133	122	114	116	109	116	78	66	64	32	**27**	
28	*Slyne Head*	317	355	351	346	328	313	287	283	261	266	251	217	199	188	180	162	158	153	139	141	133	144	103	97	95	70	75	**28**

9.12.7 MALAHIDE

Dublin **53°27'·20N 06°08'·90W** ✵✵◊◊◊✿✿✿

CHARTS AC 1468, 633, 5621; Imray C61, C62

TIDES +0030 Dover; ML 2·4; Duration 0615

Standard Port DUBLIN (NORTH WALL) (⟶)

Times				Height (metres)			
High Water		Low Water		MHWS	MHWN	MLWN	MLWS
0000	0700	0000	0500	4·1	3·4	1·5	0·7
1200	1900	1200	1700				
Differences MALAHIDE							
+0002	+0003	+0009	+0009	+0·1	–0·2	–0·4	–0·2

SHELTER Excellent in marina, dredged approx 2·3m. Visitor's berth on pontoon ***A***. Moorings preclude ⚓ in the inlet.

NAVIGATION WPT: SWM LFl 10s 53°27'·12N 06°06'·87W. The approach channel, which is well marked by 12 lit PHM and SHM, lies between drying sandbanks. The entrance is straightforward, but there is less than 1m of water below CD at some points of the chan, so adequate height of tide is required for safe entry. The flood reaches 3kn sp, the ebb 3½kn and a strong flow may be experienced through the marina at some states of the tide. Steep seas are formed in strong onshore winds against the full ebb, during which extreme caution needs to be exercised. The speed limit is 5kn in the fairway and 4kn in the marina.

LIGHTS AND MARKS The marina and apartment blocks close S of it are visible from the WPT. The marina entrance is marked by occulting red and green lights to each side.

COMMUNICATIONS (Code 01) MRCC 6620922/3; ⊜ 8746571; Police 666 4600; Dr 845 5994; ⊞ 837 7755.

Malahide Marina, Ch **M** 80 (H24). MYC, call *Yacht Base* Ch **M** (occas).

FACILITIES Marina ☎8454129, 349 inc 20 ❶ €3·90, (charge varies) (H24) Kos Ⓔ (30t)

Malahide YC ☎8453372, (for craft <5.5m, launching HW ±2).

Town Ⓑ ✈ (Dublin).

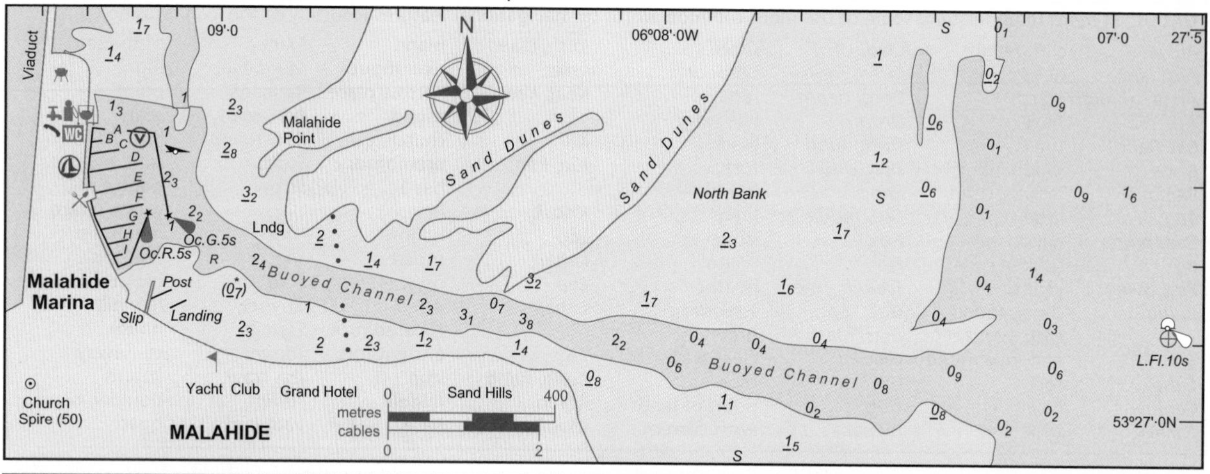

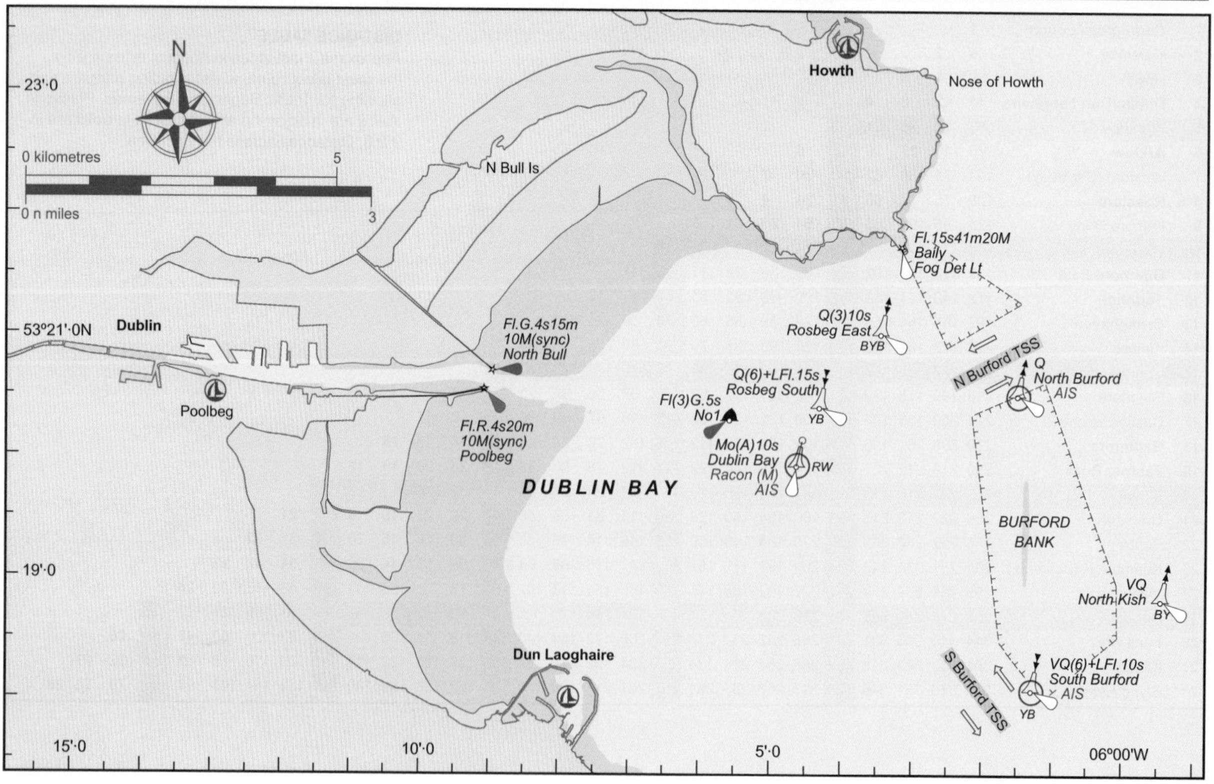

MALAHIDE TO DUN LAOGHAIRE

(AC 1468) Malahide, 4M from both Lambay Is and Howth, given adequate tidal height, can be entered in most weather except strong onshore winds. The channel, shallow at points, runs between drying banks marked by R & G fixed perches.

Ireland's Eye, a rky island which rises steeply to a height of 99m, lies about 7½ca N of Howth with reefs running SE and SW from Thulla Rk at its SE end. This provides some shelter to the ent to Howth but following strong ENE'ly winds heavy seas can pile up in the approach channel.

Ben of Howth, on N side of Dublin Bay, a prominent landmark, is steep-to, with no dangers more than 1ca offshore.

Dublin Bay is protected by the offshore shoals of Bennet and Kish Banks, the main passage between which is marked by N/S cardinal buoys. Closer inshore, SE of Baily Lt, lies Burford Bank, on which the sea breaks in E gales. Rosbeg Bank lies on the N side of Dublin Bay marked by cardinal buoys guarding the approach to the R Liffey.

A TSS ½M long at either end of the Burford Bank leads to/from an anti-clockwise 'roundabout' radius 2·3ca centred on Dublin Bay SWM lt buoy 2·75M ESE of Dublin Port. Do not impede large vessels and keep clear of the TSS and fairway.

▶ *The N-going stream begins at HW Dublin –0600, and the S-going at HW Dublin, sp rates 3kn. Strong tidal strems run SE-NW through Muglin Snd and Dalkey Snd (2.5Kn at Sp).*◀

The S part of the bay between Dublin and Dun Laoghaire is shallow but otherwise clear of obstacles. To the E Dalkey Is and Muglins (lit) lie close under Sorrento Pt. Dalkey Snd should be used only in fair weather and ⚓ made off the slip on the W shore. Muglins Snd more open, but beware rk 0.8m 1ca W of Muglins lt.

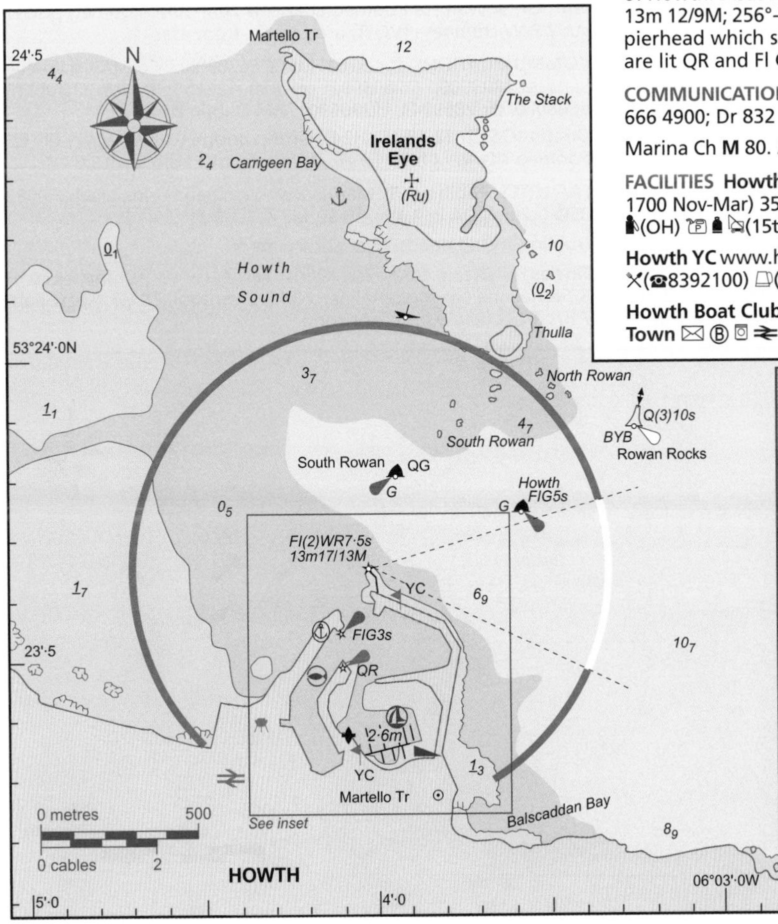

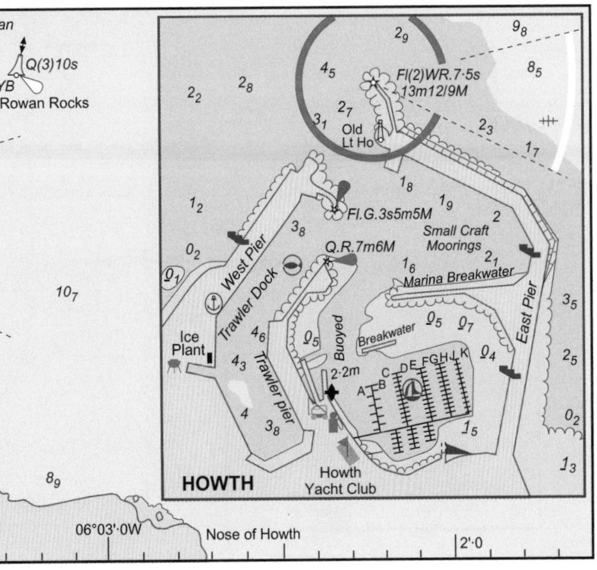

9.12.8 HOWTH

Dublin **53°23'·60N 06°04'·00W** ❀❀❀◊◊◊✿✿✿

CHARTS AC 1468, 1415, 5621; Imray C61, C62

TIDES +0025 Dover; ML 2·4; Duration 0625

Standard Port DUBLIN (NORTH WALL) (⟶)

Times				Height (metres)			
High Water		Low Water		MHWS	MHWN	MLWN	MLWS
0000	0700	0000	0500	4·1	3·4	1·5	0·7
1200	1900	1200	1700				
Differences HOWTH							
–0007	–0005	+0001	+0005	0·0	–0·1	–0·2	–0·2

SHELTER Excellent in marina, at all states of tide. After a severe ENE'ly storm, expect a dangerous scend in the app chan which has 11🅥, 6G & 5R. Caution: many moorings in E part of outer hbr. No ent to FV basin for yachts. Inside the inner hbr keep strictly to chan to avoid drying shoals either side and a substantial wavebreak (gabion). Marina depth 1·8m. R posts mark the outer limit of dredging around the marina. 4kn speed limit. There is a fair weather ⚓ in 2-3m at Carrigeen Bay, SW side of Ireland's Eye.

NAVIGATION WPT Howth SHM buoy, Fl G 5s, 53°23'·72N 06°03'·53W, 251°/0·27M to E pier lt. From the S beware Casana Rk 4ca S of the Nose of Howth and Puck's Rks extending about 50m off the Nose. Ireland's Eye is 0·6M N of hbr, with the Rowan Rks SE and SW from Thulla, marked by Rowan Rks ECM, and S Rowan SHM lt buoys. The usual approach passes S of Ireland's Eye, but beware many lobster pots between the Nose of Howth and the hbr, and rocks off both pier hds. Howth Sound has 2·4m min depth; give way to FVs (constrained by draught) in the Sound and hbr entrance. 2·5m in marina approach channel.

LIGHTS AND MARKS Baily Lt Ho, Fl 15s 41m 26M, is 1·5M S of Nose of Howth. Disused lt ho on E pier is conspic. E pier lt, Fl (2) WR 7·5s 13m 12/9M; 256°-W-295°, R elsewhere. W sector leads safely to NE pierhead which should be rounded 50m off. Trawler Dock moles are lit QR and Fl G 3s. Marina channel has 8 lit lateral marks.

COMMUNICATIONS (Code 01) MRCC 6620922/3; ⊖8746571; Police 666 4900; Dr 832 3191; 🅷 837 7755. HM 8322252.

Marina Ch **M** 80. *Howth Harbour* VHF Ch 16 (Mon-Fri 0700–2300).

FACILITIES **Howth Marina** ☎8392777 (HO 0800-2130 Apr-Oct, 0900-1700 Nov-Mar) 350 inc 🅥 €3·65 (inc ⚡) €18 wkly ♿ ⛺ ▬(H24) 🅞 ⛽(OH) 🅟 ⛽ ⛴(15t).

Howth YC www.hyc.ie ☎8322141, ♿ 🅞 Scrubbing posts <20m LOA, ✕(☎8392100) ⊐(☎8320606).

Howth Boat Club (no facilities). **Services** LB, ⛽ Kos, 🔧 ⛵ 📷 Ⓔ ⛵. **Town** ✉ Ⓑ 🅞 ⇌ ✈ (Dublin).

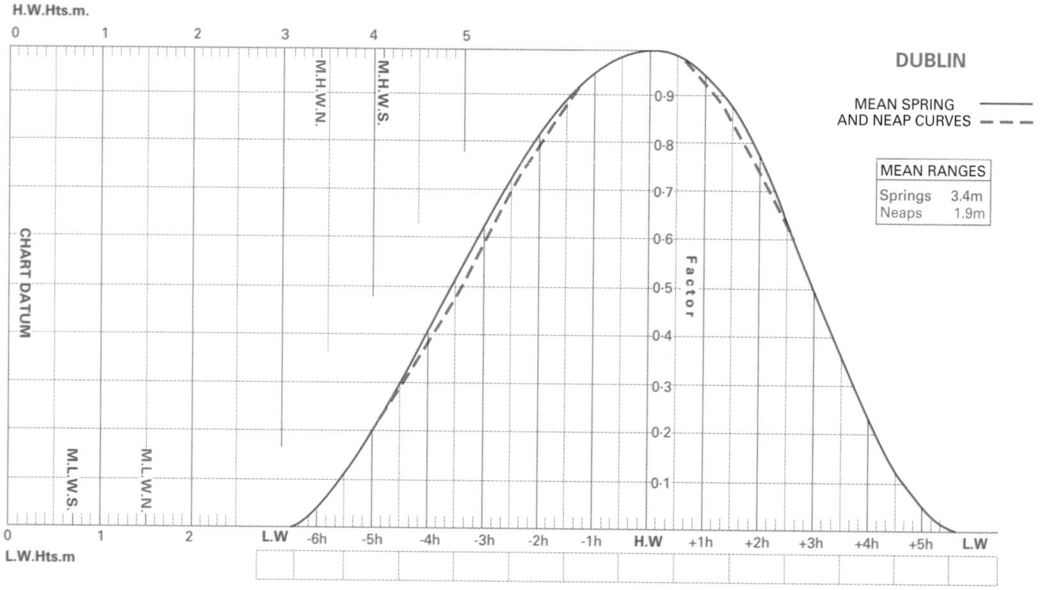

9.12.9 DUBLIN

Dublin **53°20'·85N 06°14'·80W**

CHARTS AC 1468, 1415, 1447, 5621; Imray C61, C62

TIDES +0042 Dover; ML 2·4; Duration 0640

Standard Port DUBLIN (NORTH WALL) (⟶)

Times				Height (metres)			
High Water		Low Water		MHWS	MHWN	MLWN	MLWS
0000	0700	0000	0500	4·1	3·4	1·5	0·7
1200	1900	1200	1700				
Differences DUBLIN BAR and DUN LAOGHAIRE							
–0006	–0001	–0002	–0003	0·0	0·0	0·0	+0·1
GREYSTONES (53°09'N 06°04'W)							
–0008	–0008	–0008	–0008	–0·5	–0·4	ND	ND

SHELTER Dublin Port, excellent on Poolbeg YBC Marina, S of Alexandra Basin W. City centre pontoons (no security) are W of East Link Br but availability and bridge opening schedule should be checked well in advance (+353 1 8183300).

NAVIGATION Dublin Port WPT 53°20'·50N 06°06'·71W, 275°/1·35M to hbr ent. Accessible H24, but the ent to R Liffey is rough in E'ly >F5 against ebb tide. Note Bull Wall covers 0.6 to 2.7m at HW.

For clearance to enter call *Dublin VTS* Ch 12. Conform to Dublin Port Company Small Craft Regulations (www.dublinport.ie).
Beware of shipping; small craft must keep outside fairway buoys.

LIGHTS AND MARKS Entrance, N. Bull Lt Fl G 4s 15m 10M synchro with Gt. S. Wall Hd Poolbeg Lt Fl R 4s 20m 10M. Poolbeg power stn 2 R/W chimneys (VQ R) are conspic from afar.

COMMUNICATIONS (Code 01) MRCC 6620922/3; Coast/Cliff Rescue Service 2803900; ⊜2803992; 1550 123855; Police (Dublin) 6668000; Dr 2859244; Ⓗ2806901. HM Dublin 8748771.

Dublin VTS Ch **12** 13 16 (H24). Lifting bridge (call *Eastlink*) Ch 12. *Poolbeg Marina* Ch **37** 12 16. Dublin Coast Radio Stn 16 67 83.

FACILITIES Poolbeg YBC Marina www.poolbegmarina.ie ☎6689983 35Ⓥ (<20m LOA in 2.4m) €3·80,

Dublin City, all needs, @ at library, ⇌ ✈.

Ferries Holyhead; 4/day; 3¼hrs; Irish Ferries (www.irishferries.com) & Stena Line (www.stenaline.co.uk). Liverpool; 18/wk (seasonal); 7 hrs; P&O (www.poferries.com).

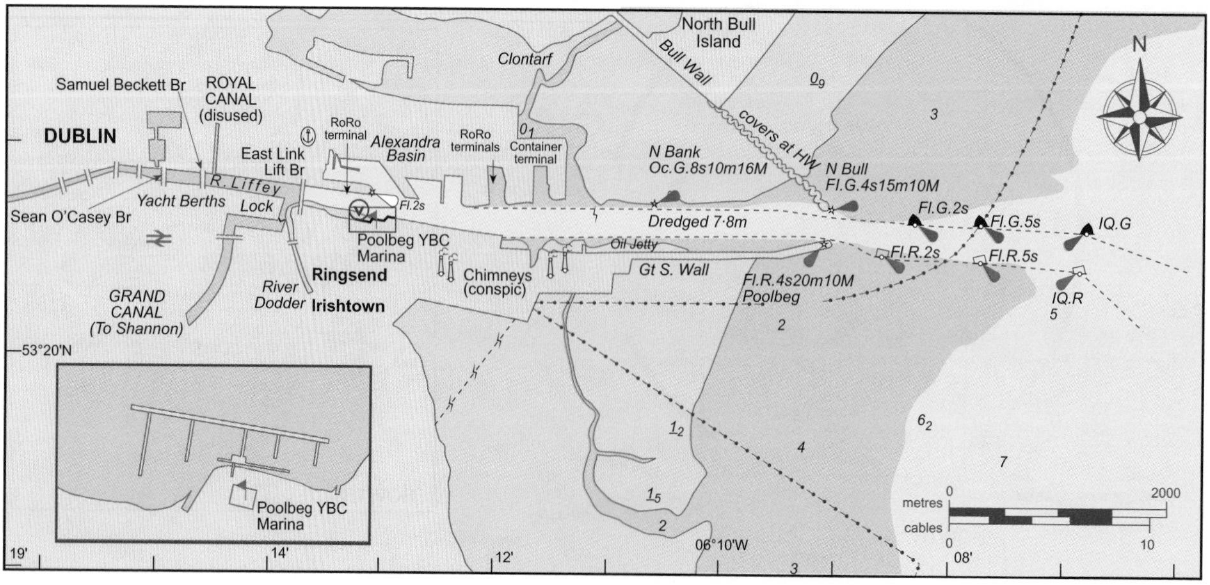

STANDARD TIME (UT)
For Summer Time add ONE hour in **non-shaded areas**

DUBLIN (NORTH WALL) LAT 53°21′N LONG 6°13′W

TIMES AND HEIGHTS OF HIGH AND LOW WATERS

Dates in red are SPRINGS
Dates in blue are NEAPS

YEAR **2018**

JANUARY

Day	Time	m	Day	Time	m
1 M	0354 1036 1620 2258	0.6 4.2 0.5 4.2	16 TU	0449 1119 1713 2342	1.1 3.9 1.0 3.7
2 TU	0441 1123 1709 ○ 2348	0.5 4.3 0.4 4.3	17 W	0520 1150 1745 ●	1.0 4.0 1.0
3 W	0527 1209 1757	0.5 4.4 0.3	18 TH	0013 0549 1221 1813	3.7 1.0 4.0 0.9
4 TH	0037 0612 1258 1846	4.2 0.5 4.4 0.3	19 F	0044 0617 1253 1841	3.7 0.9 4.0 0.9
5 F	0128 0659 1348 1937	4.1 0.7 4.3 0.4	20 SA	0118 0649 1330 1914	3.8 0.9 4.0 0.8
6 SA	0222 0750 1441 2031	4.0 0.8 4.2 0.5	21 SU	0156 0726 1410 1952	3.7 1.0 4.0 0.8
7 SU	0318 0845 1537 2127	3.9 1.0 4.1 0.7	22 M	0238 0808 1454 2036	3.7 1.0 3.9 0.9
8 M	0417 0943 1637 ◑ 2225	3.7 1.2 3.9 0.9	23 TU	0324 0854 1540 2124	3.7 1.1 3.8 0.9
9 TU	0520 1045 1741 2326	3.6 1.4 3.8 1.1	24 W	0414 0947 1630 ◐ 2218	3.6 1.2 3.7 1.0
10 W	0624 1153 1846	3.5 1.5 3.7	25 TH	0511 1047 1727 2320	3.5 1.3 3.7 1.1
11 TH	0034 0727 1307 1950	1.3 3.5 1.5 3.6	26 F	0616 1157 1834	3.5 1.3 3.6
12 F	0144 0826 1417 2052	1.3 3.6 1.5 3.6	27 SA	0033 0726 1311 1946	1.2 3.5 1.3 3.6
13 SA	0245 0920 1514 2146	1.3 3.7 1.3 3.6	28 SU	0147 0833 1419 2055	1.1 3.7 1.1 3.8
14 SU	0334 1005 1600 2231	1.2 3.8 1.2 3.7	29 M	0251 0931 1519 2156	0.9 3.9 0.8 3.9
15 M	0414 1044 1639 2308	1.1 3.9 1.1 3.7	30 TU	0346 1024 1612 2250	0.8 4.1 0.5 4.1
			31 W	0434 1112 1701 ○ 2339	0.6 4.3 0.3 4.1

FEBRUARY

Day	Time	m	Day	Time	m
1 TH	0517 1158 1747	0.5 4.4 0.2	16 F	0526 1157 1746	0.8 4.0 0.7
2 F	0025 0559 1243 1831	4.1 0.5 4.4 0.2	17 SA	0018 0552 1228 1812	3.8 0.8 4.0 0.7
3 SA	0111 0642 1329 1917	4.1 0.5 4.3 0.3	18 SU	0050 0623 1303 1845	3.8 0.7 4.0 0.6
4 SU	0156 0727 1415 2005	4.0 0.7 4.2 0.4	19 M	0126 0659 1343 1923	3.8 0.7 4.0 0.6
5 M	0243 0816 1505 2054	3.8 0.8 4.0 0.7	20 TU	0207 0739 1426 2006	3.8 0.7 4.0 0.6
6 TU	0333 0908 1557 2145	3.7 1.0 3.8 0.9	21 W	0251 0825 1512 2053	3.8 0.8 3.9 0.7
7 W	0429 1004 1656 ◑ 2240	3.5 1.2 3.6 1.2	22 TH	0339 0916 1602 2145	3.7 0.9 3.8 0.9
8 TH	0531 1106 1802 2341	3.4 1.4 3.5 1.4	23 F	0434 1015 1659 ◐ 2247	3.5 1.1 3.6 1.1
9 F	0637 1216 1910	3.3 1.5 3.4	24 SA	0539 1128 1809	3.4 1.2 3.5
10 SA	0053 0741 1341 2016	1.5 3.4 1.5 3.3	25 SU	0004 0658 1250 1931	1.3 3.4 1.2 3.5
11 SU	0214 0842 1451 2117	1.5 3.5 1.4 3.4	26 M	0129 0814 1406 2047	1.2 3.6 1.0 3.6
12 M	0312 0934 1541 2207	1.4 3.6 1.2 3.5	27 TU	0242 0919 1511 2150	1.1 3.8 0.8 3.8
13 TU	0354 1018 1619 2247	1.2 3.7 1.1 3.6	28 W	0339 1014 1605 2244	0.8 4.0 0.5 3.9
14 W	0428 1056 1651 2321	1.1 3.8 0.9 3.7			
15 TH	0458 1128 1720 ● 2351	0.9 3.9 0.8 3.7			

MARCH

Day	Time	m	Day	Time	m
1 TH	0426 1102 1651 2330	0.6 4.2 0.3 4.0	16 F	0431 1101 1648 2324	0.9 3.9 0.7 3.7
2 F	0507 1146 1733 ○	0.5 4.3 0.2	17 SA	0458 1130 1714 ● 2350	0.7 3.9 0.5 3.8
3 SA	0010 0545 1227 1814	4.0 0.4 4.3 0.2	18 SU	0525 1200 1743	0.6 4.0 0.4
4 SU	0048 0624 1307 1854	4.0 0.4 4.2 0.3	19 M	0020 0557 1237 1817	3.9 0.5 4.1 0.4
5 M	0126 0704 1348 1936	3.9 0.5 4.1 0.4	20 TU	0057 0633 1317 1856	3.9 0.4 4.1 0.4
6 TU	0206 0747 1432 2020	3.8 0.6 3.9 0.6	21 W	0138 0715 1401 1940	3.9 0.5 4.0 0.5
7 W	0249 0835 1519 2107	3.7 0.8 3.7 0.9	22 TH	0222 0802 1449 2028	3.9 0.6 3.9 0.7
8 TH	0337 0927 1612 2157	3.5 1.0 3.5 1.2	23 F	0312 0856 1541 2123	3.8 0.8 3.8 0.9
9 F	0432 1026 1717 ◑ 2255	3.4 1.3 3.3 1.4	24 SA	0408 0959 1642 ◐ 2228	3.6 0.9 3.6 1.2
10 SA	0544 1132 1831	3.2 1.4 3.2	25 SU	0515 1114 1758 2348	3.5 1.1 3.5 1.3
11 SU	0001 0657 1251 1941	1.6 3.2 1.5 3.2	26 M	0639 1237 1924	3.4 1.1 3.4
12 M	0124 0803 1417 2045	1.6 3.3 1.4 3.3	27 TU	0115 0759 1356 2041	1.3 3.5 0.9 3.6
13 TU	0241 0901 1512 2139	1.5 3.4 1.2 3.4	28 W	0230 0907 1500 2144	1.1 3.7 0.7 3.7
14 W	0327 0949 1550 2220	1.3 3.6 1.0 3.5	29 TH	0326 1004 1551 2236	0.9 3.9 0.5 3.9
15 TH	0401 1028 1621 2255	1.0 3.7 0.8 3.7	30 F	0412 1052 1636 2319	0.7 4.1 0.3 3.9
			31 SA	0452 1134 1716 ○ 2354	0.5 4.1 0.2 3.9

APRIL

Day	Time	m	Day	Time	m
1 SU	0530 1210 1754	0.5 4.1 0.3	16 M	0457 1134 1716 ● 2353	0.5 4.0 0.3 4.0
2 M	0025 0606 1246 1831	3.9 0.4 4.1 0.4	17 TU	0532 1212 1752	0.4 4.1 0.3
3 TU	0058 0643 1323 1909	3.9 0.5 4.0 0.5	18 W	0030 0611 1255 1833	4.0 0.3 4.1 0.4
4 W	0134 0723 1404 1948	3.8 0.6 3.8 0.7	19 TH	0114 0656 1342 1919	4.0 0.4 4.1 0.5
5 TH	0214 0807 1448 2032	3.7 0.8 3.7 0.9	20 F	0201 0747 1433 2010	4.0 0.5 3.9 0.7
6 F	0257 0857 1536 2120	3.6 0.9 3.5 1.2	21 SA	0253 0846 1530 2110	3.9 0.7 3.8 1.0
7 SA	0345 0953 1635 2216	3.4 1.1 3.3 1.4	22 SU	0352 0953 1636 ◐ 2217	3.7 0.8 3.6 1.2
8 SU	0447 1056 1750 ◑ 2321	3.3 1.3 3.1 1.6	23 M	0503 1107 1755 2334	3.6 0.9 3.5 1.3
9 M	0610 1206 1904	3.2 1.4 3.1	24 TU	0625 1224 1916	3.6 1.0 3.5
10 TU	0033 0723 1323 2010	1.6 3.2 1.4 3.2	25 W	0056 0742 1338 2028	1.3 3.6 0.8 3.6
11 W	0149 0824 1427 2104	1.5 3.3 1.2 3.3	26 TH	0208 0850 1440 2129	1.2 3.8 0.7 3.7
12 TH	0245 0914 1510 2148	1.3 3.5 1.0 3.5	27 F	0305 0948 1532 2220	1.0 3.9 0.5 3.8
13 F	0324 0955 1543 2223	1.1 3.7 0.8 3.7	28 SA	0352 1037 1616 2302	0.8 4.0 0.4 3.8
14 SA	0356 1029 1613 2252	0.8 3.8 0.6 3.8	29 SU	0434 1119 1656 2336	0.7 4.0 0.4 3.9
15 SU	0426 1100 1643 2320	0.6 3.9 0.4 3.9	30 M	0512 1155 1733 ○	0.6 4.0 0.5

Chart Datum: 0·20 metres above Ordnance Datum (Dublin). HAT is 4·5 metres above Chart Datum.

STANDARD TIME (UT)
For Summer Time add ONE hour in **non-shaded areas**

DUBLIN (NORTH WALL) LAT 53°21'N LONG 6°13'W

TIMES AND HEIGHTS OF HIGH AND LOW WATERS

Dates in red are SPRINGS
Dates in blue are NEAPS

YEAR **2018**

MAY

Date	Time	m	Time	m	Time	m	Time	m
1 TU	0003	3.8	0548	0.6	1227	3.9	1808	0.5
2 W	0033	3.8	0625	0.6	1302	3.9	1844	0.7
3 TH	0108	3.8	0704	0.7	1341	3.8	1921	0.8
4 F	0146	3.8	0746	0.8	1423	3.6	2002	1.0
5 SA	0227	3.7	0832	0.9	1508	3.5	2047	1.2
6 SU	0312	3.5	0924	1.1	1600	3.3	2140	1.4
7 M	0405	3.4	1023	1.2	1705	3.2	2242	1.5
8 TU	0512	3.3	1126	1.3	1819	3.1	◑ 2349	1.6
9 W	0631	3.2	1230	1.3	1926	3.2		
10 TH	0054	1.5	0736	3.3	1331	1.2	2021	3.3
11 F	0152	1.4	0829	3.5	1420	1.0	2107	3.5
12 SA	0238	1.1	0913	3.6	1501	0.8	2145	3.7
13 SU	0317	0.9	0952	3.8	1537	0.6	2218	3.8
14 M	0353	0.7	1030	4.0	1613	0.4	2252	4.0
15 TU	0431	0.5	1110	4.1	1651	0.3	● 2329	4.1
16 W	0511	0.4	1152	4.1	1732	0.3		
17 TH	0010	4.1	0554	0.3	1239	4.1	1815	0.4
18 F	0056	4.1	0643	0.4	1329	4.1	1903	0.6
19 SA	0146	4.1	0738	0.5	1424	4.0	1958	0.8
20 SU	0241	4.0	0840	0.6	1524	3.8	2058	1.0
21 M	0343	3.9	0946	0.7	1631	3.7	2204	1.2
22 TU	0453	3.8	1054	0.8	1744	3.6	◐ 2315	1.3
23 W	0609	3.7	1205	0.9	1857	3.6		
24 TH	0029	1.3	0720	3.8	1313	0.8	2005	3.6
25 F	0138	1.3	0826	3.8	1415	0.8	2105	3.7
26 SA	0238	1.1	0925	3.9	1508	0.7	2157	3.8
27 SU	0329	1.0	1016	3.9	1554	0.7	2240	3.8
28 M	0414	0.9	1100	3.9	1635	0.7	2315	3.8
29 TU	0455	0.8	1137	3.9	1713	0.7	○ 2343	3.8
30 W	0533	0.8	1210	3.8	1748	0.8		
31 TH	0012	3.8	0609	0.8	1243	3.8	1822	0.8

JUNE

Date	Time	m	Time	m	Time	m	Time	m
1 F	0046	3.9	0647	0.8	1320	3.7	1857	0.9
2 SA	0123	3.8	0726	0.9	1359	3.6	1935	1.0
3 SU	0203	3.8	0808	1.0	1442	3.5	2016	1.2
4 M	0246	3.7	0854	1.1	1528	3.4	2103	1.3
5 TU	0334	3.6	0945	1.2	1620	3.3	2158	1.4
6 W	0427	3.5	1041	1.2	1721	3.2	◑ 2259	1.5
7 TH	0528	3.4	1140	1.2	1826	3.2		
8 F	0001	1.5	0632	3.4	1238	1.2	1926	3.3
9 SA	0059	1.4	0733	3.5	1331	1.0	2018	3.5
10 SU	0151	1.2	0827	3.6	1420	0.9	2104	3.7
11 M	0239	1.0	0917	3.8	1505	0.7	2146	3.9
12 TU	0324	0.8	1004	4.0	1548	0.5	2228	4.0
13 W	0409	0.6	1050	4.1	1631	0.4	● 2311	4.2
14 TH	0454	0.4	1138	4.2	1715	0.4	2355	4.2
15 F	0542	0.3	1227	4.2	1802	0.5		
16 SA	0042	4.3	0633	0.3	1319	4.1	1850	0.6
17 SU	0134	4.2	0728	0.4	1414	4.0	1944	0.8
18 M	0229	4.1	0828	0.5	1513	3.9	2042	0.9
19 TU	0330	4.0	0930	0.6	1616	3.7	2143	1.1
20 W	0435	3.9	1033	0.7	1722	3.6	◐ 2248	1.3
21 TH	0544	3.8	1137	0.9	1828	3.6	2355	1.3
22 F	0653	3.8	1242	0.9	1933	3.6		
23 SA	0104	1.4	0757	3.8	1345	1.0	2034	3.6
24 SU	0209	1.3	0858	3.8	1442	1.0	2128	3.7
25 M	0306	1.2	0953	3.8	1532	1.0	2214	3.7
26 TU	0356	1.1	1040	3.8	1615	1.0	2251	3.8
27 W	0439	1.0	1118	3.7	1653	0.9	2323	3.8
28 TH	0517	1.0	1152	3.7	1728	0.9	○ 2353	3.9
29 F	0554	0.9	1224	3.7	1801	1.0		
30 SA	0025	3.9	0629	0.9	1258	3.7	1833	1.0

JULY

Date	Time	m	Time	m	Time	m	Time	m
1 SU	0100	3.9	0703	0.9	1335	3.6	1907	1.0
2 M	0138	3.9	0738	1.0	1414	3.6	1944	1.1
3 TU	0219	3.8	0817	1.0	1456	3.5	2026	1.2
4 W	0304	3.8	0900	1.0	1541	3.5	2112	1.2
5 TH	0351	3.7	0949	1.1	1631	3.4	2204	1.3
6 F	0443	3.6	1043	1.1	1727	3.4	◑ 2303	1.4
7 SA	0541	3.5	1143	1.1	1829	3.4		
8 SU	0006	1.4	0643	3.5	1245	1.1	1930	3.5
9 M	0109	1.3	0748	3.6	1343	1.0	2028	3.6
10 TU	0207	1.1	0848	3.8	1438	0.9	2120	3.8
11 W	0301	0.9	0944	3.9	1529	0.7	2209	4.0
12 TH	0353	0.6	1036	4.1	1617	0.6	2256	4.2
13 F	0442	0.4	1126	4.2	1703	0.5	● 2342	4.3
14 SA	0532	0.3	1215	4.2	1749	0.5		
15 SU	0029	4.3	0621	0.3	1306	4.1	1835	0.6
16 M	0118	4.3	0713	0.3	1358	4.0	1925	0.7
17 TU	0211	4.3	0808	0.4	1452	3.9	2018	0.8
18 W	0307	4.1	0905	0.6	1548	3.8	2115	1.0
19 TH	0407	4.0	1003	0.7	1648	3.6	◐ 2214	1.2
20 F	0511	3.8	1102	0.9	1751	3.5	2317	1.3
21 SA	0619	3.7	1204	1.1	1855	3.5		
22 SU	0026	1.4	0725	3.6	1311	1.2	1956	3.5
23 M	0140	1.4	0829	3.6	1415	1.3	2054	3.6
24 TU	0246	1.3	0928	3.6	1510	1.2	2144	3.7
25 W	0340	1.2	1018	3.6	1555	1.2	2226	3.8
26 TH	0423	1.1	1058	3.7	1633	1.1	2301	3.9
27 F	0501	1.0	1132	3.7	1707	1.0	○ 2333	3.9
28 SA	0535	0.9	1204	3.7	1739	1.0		
29 SU	0004	3.9	0605	0.9	1235	3.7	1808	0.9
30 M	0036	4.0	0634	0.9	1307	3.7	1838	0.9
31 TU	0111	4.0	0703	0.9	1343	3.7	1912	0.9

AUGUST

Date	Time	m	Time	m	Time	m	Time	m
1 W	0150	3.9	0739	0.9	1423	3.7	1951	1.0
2 TH	0232	3.9	0820	0.9	1505	3.6	2034	1.1
3 F	0318	3.8	0906	0.9	1552	3.6	2123	1.1
4 SA	0406	3.7	0957	1.0	1644	3.5	◑ 2217	1.2
5 SU	0501	3.6	1055	1.1	1743	3.4	2322	1.3
6 M	0606	3.5	1203	1.2	1852	3.5		
7 TU	0034	1.3	0719	3.6	1314	1.2	2000	3.6
8 W	0144	1.2	0830	3.7	1419	1.0	2101	3.8
9 TH	0247	0.9	0932	3.9	1516	0.9	2154	4.0
10 F	0343	0.6	1026	4.0	1606	0.7	2243	4.2
11 SA	0434	0.4	1115	4.1	1651	0.5	● 2328	4.3
12 SU	0521	0.2	1202	4.2	1735	0.5		
13 M	0013	4.4	0606	0.2	1248	4.1	1817	0.5
14 TU	0058	4.4	0653	0.2	1334	4.0	1902	0.6
15 W	0145	4.3	0742	0.4	1421	3.9	1950	0.7
16 TH	0235	4.1	0833	0.6	1511	3.8	2042	0.9
17 F	0330	3.9	0926	0.8	1604	3.6	2138	1.1
18 SA	0430	3.7	1022	1.1	1704	3.5	◐ 2239	1.3
19 SU	0539	3.5	1121	1.3	1810	3.4	2346	1.5
20 M	0651	3.4	1228	1.4	1917	3.4		
21 TU	0107	1.5	0759	3.4	1344	1.5	2019	3.5
22 W	0227	1.4	0904	3.5	1447	1.4	2114	3.6
23 TH	0323	1.3	0956	3.5	1534	1.3	2200	3.8
24 F	0405	1.1	1037	3.6	1612	1.1	2238	3.9
25 SA	0440	1.0	1111	3.7	1645	1.0	2311	3.9
26 SU	0510	0.9	1141	3.7	1714	0.9	○ 2340	4.0
27 M	0537	0.8	1209	3.8	1741	0.8		
28 TU	0009	4.0	0601	0.7	1239	3.8	1809	0.8
29 W	0042	4.0	0629	0.7	1312	3.8	1841	0.8
30 TH	0120	4.0	0704	0.7	1350	3.8	1919	0.8
31 F	0202	4.0	0745	0.7	1432	3.8	2002	0.9

Chart Datum: 0·20 metres above Ordnance Datum (Dublin). HAT is 4·5 metres above Chart Datum.

STANDARD TIME (UT)
For Summer Time add ONE hour in **non-shaded areas**

DUBLIN (NORTH WALL) LAT 53°21'N LONG 6°13'W

TIMES AND HEIGHTS OF HIGH AND LOW WATERS

Dates in red are SPRINGS
Dates in blue are NEAPS

YEAR **2018**

SEPTEMBER

Day	Time	m	Day	Time	m
1 SA	0246 0830 1518 2050	3.9 0.8 3.7 1.0	16 SU	0349 0941 1615 ◐ 2204	3.6 1.2 3.5 1.3
2 SU	0335 0921 1609 2146	3.8 1.0 3.6 1.2	17 M	0457 1039 1723 2310	3.4 1.4 3.4 1.5
3 M	0431 1021 1708 ◑ 2253	3.6 1.2 3.5 1.3	18 TU	0614 1145 1835	3.3 1.6 3.4
4 TU	0539 1134 1822	3.5 1.3 3.5	19 W	0029 0727 1305 1943	1.6 3.3 1.6 3.4
5 W	0013 0701 1255 1939	1.3 3.5 1.3 3.6	20 TH	0201 0835 1420 2042	1.5 3.4 1.5 3.6
6 TH	0132 0819 1408 2046	1.2 3.6 1.2 3.8	21 F	0259 0930 1509 2132	1.3 3.5 1.3 3.7
7 F	0240 0924 1508 2142	0.9 3.8 1.0 4.0	22 SA	0339 1011 1547 2212	1.1 3.6 1.2 3.9
8 SA	0336 1018 1557 2230	0.6 4.0 0.7 4.2	23 SU	0412 1045 1618 2245	0.9 3.7 1.0 4.0
9 SU	0424 1105 1640 ● 2314	0.3 4.1 0.6 4.4	24 M	0440 1116 1647 2314	0.8 3.8 0.9 4.0
10 M	0508 1147 1720 2355	0.2 4.1 0.5 4.4	25 TU	0504 1142 1713 ○ 2342	0.7 3.9 0.8 4.1
11 TU	0549 1227 1759	0.1 4.1 0.5	26 W	0529 1209 1741	0.6 3.9 0.7
12 W	0036 0631 1307 1839	4.4 0.2 4.0 0.5	27 TH	0014 0558 1242 1814	4.1 0.6 3.9 0.7
13 TH	0119 0714 1349 1923	4.2 0.4 3.9 0.7	28 F	0052 0634 1320 1853	4.1 0.6 3.9 0.7
14 F	0204 0800 1432 2011	4.1 0.6 3.8 0.9	29 SA	0134 0715 1403 1936	4.1 0.7 3.9 0.8
15 SA	0253 0849 1520 2104	3.9 0.9 3.6 1.1	30 SU	0220 0801 1450 2027	4.0 0.8 3.8 0.9

OCTOBER

Day	Time	m	Day	Time	m
1 M	0312 0855 1542 2126	3.8 1.1 3.7 1.1	16 TU	0419 1002 1636 ◐ 2237	3.4 1.5 3.5 1.4
2 TU	0411 0958 1644 ◑ 2238	3.6 1.3 3.6 1.2	17 W	0536 1107 1752 2348	3.2 1.7 3.4 1.5
3 W	0525 1116 1801	3.5 1.4 3.5	18 TH	0651 1219 1904	3.2 1.7 3.4
4 TH	0001 0653 1241 1921	1.3 3.5 1.4 3.6	19 F	0113 0759 1337 2006	1.5 3.3 1.6 3.5
5 F	0123 0811 1356 2031	1.1 3.6 1.3 3.8	20 SA	0220 0855 1433 2058	1.3 3.5 1.4 3.7
6 SA	0230 0916 1455 2129	0.8 3.8 1.1 4.0	21 SU	0304 0939 1514 2140	1.1 3.7 1.2 3.8
7 SU	0324 1009 1543 2218	0.6 4.0 0.8 4.2	22 M	0337 1015 1547 2215	0.9 3.8 1.0 3.9
8 M	0410 1053 1625 2301	0.4 4.1 0.7 4.3	23 TU	0405 1046 1616 2245	0.8 3.9 0.9 4.0
9 TU	0452 1132 1704 ● 2340	0.2 4.1 0.6 4.3	24 W	0431 1113 1645 ○ 2315	0.6 4.0 0.7 4.1
10 W	0531 1207 1742	0.3 4.1 0.5	25 TH	0500 1141 1716 2349	0.5 4.0 0.6 4.2
11 TH	0017 0609 1242 1820	4.3 0.4 4.0 0.6	26 F	0532 1215 1752	0.5 4.1 0.6
12 F	0056 0647 1319 1901	4.2 0.5 4.0 0.7	27 SA	0028 0609 1255 1832	4.2 0.6 4.1 0.6
13 SA	0139 0729 1400 1946	4.0 0.7 3.9 0.9	28 SU	0113 0651 1340 1919	4.1 0.7 4.0 0.7
14 SU	0225 0814 1445 2037	3.8 1.0 3.7 1.0	29 M	0203 0740 1429 2013	4.0 0.9 4.0 0.9
15 M	0316 0905 1534 2134	3.6 1.3 3.6 1.3	30 TU	0258 0837 1525 2117	3.8 1.1 3.8 1.0
			31 W	0402 0944 1629 ◑ 2230	3.7 1.3 3.7 1.1

NOVEMBER

Day	Time	m	Day	Time	m
1 TH	0519 1102 1745 2349	3.6 1.5 3.7 1.1	16 F	0607 1135 1813	3.2 1.7 3.4
2 F	0643 1223 1903	3.6 1.5 3.7	17 SA	0015 0714 1243 1919	1.5 3.3 1.7 3.5
3 SA	0105 0757 1336 2012	1.0 3.7 1.4 3.9	18 SU	0121 0811 1343 2014	1.4 3.4 1.6 3.6
4 SU	0211 0900 1435 2112	0.8 3.8 1.2 4.0	19 M	0213 0859 1431 2100	1.2 3.6 1.4 3.7
5 M	0306 0953 1525 2204	0.6 4.0 1.0 4.2	20 TU	0254 0938 1509 2139	1.0 3.8 1.2 3.9
6 TU	0352 1038 1609 2249	0.5 4.1 0.8 4.2	21 W	0328 1012 1544 2214	0.8 3.9 1.0 4.0
7 W	0434 1117 1649 ● 2328	0.5 4.1 0.7 4.2	22 TH	0400 1043 1618 2250	0.7 4.0 0.8 4.1
8 TH	0513 1150 1728	0.5 4.1 0.7	23 F	0434 1116 1655 ○ 2329	0.6 4.1 0.6 4.2
9 F	0003 0549 1222 1805	4.1 0.6 4.0 0.7	24 SA	0511 1153 1735	0.5 4.2 0.6
10 SA	0040 0625 1256 1845	4.0 0.7 4.0 0.8	25 SU	0012 0550 1236 1819	4.2 0.6 4.2 0.6
11 SU	0119 0703 1335 1927	3.9 0.9 4.0 0.9	26 M	0100 0635 1323 1909	4.1 0.7 4.2 0.6
12 M	0203 0745 1417 2014	3.8 1.1 3.9 1.0	27 TU	0152 0726 1415 2005	4.0 0.9 4.1 0.7
13 TU	0251 0832 1503 2106	3.6 1.3 3.7 1.2	28 W	0250 0824 1512 2108	3.9 1.1 4.0 0.9
14 W	0346 0927 1555 2204	3.4 1.5 3.6 1.4	29 TH	0355 0930 1616 2216	3.8 1.3 3.9 1.0
15 TH	0453 1029 1700 ◐ 2307	3.3 1.7 3.5 1.5	30 F	0507 1042 1727 ◑ 2327	3.7 1.4 3.9 1.0

DECEMBER

Day	Time	m	Day	Time	m
1 SA	0622 1156 1839	3.7 1.5 3.9	16 SU	0614 1147 1811	3.3 1.7 3.4
2 SU	0039 0732 1308 1948	1.0 3.7 1.4 3.9	17 M	0018 0716 1247 1913	1.4 3.4 1.6 3.5
3 M	0145 0835 1410 2050	0.9 3.8 1.3 4.0	18 TU	0115 0809 1341 2009	1.3 3.5 1.5 3.6
4 TU	0243 0931 1505 2146	0.8 3.9 1.1 4.0	19 W	0206 0855 1429 2059	1.2 3.7 1.3 3.7
5 W	0333 1019 1553 2235	0.8 4.0 1.0 4.0	20 TH	0250 0937 1512 2145	1.0 3.8 1.1 3.9
6 TH	0416 1100 1636 2317	0.7 4.0 0.9 4.0	21 F	0332 1016 1554 2230	0.8 4.0 0.8 4.0
7 F	0456 1134 1716 ● 2353	0.8 4.0 0.9 4.0	22 SA	0413 1056 1637 ○ 2315	0.7 4.2 0.6 4.1
8 SA	0533 1205 1754	0.8 4.0 0.9	23 SU	0455 1138 1722	0.6 4.3 0.5
9 SU	0026 0607 1238 1832	3.9 0.9 4.0 0.9	24 M	0001 0537 1222 1809	4.2 0.6 4.3 0.4
10 M	0103 0643 1314 1911	3.8 1.0 4.0 0.9	25 TU	0050 0623 1310 1859	4.2 0.7 4.3 0.4
11 TU	0143 0721 1353 1952	3.7 1.1 3.9 1.0	26 W	0142 0713 1402 1954	4.1 0.8 4.3 0.5
12 W	0225 0802 1435 2037	3.6 1.2 3.9 1.1	27 TH	0238 0808 1458 2052	4.0 1.0 4.2 0.6
13 TH	0312 0849 1520 2125	3.5 1.4 3.7 1.2	28 F	0339 0909 1558 2154	3.9 1.1 4.1 0.8
14 F	0405 0944 1610 2219	3.4 1.5 3.6 1.3	29 SA	0444 1013 1703 ◑ 2258	3.7 1.3 4.0 0.9
15 SA	0507 1044 1707 ◐ 2318	3.3 1.7 3.5 1.4	30 SU	0552 1122 1811	3.7 1.4 3.9
			31 M	0005 0659 1233 1919	1.0 3.6 1.4 3.8

Chart Datum: 0·20 metres above Ordnance Datum (Dublin). HAT is 4·5 metres above Chart Datum.

9.12.10 DUN LAOGHAIRE

Dublin (Port ent) **53°18'·16N 06°07'·68W** ❁❁❁◊◊◊✿✿

CHARTS AC 1468, 1415, 1447, 5621; IMRAY C61, C62

TIDES +0042 Dover; ML 2·4; Duration 0640

Standard Port DUBLIN (NORTH WALL) (⟵)

Times				Height (metres)			
High Water		Low Water		MHWS	MHWN	MLWN	MLWS
0000	0700	0000	0500	4·1	3·4	1·5	0·7
1200	1900	1200	1700				
Differences DUBLIN BAR and DUN LAOGHAIRE							
0000	0000	+0002	+0003	0·0	+0·1	0·0	0·0
GREYSTONES (53°09'N 06°04'W)							
−0008	−0008	−0008	−0008	−0·5	−0·4	ND	ND

SHELTER Excellent. Breakwaters within main hbr protect 800+ berth marina from ferry wash. Ⓥ berths on end of pontoons or as directed. Additional berths inside Western Marina Breakwater. All YCs advertise Ⓥs and/or pontoon berths.

NAVIGATION Dun Laoghaire WPT 53°18'·40N 06°07'·00W, 240°/0·47M to ent. Accessible H24. Keep clear of commercial traffic turning off St Michael's Pier. Beware drying rks around E Pier Hd.

LIGHTS AND MARKS RoRo Berth 2 x Fl.W = 'Large vessel under way; small craft keep clear of No 1 Fairway (out to 600m seaward of ent). Traffic signals (Fl W) repeated at head of E Marina Breakwater. Marina Breakwater Hds marked by sync lts Fl G 2s and Fl R 2s.

COMMUNICATIONS (Code 01) MRCC 6620922/3; Coast/Cliff Rescue Service 2803900; ⊜ 2803992; ☼ 1550 123855; Police 6665000; Dr 2859244; Ⓗ 2806901. HM Dun Laoghaire 2801130.

Dun Laoghaire Hbr VHF Ch **14** 16 (H24); Marina Ch **M** M2 16; YCs Ch M. Dublin Coast Radio Stn 16 67 83.

FACILITIES **Dun Laoghaire Harbour Marina,** www.dlmarina.com ☎2020040; 800 ⊆ inc 20Ⓥ €3.50, €5.00<6hrs, (⛽ by card) ♿ 🗊 🚿 🚿 **(call on Ch M in advance)** ⚑ wi-fi.

Town ⛽ ⛵ ✕ Ⓔ ✉ ⓑ ACA 🛒 ✕ ☐ ⇌ ✈(Dublin).

YACHT CLUBS (E→W):

Irish National SC ☎28444195.

National YC ☎2805725, ▬ ⛵ ⛽ 🚿 ⚓(12t) ✕ ☐.

Royal St George YC ☎2801811, Boatman ☎2801208; ⊆ by prior agreement, €3.60, ▬ ⛵ ⛽ 🚿 ⚓(5t) ✕ ☐.

Royal Irish YC ☎2809452, ⛵ ▬ ⛽ 🚿 ⚓(5t) ✕ ☐.

Dun Laoghaire Motor YC ☎2801371, ▬ ⊆ ⛽ ✕ ☐.

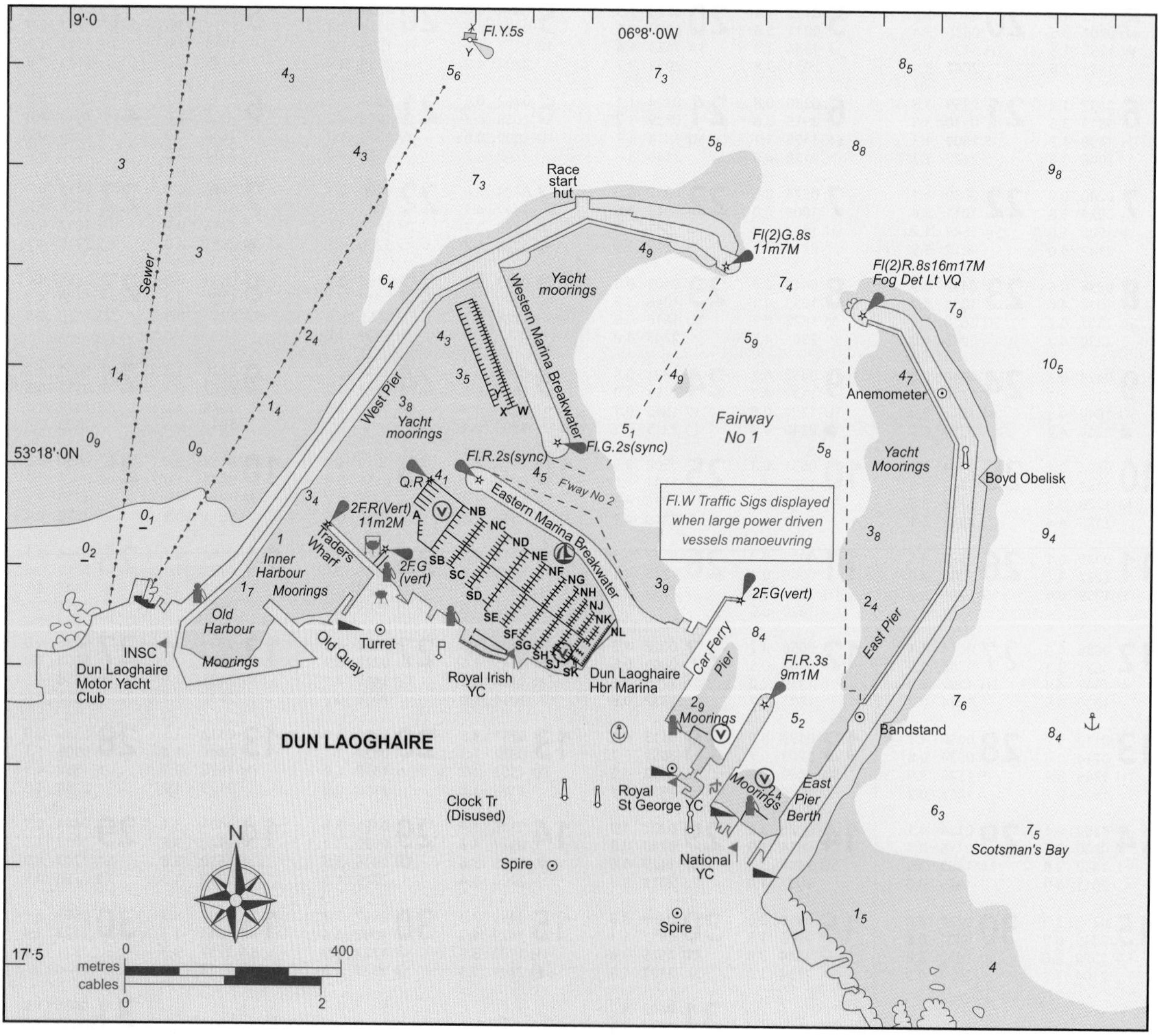

9.12.11 GREYSTONES

Greystones 53°09′·12N 06°03′·80W

CHARTS AC 1468, 633, 5621; Imray C61

TIDES +0042 Dover; ML 2·4; Duration 0640

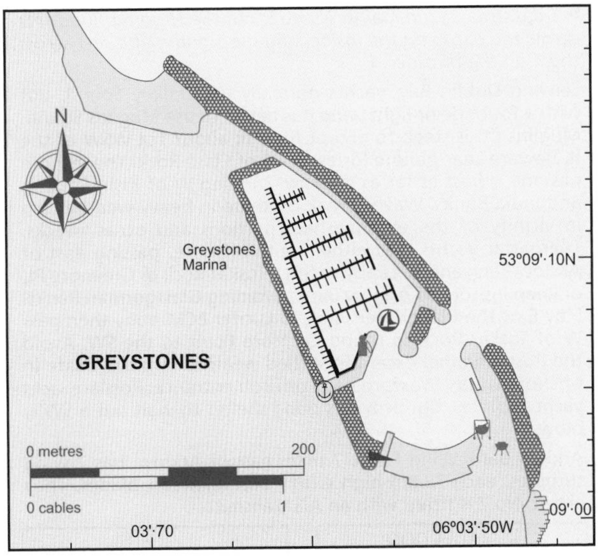

Standard Port DUBLIN (NORTH WALL) (⟵)

Times				Height (metres)			
High Water		Low Water		MHWS	MHWN	MLWN	MLWS
0000	0700	0000	0500	4·1	3·4	1·5	0·7
1200	1900	1200	1700				
GREYSTONES (53°09′N 06°04′W)							
–0008	–0008	–0008	–0008	–0·5	–0·4	ND	ND

SHELTER Midway between Dun Laoghaire and Wicklow, good shelter in all but winds from N–E. Harbour ent open to large seas in strong NE'ly winds, with large scend in outer basin, which can become untenable. Berthing on 3 of 5 pontoons in >5m. If marina full, in good weather ⚓ possible in bay N of hbr in 5-6m.

NAVIGATION If approaching from S beware Moulditch Bk marked by lit buoy Fl R 10s and sewerage outfall with Y SPM Fl Y 5s. Hbr accessible H24. Deepest water in approach lies close NE of the entrance. Pass between moles of outer hbr on a SSW'ly heading. Keeping N mole on starboard hand, a tight turn around its end gives access to the narrow ent to the marina with 'A' pontoon directly ahead.

LIGHTS AND MARKS Entrance marked by lateral bns on pier hds; Fl G 5s and Fl R 5s respectively.

COMMUNICATIONS (Code 01) MRCC 6620922/3; Coast/Cliff Rescue Service 2803900; ⊖ 2803992; 1550 123855. HM Greystones 287 3131, 086 2718161.

Marina Ch 37, **M**; Dublin Coast Radio Stn 16 67 83.

FACILITIES **Greystones Marina**, info@greystonesharbourmarina.ie ☎353 (086) 2718161; 100, Ⓥ facilities tbc in N Basin.

Town ACA.

9.12.12 WICKLOW

Wicklow **52°58′·98N 06°02′·70W**

CHARTS AC 1468, 633, 5621; Imray C61

TIDES –0010 Dover; ML 1·7; Duration 0640

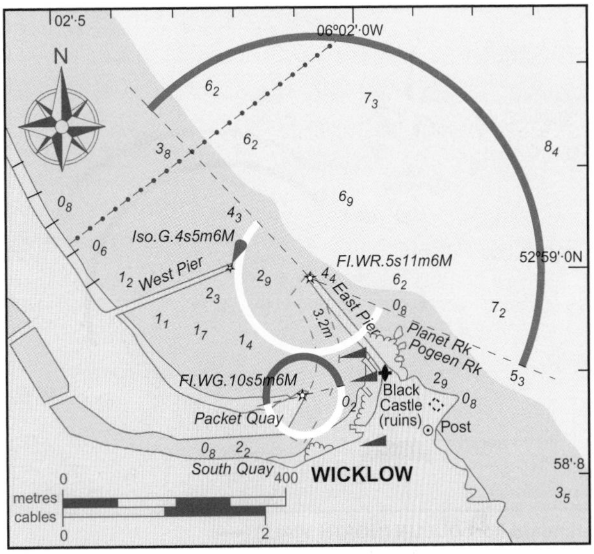

Standard Port DUBLIN (NORTH WALL) (⟵)

Times				Height (metres)			
High Water		Low Water		MHWS	MHWN	MLWN	MLWS
0000	0700	0000	0500	4·1	3·4	1·5	0·7
1200	1900	1200	1700				
Differences WICKLOW							
–0019	–0019	–0024	–0026	–1·4	–1·1	–0·4	0·0

SHELTER Very safe, access H24. Outer hbr is open to NE winds which cause a swell. Moorings in NW of hbr belong to SC and may not be used without permission. 4 berths on E Pier (2·5m) are convenient except in strong winds NW to NE, with fender boards/ladders provided. W pier is not recommended. ⚓ in hbr is restricted by ships' turning circle. Inner hbr (river) gives excellent shelter in 2·5m on N and S Quays, which are used by FVs. Packet Quay is for ships (2·5m), but may be used if none due; fender board needed. Yachts should berth on N or S quays as directed and/or space available.

NAVIGATION WPT 52°59′·20N 06°01′·80W, 220°/0·27M to ent. Appr presents no difficulty; keep in the R sector of the E pier lt to avoid Planet Rk and Pogeen Rk.

LIGHTS AND MARKS W pier head lt, Iso G 4s, is shown H24. ☆ Fl WG 10s on Packet Quay hd is vis 076°-G-256°-W-076°.

COMMUNICATIONS (Code 0404) MRCC (01) 6620922; Cliff Rescue Service 086 8686009; ⊖ 67222; Police 60140; Dr 67381. HM 67455.

Ch 12, **14**, 16. Wicklow SC Ch M 16 (occas).

FACILITIES **East Pier, S and N Quays,** €14.00/craft (bulk: see HM). **Wicklow SC** ☎67526, (except LWS).

Service Kos. **Town** Ⓑ ✈(Dublin).

9.12.13 ARKLOW

Wicklow **52°47′·60N 06°08′·20W**

CHARTS AC 1468, 633, 5621; Imray C61

TIDES –0150 Dover; ML 1·0; Duration 0640

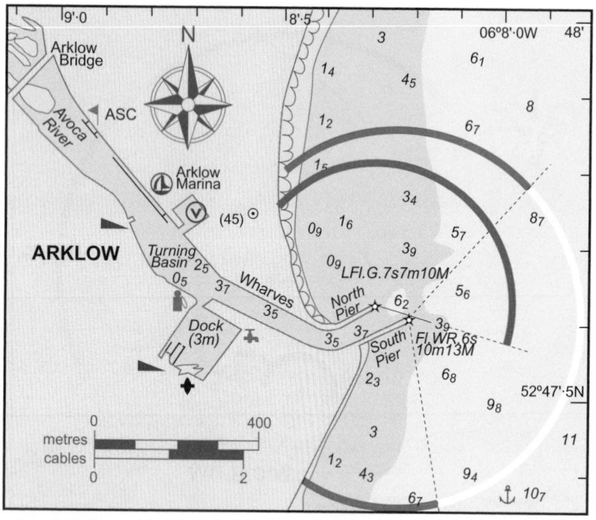

Standard Port DUBLIN (NORTH WALL) (⟵)

Times				Height (metres)			
High Water		Low Water		MHWS	MHWN	MLWN	MLWS
0000	0700	0000	0500	4·1	3·4	1·5	0·7
1200	1900	1200	1700				
Differences ARKLOW (Note small Range)							
–0315	–0201	–0140	–0134	–2·7	–2·2	–0·6	–0·1
COURTOWN							
–0328	–0242	–0158	–0138	–2·8	–2·4	–0·5	0·0

SHELTER Good, access H24. **Arklow Roadstone Hbr**, 1M S of Arklow, is not for yachts.

- Strong E'ly winds make the entrance unsafe and cause significant turbulence in the river.

A 60 berth marina lies on NE side of river. New pontoon in sheltered dock S of the river. Good ⚓ in bay; avoid whelk pots. One mooring in 1.2m at ASC quay. Moorings on SE wall of Dock (ent is 13·5m wide; 3m depth) in perfect shelter, but amidst FVs.

NAVIGATION WPT 52°47′·60N 06°07′·50W, 270°/0·40M to ent. No navigational dangers, but beware ebb setting SE across hbr ent; give S pierhd a wide berth. Ent is difficult without power, due to blanking by piers. 3kn speed limit. Night entry, see below. Caution: Upriver of Dock ent keep to NE side of river.

LIGHTS AND MARKS No ldg lts/marks, see 9.12.4 and chartlet Conspic factory chy 2·5ca NW of piers.

- Beware the Pier Hd lts are very difficult to see due to powerful orange flood lts near the root of both piers shining E/ENE onto them (to assist pilotage of departing shipping).
- Best advice to visitors is to approach from the NE with R sector just showing, or enter by day.

COMMUNICATIONS (Code 0402) MRCC (01) 6620922/3; ⊖ 67222; Cliff Rescue Service 32430; RNLI 32901; Police 32304; Dr 32421. HM 32466.

Marina Ch 16 12 (HJ); Arklow SC Ch 10.

DUN LAOGHAIRE TO TUSKAR ROCK

(AC 1468, 1787) From Dublin to Carnsore Pt as a cruising area, hbr facilities are being improved. The shallow offshore banks cause dangerous overfalls and dictate the route which is sheltered from the W winds.

▶ *Tidal streams run mainly N and S, but the N-going flood sets across the banks on the inside, and the S-going ebb sets across them on the outside.* ◀

Leaving Dublin Bay, yachts normally use Dalkey Sound, but with a foul tide or light wind it is better to use Muglins Sound. Muglins (lt) is steep-to except for a rk about 1ca WSW of the lt. Beware Leac Buidhe (dries) 1ca E of Clare Rock. The inshore passage is best as far as Wicklow running W of Kish, Codling and India Banks. Waves break on these in heavy weather esp in vicinity of the extremeshaol portions and occas wrecks. Thereafter yachts may either route offshore, passing east of Arklow Bank and its Lanby to fetch Tuskar Rock or Greenore Pt, or keep inshore of Arklow Bank, avoiding Glassgorman Banks. Stay E of the Blackwater Bank to Lucifer ECM buoy then pass W of Tuskar Rock to round Carnsore Point to the SW. Avoid the Rusk Channel except in settled weather. Arklow is safe in offshore winds; Wexford has a difficult entrance. Rosslare lacks yacht facilities, but provides good shelter to wait out a SW'ly blow.

Arklow Bank Wind Farm, 7 miles east of Arklow, has 7 wind turbines, each 72.8m high with 104m diameter blades. They are lit, No 7 is fitted with an AIS transmitter.

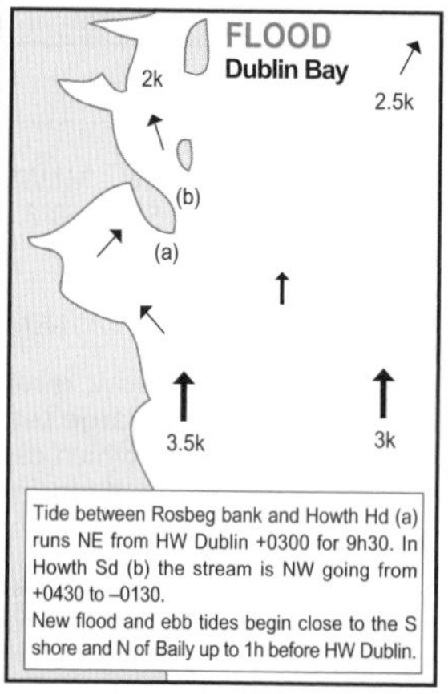

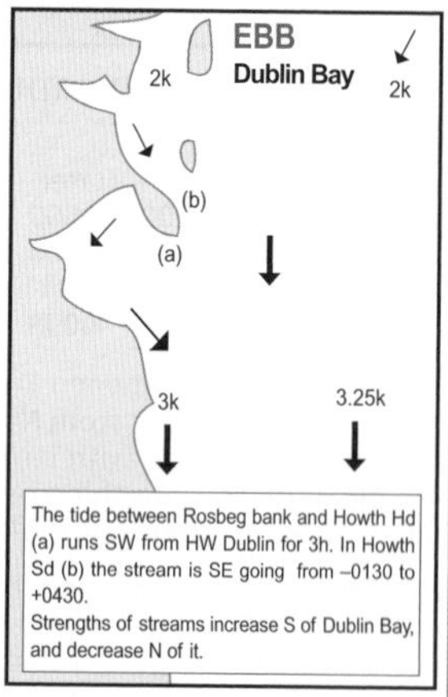

FACILITIES **Dock** €15.00/craft (2nd day free), use WC/showers in LB Ho, water (Dock ent, HO); **Arklow SC** (NE bank, 500m upriver) showers.

Marina ☎087 258 8078, 60 berths inc visitors €3·35; water, electricity, repairs, crane (20t) Kos.

Town ☎ limited, post office, bank, supermarket, restaurant, launderette, @, rail, ✈(Dublin).

MINOR HARBOURS S OF ARKLOW

COURTOWN, Wexford, **52°38′·55N 06°13′·50W**. AC 1787. 9.6M S of Arklow is feasible in settled weather and offshore winds. Caution: 10m wide ent; only 1m (maintained by local YC) at MLWS due to silting. Mooring on E wall or pick up vacant mooring.

POLDUFF PIER, Wexford, **52°34′·15N 06°11′·97W**. AC 1787. 14M S of Arklow. Pier, extends 100m NE from shore. NW side of pier has slipway from shore and 1m depth alongside. Local moorings W of pier. Good shelter for small boats in S to W winds. Swell in winds E of S. Appr in daylight only. Appr is clear from NE to E. Rks extend from shore E'ward 200m N of pier but steering along line of pier will clear them. Pub near pier. **Village** (Ballygarrett) 1·25M W.

9.12.14 WEXFORD

Wexford **52°20'·10N 06°27'·00W**

CHARTS AC 1787, 1772, 5621; Imray C61

TIDES –0450 Dover; ML 1·3; Duration 0630

Standard Port COBH (⟶)

Times				**Height (metres)**			
High Water		Low Water		MHWS	MHWN	MLWN	MLWS
0500	1100	0500	1100	4·1	3·2	1·3	0·4
1700	2300	1700	2300				
Differences WEXFORD							
+0126	+0126	+0118	+0108	–2·1	–1·7	–0·3	+0·1

SHELTER 250m of ⌒ available just below bridge though silting occurs in 50m closest to the bridge. Sheltered ⚓ off town quays in 2·3m, but streams are strong. Ⓐs are provided by WHBTC, close N of Ballast Bank (☎9122039 or Ch 16/69) or proceed to quays. FVs use a new quay on E bank with ⛽ and space for tanker. Close upstream below the bridge is an all-tide ⌞ and trailer park.

NAVIGATION Visitors are strongly advised to obtain latest information from www.wexfordharbour.com another site www.wexfordharbour.info is run by sailing enthusiasts as is WHBTC.

- Entry is hazardous in strong winds between SE and NE when the sea breaks on the bar.
- For strangers best entry is HW±2. It is difficult at any time for vessels with a draught >1.3m.
- Maintain a course on the rhumb line between marks as channel is narrow in places. Beware the S training wall (covers) and pass well S of Black Man SHM Bn at end of N training wall.
- To Wexford Bar SWM (52°19'·14N 06°19·39W): make good 214°/2·7M from North Long Buoy; from S make good 353°/3·4M from West Holdens Buoy. SWM is on 10m contour and marks the start of the buoyed channel to Wexford.

LIGHTS AND MARKS The narrow channel frequently shifts and marks are moved accordingly; positions on the chartlet are not reliable. They are sequentially numbered from 2–30. Outer channel buoys Nos 2–9 in position from Apr–Oct are removed seasonally; see www.wexfordharbour.com The 2 church spires / Opera Ho (conspic) at Wexford give useful general orientation. There are no ldg lts. Buoyage continues upstream from Wexford Br.

COMMUNICATIONS (Code 053) MRCC (01) 6620922/3; ⊜ 9133116; Police 9122333; Dr 9122524; Ⓗ 9142233. Wexford Hbr BC 9122039. HM 9122300, email: harbourmaster@wexfordcoco.ie.

Wexford Hbr listening watch VHF 16, 09 (HO).

FACILITIES HM Capt Paul Murphy, based in Ballast Office on Crescent Quay, is the Marine Officer responsible for all Co. Wexford harbours except Rosslare Europort.

Wexford Quays ⌞ ⌒(free) ⛽ delivery by road tanker.

Wexford Harbour Boat & Tennis Club, www.whbtc.ie ☎086 8131783, ⌞ (5t).

Town ✉ Ⓑ ⇌ ✈ (Waterford).

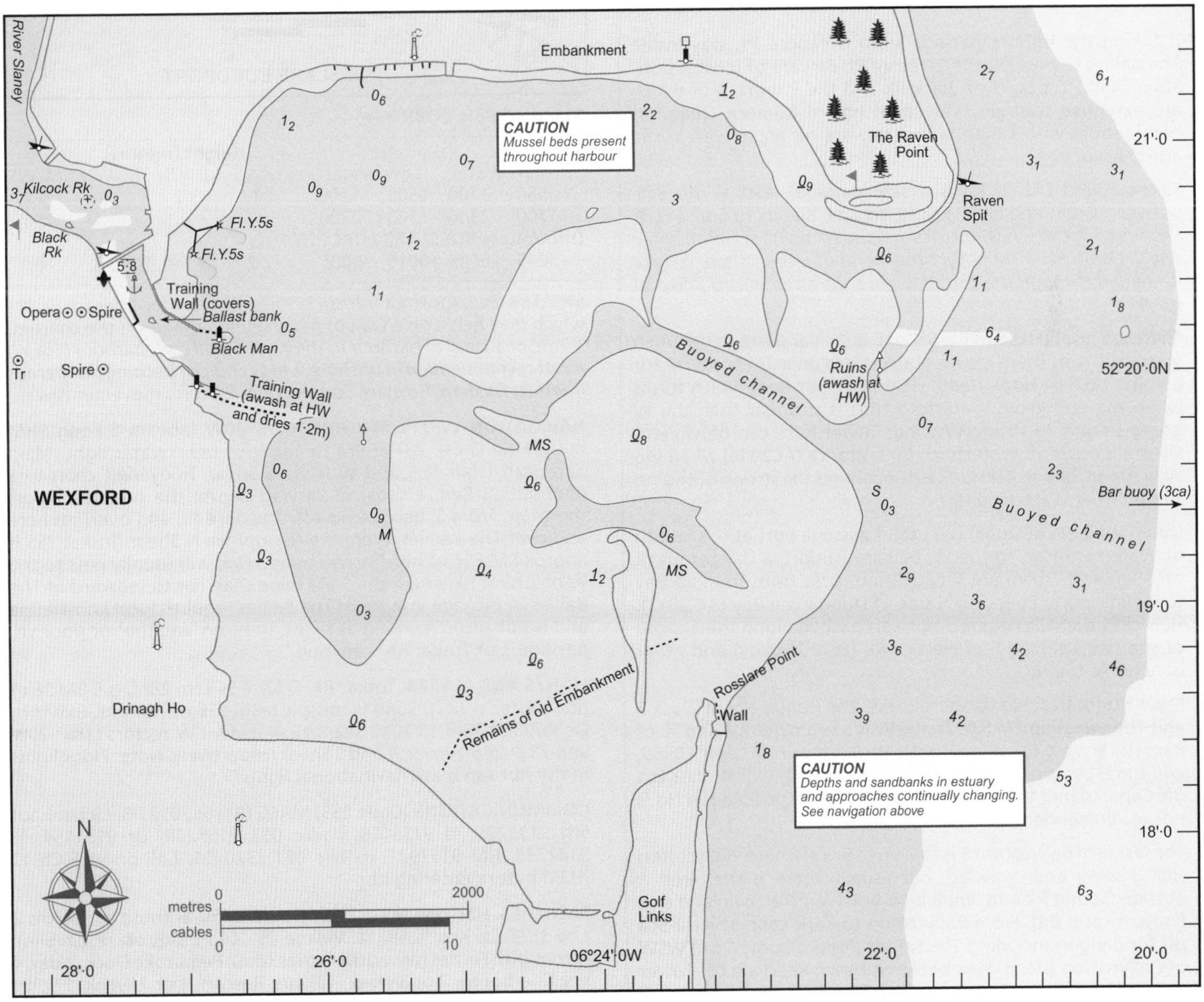

TUSKAR ROCK TO COBH

(AC 2049) Dangerous rks lie up to 2ca NW and 6½ca SSW of Tuskar Rk and there can be a dangerous race off Carnsore Pt. In bad weather or poor visibility, use the Inshore Traffic Zone of the Tuskar Rock TSS, passing to seaward of Tuskar Rk (lt), the Barrels ECM lt buoy and Coningbeg buoy.

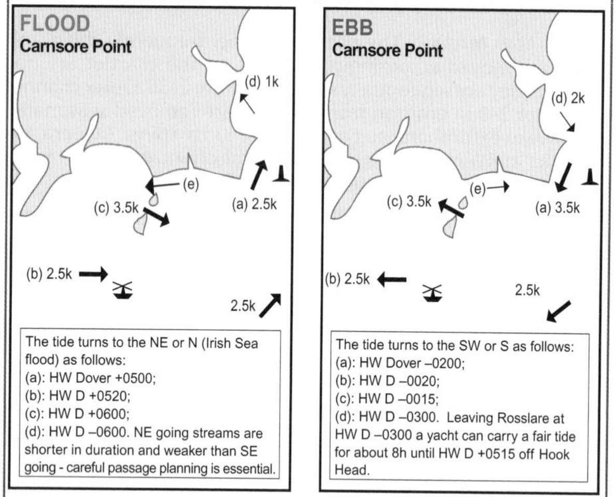

FLOOD
Carnsore Point
(d) 1k
(e)
(c) 3.5k
(a) 2.5k
(b) 2.5k
2.5k
The tide turns to the NE or N (Irish Sea flood) as follows:
(a): HW Dover +0500;
(b): HW D +0520;
(c): HW D +0600;
(d): HW D –0600. NE going streams are shorter in duration and weaker than SE going - careful passage planning is essential.
EBB
Carnsore Point
(d) 2k
(e)
(c) 3.5k
(a) 3.5k
(b) 2.5k
2.5k
The tide turns to the SW or S as follows:
(a): HW Dover –0200;
(b): HW D –0020;
(c): HW D –0015;
(d): HW D –0300. Leaving Rosslare at HW D –0300 a yacht can carry a fair tide for about 8h until HW D +0515 off Hook Head.

NOTE: The tide turns on St Patrick's Bridge (e) up to 2 hours earlier than in Saltee Sound

If taking the inshore passage from Greenore Pt, stay inside The Bailies to pass 2ca off Carnsore Pt. Beware of lobster pots. Steer WSW to pass N of Black Rk and the Bohurs, S of which are extensive overfalls. The small hbr of Kilmore Quay has been rebuilt with a marina, but beware rks and shoals in the approaches.

Saltee Sound (AC 2740) is a safe passage, least width 3ca, between Great and Little Saltee, conspic islands to S and N. ▶ *Sebber Bridge extends 7½ca N from the NE point of Great Saltee and Jackeen Rk is 1M NW of the S end of Little Saltee, so care is needed through the sound, where the stream runs 3·5kn at sp.* ◀

There are several rks S of the Saltees, but clear passage between many of them. There are no obstructions on a direct course for a point 1M S of Hook Head, clear of Tower Race which forms when the ebb (from Waterford Hbr) is stronger than the W going stream. In strong W winds Tower Race can be violent. Overfalls occur off Waterford Hbr entrance (AC2046) when the W'ly stream begins off Hook Hd and meets the strong outgoing stream from Waterford Hbr.

Dunmore East (AC 2046) is a useful passage port at the mouth of Waterford Hbr. To the W, beware Falskirt, a dangerous rk off Swines Pt. There are few offlying rocks from Tramore Bay to Ballinacourty Pt on the N side of Dungarvan Bay (AC 2017). Helvick is a small sheltered hbr approached along the S shore of the bay, keeping S of Helvick Rk (ECM lt buoy) and other dangers to the N.

Mine Hd (lt) has two dangerous rks, The Rogue about 2½ca E and The Longship 1M SW. To the W is a subm'gd rk 100m SE of Ram Hd. ▶ *Here the W-going stream starts at HW Cobh +0230, and the E-going at HW Cobh –0215, sp rates 1·5kn.* ◀ Pass 2ca off Capel Island; the sound between it and Knockadoon Hd is not recommended.

The N side of Ballycotton B is foul up to 5ca offshore. Ballycotton Hbr is small and crowded, but usually there is sheltered ⚓ outside. Sound Rk and Small Is lie between the mainland and Ballycotton Is (lit). From Ballycotton to Cork keep at least 5ca off for dangers including The Smiths (PHM lt buoy) 1·5M WSW of Ballycotton Island. Pass between Hawk Rk, close off Power Hd, and Pollock Rk (PHM lt buoy) 1.25M SE.

9.12.15 ROSSLARE

Dublin **52°15'·30N 06°20'·90W** ❁❁❁◊✿✿

CHARTS AC 1787, 1772, 5621; Imray C61, C57

TIDES –0510 Dover; ML 1·1; Duration 0640

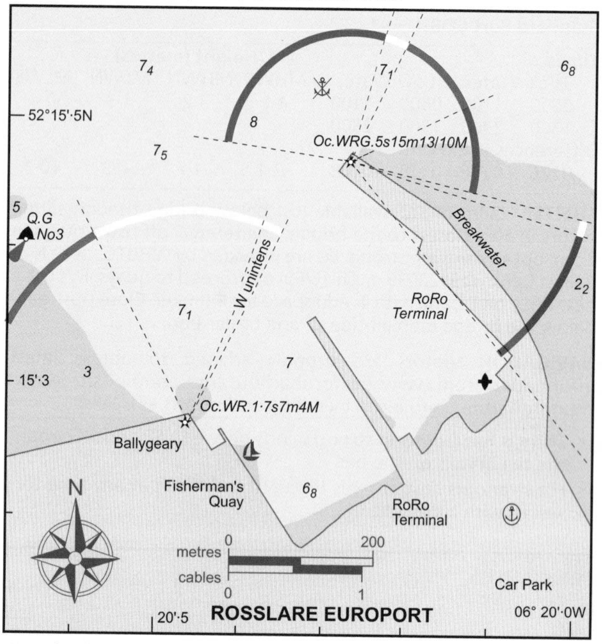

52°15'·5N
15'·3
Oc.WRG.5s15m13/10M
Breakwater
Q.G
No3
W unintens
RoRo Terminal
Oc.WR.1·7s7m4M
Ballygeary
Fisherman's Quay
RoRo Terminal
N
metres
cables
200
Car Park
20'·5
ROSSLARE EUROPORT
06° 20'·0W

Standard Port COBH (⟶)

Times				Height (metres)			
High Water		Low Water		MHWS	MHWN	MLWN	MLWS
0500	1100	0500	1100	4·1	3·2	1·3	0·4
1700	2300	1700	2300				
Differences ROSSLARE EUROPORT							
+0045	+0035	+0015	–0005	–2·2	–1·8	–0·5	–0·1

SHELTER Passage shelter from SW'lies, but few facilities for yachts which may berth on E wall of marshalling area (⛵ on the chartlet, 3·7m), or ⚓ clear of harbour to the west. ***Small craft harbour (5ca W) is not recommended in onshore winds and can become dangerous if winds freshen.*** Rosslare Europort has 80 ferry movements/wk.

NAVIGATION WPT 52°14'·70N 06°15'·80W (abeam S Long SHM buoy, Fl(2) G 6s), 287°/2·9M to 1ca N of breakwater light. Main approach from E, S and W is via S Shear, buoyed/lit chan to S of Holden's Bed, a shoal of varying depth; the tide sets across the chan. From S, beware rks off Greenore Pt, and overfalls here and over The Baillies. From the N, appr via N Shear. Tuskar TSS is approx 8M ESE of hbr. Yachts, bound N/S, will usually pass to the W of Tuskar Rk where the 3·5M wide chan lies to seaward of The Bailies. A passage inshore of The Bailies requires local knowledge and is not recommended at night. In heavy weather or poor vis, passage E of Tuskar Rk is advised.

LIGHTS AND MARKS Tuskar Rk, Q (2) 7·5s 33m 28M, is 5·8M SE of hbr. Water tr (R lt, 35m) is conspic 0·8M SSE of hbr ent. Bkwtr lt, Oc WRG 5s 15m 13/10M, see 9.12.4. Its two W sectors (188°-208° and 283°-286°) cover N and S Shear respectively. Note: Floodlights in the hbr can mask navigational lights.

COMMUNICATIONS (Code 053) MRCC (01) 6620922/3; LB Lookout Stn 9133205; ⊜ 9133116; Police 053 9165200; Dr 9131154; Ⓗ 9142233. HM 9157921, mobile 087 2320251. Call on VHF Ch **12** (H24) before entering hbr.

FACILITIES Hbr Ops ☎9157929, No dues, ⛽ (hose on berths 2 and 3) Ⓟ Ⓓ Kos 🔧 ⚙ ⛵. **Village** 🛒 ✕ ☐ ✉ Ⓑ ⇄ ✈ (Dublin). **Ferries** Irish Ferries (www.irishferries.com): Pembroke Dock, 2/day, 4 hrs; Cherbourg, 2 or 3/week, 18½hrs; Roscoff, 1 or 2/week, 17½hrs (seasonal). Stena (www.stenaline.co.uk): Fishguard, 2/day, 1¾hrs.

9.12.16 KILMORE QUAY

Wexford **52°10'·25N 06°35'·15W**

CHARTS AC 2049, 2740, 5621; Imray C61, C57

TIDES –0535 Dover; ML No data; Duration 0605

Standard Port COBH (⟶)

Times				Height (metres)			
High Water		Low Water		MHWS	MHWN	MLWN	MLWS
0500	1100	0500	1100	4·1	3·2	1·3	0·4
1700	2300	1700	2300				
Differences BAGINBUN HEAD (5M NE of Hook Hd)							
+0003	+0003	–0008	–0008	–0·2	–0·1	+0·2	+0·2
GREAT SALTEE							
+0019	+0009	–0004	+0006	–0·3	–0·4	ND	ND
CARNSORE POINT							
+0029	+0019	–0002	+0008	–1·1	–1·0	ND	ND

SHELTER Excellent in marina (3m depth) with 0.8m below CD at LAT in ent. Hbr exposed to SE'lies. FVs berth on E and W piers close S of marina.

NAVIGATION WPT 52°09'·22N 06°35'·20W, E of SWM (Apr-Sep), 000°/1·0M to pier hd lt, E of ldg line. Great (57m) and Little (35m) Saltee Islands lie respectively 3M SSW and 1·7M S, of hbr, separated by Saltee Sound. Rk 0.9m on E edge of G sector 1M S of entrance.

From the E, safest appr initially is via Saltee Sound, then N to WPT. Caution: In bad weather seas break on the Bohurs and The Bore, rks 2M E of Saltee Islands.

Beware, particularly on E-going stream, Goose Rk (2·6m) close W of Little Saltee and Murroch's Rk (2·1m) 6ca NW of Little Saltee. St Patrick's Bridge, 650m E of the WPT, is a 300m wide E/W chan used by FVs and yachts, carrying < 2m; marked by PHM, Fl R 6s and SHM, Fl G 6s (Apr to mid-Sep). Care needed in strong SW winds when a standing wave can form.

From the W, appr is clear but keep at least 5ca off Forlorn Pt to avoid Forlorn Rk (1·5m).

LIGHTS AND MARKS See 9.12.4 and chartlet. **Note**: Ldg marks lead 008° W of safe G sector and lead close to 0.9m Rk on approach.

- From W, ldg lts are obsc'd by piers until S of hbr ent. Turn 90° port into hbr ent, just past ☆ QRG at W Quay Hd; do not overshoot into shoal water ahead. The R sectors of this ☆ QRG warn of Forlorn Rock and The Lings to W of the ldg line and shingle banks drying 0·6m close E of the ldg line.

A white-gabled church is conspic from afar, as are two 20m high flood lt pylons on the E quay.

COMMUNICATIONS (Code 053) MRCC (01) 6620922/3; Emergency/Dr/Police 999; ⊜ 9133741. HM 9129955, mob 087 9001037, assistant. marineofficer@wexfordcoco.ie.

VHF Ch 16, 09 (occas).

FACILITIES www.kilmorequaymarina.com or HM ☎(0800-2000) 20Ⓥ €2.50 (€25 min) (24/7) cycle hire.

Village 3M away, (Wexford 15M).

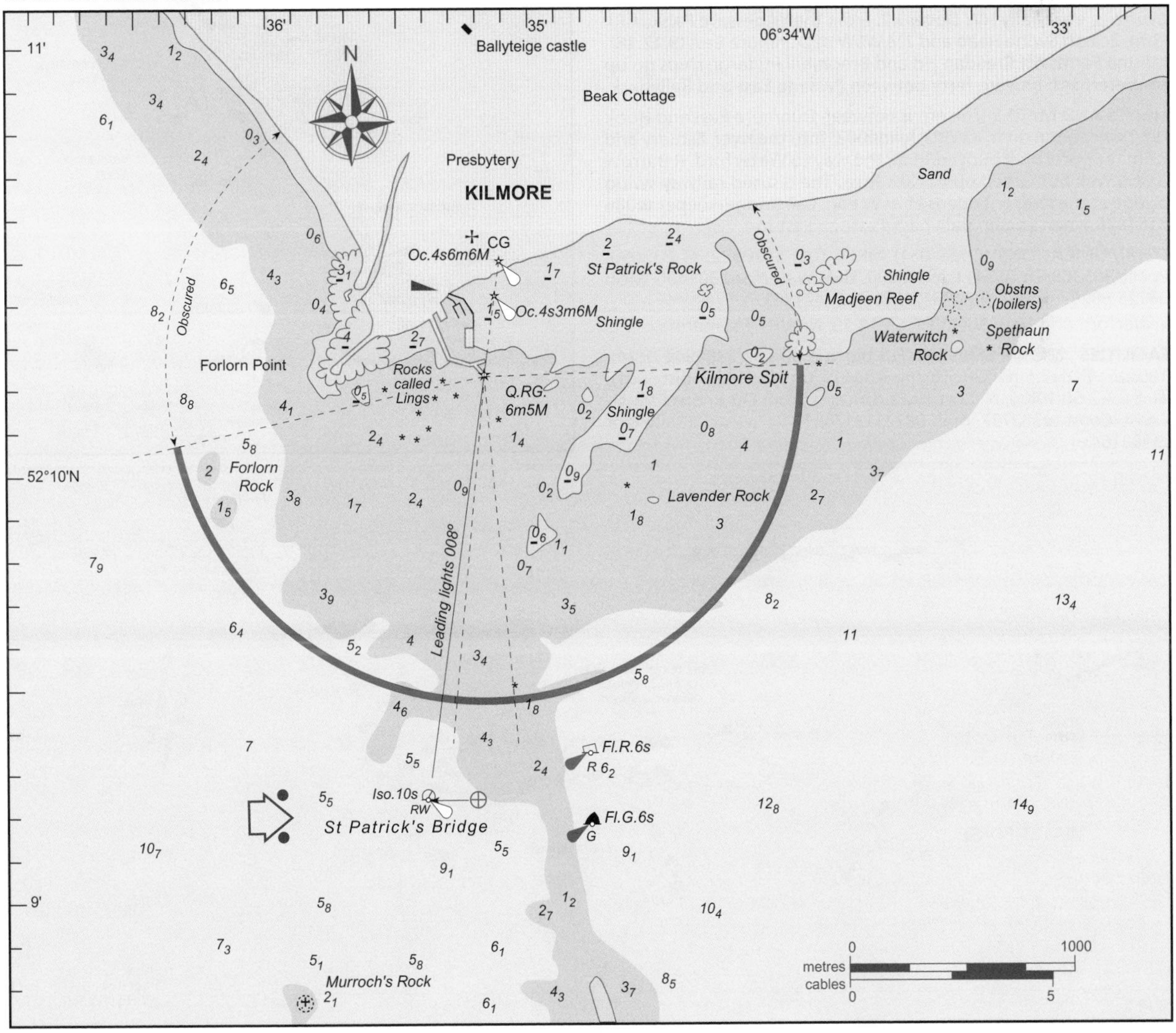

9.12.17 WATERFORD ❁❁❁◊◊✿✿

Waterford **52°15'·50N 07°06'·00W** ❁❁❁◊◊✿✿

CHARTS AC 2049, 2046, 5621, 5622; Imray C61, C57

TIDES –0520 Dover; ML 2·4; Duration 0605

Standard Port COBH (⟶)

Times				Height (metres)			
High Water		Low Water		MHWS	MHWN	MLWN	MLWS
0500	1100	0500	1100	4·1	3·2	1·3	0·4
1700	2300	1700	2300				
Differences WATERFORD							
+0053	+0032	+0015	+0100	+0·6	+0·6	+0·4	+0·2
CHEEKPOINT							
+0026	+0021	+0019	+0022	+0·5	+0·4	+0·3	+0·2
KILMOKEA POINT							
+0026	+0022	+0020	+0020	+0·2	+0·1	+0·1	+0·1
NEW ROSS							
+0100	+0030	+0055	+0130	+0·3	+0·4	+0·3	+0·4

SHELTER Very good on 4 long marina pontoons after Nanny pontoon (first one/private) on S bank, abeam cathedral spire. All tide access, but beware strong tidal stream. There are many excellent ⚓: off S side of R Suir in King's Chan (only to be entered W of Little Is); and up the R Barrow near Marsh Pt (about 2M S of New Ross) and ½M S of New Ross fixed bridge.

NAVIGATION WPT 52°06'·50N 06°58'·50W, 002°/6·7M to Dir lt at Duncannon. From the E, keep clear of Brecaun reef (2M NE of Hook Hd). Keep about 1·5M S of Hook Hd to clear Tower Race and overfalls, especially HW Dover ±2. From the W beware Falskirt Rk (3m), 2ca off Swine Head and 2M WSW of Dunmore East (9.12.18). Marine Farms off Creadan Hd and Broomhill Pt; large ships go up to Waterford; beware ferry between Passage East and Ballyhack.

LIGHTS AND MARKS The ent is between Dunmore East and Hook Hd. Duncannon dir lt, F WRG, leads 002° into the river. Estuary and R Suir are very well buoyed/lit all the way to Waterford. R Barrow is also well lit/marked up to New Ross. The disused railway swing bridge at the river ent opens at its W end. Call Bridge-keeper ☎086 8167826 when abeam Ballyhack/Passage East (no VHF).

COMMUNICATIONS (Code 051) MRCC (01) 6620922; ⊖ 832090; Police 305300; Dr 855411; Ⓗ848000. HMs Waterford 301400, Mob 08725 98297 or 08722 24961; New Ross 421303.

Waterford and New Ross VHF Ch **14** 16. No VHF for marina.

FACILITIES **Marina** ☎309900. For berth mob 087 2384944 (H24); 100 €16<7.6m>€20<10.7m>€30<13.7m (weekly discount); €2·50/10Kw, at HM's office, (from Dunmore East by Coast2Coast ☎382797, mob 0872512170) (Ballyhack ☎389164).

New Ross Marina newrossmarina@wexfordcoco.ie mob 086 388 9652; 66 €10 (€50/wk)<9.5m>€20 (€100/wk) < 10.5m>€30 (€120/wk)<13.5m; (as above) .

Waterford Boatyard (R Suir), ☎857755 or 086 1727502 will arrange Rice bridge lift on approach as will Waterford CC ☎076 1102020.

City All facilities, bus to Rosslare for UK ferries, ✈ (Waterford) for UK/Continent.

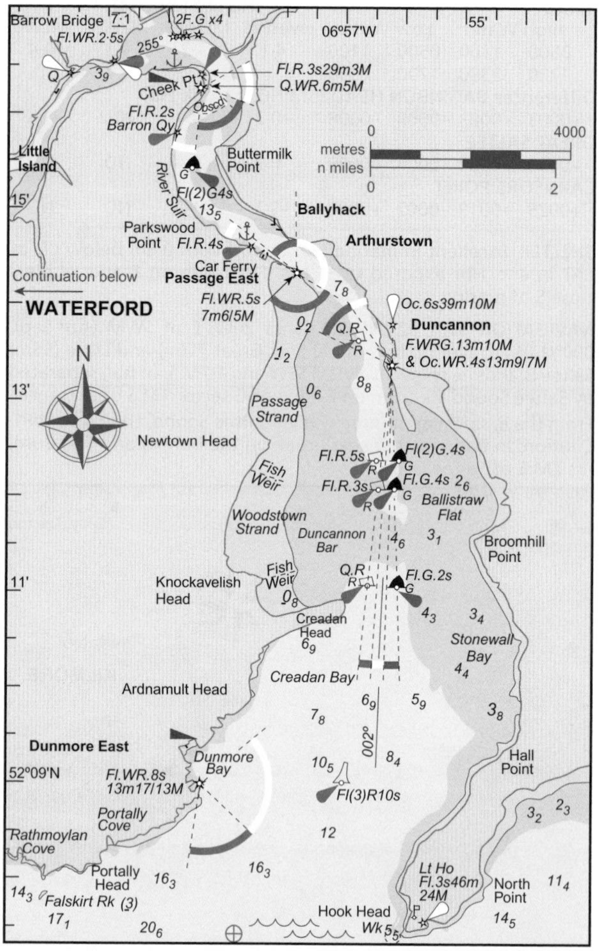

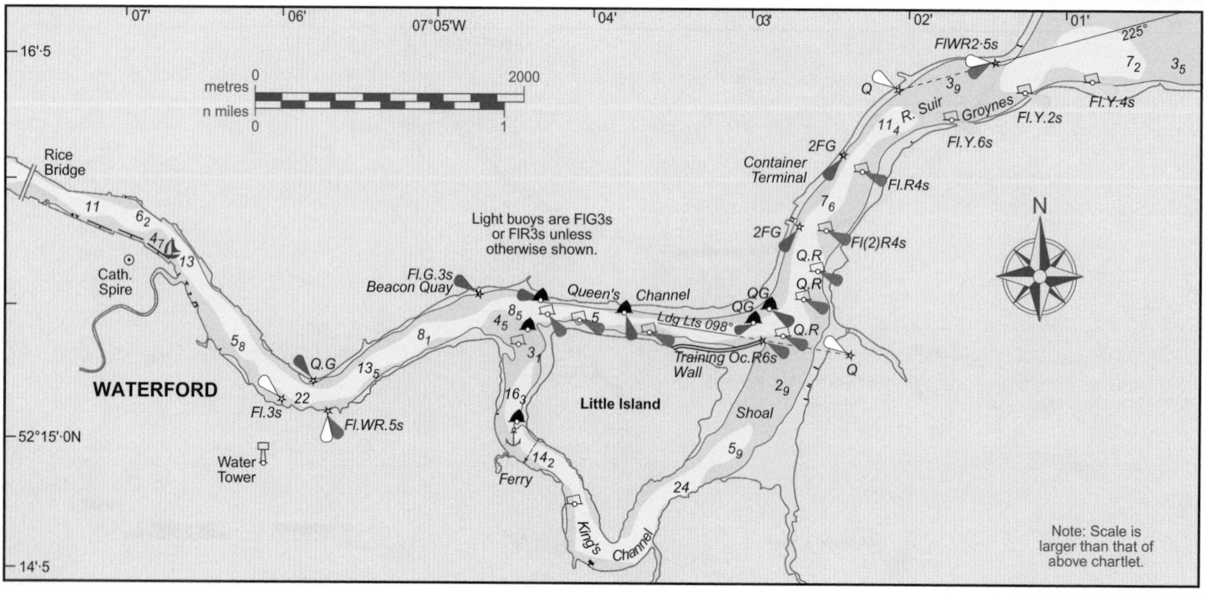

9.12.18 DUNMORE EAST

Waterford **52°08'·95N 06°59'·37W**

CHARTS AC 2049, 2046, 5621, 5622; Imray C61, C57

TIDES –0535 Dover; ML 2·4; Duration 0605

Standard Port COBH (⟶)

Times				Height (metres)			
High Water		Low Water		MHWS	MHWN	MLWN	MLWS
0500	1100	0500	1100	4·1	3·2	1·3	0·4
1700	2300	1700	2300				
Differences DUNMORE EAST							
+0008	+0003	0000	0000	+0·1	0·0	+0·1	+0·2
DUNGARVAN HARBOUR							
+0004	+0012	+0007	–0001	0·0	+0·1	–0·2	0·0

SHELTER Very good on (70m) pontoon on E pier in harbour. Moorings are open to the E or ⚓ N of the busy FV hbr. Large cruise liners ⚓ off. Waterford Harbour SC administer piers/moorings. In bad weather berth alongside FVs at W Wharf, clear of ice plant, in at least 2m or go up R Suir to Waterford (9.12.17).

NAVIGATION WPT 52°08'·00N, 06°58'·00W, 317°/1·2M to bkwtr lt. Enter under power. From E, stay 1·5M off Hook Hd to clear Tower Race; then steer for hbr in R sector of E pier lt ho. In calm weather Hook Hd can be rounded 1ca off. From W, beware Falskirt Rk (off Swines Hd, 2M WSW) dries $\underline{3}$·0m. By night track E for Hook Hd until in R sector of E pier lt, then alter to N.

LIGHTS AND MARKS Lts as chartlet 2 lit SHM in appr see 9.12.4.

COMMUNICATIONS (Code 051) MRCC (01) 6620922/3; Duty CG 0868 501764; Police 383112; ⊖ 832090; Dr 855411. HM 383166, mobile 0877 931705; Waterford Hbr SC 383230. Tugs: Fastnet shipping 051 832946, South East Tug Services 051 852819.

VHF Ch **14** 16 (Pilot Station ☎051 383119).

FACILITIES Hbr pier/pontoon (summer) €2/m/nt by road (Coast2Coast ☎051 382797, mob 0872512170) scrubbing grid, (220t).
Waterford Hbr SC if available, ✕; visitors welcome.
Village Kos ✉ Ⓒ ✕ ✈ (Waterford).

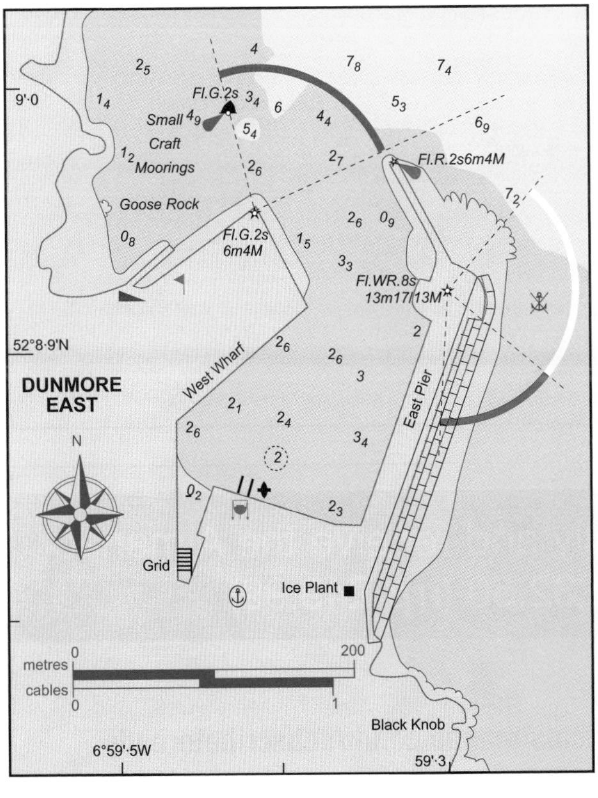

9.12.19 YOUGHAL

Cork **51°56'·54N 07°50'·20W**

CHARTS AC 2049, 2071, 5622; Imray C57

TIDES –0556 Dover; ML 2·1; Duration 0555

Standard Port COBH (⟶)

Times				Height (metres)			
High Water		Low Water		MHWS	MHWN	MLWN	MLWS
0500	1100	0500	1100	4·1	3·2	1·3	0·4
1700	2300	1700	2300				
Differences YOUGHAL							
0000	+0010	+0010	0000	–0·2	–0·1	–0·1	–0·1

SHELTER Good, but strong S'lies cause swell inside the hbr. Possible in 1.3m (drying patches just off quay); seasonal short-stay pontoon, with off landing jetty; 8 s (see chartlet), €20/night, owned by Aquatrek (call on Ch 69 or ☎086 8593482). ⚓ as chartlet; no dues. Strong tidal streams run throughout ⚓.

NAVIGATION WPT, East Bar, 51°55'·62N 07°48'·00W, 302°/1·8M to Fl WR 2·5s lt. Beware Blackball Ledge (ECM lt buoy) and Bar Rks (SCM lt buoy), both outside hbr ent in R sector of lt ho. From W, appr via West Bar (1·7m) is shorter route and E Bar has 2·0m.

- Both Bars in E to SSW'lies >F6 are likely to have dangerous seas.
- Beware salmon nets set during June-July, Mon-Thurs 0400-2100.
- Red Bank is continually changing, now further E than charted it closes off E chan at N end – obtain local knowledge.

LIGHTS AND MARKS See 9.12.4 and chartlet. Water tr is conspic from seaward; clock tr and tr within hbr. Upriver, 175° transit of convent belfry tr/town hall clears W of Red Bank.

COMMUNICATIONS (Code 024) MRCC (066) 9476109; Coast Guard 93252 or mob 0868 501769; ⊖ (021) 4325000; Police 92200; Dr 92702. HM Mobile 0872511143; Youghal Shipping 92577 (for poss).

VHF Ch 14 16 0900-1700 and when ships expected.

FACILITIES Services (☎Youghal Shipping).
Town ✉ Ⓑ ✕ Bus (Cork/W'ford) ✈(Cork).

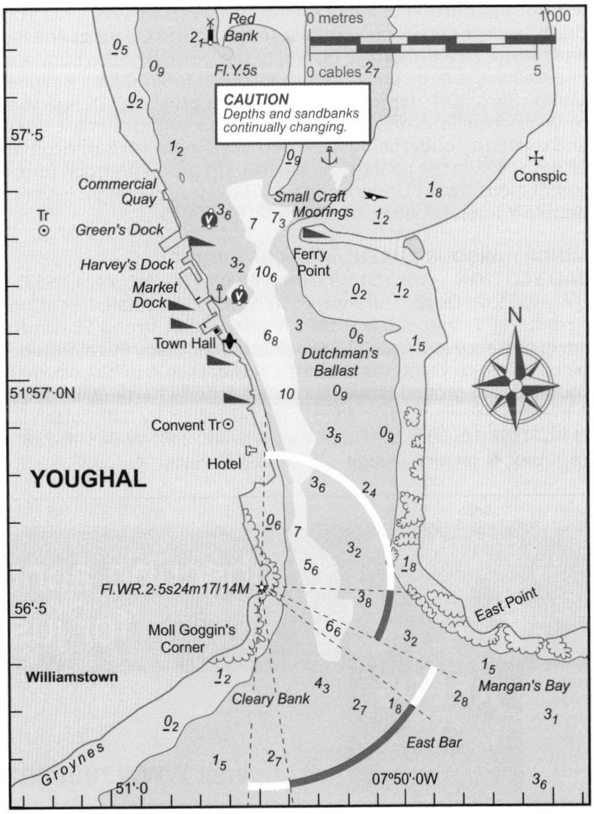

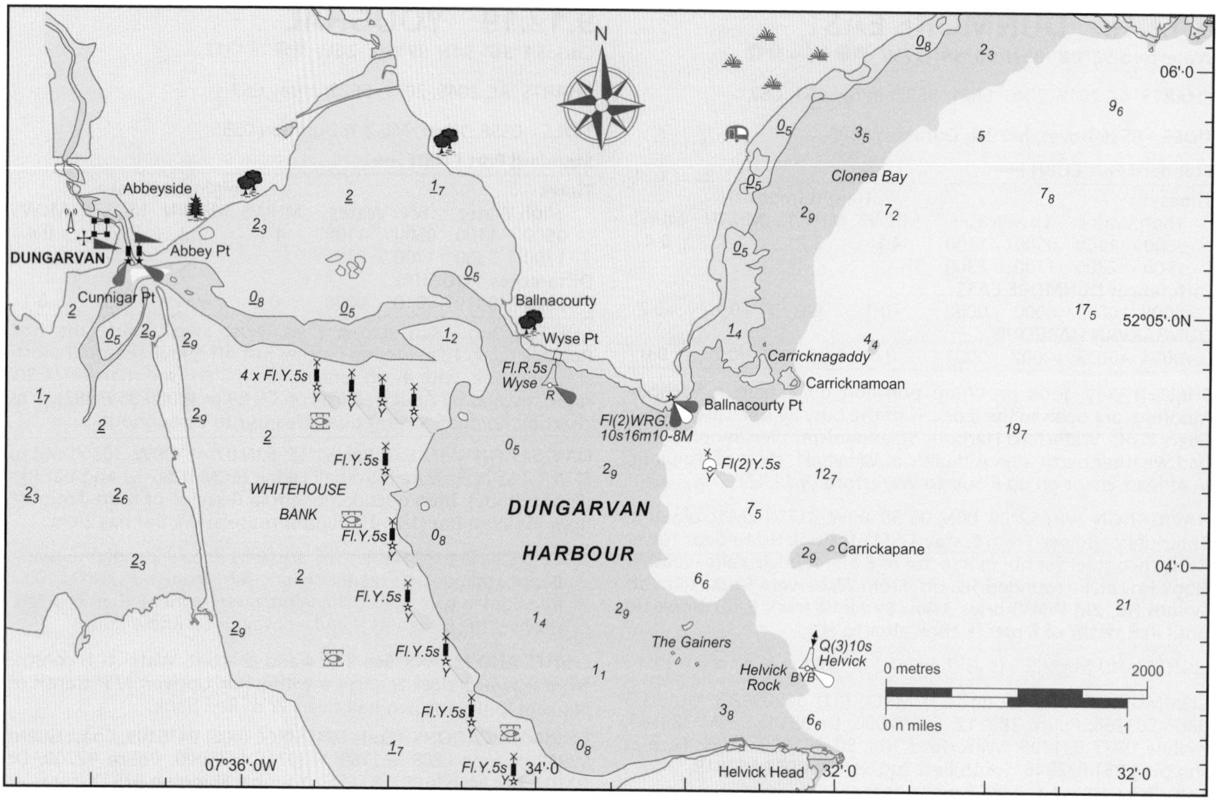

MINOR HARBOUR 16M ENE of YOUGHAL

DUNGARVAN BAY, Waterford, **52°05'·15N 07°36'·70W.** AC 2017, 5622. HW –0542 on Dover; Duration 0600. See 9.12.18. A large bay, drying to the W, entered between Helvick Hd to the S and Ballynacourty Pt to the N. Approach in W sector (274°-302°) of this lt to clear Carricknamoan islet to the N, and Carrickapane Rk and Helvick Rk (ECM buoy Q (3) 10s) to the S. 5ca W of this buoy are The Gainers, a large unmarked rocky patch (dries 0·8m). Beware salmon nets. Off Helvick harbour ⚓ in approx 4m. Dungarvan town harbour is accessible via buoyed chan which almost dries and shifts, the buoys being moved to suit. Approach is difficult in SE'lies >F6. ⚓ in the pool below the town or on pontoon (dries to soft mud), S bank below bridge; craft can stay overnight beyond double Y lines. Facilities: Kos ✉ Ⓑ ✕.

MINOR HARBOUR 15M ENE of ROCHE'S POINT

BALLYCOTTON, Cork, **51°49'·70N 08°00·19W**. AC 2424, 5622. HW –0555 on Dover; Duration 0550. See above. Small, NE-facing harbour at W end of bay suffers from scend in strong SE winds; 3m in entrance and about 1·5m against piers. Many FVs alongside piers, on which yachts should berth, rather than ⚓ in hbr, which is foul with old ground tackle. 6 Ys are outside harbour, or good ⚓ in offshore winds in 6m NE of pier, protected by Ballycotton Is. Lt ho Fl WR 10s 59m 21/17M, B tr in W walls; 238°-W-048°-R-238°. Facilities: on pier. **Village** LB, Kos ✉ Hotel ✕.

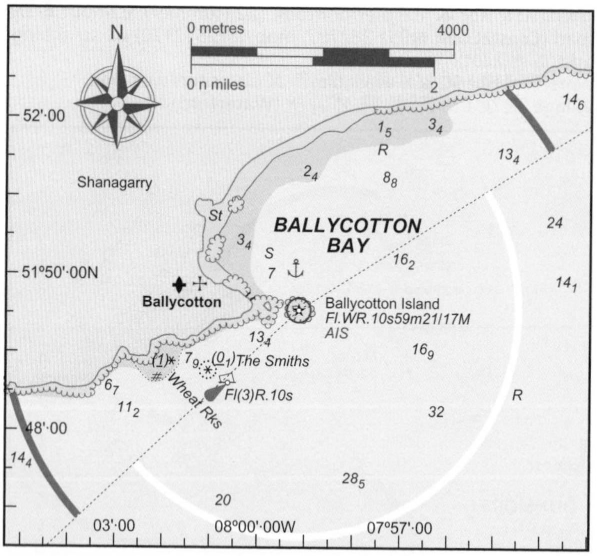

STANDARD TIME (UT)
For Summer Time add ONE hour in **non-shaded areas**

COBH LAT 51°51′N LONG 8°18′W

TIMES AND HEIGHTS OF HIGH AND LOW WATERS

Dates in red are SPRINGS
Dates in blue are NEAPS

YEAR **2018**

JANUARY

Day	Time	m	Day	Time	m
1 M	0418 1057 1645 2318	4.2 0.5 4.2 0.4	16 TU	0503 1129 1720 2344	4.0 0.8 3.9 0.8
2 TU ○	0513 1148 1737	4.3 0.3 4.3	17 W ●	0541 1200 1755	4.1 0.8 4.0
3 W	0007 0603 1237 1825	0.3 4.4 0.3 4.3	18 TH	0015 0614 1231 1826	0.7 4.1 0.8 4.0
4 TH	0055 0651 1325 1912	0.2 4.4 0.3 4.2	19 F	0045 0647 1304 1857	0.7 4.1 0.8 4.0
5 F	0142 0739 1412 1959	0.3 4.3 0.4 4.1	20 SA	0118 0720 1339 1929	0.8 4.1 0.8 3.9
6 SA	0230 0826 1500 2046	0.4 4.2 0.5 4.0	21 SU	0155 0755 1417 2005	0.8 4.0 0.9 3.9
7 SU	0319 0914 1549 2134	0.5 4.0 0.7 3.8	22 M	0234 0833 1457 2045	0.9 4.0 1.0 3.8
8 M	0410 1004 1641 ◑ 2224	0.7 3.8 0.9 3.6	23 TU	0317 0915 1540 2130	1.0 3.9 1.1 3.8
9 TU	0505 1058 1738 2321	0.9 3.6 1.1 3.4	24 W	0405 1003 1629 ◐ 2221	1.1 3.8 1.2 3.7
10 W	0605 1159 1840	1.1 3.5 1.2	25 TH	0501 1058 1728 2322	1.2 3.7 1.3 3.6
11 TH	0026 0710 1305 1945	3.4 1.2 3.4 1.2	26 F	0607 1202 1840	1.2 3.6 1.3
12 F	0135 0815 1409 2046	3.4 1.2 3.4 1.2	27 SA	0032 0720 1314 1954	3.6 1.2 3.6 1.2
13 SA	0238 0916 1506 2142	3.5 1.1 3.6 1.1	28 SU	0146 0835 1426 2106	3.6 1.0 3.7 1.0
14 SU	0333 1009 1557 2230	3.7 1.0 3.7 0.9	29 M	0259 0944 1534 2210	3.8 0.8 3.8 0.7
15 M	0421 1052 1641 2310	3.8 0.9 3.8 0.8	30 TU	0405 1045 1634 2306	4.0 0.5 4.0 0.4
			31 W	0502 1138 1726 ○ 2356	4.2 0.3 4.2 0.2

FEBRUARY

Day	Time	m	Day	Time	m
1 TH	0552 1225 1813	4.3 0.2 4.3	16 F	0556 1213 1810	4.1 0.6 4.0
2 F	0042 0637 1311 1857	0.1 4.4 0.2 4.3	17 SA	0026 0627 1245 1840	0.6 4.1 0.6 4.0
3 SA	0127 0721 1354 1940	0.1 4.3 0.2 4.2	18 SU	0058 0659 1318 1910	0.6 4.1 0.6 4.0
4 SU	0210 0804 1437 2021	0.2 4.2 0.4 4.0	19 M	0133 0732 1354 1944	0.6 4.1 0.7 4.0
5 M	0254 0846 1520 2103	0.4 4.0 0.6 3.9	20 TU	0211 0808 1432 2021	0.7 4.0 0.7 3.9
6 TU	0337 0928 1604 2145	0.6 3.8 0.8 3.7	21 W	0252 0848 1512 2102	0.7 3.9 0.8 3.9
7 W	0423 1013 1651 ◑ 2231	0.8 3.6 1.0 3.5	22 TH	0337 0932 1557 2150	0.9 3.8 1.0 3.7
8 TH	0514 1103 1745 2327	1.1 3.4 1.2 3.3	23 F	0429 1025 1652 ◐ 2249	1.0 3.6 1.1 3.6
9 F	0613 1206 1850	1.2 3.2 1.3	24 SA	0533 1130 1803	1.2 3.5 1.2
10 SA	0040 0721 1323 1959	3.2 1.3 3.2 1.3	25 SU	0001 0650 1247 1926	3.4 1.2 3.4 1.2
11 SU	0159 0832 1433 2107	3.3 1.3 3.3 1.2	26 M	0124 0813 1409 2047	3.4 1.1 3.5 1.0
12 M	0304 0937 1532 2204	3.4 1.1 3.5 1.0	27 TU	0247 0931 1522 2157	3.6 0.8 3.7 0.7
13 TU	0357 1029 1620 2249	3.7 0.9 3.7 0.8	28 W	0355 1033 1623 2254	3.9 0.5 3.9 0.4
14 W	0442 1109 1702 2326	3.9 0.8 3.8 0.7			
15 TH	0521 1142 1738 ● 2356	4.0 0.7 3.9 0.6			

MARCH

Day	Time	m	Day	Time	m
1 TH	0450 1125 1713 2342	4.1 0.2 4.1 0.2	16 F	0455 1116 1714 2331	3.9 0.6 3.9 0.5
2 F ○	0537 1210 1757	4.3 0.1 4.2	17 SA ●	0530 1148 1746	4.0 0.5 4.0
3 SA	0026 0619 1252 1838	0.1 4.3 0.1 4.3	18 SU	0002 0601 1221 1817	0.4 4.1 0.4 4.0
4 SU	0107 0659 1332 1917	0.1 4.3 0.1 4.2	19 M	0035 0634 1255 1848	0.4 4.1 0.4 4.0
5 M	0146 0737 1410 1954	0.2 4.2 0.3 4.1	20 TU	0110 0708 1331 1922	0.4 4.1 0.5 4.0
6 TU	0225 0815 1448 2030	0.3 4.0 0.5 3.9	21 W	0149 0745 1409 1959	0.5 4.0 0.5 4.0
7 W	0303 0852 1527 2107	0.5 3.8 0.7 3.7	22 TH	0231 0825 1450 2041	0.6 3.9 0.7 3.9
8 TH	0343 0930 1608 2148	0.8 3.6 0.9 3.5	23 F	0316 0911 1536 2130	0.7 3.8 0.8 3.7
9 F	0428 1014 1656 ◑ 2236	1.0 3.4 1.2 3.3	24 SA	0409 1004 1632 ◐ 2228	0.9 3.6 1.0 3.5
10 SA	0523 1108 1758 2342	1.2 3.2 1.3 3.1	25 SU	0513 1110 1743 2342	1.0 3.4 1.1 3.4
11 SU	0631 1227 1912	1.4 3.0 1.4	26 M	0631 1230 1907	1.1 3.2 1.1
12 M	0114 0745 1358 2026	3.1 1.3 3.1 1.3	27 TU	0111 0758 1357 2032	3.3 1.0 3.3 0.9
13 TU	0232 0857 1504 2131	3.3 1.2 3.3 1.1	28 W	0236 0917 1510 2144	3.5 0.7 3.6 0.6
14 W	0329 0956 1555 2221	3.5 0.9 3.5 0.8	29 TH	0341 1018 1608 2239	3.8 0.5 3.9 0.4
15 TH	0415 1040 1637 2259	3.7 0.7 3.7 0.6	30 F	0433 1107 1656 2326	4.1 0.2 4.1 0.2
			31 SA ○	0518 1150 1738	4.2 0.1 4.2

APRIL

Day	Time	m	Day	Time	m
1 SU	0006 0558 1230 1816	0.1 4.2 0.1 4.2	16 M ●	0532 1155 1750	4.1 0.3 4.0
2 M	0045 0635 1307 1852	0.1 4.2 0.2 4.1	17 TU	0011 0608 1232 1825	0.3 4.1 0.3 4.1
3 TU	0120 0710 1343 1926	0.2 4.1 0.3 4.0	18 W	0050 0646 1311 1903	0.3 4.1 0.3 4.1
4 W	0156 0744 1418 1959	0.4 3.9 0.5 3.9	19 TH	0131 0726 1353 1944	0.3 4.0 0.4 4.0
5 TH	0231 0818 1453 2034	0.6 3.8 0.7 3.7	20 F	0216 0810 1437 2029	0.4 3.9 0.5 3.9
6 F	0308 0854 1530 2113	0.8 3.6 0.9 3.6	21 SA	0304 0859 1527 2120	0.6 3.7 0.7 3.7
7 SA	0350 0934 1614 2158	1.0 3.4 1.1 3.4	22 SU	0359 0954 1624 ◐ 2219	0.8 3.5 0.9 3.5
8 SU	0442 1023 1713 ◑ 2256	1.2 3.2 1.3 3.2	23 M	0503 1100 1733 2334	0.9 3.3 1.0 3.4
9 M	0548 1129 1827	1.3 3.0 1.4	24 TU	0620 1219 1855	1.0 3.3 1.0
10 TU	0018 0700 1306 1941	3.1 1.3 3.0 1.3	25 W	0101 0744 1341 2017	3.4 0.9 3.4 0.9
11 W	0149 0810 1424 2046	3.2 1.2 3.2 1.1	26 TH	0219 0858 1450 2125	3.6 0.7 3.6 0.6
12 TH	0251 0910 1518 2139	3.4 1.0 3.4 0.9	27 F	0320 0956 1546 2219	3.8 0.5 3.8 0.4
13 F	0338 0959 1602 2222	3.6 0.8 3.7 0.7	28 SA	0411 1045 1634 2305	4.0 0.3 4.0 0.3
14 SA	0419 1041 1640 2259	3.8 0.6 3.8 0.5	29 SU	0455 1128 1716 2345	4.1 0.2 4.1 0.2
15 SU	0456 1118 1716 2334	4.0 0.4 4.0 0.4	30 M ○	0535 1206 1754	4.1 0.2 4.1

Chart Datum: 0·13 metres above Ordnance Datum (Dublin). HAT is 4·5 metres above Chart Datum.

S Ireland

STANDARD TIME (UT)
For Summer Time add ONE hour in **non-shaded areas**

COBH LAT 51°51′N LONG 8°18′W

TIMES AND HEIGHTS OF HIGH AND LOW WATERS

Dates in red are SPRINGS
Dates in blue are NEAPS

YEAR **2018**

MAY

Date	Day	Time	m	Time	m	Time	m	Time	m
1	TU	0021	0.3	0610	4.0	1242	0.3	1828	4.1
2	W	0055	0.4	0644	4.0	1316	0.4	1900	4.0
3	TH	0128	0.5	0716	3.9	1349	0.6	1932	3.9
4	F	0201	0.7	0749	3.7	1423	0.7	2007	3.8
5	SA	0237	0.8	0824	3.6	1459	0.9	2045	3.6
6	SU	0318	1.0	0904	3.5	1541	1.1	2129	3.5
7	M	0407	1.2	0950	3.3	1634	1.2	2221	3.3
8	TU	0508	1.3	1048	3.2	1742	1.3	◑ 2327	3.2
9	W	0616	1.3	1201	3.1	1852	1.3		
10	TH	0046	3.2	0722	1.2	1321	3.2	1956	1.1
11	F	0156	3.4	0822	1.0	1425	3.4	2051	0.9
12	SA	0250	3.6	0914	0.8	1515	3.6	2139	0.7
13	SU	0336	3.8	1002	0.6	1600	3.8	2224	0.5
14	M	0420	3.9	1047	0.5	1643	4.0	2307	0.4
15	TU	0502	4.0	1130	0.3	1724	4.1	● 2350	0.3
16	W	0545	4.1	1213	0.3	1806	4.1		
17	TH	0034	0.2	0628	4.1	1257	0.3	1849	4.1
18	F	0119	0.3	0714	4.1	1342	0.3	1934	4.1
19	SA	0207	0.3	0802	3.9	1431	0.4	2023	4.0
20	SU	0258	0.5	0853	3.8	1522	0.6	2116	3.8
21	M	0354	0.6	0948	3.6	1620	0.7	2216	3.6
22	TU	0456	0.8	1051	3.4	1725	0.8	◐ 2324	3.5
23	W	0607	0.9	1201	3.4	1840	0.9		
24	TH	0041	3.5	0722	0.8	1315	3.4	1954	0.8
25	F	0152	3.6	0830	0.7	1421	3.6	2058	0.7
26	SA	0252	3.7	0928	0.6	1517	3.7	2153	0.5
27	SU	0343	3.8	1018	0.5	1607	3.8	2240	0.5
28	M	0429	3.9	1103	0.5	1651	3.9	2321	0.5
29	TU	0510	3.9	1142	0.5	1730	4.0	○ 2357	0.5
30	W	0547	3.9	1218	0.5	1806	4.0		
31	TH	0030	0.6	0621	3.9	1252	0.6	1838	3.9

JUNE

Date	Day	Time	m	Time	m	Time	m	Time	m
1	F	0102	0.7	0653	3.8	1324	0.7	1911	3.9
2	SA	0134	0.8	0725	3.7	1357	0.8	1945	3.8
3	SU	0210	0.9	0801	3.7	1433	0.9	2023	3.7
4	M	0251	1.0	0840	3.6	1513	1.0	2105	3.6
5	TU	0337	1.1	0924	3.5	1601	1.1	2153	3.5
6	W	0430	1.2	1015	3.4	1658	1.2	◑ 2248	3.4
7	TH	0530	1.2	1114	3.3	1802	1.2	2351	3.4
8	F	0634	1.2	1220	3.3	1906	1.1		
9	SA	0056	3.5	0735	1.1	1326	3.5	2004	1.0
10	SU	0158	3.6	0832	0.9	1425	3.6	2100	0.8
11	M	0253	3.8	0927	0.7	1520	3.8	2153	0.6
12	TU	0346	3.9	1019	0.6	1612	4.0	2244	0.4
13	W	0437	4.0	1109	0.4	1702	4.1	● 2333	0.3
14	TH	0526	4.1	1158	0.3	1750	4.2		
15	F	0022	0.2	0615	4.1	1246	0.2	1838	4.2
16	SA	0110	0.2	0704	4.1	1334	0.2	1927	4.1
17	SU	0200	0.3	0753	4.0	1424	0.3	2017	4.0
18	M	0251	0.4	0844	3.9	1515	0.4	2109	3.9
19	TU	0345	0.5	0937	3.7	1609	0.6	2204	3.7
20	W	0442	0.7	1033	3.6	1708	0.7	◐ 2304	3.6
21	TH	0545	0.8	1134	3.5	1813	0.8		
22	F	0009	3.5	0651	0.9	1240	3.4	1920	0.8
23	SA	0116	3.5	0755	0.9	1345	3.5	2024	0.8
24	SU	0217	3.5	0855	0.8	1444	3.6	2122	0.8
25	M	0312	3.6	0949	0.8	1537	3.7	2213	0.7
26	TU	0401	3.7	1037	0.7	1625	3.8	2257	0.7
27	W	0446	3.8	1119	0.7	1707	3.9	2335	0.7
28	TH	0525	3.8	1156	0.7	1745	3.9	○	
29	F	0007	0.7	0601	3.8	1230	0.7	1820	3.9
30	SA	0039	0.7	0634	3.8	1301	0.7	1853	3.9

JULY

Date	Day	Time	m	Time	m	Time	m	Time	m
1	SU	0111	0.8	0706	3.8	1333	0.8	1927	3.9
2	M	0146	0.8	0741	3.7	1408	0.9	2003	3.8
3	TU	0225	0.9	0818	3.7	1447	0.9	2042	3.7
4	W	0307	1.0	0859	3.6	1530	1.0	2125	3.7
5	TH	0353	1.1	0944	3.6	1618	1.1	2212	3.6
6	F	0445	1.1	1036	3.5	1713	1.1	◑ 2307	3.6
7	SA	0544	1.2	1134	3.5	1815	1.1		
8	SU	0008	3.5	0648	1.1	1238	3.5	1920	1.1
9	M	0113	3.6	0753	1.0	1343	3.6	2025	0.9
10	TU	0217	3.7	0856	0.9	1447	3.7	2127	0.7
11	W	0318	3.8	0956	0.7	1548	3.9	2225	0.5
12	TH	0416	4.0	1052	0.5	1645	4.1	2320	0.3
13	F	0511	4.1	1144	0.3	1737	4.2	●	
14	SA	0010	0.2	0602	4.1	1234	0.2	1827	4.2
15	SU	0059	0.1	0651	4.2	1322	0.1	1915	4.2
16	M	0148	0.2	0740	4.1	1410	0.2	2003	4.1
17	TU	0237	0.3	0828	4.0	1459	0.3	2051	4.0
18	W	0326	0.4	0916	3.8	1548	0.4	2140	3.8
19	TH	0417	0.6	1006	3.7	1640	0.6	◐ 2232	3.7
20	F	0511	0.8	1059	3.5	1736	0.8	2328	3.5
21	SA	0610	0.9	1158	3.4	1837	1.0		
22	SU	0032	3.4	0713	1.0	1304	3.3	1942	1.0
23	M	0138	3.3	0817	1.0	1409	3.4	2047	1.0
24	TU	0240	3.4	0918	1.0	1508	3.5	2145	0.9
25	W	0334	3.5	1012	0.9	1600	3.7	2234	0.9
26	TH	0423	3.7	1058	0.8	1646	3.8	2314	0.8
27	F	0505	3.8	1136	0.7	1726	3.9	○ 2347	0.7
28	SA	0543	3.8	1208	0.7	1802	3.9		
29	SU	0017	0.7	0616	3.8	1238	0.7	1834	3.9
30	M	0048	0.7	0648	3.8	1308	0.7	1906	3.9
31	TU	0122	0.8	0720	3.8	1342	0.7	1939	3.9

AUGUST

Date	Day	Time	m	Time	m	Time	m	Time	m
1	W	0159	0.8	0754	3.8	1418	0.8	2015	3.9
2	TH	0238	0.9	0831	3.7	1458	0.9	2054	3.8
3	F	0319	1.0	0912	3.7	1541	1.0	2138	3.7
4	SA	0404	1.0	0959	3.6	1631	1.1	◑ 2228	3.7
5	SU	0457	1.1	1054	3.5	1730	1.1	2327	3.6
6	M	0603	1.2	1158	3.5	1841	1.2		
7	TU	0036	3.5	0717	1.1	1311	3.5	1954	1.1
8	W	0148	3.6	0830	1.0	1423	3.6	2106	0.9
9	TH	0258	3.7	0937	0.7	1532	3.8	2210	0.6
10	F	0402	3.9	1037	0.5	1632	4.1	2306	0.3
11	SA	0458	4.1	1130	0.2	1724	4.2	● 2357	0.2
12	SU	0548	4.2	1218	0.1	1812	4.3		
13	M	0044	0.1	0634	4.2	1305	0.1	1857	4.3
14	TU	0130	0.1	0720	4.2	1350	0.1	1941	4.2
15	W	0214	0.2	0804	4.1	1434	0.2	2025	4.1
16	TH	0259	0.4	0848	3.9	1519	0.4	2108	3.9
17	F	0345	0.6	0932	3.7	1604	0.6	2153	3.7
18	SA	0432	0.8	1018	3.5	1652	0.9	◐ 2242	3.4
19	SU	0525	1.0	1111	3.3	1749	1.1	2341	3.2
20	M	0627	1.2	1219	3.2	1855	1.2		
21	TU	0056	3.2	0737	1.2	1336	3.2	2007	1.2
22	W	0209	3.2	0846	1.1	1443	3.4	2116	1.1
23	TH	0310	3.4	0947	1.0	1538	3.6	2211	1.0
24	F	0401	3.6	1036	0.8	1624	3.8	2252	0.8
25	SA	0444	3.8	1114	0.7	1705	3.9	2325	0.7
26	SU	0522	3.9	1145	0.6	1740	4.0	○ 2354	0.6
27	M	0555	3.9	1213	0.6	1812	4.0		
28	TU	0023	0.6	0625	3.9	1242	0.6	1842	4.0
29	W	0056	0.6	0655	3.9	1314	0.6	1912	4.0
30	TH	0131	0.7	0727	3.9	1350	0.7	1946	4.0
31	F	0208	0.8	0802	3.8	1428	0.8	2023	3.9

Chart Datum: 0·13 metres above Ordnance Datum (Dublin). HAT is 4·5 metres above Chart Datum.

STANDARD TIME (UT)
For Summer Time add ONE hour in **non-shaded areas**

COBH LAT 51°51′N LONG 8°18′W

TIMES AND HEIGHTS OF HIGH AND LOW WATERS

Dates in red are SPRINGS
Dates in blue are NEAPS

YEAR **2018**

SEPTEMBER

Date	Day	Time	m	Time	m	Time	m	Time	m
1	SA	0248	0.9	0841	3.8	1511	0.9	2105	3.8
2	SU	0331	1.0	0927	3.7	1558	1.0	2155	3.7
3	M	0423	1.1	1021	3.6	1657	1.1	◑ 2255	3.5
4	TU	0529	1.2	1128	3.4	1810	1.2		
5	W	0008	3.4	0649	1.2	1248	3.4	1932	1.2
6	TH	0129	3.4	0810	1.1	1410	3.6	2050	0.9
7	F	0245	3.6	0922	0.8	1522	3.8	2157	0.6
8	SA	0349	3.9	1023	0.5	1620	4.1	2252	0.3
9	SU	0443	4.1	1115	0.2	1709	4.3	● 2340	0.2
10	M	0531	4.2	1201	0.1	1754	4.3		
11	TU	0024	0.1	0614	4.3	1244	0.0	1835	4.3
12	W	0106	0.1	0656	4.2	1325	0.1	1915	4.2
13	TH	0147	0.2	0736	4.1	1405	0.3	1954	4.1
14	F	0228	0.4	0815	3.9	1446	0.5	2033	3.9
15	SA	0309	0.6	0855	3.7	1527	0.7	2113	3.6
16	SU	0353	0.9	0937	3.5	1611	1.0	◐ 2156	3.4
17	M	0442	1.1	1025	3.3	1703	1.2	2248	3.2
18	TU	0543	1.3	1130	3.1	1809	1.4		
19	W	0004	3.1	0656	1.4	1301	3.1	1925	1.4
20	TH	0137	3.1	0812	1.3	1416	3.3	2041	1.3
21	F	0244	3.3	0917	1.1	1513	3.5	2139	1.0
22	SA	0335	3.6	1007	0.9	1559	3.8	2223	0.8
23	SU	0418	3.8	1045	0.7	1638	3.9	2257	0.7
24	M	0456	3.9	1117	0.6	1713	4.0	2327	0.6
25	TU	0529	4.0	1145	0.5	1744	4.1	○ 2357	0.6
26	W	0559	4.0	1215	0.5	1814	4.1		
27	TH	0030	0.6	0629	4.0	1248	0.6	1845	4.1
28	F	0105	0.6	0701	4.0	1324	0.6	1919	4.0
29	SA	0143	0.7	0736	3.9	1404	0.7	1957	4.0
30	SU	0223	0.8	0817	3.9	1448	0.8	2040	3.8

OCTOBER

Date	Day	Time	m	Time	m	Time	m	Time	m
1	M	0308	0.9	0904	3.7	1538	1.0	2131	3.7
2	TU	0402	1.1	1000	3.6	1637	1.2	◑ 2234	3.5
3	W	0510	1.2	1110	3.4	1752	1.3	2350	3.3
4	TH	0632	1.2	1235	3.4	1918	1.2		
5	F	0116	3.4	0756	1.1	1402	3.6	2039	0.9
6	SA	0234	3.6	0909	0.8	1511	3.8	2144	0.6
7	SU	0336	3.9	1008	0.5	1605	4.1	2236	0.4
8	M	0427	4.1	1058	0.3	1652	4.3	2322	0.2
9	TU	0512	4.3	1141	0.1	1734	4.3	●	
10	W	0003	0.2	0553	4.3	1222	0.2	1812	4.3
11	TH	0042	0.2	0632	4.2	1300	0.3	1849	4.2
12	F	0120	0.4	0709	4.1	1337	0.4	1924	4.0
13	SA	0158	0.5	0745	4.0	1414	0.6	1959	3.9
14	SU	0236	0.8	0821	3.8	1452	0.9	2036	3.7
15	M	0316	1.0	0901	3.6	1533	1.1	2116	3.5
16	TU	0401	1.2	0947	3.4	1623	1.3	◐ 2204	3.3
17	W	0500	1.4	1045	3.2	1727	1.5	2308	3.1
18	TH	0613	1.5	1211	3.1	1842	1.5		
19	F	0046	3.1	0728	1.4	1339	3.2	1955	1.4
20	SA	0207	3.3	0834	1.2	1438	3.5	2055	1.2
21	SU	0301	3.5	0926	1.0	1525	3.7	2142	0.9
22	M	0344	3.7	1008	0.8	1605	3.9	2221	0.8
23	TU	0423	3.9	1043	0.7	1640	4.0	2256	0.6
24	W	0457	4.0	1116	0.6	1714	4.1	○ 2331	0.5
25	TH	0531	4.1	1150	0.5	1747	4.2		
26	F	0006	0.5	0604	4.1	1227	0.5	1821	4.2
27	SA	0044	0.5	0640	4.1	1306	0.6	1859	4.1
28	SU	0124	0.6	0719	4.1	1348	0.7	1940	4.0
29	M	0208	0.7	0803	4.0	1435	0.8	2027	3.9
30	TU	0257	0.9	0853	3.8	1527	1.0	2120	3.7
31	W	0353	1.0	0951	3.6	1628	1.1	◑ 2223	3.5

NOVEMBER

Date	Day	Time	m	Time	m	Time	m	Time	m
1	TH	0500	1.2	1102	3.5	1742	1.2	2339	3.4
2	F	0620	1.2	1226	3.5	1906	1.2		
3	SA	0102	3.4	0742	1.0	1348	3.6	2024	1.0
4	SU	0217	3.7	0853	0.8	1452	3.9	2125	0.7
5	M	0317	3.9	0950	0.6	1545	4.1	2216	0.5
6	TU	0407	4.1	1039	0.4	1631	4.2	2301	0.4
7	W	0452	4.2	1122	0.3	1713	4.3	● 2342	0.4
8	TH	0532	4.2	1201	0.4	1751	4.2		
9	F	0019	0.4	0609	4.2	1238	0.5	1825	4.1
10	SA	0055	0.5	0645	4.1	1312	0.6	1858	4.0
11	SU	0130	0.7	0719	4.0	1346	0.8	1931	3.9
12	M	0205	0.9	0754	3.9	1422	1.0	2006	3.7
13	TU	0242	1.0	0833	3.7	1501	1.2	2044	3.6
14	W	0325	1.2	0917	3.5	1548	1.4	2130	3.4
15	TH	0418	1.4	1009	3.4	1646	1.5	◐ 2225	3.3
16	F	0525	1.5	1114	3.3	1755	1.5	2337	3.2
17	SA	0637	1.5	1234	3.3	1904	1.5		
18	SU	0102	3.3	0742	1.3	1345	3.5	2005	1.3
19	M	0209	3.5	0837	1.1	1438	3.7	2058	1.1
20	TU	0259	3.7	0925	0.9	1523	3.9	2144	0.9
21	W	0343	3.9	1009	0.8	1604	4.0	2227	0.7
22	TH	0424	4.0	1050	0.6	1644	4.1	2308	0.6
23	F	0505	4.2	1131	0.6	1723	4.2	○ 2348	0.5
24	SA	0545	4.2	1212	0.5	1804	4.2		
25	SU	0030	0.5	0626	4.2	1255	0.5	1846	4.2
26	M	0114	0.5	0710	4.2	1341	0.6	1931	4.1
27	TU	0200	0.6	0757	4.1	1429	0.7	2021	3.9
28	W	0251	0.8	0850	3.9	1523	0.9	2114	3.8
29	TH	0347	0.9	0947	3.8	1622	1.0	2215	3.6
30	F	0451	1.0	1053	3.6	1730	1.1	◑ 2323	3.5

DECEMBER

Date	Day	Time	m	Time	m	Time	m	Time	m
1	SA	0603	1.1	1206	3.6	1846	1.1		
2	SU	0037	3.5	0720	1.0	1320	3.7	1959	1.0
3	M	0149	3.6	0829	0.9	1425	3.8	2100	0.8
4	TU	0250	3.8	0927	0.7	1520	3.9	2153	0.7
5	W	0343	4.0	1018	0.6	1608	4.0	2240	0.6
6	TH	0430	4.1	1103	0.6	1652	4.1	2321	0.6
7	F	0513	4.1	1143	0.6	1730	4.1	● 2359	0.6
8	SA	0551	4.1	1218	0.7	1805	4.1		
9	SU	0034	0.7	0626	4.1	1251	0.8	1837	4.0
10	M	0107	0.8	0700	4.0	1323	0.9	1909	3.9
11	TU	0140	0.9	0734	3.9	1357	1.0	1943	3.8
12	W	0215	1.0	0811	3.8	1435	1.2	2020	3.7
13	TH	0254	1.2	0852	3.7	1517	1.3	2102	3.6
14	F	0340	1.3	0937	3.6	1607	1.4	2151	3.5
15	SA	0435	1.4	1030	3.5	1705	1.5	◐ 2248	3.4
16	SU	0539	1.4	1130	3.5	1810	1.5	2354	3.4
17	M	0645	1.4	1235	3.5	1914	1.4		
18	TU	0102	3.5	0747	1.3	1339	3.6	2013	1.2
19	W	0206	3.6	0843	1.1	1435	3.8	2108	1.0
20	TH	0301	3.8	0937	0.9	1528	3.9	2159	0.8
21	F	0353	4.0	1027	0.7	1617	4.1	2248	0.7
22	SA	0443	4.1	1116	0.6	1705	4.2	○ 2335	0.5
23	SU	0530	4.2	1202	0.5	1752	4.2		
24	M	0020	0.4	0617	4.3	1248	0.4	1838	4.2
25	TU	0106	0.4	0704	4.3	1335	0.5	1925	4.2
26	W	0154	0.5	0752	4.2	1424	0.5	2014	4.0
27	TH	0244	0.5	0843	4.1	1515	0.7	2105	3.9
28	F	0336	0.7	0936	3.9	1609	0.8	2158	3.7
29	SA	0433	0.8	1032	3.8	1708	1.0	◑ 2257	3.6
30	SU	0535	1.0	1134	3.6	1814	1.1		
31	M	0001	3.5	0644	1.0	1242	3.6	1923	1.1

Chart Datum: 0·13 metres above Ordnance Datum (Dublin). HAT is 4·5 metres above Chart Datum.

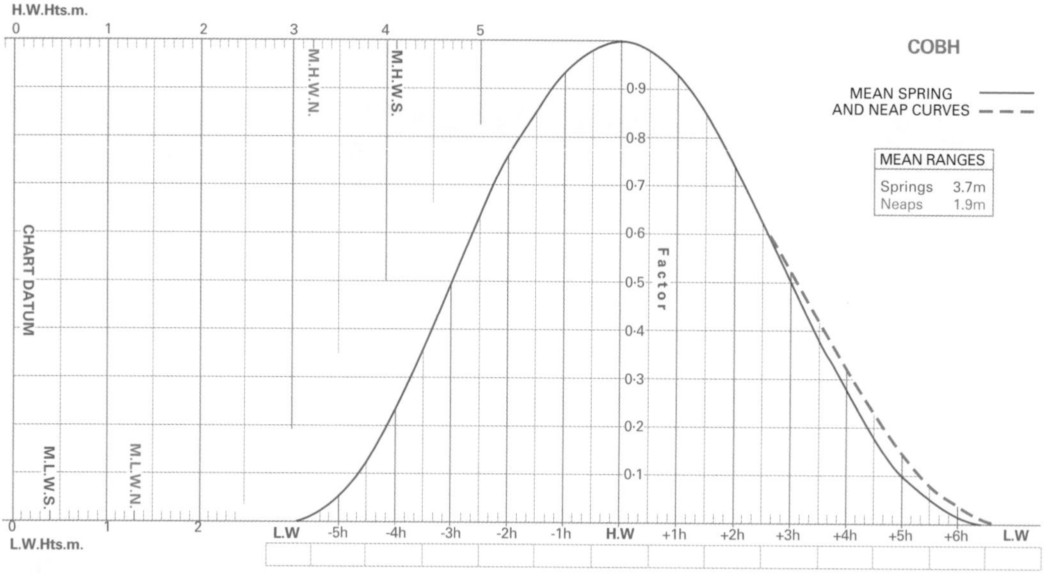
H.W.Hts.m.
0 1 2 3 4 5
M.H.W.N.
M.H.W.S.
COBH
MEAN SPRING AND NEAP CURVES
MEAN RANGES
Springs 3.7m
Neaps 1.9m
CHART DATUM
Factor
0·9
0·8
0·7
0·6
0·5
0·4
0·3
0·2
0·1
M.L.W.S.
M.L.W.N.
0 1 2
L.W.Hts.m.
L.W -5h -4h -3h -2h -1h H.W +1h +2h +3h +4h +5h +6h L.W

9.12.20 CORK HARBOUR

Cork **51°47′·50N 08°15′·54W**

CHARTS AC 1765, 1777, 1773, 5622; Imray C57, C56

TIDES –0523 Dover; ML 2·3; Duration 0555

Standard Port COBH (⟵)

Times				Height (metres)			
High Water		Low Water		MHWS	MHWN	MLWN	MLWS
0500	1100	0500	1100	4·1	3·2	1·3	0·4
1700	2300	1700	2300				
Differences BALLYCOTTON (15M ENE of Roche's Point)							
–0011	+0001	+0003	–0009	0·0	0·0	–0·1	0·0
RINGASKIDDY							
+0005	+0020	+0007	+0013	+0·1	+0·1	+0·1	+0·1
MARINO POINT							
0000	+0010	0000	+0010	+0·1	+0·1	0·0	0·0
CORK CITY							
+0005	+0010	+0020	+0010	+0·4	+0·4	+0·3	+0·2
ROBERTS COVE (approx 4M SW of Roche's Point)							
–0005	–0005	–0005	–0005	–0·1	0·0	0·0	+0·1

SHELTER Very good in all conditions, esp in Crosshaven and East Passage. There are 3 marinas at Crosshaven, plus a small marina and several ⚓s up the Owenboy River, notably at Drake's Pool. There are marinas at Cork City and at Monkstown. Cobh, Ringaskiddy and Cork City are commercial and ferry ports; contact HM/Port berthing Master for advice on berths. 100m yacht pontoon in 4·5m at Custom House Quay, Cork City.

NAVIGATION WPT 51°46′·57N, 08°15′·39W, 005°/1M to Roche's Pt lt; also on 354°ldg line. Safe hbr with no dangers for yachts; ent is deep and well marked. Sp rate is about 1½kn in ent. Main chan up to Cork and the chan to E Ferry are marked, but shoal outside navigable chan. Ent to Crosshaven/Owenboy River carries at least 3m at LWS, and the chan is buoyed.

LIGHTS AND MARKS See 9.12.4. The 24·5m high hammerhead water tr S of Crosshaven and the R/W power stn chy NE of Corkbeg Is are conspic from seaward. Two set Ldg lts/marks lead through The Sound, either side of Hbr Rk (5·2m), not a hazard for yachts; but do not impede merchant ships. The chan to Crosshaven is marked by C1 SHM lt buoy, C1A SHM lt buoy; C2A PHM lt buoy, C2 PHM lt buoy; and C4 PHM lt buoy.

Haulbowline Br connecting Is to S shore is lit. N span Iso 6s (sync), S span Iso 10s (sync). These are synchronised with Spike Is pontoon E/W ends lit Iso G 6s.

COMMUNICATIONS (Code 021) MRCC (066) 9476109; IMES 4831448; ⊖ 4311024; Police 4831222; Dr 4831716; Ⓗ 4546400. HM/Port Berthing Master 4273125, info@portofcork.ie; Port Ops 4811380.

Cork Hbr Radio (Port Ops) VHF Ch 12 14 16 (H24); *Crosshaven BY* Ch **M** (Mon–Fri: 0830–1730LT). *Royal Cork* YC Marina Ch **M** (0900–2359LT) and RCYC water taxi, *Salve Marine* Ch **M** 0830-1730.

FACILITIES Crosshaven BY Marina www.crosshavenboatyard.com ☎4831161, 100+20Ⓥ €2.50, (40t) (1½t).

Salve Marine ☎4831145, 45+12Ⓥ €2.50, Koz. **Village**.

Royal Cork YC Marina www.royalcork.com ☎4831023 mob 087 2899190, 170+30Ⓥ €3.00, wi-fi.

Crosshaven Pier/Pontoon €21.00 any size.

East Ferry Marina ☎(086) 7357785, reported closed 2015. Access all tides, max draught 5·5m reported closed 2016.

Crosshaven Village FV pier in 3·5m at Town quay, HW±4(for RIBs small power craft) Dr grid.

Cobh E of cruise liner berth 50m pontoon in 3m at 'The Quays' Restaurant for free use by patrons.

Cork Harbour Marina, www.monkstownmarina.com ☎(087) 3669009, access all tides, max length 17m, 80 inc Ⓥ €2.40, facilities under development.

Cork City Marina, 150m Ⓥ pontoon in 5m; €20 ≤12m > €35, charges inc after 3rd night.

Cork City All facilities. ⇄ ✈, Ferries: Roscoff; weekly; 13hrs; Brittany (www.brittany-ferries.ie).

Aghada Pontoon with 0.4m at LAT. (enquire at petrol stn). Appr by 2 SHM 'A1' FL G 5s and 'A2' FL(2)G 10s which should be passed close to remaining on a steady straight track. Facilities:.

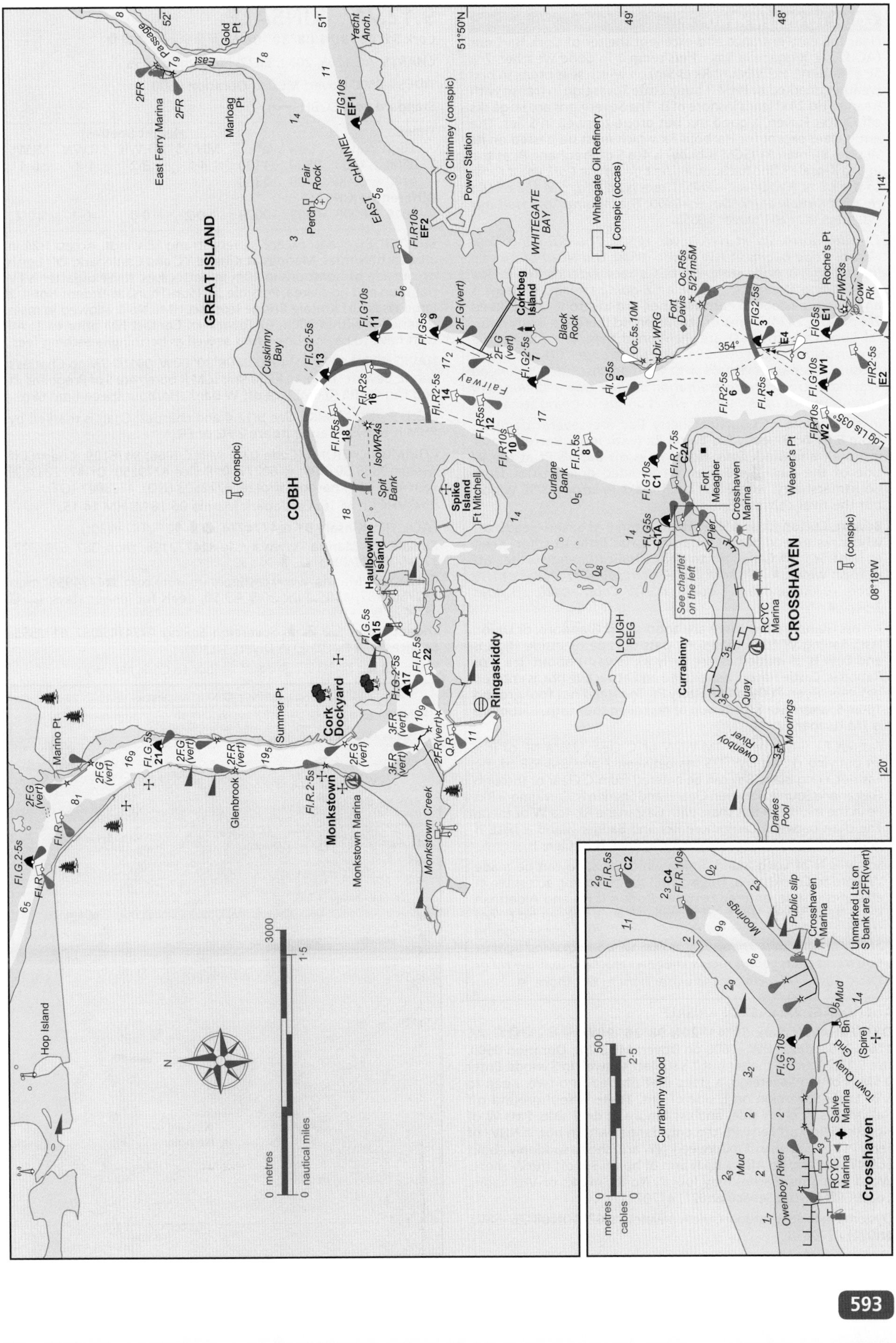
GREAT ISLAND
COBH
East Ferry Marina
Marloag Pt
Gold Pt
East Passage
Yacht Anch.
Fair Rock
Perch
EAST CHANNEL
Chimney (conspic)
Power Station
WHITEGATE BAY
Whitegate Oil Refinery
Conspic (occas)
Corkbeg Island
Black Rock
Fort Davis
Roche's Pt
Cow Rk
Cuskinny Bay
Fairway
Spit Bank
Spike Island
Ft Mitchell
Curlane Bank
Haulbowline Island
Cork Dockyard
Ringaskiddy
Summer Pt
Glenbrook
Marino Pt
Monkstown
Monkstown Marina
Monkstown Creek
Hop Island
LOUGH BEG
Currabinny
CROSSHAVEN
Crosshaven Marina
RCYC Marina
Fort Meagher
Weaver's Pt
Pier
Quay
Owenboy River
Moorings
Drakes Pool
See chartlet on the left
Ldg Lts 035°
354°
51°50'N
51'
52'
49'
48'
08°18'W
20'
14'
0 metres 3000
0 nautical miles 1·5
Currabinny Wood
Crosshaven
Salve Marina
Town Quay
Grid
Bn
(Spire)
Mud
Public slip
Unmarked Lts on S bank are 2FR(vert)
metres 0 500
cables 0 2·5

COBH TO MIZEN HEAD

Near the easy entrance and excellent shelter of Cork Harbour (AC 1777), Ringabella Bay offers temp ⚓ in good weather. 7ca SE of Robert's Hd is Daunt Rk (3·5m) on which seas break in bad weather; marked by PHM lt buoy. Little Sovereign in transit with Reanies Hd 241° leads inshore of it. The Sovereigns are large rks off Oyster Haven, a good hbr but prone to swell in S'lies. The ent is clear except for Harbour Rk which must be passed on its W side. Bulman Rk (SCM lt buoy) is 4ca S of Preghane Pt at the ent to Kinsale's fine harbour. ► *The tide on the Cork coast turns to the NE at HW Dover +0045. There is an eddy 5M ESE of Old Head of Kinsale at HW Dover +0400. The ingoing Cork Harbour tide begins at HW Dover +0055.*

The tide turns SW at HW Dover +0500. The outgoing Cork Harbour tide begins at HW Dover –0540. Old Head of Kinsale (lt, fog sig) is quite steep-to, but a race extends 1M to SW on W-going stream, and to SE on E-going stream. ◄ There is an inshore passage in light weather, but in strong winds keep 2M off. (AC 2424) From Cork to Mizen Hd there are many natural hbrs. Only the best are mentioned here. ► *Offshore the stream seldom exceeds 1·5kn, but it is stronger off headlands causing races and overfalls with wind against tide. Prolonged W winds increase the rate/duration of the E-going stream, and strong E winds have a similar effect on the W-going stream.* ◄

In the middle of Courtmacsherry Bay are several dangers, from E to W: Blueboy Rk, Barrel Rk (with Inner Barrels closer inshore), and Black Tom; Horse Rk is off Barry's Pt at the W side of the bay. These must be avoided going to or from Courtmacsherry, where the bar breaks in strong S/SE winds, but the river carries 2·3m.

Beware Cotton Rk and Shoonta Rk close E of Seven Heads, off which rks extend 50m. Clonakilty B has little to offer. Keep at least 5ca off Galley Hd to clear Dhulic Rk, and further off in fresh winds. ► *Offshore the W-going stream makes at HW Cobh +0200, and the E-going at HW Cobh –0420, sp rates 1·5kn.* ◄

Across Glandore Bay there are good ⚓s off Glandore, or Union Hall. Sailing W from Glandore, pass outside or inside High Is and Low Is; if inside beware Belly Rk (awash) about 3ca S of Rabbit Is. Castle Haven, a sheltered and attractive hbr, is entered between Reen Pt (lt) and Battery Pt. Toe Head has foul ground 100m S, and 7½ca S is a group of rks called the Stags. Baltimore is 7M further W.

Fastnet Rk (lit) is nearly 4M WSW of C Clear; 2½ca NE of it is an outlying rk. An E/W TSS lies between 2 and 8M SSE of the Fastnet. Long Island Bay can be entered from C Clear or through Gascanane Sound, between Clear Is and Sherkin Is. Carrigmore Rks lie in the middle of this chan, with Gascanane Rk 1ca W of them. The chan between Carrigmore Rks and Badger Island is best. If bound for Crookhaven, beware Bullig Reef, N of Clear Is.

Schull is N of Long Island, inside which passage can be made W'ward to Crookhaven. This is a well-sheltered hbr, accessible at all states of tide, entered between Rock Is lt Ho and Alderman Rks, ENE of Streek Hd. ⚓ off the village. ► *Off Mizen Hd (lt ho) the W-going stream starts at HW Cobh +0120, and the E-going at HW Cobh –0500. The sp rate is 4kn, which with wind against tide forms a dangerous race, sometimes reaching to Brow Hd or Three Castle Hd, with broken water right to the shore.* ◄

ANCHORAGE 2M EAST OF KINSALE

OYSTERHAVEN, Cork, **51°41'·20N 08°26'·90W**. ❁❁◊✿✿✿. AC 1765, 2053, 5622. HW –0600 on Dover; ML 2·2m; Duration 0600. Use 9.12.20. Good shelter but ⚓'s subject to swell in S winds. Enter 0·5M N of Big Sovereign, a steep islet divided into two. Keep to S of Little Sovereign on E side of ent. There is foul ground off Ballymacus Pt on W side, and off Kinure Pt on E side. Pass W of Hbr Rk (0·9m) off Ferry Pt, the only danger within hbr. ⚓ NNW of Ferry Pt in 4–6m on soft mud/weed. NW arm shoals suddenly about 5ca NW of Ferry Pt. Also ⚓ up N arm of hbr in 3m off the W shore. Weed in higher reaches may foul ⚓. No lts, marks or VHF radio. Coast/Cliff Rescue Service ☎(021) 4770711.

Oysterhaven Yacht Harbour (strictly private) 51°42'·10N 08°26'·58W, ☎(021) 4770878.

9.12.21 KINSALE

Cork **51°40'·80N 08°30'·00W** ❁❁❁◊◊◊✿✿✿

CHARTS AC 1765, 2053, 5622, 5623; Imray C56

TIDES –0600 Dover; ML 2·2; Duration 0600

Standard Port COBH (⟵)

Times				Height (metres)			
High Water		Low Water		MHWS	MHWN	MLWN	MLWS
0500	1100	0500	1100	4·1	3·2	1·3	0·4
1700	2300	1700	2300				
Differences KINSALE							
–0019	–0005	–0009	–0023	–0·2	0·0	+0·1	+0·2

SHELTER Excellent, except in very strong SE winds. Access H24 in all weathers/tides. Marinas at Kinsale YC and Castlepark; Ⓥ's berth on outside of pontoons in 10m in both cases; NNW of latter is FV pontoon and no ⚓ area. Possible ⊆ (Sun-Thurs) at Trident Hotel. 2 large Ⓥs NE of Kinsale Bridge (contact HM). No ⚓ allowed in main channel or within 700m of Town Pier. Contact HM prior to ⚓. All craft have to pay harbour dues as well as berthing/launching fees.

NAVIGATION WPT 51°40'·00N 08°30'·00W, 001°/1·7M to Charles's Fort lt. Beware: Bulman Rk (0·9m; SCM lt buoy) 4ca S of Preghane Pt and Farmer Rk (0·6m) ¾ca off W bank. Harbour speed limit 6kn.

LIGHTS AND MARKS See 9.12.4 and chartlet. Chan is marked by PHM lt buoys. Marina lts are 2 FG or FR.

COMMUNICATIONS (Code 021) MRCC (066) 9476109; Coast/Cliff Rescue 0868 501804; ⊖ 6027700; Police 4779250; Dr 4772253; Ⓗ 4546400. HM kharbour@iol.ie, 4772503 (HO), 4773047 (OT).

KYC VHF Ch M 16. Castlepark Marina 06 16 M. HM **14** 16.

FACILITIES **Kinsale BY** ☎4774774, Ⓥ ⛽ ⚒ 🔧 ⊞ (30t).

Kinsale YC Marina www.kyc.ie ☎4772196, mob 087 6787377, 170+50Ⓥ €3·20, ♿ ⛴ ⛽ ✕ ⊡.

Castlepark Marina www.castleparkmarina.com ☎4774959, mob 0877502737, 130⊆ inc 20Ⓥ €3·50, deals for longer stays, ⛴ ⊡ ⊞ ✕ ⊡ @.

Trident Hotel ⊆ ⛽ Sovereign Sailing 4774145/087 6172555.
Services ⛽ 🔧 ⊞ Ⓔ Divers (30t).

Town LB ⛴ ✉ Ⓑ ✕ ⊡ (bus to Cork, ⇌, ✈).

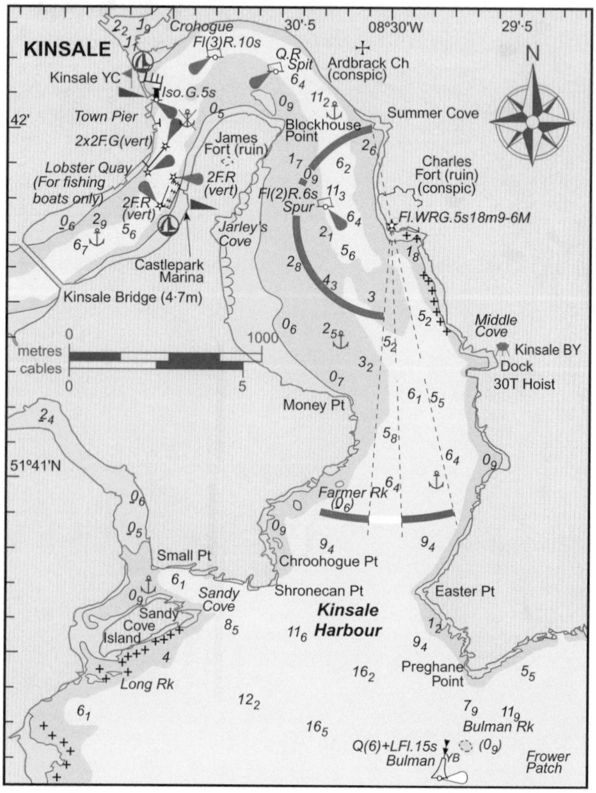

9.12.22 COURTMACSHERRY

Cork **51°38'·22N 08°40'·90W**

CHARTS AC 2092, 2081, 5622, 5623; Imray C56

TIDES HW –0610 on Dover; Duration 0545

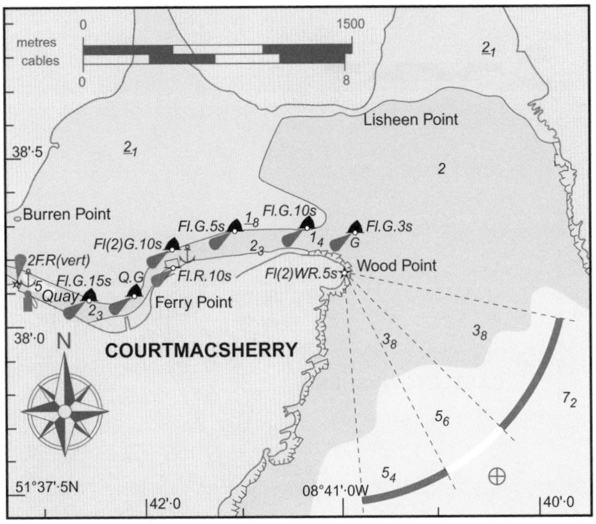

Standard Port COBH (⟵)

Times				Height (metres)			
High Water		Low Water		MHWS	MHWN	MLWN	MLWS
0500	1100	0500	1100	4·1	3·2	1·3	0·4
1700	2300	1700	2300				
Differences COURTMACSHERRY							
–0025	–0008	–0008	–0015	–0·1	–0·1	0·0	+0·1

SHELTER Good shelter upriver, but in strong S/SE winds seas break on the bar (<2m), when ent must not be attempted. Dry out in small inner hbr or afloat on jetty (FVs) or on yacht pontoon (37m). ⚓ NE of Ferry Pt in about 2·5m or N of pontoon. Weed may foul ⚓; best to moor using two ⚓s.

NAVIGATION WPT, 51°37'·50N 08°40'·17W, 324°/0·8M to Wood Pt. Appr in the W sector of Wood Pt lt, between Black Tom and Horse Rk (dries 3·6m); the latter is 3-4½ca E of Barry Pt on the W shore. Black Tom (2·3m), with SHM buoy Fl.G.5s 5ca SSE, is close NE of the appr. Further to NE, in centre of bay, Barrel Rk (dries 2·6m), has unlit perch (ruin). To NNW and E of it are Inner Barrels (0·5m) and Blueboy Rk. Hbr ent is between Wood Pt and SHM buoy 2ca NE, Fl G 3s. Chan (2m but 1·4m close inside ent) is marked by 5 SHM buoys and 1 PHM buoy (off Ferry Point). Upstream of Ferry Point there are moorings on both sides of the channel. The pier head is marked by 2 FR (vert) lights.

LIGHTS AND MARKS Wood Pt, Fl (2) WR 5s 15m 5M.

COMMUNICATIONS (023) Coast Rescue Service (Mob) 08685 01806; Dr 8846186 (HN 1850 335999); Police 8846122. HM (Mob) 0867394299; RNLI boathouse 8846600. No VHF.

FACILITIES Quay LB (min €15/craft) (Pier 0930-1800 on request). **Village** (bus to Cork).

ADJACENT ANCHORAGES

CLONAKILTY BAY 51°32'·46N 08°56'·36W Dunworthy Bay may be entered with care on its E side, avoiding Cow Rks and Horse Rk to the W. Sheltered from the N and E it is a secluded ⚓ in 8-10m of water. Appr to Clonakilty is shallow and drying. ⚓ off Ring Hd exposed in all but calmest conditions.

DIRK BAY 51°34'·90N 08°45'·52W ⚓ under bluffs to W side of bay avoiding Carrigduff Rks to E side with shallow Wk to their S.

Mill Cove and **Tralong Bay** are isolated ⚓ in narrow steep to coves, which should be approached only in fair weather with care and local advice.

9.12.23 GLANDORE/UNIONHALL

Cork, **51°33'·70N 09°07'·20W**

CHARTS AC 2092, 5622, 5623; Imray C56

TIDES Approx as for 9.12.24 Castletownshend

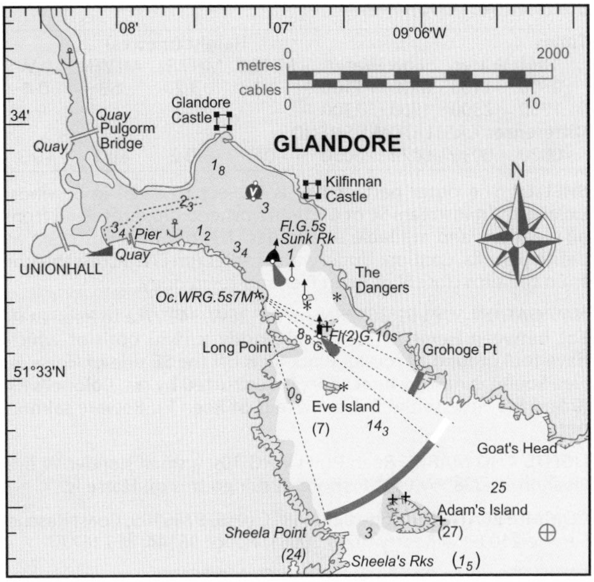

SHELTER Excellent. 12 Ys or ⚓ 1½ca E of the pier at Unionhall.

NAVIGATION WPT 51°32'·35N 09°05'·10W, 309°/1·2M to Outer Dangers. Approach between Adam Is and Goat's Hd, thence keep E of Eve Is and W of the chain of rocks: Outer, Middle and Inner Dangers and Sunk Rk. Before altering W for Unionhall, stand on to clear mudbank 1ca off S shore. Speed limit 3kn.

LIGHTS AND MARKS See 9.12.4. Galley Hd, Fl (5) 20s, is 5M E of ent. Middle and Inner Dangers are marked by 2 SHM bns; and Sunk Rk by a SHM lt buoy, Fl G 5s. Dir Lt 308° leads from W to E NW of *The Dangers*.

COMMUNICATIONS (Code 028) Coast Rescue 33115; Police (023) 23088; Dr 23456; HM Glandore/Unionhall 34737, mob 0866081944.

HM Ch 06.

FACILITIES **Glandore** GHYC, s €14.00/craft (contact Glandore Inn ☎33468/33518), Kos. **Unionhall** (outside of FVs/ drying Old Quay) €15.00/craft, D(occ on quayside) or (Leap 2M).

ADJACENT ANCHORAGES

RABBIT IS 51°32'·02N 09°07'·02W ⚓ in 8-10m of water in calm weather between Stack of Beans on Rabbit Is and shore. Ent to the E, S of Sheela's Rks. Narrow shallow passage to N of the Is should only be attempted with local knowledge.

SQUINCE HARBOUR 51°31'·81N 09°07'·75W to W of Rabbit Is best approached from Big Snd to S. Ent between Lamb Rk and South Rk with small ⚓ in pool in 7m.

9.12.24 CASTLETOWNSHEND

Cork **51°30'·90N 09°10'·70W** ❁❁❁◊◊✿✿✿

CHARTS AC 2092, 2129, 5623; Imray C56

TIDES +0605 Dover; ML 2·2; Duration 0605

Standard Port COBH (⟵)

Times				Height (metres)			
High Water		Low Water		MHWS	MHWN	MLWN	MLWS
0500	1100	0500	1100	4·1	3·2	1·3	0·4
1700	2300	1700	2300				
Differences CASTLETOWNSHEND							
−0020	−0030	−0020	−0050	−0·4	−0·2	+0·1	+0·3

SHELTER The outer part of hbr is subject to swell in S winds. Excellent ⚓ midstream SE of Castletownshend slip, protected from all weathers and available at all tides. ⚓ N of Cat Is upstream as depth permits. Caution: Underwater cables run E/W across the hbr from the slips close N of Reen Pier and town quay.

NAVIGATION WPT 51°30'·28N, 09°10'·26W, 349°/7ca to Reen Pt lt. Ent between Horse Is (35m) and Skiddy Is (9m) both of which have foul ground all round. Black Rk is off the SE side of Horse Is. Flea Sound, a narrow boat chan, is obstructed by rks. Colonel's Rk (0·5m) lies close to the E shore, 2ca N of Reen Pt. Beware salmon nets.

LIGHTS AND MARKS Reen Pt, Fl WRG 10s; a small slender W bn; vis shore-G-338°-W-001°-R-shore. A ruined tr is on Horse Is.

COMMUNICATIONS (Code 028) MRCC (066) 9746109; Coast Rescue Service 21039; ⊖ Bantry (027) 50061; Police 36144; Ⓗ 21677.

FACILITIES **Reen Pier** ↘ ⛽; **Sailing Club** ☎36100.

Village ▬ ⛽ ✉ Ⓑ(Skibbereen) 🛒 ✕ ◻ ⇄ ✈ (Cork).

ADJACENT ANCHORAGE

BARLOGE CREEK, Cork, **51°29'·57N 09°17'·58W**. AC 2129. Tides approx as Castletownshend. A narrow creek, well sheltered except from S/SE winds. Appr with Gokane Pt brg 120°. Enter W of Bullock Is, keeping to the W side to clear rks S of the island. ⚓ W of the Is in 3m but weedy. No facilities.

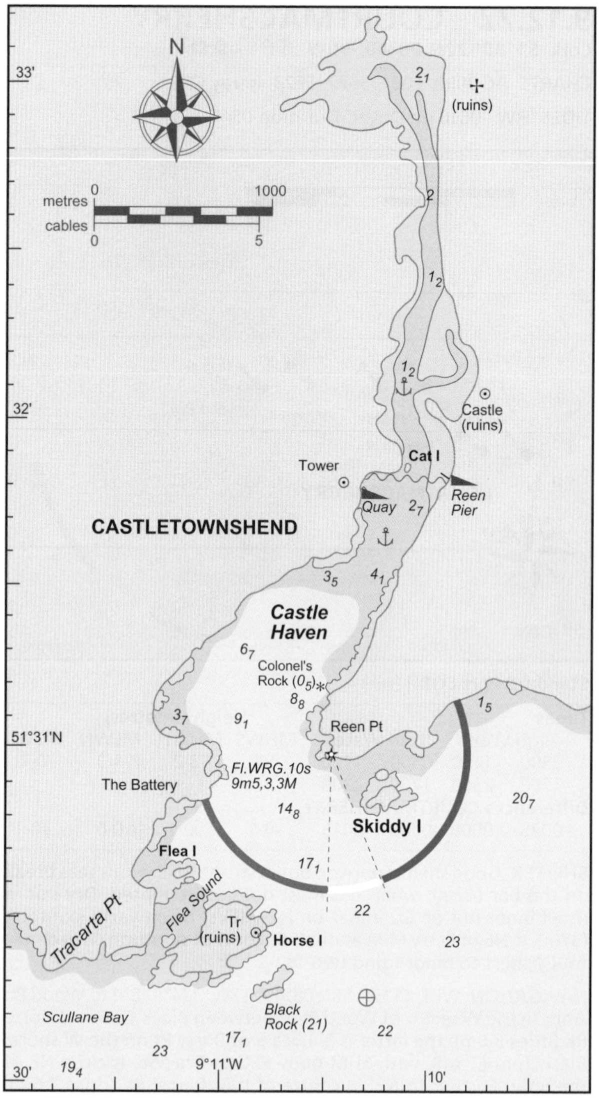

9.12.25 BALTIMORE

Cork **51°28'·30N 09°23'·40W**

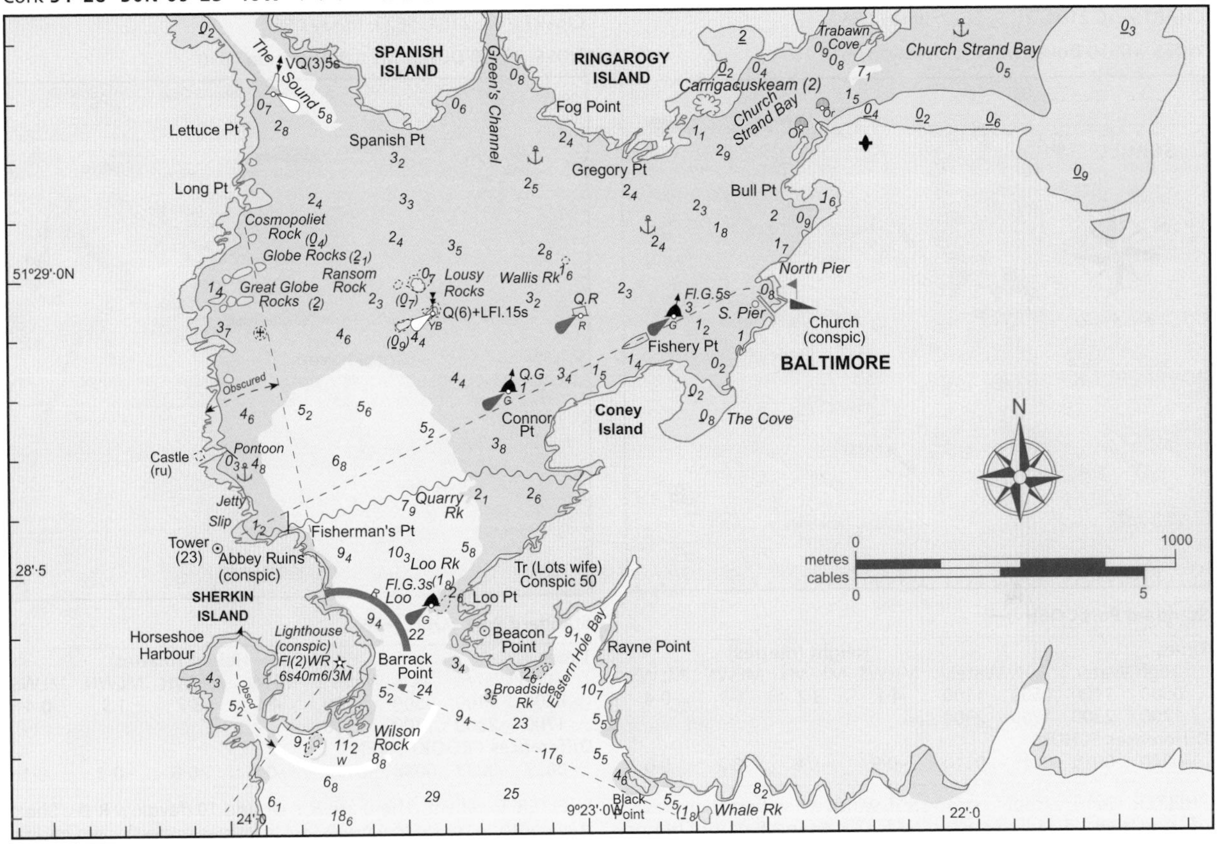

CHARTS AC 2129, 3725, 5623; Imray C56

TIDES –0605 Dover; ML 2·1; Duration 0610

Standard Port COBH (⟵)

Times				Height (metres)			
High Water		Low Water		MHWS	MHWN	MLWN	MLWS
0500	1100	0500	1100	4·1	3·2	1·3	0·4
1700	2300	1700	2300				
Differences BALTIMORE							
–0025	–0005	–0010	–0050	–0·6	–0·3	+0·1	+0·2

SHELTER Excellent. Access H24 from the S. At Baltimore, pontoon (May-Sep) on S Pier, ⊆ for up to 10 yachts rafted in 2·4m. Inner Hbr, partly dries between N and S piers, mostly used by ferries, local boats and FVs; the latter also berth on N pier. RoRo berth SE of Bull Pt. ⚓ about 200m W of S pier, or about 200m N of N Pier. Beware extensive moorings. In strong NW'lies ⚓ in Church Strand Bay. lts are required. Do not ⚓ in dredged chan between Wallis Rk buoy and N Pier, or in chan to Church Strand Bay. In strong W winds ⚓ in lee of Sherkin Is off Castle ruins or berth on pontoon (see Adjacent Anchorages, Sherkin Island).

NAVIGATION WPT 51°27'·93N 09°23'·46W, 000°/5ca to Loo Rk SHM lt buoy. No passage between buoy and mainland. Beware Lousy Rks (SCM bn) and Wallis Rk (PHM lt buoy) in middle of the bay. Cardinal buoys mark rocks in The Sound, which demands care in pilotage; AC 3725 and ICC SDs essential. SCM marks isolated rk off Inane Pt in the R Ilen, which is navigable on the flood for at least 4M above The Sound. Speed limit 6kn in R Ilen and N/NE of Wallace Rock.

LIGHTS AND MARKS See 9.12.4 and chartlet. Ent easily identified by Barrack Pt lt ho and conspic W tr (Lot's Wife) on Beacon Pt.

COMMUNICATIONS (Code 028) MRCC and Coast/Cliff Rescue Service (066) 9476109; ⊖ (027) 53210; Police 20102; Dr 23456/after hrs 1850 335999, Ⓗ 21677. HM 087 2351485.

VHF (HM) Ch 09, 16.

FACILITIES Berthing: May-Sept from €20/craft, ☎22145, 0872 351485 or www.atlanticboat.ie; ⊆ (☎20106) on pontoon; **Baltimore SC** ☎20426, visitors welcome; **Sherkin** Pontoon access to shore in season.
Services Kos (on R Ilen at Old Court), ACA.
Village bus to Cork for ⇄ ✈.

ADJACENT ANCHORAGES
SHERKIN ISLAND on W side of harbour entrance. ⚓s: Horseshoe Harbour (keep well to the W in narrow entrance; unlit); and off Castle ruins, 5ca N, where there are also some ⊆ on pontoons (and electricity) belonging to nearby Islander's Rest Hotel.

CLEAR ISLAND, N HARBOUR, 51°26'·60N 09°30'·20W. AC 2129, 5623. Tides approx as Schull, 9.12.26. A tiny, partly drying inlet on N coast of Clear Is, exposed to N'ly swell. Rks either side of outer appr 196°. Inside the narrow (30m), rky ent keep to the E. Lie to 2 ⚓s on E side in about 1·5m or drying berth in Inner Hbr clear of ferry bad weather berth. Outer (N) bkwtr rebuilt with tidal gate (2015) which will permit vessels to remain afloat, further significant work is in progress. Facilities: ✕.

ROARINGWATER BAY, Long Island Bay AC 2129, 5623. Enter between Cape Clear and Mizen Hd, extends NE into Roaringwater Bay. *Beware extensive, low-lying unlit fish farms.* Safest appr, S of Schull, is via Carthy's Sound (51°30'N 09°30'W). From the SE appr via Gascanane Sound, but beware Toorane Rks, Anima Rk and outlying rks off many of the islands. Shelter in various winds at ⚓s clockwise from Horse Island: 3ca E and 7ca NE of E tip of Horse Is; in Ballydehob B 2m (Ballydehob has a good quay for tenders and most facilities); Poulgorm B 2m; 3ca SSW of Carrigvalish Rks in 6m. Rincolisky Cas (ru) is conspic on S side of bay. The narrow chan E of Hare Is and N of Sherkin Is has two ⚓s; also leads via The Sound into Baltimore hbr. Local advice useful. Temp'y fair weather ⚓s in Carthy's Islands. Rossbrin Cove safe ⚓ 2·5M E of Schull, but many local moorings; no access from E of Horse Is due to drying Horse Ridge.

9.12.26 SCHULL

Cork **51°30'·80N 09°32'·00W** ❁❁❁◇◇✿✿✿

CHARTS AC 2184, 2129, 5623; Imray C56

TIDES +0610 Dover; ML 1·8; Duration 0610

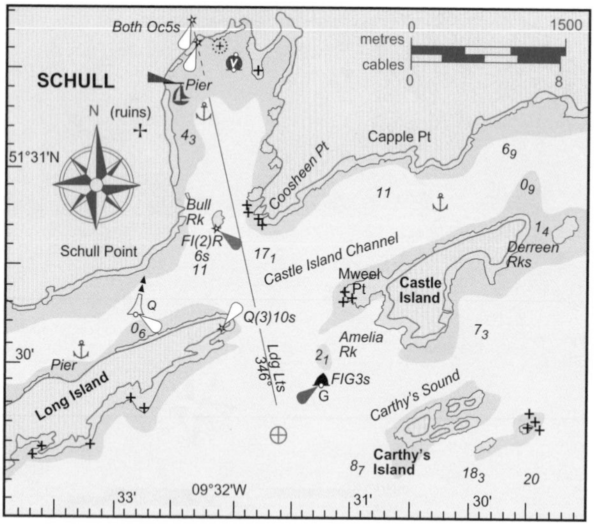

Standard Port COBH (⟵)

Times				Height (metres)			
High Water		Low Water		MHWS	MHWN	MLWN	MLWS
0500	1100	0500	1100	4·1	3·2	1·3	0·4
1700	2300	1700	2300				
Differences SCHULL							
−0040	−0015	−0015	−0110	−0·9	−0·6	−0·2	0·0

SHELTER Good, except in strong S/SE winds when best shelter is N of Long Island. Schull Hbr access H24. 12 Y ◉s in NE part of hbr or ⚓ in 3m 1ca SE of pier, usually lit by street lts all night; keep clear of fairway marked by 8 unlit lateral buoys (summer time only).

NAVIGATION WPT 51°29'·60N 09°31'·60W, 346°/2·1M to front ldg lt. In hbr ent, Bull Rk (dries 1·8m), R iron perch, can be passed either side. Beware unmarked isolated rock, 0·5m, close to the visitors' buoys.

LIGHTS AND MARKS See 9.12.4 and chartlet. Ldg lts, lead 346° between Long Is Pt, W conical tr, and Amelia Rk SHM lt buoy; thence E of Bull Rk and towards head of bay. By day in good vis 2 W radomes conspic on Mt Gabriel (2M N of Schull) lead 355° with Long Is Pt lt ho in transit.

COMMUNICATIONS (Code 028) MRCC (066) 9476109; Coast/Cliff Rescue Service 35318; Inshore Rescue Service 086 236 0206: ⊖ (027) 51562; Police 28111; Dr 28311; Ⓗ (027) 50133. Water Sports Centre 28554; HM 086 039105. No VHF.

FACILITIES **Schull Pier/Hbr** (not at LWS) FV pier/pontoon for tenders, tempy, ◉s €10/night, (by arrangement). **Sailing Club** ☎37352; **Services** Kos. **Village** (Ballydehob 5M), @, Charts, ✉ Ⓑ ✕ bus to Cork for ⇄ ✈ Ferries.

ADJACENT HARBOURS

GOLEEN (Kireal-coegea), Cork, **51°29'·65N 09°42'·21W**. AC 2184, 5623. Tides as Crookhaven. A narrow inlet 6ca N of Spanish Pt; good shelter in fair weather, except from SE. 2 churches are easily seen, but ent not visible until close. Keep to S side of ent and ⚓ fore-and-aft just below quay, where also possible. Facilities: bus to Cork ✈ ⇄.

9.12.27 CROOKHAVEN

Cork **51°28'·50N 09°42'·00W** ❁❁ ❁◇✿✿✿

CHARTS AC 2184, 5623; Imray C56

TIDES +0550 Dover; ML 1·8; Duration 0610

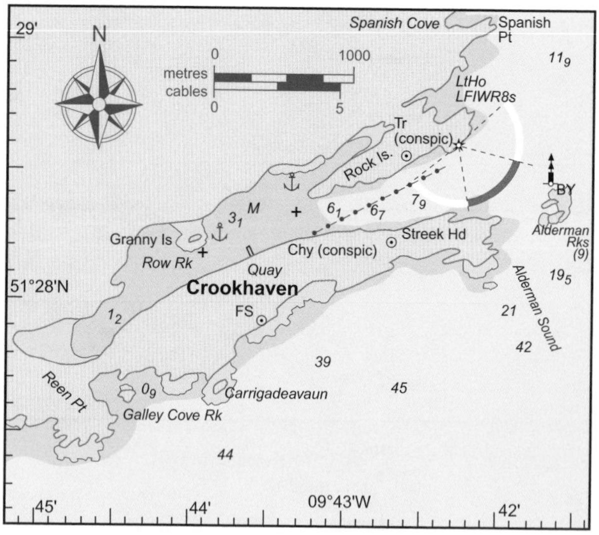

Standard Port COBH (⟵)

Times				Height (metres)			
High Water		Low Water		MHWS	MHWN	MLWN	MLWS
0500	1100	0500	1100	4·1	3·2	1·3	0·4
1700	2300	1700	2300				
Differences CROOKHAVEN							
−0057	−0033	−0048	−0112	−0·8	−0·6	−0·4	−0·1

SHELTER Excellent. There are 8 Y ◉s and 10 dayglow R ◉s. Short stay pontoon for up to 4 boats (/stores/passengers). ⚓s in middle of bay in 3m; off W tip of Rock Is; and E of Granny Is; last two are far from the village. Holding is patchy, especially in strong SW'lies; beware weed, shellfish beds around shoreline and submarine pipeline from Rock Is to Crookhaven.

NAVIGATION WPT 51°28'·50N 09°40'·50W, 274°/1M to Rock Is lt ho. Ent between this lt and NCM bn on Black Horse Rks (3½ca ESE). From S, keep 1ca E of Alderman Rks and ½ca off Black Horse Rks bn. Passage between Streek Hd and Alderman Rks is not advised for strangers. Inside the bay the shores are steep-to. 1ca WSW of West end of Rock Is beware isolated rock, which is awash at LAT.

LIGHTS AND MARKS Lt ho on Rock Is (conspic W tr) L Fl WR 8s 20m 13/11M; vis outside hbr: W over Long Is Bay-281°-R-340°; vis inside hbr: 281°-R-348°-W-shore(N).

COMMUNICATIONS (Code 028) MRCC (066) 9476109; Coast/Cliff Rescue at Goleen 35318; ⊖ (027) 50061; Dr 35148; ✉ 35200. HM (O'Sullivan's Bar) 35319. No VHF.

FACILITIES **Village** ◉s (☎086 356 7771) €8.00, pontoon for small craft ✉ Ⓑ(Schull) ✕, taxi to Goleen.

THE WEST COAST

This coast offers wonderful cruising, although exposed to the Atlantic and any swell offshore; but this diminishes mid-summer. In bad weather the sea breaks dangerously on shoals with quite substantial depths. There is often a refuge nearby, but if caught out in deteriorating weather and poor vis, a stranger may need to make an offing until conditions improve. Even in mid-summer a gale may be met in a two-week cruise. Fog is less frequent than in the Irish Sea.

▶ *Tidal streams are weak, except round headlands.* ◀

The few lights inshore render navigation unwise after dark, but coastal navigation is feasible in good visibility.

9.12.28 DUNMANUS / BANTRY BAY

Cork **51°34'N 09°57'W**

CHARTS AC 2552, 1840, 1838, 5623; Imray C56

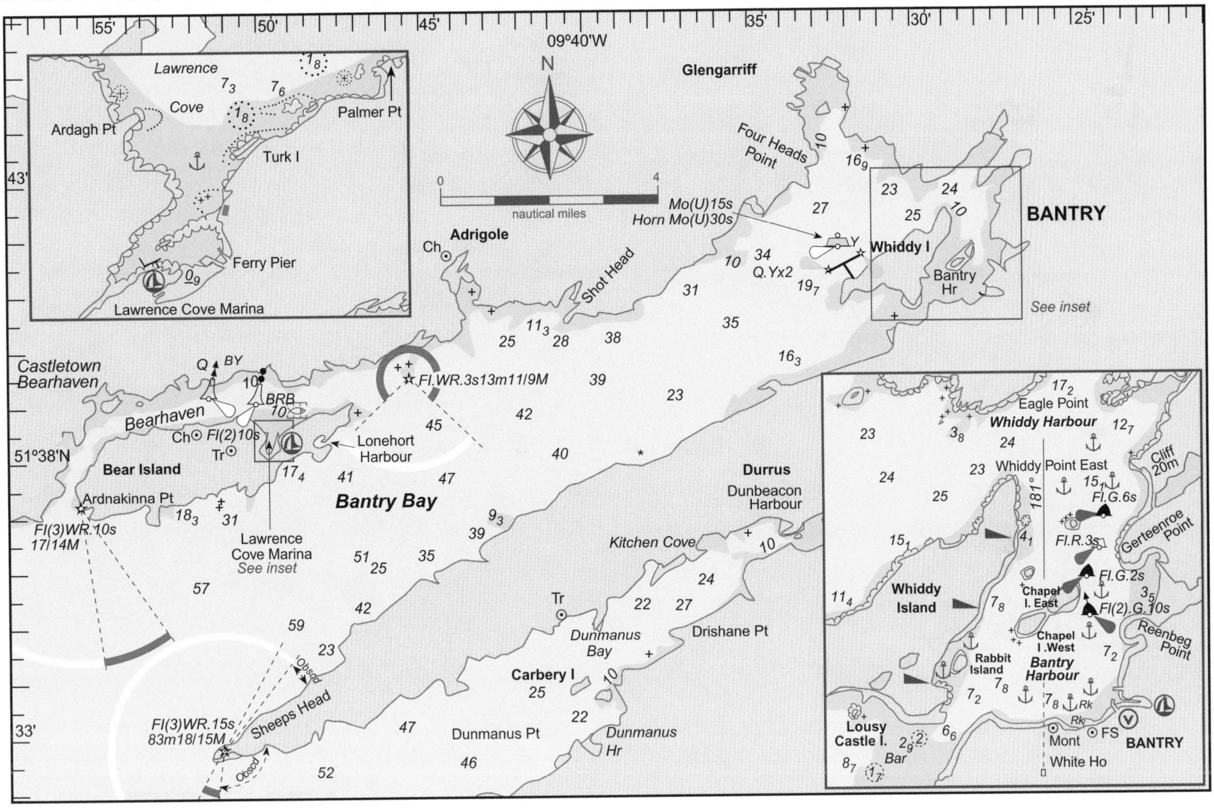

TIDES +0600 Dover; ML 1·8; Duration 0610

Standard Port COBH (⟵)

Times				Height (metres)			
High Water		Low Water		MHWS	MHWN	MLWN	MLWS
0500	1100	0500	1100	4·1	3·2	1·3	0·4
1700	2300	1700	2300				
Differences BANTRY							
–0045	–0025	–0040	–0105	–0·7	–0·6	–0·2	+0·1
CASTLETOWN (Bearhaven)							
–0048	–0012	–0025	–0101	–0·8	–0·6	–0·2	0·0
BLACK BALL HARBOUR (51°36N 10°02W)							
–0115	–0035	–0047	–0127	–0·7	–0·6	–0·1	+0·1
DUNMANUS BAY							
–0107	–0031	–0044	–0120	–0·7	–0·6	–0·2	0·0
DUNBEACON HARBOUR							
–0057	–0025	–0032	–0104	–0·8	–0·7	–0·3	–0·1

SHELTER/NAVIGATION Bantry Bay extends 20M ENE from Sheep's Hd, Fl (3) WR 15s 83m 18/15M. Access is easy, but the Bay is exposed to W'lies. The shore is clear everywhere except off Bear Is and Whiddy Is. Some of the many well-sheltered ⚓s on the N shore are detailed on this page. The S shore has few ⚓s.

DUNMANUS BAY, Cork. AC 2552, 5623. Tides see 9.12.28. Appr between Three Castle Hd and Sheep's Hd, Fl (3) WR 15s 83m 18/15M; no other lts. Ent to **Dunmanus Hbr**, 51°32'·70N 09°39'·86W, is 1ca wide; breakers both sides. ⚓ in 4m centre of B. **Kitchen Cove**, 51°35'·50N 09°38'·05W, best of the 3 hbrs; enter W of Owens Is and ⚓ 1ca NNW of it or 2ca further N in 3m. Exposed to S, but good holding. Quay at Ahakista village: (drying). **Dunbeacon Hbr**, 51°36'·35N 09°33'·60W, is shallow and rock-girt. Quay possible in 2m (used by FVs); ⚓ E or SE of Mannion Is. Durrus (¾M).

LONEHORT HARBOUR 51°38'·12N 09°47'·80W. AC 1840, 5623. At E tip of Bear Is, good shelter but keep S at ent to clear unmarked rks; then turn ENE to ⚓ in 2·7m at E end of cove. Be aware of Firing Practice Area to east of harbour entrance (full clear range procedure in force).

ADRIGOLE 51°40'·51N 09°43'·22W. AC 1840, 5623. Good shelter, but squally in W/N gales. Beware Doucallia Rk, dries 1·2m, 1M SSW of ent. Beyond the 2ca wide ent, keep E of Orthons Is (rks on W side). 7 Y 🅐s NE of Orthons Is. ⚓s to suit wind direction: off pier on E shore 4m; N or NW of Orthons Is. Drumlave (½M E): (sailing school).

Trafrask Bay, 2M east, has Y🅐 at **51°40'·8N 09°40'·1W**.

GLENGARRIFF 51°44'·20N 09°31'·90W. AC 1838, 5623. Tides as Bantry. Beautiful ⚓ S of Bark Is in 7-10m; or to NE in 3m, where there are 6 Y 🅐s. Better for yachts than Bantry hbr. Ent between Big Pt and Gun Pt. Keep 1ca E of rks off Garinish Island (Illnacullen) and Ship Is; chan marked to either side by lateral marks LFl R/G 4s. Beware marine farms. HT cables removed allowing access N of Garinish with local knowledge; but rocky chan W of should not be attempted. Facilities: Eccles hotel. **Village** (ferry berth 1800-1900) Kos.

BANTRY 51°40'·85N 09°27'·85W. AC 1838, 5623. Beware Gerane Rks ½M W of Whiddy Is. Appr via the buoyed/lit N chan to E of Horse and Chapel Is; keep 2ca off all islands to clear unlit marine farms. The S chan, fair weather only. Appr Relane Pt hdg 063° with HW mark S. Beach (seaward edge of airfield) ≠ Reenbeg Cliff (distant rounded hill) to clear Cracker Rk, then leave Blue Hill and S Beach to stbd. 🅐s call Bantry Hbr Ch 14 or ☎027 51253; VHF Ch 14 11 16 (H24). HM (027) 53277; ⊜ 50061; Police 50045; Dr 50405; Ⓗ 50133. MRCC (066) 9476109. Facilities: **Pier** (drying), Marina 40; **Bantry Bay SC** ☎51724, Kos Ⓑ bus to Cork.

9.12.29 CASTLETOWN BEARHAVEN

Cork **51°34'N 09°57'W**

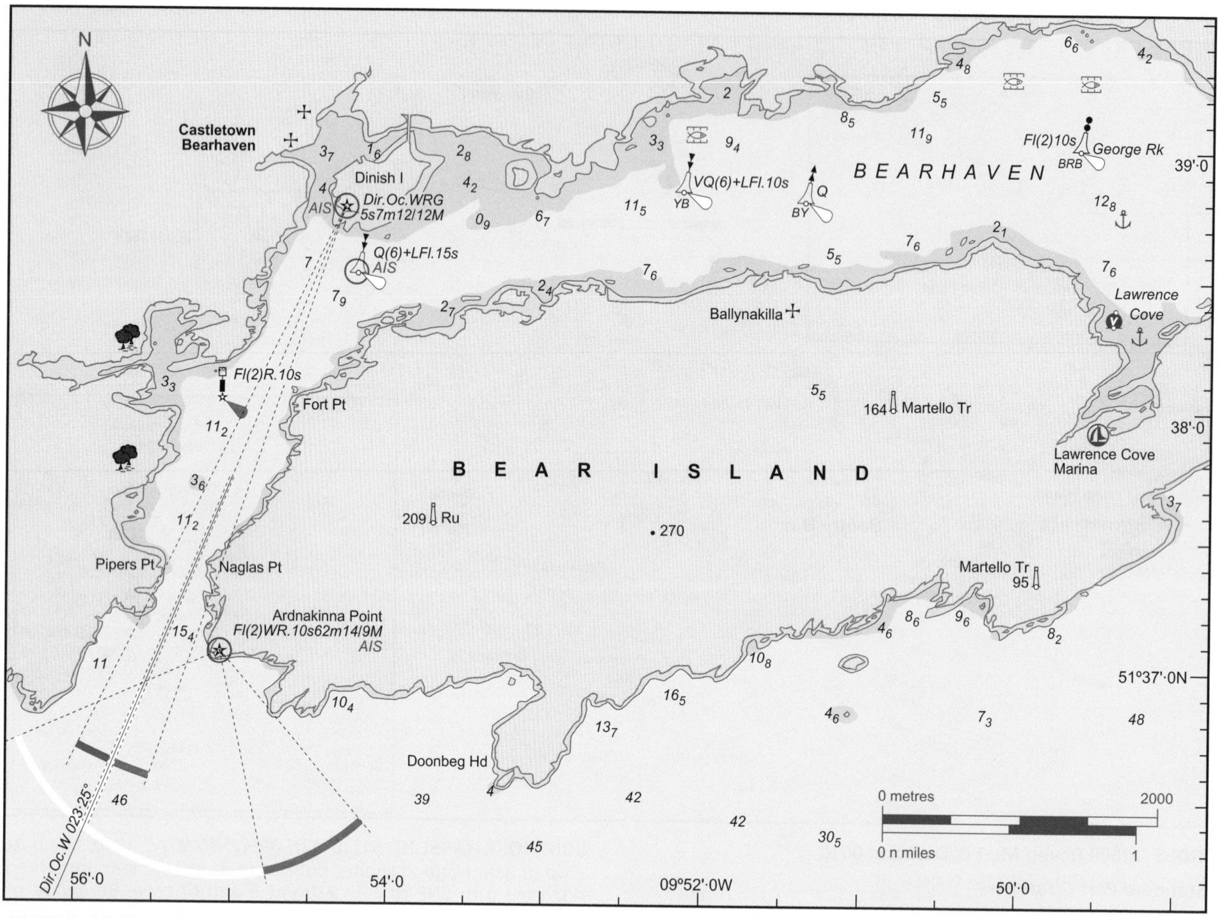
Castletown Bearhaven
Dinish I
Dir.Oc.WRG 5s7m12/12M
AIS
Q(6)+LFl.15s
Fl(2)R.10s
Fort Pt
Pipers Pt
Naglas Pt
Ardnakinna Point
Fl(2)WR.10s62m14/9M
Doonbeg Hd
Dir.Oc.W 023·25°
VQ(6)+LFl.10s
YB
Q
BY
BEARHAVEN
Fl(2)10s
George Rk
BRB
Ballynakilla
Lawrence Cove
164 Martello Tr
Lawrence Cove Marina
BEAR ISLAND
209 Ru
270
Martello Tr 95
0 metres 2000
0 n miles 1
39'·0
38'·0
51°37'·0N
56'·0
54'·0
09°52'·0W
50'·0

CHARTS AC 1840, 5623; Imray C56

TIDES +0600 Dover; ML 1·8; Duration 0610

Standard Port COBH (⟵)

Times				Height (metres)			
High Water		Low Water		MHWS	MHWN	MLWN	MLWS
0500	1100	0500	1100	4·1	3·2	1·3	0·4
1700	2300	1700	2300				
Differences CASTLETOWN (Bearhaven)							
–0048	–0012	–0025	–0101	–0·8	–0·6	–0·2	0·0

SHELTER Castletownbere Fishery Harbour lies between Dinish Is and the mainland. A pontoon with for yachts is at W end of Bere hbr, but also used by small fishing vessels. Recommend calling HM in advance(OH). ⚓ at **Dunboy Bay,** W of Piper Snd (open to E). 4 Y s are laid Apr-Sep 3ca E of Dinish Is.

NAVIGATION At W ent, Ardnakinna Pt, Fl (2) WR 10s 62m 17/14M, H24. At E ent to Bearhaven: Roancarrigmore, Fl WR 5s 13m 11/9M. Appr W of Bear Is on 023·25° Dir lt, Oc WRG 5s 7m 15/12M (023°-W-023·5°); then inner ldg lts 008°, both Oc Bu 6s 4/7m 6M, vis 005°-013°, via ent chan which narrows to 50m where it is marked by lit bcns. Beware Walter Scott Rk (2·7m), SCM lt buoy, and Carrigaglos (0·6m high) S of Dinish Is.

LIGHTS AND MARKS See 9.12.4 and chartlet.

COMMUNICATIONS (Code 028) Coast/Cliff Rescue Service 35318; Inshore Rescue Service 086 236 0206. HM (027) 70220.

VHF Ch **14** 16.

FACILITIES **Fishery Hbr** on quay; on Dinish Is.
Town Kos .
Rerrin (storage) bus to Cork.

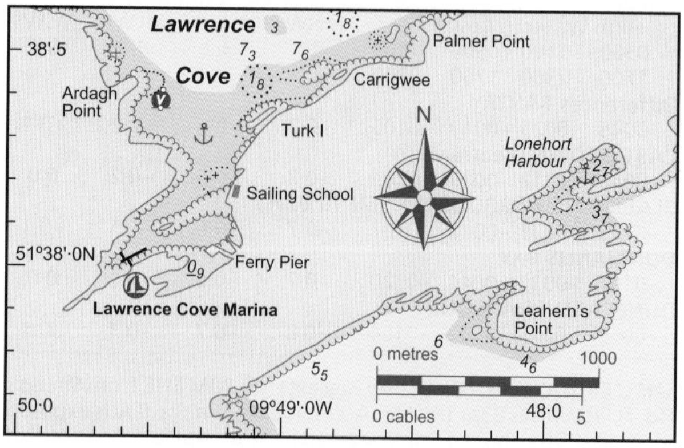
Lawrence Cove
Palmer Point
Ardagh Point
Carrigwee
Turk I
Sailing School
Lonehort Harbour
Ferry Pier
Lawrence Cove Marina
Leahern's Point
0 metres 1000
0 cables 5
38'·5
51°38'·0N
50·0
09°49'·0W
48·0

ADJACENT HARBOURS

BEAR (BERE) ISLAND Good shelter on N side of Bear Island. There are 4 yellow s in 3m close S of Ardagh Point, or ⚓ in 4m to W of Turk Is. A pontoon with for yachts is at W end of Bere hbr, but also used by small fishing vessels. Recommend calling HM in advance(OH). From E keep clear of Palmer Rock and a shoal patch, both 1·8m. Friendly welcome at the only marina between Kinsale and Cahersiveen/Dingle.

LAWRENCE COVE 51°38'·28N 09°49'·28W; Marina on S side of cove has NE/SW pontoon 90m long in 3-3·5m. ☎027 75044; VHF Ch 16 **M.** 40(€2·00), .

9.12.30 KENMARE RIVER

Kerry **51°45'·00N 10°00'·00W** ❀❀❀◊✿✿✿

CHARTS AC 2495; Imray C56

TIDES +0515 Dover; Duration Dunkerron 0620

Standard Port COBH (⟵)

Times				Height (metres)			
High Water		Low Water		MHWS	MHWN	MLWN	MLWS
0500	1100	0500	1100	4·1	3·2	1·3	0·4
1700	2300	1700	2300				
Differences BALLYCROVANE HARBOUR (Coulagh Bay)							
–0116	–0036	–0053	–0133	–0·6	–0·5	–0·1	0·0
DUNKERRON HARBOUR							
–0117	–0027	–0050	–0140	–0·2	–0·3	+0·1	0·0
WEST COVE (51°46'N 10°03'W)							
–0113	–0033	–0049	–0129	–0·6	–0·5	–0·1	0·0
BALLINSKELLIGS BAY							
–0119	–0039	–0054	–0134	–0·5	–0·5	–0·1	0·0

SHELTER Garnish Bay (S of Long I): is only good in settled weather and W'ly winds. ⚓ either W or 1ca S of the Carrigduff concrete bn.

Ballycrovane: in NE of Coulagh B is a good ⚓, but open to W'ly swell which breaks on submerged rks in SE. N and E shores are foul 5ca NE of Bird Is.

Cleanderry: ent NE of Illaunbweeheen (Yellow Is) is only 7m wide and rky. ⚓ ENE of inner hbr. Beware marine farms.

Ardgroom: excellent shelter, but intricate ent over rky bar. Appr with B bn brg 135°; then 2 W bns (front on Black Rk, rear ashore) lead 099° over bar. Alter 206° as two bns astern come in transit. When clear, steer WNW to ⚓ 0·5 ca E of Reenavade pier. Beware marine farms off Ardgroom & Kilmakilloge.

Kilmakilloge: is a safe ⚓ in all winds. Beware mussel beds and rky shoals. On appr keep S side of ent, heading W of Spanish Is until past PHM buoy, Fl(2) R 10s, then steer approx 105°. Bunaw Hbr ldg lts 041°, front Oc R 3s, rear Iso R 2s (access only near HW; ⌓ for shoal draught). Keep S side of ent; ⚓ 2ca W of Carrigwee bn; S of Eskadawer Pt; or Collorus Hbr W side only.

Ormond's Harbour: good shelter except in SW or W winds, but beware rk 2½ca ENE of Hog Is. ⚓ in S half of bay.

Kenmare: good shelter. Access only near HW via narrow ch marked by poles on S side. Poss ⌓ (☎064 664 2059 or 087 250 8803) rafted at end of pier (⛽ available) at N side of river, just below town. Beware very strong ebbs at springs and after heavy rains.

Dunkerron Harbour: ent between Cod Rks and The Boar to ⚓ 1ca NW of Fox Is in 3·2m; land at Templenoe pier. 4ca E of Reen Pt behind pier ⛽ available.

Sneem: enter between Sherky Is and Rossdohan Is. Hotel conspic NE of hbr. 4 Y 🅐s and ⚓ NE of Garinish Is, but uncomfortable if swell enters either side of Sherky Is. Beware of marine farms.

Darrynane: 1½M NW of Lamb's Hd, is appr'd from the S between Deenish and Moylaun Islands, but not with high SW swell. Enter with care on the ldg marks/lts 034°, 2 W bns, both Oc 3s 10/16m 4M. Safe ⚓ (3m) NE of Lamb's Is. Also ⚓s in Lehid Hbr (S shore), R Blackwater, Coongar Hbr & W Cove.

NAVIGATION WPT 51°40'·00N 10°17'·20W, 065°/15·6M to 0.5M S of Sherky Is. From SW, keep NW of The Bull and Dursey Is. From SE, Dursey Sound is possible in fair weather but narrow (beware Flag Rk 0·3m) and with cable car, 21m clearance. To clear dangerous rks off Coulagh Bay, keep twr on Dursey Is well open of Cod's Head 220°. From NW, there are 3 deep chans off Lamb's Head: between Scarriff Is and Deenish Is which is clear; between Deenish and Moylaun Is which has rky shoals; and between Moylaun and Two Headed Is which is clear and 4½ca wide. A night appr into the river is possible, but close appr to hbrs or ⚓s is not advised. Upriver from Sneem Hbr, keep clear of Maiden Rk(dries 0·5m); Church Rks and Lackeen Rks are unmarked; a buoyed chan lies between Carrignaronabeg and Bat Rock. Beware marine farms.

LIGHTS AND MARKS On Dursey Is: Old Watch Twr (conspic) 250m. Eagle Hill (Cod's Hd) 216m. Lights are as on chartlet.

COMMUNICATIONS (Code 064) MRCC (066) 9476109; ⊖ Bantry (027) 50061; 🄷 4108; Police 41177. No VHF.

FACILITIES

ARDGROOM Pallas Hbr ☎ ☎ Kos 🛒 ✕ 🄳 @ ✉ at Ardgoom village (2M SSW of Reenavade pier).

KILMAKILLOGE Bunaw Pier ⌓ 🛒 🄳; 2M to ☎ Kos ✉.

KENMARE ⌓. **Town** ☎ ☎ ⛽ Kos 🄷 ✉ inc @ Ⓑ ✕ 🛒 🄳 🄷 ✉ inc @ Ⓑ ⇄ (bus to Killarney) ✈ (Cork or Killarney).

SNEEM ⚓ at Hotel Parknasilla and Oysterbed Ho pier (⛽). **Town** (2M from hbr), ☎ ☎ ⛽ Kos ✉ 🛒 ✕ 🄳.

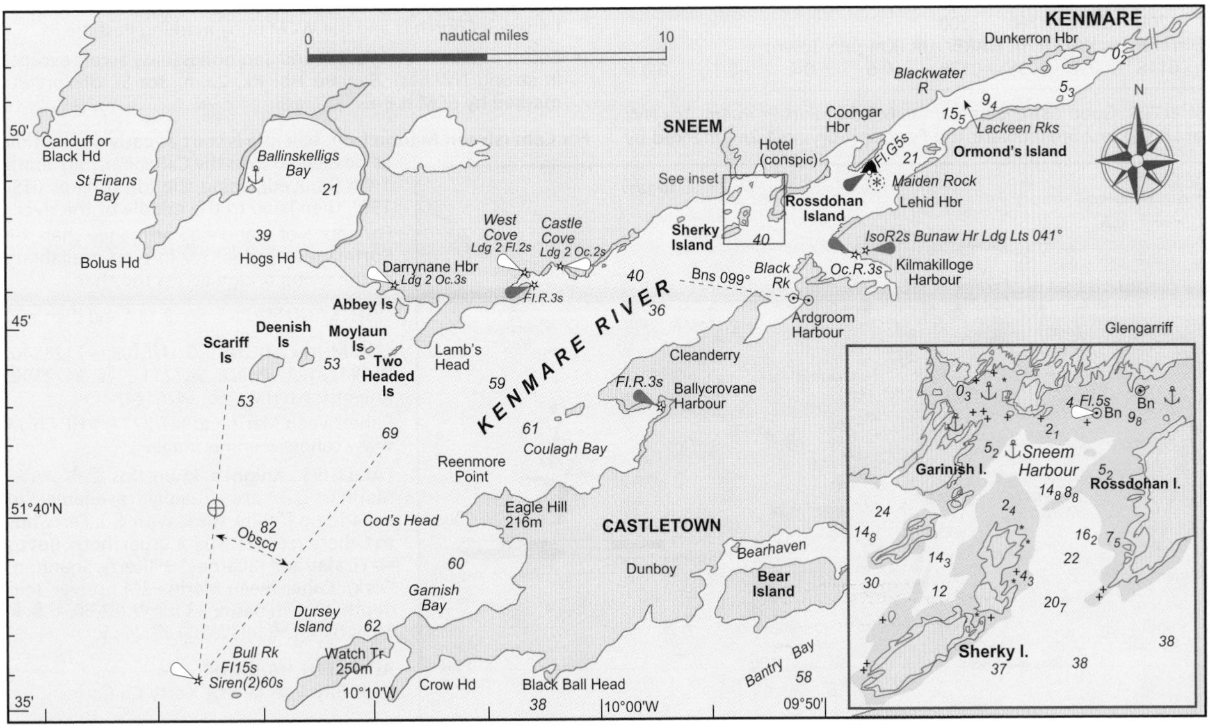

9.12.31 DINGLE BAY

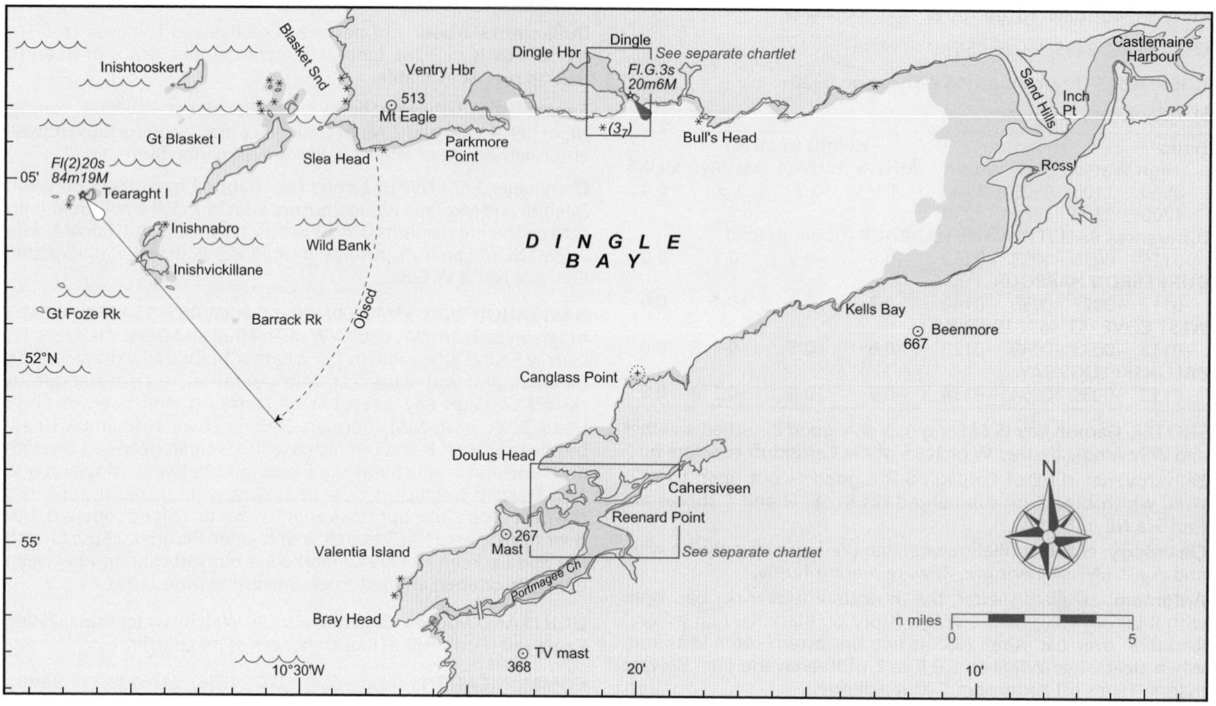

9.12.32 VALENTIA HARBOUR

Kerry **51°55'·7N 10°17'·1W**

CHARTS AC 2125; Imray C56

TIDES +0515 Dover

Standard Port COBH (⟵)

Times				Height (metres)			
High Water		Low Water		MHWS	MHWN	MLWN	MLWS
0500	1100	0500	1100	4·1	3·2	1·3	0·4
1700	2300	1700	2300				
Differences VALENTIA HARBOUR (Knight's Town)							
−0118	−0038	−0056	−0136	−0·6	−0·4	−0·1	0·0

SHELTER Good ⚓s at: Glanleam B, 6ca S of Fort Pt in 4m; 1ca NW of LB slip in 2·5m (beware The Foot, spit drying 1·2m, marked by ECM lt buoy) SE of Ferry Pier at Knight's Town (E end of the island) in 4m; in bay on the S side of Beginish Is in 3m.

NAVIGATION WPT 51°56'·84N 10°20'·15W 147°/1M to Fort Pt lt. Beware rock outcrop 2.6m 1 Ca ENE Reenadrolaun Pt and other shoal patches within 10m contour. Appr NE end of Valentia Is via:

- Doulus Bay, N of Beginish Is (avoid if swell is running). Clear Black Rks by ½ca then head for E end of Beginish Is as soon as Reenard Pt opens to port. When Lamb Is and the N point of Beginish are about to open astern, steer to keep them so till Reenard Point opens to the E of Church Is. Then steer to pass between Church Is and the WCM buoy marking Passage Rk.
- Better ent, between Fort Pt and Beginish Is (easy access except in strong NW'lies). Beware Hbr Rk, 2·6m, 3ca SE of Fort Pt marked by ECM lt Bn.

For **Cahersiveen Marina** from Valentia Is start as early on the tide as possible to cross the Caher Bar, min depth 1·4m (buoyed), using the ldg lts/lines 019-199°, then keep to the middle of the river.

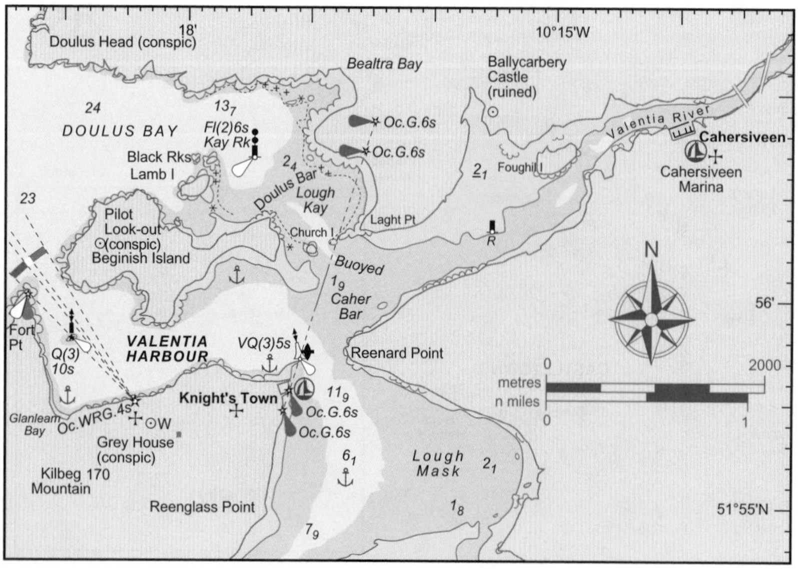

For appr S of Island via Portmagee chan see **Portmagee** overleaf for info on availability of the swing bridge across the chan.

LIGHTS AND MARKS See 9.12.4 and chartlet.

COMMUNICATIONS CG 9476109; ⊜ 7128540; Dr 9472121; Police 9472111; Ⓗ 9472100; Knightstown HM (066) 9476124;

Cahersiveen Marina ☎947 2777, VHF Ch **M** www.cahersiveenmarina.ie.

FACILITIES **Knight's Town** Kos

Marina are readily available in expanding facility, some with. Ferry/bus to Cahersiveen (2½M) for usual shops; Bus to ⇄ (Tralee and Killarney) ✈ (Kerry, Shannon, Cork). **Cahersiveen Marina** 2M upriver, min depth 2.5m in basin, 93 inc ⓥ €2.50, Ⓔ (14t) ✉ Ⓑ.

ADJACENT HARBOUR

Kells Bay 4 ⓥs laid by Kerry Co Council.

9.12.33 DINGLE

Kerry **52°07'·14N 10°15'·48W** ❁❁❁◊◊✿✿✿

CHARTS AC 2789, 2790; Imray C55, C56

TIDES +0540 Dover; ML 2·1m; Duration 0605

Standard Port COBH (⟵)

Times				Height (metres)			
High Water		Low Water		MHWS	MHWN	MLWN	MLWS
0500	1100	0500	1100	4·1	3·2	1·3	0·4
1700	2300	1700	2300				
Differences DINGLE							
–0111	–0041	–0049	–0119	–0·1	0·0	+0·3	+0·4
SMERWICK HARBOUR							
–0107	–0027	–0041	–0121	–0·3	–0·4	ND	ND

SHELTER Excellent at marina (4·5m depth) in landlocked hbr. A busy fishing port.

NAVIGATION WPT 52°06'·20N 10° 15'·48W, 360°/1·06M on Fl G 3s. Straightforward entrance H24. To SW Beware Crow Rk (dries 3·7m) and shoals lying between it and Reenbeg Pt (0·8M NE). Keep clear of rocky ledge SW of Black Pt indicated by lit SHM.

LIGHTS AND MARKS Eask Twr (195m, with fingerpost pointing E) is conspic 0·85M WSW of ent. Lit trs, Fl G 3s 20m 6M on NE side, and Fl 5s 5m 3M SW of ent. Chan, dredged 2·6m, is marked by 5 SHM lt buoys and 3 PHM lt buoys, as chartlet. Ldg lts, both Oc 3s, (W ◊s on B poles) lead from astern 182° to hbr bkwtrs. Sectored Dir lt 002° Oc RWG 4s on W side of Main Pier.

COMMUNICATIONS (Code 066) MRCC (066) 9476109; ⊖ 7121480; Dr 9152225; Ⓗ9151455; Police 9151522. Emergencies: 999 or 112.

Ch **14** 16 but no calls required. Valentia Radio (Ch 24 28) will relay urgent messages to Dingle HM.

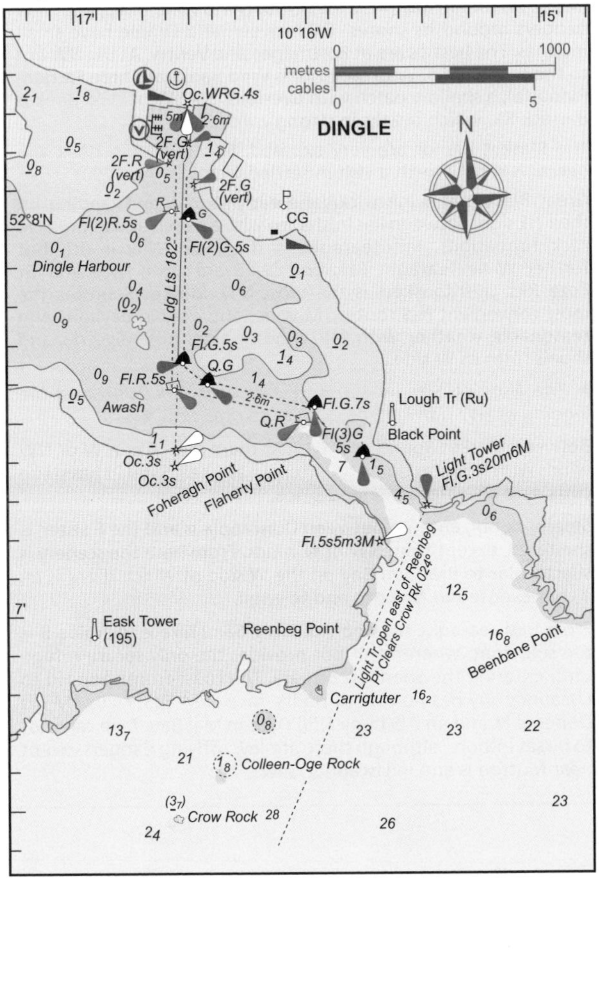

FACILITIES Marina www.dinglemarina.ie ☎087 9254115, (launch €5) 60+20 €2, (70t).

Town Kos Ⓔ Ⓑ ✕ ⇌ Tralee (by bus) ✈ (Kerry 30M).

ANCHORAGES E OF DINGLE HARBOUR

CASTLEMAIN HARBOUR, 15M E at the head of Dingle Bay, largely dries and should only be entered with local knowledge or after inspection.

ANCHORAGE SW VALENTIA ISLAND

PORTMAGEE, Kerry, **51°53'·20N 10°22'·29W**. AC 2125. HW +0550 on Dover; ML 2·0m; Duration 0610; See 9.12.32. A safe ⚓ 2·5M E of Bray Head in Portmagee Sound between the mainland and Valentia Is. The ent to the Sound often has bad seas, but dangers are visible. Care required E of Reencaheragh Pt (S side) due rks either side. Deepest water is N of mid-chan. ⚓ off the pier (S side) in 5m, opposite Skelling Heritage Centre (well worth a visit). on pier is not recommended due to strong tides. Facilities: (at hotel), ✕ Kos.

The swing bridge 1ca E of pier is currently closed; for further information check with Valentia RNLI or Valentia CG.

ANCHORAGE CLOSE W OF DINGLE HARBOUR

VENTRY Kerry, **52°06·70N 10°20'·30W**. AC 2789, 2790. HW +0540 on Dover; ML 2·1m; Duration 0605; Use 9.12.33. A pleasant harbour with entrance 1M wide 2M W of Eask Tr (conspic). Good holding on hard sand, open to swell from the SE; Sheltered from SW to N winds but in fresh w'lies prone to sharp squalls. Beware Reenvare Rocks 1ca SE of Parkmore Point; also a rocky ridge 2·9m, on which seas break, extends 2·5ca SSE of Ballymore Pt. No lts. 3 s laid by Kerry Co Council and ⚓s in about 4m off Ventry Strand (✠ brg W, the village NE); or in 3m SW side of bay, 1ca N of pier keeping clear of marine and seaweed farms. Both piers access HW±3 for landing. Facilities: Kos ✕.

ANCHORAGES BETWEEN THE BLASKETS AND KERRY HD

SMERWICK HARBOUR, Kerry, **52°13'·00N 10°24'·00W**. AC 2789. Tides 9.12.33. Adequate shelter in 1M wide bay, except from NW'ly when considerable swell runs in. Ent between The Three Sisters (150m hill) and Dunacapple Is to the NE. Beacon Fl.R.3s at pier end at Ballynagall Pt. ⚓s at: the W side close N or S of the Boat Hr in 3-10m; to the S, off Carrigveen Pt in 2·5m; or in N'lies at the bay in NE corner inside 10m line. Facilities at Ballynagall village on SE side: pier (0·5m), limited , bus.

BRANDON BAY, Kerry, **52°16'·10N 10°09'·92**W. AC 2739. Tides as Fenit 9.12.34. A 4M wide bay, very exposed to the N, but in moderate SW-W winds there is safe ⚓ in 6m close E of drying Brandon Pier, 2FG (vert). Cloghane Inlet in SW of Bay is not advised. Facilities at Brandon: limited (1M) ✕ bus.

TRALEE BAY, Kerry, **52°18'·00N 09°56'·00W**. AC 2739. HW –0612 on Dover; ML 2·6m; Duration 0605. See 9.12.34. Enter the bay passing 3M N of Magharee Islands. Pick up the W sector (W140°–152°) of Little Samphire Is lt, Fl WRG 5s 17m 16/13M; see 9.12.4 for sectors. Approach between Magharee Is and Mucklaghmore (30m high).

9.12.34 FENIT HARBOUR

Kerry **52°16'·20N 09°51'·61W**

CHARTS AC 2254, 2739; Imray C55

TIDES –0612 Dover; ML 2·6m; Duration 0605

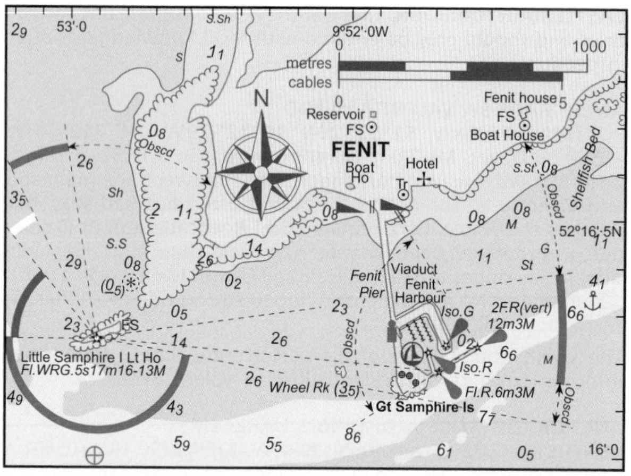

Standard Port COBH (⟵)

Times				Height (metres)			
High Water		Low Water		MHWS	MHWN	MLWN	MLWS
0500	1100	0500	1100	4·1	3·2	1·3	0·4
1700	2300	1700	2300				
Differences FENIT PIER (Tralee Bay)							
–0057	–0017	–0029	–0109	+0·5	+0·2	+0·3	+0·1

SHELTER Good shelter in marina (2.7m depth).

NAVIGATION Appr on 146° to WPT 52°16'·00N 09° 53'·00W, Little Samphire Is, conspic lt ho, Fl WRG 5s 17m 16/13M, thence 7ca E to Samphire Is; lt QR 15m 3M vis 242°–097°, leaving S breakwater bn FlR 6m 3M to N. Fenit Pier Hd 2 FR (vert) 12m 3M, vis 148°–058°. Easy ent H24.

LIGHTS AND MARKS See 9.12.4 and chartlet.

COMMUNICATIONS (Code 066) ⊜7121480. Port Manager ☎7136231; VHF Ch 16 **14 M** (0900-2100UT). Tralee SC ☎7136119. *Neptune* (Tralee SC) VHF Ch 14 16.

FACILITIES Marina www.fenitharbour.com, 130 inc 15Ⓥ; max LOA 25m, €2.30 (min €23.00/craft) (at LB stn)

Village Ⓑ.

Tralee (by bus, Fridays only) (Kerry 30M).

MIZEN HEAD TO DINGLE BAY

(AC 2423) Three Castle Hd has rks 1ca W, and seas break on S Bullig 4ca off Hd. Dunmanus B (AC 2552) has three hbrs: Dunmanus, Kitchen Cove and Dunbeacon. It is best to keep N of Carbery, Cold and Furze Is. Sheep's Hd (lt) is at the S end of Bantry Bay (AC 1838, 1840) which has excellent hbrs, notably Glengariff and Castletown. There are few dangers offshore, except around Bear and Whiddy Islands.

► *Off Blackball Hd at W entrance to Bantry B there can be a nasty race, particularly on W-going stream against the wind. Keep 3ca off Crow Is to clear dangers.* ◄

Dursey Island is steep-to; beware rk 7½ca NE of Dursey Hd and Lea Rk (1·4m) 1½ca SW. Calf and Heifer Rks are 7½ca SW of Dursey Hd, where there is often broken water and tidal streams run strogly. The Bull (lt, fog sig, Racon) and two rks W of it lie 2·5M WNW of Dursey Hd. The Cow is midway between Dursey Hd and The Bull with clear water each side.

► *2M W of The Bull the stream turns NW at HW Cobh +0150, and SE at HW Cobh –0420. Dursey Sound (chart 2495) is a good short cut, but the stream runs 4kn at Sp; W-going starts at HW Cobh +0135, and E-going at HW Cobh –0450.* ◄

Flag Rk lies almost awash in mid-chan at the narrows of Dursey Snd, which is crossed by a cable car (cables 25m above MHWS). Hold very close to the Island shore. Beware wind changes in the sound, and broken water at N entrance.

Kenmare R (AC 2495) has attractive hbrs and ⚓s, but its shores are rky, with no lights. The best places are Sneem, Kilmakilloge and Ardgroom. Off Lamb's Head, Two Headed Island is steep-to; further W is Moylaun Is with a rk 300m SW of it. Little Hog (or Deenish) Island is rky 1·5M to W, followed by Great Hog (or Scariff) Is which has a rk close N, and a reef extending 2ca W. Darrynane is an attractive, sheltered hbr NNW of Lamb Hd. The entrance has ldg lts and marks, but is narrow and dangerous in bad weather. Ballinskelligs Bay has an ⚓ N of Horse Is, which has two rks close off E end. Centre of bay is a prohib ⚓ (cables reported).

Rough water is met between Bolus Hd and Bray Hd with fresh onshore winds or swell. The SW end of Puffin Island is steep-to, but the sound to the E is rky and not advised. Great Skellig (lit) is 6M, and Little Skellig 5M WSW of Puffin Is. Lemon Rk lies between Puffin Is and Little Skellig.

► *Here the stream turns N at HW Cobh +0500, and S at HW Cobh –0110.* ◄

There is a rk 3ca SW of Great Skellig. When very calm it is possible to go alongside at Blind Man's Cove on NE side of Great Skellig, where there are interesting ruins.

DINGLE BAY TO LISCANNOR BAY

(AC 2254) Dingle Bay (AC 2789, 2790) is wide and deep, with few dangers around its shores. Cahersiveen and Dingle have small marinas. The best ⚓s are at Portmagee and Ventry. At the NW ent to the bay, 2·5M SSW of Slea Hd, is Wild Bank (or Three Fathom Pinnacle), a shallow patch with overfalls. 3M SW of Wild Bank is Barrack Rk, which breaks in strong winds.

The Blasket Islands are very exposed, ► *with strong tides and overfalls* ◄ but worth a visit in settled weather (AC 2790).

Great Blasket and Inishvickillane each have ⚓ and landing on their NE side. Between lies Inishabro with a beach and impressive rock formations. Inishtearaght is the most W'ly Is (lt), but further W lie Tearaght Rks, and 3M S are Little Foze and Gt Foze Rks. Inishtooskert is the most N'ly. Blasket Sound is the most convenient N-S route, 1M wide, and easy in daylight and reasonable weather with fair wind or tide; extensive rks and shoals form its W side.

► *The N-going stream starts at HW Galway +0430, and the S-going at HW Galway –0155, with sp rate 3kn.* ◄

Between Blasket Sound and Sybil Pt there is a race in W or NW winds with N-going tide, and often a nasty sea. Sybil Pt has steep cliffs, and offlying rks extend 3½ca.

Smerwick hbr, entered between Duncapple Is and the E Sister, is sheltered, except from NW or N winds. From here the scenery is spectacular to Brandon Bay on the W side of which there is an ⚓, but exposed to N winds and to swell.

From Inishtearaght to Loop Hd, Little Samphire Is in Tralee B is the sole light, where Fenit hbr provides the only secure refuge until entering the Shannon Estuary. The coast from Loop Hd to Liscannor Bay has no safe ⚓, no lts, save SPM Fl(5)Y 20s 3M off Donegal Pt and an AIS buoy Fl(5)Y 20s in Mal Bay. Take care not to be set inshore, although there are few offlying dangers except near Mutton Is and in Liscannor Bay.

9.12.35 SHANNON ESTUARY

Clare (N); Kerry and Limerick (S) **52°35'·00N 09°40'·00W** ❀❀❀◊◊✿✿✿

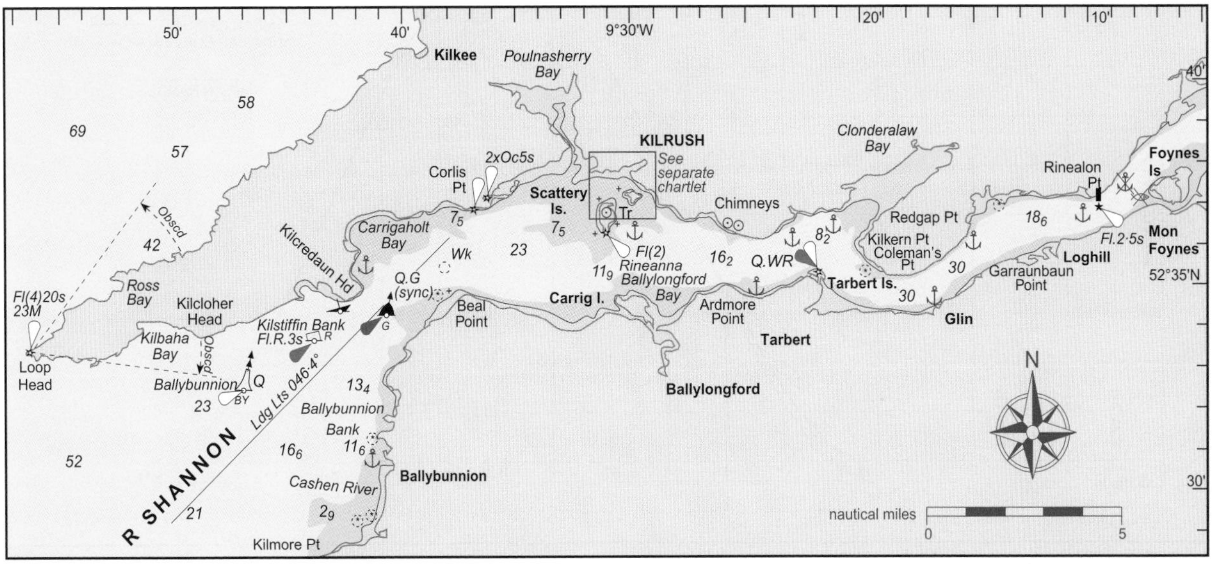

CHARTS AC 1819, 1547, 1548, 1549, 1540; L. Derg 5080; L. Ree 5078; Imray C55.

The ICC's *Sailing Directions for S & W Ireland* and/or Admiralty *Irish Coast Pilot* are essential.

TIDES

HW at	HW Tarbert Is	HW Dover
Kilbaha & Carrigaholt	–0030	+0605
Coney Island	+0045	–0500
Foynes	+0030	–0515
Limerick	+0110	–0435

At Limerick strong S-W winds increase the height and delay the times of HW; strong N-E winds do the opposite. The tides and streams have roughly equal duration and similar flood and ebb streams. In the entrance the flood stream begins at HW Tarbert Is –0555, and the ebb at HW Tarbert Is +0015. In the Shannon the stream is much affected by the wind. S and W winds increase the rate and duration of the flood stream, and reduce the ebb. Strong N or E winds have the opposite effect.

▶ *Off Kilcredaun Pt the Sp ebb reaches 4kn, and in strong winds between S and NW a race forms. This can be skirted keeping near the N shore, which is free from offlying dangers, cheating the worst of the tide. When leaving the Shannon in strong W winds, pass Kilcredaun Pt at slack water, and again keep near the N shore. Loop Hd (lt) marks the N side of Shannon Est, and should be passed 3ca off. Here the stream runs SW from HW Tarbert Is +0300, and NE from HW Tarbert Is –0300.* ◀

SHELTER The Shannon Estuary is 50M long and are tidal from its mouth between Loop Hd and Kerry Hd up to Limerick Dock, some 15M beyond the junction with R Fergus. For boats on N/S passage the nearest fine weather ⚓ is Kilbaha Bay (AC 1819), 3M inside Loop Hd; 🅐s not maintained and holding is poor. It is sheltered in winds from W to NE, but is exposed to SE and swell. 6M further E, Carrigaholt Bay (AC 1547) ent ent 1M N of Kilcredaun Pt, is sheltered from W'lies, ⚓ just N of the new quay, out of the tide; again 🅐s not maintained. In N winds ⚓ SE of Querrin Pt 4½M above Kilcredaun avoiding mussel/fish farms. At Kilrush 7M further E there are ⚓s E of Scattery Is and N of Hog Is and Kilrush Marina (9.12.36) with all facilities. From Kilcredaun Head in the W to the R Fergus ent (about 25M) there are ⚓, protected from all but E winds, at Tarbert Is, Glin, Labasheeda, Killadysert (pontoon) and among the islands in the Fergus mouth. ⚓ is prohibited between Moneypoint and Ardmore owing to submerged cables, and that reach is exposed in W'lies with overfalls on 'The Bridge' when winds are strong. There is a YC pontoon S of Foynes Is and drying quays at Ballylongford Creek (Saleen), Knock and Clarecastle (S of Ennis, off chartlet). Yachts may enter Limerick Dock, but it is primarily a commercial port.

NAVIGATION WPT 52°32'·52N 09°46'·93W, Ballybunnion NCM Q 062°/4·0M to intercept Ldg lts, Oc. 5s, 046·4° on Corlis Pt, passing between Kilcredaun PHM Q.R(sync) and Tail of Beal buoy SHM, Q.G(sync). The lower estuary between Kerry and Loop Heads is 9M wide, narrowing to 2M off Kilcredaun Pt. Here the chan is well buoyed in mid-stream and then follows the Kerry shore, S of Scattery Is. Note that there are overfalls ¾M S of Scattery Is with W winds and ebb tide. From Tarbert Is to Foynes Is the river narrows to less than 1M in places. Abeam Shannon airport at the junction with R Fergus the characteristics become more riverine, ie the flood stream is stronger than the ebb, but it runs for a shorter time. Here the buoyed channel narrows and shelves although there is a minimum of 2m at LWS. AC 1540 is essential for the final 15M stretch to Limerick.

RIVER SHANNON The Shannon, the longest navigable river in the UK or Ireland, is managed by Shannon Foynes Port Company up to Limerick. Upstream it effectively becomes an inland waterway; progress is restricted by locks and bridges. Info on navigation and facilities can be obtained from the Waterways Service, Dept of Art, Culture & the Gaeltacht, 51 St Stephen's Green, Dublin 2, ☎01-6613111; or from the Inland Waterways Association of Ireland, Kingston House, Ballinteer, Dublin 4, ☎01-983392; also from Tourist Offices and inland marinas.

LIGHTS AND MARKS See 9.12.4. There are QW (vert) aero hazard lts on tall chimneys at Money Pt power station 3M ESE of Kilrush. 2 chys at Tarbert Is are conspic (R lts).

COMMUNICATIONS Foynes Ch 12 13 16 (occas). *Shannon Estuary Radio* Ch 12 13 16 (HO).

FACILITIES Marine facilities are available at several communities on the Shannon; can be found at many villages. 🅐s are at Foynes and Glin Pier (pontoon). E of Aughanish Is on S shore, R Deal is navigable 3M to Askeaton. Deal BC may offer berths (tidal constraints). Ent, marked by RW bn, is 8ca SE of Beeves Rk with 1m in buoyed chan. at Massey's Pier ☎069 73100, 🅐s.

Facilities upstream at Foynes and Limerick inc:

Foynes Ⓑ ✕.

Foynes YC ☎(069) 65261, (pontoon) ✕.

Limerick: **Hbr Commission** ☎(069) 73100; ⊖ ☎415366.

City all usual city amenities, ⇌ ✈ (Shannon).

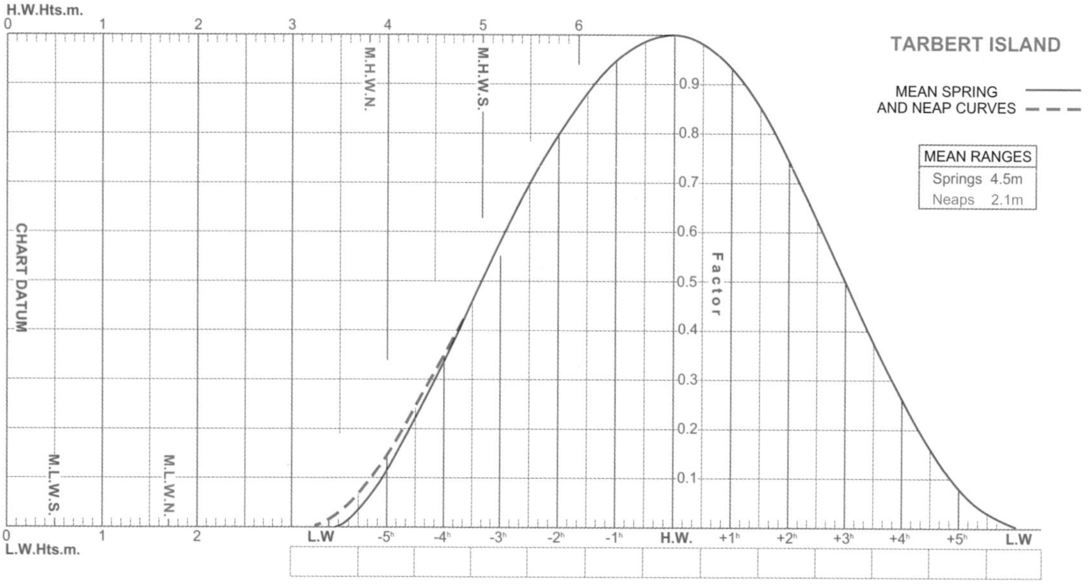

9.12.36 KILRUSH

Clare **52°37'·90N 09°29'·70W**

CHARTS AC 1819, 1547; Imray C55

TIDES –0555 Dover; ML 2·6; Duration 0610

Standard Port TARBERT ISLAND (⟶)

Times				Height (metres)			
High Water		Low Water		MHWS	MHWN	MLWN	MLWS
0500	1000	0000	0600	5·0	3·8	1·7	0·5
1700	2200	1200	1800				
Differences KILRUSH							
–0010	–0010	–0005	–0005	0·0	–0·1	0·0	0·0

SHELTER Excellent in Kilrush Marina (2·7m), access via lock (width 9m) H24. Day ⚓ in lee of Scattery Is.

NAVIGATION WPT 52°37'·18N 09°31'·64W, 063°/1M to SWM buoy. From seaward usual appr is N of Scattery Is (prominent Round Twr, 26m); beware Baurnahard Spit and Carrigillaun to the N. Follow ldg lts (355°) exactly in buoyed channel where the depth is dredged 1·5m (2016). Coming downriver between Hog Is and mainland, beware unmarked Wolf Rk.

LIGHTS AND MARKS SWM buoy, L Fl 10s, at ent to buoyed chan, with ldg lts 355°, both Oc 3s, to lock. Fl G 3s on S side of lock.

COMMUNICATIONS (Code 06590) MRCC (066) 9476109; Coast/Cliff Rescue Service 51004; ⊜ (061) 415366; (061) 62677; Police 51017; Dr (065) 51581 also 51470. Marina 52072 Mobile 086 2313870; Lock 52155. Marina Ch 80. Kilrush Ch 16, 12.

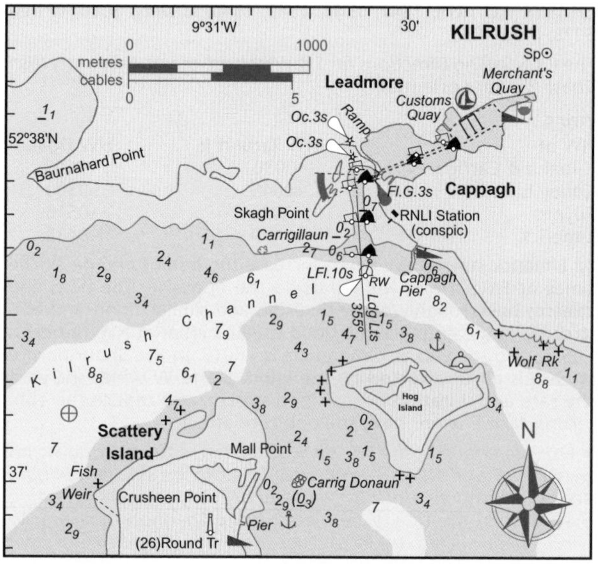

FACILITIES Marina kilrushmarina.ie ☎ 52072, lock 52155; 120 inc €1.90 (min €16.00/craft) Kos (45t) (26t) **Town** @ (bus to Limerick) (Shannon).

STANDARD TIME (UT)
For Summer Time add ONE hour in **non-shaded areas**

TARBERT ISLAND LAT 52°35′N LONG 9°21′W

TIMES AND HEIGHTS OF HIGH AND LOW WATERS

Dates in red are SPRINGS
Dates in blue are NEAPS

YEAR **2018**

JANUARY

Date	Day	Time	m	Time	m	Time	m	Time	m
1	M	0437	5.0	1052	0.5	1707	5.0	2308	0.5
2	TU	0527	5.2	1141	0.2	1758	5.1	○ 2356	0.4
3	W	0614	5.2	1229	0.1	1846	5.1		
4	TH	0042	0.4	0701	5.2	1315	0.1	1933	5.0
5	F	0128	0.5	0746	5.1	1400	0.3	2020	4.9
6	SA	0212	0.6	0832	4.9	1446	0.5	2107	4.7
7	SU	0258	0.9	0919	4.7	1535	0.8	2157	4.4
8	M	0348	1.2	1011	4.4	1629	1.1	◑ 2253	4.2
9	TU	0446	1.4	1113	4.2	1731	1.3	2359	4.0
10	W	0553	1.6	1229	4.0	1836	1.5		
11	TH	0110	4.0	0703	1.7	1346	4.0	1940	1.5
12	F	0214	4.1	0810	1.6	1448	4.1	2039	1.4
13	SA	0309	4.3	0908	1.4	1540	4.3	2130	1.3
14	SU	0356	4.5	0958	1.3	1626	4.4	2216	1.2
15	M	0437	4.6	1042	1.1	1706	4.5	2256	1.1
16	TU	0514	4.7	1122	1.0	1742	4.6	2333	1.0
17	W	0549	4.8	1159	0.9	1816	4.7	●	
18	TH	0008	1.0	0622	4.9	1233	0.8	1848	4.7
19	F	0040	1.0	0656	4.9	1305	0.8	1922	4.7
20	SA	0112	1.0	0730	4.9	1337	0.9	1956	4.6
21	SU	0146	1.1	0805	4.8	1411	1.0	2033	4.5
22	M	0222	1.2	0842	4.7	1449	1.1	2113	4.4
23	TU	0303	1.3	0924	4.5	1532	1.2	2159	4.3
24	W	0351	1.4	1015	4.3	1625	1.4	◐ 2256	4.2
25	TH	0449	1.6	1122	4.2	1729	1.5		
26	F	0006	4.1	0601	1.6	1239	4.2	1842	1.5
27	SA	0119	4.2	0723	1.5	1355	4.3	1957	1.4
28	SU	0226	4.4	0841	1.2	1502	4.5	2106	1.1
29	M	0327	4.7	0946	0.9	1602	4.7	2205	0.8
30	TU	0423	4.9	1042	0.5	1657	4.9	2258	0.6
31	W	0514	5.2	1131	0.3	1747	5.1	○ 2345	0.4

FEBRUARY

Date	Day	Time	m	Time	m	Time	m	Time	m
1	TH	0602	5.3	1217	0.1	1833	5.2		
2	F	0030	0.3	0647	5.3	1300	0.1	1917	5.2
3	SA	0112	0.4	0730	5.3	1342	0.2	1959	5.1
4	SU	0152	0.5	0811	5.1	1423	0.4	2041	4.9
5	M	0232	0.8	0853	4.9	1504	0.7	2123	4.6
6	TU	0313	1.1	0937	4.6	1548	1.1	2208	4.4
7	W	0359	1.4	1028	4.3	1640	1.5	◑ 2302	4.1
8	TH	0457	1.7	1132	4.0	1745	1.7		
9	F	0009	4.0	0610	1.9	1257	3.9	1858	1.9
10	SA	0126	4.0	0730	1.9	1415	3.9	2008	1.8
11	SU	0234	4.1	0840	1.7	1516	4.1	2107	1.6
12	M	0329	4.3	0936	1.5	1605	4.3	2156	1.4
13	TU	0414	4.5	1022	1.2	1646	4.5	2237	1.2
14	W	0453	4.7	1102	1.0	1722	4.6	2314	1.1
15	TH	0529	4.8	1139	0.8	1755	4.7	● 2349	0.9
16	F	0602	4.9	1212	0.7	1827	4.8		
17	SA	0021	0.9	0634	5.0	1244	0.7	1859	4.8
18	SU	0053	0.8	0707	5.0	1315	0.7	1932	4.8
19	M	0125	0.8	0741	5.0	1348	0.8	2007	4.8
20	TU	0159	0.9	0817	4.9	1423	0.9	2044	4.7
21	W	0237	1.0	0857	4.7	1504	1.1	2127	4.5
22	TH	0322	1.2	0945	4.5	1552	1.3	2218	4.3
23	F	0417	1.5	1048	4.2	1654	1.5	◐ 2326	4.2
24	SA	0528	1.6	1209	4.1	1812	1.7		
25	SU	0047	4.1	0658	1.6	1335	4.1	1940	1.6
26	M	0205	4.3	0828	1.3	1452	4.3	2057	1.3
27	TU	0314	4.5	0936	0.9	1555	4.6	2157	0.9
28	W	0412	4.9	1030	0.5	1647	4.9	2248	0.6

MARCH

Date	Day	Time	m	Time	m	Time	m	Time	m
1	TH	0503	5.1	1118	0.2	1734	5.1	2333	0.4
2	F	0548	5.3	1201	0.1	1817	5.3	○	
3	SA	0014	0.3	0629	5.4	1241	0.1	1857	5.3
4	SU	0052	0.3	0709	5.3	1319	0.2	1935	5.2
5	M	0128	0.4	0748	5.2	1355	0.4	2012	5.0
6	TU	0204	0.7	0826	4.9	1431	0.8	2049	4.7
7	W	0240	1.0	0905	4.6	1509	1.2	2129	4.5
8	TH	0320	1.3	0949	4.3	1553	1.6	2214	4.2
9	F	0408	1.7	1043	4.0	1648	1.9	◑ 2313	3.9
10	SA	0512	1.9	1204	3.7	1807	2.1		
11	SU	0031	3.8	0641	2.0	1336	3.7	1936	2.0
12	M	0152	3.9	0808	1.9	1446	3.9	2042	1.8
13	TU	0255	4.1	0909	1.6	1538	4.1	2132	1.6
14	W	0344	4.3	0956	1.3	1619	4.4	2212	1.3
15	TH	0425	4.6	1035	1.0	1655	4.6	2249	1.0
16	F	0501	4.8	1111	0.8	1728	4.7	2324	0.8
17	SA	0535	4.9	1145	0.6	1801	4.9	● 2358	0.7
18	SU	0609	5.1	1218	0.5	1833	5.0		
19	M	0030	0.6	0642	5.1	1251	0.5	1906	5.0
20	TU	0104	0.6	0717	5.1	1324	0.5	1942	5.0
21	W	0138	0.6	0755	5.0	1400	0.7	2020	4.9
22	TH	0216	0.8	0837	4.8	1441	0.9	2102	4.7
23	F	0300	1.0	0925	4.5	1528	1.2	2152	4.4
24	SA	0354	1.3	1027	4.2	1630	1.6	◐ 2259	4.1
25	SU	0507	1.5	1150	4.0	1755	1.7		
26	M	0022	4.0	0643	1.5	1325	4.0	1931	1.6
27	TU	0149	4.1	0816	1.2	1445	4.3	2048	1.3
28	W	0303	4.4	0922	0.8	1545	4.6	2144	0.9
29	TH	0359	4.7	1013	0.5	1634	4.9	2232	0.6
30	F	0447	5.0	1058	0.2	1717	5.1	2315	0.4
31	SA	0530	5.2	1139	0.1	1756	5.2	○ 2354	0.3

APRIL

Date	Day	Time	m	Time	m	Time	m	Time	m
1	SU	0609	5.2	1218	0.1	1834	5.2		
2	M	0030	0.3	0647	5.2	1254	0.3	1909	5.1
3	TU	0104	0.4	0723	5.1	1327	0.5	1943	5.0
4	W	0137	0.7	0758	4.9	1400	0.9	2018	4.8
5	TH	0211	0.9	0835	4.6	1434	1.2	2054	4.5
6	F	0247	1.2	0914	4.3	1513	1.6	2136	4.2
7	SA	0330	1.5	1002	3.9	1602	1.9	2227	3.9
8	SU	0424	1.8	1108	3.7	1708	2.1	◑ 2334	3.8
9	M	0539	2.0	1247	3.6	1844	2.1		
10	TU	0100	3.7	0716	1.9	1403	3.7	2003	1.9
11	W	0210	3.9	0826	1.6	1458	4.0	2056	1.6
12	TH	0304	4.1	0916	1.3	1542	4.3	2139	1.3
13	F	0348	4.4	0958	1.0	1620	4.5	2218	1.0
14	SA	0427	4.7	1037	0.7	1656	4.7	2255	0.7
15	SU	0504	4.9	1114	0.5	1731	4.9	2331	0.5
16	M	0540	5.1	1150	0.4	1806	5.1	●	
17	TU	0007	0.4	0617	5.1	1226	0.3	1842	5.1
18	W	0044	0.3	0656	5.1	1303	0.4	1920	5.1
19	TH	0121	0.4	0737	5.0	1341	0.6	2001	4.9
20	F	0202	0.5	0823	4.8	1424	0.8	2045	4.7
21	SA	0247	0.8	0914	4.5	1514	1.1	2137	4.4
22	SU	0343	1.1	1017	4.2	1618	1.5	◐ 2241	4.1
23	M	0456	1.3	1138	3.9	1744	1.6		
24	TU	0001	4.0	0627	1.3	1314	4.0	1916	1.5
25	W	0132	4.0	0752	1.1	1429	4.2	2028	1.2
26	TH	0244	4.3	0856	0.8	1526	4.5	2122	0.9
27	F	0339	4.6	0948	0.5	1613	4.8	2209	0.6
28	SA	0426	4.8	1033	0.3	1655	4.9	2252	0.4
29	SU	0508	4.9	1114	0.3	1734	5.0	2331	0.4
30	M	0547	5.0	1152	0.3	1810	5.0	○	

Chart Datum: 0·30 metres below Ordnance Datum (Dublin). HAT is 5·5 metres above Chart Datum.

S Ireland

STANDARD TIME (UT)
For Summer Time add ONE hour in **non-shaded areas**

TARBERT ISLAND LAT 52°35′N LONG 9°21′W

TIMES AND HEIGHTS OF HIGH AND LOW WATERS

Dates in red are SPRINGS
Dates in blue are NEAPS

YEAR **2018**

MAY

Date	Day	Time	m	Time	m	Time	m	Time	m
1	TU	0007	0.4	0623	5.0	1227	0.5	1843	5.0
2	W	0040	0.5	0659	4.9	1300	0.7	1917	4.9
3	TH	0113	0.7	0734	4.7	1332	0.9	1951	4.7
4	F	0146	0.9	0809	4.5	1405	1.2	2026	4.5
5	SA	0221	1.1	0846	4.2	1442	1.5	2105	4.3
6	SU	0301	1.3	0929	4.0	1526	1.7	2151	4.0
7	M	0348	1.6	1023	3.7	1621	1.9	2246	3.8
8	TU	0448	1.7	1140	3.6	1735	2.0	◑ 2357	3.7
9	W	0605	1.7	1308	3.7	1902	1.9		
10	TH	0113	3.8	0723	1.6	1410	3.9	2006	1.6
11	F	0215	4.0	0823	1.3	1459	4.2	2056	1.3
12	SA	0304	4.3	0913	1.0	1542	4.4	2141	1.0
13	SU	0349	4.6	0957	0.7	1622	4.7	2224	0.7
14	M	0431	4.8	1040	0.5	1701	4.9	2305	0.4
15	TU	0512	5.0	1122	0.3	1741	5.1	● 2346	0.3
16	W	0555	5.1	1203	0.3	1822	5.1		
17	TH	0027	0.2	0639	5.1	1245	0.3	1904	5.1
18	F	0109	0.2	0725	5.0	1328	0.5	1948	5.0
19	SA	0153	0.3	0814	4.8	1414	0.7	2035	4.7
20	SU	0241	0.5	0907	4.5	1506	1.0	2127	4.5
21	M	0337	0.8	1008	4.2	1609	1.2	2227	4.2
22	TU	0445	1.0	1123	4.0	1727	1.4	◐ 2339	4.0
23	W	0602	1.1	1250	4.0	1847	1.4		
24	TH	0103	4.0	0717	1.0	1402	4.2	1956	1.2
25	F	0216	4.2	0821	0.9	1459	4.4	2053	1.0
26	SA	0313	4.4	0915	0.7	1547	4.6	2142	0.8
27	SU	0401	4.5	1003	0.6	1631	4.7	2227	0.7
28	M	0445	4.6	1046	0.6	1710	4.8	2307	0.6
29	TU	0525	4.7	1126	0.6	1747	4.9	○ 2345	0.6
30	W	0603	4.7	1202	0.7	1821	4.8		
31	TH	0020	0.7	0638	4.6	1236	0.8	1855	4.8

JUNE

Date	Day	Time	m	Time	m	Time	m	Time	m
1	F	0054	0.7	0713	4.5	1308	1.0	1929	4.7
2	SA	0126	0.9	0747	4.4	1341	1.2	2004	4.5
3	SU	0200	1.0	0823	4.2	1417	1.3	2041	4.4
4	M	0237	1.1	0903	4.1	1457	1.5	2122	4.2
5	TU	0319	1.3	0949	3.9	1544	1.7	2209	4.0
6	W	0409	1.4	1047	3.8	1643	1.8	◑ 2306	3.9
7	TH	0509	1.5	1159	3.8	1754	1.8		
8	F	0012	3.9	0617	1.4	1312	3.9	1907	1.6
9	SA	0119	4.0	0725	1.3	1411	4.1	2010	1.4
10	SU	0218	4.2	0825	1.0	1502	4.4	2104	1.0
11	M	0311	4.5	0918	0.8	1549	4.7	2154	0.7
12	TU	0400	4.7	1009	0.6	1635	4.9	2242	0.5
13	W	0449	4.9	1057	0.4	1720	5.0	● 2328	0.3
14	TH	0538	5.0	1145	0.3	1806	5.1		
15	F	0015	0.1	0627	5.0	1232	0.3	1851	5.1
16	SA	0101	0.1	0716	4.9	1319	0.4	1938	5.0
17	SU	0147	0.2	0806	4.8	1407	0.5	2025	4.9
18	M	0235	0.3	0858	4.6	1457	0.8	2115	4.6
19	TU	0327	0.5	0955	4.4	1554	1.0	2210	4.4
20	W	0426	0.8	1059	4.2	1700	1.2	◐ 2313	4.2
21	TH	0531	1.0	1215	4.1	1810	1.3		
22	F	0026	4.0	0637	1.1	1326	4.1	1918	1.3
23	SA	0141	4.0	0742	1.1	1427	4.2	2019	1.2
24	SU	0243	4.1	0840	1.0	1519	4.4	2114	1.1
25	M	0336	4.3	0933	1.0	1606	4.5	2202	0.9
26	TU	0423	4.4	1020	0.9	1648	4.6	2246	0.9
27	W	0506	4.4	1103	0.9	1727	4.7	2326	0.8
28	TH	0545	4.5	1141	0.9	1802	4.7	○	
29	F	0003	0.8	0620	4.5	1217	1.0	1836	4.7
30	SA	0038	0.8	0655	4.5	1249	1.0	1910	4.7

JULY

Date	Day	Time	m	Time	m	Time	m	Time	m
1	SU	0110	0.8	0728	4.4	1321	1.1	1944	4.6
2	M	0142	0.9	0803	4.3	1355	1.2	2019	4.5
3	TU	0216	1.0	0839	4.2	1432	1.3	2056	4.4
4	W	0253	1.1	0919	4.1	1513	1.4	2137	4.3
5	TH	0336	1.2	1007	4.0	1602	1.6	2226	4.1
6	F	0427	1.3	1106	4.0	1701	1.6	◑ 2325	4.1
7	SA	0527	1.3	1215	4.0	1811	1.6		
8	SU	0032	4.1	0633	1.3	1324	4.1	1924	1.4
9	M	0138	4.2	0741	1.2	1425	4.3	2031	1.2
10	TU	0240	4.4	0845	1.0	1521	4.6	2130	0.9
11	W	0338	4.6	0945	0.7	1614	4.8	2225	0.6
12	TH	0433	4.8	1040	0.5	1704	5.0	2316	0.3
13	F	0527	4.9	1132	0.4	1754	5.1	●	
14	SA	0005	0.1	0618	5.0	1222	0.3	1841	5.2
15	SU	0052	0.0	0707	5.0	1309	0.3	1927	5.2
16	M	0137	0.0	0755	4.9	1355	0.4	2013	5.0
17	TU	0222	0.2	0843	4.8	1442	0.6	2059	4.8
18	W	0309	0.4	0933	4.5	1531	0.9	2148	4.6
19	TH	0359	0.7	1027	4.3	1626	1.1	◐ 2242	4.3
20	F	0454	1.0	1131	4.1	1730	1.4	2346	4.0
21	SA	0557	1.3	1243	4.0	1839	1.5		
22	SU	0101	3.9	0703	1.4	1352	4.1	1947	1.5
23	M	0213	3.9	0808	1.4	1452	4.2	2048	1.4
24	TU	0313	4.0	0907	1.4	1544	4.3	2141	1.2
25	W	0404	4.2	0959	1.3	1629	4.5	2228	1.1
26	TH	0449	4.3	1044	1.1	1709	4.6	2309	0.9
27	F	0528	4.4	1123	1.1	1744	4.7	○ 2347	0.8
28	SA	0603	4.4	1159	1.0	1818	4.8		
29	SU	0021	0.8	0635	4.5	1231	1.0	1850	4.8
30	M	0053	0.8	0707	4.5	1302	1.0	1923	4.8
31	TU	0122	0.8	0739	4.5	1333	1.0	1956	4.7

AUGUST

Date	Day	Time	m	Time	m	Time	m	Time	m
1	W	0154	0.8	0813	4.5	1407	1.1	2030	4.6
2	TH	0228	0.9	0849	4.4	1445	1.2	2107	4.5
3	F	0307	1.0	0930	4.3	1528	1.4	2152	4.3
4	SA	0352	1.2	1022	4.2	1621	1.5	◑ 2247	4.2
5	SU	0447	1.3	1128	4.1	1728	1.6	2355	4.1
6	M	0554	1.4	1244	4.1	1848	1.6		
7	TU	0109	4.1	0710	1.4	1357	4.2	2008	1.3
8	W	0220	4.2	0825	1.2	1502	4.5	2117	1.0
9	TH	0325	4.5	0933	0.9	1600	4.8	2215	0.6
10	F	0424	4.7	1031	0.6	1653	5.0	2307	0.3
11	SA	0518	4.9	1123	0.4	1743	5.2	● 2354	0.0
12	SU	0608	5.1	1210	0.2	1829	5.3		
13	M	0038	-0.1	0654	5.1	1255	0.2	1913	5.3
14	TU	0121	-0.1	0738	5.1	1337	0.3	1956	5.2
15	W	0202	0.1	0822	4.9	1419	0.5	2038	5.0
16	TH	0244	0.4	0905	4.7	1502	0.8	2122	4.7
17	F	0326	0.8	0951	4.4	1548	1.2	2210	4.3
18	SA	0414	1.2	1044	4.1	1645	1.5	◐ 2308	4.0
19	SU	0513	1.5	1153	3.9	1757	1.7		
20	M	0023	3.8	0624	1.8	1313	3.9	1916	1.8
21	TU	0144	3.8	0741	1.8	1424	4.0	2027	1.6
22	W	0252	3.9	0848	1.7	1521	4.2	2124	1.4
23	TH	0346	4.1	0942	1.5	1608	4.4	2209	1.2
24	F	0430	4.2	1025	1.3	1647	4.6	2249	1.0
25	SA	0507	4.4	1103	1.1	1722	4.7	2325	0.8
26	SU	0540	4.5	1138	0.9	1755	4.8	○ 2359	0.7
27	M	0611	4.6	1210	0.9	1827	4.9		
28	TU	0030	0.7	0641	4.7	1241	0.8	1858	4.9
29	W	0059	0.7	0713	4.7	1311	0.8	1930	4.9
30	TH	0130	0.7	0745	4.7	1343	0.9	2004	4.8
31	F	0202	0.8	0820	4.6	1419	1.0	2041	4.7

Chart Datum: 0·30 metres below Ordnance Datum (Dublin). HAT is 5·5 metres above Chart Datum.

STANDARD TIME (UT)
For Summer Time add ONE hour in **non-shaded areas**

TARBERT ISLAND LAT 52°35'N LONG 9°21'W

TIMES AND HEIGHTS OF HIGH AND LOW WATERS

Dates in red are SPRINGS
Dates in blue are NEAPS

YEAR **2018**

SEPTEMBER

Date	Day	Time	m	Time	m	Time	m	Time	m
1	SA	0239	0.9	0859	4.5	1500	1.2	2125	4.5
2	SU	0323	1.2	0947	4.3	1551	1.4	2219	4.2
3	M	0416	1.4	1051	4.1	1657	1.6	◑ 2330	4.0
4	TU	0526	1.6	1214	4.0	1825	1.6		
5	W	0052	4.0	0652	1.6	1338	4.1	1959	1.4
6	TH	0212	4.1	0820	1.4	1451	4.4	2110	1.0
7	F	0320	4.4	0929	1.0	1551	4.7	2206	0.5
8	SA	0418	4.7	1024	0.6	1643	5.0	2254	0.2
9	SU	0508	5.0	1112	0.3	1730	5.2	● 2339	0.0
10	M	0553	5.1	1156	0.2	1813	5.3		
11	TU	0020	-0.1	0635	5.2	1237	0.2	1854	5.3
12	W	0100	0.0	0716	5.1	1315	0.3	1934	5.2
13	TH	0137	0.2	0755	5.0	1353	0.5	2014	5.0
14	F	0214	0.6	0833	4.7	1430	0.8	2054	4.6
15	SA	0252	1.0	0913	4.5	1511	1.2	2138	4.3
16	SU	0333	1.4	0959	4.1	1600	1.5	◐ 2230	3.9
17	M	0424	1.7	1059	3.9	1706	1.8	2342	3.7
18	TU	0536	2.0	1225	3.7	1840	1.9		
19	W	0111	3.6	0710	2.0	1348	3.8	2001	1.8
20	TH	0225	3.8	0826	1.8	1451	4.0	2059	1.5
21	F	0320	4.0	0919	1.6	1539	4.3	2144	1.2
22	SA	0402	4.2	1000	1.3	1618	4.5	2222	1.0
23	SU	0438	4.4	1037	1.0	1654	4.7	2257	0.8
24	M	0511	4.6	1111	0.9	1727	4.8	2331	0.6
25	TU	0542	4.7	1144	0.7	1759	4.9	○	
26	W	0002	0.5	0613	4.8	1217	0.6	1831	5.0
27	TH	0034	0.5	0645	4.9	1249	0.6	1905	5.0
28	F	0106	0.6	0719	4.9	1321	0.7	1941	4.9
29	SA	0139	0.7	0756	4.8	1358	0.8	2020	4.7
30	SU	0216	0.9	0836	4.6	1440	1.0	2106	4.5

OCTOBER

Date	Day	Time	m	Time	m	Time	m	Time	m
1	M	0300	1.1	0923	4.4	1531	1.3	2202	4.2
2	TU	0355	1.4	1026	4.1	1640	1.5	◑ 2315	4.0
3	W	0509	1.7	1151	3.9	1815	1.5		
4	TH	0042	3.9	0646	1.7	1325	4.0	1951	1.3
5	F	0209	4.1	0816	1.4	1442	4.3	2058	0.9
6	SA	0314	4.4	0919	1.0	1540	4.7	2150	0.5
7	SU	0406	4.7	1010	0.6	1629	5.0	2236	0.2
8	M	0452	5.0	1055	0.3	1713	5.2	2318	0.0
9	TU	0534	5.1	1136	0.2	1754	5.3	● 2358	0.0
10	W	0613	5.2	1215	0.2	1834	5.2		
11	TH	0035	0.2	0650	5.1	1251	0.3	1911	5.1
12	F	0110	0.4	0726	5.0	1326	0.6	1949	4.9
13	SA	0144	0.7	0802	4.7	1401	0.8	2027	4.6
14	SU	0218	1.1	0838	4.5	1439	1.2	2107	4.2
15	M	0256	1.4	0920	4.2	1522	1.5	2153	3.9
16	TU	0341	1.8	1011	3.9	1618	1.8	◐ 2257	3.7
17	W	0442	2.0	1126	3.7	1741	1.9		
18	TH	0026	3.6	0615	2.1	1258	3.7	1916	1.8
19	F	0142	3.7	0744	1.9	1406	3.9	2019	1.6
20	SA	0240	3.9	0841	1.6	1459	4.1	2106	1.3
21	SU	0324	4.1	0925	1.3	1541	4.4	2146	1.0
22	M	0402	4.4	1003	1.0	1620	4.6	2223	0.7
23	TU	0437	4.6	1040	0.8	1655	4.8	2258	0.6
24	W	0511	4.8	1117	0.6	1730	4.9	○ 2333	0.5
25	TH	0545	5.0	1152	0.5	1806	5.0		
26	F	0008	0.4	0620	5.0	1228	0.5	1842	5.0
27	SA	0044	0.5	0657	5.0	1304	0.5	1922	4.9
28	SU	0120	0.6	0737	4.9	1343	0.6	2006	4.7
29	M	0200	0.8	0820	4.7	1428	0.8	2054	4.5
30	TU	0246	1.1	0910	4.4	1521	1.1	2152	4.2
31	W	0342	1.4	1011	4.1	1632	1.3	◑ 2303	3.9

NOVEMBER

Date	Day	Time	m	Time	m	Time	m	Time	m
1	TH	0500	1.6	1132	4.0	1802	1.3		
2	F	0032	3.9	0633	1.6	1308	4.0	1929	1.1
3	SA	0156	4.1	0757	1.3	1424	4.3	2034	0.8
4	SU	0257	4.4	0857	1.0	1520	4.6	2125	0.5
5	M	0347	4.7	0947	0.7	1609	4.8	2211	0.3
6	TU	0431	4.9	1032	0.5	1652	5.0	2253	0.3
7	W	0512	5.0	1114	0.4	1733	5.0	● 2332	0.3
8	TH	0550	5.0	1152	0.4	1812	5.0		
9	F	0009	0.4	0625	5.0	1228	0.5	1849	4.9
10	SA	0044	0.6	0700	4.9	1303	0.7	1926	4.7
11	SU	0116	0.9	0734	4.7	1337	0.9	2002	4.5
12	M	0150	1.1	0810	4.5	1413	1.1	2040	4.2
13	TU	0226	1.4	0849	4.3	1453	1.4	2123	4.0
14	W	0308	1.7	0935	4.1	1540	1.6	2215	3.8
15	TH	0359	1.9	1033	3.9	1642	1.8	◐ 2325	3.6
16	F	0507	2.0	1151	3.8	1806	1.8		
17	SA	0046	3.7	0636	2.0	1311	3.8	1921	1.6
18	SU	0149	3.8	0747	1.7	1410	4.0	2016	1.4
19	M	0240	4.1	0840	1.4	1459	4.3	2102	1.1
20	TU	0323	4.4	0925	1.1	1542	4.5	2145	0.8
21	W	0402	4.6	1008	0.9	1622	4.7	2225	0.6
22	TH	0441	4.8	1049	0.6	1702	4.9	2305	0.5
23	F	0519	5.0	1130	0.5	1743	5.0	○ 2345	0.4
24	SA	0559	5.1	1210	0.4	1825	5.0		
25	SU	0025	0.4	0640	5.1	1252	0.4	1908	4.9
26	M	0106	0.5	0723	5.0	1335	0.5	1955	4.8
27	TU	0150	0.7	0809	4.8	1422	0.6	2045	4.5
28	W	0238	1.0	0859	4.5	1516	0.9	2141	4.3
29	TH	0334	1.2	0957	4.3	1621	1.0	2247	4.1
30	F	0444	1.4	1108	4.1	1737	1.1	◑	

DECEMBER

Date	Day	Time	m	Time	m	Time	m	Time	m
1	SA	0008	4.0	0604	1.5	1238	4.1	1853	1.1
2	SU	0127	4.1	0722	1.3	1355	4.2	1959	0.9
3	M	0229	4.3	0826	1.1	1454	4.4	2054	0.8
4	TU	0321	4.5	0919	0.9	1545	4.6	2142	0.7
5	W	0407	4.7	1007	0.8	1631	4.7	2227	0.6
6	TH	0449	4.8	1051	0.7	1713	4.8	2308	0.6
7	F	0527	4.9	1131	0.6	1753	4.8	● 2346	0.7
8	SA	0604	4.9	1209	0.7	1831	4.7		
9	SU	0021	0.8	0638	4.9	1245	0.8	1907	4.6
10	M	0055	1.0	0713	4.8	1318	0.9	1942	4.5
11	TU	0128	1.1	0749	4.7	1353	1.0	2019	4.3
12	W	0202	1.3	0826	4.5	1430	1.2	2057	4.2
13	TH	0241	1.5	0907	4.3	1511	1.4	2141	4.0
14	F	0325	1.7	0954	4.1	1559	1.5	2234	3.9
15	SA	0418	1.8	1052	4.0	1659	1.6	◐ 2338	3.8
16	SU	0524	1.9	1202	3.9	1810	1.6		
17	M	0047	3.9	0640	1.8	1312	4.0	1917	1.5
18	TU	0148	4.1	0748	1.6	1412	4.2	2015	1.3
19	W	0240	4.3	0845	1.3	1503	4.4	2106	1.1
20	TH	0327	4.6	0936	1.0	1551	4.6	2154	0.8
21	F	0412	4.8	1025	0.8	1638	4.8	2240	0.7
22	SA	0457	5.0	1111	0.5	1724	4.9	○ 2326	0.5
23	SU	0542	5.1	1157	0.4	1811	5.0		
24	M	0011	0.5	0626	5.1	1243	0.3	1858	5.0
25	TU	0056	0.5	0712	5.1	1328	0.3	1945	4.9
26	W	0141	0.6	0758	5.0	1415	0.4	2034	4.7
27	TH	0228	0.8	0847	4.8	1505	0.6	2126	4.5
28	F	0319	1.0	0939	4.5	1600	0.8	2223	4.3
29	SA	0418	1.2	1040	4.3	1703	1.0	◑ 2330	4.2
30	SU	0526	1.4	1154	4.1	1811	1.2		
31	M	0045	4.1	0639	1.5	1317	4.1	1918	1.2

Chart Datum: 0·30 metres below Ordnance Datum (Dublin). HAT is 5·5 metres above Chart Datum.

North Ireland

Liscannor Bay clockwise to Lambay Island

9.13.1 Contents 611

9.13.2 Area map and Distance table 612

9.13.3 Tidal stream charts 614

9.13.4 Lights, buoys and waypoints 616

9.13.5 Passage information 618
Crossing the Irish Sea, crossing to/from Scotland, Liscannor Bay to Slyne Head – 618 • Slyne Head to Eagle Island, Eagle Island to Bloody Foreland – 621 • Bloody Foreland to Fair Head – 629 • Fair Head to Lambay Island – 635

9.13.6 Special notes for Ireland See *9.12.6* 619
Useful Gaelic words – 573

9.13.7 Galway Bay, tide tables/curves 619
Aran Islands • Galway Harbour

9.13.8 Westport (Clew Bay) 625
Clifden Bay • Ballynakill • Inishbofin • Killary Harbour • Inishturk • Clare Island • Blacksod Bay • Portnafrankagh • Broad Haven

9.13.9 Sligo 626
Killala Bay • Mullaghmore

9.13.10 Killybegs 627
Teelin Harbour • Inishkeel • Burtonport • Gweedore/Bunbeg • Sheep Haven • Mulroy Bay

9.13.11 Lough Swilly 628

9.13.12 Lough Foyle (River Foyle, tide tables/curves) 629

9.13.13 River Bann and Coleraine 634
Portstewart

9.13.14 Portrush 635

9.13.15 Tidal streams around Rathlin Island 636
Rathlin Island • Ballycastle • Red Bay • Carnlough • Glenarm

9.13.16 Larne 638

9.13.17 Belfast Lough, tide tables/curves 639
Carrickfergus • Belfast • Cultra • Ballyholme Bay • Groomsport Bay • Bangor • Donaghadee • Portavogie

9.13.18 Strangford Lough 645
Strangford • Portaferry • Quoile • Killyleagh • Sketrick • Kircubbin

9.13.19 Ardglass 645
Dundrum Bay • Annalong • Kilkeel

9.13.20 Carlingford Lough 646
Port Oriel • Balbriggan • Skerries

1	*Kilrush*	318	361	364	335	332	323	309	291	276	274	270	251	220	203	191	183	142	119	75	76	**1**
2	Galway	348	366	338	309	307	297	284	266	253	251	245	227	192	178	166	163	104	94	49	**2**	
3	Slyne Head	352	317	289	260	257	248	234	217	201	199	195	178	143	128	117	114	55	44	**3**		
4	Westport	337	323	295	266	249	240	226	207	193	191	187	168	137	120	108	100	57	**4**			
5	Eagle Island	297	262	234	205	198	193	175	162	147	145	136	123	88	72	62	59	**5**				
6	Sligo	281	246	218	189	179	177	156	146	123	121	117	107	72	51	30	**6**					
7	Killybegs	267	232	204	175	171	163	148	132	115	113	109	93	58	43	**7**						
8	Burtonport	218	182	153	130	130	116	108	90	74	72	68	49	18	**8**							
9	**Tory Island**	209	174	146	117	113	105	90	74	57	55	51	35	**9**								
10	L Swilly (Fahan)	200	166	138	109	104	96	81	65	48	46	42	**10**									
11	**Lough Foyle**	157	121	92	72	73	55	47	30	11	9	**11**										
12	River Bann	155	120	92	63	65	53	40	24	5	**12**											
13	**Portrush**	150	115	87	58	60	48	35	19	**13**												
14	Altacarry Head	135	102	74	45	45	31	21	**14**													
15	**Carnlough**	118	78	50	25	26	11	**15**														
16	**Larne**	108	73	45	16	16	**16**															
17	**Carrickfergus**	101	66	39	6	**17**																
18	**Bangor**	96	61	34	**18**																	
19	**Strangford L**	71	36	**19**																		
20	**Carlingford L**	50	**20**																			
21	***Dun Laoghaire***	**21**																				

DISTANCE TABLE
Approximate distances in nautical miles are by the most direct route, whilst avoiding dangers and allowing for Traffic Separation Schemes. Places in *italics* are in adjoining areas; places in **bold** are in 9.0.6, Distances across the Irish Sea.

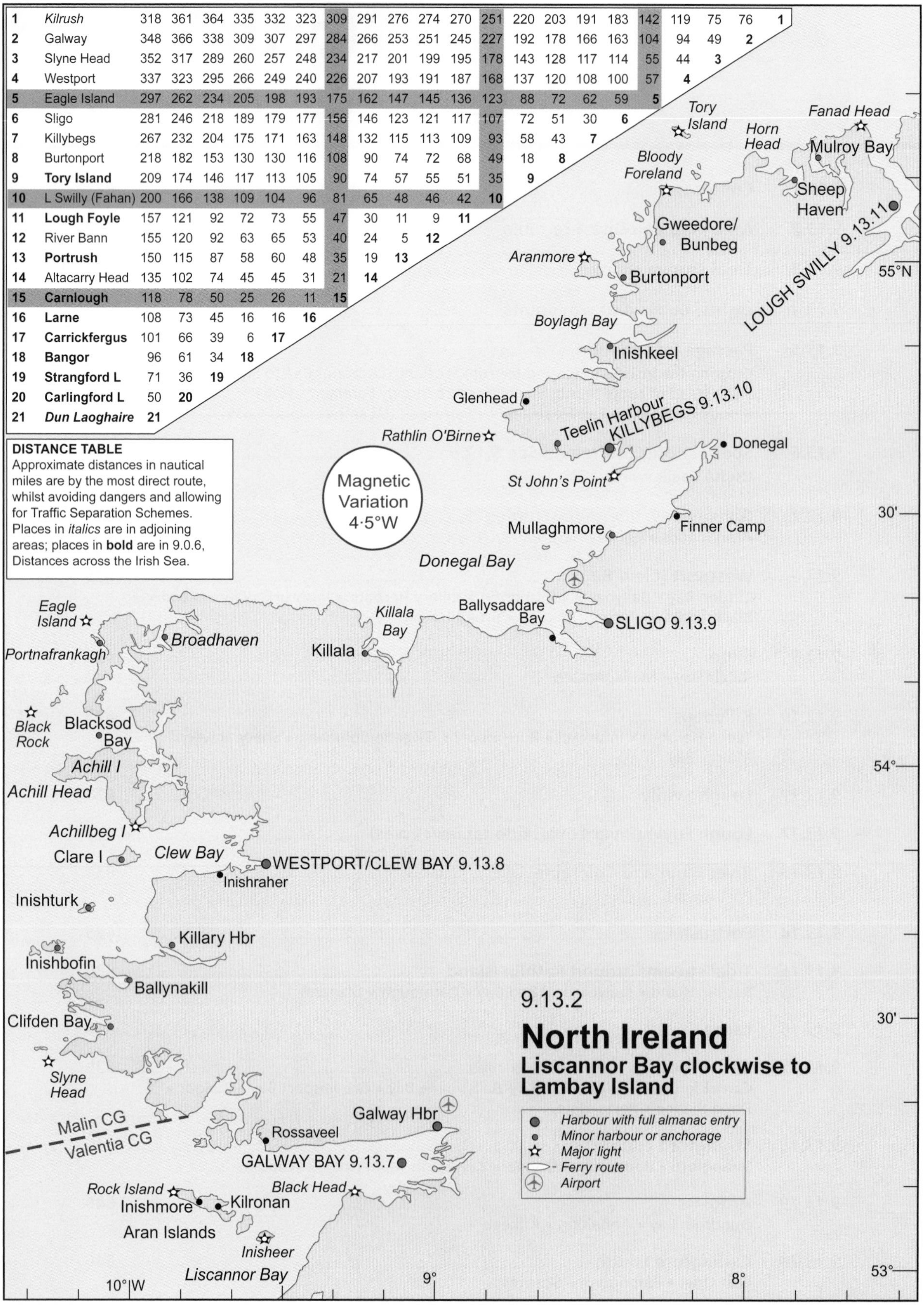
Tory Island
Fanad Head
Horn Head
Mulroy Bay
Bloody Foreland
Sheep Haven
LOUGH SWILLY 9.13.11
Gweedore/ Bunbeg
Aranmore
Burtonport
55°N
Boylagh Bay
Inishkeel
Glenhead
Teelin Harbour
KILLYBEGS 9.13.10
Rathlin O'Birne
Donegal
Magnetic Variation 4·5°W
St John's Point
30'
Mullaghmore
Finner Camp
Donegal Bay
Ballysaddare Bay
Killala Bay
SLIGO 9.13.9
Eagle Island
Broadhaven
Portnafrankagh
Killala
Black Rock
Blacksod Bay
Achill I
Achill Head
54°
Achillbeg I
Clare I
Clew Bay
WESTPORT/CLEW BAY 9.13.8
Inishraher
Inishturk
Killary Hbr
Inishbofin
Ballynakill
Clifden Bay
30'
Slyne Head
Malin CG
Valentia CG
Galway Hbr
Rossaveel
GALWAY BAY 9.13.7
Rock Island
Black Head
Inishmore
Kilronan
Aran Islands
Inisheer
Liscannor Bay
10°W
9°
8°
53°
Harbour with full almanac entry
Minor harbour or anchorage
Major light
Ferry route
Airport

9.13.2

North Ireland

Liscannor Bay clockwise to Lambay Island

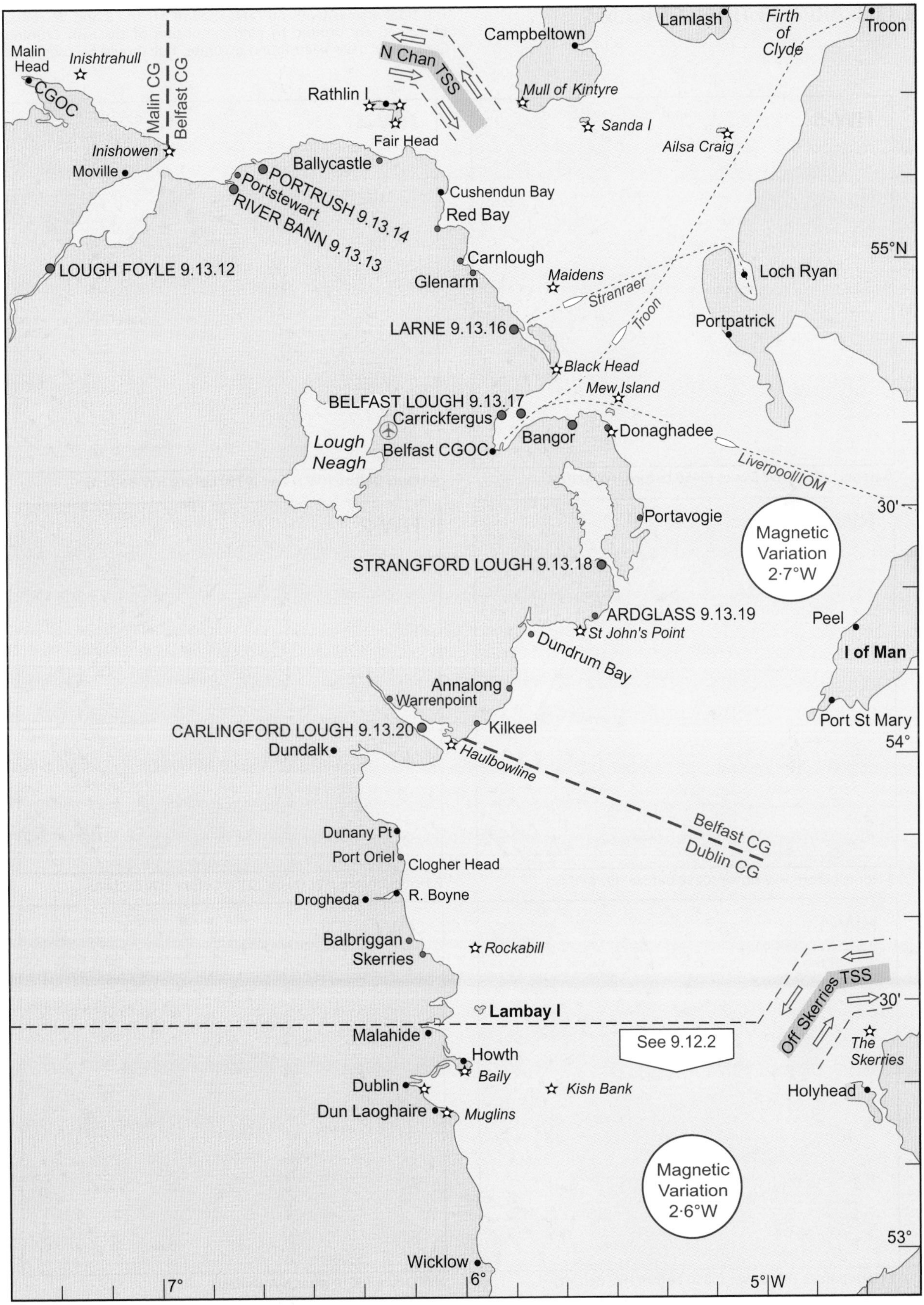
Malin Head
Inishtrahull
CGOC
Malin CG
Belfast CG
Inishowen
Moville
N Chan TSS
Rathlin I
Fair Head
Campbeltown
Lamlash
Firth of Clyde
Troon
Mull of Kintyre
Sanda I
Ailsa Craig
Ballycastle
PORTRUSH 9.13.14
Portstewart
RIVER BANN 9.13.13
Cushendun Bay
Red Bay
Carnlough
Glenarm
LOUGH FOYLE 9.13.12
Maidens
Stranraer
Troon
Loch Ryan
55°N
Portpatrick
LARNE 9.13.16
Black Head
Mew Island
BELFAST LOUGH 9.13.17
Carrickfergus
Lough Neagh
Belfast CGOC
Bangor
Donaghadee
Liverpool/IOM
30'
Portavogie
Magnetic Variation 2·7°W
STRANGFORD LOUGH 9.13.18
ARDGLASS 9.13.19
St John's Point
Peel
I of Man
Dundrum Bay
Annalong
Warrenpoint
CARLINGFORD LOUGH 9.13.20
Kilkeel
Port St Mary
54°
Dundalk
Haulbowline
Belfast CG
Dublin CG
Dunany Pt
Port Oriel
Clogher Head
Drogheda
R. Boyne
Balbriggan
Skerries
Rockabill
Off Skerries TSS
30'
Lambay I
Malahide
See 9.12.2
The Skerries
Howth
Baily
Dublin
Kish Bank
Holyhead
Dun Laoghaire
Muglins
Magnetic Variation 2·6°W
53°
Wicklow
7°
6°
5°W

9.13.3 AREA 13 TIDAL STREAMS

The tidal arrows (with no rates shown) off the S and W coasts of Ireland are printed by kind permission of the Irish Cruising Club. They have been found accurate, but should be used with caution.

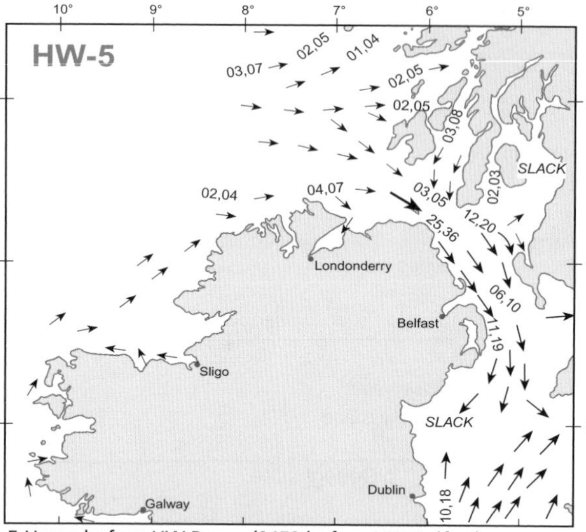

5 Hours before HW Dover (0450 before HW Belfast)

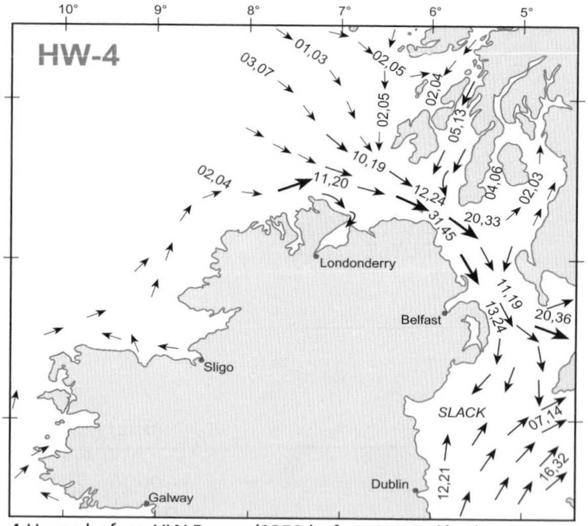

4 Hours before HW Dover (0350 before HW Belfast)

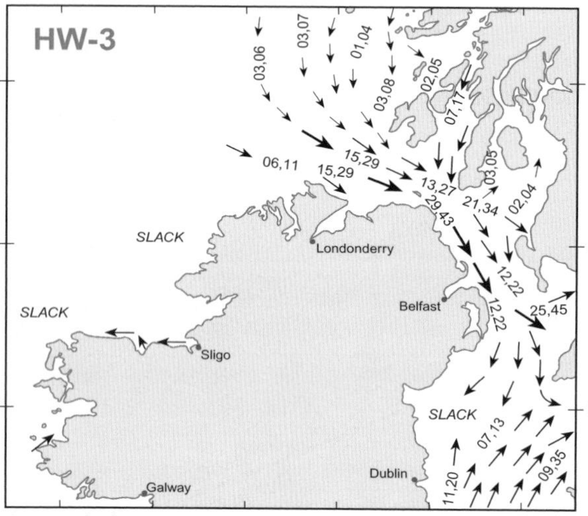

3 Hours before HW Dover (0250 before HW Belfast)

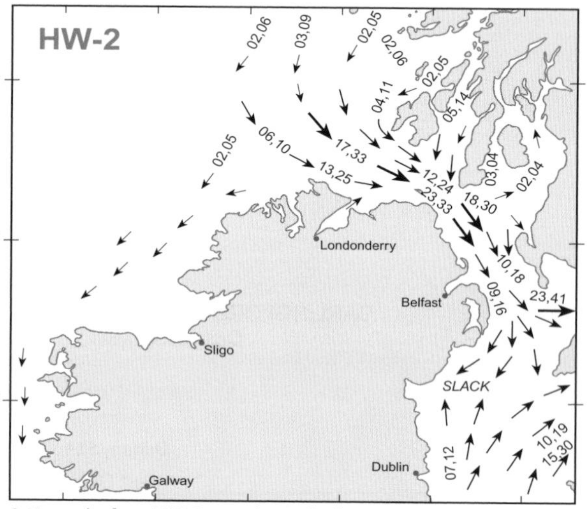

2 Hours before HW Dover (0150 before HW Belfast)

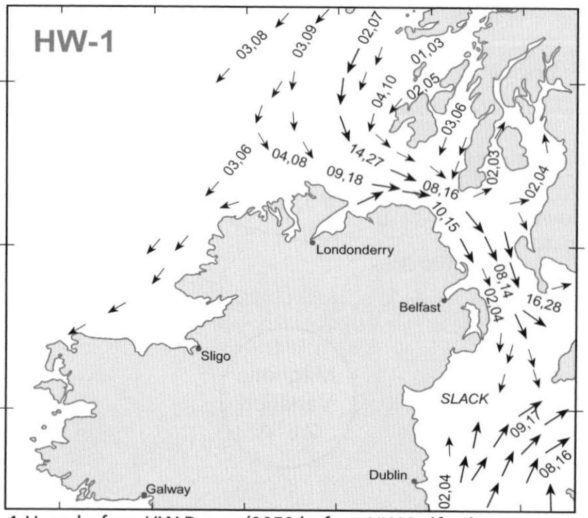

1 Hour before HW Dover (0050 before HW Belfast)

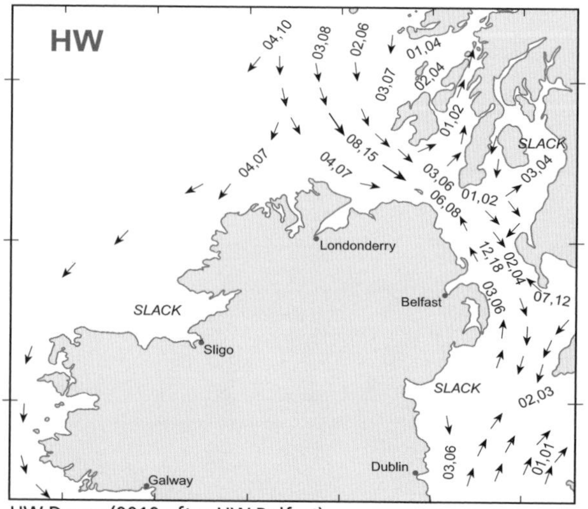

HW Dover (0010 after HW Belfast)

Rathlin Island 9.13.15
Mull of Kintyre 9.9.11
North Irish Sea 9.10.3
SW Scotland 9.9.3
South Ireland 9.12.3

The tidal arrows (with no rates shown) off the S and W coasts of Ireland are printed by kind permission of the Irish Cruising Club. They have been found accurate, but should be used with caution.

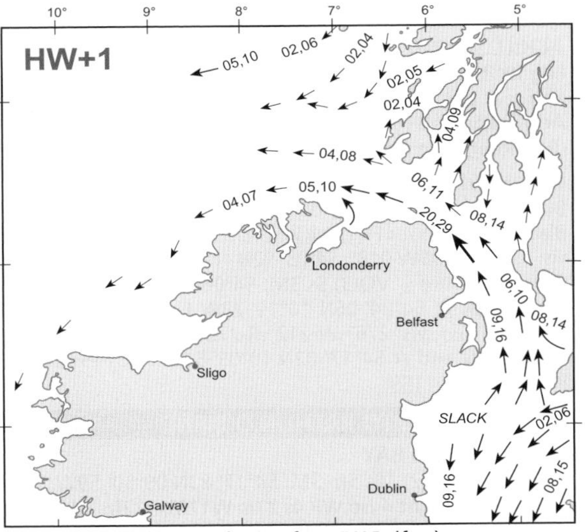

1 Hour after HW Dover (0110 after HW Belfast)

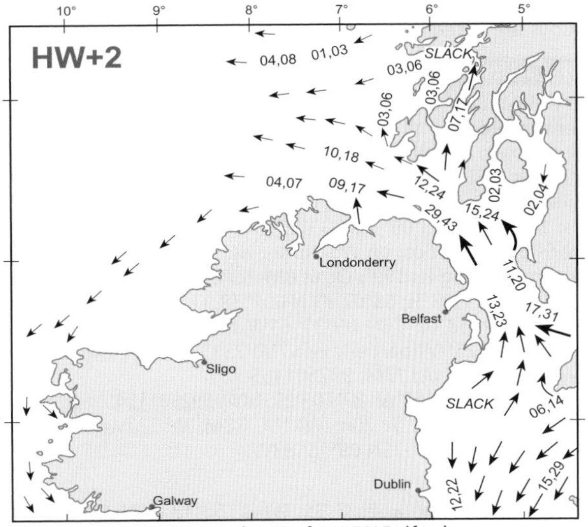

2 Hours after HW Dover (0210 after HW Belfast)

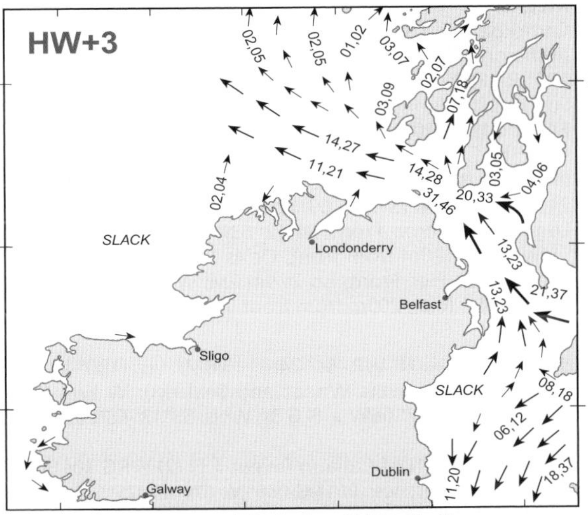

3 Hours after HW Dover (0310 after HW Belfast)

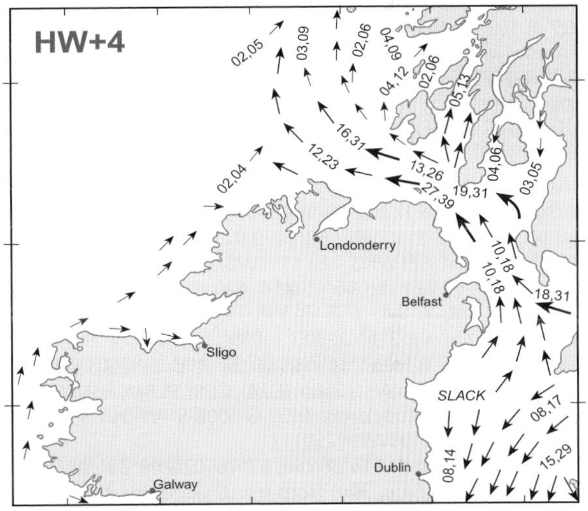

4 Hours after HW Dover (0410 after HW Belfast)

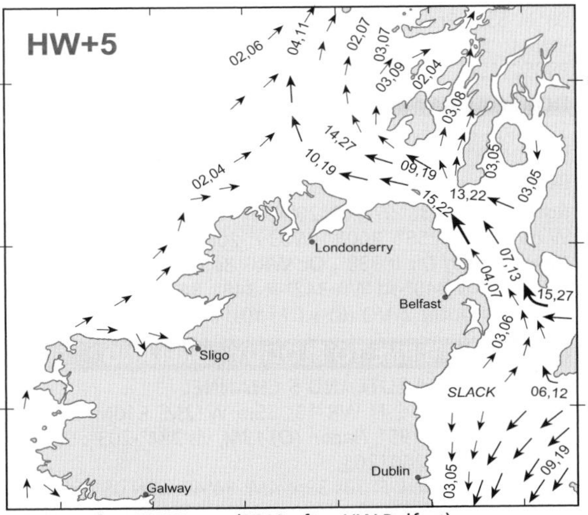

5 Hours after HW Dover (0510 after HW Belfast)

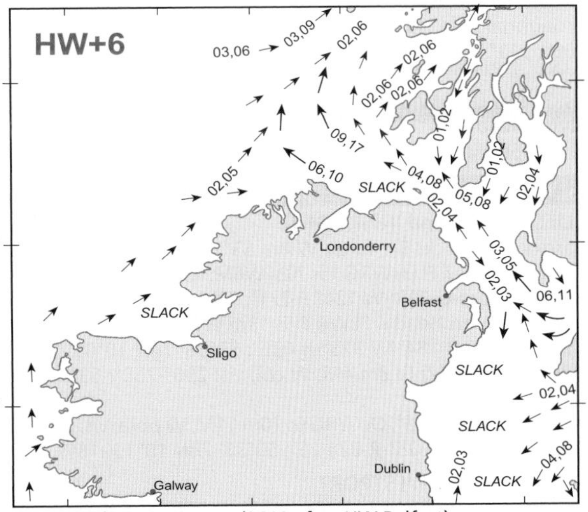

6 Hours after HW Dover (0610 after HW Belfast)

9.13.4 LIGHTS, BUOYS AND WAYPOINTS

Bold print = light with a nominal range of 15M or more. CAPITALS = place or feature. *CAPITAL ITALICS* = light-vessel, light float or Lanby. *Italics* = Fog signal. ***Bold italics*** = Racon. Many marks/ buoys are fitted with AIS, MMSI No; see relevant charts.

LISCANNOR BAY TO SLYNE HEAD

GALWAY BAY and INISHMORE

Eeragh, Rock Is ☆ 53°08'·91N 09°51'·40W Fl 15s 35m **18M**; W twr, two B bands; vis: 297°-262°; 992501172.
Straw Is ✧ Fl (2) 5s 11m 12M; W twr; 53°07'·08N 09°37'·82W.
Killeany Ldg lts 192°. Front, Oc 5s 6m 3M; W col on W □ base; vis: 142°-197°, 53°06'·25N 09°39'·74W. Rear, 43m from front, Oc 5s 8m 2M; W col on W □ base; vis: 142°-197°.
Inishmaan, Ldg lts 199°, Oc 6s 8M; 53°06'·08N 09°34'·77W.
Killeaney Fl G 3s; 53°07.33'N 009°38.37'W; 992501166.
Inisheer ☆ 53°02'·76N 09°31'·61W Iso WR 12s 34m **W16M**, R11M; vis: 225°-W(partially vis >7M)-231°, 231°-W-245°-R-269°-W-115°; ***Racon (K) 13M***; 992501165.
Finnis Q (3) 10s; 53°02'·82N 09°29'·14W, 992501164.
Black Hd ✧ Fl WR 5s 20m W11M, R8M, W □ twr; vis: 045°-R268°-276°; 53°09'·25N 09°15'·83W.

GALWAY

Margaretta Shoal Fl G 3s; *Whis;* 53°13'·68N 09°05'·99W, 992501170.
Leverets ✧ Q WRG 9m 10M; B □ twr, W bands; vis: 015°-G-058°-W-065°-R-103°-G-143·5°-W-146·5°-R-015°; 53°15'·33N 09°01'·90W.
Rinmore ✧ Iso WRG 4s 7m 5M; W □ twr; vis: 359°-G-008°-W-018°-R-027°; 53°16'·12N 09°01'·97W.
Appr Chan Dir lt 325°, WRG 7m 3M; vis: 322·25°-FG-323·75°-AlGW-324·75°-FW-325·25°-AlRW-326·25°-FR-331·25°-FlR-332·25°; 53°16'·12N 09°02'·83W.

GALWAY to SLYNE HEAD

Barna Quay Hd ✧ Fl 2 WRG 5s 6m W8M, R5M, G5M; vis:250°-G-344·5°-W-355·5°-R-090°; 53°14'·93N 09°08'·90W.
Spiddle Pier Hd ✧ Fl WRG 3·5s 11m W8M, R8M, G8M; Y col; vis: 265°-G-308°-W-024°-R-066°; 53°14'·42N 09°18'·54W.
Cashla Bay Ent, W side ✧ Fl (3) WR 10s 8m W6M, R3M; W col on concrete twr; vis: 216°-W-000°-R-069°; 53°14'·23N 09°35'·20W.
Cannon Rk Fl G 5s; 53°14'·08N 09°34'·35W, 992501173.
Lion Pt Dir lt 010°, Iso WRG 5s 6m (H24), G6M, W8M, R6M,(night), G2M, W3M, R2M(day); vis: 005°-G- 008·5°-W-011·5°-R-015°; 53°15'·83N 09°33'·98W; 992501171.
Rossaveel Pier Ldg lts 116°. Front, 53°16'·02N 09°33'·38W Oc 3s 7m 3M; W mast. Rear, 90m from front, Oc 3s 8m 3M.
Kiggaul Bay ✧ Fl WRG 3s 5m W5M, R3M, G3M; vis: 310°-G-329°-W-349°-R-059°; 53°14'·03N 09°43'·02W.
Croaghnakeela Is ✧ Fl 3·7s 7m 5M; W col; vis: 034°-045°, 218°-286°, 311°-325°; 53°19'·40N 09°58'·21W.
Inishnee ✧ Fl (2) WRG 10s 9m W5M, R3M, G3M; W col on W □ base; vis: 314°-G-017°-W-030°-R-080°-W-194°; 53°22'·75N 09°54'·53W.
Slyne Head, North twr, Illaunamid ☆ 53°23'·99N 10°14'·05W Fl (2) 15s 35m **19M**; B twr; ***Racon (T)***; 992501175.

SLYNE HEAD TO EAGLE ISLAND

CLIFDEN BAY and INISHBOFIN

Carrickrana Rocks Bn, large W Bn; 53°29'·24N 10°09'·48W.
Cleggan Point ✧ Fl (3) WRG 15s 20m W6M, R3M, G3M; W col on W hut; vis: shore-G-091°-W-124°-R-221°; 53°34'·48N 10°07'·69W.
Inishlyon Lyon Head ✧ Fl WR 7·5s 13m W7M, R4M; W post; vis: 036°-W-058°-R-184°-W-325°-R-036°; 53°36'·74N 10°09'·56W.
Gun Rock ✧ Fl (2) 6s 8m 4M; W col; vis: 296°-253°; 53°36'·59N 10°13'·23W.
Inishbofin Dir lt 021°, Oc WRG 6s 10m 11M; W pole; vis: 015·75°-G-020·75°-W-021·25°-R-026·25°; 53°36'·78N 10°13'·16W.

CLEW BAY and WESTPORT

Roonagh Quay Ldg lts 144°. Front 53°45'·75N 09°54'·23W. Rear, 54m from front, both Iso Bu 10s 9/15m.
Inishgort ✧ L Fl 10s 10M; 53°49.59'N 009°40.25'W; 992501179.
Cloughcormick Q (9) 15s; 53°50'·56N 09°43'·20W.
Achillbeg I, S Point ☆ 53°51'·51N 09°56'·84W Fl WR 5s 56m **W16M, R18M**, R11M; W ○ twr on □ building; vis: 262°-R-281°-W-342°-R-060°-W-092°-R(intens)-099°-W-118°; 992501181.

ACHILL SOUND

Ldg lts 330°, 53°52'·50N 09°56'·91W Whitestone Point. Front and rear both Oc 4s 5/6m; W ◊, B stripe.
Achill I Ldg lts 310°, Purteen, Oc 8s 5m; 53°57'·83N 10°05'·93W (PA). Rear, 46m from front Oc 8s 6m.

BLACKSOD BAY

Blacksod Q (3) 10s; 54°05'·89N 10°03'·01W.
Blacksod Pier Root ✧ Fl (2) WR 7·5s 13m W12M, R9M; W twr on bldg; vis: 189°-R-210°-W-018°; 54°05'·92N 10°03'·63W; 992501186.
Carrigeenmore VQ(3) 5s 3M; 54°06'·56N 10°03'·4W.
Black Rock ☆ 54°04'·06N 10°19'·23W Fl WR 12s 86m **W20M, R16M**; W twr; vis: 276°-W-212°-R-276°; 992501183.
Eagle Is, W end ☆ 54°17'·02N 10°05'·56W Fl (3) 15s 67m **18M**; W twr; 992501189.

EAGLE ISLAND TO RATHLIN O'BIRNE

BROAD HAVEN BAY

Rinroe Pt ✧ Fl (2) 10s 5m 3M; 54°17'·83N 09°50'·59W.
Gubacashel Point ✧ Iso WR 4s 27m **W17M**, R12M; 110°-R-133°-W-355°-R-021° W twr; 54°16'·06N 09°53'·33W.

KILLALA

Carrickpatrick Q (3) 10s; 54°15'·56N 09°09'·14W; 992501192.
Inishcrone Pier Root ✧ Fl WRG 1·5s 8m 2M; vis: 098°-W-116°-G-136°-R-187°; 54°13'·21N 09°05'·79W.
Ldg lts 230°. Rinnaun Point. Front No 1, Oc 10s 7m 5M; □ twr; 54°13'·21N 09°05'·79W. Rear, 150m from front, No 2 Oc 10s 12m 5M; □ twr.
Inch Is Dir lt 215°, Fl WRG 2s 6m 3M; □ twr; vis: 205°-G-213°-W-217°-R-225°; 54°13'·29N 09°12'·30W.
Ldg lts 196°. Kilroe. Front, 54°12'·63N 09°12'·33W Oc 4s 5m 2M; □ twr. Rear,120m from front, Oc 4s 10m 2M; □ twr.
Ldg lts 236°. Pier. Front, Iso 2s 5m 2M; W ◊ on twr; 54°13'·02N 09°12'·84W. Rear, 200m from front, Iso 2s 7m 2M; W ◊ on pole.

SLIGO

Black Rock ✧ Fl WR 5s 24m 10/8M; vis: 130°-W-107°-R-130° (R sector covers Wheat and Seal rks); W twr, B band; 54°18'·46N 08°37'·06W Fl G 3s; *Whis;* 53°13'·68N 09°05'·99W, 992501195.
Lower Rosses, (N of Cullaun Bwee) ✧ Fl (2) WRG 10s 8m 10M; W hut on piles; vis: 061°-G-066°-W-070°-R-075°; shown H24; 54°19'·73N 08°34'·41W.
Ldg lts 125° Fl (3) 6s 7M (sync). Front, Metal Man; 54°18'·24N 08°34'·55W, 3m. Rear, Oyster Is, 365m from front, 13m; H24.
Wheat Rock Q (6) + LFl 15s; 54°18'·84N 08°39'·10W; 992501196.

DONEGAL BAY and KILLYBEGS

St John's Pt ✧ Fl 6s 30m 14M; W twr; 54°34'·16N 08°27'·66W; 992501197.
Bullockmore Q (9) 15s; 54°33'·98N 08°30'·14W; 992501198.
Rotten I ☆ 54°36'·97N 08°26'·41W Fl WR 4s 20m **W15M**, R11M; W twr; vis: W255°- R008°- W039°-208°.
New Landing Dir lt 338°, Oc WRG 8s 17m; vis: 328°-G-334°-Al WG-336°-W-340°-Al WR-342°-R-348°; 54°38'·14N 08°26'·38W.
Killybegs Outer VQ (6) + L Fl 10s; 54°37'·92N 08°29'·15W.

RATHLIN O'BIRNE TO BLOODY FORELAND

S of ARAN and RUTLAND S CHANNEL

Rathlin O'Birne ✧ Fl WR 15s 35m W12M, R10M; W twr; vis: 195°-R-307°-W-195°; ***Racon (O) 13M***, vis 284°-203°. 54°39'·82N 08°49'·95W; 992501203.
Dawros Head ☆ L Fl 10s 39m 4M; 54°49'·63N 08°33'·64W.
Wyon Point ✧ Fl (2) WRG 10s 8m W6M, R3M; W □ twr; vis: shore-G-021°-W-042°-R-121°-W-150°-R-shore; 54°56'·51N 08°27'·54W.

BURTONPORT
Ldg lts 068·1°. Front , FG 17m 1M; Gy Bn, W band; 54°58′·95N 08°26′·40W. Rear, 355m from front, FG 23m 1M; Gy Bn, Y band.

N SOUND OF ARAN and RUTLAND N CHANNEL
Rutland I Ldg lts 137·6°. Front, 54°58′·97N 08°27′·68W Oc 6s 8m 1M; W Bn, B band. Rear, 330m from front, Oc 6s 14m 1M.
Inishcoo Ldg lts 119·3°. Front, Iso 6s 6m 1M; W Bn, B band; 54°59′·43N 08°29′·63W. Rear, 248m from front, Iso 6s 11m 1M.
Ldg lts 186°. Front, Oc 8s 8m 3M; B Bn, W band; 54°58′·94N 08°29′·27W. Rear, 395m from front, Oc 8s 17m 3M; B Bn.
Aranmore, Rinrawros Pt ☆ 55°00′·90N 08°33′·69W Fl (2) 20s 71m **18M**; W twr; obsc by land about 234°-007° and about 013°. Auxiliary lt Fl R 3s 61m 13M, same twr; vis: 203°-234°; 992501205.

OWEY SOUND to INISHSIRRER
Cruit Is. Owey Sound Ldg lts 068·3°. Oc 10s. Front, 55°03′·06N 08°25′·85W. Rear, 107m from front.
Rinnalea Point ☆ 55°02′·59N 08°23′·72W Fl 7·5s 19m 9M; □ twr; vis: 132°-167°.
Gola Is Ldg lts 171·2°. Oc 3s 2M (sync). Front, 9m; W Bn, B band; 55°05′·11N 08°21′·07W. Rear, 86m from front, 13m; B Bn, W band.
Glassagh. Ldg lts 137·4°. Front, Oc 8s 12m 3M; 55°06′·83N 08°18′·97W. Rear, 46m from front, Oc 8s 17m 3M; synch.
Inishsirrer, NW end ☆ Fl 3·7s 20m 4M; W □ twr vis: 083°-263°; 55°07′·40N 08°20′·93W.

BLOODY FORELAND TO INISHTRAHULL

BLOODY FORELAND to SHEEPHAVEN
Bloody Foreland ☆ Fl WG 7·5s 14m W6M, G4M; vis: 062°-W-232°-G-062°; 55°09′·51N 08°17′·03W.
Tory Island ☆ 55°16′·36N 08°14′·96W Fl (4) 30s 40m **18M**; B twr, W band; vis: 302°-277°; ***Racon (M) 12-23M***; 992501211.
West Town Ldg lts 001° ☆ Iso 2s 9m 7M △ on Y structure R stripe; 55°15′·79N 08°13′·50W. Rear Iso 2s 11m 7M ▽ ditto (sync).
Inishbofin Pier ☆ Fl 8s 3m 3M; 55°10′·14N 08°10′·01W.
Ballyness Hbr. Ldg lts 119·5°. Front, Iso 4s 25m 1M; 55°09′·06N 08°06′·98W. Rear, 61m from front, Iso 4s 26m 1M.
Portnablahy Ldg lts 125·3°. Front Oc 6s 7m 2M; B col, W bands; 55°10′·79N 07°55′·65W. Rear, 81m from front, Oc 6s 12m 2M; B col, W bands.

MULROY BAY
Limeburner Q Fl; 55°18′·54N 07°48′·40W; 992501214.
Ravedy Is ☆ Fl 3s 9m 3M; vis 177°-357°; 55°15′·14N 07°46′·90W.

LOUGH SWILLY, BUNCRANA and RATHMULLAN
Fanad Head ☆ 55°16′·57N 07°37′·92W Fl (5) WR 20s 39m **W18M**, R14M; W twr; vis 100°-R-110°-W-313°-R-345°-W-100°; 992501215.
Swillymore Fl G 3s; 55°15′·12N 07°35′·79W; 992501216.
Dunree ☆ Fl (2) WR 5s 49m W12M, R9M; vis: 320°-R-328°-W-183°-R-196°; 55°11′·89N 07°33′·24W; 992501217.
Buncrana Pier near Hd ☆ Iso WR 4s 11m W13M, R10M; R twr, W band; vis: R shore- over Inch spit, 052°-W-139°-R-shore over White Strand Rock; 55°07′·60N 07°27′·88W.
Rathmullan Pier Hd ☆ Fl G 3s 5M; vis: 206°-345°; 55°05′·70N 07°31′·66W.
Inishtrahull ☆ 55°25′·89N 07°14′·63W Fl (3) 15s 59m **19M**; W twr; obscd 256°-261° within 3M; ***Racon (T) 24M 060°-310°***. Fog Det Lt VQ; 992501229.

INISHTRAHULL TO RATHLIN ISLAND

LOUGH FOYLE
Foyle L Fl 10s; 55°15′·32N 06°52′·62W; ***Racon (M)***; 992501230.
Tuns Fl R 3s; 55°14′·00N 06°53′·46W; 992501232.
Inishowen Dunagree ☆ 55°13′·60N 06°55′·70W Fl (2) WRG 10s 28m **W18M**, R14M, G14M; W twr, 2 B bands; vis: 197°-G-211°-W-249°-R-000°. Fog Det lt VQ 16m vis: 270°.
Greencastle S Bkwtr Dir lt 042·5°. Fl (2) WRG 3s 4m W11M, R9M, G9M; vis 307°-G- 040°-W-045°-R-055°; 55°12′·17N 06°59′·13W.
McKinney's Fl R 5s; 55°10′·9N 07°00′·5W.
Moville Fl WR 2·5s 11m 4M; W house on G piles vis: 240°-W-064°-R-240°; 55°10′·98N 07°02′·13W.

RIVER BANN, COLERAINE and PORTRUSH
River Bann Ldg lts 165°. Front, Oc 5s 6m 2M; W twr; 55°09′·96N 06°46′·23W. Rear, 245m from front, Oc 5s 14m 2M; W □ twr.
W Mole ☆ Fl G 5s 4m 2M; vis: 170°-000°; 55°10′·25N 06°46′·45W.
Portstewart Point ☆ Oc R 10s 21m 5M; R □ hut; vis: 040°-220°; 55°11′·33N 06°43′·26W.
N Pier Hd ☆ Fl R 3s 6m 3M; vis: 220°-160°; 55°12′·34N 06°39′·58W.
Skerries Fl R 5s; 53°13′·90N 06°36′·90W; 992351096.

RATHLIN ISLAND
Rathlin W 0·5M NE of Bull Pt ☆ 55°18′·05N 06°16′·82W Fl R 5s 62m **22M**; W twr, lantern at base; vis: 015°-225°; H24. Fog Det Lt VQ; 992351000.
Drake Wreck 55°17′·00N 06°12′·48W Q (6) + L Fl 15s.
Manor House ☆ Oc WRG 4s 5M; vis: 020°-G-023°-W-026°-R-029°; 55°17′·52N 06°11′·73W.
Rue Pt ☆ Fl(2) 5s 16m 14M; W twr B bands; 55°15′·53N 06°11′·47W; 992351131.
Altacarry Head ☆ 55°18′·11N 06°10′·31W Fl (4) 20s 74m **26M**; W twr, B band; vis: 110°-006° and 036°-058°; ***Racon (G) 15-27M***; 992320707.

FAIR HEAD TO LAMBAY ISLAND

RED BAY, CARNLOUGH and LARNE
Red Bay Pier ☆ Fl 3s 10m 5M; 55°03′·93N 06°03′·21W.
Carnlough Hbr N Pier ☆ Fl G 3s 4m 5M; 54°59′·59N 05°59′·29W.
East Maiden ☆ Fl (3) 15s 29m **18M**; W twr, B band; ***Racon (M) 11-21M***. Auxiliary lt Fl R 5s 15m 8M; 54°55′·75N 05°43′·67W; same twr; vis:142°-182° over Russel and Highland Rks; 992351110.
N Hunter Rock Q; 54°53′·04N 05°45′·13W.
S Hunter Rock VQ(6) + LFl 10s; 54°52′·69N 05°45′·22W; 992351007.
Larne No 1 QG; 54°51′·68N 05°47′·67W; *AIS*.
Chaine Twr ☆ Iso WR 5s 23m **W16M,** R12M; Gy twr; vis: 232°-W-240°-R-000° (shore); 54°51′·27N 05°47′·90W.
Larne Ldg lts 184°, No 11 Front, 54°49′·60N 05°47′·81W Oc 4s 6m 12M; W 2 with R stripe on R pile structure; vis: 179°-189°. No 12 Rear, 610m from front, Oc 4s 14m 12M; W 2 with R stripe on R □ twr; synch with front, vis: 5° either side of Ldg line.

CARRICKFERGUS
Black Hd ☆ 54°46′·02N 05°41′·34W Fl 3s 45m **27M**; W 8-sided twr; 992351002.
Cloghan Jetty 54°44′·10N 05°41′·58W QG. Marina Ent Appr ☆ Dir Oc WRG 3s 5m 3M; vis: G308°- W317·5°- R322·5°-332°; 54°42′·58N 05°48′·78W.

BELFAST LOUGH and BANGOR
Mew Is ☆ NE end 54°41′·92N 05°30′·82W Fl (4) 30s 35m **18M**; B twr, W band; ***Racon (O) 14M***. Fog Det Lt VQ; 992351109.
Belfast Fairway Iso 4s; 54°42′·32N 05°42′·30W; ***Racon (G)***; *AIS*.
Kilroot Fl QG (sync); 54°42′·85N 05°42′·85W.
Helen's Bay QR (sync); 54°41′·86N 05°42′·85W.
No 1 Fl G 2s (sync); 54°41′·67N 05°46′·51W.
No 2 Fl R 2s (sync); 54°41′·55N 05°46′·43W.
Briggs Q; 54°41′·18N 05°53′·73W; 992351133.

DONAGHADEE
Merandoragh Fl (2) G 6s (sync); 54°39′·84N 05°32′·24W.
Foreland Spit Fl (2) R 6s (sync); 54°39′·64N 05°32′·31W.
Governor's Fl G 3s (sync); 54°39′·36N 05°31′·99W; 992351134.
Riggs Bank ⊙ V–AIS PHM; 54°38′·63N 05°27′·10W; 992356011.
Donaghadee ☆, S Pier Hd 54°38′·71N 05°31′·86W Iso WR 4s 17m **W18M**, R14M; twr; vis: shore-W-326°-R-shore; 002320792.

BALLYWATER and PORTAVOGIE

Ballywalter, Bkwtr Hd Fl WRG 3s 4m 9M; vis: 240°-G-267°-W-277°-R-314°; 54°32′·68N 05°28′·83W.

Skulmartin Fl (2) R 6s 10s; 54°31′·82N 05°24′·80W; 992351022.
Portavogie Bkwtr Hd Iso WRG 5s 9m W10M, R8M, G8M; □ twr; vis: shore-G-258°-W-275°-R-348°; 54°27′·44N 05°26′·14W.
Plough Rock 54°27′·40N 05°25′·12W Fl R 3s.
South Rock Fl (3) R 30s 9M 54°24′·48N 05°21′·99W; ***Racon (T)***; 992351004.

STRANGFORD LOUGH

Strangford L Fl 10s; 54°18′·63N 05°28′·69W; 992351028.
Bar Pladdy Q (6) + L Fl 15s; 54°19′·34N 05°30′·51W; 992351135.
Dogtail Pt Ldg lts 341°. Front, Iso 4s 2m 5M; G Bn; 54°20′·79N 05°31′·84W. Rear, Gowlands Rk, 0·8M fm front, Iso 4s 6m 5M; W twr, G top, B base.

Swan Is Q (3) 5m; BYB brick twr; 54°22′·38N 05°33′·16W.

Strangford East Ldg lts 256°. Front, Oc WRG 5s 6m W9M, R6M, G6M: vis: 190°-R-244°-G-252°-W- 260°-R-294°; 54°22′·29N 05°33′·27W. Rear, 46m from front, Oc R 5s 10m 6M; vis: 250°-264°.
Portaferry Pier Hd Oc WR 10s 9m W9M, R6M; Or mast; vis: W335°- R005°- W017°-128°; 54°22′·82N 05°33′·03W.

ARDGLASS

Inner Pier Hd Iso WRG 4s 10m W8M, R7M, G5M; twr; vis: shore-G-308°-W-314°-R-shore; 54°15′·79N 05°36′·33W.

DUNDRUM BAY

St John's Point ☆ 54°13′·61N 05°39′·61W Q (2) 7·5s 37m **25M**; B twr, Y bands. **Auxiliary Light** ☆ Fl WR 3s 14m **W15M**, R11M; same twr, vis: 064°-W-078°-R-shore; Fog Det lt VQ 14m vis: 270°; 992351005.

DZ East Fl (2) Y 10s; 54°12′·05N 05°45′·30W.
DZ West Fl Y 5s; 54°11′·84N 05°50′·82W.

ANNALONG

E Bkwtr Hd Oc WRG 5s 8m 9M; twr; vis: 204°-G-249°-W-309°-R-024°; 54°06′·51N 05°53′·73W.

KILKEEL

Pier Hd Fl WR 2s 8m 8M; vis: R296°-W313°-017°; 54°03′·46N 05°59′·30W; 992356010 (emergency AIS 992356008).

CARLINGFORD LOUGH and NEWRY RIVER

Hellyhunter Q(6) + LFl 15s; 54°00′·35N 06°02′·10W; 992351009.
Haulbowline 54°01′·19N 06°04′·74W Fl (3) 10s 32m 10M; Grey twr; 992501235.
Ldg lts 310·4° Front, Oc 3s 7m 11M; R △ on twr; vis: 295°-325°; 54°01′·80N 06°05′·43W; 992501237. Rear, 457m from front, Oc 3s 12m 11M; R ▽ on twr; vis: 295°-325°; both H24.
Newry River Ldg lts 310·4°. Front, 54°06′·37N 06°16′·51W. Rear, 274m from front. Both Iso 4s 5/15m 2M; stone cols.

DUNDALK

Imogene Fl (2) R 10s; 53°57′·41N 06°07′·02W; 992501238.
Pile Light 53°58′·56N 06°17′·71W Fl WR 15s 10m 10M; W Ho.
Dunany Fl R 3s; 53°53′·56N 06°09′·47W; 992501243.

SKERRIES BAY

Skerries Pier Hd Oc R 6s 7m 7M; W col; vis: 103°-R-154°; 53°35′·09N 06°06′·49W

DROGHEDA to LAMBAY ISLAND

Port Approach Dir lt 53°43′·30N 06°14′·73W WRG 10m **W19M, R15M**, G15M; vis: 268°-FG-269°-Al WG-269·5°-FW-270·5°-Al WR-271°-FR-272°; H24.
Balbriggan Fl (3) WRG 10s 12m W13M, R10M, G10M; W twr; vis: 159°-G-193°-W-288°-R-305°; 53°36′·76N 06°10′·80W.
Rockabill ☆ 53°35′·81N 06°00′·30W Fl WR 12s 45m **W17M, R13M;** W twr, B band; vis: 178°-W-329°-R-178°; 992501246.
Skerries Bay Pier Hd Oc R 6s 7m 7M; W col; vis: 103°-154°; 53°35′·09N 06°06′·49W.

9.13.5 PASSAGE INFORMATION

More passage information is threaded between the harbours in this area. Admiralty Leisure Folio 5612 covers Carlingford Lough to Lough Foyle.The latest editions of the Irish Cruising Club Sailing Directions are strongly recommended for all Irish waters (www.irishcruisingclub.com). Particularly useful on the N and W coast where other information is scarce they are published in two volumes, *E and N coasts of Ireland* and *S and W coasts of Ireland*. (Both available from Imray in UK or Todd Chart Services, Bangor, Co Down, ☎028 9146 6640 (www.toddchart.com).)

CROSSING THE IRISH SEA

(AC 1123, 1121, 1411) Passages across the Irish Sea range from the fairly long haul from Land's End to Cork (140M), to the relatively short hop from Mull of Kintyre to Torr Pt (11M). Such distances are deceptive, because the average cruising yacht needs to depart from and arrive at a reasonably secure hbr. See 9.0.6 for distances across the Irish Sea. Submarine exercise areas are at 9.9.18.

►*Strong tidal streams in North Channel can cause heavy overfalls.*◄

Many yachts use the Land's End/Cork route on their way to and from the delightful cruising ground along the S coast of Ireland. Penzance Bay or one of the Scilly Islands' ⚓s are convenient places from which to leave, with good lights to assist departure. Although the Celtic Sea is exposed to the Atlantic, there are no dangers on passage and the tidal streams are weak.

A landfall between Ballycotton and Old Hd of Kinsale (both have good lights) presents no offlying dangers, and in poor vis decreasing soundings indicate approach to land. Outward bound under sail, it is likely that the boat will be on the wind – a possible benefit on the return passage. If however the wind serves, and if it is intended to cruise along the southern coast, a landfall at the Fastnet with arrival at (say) Baltimore will place the yacht more to windward, for a little extra distance (170M).

From Land's End another likely destination is Dun Laoghaire. A stop at Milford Haven enables the skipper to select the best time for passing the Smalls or Bishops (see 9.11.5) and roughly divides the total passage into two equal parts of about 100M. From S Bishop onwards there are the options of making the short crossing to Tuskar Rk and going N inside the banks (theoretically a good idea in strong W winds) or of keeping to seaward.

►*But in bad weather the area off Tuskar is best avoided; apart from the Traffic Separation Scheme, the tide is strong at Sp and the sea can be very rough.*◄

The ferry route Holyhead/Dun Laoghaire is another typical crossing (56M) and with relatively straightforward landfalls either end. Beware the TSS off The Skerries and Kish Bank wind farm.

►*The tide runs hard round Anglesey at Sp, so departure just before slack water minimises the set N or S.*◄

Harbours on the Isle of Man provide convenient staging points for cruising in the Irish Sea, wherever bound.

CROSSING TO/FROM SCOTLAND

(AC 2198, 2199, 2724) Between Scotland and Ireland there are several possible routes, but much depends on weather and tide. Time of departure must take full advantage of the stream, and avoid tide races and overfalls (see 9.9.5). Conditions can change quickly, so a flexible plan is needed. The distance to Mull of Kintyre from Belfast Lough entrance is about 35M.

► *A departure at local HW (also HW Dover) provides at least 6hrs of N-going tides, and fair winds make it possible to get past the Mull or Sanda Is on one tide. To be more confident of reaching Gigha or Port Ellen, a departure from Glenarm Marina or Red Bay at HW makes a shorter passage with better stream advantage. The inshore side of the TSS coincides with the outer limit of the race S-SW off the Mull of Kintyre; this runs from HW Dover +0430 until +0610 when a local S-going stream opposes the main N-going stream.*◄

LISCANNOR BAY TO SLYNE HEAD

(AC 2173) The coast NE of Liscannor Bay is devoid of shelter. O'Brien's Tower is conspicuous just N of the 199m high Cliffs of

Moher. Eastward from Black Head there are many bays and inlets, often poorly marked, but providing shelter and exploration.

Galway is a commercial port, with a small marina. 3M SE, New Harbour (AC 1984) is a pleasant ⚓ with moorings off Galway Bay SC. The N side of Galway Bay is exposed, with no shelter. Normal approach to Galway Bay is through South Snd or North Snd. South Snd is 3M wide, with no dangers except Finnis Rock (0·4m) 5ca SE of Inisheer. North Snd is 4M wide from Eagle Rock and other dangers off Lettermullan shore, to banks on S side which break in strong winds. The other channels are Gregory Sound, 1M wide between Inishmore and Inishmaan, and Foul Sound between Inishmaan and Inisheer. The latter has one danger, Pipe Rock and the reef inshore of it, extending 3ca NW of Inisheer.

In good visibility the Connemara coast (AC 2709, 2096) and Aran Islands (AC 3339) give excellent cruising. But there are many rocks and few navigational marks. Between Slyne Hd and Roundstone Bay are many offlying dangers. If coasting, keep well seaward of Skerd Rocks. A conspicuous tower (24m) on Golam Head is a key feature. Going E the better harbours are Roundstone Bay, Cashel Bay, Killeany Bay, Greatman Bay and Cashla Bay. Kilronan (Killeany Bay) on Inishmore is the only reasonable harbour in the Aran Islands, but is exposed in E winds. Disused lighthouse on centre of island is conspicuous.

9.13.6 SPECIAL NOTES FOR IRELAND: See 9.12.6

9.13.7 GALWAY BAY

Galway **53°12'N 09°08'W**

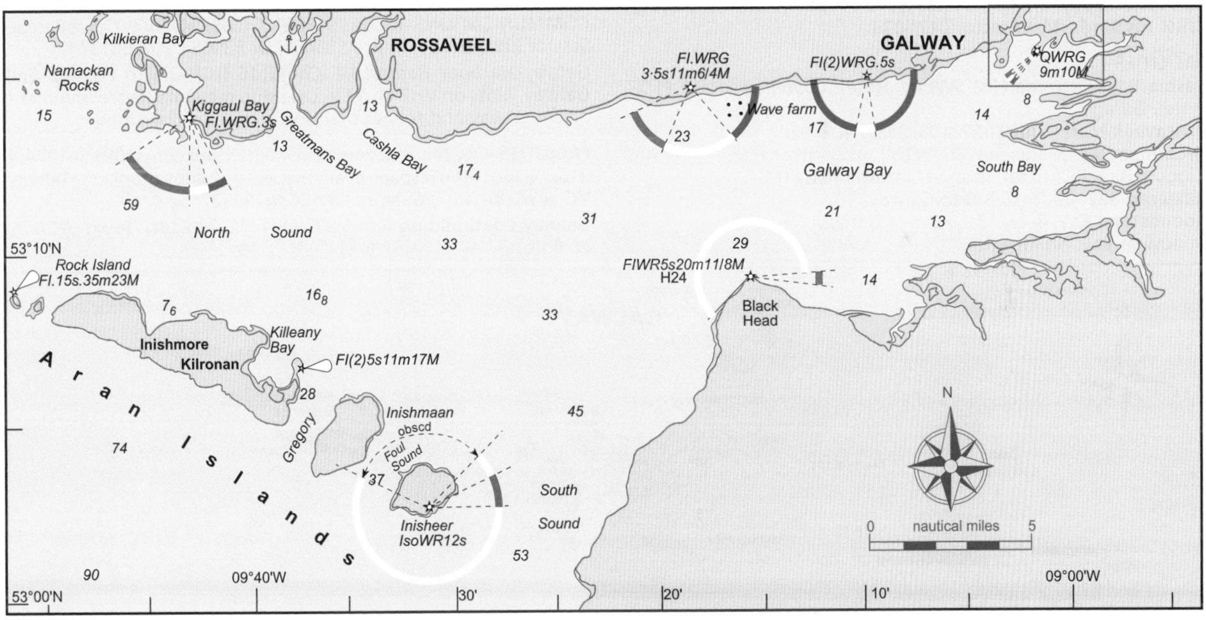

CHARTS AC 2173, 3339, 1984, 1904; Imray C55, C54

TIDES −0555 Dover; ML 2·9; Duration 0620

Standard Port GALWAY (⟶)

Times				Height (metres)			
High Water		Low Water		MHWS	MHWN	MLWN	MLWS
0600	1100	0000	0700	5·1	3·9	2·0	0·8
1800	2300	1200	1900				
Differences KILKIERAN COVE							
+0005	+0005	+0016	+0016	−0·3	−0·2	−0·1	−0·2
ROUNDSTONE BAY							
+0003	+0003	+0008	+0008	−0·7	−0·5	−0·3	−0·3
KILLEANY BAY (Aran Islands)							
0000	0000	+0001	−0001	−0·1	+0·1	+0·1	+0·2
LISCANNOR							
−0003	−0007	+0006	+0002	−0·4	−0·3	ND	ND

SHELTER Galway Bay is sheltered from large swells by Aran Is, but seas get up in the 20M between the Aran Is and Galway. Beware salmon drift nets in the apps to many bays. On the S Shore:

Bays between Black Hd and Galway have rocks and shoals, but give excellent shelter. Kinvarra B, Aughinish B, South B and Ballyvaghan B are the main ones. Enter Kinvarra B with caution on the flood; beware rks. Berth in small drying hbr. Beware fish farm in South B. Ballvaghan B, entered either side of Illaunloo Rk, leads to two piers (both dry) or ⚓ close NE in pool (3m). Best access HW±2.

On the N coast there is no safe hbr from Galway to Cashla (20M).

Cashla Bay: Easiest all-weather entry on this coast. To the East side: **Rossaveel** is a sheltered but busy fishing and ferry hbr, with small dedicated marina. To the West side: 8 Y 🅾s off Struthan Quay.

The better ⚓s in outer Galway Bay northward to Slyne Head are:

Greatman Bay: Beware English Rk (dries 1·2m), Keeraun Shoal (1.6m, seas break), Arkeena Rk, Trabaan Rk, Rin and Chapel Rks.

⚓ off Natawny Quay (E side), or on 4 Y 🟡s off Maumeen Quay (dries), ⌓ possible.

Kiggaul Bay: Easy ent, H24; ⚓ close W /NW of lt Fl WRG 3s 5/3M. Depth 3 to 4m; exposed to S/SE winds.

Kilkieran Bay: Easy ent abm Golam Tr (conspic). 12 Y 🟡s off Kilkieran. Many ⚓s in 14M long, sheltered bay.

Roundstone Bay: AC2709 (Off chartlet at 53°23'N 09°54'·5W). Safe shelter/access, except in SE'ly. 4 Y 🟡s are 5ca SSE of Roundstone, or ⚓ in 2m off N quay. Other ⚓s E in Bertraghboy and Cashel Bays.

Bunowen Bay: (53°24'·6N 10°06'·9W). Sheltered in W-NE winds; unsafe in S'ly. Easy appr with Bunowen House brg 000°, leaving Mullauncarrickscoltia Rk (1·1m) to port. ⚓ in 3-4m below conspic Doon Hill.

NAVIGATION Enter the Bay by one of four Sounds:

- North Sound between Inishmore and Golam Tr (conspic), 4½M wide, is easiest but beware Brocklinmore Bank in heavy weather.
- Gregory Sound between Inishmore and Inishmaan, is free of dangers, but give Straw Island a berth of 2-3ca.
- Foul Sound between Inishmaan and Inisheer; only danger is Pipe Rock (dries) at end of reef extending 3ca NW of Inisheer.
- South Sound between Inisheer and mainland. Finnis Rock (dries 0·4m) 4½ca SE of E point of Inisheer (marked by ECM buoy Q (3) 10s). From S, beware Kilstiffin Rocks off Liscanor Bay.

LIGHTS AND MARKS Cashla Bay: Killeen Pt Fl (3) WR 10s 6/3M; Lion Pt Dir lt 010°, Iso WRG 4s 8/6M, 008·5°-W-011·5°. Rossaveel ldg lts 116°, Oc 3s. Black Head lt Fl WR 5s 20m 11/8M H24, vis 045°-W-268°-R (covers Illanloo Rk)-276°.

Kiggaul Bay: Fl WR 3s 5m 5/3M, 329°-W-359°-R-059°.

Roundstone Bay: Croaghnakeela Is Fl 3·7s 7m 5M. Inishnee lt Fl (2) WRG 10s 9m 5/3M, W sector 017°-030°.

FACILITIES
Cashla Bay: **Carraroe** (1M SW) 🛒 Hotel. **Costelloe** (1½M E) ✉ Hotel, Garage.
Rossaveel: Marina ☎091 572108, 28⌓ 🚰 ⛽ 🔧.
Greatman Bay: Maumeen 🛒 ☏(1M) 🗑.
Kiggaul Bay: 🗑 (no ☎), shop at Lettermullen (1M).
Kilkieran Bay: ☏ 🛒 🗑 Bus to Galway.
Roundstone Bay: 🚰 ✉ 🛒 🗑 Bus to Galway.
Bunowen Bay: No facilities.

ARAN ISLANDS Shelter at **Inishmore** in Killeany Bay with harbour at Kilronan, HM ☎099 20946. 8 Y 🟡s available or ⚓ S of Kilronan pier or ⚓ E of Killeany Pt, but exposed to E/NE wind. In good weather ⚓ at Portmurvy. Facilities: ⛽ 🚰 ✉ 🛒; Ferry to Rossaveel, **Lights and marks**: Inishmore: Eeragh Island (Rk Is) Fl 15s 35m 23M, W tr, B bands. Killeany Bay: Straw Is, Fl (2) 5s 11m 17M. Ldg lts 192° Oc 5s for Killeany hbr. **Inishmaan** Ldg lts 199°, Oc 6s 8M, lead into small harbour with 3·5m and good shelter. Ferries have priority for ⌓, but do not stay overnight. Inisheer: Iso WR 12s 34m 20/16M, Racon, vis 225°-W-245° (partially obscd 225°-231° beyond 7M), R sector covers Finnis Rk.

GALWAY HARBOUR
53°16'·07N 09°02'·74W ✿✿✿✿✿✿✿✿

SHELTER Very good in Galway hbr, protected from SW'lies by Mutton Island. Dock gates open HW–2 to HW. The approach channel is dredged to 3.4m. Enter Galway Dock and secure in SW corner of basin where there is a 31-berth marina, or ask HM for waiting berth on lead-in pier. Reclamation work at Rinmore Pt has improved shelter in the 'Layby' (a dredged cut NE of New pier) where an additional 8 berths are available on a 60m pontoon. New Harbour (2·5M ESE and home of Galway Bay SC) is nearest safe ⚓ to Galway. 5 Y 🟡s in lee of Mutton Island causeway in 2-4m, may be used while waiting for the dock gates to open.

NAVIGATION Galway WPT 53°14'·80N 09°03'·40W, 061°/1·1M to Leverets lt. Shipping information see www.aislive.com.

LIGHTS AND MARKS See 9.13.4 and chartlet. Leverets Q WRG 9m 10M; B tr, W bands; Rinmore Iso WRG 4s 7m 5M; W □ tr. Appr chan 325° is defined by a Dir lt WRG 7m 3M on New Pier.

COMMUNICATIONS (Code 091) MRCC (066) 9476109; Coast Rescue Service (099) 61107; Police 538000; Dr 530054. HM 561874.
Galway Harbour Radio VHF Ch **12** 16 (HW–2½ to HW+1). Call Galway Pilots on VHF Ch **12** in case ship movements are imminent or under way and follow their instructions on berthing.

FACILITIES **City Marina**: www.galwayharbour.com ☎091 561874, ♦ 31⌓ €15(<13m) if space available, 🚰 ⚡ ⛽(by r/tanker). **Galway YC** ⛵ ⛴ 🚰 🚿 🗑; **Galway Bay SC** ☎794527, ⛵ 🚿 🗑.
Galway Boatbuilding ☎086 3379304, ⚒ ⛫ 🏗(18t). **Town** ACA ☏ ☏ ⛽ Kos 🔧 🛒 ✉ Ⓑ 🛒 ✕ 🗑 ⇌.

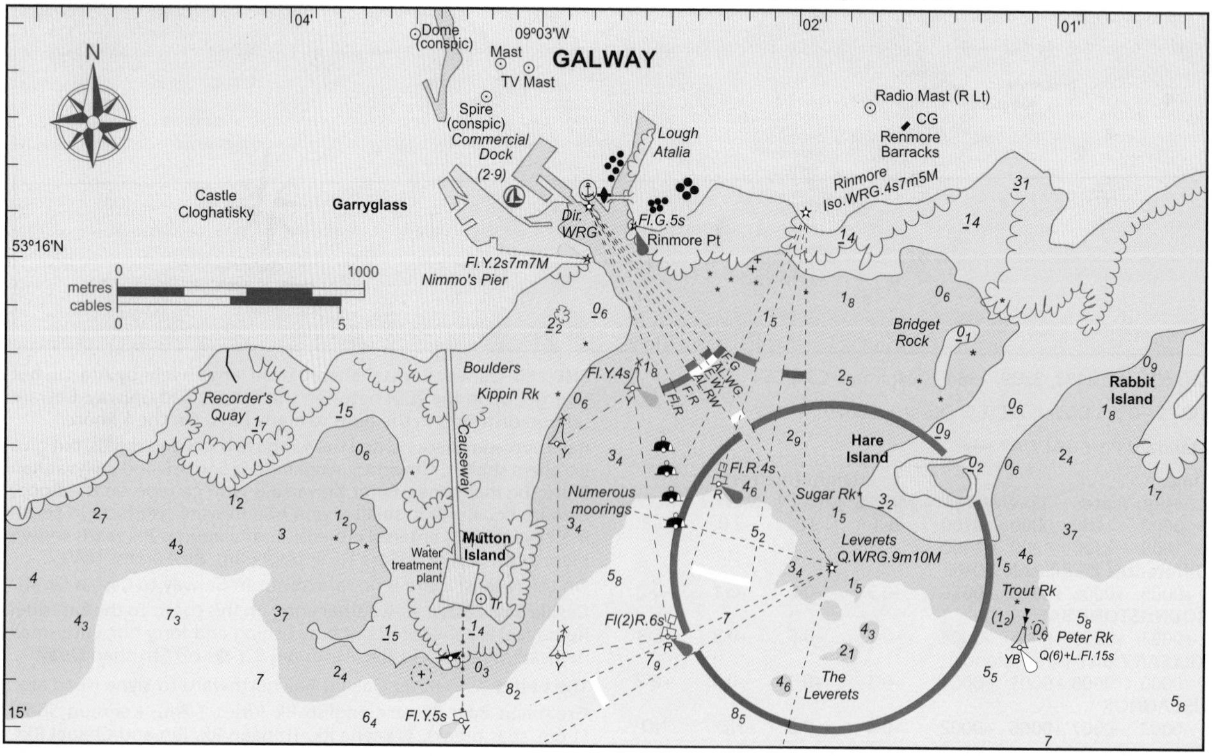

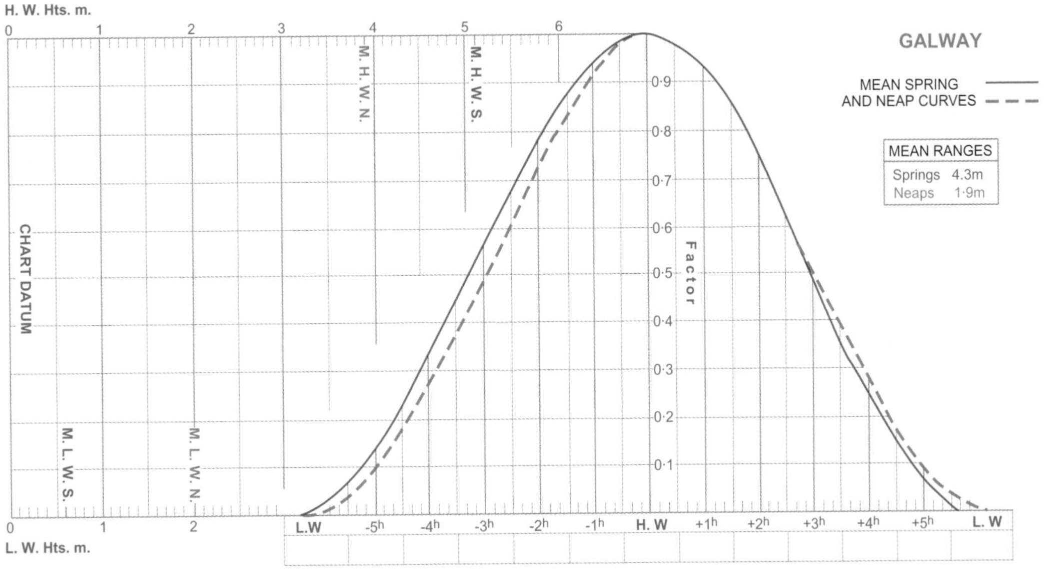
H. W. Hts. m.
GALWAY
MEAN SPRING AND NEAP CURVES
MEAN RANGES
Springs 4.3m
Neaps 1·9m
M. H. W. N.
M. H. W. S.
CHART DATUM
Factor
M. L. W. S.
M. L. W. N.
L. W. Hts. m.
L.W -5h -4h -3h -2h -1h H. W +1h +2h +3h +4h +5h L. W

SLYNE HEAD TO EAGLE ISLAND

(AC 2420) This coast has many inlets, some sheltered, but few lights. Refuelling opportunities are few and far apart.

▶ *Streams are weak offshore.* ◀

Slyne Hd Lt Ho marks SW end of the rocks and islets stretching 2M WSW from coast.

▶ *Here the stream turns N at HW Galway −0320, and S at HW Galway +0300. It runs 3kn at sp and in bad weather causes a dangerous race; keep 2M offshore.* ◀

Seas break on Barret Shoals, 3M NW of Slyne Hd. Cleggan B is moderate ⚓, open to NW but easy access. High Is Sound is usual coasting route, not Friar Is Sound or Aughrus Passage. Clifden Bay (AC 2708) has offlying dangers with breakers; enter 3ca S of Carrickrana Bn and ⚓ off Drinagh Pt, in Clifden Hbr or Ardbear Bay.

Ballynakill Hbr (AC 2706), easily entered either side of Freaghillaun South, has excellent shelter; Tully mountain is conspic to N. Beware Mullaghadrina and Ship Rk in N chan. ⚓ in Fahy, Derryinver or Barnaderg B. There is ⚓ on S side of Inishbofin (lt), but difficult access/exit in strong SW wind or swell. Rks and breakers exist E of Inishbofin and S of Inishshark; see AC 2707 for clearing lines. Lecky Rks lie 1M SSE of Davillaun. Carrickmahoy is a very dangerous rock (1·9m) between Inishbofin and Cleggan Pt.

Killary B (AC 2706) and Little Killary both have good ⚓s in magnificent scenery. Consult sailing directions, and only approach in reasonable weather and good visibility.

Clare Is has Two Fathom Rk (3·4m) 5ca off NW coast, and Calliaghcrom Rk 5ca to the N; ⚓ on NE side. In Clew Bay Newport and Westport (AC 2667, 2057) need detailed pilotage directions. S of Clare Is beware Meemore Shoal 1·5M W of Roonagh Hd. 2M further W is the isolated rk Mweelaun. The islands of Caher, Ballybeg, Inishturk (with ⚓ on E side) and Inishdalla have few hidden dangers, but the coast to the E must be given a berth of 1·5M even in calm weather; in strong winds seas break much further offshore.

Achill Sound (ACs 2667/2704) is entered close N of Achillbeg Is and extends N for about 8M to Bull's Mouth. Passage is possible at HW for shallow draught craft (<2m) via a swing bridge, which is rarely opened. ⚓s at each end of Sound, but the stream runs strongly. Rough water is likely off Achill Hd (highest cliffs in the British Islands).

Blacksod B (AC 2704) has easy ent (possible at night) and good shelter. In the appr Black Rk (lt) has rks up to 1·25M SW. From N, in good weather, there is chan between Duvillaun Beg and Gaghta Is, but in W gales beware breakers 1M SE of Duvillaun More.

Keep 5ca off Erris Hd, and further in bad weather. Unless calm, keep seaward of Eagle Is (lt) where there is race to N. Frenchport (AC 2703) is good temp ⚓ except in strong W winds. Inishkea Is (AC 2704) can be visited in good weather; ⚓ N or S of Rusheen Is. On passage keep 5ca W of Inishkea to avoid bad seas if wind over tide. The sound off Mullett Peninsula is clear, but for Pluddany Rk 6ca E of Inishkea N.

EAGLE ISLAND TO BLOODY FORELAND

Broad Haven (AC 2703) is good ⚓ and refuge, but in N/NW gales sea can break in ent. In approaches beware Slugga Rk on E side with offlier, and Monastery Rk (0·3m) on S side.

The coast E of Broad Haven is inhospitable. Only Portacloy and Belderg give a little shelter. The Stags, 1M N of Buddagh, are steep-to and high. Killala B has temp ⚓ 1M S of Kilcummin Hd, on W side. Proceeding to Killala beware St Patrick's Rks. Ent has ldg lts and marks, but bar is dangerous in strong NE winds.

In Donegal B (AC 2702) beware uncharted rks W of Teelin, a good natural hbr but exposed to S/SW swell. Killybegs has better shelter and is always accessible. Good shelter with fair access in Donegal Hbr (AC 2715). Good ⚓ or mooring via YC at Mullaghmore in fair weather; sea state is calm with winds from SE through S to NW. Inishmurray is worth a visit in good weather, ⚓ off S side. There are shoals close E and NE of the Is, and Bomore Rks 1·5M to N. Keep well clear of coast N from Sligo in onshore winds, and beware of lobster pots.

The coast and islands 15M NE from Aran Is give good cruising (AC 1883). An inshore passage avoids offlying dangers: Buniver and Brinlack shoals, which can break; Bullogconnell 1M NW of Gola Is; and Stag Rks 2M NNW of Owey Is. ⚓s include Bunbeg and Gweedore Hbr, and Cruit B which has easier access. Behind Aran Is are several good ⚓s. Use N ent, since S one is shallow (AC 2792). Rutland N Chan is main appr to Burtonport.

Boylagh B has shoals and rks N of Roaninish Is. Connell Rk (0·3m) is 1M N of Church Pool, a good ⚓, best approached from Dawros Hd 4·5M to W. On S side of Glen B a temp ⚓ (but not in W or NW winds) is just E of Rinmeasa Pt. Rathlin O'Birne Is has steps E side; ⚓ SE of them 100m offshore. Sound is 5ca wide; hold Is side to clear rks off Malin Beg Hd.

Off low-lying Bloody Foreland (lt) there is often heavy swell.

N Ireland

STANDARD TIME (UT)
For Summer Time add ONE hour in **non-shaded areas**

GALWAY LAT 53°16′N LONG 9°03′W

TIMES AND HEIGHTS OF HIGH AND LOW WATERS

Dates in red are SPRINGS
Dates in blue are NEAPS

YEAR **2018**

JANUARY

Date	Day	Time	m	Time	m	Time	m	Time	m
1	M	0359	5.3	1006	0.8	1627	5.4	2225	0.8
2	TU	0449	5.6	1052	0.6	1717	5.5	○ 2310	0.7
3	W	0537	5.7	1139	0.5	1807	5.5	2356	0.7
4	TH	0626	5.7	1225	0.5	1856	5.5		
5	F	0043	0.8	0714	5.5	1313	0.6	1945	5.3
6	SA	0131	1.0	0802	5.3	1401	0.9	2036	5.0
7	SU	0221	1.3	0853	5.0	1454	1.2	2128	4.7
8	M	0318	1.6	0946	4.7	1553	1.5	◑ 2225	4.4
9	TU	0423	1.8	1045	4.4	1700	1.7	2330	4.2
10	W	0533	2.0	1202	4.1	1809	1.9		
11	TH	0045	4.1	0640	2.0	1322	4.1	1912	1.9
12	F	0152	4.2	0742	2.0	1424	4.2	2009	1.9
13	SA	0245	4.3	0836	1.8	1514	4.3	2056	1.7
14	SU	0330	4.5	0921	1.6	1556	4.5	2136	1.6
15	M	0408	4.7	0959	1.4	1634	4.6	2214	1.4
16	TU	0445	4.9	1035	1.3	1710	4.8	2249	1.3
17	W	0522	5.0	1111	1.1	1747	4.8	● 2324	1.2
18	TH	0559	5.1	1145	1.0	1823	4.9	2358	1.2
19	F	0634	5.0	1219	1.0	1858	4.8		
20	SA	0032	1.2	0706	5.0	1254	1.0	1931	4.8
21	SU	0107	1.3	0736	4.9	1330	1.1	2003	4.6
22	M	0146	1.4	0812	4.8	1410	1.2	2041	4.5
23	TU	0228	1.5	0856	4.6	1454	1.4	2128	4.4
24	W	0316	1.7	0948	4.5	1544	1.6	◐ 2223	4.3
25	TH	0412	1.8	1047	4.3	1642	1.7	2324	4.2
26	F	0518	1.9	1154	4.3	1752	1.8		
27	SA	0034	4.3	0641	1.9	1309	4.4	1922	1.7
28	SU	0149	4.5	0811	1.6	1423	4.6	2037	1.4
29	M	0254	4.8	0911	1.2	1524	4.9	2130	1.1
30	TU	0348	5.2	1000	0.8	1617	5.3	2218	0.9
31	W	0438	5.5	1046	0.5	1707	5.5	○ 2302	0.7

FEBRUARY

Date	Day	Time	m	Time	m	Time	m	Time	m
1	TH	0526	5.7	1130	0.4	1754	5.6	2345	0.6
2	F	0612	5.7	1212	0.4	1840	5.5		
3	SA	0027	0.7	0657	5.6	1253	0.5	1924	5.4
4	SU	0109	0.8	0741	5.4	1335	0.7	2009	5.1
5	M	0152	1.1	0825	5.1	1419	1.1	2053	4.8
6	TU	0239	1.4	0910	4.8	1508	1.4	2139	4.5
7	W	0333	1.7	0958	4.4	1607	1.8	◑ 2229	4.2
8	TH	0444	2.0	1052	4.1	1721	2.0	2327	4.0
9	F	0559	2.1	1210	3.9	1831	2.1		
10	SA	0103	3.9	0705	2.1	1359	3.9	1933	2.1
11	SU	0221	4.1	0804	2.0	1457	4.1	2027	1.9
12	M	0312	4.3	0854	1.7	1541	4.3	2114	1.7
13	TU	0353	4.5	0938	1.5	1619	4.5	2155	1.5
14	W	0430	4.8	1017	1.2	1654	4.7	2233	1.3
15	TH	0505	4.9	1053	1.0	1728	4.8	● 2307	1.1
16	F	0540	5.0	1126	0.9	1802	4.9	2340	1.0
17	SA	0614	5.1	1158	0.8	1835	4.9		
18	SU	0012	0.9	0643	5.1	1232	0.7	1905	4.9
19	M	0046	0.9	0712	5.1	1307	0.8	1935	4.8
20	TU	0124	1.0	0747	5.0	1346	0.9	2012	4.7
21	W	0205	1.1	0829	4.8	1428	1.1	2056	4.6
22	TH	0251	1.3	0919	4.6	1516	1.4	2149	4.4
23	F	0344	1.6	1019	4.3	1611	1.6	◐ 2252	4.2
24	SA	0447	1.8	1129	4.1	1721	1.9		
25	SU	0007	4.1	0613	1.9	1252	4.1	1903	1.9
26	M	0134	4.3	0808	1.6	1415	4.4	2032	1.6
27	TU	0244	4.6	0908	1.2	1517	4.8	2125	1.2
28	W	0339	5.0	0955	0.8	1608	5.1	2210	0.8

MARCH

Date	Day	Time	m	Time	m	Time	m	Time	m
1	TH	0428	5.4	1037	0.5	1654	5.4	2251	0.6
2	F	0513	5.6	1116	0.3	1738	5.5	○ 2329	0.5
3	SA	0556	5.7	1152	0.3	1820	5.5		
4	SU	0006	0.5	0636	5.6	1228	0.4	1859	5.4
5	M	0043	0.6	0717	5.4	1304	0.7	1939	5.2
6	TU	0121	0.9	0756	5.1	1342	1.0	2019	4.9
7	W	0201	1.2	0838	4.7	1424	1.4	2101	4.6
8	TH	0246	1.6	0922	4.4	1511	1.8	2146	4.3
9	F	0345	1.9	1011	4.0	1627	2.1	◑ 2237	4.0
10	SA	0520	2.1	1107	3.8	1756	2.3	2336	3.8
11	SU	0631	2.1	1325	3.7	1902	2.2		
12	M	0148	3.8	0732	2.0	1437	3.9	1959	2.0
13	TU	0249	4.1	0826	1.7	1522	4.1	2049	1.7
14	W	0332	4.3	0912	1.4	1558	4.4	2132	1.4
15	TH	0408	4.6	0953	1.1	1631	4.6	2211	1.2
16	F	0442	4.8	1029	0.9	1703	4.8	2245	0.9
17	SA	0515	5.0	1102	0.7	1735	5.0	● 2316	0.8
18	SU	0547	5.1	1133	0.5	1806	5.0	2348	0.6
19	M	0618	5.2	1206	0.5	1837	5.1		
20	TU	0023	0.6	0650	5.2	1243	0.5	1910	5.0
21	W	0102	0.7	0727	5.1	1322	0.7	1948	4.9
22	TH	0144	0.8	0810	4.9	1405	0.9	2032	4.7
23	F	0230	1.1	0901	4.6	1453	1.3	2125	4.4
24	SA	0323	1.4	1001	4.3	1550	1.6	◐ 2229	4.2
25	SU	0429	1.7	1114	4.0	1703	1.9	2349	4.0
26	M	0600	1.8	1244	4.0	1901	1.9		
27	TU	0122	4.2	0804	1.5	1407	4.3	2026	1.5
28	W	0233	4.5	0900	1.1	1506	4.7	2116	1.2
29	TH	0327	4.9	0944	0.7	1554	5.0	2157	0.8
30	F	0413	5.2	1023	0.5	1637	5.3	2234	0.6
31	SA	0456	5.4	1057	0.3	1718	5.4	○ 2309	0.5

APRIL

Date	Day	Time	m	Time	m	Time	m	Time	m
1	SU	0536	5.4	1128	0.4	1756	5.4	2341	0.5
2	M	0615	5.4	1159	0.5	1833	5.3		
3	TU	0015	0.6	0652	5.2	1233	0.7	1910	5.1
4	W	0052	0.8	0730	4.9	1309	1.0	1948	4.9
5	TH	0130	1.1	0810	4.6	1347	1.4	2029	4.6
6	F	0210	1.4	0853	4.3	1428	1.7	2113	4.3
7	SA	0256	1.8	0941	4.0	1515	2.1	2202	4.1
8	SU	0430	2.0	1034	3.8	1720	2.3	◑ 2257	3.8
9	M	0557	2.1	1135	3.6	1831	2.3		
10	TU	0000	3.7	0700	2.0	1402	3.7	1929	2.1
11	W	0212	3.9	0754	1.7	1450	4.0	2020	1.8
12	TH	0259	4.1	0842	1.4	1527	4.3	2105	1.5
13	F	0337	4.4	0924	1.1	1559	4.5	2144	1.2
14	SA	0410	4.7	1001	0.8	1630	4.8	2218	0.9
15	SU	0442	4.9	1034	0.6	1701	5.0	2249	0.6
16	M	0515	5.1	1105	0.5	1734	5.1	● 2323	0.5
17	TU	0551	5.2	1140	0.4	1810	5.2		
18	W	0000	0.4	0629	5.2	1219	0.4	1848	5.2
19	TH	0042	0.5	0712	5.1	1301	0.6	1930	5.0
20	F	0126	0.6	0759	4.9	1346	0.9	2017	4.8
21	SA	0215	0.9	0852	4.6	1437	1.3	2112	4.5
22	SU	0311	1.2	0953	4.3	1538	1.6	◐ 2216	4.2
23	M	0419	1.5	1106	4.1	1655	1.9	2336	4.1
24	TU	0553	1.6	1234	4.1	1848	1.8		
25	W	0107	4.2	0744	1.4	1351	4.3	2007	1.5
26	TH	0216	4.4	0841	1.1	1447	4.6	2057	1.2
27	F	0308	4.7	0925	0.8	1534	4.9	2139	0.9
28	SA	0354	5.0	1003	0.7	1615	5.1	2215	0.7
29	SU	0435	5.1	1034	0.6	1654	5.2	2247	0.6
30	M	0515	5.1	1102	0.6	1732	5.2	○ 2317	0.6

Chart Datum: 0·20 metres below Ordnance Datum (Dublin). HAT is 5·9 metres above Chart Datum.

STANDARD TIME (UT)
For Summer Time add ONE hour in **non-shaded areas**

GALWAY LAT 53°16′N LONG 9°03′W

TIMES AND HEIGHTS OF HIGH AND LOW WATERS

Dates in red are SPRINGS
Dates in blue are NEAPS

YEAR **2018**

MAY

Day	Time	m	Time	m	Time	m	Time	m
1 TU	0553	5.1	1131	0.7	1808	5.2	2351	0.7
2 W	0630	5.0	1205	0.9	1844	5.0		
3 TH	0027	0.9	0707	4.8	1242	1.1	1921	4.9
4 F	0105	1.1	0746	4.6	1319	1.4	2002	4.6
5 SA	0145	1.3	0829	4.3	1357	1.7	2045	4.4
6 SU	0227	1.6	0914	4.1	1438	2.0	2132	4.1
7 M	0316	1.9	1004	3.9	1532	2.2	2223	3.9
8 TU	0510	2.0	1059	3.7	1753	2.3	◑ 2319	3.8
9 W	0622	2.0	1203	3.7	1855	2.1		
10 TH	0024	3.8	0719	1.8	1349	3.9	1947	1.9
11 F	0155	4.0	0808	1.5	1438	4.2	2033	1.6
12 SA	0247	4.3	0851	1.2	1514	4.5	2112	1.2
13 SU	0326	4.6	0929	0.9	1548	4.8	2147	0.9
14 M	0404	4.9	1002	0.7	1625	5.0	2222	0.7
15 TU	0444	5.1	1037	0.5	1704	5.2	● 2259	0.5
16 W	0527	5.3	1116	0.5	1746	5.3	2340	0.4
17 TH	0612	5.3	1158	0.5	1831	5.3		
18 F	0025	0.4	0659	5.2	1244	0.7	1917	5.2
19 SA	0113	0.6	0750	5.0	1332	1.0	2008	4.9
20 SU	0204	0.8	0844	4.7	1426	1.3	2103	4.7
21 M	0302	1.1	0945	4.4	1529	1.6	2206	4.4
22 TU	0409	1.3	1054	4.2	1644	1.8	◐ 2320	4.2
23 W	0532	1.4	1213	4.2	1814	1.8		
24 TH	0042	4.2	0705	1.4	1325	4.3	1933	1.6
25 F	0151	4.3	0810	1.2	1422	4.5	2030	1.4
26 SA	0245	4.5	0858	1.1	1510	4.7	2115	1.2
27 SU	0332	4.7	0938	1.0	1552	4.9	2153	1.0
28 M	0415	4.8	1010	1.0	1631	5.0	2225	0.9
29 TU	0454	4.8	1038	1.0	1708	5.0	○ 2256	0.9
30 W	0532	4.8	1109	1.0	1745	5.0	2330	0.9
31 TH	0610	4.8	1144	1.1	1822	5.0		

JUNE

Day	Time	m	Time	m	Time	m	Time	m
1 F	0007	1.0	0647	4.7	1221	1.3	1859	4.9
2 SA	0046	1.1	0726	4.6	1258	1.4	1938	4.7
3 SU	0124	1.3	0806	4.4	1335	1.6	2019	4.5
4 M	0204	1.5	0849	4.2	1414	1.8	2102	4.3
5 TU	0246	1.7	0935	4.1	1500	2.0	2149	4.1
6 W	0336	1.8	1025	3.9	1558	2.2	◑ 2240	4.0
7 TH	0444	1.9	1119	3.9	1755	2.2	2336	4.0
8 F	0623	1.8	1219	4.0	1903	2.0		
9 SA	0037	4.1	0723	1.6	1323	4.2	1953	1.7
10 SU	0142	4.3	0811	1.4	1420	4.5	2036	1.4
11 M	0240	4.6	0853	1.1	1508	4.8	2117	1.1
12 TU	0330	4.9	0934	0.9	1554	5.1	2158	0.8
13 W	0419	5.1	1015	0.7	1640	5.3	● 2241	0.5
14 TH	0508	5.3	1058	0.6	1728	5.4	2326	0.4
15 F	0557	5.3	1144	0.6	1816	5.4		
16 SA	0013	0.4	0647	5.3	1232	0.7	1905	5.4
17 SU	0103	0.5	0738	5.1	1322	0.9	1956	5.2
18 M	0154	0.7	0832	4.9	1415	1.2	2050	4.9
19 TU	0250	0.9	0929	4.6	1515	1.4	2149	4.7
20 W	0352	1.2	1031	4.4	1622	1.6	◐ 2255	4.4
21 TH	0501	1.4	1141	4.3	1737	1.7		
22 F	0009	4.3	0616	1.5	1252	4.3	1849	1.7
23 SA	0121	4.2	0727	1.5	1353	4.3	1954	1.6
24 SU	0221	4.3	0824	1.5	1445	4.5	2047	1.5
25 M	0311	4.4	0910	1.4	1530	4.6	2130	1.3
26 TU	0356	4.5	0947	1.4	1610	4.8	2206	1.2
27 W	0436	4.6	1018	1.3	1648	4.9	2239	1.1
28 TH	0515	4.7	1051	1.3	1726	4.9	○ 2314	1.1
29 F	0552	4.7	1127	1.2	1803	4.9	2350	1.0
30 SA	0630	4.7	1203	1.3	1841	4.9		

JULY

Day	Time	m	Time	m	Time	m	Time	m
1 SU	0027	1.1	0707	4.6	1239	1.4	1917	4.8
2 M	0104	1.2	0744	4.5	1315	1.5	1953	4.6
3 TU	0141	1.3	0822	4.4	1352	1.6	2030	4.5
4 W	0220	1.4	0901	4.3	1434	1.8	2112	4.3
5 TH	0303	1.5	0946	4.1	1522	1.9	2201	4.2
6 F	0353	1.7	1038	4.1	1619	2.0	◑ 2255	4.2
7 SA	0451	1.7	1134	4.1	1726	2.0	2355	4.2
8 SU	0558	1.7	1235	4.2	1848	1.8		
9 M	0059	4.3	0717	1.6	1339	4.4	2000	1.5
10 TU	0206	4.5	0822	1.3	1439	4.7	2054	1.2
11 W	0307	4.8	0913	1.1	1532	5.1	2143	0.9
12 TH	0401	5.1	1001	0.8	1623	5.3	2230	0.6
13 F	0453	5.3	1048	0.7	1713	5.5	● 2317	0.4
14 SA	0544	5.4	1134	0.6	1802	5.6		
15 SU	0003	0.3	0633	5.4	1221	0.7	1851	5.5
16 M	0051	0.4	0722	5.3	1308	0.8	1940	5.4
17 TU	0139	0.6	0812	5.1	1357	1.0	2031	5.1
18 W	0229	0.8	0904	4.8	1451	1.3	2123	4.8
19 TH	0324	1.1	0959	4.6	1551	1.6	◐ 2220	4.5
20 F	0425	1.4	1059	4.3	1659	1.8	2327	4.2
21 SA	0533	1.7	1209	4.2	1809	1.9		
22 SU	0047	4.0	0641	1.8	1322	4.1	1915	1.9
23 M	0157	4.0	0745	1.8	1422	4.2	2015	1.7
24 TU	0254	4.1	0839	1.7	1511	4.4	2105	1.6
25 W	0341	4.3	0923	1.6	1554	4.6	2145	1.4
26 TH	0422	4.4	1000	1.5	1632	4.7	2221	1.2
27 F	0459	4.6	1035	1.3	1709	4.9	○ 2257	1.1
28 SA	0535	4.7	1110	1.2	1746	4.9	2332	1.0
29 SU	0611	4.7	1145	1.2	1822	4.9		
30 M	0006	0.9	0646	4.7	1219	1.2	1856	4.9
31 TU	0041	0.9	0720	4.7	1253	1.2	1926	4.8

AUGUST

Day	Time	m	Time	m	Time	m	Time	m
1 W	0116	1.0	0751	4.6	1329	1.3	1957	4.7
2 TH	0153	1.1	0825	4.5	1408	1.4	2036	4.5
3 F	0234	1.3	0907	4.3	1453	1.6	2123	4.4
4 SA	0320	1.4	0957	4.2	1544	1.7	◑ 2219	4.3
5 SU	0413	1.6	1055	4.1	1644	1.9	2321	4.2
6 M	0514	1.7	1200	4.2	1758	1.9		
7 TU	0030	4.2	0633	1.7	1311	4.3	1935	1.7
8 W	0146	4.4	0803	1.5	1420	4.6	2043	1.3
9 TH	0254	4.7	0904	1.2	1520	5.0	2135	0.9
10 F	0350	5.0	0954	0.9	1612	5.3	2222	0.5
11 SA	0442	5.3	1039	0.7	1701	5.6	● 2307	0.3
12 SU	0530	5.4	1123	0.5	1748	5.7	2350	0.2
13 M	0617	5.5	1205	0.5	1834	5.7		
14 TU	0032	0.3	0702	5.4	1248	0.6	1919	5.5
15 W	0115	0.5	0747	5.2	1332	0.9	2005	5.2
16 TH	0159	0.8	0833	4.9	1418	1.2	2051	4.8
17 F	0247	1.2	0920	4.6	1511	1.5	2141	4.5
18 SA	0343	1.5	1010	4.3	1619	1.8	◐ 2235	4.1
19 SU	0453	1.9	1107	4.0	1734	2.0	2355	3.8
20 M	0605	2.0	1240	3.9	1842	2.0		
21 TU	0137	3.8	0710	2.1	1402	4.0	1943	1.9
22 W	0240	3.9	0808	1.9	1455	4.2	2037	1.7
23 TH	0327	4.1	0857	1.7	1538	4.5	2121	1.4
24 F	0407	4.4	0938	1.5	1616	4.7	2159	1.2
25 SA	0442	4.5	1016	1.3	1651	4.8	2236	1.0
26 SU	0516	4.7	1051	1.1	1726	5.0	○ 2310	0.8
27 M	0549	4.8	1124	1.0	1800	5.0	2343	0.7
28 TU	0622	4.8	1155	0.9	1831	5.0		
29 W	0015	0.7	0651	4.8	1229	0.9	1858	4.9
30 TH	0049	0.7	0719	4.7	1304	1.0	1927	4.8
31 F	0126	0.9	0751	4.6	1343	1.1	2006	4.7

Chart Datum: 0·20 metres below Ordnance Datum (Dublin). HAT is 5·9 metres above Chart Datum.

STANDARD TIME (UT)
For Summer Time add ONE hour in **non-shaded areas**

GALWAY LAT 53°16′N LONG 9°03′W

TIMES AND HEIGHTS OF HIGH AND LOW WATERS

Dates in red are SPRINGS
Dates in blue are NEAPS

YEAR **2018**

SEPTEMBER

Date	Day	Time	m	Time	m	Time	m	Time	m
1	SA	0206	1.0	0832	4.5	1427	1.3	2053	4.5
2	SU	0251	1.3	0922	4.3	1516	1.5	2150	4.3
3	M	0343	1.6	1022	4.2	1616	1.8	◑ 2256	4.1
4	TU	0445	1.8	1131	4.1	1732	1.9		
5	W	0011	4.0	0610	1.9	1252	4.2	1932	1.7
6	TH	0137	4.2	0800	1.7	1411	4.5	2040	1.2
7	F	0248	4.6	0859	1.3	1511	4.9	2129	0.8
8	SA	0342	5.0	0945	0.9	1601	5.3	2212	0.4
9	SU	0429	5.3	1027	0.6	1647	5.6	● 2252	0.2
10	M	0514	5.5	1107	0.4	1731	5.7	2331	0.2
11	TU	0556	5.5	1145	0.4	1814	5.6		
12	W	0008	0.2	0637	5.4	1223	0.5	1855	5.4
13	TH	0046	0.5	0718	5.2	1302	0.8	1937	5.1
14	F	0125	0.8	0759	4.9	1343	1.1	2019	4.8
15	SA	0207	1.2	0842	4.6	1430	1.5	2105	4.4
16	SU	0257	1.6	0927	4.3	1533	1.8	◐ 2154	4.0
17	M	0409	2.0	1018	4.0	1701	2.1	2252	3.7
18	TU	0533	2.2	1118	3.8	1811	2.1		
19	W	0116	3.6	0639	2.2	1337	3.9	1912	2.0
20	TH	0222	3.8	0738	2.1	1434	4.1	2006	1.7
21	F	0308	4.1	0829	1.8	1517	4.3	2053	1.4
22	SA	0346	4.3	0913	1.5	1554	4.6	2134	1.2
23	SU	0419	4.5	0952	1.2	1628	4.8	2211	0.9
24	M	0450	4.7	1027	1.0	1701	4.9	2245	0.7
25	TU	0521	4.9	1059	0.9	1732	5.0	○ 2316	0.6
26	W	0551	4.9	1130	0.8	1802	5.1	2347	0.6
27	TH	0621	5.0	1203	0.7	1831	5.0		
28	F	0022	0.6	0650	4.9	1240	0.8	1904	5.0
29	SA	0100	0.7	0724	4.8	1320	0.9	1944	4.8
30	SU	0141	1.0	0806	4.7	1405	1.1	2032	4.5

OCTOBER

Date	Day	Time	m	Time	m	Time	m	Time	m
1	M	0227	1.3	0856	4.4	1455	1.4	2131	4.2
2	TU	0320	1.6	0957	4.2	1557	1.7	◑ 2240	4.0
3	W	0427	1.9	1111	4.1	1719	1.8		
4	TH	0002	3.9	0604	2.0	1240	4.1	1931	1.6
5	F	0133	4.2	0755	1.7	1401	4.4	2032	1.2
6	SA	0239	4.5	0849	1.3	1459	4.9	2118	0.8
7	SU	0329	4.9	0932	0.9	1547	5.2	2157	0.5
8	M	0413	5.2	1011	0.6	1630	5.4	2234	0.3
9	TU	0454	5.4	1047	0.5	1712	5.5	● 2307	0.3
10	W	0534	5.5	1122	0.5	1752	5.5	2340	0.4
11	TH	0612	5.4	1157	0.6	1831	5.3		
12	F	0015	0.6	0649	5.2	1234	0.8	1910	5.0
13	SA	0052	1.0	0728	5.0	1313	1.1	1951	4.7
14	SU	0132	1.3	0809	4.7	1356	1.4	2035	4.4
15	M	0216	1.7	0854	4.4	1448	1.8	2123	4.0
16	TU	0314	2.1	0943	4.1	1621	2.1	◐ 2217	3.8
17	W	0459	2.3	1038	3.9	1739	2.1	2321	3.6
18	TH	0609	2.3	1144	3.8	1840	2.0		
19	F	0150	3.8	0708	2.1	1400	3.9	1934	1.8
20	SA	0239	4.0	0800	1.9	1446	4.2	2023	1.5
21	SU	0316	4.3	0846	1.6	1523	4.5	2105	1.2
22	M	0348	4.5	0926	1.3	1557	4.7	2143	0.9
23	TU	0418	4.7	1001	1.0	1629	4.9	2216	0.7
24	W	0447	4.9	1033	0.8	1700	5.1	○ 2247	0.6
25	TH	0518	5.1	1104	0.7	1733	5.1	2320	0.6
26	F	0551	5.1	1139	0.6	1809	5.1	2357	0.6
27	SA	0626	5.1	1218	0.7	1848	5.1		
28	SU	0037	0.7	0705	5.0	1301	0.8	1932	4.9
29	M	0121	1.0	0749	4.8	1348	1.0	2022	4.6
30	TU	0209	1.3	0841	4.6	1441	1.3	2122	4.3
31	W	0306	1.7	0943	4.3	1545	1.6	◑ 2231	4.1

NOVEMBER

Date	Day	Time	m	Time	m	Time	m	Time	m
1	TH	0417	1.9	1056	4.2	1709	1.7	2353	4.0
2	F	0555	2.0	1224	4.2	1912	1.5		
3	SA	0118	4.2	0736	1.7	1343	4.4	2012	1.2
4	SU	0221	4.6	0831	1.4	1441	4.8	2059	0.9
5	M	0310	4.9	0914	1.0	1528	5.0	2138	0.7
6	TU	0352	5.1	0953	0.8	1611	5.2	2213	0.6
7	W	0432	5.3	1027	0.7	1652	5.3	● 2244	0.6
8	TH	0510	5.3	1100	0.7	1732	5.2	2315	0.7
9	F	0548	5.3	1134	0.8	1810	5.1	2349	0.9
10	SA	0625	5.2	1210	0.9	1849	4.9		
11	SU	0026	1.2	0702	5.0	1250	1.1	1928	4.7
12	M	0105	1.4	0743	4.8	1331	1.4	2011	4.4
13	TU	0146	1.8	0826	4.5	1417	1.7	2057	4.2
14	W	0231	2.1	0913	4.3	1518	2.0	2147	4.0
15	TH	0357	2.3	1005	4.1	1654	2.1	◐ 2243	3.8
16	F	0531	2.4	1102	3.9	1802	2.0	2349	3.8
17	SA	0634	2.3	1209	3.9	1859	1.9		
18	SU	0147	3.9	0727	2.0	1351	4.1	1949	1.6
19	M	0232	4.2	0815	1.8	1439	4.3	2034	1.4
20	TU	0306	4.5	0856	1.5	1516	4.6	2113	1.1
21	W	0337	4.7	0933	1.2	1552	4.9	2147	0.9
22	TH	0410	5.0	1006	0.9	1628	5.1	2220	0.8
23	F	0446	5.2	1041	0.8	1708	5.2	○ 2256	0.7
24	SA	0526	5.3	1119	0.6	1750	5.3	2336	0.7
25	SU	0608	5.3	1202	0.6	1835	5.2		
26	M	0020	0.8	0652	5.2	1248	0.7	1923	5.0
27	TU	0107	1.0	0740	5.1	1337	0.9	2015	4.8
28	W	0158	1.3	0832	4.8	1431	1.2	2113	4.5
29	TH	0256	1.6	0932	4.6	1534	1.4	2217	4.3
30	F	0404	1.8	1040	4.4	1650	1.6	◑ 2332	4.2

DECEMBER

Date	Day	Time	m	Time	m	Time	m	Time	m
1	SA	0528	1.9	1159	4.3	1828	1.5		
2	SU	0050	4.3	0658	1.8	1316	4.4	1941	1.4
3	M	0154	4.5	0803	1.6	1417	4.6	2033	1.2
4	TU	0246	4.7	0852	1.3	1508	4.8	2117	1.1
5	W	0331	4.9	0934	1.1	1553	4.9	2153	1.1
6	TH	0412	5.1	1011	1.0	1634	5.0	2225	1.0
7	F	0450	5.1	1044	1.0	1714	5.0	● 2256	1.1
8	SA	0528	5.2	1117	1.0	1753	5.0	2330	1.2
9	SU	0605	5.1	1153	1.1	1831	4.9		
10	M	0007	1.3	0642	5.0	1232	1.2	1910	4.7
11	TU	0046	1.5	0721	4.9	1311	1.3	1950	4.6
12	W	0124	1.7	0802	4.7	1352	1.5	2032	4.4
13	TH	0203	1.9	0845	4.5	1434	1.7	2117	4.2
14	F	0247	2.1	0931	4.3	1524	1.9	2206	4.0
15	SA	0343	2.3	1022	4.1	1639	2.0	◐ 2300	4.0
16	SU	0536	2.3	1118	4.1	1807	2.0	2359	4.0
17	M	0645	2.2	1219	4.1	1908	1.9		
18	TU	0105	4.1	0738	2.0	1326	4.2	1957	1.7
19	W	0206	4.4	0824	1.7	1426	4.5	2041	1.4
20	TH	0253	4.7	0905	1.4	1515	4.8	2120	1.2
21	F	0337	5.0	0944	1.1	1601	5.1	2159	1.0
22	SA	0421	5.2	1024	0.9	1647	5.2	○ 2240	0.8
23	SU	0506	5.4	1106	0.7	1735	5.3	2323	0.8
24	M	0553	5.5	1151	0.6	1823	5.3		
25	TU	0009	0.8	0640	5.5	1238	0.6	1912	5.3
26	W	0057	0.9	0729	5.4	1327	0.7	2003	5.1
27	TH	0147	1.1	0820	5.2	1419	1.0	2057	4.8
28	F	0241	1.4	0915	4.9	1516	1.2	2155	4.6
29	SA	0343	1.6	1015	4.6	1620	1.4	◑ 2300	4.4
30	SU	0453	1.8	1125	4.4	1735	1.6		
31	M	0012	4.3	0611	1.9	1243	4.3	1855	1.7

Chart Datum: 0·20 metres below Ordnance Datum (Dublin). HAT is 5·9 metres above Chart Datum.

9.13.8 WESTPORT (CLEW BAY)

Mayo **53°47'·85N 09°35'·40W** ✿✿✿✿✿✿

CHARTS AC 2667, 2057; Imray C54

TIDES –0545 Dover; ML 2·5; Duration 0610

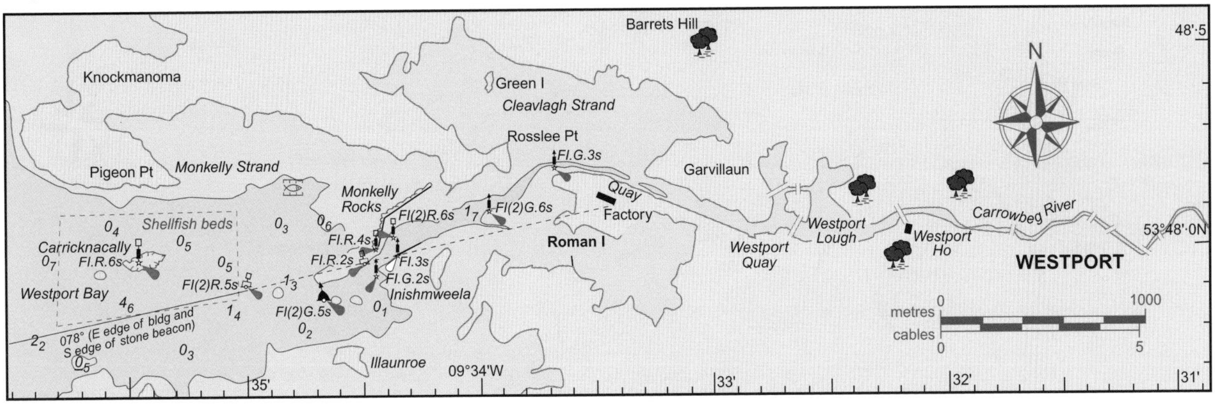

Standard Port GALWAY (⟵)

Times				Height (metres)			
High Water		Low Water		MHWS	MHWN	MLWN	MLWS
0600	1100	0000	0700	5·1	3·9	2·0	0·8
1800	2300	1200	1900				
Differences BROAD HAVEN							
+0035	+0035	+0040	+0040	–1·4	–1·0	–0·6	–0·2
BLACKSOD QUAY							
+0025	+0035	+0040	+0040	–1·2	–1·0	–0·6	–0·4
CLARE ISLAND							
+0015	+0021	+0039	+0027	–0·6	–0·4	–0·1	0·0
INISHGORT/CLEW BAY							
+0035	+0045	+0115	+0100	–0·7	–0·5	–0·2	0·0
KILLARY HARBOUR							
+0021	+0015	+0035	+0029	–1·0	–0·8	–0·4	–0·3
INISHBOFIN HARBOUR							
+0013	+0009	+0021	+0017	–1·0	–0·8	–0·4	–0·3
CLIFDEN BAY							
+0005	+0005	+0016	+0016	–0·7	–0·5	ND	ND

SHELTER Secure ⚓s amongst the islands at all times, as follows: E of Inishlyre in 2m; 2ca NE of Dorinish More, good holding in lee of Dorinish Bar (dries); 6 Ⓜs in Rosmoney Hbr 53°49'·75N 09°37'·34W; Westport Quay HW±1½, to dry out on S side; Newport Hbr (dries) can be reached above mid-flood with careful pilotage (AC 2667); dry out against N quay or ⚓ at E end of Rabbit Is.

NAVIGATION WPT 53°49'·20N 09°42'·10W, 071°/1·2M to Inishgort lt ho. Approaches to Westport Channel between Monkellys Rks and Inishmweela are well marked by lit PHMs and SHMs. Beware fish farms E of Clare I and in Newport Bay. Do not ⚓ or ground in the Carricknacally Shellfish Bed Area.

LIGHTS AND MARKS Westport Bay ent via Inishgort lt, L Fl 10s 11m 10M (H24), and a series of ldg lines, but not advised at night. Final appr line 080° towards lt bn, Fl 3s. but beware of drying patches on this lead inwards from Pigeon PHM. Chan from Westport Bay to Westport Quay, 1½M approx, is marked by bns.

COMMUNICATIONS (Code 098) MRCC (01) 6620922/3; ⊜ (094) 9021131; Police 9025555; Ⓗ (094) 9021733. No VHF.

FACILITIES Westport Quays ⛵ ⛴ ⌓ Kos ☎ Ⓔ 🛒 ✕ 🍴; **Town** ☎ ☎ ✉ Ⓑ ⇌ ✈ (Galway/Knock). **Mayo SC Rosmoney** ☎9026160, ⛴ 🍴; **Glénans Irish SC** ☎9026046 (Collanmore Is).

OTHER ANCHORAGES FROM SLYNE HEAD TO EAGLE ISLAND

CLIFDEN BAY, Galway, **53°29'·40N 10°05'·90W**. AC 1820, 2708. HW –0600 on Dover; duration 0610. Tides at 9.13.8.
Identify conspic W bn on Carrickrana Rks prior to entry; ldg marks: W bn at Fishing Pt on 080° with Clifden Castle (ruin). Avoid Coghan's and Doolick Rks to the E and beware bar 2·4m off Fishing Pt.
8 Y Ⓜs are 3ca S of Castle ruins, or ⚓ NE of Drinagh Pt. Beware ruined training wall In the drying creek to Clifden; dry out against the quay or enter Ardbear Bay to ⚓ SE of Yellow Slate Rks in 3·4m. Keep clear of fish farms. Facilities: **Town** ⛽ ☎ ☎ Kos ⛽ ✉ Ⓑ 🛒 ✕ 🍴 Dr Ⓗ bus to Galway.

BALLYNAKILL, Galway, **53°34'·95N 10°03'·00W**. AC 2706. Tides as Inishbofin/Killary. Easy appr between Cleggan Pt, Fl (3) WRG 15s and Rinvyle Pt. Then pass N of Freaghillaun South Is, E of which is good passage ⚓ in 7m. Further E, Carrigeen and Ardagh Rks lie in mid-chan. Keep N for ⚓ in Derryinver B. S chan leads to ⚓s: off Ross Pt; S of Roeillaun; in Fahy Bay with 8 Y Ⓜs sheltered by bar dries 0·2m. No facilities.

INISHBOFIN, Galway, **53°36'·60N 10°13'·20W**. AC 1820, 2707. HW –0555 on Dover; ML 1·9m. Very safe inside narrow ent. Daymarks 2 conspic W trs lead 032° and Dir RWG lt leads 021° at night to increase separation from Gun Rock, Fl (2) 6s 8m 4M, vis 296°-253°. ⚓ between new pier and Port Is. Old pier to the E now refurbished and dredged may provide ⌓. ⛴ ⛽(on both piers) 🛒 ✕ 🍴 / B&B: ☎(095) 45829.

KILLARY HARBOUR, Mayo/Galway, **53°37'·83N 09°54'·00W**, 4ca W of Doonee Is. AC 2706. Tides 9.13.8. A 7M long inlet, narrow and deep. Caution fish farms, some with Fl Y lts. Appr in good vis to identify Doonee Is and Inishbarna bns, both LFl G, ldg 099° to ent. ⚓s off Dernasliggaun, Bundorragha and, at head of inlet, Leenaun with 8 Y Ⓜs. (**Village** ⛴ 🛒 🍴 hotel.) Enter **Little Killary Bay** 4ca S of Doonee Is; drying rks at ent. Good ⚓ in 3m at head of bay.

INISHTURK, Mayo, **53°42'·3N 10°05'·2W**. 8 Y Ⓜs Garranty Hbr sheltered SW to NNW winds. ⛴ quay ✉ ✕ 🍴 6Ⓜs on E side.

CLARE ISLAND, Mayo, **53°48'·1N 09°56'·7W**. 6Ⓜs on SE side untenable in E winds. Hotel 🍴 some shops.

BLACKSOD BAY, Mayo, **54°05'·00N 10°02'·00W**. AC 2704. HW –0525 on Dover; ML 2·2m; Duration 0610. See 9.13.8. Easy appr, accessible by night. Safe ⚓s depending on wind: NW of Blacksod Pt 6 Y Ⓜs in 3m; at Elly B in 1·8m; Elly Hbr 6 Y Ⓜs; Saleen Bay (ldg lts 319°, both Oc 4s, lead to pier); N of Claggan Pt. Beware drying rk 3·5ca SSE of Ardmore Pt. Lts: Blacksod Pt, Fl (2) WR 7·5s 13m 9M, see 9.13.4. ECM buoy Q (3) 10s. Ldg lts 181°, Oc W 5s, lead to Blacksod pier hd. Few facilities; nearest town is Belmullet.

ACHILL SOUND ⚓s at each end sheltered by Achill Is. Mayo Co Council (+353 (0)97 81004) requires 2 days' notice to open bridge.

PORTNAFRANKAGH Mayo, **54°14'·95N 10°06'·00W**. AC 2703. Tides approx as Broadhaven. A safe passage ⚓, close to the coastal route, but swell enters in all winds. Appr toward Port Pt, thence keep to the N side for better water; middle and S side break in onshore winds. ⚓ in 4–5m on S side, close inshore. ⛴ ⛴ at new pier. Unlit, but Eagle Is lt, Fl (3) 15s 67m 26M H24, W tr, is 2M N. No facilities; Belmullet 4M, 🛒.

BROAD HAVEN, Mayo, **54°16'·00N 09°53'·20W**. AC 2703. A safe refuge except in N'lies. Easy appr across Broadhaven Bay to the ent between Brandy Pt and Gubacashel Pt, Iso WR 4s27m 12/9M, W tr. 7ca S of this lt is Ballyglas Fl G 3s on W side. ⚓ close N or S of Ballyglas which has pier (2m) and 8 Y Ⓜs. In E'lies ⚓ 3ca S of Inver Pt out of the tide. Further S off Barrett Pt, the inlet narrows and turns W to Belmullet. Facilities: ✉ 🛒.

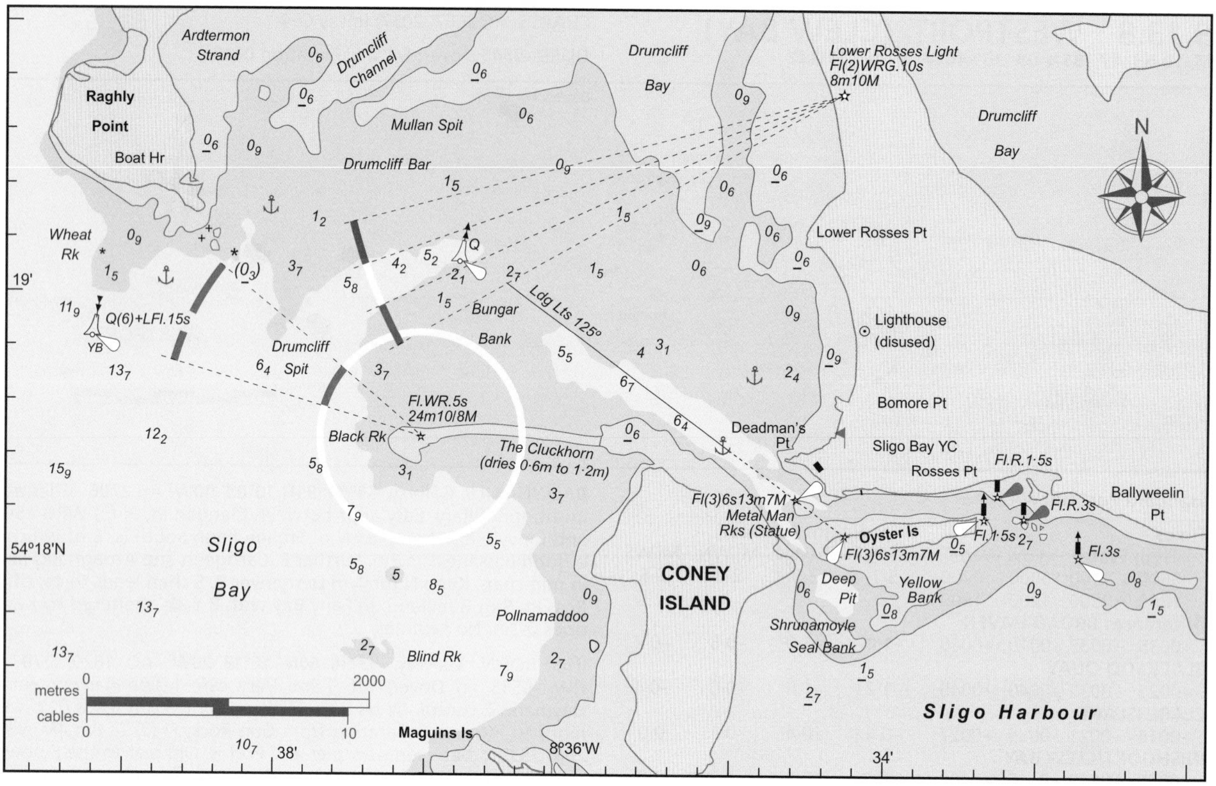

9.13.9 SLIGO

Sligo 54°18'·30N 08°34'·70W

CHARTS AC 2767, 2852; Imray C54

TIDES –0511 Dover; ML 2·3; Duration 0620

Standard Port GALWAY (⟵)

Times				Height (metres)			
High Water		Low Water		MHWS	MHWN	MLWN	MLWS
0600	1100	0000	0700	5·1	3·9	2·0	0·8
1800	2300	1200	1900				
Differences SLIGO HARBOUR (Oyster Is)							
+0043	+0055	+0042	+0054	–1·0	–0·9	–0·5	–0·3
MULLAGHMORE							
+0036	+0048	+0047	+0059	–1·4	–1·0	–0·4	–0·4
BALLYSADARE BAY (Culleenamore)							
+0059	+0111	+0111	+0123	–1·2	–0·9	ND	ND
KILLALA BAY (Inishcrone)							
+0035	+0055	+0030	+0050	–1·3	–1·2	–0·7	–0·4

SHELTER The lower hbr is fairly exposed; ⚓ along N side of Oyster Island, or proceed 4M (not at night) up to the shelter of Sligo town; 2nd berth below bridge for yachts.

NAVIGATION WPT 54°19'·15N 08°36'·77W, 125°/1·6M to front ldg lt.

- The passage between Oyster Island and Coney Island is marked 'Dangerous'.
- Pass N of Oyster Is leaving Blennick Rks to port. Passage up to Sligo town between training walls. Appr quays at HW–3 or higher.
- Some perches are in bad repair. Pilots at Raghly Pt and Rosses Pt. *Tide Tables* (based on Inishraher/Inishgort, published by Westport Hbr Comm.) available locally.

LIGHTS AND MARKS See 9.13.4 and chartlet. Channel to Sligo Deepwater Quay is well marked by lit bcns.

COMMUNICATIONS (Code 071) MRCC (01) 6620922/3; ⊖9161064; Police 9157000; Dr 9142886; Ⓗ9171111. Hbr Office 9111236, mob 086 0870767.

Pilots VHF Ch 12 16. HM Ch 16.

FACILITIES 60m visitors pontoon, 20-30ft €19.00; (15t); **Sligo YC** ☎9177168, Øs. **Services**. **Town** Ⓑ Irish Rail ☎9169888, Bus ☎9160066, ✈ Londonderry/Derry or Knock, Co Mayo (60-70M).

MINOR HARBOUR/ANCHORAGE TO THE WEST

KILLALA BAY, Sligo/Mayo, **54°13'·02N 09°12'·80W**. AC 2715. Tides, see 9.13.19. The bay, open to the N-NE, is entered between Lenadoon Pt and Kilcummin Hd, 6M to the W. 1·1M W of Kilcummin Hd are 8 Y Øs off Kilcummin pier, well sheltered from W'lies. Carrickpatrick ECM lt buoy, in mid-bay marks St Patrick's Rks to the W. Thence, if bound for Killala hbr, make good Killala SHM lt buoy, 7½ca to the SSW. The Round Tr and cathedral spire at Killala are conspic. Four sets of ldg bns/lts lead via a narrow chan between sand dunes and over the bar (0·3m) as follows:

- 230°, Rinnaun Pt lts Oc 10s 7/12m 5M, □ concrete trs.
- 215°, Inch Is, □ concrete trs; the rear has Dir lt Fl WRG 2s.
- 196°, Kilroe lts Oc 4s 5/10m 2M, W □ trs, which lead to ⚓ in Bartragh Pool, 6ca NE of Killala hbr; thence
- 236°, Pier lts Iso 2s 5/7m 2M, W ◊ daymarks, lead via narrow, dredged chan to pier where is possible in about 1·5m.

Facilities: in town ½M.

Other hbrs in the bay: R Moy leading to Ballina should not be attempted without pilot/local knowledge. Inishcrone in the SE has a pier and lt; see 9.13.4.

MINOR HARBOUR ON S SIDE OF DONEGAL BAY

MULLAGHMORE 54°27'·90N 08°26'·80W. AC 2702. Tides see 9.13.9. Pierhead lit Fl G 3s 5m 3M. Fair weather ⚓ in 2-3m off hbr ent, sheltered by Mullaghmore Head, except from N/NE winds. For Øs near hbr ent, call Rodney Lomax, ☎071 9166124, mobile 0872 727538. Keep close to N pier to avoid shingle bank drying 1m, ⅔ of the way across the ent towards the S pier. Take the ground or dry out against the piers inside hbr berth on pontoon on bkwtr (min 1m at MLWS). Access approx HW±2 when least depth is 2m. VHF Ch 16, 8, 6. Facilities: at S Pier and on bkwtr.

9.13.10 KILLYBEGS

Donegal **54°36′·90N 08°26′·80W** ❀❀❀◊◊◊✿✿✿

CHARTS AC 2702, 2792; Imray C53

TIDES –0520 Dover; ML 2·2; Duration 0620

Standard Port GALWAY (⟵)

Times				**Height (metres)**			
High Water		Low Water		MHWS	MHWN	MLWN	MLWS
0600	1100	0000	0700	5·1	3·9	2·0	0·8
1800	2300	1200	1900				
Differences KILLYBEGS							
+0040	+0050	+0055	+0035	–1·0	–0·9	–0·5	–0·2
GWEEDORE HARBOUR							
+0048	+0100	+0055	+0107	–1·3	–1·0	–0·5	–0·3
BURTONPORT							
+0042	+0055	+0115	+0055	–1·2	–1·0	–0·6	–0·3
DONEGAL HARBOUR (SALTHILL QUAY)							
+0038	+0050	+0052	+0104	–1·2	–0·9	ND	ND

SHELTER Secure natural hbr, but some swell in SSW winds. A busy fishing hbr and developing commercial port with H24 access. Sheltered marina N of Black Rk Pier or call HM and berth at pier. **Bruckless Hbr**, a pleasant ⚓ in 1·8m, 2M E at the head of McSwyne's Bay, is sheltered from all except SW winds, but is severely restricted by fish cages. Enter on 038° between rocks; ICC SDs essential.

NAVIGATION WPT 54°36′·00N 08°27′·00W, 022°/0·94M to Rotten Is lt. From W, beware Manister Rk (covers at HW; dries at LW) off Fintragh B. Keep mid-chan until off new Killybegs Fishery Centre, then follow the Dir lt or Y ◊ ldg marks 338° into hbr.

LIGHTS AND MARKS Rotten Is lt, Fl WR 4s 20m 15/11M, W tr, vis W255°-008°, R008°-039°, W039°-208°. Dir lt 338°, Oc WRG 6s 17m; W sector 336°-340° (see 9.13.4). Harbour Shoal (2·3m) is marked by a SCM and NCM lt buoy.

COMMUNICATIONS (Code 07497) MRCC (01) 6620922/3; Bundoran Inshore Rescue ☎(071) 9841713; ⊜31070; Police 31002; Dr 31148 (Surgery). HM 31032.

HM Ch **14**; essential to request a berth.

FACILITIES **Marina** 65⊆ inc 4Ⓥ €2/m (6-H24 min charge €15); short stay (<6hr) €10 (berth to be vacated by 1700), ⛽, ⛽ (card system) available from marina office (development ongoing).

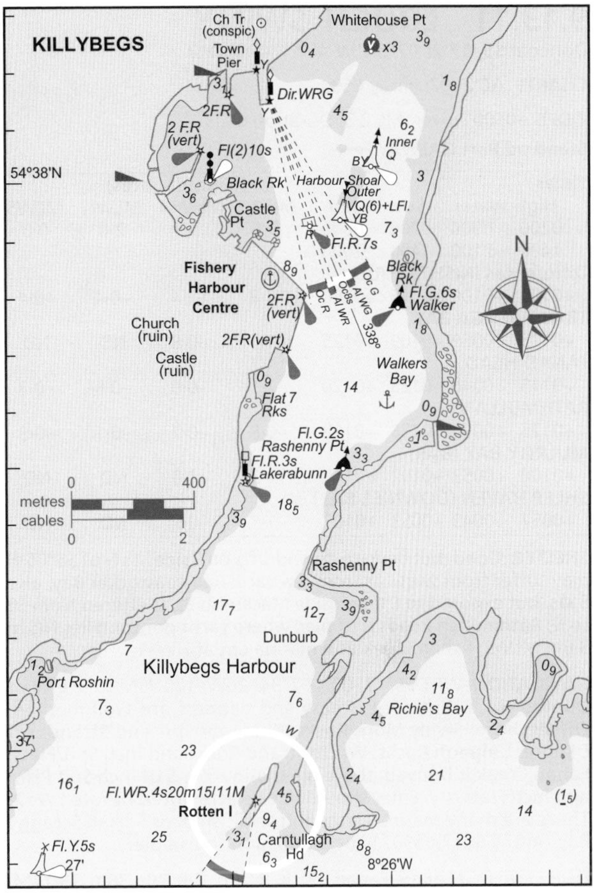

Town Pier ☎31032 ⛵ ⊆(free) ⛽ 💧 Ⓟ Kos (12t).

Black Rock Pier ⛵ ⊆ 💧.

Town ✕ 🔧 Ⓔ ✉ Ⓑ 🛒 ✕ 🍺 ⇌ (bus to Sligo).

OTHER HARBOURS AND ANCHORAGES IN DONEGAL

TEELIN HARBOUR, Donegal, **54°37′·50N 08°37′·87W**. AC 2792. Tides as 9.13.10. A possible passage ⚓, mid-way between Rathlin O'Birne and Killybegs. But Hbr is open to S'ly swell and prone to squalls in NW winds. Ent, 1ca wide, is close E of Teelin Pt lt, Fl R 10s, which is hard to see by day. 4 Y Ⓥs and ⚓ on E side in 3m to N of pier, or ⚓ on E side near pier. Many moorings and, in the NE, mussel rafts. Facilities: ⛽, 🛒 at Carrick, 3M inland.

INISHKEEL, Donegal, **54°50′·82N 08°26′·50W**. AC 2792. 6 Y Ⓥs in Church Pool, 3ca E of Inishkeel. Open to N/NE'lies.

BURTONPORT, Donegal, **54°58′·93N 08°26′·60W**. AC 1879, 2792. HW –0525 on Dover; ML 2·0m; Duration 0605. See 9.13.10. Only appr via N Chan. Ent safe in all weathers except NW gales. Hbr very full, no space to ⚓; berth on local boat at pier or go to Rutland Hbr or Aran Roads: 6 Y Ⓥs 250m NE of Black Rks, Fl R 3s. Ldg marks/lts: N Chan ldg lts on Inishcoo 119·3°, both Iso 6s 6/11m 1M; front W bn, B band; rear B bn, Y band. Rutland Is ldg lts 138°, both Oc 6s 8/14m 1M; front W bn, B band; rear B bn, Y band. Burtonport ldg lts 068°, both FG 17/23m 1M; front Gy bn, W band; rear Gy bn, Y band. HM ☎(075) 42155 (43170 home); VHF Ch 06, 12, **14**, 16. Facilities: ⛽ (root of pier), Ⓟ (½M inland). **Village** Kos ✉ 🛒 ✕ 🍺.

GWEEDORE HBR/BUNBEG, Donegal, **55°03′·75N 08°18′·87W**. AC 1883. Tides see 9.13.10. Gweedore hbr, the estuary of the R Gweedore, has sheltered ⚓s or temp ⊆ at Bunbeg Quay, usually full of FVs. Apprs via Gola N or S Sounds are not simple especially in poor visibility. N Sound is easier with ldg lts 171°, both Oc 3s 9/13m 2M, B/W bns, on the SE tip of Gola Is. (There are ⚓s on S and E sides of Gola Is.) E of Bo Is the bar 0·4m has a Fl G 3s and the chan, lying E of Inishinny Is and W of Inishcoole, is marked by a QG and 3 QR. SHM QG marks ent to Bunbeg. Night ent not advised. Facilities: ⛽ at quay; ✉ Ⓑ 🛒 🍺 at village ½M.

SHEEP HAVEN, Donegal, **55°11′·00N 07°51′·00W**. AC 2699. HW –0515 on Dover. See 9.13.11. Bay is 2M wide with many ⚓s, easily accessible in daylight, but exposed to N winds. Beware rks off Rinnafaghla Pt, and further S: Black Rk (6m) and Wherryman Rks, which dry, 1ca off E shore. ⚓ or 8 Y Ⓥs in Downies Bay to SE of pier; in Pollcormick inlet close W in 3m; in Ards Bay for excellent shelter, but beware the bar in strong winds. Lts: Breaghy Hd LFl 10s 3m 6M, Portnablahy ldg lts 125°, both Oc 6s 7/12m 2M, B col, W bands; Downies pier hd, Fl R 3s 5m 2M, R post.
Facilities: **Downies** EC Wed; ⛽ ✕ 🍺.

MULROY BAY, Donegal, **55°15′·30N 07°46′·30W**. AC 2699; HW (bar) –0455 on Dover. See 9.13.11. Beware Limeburner Rk, (NCM buoy, Q) 3M N of ent & the bar which is dangerous in swell or onshore winds. Obtain local advice as the depths on the bar change considerably. Ent at half flood (not HW); chan lies between Bar Rks (Low Bar Rk Fl G 2s) and Sessiagh Rks, it is rep'd to run along the alignment of the charted drying spit thence through First, Second (under bridge 19m) and Third Narrows to Broad Water. HW at the head of the lough is 2¼hrs later than at the bar. ⚓ Close SW of Ravedy Is (Fl 3s 9m 3M); Fanny's Bay (2m), excellent; Rosnakill Bay (3·5m) in SE side; Cranford Bay; Milford Port (3-4m). Beware cable 6m, over Moross chan, barring North Water to masted boats. Facilities: **Milford Port**, pier derelict, ⚓ 🛒; **Fanny's Bay** ✉ Mevagh Boatyard, 074 9154470 / 087 8355373, mevaghboatyard@gmail.com wooden, GRP and steel repairs, 🏗; hotel at Rosepenna (¾M).

9.13.11 LOUGH SWILLY

Donegal **55°17'N 07°34'W** ❁❁❁◊◊✿✿✿

CHARTS AC 2697; Imray C53

TIDES –0500 Dover; ML 2·3; Duration 0605

Standard Port GALWAY (⟵)

Times				Height (metres)			
High Water		Low Water		MHWS	MHWN	MLWN	MLWS
0200	0900	0200	0800	5·1	3·9	2·0	0·8
1400	2100	1400	2000				
Differences INISHTRAHULL							
+0100	+0100	+0115	+0200	–1·8	–1·4	–0·4	–0·4
TRAWBREAGA BAY							
+0115	+0059	+0109	+0125	–1·1	–0·8	ND	ND
FANAD HEAD							
+0115	+0040	+0125	+0120	–1·1	–0·9	–0·5	–0·3
RATHMULLAN							
+0125	+0050	+0126	+0118	–0·8	–0·7	–0·1	–0·3
MULROY BAY (BAR)							
+0108	+0052	+0102	+0118	–1·2	–1·0	ND	ND
SHEEP HAVEN (DOWNIES BAY)							
+0057	+0043	+0053	+0107	–1·1	–0·9	ND	ND

SHELTER Good, but beware downdrafts on E side. ⚓s N of 55°05'N may suffer from swell. ⚓s from seaward: Ballymastocker Bay, also 8 ⓿s, but exposed to E'lies; inside Macamish Pt, sheltered from SE to N; Rathmullan Roads N of pier, where yacht pontoon lies N/S in 3·6m MLWS; Fahan Creek and marina ent at HW–1.

NAVIGATION WPT 55°17'·00N 07°34'·20W, 180°/5M to 5ca W of Dunree Hd lt. Entrance is easy and dangers are well marked. Off W shore: Swilly More Rocks, Kinnegar Spit and Strand; off E shore: Colpagh Rocks, White Strand Rocks and Inch Spit/Flats. Fahan Creek is buoyed; there is a shallow bar S of Inch Spit PHM and Inch Flats dry. Entry should not be attempted before LW+2. There are many marine farms and shellfish beds S from Scraggy Bay (☎074 50172/59071 for permission to use pier).

LIGHTS AND MARKS Fanad Hd lt, Fl (5) WR 20s 38m 18/14M, touching Dunree Hd lt, Fl (2) WR 5s 46m 12/9M, leads 151° into the Lough. Thence Ballygreen Point and Hawk's Nest in line 202°.

COMMUNICATIONS (Codes: both sides of lough 074) Malin Head MRSC 9370103; Police 9153114 (Milford) and 074 9320540 (Buncrana); Dr 9158416 (Rathmullan), 1850 400911 (out of hours), and 9363611 (Buncrana); Rathmullan Pontoon 9158131, 9158315 (eves). No VHF.

FACILITIES **Portsalon** Tamney Health Centre (4M), ☎0749159060

Rathmullan Pontoon (Easter–October) ☎087 2480132, €20/craft, ⛵ ⛽ WC in Heritage Centre, Kos ✉ 🛒 Hotel ✕ ◻.

Ramelton ⌓(drying) ☎9151082, ⛽ Kos ✉ © ✕ ◻.

Lough Swilly Marina www.loughswillymarina.com ☎9360008 mob 0861082111, 200⌓ some ⓿; €3/m ⛽.

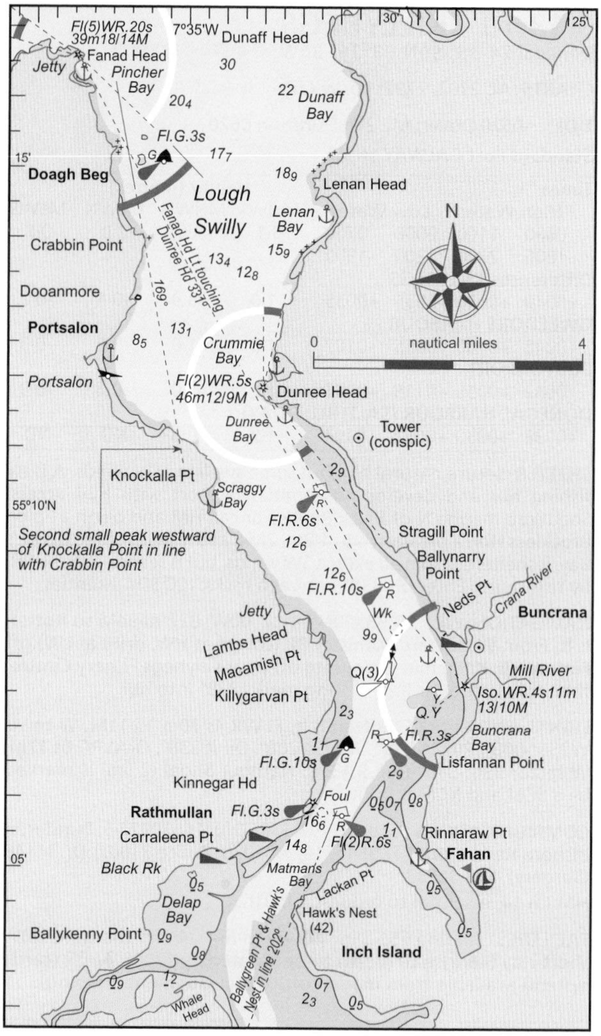

Fahan ⛽ ✕ ◻ **Lough Swilly YC** www.loughswillyyc.com (1M SE): 🛒 ⇌ ✈ (Londonderry 10M bus/taxi).

Buncrana ⌓(busy) Kos ✉ Ⓑ 🛒 Hotel ✕ ◻ @ (library).

Dunree, Small concrete pier S of Dunree Head gives access to Fort Dunree Military Museum. Tide gauge. Only use in settled weather in winds N through E to SE. Beware Dunree Skellig on approach.

BLOODY FORELAND TO FAIR HEAD

(AC 2723, 5612) This is a good cruising area, under the lee of land in SW'lies, but very exposed to NW or N. Beware fishing boats and nets in many places and the North Channel TSS.

(AC 2752) Between Bloody Foreland and Horn Head are three low-lying islands: Inishbofin, Inishdooey and Inishbeg. The first is almost part of the mainland with a temporary ⚓ on S side and a more sheltered ⚓ on NE side in Toberglassan Bay. 6M offshore is Tory Is (Fl 4 30s) with rocks for 5ca off SW side.

▶ *In Tory Sound the stream runs W from HW Galway +0230, and E from HW Galway –0530, sp rates 2kn.* ◀

Harbour in Camusmore Bay provides the best shelter on this stretch of coast (details in ICC's SDs). Enter Sheep Haven Bay between Horn Hd and Rinnafaghla Pt; good ⚓s except in strong NW or N winds. Beware Wherryman Rks, dry 1·5m, 1ca off E shore.

Between Sheep Haven and Mulroy Bay an inshore passage between Guill Rks & Carnabollion and S of Frenchman's Rock is safe in good weather, otherwise keep 1M offshore. E to Lough Swilly the coast is very foul. Beware Limeburner Rk (2m), 6·8M WNW of Fanad Hd. Mulroy Bay has good ⚓s but needs accurate pilotage (see ICC SDs).

Entrance to L Swilly is clear except for Swilly Rks off the W shore, SSE of Fanad Hd. From Dunaff Hd at ent to Lough Swilly, keep 5ca offshore to Malin Hd. Trawbreaga Lough (AC 2697) gives shelter, but is shallow, and sea can break on bar; only approach when no swell, and at half flood. **At Malin Hd the direction of buoyage changes to W.**

Garvan Is, Tor Rks and Inishtrahull lie E and NE of Malin Hd. In bad weather it is best to pass at least 3M N of Tor Rks. Inishtrahull is lit and about 1M long; rocks extend N about 3ca into Tor Sound.

▶ *W of Malin Hd a W-going eddy starts at HW Galway +0400, and an E-going one at HW. Inishtrahull Sound, between Inishtrahull and Garvan Is, is exposed; tidal streams up to 4kn sp can raise a dangerous sea with no warning. Stream also sets hard through Garvan Isles, S of which Garvan Sound can be passed safely in daylight avoiding two sunken rks, one 1½ca NE of Rossnabarton, and the other 5ca NW. The main stream runs W for only 3hrs, from HW Galway –0500 to –0200. W of Malin Hd a W-going eddy starts at HW Galway +0400, and an E-going one at HW Galway –0300.*◀

Enter Lough Foyle by either the North Chan W of The Tuns, or S chan passing 2ca N of Magilligan Pt and allowing for set towards The Tuns on the ebb (up to 3·5kn).

Proceeding to Portrush, use Skerries Sound in good weather. Beware the Storks to the E, which dry but are unmarked.

▶ *A fair tide is essential through Rathlin Sound, as sp rates reach 6kn, with dangerous overfalls. The main stream sets W from HW Dover +0030 for 5hrs, and E from HW Dover –0530 for 5hrs. The worst overfalls are S of Rue Pt (Slough-na-more) from HW Dover +0130 to +0230, and it is best to enter W-bound at the end of this period, on the last of fair tide. E-bound enter the Sound at HW Dover –0500. Close inshore between Fair Hd and Carrick-mannanon Rk a counter eddy runs W from HW Dover –0030, and an E-going eddy runs from HW Dover +0200 to +0300.* ◀

Pass outside Carrickmannanon Rk (0·3m) and Sheep Is.

There are small hbrs in Church Bay (Rathlin Is) and at Ballycastle.

9.13.12 LOUGH FOYLE

Londonderry/Donegal **55°14'N 06°54'W** ❀❀❀◊◊✿✿

CHARTS AC 2723, 2798, 2511, 2510, 5612; Imray C53, C64

TIDES
Warren Point: –0430 Dover
Moville: –0350 Dover
Londonderry: –0255 Dover
ML 1·6; Duration 0615
Standard Port RIVER FOYLE (LISAHALLY) (⟶)

Times				Height (metres)			
High Water		Low Water		MHWS	MHWN	MLWN	MLWS
0100	0800	0200	0700	2·6	1·9	0·9	0·4
1300	2000	1400	1900				
Differences WARREN LIGHTHOUSE							
–0055	–0115	–0155	–0117	–0·3	0·0	ND	ND
MOVILLE							
–0042	–0057	–0127	–0058	–0·3	0·0	+0·1	0·0
QUIGLEY'S POINT							
–0020	–0027	–0040	–0027	–0·3	–0·1	0·0	–0·1
LONDONDERRY							
+0033	+0035	+0032	+0032	+0·1	+0·2	+0·3	+0·2

SHELTER The SE side of the Lough is low lying and shallow. The NW rises steeply and has several village hbrs between the ent and Londonderry (often referred to as Derry).

White Bay: close N of Dunagree Point is a good ⚓ in settled weather on passage.

Greencastle: a busy commercial fishing hbr, open to swell in winds SW to E. No formalised ⓥ. Only advised for yachts in emergency.

Moville: a quaint resort on the western shore. A wooden pier, with 1·5m at the end, is near the village (shops closed all day Wed), but is much used by FVs. ⚓ outside hbr is exposed; inside hbr for shoal draught only. 8 Y 🅐s are about 600m upstream.

Carrickarory: pier/quay is used entirely by FVs. ⚓ in bay is sheltered in winds from SW to NNW. Plans for possible new marina.

Culmore Bay: good shelter. ⚓ 1½ca W of Culmore Pt in pleasant cove, 4M from Londonderry.

NAVIGATION WPT Tuns PHM buoy, Fl R 3s, 55°14'·00N 06°53'·49W, 235°/2·5M to Warren Pt lt, 2·5M. The Tuns bank lies 3M NE of Magilligan Pt and may dry. The main or N Chan, ¾M wide, runs NW of The Tuns; a lesser chan, min depth 4m, runs 3ca offshore around NE side of Magilligan Pt. **Beware commercial traffic.** Transiting the Loch the main channel passes NW of McKinney's Bank and the commercial ⚓ off Moville. The maintained channel leads close to the NW shore to the N of North Middle Bank and into the West Channel towards the commercial port of Lisahally. The narrows at Culmore Pt, marked by a GW Twr and medieval castle on the N shore, experience strong currents as the Loch gives way to the river proper. Upstream at Gransha the Foyle Bridge has 31m clearance before the river winds round Madams Bank following the Rosses Bay Channel, which is well marked by leading beacons. The buoyed channel leads to the city itself where further passage is limited by the Peace Bridge (clearance 3·7m) and the Craigavon Bridge (clearance 1·2m). In June and July the channel is at times obstructed by salmon nets at night. In North Chan tidal streams reach 3½kn, and upriver the ebb runs up to 6kn.

LIGHTS AND MARKS Inishowen Fl (2) WRG 10s 28m 18/14M; W tr, 2 B bands; vis 197°–G–211°–W–249°–R–000°. Warren Pt Fl 1·5s 9m 10M; W tr, G abutment; vis 232°–061°. Magilligan Pt QR 7m 4M; ✕ structure. The main chan up to Londonderry is very well lit. Foyle Bridge centre FW each side; VQ G on W pier; VQ R on E.

COMMUNICATIONS (Code 028) CGOC 9146 3933; ⊜ 7126 1937; Police 101; Dr 7126 4868; 🄷 7034 5171. HM (at Lisahally) 7186 0555. *Harbour Radio* VHF Ch **14** 12 16 (H24). Traffic and nav info Ch 14.

FACILITIES **Culdaff Bay** (10M W of Foyle SWM buoy) 6 Y 🅐s at 55°18'N 07°09'·1W, off Bunnagee Port.

Greencastle McDonald Boats, 074 9381420 / 087 0640526, mcdboats@eircom.net. Skilled wooden and GRP boatbuilders.

Lisahally is the commercial port (55°02'·6N 07°15'·6W).

Londonderry Foyle Marina (pontoon) www.londonderryport.com billmccann@londonderryport.com, ☎71860555, mob 078 41580590 ⊆ in 5-7m, £15-£21/night, ♿ ⚓ ⛽£3, adjacent to city centre. Yachts are to call *Harbour Radio* on Ch 14 for berthing directions at Foyle Marina; payments can be made at the coffee shop just outside the gate to the 'Northern' pontoon.

Prehen Boat Club (above Craigavon Bridge) ☎7034 3405.

City 🅿 ✆ 🔧 🚗 ✉ Ⓑ 🛒 ✕ 🗁 ⇌ ✈.

Continued overleaf

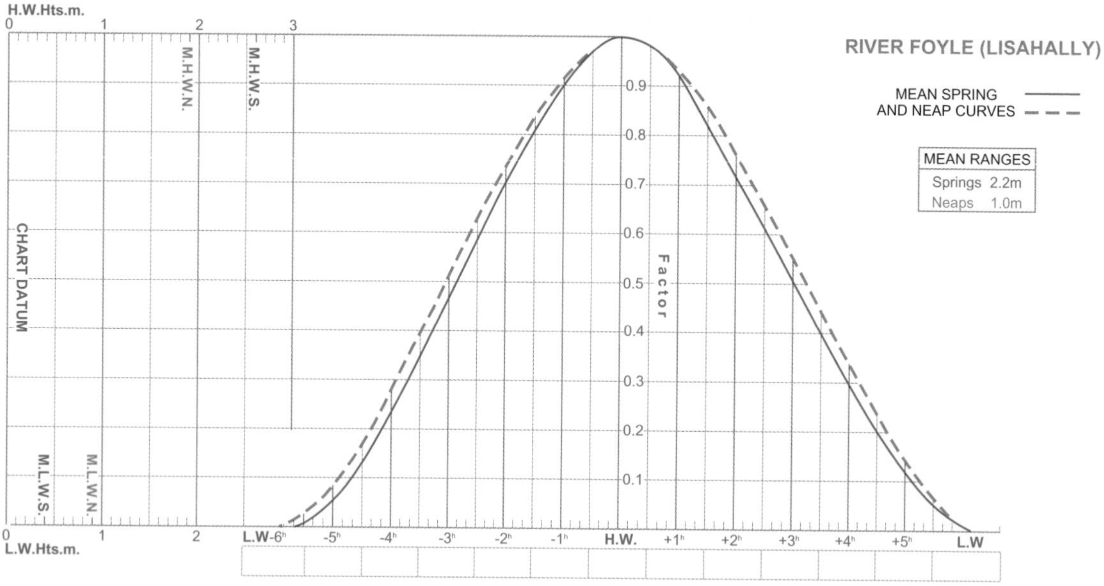
H.W.Hts.m.
0
1
2
3
M.H.W.N.
M.H.W.S.
CHART DATUM
M.L.W.S.
M.L.W.N.
0
1
2
L.W.Hts.m.
Factor
0.9
0.8
0.7
0.6
0.5
0.4
0.3
0.2
0.1
L.W.-6h
-5h
-4h
-3h
-2h
-1h
H.W.
+1h
+2h
+3h
+4h
+5h
L.W
RIVER FOYLE (LISAHALLY)
MEAN SPRING AND NEAP CURVES
MEAN RANGES
Springs 2.2m
Neaps 1.0m

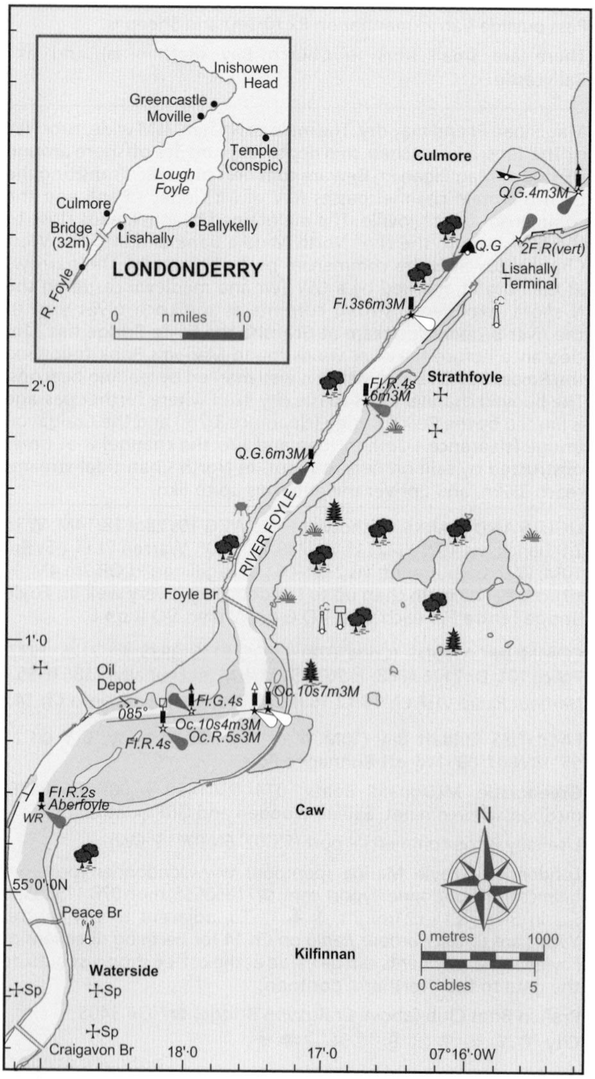
Inishowen Head
Greencastle
Moville
Temple (conspic)
Lough Foyle
Culmore
Bridge (32m)
Lisahally
Ballykelly
LONDONDERRY
R. Foyle
0 n miles 10
Culmore
Q.G.4m3M
Q.G
2F.R(vert)
Lisahally Terminal
Fl.3s6m3M
Strathfoyle
Fl.R.4s 6m3M
2'·0
Q.G.6m3M
RIVER FOYLE
Foyle Br
1'·0
Oil Depot
085°
Fl.G.4s
Oc.10s7m3M
Oc.10s4m3M
Oc.R.5s3M
Fl.R.4s
Fl.R.2s
Aberfoyle
WR
Caw
55°0'·0N
Peace Br
Waterside
Sp
Sp
Sp
Kilfinnan
0 metres 1000
0 cables 5
Craigavon Br
18'·0
17'·0
07°16'·0W

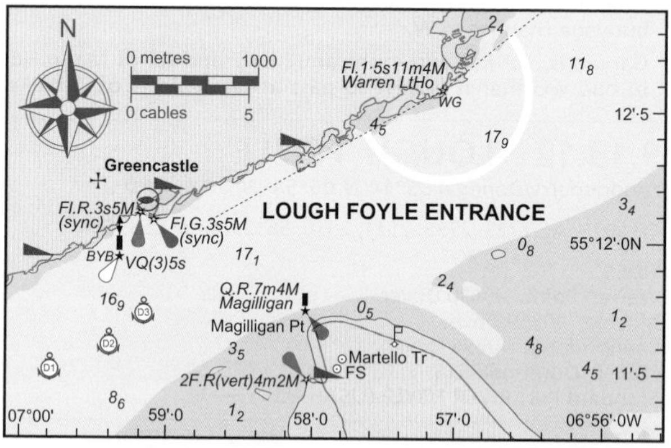
N
0 metres 1000
0 cables 5
Fl.1·5s11m4M
Warren LtHo
WG
Greencastle
Fl.R.3s5M (sync)
Fl.G.3s5M (sync)
BYB VQ(3)5s
LOUGH FOYLE ENTRANCE
Q.R.7m4M
Magilligan
Magilligan Pt
Martello Tr
FS
2F.R(vert)4m2M
D1
D2
D3
12'·5
55°12'·0N
11'·5
07°00'
59'·0
58'·0
57'·0
06°56'·0W

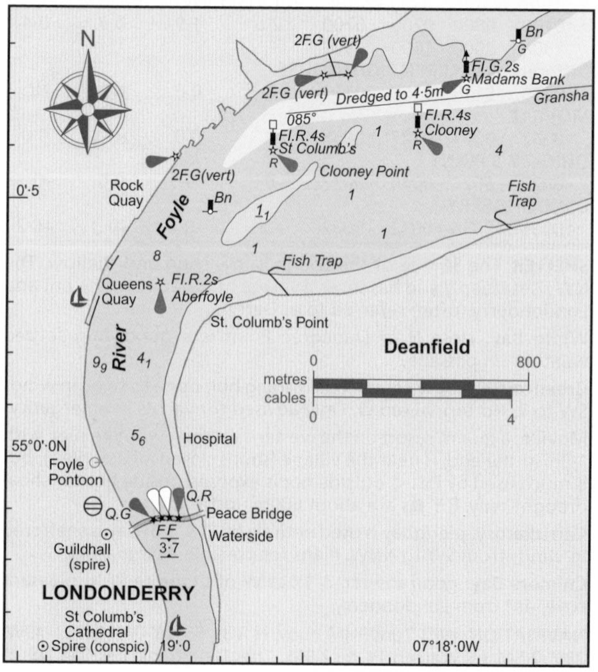
N
2F.G (vert)
Bn G
Fl.G.2s
Madams Bank
G
2F.G (vert)
Dredged to 4·5m
Gransha
085°
Fl.R.4s
St Columb's
R
Fl.R.4s
Clooney
R
Clooney Point
2F.G(vert)
0'·5
Rock Quay
Foyle
Bn
Fish Trap
Fish Trap
Queens Quay
Fl.R.2s
Aberfoyle
St. Columb's Point
River
Deanfield
0 metres 800
cables 0 4
55°0'·0N
Foyle Pontoon
Hospital
Q.G
Q.R
Peace Bridge
FF
3·7
Waterside
Guildhall (spire)
LONDONDERRY
St Columb's Cathedral
Spire (conspic)
19'·0
07°18'·0W

STANDARD TIME (UT)
For Summer Time add ONE hour in **non-shaded areas**

RIVER FOYLE LAT 55°03′N LONG 7°16′W

TIMES AND HEIGHTS OF HIGH AND LOW WATERS

Dates in red are SPRINGS
Dates in blue are NEAPS

YEAR **2018**

JANUARY

Day	Time	m	Day	Time	m
1 M	0043 0647 1316 1908	0.4 2.7 0.5 2.9	16 TU	0122 0715 1331 1934	0.6 2.6 0.7 2.3
2 TU	0130 0730 1407 ○ 1955	0.4 2.9 0.4 2.9	17 W	0158 0747 1406 ● 2002	0.5 2.6 0.7 2.3
3 W	0215 0814 1457 2042	0.3 3.0 0.4 2.8	18 TH	0231 0820 1440 2033	0.5 2.7 0.7 2.3
4 TH	0259 0859 1546 2130	0.3 3.0 0.4 2.7	19 F	0302 0855 1516 2108	0.5 2.7 0.6 2.3
5 F	0341 0945 1635 2217	0.4 2.9 0.5 2.6	20 SA	0333 0931 1553 2145	0.5 2.6 0.6 2.3
6 SA	0422 1034 1725 2305	0.4 2.8 0.6 2.4	21 SU	0406 1009 1633 2223	0.6 2.6 0.6 2.2
7 SU	0504 1127 1818 2359	0.6 2.6 0.8 2.2	22 M	0443 1051 1717 2305	0.6 2.5 0.7 2.1
8 M	0549 1234 1919 ◑	0.7 2.4 0.9	23 TU	0525 1139 1807 2354	0.7 2.3 0.7 2.0
9 TU	0103 0642 1356 2026	2.0 0.9 2.2 0.9	24 W	0617 1239 1904 ◐	0.8 2.2 0.8
10 W	0217 0750 1512 2132	1.9 1.0 2.2 0.9	25 TH	0100 0722 1356 2007	1.9 0.9 2.2 0.8
11 TH	0328 0911 1621 2230	2.0 1.0 2.2 0.9	26 F	0226 0838 1512 2115	1.9 0.9 2.2 0.8
12 F	0434 1029 1718 2320	2.1 1.0 2.2 0.8	27 SA	0348 1000 1620 2227	2.0 0.8 2.3 0.7
13 SA	0527 1127 1803	2.2 0.9 2.2	28 SU	0456 1119 1721 2334	2.2 0.7 2.4 0.6
14 SU	0004 0608 1213 1839	0.7 2.4 0.8 2.2	29 M	0551 1219 1815	2.4 0.5 2.6
15 M	0044 0643 1254 1909	0.6 2.5 0.8 2.3	30 TU	0030 0638 1313 1903	0.5 2.6 0.4 2.7
			31 W	0119 0721 1402 ○ 1948	0.4 2.8 0.3 2.7

FEBRUARY

Day	Time	m	Day	Time	m
1 TH	0204 0804 1449 2032	0.3 2.9 0.3 2.7	16 F	0217 0802 1429 2018	0.4 2.6 0.5 2.3
2 F	0246 0846 1534 2113	0.2 3.0 0.3 2.7	17 SA	0249 0835 1502 2050	0.4 2.7 0.4 2.4
3 SA	0326 0928 1616 2153	0.2 2.9 0.4 2.5	18 SU	0320 0910 1536 2123	0.4 2.7 0.4 2.4
4 SU	0404 1010 1656 2233	0.3 2.7 0.5 2.4	19 M	0352 0947 1611 2159	0.4 2.6 0.4 2.4
5 M	0441 1054 1738 2315	0.4 2.5 0.7 2.2	20 TU	0427 1026 1648 2237	0.4 2.5 0.5 2.3
6 TU	0520 1143 1825	0.6 2.3 0.8	21 W	0506 1110 1731 2319	0.5 2.4 0.6 2.1
7 W	0004 0605 1256 ◑ 1923	2.0 0.8 2.0 1.0	22 TH	0553 1204 1822	0.7 2.2 0.7
8 TH	0117 0704 1432 2036	1.9 0.9 1.9 1.0	23 F	0014 0655 1318 ◐ 1926	2.0 0.8 2.1 0.8
9 F	0243 0818 1556 2149	1.8 1.0 1.9 1.0	24 SA	0139 0815 1450 2040	1.9 0.9 2.0 0.8
10 SA	0400 0957 1703 2249	1.9 1.0 1.9 0.9	25 SU	0324 0955 1612 2204	1.9 0.8 2.1 0.8
11 SU	0503 1109 1752 2338	2.1 0.9 2.0 0.7	26 M	0444 1119 1719 2321	2.1 0.6 2.2 0.7
12 M	0550 1158 1830	2.2 0.8 2.1	27 TU	0543 1217 1812	2.3 0.5 2.4
13 TU	0022 0627 1241 1901	0.6 2.4 0.7 2.1	28 W	0017 0628 1307 1857	0.5 2.5 0.3 2.5
14 W	0104 0659 1319 1926	0.5 2.5 0.6 2.2			
15 TH	0142 0730 1355 ● 1950	0.5 2.5 0.6 2.3			

MARCH

Day	Time	m	Day	Time	m
1 TH	0105 0710 1353 1937	0.3 2.7 0.2 2.6	16 F	0119 0706 1337 1931	0.4 2.5 0.4 2.2
2 F	0148 0749 1435 ○ 2015	0.2 2.8 0.2 2.6	17 SA	0155 0738 1410 ● 1957	0.4 2.6 0.3 2.3
3 SA	0228 0827 1514 2050	0.2 2.9 0.2 2.6	18 SU	0228 0811 1442 2027	0.3 2.7 0.3 2.4
4 SU	0306 0905 1550 2125	0.1 2.8 0.3 2.5	19 M	0300 0846 1514 2100	0.3 2.7 0.2 2.5
5 M	0341 0943 1624 2200	0.2 2.7 0.4 2.4	20 TU	0333 0924 1547 2135	0.3 2.7 0.3 2.5
6 TU	0416 1021 1657 2237	0.3 2.4 0.6 2.2	21 W	0409 1004 1622 2212	0.3 2.6 0.3 2.4
7 W	0453 1101 1735 2319	0.5 2.2 0.7 2.0	22 TH	0449 1048 1701 2254	0.4 2.4 0.5 2.2
8 TH	0536 1150 1823	0.7 1.9 0.9	23 F	0537 1141 1748 2346	0.6 2.2 0.6 2.0
9 F	0018 0630 1337 ◑ 1930	1.9 0.9 1.7 1.0	24 SA	0641 1254 1850 ◐	0.7 2.0 0.8
10 SA	0201 0741 1521 2059	1.8 1.0 1.7 1.0	25 SU	0112 0809 1436 2011	1.9 0.8 1.9 0.9
11 SU	0325 0917 1637 2215	1.9 1.0 1.7 0.9	26 M	0311 0957 1602 2145	1.9 0.7 1.9 0.8
12 M	0431 1047 1730 2310	2.0 0.9 1.8 0.7	27 TU	0431 1110 1709 2302	2.1 0.5 2.1 0.6
13 TU	0522 1139 1810 2358	2.1 0.7 1.9 0.6	28 W	0528 1205 1800 2357	2.3 0.4 2.2 0.5
14 W	0602 1221 1842	2.2 0.6 2.0	29 TH	0613 1251 1842	2.5 0.2 2.4
15 TH	0040 0635 1301 1907	0.5 2.4 0.5 2.1	30 F	0044 0652 1334 1918	0.3 2.6 0.1 2.5
			31 SA	0126 0729 1413 ○ 1952	0.2 2.7 0.1 2.5

APRIL

Day	Time	m	Day	Time	m
1 SU	0205 0805 1449 2025	0.1 2.7 0.2 2.5	16 M	0200 0745 1416 ● 2003	0.2 2.7 0.2 2.5
2 M	0241 0841 1521 2057	0.1 2.6 0.2 2.5	17 TU	0235 0823 1450 2037	0.2 2.7 0.1 2.5
3 TU	0316 0917 1550 2130	0.2 2.5 0.4 2.4	18 W	0313 0904 1525 2114	0.2 2.7 0.2 2.5
4 W	0350 0952 1621 2205	0.3 2.3 0.5 2.3	19 TH	0353 0947 1601 2154	0.3 2.6 0.3 2.4
5 TH	0427 1029 1654 2246	0.5 2.1 0.6 2.1	20 F	0438 1034 1640 2239	0.4 2.4 0.4 2.3
6 F	0510 1111 1736 2338	0.6 1.8 0.8 1.9	21 SA	0531 1129 1726 2335	0.5 2.2 0.6 2.1
7 SA	0603 1212 1834	0.8 1.6 0.9	22 SU	0640 1243 1826 ◐	0.7 1.9 0.7
8 SU	0116 0710 1428 ◑ 1956	1.8 0.9 1.5 0.9	23 M	0110 0810 1417 1948	2.0 0.7 1.8 0.8
9 M	0248 0833 1550 2132	1.8 0.9 1.6 0.9	24 TU	0254 0937 1538 2120	2.0 0.6 1.9 0.8
10 TU	0351 1003 1652 2236	1.9 0.8 1.7 0.7	25 W	0407 1045 1645 2234	2.1 0.5 2.0 0.6
11 W	0443 1103 1737 2326	2.0 0.7 1.8 0.6	26 TH	0504 1140 1737 2330	2.3 0.3 2.1 0.5
12 TH	0525 1150 1810	2.1 0.5 1.9	27 F	0551 1226 1819	2.4 0.2 2.3
13 F	0009 0601 1231 1837	0.5 2.3 0.4 2.1	28 SA	0017 0631 1308 1855	0.3 2.5 0.2 2.4
14 SA	0048 0635 1308 1903	0.4 2.4 0.3 2.2	29 SU	0100 0708 1346 1928	0.2 2.5 0.2 2.5
15 SU	0124 0709 1343 1931	0.3 2.6 0.2 2.4	30 M	0139 0743 1421 ○ 2000	0.2 2.5 0.2 2.5

Chart Datum: 1·37 metres below Ordnance Datum (Belfast). HAT is 3·1 metres above Chart Datum.

N Ireland

STANDARD TIME (UT)
For Summer Time add ONE hour in **non-shaded areas**

RIVER FOYLE LAT 55°03'N LONG 7°16'W

TIMES AND HEIGHTS OF HIGH AND LOW WATERS

Dates in red are **SPRINGS**
Dates in blue are **NEAPS**

YEAR **2018**

MAY

Date	Day	Time	m	Time	m	Time	m	Time	m
1	TU	0216	0.2	0818	2.5	1452	0.3	2031	2.5
2	W	0251	0.3	0853	2.4	1521	0.3	2105	2.4
3	TH	0326	0.4	0928	2.2	1551	0.4	2141	2.3
4	F	0403	0.5	1005	2.0	1622	0.5	2221	2.2
5	SA	0447	0.6	1046	1.8	1700	0.7	2310	2.0
6	SU	0538	0.8	1136	1.7	1747	0.8		
7	M	0024	1.9	0640	0.8	1257	1.5	1853	0.9
8	TU	0159	1.8	0749	0.8	1437	1.5	◑ 2020	0.9
9	W	0302	1.9	0859	0.7	1548	1.6	2143	0.8
10	TH	0354	2.0	1005	0.6	1644	1.7	2241	0.7
11	F	0439	2.1	1102	0.5	1726	1.8	2327	0.6
12	SA	0521	2.2	1149	0.4	1800	2.0		
13	SU	0009	0.4	0600	2.4	1232	0.3	1832	2.2
14	M	0050	0.3	0640	2.5	1312	0.2	1905	2.4
15	TU	0130	0.3	0721	2.7	1350	0.1	● 1941	2.5
16	W	0212	0.2	0803	2.7	1428	0.1	2019	2.6
17	TH	0256	0.2	0847	2.7	1507	0.1	2059	2.6
18	F	0342	0.3	0935	2.6	1546	0.2	2144	2.5
19	SA	0433	0.4	1025	2.4	1628	0.3	2233	2.4
20	SU	0531	0.5	1122	2.2	1715	0.5	2335	2.2
21	M	0640	0.6	1230	2.0	1811	0.6		
22	TU	0103	2.1	0755	0.6	1348	1.9	◐ 1925	0.7
23	W	0228	2.1	0907	0.5	1502	1.9	2047	0.7
24	TH	0336	2.2	1010	0.5	1610	1.9	2200	0.6
25	F	0436	2.2	1107	0.4	1708	2.0	2300	0.5
26	SA	0527	2.3	1156	0.4	1754	2.2	2350	0.4
27	SU	0611	2.3	1239	0.3	1833	2.3		
28	M	0034	0.4	0649	2.3	1318	0.3	1906	2.4
29	TU	0115	0.4	0725	2.3	1354	0.3	○ 1939	2.4
30	W	0153	0.4	0759	2.3	1427	0.3	2011	2.5
31	TH	0229	0.4	0833	2.2	1458	0.4	2045	2.4

JUNE

Date	Day	Time	m	Time	m	Time	m	Time	m
1	F	0305	0.5	0908	2.1	1528	0.4	2122	2.4
2	SA	0343	0.6	0945	2.0	1559	0.5	2202	2.3
3	SU	0426	0.6	1026	1.9	1633	0.6	2247	2.1
4	M	0514	0.7	1111	1.8	1714	0.7	2343	2.0
5	TU	0609	0.7	1205	1.7	1806	0.8		
6	W	0055	1.9	0708	0.7	1315	1.6	◑ 1913	0.8
7	TH	0205	1.9	0808	0.7	1431	1.6	2027	0.8
8	F	0302	2.0	0907	0.6	1539	1.7	2138	0.7
9	SA	0353	2.1	1006	0.5	1636	1.8	2239	0.6
10	SU	0442	2.2	1104	0.4	1724	2.0	2331	0.5
11	M	0529	2.4	1156	0.3	1805	2.2		
12	TU	0020	0.4	0615	2.5	1243	0.2	1844	2.4
13	W	0108	0.3	0701	2.6	1328	0.2	● 1924	2.5
14	TH	0156	0.3	0748	2.6	1411	0.1	2006	2.6
15	F	0246	0.2	0836	2.6	1454	0.1	2050	2.7
16	SA	0337	0.3	0926	2.5	1536	0.2	2137	2.6
17	SU	0431	0.3	1017	2.4	1620	0.3	2229	2.5
18	M	0526	0.4	1110	2.3	1705	0.4	2328	2.4
19	TU	0626	0.5	1208	2.1	1755	0.5		
20	W	0040	2.3	0729	0.5	1313	1.9	◐ 1856	0.6
21	TH	0156	2.2	0833	0.6	1422	1.8	2009	0.7
22	F	0305	2.2	0934	0.6	1531	1.8	2124	0.7
23	SA	0409	2.2	1032	0.5	1637	1.9	2230	0.7
24	SU	0506	2.2	1125	0.5	1731	2.1	2326	0.6
25	M	0556	2.2	1211	0.5	1814	2.2		
26	TU	0014	0.5	0637	2.2	1253	0.4	1850	2.3
27	W	0057	0.5	0714	2.2	1332	0.4	1924	2.4
28	TH	0137	0.5	0748	2.1	1408	0.4	○ 1957	2.5
29	F	0215	0.5	0819	2.1	1441	0.4	2031	2.5
30	SA	0252	0.6	0852	2.1	1513	0.4	2106	2.4

JULY

Date	Day	Time	m	Time	m	Time	m	Time	m
1	SU	0329	0.6	0928	2.1	1543	0.4	2144	2.3
2	M	0409	0.6	1006	2.0	1615	0.5	2225	2.2
3	TU	0452	0.6	1047	1.9	1651	0.5	2310	2.1
4	W	0539	0.6	1131	1.8	1734	0.6		
5	TH	0004	2.0	0630	0.6	1223	1.7	1828	0.7
6	F	0108	2.0	0725	0.6	1329	1.7	◑ 1935	0.8
7	SA	0213	2.0	0822	0.6	1442	1.7	2047	0.8
8	SU	0313	2.1	0921	0.5	1552	1.8	2157	0.7
9	M	0410	2.2	1024	0.5	1653	2.0	2303	0.6
10	TU	0505	2.3	1125	0.4	1744	2.2		
11	W	0001	0.5	0558	2.4	1221	0.3	1830	2.4
12	TH	0056	0.4	0649	2.5	1311	0.2	1913	2.6
13	F	0148	0.3	0739	2.6	1358	0.2	● 1957	2.7
14	SA	0241	0.2	0828	2.6	1443	0.1	2042	2.8
15	SU	0332	0.2	0916	2.5	1526	0.1	2128	2.8
16	M	0422	0.2	1003	2.5	1607	0.2	2216	2.7
17	TU	0511	0.3	1049	2.3	1649	0.3	2307	2.5
18	W	0602	0.4	1138	2.1	1732	0.4		
19	TH	0006	2.3	0656	0.5	1233	2.0	◐ 1822	0.6
20	F	0119	2.2	0755	0.6	1339	1.8	1925	0.7
21	SA	0234	2.1	0857	0.7	1452	1.8	2044	0.8
22	SU	0346	2.0	0959	0.7	1607	1.9	2205	0.8
23	M	0451	2.0	1056	0.6	1712	2.0	2309	0.7
24	TU	0546	2.0	1146	0.6	1800	2.2		
25	W	0000	0.7	0630	2.1	1231	0.5	1839	2.3
26	TH	0045	0.6	0708	2.1	1313	0.4	1912	2.4
27	F	0126	0.6	0740	2.1	1351	0.4	○ 1944	2.5
28	SA	0205	0.6	0808	2.1	1427	0.3	2016	2.5
29	SU	0242	0.6	0836	2.1	1459	0.3	2049	2.5
30	M	0316	0.5	0908	2.1	1529	0.4	2124	2.5
31	TU	0351	0.5	0942	2.1	1558	0.4	2200	2.4

AUGUST

Date	Day	Time	m	Time	m	Time	m	Time	m
1	W	0428	0.5	1019	2.1	1631	0.5	2240	2.3
2	TH	0508	0.5	1057	2.0	1709	0.5	2325	2.2
3	F	0553	0.5	1140	1.9	1755	0.7		
4	SA	0020	2.1	0644	0.6	1236	1.8	◑ 1855	0.8
5	SU	0130	2.0	0742	0.6	1352	1.7	2009	0.8
6	M	0242	2.0	0844	0.6	1517	1.8	2129	0.8
7	TU	0349	2.1	0951	0.6	1632	1.9	2251	0.7
8	W	0453	2.2	1103	0.5	1732	2.2	2356	0.5
9	TH	0551	2.3	1206	0.4	1821	2.4		
10	F	0052	0.4	0643	2.4	1259	0.3	1904	2.6
11	SA	0144	0.3	0730	2.5	1346	0.2	● 1947	2.8
12	SU	0233	0.2	0815	2.6	1429	0.1	2028	2.9
13	M	0320	0.2	0858	2.6	1510	0.1	2111	2.9
14	TU	0404	0.2	0939	2.5	1549	0.1	2153	2.8
15	W	0446	0.3	1020	2.4	1627	0.2	2238	2.6
16	TH	0529	0.4	1102	2.2	1706	0.4	2328	2.3
17	F	0615	0.6	1150	2.0	1749	0.6		
18	SA	0035	2.1	0709	0.7	1254	1.9	◐ 1845	0.8
19	SU	0204	1.9	0816	0.8	1417	1.8	2003	0.9
20	M	0326	1.9	0925	0.8	1541	1.9	2146	0.9
21	TU	0437	1.9	1028	0.7	1652	2.0	2258	0.8
22	W	0533	2.0	1122	0.6	1743	2.2	2349	0.7
23	TH	0618	2.0	1209	0.5	1823	2.3		
24	F	0032	0.7	0654	2.1	1252	0.4	1856	2.4
25	SA	0113	0.6	0725	2.1	1332	0.4	1926	2.5
26	SU	0150	0.6	0750	2.2	1409	0.3	○ 1955	2.5
27	M	0225	0.5	0814	2.2	1441	0.3	2025	2.6
28	TU	0257	0.5	0843	2.3	1510	0.3	2058	2.6
29	W	0328	0.4	0914	2.3	1539	0.4	2132	2.5
30	TH	0400	0.4	0947	2.3	1610	0.4	2210	2.5
31	F	0435	0.5	1022	2.2	1646	0.5	2251	2.3

Chart Datum: 1·37 metres below Ordnance Datum (Belfast). HAT is 3·1 metres above Chart Datum.

STANDARD TIME (UT)
For Summer Time add ONE hour in **non-shaded areas**

RIVER FOYLE LAT 55°03'N LONG 7°16'W

TIMES AND HEIGHTS OF HIGH AND LOW WATERS

Dates in red are SPRINGS
Dates in blue are NEAPS

YEAR **2018**

SEPTEMBER

Date	Time	m	Date	Time	m
1	0515 1101 SA 1728 2341	0.5 2.1 0.6 2.2	16	0615 1206 SU 1813 ◐	0.8 2.0 0.9
2	0603 1149 SU 1825	0.6 1.9 0.8	17	0127 0720 M 1346 1928	1.8 0.9 1.9 1.0
3	0050 0700 M 1302 ◑ 1942	2.0 0.7 1.8 0.9	18	0301 0846 TU 1513 2129	1.8 1.0 1.9 1.0
4	0219 0808 TU 1453 2120	2.0 0.8 1.8 0.9	19	0413 0957 W 1622 2241	1.8 0.9 2.1 0.9
5	0338 0925 W 1620 2252	2.0 0.8 2.0 0.7	20	0510 1054 TH 1715 2329	1.9 0.7 2.2 0.8
6	0447 1048 TH 1722 2353	2.2 0.7 2.2 0.5	21	0554 1143 F 1756	2.0 0.6 2.3
7	0545 1152 F 1809	2.3 0.5 2.5	22	0011 0629 SA 1227 1829	0.7 2.1 0.5 2.4
8	0045 0633 SA 1243 1850	0.3 2.4 0.3 2.7	23	0050 0658 SU 1307 1858	0.6 2.2 0.4 2.5
9	0132 0716 SU 1328 ● 1929	0.2 2.6 0.2 2.9	24	0126 0722 M 1343 1926	0.5 2.2 0.4 2.6
10	0217 0756 M 1410 2008	0.1 2.6 0.1 2.9	25	0159 0746 TU 1415 ○ 1956	0.5 2.3 0.4 2.7
11	0258 0833 TU 1448 2047	0.1 2.6 0.1 2.9	26	0229 0814 W 1445 2029	0.4 2.4 0.3 2.7
12	0337 0910 W 1525 2126	0.2 2.6 0.1 2.8	27	0259 0844 TH 1515 2104	0.4 2.5 0.4 2.7
13	0414 0947 TH 1601 2206	0.3 2.5 0.2 2.6	28	0330 0917 F 1548 2142	0.4 2.5 0.4 2.6
14	0449 1025 F 1638 2250	0.5 2.3 0.4 2.3	29	0403 0952 SA 1625 2224	0.4 2.4 0.5 2.5
15	0528 1108 SA 1719 2345	0.7 2.1 0.6 2.0	30	0441 1031 SU 1709 2313	0.5 2.3 0.7 2.3

OCTOBER

Date	Time	m	Date	Time	m
1	0525 1117 M 1806	0.7 2.1 0.8	16	0020 0619 TU 1305 ◐ 1853	1.8 1.0 2.0 1.1
2	0022 0621 TU 1228 ◑ 1930	2.1 0.8 2.0 0.9	17	0220 0742 W 1437 2046	1.7 1.1 2.0 1.1
3	0203 0733 W 1438 2123	2.0 0.9 2.0 0.9	18	0333 0916 TH 1542 2205	1.8 1.0 2.1 1.0
4	0328 0901 TH 1603 2243	2.0 0.9 2.2 0.7	19	0433 1020 F 1634 2256	1.9 0.9 2.2 0.8
5	0435 1028 F 1703 2339	2.2 0.8 2.4 0.5	20	0519 1111 SA 1717 2338	2.0 0.8 2.3 0.7
6	0530 1131 SA 1749	2.3 0.6 2.6	21	0556 1155 SU 1752	2.1 0.7 2.4
7	0027 0615 SU 1221 1829	0.3 2.5 0.4 2.8	22	0017 0624 M 1234 1823	0.6 2.2 0.6 2.5
8	0112 0655 M 1305 1907	0.2 2.6 0.3 2.9	23	0052 0649 TU 1310 1853	0.5 2.3 0.5 2.7
9	0153 0732 TU 1345 ● 1944	0.2 2.7 0.2 2.9	24	0125 0716 W 1343 ○ 1926	0.4 2.5 0.4 2.8
10	0231 0806 W 1423 2021	0.2 2.7 0.2 2.9	25	0157 0746 TH 1416 2001	0.4 2.6 0.4 2.8
11	0306 0841 TH 1459 2058	0.3 2.7 0.3 2.8	26	0229 0818 F 1450 2039	0.4 2.7 0.4 2.8
12	0338 0916 F 1534 2136	0.4 2.6 0.4 2.5	27	0302 0853 SA 1528 2120	0.4 2.7 0.5 2.7
13	0410 0953 SA 1611 2215	0.6 2.5 0.6 2.3	28	0338 0931 SU 1610 2205	0.4 2.7 0.6 2.6
14	0444 1033 SU 1652 2300	0.7 2.3 0.8 2.0	29	0417 1013 M 1658 2257	0.5 2.5 0.7 2.3
15	0525 1125 M 1744	0.9 2.1 1.0	30	0501 1102 TU 1800	0.7 2.4 0.9
			31	0005 0554 W 1216 ◑ 1928	2.1 0.8 2.2 0.9

NOVEMBER

Date	Time	m	Date	Time	m
1	0142 0704 TH 1418 2106	2.0 0.9 2.2 0.9	16	0231 0750 F 1452 2055	1.7 1.1 2.1 1.0
2	0304 0833 F 1536 2218	2.1 0.9 2.3 0.7	17	0336 0921 SA 1545 2200	1.8 1.0 2.2 0.9
3	0411 0957 SA 1636 2314	2.2 0.8 2.5 0.5	18	0430 1024 SU 1630 2250	1.9 0.9 2.3 0.8
4	0507 1102 SU 1725	2.3 0.7 2.6	19	0511 1112 M 1709 2333	2.0 0.8 2.4 0.7
5	0002 0552 M 1154 1807	0.4 2.5 0.5 2.8	20	0545 1154 TU 1745	2.2 0.7 2.6
6	0046 0632 TU 1239 1845	0.3 2.6 0.4 2.8	21	0012 0616 W 1232 1821	0.5 2.4 0.6 2.7
7	0125 0708 W 1319 ● 1922	0.3 2.7 0.4 2.8	22	0050 0648 TH 1310 1859	0.5 2.6 0.5 2.8
8	0201 0742 TH 1358 1958	0.4 2.8 0.4 2.8	23	0127 0722 F 1350 ○ 1938	0.4 2.7 0.5 2.9
9	0235 0816 F 1434 2033	0.4 2.8 0.5 2.7	24	0204 0758 SA 1431 2020	0.4 2.8 0.5 2.9
10	0306 0850 SA 1509 2109	0.5 2.7 0.6 2.5	25	0242 0837 SU 1515 2105	0.4 2.9 0.5 2.8
11	0337 0926 SU 1546 2146	0.6 2.6 0.7 2.3	26	0321 0919 M 1602 2153	0.4 2.8 0.6 2.6
12	0409 1006 M 1627 2225	0.7 2.5 0.9 2.1	27	0403 1004 TU 1655 2247	0.5 2.7 0.7 2.4
13	0445 1052 TU 1716 2314	0.9 2.3 1.0 1.9	28	0447 1058 W 1758 2351	0.6 2.6 0.8 2.2
14	0529 1159 W 1817	1.0 2.1 1.1	29	0538 1210 TH 1915	0.8 2.4 0.9
15	0053 0628 TH 1343 ◐ 1932	1.7 1.1 2.1 1.1	30	0111 0641 F 1347 ◑ 2035	2.1 0.9 2.4 0.8

DECEMBER

Date	Time	m	Date	Time	m
1	0229 0759 SA 1504 2144	2.1 0.9 2.4 0.8	16	0210 0750 SU 1444 2044	1.8 1.1 2.2 0.9
2	0337 0920 SU 1608 2243	2.1 0.9 2.5 0.7	17	0321 0904 M 1538 2145	1.8 1.0 2.2 0.8
3	0438 1030 M 1702 2334	2.2 0.8 2.6 0.6	18	0418 1013 TU 1626 2241	2.0 0.9 2.4 0.7
4	0528 1126 TU 1748	2.4 0.7 2.6	19	0505 1110 W 1711 2332	2.1 0.8 2.5 0.6
5	0019 0610 W 1215 1828	0.5 2.5 0.6 2.7	20	0546 1159 TH 1755	2.3 0.7 2.7
6	0059 0647 TH 1258 1906	0.5 2.6 0.6 2.6	21	0018 0625 F 1246 1838	0.5 2.5 0.6 2.8
7	0136 0722 F 1337 ● 1941	0.5 2.7 0.6 2.6	22	0103 0704 SA 1332 ○ 1923	0.4 2.7 0.5 2.8
8	0210 0756 SA 1413 2014	0.5 2.8 0.6 2.5	23	0145 0744 SU 1420 2008	0.4 2.9 0.5 2.8
9	0242 0831 SU 1449 2048	0.6 2.8 0.7 2.4	24	0228 0826 M 1509 2056	0.4 2.9 0.5 2.8
10	0313 0907 M 1525 2122	0.6 2.7 0.8 2.3	25	0311 0911 TU 1559 2145	0.4 2.9 0.5 2.7
11	0343 0945 TU 1604 2159	0.7 2.6 0.9 2.1	26	0354 0959 W 1651 2236	0.4 2.9 0.6 2.5
12	0417 1026 W 1649 2240	0.8 2.4 0.9 2.0	27	0438 1050 TH 1747 2330	0.5 2.7 0.7 2.3
13	0455 1114 TH 1740 2330	0.9 2.3 1.0 1.9	28	0525 1151 F 1849	0.6 2.6 0.8
14	0541 1218 F 1838	1.0 2.2 1.0	29	0033 0617 SA 1309 ◑ 1957	2.2 0.8 2.4 0.8
15	0039 0639 SA 1339 ◐ 1941	1.8 1.0 2.1 1.0	30	0145 0722 SU 1429 2106	2.0 0.9 2.4 0.9
			31	0257 0838 M 1541 2210	2.0 0.9 2.3 0.8

Chart Datum: 1·37 metres below Ordnance Datum (Belfast). HAT is 3·1 metres above Chart Datum.

N Ireland

9.13.13 RIVER BANN AND COLERAINE

Londonderry/Antrim **55°10′·32N 06°46′·35W** ❀❀◊◊✿✿

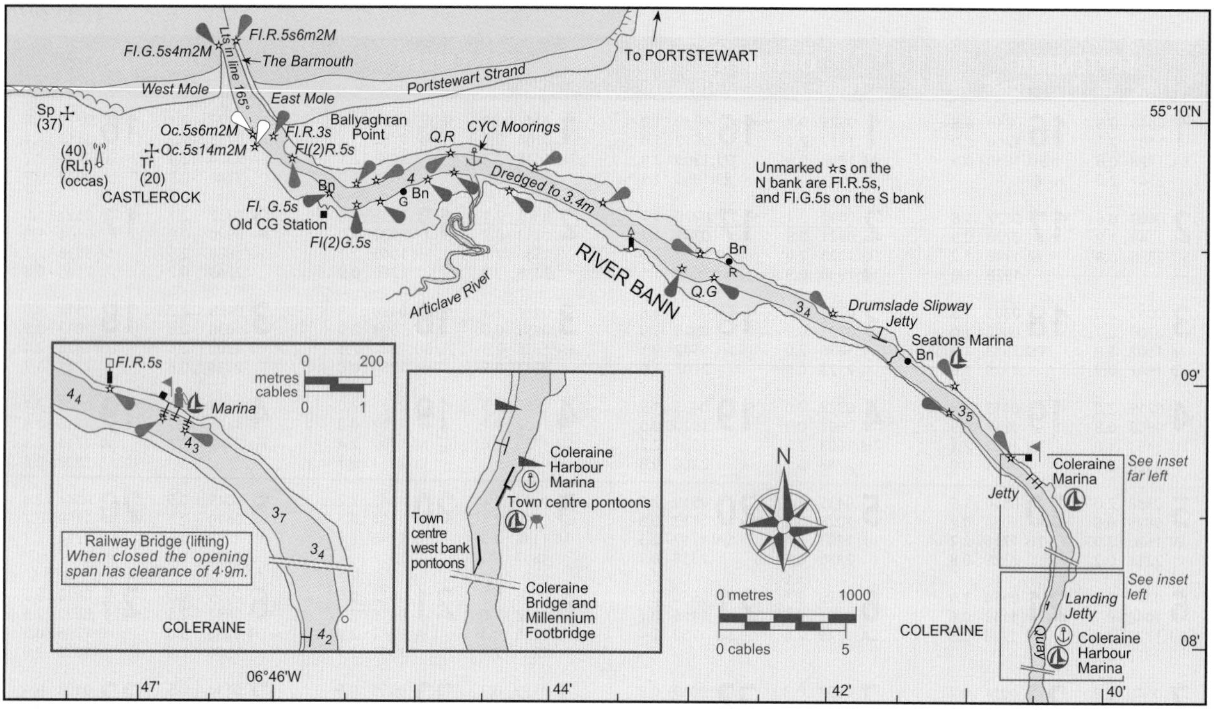

CHARTS AC 2723, 2798, 2494, 5612; Imray C53, C64

TIDES –0345 Dover (Coleraine); ML 1·1; Duration 0540

Standard Port RIVER FOYLE (⟵)

Times				Height (metres)			
High Water		Low Water		MHWS	MHWN	MLWN	MLWS
0100	0800	0200	0700	2·6	1·9	0·9	0·4
1300	2000	1400	1900				
Differences COLERAINE							
–0004	–0106	–0109	–0005	–0·4	–0·1	0·0	0·0

SHELTER Good, once inside the river ent (The Barmouth) between 2 training walls, extending 2ca N from the beaches. Do not try to enter in strong onshore winds or when swell breaks on the pierheads. If in doubt call Coleraine Hbr Radio or ring HM at Harbour Marina in town centre. ⚓ upstream of old CG stn, or berth at Seaton's, Coleraine or Town Centre marinas, 3½M, 4½M and 5M from ent, on NE bank. The last has berths on both banks between the railway and Millennium bridges.

NAVIGATION WPT 55°11′·00N, 06°46′·65W, 165°/0·72M to ent. Appr from E of N to bring ldg lts into line at bkwtr ends. The sand bar is constantly moving but ent is dredged to approx 3·5m. Beware commercial traffic, which runs up to Coleraine Harbour (town centre). This facility is accessed via the lifting railway bridge. Contact HM to arrange opening prior to arrival.

LIGHTS AND MARKS Ldg lts 165°, both Oc 5s 6/14m 2M, front on W pyramidal metal tr; rear W □ tr. Portstewart Pt, Oc R 10s, is 2M ENE.

COMMUNICATIONS (Code 028) CGOC 91463933; Police 101; Ⓗ 70344177; Dr 70344831; HM 70342012; Rly Bridge 70325400.

Coleraine Hbr Radio and Town Centre Marina Ch 12 (Mon-Fri: HO and when vessel due); Coleraine Marina Ch M.

FACILITIES **Coleraine Hbr (town centre)** ☎70342012, slip, E Bank 10 ⚓Ⓥ, W Bank 7 ⚓Ⓥ, £20; water, fuel, ⛉(35t) WC, showers.

Coleraine Marina ☎70344768, slip, 90+5Ⓥ £21, fuel(H24) ⛉(12½t).

Seatons Marina ☎07718 883099, slip(£3) ⛉(12t).

Coleraine YC ☎70344503, 🍴 ⛉.

Town ☎ ☎ fuel ✕ Ⓔ Ⓐ ✉ Ⓑ 🛒 ✕ ⇌ ✈ (Belfast).

MINOR HARBOUR TO THE EAST

Portstewart, Antrim, **55°11′·21N 06°43′·21W**. AC 2494, 5612. Tides as for Portrush. A tiny hbr 1·1ca S of Portstewart Pt lt, Oc R 10s 21m 5M, vis 040°–220°, obscd in final appr. A temp, fair weather berth (£10) at S end of inner basin in 0·8–1·7m; the very narrow ent is open to SW wind and swell. Visitors should obtain fuel at Portrush before proceeding to Portstewart. Beware rocks close to S bkwtr. Facilities: slip, water, fuel, 🛒 ✕ ⛉ @ at library.

9.13.14 PORTRUSH

Antrim **55°12′·34N 06°39′·49W** ❁❁◊◊✿✿✿

CHARTS AC 2798, 2494, 5612; Imray C53, C64

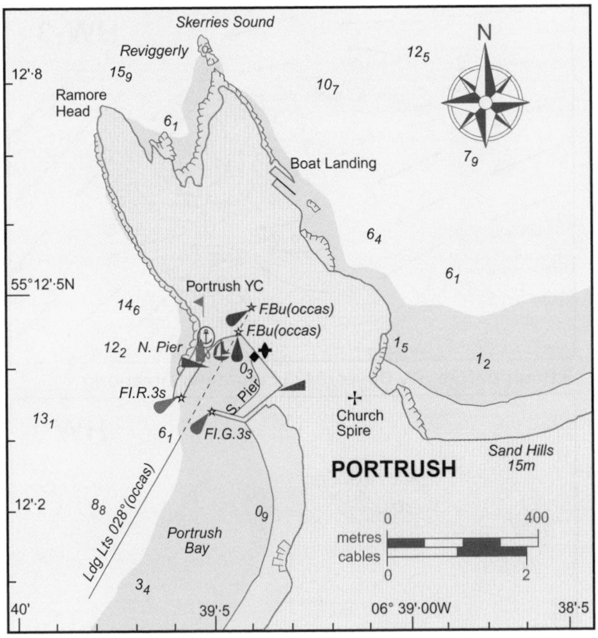

TIDES –0400 Dover; ML 1·1; Duration 0610

Standard Port RIVER FOYLE (⟵)

Times				Height (metres)			
High Water		Low Water		MHWS	MHWN	MLWN	MLWS
0100	0800	0200	0700	2·6	1·9	0·9	0·4
1300	2000	1400	1900				
Differences PORTRUSH							
–0046	–0052	–0117	–0057	–0·5	–0·3	+0·1	+0·1

SHELTER Good in hbr, except in strong NW/N winds. Berth on N pier or on pontoon at NE end of it and see HM. A ⚓ may be available, but very congested in season. ⚓ on E side of Ramore Hd in Skerries Roads 1ca S of Large Skerrie gives good shelter in most conditions, but open to NW sea/swell.

NAVIGATION WPT 55°13′·00N 06°41′·00W, 128° to N pier lt, 1·1M.

Ent with onshore winds >F 4 is difficult. Beware submerged bkwtr projecting 20m SW from N pier. Depth is 2·8m in hbr entrance.

LIGHTS AND MARKS Ldg lts 028° (occas, for LB use) both FR 6/8m 1M; R △ on metal bn and metal mast. N pier Fl R 3s 6m 3M; vis 220°-160°. S pier Fl G 3s 6m 3M; vis 220°-100°.

COMMUNICATIONS (Code 028) CGOC 9146 3933; Police 101; Dr 7082 3767; Ⓗ 7034 4177. HM 7082 2307.

VHF Ch 12 16 (0900-1700LT, Mon-Fri; extended evening hrs June-Sept; Sat-Sun: 0900–1700, June-Sept only).

FACILITIES Hbr (£3) £14, (0900-1800) Ⓔ; Portrush YC ☎7082 3932; **Town** Ⓑ @ Library ⇄ ✈ (Belfast). Giant's Causeway is 10M ENE.

FAIR HEAD TO LAMBAY ISLAND

(AC 2199/8, 2093, 44) Fair Hd is a bold 190m headland, steep-to all round, but with extensive overfalls in Rathlin Sound. The coast is fairly steep-to except in larger bays, particularly Dundalk.

▶*Streams in North Channel can reach more than 4½kn. S of Belfast Lough they are weaker, but run up to 2·5kn S of Rockabill.*◀

⚓ in offshore winds in Cushendun Bay, 5M NNW of Garron Pt, and in Red Bay 4M further S. They provide useful ⚓s on passage to/from the Clyde or Western Is. Glenarm Marina provides good shelter for small craft and is useful for on passage to the W coasts of Scotland or Ireland. (AC 2198) 4M N of Larne are the Maidens, two dangerous groups of rks extending 2·5M N/S; E Maiden is lit. Hunter Rk (0·8m), S of the Maidens, is marked by N & S cardinals.

N of Belfast Lough, Muck Island is steep-to on its E side, as is Black Hd. Three routes lead into Belfast Lough from the south:

a. E of Mew Is.

▶*Beware Ram Race (N'thly on the ebb and S'thly on the flood).*◀

b. Copeland Sound, between Mew Is and Copeland Is, is passable but not recommended.

▶*Here the stream runs SSE from HW Belfast +0420 and NW from HW Belfast –0115.*◀

c. Donaghadee Sound is buoyed and a good short cut for small craft (see AC 3709).

▶*Here the stream runs SSE from HW Belfast +0530 and NW from HW Belfast –0030, 4·5kn max. An eddy extends S to Ballyferris Pt, and about 1M offshore.*◀

From Belfast Lough to Strangford Lough, the coast has numerous rocky dangers close inshore, but is reasonably clear if keeping about 2M offshore. In fair weather and good vis, there is a passage between North Rocks and South Rock, otherwise pass to the E using South Rock superbuoy as a guide. Pass E of Butter Pladdy and 5ca off Ballyquintin Point.

▶*The tidal cycle is approx 3hrs later than in the N Channel. Flood runs for 6hrs from HW Belfast –0330 (HW Dover –0345), with a maximum rate of 7.5kn at Rue Point. The strong flow flattens the sea in onshore winds and entrance can be made in strong winds. The ebb runs for 6hrs from HW Belfast +0230 (HW Dover +0215), max rate 7.5kn, E of Angus Rk. If entering against ebb use West Channel with care. Smoothest water near Bar Pladdy Buoy when leaving.*◀

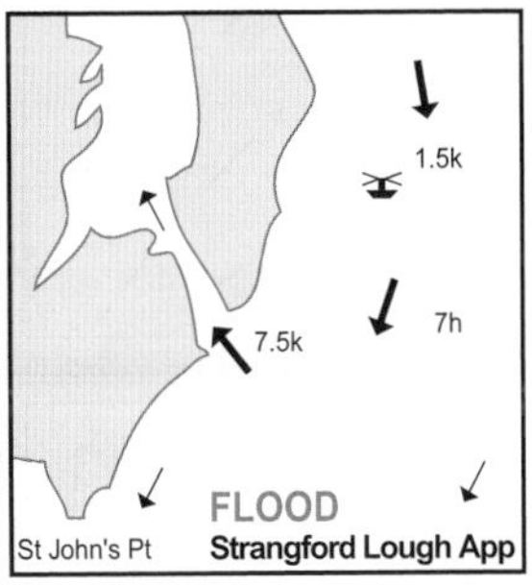

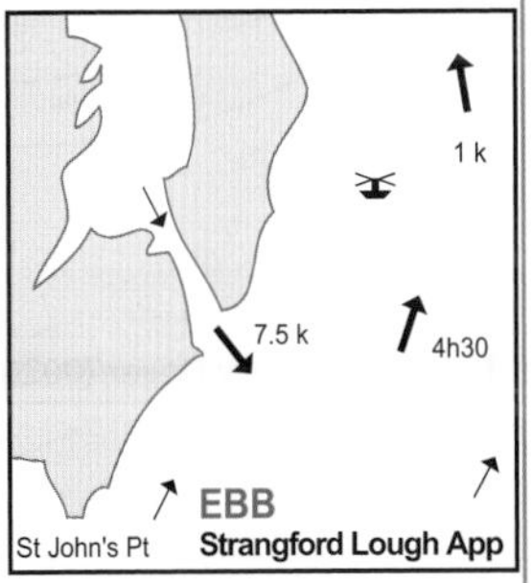

5M SSW of the entrance to Strangford Lough there is a marina at Ardglass.

There are no offshore dangers SW of Strangford to Carlingford Lough. Skerries Islands (Colt, Shenick's and St Patrick's) are 1M E and SE of Red Island, to E of Skerries hbr. Shenick's Island is connected to shore at LW. Pass between Colt and St Patrick's Islands, but the latter has offliers 3ca to S. Rockabill, two steep-to rks with lt ho, is 2·5M E of St Patrick's Island. Lambay Island is private, and steep-to except on W side, where there can be overfalls.

9.13.15 TIDAL STREAMS AROUND RATHLIN ISLAND

North Ireland 9.13.3
North Irish Sea 9.10.3
Off Mull of Kintyre 9.9.11
SW Scotland 9.9.3
South Ireland 9.12.3

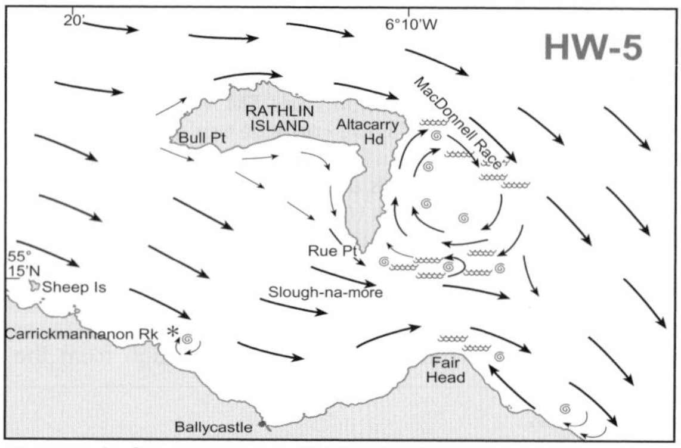

5 Hours before HW Dover (0605 after HW Greenock)

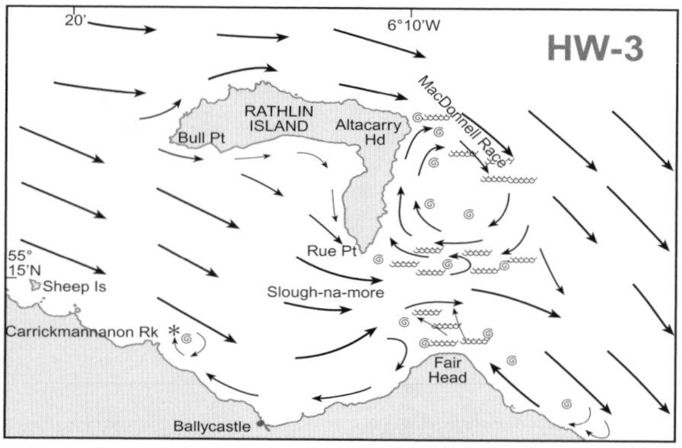

3 Hours before HW Dover (0420 before HW Greenock)

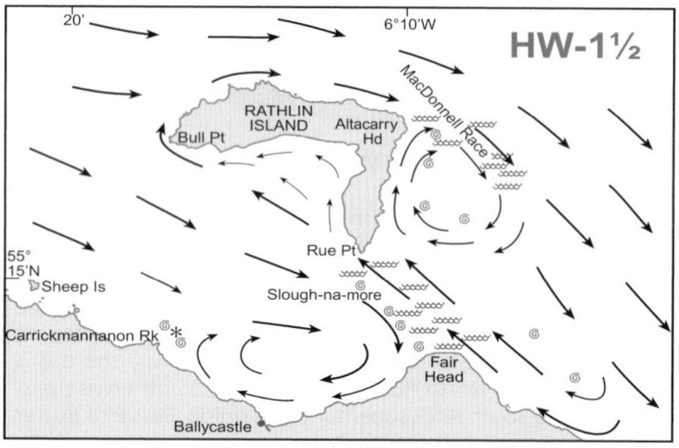

1½ Hours before HW Dover (0250 before HW Greenock)

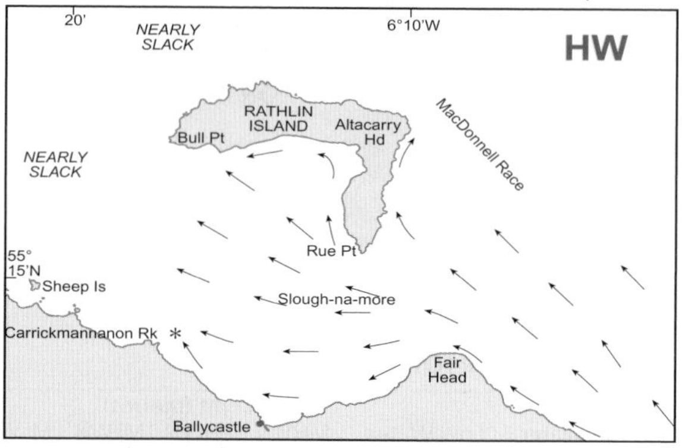

HW Dover (0120 before HW Greenock)

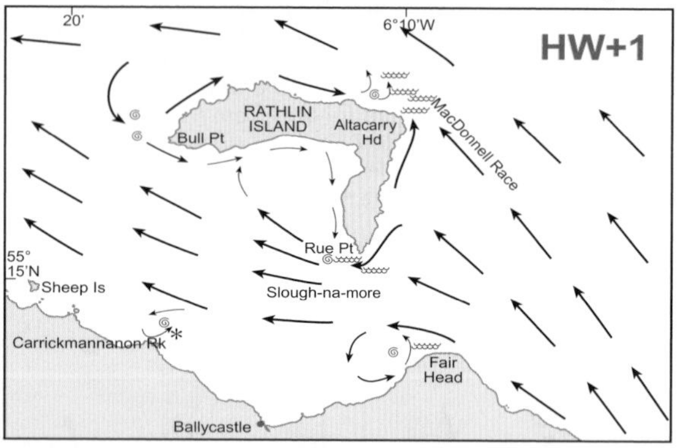

1 Hour after HW Dover (0020 before HW Greenock)

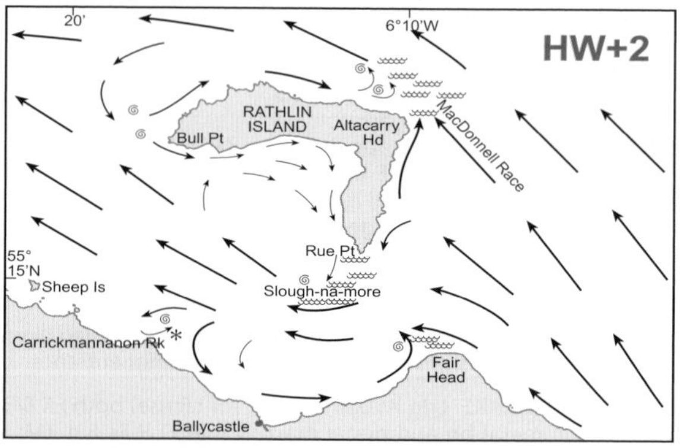

2 Hours after HW Dover (0040 after HW Greenock)

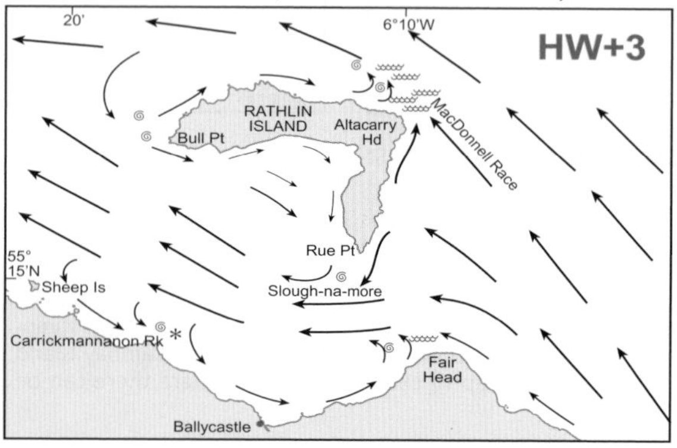

3 Hours after HW Dover (0140 after HW Greenock)

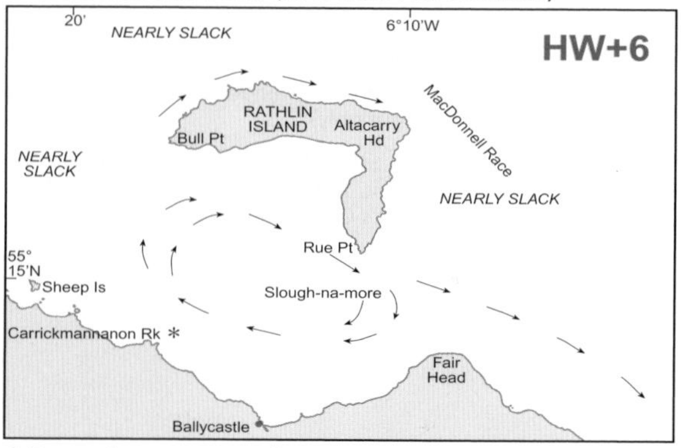

6 Hours after HW Dover (0440 after HW Greenock)

HARBOURS & ANCHORAGES BETWEEN PORTRUSH & LARNE

RATHLIN ISLAND, Antrim, **55°17'·47N 06°11'·78W**. AC 2798, 2494, 5612. HW sp –0445, nps –0200 on Dover. Small harbour in NE corner of Church Bay, sheltered from winds NW through E to SSE. Ferries run from the the Inner Harbour to Ballycastle. Beware sp streams up to 6kn in Rathlin Sound (9.13.15) and the North Channel TSS, just 2M NE of the island. Pass N or E of a wreck 6ca SW of hbr, marked on its SE side by a SCM lt buoy. When clear, appr on NNE to the W and S piers which form an outer hbr. The white sector of Manor House lt, Oc WRG 4s, leads 024·5° to Inner Harbour (2m) ent via channel dredged to 3·5m (2013). on yacht pontoons just S of Inner Harbour. ⚓ in outer hbr on NW side in about 1.2m clear of ferry ramp. Outside hbr, close to W pier ⚓ possible in about 5m, but holding poor in rock/weed. Facilities: Church Bay ✕ ferry to Ballycastle.

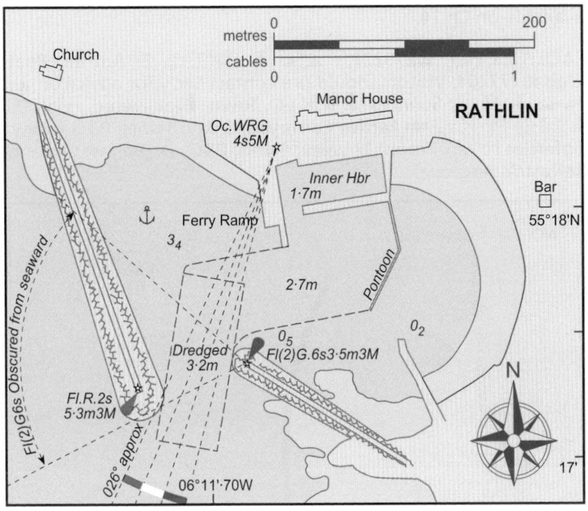

BALLYCASTLE, Antrim, **55°12'·47N 06°14'·27W**. AC 2798, 2494, 5612. Tides as for Rathlin Is; ML 0·8m; –0320 on Dover. Ferries to Rathlin Island berth inside the N breakwater; Ro-Ro disused. The marina is in the S part of the harbour with 2·3m. Outside the harbour is a fair weather ⚓ clear of strong tidal streams, but liable to sudden swell and exposed to onshore winds. Lights: see chartlet and 9.13.4. CG ☎20762226; Ⓗ 20762666. **Marina** ☎(028) 20768525, mob 07803 505084 74 £2·10, short stay £4/hr. **Town** Ⓑ ✕.

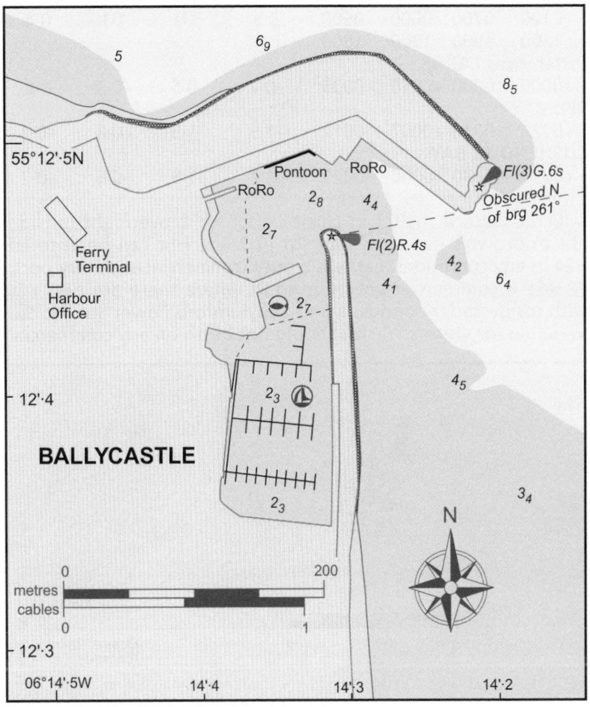

RED BAY, Antrim, **55°03´·91N 06°03´·13W**. AC 2199, 5612. HW +0010 on Dover; ML 1·1m; Duration 0625. See 9.13.16. Good holding, but open to E winds. Beware rocks, 2 ruined piers W of Garron Pt and on S side of bay, approx ½M from shore, fish farms, marked by lit buoys. Glenariff pier is lit Fl 3s 10m 5M. In S and E winds ⚓ 2ca off W stone arch near head of bay in approx 3·5m; in N or W winds ⚓ S of small pier in 2–5m, ½M NE of Glenariff (Waterfoot) village. **Waterfoot** ✕.
Cushendall (1M N of pier) ✕.

CARNLOUGH HARBOUR, Antrim, **54°59´·87N 05°59´·20W**. AC 2198, 5612. HW +0006 on Dover, +0005 on Belfast; HW –1·6m on Belfast; ML no data; Duration 0625. Good shelter, except in SE gales; do not enter in fresh/strong onshore winds. Entrance shoaling due to build up of kelp, minimum depth 1m (2004). Ldg marks 310°, Y ▽s on B/W posts. N pier lt, Fl G 3s 4m 5M; S pier Fl R 3s 6m 5M, both lts on B/W columns. Beware fish farms in the bay marked by lt buoys (unreliable); and rocks which cover at HW on either side of ent. Small harbour used by yachts and small FVs; visitors welcome. HM mob 07703 606763.
Quay £1, (see HM) (by arrangement).
Town ✕.

GLENARM, Antrim, **54°58´N 05°57´W**. AC 2198, 2199, 5612. HW +0006 on Dover, +0005 on Belfast; HW –1·6m on Belfast; ML no data; Duration 0625. Good shelter in marina, which reports 3m at LW. Hbr ent lts G.3s 3M and R.3s 3M. Beware fish farm about 0·5M NE of entrance. HM / Marina ☎028 2884 1285, Mob 07703 606763. **Marina** 40 inc 10 Ⓥ in 4-6m, £2.20.
Village .

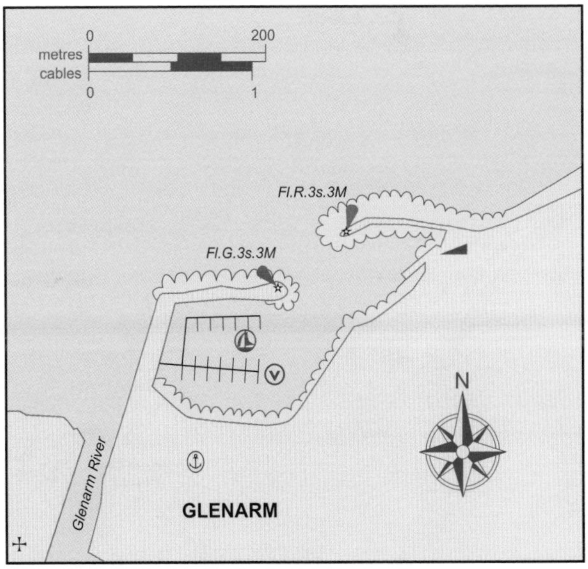

9.13.16 LARNE

Antrim **54°51′·20N 05°47′·50W** ❁❁❁◊◊✿✿

CHARTS AC 2198, 1237, 5612; Imray C62, C64, C69

TIDES +0005 Dover; ML 1·6; Duration 0620

Standard Port BELFAST (⟶)

Times				Height (metres)			
High Water		Low Water		MHWS	MHWN	MLWN	MLWS
0100	0700	0000	0600	3·5	3·0	1·1	0·4
1300	1900	1200	1800				
Differences LARNE							
+0005	0000	+0010	−0005	−0·7	−0·5	−0·3	0·0
RED BAY							
+0022	−0010	+0007	−0017	−1·9	−1·5	−0·8	−0·2
CUSHENDUN BAY							
+0010	−0030	0000	−0025	−1·7	−1·5	−0·6	−0·2

SHELTER Secure shelter in Larne Lough or ⚓ overnight outside hbr in Brown's Bay (E of Barr Pt) in 2-4m. Hbr can be entered H24 in any conditions. Larne is a busy commercial and ferry port; W side is commercial until Curran Pt where there are two YCs with congested moorings. ⚓ S of Ballylumford Power Stn. No moorings available for visitors. Yachts should not berth on any commercial quays, inc Castle Quay, without HM's permission. Boat Hbr (0·6m) 2ca S of Ferris Pt only for shoal draft craft.

NAVIGATION WPT 54°51′·70N 05°47′·47W, 184°/2·1M to front ldg lt. Beware Hunter Rk 2M NE of hbr ent. Magnetic anomalies exist near Hunter Rk and between it and the mainland. Inside the narrow ent, the recommended chan is close to the E shore. Tide in the ent runs at up to 3½kn.

LIGHTS AND MARKS No1 SHM Q G 1½ca off chartlet N edge; Ldg lts 184°, Oc 2.5s 6m / 5s14m 12M, synch and vis 179°-189°; W ◊ with R stripes. Chaine Tr and fairway lts as chartlet. Note: Many shore lts on W side of ent may be mistaken for nav lts.

COMMUNICATIONS (Code 02828) CGOC 9146 3933; Pilot 273785; Dr 275331; Police 101. HM 872100.

VHF Ch **14** 11 16 *Larne Port Control*. Traffic, weather and tidal info available on Ch 14.

FACILITIES **Pier** ☎279221, (33t); **E Antrim Boat Club** ☎277204, Visitors should pre-contact Sec'y for advice on ; ; **Services** . **Town** (delivered, tidal) Ⓑ ⇌ **Ferries** Cairnryan; 8/day; 1¾hrs; P&O (www.poferries.co.uk). Troon; 17/week; 1¾hrs; P&O. ✈ (Belfast City and Belfast/Aldergrove).

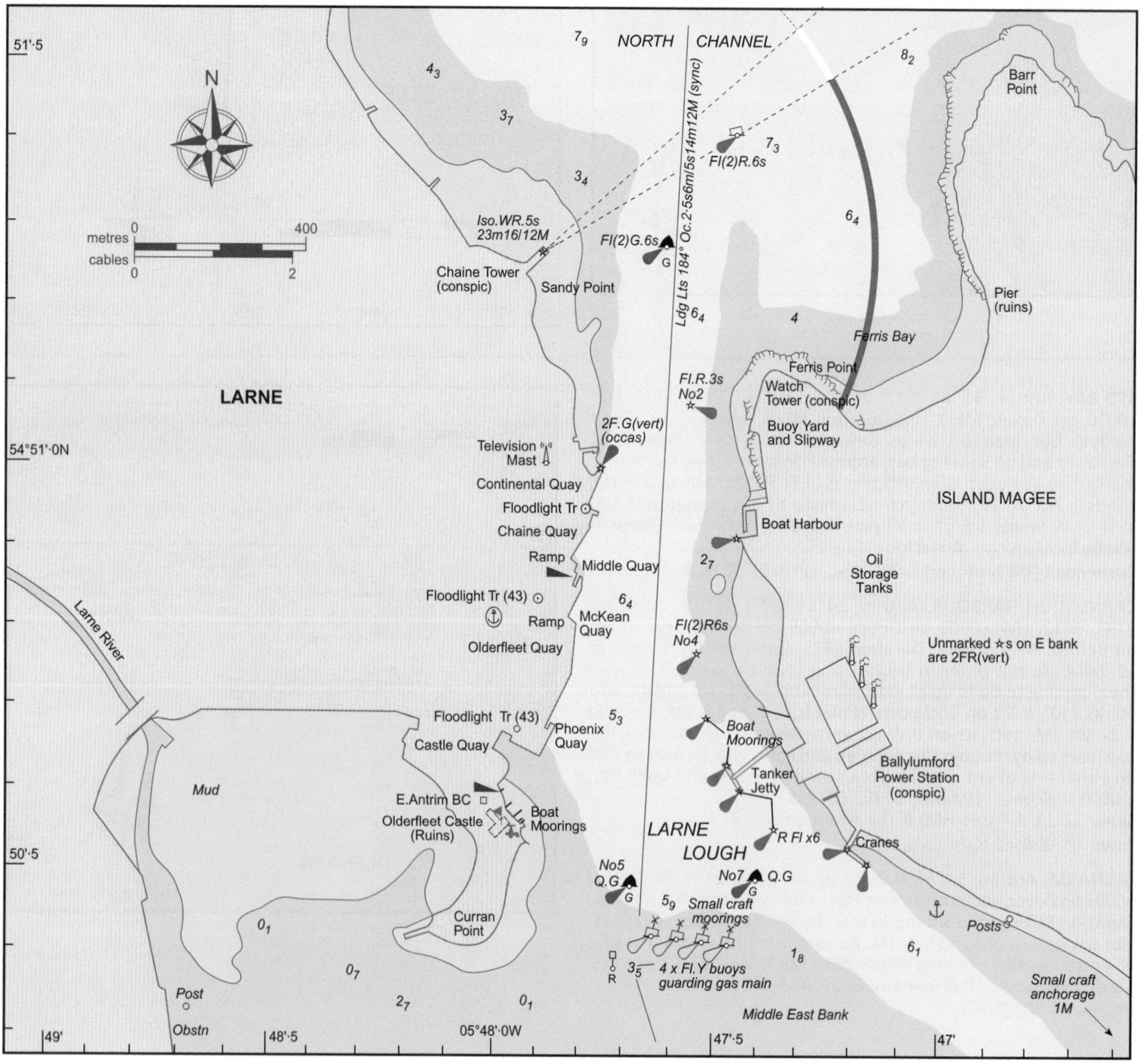

9.13.17 BELFAST LOUGH

County Down and County Antrim **54°42'N 05°45'W**
Bangor ✵✵✵◊◊◊✿✿; Carrickfergus ✵✵✵◊◊◊✿✿

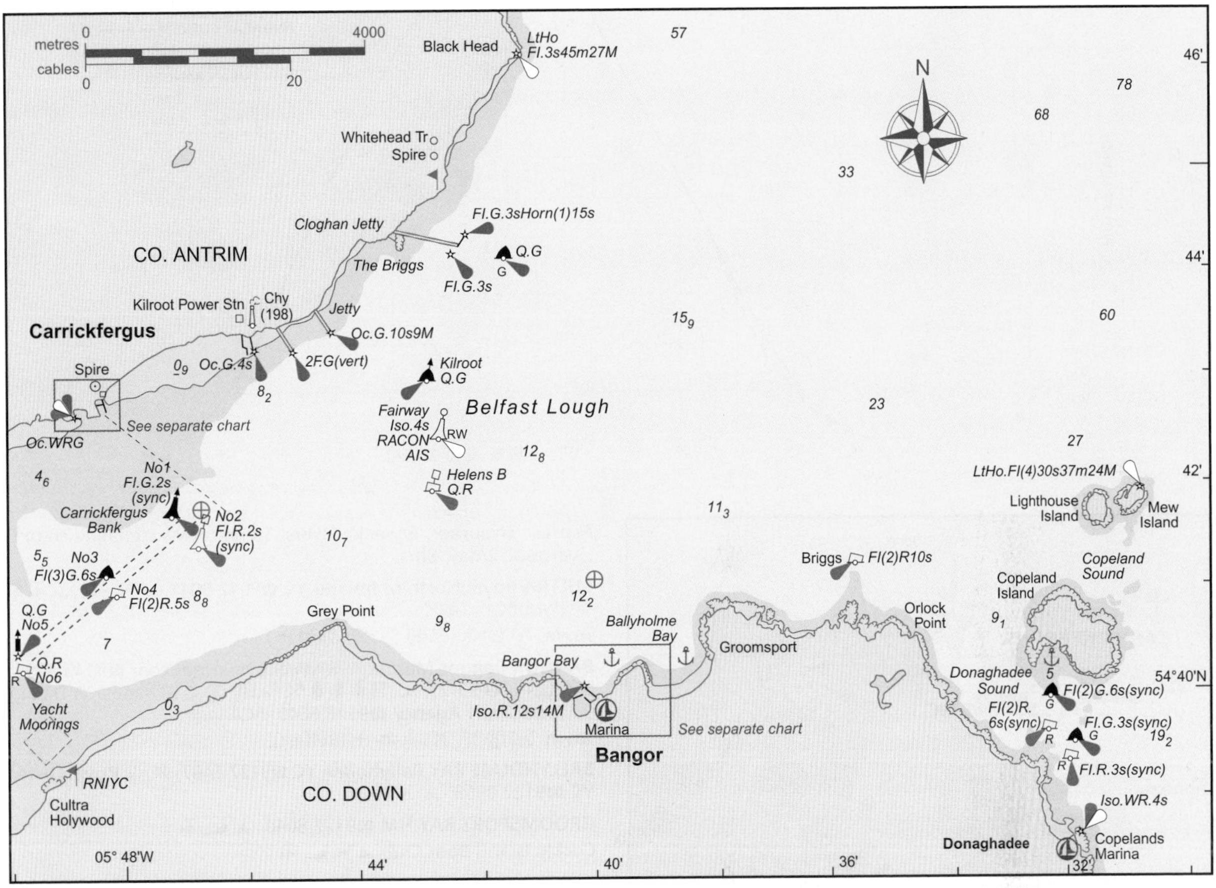

CHARTS AC 2198, 1753, 1752, 5612; Imray C62, C64, C69

TIDES +0007 Dover; ML Belfast 2·0, Carrickfergus 1·8; Duration 0620

Standard Port BELFAST (⟶)

Times				Height (metres)			
High Water		Low Water		MHWS	MHWN	MLWN	MLWS
0100	0700	0000	0600	3·5	3·0	1·1	0·4
1300	1900	1200	1800				
Differences CARRICKFERGUS							
+0005	+0005	+0005	+0005	−0·3	−0·3	−0·2	−0·1
DONAGHADEE							
+0020	+0020	+0023	+0023	+0·5	+0·4	0·0	+0·1

SHELTER Main sailing centres, clockwise around Belfast Lough, are at Bangor, Cultra and Carrickfergus.

Donaghadee: small marina at SE ent to the Lough.

Ballyholme Bay: good ⚓ in offshore winds.

Bangor: exposed to N winds, but well sheltered in marina (depths 2·9m to 2·2m). Speed limits: 4kn in marina, 8kn between Luke's Pt and Wilson's Pt.

Cultra: in offshore winds good ⚓ & moorings off RNoIYC.

Belfast Harbour is a major commercial port, but there are 40 ⌓ in Abercorn Basin, just NE of Lagan Bridge, in the River Lagan.

Carrickfergus: very good in marina, depths 1·8m to 2·3m (2015). The former commercial hbr has 10 yacht berths on the W quay. A stub bkwtr, marked by 2 PHM bns, extends NNE into the hbr from the W pier. The ent and SW part of the hbr are dredged 2·9m (2015); the NE part of the hbr dries 0·7m. Good ⚓ SSE of Carrickfergus Pier, except in E winds.

NAVIGATION Belfast Fairway SWM buoy, 54°42'·32N 05°42'·30W, Traffic passes inbound to N between SWM and Kilroot SHM, outbound between SWM and Helens Bay PHM. The Lough is well marked. WPT Carrickfergus 54°41'·71N 05°46'·16W, marks start of the buoyed chan to Belfast Hbr. It bears 121°/301° from/to Carrickfergus Marina, 1.7M. Carrickfergus Bk liable to shift. Deep draught yachts should not enter/leave before LW±2. Beware HSS ferry operation. WPT Bangor 54°41'·00N 05°40'·00W, 190°/1M to bkwtr lt. Rounding Orlock Pt beware Briggs Rks extending ¾M offshore.

LIGHTS AND MARKS Chan to Belfast Hbr is well marked/lit by buoys and bns. Beyond No 12 PHM bn it is dangerous to leave the chan. Carrickfergus is easily recognised by conspic castle to E of Marina. On Marina Bkwtr, 30m W of the ☆ QR 7m 3M, is a Dir lt 320°, Oc WRG 3s 5m 3M, (H24).

COMMUNICATIONS (Codes: Belfast 028) CGOC 91463933; ☼ (08494) 22339; Police 101; Dr 91468521. HM Bangor 91453297; HM Belfast 90553012; Belfast VTS 9055 3504. 0845 600 8000.

Bangor Marina Ch **80** M (H24); Bangor HM Ch 11 (H24). Royal N of Ireland YC (at Cultra) Ch **16**; 11 (H24) 80. *Belfast Port Control* (at Milewater Basin) Ch **12** 16 (H24); VTS provides info on request to vessels in port area. The greater part of Belfast Lough is under radar surveillance. Carrickfergus Marina Ch M, 80, M2.

FACILITIES Anti-clockwise around the Lough:

CARRICKFERGUS Marina www.carrickfergus.org/site/marina ☎93366666; entry HW±2; 300 inc Ⓥ £2.50 (2nd night free), short stay (max 6hrs) £1.00 (min charge £7.35) ⚒ ✎ ⛽ Ⓔ. **Carrick SC** ☎351402, ⚓ ⛽ ⌓. **Hbr**: 10⌓ (45t).

Town ✉ Ⓑ ✕ ⇌ ✈ (Belfast).

BELFAST Abercorn Basin www.belfast-harbour.co.uk 40⌓ £16.80 inc ⏻; short stay (5hrs) £8; ⛽ ⏻ WC.

City all facilities, ⇌ ✈.

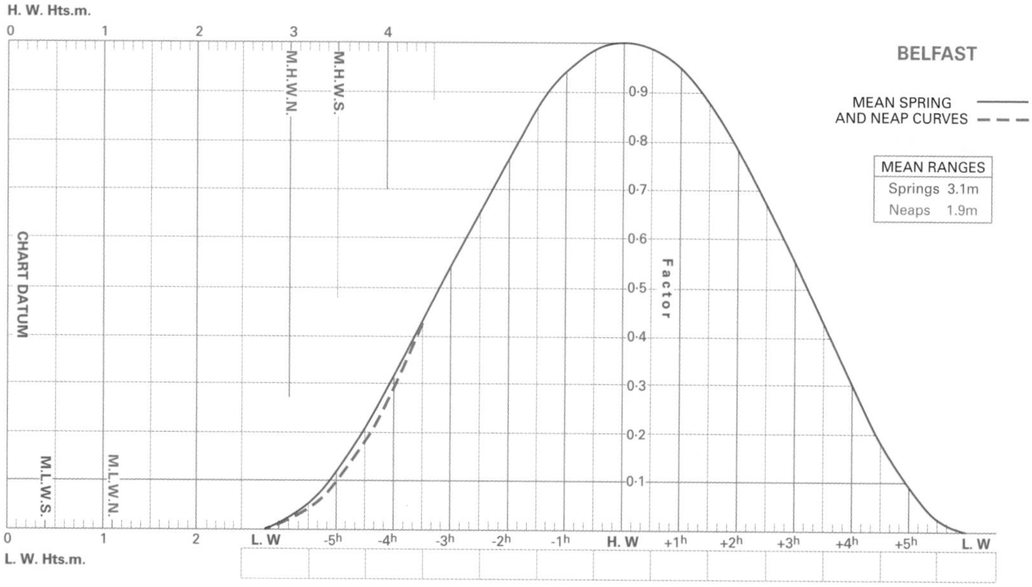

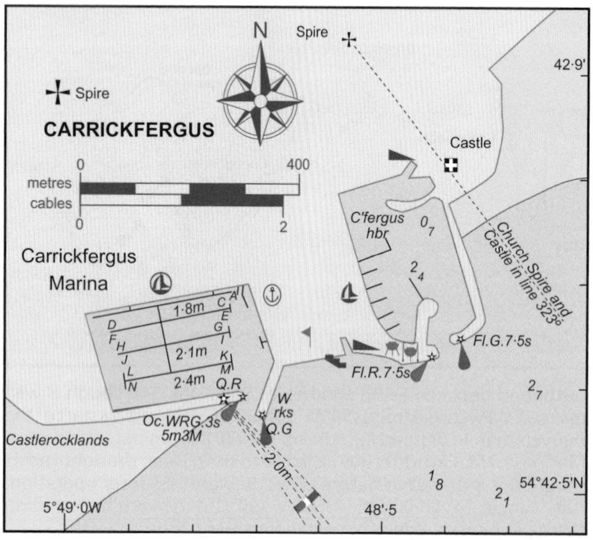

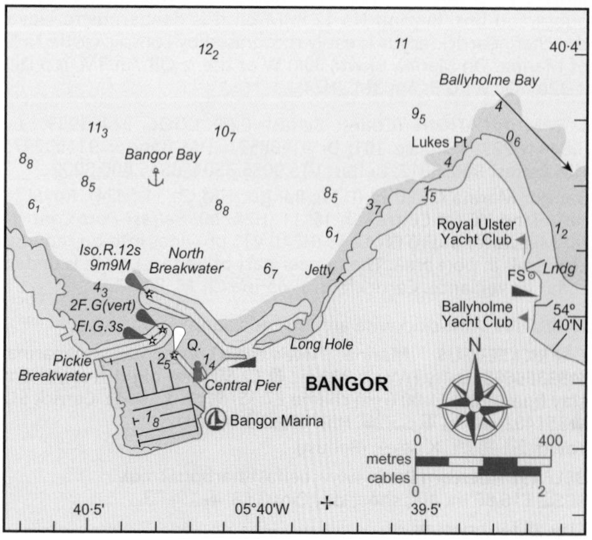

Ferries Stranraer; 6/week; 2½hrs; Stena (www.stenaline.co.uk). Liverpool; 2/day; 8hrs.

CULTRA Royal North of Ireland YC ☎9042 8041, (½M).

Town

BANGOR Bangor Marina www.quaymarinas.com ☎9145 3297, 550+40 £3·25, (40t) Diving. **Todd Chart Agency** ☎9146 6640, ACA.

Town (Belfast).

BALLYHOLME BAY Ballyholme YC ☎9127 1467; **Royal Ulster YC** ☎9127 0568.

GROOMSPORT BAY HM ☎9127 8040.

Cockle Island Boat Club

HARBOURS BETWEEN BELFAST AND STRANGFORD LOUGHS

DONAGHADEE, Down, **54°38′·71N 05°31′·85W**. AC 1753, 5612. HW +0025 on Dover; see 9.13.17; ML no data; Duration 0615. Excellent shelter and basic facilities in tiny marina, access HW±4 over sill; covers approx 1·1m at half tide. Appr on about 275° on ldg marks, orange △s to tricky ent with sharp 90° port turn into marina (pilots available). Appr in strong winds or at night not advised. 3ca to the N, the Old Hbr is small and very full; scend often sets in. Beware rocky reef with less than 2m extends 1·5ca ENE from S pier hd. Max depth in hbr is approx 2·5m, dries at SW end; best berth alongside SE quay. S pier lt, Iso WR 4s 17m 18/14M, W shore–326°, R326°–shore. HM ☎9188 2377. Police 101. Facilities: **Copelands Marina** ☎9188 2184, mob 07802 363382; VHF Ch **16** 11 80; for 6 (20t). **Old Hbr** £4. **Town** (Bangor), (Belfast).

PORTAVOGIE, Down, **54°27′·45N 05°26′·08W**. AC 2156, 5612. HW +0016 on Dover; ML 2·6m; Duration 0620. See 9.13.18. Good shelter, but hbr so full of FVs as to risk damage; best only for overnight or emergency. Entrance dangerous in strong onshore winds. Beware Plough Rks to SE marked by PHM buoy, Fl (2) R 10s, and McCammon Rks to NE of ent. Keep in W sector of outer bkwtr lt, Iso WRG 5s 9m 9M, shore-G-258°-W-275°-R-348°. Inner bkwtr 2 FG (vert) 6m 4M. Monitor VHF Ch **14** on entry/exit. (Mon-Fri: 0900-1700LT). HM ☎(028) 4277 1470. Facilities: (on central quay). **Town**

STANDARD TIME (UT)
For Summer Time add ONE hour in **non-shaded areas**

BELFAST LAT 54°36′N LONG 5°55′W

TIMES AND HEIGHTS OF HIGH AND LOW WATERS

Dates in red are SPRINGS
Dates in blue are NEAPS

YEAR **2018**

JANUARY

Day	Time	m	Time	m	Time	m	Time	m
1 M	0348	0.5	1004	3.7	1611	0.5	2229	3.6
2 TU	0435	0.5	1054	3.8	1659	0.4	○ 2321	3.6
3 W	0523	0.5	1144	3.9	1747	0.3		
4 TH	0014	3.6	0611	0.5	1235	3.9	1836	0.3
5 F	0108	3.5	0701	0.6	1326	3.9	1926	0.3
6 SA	0202	3.4	0752	0.7	1417	3.8	2018	0.4
7 SU	0256	3.3	0846	0.8	1508	3.7	2113	0.5
8 M	0350	3.2	0942	0.9	1600	3.6	◑ 2212	0.6
9 TU	0447	3.1	1044	1.0	1655	3.4	2317	0.8
10 W	0549	3.0	1150	1.1	1757	3.3		
11 TH	0022	0.9	0656	3.0	1256	1.1	1908	3.2
12 F	0124	1.0	0759	3.0	1359	1.1	2014	3.2
13 SA	0218	0.9	0853	3.1	1455	1.0	2109	3.2
14 SU	0305	0.9	0941	3.3	1542	0.9	2156	3.2
15 M	0345	0.9	1022	3.4	1622	0.8	2237	3.3
16 TU	0422	0.8	1100	3.5	1656	0.7	2315	3.3
17 W	0458	0.8	1135	3.5	1730	0.7	● 2350	3.3
18 TH	0533	0.7	1207	3.5	1805	0.6		
19 F	0021	3.2	0609	0.7	1232	3.5	1839	0.6
20 SA	0049	3.2	0645	0.7	1258	3.5	1915	0.6
21 SU	0121	3.2	0723	0.7	1332	3.5	1952	0.6
22 M	0201	3.2	0802	0.7	1413	3.5	2032	0.6
23 TU	0245	3.2	0845	0.8	1457	3.4	2116	0.6
24 W	0334	3.1	0932	0.8	1546	3.3	◐ 2208	0.7
25 TH	0431	3.0	1027	0.9	1645	3.2	2310	0.8
26 F	0535	3.0	1132	1.0	1755	3.1		
27 SA	0028	0.9	0644	3.0	1254	1.0	1911	3.1
28 SU	0145	0.8	0752	3.2	1411	0.8	2023	3.2
29 M	0246	0.7	0855	3.3	1511	0.6	2126	3.3
30 TU	0339	0.5	0951	3.5	1604	0.4	2221	3.4
31 W	0427	0.5	1042	3.7	1653	0.3	○ 2313	3.5

FEBRUARY

Day	Time	m	Time	m	Time	m	Time	m
1 TH	0514	0.4	1132	3.8	1739	0.2		
2 F	0002	3.5	0600	0.4	1220	3.9	1824	0.2
3 SA	0052	3.4	0646	0.5	1308	3.8	1909	0.2
4 SU	0140	3.3	0731	0.5	1355	3.8	1954	0.3
5 M	0228	3.3	0817	0.6	1442	3.7	2040	0.4
6 TU	0314	3.2	0905	0.7	1528	3.6	2129	0.6
7 W	0401	3.1	0958	0.8	1617	3.4	◑ 2225	0.8
8 TH	0450	3.0	1105	1.0	1709	3.2	2335	1.0
9 F	0548	2.9	1217	1.1	1811	3.0		
10 SA	0044	1.1	0705	2.9	1323	1.1	1933	2.9
11 SU	0144	1.1	0823	3.0	1423	1.0	2045	3.0
12 M	0237	1.0	0917	3.1	1516	0.8	2136	3.1
13 TU	0322	0.9	1001	3.2	1558	0.7	2219	3.1
14 W	0401	0.8	1040	3.3	1634	0.6	2257	3.2
15 TH	0438	0.7	1116	3.4	1708	0.5	● 2331	3.2
16 F	0513	0.6	1146	3.4	1742	0.5		
17 SA	0001	3.2	0548	0.6	1205	3.4	1816	0.4
18 SU	0021	3.2	0624	0.5	1229	3.5	1851	0.4
19 M	0052	3.2	0659	0.5	1305	3.5	1926	0.4
20 TU	0131	3.2	0736	0.5	1347	3.5	2004	0.4
21 W	0214	3.2	0816	0.5	1431	3.4	2047	0.5
22 TH	0302	3.2	0902	0.6	1521	3.3	2136	0.6
23 F	0356	3.1	0956	0.7	1619	3.2	◐ 2236	0.8
24 SA	0500	3.0	1101	0.9	1731	3.0	2359	0.9
25 SU	0614	3.0	1234	0.9	1853	3.0		
26 M	0130	0.9	0731	3.0	1400	0.8	2015	3.0
27 TU	0235	0.7	0842	3.2	1502	0.5	2121	3.2
28 W	0330	0.6	0940	3.4	1555	0.3	2214	3.3

MARCH

Day	Time	m	Time	m	Time	m	Time	m
1 TH	0419	0.4	1030	3.6	1643	0.2	2302	3.4
2 F	0504	0.4	1117	3.7	1726	0.1	○ 2347	3.4
3 SA	0547	0.4	1202	3.8	1807	0.1		
4 SU	0031	3.3	0627	0.4	1247	3.7	1846	0.2
5 M	0115	3.3	0706	0.4	1331	3.7	1925	0.3
6 TU	0157	3.2	0746	0.5	1414	3.6	2004	0.4
7 W	0238	3.2	0827	0.6	1457	3.5	2046	0.6
8 TH	0320	3.1	0912	0.7	1543	3.3	2132	0.8
9 F	0405	3.0	1009	0.9	1632	3.1	◑ 2230	1.0
10 SA	0457	2.9	1133	1.0	1728	2.9	2357	1.2
11 SU	0557	2.8	1246	1.0	1835	2.8		
12 M	0107	1.2	0720	2.8	1349	1.0	2013	2.8
13 TU	0206	1.1	0846	2.9	1444	0.8	2111	2.9
14 W	0255	0.9	0934	3.1	1529	0.6	2154	3.0
15 TH	0337	0.7	1012	3.2	1607	0.5	2231	3.1
16 F	0414	0.6	1046	3.3	1642	0.4	2304	3.2
17 SA	0450	0.5	1114	3.3	1716	0.3	● 2330	3.2
18 SU	0524	0.5	1131	3.4	1750	0.3	2351	3.3
19 M	0559	0.4	1200	3.4	1825	0.3		
20 TU	0024	3.3	0634	0.4	1240	3.5	1900	0.3
21 W	0105	3.3	0711	0.4	1323	3.5	1939	0.4
22 TH	0149	3.3	0753	0.4	1411	3.4	2023	0.5
23 F	0238	3.3	0840	0.5	1504	3.3	2114	0.7
24 SA	0332	3.2	0935	0.6	1606	3.1	◐ 2216	0.9
25 SU	0437	3.0	1045	0.8	1720	2.9	2344	1.0
26 M	0553	3.0	1226	0.8	1848	2.9		
27 TU	0115	0.9	0717	3.0	1348	0.7	2011	3.0
28 W	0222	0.8	0830	3.2	1450	0.4	2112	3.1
29 TH	0318	0.6	0926	3.4	1542	0.3	2202	3.3
30 F	0407	0.5	1015	3.6	1627	0.2	2246	3.3
31 SA	0450	0.4	1059	3.6	1708	0.2	○ 2328	3.3

APRIL

Day	Time	m	Time	m	Time	m	Time	m
1 SU	0530	0.4	1142	3.6	1745	0.2		
2 M	0009	3.3	0606	0.4	1224	3.6	1820	0.3
3 TU	0048	3.3	0642	0.4	1304	3.5	1855	0.4
4 W	0126	3.3	0718	0.5	1345	3.5	1931	0.5
5 TH	0204	3.3	0756	0.5	1427	3.3	2010	0.7
6 F	0244	3.2	0837	0.7	1511	3.2	2052	0.8
7 SA	0328	3.1	0926	0.8	1559	3.0	2142	1.0
8 SU	0417	3.0	1036	1.0	1653	2.8	◑ 2250	1.2
9 M	0514	2.9	1207	1.0	1755	2.7		
10 TU	0024	1.2	0618	2.8	1313	0.9	1909	2.7
11 W	0129	1.1	0739	2.8	1408	0.8	2029	2.9
12 TH	0223	1.0	0849	3.0	1455	0.6	2117	3.0
13 F	0307	0.8	0931	3.1	1535	0.5	2154	3.1
14 SA	0346	0.7	1006	3.3	1612	0.3	2227	3.2
15 SU	0422	0.5	1034	3.3	1646	0.3	2256	3.3
16 M	0457	0.4	1101	3.4	1721	0.3	● 2325	3.4
17 TU	0533	0.4	1136	3.5	1757	0.3		
18 W	0001	3.4	0610	0.3	1218	3.5	1836	0.3
19 TH	0044	3.5	0651	0.3	1306	3.5	1919	0.4
20 F	0131	3.5	0736	0.3	1358	3.4	2007	0.5
21 SA	0222	3.4	0827	0.4	1456	3.2	2102	0.7
22 SU	0319	3.3	0926	0.6	1603	3.1	◐ 2208	0.9
23 M	0423	3.2	1041	0.7	1719	2.9	2332	1.0
24 TU	0539	3.1	1213	0.7	1845	2.9		
25 W	0055	1.0	0701	3.1	1331	0.6	1957	3.0
26 TH	0204	0.8	0811	3.3	1433	0.4	2054	3.1
27 F	0301	0.7	0906	3.4	1524	0.3	2142	3.2
28 SA	0350	0.6	0955	3.5	1606	0.3	2226	3.3
29 SU	0432	0.5	1039	3.6	1644	0.3	2307	3.3
30 M	0510	0.5	1120	3.5	1719	0.4	○ 2346	3.3

Chart Datum: 2·01 metres below Ordnance Datum (Belfast). HAT is 3·9 metres above Chart Datum.

N Ireland

STANDARD TIME (UT)
For Summer Time add ONE hour in **non-shaded areas**

BELFAST LAT 54°36′N LONG 5°55′W

TIMES AND HEIGHTS OF HIGH AND LOW WATERS

Dates in red are SPRINGS
Dates in blue are NEAPS

YEAR **2018**

MAY

Day	Time	m	Time	m	Time	m	Time	m
1 TU	0546	0.5	1159	3.5	1754	0.5		
2 W	0021	3.3	0621	0.5	1238	3.4	1828	0.6
3 TH	0056	3.3	0655	0.5	1317	3.3	1903	0.7
4 F	0133	3.4	0731	0.6	1358	3.3	1941	0.8
5 SA	0213	3.3	0810	0.7	1442	3.2	2022	0.9
6 SU	0255	3.3	0855	0.8	1530	3.0	2109	1.0
7 M	0342	3.1	0950	0.9	1622	2.9	2205	1.1
8 TU	0434	3.0	1109	1.0	1720	2.8	◑ 2317	1.2
9 W	0534	2.9	1228	0.9	1824	2.8		
10 TH	0039	1.2	0639	2.9	1328	0.8	1928	2.9
11 F	0140	1.1	0745	3.0	1417	0.6	2025	3.0
12 SA	0230	0.9	0839	3.1	1500	0.5	2110	3.2
13 SU	0313	0.7	0922	3.3	1538	0.4	2148	3.3
14 M	0352	0.6	0959	3.4	1615	0.3	2225	3.4
15 TU	0430	0.5	1037	3.5	1653	0.3	● 2302	3.5
16 W	0509	0.4	1118	3.5	1733	0.3	2344	3.6
17 TH	0551	0.3	1204	3.5	1817	0.4		
18 F	0030	3.6	0636	0.3	1257	3.5	1904	0.5
19 SA	0121	3.6	0725	0.3	1354	3.4	1956	0.6
20 SU	0215	3.5	0820	0.4	1456	3.2	2054	0.8
21 M	0312	3.5	0921	0.5	1602	3.1	2200	0.9
22 TU	0413	3.4	1033	0.6	1714	3.0	◐ 2313	1.0
23 W	0523	3.3	1151	0.6	1828	3.0		
24 TH	0027	1.0	0638	3.2	1305	0.5	1933	3.0
25 F	0135	0.9	0746	3.3	1407	0.5	2029	3.1
26 SA	0236	0.8	0842	3.4	1458	0.5	2119	3.2
27 SU	0327	0.7	0932	3.4	1541	0.5	2204	3.3
28 M	0412	0.6	1018	3.4	1619	0.5	2245	3.3
29 TU	0451	0.6	1059	3.4	1655	0.6	○ 2323	3.3
30 W	0527	0.6	1137	3.4	1730	0.7	2358	3.4
31 TH	0602	0.6	1213	3.3	1805	0.7		

JUNE

Day	Time	m	Time	m	Time	m	Time	m
1 F	0031	3.4	0636	0.6	1250	3.3	1839	0.8
2 SA	0107	3.4	0711	0.6	1330	3.2	1916	0.8
3 SU	0145	3.4	0748	0.7	1414	3.1	1957	0.9
4 M	0225	3.4	0829	0.7	1500	3.1	2042	0.9
5 TU	0306	3.3	0916	0.8	1550	3.0	2131	1.0
6 W	0351	3.2	1011	0.9	1645	2.9	◑ 2227	1.1
7 TH	0444	3.0	1117	0.9	1743	2.9	2330	1.1
8 F	0546	3.0	1230	0.8	1842	2.9		
9 SA	0038	1.1	0651	3.0	1331	0.7	1937	3.0
10 SU	0142	1.0	0751	3.1	1420	0.6	2028	3.2
11 M	0235	0.8	0843	3.3	1504	0.5	2114	3.3
12 TU	0322	0.6	0931	3.4	1547	0.4	2158	3.5
13 W	0406	0.5	1017	3.5	1629	0.3	● 2242	3.6
14 TH	0451	0.4	1105	3.5	1714	0.4	2330	3.6
15 F	0537	0.3	1156	3.5	1801	0.4		
16 SA	0020	3.7	0625	0.2	1251	3.5	1852	0.5
17 SU	0112	3.7	0716	0.2	1348	3.4	1946	0.6
18 M	0206	3.7	0811	0.3	1448	3.3	2043	0.7
19 TU	0301	3.6	0909	0.4	1550	3.2	2144	0.8
20 W	0357	3.5	1013	0.5	1654	3.1	◐ 2248	0.9
21 TH	0458	3.4	1123	0.6	1759	3.0	2354	0.9
22 F	0606	3.3	1231	0.6	1903	3.0		
23 SA	0101	0.9	0715	3.3	1334	0.6	2001	3.1
24 SU	0204	0.9	0816	3.3	1428	0.7	2053	3.2
25 M	0301	0.8	0909	3.3	1514	0.7	2141	3.2
26 TU	0350	0.7	0957	3.3	1555	0.7	2224	3.3
27 W	0432	0.7	1040	3.3	1632	0.7	2303	3.4
28 TH	0509	0.7	1118	3.3	1708	0.8	○ 2338	3.4
29 F	0544	0.6	1153	3.2	1743	0.8		
30 SA	0011	3.4	0617	0.6	1229	3.2	1818	0.8

JULY

Day	Time	m	Time	m	Time	m	Time	m
1 SU	0044	3.4	0651	0.6	1305	3.2	1854	0.8
2 M	0118	3.4	0725	0.6	1345	3.1	1933	0.8
3 TU	0152	3.4	0803	0.6	1426	3.1	2015	0.8
4 W	0228	3.4	0844	0.7	1511	3.1	2059	0.9
5 TH	0308	3.3	0930	0.7	1601	3.0	2148	0.9
6 F	0355	3.2	1022	0.8	1656	3.0	◑ 2241	1.0
7 SA	0452	3.1	1124	0.8	1754	3.0	2342	1.0
8 SU	0559	3.1	1235	0.8	1853	3.0		
9 M	0051	1.0	0708	3.1	1342	0.7	1949	3.2
10 TU	0201	0.9	0812	3.2	1437	0.6	2043	3.3
11 W	0259	0.7	0909	3.4	1526	0.5	2135	3.5
12 TH	0350	0.5	1002	3.5	1613	0.4	2225	3.6
13 F	0439	0.3	1054	3.5	1700	0.4	● 2316	3.7
14 SA	0527	0.2	1146	3.5	1749	0.5		
15 SU	0007	3.8	0614	0.2	1240	3.4	1838	0.5
16 M	0059	3.8	0704	0.2	1334	3.4	1930	0.6
17 TU	0150	3.8	0755	0.2	1430	3.3	2023	0.6
18 W	0242	3.7	0847	0.3	1525	3.2	2118	0.7
19 TH	0333	3.6	0944	0.4	1621	3.1	◐ 2217	0.8
20 F	0427	3.5	1047	0.6	1720	3.0	2321	0.9
21 SA	0526	3.3	1154	0.7	1823	3.0		
22 SU	0027	1.0	0634	3.1	1259	0.8	1928	3.0
23 M	0132	1.0	0746	3.1	1357	0.9	2026	3.1
24 TU	0234	0.9	0847	3.1	1448	0.9	2118	3.2
25 W	0328	0.8	0938	3.2	1531	0.8	2203	3.3
26 TH	0413	0.7	1022	3.2	1610	0.8	2243	3.4
27 F	0449	0.7	1101	3.2	1645	0.8	○ 2320	3.4
28 SA	0522	0.6	1137	3.2	1720	0.8	2352	3.4
29 SU	0554	0.6	1209	3.2	1755	0.8		
30 M	0021	3.4	0627	0.6	1240	3.2	1831	0.7
31 TU	0046	3.4	0700	0.6	1311	3.2	1907	0.7

AUGUST

Day	Time	m	Time	m	Time	m	Time	m
1 W	0117	3.4	0735	0.6	1346	3.2	1946	0.7
2 TH	0153	3.4	0812	0.6	1427	3.1	2026	0.7
3 F	0234	3.4	0853	0.6	1514	3.1	2111	0.8
4 SA	0320	3.3	0940	0.7	1607	3.1	◑ 2201	0.9
5 SU	0413	3.2	1036	0.8	1707	3.0	2259	1.0
6 M	0519	3.1	1144	0.9	1812	3.0		
7 TU	0010	1.0	0634	3.1	1310	0.9	1917	3.1
8 W	0137	0.9	0748	3.1	1418	0.7	2020	3.3
9 TH	0245	0.7	0854	3.2	1513	0.6	2117	3.5
10 F	0340	0.5	0952	3.4	1603	0.5	2211	3.6
11 SA	0430	0.3	1044	3.5	1650	0.5	● 2301	3.8
12 SU	0516	0.2	1134	3.5	1736	0.5	2350	3.8
13 M	0601	0.1	1223	3.4	1822	0.5		
14 TU	0040	3.8	0646	0.1	1313	3.4	1908	0.5
15 W	0129	3.8	0731	0.2	1403	3.3	1956	0.6
16 TH	0217	3.7	0817	0.3	1453	3.2	2045	0.7
17 F	0305	3.6	0905	0.5	1542	3.2	2139	0.8
18 SA	0354	3.4	1000	0.7	1632	3.1	◐ 2243	0.9
19 SU	0446	3.2	1109	0.9	1727	3.0	2353	1.0
20 M	0546	3.0	1221	1.1	1836	2.9		
21 TU	0101	1.1	0707	2.9	1324	1.1	1955	3.0
22 W	0205	1.0	0825	2.9	1420	1.1	2054	3.1
23 TH	0302	0.9	0919	3.0	1507	1.0	2141	3.3
24 F	0348	0.7	1003	3.1	1546	0.9	2221	3.4
25 SA	0424	0.6	1041	3.2	1622	0.8	2257	3.4
26 SU	0456	0.6	1116	3.2	1656	0.7	○ 2329	3.4
27 M	0528	0.5	1147	3.2	1731	0.7	2351	3.4
28 TU	0600	0.5	1210	3.2	1805	0.7		
29 W	0010	3.4	0632	0.5	1235	3.2	1839	0.7
30 TH	0043	3.5	0705	0.5	1310	3.3	1915	0.6
31 F	0122	3.5	0740	0.5	1352	3.3	1954	0.7

Chart Datum: 2·01 metres below Ordnance Datum (Belfast). HAT is 3·9 metres above Chart Datum.

STANDARD TIME (UT)
For Summer Time add ONE hour in **non-shaded areas**

BELFAST LAT 54°36′N LONG 5°55′W

TIMES AND HEIGHTS OF HIGH AND LOW WATERS

Dates in red are SPRINGS
Dates in blue are NEAPS

YEAR **2018**

SEPTEMBER

Date	Day	Time	m	Time	m	Time	m	Time	m
1	SA	0205	3.5	0819	0.6	1438	3.3	2038	0.7
2	SU	0252	3.4	0905	0.7	1529	3.2	2128	0.8
3	M	0345	3.2	1000	0.9	1630	3.1	◑ 2227	1.0
4	TU	0453	3.1	1109	1.0	1740	3.1	2343	1.0
5	W	0613	3.0	1251	1.0	1853	3.1		
6	TH	0125	0.9	0734	3.0	1406	0.9	2003	3.3
7	F	0234	0.7	0848	3.2	1502	0.7	2105	3.5
8	SA	0329	0.4	0945	3.3	1552	0.6	2158	3.7
9	SU	0418	0.3	1033	3.5	1637	0.5	● 2246	3.8
10	M	0501	0.2	1119	3.5	1720	0.5	2332	3.8
11	TU	0542	0.2	1204	3.5	1801	0.5		
12	W	0018	3.8	0622	0.2	1249	3.4	1842	0.5
13	TH	0105	3.8	0701	0.3	1334	3.4	1925	0.6
14	F	0150	3.7	0742	0.5	1418	3.3	2009	0.7
15	SA	0236	3.6	0824	0.7	1503	3.3	2056	0.8
16	SU	0322	3.4	0911	0.9	1549	3.2	◐ 2154	1.0
17	M	0411	3.2	1007	1.1	1639	3.1	2314	1.1
18	TU	0506	3.0	1133	1.3	1737	3.0		
19	W	0026	1.1	0613	2.8	1247	1.3	1855	3.0
20	TH	0131	1.1	0756	2.8	1347	1.2	2022	3.1
21	F	0229	0.9	0856	3.0	1438	1.1	2113	3.2
22	SA	0316	0.8	0939	3.1	1520	1.0	2153	3.3
23	SU	0354	0.6	1016	3.2	1556	0.8	2228	3.4
24	M	0427	0.6	1049	3.3	1630	0.7	2257	3.4
25	TU	0459	0.5	1118	3.3	1704	0.7	○ 2315	3.5
26	W	0531	0.5	1138	3.4	1738	0.6	2338	3.5
27	TH	0603	0.5	1204	3.4	1812	0.6		
28	F	0014	3.5	0636	0.5	1241	3.4	1847	0.6
29	SA	0056	3.5	0712	0.5	1323	3.4	1927	0.6
30	SU	0141	3.5	0753	0.6	1410	3.4	2012	0.7

OCTOBER

Date	Day	Time	m	Time	m	Time	m	Time	m
1	M	0231	3.4	0840	0.8	1503	3.3	2104	0.8
2	TU	0329	3.2	0937	1.0	1605	3.2	◑ 2207	0.9
3	W	0440	3.0	1050	1.2	1717	3.1	2333	1.0
4	TH	0603	3.0	1237	1.2	1835	3.2		
5	F	0113	0.9	0731	3.0	1351	1.0	1951	3.3
6	SA	0220	0.7	0841	3.2	1449	0.8	2053	3.5
7	SU	0314	0.4	0934	3.4	1538	0.7	2144	3.7
8	M	0401	0.3	1019	3.5	1622	0.6	2230	3.8
9	TU	0442	0.3	1102	3.5	1702	0.6	● 2314	3.8
10	W	0519	0.3	1143	3.5	1741	0.6	2357	3.8
11	TH	0556	0.4	1224	3.5	1818	0.6		
12	F	0040	3.7	0632	0.5	1305	3.5	1857	0.7
13	SA	0123	3.6	0710	0.7	1345	3.4	1938	0.7
14	SU	0207	3.5	0750	0.8	1427	3.4	2021	0.9
15	M	0251	3.3	0832	1.0	1511	3.3	2112	1.0
16	TU	0339	3.2	0921	1.2	1600	3.2	◐ 2222	1.1
17	W	0433	3.0	1026	1.4	1655	3.1	2346	1.2
18	TH	0534	2.8	1200	1.4	1759	3.0		
19	F	0052	1.1	0650	2.8	1308	1.4	1917	3.0
20	SA	0150	1.0	0815	3.0	1403	1.2	2029	3.2
21	SU	0239	0.8	0903	3.1	1449	1.1	2115	3.3
22	M	0319	0.7	0941	3.3	1527	0.9	2151	3.4
23	TU	0354	0.6	1015	3.4	1603	0.8	2221	3.5
24	W	0428	0.5	1044	3.5	1637	0.7	○ 2244	3.5
25	TH	0501	0.5	1110	3.5	1711	0.6	2313	3.6
26	F	0535	0.5	1140	3.6	1747	0.6	2351	3.6
27	SA	0611	0.6	1218	3.6	1826	0.6		
28	SU	0036	3.6	0650	0.6	1303	3.6	1908	0.6
29	M	0125	3.5	0735	0.8	1352	3.6	1957	0.7
30	TU	0220	3.4	0826	0.9	1447	3.5	2052	0.8
31	W	0323	3.2	0927	1.1	1550	3.4	◑ 2200	0.9

NOVEMBER

Date	Day	Time	m	Time	m	Time	m	Time	m
1	TH	0436	3.1	1044	1.2	1701	3.3	2325	0.9
2	F	0601	3.0	1215	1.2	1821	3.3		
3	SA	0052	0.8	0722	3.1	1330	1.1	1935	3.4
4	SU	0200	0.7	0824	3.2	1430	0.9	2035	3.6
5	M	0254	0.5	0915	3.4	1520	0.8	2126	3.7
6	TU	0339	0.5	1001	3.5	1604	0.7	2212	3.8
7	W	0419	0.5	1043	3.5	1644	0.7	● 2256	3.7
8	TH	0456	0.5	1123	3.6	1722	0.7	2337	3.7
9	F	0532	0.6	1201	3.6	1759	0.7		
10	SA	0018	3.6	0607	0.7	1239	3.6	1836	0.7
11	SU	0058	3.5	0644	0.9	1316	3.6	1915	0.8
12	M	0139	3.4	0722	1.0	1356	3.5	1955	0.9
13	TU	0223	3.3	0803	1.1	1439	3.5	2040	1.0
14	W	0310	3.2	0849	1.2	1526	3.4	2134	1.1
15	TH	0402	3.0	0943	1.3	1618	3.2	◐ 2246	1.2
16	F	0459	2.9	1050	1.4	1716	3.1		
17	SA	0004	1.2	0602	2.9	1213	1.4	1820	3.1
18	SU	0106	1.1	0710	3.0	1319	1.3	1926	3.1
19	M	0158	0.9	0811	3.1	1410	1.2	2024	3.2
20	TU	0242	0.8	0858	3.3	1454	1.0	2109	3.4
21	W	0320	0.7	0937	3.4	1533	0.8	2146	3.5
22	TH	0356	0.6	1013	3.5	1610	0.7	2220	3.6
23	F	0433	0.5	1046	3.6	1649	0.6	○ 2256	3.6
24	SA	0511	0.5	1123	3.7	1729	0.6	2338	3.6
25	SU	0552	0.6	1204	3.7	1812	0.5		
26	M	0026	3.6	0636	0.7	1252	3.7	1858	0.5
27	TU	0119	3.5	0725	0.8	1343	3.7	1949	0.6
28	W	0218	3.4	0819	0.9	1439	3.6	2047	0.7
29	TH	0322	3.2	0920	1.1	1539	3.5	2153	0.7
30	F	0433	3.1	1030	1.2	1646	3.4	◑ 2307	0.8

DECEMBER

Date	Day	Time	m	Time	m	Time	m	Time	m
1	SA	0549	3.1	1146	1.2	1801	3.4		
2	SU	0023	0.8	0659	3.1	1259	1.1	1911	3.4
3	M	0131	0.7	0800	3.2	1403	1.0	2013	3.5
4	TU	0228	0.7	0853	3.3	1458	0.9	2106	3.6
5	W	0315	0.6	0941	3.4	1545	0.8	2155	3.6
6	TH	0357	0.7	1025	3.5	1628	0.7	2239	3.6
7	F	0435	0.7	1106	3.5	1707	0.7	● 2321	3.5
8	SA	0512	0.8	1143	3.6	1745	0.7	2359	3.5
9	SU	0548	0.9	1218	3.6	1821	0.8		
10	M	0036	3.4	0623	0.9	1254	3.6	1857	0.8
11	TU	0116	3.3	0700	1.0	1332	3.6	1934	0.8
12	W	0158	3.3	0739	1.0	1412	3.5	2014	0.9
13	TH	0243	3.2	0822	1.1	1454	3.5	2059	0.9
14	F	0331	3.1	0909	1.1	1538	3.3	2150	1.0
15	SA	0424	3.0	1003	1.2	1629	3.2	◐ 2250	1.0
16	SU	0521	3.0	1103	1.3	1729	3.1		
17	M	0001	1.0	0621	3.0	1212	1.3	1832	3.1
18	TU	0107	1.0	0720	3.1	1320	1.2	1933	3.2
19	W	0200	0.8	0814	3.2	1416	1.1	2027	3.3
20	TH	0247	0.7	0901	3.4	1504	0.9	2115	3.4
21	F	0329	0.6	0944	3.5	1548	0.7	2200	3.5
22	SA	0411	0.6	1026	3.6	1631	0.6	○ 2244	3.6
23	SU	0453	0.6	1109	3.7	1716	0.5	2331	3.6
24	M	0538	0.6	1155	3.8	1802	0.4		
25	TU	0022	3.5	0625	0.6	1245	3.8	1850	0.4
26	W	0117	3.5	0715	0.7	1336	3.8	1942	0.4
27	TH	0214	3.4	0809	0.8	1430	3.8	2037	0.4
28	F	0314	3.3	0906	0.9	1526	3.7	2136	0.5
29	SA	0416	3.2	1007	1.0	1625	3.6	◑ 2241	0.6
30	SU	0522	3.1	1114	1.0	1731	3.5	2350	0.7
31	M	0629	3.1	1224	1.0	1841	3.4		

Chart Datum: 2·01 metres below Ordnance Datum (Belfast). HAT is 3·9 metres above Chart Datum.

STRANGFORD LOUGH

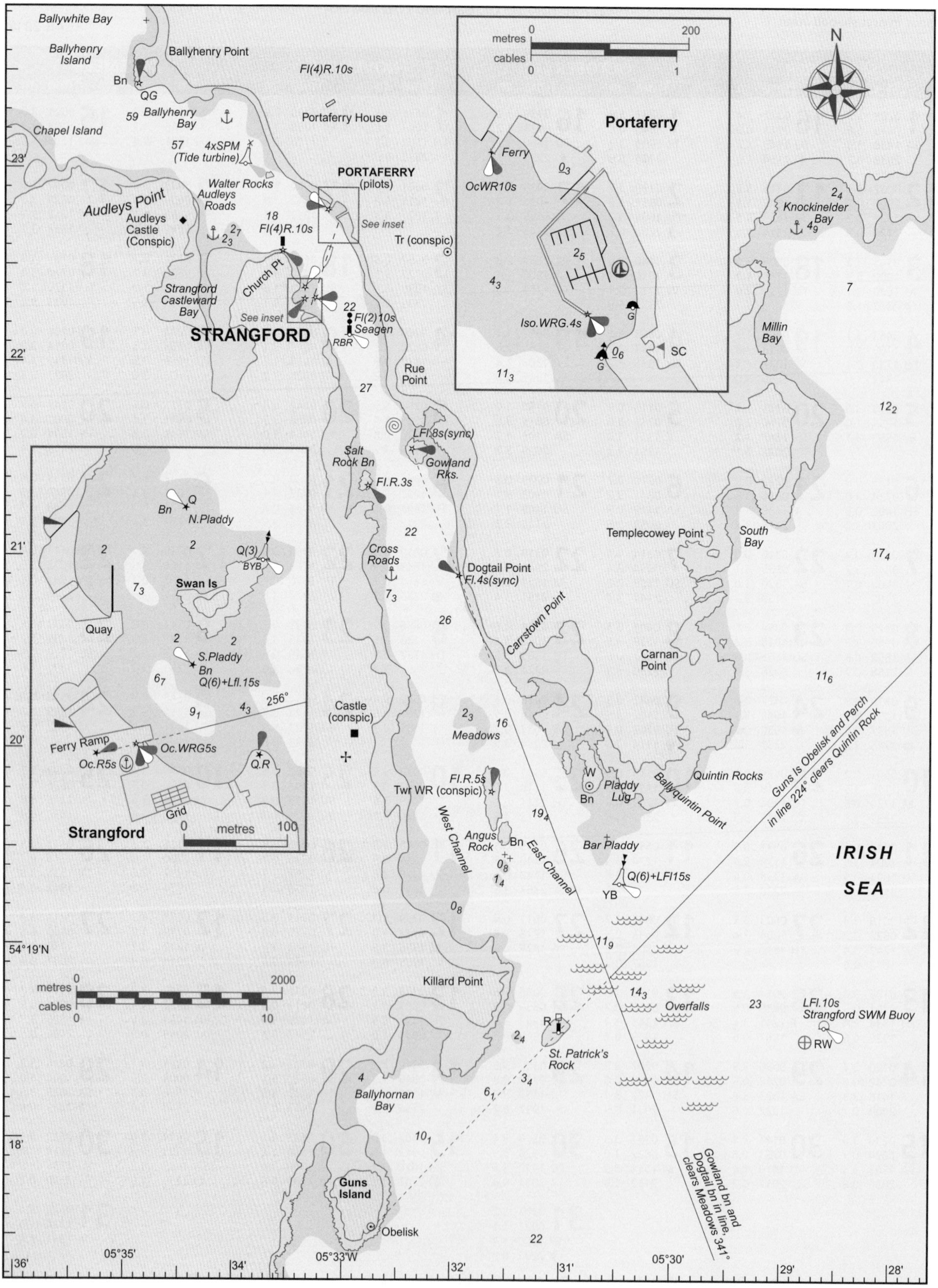

Ballywhite Bay
Ballyhenry Island
Bn
QG
Ballyhenry Point
Fl(4)R.10s
Portaferry House
59
Ballyhenry Bay
Chapel Island
57
4xSPM (Tide turbine)
23'
Walter Rocks
Audleys Roads
PORTAFERRY (pilots)
Audleys Point
Audleys Castle (Conspic)
18
Fl(4)R.10s
See inset
Tr (conspic)
Church Pt
Strangford Castleward Bay
See inset
22
Fl(2)10s
Seagen
RBR
STRANGFORD
22'
Rue Point
27
LFl.8s(sync)
Salt Rock Bn
Gowland Rks.
Fl.R.3s
22
Cross Roads
Dogtail Point
Fl.4s(sync)
26
Carrstown Point
21'
Castle (conspic)
Meadows
16
20'
Fl.R.5s
Twr WR (conspic)
West Channel
East Channel
Angus Rock
Bn
Pladdy Lug
Ballyquintin Point
Quintin Rocks
Bar Pladdy
Q(6)+LFl15s
YB
Overfalls
Killard Point
St. Patrick's Rock
Ballyhornan Bay
Guns Island
Obelisk
22
54°19'N
18'
metres
cables
0
2000
10
Gowland bn and Dogtail bn in line, clears Meadows 341°
Guns Is Obelisk and Perch in line 224° clears Quintin Rock
IRISH SEA
23
LFl.10s
Strangford SWM Buoy
RW
Knockinelder Bay
Millin Bay
Templecowey Point
South Bay
Carnan Point
36'
05°35'
34'
05°33'W
32'
31'
05°30'
29'
28'
N
Portaferry
metres
cables
0
200
1
Ferry
OcWR10s
Iso.WRG.4s
G
SC
Bn
Q
N.Pladdy
Q(3)
BYB
Swan Is
Quay
S.Pladdy
Bn
Q(6)+Lfl.15s
256°
Ferry Ramp
Oc.R5s
Oc.WRG5s
Q.R
Grid
Strangford
metres
100

9.13.18 STRANGFORD LOUGH

Down **54°19'·33N 05°30'·85W** (Narrows)

CHARTS AC 2156, 2159, 5612; Imray C62, C69

TIDES Killard Pt 0000, Strangford Quay +0200 Dover; ML 2·0; Duration 0610

Standard Port BELFAST (⟵)

Times				Height (metres)			
High Water		Low Water		MHWS	MHWN	MLWN	MLWS
0100	0700	0000	0600	3·5	3·0	1·1	0·4
1300	1900	1200	1800				
Differences STRANGFORD (The Narrows)							
+0147	+0157	+0148	+0208	+0·1	+0·1	–0·2	0·0
KILLARD POINT (Entr)							
+0011	+0021	+0005	+0025	+1·0	+0·8	+0·1	+0·1
QUOILE BARRIER							
+0150	+0200	+0150	+0300	+0·2	+0·2	–0·3	–0·1
KILLYLEAGH							
+0157	+0207	+0211	+0231	+0·3	+0·3	ND	ND
SOUTH ROCK							
+0023	+0023	+0025	+0025	+1·0	+0·8	+0·1	+0·1
PORTAVOGIE							
+0010	+0020	+0010	+0020	+1·2	+0·9	+0·3	+0·2

SHELTER Excellent; largest inlet on E coast. ⚓ in the Narrows at Cross Roads, off Strangford clear of moorings, in Audley Roads (in about 5m) and in Ballyhenry Bay. Limited berths at Strangford; moorings may be available in Audley Roads (check with Sailing Club). Small marina at Portaferry, where stream runs fast; best to enter near slack water. Many good ⚓ (NB Marine Nature Reserve) and some buoys up the lough, by villages and YCs.

NAVIGATION WPT: SWM buoy, L Fl 10s, 54°18'·63N 05°28'·69W, 306°/2·04M to Angus Rk lt twr Fl R 5s 5M. Visitors should use E Chan. Disregard W Chan ≠ 320·5° shown on old editions of AC 2159. Beware St Patricks Rk, Bar Pladdy and Pladdy Lug; overfalls occur in the SE apprs and at the bar, which can be dangerous when ebb meets the NW set outside. Strong tidal streams (7kn at sp) in the Narrows. The bar is passable during the flood; best to enter on young flood or at slack water. The flood starts in the Narrows at HW Belfast –3½ and runs for about 6hrs; the ebb starts at HW Belfast +2½. Beware car ferry between Strangford, S and E of Swan Is, and Portaferry. Swan Island, seen as a grassy mound at HW, is edged with rks and a reef extends 32m E ending at W bn, Q (3). Further up the lough, despite improved marks and lights, unmarked drying shoals (pladdies) abound; AC 2156 or equivalent is essential.

LIGHTS AND MARKS Off Strangford *Seagen* tide turbine pile marked as IDM, Fl(2)10s; turbine decommissioned. Further turbine 1¾ca WNW of Walter Rks marked by 2 pair Y SPM; outer pr Fl(2)Y 10s, inner pr FlY 5s.

COMMUNICATIONS (Code 028) CGOC 91463933; Police 101; Medical Clinic 4488 1209. HM at Strangford Ferry Terminal 4488 1637.
HM Ch 16 (Mon-Fri 0900-1700). Some YCs Ch **80** M.

FACILITIES Strangford, Portaferry and Killyleagh are easy to access and offer good shops, pubs and restaurants.

STRANGFORD 25m pontoon; Cuan Inn.

PORTAFERRY Marina portaferrymarina.co.uk, mob 7703 209780, (limited) £1·50. **Village**

Cook St Pier (2ca S), limited.

QUOILE RIVER: Quoile YC ☎4461 2266.

KILLYLEAGH Kos (Irish Spars & Rigging ☎9751 2830).

Killyleagh YC ☎07801 291410, N of village.

East Down YC ☎4482 8375, (about 1M NE of town).

RINGHADDY QUAY CC, drying.

SKETRICK ISLAND In White Rk B,

Strangford Lough YC ☎9754 1883.

Down CC (Old Lightship to NW in Dorn).

KIRCUBBIN (tidal).

9.13.19 ARDGLASS

Down 54°15'·63N 05°35'·96W

CHARTS AC 2093, 633, 5612; Imray C62

TIDES HW +0025 Dover; ML 3·0; Duration 0620

Standard Port BELFAST (⟵)

Times				Height (metres)			
High Water		Low Water		MHWS	MHWN	MLWN	MLWS
0100	0700	0000	0600	3·5	3·0	1·1	0·4
1300	1900	1200	1800				
Differences KILKEEL							
+0040	+0030	+0010	+0010	+1·2	+1·1	+0·4	+0·4
NEWCASTLE							
+0025	+0035	+0020	+0040	+1·6	+1·1	+0·4	+0·1
KILLOUGH HARBOUR							
0000	+0020	ND	ND	+1·8	+1·6	ND	ND
ARDGLASS							
+0010	+0015	+0005	+0010	+1·7	+1·2	+0·6	+0·3

SHELTER Good, except in strong winds from E to S. It is the only all-weather, all-tide shelter between Howth and Bangor. Phennick Cove/Ardglass marina is on W side of hbr, with depths 1·0m to 2·8m. Visitors should check depth of berth offered by marina against depth drawn. The busy fishing port is in South Hbr, with quays (2·1m) on inside of extended S pier. At NW end of hbr, old drying N Dock is also used by FVs.

NAVIGATION WPT 54°15'·30N 05°35'·32W, 131°/5ca to hbr ent. Appr 311° in W sector of WRG Dir lt. Depth in chan 2·4m. Off the tip of the inner breakwater the buoyed marina channel commences in a depth of 1.3m. It is marked by lit PHM and SHM (not shown on chartlet) and turns sharply to port to approach the marina on a heading of 230°. Do not cross the drying SW portion of inner bkwtr, marked by two unlit SCM perches.

LIGHTS AND MARKS Dir lt, 311°, conspic W tr at inner hbr, Iso WRG 4s 10m 8/7/5M, 308°-W-314°; reported hard to see against shore lts. S bkwtr Fl R 3s 10m 5M. W roof of shed on S bkwtr is conspic. If entering S Hbr, avoid Churn Rk, unlit SCM bn. Entrance to marina is buoyed. Castle, spire and water tr (off plan) are conspic to W.

COMMUNICATIONS (Code 028) CGOC 91463933; Police 101; Dr 9084 1242. HM 4484 1291, mob 07790 648274.

Monitor VHF Ch **12** on entry/exit. Marina Ch 80.

FACILITIES

Ardglass Marina www.ardglassmarina.co.uk ☎44 842332, (£8·00) 55 inc 22 £2·40+£1/day.

Town

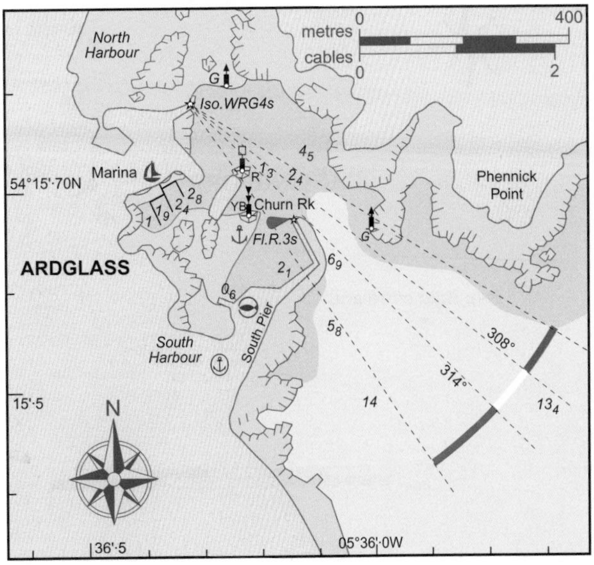

MINOR HARBOURS SOUTH OF ARDGLASS

DUNDRUM BAY, Down. AC 44, 5612. Tides see 9.13.19. This 8M wide bay to the W of St John's Pt is shoal to 5ca offshore and unsafe in onshore winds. The small drying hbr at **Newcastle** (54°11'·8N 05°53'·0W) is for occas use in fair weather. HM ☎(02843) 722804, mob 07803 832515. **Dundrum Hbr (54°14'·2N 05°49'·4W)** No longer used by commercial tfc and only to be used with caution, provides ⚓ in 2m for shoal draught; the bar carries about 0·3m. A steep sea can run at the bar in onshore winds. HW Dundrum is approx that of HW Liverpool; see also 9.13.19 Newcastle. *The Irish Cruising Club's Sailing Directions* are essential for the 1M long, buoyed approach channel. 2 lit DZ buoys offshore are part of the Ballykinler firing range, 2M E of hbr; R flag/lts indicate range active.

ANNALONG HBR, Down, **54°06'·50N 05°53'·65W**. AC 44, 5621, 5612. Tides as Kilkeel, see 9.13.8. Slight silting rep't 2006. Entry HW ±2. Excellent shelter in small drying hbr, dredged to 1·5m 80m beyond pier with 30m pontoon (£12/craft). Appr in W sector of S breakwater light, Oc WRG 5s 8m 9M, vis 204°-G-249°-W-309°-R-024°. Hug N side of the breakwater to avoid rocky shore to starboard. Surge gate at harbour entrance may be closed in SE winds (3R lts vert shown). IPTS shown at entrance. HM mob 07739 527036. Facilities:

KILKEEL, Down, **54°03'·47N 05°59'·26W**. AC 44, 2800, 5612. HW +0015 on Dover; ML 2·9m; Duration 0620. See 9.13.19. Do not appr in E-SW winds >F4. Inner basin is sheltered, but crowded by FVs; depth off quays approx 1m. Secure in inner basin and see HM. There are drying banks both sides of ent chan and SW gales form a sandbank across ent. This is dredged or slowly eroded in E winds. S bkwtr lt Fl WR 2s 8m 8M, 296°-R-313°-W-017°, storm sigs. Meeney's pier (N bkwtr) Fl G 3s 6m 2M. Monitor VHF Ch **12** on entry/exit. HM ☎(028 417) 62287. Facilities: on quay, (between fish market and dock). **Town** (¾M)

9.13.20 CARLINGFORD LOUGH

Louth/Down **54°01'·25N 06°04'·30W**

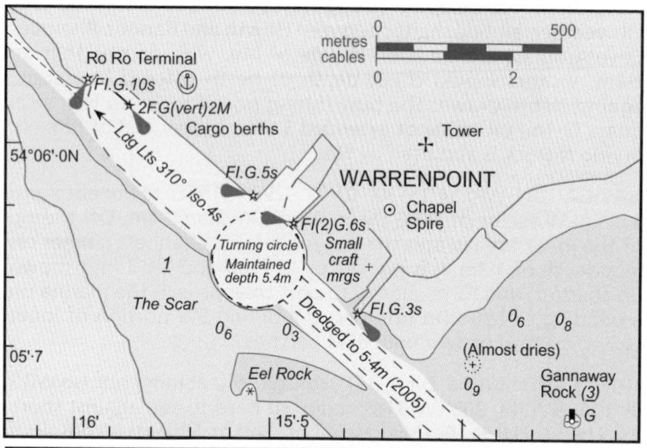

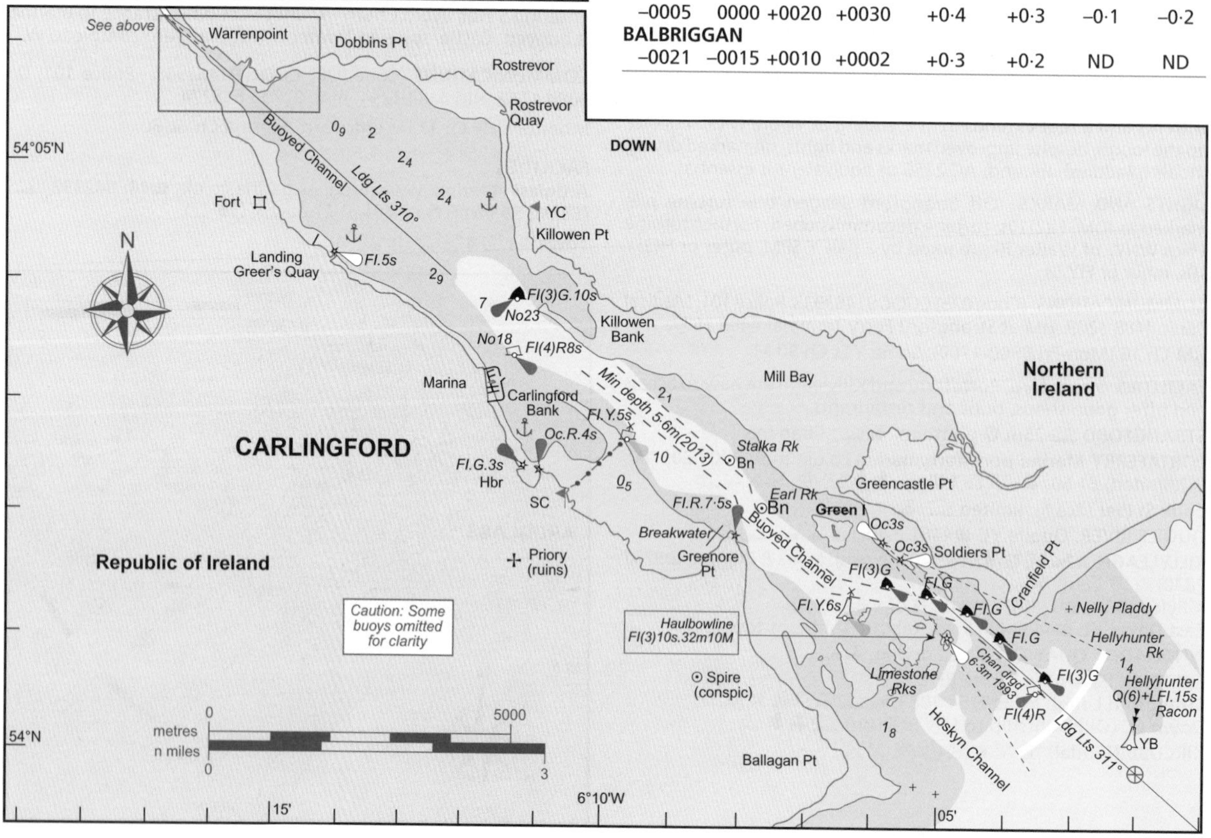

CHARTS AC 44, 2800, 5621, 5612; Imray C62

TIDES Cranfield Pt +0025 and Warrenpoint +0035 Dover; ML 2·9; Duration Cranfield Pt 0615, Warrenpoint 0540

Standard Port DUBLIN (NORTH WALL – AREA 12) (←)

Times				Height (metres)			
High Water		Low Water		MHWS	MHWN	MLWN	MLWS
0000	0700	0000	0500	4·1	3·4	1·5	0·7
1200	1900	1200	1700				
Differences CRANFIELD POINT							
–0027	–0011	+0005	–0010	+0·7	+0·9	+0·3	+0·2
WARRENPOINT							
–0020	–0010	+0025	+0035	+1·0	+0·7	+0·2	0·0
NEWRY (VICTORIA LOCK)							
+0005	+0015	+0045	Dries	+1·2	+0·9	+0·1	DR
DUNDALK (SOLDIERS POINT)							
–0010	–0010	0000	+0045	+1·0	+0·8	+0·1	–0·1
DUNANY POINT							
–0028	–0018	–0008	–0006	+0·7	+0·9	ND	ND
RIVER BOYNE BAR							
–0005	0000	+0020	+0030	+0·4	+0·3	–0·1	–0·2
BALBRIGGAN							
–0021	–0015	+0010	+0002	+0·3	+0·2	ND	ND

SHELTER

Carlingford Marina is protected on S side by sunken barge; depths 1·5m at LW (check with Marina). Appr from N with Nos 18 and 23 buoys in transit astern 012°, to clear the tail of Carlingford Bank (dries) and beware of marine farms in vicinity.

Carlingford Hbr (dries 2·2m), at piers.

Warrenpoint has pontoons on NW side of breakwater (Fl G 3s); access dredged 1·1m. ⚓s clockwise from ent include: off Greenore Pt, between SW end of quay and bkwtr, in 3m clear of commercial traffic; off Greer's Quay in 2m; off Rostrevor Quay, Killowen Pt (YC) and off derelict pier at Greencastle Pt (beware rks). Limited space may be available for short-stay visiting craft in the mussel fishing complex (approx £15/night). Call at least 24hrs before arrival.

NAVIGATION WPT 54°00´·09N 06°02´·00W, (2½ ca S of Hellyhunter SCM lt buoy) 311°/1M to first chan buoys. The main chan is Carlingford Cut (6·3m), about 3ca SW of Cranfield Pt, and passing 2ca NE of Haulbowline lt ho. Drying rocks and shoals obstruct most of the entrance. Small craft should at all times keep clear of commercial shipping in the narrow dredged channel. The ent is impassable in strong onshore winds. The NE bank is **Northern Ireland**, SW bank is **Republic of Ireland**.

The lough becomes choppy in S'ly winds and, due to the funnelling effect of the mountains, NW winds can cause a higher sea state within the lough than outside it.

Tides run up to 5kn off Greenore Pt through a channel with a minimum depth of 5.6m. Entry is impracticable against the ebb. Beware sudden squalls and waterspouts.

Extensive shellfish beds exist along the NE side of the lough; beware fishing vessels on both sides of the channel, and give them a wide berth.

LIGHTS AND MARKS Haulbowline Fl (3) 10s 32m 10M; granite tower. Ldg lts 310°26': both Oc 3s 7/12m 11M, vis 295°-325°; R △ front, ▽ rear, on framework trs. Greenore Pier Fl R 7·5s 10m 5M. Newry R: Ldg lts 310°, both Iso 4s 5/15m 2M, stone columns. Channel from Green Is to Warren Pt marked by lit lateral buoys.

COMMUNICATIONS (Code Greenore/Carlingford 042; Warrenpoint 028). MRCC (01) 6620922/3 or (02891) 463933; Irish ⊖: Dundalk (042) 34114; Dr (042) 73110; H Newry (028) 3026 5511, Dundalk (042) 34701; Police Newry 101, Dundalk (042) 9373102.

Greenore (*Ferry Greenore*) Ch 12 16 (HJ). Carlingford Marina Ch M 16. Warrenpoint Ch 12 16 (H24); call Ch 12 at By No 23 to enter dredged chan. Dundalk Ch 14 16 (HW±3).

FACILITIES **Carlingford Marina** www.carlingfordmarina.com ☎0429373072, mob 0872 321567, 290 inc Ⓥ €4.00 (min€20), short stay <5hrs €12.50, (0900-2100) (50t) @.

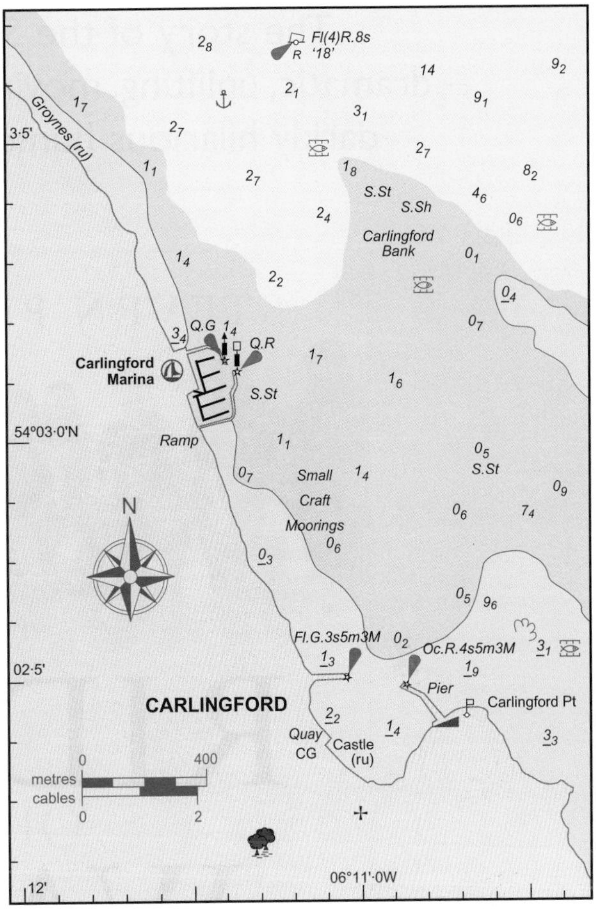

Services ☎0872 301319, ☎(048)44 828882, Divers.

Carlingford YC ☎(041) 685 1951.

Carlingford Hbr Kos.

Village Ⓑ.

Warrenpoint HM ☎(02841) 752878; (but no access at LW) also at Rostrevor, Ⓑ also Dundalk, ⇌ (Dundalk, Newry), ✈ (Dublin).

MINOR HARBOURS AND ANCHORAGES BETWEEN CARLINGFORD LOUGH AND LAMBAY ISLAND

PORT ORIEL, Louth, **53°47'·94N 06°13'·37W.** AC 44. Tides see 9.13.20 (Dunany Pt). Good shelter in small new harbour except in strong ENE winds when a dangerous scend can enter the harbour. Entry reported to be difficult in strong NE winds. Approach from NE on leading marks 174·9°, front and rear Fl 3s (sync) avoiding Wk 1·6m 2.7ca from entrance; Pier Head Light Mo(A) R 9s. on pier in 4m, €25.00/craft, or dry out in inner harbour. HM ☎087 2628777. No facilities; by tanker, in Clogher Head village (1·2M).

BALBRIGGAN, Dublin, **53°36'·76N 06°10'·84W**. AC 44, 1468. Tides see 9.13.20. Good shelter in small harbour which dries about 1m. Harbour often crowded with FVs and is not recommended for yachts. Approach from E to open the outer harbour; enter from NE but beware severe shoaling on W side of harbour mouth and on both sides of outer harbour. Thence to on SE quay in inner harbour. Lt, Fl (3) WRG 10s 12m 13/10M, conspic W tr on East breakwater head, vis 159°-G193°-W-288°-R-305°. Facilities: (by tanker from Skerries) (HW±2).

SKERRIES, Dublin, **53°35'·09N 06°06'·49W**. AC 633. Tides as Balbriggan, 9.13.20. E & SE of Red Island (a peninsula) lie Colt, Shenick's and St Patrick's Islands, the latter foul to S and SW. Inshore passage between Colt and St Patrick's Is uses transit/brg as on chart to clear dangers. Good shelter and holding in 3m at Skerries Bay, W of Red Is. Approach from E or NE outside PHM buoy, Fl R 10s, off Red Is. ⚓ WNW of pier, Oc R 6s 7m 7M, vis 103°-154°; clear of moorings. Most facilities; Skerries SC ☎1-849 1233, (HW±3). Rockabill Lt, Fl WR 12s 45m 17/13M, is conspic 2·4M ENE of St Patrick's Is.

West Denmark

Skagen to Rømø

9.14.1 Contents 649

9.14.2 Area map and Distance table 650

9.14.3 Tidal stream charts see Area 15 Tidal stream charts

9.14.4 Lights, buoys and waypoints 651

9.14.5 Passage information 653
Skagen to Hanstholm – 653 • Hanstholm to Thyborøn,
Thyborøn to Hvide Sande – 656 • Hvide Sande to Esbjerg – 658 •
Esbjerg to Rømø, Crossing the North Sea – 658

9.14.6 Special notes for West Denmark 653

9.14.7 Skagen 654

9.14.8 Hirtshals 655

9.14.9 Hanstholm 655

9.14.10 Thyborøn (Western Entrance to Limfjord) 656

9.14.11 Thorsminde 657

9.14.12 Hvide Sande 658
Horns Rev • Grådyb

9.14.13 Esbjerg, tide tables/curves 660

9.14.14 Nordby (Fanø Island) 664

9.14.15 Havneby (Rømø Island) 664

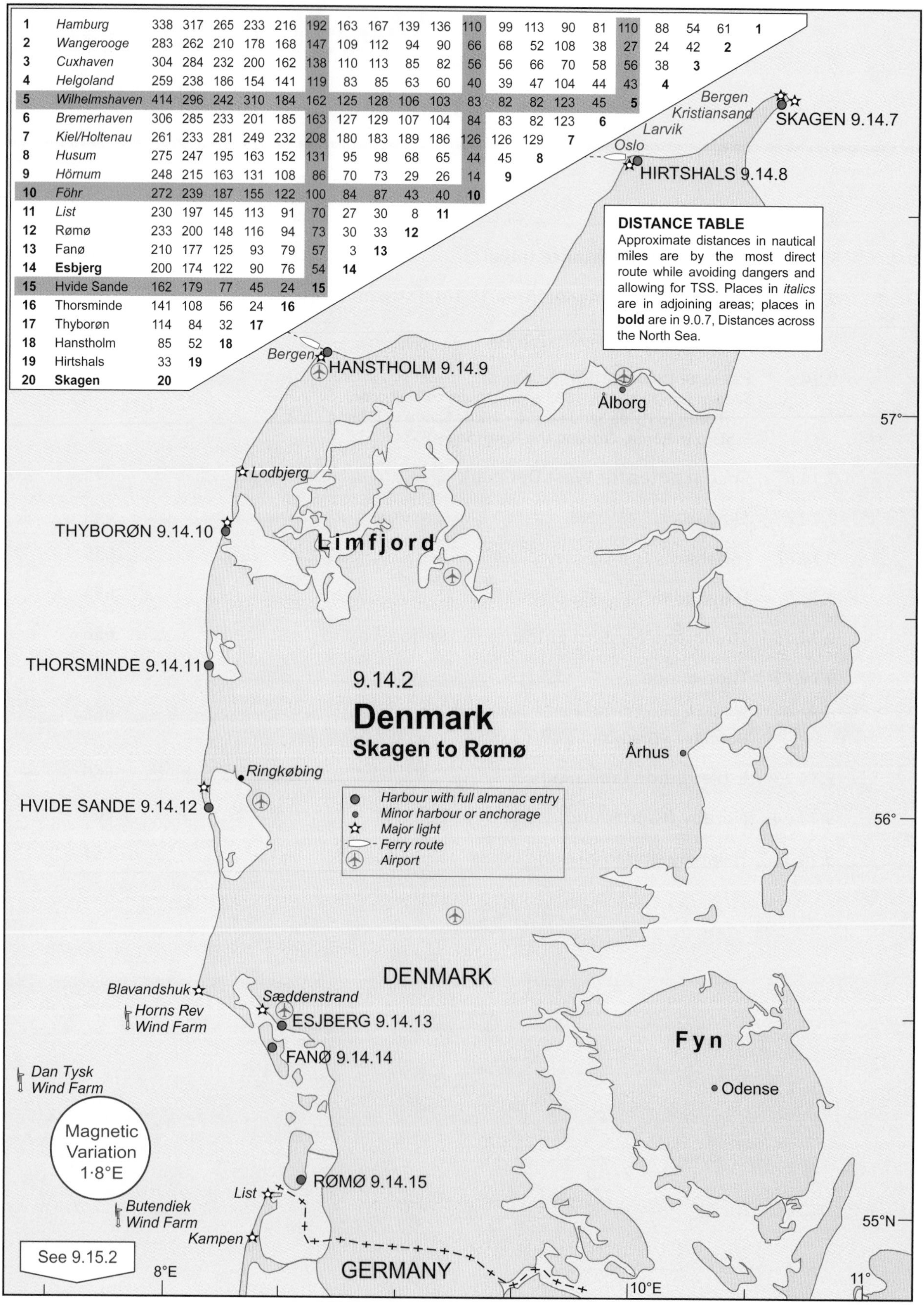
Bergen
Kristiansand
Larvik
Oslo
SKAGEN 9.14.7
HIRTSHALS 9.14.8
Bergen
HANSTHOLM 9.14.9
Ålborg
57°
Lodbjerg
THYBORØN 9.14.10
Limfjord
THORSMINDE 9.14.11
9.14.2
Denmark
Skagen to Rømø
Århus
Ringkøbing
HVIDE SANDE 9.14.12
Harbour with full almanac entry
Minor harbour or anchorage
Major light
Ferry route
Airport
56°
Blavandshuk
Horns Rev Wind Farm
Sæddenstrand
ESBJERG 9.14.13
DENMARK
FANØ 9.14.14
Fyn
Dan Tysk Wind Farm
Odense
Magnetic Variation 1·8°E
RØMØ 9.14.15
List
Butendiek Wind Farm
Kampen
55°N
See 9.15.2
8°E
GERMANY
10°E
11°

1	*Hamburg*	338	317	265	233	216	192	163	167	139	136	110	99	113	90	81	110	88	54	61	**1**
2	*Wangerooge*	283	262	210	178	168	147	109	112	94	90	66	68	52	108	38	27	24	42	**2**	
3	*Cuxhaven*	304	284	232	200	162	138	110	113	85	82	56	56	66	70	58	56	38	**3**		
4	*Helgoland*	259	238	186	154	141	119	83	85	63	60	40	39	47	104	44	43	**4**			
5	*Wilhelmshaven*	414	296	242	310	184	162	125	128	106	103	83	82	82	123	45	**5**				
6	*Bremerhaven*	306	285	233	201	185	163	127	129	107	104	84	83	82	123	**6**					
7	*Kiel/Holtenau*	261	233	281	249	232	208	180	183	189	186	126	126	129	**7**						
8	*Husum*	275	247	195	163	152	131	95	98	68	65	44	45	**8**							
9	*Hörnum*	248	215	163	131	108	86	70	73	29	26	14	**9**								
10	*Föhr*	272	239	187	155	122	100	84	87	43	40	**10**									
11	*List*	230	197	145	113	91	70	27	30	8	**11**										
12	Rømø	233	200	148	116	94	73	30	33	**12**											
13	Fanø	210	177	125	93	79	57	3	**13**												
14	**Esbjerg**	200	174	122	90	76	54	**14**													
15	Hvide Sande	162	179	77	45	24	**15**														
16	Thorsminde	141	108	56	24	**16**															
17	Thyborøn	114	84	32	**17**																
18	Hanstholm	85	52	**18**																	
19	Hirtshals	33	**19**																		
20	**Skagen**	**20**																			

DISTANCE TABLE
Approximate distances in nautical miles are by the most direct route while avoiding dangers and allowing for TSS. Places in *italics* are in adjoining areas; places in **bold** are in 9.0.7, Distances across the North Sea.

9.14.3 TIDAL STREAM CHARTS SEE 9.15.3

9.14.4 LIGHTS, BUOYS AND WAYPOINTS

Bold print = light with a nominal range of 15M or more. CAPITALS = place or feature. *CAPITAL ITALICS* = light-vessel, light float or Lanby. *Italics* = Fog signal. ***Bold italics*** = Racon. Many marks/buoys are fitted with AIS (MMSI No); see relevant charts.

SKAGEN TO THYBORØN

SKAGEN

Skagen W ☆ Fl (3) WR 10s 31m **W17M**/R12M; 053°-W-248°-R-323°; W ○ twr; 57°44′·94N 10°35·70E.
Skagen ☆ Fl 4s 44m **23M**; Gy ○ twr; ***Racon G, 20M***; 57°44′·14N 10°37′·81E.
Skagen No 1A L Fl 10s; ***Racon N***; 57°43′·46N 10°53′·55E. (Route T)
Skagen No 2 L Fl 10s; 57°37′·61N 11°05′·51E. (Route T)
Skagens Rev Q; 57°45′·97N 10°43′·74E.
Q (3) 10s; 57°43′·87N 10°42′·31E.
Skagen Harbour S bkwtr root, Dir Oc WRG 5s 20m W11/RG10M, 267°-W- 271°; Gy lattice twr; 57°42′·77N 10°34′·99E.
S bkwtr head Fl R 3s 4m 5M; 57°42′·72N 10°35′·99E.
N bkwtr head Fl G 3s 4m 5M; 57°42′·92N 10°35′·91E.
Inner hbr ent SW side Fl R 5s
Inner hbr ent NE side Fl G 5s

HIRTSHALS

Hirtshals ☆ F Fl 30s 57m **F 18M; Fl 25M**; W ○ twr, approx 1M SSW of hbr ent; 57°35′·10N 09°56′·55E.
Ldg lts 166°, both 156°-176°. Front, Iso R 2s 10m 11M; R △ on twr; 57°35′·69N 09°57′·64E; marina ent is close N of this lt. Rear, Iso R 4s 18m 11M; R ▽ on twr; 330m from front.
Approach chan Fl (3) G 10s; 57°36′·18N 09°56·94E.
Fl R 3s; 57°36′·44N 09°57′·67E.
Fl (5) Y 20s; 57°36′·43N 09°57′·72E.
Fl G 5s; 57°36′·11N 09°57·14E.
Outer W mole Fl G 3s 14m 6M; G mast; *Horn 15s*; 57°35′·97N 09°57′·37E.
W mole spur Fl G 5s 9m 4M; G mast; 57°35′·77N 09°57′·51E.
E mole Fl R 5s 9m 6M; G mast; 57°35′·85N 09°57′·61E.

LØKKEN

Lee bkwtr Fl 5s 5m 5M; 57°22′·39N 09°42′·11E.

TRANUM STRAND (Firing ranges)

Tranum No 1 ☆ Al Fl WR 4s 19m W7M, R7M; twr; by day Q 4M; shown when firing in progress; 57°12′·43N 09°30′·34E.
Tranum No 2 ☆ light as per No 1; 57°10′·57N 09°26′·22E.

LILD STRAND

Bragerne Fl G 5s; 57°10′·67N 08°56′·35E.
Ldg lts 138°, three : F 12/22m 7/8M; 127°-149°; 3 masts. Front 57°09′·22N 08°57′·75E.

HANSTHOLM

Hanstholm ☆ Fl (3) 20s 65m **24M**; shown by day in poor vis; W 8-sided twr; 57°06′·77N 08°35′·92E, approx 1M S of the hbr ent.
Hanstholm LFl 10s; 57°08′·06N 08°34′·87E.
Ldg lts 142·6°, both Iso 2s 37/45m 13M; synch; 127·6°-157·6°; R △ on mast. Front, 57°07′·12N 08°36′·15E. Rear, 170m from front, R ▽ on mast.
Note: The 4 outer/inner mole heads are floodlit.
W outer mole Fl G 3s 11m 9M; G pillar; 57°07′·56N 08°35′·45E. E outer mole Fl R 3s 11m 9M; R pillar; 57°07′·61N 08°35′·57E.
Roshage Fl 5s 7m 5M; 57°07′·75N 08°37′·25E (1M E of hbr).

NØRRE VORUPØR

Mole Fl G 5s 6m 5M; 56°57′·75N 08°21′·679E.
Ldg lts, both Iso R 4s 20/30m 9M, indicate safest landing place for FVs; vis 22·5° either side of ldg line; synch. Front 57°57′·46N 08°22′·10E. Rear, 80m from front.
Lodbjerg ☆ Fl (2) 20s 48m **23M**; ○ twr; 56°49′·40N 08°15′·76E.

THYBORØN

Landfall L Fl 10s; ***Racon T, 10m***; 56°42′·54N 08°08′·69E.
Agger Tange ldg lts 082°: Front, Iso WRG 4s 8m W11M, R/G8M; 074·5°-G-079·5°-W-084·5°-R-089·5°; R △ on bcn; 56°42′·97N 08°14′·14E. Rear, Iso 4s 17m 11M; 075°-089°; synch; R ▽ on Gy twr; 804m from front.
Off Havmolen 56°43′·25N 08°12′·52E.
Approach ☆ Fl (3) 10s 24m 12M; intens 023·5°-203·5°; also lit by day in poor vis; lattice twr; 56°42′·49N 08°12′·91E (S side of ent).
Langholm ldg lts 120°, both Iso 2s 7/13m 11M; synch; 113°-127°. Front, R △ on R hut, 56°42′·45N 08°14′·54E. Rear, R ▽ on Gy twr.
Thyborøn Havn Oc (2) WRG 12s 6m W11M, R/G8M; 122·5°-G-146·5°- W-150°- R-211·3°-G-337·5°- W-340°-R-344°; W twr R band; 56°42′·35N 08°13′·39E (680m N of ent to Yderhavn and Basins).
Yderhavn approach Dir Iso WRG 2s 21m 5M (0.5M by day); 213°-G-218°-W-223°-R-228°; 56°41′·85N 08°13′·32E
N mole Fl G 3s 6m 4M; G pedestal; 56°42′·02N 08°13′·52E.
S mole Fl R 3s 6m 4M; R pedestal; 56°41′·97N 08°13′·53E.

LIMFJORD (Limited coverage eastward, only to 08°42′E)

Sælhundeholm Løb, into Nissum Bredning ('Broad').
No 1 Fl (2) G 5s; 56°41′·14N 08°14′·17E.
No 3 Fl G 3s; 56°40′·75N 08°13′·79E.
No 7 Fl G 3s; 56°40′·31N 08°13′·52E.
No 11 Fl G 3s; 56°39′·83N 08°13′·59E.
No 16 Fl R 3s; 56°38′·51N 08°13′·89E.
No 18 Fl (2) R 5s; 56°38′·20N 08°14′·34E.
No 21 Fl G 3s; 56°38′·98N 08°14′·71E.
No 26 Fl R 3s; 56°38′·71N 08°15′·38E.
No 29 Fl G 3s; 56°38′·40N 08°15′·94E.

APPROACHES TO LEMVIG (Marina and Havn)

Toftum Dir 120°, Iso WRG 4s 24m, W12M, R/G 8M; 110°-G-120°-W-137°-R-144°; hut; 56°33′·09N 08°18′·33E.
Rønnen Fl G 3s; 56°36′·71N 08°21′·74E.
Søgard Mark ldg lts 243·5°: both FR 20/30m 5M; vis 90° either side of ldg line. Front, R △ on W bcn; 56°34′·39N 08°17′·29E. Rear, R ▽ on W post; 235m from front.
Chan 56°33′·27N 08°18′·31E.
Ldg lts, W of hbr 177·7°, both FR 8/20m 5M; 153°-203°. Front R △ on twr; 56°33′·04N 08°18′·16E. Rear, R ▽ on W post; 184m from front.
Vinkel Hage Marina, N mole FG 3m 5M; 56°33′·09N 08°18′·33E. S mole, FR 3m 4M. Marina is 9ca N of the Havn on the W side.
Ostre Havn 56°33′·17N 08°18′·40E. Havn ent, FG/FR 4m 5M.

THISTED HAVN (Marina)

Outer W mole Fl R 3s 4m 2M; 56°57′·10N 08°41′·90E.
Outer E mole Fl G 3s 4m 2M; 56°57′·10N 08°41′·95E.
Thisted Bredning Aero 3 Fl R 1·5s (vert; 45m apart) 183m 10M; TV mast; 56°58′·52N 08°41′·15E, 1·55M NNW of hbr ent.

THYBORØN TO BLÅVANDS HUK

Bovbjerg ☆ Fl (2) 15s 62m 16M; 56°30′·79N 08°07′·18E.
Wave recorder buoy Fl (5) Y 20s; 56°28′·49N 08°03′·35E.

THORSMINDE HAVN

(All Lat/Longs for this harbour are approximate)
Lt ho F 30m 13M; Gy twr; 56°22′·34N 08°06′·99E.
Groyne, N Fl 5s 8m 5M; Gy hut; 56°22′·46N 08°06′·82E.
N mole Iso R 2s 9m 4M; R hut; 56°22′·36N 08°06′·62E.
S mole Iso G 2s 9m 4M; G hut; 56°22′·26N 08°06′·92E.
West hbr, W mole FG 5m 2M; Gy post; 56°22′·36N 08°07′·12E.
E mole FR 5m 2M; Gy post; 56°22′·26N 08°07′·18E.
NW dolphin FG 5m 4M; Gy post; 56°22′·26N 08°07′·22E.
SE dolphin FG 5m 4M; Gy post; 56°22′ 26N 08°07′ 26E.
Lock, E side Iso 4s 12m 4M; Gy mast; 020°-160°; 56°22′·36N 08°07′·22E.
Road bridge Iso 4s 5m 4M; 200°-340°; 56°22′·36N 08°07′·26E.

HVIDE SANDE

Lyngvig ☆ Fl 5s 53m **23M** (may have Y tint); W ○ twr; 56°02'·99N 08°06'·22E.
N outer bkwtr Fl R 3s 7m 8M; R hut; 55°59'·94N 08°06'·55E.
N mole Fl R 5s 10m 6·5M; R floodlit edifice; 55°59'·98N 08°06'·84E.
S mole Fl G 5s 10m 6M; 55°59'·96N 08°06'·98E.
Lt ho F 27m 14M; Gy twr; 56°00'·00N 08°07'·35E.
Nordhavn, E pier FG 4m 4M; 56°00'·16N 08°07'·42E.
W pier 2 FR 3m 2M; W posts; 060°-035°; 56°00'·07N 08°07'·12E.
Sydhavn, W pier FG 4m 2M; 56°00'·06N 08°07'·52E.
E Pier FR 4m 2M; Gy post; 56°00'·06N 08°07'·53E.
Lock entrance ldg lts 293·5°: both FR 11/14m 2M; 201·6°-021·6°. Front, R △ on Gy tr, 56°00'·0N 08°07'·8E. Rear, R ▽ on Gy twr, 72m from front.
Fjordhavn ldg lts 246·6° (both vis 7·5° either side of ldg line): Front, Iso G 2s 4m 4M; Or △ on mast; 56°00'·5N 08°07'·9E. Rear, Iso G 4s 6m 4M, Or ▽ on mast, 128m from front.

HORNS REV (marks westward from coast)

Oskbøl firing range. Two lights (4M apart) both AlFl WR 4s 35m **16M**, R13M, (by day Q 10M) are shown when firing is in progress: North ☆ 55°37'·24N 08°07'·04E. South ☆ 55°33'·53N 08°04'·67E.
Range safety buoys: Fl Y 5s; 55°42'·32N 08°06'·92E. Fl Y 3s; 55°38'·63N 07°50'·91E. Fl Y 3s; 55°37'·35N 07°56'·98E. 55°36'·02N 08°02'·49E.

Blåvands Huk ☆ Fl (3) 20s 55m **23M**; W □ twr; 55°33'·46N 08°04'·95E.

Horns Rev is encircled by:
Tuxen Q; 55°34'·22N 07°41'·92E on the N side.
Vyl Q (6) + L Fl 15s; 55°26'·22N 07°49'·99E on the S side.
No 2 L Fl 10s; 55°28'·74N 07°36'·49E on the SW side.
Horns Rev W Q (9) 15s; 55°34'·47N 07°26'·05E, off the W end.

Slugen Channel (crosses Horns Rev ESE/WNW)
L Fl G 10s; 55°33'·99N 07°49'·38E.
Fl G 3s; 55°32'·26N 07°53'·65E.
Fl (2) R 5s; 55°31'·46N 07°52'·88E.
Fl (2) G 5s; 55°30'·52N 07°59'·20E.
Fl (3) R 10s; 55°29'·42N 08°02'·56E.

Søren Bovbjergs Dyb (unlit N/S side channel off Slugen Chan)
55°33'·57N 07°55'·55E.
55°32'·80N 07°55'·30E.
55°32'·19N 07°56'·29E.
55°31'·24N 07°57'·46E.

BLÅVANDS HUK TO RØMØ

APPROACHES TO ESBJERG

Grådyb L Fl 10s; ***Racon G, 10M***; 55°24'·63N 08°11'·59E.
Sædding Strand 053·8° triple ldg lts: valid up to Nos 7/8 buoys; H24:
Front Iso 2s 13m **21M**; 052°-056°; R bldg; 55°29'·74N 08°23'·87E.
Middle Iso 4s 26m **21M**; 051°-057°; R twr, W bands; 55°29'·94N 08°24'·33E, 630m from front.
Rear F 37m **18M**; 052°-056°; R twr; 55°30'·18N 08°24'·92E, 0·75M from front.
No 1 Q; 55°25'·49N 08°13'·89E.
No 2 Fl (3) R 10s; 55°25'·62N 08°13'·73E.
No 3 Fl G 3s; 55°25'·93N 08°14'·84E.
No 4 Fl R 3s; 55°26'·02N 08°14'·72E.
Tide Gauge Fl (5) Y 20s 8m 4M; 55°26'·05N 08°15'·93E.
No 5 Fl G 5s; 55°26'·32N 08°15'·83E.
No 6 Fl R 5s; 55°26'·44N 08°15'·70E.
No 7 Q; 55°26'·76N 08°16'·91E.
No 8 Fl (2) R 5s; 55°26'·89N 08°16'·81E.
Ldg lts 067°, valid up to Nos 9/10 buoys. Both FG 10/25m **16M**, H24. Front, Gy tripod; rear, Gy twr, 55°28'·76N 08°24'·70E.
No 9 Fl (2) G 10s; 55°27'·04N 08°18'·21E.
No 10 Fl (2) R 10s; 55°27'·20N 08°18'·04E.
Ldg lts 049°, valid up to No 16 buoy/Jerg. Both FR 16/27m **16M**, H24. Front, W twr; rear, Gy twr, 55°29'·92N 08°23'·75E.
No 11 Fl G 3s; 55°27'·71N 08°19'·59E.
No 12 Fl R 3s; 55°27'·88N 08°19'·39E.
No 13 Fl G 5s; 55°28'·40N 08°20'·99E.
No 14 Fl R 5s; 55°28'·57N 08°20'·73E.
Jerg Fl G 3s 7m 5M; G twr, Y base; 55°28'·88N 08°22'·00E.
No 16 Q (6) + L Fl 15s; 55°29'·04N 08°21'·80E.
No 15A Fl (2) G 5s; 55°29'·01N 08°22'·47E.
No 18 Fl (2) R 5s; 55°29'·19N 08°22'·71E.
Fovrfelt N Oc (2) WRG 6s 7m W6M, R/G4M; 066·5°-G-073°-W-077°-R-085·5°; 327°-G-331°- W-333·5°-R-342°; Y twr; 55°29'·29N 08°23'·79E.
Fovrfelt Fl (2) R 10s 11m 6M; R twr; 55°29'·03N 08°23'·75E.
No 15B Fl (2) G 10s; 55°28'·83N 08°23'·65E.

ESBJERG HAVN

Strandby, shelter mole, NW corner Oc WRG 5s 6m W13M, R/G9M; 101·7°-G-105·5°-W-109·5°-R-111·7°; W bldg, R band; 55°28'·76N 08°24'·63E.
Industrifiskerihavn, W mole Fl R 5s 6m 4M; R structure; 55°28'·57N 08°24'·89E.
E mole Fl G 5s 7m 4M; G structure; 55°28'·52N 08°25'·03E.
Nordsøkai Q (9) 15s 5m; Y twr, B band; 55°28'·45N 08°25'·04E.
Konsumfiskerihavn, W mole FlR 3s 6m; 203°-119°; R twr; 55°28'·31N 08°25'·33E. Yacht hbr in SSE part of Basin II.
E mole Fl G 3s 6m; 023°-256°; G tr; 55°28·31N 08°25·40E.
Trafikhavn, NW corner, Oc (2) WRG 12s 6m W11M, R/G8M; 118°-G-124·5°-W-129°-R-131°; W bldg, R band; 55°28·22N 08°25·43E.
N mole FR 8m 5M; 232°-135°; R bldg; 55°28'·13N 08°25'·46E.
S mole FG 8m 4M; 045°-276°; G bldg; 55°28'·08N 08°25'·51E.
No 22 Fl (2) R 5s; 55°27'·62N 08°25'·50E.
Sønderhavn (industrial) W mole FR 9m 4M; 55°27'·49N 08°26'·12E. E mole FG 9m 4M; 55°27'·43N 08°26'·31E.
Aero 3 x Fl 1·5s (vert, 82m apart) 251m 12M, H24; on chimney; 55°27'·27N 08°27'·32E (1200m ESE of Sønderhavn ent).

FANØ

Slunden outer ldg lts 242°, both Iso 2s 5/8m 3M; 227°-257°. Front, twr; 55°27'·20N 08°24'·53E. Rear, twr, 106m from front.
E shore, reciprocal ldg lts 062°, both FR 10/13m 3M; 047°-077°. Front, twr; 55°27'·65N 08°26'·01E. Rear, twr, 140m from front.
No 1 Fl (2) G l0s 5m 2M; G pile; 55°27'·45N 08°25'·28E.
No 2 Fl (2+1) Y 5s 5m 2M; Y pile; 55°27'·42N 08°25'·32E.
No 3 Fl G 3s 5m 2M; G pile; 55°27'·39N 08°25'·07E.
No 4 Fl R 3s 5m 2M; R pile; 55°27'·35N 08°25'·10E.
Nordby ldg lts 214°, both FR 7/9m 4M; 123·7°-303·7°. Front, W mast;55°26'·94N 08°24'·44E. Rear, Gy twr, 84m from front.
Kremer Sand FG 5m 3M; G dolphin; 55°27'·3N 08°24'·9E.
Næs Søjord FR 5m 3M; R pile; 55°27'·27N 08°24'·86E.
Nordby marina 55°26'·65N 08°24'·53E.

KNUDEDYB

G 55°20'·50N 08°24'·28E.
K 55°18'·92N 08°20'·06E.
No 2 55°18'·82N 08°21'·33E.
No 4 55°18'·81N 08°22'·21E.
No 6 55°18'·38N 08°24'·63E.
No 10 55°18'·68N 08°28'·50E.
Knoben 55°18'·71N 08°30'·60E.

JUVRE DYB

No 4 55°13'·76N 08°24'·73E.
No 6 55°13'·41N 08°26'·60E.
No 8 55°12'·69N 08°26'·83E.
No 10 55°12'·55N 08°28'·72E.
Rejsby Stjært 55°13'·15N 08°30'·55E.

OUTER APPROACH (Lister Tief) TO RØMØ

See also Area 15 for details of lights on Sylt.
Rode Klit Sand, Recording stn Fl (3) Y 15s, 55°08'·40N 08°07'·25E.
Lister Tief Iso 8s, *Whis;* 55°05'·32N 08°16'·80E.
No 1 55°05'·48N 08°18'·50E.
No 3 Fl G 4s; 55°05'·36E 08°20'·14E.
No 2 Fl (3) R 10s; 55°03'·92N 08°21'·22E.
No 9 Fl (2) G 9s; 55°03'·76N 08°23'·05E.
Lister Landtief No 5 55°03'·68N 08°24'·73E.
No 4 FL (2) R 5s; 55°03'·84N 08°25'·29E.
G1 Fl Y 4s; 55°03'·27N 08°28'·32E.

RØMØ DYB and HAVN

No 1 Fl (2) G 10s; 55°03'·23N 08°30'·30E.
No 10 Fl (2) R 10s 5m 3M; R pole; 55°03'·50N 08°31'·10E.
No 14 Fl R 3s 6m 2M; R pole; 55°03'·85N 08°32'·55E.
No 20 Fl R 5s 5m 2M; R pole; 55°04'·79N 08°34'·13E.
No 9 55°04'·79N 08°34'·63E.
No 11 55°05'·17N 08°34'·69E.
Rømø Hbr:
S mole Fl R 3s 7m 2M; Gy twr; 55°05'·19N 08°34'·31E.
N mole Fl G 3s 7m 2M; Gy twr; 55°05'·23N 08°34'·30E.
Inner S mole FR 4m 1M; 55°05'·2N 08°34'·2E.

9.14.5 PASSAGE INFORMATION

More passage information is threaded between successive harbours in this Area. **Bibliography:** *North Sea (East) Pilot* (NP 55); *Cruising Guide to Germany and Denmark* (Imray/Navin).

SKAGEN TO HANSTHOLM

(AC 1402) From/to **Skagen** keep outside the cardinal buoys marking Skagen Rev. In Jammerbugt (The Bay of Woe: Hirtshals to Hanstholm) a firing practice area extends 7M off Tranum Strand, 57°10'N 09°25'E. (See 5.11.4.)

Jutland's low, sandy W coast is not a notable cruising ground and lacks genuine harbours of refuge in strong onshore winds. Even **Thyborøn** should not be approached on the ebb with onshore winds >F5. **Esbjerg** is made difficult by a bar on which seas break heavily in strong W or SW winds. But in settled weather, these and other ports may break the long passage to the Skagerrak or round **Skagen** (The Skaw) into the Kattegat.

Coastal dangers include: Horns Rev, a large shoal (3m-5m) extending about 22M W of Blåvands Huk, with wind farms Horns Rev 1, 80 turbines, and Horns Rev 2, 91 turbines, located on it. Both show FR lts and Fl Y on perimeters. The main buoyed Slugen channel lies some 5M offshore; further inshore, extensive sand ridges lie parallel to the coast up to 5ca from the shore, with depths of 1m to 5.5m. There are many coastal nature reserves, as charted, into which entry is either restricted or prohibited; but they do not deny access to hbrs.

►*Tidal streams are weak as far N as Thyborøn and imperceptible further N, but expect wind-driven currents such as the N-going Stryget.*◄

The general direction of buoyage is northerly. Navigational marks are excellent. There is much fishing activity, including pair-trawling.

9.14.6 SPECIAL NOTES FOR W DENMARK

VOCABULARY A few Danish words which may be useful:

Ashore	***Paa Lan***	**Nautical**	
Hello	*Goodag*	Harbourmaster	*Havnefoged*
Goodbye	*Farvel*	Customs	*Told*
Please	*Vaer so gud*	Hbr Police	*Havnepoliti*
Thank you	*Tak*	Boat name	*Bådenavn*
Yes	*Ja*	Length	*Længde*
No	*Nej*	Beam	*Bredde*
Sorry	*Undskyld*	Draught	*Dybgang*
How much ..?	*Hvor meget*	Water, fresh	*Vand*
	koster ..?	Electricity	*Electricitet*
Where is ..?	*Hvor er ..?*	Petrol	*Benzin*
Left	*Venstre*	Shower	*Bruser*
Right	*Højre*	Red	*Rød*
Doctor	*Læge*	Green	*Grøn*
Dentist	*Tandlæge*	White	*Hvid*
Hospital	*Hospitalet*	Anchorage	*Ankerplads*
Chemist	*Apotek*	Prohibited	*Forbudt*
Laundry	*Vaskeri*	High water	*Højvande*
Post office	*Postkontoret*	Low water	*Lavvande*
Bus	*Bussen*	Chart datum	*Kortdatum*
Train	*Toget*	Forecast	*Vejrudsigt*
Ticket, single	*enkeltbillet*	Low	*Lavtryk*
Open	*Åben*	High	*Høj*
Closed	*Lukket*	Gale	*Hård kuling*
Market	*Marked*	Squall	*Byge*
Milk	*Mœlk*	Rough sea	*Grov sø*
Bread	*Brød*	Rain	*Regn*
Meat	*Kød*	Fog	*Tåge*

LANGUAGES English and German are widely spoken.

AMTSKOMMUNERS are given in lieu of 'counties' in the UK.

TIME ZONE is –0100 (subtract 1 hour for UT). DST is kept from the last Sunday in March until the last Sunday in October.

CHARTS Danish charts are issued by Kort-og Matrikelstyrelsen, Rentemestervej 8, DK-2400 København. Those prefixed 'DK' are standard Danish nautical charts. Leisure charts for W Jutland are not available. British Admiralty charts are mostly small scale.

LIGHTS Navigational marks, buoys and lights are excellent.

HARBOURS Most yacht hbrs are owned by the state or community and run by a local Yacht Club (as in Germany).

TRAFFIC SEPARATION SCHEMES There are none off West Jutland, but off Skagen heavy traffic between the Skaggerak and Kattegat follows Transit Routes T or B; see chartlet overleaf.

SIGNALS Local port, tidal, distress and traffic signals are given where possible. When motor sailing, always display a motoring ▼.

TELEPHONES To call UK from Denmark: dial 00 44, then the UK area code, minus the initial zero; followed by the number required. To call Denmark, which has no area codes, from the UK: dial 00 (or +) 45, then the required 8 digit number.

EMERGENCIES Police, Fire and Ambulance: dial 112.

PUBLIC HOLIDAYS New Year's Day, Maundy Thurs (Thu before Easter) thru' to Easter Monday, Common Prayer Day (4th Fri after Easter) Ascension Day, Whit Monday, Constitution Day (5 Jun) Christmas Eve to Boxing Day. Local festivals are common.

CURRENCY The Danish krone (Dkr) = 100 øre. Rate of exchange June 2016: £1.00 = approx Dkr 9.76; 1 Dkr = approx £0.1. VAT (MOMS) is 25%, on everything. Banks with ATMs are as common as in the UK. All major credit cards are accepted.

GAS Propane is the norm. Camping Gaz (butane) is available, but Calor gas, whether butane or propane, is not.

USEFUL ADDRESSES Danish Tourist Board, 55 Sloane St, London SW1X 9SY; ☎020 7259 5959; dtb.london@dt.dk. The Embassy is at the same address.

Denmark: The main Tourist Office is Vesterbrogade 6D, 1620 København V; ☎33 11 14 15; dt@dt.dk; www.dt.dk. There are excellent and very helpful TOs in most fair-sized towns.

British Embassy, Kastelsvej 36-40, DK-2100 København Ø; ☎35 44 52 00.

For other addresses see Chapter 1.

TRANSPORT Ferries run from Hirtshals to Oslo, Larvik and Kristiansand or Hanstholm to Bergen, the Faroe Is and Iceland.

UK scheduled and low-cost flights go to Billund (35M NE of Esbjerg) and Copenhagen. 'Norwegian' have regular budget flights to/from Aalborg (107M NE of Thyboron) to Gatwick and many other domestic and international destinations. Internal flights are limited as Denmark is compact with reliable and fast trains, (DSB) and a broad fare structure. Buses are also widespread and reliable. Bicycles are very popular and easy to hire.

SHOPPING Most towns have a market day on either Wed or Sat and launderettes (*montvaskeri*) coin or token-operated.

9.14.7 SKAGEN

Nordjylland **57°42'·86N 10°35'·63E**

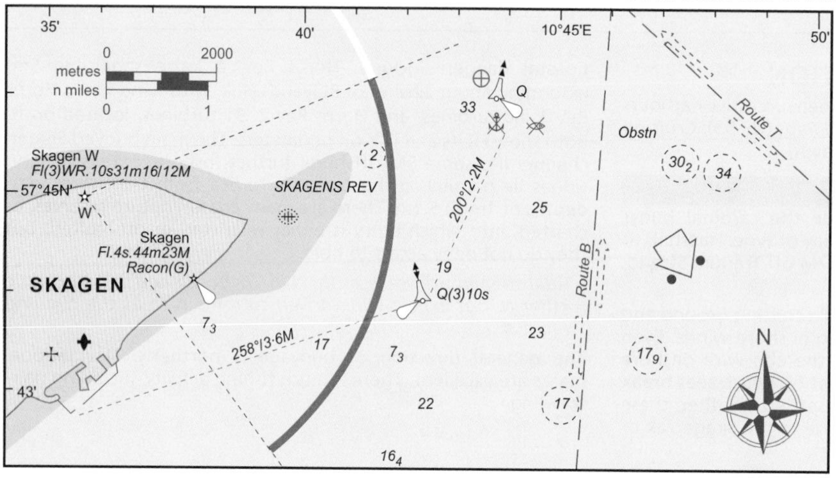

CHARTS AC 1402, 2107 with 1:12,500 hbr inset

TIDES Variations in heights are minimal and largely generated by wind. For all practical purposes Hirtshals differences are adequate. HW heights are: MHWS 0·2m, MHWN 0·1m.

TIDAL STREAMS are perceptible only in calm conditions. Wind influence usually creates a NE-going current for 75% of the year.

SHELTER is good, access at all tides/weather. Yachts berth in 4m between Old Pier and Pier 1, NE of the central pontoon. FVs berth either side of Pier 1. There are also quieter berths at the YC pontoons in 3·5m on S side of Bundgarns Bassin.

NAVIGATION From the W, the WPT is 57°45'·98N 10°43'·74E, a NCM buoy Q, off the NE tip of Skagens Rev. Thence 200°/2·2M to an ECM buoy, Q(3) 10s, at 57°43'·87N 10°42'·35E; thence 258°/3·6M to hbr ent. Buoyed routes B and T are for transit shipping. Avoid restricted area in hbr approach.

LIGHTS AND MARKS As chartlet and 9.14.4. The R sector of Skagen West lt ho shows over Skagens Rev. Skagen lt ho is 1·7M NE of the hbr ent, with Racon G, 20M. Use Dir ☆ Oc WRG 5s (267°-W- 271°) for harbour approach.

COMMUNICATIONS Coast Guard 89 43 30 99; LB Station 98 45 07 57; H 70 15 03 00; Police, 96 22 14 48, (emergency 112); Dr 70 15 03 00, (emergency 112); HM 98 44 13 46 (H24) VHF Ch 16, 12; Taxi 98 43 34 34; Tourist Info 98 44 13 77.

FACILITIES <11.9m 200Dkr/night, 12·1m-14·9m, 280Dkr/night. WC. **YC Skagen Sejl Klub** ☎23 23 38 45/25 12 19 97, call ahead, max LOA <12m 200Dkr/night, WC. **Town** (Aalborg) ☎98 17 33 11.

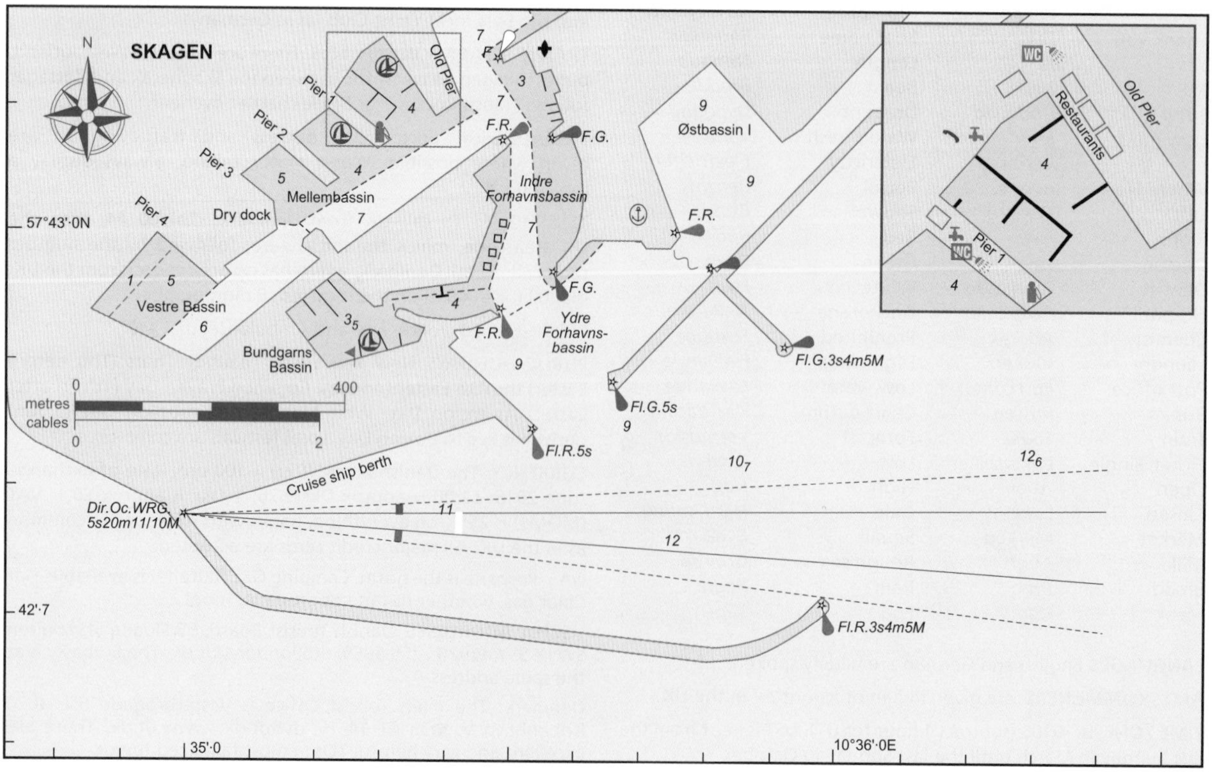

9.14.8 HIRTSHALS

Nordjylland **57°35'·90N 09°57'·54E** ✵✵✵◇◇✿

CHARTS AC 1402 with 1:12,500 hbr inset; DK92; D 63

TIDES +0600 Dover, ML 0·0, Duration 0625

Standard Port ESBJERG (⟶)

Times				Height (metres)			
High Water		Low Water		MHWS	MHWN	MLWN	MLWS
0300	0700	0100	0800	2·0	1·6	0·6	0·2
1500	1900	1300	2000				
Differences HIRTSHALS							
+0055	+0320	+0340	+0100	–1·7	–1·4	–0·5	–0·2

SHELTER Good. Yachts berth in a small marina to stbd and close S of the hbr ent. For possible berth on pontoon in Vestbassin, mostly locals, call HM. Hirtshals is a commercial and fishing hbr which in theory foreign yachts may use only with HM's prior approval. It is not advisable to attempt entrance in strong onshore winds from N to NW due to heavy seas and strong E-going current. In E gales water levels are lowered by up to 1·0m.

NAVIGATION WPT 57°36'·39N 09°57'·32E, 166°/7ca to marina ent in front of rear 166° ldg lt. The outer PHM and SHM buoys funnel vessels into the entrance. Inbound vessels have precedence over outbound. Turn to stbd before reaching the Inner Hbr lt FG. Caution: FVs and fast ferries to Norway. Speed limit 3kn.

LIGHTS AND MARKS As chartlet and 9.14.4. 166° ldg bcns: front, R ▲ on frame twr; rear, R ▼ on frame twr. The white lt ho is approx 1M SW of the hbr ent.

COMMUNICATIONS Coast Guard 98 92 22 22; Police 96 23 14 48, (emergency 112); Ⓗ 70 15 03 00; Ⓗ (Hjørring) 98 92 72 44; Dr 98 94 11 77; HM 98 94 14 22, VHF Ch 16, 12, 13, HX; Taxi 98 92 47 00.

FACILITIES <10m, 140Dkr, >10m, 160Dkr, WC ☎98 94 12 27.

Town ✕ ⊠, ⇄ ✈ (Aalborg) ☎98 17 33 11. Ferries to Bergen, Oslo, Larvik and Kristiansand.

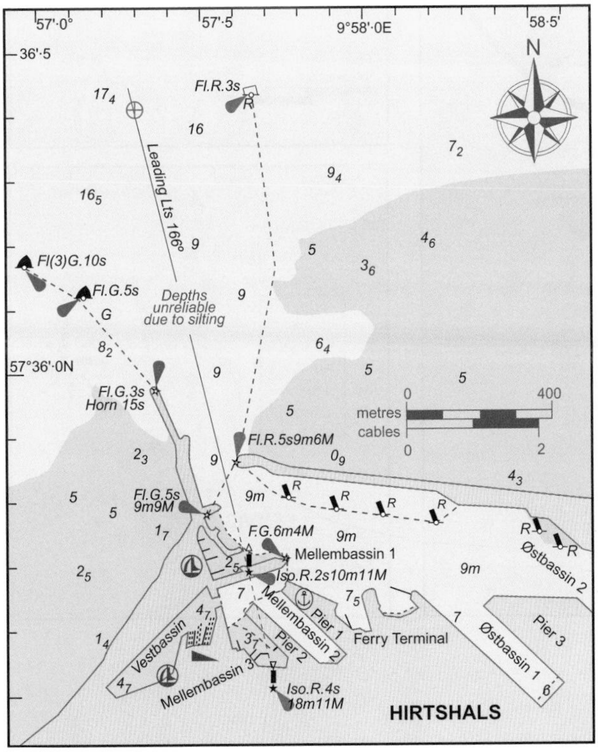

9.14.9 HANSTHOLM

Viborg **57°07'·57N 08°35'·51** ✵✵✵✵◇◇✿

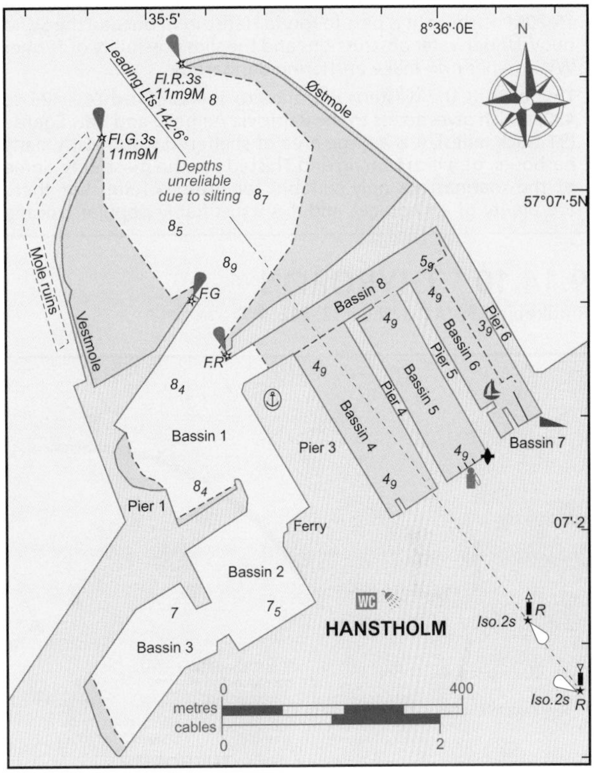

CHARTS AC 1402 with 1:12,500 hbr inset; DK92, 104; D 82

TIDES +0600 Dover, ML 0.0, Duration 0630

Standard Port ESBJERG (⟶)

Times				Height (metres)			
High Water		Low Water		MHWS	MHWN	MLWN	MLWS
0300	0700	0100	0800	2·0	1·6	0·6	0·2
1500	1900	1300	2000				
Differences HANSTHOLM							
+0100	+0340	+0340	+0130	–1·7	–1·3	–0·5	–0·2

SHELTER Good. The port is a commercial and fishing hbr which in theory foreign yachts may use only with the HM's prior approval. Yachts berth at the SW corner of Bassin 6 or as directed. S of the FG/FR inner mole heads speed limit 3kn.

NAVIGATION WPT 57°08'·10N 08°34'·94E (SWM buoy, L Fl 10s) 142° about 6ca to the hbr entrance. The approach is clear. Ldg marks 142·6° front, R ▲ on mast; rear, R ▼ on mast, lead between the outer moles.

- Charted depths are unreliable due to silting and particularly after E gales when levels may be lowered by up to 1·3m.
- Check on VHF that the entrances are clear of departing ships which may be hidden behind the moles. Inbound vessels have precedence over outbound.

LIGHTS AND MARKS As chartlet and 9.14.4. Hanstholm lt ho, a W 8-sided twr with R top, is approx 7ca S of the hbr ent and visible by day from seaward, rising above the flat terrain. The outer and inner mole heads are floodlit.

COMMUNICATIONS Coast Guard 97 92 22 22; Police (Emergency) 112; Ⓗ (Thisted) 97 92 44 00, (Skagen) 70 15 03 00; HM 97 96 18 33/96 55 07 10, VHF Ch 16; 12 13, HX; Taxi 97 96 17 11.

FACILITIES Diver ☎97 96 27 00. **Town** ✕ ⇄ (Thisted) ✈ (Thisted) ☎97 96 51 66. Ferries to Bergen, the Faroe Is and Iceland.

HANSTHOLM TO THYBORØN

(AC 1422) Off **Hanstholm** S/SW winds may cause currents up to 4kn in rough weather, but tidal streams are imperceptible for 15-20M offshore. It is best to round Hanstholm outside the SWM buoy. Underwater obstructions and the slim possibility of former WW2 mines may make anchoring dangerous.

Thyborøn is the western entrance to the **Limfjord** (AC 426 to 430) which gives access to the Baltic via Aalborg and Hals/Egense (91 track miles). It is a large area of sheltered water with many harbours, of which **Lemvig** and Thisted are the most W'ly. Some of the marinas are only suitable for drafts <1·5m, but there are plenty of anchorages and it is a justifiably popular cruising ground. The Danish word 'Bredning', meaning a Broad (as in Norfolk), aptly describes the stretches of water linked by narrow sounds; least depths are 4m.

THYBORØN TO HVIDE SANDE

(AC 1422) 'Dangerous anchoring' areas fringe the coast to 1M offshore. Bovbjerg lt ho, a red tower on a 38m high sand dune, is conspic. **Thorsminde** is a FV hbr between the sea and Nissum Fjord. S of here coastal dunes are high enough to obscure the houses behind them. ▶*Tidal streams (such as they are) divide off Lyngvig lt ho, ie to the S the in-going stream sets S and the out-going stream sets N; the reverse occurs N of Lyngvig.*◀

9.14.10 THYBORØN

Ringkøbing **56°42'·87N 08°12'·81E**

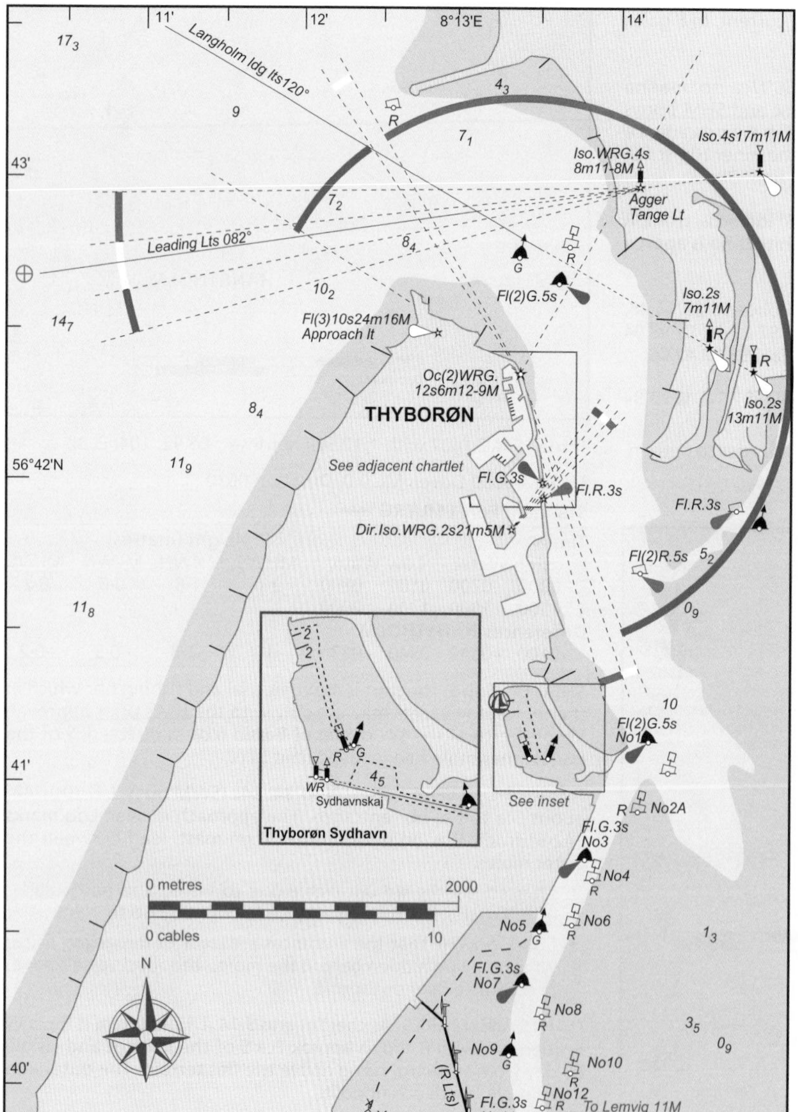

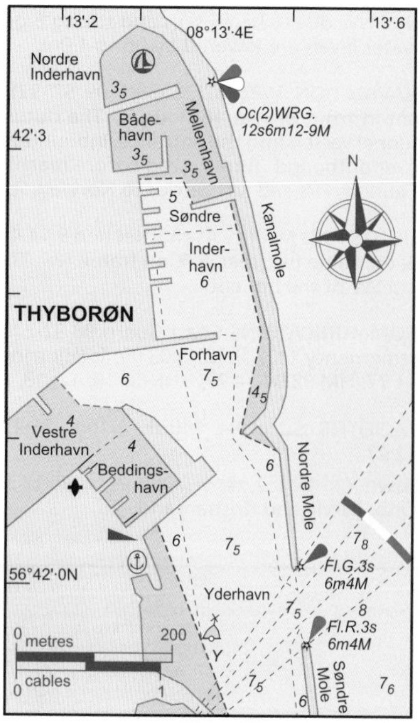

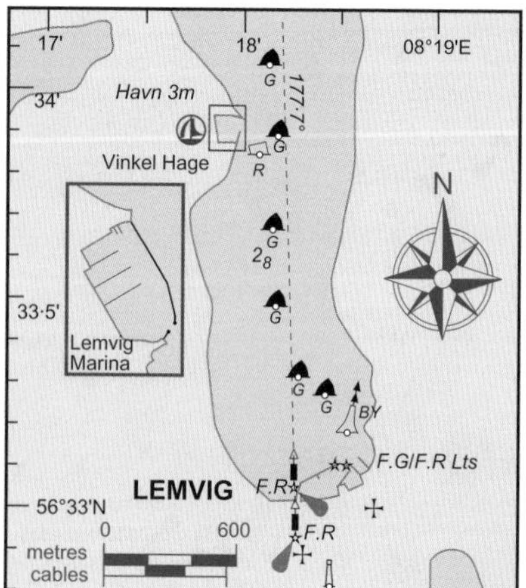

THYBORØN *continued*

CHARTS AC 426 (inc 2 hbr plans); DK108S; D 81

TIDES +0530 Dover; ML 0·0; Duration 0620

Standard Port ESBJERG (⟶)

Times				Heights (metres)			
High Water		Low Water		MHWS	MHWN	MLWN	MLWS
0300	0700	0100	0800	2·0	1·6	0·6	0·2
1500	1900	1300	2000				
Differences THYBORØN							
+0120	+0230	+0410	+0210	−1·6	−1·3	−0·5	−0·2

SHELTER inside is good. Yachts berth in the N'most basin, Nordre Inderhavn, (aka Thyborøn Marina) in 3·5m or as directed. Just over 1M south of hbr Thyborøn Lystbådehavn has limited space on two 45m long pontoons in 2m (see chartlet inset).

NAVIGATION Entry can be dangerous in near gale force onshore winds which cause breaking seas and violent eddies. Least depth is usually about 6m on appr and 5–8m within the bar.

WPT 56°42'·55N 08°08'·70E (SWM buoy L Fl 10s, Racon T) 082°/2·5M to abeam unlit SHM buoy at ent. Here turn stbd SSE, past a SHM buoy Fl (2) G 5s, into the main fairway to the Yderhavn ent. Inside the ent turn 90° stbd to Nordre Inderhavn 4 cables N.

LIGHTS AND MARKS As on chartlet and 9.14.4. The Appr lt, Fl (3) 10s, is an all-round lt ho; in poor vis shown by day. The E mole lt, Oc (2) WRG 12s, has a W sector covering a 148·2° approach from NNW. Yderhavn ent, W sector, Dir Iso WRG 2s.

Outer 082° ldg marks: front, Agger Tange R ▲ on bn; rear, R ▼ on grey frame twr. Langholm 120° ldg marks: front, R ▲ on R hut; rear, R ▼ on grey frame twr. Caution: light sectors and buoys in the approach chans are moved to reflect changes in depths.

COMMUNICATIONS Coast Guard 97 82 13 22; Ⓗ (Thisted) 97 92 44 00; HM 97 83 10 50, VHF Ch 16; 12 13, H24; Taxi 97 83 25 11.

FACILITIES or bow/stern on piles and quay<9.4m 100Dkr, 9.4m to <12.4m 150Dkr, >12.4m 170Dkr, inc ☎97 83 11 26, ☎97 83 11 25.

Town ✕ ✉ ⇌ ✈(Thisted) ☎97 96 51 66.

Limfjord cuts across Jutland via Aalborg to the E ent at Hals in the Kattegat, approx 91M; saving about 90M over the offshore route via Skagen. Thyborøn is the W ent to Limfjord, a notable cruising ground in its own right.

Lemvig (see chartlet opposite) is 13M SSE of Thyborøn. Note: WIP 2014 to enlarge hbr. **Lemvig Marina** is at Vinkel Hage, 56°33'·93N 08°17'·86E, (W bank) 9ca N of Lemvig; www.lemvig-marina.dk

9.14.11 THORSMINDE (TORSMINDE)

Ringkøbing **56°22'·32N 08°06'·82E**

CHARTS AC 1422; DK93; D 82

TIDES +0425 Dover; ML 0·1; Duration 0605

Standard Port ESBJERG (⟶)

Times				Height (metres)			
High Water		Low Water		MHWS	MHWN	MLWN	MLWS
0300	0700	0100	0800	2·0	1·6	0·6	0·02
1500	1900	1300	2000				
Differences THORSMINDE							
+0045	+0050	+0040	+0010	−1·4	−1·1	−0·5	−0·2

SHELTER Shelter is good inside, but see the notes below. Yachts berth in the Vesthavn between piers 3 and 4. There is no access into Nissum Fjord due to drainage sluices which close off the hbr immediately W of the road bridge.

NAVIGATION WPT 56°22'·34N 08°05'·49E, approx 090°/1M to hbr ent, which is dredged 4m except during onshore gales. Approach directly from seaward and turn stbd into Vesthavn.

Even moderate winds can cause breakers over the bar which normally has less than 2·7m below MSL and the Hbr may have less water than charted due to silting.

WATER LEVEL AND CURRENT

Strong W'lies can raise the water level by up to 3·0m and E'lies lower it by up to 1·8m. Levels are said to be signalled by a complex array of R & W lts, but before approaching, check conditions with the HM and request a berth.

Sluicing causes currents into and out of the hbr; warning signals, as in Hvide Sande, are shown from masts by the sluices.

LIGHTS AND MARKS Lt ho 56°22'·5N 08°07'·2E, F 30m 14M, grey frame tr. Other lts as chartlet and 9.14.4.

TELEPHONE Coast Guard 97 41 22 22; Ⓗ (Holstebro) 97 41 42 00; Police (Emergency) 112; HM 97 49 72 44, VHF Ch **13** 16, 0300-1300 1400-2400 LT; Taxi 97 82 14 15.

FACILITIES 100Dkr all LOA. **Town** ✕ ⇌ (Ramme, Holstebro, Ringkøbing) ✈(Karup) ☎97 10 12 18.

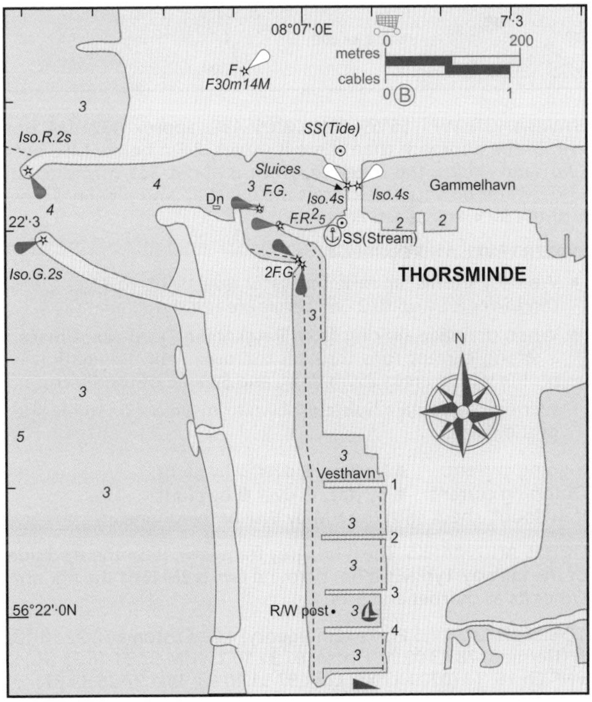

9.14.12 HVIDE SANDE

Ringkøbing **55°59'·89N 08°06'·56E**

CHARTS AC 1422; DK93, 99; D 82

TIDES +0345 Dover, ML 0·2, Duration 0550. Mean range is about 0·75m.

Standard Port ESBJERG (→)

Times				Height (metres)			
High Water		Low Water		MHWS	MHWN	MLWN	MLWS
0300	0700	0100	0800	2·0	1·6	0·6	0·2
1500	1900	1300	2000				
Differences HVIDE SANDE							
0000	+0010	–0015	–0025	–1·2	–0·9	–0·4	–0·2

SHELTER ***Strong W winds can cause breakers over the bar rendering the entrance dangerous.*** Good shelter inside, but see notes on Water level and Current. No ⚓ in the hbr channels.

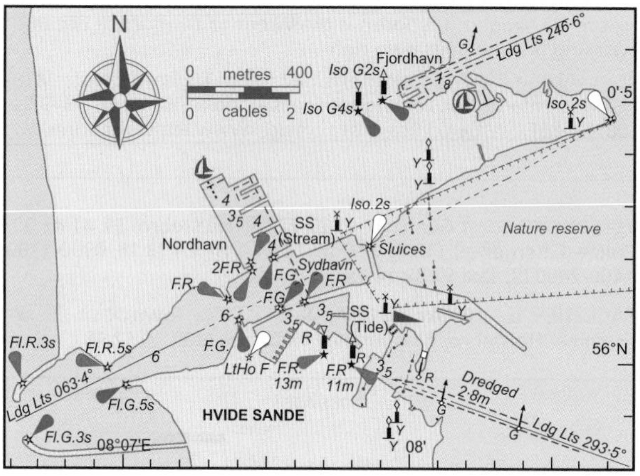

NAVIGATION WPT 55°59'·80N 08°05'·49E, approx 072°/1M Hbr ent. In the approach chan there is usually 2·5m below MSL over two sand ridges, the outer of which is about 3ca offshore. An underwater power cable crosses the ent chan and pipelines cross E of the lock. Hbr speed limit is 3kn.

WATER LEVEL AND CURRENT

- Westerly storms can raise the water level by up to 3·5m, E'lies can lower it by up to 2·0m. Levels are not signalled.
- When drainage sluicing from Ringkøbing Fjord takes place, a strong current runs through the outer hbr. Navigation is prohib within areas 250m W of, and 500m E of the sluices.
- Warning signals are hoisted/shown from a mast on the N side of the sluice:

Ingoing current: ▲ by day; ● over ○ by night.
Outgoing current: ▼ by day; ○ over ● by night.
If in doubt, check with the HM by VHF or telephone.

LIGHTS AND MARKS The lt ho, grey frame twr, is on the stbd side of the fairway. Lyngvig lt ho, W round twr, is 3M N of the hbr ent. Other lts as chartlet and 9.14.4.

COMMUNICATIONS Police (Emergency) 112; Customs 72 22 18 18; Ⓗ (Herning) 78 43 00 00; Doctor 97 31 10 23; HM 97 31 16 33 (H24) VHF Ch 16, 12 (0700-1700); Lock 97 31 10 93; Taxi 97 35 33 77.

FACILITIES While the harbour is mainly a fishing port, it also gives access to Ringkøbing Fjord, which is drained by sluices at the E end of the Outer Hbr, and is a popular tourist destination.

Yachts berth on a pontoon in the Sydhavn (first turning to stbd) or as directed by the HM. Or lock through to the Østhavn to enter appr chan (1·8m) and berth in Fjordhavn marina (1·6m). by bowser, contact HM, WC. ☎97 31 15 22.

Town ✕ ✉ ⇌ (Ringkøbing) ✈ (Esbjerg).

HVIDE SANDE TO ESBJERG

(AC 3766, 3768, Danish 99) Firing practice areas extend 9M W and 8M NNW from a pos 4M N of Blåvands Huk lt ho; and 7-10M to seaward of Nyminde Gab 55°49'N 08°12'E.(see 5.11.4). Charts warn of the dangers of anchoring and fishing due to wrecks and underwater explosives.

Entrance to **Hvide Sande** can be difficult when sluicing causes strong currents in the entrance. Thence Ringkøbing Fjord, a lagoon 15M long by 6M wide, is entered via a lock. There are several attractive hbrs/marinas (Ringkøbing, Bork, Skaven and Stavning) and ⚓s, but also shallows and conservation areas with prohibited access – see Danish AC 99.

Off Blåvands Huk (AC 3766) Slugen is the buoyed/lit and deep inshore channel through the shallow banks of **Horns Rev**. See Fig 14(1). The general direction of buoyage is NW.

Close SW of Slugen Horns Rev 1 wind farm, is centred on 55°29'·22N 07° 50'·21E: 80 turbines all R lts, 12 perimeter turbines Fl Y. NE/SW turbines, ***Racon (U)***; in fog: Mo U 15s.

NW of this wind farm a 12M x 3·5M rectangular area is dangerous for ⚓ing, fishing and seabed ops. It was formerly mined.

11M NW of Horns Rev 1, Horns Rev 2 wind farm, centred on 55°36'·08N 07°34'·78E has 91 turbines, all R lts, perimeter turbines Fl Y; NW turbine ***Racon (U)***. In fog: Mo U 15s.

ESBJERG TO RØMØ

(AC 3767, 3768) Grådyb, the ent channel to **Esbjerg**, is well buoyed. See Fig 14(2). ►*In Esbjerg Roads the tide sets ESE from HW Helgoland –0305 and WSW from +0315. Streams in the Fanø Bugt are shown in tables on AC 3768. In the open sea the flood is SE-going and the ebb NW-going; there is no slack water, just a turning of the stream, usually anti-clockwise. The rate is 1½kn at the change; the ebb is often stronger than the flood.*

Abeam Rømø Havn the ingoing stream begins at HW Helgoland –0215 and runs NNE across the hbr entrance; the outgoing stream begins at +0345 and runs SSW across the entrance; max rate in each direction is about 2kn.◄

From Grådyb SWM buoy/Racon to Lister Tief SWM is 171°/19·5M. A firing practice range extends 12M seaward of Rømø. (See 5.11.4.) Approach Rømø via the buoyed channel.

Butendiek wind farm, centred on 55°01'·00N 07°46'·40E, 80 turbines, lies 25M WSW of Rømø. Dan Tysk wind farm, centred on 55°09'·00N 07°12'·00E, 80 turbines, lies 44M W of Rømø. Sandbank wind farm 55°13'·88N 06°50'·82E, 72 turbines, is 13M WNW of Dan Tysk. Turbines on all farms show R lts, and Fl Y on perimeters.

CROSSING THE NORTH SEA

(AC 2182A, 2182B, 2182C) Important considerations include:

- Distances which are considerable. Harwich to Esbjerg is 330M and Harwich to Skagen is 483M. Experienced crew used to night passages, and a well found yacht, are essential. See 9.0 for distances across the North Sea.
- The many oil/gas rigs must be identified and avoided.
- The extensive Dutch and German TSS south of 54°12'N, and west of Helgoland, must be avoided or carefully negotiated.

From the English S coast it may be prudent to coast-hop via the Netherlands and the Frisian Islands, then make for Helgoland, dependent on weather. A suitable departure point from the Thames estuary is S Galloper SCM, and from Lowestoft, Smiths Knoll SCM. From further N, ie Hartlepool to the Firth of Forth, a track to Esbjerg avoids Dogger Bank and the densest oil/gas rig concentrations. See also Special notes in Areas 15 and 16.

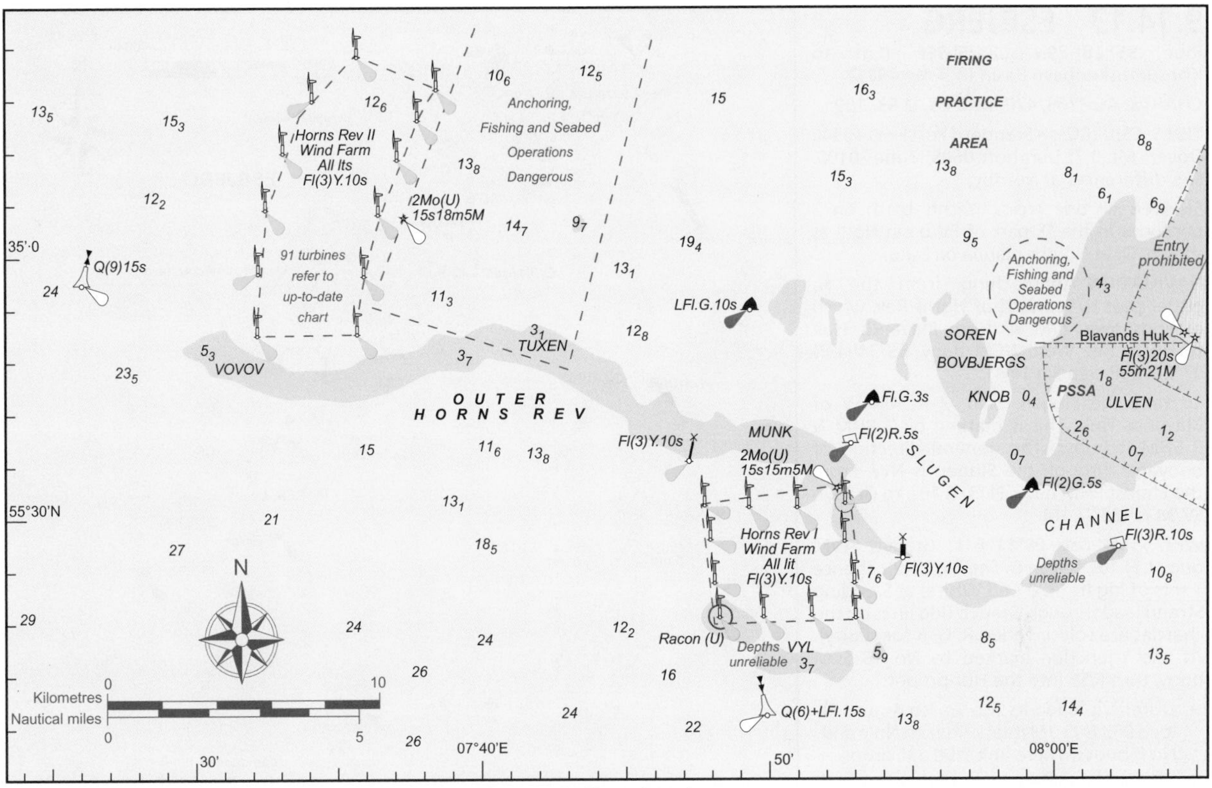

Fig 14(1) Horns Rev, wind farms, and Slugen Channel west of Blåvands Huk

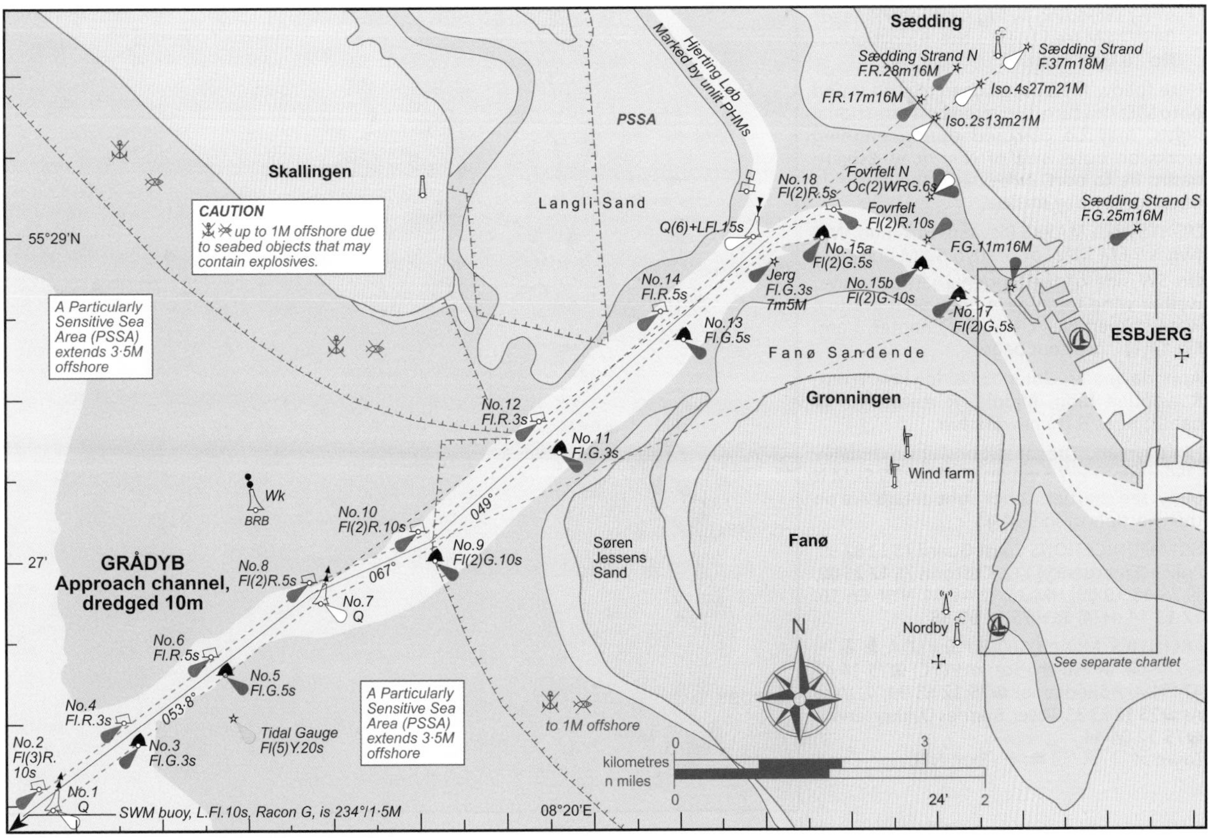

Fig 14(2) Grådyb: Outer approach to Esbjerg

9.14.13 ESBJERG

Ribe **55°28′·29N 08°25′·36E** (Ent to Konsumfiskerihavn Basin II)

CHARTS AC 3766, 420; DK94/5; D 83, 109

TIDES ESBJERG is a Standard Port (⟶) +0340 Dover; ML 0·7; Duration 0605; Zone -0100. See differences at Nordby.

SHELTER All tide access. Yachts berth on 2 pontoons in the SE part of FV basin No II as shown. Or at Nordby marina on Fanø.

NAVIGATION Approaching from the N, either pass to seaward of Horns Rev, which extends over 21M W from Blåvands Huk to Horns Rev West WCM buoy, 55°34′·49N 07°26′·08E. See Fig 14(1).

Or take the Slugen chan, 9 to 4M W of Blåvands Huk. This is marked by 2 PHM & 3 SHM lt buoys. The general direction of buoyage through the Slugen is NW. From the E'most PHM buoy, Fl (3) R 10s, to Grådyb SWM is 132°/7·1M.

WPT 55°24′·63N 08°11′·61E, Grådyb SWM buoy L Fl 10s, Racon G. See Fig 14(2). Thence 3 sets of ldg lts (R, G and White) at Sædding Strand lead through Grådyb (ldg lines on the chartlet are colour-coded R, G, B for clarity). At the Y-junction marked by No 16 SCM buoy, turn E/SE into the Hbr proper:

- Outer triple ldg lts (Iso 2s, Iso 4s and F) lead 053·8°/3·7M (black line) to No 7 and No 8 buoys. There jink stbd 13° onto:
- Middle (Sædding S) ldg lts, both FG, 067°/8ca (green line) to Nos 9 & 10 buoys. Thence jink 16° port onto:
- Inner (Sædding N) ldg lts, both FR, lead 049°/2·8M (red line) to the Y-junction at No 16 SCM buoy.

Here follow the buoyed chan to stbd round onto SSE; this turn is covered by 4 directional lights, may be obscured during ongoing works on outer side of N'ly quay. Esbjerg basins lie to port, or deviate stbd at No 21 buoy for Nordby marina.

LIGHTS AND MARKS Blåvands Huk lt ho, W □ twr, is 9·6M NNW of Gradyb SWM buoy.

On SW side of the Slugen chan extensive, well-lit wind farms have been built in shoal waters; keep well clear. See Chapter 3 and Fig 14(1) – previous page.

Appr daymarks. Outer 053·8° ldg line: Front, R wooden bldg; Middle, R metal twr W bands; Rear, R framework twr.

Hbr daymark: The conspic power stn chimney (250m high) is 7·5 cables E of No 25 SHM lt buoy; see chartlet. Other light details are on the chartlets or in 9.14.4.

COMMUNICATIONS Coast Guard 75 12 82 99; Police (Emergency) 112; Customs 75 12 25 00; Ⓗ 75 18 19 00; HM 75 12 41 44, VHF Ch 16: 12 13 14, H24; Taxi 75 12 69 88.

FACILITIES Marina, 100Dkr any LOA, at Esbjerg Søsport (YC) ☎75 14 47 47; A-Z Snedkeriet ☎75 12 65 99; Vase As ☎75 12 33 33; Diver, Bjarnes Dykkerservice ☎75 12 04 44.

Town (8km NE).

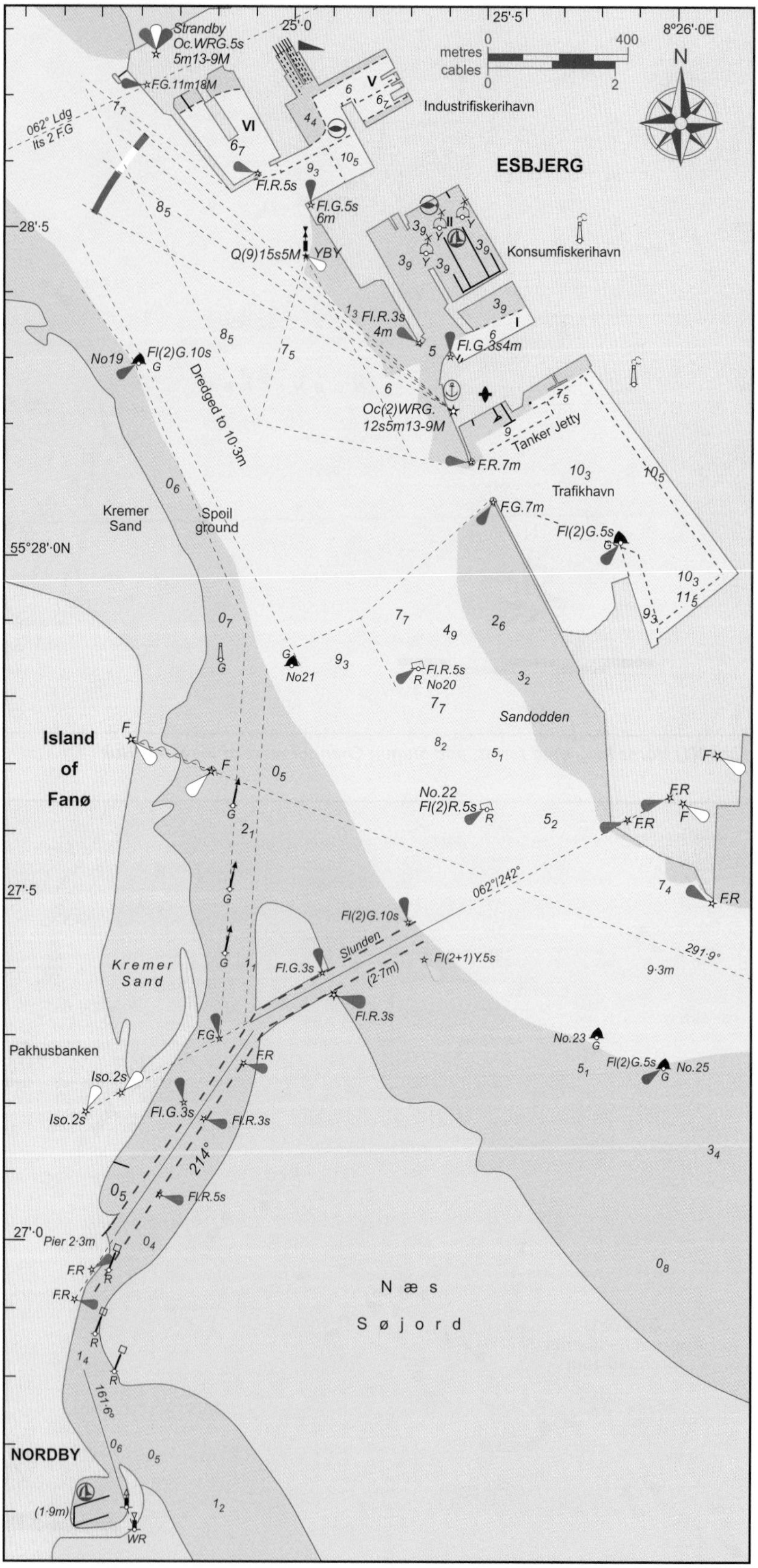

STANDARD TIME UT –01
Subtract 1 hour for UT
For Danish Summer Time add ONE hour in **non-shaded areas**

ESBJERG LAT 55°28′N LONG 8°27′E

TIMES AND HEIGHTS OF HIGH AND LOW WATERS

Dates in red are SPRINGS
Dates in blue are NEAPS

YEAR **2018**

JANUARY

Day	Time	m	Day	Time	m
1 M	0136	2.1	16 TU	0229	2.1
	0730	0.5		0825	0.5
	1403	2.2		1452	2.0
	1958	0.5		2039	0.6
2 TU ○	0230	2.2	17 W ●	0310	2.1
	0824	0.4		0905	0.5
	1500	2.2		1531	2.0
	2047	0.5		2115	0.6
3 W	0320	2.2	18 TH	0344	2.1
	0915	0.4		0941	0.5
	1551	2.1		1603	2.0
	2135	0.4		2148	0.5
4 TH	0407	2.3	19 F	0411	2.1
	1004	0.3		1014	0.5
	1640	2.1		1629	2.0
	2221	0.4		2220	0.5
5 F	0451	2.3	20 SA	0436	2.1
	1052	0.3		1046	0.5
	1727	2.1		1656	2.0
	2307	0.5		2253	0.5
6 SA	0536	2.3	21 SU	0504	2.2
	1140	0.4		1120	0.4
	1813	2.0		1727	2.0
	2354	0.5		2329	0.5
7 SU	0622	2.3	22 M	0537	2.2
	1230	0.4		1158	0.4
	1900	2.0		1804	2.0
8 M ◑	0042	0.5	23 TU	0008	0.4
	0711	2.2		0616	2.2
	1321	0.5		1239	0.4
	1952	1.9		1846	2.0
9 TU	0133	0.6	24 W ◐	0052	0.4
	0806	2.2		0702	2.2
	1416	0.5		1326	0.4
	2050	1.9		1933	2.0
10 W	0230	0.6	25 TH	0141	0.5
	0908	2.1		0753	2.2
	1516	0.6		1418	0.5
	2153	1.9		2028	1.9
11 TH	0333	0.7	26 F	0237	0.5
	1016	2.1		0852	2.1
	1621	0.6		1517	0.5
	2256	2.0		2130	1.9
12 F	0442	0.7	27 SA	0341	0.6
	1122	2.1		1001	2.0
	1725	0.6		1625	0.6
	2356	2.0		2245	1.9
13 SA	0548	0.6	28 SU	0455	0.6
	1222	2.1		1123	2.0
	1823	0.6		1736	0.6
14 SU	0052	2.1	29 M	0004	1.9
	0647	0.6		0608	0.5
	1317	2.1		1243	2.0
	1914	0.6		1841	0.5
15 M	0143	2.1	30 TU	0114	2.0
	0739	0.5		0713	0.4
	1408	2.1		1351	2.0
	1959	0.6		1939	0.5
			31 W ○	0214	2.1
				0810	0.3
				1449	2.0
				2031	0.4

FEBRUARY

Day	Time	m	Day	Time	m
1 TH	0306	2.2	16 F	0320	2.1
	0901	0.3		0918	0.4
	1540	2.0		1542	1.9
	2119	0.4		2125	0.4
2 F	0354	2.2	17 SA	0351	2.1
	0950	0.2		0951	0.4
	1627	2.0		1612	1.9
	2204	0.3		2159	0.4
3 SA	0438	2.2	18 SU	0419	2.1
	1036	0.2		1024	0.3
	1709	2.0		1640	1.9
	2248	0.3		2233	0.3
4 SU	0520	2.2	19 M	0448	2.1
	1121	0.2		1059	0.3
	1749	2.0		1711	1.9
	2332	0.3		2309	0.3
5 M	0601	2.2	20 TU	0521	2.1
	1205	0.3		1136	0.3
	1830	1.9		1744	1.9
				2348	0.3
6 TU	0017	0.4	21 W	0559	2.1
	0644	2.2		1216	0.3
	1251	0.4		1823	1.9
	1912	1.9			
7 W ◑	0103	0.4	22 TH	0031	0.3
	0730	2.1		0642	2.1
	1339	0.5		1301	0.3
	1959	1.9		1907	1.9
8 TH	0153	0.5	23 F ◐	0118	0.3
	0823	2.0		0731	2.0
	1431	0.6		1350	0.4
	2054	1.8		1958	1.9
9 F	0251	0.6	24 SA	0212	0.4
	0926	1.9		0829	2.0
	1532	0.6		1447	0.5
	2201	1.8		2058	1.8
10 SA	0359	0.6	25 SU	0316	0.5
	1037	1.9		0940	1.9
	1641	0.7		1556	0.6
	2310	1.9		2214	1.8
11 SU	0514	0.6	26 M	0433	0.5
	1145	1.9		1111	1.8
	1748	0.6		1713	0.6
				2343	1.8
12 M	0014	1.9	27 TU	0552	0.4
	0621	0.6		1234	1.8
	1245	1.9		1823	0.5
	1845	0.6			
13 TU	0110	2.0	28 W	0058	1.9
	0716	0.5		0659	0.3
	1338	1.9		1341	1.9
	1933	0.5		1922	0.4
14 W	0200	2.0			
	0802	0.5			
	1426	1.9			
	2015	0.5			
15 TH ●	0243	2.1			
	0842	0.4			
	1507	1.9			
	2051	0.5			

MARCH

Day	Time	m	Day	Time	m
1 TH	0158	2.0	16 F	0210	2.0
	0755	0.2		0812	0.3
	1436	1.9		1438	1.9
	2014	0.3		2023	0.4
2 F ○	0251	2.1	17 SA ●	0250	2.0
	0845	0.2		0849	0.3
	1525	2.0		1516	1.9
	2101	0.2		2059	0.3
3 SA	0338	2.1	18 SU	0326	2.0
	0932	0.1		0924	0.2
	1608	2.0		1550	1.9
	2145	0.2		2135	0.2
4 SU	0420	2.2	19 M	0358	2.0
	1015	0.1		0959	0.2
	1647	1.9		1621	1.9
	2227	0.2		2211	0.2
5 M	0500	2.1	20 TU	0430	2.0
	1057	0.2		1035	0.2
	1722	1.9		1652	1.9
	2309	0.2		2249	0.2
6 TU	0537	2.1	21 W	0505	2.0
	1138	0.2		1113	0.2
	1756	1.9		1725	1.9
	2350	0.2		2329	0.1
7 W	0614	2.0	22 TH	0543	2.0
	1218	0.3		1154	0.2
	1830	1.9		1803	1.9
8 TH	0032	0.3	23 F	0012	0.2
	0652	2.0		0626	2.0
	1259	0.4		1238	0.3
	1909	1.8		1845	1.9
9 F ◑	0117	0.4	24 SA ◐	0059	0.2
	0736	1.9		0716	1.9
	1344	0.5		1327	0.4
	1954	1.8		1935	1.8
10 SA	0207	0.5	25 SU	0154	0.3
	0829	1.8		0815	1.8
	1436	0.6		1424	0.5
	2051	1.8		2036	1.8
11 SU	0309	0.6	26 M	0300	0.4
	0938	1.7		0933	1.7
	1543	0.7		1534	0.6
	2206	1.8		2157	1.7
12 M	0430	0.6	27 TU	0420	0.4
	1058	1.7		1108	1.7
	1702	0.7		1654	0.6
	2325	1.8		2329	1.8
13 TU	0546	0.6	28 W	0538	0.4
	1206	1.7		1225	1.8
	1808	0.6		1804	0.5
14 W	0029	1.8	29 TH	0042	1.9
	0644	0.5		0643	0.2
	1304	1.8		1326	1.8
	1900	0.5		1903	0.4
15 TH	0123	1.9	30 F	0141	2.0
	0731	0.4		0738	0.1
	1354	1.8		1419	1.9
	1944	0.4		1954	0.2
			31 SA ○	0233	2.1
				0826	0.1
				1505	1.9
				2041	0.2

APRIL

Day	Time	m	Day	Time	m
1 SU	0319	2.1	16 M ●	0256	2.0
	0910	0.1		0855	0.1
	1546	1.9		1523	1.9
	2124	0.1		2109	0.2
2 M	0401	2.1	17 TU	0334	2.0
	0952	0.1		0933	0.1
	1622	1.9		1558	1.9
	2205	0.1		2148	0.1
3 TU	0438	2.0	18 W	0411	2.0
	1031	0.1		1012	0.1
	1654	1.9		1632	1.9
	2245	0.1		2229	0.1
4 W	0511	2.0	19 TH	0449	2.0
	1109	0.2		1052	0.1
	1724	1.9		1708	1.9
	2324	0.2		2311	0.1
5 TH	0543	1.9	20 F	0530	1.9
	1145	0.3		1134	0.2
	1753	1.8		1746	1.9
				2356	0.1
6 F	0003	0.2	21 SA	0615	1.9
	0616	1.8		1219	0.3
	1222	0.4		1830	1.8
	1826	1.8			
7 SA	0043	0.3	22 SU ◐	0046	0.2
	0653	1.8		0707	1.8
	1300	0.5		1309	0.4
	1906	1.8		1921	1.8
8 SU ◑	0127	0.4	23 M	0142	0.3
	0739	1.7		0811	1.7
	1344	0.5		1407	0.5
	1956	1.8		2024	1.8
9 M	0221	0.5	24 TU	0250	0.3
	0837	1.6		0934	1.6
	1439	0.6		1517	0.5
	2057	1.7		2147	1.8
10 TU	0332	0.6	25 W	0407	0.3
	0953	1.6		1059	1.7
	1556	0.6		1633	0.5
	2215	1.7		2313	1.8
11 W	0455	0.5	26 TH	0521	0.3
	1116	1.6		1208	1.7
	1715	0.6		1742	0.4
	2335	1.8			
12 TH	0600	0.4	27 F	0022	1.9
	1222	1.7		0623	0.2
	1816	0.5		1306	1.8
				1841	0.3
13 F	0038	1.8	28 SA	0120	2.0
	0652	0.3		0717	0.1
	1316	1.8		1357	1.9
	1906	0.4		1932	0.2
14 SA	0130	1.9	29 SU	0212	2.0
	0736	0.3		0804	0.1
	1404	1.8		1442	1.9
	1949	0.3		2019	0.1
15 SU	0215	1.9	30 M ○	0259	2.0
	0816	0.2		0848	0.1
	1446	1.9		1523	1.9
	2029	0.2		2103	0.1

Chart Datum: 0·69 metres below Dansk Normal Null. HAT is 2·2 metres above Chart Datum.

STANDARD TIME UT –01
Subtract 1 hour for UT
For Danish Summer Time add ONE hour in **non-shaded areas**

ESBJERG LAT 55°28′N LONG 8°27′E

TIMES AND HEIGHTS OF HIGH AND LOW WATERS

Dates in red are SPRINGS
Dates in blue are NEAPS

YEAR **2018**

MAY

Date	Day	Time	m	Time	m	Time	m	Time	m
1	TU	0340	2.0	0928	0.1	1559	1.9	2144	0.1
2	W	0416	1.9	1006	0.2	1630	1.9	2223	0.1
3	TH	0448	1.9	1042	0.3	1656	1.9	2301	0.2
4	F	0516	1.8	1115	0.3	1722	1.8	2337	0.3
5	SA	0544	1.7	1148	0.4	1752	1.8		
6	SU	0014	0.3	0618	1.7	1223	0.4	1830	1.8
7	M	0054	0.4	0701	1.6	1304	0.5	1915	1.8
8	TU	0142	0.4	0752	1.6	1353	0.5	◑ 2009	1.8
9	W	0240	0.5	0856	1.6	1455	0.6	2113	1.8
10	TH	0352	0.5	1012	1.6	1611	0.6	2227	1.8
11	F	0504	0.4	1128	1.7	1722	0.5	2341	1.8
12	SA	0604	0.3	1231	1.7	1821	0.4		
13	SU	0044	1.9	0655	0.2	1325	1.8	1912	0.3
14	M	0137	1.9	0741	0.2	1412	1.9	1959	0.2
15	TU	0226	2.0	0825	0.1	1455	1.9	● 2043	0.2
16	W	0311	2.0	0907	0.1	1536	1.9	2127	0.1
17	TH	0354	1.9	0949	0.1	1614	1.9	2211	0.1
18	F	0437	1.9	1032	0.2	1653	1.9	2256	0.1
19	SA	0522	1.9	1116	0.2	1735	1.9	2344	0.1
20	SU	0610	1.8	1203	0.3	1820	1.9		
21	M	0035	0.2	0704	1.7	1254	0.4	1913	1.9
22	TU	0132	0.2	0808	1.7	1351	0.4	◐ 2017	1.8
23	W	0237	0.3	0924	1.6	1457	0.5	2134	1.8
24	TH	0348	0.3	1038	1.7	1608	0.5	2250	1.9
25	F	0457	0.3	1142	1.7	1715	0.4	2357	1.9
26	SA	0558	0.2	1239	1.8	1816	0.3		
27	SU	0056	2.0	0652	0.2	1331	1.9	1909	0.2
28	M	0149	2.0	0741	0.1	1418	1.9	1958	0.2
29	TU	0237	2.0	0825	0.2	1500	1.9	○ 2044	0.2
30	W	0320	1.9	0906	0.2	1537	1.9	2126	0.2
31	TH	0357	1.9	0943	0.3	1609	1.9	2205	0.2

JUNE

Date	Day	Time	m	Time	m	Time	m	Time	m
1	F	0429	1.8	1018	0.3	1636	1.9	2241	0.3
2	SA	0454	1.7	1050	0.4	1700	1.9	2316	0.3
3	SU	0520	1.7	1122	0.4	1727	1.9	2350	0.4
4	M	0551	1.7	1156	0.4	1802	1.9		
5	TU	0028	0.4	0631	1.7	1234	0.4	1844	1.9
6	W	0111	0.4	0718	1.7	1320	0.5	◑ 1933	1.9
7	TH	0202	0.4	0813	1.7	1414	0.5	2029	1.9
8	F	0301	0.4	0917	1.7	1518	0.5	2133	1.9
9	SA	0407	0.4	1028	1.7	1627	0.5	2244	1.9
10	SU	0513	0.4	1140	1.7	1735	0.5	2355	1.9
11	M	0613	0.3	1243	1.8	1835	0.4		
12	TU	0100	1.9	0707	0.3	1339	1.9	1929	0.3
13	W	0158	1.9	0757	0.2	1429	1.9	● 2020	0.2
14	TH	0251	2.0	0844	0.2	1515	2.0	2108	0.2
15	F	0340	1.9	0930	0.2	1559	2.0	2156	0.1
16	SA	0428	1.9	1015	0.2	1642	2.0	2244	0.1
17	SU	0515	1.9	1101	0.3	1726	2.0	2332	0.1
18	M	0604	1.8	1148	0.3	1813	2.0		
19	TU	0023	0.2	0656	1.8	1238	0.4	1904	2.0
20	W	0117	0.2	0754	1.7	1332	0.4	◐ 2003	2.0
21	TH	0216	0.3	0858	1.7	1431	0.5	2110	2.0
22	F	0320	0.3	1005	1.7	1537	0.5	2221	2.0
23	SA	0426	0.3	1108	1.8	1644	0.4	2328	2.0
24	SU	0529	0.3	1207	1.8	1748	0.4		
25	M	0029	2.0	0626	0.3	1301	1.9	1847	0.3
26	TU	0124	2.0	0717	0.3	1351	2.0	1939	0.3
27	W	0215	2.0	0804	0.3	1437	2.0	2027	0.3
28	TH	0300	1.9	0845	0.3	1518	2.0	○ 2109	0.3
29	F	0339	1.9	0923	0.4	1552	2.0	2148	0.3
30	SA	0412	1.8	0958	0.4	1620	2.0	2224	0.4

JULY

Date	Day	Time	m	Time	m	Time	m	Time	m
1	SU	0439	1.8	1029	0.4	1644	2.0	2256	0.4
2	M	0503	1.8	1101	0.4	1709	2.0	2329	0.4
3	TU	0531	1.8	1134	0.4	1741	2.0		
4	W	0005	0.4	0607	1.8	1211	0.4	1819	2.0
5	TH	0044	0.4	0649	1.8	1254	0.4	1904	2.0
6	F	0130	0.4	0738	1.8	1343	0.4	◑ 1955	2.0
7	SA	0221	0.4	0834	1.8	1438	0.5	2053	2.0
8	SU	0320	0.4	0936	1.8	1541	0.5	2158	2.0
9	M	0426	0.5	1047	1.8	1651	0.5	2313	1.9
10	TU	0534	0.4	1200	1.8	1801	0.5		
11	W	0028	1.9	0636	0.4	1307	1.9	1904	0.4
12	TH	0136	2.0	0733	0.4	1405	2.0	2001	0.3
13	F	0235	2.0	0825	0.3	1457	2.0	● 2053	0.2
14	SA	0329	2.0	0913	0.3	1545	2.1	2142	0.2
15	SU	0419	2.0	1000	0.3	1631	2.1	2231	0.2
16	M	0505	1.9	1045	0.3	1715	2.1	2318	0.2
17	TU	0551	1.9	1131	0.3	1800	2.1		
18	W	0006	0.2	0637	1.9	1218	0.3	1848	2.1
19	TH	0056	0.3	0726	1.8	1308	0.4	◐ 1940	2.1
20	F	0148	0.4	0820	1.8	1402	0.4	2039	2.1
21	SA	0245	0.4	0921	1.8	1502	0.5	2145	2.0
22	SU	0348	0.5	1026	1.8	1609	0.5	2254	2.0
23	M	0455	0.5	1130	1.9	1719	0.5	2359	2.0
24	TU	0557	0.5	1229	1.9	1824	0.5		
25	W	0057	2.0	0653	0.5	1323	2.0	1920	0.4
26	TH	0150	2.0	0742	0.5	1412	2.0	2009	0.4
27	F	0238	2.0	0825	0.5	1456	2.1	○ 2053	0.4
28	SA	0320	1.9	0904	0.5	1534	2.1	2130	0.4
29	SU	0355	1.9	0938	0.5	1604	2.1	2204	0.4
30	M	0423	1.9	1009	0.5	1629	2.1	2236	0.4
31	TU	0447	1.9	1041	0.5	1653	2.1	2307	0.4

AUGUST

Date	Day	Time	m	Time	m	Time	m	Time	m
1	W	0513	1.9	1114	0.4	1722	2.1	2341	0.4
2	TH	0545	1.9	1150	0.4	1757	2.2		
3	F	0019	0.4	0623	1.9	1230	0.4	1839	2.2
4	SA	0101	0.4	0707	1.9	1315	0.4	◑ 1926	2.1
5	SU	0149	0.4	0757	1.9	1407	0.5	2021	2.1
6	M	0243	0.5	0855	1.9	1506	0.5	2124	2.0
7	TU	0347	0.6	1002	1.9	1617	0.6	2241	2.0
8	W	0459	0.6	1122	1.9	1734	0.6		
9	TH	0007	2.0	0610	0.6	1241	2.0	1844	0.5
10	F	0121	2.0	0713	0.5	1346	2.0	1945	0.4
11	SA	0223	2.0	0807	0.5	1441	2.1	● 2038	0.3
12	SU	0317	2.1	0856	0.4	1531	2.2	2127	0.2
13	M	0405	2.1	0942	0.3	1617	2.3	2214	0.2
14	TU	0449	2.1	1027	0.3	1700	2.3	2259	0.2
15	W	0530	2.0	1111	0.3	1742	2.3	2343	0.3
16	TH	0610	2.0	1155	0.3	1825	2.2		
17	F	0028	0.4	0651	2.0	1241	0.4	1910	2.2
18	SA	0115	0.5	0737	1.9	1330	0.5	◐ 2001	2.1
19	SU	0206	0.6	0829	1.9	1425	0.6	2102	2.0
20	M	0304	0.7	0933	1.9	1531	0.7	2213	2.0
21	TU	0413	0.7	1045	1.9	1647	0.7	2324	2.0
22	W	0524	0.7	1152	2.0	1759	0.7		
23	TH	0027	2.0	0626	0.7	1251	2.0	1858	0.6
24	F	0123	2.0	0717	0.6	1343	2.1	1948	0.5
25	SA	0212	2.0	0801	0.6	1430	2.2	2030	0.5
26	SU	0255	2.0	0840	0.6	1509	2.2	○ 2107	0.5
27	M	0332	2.0	0914	0.5	1542	2.2	2140	0.5
28	TU	0402	2.0	0947	0.5	1609	2.2	2211	0.5
29	W	0429	2.0	1019	0.5	1635	2.2	2243	0.4
30	TH	0455	2.1	1052	0.5	1704	2.2	2317	0.4
31	F	0525	2.1	1128	0.4	1738	2.2	2354	0.4

Chart Datum: 0·69 metres below Dansk Normal Null. HAT is 2·2 metres above Chart Datum.

STANDARD TIME UT –01
Subtract 1 hour for UT
For Danish Summer Time add ONE hour in **non-shaded areas**

ESBJERG LAT 55°28′N LONG 8°27′E

TIMES AND HEIGHTS OF HIGH AND LOW WATERS

Dates in red are SPRINGS
Dates in blue are NEAPS

YEAR **2018**

SEPTEMBER

Date	Day	Time	m	Time	m	Time	m	Time	m
1	SA	0600	2.1	1208	0.4	1818	2.2		
2	SU	0035	0.5	0641	2.1	1252	0.5	1904	2.2
3	M	0121	0.5	0728	2.1	1342	0.5	◑ 1957	2.1
4	TU	0213	0.6	0822	2.0	1440	0.6	2101	2.0
5	W	0316	0.7	0929	2.0	1553	0.7	2223	2.0
6	TH	0432	0.8	1054	2.0	1715	0.7	2356	2.0
7	F	0549	0.8	1221	2.0	1829	0.6		
8	SA	0110	2.0	0654	0.7	1328	2.2	1929	0.5
9	SU	0210	2.1	0748	0.6	1424	2.3	● 2021	0.4
10	M	0301	2.2	0837	0.5	1514	2.3	2109	0.3
11	TU	0346	2.2	0923	0.4	1559	2.4	2153	0.3
12	W	0427	2.2	1006	0.4	1640	2.4	2236	0.3
13	TH	0504	2.2	1049	0.4	1719	2.3	2317	0.4
14	F	0539	2.1	1131	0.4	1758	2.3	2359	0.5
15	SA	0615	2.1	1214	0.5	1838	2.2		
16	SU	0041	0.6	0653	2.1	1259	0.5	1922	2.1
17	M	0125	0.7	0737	2.0	1349	0.7	◐ 2014	2.0
18	TU	0216	0.8	0832	2.0	1450	0.8	2121	2.0
19	W	0321	0.9	0944	2.0	1608	0.8	2241	1.9
20	TH	0439	0.9	1104	2.0	1727	0.8	2350	2.0
21	F	0549	0.9	1211	2.1	1828	0.7		
22	SA	0049	2.0	0645	0.8	1307	2.2	1918	0.6
23	SU	0140	2.1	0730	0.7	1356	2.2	2000	0.6
24	M	0224	2.1	0810	0.6	1438	2.3	2037	0.5
25	TU	0303	2.2	0846	0.6	1514	2.3	○ 2111	0.5
26	W	0337	2.2	0921	0.5	1545	2.3	2144	0.5
27	TH	0406	2.2	0955	0.5	1614	2.3	2218	0.5
28	F	0435	2.2	1030	0.5	1646	2.3	2253	0.5
29	SA	0506	2.2	1108	0.5	1721	2.3	2331	0.5
30	SU	0540	2.2	1149	0.5	1801	2.3		

OCTOBER

Date	Day	Time	m	Time	m	Time	m	Time	m
1	M	0013	0.5	0619	2.2	1233	0.5	1847	2.2
2	TU	0058	0.6	0705	2.1	1324	0.6	◑ 1942	2.1
3	W	0151	0.7	0759	2.1	1424	0.7	2049	2.0
4	TH	0255	0.8	0908	2.1	1539	0.7	2219	2.0
5	F	0412	0.9	1039	2.1	1701	0.7	2348	2.0
6	SA	0529	0.8	1204	2.2	1812	0.6		
7	SU	0055	2.1	0633	0.7	1309	2.3	1910	0.5
8	M	0152	2.2	0728	0.6	1405	2.4	2001	0.4
9	TU	0241	2.2	0816	0.5	1454	2.4	● 2047	0.4
10	W	0324	2.3	0902	0.4	1539	2.4	2130	0.4
11	TH	0403	2.3	0945	0.4	1619	2.4	2211	0.4
12	F	0438	2.2	1026	0.4	1656	2.3	2251	0.5
13	SA	0510	2.2	1107	0.5	1731	2.3	2329	0.6
14	SU	0541	2.2	1148	0.5	1806	2.2		
15	M	0007	0.7	0614	2.2	1230	0.6	1843	2.1
16	TU	0047	0.8	0653	2.2	1315	0.7	◐ 1928	2.0
17	W	0131	0.9	0740	2.1	1409	0.8	2024	2.0
18	TH	0224	1.0	0839	2.1	1518	0.9	2139	1.9
19	F	0337	1.0	0956	2.1	1639	0.9	2300	2.0
20	SA	0457	1.0	1117	2.1	1745	0.8		
21	SU	0005	2.0	0600	0.9	1220	2.2	1838	0.7
22	M	0100	2.1	0650	0.8	1314	2.2	1922	0.6
23	TU	0148	2.2	0734	0.7	1400	2.3	2001	0.6
24	W	0230	2.2	0814	0.6	1441	2.3	○ 2039	0.5
25	TH	0308	2.2	0852	0.6	1518	2.3	2115	0.5
26	F	0342	2.2	0930	0.5	1554	2.3	2152	0.5
27	SA	0414	2.2	1009	0.5	1630	2.3	2231	0.5
28	SU	0448	2.2	1050	0.5	1708	2.3	2311	0.6
29	M	0524	2.2	1133	0.5	1750	2.2	2354	0.6
30	TU	0604	2.2	1220	0.5	1839	2.1		
31	W	0041	0.7	0651	2.2	1313	0.6	◑ 1936	2.1

NOVEMBER

Date	Day	Time	m	Time	m	Time	m	Time	m
1	TH	0135	0.8	0748	2.2	1415	0.7	2047	2.0
2	F	0239	0.9	0859	2.1	1528	0.7	2215	2.0
3	SA	0353	0.9	1026	2.2	1644	0.7	2332	2.0
4	SU	0506	0.8	1144	2.2	1751	0.6		
5	M	0035	2.1	0609	0.7	1248	2.3	1848	0.5
6	TU	0129	2.2	0705	0.6	1344	2.4	1938	0.5
7	W	0218	2.2	0754	0.5	1434	2.4	● 2024	0.4
8	TH	0301	2.3	0841	0.5	1519	2.4	2107	0.5
9	F	0340	2.3	0924	0.5	1559	2.3	2148	0.5
10	SA	0415	2.3	1006	0.5	1635	2.3	2226	0.6
11	SU	0445	2.2	1046	0.5	1707	2.2	2302	0.7
12	M	0514	2.2	1125	0.6	1737	2.1	2337	0.7
13	TU	0543	2.2	1204	0.7	1810	2.0		
14	W	0013	0.8	0618	2.2	1246	0.7	1850	2.0
15	TH	0053	0.9	0701	2.2	1332	0.8	◐ 1938	2.0
16	F	0139	0.9	0753	2.2	1427	0.8	2038	1.9
17	SA	0237	0.9	0853	2.1	1535	0.9	2151	1.9
18	SU	0349	1.0	1005	2.1	1645	0.8	2307	2.0
19	M	0501	0.9	1119	2.2	1746	0.7		
20	TU	0011	2.1	0601	0.8	1222	2.2	1837	0.7
21	W	0105	2.1	0653	0.7	1317	2.2	1923	0.6
22	TH	0154	2.2	0740	0.7	1406	2.3	2006	0.5
23	F	0237	2.2	0824	0.6	1452	2.3	○ 2048	0.5
24	SA	0318	2.3	0908	0.5	1535	2.3	2129	0.5
25	SU	0356	2.3	0951	0.5	1617	2.2	2211	0.5
26	M	0433	2.3	1035	0.5	1700	2.2	2254	0.6
27	TU	0513	2.3	1121	0.5	1745	2.1	2339	0.6
28	W	0556	2.3	1210	0.5	1836	2.1		
29	TH	0028	0.7	0644	2.2	1304	0.5	1933	2.0
30	F	0121	0.7	0742	2.2	1404	0.6	◑ 2042	2.0

DECEMBER

Date	Day	Time	m	Time	m	Time	m	Time	m
1	SA	0222	0.8	0850	2.2	1511	0.6	2157	2.0
2	SU	0329	0.8	1008	2.2	1620	0.6	2307	2.0
3	M	0439	0.8	1120	2.3	1725	0.6		
4	TU	0008	2.1	0543	0.7	1224	2.3	1823	0.5
5	W	0103	2.2	0641	0.6	1321	2.3	1915	0.5
6	TH	0153	2.2	0734	0.5	1413	2.3	2002	0.5
7	F	0238	2.3	0822	0.5	1500	2.3	● 2046	0.5
8	SA	0319	2.3	0907	0.5	1542	2.2	2127	0.6
9	SU	0356	2.2	0949	0.5	1618	2.1	2204	0.6
10	M	0427	2.2	1029	0.6	1649	2.1	2239	0.7
11	TU	0454	2.2	1106	0.6	1716	2.0	2313	0.7
12	W	0520	2.2	1142	0.7	1744	2.0	2346	0.7
13	TH	0552	2.2	1219	0.7	1819	2.0		
14	F	0023	0.7	0630	2.2	1259	0.7	1902	2.0
15	SA	0105	0.8	0716	2.2	1346	0.7	◐ 1953	2.0
16	SU	0154	0.8	0809	2.2	1439	0.7	2052	2.0
17	M	0253	0.8	0908	2.2	1541	0.7	2159	2.0
18	TU	0359	0.8	1015	2.1	1647	0.7	2311	2.0
19	W	0507	0.8	1127	2.1	1749	0.7		
20	TH	0017	2.0	0610	0.7	1234	2.2	1845	0.6
21	F	0115	2.1	0707	0.6	1334	2.2	1936	0.6
22	SA	0207	2.2	0759	0.6	1429	2.2	○ 2024	0.5
23	SU	0255	2.2	0848	0.5	1519	2.2	2109	0.5
24	M	0339	2.2	0935	0.4	1607	2.2	2154	0.5
25	TU	0422	2.2	1022	0.4	1654	2.1	2239	0.5
26	W	0505	2.3	1110	0.4	1741	2.1	2325	0.5
27	TH	0549	2.3	1159	0.4	1829	2.0		
28	F	0013	0.6	0637	2.3	1251	0.4	1922	2.0
29	SA	0104	0.6	0731	2.2	1346	0.5	◑ 2021	2.0
30	SU	0200	0.6	0833	2.2	1446	0.5	2126	1.9
31	M	0301	0.7	0942	2.2	1550	0.6	2233	2.0

Chart Datum: 0·69 metres below Dansk Normal Null. HAT is 2·2 metres above Chart Datum.

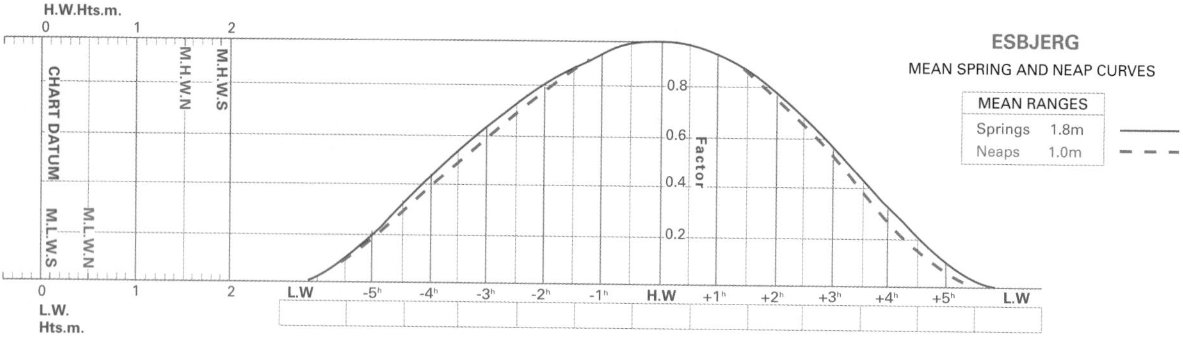

9.14.14 NORDBY (FANØ ISLAND)

Ribe **55°27'·37N 08°25'·09E**

CHARTS AC 3766, 420

TIDES +0340 Dover; ML 0·7; Duration 0605

Standard Port ESBJERG (⟶)

Times				Height (metres)			
High Water		Low Water		MHWS	MHWN	MLWN	MLWS
0300	0700	0100	0800	2·0	1·6	0·6	0·2
1500	1900	1300	2000				
Differences BLÅVANDS HUK (55°33'·0N 08°05'·0E)							
−0120	−0110	−0050	−0100	−0·2	−0·2	−0·3	−0·2
GRÅDYB BAR (55°26'·0N 08°15'·0E)							
−0130	−0115	ND	ND	−0·5	−0·4	−0·3	−0·2

SHELTER Good at Nordby Marina in 1·8m; access at all tides.

NAVIGATION As for Esbjerg (see Chartlet 9.14.13) until nearing No 21 buoy then 154° for 4ca until ldg lts 242° Iso 2s are abeam to stbd, take Slunden chan (dredged 2·0m) for 3ca thence turn to 214° for FR ldg lts at Nordby. The final appr is on 161·6° transit of two WR bns in the marina.

LIGHTS AND MARKS As Esbjerg and see 9.14.4 for lt details.

COMMUNICATIONS CG 75 16 36 66; Police (Emergency) 112; Customs (Esbjerg) 75 12 25 00; Ⓗ (Esbjerg) 75 18 19 00; HM 75 16 31 00.

FACILITIES Pontoons with WC at SC or tie up on jetty wall 100m S of ferry terminal.

Town limited at Nordby, ✕. Full services at Esbjerg via regular ferries.

9.14.15 HAVNEBY (RØMØ ISLAND)

Sønderjylland **55°05'·21N 08°34'·31E**

CHARTS AC 3766, 3767; DK 94; BSH 1440

TIDES +0315 Dover; ML 0·9; Duration 0620

Standard Port ESBJERG (⟶)

Times				Height (metres)			
High Water		Low Water		MHWS	MHWN	MLWN	MLWS
0300	0700	0100	0800	2·0	1·6	0·6	0·2
1500	1900	1300	2000				
Difference RØMØ HAVN							
−0040	−0005	0000	−0020	−0·1	0·0	−0·3	−0·3
HOJER (54°58'·0N 08°40'·0E)							
−0020	+0015	ND	ND	+0·4	+0·5	−0·2	−0·2

SHELTER Good, access at all tides. Havneby hbr is on the SE tip of Rømø. ⚓ outside the hbr, close N of the entrance.

NAVIGATION WPT 55°05'·33N 08°16'·83E, Lister Tief SWM buoy, 107°/7M via buoyed channel to G1 Pillar buoy Fl Y 4s. Here enter Rømø Dyb (deep water) marked by 3 PHM lt dolphins and by No 1 SHM lt buoy and 5 unlit SHM buoys to the hbr ent.

LIGHTS AND MARKS Rømø has no major lights. On the N end of Sylt: List West (Ellenbogen) Oc WRG 6s, provides a narrow W sector to mark the outer part of Rømø Dyb. The inner part is marked by a narrow W sector from List Land lt Oc WRG 3s, W mast, R band. List Ost, Iso WRG 6s, W twr, R band, R lantern is the 3rd major light. See Area 15 for lt sectors. Hbr lts as on chartlet.

COMMUNICATIONS Coast Guard 74 75 22 22; Police (Emergency) 112; Ⓗ; (Esbjerg) 75 18 19 00; HM 74 75 55 92, VHF Ch 10, 12, 13, 16 HX; Taxi 74 75 11 00, 74 75 53 94.

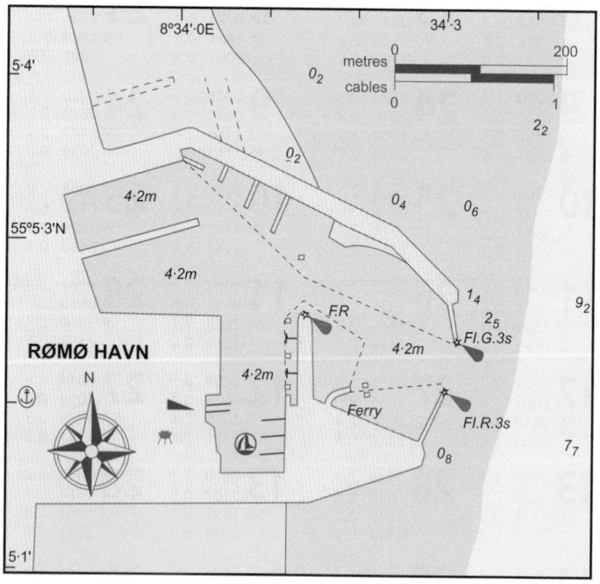

FACILITIES Essentially an isolated fishing and ferry port. Yachts berth at 3 pontoons in about 4m on S side of inner hbr. in FV hbr, WC at SC on N pier.

Havneby town. Ferry, every 2hrs by day, 45 mins to List. Rail at Ribe (mainland, 32km by road). ✈ (Esbjerg).

Germany

Sylt to Emden

9.15.1	**Contents**	665
9.15.2	**Area map, Distance table and Inland waterways**	666
9.15.3	**Tidal stream charts**	668
9.15.4	**Lights, buoys and waypoints**	670
9.15.5	**Passage information** North Frisian Islands, River Eider and Schleswig-Holstein, Helgoland to the River Elbe – 672 • From the German Bight to the UK – 676 • River Weser – 689 • River Jade, The East Frisians, River Jade to River Ems – 690 • East Frisian Islands Passage Information – 695 • River Ems – 700	672
9.15.6	**Special notes for Germany**	672
9.15.7	**North Frisian Islands** Sylt (List & Hörnum) • Föhr (Wyk) • Amrum-Hafen • Pellworm • Husum • Tönning	673
9.15.8	**Büsum**	675
9.15.9	**Helgoland, tide tables/curves**	675
9.15.10	**River Elbe**	680
9.15.11	**Cuxhaven (R Elbe), tide tables/curves** Otterndorf	682
9.15.12	**Brunsbüttel (R Elbe)**	686
9.15.13	**Nord-Ostsee Kanal (Kiel Canal)**	686
9.15.14	**Hamburg (R Elbe)**	687
9.15.15	**Bremerhaven (R Weser)**	688
9.15.16	**Hooksiel (R Jade)**	689
9.15.17	**Wilhelmshaven (R Jade), tide tables/curves**	691
9.15.18	**East Frisian Islands**	695
9.15.19	**Wangerooge** Harlesiel	696
9.15.20	**Spiekeroog** Neuharlingersiel • Bensersiel	697
9.15.21	**Accumersiel**	697
9.15.22	**Langeoog** Baltrum • Nessmersiel	698
9.15.23	**Norderney** Norddeich • Juist • Greetsiel	698
9.15.24	**Borkum**	699
9.15.25	**Emden (R Ems)**	700

9.15.2
Germany
Danish Border to Emden

1	***Den Helder***	378	322	187	213	192	198	180	229	200	245	192	175	180	159	150	153	148	138	130	132	115	125	95	115	**1**
2	***Delfzijl***	327	222	155	140	119	127	107	159	130	173	120	105	100	89	83	81	65	54	56	58	41	10	22	**2**	
3	Borkum	305	200	133	128	97	105	94	104	75	163	110	95	88	80	71	67	55	45	46	48	31	32	**3**		
4	Emden	337	232	165	142	129	137	111	174	145	190	137	120	115	106	97	85	80	71	63	65	47	**4**			
5	Norderney	291	186	123	110	77	85	70	81	52	137	84	69	62	53	44	44	29	23	18	20	**5**				
6	Accumersiel	310	206	121	99	74	79	63	116	88	132	79	62	49	44	36	37	23	15	2	**6**					
7	Langeoog	308	204	119	98	72	77	61	114	85	130	77	60	47	43	34	35	21	13	**7**						
8	Spiekeroog	301	188	119	98	70	61	53	101	72	119	64	52	47	37	29	32	9	**8**							
9	Wangerooge	283	178	109	88	60	52	47	61	32	108	55	42	38	27	19	24	**9**								
10	**Helgoland**	259	154	83	64	38	47	34	88	59	104	51	38	44	43	35	**10**									
11	Hooksiel	405	301	116	96	69	73	46	101	72	117	64	47	36	9	**11**										
12	**Wilhelmshaven**	414	310	125	104	78	82	54	110	81	123	70	56	45	**12**											
13	**Bremerhaven**	306	201	127	107	80	82	55	81	52	131	78	58	**13**												
14	Cuxhaven	304	200	110	82	63	66	25	54	25	70	17	**14**													
15	**Brunsbüttel**	301	196	126	97	75	76	35	37	8	53	**15**														
16	Kiel/Holtenau	231	249	179	153	128	129	85	90	61	**16**															
17	Gluckstadt	309	204	134	111	83	84	47	29	**17**																
18	Hamburg	338	233	163	138	112	113	73	**18**																	
19	Busum	286	180	97	72	48	43	**19**																		
20	Husum	268	163	95	70	48	**20**																			
21	**Hörnum Lt (Sylt)**	225	120	47	26	**21**																				
22	List	220	110	36	**22**																					
23	***Esbjerg***	195	90	**23**																						
24	*Thyborøn*	104	**24**																							
25	***Skagen***	**25**																								

DISTANCE TABLE
Approximate distances in nautical miles are by the most direct route while avoiding dangers and allowing for TSS. Places in *italics* are in adjoining areas; places in **bold** are in 9.0.7, Distances across the North Sea.

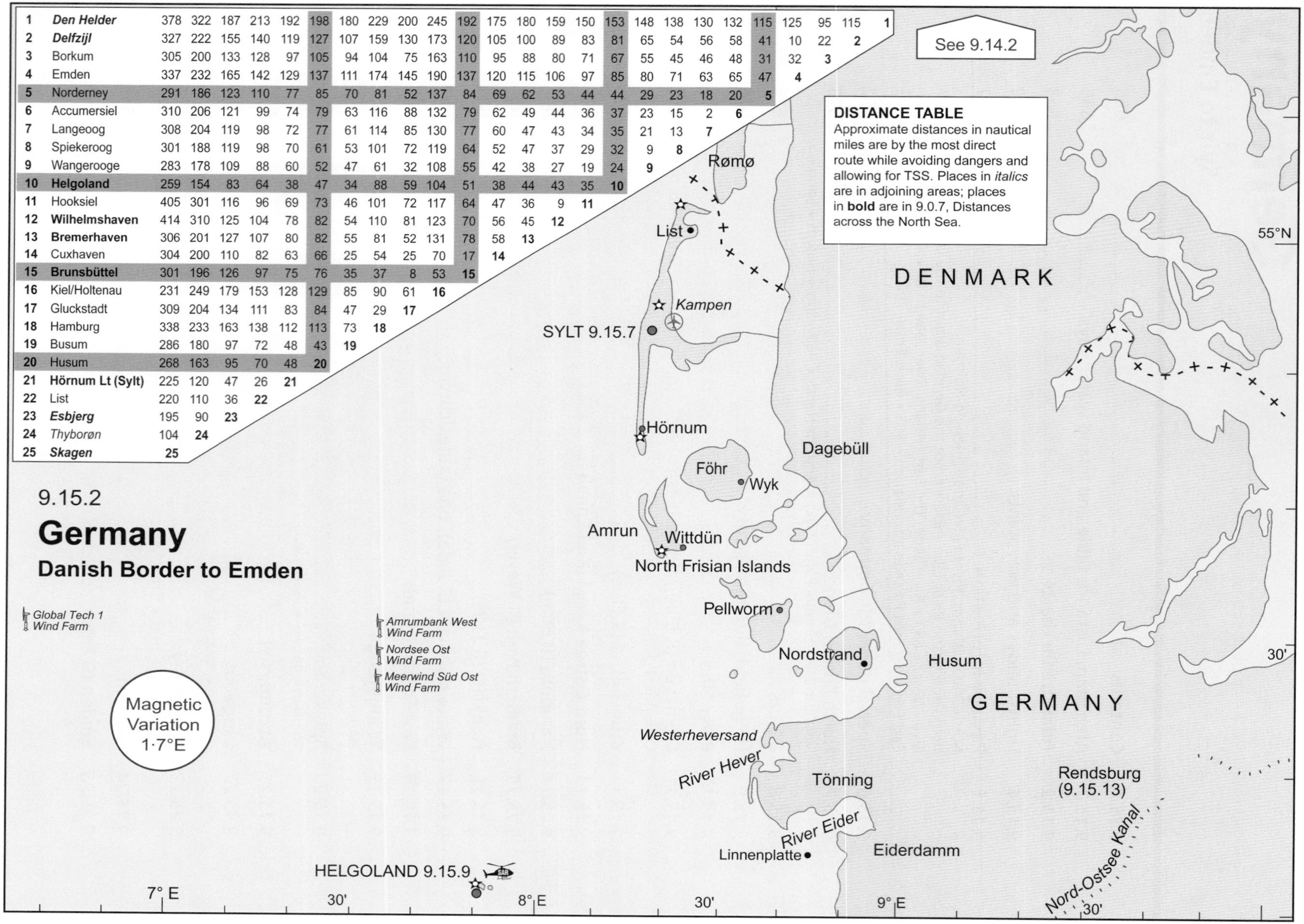

See 9.14.2
DENMARK
GERMANY
Rømø
List
Kampen
SYLT 9.15.7
Hörnum
Föhr
Wyk
Dagebüll
Amrun
Wittdün
North Frisian Islands
Pellworm
Nordstrand
Husum
Westerheversand
River Hever
Tönning
River Eider
Linnenplatte
Eiderdamm
Rendsburg
(9.15.13)
Nord-Ostsee Kanal
HELGOLAND 9.15.9
Global Tech 1
Wind Farm
Amrumbank West
Wind Farm
Nordsee Ost
Wind Farm
Meerwind Süd Ost
Wind Farm
Magnetic
Variation
1·7°E
55°N
30'
7° E
30'
8° E
30'
9° E
30'

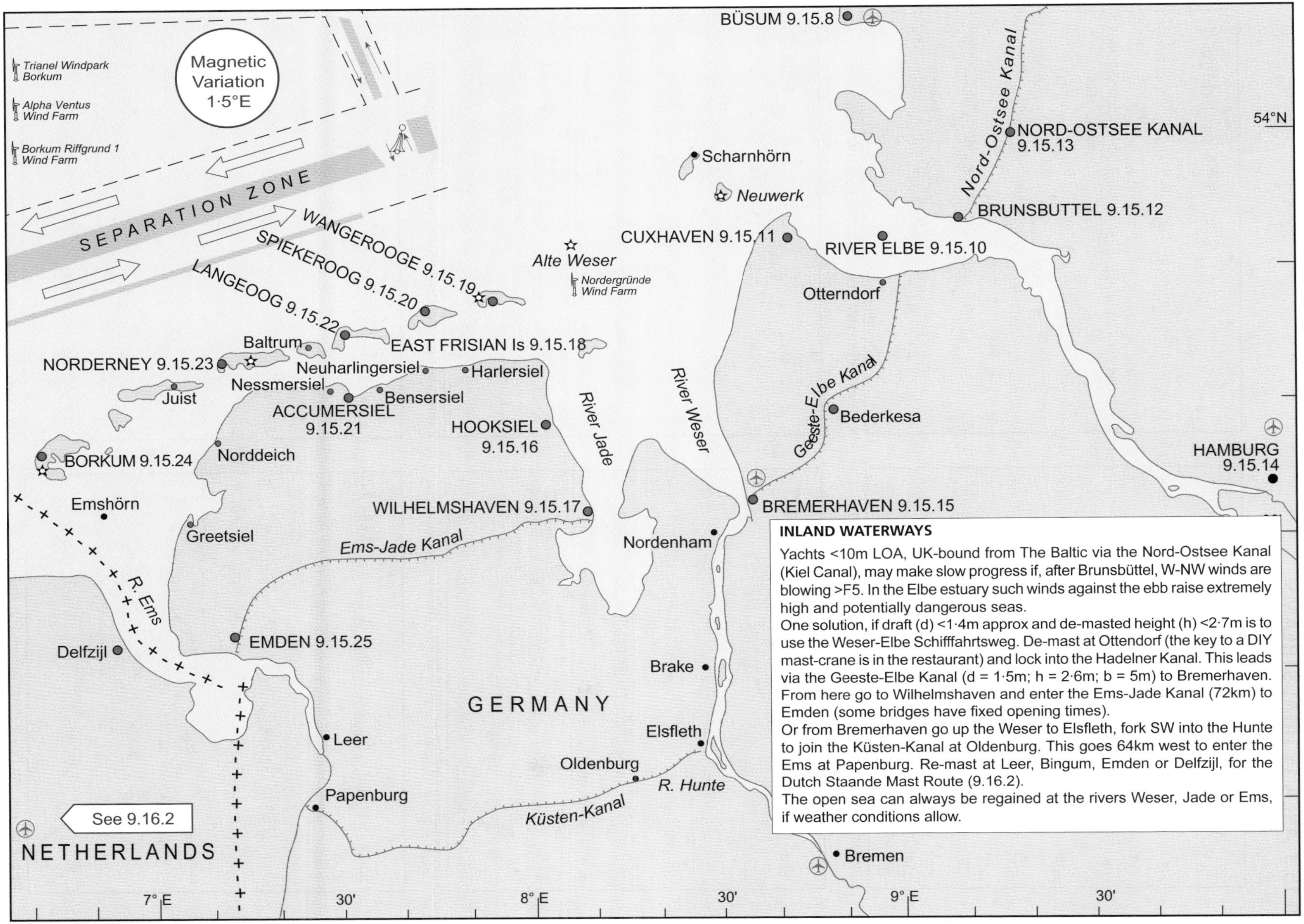
Trianel Windpark Borkum
Alpha Ventus Wind Farm
Borkum Riffgrund 1 Wind Farm
Magnetic Variation 1·5°E
SEPARATION ZONE
BÜSUM 9.15.8
Nord-Ostsee Kanal
NORD-OSTSEE KANAL 9.15.13
54°N
Scharnhörn
Neuwerk
BRUNSBUTTEL 9.15.12
CUXHAVEN 9.15.11
RIVER ELBE 9.15.10
WANGEROOGE 9.15.19
SPIEKEROOG 9.15.20
LANGEOOG 9.15.22
Alte Weser
Nordergründe Wind Farm
Otterndorf
Baltrum
EAST FRISIAN Is 9.15.18
NORDERNEY 9.15.23
Neuharlingersiel
Harlersiel
Nessmersiel
Bensersiel
Juist
ACCUMERSIEL 9.15.21
HOOKSIEL 9.15.16
River Jade
River Weser
Geeste-Elbe Kanal
Bederkesa
BORKUM 9.15.24
Norddeich
HAMBURG 9.15.14
Emshörn
WILHELMSHAVEN 9.15.17
BREMERHAVEN 9.15.15
Greetsiel
Ems-Jade Kanal
Nordenham
R. Ems
EMDEN 9.15.25
Delfzijl
Brake
GERMANY
Elsfleth
Leer
Oldenburg
R. Hunte
Papenburg
Küsten-Kanal
See 9.16.2
NETHERLANDS
Bremen
7° E
30'
8° E
30'
9° E
30'

INLAND WATERWAYS

Yachts <10m LOA, UK-bound from The Baltic via the Nord-Ostsee Kanal (Kiel Canal), may make slow progress if, after Brunsbüttel, W-NW winds are blowing >F5. In the Elbe estuary such winds against the ebb raise extremely high and potentially dangerous seas.

One solution, if draft (d) <1·4m approx and de-masted height (h) <2·7m is to use the Weser-Elbe Schifffahrtsweg. De-mast at Ottendorf (the key to a DIY mast-crane is in the restaurant) and lock into the Hadelner Kanal. This leads via the Geeste-Elbe Kanal (d = 1·5m; h = 2·6m; b = 5m) to Bremerhaven. From here go to Wilhelmshaven and enter the Ems-Jade Kanal (72km) to Emden (some bridges have fixed opening times).

Or from Bremerhaven go up the Weser to Elsfleth, fork SW into the Hunte to join the Küsten-Kanal at Oldenburg. This goes 64km west to enter the Ems at Papenburg. Re-mast at Leer, Bingum, Emden or Delfzijl, for the Dutch Staande Mast Route (9.16.2).

The open sea can always be regained at the rivers Weser, Jade or Ems, if weather conditions allow.

9.15.3 AREA 15 TIDAL STREAMS

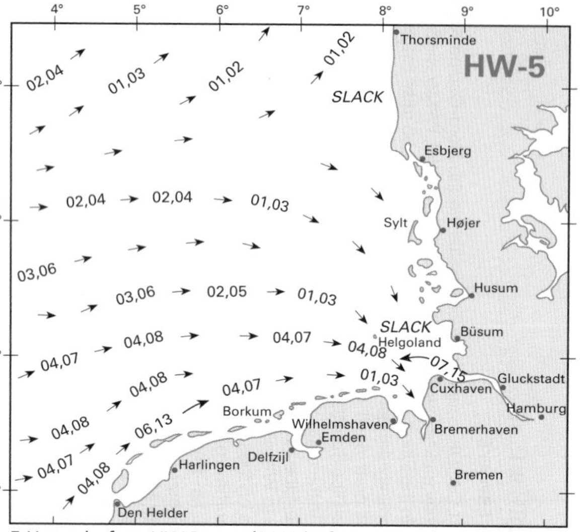

5 Hours before HW Dover (0440 before HW Helgoland)

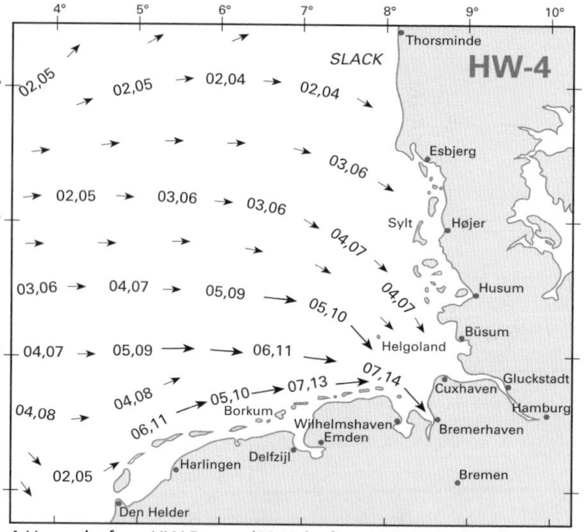

4 Hours before HW Dover (0340 before HW Helgoland)

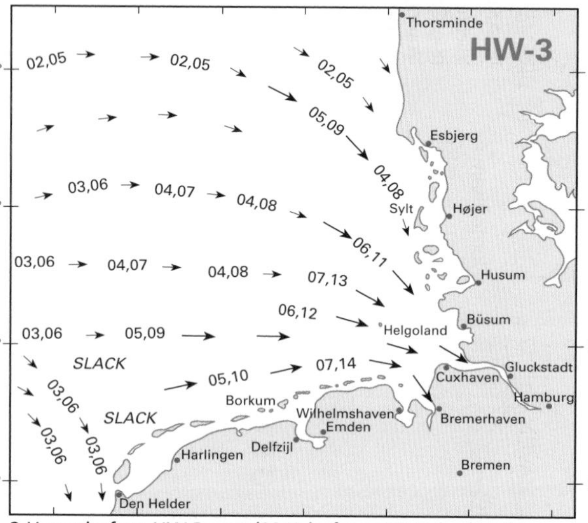

3 Hours before HW Dover (0240 before HW Helgoland)

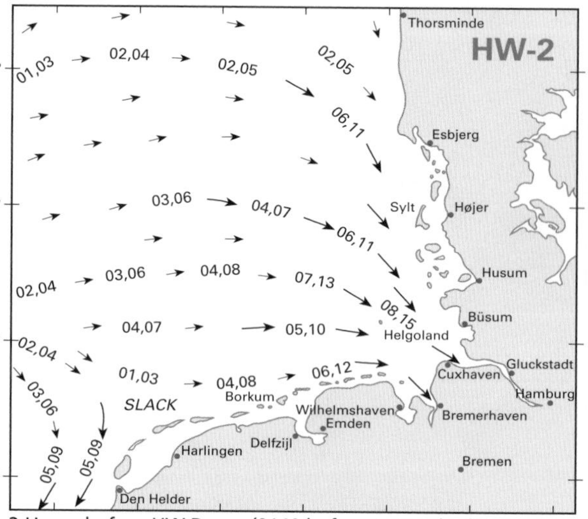

2 Hours before HW Dover (0140 before HW Helgoland)

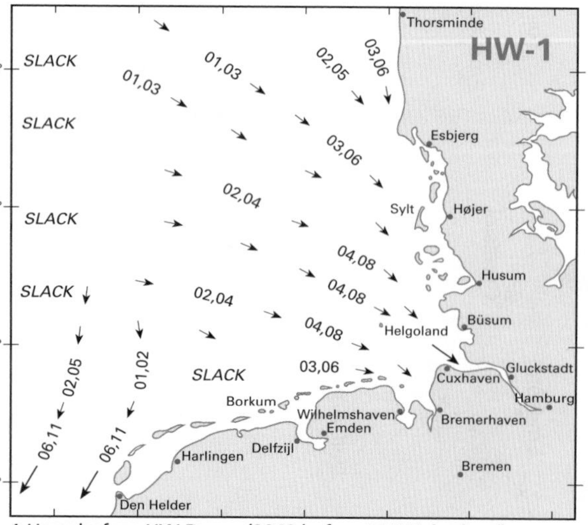

1 Hour before HW Dover (0040 before HW Helgoland)

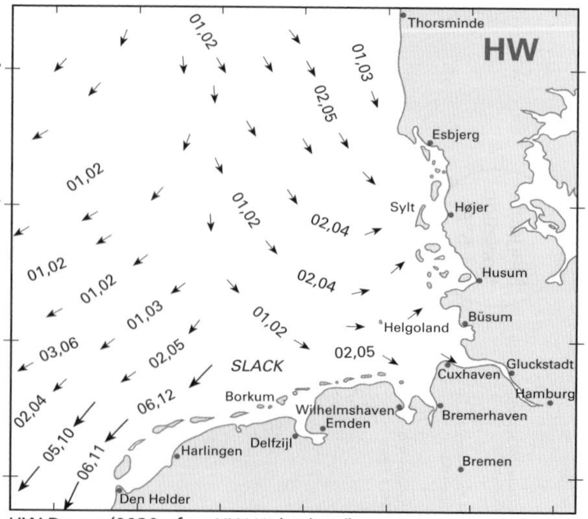

HW Dover (0020 after HW Helgoland)

South-westward 9.16.3

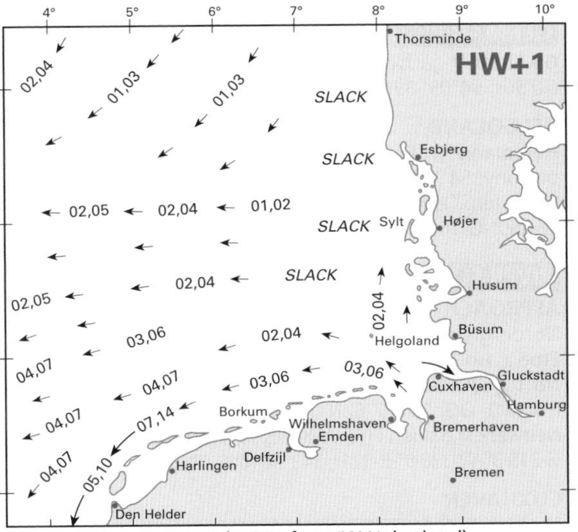

1 Hour after HW Dover (0120 after HW Helgoland)

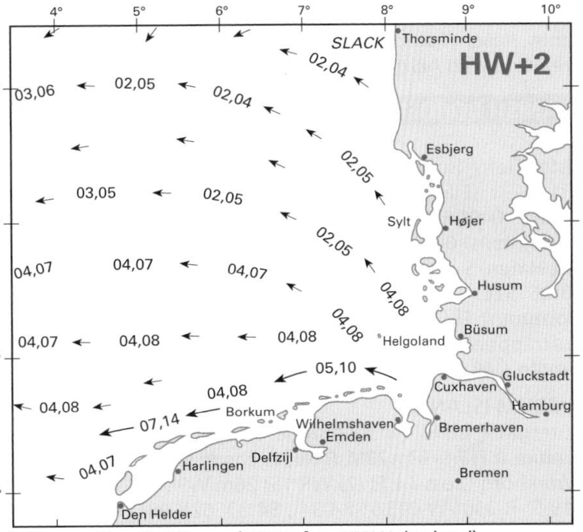

2 Hours after HW Dover (0220 after HW Helgoland)

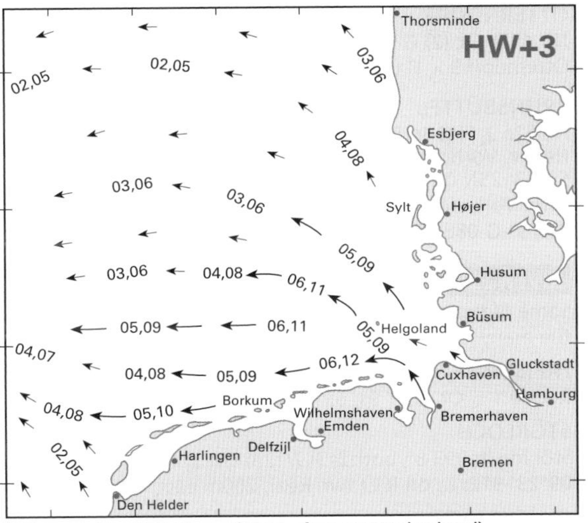

3 Hours after HW Dover (0320 after HW Helgoland)

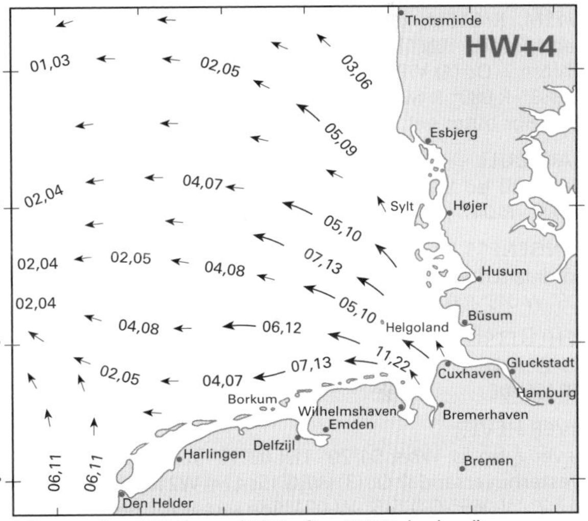

4 Hours after HW Dover (0420 after HW Helgoland)

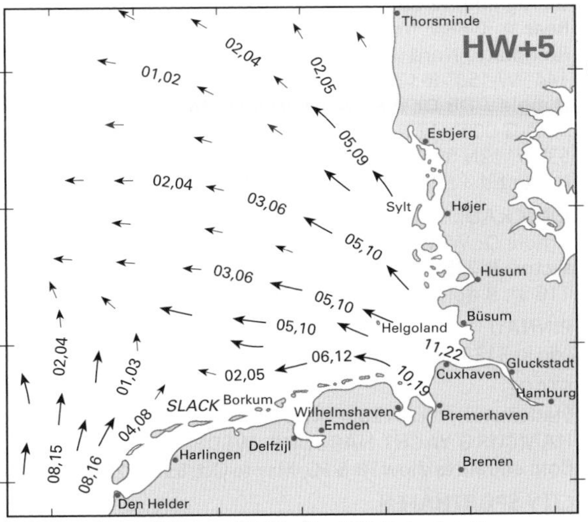

5 Hours after HW Dover (0520 after HW Helgoland)

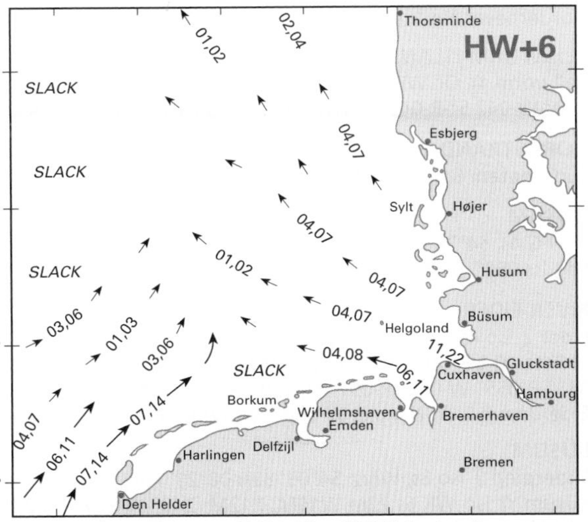

6 Hours after HW Dover (0620 after HW Helgoland)

9.15.4 LIGHTS, BUOYS AND WAYPOINTS

Bold print = light with a nominal range of 15M or more. CAPITALS = place or feature. *CAPITAL ITALICS* = light-vessel, light float or Lanby. *Italics* = Fog signal. ***Bold italics*** = Racon. Many marks/buoys are fitted with AIS (MMSI No); see relevant charts.

DANISH BORDER TO BÜSUM

SYLT

Lister Tief Iso 8s; *Whis;* 55°05'·33N 08°16'·79E.
List West (Ellenbogen) Oc WRG 6s 19m W14M, R11M, G10M; 040°-R-133°-W-227°-R-266·4°-W-268°-G-285°-W-310°-W(unintens)-040°; W twr, R lantern; 55°03'·15N 08°24'·00E.
List Hafen, S mole FR 5m 4M; 218°-353°; R mast; 55°01'·01N 08°26'·51E.
Hörnum ☆ Fl (2) 9s 48m **20M**; 54°45'·23N 08°17'·47E.
Vortrapptief Iso 4s; 54°34'·80N 08°14'·36E, toward Hörnum.
S mole FR 7m 4M; 54°45'·57N 08°17'·97E.

AMRUM ISLAND

Rütergat Iso 8s; 54°30'·08N 08°12'·32E.
Amrum ☆ Fl 7·5s 63m **23M**; R twr, W bands; 54°37'·84N 08°21'·23E.
Wriakhorn Cross L Fl (2) WR 15s 26m W9M, R7M; 297·5°-W-319·5°-R-330°-W-005·5°-R-034°; 54°37'·62N 08°21'·22E.

FÖHR ISLAND

Nieblum Dir lt showing over Rütergat. ☆ Oc (2) WRG 10s 11m **W19M, R/G15M**; 028°-G-031°-W-032·5°-R-035·5°; R twr, W band; 54°41'·10N 08°29'·20E.
Ohlörn Oc (4) WR 15s 10m 13/10M, 208°-W-237·5°- R-298°-W-353°- R-080°; R twr, Gy lantern; 54°40'·85N 08°34'·00E (SE Föhr).
Wyk Hbr outer ent, FR 54°41'·55N 08°34'·69E; and FG.

DAGEBÜLL

Dagebüll Iso WRG 8s 23m **W18M, R/G15M**; 042°-G-043°-W-044·5°- R-047°; 54°43'·82N 08°41'·43E. FW lts on ent moles.

LANGENESS ISLAND

Nordmarsch L Fl (3) WR 20s 13m W14M, R11M; 268°-W-279°-R-306°-W-045°-R-070°-W-218°; dark brown twr; 54°37'·58N 08°31'·85E.

SCHLÜTTSIEL

No 2/SA 26 54°36'·84N 08°38'·95E. Hbr ent 54°40'·89N 08°45'·10E.

RIVER HEVER

Hever Iso 4s; *Whis;* 54°20'·41N 08°18'·82E.
Westerheversand ☆ Oc (3) WRG 15s 41m **W21M, R17M, G16M**; 012·2°-W-069°-G-079·5°-W-081°(ldg sector for Hever) -R-107°-W-150°-R-207°-W-233°-R-248°; R twr, W bands; 54°22'·37N 08°38'·36E.
Norderhever No 1 Fl (2+1) R 15s; 54°22'·46N 08°30'·83E.

PELLWORM ISLAND

Pellworm ☆ Oc WRG 5s 38m **20M, R 16M, G 15M**; 037·5°-G-040°-W-042·5°-R-045°; R twr, W band; 54°29'·78N 08°39'·98E.

NORDSTRAND

Suderhafen, S mole 54°28'·07N 08°55'·62E.

HUSUM

Fl G 4s, 54°28'·80N 08°58'·60E, start of access chan.
Ldg lts 090°, both Iso G 8s 7/9m 3M.

RIVER EIDER

Eider Iso 4s; 54°15'·70N 08° 29'·20E.
St Peter ☆ L Fl (2) WR 15s 23m **W15M**, R12M; 271°-R-280·5°-W-035°-R-055°-W-068°-R-091°-W-120°; 54°17'·24N 08°39'·10E.
Eiderdamm lock, N mole, W end Oc (2) R 12s 8m 5M; W twr.

BÜSUM

Süderpiep Iso 8s; *Whis;* 54°05'·82N 08°25'·70E.
Büsum ☆ Iso WR 6s 22m **W19M**, R12M; 248°-W-317°-R-024°-W-148°; 54°07'·60N 08°51'·48E.
E mole Oc (3) G 12s 10m 4M; vis 260°-168°; G twr; 54°07'·19N 08°51'·65E.

GERMAN BIGHT TO RIVER ELBE

GB Light V Iso 8s 12m **17M**; R hull marked G-B; *Horn Mo (R) 30s*; 54°09'·89N 06°20'·84E.

HELGOLAND

Helgoland ☆ Fl 5s 82m **28M**; brown □ twr, B lantern, W balcony; 54°10'·91N 07°52'·93E.
Vorhafen. Ostmole, S elbow Oc WG 6s 5m W6M, G3M; 203°-W-250°-G-109°; G post; fog det lt; 54°10'·31N 07°53'·94E.

RIVER ELBE (LOWER)

APPROACHES

Nordergründe N VQ; 53°57'·06N 08°00'·12E.
Elbe Iso 10s; ***Racon T, 8M***; 53°59'·95N 08°06'·49E.
No 1 QG; 53°59'·21N 08°13'·20E.
No 25 QG; 53°56'·62N 08°38'·25E.
Neuwerk ☆, S side, L Fl (3) WRG 20s 38m **W16M**, R12M, G11M; 165·3°-G-215·3°-W-238·8°-R-321°; 343°-R-100°; 53°54'·92N 08°29'·73E.

CUXHAVEN

No 31 Fl G 4s; 53°53'·93N 08°41'·21E.
Yacht hbr ent, F WR and F WG lts; 53°52'·43N 08°42'·49E.

OTTERNDORF

No 43 Oc (2) G 9s; 53°50'·23N 08°52'·24E.
Otterndorf 3 Fl (3) G 12s; 53°50'·22N 08°53'·94E.

BRUNSBÜTTEL

No 57a Fl G 4s; 53°52'·62N 09°07'·93E, 030°/ 8 cables to lock.
Neuer Vorhafen ent, mole 3 head 2FG (vert); 10m 7M, 53°53'·25N 09°08'·07E.
Alter Vorhafen ent, mole 1 F WG 14m W10M, G6M; 266·3°-W-273·9°-G-088·8° (FW in fog), floodlit; 53°53'·27N 09°08'·59E.

RIVER ELBE (BRUNSBÜTTEL TO HAMBURG)

Some of the more accessible yacht hbrs are listed below, but not the many ldg lts and dir lts which define the main river fairway.

FREIBURG

Reede 1 Oc (2) Y 9s; 53°50'·41N 09°19'·45E, off ent.

STÖRLOCH

Stör ldg lts 093·8°, both Fl 3s 7/12m 6M; synch. Front, 53°49'·29N 09°23'·91E; △ on R ○ twr. Rear, 200m east; ▽ on white mast.

GLÜCKSTADT

Glückstadt ldg lts 131·8°, both Iso 8s 15/30m **19/21M**; intens on ldg line; W twrs, R bands. **Front** ☆, 53°48'·31N 09°24'·24E. **Rear** ☆, 0·68M from front.
Rhinplatte Nord Oc WRG 6s 11m W6M, R4M, G3M; 122°-G-144°-W-150°-R-177°- W-122°; 53°48'·09N 09°23'·36E.
N mole Dir Oc WRG 6s 9m W9M R7M, G6M; 330°-R-343°-W-346°-G-008°; 123°-G-145°-W-150°-R-170°; W twr with gallery; 53°47'·12N 09°24'·53E.
N pier hd FR 5m 5M; 53°47'·10N 09°24'·50E. (S mole hd, FG).

KRUCKAU

S mole Oc WRG 6s 8m, W6M, R4M, G3M; 116·3°-W-120·7° (ldg sector)-R-225°-G-315°-R-331·9°-W-335·4° (ldg sector)-335·4°-G-116·3°; B dolphin; 53°42'·85N 09°30'·72E.

PINNAU

Ldg lts 112·7°, both Iso 4s 8/13m 6M. Front, 53°40'·08N 09°34'·02E.

STADE

Stadersand Iso 8s 20m 14M; 53°37'·69N 09°31'·64E (at ent).

HAMBURG YACHT HARBOUR, WEDEL

Both entrances show FR & FG, May to Oct; 53°34'·25N 09°40'·77E.

CITY SPORTHAFEN

Brandenburger Hafen Ent Iso Or 2s; 53°32'·52N 09°58'·81E.

WESER ESTUARY

ALTE WESER

Alte Weser Dir ☆ F WRG 33m **W23M, R19M, G18M**; 288°-FW-352°-FR-003°-FW-017°(ldg sector for Alte Weser) 017°-FG-045°-FW-074°-FG-118°-FW-123° (ldg sector for Alte Weser)123°-FR-140°-FG-175°-FW-183°-FR-196°-FW-238°; R ○ twr, 2 W bands, B base, floodlit; Fog det lt; *Horn Mo (AL) 60s;* 53°51'·80N 08°07'·65E.

16/A15 Fl (2+1) R 15s; 53°49'·66N 08°06'·44E (junction with Neuwe Weser).

NEUE WESER

Tegeler Plate, N end, Dir ☆ Occ (3) WRG 12s 21m **W21M, G17M R18M R17M** ; 329°-W-340°-R-014°-W-100°-G-116°-W-119° (ldg sector for Neue Weser).119°-R-123°-G-144°-W-147° (ldg sector for Alte Weser).148°-R(17M)- 264°; R ○ twr, gallery, W lantern, R roof; Fog det lt; Ra refl; 53°47'·87N 08°11'·46E.

BREMERHAVEN

No 61 QG; 53°32'·26N 08°33'·93E (Km 66·0).

Vorhafen N pier FR 15m 5M; 245°-166°; F in fog; 53°32'·15N 08°34'·50E.

RIVER JADE

1b/Jade1 Oc G 4s; 53°52'·40N 07°44'·02E.

Mellumplate ☆ FW 28m **24M**; 116·1°-116·4° (ldg sector for outer part of Wangerooger Fahrwasser); R □ twr, W band; 53°46'·28N 08°05'·51E.

No 19 QG; 53°47'·10N 08°01'·83E.

No 31/P-Reede/W Siel 1 Oc (3) G 12s; 53°41'·59N 08°04'·51E.

HOOKSIEL

No 37/Hooksiel 1 IQ G 13s; 53°39'·37N 08°06'·58E.

Vorhafen ent L Fl R 6s 9m 3M; 53°38'·63N 08°05'·25E.

WILHELMSHAVEN

Fluthafen N mole F WG 9m,W6M, G3M; 216°-W-280°-G-010°-W-020°-G-130°; G twr; 53°30'·86N 08°09'·32E.

EAST FRISIAN ISLANDS

NORTH EDGE OF INSHORE TRAFFIC ZONE

TG9/Weser 2 Fl (2+1) G 15s; 53°55'·0N 07°44'·60E.

TG13 Oc (3) G 12s; 53°50'·85N 07°15'·43E.

TG7 Fl (2) G 9s; 53°47'·24N 06°49'·65E.

TG1 Oc (3) G 12s; 53°44'·90N 06°33'·20E.

WANGEROOGE

Harle Iso 8s; 53°49'·25N 07°50'·47E.

Wangerooge, W end ☆ Fl R 5s 60m **23M**; R ○ twr, 2 W bands; 53°47'·40N 07°51'·37E.

Dir lt 145·5°, Dir WRG 24m W22M G18M R17M; 119·4°-G-138·8°-W-152·2°-R-159·9°.

Buhne H VQ (9) 10s; 53°46'·86N 07°49'·65E.

W2 ; 53°46'·25N 07°51'·89E, off hbr ent.

SPIEKEROOG

Otzumer Balje Iso 4s; 53°48'·29N 07°38'·00E (often moved).

Spiekeroog FR 6m 4M; 197°-114°; R mast; 53°45'·0N 07°41'·3E.

LANGEOOG

Accumer Ee Iso 8s; 53°47'·09N 07°26'·62E (frequently moved).

W mole head Oc WRG 6s 8m W7M, R5M, G4M; 064°-G-070°-W-074°-R-326°-W-330°-G-335°-R-064°; R basket on R mast; *Horn Mo (L) 30s* (0730-1800LT); 53°43'·42N 07°30'·13E.

BALTRUM

Groyne hd Oc WRG 6s 6m; W6M, R4M, G3M; 074·5°-G-090°-W-095°-R-074·5°; 53°43'·3N 07°21'·7E.

NORDERNEY

Norderney ☆ Fl (3) 12s 59m **23M**; unintens 067°-077° and 270°-280°; R 8-sided twr; 53°42'·54N 07°13'·79E.

Dovetief Iso 4s; 53°45'·47N 07°12'·70E.

Schluchter Iso 8s; 53°44'·50N 07°02'·13E.

W mole head Oc (2) R 9s 13m 4M; 53°41'·9N 07°09'·9E.

JUIST

Juist-N VQ; 53°43'·82N 06°55'·42E.

Training wall, S end Oc (2) R 9s 7m 3M; 53°39'·65N 06°59'·81E.

MAINLAND HARBOURS: RIVER JADE TO RIVER EMS

HARLESIEL

Carolinensieler Balje, Leitdamm L Fl 8s 7m 6M; G mast; 53°44'·13N 07°50'·10E.

Ldg lts 138°, both Iso 6s 12/18m 9M, intens on ldg line; Front 53°40'·70N 07°34'·50E. Rear 167m from front.

N mole head Iso R 4s 6m 7M; 53°42'·58N 07°48'·64E.

NEUHARLINGERSIEL

Training wall head Oc 6s 6m 5M; 53°43'·22N 07°42'·30E.

BENSERSIEL

E training wall head Oc WRG 6s 6m W5M, R3M, G2M; 110°-G-119°-W-121°-R-110°; R post & platform; 53° 41'·80N 07°32'·84E.

DORNUMER-ACCUMERSIEL

W bkwtr head, approx 53°41'·04N 07°29'·30E.

NESSMERSIEL

N mole head Oc 4s 6m 5M; G mast; 53°41'·9N 07°21'·7E.

NORDDEICH

W trng wall head FG 8m 4M, 021°-327°; G framework twr; 53°38'·62N 07°09'·0E.

GREETSIEL

Meßstation lt bcn, Fl Y 4s 15m 3M; 53°32'·94N 07°02'·18E.

RIVER EMS

APPROACHES

GW/EMS Iso 8s 14m **17M** (H24); Emergency Lt, FR, occas. 2 FR vert; R Lt vessel, floodlit; *Horn Mo (R) 30s (H24);* 54°09'·98N 06°20'· 85E.

Borkumriff Oc 4s; 53°47'·48N 06°22'·27E.

Osterems Iso 4s; 53°41'·91N 06°36'·17E.

Riffgat Iso 8s; 53°38'·96N 06°27'·10E.

Westerems Iso 4s; 53°36'·93N 06°19'·39E.

H1 53°34'·91N 06°17'·97E.

BORKUM

Borkum Grosser ☆ Fl (2) 12s 63m **24M**; brown ○ twr; 53°35'·32N 06°39'·64E. Same twr, F WRG 46m **W19M, R/G15M**; 107·4°-G-109°-W-111·2°- R-112·6°.

Fischerbalje Oc (2) 16s 15m **3M**; 260°-W-123°. Fog det lt; R/W ○ twr on tripod; 53°33'·18N 06°42'·90E.

Schutzhafen, E mole hd FG10m 4M; 53°33'·48N 06°45'·02E. W mole hd, FR 8m 4M.

RIVER EMS (LOWER)

No 27 Fl G 4s; 53°30'·24N 06°47'·52E.

No 35 Fl G 4s; 53°27'·03N 06°52'·80E.

No 37 QG; 53°26'·01N 06°54'·85E.

No 41 Fl (2) G 9s; 53°24'·25N 06°56'·68E.

No 49 Oc (2) G 9s; 53°19'·95N 06°59'·71E.

KNOCK

Knock F WRG 28m W12M,R9M, G8M; 270°-W-299°-R-008·3°-G-023°-W-026·8°-R-039°-W-073°-R-119°-W-154°; fog det lt; Gy twr, white conical radar antenna; 53°20'·32N 07°01'·40E.

EMDEN

No 59 Oc (2) G 9s; 53°19'·41N 07°03'·86E.

No 65 Fl (2) G 9s; 53°19'·82N 07°06'·56E.

Outer hbr, W pier FR 10m 4M; R 8-sided twr; *Horn Mo (ED) 30s;* 53°20'·06N 07°10'·49E.

E pier FG 7m 5M; G mast on pedestal; 53°20'·05N 07°10'·84E.

9.15.5 PASSAGE INFORMATION

More passage information is threaded between successive harbours in this Area. **Bibliography**: NP 55 *North Sea (East);* 3rd ed 2006. *Cruising Guide to Germany and Denmark* (Imray/Navin) 4th ed 2012. The *Hafenhandbuch, Nord See* (DSV-Verlag) is an annual guide, covering Calais to Trondheim and the Lofoten Islands.

NORTH FRISIAN ISLANDS

All the channels from the open sea on this coast are challenging for yachts when the wind is W/NW 4 and start becoming dangerous at F5 and above. From seaward, Butendiek wind farm, centred on 55°01'·00N 07°46'·40E, 80 turbines, all FR and Fl Y on perimeters, lies 22M W of List West ⚹ NW Sylt.

Lister Tief is the chan between the Danish island of Rømø and the N end of Sylt; it gives access to **List Roads** and hbr as well as to Danish hbrs (AC 1875, 3767). Lister Tief is well buoyed; least depth over the bar is about 4m. Relatively it is the safest chan on this coast (after Süderpiep) for yachts seeking anch under the lee of Sylt in strong W winds, (beware big swell over the bar on ebb, and buoyed obstructions (ODAS) 18M WSW of List West lt ho.

Sylt is the largest of the N Frisian Islands, almost 20M long from S to N. It has a straight seaward coast, and on its E side is connected by the Hindenburgdamm to the mainland. Vortrapptief is the NNE chan inward between Amrum and Sylt, leading to **Hörnum** Hafen. It has a depth > 10m (but subject to frequent change, and may be < 4m on the bar) and is buoyed and lit. ***The area should not be approached in strong W winds.*** ▶*The flood (ESE-going) stream begins at HW Helgoland –0350, and the ebb (WNW-going) at HW Helgoland +0110, sp rates 2·5kn.*◀

A large complex of wind farms, centred on 54°26'·03N 07°42'·77E Amrumbank West and Meerwind Sud/Ost, both 80 turbines, and Noordsee Ost, 48 turbines, lies 25M SW of **Amrum** and 18M NNW of **Helgoland.** All turbines show FR lts, Fl Y on perimeters, see AC 1423.

Rütergat and Schmaltief give access to **Amrum** (Wittdün hbr on SE side) to Wyk on the SE corner of **Fohr** and to Dagebüll (ferry port). The R. Hever consists of several chans on the N side of Eiderstedt Peninsula, and S of the North Frisian Islands of **Süderoogsand** and **Pellworm**. Mittelhever is the most important of the three buoyed chans through the outer grounds, all of which meet SE of Süderoogsand. Here they separate into Norderhever, which runs NE between Pellworm and Nordstrand into a number of chans, with Heverstrom leading to Husum.

RIVER EIDER AND SCHLESWIG-HOLSTEIN

Approaching the R Eider from seaward, the Eider SWM lt buoy, is about 1·2M W of the buoyed ent chan. ***The ent can be rough in W winds, and dangerous in onshore gales.*** St Peter lt ho can be seen above the dyke. Here the estuary winds up to the Eiderdamm, a storm barrage with a lock (H24) and sluices. **Tönning** is about 5M upriver. The upper Eider parallels the Nord-Ostsee Kanal which it joins at Gieselau Lock.

The W coast of Schleswig-Holstein is flat, marshy, and drying banks extend 5–10M offshore. Between the banks and islands, the chans shift frequently. Süderpiep and Norderpiep join allowing access to **Büsum** and Meldorfer Hafen (marina). Norderpiep has a bar (depth 3m) and is unlit; Süderpiep is deeper and preferable in W'lies, but avoid in strong ground seas. Landmarks are Tertius and Blauortsand bns, and a conspic silo and tall building at Büsum.

HELGOLAND TO THE RIVER ELBE

Helgoland is a useful staging post for yachts entering the Elbe bound for **Cuxhaven** (38M) or direct **Brunsbüttel** (51M) at the ent to the **Nord-Ostsee Kanal** (AC 2469). From the E end of the TSS the Elbe channel is well marked by buoys and beacon trs. Commercial traffic is very heavy. For further details see R Elbe.

▶*At Elbe SWM buoy the E-going (flood) stream begins at HW Helgoland –0500, and the W-going (ebb) stream at HW Helgoland +0050, sp rates 2kn. The stream runs harder N of Scharhörn, up to 4kn on the ebb, when the Elbe estuary is dangerously rough in strong W or NW winds and must not be attempted.*◀

Entering the Elbe estuary (AC 3619, 3625, 3267, 3268) Scharhörn and Neuwerk are islets. The latter features in *Riddle of the Sands,* Erskine Childer's classic sailing and spy thriller.

9.15.6 SPECIAL NOTES FOR GERMANY

LANDS are given in lieu of 'counties' in the UK.

TIME ZONE is –0100 (subtract 1 hour for UT). DST is kept from the last Sunday in March to the last Sunday in October.

CHARTS: German charts are issued by the Bundesamt für Seeschifffahrt und Hydrographie (BSH) Hamburg. Large A0 size (118x84 cm) German *seekarten,* prefixed D in this almanac are intended for deep water vessels and increasingly do not show depths inside the 5m contour, except in harbour plans.
Medium/large scale A1 size charts (84x59cm) prefixed BSH, are for coastal waters and inshore areas. All charts are referred to WGS 84 and are corrected by *Nachrichten für Seefahrer* (NfS) = Notices to Mariners. Further details: http://www.bsh.de/de/Produkte/Karten/Seekarten/Deutsche_Bucht_Regionale_A1-Karten/index.jsp
Where possible the AC, Imray and Dutch chart numbers are also quoted.

TIDES: Admiralty charts of German coastal waters are now referred to LAT (not MLWS) as are German charts. Depths in the shallow estuaries and the North and East Frisian islands vary annually, and can be noticeably affected by wind strength and direction on a daily basis. Obtain the latest chart updates from BSH and treat tidal predictions with caution, height differences due to meteorological factors are updated by BSH four times a day at www.bsh.de/aktdat/wvd/wahome.htm

LIGHTS: In coastal waters considerable use is made of sectored lights. A leading or directional sector (usually W, and often intens) may be flanked by warning sectors to show the side to which the vessel has deviated: If to port, a FR lt or a Fl W lt with an even number of flashes; if to starboard, a FG lt or a Fl W lt with an odd number of flashes. Crossing lts with R, W and G sectors indicate (eg) the limits of roadsteads, bends in chans etc.

SIGNALS: IPTS are widely used in major ports. Local port, tidal, distress and traffic signals are given where possible. Visual storm warning signals are not used. When motoring under sail, always display a black motoring cone (▼). Rule 25e is strictly enforced and non-compliance will incur a fine.

Lights at bridges and locks

●●	=	Passage/entry prohib.
●	=	Prepare to pass or enter; exit from lock prohib.
●	=	Exit from lock permitted.
○ ●●	=	Passage or entry permitted if there is sufficient clearance; beware of oncoming traffic which has right of way.
○○ ●●	=	Lifting bridge is at first lift position; and may be passed by vessels for which the vertical clearance is safe.
●●	=	Passage/entry permitted; oncoming traffic stopped.
○ ●●	=	Passage or entry permitted, but beware oncoming traffic which may have right of way.
● ●	=	Bridge, lock or flood barrage closed to navigation.

Signals hoisted at masts

By day	*By night*	*Meaning*
R cylinder	○ ● ○	Reduce speed to minimise wash.
● ● ▼	● ● ●	Unusual obstruction to navigation.
● ▼ ▲	● ● ● ○	Long-term closure of waterway.

HARBOURS: Most marinas are owned by the state or community and run by a local YC (as in Belgium and the Netherlands).

TRAFFIC SEPARATION SCHEMES: The extensive TSS (off Terschelling in the German Bight and in the approaches to the Rivers Jade and Elbe) link up with the various Dutch TSS. Information broadcasts by VTS centres and their associated communications are given in Areas 15 and 16.

Caution: Although the TSS may be crossed in accordance with the IRPCS, vessels in the ITZ should not approach the S edge of the E-bound lane of the Terschelling-German Bight TSS (well marked by buoys TG1 to TG7) closer than 1M, unless in emergency or due to stress of weather. The German Marine Police can impose on-the-spot fines or confiscate equipment to the value of €1000 pending payment of the fine.

Navigators are strongly advised to:

- Be mindful of the value of GPS navigation in these waters.
- Log positions, times, courses, speeds, wind, weather, seastate, other traffic and use of sail or engine. Such records can be important in any dispute or litigation and also keep the skipper alert to any consequences. In addition, they can demonstrate that the boat is being responsibly navigated.
- Always monitor the appropriate VTS channel: Ch 80 in E part of Inner German Bight; Ch 79 in W part. If a deviation from the rules is necessary, inform the VTS traffic centre.
- Beware of deep-draught vessels S-bound from the German Bight lt vessel in the Jade approach TSS and crossing E-bound traffic in the Terschelling-German Bight TSS. The former have right of way over E-bound traffic. Yachts either E- or W-bound must take this into account.

HIGH SPEED CRAFT: High speed craft ply between Emden and Borkum, from Hamburg to Stadersand, Cuxhaven and Helgoland, and from an increasing number of ports. Keep a good lookout.

TELEPHONES: To call UK from Germany: dial 00 44; then the UK area code, minus the initial zero; then the number required. To call Germany from UK: dial 00 49; then area code minus initial zero; then desired number. Mobile numbers begin with 015, 016, 017; number of digits varies depending on Service provider.

EMERGENCIES: Police: dial 110. Fire, Ambulance: dial 112.

PUBLIC HOLIDAYS: New Year's Day, Good Friday, Easter Monday, Labour Day (1 May), Ascension Day, Whit Monday, Day of German Unity (3 Oct), Reformation Day (13 Oct), Christmas Day and Boxing Day.

NATIONAL WATER PARKS exist in the Wadden Sea areas (tidal mud flats) of Lower Saxony (excluding the Jade and Weser rivers and the Ems-Dollart estuary) and along the west coast of Schleswig-Holstein to the Germany/Denmark border. *These conservation areas have the status of Particularly Sensitive Sea Areas (PSSA), vessels should take the utmost care to avoid damaging the marine environment and marine organisms living therein. See Chapter 9 Introduction on Environmental Guidance.* The Parks (shown on AC & BSH charts) are divided into 3 zones:

Zone 1: comprises the most sensitive areas (about 30%) where yachts must keep to buoyed chans, except HW±3. Speed limit 8kn.

Zone 2: is a buffer zone.

Zone 3: is the remainder. No special constraints exist in Zones 2 and 3.

CUSTOMS: Ports of entry are: Borkum, Norderney, Norddeich, Wilhelmshaven, Bremerhaven, Cuxhaven; but not Helgoland.

GAS: Calor gas bottles can sometimes be re-filled. German 'Flüssig' gas can be used with Calor regulators.

CURRENCY is the Euro (€). VAT (MWST) is 19%.

VISITOR'S TAX (KURTAXE) is used to fund local amenities in tourist areas. It is approx €2–€3 per person per day and may be payable in addition to berthing fees.

9.15.7 NORTH FRISIAN ISLANDS

Schleswig-Holstein **54°45'·51N 08°17'·83E** (Hörnum hbr)

CHARTS AC 3767; D 107, D 108; BSH 1440 List, 1430 Hörnum. Up-to-date charts are essential for these waters.

TIDES +0110 Dover; ML 1·8; Duration 0540

Standard Port HELGOLAND (⟶)

Times				Height (metres)			
High Water		Low Water		MHWS	MHWN	MLWN	MLWS
0100	0600	0100	0800	3·1	2·8	0·8	0·4
1300	1800	1300	2000				
Differences LIST							
+0252	+0240	+0201	+0210	–0·7	–0·6	–0·2	0·0
HÖRNUM							
+0223	+0218	+0131	+0137	–0·4	–0·3	–0·2	0·0
AMRUM-HAFEN							
+0138	+0137	+0128	+0134	+0·3	+0·3	0·0	0·0
DAGEBÜLL							
+0226	+0217	+0211	+0225	+0·7	+0·8	+0·1	+0·1
SUDEROOGSAND							
+0116	+0102	+0038	+0122	+0·5	+0·6	+0·1	+0·1
HUSUM							
+0205	+0152	+0118	+0200	+1·2	+1·2	+0·1	+0·1

Die nordfriesische Küste comprises four main islands (Sylt, Amrum, Föhr, Pellworm) many small islets and the adjacent mainland.

SYLT Westerland (the capital) is central, where the Hindenburgdamm links to the mainland. Most of it is nature reserve (landing prohib). Two main hbrs: List and Hörnum, two other hbrs which both dry (soft mud) are Munkmarsch and Rantum; accessible only towards the top of the tide.

FACILITIES WESTERLAND: (04651) CG 85199; Police/Marine police 70470. Ⓗ 04651 840. **Town** ✕ ⊜ 8356333, ✉ Ⓑ; ⇌ ✈.

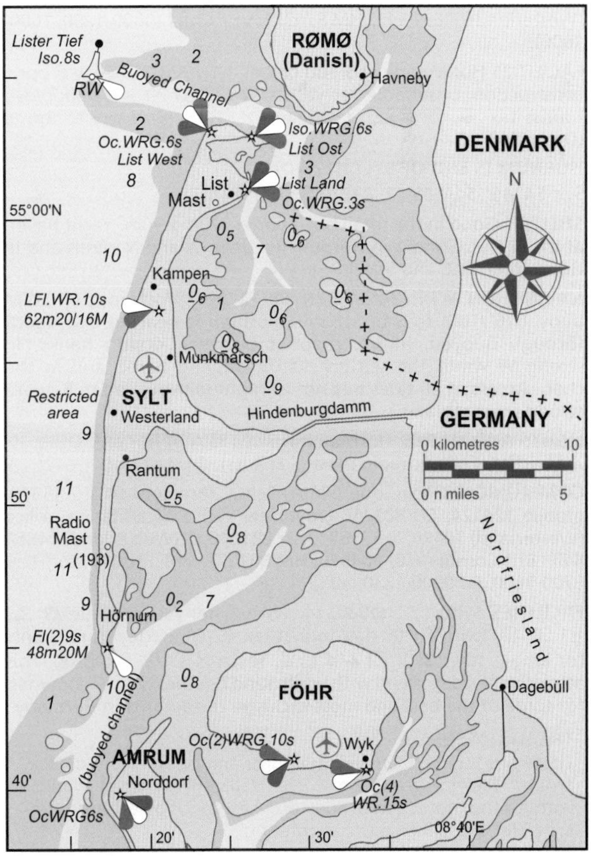

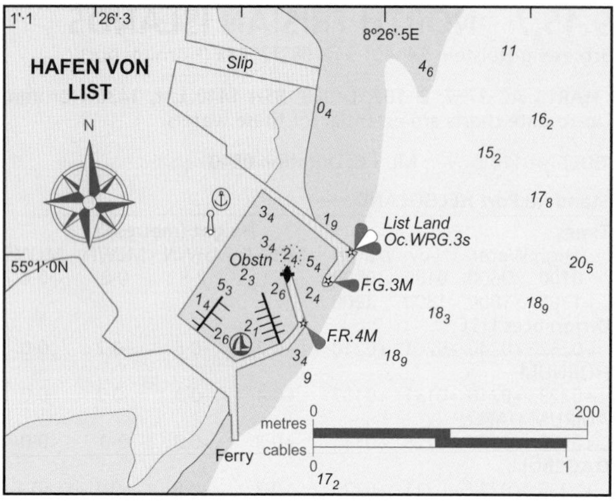

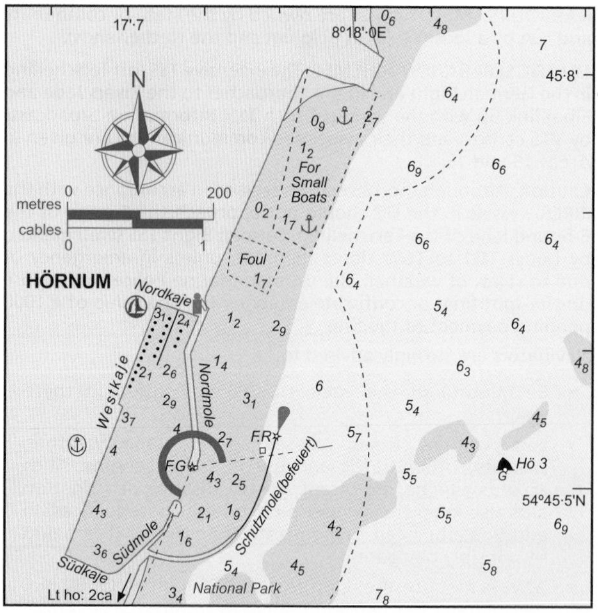

LIST (N END OF SYLT ISLAND)

Sylt **55°00'·99N 08°26'·45E**

SHELTER The small hbr/marina is sheltered except from NE/E winds.

NAVIGATION WPT 55°05'·32N 08°16'·67E Lister Tief SWM buoy, 111°/7·0M to No 13 SHM buoy. ***Strong W/NW winds cause a heavy swell over the bar (depth 3m) on the ebb, which sets on to Salzsand.*** Thence 214°/2·0M to the hbr via buoyed chan and W sector of List Land dir lt. Access by day at all tides, but beware strong cross-streams. Ent is 25m wide. Enter hbr from SE, keeping List Land lt ho between the mole heads.

LIGHTS AND MARKS Hbr lts as on the chartlet. See 9.15.4 for lts at List West, List Ost, List Land (overlooks List hbr) and Kampen, 5.4M SW. Rømø church, 7M NNE, is conspic.

COMMUNICATIONS (Code 04651 for the whole of Sylt) CG 870365; Police/Marine police (Westerland) 70470; Dr 870350; Ⓗ (Westerland) 04651 840; HM 870374, VHF Ch **11** (0800-1200, 1600-1800).

FACILITIES Hbr Marina at S end carries 1·1-2·6m. NE quay is open construction, unsuitable for yachts. Ⓥ €1·20 + €2·60pp/day tourist tax, SC. **Village** Ⓑ. Ferry to Rømø (Denmark).

HÖRNUM (S END OF SYLT ISLAND)

Sylt **54°45'·51N 08°17'·83E**

SHELTER Good in the small hbr, approx 370m x 90m. Yacht haven at the N end. Good ⚓ in Hörnum Reede in W and N winds and in Hörnumtief in E and S winds.

NAVIGATION WPT: 54°34'·87N 08°12'·97E, Vortrapptief SWM buoy, 016°/10M to S tip of Sylt. Hörnum lt bearing 012° leads through buoyed, lit Vortrapptief between drying banks. In strong W winds the sea breaks on offlying banks and in the chan. Access at all tides but not at night without radar. Beware strong cross-streams.

LIGHTS AND MARKS Hörnum lt is 3½ca SSW of hbr ent. Other lts as chartlet. Conspic radio mast (5 Fl R lts) 3M N of hbr.

COMMUNICATIONS (Code 04651) MRCC (Bremen) 04215 36870, mobile 124124; CG 881256 (volunteer svc); Police/Marine police (Westerland) 70470; ⊖ 8356333; Dr 881016; Ⓗ (Westerland) 04651 840; Brit Consul (030) 204570; HM 881027, VHF Ch 67, Mon-Thu 0700-1600; Fri 0700-1230, all LT.

FACILITIES Sylter YC ☎880274, www.sylter-yachtclub.de Ⓥ €1·50; /wi-fi €3·00 day, tourist tax €2·60 pp/day usually only for longer stays; **Town** Ⓑ. This attractive holiday island with white sand beaches is also renowned for some of the best and most exclusive restaurants in Germany.

THE HALLIGEN

There are ten German Hallig islands, and one Danish, dotted around *Die nordfriesische Küste*. Halligen are small islands, without the protection of coastal dykes. Lacking harbours they are of little real interest to yachtsmen.

OTHER HARBOURS IN THE NORTH FRISIAN ISLANDS

WYK AUF FÖHR, 54°41'·66N 08°34'·72E. AC 3767; D 107; BSH 1410. HW +0107 on Dover (UT); +0212 on Helgoland (zone –0100); ML 2·8. Good yacht hbr (1·2-1·7m) to N of ent, sheltered in all winds; access H24; visitors berth on pontoon 1. Inner hbr berths are for locals. Ferry hbr (4m). Lts see 9.15.4: Olhörn (SE point of Föhr) R twr. Mole heads, FR, R mast and FG, G mast. Port VHF Ch **11** 16. Yacht hbr HM ☎04681 3030; Commercial HM ☎500430; Marine Police ☎1280; ⊖ ☎2594; Dr ☎8558; Facilities: **Hbr road** (500m); **Yacht Hbr** Ⓥ €2·00 + €2·60 pp/day tourist tax, €1·00; free wi-fi, (15t); **W Quay**.

AMRUM-HAFEN, 54°37'·90N 08°23'·04E. AC 3767; D 107; BSH 1410. HW +0107 on Dover (UT); +0137 on Helgoland (zone –0100); ML 2·7m; Duration 0540. See N Frisian Islands. Appr via Rütergat and Norderaue. Make good RGR buoy No 26/AH1, Fl(2+1)R 15s, at 54°37'·76N 08°24'·80E where the hbr chan starts; it carries 2·5m and is marked by PHM withies. Yachts berth S of stone quay, pontoon. Good shelter except in E winds. Ferry quay is 800m to the E. Lt ho Fl 7·5s, R tr, W bands is same location as rear ldg lt. Wriakhörn, Cross lt, is 1M WSW of hbr, see 9.15.4. It is not advisable to enter at night. HM ☎04682 2294; ⊖ ☎2026; Dr☎531; Facilities: Ⓥ €1·75 + €2·60 pp/day tourist tax, (at Nebel); **Amrum YC** ☎2054.

PELLWORM, 54°31'·27N 08°41'·16E. AC 3767; D 106; BSH 1330. Tides: see Suderoogsand/Husum. Outer appr via Norderhever to NH18 RGR buoy, Fl (2+1) R 15s, at the mouth of the ent chan which has a limiting depth of 0·2m over datum and is marked by withies. VHF Ch 11, 0700-1700. Small yacht hbr dries to soft mud, if you berth on the wall you will need a fender board; 2·8m at MHW. €1·00. **Village** 600m N/W.

MAINLAND HARBOUR 12 MILES EAST OF PELLWORM

HUSUM, Schleswig-Holstein, **54°28'·74N 08°59'·92E**. AC 3767; D106; BSH 1330. HW + 0036 on Dover (UT); ML 1·9m; Duration 0555. See N Frisian Islands. SHM bcn, Fl G 4s, 54°28'·80N 08°58'·60E, marks start of access chan; also marked by two PHM bcns, both Fl (2) R 9s. A sluice/lock, 7ca W of rly bridge, is shut when level > 0·3m over MHW, as shown by ●. Beware the canal effect when meeting big ships in the narrow appr chan. In the outer hbr yachts should turn stbd just before rly bridge for pontoons on S bank, or pass through bridge (clnce 5m when shut) to inner hbr by SC Nordsee; both dry. VHF call *Husum Port* Ch 11. Tfc reports broadcast on Ch 11 every H +00 from HW –4 to HW +2. See 9.15.4 for hbr lts. Night entry not advised. ⊖ ☎61759; HM ☎04841 667218; Sluice ☎2565; **Husum YC** ☎65670; **SC Nordsee** ☎3436, €1·00, (at hbr).

MAINLAND (RIVER EIDER) HARBOUR 9 MILES NORTH OF BÜSUM
TÖNNING, Schleswig-Holstein, **54°19'·00N 08°57'·00E**. AC 3767 (only appr from Eider SWM buoy); D 103, BSH 104. Eiderdamm lock, 5·5M downriver, opens H24; VHF Ch 14. Lts, see 9.15.4. Above the dam, beware strong currents when sluices are operated HW +3 to HW+½. on S side of drying marina (3m at MHW) or on less-comfortable river quays if marina full. Upriver, bridge (clnce 5·6m) opens on request Mon-Sat 0600-SS. HM ☎(04861) 1400; Ⓗ ☎706; Dr ☎389; Facilities: **Quay** €1·00, (5t); **YC** ☎754 (all welcome). **Town** Ⓑ. Tönning is linked to the Kiel Canal and Rendsburg by the R Eider and the Gieselau Kanal (BSH 3009.7/.6/.5/.2).

9.15.8 BÜSUM

Schleswig-Holstein **54°07'·16N 08°51'·52E**

CHARTS AC 1875, 3767; D 105, BSH 1360

TIDES HW +0036 on Dover (UT); ML 1·9m; Duration 0625

Standard Port HELGOLAND (⟶)

Times				Height (metres)			
High Water		Low Water		MHWS	MHWN	MLWN	MLWS
0100	0600	0100	0800	3·1	2·7	0·8	0·4
1300	1800	1300	2000				
Differences BÜSUM							
+0054	+0049	–0001	+0027	+0·9	+0·9	+0·1	0·0
LINNENPLATE 54°13'·0N 08°40'·0E							
+0047	+0046	+0034	+0046	+0·7	+0·6	0·0	0·0
SÜDERHÖFT 54°16'·0N 08°41'·8E							
+0103	+0056	+0051	+0112	+0·7	+0·6	–0·2	0·0
EIDERSPERRWERK 54°16'·0N 08°50'·7E							
+0120	+0115	+0130	+0155	+0·7	+0·5	–0·1	0·0

SHELTER May be uncomfortable in strong W'ly winds. Beware strong cross-tides and sudden winds over moles. Barrage closes when level >MHW, but craft <30m LOA can enter via lock. For opening (H24) call VHF or sound 1 long blast in appr chan; 2 long blasts at lock if not already open; obey R/G lts. Turn 90° stbd into marina (1·8m LW) Basin IV. Isolated Meldorf marina is 4M ESE, 2-6m. Appr via Kronenloch (1·1m); enter via barrage/lock.

NAVIGATION WPT 54°05'·82N 08°25'·70E, Süderpiep SWM buoy Iso 8s, 096°/1·0M to No 1 SHM buoy, Fl G 4s. Chan is lit/well-buoyed. Norderpiep is buoyed, but unlit; beware bar if wind-over-tide. Both are approx 15M long; night appr not advised.

LIGHTS AND MARKS Lt ho, ldg lts 355·1° and hbr lts as chartlet. A 22 storey bldg is conspic 8ca NW of hbr; silo is conspic in hbr.

COMMUNICATIONS (Code 04834) Coast Guard 2246; Customs 2376; Doctor 2088; HM 2183, Call *Büsum Port* Ch 11 16 for lock opening; YC 2997.

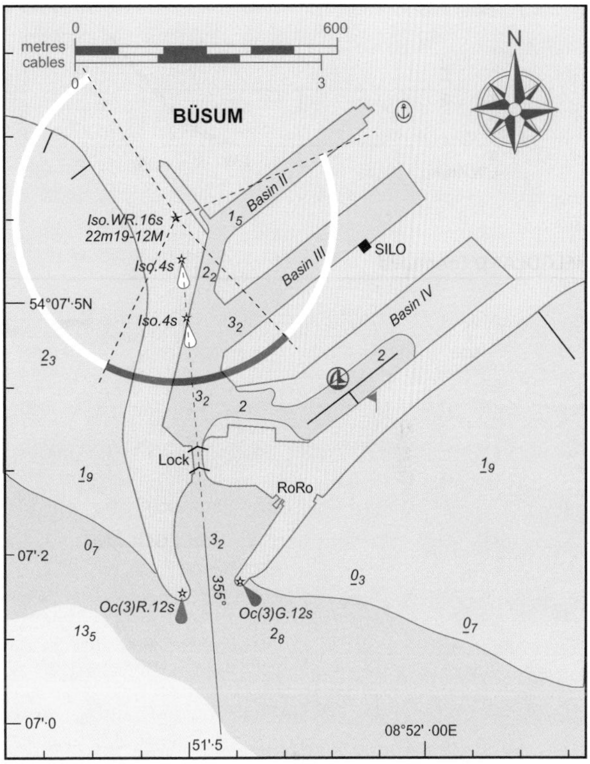

FACILITIES **Yacht hbr** €1·30. **Town** Ⓑ Ⓗ ✈ (Hamburg).

9.15.9 HELGOLAND

Schleswig-Holstein **54°10'·28N 07°53'·93E**

CHARTS AC 1635, 1875; Imray C26; D 3, 88; BSH 1310,1311

TIDES –0030 Dover; ML 1·4; Duration 0540
HELGOLAND is a Standard Port (⟶).

SHELTER Good in safe artificial hbr (5m); yachts berth on pontoons on the NE side of the Südhafen which gets very crowded, rafting 12 or more deep. Ostkaje now finished, with pontoons and coin operated power. Or ⚓ in the SW part of the Vorhafen, sheltered except in SE'lies; ask permission from Port Control Ch 67.

NAVIGATION WPT 54°08'·96N 07°53'·49E (Helgoland-O ECM buoy, Q (3) 10s, Whis) 020°/1·3M to abeam No 3 buoy. Beware: the Hogstean shoal (1m) 4ca S of Sudmole head lt, and other rky shoals either side of chan; lobster pots around Düne and fast ferries using the S appr chan and ent. Passage between Düne and Helgoland is inadvisable at night or in heavy weather.

- *Between Helgoland and Düne the general direction of buoyage changes at approx 54°11'N; see chartlet overleaf.*
- Entry is prohib at all times into Nature Reserves close to either side of the appr chans from SSW and NW.

Reserves extend about 2·9M NE and SW of Helgoland; limits marked by 7 card buoys, actively policed. Smaller reserve, lying to the N, E and S of Düne, is a prohib ⚓, with other restrictions. See BSH 1311, AC 1635 and 1875 (plan) for limits.

LIGHTS AND MARKS Helgoland is a 60m high red sandstone plateau; in contrast Düne is a low sandy islet. The lt ho is a brown □ twr, B lantern, W balcony. Close S a R/W radio mast and Sig stn are conspic. Düne rear ldg lt is on a red twr with W band.

COMMUNICATIONS (Code 04725) Coast Guard 210; SAR 811305; Met 811007; Police 607; ⊖ 1537 or 304; Brit Consul (030) 204570; Ⓗ 8030; Ambulance 7723; Dr 7345; HM 81593583, or dial 81593-0 and ask for extension; *Helgoland Port Radio* Ch 67, 16 (**1/5–31/8**: Mon-Thur 0700-1200,1300-2000; Fri/Sat 0700-2000; Sun 0700-1200LT. **1/9–30/4**: Mon-Thur 0700-1200, 1300-1600; Fri 0700-1200).

FACILITIES *Yachts must not enter the Nordost hafen and Dünen hafen nor land on Düne island.*

NOTE: Helgoland is not a port of entry into Germany. Customs in Helgoland are for passport control. Duty free goods are obtainable; hence many day-trippers by ferry. €2.75/pp/day tax. Useful webcam www.rickmers-online.de/webcam.html.

Vorhafen ⚓. **Südhafen** €1·32. Met offfice above HM. on Westkaje, limit 70 litres, €0·50, (coins) (mobile 12t).

Nordkaje €1·00 (coins).

Binnenhafen closed except for fuel, no at fuel station.

Wasser Sport Club ☎7422, Berthing <10m with permission; (12t).

Town Ⓑ ✈ to Bremen, Hamburg, Cuxhaven.

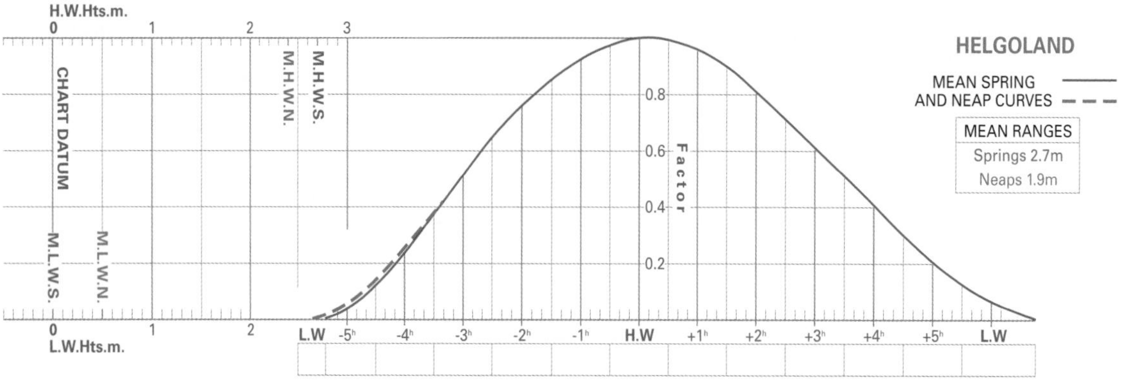

HELGOLAND *continued*

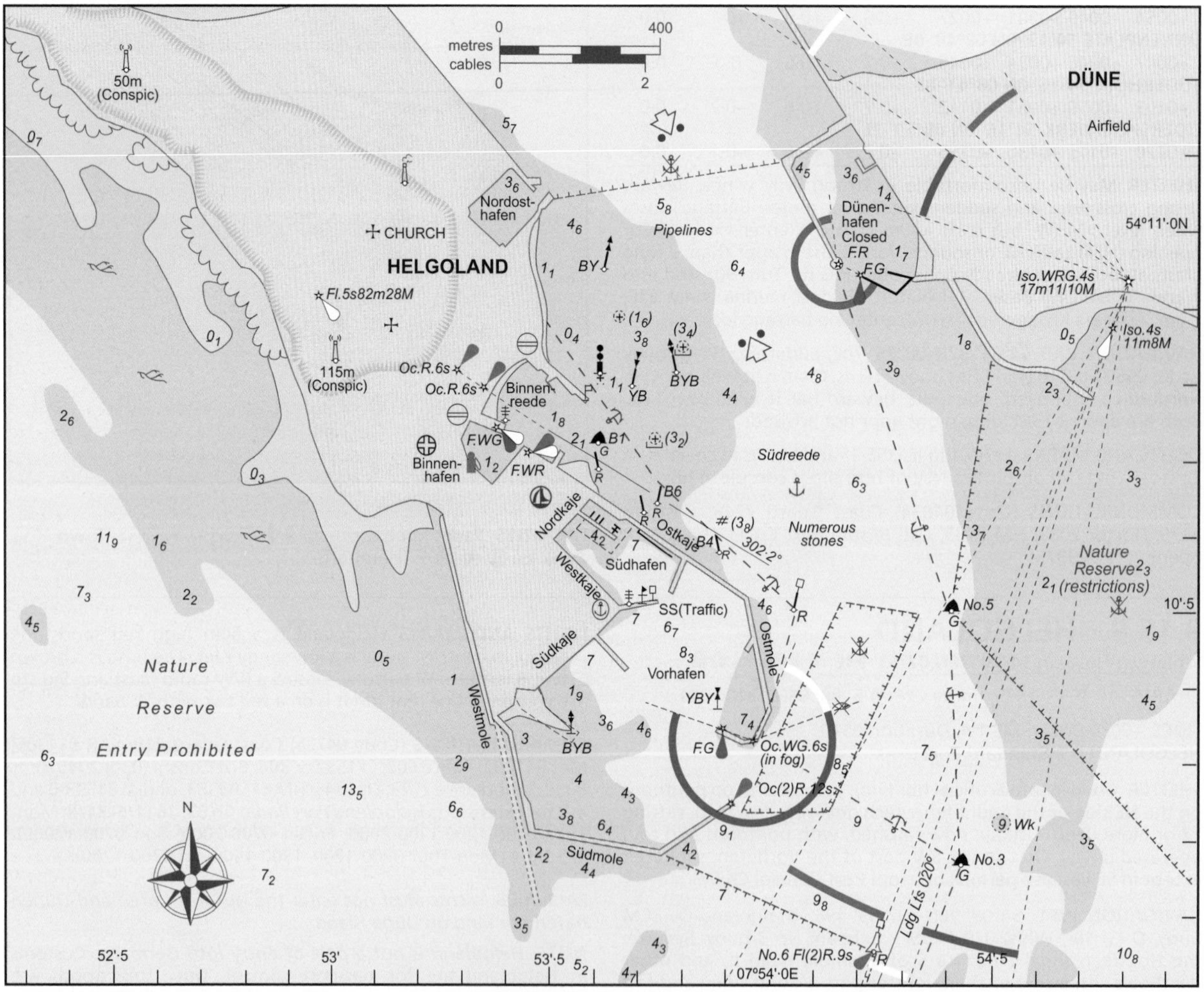

FROM THE GERMAN BIGHT TO THE UK

(AC 2182A, 1423, 1405, 1635) From the Elbe, Weser and Jade estuaries, skirt the E ends of the German Bight western approaches TSS to depart from the vicinity of Helgoland or the GB Lt Vessel.

▶*West of German Bight streams run approx E/W, spring rates <1kn.*◀ Thence parallel the N side of TSS, towards Botney Ground (BG2 buoy) if heading north of Flamborough Head. A WNW track towards the Firth of Forth avoids the areas most densely obstructed by offshore oil and gas installations.

If bound for East Anglia and the Thames Estuary, follow the ITZ westwards until S of Den Helder and Off Texel TSS in about Lat 52° 50′N; thence head west, avoiding areas of offshore industrial activity and the heavy traffic concentrations off the Maas and Westerschelde.

For the English Channel it is best to stay inshore until Cap Gris Nez. For North Sea distances, see Chapter 9, Introduction.

Note: When planning consider that Helgoland is the only all weather harbour of refuge on this coast.

STANDARD TIME UT –01
Subtract 1 hour for UT
For German Summer Time add ONE hour in **non-shaded areas**

HELGOLAND LAT 54°11'N LONG 7°53'E

TIMES AND HEIGHTS OF HIGH AND LOW WATERS

Dates in red are SPRINGS
Dates in blue are NEAPS

YEAR **2018**

JANUARY

Date	Day	Time	m	Time	m	Time	m	Time	m	Moon
1	M	0513	0.5	1049	3.1	1738	0.5	2318	3.1	
2	TU	0608	0.4	1143	3.1	1829	0.4			○
3	W	0007	3.2	0700	0.4	1234	3.1	1919	0.5	
4	TH	0056	3.2	0752	0.4	1327	3.1	2010	0.5	
5	F	0147	3.3	0845	0.4	1419	3.1	2059	0.5	
6	SA	0235	3.3	0933	0.4	1507	3.0	2143	0.5	
7	SU	0320	3.3	1017	0.5	1552	2.9	2226	0.6	
8	M	0404	3.2	1102	0.6	1640	2.8	2311	0.7	◑
9	TU	0453	3.1	1148	0.6	1730	2.8			
10	W	0001	0.8	0545	3.0	1238	0.7	1825	2.7	
11	TH	0059	0.8	0647	2.9	1339	0.8	1929	2.7	
12	F	0209	0.9	0759	2.9	1450	0.9	2039	2.8	
13	SA	0324	0.9	0912	2.9	1559	0.8	2143	2.9	
14	SU	0430	0.8	1014	2.9	1655	0.8	2236	3.0	
15	M	0523	0.7	1103	3.0	1740	0.7	2320	3.0	
16	TU	0605	0.6	1143	3.0	1819	0.7	2358	3.1	
17	W	0642	0.6	1219	3.0	1854	0.6			●
18	TH	0032	3.1	0716	0.5	1253	3.0	1928	0.6	
19	F	0105	3.1	0749	0.5	1326	3.0	1959	0.6	
20	SA	0136	3.2	0821	0.5	1358	3.0	2029	0.6	
21	SU	0207	3.2	0853	0.6	1432	2.9	2102	0.6	
22	M	0242	3.2	0930	0.6	1510	2.9	2141	0.7	
23	TU	0322	3.2	1011	0.6	1551	2.9	2221	0.7	
24	W	0403	3.1	1050	0.6	1630	2.9	2259	0.8	◐
25	TH	0444	3.1	1129	0.7	1713	2.8	2348	0.8	
26	F	0535	3.0	1224	0.8	1812	2.8			
27	SA	0057	0.9	0647	2.9	1338	0.8	1929	2.8	
28	SU	0221	0.8	0809	2.9	1502	0.7	2049	2.9	
29	M	0344	0.6	0927	2.9	1619	0.6	2202	2.9	
30	TU	0457	0.5	1036	3.0	1724	0.5	2304	3.1	
31	W	0558	0.4	1135	3.0	1820	0.4	2356	3.2	○

FEBRUARY

Date	Day	Time	m	Time	m	Time	m	Time	m	Moon
1	TH	0652	0.3	1227	3.0	1910	0.4			
2	F	0045	3.3	0743	0.3	1316	3.1	1959	0.4	
3	SA	0133	3.3	0832	0.3	1403	3.0	2046	0.4	
4	SU	0219	3.3	0917	0.4	1448	3.0	2127	0.4	
5	M	0302	3.3	0957	0.4	1528	2.9	2204	0.4	
6	TU	0341	3.2	1033	0.5	1608	2.9	2241	0.5	
7	W	0420	3.1	1109	0.6	1648	2.8	2319	0.6	◑
8	TH	0502	3.0	1146	0.7	1731	2.7			
9	F	0005	0.7	0552	2.8	1236	0.8	1827	2.7	
10	SA	0109	0.8	0702	2.7	1348	0.9	1940	2.7	
11	SU	0232	0.9	0824	2.7	1511	0.9	2100	2.8	
12	M	0353	0.8	0941	2.8	1622	0.8	2206	2.9	
13	TU	0457	0.7	1040	2.8	1716	0.7	2256	3.0	
14	W	0544	0.6	1123	2.9	1758	0.7	2336	3.1	
15	TH	0622	0.5	1200	3.0	1835	0.6			●
16	F	0012	3.1	0658	0.5	1233	3.0	1910	0.5	
17	SA	0045	3.1	0732	0.4	1306	3.0	1943	0.5	
18	SU	0117	3.1	0804	0.4	1340	2.9	2015	0.5	
19	M	0150	3.1	0838	0.4	1414	2.9	2049	0.5	
20	TU	0227	3.1	0915	0.4	1452	3.0	2128	0.5	
21	W	0307	3.2	0955	0.5	1531	3.0	2206	0.5	
22	TH	0346	3.1	1030	0.5	1606	3.0	2240	0.6	
23	F	0422	3.1	1103	0.6	1642	2.9	2320	0.6	◐
24	SA	0506	2.9	1150	0.7	1736	2.8			
25	SU	0026	0.7	0616	2.8	1306	0.8	1856	2.8	
26	M	0156	0.7	0746	2.8	1439	0.8	2027	2.8	
27	TU	0329	0.6	0915	2.8	1605	0.6	2148	3.0	
28	W	0448	0.4	1028	2.9	1715	0.5	2252	3.1	

MARCH

Date	Day	Time	m	Time	m	Time	m	Time	m	Moon
1	TH	0550	0.3	1126	3.0	1810	0.4	2345	3.2	
2	F	0641	0.3	1215	3.0	1859	0.4			○
3	SA	0031	3.2	0728	0.2	1300	3.0	1944	0.3	
4	SU	0115	3.3	0812	0.3	1342	3.0	2026	0.3	
5	M	0158	3.3	0853	0.3	1422	3.0	2104	0.3	
6	TU	0238	3.2	0929	0.4	1500	3.0	2138	0.3	
7	W	0314	3.1	1001	0.4	1534	2.9	2210	0.4	
8	TH	0348	3.0	1030	0.5	1608	2.8	2242	0.5	
9	F	0423	2.9	1059	0.6	1643	2.8	2318	0.6	◑
10	SA	0505	2.7	1140	0.8	1731	2.7			
11	SU	0015	0.7	0608	2.6	1247	0.9	1842	2.6	
12	M	0137	0.8	0732	2.5	1416	0.9	2008	2.7	
13	TU	0308	0.8	0859	2.6	1541	0.9	2127	2.8	
14	W	0423	0.7	1007	2.7	1644	0.7	2224	2.9	
15	TH	0515	0.6	1055	2.8	1730	0.6	2307	3.0	
16	F	0555	0.5	1133	2.9	1809	0.5	2344	3.1	
17	SA	0632	0.4	1208	2.9	1846	0.5			●
18	SU	0019	3.1	0708	0.3	1243	3.0	1921	0.4	
19	M	0054	3.1	0743	0.3	1317	3.0	1956	0.3	
20	TU	0130	3.1	0819	0.3	1354	3.0	2033	0.4	
21	W	0209	3.1	0856	0.3	1431	3.0	2111	0.4	
22	TH	0248	3.1	0934	0.4	1508	3.0	2149	0.4	
23	F	0327	3.1	1009	0.5	1544	3.0	2225	0.4	
24	SA	0406	3.0	1044	0.6	1623	2.9	2308	0.5	◐
25	SU	0454	2.9	1134	0.7	1719	2.8			
26	M	0015	0.6	0604	2.7	1252	0.8	1841	2.8	
27	TU	0147	0.6	0736	2.7	1427	0.8	2015	2.9	
28	W	0322	0.5	0907	2.8	1555	0.7	2136	3.0	
29	TH	0438	0.4	1018	2.9	1702	0.5	2237	3.1	
30	F	0535	0.2	1111	2.9	1754	0.4	2326	3.1	
31	SA	0623	0.2	1157	3.0	1841	0.4			○

APRIL

Date	Day	Time	m	Time	m	Time	m	Time	m	Moon
1	SU	0012	3.2	0707	0.2	1239	3.0	1924	0.3	
2	M	0055	3.2	0748	0.2	1318	3.0	2003	0.3	
3	TU	0134	3.2	0825	0.3	1355	3.0	2038	0.2	
4	W	0211	3.1	0858	0.3	1429	3.0	2110	0.3	
5	TH	0245	3.0	0927	0.4	1501	2.9	2141	0.3	
6	F	0318	2.9	0954	0.4	1532	2.9	2211	0.4	
7	SA	0350	2.8	1021	0.6	1605	2.8	2244	0.5	
8	SU	0429	2.6	1057	0.7	1648	2.7	2332	0.7	◑
9	M	0523	2.5	1155	0.9	1750	2.7			
10	TU	0045	0.8	0640	2.5	1319	0.9	1913	2.7	
11	W	0215	0.7	0806	2.5	1448	0.9	2036	2.8	
12	TH	0336	0.6	0921	2.7	1600	0.7	2140	2.9	
13	F	0434	0.5	1016	2.8	1652	0.6	2228	3.0	
14	SA	0518	0.4	1058	2.9	1735	0.5	2309	3.1	
15	SU	0559	0.3	1138	3.0	1816	0.4	2349	3.1	
16	M	0639	0.3	1215	3.0	1855	0.3			●
17	TU	0028	3.1	0717	0.2	1251	3.0	1934	0.3	
18	W	0107	3.1	0755	0.3	1329	3.0	2013	0.3	
19	TH	0147	3.1	0833	0.3	1408	3.1	2053	0.3	
20	F	0229	3.1	0912	0.4	1447	3.1	2133	0.3	
21	SA	0311	3.0	0951	0.5	1528	3.1	2217	0.4	
22	SU	0358	2.9	1035	0.6	1615	3.0	2308	0.5	◐
23	M	0453	2.8	1132	0.7	1716	3.0			
24	TU	0017	0.5	0604	2.7	1248	0.8	1835	2.9	
25	W	0143	0.5	0730	2.7	1418	0.7	2002	3.0	
26	TH	0311	0.5	0854	2.8	1539	0.6	2118	3.0	
27	F	0421	0.3	0959	2.9	1641	0.5	2215	3.1	
28	SA	0511	0.2	1048	2.9	1730	0.4	2303	3.1	
29	SU	0557	0.2	1133	2.9	1817	0.4	2349	3.1	
30	M	0641	0.2	1216	3.0	1901	0.3			○

Chart Datum: 1·68 metres below Normal Null (German reference level). HAT is 3·0 metres above Chart Datum.

STANDARD TIME UT –01
Subtract 1 hour for UT
For German Summer Time add ONE hour in **non-shaded areas**

HELGOLAND LAT 54°11′N LONG 7°53′E

TIMES AND HEIGHTS OF HIGH AND LOW WATERS

Dates in red are SPRINGS
Dates in blue are NEAPS

YEAR **2018**

MAY

Date	Day	Time	m	Time	m	Time	m	Time	m
1	TU	0032	3.1	0722	0.2	1254	3.0	1939	0.2
2	W	0109	3.1	0755	0.3	1327	3.0	2011	0.2
3	TH	0143	3.0	0826	0.3	1359	3.0	2043	0.2
4	F	0216	2.9	0854	0.4	1431	3.0	2114	0.3
5	SA	0250	2.8	0923	0.4	1503	2.9	2145	0.4
6	SU	0325	2.7	0952	0.6	1537	2.9	2219	0.5
7	M	0403	2.7	1027	0.7	1617	2.9	2302	0.7
8	TU	0450	2.6	1117	0.9	1709	2.8	◑	
9	W	0002	0.7	0552	2.6	1226	0.9	1818	2.8
10	TH	0118	0.7	0709	2.6	1348	0.9	1936	2.8
11	F	0237	0.6	0824	2.6	1504	0.8	2046	2.9
12	SA	0342	0.5	0927	2.8	1605	0.6	2143	3.0
13	SU	0435	0.5	1018	2.9	1656	0.5	2231	3.1
14	M	0522	0.4	1103	3.0	1744	0.5	2317	3.1
15	TU	0607	0.3	1144	3.0	1828	0.4	● 2359	3.1
16	W	0649	0.3	1223	3.1	1909	0.3		
17	TH	0042	3.1	0730	0.3	1303	3.1	1953	0.3
18	F	0127	3.1	0813	0.3	1347	3.1	2039	0.3
19	SA	0214	3.0	0856	0.4	1432	3.1	2125	0.3
20	SU	0303	3.0	0941	0.5	1519	3.1	2215	0.4
21	M	0355	2.9	1032	0.6	1612	3.1	2311	0.5
22	TU	0454	2.8	1131	0.7	1713	3.1	◐	
23	W	0017	0.5	0601	2.7	1241	0.7	1824	3.0
24	TH	0130	0.5	0714	2.7	1358	0.7	1939	3.0
25	F	0246	0.4	0828	2.8	1511	0.6	2050	3.0
26	SA	0351	0.4	0931	2.8	1612	0.5	2148	3.1
27	SU	0443	0.4	1021	2.9	1703	0.5	2238	3.1
28	M	0528	0.3	1106	3.0	1751	0.4	2325	3.1
29	TU	0613	0.3	1150	3.0	1836	0.3	○	
30	W	0009	3.0	0654	0.3	1229	3.0	1914	0.3
31	TH	0046	3.0	0728	0.3	1302	3.0	1947	0.3

JUNE

Date	Day	Time	m	Time	m	Time	m	Time	m
1	F	0119	3.0	0758	0.4	1333	3.0	2018	0.3
2	SA	0152	2.9	0828	0.4	1406	3.1	2051	0.4
3	SU	0227	2.9	0858	0.5	1439	3.1	2124	0.5
4	M	0303	2.8	0930	0.6	1514	3.0	2159	0.6
5	TU	0341	2.8	1006	0.7	1553	3.0	2239	0.7
6	W	0424	2.7	1049	0.8	1637	3.0	◑ 2327	0.7
7	TH	0514	2.7	1143	0.9	1732	2.9		
8	F	0027	0.7	0615	2.7	1251	0.8	1839	2.9
9	SA	0136	0.6	0725	2.7	1405	0.8	1950	2.9
10	SU	0245	0.6	0833	2.8	1514	0.7	2055	3.0
11	M	0348	0.5	0933	2.9	1615	0.6	2152	3.1
12	TU	0444	0.4	1026	3.0	1711	0.5	2245	3.1
13	W	0536	0.3	1113	3.0	1801	0.3	● 2334	3.1
14	TH	0622	0.3	1158	3.1	1848	0.3		
15	F	0022	3.1	0709	0.3	1243	3.2	1938	0.2
16	SA	0113	3.1	0758	0.4	1333	3.2	2030	0.3
17	SU	0205	3.0	0848	0.4	1423	3.2	2121	0.3
18	M	0257	3.0	0936	0.4	1511	3.2	2211	0.3
19	TU	0348	2.9	1026	0.5	1603	3.2	2305	0.4
20	W	0444	2.8	1120	0.6	1700	3.2	◐	
21	TH	0002	0.5	0543	2.8	1220	0.7	1801	3.1
22	F	0102	0.5	0645	2.7	1323	0.7	1906	3.0
23	SA	0206	0.5	0750	2.8	1431	0.6	2014	3.0
24	SU	0311	0.5	0854	2.8	1537	0.6	2118	3.0
25	M	0410	0.5	0951	2.9	1636	0.6	2214	3.0
26	TU	0501	0.5	1039	3.0	1727	0.5	2303	3.0
27	W	0547	0.5	1124	3.0	1812	0.4	2347	3.0
28	TH	0628	0.4	1205	3.1	1851	0.4	○	
29	F	0025	3.0	0704	0.4	1240	3.1	1926	0.4
30	SA	0059	3.0	0737	0.4	1313	3.1	1959	0.4

JULY

Date	Day	Time	m	Time	m	Time	m	Time	m
1	SU	0133	3.0	0808	0.5	1346	3.2	2032	0.5
2	M	0207	2.9	0838	0.6	1418	3.2	2104	0.5
3	TU	0241	2.9	0910	0.6	1452	3.1	2140	0.6
4	W	0319	2.9	0948	0.7	1531	3.1	2219	0.6
5	TH	0401	2.8	1029	0.8	1613	3.1	2301	0.7
6	F	0444	2.8	1111	0.8	1657	3.0	◑ 2345	0.7
7	SA	0531	2.8	1203	0.8	1750	3.0		
8	SU	0041	0.7	0630	2.8	1309	0.8	1857	3.0
9	M	0150	0.7	0738	2.8	1423	0.8	2009	3.0
10	TU	0302	0.6	0847	2.9	1536	0.6	2117	3.0
11	W	0409	0.5	0951	2.9	1642	0.5	2219	3.0
12	TH	0510	0.4	1049	3.0	1741	0.3	2316	3.1
13	F	0604	0.4	1141	3.1	1835	0.3	●	
14	SA	0010	3.1	0656	0.4	1231	3.2	1928	0.3
15	SU	0103	3.1	0748	0.4	1321	3.3	2022	0.3
16	M	0156	3.1	0839	0.4	1412	3.3	2113	0.3
17	TU	0246	3.0	0926	0.4	1459	3.3	2200	0.3
18	W	0333	2.9	1011	0.4	1546	3.3	2246	0.4
19	TH	0422	2.9	1058	0.5	1636	3.2	◐ 2333	0.5
20	F	0512	2.8	1146	0.6	1728	3.1		
21	SA	0021	0.6	0604	2.8	1239	0.7	1824	3.0
22	SU	0115	0.7	0702	2.8	1342	0.7	1930	2.9
23	M	0222	0.7	0809	2.8	1456	0.8	2042	2.9
24	TU	0332	0.8	0917	2.9	1607	0.7	2150	2.9
25	W	0434	0.7	1015	3.0	1705	0.6	2244	2.9
26	TH	0523	0.6	1102	3.0	1751	0.5	2328	2.9
27	F	0606	0.6	1143	3.1	1831	0.5	○	
28	SA	0007	3.0	0643	0.6	1221	3.1	1907	0.5
29	SU	0042	3.0	0718	0.5	1255	3.2	1942	0.5
30	M	0115	3.0	0750	0.5	1326	3.2	2013	0.5
31	TU	0147	3.0	0820	0.5	1357	3.2	2044	0.5

AUGUST

Date	Day	Time	m	Time	m	Time	m	Time	m
1	W	0220	3.0	0851	0.6	1431	3.2	2119	0.6
2	TH	0257	2.9	0929	0.6	1510	3.2	2159	0.6
3	F	0338	2.9	1009	0.7	1552	3.2	2237	0.6
4	SA	0417	2.9	1046	0.7	1630	3.1	◑ 2312	0.7
5	SU	0454	2.9	1125	0.8	1712	3.0	2355	0.7
6	M	0542	2.8	1222	0.8	1812	2.9		
7	TU	0101	0.8	0650	2.8	1341	0.8	1930	2.9
8	W	0222	0.8	0810	2.8	1506	0.7	2051	2.9
9	TH	0343	0.7	0926	2.9	1623	0.5	2203	3.0
10	F	0453	0.5	1033	3.0	1729	0.4	2306	3.0
11	SA	0553	0.4	1129	3.2	1826	0.3	●	
12	SU	0001	3.1	0646	0.4	1220	3.3	1918	0.3
13	M	0052	3.1	0737	0.4	1308	3.3	2008	0.3
14	TU	0141	3.1	0825	0.4	1355	3.3	2056	0.3
15	W	0227	3.1	0909	0.4	1440	3.3	2138	0.3
16	TH	0310	3.0	0949	0.4	1523	3.3	2217	0.4
17	F	0352	2.9	1028	0.5	1606	3.2	2256	0.6
18	SA	0434	2.9	1108	0.6	1650	3.1	◐ 2334	0.7
19	SU	0517	2.8	1152	0.7	1739	2.9		
20	M	0020	0.8	0609	2.8	1250	0.8	1842	2.8
21	TU	0126	0.9	0718	2.8	1409	0.9	2002	2.8
22	W	0247	1.0	0837	2.8	1533	0.8	2122	2.8
23	TH	0404	0.9	0948	2.9	1643	0.7	2225	2.9
24	F	0501	0.8	1041	3.0	1731	0.6	2310	2.9
25	SA	0544	0.7	1122	3.1	1809	0.6	2346	3.0
26	SU	0621	0.6	1158	3.1	1845	0.5	○	
27	M	0021	3.0	0657	0.6	1232	3.2	1919	0.5
28	TU	0054	3.0	0730	0.5	1304	3.2	1951	0.5
29	W	0125	3.0	0801	0.5	1336	3.2	2023	0.5
30	TH	0158	3.0	0832	0.5	1410	3.2	2057	0.5
31	F	0233	3.0	0908	0.6	1448	3.2	2135	0.6

Chart Datum: 1·68 metres below Normal Null (German reference level). HAT is 3·0 metres above Chart Datum.

STANDARD TIME UT –01
Subtract 1 hour for UT
For German Summer Time add ONE hour in **non-shaded areas**

HELGOLAND LAT 54°11'N LONG 7°53'E

TIMES AND HEIGHTS OF HIGH AND LOW WATERS

Dates in red are SPRINGS
Dates in blue are NEAPS

YEAR **2018**

SEPTEMBER

Date	Time	m	Date	Time	m
1 SA	0312 0946 1528 2211	3.0 0.6 3.2 0.6	16 SU	0354 1030 1611 2248	2.9 0.6 3.0 0.8
2 SU	0348 1021 1604 2242	3.0 0.7 3.1 0.7	17 M	0432 1108 1656 ◐ 2328	2.9 0.7 2.8 0.9
3 M	0421 1056 1643 ◑ 2321	2.9 0.7 3.0 0.8	18 TU	0519 1201 1755	2.8 0.9 2.7
4 TU	0507 1151 1742	2.8 0.8 2.9	19 W	0030 0626 1319 1916	1.1 2.7 1.0 2.6
5 W	0027 0617 1314 1907	0.9 2.8 0.8 2.8	20 TH	0156 0751 1450 2044	1.1 2.8 0.9 2.7
6 TH	0157 0747 1449 2038	0.9 2.9 0.7 2.9	21 F	0324 0912 1610 2155	1.1 2.9 0.8 2.8
7 F	0328 0913 1613 2156	0.8 3.0 0.6 2.9	22 SA	0431 1012 1703 2244	0.9 3.0 0.7 2.9
8 SA	0443 1022 1720 2257	0.7 3.1 0.4 3.0	23 SU	0516 1053 1741 2319	0.8 3.1 0.6 2.9
9 SU	0542 1117 1814 ● 2349	0.5 3.2 0.3 3.1	24 M	0553 1129 1815 2354	0.7 3.1 0.5 3.0
10 M	0633 1206 1903	0.5 3.3 0.3	25 TU	0629 1204 1851 ○	0.6 3.2 0.5
11 TU	0036 0720 1251 1948	3.1 0.4 3.3 0.3	26 W	0028 0705 1239 1925	3.0 0.6 3.2 0.5
12 W	0120 0804 1335 2031	3.1 0.4 3.3 0.3	27 TH	0102 0738 1313 1959	3.0 0.5 3.2 0.5
13 TH	0202 0844 1417 2110	3.1 0.4 3.3 0.4	28 F	0135 0812 1348 2032	3.1 0.5 3.2 0.5
14 F	0241 0921 1456 2144	3.1 0.4 3.2 0.5	29 SA	0209 0846 1425 2107	3.1 0.6 3.2 0.6
15 SA	0318 0956 1533 2216	3.0 0.5 3.1 0.6	30 SU	0243 0922 1503 2142	3.1 0.6 3.1 0.7

OCTOBER

Date	Time	m	Date	Time	m
1 M	0319 0958 1542 2216	3.1 0.7 3.1 0.8	16 TU	0354 1032 1619 ◐ 2246	2.9 0.7 2.7 1.0
2 TU	0357 1038 1627 ◑ 2301	3.0 0.7 2.9 0.9	17 W	0438 1120 1714 2341	2.9 0.9 2.6 1.1
3 W	0448 1138 1731	2.9 0.8 2.8	18 TH	0538 1229 1826	2.8 1.0 2.6
4 TH	0011 0603 1304 1858	1.0 2.9 0.9 2.8	19 F	0100 0657 1356 1951	1.2 2.8 1.0 2.6
5 F	0144 0735 1442 2031	1.0 2.9 0.8 2.9	20 SA	0229 0820 1519 2108	1.2 2.9 0.9 2.7
6 SA	0317 0902 1605 2148	0.9 3.1 0.6 2.9	21 SU	0344 0928 1621 2204	1.0 3.0 0.8 2.8
7 SU	0431 1009 1706 2244	0.8 3.2 0.5 3.0	22 M	0437 1016 1703 2245	0.9 3.0 0.7 2.9
8 M	0526 1100 1756 2332	0.6 3.2 0.4 3.0	23 TU	0518 1055 1741 2323	0.8 3.1 0.6 3.0
9 TU	0614 1147 1842 ●	0.5 3.3 0.4	24 W	0558 1134 1819 ○	0.7 3.2 0.5
10 W	0016 0659 1232 1924	3.1 0.5 3.3 0.4	25 TH	0000 0636 1211 1856	3.1 0.6 3.2 0.5
11 TH	0057 0740 1313 2003	3.1 0.4 3.3 0.4	26 F	0034 0713 1248 1931	3.1 0.6 3.2 0.5
12 F	0135 0817 1351 2038	3.1 0.4 3.2 0.5	27 SA	0109 0750 1325 2007	3.1 0.5 3.2 0.6
13 SA	0211 0852 1427 2109	3.1 0.4 3.1 0.6	28 SU	0144 0826 1403 2043	3.2 0.6 3.2 0.6
14 SU	0244 0924 1502 2138	3.0 0.5 3.0 0.6	29 M	0220 0904 1443 2120	3.2 0.6 3.1 0.7
15 M	0318 0957 1538 2208	3.0 0.6 2.8 0.8	30 TU	0259 0945 1528 2202	3.2 0.6 3.0 0.8
			31 W	0344 1034 1622 ◑ 2255	3.1 0.7 2.9 1.0

NOVEMBER

Date	Time	m	Date	Time	m
1 TH	0441 1137 1729	3.1 0.8 2.8	16 F	0455 1144 1737	2.9 1.0 2.6
2 F	0006 0555 1259 1851	1.0 3.0 0.8 2.8	17 SA	0005 0600 1255 1850	1.2 2.9 1.0 2.6
3 SA	0133 0722 1429 2017	1.0 3.0 0.7 2.8	18 SU	0124 0716 1414 2006	1.2 2.9 0.9 2.7
4 SU	0300 0844 1548 2131	0.9 3.1 0.6 2.9	19 M	0243 0830 1523 2112	1.1 2.9 0.8 2.8
5 M	0410 0949 1645 2225	0.8 3.2 0.5 3.0	20 TU	0347 0929 1617 2204	0.9 3.0 0.8 2.9
6 TU	0503 1040 1732 2310	0.7 3.2 0.5 3.0	21 W	0438 1017 1702 2247	0.8 3.1 0.7 3.0
7 W	0551 1127 1817 ● 2354	0.6 3.2 0.5 3.1	22 TH	0524 1101 1745 2328	0.8 3.1 0.6 3.1
8 TH	0637 1211 1859	0.5 3.2 0.5	23 F	0607 1142 1825 ○	0.7 3.2 0.5
9 F	0033 0716 1250 1935	3.1 0.5 3.2 0.5	24 SA	0005 0647 1222 1904	3.1 0.6 3.2 0.5
10 SA	0108 0751 1325 2007	3.1 0.4 3.1 0.5	25 SU	0043 0729 1304 1945	3.2 0.5 3.2 0.6
11 SU	0142 0824 1400 2037	3.1 0.5 3.0 0.6	26 M	0125 0812 1349 2028	3.2 0.5 3.1 0.6
12 M	0215 0857 1435 2107	3.1 0.5 2.9 0.7	27 TU	0207 0856 1435 2110	3.2 0.5 3.1 0.7
13 TU	0249 0930 1511 2138	3.1 0.6 2.8 0.8	28 W	0250 0942 1523 2157	3.2 0.6 3.0 0.8
14 W	0325 1006 1551 2214	3.0 0.7 2.7 1.0	29 TH	0338 1035 1619 2253	3.2 0.6 2.9 0.9
15 TH	0405 1048 1638 ◐ 2301	3.0 0.9 2.7 1.1	30 F	0435 1137 1723 ◑ 2358	3.2 0.7 2.8 0.9

DECEMBER

Date	Time	m	Date	Time	m
1 SA	0543 1247 1834	3.1 0.7 2.8	16 SU	0509 1159 1751	3.0 0.9 2.7
2 SU	0113 0659 1404 1950	0.9 3.1 0.7 2.8	17 M	0022 0612 1305 1859	1.1 2.9 0.9 2.7
3 M	0230 0816 1517 2101	0.9 3.1 0.7 2.9	18 TU	0135 0725 1416 2010	1.1 2.9 0.9 2.8
4 TU	0340 0923 1617 2159	0.8 3.1 0.6 3.0	19 W	0248 0835 1523 2113	1.0 3.0 0.8 2.9
5 W	0438 1018 1707 2247	0.8 3.2 0.6 3.0	20 TH	0353 0935 1621 2207	0.9 3.0 0.7 3.0
6 TH	0529 1106 1753 2331	0.7 3.2 0.6 3.1	21 F	0449 1028 1712 2255	0.7 3.1 0.6 3.0
7 F	0615 1151 1835 ●	0.6 3.1 0.5	22 SA	0539 1115 1759 ○ 2339	0.6 3.1 0.5 3.1
8 SA	0011 0655 1229 1910	3.1 0.5 3.1 0.5	23 SU	0626 1201 1844	0.5 3.1 0.5
9 SU	0045 0728 1304 1942	3.1 0.5 3.0 0.6	24 M	0023 0714 1250 1932	3.2 0.5 3.1 0.5
10 M	0119 0802 1339 2014	3.1 0.5 3.0 0.6	25 TU	0111 0805 1341 2021	3.2 0.5 3.1 0.5
11 TU	0153 0836 1415 2045	3.1 0.5 2.9 0.7	26 W	0159 0855 1430 2108	3.3 0.4 3.0 0.6
12 W	0227 0910 1450 2116	3.1 0.6 2.9 0.8	27 TH	0245 0943 1519 2154	3.3 0.4 3.0 0.6
13 TH	0301 0944 1526 2150	3.1 0.7 2.8 0.9	28 F	0331 1032 1610 2245	3.3 0.5 2.9 0.7
14 F	0338 1022 1607 2231	3.1 0.8 2.8 1.0	29 SA	0424 1126 1706 ◑ 2341	3.2 0.5 2.8 0.7
15 SA	0419 1106 1654 ◐ 2320	3.0 0.9 2.7 1.1	30 SU	0522 1222 1806	3.1 0.6 2.8
			31 M	0041 0626 1325 1911	0.8 3.1 0.7 2.7

Chart Datum: 1·68 metres below Normal Null (German reference level). HAT is 3·0 metres above Chart Datum.

Germany

9.15.10 RIVER ELBE

Niedersachsen/Schleswig-Holstein

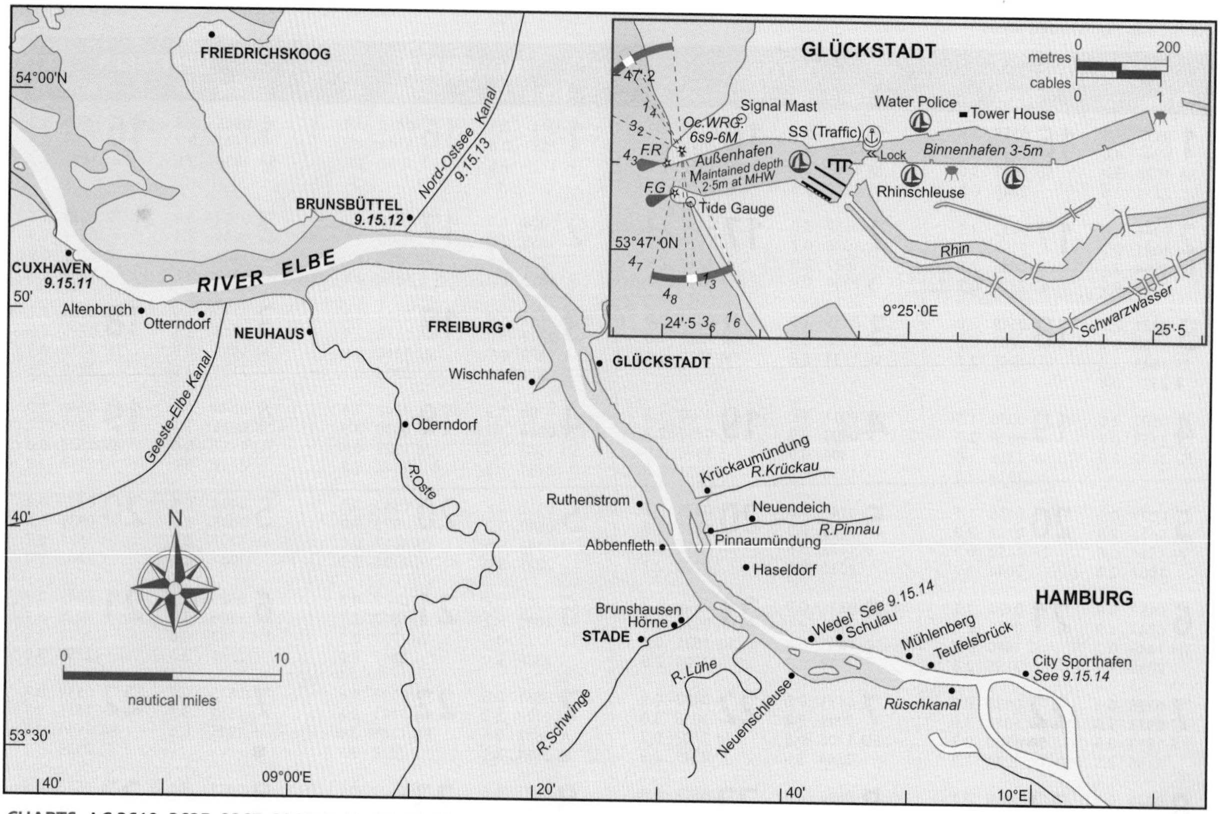

CHARTS AC 3619, 3625, 3267, 3268; D 44, 46, 47, 48; BSH 1610-60

TIDES

Standard Port CUXHAVEN (⟶)

Times				Height (metres)			
High Water		Low Water		MHWS	MHWN	MLWN	MLWS
0200	0800	0200	0900	3·7	3·3	0·8	0·4
1400	2000	1400	2100				
Differences SCHARHÖRN (11M NW of Cuxhaven)							
−0045	−0047	−0101	−0103	0·0	0·0	0·0	0·0
GROßER VOGELSAND							
−0044	−0046	−0101	−0103	+0·1	0·0	+0·1	+0·1
OTTERNDORF							
+0029	+0029	+0027	+0027	0·0	−0·1	0·0	+0·1
GLÜCKSTADT							
+0205	+0214	+0220	+0213	−0·1	0·0	0·0	+0·1
STADERSAND							
+0241	+0245	+0300	+0254	+0·1	+0·2	−0·1	+0·1
SCHULAU							
+0304	+0315	+0337	+0321	+0·3	+0·3	−0·2	0·0
SEEMANNSHÖFT (53°32'·5N 09°52'·7E)							
+0324	+0332	+0403	+0347	+0·4	+0·5	−0·3	−0·1
HAMBURG							
+0338	*+0346*	*+0422*	*+0406*	*+0·5*	*+0·5*	*−0·3*	*−0·2*

NAVIGATION Distances: Elbe SWM buoy to Cuxhaven = 24M; Cuxhaven to Wedel Yacht Haven = 45M; Wedel to City Sport Hafen = 11·5M. The river is 13m deep up to Hamburg and tidal to Geesthacht, 24M above Hamburg.

Strong W winds can raise the level by as much as 4m. Do not try to enter in strong W/NW winds against the ebb. It is a very busy waterway and at night the many lights can be confusing. Yachts should keep to stbd, just outside the marked chan.

SHELTER AND FACILITIES This inland area is well worth exploring, the following list of marinas and harbours offers a varied choice:

FREIBURG: 7M above Brunsbüttel on the SW bank. Enter at HW, but mainly commercial at Freiburg Reede; dries, little space for small craft. ML 2·2m. HM ☎(04779) 8314. Facilities: ; **Jugendheim & YC Klubheim** .

STÖRLOCH/BORSFLETH: Ent approx 600m above locks on E bank. ML 2·8m. HM ☎(04124) 71437. Facilities: YC. Stör Bridge VHF Ch 09, 16.

STÖR/BEIDENFLETH: ML 2·8m. **Langes Rack YC**.

GLÜCKSTADT: E bank, mouth of R Rhin (see inset). Good shelter: 1 marina in outer hbr, 5.8m at MHW. Or via entry gate, opens HW −2 to +½, into inner hbr for 3 marinas in 3-4·5m. VHF Ch 11. HM ☎(04124) 2087; ⊖ ☎2171. YC.

WISCHHAFEN: HM☎(04770) 334; ⊖ 3014 ML 2·7m. Dries.

RUTHENSTROM: 197° ldg bns 2 Oc G 3s with △ topmarks into hbr. ML 2·6m. HM ☎(04143) 5282, . Partially dries, hard ground.

KRÜCKAUMÜNDUNG JACHTHAFEN: Entrance via lock gate; ☎(04125) 1521 . ML 2·7m. ⊖ ☎20551).

PINNAUMÜNDUNG JACHTHAFEN: Ent via lock gate on N bank after passing through main locks. ML 2·5m. HM ☎(04101) 22447, YC, .

PINNAU-NEUENDEICH: Drying marina 1½M up the Pinnau from main locks and another at approx 2M.

ABBENFLETH: Ent marked by two bns in line 221° with △ topmarks. Dries.

HASELDORF Hafen: HM ☎(04129) 268, YC. Dries.

R SCHWINGE on SW bank, 12M up-river from Glückstadt: **BRUNSHAUSEN** ☎(04141) 3085. ML 1·1; Duration 0510.

HÖRNE/WÖHRDEN ML 2·8m.

STADE HM ☎(04141) 101275, ⊖ ☎3014, YC, . Very good shelter in scenic town.

LÜHE: Hafen in town of Lühe.

RIVER ELBE, VESSEL TRAFFIC SERVICE

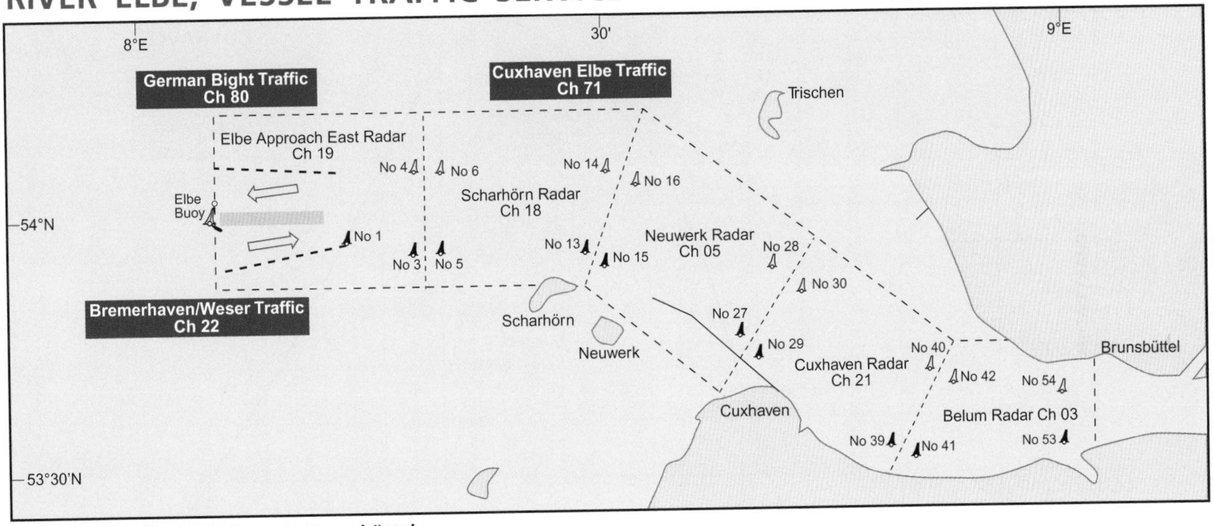
8°E
30'
9°E
German Bight Traffic Ch 80
Cuxhaven Elbe Traffic Ch 71
Trischen
Elbe Approach East Radar Ch 19
No 4
No 6
No 14
No 16
Scharhörn Radar Ch 18
Elbe Buoy
54°N
No 1
No 3
No 5
No 13
No 15
Neuwerk Radar Ch 05
No 28
No 30
Bremerhaven/Weser Traffic Ch 22
Scharhörn
Neuwerk
No 27
No 29
Cuxhaven Radar Ch 21
No 40
No 42
No 54
Brunsbüttel
Cuxhaven
Belum Radar Ch 03
No 39
No 41
No 53
53°30'N

Fig 9.15.10A. Elbe SWM buoy to Brunsbüttel

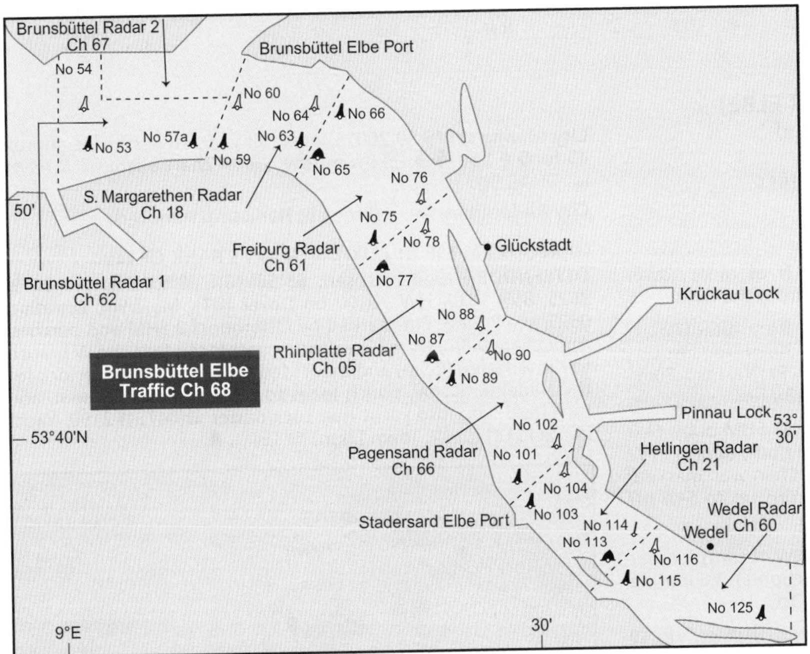
Brunsbüttel Radar 2 Ch 67
Brunsbüttel Elbe Port
No 54
No 60
No 64
No 66
No 53
No 57a
No 63
No 59
No 65
No 76
S. Margarethen Radar Ch 18
50'
No 75
No 78
Glückstadt
Freiburg Radar Ch 61
No 77
Brunsbüttel Radar 1 Ch 62
Krückau Lock
No 88
No 87
No 90
Rhinplatte Radar Ch 05
No 89
Brunsbüttel Elbe Traffic Ch 68
Pinnau Lock
53° 30'
No 102
53°40'N
Pagensand Radar Ch 66
No 101
Hetlingen Radar Ch 21
No 104
No 103
Wedel Radar Ch 60
Stadersard Elbe Port
No 114
Wedel
No 113
No 116
No 115
No 125
9°E
30'

Fig 9.15.10B. Brunsbüttel to 2M east of Wedel

Elbe VTS is not mandatory for yachts, but it is sensible to monitor the 3 Traffic Centres (callsigns and channels below) on your way upriver.

Cuxhaven Elbe Traffic	Ch 71
Brunsbüttel Elbe Traffic	Ch 68
Hamburg Port Traffic	Ch 14/74

Broadcasts of navigational, weather and traffic info are detailed in each port entry.

If radar guidance is required in English, request it from the relevant Traffic Centre.

The radar stations, their areas of coverage and VHF channels are stated for sectors:

Elbe Lt Float-buoy 53	See Cuxhaven
Buoys 51-125	See Brunsbüttel
Then continue with *Hamburg Radar:*	
Buoys 125-129	Ch 19
Buoys 129-Seemanshöft (09°53'E)	Ch 03
Seemanshöft-Vorhafen (09°57'E)	Ch 63
09°57'E-Norderelbe bridges	Ch 05

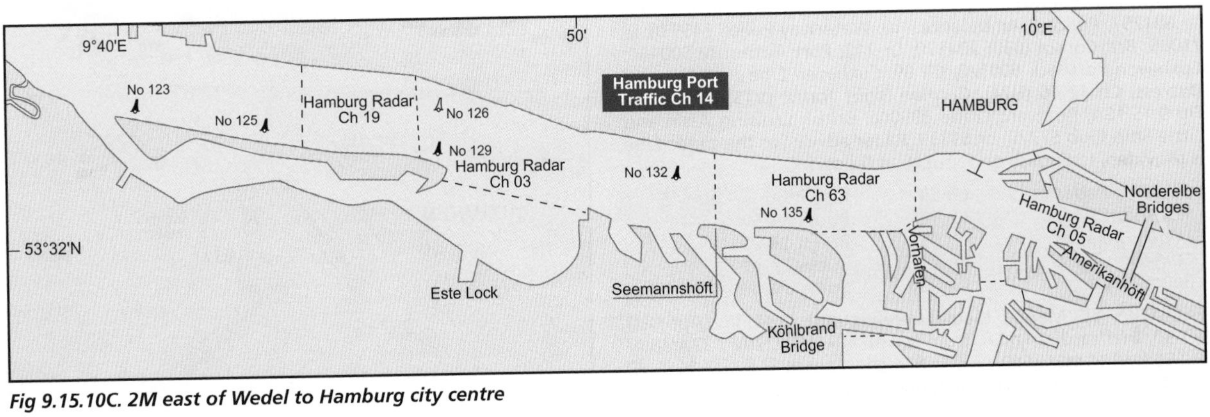
9°40'E
50'
10°E
No 123
Hamburg Radar Ch 19
No 126
Hamburg Port Traffic Ch 14
HAMBURG
No 125
No 129
Hamburg Radar Ch 03
No 132
Hamburg Radar Ch 63
Norderelbe Bridges
No 135
Hamburg Radar Ch 05
53°32'N
Vorhafen
Amerikanhöft
Este Lock
Seemannshöft
Köhlbrand Bridge

Fig 9.15.10C. 2M east of Wedel to Hamburg city centre

Germany

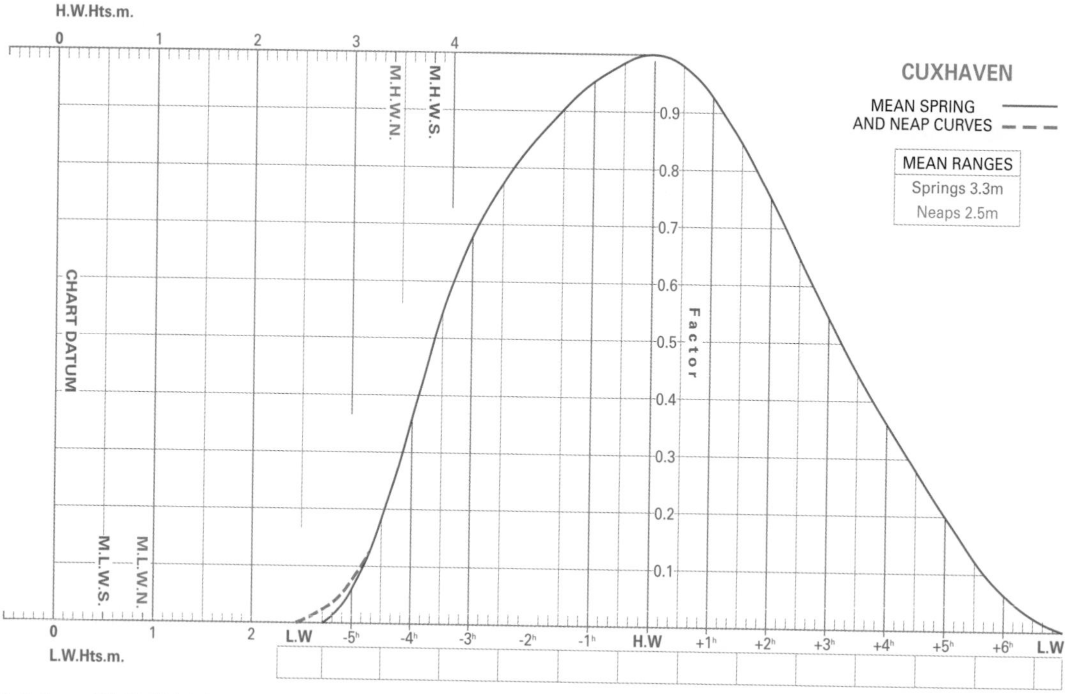

9.15.11 CUXHAVEN (RIVER ELBE)

Niedersachsen **53°52'·43N 08°42'·49E** (Marina ent)

CHARTS AC 3619; Imray C26; D 44; BSH 1610,1611

TIDES +0103 Dover; ML 1·7; Duration 0535

CUXHAVEN is a Standard Port (⟶)

SHELTER Good in both marinas: YC marina N of radar tower (2·5–3·5m) is open H24 Apr-Oct, direct access from the river.

City Marina, close S of radio mast, is entered from Alter Hafen via bridge which opens (0500-2300) H and H+30, on request Ch 69 *Cuxhaven Lock*, not at night nor in winds > F7. Yachts > 30m LOA berth in the Alter Hafen or Alter Fischereihafen.

NAVIGATION WPT 53°53'·92N 08°41'·20E [No 31 SHM buoy, Fl G 4s], 152°/1·7M to marina ent. From No 27 SHM buoy, appr is in W sector (149°-154°) of Baumrönne ldg lt Iso 4s. Chan well marked/lit, see Lights, buoys & waypoints. *The ebb runs up to 5kn off Cuxhaven. There is much commercial shipping.*

LIGHTS AND MARKS Ent to YC Marina is close NW of conspic radar tr, and N of disused lt ho (dark R with copper cupola). YC marina ent, N side FWG; S side FWR, shown 1 Apr-31 Oct.

COMMUNICATIONS (Code 04721) CG 38011/12, VHF Ch 16; LB 34622, VHF Ch 16; **Cuxhaven Elbe Traffic** (VTS) 567380, broadcasts nav/tfc/weather info for sector Cuxhaven-Brunsbüttel on Ch 71 in German & English every H + 35, yachts should monitor Ch **71**; 681757; Police & Ambulance 110; Waterway Police 745930; 21085; Brit Consul (030) 204570; Dr 112; Port Authority 500150; Cuxhaven Port/lock 500120, Ch 69. *Cuxhaven Elbe Port* (Sig stn/ Distress) Ch **12** 16 (H24). *German Bight Traffic* (VTS) Ch 80; see Fig 9.15.16A; Boatyard/Crane 399000; British Cruising Ass'n and Little Ship Club 57270, or 51339. Radar advice for the outer Elbe is provided, in English on request, as follows:

Elbe East Radar	Ch 19	Elbe lt buoy – buoy 5.
Scharhörn Radar	Ch 18	Buoys 3–15.
Neuwerk Radar	Ch 05	Buoys 13–29.
Cuxhaven Radar	Ch 21	Buoys 27–41.
Belum Radar	Ch 03	Buoys 39–53.

FACILITIES **YC Marina (Segler-Vereinigung)** ☎34111 (Apr-Oct) €1·50, (cr/card only) (from town) (16A/220V / 32A/380V €0·50/kW) ✕ ☎663650, chart agent (10t) courtesy bikes available.

City Marina ☎175 90 20015, open all year, 90 berths inc approx 45 for Ⓥ €1·50. (from town) chart agent (25t).

City All facilities, ⇄ ✈ (Bremen, Hamburg, Hanover).

HARBOUR 7M ESE OF CUXHAVEN, ON S BANK OF ELBE

OTTERNDORF, Niedersachsen, **53°50'·10N 08°53'·84E**. AC 3619, 3625; BSH 1610. HW +0100 on Dover (UT); ML 2·9m; Duration 0525; see R Elbe. Ent marked by Otterndorf 3 SHM and perches. Appr chan (0·8m) from Elbe divides: yachts can take the W branch to Kutterhafen (0·9m) and the R Medem; or to E, through lock for the Hadelner Kanal, which leads to the Geeste-Elbe Kanal, and turn hard stbd into yacht hbr. Lockmaster ☎(04751) 2190; Yacht hbr ☎13131, . **Town** (3km) .

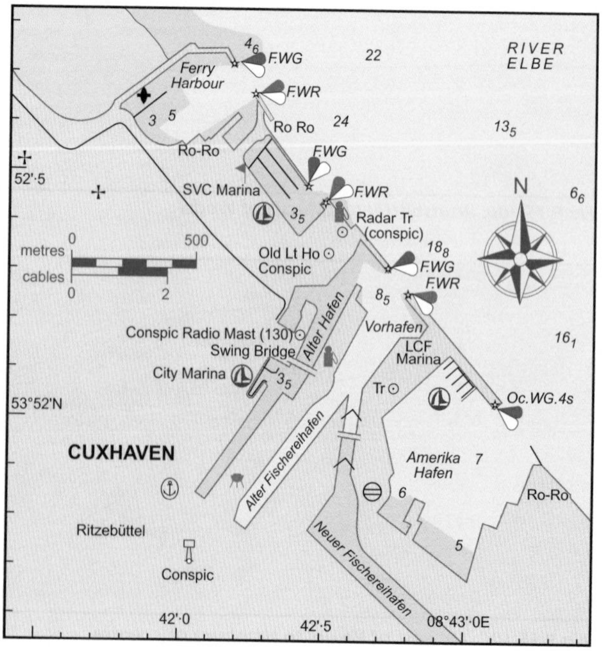

STANDARD TIME UT –01
Subtract 1 hour for UT
For German Summer Time add ONE hour in **non-shaded areas**

CUXHAVEN LAT 53°52′N LONG 8°43′E

TIMES AND HEIGHTS OF HIGH AND LOW WATERS

Dates in red are SPRINGS
Dates in blue are NEAPS

YEAR **2018**

JANUARY

Date	Day	Time	m	Time	m	Time	m	Time	m	Moon
1	M	0637	0.5	1201	3.6	1901	0.4			
2	TU	0033	3.6	0734	0.4	1256	3.6	1953	0.4	○
3	W	0123	3.7	0825	0.4	1349	3.6	2043	0.4	
4	TH	0211	3.8	0917	0.4	1443	3.6	2134	0.5	
5	F	0301	3.9	1010	0.4	1535	3.6	2223	0.5	
6	SA	0349	3.9	1059	0.4	1624	3.5	2307	0.5	
7	SU	0434	3.9	1142	0.5	1710	3.4	2348	0.6	
8	M	0520	3.8	1224	0.5	1757	3.3			◑
9	TU	0030	0.6	0607	3.7	1307	0.6	1845	3.3	
10	W	0116	0.7	0659	3.6	1354	0.7	1939	3.2	
11	TH	0210	0.8	0759	3.5	1454	0.8	2042	3.2	
12	F	0320	0.9	0910	3.5	1606	0.8	2152	3.3	
13	SA	0437	0.9	1022	3.5	1716	0.8	2257	3.4	
14	SU	0547	0.8	1124	3.5	1815	0.8	2350	3.5	
15	M	0644	0.7	1215	3.5	1901	0.7			
16	TU	0033	3.6	0728	0.6	1257	3.5	1941	0.6	
17	W	0111	3.6	0805	0.5	1334	3.5	2017	0.6	●
18	TH	0145	3.7	0840	0.5	1408	3.5	2051	0.5	
19	F	0217	3.7	0914	0.5	1442	3.5	2123	0.5	
20	SA	0249	3.7	0947	0.5	1514	3.5	2153	0.5	
21	SU	0321	3.7	1018	0.5	1547	3.5	2224	0.6	
22	M	0357	3.7	1054	0.6	1624	3.5	2301	0.6	
23	TU	0436	3.7	1134	0.6	1704	3.5	2340	0.7	
24	W	0515	3.7	1211	0.6	1743	3.4			◐
25	TH	0017	0.7	0556	3.7	1248	0.7	1826	3.4	
26	F	0102	0.8	0647	3.5	1339	0.7	1925	3.3	
27	SA	0208	0.8	0756	3.5	1452	0.8	2041	3.3	
28	SU	0333	0.8	0917	3.4	1616	0.7	2201	3.4	
29	M	0500	0.6	1036	3.5	1737	0.6	2314	3.5	
30	TU	0618	0.4	1147	3.5	1845	0.4			
31	W	0018	3.6	0723	0.3	1248	3.6	1943	0.4	○

FEBRUARY

Date	Day	Time	m	Time	m	Time	m	Time	m	Moon
1	TH	0111	3.8	0817	0.3	1342	3.6	2034	0.4	
2	F	0200	3.9	0908	0.3	1432	3.6	2123	0.4	
3	SA	0247	3.9	0957	0.3	1520	3.6	2210	0.4	
4	SU	0333	3.9	1043	0.4	1605	3.6	2251	0.4	
5	M	0416	3.9	1122	0.4	1647	3.5	2327	0.4	
6	TU	0457	3.8	1157	0.5	1726	3.4			
7	W	0001	0.5	0536	3.7	1229	0.6	1804	3.3	◑
8	TH	0035	0.6	0616	3.5	1301	0.7	1845	3.2	
9	F	0115	0.7	0705	3.4	1347	0.8	1940	3.2	
10	SA	0216	0.8	0812	3.3	1457	0.9	2052	3.2	
11	SU	0339	0.8	0933	3.3	1621	0.9	2211	3.3	
12	M	0505	0.8	1049	3.3	1737	0.8	2318	3.4	
13	TU	0614	0.7	1149	3.4	1834	0.7			
14	W	0008	3.5	0704	0.6	1235	3.5	1918	0.6	
15	TH	0047	3.6	0744	0.5	1313	3.5	1957	0.5	●
16	F	0123	3.7	0820	0.5	1349	3.5	2033	0.5	
17	SA	0156	3.7	0855	0.4	1422	3.5	2107	0.4	
18	SU	0229	3.7	0928	0.4	1455	3.5	2139	0.4	
19	M	0303	3.7	1001	0.4	1530	3.5	2212	0.4	
20	TU	0340	3.7	1038	0.4	1607	3.5	2249	0.5	
21	W	0420	3.8	1117	0.5	1645	3.6	2327	0.5	
22	TH	0458	3.8	1152	0.5	1720	3.5	2359	0.5	
23	F	0534	3.7	1221	0.6	1755	3.4			◐
24	SA	0035	0.6	0618	3.5	1304	0.7	1849	3.3	
25	SU	0135	0.7	0726	3.3	1416	0.7	2008	3.3	
26	M	0304	0.7	0854	3.3	1550	0.7	2138	3.4	
27	TU	0442	0.6	1024	3.4	1721	0.6	2259	3.5	
28	W	0606	0.4	1140	3.4	1834	0.5			

MARCH

Date	Day	Time	m	Time	m	Time	m	Time	m	Moon
1	TH	0005	3.6	0713	0.3	1241	3.5	1932	0.4	
2	F	0059	3.8	0806	0.2	1332	3.6	2022	0.3	○
3	SA	0145	3.8	0852	0.2	1417	3.6	2107	0.3	
4	SU	0229	3.9	0936	0.3	1459	3.6	2149	0.3	
5	M	0312	3.9	1017	0.3	1540	3.6	2227	0.3	
6	TU	0353	3.8	1054	0.4	1618	3.5	2301	0.3	
7	W	0430	3.7	1125	0.4	1652	3.5	2331	0.4	
8	TH	0504	3.6	1150	0.5	1723	3.4	2359	0.5	
9	F	0537	3.4	1214	0.6	1756	3.3			◑
10	SA	0030	0.6	0618	3.2	1248	0.7	1843	3.1	
11	SU	0119	0.7	0718	3.1	1351	0.8	1953	3.1	
12	M	0239	0.8	0841	3.1	1520	0.9	2118	3.2	
13	TU	0414	0.7	1006	3.1	1650	0.8	2237	3.3	
14	W	0536	0.6	1115	3.3	1759	0.6	2335	3.5	
15	TH	0633	0.5	1205	3.4	1848	0.5			
16	F	0017	3.6	0716	0.4	1246	3.5	1930	0.5	
17	SA	0055	3.7	0754	0.4	1323	3.5	2009	0.4	●
18	SU	0130	3.7	0830	0.3	1359	3.5	2045	0.3	
19	M	0206	3.7	0905	0.3	1433	3.5	2120	0.3	
20	TU	0242	3.7	0940	0.3	1509	3.6	2156	0.3	
21	W	0321	3.7	1018	0.3	1547	3.6	2233	0.3	
22	TH	0401	3.7	1056	0.4	1624	3.6	2310	0.4	
23	F	0440	3.7	1130	0.4	1659	3.6	2344	0.4	
24	SA	0519	3.6	1202	0.5	1737	3.5			◐
25	SU	0022	0.5	0607	3.4	1247	0.6	1833	3.4	
26	M	0124	0.6	0717	3.3	1401	0.7	1954	3.4	
27	TU	0255	0.6	0848	3.3	1538	0.7	2127	3.4	
28	W	0434	0.5	1019	3.3	1710	0.6	2248	3.6	
29	TH	0556	0.4	1132	3.4	1820	0.5	2350	3.7	
30	F	0656	0.2	1227	3.5	1914	0.4			
31	SA	0040	3.7	0746	0.2	1314	3.5	2002	0.3	○

APRIL

Date	Day	Time	m	Time	m	Time	m	Time	m	Moon
1	SU	0126	3.8	0831	0.2	1356	3.6	2046	0.3	
2	M	0209	3.8	0911	0.2	1435	3.6	2126	0.3	
3	TU	0249	3.8	0948	0.3	1512	3.6	2201	0.3	
4	W	0326	3.7	1021	0.3	1546	3.5	2232	0.3	
5	TH	0401	3.6	1049	0.4	1617	3.5	2301	0.3	
6	F	0433	3.4	1113	0.4	1647	3.4	2328	0.3	
7	SA	0505	3.3	1135	0.5	1718	3.3	2357	0.5	
8	SU	0542	3.1	1206	0.7	1800	3.2			◑
9	M	0038	0.6	0635	3.0	1259	0.8	1902	3.1	
10	TU	0148	0.7	0751	3.0	1421	0.9	2024	3.2	
11	W	0319	0.7	0916	3.1	1554	0.8	2146	3.3	
12	TH	0446	0.6	1031	3.2	1712	0.6	2251	3.4	
13	F	0551	0.5	1127	3.3	1809	0.5	2340	3.6	
14	SA	0638	0.4	1212	3.4	1856	0.5			
15	SU	0022	3.6	0720	0.3	1253	3.5	1939	0.4	
16	M	0102	3.7	0800	0.3	1331	3.6	2019	0.3	●
17	TU	0141	3.7	0838	0.2	1408	3.6	2057	0.3	
18	W	0220	3.7	0916	0.3	1445	3.6	2136	0.3	
19	TH	0300	3.7	0955	0.3	1524	3.6	2215	0.3	
20	F	0343	3.7	1034	0.4	1604	3.7	2255	0.3	
21	SA	0426	3.6	1113	0.4	1645	3.6	2336	0.4	
22	SU	0513	3.5	1153	0.5	1731	3.6			◐
23	M	0024	0.5	0609	3.4	1245	0.7	1831	3.6	
24	TU	0129	0.5	0720	3.3	1358	0.7	1949	3.5	
25	W	0254	0.5	0845	3.2	1528	0.7	2115	3.5	
26	TH	0424	0.5	1009	3.3	1654	0.6	2231	3.6	
27	F	0538	0.3	1116	3.4	1758	0.5	2328	3.7	
28	SA	0632	0.3	1205	3.5	1849	0.4			
29	SU	0016	3.7	0719	0.2	1249	3.5	1937	0.3	
30	M	0103	3.7	0804	0.2	1332	3.6	2023	0.3	○

Chart Datum: 2·06 metres below Normal Null (German reference level). HAT is 4·1 metres above Chart Datum.

STANDARD TIME UT –01
Subtract 1 hour for UT
For German Summer Time add
ONE hour in **non-shaded areas**

CUXHAVEN LAT 53°52′N LONG 8°43′E

TIMES AND HEIGHTS OF HIGH AND LOW WATERS

Dates in red are SPRINGS
Dates in blue are NEAPS

YEAR **2018**

MAY

Date	Day	Time	m	Time	m	Time	m	Time	m
1	TU	0147	3.7	0844	0.2	1410	3.6	2101	0.3
2	W	0226	3.6	0917	0.2	1443	3.6	2134	0.2
3	TH	0300	3.6	0947	0.3	1514	3.6	2204	0.2
4	F	0332	3.5	1014	0.3	1545	3.5	2234	0.3
5	SA	0405	3.4	1040	0.4	1617	3.5	2304	0.3
6	SU	0439	3.2	1107	0.5	1651	3.4	2335	0.5
7	M	0517	3.2	1139	0.7	1731	3.4		
8	TU	0014	0.6	0604	3.1	1224	0.8	◑ 1823	3.3
9	W	0109	0.7	0707	3.0	1331	0.9	1932	3.3
10	TH	0226	0.6	0823	3.1	1455	0.8	2049	3.3
11	F	0348	0.6	0938	3.2	1615	0.7	2159	3.5
12	SA	0458	0.5	1041	3.3	1721	0.6	2257	3.6
13	SU	0554	0.4	1133	3.4	1816	0.5	2345	3.6
14	M	0643	0.4	1219	3.6	1906	0.4		
15	TU	0031	3.7	0729	0.3	1300	3.6	● 1951	0.4
16	W	0113	3.7	0810	0.3	1339	3.7	2032	0.3
17	TH	0156	3.7	0851	0.3	1420	3.7	2116	0.3
18	F	0241	3.7	0934	0.3	1504	3.7	2201	0.3
19	SA	0329	3.6	1018	0.4	1550	3.7	2247	0.3
20	SU	0419	3.5	1103	0.4	1636	3.7	2335	0.4
21	M	0512	3.5	1151	0.6	1728	3.7		
22	TU	0029	0.5	0612	3.4	1247	0.7	◐ 1828	3.7
23	W	0132	0.5	0719	3.3	1353	0.7	1939	3.6
24	TH	0245	0.5	0833	3.3	1509	0.6	2055	3.6
25	F	0402	0.4	0946	3.3	1625	0.6	2206	3.6
26	SA	0509	0.4	1049	3.4	1728	0.5	2303	3.7
27	SU	0602	0.4	1139	3.5	1821	0.5	2353	3.7
28	M	0649	0.4	1223	3.6	1911	0.4		
29	TU	0040	3.7	0736	0.3	1306	3.6	○ 1958	0.3
30	W	0125	3.6	0817	0.3	1345	3.6	2037	0.3
31	TH	0203	3.5	0849	0.3	1418	3.6	2109	0.3

JUNE

Date	Day	Time	m	Time	m	Time	m	Time	m
1	F	0236	3.5	0918	0.3	1448	3.6	2140	0.3
2	SA	0309	3.4	0947	0.4	1520	3.6	2212	0.4
3	SU	0343	3.4	1016	0.5	1554	3.6	2245	0.4
4	M	0419	3.3	1047	0.6	1630	3.6	2320	0.5
5	TU	0457	3.3	1122	0.7	1709	3.6	2358	0.6
6	W	0540	3.2	1203	0.8	1754	3.5	◑	
7	TH	0043	0.7	0630	3.2	1254	0.8	1848	3.4
8	F	0140	0.6	0732	3.2	1401	0.8	1954	3.4
9	SA	0249	0.6	0842	3.2	1516	0.8	2105	3.5
10	SU	0400	0.6	0949	3.3	1629	0.7	2210	3.6
11	M	0505	0.5	1049	3.5	1734	0.6	2307	3.6
12	TU	0604	0.4	1141	3.6	1832	0.4	2359	3.7
13	W	0657	0.3	1229	3.6	1924	0.3	●	
14	TH	0048	3.7	0745	0.3	1314	3.7	2011	0.3
15	F	0137	3.7	0831	0.3	1401	3.7	2100	0.3
16	SA	0228	3.7	0920	0.3	1450	3.8	2153	0.3
17	SU	0322	3.6	1010	0.4	1540	3.8	2244	0.3
18	M	0415	3.6	1058	0.4	1629	3.8	2333	0.3
19	TU	0508	3.5	1146	0.5	1720	3.8		
20	W	0026	0.4	0604	3.4	1239	0.6	◐ 1816	3.8
21	TH	0121	0.5	0703	3.3	1335	0.6	1917	3.7
22	F	0220	0.5	0804	3.3	1436	0.6	2022	3.6
23	SA	0323	0.5	0909	3.3	1543	0.6	2130	3.6
24	SU	0429	0.5	1012	3.4	1651	0.6	2234	3.6
25	M	0529	0.5	1109	3.5	1753	0.6	2330	3.6
26	TU	0621	0.5	1157	3.6	1847	0.5		
27	W	0019	3.6	0708	0.5	1241	3.6	1934	0.4
28	TH	0104	3.5	0749	0.4	1321	3.6	○ 2014	0.4
29	F	0142	3.5	0825	0.4	1356	3.7	2049	0.4
30	SA	0217	3.5	0857	0.4	1429	3.7	2122	0.4

JULY

Date	Day	Time	m	Time	m	Time	m	Time	m
1	SU	0251	3.5	0929	0.5	1501	3.7	2155	0.5
2	M	0324	3.5	0959	0.5	1534	3.7	2227	0.5
3	TU	0358	3.4	1030	0.6	1609	3.7	2303	0.6
4	W	0436	3.4	1106	0.7	1648	3.7	2342	0.6
5	TH	0517	3.4	1146	0.7	1730	3.7		
6	F	0022	0.6	0600	3.4	1228	0.8	◑ 1814	3.6
7	SA	0104	0.6	0649	3.3	1317	0.8	1907	3.6
8	SU	0157	0.6	0748	3.3	1421	0.8	2012	3.5
9	M	0303	0.7	0855	3.3	1536	0.7	2123	3.5
10	TU	0416	0.6	1003	3.4	1651	0.6	2230	3.6
11	W	0526	0.5	1106	3.5	1801	0.4	2332	3.6
12	TH	0630	0.4	1204	3.6	1903	0.3		
13	F	0031	3.6	0726	0.3	1257	3.7	● 1958	0.3
14	SA	0126	3.7	0819	0.3	1348	3.8	2051	0.3
15	SU	0220	3.7	0911	0.4	1438	3.9	2145	0.3
16	M	0314	3.6	1003	0.4	1528	3.9	2237	0.3
17	TU	0405	3.6	1049	0.4	1616	3.9	2324	0.3
18	W	0454	3.5	1133	0.4	1704	3.8		
19	TH	0009	0.4	0543	3.4	1218	0.5	◐ 1753	3.8
20	F	0055	0.5	0632	3.4	1304	0.6	1845	3.7
21	SA	0141	0.6	0723	3.3	1353	0.7	1940	3.6
22	SU	0232	0.7	0821	3.3	1453	0.7	2046	3.5
23	M	0337	0.7	0927	3.3	1607	0.8	2159	3.5
24	TU	0448	0.8	1034	3.4	1721	0.7	2306	3.5
25	W	0552	0.7	1132	3.5	1824	0.6		
26	TH	0001	3.5	0643	0.6	1219	3.6	1912	0.5
27	F	0045	3.5	0725	0.6	1300	3.6	○ 1953	0.5
28	SA	0124	3.5	0804	0.5	1337	3.7	2030	0.5
29	SU	0159	3.5	0840	0.5	1410	3.7	2105	0.5
30	M	0233	3.5	0913	0.5	1442	3.8	2137	0.5
31	TU	0304	3.5	0943	0.5	1513	3.8	2208	0.5

AUGUST

Date	Day	Time	m	Time	m	Time	m	Time	m
1	W	0337	3.5	1013	0.6	1547	3.7	2242	0.6
2	TH	0413	3.5	1049	0.6	1626	3.7	2322	0.6
3	F	0454	3.5	1129	0.7	1707	3.8		
4	SA	0000	0.6	0533	3.5	1206	0.7	◑ 1745	3.7
5	SU	0033	0.6	0610	3.4	1242	0.7	1828	3.6
6	M	0112	0.7	0659	3.3	1335	0.8	1927	3.5
7	TU	0213	0.7	0807	3.3	1451	0.8	2043	3.4
8	W	0334	0.7	0926	3.4	1618	0.6	2204	3.5
9	TH	0457	0.6	1042	3.5	1740	0.5	2318	3.5
10	F	0612	0.5	1149	3.6	1851	0.4		
11	SA	0023	3.6	0715	0.4	1246	3.7	● 1950	0.3
12	SU	0119	3.6	0810	0.4	1337	3.8	2043	0.3
13	M	0211	3.6	0901	0.4	1425	3.9	2133	0.3
14	TU	0300	3.6	0949	0.4	1512	3.9	2220	0.3
15	W	0347	3.6	1033	0.4	1557	3.9	2303	0.4
16	TH	0431	3.5	1112	0.4	1641	3.8	2342	0.4
17	F	0513	3.5	1150	0.5	1724	3.7		
18	SA	0018	0.6	0554	3.4	1227	0.6	◐ 1806	3.6
19	SU	0053	0.7	0635	3.3	1306	0.7	1854	3.5
20	M	0135	0.8	0726	3.3	1359	0.8	1956	3.3
21	TU	0237	0.9	0834	3.2	1516	0.9	2116	3.3
22	W	0359	0.9	0953	3.3	1644	0.8	2236	3.3
23	TH	0518	0.9	1104	3.5	1758	0.7	2340	3.4
24	F	0618	0.7	1157	3.6	1851	0.6		
25	SA	0026	3.4	0703	0.6	1237	3.6	1931	0.5
26	SU	0103	3.5	0742	0.6	1313	3.7	○ 2007	0.5
27	M	0138	3.5	0819	0.5	1347	3.7	2042	0.5
28	TU	0211	3.5	0854	0.5	1420	3.7	2115	0.4
29	W	0243	3.5	0925	0.5	1452	3.8	2146	0.5
30	TH	0315	3.5	0955	0.5	1526	3.8	2219	0.5
31	F	0349	3.6	1030	0.6	1603	3.8	2257	0.6

Chart Datum: 2·06 metres below Normal Null (German reference level). HAT is 4·1 metres above Chart Datum.

STANDARD TIME UT –01
Subtract 1 hour for UT
For German Summer Time add ONE hour in **non-shaded areas**

CUXHAVEN LAT 53°52′N LONG 8°43′E

TIMES AND HEIGHTS OF HIGH AND LOW WATERS

Dates in red are SPRINGS
Dates in blue are NEAPS

YEAR **2018**

SEPTEMBER

Date	Day	Time	m	Time	m	Time	m	Time	m	Moon
1	SA	0427	3.6	1107	0.6	1641	3.8	2333	0.6	
2	SU	0503	3.6	1141	0.6	1717	3.7			
3	M	0002	0.7	0537	3.5	1214	0.7	1757	3.5	◑
4	TU	0037	0.8	0622	3.4	1303	0.8	1857	3.4	
5	W	0138	0.8	0733	3.3	1423	0.8	2020	3.3	
6	TH	0307	0.8	0902	3.4	1601	0.7	2152	3.4	
7	F	0442	0.7	1028	3.5	1731	0.5	2312	3.5	
8	SA	0602	0.6	1138	3.6	1842	0.4			
9	SU	0016	3.5	0704	0.5	1234	3.8	1939	0.3	●
10	M	0109	3.6	0757	0.4	1323	3.8	2028	0.3	
11	TU	0156	3.6	0845	0.4	1408	3.9	2113	0.3	
12	W	0240	3.6	0929	0.4	1452	3.9	2156	0.3	
13	TH	0322	3.6	1009	0.4	1534	3.8	2235	0.4	
14	F	0402	3.6	1045	0.4	1614	3.7	2308	0.5	
15	SA	0438	3.5	1117	0.5	1651	3.6	2337	0.6	
16	SU	0512	3.4	1149	0.6	1727	3.4			
17	M	0005	0.7	0547	3.3	1222	0.7	1809	3.3	◐
18	TU	0040	0.9	0634	3.2	1309	0.8	1907	3.1	
19	W	0138	1.0	0740	3.2	1423	0.9	2028	3.1	
20	TH	0303	1.1	0905	3.2	1557	0.9	2156	3.2	
21	F	0434	1.0	1026	3.4	1723	0.8	2309	3.3	
22	SA	0546	0.8	1127	3.5	1822	0.7	2359	3.4	
23	SU	0635	0.7	1208	3.6	1902	0.6			
24	M	0037	3.4	0714	0.6	1243	3.6	1938	0.5	
25	TU	0111	3.5	0753	0.6	1319	3.7	2014	0.5	○
26	W	0145	3.5	0829	0.5	1354	3.7	2048	0.4	
27	TH	0218	3.5	0904	0.5	1429	3.7	2121	0.5	
28	F	0251	3.6	0936	0.5	1503	3.7	2155	0.5	
29	SA	0325	3.6	1009	0.5	1539	3.7	2229	0.6	
30	SU	0359	3.6	1044	0.6	1616	3.7	2304	0.6	

OCTOBER

Date	Day	Time	m	Time	m	Time	m	Time	m	Moon
1	M	0434	3.6	1118	0.6	1654	3.6	2336	0.7	
2	TU	0512	3.5	1155	0.7	1740	3.5			◑
3	W	0017	0.9	0602	3.4	1250	0.8	1845	3.3	
4	TH	0123	1.0	0717	3.4	1414	0.8	2012	3.3	
5	F	0255	1.0	0849	3.5	1554	0.8	2146	3.3	
6	SA	0432	0.9	1017	3.6	1724	0.6	2306	3.4	
7	SU	0550	0.7	1125	3.7	1829	0.5			
8	M	0004	3.5	0648	0.6	1217	3.8	1921	0.4	
9	TU	0052	3.6	0737	0.5	1304	3.8	2007	0.4	●
10	W	0135	3.6	0824	0.4	1348	3.8	2050	0.4	
11	TH	0216	3.6	0906	0.4	1430	3.8	2128	0.4	
12	F	0254	3.6	0943	0.4	1509	3.7	2202	0.5	
13	SA	0329	3.6	1016	0.4	1545	3.6	2232	0.5	
14	SU	0402	3.5	1046	0.5	1619	3.5	2258	0.6	
15	M	0433	3.5	1116	0.5	1653	3.3	2324	0.7	
16	TU	0507	3.4	1148	0.7	1732	3.2	2356	0.9	◐
17	W	0550	3.3	1230	0.8	1825	3.1			
18	TH	0048	1.1	0651	3.2	1335	1.0	1937	3.0	
19	F	0205	1.2	0809	3.2	1502	1.0	2103	3.1	
20	SA	0338	1.1	0932	3.3	1631	0.9	2221	3.2	
21	SU	0458	0.9	1041	3.5	1739	0.7	2320	3.3	
22	M	0556	0.8	1130	3.5	1825	0.6			
23	TU	0003	3.4	0640	0.7	1209	3.6	1903	0.5	
24	W	0041	3.5	0722	0.6	1248	3.7	1942	0.5	○
25	TH	0117	3.6	0802	0.6	1326	3.7	2019	0.5	
26	F	0151	3.6	0839	0.5	1403	3.7	2055	0.5	
27	SA	0224	3.6	0915	0.5	1440	3.7	2130	0.5	
28	SU	0300	3.7	0950	0.5	1518	3.7	2206	0.6	
29	M	0337	3.7	1026	0.5	1558	3.6	2242	0.6	
30	TU	0415	3.7	1104	0.6	1642	3.5	2322	0.8	
31	W	0459	3.6	1151	0.7	1735	3.4			◑

NOVEMBER

Date	Day	Time	m	Time	m	Time	m	Time	m	Moon
1	TH	0011	0.9	0554	3.6	1252	0.8	1843	3.3	
2	F	0119	1.0	0708	3.5	1412	0.8	2006	3.2	
3	SA	0246	1.0	0835	3.5	1545	0.7	2133	3.3	
4	SU	0416	0.9	0958	3.6	1707	0.6	2248	3.4	
5	M	0529	0.8	1104	3.7	1809	0.5	2344	3.5	
6	TU	0625	0.7	1155	3.8	1857	0.5			
7	W	0029	3.6	0714	0.6	1243	3.8	1943	0.4	●
8	TH	0111	3.6	0801	0.5	1328	3.7	2025	0.4	
9	F	0151	3.6	0842	0.4	1407	3.7	2100	0.4	
10	SA	0225	3.6	0917	0.4	1443	3.6	2130	0.5	
11	SU	0257	3.6	0948	0.4	1517	3.5	2159	0.5	
12	M	0329	3.6	1019	0.5	1551	3.4	2226	0.6	
13	TU	0402	3.5	1050	0.5	1626	3.3	2254	0.7	
14	W	0437	3.5	1123	0.7	1704	3.2	2327	0.9	
15	TH	0518	3.4	1202	0.8	1750	3.1			◐
16	F	0010	1.0	0608	3.4	1255	0.9	1848	3.1	
17	SA	0113	1.1	0712	3.3	1406	0.9	2002	3.1	
18	SU	0233	1.1	0828	3.3	1527	0.9	2119	3.1	
19	M	0355	1.0	0942	3.4	1640	0.8	2226	3.3	
20	TU	0505	0.9	1042	3.5	1737	0.7	2319	3.4	
21	W	0600	0.8	1131	3.6	1825	0.6			
22	TH	0004	3.5	0648	0.7	1214	3.7	1909	0.6	
23	F	0044	3.6	0732	0.6	1256	3.7	1949	0.5	○
24	SA	0121	3.7	0812	0.5	1336	3.7	2028	0.5	
25	SU	0159	3.7	0853	0.5	1419	3.7	2109	0.5	
26	M	0240	3.7	0937	0.5	1504	3.7	2151	0.6	
27	TU	0323	3.8	1020	0.5	1550	3.6	2233	0.6	
28	W	0406	3.8	1103	0.5	1639	3.5	2318	0.7	
29	TH	0453	3.8	1153	0.6	1734	3.4			
30	F	0010	0.8	0549	3.7	1253	0.7	1837	3.3	◑

DECEMBER

Date	Day	Time	m	Time	m	Time	m	Time	m	Moon
1	SA	0113	0.9	0655	3.6	1403	0.7	1949	3.2	
2	SU	0226	0.9	0811	3.6	1521	0.7	2106	3.3	
3	M	0345	0.9	0928	3.6	1636	0.7	2217	3.4	
4	TU	0457	0.8	1035	3.7	1740	0.6	2316	3.5	
5	W	0558	0.7	1131	3.7	1831	0.6			
6	TH	0004	3.6	0650	0.7	1221	3.7	1918	0.6	
7	F	0047	3.6	0739	0.5	1307	3.6	2000	0.5	●
8	SA	0126	3.6	0820	0.5	1347	3.6	2034	0.5	
9	SU	0200	3.6	0854	0.4	1422	3.5	2104	0.5	
10	M	0232	3.6	0926	0.5	1456	3.5	2135	0.6	
11	TU	0305	3.6	0959	0.5	1531	3.4	2205	0.6	
12	W	0339	3.6	1032	0.6	1605	3.3	2235	0.7	
13	TH	0414	3.6	1106	0.7	1641	3.3	2307	0.8	
14	F	0452	3.6	1142	0.8	1720	3.2	2344	0.9	
15	SA	0533	3.5	1223	0.9	1806	3.2			◐
16	SU	0031	1.0	0622	3.4	1314	0.9	1903	3.2	
17	M	0132	1.0	0724	3.4	1419	0.9	2011	3.2	
18	TU	0246	1.0	0835	3.4	1532	0.8	2122	3.3	
19	W	0403	0.9	0945	3.5	1640	0.8	2226	3.4	
20	TH	0511	0.8	1046	3.6	1741	0.7	2321	3.5	
21	F	0611	0.7	1138	3.6	1834	0.6			
22	SA	0009	3.6	0703	0.6	1227	3.6	1922	0.5	○
23	SU	0054	3.7	0750	0.5	1314	3.7	2007	0.5	
24	M	0138	3.7	0838	0.4	1404	3.7	2056	0.5	
25	TU	0226	3.8	0929	0.4	1456	3.6	2145	0.5	
26	W	0314	3.9	1020	0.4	1546	3.6	2232	0.5	
27	TH	0359	3.9	1106	0.4	1636	3.5	2317	0.6	
28	F	0446	3.8	1153	0.5	1727	3.4			
29	SA	0005	0.6	0538	3.8	1245	0.5	1822	3.3	◑
30	SU	0057	0.7	0635	3.7	1340	0.6	1921	3.3	
31	M	0155	0.8	0738	3.6	1442	0.6	2025	3.2	

Chart Datum: 2·06 metres below Normal Null (German reference level). HAT is 4·1 metres above Chart Datum.

9.15.12 BRUNSBÜTTEL (RIVER ELBE)

Schleswig-Holstein **53°53'·27N 09°08'·48E**

CHARTS AC 2469, 3625; Imray C26; D 42; BSH 1620, 1711

TIDES +0203 Dover; ML 1·4; Duration 0520

Standard Port CUXHAVEN (⟵)

Times				Height (metres)			
High Water		Low Water		MHWS	MHWN	MLWN	MLWS
0200	0800	0200	0900	3·7	3·3	0·8	0·4
1400	2000	1400	2100				
Differences *BRUNSBÜTTEL*							
+0057	*+0105*	*+0121*	*+0112*	*–0·1*	*–0·2*	*–0·1*	*+0·1*

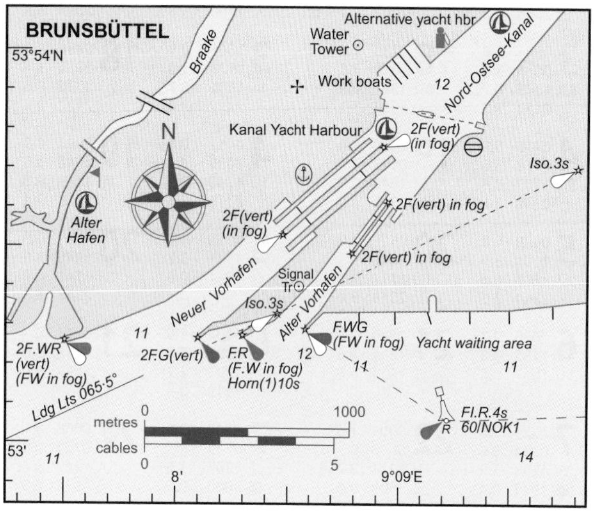

SHELTER Good in the Alter Hafen yacht harbour W of the locks, but HW pontoons dry at LW (soft mud). Waiting area is close E of FWG ☆ at ent to Alter Vorhafen. No smoking in locks area. Once locked through, good shelter, but noisy and crowded in Kanal-Yachthafen, close NW of the larger Neue locks.

NAVIGATION WPT 53°53'·01N 09°08'·14E, 039°/6ca to Alte Schleusen (the smaller SE locks, usually for yachts). No navigational dangers in the near apprs, but commercial traffic is heavy. The stream sets strongly across access chan to locks.

Lock Entry Sigs: see Nord-Ostsee Kanal; await White signal or loudspeaker.

LIGHTS AND MARKS Lights as chartlet. Ldg lts 065·5° direct large ships from the main fairway to the lock Approach areas.

COMMUNICATIONS (Code 04852) **VTS**, see River Elbe. *Brunsbüttel Elbe Traffic* broadcasts weather info every H + 05 on Ch 68 in English and German for the inner Elbe. Monitor Ch 68 when underway between buoys 53 and 125; 36400; Police 112; 83000; Brit Consul (030) 204570; Ⓗ 9800; WSA (hbr info) 8850 request *Kiel Kanal I* on Ch 13 for a locking allocation 15 mins before arrival; see Nord-Ostsee Kanal. Radar cover of the inner Elbe is as follows:

Brunsbüttel Radar I	Ch 62	Buoys 51–59;
Brunsbüttel Radar II	Ch 67	Buoys 60–Elbehafen;
(call if entering locks in dense fog)		
S Margarethen Radar	Ch 18	Buoys 57a–65;
Freiburg Radar	Ch 61	Buoys 63–77;
Rhinplate Radar	Ch 05	Buoys 75–89;
Pagensand Radar	Ch 66	Buoys 87–89;
Hetlingen Radar	Ch 21	Buoys 101–115;
Wedel Radar	Ch 60	Buoys 113–125.

FACILITIES **Alter Hafen** ☎ +49 1629630958, €1·10, SC; **YC SVB** ☎3348, www.svb-bru.de

Town (as shown on chartlet, 0800-1800 ☎2001) Ⓑ Ⓗ (Hamburg).

9.15.13 NORD-OSTSEE KANAL (KIEL CANAL) SCHLESWIG-HOLSTEIN

CHARTS AC 2469; Kieler Förde, inner part 2344, outer part 2341; D42

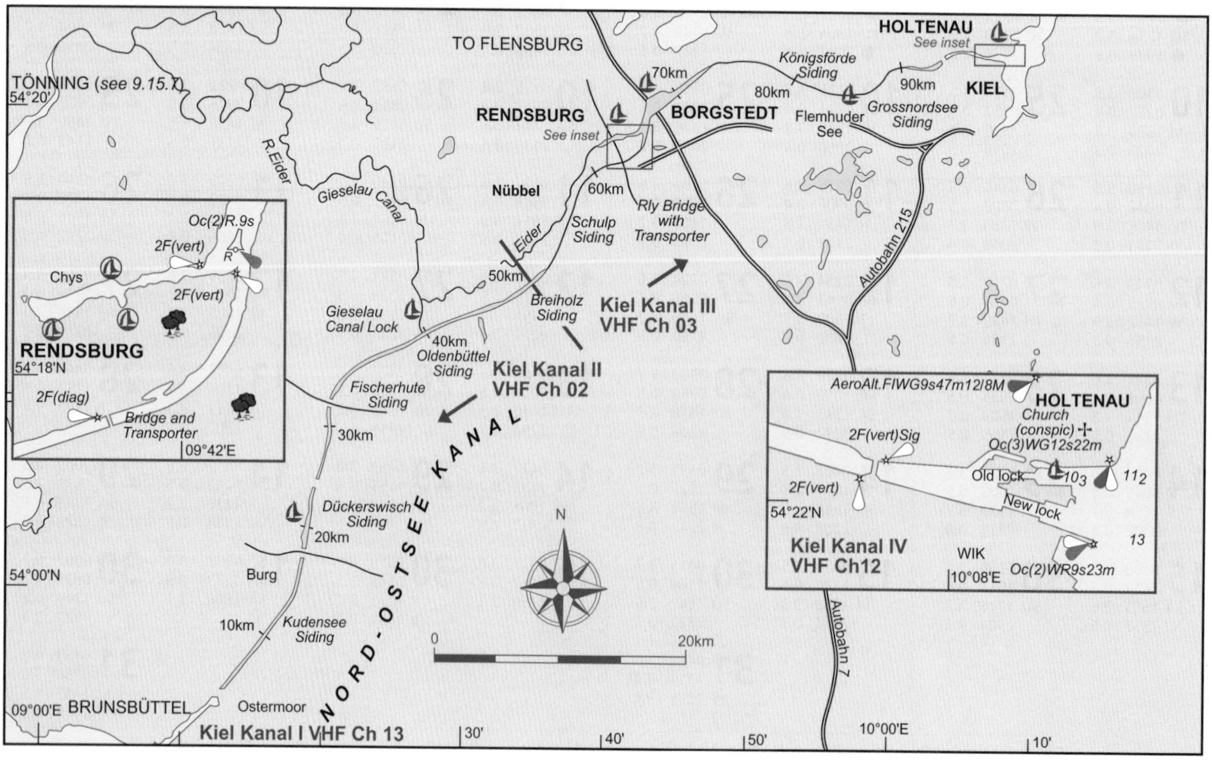

SIGNALS Two sets of Occulting lights must be obeyed: a. those to move from the Waiting Area (Brunsbüttel) and enter the Approach Area, shown from mast at the lock island; and b. those to enter the lock, shown from a mast at the lock:

○	=	No entry.
○ ●	=	Prepare to enter.
○ ●	=	Ships exempt from pilotage enter; secure on central island.
○ Oc	=	**Yachts should enter outer hbr and lock** (berth on low, narrow pontoons).

In the canal Sidings, the following traffic sigs apply to yachts:

● QR	=	Entry into a Siding is prohib.
●●● (Oc R, vert)	=	Exit from a Siding is prohib.

COMMUNICATIONS Before entering, yachts should request a lock clearance: **at Brunsbüttel** from *Kiel Kanal I* on Ch 13, or **at Holtenau** from *Kiel Kanal IV* on Ch 12. **In the Canal**. Maintain listening watch as follows:

Kiel Kanal I	Ch **13**	Brunsbüttel approaches and lock area.
Kiel Kanal II	Ch **02**	Brunsbüttel to Breiholz.
Kiel Kanal III	Ch **03**	Breiholz to Holtenau.
Kiel Kanal IV	Ch **12**	Holtenau approaches and lock area.

Info broadcasts by *Kiel Kanal II* on Ch 02 at H+15, H+45; and by *Kiel Kanal III* on Ch 03 at H+20, H+50. Vessels should monitor these broadcasts and avoid calling the station if possible. Non AIS-fitted yachts >20m are required to carry an AIS Class B transponder, or a portable Class A transponder which can be hired from the lock master.

NAVIGATION The Canal runs 53·3NM (98·7 km) from Brunsbüttel to Kiel-Holtenau; it is 103-162m wide and 11m deep. For *Navigation Rules Kiel Canal* in English/German, see www.kiel-canal.org/english. Speed limit 8kn. All 8 bridges have 40m clearance. Yachts may only use the Canal and its ents in official daylight hours (next para) and in good visibility (unless going to Brunsbüttel's Alter or Inner Hbrs, or Holtenau's yacht hbr). Motoring or motor-sailing (hoist a B ▼, or a B pennant) is the norm. Pure sailing (no engine) is prohib.

Daylight hours (LT) for Kiel Canal are: 1-15 May, 0430-2200; 16-31 May, 0400-2230; 1 June-15 July, 0330-2300; 16-31 July, 0400-2230; 1-15 Aug, 0430-2200; 16-31 Aug 0500-2130; 1-15 Sep, 0530-2100; 16-30 Sep, 0600-2030. See: www. WSV.de (Guidance for operators of pleasure craft, Kiel Canal).

Canal dues (approx €18 <12m) E or W-bound, are paid at Kiel-Holtenau to the Lockmaster if using the Old lock; or at the newspaper stand if using the New lock. Credit cards not accepted.

SHELTER As well as Brunsbüttel and Holtenau, berthing is only permitted in the 5 sidings or *weichen* listed below which must be reached by pleasure craft during **daylight hours** (shown above).

- *Dückerswisch siding (km 20·5); W side in turning area.
- *Oldenbüttel siding (km 40·5) off Gieselau Canal lock (links Kiel Canal to R Eider/ N. Sea, via Tönning).
- Rendsburg (ent at km 66). All facilities and 3 marinas in Lake Obereider; the W'most is nearest town centre.
- The Borgstedter See, entrances at km 67.5 and 70.
- Flemhudersee (km 85.4). Designated small craft anchorage within is marked by yellow bys, the anchoring prohib. sign at ent. only applies to ships. Note:*Usually for one night only.

KIEL-HOLTENAU (km 98·7) a major port, has two pairs of locks leading into Kieler Förde, almost tideless, and nearly level with the canal. Monitor Ch 68 *Kiel Traffic* for VTS info. Yachts usually use smaller Old locks (no smoking); signals/ pontoons as at Brunsbüttel. Small Yacht Hbr (max 4 days) is on the N bank (E of Old locks) no ⛽. HM ☎(0431) 363830. Fuel barge E of locks. At Wik (S of locks) **Nautischer Dienst** ☎0431 331772, ACA and BSH Agents.

Conveniently **Sport Harbour Stickenhörn** is 1·5M NNE of lock, HM ☎0431 26048424, www.sporthafen-kiel.de/sporthaefen/ sporthafen-stickenhoern stickenhoern@sporthafen-kiel.de 460 berths inc Ⓥ max 20m LOA €3·50/m inc ⛽; ✕ €1·00 WC; (mast) free wi-fi. Nearest see: barge, above. For other **Marinas** nearby visit: www.sporthafen-kiel.de/sporthaefen. **Town,** 15min walk ✕ ✉ Ⓑ. Kiel city, S of Wik, 30 mins bus ride.

9.15.14 HAMBURG (RIVER ELBE)

Schleswig-Holstein **53°32'·52N 09°58'·84E**

CHARTS AC 3625, 3267, 3268; D 48; BSH 1661, 1662

TIDES See River Elbe. ML 1·3; Duration 0435

SHELTER A busy commercial port with several marinas. Visitors usually berth at Wedel in Hamburger Yachthafen, 12M W of Hamburg, or in the city centre at City Sporthafen.

COMMUNICATIONS (Code 40) Met 3190 8826/7; Auto 0190 116456; Brit Consul (030) 204570; *Hamburg Port Traffic* and Hbr Control vessel Ch 13 14 **73** (H24) all monitor Ch 74. AC Agent 374 8110.

FACILITIES HAMBURGER YACHTHAFEN (53°34'·28N 09°40'·53E, N bank). HM ☎(4103) 4438 (office); HM (east) ☎0172 6423227; HM (west) ☎ 0171 2766300; ☎0172 6423228; www.hamburger-yachthafen.de Conspic 50m radar twr at SW corner of hbr. Very good shelter, access H24, via 2 ents. 2100 €1·14. (shut Tues) ✕ Ⓔ SC, (16t) (15t) (masts).

SCHULAUER HAVEN, Good shelter, 7ca E of Wedel. Beware strong tide across ent, marked by FR and FG lts. Although re-opened in 2015, progress on this waterfront regeneration for the town of Wedel has been slow and the anticipated facilities for visiting craft have not yet appeared. HM☎ 2422.

MÜHLENBERG. 53°33'·19N 09°49'·38E, N bank. 250 ⛽ SC. Yachts < 9m; partially dries.

TEUFELSBRÜCK. 53°32'·82N 09°52'·06E, N bank, E of ferry pier. Good shelter in small hbr; partially dries. SC.

RÜSCHKANAL. 53°32'·57N 09°51'·34E, S bank, narrow ent. ; 4 SCs, pontoons NE side in 3·6m.

CITY SPORTHAFEN. 53°32'·52N 09°58'·84E HM ☎364297, mob 170 805 2004, out of hrs 227 7651. www.city-sporthafen-hamburg.de hafen@city-sporthafen-hamburg.de 80-120 most <20m LOA, max draft 2·5-4m, max LOA 50m Ⓥ€1·75, €0·90 pay 6 days, 7th free; ⛽ small amounts free; €0·50 per kWh; €1·00, wi-fi free. **Town** All facilities, ✈ (Hamburg).

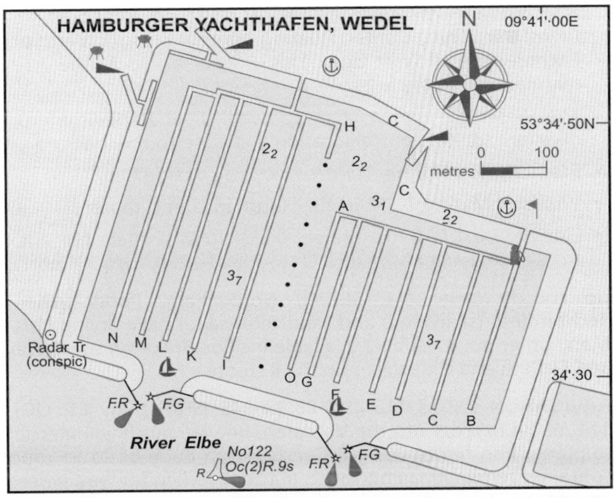

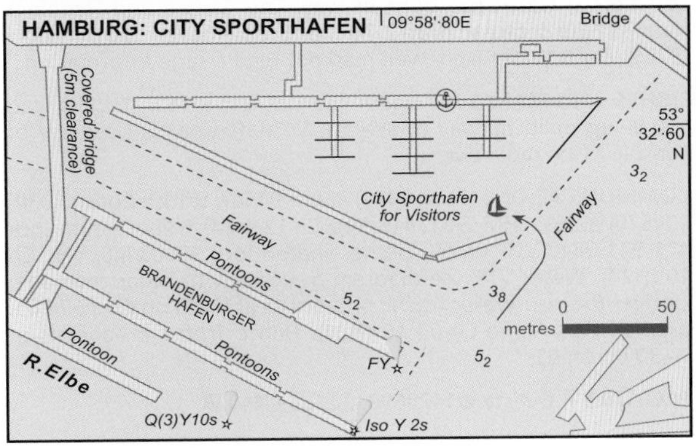

9.15.15 BREMERHAVEN (RIVER WESER)

Federal State of Bremen **53°32′·12N 08°34′·50E**

CHARTS AC 3617, 3621 plans A & B; Imray C26; D 4

TIDES +0051 Dover; ML 2·0; Duration 0600

Standard Port WILHELMSHAVEN (⟶)

Times				Height (metres)			
High Water		Low Water		MHWS	MHWN	MLWN	MLWS
0200	0800	0200	0900	4·7	4·2	1·0	0·5
1400	2000	1400	2100				
Differences ALTE WESER LT HO (53°51′·8N 08°07′·6E)							
–0055	–0048	–0015	–0029	–0·1	–0·1	–0·1	–0·1
DWARSGAT (53°43′·0N 08°18′·0E)							
–0015	+0002	–0006	–0001	–0·5	–0·5	–0·1	–0·1
ROBBENSUDSTEERT (53°38′·0N 08°27′·0E)							
–+0009	+0026	+0015	+0020	–0·3	–0·3	–0·1	–0·1
BREMERHAVEN							
+0029	*+0046*	*+0033*	*+0038*	*–0·1*	*0·0*	*–0·1*	*0·0*
NORDENHAM							
+0051	+0109	+0055	+0058	0·0	+0·1	–0·1	–0·1
BRAKE							
+0120	+0119	+0143	+0155	–0·1	–0·1	–0·4	–0·3
ELSFLETH							
+0137	+0137	+0206	+0216	–0·2	–0·2	–0·4	–0·3
VEGESACK							
+0208	+0204	+0250	+0254	–0·1	–0·1	–0·5	–0·3
BREMEN							
+0216	+0211	+0311	+0314	0·0	0·0	–0·5	–0·3

SHELTER There are 6 options for visitors. The first three are most suitable and nearest the city centre, on the upper chartlet:

- Berth in R Geeste downstream of Kennedy fixed bridge (clearance 5·5m) on pontoons, but short stay only as it is noisy and exposed to swell/wash. If able to transit the bridge (flood barrage is normally open) berth on quay upstream.
- Lock into the Schleusenhafen via the smaller W lock. Operational H24, but call *Fischereihafenschleuse* Ch 10 for current opening times; ●●○ (vert) = enter. Floating pontoons in lock. Berth at Fischereihafen II West Quay. This gives access to 2 other YC/ marinas well to the S.
- The Weser YC marina in Hauptkanal (E of Handelshafen); excellent shelter, central location and close to the lock.
- Bremerhaven Marina, 1·3M S of lock on W side (3m).
- Wulsdorf Marina, 0·5M further south in Luneorthafen.
- Lloyd Marina in Neuer Hafen, 0·6M NNW of main hbr ent. Access via Neuer Hafen lock Ch 69, 0600–2200, turn 90° port.

Up the R Weser (AC 3622/3) Nordenham, Rodenkirchen, Rechtenfleth (sand/mud) and Sandstedt (sand) have drying hbrs. Many other non-tidal hbrs available include Brake on the Weser and Elsfleth and Oldenburg on the R Hunte.

NAVIGATION WPT 53°32′·25N 08°33′·94E [SHM buoy 61, QG], 111°/650m to cross into the Vorhafen. Beware much commercial shipping; also ferries using R Geeste. From buoy 51 to 61 (opp container terminal) sailing yachts may not tack in fairway, where commercial traffic has right of way. The Geeste and Hadelner Kanals (1·5m depth; air draft 2·7m) link Bremerhaven to Otterndorf (32M). For R Weser (very well marked) see Passage Information.

LIGHTS AND MARKS See upper chartlet and 9.15.4. Ldg lts lead 150.8° up main fairway (R Weser). Vorhafen ent is close SW of conspic 112m radio twr.

COMMUNICATIONS (Code 0471) Police 94667; British Consul (030) 204570; Ⓗ 2991; HM 59613416, VHF Ch 12 (H24); Neuer Hafen lock 471 941 2840 VHF Ch 69; Fischereihafen lock 59603440, VHF Ch 10 (H24). Weser VTS, see diagram overleaf with radar coverage. Upriver *Bremen-Weser Traffic* broadcasts at H+30 on Ch 19 78 81. *Bremen Port Radio* Ch 03 16 (H24). *Hunte Traffic* broadcasts at H+30 on Ch 63.

FACILITIES R Geeste ☎1428690, 20 + 440 Ⓥ.

Lloyd Marina ☎1428690, 180 €1·19. VHF Ch 69. www.im-jaich.de ✕.

Weser YC ☎23531, 150 + 20 Ⓥ, €1·29, ✕. www.weser-yacht-club.de

Fischereihafen II W Quay ☎76189.

Bremerhaven Marina ☎77555, 280 + 30 Ⓥ (13t).

Wulsdorf Marina ☎73268, 150 Ⓥ on request.

City All facilities: ACA ✈.

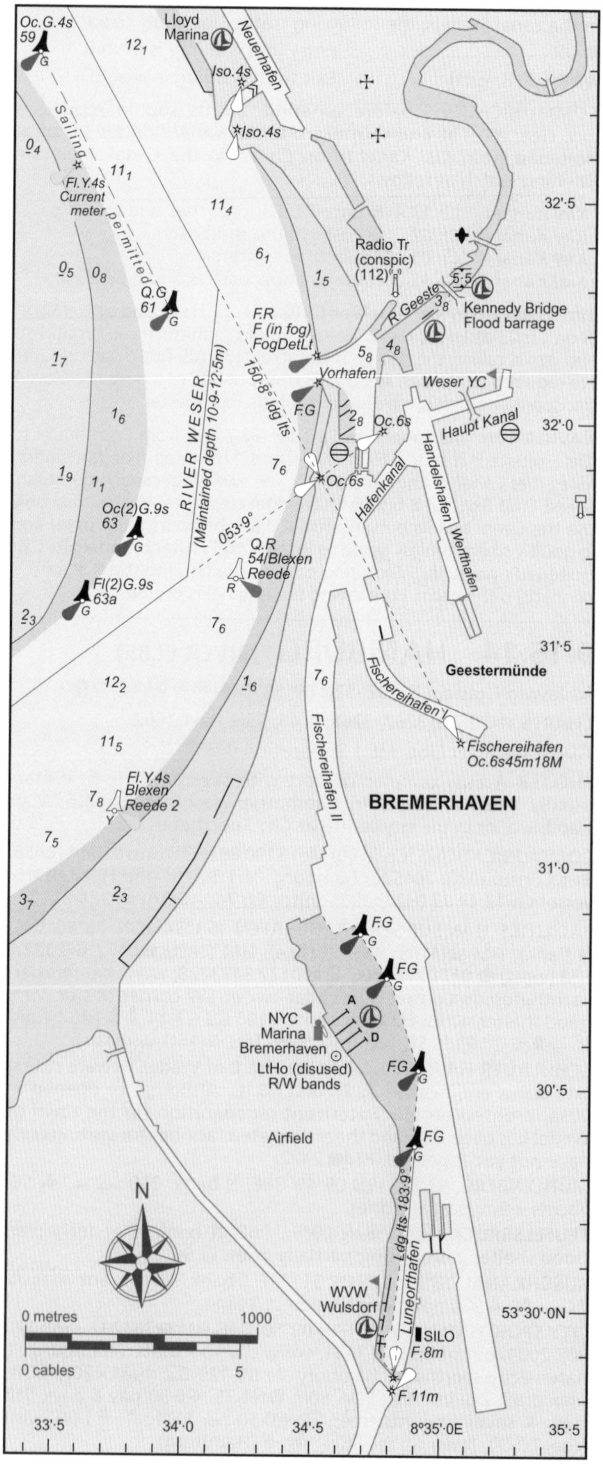

RIVER WESER

(AC 1875, 3617, 3622, 3623) The R Weser is a major waterway leading to **Bremerhaven, Nordenham, Brake,** and **Bremen** where it connects with the inland waterways. The upper reaches, *Unterweser*, run from Bremen to Bremerhaven and then the *Aussenweser* flows into a wide estuary (split by two main chans: *Neue Weser* and *Alte Weser*). The position and extent of sandbanks vary: the W side tends to be steep-to, the E side has extensive drying shoals (eg Tegeler Plate).

The Jade-Weser SWM lt buoy marks the approach from NW to Neue Weser (the main fairway, recommended) and Alte Weser (not well lit) which are separated by Roter Sand and Roter Grund, marked by the disused Roter Sand lt tr (conspic). Both chans are well marked and converge about 3M S of Alte Weser lt tr (conspic). From this junction *Hohewegrinne* (buoyed) leads inward in a SE direction past Tegeler Plate lt tr (conspic) on the NE side and Hohe Weg lt tr (conspic) to the SSE. The Nordegründe Windfarm (WIP 2017/18, 18 turbines, 53°50'·07N 08°10'·17E) lies midway between Alte Weser and Tegeler Plate lt twrs. From Robbenplate to Wremer ief (part way towards Bremerhaven) it is constrained by training walls, which may cause tidal accelerations. ►*In the Aussenweser the stream (> 3kn at sp) often sets towards the banks and the branch chans which traverse them.*◄

The Weser-Elbe Wattfahrwasser is a demanding, extremely shallow inshore passage between R Weser and R Elbe. It leads NNE from the Wurster Arm (E of Hohe Weg) keeping about 3M offshore; SE of Neuwerk and around Cuxhaven training wall. It is tricky, normally requires two or three spring tides for a vessel drawing up to 1·2m, and is not recommended for visitors.

9.15.16 HOOKSIEL (RIVER JADE)

Niedersachsen **53°38'·61N 08°05'·19E** ☸☸◊◊✿✿

CHARTS AC 3618; Imray C26; D 7

TIDES +0034 Dover; ML no data; Duration 0605

Standard Port WILHELMSHAVEN (⟶)

Times				**Height (metres)**			
High Water		Low Water		MHWS	MHWN	MLWN	MLWS
0200	0800	0200	0900	4·7	4·2	1·0	0·5
1400	2000	1400	2100				
Differences HOOKSIEL							
−0023	−0022	−0008	−0012	−0·5	−0·4	−0·1	0·0
SCHILLIG							
−0031	−0025	−0006	−0014	−0·6	−0·6	−0·1	0·0

SHELTER Temp ⚓ in the Vorhafen (approx 1m at MLWS) but it is very commercial and uncomfortable in E winds. Beyond the lock there is complete shelter in the Binnentief, 2M long and 2·0-3·5m deep. Best for visitors is Alter Hafen Yacht Hbr in the town; max draft 2m. Larger yachts go to YCs; see lockmaster. Do not enter Watersports Area due to water-ski cables.

NAVIGATION WPT 53°39'·33N 08°06'·52E (No 37/Hooksiel 1 SHM buoy, IQ G 13s), 217°/9ca to H3 SHM buoy, Fl G 4s, approx 350m E of the ent. Caution: aquaculture N of H3, seasonal HS ferry, strong cross-tide, transhipment pier and restricted area to SE of ent.

Appr via chan 2·1m deep to Vorhafen (beware shoaling) enclosed by two moles. Inner ldg daymarks 276·5°, two RW bcns, lead through ent, but are obsc'd when ferry berthed on N pier.

Lock and opening bridge, see www. marinahooksiel.de/ Schleusenzeiten for times. Secure well in lock; climb up to control office to pay €1·00/ metre (each way).

LIGHTS AND MARKS Ldg lts 164·5°, as chartlet. Conspic chys of chemical works and oil refinery SSE of lock. ☆ L Fl R 6s on dayglo R pile on S mole and street lamp on N mole. R/G tfc lts at lock.

COMMUNICATIONS (Code 04425) Coast Guard (0421) 5550555; ☼ (0190) 116047; Police 269; ⊖ 1302; Brit Consul (030) 204570; Ⓗ (04421) 2080; Dr 1080; HM/Lockmaster, no VHF, ☎430. Jade VTS VHF Ch 63.

FACILITIES **Werft BY** ☎95850, ⚑(25t) ⟝. **Wilhelmshaven YC** ☎ 04421 22983, 50 Ⓥ berths (⚓) €1·00, ⛉. **Alter Hafen** Ⓥ berth on quays, first night free then €1·00. **Marina Hooksiel** ☎958050 hafenmeister@wangerland.de www.marinahooksiel.de. €1·20. **Town** ⛽ ✕ ⛉ ⓑ ✉ ⇄ ✈ (Wilhelmshaven and Bremen). **Wangersiel**, 3·4M NNW (53°41'·0N 8°01'·5E) has small marina ☎(04463) 1515, ✕ ⛉ Ⓛ.

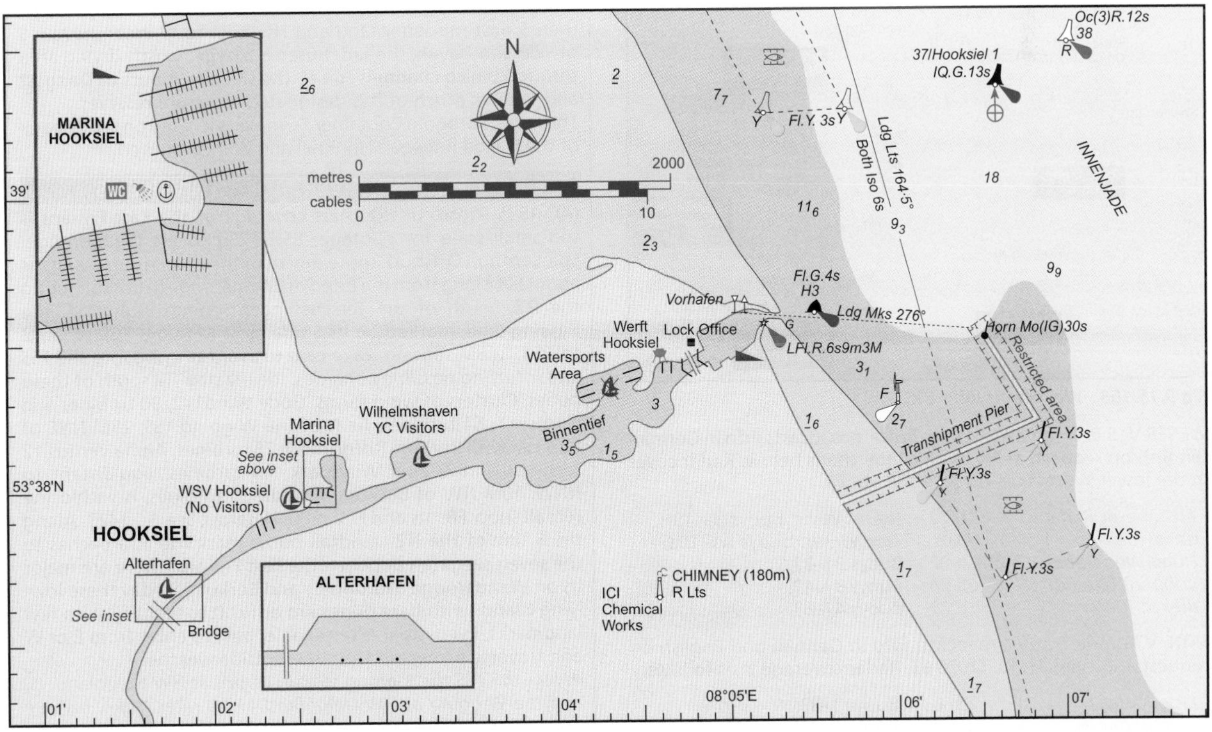

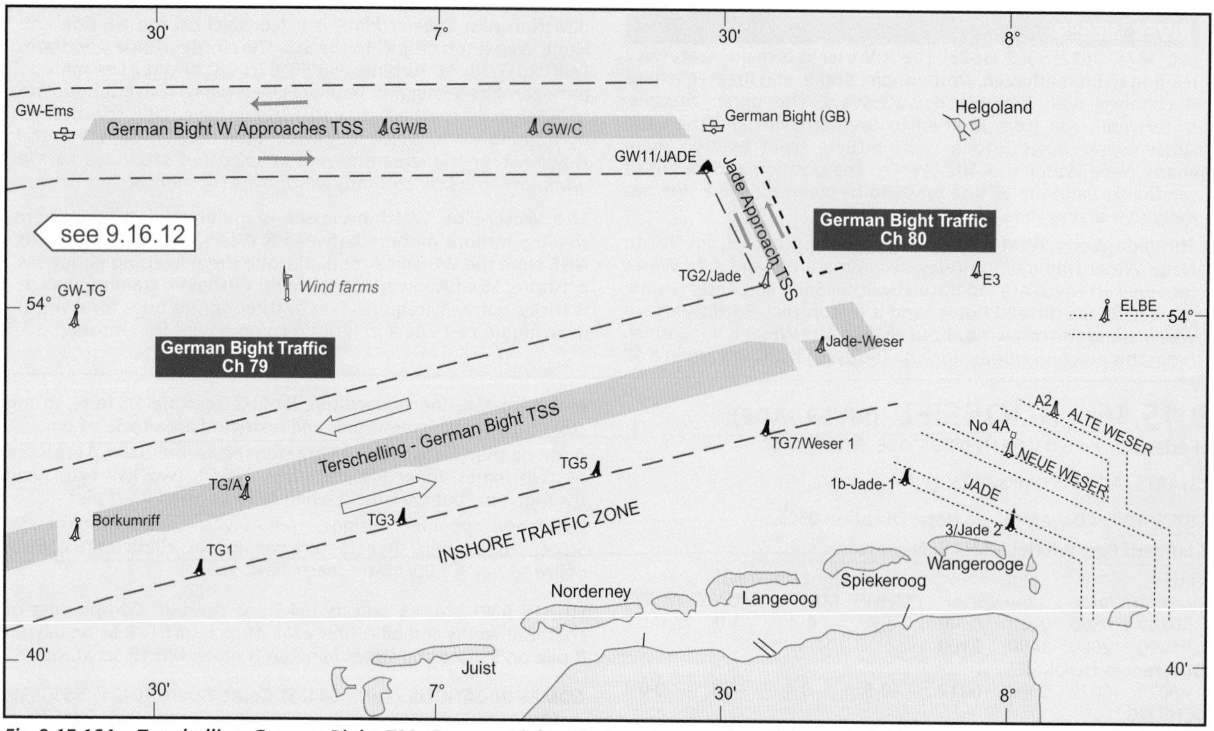

Fig 9.15.16A. ***Terschelling-German Bight TSS, German Bight Western Approaches TSS and Jade Approach TSS.*** German Bight VTS: *German Bight Traffic* broadcasts safety and weather info Ch 80 every hour in German/English.

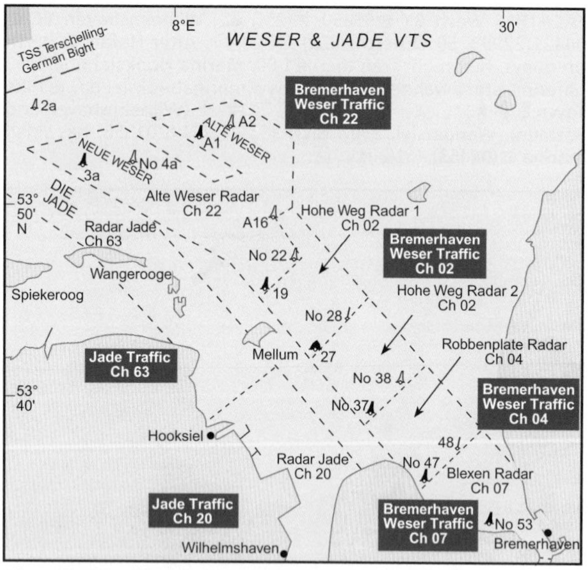

Fig 9.15.16B. ***Weser and Jade VTS***

WESER VTS *Bremerhaven Weser Traffic* broadcasts info in German (English on request) at H+20 on all the chans below. Radar cover in the lower Weser is as Fig 9.15.16B above.

Alte Weser Radar	Ch 22	Neue Weser: buoys 3a–19H.
ditto	ditto	Alte Weser: buoys A1–16a.
Hohe Weg Radar 1 & 2	Ch 02	Buoys 21–37.
Robbenplate Rdr	Ch 04	Buoys 37–47.
Blexen Radar	Ch 07	Buoys 47–63.

JADE VTS *Jade Traffic* broadcasts info in German and English on request and every H+10, Ch 20 63. Radar coverage is as follows:

Jade Radar I	Ch 63	Buoys 1–33;
Jade Radar II	Ch 20	Buoys 33–58.

RIVER JADE

(AC 3617, 3618) The estuaries of the River Weser and River Jade flow seaward between Cuxhaven and Wangerooge.

►*The outer parts of the rivers Weser and Jade can become very rough with wind against tide, and are dangerous on the ebb in strong NW winds.*◄

Enter from 1b/Jade 1 buoy via Wangerooger Fahrwasser (buoyed fairway) which leads ESE to the N of Wangerooge, then S past Minsener Oog and Hooksiel to Wilhelmshaven. S of Wilhelmshaven, the Jadebusen is a large, mostly drying area through which channels run to the small harbours of Dangast and Vareler. Much of it is designated as nature reserves.

The large, Eurogate Container Terminal is located on the W bank of the R Jade between Hooksiel and Wilhelmshaven.

THE EAST FRISIANS, RIVER JADE TO RIVER EMS

(AC 1635. Note: UKHO chart coverage of the East Frisians is too small scale for pilotage. BSH 1230 covers Wangerooge/Spiekeroog.) Offshore route, north of the East Frisian Islands, is about 50M long from the E end of Wangerooge to Borkum, using the ITZ, south of the Terschellinger-German Bight TSS, the E-going lane marked on its S side by SHM buoys TG9/Weser 2 to TG1, at 5M spacing. *Take care to avoid straying into the TSS and incurring possible penalties,* ideally stay 1M south of these buoys. Clusters of wind farms, Gode Wind1+2, 90 turbines and Nordsee1, 54 turbines, lie N of the W-going TSS, 25M NNE of Borkum with Borkum Riffgrund 1, 78 turbines, Alpha Ventus, 12 turbines and Trianel Windpark, 40 turbines, equidistant to NNW. 10M NW of Borkum, Riffgat, 30 turbines, is within the ITZ; all show FR lts and Fl Y on perimeters, see AC 1423. Along the S side of the ITZ landfall buoys mark the approaches to the seven seegaten between the East Frisians. There are major lts on Wangerooge, Norderney and Borkum. By day these low-lying islands with bare dunes are difficult to identify, with few landmarks. Even radar is unreliable, best to enter from E or W and traverse protected from the outside weather.

►*Near the TSS the E-going stream begins at HW Helgoland –5, and the W-going at HW Helgoland +1, sp rates 1·2kn. Inshore the stream is influenced by the flow through the seegaten.*◄

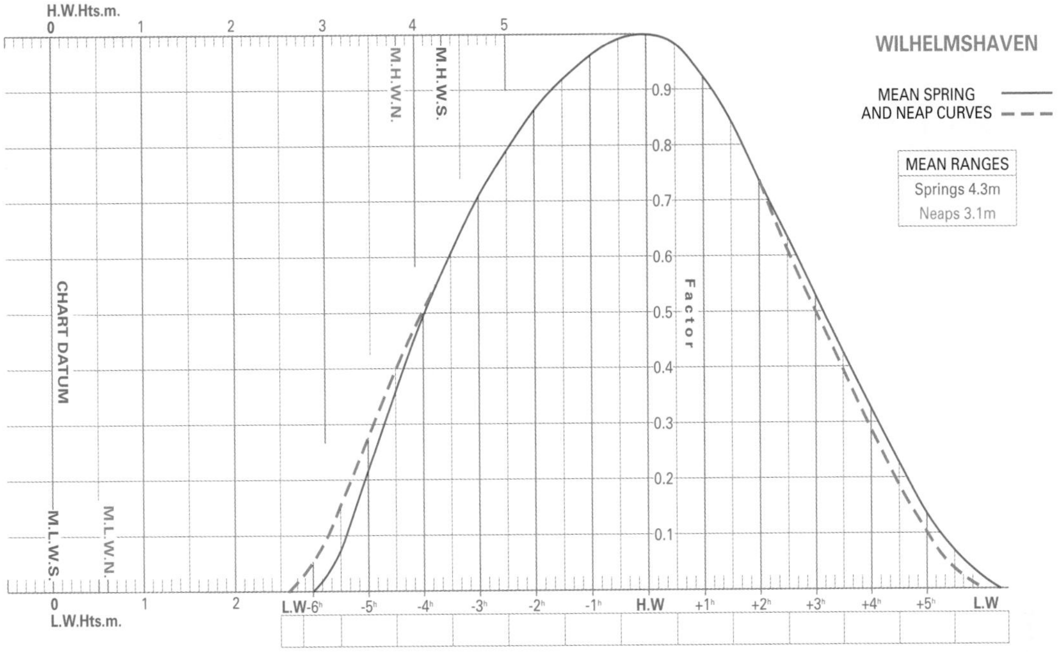

9.15.17 WILHELMSHAVEN (R. JADE)

Niedersachsen **53°30'·80N 08°09'·17E**

CHARTS AC 3617, 3618; Imray C26; D 7

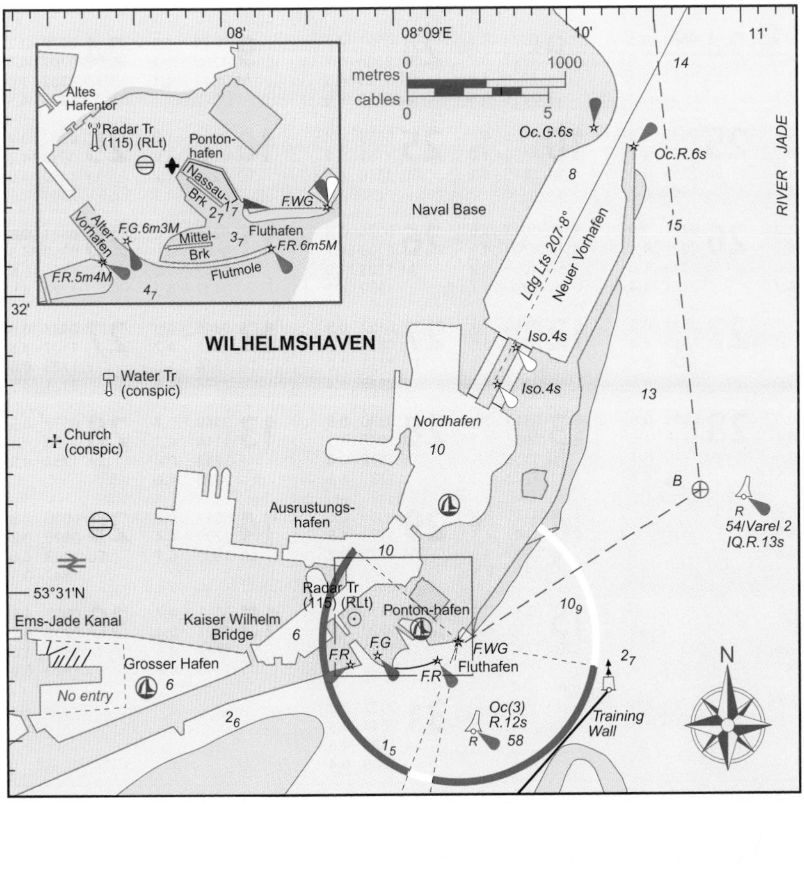

TIDES +0050 Dover; ML 2·3; Duration 0615
WILHELMSHAVEN is a Standard Port (→).

SHELTER Good in yacht hbrs at Nordhafen (rather remote) and Großer Hafen. Access via sea lock which opens H24 at 1hr's notice. No yacht berths in Neuer Vorhafen (naval port). Nassauhafen in the tidal hbr (*Fluthafen*) has yacht pontoons in about 1·7m, access H24.

NAVIGATION WPT 'A' 53°35'·71N 08°09'·98E (No 45 SHM buoy, QG) 175°/4.4M to WPT 'B' 53°31'·34N 08°10'·57E whence the Fluthafen ent bears 235°/9ca. The fairway is deep, wide and well marked.

Ems-Jade Canal: 39M from Großer Hafen to Emden, can be used by de-masted yachts; max draft 1·7m, min air clearance 3·75m. It has 6 locks. Max speed 4kn.

LIGHTS AND MARKS Principal lts on R Jade, see 9.15.4. Other lts on chartlet.

COMMUNICATIONS (Code 04421) Bremerhaven 72220; Water Police 942358; Customs 480723; Brit Consul (030) 204570; HM 154580, VHF Ch **11** 16 (H24); Naval base/Port Captain 684923 (operator); VTS 4891281, see Fig. 9.15.16B above for VTS, broadcast info, radar assistance; Sealock 7557620, VHF Ch **13;** Bridge opening VHF Ch **11**.

FACILITIES Berthing fee at all marinas is €1·70/m. **Nassauhafen Marina** ☎41439, 28 + 100Ⓥ. **Wiking Sportsboothafen** ☎41301, 30. **Hochsee YC Germania** ☎44121. There are 16 YCs in the area. **City** Ⓑ.

Germany

STANDARD TIME UT –01
Subtract 1 hour for UT
For German Summer Time add ONE hour in **non-shaded areas**

WILHELMSHAVEN LAT 53°31′N LONG 8°09′E

TIMES AND HEIGHTS OF HIGH AND LOW WATERS

Dates in red are SPRINGS
Dates in blue are NEAPS

YEAR **2018**

JANUARY

Date	Day	Time	m
1	M	0535 1149 1802	0.7 4.6 0.6
2	TU	0020 0634 1245 ○ 1857	4.7 0.5 4.7 0.5
3	W	0110 0727 1339 1949	4.8 0.5 4.7 0.5
4	TH	0158 0820 1432 2041	4.9 0.5 4.7 0.6
5	F	0248 0912 1525 2129	5.0 0.5 4.6 0.6
6	SA	0336 0959 1612 2211	5.0 0.5 4.6 0.6
7	SU	0421 1041 1657 2251	4.9 0.5 4.5 0.7
8	M	0505 1122 1742 ◑ 2333	4.8 0.7 4.3 0.8
9	TU	0552 1206 1828	4.7 0.8 4.2
10	W	0018 0642 1255 1920	1.0 4.6 0.9 4.1
11	TH	0112 0741 1354 2022	1.1 4.5 1.0 4.1
12	F	0219 0852 1506 2132	1.2 4.4 1.1 4.2
13	SA	0335 1004 1617 2238	1.2 4.5 1.1 4.4
14	SU	0447 1107 1717 2332	1.1 4.5 1.0 4.5
15	M	0544 1158 1805	0.9 4.5 0.9
16	TU	0016 0629 1240 1845	4.6 0.8 4.5 0.8
17	W	0055 0708 1317 ● 1922	4.6 0.7 4.5 0.7
18	TH	0129 0744 1352 1957	4.7 0.7 4.5 0.7
19	F	0202 0820 1426 2031	4.7 0.6 4.5 0.7
20	SA	0233 0853 1458 2102	4.8 0.6 4.5 0.7
21	SU	0305 0925 1531 2133	4.8 0.6 4.4 0.7
22	M	0340 1000 1608 2209	4.7 0.7 4.4 0.8
23	TU	0420 1038 1648 2247	4.7 0.7 4.4 0.8
24	W	0500 1115 1726 ◐ 2323	4.7 0.8 4.4 0.9
25	TH	0539 1151 1808	4.7 0.8 4.3
26	F	0006 0629 1240 1906	1.0 4.5 1.0 4.3
27	SA	0108 0739 1351 2022	1.1 4.4 1.0 4.3
28	SU	0230 0901 1514 2144	1.1 4.4 1.0 4.4
29	M	0356 1023 1635 2259	0.9 4.5 0.8 4.5
30	TU	0514 1135 1745	0.6 4.5 0.6
31	W	0004 0621 1238 ○ 1846	4.7 0.5 4.6 0.5

FEBRUARY

Date	Day	Time	m
1	TH	0059 0719 1333 1941	4.8 0.4 4.6 0.5
2	F	0147 0810 1423 2030	4.9 0.4 4.6 0.5
3	SA	0235 0900 1511 2116	5.0 0.4 4.6 0.5
4	SU	0322 0945 1556 2156	5.0 0.4 4.6 0.5
5	M	0404 1023 1635 2232	4.9 0.5 4.5 0.5
6	TU	0444 1058 1712 2306	4.8 0.6 4.4 0.6
7	W	0522 1132 1747 ◑ 2339	4.7 0.7 4.3 0.8
8	TH	0601 1206 1826	4.5 0.8 4.2
9	F	0019 0649 1252 1920	0.9 4.3 1.0 4.1
10	SA	0117 0755 1400 2034	1.1 4.2 1.2 4.1
11	SU	0238 0917 1523 2154	1.2 4.2 1.2 4.3
12	M	0404 1034 1640 2301	1.1 4.3 1.1 4.4
13	TU	0514 1134 1737 2351	0.9 4.4 0.9 4.5
14	W	0604 1219 1822	0.8 4.5 0.8
15	TH	0032 0646 1258 ● 1902	4.6 0.7 4.5 0.7
16	F	0109 0724 1335 1939	4.7 0.6 4.5 0.6
17	SA	0143 0801 1410 2014	4.7 0.5 4.5 0.6
18	SU	0217 0834 1444 2047	4.8 0.5 4.5 0.5
19	M	0251 0907 1517 2120	4.8 0.5 4.5 0.5
20	TU	0327 0944 1554 2157	4.8 0.5 4.5 0.6
21	W	0407 1022 1632 2234	4.8 0.6 4.5 0.6
22	TH	0445 1057 1706 2305	4.8 0.6 4.5 0.7
23	F	0519 1126 1740 ◐ 2339	4.7 0.7 4.4 0.8
24	SA	0603 1207 1832	4.5 0.9 4.3
25	SU	0035 0711 1316 1951	0.9 4.3 1.0 4.3
26	M	0201 0841 1449 2122	1.0 4.3 1.0 4.4
27	TU	0337 1012 1620 2246	0.8 4.4 0.8 4.5
28	W	0503 1129 1736 2353	0.6 4.5 0.7 4.7

MARCH

Date	Day	Time	m
1	TH	0612 1232 1837	0.4 4.6 0.5
2	F	0048 0708 1324 ○ 1929	4.8 0.4 4.6 0.5
3	SA	0135 0756 1410 2015	4.9 0.3 4.6 0.4
4	SU	0220 0840 1453 2056	4.9 0.3 4.6 0.4
5	M	0304 0921 1533 2133	4.9 0.4 4.6 0.4
6	TU	0344 0958 1608 2207	4.9 0.4 4.5 0.4
7	W	0420 1029 1639 2237	4.8 0.5 4.5 0.5
8	TH	0453 1056 1708 2304	4.6 0.6 4.4 0.6
9	F	0524 1121 1739 ◑ 2335	4.4 0.7 4.2 0.8
10	SA	0603 1156 1825	4.2 1.0 4.1
11	SU	0023 0703 1256 1936	1.0 4.0 1.2 4.1
12	M	0140 0825 1423 2103	1.1 4.0 1.3 4.2
13	TU	0313 0952 1553 2222	1.1 4.1 1.1 4.3
14	W	0435 1101 1702 2320	0.9 4.3 0.9 4.5
15	TH	0533 1152 1752	0.7 4.4 0.8
16	F	0004 0616 1233 1834	4.6 0.6 4.5 0.7
17	SA	0043 0656 1312 ● 1914	4.7 0.5 4.5 0.6
18	SU	0120 0735 1349 1952	4.7 0.4 4.5 0.5
19	M	0157 0810 1425 2028	4.8 0.3 4.5 0.4
20	TU	0234 0846 1501 2104	4.8 0.3 4.6 0.4
21	W	0312 0924 1537 2141	4.8 0.4 4.6 0.4
22	TH	0351 1003 1613 2216	4.8 0.5 4.6 0.5
23	F	0429 1037 1647 2249	4.7 0.5 4.6 0.5
24	SA	0507 1108 1723 ◐ 2326	4.6 0.7 4.5 0.6
25	SU	0553 1151 1818	4.4 0.9 4.4
26	M	0024 0703 1303 1939	0.8 4.2 1.0 4.3
27	TU	0152 0835 1438 2113	0.9 4.2 1.0 4.4
28	W	0330 1008 1612 2237	0.8 4.3 0.8 4.6
29	TH	0454 1123 1725 2340	0.6 4.5 0.7 4.7
30	F	0556 1220 1820	0.4 4.5 0.5
31	SA	0032 0648 1308 ○ 1909	4.8 0.3 4.6 0.4

APRIL

Date	Day	Time	m
1	SU	0119 0734 1352 1954	4.8 0.3 4.6 0.4
2	M	0202 0816 1430 2032	4.8 0.3 4.6 0.3
3	TU	0243 0853 1505 2106	4.8 0.3 4.6 0.3
4	W	0320 0926 1537 2138	4.7 0.4 4.6 0.3
5	TH	0353 0954 1605 2207	4.6 0.5 4.5 0.4
6	F	0423 1019 1633 2233	4.5 0.5 4.4 0.5
7	SA	0453 1043 1702 2301	4.3 0.7 4.3 0.6
8	SU	0528 1114 1742 ◑ 2343	4.1 0.9 4.2 0.9
9	M	0619 1206 1844	4.0 1.1 4.1
10	TU	0051 0734 1326 2008	1.0 3.9 1.2 4.1
11	W	0219 0900 1457 2132	1.0 4.0 1.2 4.3
12	TH	0345 1017 1614 2238	0.9 4.2 1.0 4.4
13	F	0449 1114 1712 2328	0.7 4.3 0.8 4.6
14	SA	0537 1200 1800	0.6 4.4 0.7
15	SU	0011 0621 1243 1845	4.7 0.4 4.5 0.6
16	M	0053 0704 1324 ● 1926	4.8 0.3 4.6 0.4
17	TU	0133 0744 1402 2005	4.8 0.3 4.6 0.3
18	W	0213 0823 1439 2044	4.8 0.3 4.7 0.3
19	TH	0254 0903 1516 2122	4.8 0.4 4.7 0.3
20	F	0335 0942 1554 2200	4.7 0.4 4.7 0.4
21	SA	0417 1019 1633 2239	4.6 0.5 4.6 0.5
22	SU	0502 1059 1718 ◐ 2326	4.5 0.7 4.6 0.6
23	M	0556 1150 1817	4.4 0.9 4.5
24	TU	0028 0707 1302 1936	0.7 4.3 1.0 4.5
25	W	0151 0833 1430 2104	0.7 4.2 1.0 4.5
26	TH	0321 0959 1556 2222	0.6 4.3 0.8 4.6
27	F	0437 1107 1703 2321	0.5 4.5 0.6 4.7
28	SA	0532 1158 1754	0.3 4.5 0.5
29	SU	0010 0620 1243 1842	4.8 0.3 4.6 0.5
30	M	0057 0707 1327 ○ 1929	4.8 0.3 4.6 0.4

Chart Datum: 2·70 metres below Normal Null (German reference level). HAT is 5·1 metres above Chart Datum.

STANDARD TIME UT –01
Subtract 1 hour for UT
For German Summer Time add ONE hour in **non-shaded areas**

WILHELMSHAVEN LAT 53°31′N LONG 8°09′E

TIMES AND HEIGHTS OF HIGH AND LOW WATERS

Dates in red are **SPRINGS**
Dates in blue are **NEAPS**

YEAR **2018**

MAY

Date	Day	Time	m	Time	m	Time	m	Time	m
1	TU	0142	4.7	0749	0.3	1405	4.6	2007	0.3
2	W	0220	4.7	0823	0.3	1436	4.6	2039	0.3
3	TH	0253	4.6	0852	0.4	1506	4.6	2109	0.3
4	F	0325	4.5	0920	0.5	1535	4.6	2139	0.4
5	SA	0356	4.4	0947	0.5	1603	4.5	2209	0.4
6	SU	0427	4.3	1016	0.7	1634	4.5	2240	0.6
7	M	0502	4.2	1049	0.9	1712	4.4	2320	0.8
8	TU	0546	4.0	1133	1.1	1805	4.3	◑	
9	W	0015	0.9	0648	4.0	1237	1.2	1915	4.2
10	TH	0128	0.9	0805	4.0	1358	1.1	2035	4.3
11	F	0247	0.8	0922	4.1	1518	1.0	2147	4.5
12	SA	0357	0.7	1027	4.3	1624	0.8	2245	4.6
13	SU	0454	0.6	1121	4.4	1720	0.7	2335	4.7
14	M	0544	0.5	1210	4.6	1812	0.6		
15	TU	0022	4.8	0633	0.4	1255	4.7	● 1857	0.4
16	W	0107	4.8	0717	0.3	1335	4.7	1938	0.3
17	TH	0150	4.8	0759	0.3	1415	4.7	2021	0.3
18	F	0236	4.7	0842	0.4	1457	4.8	2106	0.3
19	SA	0324	4.7	0926	0.4	1540	4.8	2150	0.3
20	SU	0412	4.6	1009	0.5	1625	4.8	2236	0.4
21	M	0502	4.5	1055	0.7	1716	4.8	2329	0.6
22	TU	0600	4.4	1151	0.8	1816	4.7	◐	
23	W	0031	0.6	0706	4.3	1257	0.9	1927	4.7
24	TH	0142	0.6	0820	4.3	1412	0.9	2044	4.6
25	F	0259	0.6	0935	4.3	1527	0.7	2155	4.7
26	SA	0408	0.5	1039	4.4	1631	0.6	2254	4.7
27	SU	0503	0.4	1129	4.5	1725	0.6	2345	4.7
28	M	0551	0.4	1214	4.6	1815	0.5		
29	TU	0033	4.7	0639	0.4	1258	4.6	○ 1902	0.4
30	W	0118	4.7	0722	0.4	1338	4.7	1942	0.3
31	TH	0156	4.6	0755	0.3	1410	4.7	2014	0.3

JUNE

Date	Day	Time	m	Time	m	Time	m	Time	m
1	F	0229	4.6	0824	0.4	1440	4.7	2045	0.4
2	SA	0301	4.5	0854	0.5	1510	4.7	2118	0.4
3	SU	0333	4.4	0924	0.6	1540	4.7	2151	0.5
4	M	0406	4.3	0956	0.7	1613	4.6	2226	0.6
5	TU	0441	4.3	1032	0.8	1651	4.6	2305	0.8
6	W	0522	4.2	1112	1.0	1736	4.5	◑ 2349	0.8
7	TH	0611	4.1	1202	1.0	1832	4.4		
8	F	0044	0.8	0714	4.1	1306	1.1	1939	4.4
9	SA	0151	0.8	0825	4.2	1420	1.0	2051	4.5
10	SU	0302	0.8	0934	4.3	1533	0.9	2157	4.6
11	M	0407	0.7	1037	4.5	1637	0.7	2256	4.7
12	TU	0506	0.6	1133	4.6	1736	0.6	2351	4.7
13	W	0600	0.4	1224	4.7	1828	0.4	●	
14	TH	0042	4.8	0650	0.3	1310	4.8	1915	0.3
15	F	0132	4.8	0739	0.3	1355	4.8	2005	0.3
16	SA	0224	4.7	0828	0.4	1443	4.9	2057	0.3
17	SU	0317	4.7	0917	0.4	1531	4.9	2147	0.3
18	M	0408	4.6	1004	0.5	1619	4.9	2235	0.4
19	TU	0459	4.5	1051	0.6	1710	4.9	2325	0.5
20	W	0553	4.4	1142	0.7	1805	4.8	◐	
21	TH	0020	0.6	0650	4.3	1239	0.8	1905	4.7
22	F	0119	0.6	0750	4.3	1340	0.8	2010	4.7
23	SA	0223	0.6	0855	4.3	1446	0.8	2118	4.6
24	SU	0329	0.6	0959	4.4	1553	0.8	2222	4.6
25	M	0431	0.7	1056	4.5	1655	0.7	2319	4.7
26	TU	0524	0.6	1145	4.6	1750	0.6		
27	W	0010	4.6	0612	0.6	1231	4.6	1837	0.5
28	TH	0055	4.6	0656	0.5	1312	4.7	○ 1919	0.4
29	F	0134	4.6	0732	0.5	1347	4.7	1954	0.4
30	SA	0208	4.6	0805	0.5	1419	4.8	2029	0.5

JULY

Date	Day	Time	m	Time	m	Time	m	Time	m
1	SU	0242	4.5	0837	0.6	1450	4.8	2103	0.5
2	M	0314	4.5	0909	0.6	1521	4.8	2136	0.6
3	TU	0346	4.4	0940	0.7	1554	4.7	2211	0.7
4	W	0421	4.4	1017	0.8	1633	4.7	2249	0.7
5	TH	0501	4.3	1057	0.9	1714	4.7	2329	0.7
6	F	0543	4.3	1137	0.9	1757	4.6	◑	
7	SA	0010	0.8	0631	4.3	1225	1.0	1850	4.5
8	SU	0101	0.8	0730	4.3	1327	1.0	1956	4.5
9	M	0207	0.8	0839	4.3	1440	1.0	2108	4.6
10	TU	0320	0.8	0950	4.4	1554	0.8	2219	4.6
11	W	0429	0.7	1057	4.5	1702	0.6	2324	4.6
12	TH	0532	0.5	1157	4.6	1805	0.4		
13	F	0025	4.7	0631	0.4	1251	4.8	● 1902	0.3
14	SA	0121	4.7	0727	0.4	1341	4.9	1956	0.3
15	SU	0215	4.7	0820	0.4	1431	5.0	2050	0.3
16	M	0309	4.7	0911	0.4	1521	5.0	2141	0.3
17	TU	0359	4.6	0956	0.4	1608	5.0	2226	0.3
18	W	0446	4.6	1039	0.5	1655	4.9	2310	0.5
19	TH	0532	4.5	1123	0.6	1743	4.8	◐ 2357	0.6
20	F	0619	4.4	1209	0.7	1832	4.7		
21	SA	0044	0.7	0707	4.3	1258	0.8	1926	4.6
22	SU	0136	0.8	0803	4.3	1357	0.9	2031	4.5
23	M	0241	0.9	0909	4.3	1509	1.0	2144	4.5
24	TU	0352	0.9	1018	4.4	1624	0.9	2252	4.5
25	W	0458	0.9	1118	4.5	1727	0.8	2348	4.5
26	TH	0550	0.8	1206	4.6	1816	0.6		
27	F	0034	4.5	0634	0.7	1247	4.7	○ 1858	0.6
28	SA	0113	4.5	0714	0.6	1325	4.7	1937	0.6
29	SU	0149	4.6	0750	0.6	1359	4.8	2014	0.5
30	M	0223	4.6	0823	0.6	1431	4.8	2047	0.5
31	TU	0255	4.5	0854	0.6	1502	4.8	2119	0.6

AUGUST

Date	Day	Time	m	Time	m	Time	m	Time	m
1	W	0326	4.5	0924	0.7	1535	4.8	2152	0.6
2	TH	0401	4.5	1000	0.7	1613	4.8	2230	0.7
3	F	0440	4.5	1040	0.8	1652	4.8	2308	0.7
4	SA	0517	4.5	1116	0.8	1729	4.7	◑ 2340	0.7
5	SU	0553	4.4	1151	0.9	1810	4.6		
6	M	0019	0.8	0641	4.3	1241	1.0	1909	4.5
7	TU	0119	0.9	0749	4.3	1354	1.0	2027	4.4
8	W	0238	0.9	0910	4.4	1519	0.9	2151	4.5
9	TH	0401	0.8	1029	4.5	1641	0.6	2307	4.5
10	F	0516	0.6	1138	4.6	1753	0.5		
11	SA	0014	4.6	0621	0.5	1237	4.8	● 1855	0.4
12	SU	0112	4.7	0720	0.5	1328	4.9	1949	0.3
13	M	0205	4.7	0812	0.4	1417	5.0	2040	0.3
14	TU	0255	4.7	0859	0.4	1504	5.0	2127	0.3
15	W	0341	4.7	0941	0.4	1550	5.0	2209	0.4
16	TH	0423	4.6	1019	0.5	1632	4.9	2247	0.5
17	F	0502	4.5	1056	0.6	1713	4.8	2324	0.7
18	SA	0539	4.4	1133	0.7	1753	4.6	◐	
19	SU	0001	0.8	0617	4.3	1213	0.9	1838	4.5
20	M	0043	1.0	0706	4.2	1305	1.0	1939	4.3
21	TU	0144	1.2	0814	4.2	1420	1.1	2059	4.3
22	W	0305	1.2	0935	4.3	1546	1.1	2220	4.3
23	TH	0425	1.1	1047	4.5	1702	0.9	2325	4.4
24	F	0527	0.9	1141	4.6	1755	0.8		
25	SA	0012	4.4	0612	0.8	1222	4.7	1836	0.7
26	SU	0050	4.5	0652	0.7	1259	4.7	○ 1915	0.6
27	M	0126	4.5	0730	0.7	1335	4.8	1952	0.6
28	TU	0200	4.6	0805	0.6	1408	4.8	2026	0.5
29	W	0233	4.5	0837	0.6	1441	4.8	2057	0.5
30	TH	0305	4.5	0908	0.6	1514	4.8	2130	0.6
31	F	0338	4.5	0942	0.7	1551	4.8	2206	0.7

Chart Datum: 2·70 metres below Normal Null (German reference level). HAT is 5·1 metres above Chart Datum.

STANDARD TIME UT –01
Subtract 1 hour for UT
For German Summer Time add ONE hour in **non-shaded areas**

WILHELMSHAVEN LAT 53°31'N LONG 8°09'E

TIMES AND HEIGHTS OF HIGH AND LOW WATERS

Dates in red are SPRINGS
Dates in blue are NEAPS

YEAR **2018**

SEPTEMBER

Date	Day	Time	m	Time	m	Time	m	Time	m
1	SA	0415	4.6	1019	0.7	1628	4.8	2241	0.7
2	SU	0449	4.5	1052	0.8	1702	4.7	2311	0.8
3	M	0520	4.5	1123	0.8	1739	4.5	◑ 2345	0.9
4	TU	0603	4.3	1209	1.0	1838	4.4		
5	W	0044	1.1	0713	4.3	1326	1.1	2002	4.3
6	TH	0211	1.1	0843	4.3	1501	1.0	2136	4.4
7	F	0346	1.0	1011	4.5	1632	0.8	2258	4.5
8	SA	0507	0.8	1124	4.7	1745	0.6		
9	SU	0005	4.6	0613	0.7	1223	4.8	● 1844	0.4
10	M	0100	4.7	0708	0.5	1313	4.9	1936	0.4
11	TU	0149	4.7	0757	0.5	1359	5.0	2022	0.3
12	W	0234	4.7	0840	0.4	1443	5.0	2104	0.4
13	TH	0315	4.7	0919	0.4	1526	4.9	2143	0.4
14	F	0352	4.6	0954	0.5	1604	4.8	2217	0.6
15	SA	0425	4.5	1026	0.6	1640	4.7	2246	0.7
16	SU	0456	4.4	1056	0.7	1714	4.5	2315	0.9
17	M	0529	4.3	1129	0.9	1753	4.3	◐ 2351	1.1
18	TU	0612	4.2	1216	1.1	1849	4.1		
19	W	0047	1.3	0718	4.1	1328	1.3	2008	4.0
20	TH	0210	1.5	0843	4.2	1500	1.2	2136	4.1
21	F	0341	1.4	1006	4.4	1625	1.1	2250	4.2
22	SA	0454	1.1	1108	4.5	1725	0.9	2341	4.4
23	SU	0543	0.9	1150	4.6	1806	0.7		
24	M	0020	4.4	0623	0.8	1228	4.7	1843	0.6
25	TU	0056	4.5	0702	0.7	1305	4.7	○ 1922	0.6
26	W	0133	4.6	0740	0.6	1341	4.8	1958	0.5
27	TH	0207	4.6	0816	0.6	1416	4.8	2032	0.5
28	F	0240	4.6	0849	0.6	1451	4.8	2106	0.6
29	SA	0313	4.6	0921	0.6	1526	4.8	2140	0.7
30	SU	0346	4.6	0954	0.7	1603	4.7	2213	0.8

OCTOBER

Date	Day	Time	m	Time	m	Time	m	Time	m
1	M	0419	4.6	1027	0.7	1639	4.6	2245	0.9
2	TU	0454	4.5	1103	0.9	1723	4.4	◑ 2324	1.1
3	W	0542	4.4	1155	1.0	1825	4.3		
4	TH	0028	1.2	0656	4.4	1316	1.1	1952	4.2
5	F	0159	1.3	0829	4.4	1454	1.0	2127	4.3
6	SA	0337	1.1	0958	4.6	1624	0.8	2249	4.5
7	SU	0457	0.9	1108	4.7	1732	0.6	2350	4.6
8	M	0557	0.8	1203	4.8	1825	0.5		
9	TU	0041	4.6	0647	0.6	1252	4.9	● 1914	0.4
10	W	0126	4.6	0734	0.5	1337	4.9	1958	0.4
11	TH	0207	4.7	0816	0.5	1419	4.9	2037	0.5
12	F	0244	4.7	0851	0.5	1458	4.8	2111	0.5
13	SA	0317	4.6	0924	0.5	1534	4.7	2141	0.6
14	SU	0348	4.6	0954	0.6	1606	4.5	2207	0.7
15	M	0417	4.5	1022	0.7	1638	4.3	2234	0.9
16	TU	0448	4.4	1053	0.9	1715	4.2	◐ 2308	1.1
17	W	0528	4.3	1136	1.1	1804	4.0	2358	1.4
18	TH	0626	4.2	1240	1.3	1914	4.0		
19	F	0113	1.6	0746	4.2	1405	1.3	2039	4.0
20	SA	0242	1.5	0911	4.3	1532	1.2	2158	4.1
21	SU	0403	1.3	1021	4.4	1639	1.0	2257	4.3
22	M	0501	1.1	1110	4.5	1726	0.8	2342	4.4
23	TU	0547	0.9	1151	4.6	1807	0.7		
24	W	0022	4.5	0631	0.8	1232	4.7	○ 1848	0.6
25	TH	0102	4.6	0712	0.7	1311	4.8	1928	0.6
26	F	0138	4.6	0750	0.6	1349	4.8	2005	0.6
27	SA	0213	4.7	0826	0.6	1426	4.8	2041	0.6
28	SU	0247	4.7	0900	0.6	1505	4.7	2116	0.7
29	M	0322	4.7	0935	0.6	1544	4.6	2151	0.8
30	TU	0358	4.7	1011	0.7	1627	4.5	2228	1.0
31	W	0441	4.6	1056	0.9	1718	4.4	◑ 2317	1.2

NOVEMBER

Date	Day	Time	m	Time	m	Time	m	Time	m
1	TH	0535	4.6	1154	1.0	1824	4.3		
2	F	0023	1.3	0648	4.5	1312	1.0	1946	4.2
3	SA	0149	1.3	0815	4.5	1442	1.0	2114	4.3
4	SU	0319	1.2	0939	4.6	1606	0.8	2230	4.4
5	M	0434	1.0	1046	4.7	1710	0.7	2328	4.5
6	TU	0531	0.8	1139	4.8	1800	0.6		
7	W	0015	4.6	0621	0.7	1228	4.8	● 1847	0.6
8	TH	0059	4.6	0708	0.6	1314	4.8	1931	0.5
9	F	0138	4.6	0749	0.5	1355	4.7	2007	0.5
10	SA	0212	4.6	0822	0.5	1430	4.6	2038	0.6
11	SU	0244	4.6	0853	0.5	1504	4.5	2107	0.7
12	M	0314	4.6	0925	0.6	1537	4.4	2135	0.7
13	TU	0345	4.6	0956	0.7	1609	4.3	2203	0.9
14	W	0417	4.5	1029	0.9	1644	4.2	2237	1.1
15	TH	0454	4.4	1108	1.1	1727	4.1	◐ 2321	1.4
16	F	0543	4.3	1200	1.3	1824	4.0		
17	SA	0020	1.5	0649	4.3	1309	1.3	1937	4.0
18	SU	0137	1.5	0806	4.3	1426	1.2	2054	4.1
19	M	0258	1.4	0921	4.4	1539	1.1	2202	4.2
20	TU	0408	1.2	1021	4.5	1638	0.9	2257	4.4
21	W	0505	1.0	1111	4.6	1727	0.8	2345	4.5
22	TH	0554	0.9	1157	4.7	1813	0.7		
23	F	0028	4.6	0640	0.8	1240	4.7	○ 1856	0.6
24	SA	0107	4.7	0720	0.6	1322	4.7	1937	0.6
25	SU	0145	4.7	0801	0.6	1405	4.7	2018	0.6
26	M	0226	4.8	0844	0.6	1451	4.7	2100	0.7
27	TU	0307	4.8	0926	0.6	1537	4.6	2141	0.8
28	W	0349	4.8	1007	0.7	1625	4.5	2223	0.9
29	TH	0436	4.8	1055	0.8	1718	4.4	2314	1.1
30	F	0532	4.7	1152	0.9	1821	4.3	◑	

DECEMBER

Date	Day	Time	m	Time	m	Time	m	Time	m
1	SA	0016	1.2	0638	4.7	1300	0.9	1932	4.2
2	SU	0128	1.2	0753	4.6	1417	0.9	2048	4.2
3	M	0245	1.1	0910	4.6	1533	0.8	2159	4.4
4	TU	0359	1.0	1017	4.7	1639	0.8	2257	4.5
5	W	0501	0.9	1114	4.8	1732	0.7	2346	4.6
6	TH	0554	0.8	1205	4.7	1820	0.7		
7	F	0031	4.6	0642	0.7	1252	4.7	● 1904	0.6
8	SA	0111	4.6	0723	0.6	1332	4.6	1940	0.6
9	SU	0146	4.6	0757	0.5	1407	4.5	2010	0.6
10	M	0217	4.7	0829	0.6	1441	4.5	2042	0.7
11	TU	0249	4.7	0904	0.6	1514	4.4	2113	0.8
12	W	0321	4.7	0938	0.7	1547	4.3	2143	0.9
13	TH	0354	4.6	1012	0.8	1620	4.3	2216	1.0
14	F	0429	4.6	1048	1.0	1658	4.2	2254	1.2
15	SA	0511	4.5	1129	1.1	1743	4.1	◐ 2339	1.3
16	SU	0601	4.4	1218	1.1	1839	4.1		
17	M	0037	1.4	0703	4.4	1320	1.2	1947	4.1
18	TU	0149	1.4	0815	4.4	1431	1.1	2059	4.2
19	W	0305	1.3	0925	4.5	1541	1.0	2205	4.4
20	TH	0413	1.1	1027	4.5	1642	0.9	2302	4.5
21	F	0513	0.9	1122	4.6	1736	0.7	2354	4.6
22	SA	0605	0.7	1213	4.7	1825	0.6	○	
23	SU	0040	4.7	0653	0.6	1302	4.7	1913	0.6
24	M	0124	4.8	0742	0.6	1352	4.7	2003	0.6
25	TU	0211	4.8	0833	0.5	1444	4.6	2052	0.6
26	W	0259	4.9	0923	0.5	1535	4.6	2138	0.7
27	TH	0345	4.9	1007	0.5	1623	4.5	2220	0.7
28	F	0432	4.9	1052	0.6	1714	4.4	2307	0.8
29	SA	0524	4.8	1142	0.7	1808	4.3	◑ 2359	0.9
30	SU	0621	4.7	1237	0.8	1905	4.2		
31	M	0056	1.0	0722	4.6	1339	0.8	2007	4.2

Chart Datum: 2·70 metres below Normal Null (German reference level). HAT is 5·1 metres above Chart Datum.

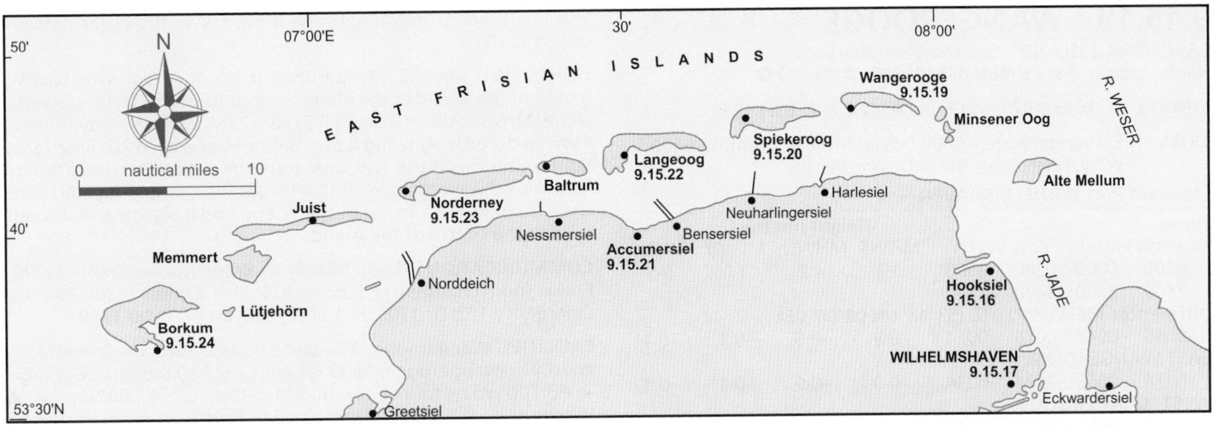

9.15.18 EAST FRISIAN ISLANDS

CHARTS AC 1635, 1875 and 3631 cover the E Frisians at small to medium scales. D 2, 89, 90; BSH 1230 (Wangerooge and Spiekeroog only). The *Hafenhandbuch Nordsee* is the most detailed harbour guide with excellent chartlets and aerial shots. Its full coverage extends from Calais to Trondheim, Norway.

GEOGRAPHY The East Frisians (*Die Ostfriesischen Küste*) lie from 3 to 11M off the German coast and were once the N coast of the German mainland. Shoals extend seaward for 2 or more miles in places. Groynes and sea defences are on their W and NW sides. Their bare sand dunes are not easy to identify, so the few conspic landmarks must be carefully selected.

The gaps between the islands are called ***Seegats***. They vary in position and depth, and all of them are dangerous on the ebb tide, even in a moderate onshore wind, or in winds >F4 with any N in them. The area between the low-lying islands and the mainland coast is called the ***Wattenmeer***, *wattfahrenwassern* (abbrev: *watt*) being the generic name for tidal channels. Where the *watts* meet (having swept both ways round the island, usually about ⅓ of the way from the E end) are called *Wattenhochs*.

Cruising between the islands and the mainland is generally only for shoal-draft boats able to take the ground. Vessels drawing more than 1·4m are likely to be constrained by their draft (see www.wattenschipper.de/Aktuelles.htm). For navigating inside the islands in the shoal or partly drying *watts*, the large-scale German BSH A1 charts are essential.

TIDES The general strategy, whether E- or W-bound, is to leave as early as possible on the flood (dependent on distance) so as to reach your destination or negotiate the shallowest part of the *watts* near HW. Springs occur around midday and give approx 0·5m more water than neaps.

▶*Streams are very slack over the watts but very strong in the seegats, especially on a sp ebb.*◀

Persistent strong W/NW winds may raise the sea level by > 0·75m (exceptionally by 3m); against the ebb they cause steep dangerous seas over the bars near the entrance to the seegats. Strong E/SE winds can lower sea levels, the difference between predicted and expected heights are in German weather forecasts.

WITHIES (*pricken*) are used to mark the *watts*, usually these are PHMs, unbound withies (ᛉ, twigs pointing up) often marked with red reflective tape; bound withies (ᛦ, twigs pointing down) are less common (except in ent chans) SHMs.

The **conventional direction of buoyage is always E'ward**, though in places this may conflict with the actual direction of the flood.

NATURE RESERVES inshore of most of the islands must not be entered. Seal and Bird reserves are closed as shown on the charts, but channels are excluded. The *Nationalpark Niedersächsisches Wattenmeer* extends from the mainland to the seaward margin of the drying flats.

National Parks are marked on the charts. Within them Zones 1 are closed from HW +3 to HW –3; landing is prohib year round.

PASSAGE INFORMATION

Generally, the Seegats between the islands should be avoided. Vessels small enough to use the Wattenmeer are best advised to enter at the E or W ends and stay inside, enjoying the protection the islands afford from the sea outside.

Alte Mellum, 6M SE of Wangerooge, where the Weser and Jade meet, is part of a bird sanctuary; landing prohib.

Minsener Oog, 1-2·5M SE of Wangerooge, is two small islets linked by a causeway and with many groynes and a conspic radar twr. Beware overfalls in strong NW'lies. Blaue Balje, between Minsener Oog and Wangerooge, is marked by buoys (prefixed 'B' and moved as necessary) but has strong tides and is dangerous in strong W/N winds. Seal (RSG) and Bird (VSG) reserves off the E end of Wangerooge are prohib areas (1/5–1/10 and 1/4–1/10 respectively).

Between **Spiekeroog** and **Langeoog**, the Otzumer Balje (buoys OB1-28/AH2) and unmarked Westerbalje chans lead inward. The former is usually deeper (min 3·5m) but both chans may silt up and unmarked channels are not in any case advised, even in good weather and on a rising tide.

Acummer Ee, leads east of **Baltrum** to **Langeoog** and to **Bensersiel** and **Dornumer-Accumersiel** on the mainland. It is buoyed (A1-A32, moved as required). Shoals extend 2M offshore, chan depths vary greatly, prone to silting. *In onshore winds the sea breaks on the bar (0·8m) between A1 and A1a.*

Norderneyer Seegat, lies between **Norderney** and **Juist**, but is approached across dangerous offshore shoals (Norder-gründe and Nordwestgründe) via two shallow buoyed channels, Dovetief and Schluchter. Dovetief, from the NNE (buoys D1-44) is the main chan, but Schluchter from the WNW (buoys S1-D5/S8) is better protected in NE'lies. *Depths vary considerably and at times the channels silt up and buoys are lifted. Neither channel should be used in strong winds.* Further inshore, Dovetief, now 14–11m deep, hugs the W end of the island and round to Norderney harbour. Beware groynes along the shore.

SW of Norderney, Busetief (buoys B1-24) is deeper than Dovetief and Schluchter. It leads generally S'ward to **Norddeich**, a tidal mainland hbr (2·0m).

▶*The flood begins at HW Helgoland –0605, and the ebb at HW Helgoland –0040, sp rates 1kn.*◀

Juist is the last of the chain of similar, long, narrow and low-lying islands. It has a small drying marina in the hbr midway along its southern side.

Memmert and **Kachelot**, S of Juist's W tip, and Lütje Horn, an islet E of Borkum, are bird sanctuaries; landing is prohibited.

Borkum (AC 3631) lies between Osterems and Westerems channels, with high dunes each end so that at a distance it looks like two separate islands. Round the W end of Borkum are unmarked groynes, some extending 3ca offshore. Conspic landmarks, all at the W end of the island, include: Grosse and Neue beacons, a water tower, Borkum Grosser lt ho and two disused lt houses.

9.15.19 WANGEROOGE

EAST FRISIAN ISLANDS. See overview chartlet
Niedersachsen **53° 46'·46N 07° 52'·10E**

CHARTS AC 1635, 1875, 3617; Imray C26; D 2; BSH 1230

TIDES E Wangerooge, –0009 Dover; ML 1·9. Duration 0600
W Wangerooge, –0014 Dover; ML 1·5

Standard Port WILHELMSHAVEN (⟵)

Times				Height (metres)			
High Water		Low Water		MHWS	MHWN	MLWN	MLWS
0200	0800	0200	0900	4·7	4·2	1·0	0·5
1400	2000	1400	2100				
Differences MELLUMPLATE (53°46'·0N 08°06'·0E)							
–0046	–0042	–0016	–0024	–0·9	–0·8	–0·1	–0·1
EAST WANGEROOGE							
–0058	–0053	–0024	–0034	–0·9	–0·9	–0·1	–0·1
WEST WANGEROOGE							
–0101	–0058	–0035	–0045	–1·0	–1·0	–0·1	–0·1

SHELTER Good in most winds, but SW gales, and S'lies at HW, cause heavy swell and difficult conditions in hbr when **Harlesiel**, 5M SSW via Carolinensieler Balje, will be safer. Yachts on marina pontoons at E side (HM) of hbr have 1·3–1·8m depth; rafting three or four deep, beware shallower spots. The W jetty (YC) is mainly for ferries but yachts >12m may request a berth.

NAVIGATION WPT 53°49'·25N 07°50'·47E Harle SWM buoy, Iso 8s, 122°/8½ca to H2 buoy; 207°/1·4M to H10 buoy; 154°/8ca to Buhne H WCM buoy, VQ (9) 10s; lastly 141°/1M to H7/OB42 buoy and to hbr ent via D4. The Harle chan has least depth 0·4m near H4 buoy; it shifts and buoys are moved accordingly. Beware Buhne (groyne) H, extending 7½ca, marked by WCM lt buoy and in FR sector of Wangerooge lt ho, F WR; the outer portion covers at HW.

LIGHTS AND MARKS Wangerooge lt ho, a R twr with two W bands, at the W end of the island has 3 co-located lts with separate characteristics: the main lt, Fl R 5s 60m 23M, with 360° coverage; a F WR sectored lt, showing R over Buhne H; and a F WRG directional light visible from the NW over Harleriff, whose sectors are not shown on the chartlet. See 9.15.4 for details. Conspic daymarks are the 52m high West Tower at the W end and a Sig Stn and disused lt ho in the centre of the island.

COMMUNICATIONS (Code 04469) Bremerhaven (0471) 72220; Police (non emergency) 205; ⊖ 519; Brit Consul (030) 204570; Emergency 112; Dr 1700; HM 1322, VHF Ch 17, 0700-1700.

FACILITIES **Wangerooge YC** ☎0151-23457106; or 044691322; www.wyc-wangerooge.de; €1·40m + €1·50 p/d service charge + €3·50p/p/day tourist tax mid-Mar–Oct. €3·00/day. **Village** (ferry to Harlesiel) ✈ (to Harle and Helgoland). **Ferry** Hamburg-Harwich.

MAINLAND HARBOUR 5M SSW OF WANGEROOGE

HARLESIEL, Niedersachsen, **53°42'·60N 07°48'·63E**. AC 1875, 3617; BSH 1230. HW –0100 on Dover (UT); HW (zone –0100) –0005 and ht +0·5m on Helgoland. Appr via Carolinensieler Balje which dries S of the training wall lt, L Fl 8s. Excellent shelter S of lock which has set opening times. 120 pontoon berths to W by village or at to E after passing through lock on W side of dyke. Call *Harle Lock*, VHF Ch 17, 0800-2000 or ☎(04464) 472 (Lock & HM). Berthing fees similar to Wangerooge, lock costs depend on how many vessels in lock, max,€13·30, min, €5·15 ⊖ ☎(04462) 6154; **YC** ☎1473; Facilities: .

Town ✈ and ferry to Wangerooge.

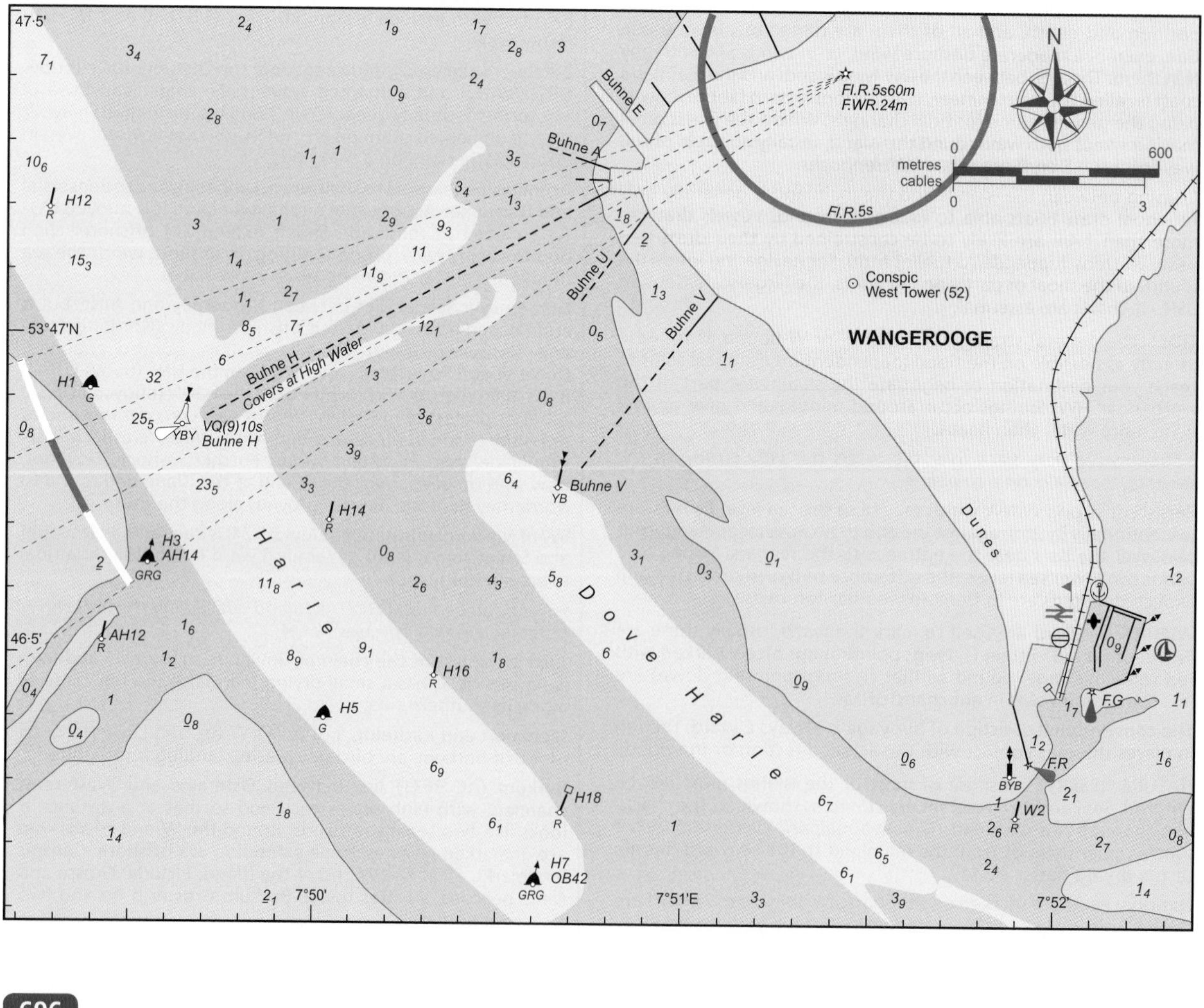

9.15.20 SPIEKEROOG

EAST FRISIAN ISLANDS
Niedersachsen **53°45'·00N 07°41'·27E** (ent to inner chan) ❀◊◊✿✿

CHARTS AC 1635, 1875; Imray C26; D 2, 89; BSH 1230

TIDES HW –0008 on Dover; ML 1·3m; Duration 0555

Standard Port HELGOLAND (⟵) See differences Langeoog.

SHELTER Good, *but S/SW winds cause heavy swell*. 3 yacht pontoons to the E of ferry berth almost dry to soft mud. Yachts >12m LOA should request a berth on the W jetty.

NAVIGATION WPT 53°48'·29N 07°38'·00E (Otzumer Balje SWM buoy, Iso 4s; often moved) 180°/0·2M to OB1 SHM buoy. Least depth on the bar (between OB2 and OB4) is about 3·5m (reported less 2017). Otzumer Balje is well buoyed, but only 4 buoys are lit. The chan skirts the SW end of the island into Schillbalje and to ☆ FR, R mast (lat/long below title) at the ent to inner chan, marked by withies, which leads 020°/1M to small ferry hbr (0·8m). Westerbalje, a shallow, unbuoyed secondary chan, is not advised.

Spiekeroog can also be approached from E and W via the Harlesieler and Neuharlingersieler Wattfahrwassern respectively.

LIGHTS AND MARKS Sand dunes near the W end of the island are up to 24m high, but the E end is low-lying (3m). Two bcns with spherical topmarks are near the centre and E end of island.

COMMUNICATIONS (Code 04976) British Consul (030) 204570; HM 178 879 7741 Mob (0800-1800).

FACILITIES **Hbr** is run by YC: www.ssc-spiekeroog.de 130Ⓥ €1·66 multihulls + 100% extra, <4hrs €5·00, ⊕ €3·00/day; new 🚿 WC adults €2·00/day, ✕ no wi-fi, ⛴(15t). **Town** ½M from hbr. Neuharlingersiel by ferry.

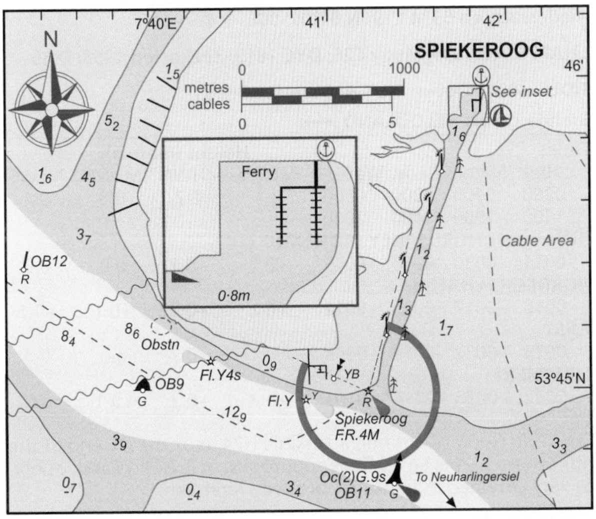

MAINLAND HARBOURS S AND SW OF SPIEKEROOG

NEUHARLINGERSIEL, Niedersachsen, **53°42'·10N 07°42'·29E**. AC 1635, 1875. HW 0000 on Dover (UT); see differences under Langeoog. Appr via Otzumer Balje and Schillbalje to N end of trng wall, Oc 6s. Training wall, 1M long, covers at HW and is marked by SHM withies ⇞. Beware strong tidal streams across the ent. Neuharlinger YC hbr, yachts lie in NE corner of hbr, limited Ⓥ €1·00/m + €2·00 per person tourist tax, pay at ferry terminal café. Inner berths <1·2m draught. HM ☎(04974) 289. Facilities: **Quay** ⛽. **Village** (picturesque) ✕ 🛒. Ferry to Spiekeroog (35 mins).

BENSERSIEL, Niedersachsen, **53°40'·81N 07°34'·20E**. AC 1635, 1875; D 89. HW –0024 on Dover (UT); +0005 on Helgoland (zone –0100); HW ht +0·4m on Helgoland. Appr as for Langeoog thence lit/buoyed Rute chan to training walls with depth of 1·4m to ferry berth, but covering at HW. Very good shelter in the yacht hbr (dries) to stbd just before inner hbr ent (1·0m); also berths on the SW side of main hbr. Lts as 9.15.4. HM VHF Ch 17, ☎(04971) 2502; Facilities: ⛽ ⛴(8t) ⛽(on E pier) ☎ 🛒 ⚒ ✕. **Town** Ⓑ ✕ 🛒 ✉ ≹ 🛒 ⛽. Ferry to Langeoog.

9.15.21 ACCUMERSIEL

Niedersachsen **53°40'·90N 07°29'·25E** ❀❀◊◊✿✿

CHARTS AC 1635, 1875; Imray C26; D 89

TIDES –0040 Dover; ML 1·4; Duration 0600

Standard Port HELGOLAND (⟵) Use differences Langeoog.

SHELTER The marina provides complete shelter in all winds; LW depth, 0.5m-dries in places, very soft mud. Ent is narrow; keep to W of chan on entering. Marina is fenced; obtain a gate key on arrival.

NAVIGATION Appr through Accumer Ee (see Langeoog) leading into Accumersieler Balje and to AB3 SHM buoy, IQ G 13s, 53°41'·44N 07°29'·27E. From here leave all withies ⇞ and posts to stbd. Note warnings on German chart D89. Least depth 0·3m. Locals advise HW, approx 2·0m-2.5m in chan and marina.

LIGHTS AND MARKS None.

COMMUNICATIONS (Code 04933) LB (04972) 247; ⛅ 0190 116048; Police 2218; Customs (04971) 7184; Brit Consul (030) 204570; H 04941-940; HM 2440; Deputy HM 441; *German Bight Tfc* (VTS) broadcasts traffic and weather VHF Ch 80 every H in German/English.

FACILITIES **Dornumer Yacht Haven, YC** ☎2440, mob 0160 2293046. www.ycacc.de All facilities: 250 ⛵ Ⓥ €1·10, 🚿 WC €2·00/day, ⛽ ✕ ⚒ 🛒 ⚒ ⛴(15t); pontoons are lifted out of season. **Town** ✕ 🛒 🛒 ✉ Ⓑ ≹ (Harlesiel) ✈ (Bremen).

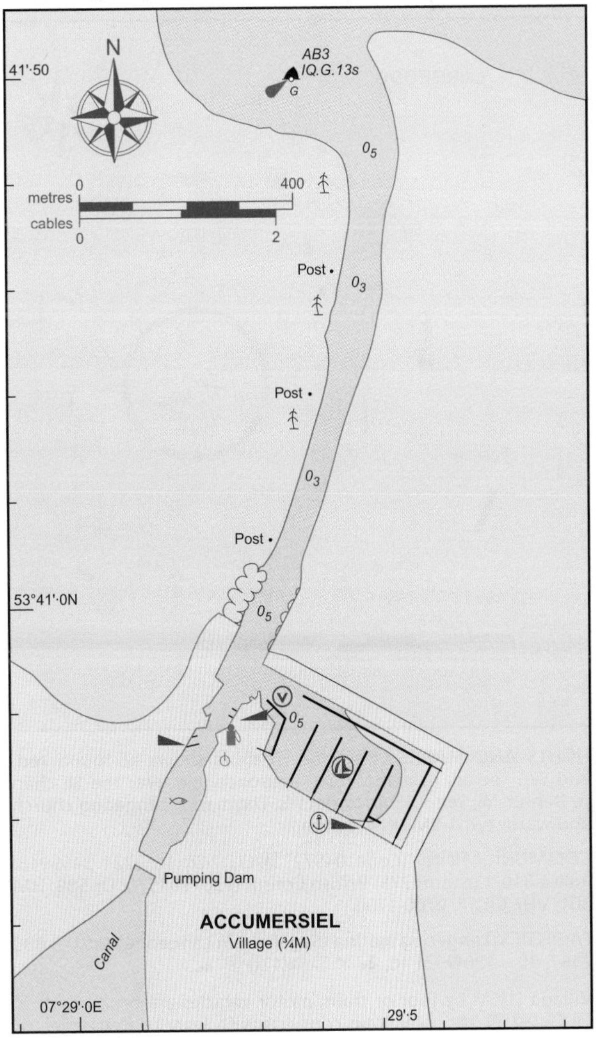

9.15.22 LANGEOOG

EAST FRISIAN ISLANDS
Niedersachsen **53°43'·38N 07°30'·12E**

CHARTS AC 1635, 1875; Imray C26; D 89

TIDES –0010 Dover; ML No data; Duration 0600

Standard Port HELGOLAND (⟵)

Times				Height (metres)			
High Water		Low Water		MHWS	MHWN	MLWN	MLWS
0200	0700	0200	0800	3·1	2·7	0·8	0·4
1400	1900	1400	2000				
Differences LANGEOOG							
+0003	–0001	–0034	–0018	+0·3	+0·3	0·0	0·0
SPIEKEROOG							
+0003	–0003	–0031	–0012	+0·4	+0·4	+0·1	0·0
NEUHARLINGERSIEL							
+0014	+0008	–0024	–0013	+0·5	+0·5	+0·1	0·0

SHELTER Hbr is well sheltered by 20m high sand dunes, but is open to the S. Marina dredged 1m; E part of hbr dries 1·5m; chan to ferry pier and marina and is marked by several (8+) SHM withies.

NAVIGATION WPT 53°46'·92N 07°25'·92E (Accumer Ee SWM buoy, Iso 8s; moves frequently) approx 180°/5ca to A1–2 chan buoys; thence via by'd chan to A9/B26 GRG by, Fl (2+1) G 15s. W sector of W mole lt leads 072°/1·4M to hbr ent. Ice protectors extend about 40m E of E mole, awash at HW, marked by card buoys. *Buoys shift frequently, call vess Berhard Gruben (Ch 16) for latest info.*

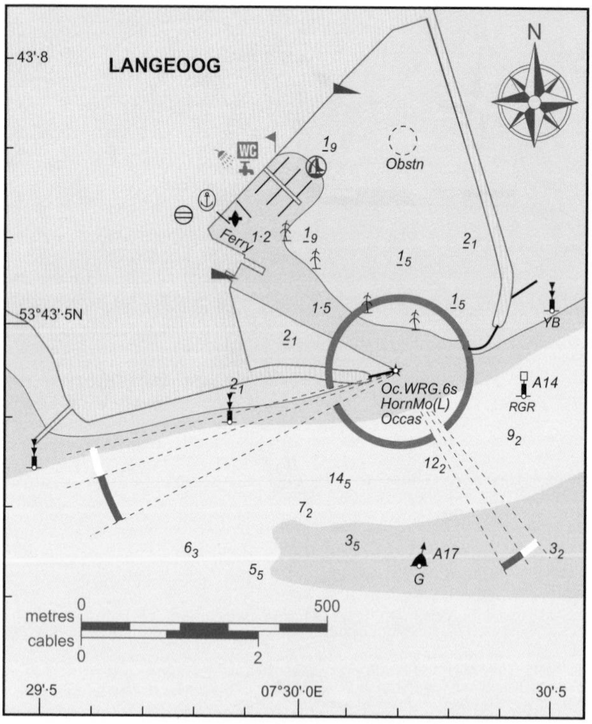

LIGHTS AND MARKS Lt twr on W mole shows all-round red, and WG sectors over the WSW approach and over the SE chan to Bensersiel; see 9.15.4 for details. Daymarks: Langeoog church and water twr 1·5M NNW of hbr.

COMMUNICATIONS (Code 04972) LB/CG 247; 0221 3459918; Police 810; Customs 275; British Consul (030) 204570; Dr 589; HM 301, VHF Ch 17, 0700-1700.

FACILITIES Langeoog marina (Segelverein Langeoog) ☎0173 883 2567, 70 + 130Ⓥ €1·40.

Village (1½M by foot or train; motor vehicles are prohibited) Ⓑ. Local train connects with ferry to Bensersiel. ✈ Bremen.

ISLAND HARBOUR 3M NORTH OF NESSMERSIEL

BALTRUM, Niedersachsen, **53°43'·26N 07°21'·80E**. AC 1635, 1875. HW –0040 on Dover (UT); Use differences Langeoog. The island is about 3 sq miles, 2·5M long, very low in the E and rising in the W to dunes about 15m high. Shelter is good except in strong SW'lies. Approach at HW via the Norderneyer Wattfahrwasser (which also gives access to Neßmersiel) running W-E, S of Norderney. The appr from seaward via the Wichter Ee is dangerous and is shunned even by locals. Yacht pontoons in 1·5m in the Bootshafen at the E end of the tiny hbr. HM ☎(04939) 448; ☎(04939) 668.

Facilities: Hbr; Baltrumer Bootsclub YC. **Village** (¼M NNE). No fuel. Ferry from Nessmersiel.

MAINLAND HARBOUR 5M WEST OF DORNUMER-ACCUMER

NESSMERSIEL, Niedersachsen, **53°41'·14N 07°21'·68E**. AC 1635; D89. HW –0040 on Dover (UT); –0020 on Helgoland (zone –0100); HW ht –0·2m on Helgoland. Appr as for Baltrum above, thence via the buoyed Nessmersieler Balje, chan marked by N3–N11 SHM buoys leading to end of trng wall, covers at HW. Here, a lt bn, Oc 4s 5M, and SHM and PHM mark the 6ca long trng wall. Yachthafen with pontoons is on W side, beyond ferry quay. Good shelter in all weathers. Hbr dries (2m at HW). HM ☎(04933) 1780.

Facilities: **Nordsee YC Nessmersiel**; but no supplies. **Village** (1M to S) has only limited facilities. Ferry to Baltrum.

9.15.23 NORDERNEY

EAST FRISIAN ISLANDS
Niedersachsen **53°41'·90N 07°09'·90E**

CHARTS AC 1635; Imray C26; DYC 1812; Zeekarten 1353; D 89

TIDES –0042 Dover; ML 1·4; Duration 0605

Standard Port HELGOLAND (⟵)

Times				Height (metres)			
High Water		Low Water		MHWS	MHWN	MLWN	MLWS
0200	0700	0200	0800	3·1	2·7	0·8	0·4
1400	1900	1400	2000				
Differences NORDERNEY (RIFFGAT)							
–0024	–0030	–0056	–0045	+0·1	+0·1	0·0	0·0
NORDDEICH HAFEN							
–0018	–0017	–0029	–0012	+0·2	+0·2	+0·1	+0·1
JUIST							
–0026	–0032	–0019	–0008	+0·1	+0·2	0·0	0·0
MEMMERT							
–0032	–0038	–0114	–0103	+0·2	+0·2	+0·1	0·0

SHELTER Good. Yacht hbr, accessible H24, is at the NE end of the hbr, where yachts lie on finger pontoons; or on W wall of hbr, as very crowded in Jul/Aug. Hbr speed limit 3kn.

NAVIGATION Tidal streams set across, not along, the Dovetief and Schlucter. **From N/E**, WPT 53°45'·48N 07°12'·70E (Dovetief SWM buoy, Iso 4s) 227°/2·7M to D8 PHM buoy, Oc (2) R 9s. Ent through the Dovetief (see Passage Information) well buoyed but the bar (3·1m) *can be dangerous in onshore winds and following seas which break on it, esp. on the ebb.*

From W, WPT 53°44'·80N 07°06'·00E (Schlucter SWM buoy, Iso 8s) 121°/2·1M to S1 SHM buoy, Oc (2) G 9s. *Ent at night is dangerous.* Both chans meet at D5/S8 GRG buoy, Fl (2+1) G 15s.

LIGHTS AND MARKS Lts, see 9.15.4. Landmarks: lt ho, 8-sided R brick twr, near centre of island. Conspic water twr in town.

COMMUNICATIONS (Code 04932) Coast Guard 2293; 549; Police 788; Customs 2386; British Consul (030) 204570; Ⓗ 477 and 416; HM 83545, 0175 2785687, VHF Ch 17, Wed–Sun 0700 (0900 Tue)–1200; 1230–1900 (1730 Mon).

FACILITIES Yacht Hbr (10t); **Yacht Club**. **Town** Ⓑ. (ferry to Norddeich) ✈ (to Bremen). Ferry Hamburg–Harwich.

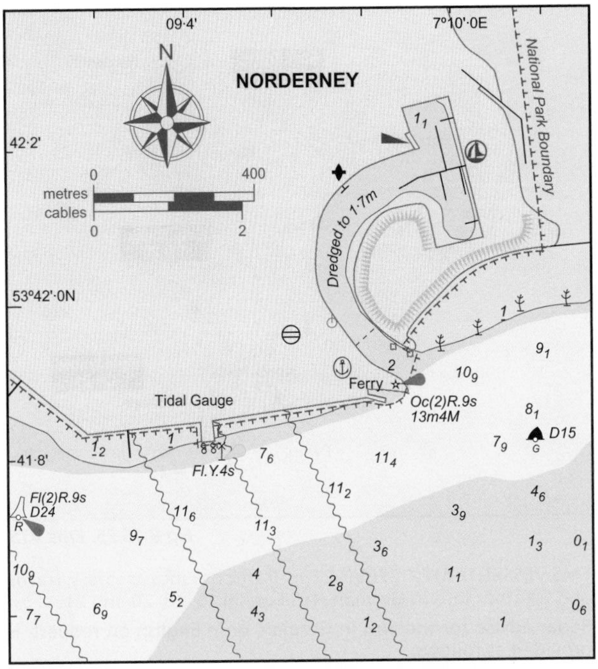

MAINLAND HARBOUR 4·5M SOUTH OF NORDERNEY

NORDDEICH, Niedersachsen, **53°38'·71N 07°08'·88E** (trng wall). AC 1635. HW –0030 on Dover (UT); See Norderney. Appr as for Norderney, then via buoyed/lit Busetief to two training walls (Lat/Long as above) which cover at HW and are marked by ⫯s. The chan is 100m wide, 2·0m deep and 1·2M long. Much ferry activity can make things interesting at LW. Very good shelter in hbr, divided by central mole. Yacht pontoons and ferry in W hbr; a few yacht berths in Osthafen; FVs in E hbr. Lts as in 9.15.4. HM VHF Ch 17, ☎(04931) 81317; ⊖ ☎(04931) 8435; YC ☎3560; Facilities: ☎2721, BSH agent (5t). **Town** Ⓑ Dr, . Ferries: Juist and Norderney.

ISLAND HARBOUR 6M WEST OF NORDERNEY

JUIST, Niedersachsen, **53°39'·66N 06°59'83E**. AC 3631; D90. HW –0105 on Dover (UT); HW –0035 and +0·1 on Helgoland; or use differences Memmert (see Norderney). Off the W end of Juist the unmarked, shallow and twisting Haaksgat leads into Juister Balje which then runs E for about 6M to Juist hbr.

The safer approach is via Norderney passing the E tip of Juist and into Memmert and Juister Wattfahrwasseren. Enter hbr via a narrow chan running N into the centre of the S side of island, marked by a red post, Oc (2) R 9s, and by ECM perches to port.

Conspic marks are: West bn, on Haakdünen at W end of island, Juist water twr in centre and East bn, 1M from E end of island. Aero lt Fl 5s at the airfield, see 9.15.4.

There is a small, drying yacht hbr, or yachts can berth in 0.6m alongside quay in ferry hbr. There are extensive No ⚓ areas and underwater power cables, but many drying moorings close E of the hbr. HM ☎(04935) 724; ⊖ ☎1321. Facilities: ; villages of Ostdorf, Westdorf and Loog in centre of island have limited facilities. Ferry to Norddeich.

MAINLAND HARBOUR 14M SOUTH EAST OF BORKUM

GREETSIEL, Niedersachsen, **53°32'·86N 07°02'·07E**. AC 1635, 3631; D 89. HW –0400 on Dover (UT) –0010 on Helgoland; ML 2·6m. WPT 53°41'·91N 06°36'·17E (Osterems SWM buoy, Iso 4s) 118°/1·2M to chan buoys (O1/O2) passing between Memmert and Borkum. Follow the Osterems chan for 17.5M to O30/L2 buoy; here turn ENE into the Ley chan for 2½M to L8 buoy. Turn 90° stbd to track 165°/7ca, between trng walls to lock which opens HW -4 to +3 (from 0500 to 2200) call *Leysiel Lock* on Ch 17. Thence 4M chan in 3m depths to Greetsiel, FV hbr and on marina pontoons (2m). HM ☎(04926) 990371; ⊖ ☎(04931) 2764. **Village** YC .

9.15.24 BORKUM

EAST FRISIAN ISLANDS
Niedersachsen **53°33'·48N 06°45'·00E**

CHARTS AC 1635, 3631; Imray C26; D 90; DYC 1812.5; ANWB A

TIDES –0105 Dover; ML 1·4; Duration 0610

Standard Port HELGOLAND (⟵)

Times				Height (metres)			
High Water		Low Water		MHWS	MHWN	MLWN	MLWS
0200	0700	0200	0800	3·1	2·7	0·8	0·4
1400	1900	1400	2000				
Differences BORKUM (FISCHERBALJE)							
–0048	–0052	–0124	–0105	0·0	+0·1	0·0	0·0

SHELTER Good except in strong winds from S; access H24. Yacht Marina is reported to be silting up, so berth in Burkana Hafen on quays 4 and 5 opposite the ent in 4·1m. Yachts are not allowed to use the ferry berth (*Fährhafen*). The YC in the Schutzhafen has no Ⓥ.

NAVIGATION From the N, WPT 53°38'·96N 06°27'·10E (Riffgat

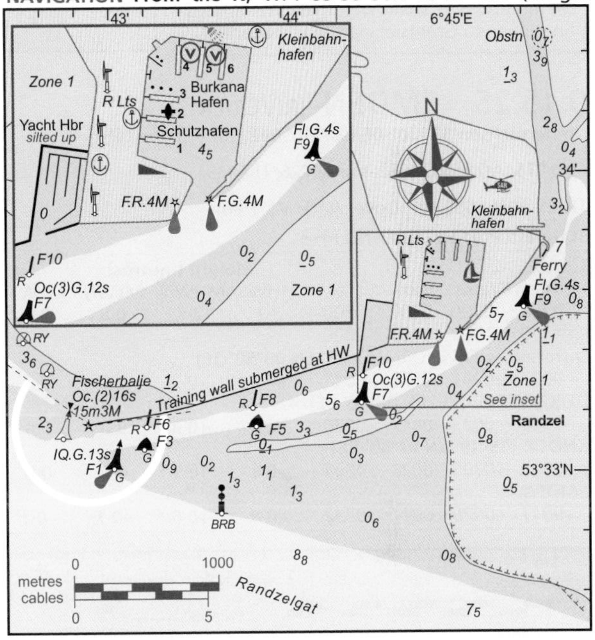

SWM buoy, Iso 8s) about 122°/11M to Fischerbalje lt. See also N Netherlands TSS. **From the W** appr via the Westerems SWM buoy, Iso 4s, Racon (T) (53°36'·93N 06°19'·39E) to join Riffgat which is covered by the 127° W sector of Campen lt, Dir F. (Hubertgat is still marked (unlit R/W buoys H1-H5) least depths around 9m but prone to silting.) Many groynes extend 400m off W end of Borkum. Make for Fischerbalje lt (see 9.15.4 for sectors) at the end of the trng wall which covers at HW. Use the dredged ferry channel and do not cut corners. Beware strong SW'lies and strong currents across the Fischerbalje chan (F1–9 buoys/partly lit). Speed limit in hbrs is 5kn.

LIGHTS AND MARKS Daymarks all WNW of hbr: Water twr, Grosser lt ho (brown brick twr) and disused Kleiner lt ho, R twr with W bands. 3 wind turbines and café immed. NNE of Yacht Hbr ent.

COMMUNICATIONS (Code 4922) Police 91860; Customs 2287; British Consul (030) 204570; Ⓗ 813; Port HM 912828, *Borkum Port* VHF Ch 14 (In season: Mon-Fri 0700-2200; Sat 0800-2100; Sun 0700-2000); *Burkana Hafen* VHF Ch 17.

FACILITIES WSVB Burkana Hafen ☎7877, 80 (max 12m LOA) €1·20+ €2·50 pp/day (via ☎7877).
Yacht Hbr (currently not recommended due to silting) ☎7773, 50 + 200 Ⓥ €1·20.
Town (7km WNW) Ⓑ. Ferry to Emden (& Bremen). S part of island is a Nature Reserve.

RIVER EMS

(AC 3631, 3632) The Ems forms the Dutch-German border and is a major waterway leading to Eemshaven, Delfzijl, Emden, Leer and Papenburg. Approach via Hubertgat or Westerems, which meet W of Borkum; the former is unlit and sparsely buoyed. ▶*Both can be dangerous with a strong W/NW wind against the ebb. The flood begins at HW Helgoland +0530, and the ebb at HW −0030, sp rates 1·5kn.*◀

Close SW of Borkum the chan divides: Randzel Gat to the NE side and Alte Ems parallel to it on the SW side – as far as Eemshaven on the S bank; here the stream runs 2-3kn. Keep in Ostfriesisches Gatje, the main chan, for Delfzijl and beyond.

Osterems is the unlit E branch of the Ems estuary, passing between Borkum and Memmert. It is shallower than Westerems and leads to Greetsiel via the Ley channel.

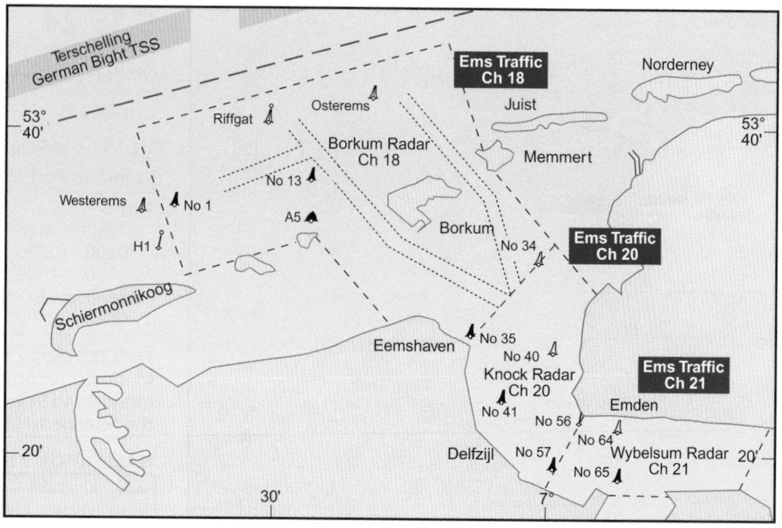

Fig 9.15.25. Ems VTS

9.15.25 EMDEN (RIVER EMS)

Niedersachsen **53°20'·06N 07°10'·69E** Hbr ent

CHARTS AC 3631, 3632; Imray C26; D 90, 91

TIDES HW +0022 on Dover (UT); ML 1·9m

Standard Port HELGOLAND (⟵)

Times				Height (metres)			
High Water		Low Water		MHWS	MHWN	MLWN	MLWS
0200	0700	0200	0800	3·1	2·7	0·8	0·4
1400	1900	1400	2000				
Differences EMSHÖRN (53°29'·6N 06°50'·5E)							
−0037	−0041	−0108	−0047	+0·2	+0·3	0·0	0·0
DUKEGAT (53°26'·0N 06°56'·0E)							
−0019	−0023	−0047	−0028	+0·3	+0·4	0·0	0·0
KNOCK (53°19'·6N 07°00'·8E)							
+0018	+0005	−0028	+0004	+0·6	+0·7	0·0	0·0
EMDEN							
+0041	*+0028*	*−0011*	*+0022*	*+0·8*	*+0·8*	*−0·1*	*−0·1*

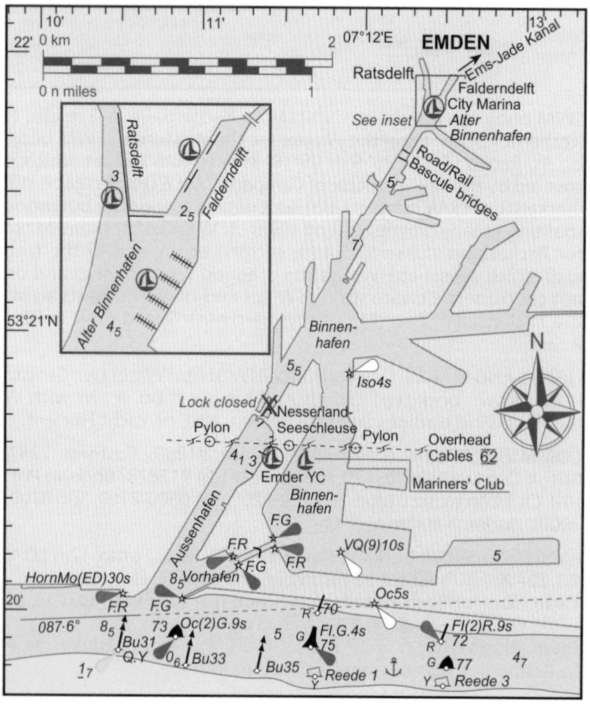

EMS VESSEL TRAFFIC SERVICE *Ems Traffic* broadcasts safety, traffic and weather info in German H+50 on Ch 15, 18, 20 and 21.

Radar advice for the Ems in German, or in English on request, is provided as follows:

Borkum Radar	Ch 18	Buoys 1–35;
Knock Radar	Ch 20	Buoys 35–57;
Wybelsum Radar	Ch 21	Buoy 57–Emden hbr.

SHELTER Good, although the Emder YC marina may be exposed to SSW winds.

NAVIGATION See Borkum and Delfzijl for outer approaches via well buoyed/lit R Ems to No 53 buoy 53°19'·34N 07°01'·15E, south abeam Knock lt ho. Thence 6M east to the hbr ent via Emder Fahrwasser (dredged 8·6m) with drying banks and training walls close outboard of chan buoys. Beware of fast catamaran ferries (*Hochgeschwindigkeitsfahrzeuge*).

Nesserland lock is closed due to major works. Enter Binnenhafen via *Borsummer Schleuse* ☎897265 (Ch 13) which opens on request for small craft between 0800-1230 and 1330-1730.

LIGHTS AND MARKS Fahrwasser outer ldg lts 075°, both Oc (2) 12s 16/28m 12M (at Logum, off chartlet). Inner ldg lts 088°, both Oc 5s 14/30m 12M, lead to hbr ent, marked by FR and FG lts and between Nos 71 and 73 buoys. HT cables on 3 conspic pylons (100m) cross the Außenhafen and Binnenhafen.

COMMUNICATIONS (Code 04921) Police 110; Fire/Ambulance 112; Customs 9279-0; Brit Consul (030) 204570; HM 897260 (H24) Emden Hbr and Locks VHF Ch 13 (H24); Nesserlander lock ☎897270; Ems VTS see above; Tourist Info 97400; no VHF at individual marinas.

FACILITIES Berthing options from seaward:

Emder YC marina (3m) in the Außenhafen, just before Nesserland sealock. HM ☎0175 7528918, 12 ⓥ (May–Oct)€0·90, 3 pontoons, most facilities.

Through the large Vorhafen sealock to:

Mariners Club, small marina ☎0175 7112027, €0·51; no .

City Marina, access via two road/rail bridges opening 0650, 0855, 0955, 1140, 1335, 1555, 1735, 1820 and 2140LT on request. For opening sound M (– –). Marina, ☎8907211 or mob 0160 3624744, comprises Alter Binnenhafen (4·5m) Falderndelft (3m) Ratsdelft (3m); all near the city centre. The first two are best for yachts <12m. €0·80, barge, for location in the hbr call ☎0171 324 4337. **City** All amenities. Ferry to Borkum.

CANALS The Ems-Jade canal, 39M to Wilhelmshaven, is usable by yachts with lowering masts and max draft 1·7m. Access at Emden via the Falderndelft. Min bridge clearance 3·75m. It has 6 locks. Speed limit 4kn.

Netherlands & Belgium

Delfzijl to Nieuwpoort

9.16.1	Contents	701
9.16.2	Area map. 9.16.2A Staande Mastroute (Distance table p 742)	702
9.16.3	Tidal stream chartlets	704
9.16.4	Lights, buoys and waypoints	706
9.16.5	Passage information Charts, PSSA and TSS – 710 • Crossing the North Sea to the UK – 710 • The West Frisian Islands – 713 • Delfzijl to Ameland – 713 • Terschelling to Texel and Den Helder – 714 • Den Helder to Scheveningen – 724 • Hoek van Holland to the Westerschelde – 724 • Hoek van Holland to the South East UK – 728 • The Belgian Coast – 740 • Crossing the North Sea from Belgium – 746	710
9.16.6	Special notes for the Netherlands	710
9.16.7	TSS off the Northern Netherlands	711
9.16.8	Delfzijl, Termunterzijl • Eemshaven	712
9.16.9	Lauwersoog, Zoutkamp • Oostmahorn • Schiermonnikoog • Nes (Ameland)	712
9.16.10	Het Vlie (Zeegat van Terschelling)	714
9.16.11	West Terschelling	715
9.16.12	Vlieland	715
9.16.13	Harlingen	716
9.16.14	Oudeschild	716
9.16.15	Den Helder	717
9.16.16	IJsselmeer	718
9.16.17	IJmuiden	720
9.16.18	Noordzeekanaal	721
9.16.19	Amsterdam	721
9.16.20	Scheveningen	723
9.16.21	TSS and VTS off South Netherlands and Belgium	724
9.16.22	Hoek van Holland tides and Maas TSS	725
9.16.23	Hoek van Holland and Nieuwe Waterweg VTS	729
9.16.24	Rotterdam	730
9.16.25	Haringvliet (Stellendam and Hellevoetsluis)	731
9.16.26	Roompotsluis (Oosterschelde)	732
9.16.27	Westerschelde Ellewoutsdijk • Hoedekenskerke • Hansweert • Walsoorden • Paal • Doel • Lillo	733
9.16.28	Vlissingen, tide tables/curves	734
9.16.29	Breskens	739
9.16.30	Terneuzen	739
9.16.31	Special notes for Belgium	740
9.16.32	Antwerpen	740
9.16.33	Zeebrugge, tide tables/curves Brugge	741
	Area distance table	742
9.16.34	Blankenberge	746
9.16.35	Oostende	746
9.16.36	Nieuwpoort	748

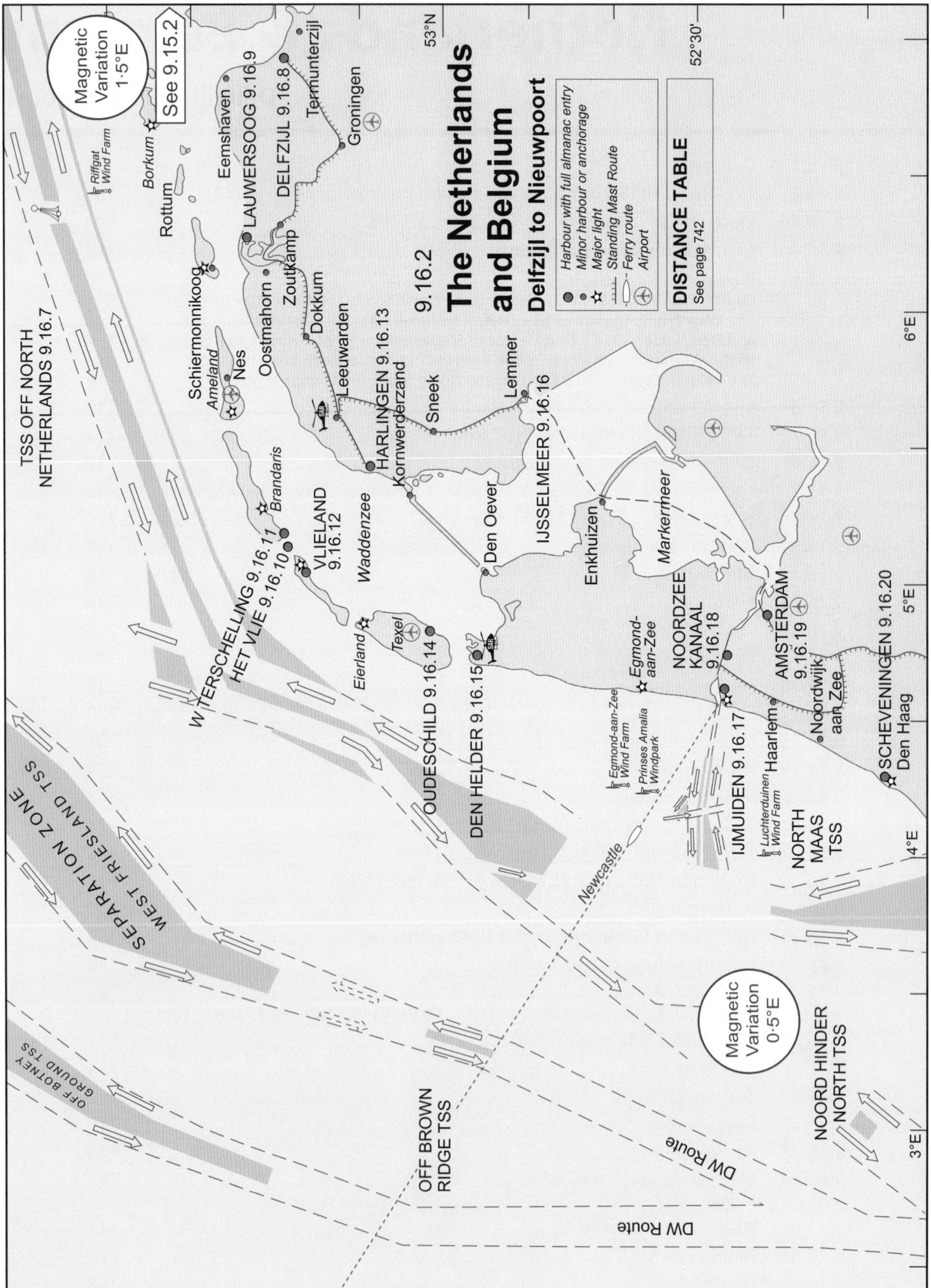
9.16.2
The Netherlands and Belgium
Delfzijl to Nieuwpoort
Harbour with full almanac entry
Minor harbour or anchorage
Major light
Standing Mast Route
Ferry route
Airport
DISTANCE TABLE
See page 742
Magnetic Variation 1·5°E
Magnetic Variation 0·5°E
See 9.15.2
53°N
52°30'
3°E
4°E
5°E
6°E
TSS OFF NORTH NETHERLANDS 9.16.7
WEST FRIESLAND TSS
SEPARATION ZONE
OFF BOTNEY GROUND TSS
OFF BROWN RIDGE TSS
NOORD HINDER NORTH TSS
NORTH MAAS TSS
DW Route
DW Route
Newcastle
Riffgat Wind Farm
Borkum
Rottum
Schiermonnikoog
Ameland
Nes
Eemshaven
LAUWERSOOG 9.16.9
DELFZIJL 9.16.8
Termunterzijl
Groningen
Oostmahorn
Zoutkamp
Dokkum
Leeuwarden
HARLINGEN 9.16.13
Kornwerderzand
Sneek
Lemmer
Brandaris
W TERSCHELLING 9.16.11
HET VLIE 9.16.10
VLIELAND 9.16.12
Waddenzee
Texel
Eierland
OUDESCHILD 9.16.14
DEN HELDER 9.16.15
Den Oever
IJSSELMEER 9.16.16
Enkhuizen
Markermeer
Egmond-aan-Zee
Egmond-aan-Zee Wind Farm
Prinses Amalia Windpark
NOORDZEE KANAAL 9.16.18
AMSTERDAM 9.16.19
IJMUIDEN 9.16.17
Haarlem
Noordwijk aan Zee
SCHEVENINGEN 9.16.20
Den Haag
Luchterduinen Wind Farm

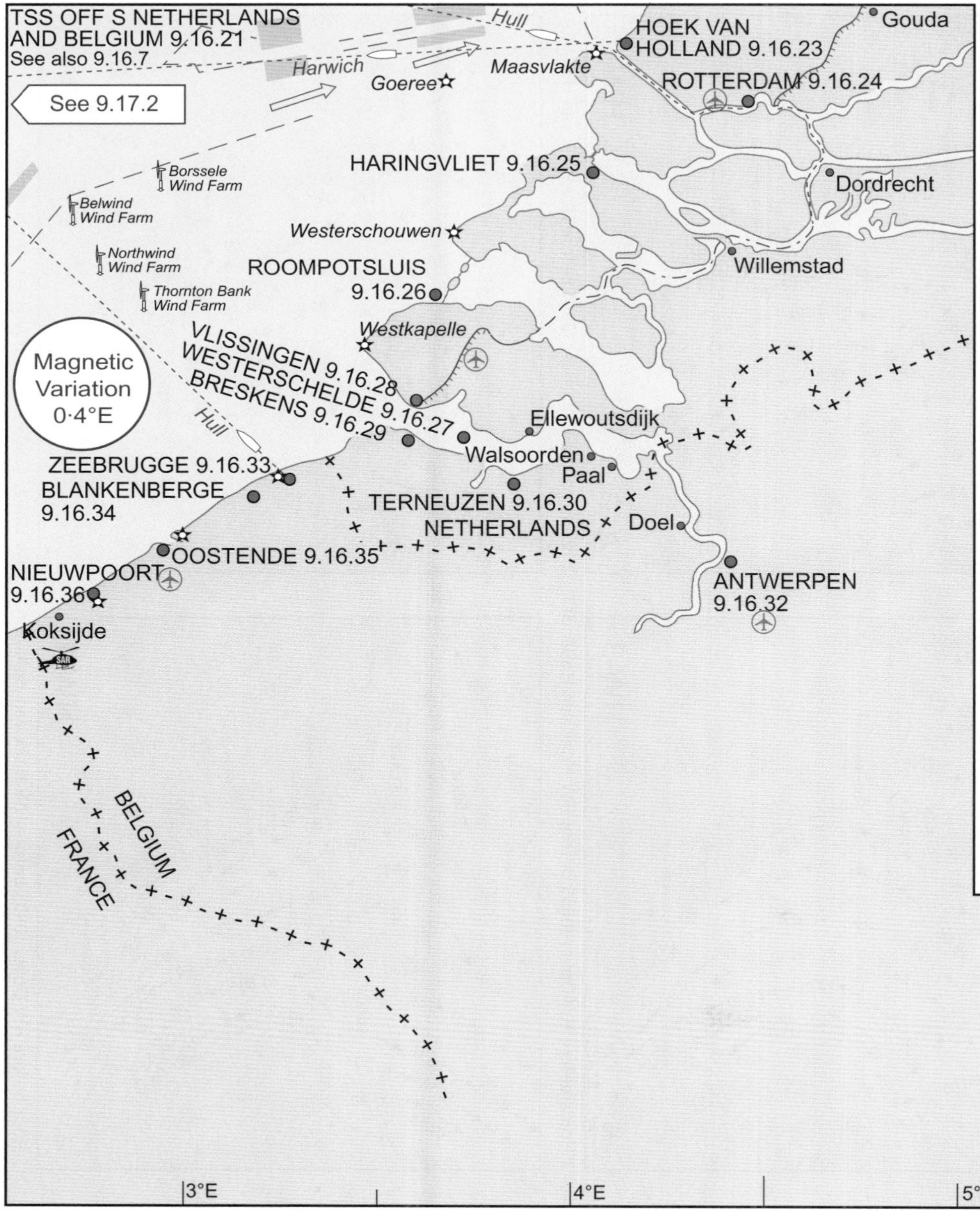

9.16.2A THE STAANDE MASTROUTE

The Standing Mast Route (SMR) which does not require masts to be lowered as there are no fixed bridges, can be a useful means of progressing, especially to windward, through the Dutch inland waterways when conditions at sea make this difficult or impossible. Inland the wind may be one or two Forces less and there is usually insufficient fetch to raise a bad sea. The open sea can always be regained at many points. It is a rewarding route and the added interest of progressing through the Dutch countryside and towns is a special bonus.

Pre-planning. To minimise delays at bridges and locks and to have a fair idea of your next night-stop, buy the special SMR chart (wire-bound booklet) published by ANWB at €19.95; it contains detailed information in Dutch but the gist is clear. Michelin road maps give a broader 1: 200,000 perspective. The website: www.varendoejesamen.nl also provides a useful overview and up-to-date information regarding the route.

For the IJsselmeer see ANWB Wateralmanak, Vols 1 and 2 in Dutch.

An International Certificate of Competence (ICC) is required endorsed for Inland Waters, ie CEVNI.

The Route falls broadly into a northern and a southern part, divided by the IJsselmeer/Markermeer. From Delfzijl the Eemskanaal leads to Groningen, thence via the Reitdiep (river) to Zoutkamp and across the Lauwersmeer. Leave via Dokkumer Ee to Leeuwarden where the sea can be regained at Harlingen. If not, continue S past Sneek to enter the IJsselmeer at Lemmer. Cross via Enkhuizen to Amsterdam.

Getting through Amsterdam is complicated by severe restrictions on when bridges may open (due to heavy road/rail traffic). One option is a night convoy through the centre and suburbs. From Het IJ (9.16.19) enter the Westerkanaal near IJ2 buoy. Head SSW past Schiphol airport, Gouda and Rotterdam, thence to Dordrecht.

A simpler daytime option is to detour west via the Noordzeekanaal, turn south at Zijkanaal C through Haarlem and/or Leiden to resume the main route north of Gouda; thence via Rotterdam to Dordrecht.

S of Dordrecht enter Hollandsdiep at which point the SMR has virtually ended. Continue past Willemstad into Volkerak, thence across the Oosterschelde into Veerse Meer and down the Walcheren canal to Vlissingen.

9.16.3 AREA 16 TIDAL STREAMS

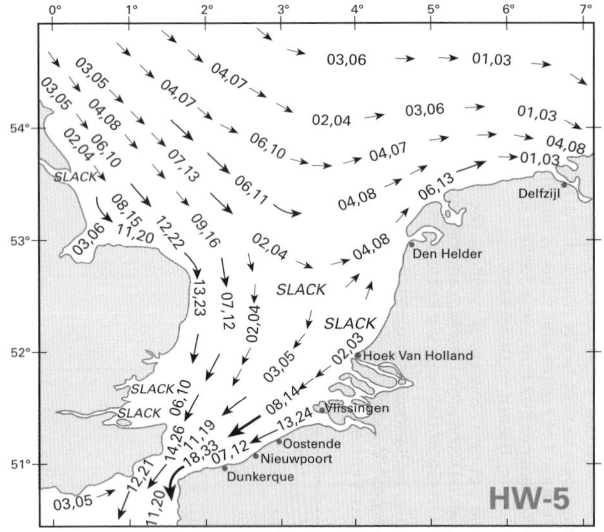

5 Hours before HW Dover (0420 after HW Hoek van Holland)

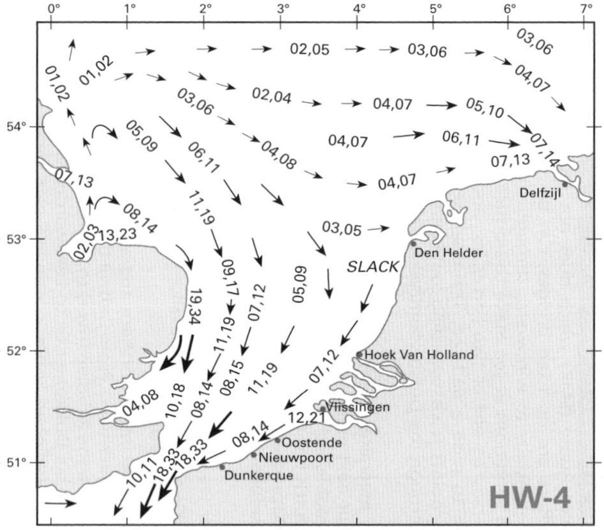

4 Hours before HW Dover (0520 after HW Hoek van Holland)

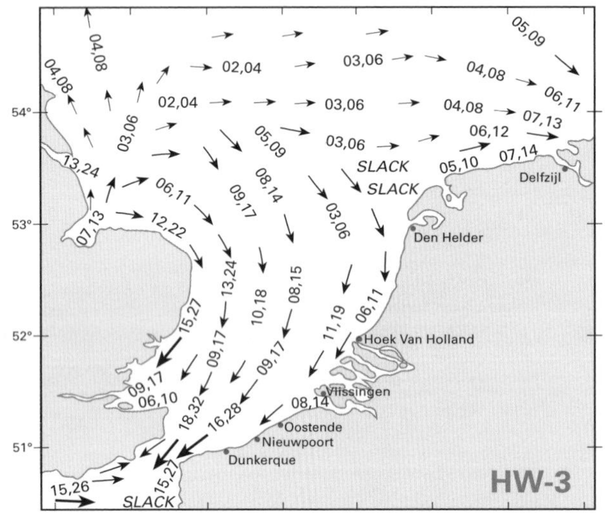

3 Hours before HW Dover (0605 before HW Hoek van Holland)

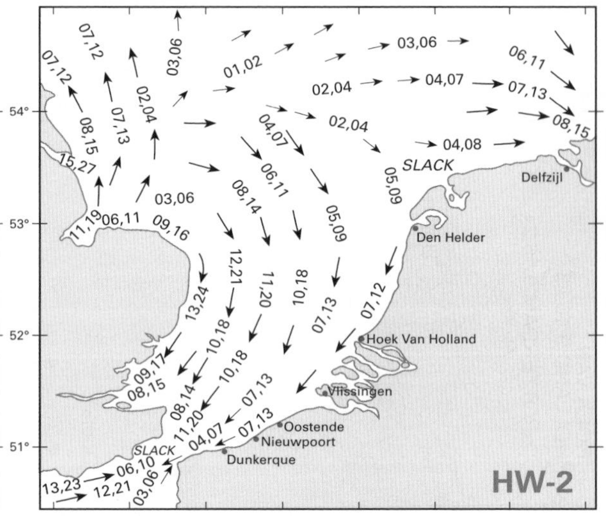

2 Hours before HW Dover (0505 before HW Hoek van Holland)

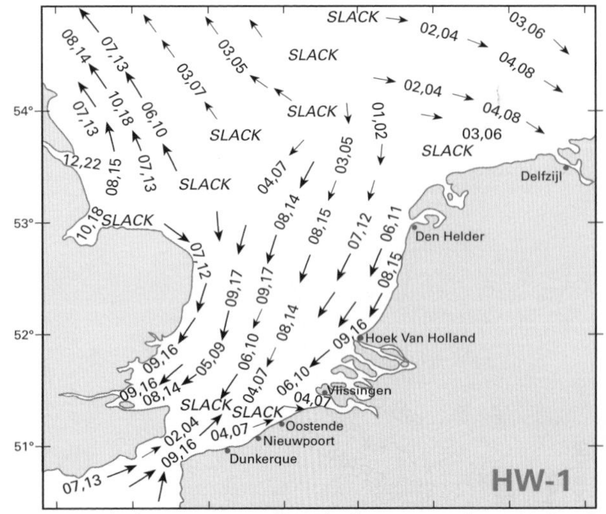

1 Hour before HW Dover (0405 before HW Hoek van Holland)

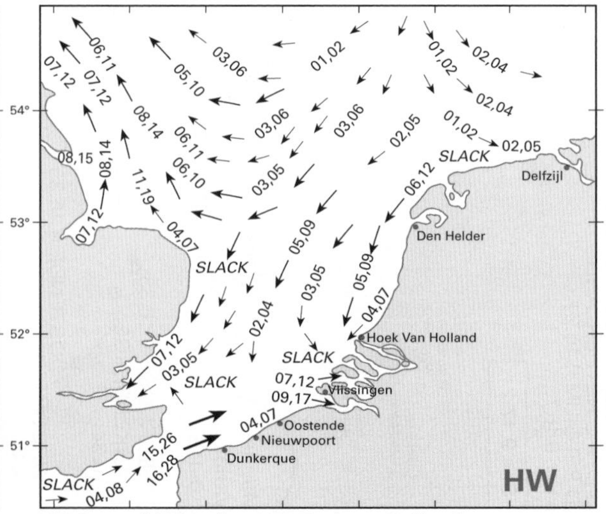

HW Dover (0305 before HW Hoek van Holland)

South-westward 9.17.3 North-westward 9.4.3 North-eastward 9.15.3

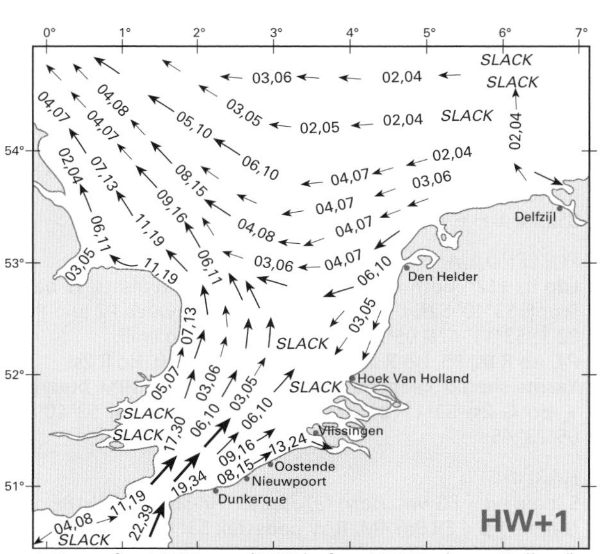

1 Hour after HW Dover (0205 before HW Hoek van Holland)

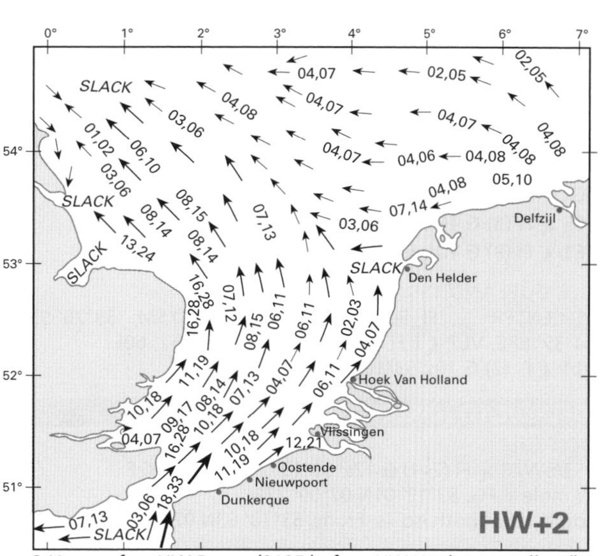

2 Hours after HW Dover (0105 before HW Hoek van Holland)

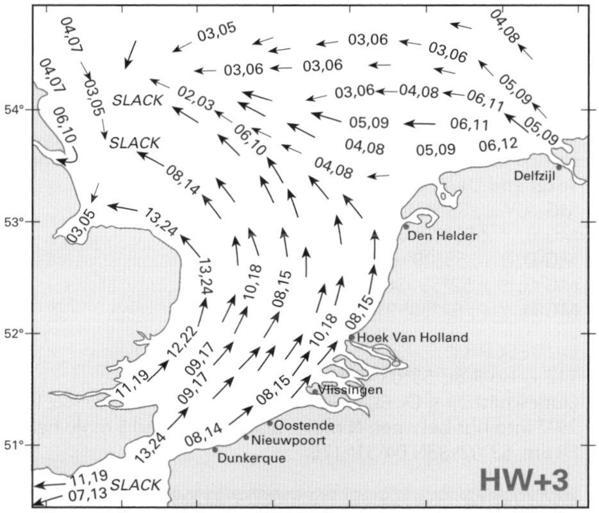

3 Hours after HW Dover (0005 after HW Hoek van Holland)

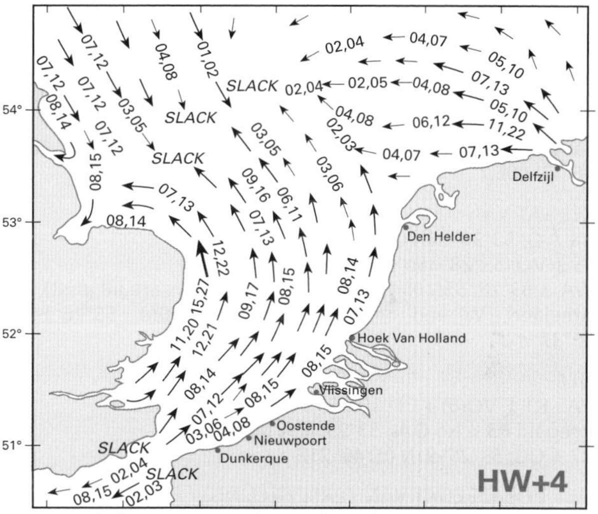

4 Hours after HW Dover (0055 after HW Hoek van Holland)

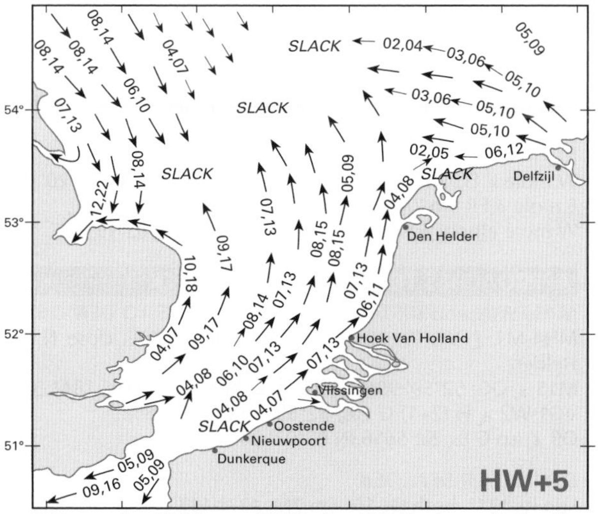

5 Hours after HW Dover (0155 after HW Hoek van Holland)

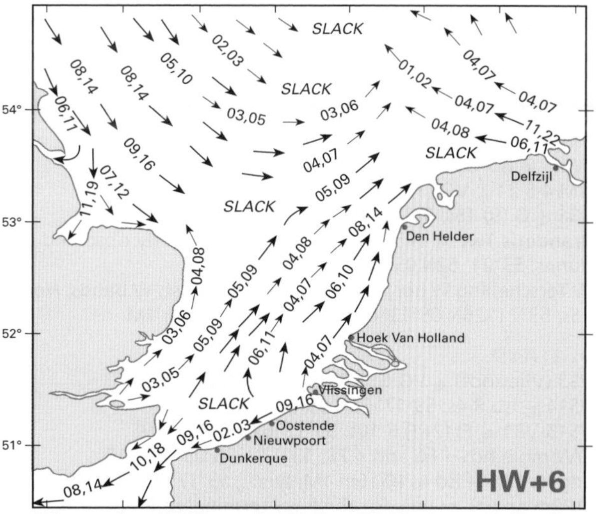

6 Hours after HW Dover (0255 after HW Hoek van Holland)

9.16.4 LIGHTS, BUOYS AND WAYPOINTS

Bold print = light with a nominal range of 15M or more. CAPITALS = place or feature. *CAPITAL ITALICS* = light-vessel, light float or Lanby. *Italics* = Fog signal. ***Bold italics*** = Racon. Many marks/buoys are fitted with AIS (MMSI No); see relevant charts.

TSS OFF NORTHERN NETHERLANDS

TERSCHELLING-GERMAN BIGHT TSS

TG1/Ems IQ G 13s; 53°43'·33N 06°22'·24E.
TE5 Fl (3) G 10s; 53°37'·79N 05°53'·69E.
TE1 Fl (3) G 10s; 53°29'·58N 05°11'·31E.

OFF VLIELAND TSS

VL-CENTER Fl 5s 12M; ***Racon C, 12–15M***; 53°26'·93N 04°39'·88E. VL7 L Fl G 10s; 53°26'·40N 04°57'·60E.
VL1 Fl (2) G 10s; 53°10'·96N 04°35'·31E.

DELFZIJL TO HARLINGEN

DELFZIJL

PS3/BW26 Fl (2+1) G 12s; 53°19'·25N 07°00'·32E.
W mole FG; 53°19'·01N 07°00'·27E.
Ldg lts 203° both Iso 4s. Front, 53°18'·63N 07°00'·17E.

SCHIERMONNIKOOG AND LAUWERSOOG

WG (Westgat) Iso 8s; ***Racon N***; 53°31'·96N 06°01'·84E .
WRG Q; 53°32'·87N 06°03'·24E.AM VQ; 53°30'·95N 05°44'·72E.
Schiermonnikoog ☆ Fl (4) 20s 43m **28M**; dark R ○ twr. Same twr: F WR 29m **W15M,** R12M; 210°-W-221°-R-230°. 53°29'·20N 06°08'·79E.
Lauwersoog W mole FG; *Horn (2) 30s;* 53°24'·68N 06°12'·00E.

ZEEGAT VAN AMELAND

BR Q; 53°30'·66N 05°33'·52E.
TS VQ; 53°28'·15N 05°21'·53E.
WA 53°28'·35N 05°28'·64E. (Westgat buoys are all unlit)
Ameland, W end ☆ Fl (3) 15s 57m **30M**; 53°26'·89N 05°37'·42E.

NES

VA2-R1 VQ(6) + L Fl 10s; 53°25'·71N 05°45'·88E.
Reegeul R3 Iso G 4s; 53°25'·80N 05°45'·93E.
R7 QG; 53°25'·91N 05°46'·21E.

HET VLIE (ZEEGAT VAN TERSCHELLING)

ZS (Zuider Stortemelk) Iso 4s; ***Racon T***; 53°18'·28N 04°56'·23E.
ZS1 VQ G; 53°18'·58N 04°57'·54E.
ZS3 QG; 53° 19'·29N 04° 59'·49E
ZS5 L Fl G 8s; 53°18'·55N 05°00'·83E.
ZS11-VS2 Q (9) 15s; 53°18'·63N 05°05'·94E.

NOORD MEEP/SLENK TO WEST TERSCHELLING

WM3 Iso G 2s; 53°17'·45N 05°12'·28E.
NM 4-S 21 VQ (3) 5s; 53°19'·02N 05°15'·47E.
SG1 Q (9) 15s; 53°20'·44N 05°11'·70E.
Brandaris Twr ☆ Fl 5s 54m **29M**; Y □ twr partly obscured by dunes; 53°21'·62N 05°12'·86E.
W Terschelling W hbr mole FR 5m 5M; R post, W bands; *Horn 15s;* 53°21'·26N 05°13'·09E. E pier hd FG 4m 4M.

VLIELAND

VS3 (Vliesloot) VQ G; 53°18'·27N 05°06'·25E.
VS14 Iso R 4s; 53°17'·58N 05°05'62E.
VS16-VB1 Fl (2+1) R 10s; 53°17'·62N 05°05'·19E.
E/W mole hds FG and FR; 53°17'·68N 05°05'·51E.
Ldg lts 282° Iso 4s 10/16m 1M, synch; 53°17'·75N 05°04'·47W (100m apart); mainly for the ferry terminal at E Vlieland.
E Vlieland (Vuurduin) ☆ Iso 4s 54m **20M**; 53°17'·75N 05°03'·49E.

APPROACHES TO HARLINGEN (selected marks):

VLIESTROOM buoys are frequently moved.
VL1 QG; 53°18'·99N 05°08'·82E. VL 2 QR; 53°19'·40N 05°09'·19E.
VL 11 Iso G 8s; 53°16'·42N 05°09'·70E.

BLAUWE SLENK

BS1-IN2 VQ (3) 5s; 53°15'·41N 05°09'·41E.
BS13 QG; 53°13'·31N 05°17'·13E. BS19 VQ G; 53°11'·90N 05°18'·28E.
BS23 L Fl G 8s; 53°11'·42N 05°19'·60E.

POLLENDAM

Ldg lts 112°, both Iso 6s 8/19m 13M (H24); B masts, W bands. Front, 53°10'·52N 05°24'·19E. Use only between P2 and P6.
P2 ; 53°11'·47N 05°20'·38E on the training wall.
P4, Iso R 8s; P6, Iso R 4s; P8, Iso R 8s; and P10, Iso R 2s.
Yachts should keep outboard of P1 thru 7 SHM buoys. P1 Iso G 2s; 53°11'·39N 05°20'·32E. P7 VQ G; 53°10'·68N 05°23'·45E.

HARLINGEN

S mole hd FG 9m; *Horn (3) 30s;* 53°10'·56N 05°24'·18E.
N mole hd FR 9m 4M; R/W pedestal; 53°10'·59N 05°24'·32E.

TEXEL AND THE WADDENZEE

TEXEL (from NW and W)

Eierland ☆ Fl (2) 10s 52m **29M**; R ○ twr; 53°10'·93N 04°51'·31E.
TX Q(9) 15s; 53°06'·81N 04°41'·19E

MOLENGAT (from the N)

Note: Positions/depths unreliable, see: 712, Pl Terschelling to Texel and Den Helder.
MG-A,Y ; 53°02'·54N 04°41'·88E.
MG-B, Y ; 53°02'·00N 04°42'·11E
MG-D, Y ; 53°00'·90N 04°42'·04E;
MG-G, Y ; 52°59'·30N 04°42'·56E;
MG-H, Y ; 52°58'·91N 04°43'·10E.

OUDESCHILD

T12 Iso R 8s; 53°02'·23N 04°51'·52E.
Oudeschild Dir Oc 6s; intens 291°; 53°02'·40N 04°50'·94E; leads 291° into hbr between N mole head FG 6m; and S mole head FR 6m; 53°02'·33N 04°51'·17E.

APPROACHES TO KORNWERDERZAND SEALOCK

DOOVE BALG (From Texelstroom eastward)

T23 VQ G; 53°03'·60N 04°55'·85E, 066°/3M from Oudeschild.
T29 53°03'·25N 05°00'·05E.
D1 Iso G 4s; 53°02'·18N 05°03'·42E.
D21 Iso G 8s; 53°03'·55N 05°15'·71E.
BO2-WG1 Q (6) + L Fl 10s; 53°05'·00N 05°17'·91E.

KORNWERDERZAND SEALOCK

W mole FG 9m 7M; *Horn Mo(N) 30s;* 53°04'·78N 05°20'·03E.
E mole FR 9m 7M; 53°04'·70N 05°20'·08E.
W mole elbow Iso G 6s 6m 7M; 53°04'·61N 05°19'·90E.

APPROACHES TO DEN OEVER SEALOCK

MALZWIN and VISJAGERSGAATJE CHANS TO DEN OEVER

MH4-M1 VQ (9) 10s; 52°58'·14N 04°47'·49E, close N Den Helder.
M15 QG; 52°59'·39N 04°55'·48E (hence use DYC 1811.3).
VG1-W2 Fl (2+1) G 10s; 52°59'·00N 04°56'·85E.
O9 Iso G 8s; 52°56'·63N 05°02'·38E.

DEN OEVER SEALOCK

Ldg lts 131°, both Oc 10s 6m 7M; 127°-137°. Front, 52°56'·32N 05°02'·98E. Rear, 280m from front.

E end of swing bridge, Iso WRG 5s 14m 10/7M; 226°-G-231°-W-235°-R-290°-G-327°-W-335°-R-345°; 52°56'·12N 05°02'·52E.

ZEEGAT VAN TEXEL AND DEN HELDER

OFFSHORE MARKS W and SW OF DEN HELDER

NH (Noorderhaaks) VQ; 53°00'·24N 04°35'·37E.
MR Q (9) 15s; 52°56'·77N 04°33'·82E.
ZH (Zuiderhaaks) VQ (6) + L Fl 10s; 52°54'·65N 04°34'·72E.
Vinca G wreck Q (9) 15s; ***Racon D***; 52°45'·93N 04°12'·31E.

SCHULPENGAT (from the SSW)

Schulpengat Dir ☆ 026·5°, Dir WRG, Al WR, Al WG, **W22M R/G18M**, church spire; 025.1°–FG–025.6°–AlWG–026.3°–FW–026.7°–Al WR–027.4°–F R–027.9°; shown H24.
Schilbolsnol F WRG 27m W8-3M, R8M, G5M; 333°-W-026°-G-033°-W (Ldg sector for Schulpengat)- 038°-R-070°; Obsc 070°-333°; Post; 53°00'·50N 04°45'·70E (on Texel).
SG Mo (A) 8s; ***Racon Z***; 52°52'·90N 04°37'·90E.
S1 Iso G 4s; 52°53'·53N 04°38'·82E.
S7 QG; 52°56'·25N 04°40'·92E. S6A QR; 52°56'·52N 04°40'·51E.
S10 Iso R 8s; 52°57'·59N 04°41'·57E. S14-MG17, see Molengat.
S11 Iso G 8s; 52°57'·55N 04°43'·25E.
Huisduinen F WR 26m W14M, R11M; 070°-W-113°-R-158°-W-208°; □ twr; 52°57'·14N 04°43'·30E (abeam S10 PHM buoy).
Kijkduin ☆ Fl (4) 20s 56m **30M**; vis 360°, except where obsc'd by dunes on Texel; brown twr; 52°57'·33N 04°43'·58E (mainland).

MARSDIEP and DEN HELDER

T1 Fl (3) G 10s; 52°57'·99N 04°44'·62E.
T3 Iso G 8s; 52°58'·07N 04°46'·42E.
Den Helder ldg lts 191°, both Oc G 5s 16/25m 3M, synch. Front, vis 183·5°-198·5°; B ▽ on bldg; 52°57'·37N 04°47'·08E.
Marinehaven, W bkwtr head QG 11m 8M; *Horn 20s;* 52°57'·95N 04°47'·07E (Harssens Island).
W side, Fl G 5s 9m 4M (H24); 180°-067°; 52°57'·78N 04°47'·08E.
Yacht hbr (KMYC) ent FR & FG; 165m SW of Fl G 5s, above.
E side, MH6 Iso R 4s; 52°57'·99N 04°47'·41E.
Ent E side, QR 9m 4M (H24); 52°57'·77N 04°47'·37E.

DEN HELDER TO AMSTERDAM

Zanddijk Grote Kaap Oc WRG 10s 30m 8M; 041°-G-088°-W-094°-R-120°; brown twr; 52°52'·86N 04°42'·88E.
Petten VQ (9) 10s; 52°47'·33N 04°36'·78E (Power stn outfall).
Egmond-aan-Zee ☆ Iso WR 10s 36m **W18M**, R14M; 010°-W-175°-R-188°; W ○ twr; 52°36'·99N 04°37'·16E.

IJMUIDEN

Baloeran Q (9) 15s; 52°29'·21N 04°32'·00E.
IJmuiden Mo (A) 8s; ***Racon Y, 10M***; 52°28'·45N 04°23'·92E.
Ldg lts 100·5° (FW 5M by day; 090·5°-110·5°). **Front** ☆ F WR 30m **W16M**, R13M; 050°-W-122°-R-145°-W-160°; (Tidal and traffic sigs); dark R ○ twrs; 52°27'·70N 04°34'·47E. **Rear** ☆ Fl 5s 52m **29M**; 019°-199° (FW 5M by day; 090·5°-110·5°); 560m from front.
S bkwtr hd FG 14m 10M (in fog Fl 3s); W twr, G bands; 52°27'·82N 04°31'·93E.
N bkwtr hd FR 15m 10M; 52°28'·05N 04°32'·55E.
IJM1 Iso G 4s; 52°27'·75N 04°33'·59E.
S outer chan Iso G 6s, 52°27'·75N 04°33'·81E. Iso R 6s, 52°27'·84N 04°34'·39E (Forteiland). Kleine Sluis 52°27'·84N 04°35'·43E.

AMSTERDAM

IJ8 Iso R 8s (for Sixhaven marina); 52°22'·86N 04°54'·37E.
Oranjesluizen, N lock 52°22'·93N 04°57'·60E (for IJsselmeer).

AMSTERDAM TO ROTTERDAM

Noordwijk-aan-Zee ☆ Oc (3) 20s 32m **18M**; W□twr; 52°14'·88N 04°26'·02E.

SCHEVENINGEN

Lighthouse ☆ Fl (2) 10s 48m **29M**; 014°-244°; brown twr; 52°06'·23N 04°16'·13E, 5ca E of hbr ent.
Ldg lts 156°, both Iso 4s 14M, H24; synch; Gy masts. Front 52°05'·99N 04°15'·44E; rear 250m from front. Intens at night.
SCH Iso 4s; 52°07'·76N 04°14'·12E.
KNS Q (9)15s; 52°06'·41N 04°15'·32E.
W mole FG 12m 9M; G twr, W bands; 52°06'·23N 04°15'·16E.
E mole , FR 12m 9M; R twr, W bands; 52°06'·24N 04°15'·37E.
Inner ldg lts 131°: both Iso G 4s synch; Gy posts. Front 52°05'·81N 04°15'·89E. Rear, 34m from front.

NOORD HINDER N & S TSS and JUNCTION

NHR-N L Fl 8s; ***Racon K, 10M***; 52°10'·91N 03°04'·76E.
Noord Hinder Fl (2) 10s; *Horn (2) 30s*; ***Racon T, 12-15M***; 52°00'·10N 02° 51'·11E.
NHR-S Fl Y 10s; 51°49'·53N 02°25'·95E.
NHR-SE Fl G 5s; 51°43'·43N 02°37'·18E.
Birkenfels Q (9) 15s; 51°38'·96N 02°32'·03E.
Twin Fl (3) Y 9s; 51°32'·05N 02°22'·62E.
Garden City Q (9) 15s; 51°29'·12N 02°17'·92E.

APPROACHES TO HOEK VAN HOLLAND

Europlatform Mo (U) 15s; W structure, R bands; helicopter platform; *Horn Mo(U) 30s;* 51°59'·89N 03°16'·46E.
Goeree ☆ Fl (4) 20s 32m **28M**; R/W chequered twr on platform; helicopter platform; *Horn (4) 30s*; ***Racon T, 12-15M***; 51°55'·42N 03°40'·03E.
Maasvlakte ☆ Fl (5) 20s 67m **28M**, H24; 340°-267°; W twr, B bands; 51°58'·20N 04°00'·84E, 1·5M SSW of Maas ent.
Maas Center Iso 4s; ***Racon M, 10M***; 52°00'·92N 03°48'·79E.
MO Mo (A) 8s; 52°01'·10N 03°58'·19E.
MN3 Fl (3) G 10s; 52°07'·04N 04°00'·00E.
MN1 Fl G 5s; 52°02'·23N 04°01'·91E.

HOEK VAN HOLLAND

Maasmond ldg lts 112° (for deep draught vessels): both Iso 4s 30/46m **21M**; 101°-123°, synch; W twr, B bands. **Front**, 51°58'·88N 04°04'·88E (NW end of Splitsingsdam). **Rear**, 0·6M from front.
Indusbank N VQ; 52°02'·89N 04°03'·57E.
MVN VQ; 51°59'·61N 04°00'·23E.
MV Q (9) 15s; 51°58'·40N 03°56'·58E.
Maas 1 L Fl G 5s; 51°59'·35N 04°01'·68E.
Nieuwe Waterweg ldg lts 107°: both Iso R 6s 29/43m **18M**; 099.5°-114.5°; R twr, W bands. Front, 51°58'·55N 04°07'·52E. Rear, 450m from front.
Noorderdam Head FR 25m 10M (In fog Al Fl WR 6s; 278°-255°); R twr, W bands; 51°59'·67N 04°02'·80E.
Nieuwe Zuiderdam FG 25m 10M, 330°-307°; (In fog Al Fl WG 6s); G twr, W bands; 51°59'·14N 04°02'·49E.

ROTTERDAM

Maassluis FG 6m; 51°54'·94N 04°14'·81E; and FR.
Vlaardingen FG; 51°53'·99N 04°20'·95E; and FR.
Spuihaven, W ent FR; 51°53'·98N 04°23'·97E.
Veerhaven, E ent FG; 51°54'·42N 04°28'·75E; and FR.
City marina ent, 51°54'·64N 04°29'·76E.

APPROACHES TO HARINGVLIET

Buitenbank , Iso 4s; 51°51'·16N 03°25'·71E.
Hinder Q (9) 15s; 51°54'·55N 03°55'·42E.
SH VQ (9) 10s; 51°49'·49N 03°45'·79E.
Westhoofd ☆ Fl (3) 15s 55m **30M**; R □ tr; 51°48'·79N 03°51'·85E.
Ooster Q (9) 15s; 51°47'·90N 03°41'·27E.

SLIJKGAT

SG Iso 4s; 51°51'·95N 03°51'·42E.
SG 2 Iso R 4s; 51°51'·71N 03°53'·45E.
SG 5 Iso G 4s; 51°50'·00N 03°55'·56E.
SG 11 Iso G 4s; 51°50'·81N 03°58'·52E.
P1 Iso G 4s; 51°51'·30N 04°01'·12E.
P3 Iso G 8s; 51°51'·12N 04°01'·45E.
P9 Iso G 8s; 51°49'·98N 04°02'·15E.

STELLENDAM
N mole ☆ FG; *Horn (2) 15s;* 51°49'·88N 04°02'·03E.
Buitenhaven ☆ Oc 6s; 51°49'·73N 04°01'·75E.

APPROACHES TO OOSTERSCHELDE

OUTER APPROACHES
Schouwenbank Mo (A) 8s; ***Racon O, 10M***; 51°44'·94N 03°14'·32E.
Middelbank Iso 8s; 51°40'·86N 03°18'·20E.
MW Q (9) 15s; 51°44'·55N 03°24'·04E (Schouwendiep).
MD 3 Fl G 5s; 51°42'·70N 03°26'·98E.
SW Thornton Iso 8s; 51°30'·98N 02°50'·90E.
Rabsbank Iso 4s; 51°38'·25N 03°09'·93E.
Westpit Iso 8s; 51°33'·65N 03°09'·92E.
ZSB VQ (9) 10s; 51°36'·57N 03°15'·62E.
OG1 QG; 51°36'·14N 03°20'·08E.

WESTGAT, OUDE ROOMPOT and ROOMPOTSLUIS
West Schouwen ☆ Fl (2+1)15s 57m **30M**; Gy twr, R diagonals on upper part; 51°42'·52N 03°41'·50E, 5·8M N of Roompotsluis.
OG-WG VQ (9) 10s; 51°37'·18N 03°23'·82E.
WG1 Iso G 8s; 51°38'·00N 03°26'·24E.
WG4 ☆ L Fl R 8s; 51°38'·62N 03°28'·78E.
WG7 Iso G 4s 51°39'·40N 03°32'·67E.
WG-GB (Geul van de Banjaard) 51°39'·72N 03°32'·69E.
OR1 51°39'·15N 03°33'·59E.
OR5 Iso G 8s; 51°38'·71N 03°35'·53E.
OR11 Iso G 4s; 51°36'·98N 03°38'·40E.
OR12 Iso R 4s; 51°37'·27N 03°39'·25E.
OR-R VQ (3) 5s; 51°36'·41N 03°38'·96E.
Roompotsluis ldg lts 073·5°, both Oc G 5s; synch. Front, 51°37'·33N 03°40'·75E. Rear, 280m from front.
N bkwtr ☆ FR 7m; 51°37'·31N 03°40'·09E.

WESTKAPELLE TO VLISSINGEN

OOSTGAT
Ldg lts 149·5°: Front, Noorderhoofd Oc WRG 10s 20m; W13M, R/G10M; 353°-R-008°-G-029°-W-169°; R ○ twr, W band; 51°32'·40N 03°26'·21E, 0·73M from rear (Westkapelle).
Westkapelle ☆, rear, Fl 3s 50m **28M**; obsc'd by land on certain brgs; □ twr, R top; 51°31'·75N 03°26'·83E.
Kaloo Iso 8s; 51°35'·55N 03°23'·24E. Chan is well buoyed/lit.
OG5 Iso G 8s; 51°34'·10N 03°23'·88E.
OG-GR VQ (3) 5s; 51°32'·74N 03°24'·71E.
Molenhoofd ☆ Oc WRG 6s 10m; 311·5°-R-330·5°-W-348·5°-R-008°-G-034·5°-W-036·5°-G-147.5°-W-168.5°-R-198°; W mast R bands; 51°31'·58N 03°26'·05E.
Zoutelande F 22m 12M; 321°-352°; R □ twr; 51°30'·28N 03°28'·41E.
Kaapduinen, ldg lts 130°: both Oc 5s 25/34m 13M; synch; Y □ twrs, R bands. Front, 115°-145°; 51°28'·47N 03°30'·99E. Rear, 107·5°-152·5°; 220m from front.
Fort de Nolle ☆ Oc WRG 9s 11m W6M, R/G4M; 293°-R-309°-W-324·5°-G-336·5°-R-014°-G-064°-R-099·5°-W-110·5°-G-117°-R-130°; W col, R bands; 51°26'·94N 03°33'·12E.
Ldg lts 117°: Front, Leugenaar, Oc R 5s 6m 7M; intens 108°-126°; W&R pile; 51°26'·43N 03°34'·14E.
Rear, Sardijngeul ☆ Oc WR 5s 10m 8M, synch; 245°-R-273°-W-123.5°-R-147°; R △, W bands on R & W mast; 550m from front; 51°26'·30N 03°34'·55E.

OFFSHORE: W HINDER TSS TO SCHEUR CHANNEL

West Hinder ☆ Fl (4) 30s 23m 13M; *Horn Mo (U) 30s*; ***Racon W***; 51°23'·30N 02°26'·27E.
WH Zuid Q (6) + L Fl 15s; 51°22'·78N 02°26'·25E.
OostdyckBk Q; 51°21'·38N 02°31'·12E.
BerguesBk-N Q; 51°19'·95N 02°24'·50E.
Oost-Dyck West Q (9) 15s; 51°17'·15N 02°26'·32E.
Oostdyck radar twr; ☆ Mo (U) 15s 15m 12M on 4 corners; *Horn Mo (U) 30s; **Racon O***. R twr, 3 W bands, with adjacent red twr/helipad; 51°16'·49N 02°26'·85E.
A-N Fl (4) R 20s; 51°23'·45N 02°36'·90E.
AS Fl (3) G 10s; 51°21'·15N 02°36'·92E.
KB2 VQ; 51°21'·04N 02°42'·22E.
KB Q; ***Racon K***; 51°21'·03N 02°42'·83E.
MBN Q; 51°20'·82N 02°46'·29E.
Akkaert-SW Q (9) 15s; 51°22'·28N 02°46'·34E.
VG Q ; 51°23'·38N 02°46'·21E, Vaargeul 1.
VG1 VQ G; 51°25'·03N 02°49'·04E.
VG2 Q (6) + L Fl R 15s; ***Racon V***; 51°25'·96N 02°48'·16E.
VG3 QG; 51°25'·05N 02°52'·92E.
VG5 Fl G 5s; 51°24'·63N 02°57'·92E.
SVG Q ; 51°24'·53N 02°59'·92E.
Goote Bank Q (3) 10s; 51°26'·95N 02°52'·72E.
A1 Iso 8s; 51°22'·36N 02°53'·33E.
A1bis L Fl 10s; 51°21'·68N 02°58'·02E.

WESTERSCHELDE APPROACHES

SCHEUR CHANNEL
S1 Fl G 5s; 51°23'·14N 03°00'·12E.
S3 Q; 51°24'·30N 03°02'·92E.
MOW 0 ⊙ Fl (5) Y 20s; ***Racon S, 10M***; 51°23'·67N 03°02'·75E.
S5 Fl G 5s; 51°23'·70N 03°06'·30E.
S7 Fl G 5s; 51°23'·98N 03°10'·42E.
S9 QG; 51°24'·42N 03°14'·99E.
S12 Fl (4) R 10s; 51°24'·67N 03°18'·22E.
S-W Q; 51°24'·13N 03°18'·22E, here Wielingen chan merges.
S14 Fl R 5s; 51°24'·58N 03°19'·67E.

WIELINGEN CHANNEL
BVH Q (6) + L Fl R 15s; 51°23'·15N 03°12'·04E.
MOW3 tide gauge ☆ Fl (5) Y 20s; ***Racon H, 10M***; 51°23'·38N 03°11'·92E.
W Fl (3) G 15s; 51°23'·27N 03°14'·92E.
W1 Fl G 5s; 51°23'·48N 03°18'·22E.
Fort Maisonneuve VQ (9) 10s; wreck; 51°24'·20N 03°21'·50E.
W3 Iso G 4s; 51°26'·29N 03°39'·04E.
W5 Iso G 8s; 51°26'·26N 03°39'·89E.
W7 Iso G 8s; 51°25'·68N 03°40'·91E.
W9 Q G; 51°25'·11N 03°41'·86E.
Nieuwe Sluis ☆ Oc WRG 10s 26m W14M, R11M, G10M; 055°-R-089°-W-093°-G-105°-R-134°-W-136·5°-G-156·5°-W-236·5°-G-243°-W-254°-R-292°-W-055°; B 8-sided twr, W bands; 51°24'·41N 03°31'·29E.
Songa QG; 51°25'·26N 03°33'·66E.
W10 QR; 51°25'·85N 03°33'·28E.

VLISSINGEN
Koopmanshaven, W mole root, ☆ Iso WRG 3s 16m 8M; 253°-R-277°-W-284°-R-297°-W-306·5°-G-013°-W-024°-G-033°-W-035°-G-039°-W-055°-G-084·5°-R-092°-G-111°-W-114°; R pylon; 51°26'·37N 03°34'·52E.
Sardijngeul ☆ Oc WR 5s; 51°26'·30N 03°34'·55E: see OOSTGAT last 3 lines. E mole head, ☆ FG 7m; W mast; 51°26'·32N 03°34'·67E.
Buitenhaven ent, W side ☆ FR 10m 5M; also Iso WRG 4s 6M: W073°-324°, G324°-352°, W352°-017°, G017°-042°, W042°-056°, R056°-073°; W post, R bands; tfc sigs; 51°26'·38N 03°36'·06E.
Buitenhaven ent, E side ☆ FG 7m 4M; 51°26'·41N 03°36'·38E.
Schone Waardin ☆ Oc WRG 9s 10m W13M, R10M, G9M; 235°-R-271°-W-288°-G-335°-R-341°-G-026°-W-079°-R-091°; R mast, W bands; 51°26'·54N 03°37'·91E (1M E of Buitenhaven ent).

BRESKENS
Nieuwe Sluis ☆ Oc 10s 28m 14M (priv); B/W banded 8 sided tr; 51°24'·43N 03°31'·26E.

ARV-VH Q; 51°24′·71N 03°33′·89E.
VH2 (Vaarwaterlangs Hoofdplaat) 51°24′·34N 03°33′·90E.
Yacht hbr, W mole FG 7m; in fog FY; Gy post; 51°24′·03N 03°34′·06E. E mole FR 6m; Gy mast; 51°23′·95N 03°34′·09E.

WESTERSCHELDE: TERNEUZEN TO PAAL

TERNEUZEN

Nieuw Neuzenpolder ldg lts 125°, both Oc 5s 6/16m 9/13M; intens 117°-133°; synch. Front, W col, B bands; 51°20′·97N 03°47′·24E. Rear, B & W twr; 365m from front.
Oost Buitenhaven E mole FR 5M; 51°20′·56N 03°49′·19E.
Veerhaven (former ferry hbr, W part) & marinas (E part) W mole head FG, Gy mast; 51°20′·57N 03°49′·64E. E mole, FR.
W mole Oc WRG 5s 15m W9M, R7M, G6M; 090°-R-115°-W-120°-G-130°-W-245°-G-249°-W-279°-R-004°; B & W post; 51°20′·54N 03°49′·58E, close SW of FG.

HANSWEERT

W mole Oc WRG 10s 9m W6M, R6M, G6M; (in fog FY); 288°-R-311°-G-320°-W-332·5°-G-348·5°-W-042·5°-R-061·5°-W-078°-G-099°-W-114·5°-R-127·5°-W-288°; R twr, W bands; 51°26′·42N 04°00′·53E.

BELGIUM
ZANDVLIET TO ANTWERPEN

ZANDVLIET

Dir 118·3°,WRG 20m W4M, R/ G3M; 116·63°-Oc G-117·17°- FG-117·58°-Alt GW-118·63°-F-118·63°-Alt RW-119·18°-FR-119·58°-Oc R-120·13°; 51°20′·61N 04°16′·47E, near Zandvliet locks.

ANTWERPEN

No 107 Iso G 8s, 51°14′·12N 04°23′·80E (Kattendijksluis for Willemdok).
Royerssluis, ldg lts 091°, both FR. Ent FR/FG.
No 109 Iso G 8s; 51°13′·88N 04°23′·87E, (off Linkeroever).
Linkeroever marina F WR 9m W3M, R2M; shore-W-283°- R-shore; B ⊙, R lantern; 51°13′·91N 04°23′·70E. Marina ent, FR/FG.

COASTAL MARKS

AW2 Fl (4) R 20s; 51°21′·95N 03°00′·94E; Wandelaar.
AW1 QG; 51°21′·50N 03°02′·59E; Wandelaar.
Oostende Bank N Q; 51°21′·20N 02°52′·93E.
Wenduine Bank E QR; 51°18′·83N 03°01′·64E.
Wenduine Bank W Q (9) 15s; 51°17′·23N 02°52′·76E.
Nautica Ena wreck Q; 51°18′·08N 02°52′·79E.
Oostendebank E Fl G 5s; 51°17′·35N 02°51′·92E.
Oostendebank W Q (9)15s; 51°16′·20N 02°44′·74E.
LST 420 Q (9)15s; 51°15′·45N 02°40′·67E.
MBN Q; 51°20′·82N 02°46′·29E.
Middelkerke Bank Fl G 5s; 51°18′·19N 02°42′·75E.
Middelkerke Bank S Q (9) R 15s; 51°14′·73N 02°41′·89E.
D1 Q (3) 10s; 51°13′·95N 02°38′·59E.
BT Ratel Fl (4) R 15s; 51°11′·63N 02°27′·92E; Buiten Ratel.

ZEEBRUGGE TO THE FRENCH BORDER

ZEEBRUGGE

AW Iso 8s; 51°22′·41N 03°07′·05E.
Ldg lts 136°, both Oc 5s 22/45m 8M; 131°-141°; H24, synch; W cols, R bands. Front, 51°20′·71N 03°13′·11E. Rear, 890m SE.
SZ Q (3) 10s; 51°23′·30N 03°08′·65E (Scheur Channel).
Z QG; 51°22′·48N 03°09′·95E.
WZ Q (9) 15s; 51°22′·57N 03°10′·72E.
W outer mole Oc G 7s 31m 7M; G vert strip lts visible from seaward; 057°-267°; *Horn (3) 30s;* IPTS; 51°21′·74N 03°11′·17E.
E outer mole Oc R 7s 31m 7M; R vert strip lts visible from seaward; 087°-281°; *Bell 25s;* 51°21′·78N 03°11′·86E.
Ldg lts 154°: Front, Oc WR 6s 20m 3M, 135°-W-160°-R-169°; W pylon, R bands; 51°20′·33N 03°12′·89E. Rear, Oc 6s 38m 3M, H24, synch; 520m from front.
Leopold II mole ☆ Oc WR 15s 22m, **W20M, R18M**; 068°-W-145°-R-212°-W-296°; IPTS; *Horn (3+1) 90s;* 51°20′·85N 03°12′·17E.
Entrance to Marina and FV hbr 51°19′·88N 03°11′·85E.

BLANKENBERGE

Promenade pier Fl (3) Y 20s, 8m 4M; 51°19′·28N 03°08′·18E.
Lt ho ☆ Fl (2) 8s 30m **20M**; 065°-245°; W twr, B top; 51°18′·76N 03°06′·87E.
Ldg lts 134°, both FR 5/9m 3/10M, R cross (X) topmarks on masts; front 51°18′·70N 03°08′·82E; rear 81m from front.
E pier FR 12m 11M; R290°-245°(315°); W ○ twr; 51°18′·91N 03°06′·56E.
W pier FG 14m 11M; intens 065°-290°, unintens 290°-335°; W ○ twr; 51°18′·89N 03°06′·42E.
OBST 4 – OBST 14 are eleven s Q approx 3ca offshore, marking Spoil Ground between Blankenberge and Oostende.

OOSTENDE

Wenduinebank West Q (9) 15s; 51°17′·23N 02°52′·76E.
Buitenstroombank Q; 51°15′·17N 02°51′·71E.
Binnenstroombank Q (3) 10s; 51°14′·47N 02°53′·65E.
Ldg lts 143°: both Iso 4s (triple vert) 36/46m 4M, 068°-218°; X on metal mast, R/W bands. Front, 51°13′·80N 02°55′·89E.
Oostende lt ho ☆ Fl (3) 10s 65m **27M**; obsc 069·5°-071°; Gy twr, 2 sinusoidal Bu bands; 51°14′·18N 02°55′·84E.
W bkwtr Hd FG 9m 3M G mast; 51°14′·44N 02° 54′·97E.
E bkwtr Hd FR 9m 3M; R mast; 51°14′·51N 02° 55′·18E.
IPTS at inner E bkwtr Hd, Radar tr, G,R top; 51° 14′·51 02° 55′·19E.
Inner W bkwtr Hd FG 12m 10M, G057°-327°(270°); W ○ twr; 51°14′·31N 02°55′·03E.

NIEUWPOORT

Zuidstroombank Fl R 5s; 51°12′·28N 02°47′·37E.
Weststroombank Fl (4) R 20s; 51°11′·34N 02°43′·03E.
Wreck 4 Q (6) + L Fl 15s; 51°10′·98N 02°40′·10E.
Nieuwpoort Bank Q (9) 15s; 51°10′·16N 02°36′·09E.
Whitley Q; 51°09′·15N 02°39′·44E.
Lt ho ☆ Fl (2) R 14s 28m **16M**; R/W twr; 51°09′·27N 02°43′·79E.
E pier FR 10m 10M; R025°-250°(225°) R307°-347°(40°); W ○ twr; 51°09′·41N 02°43′·08E.
W pier FG 10m 9M; G025°-250°(225°) G284°-324°(40°); W ○ twr; 51°09′·35N 02°43′·00E.
QG 51°08′·65N 02°44′·31E marks the Y-junction where the channel forks stbd for KYCN and port for WSKLM and VVW-N.

WESTDIEP and PASSE DE ZUYDCOOTE

Den Oever wreck 2 Q; 51°08′·11N 02°37′·43E.
Wreck 1 Q; 51°08′·32N 02°35′·03E (adjacent to next line).
Wave recorder Fl (5) Y 20s; 51°08′·25N 02°34′·98E.
Trapegeer Fl G 10s; 51°08′·41N 02°34′·36E.
E12 VQ (6) + L Fl 10s; 51°07′·92N 02°30′·61E.

French waters, for continuity (see also Area 17):
CME Q (3) 10s; 51°07′·30N 02°30′·00E.
E11 Fl G 4s; 51°06′·85N 02°30′·83E.
E10 Fl (2) R 6s; 51°06′·26N 02°30′·40E.
E9 Fl (2) G 6s; 51°05′·61N 02°29′·60E.
E8 Fl (3) R 12s; 51°05′·12N 02°28′·60E.

9.16.5 PASSAGE INFORMATION

More passage information is threaded between harbours in this Area. **Bibliography**: *N Sea Passage Pilot* (Imray/Navin). *Cruising Guide to the Netherlands* (Imray/Navin). NP 55 *N Sea (East) Pilot*. NP 28 *Dover Strait Pilot*. *Hafenhandbuch Nordsee* (DSV-Verlag).

CHARTS, PSSA AND TSS

While AC 2182A, 1405/06/08, 1630/31/32/33, 1872 suffice for coastal passages and entry to the main ports, larger scale **Dutch yacht charts** (1800 series) are essential for exploring the cruising grounds along this coast or entering the smaller hbrs. Inland, the ANWB booklet-style chart (€19.95) of the *Staande-Mast Route* (Fixed Mast Route; see Stande Maastroute) is very detailed with copious, but intelligible, notes in Dutch.

From the Ems estuary west to Den Helder a **Particularly Sensitive Sea Area** (PSSA) extends 3M seaward from the West Frisian Islands. Yachts should carefully avoid damaging the maritime environment and marine organisms living in it.

The Terschelling-German Bight TSS, Off Vlieland TSS and Off Texel TSS lie between 5 and 10M to seaward of the West Frisian Islands. Cruising yachts are advised to navigate within this relatively narrow ITZ. Further offshore, and particularly in and near the Off Vlieland TSS, West Friesland TSS and Botney Ground TSS, navigation is further complicated by the many oil and gas fields. For general notes on North Sea oil & gas installations, see Chapter 3 and Area 5. Up to date charts are essential, particularly AC 1406,1408 and 1423.

CROSSING THE NORTH SEA TO THE UK

From ports S of Hoek van Holland make for NHR-SE, to cross the TSS for destinations between Harwich and Great Yarmouth (AC 1406, 1408, 1872, 2449, 3371). From ports N of Hoek van Holland passages can be more problematic. For example, a route from IJmuiden to the Humber crosses two DW routes, N and NW of Brown Ridge, and then runs into extensive offshore Gas Fields. These might cause you to opt for two shorter legs, stopping a night at Great Yarmouth. Similar thinking might apply if coming out of Den Helder, even if a stop at Great Yarmouth might incur some southing. From east of Den Helder, make ground west via the ITZ before taking departure.

9.16.6 SPECIAL NOTES: NETHERLANDS

PROVINCES are given in lieu of UK 'counties'.

CHARTS The following types of chart are available from agents. The Chart catalogue (HP7) is downloadable from www.hydro.nl:

- Zeekaarten (equivalent to AC) are issued by the Royal Netherlands Navy Hydrographer and corrected by Notices to Mariners (*Berichten aan Zeevarenden or BaZ*).
- 1800 series *voor Kust-en Binnenwateren* (coastal and inland waters) are yacht charts (DYC) issued annually in March by the Hydrographer in 8 folios (1801-1812, excluding 1802/4/6 & 8); about 9 loose double-sided sheets (54 x 38cm) per folio.

TIME ZONE is –0100, but add 1 hr for DST in the summer months.

TIDES HP 33 *Waterstanden & Stromen* (Tide tables and tidal streams in **English** and Dutch, £16·90 www.bookharbour.com) is useful if cruising Dutch waters for any length of time. It contains tide tables for 15 Dutch and 2 Belgian coastal ports; and 8 tidal stream atlases, including Westerschelde, Oosterschelde and the Maas.

REGULATIONS Discharge of toilet waste from recreational boats is forbidden in all Dutch waters, including inland waterways, lakes and the Waddenzee. Carry evidence (receipts) that any red diesel in your tanks is duty paid.

MARINAS Most marinas are private YCs or Watersport Associations (WSV or WV): *Gemeentelijke (Gem)* = municipal. Marinas with >50 berths must have a pump-out unit ⛽. Sometimes (in Belgium also) berth-holders show a green tally if a berth is free, or a red tally if returning same day, but check with HM. Duty-free fuel (coloured red) is not available for leisure craft and may only be carried in the tank, NOT in cans. A tourist tax (Touristenbelasting) of €0.55–€1.82/head/night is often levied. VAT (BTW) is 21%. A useful website covering other marinas is www.allejachthavens.nl

CUSTOMS Ports of entry are: Delfzijl, Lauwersoog, W Terschelling, Vlieland*, Harlingen, Kornwerderzand, Den Helder, IJmuiden, Scheveningen, Hoek van Holland, Maassluis, Schiedam, Vlaardingen, Rotterdam, Roompot*, Vlissingen, Terneuzen and Breskens. *Summer only. Den Oever and Stellendam are *not* Ports of entry.

FERRIES TO THE UK IJmuiden-Newcastle; Hoek van Holland-Harwich; Rotterdam (Europort)-Hull.

BUOYAGE Buoys are often named by the abbreviations of the banks or chans which they mark (eg VL = Vliestroom). A division buoy has the abbreviations of both chans meeting there, eg VL2-SG2 = as above, plus Schuitengat.

Some minor, tidal channels are marked by withies: SHM bound ⚳; PHM unbound ⚳. On tidal flats (eg Friesland) where the direction of main flood stream is uncertain, bound withies are on the S side of a chan and unbound on the N side; the banks thus marked are steep-to. In minor chans the buoyage may be moved without notice to accommodate changes.

The SIGNI buoyage system is used in the IJsselmeer, but not in the Eems, Waddenzee and Westerschelde.

SIGNALS When **motor-sailing** yachts must by law hoist a ▼ and when **at anchor** a black ball ●; these laws are rigidly enforced.

IPTS are widely used at coastal ports. Local signals, if any, are given where possible.

Sluicing signals may be shown by day: A blue board, with the word 'SPUIEN' on it; by night 3 ● in a △; sometimes both at once.

Storm warning signals, lts only, are shown by day & night at West Terschelling, Den Helder and IJmuiden; see Chapter 6.

R/T In emergency call *Den Helder Rescue* Ch 16 for Netherlands CG (see Chapter 7); or the working channel of a VTS sector or nearest lock or bridge. Monitor TSS info broadcasts and VTS sector channels. Ch 30/31 is for Dutch marinas (UK VHF sets need to be modified). Note: Do not use Ch M in Dutch waters, where it is a salvage frequency. Ch 13 is for commercial ship-ship calling. English is the second language and widely spoken.

TELEPHONE To call UK from the Netherlands, dial 00-44; then the UK area code minus the prefix 0, followed by the number required. To call the Netherlands from UK dial 00-31 then the area code minus the prefix 0 followed by two or three digits, followed by a 7 or 6 digits subscriber. No Mobile phone Nos start 06.

Emergency: Fire, Police, Ambulance, dial 112 (free); Non-emergency 0900 8844 (local tariff).

PUBLIC HOLIDAYS New Year's Day, Easter Sun and Mon, King's Birthday (27 April) Liberation Day (5 May) Ascension Day, Whit Mon, Christmas and Boxing Days.

BRITISH CONSULS Contact British Consulate-General, Koningslaan 44, 1075 AE Amsterdam; ☎020 676 4343. Or British Embassy, Lange Voorhout 10, 2514 ED The Hague; ☎070 4270 427.

INLAND WATERWAYS The sealocks at Kornwerderzand, Den Oever (IJsselmeer) IJmuiden, Stellendam and Roompotsluis are fully covered. The Staandemast (mast-up) route (Area map) and the IJsselmeer are outlined. Lack of space precludes detailed coverage of other harbours in the very extensive and enjoyable inland seas, waterways and canals.

Regulations. All craft must carry a copy of waterway regulations, *Binnenvaartpolitiereglement (BPR)*, as given in Dutch in the annual ANWB *Wateralmanak Vol 1* or available separately. Vol 2, also in Dutch, is essential reading; it gives pictograph details of marinas and the opening hours of bridges and locks.

Qualifications. Craft >15m LOA or capable of more than 20kph (11kn) must be skippered by the holder of an RYA Coastal Skipper's Certificate or higher qualification; *plus* an International Certificate of Competence (ICC) endorsed for Inland waterways, ie CEVNI.

Bridges and locks mostly work VHF Ch 18, 20 or 22, but CEVNI light signals (shown up/down-stream) largely negate the need for R/T. The most commonly seen signals include:

● = Bridge closed (opens on request).

To request bridges to open, call on VHF low power (1 watt) or sound 'K' (–•–).

● over ● = Bridge about to open. ● = Bridge open.

● over ● = No service.

9.16.7 TSS OFF THE NORTHERN NETHERLANDS

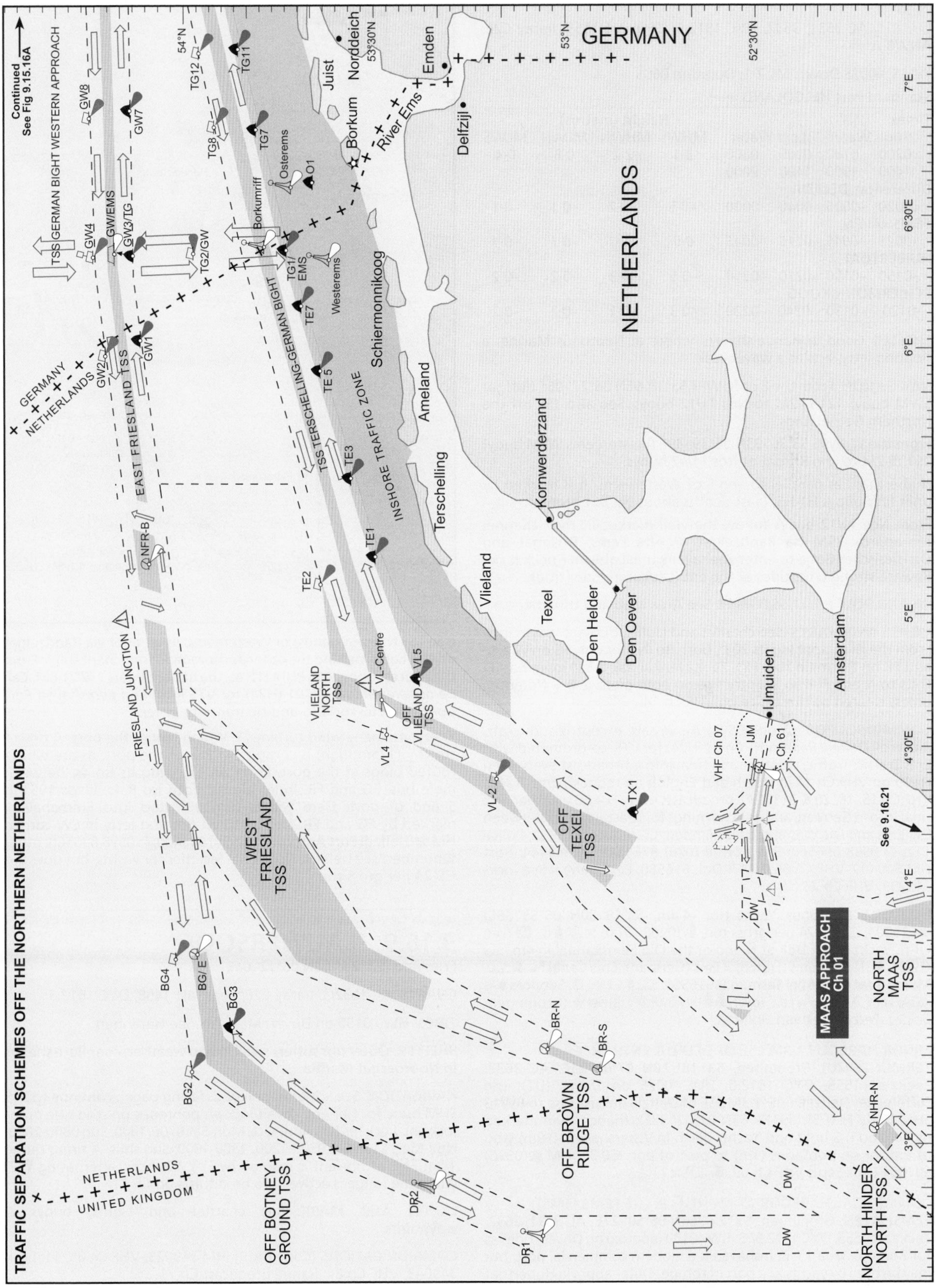

9.16.8 DELFZIJL

Groningen **53°18'·99N 07°00'·45E**

CHARTS AC 3631, 3632; DYC 1812.6; Zeekaart 1555; Imray C26; ANWB A

TIDES –0025 Dover; ML 2·1; Duration 0605

Standard Port HELGOLAND (⟵)

Times				**Height (metres)**			
High Water		Low Water		MHWS	MHWN	MLWN	MLWS
0200	0700	0200	0800	3·1	2·7	0·8	0·4
1400	1900	1400	2000				
Differences DELFZIJL							
+0020	–0005	–0040	0000	+0·5	+0·7	–0·1	–0·1
EEMSHAVEN							
–0025	*–0045*	*–0115*	*–0045*	*0·0*	*+0·1*	*–0·1*	*–0·1*
HUIBERTGAT							
–0150	–0150	–0210	–0210	–0·5	–0·3	–0·2	–0·2
SCHIERMONNIKOOG							
–0120	–0130	–0240	–0220	–0·3	–0·1	–0·2	–0·2

SHELTER Good in Handelshaven, where at Neptunus Marina, a floating jetty, acts as a wavebreak.

NAVIGATION From the E or N, WPT 53°38'·96N 06°27'·06E (Riffgat SWM buoy) 121°/4·2M to Nos 11/12 buoys. See also TSS off the Northern Netherlands.

From the W, WPT 53°36'·93N 06°19'·39E (Westereems SWM buoy) 091°/8·2M to join Riffgat at Nos 11/12 buoys.

Huibertgat lies parallel to and S of Westereems. It is marked by unlit R/W buoys H1-H5, least depths about 9m but prone to silt.

From Nos 11/12 buoys follow the well marked/lit river channel for approx 25M via Randzelgat or Alte Eems, Dukegat and Ostfriesisches Gatje to enter Zeehavenkanaal abeam Knock lt ho. Beware strong cross tides at the ent (Lat/Long under title).

INLAND ROUTE TO IJSSELMEER See Area Map and IJsselmeer.

LIGHTS AND MARKS See chartlet and Lights, buoys & waypoints. From the river, appr ldg lts 203°, both Iso 4s. Hbr ent, FG on W arm and FR on E arm (in fog, FY). Zeehavenkanaal, 2·5M long, has Fl G lts to N and Fl R to S. Entry sigs on both piers: 2 ● = No entry, unless cleared by Hbr office on VHF Ch 14.

COMMUNICATIONS (Code 0596) All vessels, except leisure craft, must call *Delfzijl Radar* VHF Ch 03 (H24) for VTS, co-ordinated with Ems Traffic; Traffic, weather and tidal info is broadcast every even H+10 on VHF Ch 14 in Dutch and English on request; *Ems Traffic* VHF Ch 15, 18, 20 & 21 (H24) broadcasts every H + 50 weather and tidal info in German, and gale warnings for coastal waters between Die Ems and Die Weser, see also Emden; CG (Police) 613831; Police 112; ⊖ 0598 696560; Brit Consul (020) 6764343; Ⓗ 644444; Port HM 640400, VHF Ch 66; HM 't Dok 616560; Eemskanaal Sea locks 613293, VHF Ch 26.

FACILITIES **Neptunus Yacht Hbr** (4·4m, 53°19'·80N 06°55'·86E) ☎615004, €0·24 per gross ton, (0900-1700) free wi-fi. **Yacht Hbr 't Dok** at N end of the Old Eemskanaal in 4m, €0·41, . Note: Eems (Dutch) = Ems (German). **Ems Canal** . **Motor Boat Club Abel Tasman** ☎616560, . **Services** ACA, DYC Agent, . **Town** (Groningen/ Eelde). **Ferry** Hoek van Holland.

MINOR HARBOUR 1·3M ESE OF DELFZIJL ENTRANCE

TERMUNTERZIJL Groningen, **53°18'·20N 07°02'·21E**. AC 3632; Zeekaart 1555; DYC 1812.6. HW –0025 on Dover (UT); use Differences Delfzijl. Ent (1·3M ESE of Delfzijl ent) is close to BW13 SHM buoy Fl G 5s (53°18'·63N 07°02'·32E); thence chan marked by 7 R and 7 G unlit bns. Yachts berth in Vissershaven (0·9m) stbd of ent, or on pontoons (1m) to port of ent, €0·36. HM ☎(0596) 601891 (Apr-Sept) VHF Ch 09, .

COMMERCIAL HARBOUR AT MOUTH OF THE EEMS (EMS)

EEMSHAVEN, Groningen, **53°27'·66N 06°50'·27E**. AC 3631, 3632, Zeekaart 1555, DYC 1812.5/.6. HW –0100 (approx) on Dover. Tides as for Borkum Area 15. Eemshaven is a modern commercial port, but may be used by yachts as a port of refuge. Outer appr via Hubertgat

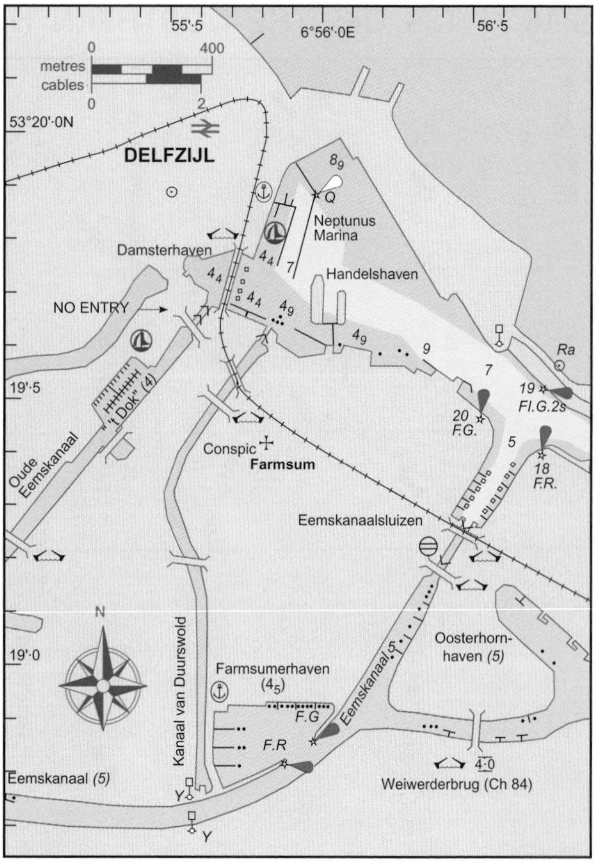

(see TSS N Netherlands) or Westereems; inner appr via Randzelgat or Alte Eems, passing the outer anchorage for merchant ships. From the nearest buoy, A16 PHM Fl R 4s, the hbr ent bears 137°/1·6M. Call *Eemshaven Radar* Ch 01 (H24) for VTS info; and *Eemshaven Port Control* Ch 66 for info and clearance to enter.

There are many wind turbines S, W and NW of the port. A power stn chy (128m high) is conspic 2M ESE of the port; as are white-roofed bldgs at the port. Enter on 175°, ldg lts Iso 4s, between mole hds, FG and FR. Inner ldg lts, both Iso R 4s, leads 195° to S end of port. Here yachts turn 90° stbd into Emmahaven, marked by FG and FR, and berth on floating jetty in SW corner. HM ☎(Delfzijl Port Authority) (0596) 640400; ⊖ 0598 696560; other ☎numbers see Delfzijl. No special facilities for yachts, but dues are €0·24 per gross ton.

9.16.9 LAUWERSOOG

Friesland, **53°24'·68N 06°12'·04E**

CHARTS AC 1632/3; Imray C26; Zeekaart 1458; DYC 1812.3

TIDES HW –0150 on Dover; ML 1·7m. See Harlingen.

SHELTER Outer hbr suffers swell in bad weather; complete shelter in Noordergat Marina.

NAVIGATION See Schiermonnikoog (facing page); continue to Z15 SHM buoy for hbr ent. Await lock on pontoons on stbd side outer lock ent. Lock hrs (LT) **April-Oct**: Mon-Sat 0700-1900; Sun 0800-2000. **Nov-Mar**: Mon-Sat 0700-1200, 1300-1800; Sun shut. A firing range 1·5m ENE of hbr ent is marked by Fl Y 10s bcns, alternating W/R when the range is active; info broadcasts on Ch 71.

LIGHTS AND MARKS See chartlet and Lights, buoys & waypoints.

COMMUNICATIONS (Code 0519) HM 349023, VHF Ch 05, 11; Lock 349043, VHF Ch 84; Range broadcast Ch 71.

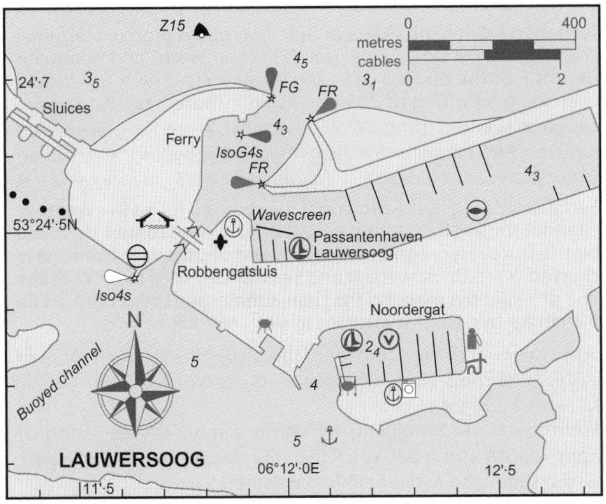

FACILITIES **Noordergat Marina**, ☎349040; www.noordergat.nl (2·4m-2·8m). Ⓥs berth on first pontoon, €1·10 + €1·15 pp/day tax. (E end of hbr); (ferry terminal, W end of hbr) ✕ (30t) YC. **Passantenhaven Lauwersoog**, ☎349023, 60 berths (visitors only) €1.50. The Staande Mastroute (Area map, Delfzijl-Harlingen) can be entered from the Lauwersmeer at Dokkum.

OTHER HARBOURS IN THE LAUWERSMEER

ZOUTKAMP, Groningen, **53°20'·38N 06°17'·55E**. AC 2593, Zeekaarten 1458, DYC 1812·4; non-tidal. Appr down the Zoutkamperril (2·6-4·5m); approx 2ca before lock/bridge, Hunzegat marina (1·5-2·1m) is to port. ☎(0595) 402875, SC. Beyond the lock (FR lts) and close to port is Oude Binnenhaven marina (2m) €1·25 + €1·15 pp/day tax. (20t).

Town ✕ Dr.

OOSTMAHORN, Friesland, **53°22'·94N 06°09'·63E**. AC 2593, Zeekaarten 1458, DYC 1812·4. Non-tidal hbr on W side of Lauwersmeer; lock in as for Lauwersoog. Floating bns with Y flags mark fishing areas. Main hbr with FR and FG lts at ent has marina (2·2-3·0m). VHF Ch 10. HM ☎(0511) 408100, €0·91, ✕ (15t). Approx 450m to the SSE, next to the Voorm Veerhaven (ferry hbr) is a tiny marina with 1·5–2m.

MINOR HARBOURS IN THE WEST FRISIAN ISLANDS

SCHIERMONNIKOOG, Friesland, **53°28'·07N 06°10'·05E**. AC 3761; Zeekaart 1458; DYC 1812.3. HW –0150 on Dover. See Delfzijl. WPT 53°31'·96N 06°01'·84E (WG SWM buoy, Iso 8s, Racon N) 150°/1·0M to WG1 SHM buoy, VQ G, at ent to Westgat; though buoyed/lit, this approach should only be attempted by strangers in gentle, settled conditions and avoided completely in winds W-N-NE >F4, when the fast shifting shoals and chan make it very dangerous. **It is essential to call Schiermonnikoog ☆ on VHF Ch 05 for latest update**. Follow Westgat chan into Zoutkamperlaag either to Lauwersoog or Schiermonnikoog; leave at Z4 & Z6 bys, then use GVS chan bys for Gat van Schiermonnikoog. Follow GVS bys to ent of Groote Siege (GS bys), turn port at GS6 into Reegeul chan (aka Harms Geultje), R&G lateral bys (unlit), and east to the small drying yacht hbr of Schiermonnikoog, (1·3-1·5m) 1·5m max at HW in apprs, silting rptd 2016. Picturesque, busy in season, €2·00/m. HM VHF Ch 31; ☎(0519) 531544 (May-Sept). Facilities: ✕. Note: Lt ho Fl (4) 20s, R twr, conspic 1.35M NNW of yacht hbr. CG at lt ho, 48M radius radar surveillance of the Terschelling/German Bight TSS and coordinates local SAR operations. VHF Ch **05**, 10, 16, 67 and 37 (all H24); ☎0519 531247.

NES, Ameland, Friesland, **53°26'·22N 05°46'·53E**. AC 2593, Zeekaart 1458, DYC 1811.10 & .2. HW –0155 on Dover; ML 1·6m; Duration 0625. See Harlingen. Shelter in all but E/S winds. Appr from WA SWM buoy via Westgat, Borndiep and Molengat to VA2-R1 SCM lt perch, VQ(6) + L Fl 10s, beware sandbanks; dangerous in >F6 from SW-N-NE. Lts: see Lights, buoys and waypoints. **Yacht hbr** ('t Leije Gat) HM ☎(0519) 542159. 140 berths, €0·66/m^2 + €1·18 pp/day tax. L Fl R 8s and L Fl G 8s piles at ent. Pontoons N end hbr (0·8m) beyond ferry; W side dries. Facilities: YC.

THE WEST FRISIAN ISLANDS

These islands stretch from the R Ems estuary W and SSW for some 85M along the Dutch coast to Den Helder (AC 1632, 1633). They have similar characteristics – being long, low and narrow, with the major axis parallel to the coast. Texel is the largest and, with Vlieland and Terschelling, lies furthest offshore.

Between the islands, narrow channels (*zeegat* in Dutch, *Seegat* in German) give access to/from the North Sea. Most of these channels are shallow for part of their length, and in these shoal areas a dangerous sea builds up in a strong onshore wind against the outgoing (ebb) tide. The Westerems and the Zeegaten van Terschelling and van Texel are safe for yachts in W–NE winds up to force 6. The rest are unsafe in strong onshore winds.

▶*The flood stream along this coast is E-going, so it starts to run in through the zeegaten progressively from W to E. Where the tide meets behind each island, as it flows in first at the W end and a little later at the E end, a bank is formed, called a wantij (Dutch) or Wattenhoch (German).*◀

These banks between the islands and the coast are major obstacles to E/W progress inside the islands. The chans are narrow and winding, marked by buoys and/or withies in the shallower parts, and they mostly dry; so that it is essential to time the tide correctly.

This is an area most suited to shallow-draft yachts that can take the ground easily. Whilst the zeegaten are described briefly below, the many channels inside the islands and across the Waddenzee are mentioned only for general orientation.

DELFZIJL TO AMELAND

The Ems estuary (AC 1633, 3631) flows seaward past the SW side of the German island of Borkum giving access to **Delfzijl**, **Termunterzijl** and **Emden**. Hubertgat, which runs parallel to and S of the main Westerems chan, though sparsely buoyed and unlit, is fine for yachts in fair weather and slightly more direct when bound to/from the W. In strong NW winds against the ebb both chans produce a dangerous sea.

Further offshore, the growing string of wind farms continues W with the Gemini 'twins' BuitenGaats and ZeeEnergie, 150 turbines, 34M due north of Ameland.

▶*The E-going (flood) stream begins at HW Helgoland +0530, and the W-going (ebb) stream begins at HW Helgoland –0030, sp rates 1·5kn.*◀

Friesche Zeegat (DYC 1812.3 & .9) between Schiermonnikoog and Ameland, contains two channels: Westgat is marked by 'WG' buoys, but shoaling and shifting channels have made it increasingly hazardous without local knowledge and Plaatgat, an unmarked channel, which is dangerous. In strong winds the sea breaks across the whole estuary. Westgat trends SE past Wierumergronden and N7-FA-1 platform, the S past Het Rif and Engelsmanplaat (a prominent sandbank) into Zoutkamperlaag, the main channel (buoys prefixed 'Z') to **Lauwersoog**. Here locks give access to the Lauwersmeer and inland waterways.

Zeegat van Ameland (DYC 1811.6) between Ameland and Terschelling is fronted by the sandbank of Bornrif about 3M offshore. The main entrance is also called Westgat, with buoys prefixed by letters 'WA', all unlit except WA12 QR. The channel runs ESE close N of Terschelling, and divides into Boschgat (BG) at the E end of West Terschelling and Borndiep (BB) the wider, deeper channel. This skirts the W end of Ameland and at WA22-WG1 buoy gives access via the Molengat to the small ferry port and yacht hbr at Nes.

▶*In Westgat the flood stream begins at HW Helgoland +0425, and the ebb stream at HW Helgoland –0150, sp rates 2kn.*◀ A dangerous sea develops in strong onshore winds.

TERSCHELLING TO TEXEL AND DEN HELDER

Zeegat Het Vlie, aka Zeegat van Terschelling (AC 112 and DYC 1811.4, .5 and .9) between Terschelling and Vlieland, gives access to the hbrs of **Vlieland, West Terschelling and Harlingen**; it is also a northern approach to the sealock at Kornwerderzand. Shallow banks extend more than 5M seaward narrowing the ITZ to only 4M wide.

▶*The E-going (flood) stream begins at HW Helgoland +0325, while the W-going (ebb) stream begins at HW Helgoland –0230, sp rates 2·5kn.*◀

The main chan (buoyed/lit) through the banks is Zuider Stortemelk (buoys prefixed 'ZS') running ESE close N of Vlieland into Vliesloot (VS) which leads to **Oost Vlieland** hbr. The Stortmelk (SM) forks eastward at SM1-ZS10 buoy towards the deeper wider channel of Vliestroom.

In fair weather, and daylight, approach **West Terschelling** via the Schuitengat-Zuid, R and G lateral buoys (unlit), beginning at the RGR (preferred chan to stbd) VL2-SG1 buoy. At night, or in strong W or NW'lies and swell, it is advisable to go via Meep and Slenk. From Zuider Stortemelk the Vliestroom, a deep well-buoyed chan (buoys prefixed 'VL') runs S for about 4M to its junction with Blauwe Slenk (BS) and Inschot (IN). Blauwe Slenk runs ESE to **Harlingen**; from Harlingen a S-going channel 'Boontjes' leads via the locks at Kornwerderzand into the IJsselmeer.

Eierlandsche Gat (DYC 1811.7) between Vlieland and Texel, consists of dangerous shoals, shallow and unmarked chans used only by fishermen, *and should not be attempted by strangers*.

Zeegat van Texel (AC 1546/DYC 1811.2), lies between Texel and Den Helder, and gives access to the **Waddenzee** and IJsselmeer via locks at Den Oever or Kornwerderzand. Haaksgronden shoals extend 5M seaward. The 2 appr channels are: Molengat from the N along the Texel shore (see next para) and from the SSW the well-marked/lit main chan Schulpengat, buoys prefixed 'S'.Small craft bound for Den Helder will find clear water and adequate depths E of the buoyed chan and, closing Kijkduin lt ho, should then keep an offing of 200m to avoid inshore hazards. Beware rough seas with strong SW wind against. ▶*the SW-going (ebb) stream which begins at HW Helgoland –0330, while the NE-going (flood) stream begins at HW Helgoland +0325, sp rates 1·5kn.*◀

Serious shoaling in the Molengat has reduced it to a fair weather channel for small craft in daylight only. It is no longer surveyed by the Dutch Hydrographic Service, and depths vary from those charted. Y SPM's mark the N and S entrances; keep close W of the line of Y spar bys marking the chan, submerged WWII bunkers lie E of these bys. Do not attempt in fresh NW'lies or swell.

▶*In Molengat the N-going (ebb) stream begins at HW Helgoland –0145, and the S-going (flood) stream at HW Helgoland +0425, sp rates 1·25kn.*◀

From the N the Schulpengat involves a southerly deviation of approx 15M and leads W of the very dangerous Zuider Haaks which should be avoided in bad weather.

E of **Den Helder** and the Marsdiep, the flood makes in three main directions through the SW Waddenzee:

- to E and SE through Malzwin and Visjagersgaatje (keeping to the ctr of the channel) to **Den Oever** (where the lock into IJsselmeer is only available during daylight hours); thence NE along the Afsluitdijk, and then N towards Harlingen;
- to NE and E through Texelstroom and Doove Balg towards Kornwerderzand; and
- from Texelstroom, NE and N through Scheurrak, Omdraai and Inschot, where it meets the flood stream from Zeegat van Terschelling. The ebb runs in reverse. The **Kornwerderzand** locks (available H24), near NE end of Afsluitdijk, also give access to the IJsselmeer.

9.16.10 HET VLIE (ZEEGAT VAN TERSCHELLING)

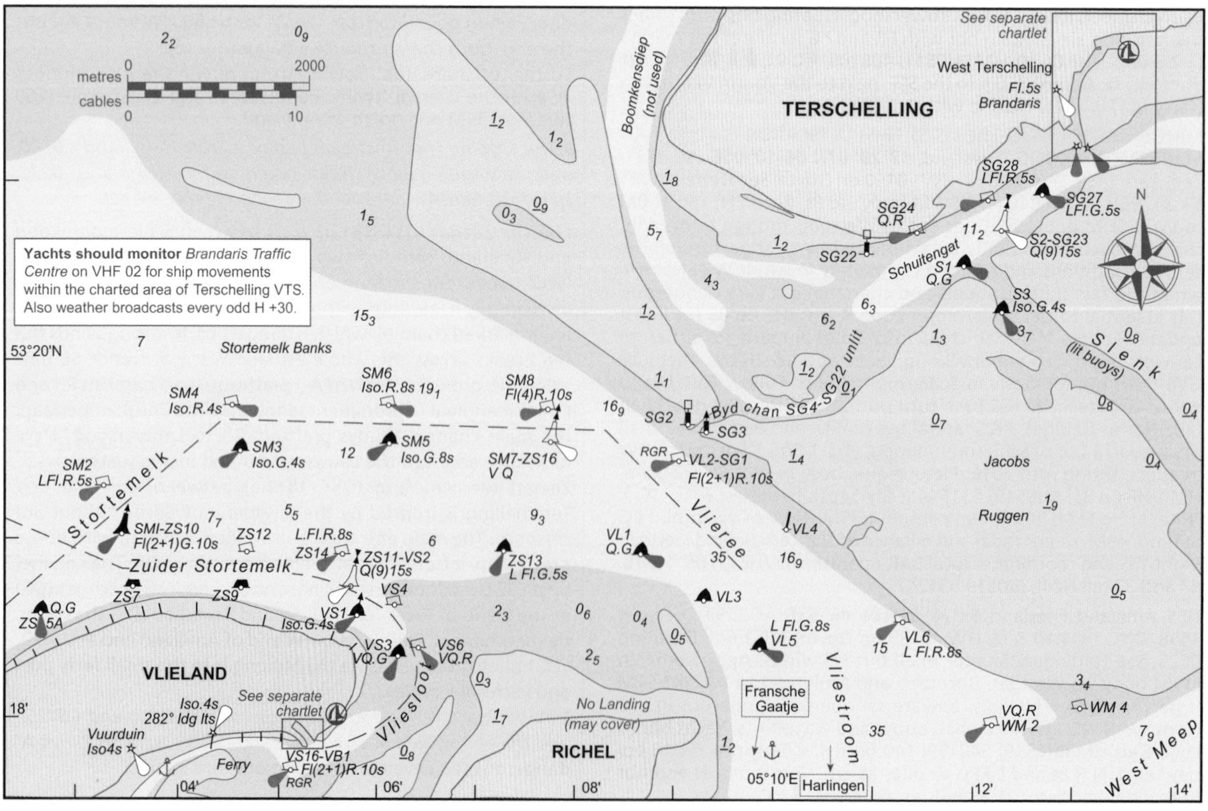

9.16.11 WEST TERSCHELLING

WEST FRISIAN ISLANDS **53°21'·26N 05°13'·13E**

CHARTS AC 1633, 112; Zeekaart 1456; DYC 1811.4/.5; Imray C25

TIDES –0300 Dover; ML 1·4; Duration No data

Standard Port HELGOLAND (⟵)

Times				**Height (metres)**			
High Water		Low Water		MHWS	MHWN	MLWN	MLWS
0200	0700	0200	0800	3·1	2·7	0·8	0·4
1400	1900	1400	2000				
Differences WEST TERSCHELLING							
–0220	–0250	–0335	–0310	–0·8	–0·6	–0·3	–0·2
VLIELAND-HAVEN							
–0250	–0320	–0355	–0330	–0·8	–0·6	–0·3	–0·3

SHELTER Good in the marina; very crowded in season.

NAVIGATION WPT 53°19'·58N 04°55'·77E (ZS buoy) 099°/6·2M to ZS11-VS2 buoy via Zuider Stortemelk which is well marked/lit. In strong W/NW'lies beware dangerous seas from ZS to ZS5/6 buoys. Stortemelk, the deeper N'ly route, is no shorter and is more exposed.

In daylight use fair weather approach to West Terschelling via Schuitengat-Zuid from RGR (preferred chan to stbd) VL2-SG1 buoy and subsequent numbered R and G SG lateral bys SG3 to SG 31 (unlit until SG 23). In darkness, or strong W or NW'lies and swell, it is essential to go via West Meep and Slenk, longer, but wide, safe (3·2m) and much easier for visitors. Route: WM2, 4 & 6 buoys, NM4–S21 buoy to enter Slenk buoyed/lit chan (note: SHMs to port for this approach) leading NW into the Schuitengat (11m) at SG 23 buoy. (SHMs then to stbd to West Terschelling.) Expect much commercial traffic and ferries in Slenk.

Ameland can be reached if draft <1.5m by the inshore channels across the Waddenzee (Meep, Noorder Balgen and Oosterom; DYC 1811.4 & .6). Leave at HW –3 to arrive at HW.

LIGHTS AND MARKS Hbr lts as chartlet and Lights, buoys & waypoints. The square, yellow Brandaris light tower dominates the town and hbr.

COMMUNICATIONS (Code 0562) Coast Guard 442341; *Brandaris* (VTS) Ch 02, 04 broadcasts weather, visibility, traffic, tidal data at H+30 in Dutch and English. Yachts must monitor Ch 02; ⊖ 442884; Dr 442181; Port HM 443337 (H24) VHF Ch 12; Marina Ch 31 HO.

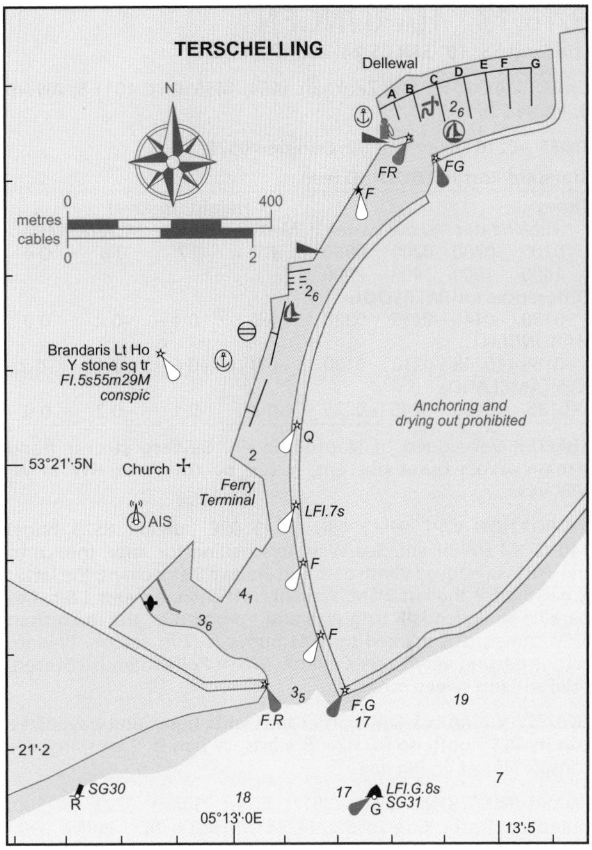

FACILITIES **Marina Stichting Passantenhaven** ☎443337 (H24 Apr-Oct) info@jachthaventerschelling.nl. www.waddenhavens.nl. Notices on pontoons A-G indicate berths by LOA and type of boat (yacht, motor cruiser or traditional craft). 500 berths €0·70/m² + €1·30 pp/day tax, inc; at marina ent, @, chart agent.

Village is an easy walk: (5km). ✈ Amsterdam. Ferry to Harlingen, thence ⇌ for Hook-Harwich.

9.16.12 VLIELAND

WEST FRISIAN ISLANDS

Friesland **53°17'·68N 05°05'·49E**

CHARTS AC 1633, 112; Zeekaart 1456; DYC 1811.4/.5; Imray C26

TIDES –0300 Dover; ML 1·4; Duration 0610. See West Terschelling. The Dutch use Harlingen as a Standard Port.

SHELTER Good in yacht hbr. Two ⚓s, both affected by swell in strong SE-SW'lies near HW: (a) in up to 3m ½M S of the hbr or (b) in 4-9m 1M W of the hbr (beyond the ferry pier). Do not ⚓ in buoyed chan from hbr ent to ferry pier (no berths).

NAVIGATION From ZS buoy (WPT) follow W Terschelling Navigation, lines 1-3. At ZS11-VS2 and VS1 buoys turn S into Vliesloot (narrow and in places only 2·5m MLWS). Keep in mid-chan past VS3-VS7 buoys to hbr ent (strong current across); tight berths difficult in SW wind.

LIGHTS AND MARKS A dk R lt ho (W lantern, R top) stands on Vuurduin, 1·2M W of hbr. Hbr lts as chartlet. Tfc sigs: R Flag or ●● at ent = hbr closed (full). The 282° ldg lts (Lights, bys & waypoints & W Terschelling) lead toward the ferry terminal in E Vlieland.

COMMUNICATIONS (Code 0562) CG 442341; All vessels in Zeegat van Terschelling and N Waddenzee must monitor Ch 02 for *Brandaris Traffic Centre VTS;* Police 451312; ⊖ 058 2949488 (Leeuwarden); Brit Consul (020) 6764343; Dr 451307; HM 451729, mob 06 201 33086, VHF Ch 12.

FACILITIES **Yacht Hbr** ☎451729. www.waddenhavens.nl 300 inc Ⓥ; finger berths on all pontoons in 2m. €0·70 per m² + €1·35 pp/day tax; (10 mins); at Harlingen and Terschelling.

Village @ ✈(Amsterdam). **Ferry** see West Terschelling.

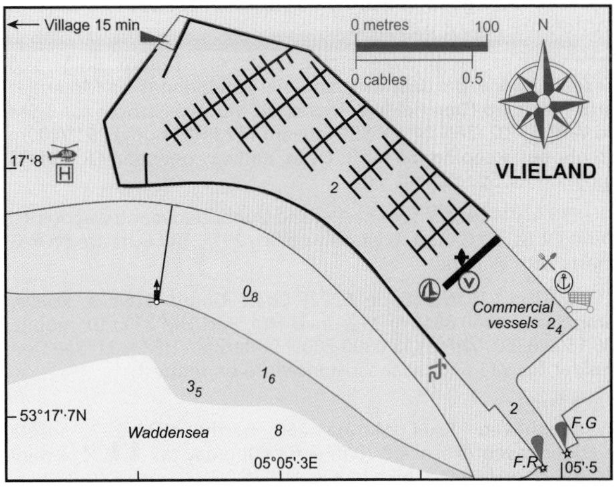

9.16.13 HARLINGEN

Friesland **53°10'·58N 05°24'·23E**

CHARTS AC 1633, 112; Zeekaart 1454, 1456; DYC 1811·5; ANWB B; Imray C26

TIDES –0210 Dover; ML 1·2; Duration 0520

Standard Port HELGOLAND (⟵)

Times				Height (metres)			
High Water		Low Water		MHWS	MHWN	MLWN	MLWS
0200	0700	0200	0800	3·1	2·7	0·8	0·4
1400	1900	1400	2000				
Differences LAUWERSOOG							
–0130	–0145	–0235	–0220	–0·3	–0·1	–0·2	0·0
HARLINGEN							
–0155	–0245	–0210	–0130	–0·8	–0·6	–0·4	–0·2
NES (AMELAND)							
–0135	–0150	–0245	–0225	–0·3	–0·1	–0·2	0·0

SHELTER Very good in Noorderhaven. Beware strong flood stream across outer hbr ent; it can be rough at HW in W/NW'lies.

NAVIGATION WPT 53°11'·48N 05°19'·63E (abeam BS23 buoy) 110°/2·8M to hbr ent. See West Terschelling for appr, thence to the WPT via buoyed Vliestroom and Blauwe Slenk chans; the latter is narrow for the last 2½M. A small craft chan, at least 1·8m, lies parallel to Pollendam trng wall and outboard of the main chan SHM buoys; it is marked by SPM buoys A–N in season. Beware ferries passing very close. Caution: When Pollendam is covered, tidal streams sweep across it.

LIGHTS AND MARKS See chartlet and Lights, buoys and waypoints. Ldg lts 111°, both Iso 6s, H24; B masts, W bands. 2 ch spires are conspic almost on ldg line.

COMMUNICATIONS (Code 0517) Coast Guard 0223 542300; Brandaris Traffic Ctre (0562) 442341, VHF Ch 02; Police 0900 8844/112; ⊖ 088 151444; British Consul (020) 6764343; Ⓗ 058 2866666; Doctor 412544; Harlingen Port Control 412512, VHF Ch 11; HM 492300, VHF Ch 11 (not on Sun); Harinxma Canal locks VHF Ch 22.

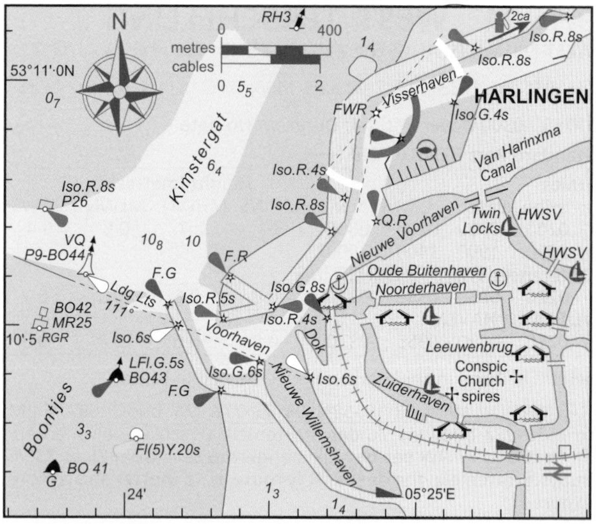

FACILITIES Lifting bridges across the Oude Buitenhaven and Noorderhaven open in unison 2 x per hr 0600-2200 in season (on request in winter) but are shut at times of boat trains/ferries and at a tidal height exceeding LAT + 2·54m. Fuel available in the NE corner of the Nieuwe Industriehaven.

Noorderhaven Yacht Hbr ☎415666, Ⓔ Diving/salvage (by arrangement).

Harlinger Watersportverenigingen (HWSV) ☎416898 info@harlingerwatersportverenigingen.nl, useful small marina just inside the locks, 100+ inc €1·10 + €0·75 pp/day tax, inc @. **Town** Ⓑ ✈ (Amsterdam). **Ferry** see Hoek van Holland.

9.16.14 OUDESCHILD

Texel, **53°02'·35N 04°51'·18E**

CHARTS AC 1631, 1546; Zeekaart 1546, 1454; DYC 1811·3

TIDES –0355 Dover; ML 1·1m; Duration 0625

Standard Port HELGOLAND (⟵)

Times				Height (metres)			
High Water		Low Water		MHWS	MHWN	MLWN	MLWS
0200	0700	0200	0800	3·1	2·8	0·8	0·4
1400	1900	1400	2000				
Differences OUDESCHILD							
–0310	–0420	–0445	–0400	–1·4	–1·1	–0·4	–0·2

SHELTER Very good in marina (2·4m) in far NE basin. ⚓ prohib. Visitors are always welcome.

NAVIGATION From Waddenzee appr via Doove Balg and Texelstroom. From seaward, app via Schulpengat or Molengat into Marsdiep (Den Helder). Thence NE via Texelstroom for 3·5M to WPT 53°02'·26N 04°51'·55E (abeam T12 PHM buoy) 291°/400m to hbr ent, keeping the dir lt, Oc 6s, midway between FR and FG mole hd lts. Speed limit 5kn.

LIGHTS AND MARKS See chartlet and Lights, buoys and waypoints. Dir lt Oc 6s, on G mast, is vis only on brg 291°. FR/FG lts are on R/G masts with W bands.

COMMUNICATIONS (Code 0222) Coast Guard 316270; Police/ambulance 0900 8844 or 112; ⊖ via HM; Port HM 312710, mobile 06 1502 8380, VHF Ch 12 0800-2000LT; Marina VHF Ch 31; See Den Helder for VTS and radar assistance/info on request.

FACILITIES

Waddenhaven Texel Marina 250 berths ☎321227. info@waddenhaventexel.nl €0·70/m² + €1·60pp/day tax mini in season @ bike hire.

YC WSV Texel, members only. Dry dock (FVs only).

Village (walking distance) Ⓑ. Ferry from 't Horntje to Den Helder. UK ferries from Hook/Rotterdam. ✈ Amsterdam.

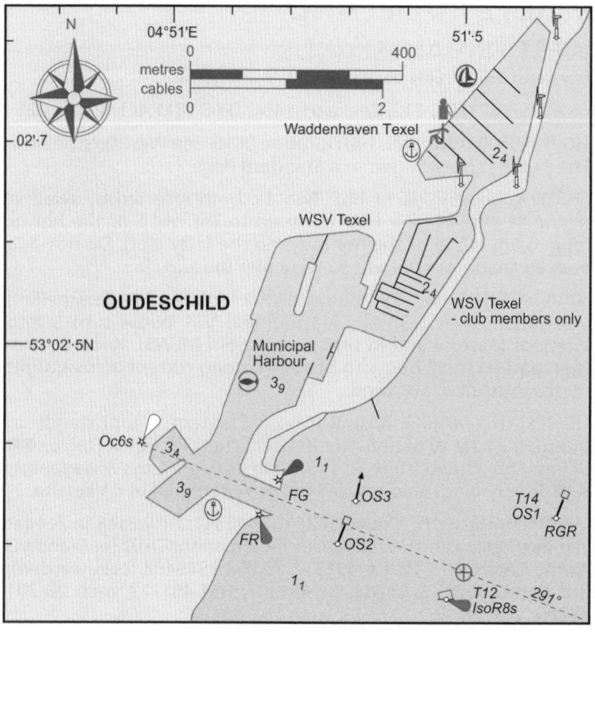

9.16.15 DEN HELDER

Noord Holland **52°57'·94N 04°47'·24E**

CHARTS AC 1408, 1631, 1546, 126; Zeekaart 1454, 1546; DYC 1811.2, 1801.10; ANWB F; Imray C25

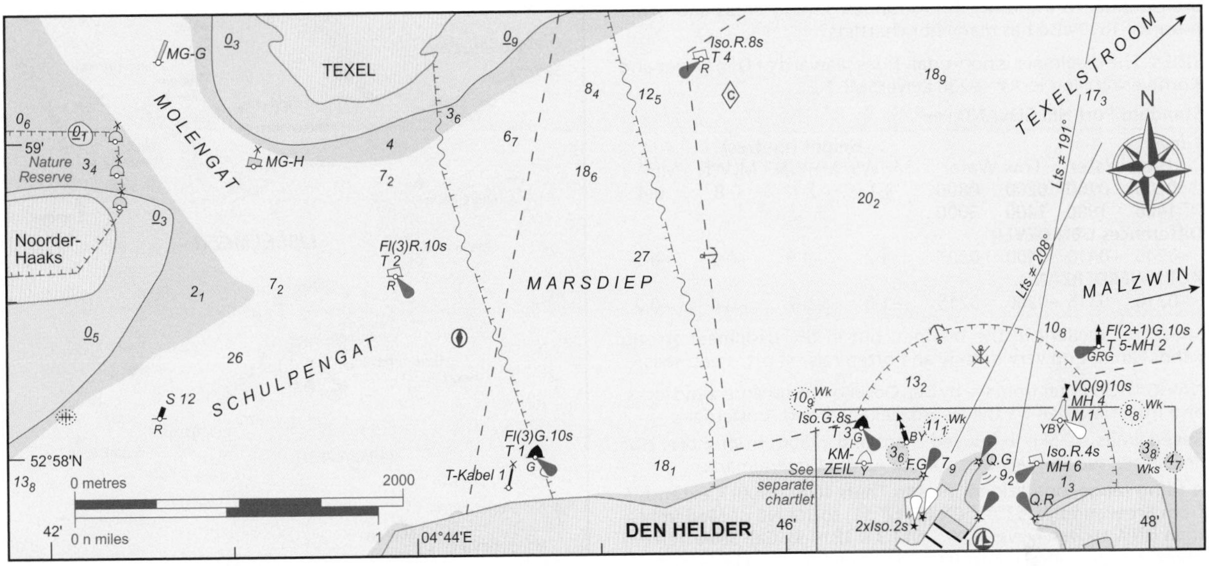

TIDES –0430 Dover; ML 1·1; Duration 0540

Standard Port HELGOLAND (⟵)

Times				Height (metres)			
High Water		Low Water		MHWS	MHWN	MLWN	MLWS
0200	0700	0200	0800	3·1	2·7	0·8	0·4
1400	1900	1400	2000				
Differences *DEN HELDER*							
–0410	*–0520*	*–0520*	*–0430*	*–1·3*	*–1·1*	*–0·4*	*–0·2*
K13A PLATFORM (53°13'·0N 03°13'·1E; 58M WNW of Den Helder)							
–0420	–0430	–0520	–0530	–1·4	–1·3	–0·3	–0·3

SHELTER Good in all yacht hbrs (see Facilities). Hbr speed limit 5kn. Den Helder is the main base of the Royal Netherlands Navy which manages the Marinehaven Willemsoord and KMYC.

NAVIGATION Caution: fast ferries to/from Texel, many FVs and offshore service vessels, strong tidal streams across the hbr ent.

Schulpengat leads into Marsdiep for the hbr ent. It is well marked/lit. WPT 52°52'·90N 04°37'·90E (SG (SWM) buoy, Mo (A) 8s, Racon Z) 026·5°/6M towards S14/MG17 SCM lt buoy.

Although closed as a shipping chan due to silting, the Molengat remains a viable fair weather chan for smaller craft, but depths are now unreliable as regular hydrographic surveys have been discontinued. Keep close W of Y bys marking E side. Do not attempt at night or in fresh NW-N wind or swell.

LIGHTS AND MARKS See chartlet and Lights, buoys and waypoints. Schulpengat: Dir lt Al WRG and F WRG. Kijkduin lt ho, R twr, is conspic 2·3M WSW of hbr. Hbr 191° ldg lts; front B ▲ on bldg; rear B ▼ on B lattice twr. A 60m radar twr is conspic on E side of hbr.

Entry sigs, from Hbr Control twr (W side of ent): ring of R lts = No entry/exit, except for the vessel indicated by Hbr Control Ch 62.

Bridges: Moorman bridge operates H24 7/7, except 0700-0845, 1200-1230, 1600-1700, giving access to Nieuwe Diep, Koopvaarder Lock and N Holland Canal.

Van Kinsbergen bridge is operated by HM, on request, Mon-Fri. All bridges are closed 0705-0810, 1200-1215, 1245-1300, 1600-1700, Mon-Fri. All LT.

COMMUNICATIONS (Code 0223) VTS 657522, monitor VHF Ch 62 *Den Helder Traffic* (VTS) in the Schulpengat and Marsdiep; info on request; Police 112/09008844; Water Police 616767; ⊜ 0255 566707; Immigration 08000543; British Consul (020) 676 4343; Ⓗ 696969; HM 613955, VHF Ch 14 (H24) also remote control of van Kinsbergen bridge; *Koopvaarders Lock* VHF Ch 22 (H24) also remote control of Burgemeester Vissersbrug; Moorman bridge VHF Ch 18 (H24).

FACILITIES **KMJC** is hard to stbd on entering Naval Hbr. ☎652645, mob 0651007528, VHF Ch 31, www.kmjc.eu €2·10 + €1·24 pp/day tax draught <4m.

Willemsoord Marina through Zeedoksluis by arrangement with HM (Ch 14) 0800-1700, expect wait of 1-1·5 hours. ☎616100, www.willemsoord.nl €1·65 + €1·24pp/day tax.

In or near **Binnenhaven**, YCs/marinas (MWV, HWN and Breewijd) can only be reached via the Rijkshaven, Moorman bridge, Nieuwe Diep and lock: **MWV YC** ☎652173, www.marinewatersport.nl €1·40 + €1·24pp/day tax. **HWN YC** ☎624422, www.wsvhwn.nl €1·00 + €1·24pp/day tax. **YC WSOV Breewijd** ☎615500 €0·75 + €1·20pp/day tax. **Council harbour** ☎613955 €1·30 + €1·24pp/day tax.

Services Floating dock. **Boatyard** Jachtwerf Den Helder ☎636964, (40t).

Town (Amsterdam). **Ferry** Hook-Harwich; Rotterdam-Hull, IJmuiden-Newcastle.

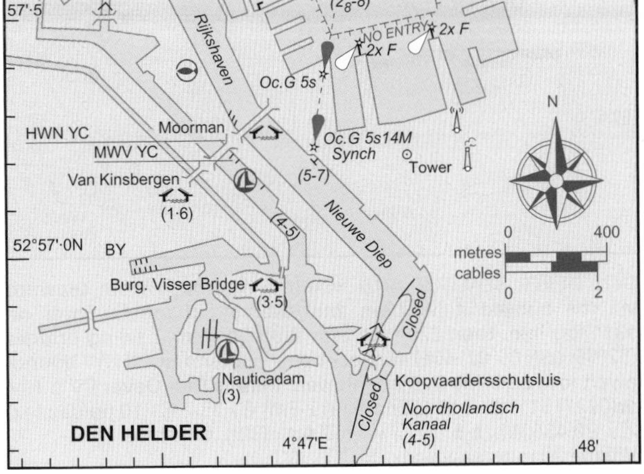

9.16.16 IJSSELMEER

CHARTS Zeekaart 1351, 1454; In-date DYC 1810, sheets 3-5, are essential to avoid live firing ranges, fishing areas and other hazards; 1810 also has many hbr chartlets.

TIDES The IJsselmeer is non-tidal. Tides seaward of Den Oever and Kornwerderzand locks: –0230 Dover; ML 1·2

Standard Port HELGOLAND (⟵)

Times				Height (metres)			
High Water		Low Water		MHWS	MHWN	MLWN	MLWS
0200	0700	0200	0800	3·1	2·7	0·8	0·4
1400	1900	1400	2000				
Differences DEN OEVER							
–0245	–0410	–0400	–0305	–1·2	–0·9	–0·5	–0·2
KORNWERDERZAND							
–0210	–0315	–0300	–0215	–1·0	–0·7	–0·4	–0·2

SHELTER Excellent in the marinas, but in the IJsselmeer strong winds can get up very quickly and often raise short, steep seas.

NAVIGATION Enter from sea by Den Oever or Kornwerderzand locks; also from IJmuiden via the Noordzeekanaal and Amsterdam.

Speed limits: 10·5kn in buoyed chans and <250m from shore. Hbr limits vary; see Special notes for the ANWB *Wateralmanak*.

A firing range, operational Tues to Thurs 1000–1900LT, extends S from Breezanddijk (53°01′·0N 05°12′·5E) to 3M NE of Medemblik then NNW to Den Oever (DYC 1811.3 & 1810.3). Call *Schietterrein Breezanddijk* (range control) Ch 71. Firing times are broadcast on VHF Ch 01 by Centrale Meldpost at H +15 on the day of firing, after weather forecasts.

R/T Nav info VHF Ch 01. Sealocks: Kornwerderzand 18; Den Oever 20. Enkhuizen naviduct 22; Lelystad 20; Oranjesluizen 18.

SEALOCKS Standard signals, see Special notes.

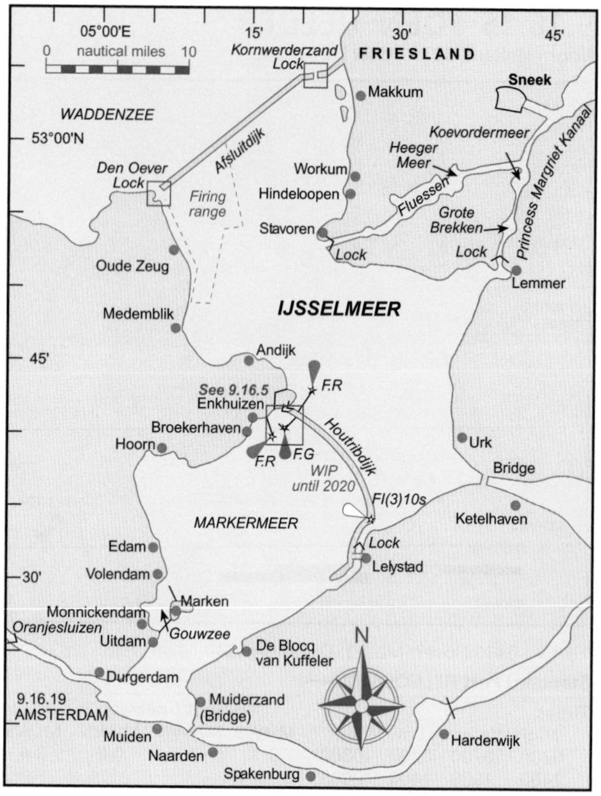

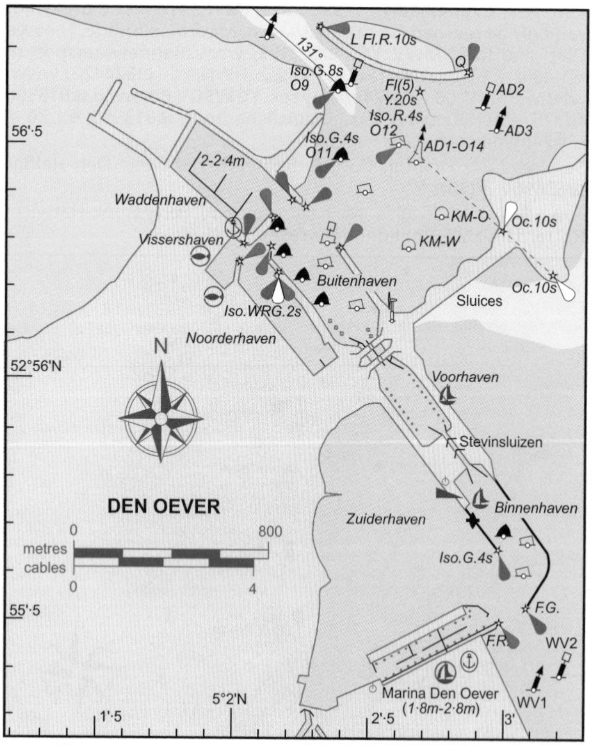

DEN OEVER SEALOCK AND MARINA Approach from seaward via the buoyed/lit Malzwin and Wierbalg channels. Enter on 131° ldg line, then 220° towards Buitenhaven. 2 swing bridges (52°56′·05N 05°02′·50E) and lock open in unison HO. If NW-bound, await lock opening in Binnenhaven. **Marina Den Oever BV** ⚓ HM ☎(0227) 511789, 310 ⊆inc Ⓥ (in 2-3m) €1·75 + €1·10 pp/day tax, ⚡ €0·45/kWh, 🚿 wi-fi 🔲 ⛽ ⛵(30t), bike hire.
Village 20 mins easy walk, ✕ 🛒 Ⓑ ✉.

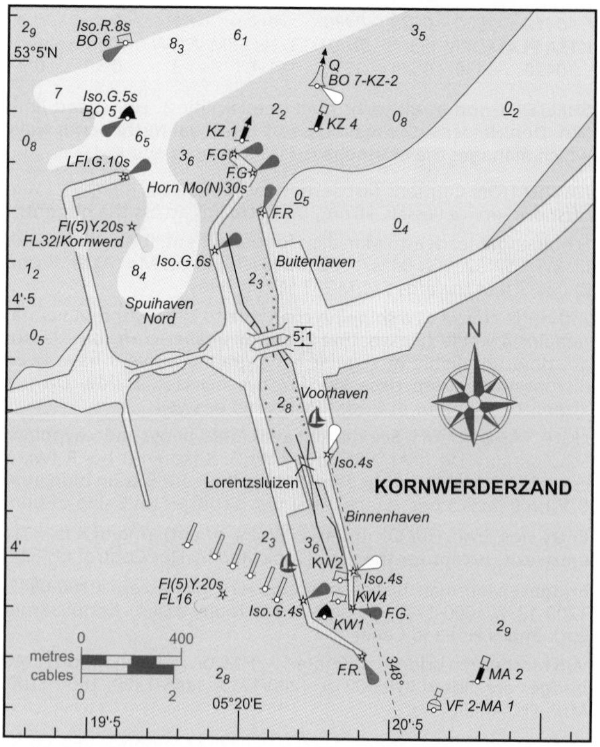

KORNWERDERZAND SEALOCK From seaward approach from the W via Doove Balg; from NW via shallow Inschot chan; or from N via Boontjes. Entrance to Buitenhaven has FR/G and Iso G 6s lts. When two road bridges (53°04′·44N 05°20′·09E) have opened, yachts enter the smaller Lorentz E lock, operates H24. N-bound, follow 348° ldg lts, Iso 4s, to FR/G at ent. Await lock in Binnenhaven (3·6m). HM ☎(0517) 578170. ⊖ 058 2949444.

FACILITIES clockwise from Kornwerderzand. Overnight fees range from approx €0·80 – €1·80/metre LOA. Most berths are bows on to a pontoon, stern lines to piles; there are few ⚓s.

IJSSELMEER EASTERN SHORE

MAKKUM: 1M SE of Kornwerderzand, MA5 SHM by, Iso G4s, marks the byd chan. FR/FG lts lead 090·5° into Makkum. To stbd, **Marina Makkum** (2·5-2·8m) ☎(0515) 232828, . 5 more marinas/YCs are to E; (40t) (30t). **Town** Ⓑ Dr.

WORKUM: 5M S of Makkum; FW ldg lts 081° along buoyed chan to **It Soal Marina** ☎(0515) 542937, .

HINDELOOPEN: **WV Hylper Haven** HM ☎(0514) 522009, . **Old Hbr** . **Jachthaven Hindeloopen** (500) HM ☎ 088 0504140. (65t).

STAVOREN: Ent Buitenhaven 048° on Dir lt Iso 4s between FR/G. Marina, €1·00, E of ent in Oudehaven; ☎(0514) 681216, VHF Ch 74. Or, 1km S, ent Nieuwe Voorhaven (FR/G & Fl 5s Dir lt) then via lock to **Marina Stavoren** (3m) ☎088 0504122. (65t); **Outer Marina** (3·5m) close S of Nieuwe Voorhaven. Also 3 other marinas. **Town** Ⓑ Dr.

LEMMER: Appr on ldg lts 038°, Iso 8s, to KL5/VL2 By; then ldg lts 083°, Iso 8s, through Lemstergeul. Lastly FG and Iso G 4s lead 065° into town and some 14 marinas. **Jachthaven Friese Hoek** (275) HM ☎ 088 0504130. (30t).

URK: Hbr ent ½M SE of lt ho. Dir lt Iso G 4s to hbr ent, FR/G. Hbr has 4 basins; keep NNW to berth in Nieuwe Haven, Westhaven or Oosthaven (3·3m). HM ☎(0527) 689970. **Westhaven** ; **Oosthaven** Ⓔ. **Town** EC Tues; Ⓑ Dr.

KETELHAVEN, E of Ketel bridge, (opens H+20/+50), for buoyed access chan to **Yachthaven Ketelmeer** ☎, 0321 312271, 300 inc in 3m most pile/ pontoon, some €1·27. wi-fi.

LELYSTAD: **Flevo** is 2M NNE of lock. (550) ☎(0320) 279800, (50t) . **Deko Marina** is close N of the lock; ☎(0320) 269000, . **WV Lelystad, Houtribhaven** (560) HM ☎(0320) 260198, (20t). S of lock **Bataviahaven** (150) Ch 14, HM ☎06 511 77049. **Marina Lelystadhaven** ☎(0320) 260326.

IJSSELMEER WESTERN SHORE

ENKHUIZEN: 036° ldg lts Iso 4s; 230° ldg lts Iso 8s. Here, the 13M Houtribdijk causeway between the Ijsselmeer and Markermeer is crossed by a double chamber lock above a road tunnel, minimising delays for boat and road traffic; call Ch 22. Boats <6m air clearance use Krabbersgat lock and bridge. **Compagnieshaven** (500) HM ☎(0228) 313353, (12); **Buyshaven** (195) ☎315660, ; **Buitenhaven** ☎312444. **Town** EC Mon; Market Wed; Ⓑ Dr .

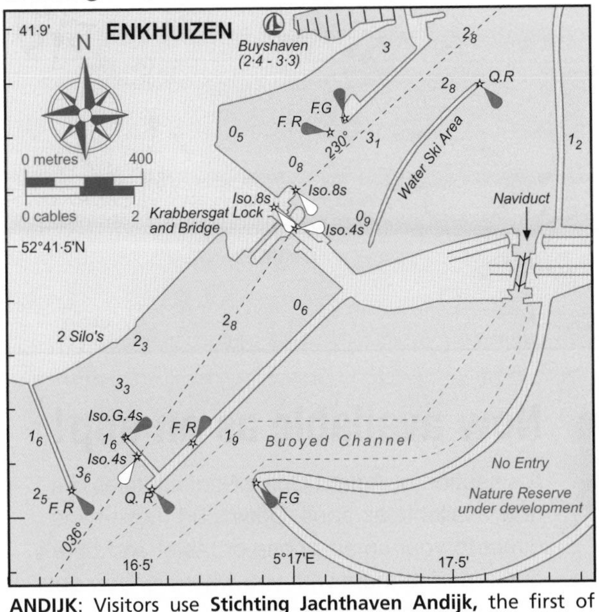

ANDIJK: Visitors use **Stichting Jachthaven Andijk,** the first of 2 marinas; (600) ☎(0228) 593075, narrow ent with tight turn between FR/G lts. (20t).

MEDEMBLIK: Ent on 232°, Dir lt Oc 5s between FR/G. Thence via Oosterhaven into Middenhaven (short stay) and via bridge to Westerhaven. **Pekelharinghaven** (120) HM ☎06 12335841; ent is to port by Castle, . **Middenhaven** HM ☎541686, **Stichting Jachthaven** HM ☎541681 in Westerhaven, . **Town** Ⓑ Dr. **Regatta Centre** 0·5M S of hbr entr. HM ☎(0227) 547781, 450, (20t).

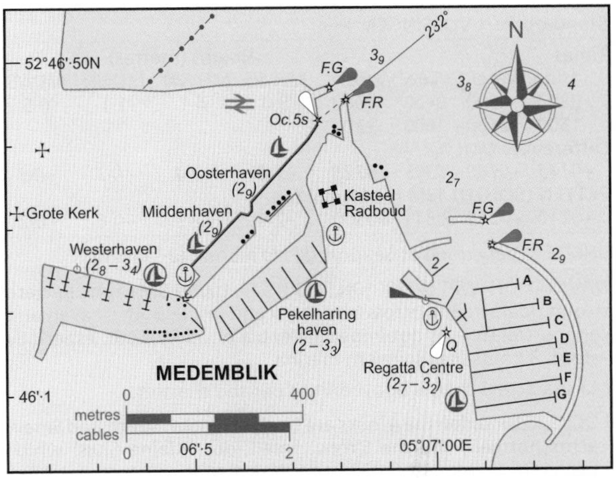

MARKERMEER is accessed from the sea via IJmuiden, Noordzeekanaal, or Amsterdam/Oranjesluizen. On the S side of Houtribdijk there is WIP until 2020 creating the artificial Marken Wadden islands nature reserve. Hbrs clockwise from Lelystad to Broekerhaven:

DE BLOCQ VAN KUFFELER: (8·5M SW Lelystad) ☎06 2751 2497.

MUIDERZAND: Ent 1M N of Hollandsebrug (12·7m cl'nce at SE corner of Markermeer) at buoys IJM5 & IJM7/JH2. **Marina** ☎(036) 5369151.

MUIDEN: Ldg lts Q 181° into **KNZ & RV Marina** (2·6m) W of ent; home of Royal Netherlands YC (150 berths). HM ☎(0294) 261450, www.knzrv.nl €1·95. On E bank **Stichting Jachthaven** (70) ☎(0294) 261223, €1·60.

DURGERDAM: ½M E of overhead power lines (70m); convenient for Oranjesluizen. Keep strictly in buoyed chan. **WV Durgerdam** Berth to stbd of ent (1·8m). ☎ 06 51628873.

UITDAM Appr from MIJ5 buoy Fl Y 5s via buoyed chan to FR/FG at ent. (9t). HM (020) 4031433.

MARKEN (picturesque show piece): Ent Gouwzee from N, abeam Volendam, thence via buoyed chan; Dir FW lt 116° between FR/G at hbr (2·2m). Lt ho, conspic, Oc 8s 16m 9M, on E end of island. HM ☎(0299) 601253, free on quay, Ⓑ.

MONNICKENDAM: Appr as for Marken, then W to MO10 Iso R 8s and 236° ldg lts FR. **Hemmeland Marina** ☎(0299) 655555, (2·0m) C. **Waterland Marina** ☎652000, (2·5m) (15t) www.jachthavenwaterland.nl. **Marina Monnickendam** ☎652595, (2·0m) C. **Zeilhoek Marina** ☎651463, (2·5m).

VOLENDAM: Fork stbd to old hbr (2·4m). Dir lt Fl 5s 313°. FR/FG at ent. ☎06 51337494, . Fork port via unlit buoyed chan to **Marina Volendam** (2·7m) HM (0299) 320262, Ⓑ (16t).

EDAM: Appr via unlit chan keeping Iso W 8s between FG /R at narrow ent; beware commercial traffic. **Jachthaven WSV De Zeevang** (2·2m) S side of outer hbr. ☎(0299) 350174. Or lock into the Oorgat and via S canal to Nieuwe Haven. **Town** Ⓑ.

HOORN: Radio twr (80m) 1·5M ENE of hbr. Iso 4s 15m 10M and FR/FG at W Hbr ent. Four options: To port **Grashaven** (700) HM ☎(0229) 215208. To stbd ⚓ in **Buitenhaven** (1.6m). Ahead & to stbd **WSV Hoorn,** (100) ☎213540. Ahead to **Binnenhaven** (2·5m) via narrow lock (open H24) . **Town** Ⓑ Dr.

BROEKERHAVEN: Small yacht hbr 1·5M SW of Enkhuizen. Appr from KG15-BR2 buoy. WSV de Broekerhaven ☎(0228) 518798.

9.16.17 IJMUIDEN

N Holland **52°27'·94N 04°32'·39E** (Hbr ent) SPM ❀❀◇◇◇✿✿

CHARTS AC 1631, 124; Zeekaart 1450, 1543, 1035, 1350; DYC 1801.8; Imray C25

TIDES +0400 Dover; ML 1·0. Noordzeekanaal level may be above or below sea level

Standard Port VLISSINGEN (⟶)

Times				Height (metres)			
High Water		Low Water		MHWS	MHWN	MLWN	MLWS
0300	0900	0400	1000	5·0	4·1	1·1	0·5
1500	2100	1600	2200				
Differences *IJMUIDEN*							
+0145	*+0140*	*+0305*	*+0325*	*–2·8*	*–2·4*	*–0·7*	*–0·3*
PETTEN (SOUTH) 18M N of IJmuiden							
+0210	+0215	+0345	+0500	–2·9	–2·3	–0·6	–0·2

SHELTER Very good at Seaport (SPM) marina (2·9-4·8m).

NAVIGATION WPT 52°28'·10N 04°30'·94E, 100°/0·9M to ent. Beware strong tidal streams across hbr ent, scend inside Buitenhaven and commercial tfc – do not impede. Keep a good lookout, especially astern. 3 knots max speed in marina.

Marina access chan is buoyed/lit as per the chartlet.

LOCKS In IJmuiden the 4 locks are North, Middle, South and Small. Yachts normally use the S'most Small lock (Kleine Sluis) which opens H24 on request Ch 22; wait W or E of it.

Lock signals shown W and E from each lock are standard, ie:

●● = Lock not in use; no entry. ● = No entry/exit.

●● = Prepare to enter/exit. ● = Enter or exit.

Tidal & sluicing sigs may be shown from or near the conspic Hbr Ops Centre (HOC) bldg, near the front 100·5° ldg lt:

Tidal signals: ● over Ⓦ = rising tide; Ⓦ over ● = falling tide.

Sluicing sigs are a △ of 3 horiz lts and 1 lt at the apex. The sluices are N of the N lock, so unlikely to affect yachts.

LIGHTS AND MARKS Both ldg lt ho's 100·5° for Zuider Buitenkanaal are dark R twrs. The HOC bldg is conspic next to front lt; so are 6 chimneys (138-166m high) 7ca N and ENE of Small lock.

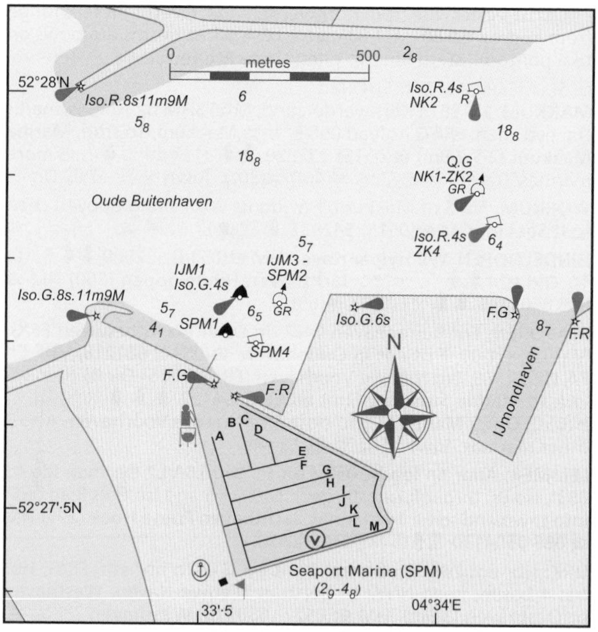

COMMUNICATIONS (Code 0255) Coast Guard 537644; Tfc Centre IJmuiden 564500, VHF Ch 07, see also VTS overleaf; Police 0900 8844; ⊖ 020 5813614; British Consul (020) 6764343; Ⓗ (023) 5453200; Hbr Ops 523934; Seaport Marina call *SPM* VHF Ch 74; Pilot 564503.

FACILITIES Seaport Marina (SPM) ☎560300. www.marinaseaport.nl info@ marinaseaport.nl ⓐ 600 inc♥ €2·20 inc. Berth as directed, or on M pontoon in a slot with green tally. (70t). Buses to Amsterdam and Haarlem in summer.

Town ✕ @ ✉ Ⓑ ⇌ (bus to Beverwijk) ✈ Amsterdam. **Ferry** IJmuiden-Newcastle.

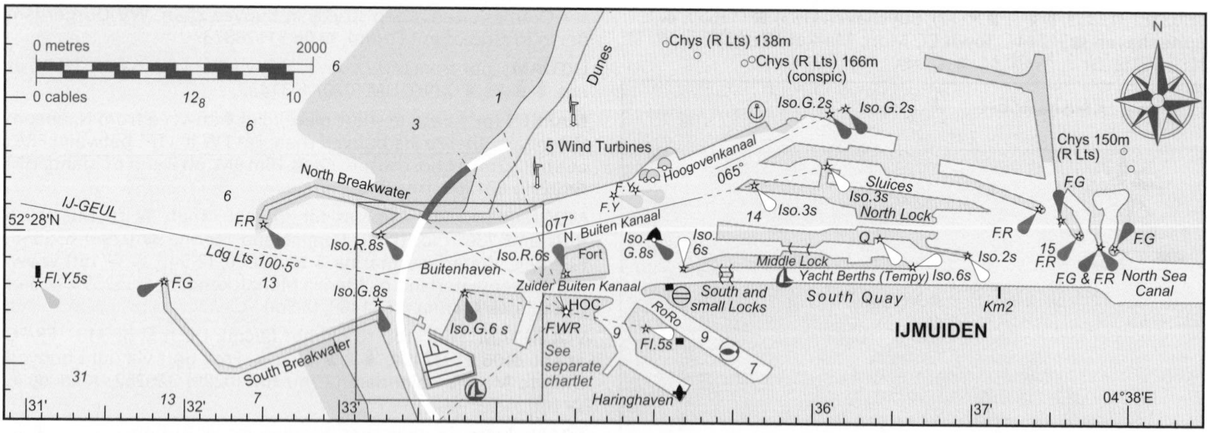

9.16.18 NOORDZEEKANAAL

VTS Monitor the following VTS stns (H24) in sequence to approach, enter and transit the canal (see diagram below):

• *IJmuiden Traffic Centre*	Ch 07	W of IJM C buoy
• *IJmuiden Port Control*	Ch 61	IJM buoy to locks
• *IJmuiden Locks*	Ch 22	at the locks
• *Noordzeekanaal Traffic Centre*	Ch 03	Locks to km 11
• *Amsterdam Port Control*	Ch 68	Km 11 – Amsterdam
• *Sector Schellingwoude*	Ch 60	City centre (04°55'E) to Buiten IJ

Radar surveillance is available on request Ch 07. Visibility reports are broadcast on all VHF chans every H+00 when vis <1000m.

NAVIGATION Canal speed limit is 9kn. The 13·5M transit is simple, but there is much commercial traffic. Keep as far to stbd as possible. Keep a good lookout for vessels emerging from dock basins and side canals. The banks and ents to basins and side canals are well lit, so night navigation need be no problem apart from the risk of not being seen by other vessels against shore lights.

FACILITIES There are small marinas at IJmond beyond lifting bridge (Ch 18) in Zijkanaal Km 10 (S bank); and at Nauerna (Zijkanaal Km 12) (N bank).

WV IJmond . Ch 31, HM ☎(023) 5375003, €1.10. (20t) ✕.

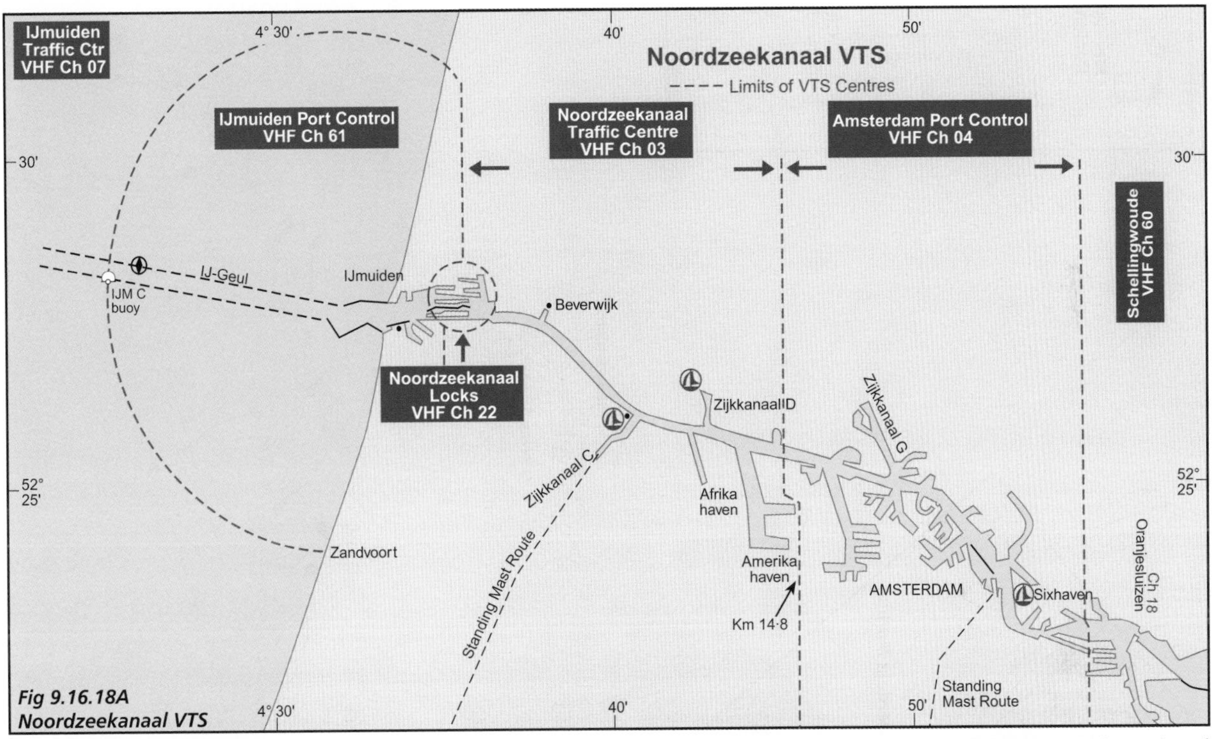

Fig 9.16.18A
Noordzeekanaal VTS

9.16.19 AMSTERDAM

Noord Holland **52°22'·97N 04°53'·92E** Marinas

CHARTS AC 124; DYC 1801.8, 1810.2; ANWB G, I

NAVIGATION Het IJ (pronounced eye) is the well-lit/buoyed chan through the city centre. From IJ 10/11 to IJ 14/15 buoys yachts must keep out of Het IJ, using a yacht chan between the lateral buoys and RW (N side) or GW (S side) buoys further outboard. A second recreational fairway, 100m wide and 5.5m deep (NAP), runs between IJ2 and IJ6.

Two yacht crossing points by YM 14-15 lead to Oranjesluizen, use the N lock, marked 'SPORT'; Ch 18, H24. Waiting piers/jetties either side. The Schellingwoude bridge (9m) opens on the hour and ±20 mins, except Mon-Fri 0600-0900 and 1600-1800; VHF Ch 18.

COMMUNICATIONS (Code 020) Emergency 112; Police 0900 8844; 5867511; Brit Consul 6764343; Dr 0880 030600; Traffic Info VHF Ch 68; Port Control (East) 6221515; Port Control (West) 0255 514457; Port Info VHF Ch 14; Westerdoks-brug 6241457, VHF Ch 22; Oranjesluizen VHF Ch 18; Amsterdam Marina VHF Ch 31.

FACILITIES Complete shelter in all yacht hbrs/marinas.

Amsterdam Marina (52°24'·12N 04°53'·10E) VHF Ch 31, ☎6310767. info@marinaamsterdam.com www.marinaamsterdam.com 250+100Ⓥ, max LOA 30m, €2·50 inc ✕.

City Marina IJdock 52°23'·04N 04°53'·63E, is centrally located in approach to Westerdok, due W of IJ6 buoy, within the IJdock high rise complex. Access through bridge opening on request, VHF Ch 22. Essential to book, HM ☎ 0687478290, www.citymarina.nl citymarina@outlook.com. 60 inc Ⓥ, €3·00 inc ; ✕ 5 mins walk to Haarlemmerstraat shopping centre and ⇌. Reports welcome.

Marina Het Realeneiland 52°23'·28N 04°53'·43E, in the Westerdok, ent lies W of Noordzee Canal IJ8 buoy, the two bridges open simultaneously on request: VHF Ch 22 or ☎0206241457. Must pre-book berth. No VHF, ☎6238855 or hetrealeneiland@upcmail.nl 50 incⓋ max LOA 30m. €2·50, hose/cable from HM, no on site but possible at local squash club. All facilities nearby, easy walk, 5 mins. Access by locked gate, key provided.

WVDS Sixhaven 52°22'·90N 04°54'·40E, close NE of IJ8 buoy and NE of conspic Central ⇌ Stn, is small, popular, and often full in season 1800-1100. ☎6329429, www.sixhaven.nl 100 +Ⓥ max LOA 15m. €1·50 inc (w/e) . WIP, due to end 2017, on adjacent new Metro N-S line detracts only slightly. Free ferries to N bank.

WV Aeolus 52°22'·91N 04°55'·17E. Few Ⓥ berths, rafting is strictly controlled. ☎6360791. Often full in season, no pre-booking, berth as directed. 45 + 8Ⓥ €1·10, YC. Free ferries to N bank.

Aquadam Twellegea 52°23'·04N 04°56'·63E, ent to Zijkanaal K. ☎6320616. €2·50, (30t). www.aquadam.nl Full facilities.

WV Zuiderzee 52°22'·95N 04°57'·77E, 140m NE of Oranjesluizen. ☎6946884, www.wsv-dezuiderzee.nl €1·10, YC.

City All needs; Ⓔ ACA, DYC Agent, Ⓑ @ ⇌ ✈. Amsterdam gives access to the N Holland and Rijn canals.

AMSTERDAM *continued*

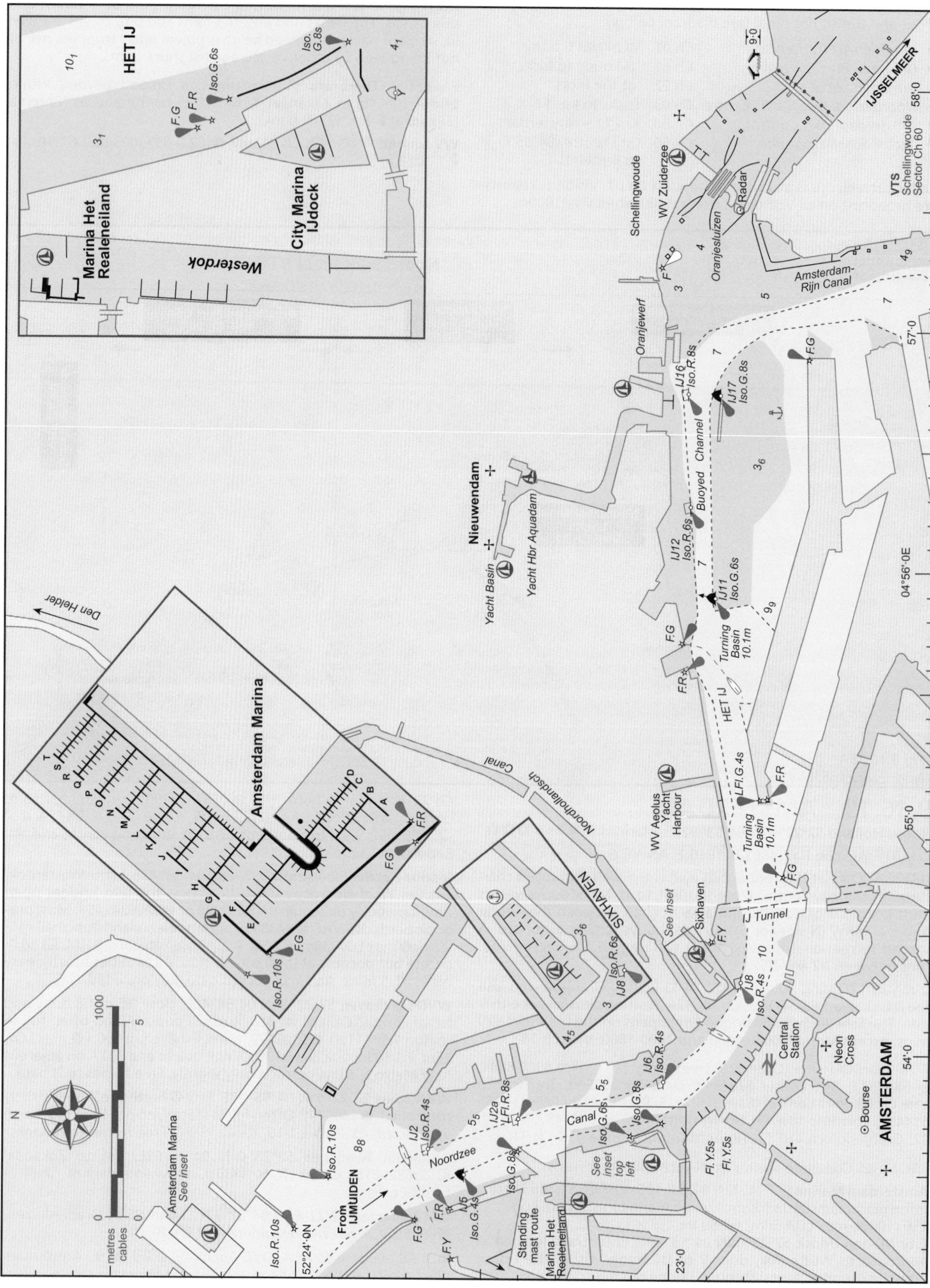
HET IJ
Marina Het Realeneiland
City Marina IJdock
Westerdok
Iso. G.8s
Iso.G.6s
F.R
F.G
Amsterdam Marina
Den Helder
Noordhollandsch Canal
SIXHAVEN
Nieuwendam
Yacht Basin
Yacht Hbr Aquadam
Oranjewerf
Schellingwoude
WV Zuiderzee
Oranjesluizen
Radar
Amsterdam-Rijn Canal
VTS
Schellingwoude
Sector Ch 60
IJSSELMEER
IJ16 Iso.R.8s
IJ17 Iso.G.8s
Buoyed Channel
IJ12 Iso.R.6s
IJ11 Iso.G.6s
Turning Basin 10.1m
WV Aeolus Yacht Harbour
LFl.G.4s
See inset
Sixhaven
F.Y
IJ Tunnel
IJ8 Iso.R.4s
IJ6 Iso.R.4s
Central Station
Neon Cross
Bourse
AMSTERDAM
IJ2 Iso.R.4s
IJ2a LFl.R.8s
Noordzee
Canal
See inset top left
IJ5 Iso.G.4s
Iso.G.8s
Fl.Y.5s
From IJMUIDEN
Iso.R.10s
Amsterdam Marina See inset
Standing mast route
Marina Het Realeneiland
metres
cables
N
52°24'·0N
23'·0
54'·0
55'·0
04°56'·0E
57'·0
58'·0

9.16.20 SCHEVENINGEN

Zuid Holland **52°06′·24N 04°15′·26E**

CHARTS AC 1630, 125, 122; Zeekaart 1035, 1349, 1350, 1449; DYC 1801.7; ANWB H/J; Imray C25

TIDES +0320 Dover; ML 0·9; Duration 0445

Standard Port VLISSINGEN (⟶)

Times				Height (metres)			
High Water		Low Water		MHWS	MHWN	MLWN	MLWS
0300	0900	0400	1000	5·0	4·1	1·1	0·5
1500	2100	1600	2200				
Differences *SCHEVENINGEN*							
+0105	*+0100*	*+0220*	*+0245*	*–2·7*	*–2·3*	*–0·7*	*–0·2*

SHELTER Very good in marina. Ent difficult in SW-N F6 winds, and dangerous in NW F6-8 which cause scend in outer hbr.

NAVIGATION WPT 52°07′·75N 04°14′·12E (SCH buoy) 156°/1·6M to ent; access H24. Close west of the 156° leading line and 1M from the hbr ent, outfalls are marked by E and W cardinal light buoys and by 2 SPM buoys (off chartlet). The promenade pier, Iso 5s, is 1·2M NE of the hbr ent. Caution: Strong tidal streams set across the ent. Slack water is about HW Scheveningen –2 and +3. Beware large ships and FVs entering/leaving.

LIGHTS AND MARKS Daymarks include: the reddish-brown lt ho (5ca E of hbr ent); twr bldgs in Scheveningen and Den Haag.

Traffic signals (from signal mast, N side of ent to Voorhaven):

● over ○ = No entry. ○ over ● = No exit.

Fl ● = One or more large vessels are leaving the port.

Tide sigs (same mast): ● over ○ = tide rising. ○ ● = tide falling.

Shown from SE end of narrow chan between 1st and 2nd Hbrs: ● = vessels must not leave the 2nd Hbr. The chan is generally blind, so go slowly and sound horn.

COMMUNICATIONS (Code 070) Call *Traffic Centre Scheveningen* Ch 21 (H24) prior to entry/departure to avoid FVs; Police 0900 8844; ⊖ 020 5813614; Brit Consul (020) 6764343; Dr 3450650; Port HM 3527711; Radar (info only) on request VHF Ch 21; When in 2nd Hbr call *Yacht Club Scheveningen* VHF Ch 31 for a berth.

FACILITIES **YC Scheveningen** ☎3520017, mob 0653 293137. www.jachtclubscheveningen.com info@jachtclubscheveningen.com 223 + 100Ⓥ €2·00 + €2·05 pp/day tax. Visitors *must* turn to berth/raft bows NE, for fire safety reasons. ✕ ☎3520308.

2nd Harbour Fuel barge GEO (0630-1600) only. DYC agent;

Town Rotterdam and Amsterdam. The town is effectively merged with Den Haag (The Hague), seat of Dutch government and well worth a visit by bus.

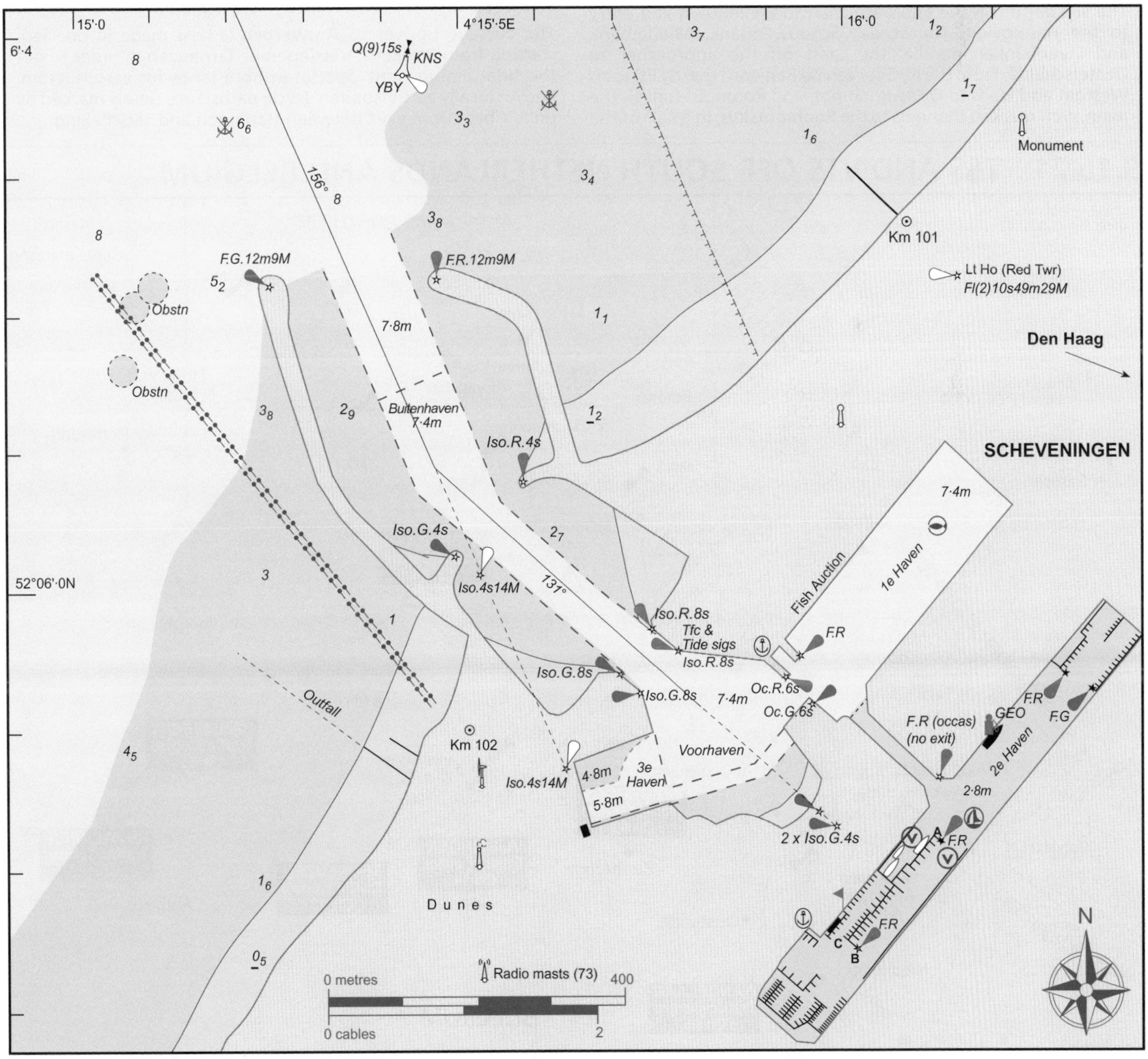

DEN HELDER TO SCHEVENINGEN

South of Den Helder the coast is low, and, like most of the Dutch coast, not readily visible from seaward. Conspic landmarks include: chimneys of nuclear power station 1·5M NNE of Petten; Egmond aan Zee lighthouse; chimneys of steelworks N of IJmuiden; two light houses at IJmuiden; big hotels at Zandvoort; Noordwijk aan Zee light house; and Scheveningen lighthouse and big hotels.

Egmond aan Zee wind farm, 36 turbines, 52°36′·03N 04°26′·47E (about 6·7M W of the town it is named after) and 8M further W Prinses Amalia Windpark, 60 turbines, is centred on 52°35′·27N 04°13′·55E. Luchterduinen wind farm, 43 turbines, centred on 52°40′·20N 04°16′·22E is 14M WSW of IJmuiden. All show FR lts and Fl Y on perimeters: see AC 1631 and AC 1408.

▶*3M W of IJmuiden the N-going stream begins at HW Hoek van Holland –0120, and the S-going at HW Hoek van Holland +0430, sp rates about 1·5kn. Off ent to IJmuiden the stream turns about 1h earlier and is stronger, and in heavy weather there may be a dangerous sea.*◀ From **IJmuiden** the **Noordzeekanaal** leads east to **Amsterdam** and the **IJsselmeer**.

HOEK VAN HOLLAND TO THE WESTERSCHELDE

Off Hoek van Holland at the ent to Europoort and **Rotterdam** shipping is dense and fast-moving. Yachts must go upriver via the Nieuwe Waterweg which near Vlaardingen becomes the Nieuwe Maas.

The Slijkgat (lit) is the approach chan to **Stellendam** and entry to the Haringvliet. The Schaar, Schouwenbank, Middelbank and Steenbanken parallel the coast off the approaches to Oosterschelde. From the N, Geul van de Banjaard (partly lit) joins Westgat and leads to Oude Roompot, and Roompot (unlit) the main, well-marked channels to the **Roompotsluis**, in S half of the barrage. Here the Oosterschelde (AC 192) is entered.

Rounding Walcheren via the Oostgat, close inshore, Westkapelle lt ho is conspic with two smaller lts nearby: Molenhoofd 5ca WSW and Noorderhoofd 7ca NNW. The Oostgat is the inshore link between Oosterschelde and Westerschelde and also the N approach to the latter.

Deurloo and Spleet are unlit secondary channels parallel to Oostgat and a mile or so to seaward. By day they keep yachts clear of commercial traffic in the Oostgat.

All channels converge between **Vlissingen** and **Breskens.** This bottleneck is declared a Precautionary Area where yachts have no rights of way over other vessels. An above-average lookout, and traffic avoidance is essential. Vessels <20m must give way to larger craft; yachts <12m must stay outside the buoyed chans.

The main approach chan to the Westerschelde from the W is the Scheur, which yachts may follow just outside the fairway. From **Zeebrugge** and the SW use the Wielingen chan, keeping close to S side of estuary until past **Breskens**.

If crossing the Scheur there are two recommended routes. The W route runs to the W of Songa with a dogleg at W10 towards SG-W. The E route from Breskens, head up channel from ARV-VH, staying S of the G bys, turning N to cross the mini-TSS which runs E/W close off Vlissingen. Ensure you cross at right angles. The tide runs hard in the estuary, causing a bad sea in chans and overfalls on some banks in strong winds. There is shoaling.

The passage upriver to **Antwerpen** is best made in one leg, starting from Breskens, Vlissingen or **Terneuzen** in order to get the tidal timing right. Special inshore lanes for vessels <15m, known locally as 'fietspaden' (cycle paths!) are clearly marked by unlit Y bys. More exist between Harlingen and Terschelling.

9.16.21 TSS AND VTS OFF SOUTH NETHERLANDS AND BELGIUM

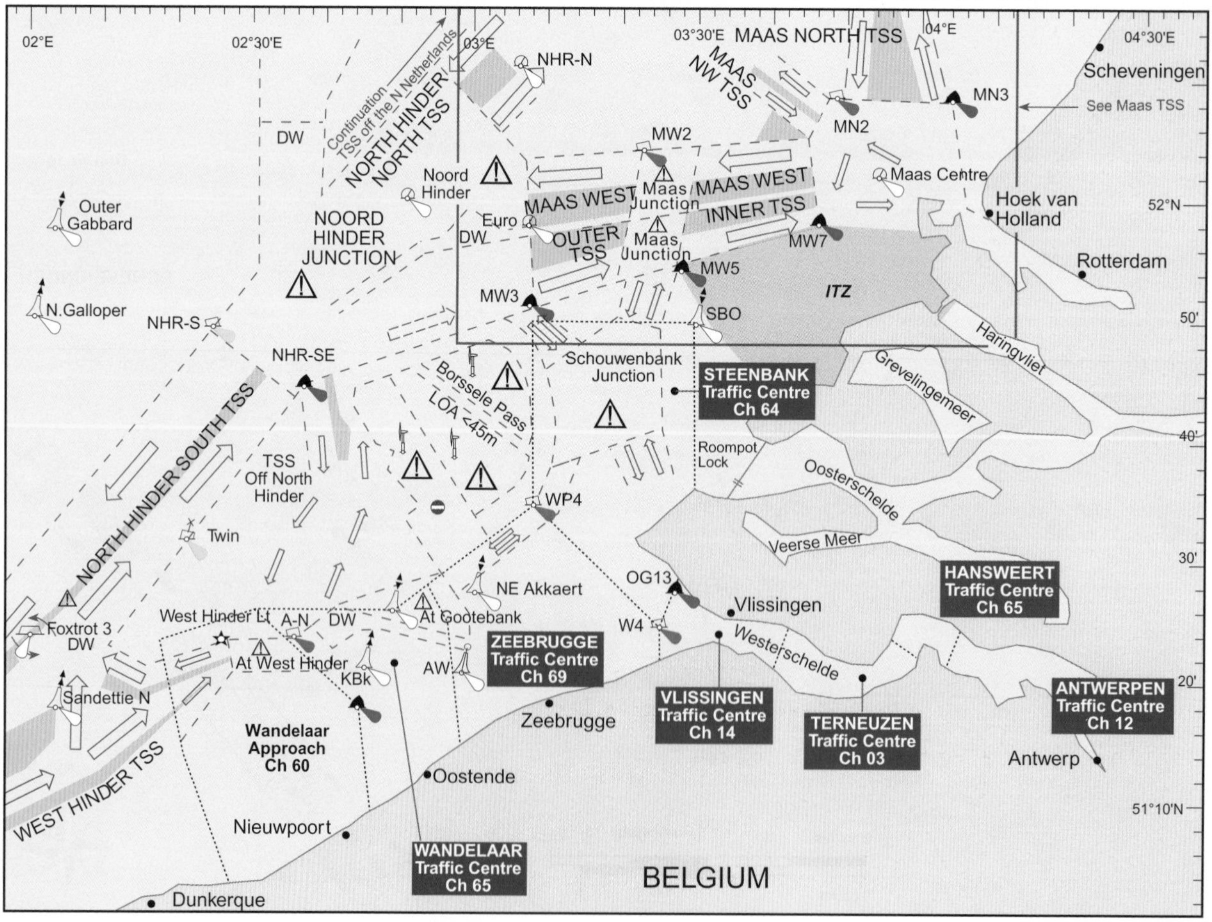

STANDARD TIME UT –01
Subtract 1 hour for UT
For Dutch Summer Time add ONE hour in **non-shaded areas**

HOEK VAN HOLLAND LAT 51°59′N LONG 4°07′E

TIMES AND HEIGHTS OF HIGH AND LOW WATERS

Dates in red are SPRINGS
Dates in blue are NEAPS

YEAR **2018**

JANUARY

Date	Time	m	Date	Time	m
1	0132	2.3	16	0236	2.1
	0656	0.4		0806	0.3
M	1355	2.3	TU	1445	2.1
	1909	0.3		2050	0.5
2	0222	2.3	17	0304	2.1
	0731	0.4		0824	0.3
TU	1441	2.4	W	1519	2.2
	○ 1955	0.4		● 2204	0.5
3	0308	2.3	18	0339	2.1
	0815	0.3		0849	0.3
W	1527	2.4	TH	1555	2.2
	2035	0.4		2300	0.5
4	0355	2.2	19	0411	2.1
	0858	0.2		0926	0.2
TH	1612	2.4	F	1625	2.2
				2344	0.5
5	0024	0.5	20	0445	2.1
	0445	2.2		0955	0.2
F	0945	0.2	SA	1701	2.2
	1657	2.4			
6	0114	0.5	21	0046	0.5
	0531	2.1		0520	2.1
SA	1035	0.2	SU	1024	0.2
	1748	2.4		1735	2.2
7	0226	0.5	22	0126	0.5
	0626	2.1		0549	2.0
SU	1129	0.1	M	1110	0.2
	1845	2.3		1808	2.2
8	0305	0.5	23	0205	0.5
	0714	2.0		0629	2.0
M	1229	0.1	TU	1144	0.1
	◑ 1946	2.2		1856	2.2
9	0416	0.5	24	0234	0.5
	0813	1.9		0716	2.0
TU	1346	0.2	W	1234	0.1
	2050	2.1		◐ 1945	2.1
10	0246	0.5	25	0220	0.5
	0915	1.9		0815	2.0
W	1434	0.3	TH	1344	0.1
	2206	2.0		2056	2.1
11	0334	0.5	26	0306	0.5
	1041	1.8		0926	1.9
TH	1604	0.3	F	1455	0.2
	2316	1.9		2206	2.0
12	0435	0.5	27	0354	0.5
	1139	1.9		1035	1.9
F	1726	0.4	SA	1616	0.2
				2315	2.0
13	0015	2.0	28	0455	0.5
	0535	0.5		1146	2.0
SA	1240	1.9	SU	1715	0.3
	1815	0.4			
14	0104	2.0	29	0022	2.0
	0915	0.4		0549	0.4
SU	1325	2.0	M	1248	2.1
	1905	0.4		1815	0.3
15	0206	2.0	30	0119	2.1
	0714	0.4		0635	0.4
M	1404	2.1	TU	1339	2.2
	1955	0.5		1859	0.4
			31	0208	2.1
				0715	0.3
			W	1427	2.3
				○ 2240	0.4

FEBRUARY

Date	Time	m	Date	Time	m
1	0256	2.2	16	0319	2.1
	0759	0.2		0824	0.2
TH	1512	2.4	F	1536	2.2
	2325	0.4		2250	0.5
2	0345	2.2	17	0348	2.1
	0846	0.2		0855	0.2
F	1557	2.4	SA	1606	2.3
				2335	0.4
3	0015	0.4	18	0421	2.1
	0427	2.2		0925	0.2
SA	0925	0.1	SU	1637	2.3
	1642	2.4			
4	0105	0.4	19	0015	0.4
	0510	2.2		0458	2.1
SU	1016	0.1	M	0959	0.1
	1731	2.4		1716	2.2
5	0154	0.4	20	0054	0.4
	0559	2.1		0528	2.1
M	1059	0.1	TU	1040	0.1
	1819	2.3		1747	2.2
6	0250	0.4	21	0145	0.4
	0646	2.1		0605	2.1
TU	1155	0.1	W	1115	0.1
	1905	2.2		1827	2.2
7	0055	0.5	22	0210	0.4
	0736	2.0		0649	2.1
W	1253	0.2	TH	1203	0.1
	◑ 2006	2.0		1915	2.1
8	0144	0.4	23	0029	0.4
	0830	1.9		0739	2.0
TH	1404	0.2	F	1314	0.1
	2105	1.9		◐ 2020	2.0
9	0255	0.4	24	0224	0.4
	0935	1.8		0845	1.9
F	1530	0.3	SA	1435	0.2
	2225	1.7		2136	1.9
10	0426	0.4	25	0336	0.4
	1100	1.7		1010	1.9
SA	1654	0.4	SU	1545	0.3
	2350	1.7		2256	1.8
11	0525	0.4	26	0425	0.4
	1210	1.8		1131	1.9
SU	1800	0.4	M	1705	0.3
12	0050	1.8	27	0010	1.8
	0615	0.3		0535	0.4
M	1305	1.9	TU	1231	2.0
	1854	0.4		2040	0.3
13	0133	1.9	28	0109	1.9
	0659	0.3		0619	0.3
TU	1349	2.0	W	1326	2.2
	2154	0.4		2140	0.3
14	0220	2.0			
	0740	0.3			
W	1425	2.1			
	2234	0.5			
15	0255	2.0			
	0816	0.3			
TH	1454	2.2			
	● 2237	0.5			

MARCH

Date	Time	m	Date	Time	m
1	0158	2.0	16	0226	1.9
	0701	0.2		0734	0.3
TH	1416	2.3	F	1431	2.2
	2225	0.4		2256	0.4
2	0242	2.1	17	0251	2.0
	0745	0.2		0755	0.2
F	1457	2.3	SA	1506	2.2
	○ 2254	0.4		● 2250	0.4
3	0326	2.1	18	0320	2.1
	0822	0.1		0825	0.2
SA	1541	2.4	SU	1539	2.3
	2345	0.4		2305	0.4
4	0407	2.2	19	0356	2.1
	0901	0.1		0855	0.1
SU	1622	2.4	M	1610	2.3
				2345	0.4
5	0045	0.4	20	0431	2.1
	0448	2.2		0935	0.1
M	0945	0.1	TU	1647	2.3
	1707	2.3			
6	0145	0.4	21	0034	0.3
	0528	2.2		0507	2.1
TU	1410	0.1	W	1011	0.1
	1748	2.2		1727	2.2
7	0220	0.4	22	0114	0.3
	0611	2.1		0545	2.1
W	1125	0.2	TH	1056	0.1
	1835	2.1		1807	2.1
8	0255	0.4	23	0200	0.3
	0656	2.1		0626	2.1
TH	1224	0.2	F	1144	0.1
	1925	1.9		1856	2.0
9	0110	0.3	24	0004	0.3
	0746	1.9		0718	2.1
F	1325	0.2	SA	1330	0.2
	◑ 2016	1.8		◐ 1956	1.9
10	0210	0.3	25	0200	0.3
	0846	1.8		0826	1.9
SA	1457	0.3	SU	1434	0.2
	2115	1.6		2104	1.7
11	0405	0.3	26	0316	0.3
	1000	1.7		0955	1.9
SU	1624	0.4	M	1556	0.3
	2304	1.5		2234	1.6
12	0506	0.3	27	0405	0.3
	1135	1.7		1116	1.9
M	1735	0.4	TU	1910	0.3
13	0014	1.6	28	0000	1.7
	0554	0.3		0515	0.3
TU	1240	1.8	W	1225	2.0
	1840	0.4		2034	0.3
14	0104	1.7	29	0059	1.8
	0635	0.3		0855	0.2
W	1326	2.0	TH	1315	2.1
	2120	0.4		2115	0.3
15	0149	1.9	30	0145	1.9
	0720	0.3		0955	0.2
TH	1405	2.1	F	1358	2.2
	2205	0.4		2206	0.3
			31	0229	2.0
				0726	0.2
			SA	1441	2.3
				○ 2245	0.4

APRIL

Date	Time	m	Date	Time	m
1	0307	2.1	16	0251	2.1
	0759	0.2		0756	0.2
SU	1520	2.3	M	1510	2.3
	2336	0.4		● 2019	0.4
2	0345	2.1	17	0329	2.2
	0845	0.2		0836	0.1
M	1602	2.3	TU	1547	2.3
				2340	0.3
3	0025	0.3	18	0405	2.2
	0425	2.2		0910	0.1
TU	1245	0.2	W	1625	2.3
	1646	2.2			
4	0116	0.3	19	0014	0.3
	0505	2.2		0445	2.2
W	1346	0.2	TH	0949	0.2
	1726	2.1		1706	2.2
5	0156	0.3	20	0105	0.3
	0541	2.1		0526	2.2
TH	1415	0.2	F	1034	0.2
	1806	2.0		1750	2.1
6	0220	0.3	21	0145	0.3
	0626	2.1		0607	2.2
F	1230	0.3	SA	1330	0.2
	1845	1.9		1840	1.9
7	0015	0.3	22	0005	0.2
	0706	2.0		0659	2.1
SA	1320	0.3	SU	1344	0.2
	1923	1.7		◐ 1945	1.8
8	0115	0.2	23	0125	0.2
	0800	1.8		0810	2.0
SU	1440	0.4	M	1434	0.3
	◑ 2035	1.6		2105	1.6
9	0337	0.2	24	0245	0.2
	0910	1.7		0935	1.9
M	1605	0.4	TU	1534	0.3
	2125	1.5		2230	1.6
10	0446	0.2	25	0350	0.2
	1034	1.7		1059	1.9
TU	1714	0.4	W	1904	0.3
	2330	1.5		2346	1.7
11	0535	0.2	26	0450	0.2
	1206	1.8		1203	2.0
W	1820	0.4	TH	2020	0.3
12	0036	1.6	27	0039	1.8
	0614	0.2		0824	0.2
TH	1245	1.9	F	1255	2.1
	2025	0.4		2110	0.3
13	0116	1.8	28	0129	1.9
	0654	0.2		0915	0.2
F	1325	2.1	SA	1338	2.2
	2140	0.3		2140	0.3
14	0145	1.9	29	0205	2.0
	0659	0.2		0706	0.2
SA	1405	2.2	SU	1420	2.2
	2215	0.3		2226	0.3
15	0215	2.0	30	0247	2.1
	0726	0.2		0745	0.2
SU	1430	2.3	M	1505	2.2
	2300	0.4		○ 2306	0.3

Chart Datum is 0·92 metres below NAP Datum. HAT is 2·5 metres above Chart Datum.

STANDARD TIME UT –01
Subtract 1 hour for UT
For Dutch Summer Time add ONE hour in **non-shaded areas**

HOEK VAN HOLLAND LAT 51°59′N LONG 4°07′E

TIMES AND HEIGHTS OF HIGH AND LOW WATERS

Dates in red are SPRINGS
Dates in blue are NEAPS

YEAR **2018**

MAY

Date	Time	m	Time	m	Time	m	Time	m
1 TU	0322	2.1	0826	0.3	1540	2.2	2356	0.3
2 W	0405	2.2	1205	0.2	1618	2.1		
3 TH	0035	0.2	0438	2.2	1254	0.3	1659	2.0
4 F	0125	0.2	0515	2.1	1346	0.3	1738	1.9
5 SA	0135	0.2	0555	2.1	1340	0.4	1804	1.8
6 SU	0205	0.2	0636	2.0	1357	0.4	1856	1.8
7 M	0040	0.2	0715	1.9	1440	0.4	1945	1.7
8 TU	0135	0.2	0836	1.8	1555	0.4	◑ 2044	1.6
9 W	0421	0.2	0934	1.7	1644	0.4	2205	1.5
10 TH	0505	0.2	1105	1.8	1744	0.4	2314	1.6
11 F	0554	0.2	1200	1.9	1950	0.4		
12 SA	0026	1.7	0750	0.2	1246	2.1	2106	0.3
13 SU	0105	1.9	0615	0.2	1325	2.2	2144	0.3
14 M	0146	2.0	0649	0.2	1401	2.3	2225	0.3
15 TU	0222	2.1	0730	0.2	1440	2.3	● 1956	0.3
16 W	0301	2.2	0805	0.2	1526	2.3	2024	0.3
17 TH	0342	2.2	0845	0.2	1603	2.2	2109	0.3
18 F	0426	2.3	0929	0.2	1647	2.1	2155	0.2
19 SA	0505	2.3	1300	0.3	1736	2.0	2250	0.2
20 SU	0555	2.2	1340	0.3	1825	1.9	2349	0.1
21 M	0649	2.1	1347	0.3	1924	1.8		
22 TU	0055	0.1	0805	2.0	1415	0.3	◐ 2049	1.7
23 W	0205	0.1	0926	2.0	1715	0.3	2205	1.7
24 TH	0325	0.2	1035	2.0	1840	0.3	2320	1.7
25 F	0655	0.2	1146	2.1	1945	0.3		
26 SA	0016	1.8	0754	0.2	1235	2.1	2035	0.3
27 SU	0101	1.9	0844	0.2	1321	2.1	2117	0.3
28 M	0145	2.0	0655	0.3	1402	2.1	2205	0.3
29 TU	0228	2.1	0740	0.3	1445	2.1	○ 2240	0.3
30 W	0305	2.1	0819	0.3	1525	2.1	2335	0.3
31 TH	0341	2.1	1120	0.3	1605	2.0		

JUNE

Date	Time	m	Time	m	Time	m	Time	m
1 F	0016	0.2	0417	2.2	1210	0.4	1634	2.0
2 SA	0035	0.2	0455	2.1	1250	0.4	1715	1.9
3 SU	0120	0.1	0536	2.1	1317	0.4	1756	1.9
4 M	0145	0.1	0604	2.0	1400	0.4	1819	1.8
5 TU	0225	0.1	0644	2.0	1425	0.4	1905	1.8
6 W	0055	0.1	0756	1.9	1520	0.4	◑ 2016	1.7
7 TH	0155	0.1	0856	1.9	1610	0.4	2116	1.7
8 F	0249	0.2	1000	1.9	1657	0.4	2226	1.7
9 SA	0354	0.2	1055	2.0	1750	0.4	2330	1.8
10 SU	0444	0.2	1155	2.1	2007	0.4		
11 M	0026	1.9	0535	0.2	1250	2.2	2126	0.3
12 TU	0112	2.0	0626	0.2	1336	2.2	1855	0.3
13 W	0155	2.2	0705	0.2	1417	2.3	● 1928	0.3
14 TH	0240	2.2	0750	0.2	1506	2.2	2009	0.2
15 F	0322	2.3	0829	0.3	1547	2.2	2056	0.2
16 SA	0407	2.3	0915	0.4	1632	2.1	2139	0.2
17 SU	0455	2.3	1255	0.4	1720	2.0	2236	0.1
18 M	0540	2.3	1354	0.3	1819	1.9	2325	0.1
19 TU	0635	2.2	1454	0.4	1914	1.9		
20 W	0035	0.1	0745	2.1	1600	0.4	◐ 2030	1.8
21 TH	0133	0.1	0855	2.1	1716	0.4	2136	1.8
22 F	0244	0.1	1005	2.0	1755	0.4	2246	1.8
23 SA	0345	0.2	1116	2.0	1910	0.4	2346	1.8
24 SU	0715	0.2	1216	2.0	2007	0.4		
25 M	0035	1.9	0554	0.3	1305	2.1	2115	0.3
26 TU	0126	2.0	0649	0.3	1344	2.1	1914	0.3
27 W	0209	2.0	0750	0.4	1436	2.1	1945	0.3
28 TH	0249	2.1	0850	0.4	1508	2.0	○ 2035	0.2
29 F	0325	2.1	1010	0.4	1545	2.0	2055	0.2
30 SA	0406	2.2	1120	0.5	1625	2.0		

JULY

Date	Time	m	Time	m	Time	m	Time	m
1 SU	0010	0.2	0435	2.2	1214	0.4	1655	2.0
2 M	0040	0.2	0515	2.1	1245	0.4	1725	1.9
3 TU	0114	0.1	0545	2.1	1335	0.4	1759	1.9
4 W	0200	0.1	0625	2.1	1415	0.4	1834	1.9
5 TH	0015	0.1	0706	2.0	1454	0.4	1925	1.8
6 F	0104	0.1	0755	2.0	1510	0.5	◑ 2036	1.8
7 SA	0155	0.1	0910	2.0	1524	0.4	2135	1.8
8 SU	0305	0.1	1016	2.0	1605	0.4	2246	1.9
9 M	0416	0.2	1121	2.1	1704	0.4	2346	1.9
10 TU	0505	0.2	1216	2.1	1755	0.4		
11 W	0041	2.1	0605	0.2	1312	2.2	1836	0.3
12 TH	0136	2.2	0649	0.3	1359	2.2	1916	0.3
13 F	0222	2.3	0735	0.3	1445	2.2	● 1956	0.2
14 SA	0306	2.3	0818	0.4	1535	2.2	2038	0.2
15 SU	0350	2.4	1154	0.4	1617	2.1	2119	0.1
16 M	0437	2.4	1306	0.4	1707	2.1	2209	0.1
17 TU	0527	2.4	1356	0.4	1759	2.0	2305	0.1
18 W	0619	2.3	1434	0.4	1856	2.0	2359	0.1
19 TH	0715	2.2	1535	0.4	1955	1.9	◐	
20 F	0104	0.1	0820	2.1	1625	0.5	2044	1.9
21 SA	0205	0.1	0925	2.0	1509	0.4	2206	1.8
22 SU	0315	0.2	1035	1.9	1626	0.4	2310	1.8
23 M	0434	0.3	1156	1.9	1714	0.4		
24 TU	0009	1.9	0535	0.3	1245	2.0	1809	0.4
25 W	0103	2.0	0634	0.4	1340	2.0	1854	0.3
26 TH	0156	2.0	0725	0.4	1419	2.0	1934	0.3
27 F	0235	2.1	0820	0.5	1459	2.0	○ 2015	0.3
28 SA	0309	2.2	0920	0.5	1535	2.0	2035	0.2
29 SU	0345	2.2	1044	0.5	1606	2.1	2103	0.2
30 M	0415	2.2	1135	0.5	1635	2.1	2139	0.2
31 TU	0448	2.2	1236	0.5	1710	2.0	2216	0.2

AUGUST

Date	Time	m	Time	m	Time	m	Time	m
1 W	0525	2.2	1304	0.5	1735	2.0	2249	0.2
2 TH	0555	2.2	1344	0.5	1816	2.0	2330	0.1
3 F	0636	2.2	1436	0.5	1849	2.0		
4 SA	0004	0.1	0720	2.1	1434	0.5	◑ 1945	2.0
5 SU	0115	0.1	0813	2.1	1440	0.5	2045	1.9
6 M	0224	0.2	0930	2.0	1536	0.4	2159	1.9
7 TU	0346	0.2	1039	2.0	1629	0.4	2315	2.0
8 W	0450	0.3	1149	2.0	1725	0.4		
9 TH	0019	2.1	0545	0.3	1251	2.1	1820	0.3
10 F	0115	2.2	0640	0.4	1348	2.1	1855	0.3
11 SA	0206	2.3	0719	0.4	1435	2.2	● 1940	0.2
12 SU	0251	2.4	0759	0.5	1519	2.2	2015	0.2
13 M	0335	2.4	1156	0.5	1602	2.2	2059	0.1
14 TU	0419	2.4	1246	0.5	1647	2.2	2146	0.1
15 W	0507	2.4	1325	0.5	1736	2.1	2235	0.1
16 TH	0552	2.3	1436	0.5	1825	2.1	2325	0.2
17 F	0645	2.2	1515	0.5	1904	2.1		
18 SA	0029	0.2	0739	2.1	1325	0.5	◐ 2005	2.0
19 SU	0134	0.2	0840	2.0	1430	0.5	2116	1.9
20 M	0254	0.3	0944	1.8	1545	0.4	2235	1.8
21 TU	0415	0.4	1120	1.8	1654	0.4	2350	1.9
22 W	0524	0.4	1225	1.9	1755	0.4		
23 TH	0044	2.0	0625	0.5	1326	1.9	1835	0.3
24 F	0135	2.1	0944	0.5	1405	2.0	1920	0.3
25 SA	0215	2.1	1036	0.5	1439	2.0	1955	0.3
26 SU	0245	2.2	0820	0.6	1509	2.1	○ 2015	0.3
27 M	0319	2.3	0834	0.6	1539	2.1	2034	0.3
28 TU	0356	2.3	1104	0.6	1609	2.1	2104	0.2
29 W	0425	2.3	1206	0.5	1646	2.1	2146	0.2
30 TH	0458	2.3	1246	0.5	1711	2.1	2215	0.2
31 F	0529	2.2	1325	0.5	1745	2.1	2255	0.2

Chart Datum is 0·92 metres below NAP Datum. HAT is 2·5 metres above Chart Datum.

STANDARD TIME UT –01
Subtract 1 hour for UT
For Dutch Summer Time add ONE hour in **non-shaded areas**

HOEK VAN HOLLAND

LAT 51°59′N LONG 4°07′E

TIMES AND HEIGHTS OF HIGH AND LOW WATERS

Dates in red are SPRINGS
Dates in blue are NEAPS

YEAR **2018**

SEPTEMBER

Date	Time	m	Date	Time	m
1 SA	0606 1405 1821 2334	2.2 0.5 2.1 0.2	16 SU	0659 1225 1919	2.1 0.5 2.1
2 SU	0648 1154 1910	2.2 0.5 2.1	17 M	0054 0749 1340 ◐ 2015	0.4 1.9 0.5 1.9
3 M	0035 0739 1310 ◑ 2008	0.2 2.1 0.5 2.0	18 TU	0215 0849 1536 2135	0.4 1.8 0.4 1.8
4 TU	0155 0856 1445 2125	0.3 2.0 0.5 2.0	19 W	0404 1045 1640 2320	0.5 1.6 0.4 1.8
5 W	0314 1016 1605 2244	0.3 1.9 0.5 2.0	20 TH	0504 1206 1735	0.5 1.7 0.4
6 TH	0435 1129 1710	0.4 1.9 0.4	21 F	0025 0604 1253 1820	1.9 0.5 1.8 0.4
7 F	0006 0535 1239 1800	2.1 0.4 2.0 0.4	22 SA	0105 0916 1334 1854	2.1 0.5 1.9 0.4
8 SA	0058 0915 1336 1835	2.2 0.4 2.1 0.3	23 SU	0144 1006 1409 1930	2.2 0.5 2.0 0.4
9 SU	0149 1000 1419 ● 1915	2.3 0.5 2.1 0.3	24 M	0219 1045 1439 1945	2.2 0.6 2.1 0.3
10 M	0236 1046 1500 1958	2.4 0.5 2.2 0.2	25 TU	0248 0805 1509 ○ 2009	2.3 0.6 2.2 0.3
11 TU	0317 1130 1546 2038	2.5 0.6 2.2 0.2	26 W	0326 0835 1538 2046	2.4 0.6 2.2 0.3
12 W	0359 1226 1626 2119	2.5 0.6 2.2 0.2	27 TH	0355 1136 1610 2116	2.4 0.6 2.2 0.3
13 TH	0442 1316 1705 2205	2.4 0.5 2.2 0.2	28 F	0427 1225 1647 2145	2.4 0.5 2.2 0.3
14 F	0527 1406 1749 2300	2.3 0.5 2.2 0.3	29 SA	0506 1254 1723 2230	2.3 0.5 2.3 0.3
15 SA	0615 1446 1836 2355	2.2 0.5 2.2 0.3	30 SU	0543 1050 1759 2315	2.3 0.5 2.3 0.3

OCTOBER

Date	Time	m	Date	Time	m
1 M	0625 1135 1846	2.2 0.4 2.2	16 TU	0040 0704 1256 ◐ 1946	0.5 1.9 0.4 2.0
2 TU	0009 0716 1235 ◑ 1939	0.3 2.0 0.4 2.1	17 W	0200 0805 1440 2056	0.6 1.8 0.4 1.8
3 W	0216 0836 1430 2105	0.4 1.9 0.5 2.0	18 TH	0337 0916 1620 2214	0.6 1.6 0.4 1.8
4 TH	0315 0956 1534 2236	0.4 1.8 0.5 2.0	19 F	0455 1126 1710 2345	0.6 1.6 0.4 1.9
5 F	0414 1120 1635 2350	0.5 1.8 0.4 2.1	20 SA	0550 1226 1754	0.6 1.7 0.4
6 SA	0755 1225 1736	0.5 1.9 0.4	21 SU	0035 0807 1259 1835	2.0 0.6 1.9 0.4
7 SU	0045 0906 1315 1815	2.2 0.5 2.0 0.4	22 M	0116 0925 1336 1900	2.2 0.5 2.0 0.4
8 M	0136 0940 1358 1855	2.3 0.5 2.1 0.3	23 TU	0148 1010 1405 1904	2.3 0.5 2.1 0.4
9 TU	0216 1020 1441 ● 1936	2.4 0.5 2.2 0.3	24 W	0218 0734 1435 ○ 1945	2.4 0.6 2.2 0.3
10 W	0257 1100 1521 2016	2.4 0.6 2.3 0.3	25 TH	0251 0806 1508 2011	2.4 0.5 2.3 0.3
11 TH	0339 1150 1600 2058	2.4 0.5 2.3 0.3	26 F	0327 0838 1546 2050	2.4 0.5 2.3 0.3
12 F	0419 1246 1641 2139	2.4 0.5 2.3 0.4	27 SA	0403 0909 1623 2130	2.4 0.5 2.3 0.3
13 SA	0500 1335 1718 2229	2.3 0.5 2.3 0.4	28 SU	0442 0950 1702 2209	2.3 0.4 2.3 0.4
14 SU	0545 1044 1805 2336	2.1 0.5 2.2 0.5	29 M	0525 1035 1741 2259	2.2 0.4 2.3 0.4
15 M	0626 1145 1845	2.0 0.4 2.1	30 TU	0608 1125 1828	2.1 0.4 2.3
			31 W	0130 0706 1224 ◑ 1926	0.5 2.0 0.4 2.1

NOVEMBER

Date	Time	m	Date	Time	m
1 TH	0216 0815 1406 2056	0.5 1.8 0.4 2.0	16 F	0310 0835 1555 2126	0.6 1.7 0.4 1.8
2 F	0254 0935 1504 2215	0.5 1.7 0.4 2.0	17 SA	0426 0925 1645 2224	0.6 1.6 0.4 1.9
3 SA	0630 1054 1615 2329	0.6 1.8 0.4 2.1	18 SU	0514 1045 1746 2346	0.6 1.7 0.4 2.0
4 SU	0756 1210 2000	0.5 1.9 0.4	19 M	0620 1155 1840	0.6 1.8 0.4
5 M	0025 0850 1255 2055	2.2 0.5 2.0 0.4	20 TU	0024 0846 1250 2046	2.1 0.5 2.0 0.4
6 TU	0115 0926 1342 1834	2.3 0.5 2.1 0.4	21 W	0110 0924 1326 1834	2.2 0.5 2.1 0.4
7 W	0157 0950 1421 ● 1919	2.4 0.5 2.2 0.4	22 TH	0145 1026 1405 1911	2.3 0.5 2.2 0.3
8 TH	0238 1035 1501 2005	2.4 0.5 2.3 0.4	23 F	0222 0734 1446 ○ 1949	2.4 0.5 2.3 0.3
9 F	0321 1114 1541 2045	2.3 0.5 2.3 0.4	24 SA	0302 0816 1520 2030	2.4 0.4 2.4 0.3
10 SA	0401 1215 1617	2.3 0.4 2.3	25 SU	0346 0856 1602 2116	2.4 0.4 2.4 0.4
11 SU	0046 0441 1306 1657	0.5 2.2 0.4 2.3	26 M	0426 0936 1645 2155	2.3 0.4 2.4 0.4
12 M	0115 0519 1023 1738	0.5 2.1 0.4 2.2	27 TU	0508 1019 1727	2.2 0.3 2.4
13 TU	0206 0555 1114 1820	0.6 2.0 0.4 2.2	28 W	0110 0556 1111 1818	0.5 2.1 0.3 2.3
14 W	0107 0635 1204 1916	0.6 1.9 0.3 2.0	29 TH	0140 0651 1214 1919	0.5 1.9 0.3 2.2
15 TH	0150 0726 1304 ◐ 2010	0.6 1.8 0.4 1.9	30 F	0204 0810 1324 ◑ 2035	0.5 1.8 0.3 2.1

DECEMBER

Date	Time	m	Date	Time	m
1 SA	0244 0915 1434 2156	0.6 1.8 0.3 2.1	16 SU	0340 0845 1419 2130	0.6 1.8 0.3 1.9
2 SU	0610 1036 1545 2316	0.6 1.8 0.4 2.1	17 M	0427 0944 1515 2236	0.6 1.8 0.4 2.0
3 M	0724 1134 1936	0.5 1.9 0.3	18 TU	0520 1100 1625 2335	0.6 1.8 0.4 2.1
4 TU	0005 0824 1235 2025	2.2 0.5 2.0 0.4	19 W	0640 1206 1724	0.6 1.9 0.4
5 W	0056 0904 1319 1830	2.2 0.5 2.1 0.4	20 TH	0030 0905 1255 1805	2.2 0.5 2.1 0.4
6 TH	0141 0946 1401 1915	2.3 0.5 2.2 0.4	21 F	0118 0639 1335 1856	2.3 0.5 2.2 0.4
7 F	0225 0735 1445 ● 1954	2.3 0.5 2.2 0.5	22 SA	0158 0719 1419 ○ 1936	2.3 0.4 2.3 0.4
8 SA	0305 0815 1525 2240	2.2 0.4 2.3 0.5	23 SU	0246 0755 1502 2015	2.3 0.4 2.4 0.4
9 SU	0345 1156 1601 2350	2.2 0.4 2.3 0.5	24 M	0325 0835 1545 2100	2.3 0.3 2.4 0.4
10 M	0425 1235 1638	2.1 0.3 2.3	25 TU	0410 0918 1631 2146	2.2 0.3 2.4 0.5
11 TU	0050 0506 1015 1715	0.5 2.1 0.3 2.2	26 W	0457 1005 1715	2.2 0.2 2.4
12 W	0110 0535 1055 1755	0.6 2.0 0.3 2.2	27 TH	0126 0546 1055 1805	0.5 2.1 0.2 2.3
13 TH	0130 0616 1139 1840	0.6 2.0 0.3 2.1	28 F	0210 0646 1156 1905	0.5 2.0 0.2 2.3
14 F	0200 0649 1224 1925	0.6 1.9 0.3 2.0	29 SA	0250 0745 1300 ◑ 2016	0.5 1.9 0.2 2.2
15 SA	0240 0746 1315 ◐ 2025	0.6 1.8 0.3 2.0	30 SU	0215 0855 1416 2119	0.6 1.9 0.2 2.1
			31 M	0534 1007 1515 2229	0.6 1.8 0.3 2.1

Chart Datum is 0·92 metres below NAP Datum. HAT is 2·5 metres above Chart Datum.

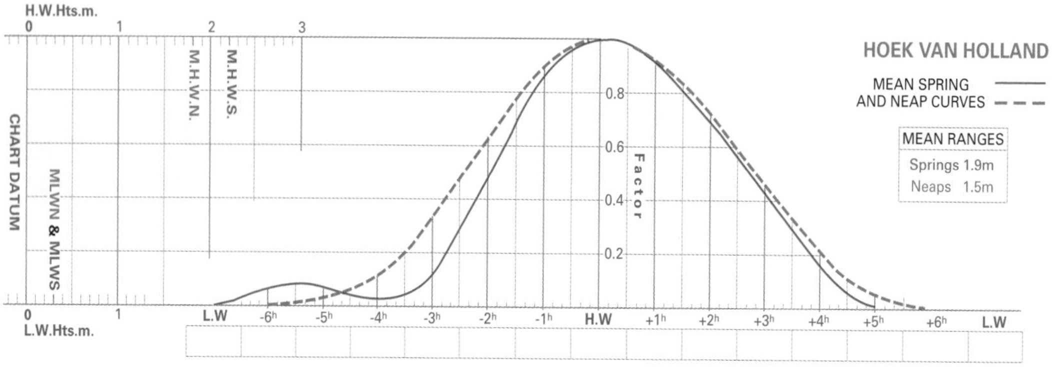

9.16.22 MAAS TSS

Large ships bound up-Channel for Europoort route via the Dover Strait and the Noord Hinder South TSS to Noord Hinder Junction (a large pentagon roughly centred on 52°N 02°51'·1E). Here ships enter the MAAS TRAFFIC SEPARATION SCHEME.

Maas West Outer TSS starts some 33M offshore and funnels large ships 083°/27M via the TSS lanes or Eurogeul (DW route dredged 24·5m) towards a second pentagon 'Maas Precautionary Area' clear of Maas West Inner TSS and 10M offshore. When abeam Maas Centre SWM buoy, ships enter the Maasgeul (Maas narrows) and track inbound 5·5M on the 112° leading lights to the Maasmond (Maas mouth, ie the harbour entrance).

Yachts should avoid the whole complex by using the ITZ and/or crossing the Maasgeul via the recommended track (see Hoek van Holland and www.maasvlakte2.com/uploads/crossing_route.pdf). Knowing the above is to be aware of what you are avoiding.

HOEK VAN HOLLAND TO THE SOUTH EAST UK

Yachts out of Rotterdam/Hoek van Holland bound for the southern Thames Estuary should route 254°/52M from MV-N buoy to NHR-SE buoy, passing MW5, Goeree tower, MW3 and MW1 buoys. Cross the Noord Hinder South TSS between NHR-SE and NHR-S buoys. Thence depending on destination, set course 242°/44M to Outer Tongue for the R Thames; or 228°/46M to NE Goodwin for Ramsgate or points S.

If bound for the R Orwell or adjacent rivers, it may be best to pass N (rather than S) of the large and busy Sunk Outer and Inner Precautionary Areas and their associated TSS. From NHR-S buoy route via West Gabbard, North Inner Gabbard, S Shipwash and Rough buoys to pick up the recommended yacht track at Cork Sand Yacht beacon; it is a less direct route than going S via Galloper, but it avoids the worst of the commercial traffic.

9.16.22A MAAS TSS, PRECAUTIONARY AREA AND MAASGEUL

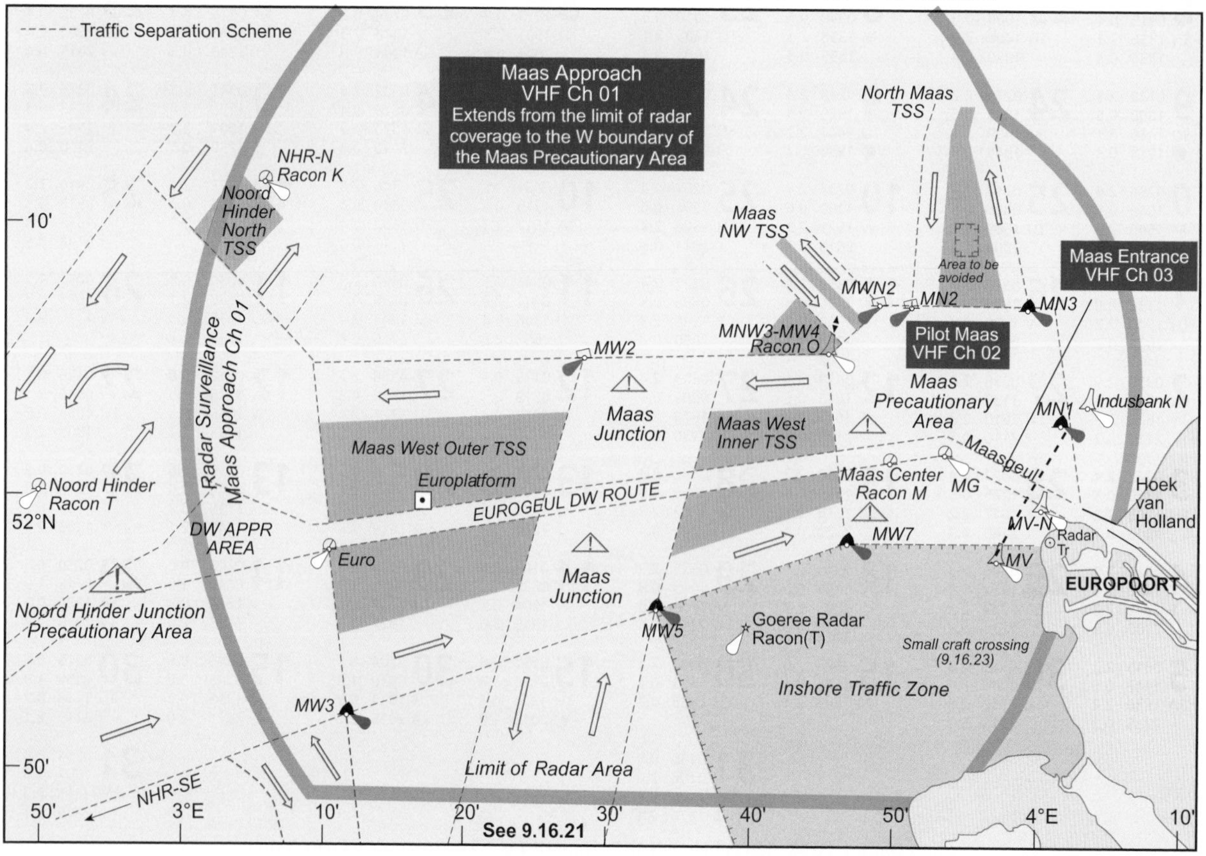

9.16.23 HOEK VAN HOLLAND AND NIEUWE WATERWEG VTS

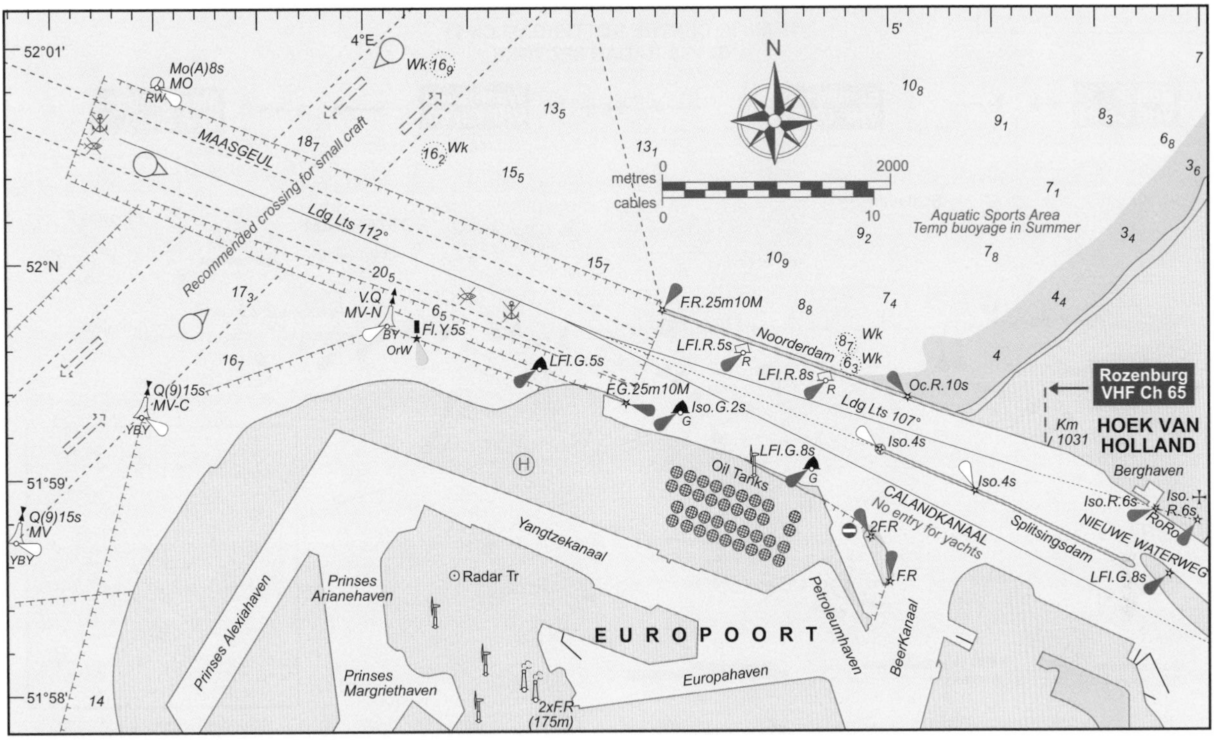

CROSSING THE MAASGEUL To cross the entrance (ie seaward of the bkwtrs) coasting yachts should advise *Maas Ent* Ch 03 of position/course/speed, then monitor Ch 03. Cross on the recommended track, 046° (226°) under power; see chartlet. Beware strong cross-tides. Keep a keen lookout for fast-moving merchantmen; Rules 18 d (ii) and 28.

HOEK VAN HOLLAND

CHARTS AC 122, 132; Zeekaart 1540, 1349, 1350, 1449; DYC 1801.6, 1801.7; Imray C30, Y5

TIDES +0251 Dover; ML 0·9; Duration 0505. HOEK VAN HOLLAND is a Standard Port (⟵), but has no Secondary ports; see also Rotterdam. Double LWs occur, more obviously at sp; in effect a LW stand. The 1st LW is about 5½hrs after HW and the 2nd LW about 4¼hrs before the next HW. Predictions are for the *lower* LW. Prolonged NW gales can raise levels by up to 3m.

SHELTER Entry safe, but in strong onshore winds heavy seas/swell develop. The first adequate shelter is 6M upriver at Maassluis (3m). Complete shelter 10-19M further E at Rotterdam.

NAVIGATION From N, WPT 52°02'·89N 04°03'·57E (Indusbank NCM lt buoy, Q) 190°/3·2M to Noorderdam lt, FR.

From S, WPT 51°59'·61N 04°00'·20E (MV-N buoy) 101°/3·0M to ent to Nieuwe Waterweg. *Yachts must on no account enter the Calandkanaal or Europoort. Stay in the Nieuwe Waterweg.*

LIGHTS AND MARKS See chartlet and Lights, buoys and waypoints for details. Outer ldg lts 112° to ent; then 107° R (ie keep to port) ldg lts into Nieuwe Waterweg, both R trs, W bands.

Hbr patrol vessels show a Fl Bu lt; additionally a Fl R lt = 'Stop'.

COMMUNICATIONS (Code 0174) TC/Port Authority (010) 2522801; Police (0900) 8844; Brit Consul (020) 6764343; Ⓗ 4112800.

FACILITIES Berghaven, use only in emergencies, HM 638850.

Hoek van Holland 🚿 🚻 ✕ 🛒 ✉ Ⓑ ⇌ ✈ (Rotterdam). **Ferries** Hook-Harwich; Rotterdam (Vlaardingen)-Hull.

Maasluis Binnenhaven, bridge, (HM 5912852 Ch 68) quay, picturesque town centre, only charge €6 for bridge transit.

NIEUWE WATERWEG VTS

Arrival procedure for yachts First report to *Maas Approach* or *Pilot Maas*, depending on distance offshore (or *Maas Ent* if within 4M of hbr ent) stating name/type of vessel, position and destination. Obey any instructions, monitoring the relevant Radar Ch's (limits as shown by W☐ signboards on the riverbanks; Km signs are similar).

Rules for yachts in Nieuwe Waterweg/Nieuwe Maas:
Crossing the Nieuwe Waterweg S to N or vice versa is not permitted without VTS permission. Monitor VTS channels (see below); transmit only in emergency or if obliged to deviate from the usual traffic flow. Keep to extreme stbd limit of buoyed line, avoiding debris between buoys and bank. No tacking/beating; no ⚓. Engine ready for instant start. Able to motor at 3·24kn (6km/hr). Hoist a radar reflector, esp in poor vis or at night. Cross chan quickly at 90°. All docks are prohib to yachts, except to access a marina. *Keep a good lookout, especially astern.*

The 3 **Traffic Centres (TC)** oversee their Radar surveillance stations and sub-sectors *(italics)*, on dedicated VHF chans below:

- **TC Hoek van Holland (VCH)** Ch 11. (See diagram above)

Maas Approach	*Ch 01*	*38 – 11M W of Hoek;*
Pilot Maas	*Ch 02*	*11 – 4M W of Hoek;*
Maas Entrance	*Ch 03*	*4M – km 1031.*

  English is the primary language on Ch 01, 02 and 03.

Rozenburg	*Ch 65*	*km 1031 – 1028;*
Maasluis	*Ch 80*	*km 1028 – 1017.*

- **Botlek Information & Tracking system** Ch 14.

Botlek	*Ch 61*	*km 1017 – 1011;*
Eemhaven	*Ch 63*	*km 1011 – 1007.*

- **TC Rotterdam (VCR)** *Ch 11.*

Waalhaven	*Ch 60*	*km 1007 – 1003·5;*
Maasbruggen	*Ch 81*	*km 1003·5 – 998;*
Brienenoord	*Ch 81*	*km 998 – 993.*

Harbour Coordination Centre (HCC) administers and controls Rotterdam port, Ch 19 (H24).
MSI broadcasts by TCs Ch 11 and on request by Radar stns.

Nieuwe Waterweg VTS and Nieuwe Maas into central Rotterdam *continued*

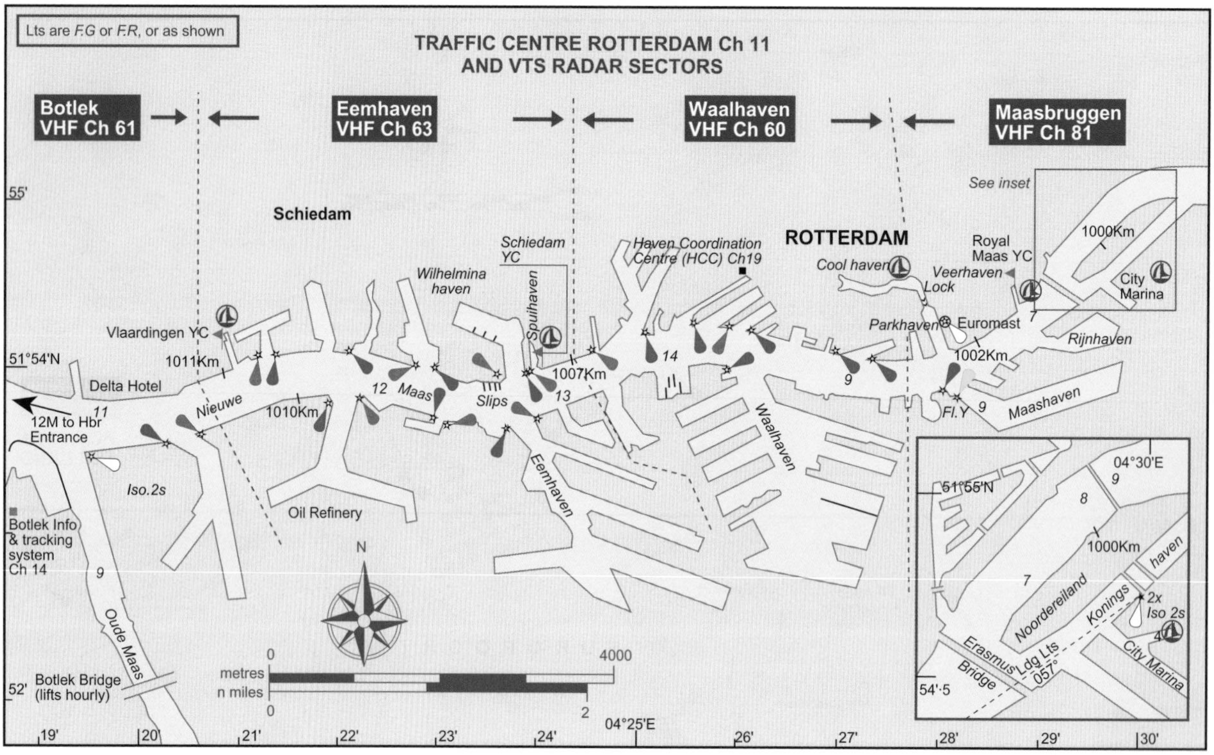

9.16.24 ROTTERDAM

Zuid Holland **51°54'·00N 04°28'·00E** (610m S of Euromast)

CHARTS AC 122, 132, 133; Zeekaart 1540/1/2; DYC 1809.4, 1809.5

TIDES +0414 Dover; ML 0·9; Duration 0440

Standard Port VLISSINGEN (⟶)

Times				Height (metres)			
High Water		Low Water		MHWS	MHWN	MLWN	MLWS
0300	0900	0400	1000	5·0	4·1	1·1	0·5
1500	2100	1600	2200				
Differences EUROPLATFORM (30M W of Hoek van Holland)							
+0005	–0005	–0030	–0055	–2·8	–2·3	–0·6	–0·1
MAASSLUIS (Km 1019)							
+0155	*+0115*	*+0100*	*+0310*	*–2·9*	*–2·4*	*–0·8*	*–0·3*
VLAARDINGEN (Km 1011)							
+0150	+0120	+0130	+0330	–2·9	–2·4	–0·8	–0·3

NOTE: Double LWs occur. Maasluis and Vlaardingen are referenced to Vlissingen, in UK ATT as above. The Dutch HP33 *Tidal heights and streams in Dutch coastal waters* shows the time differences below, relative to HW and the first LW at Hoek van Holland:

HOEK VAN HOLLAND	HW	1st LW
Maasluis	+0102	+0308
Vlaardingen	+0103	+0333
Rotterdam	+0111	+0341

SHELTER Good in the yacht hbrs where visitors are welcome (see Facilities). There is always a considerable chop/swell in the river due to constant heavy traffic to/from Europoort and Rotterdam.

NAVIGATION See 9.16.23 for WPTs (to enter Nieuwe Waterweg) and Yacht Rules. From the hbr ent to the conspic Euromast (51°54'·33N 04°28'·00E) is about 18M (33km). 6M W of the Euromast, the very busy Oude Maas joins at km 1013, giving access to Dordrecht and the Delta network of canals/lakes.

COMMUNICATIONS (Code 010) See chartlet above for VTS in central Rotterdam. In emergency call Rotterdam Tfc Centre Ch 11; Police (0900) 8844; ⊜ 2442266; Brit Consul (020) 676 4343; Ⓗ 4112800; Hbr Coordination Centre (HCC) 2522601, also Emergency; see Facilities for VHF Chans at locks/bridges, English is the second language.

FACILITIES Marinas/yacht harbours from seaward:

Vlaardingen YC, 51°53'·98N 04°20'·93E, 400m E of Delta Hotel in Buitenhaven. (3·6-4·4m) or lock (Ch 20) into Oude Haven (2·7m). HM ☎2484333.

Spuihaven, 51°54'·00N 04°24'·00E, immediately E of the ent to Wilhelmina Haven. €1.25/m. No lock/bridge to transit. Schiedam YC mob 0644326722, (1·6-2·8m).

Coolhaven Yacht Hbr, 51°54'·12N 04°28'·00E; next to Euromast 185m. Access through Parkhaven via lock (Ch 22). ☎4764146, (2·7m).

Veerhaven. 51°54'·39N 04°28'·76E, 5ca E of Euromast. ☎ 4365446, mob 0653536107, www.veerhavenrotterdam.nl info@veerhavenrotterdam.nl Centre for traditional sea-going vessels. Ⓥ welcome, €2·20, €3·00 p/d. (3·9m) 350m N, water taxi to S bank. **Royal Maas YC** ☎4137681 (clubhouse, members only).

City Marina, 51°54'·64N 04°29'·76E. Go under Erasmus bridge (Ch 18) via lifting section at SE end which only opens 1000, 1100, 1330, 1530 & 1900LT or on request Ch 18 2030-0700 1hr before req'd (11m clearance under fixed span). Ldg lts 056·7°, both Iso 2s; then 2nd ent to stbd, via lifting bridge. ☎4854096, mob 0622 215761, www.citymarinarotterdam.nl info@citymarinarotterdam.nl 130 +40 Ⓥ in 4m. €2·00 night for 2 nights; €1·50 3rd-7th nights; €1·25 7 nights, €3·30 p/d. YC, water taxi to N bank, @.

WSV IJsselmonde, 51°54'·24N 04°33'·34E, on S bank at km 994, 800m E of Brienenoordbrug, Ch 20 (off chartlet). ☎4828333, (1·3–2·1m).

City All facilities, ACA, DYC Agent. **Ferry** Rotterdam (Vlaardingen) -Hull; Hook-Harwich.

9.16.25 HARINGVLIET (Stellendam and Hellevoetsluis)

Zuid Holland **51°49'·46N 04°02'·29E (Goereesesluis).** Stellendam ❁❁⛵⛵✿

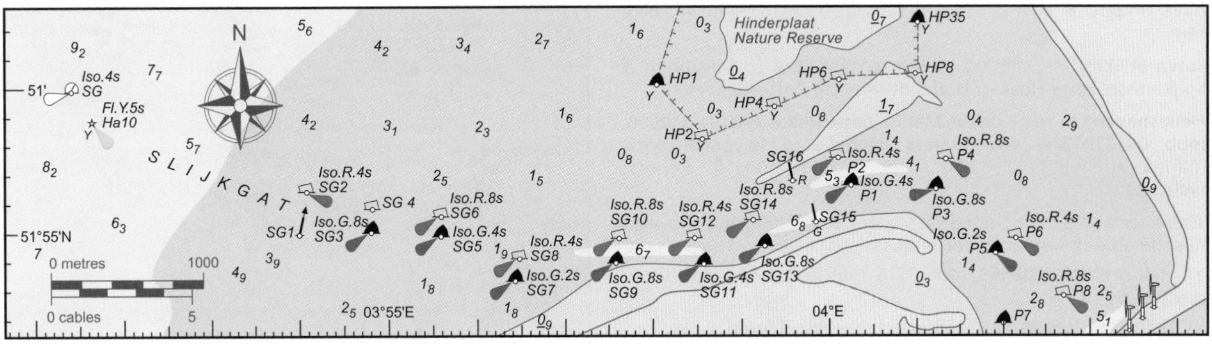

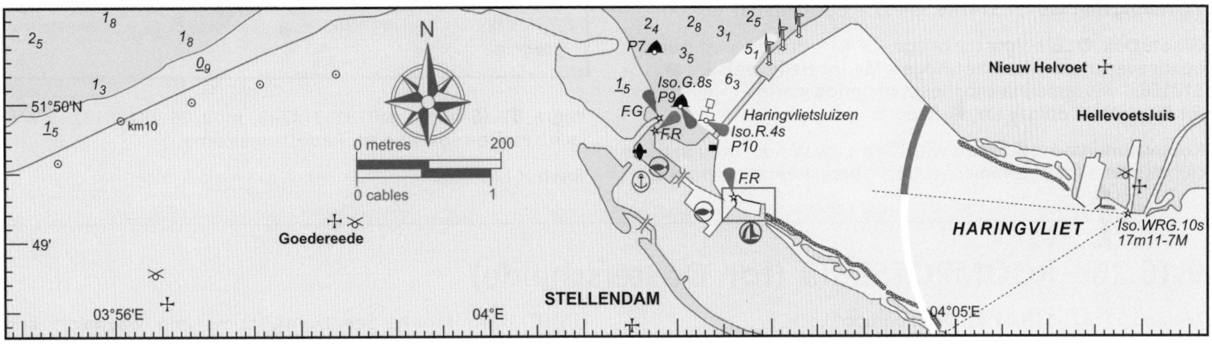

CHARTS AC 1630, 110; Zeekaart 1447, 1448; DYC 1801.6, 1807.6; Imray C30

TIDES +0300 Dover; ML 1·2; Duration 0510

Standard Port VLISSINGEN (⟶)

Times				Height (metres)			
High Water		Low Water		MHWS	MHWN	MLWN	MLWS
0300	0900	0400	1000	5·0	4·1	1·1	0·5
1500	2100	1600	2200				
Differences HARINGVLIETSLUIZEN							
+0015	+0015	+0015	–0020	–2·0	–1·9	–0·7	–0·2

NOTE: Double LWs occur. The rise after the 1st LW is called the Agger. Water levels on this coast are much affected by weather. Prolonged NW gales can raise levels by up to 3m. Water levels in the Haringvliet can drop by 0·5m an hour when the sluices are open.

SHELTER Good in all the marinas. The entrance to the Slijkgat can be rough in W/NW winds stronger than Force 6, and also with wind against tide. When there is heavy swell, entry into the Slijkgat is not advisable. Call Post Ouddorp, VHF Ch 25 if in doubt. (No service Sunday.)

NAVIGATION WPT 51°51'·95N 03°51'·42E (SG SWM buoy, Iso 4s) 110°/2·7M to SG5/6 chan buoys. Note 1·4m shoal close N bys SG5/8, 7/8 and 9/10. Call Post Ouddorp VHF (see Comms) for latest silting info.Thence 2·4M via the well-buoyed/lit Slijkgat chan to SG15/16 bns. Follow Pampus chan P1,3,5,7,9 SHM buoys SSE for 2·2M to the Buitenhaven, avoiding the no-entry sluicing area, marked by 4 SPM buoys.

Access is via a lock which operates 24/7 and has recessed bollards. 2 bridges lift in sequence to minimise road tfc delays. Note: the W bridge has 14m vertical clearance when down (with digital clearance gauge outside) the E bridge only 5·4m.

Hellevoetsluis is 2·6M E of Stellendam marina on the N bank. Three hbrs from W: Heliushaven, Het Groote Dok and Koopvaardijhaven, a lt ho (see below) marks ent to Groote Dok.

LIGHTS AND MARKS Haringvlietsluizen: 3 ● in △ are shown from pier heads on dam when sluicing in progress. Groote Dok LtHo: Iso WRG 10s 16m W11M, R8M, G7M; W tower, R top; 266°-G-275°-W-294°-R-316°-W036°-G-058°-W-095°-R-140°.

COMMUNICATIONS Post Ouddorp (lighthouse) VHF Ch 25 for weather, advice & assistance daily, except Sun, (01/04-01/10), 0800-2200, (01/11-31/03), (0800-1600); ⊖ Rotterdam (010) 4298088 or Vlissingen (0118) 484600; Emergencies 112; Brit Consul (020) 676 4343; Stellendam Port HM 0187 491000; Lock (Walcheren Canal) (0118) 412840; Lock 0187 497350, *Goereese Sluis* VHF Ch 20 for bridges and lock; Hellevoetsluis HM (and locks) VHF Ch 74.

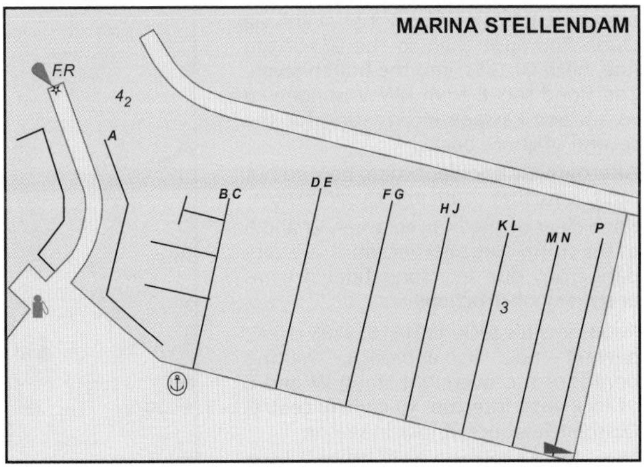

FACILITIES **Stellendam Marina** ☎0187 493769, VHF Ch 31. www.marinastellendam.nl info@marinastellendam.nl 200 inc Ⓥ €2·00 inc tourist tax. Berth as directed in 3m; all pontoons have fingers. (20t) ☎0187 492344, bike hire.

Town (4½km) ✕. ✈ (Rotterdam). Bus to Vlissingen & Spijkenisse. **Ferry** Hoek of Holland-Harwich; Rotterdam-Hull.

Heliushaven On the E side is **Marina Cape Helius** ☎0181 310056, mob 0613181974. www.marina-capehelius.nl havenkantoor@marina-capehelius.nl €1·50 + €0·70 pp/day tax. Reports welcome.

There are also 3 YCs situated on the W side of Heliushaven which may be able to help with berthing.

YC Helius ☎0181 316563, mob 0616 756515; €1·40 + €0·70 pp/day tax.

YC Hellevoetsluis ☎0181 315868, €1·40 + €0·70 pp/day tax.

YC Haringvliet ☎0181 314748, €1·35 + €0·70 pp/day tax.

Groote Dok. Ⓥ before the bridge. In summer the bridge opens every hour. After the bridge is **Marina Hellevoetsluis** ☎0181 312166. www.marina-capehelius.nl info@marina-capehelius.nl €1·50 + €0·70 pp/day tax. Reports welcome.

Koopvaardijhaven. Ⓥ berths with on the W side, though there can also be a lot of commercial traffic here. Reports welcome.

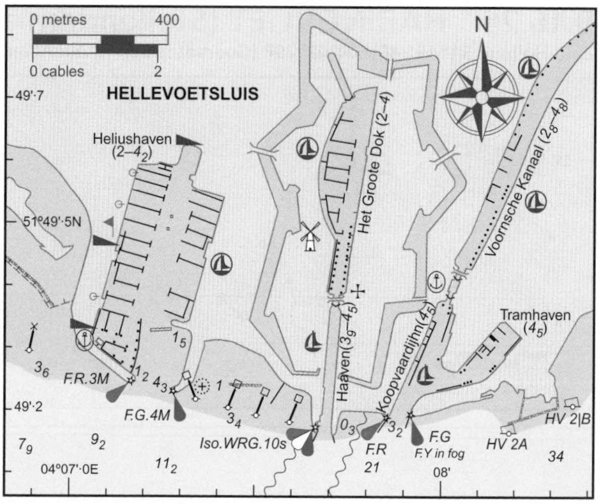

Yagra BY (E bank) ☎0181 314748, mob 06 29403177. www.jachtservice-reparatie.nl Reports welcome.

Town ✕.

9.16.26 ROOMPOTSLUIS (for Oosterschelde)

Zeeland **51°37'·11N 03°41'·08E** Roompot Lock

CHARTS AC 1630, 110; Zeekaart 1448; DYCs 1805.8, 1801.5; Imray C30

TIDES +0230 Dover

Standard Port VLISSINGEN (⟶)

Times				Height (metres)			
High Water		Low Water		MHWS	MHWN	MLWN	MLWS
0300	0900	0400	1000	5·0	4·1	1·1	0·5
1500	2100	1600	2200				
Differences ROOMPOT BUITEN							
−0015	+0005	+0005	−0020	−1·3	−1·1	−0·4	−0·1

SHELTER An approach in strong SW through NW winds is not advised. The Buitenhaven's inner part is sheltered.

NAVIGATION WPT 51°39'·35N 03°33'·65E (abeam OR1 SHM buoy) 122°/4·2M via Oude Roompot chan to the 073·5° ldg line, both Oc G 5s, into the Buitenhaven. The flood sets E from HW Vlissingen −3 to +1. See Passage information for the several offshore banks.

Alternatively Roompot chan, buoyed but unlit, is further south and closer inshore.

Keep clear of the buoyed areas, W and E of the storm-surge barrier, which are very dangerous due to strong tidal streams and many obstructions.

Roompotsluis lock, ☎0111659265 (H24), beware tide in approach, waiting pontoons (no overnight stays) W and E of lock with intercom to control centre. Custom clearance at lock in season.

The fixed bridge has 18·2m least clearance. At LW clearance is approx 21m. Check with tide gauges or lock-keeper if in doubt. Small bollards, fixed at vertical intervals, are recessed into the lock walls. Ent to/exit from the lock is controlled by R/G traffic lights.

LIGHTS AND MARKS See Lights, buoys and waypoints and chartlet.

COMMUNICATIONS Lock *Roompotsluis* Ch 18. Roompot Marina Ch 31. Monitor Ch 68 which broadcasts local forecasts at H+15.

FACILITIES **Roompot Marina** Good shelter, 1·5M SE of lock. ☎(0113) 374125, marina@roompot.nl. 250 + 80 Ⓥ, €2·00 + €1·60pp/day tax, Ⓑ Dr ☎372565; 0118 484600.

Alternatively, follow G3-G17 buoys into **Betonhaven** about 1M NE of the lock. ⚓ in 3-6m, good holding in sticky black mud. Easy walk to the Delta Expo.

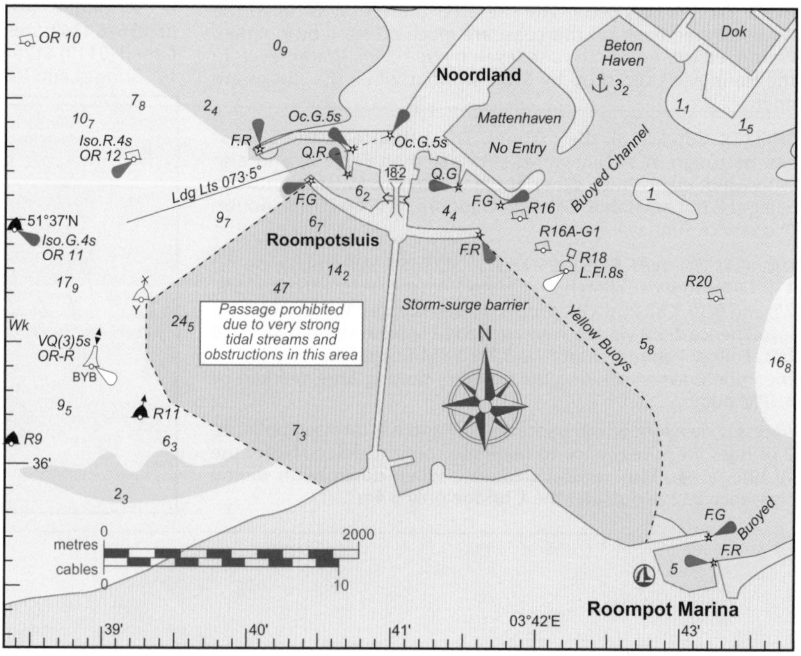

9.16.27 WESTERSCHELDE

Zeeland mostly, but Belgium for the last 12M to Antwerpen

CHARTS AC 1874, 120, 128; Zeekaart 1443; BE 103, 104; DYC 1803; Imray C30

TIDES +0200 Dover; ML Hansweert 2·7, Westkapelle 2·0, Bath 2·8; Duration 0555

Standard Port VLISSINGEN (⟶)

Times				Height (metres)			
High Water		Low Water		MHWS	MHWN	MLWN	MLWS
0300	0900	0400	1000	5·0	4·1	1·1	0·5
1500	2100	1600	2200				
Differences WESTKAPELLE (8M NW of Vlissingen)							
−0025	−0015	−0010	−0025	−0·7	−0·6	−0·2	−0·1
HANSWEERT							
+0100	+0050	+0040	+0100	+0·6	+0·6	0·0	0·0
BATH							
+0125	+0115	+0115	+0140	+1·0	+1·0	0·0	+0·1

SHELTER In strong winds a bad sea can be met in the estuary mouth. Conditions become easier further upriver. See Facilities.

NAVIGATION Westerschelde is the waterway to Antwerpen (and via canal to Gent) very full of ships and barges, especially in the last 15M. The main channel winds through a mass of well-marked sandbanks. It is essential to work the tides, which average 2½kn, more at springs. Best timing is most easily achieved by starting from Vlissingen, Breskens or Terneuzen. Yachts should keep to the edge of main chan. Use alternative chans with caution; Vaarwater langs Hoofdplat and de Paulinapolder/Thomasgeul are buoyed shortcuts popular with yachtsmen, but note that channels shift regularly.

Commercial shipping: Yachts should keep just outside the busy shipping chans, ie Wielingen from the SW, Scheur from the W, and Oostgat from the NW. A listening watch on Ch 10 (ship-to-ship) is compulsory above buoy 100 (near Antwerpen).

Be aware of large ship anchorages: Wielingen Noord and Zuid, either side of the fairway, as defined by buoys W6-Trawl-WN6 and W9-Songa. Further E, Flushing Roads anchorage is defined by Songa, SS1, SS5 and ARV-VH buoys. Ocean-going ships often manoeuvre off Vlissingen to transfer pilots.

S of Vlissingen (see Breskens) an E-W TSS (part of a Precautionary area) is best avoided by yachts which should cross the fairway via the recommended N-S track between Buitenhaven and ARV3 SPM lt buoy. Fast ferries, which have right of way, ply half-hourly from Vlissingen Buitenhaven to Breskens. *Keep a sharp lookout*.

Recommended small craft routes: **From the SW** there are few dangers. After Zeebrugge, keep S of the Wielingen chan buoys (W1-9). Off Breskens avoid fast ferries to/from Vlissingen; continue E to SS1 buoy, then cross to Vlissingen on a N'ly track.

From the W, keep clear of the Scheur chan by crossing to the S of Wielingen as soon as practicable.

From the N, the narrow, busy Oostgat can be used with caution, keeping just outside the SW edge of the buoyed/lit chan.

Three lesser, unlit day-only N'ly routes which avoid Oostgat are:

- From Kaloo or DR1 buoys, follow the Geul van de Rassen, Deurloo & Spleet chans to SP4 buoy. Thence E via WN6 buoy.
- Or continue down Deurloo from DL5 by to join Oostgat at OG19 by; thence cross to the N shore when Oostgat tfc permits.
- Another route, slightly further offshore, is to skirt the NW side of Kaloo bank to Botkil-W buoy, thence SE via Geul van de Walvischstaart (PHM buoys only) to Trawl SCM buoy.

LIGHTS AND MARKS The apprs are well lit by lighthouses: on the S shore at Nieuwe Sluis, and on the N shore at Westkapelle; see Lights, buoys and waypoints. The main fairways are, for the most part, defined by ldg lts and by the W sectors of the many Dir lts.

SCHELDEMOND VTS (www.vts-scheldt.net) covers from the North Sea outer approaches upriver to Antwerpen; see the diagram below and TSS off S Netherlands. Yachts should monitor at all times the VHF Ch for the area in which they are, so as to be aware of other shipping and to be contactable if required. Do not transmit, unless called. 7 **Traffic Centres** control the Areas below, within which radar stations provide radar, weather and hbr info, as shown below:

Outer approaches: (*Traffic Centre* is the callsign prefix)		
Wandelaar	Ch 65	*Zeebrugge Radar* Ch 04.
Zeebrugge	Ch 69	*Radar* as in line above.
Steenbank	Ch 64	*Radar* also on Ch 64.
In the Westerschelde: (*Centrale* is the callsign prefix)		
Vlissingen	Ch 14	*Radar* Ch 21. Vlissingen to E2A/PvN SPR buoys (51°24'N 03°44'E).
Terneuzen	Ch 03	*Radar* Ch 03. Thence to Nos 32/35 buoys (51°23'N 03°57'E). Ch 11 Terneuzen-Gent Canal.
Hansweert	Ch 65	*Radar* Ch 65. Thence to Nos 46/55 buoys (51°24'N 04°02'E).
Zandvliet	Ch 12	Thence to Antwerpen. *Radar Waarde* 19; *Saeftinge* 21; *Zandvliet* 04; *Kruisschans* 66.

In **emergency**, call initially on the working channel in use; state yacht's name, position and the nature of the problem. You may then be switched to Ch **67 (Emergency)** or another VHF channel.

Broadcasts of visibility, Met, tidal data and ship movements are made in Dutch at: H +00 by *Terneuzen* Ch 11; H +10 by *Zeebrugge* Ch 69; H +30 by *Zandvliet* Ch 12; H +50 by *Centrale Vlissingen* Ch 14; **H +55 by Radar Vlissingen Ch 21 in English**.

FACILITIES Some minor hbrs from Terneuzen to Antwerpen (38M) are listed below. They may be useful in emergency or offer shelter, but most dry. Yachts usually go non-stop to Antwerpen.

ELLEWOUTSDIJK, 51°23'·10N 03°49'·05E. BE 103; DYC 1803.2. HW +2 and +0·3m on Vlissingen; ML 2·6m. Small, unlit hbr, 27 ⛵ voluntary donation. 1·5m at MLWS. Strong cross-eddy on ebb. HM ☎(0113) 548431/06 251154766, ⛽ @ ⚓(10t) YC.

HOEDEKENSKERKE, 51°25'·11N 03°54'·90E. BE 103; DYC 1803.3. Disused ferry hbr (dries) abeam MG13 SHM buoy (Iso G 4s).

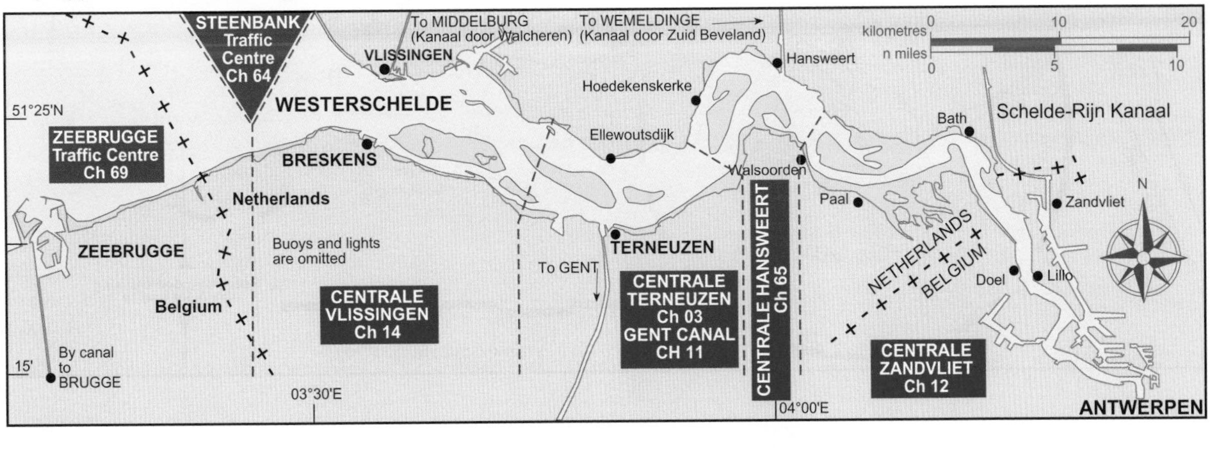

€1·00/m (min €8·00/night) inc. **YC WV Hoedekenskerke** ☎(0113) 639278, mob 0653794069. 33 + 6 at campsite 400m. **Town** (Goes).

HANSWEERT, 51°26'·37N 04°00'·66E. BE 103; DYC 1803.3. Tidal differences above. Temporary stop, but it is the busy ent to Zuid Beveland canal, lock Ch 22. Lt Oc WRG 10s, R lattice tr, W band, at ent. Waiting berths outside lock on E side. **No smoking or naked flames in, or near lock**. Services: (17t). **Town** (Kruiningen-Yerseke).

WALSOORDEN, 51°22'·93N 04°02'·10E. BE 103; DYC 1803.3. HW is +0110 and +0·7m on Vlissingen; ML 2·6m. Prone to swell. SHM buoy 57, Iso G 8s, is 500m N of ent where 16 silos are conspic. Ldg lts 220° both Oc 3s. Hbr ent FG & FR. Unmarked stone pier just outside E hbr pier, partly dries at LW. Yacht basin dead ahead on ent to hbr, depths 2 to 2·8m. 4/5 €0·30/m, max stay H24. *Zandvliet Radio* VHF Ch 12. WSV d'Ouwe Haven ☎(0114) 681235, (16t). **Town**.

PAAL, 51°21'·25N 04°06'·65E. BE 103; DYC 1803.3. HW +0120 and +0·8m on Vlissingen; ML 2·7m. Appr via No 63 SHM buoy and tide gauge, across drying Speelmansgat. Unlit, drying yacht hbr on S bank at river mouth, ent marked by withy. HM ☎(0114) 314974, 0611 028174. *Zandvliet Radio* Ch 12. **Jachthaven** 150 €0·50, @ in YC. (10 mins walk). **Yachtclub** ☎(0114) 315548; www.wv-saeftinghe.nl

DOEL, 51°18'·67N 04°16'·11E. BE 103; DYC 1803.5. HW +0100 and +0·7m on Vlissingen. Small drying hbr next to 'ghost town' on W bank. Ldg lts 188·5°: front Fl WR 3s on N pier hd; rear Fl 3s, synch. HM ☎(03) 5758103; **YC de Noord** ☎7733669, open to visitors.

LILLO, 51°18'·16N 04°17'·30E. BE 103; DYC 1803.5. 1M SE of Doel on opp bank; small drying hbr for shoal-draft only; Customs base. T-jetty has Oc WRG 10s. HM (035) 686456; small YC, Scaldis, is named after local restaurant original members used for meetings.

9.16.28 VLISSINGEN (FLUSHING)

Zeeland **51°26'·31N 03°34'·61E** Koopmanshaven

CHARTS AC 1872, 1874, 120; Zeekaart 1442, 1443, 1533; BE 103; DYC 1803.2, 1801.4; Imray C30

TIDES +0210 Dover; ML 2·3; Duration 0555. Note: Vlissingen is a Standard Port (⟶)

SHELTER Very good in both yacht hbrs.

NAVIGATION WPT 51°25'·16N 03°33'·66E (Songa SHM buoy, QG) 027°/1·29M to Koopmanshaven ent. Keep to W pier side, strong crossflow until piers. Study Westerschelde (previous page.

LIGHTS AND MARKS From North West, Oostgat 117° ldg lts: Front RW pile; rear Sardijngeul, Oc WR 5s, R/W banded mast, R △. Note: Conspic radar twr (close NW of Koopmanshaven) shows a Fl Y lt to warn when ships are approaching in the blind NW arc through the well buoyed Oostgat-Sardijngeul chan.

A conspic, floodlit R/W metal framework tr (50m) near de Ruyter Marina indicates the appr. Buitenhaven traffic signals from mole W side of ent: R flag or extra ● near FR on W mole hd = No entry.

COMMUNICATIONS (Code 0118) Emergency 112; Schelde Traffic Coordination Centre 424760; Police 0900-8844; ⊖ 484600; Brit Consul (020) 676 4343; Dr 412233; Port HM 414498, VHF Ch 14; Sealock VHF Ch 18; Canal bridges VHF Ch 22, see also Westerschelde; Michiel de Ruyter and Schelde Marinas, no VHF; use mobile.

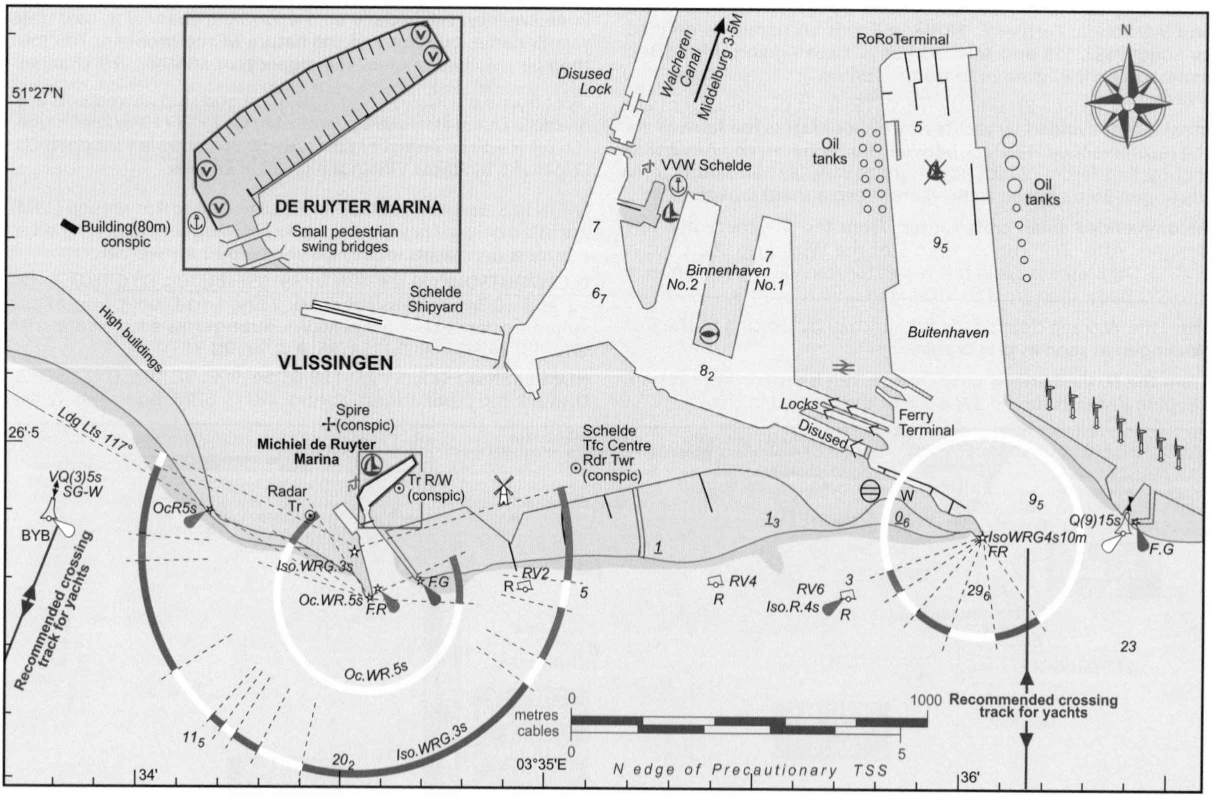

FACILITIES

Michiel de Ruyter Marina (2·9m) ☎414498, *Pre-booking in season is strongly advised.* 100 + 40Ⓥ €2·20/m + €1·45 pp/day tax. ✕ Ⓓ @ free wi-fi; info@brasserieevertsen.nl www. brasserieevertsen.nl

Ent is 6m narrow, over a sill with 1·2m water at MLWS. Access HW±4. Check depth gauge on outer wall or with HM. 2 small footbridges (R/G tfc lts) are swiftly swung open by HM 0800-2200LT. They stay open 2200–0800LT, but only for yachts to leave; ●● (vert) tfc lts prohibit arrival from sea. Storm barrier is open 1/4-1/11.

Beware high speed Pilot boats using the adjacent inlet.

VVW Schelde (2·8-4·1m) ☎465912, HM mob 0615538515. www. vvwschelde.nl 90 + 50Ⓥ €1·75 + €1·45 pp/day tax. €1·00/4kWh. 500m walk to ferry. ✕ (12t max), bike hire, free wi-fi. At ent to the Buitenhaven beware ferries; keep to port, pass S of the ferry terminal for the most N'ly and smallest sealock, which operates H24. Waiting possible on piles to SE.

Town ✕ Ⓑ ✈ Antwerpen). Foot ferry to Breskens; road tunnel to Terneuzen. At Middelburg: .

MARINA 8M WSW OF VLISSINGEN, Marina Cadzand-Bad, 51°22'·90N 03°22'·88E. ☎+32 3 3037557; www.yachtatcadzandbad. nl cadzand@rycb.be. 125 incⓋ €1·57/m + €1·15 pp/day tax; €3·00/day. Free wi-fi; ✕. With easy sea access, this new facility (April 2017) next to a popular tourist resort and vast sandy beach is managed by the Royal YC of Belgium. Reports welcome.

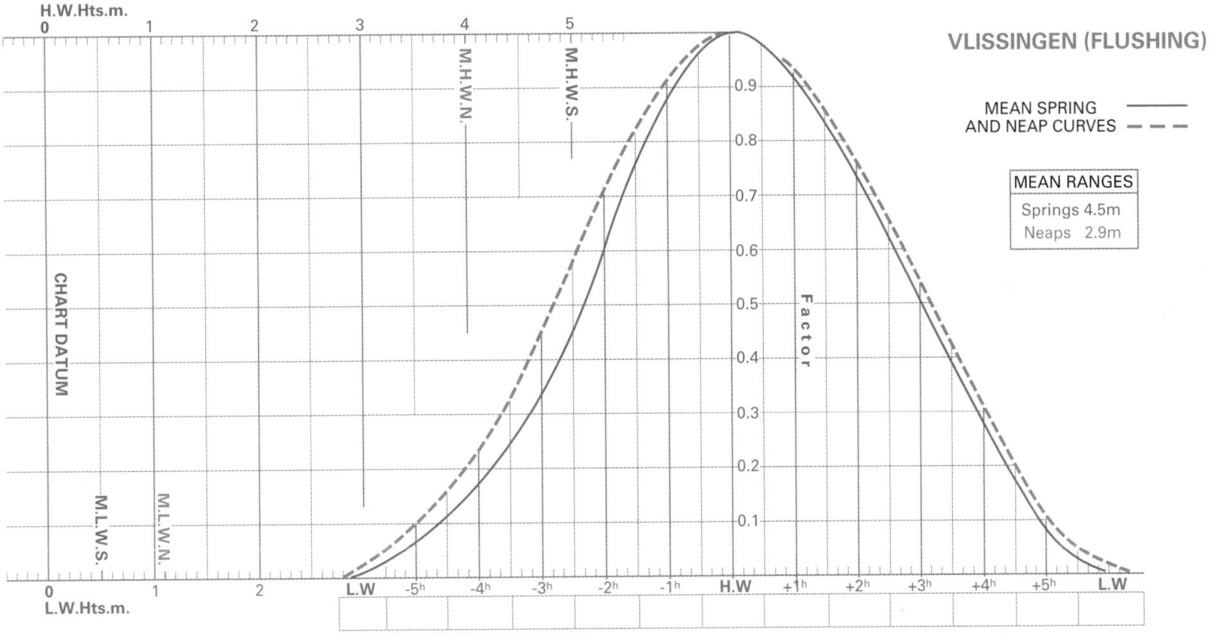

STANDARD TIME UT –01
Subtract 1 hour for UT
For Dutch Summer Time add ONE hour in **non-shaded areas**

VLISSINGEN LAT 51°27'N LONG 3°36'E

TIMES AND HEIGHTS OF HIGH AND LOW WATERS

Dates in red are SPRINGS
Dates in blue are NEAPS

YEAR **2018**

JANUARY

Date	Time	m	Date	Time	m
1 M	0047	5.0	16 TU	0145	4.6
	0712	0.7		0755	0.8
	1305	5.1		1359	4.7
	1938	0.5		2008	0.9
2 TU	0136	5.1	17 W	0219	4.7
	0806	0.5		0836	0.7
	1353	5.2		1435	4.8
	○ 2025	0.5		● 2046	0.9
3 W	0223	5.1	18 TH	0248	4.7
	0856	0.5		0909	0.6
	1441	5.3		1506	4.8
	2112	0.5		2121	0.9
4 TH	0308	5.1	19 F	0325	4.8
	0946	0.4		0946	0.6
	1529	5.3		1538	4.9
	2156	0.6		2156	0.9
5 F	0356	5.0	20 SA	0356	4.8
	1030	0.4		1026	0.6
	1616	5.2		1611	4.8
	2246	0.7		2231	0.9
6 SA	0445	5.0	21 SU	0429	4.7
	1118	0.4		1100	0.6
	1707	5.1		1646	4.8
	2328	0.8		2306	0.9
7 SU	0536	4.8	22 M	0503	4.7
	1205	0.5		1135	0.6
	1800	4.9		1718	4.7
				2340	1.0
8 M	0015	0.9	23 TU	0542	4.6
	0627	4.7		1209	0.6
	1255	0.6		1802	4.7
	◑ 1902	4.7			
9 TU	0105	1.1	24 W	0020	1.0
	0725	4.5		0627	4.6
	1350	0.7		1255	0.7
	2006	4.5		◐ 1856	4.5
10 W	0206	1.2	25 TH	0110	1.0
	0831	4.3		0721	4.4
	1444	0.9		1345	0.8
	2110	4.3		2007	4.4
11 TH	0315	1.3	26 F	0216	1.1
	0940	4.2		0836	4.3
	1555	1.0		1456	0.8
	2227	4.2		2116	4.4
12 F	0446	1.3	27 SA	0326	1.1
	1050	4.2		0946	4.3
	1720	1.0		1605	0.9
	2330	4.3		2228	4.4
13 SA	0539	1.2	28 SU	0440	1.1
	1150	4.3		1056	4.5
	1816	1.0		1726	0.8
				2336	4.5
14 SU	0025	4.4	29 M	0556	0.9
	0635	1.0		1157	4.7
	1239	4.4		1830	0.7
	1855	1.0			
15 M	0105	4.5	30 TU	0032	4.7
	0715	0.9		0658	0.7
	1321	4.5		1252	4.9
	1932	0.9		1921	0.6
			31 W	0122	4.9
				0753	0.5
				1343	5.1
				○ 2012	0.6

FEBRUARY

Date	Time	m	Date	Time	m
1 TH	0210	5.0	16 F	0232	4.7
	0843	0.4		0849	0.6
	1428	5.2		1447	4.9
	2058	0.6		2056	0.8
2 F	0256	5.1	17 SA	0301	4.8
	0927	0.3		0926	0.5
	1516	5.3		1517	5.0
	2141	0.6		2135	0.7
3 SA	0340	5.1	18 SU	0336	4.9
	1015	0.3		1006	0.4
	1600	5.2		1547	5.0
	2225	0.7		2209	0.7
4 SU	0425	5.1	19 M	0407	4.9
	1058	0.3		1039	0.4
	1646	5.1		1622	4.9
	2308	0.7		2246	0.7
5 M	0509	5.0	20 TU	0442	4.8
	1146	0.4		1118	0.4
	1735	4.9		1656	4.9
	2348	0.8		2322	0.8
6 TU	0555	4.8	21 W	0517	4.8
	1226	0.5		1156	0.5
	1826	4.7		1740	4.8
				2354	0.8
7 W	0035	0.9	22 TH	0559	4.7
	0645	4.6		1236	0.6
	1308	0.7		1827	4.6
	◑ 1915	4.4			
8 TH	0119	1.1	23 F	0045	0.9
	0740	4.3		0652	4.6
	1400	0.9		1326	0.7
	2015	4.1		◐ 1930	4.4
9 F	0236	1.2	24 SA	0146	1.0
	0845	4.1		0759	4.4
	1506	1.1		1426	0.8
	2130	3.9		2045	4.2
10 SA	0340	1.3	25 SU	0255	1.1
	1011	3.9		0920	4.3
	1630	1.2		1534	1.0
	2255	3.9		2206	4.1
11 SU	0453	1.3	26 M	0414	1.1
	1126	4.0		1038	4.3
	1735	1.2		1706	1.0
	2356	4.1		2320	4.3
12 M	0605	1.1	27 TU	0546	0.9
	1215	4.2		1148	4.5
	1830	1.1		1821	0.8
13 TU	0045	4.3	28 W	0018	4.5
	0655	1.0		0649	0.7
	1306	4.4		1242	4.8
	1909	1.0		1912	0.7
14 W	0125	4.4			
	0740	0.8			
	1345	4.6			
	1946	0.9			
15 TH	0159	4.6			
	0816	0.7			
	1416	4.7			
	● 2026	0.9			

MARCH

Date	Time	m	Date	Time	m
1 TH	0110	4.7	16 F	0131	4.5
	0746	0.4		0749	0.7
	1332	5.0		1350	4.8
	2000	0.6		1955	0.8
2 F	0155	4.9	17 SA	0202	4.7
	0830	0.3		0826	0.5
	1415	5.2		1419	4.9
	○ 2046	0.6		● 2032	0.7
3 SA	0239	5.0	18 SU	0233	4.9
	0916	0.2		0900	0.4
	1459	5.2		1450	5.0
	2126	0.6		2110	0.6
4 SU	0320	5.1	19 M	0306	5.0
	0957	0.2		0938	0.3
	1542	5.2		1523	5.1
	2207	0.6		2151	0.6
5 M	0402	5.1	20 TU	0340	5.0
	1035	0.3		1015	0.3
	1626	5.1		1559	5.0
	2246	0.7		2225	0.6
6 TU	0446	5.0	21 W	0415	5.0
	1111	0.4		1056	0.4
	1706	4.9		1636	5.0
	2319	0.7		2305	0.6
7 W	0526	4.8	22 TH	0456	4.9
	1150	0.6		1136	0.4
	1747	4.7		1717	4.8
				2345	0.7
8 TH	0001	0.8	23 F	0537	4.8
	0608	4.6		1216	0.5
	1226	0.8		1805	4.6
	1828	4.4			
9 F	0040	1.0	24 SA	0029	0.7
	0656	4.4		0630	4.6
	1310	1.0		1302	0.7
	◑ 1919	4.1		◐ 1905	4.3
10 SA	0125	1.2	25 SU	0130	0.9
	0750	4.0		0734	4.3
	1415	1.2		1406	0.9
	2020	3.8		2027	4.1
11 SU	0254	1.3	26 M	0245	1.0
	0917	3.8		0906	4.2
	1540	1.3		1526	1.0
	2205	3.6		2146	4.0
12 M	0426	1.3	27 TU	0404	1.0
	1046	3.8		1025	4.3
	1701	1.3		1655	1.0
	2326	3.8		2306	4.1
13 TU	0524	1.1	28 W	0535	0.8
	1149	4.1		1138	4.5
	1755	1.2		1810	0.9
14 W	0021	4.1	29 TH	0007	4.4
	0635	1.0		0639	0.6
	1235	4.3		1235	4.8
	1846	1.0		1859	0.7
15 TH	0100	4.3	30 F	0055	4.6
	0716	0.8		0728	0.4
	1318	4.6		1317	5.0
	1926	0.9		1946	0.6
			31 SA	0139	4.8
				0815	0.3
				1359	5.1
				○ 2026	0.6

APRIL

Date	Time	m	Date	Time	m
1 SU	0219	5.0	16 M	0206	4.9
	0853	0.2		0829	0.4
	1440	5.1		1422	5.1
	2106	0.5		● 2046	0.5
2 M	0259	5.0	17 TU	0236	5.0
	0931	0.3		0912	0.3
	1521	5.1		1456	5.1
	2143	0.5		2125	0.5
3 TU	0336	5.0	18 W	0316	5.1
	1012	0.4		0952	0.3
	1559	5.0		1536	5.1
	2219	0.6		2208	0.5
4 W	0417	5.0	19 TH	0355	5.1
	1045	0.5		1033	0.3
	1637	4.8		1616	5.0
	2258	0.7		2251	0.5
5 TH	0456	4.8	20 F	0435	5.0
	1120	0.7		1115	0.4
	1716	4.6		1701	4.8
	2329	0.8		2336	0.6
6 F	0531	4.6	21 SA	0523	4.9
	1156	0.8		1201	0.6
	1755	4.4		1751	4.6
7 SA	0006	0.9	22 SU	0026	0.6
	0615	4.4		0618	4.6
	1226	1.0		1250	0.7
	1836	4.1		◐ 1856	4.3
8 SU	0045	1.0	23 M	0119	0.7
	0705	4.1		0736	4.4
	1305	1.3		1355	0.9
	◑ 1930	3.8		2016	4.1
9 M	0225	1.2	24 TU	0236	0.8
	0821	3.8		0856	4.3
	1500	1.4		1504	1.1
	2045	3.6		2135	4.0
10 TU	0334	1.2	25 W	0354	0.9
	0956	3.7		1012	4.3
	1621	1.3		1646	1.0
	2236	3.6		2250	4.1
11 W	0450	1.1	26 TH	0526	0.7
	1110	4.0		1125	4.5
	1715	1.2		1756	0.9
	2341	3.9		2349	4.4
12 TH	0555	0.9	27 F	0622	0.5
	1202	4.3		1220	4.8
	1810	1.0		1846	0.7
13 F	0026	4.2	28 SA	0036	4.6
	0640	0.8		0710	0.4
	1241	4.6		1305	4.9
	1856	0.9		1925	0.6
14 SA	0058	4.5	29 SU	0118	4.8
	0715	0.6		0752	0.3
	1316	4.8		1340	5.0
	1925	0.8		2006	0.6
15 SU	0128	4.7	30 M	0157	4.9
	0751	0.5		0829	0.3
	1347	5.0		1420	5.0
	2006	0.6		○ 2043	0.5

Chart Datum is 2·56 metres below NAP Datum. HAT is 5·4 metres above Chart Datum.

STANDARD TIME UT –01
Subtract 1 hour for UT
For Dutch Summer Time add ONE hour in **non-shaded areas**

VLISSINGEN LAT 51°27'N LONG 3°36'E

TIMES AND HEIGHTS OF HIGH AND LOW WATERS

Dates in red are **SPRINGS**
Dates in blue are **NEAPS**

YEAR **2018**

MAY

Date	Time	m	Time	m	Time	m	Time	m
1 TU	0236	4.9	0907	0.4	1457	5.0	2126	0.5
2 W	0315	5.0	0943	0.5	1537	4.9	2200	0.5
3 TH	0350	4.9	1021	0.6	1612	4.7	2235	0.6
4 F	0427	4.8	1056	0.8	1647	4.6	2304	0.7
5 SA	0506	4.6	1126	0.9	1726	4.4	2339	0.8
6 SU	0545	4.4	1156	1.1	1806	4.2		
7 M	0014	0.9	0625	4.2	1246	1.2	1856	4.0
8 TU	0115	1.1	0735	4.0	1410	1.4	◑ 2006	3.8
9 W	0306	1.1	0849	3.9	1530	1.3	2115	3.7
10 TH	0405	1.0	1009	4.0	1636	1.2	2246	3.9
11 F	0459	0.9	1115	4.3	1726	1.0	2336	4.2
12 SA	0556	0.7	1159	4.6	1816	0.9		
13 SU	0016	4.5	0635	0.6	1239	4.8	1856	0.7
14 M	0053	4.8	0720	0.5	1315	5.0	1939	0.6
15 TU	0133	5.0	0802	0.4	1355	5.1	● 2018	0.5
16 W	0213	5.1	0846	0.3	1435	5.2	2103	0.4
17 TH	0254	5.1	0928	0.3	1516	5.1	2148	0.4
18 F	0336	5.1	1012	0.4	1600	5.0	2235	0.4
19 SA	0420	5.0	1057	0.5	1648	4.8	2326	0.4
20 SU	0509	4.9	1141	0.6	1740	4.6		
21 M	0015	0.5	0609	4.7	1236	0.8	1848	4.4
22 TU	0116	0.6	0725	4.5	1340	0.9	◐ 1956	4.2
23 W	0226	0.7	0836	4.4	1455	1.0	2105	4.1
24 TH	0334	0.7	0949	4.4	1614	1.0	2219	4.2
25 F	0506	0.6	1059	4.6	1730	0.9	2325	4.4
26 SA	0555	0.5	1155	4.7	1820	0.8		
27 SU	0010	4.5	0646	0.5	1241	4.8	1905	0.7
28 M	0057	4.7	0728	0.5	1325	4.8	1945	0.6
29 TU	0138	4.8	0805	0.5	1406	4.8	○ 2022	0.6
30 W	0217	4.8	0842	0.6	1438	4.8	2102	0.5
31 TH	0256	4.8	0918	0.6	1518	4.8	2140	0.5

JUNE

Date	Time	m	Time	m	Time	m	Time	m
1 F	0336	4.8	0955	0.7	1551	4.7	2221	0.6
2 SA	0407	4.7	1031	0.8	1628	4.6	2256	0.7
3 SU	0442	4.6	1100	1.0	1702	4.4	2330	0.7
4 M	0518	4.5	1136	1.1	1740	4.3	2355	0.8
5 TU	0605	4.3	1204	1.2	1826	4.2		
6 W	0045	0.9	0700	4.2	1306	1.2	◑ 1926	4.0
7 TH	0150	0.9	0806	4.1	1415	1.3	2026	4.0
8 F	0255	0.9	0916	4.2	1546	1.2	2135	4.1
9 SA	0406	0.8	1016	4.3	1636	1.1	2242	4.3
10 SU	0505	0.7	1111	4.6	1731	0.9	2336	4.5
11 M	0558	0.6	1206	4.8	1815	0.8		
12 TU	0021	4.8	0648	0.5	1248	5.0	1911	0.6
13 W	0105	5.0	0736	0.4	1332	5.1	● 1955	0.5
14 TH	0150	5.1	0822	0.4	1416	5.1	2048	0.4
15 F	0235	5.2	0907	0.4	1500	5.1	2136	0.4
16 SA	0320	5.2	0953	0.5	1548	5.0	2225	0.3
17 SU	0408	5.1	1040	0.6	1637	4.8	2311	0.3
18 M	0459	5.0	1130	0.7	1731	4.7		
19 TU	0005	0.4	0558	4.9	1219	0.8	1829	4.6
20 W	0059	0.4	0701	4.7	1320	0.9	◐ 1931	4.4
21 TH	0154	0.5	0810	4.6	1414	1.0	2038	4.3
22 F	0305	0.6	0918	4.5	1535	1.1	2145	4.3
23 SA	0426	0.7	1028	4.5	1650	1.0	2252	4.3
24 SU	0531	0.7	1128	4.6	1745	0.9	2348	4.5
25 M	0618	0.7	1219	4.6	1840	0.8		
26 TU	0039	4.6	0659	0.7	1308	4.7	1922	0.7
27 W	0126	4.7	0739	0.7	1350	4.7	2005	0.7
28 TH	0205	4.7	0818	0.7	1426	4.7	○ 2046	0.6
29 F	0238	4.8	0851	0.8	1458	4.7	2119	0.6
30 SA	0315	4.8	0930	0.8	1535	4.7	2155	0.6

JULY

Date	Time	m	Time	m	Time	m	Time	m
1 SU	0348	4.8	1005	0.9	1606	4.7	2235	0.6
2 M	0425	4.7	1040	1.0	1646	4.6	2309	0.7
3 TU	0502	4.6	1112	1.0	1715	4.5	2345	0.7
4 W	0536	4.5	1150	1.1	1755	4.4		
5 TH	0025	0.7	0620	4.4	1230	1.1	1840	4.3
6 F	0105	0.8	0715	4.4	1325	1.1	◑ 1934	4.2
7 SA	0206	0.8	0814	4.3	1436	1.1	2048	4.2
8 SU	0305	0.8	0926	4.4	1540	1.1	2155	4.3
9 M	0416	0.8	1036	4.5	1646	1.0	2255	4.5
10 TU	0526	0.7	1132	4.7	1751	0.8	2355	4.7
11 W	0626	0.6	1226	4.9	1849	0.7		
12 TH	0046	4.9	0712	0.5	1313	5.0	1939	0.5
13 F	0133	5.1	0803	0.5	1403	5.1	● 2032	0.4
14 SA	0220	5.2	0849	0.5	1446	5.1	2122	0.3
15 SU	0306	5.2	0938	0.6	1536	5.0	2210	0.3
16 M	0355	5.2	1026	0.6	1622	5.0	2255	0.3
17 TU	0445	5.1	1112	0.7	1712	4.9	2345	0.3
18 W	0537	5.0	1158	0.8	1805	4.8		
19 TH	0036	0.4	0635	4.8	1248	0.9	◐ 1859	4.6
20 F	0126	0.5	0736	4.7	1346	1.0	2000	4.5
21 SA	0225	0.7	0840	4.5	1445	1.1	2106	4.3
22 SU	0325	0.9	0950	4.3	1555	1.1	2221	4.2
23 M	0445	0.9	1100	4.3	1720	1.1	2321	4.3
24 TU	0550	0.9	1159	4.4	1815	1.0		
25 W	0026	4.4	0635	0.9	1249	4.5	1905	0.8
26 TH	0109	4.6	0720	0.9	1336	4.6	1948	0.7
27 F	0152	4.7	0758	0.9	1409	4.7	○ 2021	0.7
28 SA	0225	4.7	0836	0.9	1445	4.7	2059	0.6
29 SU	0257	4.8	0906	0.9	1516	4.8	2136	0.6
30 M	0328	4.8	0942	0.9	1548	4.8	2215	0.6
31 TU	0406	4.8	1021	0.9	1617	4.8	2249	0.6

AUGUST

Date	Time	m	Time	m	Time	m	Time	m
1 W	0435	4.8	1056	1.0	1649	4.7	2326	0.6
2 TH	0507	4.7	1126	1.0	1726	4.6	2356	0.7
3 F	0545	4.7	1206	1.0	1806	4.6		
4 SA	0035	0.7	0627	4.6	1246	1.0	◑ 1855	4.5
5 SU	0126	0.7	0730	4.5	1334	1.1	1954	4.4
6 M	0226	0.8	0842	4.4	1444	1.1	2116	4.4
7 TU	0336	0.9	0956	4.4	1605	1.1	2226	4.4
8 W	0450	0.8	1102	4.5	1722	0.9	2332	4.6
9 TH	0601	0.8	1206	4.7	1832	0.7		
10 F	0027	4.9	0658	0.7	1259	4.9	1928	0.6
11 SA	0116	5.1	0748	0.6	1346	5.0	● 2017	0.4
12 SU	0206	5.2	0835	0.6	1433	5.1	2105	0.3
13 M	0252	5.3	0922	0.6	1516	5.1	2153	0.3
14 TU	0336	5.3	1005	0.7	1602	5.1	2236	0.3
15 W	0425	5.2	1048	0.7	1647	5.1	2326	0.4
16 TH	0512	5.1	1129	0.8	1736	4.9		
17 F	0006	0.5	0606	4.9	1216	0.9	1825	4.8
18 SA	0045	0.6	0655	4.6	1306	1.0	◐ 1920	4.5
19 SU	0135	0.9	0751	4.3	1406	1.2	2019	4.3
20 M	0245	1.1	0906	4.1	1515	1.3	2140	4.1
21 TU	0354	1.2	1025	4.0	1634	1.2	2255	4.1
22 W	0515	1.2	1136	4.2	1750	1.1		
23 TH	0006	4.3	0609	1.1	1229	4.4	1846	0.9
24 F	0055	4.5	0655	1.0	1315	4.5	1936	0.8
25 SA	0136	4.7	0735	1.0	1349	4.7	2005	0.7
26 SU	0205	4.8	0808	0.9	1419	4.8	○ 2035	0.7
27 M	0236	4.9	0846	0.9	1449	4.9	2116	0.6
28 TU	0307	5.0	0915	0.8	1521	4.9	2145	0.5
29 W	0337	5.0	0956	0.8	1552	4.9	2226	0.5
30 TH	0407	5.0	1030	0.9	1623	4.9	2255	0.6
31 F	0441	4.9	1106	0.9	1657	4.9	2332	0.6

Chart Datum is 2·56 metres below NAP Datum. HAT is 5·4 metres above Chart Datum.

STANDARD TIME UT –01
Subtract 1 hour for UT
For Dutch Summer Time add ONE hour in **non-shaded areas**

VLISSINGEN LAT 51°27′N LONG 3°36′E

TIMES AND HEIGHTS OF HIGH AND LOW WATERS

Dates in red are SPRINGS
Dates in blue are NEAPS

YEAR **2018**

SEPTEMBER

Date	Day	Time	m	Time	m	Time	m	Time	m
1	SA	0517	4.8	1141	0.9	1733	4.8		
2	SU	0005	0.7	0557	4.7	1215	1.0	1820	4.7
3	M	0056	0.8	0655	4.5	1310	1.0	◑ 1919	4.5
4	TU	0150	0.9	0806	4.3	1420	1.1	2045	4.3
5	W	0305	1.0	0926	4.2	1546	1.1	2202	4.4
6	TH	0431	1.0	1046	4.3	1705	1.0	2316	4.5
7	F	0546	0.9	1148	4.5	1820	0.8		
8	SA	0018	4.8	0646	0.8	1245	4.8	1915	0.6
9	SU	0107	5.1	0735	0.7	1331	5.0	● 2005	0.4
10	M	0150	5.2	0820	0.7	1413	5.1	2050	0.3
11	TU	0233	5.3	0906	0.7	1455	5.2	2133	0.3
12	W	0316	5.3	0946	0.7	1536	5.2	2216	0.4
13	TH	0400	5.2	1025	0.7	1620	5.1	2255	0.5
14	F	0446	5.1	1106	0.8	1703	5.0	2332	0.6
15	SA	0527	4.8	1142	0.9	1745	4.8		
16	SU	0010	0.8	0611	4.6	1225	1.0	1836	4.5
17	M	0055	1.0	0701	4.3	1327	1.2	◐ 1936	4.2
18	TU	0156	1.3	0806	4.0	1445	1.3	2045	4.0
19	W	0326	1.4	0945	3.8	1600	1.3	2225	4.0
20	TH	0435	1.4	1108	3.9	1716	1.2	2336	4.2
21	F	0546	1.3	1201	4.2	1815	1.0		
22	SA	0025	4.5	0624	1.2	1248	4.4	1906	0.9
23	SU	0106	4.7	0710	1.0	1322	4.6	1935	0.8
24	M	0136	4.8	0746	1.0	1349	4.8	2010	0.7
25	TU	0205	5.0	0815	0.9	1418	4.9	○ 2042	0.6
26	W	0236	5.1	0849	0.8	1449	5.1	2116	0.5
27	TH	0307	5.1	0928	0.8	1523	5.1	2156	0.5
28	F	0340	5.1	1006	0.8	1556	5.1	2232	0.5
29	SA	0415	5.0	1040	0.8	1633	5.0	2311	0.6
30	SU	0453	4.9	1121	0.8	1710	5.0	2348	0.7

OCTOBER

Date	Day	Time	m	Time	m	Time	m	Time	m
1	M	0535	4.8	1206	0.9	1757	4.8		
2	TU	0032	0.8	0628	4.5	1256	1.0	◑ 1856	4.5
3	W	0130	1.0	0746	4.2	1406	1.1	2019	4.3
4	TH	0246	1.2	0906	4.1	1525	1.2	2145	4.3
5	F	0409	1.2	1025	4.2	1656	1.0	2301	4.5
6	SA	0536	1.1	1135	4.4	1816	0.8		
7	SU	0006	4.8	0629	0.9	1227	4.7	1902	0.6
8	M	0051	5.1	0720	0.8	1310	4.9	1947	0.4
9	TU	0135	5.2	0759	0.7	1353	5.1	● 2027	0.4
10	W	0215	5.3	0842	0.7	1436	5.2	2110	0.4
11	TH	0256	5.3	0922	0.7	1516	5.2	2147	0.5
12	F	0338	5.2	1002	0.7	1556	5.1	2225	0.6
13	SA	0417	5.0	1040	0.8	1636	5.0	2306	0.8
14	SU	0455	4.8	1115	0.9	1716	4.8	2336	1.0
15	M	0537	4.5	1156	1.0	1756	4.5		
16	TU	0016	1.2	0619	4.3	1234	1.2	◐ 1850	4.2
17	W	0054	1.4	0712	4.0	1354	1.3	2000	4.0
18	TH	0235	1.6	0820	3.7	1520	1.4	2130	3.8
19	F	0356	1.5	1021	3.7	1636	1.3	2256	4.0
20	SA	0454	1.4	1122	4.0	1736	1.1	2350	4.3
21	SU	0556	1.2	1205	4.3	1826	0.9		
22	M	0030	4.6	0636	1.1	1241	4.6	1902	0.8
23	TU	0105	4.8	0709	1.0	1316	4.8	1936	0.7
24	W	0132	5.0	0745	0.9	1347	5.0	○ 2009	0.6
25	TH	0206	5.2	0826	0.8	1418	5.1	2046	0.5
26	F	0240	5.2	0906	0.7	1456	5.2	2128	0.5
27	SA	0316	5.2	0942	0.7	1534	5.2	2206	0.5
28	SU	0355	5.1	1026	0.7	1612	5.1	2245	0.6
29	M	0435	5.0	1106	0.7	1653	5.0	2331	0.8
30	TU	0522	4.7	1150	0.8	1741	4.8		
31	W	0016	0.9	0615	4.5	1246	0.9	◑ 1846	4.5

NOVEMBER

Date	Day	Time	m	Time	m	Time	m	Time	m
1	TH	0116	1.1	0731	4.2	1355	1.0	2010	4.4
2	F	0225	1.3	0851	4.1	1521	1.1	2125	4.4
3	SA	0355	1.3	1008	4.2	1634	1.0	2246	4.5
4	SU	0526	1.2	1115	4.4	1749	0.8	2346	4.8
5	M	0616	1.0	1206	4.6	1842	0.6		
6	TU	0036	5.0	0700	0.8	1250	4.8	1925	0.5
7	W	0117	5.1	0746	0.8	1335	5.0	● 2006	0.5
8	TH	0156	5.1	0822	0.7	1413	5.1	2045	0.5
9	F	0237	5.1	0902	0.7	1456	5.1	2126	0.6
10	SA	0317	5.0	0939	0.7	1532	5.1	2200	0.7
11	SU	0356	4.9	1021	0.7	1611	5.0	2236	0.9
12	M	0430	4.7	1056	0.8	1652	4.8	2311	1.1
13	TU	0510	4.5	1130	1.0	1729	4.6	2334	1.2
14	W	0550	4.3	1205	1.1	1816	4.3		
15	TH	0020	1.4	0636	4.1	1255	1.2	◐ 1911	4.1
16	F	0124	1.6	0735	3.9	1436	1.3	2025	3.9
17	SA	0311	1.6	0846	3.8	1540	1.3	2156	4.0
18	SU	0410	1.5	1016	3.9	1634	1.2	2256	4.2
19	M	0506	1.3	1115	4.2	1736	1.0	2341	4.5
20	TU	0555	1.2	1200	4.5	1820	0.8		
21	W	0022	4.8	0637	1.0	1238	4.7	1855	0.7
22	TH	0059	5.0	0716	0.8	1316	5.0	1938	0.6
23	F	0136	5.2	0755	0.7	1353	5.1	○ 2023	0.5
24	SA	0215	5.2	0838	0.6	1433	5.2	2106	0.5
25	SU	0255	5.2	0925	0.6	1514	5.2	2145	0.6
26	M	0336	5.1	1008	0.6	1556	5.2	2228	0.6
27	TU	0423	5.0	1056	0.6	1643	5.1	2316	0.8
28	W	0511	4.8	1146	0.7	1736	4.9		
29	TH	0001	0.9	0606	4.5	1240	0.7	1839	4.7
30	F	0059	1.1	0716	4.3	1345	0.8	◑ 1956	4.5

DECEMBER

Date	Day	Time	m	Time	m	Time	m	Time	m
1	SA	0210	1.2	0825	4.2	1455	0.9	2105	4.5
2	SU	0325	1.3	0940	4.2	1616	0.9	2215	4.5
3	M	0450	1.2	1045	4.3	1726	0.8	2326	4.6
4	TU	0550	1.1	1141	4.5	1820	0.7		
5	W	0016	4.8	0640	0.9	1231	4.7	1906	0.6
6	TH	0058	4.9	0722	0.8	1317	4.8	1945	0.6
7	F	0142	4.9	0801	0.7	1357	4.9	● 2025	0.7
8	SA	0220	4.9	0846	0.7	1435	5.0	2100	0.7
9	SU	0301	4.9	0922	0.6	1515	5.0	2138	0.8
10	M	0336	4.8	0959	0.7	1556	4.9	2216	0.9
11	TU	0412	4.7	1040	0.7	1632	4.8	2245	1.1
12	W	0450	4.6	1115	0.8	1710	4.6	2320	1.2
13	TH	0526	4.5	1150	0.9	1750	4.4	2356	1.3
14	F	0605	4.3	1225	1.0	1836	4.3		
15	SA	0036	1.4	0655	4.2	1315	1.1	◐ 1936	4.1
16	SU	0125	1.5	0756	4.0	1436	1.1	2035	4.1
17	M	0254	1.5	0906	4.0	1536	1.1	2146	4.2
18	TU	0410	1.3	1009	4.2	1636	1.0	2250	4.4
19	W	0505	1.2	1112	4.4	1735	0.9	2345	4.7
20	TH	0556	1.0	1202	4.7	1825	0.7		
21	F	0030	4.9	0649	0.9	1247	4.9	1916	0.6
22	SA	0116	5.0	0736	0.7	1331	5.1	○ 1955	0.6
23	SU	0155	5.1	0819	0.6	1413	5.2	2046	0.5
24	M	0241	5.1	0908	0.5	1458	5.2	2128	0.6
25	TU	0325	5.1	0958	0.5	1543	5.2	2213	0.6
26	W	0410	5.0	1046	0.4	1630	5.1	2302	0.7
27	TH	0459	4.9	1135	0.5	1723	5.0	2350	0.8
28	F	0555	4.7	1231	0.5	1822	4.8		
29	SA	0045	1.0	0656	4.6	1322	0.6	◑ 1930	4.7
30	SU	0139	1.1	0755	4.4	1425	0.8	2035	4.5
31	M	0246	1.2	0906	4.3	1536	0.9	2145	4.4

Chart Datum is 2·56 metres below NAP Datum. HAT is 5·4 metres above Chart Datum.

9.16.29 BRESKENS

Zeeland **51°24'·00N 03°34'·08E**

CHARTS AC 1874, 1872, 120; Zeekaart 120, 101; BE 103; DYC 1801.4, 1803.2; Imray C30

TIDES +0210 Dover; ML no data; Duration 0600

Standard Port VLISSINGEN (←) Use Vlissingen data.

SHELTER Good in all winds except N/NW. In fine weather ⚓ off Plaat van Breskens or in peaceful Vaarwater langs Hoofdplaat; no ⚓ in commercial/fishing hbr.

NAVIGATION WPT 51°24'·71N 03°33'·90E (ARV-VH NCM buoy, Q), 170°/7ca to hbr ent. Beware fast ferries and strong tides across the ent. Do not confuse the ent with the ferry port ent, 0·7M WNW, where yachts are prohib.

LIGHTS AND MARKS Large bldg/silo on centre pier in hbr and three apartment blocks (30m) SE of marina are conspic. See chartlet and Lights, buoys and waypoints. Nieuwe Sluis lt ho, a 28m B/W banded 8-sided twr, is 1·8M W of marina.

COMMUNICATIONS (Code 0117); Police 0900 8844; ⊖ (0118) 484614/484624; British Consul (020) 676 4343; Ⓗ (0117) 459000; Dr 384010, at night/weekends (0115) 643000; Marina VHF Ch 31.

FACILITIES **Marina** jachthavenbreskens@zonnet.nl ☎381902. www.jachthavenbreskens.nl 580 inc Ⓥ €1·90 + €1·15 pp/day tax. Enter marina between two wavebreak barges; access H24, 5m at ent. Berth on 1st pontoon where HM assigns a berth via an intercom ☎. (fuel berth in FV hbr) ACA Ⓔ (70t) (30t) . **YC Breskens** ☎383278, (book early) @.

Town Ⓑ ✈ (Oostende, Antwerp or Brussels). Pedestrian & bike ferry or car tunnel to Vlissingen for ≷.

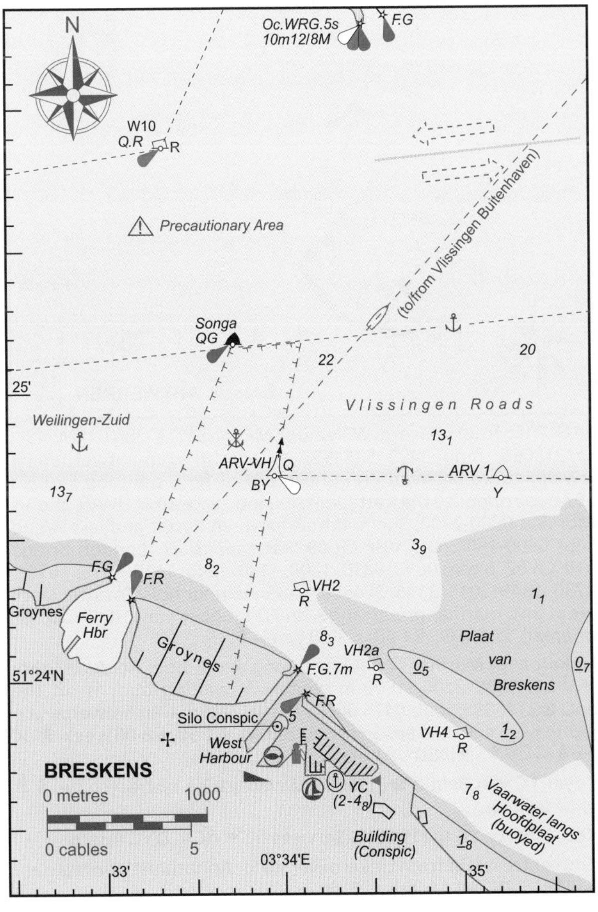

9.16.30 TERNEUZEN

Zeeland **51°20'·58N 03°49'·69E**

CHARTS AC 120; Zeekaart 1443; BE 103, 105; DYC 1803.2; Imray C30

TIDES +0230 Dover; ML 2·5; Duration 0555

Standard Port VLISSINGEN (←)

Times				Height (metres)			
High Water		Low Water		MHWS	MHWN	MLWN	MLWS
0300	0900	0400	1000	5·0	4·1	1·1	0·5
1500	2100	1600	2200				
Differences *TERNEUZEN*							
+0020	*+0020*	*+0020*	*+0030*	*+0·4*	*+0·3*	*+0·1*	*0·0*

SHELTER Very good except in strong N'lies. Exposed ⚓ on N side of fairway between buoys WPT4, WPT6, PvT-ZE & ZE5. Strong currents.

NAVIGATION WPT 51°20'·82N 03°47'·96E (25B SHM buoy), 101°/1M, keep well to stbd and call *Traffic Centre Terneuzen* Ch 03 when 1·5M from hbr ent (and also when departing). Fairway only 500m wide and large ships pass very close; maintain a constant lookout E and W. Very busy traffic to/from the locks; call *Port Control Terneuzen*, Ch 11. If S-bound via Gent Canal transit the E lock to berth in Zijkanaal A. Strong eddy during ebb at Veerhaven ent.

LIGHTS AND MARKS Dow Chemical works and storage tanks are conspic 2M W of hbr. Lt Oc WRG 5s, B/W post, on W mole is a conspic mark for the Veerhaven.

When entry to E Buitenhaven is prohib, a second ● is shown below FR on E mole. For E lock: ● = no entry; ●● (vert) = get ready; ● = go. No yachts in W Buitenhaven, Middle and W locks.

COMMUNICATIONS (Code 0115) Police 0900 8844; ⊖ (0118) 484600; British Consul (020) 676 4343; Ⓗ 688000; Dr 616262; Port HM 612161, call *Port Control* Ch 11 (H24) for locks and Gent canal; also info broadcasts every H+00; East lock VHF Ch 18; No marina VHF.

FACILITIES Two marinas in SE corner of Veerhaven (former ferry hbr, 0·5M E of main hbr ent): **WV Honte Marina** where berths are more likely. ☎697089, mob 0651 168987. www.jachthaventerneuzen.nl 130 inc Ⓥ €1·50. (230v) €1·25, (6t).

WV Neusen Marina is close ESE (and in Zijkanaal A) ☎696331; mob 0652182564 www.wvneusen.nl 100 €1·00, wi-fi. Boatyards: **Aricom** www.aricom.nl ☎614577, €1·00, (50t). **Vermeulen's Yachtwerf** ☎612716, €0·75, (50t).

Town Ⓑ ✈ (Antwerpen). Foot ferry Breskens to Vlissingen. Cars by Schelde tunnel Terneuzen-Ellewoutsdijk.

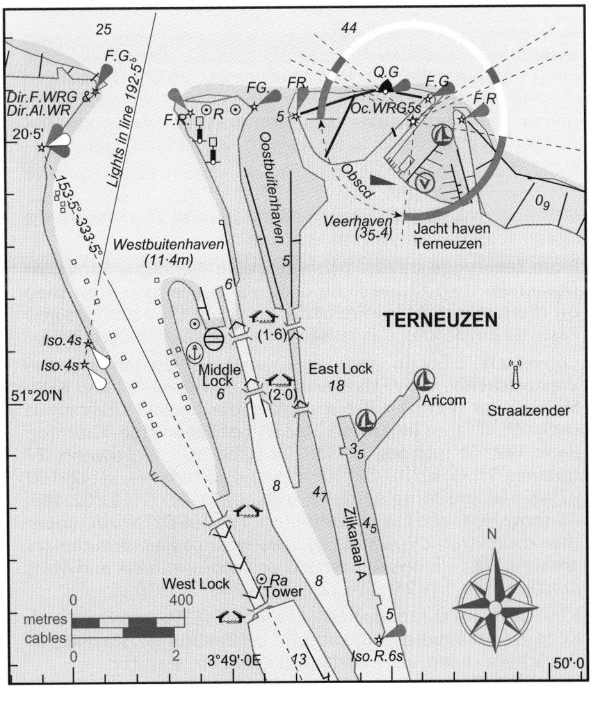

9.16.31 SPECIAL NOTES FOR BELGIUM

PROVINCES are given in lieu of UK 'counties'.

LANGUAGES Flemish, ie Dutch as spoken in Flanders, is the 1st language along the coast and N of Brussels. English is also widely spoken. French, the 2nd language, is spoken in and S of Brussels.

CURRENCY is the Euro €. VAT (BTW/TVA) is 21%.

CHARTS *'Vlaamse Banken'* (BE) issued by the Hydrografische Dienst der Kust are most widely used. Dutch yacht charts (DYC 1800 series) cover all Belgian ports. Imray C30 is also popular.

TIME ZONE is –0100, which is allowed for in tidal predictions but no provision is made for daylight saving schemes.

HARBOURS Ports of entry are Nieuwpoort, Oostende and Zeebrugge; Blankenberge, early April–late Sep. Berths and moorings are administered by local YCs and municipal authorities.

SIGNALS At Oostende and Zeebrugge IPTS are used, and small craft wind warnings (also at Nieuwpoort and Blankenberge). They apply only to craft <6m LOA and indicate onshore wind >F3; offshore wind >F4. Day, 2 ▼s, points together; night, Fl Bu lt.

TELEPHONE To call UK from Belgium, dial 00 44 then the UK area code minus the prefix 0, followed by the number called. To call Belgium from UK, dial 00 32 then the code and 6/7 digit number.

Emergency: ☎101 Police; ☎100 Fire, Ambulance and Marine. ☎112 (EU emergency number) is also operational.

CONSUL British Embassy, Brussels, (consular) 02 287 6248.

MRCC Oostende co-ordinates SAR operations (5.14). If no contact, call *Oostende Radio* VHF Ch 16 or ☎100. For medical advice call *Radiomédical Oostende* on Ch 16.

PUBLIC HOLIDAYS New Year's Day, Easter Mon, Labour Day (1 May) Ascension Day, Whit Mon, National Day (21 July) Feast of the Assumption (15 Aug) All Saints' Day (1 Nov) Armistice Day (11 Nov) King's Birthday (15 Nov) Christmas Day.

RULES A ▼ when motor-sailing and a black ball ● at ⚓ are strictly enforced. Navigation within 200m of shore (MLWS) and transit through restricted areas around wind farms is prohibited. Red diesel in pleasure craft is illegal in Belgium, see 2.3.2. Ship Radio Licences must be up-to-date and cover all relevant equipment including radar.

INLAND WATERWAYS At www.mobilit.fgov.be download CEVNI-based regulations in French or Dutch. Licence plates (*Immatriculatieplaat*) are required on Belgian waterways. Helmsman's Competence criteria are as for the Netherlands.

THE BELGIAN COAST

Long shoals parallel this 36M coastline (AC 1872). The buoyed channels mostly run within 3M of the shore, the outer shoals giving some protection from strong W or SW winds, but dangerous in strong W to NE'lys with wind against tide.

▶*Off the Belgian coast the E-going stream begins at HW Vlissingen –0320 (HW Dover –0120), and the W-going at HW Vlissingen +0240 (HW Dover +0440), sp rates 2kn. Mostly the streams run parallel with the coast.*◀

From **Zeebrugge** stay 1M offshore inside Wenduine Bank past **Oostende**, then Kleine Rede or Grote Reede into West Diep off **Nieuwpoort**. At the French border West Diep narrows into Passe de Zuydcoote; stay close inshore for 25M to Dyck PHM.

Conversely, E-bound from the Thames, for **Oostende** or the **Westerschelde**, use W Hinder lt. From N, use NHR-S and NHR-SE buoys or N Hinder lt buoy. Enter the buoyed channels at Dyck. Wind farms lie 13M to 24M NW of Zeebrugge: Thornton Bank 1+2, 48 turbines, 51°31'·25N 02°55'·69E, Northwind, 72 turbines, 51°35'·82N 02°52'·10E, Belwind, 55 turbines, 51°42'·16N 02°48'·54E, and Borssele 1+2, 196 turbines, 51°42'·77N 03°02'·18E. All show FR lts and Fl Y at perimeters. The TSS *Off North Hinder* then routes traffic W, S and E of these hazards via precautionary areas *At West Hinder*, *At Gootebank*, *Schouwenbank* and *Maas junctions*, see 9.16.21, 9.16.22A and AC 1872, 1630.

E bound, leave Oostende ▶*HW Vlissingen –0300 on a fair tide*◀. Keep 2M off **Blankenberge** and 1M off **Zeebrugge**, staying S of the Scheur channel to avoid much commercial traffic.

9.16.32 ANTWERPEN

Belgium, Antwerpen **51°13'·66N 04°23'·79E**

CHARTS AC 128; Zeekaart 1443; BE 103, 104; DYC 1803.5

TIDES +0342 Dover; ML 2·9; Duration 0605

Standard Port VLISSINGEN (←)

Times				Height (metres)			
High Water		Low Water		MHWS	MHWN	MLWN	MLWS
0300	0900	0400	1000	5·0	4·1	1·1	0·5
1500	2100	1600	2200				
Differences *ANTWERPEN*							
+0128	*+0116*	*+0121*	*+0144*	*+1·2*	*+1·0*	*+0·1*	*+0·1*

SHELTER Excellent in both marinas. ⚓ in the river is not advised.

NAVIGATION See Westerschelde. Best to check off the buoys coming upriver. There is a gap of 1·4M between No 116 PHM buoy and No 107 SHM buoy. Entrance to the Willemdok marina via Royersluis and Siberia bridge is permitted, but not recommended. Use the Kattendijksluis (abeam buoy 107). VHF 69, operating if tide between TAW 2.2–5.0m, or approximately 3±HW.

COMMUNICATIONS (Code 03) VTS, Zandvliet Centre VHF Ch 12, lock Ch 79; Radar VHF Ch 04, 66 ⊖ 2292004; Police 5460730; Ⓗ 2852000 (W Bank) 234111 (E Bank); Antwerp Port Ops Ch 74 (H24); Royerssluis VHF Ch 22; Access bridges VHF Ch 62; Willemdok VHF Ch 23; Linkeroever VHF Ch 09 (HW±1).

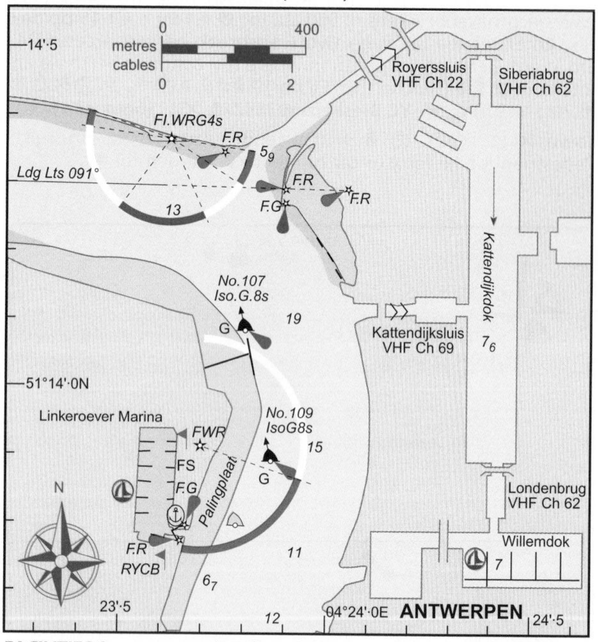

FACILITIES from seaward: **Willemdok Marina** 51°13'·78N 04°24'·43E. ☎2315066, mob 0495 535455. www.jachthaven-antwerpen.be jaw@pandora.be. Wait on inshore side of ferry pontoon S of No 107 buoy opposite the Kattendijksluis lock, accessible HW-/+ 3hours Mon-Sat 0600-2200; Sun and hols between Easter and last w/end Sept 0900-1900. Call VHF Ch 69 *'kattendijksluis'*. London bridge VHF Ch 62, opens 0630, 0830, 1000, 1130, 1245, 1415, 1515, 1615*, 1730, 1845, 2015, 2145, 2245LT.*Sat/Sun/Public hols. To enter Dock areas and marina, pre-arrange an FD number via VHF Ch 20, ☎, or email. 200 + ⓥ, €1·50, €8·00 week.

Linkeroever Marina (W bank); lat/long under title. Access by gate HW ±1, 0800–2200 (1800 in winter). Y waiting buoy is off the ent. ☎2190895, mob 0475 643957. www.jachthaven-antwerpen.be jachthaven_linkeroever@skynet.be 200+ⓥ, €1·50, €8·00 week. (38t) (1·5t).

Royal YC van België ☎2195231. www.rycb.be rycb@rycb.be.

Kon. Liberty YC ☎2191147. **Services** ACA, DYC Agent.

City centre is ¾M from Linkeroever via St. Annatunnel (pedestrian) 51°13'·22N. All facilities, @ ⇄ ✈.

9.16.33 ZEEBRUGGE

Belgium, West Flanders **51°21'·83N 03°11'·39E**

CHARTS AC 2449, 3371, 1872, 1874; Zeekaart 1441; BE 104; DYC 1801.3, 1803; Imray C30

TIDES +0135 Dover; ML 2·4; Duration 0535. Note: Zeebrugge is a Standard Port (⟶)

SHELTER Very good in the marina, access H24.

NAVIGATION WPT 51°22'·48N 03°09'·95E (Z SHM buoy, QG), 129°/1·1M to ent (lat/long under title). Lts on outer bkwtr heads show high-vis strip lts to seaward. Beware strong currents in hbr apprs (up to 4kn at HW –1). Caution on ent/dep due to limited vis; give all jetties a wide berth. A busy commercial, naval and fishing port and a ferry terminal. An inner WPT 51°20'·85N 03°12'·29E off Leopold II Dam head is useful to avoid getting 'lost' inside the vast outer hbr, especially in poor vis; see chartlet.

LIGHTS AND MARKS Big ship ldg marks (hard to see by day) and lts (as chartlet) lead in sequence to Vissershaven and the marina:

- 136°: Both W cols, R bands.
- 154°: Front, W pylon, R bands; rear, W bldg, R bands.
- 220°: Both W cols, B bands. • 193°: Both W cols, R bands.

IPTS are shown prominently from E and W outer bkwtrs and Leopold II Dam. Extra sigs: 3 Fl Y lts (vert) + IPTS No 2 or 5 = LNG tanker entering/leaving. No exit/entry without specific permission from Port Control.

COMMUNICATIONS (Code 050) Coast Guard 545072; Sea Saving Service 544007; Police 544148; ⊜ 545455; British Consul 02 287 6248; Dr 544590; Port HM 543241; Port Control 546867/550801, VHF Ch 71 (H24); Lock 543231, VHF Ch 68; Marina VHF Ch 23.

FACILITIES **Royal Belgian SC (VZW)** ☎544903, mob 0496 789053. havenmeester@rbsc.be www.rbsc.be 100 + 100Ⓥ €2·64 inc free wi-fi, (on coin meter) (0830-1200, 1300-1800) (Clubhouse Alberta) ☎544197.

BZYC Tijdokhaven Marina, HM ☎734738. www.bzyc.be info@bzyc.be 94 inc Ⓥ (max 20m) €2·68 inc wi-fi.

Town Ⓑ. ⇌ 15 mins to Brugge. Tram to Oostende for ✈. Ferries to Hull and Rosyth (Edinburgh).

BRUGGE Masted yachts can transit Zeebrugge's eastern sealock to go 6M S via the Boudewijnkanaal (Ch 68) & 2 lifting bridges to Brugge docks. **Brugse Zeil en Yacht Club (BZYC)** is on the E bank: ☎(0478) 711301. www.bzyc.be info@bzyc.be €1·00/m; & €2·00/day. 15 min's walk to city centre. Unmasted boats can go clockwise on the Oostende-Gent Canal (Ch 18) to **Flandria Marina** (S of city): ☎380866, mob 0477 384456. www.yachtclubflandria.be 10 min walk to city centre; close to ⇌ (quick and easy by train).

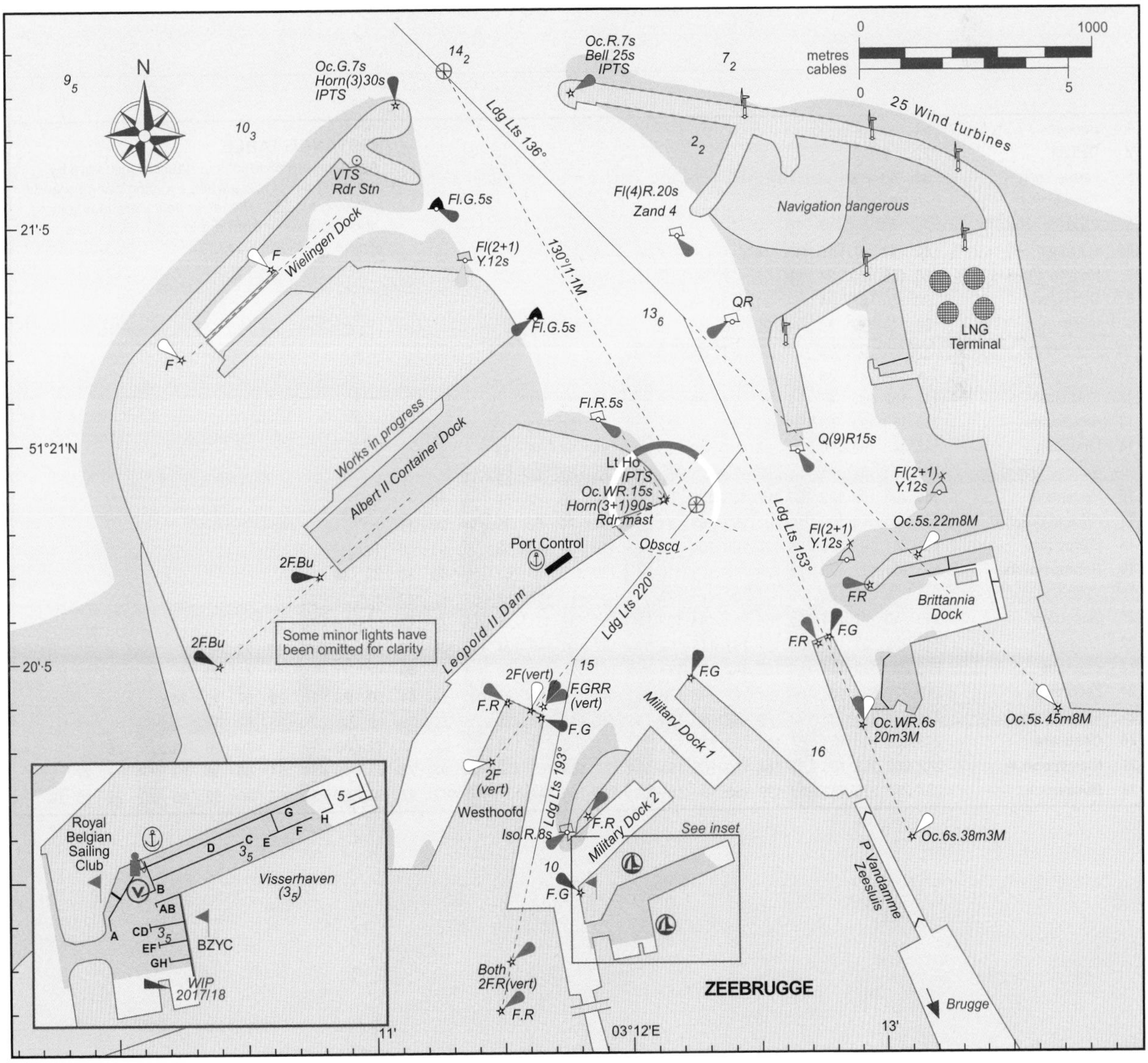

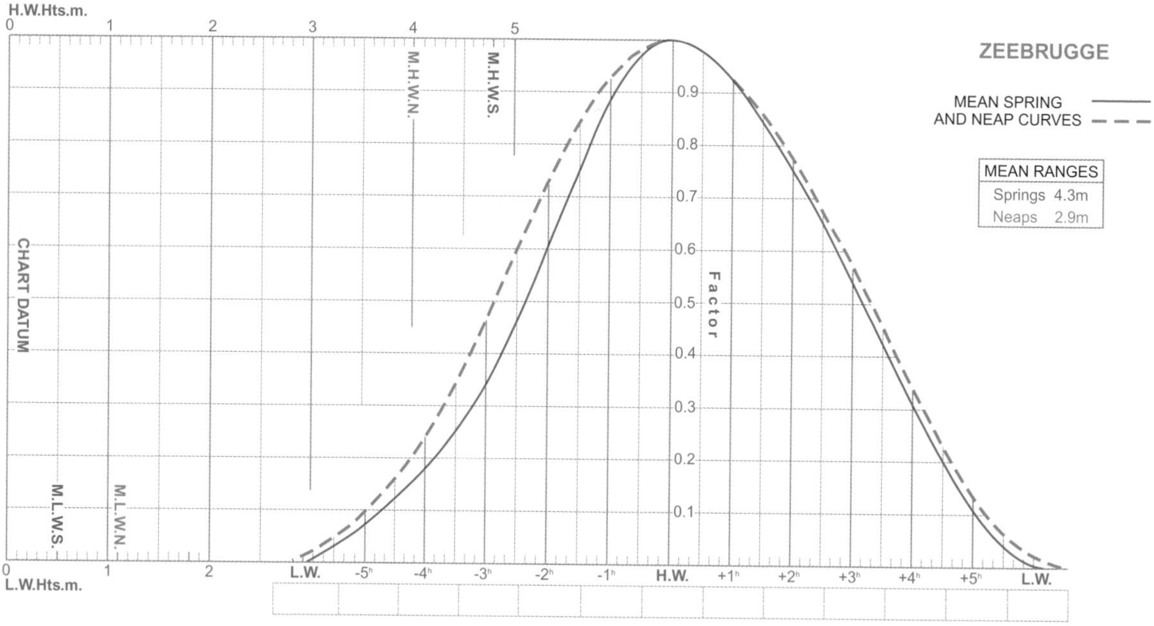

H.W.Hts.m.
ZEEBRUGGE
MEAN SPRING AND NEAP CURVES
MEAN RANGES
Springs 4.3m
Neaps 2.9m
M.H.W.N.
M.H.W.S.
M.L.W.S.
M.L.W.N.
CHART DATUM
Factor
0.9
0.8
0.7
0.6
0.5
0.4
0.3
0.2
0.1
L.W.Hts.m.
L.W. -5h -4h -3h -2h -1h H.W. +1h +2h +3h +4h +5h L.W.

DISTANCE TABLE

Approximate distances in nautical miles are by the most direct route while avoiding dangers and allowing for TSS. Places in *italics* are in adjoining areas; places in **bold** are in 9.0.7, Distances across the North Sea.

1	*Borkum*	**1**																											
2	**Delfzijl**	22	**2**																										
3	Lauwersoog	30	46	**3**																									
4	Terschelling	65	85	43	**4**																								
5	Vlieland	72	92	52	7	**5**																							
6	Harlingen	80	102	67	19	18	**6**																						
7	Kornwerderzand	86	106	70	24	19	7	**7**																					
8	Den Oever	90	110	88	34	33	21	13	**8**																				
9	Oudeschild	94	114	79	38	34	25	18	10	**9**																			
10	**Den Helder**	95	115	81	39	33	30	24	11	5	**10**																		
11	Medemblik	104	124	99	39	40	27	20	12	22	24	**11**																	
12	Enkhuizen	112	132	106	47	41	28	23	18	28	29	10	**12**																
13	Amsterdam	139	159	123	83	84	81	47	62	52	51	38	26	**13**															
14	**IJmuiden**	126	146	109	70	71	68	57	49	38	38	58	37	13	**14**														
15	**Scheveningen**	151	171	132	95	96	93	79	74	60	63	80	62	38	25	**15**													
16	Rotterdam	185	205	159	129	130	127	113	108	94	97	114	96	72	59	34	**16**												
17	Hook of Holland	165	185	146	109	110	107	93	88	74	77	94	76	52	39	14	20	**17**											
18	Stellendam	181	201	157	125	126	123	109	104	90	93	110	92	68	55	30	36	16	**18**										
19	**Roompotsluis**	193	204	177	128	124	129	118	109	110	97	130	112	90	63	50	49	29	27	**19**									
20	**Vlissingen**	211	222	190	146	143	147	137	128	121	115	141	123	108	82	61	67	47	45	21	**20**								
21	Terneuzen	220	240	202	164	165	162	152	143	133	132	153	135	111	98	73	79	59	57	36	12	**21**							
22	Antwerpen	249	269	221	193	194	191	181	172	162	161	182	164	140	127	102	108	88	86	65	41	31	**22**						
23	Breskens	202	230	192	154	155	152	142	133	123	122	143	125	101	88	63	69	49	47	21	3	12	45	**23**					
24	**Zeebrugge**	219	239	194	163	164	161	147	142	128	131	148	130	106	93	68	74	54	50	25	16	28	57	13	**24**				
25	Blankenberge	224	244	196	168	169	166	152	147	133	136	153	135	111	98	73	79	59	55	33	21	33	62	18	5	**25**			
26	**Oostende**	233	239	205	163	164	161	160	142	141	131	161	143	110	106	81	87	67	72	36	27	41	70	26	13	9	**26**		
27	**Nieuwpoort**	242	262	215	186	187	184	170	165	151	154	171	153	129	116	91	97	77	83	46	39	51	80	36	23	18	9	**27**	
28	***Dunkerque***	257	277	228	201	202	199	185	180	166	169	186	168	144	131	106	112	92	90	57	50	67	96	52	40	35	26	15	**28**

STANDARD TIME UT –01
Subtract 1 hour for UT
For Belgian Summer Time add ONE hour in **non-shaded areas**

ZEEBRUGGE LAT 51°21′N LONG 3°12′E

TIMES AND HEIGHTS OF HIGH AND LOW WATERS

Dates in red are SPRINGS
Dates in blue are NEAPS

YEAR **2018**

Belgium

JANUARY

Date	Day	Time	m	Time	m	Time	m	Time	m
1	M	0023	4.7	0646	0.7	1244	4.8	1908	0.6
2	TU	0111	4.8	0734	0.6	1332	4.9	○ 1955	0.6
3	W	0157	4.8	0820	0.5	1418	5.0	2041	0.6
4	TH	0241	4.8	0906	0.4	1504	5.0	2126	0.7
5	F	0327	4.8	0953	0.4	1552	4.9	2213	0.7
6	SA	0414	4.7	1042	0.4	1642	4.9	2301	0.8
7	SU	0503	4.6	1132	0.4	1735	4.7	2352	1.0
8	M	0557	4.5	1227	0.6	1833	4.5	◑	
9	TU	0048	1.1	0657	4.3	1326	0.7	1937	4.3
10	W	0151	1.2	0803	4.2	1431	0.9	2045	4.2
11	TH	0302	1.3	0913	4.1	1539	1.0	2156	4.1
12	F	0416	1.3	1025	4.1	1647	1.0	2304	4.2
13	SA	0526	1.2	1129	4.2	1749	1.0	2359	4.3
14	SU	0621	1.0	1220	4.3	1838	1.0		
15	M	0045	4.4	0704	0.9	1302	4.4	1916	1.0
16	TU	0123	4.4	0738	0.9	1338	4.4	1945	1.0
17	W	0156	4.4	0806	0.8	1409	4.5	● 2010	1.0
18	TH	0225	4.4	0833	0.7	1439	4.5	2038	0.9
19	F	0252	4.5	0903	0.7	1508	4.6	2111	0.9
20	SA	0321	4.5	0937	0.6	1540	4.6	2146	0.8
21	SU	0354	4.6	1014	0.6	1616	4.7	2225	0.9
22	M	0431	4.6	1054	0.6	1656	4.7	2306	0.9
23	TU	0513	4.6	1137	0.6	1743	4.6	2353	1.0
24	W	0602	4.5	1229	0.7	1837	4.5	◐	
25	TH	0048	1.1	0701	4.3	1331	0.8	1942	4.3
26	F	0159	1.2	0810	4.2	1445	0.9	2054	4.2
27	SA	0319	1.2	0923	4.2	1556	0.9	2205	4.2
28	SU	0432	1.1	1034	4.2	1702	0.9	2312	4.3
29	M	0537	1.0	1138	4.4	1802	0.8		
30	TU	0010	4.4	0633	0.8	1232	4.6	1854	0.8
31	W	0059	4.5	0722	0.6	1320	4.8	○ 1941	0.7

FEBRUARY

Date	Day	Time	m	Time	m	Time	m	Time	m
1	TH	0143	4.7	0807	0.4	1405	4.9	2025	0.7
2	F	0226	4.8	0852	0.3	1449	5.0	2109	0.6
3	SA	0309	4.9	0937	0.2	1534	5.0	2153	0.6
4	SU	0354	4.9	1022	0.2	1621	4.9	2238	0.7
5	M	0440	4.8	1109	0.3	1709	4.8	2323	0.8
6	TU	0528	4.7	1157	0.4	1800	4.6		
7	W	0011	0.9	0619	4.4	1249	0.7	◑ 1854	4.3
8	TH	0106	1.2	0717	4.2	1351	1.0	1957	4.0
9	F	0219	1.3	0826	3.9	1501	1.2	2110	3.8
10	SA	0339	1.4	0945	3.8	1612	1.3	2228	3.8
11	SU	0453	1.3	1059	3.9	1719	1.2	2333	3.9
12	M	0556	1.2	1157	4.1	1815	1.2		
13	TU	0022	4.1	0644	1.0	1241	4.2	1856	1.1
14	W	0101	4.3	0719	0.9	1316	4.4	1922	1.0
15	TH	0132	4.4	0745	0.8	1346	4.5	● 1947	0.9
16	F	0200	4.5	0811	0.6	1415	4.6	2016	0.8
17	SA	0228	4.6	0843	0.5	1445	4.7	2051	0.7
18	SU	0259	4.7	0918	0.4	1519	4.8	2129	0.6
19	M	0333	4.8	0956	0.4	1555	4.9	2208	0.6
20	TU	0410	4.8	1036	0.4	1635	4.8	2248	0.7
21	W	0451	4.7	1117	0.5	1718	4.7	2331	0.8
22	TH	0536	4.6	1202	0.6	1807	4.5		
23	F	0019	1.0	0629	4.5	1257	0.8	◐ 1905	4.3
24	SA	0121	1.1	0734	4.2	1410	1.0	2018	4.0
25	SU	0248	1.3	0854	4.0	1531	1.1	2141	3.9
26	M	0411	1.2	1017	4.1	1644	1.1	2257	4.0
27	TU	0521	1.0	1127	4.3	1748	1.0	2358	4.2
28	W	0619	0.8	1222	4.5	1841	0.8		

MARCH

Date	Day	Time	m	Time	m	Time	m	Time	m
1	TH	0045	4.4	0708	0.5	1307	4.7	1926	0.7
2	F	0127	4.6	0751	0.3	1349	4.9	○ 2008	0.6
3	SA	0208	4.8	0834	0.2	1431	5.0	2049	0.5
4	SU	0249	4.9	0916	0.1	1514	5.0	2131	0.5
5	M	0331	5.0	0959	0.1	1557	5.0	2213	0.5
6	TU	0415	4.9	1042	0.2	1641	4.8	2254	0.6
7	W	0458	4.7	1124	0.4	1725	4.5	2334	0.8
8	TH	0542	4.5	1207	0.8	1811	4.2		
9	F	0016	1.1	0630	4.2	1259	1.1	◑ 1903	3.9
10	SA	0118	1.3	0730	3.8	1419	1.4	2016	3.6
11	SU	0259	1.5	0856	3.6	1533	1.5	2142	3.5
12	M	0411	1.4	1019	3.6	1639	1.4	2255	3.7
13	TU	0516	1.3	1123	3.8	1738	1.3	2348	3.9
14	W	0608	1.1	1209	4.1	1821	1.2		
15	TH	0029	4.1	0646	0.9	1245	4.3	1851	1.0
16	F	0101	4.3	0714	0.7	1316	4.5	1919	0.8
17	SA	0130	4.5	0744	0.5	1347	4.7	● 1952	0.7
18	SU	0200	4.7	0818	0.4	1419	4.9	2030	0.5
19	M	0234	4.8	0856	0.3	1455	5.0	2109	0.5
20	TU	0310	4.9	0935	0.3	1533	5.0	2149	0.5
21	W	0348	4.9	1015	0.3	1612	4.9	2229	0.6
22	TH	0429	4.8	1056	0.4	1655	4.7	2311	0.7
23	F	0514	4.7	1140	0.6	1741	4.5	2357	0.9
24	SA	0605	4.5	1232	0.9	1837	4.2	◐	
25	SU	0057	1.1	0709	4.2	1345	1.1	1952	3.9
26	M	0227	1.2	0835	4.0	1511	1.2	2123	3.8
27	TU	0350	1.1	1003	4.0	1625	1.2	2241	3.9
28	W	0501	0.9	1114	4.3	1731	1.0	2341	4.2
29	TH	0601	0.7	1208	4.5	1824	0.9		
30	F	0028	4.4	0650	0.5	1251	4.7	1908	0.7
31	SA	0108	4.6	0732	0.3	1331	4.9	○ 1948	0.6

APRIL

Date	Day	Time	m	Time	m	Time	m	Time	m
1	SU	0148	4.8	0813	0.2	1411	5.0	2028	0.5
2	M	0228	4.9	0854	0.1	1452	5.0	2108	0.4
3	TU	0309	4.9	0934	0.2	1533	4.9	2147	0.5
4	W	0349	4.9	1014	0.3	1613	4.7	2225	0.6
5	TH	0429	4.7	1051	0.6	1652	4.4	2300	0.8
6	F	0508	4.4	1125	0.9	1730	4.2	2334	1.0
7	SA	0547	4.1	1200	1.2	1809	3.9		
8	SU	0014	1.2	0633	3.8	1250	1.5	◑ 1905	3.6
9	M	0210	1.5	0755	3.6	1448	1.6	2045	3.4
10	TU	0327	1.4	0927	3.5	1553	1.5	2204	3.5
11	W	0426	1.3	1036	3.8	1648	1.4	2302	3.8
12	TH	0519	1.1	1127	4.1	1735	1.2	2347	4.0
13	F	0601	0.8	1207	4.4	1813	1.0		
14	SA	0023	4.3	0637	0.6	1242	4.6	1849	0.7
15	SU	0056	4.6	0713	0.4	1317	4.8	1927	0.6
16	M	0131	4.8	0751	0.3	1353	5.0	● 2007	0.4
17	TU	0208	4.9	0832	0.2	1431	5.0	2048	0.4
18	W	0247	5.0	0913	0.2	1510	4.9	2130	0.4
19	TH	0327	4.9	0955	0.4	1551	4.8	2212	0.5
20	F	0410	4.8	1037	0.5	1635	4.6	2255	0.7
21	SA	0456	4.7	1122	0.7	1722	4.3	2343	0.8
22	SU	0548	4.4	1216	1.0	1819	4.1	◐	
23	M	0046	1.0	0656	4.2	1329	1.2	1937	3.8
24	TU	0210	1.0	0822	4.0	1450	1.2	2104	3.8
25	W	0327	1.0	0946	4.1	1602	1.2	2219	3.9
26	TH	0436	0.8	1055	4.3	1708	1.0	2319	4.2
27	F	0537	0.6	1148	4.6	1804	0.9		
28	SA	0007	4.4	0628	0.4	1233	4.7	1848	0.7
29	SU	0049	4.6	0711	0.3	1313	4.8	1928	0.6
30	M	0128	4.8	0751	0.3	1352	4.8	○ 2007	0.5

Chart Datum is 0·23 metres below TAW Datum. HAT is 5·6 metres above Chart Datum.

STANDARD TIME UT –01
Subtract 1 hour for UT
For Belgian Summer Time add ONE hour in **non-shaded areas**

ZEEBRUGGE LAT 51°21′N LONG 3°12′E

TIMES AND HEIGHTS OF HIGH AND LOW WATERS

Dates in red are SPRINGS
Dates in blue are NEAPS

YEAR **2018**

MAY

Date	Day	Time	m	Time	m	Time	m	Time	m
1	TU	0208	4.8	0831	0.3	1431	4.8	2045	0.5
2	W	0248	4.8	0909	0.4	1510	4.7	2123	0.5
3	TH	0326	4.7	0945	0.6	1548	4.5	2158	0.6
4	F	0404	4.5	1018	0.8	1623	4.3	2230	0.8
5	SA	0438	4.3	1048	1.0	1655	4.1	2302	0.9
6	SU	0513	4.1	1118	1.2	1728	3.9	2338	1.1
7	M	0553	3.9	1158	1.4	1812	3.7		
8	TU	0032	1.3	0653	3.7	1312	1.6	◑ 1931	3.5
9	W	0236	1.3	0828	3.7	1501	1.5	2104	3.6
10	TH	0336	1.2	0941	3.8	1559	1.4	2208	3.8
11	F	0428	1.0	1038	4.1	1649	1.1	2259	4.0
12	SA	0516	0.8	1125	4.4	1735	0.9	2343	4.3
13	SU	0600	0.6	1207	4.7	1819	0.7		
14	M	0023	4.6	0642	0.4	1247	4.8	1901	0.6
15	TU	0103	4.8	0725	0.3	1327	4.9	● 1945	0.5
16	W	0144	4.9	0808	0.3	1408	4.9	2028	0.4
17	TH	0226	4.9	0852	0.3	1450	4.8	2112	0.4
18	F	0309	4.9	0935	0.5	1534	4.7	2156	0.5
19	SA	0355	4.8	1020	0.6	1619	4.5	2243	0.6
20	SU	0443	4.6	1108	0.8	1709	4.3	2335	0.7
21	M	0539	4.5	1204	1.0	1808	4.1		
22	TU	0038	0.8	0646	4.3	1312	1.1	◐ 1920	4.0
23	W	0151	0.8	0804	4.2	1424	1.2	2038	3.9
24	TH	0300	0.8	0920	4.2	1533	1.1	2149	4.1
25	F	0406	0.7	1028	4.4	1640	1.0	2252	4.2
26	SA	0510	0.6	1125	4.5	1740	0.9	2344	4.4
27	SU	0605	0.5	1213	4.6	1829	0.8		
28	M	0030	4.6	0650	0.5	1256	4.7	1911	0.7
29	TU	0112	4.6	0731	0.5	1335	4.7	○ 1949	0.6
30	W	0151	4.7	0809	0.6	1414	4.6	2026	0.6
31	TH	0230	4.6	0844	0.7	1451	4.5	2101	0.6

JUNE

Date	Day	Time	m	Time	m	Time	m	Time	m
1	F	0307	4.5	0917	0.8	1526	4.4	2134	0.7
2	SA	0341	4.4	0947	0.9	1558	4.3	2206	0.8
3	SU	0414	4.3	1017	1.0	1628	4.2	2239	0.8
4	M	0447	4.2	1050	1.1	1701	4.1	2315	0.9
5	TU	0526	4.1	1129	1.2	1742	4.0	2359	1.0
6	W ◑	0618	4.1	1222	1.3	1840	3.9		
7	TH	0121	1.1	0728	4.0	1351	1.4	1959	3.8
8	F	0242	1.0	0844	4.0	1507	1.3	2111	3.9
9	SA	0340	0.9	0947	4.2	1605	1.1	2211	4.1
10	SU	0434	0.8	1043	4.4	1659	0.9	2304	4.3
11	M	0525	0.6	1133	4.6	1749	0.8	2352	4.6
12	TU	0613	0.5	1220	4.7	1838	0.6		
13	W	0038	4.7	0701	0.4	1305	4.8	● 1925	0.5
14	TH	0124	4.8	0747	0.4	1349	4.8	2011	0.5
15	F	0209	4.9	0832	0.5	1433	4.7	2056	0.5
16	SA	0255	4.9	0918	0.6	1519	4.7	2143	0.5
17	SU	0342	4.8	1005	0.7	1606	4.6	2232	0.5
18	M	0432	4.7	1054	0.8	1656	4.4	2325	0.5
19	TU	0527	4.6	1148	0.9	1752	4.3		
20	W	0022	0.6	0629	4.5	1248	1.0	◐ 1856	4.2
21	TH	0125	0.6	0738	4.4	1352	1.1	2005	4.2
22	F	0229	0.7	0847	4.3	1459	1.1	2114	4.2
23	SA	0334	0.7	0955	4.3	1608	1.1	2221	4.2
24	SU	0440	0.7	1059	4.4	1715	1.0	2321	4.3
25	M	0541	0.7	1154	4.5	1811	0.9		
26	TU	0013	4.4	0632	0.7	1240	4.5	1856	0.8
27	W	0058	4.5	0714	0.8	1321	4.5	1935	0.8
28	TH	0137	4.5	0750	0.8	1358	4.5	○ 2010	0.7
29	F	0214	4.5	0822	0.9	1433	4.4	2042	0.7
30	SA	0248	4.5	0851	0.9	1505	4.4	2113	0.7

JULY

Date	Day	Time	m	Time	m	Time	m	Time	m
1	SU	0321	4.4	0921	1.0	1535	4.3	2145	0.7
2	M	0352	4.4	0953	1.0	1605	4.3	2219	0.7
3	TU	0425	4.4	1028	1.0	1638	4.3	2257	0.7
4	W	0503	4.4	1107	1.0	1718	4.3	2340	0.8
5	TH	0549	4.4	1154	1.1	1807	4.3		
6	F	0033	0.8	0644	4.3	1253	1.2	◑ 1908	4.2
7	SA	0141	0.9	0751	4.3	1408	1.2	2018	4.2
8	SU	0252	0.9	0859	4.3	1521	1.1	2125	4.2
9	M	0355	0.8	1003	4.4	1625	1.0	2228	4.3
10	TU	0453	0.7	1103	4.4	1724	0.9	2326	4.5
11	W	0549	0.7	1157	4.6	1818	0.8		
12	TH	0019	4.6	0640	0.6	1247	4.6	1908	0.6
13	F	0107	4.8	0728	0.6	1333	4.7	● 1955	0.5
14	SA	0154	4.9	0815	0.6	1418	4.7	2042	0.4
15	SU	0241	4.9	0902	0.6	1503	4.8	2129	0.3
16	M	0328	5.0	0948	0.7	1549	4.7	2218	0.3
17	TU	0417	4.9	1036	0.7	1638	4.7	2307	0.3
18	W	0508	4.8	1126	0.8	1730	4.6	2359	0.4
19	TH ◐	0604	4.7	1218	0.9	1826	4.5		
20	F	0055	0.5	0704	4.5	1316	1.0	1928	4.3
21	SA	0156	0.7	0809	4.3	1422	1.2	2035	4.2
22	SU	0302	0.8	0918	4.2	1535	1.2	2147	4.1
23	M	0411	0.9	1030	4.2	1649	1.2	2258	4.2
24	TU	0517	1.0	1133	4.2	1752	1.0	2356	4.3
25	W	0613	1.0	1223	4.3	1842	0.9		
26	TH	0043	4.4	0657	1.0	1305	4.4	1921	0.8
27	F	0122	4.4	0732	1.0	1341	4.4	○ 1954	0.8
28	SA	0156	4.5	0759	1.0	1412	4.4	2023	0.7
29	SU	0227	4.5	0826	1.0	1442	4.5	2052	0.7
30	M	0258	4.6	0857	0.9	1511	4.5	2124	0.6
31	TU	0329	4.6	0931	0.8	1542	4.6	2159	0.6

AUGUST

Date	Day	Time	m	Time	m	Time	m	Time	m
1	W	0402	4.7	1008	0.8	1616	4.6	2237	0.6
2	TH	0439	4.7	1047	0.8	1654	4.6	2317	0.6
3	F	0521	4.7	1129	0.9	1738	4.6	2359	0.7
4	SA ◑	0609	4.6	1218	1.0	1830	4.5		
5	SU	0055	0.8	0706	4.4	1318	1.1	1932	4.3
6	M	0204	0.9	0814	4.3	1437	1.2	2044	4.2
7	TU	0320	0.9	0927	4.2	1555	1.2	2158	4.2
8	W	0428	0.9	1038	4.2	1702	1.0	2306	4.4
9	TH	0529	0.9	1140	4.4	1801	0.8		
10	F	0004	4.6	0624	0.8	1232	4.5	1853	0.7
11	SA	0054	4.8	0713	0.7	1318	4.7	● 1941	0.5
12	SU	0140	5.0	0759	0.7	1401	4.8	2026	0.3
13	M	0225	5.1	0844	0.6	1445	4.9	2112	0.2
14	TU	0310	5.1	0929	0.6	1529	5.0	2158	0.1
15	W	0356	5.1	1014	0.6	1615	5.0	2244	0.2
16	TH	0444	5.0	1100	0.7	1703	4.9	2332	0.3
17	F	0534	4.8	1147	0.8	1753	4.7		
18	SA	0022	0.5	0627	4.5	1237	1.0	◐ 1848	4.4
19	SU	0119	0.8	0726	4.2	1342	1.2	1953	4.2
20	M	0228	1.1	0837	4.0	1503	1.3	2111	4.0
21	TU	0340	1.2	0956	3.9	1619	1.3	2230	4.0
22	W	0449	1.2	1107	4.0	1726	1.2	2334	4.1
23	TH	0550	1.2	1201	4.2	1820	1.0		
24	F	0022	4.3	0636	1.1	1242	4.3	1901	0.9
25	SA	0100	4.5	0709	1.1	1317	4.4	1931	0.8
26	SU	0132	4.6	0734	1.0	1347	4.5	○ 1958	0.7
27	M	0202	4.7	0802	0.9	1415	4.6	2027	0.6
28	TU	0232	4.8	0834	0.8	1445	4.8	2101	0.5
29	W	0303	4.9	0910	0.7	1517	4.8	2137	0.4
30	TH	0338	4.9	0948	0.7	1551	4.9	2215	0.4
31	F	0414	4.9	1026	0.7	1629	4.9	2253	0.5

Chart Datum is 0·23 metres below TAW Datum. HAT is 5·6 metres above Chart Datum.

STANDARD TIME UT –01
Subtract 1 hour for UT
For Belgian Summer Time add ONE hour in **non-shaded areas**

ZEEBRUGGE LAT 51°21′N LONG 3°12′E

TIMES AND HEIGHTS OF HIGH AND LOW WATERS

Dates in red are SPRINGS
Dates in blue are NEAPS

YEAR **2018**

SEPTEMBER

Date	Day	Time	m	Time	m	Time	m	Time	m	Moon
1	SA	0454	4.9	1106	0.8	1711	4.8	2334	0.6	
2	SU	0539	4.7	1150	0.9	1759	4.7			
3	M	0023	0.8	0631	4.5	1243	1.1	1857	4.4	◑
4	TU	0126	1.0	0736	4.2	1400	1.2	2012	4.2	
5	W	0252	1.1	0859	4.0	1532	1.2	2137	4.2	
6	TH	0407	1.1	1020	4.1	1644	1.1	2252	4.3	
7	F	0512	1.0	1125	4.3	1746	0.8	2351	4.6	
8	SA	0609	0.9	1216	4.5	1838	0.6			
9	SU	0040	4.9	0657	0.8	1300	4.7	1924	0.4	●
10	M	0124	5.1	0741	0.7	1342	4.9	2008	0.2	
11	TU	0206	5.2	0824	0.6	1424	5.1	2051	0.1	
12	W	0249	5.2	0907	0.5	1507	5.2	2135	0.1	
13	TH	0333	5.2	0950	0.5	1551	5.1	2219	0.2	
14	F	0418	5.0	1033	0.6	1636	5.0	2302	0.4	
15	SA	0503	4.8	1115	0.8	1721	4.7	2346	0.7	
16	SU	0550	4.5	1158	1.0	1809	4.4			
17	M	0036	1.0	0641	4.1	1253	1.3	1908	4.1	◐
18	TU	0149	1.3	0749	3.8	1429	1.5	2029	3.8	
19	W	0308	1.5	0915	3.7	1545	1.4	2155	3.8	
20	TH	0415	1.5	1031	3.8	1650	1.3	2302	4.0	
21	F	0516	1.4	1129	4.0	1747	1.1	2352	4.3	
22	SA	0605	1.2	1212	4.3	1829	0.9			
23	SU	0030	4.5	0638	1.1	1247	4.5	1900	0.8	
24	M	0103	4.7	0706	0.9	1317	4.6	1929	0.6	
25	TU	0133	4.9	0736	0.8	1346	4.8	2000	0.5	○
26	W	0204	5.0	0811	0.6	1417	4.9	2036	0.4	
27	TH	0237	5.1	0848	0.5	1451	5.0	2113	0.3	
28	F	0313	5.1	0927	0.6	1528	5.0	2152	0.4	
29	SA	0350	5.0	1006	0.6	1606	5.0	2231	0.5	
30	SU	0430	4.9	1045	0.7	1648	4.9	2311	0.7	

OCTOBER

Date	Day	Time	m	Time	m	Time	m	Time	m	Moon
1	M	0513	4.7	1128	0.9	1735	4.7	2358	0.9	
2	TU	0603	4.4	1220	1.1	1832	4.4			◑
3	W	0102	1.2	0709	4.1	1340	1.3	1951	4.2	
4	TH	0231	1.3	0839	3.9	1513	1.2	2122	4.2	
5	F	0349	1.3	1002	4.0	1625	1.0	2238	4.4	
6	SA	0455	1.1	1108	4.3	1727	0.8	2337	4.7	
7	SU	0552	1.0	1158	4.6	1820	0.5			
8	M	0024	4.9	0640	0.8	1242	4.8	1905	0.4	
9	TU	0106	5.1	0723	0.7	1323	5.0	1948	0.2	●
10	W	0147	5.2	0804	0.6	1404	5.1	2030	0.2	
11	TH	0229	5.2	0846	0.5	1446	5.2	2112	0.2	
12	F	0311	5.1	0927	0.5	1528	5.1	2153	0.4	
13	SA	0353	4.9	1007	0.6	1610	4.9	2233	0.6	
14	SU	0434	4.7	1045	0.8	1652	4.7	2311	0.9	
15	M	0515	4.4	1123	1.0	1734	4.4	2349	1.2	
16	TU	0558	4.1	1205	1.3	1824	4.1			◐
17	W	0042	1.5	0655	3.8	1347	1.5	1940	3.8	
18	TH	0229	1.7	0825	3.6	1506	1.5	2108	3.7	
19	F	0335	1.6	0944	3.7	1608	1.3	2219	3.9	
20	SA	0433	1.5	1046	3.9	1702	1.2	2312	4.2	
21	SU	0522	1.3	1132	4.2	1747	0.9	2354	4.5	
22	M	0601	1.1	1210	4.4	1823	0.7			
23	TU	0029	4.7	0635	0.9	1243	4.7	1857	0.6	
24	W	0103	4.9	0710	0.7	1316	4.9	1933	0.4	○
25	TH	0137	5.1	0747	0.6	1351	5.0	2011	0.4	
26	F	0212	5.1	0827	0.5	1427	5.1	2050	0.4	
27	SA	0250	5.1	0907	0.5	1506	5.1	2130	0.5	
28	SU	0328	5.0	0947	0.6	1546	5.0	2211	0.6	
29	M	0409	4.8	1029	0.7	1630	4.8	2253	0.8	
30	TU	0454	4.6	1114	0.9	1718	4.6	2342	1.0	
31	W	0545	4.3	1209	1.0	1818	4.4			◑

NOVEMBER

Date	Day	Time	m	Time	m	Time	m	Time	m	Moon
1	TH	0047	1.3	0653	4.0	1329	1.1	1939	4.2	
2	F	0212	1.4	0821	3.9	1452	1.1	2106	4.2	
3	SA	0326	1.3	0940	4.0	1601	0.9	2219	4.4	
4	SU	0433	1.2	1045	4.3	1704	0.7	2318	4.7	
5	M	0533	1.0	1138	4.6	1759	0.5			
6	TU	0007	4.9	0623	0.8	1224	4.8	1846	0.4	
7	W	0049	5.0	0706	0.7	1305	4.9	1929	0.3	●
8	TH	0130	5.1	0747	0.6	1346	5.0	2010	0.4	
9	F	0211	5.0	0826	0.6	1427	5.0	2050	0.5	
10	SA	0251	4.9	0906	0.6	1508	4.9	2128	0.6	
11	SU	0331	4.8	0944	0.7	1548	4.8	2204	0.8	
12	M	0409	4.6	1019	0.8	1627	4.6	2237	1.1	
13	TU	0446	4.3	1054	1.0	1705	4.3	2310	1.3	
14	W	0522	4.1	1131	1.2	1747	4.1	2348	1.5	
15	TH	0606	3.9	1227	1.4	1846	3.9			◐
16	F	0100	1.7	0720	3.7	1419	1.4	2011	3.8	
17	SA	0246	1.7	0846	3.7	1520	1.3	2124	3.9	
18	SU	0344	1.5	0951	3.8	1614	1.2	2223	4.2	
19	M	0436	1.3	1044	4.1	1702	1.0	2311	4.4	
20	TU	0522	1.1	1129	4.4	1745	0.8	2353	4.7	
21	W	0604	0.9	1209	4.6	1826	0.6			
22	TH	0032	4.9	0645	0.7	1247	4.8	1906	0.5	
23	F	0111	5.0	0726	0.6	1326	5.0	1947	0.4	○
24	SA	0150	5.0	0808	0.5	1406	5.0	2029	0.5	
25	SU	0230	5.0	0850	0.5	1448	5.0	2111	0.6	
26	M	0311	4.8	0933	0.6	1531	4.9	2154	0.7	
27	TU	0354	4.7	1017	0.7	1617	4.8	2240	0.9	
28	W	0441	4.5	1106	0.8	1709	4.6	2331	1.1	
29	TH	0535	4.3	1204	0.9	1810	4.5			
30	F	0035	1.2	0641	4.1	1314	0.9	1925	4.3	◑

DECEMBER

Date	Day	Time	m	Time	m	Time	m	Time	m	Moon
1	SA	0147	1.3	0758	4.1	1426	0.9	2042	4.3	
2	SU	0258	1.3	0912	4.1	1533	0.8	2153	4.4	
3	M	0406	1.2	1019	4.3	1639	0.7	2256	4.6	
4	TU	0512	1.1	1117	4.5	1739	0.6	2350	4.7	
5	W	0607	0.9	1208	4.7	1829	0.6			
6	TH	0036	4.8	0652	0.8	1252	4.8	1913	0.6	
7	F	0118	4.8	0733	0.7	1334	4.8	1953	0.6	●
8	SA	0158	4.8	0812	0.7	1414	4.8	2031	0.7	
9	SU	0236	4.7	0849	0.7	1453	4.7	2106	0.8	
10	M	0313	4.6	0925	0.7	1530	4.6	2139	1.0	
11	TU	0349	4.5	0959	0.8	1606	4.5	2209	1.1	
12	W	0422	4.3	1032	0.9	1641	4.4	2241	1.2	
13	TH	0455	4.2	1108	1.0	1719	4.2	2317	1.3	
14	F	0533	4.1	1152	1.1	1805	4.1			
15	SA	0004	1.4	0623	4.0	1300	1.2	1907	4.0	◐
16	SU	0119	1.5	0734	3.9	1422	1.2	2021	4.0	
17	M	0246	1.5	0848	3.9	1523	1.1	2127	4.1	
18	TU	0348	1.4	0951	4.0	1617	1.0	2224	4.3	
19	W	0443	1.2	1046	4.3	1708	0.8	2316	4.5	
20	TH	0534	1.0	1135	4.5	1756	0.7			
21	F	0004	4.7	0621	0.8	1222	4.7	1842	0.6	
22	SA	0048	4.8	0707	0.7	1306	4.8	1927	0.6	○
23	SU	0131	4.8	0751	0.6	1350	4.9	2011	0.6	
24	M	0214	4.8	0836	0.5	1434	4.9	2056	0.7	
25	TU	0257	4.8	0921	0.5	1519	4.9	2141	0.7	
26	W	0342	4.7	1008	0.5	1607	4.9	2228	0.8	
27	TH	0430	4.6	1058	0.5	1659	4.8	2319	1.0	
28	F	0522	4.5	1153	0.6	1756	4.6			
29	SA	0015	1.1	0621	4.4	1252	0.6	1902	4.5	◑
30	SU	0117	1.2	0728	4.3	1356	0.7	2011	4.4	
31	M	0224	1.2	0838	4.2	1502	0.8	2122	4.3	

Chart Datum is 0·23 metres below TAW Datum. HAT is 5·6 metres above Chart Datum.

9.16.34 BLANKENBERGE

Belgium, West Flanders **51°18'·90N 03°06'·48E**

CHARTS AC 2449, 1872, 1874; DYC 1801.3; Imray C30

TIDES +0130 Dover; ML 2·5; Duration 0535

Standard Port ZEEBRUGGE (⟵)

Times				Height (metres)			
High Water		Low Water		MHWS	MHWN	MLWN	MLWS
0300	0900	0300	0900	4·8	3·9	1·1	0·5
1500	2100	1500	2100				
Differences BLANKENBERGE							
–0007		–0002		+0·1	+0·1	0·0	0·0

SHELTER Good, but entry is dangerous in NW'lies F6 and above.

NAVIGATION WPT 51°19'·60N 03°05'·31E, 134°/1M to pierheads. Caution: 4 unlit Y SPM buoys and one Fl (3) Y 20s lie E and W of hbr ent about 400m offshore. Beware strong tides (& fishing lines) across ent. Said to be dredged 2·5m during the season; but out of season it silts badly between piers and dries at LW. Do not try to ent/exit around low water, especially at springs and from Oct-end May, unless depths have been pre-checked. Call dredger Ch 10 for clearance to pass.

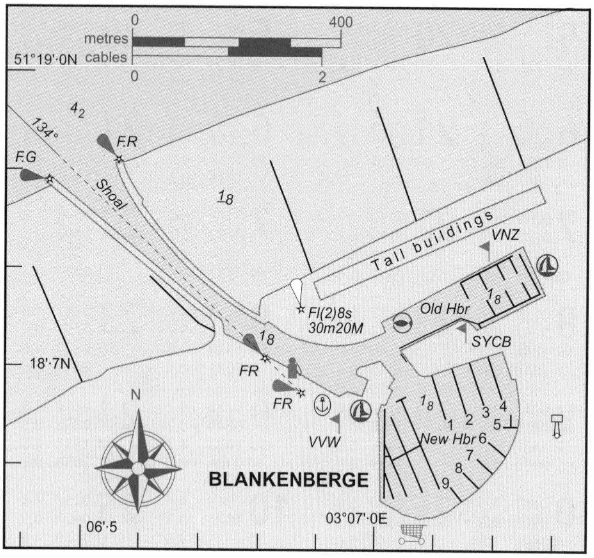

LIGHTS AND MARKS Conspic high-rise blocks E of lt ho, W twr B top. Ldg lts 134°, both FR, (Red X on front mast) show the best water. FG on W pier is more visible than FR (E pier). A water twr is conspic on E side of new Hbr. See also Lights, buoys and waypoints and chartlet.

COMMUNICATIONS (Code (0)50) *Blankenberge Rescue* Ch 08 or relay via Zeebrugge Traffic Centre VHF Ch 69; ⊜ 544223; Police 429842; Dr 333668; Ⓗ 413701; Brit Consul (02) 287 6248; VNZ, SYCB and VVW marinas VHF Ch 23; Dredger VHF Ch 10.

FACILITIES A Port of Entry, with Customs early Apr–late Sept.

Keep to port, past the FV hbr, for the old Yacht Hbr (1·8m); VNZ pontoons are on N side and SYCB to the E. Or turn 90° stbd into new Hbr/marina (2·5m); 12 pontoons, run by VNZ, SYCB & VVW.

VNZ (YC Vrije Noordzeezeilers) ☎425292, mob 0497 565565. www.vnzblankenberge.be vnz@skynet.be 120 inc Ⓥ, €2·50 inc wi-fi, multihulls €3·80.

SYCB (Scarphout Royal YC) ☎411420, mob 0476971692 www.scarphout.be scarphout@skynet.be 250 inc Ⓥ, €2·40 inc wi-fi coin meters, multihulls +50%. (10·5t).

VVW Marina ☎417536, mob 0495527536. www.vvwblankenberge.be info@vvweblankenberge.be 350 inc Ⓥ, €1·90 inc wi-fi, €2·00 p/d, multihulls +50%, (20t).

Town Ⓑ Ⓒ ⇄ ✈Oostende.

9.16.35 OOSTENDE

Belgium, West Flanders **51°14'·35N 02°55'·09E**

CHARTS AC 2449, 1872, 1874, 1873; SHOM 7214; Navi 1010; DYC 1801.2; Imray C30; BE D11

TIDES +0115 Dover; ML 2·79; Duration 0530

Standard Port ZEEBRUGGE (⟵)

Times				Height (metres)			
High Water		Low Water		MHWS	MHWN	MLWN	MLWS
0300	0900	0300	0900	4·8	3·9	1·1	0·5
1500	2100	1500	2100				
Differences *OOSTENDE*							
–0019	*–0019*	*–0008*	*–0008*	*+0·4*	*+0·2*	*+0·2*	*+0·1*

SHELTER Very good in Mercator Marina (5·0m) and Royal North Sea YC (2.2m). RYCO (2·7m) may be exposed in strong W/NW'lies.

NAVIGATION WPT 51° 15'·2N 02° 54'·23E, 143°/1M to ent. Avoid the offshore banks esp in bad weather: From the NE stay to seaward of Wenduinebank, except in calm weather. From the NW keep S of W Hinder TSS and approach from MBN buoy. From the SW appr via West Diep and Kleine Rede, inside Stroombank.

LIGHTS AND MARKS Europa Centrum bldg (105m; twice as high as other bldgs) is conspic 4ca SSW of ent. W lt ho, 5ca ESE of the ent, is conspic with 2 sinusoidal blue bands. 143° ldg marks are lattice masts with R/W bands and X topmarks. See chartlet and Lights, buoys and waypoints for lt details.

IPTS from E pier. At blind exit from Montgomerydok, green and red arrows regulate exit.

COMMUNICATIONS (Code 059) VHF Ch 27 at 0820 & 1720 UT (English and Dutch); Police 701111; ⊜ 242070; Brit Consul (02) 287 6248; Ⓗ 552000; HM 321687, Ch 09 (H24); Mercator lock 705762, VHF Ch 14; Marina VHF Ch 14 (lock hrs); Demey lock (VHF Ch 84) gives access to Oostende-Brugge canal.

FACILITIES from seaward: **Royal North Sea YC** (RNSYC) ☎430694 HM 474688278. www.rnsyc.be simon@rnsyc.be No VHF. 150+50Ⓥ €2·70/m inc (M/Cruisers €3.25/m). wi-fi, grid.

Mercator lock Must pre-call Ch 14 for lock-in time and berth. Waiting pontoon N of lock. No freeflow. R/G tfc lts. Hrs (times in brackets are Fri-Sun & public hols): May/Jun 0800-2000 (2100); Jul/Aug 0700-2200, 7/7; Sep 0800-1800 (2000). Oct–Apr, see web.

Mercator Marina ☎+32597705762.www.mercatormarina.be info@mercatormarina.be 300+50Ⓥ €2·20, (vessels >13.75m +€1·10/m p/d surcharge), €1·20 €1·00 €1·00/1kw; pay cash/card before entering lock outbound.

Royal YC Oostende (RYCO) ☎32477 676391(Dockmaster). ryco@telenet.be www.ryco.be No VHF. 160 + 35Ⓥ €2·60 inc ; €3·50/day. (10t) grid (½t).

Town All needs, only, ⇄ ✈.

CROSSING THE NORTH SEA FROM BELGIUM

(AC 1406, 323) There are so many permutations that it is better to try to apply just four broad principles:

- Avoid the N Hinder-Maas and W Hinder-Sandettie complexes.
- Cross TSS at their narrowest parts, ie between NHR-SE and Fairy W; and SW of Sandettie.
- Plan to cross the many offshore ridges at their extremities, zigzagging as necessary to achieve this.
- If bound for Dover or down-Channel use the coastal passage W to Dyck, then via MPC to SW Goodwin buoy. Or route via Sandettie to NE Goodwin buoy and into the southern Thames Estuary.

From the Scheur chan off Zeebrugge a fairly direct course via Track Ferry and S Galloper leads into the N Thames Estuary or towards the Suffolk ports. Avoid shoals, particularly in rough weather when the sea-state and under-keel clearance may be crucial problems. For N Sea distances see Chapter 9, Introduction.

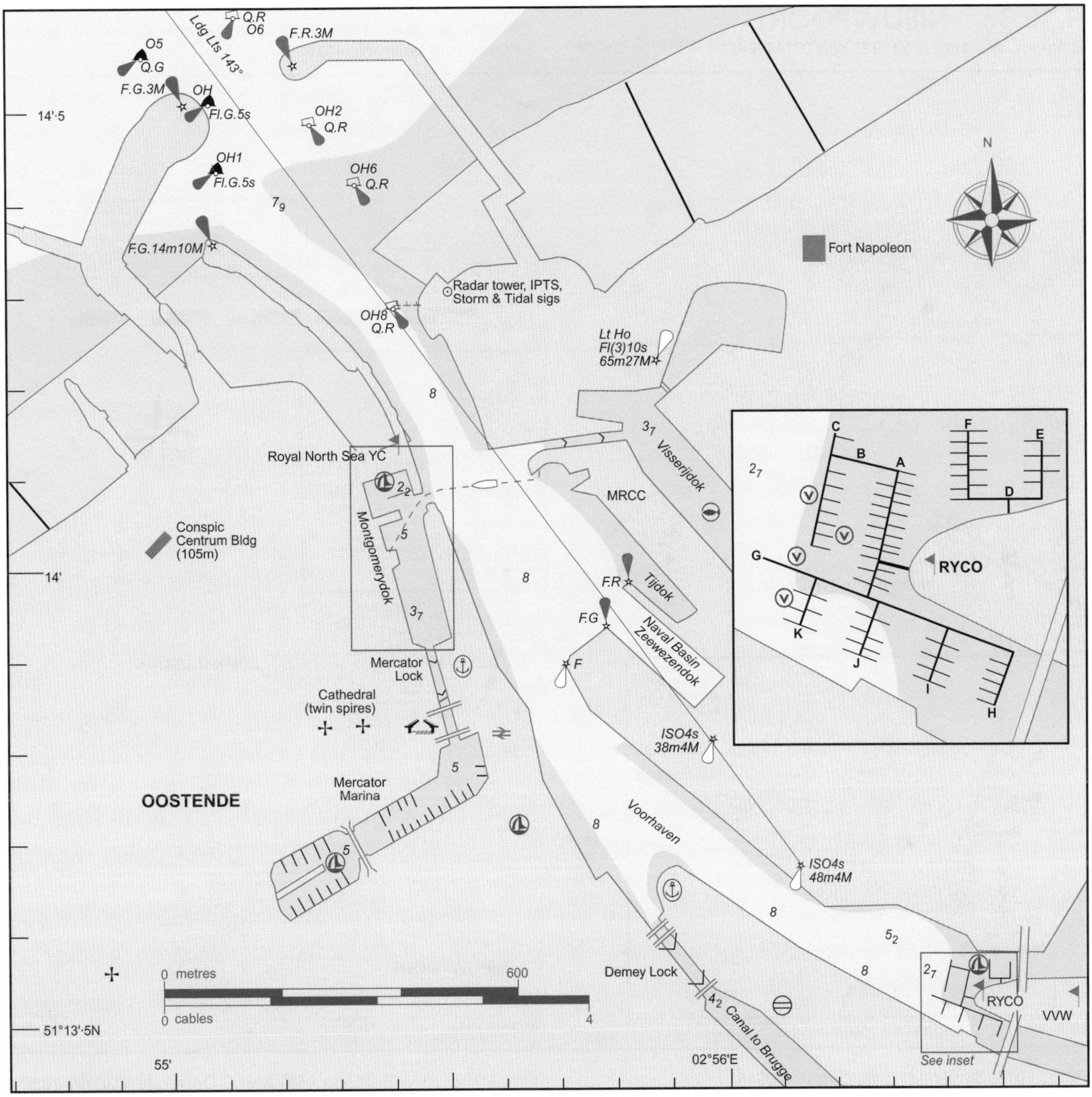
Q.R
O6
O5
Q.G
F.R.3M
Ldg Lts 143°
F.G.3M
OH
Fl.G.5s
OH2
Q.R
OH1
Fl.G.5s
OH6
Q.R
14'·5
N
F.G.14m10M
Fort Napoleon
Radar tower, IPTS, Storm & Tidal sigs
OH8
Q.R
Lt Ho
Fl(3)10s
65m27M
Vissersdok
Royal North Sea YC
MRCC
Conspic Centrum Bldg (105m)
Montgomerydok
14'
F.R
Tijdok
F.G
Naval Basin Zeewezendok
F
Mercator Lock
Cathedral (twin spires)
ISO4s
38m4M
Mercator Marina
OOSTENDE
Voorhaven
ISO4s
48m4M
0 metres
600
0 cables
4
Demey Lock
Canal to Brugge
RYCO
VVW
See inset
51°13'·5N
55'
02°56'E
C
B
A
F
E
D
G
K
J
I
H

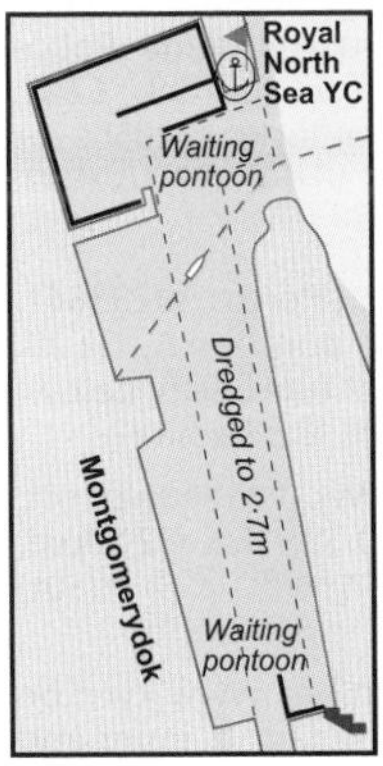
Royal North Sea YC
Waiting pontoon
Dredged to 2·7m
Montgomerydok
Waiting pontoon

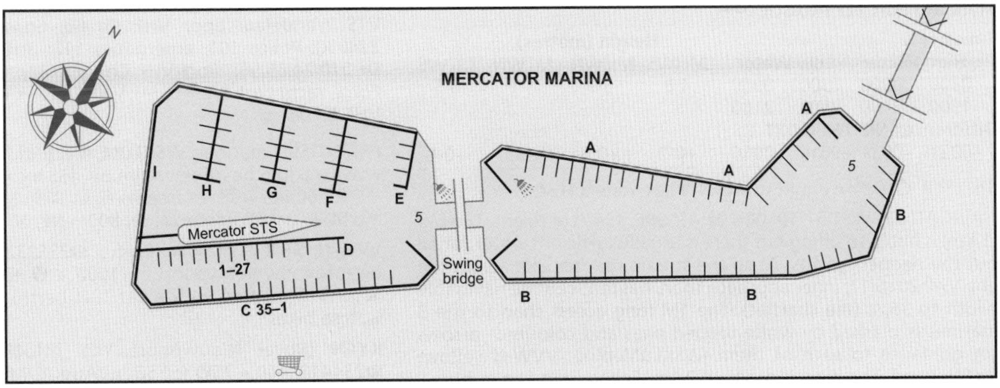
N
MERCATOR MARINA
A
A
A
I
H
G
F
E
5
Mercator STS
D
1–27
C 35–1
Swing bridge
B
B
B
5

9.16.36 NIEUWPOORT

Belgium, W Flanders **51°09'·38N 02°43'·04E** ❀❀❀◊◊◊✿✿✿

CHARTS AC 2449, 1872, 1873; Belgian 101, D11; DYC 1801.2; SHOM 7214; Navicarte 1010; Imray C30

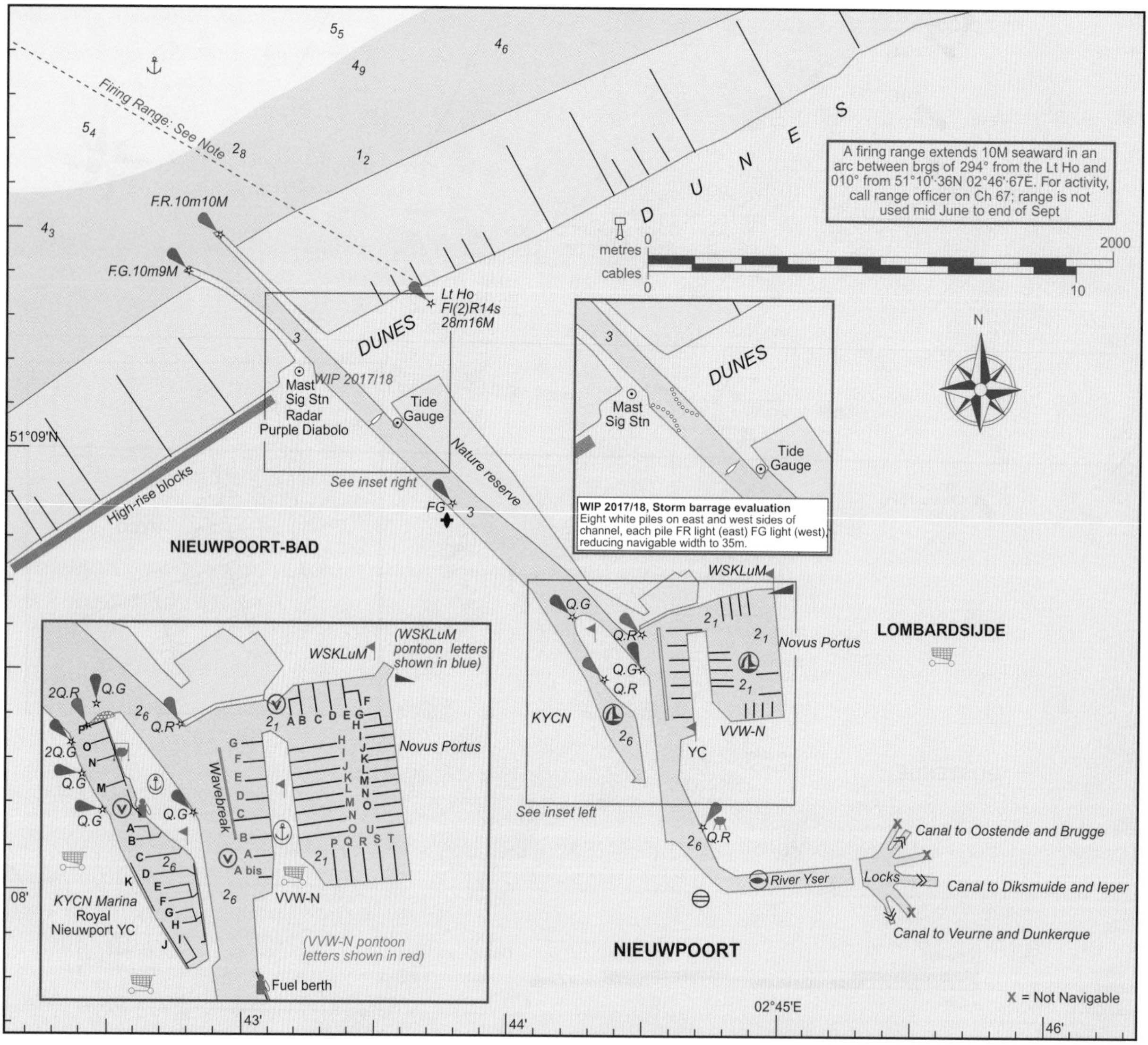

TIDES +0105 Dover; ML 2·96; Duration 0515

Standard Port ZEEBRUGGE (⟵)

Times				Height (metres)			
High Water		Low Water		MHWS	MHWN	MLWN	MLWS
0300	0900	0300	0900	4·8	3·9	1·1	0·5
1500	2100	1500	2100				
Differences NIEUWPOORT							
–0031	–0031	–0010	–0010	+0·7	+0·6	+0·3	+0·1

SHELTER Good except in strong NW'lies. Access H24.

NAVIGATION WPT 51°10'·08N 02°41'·90E, 134°/1M to ent. The bar (1·5m) is liable to silting but there is usually sufficient water for all but the deepest yachts. At sp the stream reaches 2kn across the ent. WIP 2016/17, inner approach chan, has reduced the navigable width to 35m; (see chartlet). The 1M long access chan to the 3 marinas is marked by white-topped piles and coloured arrows for guidance to each of them (WSKLuM–blue; VVW-N–yellow; KYCN–grey). The chan is dredged 3·1m. Speed limit 5kn in hbr.

LIGHTS AND MARKS The high-rise blocks W of the entrance are in stark contrast to the sand dunes and flatlands to the E. The lt ho is a conspic 28m R twr, W bands; see chartlet and Lights, buoys & waypoints. The central, pyramidal white HM bldg at VVW-N is conspic.

COMMUNICATIONS (Code 058) MRCC Oostende VHF Ch 16,67; (059) 701000, emergency direct line, SAR support ship 243936; VTS Wandelaar appr VHF Ch 60; Coast Guard/Marine Police 224030; Police 101, emergency 112; Brit Consul (02) 287 6248; Dr 070/24.65.55; Port VHF Ch 60 (H24); Canal locks 233050; *Air Force Yacht Club* (WSKLuM): VHF Ch 72. KYCN: VHF Ch 23. VVW-N: VHF Ch 08.

FACILITIES 3 marinas: **WSKLuM**, N & E of Novus Portus. ☎233641, www.wsklum.be info@wsklm.be 453 inc Ⓥ on pontoon A, €2·20. ⏻ €2·60p/d, free wi-fi, (at fuel berth, below) (25t) . At Lombardsijde, 800m NE, bike hire.

VVW-N, S & W of Novus Portus. ☎235232, www.vvwnieuwpoort.be info@vvwnieuwpoort.be 1000 + Ⓥ €1·90. ⏻16A €2·50p/d, **free wi-fi** (at fuel berth) Ⓔ (50t) free bikes.

KYCN (Royal Nieuwpoort YC). info@kycn.be www.kycn.be ☎234413, 440 + 75Ⓥ €2·58 Jul/Aug, ⏻ €2·14/day. inner end Ⓥ pontoon. free wi-fi (25t) .

Fuel available alongside S of VVW-N on the E bank of the river, see inset, at KYCN. The river accesses the N Belgian canals.

Town Ⓑ ⇌ ✈ (Oostende).

North France

Dunkerque to Cap de la Hague

9.17.1 Contents 749
9.17.2 Area map and Distance table 750
9.17.3 Tidal stream charts 752
9.17.4 Lights, buoys and waypoints 754
9.17.5 Passage information 757
North East France – 757 • Dunkerque to Boulogne – 757 • Boulogne to Dieppe – 757 • Dieppe to Le Havre – 769 • The Seine Estuary – 775 • Deauville to Grandcamp – 784 • Grandcamp to Pointe de Barfleur – 787 • Pointe de Barfleur to Cap de la Hague – 787
9.17.6 Special notes for France 757
9.17.7 Dunkerque, tide tables/curves, Port Est 759
9.17.8 Gravelines 763
9.17.9 Calais, tidal coefficients 764
9.17.10 Boulogne-sur-Mer 766
9.17.11 Étaples 766
Le Touquet
9.17.12 St Valéry-sur-Somme 767
Le Hourdel • Le Crotoy
9.17.13 Le Tréport 768
9.17.14 Dieppe, tide tables/curves 768
9.17.15 St Valéry-en-Caux 773
9.17.16 Fécamp 774
9.17.17 Le Havre, tide tables/curves 774
9.17.18 Honfleur 779
9.17.19 River Seine 780
Rouen
9.17.20 Paris 781
9.17.21 Deauville/Trouville 782
9.17.22 Dives-sur-Mer 783
9.17.23 Ouistreham 784
Caen
9.17.24 Courseulles-sur-Mer 785
Arromanches
9.17.25 Port-en-Bessin 786
9.17.26 Grandcamp 787
9.17.27 Carentan 788
Isigny • Iles St Marcouf
9.17.28 St Vaast-la-Hougue 789
9.17.29 Barfleur 789
9.17.30 Cherbourg, tide tables/curves, tidal coefficients 790
Port de Lévi • Port du Becquet
9.17.31 Omonville-la-Rogue 796
Anse de St Martin

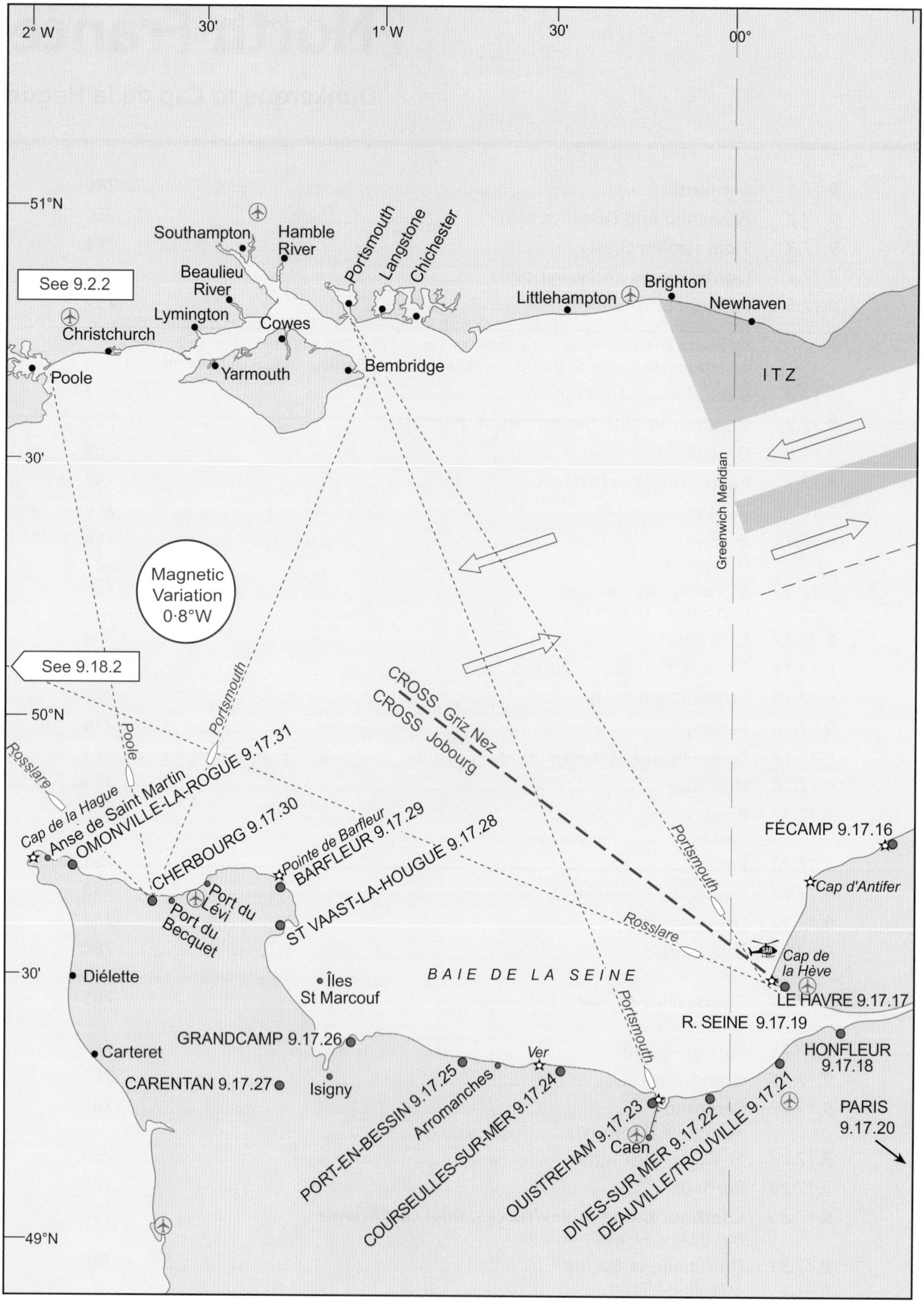
2° W
30'
1° W
30'
00°
51°N
30'
50°N
30'
49°N
See 9.2.2
See 9.18.2
Southampton
Hamble River
Portsmouth
Langstone
Chichester
Beaulieu River
Lymington
Cowes
Christchurch
Poole
Yarmouth
Bembridge
Littlehampton
Brighton
Newhaven
ITZ
Greenwich Meridian
Magnetic Variation 0·8°W
Portsmouth
Poole
Rosslare
CROSS Griz Nez
CROSS Jobourg
Cap de la Hague
Anse de Saint Martin
OMONVILLE-LA-ROGUE 9.17.31
CHERBOURG 9.17.30
Pointe de Barfleur
BARFLEUR 9.17.29
ST VAAST-LA-HOUGUE 9.17.28
Port du Lévi
Port du Becquet
Diélette
Carteret
Îles St Marcouf
BAIE DE LA SEINE
GRANDCAMP 9.17.26
CARENTAN 9.17.27
Isigny
PORT-EN-BESSIN 9.17.25
Arromanches
Ver
COURSEULLES-SUR-MER 9.17.24
OUISTREHAM 9.17.23
Caen
DIVES-SUR MER 9.17.22
DEAUVILLE/TROUVILLE 9.17.21
HONFLEUR 9.17.18
PARIS 9.17.20
R. SEINE 9.17.19
LE HAVRE 9.17.17
Cap de la Hève
Cap d'Antifer
FÉCAMP 9.17.16
Portsmouth
Rosslare
Portsmouth

9.17.2 North France
Dunkerque to Cap de la Hague

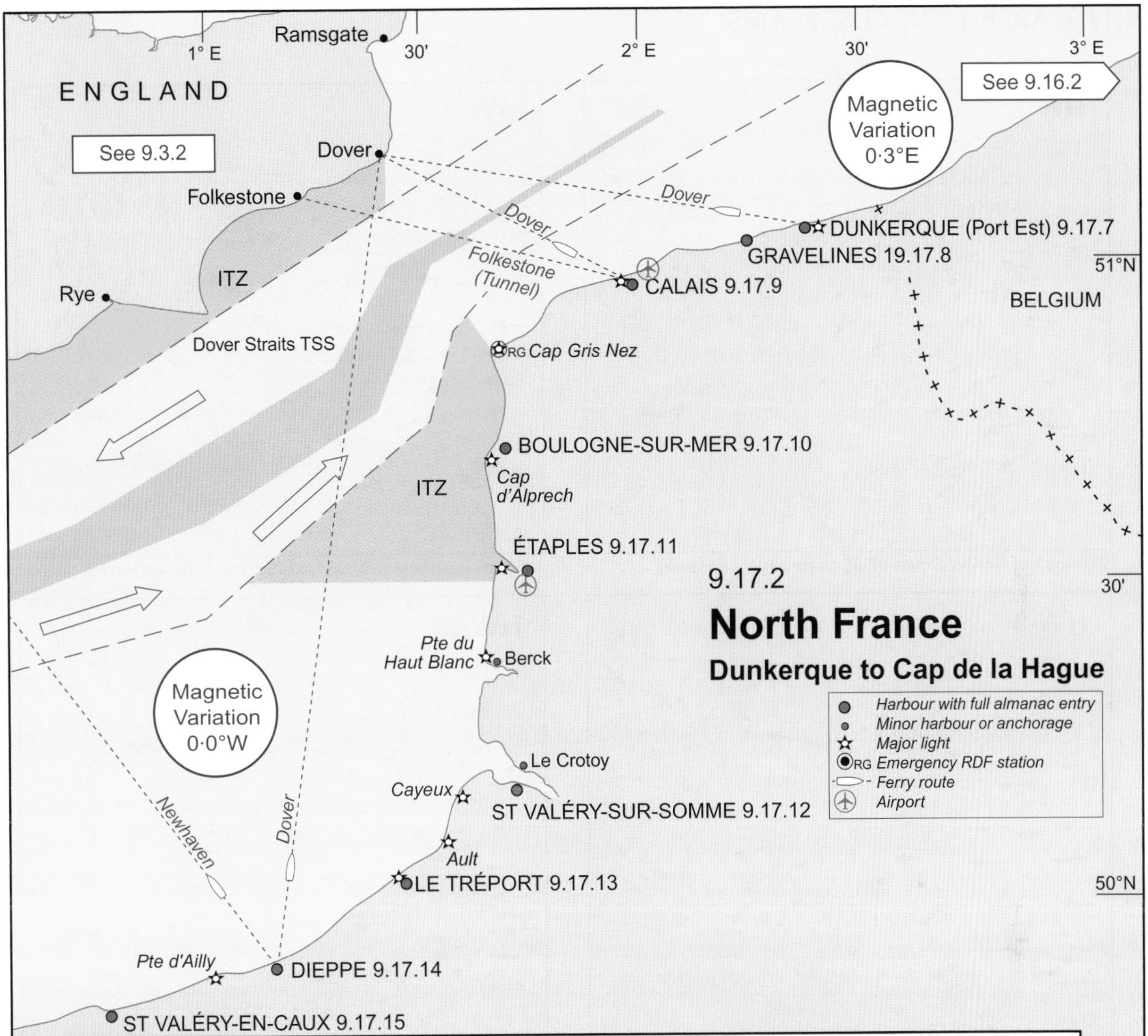

1° E
30'
2° E
30'
3° E
Ramsgate
ENGLAND
See 9.3.2
Dover
Folkestone
Rye
ITZ
Dover Straits TSS
Magnetic Variation 0·3°E
See 9.16.2
Dover
Dover/Folkestone (Tunnel)
DUNKERQUE (Port Est) 9.17.7
GRAVELINES 19.17.8
CALAIS 9.17.9
51°N
BELGIUM
RG Cap Gris Nez
BOULOGNE-SUR-MER 9.17.10
Cap d'Alprech
ITZ
ÉTAPLES 9.17.11
30'
Pte du Haut Blanc
Berck
Magnetic Variation 0·0°W
Harbour with full almanac entry
Minor harbour or anchorage
Major light
RG Emergency RDF station
Ferry route
Airport
Le Crotoy
Cayeux
ST VALÉRY-SUR-SOMME 9.17.12
Newhaven
Dover
Ault
LE TRÉPORT 9.17.13
50°N
Pte d'Ailly
DIEPPE 9.17.14
ST VALÉRY-EN-CAUX 9.17.15
30'
49°N

DISTANCE TABLE

Approximate distances in nautical miles are by the most direct route while avoiding dangers and allowing for TSS. Places in *italics* are in adjoining areas; places in **bold** are in 9.0.5, Cross-Channel Distances; place underlined are in 9.0.7, Distances across the North Sea.

Routes to the Mediterranean
See 9.17.6

1	***Nieuwpoort***	1																								
2	Dunkerque-Est	16	2																							
3	Gravelines	29	15	3																						
4	**Calais**	44	28	14	4																					
5	**Boulogne**	65	49	35	21	5																				
6	Étaples	73	58	48	37	17	6																			
7	St Valéry/Somme	102	86	72	58	41	30	7																		
8	Le Tréport	107	90	76	62	43	34	21	8																	
9	**Dieppe**	115	100	88	74	54	46	30	15	9																
10	St Valéry/Caux	124	109	95	81	62	56	42	28	16	10															
11	**Fécamp**	137	121	107	93	76	70	57	44	32	17	11														
12	**Le Havre**	163	148	135	121	103	97	84	71	61	47	27	12													
13	Rouen	228	213	200	186	168	162	149	136	126	112	92	77	13												
14	Honfleur	173	157	143	129	108	103	92	80	67	51	35	13	78	14											
15	**Deauville/Trouville**	167	152	139	125	108	101	91	79	61	53	34	9	74	13	15										
16	Dives/Mer	170	155	143	129	110	106	94	83	66	55	38	16	81	19	9	16									
17	**Ouistreham**	175	160	152	138	115	109	97	85	73	59	41	20	85	24	15	9	17								
18	Courseulles/Mer	177	162	150	136	115	111	100	87	75	60	44	24	89	30	23	18	14	18							
19	Port-en-Bessin	183	168	160	149	126	119	109	95	82	67	51	36	101	40	32	28	25	15	19						
20	Grandcamp	192	177	164	150	130	127	118	104	94	80	62	47	112	52	45	41	37	27	14	20					
21	Carentan	203	187	173	159	139	135	126	112	100	85	69	56	121	61	55	50	45	36	23	13	21				
22	**St Vaast**	194	179	165	151	131	127	120	107	96	80	65	54	119	61	54	50	46	35	25	16	20	22			
23	Barfleur	191	175	161	147	128	125	118	105	94	78	64	56	121	62	57	53	48	39	28	21	26	10	23		
24	**Cherbourg**	205	188	174	160	142	139	131	120	108	94	80	71	136	77	73	69	66	57	48	40	44	28	21	24	
25	Dielette	232	215	201	187	169	166	158	147	135	121	107	98	163	104	100	96	93	84	71	67	71	55	48	32	25

9.17.3 AREA 17 TIDAL STREAMS

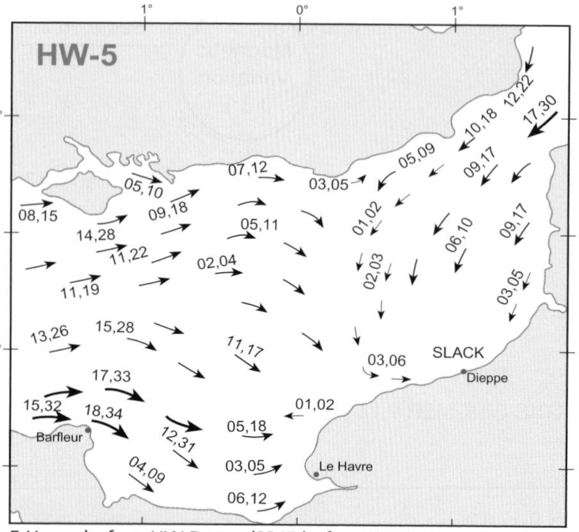

5 Hours before HW Dover (0345 before HW Le Havre)

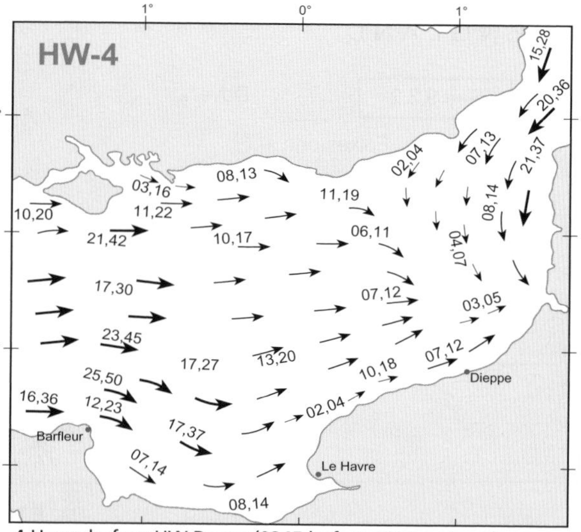

4 Hours before HW Dover (0245 before HW Le Havre)

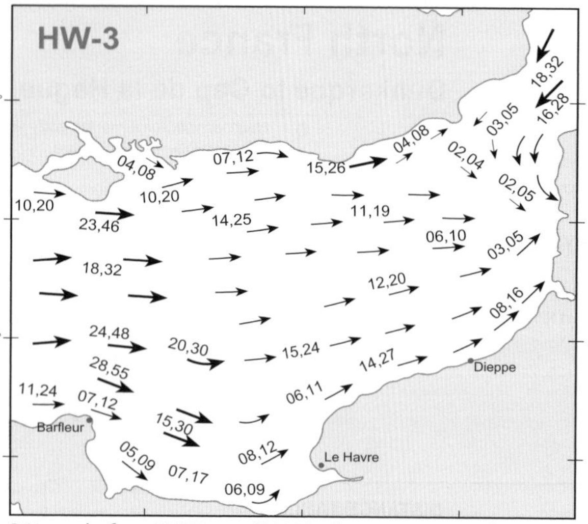

3 Hours before HW Dover (0145 before HW Le Havre)

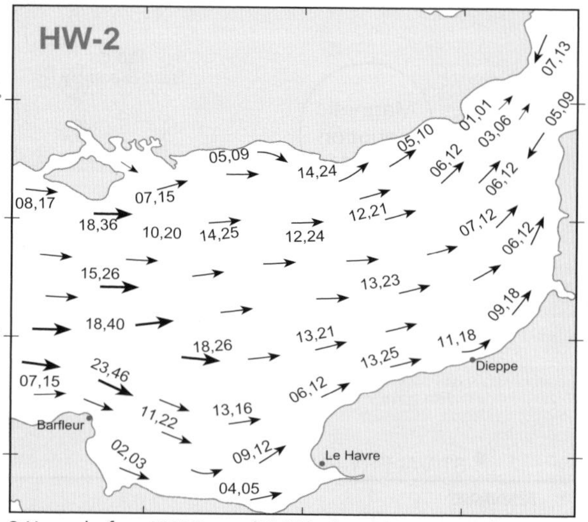

2 Hours before HW Dover (0045 before HW Le Havre)

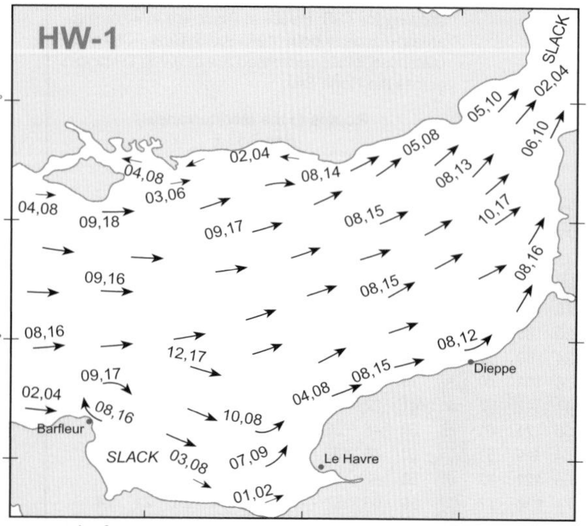

1 Hour before HW Dover (0015 after HW Le Havre)

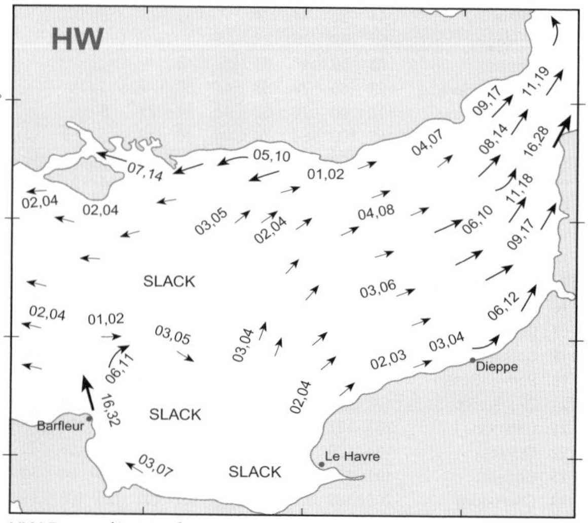

HW Dover (0115 after HW Le Havre)

Westward 9.18.3 Channel Is 9.19.3 Northward 9.2.3 North-eastward 9.3.3 Eastward 9.16.3

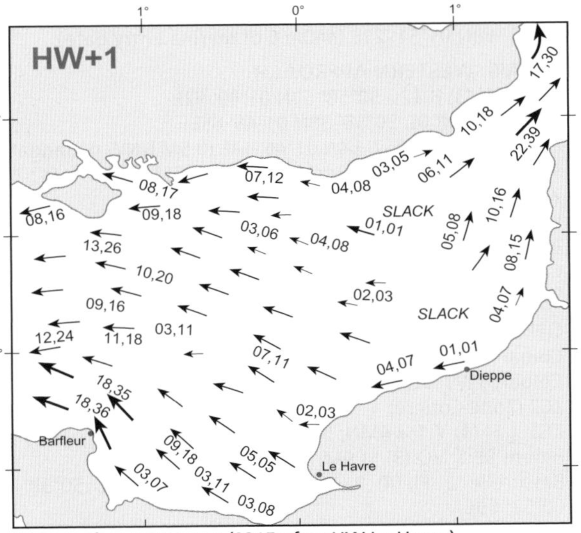

1 Hour after HW Dover (0215 after HW Le Havre)

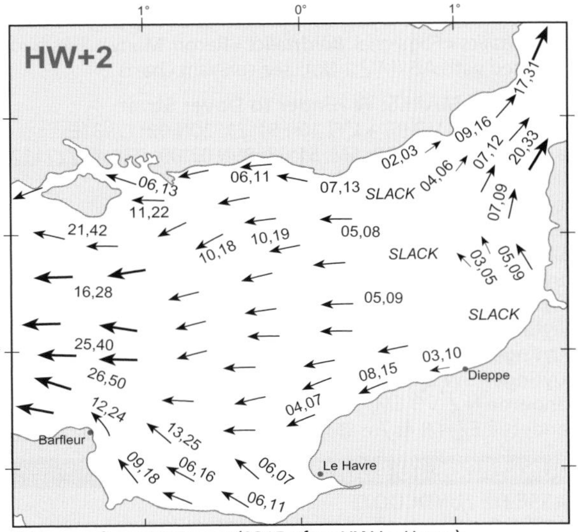

2 Hours after HW Dover (0315 after HW Le Havre)

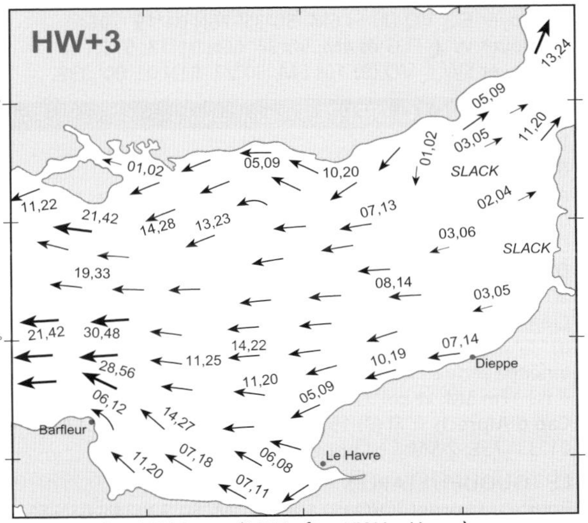

3 Hours after HW Dover (0415 after HW Le Havre)

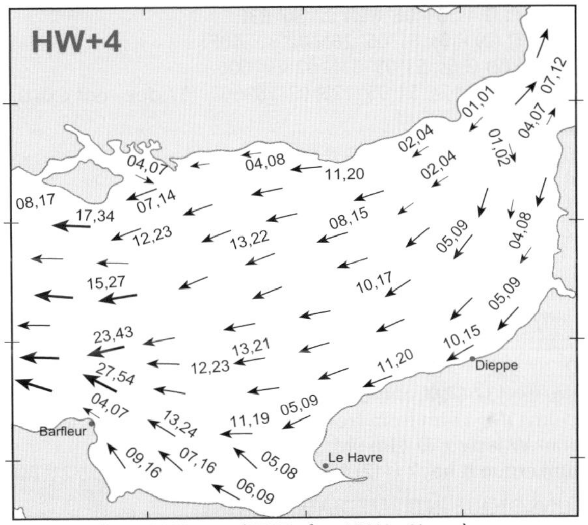

4 Hours after HW Dover (0515 after HW Le Havre)

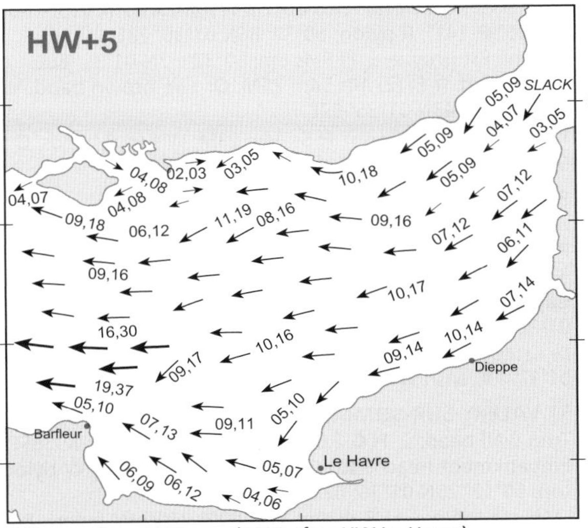

5 Hours after HW Dover (0615 after HW Le Havre)

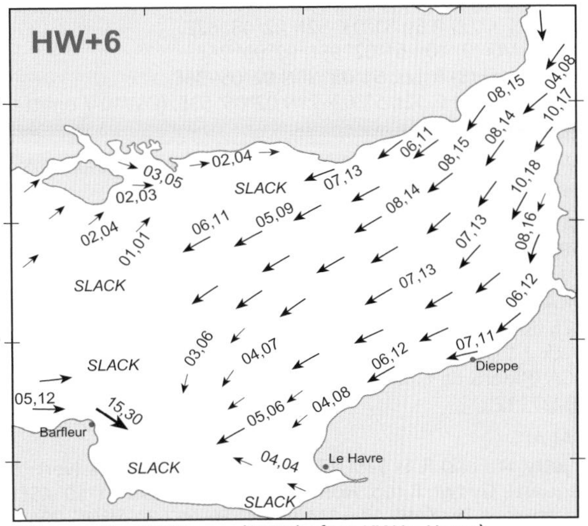

6 Hours after HW Dover (0510 before HW Le Havre)

9.17.4 LIGHTS, BUOYS AND WAYPOINTS

Bold print = light with a nominal range of 15M or more. CAPITALS = place or feature. *CAPITAL ITALICS* = light-vessel, light float or Lanby. *Italics* = Fog signal. ***Bold italics*** = Racon. Many marks/buoys are fitted with AIS (MMSI No); see relevant charts.

OFFSHORE MARKS: W Hinder to Dover Strait

Fairy South VQ (6) + L Fl 10s; 51°21'·20N 02°17'·31E.
Fairy West VQ (9) 10s 6M; 51°23'·89N 02°09'·27E. 992271127.
Hinder 1 Fl (2) 6s; 51°20'·80N 02°10'·93E.
Bergues Fl G 4s 7m 4M; 51°17'·14N 02°18'·63E.
Bergues S Q (6) + L Fl 15s; 51°15'·09N 02°19'·42E.
Ruytingen E VQ; 51°14'·55N 02°17'·93E.
Ruytingen N VQ 4M; 51°13'·16N 02°10'·28E.
Ruytingen SE VQ (3) 15s; 51°09'·20N 02°08'·94E.992271126.
Ruytingen NW Fl G 4s 3M; 51°09'·11N 01°57'·30E.
Ruytingen W VQ 4M; 51°06'·93N 01°50'·45E.
Ruytingen SW Fl (3) G 12s 3M; 51°04'·33N 01°45'·84E.
Sandettié N VQ 6M; 51°18'·35N 02°04'·73E.
Sandettié E Fl R 4s 7m 3M;51°14'·88N 02°02'·65E.992271119.

DUNKERQUE TO BOULOGNE

PASSE DE ZUYDCOOTE

E12 VQ (6) + L Fl 10s; 51°07'·92N 02°30'·61E.(Belgium).
CME Q (3) 10s; 51°07'·30N 02°30'·00E.
E11 Fl G 4s; 51°06'·85N 02°30'·83E.
E10 Fl (2) R 6s; 51°06'·26N 02°30'·40E.
E9 Fl (2) G 6s; 51°05'·61N 02°29'·60E.
E8 Fl (3) R 12s; 51°05'·12N 02°28'·60E. (E7 does not exist)

PASSE DE L'EST

E6 QR; 51°04'·86N 02°27'·08E.
E4 Fl R 4s; 51°04'·58N 02°24'·52E.
E1 Fl (2) G 6s; 51°04'·12N 02°23'·04E.
E2 Fl (2) R 6s; 51°04'·35N 02°22'·31E.
Q (6) + L Fl 15s; 51°04'·28N 02°21'·73E.

DUNKERQUE PORT EST

E jetty ☆ Fl (2) R 6s 12m 10M; R □, W pylon; 51°03'·59N 02°21'·20E.
W jetty ☆ Fl (2) G 6s 35m 11M; W twr, brown top; 51°03'·63N 02°20'·95E.
Ldg lts 137·5°, front Q7m11M 51°02'·98N 02°22'·05E, rear, Q10m11M, 114m from front, both W cols, R tops, synched.
Inner W jetty Q 11m 9M; 51°03'·33N 02°21'·43E.
Dunkerque lt ho ☆ Fl (2) 10s 59m **26M**; 51°02'·93N 02°21'·86E.

DUNKERQUE INTERMEDIATE CHANNEL

DW30 QR; 51°04'·14N 02°20'·16E.
DW29 QG; 51°03'·85N 02°20'·21E.
DW16 Fl (2) R 6s; 51°03'·52N 02°08'·62E.
DKB VQ (9) 10s; 51°02'·95N 02°09'·26E.
DW12 Fl (3) R 12s; 51°03'·38N 02°05'·36E.
DW11 Fl (3) G 12s; 51°02'·79N 02°05'·53E. (DW10-7 omitted)

GRAVELINES

W jetty ☆ Fl (2) WG 6s 9m W/G4M; 085°-W-224°-G-085°; Y ○ twr, G top; 51°00'·94N 02°05'·49E.

PASSE DE L'OUEST

DW6 VQ R; 51°02'· 81N 02°00'· 80E.
DW5 QG; 51°02'·20N 02°00'·92E.
DKA L Fl 10s; 51°02'·55N 01°56'·96E.
RCE (Ridens de Calais East) Fl G 4s; 51°02'·29N 01°52'·98E.
Dyck Fl R 4s; ***Racon B***; 51° 02'·90N 01°51'·80E.
RCA (Ridens de Calais Approach) Q; 51°01'·00N 01°48'·53E. 992271125.

CALAIS

E jetty ☆ Fl (2) R 6s 12m **17M**; (in fog two Fl (2) 6s (vert) on request); Gy twr, R top; *Horn (2) 40s;* 50°58'·39N 01°50'·45E.
E Jetty root, Dir ☆ WG 12m 1M; 089·4°-FG-093·7°-Al WG-094°·3-FW-098·6°; metal structure; 50°58'·25N 01°51'·20E.
W jetty ☆ Iso G 3s 12m 9M; (in fog Fl 5s on request); W twr, G top; *Bell 5s;* 50°58'·24N 01°50'·40E.
Calais ☆ Fl (4) 15s 59m **22M**; vis 073°-260°; W 8-sided twr, B top; 50°57'·68N 01°51'·21E (440m E of marina entry gate).

CALAIS, WESTERN APPROACH

CA6 Fl (3) R 12s; 50°58'·63N 01°49'·92E.
CA4 Fl (2)R 6s; 50°58'·38N 01°48'·65E.
CA1 Fl G 4s; 50°57'·64N 01°46'·14E (0·5M NNW of Sangatte).
Sangatte ☆ Oc WG 4s 13m W8M, G5M; 065°-G-089°-W-152°-G-245°; W pylon, B top; 50°57'·19N 01°46'·50E.
Les Quénocs VQ; 50°56'·85N 01°41'·12E.
Abbeville wreck VQ (9) 10s; 50°56'·08N 01°37'·58E.
Cap Gris-Nez ☆ Fl 5s 72m **29M**; 005°-232°; W twr, B top; 50°52'·09N 01°34'·96E.

OFFSHORE MARKS: DOVER STRAIT TSS, French side

Colbart N Q 6M; 50°57'·50N 01°23'·30E. 992271121.
Colbart SW VQ (6) + L Fl 10s 8m; 50°48'·87N 01°16'·32E.
ZC2 (Zone Cotière) Fl (2+1) Y 15s 5M; 50°53'·54N 01°30'·89E.
ZC1 Fl (4) Y 15s 4MN; 50°44'·99N 01°27'·21E.
Ridens SE VQ (3) 5s 6M; 50°43'·48N 01°18'·87E.
Bassurelle Fl (4) R 15s 6M; ***Racon B, 5-8M***; 50°32'·74N 00°57'·69E.
Vergoyer N VQ 5M; 50°39'·67N 01°22'·21E.
Vergoyer NW Fl (2) G 6s 4M; 50°37'·16N 01°17'·85E.
Vergoyer E VQ (3) 5s 6M; 50°35'·76N 01°19'·70E.
Vergoyer W Fl G 4s 4M; 50°34'·66N 01°13'·57E.
Vergoyer SW VQ (9) 10s 6M; 50°27'·01N 01°00'·03E.

BOULOGNE TO DIEPPE

BOULOGNE

Bassure de Baas VQ; 50°48'·53N 01°33'·05E.
Approches Boulogne VQ (6) + L Fl 10s 8m 6M; 50°45'·31N 01°31'·07E.
Digue N (detached) ☆ Fl (2) R 6s 10m 7M; 50°44'·71N 01°34'·18E.
Digue S (Carnot) ☆ Fl (2+1) 15s 25m **19M**; W twr, G top; 50°44'·44N 01°34'·05E.
Clearing brg 122·4° : Front, FG in a neon ▽ 4m 5M; 50°43'·71N 01°35'·66E. Rear, FR 44m 11M; intens 113°-133°; 560m from front.
Inner NE jetty ☆ FR 11m 7M; 50°43'·91N 01°35'·24E. Inner SW jetty ☆ FG 17m 5M; W col, G top; *Horn 30s;* 50°43'·90N 01°35'·11E.
Cap d'Alprech ☆ Fl (3) 15s 62m **23M**; W twr, B top; 50°41'·91N 01°33'·75E, 2·5M S of hbr ent.

LE TOUQUET/ÉTAPLES

Pointe de Lornel VQ (9) 10s 6m 3M; 50°33'·24N 01°35'·12E.
Mérida wreck 50°32'·85N 01°33'·44E.
Camiers lt ho ☆ Oc (2) WRG 6s 17m W10M, R/G7M; 015°-G-090°-W-105°-R-141°; R pylon; 50°32'·86N 01°36'·28E.
Canche Est groyne Fl R 4s 8m; 50°32'·57N 01°35'·66E.
Le Touquet ☆ Fl (2) 10s 54m **25M**; Or twr, brown band, W&G top; 50°31'·43N 01°35'·52E.
Pointe du Haut-Blanc ☆ Fl 5s 44m **23M**; W twr, R bands, G top; 50°23'·90N 01°33'·67E (Berck).

BAIE DE LA SOMME

ATSO Mo (A) 12s; 50°14'·00N 01°28'·08E (shifts frequently).
Pte du Hourdel ☆ Oc (3) WG 12s 19m, W12M, G9M; 053°-W-248°-G-323°; tidal sigs; *Horn (3) 30s*; W twr, G top; 50°12'·90N 01°33'·98E.
Cayeux-sur-Mer ☆ Fl R 5s 32m **22M**; W twr, R top; 50°11'·65N 01°30'·72E.
Le Crotoy ☆ Oc (2) R 6s 19m 8M; 285°-135°; W pylon; 50°12'·91N 01°37'·40E. Marina ☆ Fl R & Fl G 2s 4m 2M; 50°12'·98N 01°38'·20E.

ST VALÉRY-SUR-SOMME

Trng wall head, Fl G 2.5s 2m 1M; 50°12'·25N 01°35'·85E,.
Embankment head ☆ Iso G 4s 9m 9M; 347°-222°; W pylon, G top; 50°12'·25N 01°36'·02E.
La Ferté môle ☆ Fl R 4s 9m 9M; 000°-250°; W pylon, R top; 50°11'·18N 01°38'·14E (ent to marina inlet).

LE TRÉPORT

Ault ☆ Oc (3) WR 12s 95m **W15M**, R11M; 040°-W-175°-R-220°; W twr, R top; 50°06'·28N 01°27'·23E (4M NE of Le Tréport).
W jetty ☆ Fl (2) G 10s 15m **20M**; W twr, G top; 50°03'·88N 01°22'·14E.

DIEPPE

W jetty ☆ Iso G 4s 11m 8M; W twr, G top; *Horn 30s;* 49°56'·27N 01°04'·97E.
Quai de la Marne QR 12m 3M; 49°55'·93N 01°05'·20E, E quay.
Pointe d'Ailly ☆ Fl (3) 20s 95m **31M**; W □ twr, G top; *Horn (3) 60s;* 49°54'·96N 00°57'·50E.

DIEPPE TO LE HAVRE

SAINT VALÉRY-EN-CAUX

W jetty ☆ Fl (2) G 6s 13m 11M; W twr, G top; 49°52'·40N 00°42'·54E.
Paluel power station, restricted area, Paluel 2 Fl Y 4s; 49°52'·33N 00°38'·45E; Wave recorder Fl(5) Y 20s; 49°52'·30N 00°37'·87E; Paluel 1 Fl Y 4s; 49°52'·33N 00°37'·53E.

FÉCAMP

N jetty ☆ Fl (2) 10s 15m **16M**; Gy twr, R top; 49°45'·94N 00°21'·80E.
Fécamp NW, Met Mast FECO1-YO2 ☆ Mo(U) W 15s 13m 10M, Aero F R 36m, Aero UQ R 60m, Aero UQ W 60m(day) Gy pylon, Y platform; Horn Mo(U) 30s; 49°50'·85N 00°13'·14E. 992271122.

PORT DU HAVRE-ANTIFER

Cap d'Antifer ☆ Fl 20s 128m **29M**; 021°-222°; Gy 8-sided twr, G top, on 90m cliffs; 49°41'·01N 00°09'·93E.
A17 Iso G 4s; 49°41'·53N 00°01·75E.
A18 QR; 49°42'·02N 00°02'·18E. Cross the chan W of A17/18.
Ldg lts 127·5°, both Dir Oc 4s 113/135m **22M**; 127°-128°; by day F **33M** 126·5°-128·5° occas. **Front** ☆, 49°38'·31N 00°09'·12E.

LE HAVRE, APPROACH CHANNEL

Cap de la Hève ☆ Fl 5s 123m **24M**; 225°-196°; W 8-sided twr, R top; 49°30'·74N 00°04'·16E.
LHA Mo (A) 12s 10m 6M; R&W; ***Racon, 8-10M*** (a series of 8 dots, or 8 groups of dots; distance between each dot or group represents 0·3M); 49°31'·38N 00°09'·86W. Reserve lt Mo (A).
Ldg lts 106·8°, both Dir F 36/78m **25M** (H24); intens 106°-108°; Gy twrs, G tops. Front, 49°28'·91N 00°06'·50E; rear, 0·73M from front.
LH3 QG; 49°30'·84N 00°04'·02W. (LH1 & 2 buoys do not exist).
LH4 QR; 49°31'·11N 00°03'·90W.
LH7 Iso G 4s; 49°30'·25N 00°00'·82W.
LH8 Fl (2) R 6s; 49°30'·44N 00°00'·70W.
Note the W-E longitude change. (LH9 buoy does not exist).
LH13 Fl G 4s; 49°29'·32N 00°03'·62E (Ent to Port 2000).
LH14 Fl R 4s; 49°29'·67N 00°03'·43E; 1m shoal depth close W.
LH16 Fl (2) R 6s; 49°29'·45N 00°04'·28E.
LH 2000 VQ (9) 10s; 49°29'·14N 00°04'·78E (Ent to Port 2000).

LE HAVRE

Digue N ☆ Fl R 5s 15m **21M**; IPTS; W ○ twr, R top; *Horn 15s;* 49°29'·19N 00°05'·44E.
Digue S ☆ VQ (3) G 2s 15m 11M; W twr, G top; 49°29'·05N 00°05'·38E.
Marina ent, W spur ☆ Fl (2) R 6s 3M; 49°29'·22N 00°05'·53E.

THE SEINE ESTUARY UP TO HONFLEUR

CHENAL DE ROUEN

Nord du Mouillage Fl (4) Y 15s; 49°28'·80N 00°00'·22E.
No 2 QR; ***Racon T***; 49°27'·70N 00°00'·60E.
No 4 Fl R 2·5s; 49°27'·19N 00°01'·97E. Yachts keep N of chan.
Amfard SW QR; 49°26'·30N 00°04'·82E.
No 10 Fl R 4s; 49°26'·10N 00°06'·39E.
Digue du Ratier VQ 10m 4M; 49°25'·94N 00°06'·59E.
Falaise des Fonds ☆ Fl (3) WRG 12s 15m, **W17M**, R/G13M; 040°-G-080°-R-084°-G-100°- W-109°-R-162°-G-260°; W twr, G top; 49°25'·47N 00°12'·85E.
No 20 Fl (2) R 6s; 49°25'·85N 00°13'·71E. (over to Honfleur)

HONFLEUR

Digue Ouest ☆ QG 10m 6M; 49°25'·67N 00°13'·83E.
Digue Est ☆ Q 9m 8M; *Horn (5) 40s;* 49°25'·67N 00°13'·95E.
Inner E jetty head, ☆ Fl R 2M; 49°25'·40N 00°14'·10E.
No 22 Fl R 4s; 49°25'·85N 00°15'·37E.

TROUVILLE TO COURSEULLES

CHENAL DE ROUEN TO DEAUVILLE and TROUVILLE

Ratelets Q (9) 15s; 49°25'·29N 00°01'·71E.
Semoy VQ (3) 5s; 49°24'·15N 00°02'·35E, close to 148° ldg line.
Trouville SW VQ (9) 10s; 49°22'·54N 00°02'·56E.

DEAUVILLE and TROUVILLE

Ldg lts 145°, both Oc R 4s 11/17m 12/10M: Front, East inner jetty (*estacade*); 330°-150°; W twr, R top; 49°22'·03N 00°04'·48E.
Rear, Pte de la Cahotte; synch; 120°-170°; 49°21'·93N 00°04'·58E.
W trng wall ☆ Fl WG 4s 10m W9M, G6M; 005°-W-176°-G-005°; B pylon, G top; 49°22'·37N 00°04'·11E. Also 4 unlit SHM bcns.
E trng wall ☆ Fl (4) WR 12s 8m W7M, R4M; 131°-W-175°-R-131°; W pylon, R top; 49°22'·22N 00°04'·33E. Also 3 unlit PHM bcns.
W outer bkwtr ☆ Iso G 4s 9m 5M; 49°22'·11N 00°04'·33E.
West inner jetty (*estacade*) ☆ QG 11m 9M; 49°22'·03N 00°04'·43E.

DIVES-SUR-MER *Note the E-W longitude change.*

DI Iso 4s; 49°19'·17N 00°05'·86W.
No 1 VQ G; 49°18'·50N 00°05'·67W. Ch bys freq moved.
No 2 VQ R; 49°18'·51N 00°05'·56W.
No 3 QG 7m 4M; W pylon, G top; 49°18'·30N 00°05'·55W.
No 5 Fl G 4s 8m 4M; W pylon, G top; 49°18'·09N 00°05'·50W.
Bcns 3 & 5, if damaged, may be temporarily replaced by buoys.
No 7 Fl G 4s; 49°17'·65N 00°05'·31W.

OUISTREHAM and CAEN

Merville VQ; 49°19'·65N 00°13'·39W; spoil ground buoy.
Ouistreham VQ (3) 5s; wreck buoy; 49°20'·42N 00°14'·81W.
Ldg lts 185°, both Dir Oc (3+1) R 12s 10/30m **17M**; intens 183·5°-186·5°, synch. **Front** ☆, E jetty, W mast, R top, 49°16'·99N 00°14'·81W. **Rear** ☆, 610m from front, tripod, R top.
No 1 QG; 49°19'·19N 00°14'·67W.
No 2 QR; 49°19'·17N 00°14'·43W.
Barnabé ☆ QG 7m 5M; W pylon, G top; 49°18'·02N 00°14'·76W.
St-Médard ☆ QR 7m 5M; 49°18'·02N 00°14'·62W.
Riva ☆ Fl G 4s 9m 3M; W pylon, G top; 49°17'·73N 00°14'·79W.
Quilbé ☆ Fl R 4s 9m 3M; W pylon, R top; 49°17'·72N 00°14'·67W.
Ouistreham lt ho ☆ Oc WR 4s 37m **W17M**, R13M; 115°-R-151°-W-115°; W twr, R top; 49°16'·79N 00°14'·87W.

COURSEULLES-SUR-MER

Courseulles Iso 4s; 49°21'·28N 00°27'·68W.
W jetty ☆ Iso WG 4s 7m; W9M, G6M; 135°-W-235°-G-135°; brown pylon on dolphin, G top; 49°20'·41N 00°27'·37W.
E jetty ☆ Oc (2) R 6s 9m 7M; 49°20'·26N 00°27'·39W.

COURSEULLES TO ST VAAST

Ver ☆ Fl (3)15s 42m **26M**; obsc'd by cliffs of St Aubin when brg >275°; conspic lt ho, W twr, Gy top; 49°20'·41N 00°31'·13W.

ARROMANCHES

Ent buoys: 49°21'·35N 00°37'·26W; 49°21'·25N00°37'·30W.
Bombardons wreck buoys; 49°21'·66N 00°38'·97W.

PORT-EN-BESSIN

Ldg lts 204°, both Oc (3) 12s 25/42m 10/11M; synch. Front, 069°-339°, W pylon, G top; 49°20'·96N 00°45'·53W. Rear; 114°-294°, W and Gy ho; 93m from front.
E mole ☆ Oc R 4s 14m 7M, R pylon; 49°21'·12N 00°45'·38W.
W mole ☆ Fl WG 4s 14m, W10M, G7M; G065°-114·5°, W114·5°-065°; G pylon; 49°21'·17N 00°45'·43W.

COASTAL MARKS
Omaha Beach, 1M off : 49°22′·66N 00°50′·28W; 49°23′·17N 00°51′·93W; 49°23′·66N 00°53′·74W.
Broadsword Q (3) 10s, wreck buoy; 49°25′·34N 00°52′·96W.
Est du Cardonnet VQ (3) 5s; 49°26′·83N 01°01′·10W.

GRANDCAMP
Les Roches de Grandcamp: No 1 49°24′·72N 01°01′·75W; No 3 49°24′·92N 01°03′·70W; No 5 49°24′·78N 01°04′·98W.
Ldg lts 146°, both Dir Q 9/12m **15M**, 144·5°-147·5°. **Front** ☆, 49°23′·42N 01°02′·90W. **Rear** ☆,102m from front.
Jetée Est Oc (2) R 6s 9m 9M; *Horn Mo(N) 30s;* 49°23′·53N 01°02′·96W.
Jetée Ouest Fl G 4s 9m 6M; 49°23′·47N 01°02′·96W.

ISIGNY-SUR-MER
IS, small B/Y, no topmark (on AC 2135); 49°24′·28N 01°06′·37W.
No 1, Fl R 4s; 49°23′·60N 01°07·27W
Dir lts 173°, both Dir Q WRG 7m 9M; 49°19′·57N 01°06·78W.
Training wall heads Fl G 4s; 49°21′·40N 01°07′·20W; Fl R 4s, 49°21′·40N 01°07′·10W, off Pte du Grouin.

CARENTAN
C-I Iso 4s; 49°25′·44N 01°07′·08W; 210°/1·76M to 1 & 2 bys.
No 1 Fl G 2·5s; 49°23′·93N 01°08′·52W.
No 2 Fl R 2·5s; 49°23′·88N 01°08′·37W.
Trng wall Fl (4) G 15s; G △ on G bcn;49°21′·96N 01°09′·95W.
Trng wall Fl (4) R 15s; R ☐ on R bcn;49°21′·93N 01°09′·878W.
Ldg lts 209·5°. **Front** ☆ Dir Oc (3) R 12s 6m **18M**; intens 208·2°-210·7°; W mast, R top; 49°20′·47N 01°11′·17W. Rear, Dir Oc (3) 12s 14m 10M; vis 120°-005°; W gantry, G top; 723m from front.

ÎLES SAINT-MARCOUF
Iles St-Marcouf VQ (3) 5s 18m 8M; ☐ Gy twr, G top; 49°29′·86N 01°08′·81W.
Ouest-Saint-Marcouf Q (9) 15s; 49°29′·73N 01°11′·97W.
Saint Floxel 49°30′·64N 01°13′·94W.
Quineville Q (9) 10s, wreck buoy; 49°31′·79N 01°12′·38W.

ST VAAST TO POINTE DE BARFLEUR

ST VAAST-LA-HOUGUE
Ldg lts 267°: Front, La Hougue Oc 4s 9m 10M; W pylon, G top; 49°34′·25N 01°16′·37W. Rear, Morsalines Oc (4) WRG 12s 90m, W11M, R/G8M; 171°-W-316°-G-321°-R-342°-W-355°; W 8-sided twr, G top; 49°34′·16N 01°19′·10W, 1·8M from front.
Le Manquet 49°34′·26N 01°15′·56W.
Le Bout du Roc 49°34′·68N 01°15′·27W.
La Dent 49°34′·57N 01°14′·20W.
Le Gavendest Q (6) + L Fl 15s; 49°34′·36N 01°13′·89W.
Jetty Dir Oc (2) WRG 6s 12m W10M, R/G7M; 219°-R-237°-G-310°-W-350°-R-040°; W 8-sided twr, R top; 49°35′·17N 01°15′·41W.
Pte de Saire Oc (2+1) 10s 11m 10M; squat W twr, G top; 49°36′·36N 01°13′·78W.

BARFLEUR
Ldg lts 219·5°, both Oc (3) 12s 7/13m 10M; synch. Front, W ☐ twr;49°40′·18N 01°15′·61W. Rear, 085°-355°; Gy and W ☐ twr, G top; 288m from front.
La Grotte 49°41′·06N 01°14′·86W.
Roche-à-l'Anglais 49°40′·78N 01°14′·93W.
La Vimberge 49°40′·54N 01°15′·25W.
W jetty Fl G 4s 8m 6M; 49°40′·32N 01°15′·57W.
E jetty Oc R 4s 5m 6M; 49°40′·31N 01°15′·47W.
La Jamette 49°41′·87N 01°15′·59W.
Pte de Barfleur ☆ Fl (2) 10s 72m **25M**; obsc when brg less than 088°; Gy twr, B top; 49°41′·78N 01°15′·96W.

POINTE DE BARFLEUR TO CAP DE LA HAGUE
Les Équets Q 8m 3M; 49°43′·62N 01°18′·36W.
Basse du Rénier VQ 8m 4M; 49°44′·84N 01°22′·09W.
Les Trois Pierres 49°42′·90N 01°21′·80W.
Anse de Vicq, 158° ldg lts; both Iso R 4s 8/14m 6M; front 49°42′·20N 01°23′·95W.
La Pierre Noire Q (9) 15s 8m 4M;49°43′·54N 01°29′·07W.

PORT DU LÉVI
Cap Lévi ☆ Fl R 5s 36m **17M**; Gy ☐ twr; 49°41′·75N 01°28′·38W.
Port Lévi Oc (2) WRG 6s 7m 7M; 055°-G-083°-W-105°-R-163°; W & Gy hut, W lantern; 49°41′·24N 01°28′·34W.

PORT DU BECQUET
Ldg lts 186·3°, both intens 183°-189·3°; synch. Front, Dir Oc (3) 12s 8m 10M; W 8-sided twr; 49°39′·23N 01°32′·84W. Rear, Dir Oc (3) 12s 13m 7M. W 8-sided twr, R top; 49m from front.

CHERBOURG, EASTERN ENTRANCES
Passe Collignon Fl (2) R 6s 5m 4M; 49°39′·59N 01°34′·24W.
Passe de l'Est, Jetée des Flamands ldg lts 189°, both Q 9/16m 13M. Front, 49°39′·33N 01°35′·94W . Rear, 516m from front.
Roches du Nord-Ouest Fl R 2·5s; 49°40′·64N 01°35′·28W.
La Truite Fl (4) R 15s; 49°40′·33N 01°35′·49W.
Fort d'Île Pelée Oc (2) WR 6s 19m; W10M, R7M; 055°-W-120°-R-055°; W & R pedestal; 49°40′·21N 01°35′·08W.
Fort de l'Est 49°40′·28N 01°35′·92W, Iso G 4s 19m 9M.
Fort Central VQ (6) + L Fl 10s 5m 4M; 322°-032°; 49°40′·40N 01°37′·04W.

CHERBOURG, PASSE DE L'OUEST
CH1 ⊙; V-AIS; 49°43′·24N 01°42′·09W.
Passe de l'Ouest, Dir Q , lights in line140·3°; Front, Jetée du Homet 5m **17M**; W △; 49° 39′·54N 01°37′·97W. Rear, Gare Maritime, 0.99M from front; 35m **17M**; intens 138·8° - 141·8°, shows 24H, sync with front; W △ on Gy pylon; 49°38′·78N 01°37′·00W.
Fort de l'Ouest ☆ Fl (3) WR 15s 19m **W24M, R20M**; 122°-W-355°-R-122°; Gy twr, R top; 49°40′·45N 01°38′·87W.
Fort de l'Ouest Fl R 4s; 49°40′·39N 01°38′·89W.
Q (6) + L Fl 15s; 49°40′·34N 01°38′·65W.
Digue de Querqueville Fl (2) G 6s 8m 6M; W col, G top; 49°40′·30N 01°39′·80W.
Inner ldg lts 124·3°; both intens 114·3°-134·3°: Front, Digue du Homet head, QG 10m 6M; 49°39′·48N 01°36′·96W. Rear, Dir Iso G 4s 16m 10M; W col, B bands, 397m from front.
La Ténarde VQ 8m 4M; 49°39′·74N 01°37′·75W.

CHERBOURG, PETITE RADE and MARINA
Entrance, W side, Digue du Homet QG 10m 8M; intens 114·3°-134·3°; W pylon, G top; 49°39′·48N 01°36′·96W.
E side, Q R, off Jetée des Flamands; 49°39′·44N 01°36′·60W.
Marina ent, E side, Fl (3) R 12s 6m 6M; W col, R lantern; 49°38′·91N 01°37′·08W.
W mole Fl (3) G 12s 7m 6M; G pylon; 49°38′·87N 01°37′·15W.
E quay Fl (4) R 15s 3m 3M; R bcn; 49°38′·79N 01°37′·12W.
Wavescreen pontoon, N end Fl (4) G 15s 4m 2M; W post, G top.

CHERBOURG TO CAP DE LA HAGUE
Raz de Bannes 49°41′·32N 01°44′·53W.
Omonville Dir lt 257°: Iso WRG 4s13m; W10M, R/G7M; 180°-G-252°-W-262°-R-287°; W pylon, G top; 49°42′·24N 01°50′·15W.
L'Étonnard 49°42′·33N 01°49′·84W.
Basse Bréfort VQ 8m 4M; 49°43′·90N 01°51′·15W.
Jobourg Nuclear plant chimney, R lts; 49°40′·80N 01°52′·91W.
La Plate Fl (2+1) WR 10s 11m; W9M, R6M; 115°-W-272°-R-115°; Y 8-sided twr, with B top; 49°43′·97N 01°55′·74W.
Cap de la Hague (Gros du Raz) ☆ Fl 5s 48m **23M**; Gy twr, W top; *Horn 30s;* 49°43′·31N 01° 57′·26W.
La Foraine VQ (9) 10s, 12m 6M; 49°42′·90N 01°58′·31W.

9.17.5 PASSAGE INFORMATION

More passage information is threaded between harbours in this Area. **Bibliography**: *Shell Channel Pilot* (Imray/Cunliffe). *Dover Strait NP28* and *Channel NP27 Pilots*. *Channel Havens* (ACN/Endean).

NORTH EAST FRANCE

The coasts of Picardy and Normandy are hardly more than an overnight passage from harbours on the UK's S coast – eg, Brighton to Fécamp is only 65M. However some of the harbours dry, so a boat which can take the ground is an advantage. For a chart of the Dover Strait TSS, see Area 3. Notes on the English Channel and on cross-Channel passages appear below and in Area 3. See Chapter 9, Introduction for cross-Channel distances. For a French glossary, see Chapter 1.

DUNKERQUE TO BOULOGNE

Offshore, a series of banks lies roughly parallel with the coast (AC 323, 1892, 2451): Sandettié bank, Outer Ruytingen midway between Sandettié and the coast, and the Dyck banks which extend NE'wards for 30M from a point 5M NE of Calais. There are well-buoyed channels between some of these banks, but great care is needed in poor visibility. In general the banks are steep-to on the inshore side, and slope to seaward. In bad weather the sea breaks on the shallower parts.

Dunkerque Port Est, the old port, has several good yacht marinas and all facilities. Dunkerque Port Ouest is a commercial/ferry port which yachts should not enter. About 3M SW is the drying hbr of **Gravelines**, which should not be entered in strong onshore winds. If E-bound, the Passe de Zuydcoote (4·4m) is a popular inshore link to West Diep and the Belgian ports.

The sea breaks heavily in bad weather on Ridens de Calais, 3M N of **Calais** (AC 1351) and also on Ridens de la Rade immediately N and NE of the harbour where the least charted depth is 0·1m.

The NE-bound traffic lane of the Dover Strait TSS is only 3M off C Gris Nez. Keep a sharp lookout not only for coastal traffic in the ITZ, but also cross-Channel ferries. ▶*1M NW of C Gris Nez the NE-going stream begins at HW Dieppe –0150, and the SW-going at HW Dieppe +0355, sp rates 4kn.*◀ Between C Gris Nez (lt, fog sig) and Boulogne the coastal bank dries about 4ca offshore.

BOULOGNE TO DIEPPE

In the approaches to Pas de Calais a number of shoals lie offshore (AC 2451): The Ridge (or Le Colbart) Les Ridens, Bassurelle, Vergoyer, Bassure de Baas and Battur. In bad weather, and particularly with wind against tide, the sea breaks heavily on all these shoals.

From **Boulogne** (AC 438) to Pte de Lornel the coast dries up to 5ca offshore. ▶*Off Boulogne's Digue Carnot the N-going stream begins HW Dieppe –0130, and the S-going at HW Dieppe +0350, sp rates 1·75kn.*◀

Le Touquet and **Étaples** lie in the Embouchure de la Canche, entered between Pte de Lornel and Pte du Touquet, and with a drying bank extending 1M seaward of a line joining these two points. Le Touquet-Paris-Plage lt is shown from a conspic twr, 1M S of Pte du Touquet.

▶*Off the estuary entrance the N-going stream begins about HW Dieppe –0335, sp rate 1·75kn; and the S-going stream begins about HW Dieppe +0240, sp rate 1·75kn.*◀

From Pte du Touquet the coast runs 17M S to Pte de St Quentin, with a shallow coastal bank which dries to about 5ca offshore, except in the approaches to the dangerous and constantly changing Embouchure de l'Authie (Pte du Haut-Blanc, about 10M S) where it dries up to 2M offshore.

Baie de la Somme, between Pte de St Quentin and Pte du Hourdel (lt) is a shallow, drying area of shifting sands. The access channel to **St Valéry-sur-Somme** and **Le Crotoy**, which runs close to Pte du Hourdel, is well buoyed, but the whole estuary dries out 3M to seaward, and should not be approached in strong W/NW winds.

Offshore there are two shoals, Bassurelle de la Somme and Quémer, on parts of which the sea breaks in bad weather. ▶*4·5M NW of Cayeux-sur-Mer (lt) the stream is rotatory anti-clockwise. The E-going stream begins about HW Dieppe –0200, and sets 070° 2·5kn at sp: the W-going stream begins about HW Dieppe +0600, and sets 240° 1·5kn at sp.*◀

S of Ault (lt) the coast changes from low sand dunes to medium-height cliffs. Between **Le Tréport** and Dieppe, 14M SW, rky banks, drying in places, extend 5ca offshore. Banc Franc-Marqué (3·6m) lies 2M offshore, and some 3M N of Le Tréport. About 3M NW of Le Tréport, Ridens du Tréport (5·1m) should be avoided in bad weather. A prohibited area extends 6ca off Penly nuclear power station and is marked by 2 SPM lt buoys.

9.17.6 SPECIAL NOTES FOR FRANCE

Instead of 'County' the 'Département' is given. For details of documentation apply to the French Tourist Office, 300 High Holborn, London, WC1V 7JH; ☎020 7061 6631; info.uk@franceguide.com www.franceguide.com.

STANDARD TIME is –0100, to which DST should be added.

VOCABULARY See Chapter 1.

AFFAIRES MARITIMES is a part of the central government Ministry of Transport. It oversees all maritime activities (commercial, fishing, pleasure) and helps them develop harmoniously. Information on navigation and other maritime issues can be supplied by a representative whose ☎ is given under each port; he may be based at the nearest commercial or fishing port. The Head Office is: Ministère des Transports et de la Mer, Bureau de la Navigation de Plaisance, 3 Place de Fontenoy, 75700 Paris, ☎01·44·49·80·00. www.mer.gouv.fr

CHARTS Official charts are issued by SHOM (*Service Hydrographique et Oceanographique de la Marine*), the Navy's Hydrographer. (See Chapter 1 for contact details.) SHOM charts are excellent for the smaller French ports not covered by UKHO. A free, annual chart catalogue *Le petit catalogue* is downloadable from www.shom.fr. It includes chart agents and mail order specialists. In this Almanac under 'Facilities', SHOM means a chart agent. Any new edition of a SHOM chart receives a new, different chart number.

TIDAL LEVELS SHOM charts refer elevations of lights to MHWS. Heights of other features are referred to Mean Sea Level (*Niveau moyen*) or as indicated on the chart; it is important to check the chart's title block. Clearance under bridges etc is referred to MSL, MHWS or HAT depending on the recency of the chart.
Useful French tidal terms:

LAT	Plus basse mer astronomique (PBMA)
MHWS	Pleine mer moyenne de VE (PMVE)
MHWN	Pleine mer moyenne de ME (PMME)
MLWN	Basse mer moyenne de ME (BMME)
MLWS	Basse mer moyenne de VE (BMVE)
ML/MSL	Niveau moyen (NM)
HW	Vive-eau (VE)
LW	Morte-eau (ME)

TIDAL COEFFICIENTS Popular and much used in France, these are included for a selection of strategic ports, Calais, Cherbourg, St Malo, Brest and Port Bloc, together with explanatory notes.

PUBLIC HOLIDAYS New Year's Day, Easter Sunday and Monday, Labour Day (1 May), Ascension Day, Armistice Day 1945 (8 May), Whit Sunday and Monday, National (Bastille) Day (14 July), Feast of the Assumption (15 Aug), All Saints' Day (1 Nov), Remembrance Day (11 Nov), Christmas Day.

REGULATIONS Flares must be in-date. Carry original ship's registration papers. Yachts built since 2007 must have black water tank(s) or a treatment system. Mandatory boat equipment in French waters is listed at www.developpement-durable.gouv.fr/spip.php?page=article&id_article=5476.

FACILITIES The cost of a visitor's overnight berth is based on high season rates, mostly quoted as €/metre LOA, although sometimes beam may also be taken into account. Low season rates and concessions can be a big saving. The fee usually includes electricity, but rarely showers which range between €1·20 and €2. VAT (TVA) is 20%. Port à Sec offers savings for longer stays if not living aboard. **Fuel** can be obtained H24 in many marinas, self-service, using credit cards to activate/pay at the pumps. Lacking a suitable card, payments can always be made during office hours at the Capitainerie.

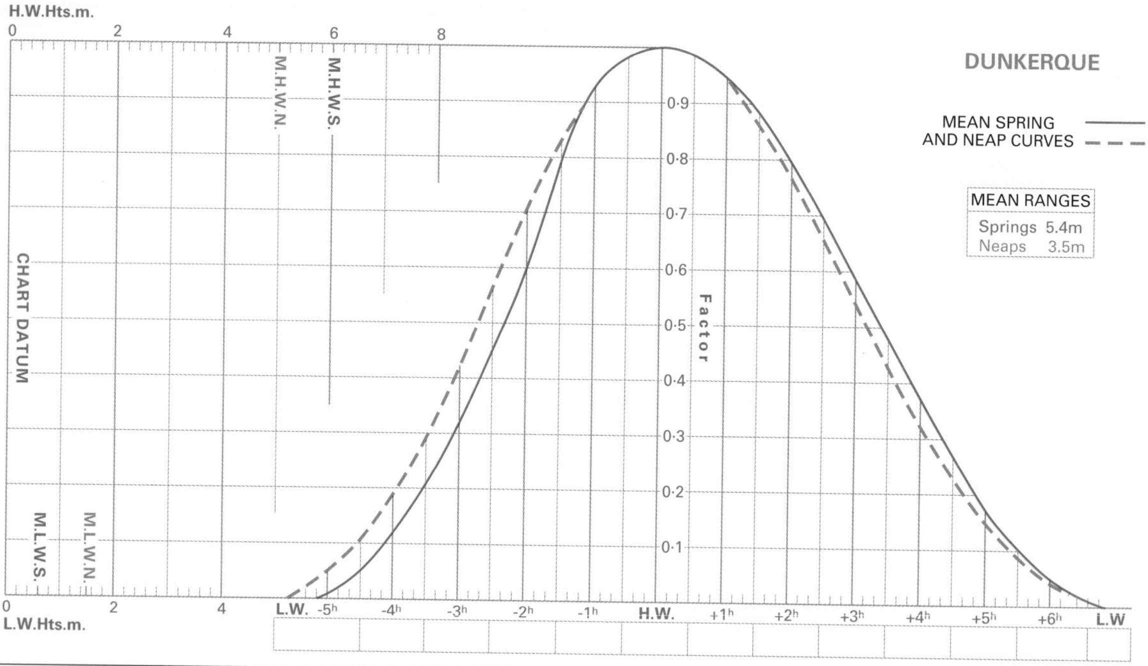

TELEPHONES ☎ numbers contain 10 digits, the first 2 digits being Zone codes (01 to 05) as appropriate to location. Mobile numbers are prefixed 06. Info Nos, eg the recorded weather (Auto) are prefixed 08. The ringing tone is long, equal on/off tones (slower than UK engaged tone). Rapid pips mean the call is being connected. Engaged tone is like that in UK.

To call France from UK, dial + (or 00) 33, then the 9 digit number, omitting the 0 from the Zone code prefix. To call UK from France dial + (or 00) 44 followed by the Area Code (omitting the first 0) and the number. Phonecards for public phones may be bought at the PTT, many Hbr offices, cafés and tabacs. Cheap rates are 2130-0800 Mon-Fri 1330-0800 Sat–Mon.

⚠ Emergencies, dial:
15 Ambulance (SAMU), better than a doctor;
17 Police, better than a gendarmerie;
18 Fire (also divers)
112 CROSS & general emergencies

BRITISH CONSULS IN FRANCE
The British Consular service assists UK nationals who are travelling abroad and have encountered difficulties or distress ranging from loss of passport or money to the death of or serious injury to a crew member or fellow traveller.

British Consuls at harbours on the Channel and Atlantic coasts are *the first port of call when help is needed*. The relevant Tel No is given under each hbr in Areas 17-22.

SIGNALS International Port Traffic Signals (Chapter 5) and Storm warning signals (Chapter 6) are used in many French ports. Tidal signals are now rarely seen in French ports.

INLAND WATERWAYS

TOLLS are due on waterways managed by Voies Navigable de France (VNF). Licence discs (*vignettes*) must be visibly displayed stbd side forward. They are obtainable:

- Online from www.vnf.fr/vignettesVNF/ in English. Pay on line by Visa, Mastercard or Eurocard.
- By post from VNF offices listed on the website. Allow 2 weeks.
- Over the counter (cash only) from 35 listed VNF offices.

Licence fees, 2017, were calculated with a set charge per metre depending on length of stay and LOA added to a fixed fee depending on four classes of size. Validity was for either 1 year, (Jan-Dec) 1 month (30 days) or 7 days. Note: All time periods are consecutive. 1 day licences are also available on request.

Duration	LOA x €/m	<8m	8–11m	11–14m	>14m
1 year	€8·30/m	+€85·80	+€196·90	+€375·10	+€489·70
30 days	€7·40/m	+€27·20	+€39·60	+€51·90	+€66·30
7 days	€3·80/m	+€15·00	+€22·80	+€30·30	+€37·70

e.g. 10m yacht for 30 days = (€7·40 x 10) + €39·60 = €113·60.

See: www.french-waterways.com for additional information.

CLOSURES
Dates of closures (*chomages*) plus lock hours, water levels and other practicalities, can be obtained from www.vnf.fr or the French National Tourist Office in London (see overleaf).

VNF Head Office, 175 Rue Ludovic Boutleux, BP 820, 62400 Bethune. ☎03·21·63·24·30. www.vnf.fr

QUALIFICATIONS
Helmsmen of craft <15m LOA and not capable of >20 kph (11kn) must have an International Certificate of Competence validated for inland waterways, plus a copy of the CEVNI rules. For larger, faster craft the requirements are under review. Copies of police regs for inland waterways must be on board (electronic if easy to access). Download general regs (RGPNI) at: www.developpement-durable.gouv.fr/Police-de-la-navigation and special regs (RPP) at: www. vnf.fr/vnf/content.vnf?action=content&occ_id=37793.

INLAND WATERWAYS TO THE MEDITERRANEAN
The quickest route is R Seine - Paris (see 9.17.19), Paris - St Mammès – Canal du Loing – Canal de Briare – Canal Latéral à la Loire – Canal du Centre – Saône – Rhône. Approx 1318km (824M) 182 locks; allow 4 weeks. Max dimensions: LOA 38·5m, beam 5m, draft 1·8m, air draft 3·5m.

Alternatives above St Mammès: R Yonne-Laroche, then either Canal de Bourgogne – Saône; or Canal du Nivernais – Canal du Centre – Saône. Both are slowed by many locks.

There are other routes via R Oise/Aisne or R Marne, both continuing via Canal de la Marne à la Saône.

The Saône can also be accessed via the canals of N France, entered at Calais, Dunkerque or Belgian and Dutch ports.

CANALS IN WESTERN FRANCE
See (9.18.14) Inland Waterways, especially the Ille et Rance Canal/ Vilaine River from St Malo to Arzal/Camoel in S Brittany and (9.22.22-.25) R Gironde, Canal Latéral à la Garonne and Canal du Midi.

STANDARD TIME UT –01
Subtract 1 hour for UT
For French Summer Time add ONE hour in **non-shaded areas**

DUNKERQUE LAT 51°03′N LONG 2°22′E

TIMES AND HEIGHTS OF HIGH AND LOW WATERS

Dates in red are SPRINGS
Dates in blue are NEAPS

YEAR **2018**

JANUARY

Day		Time	m	Time	m	Time	m	Time	m	Moon
1	M	0625	0.8	1143	6.0	1853	0.6			
2	TU	0013	6.1	0716	0.6	1233	6.2	1942	0.5	○
3	W	0101	6.2	0805	0.4	1322	6.3	2031	0.5	
4	TH	0150	6.2	0854	0.3	1413	6.3	2118	0.5	
5	F	0238	6.1	0942	0.3	1503	6.2	2206	0.7	
6	SA	0326	6.0	1030	0.4	1553	6.0	2253	0.9	
7	SU	0414	5.8	1118	0.6	1643	5.8	2341	1.1	
8	M	0503	5.6	1209	0.9	1737	5.5			◑
9	TU	0033	1.3	0559	5.3	1304	1.1	1840	5.2	
10	W	0131	1.5	0707	5.1	1406	1.3	1952	5.0	
11	TH	0236	1.6	0820	5.0	1513	1.4	2059	5.0	
12	F	0347	1.6	0924	5.0	1623	1.4	2158	5.0	
13	SA	0456	1.5	1023	5.1	1725	1.3	2252	5.2	
14	SU	0552	1.3	1114	5.3	1813	1.2	2338	5.4	
15	M	0636	1.1	1159	5.5	1852	1.1			
16	TU	0018	5.5	0713	1.0	1237	5.6	1925	1.0	
17	W	0053	5.6	0746	0.9	1311	5.7	1959	0.9	●
18	TH	0123	5.7	0820	0.8	1342	5.8	2033	0.9	
19	F	0153	5.8	0855	0.8	1414	5.8	2108	0.9	
20	SA	0226	5.8	0929	0.7	1449	5.8	2141	0.9	
21	SU	0300	5.7	1002	0.8	1523	5.7	2215	1.0	
22	M	0333	5.6	1036	0.8	1558	5.6	2251	1.1	
23	TU	0406	5.5	1114	0.9	1635	5.5	2331	1.2	
24	W	0449	5.4	1157	1.1	1727	5.3			◐
25	TH	0018	1.3	0547	5.3	1250	1.2	1832	5.2	
26	F	0119	1.5	0657	5.2	1401	1.3	1942	5.1	
27	SA	0238	1.5	0810	5.2	1522	1.3	2058	5.2	
28	SU	0357	1.4	0928	5.3	1637	1.1	2215	5.4	
29	M	0509	1.1	1040	5.6	1744	0.9	2317	5.7	
30	TU	0612	0.8	1137	5.9	1842	0.7			
31	W	0008	5.9	0707	0.5	1228	6.1	1933	0.5	○

FEBRUARY

Day		Time	m	Time	m	Time	m	Time	m	Moon
1	TH	0055	6.1	0755	0.3	1315	6.3	2019	0.5	
2	F	0139	6.2	0842	0.2	1401	6.3	2104	0.5	
3	SA	0223	6.2	0927	0.2	1447	6.2	2147	0.6	
4	SU	0306	6.1	1011	0.3	1531	6.1	2229	0.7	
5	M	0348	6.0	1053	0.5	1614	5.8	2310	0.9	
6	TU	0430	5.8	1135	0.7	1659	5.6	2352	1.2	
7	W	0516	5.5	1219	1.0	1748	5.2			◑
8	TH	0039	1.4	0610	5.2	1311	1.3	1850	4.9	
9	F	0138	1.6	0721	4.9	1415	1.6	2006	4.7	
10	SA	0249	1.8	0840	4.7	1529	1.7	2120	4.7	
11	SU	0411	1.7	0951	4.8	1648	1.6	2224	4.8	
12	M	0524	1.5	1051	5.0	1748	1.4	2317	5.1	
13	TU	0615	1.2	1140	5.3	1831	1.2			
14	W	0000	5.4	0653	1.0	1220	5.5	1906	1.0	
15	TH	0035	5.6	0726	0.8	1254	5.7	1939	0.9	●
16	F	0106	5.7	0800	0.7	1324	5.8	2013	0.8	
17	SA	0135	5.8	0834	0.6	1355	5.9	2048	0.7	
18	SU	0205	5.9	0909	0.5	1427	5.9	2122	0.7	
19	M	0237	5.9	0943	0.5	1458	5.9	2155	0.7	
20	TU	0308	5.8	1017	0.6	1530	5.8	2229	0.8	
21	W	0340	5.8	1052	0.7	1606	5.7	2306	0.9	
22	TH	0421	5.7	1132	0.8	1653	5.5	2350	1.1	
23	F	0514	5.5	1220	1.1	1757	5.2			◐
24	SA	0047	1.3	0625	5.2	1328	1.3	1913	5.0	
25	SU	0206	1.5	0745	5.1	1455	1.4	2040	5.0	
26	M	0334	1.4	0918	5.2	1619	1.2	2208	5.2	
27	TU	0455	1.1	1035	5.5	1734	1.0	2311	5.5	
28	W	0602	0.8	1132	5.8	1832	0.7			

MARCH

Day		Time	m	Time	m	Time	m	Time	m	Moon
1	TH	0001	5.8	0655	0.5	1219	6.1	1920	0.5	
2	F	0043	6.0	0742	0.3	1303	6.2	2004	0.5	○
3	SA	0122	6.1	0825	0.2	1344	6.2	2045	0.5	
4	SU	0202	6.2	0907	0.2	1425	6.2	2124	0.5	
5	M	0241	6.1	0946	0.3	1505	6.1	2202	0.6	
6	TU	0319	6.0	1024	0.4	1543	5.9	2238	0.8	
7	W	0358	5.8	1100	0.7	1621	5.6	2315	1.0	
8	TH	0437	5.6	1137	1.0	1702	5.3	2355	1.3	
9	F	0524	5.2	1221	1.3	1753	4.9			◑
10	SA	0045	1.6	0624	4.8	1319	1.6	1904	4.6	
11	SU	0153	1.8	0747	4.6	1435	1.8	2031	4.4	
12	M	0319	1.9	0913	4.6	1602	1.8	2149	4.6	
13	TU	0444	1.6	1022	4.8	1714	1.5	2248	4.9	
14	W	0543	1.3	1115	5.2	1803	1.2	2334	5.2	
15	TH	0625	1.0	1156	5.5	1840	1.0			
16	F	0011	5.5	0700	0.8	1231	5.7	1913	0.8	
17	SA	0042	5.7	0734	0.6	1301	5.8	1948	0.7	●
18	SU	0111	5.8	0809	0.5	1330	5.9	2023	0.6	
19	M	0140	5.9	0845	0.4	1401	6.0	2059	0.5	
20	TU	0211	6.0	0921	0.4	1432	6.0	2134	0.5	
21	W	0243	6.0	0956	0.4	1507	5.9	2210	0.6	
22	TH	0320	5.9	1032	0.6	1546	5.8	2248	0.8	
23	F	0402	5.8	1112	0.8	1635	5.5	2332	1.0	
24	SA	0459	5.6	1202	1.0	1741	5.2			◐
25	SU	0030	1.2	0611	5.3	1311	1.3	1858	5.0	
26	M	0151	1.4	0735	5.1	1442	1.4	2032	4.9	
27	TU	0320	1.3	0913	5.1	1608	1.3	2157	5.1	
28	W	0442	1.0	1026	5.5	1721	1.0	2257	5.5	
29	TH	0548	0.7	1120	5.8	1817	0.7	2345	5.7	
30	F	0639	0.4	1205	6.0	1902	0.6			
31	SA	0025	5.9	0723	0.3	1244	6.1	1943	0.5	○

APRIL

Day		Time	m	Time	m	Time	m	Time	m	Moon
1	SU	0101	6.0	0804	0.3	1322	6.1	2022	0.5	
2	M	0137	6.1	0842	0.3	1400	6.1	2059	0.5	
3	TU	0215	6.1	0919	0.4	1437	6.0	2134	0.6	
4	W	0252	6.0	0954	0.5	1513	5.8	2209	0.7	
5	TH	0328	5.8	1027	0.7	1548	5.6	2244	0.9	
6	F	0405	5.6	1102	1.0	1625	5.3	2320	1.2	
7	SA	0448	5.3	1141	1.3	1711	5.0			
8	SU	0003	1.5	0543	4.9	1231	1.6	1814	4.6	◑
9	M	0102	1.7	0656	4.6	1341	1.9	1933	4.4	
10	TU	0223	1.9	0821	4.5	1510	1.9	2059	4.5	
11	W	0352	1.7	0941	4.7	1629	1.6	2207	4.8	
12	TH	0459	1.4	1038	5.1	1724	1.3	2258	5.2	
13	F	0547	1.0	1123	5.4	1806	1.0	2337	5.5	
14	SA	0626	0.8	1159	5.7	1843	0.8			
15	SU	0011	5.7	0703	0.6	1231	5.8	1919	0.6	
16	M	0040	5.8	0740	0.5	1301	6.0	1957	0.5	●
17	TU	0111	6.0	0819	0.4	1334	6.0	2035	0.5	
18	W	0146	6.1	0857	0.3	1410	6.0	2114	0.4	
19	TH	0224	6.1	0937	0.4	1450	6.0	2154	0.5	
20	F	0306	6.0	1017	0.5	1534	5.8	2236	0.6	
21	SA	0356	5.8	1101	0.8	1630	5.5	2324	0.9	
22	SU	0457	5.6	1155	1.1	1736	5.3			◐
23	M	0025	1.1	0607	5.3	1308	1.3	1849	5.0	
24	TU	0145	1.2	0729	5.1	1433	1.4	2020	4.9	
25	W	0308	1.2	0901	5.2	1553	1.3	2138	5.2	
26	TH	0425	0.9	1008	5.5	1702	1.0	2236	5.4	
27	F	0528	0.7	1101	5.7	1756	0.8	2322	5.7	
28	SA	0617	0.5	1145	5.8	1840	0.7			
29	SU	0001	5.8	0700	0.5	1222	5.9	1920	0.7	
30	M	0037	5.9	0740	0.5	1259	6.0	1957	0.6	○

Chart Datum is 2·69 metres below IGN Datum. HAT is 6·4 metres above Chart Datum.

STANDARD TIME UT –01
Subtract 1 hour for UT
For French Summer Time add ONE hour in **non-shaded areas**

DUNKERQUE LAT 51°03'N LONG 2°22'E

TIMES AND HEIGHTS OF HIGH AND LOW WATERS

Dates in red are **SPRINGS**
Dates in blue are **NEAPS**

YEAR **2018**

MAY

Date	Time	m	Date	Time	m
1 TU	0114 0816 1335 2033	6.0 0.5 5.9 0.6	16 W	0044 0753 1309 2013	6.0 0.4 6.0 0.4
2 W	0151 0852 1411 2109	6.0 0.6 5.9 0.6	17 TH	0125 0836 1352 2057	6.1 0.4 6.1 0.4
3 TH	0227 0926 1446 2144	5.9 0.7 5.8 0.7	18 F	0210 0921 1439 2142	6.1 0.4 6.0 0.4
4 F	0303 1000 1520 2218	5.8 0.9 5.6 0.9	19 SA	0300 1007 1531 2230	6.1 0.6 5.8 0.5
5 SA	0340 1034 1558 2254	5.6 1.1 5.4 1.1	20 SU	0355 1057 1628 2322	5.9 0.8 5.6 0.7
6 SU	0422 1111 1643 2333	5.3 1.3 5.1 1.3	21 M	0455 1154 1728	5.7 1.0 5.4
7 M	0514 1156 1740	5.0 1.6 4.8	22 TU	0023 0558 1302 ◐ 1835	0.9 5.5 1.2 5.2
8 TU	0023 0617 1254 ◑ 1846	1.5 4.8 1.8 4.6	23 W	0135 0715 1416 1957	1.0 5.3 1.3 5.1
9 W	0128 0727 1411 1959	1.7 4.6 1.8 4.6	24 TH	0248 0838 1528 2110	1.0 5.3 1.2 5.2
10 TH	0252 0842 1534 2112	1.6 4.8 1.6 4.8	25 F	0359 0943 1635 2207	0.9 5.4 1.1 5.4
11 F	0406 0949 1637 2210	1.4 5.0 1.3 5.1	26 SA	0502 1036 1730 2255	0.8 5.5 1.0 5.5
12 SA	0502 1040 1726 2256	1.1 5.4 1.1 5.4	27 SU	0553 1120 1816 2336	0.7 5.6 0.9 5.7
13 SU	0549 1121 1809 2333	0.8 5.6 0.8 5.6	28 M	0637 1200 1857	0.7 5.7 0.8
14 M	0631 1156 1850	0.6 5.8 0.7	29 TU	0015 0716 1237 ○ 1935	5.7 0.7 5.8 0.8
15 TU	0007 0712 1231 ● 1931	5.8 0.5 6.0 0.6	30 W	0054 0752 1315 2011	5.8 0.7 5.8 0.7
			31 TH	0132 0827 1351 2047	5.8 0.8 5.8 0.7

JUNE

Date	Time	m	Date	Time	m
1 F	0208 0902 1424 2123	5.8 0.8 5.7 0.8	16 SA	0201 0908 1432 2132	6.2 0.5 6.0 0.3
2 SA	0244 0937 1500 2158	5.7 0.9 5.6 0.9	17 SU	0255 0958 1525 2223	6.2 0.6 5.9 0.4
3 SU	0322 1012 1538 2233	5.6 1.1 5.4 1.0	18 M	0349 1049 1617 2315	6.0 0.7 5.8 0.5
4 M	0403 1048 1621 2310	5.4 1.2 5.2 1.2	19 TU	0444 1144 1712	5.9 0.9 5.6
5 TU	0450 1128 1711 2353	5.2 1.4 5.0 1.3	20 W	0012 0542 1243 ◐ 1811	0.7 5.6 1.1 5.4
6 W	0544 1217 1807 ◑	5.0 1.5 4.9	21 TH	0113 0650 1347 1923	0.8 5.4 1.2 5.2
7 TH	0046 0642 1317 1907	1.4 4.9 1.6 4.8	22 F	0218 0804 1453 2033	0.9 5.3 1.3 5.2
8 F	0151 0744 1431 2011	1.5 4.9 1.6 4.9	23 SA	0325 0909 1559 2133	1.0 5.3 1.3 5.3
9 SA	0308 0848 1544 2113	1.3 5.0 1.4 5.1	24 SU	0430 1005 1701 2226	1.0 5.3 1.2 5.4
10 SU	0414 0948 1643 2208	1.1 5.3 1.2 5.3	25 M	0527 1055 1753 2314	1.0 5.4 1.1 5.5
11 M	0509 1039 1734 2255	0.9 5.5 1.0 5.6	26 TU	0615 1140 1838 2358	1.0 5.5 1.0 5.6
12 TU	0559 1124 1822 2339	0.7 5.7 0.8 5.8	27 W	0655 1221 1917	0.9 5.6 0.9
13 W	0646 1206 1909 ●	0.6 5.9 0.6	28 TH	0039 0732 1300 ○ 1954	5.7 0.9 5.6 0.8
14 TH	0024 0733 1252 1955	6.0 0.5 6.0 0.4	29 F	0118 0807 1335 2029	5.7 0.9 5.7 0.8
15 F	0111 0820 1340 2043	6.1 0.4 6.1 0.3	30 SA	0154 0843 1407 2105	5.7 0.9 5.7 0.8

JULY

Date	Time	m	Date	Time	m
1 SU	0228 0918 1441 2140	5.7 1.0 5.6 0.8	16 M	0244 0945 1509 2210	6.3 0.5 6.1 0.2
2 M	0303 0952 1517 2214	5.6 1.0 5.5 0.9	17 TU	0335 1033 1558 2259	6.1 0.6 5.9 0.3
3 TU	0342 1026 1557 2248	5.5 1.1 5.4 1.0	18 W	0425 1122 1647 2348	6.0 0.8 5.8 0.5
4 W	0423 1103 1638 2326	5.4 1.2 5.3 1.1	19 TH	0516 1213 1739 ◐	5.7 1.0 5.6
5 TH	0508 1145 1724	5.2 1.3 5.1	20 F	0041 0613 1308 1839	0.8 5.4 1.2 5.3
6 F	0011 0558 1234 ◑ 1818	1.2 5.1 1.4 5.0	21 SA	0139 0720 1410 1949	1.0 5.2 1.4 5.2
7 SA	0104 0654 1334 1918	1.3 5.1 1.5 5.0	22 SU	0242 0828 1517 2057	1.2 5.0 1.5 5.1
8 SU	0211 0755 1449 2020	1.3 5.1 1.5 5.1	23 M	0351 0932 1628 2159	1.3 5.0 1.4 5.1
9 M	0326 0859 1600 2125	1.2 5.2 1.3 5.3	24 TU	0459 1031 1731 2255	1.3 5.1 1.3 5.3
10 TU	0432 1003 1703 2226	1.0 5.4 1.1 5.5	25 W	0555 1123 1821 2344	1.2 5.3 1.1 5.4
11 W	0532 1100 1800 2321	0.9 5.6 0.9 5.8	26 TH	0639 1207 1902	1.1 5.4 1.0
12 TH	0627 1152 1852	0.7 5.8 0.6	27 F	0027 0715 1245 ○ 1937	5.6 1.0 5.6 0.9
13 F	0012 0718 1241 ● 1943	6.0 0.6 6.0 0.4	28 SA	0104 0749 1319 2011	5.7 1.0 5.7 0.8
14 SA	0102 0808 1330 2032	6.2 0.5 6.1 0.3	29 SU	0137 0823 1349 2045	5.7 0.9 5.7 0.7
15 SU	0152 0857 1420 2121	6.3 0.5 6.1 0.2	30 M	0208 0858 1420 2119	5.8 0.9 5.7 0.7
			31 TU	0241 0931 1453 2152	5.8 0.9 5.7 0.7

AUGUST

Date	Time	m	Date	Time	m
1 W	0315 1004 1527 2225	5.7 1.0 5.6 0.8	16 TH	0357 1053 1614 2318	6.0 0.8 5.9 0.6
2 TH	0350 1037 1559 2259	5.6 1.1 5.5 0.9	17 F	0442 1137 1701	5.7 1.0 5.7
3 F	0424 1114 1633 2338	5.5 1.1 5.4 1.0	18 SA	0003 0531 1224 ◐ 1754	0.9 5.4 1.3 5.4
4 SA	0505 1157 1722 ◑	5.3 1.3 5.3	19 SU	0053 0629 1321 1901	1.2 5.1 1.5 5.1
5 SU	0025 0604 1250 1828	1.1 5.2 1.4 5.2	20 M	0154 0742 1430 2018	1.5 4.8 1.7 4.9
6 M	0125 0710 1401 1938	1.3 5.1 1.5 5.1	21 TU	0307 0857 1551 2131	1.7 4.8 1.7 4.9
7 TU	0244 0822 1524 2053	1.3 5.1 1.5 5.2	22 W	0429 1006 1707 2236	1.6 4.9 1.5 5.1
8 W	0402 0940 1638 2210	1.2 5.2 1.2 5.4	23 TH	0533 1104 1801 2328	1.4 5.1 1.2 5.3
9 TH	0512 1050 1744 2313	1.0 5.5 0.9 5.8	24 F	0619 1149 1843	1.2 5.4 1.0
10 F	0614 1145 1841	0.8 5.8 0.6	25 SA	0010 0656 1226 1917	5.6 1.1 5.6 0.9
11 SA	0005 0708 1233 ● 1932	6.1 0.6 6.0 0.4	26 SU	0046 0728 1258 ○ 1948	5.7 1.0 5.7 0.7
12 SU	0052 0756 1318 2019	6.3 0.5 6.1 0.2	27 M	0116 0800 1326 2021	5.8 0.9 5.8 0.7
13 M	0139 0842 1402 2105	6.3 0.5 6.2 0.1	28 TU	0145 0833 1354 2055	5.9 0.9 5.9 0.6
14 TU	0226 0927 1446 2150	6.3 0.5 6.2 0.2	29 W	0214 0907 1424 2128	5.9 0.8 5.9 0.6
15 W	0312 1010 1531 2234	6.2 0.6 6.1 0.3	30 TH	0245 0939 1453 2200	5.9 0.9 5.8 0.7
			31 F	0314 1011 1523 2233	5.8 0.9 5.7 0.8

Chart Datum is 2·69 metres below IGN Datum. HAT is 6·4 metres above Chart Datum.

STANDARD TIME UT –01
Subtract 1 hour for UT
For French Summer Time add ONE hour in **non-shaded areas**

DUNKERQUE

LAT 51°03'N LONG 2°22'E

TIMES AND HEIGHTS OF HIGH AND LOW WATERS

Dates in red are SPRINGS
Dates in blue are NEAPS

YEAR **2018**

SEPTEMBER

Date	Day	Time	m	Time	m	Time	m	Time	m	Moon
1	SA	0345	5.7	1046	1.0	1556	5.7	2309	0.9	
2	SU	0423	5.5	1126	1.2	1642	5.5	2353	1.1	
3	M	0519	5.3	1216	1.4	1749	5.3			◑
4	TU	0050	1.4	0637	5.1	1327	1.6	1910	5.1	
5	W	0213	1.5	0759	5.0	1458	1.5	2039	5.1	
6	TH	0342	1.4	0931	5.1	1621	1.3	2205	5.4	
7	F	0500	1.2	1042	5.5	1733	0.9	2306	5.8	
8	SA	0604	0.9	1136	5.8	1829	0.6	2356	6.1	
9	SU	0655	0.7	1220	6.1	1918	0.3			●
10	M	0039	6.3	0740	0.6	1259	6.2	2002	0.2	
11	TU	0121	6.4	0822	0.5	1339	6.3	2045	0.2	
12	W	0202	6.3	0903	0.6	1419	6.2	2126	0.3	
13	TH	0244	6.2	0943	0.7	1500	6.1	2206	0.5	
14	F	0325	6.0	1022	0.8	1541	6.0	2244	0.7	
15	SA	0405	5.8	1101	1.1	1623	5.7	2323	1.0	
16	SU	0448	5.4	1142	1.3	1711	5.4			
17	M	0007	1.4	0539	5.1	1232	1.6	1812	5.0	◐
18	TU	0103	1.7	0648	4.7	1339	1.9	1933	4.7	
19	W	0218	1.9	0815	4.6	1507	1.9	2059	4.7	
20	TH	0350	1.9	0935	4.7	1633	1.7	2210	4.9	
21	F	0503	1.6	1036	5.0	1732	1.3	2304	5.3	
22	SA	0552	1.4	1123	5.3	1816	1.1	2345	5.6	
23	SU	0629	1.1	1200	5.6	1850	0.9			
24	M	0020	5.8	0701	1.0	1231	5.8	1921	0.7	
25	TU	0050	5.9	0733	0.9	1258	5.9	1953	0.6	○
26	W	0117	6.0	0806	0.8	1325	6.0	2027	0.6	
27	TH	0144	6.0	0840	0.8	1353	6.0	2101	0.6	
28	F	0213	6.0	0914	0.8	1423	6.0	2135	0.7	
29	SA	0244	5.9	0948	0.9	1456	5.9	2209	0.8	
30	SU	0318	5.8	1023	1.0	1533	5.8	2246	1.0	

OCTOBER

Date	Day	Time	m	Time	m	Time	m	Time	m	Moon
1	M	0400	5.6	1104	1.1	1621	5.6	2330	1.2	
2	TU	0457	5.3	1155	1.4	1732	5.3			◑
3	W	0030	1.5	0619	5.0	1309	1.6	1857	5.1	
4	TH	0158	1.6	0746	4.9	1442	1.6	2033	5.1	
5	F	0330	1.5	0922	5.1	1608	1.3	2156	5.5	
6	SA	0448	1.2	1029	5.5	1718	0.9	2254	5.9	
7	SU	0549	0.9	1120	5.8	1813	0.6	2341	6.1	
8	M	0637	0.7	1201	6.0	1859	0.4			
9	TU	0021	6.3	0720	0.7	1237	6.2	1941	0.3	●
10	W	0059	6.3	0800	0.7	1314	6.2	2021	0.4	
11	TH	0137	6.3	0838	0.7	1352	6.2	2100	0.5	
12	F	0215	6.2	0916	0.8	1431	6.1	2136	0.6	
13	SA	0253	6.0	0952	0.8	1510	6.0	2212	0.9	
14	SU	0331	5.7	1029	1.1	1550	5.7	2248	1.2	
15	M	0409	5.5	1107	1.3	1633	5.4	2327	1.5	
16	TU	0455	5.1	1150	1.6	1729	5.0			◐
17	W	0016	1.8	0556	4.7	1248	1.9	1842	4.7	
18	TH	0124	2.1	0717	4.5	1411	2.0	2010	4.6	
19	F	0257	2.1	0847	4.6	1543	1.9	2131	4.8	
20	SA	0418	1.8	0956	4.9	1650	1.5	2228	5.2	
21	SU	0513	1.5	1046	5.2	1738	1.2	2312	5.5	
22	M	0554	1.2	1126	5.5	1815	0.9	2348	5.7	
23	TU	0629	1.0	1158	5.7	1849	0.8			
24	W	0018	5.9	0703	0.9	1226	5.9	1923	0.7	○
25	TH	0045	6.0	0738	0.8	1254	6.0	1959	0.6	
26	F	0114	6.1	0814	0.7	1325	6.1	2036	0.6	
27	SA	0147	6.1	0851	0.7	1400	6.1	2113	0.7	
28	SU	0222	6.0	0929	0.8	1438	6.1	2151	0.8	
29	M	0303	5.9	1008	0.9	1523	5.9	2232	1.0	
30	TU	0350	5.6	1053	1.1	1618	5.7	2320	1.3	
31	W	0455	5.3	1148	1.3	1730	5.4			◑

NOVEMBER

Date	Day	Time	m	Time	m	Time	m	Time	m	Moon
1	TH	0024	1.5	0609	5.1	1303	1.5	1848	5.2	
2	F	0150	1.7	0733	5.0	1430	1.4	2022	5.2	
3	SA	0315	1.6	0904	5.1	1550	1.2	2139	5.5	
4	SU	0429	1.3	1008	5.5	1659	0.9	2235	5.8	
5	M	0529	1.0	1058	5.8	1753	0.6	2322	6.0	
6	TU	0617	0.9	1139	5.9	1838	0.5			
7	W	0001	6.1	0659	0.8	1215	6.1	1919	0.5	●
8	TH	0037	6.1	0737	0.8	1252	6.1	1958	0.6	
9	F	0113	6.1	0815	0.8	1330	6.1	2034	0.7	
10	SA	0150	6.0	0851	0.8	1408	6.1	2110	0.8	
11	SU	0227	5.9	0928	0.9	1446	5.9	2145	1.0	
12	M	0303	5.7	1003	1.1	1524	5.7	2219	1.2	
13	TU	0340	5.5	1040	1.3	1606	5.4	2256	1.5	
14	W	0422	5.2	1119	1.5	1655	5.1	2339	1.8	
15	TH	0516	4.9	1207	1.7	1757	4.8			◐
16	F	0034	2.0	0622	4.7	1310	1.9	1908	4.7	
17	SA	0149	2.1	0737	4.6	1436	1.9	2027	4.7	
18	SU	0317	1.9	0854	4.8	1553	1.6	2136	5.0	
19	M	0422	1.6	0956	5.1	1649	1.3	2227	5.3	
20	TU	0511	1.4	1042	5.4	1735	1.1	2308	5.6	
21	W	0553	1.1	1120	5.6	1815	0.9	2343	5.8	
22	TH	0632	1.0	1153	5.8	1853	0.7			
23	F	0015	6.0	0711	0.8	1226	6.0	1933	0.7	○
24	SA	0049	6.1	0751	0.7	1303	6.1	2014	0.6	
25	SU	0127	6.1	0833	0.7	1345	6.2	2056	0.7	
26	M	0210	6.1	0916	0.7	1430	6.2	2140	0.8	
27	TU	0257	5.9	1001	0.7	1521	6.0	2226	1.0	
28	W	0350	5.7	1051	0.9	1619	5.8	2318	1.2	
29	TH	0449	5.5	1147	1.1	1722	5.6			
30	F	0021	1.4	0553	5.3	1255	1.2	1832	5.4	◑

DECEMBER

Date	Day	Time	m	Time	m	Time	m	Time	m	Moon
1	SA	0135	1.5	0709	5.1	1411	1.2	1958	5.3	
2	SU	0250	1.5	0834	5.2	1524	1.1	2112	5.4	
3	M	0401	1.4	0938	5.4	1632	1.0	2210	5.6	
4	TU	0503	1.2	1031	5.6	1730	0.8	2259	5.7	
5	W	0555	1.1	1116	5.7	1817	0.8	2341	5.8	
6	TH	0638	1.0	1156	5.8	1859	0.8			
7	F	0018	5.9	0718	0.9	1235	5.9	1937	0.8	●
8	SA	0056	5.9	0756	0.8	1314	6.0	2013	0.9	
9	SU	0133	5.9	0833	0.8	1352	5.9	2049	0.9	
10	M	0209	5.8	0909	0.9	1429	5.8	2123	1.1	
11	TU	0243	5.7	0944	1.0	1505	5.7	2158	1.2	
12	W	0319	5.6	1019	1.1	1544	5.5	2233	1.4	
13	TH	0358	5.4	1055	1.3	1627	5.3	2311	1.6	
14	F	0443	5.1	1134	1.5	1718	5.1	2355	1.7	
15	SA	0537	4.9	1223	1.6	1816	4.9			◐
16	SU	0049	1.8	0638	4.8	1323	1.7	1919	4.8	
17	M	0159	1.9	0743	4.8	1441	1.6	2025	4.9	
18	TU	0318	1.7	0850	4.9	1552	1.5	2129	5.1	
19	W	0421	1.5	0949	5.2	1650	1.2	2223	5.4	
20	TH	0514	1.3	1039	5.5	1740	1.0	2309	5.6	
21	F	0602	1.1	1123	5.7	1827	0.8	2350	5.8	
22	SA	0648	0.9	1205	6.0	1912	0.7			○
23	SU	0032	6.0	0733	0.7	1249	6.1	1957	0.6	
24	M	0116	6.1	0820	0.5	1336	6.2	2044	0.6	
25	TU	0202	6.1	0907	0.5	1425	6.2	2132	0.7	
26	W	0251	6.0	0956	0.5	1517	6.1	2220	0.8	
27	TH	0342	5.9	1046	0.6	1609	6.0	2311	1.0	
28	F	0434	5.7	1139	0.7	1705	5.7			
29	SA	0006	1.2	0530	5.5	1237	0.9	1807	5.5	◑
30	SU	0107	1.4	0635	5.3	1342	1.1	1922	5.3	
31	M	0214	1.5	0752	5.2	1449	1.1	2036	5.2	

Chart Datum is 2·69 metres below IGN Datum. HAT is 6·4 metres above Chart Datum.

N France

9.17.7 DUNKERQUE (PORT EST)

Nord **51°03'·62N 02°21'·09E** ✿✿✿♪♪♪✿✿

CHARTS AC 323, 1872, 1350, 5605.11; SHOM 6651, 7057; Navi 1010; Imray C30

TIDES Dunkerque is a Standard Port (⟵). +0050 Dover; ML 3·2; Duration 0530. See Gravelines for Dunkerque Port Ouest.

SHELTER Good; access at all tides/weather, but fresh NW–NE winds cause heavy seas at ent and scend in hbr.

NAVIGATION Yachts must not use the W Port. From the east, WPT 51°04'·29N 02°21'·72E (SCM lt buoy) 210°/0·8M to hbr ent. From Nieuwpoort Bank WCM lt buoy, the E1-12 buoys (Lights, buoys and waypoints) lead S of Banc Hills but shore lights make navlights and shipping hard to see. Avoid very large ships manoeuvring into/out of Charles de Gaulle lock.

From the west, WPT 51°03'·83N 02°20'·25E (DW29 lt buoy) 111°/0·6M to hbr ent. Fetch Dyck PHM buoy, 5M N of Calais, thence to DKA SWM buoy, and via DW channel lt buoys past W Port to WPT. Streams reach about 3½kn.

LIGHTS AND MARKS A chimney (116m) 1M WSW of hbr ent and other industrial structures are conspic. The W jetty lt ho is a distinctive, brown brick twr, green top. The E jetty lt pylon is small, slender and less obvious; the jetty covers at HW but is lit by 9 bright sodiums. The ldg lts, W cols, R tops, and the tall lt ho, W tr with B top, lead 137°/1M towards the marinas. (The F Vi(olet) 179° and 185° ldg lts define big ship turning circles.)

IPTS (full) E jetty head and seaward of Port du Grand Large.

Lock Enter Trystram lock (5m) for marinas in Bassin du Commerce and Bassin de la Marine via 3 bridges: (a) at S end of the lock; (b) at SE side of Darse No 1; and (c) at ent to Bassin du Commerce.

The daily schedule (1 Apr–3 Sep, 7/7, LT) for lock and bridges is:

Outward
Bridges (c) and (b) both open 0815, 1045, 1415, 1615, 1830.
Bridge (a) and lock open 0850, 1105, 1435, 1635, 1900.

Inward
Lock opens 1020, 1530, 1830, 2100. Bridge (a) opens 30 mins later. Bridges (b) and (c) open 20 mins after (a); the 1110 opening is only on Sat/Sun.

Lock/bridge, light and sound signals: ● ● = No entry
2 long blasts = Request open lock or bridge
● + Fl ● = Standby to secure on the side of the Fl ●
● + Fl ● = Enter lock and secure on side of the Fl ●

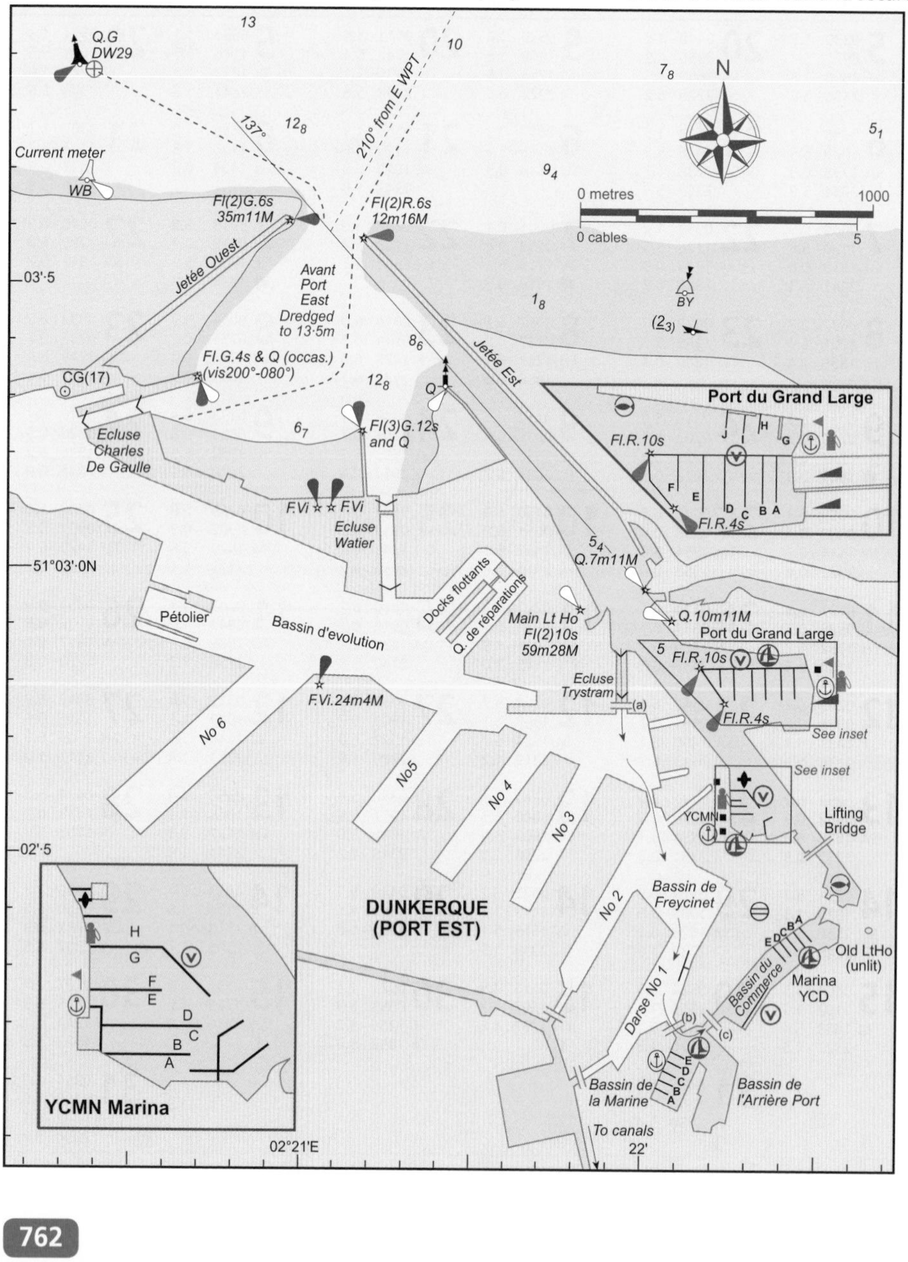

COMMUNICATIONS Monitor *Dunkerque VTS* Ch **73** (H24) for traffic info (English spoken); CROSS 03·21·87·21·87, VHF Ch 16; ⛅ 03·28·66·45·25; Auto 08·92·68·08·59; Police 03·28·59·13·22; ⊖ 03·28·29·25·50; Brit Consul 01·44·51·31·00; H 03·28·66·70·01; HM 03·28·28·75·96. www.portdedunkerque.fr Port Control 03·28·28·78·78; Aff Mar 03·28·63·13·93; Locks VHF Ch 14. Marinas VHF Ch 09.

FACILITIES from seaward: The 3 *marinas are municipal and ⓥ berths are at different rates; all on the same website www.dunkerque-marina.com

***Port du Grand Large** H24 access (3m). ☎03.28.63.23.00. 315+25ⓥ €2·40. (0800-1200, 1400-1830 daily) (30t) ✕ YC.

YC Mer du Nord (YCMN) ☎ 03·28·66·79·90. 250+50ⓥ €2·40 plus €0·20 pp/day tax, €1·00. H24 access (3m). secreteriat@ycmn.com www.ycmn.com 0800-1200, 1400-1800 daily, ✕ wi-fi (7t).

***Bassin de la Marine** 170 incⓥ €2·40. ☎03·28·24·58·80. Access to/from canals via lock at SW end of Darse No 1.

***Bassin du Commerce** 140+30ⓥ €1·90. Quai des Hollandais (SE bank pontoon) €1·15. YC de Dunkerque (YCD) marina (5m) ☎03.28.21.13.77.

Town ✕ SHOM Ⓔ ✉ Ⓑ ⇄ ✈ (Lille). Vehicle ferry (no foot passengers) to Dover.

9.17.8 GRAVELINES

Nord **51°00'·94N 02°05'·55E** ✿✿✿✿✿

CHARTS AC 323, 5605.11, 1350; SHOM 6651, 7057; Navi 1010

TIDES HW +0045 on Dover (UT); ML 3·3m; Duration 0520

Standard Port DUNKERQUE (⟵)

Times				**Height (metres)**			
High Water		Low Water		MHWS	MHWN	MLWN	MLWS
0200	0800	0200	0900	6·0	5·0	1·5	0·6
1400	2000	1400	2100				
Differences GRAVELINES (3M SW of Dunkerque Ouest)							
−0010	−0015	−0010	−0005	+0·5	+0·3	+1·0	0·0
DUNKERQUE PORT OUEST (3M ENE of Gravelines)							
−0010	−0015	−0010	−0005	+0·4	+0·3	0·0	0·0

SHELTER Good, but do not enter in strong winds. Appr chan has only 0·5m at LWS. Access approx HW ±3 for shoal draft, ±2 if draft >1·5m; max draft 2·5m. For a first visit HW is recommended.

In strong NE or SW winds the ancient, manually operated bridge over the entry gate cannot be swung, stopping entry and exit to/from the basin.

NAVIGATION WPT 51°01'·30N 02°05'·13E, 142°/0·43M to bkwtr heads; old lt ho (unlit, conspic B/W spiral) in transit with wine-glass shaped water twr 142°. Beware strong E-going stream across ent near HW.

There is often a dredger working at entrance. Do not cut between the E bkwtr head and a NCM lt bcn close N of it.

The approach chan dries to soft mud, all but a trickle; it is about 15m wide and marked by lateral dolphins. Keep to the W on entry and to the E when inside. 650m before the ent to Bassin Vauban the chan turns 60° stbd.

Use pontoon (waiting only) on port hand side of approach to ent, the entry gate into the marina stays open approx HW ±3 in season, HW ±1½ out of season. A digital gauge shows depth over the sill which dries 0·6m. Ⓥ berth to stbd.

The River Aa, pronounced Ar-Ar, flows through the Bassin via sluice gates upstream which are usually shut.

LIGHTS AND MARKS Lts as chartlet and Lights, buoys and waypoints. A nuclear power stn with 6 towers (63m) is 1M NE. 1·8M further NE is the ent to Dunkerque Ouest, commercial & ferry port.

The disused lt ho, with continuous black and white spiral band, is very distinctive. The W bkwtr lt shows an approach lt across a sector of arc 139° (085°-224°) G landwards.

COMMUNICATIONS 08·92·68·02·59; Police 03·28·23·15·17/ 03·28·24·56·45; Brit Consul 01·44·51·31·00; Aff Mar 03·28·26·73·00. Entry gate 03·28·23·13·42, VHF Ch 09 (HO); Marina VHF Ch 09 (HO); Tourist Office 03·28·51·94·00.

FACILITIES

Bassin Vauban General Council Harbour Office, ☎03·28·65·45·24. port.de.plaisance.gravelines@wanadoo.fr www.portvaubangravelines.com M-F 0800-1200, 1345-1715, 430+20Ⓥ, €1·90. Max LOA 15m, max beam for entry gate 9·8m. ✕ free wi-fi, bike/car hire. Large well equipped (10t, 3t) (7t).

Berth on Ⓥ pontoon No 1, first to stbd, or as directed. The marina almost dries, but fin keelers sink upright into soft, glorious mud. It may be advisable to close the engine cooling water seacock after shutting down and to clean the water strainer thereafter.

Town (H24 Super-U 600m) ✕ Ⓑ ⇄.

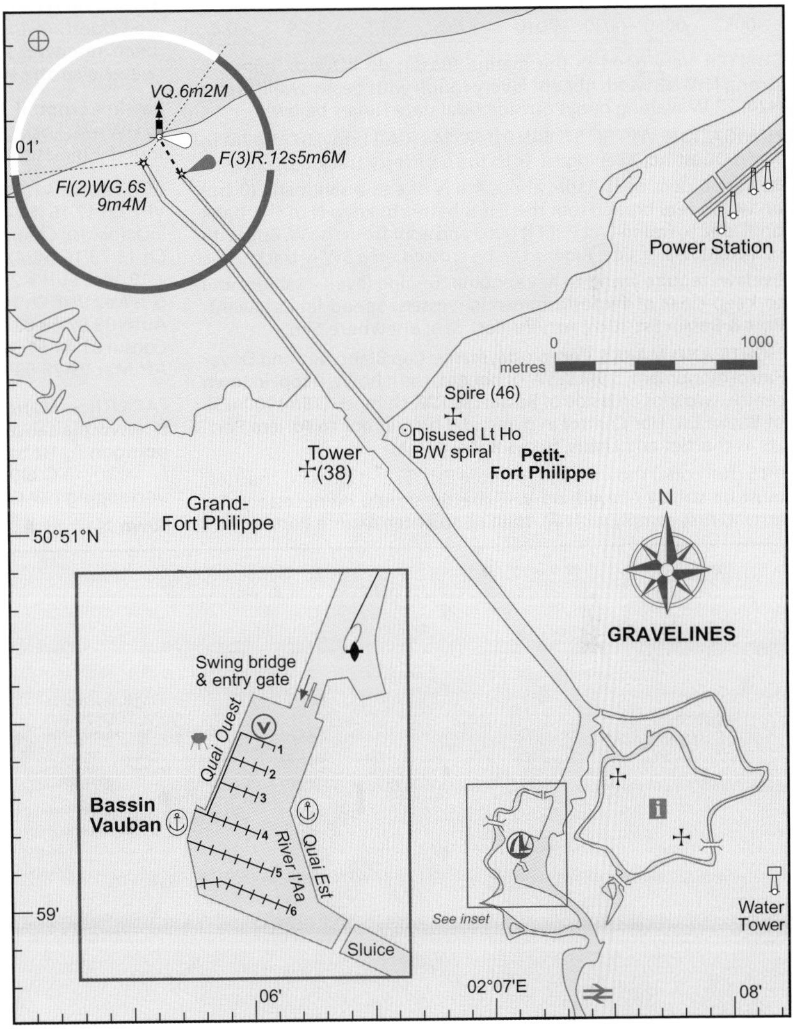

9.17.9 CALAIS

Pas de Calais **50°58'·33N 01°50'·42E**

CHARTS AC 1892, 323, 1351, 5605.10; SHOM 7323, 6651, 7258; Navi 1010; Imray C8

TIDES +0048 Dover; ML 4·0; Duration 0525

Standard Port DUNKERQUE (⟵)

Times				**Height (metres)**			
High Water		Low Water		MHWS	MHWN	MLWN	MLWS
0200	0800	0200	0900	6·0	5·0	1·5	0·6
1400	2000	1400	2100				
Differences *CALAIS*							
–0020	*–0030*	*–0015*	*–0005*	*+1·3*	*+1·0*	*+0·5*	*+0·2*
SANDETTIE BANK (11M N of Calais)							
–0010	–0015	–0015	–0010	–0·6	–0·6	–0·2	–0·1
WISSANT (8M WSW of Calais)							
–0035	–0050	–0030	–0010	+2·0	+1·5	+0·9	+0·4

SHELTER Very good in the marina (Bassin de l'Ouest, 3-6m). In strong NW-NE winds hbr ent is very rough with heavy swell; access H24. 22 W waiting buoys outside tidal gate (times below).

NAVIGATION WPT 50°57'·64N 01°46'·14E (CA 1 buoy) 077°/2·7M to Jetée Ouest hd, keeping clear to the S of ferry track 083°/263°.

Beware Ridens de la Rade, about 4ca N of ent, a sandbank (0·1m) on which seas break. From the E it is better to keep N of this bank until able to round CA4 PHM lt buoy and appr from the W. But, with sufficient rise of tide, Ridens can be crossed on a SW'ly track.

Byelaws require yachts to have engine running (even if sailing) and to keep clear of ferries/commercial vessels. Speed limits: Avant-Port & Bassin Est 10kn; Arrière-Port 8kn; elsewhere 5kn.

LIGHTS AND MARKS Conspic daymarks: Cap Blanc-Nez and Dover Patrol monument, 5·5M WSW of hbr ent; the lt ho(W, B top) in town centre; two silos on N side of Bassin Est; R/W chimney (78m) 700m SE of Bassin Est; Hbr Control in pyramidal bldg at ent to Arrière Port. Lts as chartlet and Lights, buoys & waypoints.

IPTS (full code) shown from Ⓐ (Jetée Est) Ⓑ and Ⓒ as on chartlet, must be strictly obeyed; no VHF chatter should be necessary. On arrival, first comply with Ⓐ, then Ⓑ to enter Arrière Port.

If no sigs are shown (ie no ferries under way) yachts may enter/exit. Or follow a ferry entering, keeping to the stbd side of the fairway and not impeding said ferry. Keep a very sharp lookout, especially for ferries closing fast from astern.

One ● (alongside lowest IPTS lt) = dredger working.

On leaving, first comply with Ⓒ, then Ⓑ, Ⓐ for seaward. Yachts are often cleared outward as a convoy; monitor Ch 17.

Bassin de l'Ouest (marina). 17m wide entry gate (sill 2m above CD) stays open HW –2 to +2½. Gate signals:

●	=	All movements prohib.
●	=	10 mins before gate opens.
●	=	Movement authorised.
4 blasts	=	Request permission to enter.

The co-located Hénon swing bridge opens at HW –2, –1, HW, +1¼, +2½. Times are usually strictly observed. The monthly schedule is posted on www.plaisance-opale.com. The lock gates to Bassin de l'Ouest, giving access to the marina, are reported as having been removed until further notice. A gauge shows depth of water over the sill.

Bassin Carnot: If bound for the canals, lock gates open HW –1½ to HW +¾. Lock sigs are as per the CEVNI code. Call VHF Ch 17 or sound 2 blasts to request permission to enter.

COMMUNICATIONS Whilst underway in apprs and hbr, monitor VHF Ch **17** 16 (H24) *Calais Port Control* for VTS, marina and Carnot lock (occas); Channel Navigation Info Service (CNIS): *Gris Nez Traffic* Ch **13** 79 16 (H24). Info broadcasts in English & French Ch 79, at H + 10, also at H + 25 when vis is < 2M; CROSS 03·21·87·21·87, *CROSS Gris Nez* VHF Ch 15, 67, **68**, 73; 03·21·96·31·20; 03·21·33·24·25; Auto 08·92·68·02·62; Police 03·21·34·86·00; 03·21·34·75·40; Brit Consul 01·44·51·31·00; 03·21·46·33·33; HM (Port) 03·21·96·31·20; Aff Mar 03·28·59·19·33.

FACILITIES **Marina** ☎03·21·34·55·23 calais-marina@calais-port.fr www.plaisance-opale.com; 250 + 30 Ⓥ €2·36 Berth/raft on pontoon A, 1st to stbd, or on fingers S side of B pontoon. (9t). **YC** ☎03·21·82·28·05, www.calais-voile.fr. For mast unstepping call Calais Nautic, ☎03·21·96·07·57.

Town Ⓑ ferries to Dover.

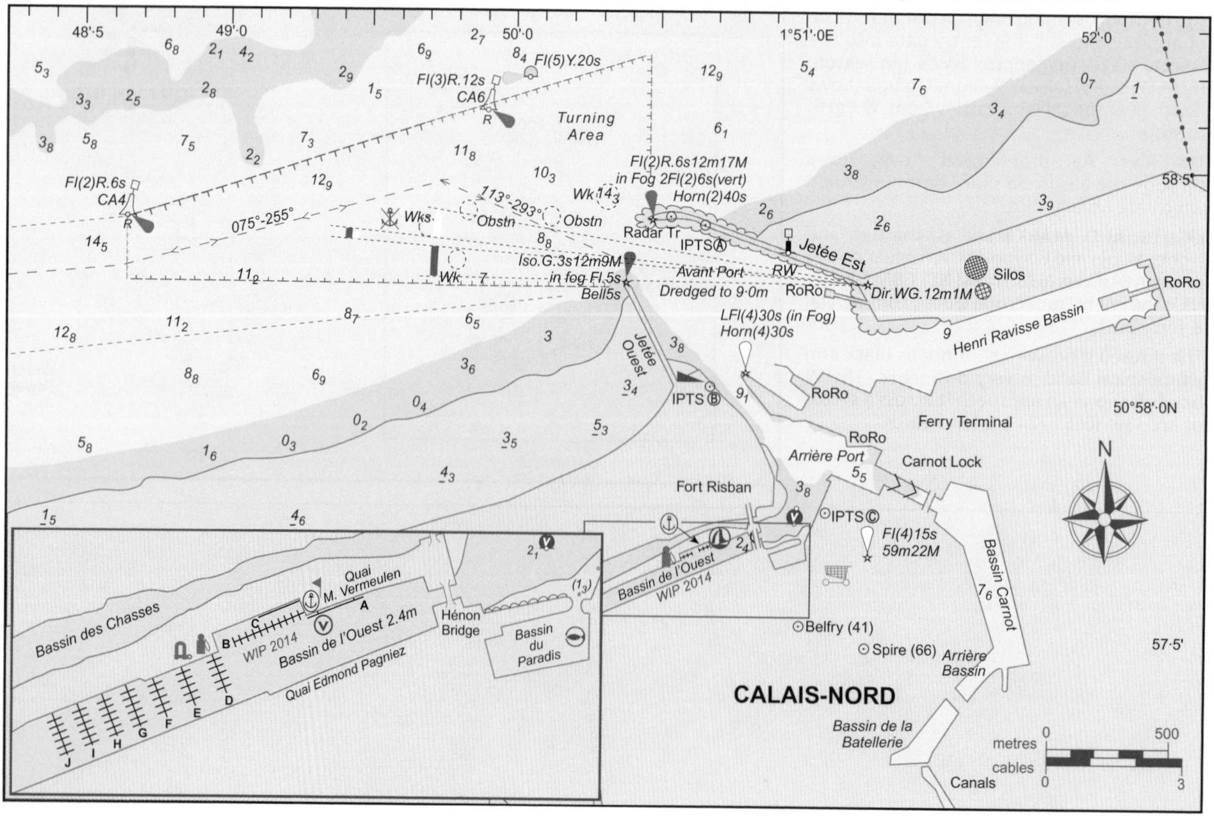

CALAIS TIDAL COEFFICIENTS 2018

Date	Jan		Feb		Mar		Apr		May		June		July		Aug		Sept		Oct		Nov		Dec	
	am	pm	am	pm	am	pm	am	pm	am	pm	am	pm	am	pm	am	pm	am	pm	am	pm	am	pm	am	pm
1	92	97	103	107	97		104	105	95	94	80	77	75	73	76	74	74	70	69	63	51	48	55	56
2	101		109	109	102	106	105	103	92	89	74	71	72	70	72	69	65	60	57	52	49	52	58	61
3	104	106	108	106	109	110	100	96	86	82	68	64	67	64	66	62	55	51	47	44	57	63	64	69
4	107	106	103	98	109	108	92	86	77	72	60	56	62	59	59	55	47	45	45	48	69	76	73	77
5	104	101	92	85	104	100	80	74	67	61	52	49	56	53	52	49	45	48	54	62	82	87	80	83
6	96	91	78	71	94	88	67	60	56	50	45	43	50	48	48	47	54	61	70	78	92	95	85	86
7	85	79	63	56	81	74	53	46	45	40	41	41	47	46	49	52	69	77	85		97		87	
8	72	65	49	43	66	58	40	35	37	34	41	44	47	50	57	64	85		92	98	99	99	87	86
9	59	54	39	36	51	44	31	29	34	35	47	52	53	58	70	78	93	99	103	106	97	95	85	83
10	49	46	35	37	38	33	30	34	39	43	57	63	63	69	85		105	108	107	108	93	89	80	78
11	44	44	40	45	30	30	39	45	49	55	69	76	75	82	92	97	111	111	106	104	84	79	74	71
12	46	49	50	55	33	37	52	59	62	68	81		87		103	106	110	108	100	95	74	68	67	63
13	52	55	60	65	43	49	65		75		87	92	93	97	109	109	104	99	89	83	62	56	58	54
14	59	63	69		55	62	72	78	81	86	96	99	101	103	109	107	92	85	75	68	50	45	50	46
15	66	69	74	78	68	74	84	89	91	96	101	102	104	105	103	98	77	69	61	53	40	35	42	40
16	72		81	84	79		93	97	99	101	101	100	103	101	92	85	61	53	46	40	33	32	38	37
17	75	77	87	88	84	88	100	101	102	102	98	94	97	93	78	70	46	39	34	30	33	36	39	41
18	79	80	90	90	92	94	102	101	100	98	90	85	88	82	62	55	34	31	29	30	40	45	45	50
19	81	81	90	89	96	98	99	96	94	90	80	75	75	69	48	43	31	33	34	39	51	57	55	61
20	81	80	87	84	98	97	92	87	84	79	69	65	63	57	39	37	38	43	45	51	63	69	67	73
21	79	77	81	77	95	92	81	75	72	67	61	58	52	49	38	40	49	55	57	63	75	81	79	85
22	75	72	72	67	88	84	68	62	62	58	56	55	47	47	44	48	61		69		85	90	89	
23	69	66	62	57	78	72	56	52	56	55	56	57	48	50	53	58	66	71	75	80	93		93	97
24	62	58	52	49	66	59	50	51	57	59	59	62	53	56	63		76	80	84	88	95	97	99	100
25	55	52	48	49	53	49	55	59	62	66	64	67	60		67	71	84	87	91	94	98	97	100	99
26	50	50	54	60	47	48	65	71	70	73	69		63	66	75	78	89	91	95	96	95	93	97	94
27	51	54	67	75	52	58	77	82	77		71	73	69	71	80	83	92	92	96	94	89	85	90	86
28	59	65	83	90	66	73	87		79	81	74	75	74	75	84	85	91	90	92	88	80	74	81	75
28	72	79			81		91	93	83	84	76	76	77	78	86	85	87	84	84	79	69	64	70	65
30	86	93			88	94	95	96	84	84	76	76	78	78	85	83	80	75	73	67	60	57	61	58
31	99				98	102			83	81			78	77	81	77			61	55			56	55

Tidal coefficients indicate the magnitude of the tide on any particular day, without having to look up and calculate the range, and thus determine whether it is springs, neaps or somewhere in between. This table is valid for all areas covered by this Almanac. Typical values are:

120	Very big spring tide
95	**Mean spring tide**
70	Average tide
45	**Mean neap tide**
20	Very small neap tide

See also coefficients for Cherbourg (p 792), St Malo (p 811), Brest (p 879) and Pointe de Grave (p 942).

9.17.10 BOULOGNE-SUR-MER

Pas de Calais 50°44'·58N 01°34'·10E (hbr ent) ❁❁◊◊✿✿

CHARTS AC 1892, 2451, 438; SHOM 6824, 7247, 7416,7323; Navi 1010, 1011; Imray C8, C31

TIDES 0000 Dover; ML 4·9; Duration 0515

Standard Port DUNKERQUE (⟵)

Times				Height (metres)			
High Water		Low Water		MHWS	MHWN	MLWN	MLWS
0200	0800	0200	0900	6·0	5·0	1·5	0·6
1400	2000	1400	2100				
Differences *BOULOGNE*							
–0045	*–0100*	*–0045*	*–0025*	*+2·8*	*+2·2*	*+1·1*	*+0·5*

SHELTER Good, except in strong NW'lies. Entry H24 at all tides and in most weather. Exposed ⚓ in N part of outer hbr; no ⚓ SW of pecked magenta line.

NAVIGATION WPT 50°44'·71N 01°33'·00E, 100°/0·71M to hbr ent. No navigational dangers, but keep W and S of the free-standing head of Digue Nord, as outer part of bkwtr covers at HW. After rounding Digue Carnot, head S for 325m to a white □ mark (often faded) on bkwtr, thence track 123° to inner ent; caution drying banks on either side. Obey IPTS; keep clear of FVs. Yachts must call Port Ctrl, VHF Ch 12, on entry and departure.

LIGHTS AND MARKS 'Approches Boulogne' SCM buoy is 295°/ 2·1M from Digue Carnot lt. Cap d'Alprech lt ho is 2·5M S of hbr ent. Monument is conspic 2M E of hbr ent. Cathedral dome is conspic, 0·62M E of marina. There are no ldg lts/marks.

IPTS are shown from SW jetty hd (FG ☆) and from Quai Gambetta, opposite ☆ 3FG ▽, visible from marina. A Y lt ● by top IPTS = dredger working, but does not prohibit movements.

COMMUNICATIONS CROSS 03·21·87·21·87; ☁ 08·92·68·02·62; Auto 08·92·65·08·08; Forecasts by CROSS Gris Nez VHF Ch 79 at H+10 (078-1910LT); Maritime Police 03·21·30·87·09; Emergency 17; ⊖ 03·21·80·89·90; Brit Consul 01·44·51·31·00; 🄷 03·21·99·33·33; AffMar 03·21·30·53·23; Dr 03·21·71·33·33; Controltwr 03·21·10·35·47, VHF Ch 12 (H24); Lock into Bassin Napoléon VHF Ch 12 (H24); Marina Ch 09.

FACILITIES Visitors berth in marina (2·7m) on W side of river. FVs berth opposite at Quai Gambetta. Beware turbulence when R Liane is sluicing; indicated at night by 2 Bu lts (hor) S of marina.

Marina ☎03·21·99·66·50 www.portboulogne.com 130 inc 70Ⓥ €2·00 plus €0·20pp/day tax. ⛽ HW±3, WC(card access) Ⓔ 🔧 ⛟ ⛵ ⛴(20t). Flagler ⛿ ☎03·21·33·90·75, also for sail repairs and ⛽. YC Boulonnais ☎03·21·31·80·67, ✕ ⛟ ⛴.

Bassin Napoléon pontoons are for locals and long-stay Ⓥ (week or month; 12-25m LOA) by arrangement. Sanson lock (Ch 12) works HW–3¼ to HW+4½ with ent/exits approx every 35 mins, and freeflow HW –2 to +¼. Daily schedules from HM or website.

Town ✕ ⛟ 🛒 ⛿ SHOM ✉ Ⓑ ⥱ ✈ Le Touquet.

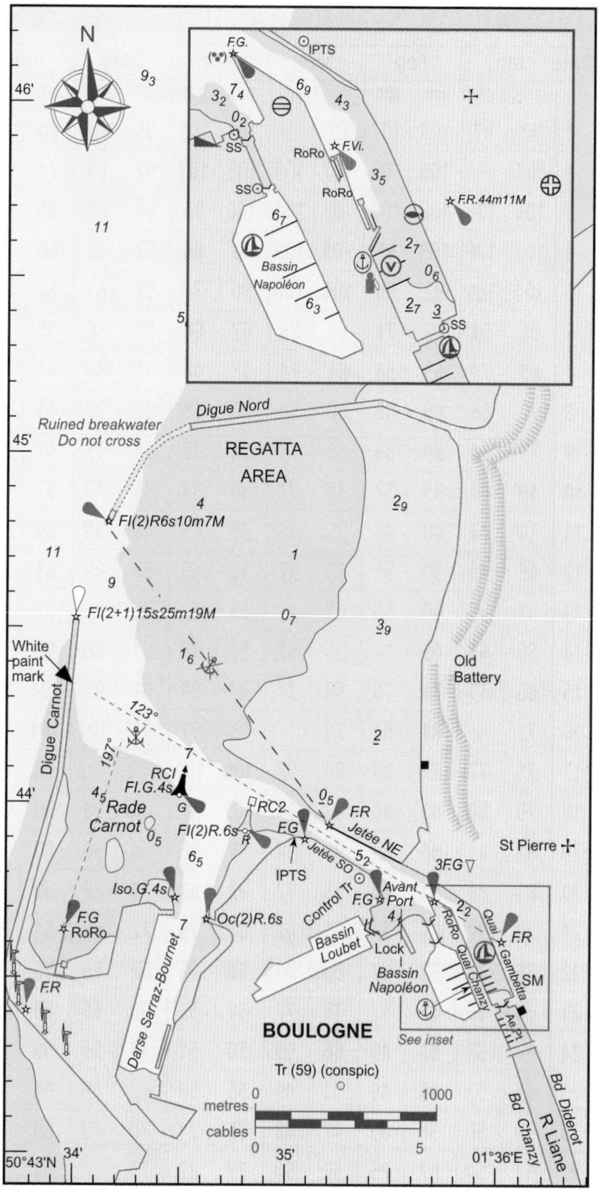

9.17.11 ÉTAPLES

Pas de Calais **50°31'·00N 01°38'·00E** ❁❁◊◊✿✿

CHARTS AC 2451; SHOM 7416; Navi 1011; Imray C31

TIDES –0010 Dover; ML 5·3; Duration 0520

Standard Port DIEPPE (⟶)

Times				Height (metres)			
High Water		Low Water		MHWS	MHWN	MLWN	MLWS
0100	0600	0100	0700	9·3	7·4	2·5	0·8
1300	1800	1300	1900				
Differences LE TOUQUET (ÉTAPLES)							
+0010	+0015	+0030	+0030	+0·2	+0·2	+0·3	+0·4
BERCK							
+0005	+0015	+0025	+0030	+0·4	+0·5	+0·3	+0·4

SHELTER Good, except in strong W/NW'lies.

NAVIGATION WPT 50°32'·88N 01°32'·36E is on the boundary between W and G sectors of Camiers lt; 090°/0·7M to Mérida unlit

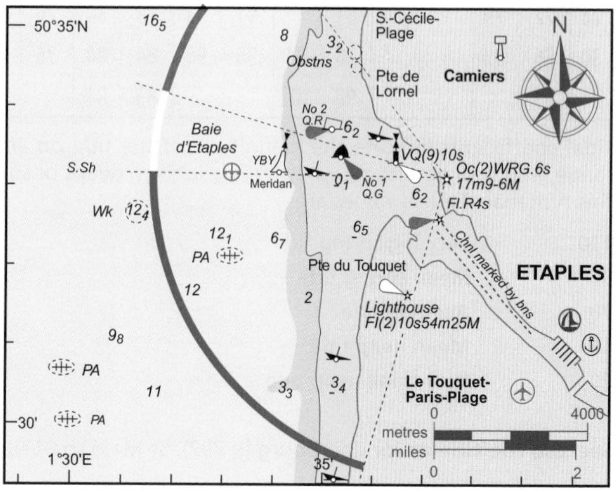

ÉTAPLES *continued*

WCM buoy (50°32'·88N 01°33'·47E) marking a drying wreck 2M NW of Le Touquet lt ho. Estuary dries 1M offshore; do not attempt entry in even moderate SW/W winds, when seas break heavily a long way out. Careful identification of marks is essential.

The outer part of the buoyed chan constantly shifts, such that the chan ent may lie N or S of the ⊕. Nos 1 & 2 buoys (QG and QR) should be visible from the WPT. Bcn, Fl R 4s, 4ca SW of Camiers lt, marks NE end of covering training wall (also marked by posts).

LIGHTS AND MARKS See Lights, buoys and waypoints. Le Touquet is at the S end of 175m high hills, visible for 25M. Le Touquet lt ho, orange with brown band, is conspic; Camiers' R pylon is hard to see by day.

COMMUNICATIONS CROSS 03·21·87·21·87; Auto 08·36·68·08·62; ⊜ 03·21·05·01·72; Brit Consul 01·44·51·31·00; Dr 03·21·05·14·42; Aff Mar Étaples 03·21·94·61·50; HM VHF Ch 09.

FACILITIES **Marina** ☎03·21·84·54·33. cn.canche@wanadoo.fr 182 + 18Ⓥ €2·04. (1·2m) close downriver of low bridge; beware up to 5kn current. Best to berth on first pontoon hammerhead near HW slack. (8t); Quay (130t). **YC** ☎03.21.94.74.26.

Town Le Touquet.

Le Touquet Drying moorings to stbd off Le Touquet YC. VHF Ch 09, 77. **Cercle Nautique du Touquet** ☎03·21·05·12·77. **Services** . **Town** .

9.17.12 ST VALÉRY-SUR-SOMME

Somme **50°11'·34N 01°38'·90E**

CHARTS AC 2451; SHOM 7416; Navi 1011; Imray C31

TIDES LE HOURDEL –0010 Dover; ML —.

Standard Port DIEPPE (⟶)

Times				**Height (metres)**			
High Water		Low Water		MHWS	MHWN	MLWN	MLWS
0100	0600	0100	0700	9·3	7·4	2·5	0·8
1300	1800	1300	1900				
Differences ST VALÉRY-SUR-SOMME							
+0035	+0035	ND	ND	+0·9	+0·7	ND	ND
LE HOURDEL							
+0020	+0020	ND	ND	+0·8	+0·6	ND	ND
CAYEUX							
+0000	+0005	+0015	+0010	+0·5	+0·6	+0·4	+0·4

SHELTER The 3 hbrs (Le Hourdel, Le Crotoy and St Valéry-sur-Somme) are well sheltered.

NAVIGATION WPT 50°14'·00N 01°28'·08E ('ATSO' SWM buoy, Mo (A) 12s). The estuary dries up to 3M seaward of Le Hourdel. It is open to the W and can be dangerous in onshore winds >F6. Silting is a major problem. The sands build up in ridges offshore, but inside Pte du Hourdel are mostly flat, except where R Somme and minor streams scour their way to the sea. If Dover tidal range >4·4m, there is enough water at HW ±1 for vessels <1·5m draft.

Leave 'ATSO' buoy at HW St Valéry –2, then head SE twds R/W lt ho on dunes near Cayeux-sur-Mer to beginning of buoyed chan (S1) Follow chan buoys S1 to S50 (some lit) in strict order (no corner-cutting!) to small unlit WCM BIFurcation buoy, E of Pte du Hourdel. Here fork stbd to St Valéry and its covering training wall with four light beacons; as chartlet and Lights, buoys & waypoints. Continue between the tree-lined promenade to stbd and a covering dyke marked by PHM bns. Bias your track towards the town side, but comply with any buoys. At W lt bcn on head of Digue du Nord turn stbd past town quay into marina, dredged 2m. Enter St Valéry Marina (max draft 2·0m) at HW ±1; usually met and given a berth on pontoons 4–6. If N-bound leave St Valéry HW–2 for a fair tide.

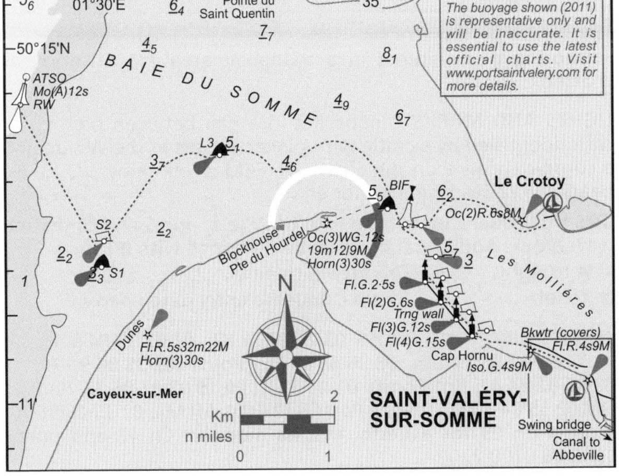

Abbeville Canal (max draft 2·0m) is navigable, by day only, to Abbeville. Lock 03·22·60·80·23; pre-call Amiens ☎06·74·83·60·69.

LIGHTS AND MARKS Cayeux-sur-Mer lt ho (W + R top, Fl R 5s) and Le Crotoy water twr are conspic. Pte du Hourdel lt ho is partly obscured by dunes until close to. See also Lights, buoys and waypoints.

COMMUNICATIONS CROSS 03·21·87·21·87; Auto 08·92·68·08·80; Police 17 or 03·22·60·82·08; ⊜ 03·22·24·04·75; British Consul 01·44·51·31·00; Dr 03·22·26·92·25; Aff Mar 03·21·30·87·19 (Boulogne); HM VHF Ch 09 (St Valéry HW ±2); Le Crotoy YC (Jul/Aug only).

FACILITIES **Marina/YC Sport Nautique Valéricain** ☎03·22·60·24·80. snval@wanadoo.fr www.portsaintvalery.com Access HW ±2 for 1·5m draft. 250 + 30Ⓥ €2·35, multihulls €2·80. (€5·00) free wi-fi, (10t).

Town (500m) and ✈ (Abbeville). **Ferry** see Dieppe, Boulogne or Calais.

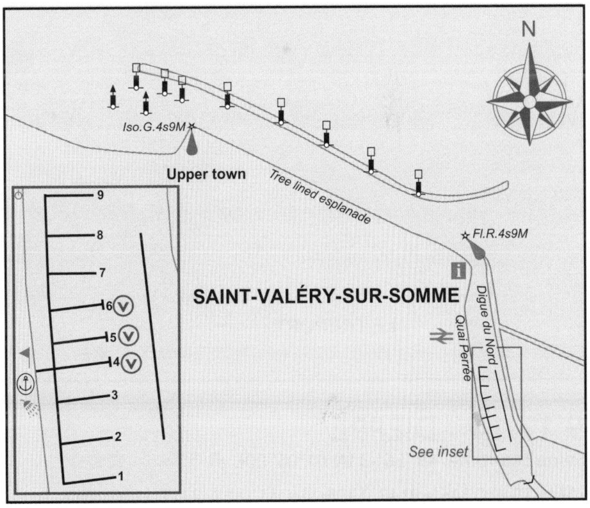

ADJACENT HARBOURS

LE HOURDEL A basic FV hbr. Access HW±1½ for 1·5m draft. After lt ho, head SW via unmarked side chan to hug the end of shingle spit. Dry out on hard sand. Impossible to leave before HW –2.

LE CROTOY Somme **50°13'·07N 01°37'·99E**
From the BIF buoy follow the chan E, marked by buoys C1-C10. Enter hbr very close to FV stages (port-side). The badly silted marina can be entered by max draft 0·8m when tidal range at Dover >4·4m (approx Coeff 85). Secure at last FV stage and ask YC for berth on the two drying pontoons. Departure impossible before HW–2. **Marina** (280) ☎03·22·27·83·11 (office in YC bldg), (6t).
YC Nautique de la Baie de Somme ☎03·22·27·83·11.
Town .

9.17.13 LE TRÉPORT

Seine Maritime **50°03'·89N 01°22'·20E**

CHARTS AC 2451, 1354; SHOM 7207, 7416, 7417; Navi 1011; Imray C31

TIDES –0025 Dover; ML 5·0; Duration 0530

Standard Port DIEPPE (⟶)

Times				**Height (metres)**			
High Water		Low Water		MHWS	MHWN	MLWN	MLWS
0100	0600	0100	0700	9·3	7·4	2·5	0·8
1300	1800	1300	1900				
Differences LE TRÉPORT							
+0005	+0000	+0005	+0015	+0·3	+0·2	+0·1	+0·1

SHELTER Good in marina, E of FVs at S side of S Basin (3·7m).

NAVIGATION WPT 50°04'·27N 01°21'·90E, 146°/0·4M to ent. Coast dries to approx 300m off the pier hds. Shingle spit extends NW from E pier hd; keep well to the W. Entry difficult in strong onshore winds which cause scend in Avant Port. Strong cross-current at entrance; 5kn speed limit. Ent chan and most of Avant Port dry; S chan is dredged $\underline{1}$·5m, but prone to silting; avoid grounding on the triangle between the two channels. Lock opens HW±4; yachts can wait against Quai Francois I with sufficient rise of tide. Berth, if possible, on smooth S wall of lock; vert wires rigged for warps. N wall is corrugated steel shuttering on which fenders can snag. Beware current when leaving.

LIGHTS AND MARKS Le Tréport lies between high chalk cliffs, with crucifix (floodlit) 101m above town and conspic church S of hbr. IPTS at the root of the E Jetty. There are 150° ldg marks, but they are hard to see and not strictly necessary.

Lock sigs shown from head of piled ent chan: 3 ● (vert) = enter; 3 ● (vert) = no entry.

COMMUNICATIONS LB 02·35·86·30·27; CROSS 03·21·87·21·87; Auto 06·70·63·43·40; Police 02·35·86·12·11; ⊖ 02·35·86·15·34; Brit Consul 01·44·51·31·00; Dr 02·35·86·16·23; Port HM 06·87·70·30·90; *Capitainerie Le Tréport* VHF Ch 12 (HW ±4) for lock/marina; Aff Mar 02·35·06·96·70.

FACILITIES **Marina/lock** ☎02·35·50·63·06. www.treport.cci.fr accueilcci@treport.cci.fr 110+15Ⓥ €2·13, Ⓔ. **Port de Commerce** is an overflow; half-price rates for yachts. (10t). **YC de la Bresle** ☎02·35·50·17·60. **Town** Ⓑ ⇌, ✈ Dieppe.

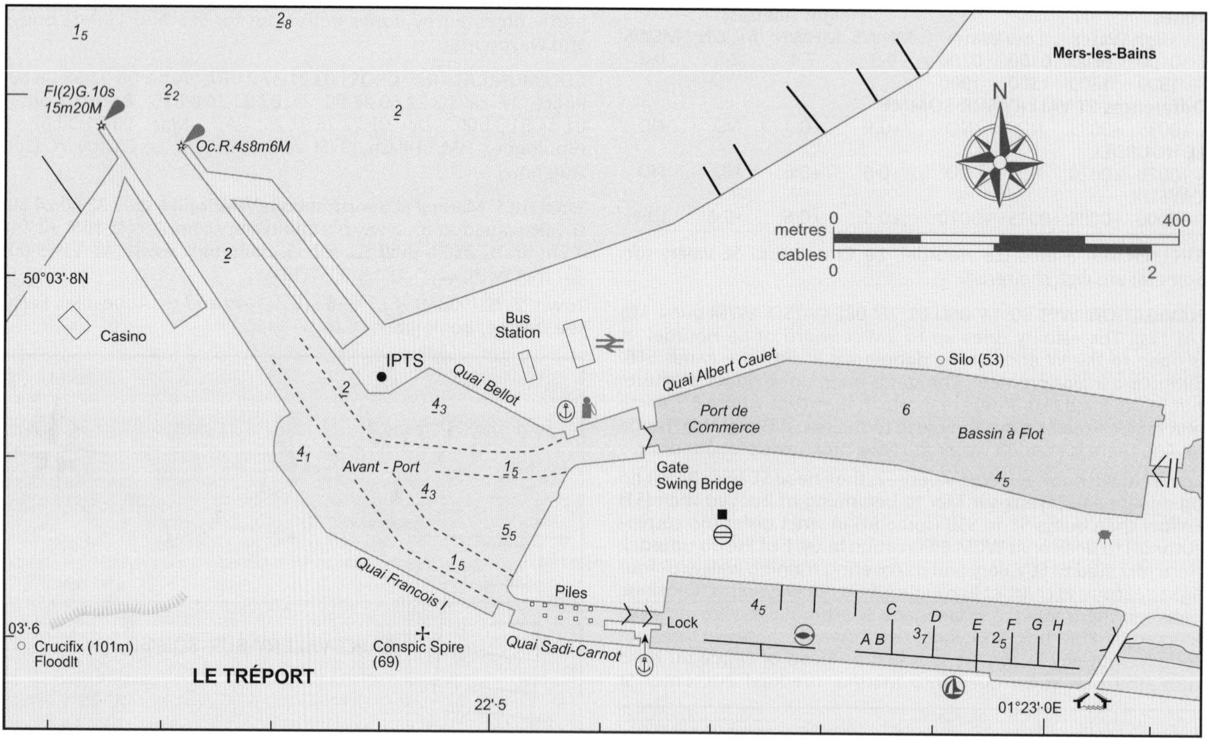

9.17.14 DIEPPE

Seine Maritime **49°56'·31N 01°05'·00E**

CHARTS AC 2451, 2148, 1355; SHOM 7417, 7317; Navi 1011, 1012; Imray C31

TIDES –0011 Dover; ML 4·9; Duration 0535; Standard Port (⟶)

SHELTER Very good. Access all tides, but ent exposed to NW-NE winds, which cause a heavy scend. A fixed wavebreak at the E end of the marina is effective. 3kn max speed in marina.

NAVIGATION WPT 49°56'·66N 01°04'·83E (off chartlet) 167°/4ca to W jetty head. Ent to hbr is simple, but beware strong stream across ent. Ent chan and Avant Port are dredged 4·5m. Be alert for ferry at the outer hbr, and small coasters or FVs in the narrow chan between outer hbr and marina.

Due to restricted visibility, monitor Ch 12 during arr/dep. It is vital to comply precisely with IPTS (below) both entering and leaving. Anchoring is prohibited in a triangular area 7ca offshore, as charted.

LIGHTS AND MARKS Dieppe lies in a gap between high chalk cliffs, identified by a castle with pinnacle roofs at the W side and a conspic ch spire on the E cliff. DI, ECM wreck buoy, VQ (3) 5s, bears 288°/2·5M from the hbr ent.

IPTS (full code) shown from root of W jetty and S end of marina wavebreak. Additional sigs may be combined with IPTS:

● to right	=	Dredger in channel.
Ⓦ to left	=	Bassin Duquesne entry gate open.

COMMUNICATIONS CROSS 03·21·87·21·87; LB 02·35·84·8·55; 03·21·31·52·23; Auto 08·36·68·08·76; Police 02·35·06·96·74; ⊖ 02·35·82·24·47; Brit Consul 01·44·51·31·00; Ⓗ 02·35·06·76·76; Port HM 02·35·84·10·55, *Dieppe Port* Ch **12** (HO); Aff Mar 02·35·06·96·70; Marina Ch 09 for a berth. Marina monitors Ch 12 and opens 1/7-24/8 0700-2200.

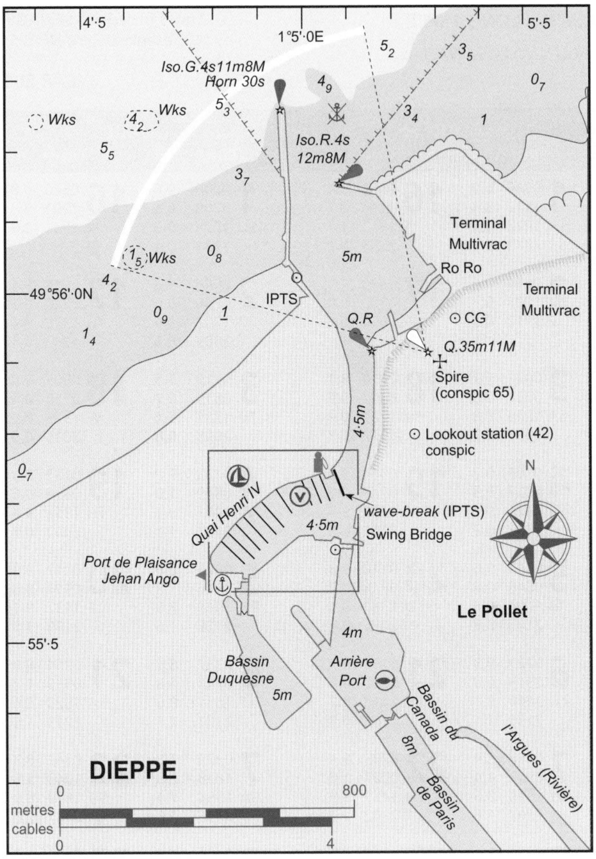

FACILITIES

Marina Jehan Ango ☎02·35·84·10·55. smpd-plaisance@portdedieppe.fr www.portdedieppe.fr 450 ⌓ inc 50Ⓥ €3·04, on pontoons 10, 9, 8 in about 4·5m but not on hammerheads. If 10 & 9 are full, late arrivals ⌓/raft on E side of pontoon 8; Pontoon 1 W side finger is for boats >14m LOA. Use gangway intercom for shore access code number (if arriving out of hrs, for code call Ch 12). cr/card H24, call Ch 09 if unmanned. Ⓔ (12t).

Cercle de la Voile de Dieppe ☎02·35·84·32·99, WC(code access).

Bassin Duquesne (70 ⌓) access via lifting bridge/entry gate, and **Bassin de Paris** (70 ⌓) are only for local yachts.

Town @ Ⓑ ⇌ ✈. Ferry Dieppe-Newhaven; www.transmancheferries.co.uk

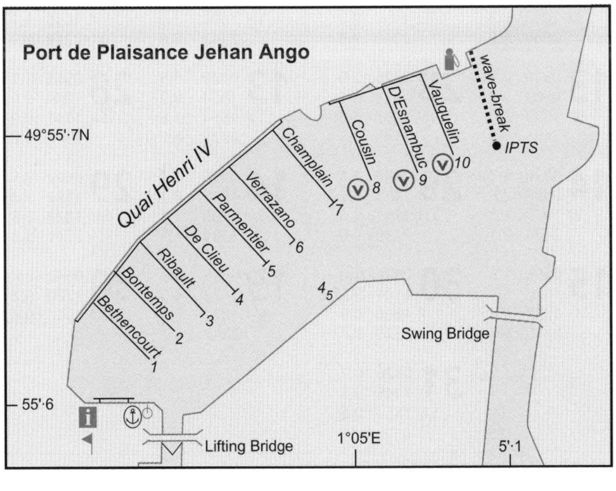

DIEPPE TO LE HAVRE

From **Dieppe** to Pte d'Ailly light house the coast (AC 2451) is fringed by a bank, drying in places, up to 4ca offshore.

▶*Off Dieppe the ENE-going stream begins about HW Dieppe –0505, and the WSW-going at about HW Dieppe +0030, sp rates 2kn. E of Pte d'Ailly an eddy runs W close inshore on the first half of the E-going stream.*◀

Drying rks extend 5ca off Pte d'Ailly, including La Galère, a rk which dries 6·8m, about 3ca N of the Pointe (AC 2147). Dangerous wrecks lie between about 1·5M NNW and 1·2M WNW of the lighthouse, the former marked by a NCM light buoy. About 6M N of Pte d'Ailly, Grands and Petits Écamias are banks with depths of 11m, dangerous in a heavy sea.

Between Pte d'Ailly and **St Valéry-en-Caux** (lighthouse) there are drying rks 4ca offshore in places. About 1·5M E of Pte de Sotteville a rocky bank (4·2m) extends about 1M NNW; a strong eddy causes a race, Raz de Saint-Michel, over this bank.

There are rky ledges, extending 4ca offshore in places. Immediately E of St Valéry-en-Caux shallow sandbanks, Les Ridens, with a least depth of 0·6m, extend about 6ca offshore.

▶*At St Valéry-en-Caux entrance the E-going stream begins about HW Dieppe –0550, and the W-going stream begins about HW Dieppe –0015, sp rates 2·75kn. E of the ent a small eddy runs W on the E-going stream.*◀

From St Valéry-en-Caux to **Fécamp**, 15M WSW, the coast consists of high, sheer chalk cliffs broken by valleys. 3M W of St Valéry-en-Caux, Paluel nuclear power station is conspicuous with the NE/NW limits of its seaward prohibited area marked by two SPM lt buoys. Close NE of Fécamp off Pte Fagnet, Les Charpentiers are unmarked drying rocks extending almost 2ca offshore.

▶*At Fécamp pierheads the NNE-going stream begins about HW Le Havre –0340, up to 2·9kn sp; the SSW-going about HW Le Havre +0220, much weaker. Diamond A on AC 1354 gives tidal stream data about 9ca WNW of the entrance.*◀

From Fécamp to Cap d'Antifer light house drying rocks extend up to 2½ca offshore. L'Aiguille, a prominent (51m) pinnacle rock is just off Étretat, 1·7M NNE of Cap d'Antifer. A large offshore wind farm (WIP 2017/18) is being built 7·5M NW of Fécamp.

Port du Havre-Antifer, a VLCC harbour lies, 1·5M S of Cap d'Antifer (AC 2146, 2990). A 2M long breakwater extends about 1·5M seaward, and should be given a berth of about 1·5M, or more in heavy weather with wind against tide when there may be a race.

The buoyed approach channel starts 11M NW of the harbour. Commercial vessels in it have priority. Yachts should cross it 3·8M to the NW at A17/A18 lt buoys; at 90° to its axis; as quickly as possible, keeping well clear of ships in the channel. Crossing vessels should contact *Le Havre d'Antifer* and any priority vessel on VHF Ch 22.

▶*Off Cap d'Antifer the NE-going stream begins about HW Le Havre –0430, and the SW-going at about HW Le Havre +0140. There are eddies close inshore E of Cap d'Antifer on both streams.*◀

Le Havre is a large commercial port, as well as a yachting centre. From the NW, the most useful mark is the Le Havre Lanby 'LHA' 9M W of C de la Hève (lt). The well-buoyed/lit access channel runs 6M ESE from LH 3/4 buoys to the hbr ent.

Strong W'lies cause rough water over shoal patches either side of the channel. Coming from the N or NE, there is deep water close off C de la Hève, but from here steer S to join the main ent chan. Beware Banc de l'Éclat (1·0m) which lies on N side of main channel near LH 14 buoy about 1·5M from harbour entrance.

W and S of Digue Sud yachts should not impede vessels entering/leaving Port 2000, a container terminal. If inbound to the marina it is best to cross early to the N side of the channel.

STANDARD TIME UT –01
Subtract 1 hour for UT
For French Summer Time add ONE hour in **non-shaded areas**

DIEPPE LAT 49°56′N LONG 1°05′E

TIMES AND HEIGHTS OF HIGH AND LOW WATERS

Dates in red are SPRINGS
Dates in blue are NEAPS

YEAR **2018**

JANUARY

Date	Time	m	Date	Time	m
1	0517 1045 M 1749 2313	1.1 9.3 0.8 9.3	16	0557 1123 TU 1819 2344	1.7 8.6 1.4 8.6
2	0613 1136 TU 1844 ○	0.8 9.6 0.5	17	0635 1158 W 1856 ●	1.5 8.8 1.3
3	0005 0706 W 1226 1936	9.6 0.7 9.7 0.4	18	0018 0710 TH 1233 1931	8.7 1.4 8.9 1.2
4	0054 0757 TH 1315 2025	9.7 0.6 9.8 0.4	19	0052 0744 F 1307 2004	8.8 1.4 8.9 1.2
5	0143 0844 F 1403 2111	9.6 0.7 9.6 0.6	20	0126 0817 SA 1341 2036	8.8 1.4 8.9 1.2
6	0230 0929 SA 1449 2155	9.4 1.0 9.3 0.9	21	0200 0850 SU 1415 2109	8.8 1.5 8.7 1.3
7	0317 1013 SU 1536 2237	9.0 1.3 8.8 1.3	22	0234 0923 M 1451 2143	8.6 1.6 8.5 1.5
8	0404 1057 M 1625 ◑ 2321	8.5 1.8 8.3 1.8	23	0311 1000 TU 1530 2220	8.4 1.8 8.2 1.8
9	0454 1146 TU 1718	8.1 2.2 7.8	24	0352 1043 W 1614 ◐ 2305	8.1 2.1 7.9 2.0
10	0012 0551 W 1243 1822	2.2 7.6 2.5 7.4	25	0440 1135 TH 1710	7.9 2.3 7.7
11	0112 0659 TH 1350 1936	2.5 7.4 2.6 7.2	26	0001 0543 F 1239 1824	2.2 7.7 2.4 7.5
12	0221 0813 F 1501 2047	2.6 7.4 2.5 7.4	27	0112 0705 SA 1400 1948	2.3 7.7 2.3 7.7
13	0330 0915 SA 1604 2144	2.4 7.7 2.2 7.7	28	0236 0824 SU 1522 2101	2.1 8.0 1.9 8.1
14	0428 1005 SU 1655 2229	2.2 8.0 1.9 8.0	29	0353 0931 M 1631 2205	1.7 8.5 1.3 8.7
15	0515 1046 M 1739 2308	1.9 8.4 1.6 8.3	30	0458 1031 TU 1734 2302	1.3 9.0 0.9 9.1
			31	0559 1126 W 1832 ○ 2355	0.9 9.4 0.5 9.5

FEBRUARY

Date	Time	m	Date	Time	m
1	0655 1216 TH 1926	0.6 9.7 0.3	16	0653 1215 F 1914	1.3 9.0 1.0
2	0043 0746 F 1303 2013	9.7 0.5 9.8 0.2	17	0034 0728 SA 1249 1948	9.0 1.1 9.1 0.9
3	0128 0832 SA 1347 2056	9.7 0.5 9.7 0.3	18	0107 0802 SU 1323 2021	9.1 1.0 9.2 0.8
4	0211 0912 SU 1429 2134	9.6 0.7 9.5 0.7	19	0141 0835 M 1357 2053	9.1 1.0 9.1 0.9
5	0252 0949 M 1509 2208	9.2 1.1 9.1 1.1	20	0215 0909 TU 1432 2126	9.0 1.1 8.9 1.1
6	0331 1022 TU 1550 2241	8.8 1.5 8.5 1.6	21	0250 0943 W 1509 2159	8.8 1.4 8.7 1.4
7	0412 1059 W 1633 ◑ 2319	8.2 2.0 7.9 2.2	22	0327 1021 TH 1550 2239	8.5 1.6 8.3 1.7
8	0457 1146 TH 1725	7.6 2.5 7.3	23	0411 1107 F 1641 ◐ 2331	8.2 2.0 7.9 2.1
9	0010 0557 F 1249 1837	2.7 7.1 2.8 6.8	24	0509 1208 SA 1752	7.7 2.3 7.5
10	0120 0717 SA 1408 2004	3.0 6.9 2.9 6.8	25	0041 0633 SU 1330 1925	2.4 7.5 2.4 7.5
11	0243 0839 SU 1526 2115	2.9 7.1 2.6 7.2	26	0211 0804 M 1502 2048	2.4 7.7 2.0 7.9
12	0356 0939 M 1628 2206	2.6 7.6 2.2 7.7	27	0336 0920 TU 1617 2156	1.9 8.2 1.5 8.5
13	0451 1025 TU 1717 2247	2.1 8.0 1.7 8.2	28	0446 1022 W 1723 2253	1.4 8.8 0.9 9.1
14	0536 1104 W 1759 2324	1.7 8.4 1.4 8.5			
15	0616 1140 TH 1838 ● 2359	1.5 8.7 1.2 8.8			

MARCH

Date	Time	m	Date	Time	m
1	0549 1116 TH 1822 2343	0.9 9.3 0.5 9.5	16	0551 1116 F 1812 2335	1.4 8.7 1.1 8.9
2	0644 1203 F 1912 ○	0.6 9.7 0.3	17	0630 1152 SA 1850 ●	1.1 9.0 0.8
3	0027 0731 SA 1246 1955	9.7 0.5 9.8 0.2	18	0010 0707 SU 1227 1927	9.1 0.9 9.2 0.7
4	0109 0812 SU 1326 2033	9.7 0.5 9.7 0.3	19	0044 0743 M 1302 2001	9.3 0.8 9.4 0.6
5	0147 0848 M 1404 2107	9.6 0.6 9.5 0.6	20	0118 0818 TU 1337 2035	9.3 0.7 9.4 0.7
6	0223 0919 TU 1440 2135	9.3 0.9 9.1 1.1	21	0153 0852 W 1413 2108	9.3 0.8 9.2 0.8
7	0258 0947 W 1515 2202	8.9 1.4 8.6 1.6	22	0229 0927 TH 1451 2142	9.1 1.0 8.9 1.2
8	0332 1017 TH 1551 2233	8.3 1.8 8.0 2.1	23	0307 1005 F 1533 2222	8.8 1.4 8.5 1.6
9	0408 1056 F 1634 ◑ 2317	7.7 2.4 7.3 2.7	24	0351 1051 SA 1624 ◐ 2314	8.3 1.8 7.9 2.1
10	0457 1151 SA 1737	7.1 2.9 6.7	25	0450 1151 SU 1738	7.7 2.2 7.4
11	0020 0614 SU 1310 1912	3.2 6.6 3.1 6.5	26	0025 0617 M 1315 1915	2.5 7.4 2.3 7.4
12	0152 0755 M 1442 2040	3.3 6.7 2.9 6.9	27	0159 0753 TU 1450 2040	2.4 7.6 2.0 7.8
13	0319 0907 TU 1553 2136	2.9 7.2 2.4 7.5	28	0325 0911 W 1607 2146	2.0 8.1 1.5 8.5
14	0420 0957 W 1647 2220	2.3 7.8 1.9 8.1	29	0436 1011 TH 1711 2239	1.4 8.7 1.0 9.0
15	0508 1038 TH 1732 2258	1.8 8.3 1.4 8.5	30	0536 1101 F 1806 2325	1.0 9.2 0.6 9.4
			31	0626 1145 SA 1851 ○	0.7 9.5 0.5

APRIL

Date	Time	m	Date	Time	m
1	0006 0709 SU 1225 1931	9.6 0.6 9.6 0.4	16	0640 1201 M 1901 ●	0.8 9.3 0.6
2	0044 0746 M 1302 2005	9.6 0.6 9.6 0.5	17	0018 0720 TU 1238 1939	9.4 0.7 9.4 0.5
3	0119 0819 TU 1337 2035	9.5 0.7 9.4 0.8	18	0055 0758 W 1316 2015	9.5 0.6 9.5 0.6
4	0153 0849 W 1411 2102	9.2 1.0 9.1 1.1	19	0133 0836 TH 1356 2052	9.5 0.6 9.4 0.8
5	0225 0916 TH 1444 2128	8.9 1.3 8.6 1.6	20	0212 0914 F 1437 2130	9.3 0.8 9.1 1.1
6	0257 0944 F 1517 2157	8.4 1.8 8.0 2.1	21	0254 0955 SA 1523 2213	8.9 1.2 8.6 1.6
7	0329 1018 SA 1554 2236	7.8 2.3 7.4 2.6	22	0342 1043 SU 1619 ◐ 2307	8.3 1.6 8.0 2.0
8	0411 1105 SU 1647 ◑ 2332	7.2 2.8 6.8 3.1	23	0444 1145 M 1735	7.8 2.0 7.6
9	0515 1213 M 1813	6.6 3.1 6.5	24	0020 0610 TU 1309 1903	2.4 7.5 2.2 7.6
10	0054 0656 TU 1345 1949	3.3 6.5 3.1 6.7	25	0150 0738 W 1436 2023	2.3 7.6 1.9 7.9
11	0228 0821 W 1505 2055	3.0 6.9 2.6 7.3	26	0310 0853 TH 1549 2127	1.9 8.1 1.5 8.5
12	0337 0918 TH 1604 2143	2.5 7.6 2.0 8.0	27	0418 0951 F 1650 2218	1.4 8.6 1.1 8.9
13	0429 1004 F 1654 2225	1.9 8.2 1.5 8.5	28	0515 1040 SA 1741 2302	1.1 9.0 0.9 9.2
14	0516 1045 SA 1739 2304	1.4 8.7 1.1 8.9	29	0602 1122 SU 1824 2341	0.9 9.2 0.8 9.3
15	0559 1123 SU 1821 2342	1.1 9.0 0.8 9.2	30	0642 1200 M 1900 ○	0.9 9.2 0.8

Chart Datum is 4·43 metres below IGN Datum. HAT is 10·1 metres above Chart Datum.

STANDARD TIME UT –01
Subtract 1 hour for UT
For French Summer Time add ONE hour in **non-shaded areas**

DIEPPE LAT 49°56'N LONG 1°05'E

TIMES AND HEIGHTS OF HIGH AND LOW WATERS

Dates in red are SPRINGS
Dates in blue are NEAPS

YEAR **2018**

MAY

Date	Day	Time	m	Time	m	Time	m	Time	m
1	TU	0017	9.3	0717	0.8	1236	9.2	1933	0.9
2	W	0051	9.2	0750	0.9	1310	9.1	2005	1.0
3	TH	0124	9.1	0821	1.1	1344	8.9	2034	1.3
4	F	0157	8.8	0850	1.3	1417	8.5	2102	1.6
5	SA	0229	8.4	0918	1.7	1450	8.1	2131	2.1
6	SU	0302	7.9	0951	2.1	1527	7.6	2207	2.5
7	M	0340	7.4	1033	2.5	1613	7.1	2257	2.9
8	TU	0435	6.9	1130	2.8	1721	6.8	◑	
9	W	0004	3.1	0554	6.7	1245	2.9	1847	6.8
10	TH	0126	3.0	0722	6.9	1405	2.6	2001	7.3
11	F	0241	2.5	0829	7.4	1512	2.1	2058	7.8
12	SA	0341	2.0	0921	8.0	1608	1.6	2146	8.4
13	SU	0434	1.5	1008	8.5	1659	1.2	2229	8.8
14	M	0524	1.2	1051	8.9	1747	0.9	2311	9.1
15	TU	0611	0.9	1134	9.2	1833	0.7	● 2352	9.4
16	W	0656	0.7	1216	9.4	1916	0.6		
17	TH	0033	9.5	0740	0.5	1258	9.5	1957	0.6
18	F	0116	9.5	0822	0.5	1343	9.4	2039	0.7
19	SA	0200	9.3	0905	0.7	1429	9.1	2122	1.0
20	SU	0246	9.0	0950	1.0	1519	8.7	2209	1.4
21	M	0339	8.5	1041	1.4	1617	8.3	2305	1.8
22	TU	0442	8.0	1142	1.7	1725	7.9	◐	
23	W	0014	2.1	0555	7.7	1256	1.9	1840	7.8
24	TH	0131	2.1	0712	7.7	1410	1.8	1953	8.0
25	F	0243	1.9	0824	8.0	1518	1.6	2057	8.3
26	SA	0348	1.6	0924	8.3	1619	1.4	2151	8.6
27	SU	0445	1.4	1015	8.6	1710	1.3	2236	8.8
28	M	0532	1.3	1058	8.7	1752	1.2	2316	8.9
29	TU	0612	1.2	1136	8.8	1829	1.2	○ 2352	8.9
30	W	0648	1.1	1212	8.8	1904	1.2		
31	TH	0026	8.9	0723	1.1	1247	8.8	1938	1.3

JUNE

Date	Day	Time	m	Time	m	Time	m	Time	m
1	F	0059	8.8	0757	1.2	1321	8.7	2011	1.4
2	SA	0133	8.7	0829	1.4	1356	8.5	2041	1.7
3	SU	0207	8.4	0859	1.6	1430	8.2	2111	2.0
4	M	0241	8.1	0931	1.9	1506	7.9	2146	2.3
5	TU	0319	7.7	1010	2.2	1548	7.5	2230	2.5
6	W	0405	7.3	1058	2.4	1640	7.3	◑ 2325	2.7
7	TH	0504	7.1	1158	2.6	1745	7.1		
8	F	0030	2.8	0616	7.1	1306	2.5	1858	7.3
9	SA	0141	2.5	0730	7.3	1416	2.2	2005	7.7
10	SU	0250	2.1	0834	7.8	1520	1.8	2102	8.2
11	M	0351	1.7	0929	8.3	1619	1.4	2153	8.6
12	TU	0448	1.3	1020	8.7	1714	1.1	2241	9.0
13	W	0542	1.0	1108	9.1	1806	0.9	● 2328	9.3
14	TH	0634	0.7	1156	9.3	1855	0.7		
15	F	0015	9.5	0724	0.5	1244	9.5	1943	0.6
16	SA	0103	9.5	0812	0.5	1333	9.5	2031	0.7
17	SU	0151	9.4	0859	0.5	1422	9.3	2118	0.9
18	M	0241	9.2	0947	0.8	1513	9.0	2206	1.2
19	TU	0333	8.8	1037	1.1	1606	8.6	2259	1.5
20	W	0428	8.4	1130	1.4	1703	8.2	◐ 2356	1.8
21	TH	0528	8.0	1229	1.7	1806	8.0		
22	F	0059	2.0	0635	7.8	1333	1.9	1913	7.8
23	SA	0205	2.0	0746	7.7	1438	2.0	2021	7.9
24	SU	0310	1.9	0852	7.9	1540	1.9	2120	8.1
25	M	0410	1.8	0948	8.1	1635	1.7	2210	8.3
26	TU	0501	1.6	1035	8.3	1721	1.6	2252	8.5
27	W	0544	1.5	1116	8.4	1802	1.5	2330	8.6
28	TH	0624	1.4	1152	8.5	1840	1.4	○	
29	F	0005	8.7	0701	1.3	1228	8.6	1917	1.4
30	SA	0040	8.7	0737	1.3	1302	8.6	1952	1.5

JULY

Date	Day	Time	m	Time	m	Time	m	Time	m
1	SU	0114	8.7	0812	1.3	1337	8.6	2024	1.6
2	M	0149	8.5	0843	1.5	1412	8.4	2055	1.7
3	TU	0223	8.3	0915	1.6	1446	8.2	2128	1.9
4	W	0259	8.1	0950	1.8	1523	8.0	2207	2.1
5	TH	0339	7.8	1031	2.0	1605	7.7	2252	2.3
6	F	0425	7.6	1118	2.2	1656	7.6	◑ 2345	2.5
7	SA	0522	7.4	1215	2.3	1758	7.5		
8	SU	0048	2.5	0631	7.4	1322	2.3	1910	7.6
9	M	0200	2.3	0746	7.6	1435	2.1	2020	8.0
10	TU	0312	1.9	0853	8.0	1544	1.7	2121	8.4
11	W	0417	1.4	0953	8.5	1646	1.3	2217	8.8
12	TH	0518	1.1	1048	9.0	1744	1.0	2310	9.2
13	F	0616	0.7	1142	9.3	1839	0.8	●	
14	SA	0002	9.5	0711	0.5	1233	9.5	1933	0.6
15	SU	0052	9.6	0804	0.4	1323	9.6	2024	0.6
16	M	0141	9.6	0853	0.4	1411	9.5	2111	0.7
17	TU	0229	9.4	0939	0.5	1458	9.3	2156	0.9
18	W	0316	9.1	1022	0.9	1545	8.9	2240	1.3
19	TH	0404	8.6	1106	1.3	1633	8.5	◐ 2326	1.7
20	F	0455	8.1	1153	1.8	1725	8.0		
21	SA	0018	2.1	0553	7.7	1247	2.2	1827	7.6
22	SU	0119	2.3	0702	7.4	1352	2.4	1938	7.5
23	M	0228	2.4	0817	7.3	1500	2.4	2048	7.6
24	TU	0335	2.2	0923	7.6	1603	2.2	2146	7.9
25	W	0433	1.9	1015	7.9	1656	1.9	2232	8.2
26	TH	0522	1.7	1058	8.2	1741	1.7	2312	8.4
27	F	0604	1.5	1135	8.4	1821	1.6	○ 2348	8.6
28	SA	0643	1.3	1210	8.6	1859	1.4		
29	SU	0022	8.7	0720	1.2	1244	8.7	1934	1.4
30	M	0056	8.8	0754	1.2	1318	8.8	2007	1.4
31	TU	0130	8.8	0826	1.2	1351	8.7	2039	1.5

AUGUST

Date	Day	Time	m	Time	m	Time	m	Time	m
1	W	0203	8.7	0858	1.3	1424	8.6	2110	1.6
2	TH	0237	8.5	0930	1.5	1458	8.4	2144	1.8
3	F	0313	8.3	1004	1.7	1535	8.2	2223	2.0
4	SA	0353	8.0	1044	2.0	1617	7.9	◑ 2308	2.2
5	SU	0441	7.7	1134	2.2	1710	7.7		
6	M	0006	2.4	0543	7.5	1238	2.4	1822	7.5
7	TU	0118	2.4	0706	7.5	1357	2.3	1945	7.7
8	W	0241	2.1	0827	7.8	1517	2.0	2058	8.2
9	TH	0355	1.6	0935	8.4	1626	1.5	2201	8.7
10	F	0500	1.1	1036	8.9	1728	1.1	2258	9.2
11	SA	0602	0.7	1131	9.3	1828	0.8	● 2351	9.5
12	SU	0700	0.4	1221	9.6	1922	0.6		
13	M	0040	9.7	0752	0.3	1309	9.8	2011	0.5
14	TU	0126	9.8	0838	0.3	1353	9.7	2055	0.6
15	W	0210	9.6	0920	0.5	1435	9.5	2135	0.8
16	TH	0252	9.3	0957	0.9	1516	9.1	2211	1.3
17	F	0333	8.8	1032	1.4	1557	8.6	2248	1.7
18	SA	0417	8.2	1110	1.9	1642	8.0	◐ 2332	2.3
19	SU	0507	7.5	1157	2.5	1737	7.4		
20	M	0030	2.7	0613	7.0	1302	2.9	1851	7.0
21	TU	0145	2.8	0740	6.9	1422	2.9	2016	7.1
22	W	0303	2.6	0859	7.2	1536	2.6	2124	7.5
23	TH	0408	2.2	0955	7.7	1635	2.2	2212	7.9
24	F	0500	1.8	1038	8.1	1722	1.8	2252	8.3
25	SA	0544	1.5	1114	8.5	1803	1.5	2328	8.6
26	SU	0623	1.3	1149	8.7	1840	1.4	○	
27	M	0002	8.8	0700	1.1	1222	8.9	1914	1.3
28	TU	0035	9.0	0733	1.1	1255	9.0	1947	1.2
29	W	0108	9.0	0806	1.0	1327	9.0	2019	1.2
30	TH	0140	9.0	0837	1.1	1359	8.9	2051	1.3
31	F	0213	8.8	0908	1.3	1432	8.8	2123	1.5

Chart Datum is 4·43 metres below IGN Datum. HAT is 10·1 metres above Chart Datum.

STANDARD TIME UT –01
Subtract 1 hour for UT
For French Summer Time add ONE hour in **non-shaded areas**

DIEPPE LAT 49°56′N LONG 1°05′E

TIMES AND HEIGHTS OF HIGH AND LOW WATERS

Dates in red are SPRINGS
Dates in blue are NEAPS

YEAR **2018**

SEPTEMBER

Date	Time m	Date	Time m
1	0248 8.6 0940 1.5 SA 1507 8.5 2157 1.8	16	0339 8.1 1026 2.1 SU 1559 7.9 2246 2.4
2	0326 8.3 1016 1.9 SU 1547 8.2 2239 2.1	17	0422 7.5 1108 2.7 M 1647 7.3 ◐ 2339 2.9
3	0411 7.9 1103 2.2 M 1637 7.8 ◑ 2334 2.4	18	0523 6.8 1212 3.2 TU 1759 6.7
4	0512 7.5 1206 2.5 TU 1749 7.4	19	0056 3.2 0656 6.6 W 1342 3.3 1938 6.7
5	0048 2.5 0641 7.3 W 1332 2.6 1923 7.5	20	0227 3.0 0829 6.9 TH 1507 2.9 2054 7.2
6	0221 2.3 0812 7.7 TH 1501 2.2 2045 8.0	21	0338 2.5 0927 7.5 F 1608 2.4 2145 7.8
7	0342 1.7 0925 8.3 F 1613 1.6 2151 8.6	22	0432 2.0 1009 8.1 SA 1655 1.9 2225 8.3
8	0449 1.1 1026 9.0 SA 1717 1.1 2248 9.2	23	0516 1.6 1047 8.6 SU 1736 1.5 2302 8.7
9	0551 0.7 1118 9.5 SU 1816 0.7 ● 2338 9.6	24	0556 1.3 1122 8.9 M 1814 1.3 2337 9.0
10	0646 0.4 1205 9.7 M 1907 0.5	25	0633 1.1 1155 9.1 TU 1850 1.1 ○
11	0023 9.8 0734 0.3 TU 1248 9.8 1952 0.5	26	0010 9.1 0708 1.0 W 1228 9.2 1924 1.1
12	0106 9.8 0816 0.3 W 1329 9.8 2032 0.6	27	0043 9.2 0741 0.9 TH 1301 9.2 1957 1.0
13	0146 9.6 0853 0.6 TH 1407 9.5 2106 0.9	28	0116 9.2 0814 1.0 F 1333 9.2 2030 1.1
14	0224 9.3 0925 1.0 F 1444 9.1 2138 1.3	29	0150 9.1 0846 1.1 SA 1408 9.0 2103 1.3
15	0301 8.8 0954 1.5 SA 1520 8.6 2208 1.8	30	0226 8.9 0919 1.4 SU 1444 8.7 2138 1.6

OCTOBER

Date	Time m	Date	Time m
1	0306 8.5 0956 1.8 M 1525 8.3 2221 2.0	16	0344 7.5 1027 2.8 TU 1603 7.3 ◐ 2253 2.9
2	0352 8.0 1044 2.3 TU 1616 7.8 ◑ 2315 2.4	17	0436 6.9 1123 3.3 W 1707 6.7
3	0456 7.5 1149 2.7 W 1733 7.4	18	0001 3.3 0600 6.5 TH 1249 3.5 1844 6.5
4	0032 2.6 0632 7.3 TH 1320 2.7 1913 7.4	19	0135 3.3 0738 6.8 F 1422 3.2 2009 6.9
5	0211 2.4 0804 7.7 F 1452 2.2 2035 8.0	20	0254 2.8 0844 7.3 SA 1528 2.6 2105 7.5
6	0332 1.7 0915 8.4 SA 1603 1.6 2140 8.7	21	0352 2.2 0931 8.0 SU 1618 2.0 2150 8.2
7	0438 1.1 1012 9.0 SU 1705 1.1 2233 9.2	22	0439 1.7 1012 8.5 M 1701 1.6 2229 8.6
8	0535 0.7 1100 9.5 M 1759 0.8 2319 9.6	23	0521 1.3 1049 8.9 TU 1742 1.3 2306 9.0
9	0626 0.5 1144 9.7 TU 1846 0.6 ●	24	0601 1.1 1125 9.1 W 1821 1.1 ○ 2342 9.2
10	0002 9.7 0709 0.5 W 1224 9.8 1927 0.6	25	0639 1.0 1200 9.3 TH 1858 1.0
11	0041 9.7 0747 0.6 TH 1302 9.7 2003 0.8	26	0017 9.3 0716 0.9 F 1234 9.4 1935 0.9
12	0119 9.5 0821 0.9 F 1338 9.4 2035 1.0	27	0053 9.4 0751 0.9 SA 1310 9.4 2011 1.0
13	0155 9.2 0851 1.2 SA 1412 9.0 2105 1.4	28	0131 9.3 0826 1.1 SU 1348 9.2 2048 1.1
14	0229 8.7 0919 1.7 SU 1446 8.5 2134 1.9	29	0210 9.0 0903 1.4 M 1428 8.9 2127 1.4
15	0305 8.1 0948 2.2 M 1521 7.9 2207 2.4	30	0253 8.6 0944 1.8 TU 1512 8.4 2211 1.8
		31	0344 8.1 1035 2.2 W 1609 7.9 ◑ 2308 2.2

NOVEMBER

Date	Time m	Date	Time m
1	0453 7.6 1143 2.6 TH 1729 7.5	16	0504 6.8 1150 3.4 F 1739 6.7
2	0026 2.5 0624 7.5 F 1313 2.6 1900 7.6	17	0027 3.2 0629 6.8 SA 1314 3.3 1905 6.8
3	0159 2.2 0747 7.9 SA 1438 2.1 2017 8.0	18	0149 3.0 0745 7.2 SU 1430 2.9 2013 7.3
4	0315 1.7 0855 8.4 SU 1547 1.6 2121 8.6	19	0257 2.5 0843 7.7 M 1529 2.3 2106 7.9
5	0419 1.3 0951 9.0 M 1645 1.2 2213 9.0	20	0352 2.0 0930 8.3 TU 1619 1.8 2151 8.4
6	0513 1.0 1038 9.3 TU 1736 1.0 2258 9.3	21	0441 1.6 1013 8.7 W 1706 1.4 2233 8.8
7	0600 0.9 1120 9.5 W 1821 0.9 ● 2339 9.4	22	0526 1.2 1053 9.1 TH 1750 1.1 2313 9.1
8	0641 0.9 1159 9.5 TH 1859 0.9	23	0609 1.0 1132 9.3 F 1833 0.9 ○ 2353 9.3
9	0017 9.4 0716 1.0 F 1235 9.4 1934 1.0	24	0651 0.9 1211 9.4 SA 1915 0.8
10	0053 9.3 0750 1.1 SA 1310 9.2 2007 1.1	25	0034 9.4 0732 0.9 SU 1252 9.5 1956 0.8
11	0128 9.0 0821 1.4 SU 1344 9.0 2038 1.4	26	0116 9.4 0812 1.0 M 1334 9.4 2037 0.9
12	0203 8.7 0851 1.8 M 1418 8.5 2107 1.8	27	0201 9.2 0855 1.2 TU 1419 9.1 2121 1.2
13	0238 8.2 0920 2.2 TU 1452 8.0 2139 2.3	28	0249 8.8 0940 1.6 W 1509 8.6 2209 1.5
14	0315 7.7 0956 2.7 W 1531 7.5 2218 2.7	29	0343 8.4 1033 2.0 TH 1608 8.2 2306 1.9
15	0400 7.2 1043 3.1 TH 1623 7.0 ◐ 2312 3.1	30	0448 8.0 1138 2.3 F 1718 7.8 ◑

DECEMBER

Date	Time m	Date	Time m
1	0016 2.1 0603 7.8 SA 1255 2.3 1834 7.7	16	0518 7.1 1205 3.0 SU 1750 7.0
2	0134 2.1 0717 7.9 SU 1412 2.1 1948 7.9	17	0036 2.8 0631 7.1 M 1316 2.9 1906 7.1
3	0247 1.9 0826 8.2 M 1520 1.8 2054 8.3	18	0148 2.7 0743 7.4 TU 1428 2.6 2013 7.5
4	0351 1.6 0924 8.6 TU 1619 1.5 2149 8.6	19	0256 2.3 0843 7.9 W 1532 2.1 2110 8.0
5	0446 1.4 1014 8.9 W 1711 1.3 2236 8.8	20	0357 1.9 0935 8.4 TH 1629 1.6 2200 8.5
6	0532 1.3 1057 9.1 TH 1754 1.2 2318 8.9	21	0451 1.5 1022 8.8 F 1721 1.3 2247 8.9
7	0612 1.3 1136 9.1 F 1833 1.1 ● 2356 9.0	22	0542 1.2 1108 9.2 SA 1810 1.0 ○ 2333 9.2
8	0648 1.3 1212 9.1 SA 1909 1.1	23	0630 1.0 1153 9.4 SU 1859 0.7
9	0032 9.0 0724 1.3 SU 1247 9.0 1944 1.2	24	0019 9.4 0718 0.9 M 1239 9.6 1946 0.6
10	0107 8.9 0758 1.5 M 1321 8.9 2017 1.4	25	0107 9.5 0805 0.8 TU 1326 9.5 2033 0.6
11	0142 8.7 0831 1.7 TU 1356 8.6 2048 1.7	26	0155 9.4 0852 1.0 W 1415 9.4 2120 0.8
12	0217 8.4 0901 2.0 W 1431 8.2 2119 2.0	27	0244 9.2 0939 1.2 TH 1505 9.0 2208 1.1
13	0252 8.0 0933 2.4 TH 1507 7.8 2153 2.3	28	0336 8.8 1029 1.5 F 1557 8.6 2258 1.4
14	0330 7.6 1013 2.7 F 1549 7.4 2236 2.6	29	0430 8.4 1124 1.8 SA 1655 8.2 ◑ 2354 1.8
15	0417 7.3 1103 2.9 SA 1642 7.1 ◐ 2331 2.8	30	0531 8.1 1225 2.1 SU 1759 7.9
		31	0057 2.1 0637 7.9 M 1333 2.2 1910 7.7

Chart Datum is 4·43 metres below IGN Datum. HAT is 10·1 metres above Chart Datum.

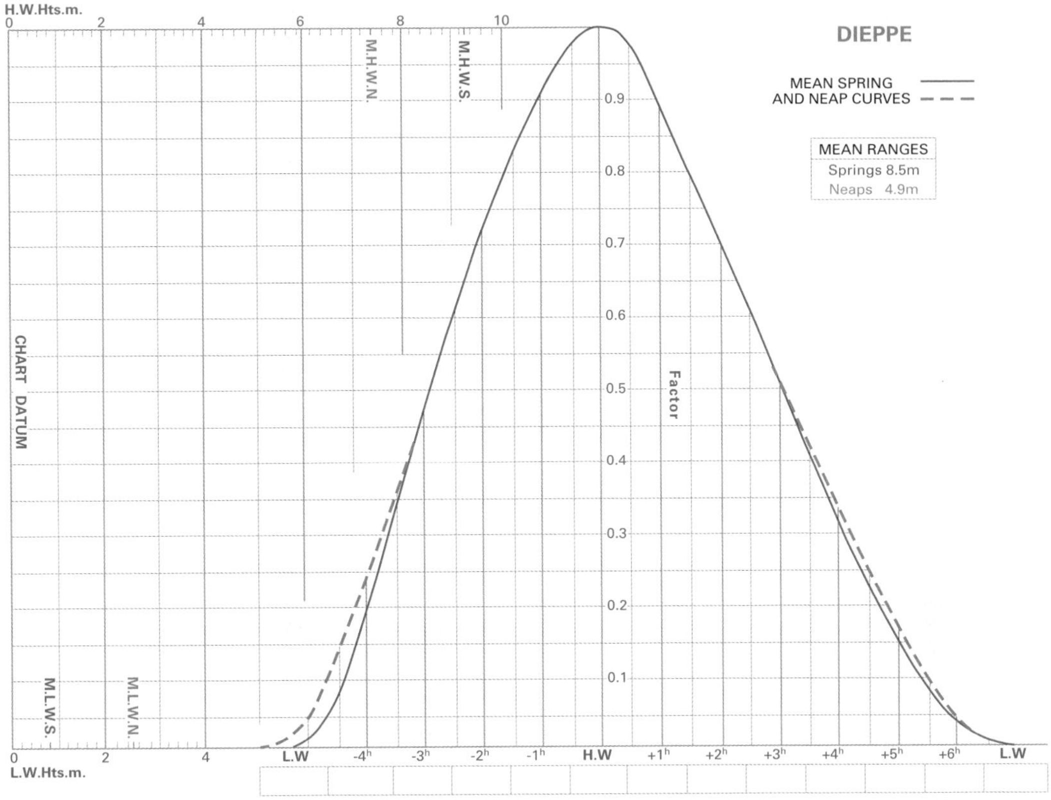

9.17.15 ST VALÉRY-EN-CAUX

Seine Maritime **49°52'·48N 00°42'·64E**

CHARTS AC 2451; SHOM 7417; Navi 1012; Imray C31

TIDES –0044 Dover; ML 4·6; Duration 0530

Standard Port DIEPPE (←)

Times				Height (metres)			
High Water		Low Water		MHWS	MHWN	MLWN	MLWS
0100	0600	0100	0700	9·3	7·4	2·5	0·8
1300	1800	1300	1900				
Differences ST VALÉRY-EN-CAUX							
–0005	–0005	–0015	–0015	–0·5	–0·4	–0·1	–0·1

SHELTER Good, but confused seas break at entrance in fresh W-NE'lies.

NAVIGATION WPT 49°52'·97N 00°42'·14E, 155°/6ca to W pier. Ent is easy, but tidal streams across ent are strong. Shingle builds up against W wall; hug the E side. Inside the pier hds, wave-breaks (marked by posts) reduce the surge. Avant Port dries 3m. 5 W waiting buoys are in the pool NE of gate.

Gate is open HW ±2½ if coeff >79; if coeff < 41 gate is open HW –2½ to HW+1¾ (bridge opens H & H+30 in these periods). When entry gate first opens, strong current may complicate berthing on Ⓥ pontoon W side; best to wait >15 mins (i.e. second bridge opening). Ⓥ also berth on 'A' pontoon. Traffic sigs at the bridge/gate are coordinated to seaward/inland: ● = ent/exit; ● = no ent/exit; ● + ● = no movements.

LIGHTS AND MARKS From N or W Paluel nuclear power stn is conspic 3M W of ent. From E a TV mast is 1M E of ent. Hbr is hard to see between high chalk cliffs, but lt ho (W twr, G top) on W pierhead is fairly conspic. Lts as on chartlet and LBW.

COMMUNICATIONS CROSS 03·21·8728.76; Police 02·35·97·00·17; British Consul 01·44·51·31·00; Ⓗ 02·35·97·00·11; Doctor 02·35·97·05·99; Aff Mar 02·35·10·34·34; HM VHF Ch 09 (French only).

FACILITIES **Marina** ☎02·35·97·01·30, mob 06·07·31·56·95. www.ville-saint-valery-en-caux.fr 575 + 20 Ⓥ €2·20; max LOA 14m. (5/10t). **CN Valeriquais** ☎02.35.97.25.49, . **Town** Ⓑ bus to ≷ at Yvetot; ✈ and ferry Dieppe.

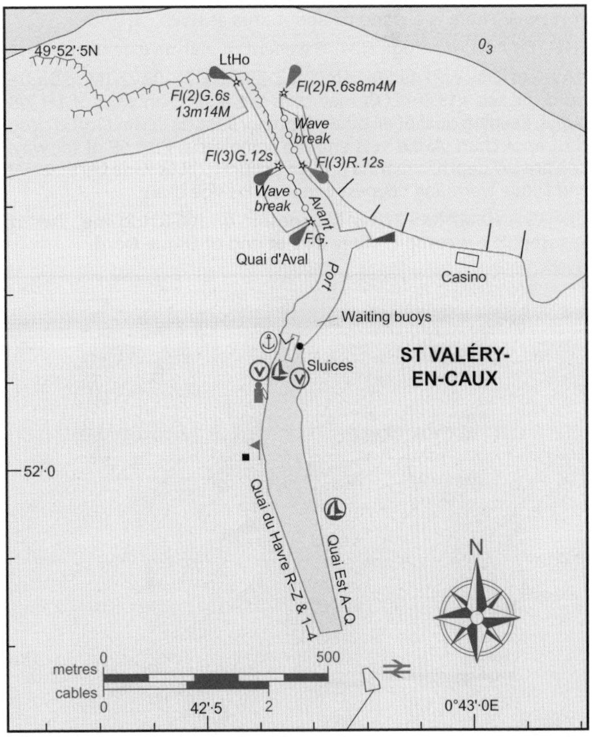

9.17.16 FÉCAMP

Seine Maritime **49°45'·92N 00°21'·80E**

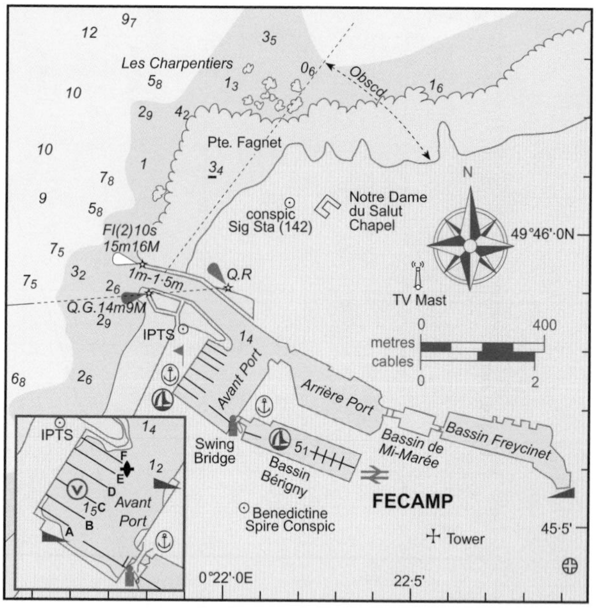

CHARTS AC 2451, 2148, 1354; SHOM 6857, 7417, 7207; Navi 1012; Imray C31

TIDES –0044 Dover; ML 4·9; Duration 0550

Standard Port DIEPPE (⟵)

Times				Height (metres)			
High Water		Low Water		MHWS	MHWN	MLWN	MLWS
0100	0600	0100	0700	9·3	7·4	2·5	0·8
1300	1800	1300	1900				
Differences FÉCAMP							
–0015	–0010	–0030	–0040	–0·8	–0·5	+0·3	+0·4
ETRETAT 49°42'·6N 00°12'·0E							
–0020	–0015	–0050	–0050	–1·1	–0·8	+0·3	+0·4

SHELTER Excellent in basins, but in even moderate W/NW winds a considerable surf runs off the ent and scend can make the Avant Port uncomfortable. Access difficult in onshore winds >F5; do not attempt >F7. Bassin Bérigny for long stay; see HM.

NAVIGATION WPT 49°46'·01N 00°21'·36E, 107°/3ca to hbr ent. Beware the Charpentier Rks off Pte Fagnet and strong cross currents, depending on tides. Ent chan (1·5m) is prone to silting; best water is close to N jetty.

LIGHTS AND MARKS Ent lies SW of conspic ✠, sig stn, TV mast and 5 wind turbines (2 Q) on Pte Fagnet cliff, 142m high. See chartlet and Lights, buoys & waypoints for lts. Pilots use the QR aligned with QG as a 082° ldg line.

IPTS on column at root of S jetty; a W lt is shown next to top lt when Bassin Bérigny gate is open.

COMMUNICATIONS CROSS 03·21·87·21·87; 02·35·28·00·91; Police 02·35·10·45·00; ⊜ 02·35·28·19·40; British Consul 01·44·51·31·00; Ⓗ 02·35·28·05·13; HM 02·35·28·25·53, VHF Ch **12** 16 (HW –3 to +1); Marina VHF Ch 09 & Écluse Bérigny.

FACILITIES **Marina** ☎02·35·28·13·58 plaisance@portdefecamp.fr www.portdefecamp.fr. 725 + 75 ♥ fingers at pontoon C, €2·40. (H24 with any cr/card) Ⓔ (mob 20t). **Société des Régates de Fécamp** ☎02·35·28·08·44.

Bassin Bérigny is entered via a gate & swing bridge, HW –2½ to HW +¾; max LOA for visitors is 45m. ☎02.35.28.23.76, (30t).

Town Ⓑ ⇌. ✈ Le Havre.

9.17.17 LE HAVRE

Seine Maritime **49°29'·12N 00°05'·43E**

CHARTS AC 2613, 2146, 2990; SHOM 7418, 6683; Navi 526, 1012; Imray C31

TIDES –0103 Dover; ML 4·9; Duration 0543. Le Havre is a Standard Port (⟵). There is a stand of about 3hrs at HW.

SHELTER Port of refuge H24. Excellent in marina (see overleaf).

NAVIGATION WPT 49°29'·86N 00°02'·33E (LH12) 108°/2·1M to Digue Nord. Vessels <19.8m LOA may cross the appr chan west of LH 7/8 buoys, keeping clear of all other shipping. Banc de l'Éclat (1m) is close N of appr chan. Avoid vess ent/dep commercial Port SE of fairway. Beware LW depth in marina ent, give spur Fl(2)R 6s wide berth; at W end Digue Normand deepest water on PH side chan.

LIGHTS AND MARKS 2 chys, RW conspic, on 106·8° ldg line. Twr of St Joseph's ✠ is conspic. Obey IPTS at end of Digue Nord.

COMMUNICATIONS CROSS 02·33·52·16·16; 02·35·42·21·06; Auto 08·92·68·08·76; ⊜ 02·35·41·33·51; Brit Consul 01·44·51·31·00; Dr 02·35·41·23·61; HM 02·35·21·23·95; Port Control & Radar VHF Ch **12**, 20; Aff Mar 02·35·19·29·99; Marina VHF Ch 09; Sas Quinette (lock) VHF Ch 88.

FACILITIES **Marina** ☎02·35·21·23·95. www.lehavreplaisance.com capitainerie@lehavre-plaisance.fr 973 + 60♥ pontoons O or A, €3·00, Ⓔ SHOM ACA (16t) de-mast (6t) **Port Vauban**, berthing by arrangement with HM, 3+days min. stay, see website for opening times of bridge & lock (twice per day) €3·20, comfortable berth in centre of main shopping centre/facilities.

Sport Nautique et Plaisance du Havre (SNPH) ☎02·35·21·01·41, www.snph.org/.

Sté Régates du Havre (SRH) ☎02·35·42·41·21, (shut Aug).

City All facilities.

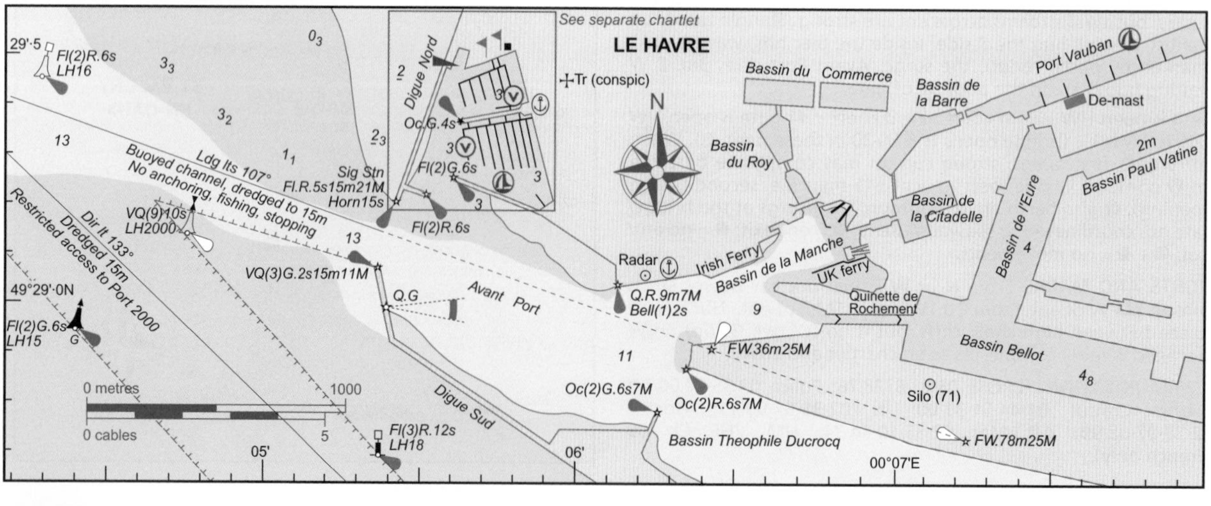

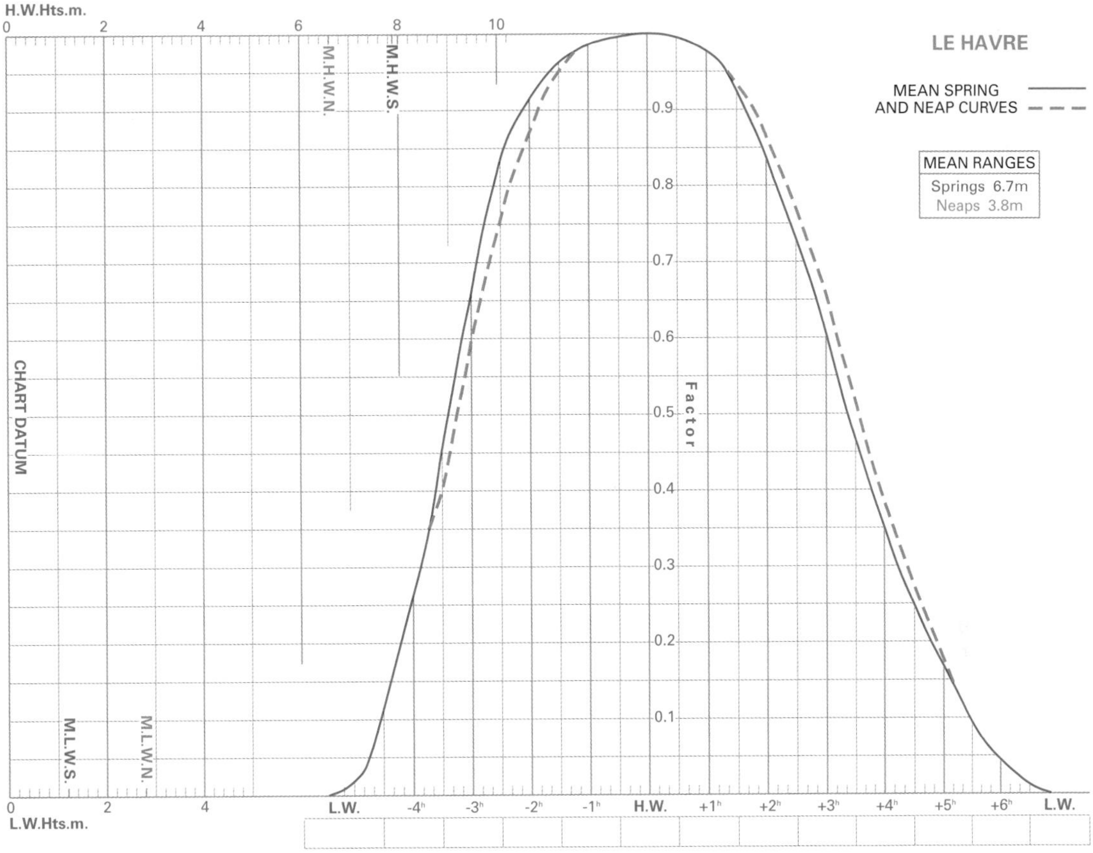

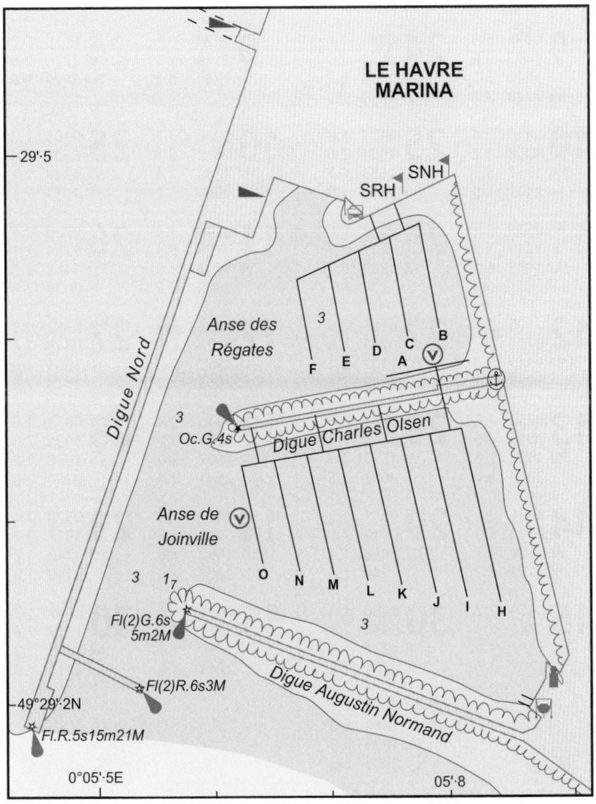

THE SEINE ESTUARY

The Seine estuary is entered between Le Havre and Deauville, and is encumbered by shallow and shifting banks which extend seawards to Banc de Seine, 15M W of Le Havre. With wind against tide there is a heavy sea on this bank. N and E of it there are 4 big ship waiting anchorages. The estuary is carefully regulated by the port authorities at Le Havre and Rouen. Given the large amount of commercial traffic to/from both these ports, it is sensible for yachtsmen to study AC 2146, 2990 carefully prior to entering the area, so as to gain a sound working knowledge of their routes and the general layout. **Note that the Greenwich Meridian lies about 2·7M W of Cap de la Hève and Deauville; extra caution is necessary in this area to ensure you are using the correct longitude sign (E/W) for your navigation.**

Yachts leaving **Le Havre** Marina near LW should give the inner spur, Fl (2) R 6s, a wide berth due to shoal ground. If bound for **Honfleur, Rouen** or **Paris**, do not try a short cut east of PHM No 2 (Q R pillar buoy at 49°27'·70N 00°00'·60E); to do so risks grounding on Spoil Ground (0·4m). ▶*The SW-going stream begins at HW Le Havre +0400, and the NE-going at HW Le Havre –0300, sp rates 1·5kn.*◀ Between Deauville and Le Havre the sea can be rough in W winds. The inshore **Passage des Pêcheurs,** over the Digue du Ratier, between Honfleur and Deauville is only good HW±2 and requires local knowledge.

Chenal du Rouen is the main chan into R. Seine, and carries much commercial tfc. The S side of the chan is defined by Digue du Ratier, a training wall which extends E to Honfleur. Yachts should stay on the N side of the channel, just outside the PHM buoys, whether east or west bound. This rule applies between No 2 buoy and Tancarville bridge.

With 24hrs access/exit, **Honfleur** is a useful starting port when bound upriver. See routes to the Mediterranean (Special notes), R Seine, Rouen and Paris.

STANDARD TIME UT –01
Subtract 1 hour for UT
For French Summer Time add ONE hour in **non-shaded areas**

LE HAVRE

LAT 49°29′N LONG 0°07′E

TIMES AND HEIGHTS OF HIGH AND LOW WATERS

Dates in red are SPRINGS
Dates in blue are NEAPS

YEAR **2018**

JANUARY

Date	Day	Time	m	Time	m	Time	m	Time	m
1	M	0428	1.4	0949	8.0	1701	1.2	2219	8.1
2	TU	0523	1.2	1039	8.2	1756	0.9	○ 2309	8.2
3	W	0618	1.0	1127	8.3	1848	0.7	2358	8.3
4	TH	0709	1.0	1215	8.3	1938	0.7		
5	F	0046	8.2	0757	1.1	1302	8.2	2025	0.9
6	SA	0134	8.1	0842	1.4	1349	8.0	2108	1.2
7	SU	0222	7.8	0926	1.8	1436	7.6	2151	1.7
8	M	0311	7.4	1009	2.2	1527	7.3	◑ 2234	2.2
9	TU	0404	7.1	1056	2.6	1624	6.9	2322	2.6
10	W	0504	6.9	1151	2.9	1730	6.7		
11	TH	0020	2.9	0610	6.8	1256	3.0	1843	6.6
12	F	0128	2.9	0720	6.8	1408	2.9	1956	6.7
13	SA	0237	2.8	0822	7.0	1512	2.6	2054	6.9
14	SU	0336	2.5	0911	7.2	1605	2.3	2138	7.2
15	M	0425	2.3	0950	7.4	1650	2.0	2215	7.4
16	TU	0508	2.0	1025	7.6	1730	1.8	2249	7.5
17	W	0547	1.9	1059	7.7	1808	1.6	● 2322	7.6
18	TH	0622	1.8	1132	7.7	1842	1.6	2356	7.6
19	F	0656	1.8	1205	7.8	1915	1.5		
20	SA	0029	7.6	0729	1.8	1239	7.7	1948	1.6
21	SU	0104	7.5	0803	1.9	1315	7.6	2021	1.7
22	M	0141	7.4	0838	2.0	1354	7.4	2056	1.9
23	TU	0221	7.3	0914	2.2	1435	7.2	2133	2.2
24	W	0303	7.1	0955	2.5	1521	7.0	◐ 2216	2.4
25	TH	0353	6.9	1044	2.7	1618	6.8	2310	2.6
26	F	0457	6.8	1146	2.8	1733	6.7		
27	SA	0021	2.7	0617	6.9	1312	2.7	1859	6.9
28	SU	0152	2.5	0735	7.1	1436	2.3	2014	7.2
29	M	0307	2.1	0841	7.5	1544	1.7	2115	7.6
30	TU	0410	1.6	0936	7.9	1646	1.3	2208	7.9
31	W	0512	1.3	1027	8.1	1747	0.9	○ 2257	8.2

FEBRUARY

Date	Day	Time	m	Time	m	Time	m	Time	m
1	TH	0611	1.0	1115	8.3	1841	0.6	2345	8.3
2	F	0702	0.9	1201	8.3	1928	0.6		
3	SA	0030	8.3	0746	0.9	1245	8.3	2010	0.7
4	SU	0114	8.1	0826	1.1	1328	8.1	2048	1.0
5	M	0156	7.9	0902	1.5	1409	7.8	2122	1.5
6	TU	0237	7.5	0936	1.9	1450	7.4	2156	2.0
7	W	0318	7.2	1012	2.4	1536	6.9	◑ 2233	2.6
8	TH	0408	6.8	1056	2.9	1635	6.6	2321	3.0
9	F	0512	6.5	1155	3.2	1751	6.3		
10	SA	0028	3.3	0629	6.4	1314	3.3	1920	6.3
11	SU	0153	3.2	0750	6.6	1436	3.0	2033	6.6
12	M	0307	2.9	0849	6.8	1538	2.6	2120	6.9
13	TU	0403	2.5	0931	7.2	1629	2.2	2157	7.2
14	W	0449	2.1	1007	7.4	1713	1.8	2231	7.5
15	TH	0530	1.9	1041	7.6	1751	1.6	● 2304	7.6
16	F	0607	1.7	1114	7.7	1827	1.4	2337	7.7
17	SA	0642	1.5	1148	7.8	1900	1.3		
18	SU	0011	7.7	0714	1.5	1223	7.9	1933	1.3
19	M	0046	7.8	0748	1.5	1259	7.8	2006	1.3
20	TU	0122	7.7	0822	1.6	1336	7.7	2040	1.5
21	W	0159	7.5	0857	1.8	1415	7.5	2114	1.8
22	TH	0238	7.3	0933	2.1	1458	7.2	2152	2.2
23	F	0322	7.0	1016	2.4	1550	6.9	◐ 2241	2.5
24	SA	0421	6.8	1114	2.7	1705	6.7	2350	2.8
25	SU	0547	6.7	1242	2.8	1843	6.7		
26	M	0129	2.7	0719	6.9	1417	2.4	2003	7.1
27	TU	0249	2.3	0828	7.3	1529	1.9	2105	7.5
28	W	0359	1.8	0925	7.7	1638	1.4	2156	7.9

MARCH

Date	Day	Time	m	Time	m	Time	m	Time	m
1	TH	0506	1.4	1014	8.0	1739	0.9	2243	8.1
2	F	0602	1.0	1059	8.1	1829	0.6	○ 2327	8.2
3	SA	0648	0.8	1142	8.2	1911	0.6		
4	SU	0009	8.2	0727	0.8	1224	8.2	1948	0.7
5	M	0049	8.1	0802	1.0	1303	8.0	2021	1.0
6	TU	0126	7.9	0833	1.3	1340	7.8	2050	1.5
7	W	0201	7.6	0902	1.8	1416	7.4	2118	2.0
8	TH	0236	7.2	0931	2.3	1453	7.0	2147	2.6
9	F	0314	6.8	1005	2.8	1540	6.5	◑ 2228	3.1
10	SA	0410	6.4	1058	3.2	1657	6.1	2331	3.5
11	SU	0535	6.2	1213	3.5	1833	6.1		
12	M	0100	3.6	0704	6.2	1349	3.3	1959	6.3
13	TU	0232	3.2	0816	6.5	1505	2.8	2052	6.7
14	W	0335	2.7	0904	6.9	1600	2.3	2131	7.1
15	TH	0424	2.2	0941	7.3	1647	1.9	2205	7.4
16	F	0507	1.8	1016	7.6	1727	1.6	2239	7.6
17	SA	0545	1.6	1051	7.8	1804	1.3	● 2313	7.8
18	SU	0620	1.4	1126	7.9	1838	1.1	2348	7.9
19	M	0655	1.2	1202	8.0	1912	1.1		
20	TU	0023	7.9	0729	1.2	1239	8.0	1947	1.1
21	W	0100	7.9	0804	1.2	1318	7.9	2021	1.3
22	TH	0138	7.7	0839	1.5	1358	7.6	2055	1.7
23	F	0217	7.4	0915	1.8	1442	7.3	2132	2.1
24	SA	0301	7.1	0957	2.3	1536	6.9	◐ 2220	2.6
25	SU	0401	6.8	1054	2.6	1653	6.7	2332	2.9
26	M	0531	6.6	1227	2.8	1835	6.7		
27	TU	0115	2.8	0705	6.8	1402	2.4	1952	7.1
28	W	0237	2.4	0814	7.2	1517	1.9	2051	7.5
29	TH	0351	1.9	0910	7.5	1628	1.4	2140	7.8
30	F	0456	1.4	0957	7.8	1724	1.0	2224	7.9
31	SA	0546	1.1	1040	8.0	1809	0.8	○ 2305	8.0

APRIL

Date	Day	Time	m	Time	m	Time	m	Time	m
1	SU	0627	1.0	1120	8.0	1846	0.8	2343	8.0
2	M	0702	1.0	1159	8.0	1919	0.9		
3	TU	0020	8.0	0733	1.1	1235	7.9	1949	1.2
4	W	0054	7.8	0802	1.4	1310	7.7	2017	1.6
5	TH	0127	7.6	0829	1.8	1344	7.3	2043	2.1
6	F	0159	7.3	0855	2.2	1418	7.0	2109	2.6
7	SA	0232	6.9	0924	2.7	1456	6.6	2145	3.1
8	SU	0315	6.5	1009	3.1	1557	6.2	◑ 2243	3.5
9	M	0429	6.1	1120	3.5	1740	6.0		
10	TU	0006	3.7	0610	6.1	1248	3.4	1905	6.2
11	W	0140	3.4	0726	6.3	1414	3.0	2008	6.6
12	TH	0252	2.9	0823	6.7	1517	2.5	2053	7.0
13	F	0345	2.3	0906	7.1	1607	2.0	2131	7.4
14	SA	0431	1.9	0945	7.5	1652	1.6	2208	7.6
15	SU	0513	1.6	1023	7.7	1733	1.3	2244	7.8
16	M	0552	1.3	1101	7.9	1811	1.1	● 2321	7.9
17	TU	0630	1.1	1139	8.0	1849	1.0	2359	8.0
18	W	0708	1.0	1220	8.0	1926	1.0		
19	TH	0038	8.0	0746	1.1	1301	7.9	2002	1.3
20	F	0119	7.8	0823	1.3	1345	7.7	2039	1.6
21	SA	0201	7.6	0901	1.7	1432	7.4	2118	2.1
22	SU	0249	7.3	0944	2.1	1528	7.0	◐ 2209	2.5
23	M	0351	6.9	1046	2.5	1649	6.8	2327	2.9
24	TU	0519	6.7	1220	2.6	1820	6.8		
25	W	0103	2.8	0646	6.8	1344	2.4	1932	7.1
26	TH	0220	2.4	0754	7.1	1458	2.0	2030	7.4
27	F	0332	2.0	0849	7.4	1605	1.6	2118	7.6
28	SA	0433	1.6	0935	7.6	1658	1.4	2200	7.8
29	SU	0520	1.4	1017	7.7	1740	1.2	2240	7.8
30	M	0558	1.3	1057	7.8	1815	1.2	○ 2316	7.8

Chart Datum is 4·38 metres below IGN Datum. HAT is 8·4 metres above Chart Datum.

STANDARD TIME UT –01
Subtract 1 hour for UT
For French Summer Time add ONE hour in **non-shaded areas**

LE HAVRE LAT 49°29′N LONG 0°07′E

TIMES AND HEIGHTS OF HIGH AND LOW WATERS

Dates in red are SPRINGS
Dates in blue are NEAPS

YEAR **2018**

MAY

Date	Day	Time	m	Time	m	Time	m	Time	m
1	TU	0632	1.3	1134	7.8	1847	1.3	2351	7.8
2	W	0703	1.3	1209	7.7	1918	1.5		
3	TH	0024	7.7	0733	1.5	1244	7.5	1946	1.8
4	F	0057	7.5	0800	1.8	1317	7.3	2014	2.1
5	SA	0128	7.3	0827	2.1	1351	7.0	2041	2.5
6	SU	0201	7.0	0855	2.5	1427	6.7	2114	3.0
7	M	0240	6.7	0934	2.9	1515	6.4	2204	3.3
8	TU	0335	6.3	1033	3.2	1632	6.2	◑ 2316	3.5
9	W	0502	6.2	1151	3.3	1804	6.3		
10	TH	0037	3.4	0626	6.3	1309	3.1	1912	6.6
11	F	0152	3.0	0730	6.6	1419	2.6	2006	7.0
12	SA	0253	2.5	0822	7.0	1517	2.2	2051	7.3
13	SU	0346	2.0	0908	7.3	1609	1.8	2133	7.6
14	M	0435	1.7	0951	7.6	1657	1.5	2214	7.8
15	TU	0521	1.3	1034	7.8	1742	1.2	● 2255	8.0
16	W	0606	1.1	1117	8.0	1825	1.1	2337	8.0
17	TH	0649	1.0	1202	8.0	1907	1.1		
18	F	0020	8.0	0731	1.0	1247	8.0	1948	1.3
19	SA	0104	7.9	0812	1.2	1334	7.8	2029	1.6
20	SU	0150	7.7	0855	1.5	1425	7.5	2114	2.0
21	M	0241	7.4	0944	1.9	1523	7.2	2209	2.4
22	TU	0342	7.1	1049	2.3	1636	7.0	◐ 2325	2.6
23	W	0500	6.9	1206	2.4	1753	6.9		
24	TH	0041	2.6	0617	6.9	1317	2.3	1902	7.1
25	F	0150	2.4	0724	7.0	1424	2.1	2001	7.3
26	SA	0257	2.2	0822	7.2	1528	2.0	2051	7.4
27	SU	0358	1.9	0911	7.3	1622	1.8	2135	7.6
28	M	0446	1.8	0955	7.4	1705	1.7	2214	7.6
29	TU	0525	1.6	1034	7.5	1742	1.7	○ 2251	7.7
30	W	0601	1.6	1111	7.5	1816	1.7	2325	7.7
31	TH	0635	1.6	1146	7.5	1849	1.8	2358	7.6

JUNE

Date	Day	Time	m	Time	m	Time	m	Time	m
1	F	0707	1.6	1221	7.4	1921	1.9		
2	SA	0031	7.5	0737	1.8	1255	7.3	1951	2.1
3	SU	0104	7.4	0806	2.0	1329	7.1	2021	2.4
4	M	0138	7.2	0836	2.3	1405	6.9	2054	2.7
5	TU	0216	6.9	0911	2.6	1447	6.7	2136	3.0
6	W	0303	6.7	0957	2.8	1541	6.5	◑ 2232	3.2
7	TH	0403	6.5	1059	3.0	1652	6.5	2339	3.2
8	F	0517	6.5	1207	2.9	1806	6.6		
9	SA	0049	3.0	0629	6.6	1318	2.7	1910	6.9
10	SU	0158	2.6	0732	6.9	1426	2.3	2006	7.2
11	M	0301	2.2	0829	7.2	1527	2.0	2057	7.5
12	TU	0358	1.8	0921	7.5	1622	1.6	2144	7.7
13	W	0452	1.4	1010	7.7	1714	1.4	● 2231	7.9
14	TH	0543	1.2	1059	7.9	1804	1.2	2317	8.1
15	F	0632	1.0	1147	8.0	1852	1.1		
16	SA	0004	8.1	0721	0.9	1235	8.0	1940	1.2
17	SU	0052	8.0	0809	1.0	1325	7.9	2028	1.4
18	M	0140	7.9	0857	1.3	1415	7.7	2117	1.8
19	TU	0231	7.6	0947	1.6	1510	7.4	2210	2.1
20	W	0326	7.3	1041	2.0	1610	7.2	◐ 2307	2.4
21	TH	0430	7.0	1139	2.2	1716	7.0		
22	F	0008	2.5	0538	6.9	1239	2.4	1822	7.0
23	SA	0111	2.5	0647	6.9	1342	2.4	1925	7.0
24	SU	0215	2.5	0752	6.9	1443	2.4	2022	7.2
25	M	0315	2.3	0848	7.1	1540	2.3	2110	7.3
26	TU	0408	2.1	0935	7.2	1629	2.1	2152	7.4
27	W	0453	2.0	1016	7.3	1711	2.0	2229	7.5
28	TH	0533	1.8	1053	7.4	1750	1.9	○ 2303	7.6
29	F	0611	1.7	1128	7.4	1826	1.9	2337	7.6
30	SA	0646	1.7	1202	7.4	1901	2.0		

JULY

Date	Day	Time	m	Time	m	Time	m	Time	m
1	SU	0010	7.6	0718	1.8	1236	7.3	1933	2.1
2	M	0044	7.5	0750	1.9	1310	7.3	2005	2.2
3	TU	0118	7.4	0822	2.0	1345	7.2	2038	2.4
4	W	0156	7.2	0855	2.2	1424	7.0	2115	2.6
5	TH	0237	7.0	0932	2.4	1508	6.9	2158	2.8
6	F	0325	6.8	1018	2.6	1600	6.8	◑ 2250	2.9
7	SA	0422	6.7	1115	2.7	1703	6.7	2352	2.9
8	SU	0530	6.7	1221	2.7	1813	6.8		
9	M	0105	2.7	0643	6.8	1339	2.5	1922	7.0
10	TU	0223	2.4	0754	7.0	1453	2.2	2025	7.4
11	W	0328	1.9	0857	7.4	1554	1.8	2121	7.7
12	TH	0427	1.5	0953	7.7	1652	1.5	2213	7.9
13	F	0524	1.2	1044	7.9	1748	1.3	● 2302	8.1
14	SA	0621	0.9	1134	8.1	1844	1.1	2351	8.2
15	SU	0714	0.8	1223	8.1	1936	1.1		
16	M	0039	8.2	0804	0.8	1311	8.1	2024	1.2
17	TU	0127	8.0	0850	1.0	1359	7.9	2109	1.5
18	W	0214	7.8	0934	1.3	1447	7.6	2152	1.8
19	TH	0301	7.5	1016	1.8	1536	7.3	◐ 2237	2.2
20	F	0353	7.1	1101	2.2	1631	7.0	2327	2.6
21	SA	0454	6.8	1153	2.6	1734	6.8		
22	SU	0027	2.8	0604	6.6	1256	2.8	1843	6.8
23	M	0133	2.8	0720	6.6	1403	2.8	1952	6.9
24	TU	0238	2.7	0828	6.8	1506	2.7	2049	7.1
25	W	0336	2.4	0920	7.0	1600	2.5	2134	7.3
26	TH	0427	2.2	1002	7.2	1648	2.2	2212	7.4
27	F	0511	2.0	1037	7.3	1730	2.1	○ 2245	7.6
28	SA	0552	1.8	1110	7.4	1809	1.9	2318	7.6
29	SU	0628	1.7	1143	7.5	1844	1.9	2351	7.7
30	M	0702	1.7	1216	7.5	1917	1.9		
31	TU	0025	7.7	0733	1.7	1249	7.5	1949	1.9

AUGUST

Date	Day	Time	m	Time	m	Time	m	Time	m
1	W	0059	7.6	0805	1.7	1323	7.4	2021	2.0
2	TH	0135	7.5	0837	1.9	1400	7.3	2055	2.2
3	F	0213	7.3	0911	2.1	1439	7.1	2132	2.4
4	SA	0255	7.1	0949	2.4	1522	7.0	◑ 2215	2.6
5	SU	0344	6.9	1036	2.6	1617	6.8	2309	2.8
6	M	0448	6.7	1137	2.8	1727	6.8		
7	TU	0021	2.8	0608	6.7	1300	2.8	1849	6.9
8	W	0153	2.6	0732	6.9	1428	2.4	2004	7.2
9	TH	0307	2.1	0842	7.3	1535	2.0	2106	7.6
10	F	0409	1.6	0940	7.7	1637	1.6	2159	7.9
11	SA	0512	1.2	1031	8.0	1739	1.3	● 2249	8.2
12	SU	0612	0.9	1120	8.2	1836	1.0	2336	8.3
13	M	0705	0.7	1206	8.2	1925	0.9		
14	TU	0022	8.3	0750	0.7	1252	8.2	2008	1.0
15	W	0106	8.2	0831	0.9	1335	8.0	2047	1.3
16	TH	0149	7.9	0908	1.3	1417	7.7	2123	1.7
17	F	0231	7.6	0942	1.8	1458	7.4	2158	2.2
18	SA	0314	7.2	1017	2.4	1543	7.0	◐ 2239	2.7
19	SU	0407	6.7	1101	2.9	1642	6.7	2335	3.1
20	M	0518	6.4	1205	3.3	1757	6.5		
21	TU	0049	3.2	0646	6.3	1325	3.3	1921	6.6
22	W	0205	3.0	0809	6.5	1439	3.1	2029	6.8
23	TH	0310	2.7	0904	6.9	1539	2.7	2115	7.1
24	F	0405	2.3	0943	7.2	1629	2.3	2152	7.4
25	SA	0452	2.0	1017	7.4	1713	2.0	2225	7.6
26	SU	0533	1.8	1048	7.5	1751	1.9	○ 2257	7.7
27	M	0609	1.6	1120	7.6	1825	1.7	2330	7.8
28	TU	0642	1.5	1153	7.7	1857	1.7		
29	W	0003	7.8	0713	1.5	1226	7.7	1929	1.6
30	TH	0037	7.8	0745	1.5	1300	7.7	2001	1.7
31	F	0113	7.7	0817	1.7	1335	7.5	2035	1.9

Chart Datum is 4·38 metres below IGN Datum. HAT is 8·4 metres above Chart Datum.

STANDARD TIME UT –01
Subtract 1 hour for UT
For French Summer Time add ONE hour in **non-shaded areas**

LE HAVRE LAT 49°29′N LONG 0°07′E

TIMES AND HEIGHTS OF HIGH AND LOW WATERS

Dates in red are SPRINGS
Dates in blue are NEAPS

YEAR **2018**

SEPTEMBER

Date	Day	Time	m	Time	m	Time	m	Time	m
1	SA	0151	7.5	0850	1.9	1412	7.3	2109	2.2
2	SU	0231	7.2	0925	2.2	1453	7.1	2148	2.5
3	M	0318	6.9	1008	2.6	1544	6.9	◑ 2238	2.8
4	TU	0422	6.7	1106	2.9	1658	6.7	2350	2.9
5	W	0552	6.6	1235	3.0	1832	6.8		
6	TH	0135	2.7	0724	6.9	1413	2.6	1952	7.2
7	F	0252	2.1	0833	7.4	1522	2.1	2054	7.6
8	SA	0357	1.6	0928	7.8	1627	1.6	2146	8.0
9	SU	0502	1.1	1016	8.1	1730	1.2	● 2233	8.2
10	M	0559	0.8	1102	8.2	1822	1.0	2318	8.3
11	TU	0647	0.7	1145	8.3	1906	0.9		
12	W	0001	8.3	0728	0.7	1227	8.2	1944	1.0
13	TH	0042	8.2	0803	1.0	1307	8.0	2018	1.3
14	F	0121	7.9	0835	1.4	1344	7.8	2049	1.7
15	SA	0159	7.6	0904	1.9	1420	7.4	2118	2.2
16	SU	0237	7.2	0932	2.5	1459	7.0	2151	2.8
17	M	0323	6.7	1010	3.1	1550	6.6	◐ 2241	3.2
18	TU	0433	6.3	1112	3.5	1711	6.3	2357	3.5
19	W	0608	6.2	1242	3.7	1842	6.3		
20	TH	0129	3.4	0739	6.4	1411	3.3	1959	6.6
21	F	0243	2.9	0837	6.8	1514	2.8	2048	7.0
22	SA	0338	2.4	0916	7.2	1604	2.4	2126	7.3
23	SU	0426	2.0	0949	7.5	1648	2.0	2159	7.6
24	M	0507	1.7	1021	7.7	1726	1.8	2232	7.8
25	TU	0543	1.5	1054	7.8	1801	1.6	○ 2306	7.9
26	W	0617	1.4	1127	7.8	1833	1.5	2340	7.9
27	TH	0649	1.3	1200	7.9	1906	1.4		
28	F	0015	7.9	0722	1.4	1235	7.8	1940	1.5
29	SA	0052	7.8	0756	1.5	1312	7.7	2015	1.7
30	SU	0132	7.6	0830	1.8	1350	7.5	2050	2.0

OCTOBER

Date	Day	Time	m	Time	m	Time	m	Time	m
1	M	0214	7.4	0905	2.2	1432	7.2	2128	2.4
2	TU	0304	7.0	0948	2.6	1526	6.9	◑ 2218	2.7
3	W	0411	6.8	1047	3.0	1644	6.7	2333	3.0
4	TH	0547	6.7	1227	3.1	1823	6.8		
5	F	0124	2.7	0715	7.0	1402	2.7	1941	7.2
6	SA	0240	2.1	0819	7.5	1511	2.1	2040	7.6
7	SU	0345	1.6	0911	7.8	1616	1.6	2129	8.0
8	M	0447	1.2	0957	8.1	1713	1.2	2214	8.2
9	TU	0539	0.9	1040	8.2	1801	1.1	● 2256	8.2
10	W	0622	0.9	1121	8.2	1840	1.0	2337	8.2
11	TH	0659	1.0	1159	8.1	1915	1.2		
12	F	0016	8.1	0732	1.2	1236	8.0	1947	1.4
13	SA	0053	7.9	0801	1.6	1311	7.7	2016	1.8
14	SU	0129	7.5	0829	2.1	1345	7.4	2043	2.3
15	M	0205	7.1	0856	2.6	1420	7.1	2113	2.7
16	TU	0246	6.7	0930	3.2	1504	6.6	◐ 2156	3.2
17	W	0346	6.3	1026	3.6	1618	6.3	2306	3.6
18	TH	0523	6.2	1151	3.8	1755	6.2		
19	F	0035	3.5	0647	6.3	1326	3.6	1910	6.4
20	SA	0200	3.1	0752	6.7	1437	3.0	2008	6.8
21	SU	0300	2.6	0837	7.1	1529	2.5	2050	7.2
22	M	0349	2.2	0914	7.5	1613	2.1	2128	7.6
23	TU	0432	1.8	0949	7.7	1654	1.8	2204	7.8
24	W	0511	1.6	1024	7.9	1731	1.6	○ 2240	7.9
25	TH	0547	1.4	1059	8.0	1807	1.4	2317	8.0
26	F	0623	1.3	1135	8.0	1844	1.3	2354	8.0
27	SA	0700	1.3	1212	8.0	1921	1.3		
28	SU	0035	8.0	0736	1.5	1252	7.9	1958	1.5
29	M	0117	7.8	0812	1.8	1333	7.7	2035	1.8
30	TU	0203	7.5	0850	2.2	1420	7.4	2116	2.2
31	W	0257	7.2	0936	2.6	1517	7.1	◑ 2208	2.6

NOVEMBER

Date	Day	Time	m	Time	m	Time	m	Time	m
1	TH	0406	6.9	1039	3.0	1636	6.8	2330	2.8
2	F	0539	6.9	1222	3.0	1808	6.9		
3	SA	0110	2.6	0657	7.1	1347	2.6	1921	7.2
4	SU	0222	2.1	0759	7.5	1454	2.1	2020	7.5
5	M	0326	1.7	0850	7.8	1556	1.7	2109	7.8
6	TU	0423	1.4	0935	8.0	1650	1.4	2153	8.0
7	W	0512	1.3	1017	8.1	1734	1.3	● 2235	8.0
8	TH	0552	1.2	1056	8.1	1812	1.3	2314	8.0
9	F	0628	1.3	1133	8.0	1845	1.4	2352	7.9
10	SA	0700	1.5	1208	7.9	1918	1.5		
11	SU	0028	7.7	0731	1.8	1242	7.7	1948	1.8
12	M	0104	7.5	0801	2.2	1316	7.5	2017	2.2
13	TU	0139	7.2	0830	2.6	1350	7.2	2046	2.6
14	W	0217	6.9	0903	3.0	1429	6.8	2124	3.0
15	TH	0304	6.5	0950	3.4	1523	6.5	◐ 2220	3.3
16	F	0423	6.3	1059	3.7	1652	6.3	2334	3.5
17	SA	0548	6.4	1218	3.6	1813	6.4		
18	SU	0052	3.3	0654	6.6	1336	3.2	1915	6.7
19	M	0203	2.9	0748	7.0	1439	2.8	2007	7.0
20	TU	0301	2.4	0834	7.3	1531	2.3	2052	7.4
21	W	0350	2.0	0914	7.6	1616	1.9	2133	7.7
22	TH	0435	1.7	0953	7.8	1700	1.6	2214	7.9
23	F	0518	1.5	1032	8.0	1742	1.4	○ 2255	8.0
24	SA	0559	1.3	1112	8.1	1824	1.2	2337	8.1
25	SU	0641	1.3	1154	8.1	1905	1.2		
26	M	0022	8.0	0721	1.4	1237	8.0	1947	1.3
27	TU	0108	7.9	0802	1.7	1323	7.8	2028	1.6
28	W	0157	7.7	0844	2.0	1413	7.6	2113	1.9
29	TH	0251	7.4	0933	2.4	1510	7.3	2209	2.3
30	F	0357	7.1	1040	2.7	1621	7.0	◑ 2325	2.5

DECEMBER

Date	Day	Time	m	Time	m	Time	m	Time	m
1	SA	0515	7.0	1204	2.8	1741	7.0		
2	SU	0044	2.5	0628	7.1	1319	2.6	1852	7.1
3	M	0153	2.2	0731	7.3	1426	2.3	1954	7.3
4	TU	0256	2.0	0825	7.6	1528	2.0	2047	7.5
5	W	0354	1.8	0912	7.7	1622	1.8	2134	7.7
6	TH	0442	1.7	0955	7.8	1706	1.6	2217	7.7
7	F	0523	1.7	1034	7.9	1744	1.5	● 2256	7.8
8	SA	0559	1.7	1110	7.9	1820	1.5	2333	7.7
9	SU	0634	1.7	1145	7.8	1854	1.6		
10	M	0008	7.6	0708	1.9	1219	7.7	1926	1.8
11	TU	0043	7.5	0740	2.1	1253	7.5	1958	2.0
12	W	0118	7.3	0812	2.4	1327	7.3	2029	2.3
13	TH	0154	7.1	0845	2.7	1403	7.1	2103	2.6
14	F	0233	6.8	0923	3.0	1446	6.8	2145	2.9
15	SA	0322	6.6	1013	3.3	1541	6.6	◐ 2239	3.1
16	SU	0432	6.5	1114	3.4	1657	6.5	2343	3.1
17	M	0547	6.6	1221	3.3	1812	6.6		
18	TU	0050	3.0	0651	6.8	1332	3.0	1915	6.8
19	W	0201	2.7	0747	7.1	1441	2.6	2012	7.1
20	TH	0306	2.3	0838	7.4	1539	2.1	2103	7.4
21	F	0401	1.9	0925	7.7	1631	1.7	2151	7.7
22	SA	0451	1.6	1010	7.9	1720	1.4	○ 2238	7.9
23	SU	0539	1.4	1055	8.1	1808	1.1	2324	8.1
24	M	0627	1.3	1141	8.2	1856	1.0		
25	TU	0012	8.1	0714	1.3	1228	8.2	1943	1.0
26	W	0100	8.1	0801	1.4	1315	8.1	2030	1.2
27	TH	0149	7.9	0848	1.7	1405	7.8	2118	1.5
28	F	0241	7.7	0938	2.0	1457	7.6	2208	1.8
29	SA	0337	7.4	1032	2.3	1556	7.3	◑ 2304	2.2
30	SU	0441	7.2	1133	2.5	1704	7.0		
31	M	0006	2.4	0549	7.1	1240	2.6	1816	6.9

Chart Datum is 4·38 metres below IGN Datum. HAT is 8·4 metres above Chart Datum.

9.17.18 HONFLEUR

Calvados **49° 25′·69N 00° 13′·90E** ❁❁❁◊◊◊✿✿✿

CHARTS AC 2146, 2990, 2879, 1349; SHOM 7418, 6683, 7420; Navi 1012; Imray C31

TIDES –0135 Dover; ML 5·0; Duration 0540

Standard Port LE HAVRE (⟵)

Times				Height (metres)			
High Water		Low Water		MHWS	MHWN	MLWN	MLWS
0000	0500	0000	0700	8·0	6·7	2·9	1·2
1200	1700	1200	1900				
LE HAVRE-ANTIFER (49°39′·5N 00°06′·8E)							
+0025	+0015	+0005	–0005	+0·1	0·0	0·0	0·0
CHENAL DE ROUEN (49°26′N 00°07′E)							
0000	0000	0000	+0015	0·0	–0·1	0·0	–0·1
HONFLEUR							
–0150	–0135	+0025	+0040	0·0	0·0	+0·1	+0·4

In the Seine a HW stand lasts about 2hrs 50 mins. The HW time differences refer to the beginning of the stand.

SHELTER Excellent in the Vieux Bassin and Bassin de l'Est.

NAVIGATION WPT No 2 PHM buoy, QR, 49°27′·70N 00°00′·60E, 9M to Honfleur. Begin appr between LW+1½ to HW–1½ to avoid foul tide. From WPT keep to the N of the Chenal de Rouen between PHM buoys and posts marking Digue basse du Nord; there is no room for E-bound yachts to navigate S of the chan. Beware risk of collision in low vis with W-bound yachts. This rule applies from No 2 buoy to Tancarville bridge.

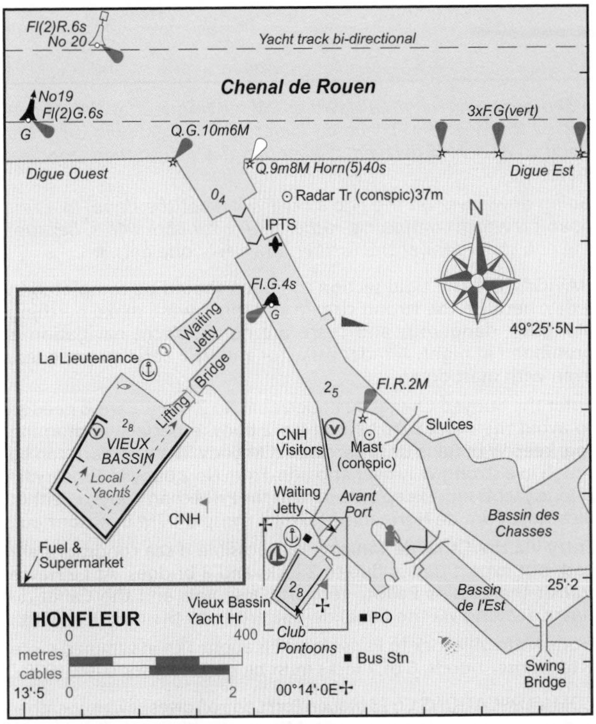

After No 20 PHM buoy cross to the ent. Caution: strong stream across ent, shoal patches reported at 'shoulders' of lock chamber.

Rouen is 60M and Paris 192M upriver.

LIGHTS AND MARKS See chartlet and Lights, buoys and waypoints. The radar tower by the lock and the Pont de Normandie 1·6M upriver are highly conspic; slightly less so are the wooded hills SW of Honfleur.

COMMUNICATIONS CROSS 02·33·52·16·16; LB 02·31·89·20·17; Honfleur Radar Ch **73** (H24); Auto (local) 08·92·68·08·14; Auto (regional) 08·92·68·08·76; Auto (offshore) 08·92·68·08·08; Police 02·31·14·44·45; ⊖ 02·31·14·44·30; Brit Consul 01·44·51·31·00; Dr 02·31·89·34·05; H 02·31·89·89·89; Port HM 02·31·49·19·19, VHF Ch **17**; Aff Mar 02·31·53·66·50; Lock VHF **17** (H24); Vieux Bassin VHF Ch 09.

THE LOCK operates H24 and opens at H, every hour for arrivals; and every H +30 for departures. It is 23m wide and has recessed floating bollards, no pontoons. **IPTS** in force. Freeflow operates from HW Le Havre –1½ to HW.

THE ROAD BRIDGE at the Vieux Bassin lifts at times (LT) below. Inbound yachts can wait on E side of the jetty immediately outside the Vieux Bassin. Departing yachts take priority over arrivals; be ready 5 mins in advance.

1 May to 31 Aug
Every day: 0830, 0930, 1030, 1130. 1630, 1730, 1830, 1930.

1 Jan to 30 Apr and 1 Sep to 31 Dec
Every day: 0830, ***0930***, ***1030***, 1130. 1430, ***1530***, ***1630***, 1730.
Times in ***bold italic*** must be requested, Mon-Fri.

FACILITIES **The Avant Port's** W wall, close N of the waiting jetty, can be a temp'y (max 24hrs) berth, useful for locking out before the Vieux Bassin's 0830 bridge lift or to await the next lock time.

Vieux Bassin ☎02·31·98·87·13 (CNH). info@ville-honfleur.fr 120 +30Ⓥ max LOA 20m, €2·60; €2·30 Avant-Port; multihulls and large motor yachts +50%. Ⓥ raft on pontoons on NW side; or in a CNH berth as assigned by CNH dory which meets and directs all arrivals.

Cercle Nautique d'Honfleur (CNH) www.cnh-honfleur.net controls all yacht berthing. Berthing fees and ⛽ tokens (€2·00) paid for here. ☎02·31·98·87·13. cnh14@wanadoo.fr ⛵ **Bassin de l'Est** can be used by yachts >20m LOA; see HM. ⚒ ✕ Ⓔ ⛭(10t and for masting) ▬.

Town ✕ ⛾ 🛒 ⛝ ⛟ ⛟ ⛽ @ ✉ Ⓑ ⇌ ✈ Deauville.

9.17.19 RIVER SEINE

CHARTS AC 2146, 2990, 2879; SHOM 6683, 6796, 6117; Imray C31; *Fluviacarte No 1.*

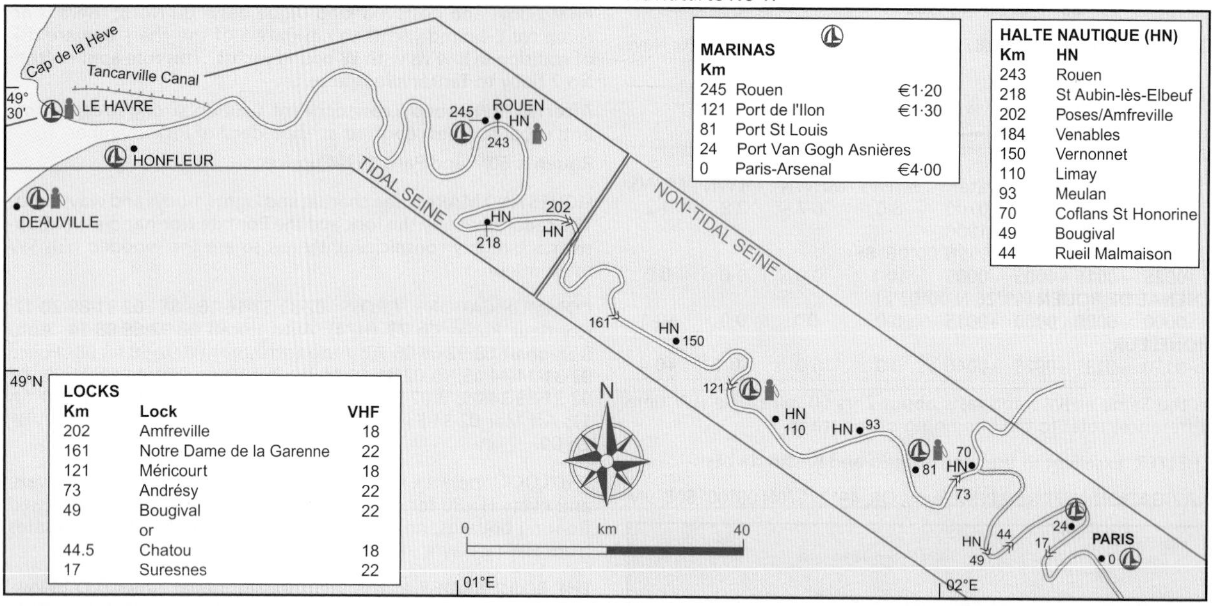

Cap de la Hève
Tancarville Canal
49° 30'
LE HAVRE
HONFLEUR
DEAUVILLE
ROUEN
245
HN
243
TIDAL SEINE
NON-TIDAL SEINE
202
HN
218
161
HN
150
121
HN
110
HN 93
81
70
HN
73
HN
44
49
17
24
PARIS
0
49°N
01°E
02°E
N
0
km
40
MARINAS
Km
245 Rouen €1·20
121 Port de l'Ilon €1·30
81 Port St Louis
24 Port Van Gogh Asnières
0 Paris-Arsenal €4·00
HALTE NAUTIQUE (HN)
Km HN
243 Rouen
218 St Aubin-lès-Elbeuf
202 Poses/Amfreville
184 Venables
150 Vernonnet
110 Limay
93 Meulan
70 Coflans St Honorine
49 Bougival
44 Rueil Malmaison
LOCKS
Km Lock VHF
202 Amfreville 18
161 Notre Dame de la Garenne 22
121 Méricourt 18
73 Andrésy 22
49 Bougival 22
or
44.5 Chatou 18
17 Suresnes 22

TIDES **Standard Port LE HAVRE (⟵)**

Times				Height (metres)			
High Water		Low Water		MHWS	MHWN	MLWN	MLWS
0000	0500	0000	0700	7·9	6·6	2·8	1·2
1200	1700	1200	1900				
Differences TANCARVILLE* *(Km 338. 49°28'·35N 00°27'·88E)*							
–0135	–0120	+0030	+0145	+0·1	+0·1	+0·3	+1·0
QUILLEBEUF* *(Km 332. 49°28'·25N 00°32'·00E)*							
–0055	–0110	+0105	+0210	+0·1	+0·1	+0·5	+1·4
VATTEVILLE* *(Km 317. 49°28'·89N 00°40'·01E)*							
–0015	–0040	+0205	+0240	–0·1	–0·1	+0·9	+2·2
CAUDEBEC* *(Km 309. 49°31'·35N 00°43'·66E)*							
–0005	–0030	+0220	+0300	–0·1	–0·1	+1·0	+2·3
HEURTEAUVILLE* *(Km 295. 49°25'·70N 00°48'·17E)*							
+0055	+0005	+0250	+0330	–0·2	–0·1	+1·2	+2·6
DUCLAIR* *(Km 278. 49°28'·73N 00°52'·38E)*							
+0210	+0145	+0350	+0410	–0·2	0·0	+1·5	+3·2
ROUEN *(Km 245. 49°26'·50N 01°03'·13E)*							
+0305	+0240	+0505	+0515	–0·1	+0·2	+1·6	+3·3

*HW time differences refer to the start of a stand lasting about 2¾hrs up to Vatteville, decreasing to about 1¾hrs at Duclair.

SHELTER Marinas/Haltes Nautiques (HN)/fuel, see above. Masts can be lowered at Dives, Deauville, Le Havre, Honfleur and Rouen.

TIDAL STREAMS require careful study; see *N France and Belgium Cruising Companion* (Featherstone/Fernhurst) for tidal stream graphs and a detailed analysis, plus Rouen and Paris. ▶*At Ratier NW SHM buoy the flood starts at LW Le Havre +1 and at La Roque (Km 342) at LW+2, and progressively later further upriver. So even a 5kn boat which left Le Havre at LW (or Honfleur at LW+1) and passed the W end of Digue du Ratier at LW+15, should carry the flood to Rouen. If delayed, try another day rather than stopping en route.*

Going downriver on the ebb a boat will meet the flood. In a fast boat it is worth continuing, rather than ⚓ for about 4hrs, because the ebb starts sooner the further downriver one gets.◀

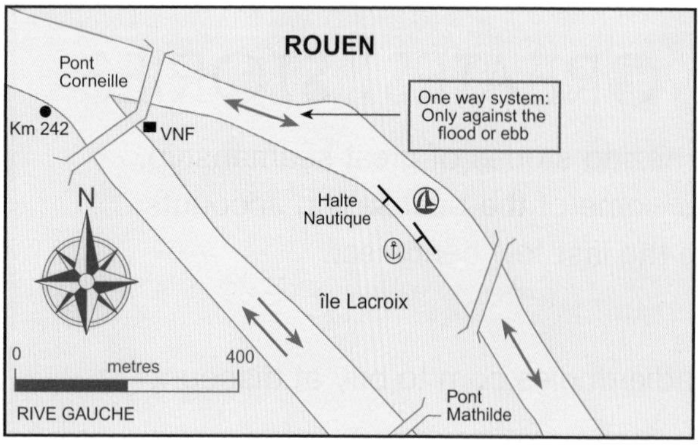

ROUEN
Pont Corneille
Km 242
VNF
One way system: Only against the flood or ebb
N
Halte Nautique
Île Lacroix
0
metres
400
RIVE GAUCHE
Pont Mathilde

NAVIGATION The tidal section to Rouen should be completed in 1 day, because the strong stream and ships' wash make berthing alongside dangerous and there are no ⚓s. Yacht navigation is prohibited at night. A radar reflector and VHF aerial are needed, even with mast down.

Enter the buoyed Chenal de Rouen abm No 2 buoy. Care is needed to avoid the shoal banks NE of No 2 buoy, especially in morning fog; keep W of Rade de la Carosse WCM buoy. The approach can be rough in a strong W'ly over ebb tide. From No 2 buoy to Tancarville bridge yachts must keep outboard of the PHM chan buoys, in either direction. Pont de Normandie (52m) is conspic 1·7M E of Honfleur.

Entry via the Canal de Tancarville is possible if sea conditions are bad, but expect delays due to 2 locks and 8 bridges. At Le Havre transit the Bassins Bellot, Vétillart, Despujols and the Canal du Havre, leading via the Canal de Tancarville to the lock (Km 338).

From Amfreville lock to Paris current is about 1kn in summer, more after winter floods. 6 of 7 locks must be transited; foc 0700-1900.

COMMUNICATIONS Ch 73 (*Rouen Port Control*) gives nav, vis, weather and water level info on request. Monitor Ch 73 for tfc info. Ch 82 broadcasts water levels from Le Havre to Caudebec every 5 mins.

ROUEN, Seine Maritime, **49°26'·07N 01°06'·24E**. AC 2879; SHOM 6796, 6117. Yacht navigation prohib SS+½ to SR–½. ⊆ in the Halte Nautique, NE side of Île Lacroix, Km 241 (lat/long above) or **Marina Bassin St Gervais**, N bank, Km 245, see below. A one-way system in the chan NE of Île Lacroix only allows navigation *against* the stream. For example, if leaving on the young flood to go upriver, you must first go downriver to the NW tip of the island, then turn upriver via the SW chan. *Rouen Port* VHF Ch **73** 68. HM 02·35·52·54·56; Aff Mar 02·35·98·53·98; ⊖ 02·35·98·27·60; ☼ 02·35·80·11·44.

Facilities: **Marina Bassin St Gervais**, ☎02·35·08·30·59, www.la-crea.fr/port-de-plaisance-de-la-crea.html; €1·20. Mast down/up at pontoon SE side; (25t,3t).

Halte Nautique ☎02·35·07·33·94, www.rouen.fr/adresse/halte-nautique 50 ⊆ (Ⓔ) (3t). from barge at Km 239.

9.17.20 PARIS

Île-de-France, **48°50'·84N 02°22'·02E** (Paris-Arsenal marina).

CHARTS AC & SHOM charts do not cover the Seine E of Rouen, but Fluviacarte No 1 covers Le Havre to Paris in detail.

SHELTER Complete in Paris-Arsenal Marina.

NAVIGATION Between Eiffel Tower and Notre Dame the wash of many *vedettes* can raise quite a chop.

A traffic system (chartlet) around Île de la Cité and Île St Louis must be understood and obeyed. Going upriver, the simpler route is: Hug the S bank in the narrowish one-way Bras de la Monnaie, leaving Notre Dame to port. Or take the wider, two-way N bank chan, noting that this route is only available H to H+20; is regulated by R/G tfc lts on Pont au Change; and requires two cross-overs where shown below.

Going downriver, make good a window H+35 to H+50, obey R/G tfc lts on Pont de Sully, then leave Île St Louis to stbd and Notre Dame to port. Cross-over twice where indicated.

By 2020 Paris should be joined to Cambrai in N France by the 66-mile long Seine-Nord Europe canal, which will be open to leisure craft.

LIGHTS AND MARKS Eiffel Tower and Notre Dame. Check off other landmarks and all bridges carefully; obey cross-overs.

COMMUNICATIONS Brit Consul 01·44·51·31·00; Monitor VHF Ch 10 on the river (mandatory); at the lock to Arsenal talk direct to HM via intercom, CCTV monitors; Marina VHF Ch 09; Canal St Martin VHF Ch 20; Taxi 01·45·85·85·85.

FACILITIES

Paris-Arsenal Marina 11 Blvd de la Bastille, 75012 Paris, ☎01·43·41·39·32. www.fayollemarine.fr No reservations 1/6-30/9, but contact marina several days before arrival. Enter 0800-1900 (2000: w/e, and Jul/Aug) via small lock, with waiting pontoon outside; obey R/G tfc lts signed 'Plaisance'. Air clearance in lock is 5·2m, least depth 1·9m. Inside, HM and office are to stbd; berth as directed. 176 €4·00; max LOA 25m. (plus on marina trolley, 750m SE) (7t). Metro stns: Quai de la Rapée (Line 5) at S end of marina and Bastille (Lines 1, 5 & 8) at the N end. Numerous buses from Bastille. Tourist Office at Gare de Lyon (550m).

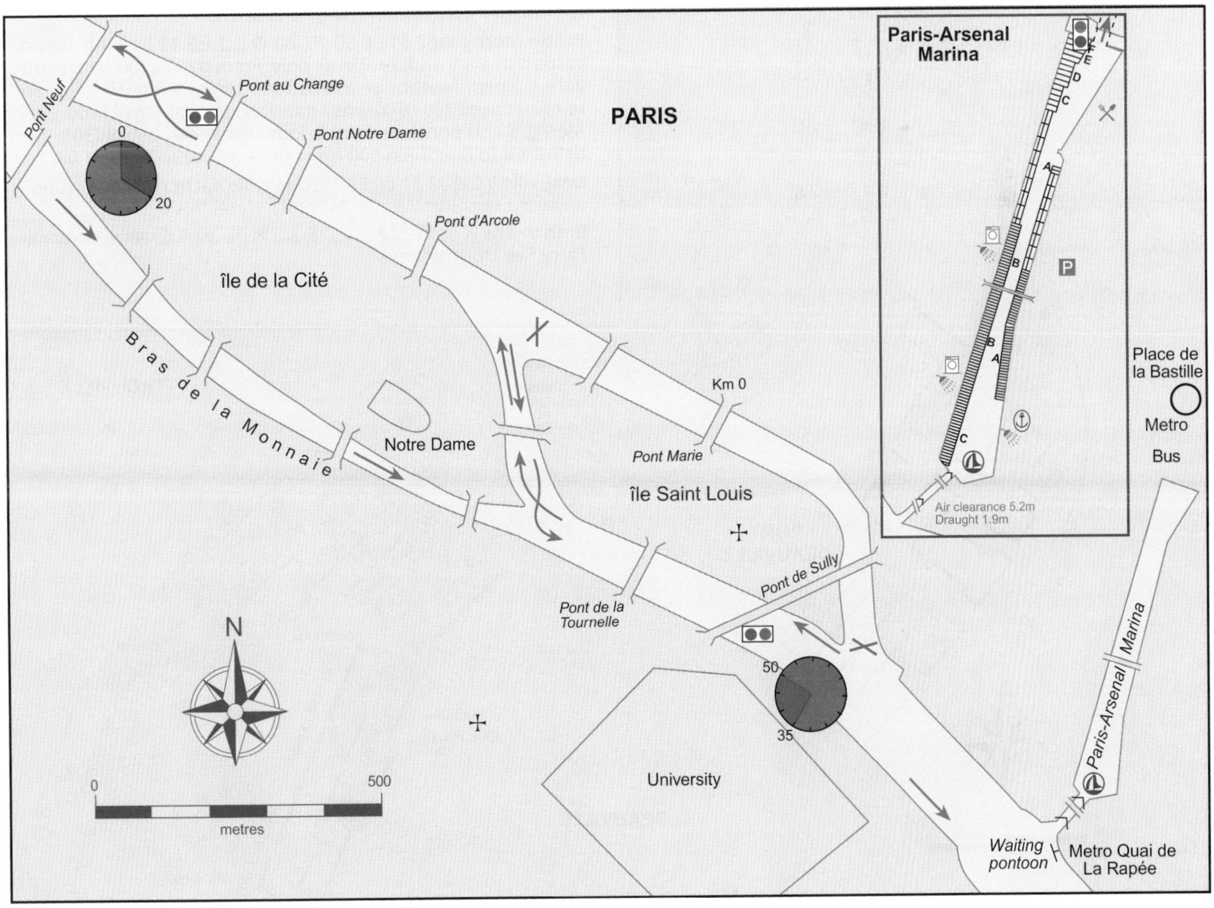
PARIS
Pont Neuf
Pont au Change
Pont Notre Dame
Pont d'Arcole
0
20
île de la Cité
Bras de la Monnaie
Notre Dame
Km 0
Pont Marie
île Saint Louis
Pont de Sully
Pont de la Tournelle
50
35
University
N
0
500
metres
Paris-Arsenal Marina
A
B
C
D
E
P
Air clearance 5.2m
Draught 1.9m
Place de la Bastille
Metro
Bus
Paris-Arsenal Marina
Waiting pontoon
Metro Quai de La Rapée

9.17.21 DEAUVILLE/TROUVILLE

Calvados **49° 22'·38N 00° 04'·15E** ✵✵◊◊◊✿✿✿

CHARTS AC 2613, 2146, 1349; SHOM 7418, 7420; Navi 526; Imray C32

TIDES –0130 Dover; ML 5·1; Duration 0510

Standard Port LE HAVRE (⟵)

Times				Height (metres)			
High Water		Low Water		MHWS	MHWN	MLWN	MLWS
0000	0500	0000	0700	8·0	6·7	2·9	1·2
1200	1700	1200	1900				
Differences TROUVILLE							
–0100	–0010	0000	+0005	+0·4	+0·3	+0·3	+0·1

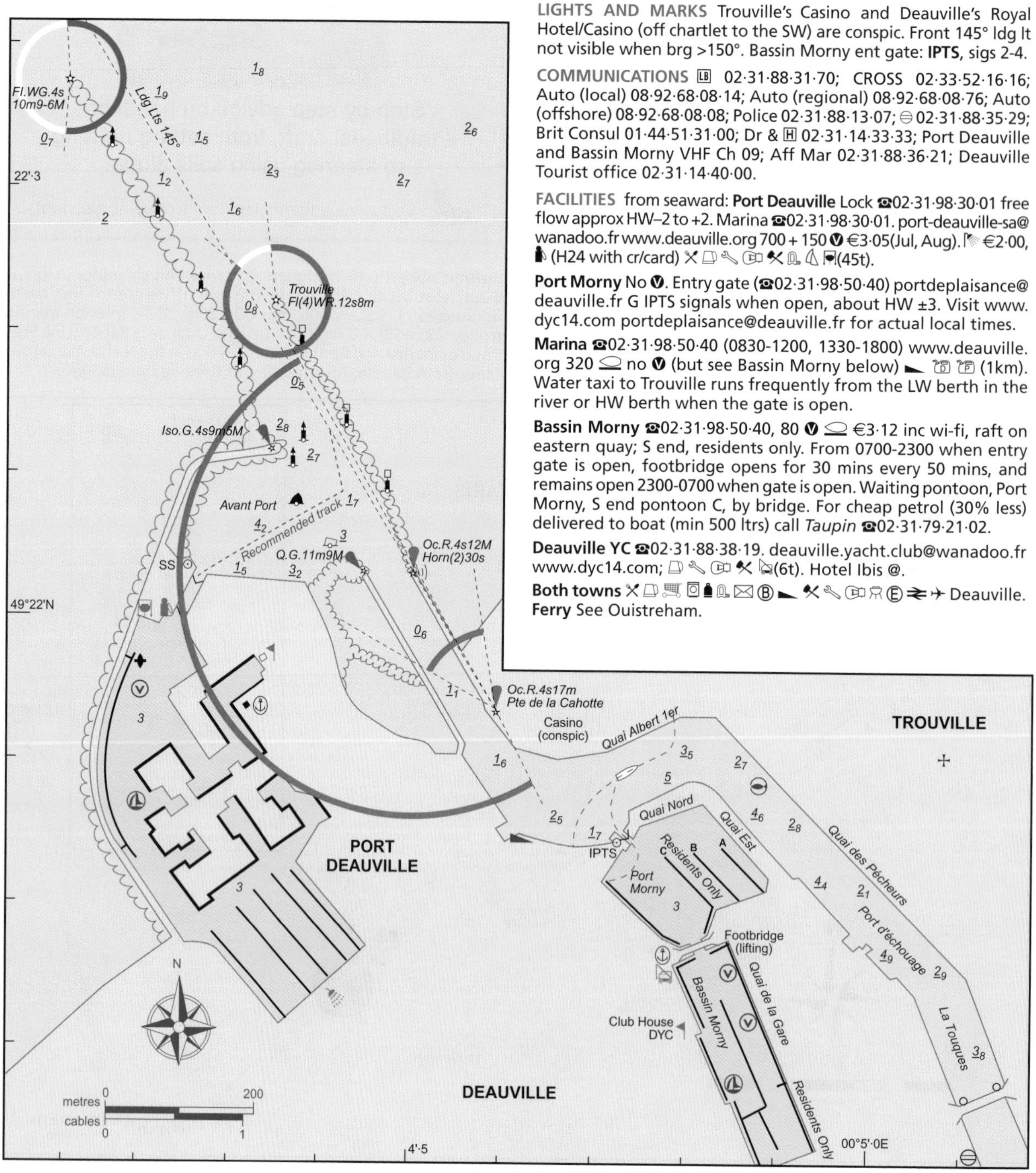

NOTE: There is a double HW at Trouville. The HW time differences, when referred to the time of HW Le Havre, give the times of the first HW.

SHELTER Access difficult in NW/N winds >F5. Best shelter in Bassin Morny (3m) Port Deauville outer basin (2·8m) can be uncomfortable during freeflow, again in strong winds from the N quadrant. Only FVs berth at Trouville.

NAVIGATION WPT 49°22'·94N 00°03'·62E,145°/0·65M to abeam W training wall lt, Fl WG 4s, beware drying shoal extending E from the training wall, keep well to stbd. Do not appr from E of N due to Les Ratelets drying shoal and Banc de Trouville. Trouville SW WCM buoy is 1M WNW of ent. Chan and river dry 2·4m; no access LW±2½, for 2m draft, less water than charted reported in Avant Port.

LIGHTS AND MARKS Trouville's Casino and Deauville's Royal Hotel/Casino (off chartlet to the SW) are conspic. Front 145° ldg lt not visible when brg >150°. Bassin Morny ent gate: **IPTS**, sigs 2-4.

COMMUNICATIONS 02·31·88·31·70; CROSS 02·33·52·16·16; Auto (local) 08·92·68·08·14; Auto (regional) 08·92·68·08·76; Auto (offshore) 08·92·68·08·08; Police 02·31·88·13·07; ⊖ 02·31·88·35·29; Brit Consul 01·44·51·31·00; Dr & Ⓗ 02·31·14·33·33; Port Deauville and Bassin Morny VHF Ch 09; Aff Mar 02·31·88·36·21; Deauville Tourist office 02·31·14·40·00.

FACILITIES from seaward: **Port Deauville** Lock ☎02·31·98·30·01 free flow approx HW–2 to +2. Marina ☎02·31·98·30·01. port-deauville-sa@wanadoo.fr www.deauville.org 700 + 150 Ⓥ €3·05(Jul, Aug). €2·00, (H24 with cr/card) (45t).

Port Morny No Ⓥ. Entry gate (☎02·31·98·50·40) portdeplaisance@deauville.fr G IPTS signals when open, about HW ±3. Visit www.dyc14.com portdeplaisance@deauville.fr for actual local times.

Marina ☎02·31·98·50·40 (0830-1200, 1330-1800) www.deauville.org 320 no Ⓥ (but see Bassin Morny below) (1km). Water taxi to Trouville runs frequently from the LW berth in the river or HW berth when the gate is open.

Bassin Morny ☎02·31·98·50·40, 80 Ⓥ €3·12 inc wi-fi, raft on eastern quay; S end, residents only. From 0700-2300 when entry gate is open, footbridge opens for 30 mins every 50 mins, and remains open 2300-0700 when gate is open. Waiting pontoon, Port Morny, S end pontoon C, by bridge. For cheap petrol (30% less) delivered to boat (min 500 ltrs) call *Taupin* ☎02·31·79·21·02.

Deauville YC ☎02·31·88·38·19. deauville.yacht.club@wanadoo.fr www.dyc14.com; (6t). Hotel Ibis @.

Both towns ✕ ✉ Ⓑ Ⓔ ✈ Deauville. **Ferry** See Ouistreham.

9.17.22 DIVES-SUR-MER

Calvados **49°17'·68N 00°05'·63W** (entry gate)

CHARTS AC 2146, 1349; SHOM 7418, 7420 (the preferred chart); Navi 526; Imray C32

TIDES –0135 Dover; ML 5·1m

Standard Port LE HAVRE (⟵)

Times				Height (metres)			
High Water		Low Water		MHWS	MHWN	MLWN	MLWS
0000	0500	0000	0700	8·0	6·7	2·9	1·2
1200	1700	1200	1900				
Differences DIVES-SUR-MER							
–0100	–0010	0000	0000	+0·3	+0·2	+0·2	+0·1
OUISTREHAM							
–0045	–0010	–0005	0000	–0·3	–0·3	–0·2	–0·3

NOTE: There is a double HW at Dives. HW time differences, referred to the time of HW Le Havre, give times of the first HW.

SHELTER Excellent inside. Appr can be difficult in NW/NE >F5 when a bad sea can build quickly.

NAVIGATION WPT WPT 49°19'·18N 00°05'·85W, SWM buoy 'DI' (off chartlet) Iso 4s, 168°/7ca to Nos 1/2 buoys; thence follow the buoyed chan between sandbanks (drying 4·2m). Appr dries to 1M offshore. See FACILITIES for access times.

4 PHM and SHM buoy/bns are moved to suit shifting chan; Nos 1 (SHM) and 2 (PHM) are the only lit lateral buoys; Nos 3 and 5 SHMs are fixed lt bns which should be given a wide berth. Caution: Buoys/bns may lack numbers.

After last chan buoys (7 & 8) keep to port for the marina ent (400m W of lt ho). Or fork stbd to follow drying Dives river to YC's pontoon (2 Ⓥ berths) E of footbridge.

LIGHTS AND MARKS See Lights, buoys and waypoints and the chartlet. Wooded hills E of Dives and Houlgate church spire help locate the marina.

COMMUNICATIONS CROSS/ 02·31·88·11·13; via HM; Auto 08·92·68·08·14; Police 02·31·28·23·00; Brit Consul 01·44·51·31·00; Dr 02·31·91·60·17; HM VHF Ch 09 (H24).

FACILITIES **Marina** ☎02·31·24·48·00. sncport guillaume@cegetel.net www.calvados-nautisme.com Access via entry gate HW±3; HW±2½ for draft >1·5m; HW±1½ in bad conditions. Note: unless recently dredged, craft with draft >1.8m should only attempt entry HW±2. Sill below gate is 2·5m above CD; gate opens when tide 4·5m above CD and at springs may create a 4–5kn current for the first 45 mins. 550+50 Ⓥ €2·85, max LOA 15m, draft 1·9m. Office hrs: H24 summer; 0900-1200, 1400-1800 winter. H24, (30t) demasting (1·5t). No @ or wi-fi.

Cabourg YC ☎02·31·91·23·55. cabourg.yacht.club@wanadoo.fr .

Town ✈ (Deauville). **Ferry** Ouistreham.

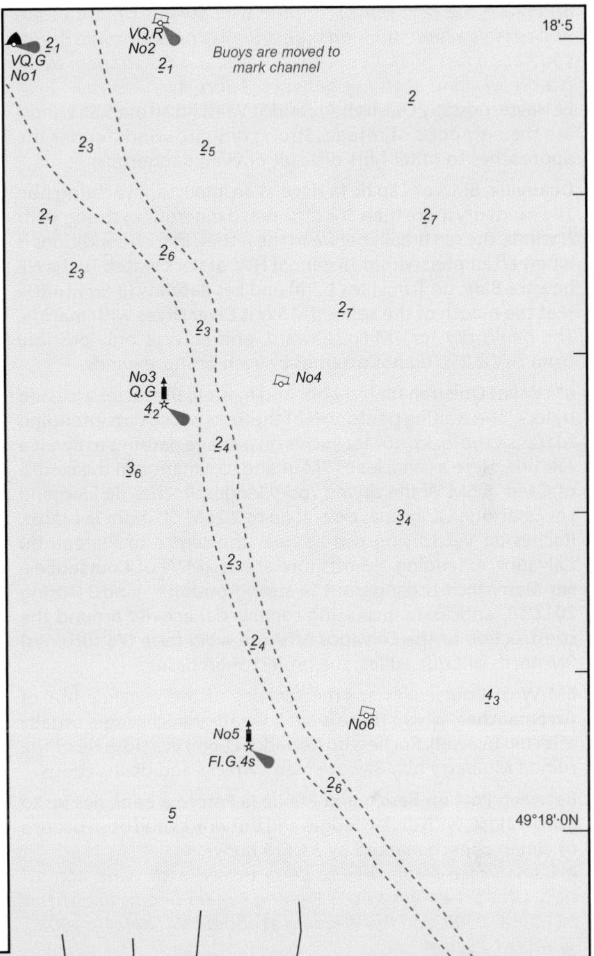

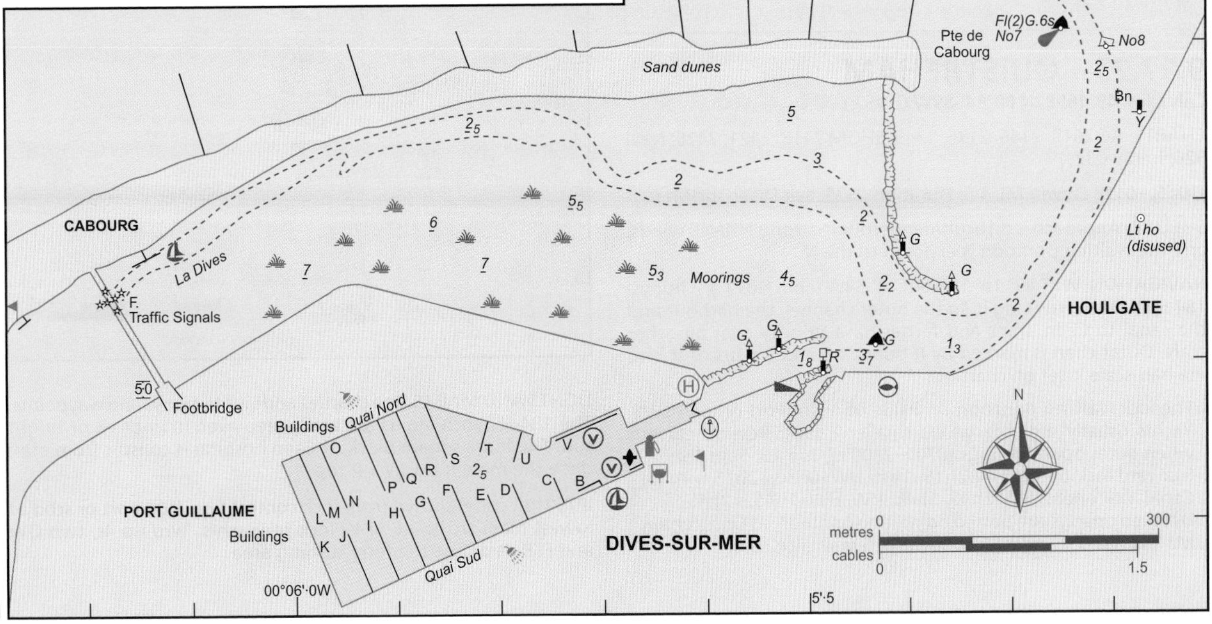

DEAUVILLE TO GRANDCAMP

(AC 2146, 2136). Since access to all the hbrs along this coast is to some extent tidally limited, it is best to cruise this area from W to E, so as to take advantage of the main Channel flood. ►*Thus you can leave one harbour at the start of the tidal window and reach the next hbr before the window has closed; in the opposite direction this is difficult and may be impossible unless you have a fast boat. Between Le Havre and Ouistreham there is a useful stand at HW of between 2-3hrs.*◄
Le Havre, possibly Ouistreham, and St Vaast (in all but S/SE winds) are the only ports of refuge. Strong onshore winds render the approaches to other hbrs difficult or even dangerous.

Deauville, 8M S of Cap de la Hève, is an important yachting hbr. The sands dry more than 5ca offshore; dangerous in strong W or N winds, the sea breaks between the jetties. In such conditions it is best attempted within 15 mins of HW, at slack water. To the NE beware Banc de Trouville (1·7m) and Les Ratelets (0·9m) to the N at the mouth of the Seine. 7M SW is **River Dives** with marina. The banks dry for 1M to seaward, and entry is only possible from HW ± 2½; do not attempt in fresh onshore winds.

6M W lies **Ouistreham** ferry hbr and marina, the latter accessed by lock. The waiting pontoon N of the locks is for boats intending to transit the locks, not for yachts on passage pausing to await a fair tide. Here a canal leads 7M inland to a marina in the centre of Caen. 2-6M W the drying rocky ledges, Roches de Lion and Les Essarts de Langrune, extend up to 2·25M offshore in places. Roches de Ver (drying rks) lie near the centre of Plateau du Calvados, extending 1M offshore about 2M W of **Courseulles-sur-Mer** which is dangerous in strong onshore winds. During 2017/18, anticipate increasing commercial activity around the construction of the Calvados offshore wind farm (75 turbines) 9M north of Courseulles, the project shorebase.

5M W of Courseulles are the remains of the wartime hbr of **Arromanches**, where there is a fair weather anchorage, usually affected by swell. Rochers du Calvados (1·6m) lies close NE of the ruined Mulberry hbr. Beware many wrecks and obstructions.

Between **Port-en-Bessin** and Pte de la Percée a bank lies up to 3ca offshore, with drying ledges and the wrecks and obstructions of Omaha Beach marked by 3 NCM buoys.
►*A small race forms off Pte de la Percée with wind against tide. Off Port-en-Bessin the E-going stream begins about HW Le Havre –0500, and the W-going at about HW Le Havre +0050, sp rates 1·25kn.*◄

9.17.23 OUISTREHAM

Calvados **49°16'·82N 00°14'·89W** (E lock)

CHARTS AC 2613, 2146, 2136, 1349; SHOM 7418, 7421, 7420; Navi 526; Imray C32

TIDES –0118 Dover; ML 4·6; Duration 0525. See Dives-sur-Mer.

SHELTER Approach is difficult/dangerous in strong NW-NE winds, and the waiting pontoon is exposed to the N.

NAVIGATION WPT 49° 19'·18N 00° 14'·54W (abm Nos 1 & 2 buoys) 184·5°/2·1M to front ldg lt. In the outer channel, the harbour and the canal to Caen, ships and ferries have priority over all other craft. Outer chan is marked by lt buoys 1-6 and 3 pairs of lt bns; see half-scale inset on chartlet.

The lock waiting pontoon on E side of Avant Port dries at LWS. Yachts usually enter canal via smaller E lock. Beware current when gates open. Timings (0700 -2100 LT, Jun 15 -Sept 15):
Seaward lock opens: HW-2h15,-1h15,HW+0h30,+2h15, +3h15.
Canal lock opens: HW-2h45,-1h45, HW, HW+1h45, +2h45.
Detailed timings are posted on waiting pontoon, at Ouistreham Marina (Ch 09) and www.ouistreham-plaisance.com.

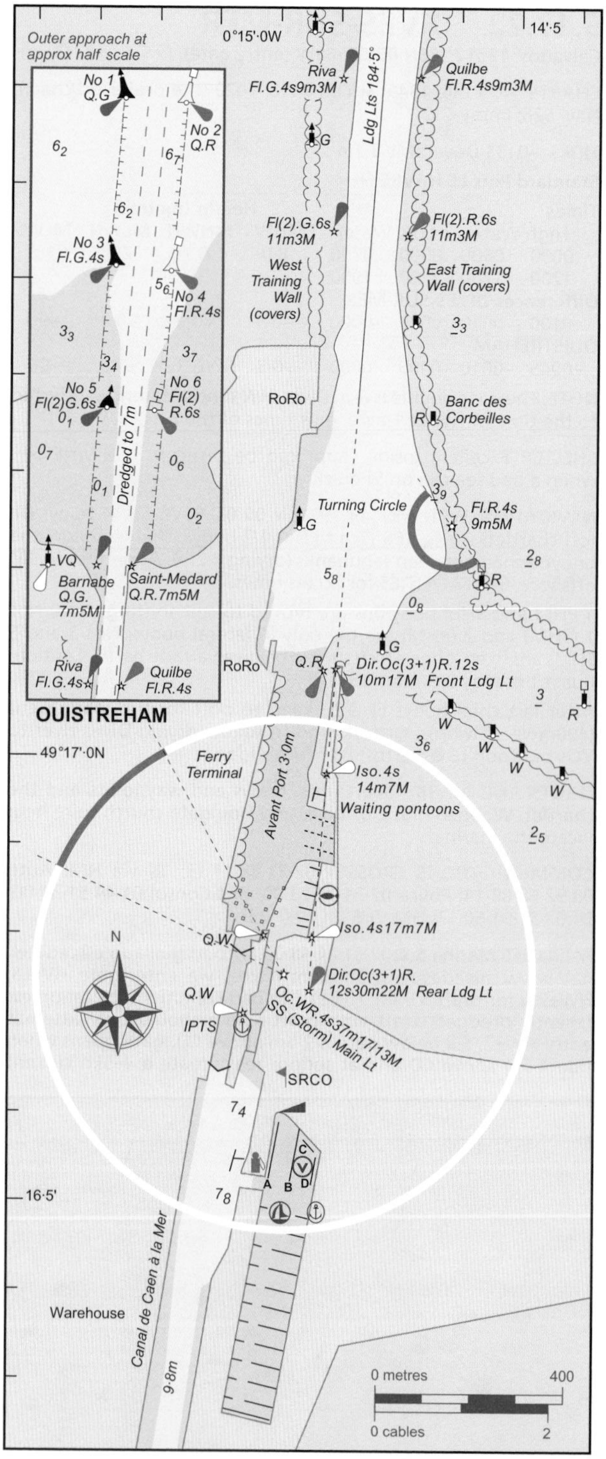

LIGHTS AND MARKS See chartlet and Lights, buoys and waypoints. The 184·5° synch ldg lts are easily seen even in poor vis or bright sun. The huge square block of Caen hospital is conspic from afar; ditto the main lt ho, W + R top.

IPTS (full code) shown from lock control twr. A Ⓦ port or stbd of lowest main tfc lt, = E or W lock for yachts. Two Iso 4s, two QW and Fl R 4s define the ferry turning area.

COMMUNICATIONS CROSS/LB 02·33·52·16·16; Police 02·31·36·22·70; ⊖ 09·70·27·44·50; Dr 02·31·97·18·45; H(Caen) 02·31·27·27·27; British Consul 01·44·51·31·00; Port HM and Lock 02·31·36·22·00; Call *Ouistreham Port* or *Ouistreham Lock* VHF Ch 74 (HW -2 to HW+3); Marina VHF Ch 09; Sté des Régates VHF Ch 09 office hours; 08·99·71·02·14; Auto 08·92·68·08·77; Aff Mar 02·31·53·66·50; Taxi 02·31·97·39·41; Ferry terminal 02·31·36·36·36.

FACILITIES

Marina ☎02·31·96·91·37. www.ouistreham-plaisance.com 650 inc 100 Ⓥ €3·10. Ⓥ raft on pontoon D, in 3·5m. (H24) Ⓔ SHOM wi-fi (14t).

Société des Régates de Caen-Ouistreham (SRCO) www.srco.fr ☎02·31·96·13·30. **Town** Ⓑ (bus to Caen) ✈ (Caen). Ferry to Portsmouth.

HARBOUR AT SOUTH END OF OUISTREHAM CANAL

CAEN 49°10′·95N 00°21′·17W. Charts: AC 1349, SHOM 7420.

NAVIGATION The 8M canal passage is simple and takes approx 1½hrs. Depths 2·5m to 9·8m; max speed 7kn; no overtaking. The 3 opening bridges are: Bénouville (Pegasus) (2½M S of Ouistreham) Colombelles (5M) and La Fonderie, Caen (8M). Tfc lts are not used; N-bound vessels have right of way at bridges.

Bridges open free for boats which transit at the scheduled times, 1/4-30/9, fees due at other times. S-bound: Dep Bénouville bridge 1010, 1330, 1630. (Allow ½hr from Ouistreham lock/marina). N-bound dep La Fonderie bridge: 0845, 1200, 1500. Times can vary; check with marina or the website below.

R/T Monitor Ch 68 in the canal. *Caen Port* Ch **74**, 68.

Marina ☎02·31·95·24·47. www.caen-plaisance.com After La Fonderie bridge turn 90° stbd for marina (4m) at Bassin St Pierre in city centre. Ⓥ berths on pontoon E or as directed. 76+16Ⓥ €2·27, max LOA 25m, draft 3.8m.

City Ⓗ Ⓑ @ ✈ Caen-Carpiquet.

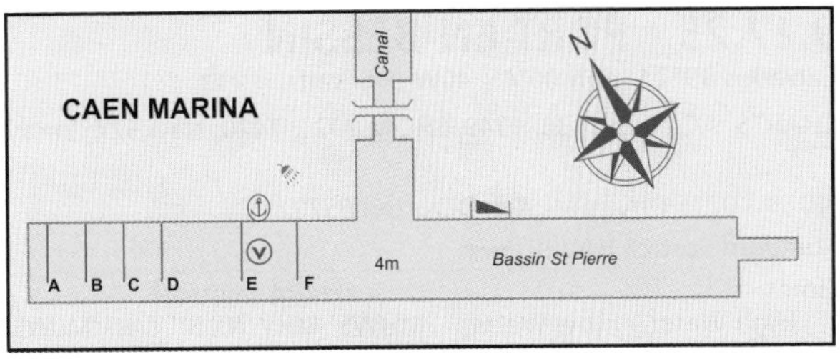

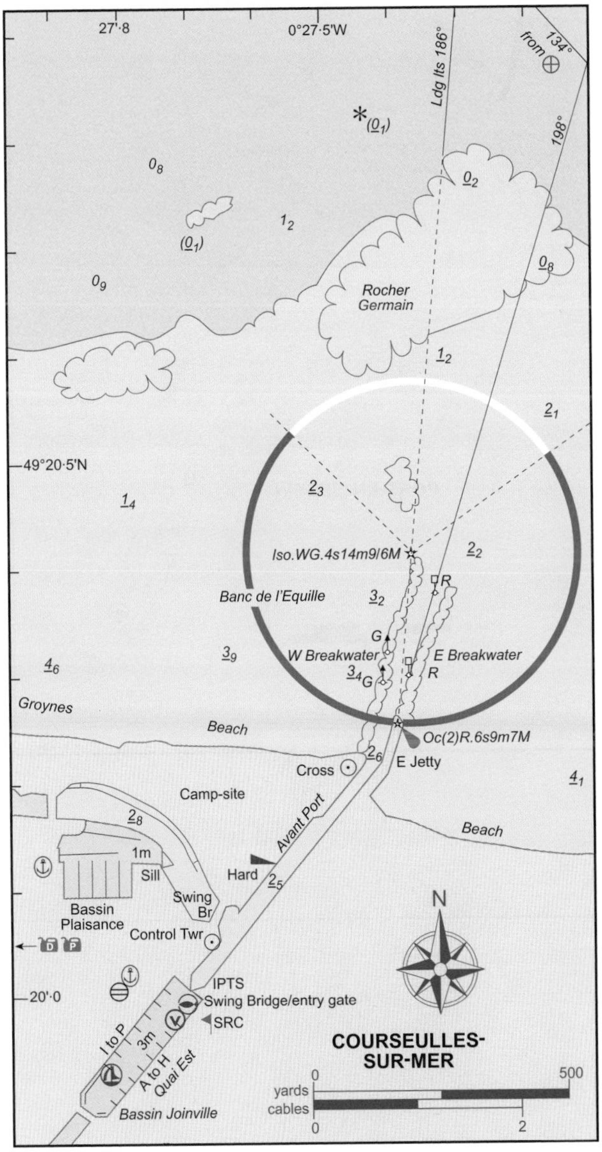

9.17.24 COURSEULLES-SUR-MER

Calvados **49°20′·40N 00°27′·32W**

CHARTS AC 2613, 2136, 1349; SHOM 7421, 7420; Navi 526; Imray C32

TIDES –0145 Dover; ML 4·6; Duration No data. See Port-en-Bessin.

SHELTER Good in Bassin Joinville (3m) but appr becomes difficult in strong N to NE winds. Exposed offshore ⚓ (3-5m) at L'Anneau de la Marguerite, 134°/0·4M from SWM buoy.

NAVIGATION WPT 49° 21′·28N 00° 27′·69W (SWM buoy Iso 4s). From waypoint steer 134° 5ca, (use outer ldg marks, front, Bernières tower ≠ 134° with rear, twin spires of Douvres-La-Déliverande church, (partly obsc'd by trees and below skyline close in) then steer 198° 5ca direct to E Jetty hd. At night the two bkwtr lights ≠ 186° form a useful leading line. Beware: Plateau du Calvados extending 2M seaward of the hbr, with drying banks for >0·6M; also oyster beds to the west marked by a line of unlit Y bys running parallel to the shore between Ver-sur-Mer and Asnelles.

The Avant Port dries 2·5m; best ent at HW –1, keep to the E side. Entry gate into Bassin Joinville stays open approx HW ±2. (A detailed timetable of gate opening/closing times for every day of the year can be downloaded at www.courseulles-sur-mer.com/leport). The Control Twr opens the swing bridge above it on request Ch 09 or when an arriving yacht is spotted, usually quite quickly. **IPTS** in use. There is space at the SW end of the Bassin to turn a boat round.

LIGHTS AND MARKS See chartlet and Lights, buoys and waypoints. Both drying bkwtrs and their perches are easily seen, as is a conspic crucifix at root of the W bkwtr. A Cross of Lorraine is 4ca, and Pte de Ver lt ho is 2·5M W of the hbr ent.

COMMUNICATIONS CROSS 02·33·52·16·16,(Emergency 196); LB 02·31·37·45·47; 08·92·68·08·14; Auto 08·92·68·32·50; Police 02·31·29·55·20 or 17; ⊖ 02·31·21·71·09 @ Port-en-Bessin; Brit Consul 01·44·51·31·00 (Paris); H 02·31·27·27·27 (Caen); Dr 02·31·37·45·24; Ambulance 02·31·44·88·88 or 15; Fire 18; Control twr 02·31·37·46·03, VHF Ch 09 HW±2; Aff Mar (@Caen) 02·31·53·66·50; Tourist Info 02·31·37·46·80.

FACILITIES Bassin Plaisance local shoal draft boats in 1m; no Ⓥ. **Bassin Joinville** ☎02·31·37·51·69. Marina hours: All year, Mon-Sat 0900-1200, + Sun and hols, April-Aug, + July-Aug, 1400-2000 at HW times. 730+20Ⓥ berth as directed by HM, or if absent, on pontoon X on E Quay. €3·10 and €0·20pp/day tax. 11m max LOA. (600m) Ⓔ (25t).

Société des Régates de Courseulles (SRC) ☎02.31.37.47.42.

Town @ Ⓑ (via bus to Caen) ✈ (Caen-Carpiquet). Taxi ☎02·31·37·90·37. Ferry Ouistreham.

MULBERRY ANCHORAGE 6·5M WEST OF COURSEULLES

ARROMANCHES, Calvados, **49°21'·36N 00°37'·25W**. AC 2613, 2136; SHOM 7421; Navi 527. Tides, see Port-en-Bessin. Strictly a fair weather anchorage, with limited shelter from the ruined WW II Mulberry caissons which are conspicuous especially at LW. Swell intrudes and can make anchoring uncomfortable. Rochers du Calvados, 7ca ENE of the entrance, dries 1·6m but can be crossed near HW.

There are many obstructions within the harbour and offshore: 3 to the W and N are marked by a WCM and two ECM buoys. From the more N'ly ECM buoy (Roseberry, 49°23'·10N 00°36'·49W) the entrance (lat/long as line 1) bears approx 196°/1·8M; it is marked by a small unlit SHM and PHM buoy.

Enter on about 245° for charted anchorage in 3-5m to S of the caissons, or sound closer inshore with caution. Entry from E or W is not advised due to uncharted obstructions. Caution: rocky plateau (3·4m) and further obstructions W of the dinghy landing area.

Facilities: YC Port Winston ☎02·31·22·31·01, 2 dinghy slips. Worth going ashore for D-Day museums and the panoramic view from the clifftops, but very crowded in season.

9.17.25 PORT-EN-BESSIN

Calvados **49°21'·16N 00°45'·40W** (Hbr ent)

CHARTS AC 2613, 2136, 1349; SHOM 7421, 7420; Navi 527; Imray C32

TIDES –0215 Dover; ML 4·4; Duration 0520

Standard Port LE HAVRE (⟵)

Times				Height (metres)			
High Water		Low Water		MHWS	MHWN	MLWN	MLWS
0000	0500	0000	0700	8·0	6·7	2·9	1·2
1200	1700	1200	1900				
Differences COURSEULLES-SUR-MER							
–0100	–0055	–0015	–0025	–0·6	–0·6	–0·3	–0·1
PORT-EN-BESSIN							
–0055	–0030	–0030	–0035	–0·7	–0·7	–0·2	–0·1
ARROMANCHES							
–0055	–0025	–0025	–0035	–0·6	–0·6	–0·2	–0·2

SHELTER Good. Ent difficult in strong N/NE'lies and dangerous in F8+. No ⚓ in outer hbr nor 1ca either side of 204° ldg line.

NAVIGATION WPT 49°21'·62N 00°45'·09W, 204°/0·5M to hbr ent. Avoid G sector of W mole hd Fl WG 4s which covers the inshore dangers off Omaha Beach, 3 to 6M to the WNW. In the outer hbr beware submerged jetty (marked by R bcn) to E of ent chan.

LIGHTS AND MARKS Conspic marks: a water twr (104m) 1·7M ESE of the hbr; a Sig Stn 7 cables W of hbr. Ldg lts 204°: Front, W pylon, G top, at bottom of hill; rear, W house/grey roof near top of the hillside. See chartlet and Lights, buoys & waypoints.

IPTS control entry to the basins. Entry gate opens HW ±2. While gate stays open, swing bridge opens whenever possible to suit yachts and FVs; there is little road traffic. When shut the bridge shows FR in the middle.

COMMUNICATIONS CROSS 02·33·52·16·16; Sig Stn/LB 02·31·21·81·51; Auto 08·92·68·08·14; Police 02·31·21·70·10; ⊖ 02·31·21·71·09; Brit Consul 01·44·51·31·00; H 02·31·51·51·51; Dr 02·31·21·74·26; HM 02·31·21·70·49, VHF Ch 18 (HW ±2) for gate opening H24; Aff Mar 02·31·21·71·52; Mairie 02·31·21·72·12.

FACILITIES A major FV port. **Outer Hbr** dries up to 3·7m; slip L. Drying on E side Quai de L'Epi, no charge.

Bassin 1: Inside the entry gate, tight turn 90° stbd, **V** berth/raft alongside 25m pontoon in NNW corner. €0·77 + €0·20pp/day tax, WC €3·00 pp/day, code access (free, children <10 yrs) at Tourist Office opp on E quay. Yachts may stay only 24-48hrs, due to limited space. No berthing on sloping E wall. Call Gatemaster ☎02·31·21·71·77 (HW ±2) to pre-book gate time if leaving early.

Bassin 2, no entry. **Services** slip (E) (4t).

Town ✕ ✉ (B) ≠ (bus to Bayeux) ✈ (Caen, ☎ 02·31·26·58·00). **Ferry** see Ouistreham.

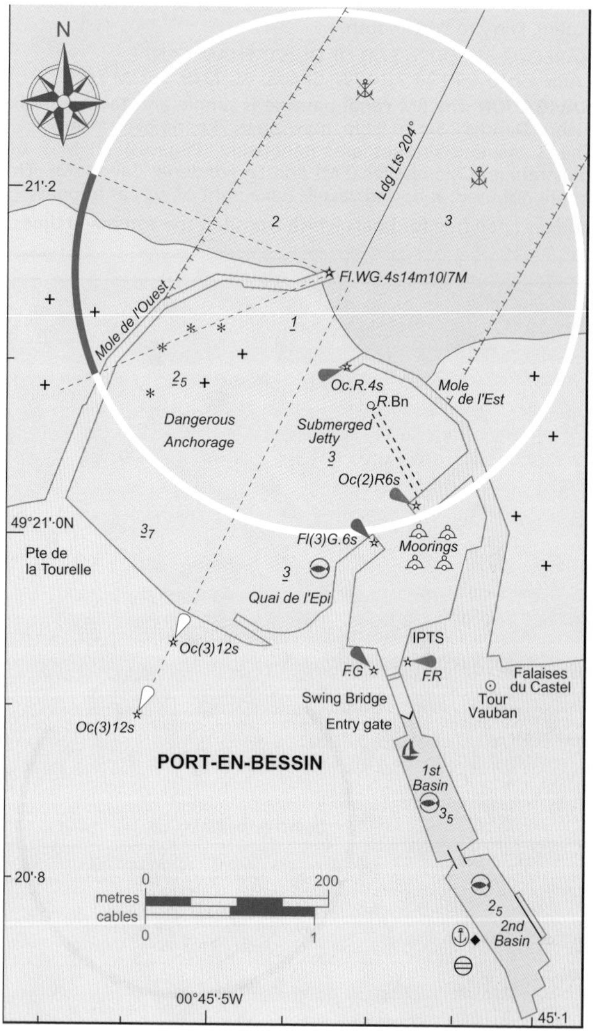

9.17.26 GRANDCAMP

Calvados **49°23'·51N 01°02'·99W** (Pierheads)

CHARTS AC 2613, 2135, 1349; SHOM 7422, 7420; Navi 527; Imray C32

TIDES –0220 Dover; ML Rade de la Capelle 4·4; Duration 0510

Standard Port CHERBOURG (⟶)

Times				Height (metres)			
High Water		Low Water		MHWS	MHWN	MLWN	MLWS
0300	1000	0400	1000	6·4	5·1	2·6	1·1
1500	2200	1600	2200				
Differences RADE DE LA CAPELLE (3M to NW)							
+0125	+0050	+0125	+0110	+0·7	+0·7	0·0	+0·1
ILES SAINT MARCOUF							
+0130	+0055	+0120	+0110	+0·5	+0·5	0·0	0·0

SHELTER Good, but approach is difficult in NW-NE winds >F6.

NAVIGATION WPT 49°24'·82N 01°04'·33W, 146°/1·6M to E pier head. Nos 1, 3 & 5 NCM buoys mark the seaward limit of Les Roches de Grandcamp, a large plateau of flat rock extending about 1½M offshore and drying approx 1·5m; heavy kelp can cause echosounders to under-read. It can be crossed from most directions, given adequate rise of tide.

Watch out for FVs in the narrow access chan. 14·3m wide gate into wet basin stays open approx HW ±2½; entry is controlled by IPTS. HW –2½ is the same as LW Dunkerque and HW +2½ is the same as HW Dunkerque.

LIGHTS AND MARKS Nos 1, 3 and 5 unlit NCM buoys are 1·4-1·7M NE to NW of the hbr. The 221° ldg lts are primarily for FVs. Maisy's modern church twr is conspic 6ca SSW of hbr ent. See chartlet and Lights, buoys and waypoints and Carentan for other data.

COMMUNICATIONS CROSS 02·33·52·16·16; LB 02·31·22·67·12; 02·21·33·25·26; Auto 08·92·68·08·14; Police 02·31·22·00·18; Brit Consul 01·44·51·31·00; Dr 02·31·22·60·44; Hbr/marina VHF Ch 09; Aff Mar 02·31·22·60·65.

FACILITIES **Marina** ☎02·31·22·63·16. 240 + 10Ⓥ €2·00 (no cr/cards). Ⓥ berths in 2·5m at E end of pontoon C, either side; or as directed. (5t) YC ☎02.31.22.14.35.
Town Ⓑ ⇌ (Carentan) ✈ (Caen). **Ferry** Cherbourg, Ouistreham.

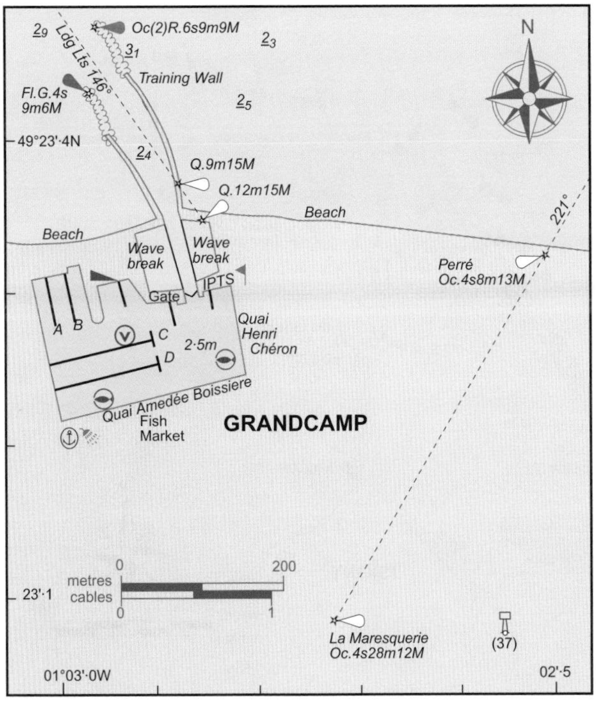

GRANDCAMP TO POINTE DE BARFLEUR

(AC 2135) On E side of B du Grand Vey, Roches de Grandcamp (dry) extend more than 1M offshore, N and W of **Grandcamp**, but they are flat and can be crossed from the N in normal conditions HW±1½. Three NCM buoys mark the N edge of this ledge. Heavy kelp can give false echo-sounder readings.

At the head of B du Grand Vey, about 10M S of Îles St Marcouf, are the (very) tidal hbrs of Carentan and Isigny; entry is only possible near HW and should not be attempted in strong onshore winds. The **Carentan** chan is well buoyed and adequately lit. It trends SSW across sandbanks for about 4M, beyond which it runs between two training walls leading to a lock, and thence into the canal to Carentan's popular marina. The **Isigny** chan is slightly deeper, but the hbr dries to steepish mudbanks.

Îles St Marcouf lie 7M SE of St Vaast-la-Hougue, about 4M offshore, and consist of Île du Large (lt) and Île de Terre about ¼M apart. The Banc du Cardonnet, with depths of 5·2m and many wks, extends for about 5M ESE from the islands. Banc de St Marcouf, with depths of 2·4m and many wks, extends 4·5M NW from the isles, and the sea breaks on it in strong N/NE winds.

Approach **St Vaast-la-Hougue** S of Île de Tatihou, but beware drying rks: La Tourelle (unmarked) Le Gavendest and La Dent, which lie near the approaches and are buoyed. 2M N is Pte de Saire with rks and shoals up to 1M offshore. From Pte de Saire the coast runs 4M NNW to drying **Barfleur**.

Raz de Barfleur, in which the sea breaks heavily, must be avoided in bad weather, particularly with NW or SE winds against the tide, by passing 5-7M seaward of Pte de Barfleur.

▶*In calmer weather it can be taken at slack water (HW Cherbourg –4½ and +2) via an inshore passage, 3ca NE of La Jamette ECM beacon. Expect some turbulence.*◀

Pte de Barfleur marks the W end of Baie de Seine, 56M west of Cap d'Antifer. There are no obstructions on a direct course across the Bay, but a transhipment area for large tankers is centred about 10M ESE of Pte de Barfleur. Be advised: The W end of the Baie de Seine has at times been affected by floating Sargassum weed; in harbours from Grandcamp to St Vaast propellers may be fouled.

POINTE DE BARFLEUR TO CAP DE LA HAGUE

(AC 1114) The N coast of the Cotentin peninsula runs E/W for 26M, bordered by rks which extend 2·5M offshore from Pte de Barfleur to C. Lévi, and 1M offshore between Pte de Jardeheu and C. de la Hague. ▶*Tidal streams reach 5kn at sp, and raise a steep, stopping sea with wind against tide.*◀ Between Pte de Barfleur and Cherbourg, yachts route via Les Equets and Basse du Rénier NCM buoys and La Pierre Noire WCM buoy; keep a lookout for oncoming traffic using same Wpts.

The inshore passage between Pte de Barfleur and C. Lévi, well S of the above 3 cardinal buoys, is not advised except in fair weather and good visibility. Numerous depths were reported (2017) to be less than those shown on AC 1114, 2135 and 2613, the most significant, 1·8m at 49°44'·08N 01°21'·83W. SHOM 7444 and due caution are essential. Port Lévi and Port de Becquet are two small drying hbrs E of Cherbourg. ▶*Tidal streams run strongly with considerable local variations. Off C. Lévi a race develops with wind against tide, and extends nearly 2M N. Off Cherbourg the stream is E-going from about HW –0430 and W-going from HW +0230.*◀

Cherbourg is a port of refuge, hugely popular with British yachtsmen which will become increasingly busy during 2017/18 as the assembly hub for offshore wind farms and tidal energy turbines along the N French coast.

If not catered for, the tidal streams are strong enough to set you downtide of Cherbourg. Do your sums and bias the approach to be uptide of the harbour. At night positively identify the leading lights through either entrance, *before* entering.

▶*Close inshore between Cherbourg and C. de la Hague a back eddy runs W.*◀ West of **Omonville** and about 2M E of C. de la Hague there is an anchorage off Port Racine in Anse de St Martin, guarded by at least 3 groups of rocks. It is open to the N, but useful to await a fair tide through the Alderney Race.

9.17.27 CARENTAN

Manche **49°19'·09N 01°13'·53W**

CHARTS AC 2613, 2135; SHOM 7056, 7422; Navi 527; Imray C32

TIDES –0225 Dover; ML Rade de la Capelle 4·4; Duration 0510

Standard Port CHERBOURG (⟶) Use differences **RADE DE LA CAPELLE** (Grandcamp). HW Carentan = HW Cherbourg +0110.

SHELTER Complete shelter in the land-locked marina (3kn max) but do not attempt to approach in onshore winds >F5.

NAVIGATION WPT 49°25'·45N 01°07'·07W (C-I SWM buoy) 210°/1·8M to Nos 1/2 buoys, not to be confused with the unlit Isigny chan bys 1/2 to the ESE. Start from WPT at HW –2 to –1½. Graph inset gives approx availability. Shallowest water is typically in the area between bys 7-10, but channels in the bay are broad and fairly flat. Once inside trng walls chan deepens.

Appr protected from prevailing S to W winds. Drying out on the hard sands of the estuary is not advised; nor is an early approach, as a bore (*mascaret*) may occur in the river chans between HW –3 and HW–2½ especially at springs. Chan is liable to vary in both depth and direction; buoys are moved accordingly. All buoys have R or G reflective panels; 6 are lit as on chartlet. After about 2·2M the chan lies between 2 training walls, marked by lt bns.

3·8M SW a small pool is formed where R Taute and Douve meet. Ahead, the little lock (room for about 6 boats) opens HW –2 to HW+3. Lock sigs: ● = open, ● = shut (use phone at lock office if lock-keeper absent). Small waiting pontoons are on E side, down- and upstream of the lock. A magnetic anomaly has been reported in the vicinity of the N13 underpass. Electronic autopilots should not be relied upon for steering in this area.

LIGHTS AND MARKS See chartlet and Lights, buoys and waypoints. Maisy Ch twr is a good landmark initially. Ldg lts 209·5° are only valid from the training wall bcns to the front lt, ie not in the buoyed chan.

COMMUNICATIONS CROSS 02·33·52·16·16; Auto 08·92·68·08·50; Police 02·33·42·00·17; ⊖ 02·31·21·71·09; Brit Consul 01·44·51·31·00; Ⓗ 02·33·42·14·12; Dr 02·33·42·33·21; Lockmaster 02·33·71·10·85; *Écluse de Carentan* VHF Ch 09 (0800-1200, 1400-1600LT & lock opening hrs); Aff Mar 02·33·44·00·13.

FACILITIES **Marina** ☎02·33·42·24·44, mob 06·89·13·15·56. port-carentan@orange.fr www.cc-carentan-cotentin.fr. 310 + 50Ⓥ fees based on m², so approx fee €2·07/m. Max/min depths 3·5/3m. Ⓥ berths normally on pontoon K. (daily: 0900-1000, 1500-1600) (35t) (50t). Additional space for wintering ashore at Top Nautique ☎02·33·42·23·87.

YC Croiseurs Côtiers de Carentan ☎02·33·42·06·61.

Town Ⓑ @ in ✈ and ferry Cherbourg.

ISIGNY-SUR-MER 49°19'·31N 01°06'·24W

SHELTER Good in town, but the drying river bed shelves steeply there, soft mud. Cautions in outer approaches as for Carentan, though the Isigny chan is somewhat deeper.

NAVIGATION Leave C-I WPT at HW –2½ tracking 158°/1·25M to IS, a very small unlit NCM buoy at 49°24'·29N 01°06'·37W, near ent to unlit buoyed chan.

From IS buoy track about 220°/0·9M to first unlit chan buoys. Pairs of buoys are spaced at approx 3ca intervals, but between Nos 9/10 and 11/12 the interval is 6ca, with an IDM bn midway.

From Pte du Grouin, ldg lts lead 172·5°/1·9M (as chartlet) between training walls to a Y-junction. Here turn port into R l'Aure for 4ca to town quays on SW bank.

COMMUNICATIONS Ch 09 (0900-1200 & 1400-1800LT).

FACILITIES **HM** ☎02·31·51·24·01; **Quay** (dries) 40+5 Ⓥ. Drying pontoons on SW bank; berth bows-in/stern to buoys. Pay fees at town-hall; (8t). **Town** Ⓑ.

ADJACENT ANCHORAGE

ILES ST MARCOUF, Manche, **49°29'·78N 01°08'·92W**, the charted ⚓. AC 2613, 2135; SHOM 7422. Tides, Grandcamp. A fair weather ⚓ only, no shelter in S'lies. The two islands, Île du Large and SW of it, Île de Terre, look from afar like ships at ⚓. The former is a fort with a small dinghy hbr on its SW side; the latter is a bird sanctuary, closed to the public. ⚓ SW or SE of Île du Large or SE or NE of Île de Terre. Holding is poor on pebbles and kelp. Île du Large lt, VQ (3) 5s 18m 8M, on top of the fort. Both islands are surrounded by drying rks, uninhabited and have no facilities.

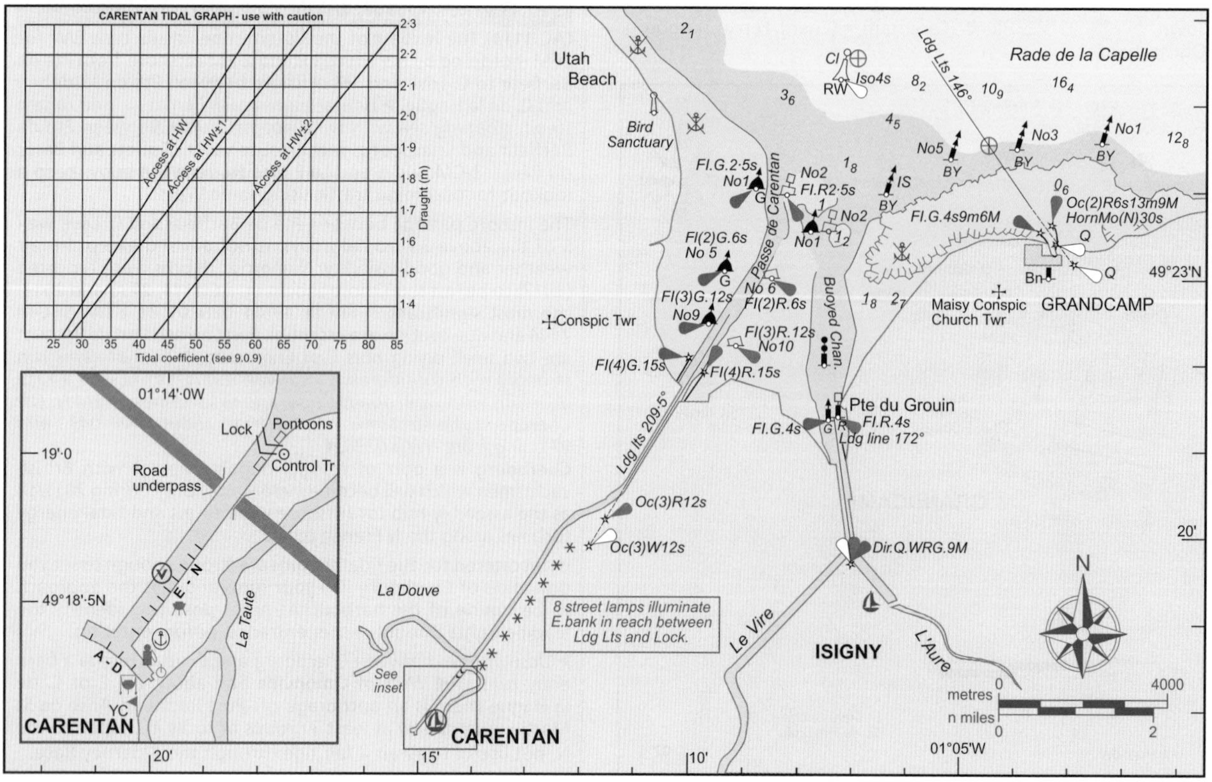

9.17.28 ST VAAST-LA-HOUGUE

Manche **49°35'·17N 01°15'·41W** (Jetty head)

CHARTS AC 2613, 2135; SHOM 7422, 7120, 7090; Navi 527, 528; Imray C32

TIDES −0240 Dover; ML 4·1; Duration 0530

Standard Port CHERBOURG (⟶)

Times				**Height (metres)**			
High Water		Low Water		MHWS	MHWN	MLWN	MLWS
0300	1000	0400	1000	6·4	5·1	2·6	1·1
1500	2200	1600	2200				
Differences ST VAAST-LA-HOUGUE							
+0115	+0045	+0120	+0110	+0·3	+0·3	−0·2	−0·1

SHELTER Excellent in marina especially in W'lies. If full, or awaiting entry, ⚓ off between brgs of 330° and 350° on jetty lt, but this ⚓ becomes untenable in strong E-S winds.

NAVIGATION WPT 49°34'·36N 01°13'·88W (Le Gavendest buoy) 310°/1·3M to main jetty lt, Oc (2) WRG 6s; appr in its wide, well marked W sector, dries 1·8m. Beware boats at ⚓ and cross-currents. 'Le Run' appr is only feasible (over extensive oyster beds) if draft <1·2m and when the entry gate is open, HW −2¼ to HW +3½. If barometer is high and Coeff 40-50, gate may close 30 mins early; and 1-1¼hrs early if Coeff <40. Gate times are on the website.

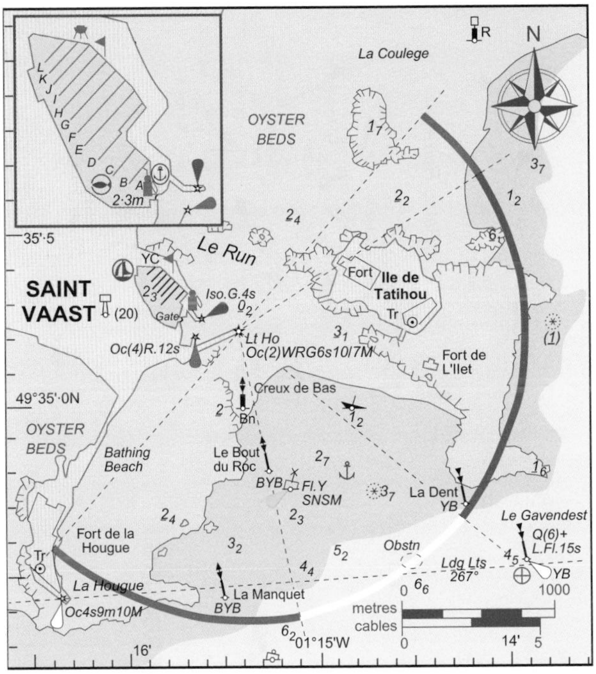

LIGHTS AND MARKS By day do not confuse similar twrs on Ile de Tatihou and Fort de la Hougue. From N, Pte de Saire is a squat white lt ho/G top. From E, ldg lts 267°: front La Hougue; rear, Morsalines in W sector. Main jetty hd lt is a conspic white twr/R top; W sector covers the bay. See chartlet, Lights, buoys and waypoints.

COMMUNICATIONS CROSS 02·33·52·72·13; 08·99·71·08·08; Police 17 or 02·33·23·31·90; 02·33·23·34·01; British Consul 01·44·51·31·00; Ambulance (SAMU) 15; Aff Mar 02·33·54·51·74; Semaphone stn (Fort de la Hougue) VHF Ch 16; Marina VHF Ch 09; Tourist Office 02·33·23·19·32.

FACILITIES **Marina** ☎02·33·23·61·00. www.saint-vaast-reville.com port-st-vaast@saint-vaast-reville.com Season 0900-1200, 1400-1700. 604 + 100 Ⓥ in 2·3m, €2·83 + €0·22pp/day tax, multihulls +50%. Ⓥ berths by LOA: B >14m; C 12-14m; D no Ⓥ; E (outer part) <12m. (pontoon A) (45t).

YC de St Vaast ☎02·33·44·07·87, (3t). **Town** (closed Mondays) Ⓑ (bus to Valognes) Cherbourg ✈ ferry.

9.17.29 BARFLEUR

Manche **49°40'·34N 01°15'·48W**

CHARTS AC 2613, 2135, 1114; SHOM 7422, 7120; Navi 528; Imray C32

TIDES −0208 Dover; ML 3·9; Duration 0550

Standard Port CHERBOURG (⟶)

Times				**Height (metres)**			
High Water		Low Water		MHWS	MHWN	MLWN	MLWS
0300	1000	0400	1000	6·4	5·1	2·6	1·1
1500	2200	1600	2200				
Differences BARFLEUR							
+0115	+0050	+0045	+0050	+0·2	+0·1	0·0	+0·1

SHELTER Excellent, except in fresh NE/E winds when ent is difficult and berths uncomfortable. Hbr dries. Rks/shoals in SE of hbr. Safe to ⚓ outside hbr in offshore winds.

NAVIGATION WPT 49°41'·13N 01°14'·41W, 219·5°/1·0M to hbr ent. Positively identify Roche à l'Anglais SHM and Le Hintar PHM buoys before closing the hbr any further. Beware cross-currents.

In rough weather, esp wind against tide, keep 5M off Pte de Barfleur to clear the Race; see Passage information. If using the inshore passage, identify La Jamette ECM bn and La Grotte SHM buoy. From the S, keep seaward of Pte Dranguet and Le Moulard, both ECM bns.

LIGHTS AND MARKS Pte de Barfleur lt ho is conspic 1½M NNW of hbr, a 72m high, grey twr/B top. The squat church twr is a conspic daymark. Ldg lts 219·5°: both W □ twrs, not easy to see by day. Light details as chartlet and Lights, buoys and waypoints.

COMMUNICATIONS CROSS 02·33·52·72·13; 02·33·23·10·10; 02·33·10·16·10; Auto 08·92·68·02·50; Police 17; 02·33·23·34·01; Brit Consul 01·44·51·31·00; SAMU 15; Dr 02·33·43·73·55; Dentist 02·33·54·49·31; HM 02·33·54·08·29; Aff Mar 02·33·23·36·00.

FACILITIES

NW Quay Yachts dry out on firm, level sand/mud or at SW end of quay, but space may be restricted by FVs. Ⓥ 6x 0m-14.99m €1·84, 6x7m- 9.99m, rafting, €1·53. (needs long cable), nearby at La Blanche Nef camping/caravan site on presentation of berthing fee receipt. **SC** ☎02·33·54·79·08.

Town www.ville-barfleur.fr (Montfarville: 1km S) Ⓑ no wi-fi, bus to Cherbourg for ✈ ferry.

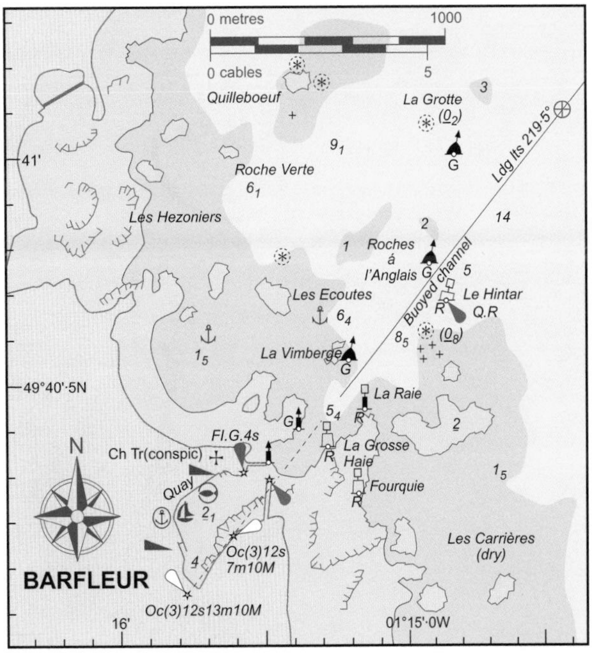

9.17.30 CHERBOURG

Manche **49°38'·94N 01°37'·11W** (Marina ent) ❁❁❁⚓⚓⚓✿✿

CHARTS AC 2656, 2669, 1114, 1112; SHOM 7120, 7092, 7086; Navi 528, 1014; Imray C32, C33A

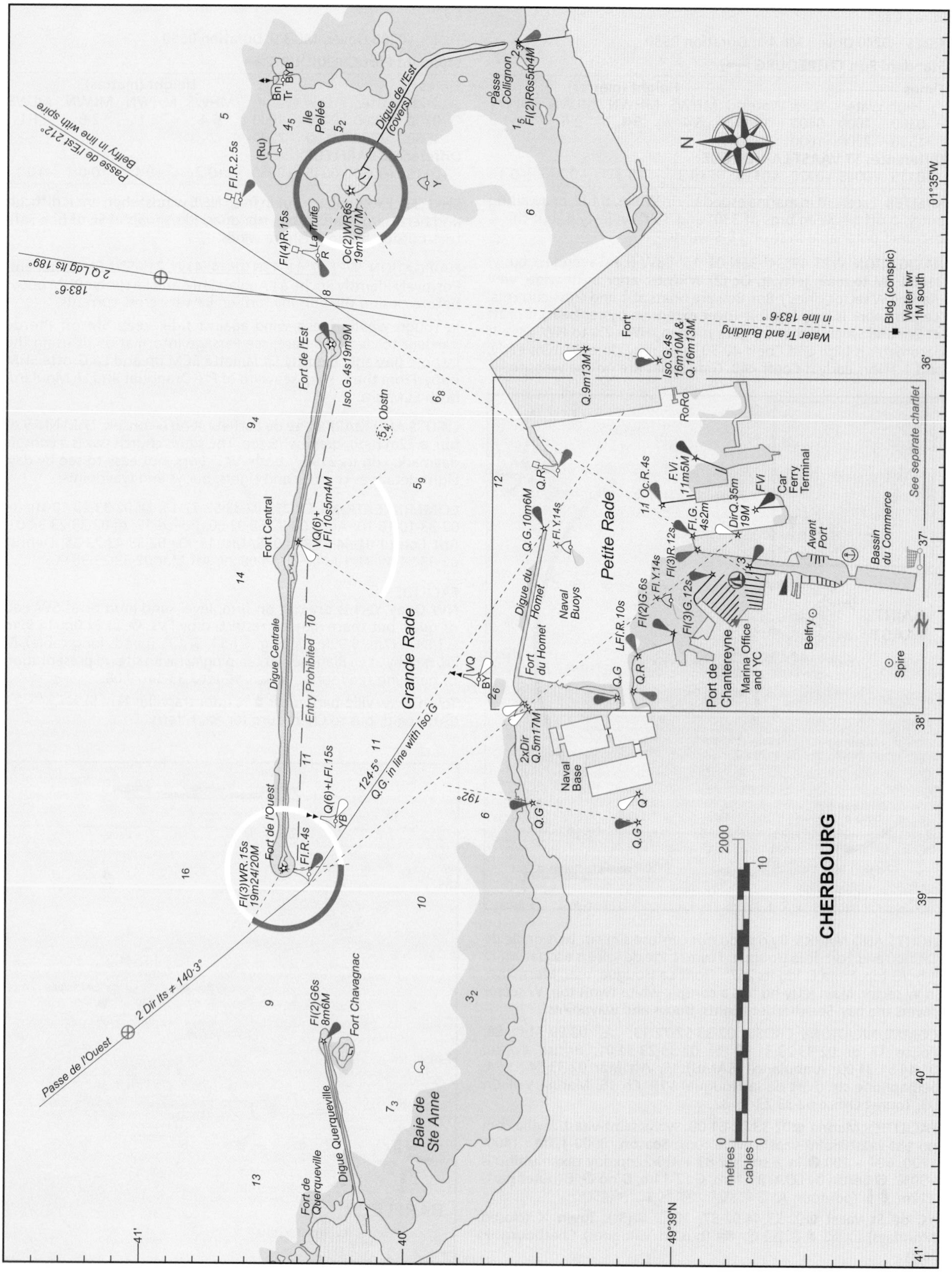

TIDES Cherbourg is a Standard Port (⟶). –0308 Dover; ML 3·8; Duration 0535

SHELTER Excellent; a port of refuge available H24 in all tides and weather. Small craft ⚓ N of marina bkwtr in 2·3m, keeping clear of the charted limits of the military port, close N and W.

NAVIGATION For coastal features from Pte de Barfleur to Cap de la Hague see Passage Information. Enter the Grande Rade via:

- **Passe de l'Ouest** (W ent). WPT 49°41´·05N 01°39´·86W, 140°/0·85M to abeam Fort de l'Ouest. Rks, marked by a PHM buoy, Fl R 4s, off Fort de l'Ouest, extend about 80m off each bkwtr. From W, the white sector of Fort de l'Ouest lt (or by day bearing >122°) keeps clear of offlying dangers E of Cap de la Hague. From CH1 SWM buoy, L Fl 10s, Fort de l'Ouest bears 145°/3·5M.
- **Passe de l'Est** (E ent, least depth 8m). WPT 49°40´·91N 01°35´·55W, 189°/0·65M to abeam Fort de l'Est. Keep to W side of chan (but at least 80m off Fort de l'Est) to avoid dangers W and NW of Ile Pelée marked by two PHM lt buoys. N/NE of Ile Pelée an extensive drying area is marked by 2 unlit bn trs.
- **Passe Collignon** is a shallow (2m) chan, 93m wide, through Digue de l'Est (covers) near the shore. Tidal stream reaches 3·4kn. Only advised in good conditions, near HW.

No anchoring in the Passe de L'Ouest and Passe de L'Est. Speed limits: Grande Rade 14kn; Petite Rade 8kn; Marina 3kn. No entry to: the area S of the Digue Centrale due to fish farms, nor to the area east of the Port Militaire. Keep clear of ferries and shipping using the large N and E extension of the commercial port, the base for offshore wind farm turbine and tidal turbine assembly.

LIGHTS AND MARKS Daymarks include the chimney of Jobourg nuclear plant, 10M W; the cranes of the naval base; and higher ground S of the city. Five powerful lights assist a good cross-Channel landfall:

- 13M E, Pte de Barfleur, Fl (2) 10s 29M
- 5M ENE, Cap Lévi, Fl R 5s 22M
- 12M WNW, Cap de la Hague, Fl 5s 23M
- 28M W, Casquets, Fl (5) 30s 24M

See also Lights, buoys and waypoints (LBW) and Area 19.

Passe de l'Ouest ldg lts 140·3° are a Dir Q rear ldg lt aligned between two Q front ldg lts (horizontally disposed) at base of Digue du Homet. Other lts as on chartlet and LBW.

On entering the Petite Rade make good 200° for marina ent, Fl (3) R 12s and Fl (3) G 12s. Shore lights may confuse and mask navigational lights.

COMMUNICATIONS CROSS 02·33·52·16·16 or 112; *Jobourg Traffic* Ch **13** 80 (H24) provides radar surveillance of the Casquets TSS and ITZ and Mont St Michel to Cap d'Antifer. Radar assistance available on request, Ch 80, to vessels in the 270° sector from S clockwise to E, radius 40M from CROSS Jobourg at 49°41'·1N 01°54'·5W. Jobourg broadcasts nav, weather and traffic info in English and French Ch 80 at H+20 & H+50; ☁ 08·92·68·32·50; Police 02·33·92·70·00; ⊖ 02·33·23·34·02; Brit Consul 01·44·51·31·00; Ⓗ 02·33·20·70·00; Dr 02·33·01·58·58; HM (Port & Lock) 02·33·20·41·25; Aff Mar 02·33·23·36·00; Marina: *Chantereyne* VHF Ch 09; lock into Bassin du Commerce (long stay/>25m) VHF Ch 06.

FACILITIES Port Chantereyne Marina ☎ 02·33·87·65·70. www.portchantereyne.fr portchantereyne@ville-cherbourg.fr Access H24. 1310 + 250 Ⓥ €2·77 on pontoons J,N,P, Q, N side of detached pontoon H and W side of K; max LOA 25m; max draught 3m: ⛽ (HO) or (H24) cr/debit card. max fill €120·00. @ Ⓔ SHOM, (30t).

YC de Cherbourg ☎02·33·53·02·83, ✕ .

Bassin du Commerce is for permanent residents only/>25m LOA.

City ✕ ✉ Ⓑ ⇌. Cherbourg (Maupertus) ✈ ☎ 02·33·88·57·60. Ferry: Portsmouth, Poole.

MINOR HARBOURS EAST OF CHERBOURG

PORT DE LÉVI, Manche, **49°41´·23 N 01°28´·46W**. AC 1114; SHOM 7120, 5609, 7092; HW –0310 on Dover (UT); +0024 on Cherbourg. HW ht +0·2m on Cherbourg. Shelter good except in SW to N winds. By day appr on 094° keeping the white wall and lt between the white marks on each pier hd. Lt is Oc (2) WRG 6s; see Lights, buoys and waypoints. Keep in W sector (083°-105°) but night entry not advised due to many pot floats. Berth bows on to NE side below white wall, amongst small FVs. Dries to clean sand. Facilities: Peace. Fermanville (1·5M) has ✕ .

PORT DU BECQUET, Manche, **49°39´·304N 01°32´·81W**. AC 1114; SHOM 7120, 7092. Tides as Cherbourg. Ldg lts/marks 186·3°: Both Dir Oc (3) 12s (front lt White; rear lt Red) W 8-sided twrs; see LBW. Large PHM bcn twr, La Tounette, marks rks close E. Shelter good except from N to E when a strong scend enters. Dries, clean sand. Secure to S of the E/W jetty (little space). Facilities: very few; all facilities at Cherbourg 2·5M.

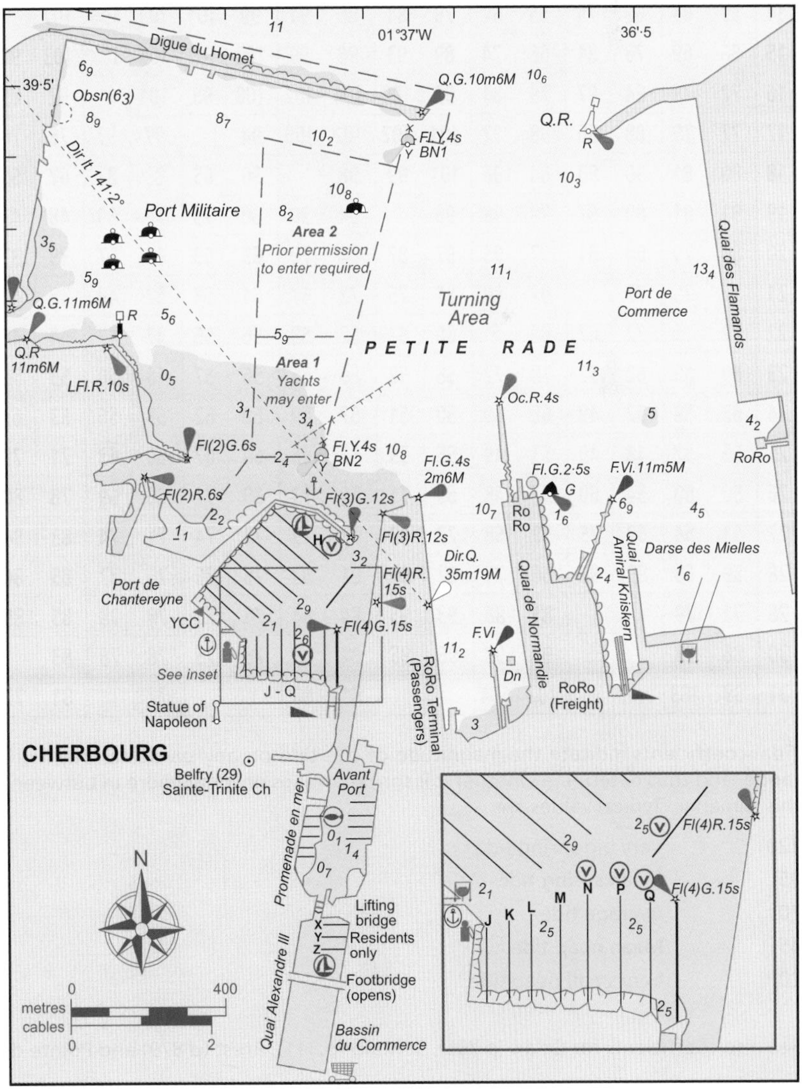

CHERBOURG TIDAL COEFFICIENTS 2018

Date	Jan		Feb		Mar		Apr		May		June		July		Aug		Sept		Oct		Nov		Dec	
	am	pm	am	pm	am	pm	am	pm	am	pm	am	pm	am	pm	am	pm	am	pm	am	pm	am	pm	am	pm
1	92	97	107	109	97	102	105	105	94	92	77	74	73	72	76	74	74	70	69	63	51	48	55	56
2	101	104	109	108	106	109	103	100	89	86	71		70		72	69	65	60	57	52	49	52	58	61
3	106	107	106	103	110	109	96		82		68	64	67	64	66	62	55	51	47	44	57	63	64	69
4	106	104	98		108	104	92	86	77	72	60	56	62	59	59	55	47	45	45	48	69	76	73	77
5	101	96	92	85	100	94	80	74	67	61	52	49	56	53	52	49	45	48	54	62	82	87	80	83
6	91		78	71	88		67	60	56	50	45	43	50	48	48	47	54	61	70	78	92	95	85	86
7	85	79	63	56	81	74	53	46	45	40	41	41	47	46	49	52	69	77	85	92	97	99	87	87
8	72	65	49	43	66	58	40	35	37	34	41	44	47	50	57	64	85	93	98	103	99	97	86	85
9	59	54	39	36	51	44	31	29	34	35	47	52	53	58	70	78	99	105	106	107	95	93	83	80
10	49	46	35	37	38	33	30	34	39	43	57	63	63	69	85	92	108	111	108	106	89	84	78	74
11	44	44	40	45	30	30	39	45	49	55	69	76	75	82	97	103	111	110	104	100	79	74	71	67
12	46	49	50	55	33	37	52	59	62	68	81	87	87	93	106	109	108	104	95	89	68	62	63	58
13	52	55	60	65	43	49	65	72	75	81	92	96	97	101	109	109	99		83		56		54	
14	59	63	69	74	55	62	78	84	86	91	99	101	103	104	107		92	85	75	68	50	45	50	46
15	66	69	78	81	68	74	89	93	96	99	102	101	105	103	103	98	77	69	61	53	40	35	42	40
16	72	75	84	87	79	84	97	100	101	102	100	98	101		92	85	61	53	46	40	33	32	38	37
17	77	79	88	90	88	92	101	102	102	100	94		97	93	78	70	46	39	34	30	33	36	39	41
18	80	81	90	90	94	96	101	99	98		90	85	88	82	62	55	34	31	29	30	40	45	45	50
19	81	81	89	87	98	98	96		94	90	80	75	75	69	48	43	31	33	34	39	51	57	55	61
20	80	79	84	81	97	95	92	87	84	79	69	65	63	57	39	37	38	43	45	51	63	69	67	73
21	77	75	77		92	88	81	75	72	67	61	58	52	49	38	40	49	55	57	63	75	81	79	85
22	72		72	67	84		68	62	62	58	56	55	47	47	44	48	61	66	69	75	85	90	89	93
23	69	66	62	57	78	72	56	52	56	55	56	57	48	50	53	58	71	76	80	84	93	95	97	99
24	62	58	52	49	66	59	50	51	57	59	59	62	53	56	63	67	80	84	88	91	97	98	100	100
25	55	52	48	49	53	49	55	59	62	66	64	67	60	63	71	75	87	89	94	95	97	95	99	97
26	50	50	54	60	47	48	65	71	70	73	69	71	66	69	78	80	91	92	96	96	93	89	94	90
27	51	54	67	75	52	58	77	82	77	79	73	74	71	74	83	84	92	91	94	92	85	80	86	
28	59	65	83	90	66	73	87	91	81	83	75	76	75	77	85	86	90	87	88	84	74		81	75
28	72	79			81	88	93	95	84	84	76	76	78	78	85	85	84		79	73	69	64	70	65
30	86	93			94	98	96	95	84	83	76	75	78	78	83		80	75	67		60	57	61	58
31	99	103			102	104			81	80			77		81	77			61	55			56	55

Tidal coefficients indicate the magnitude of the tide on any particular day, without having to look up and calculate the range, and thus determine whether it is springs, neaps or somewhere in between. This table is valid for all areas covered by this Almanac. Typical values are:

120	Very big spring tide
95	**Mean spring tide**
70	Average tide
45	**Mean neap tide**
20	Very small neap tide

See also coefficients for Calais (p 765), St Malo (p 811), Brest (p 879) and Pointe de Grave (p 942).

STANDARD TIME UT –01
Subtract 1 hour for UT
For French Summer Time add ONE hour in **non-shaded areas**

CHERBOURG LAT 49°39'N LONG 1°38'W

TIMES AND HEIGHTS OF HIGH AND LOW WATERS

Dates in red are SPRINGS
Dates in blue are NEAPS

YEAR **2018**

JANUARY

Date	Day	Time	m	Time	m	Time	m	Time	m
1	M	0212	1.4	0750	6.5	1445	1.2	2021	6.5
2	TU	0306	1.1	0841	6.7	1538	0.9	○ 2114	6.6
3	W	0358	1.0	0931	6.8	1629	0.7	2205	6.7
4	TH	0447	1.0	1020	6.9	1718	0.7	2254	6.6
5	F	0535	1.1	1107	6.7	1805	0.9	2342	6.4
6	SA	0622	1.3	1154	6.5	1851	1.2		
7	SU	0028	6.1	0708	1.7	1239	6.1	1937	1.5
8	M	0114	5.8	0756	2.0	1327	5.8	◑ 2025	1.9
9	TU	0203	5.5	0849	2.4	1420	5.4	2120	2.3
10	W	0301	5.2	0952	2.6	1524	5.1	2225	2.5
11	TH	0409	5.1	1103	2.6	1637	5.0	2335	2.5
12	F	0519	5.2	1211	2.5	1749	5.1		
13	SA	0038	2.4	0620	5.4	1309	2.3	1847	5.3
14	SU	0131	2.2	0709	5.6	1358	2.1	1935	5.6
15	M	0216	2.0	0751	5.9	1440	1.8	2015	5.7
16	TU	0256	1.9	0829	6.0	1518	1.6	2052	5.9
17	W	0333	1.7	0905	6.2	1553	1.5	● 2126	6.0
18	TH	0407	1.7	0938	6.2	1627	1.4	2159	6.0
19	F	0441	1.6	1010	6.3	1701	1.4	2231	6.0
20	SA	0514	1.7	1043	6.2	1734	1.4	2305	6.0
21	SU	0548	1.7	1118	6.1	1808	1.5	2340	5.9
22	M	0623	1.9	1155	6.0	1843	1.7		
23	TU	0018	5.7	0701	2.0	1233	5.8	1924	1.9
24	W	0058	5.5	0746	2.2	1317	5.5	◐ 2012	2.1
25	TH	0147	5.3	0842	2.4	1412	5.3	2112	2.3
26	F	0251	5.2	0952	2.5	1526	5.2	2228	2.3
27	SA	0415	5.2	1113	2.4	1658	5.3	2347	2.2
28	SU	0536	5.5	1228	2.1	1813	5.6		
29	M	0057	1.9	0641	5.9	1335	1.6	1916	6.0
30	TU	0200	1.5	0737	6.3	1435	1.2	2013	6.3
31	W	0257	1.2	0831	6.6	1530	0.8	○ 2106	6.5

FEBRUARY

Date	Day	Time	m	Time	m	Time	m	Time	m
1	TH	0350	1.0	0922	6.8	1620	0.6	2156	6.7
2	F	0438	0.9	1010	6.9	1706	0.6	2242	6.7
3	SA	0522	0.9	1054	6.8	1749	0.7	2324	6.5
4	SU	0604	1.1	1135	6.6	1829	1.0		
5	M	0003	6.3	0644	1.4	1214	6.3	1908	1.3
6	TU	0040	5.9	0723	1.8	1252	5.8	1946	1.8
7	W	0119	5.6	0804	2.2	1333	5.4	◑ 2029	2.3
8	TH	0204	5.2	0854	2.5	1426	5.0	2123	2.6
9	F	0305	4.9	1002	2.8	1541	4.8	2240	2.8
10	SA	0428	4.8	1125	2.8	1713	4.8		
11	SU	0000	2.8	0549	5.0	1237	2.6	1826	5.0
12	M	0105	2.5	0646	5.3	1334	2.2	1916	5.3
13	TU	0156	2.2	0731	5.6	1420	1.9	1957	5.6
14	W	0239	2.0	0810	5.9	1459	1.7	2035	5.8
15	TH	0316	1.7	0847	6.1	1535	1.4	● 2110	6.0
16	F	0350	1.5	0921	6.2	1609	1.3	2142	6.1
17	SA	0424	1.4	0954	6.3	1643	1.2	2214	6.2
18	SU	0457	1.3	1027	6.4	1716	1.2	2247	6.2
19	M	0530	1.4	1101	6.3	1749	1.2	2321	6.1
20	TU	0604	1.5	1136	6.2	1822	1.4	2355	6.0
21	W	0640	1.6	1212	6.0	1900	1.6		
22	TH	0032	5.7	0721	1.9	1252	5.7	1944	1.9
23	F	0115	5.5	0812	2.2	1342	5.4	◐ 2041	2.3
24	SA	0213	5.2	0919	2.4	1456	5.1	2158	2.5
25	SU	0342	5.1	1047	2.4	1643	5.1	2327	2.4
26	M	0519	5.3	1213	2.1	1805	5.4		
27	TU	0046	2.1	0629	5.7	1325	1.7	1909	5.8
28	W	0152	1.6	0728	6.1	1426	1.2	2005	6.2

MARCH

Date	Day	Time	m	Time	m	Time	m	Time	m
1	TH	0249	1.3	0822	6.5	1519	0.8	2055	6.5
2	F	0339	1.0	0910	6.7	1606	0.6	○ 2140	6.6
3	SA	0423	0.8	0954	6.8	1648	0.6	2221	6.7
4	SU	0503	0.8	1034	6.8	1726	0.7	2258	6.5
5	M	0540	1.0	1110	6.6	1801	0.9	2332	6.3
6	TU	0615	1.2	1145	6.3	1834	1.3		
7	W	0005	6.0	0648	1.6	1217	5.9	1907	1.8
8	TH	0037	5.6	0724	2.0	1251	5.4	1943	2.2
9	F	0113	5.3	0805	2.4	1334	5.0	◑ 2028	2.7
10	SA	0203	4.9	0902	2.8	1440	4.6	2138	3.0
11	SU	0324	4.6	1029	2.9	1628	4.5	2317	3.0
12	M	0507	4.7	1158	2.7	1759	4.8		
13	TU	0035	2.8	0616	5.0	1302	2.4	1851	5.1
14	W	0130	2.4	0704	5.4	1351	2.0	1932	5.5
15	TH	0214	2.0	0745	5.7	1432	1.7	2010	5.8
16	F	0252	1.7	0823	6.0	1509	1.4	2045	6.0
17	SA	0327	1.4	0858	6.3	1544	1.2	● 2119	6.2
18	SU	0401	1.2	0933	6.4	1619	1.0	2152	6.3
19	M	0436	1.1	1006	6.5	1653	1.0	2225	6.4
20	TU	0510	1.1	1041	6.5	1727	1.0	2259	6.3
21	W	0545	1.2	1117	6.3	1802	1.2	2334	6.2
22	TH	0621	1.4	1155	6.1	1839	1.5		
23	F	0011	5.9	0703	1.7	1236	5.8	1924	1.9
24	SA	0055	5.6	0754	2.0	1328	5.4	◐ 2020	2.3
25	SU	0153	5.3	0902	2.3	1447	5.0	2141	2.6
26	M	0326	5.0	1033	2.4	1637	5.0	2316	2.5
27	TU	0505	5.2	1203	2.1	1757	5.3		
28	W	0037	2.2	0617	5.6	1314	1.7	1859	5.8
29	TH	0142	1.7	0716	6.0	1412	1.3	1951	6.1
30	F	0235	1.3	0806	6.3	1501	0.9	2037	6.4
31	SA	0321	1.1	0851	6.5	1544	0.8	○ 2117	6.5

APRIL

Date	Day	Time	m	Time	m	Time	m	Time	m
1	SU	0402	0.9	0931	6.6	1623	0.8	2154	6.6
2	M	0439	0.9	1008	6.6	1658	0.9	2228	6.5
3	TU	0513	1.0	1042	6.4	1730	1.1	2300	6.3
4	W	0545	1.3	1114	6.2	1801	1.4	2330	6.0
5	TH	0616	1.6	1145	5.8	1832	1.8		
6	F	0000	5.7	0649	1.9	1217	5.4	1905	2.3
7	SA	0032	5.3	0724	2.3	1254	5.0	1945	2.7
8	SU	0114	5.0	0812	2.7	1349	4.7	◑ 2045	3.0
9	M	0222	4.7	0928	2.9	1525	4.5	2220	3.1
10	TU	0404	4.6	1104	2.8	1713	4.7	2351	2.9
11	W	0530	4.8	1217	2.5	1812	5.0		
12	TH	0051	2.5	0625	5.2	1310	2.2	1856	5.4
13	F	0137	2.1	0709	5.6	1354	1.8	1935	5.8
14	SA	0218	1.8	0750	5.9	1434	1.4	2013	6.1
15	SU	0256	1.4	0828	6.2	1512	1.2	2050	6.3
16	M	0333	1.2	0906	6.4	1550	1.0	● 2125	6.4
17	TU	0411	1.0	0943	6.5	1628	0.9	2201	6.5
18	W	0449	1.0	1021	6.5	1706	1.0	2238	6.5
19	TH	0527	1.0	1101	6.4	1744	1.2	2316	6.3
20	F	0608	1.2	1142	6.1	1825	1.5	2357	6.1
21	SA	0652	1.5	1228	5.8	1913	1.9		
22	SU	0044	5.7	0746	1.9	1324	5.4	◐ 2014	2.3
23	M	0145	5.4	0855	2.2	1446	5.1	2133	2.5
24	TU	0314	5.1	1022	2.3	1623	5.1	2304	2.5
25	W	0446	5.2	1147	2.1	1739	5.4		
26	TH	0021	2.2	0556	5.5	1254	1.7	1838	5.7
27	F	0122	1.8	0653	5.9	1350	1.4	1927	6.0
28	SA	0213	1.5	0743	6.1	1437	1.2	2011	6.2
29	SU	0258	1.3	0826	6.3	1518	1.1	2049	6.4
30	M	0337	1.2	0905	6.3	1554	1.1	○ 2124	6.4

Chart Datum is 3·33 metres below IGN Datum. HAT is 7·0 metres above Chart Datum.

STANDARD TIME UT –01
Subtract 1 hour for UT
For French Summer Time add ONE hour in **non-shaded areas**

CHERBOURG LAT 49°39′N LONG 1°38′W

TIMES AND HEIGHTS OF HIGH AND LOW WATERS

Dates in red are **SPRINGS**
Dates in blue are **NEAPS**

YEAR **2018**

MAY

Date	Time	m	Date	Time	m
1	0412	1.2	16	0346	1.0
	0940	6.3		0920	6.5
	TU 1628	1.2		W 1604	1.0
	2157	6.3		2138	6.6
2	0445	1.2	17	0429	0.9
	1014	6.2		1004	6.5
	W 1700	1.4		TH 1647	1.0
	2229	6.2		2220	6.6
3	0517	1.4	18	0513	1.0
	1046	6.0		1048	6.4
	TH 1731	1.6		F 1731	1.2
	2300	6.0		2302	6.4
4	0549	1.6	19	0559	1.1
	1118	5.8		1134	6.2
	F 1802	1.9		SA 1817	1.5
	2331	5.8		2348	6.2
5	0621	1.9	20	0648	1.4
	1150	5.5		1224	5.9
	SA 1835	2.3		SU 1909	1.8
6	0003	5.5	21	0038	5.9
	0655	2.2		0743	1.7
	SU 1226	5.1		M 1322	5.5
	1914	2.6		2009	2.2
7	0042	5.2	22	0139	5.5
	0739	2.5		0848	2.0
	M 1315	4.9		TU 1435	5.3
	2006	2.9		◐ 2121	2.4
8	0138	4.9	23	0256	5.3
	0837	2.7		1003	2.1
	TU 1427	4.7		W 1555	5.2
	◑ 2121	3.0		2241	2.4
9	0258	4.7	24	0415	5.3
	0958	2.8		1119	2.0
	W 1558	4.7		TH 1706	5.4
	2249	3.0		2352	2.2
10	0423	4.8	25	0524	5.4
	1117	2.6		1224	1.9
	TH 1715	5.0		F 1806	5.6
	2357	2.6			
11	0531	5.1	26	0053	2.0
	1218	2.3		0623	5.6
	F 1808	5.3		SA 1319	1.7
				1856	5.8
12	0050	2.3	27	0144	1.7
	0623	5.5		0714	5.8
	SA 1309	1.9		SU 1407	1.6
	1853	5.7		1941	6.0
13	0136	1.9	28	0229	1.6
	0710	5.8		0759	6.0
	SU 1354	1.6		M 1448	1.5
	1936	6.0		2021	6.1
14	0220	1.5	29	0309	1.5
	0754	6.1		0839	6.0
	M 1438	1.3		TU 1526	1.5
	2017	6.3		○ 2056	6.2
15	0303	1.2	30	0345	1.4
	0837	6.3		0915	6.0
	TU 1521	1.1		W 1600	1.5
	● 2057	6.5		2130	6.2
			31	0420	1.4
				0950	6.0
				TH 1634	1.6
				2203	6.1

JUNE

Date	Time	m	Date	Time	m
1	0453	1.5	16	0503	0.9
	1023	5.9		1040	6.4
	F 1706	1.8		SA 1722	1.2
	2236	6.0		2253	6.6
2	0526	1.6	17	0552	0.9
	1056	5.7		1129	6.3
	SA 1739	2.0		SU 1811	1.4
	2308	5.8		2342	6.4
3	0559	1.8	18	0642	1.1
	1130	5.5		1220	6.1
	SU 1813	2.2		M 1903	1.6
	2342	5.6			
4	0633	2.0	19	0032	6.1
	1206	5.3		0735	1.4
	M 1850	2.4		TU 1313	5.8
				1958	1.9
5	0021	5.4	20	0127	5.8
	0713	2.2		0831	1.7
	TU 1249	5.1		W 1411	5.5
	1936	2.6		◐ 2058	2.2
6	0108	5.2	21	0228	5.5
	0802	2.4		0933	2.0
	W 1343	5.0		TH 1516	5.3
	◑ 2034	2.8		2206	2.3
7	0207	5.0	22	0336	5.3
	0901	2.5		1040	2.1
	TH 1450	4.9		F 1622	5.3
	2143	2.8		2314	2.3
8	0316	5.0	23	0444	5.3
	1012	2.5		1145	2.2
	F 1603	5.0		SA 1726	5.4
	2256	2.7			
9	0426	5.1	24	0017	2.2
	1121	2.3		0548	5.4
	SA 1710	5.2		SU 1244	2.1
	2359	2.4		1823	5.6
10	0531	5.3	25	0113	2.1
	1221	2.0		0645	5.5
	SU 1807	5.6		M 1335	2.0
				1912	5.7
11	0054	2.0	26	0201	1.9
	0628	5.7		0735	5.6
	M 1315	1.7		TU 1420	1.9
	1857	5.9		1955	5.9
12	0145	1.6	27	0244	1.7
	0721	6.0		0818	5.7
	TU 1406	1.4		W 1501	1.8
	1945	6.2		2033	6.0
13	0235	1.3	28	0322	1.6
	0811	6.2		0856	5.8
	W 1456	1.2		TH 1538	1.8
	● 2032	6.4		○ 2109	6.0
14	0325	1.1	29	0358	1.6
	0901	6.4		0931	5.8
	TH 1544	1.1		F 1613	1.8
	2119	6.6		2143	6.1
15	0414	0.9	30	0433	1.5
	0950	6.5		1005	5.8
	F 1633	1.1		SA 1647	1.8
	2206	6.6		2216	6.0

JULY

Date	Time	m	Date	Time	m
1	0506	1.6	16	0543	0.8
	1038	5.8		1120	6.5
	SU 1720	1.9		M 1801	1.2
	2249	6.0		2333	6.6
2	0540	1.7	17	0630	0.9
	1111	5.7		1207	6.3
	M 1754	2.0		TU 1848	1.4
	2324	5.8			
3	0614	1.8	18	0019	6.3
	1147	5.6		0716	1.2
	TU 1829	2.2		W 1252	6.0
				1936	1.7
4	0001	5.7	19	0105	6.0
	0649	1.9		0803	1.6
	W 1225	5.4		TH 1338	5.7
	1908	2.3		◐ 2026	2.1
5	0041	5.5	20	0153	5.6
	0731	2.1		0854	2.0
	TH 1308	5.3		F 1430	5.4
	1955	2.5		2123	2.3
6	0128	5.3	21	0250	5.3
	0820	2.3		0953	2.3
	F 1400	5.2		SA 1531	5.2
	◑ 2052	2.6		2229	2.5
7	0223	5.2	22	0358	5.1
	0918	2.4		1101	2.5
	SA 1501	5.1		SU 1642	5.1
	2159	2.6		2339	2.5
8	0328	5.1	23	0513	5.0
	1028	2.4		1208	2.5
	SU 1611	5.2		M 1751	5.3
	2310	2.4			
9	0441	5.2	24	0042	2.3
	1138	2.2		0621	5.2
	M 1723	5.4		TU 1307	2.3
				1847	5.5
10	0017	2.1	25	0136	2.1
	0553	5.5		0715	5.4
	TU 1243	1.9		W 1357	2.2
	1825	5.8		1934	5.7
11	0117	1.8	26	0222	1.9
	0656	5.8		0800	5.6
	W 1341	1.6		TH 1441	2.0
	1921	6.1		2014	5.9
12	0214	1.4	27	0303	1.7
	0753	6.1		0839	5.7
	TH 1437	1.4		F 1520	1.9
	2013	6.4		○ 2051	6.0
13	0309	1.1	28	0339	1.6
	0847	6.4		0914	5.8
	F 1531	1.2		SA 1555	1.8
	● 2105	6.6		2125	6.1
14	0403	0.9	29	0414	1.5
	0940	6.5		0947	5.9
	SA 1623	1.0		SU 1629	1.7
	2156	6.7		2158	6.2
15	0454	0.7	30	0447	1.5
	1032	6.5		1019	5.9
	SU 1713	1.0		M 1702	1.7
	2245	6.7		2230	6.2
			31	0520	1.5
				1051	5.9
				TU 1734	1.8
				2304	6.1

AUGUST

Date	Time	m	Date	Time	m
1	0552	1.6	16	0649	1.2
	1125	5.8		1223	6.1
	W 1806	1.9		TH 1906	1.6
	2339	6.0			
2	0624	1.7	17	0035	6.1
	1200	5.7		0729	1.6
	TH 1842	2.0		F 1301	5.8
				1948	2.0
3	0015	5.8	18	0115	5.6
	0701	1.9		0810	2.1
	F 1237	5.6		SA 1343	5.4
	1922	2.2		◐ 2036	2.4
4	0054	5.6	19	0204	5.2
	0743	2.1		0901	2.5
	SA 1319	5.4		SU 1438	5.1
	◑ 2011	2.4		2139	2.7
5	0142	5.3	20	0310	4.9
	0835	2.3		1011	2.8
	SU 1412	5.2		M 1554	4.9
	2113	2.5		2259	2.8
6	0243	5.2	21	0439	4.8
	0943	2.4		1133	2.8
	M 1522	5.2		TU 1720	5.0
	2231	2.5			
7	0405	5.1	22	0013	2.6
	1104	2.4		0601	5.0
	TU 1650	5.3		W 1243	2.6
	2350	2.3		1825	5.3
8	0533	5.3	23	0113	2.3
	1220	2.2		0658	5.2
	W 1805	5.6		TH 1338	2.4
				1914	5.6
9	0059	1.9	24	0201	2.0
	0642	5.7		0741	5.5
	TH 1325	1.8		F 1422	2.1
	1906	6.0		1954	5.8
10	0201	1.4	25	0242	1.8
	0741	6.1		0819	5.8
	F 1425	1.5		SA 1501	1.9
	2001	6.4		2031	6.1
11	0258	1.1	26	0318	1.6
	0837	6.4		0854	6.0
	SA 1521	1.2		SU 1535	1.7
	● 2054	6.7		○ 2105	6.2
12	0352	0.8	27	0352	1.4
	0929	6.6		0926	6.1
	SU 1612	1.0		M 1608	1.6
	2144	6.9		2138	6.3
13	0441	0.6	28	0425	1.3
	1018	6.7		0957	6.1
	M 1700	0.9		TU 1640	1.5
	2231	6.9		2209	6.4
14	0527	0.6	29	0457	1.3
	1103	6.6		1028	6.2
	TU 1744	1.0		W 1712	1.5
	2315	6.7		2241	6.3
15	0609	0.8	30	0528	1.4
	1144	6.4		1100	6.1
	W 1825	1.2		TH 1743	1.6
	2356	6.5		2315	6.2
			31	0600	1.5
				1134	6.0
				F 1816	1.7
				2350	6.0

Chart Datum is 3·33 metres below IGN Datum. HAT is 7·0 metres above Chart Datum.

STANDARD TIME UT –01
Subtract 1 hour for UT
For French Summer Time add ONE hour in **non-shaded areas**

CHERBOURG LAT 49°39'N LONG 1°38'W

TIMES AND HEIGHTS OF HIGH AND LOW WATERS

Dates in red are SPRINGS
Dates in blue are NEAPS

YEAR **2018**

SEPTEMBER

Day	Time	m	Day	Time	m
1	0634	1.7	16	0038	5.6
	1208	5.8		0728	2.2
	SA 1854	2.0		SU 1259	5.5
				1951	2.4
2	0027	5.8	17	0120	5.2
	0713	2.0		0812	2.7
	SU 1247	5.6		M 1347	5.1
	1940	2.2		◐ 2047	2.8
3	0112	5.5	18	0223	4.8
	0803	2.3		0918	3.1
	M 1337	5.3		TU 1503	4.8
	◑ 2040	2.5		2211	3.0
4	0214	5.2	19	0401	4.6
	0912	2.6		1057	3.1
	TU 1450	5.1		W 1644	4.8
	2203	2.6		2340	2.8
5	0349	5.1	20	0538	4.8
	1043	2.6		1216	2.9
	W 1633	5.2		TH 1759	5.1
	2334	2.4			
6	0526	5.3	21	0045	2.5
	1207	2.3		0634	5.2
	TH 1754	5.6		F 1313	2.5
				1848	5.5
7	0048	1.9	22	0134	2.2
	0635	5.7		0715	5.5
	F 1316	1.9		SA 1357	2.2
	1855	6.0		1928	5.8
8	0151	1.4	23	0215	1.8
	0732	6.1		0752	5.9
	SA 1416	1.5		SU 1435	1.9
	1950	6.4		2005	6.1
9	0247	1.0	24	0251	1.6
	0825	6.5		0827	6.1
	SU 1509	1.1		M 1509	1.7
	● 2041	6.8		2040	6.3
10	0337	0.7	25	0325	1.4
	0913	6.7		0900	6.2
	M 1557	0.9		TU 1542	1.5
	2128	6.9		○ 2113	6.4
11	0422	0.6	26	0358	1.3
	0957	6.8		0931	6.3
	TU 1640	0.9		W 1615	1.4
	2211	6.9		2145	6.5
12	0504	0.7	27	0431	1.2
	1037	6.7		1002	6.4
	W 1720	1.0		TH 1648	1.4
	2250	6.8		2218	6.5
13	0542	0.9	28	0504	1.3
	1114	6.5		1035	6.3
	TH 1757	1.2		F 1721	1.4
	2327	6.5		2252	6.4
14	0617	1.3	29	0536	1.4
	1149	6.2		1108	6.2
	F 1833	1.6		SA 1755	1.6
				2329	6.2
15	0002	6.1	30	0612	1.7
	0652	1.7		1144	6.0
	SA 1222	5.8		SU 1833	1.8
	1909	2.0			

OCTOBER

Day	Time	m	Day	Time	m
1	0008	5.9	16	0043	5.2
	0651	2.0		0731	2.8
	M 1225	5.7		TU 1304	5.2
	1920	2.2		◐ 2002	2.8
2	0056	5.5	17	0140	4.8
	0742	2.4		0829	3.1
	TU 1317	5.4		W 1411	4.8
	◑ 2022	2.5		2114	3.0
3	0204	5.2	18	0311	4.6
	0854	2.7		1005	3.3
	W 1436	5.2		TH 1550	4.7
	2149	2.6		2252	3.0
4	0349	5.1	19	0456	4.8
	1032	2.7		1137	3.1
	TH 1625	5.2		F 1716	5.0
	2324	2.4			
5	0520	5.4	20	0004	2.7
	1159	2.4		0557	5.1
	F 1743	5.6		SA 1237	2.7
				1811	5.3
6	0038	1.9	21	0056	2.3
	0625	5.8		0639	5.5
	SA 1307	1.9		SU 1322	2.3
	1843	6.1		1854	5.7
7	0138	1.4	22	0138	2.0
	0718	6.2		0717	5.9
	SU 1403	1.5		M 1401	2.0
	1935	6.5		1933	6.0
8	0230	1.1	23	0216	1.7
	0806	6.5		0754	6.1
	M 1452	1.2		TU 1438	1.7
	2023	6.7		2010	6.3
9	0316	0.9	24	0252	1.4
	0850	6.7		0829	6.3
	TU 1536	1.0		W 1513	1.4
	● 2106	6.9		○ 2045	6.5
10	0358	0.8	25	0328	1.3
	0930	6.8		0902	6.5
	W 1616	1.0		TH 1549	1.3
	2146	6.8		2120	6.6
11	0436	0.9	26	0404	1.2
	1007	6.7		0936	6.5
	TH 1653	1.1		F 1625	1.2
	2222	6.7		2156	6.6
12	0511	1.1	27	0440	1.2
	1041	6.5		1011	6.5
	F 1728	1.3		SA 1702	1.3
	2257	6.4		2234	6.5
13	0544	1.5	28	0517	1.4
	1114	6.2		1048	6.4
	SA 1801	1.6		SU 1740	1.4
	2331	6.0		2314	6.3
14	0616	1.9	29	0555	1.7
	1146	5.9		1128	6.2
	SU 1835	2.0		M 1822	1.7
				2358	6.0
15	0005	5.6	30	0640	2.0
	0650	2.3		1213	5.9
	M 1221	5.5		TU 1912	2.0
	1913	2.4			
			31	0051	5.6
				0734	2.4
				W 1310	5.6
				◑ 2016	2.3

NOVEMBER

Day	Time	m	Day	Time	m
1	0203	5.3	16	0214	4.8
	0850	2.7		0902	3.2
	TH 1430	5.3		F 1444	4.8
	2140	2.5		2141	2.9
2	0342	5.2	17	0343	4.8
	1022	2.7		1032	3.1
	F 1609	5.3		SA 1608	4.9
	2310	2.3		2303	2.8
3	0504	5.4	18	0500	5.0
	1145	2.4		1144	2.9
	SA 1724	5.6		SU 1717	5.2
4	0021	1.9	19	0005	2.5
	0605	5.8		0553	5.4
	SU 1249	2.0		M 1237	2.5
	1823	6.0		1809	5.5
5	0118	1.6	20	0054	2.1
	0657	6.2		0637	5.7
	M 1343	1.6		TU 1321	2.1
	1914	6.3		1854	5.8
6	0208	1.3	21	0137	1.8
	0743	6.4		0717	6.1
	TU 1431	1.4		W 1403	1.8
	2001	6.5		1936	6.1
7	0252	1.1	22	0218	1.5
	0825	6.6		0756	6.3
	W 1513	1.2		TH 1443	1.5
	● 2042	6.6		2017	6.4
8	0332	1.1	23	0259	1.3
	0903	6.6		0835	6.5
	TH 1551	1.2		F 1524	1.3
	2120	6.6		○ 2058	6.5
9	0408	1.2	24	0340	1.2
	0938	6.6		0913	6.6
	F 1627	1.3		SA 1605	1.2
	2156	6.4		2139	6.6
10	0442	1.4	25	0421	1.2
	1011	6.4		0953	6.6
	SA 1701	1.4		SU 1648	1.2
	2230	6.2		2221	6.5
11	0515	1.7	26	0503	1.3
	1045	6.2		1035	6.6
	SU 1734	1.6		M 1731	1.3
	2304	6.0		2306	6.3
12	0548	2.0	27	0548	1.6
	1118	6.0		1119	6.4
	M 1808	1.9		TU 1818	1.5
	2339	5.7		2354	6.1
13	0622	2.3	28	0637	1.9
	1152	5.7		1208	6.1
	TU 1844	2.3		W 1910	1.7
14	0016	5.3	29	0049	5.8
	0700	2.7		0734	2.2
	W 1231	5.3		TH 1305	5.8
	1926	2.6		2012	2.0
15	0104	5.0	30	0157	5.5
	0751	3.0		0841	2.5
	TH 1325	5.0		F 1418	5.5
	◐ 2024	2.8		◑ 2124	2.2

DECEMBER

Day	Time	m	Day	Time	m
1	0318	5.4	16	0229	4.9
	1000	2.5		0917	3.0
	SA 1540	5.4		SU 1453	5.0
	2243	2.2		2148	2.7
2	0433	5.5	17	0341	5.0
	1118	2.4		1031	2.9
	SU 1653	5.6		M 1605	5.0
	2353	2.0		2300	2.6
3	0536	5.7	18	0451	5.2
	1223	2.1		1139	2.7
	M 1756	5.8		TU 1714	5.3
4	0052	1.8	19	0003	2.3
	0630	5.9		0549	5.5
	TU 1319	1.9		W 1237	2.3
	1850	6.0		1812	5.6
5	0142	1.6	20	0057	2.0
	0717	6.2		0640	5.8
	W 1407	1.6		TH 1328	1.9
	1938	6.1		1904	5.9
6	0227	1.5	21	0147	1.7
	0800	6.3		0726	6.2
	TH 1450	1.5		F 1416	1.6
	2021	6.2		1952	6.2
7	0307	1.5	22	0234	1.4
	0839	6.4		0811	6.4
	F 1529	1.4		SA 1504	1.3
	● 2100	6.2		○ 2040	6.4
8	0344	1.5	23	0321	1.3
	0914	6.4		0856	6.6
	SA 1605	1.4		SU 1551	1.1
	2136	6.2		2127	6.5
9	0419	1.6	24	0408	1.2
	0949	6.3		0941	6.7
	SU 1640	1.5		M 1638	1.0
	2211	6.1		2214	6.5
10	0453	1.8	25	0456	1.2
	1023	6.2		1027	6.7
	M 1714	1.6		TU 1726	1.0
	2245	5.9		2302	6.5
11	0527	2.0	26	0544	1.3
	1057	6.1		1115	6.6
	TU 1748	1.8		W 1815	1.1
	2319	5.7		2352	6.3
12	0601	2.2	27	0633	1.5
	1131	5.8		1204	6.4
	W 1823	2.0		TH 1905	1.3
	2355	5.5			
13	0637	2.5	28	0043	6.0
	1207	5.6		0725	1.8
	TH 1900	2.3		F 1257	6.1
				1959	1.6
14	0035	5.3	29	0139	5.7
	0720	2.7		0822	2.1
	F 1251	5.3		SA 1355	5.7
	1944	2.5		◑ 2058	1.9
15	0125	5.1	30	0242	5.5
	0812	2.9		0927	2.3
	SA 1346	5.1		SU 1502	5.5
	◐ 2040	2.7		2204	2.1
			31	0350	5.4
				1039	2.4
				M 1614	5.4
				2315	2.2

Chart Datum is 3·33 metres below IGN Datum. HAT is 7·0 metres above Chart Datum.

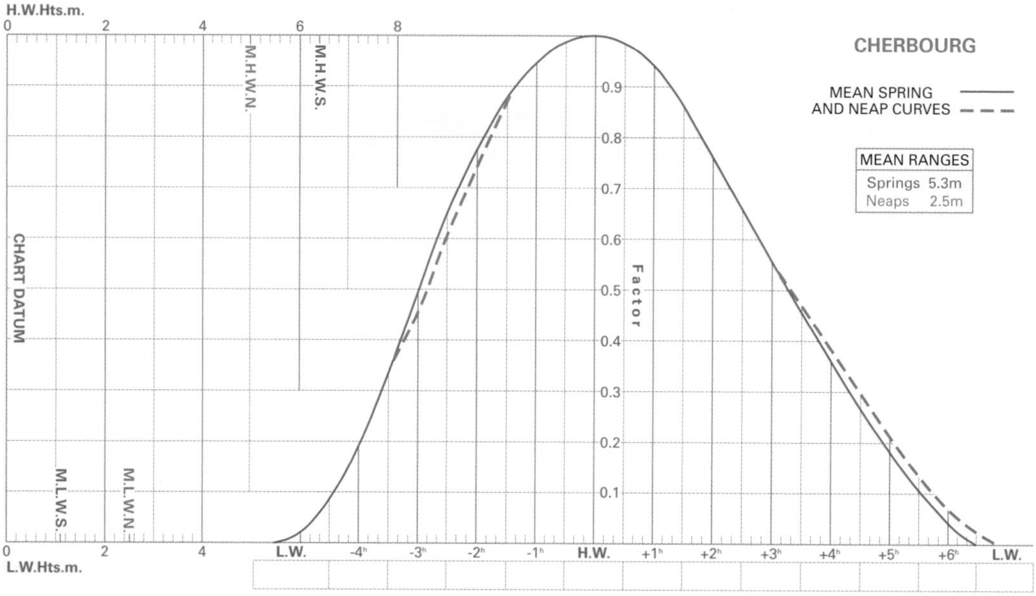

9.17.31 OMONVILLE-LA-ROGUE

Manche **49°42'·29N 01°49'·84W** ❁❁⛵⛵✿✿

CHARTS AC 2669, 1114; SHOM 7120, 7158, 5636; Navi 528, 1014; Imray C33A

TIDES –0330 Dover; ML 3·8; Duration 0545

Standard Port CHERBOURG (⟵)

Times				**Height (metres)**			
High Water		Low Water		MHWS	MHWN	MLWN	MLWS
0300	1000	0400	1000	6·4	5·1	2·6	1·1
1500	2200	1600	2200				
Differences OMONVILLE							
–0015	–0010	–0015	–0015	–0·1	–0·1	0·0	0·0
GOURY							
–0100	–0040	–0105	–0120	+1·2	+1·3	+0·7	0·0

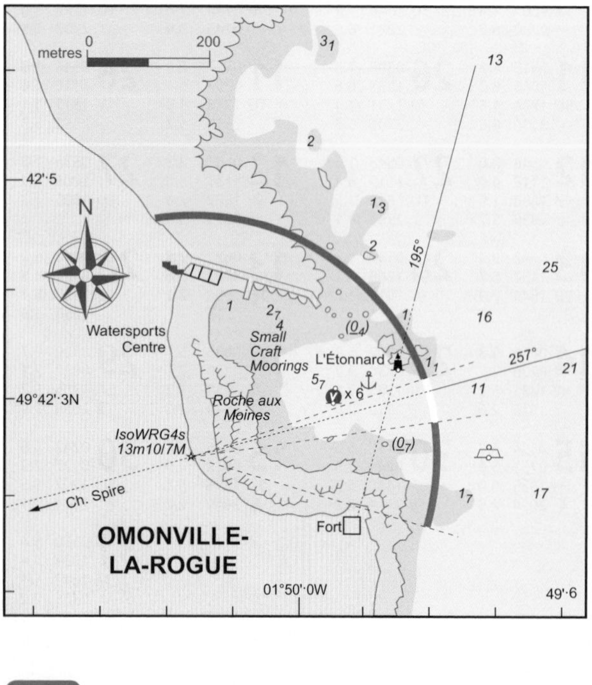

SHELTER Good, except in moderate/fresh N to SE winds when it may become untenable. Swell tends to work in.

NAVIGATION WPT 49°42'·47N 01°48'·66W, 257°/1·0M to Omonville dir lt. From W or N, keep clear of Basse Bréfort (depth 1m, marked by NCM buoy, VQ) 0·6M N of Pte Jardeheu. Appr on 195° transit (below) passing 100m E of L'Étonnard and into W sector of lt before turning stbd 290° for Ⓥs.

From E, appr on 257° transit with church spire and in W sector of lt, until S of L'Étonnard.

Harbour entrance is 100m wide: rocks extend N from Omonville Fort, and ESE from bkwtr to L'Étonnard, G bcn twr.

LIGHTS AND MARKS Omonville lt, on W framework tr with R top, Iso WRG 4s 13m 10/7M, vis 180°-G-252°-W-262°-R-287°. Lt in transit 257° with ⛪ steeple (hard to see) 650m beyond, leads S of L'Étonnard, 200m SE of which is a large unlit mooring buoy. From N, L'Étonnard in transit 195° with fort just clears Les Tataquets rocks. Street lights adequately illuminate the hbr area.

COMMUNICATIONS CROSS 02·33·52·16·16; ☁ 02·33·10·16·10; Auto 08·92·68·02·50; Police (Beaumont Hague) 02·33·01·89·30 or 17; Brit Consul 01·44·51·31·02; Samu (emergency medical) 15; Doctor 0 2·33·52·73·07/02·33·01·87·00/02·33·01·09·42.; Fire (*pompiers*, inc. divers) 18; Aff Mar 02·33·23·36·00.

FACILITIES **Harbour** There are 6 large W conical Ⓥs or ⚓ inside bkwtr; beware rocks off outer end.

Village ✕ at l'Association du Camping in village centre and at Watersports Centre; (at Beaumont-Hague 5km) ✉ Ⓑ ⇄ (bus to Cherbourg) ✈. Free historical tour www.visiteomonvillelarogue.fr **Ferry** see Cherbourg.

MINOR HARBOUR 2M EAST OF CAP DE LA HAGUE

ANSE DE ST MARTIN, Manche, **49°42'·72N 01°53'·78W**. AC 1114, 3653; SHOM 7120, 5636. Tides as Omonville-la-Rogue. From N, appr with conspic chy (279m) at Jobourg nuclear plant brg 175°; or from NE via Basse Bréfort NCM buoy, VQ, on with Danneville spire brg 237°. Both lines clear La Parmentière rks awash in centre of bay and Les Herbeuses and Le Grun Rk (1·9m) to W and SE respectively. Care needed, especially in poor visibility.

This bay, 2M E of Cap de la Hague, has ⚓s sheltered from all but onshore winds. Port Racine (said to be the smallest hbr in France) is in the SW corner of Anse de St Martin. ⚓ or moor off the hbr which is obstructed by lines; landing by dinghy.

Central North France

Cap de la Hague to St Quay-Portrieux

9.18.1 **Contents** 797

9.18.2 **Area map and Distance table** 798

9.18.3 **Tidal stream charts** 800

9.18.4 **Lights, buoys and waypoints** 802

9.18.5 **Passage information** 804
The West Coast of the Cotentin Peninsula – 804 • Cap de la Hague to Mont St Michel – 804 • Mont St Michel to St Malo – 808 • St Malo to L'Ost Pic and Beyond – 808

9.18.6 **Special notes for France, see Area 17**

9.18.7 **Diélette** 804
Goury

9.18.8 **Carteret** 805

9.18.9 **Portbail** 806

9.18.10 **Granville** 806
Regnéville

9.18.11 **Îles Chausey** 807

9.18.12 **St Malo, tidal coefficients, tide tables/curves** 808
Cancale • Rotheneuf • Dinard

9.18.13 **River Rance** 815
Plouër • Lyvet • Dinan

9.18.14 **Inland waterways of Brittany** 816

9.18.15 **St Cast Le Guildo** 817
Saint Briac • Erquy

9.18.16 **Dahouet** 817

9.18.17 **Saint-Brieuc Le Légué** 818

9.18.18 **Binic** 819

9.18.19 **St Quay-Portrieux** 820

DISTANCE TABLE
Approximate distances in nautical miles are by the most direct route while avoiding dangers and allowing for TSS. Places in *italics* are in adjoining areas; places in **bold** are in 9.0.5, Cross-Channel Distances.

1	***Calais***	**1**																						
2	Barfleur	148	**2**																					
3	**Cherbourg**	160	20	**3**																				
4	Omonville	163	27	10	**4**																			
5	Cap de la Hague	167	32	18	6	**5**																		
6	*Braye (Alderney)*	172	41	25	15	9	**6**																	
7	***St Peter Port***	193	60	44	34	28	23	**7**																
8	*Creux (Sark)*	190	55	37	29	23	22	10	**8**															
9	***St Helier***	213	77	64	51	45	46	29	24	**9**														
10	Dielette	187	48	32	20	12	18	29	22	40	**10**													
11	Carteret	192	55	41	29	23	28	31	23	26	17	**11**												
12	Portbail	196	59	49	33	27	32	35	27	25	21	5	**12**											
13	Iles Chausey	222	87	69	61	55	58	48	43	25	48	33	30	**13**										
14	Granville	227	93	75	67	61	66	55	50	30	49	38	35	9	**14**									
15	Dinan	250	117	102	91	85	85	66	64	50	72	62	59	29	35	**15**								
16	**St Malo**	238	105	90	79	73	73	54	52	38	59	50	47	17	23	12	**16**							
17	St Cast	246	102	86	77	71	76	52	49	38	62	51	49	23	30	24	12	**17**						
18	Dahouet	240	106	88	80	74	72	54	52	41	69	60	59	37	45	41	29	22	**18**					
19	St-Brieuc Le Légué	244	110	96	86	78	76	57	56	46	73	69	69	41	49	45	33	32	8	**19**				
20	Binic	244	115	95	84	78	75	56	55	46	72	70	70	43	51	45	33	28	10	8	**20**			
21	**St Quay-Portrieux**	244	106	88	80	74	73	56	51	46	68	64	64	47	54	47	35	29	11	7	4	**21**		
22	Paimpol	248	104	88	79	73	70	48	51	45	68	64	64	49	58	55	43	36	25	25	20	16	**22**	
23	***Lézardrieux***	238	106	88	80	74	68	48	38	47	68	68	71	53	54	61	49	40	33	32	30	21	14	**23**

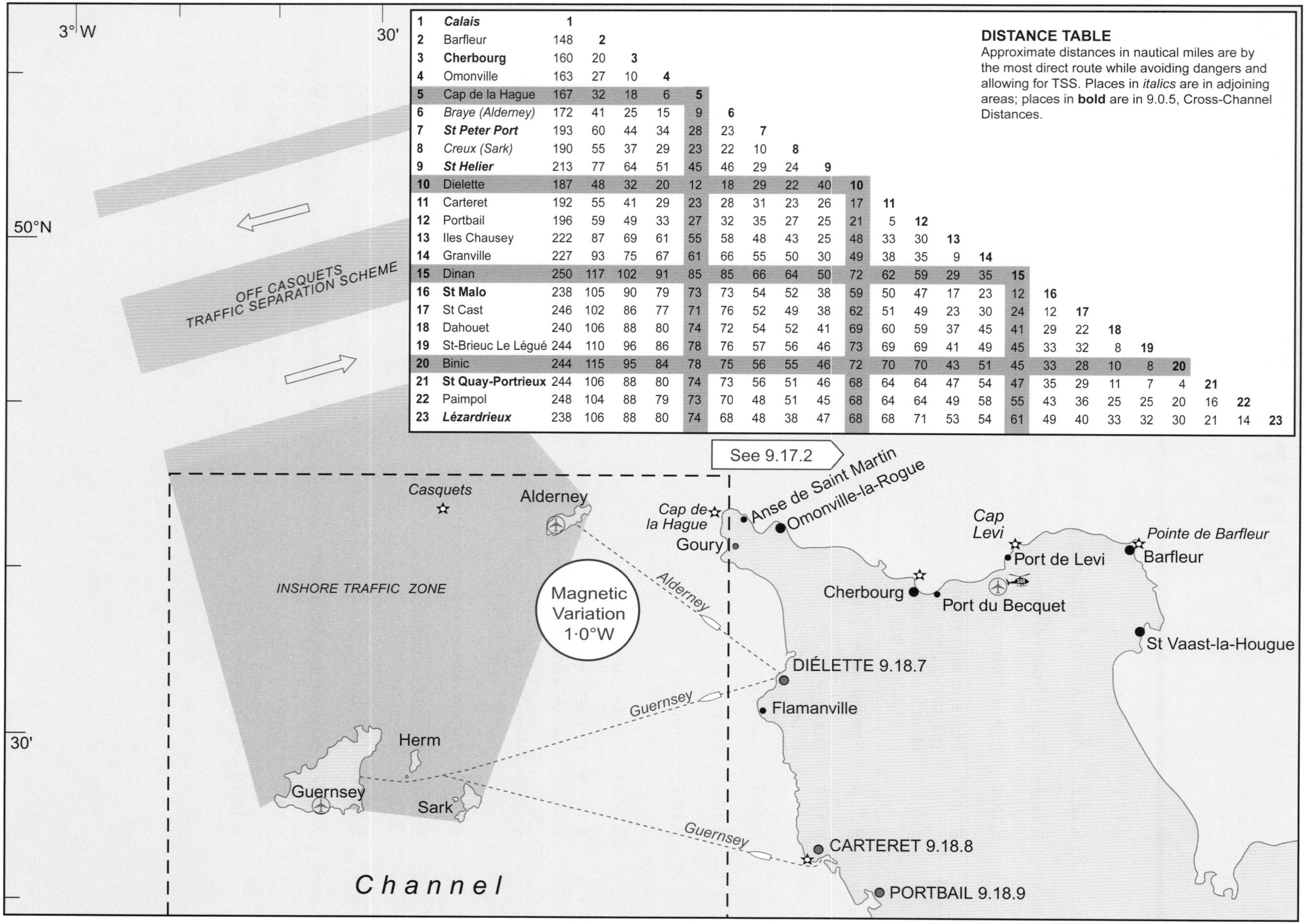
3° W
30'
50°N
30'
OFF CASQUETS TRAFFIC SEPARATION SCHEME
INSHORE TRAFFIC ZONE
Casquets
Alderney
Magnetic Variation 1·0°W
Herm
Guernsey
Sark
Channel
Alderney
Guernsey
Guernsey
See 9.17.2
Cap de la Hague
Goury
Anse de Saint Martin
Omonville-la-Rogue
Cherbourg
Port du Becquet
Cap Levi
Port de Levi
Pointe de Barfleur
Barfleur
St Vaast-la-Hougue
DIÉLETTE 9.18.7
Flamanville
CARTERET 9.18.8
PORTBAIL 9.18.9

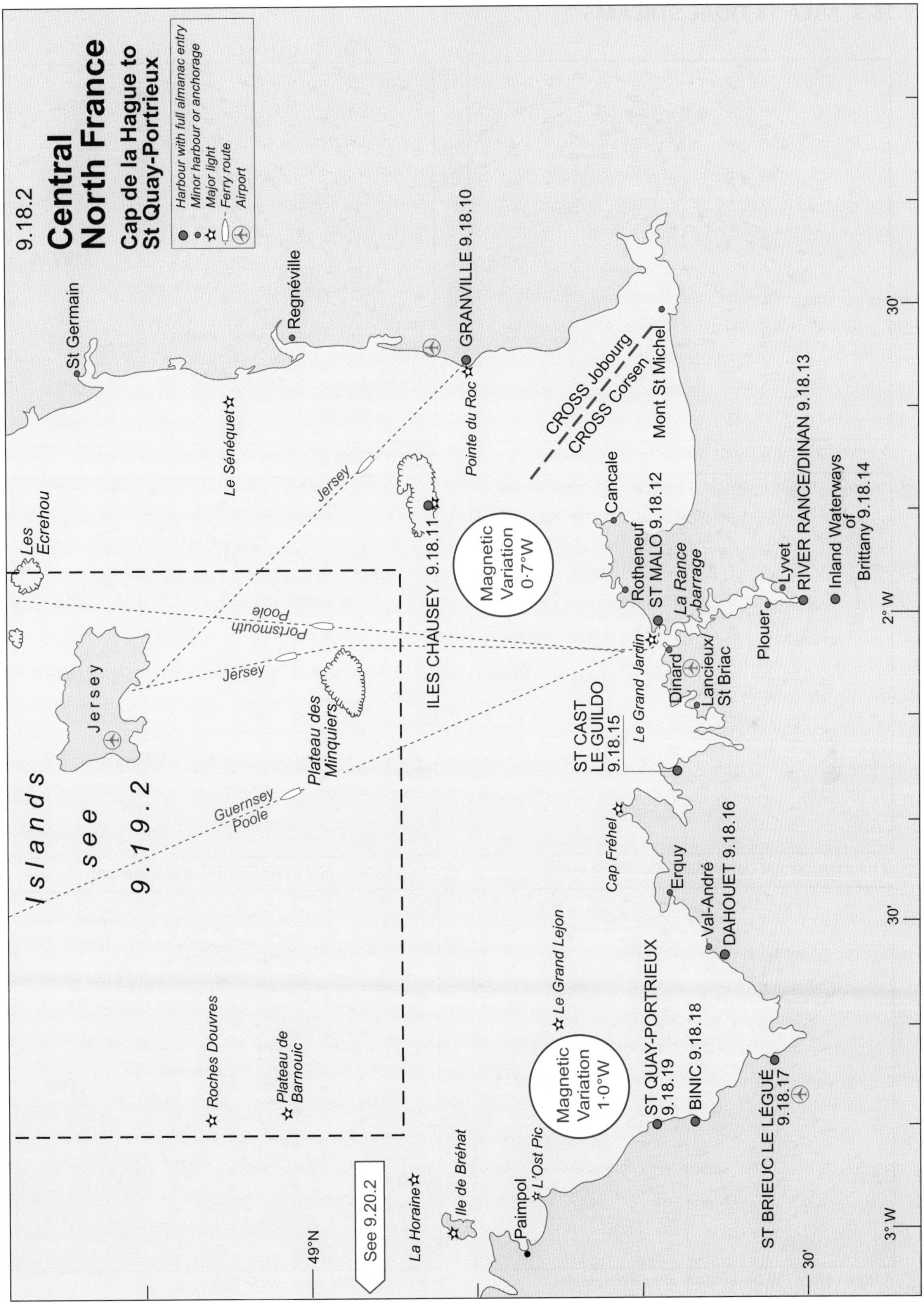
9.18.2
Central North France
Cap de la Hague to St Quay-Portrieux
Harbour with full almanac entry
Minor harbour or anchorage
Major light
Ferry route
Airport
St Germain
Regnéville
GRANVILLE 9.18.10
Pointe du Roc
Le Sénéquet
Les Ecrehou
Jersey
Jersey
Portsmouth
Poole
Guernsey
Poole
Islands
see
9.19.2
Plateau des Minquiers
ILES CHAUSEY 9.18.11
Magnetic Variation 0·7°W
CROSS Jobourg
CROSS Corsen
Mont St Michel
Cancale
Rotheneuf
ST MALO 9.18.12
La Rance barrage
Lyvet
RIVER RANCE/DINAN 9.18.13
Inland Waterways of Brittany 9.18.14
Plouer
Le Grand Jardin
Dinard
Lancieux
St Briac
ST CAST LE GUILDO 9.18.15
Cap Fréhel
Erquy
Val-André
DAHOUET 9.18.16
Le Grand Lejon
Roches Douvres
Plateau de Barnouic
Magnetic Variation 1·0°W
ST QUAY-PORTRIEUX 9.18.19
BINIC 9.18.18
ST BRIEUC LE LÉGUÉ 9.18.17
Ile de Bréhat
La Horaine
L'Ost Pic
Paimpol
See 9.20.2
49°N
30'
3° W
30'
2° W
30'

9.18.3 AREA 18 TIDAL STREAMS

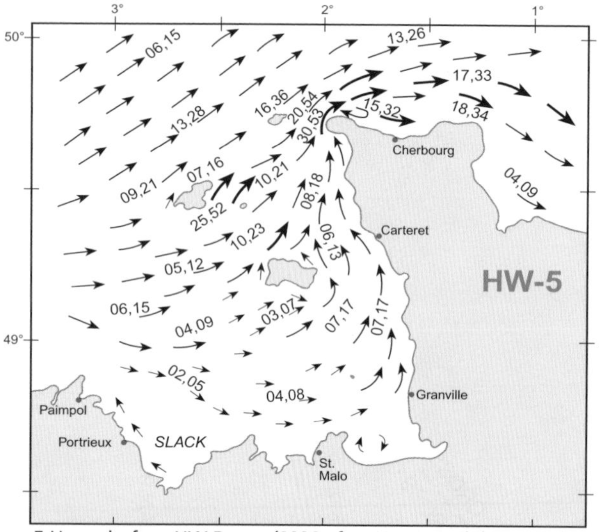

5 Hours before HW Dover (0006 after HW St Malo)

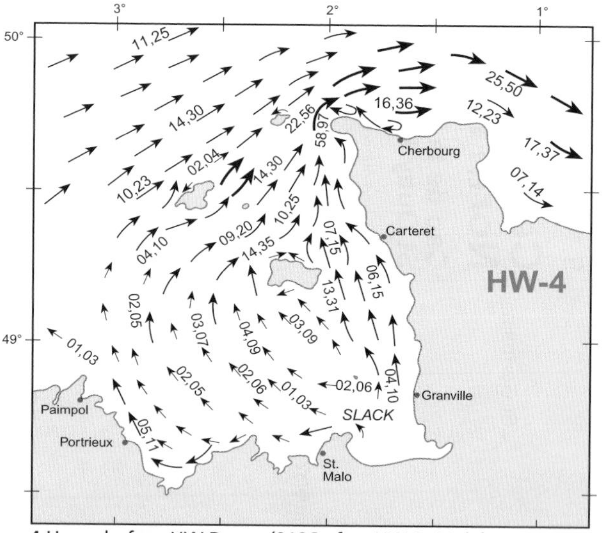

4 Hours before HW Dover (0106 after HW St Malo)

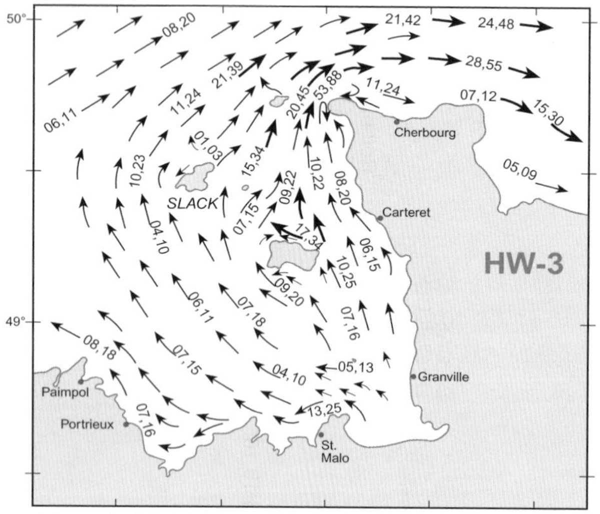

3 Hours before HW Dover (0206 after HW St Malo)

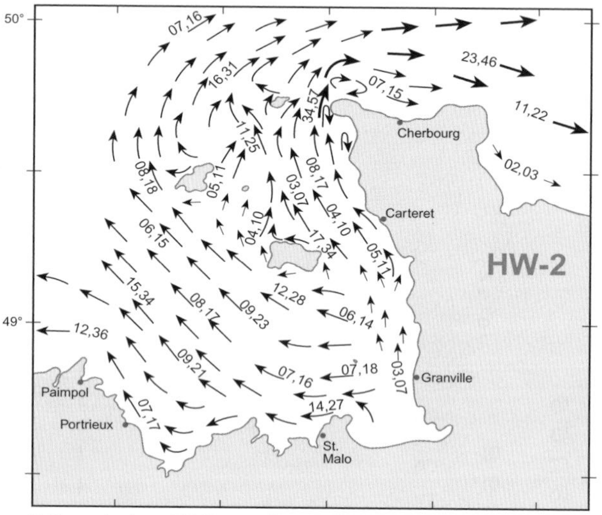

2 Hours before HW Dover (0306 after HW St Malo)

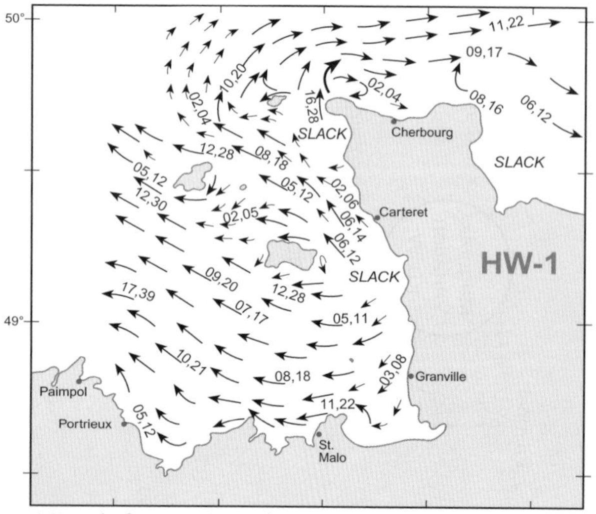

1 Hour before HW Dover (0406 after HW St Malo)

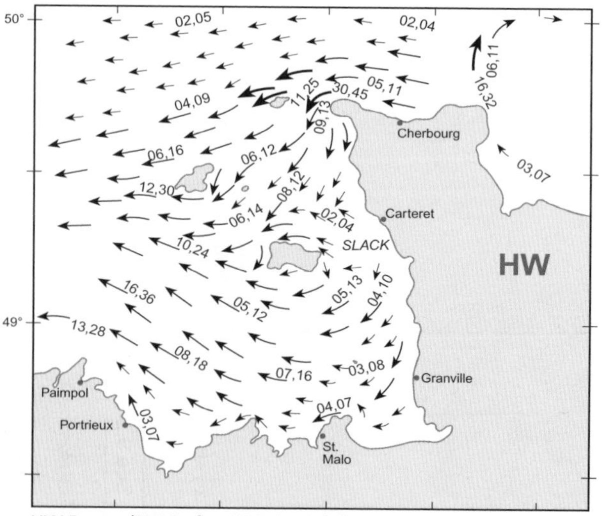

HW Dover (0506 after HW St Malo)

Westward 9.20.3 Channel Islands 9.19.3 Eastward 9.17.3 Northward 9.2.3

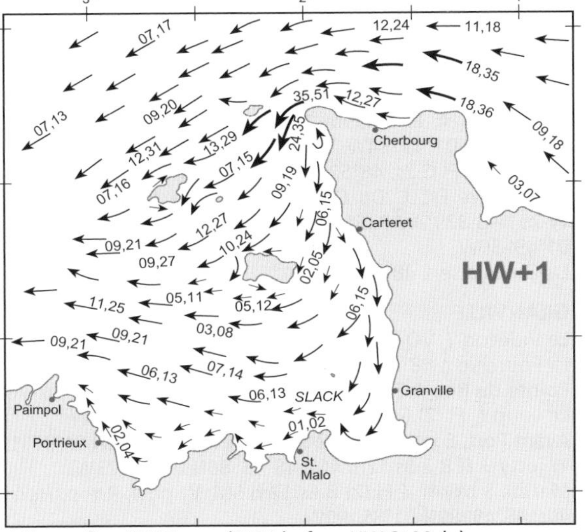

1 Hour after HW Dover (0554 before HW St Malo)

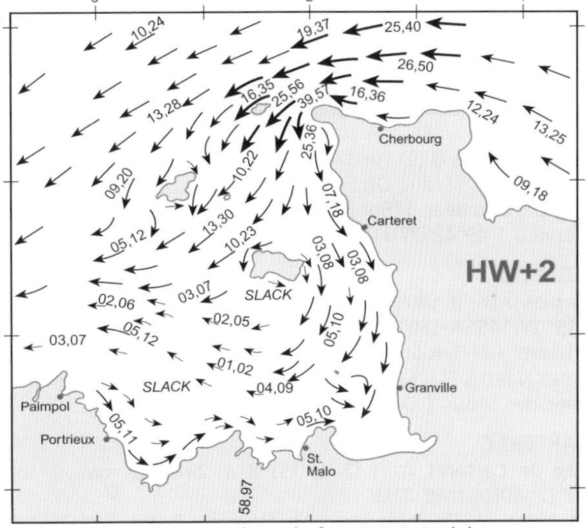

2 Hours after HW Dover (0454 before HW St Malo)

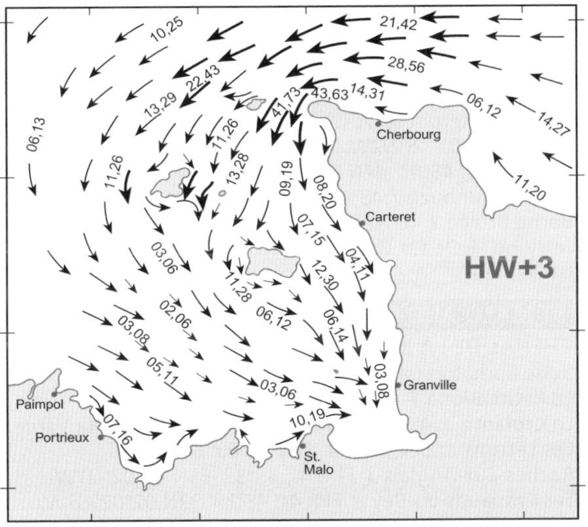

3 Hours after HW Dover (0354 before HW St Malo)

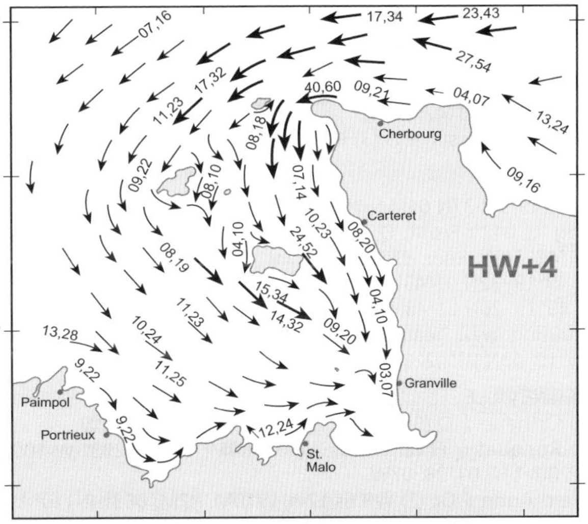

4 Hours after HW Dover (0254 before HW St Malo)

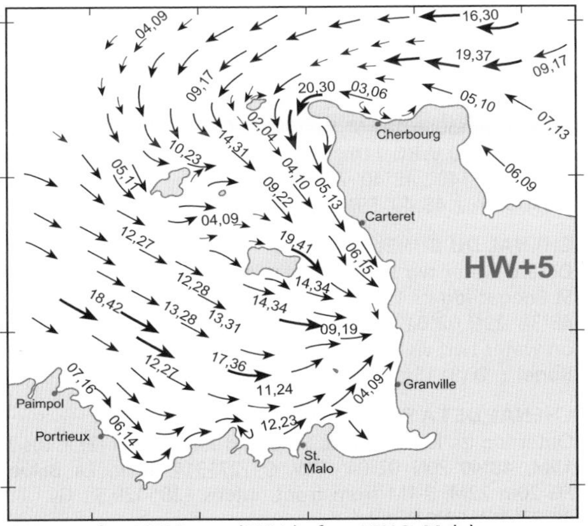

5 Hours after HW Dover (0154 before HW St Malo)

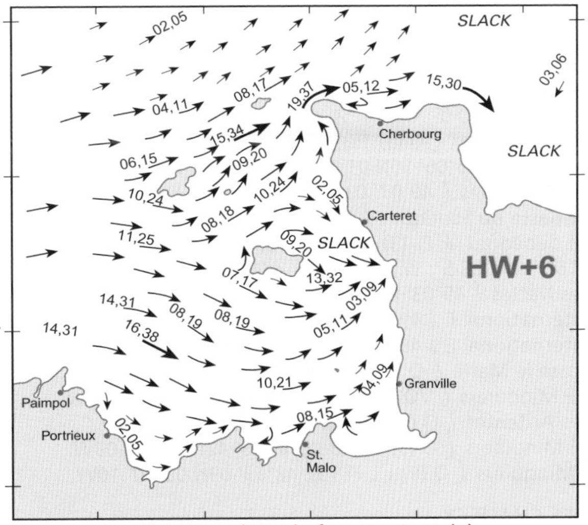

6 Hours after HW Dover (0054 before HW St Malo)

9.18.4 LIGHTS, BUOYS AND WAYPOINTS

Bold print = light with a nominal range of 15M or more. CAPITALS = place or feature. *CAPITAL ITALICS* = light-vessel, light float or Lanby. *Italics* = Fog signal. ***Bold italics*** = Racon. Many marks/buoys are fitted with AIS (MMSI No); see relevant charts.

CAP DE LA HAGUE TO ST MALO

GOURY

La Foraine VQ (9) 10s 12m 6M; 49°42'·90 N 01°58'·32W.
Ldg lts 065·2°: Front, QR 5m 7M; R □ in W □ on pier, 49°42'·89N 01°56'·70W. Rear, 116m from front, Q 11m 7M; W pylon/hut.
Hervieu 49°42'·77N 01°56'·92W.

DIELETTE

W bkwtr Dir lt 140°, Iso WRG 4s 12m W10M, R/G7M; 070°-G-135°-W-145°-R-180°; W twr, G top ;49°33'·18N 01°51'·81W.
E bkwtr Fl R 4s 6m 2M; 49°33'·21N 01°51'·78W.
Inner N jetty, Fl (2) R 6s. Inner S jetty, Fl (2) G 6s; bth 6m 1M.
Banc des Dious Q (9) 15s; 49°32'·58N 01°54'·02W.

CARTERET

Cap de Carteret ☆ Fl (2+1) 15s 81m **26M**; Gy twr, G top; 49°22'·40N 01°48'·41W.
W bkwtr Oc R 4s 7m 7M; W post, R top; 49°22'·07N 01°47'·32W.
E training wall Fl G 2·5s 4m 2M; W post, G top; 49°22'·17N 01°47'·30W.
Channel bend Fl (2) R 6s 5m 1M; R pylon; 49°22'·58N 01°47'·23W. Inside the bend: Fl (2) G 6s 5m 1M; G pylon; 49°22'·55N 01°47'·20W.
Marina entry sill: Fl (3) R 12s and Fl (3) G 12s; R & G pylons.

PORTBAIL

PB 49°18'·37N 01°44'·75W.
Ldg lts 042°: Front, Q 14m 10M; W pylon, R top, 49°19'·75N 01°42'·50W. Rear, 870m frm front, Oc 4s 20m 10M; ch belfry.
49°19'·32N 01°43'·16W.
49°19'·20N 01°43'·00W.
Training wall head Fl (2) R 5s 5m 4M; W mast, R top; 49°19'·43N 01°42'·99W.

REGNÉVILLE

La Catheue Q (6) + L Fl 15s, 48°57'·67N 01°42'·23W.
Le Ronquet Fl (2) WR 6s, W6M, R4M; 100°-R-293°-W-100°; 49°00'·11N 01°38'·07W.
Pte d'Agon Oc (2) WR 6s 12m, W10M, R7M; 063°-R-110°-W-063°; W twr, R top, W dwelling; 49°00'·18N 01°34'·63W.
Dir lt 028°, Oc WRG 4s 9m, W12M, R/G9M; 024°-G-027°-W-029°-R-033°; house; 49°00'·63N 01°33'·36W.

PASSAGE DE LA DÉROUTE

Les Trois-Grunes Q (9) 15s, 49°21'·84N 01°55'·21W.
Écrévière Q (6) + L Fl 15s; *Bell;* 49°15'·27N 01°52'·16W.
Basse Jourdan Q (3) 10s; 49°06'·85N 01°43'·96W.
Le Boeuf 49°06'·56N 01°47'·17W.
Les Boeuftins 49°07'·03N 01°45'·96W.
La Basse du Sénéquet 49°05'·96N 01°41'·11W.
Le Sénéquet Fl (3) WR 12s 18m W13M, R10M; 083·5°-R-116·5°-W-083·5°; W twr; 49°05'·48N 01°39'·73W.
Les Nattes 49°03'·46N 01°41'·81W.
International F 49°02'·16N 01°42'·98W.
International E 49°02'·08N 01°47'·21W.
Basse le Marié Q (9) 15s; 49°01'·79N 01°48'·57W.
NE Minquiers VQ (3) 5s; *Bell;* 49°00'·85N 01°55'·30W.
Les Ardentes Q (3) 10s; 48°57'·89N 01°51'·53W.
SE Minquiers Q (3) 10s; *Bell;* 48°53'·42N 02°00'·09W.
S Minquiers Q (6) + L Fl 15s; 48°53'·09N 02°10'·10W.

ÎLES CHAUSEY

La Pointue 48°54'·44N 01°50'·92W.
L'Enseigne, W twr, B top; 48°53'·67N 01°50'·37W.
L'Etat, BW, 48°54'·67N 01°46'·21W.
Anvers wreck 48°53'·91N 01°41'·07W.
Le Founet Q (3) 10s; 48°53'·25N 01°42'·34W.
Le Pignon Fl (2) WR 6s 10m, W9M, R6M; 005°-R-150°-W-005°; B twr, W band; 48°53'·49N 01°43'·36 W.
La Haute Foraine 48°52'·89N 01°43'·66W.
Grande Île ☆ Fl 5s 39m **23M**; Gy □ twr, G top; *Horn 30s;* 48°52'·17N 01°49'·34W.
Channel Fl G 2s; 48°52'·07N 01°49'·08W.
La Crabière Est Dir Oc(3)WRG 12s 5m, W9M, R/G6M;079°-W-291°-G-329°-W-335°-R-079°; B beacon, Y top; 48°52'·46N 01°49'·39W.
La Cancalaise 48°51'·90N 01°51'·11W.

GRANVILLE

Le Videcoq VQ (9) 10s; 48°49'·66N 01°42'·06W.
La Fourchie 48°50'·15N 01°37'·00W.
Pointe du Roc ☆ Fl (4) 15s 49m **23M;** 48°50'·06N 01°36'·78W.
Le Loup Fl (2) 6s 8m 11M; 48°49'·57N 01°36'·24W.
Avant Port, E jetty Fl G 2·5s 11m 4M; 48°49'·93N 01°36'·19W.
W jetty Fl R 2·5s 12m 4M; 48°49'·86N 01°36'·23W.
Marina S bkwtr Fl (2) R 6s 12m 5M; W post, R top; *Horn (2) 40s;* 48°49'·89N 01°35'·90W.
N bkwtr Fl (2) G 6s 4m 5M; 48°49'·93N 01°35'·90W.
Sill, W side, QR 2M, E side QG 2M; Gy pylons topped R (W) and G (E).

CANCALE

La Fille 48°44'·16N 01°48'·46W.
Pierre-de-Herpin ☆ Oc (2) 6s 20m 13M; W twr, B top and base; 48°43'·77N 01°48'·92W.
Ruet *Bell;* 48°43'·44N 01°50'·11W.
Grande Bunouze 48°43'·17N 01°50'·95W.
Barbe Brûlée 48°42'·11N 01°50'·57W.
Jetty hd Oc (3) G 12s 9m 3M; W pylon B top; 48°40'·10N 01°51'·11W.

ST MALO AND RIVER RANCE

CHENAL DE LA BIGNE

Basse Rochefort (aka Basse aux Chiens) 48°42'·69N 01°57'·31W.
La Petite Bigne 48°41'·66N 01°58'·72W.
La Crolante ; 48°41'·01N 01°59'·51W, off Pte de la Varde.
Les Létruns ; *Bell;* 48°40'·71N 02°00'·61W.
Roches-aux-Anglais Fl G 4s; 48°39'·65N 02°02'·27W.
Les Crapauds-du-Bey Fl R 4s; 48°39'·37N 02°02'·57W.

CHENAL DES PETITS POINTUS

Dinard ch spire (74m) brg 203° to right of Le Petit Bé rocks.
La Saint-Servantine Fl G 2·5s; *Bell;* 48°41'·93N 02°00'·94W.
Les Petits Pontus 48°41'·30N 02°00'·86W.

CHENAL DE LA GRANDE CONCHÉE

Villa Brisemoulin 181·5°, on with LH edge of Le Petit Bé rocks.
La Plate Q WRG 11m, W10M, R/G7M; 140°-W-203°-R-210°-W-225°-G-140°; 48°40'·78N 02°01'·91W.
Le Bouton 48°40'·59N 02°01'·85W.

CHENAL DU BUNEL

Dinard water twr lt 158·2° on with St Énogat lts.
St Énogat ldg lts 158·2°; both Iso 4s 3/85m 6/8M, synch. Front 48°38'·29N 02°04'·11W, vis 126°-236°. Rear, 1.4M from front, on water twr; vis 143°-210°.
Bunel Q (9) 15s; 48°40'·84N 02°05'·38W.

CHENAL DE LA PETITE PORTE

Outer ldg lts 129·7°: **Front, Le Grand Jardin** ☆ Fl (2) R 10s 24m **15M,** 48°40'·20N 02°04'·97W. 992271314. Rear, **La Balue** ☆ FG 20m **22M**; 3·1M from front; intens 128°-129·5°; Gy □ twr; 48°38'·16N 02°01'·30W.
Vieux-Banc E Q; 48°42'·38N 02°09'·12W.

Vieux-Banc W VQ (9) 10s; 48°41'·84N 02°10'·20W.
St Malo Atterrisage (Fairway) Iso 4s; 48°41'·39N 02°07'·28W.
Les Courtis Fl G 4s 14m 7M; 48°40'·46N 02°05'·80W.

Nearing Le Grand Jardin, move stbd briefly onto Ch du Bunel 152·8° ldg lts to pick up: Inner ldg lts 128·6°, both Dir FG 20/69m **22/25M**; H24. Front, **Les Bas Sablons** ☆, intens 127·2°-130·2°; W □ twr, B top; 48°38'·16N 02°01'·30W. 992271312. Rear, **La Balue** ☆, 0·9M from front; intens 128°-129·5°; Gy □ twr; 48°37'·60N 02°00'·24W. 992271313.
Basse du Nord No 5 48°39'·98N 02°05'·04W.
Les Pierres-Garnier No 8 48°39'·98N 02°04'·41W.
Les Patouillets Fl (3) G 12s, 48°39'·68N 02°04'·30W.
Clef d'Aval No 10 48°39'·72N 02°03'·91W.
Basse du Buron No 12 Fl (4) R 15s, 48°39'·42N 02°03'·51W.
Le Buron Fl (4) G 15s 15m 7M; G twr, 48°39'·32N 02°03'·66W.
Les Grelots VQ (6) + L Fl 10s, 48°39'·16N 02°03'·03W.

CHENAL DE LA GRANDE PORTE
Banchenou VQ, 48°40'·44N 02°11'·48W.
Outer ldg lts 089·1°: **Front, Le Grand Jardin** ☆ Fl (2) R 10s 24m **15M,** 48°40'·20N 02°04'·97W.
Rear, **Rochebonne** ☆ Dir FR 40m **24M**; intens 088·2°-089·7°; Gy □ twr, R top, 4·2M from front; 48°40'·26N 01°58'·71W. 992271311.
Buharats W No 2 Fl R 2·5s, 48°40'·22N 02°07'·50W.
Buharats E No 4 *Bell;* 48°40'·24N 02°07'·20W.
Bas du Boujaron No 1 Fl (2) G 6s, 48°40'·17N 02°05'·97W.
Le Sou VQ (3) 5s; 48°40'·11N 02°05'·30W.
Continue on inner 128·6° ldg line: see Chenal de la Petite Porte.

RADE DE ST MALO
Plateau Rance Nord VQ, 48°38'·64N 02°02'·35W.
Plateau Rance Sud Q (6) + L Fl 15s, 48°38'·43N 02°02'·28W.
Crapaud de la Cité QG, 48°38'·34N 02°02'·01W.

ST MALO
Môle des Noires hd VQ R 11m 6M; W twr, R top; *Horn (2) 20s*; 48°38'·52N 02°01'·91W.
Écluse du Naye ldg lts 070·4°, both FR 7/23m 3/7M. Front, 48°38'·58N 02°01'·48W. Rear, 030°-120°.
Ferry jetty hd, VQ G 6M; 48°38'·44N 02°01'·82W (128·6° ldg line). Ferry jetty, Fl R 4s 3m 1M; 260°-080°; 48°38'·44N 02°01'·76W.
Bas-Sablons marina, mole head Fl G 4s 7m 5M; Gy mast; 48°38'·42N 02°01'·70W.

LA RANCE BARRAGE
La Jument Fl G 4s 6m 4M; G twr, 48°37'·44N 02°01'·76W.
ZI 12 Fl R 4s, 48°37'·47N 02°01'·62W.
NE dolphin Fl (2) R 6s 6m 5M; 040°-200°, 48°37'·09N 02°01'·71W.
Barrage lock, NW wall Fl (2) G 6s 6m 5M,191°-291°; G pylon, 48°37'·06N 02°01'·73W.
Barrage lock, SW wall, Fl (3) G 12s, 48°37'·00N 02°01'·70W.
SE dolphin Fl (3) R 12s, 48°36'·97N 02°01'·66W.
ZI 24 Fl (2) R 6s, 48°36'·63N 02°01'·33W.

ST MALO TO ST QUAY-PORTRIEUX

ST BRIAC
R. Frémur mouth. Dir lt 125° Iso WRG 4s 10m, W13M, R/G 11M; 121·5°-G-124·5°-W-125·5°-R-129·5°; W mast on hut, 48°37'·07N 02°08'·20W.

ST CAST
Les Bourdinots 48°39'·01N 02°13'·48W.
St Cast môle Iso WG 4s 12m, W9M, G6M; 180°-G-206°-W-217°-G-235°-W-245°-G-340°; G&W structure; 48°38'·41N 02°14'·61W.
Laplace , 48°39'·73N 2°16'·45W; 5ca SE of Pte de la Latte.
Cap Fréhel ☆ Fl (2) 10s 85m **29M**; Gy □ twr, G lantern; 48°41'·05N 02°19'·13W. Reserve lt range **15M**.

CHENAL and PORT D'ERQUY
Les Justières Q (6) + L Fl 15s; 48°40'·56N 02°26'·48W.
Basses du Courant VQ (6) + L Fl 10s; 48°39'·21N 02°29'·16W.
L'Evette 48°38'·51N 02°31'·45W.
S môle Fl (2) WRG 6s 11m W10M, R/G7M; 055°-R-081°-W-094°-G-111°-W-120°-R-134°; W twr; 48°38'·06N 02°28'·68W.
Inner jetty Fl (3) R 12s 10m 3M; R/W twr; 48°38'·09N 02°28'·39W.

DAHOUET
Petit Bignon 48°36'·82N 02°35'·06W.
Le Dahouet 48°35'·15N 02°35'·43W.
La Petite Muette Fl WRG 4s 10m W9M, R/G6M; 055°-G-114°-W-146°-R-196°; W twr, G band; 48°34'·82N 02°34'·30W.
Entry chan, Fl (2) G 6s 5m 1M; 156°-286°; 48°34'·71N 02°34'·19W.

BAIE DE ST BRIEUC
Grand Léjon ☆ Fl (5) WR 20s 17m **W18M**, R14M; 015°-R-058°-W-283°-R-350°-W-015°; R twr, W bands; 48°44'·91N 02°39'·87W. 992271325.
Petit Léjon ; 48°41'·80N 02°37'·55W.
Les Landas Q, 48°41'·43N 02°31'·29W.
Le Rohein Q (9) WRG 15s 13m, W8M, R/G5M; 072°-R-105°-W-180°-G-193°-W-237°-G-282°-W-301°-G-330°-W-072°; Y twr, B band; 48°38'·80N 02°37'·77W.

SAINT-BRIEUC LE LÉGUÉ
Tra-Hillion 48°33'·38N 02°38'·50W.
Le Légué Mo (A)10s; 48°34'·32N 02°41'·15W.
No 1 Fl G 2·5s; 48°32'·42N 02°42'·51W.
No 2 Fl R 2·5s; 48°32'·37N 02°42'·40W.
No 3 Fl (2) G 6s; 48°32'·27N 02°42'·78W.
No 4 Fl (2) R 6s; 48°32'·23N 02°42'·70W.
No 5 Fl (3) G 12s; 48°32'·18N 02°42'·92W.
No 6 Fl (3) R 12s; 48°32'·14N 02°42'·90W.
NE jetty VQ R 4M; 48°32'·12N 02°42'·88W.
Pte à l'Aigle jetty VQ G 13m 8M; 160°-070°; W twr, G top; 48°32'·12N 02°43'·11W.
No 7 Fl (4) G 15s; 48°32'·11N 02°43'·08W.
No 8 Fl R 2·5s; 48°32'·01N 02°43'·16W.
No 9 Fl (2) G 6s; 48°31'·96N 02°43'·29W.
No 10 Fl (2) R 6s; 48°31'·91N 02°43'·31W.
Jetty Iso G 4s 6m 2M; W cols, G top; 48°31'·90N 02°43'·43W.
No 11 Fl (3) G 12s; 48°31'·90N 02°43'·43W.
No 13 Fl (4) G 15s; 48°31'·76N 02°43'·56W.
No 14 Fl (4) R 15s; 48°31'·70N 02°43'·61W.

BINIC
N môle Oc (3) 12s 12m 11M; unintens 020°-110°; W twr, G lantern; 48°36'·07N 02°48'·92W.

ST QUAY-PORTRIEUX
Les Hors 48°39'·60N 02°44'·04W.
Caffa Q (3) 10s; 48°37'·82N 02°43'·08W.
La Longue 48°37'·88N 02°44'·68W.
La Roselière VQ (6) + L Fl 10s; 48°37'·31N 02°46'·19W.
Herflux Dir 130°, Fl (2) WRG 6s 10m, W 8M, R/G 5M; 115°-G-125°-W-135°-R-145°; 48°39'·07N 02°47'·95W. 992271323.
Île Harbour (Roches de Saint-Quay) Fl WRG 4s 16m, W9M, R/G 6M; 011°-R-133°-G-270°-R-306°-G-358°-W-011°; W twr & dwelling, R top; 48°39'·99N 02°48'·49W. 992271321.
Madeux 48°40'·41N 02°48'·81W.
Grandes Moulières de St Quay 48°39'·76N 02°49'·91W.
Moulières de Portrieux 48°39'·26N 02°49'·21W.
Les Noirs 48°39'·09N 02°48·46W.
Marina, **NE mole elbow**, Dir lt 318·2°: Iso WRG 4s 16m **W15M**, R/G11M; W159°-179°, G179°-316°, W316°-320·5°, R320·5° -159°; Reserve lt ranges 11/8M; 48°38'·99N 02°49'·09W. 992271322.
NE môle hd Fl (3) G 12s 10m 2M; 48°38'·84N 02°48'·91W.
S môle hd Fl (3) R 12s 10m 2M; 48°38'·83N 02°49'·03W.
Old hbr ent: N side, Fl G 2.5s 11m 2M; 48°38'·71N 02°49'·36W.
S side, Fl R 2.5s 8m 2M; 48°38'·67N 02°49'·35W.

9.18.5 PASSAGE INFORMATION

More passage information is threaded between successive harbours in this Area. **Bibliography**: The Channel Islands (Imray/RCC/Carnegie) ; *Shell Channel Pilot* (Imray/Cunliffe); *North Brittany and Channel Islands CC* (Fernhurst/Cumberlidge); *North Brittany* (Imray/RCC/Lawson); *Channel Pilot* (NP 27); *Channel Havens* (ACN/Endean).

THE WEST COAST OF THE COTENTIN PENINSULA

This coast is exposed and often a lee shore (AC 3653, 3655, 3656, 3659). North of Carteret it is mostly rocky. Southward to Mont St Michel and W to St Malo the coast changes to extensive offshore shoals, sand dunes studded with rocks and a series of drying hbrs; there is little depth of water, so that a nasty sea can build.

▶*The seas around this coast are dominated by powerful tidal streams rotating anti-clockwise; and a very large tidal range. In the Alderney Race the main English Channel tidal streams are rectilinear NE/SW. Tidal streams need to be worked carefully; neaps are best, particularly for a first visit. The Admiralty tidal stream atlas NP 264 covers the French coast and Channel Islands. The equivalent SHOM 562-UJA gives more details.*◀

CAP DE LA HAGUE TO MONT ST MICHEL

Cap de La Hague is low-lying, but rises steeply to the south. Between the coast and Gros du Raz lt ho a difficult and narrow passage leads S to Goury. It is sheltered when the Alderney Race is fully exposed, but not for the inexperienced. Pylons and Jobourg nuclear plant are conspic 3·7M SE. CROSS Jobourg is adjacent.

5M S of Cap de la Hague beware Les Huquets de Jobourg, an extensive unmarked bank of drying (2·1m) and submerged rks, and Les Huquets de Vauville (5·4m) close SE of them.

The drying hbrs at **Goury, Carteret and Portbail** are more readily accessible if cruising from S to N on the flood. The marinas at **Diélette** and **Carteret** are non-tidal. The former has H24 access for 1·5m draught if coefficient is <80.

Déroute de Terre and Passage de la Déroute are coastal chans, poorly marked, shallow in places and not advised at night.

Déroute de Terre (not shown on AC 2669 and 3655) passes W of Plateau des Trois Grunes; Basses de Portbail; La Basse du Sénéquet WCM buoy; Les Nattes WCM buoy; Roches d'Agon; E of La Catheue SCM lt buoy; E of Iles Chausey; and W of Pte du Roc (Granville). Between Granville and Îles Chausey it carries <1m in places, but with adequate rise of tide this is not a problem for small craft; the *Channel Pilot* gives directions.

Passage de la Déroute is used by ferries from the UK to St Malo. It passes W of Les Trois Grunes; between Basses de Taillepied and Les Écrehou; Chaussée des Boeufs and Plateau de l'Arconie; E of Les Minquiers and Les Ardentes; thence NW of Îles Chausey via Entrée de la Déroute, a side channel.

Granville has an excellent but very crowded half-tide marina. **Iles Chausey**, 8·3M WNW of Granville, is a popular and attractive archipelago. The Sound can be entered from the S or N with careful pilotage and sufficient rise of tide.

The drying expanse of Baie du Mont St Michel should not be entered by sea, but is an enjoyable visit from the mainland.

9.18.6 SPECIAL NOTES FOR FRANCE: see Area 17

MINOR HARBOUR CLOSE SOUTH OF CAP DE LA HAGUE

GOURY, Manche, **49°42'·85N 01°56'·83W**. AC 1114, 3653, 5604.2; SHOM 7158, 5636, 7133 (essential). HW –0410 on Dover (UT); ML 5·1m. See Omonville-la-Rogue. For visitors, appr at slack water nps with no swell and good vis; a fair weather hbr only, dries to flattish shingle. At tidal diamond M, 1·3M W, the N-S stream reaches 9·7kn at sp, 5·8kn at nps.

Cap de la Hague (Gros du Raz) lt ho is 0·5M NW of hbr; La Foraine WCM lt bn is 1·0M to the W. 065° ldg lts, by day: Front W patch with R ■ at end of bkwtr; rear, W pylon, lead between Diotret to S and Les Grios to N. ⚓ W of the 2 LB slips in 1·7m or dry out on shingle banks SE of the bkwtr.

☎02·33·52·85·92. Facilities: ✕ at Auderville (0·5M).

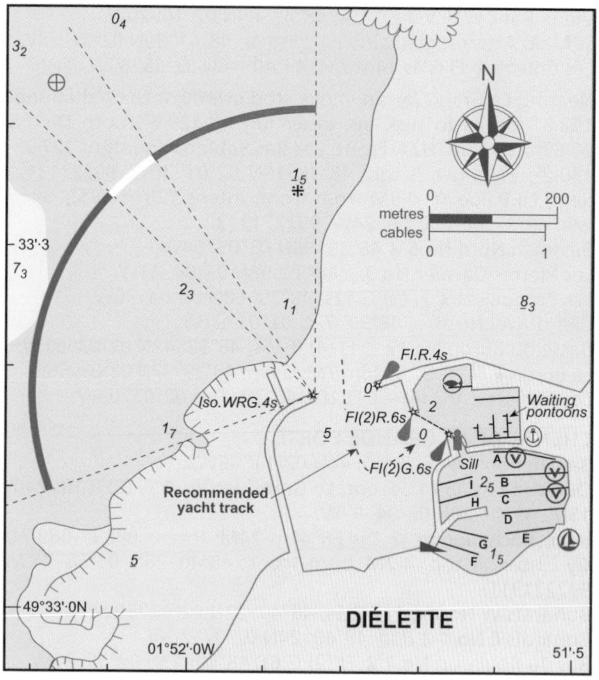

9.18.7 DIÉLETTE

Manche, **49°33'·20N 01°51'·79W**

CHARTS AC 2669, 3653; SHOM 7158, 7133; Navi 528, 1014; Imray C33A

TIDES HW –0430 on Dover (UT); ML 5·4m

Standard Port ST MALO (⟶)

Times				**Height (metres)**			
High Water		Low Water		MHWS	MHWN	MLWN	MLWS
0100	0800	0300	0800	12·2	9·3	4·2	1·5
1300	2000	1500	2000				
Differences DIÉLETTE							
+0045	+0035	+0020	+0035	–2·5	–1·9	–0·7	–0·3

SHELTER Good in marina, but when retaining wall covers, boats surge fore and aft; rig good springs. No entry in strong W'lies.

NAVIGATION WPT 49°33'·45N 01°52'·16W, 140°/650m to W bkwtr lt. Appr is exposed to W'ly winds/swell; 2kn cross tide at hbr ent. Caution: drying rks 3ca E of ⊕, marked by unlit WCM buoy. 1·5M WSW, keep seaward of WCM lt buoy off Flamanville power stn. Outer hbr ent dredged CD +0.5m; with Coefficient <55 accessible for 2m draft. W side of outer hbr dries approx 5m.

LIGHTS AND MARKS The power stn is conspic from afar 1·2M to SW, with pylons on the skyline. W bkwtr Lt ho, W twr/G top. Lts as chartlet.

COMMUNICATIONS CROSS 02·33·52·16·16; LB 02·33·04·93·17; 08·92·68·08·50; Emergency 15; ⊖ 02·33·23·34·00; Brit Consul 01·44·51·31·00; Dr 02·33·52·99·00; HM VHF Ch 09, summer 0800-1300, 1330-2000LT, winter 0800-1200, 1330-1700LT; Aff Mar 02·33·23·36·00; YC 02·33·04·14·78; Tourist office ☎02·33·52·81·60.

FACILITIES **Bassin de Commerce,** Ⓥ waiting pontoons, E side; fuel berth H24 cr/debit cards, W side by Marina cill, both in 2m. **Marina** ☎02·33·53·68·78. portdielette@cc-lespieux.com www.cc-lespieux.fr 420+70 Ⓥ €3·00. Enter about HW±3, tide gate over sill (CD+3·5m) drops when tide reaches CD+5m, to show 1·5m depth, on tide gauge by sill; Ⓥ berths pontoons A and E, ends of B (S side) and C (N side). Rig springs to minimise surging around HW. free wi-fi (40t). Ferry to CI.
Village basic foods, mkt Sun am, ✕. **Flamanville**, where third 1750MW reactor is being built, 15 mins' walk. ✉.
Les Pieux ✕ ✉ Ⓑ. Free daytime shuttle bus, Marina/ Flamanville/ Les Pieux, Jul/Aug, every 2 or 2½hrs.

9.18.8 CARTERET

Manche **49°22'·08N 01°47'·33W**

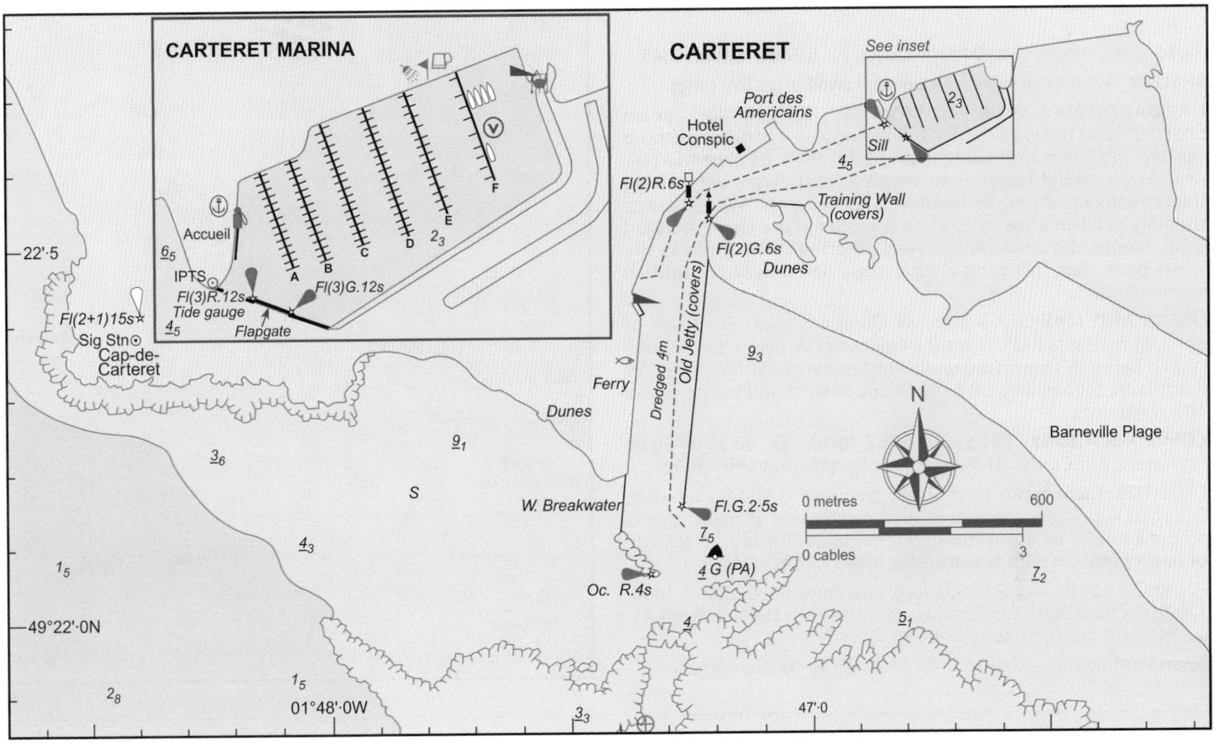

CHARTS AC 2669, 3655; SHOM 7157, 7158, 7133; Navi 1014; Imray C33A

TIDES –0440 Dover; ML 5·9; Duration 0545

Standard Port ST MALO (⟶)

Times				Height (metres)			
High Water		Low Water		MHWS	MHWN	MLWN	MLWS
0100	0800	0300	0800	12·2	9·3	4·2	1·5
1300	2000	1500	2000				
Differences CARTERET							
+0030	+0020	+0015	+0030	–1·6	–1·2	–0·7	–0·3
PORTBAIL							
+0030	+0025	+0025	+0030	–0·8	–0·6	–0·2	–0·1
ST GERMAIN-SUR-AY 49°13'·6N 01°39'·3W							
+0025	+0025	+0035	+0035	–0·7	–0·5	0·0	+0·1
LE SÉNÉQUET 49°05'·9N 01°41'·0W							
+0015	+0015	+0025	+0025	–0·3	–0·3	+0·1	+0·1

SHELTER Good in marina, but very crowded at weekends and in season. No safe ⚓s offshore.

NAVIGATION WPT 49°21'·86N 01°47'·36W, 006°/420m to W bkwtr lt. From N/NW, keep well off shore on appr to avoid rks 1M N of Cap de Carteret extending about 7ca from coast. From W beware Trois Grune Rks (dry 1·6m) about 4M offshore, marked by WCM lt buoy. Appr dries ½M offshore and is exposed to fresh W/SW winds which can make ent rough. Caution: strong cross-streams on the flood.

Best appr at HW–1 to avoid max tidal stream, 4½kn sp. The outer end of W bkwtr covers at big springs. Bar, at right angles to W bkwtr, dries 4m; a SHM buoy east of the W bkwtr marks a shifting shoal patch. Best water is to port of a mid-channel course. The chan dries progressively to firm sand, and is dredged to 4m and 4.5m just W of the marina.

LIGHTS AND MARKS Cap de Carteret, grey lt twr, G top, and conspic Sig stn are 8ca 295° from the ent. Breakwater and channel lts as chartlet. Marina sill is marked by PHM/SHM lt bcns, and Y poles on the retaining wall.

COMMUNICATIONS CROSS/LB 02·33·52·16·16; 02·33·22·91·77; Auto 08·92·68·02·50; Police 02·33·53·80·17; 02·33·04·90·08; Brit Consul 01·44·51·31·00; H (Valognes) 02·33·40·14·39; Signal station VHF 09, 16; Marina VHF Ch 09; Tourist Office 02·33·04·90·58.

FACILITIES

Marina ☎02·33·04·70·84. www.barneville-carteret.net barneville-carteret @wanadoo.fr 311 + 60Ⓥ €2·95 (Apr-Sep; discounts possible Mon-Thu). Access HW ±2½ for 1·5m draft over sill 5m; lifting flapgate retains 2·3m within. IPTS N side of marina ent control ent/exit (sigs 2 & 4). Cross the sill squarely, ie heading NE, to clear the concrete bases each side. Ⓥ /rafted on E side only of pontoon F (no need to stop at accueil pontoon).

at accueil pontoon (limited hrs, displayed on the pumps) (35t) (24t). **YC** ☎02·33·52·60·73.

West quay Possible waiting berth clear of ferry, if too late for the marina. A 1·5m draft boat can stay afloat for 6hrs np, 9hrs sp. free for 6hrs then at 50% of marina rates.

Other options: Dry out in the tiny Port des Américains and basin close W of marina (up to 5m at HW); or on fine sand SW of marina.

Town Ⓑ ⇌ (Valognes) ✈ (Cherbourg). **Ferry** Cherbourg, Jersey.

9.18.9 PORTBAIL

Manche **49°19'·72N 01°42'·42W** (Basin ent)

CHARTS AC 2669, 3655; SHOM 7157, 7133; Navi 1014; Imray C33A

TIDES See Carteret. HW –0440 on Dover; ML 6·3m; Duration 0545

SHELTER Good in all winds. Occasional swell after SW gales.

NAVIGATION WPT 49°18'·25N 01°44'·58W (off chartlet, abeam unlit 'PB' SWM buoy) 042°/1·5M to training wall lt bcn. 7ca offshore the 042° ldg line crosses banks drying 5.3m, thence between a pair of unlit PHM/SHM buoys, least depth 8.1m. Beware very strong tidal stream, esp during sp flood (4-5k) at basin ent. When base of training wall bcn is covered, there is > 2·5m in the chan, dredged 5·2m. Frequent inundations of sand reported, Y buoy marks the worst bank, but following a local vessel (of similar draught) is recommended.

LIGHTS AND MARKS A water twr (38m) is conspic 6ca NNW of ent. Ldg marks/lts 042°: Front (La Caillourie) W pylon, R top; rear, church belfry in town. Trng wall, which covers near HW, head: W mast/R top, followed by 2 R perches. See chartlet and Lights, buoys and waypoints.

COMMUNICATIONS CROSS 02·33·52·16·16; ⊜ 02·33·04·90·08 (Carteret); Brit Consul 01·44·51·31·00; Port/marina VHF Ch 09.

FACILITIES **Yacht basin** dries 7·0m, frequent dredging needed. Enlarged Ⓥ pontoon parallel to road on NW side of basin; also Ⓥ on the E side of adjacent stone FV jetty; or as directed. At NE side of basin pontoon with fingers is for locals <7.5m LOA.

HM ☎02·33·04·83·48 (15 Jun-31 Aug, tide times; 0830-1200 & 1400-1700). portbail@wanadoo.fr www.portbail.com 160 + 30Ⓥ €1·41. (5t). **YC** ☎02·33·04·86·15.

Town (½M by causeway) (Valognes).

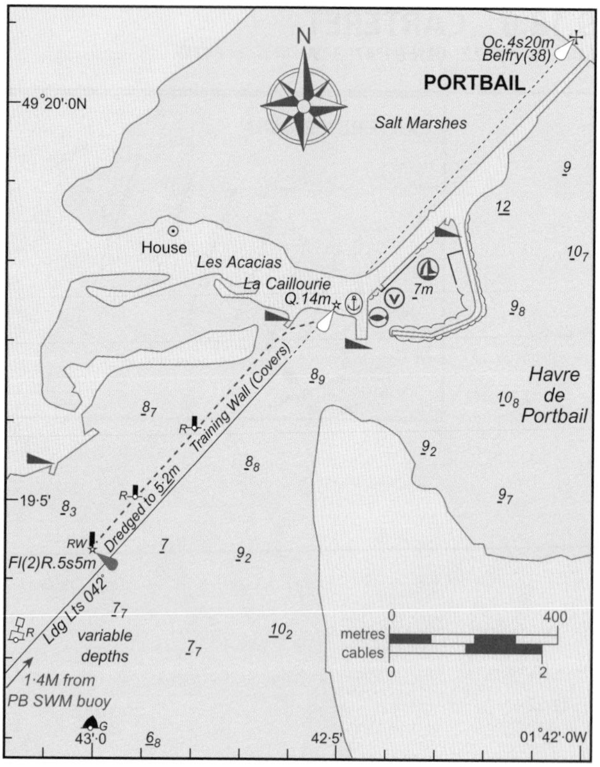

9.18.10 GRANVILLE

Manche **48°49'·94N 01°35'·93W** (Marina ent)

See chartlet opposite

CHARTS AC 3656, 3659; SHOM 7156, 7341; Navi 534, 535; Imray C33B

TIDES –0510 Dover; ML 7·1; Duration 0525

Standard Port ST MALO (⟶)

Times				Height (metres)			
High Water		Low Water		MHWS	MHWN	MLWN	MLWS
0100	0800	0300	0800	12·2	9·3	4·2	1·5
1300	2000	1500	2000				
Differences REGNÉVILLE-SUR-MER							
+0010	+0010	+0030	+0020	+0·5	+0·4	+0·2	0·0
GRANVILLE							
+0010	+0005	+0025	+0015	+0·7	+0·4	+0·3	0·0
CANCALE							
0000	0000	+0010	+0010	+0·8	+0·6	+0·3	+0·1

SHELTER Good in the marina. Appr is rough in strong W winds. ⚓ in 2m about 4ca WSW of Le Loup to await the tide.

NAVIGATION WPT 48°49'·60N 01°36'·30W (abm Le Loup IDM) 042°/0·40M to S bkwtr lt. Beware rks seaward of La Fourchie WCM bcn twr, pot markers off Pte du Roc and 0·4m patches on Banc de Tombelaine, 1M SSW of Le Loup lt. At night best to keep at least 8ca W of Pte du Roc to avoid these dangers.

At bkwtr hd turn port wide into marina ent to avoid yachts leaving; cross the sill between R/G piles. Ent/exit under power; speed limit 5kn in the near approach, 3kn in hbr. The 5 R piles, Fl Y 2.5s, mark the covering wall of a windsurfing/dinghy area to stbd.

LIGHTS AND MARKS Pte du Roc is a conspic headland with large old bldgs and lt ho, grey twr, R top; the Sig stn and church spire are also obvious. The twin domes of St Paul's church in transit 034° with Le Loup lead towards the marina ent. No ldg lts, but S bkwtr hd on with TV mast leads 057° to ent; hbr lts are hard to see against town lts. 3·5M W of Pte du Roc, Le Videcoq rock drying 0·8m, is marked by a WCM lt buoy. See chartlet and Lights, buoys and waypoints for lt details.

COMMUNICATIONS CROSS 02·33·52·16·16; 02·33·61·26·51; Auto 08·92·68·08·50; Police 02·33·91·27·50; ⊜ 02·33·50·19·90; Brit Consul 01·44·51·31·00; Ⓗ 02·33·91·50·00; Dr 02·33·50·00·07; Port HM 02·33·50·20·06, VHF Ch **09**, 16 (HW±1½); Aff Mar 02·33·91·31·40; Marina VHF Ch 09, 0800-2200 Apr-Oct.

FACILITIES

Hérel Marina ☎02·33·50·20·06. www.granville.cci.fr/herel herel@granville.cci.fr. Depth over sill shown on digital display atop S bkwtr: eg 76 = 7·6m; 00 = no entry. 850+150 Ⓥ Jun-Sep, €3·34 in least depth 2.5m as indicated on SW side pontoon G & NW side pontoon H; in 1.5m pontoon V; (vessels >15m +€4·05 p/d, per additional metre); multihulls +50%. Ⓔ SHOM, free wi-fi, (12t) (1·5t).

YC de Granville ☎02·33·50·04·25, Port á Sec, St Nicolas ☎02·33·61·81·53; STL Nautisme ☎02·33·69·22·75.

Town Ⓑ (Dinard). **Ferry** UK via Jersey or Cherbourg.

MINOR HARBOUR 10M NORTH OF GRANVILLE

REGNÉVILLE, Manche, **48°59'·72N 01°34'·05W** (SHM buoy abeam Pte d'Agon). AC 2669, 3656; SHOM 7156, 7133. HW –0500 on Dover (UT); ML 7·0m; Duration 0535. See Granville. A seriously drying hbr on the estuary of R. La Sienne; few yachts visit, a magnet for hardy adventurers seeking sand and solitude.

From 48°57'·65N 01°38'·86W (2·2M E of La Catheue SCM buoy) identify Pte d'Agon lt ho, W twr/R top, and Regnéville's 028° dir lt, both 4M NE at the river mouth (see Lights, buoys & waypoints). Thence track 056°/3·8M across the drying estuary to the SHM buoy (Lat/Long in line 1) marking a drying mole extending SW from the sandspit with landing stages to stbd; a small pontoon at Regnéville is 1·2M NNE. Drying heights are from 9m-12·7m off Pte d'Agon.

Access HW –1 to +2 for 1·3m draft. Approx 80 moorings inc Ⓥs. YC ☎02·33·46·36·76 cnregnevillais@free.fr. Facilities: Quay, (25t).

Town Ⓑ Tourist office ☎02·33·45·88·71.

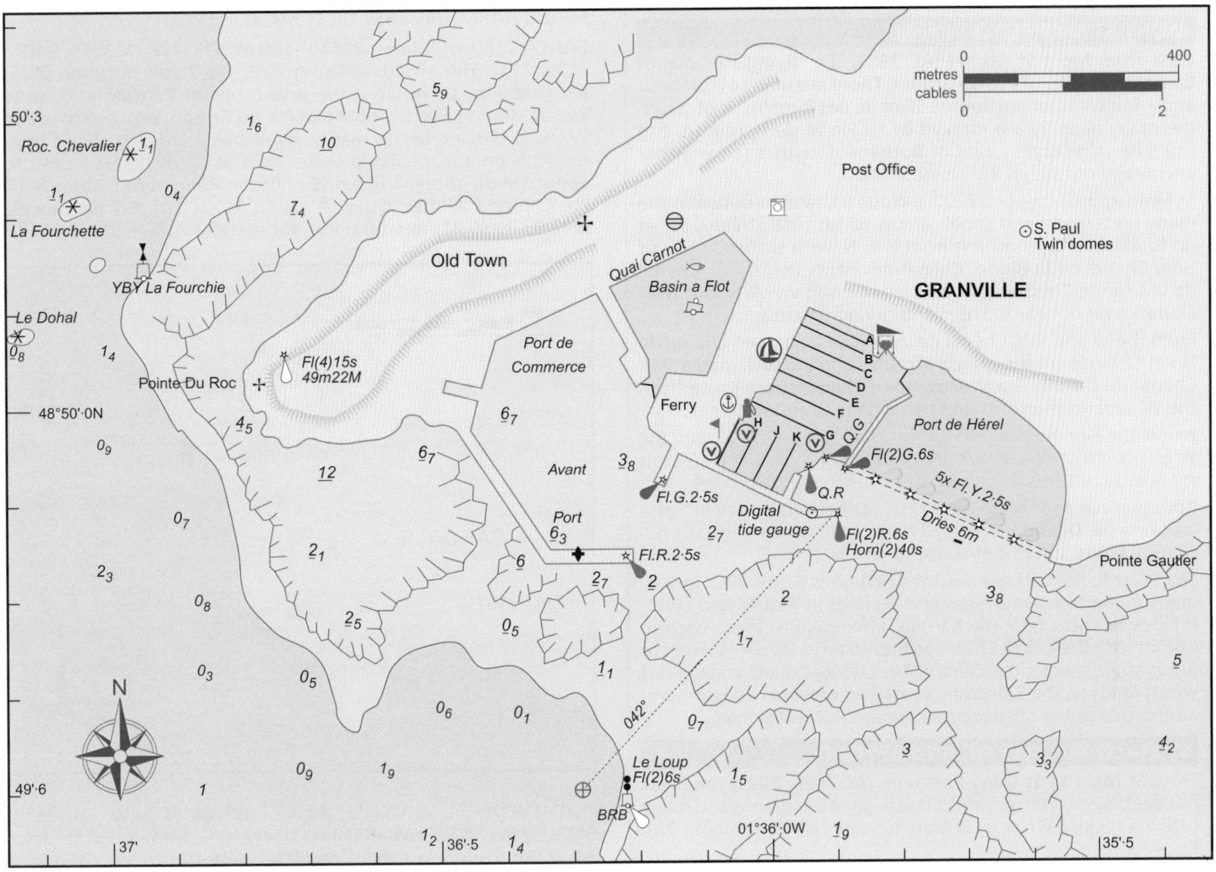
metres
cables
0
400
0
2
Roc. Chevalier
La Fourchette
YBY La Fourchie
Le Dohal
Pointe Du Roc
Fl(4)15s
49m22M
Old Town
Quai Carnot
Basin a Flot
Post Office
S. Paul
Twin domes
GRANVILLE
Port de
Commerce
Ferry
Avant
Port
Fl.G.2·5s
Fl.R.2·5s
Digital
tide gauge
Q.R
Q.G
Fl(2)G.6s
5x Fl.Y.2·5s
Dries 6m
Fl(2)R.6s
Horn(2)40s
Port de Hérel
Pointe Gautier
042°
Le Loup
Fl(2)6s
BRB
01°36'·0W
50'·3
48°50'·0N
49'·6
37'
36'·5
35'·5
N

9.18.11 ÎLES CHAUSEY

Manche **48°52'·08N 01°49'·08W** SHM By, S ent

CHARTS AC 3656, 3659; SHOM 7156, 7155, 7161, 7134; Navi 534, 535; Imray C33B

TIDES –0500 Dover; ML 7·4; Duration 0530

Standard Port ST MALO (⟶)

Times				Height (metres)			
High Water		Low Water		MHWS	MHWN	MLWN	MLWS
0100	0800	0300	0800	12·2	9·3	4·2	1·5
1300	2000	1500	2000				
Differences ÎLES CHAUSEY (Grande Île)							
+0005	+0005	+0015	+0015	+0·8	+0·7	+0·6	+0·4
LES ARDENTES (48°58'N 01°52'W, 6M NNW of Grande Île)							
+0010	+0010	+0020	+0010	0·0	–0·1	0·0	–0·1

SHELTER Good except in strong NW or SE winds. Grande Île is privately owned, but may be visited; it is not a Port of Entry.

NAVIGATION WPT 48°51'·43N 01°48'·55W, 332°/1·1M to Crabière lt. In transit with L'Enseigne, W bn tr, B top, leads 332° to Sound. 1 SHM lt buoy, thence between unlit cardinal bns.

The N chan needs adequate ht of tide (max drying ht 5·3m) SHOM 7134, a good Pilot and/or local knowledge, plus careful pilotage. L'Enseigne ≠ Grande Île lt ho leads 156° to the N ent; thence follow charted dogleg. No access 1/4–30/6 to a bird sanctuary, ie all E of line from Grande Île lt ho to L'Enseigne bcn twr (except Aneret).

LIGHTS AND MARKS Grande Île lt ho is conspic. La Crabière lt is on blackish stilts with Y top. See chartlet and Lights, bys & w'points.

COMMUNICATIONS CROSS 02·33·52·16·16; LB 02·33·50·28·33; Auto 08·92·68·08·50; Police 02·33·52·72·02.

FACILITIES Moor fore-and-aft to W buoys, free, in about 1·3m; some dry at sp. Very crowded w/ends in season, especially as drying out in Port Homard (W side of Grande Île) is discouraged. Tidal streams are moderate. **Village** (limited).

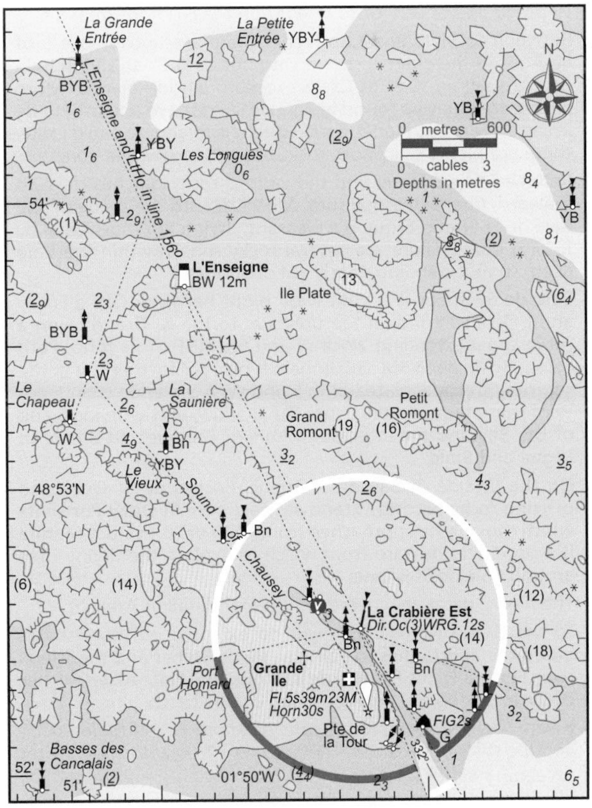
La Grande
Entrée
La Petite
Entrée YBY
BYB
L'Enseigne and Lt Ho in line 156°
YBY
Les Longues
YB
0 metres 600
0 cables 3
Depths in metres
YB
54'
L'Enseigne
BW 12m
Ile Plate
BYB
W
Le
Chapeau
La
Saunière
Petit
Romont
Grand
Romont
Bn
Le
Vieux
YBY
Sound
48°53'N
Bn
Chausey
La Crabière Est
Dir.Oc(3)WRG.12s
Bn
Port
Homard
Grande
Ile
Fl.5s39m23M
Horn30s
Pte de
la Tour
FlG2s
G
332°
Basses des
Cancalais
52'
51'
01°50'W
N

Central N France

MONT ST MICHEL TO ST MALO

West from Mont St Michel (AC 3659) the drying harbour of **Cancale** lies 4M S of Pte du Grouin. There are many oyster beds and a fair weather anchorage SE of Île des Rimains, N of which the many dangers are marked by La Pierre-de-Herpin (lt, fog sig). The large drying inlet of **Rothéneuf**, with a fair weather anchorage outside, is 4M NE of St Malo.

St Malo approaches (AC 2700) include 6 channels between the many islets, rocks and shoals across which tidal streams set at up to 4kn sp. Approaching from E or N, with sufficient rise of tide, Chenal de la Bigne, Chenal des Petits Pointus or Chenal de la Grande Conchée can be used in good visibility, but they all pass over or near to shoal and drying patches.

From the W and NW, Chenal de la Grande Porte and Chenal de la Petite Porte are the principal routes and are well marked/lit. Chenal du Décollé is a shallow, ill-marked inshore route from the W, and no shorter than Chenal de la Grande Porte.

▶*Here the E-going stream begins at HW St Helier –0510, and the W-going at HW St Helier +0030, max sp rates 3·75kn. The streams set across the Chenal between Grand Jardin and Buron.*◀

Both marinas at St Malo have tidal restrictions due to either a lock or a sill. **Dinard** has a small basin 2·0m which is usually full of local boats, but it is pleasant to visit by ferry.

The **River Rance** barrage (SHOM 4233) gives access via a lock to many delightful anchorages and marinas at Plouër and Lyvet. It helps to know how the barrage affects water levels upriver. Continue to the lock at Châtelier, thence on to Dinan – subject to draught. Here enter the Canal d'Ille et Rance (Inland waterways) which leads to the S Brittany coast and provides a fascinating alternative to the offshore passage around NW Brittany.

ST MALO TO L'OST PIC AND BEYOND

From **St Malo to St Quay-Portrieux** (AC 2028, 2029) the coast has deep bays (often drying) a few rugged headlands and many offlying rocks. 6M NW of St Malo beware Le Vieux-Banc (1·2m) buoyed.

▶*Here the ESE-going stream begins at HW St Helier –0555, and the NW-going at HW St Helier –0015, sp rates 2·5kn. There are W-going eddies very close inshore on the E-going stream.*◀

Between St Malo and Cap Fréhel there are anchorages S of Île Agot in the apprs to the drying hbr of St Briac and in Baie de l'Arguenon, SE of **St Cast's** excellent all-tide marina. More anchorages may be found in Baie de la Fresnaye and off Pte de la Latte. From Cap Fréhel, a bold steep headland, to Cap d'Erquy there are plenty of inshore rocks but no worthwhile hbrs.

Between Cap d'Erquy and the various rocky patches close to seaward, Chenal d'Erquy runs WSW/ENE into the E side of the Baie de St Brieuc. **Erquy** is a pleasant, drying hbr much used by fishing boats. There are several rocky shoals within the Baie itself, some extending nearly 2M offshore.

Baie de St Brieuc is a 20M wide bight between Cap d'Erquy and L'Ost Pic. Principal features are: to the N, Grand Léjon a rocky shoal extending 2½ca W and 8ca NNE of its lt ho. Petit Léjon (3·1m) lies 3·5M SSE. Rohein lt bcn, 3M further S, is in the centre with rocky plateaux to E and W. A 3M wide chan leads W of these features and S into the shallow, partly-drying S end of the Bay and the interesting hbrs of **Dahouet, St-Brieuc Le Légué and Binic**.

On the W side of Bay de St-Brieuc, Roches de St Quay and offlying rocky patches extend 4M east from **St Quay-Portrieux** which can only be approached from NNW or SE. St Quay Marina is a good all-tide base from which to explore the drying hbrs around Baie de St Brieuc.

The next 2 paras are covered in greater detail in Area 20:

To the N and NE of L'Ost-Pic lt ho extensive offshore shoals guard the approaches to Paimpol, Ile de Bréhat and the Trieux river. Further N, the Plateau de Barnouic and Plateau des Roches Douvres (lt, fog sig) must be given a wide berth.

▶*Here the E-going stream begins at about HW St Malo –0400 and the W-going at about HW St Malo +0100 with Spring rates exceeding 4kn.*◀

MINOR HARBOURS EAST OF ST MALO

CANCALE, Ille-et-Vilaine, **48°40'·10N 01°51'·11W**. AC 3659; SHOM 7155, 7131. HW –0510 on Dover (UT); ML 7·2m; Duration 0535; see Granville. La Houle is the drying hbr of Cancale just inside Bay of Mont St Michel, 2·6M S of Pte du Grouin; exposed to winds SW to SE. Drying berths may be available. Pier hd lt, obsc'd from the N, is on a mast. Avoid oyster beds at all costs. Area dries to about 1M off-shore. ⚓ in 4m SE of Île des Rimains or further N off Pte Chatry. Facilities: **Quay** (1·5t). **CN de Cancale** ☎02·99·89·90·22. **Town** (famous for oysters) Ⓑ.

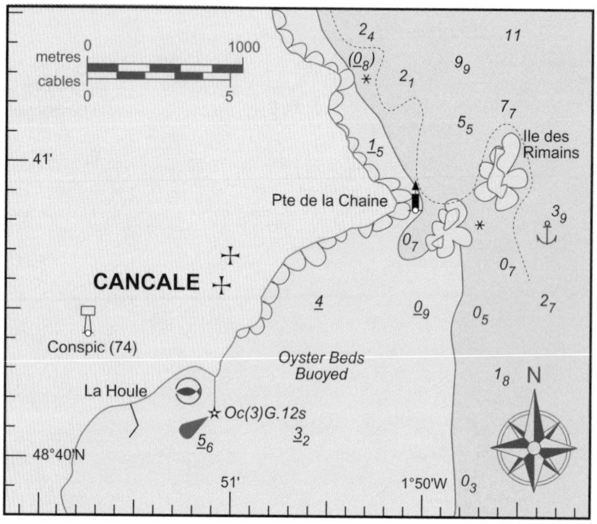

ROTHENEUF, Ille-et-Vilaine, **48°41'·38N 01°57'·64W**. AC 3659; SHOM 7155, 7131. HW –0510 on Dover (UT); Tides as for St Malo; ML 7·0m; Duration 0540. Complete shelter in quiet, delightful sandy hbr which dries up to 8·6m. ⚓ outside in 4m just N of SHM bn marking ent. Rks on both sides of ent which is barely 230m wide. Safest to enter when rks uncovered. Ldg line at 163°, W side of Pte Benard and old windmill (white twr). There are no lts. Facilities: **Village**.

9.18.12 ST MALO

Ille et Vilaine **48°38'·48N 02°01'·91W**
Bassin Vauban and Bas Sablons Marinas

CHARTS AC 2669, 3659, 2700; SHOM 7155, 7156, 7130; Navi 535; Imray C33B

TIDES –0506 Dover; ML 6·8; Duration 0535

SHELTER Good at Bas Sablons Marina, but in fresh W/NW'lies Ⓥ berths at outer ends of A & B pontoons are very uncomfortable. Excellent shelter in Bassin Vauban near the walled city.

NAVIGATION Care is needed due to strong tidal streams and many dangerous rocks close to the appr chans, which from W to E (see chartlet and Lights, buoys and waypoints) are:

1. Grande Porte, from the W, lit. WPT 48°40'·17N 02°08'·49W.
2. Petite Porte, the main lit chan from NW. WPT 48°42'·44N 02°09'·04W (abm Vieux-Banc Est NCM buoy, Q).
3. Bunel, from NNW, lit. WPT 48°42'·29N 02°06'·51W.

The above chans converge at or near Le Grand Jardin lt ho, 48°40'·20N 02°04'·97W. Thence continue in the main fairway 129°/2·8M to Môle des Noires.

4. Grande Conchée, from N, unlit. WPT 48°42'·15N 02°02'·12W.
5. Petits Pointus, from NNE, unlit. WPT 48°42'·34N 02°00'·38W.
6. La Bigne, from NE, unlit. WPT 48°42'·67N 01°57'·25W.

The above chans converge at or near Roches aux Anglais SHM buoy, 48°39'·66N 02°02'·22W. Thence continue 221°/8ca to enter the main 129° fairway.

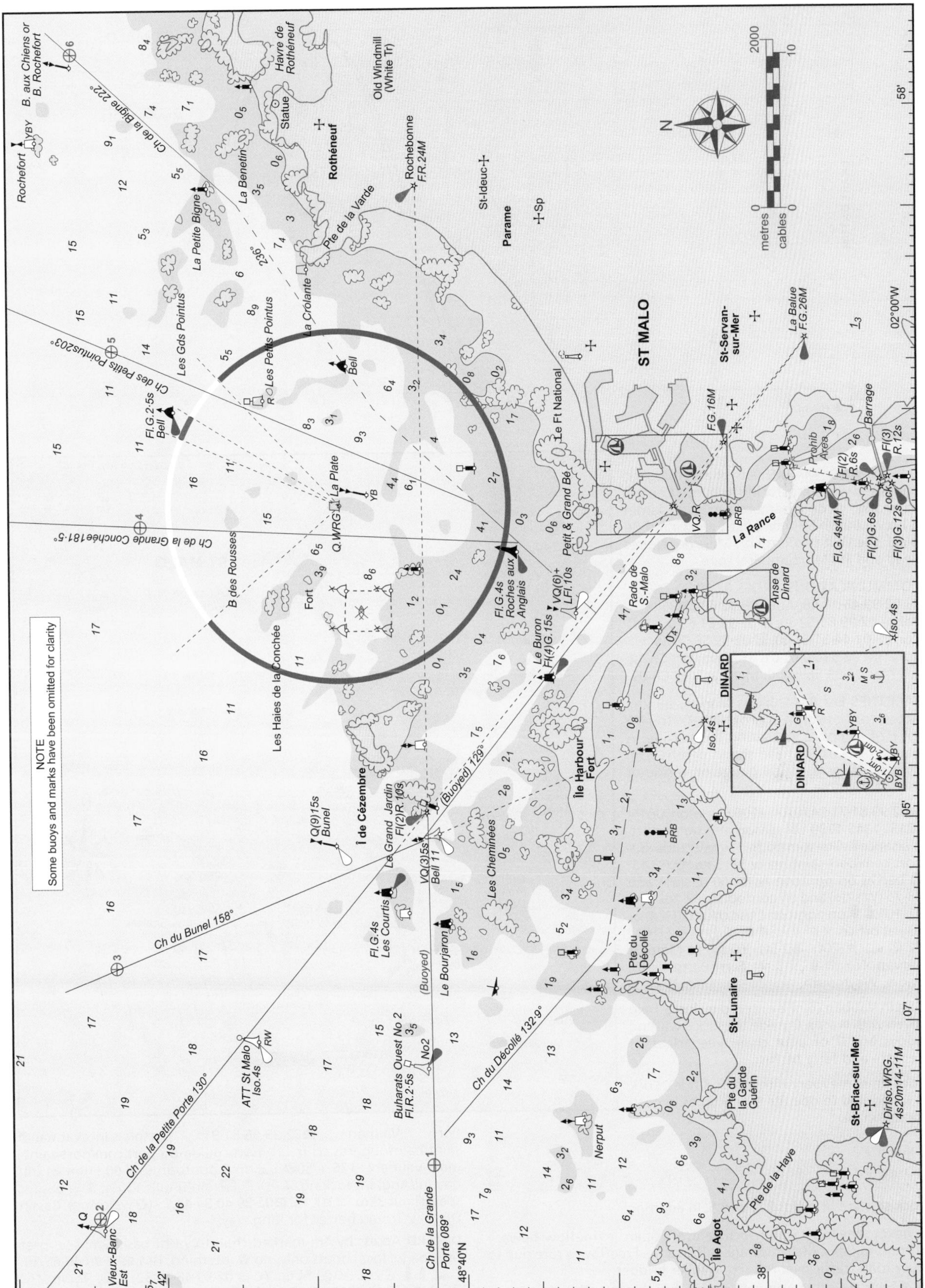
NOTE
Some buoys and marks have been omitted for clarity
ST MALO
St-Servan-sur-Mer
Parame
Rothéneuf
DINARD
St-Lunaire
St-Briac-sur-Mer
Île Agot
Î de Cézembre
Île Harbour Fort
Petit & Grand Bé
Le Ft National
La Rance
Anse de Dinard
Rade de S.-Malo
Barrage
Lock
Prohib Area
Ch de la Grande Porte 089°
Ch de la Petite Porte 130°
Ch du Bunel 158°
Ch du Décollé 132·9°
Ch de la Grande Conchée 181·5°
Ch des Petits Pointus 203°
Ch de la Bigne 222°
(Buoyed) 129°
(Buoyed)
Vieux-Banc Est
Q
ATT St Malo Iso.4s
RW
Buharats Ouest No 2 Fl.R.2·5s
No2
Le Bourjaron
Fl.G.4s Les Courtis
Q(9)15s Bunel
Le Grand Jardin Fl(2)R.10s
VQ(3)5s Bell 11
Les Cheminées
Pte du Décollé
Pte du la Garde Guérin
Pte de la Haye
Dir Iso.WRG. 4s20m14-11M
Nerput
Le Buron Fl(4)G.15s
VQ(6)+ LFl.10s
Fl.G.4s Roches aux Anglais
Fort
Les Haies de la Conchée
B des Rousses
Q.WRG La Plate
YB
Bell
Fl.G.2·5s Bell
Les Gds Pointus
Les Petits Pointus
La Crolante
Pte de la Varde
Rochebonne F.R.24M
La Petite Bigne
La Benetin
Statue
Havre de Rothéneuf
Old Windmill (White Tr)
Rochefort
YBY
B. aux Chiens or B. Rochefort
St-Ideuc
Sp
VQ.R
F.G.16M
BRB
Fl.G.4s4M
Fl(2)G.6s
Fl(3)G.12s
Fl(2) R.6s
Fl(3) R.12s
La Balue F.G.26M
Iso.4s
metres
cables
2000
10
0
N
48°40'N
42'
38'
07'
05'
02°00'W
58'

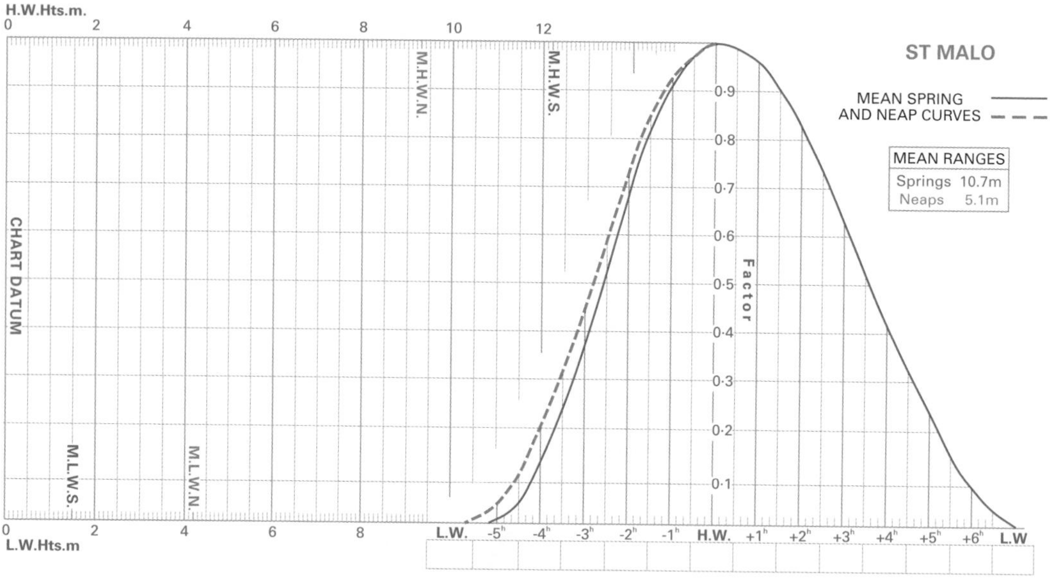

LIGHTS AND MARKS See chartlets/Lights, buoys and waypoints for ldg lts/buoys. Conspic daymarks: Île de Cézembre, Le Grand Jardin lt ho, Le Buron SHM twr, Petit and Grand Bé islets, the W lt twr/R top on Mole des Noires head and St Malo cathedral spire.

COMMUNICATIONS CROSS 02·98·89·31·31; 02·99·46·10·46; Auto 08·92·68·08·35; Police 02·99·81·52·30; ⊖ 02·99·81·65·90; Brit Consul 01·44·51·31·00; Ⓗ 02·99·56·56·19; Port HM 02·99·20·63·01, *St Malo Port* Ch **12**; Aff Mar 02·99·56·87·00; Marinas VHF Ch 09.

FACILITIES Les Bas-Sablons Marina, sill 2m. Access for 1·5m draft approx HW–3½ to +4½ sp; H24 at nps. 2 W waiting bys outside. A gauge on S bkwtr head shows depths <3m over sill. A large digital gauge on N side of marina is visible from all berths.

☎02·99·81·71·34.(0700-2100 in season, 0815-1215, 1345-1730 off season and hols). port.plaisance@ville-st-malo.fr www.guide-du-port.com/port-saint-malo/ 1216 + 64Ⓥ €3·15. Ⓥ berths on pontoon A: 32-66 (E side) and 43-75 (W side) and on pontoon B: 92-102 and 91-101. on pontoon I; use cr/card (H24) or pay at office. Ⓔ SHOM (20t) (2·5t). **YC** . **St Malo/St Servan** Ⓑ. **Ferry** Portsmouth, Poole, Weymouth.

Bassin Vauban (6m) is entered by lock; help given with warps. Outside the lock 3 waiting buoys are N of appr chan; keep clear of vedette and ferry berths.

Lock times may vary with traffic & tides. Lock is scheduled to operate 5 or 6 times in each direction, ie:

Inward	–2½	–1½	–½	+½	+1½	+2½
Outward	–2	–1	HW	+1	+2	

Lock sigs are IPTS Nos 2, 3 and 5. In addition:

● next to the top lt = both lock gates are open, ie freeflow, beware current initially. Main message is the same. Freeflow is rare due to busy road traffic over retracting roller bridges.

● ● over ● = all movements prohib, big ship is outbound.

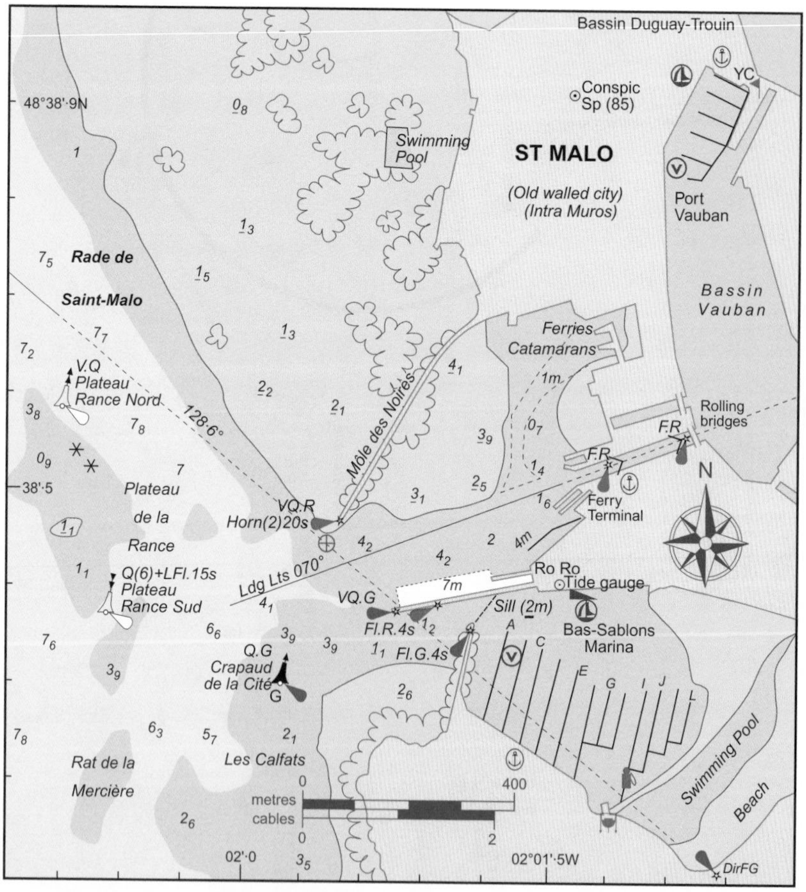

Port Vauban ☎02·99·56·51·91 portplaisancevauban@saintmalofougeres.cci.fr www.guide-du-port.com/port-saint-malo-vauban; 175 + 50Ⓥ on S pontoon, €46·00 (10m <12m/day Jul/Aug) inc locking, multihulls +50%. in basins; speed limit 3kn. (1t). **YC** ☎02·99·40·84·42, (Ⓥ welcome). Bassin Duguay-Trouin better for long stay.

DINARD Access by 1m marked chan to yacht basin 2m; see inset prev page, local boats only, no Ⓥ berthing. **HM** ☎02·99·46·65·55, Ⓔ. **YC** ☎ 02·99·46·14·32, . **Town** Ⓑ Ⓗ 02·99·46·18·68. . Ferries to St Malo.

ST MALO TIDAL COEFFICIENTS 2018

Date	Jan		Feb		Mar		Apr		May		June		July		Aug		Sept		Oct		Nov		Dec	
	am	pm	am	pm	am	pm	am	pm	am	pm	am	pm	am	pm	am	pm	am	pm	am	pm	am	pm	am	pm
1	92	97	107	109	97	102	105	105	94	92	77	74	73	72	74	72	70	65	63	57	51	48	55	56
2	101	104	109	108	106	109	103	100	89	86	71	68	70	67	69	66	60		52		49	52	58	61
3	106	107	106	103	110	109	96	92	82	77	64	60	64	62	62	59	55	51	47	44	57	63	64	69
4	106	104	98	92	108	104	86	80	72	67	56	52	59	56	55		47	45	45	48	69	76	73	77
5	101	96	85	78	100	94	74	67	61	56	49		53		52	49	45	48	54	62	82	87	80	83
6	91	85	71	63	88	81	60	53	50	45	45	43	50	48	48	47	54	61	70	78	92	95	85	86
7	79	72	56		74	66	46		40		41	41	47	46	49	52	69	77	85	92	97	99	87	87
8	65		49	43	58	51	40	35	37	34	41	44	47	50	57	64	85	93	98	103	99	97	86	85
9	59	54	39	36	44	38	31	29	34	35	47	52	53	58	70	78	99	105	106	107	95	93	83	80
10	49	46	35	37	33		30	34	39	43	57	63	63	69	85	92	108	111	108	106	89	84	78	74
11	44	44	40	45	30	30	39	45	49	55	69	76	75	82	97	103	111	110	104	100	79	74	71	67
12	46	49	50	55	33	37	52	59	62	68	81	87	87	93	106	109	108	104	95	89	68	62	63	58
13	52	55	60	65	43	49	65	72	75	81	92	96	97	101	109	109	99	92	83	75	56	50	54	50
14	59	63	69	74	55	62	78	84	86	91	99	101	103	104	107	103	85	77	68	61	45	40	46	42
15	66	69	78	81	68	74	89	93	96	99	102	101	105	103	98	92	69	61	53	46	35		40	
16	72	75	84	87	79	84	97	100	101	102	100	98	101	97	85	78	53		40		33	32	38	37
17	77	79	88	90	88	92	101	102	102	100	94	90	93	88	70		46	39	34	30	33	36	39	41
18	80	81	90	90	94	96	101	99	98	94	85	80	82		62	55	34	31	29	30	40	45	45	50
19	81	81	89	87	98	98	96	92	90	84	75		75	69	48	43	31	33	34	39	51	57	55	61
20	80	79	84	81	97	95	87	81	79	72	69	65	63	57	39	37	38	43	45	51	63	69	67	73
21	77	75	77	72	92	88	75	68	67		61	58	52	49	38	40	49	55	57	63	75	81	79	85
22	72	69	67	62	84	78	62		62	58	56	55	47	47	44	48	61	66	69	75	85	90	89	93
23	66	62	57		72	66	56	52	56	55	56	57	48	50	53	58	71	76	80	84	93	95	97	99
24	58	55	52	49	59	53	50	51	57	59	59	62	53	56	63	67	80	84	88	91	97	98	100	100
25	52		48	49	49		55	59	62	66	64	67	60	63	71	75	87	89	94	95	97	95	99	97
26	50	50	54	60	47	48	65	71	70	73	69	71	66	69	78	80	91	92	96	96	93	89	94	90
27	51	54	67	75	52	58	77	82	77	79	73	74	71	74	83	84	92	91	94	92	85	80	86	81
28	59	65	83	90	66	73	87	91	81	83	75	76	75	77	85	86	90	87	88	84	74	69	75	70
28	72	79			81	88	93	95	84	84	76	76	78	78	85	85	84	80	79	73	64	60	65	
30	86	93			94	98	96	95	84	83	76	75	78	78	83	81	75	69	67	61	57		61	58
31	99	103			102	104			81	80			77	76	77	74			55				56	55

Tidal coefficients indicate the magnitude of the tide on any particular day, without having to look up and calculate the range, and thus determine whether it is springs, neaps or somewhere in between. This table is valid for all areas covered by this Almanac. Typical values are:

120	Very big spring tide
95	**Mean spring tide**
70	Average tide
45	**Mean neap tide**
20	Very small neap tide

See also coefficients for Calais (p 765), Cherbourg (p 792), Brest (p 879) and Pointe de Grave (p 942).

STANDARD TIME UT –01
Subtract 1 hour for UT
For French Summer Time add ONE hour in **non-shaded areas**

ST MALO LAT 48°38'N LONG 2°02'W

TIMES AND HEIGHTS OF HIGH AND LOW WATERS

Dates in red are SPRINGS
Dates in blue are NEAPS

YEAR **2018**

JANUARY

Date	Day	Time	m	Time	m	Time	m	Time	m
1	M	0033	1.9	0604	12.0	1305	1.6	1834	12.1
2	TU	0131	1.3	0656	12.6	1401	1.1	○ 1927	12.5
3	W	0225	1.0	0746	12.9	1454	0.8	2017	12.7
4	TH	0315	1.0	0833	12.9	1543	0.8	2104	12.6
5	F	0400	1.1	0919	12.7	1629	1.1	2149	12.2
6	SA	0444	1.6	1003	12.2	1712	1.7	2233	11.6
7	SU	0525	2.2	1047	11.5	1753	2.4	2316	10.9
8	M	0606	2.9	1131	10.7	1835	3.1	◑	
9	TU	0002	10.1	0651	3.6	1222	10.0	1922	3.8
10	W	0058	9.5	0745	4.2	1325	9.4	2021	4.2
11	TH	0209	9.2	0853	4.4	1443	9.2	2132	4.3
12	F	0326	9.3	1009	4.2	1556	9.4	2242	4.0
13	SA	0429	9.7	1113	3.8	1655	9.8	2340	3.6
14	SU	0520	10.3	1206	3.3	1743	10.3		
15	M	0028	3.2	0604	10.8	1251	2.9	1825	10.7
16	TU	0111	2.8	0643	11.1	1333	2.5	1902	11.0
17	W	0149	2.5	0718	11.4	1411	2.3	● 1937	11.2
18	TH	0225	2.4	0752	11.6	1446	2.1	2011	11.4
19	F	0259	2.3	0825	11.7	1520	2.1	2044	11.4
20	SA	0332	2.3	0857	11.6	1554	2.2	2117	11.3
21	SU	0405	2.4	0931	11.4	1627	2.3	2151	11.1
22	M	0437	2.7	1005	11.1	1701	2.6	2225	10.7
23	TU	0512	3.1	1041	10.7	1737	3.0	2303	10.3
24	W	0551	3.5	1122	10.2	1820	3.5	◐ 2349	9.8
25	TH	0640	3.9	1217	9.7	1915	3.8		
26	F	0053	9.5	0746	4.1	1333	9.5	2029	4.0
27	SA	0215	9.5	0912	4.0	1500	9.6	2153	3.7
28	SU	0338	9.9	1034	3.4	1620	10.2	2309	3.0
29	M	0450	10.7	1146	2.6	1727	11.0		
30	TU	0018	2.2	0552	11.6	1252	1.8	1826	11.8
31	W	0119	1.6	0647	12.3	1352	1.2	○ 1919	12.4

FEBRUARY

Date	Day	Time	m	Time	m	Time	m	Time	m
1	TH	0214	1.0	0737	12.8	1445	0.7	2007	12.7
2	F	0304	0.8	0823	13.1	1533	0.6	2052	12.8
3	SA	0349	0.8	0906	13.0	1615	0.7	2133	12.5
4	SU	0429	1.1	0946	12.6	1653	1.3	2211	12.0
5	M	0504	1.7	1023	11.9	1727	2.0	2247	11.3
6	TU	0537	2.5	1059	11.0	1759	2.9	2323	10.4
7	W	0611	3.3	1138	10.1	1834	3.7	◑	
8	TH	0003	9.6	0651	4.1	1225	9.3	1919	4.4
9	F	0100	9.0	0749	4.7	1339	8.7	2029	4.8
10	SA	0230	8.6	0914	4.8	1516	8.6	2157	4.7
11	SU	0357	9.0	1039	4.4	1630	9.1	2310	4.2
12	M	0457	9.6	1140	3.8	1722	9.7		
13	TU	0005	3.6	0544	10.3	1229	3.1	1805	10.4
14	W	0051	3.0	0624	10.9	1312	2.6	1844	10.9
15	TH	0132	2.6	0701	11.3	1353	2.2	● 1920	11.3
16	F	0210	2.2	0736	11.7	1430	1.9	1954	11.6
17	SA	0245	1.9	0809	11.9	1506	1.7	2028	11.8
18	SU	0320	1.8	0842	12.0	1540	1.6	2100	11.8
19	M	0353	1.8	0915	12.0	1613	1.7	2133	11.7
20	TU	0425	2.0	0948	11.7	1645	2.0	2206	11.3
21	W	0457	2.4	1022	11.2	1719	2.5	2240	10.8
22	TH	0532	2.9	1059	10.6	1757	3.1	2321	10.2
23	F	0614	3.5	1146	9.9	1845	3.7	◐	
24	SA	0016	9.6	0714	4.0	1257	9.3	1956	4.1
25	SU	0140	9.3	0842	4.2	1439	9.2	2128	4.0
26	M	0320	9.5	1017	3.7	1611	9.8	2255	3.4
27	TU	0441	10.3	1136	2.8	1721	10.7		
28	W	0007	2.5	0543	11.3	1243	1.9	1818	11.6

MARCH

Date	Day	Time	m	Time	m	Time	m	Time	m
1	TH	0108	1.7	0636	12.1	1341	1.2	1907	12.3
2	F	0202	1.1	0723	12.7	1432	0.7	○ 1952	12.7
3	SA	0248	0.7	0806	13.0	1516	0.5	2032	12.8
4	SU	0330	0.7	0846	13.0	1554	0.7	2109	12.6
5	M	0407	1.0	0922	12.6	1627	1.2	2143	12.2
6	TU	0438	1.6	0955	12.0	1656	1.9	2215	11.5
7	W	0506	2.3	1027	11.1	1722	2.8	2244	10.7
8	TH	0532	3.2	1058	10.2	1748	3.7	2316	9.8
9	F	0603	4.0	1134	9.3	1822	4.5	◑ 2359	9.0
10	SA	0650	4.7	1232	8.5	1921	5.1		
11	SU	0119	8.3	0811	5.2	1423	8.1	2105	5.3
12	M	0316	8.4	1001	4.9	1559	8.6	2238	4.8
13	TU	0428	9.1	1110	4.2	1656	9.3	2337	4.0
14	W	0516	9.9	1201	3.4	1739	10.1		
15	TH	0025	3.2	0558	10.6	1246	2.7	1818	10.8
16	F	0107	2.6	0636	11.3	1328	2.2	1856	11.4
17	SA	0147	2.1	0713	11.8	1408	1.7	● 1931	11.8
18	SU	0225	1.7	0748	12.1	1445	1.4	2006	12.1
19	M	0301	1.4	0822	12.3	1521	1.3	2039	12.2
20	TU	0336	1.4	0856	12.3	1555	1.3	2113	12.1
21	W	0409	1.6	0930	12.1	1628	1.7	2146	11.8
22	TH	0442	2.0	1005	11.5	1701	2.2	2222	11.2
23	F	0516	2.6	1043	10.8	1738	2.9	2302	10.5
24	SA	0558	3.3	1131	10.0	1826	3.7	◐ 2357	9.7
25	SU	0657	3.9	1243	9.2	1937	4.3		
26	M	0123	9.2	0827	4.2	1431	9.1	2114	4.3
27	TU	0308	9.4	1006	3.8	1604	9.7	2244	3.6
28	W	0429	10.2	1126	2.9	1710	10.6	2354	2.7
29	TH	0529	11.2	1230	2.0	1802	11.5		
30	F	0053	1.9	0619	11.9	1324	1.3	1847	12.2
31	SA	0144	1.3	0703	12.5	1411	1.0	○ 1929	12.5

APRIL

Date	Day	Time	m	Time	m	Time	m	Time	m
1	SU	0227	1.0	0744	12.7	1451	0.9	2007	12.6
2	M	0305	1.0	0821	12.6	1526	1.1	2041	12.5
3	TU	0339	1.2	0855	12.3	1555	1.5	2113	12.1
4	W	0407	1.7	0926	11.8	1622	2.1	2142	11.5
5	TH	0434	2.3	0955	11.1	1646	2.8	2210	10.8
6	F	0459	3.1	1024	10.3	1709	3.6	2239	10.0
7	SA	0527	3.8	1056	9.4	1739	4.4	2314	9.2
8	SU	0606	4.6	1143	8.6	1827	5.1	◑	
9	M	0015	8.4	0710	5.1	1317	8.1	1955	5.5
10	TU	0213	8.2	0856	5.1	1507	8.3	2149	5.1
11	W	0341	8.7	1026	4.5	1614	9.1	2256	4.3
12	TH	0436	9.5	1121	3.7	1702	9.9	2346	3.5
13	F	0521	10.4	1209	2.9	1744	10.7		
14	SA	0031	2.7	0603	11.1	1254	2.2	1824	11.4
15	SU	0115	2.1	0642	11.7	1337	1.7	1902	11.9
16	M	0157	1.6	0721	12.2	1418	1.3	● 1939	12.3
17	TU	0238	1.3	0758	12.4	1458	1.2	2015	12.5
18	W	0316	1.2	0835	12.4	1535	1.2	2052	12.4
19	TH	0353	1.3	0913	12.2	1611	1.5	2129	12.1
20	F	0429	1.8	0952	11.7	1647	2.1	2208	11.5
21	SA	0507	2.4	1035	10.9	1728	2.9	2253	10.7
22	SU	0553	3.1	1127	10.1	1818	3.6	◐ 2351	9.9
23	M	0654	3.8	1242	9.4	1930	4.2		
24	TU	0115	9.4	0819	4.0	1418	9.2	2101	4.2
25	W	0249	9.6	0951	3.7	1544	9.8	2226	3.6
26	TH	0406	10.2	1105	3.0	1647	10.5	2332	2.8
27	F	0505	10.9	1206	2.3	1737	11.3		
28	SA	0029	2.2	0554	11.6	1258	1.8	1821	11.8
29	SU	0117	1.8	0638	11.9	1343	1.6	1901	12.1
30	M	0159	1.6	0718	12.1	1421	1.5	○ 1938	12.2

Chart Datum is 6·29 metres below IGN Datum. HAT is 13·6 metres above Chart Datum.

STANDARD TIME UT –01
Subtract 1 hour for UT
For French Summer Time add ONE hour in **non-shaded areas**

ST MALO LAT 48°38'N LONG 2°02'W

TIMES AND HEIGHTS OF HIGH AND LOW WATERS

Dates in red are SPRINGS
Dates in blue are NEAPS

YEAR **2018**

MAY

Date	Day	Time	m	Time	m	Time	m	Time	m	Moon
1	TU	0236	1.6	0754	12.1	1453	1.7	2012	12.1	
2	W	0309	1.7	0827	11.9	1522	1.9	2043	11.8	
3	TH	0337	2.0	0858	11.5	1549	2.3	2112	11.4	
4	F	0405	2.4	0927	11.0	1615	2.9	2141	10.9	
5	SA	0432	3.0	0958	10.3	1641	3.5	2211	10.2	
6	SU	0501	3.6	1031	9.7	1710	4.2	2246	9.5	
7	M	0537	4.2	1113	9.0	1752	4.8	2337	8.8	
8	TU	0629	4.7	1221	8.5	1858	5.2			◑
9	W	0104	8.5	0746	4.9	1357	8.4	2034	5.2	
10	TH	0235	8.7	0916	4.6	1515	8.9	2156	4.6	
11	F	0342	9.3	1025	3.9	1613	9.7	2256	3.8	
12	SA	0435	10.1	1121	3.2	1702	10.5	2348	3.0	
13	SU	0523	10.8	1212	2.5	1747	11.2			
14	M	0037	2.3	0608	11.5	1302	1.9	1829	11.8	
15	TU	0126	1.8	0651	12.0	1349	1.5	1911	12.3	●
16	W	0212	1.4	0734	12.3	1434	1.2	1952	12.5	
17	TH	0256	1.2	0816	12.4	1516	1.2	2033	12.5	
18	F	0339	1.3	0859	12.2	1557	1.5	2116	12.3	
19	SA	0421	1.6	0944	11.8	1639	2.0	2200	11.7	
20	SU	0504	2.1	1032	11.1	1723	2.7	2249	11.0	
21	M	0553	2.8	1126	10.4	1815	3.3	2347	10.3	
22	TU	0652	3.4	1232	9.8	1920	3.8			◐
23	W	0058	9.8	0804	3.7	1351	9.6	2037	3.9	
24	TH	0219	9.8	0922	3.6	1509	9.8	2154	3.6	
25	F	0333	10.1	1032	3.2	1614	10.3	2300	3.2	
26	SA	0434	10.5	1133	2.8	1706	10.8	2356	2.7	
27	SU	0525	11.0	1225	2.5	1752	11.2			
28	M	0045	2.4	0610	11.3	1309	2.3	1833	11.5	
29	TU	0127	2.2	0651	11.4	1348	2.2	1910	11.6	○
30	W	0205	2.2	0728	11.4	1421	2.3	1945	11.6	
31	TH	0239	2.2	0802	11.4	1452	2.4	2017	11.5	

JUNE

Date	Day	Time	m	Time	m	Time	m	Time	m	Moon
1	F	0310	2.3	0834	11.2	1523	2.6	2047	11.3	
2	SA	0341	2.5	0905	10.9	1552	2.9	2119	11.0	
3	SU	0412	2.9	0938	10.5	1621	3.4	2151	10.5	
4	M	0443	3.3	1013	10.0	1652	3.8	2228	10.0	
5	TU	0518	3.8	1052	9.5	1730	4.3	2311	9.5	
6	W	0601	4.2	1143	9.1	1821	4.6			◑
7	TH	0010	9.1	0658	4.4	1251	8.9	1929	4.8	
8	F	0126	9.0	0808	4.4	1407	9.0	2048	4.5	
9	SA	0239	9.3	0923	4.0	1515	9.5	2200	4.0	
10	SU	0343	9.9	1031	3.4	1614	10.2	2302	3.3	
11	M	0440	10.5	1131	2.8	1707	10.9			
12	TU	0000	2.6	0533	11.2	1227	2.2	1757	11.6	
13	W	0055	2.0	0624	11.7	1321	1.7	1846	12.1	●
14	TH	0148	1.5	0713	12.1	1412	1.4	1933	12.5	
15	F	0239	1.3	0802	12.3	1501	1.3	2020	12.6	
16	SA	0328	1.2	0850	12.3	1547	1.4	2107	12.5	
17	SU	0415	1.4	0938	12.0	1633	1.7	2154	12.1	
18	M	0502	1.8	1027	11.5	1719	2.3	2243	11.5	
19	TU	0549	2.3	1117	10.9	1807	2.9	2334	10.8	
20	W	0640	2.9	1211	10.3	1901	3.4			◐
21	TH	0032	10.3	0736	3.4	1312	9.8	2003	3.8	
22	F	0138	9.9	0840	3.7	1423	9.7	2113	3.9	
23	SA	0250	9.8	0948	3.7	1532	9.8	2219	3.7	
24	SU	0357	10.0	1052	3.5	1632	10.2	2319	3.4	
25	M	0454	10.3	1148	3.2	1723	10.6			
26	TU	0011	3.0	0544	10.6	1236	3.0	1807	10.9	
27	W	0057	2.8	0627	10.8	1318	2.8	1847	11.1	
28	TH	0138	2.6	0707	10.9	1355	2.7	1923	11.3	○
29	F	0215	2.5	0742	11.0	1430	2.6	1957	11.3	
30	SA	0249	2.4	0816	11.0	1503	2.6	2029	11.3	

JULY

Date	Day	Time	m	Time	m	Time	m	Time	m	Moon
1	SU	0323	2.5	0848	11.0	1535	2.8	2102	11.2	
2	M	0355	2.6	0921	10.8	1606	3.0	2135	10.9	
3	TU	0427	2.9	0956	10.5	1637	3.3	2210	10.6	
4	W	0501	3.2	1031	10.2	1712	3.6	2247	10.2	
5	TH	0538	3.5	1111	9.8	1753	4.0	2331	9.7	
6	F	0623	3.8	1200	9.5	1844	4.2			◑
7	SA	0027	9.4	0718	4.0	1304	9.3	1949	4.3	
8	SU	0138	9.4	0827	4.0	1417	9.5	2107	4.1	
9	M	0252	9.6	0944	3.7	1528	9.9	2222	3.6	
10	TU	0401	10.2	1054	3.1	1633	10.6	2328	2.9	
11	W	0505	10.8	1158	2.5	1733	11.3			
12	TH	0031	2.2	0604	11.4	1259	2.0	1828	12.0	
13	F	0131	1.6	0700	12.0	1357	1.5	1920	12.5	●
14	SA	0227	1.2	0752	12.3	1451	1.2	2010	12.8	
15	SU	0320	1.0	0842	12.5	1540	1.2	2058	12.8	
16	M	0408	1.0	0929	12.4	1625	1.4	2144	12.5	
17	TU	0453	1.3	1014	12.0	1708	1.8	2228	12.0	
18	W	0536	1.9	1057	11.4	1750	2.4	2312	11.3	
19	TH	0617	2.6	1141	10.7	1833	3.1	2358	10.5	◐
20	F	0700	3.3	1230	10.0	1921	3.7			
21	SA	0053	9.8	0752	3.9	1330	9.5	2021	4.2	
22	SU	0202	9.4	0856	4.2	1445	9.3	2136	4.3	
23	M	0319	9.3	1008	4.2	1559	9.5	2245	4.0	
24	TU	0427	9.6	1114	3.9	1658	10.0	2343	3.6	
25	W	0522	10.0	1208	3.5	1747	10.5			
26	TH	0032	3.1	0608	10.4	1254	3.1	1828	10.9	
27	F	0116	2.8	0648	10.7	1335	2.9	1906	11.2	○
28	SA	0156	2.5	0725	11.0	1412	2.7	1940	11.4	
29	SU	0232	2.4	0759	11.1	1447	2.5	2013	11.5	
30	M	0306	2.3	0831	11.2	1519	2.5	2045	11.5	
31	TU	0339	2.3	0903	11.2	1551	2.5	2117	11.4	

AUGUST

Date	Day	Time	m	Time	m	Time	m	Time	m	Moon
1	W	0411	2.4	0936	11.1	1621	2.7	2150	11.2	
2	TH	0442	2.6	1008	10.8	1653	3.0	2223	10.8	
3	F	0516	3.0	1043	10.4	1728	3.4	2259	10.3	
4	SA	0553	3.4	1122	10.0	1810	3.8	2344	9.8	◑
5	SU	0640	3.8	1214	9.6	1905	4.2			
6	M	0048	9.5	0742	4.1	1327	9.4	2023	4.3	
7	TU	0212	9.4	0905	4.0	1453	9.6	2151	3.9	
8	W	0337	9.8	1028	3.6	1611	10.2	2307	3.2	
9	TH	0451	10.5	1139	2.8	1719	11.1			
10	F	0015	2.3	0554	11.3	1245	2.1	1817	11.9	
11	SA	0119	1.6	0651	12.0	1346	1.5	1910	12.6	●
12	SU	0217	1.0	0742	12.5	1440	1.0	1959	13.0	
13	M	0309	0.7	0829	12.8	1528	0.9	2044	13.1	
14	TU	0355	0.7	0912	12.7	1611	1.0	2126	12.9	
15	W	0436	1.0	0953	12.3	1649	1.5	2206	12.3	
16	TH	0512	1.7	1030	11.7	1724	2.2	2243	11.5	
17	F	0546	2.5	1107	10.9	1758	3.0	2321	10.6	
18	SA	0619	3.4	1146	10.1	1836	3.8			◐
19	SU	0006	9.7	0700	4.2	1236	9.3	1928	4.5	
20	M	0109	9.0	0800	4.7	1354	8.8	2046	4.8	
21	TU	0241	8.7	0926	4.9	1528	8.9	2215	4.6	
22	W	0405	9.0	1046	4.5	1637	9.5	2320	4.0	
23	TH	0503	9.6	1146	3.8	1727	10.2			
24	F	0011	3.3	0549	10.2	1234	3.3	1808	10.8	
25	SA	0055	2.8	0628	10.8	1316	2.8	1846	11.3	
26	SU	0136	2.4	0704	11.2	1354	2.5	1920	11.6	○
27	M	0213	2.2	0738	11.4	1429	2.3	1953	11.8	
28	TU	0247	2.0	0811	11.6	1502	2.1	2025	11.9	
29	W	0320	1.9	0842	11.7	1533	2.1	2056	11.9	
30	TH	0352	2.0	0913	11.6	1604	2.2	2127	11.7	
31	F	0422	2.2	0944	11.4	1634	2.6	2159	11.3	

Chart Datum is 6·29 metres below IGN Datum. HAT is 13·6 metres above Chart Datum.

STANDARD TIME UT –01
Subtract 1 hour for UT
For French Summer Time add ONE hour in **non-shaded areas**

ST MALO LAT 48°38′N LONG 2°02′W

TIMES AND HEIGHTS OF HIGH AND LOW WATERS

Dates in red are SPRINGS
Dates in blue are NEAPS

YEAR **2018**

SEPTEMBER

Date	Day	Time	m	Time	m	Time	m	Time	m
1	SA	0453	2.6	1016	10.9	1706	3.0	2233	10.7
2	SU	0528	3.2	1052	10.4	1744	3.6	2314	10.1
3	M ◑	0611	3.7	1139	9.8	1835	4.1		
4	TU	0013	9.4	0710	4.2	1252	9.3	1952	4.4
5	W	0149	9.1	0839	4.4	1433	9.4	2133	4.1
6	TH	0329	9.5	1012	3.9	1602	10.1	2257	3.3
7	F	0446	10.4	1130	3.0	1710	11.0		
8	SA	0007	2.3	0546	11.4	1234	2.1	1807	12.0
9	SU	0109	1.5	0638	12.2	1332	1.4	● 1856	12.7
10	M	0203	0.9	0725	12.7	1423	0.9	1942	13.1
11	TU	0251	0.6	0809	13.0	1509	0.8	2024	13.2
12	W	0334	0.7	0849	12.9	1549	1.0	2103	12.9
13	TH	0410	1.1	0925	12.5	1623	1.5	2139	12.3
14	F	0442	1.8	0959	11.8	1654	2.2	2212	11.5
15	SA	0509	2.6	1030	11.0	1722	3.1	2245	10.6
16	SU	0536	3.6	1103	10.1	1753	3.9	2321	9.6
17	M ◐	0609	4.4	1145	9.3	1836	4.7		
18	TU	0015	8.7	0702	5.1	1258	8.6	1952	5.2
19	W	0158	8.3	0840	5.4	1454	8.5	2142	5.0
20	TH	0339	8.6	1019	4.9	1611	9.1	2253	4.3
21	F	0439	9.4	1121	4.2	1701	9.9	2345	3.5
22	SA	0523	10.1	1208	3.4	1742	10.7		
23	SU	0028	2.9	0601	10.8	1249	2.8	1819	11.3
24	M	0109	2.4	0638	11.4	1328	2.4	1855	11.8
25	TU	0148	2.0	0712	11.7	1405	2.1	○ 1929	12.1
26	W	0223	1.8	0745	12.0	1440	1.9	2002	12.2
27	TH	0257	1.7	0817	12.1	1513	1.8	2034	12.2
28	F	0330	1.7	0849	12.0	1545	1.9	2106	12.0
29	SA	0402	2.0	0921	11.8	1616	2.3	2138	11.6
30	SU	0434	2.4	0954	11.3	1648	2.8	2214	10.9

OCTOBER

Date	Day	Time	m	Time	m	Time	m	Time	m
1	M	0508	3.1	1031	10.7	1727	3.4	2257	10.2
2	TU	0551	3.8	1120	9.9	1819	4.1	◑ 2359	9.4
3	W	0653	4.4	1237	9.3	1939	4.5		
4	TH	0144	9.0	0827	4.6	1425	9.3	2125	4.2
5	F	0325	9.5	1005	4.0	1553	10.1	2248	3.3
6	SA	0436	10.5	1119	3.0	1657	11.1	2355	2.3
7	SU	0531	11.5	1220	2.1	1750	12.0		
8	M	0052	1.5	0619	12.2	1314	1.4	1837	12.7
9	TU	0143	1.0	0703	12.7	1402	1.1	● 1920	13.0
10	W	0227	0.9	0744	12.9	1444	1.0	2000	13.0
11	TH	0306	1.0	0821	12.7	1522	1.2	2036	12.7
12	F	0339	1.4	0855	12.4	1553	1.7	2110	12.1
13	SA	0407	2.0	0926	11.8	1622	2.3	2141	11.4
14	SU	0433	2.8	0956	11.1	1649	3.1	2211	10.5
15	M	0458	3.6	1026	10.2	1717	3.9	2245	9.7
16	TU	0527	4.4	1102	9.4	1755	4.6	◐ 2330	8.8
17	W	0612	5.2	1202	8.6	1858	5.2		
18	TH	0101	8.2	0738	5.6	1359	8.3	2043	5.3
19	F	0253	8.4	0934	5.3	1529	8.8	2213	4.7
20	SA	0400	9.1	1043	4.5	1623	9.6	2307	3.9
21	SU	0447	9.9	1131	3.7	1706	10.4	2352	3.1
22	M	0527	10.7	1214	3.0	1746	11.2		
23	TU	0035	2.5	0605	11.4	1255	2.4	1824	11.7
24	W	0115	2.0	0642	11.9	1335	2.0	○ 1901	12.1
25	TH	0154	1.7	0717	12.2	1414	1.7	1936	12.3
26	F	0232	1.5	0752	12.4	1451	1.6	2011	12.4
27	SA	0309	1.6	0826	12.3	1527	1.7	2047	12.2
28	SU	0344	1.8	0902	12.1	1602	2.0	2124	11.8
29	M	0419	2.3	0940	11.6	1639	2.6	2205	11.1
30	TU	0457	3.0	1022	10.9	1721	3.2	2253	10.3
31	W ◑	0544	3.7	1116	10.1	1817	3.9		

NOVEMBER

Date	Day	Time	m	Time	m	Time	m	Time	m
1	TH	0001	9.6	0648	4.3	1233	9.6	1937	4.2
2	F	0136	9.3	0818	4.4	1410	9.6	2112	4.0
3	SA	0307	9.7	0950	3.9	1533	10.2	2231	3.2
4	SU	0415	10.5	1059	3.1	1636	11.0	2334	2.4
5	M	0509	11.3	1158	2.3	1728	11.7		
6	TU	0029	1.8	0555	12.0	1250	1.8	1814	12.2
7	W	0117	1.5	0638	12.3	1336	1.5	● 1856	12.4
8	TH	0159	1.4	0717	12.5	1416	1.5	1935	12.4
9	F	0235	1.6	0753	12.4	1453	1.7	2010	12.2
10	SA	0307	1.9	0826	12.1	1523	2.0	2043	11.8
11	SU	0335	2.3	0858	11.7	1553	2.4	2115	11.3
12	M	0403	2.9	0928	11.1	1622	3.0	2146	10.6
13	TU	0430	3.5	0959	10.4	1652	3.7	2219	9.9
14	W	0459	4.2	1034	9.7	1727	4.3	2300	9.1
15	TH ◐	0539	4.9	1122	9.0	1817	4.9		
16	F	0003	8.6	0640	5.3	1245	8.6	1930	5.1
17	SA	0139	8.5	0813	5.4	1421	8.7	2100	4.9
18	SU	0300	8.9	0941	4.9	1529	9.3	2211	4.2
19	M	0358	9.6	1040	4.1	1621	10.0	2306	3.5
20	TU	0445	10.4	1130	3.3	1707	10.8	2353	2.8
21	W	0528	11.1	1217	2.6	1750	11.4		
22	TH	0039	2.2	0609	11.7	1303	2.1	1831	11.9
23	F	0124	1.8	0649	12.2	1347	1.7	○ 1912	12.2
24	SA	0208	1.5	0729	12.4	1431	1.5	1952	12.3
25	SU	0250	1.5	0808	12.5	1513	1.5	2034	12.3
26	M	0330	1.7	0850	12.3	1554	1.8	2117	11.9
27	TU	0411	2.1	0933	11.9	1637	2.2	2203	11.4
28	W	0455	2.6	1020	11.3	1724	2.8	2255	10.7
29	TH	0544	3.3	1115	10.6	1820	3.3	2357	10.0
30	F ◑	0645	3.8	1222	10.1	1927	3.7		

DECEMBER

Date	Day	Time	m	Time	m	Time	m	Time	m
1	SA	0113	9.7	0759	4.0	1341	9.9	2045	3.7
2	SU	0233	9.8	0920	3.8	1500	10.1	2159	3.4
3	M	0343	10.2	1029	3.3	1606	10.6	2304	2.9
4	TU	0440	10.8	1129	2.8	1701	11.1		
5	W	0000	2.5	0529	11.3	1223	2.4	1749	11.5
6	TH	0048	2.2	0613	11.7	1308	2.1	1833	11.7
7	F	0130	2.1	0653	11.9	1349	2.0	● 1913	11.7
8	SA	0206	2.1	0730	11.9	1426	2.0	1949	11.7
9	SU	0239	2.2	0804	11.8	1459	2.2	2023	11.5
10	M	0311	2.4	0836	11.6	1531	2.4	2055	11.2
11	TU	0342	2.8	0908	11.2	1603	2.8	2128	10.8
12	W	0412	3.2	0941	10.8	1635	3.2	2201	10.3
13	TH	0442	3.7	1015	10.2	1708	3.7	2238	9.7
14	F	0516	4.2	1055	9.6	1747	4.2	2323	9.2
15	SA ◐	0601	4.7	1146	9.2	1837	4.5		
16	SU	0024	8.9	0702	4.9	1259	8.9	1942	4.6
17	M	0142	8.9	0818	4.9	1418	9.0	2058	4.4
18	TU	0256	9.2	0936	4.4	1526	9.5	2209	3.9
19	W	0357	9.9	1041	3.7	1623	10.2	2309	3.2
20	TH	0449	10.6	1138	3.0	1715	10.9		
21	F	0004	2.5	0538	11.3	1232	2.4	1804	11.5
22	SA	0057	2.0	0625	11.9	1324	1.8	○ 1852	12.0
23	SU	0147	1.6	0711	12.4	1415	1.5	1940	12.3
24	M	0235	1.4	0757	12.6	1503	1.3	2027	12.4
25	TU	0322	1.4	0843	12.6	1551	1.3	2114	12.2
26	W	0408	1.6	0929	12.4	1638	1.6	2201	11.9
27	TH	0454	2.0	1017	11.9	1725	2.0	2250	11.3
28	F	0541	2.5	1106	11.3	1813	2.6	2341	10.7
29	SA ◑	0632	3.1	1200	10.6	1906	3.2		
30	SU	0038	10.1	0729	3.6	1303	10.1	2007	3.6
31	M	0146	9.7	0836	3.9	1417	9.8	2116	3.7

Chart Datum is 6·29 metres below IGN Datum. HAT is 13·6 metres above Chart Datum.

9.18.13 RIVER RANCE

Ille-et-Vilaine **48°37'·04N 02°01'·71W** (Barrage)

CHARTS AC 3659, 2700; SHOM 7130, 4233; Imray C33B

TIDES Standard Port ST MALO (⟵)
Water levels upriver of the Rance hydro-electric tidal barrage are strongly affected by the operation of the sluice gates and occasional use of the turbines as pumps. On most days from 0700–2100LT, 4m above CD is maintained. There is generally 8·5m above CD for a period of 4hrs between 0700–2000LT. A French language pamphlet, issued by Électricité de France (EDF) should be obtained from HMs at St Malo or Bas Sablons, or from the office at the barrage lock. It gives forecasts for the summer months of when heights of 4m and 8·5m above CD will occur in the period 0700–2000LT. The local daily paper *Ouest France* gives a forecast for the next day of HW and LW upstream of the barrage, under the heading *Usine Marémotrice de la Rance*.

SHELTER Good shelter upriver dependent on wind direction. The principal ⚓s/moorings on the E bank are at St Suliac and Mordreuc, and at La Richardais, La Jouvente, Le Minihic and La Pommeraie on the W bank. Marinas at Plouër, Lyvet (E bank, beyond Chatelier lock) and Dinan: see next column.

NAVIGATION From St Malo/Dinard, appr the lock (at the W end of the barrage) between Pte de la Jument to stbd and a prohib sluicing zone to port, marked by PHM buoys linked by wire cables. 4 W waiting buoys lie on the E side of the appr chan, close to the prohibited zone, with 4 W waiting buoys upstream of the lock.

Barrage lock opens day/night (on request 2030–0430) on the hour, every hour provided the level is at least 4m above CD on both sides of the barrage see: *www.plouer-sur-rance.fr/fr/horairesdesmarees.* Yachts should arrive at H–20 mins. An illuminated display board gives access times in French/English. Lock entry sigs are **IPTS** sigs 2, 3 and 5. Masted boats entering from sea should berth at the S end of the lock so that the bridge can close astern of them. Vertical wires assist berthing/warp-handling. The lifting road-bridge across the lock opens only between H and H +15. Upstream of the lock a further prohib area to port is marked as above.

The chan upriver is marked by perches; binoculars needed. The 3M chan to St Suliac has min depth of 2m. The next 6M to the Chatelier lock partially dries and is buoyed; keep to the outside of bends. The suspension bridge and road bridge at Port St Hubert have 20m clearance. A viaduct 1M beyond Mordreuc has 19m clearance. Allow 2–3hrs from the barrage to Chatelier.

Chatelier lock and swing bridge operate 0600-2100LT, provided there is at least 8·5m rise of tide. HW Chatelier is 2–3hrs after HW St Malo depending on the barrage. Entry is controlled by CEVNI sigs (variations on a R and G theme).

The final 3M to Dinan has a published min depth in the marked chan of 1·4m; check with lock-keeper. Dinan gives access to Ille et Rance Canal and River Vilaine to Biscay (see Inland waterways).

LIGHTS AND MARKS Approaching the barrage from seaward: Pte de la Jument bn tr, Fl G 4s 6m 4M; PHM buoy opposite, Fl R 4s (prohib zone). The lock control twr is conspic. NW side of lock, Fl (2) G 6s, with G ▲ on W □. First dolphin, Fl (2) R 6s, with R ■ on W □.

Approaching from Dinan: PHM buoy, Fl (2) R 6s, at S end of prohib zone; leave to stbd. First dolphin, Fl (3) R 12s, with R ■ on W □. SW side of lock, Fl (3) G 12s, G ▲ on W □.

COMMUNICATIONS 02·99·46·10·46; Auto 08·92·68·08·35; Police 02·99·81·52·30; Brit Consul 01·44·51·31·00; Aff Mar 02·96·39·56·44; Water levels/navigation 02·99·46·14·46; Barrage/lock info 02·99·46·21·87, *Barrage de la Rance* (lock) VHF Ch 13; Chatelier lock 02·96·39·55·66, VHF Ch 14.

FACILITIES St Suliac Divers (Convoimer). **Mordreuc**.

La Richardais HM ☎02·99·46·24·20, ⑧. **La Jouvente**. **Le Minihic**.

La Cale de Plouër SC.

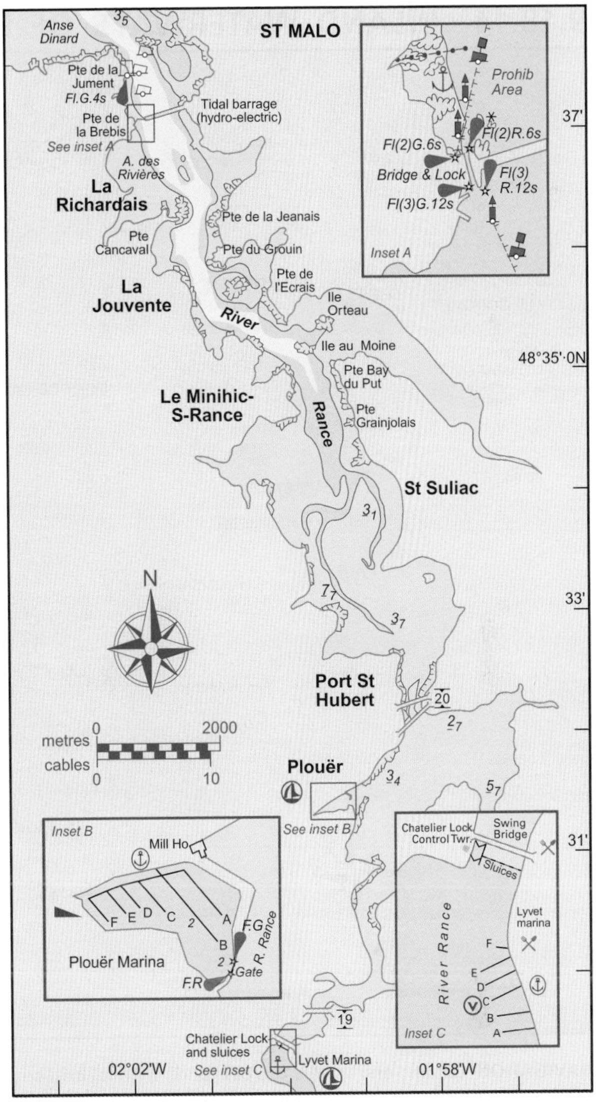

MARINAS ON THE RIVER RANCE
(NB: Berthing space limited, visitors are advised to call ahead.)
PLOUËR, Côtes d'Armor, **48°31'·54N 01°58'·95W.** On W bank of R Rance, 6M S of the barrage and 2M N of Chatelier lock. Tide 8m above CD gives 1·5m water over rising gate. Appr with Plouër ✠ spire brg 285°. Off S end bkwtr unlit PHM and SHM perches are 30m from narrow ent between 2 metal lattice pylons marking sill; access when FG/FR lts lit, day/night. Floodlit depth gauge (hard to read).
Marina plouer.portplaisance@wanadoo.fr www.plouer-sur-rance.fr/fr/portdeplaisance ☎02·96·86·83·15; 02·96·89·11·00. Ch 09. HM, Mlle Liliane Faustin is very helpful. 230 +10 Ⓥ pontoon B, €2·53. elec bike hire (14t). **Village** 1M.

LYVET, 48°29'·40N 02°00'·00W, on E bank just S of Chatelier lock. **La Vicomté Marina** ☎02·96·83·35·57. 210+25Ⓥ €2·00. Berth in 2m on pontoon D, or as directed. limited. Draught restricted trot moorings at La Hisse (opp Lyvet), contact La Mairie at Sampson-sur-Rance.

DINAN . **Marina** ☎02·96·39·56·44. line the W bank of the river, with fingers (€1·50) near to the Port in about 1·5m. for de-masting. Low bridge beyond Port has 2·5m headroom, giving access to the Ille et Rance canal. **Town** (75m above river) Ⓑ ✈ (Dinard). Also on Quai du Tallard, Lanvally (opp Dinan).

Ille et Rance Canal (opposite): Tolls (see Special notes) are not levied on Breton canals. A CEVNI is required, unless <5m LOA *and not capable* of more than 20kph/11kn.

9.18.14 INLAND WATERWAYS OF BRITTANY

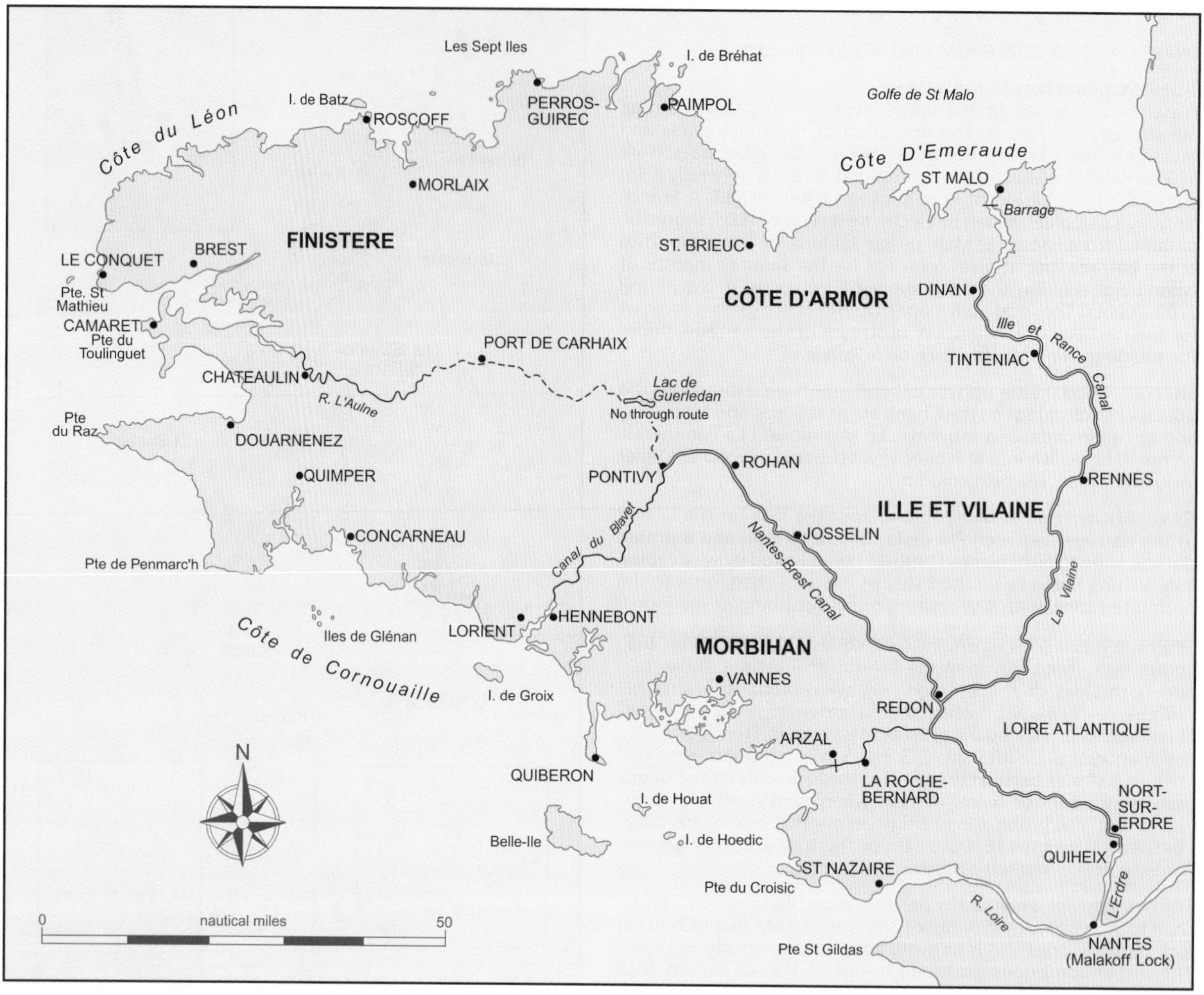

NAVIGATION Canals and rivers across and within Brittany enable boats of limited water and air draughts to go from the English Channel to the Bay of Biscay avoiding the passage around Finistère. Distances, number of locks, boat size and speed limits are summarised below. Dinan-Arzal takes about 5 days. Despite the many locks it can be a thoroughly enjoyable trip through unspoiled countryside and some interesting towns. Most overnight stops are free or at nominal cost.

LOCKS From Apr to Sept locks are worked 7 days a week 0800–1930LT, closing for lunch 1230-1330 approx. All locks are attended, but a fair measure of self-help is the order of the day. In Jul/Aug, in order to conserve water, locks may open on the hour only (and at H+30 if traffic demands).

ACCESS For prior estimate of max possible draught, contact: Equipement, Ille et Vilaine, 1 Avenue de Mail, 35000 Rennes, ☎02·99·59·20·60; or obtain recorded information update on ☎02·99·59·11·12. For latest info on the Ille et Rance Canal/R Vilaine, contact: Rennes ☎02·99·59·20·60 or Redon ☎02·99·71·03·78. For the Lorient-Nantes Canal, contact: Lorient ☎02·97·21·21·54; Hennebont ☎02·97·85·15·15; Pontivy ☎02·97·25·55·21; Nantes ☎02·40·71·02·00. Closures *(Chômages)* for maintenance are scheduled every Wed from approx first week in Nov to last week in March.

INFORMATION *Cruising French Waterways* (McKnight/ACN) *Through the French Canals* (Jefferson/ACN) and *Navicarte Guide No 12 (Bretagne)*.

TOLLS may be due on the R Loire only; see Area 17, Special Notes for France, for rates.

SUMMARY	Length km	No of locks	Max draft m	Max air draft m	Max LOA m	Max beam m	Speed limit kn
St MALO–ARZAL (Ille et Rance Canal and La Vilaine river)							
R Rance-Dinan	29·0	1	1·3	19	25	–	5·4
Ille et Rance Canal							
Dinan-Rennes	79·0	48	1·2	2·5	25	4·5	4·3
Rennes-Redon	89·0	13	1·2	3·2/2·6*	25	4·5	4·3
Redon-Arzal	42·0	1	1·3	–			
*Depending on water level							
LORIENT–NANTES							
Canal du Blavet (See Lorient)							
Lorient-Pontivy	70	28	1·4	2·6	25	4·6	4·3
Nantes-Brest Canal	184·3	106	–	3	25	4·6	4·3
Pontivy-Rohan			0·8 (possible closure)				
Rohan-Josselin			1·0				
Josselin-Redon			1·4				
Redon-Quiheix			1·1				
L'Erdre River	27·6	1	1·4	3·8	400	6·2	13·5
R Loire, above Nantes (St Nazaire) may be navigable to Angers.							
R L'AULNE (See Brest)							
Brest-Chateaulin	42	1	3·0	N/A	25	–	–
Chateaulin-Carhaix	72	33	1·1	2·5	25	4·6	4·3

MINOR HARBOUR BETWEEN ST MALO AND ST CAST LE GUILDO

ST BRIAC 48°37´·31N 02°08´·71W. AC 3659, 2700; SHOM 7155, 7130, 7129. HW –0515 on Dover (UT); ML 6·8m;-Duration 0550. Tides as Dahouet; use Ile des Hébihens. Drying hbr (6m) open to SW-NW. A Dir Iso WRG 4s lt leads 125° between offlying drying and beaconed rocks/islets. The last 6ca are marked by 4 PHM and 3 SHM perches. 10 ⚓s in Le Bechet cove or ⚓ on sand W of Ile du Perron in 3-5m. HM ☎02·99·88·01·75. **YC de St Briac** ☎02·99·88·31·45. **Town** ✕ 🛒.

9.18.15 ST CAST LE GUILDO

Côtes d'Armor **48°38´·39N 02°14´·76W**

CHARTS AC 2669, 3659; SHOM 71, 7129, 7155; Navi 535/6; Imray C33B

TIDES –0520 Dover; ML 6·3; Duration 0550

Standard Port ST MALO (⟵)

Times				Height (metres)			
High Water		Low Water		MHWS	MHWN	MLWN	MLWS
0100	0800	0300	0800	12·2	9·3	4·2	1·5
1300	2000	1500	2000				
Differences SAINT CAST							
0000	0000	–0005	–0005	–0·2	–0·2	–0·1	–0·1
ERQUY							
0000	–0005	–0020	–0010	–0·8	–0·6	–0·2	–0·2

SHELTER Good shelter in marina, access all states of tide, but exposed shoaling approach in strong NE/E/SE conditions. No anchoring.

NAVIGATION. WPT 48°39´·00N 02°13´·25W E of ECM Les Bourdinots (¾M NE of Pte de St Cast, marks 2m patch) then 225° for 1M to marina ent chan, R & G bys. Beware west mole, submerged HW.

LIGHTS AND MARKS Iso WG 4s 11/8M (appr on W sectors to clear Les Bourdinots) Bright shore lights confusing until within 2M.

COMMUNICATIONS CROSS Corsen 02·98·89·31·31; LB 02·96·41·76·61; Police 02·99·81·52·30; British Consul 01·44·51·31·00; H St Malo 02·99·56·56·19; HM 02·96·70·88·30, VHF Ch 09, 16; Semaphore 02·96·41·85·30; Affaires Maritime 02·96·81·04·43.

FACILITIES Port d'Armor Marina ☎02·96·81·04·43 www.cotesdarmor.cci.fr stcast.plaisance@cotesdarmor.cci.fr; 772 + 50 Ⓥ €3·10 + €0·20pp/day tax; pontoon D or Z, berth as indicated for LOA, or as instructed. (H24 cr/card only) ✕ (20t) (2·5t, masts). **YC** ☎02·96·41·71·71. **Town** (10 mins) ✕ 🛒 ✉ Ⓑ ⇌ (Lamballe) ✈ (St Brieuc). **Ferry** St Malo.

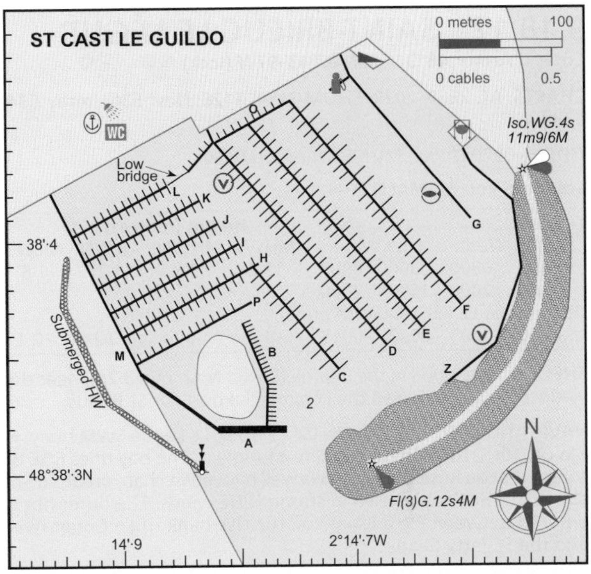

MINOR HARBOUR BETWEEN ST CAST LE GUILDO AND DAHOUET

ERQUY (pronounced Erky) **48°38´·04N 02°28´·69W.** AC 2669, 2029; SHOM 7154, 7310. HW –0515 on Dover (UT); ML 6·5m; Duration 0550; see St Cast Le Guildo. Sheltered from E, but open to SW/W'lies. An active FV hbr, but yachts can dry out E of the inner jetty hd Fl (3) R 12s; or ⚓ on sand 3ca SW of the outer mole. Beware Plateau des Portes d'Erquy (dry) about 2M to W. Beware rks off Pte de Lahoussaye. Mole hd lt Fl (2) WRG 6s 11m W10M, R/G7M; approach in either W sector (see Lights, buoys and waypoints). HM & ☎02·96·72·19·32. **YC** ☎02·96·72·32·40. Facilities: Ⓥ (drying) €0·56, **Quay** (3·5t). **Town** ✕ 🛒.

9.18.16 DAHOUET

Côtes d'Armor **48°34´·79N 02°34´·39W**

CHARTS AC 2669, 2029; SHOM 7154, 7310; Navi 536; Imray C33B, C34

TIDES –0520 Dover; ML 6·3; Duration 0550

Standard Port ST MALO (⟵)

Times				Height (metres)			
High Water		Low Water		MHWS	MHWN	MLWN	MLWS
0100	0800	0300	0800	12·2	9·3	4·2	1·5
1300	2000	1500	2000				
Differences ÎLE DES HÉBIHENS (7M W of St Malo)							
0000	0000	–0005	–0005	–0·2	–0·2	–0·1	–0·1
DAHOUET							
–0005	0000	–0025	–0010	–0·8	–0·7	–0·2	–0·1

SHELTER Good, but ent (dries 4m) has strong currents and is unsafe in fresh/strong NW'lies, when a bar may form.

NAVIGATION WPT 48°35´·15N 02°35´·44W, unlit NCM buoy, 117°/0·8M to La Petite Muette (LPM) lt tr. Appr in W sector, crossing into the R until LPM bears 160°. Enter the narrow break in the cliffs on that track leaving LPM to stbd, 1st R pole to port, then 3 remaining R poles to port, to clear slipway/wall below the shrine on headland. It is dangerous to enter S of LPM, due to rocks. At SHM bcn the chan turns E, then SE to the marina sill marked by PHM/SHM perches. Night entry not advised without prior day experience.

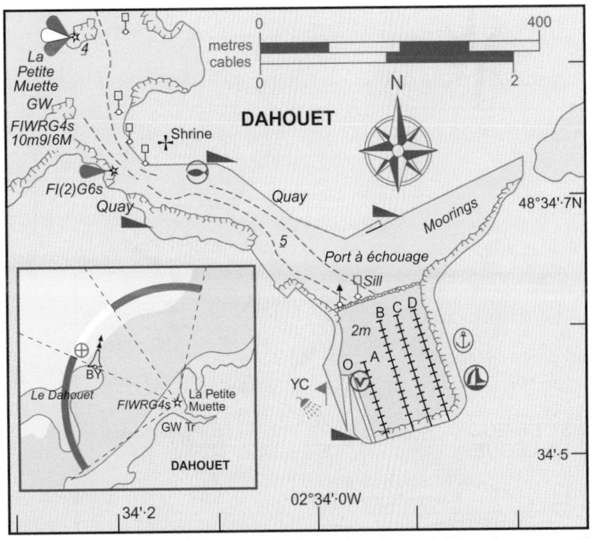

LIGHTS AND MARKS La Petite Muette (see Lights, buoys and waypoints) is the key feature. Conspic daymarks: the wide beach NE at Val André and, in the hbr ent, a pagoda-like shrine. See also St Brieuc.

Central N France

DAHOUET *continued*

COMMUNICATIONS CROSS 02·96·70·42·18; 02·36·65·02·22; Auto 08·92·68·02·22; Police 02·96·72·22·18; 02·96·74·75·32; British Consul 01·44·51·31·00; Ⓗ 02·96·45·23·28; HM VHF Ch 09, 16; Affaires Maritimes 02·96·72·31·42.

FACILITIES Outer hbr (FVs) dries 5·5m. **Marina**, min depth 2m, is entered over 5·5m sill, with depth gauge. Very crowded in season. ☎02·96·72·82·85, 318+25 Ⓥ berths on 'O' pontoon in about 1·6-2·0m, €2·25. (8t mobile) **YC du Val-André** ☎02·96·72·21·68.
Town (Lamballe) (St Brieuc). **Ferry** St Malo.

9.18.17 SAINT-BRIEUC LE LÉGUÉ

Côtes d'Armor **48°31´·68N 02°43´·97W (lock)**

CHARTS AC 2669, 2029; SHOM 7154, 7128; Navi 536; Imray C34, C33B

TIDES –0520 Dover; ML 6·5; Duration 0550

Standard Port ST MALO (⟵)

Times				Height (metres)			
High Water		Low Water		MHWS	MHWN	MLWN	MLWS
0100	0800	0300	0800	12·2	9·3	4·2	1·5
1300	2000	1500	2000				
Differences LE LÉGUÉ (SWM buoy)							
–0010	–0005	–0020	–0015	–0·8	–0·5	–0·2	–0·1

SHELTER Very good in the marina (Bassin No 2, min 3·2m) near the viaduct. Le Légué is also the commercial port for St Brieuc.

NAVIGATION WPT 48°34´·33N 02°41´·15W, Le Légué SWM buoy, Fl Mo (A) 10s, 210°/2·6M to abm Pte à l'Aigle lt. The bay dries E/SE of conspic Pte du Roselier. Access via well buoyed/lit chan, dredged 5m above CD; but not advised in strong N/NE winds. The outer hbr is entered between Pte à l'Aigle on the NW bank of Le Gouet river and the SE jetty head.

Lock opens, relative to height of tide at St Malo, *at local HW*:

(MHWN 9·3m)	<9·4m	±1
	9·4-10·3m	±1¼
	10·3-10·8m	±1½
(MHWS 12·2m)	>10·8m	–2 to +1½

The lock is 85m x 14m; sill dries 5·0m. Lock staff help with warps. Commercial ships take priority. A low swing bridge at the ent to Bassin No 2 opens when the lock is in use. A sliding footbridge gives access further upstream (no Ⓥ).

LIGHTS AND MARKS Conspic marks: Le Verdelet Is (42m) from E; Rohein twr, from N; Pte du Roselier in near appr; St Brieuc.

COMMUNICATIONS CROSS 02·98·89·31·31; 02·96·88·35·47; 02·99·46·10·46; Auto 08·92·68·08·22; Police 02·96·61·22·61; 02·96·74·75·32; Brit Consul 01·44·51·31·00; Dr 02·96·61·49·07; Port HM 02·96·33·35·41, *Le Légué Port* VHF Ch 12, 16 (approx HW–2 to +1½); Aff Mar 02·96·68·30·70.

FACILITIES **Marina** ☎02·96·77·49·85, mob 06·75·91·67·63, legue.plaisance@cotesdarmor.cci.fr/ www.cotesdarmor.cci.fr 250 + 20Ⓥ €2·10. Berth by HM's office on S quay for directions. YC (20t) (2t for de-masting).

Ship Repair Yard ☎06·76·33·56·66, (350t).

Town Ⓑ @. **Ferry** St Malo, Roscoff.

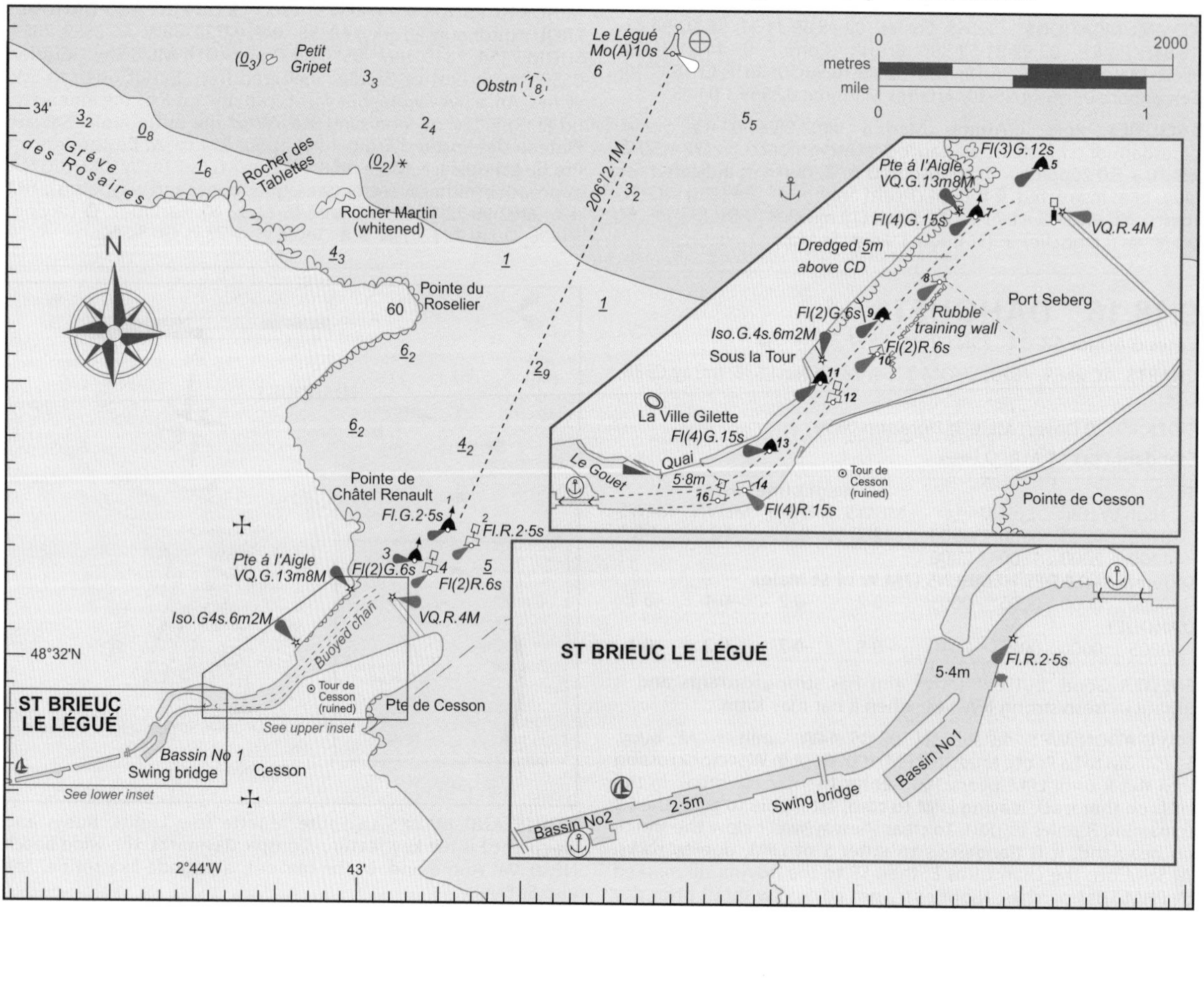

9.18.18 BINIC

Côtes d'Armor **48°36´·06N 02°48´·99W** ✪✪✪✪✪✪✪

CHARTS AC 2648, 2669, 2029; SHOM 7154, 7128; Navi 536; Imray C33B, C34

TIDES –0525 Dover; ML 6·3; Duration 0550

Standard Port ST MALO (⟵)

Times				Height (metres)			
High Water		Low Water		MHWS	MHWN	MLWN	MLWS
0100	0800	0300	0800	12·2	9·3	4·2	1·5
1300	2000	1500	2000				
Differences BINIC							
–0005	–0005	–0025	–0015	–0·8	–0·6	–0·2	–0·1

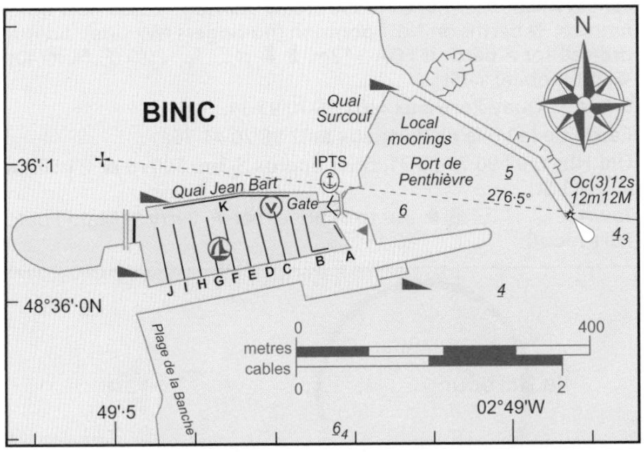

SHELTER Good in marina. Appr not advised in strong E/NE'lies.

NAVIGATION WPT 48°35´·86N 02°46´·68W, 276·5°/1·5M to ent. Appr dries 7ca offshore. From E, appr via Caffa ECM buoy, whence ent bears 246°/4·2M; or from N through Rade de St Quay-Portrieux.

Avant Port dries 5·5m, is easy day/night, except in E'lies. IPTS, sigs 2 & 3, control entry H24 to the marina via hydraulic flapgate and retracting bridge (office manned only when tide is sufficient). Gate opens when height of tide >8·5m. Times vary (see www.ville-binic.fr) with coefficient/barometer:

Coeff 40	<8·5m	=	No entry; no exit, ie neaped
40-50	8·5m	=	HW –1 to HW +1
50-60	9·15m	=	HW –1½ to HW + 1½
60-80	9·5m	=	HW –2 to HW + 2
>80	10·6m	=	HW –2¼ to HW + 2¼

Outbound vessels have priority. Beware strong current (up to 5kn) in the ent for 20 mins after the gate first opens.

LIGHTS AND MARKS Ldg line 276·5°: N mole lt, W twr, G gallery, ≠ church spire. A water twr is conspic 8ca N of hbr.

COMMUNICATIONS CROSS 02·98·89·31·31; ⊜ 02·96·74·75·32; ☁ 08·92·68·08·08; Ⓗ 02·96·94·31·71; SAMU 15; Fire 18; Call Port/marina VHF Ch 09 to check tide height and to advise of boat size and length of stay; Aff Mar 02·96·68·30·70.

FACILITIES **Marina** ☎02·96·73·61·86. English spoken. port@ville-binic.fr www.ville-binic.fr 350 + 50Ⓥ €2·05. Ⓥ berth/raft on pontoon K, to stbd on entry (1·5-2·5m). SHOM Ⓔ SC (20t mobile), hire car available. At St Quay-Portrieux and nearby.

Town @ ✉ Ⓑ. Bus to St Brieuc ⇄. **Ferry** St Malo.

9.18.19 ST QUAY-PORTRIEUX

Côtes d'Armor **48°38´·84N 02°48´·97W**

CHARTS AC 2648, 2669, 3674; SHOM 7154, 7128; Navi 536, 537; Imray C33B, C34

TIDES –0520 Dover; ML 6·3; Duration 0550

Standard Port ST MALO (⟵)

Times				Height (metres)			
High Water		Low Water		MHWS	MHiWN	MLWN	MLWS
0100	0800	0300	0800	12·2	9·3	4·2	1·5
1300	2000	1500	2000				
Differences ST QUAY-PORTRIEUX							
–0010	–0010	–0030	–0010	–0·9	–0·7	–0·2	–0·1

SHELTER Excellent in marina. ⚓ in the Rade de St Quay-Portrieux, sheltered by Roches de St Quay, but open to NW & SE winds.

NAVIGATION From E and SE appr via Caffa ECM lt buoy to WPT 48°37'·08N 02°46'·18W (2ca S of La Roselière SCM buoy VQ (6) + L Fl 10s); thence 314°/2·5M to NE mole head.

From the N, WPT 48°40´·94N 02°49´·69W, 169°/2·0M to NE mole elbow. At night, to avoid rocks/shoals, follow the white sectors of 4 Dir lts (see chartlet and tinted box) tracking 169°, 130°, 185° (astern) and 318° in sequence to the marina ent:

- NE mole elbow lt, **W159°-179°**. White concrete twr.
- Herflux lt, **W125°-135°**. A white bcn twr on drying rock.
- Ile Harbour lt, **W358°-011°**. Short W twr/R top on an islet.
- NE mole elbow lt (as first • above) **W316°-320·5°**.

LIGHTS AND MARKS See chartlet and Lights, buoys & waypoints. Signal stn at Pointe de St Quay, NNW of the marina, is conspic. N of the marina Moulières de Portrieux, ECM bcn twr is unlit. E of the marina an unlit WCM buoy marks Les Noirs rks (2·4m).

COMMUNICATIONS CROSS 02·98·89·31·31; 02·96·76·76·80; Auto 08·92·68·08·22; Police 02·96·70·61·24; 02·96·33·33·03; Brit Consul 01·44·51·31·00; Dr 02·96·70·41·31; HM (Old Hbr) 02·96·70·95·31; Aff Mar 02·96·68·30·73; Marina VHF Ch 09 (H24).

FACILITIES **Marina** ☎02·96·70·81·30. welcome@port-armor.com www.port-armor.com 900+100 Jul/Aug, €3·00, less other months. berths on No 7 pontoon (no fingers NW side). Jul/Aug pre-call for a berth if LOA >12m. (40t) (20t mobile) (5t).

SN de St Quay-Portrieux ☎02·96·70·93·34.

Cercle de la Voile de Portrieux ☎02·96·70·41·76.

Old Hbr ☎02·96·70·95·31, dries approx 5·3m. 500+8 €1·50. (1·5t).

Town Ⓑ. Bus to St Brieuc ✈. **Ferry** St Malo-Poole, Portsmouth.

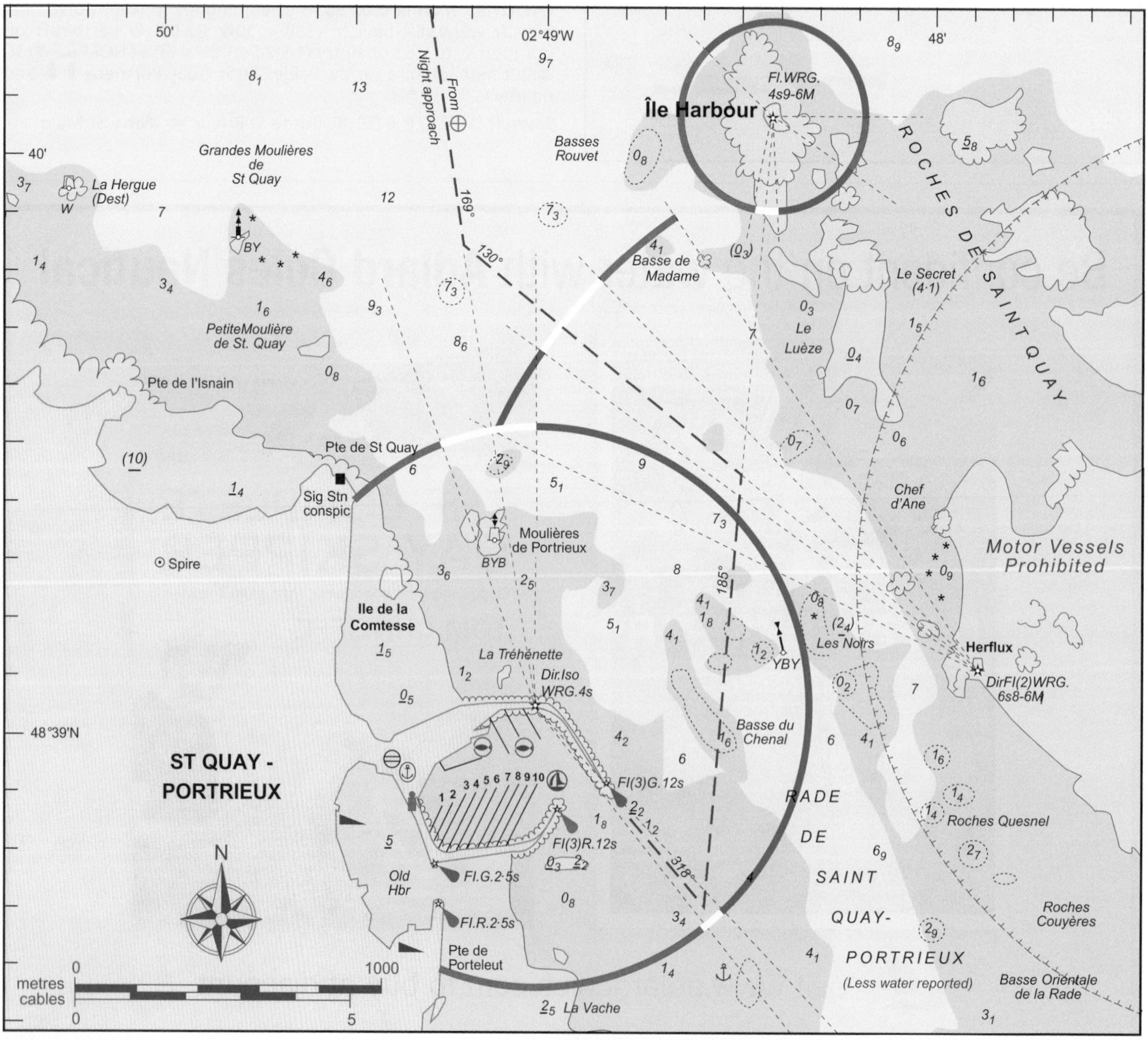

Channel Islands

Alderney to Jersey

9.19.1 Contents 821

9.19.2 Area map and Distance table 822

9.19.3 Tidal stream charts 824

9.19.4 Lights, buoys and waypoints 826

9.19.5 Passage information 828
The Channel Islands – 828 • The Casquets and Ortac Channel – 828 • Alderney and the Swinge – 828 • The Alderney Race – 828 • Approaches to Guernsey – 831 • Jersey – 840

9.19.6 Special notes for The Channel Islands 829

9.19.7 Alderney 829
Saye Bay • Corblets Bay • Longy Bay • La Tchue • Telegraph Bay • Hannaine Bay • Platte Saline Bay • Burhou

9.19.8 Braye Harbour (Alderney) 830

9.19.9 Little Russel Channel (Guernsey/Herm) 831

9.19.10 Beaucette (Guernsey) 832

9.19.11 St Peter Port (Guernsey), tide tables/curves 832
Minor harbours and anchorages around Guernsey:
Bordeaux Harbour • St Sampson • Havelet Bay • Soldier's Bay • Fermain Bay • Petit Port • Moulin Huet • Saints Bay • Icart Bay • Jaonnet • Petit Bôt Bay • Portelet • Portelet Harbour • Lihou Island • Perelle Bay • Vazon Bay • Cobo Bay • Grande Havre • L'Ancresse Bay • Fontenelle Bay

9.19.12 Herm 838

9.19.13 Sark 838
Saignie Bay • Port à la Jument • Havre Gosselin • Port és Saies • La Grande Grève • Port Gorey • Rouge Terrier • Dixcart Bay • Derrible Bay • Grève de la Ville • Les Fontaines

9.19.14 St Helier (Jersey) 840
Minor harbours and anchorages around Jersey:
St Aubin • Belcroute Bay • Portelet Bay • St Brelade • Grève au Lancon • Grève de Lecq • Bonne Nuit Bay • Bouley Bay • Rozel Bay • St Catherine • La Rocque • Les Écrehou • Plateau des Minquiers

9.19.15 Gorey (Jersey) 842

St Helier (Jersey), tide tables/curves 843

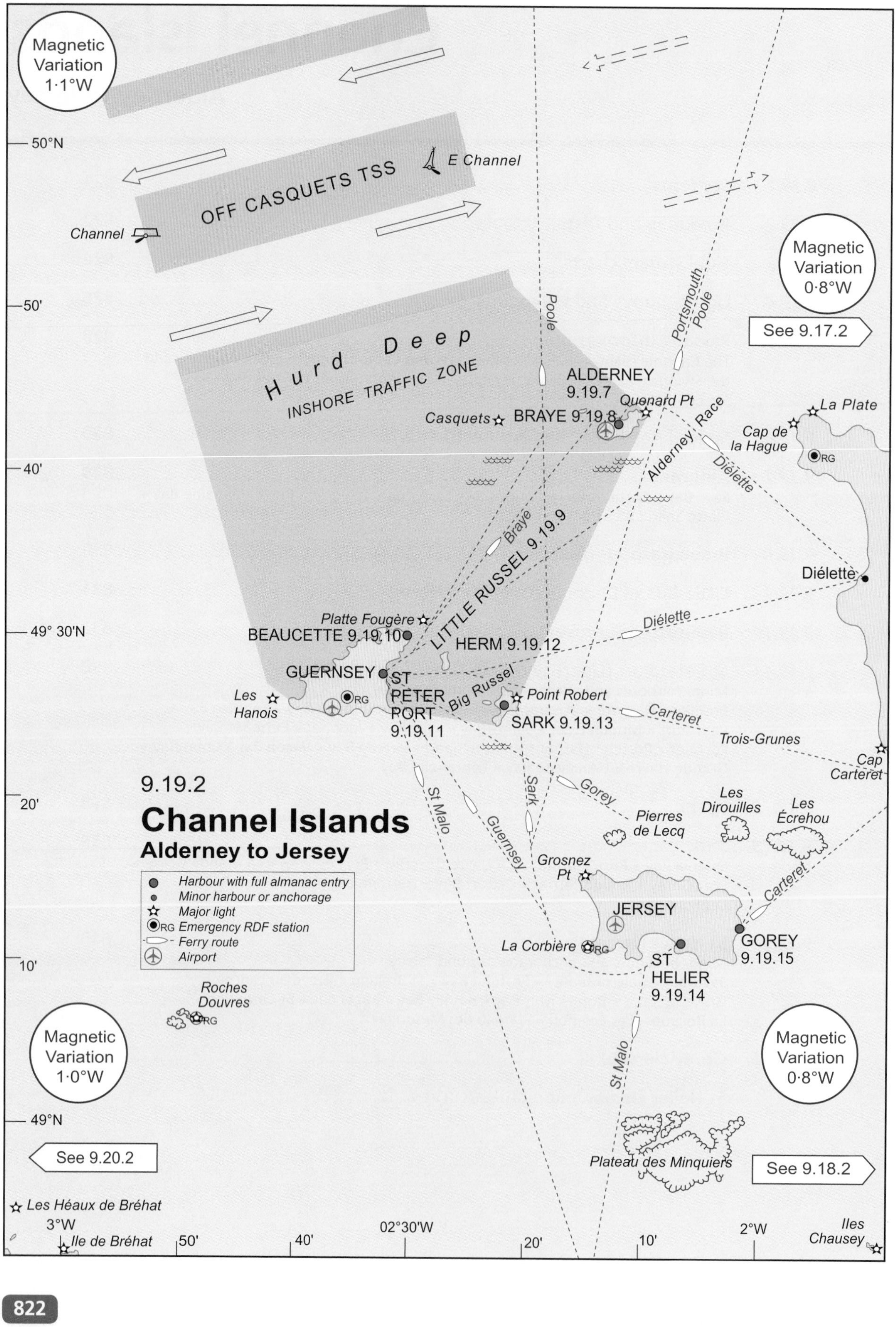

9.19.2
Channel Islands
Alderney to Jersey
Harbour with full almanac entry
Minor harbour or anchorage
Major light
RG Emergency RDF station
Ferry route
Airport
Magnetic Variation 1·1°W
Magnetic Variation 0·8°W
Magnetic Variation 1·0°W
Magnetic Variation 0·8°W
See 9.17.2
See 9.20.2
See 9.18.2
OFF CASQUETS TSS
E Channel
Channel
Hurd Deep
INSHORE TRAFFIC ZONE
Poole
Portsmouth
Poole
ALDERNEY
9.19.7
Quenard Pt
Casquets
BRAYE 9.19.8
Alderney Race
La Plate
Cap de la Hague
RG
Diélette
Diélette
Braye
LITTLE RUSSEL 9.19.9
Platte Fougère
BEAUCETTE 9.19.10
HERM 9.19.12
Diélette
GUERNSEY
ST PETER PORT 9.19.11
Les Hanois
RG
Big Russel
Point Robert
SARK 9.19.13
Carteret
Trois-Grunes
Cap Carteret
St Malo
Guernsey
Sark
Gorey
Pierres de Lecq
Les Dirouilles
Les Écrehou
Grosnez Pt
JERSEY
Carteret
La Corbière
RG
ST HELIER
9.19.14
GOREY
9.19.15
Roches Douvres
RG
St Malo
Plateau des Minquiers
50°N
50'
40'
49° 30'N
20'
10'
49°N
Les Héaux de Bréhat
3°W
Ile de Bréhat
50'
40'
02°30'W
20'
10'
2°W
Iles Chausey

1	***L'Aberwrac'h***	145	131	126	128	116	115	122	107	103	93	109	110	123	103	91	88	84	72	32	**1**
2	***Roscoff***	117	103	95	96	84	87	94	77	73	63	79	80	93	71	59	58	54	41	**2**	
3	***Tréguier***	94	80	72	72	60	66	72	56	52	42	58	53	63	58	30	29	22	**3**		
4	***Lézardrieux***	88	74	68	54	49	65	68	52	48	42	38	47	55	33	21	14	**4**			
5	*Paimpol*	91	77	65	56	42	67	70	54	50	45	50	45	53	24	24	**5**				
6	***St Quay-Portrieux***	88	74	64	54	35	71	73	55	56	48	51	46	52	12	**6**					
7	*Dahouet*	88	74	62	44	28	70	72	62	58	57	53	41	47	**7**						
8	Gorey (Jersey)	47	33	16	29	38	36	35	32	29	35	20	13	**8**							
9	**St Helier**	59	45	28	30	38	43	46	33	29	32	24	**9**								
10	Creux (Sark)	37	23	23	50	52	18	22	11	10	16	**10**									
11	Les Hanois	49	35	37	58	56	23	29	14	10	**11**										
12	**St Peter Port**	42	28	31	55	54	18	23	4	**12**											
13	Beaucette	39	25	34	59	58	15	19	**13**												
14	**Braye (Alderney)**	23	9	26	66	73	8	**14**													
15	Casquets	31	17	32	63	70	**15**														
16	***St Malo***	*87*	*73*	*49*	*23*	**16**															
17	*Granville*	75	61	38	**17**																
18	*Carteret*	41	23	**18**																	
19	*Cap de la Hague*	14	**19**																		
20	***Cherbourg***	**20**																			

DISTANCE TABLE
Approximate distances in nautical miles are by the most direct route while avoiding dangers and allowing for TSS. Places in *italics* are in adjoining areas; places in **bold** are in 9.0.5, Cross-Channel Distances.

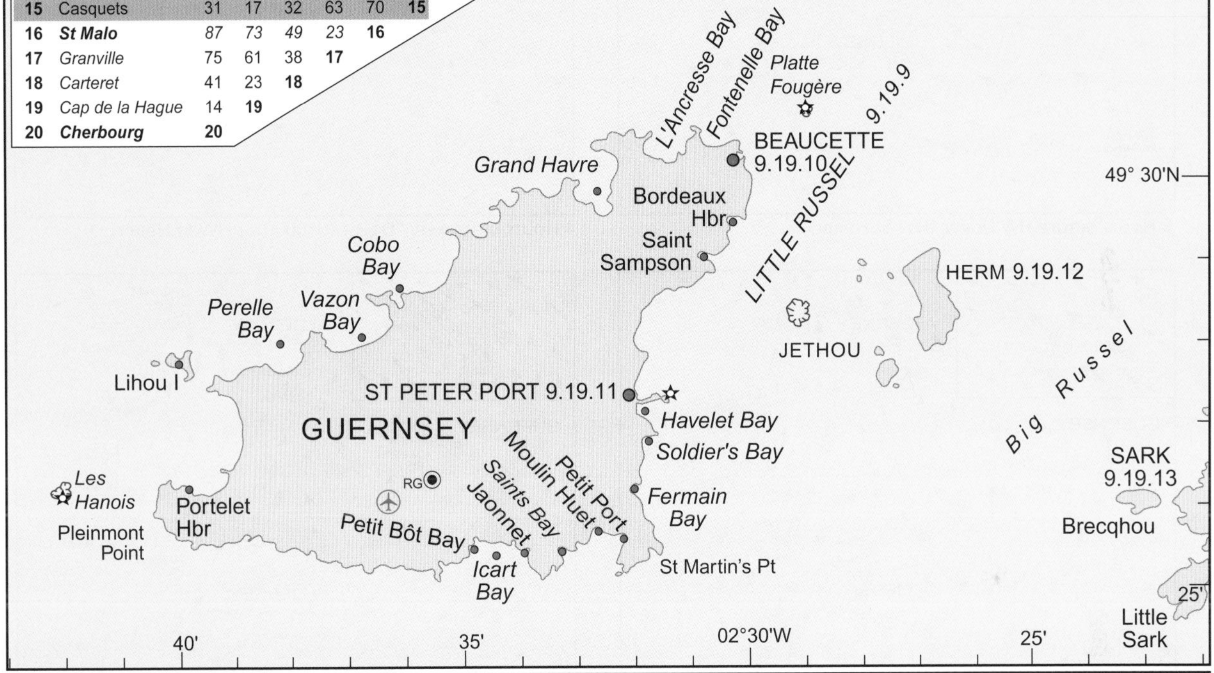

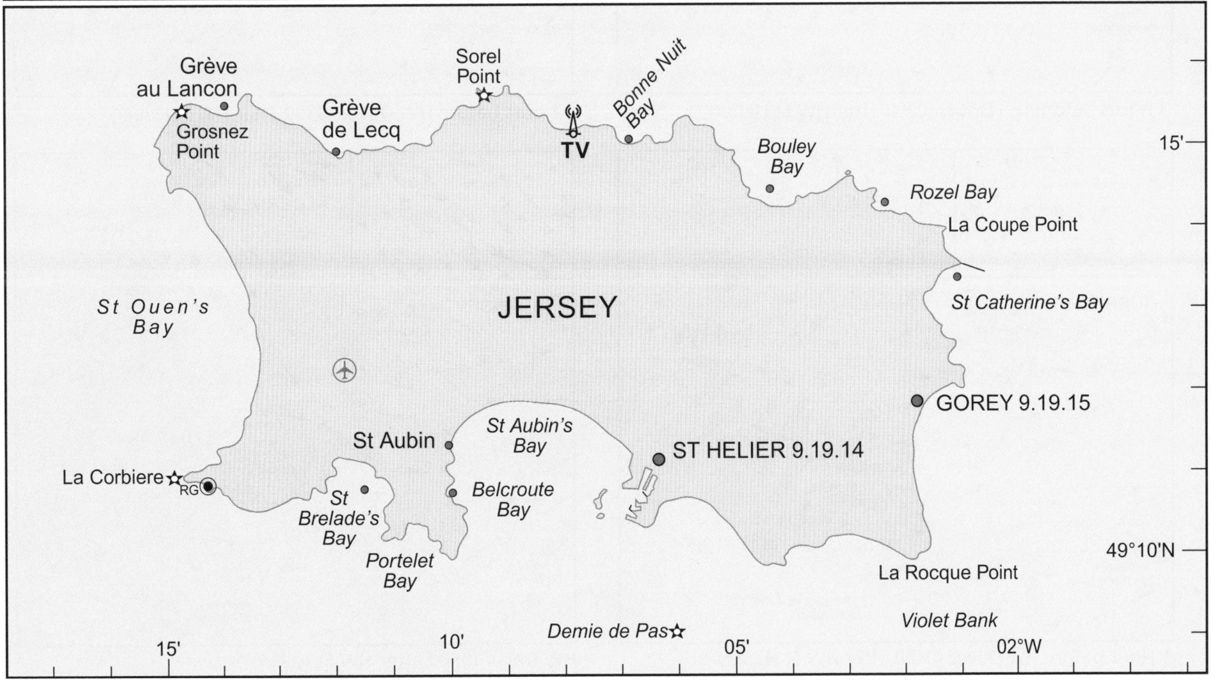

9.19.3 AREA 19 TIDAL STREAMS

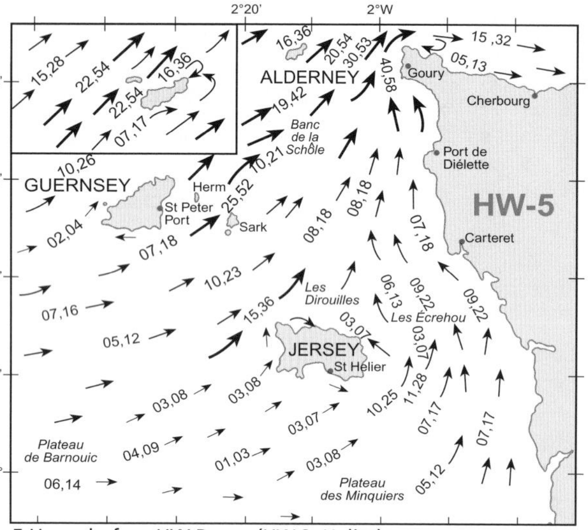

5 Hours before HW Dover (HW St Helier)

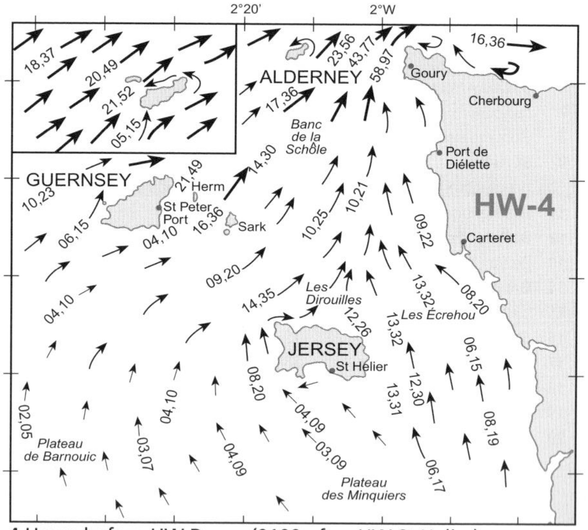

4 Hours before HW Dover (0100 after HW St Helier)

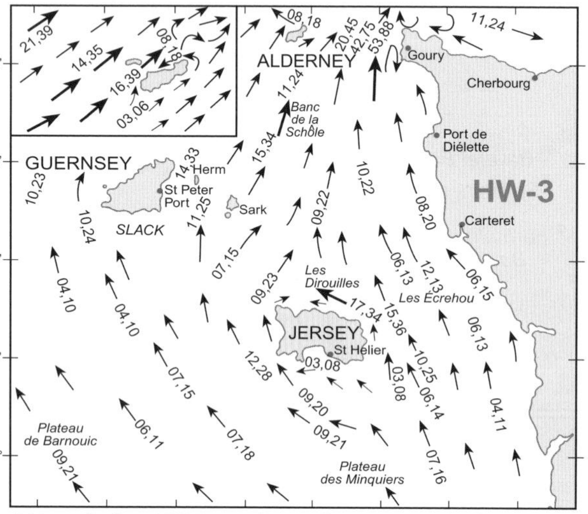

3 Hours before HW Dover (0200 after HW St Helier)

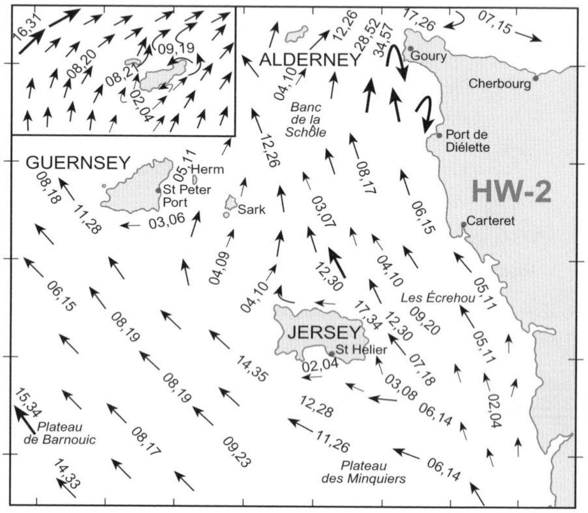

2 Hours before HW Dover (0300 after HW St Helier)

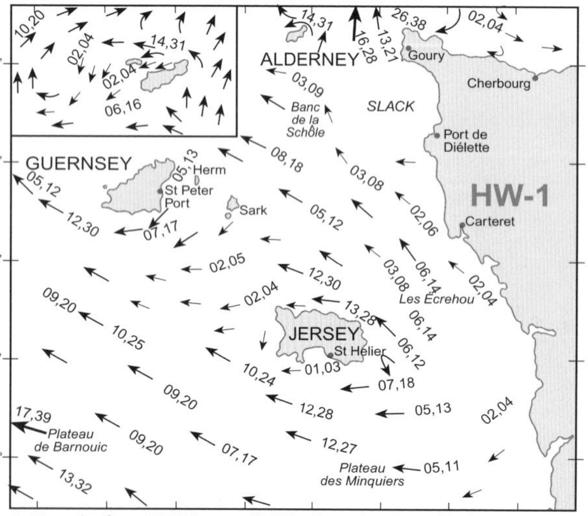

1 Hour before HW Dover (0400 after HW St Helier)

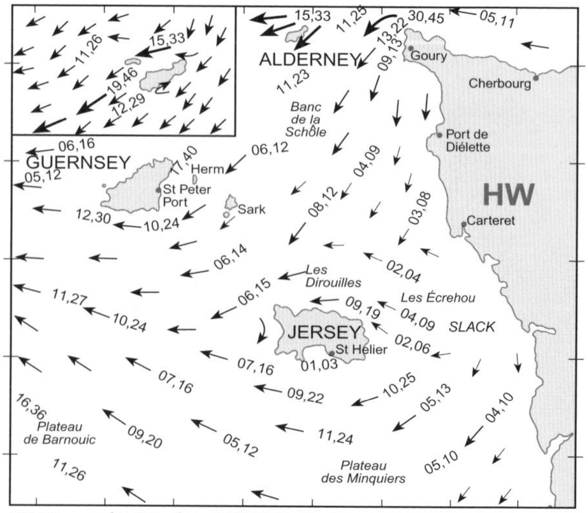

HW Dover (0500 after HW St Helier)

Westward 9.20.3   Southward 9.18.3   Northward 9.2.3   Eastward 9.17.3

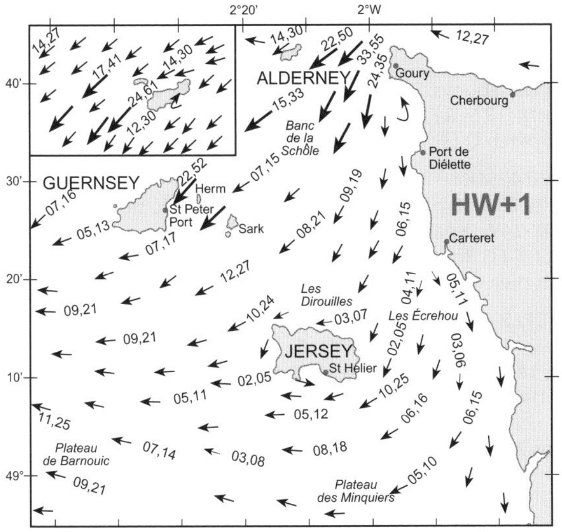

1 Hour after HW Dover (0600 after HW St Helier)

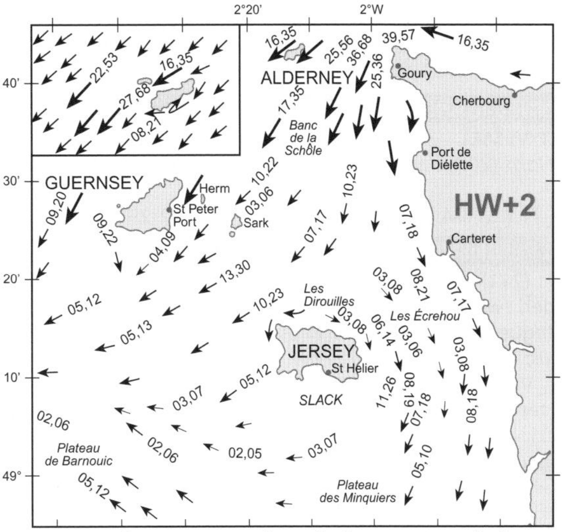

2 Hours after HW Dover (0530 before HW St Helier)

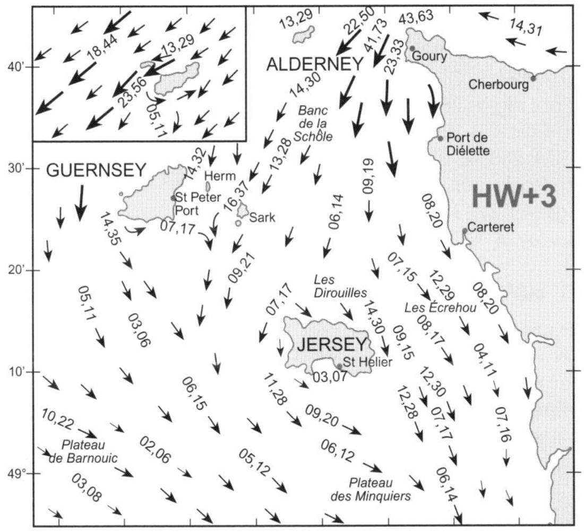

3 Hours after HW Dover (0430 before HW St Helier)

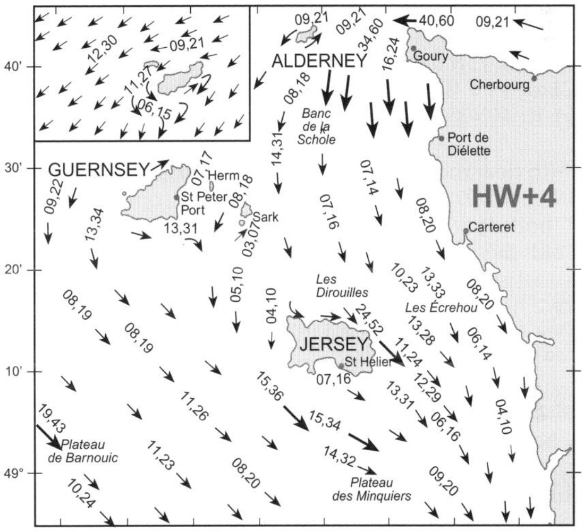

4 Hours after HW Dover (0330 before HW St Helier)

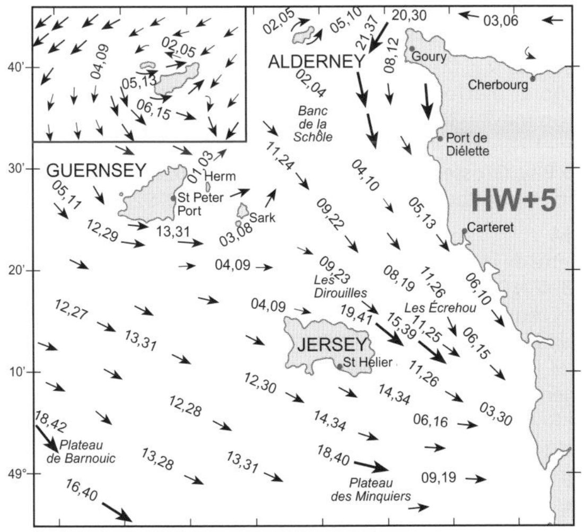

5 Hours after HW Dover (0230 before HW St Helier)

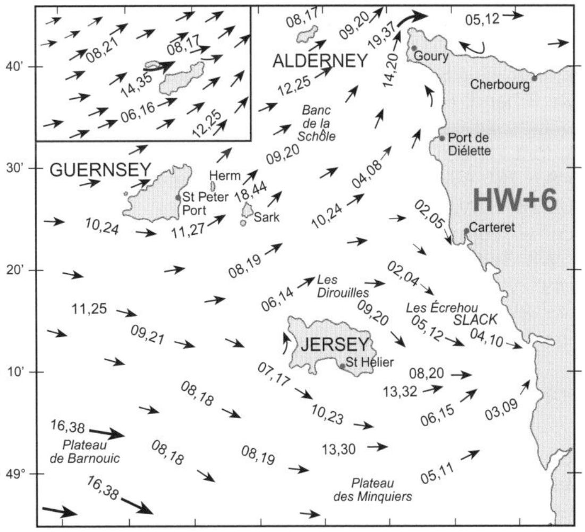

6 Hours after HW Dover (0130 before HW St Helier)

9.19.4 LIGHTS, BUOYS AND WAYPOINTS

Bold print = light with a nominal range of 15M or more. CAPITALS = place or feature. *CAPITAL ITALICS* = light-vessel, light float or Lanby. *Italics* = Fog signal. ***Bold italics*** = Racon. Many marks/buoys are fitted with AIS (MMSI No); see relevant charts.

MID-CHANNEL MARKS

CHANNEL LT VESSEL Fl 15s 12m **15M**; R hull with lt twr amidships; *Horn (20s)*; ***Racon O, 15M***; 49°54'·46N 02°53'·74W; 992351028.

E Channel Fl Y 5s 6M; ***Racon T, 10M***; 49°58'·67N 02°29'·01W.

COTENTIN PENINSULA (NW COAST)

La Plate Fl (2+1) WR 10s 11m; W9M, R6M; 115°-W-272°-R-115°; Y 8-sided twr, with B top; 49°43'·98N 01°55'·76W.

Cap de la Hague (Gros du Raz) ☆ Fl 5s 48m **23M**; Gy twr, W top; *Horn 30s;* 49°43'·31N 01° 57'·27W.

La Foraine VQ (9) 10s 12m 6M; 49°42'·90 N 01°58'·32W.

Cap de Carteret ☆ Fl (2+1) 15s 81m **26M**; Gy twr, G top; 49°22'·41N 01°48'·41W.

THE CASQUETS AND ALDERNEY

Casquets ☆ Fl (5) 30s 37m **18M**, H24; W twr, 2 R bands; NW'most of three; ***Racon T, 25M***; 49°43'·32N 02°22'·63W. 992351121.

Ortac rock, unlit; 49°43'·40N 02°17'·44W.

Pierre au Vraic, unmarked rk 1·2m; 49°41'·61N 02°16'·94W.

Quenard Pt (Alderney) Fl (4) 15s 37m 12M; 085°-027°; W ○ twr, B band; 49°43'·75N 02°09'·86W.

Château à L'Étoc Pt Iso WR 4s 20m W10M, R7M; 071·1°-R-111·1°-W-151·1°; 49°43'·94N 02°10'·63W.

BRAYE

Ldg bns 142° (to clear the submerged Adm'ty bkwtr). Front, W, 49°43'·90N 02°10'·97W. Rear, BW; 720m from front.

Ldg lts 215°: both Q 8/17m 9/12M, synch; 210°-220°; orange △s. Front, old pier elbow, 49°43'·40N 02°11'·91W. Rear, 215°/335m.

Admiralty bkwtr head L Fl 10s 7m 5M; 49°43'·82N 02°11'·67W.

Fairway No 1 QG; 49°43'·72N 02°11'·72W.

No 2 QR; 49°43'·60N 02°11'·75W.

Inner fairway Q (2) G 5s; 49°43'·58N 02°11'·98W.

Braye quay 2 FR (vert) 8m 5M; 49°43'·53N 02°12'·00W.

Little Crabby hbr ent FG & FR 5m 2M; 49°43'·45N 02°12'·12W.

GUERNSEY, NORTHERN APPROACHES

LITTLE RUSSEL CHANNEL

Grande Amfroque, two unlit bcn twrs: larger, BW-banded; smaller, white; 49°30'·57N 02°24'·62W.

Tautenay Q (3) WR 6s 7m W7M, R6M; 050°-W-215°- R-050°; B & W striped bcn 49°30'·11N 02°26'·84W.

Platte Fougère ☆ Fl WR 10s 15m **16M**; 155°-W-085°-R-155°; W 8-sided twr, B band; *Horn 45s* **TD 2017**; ***Racon P***; 49°30'·83N 02°29'·14W.

Corbette d'Amont Y bcn twr, topmark; 49°29'·64N 02°29'·38W.

Roustel Q 8m 7M; BW chequered base, W framework col; 49°29'·23N 02°28'·79W.

Rousse, Y bcn twr, topmark; 49°28'·98N 02°28'·36W.

Platte, Fl WR 3s 6m, W7M, R5M; 024°-R-219°-W-024°; G conical twr; 49°29'·08N 02°29'·57W.

Vivian bcn twr, BW bands, 49°28'·45N 02°30'·66W.

Brehon Iso 4s 19m 9M; bcn on ○ twr, 49°28'·28N 02°29'·28W.

Demie Flieroque, Y bcn twr, topmark F; 49°28'·13N 02°31'·38W.

BIG RUSSEL

Noire Pute Fl (2) WR 15s 8m 6M; 220°-W-040°-R-220°; on 2m high rock; 49°28'·21N 02°25'·02W; unreliable.

Fourquies Q; 49°27'·34N 02°26'·47W.

Lower Heads Q (6) + L Fl 15s; *Bell;* 49°25'·85N 02°28'·55W.

GUERNSEY, HERM AND SARK

BEAUCETTE MARINA

Petite Canupe Q (6) + L Fl 15s; 49°30'·20N 02°29'·14W.

Ldg lts 277°: Both FR. Front, W □, R stripe; 49°30'·19N 02°30'·23W. Rear, R □, W stripe; 185m from front.

Appr chan buoys: SWM L Fl 10s 49°30'·15N 02°29'·66W. SHM Fl G 5s, PHM Fl R 5s & Fl (3) R 5s. NCM perch Q 49°30'·165N 02°30'·06W. SHM perch Q (3) G 5s at ent; 49°30'·18N 02°30'·24W.

ST SAMPSON

Ldg lts 286°: Front, FR 3m 5M; 230°-340°; tfc sigs; 49°28'·90N 02°30'·74W. Rear, FG 13m; clock twr, 390m from front.

N Pier FG 3m 5M; 230°-340°; 49°28'·92N 02°30'·71W.

Crocq pier FR 11m 5M; 250°-340°; 49°28'·98N 02°31'·00W.

ST PETER PORT

Outer ldg lts 220°: **Front**, Castle bkwtr, Al WR 10s 14m **16M**; 187°-007°; dark ○ twr, W on NE side; *Horn 15s;* 49°27'·31N 02°31'·45W.

Rear 220° ldg lt, Belvedere, Oc 10s 61m 14M; 179°-269°; intens 217°-223°; W □ on W twr; 980m from front. The lts are synchronised so that the rear lt is on when the front is W, and the off when the front is R.

Queen Elizabeth II marina, 270° Dir Oc WRG 3s 5m 6M; 258°-G-268°-W-272°-R-282°; 49°27'·73N 02°31'·87W.

Refféе Q (6) + L Fl 15s; 49°27'·74N 02°31'·27W.

Appr buoys: outer pair QG; 49°27'·83N 02°31'·54W. QR; 49°27'·71N 02°31'·52W. Inner pair: QG; 49°27'·76N 02°31'·74W. QR; 49°27'·72N 02°31'·74W.

The Pool ldg lts 265° (*not* into moorings): Front, Victoria marina, S Pier, Oc R 5s 10m 14M; 49°27'·32N 02°32'·03W. Rear, Iso R 2s 22m 3M; 260°-270°; on Creasey's bldg, 160m from front.

White Rock pier Oc G 5s 11m 14M; intens 174°-354°; ○ twr; tfc sigs; 49°27'·38N 02°31'·59W.

S Fairway QG; 49°27'·30N 02°31'·76W; N of fuel pontoon W of buoy 3 x Fl R; 49°27'·28N 02°31'·74W. 49°27'·27N 02°31'·80W. 49°27'·27N 02°31'·86W.

HAVELET BAY

Oyster Rock Y bcn, topmark 'O'; 49°27'·09N 02°31'·46W.

Oyster Rock QG; 49°27'·04N 02°31'·47W.

Moulinet QR; 49°26'·97N 02°31'·54W.

Moulinet Y bcn, topmark 'M'; 49°26'·95N 02°31'·58W.

GUERNSEY, SOUTH-EAST and SOUTH COASTS

Anfré, Y bcn, topmark 'A'; 49°26'·45N 02°31'·48W.

Longue Pierre, Y bcn, topmark 'LP'; 49°25'·36N 02°31'·48W.

St Martin's Pt Fl (3) WR 10s 15m 14M; 185°-R-191°-W-011°-R-061·5°; flat-topped, W bldg. *Horn (3) 30s;* 49°25'·30N 02°31'·70W.

GUERNSEY, NORTH-WEST COAST

Les Hanois ☆ Fl (2) 13s 33m **20M**; 294°-237°; Gy ○ twr, B lantern, helicopter platform; *Horn (2) 60s.* 49°26'·10N 02°42'·15W.

4 FR on mast 1·3M ESE of Les Hanois lt ho.

Portelet Hbr, bkwtr bcn, 49°26'·16N 02°39'·84W.

Cobo Bay, Grosse Rock, B bcn 11m; 49°29'·02N 02°36'·19W.

Grand Havre, Rousse Point bkwtr, B bcn; 49°29'·92N 02°33'·05W.

HERM

Corbette de la Mare, Wh disc (W side) and R disc (E side) on Y pole, 49°28'·48N 02°28'·72W.

Petit Creux QR; red 'C' on red pole; 49°28'·09N 02°28'·72W.

Alligande Fl (3) G 5s; B pole, Or 'A'; 49°27'·86N 02°28'·78W.

Épec Fl G 3s; black 'E' on G mast; 49°27'·98N 02°27'·89W.

Vermerette Fl (2) Y 5s; Or 'V' on bcn; 49°28'·12N 02°27'·75W.

Gate Rock (Percée Pass) Q (9) 15s; 49°27'·88N 02°27'·54W.

Hbr ldg lts 078°: White drums. 2F occas; 49°28'·25N 02°27'·11W.

Hbr pier, N end 2 FG; G □ on G bcn; 49°28'·21N 02°27'·26W.

SARK

Courbée du Nez Fl (4) WR 15s 14m 8M; 057°-W-230°-R-057°; W structure on rock; 49°27'·09N 02°22'·17W.

Point Robert ☆ Fl 15s 65m **20M**; vis 138°-353°; W 8-sided twr; *Horn (2) 30s;* 49°26'·19N 02°20'·75W.
Founiais, topmark 'F'; 49°26'·02N 02°20'·36W.
Blanchard Q (3) 10s; *Bell;* 49°25'·36N 02°17'·42W.
Pilcher monument (070° appr brg); 49°25'·71N 02°22'·44W.

JERSEY, WEST AND SOUTH COASTS

Desormes Q (9) 15s; 49°18'·94N 02°17'·98W.
Grosnez Point ☆ Fl (2) WR 15s 50m **W19M, R17M**; 081°-W-188°-R-241°; W hut; 49°15'·50N 02°14'·80W.
L a Rocco twr (conspic) 15m; 49°11'·90N 02°14'·05W.
La Frouquie (seasonal); 49°11'·30N 02°15'·38W.
La Corbière ☆ Iso WR 10s 36m **W18M, R16M**; shore-W-294°-R-328°-W-148°-R-shore; W ○ twr; *Horn Mo (C) 60s;* 49°10'·79N 02°15'·01W.
Pt Corbière FR; R □, W stripe; 49°10'·87N 02°14'·38W.

WESTERN PASSAGE

Ldg lts 082°. Front, La Gréve d'Azette Oc 5s 23m 14M; 034°-129°; 49°10'·16N 02°05'·09W. Rear, Mont Ubé, Oc R 5s 46m 12M; 250°-095°; 1M from front.
Passage Rock VQ; 49°09'·54N 02°12'·26W.
Les Fours Q; 49°09'·59N 02°10'·16W.
Noirmont Pt Fl (4) 12s 18m 10M; B twr, W band; 49°09'·91N 02°10'·08W.
Pignonet 49°09'·88N 02°09'·70W.
Ruaudière Rock Fl G 3s; *Bell;* 49°09'·74N 02°08'·62W.

ST AUBIN'S BAY and HARBOUR

Les Grunes du Port 49°10'·02N 02°09'·14W.
Diamond Rock Fl (2) R 6s; 49°10'·12N 02°08'·64W.
Castle pier Fl R 4s 8m 1M; 49°11'·13N 02°09'·634W.
North pier, Dir lt 254° F WRG 5m, 248°-G-253°-W-255°-R-260°; 49°11'·22N 02°10'·03W. Same col, Iso R 4s 12m 10M.
Beach Rock 49°11'·29N 02°08'·42W, (Apr-Oct).
Rocquemin 49°10'·64N 02°07'·95W.
Baleine 49°10'·41N 02°08'·23W.

ST HELIER

Elizabeth marina, west appr: Dir 106°: F WRG 4m 1M; 096°-G-104°-W-108°-R-119°; R dayglo □, B stripe; 49°10'·76N 02°07'·12W.
La Vrachiére 49°10'·90N 02°07'·59W, Fl (2) 5s 1M.
Fort Charles North 49°10'·81N 02°07'·50W.
Marina ent Oc G & Oc R, both 4s 2M; 49°10'·83N 02°07'·13W.
Red & Green Passage, ldg lts 022·7° on dayglo R dolphins: Front, Elizabeth E berth Dn Oc G 5s 10m 11M; 49°10'·63N 02°06'·94W.
Rear, Albert Pier root Oc R 5s 18m 12M; synch; 230m SSW.
East Rock QG; 49°09'·96N 02°07'·28W.
Dog's Nest Rk Fl Y 3s 3M; Y cross on bcn; 49°09'·99N 02°06'·95W.
Oyster Rocks, R/W bcn, topmark 'O'; 49°10'·10N 02°07'·49W.
Platte Rock Fl R 1·5s 6m 5M; R col; 49°10'·16N 02°07'·34W.
Small Road No 2 QR; 49°10'·39N 02°07'·24W.
No 4 QR; 49°10'·53N 02°07'·12W.
Elizabeth marina, S appr: E1 Fl G 3s; 49°10'·59N 02°07'·09W.
E2 Fl R 2s; 49°10'·58N 02°07'·13W.
E5 Fl G 5s; 49°10'·70N 02°07'·17W.
E6 Fl R 2s; 49°10'·69N 02°07'·21W.
Fort Charles East Q (3) 5s 2m 1M; 49°10'·74N 02°07'·26W.
La Collette basin QR; 49°10'·54N 02°06'·91W. 49°10'·52N 02°06'·90W.
St Helier Hbr, ldg lts 078°, both FG on W cols. Front, 49°10'·62N 02°06'·66W. Rear, 80m from front.
Victoria pier hd, Port control twr; IPTS; 49°10'·57N 02°06'·88W.

JERSEY, SOUTH-EAST AND EAST COASTS

Hinguette QR; 49°09'·33N 02°07'·32W.
Hettich Fl Y 5s; 49°08'·10N 02°09'·00W.
South Pier Marine Fl Y 5s; 49°09'·10N 02°06'·30W.
Demie de Pas Mo (D) WR 12s 11m, W14M, R10M; 130°-R-303°-W-130°; *Horn (3) 60s*; ***Racon T, 10M***; B bn twr, Y top; 49°09'·01N 02°06'·15W. Icho Tower (conspic, 14m) 49°08'·89N 02°02'·90W.
Canger Rock Q (9) 15s; 49°07'·35N 02°00'·38W.
La Conchière Q (6) + L Fl 15s 2M; 49°08'·22N 02°00'·17W.
Frouquier Aubert Q (6) + L Fl 15s; 49°06'·08N 01°58'·84W.
Violet L Fl 10s; 49°07'·81N 01°57'·14W.
Petite Anquette; SCM; 49°08'·47N 01°56'·29W.
Grande Anquette VQ(9) 10s; 49°08'·32N 01°55'·20W.
Le Cochon 49°09'·77N 01°58'·80W.
La Noire 49°10'·13N 01°59'·23W.
Le Giffard Fl R 3s 49°10'·59N 01°58'·99W.

GOREY

Pier Hd Occ WRG 5s 8m 8M; 228°-G-296·5°-W-299·5°-R-299·5°-008°; W twr on pierhead; 49°11'·81N 02°01'·33W.
Horn Rock, topmark 'H'; 49°10'·96N 01°59'·85W.
Les Burons, R bcn, topmark 'B'; 49°11'·33N 02°00'·81W.
Fairway QG; 49°11'·50N 02°00'·34W.
Écureuil Rock 49°11'·67N 02°00'·78W.
Equerrière Rk, bcn 'fishtail' topmark; 49°11'·80N 02°00'·67W.
Les Arch, BW bcn, 'A' topmark; 49°12'·02N 02°00'·60W.

ST CATHERINE BAY

St Catherine Bay, Le Fara Q (3) 10s 3M; 49°12'·85N 02°00'·48W.
Archirondel Tower (conspic, 16m) 49°12'·72N 02°01'·42W.
Verclut bkwtr Fl 1·5s 18m 13M; 49°13'·34N 02°00'·64W. In line 315° with unlit turret, 49°13'·96N 02°01'·57W, on La Coupe Pt.

JERSEY, NORTH COAST

Rozel Bay Dir lt 245°, F WRG 11m 5M; 240°-G-244°-W-246°-R-250°; W col; 49°14'·21N 02°02'·76W.
Bonne Nuit Bay ldg lts 223°: both FG 7/34m 6M. Front, Pier 49°15'·10N 02°07'·17W. Rear, 170m from front.
Demie Rock 49°15'·56N 02°07'·36W.
Sorel Point ☆ L Fl WR 7·5s 50m **15M**; 095°-W-112°-R-173°-W-230°-R-269°-W-273°; W ○ twr, only 3m high; 49°15'·60N 02°09'·54W.

OFFLYING ISLANDS

LES ÉCREHOU

Écrevière Q (6) + L Fl 15s; 49°15'·26N 01°52'·15W.
Mâitre Ile 49°17'·08N 01°55'·60W.

PLATEAU DES MINQUIERS

N Minquiers Q; 49°01'·64N 02°00'·58W.
NE Minquiers VQ (3) 5s; *Bell;* 49°00'·85N 01°55'·30W.
SE Minquiers Q (3) 10s; *Bell;* 48°53'·42N 02°00'·09W.
S Minquiers Q (6) + L Fl 15s; 48°53'·09N 02°10'·10W.
SW Minquiers Q (9) 15s 5M; *Whis;* 48°54'·35N 02°19'·41W.
NW Minquiers Q 5M; *Whis;* 48°59'·63N 02°20'·59W.
Refuge; B/W bcn; 49°00'·13N 02°10'·16W.
Demie de Vascelin Fl G 3s, 49°00'·81N 02°05'·17W.
Grand Vascelin, BW bcn 48°59'·97N 02°07'·26W.
Maitresse Ile, Puffin B&W bcn twr 48°58'·33N 02°03'·65W.
Le Coq Reef, Q (3) 10s 6m 3M; 48°57'·88N 02°01'·29W.

FRENCH MARKS NORTH OF ILE DE BRÉHAT

Roches Douvres ☆ Fl 5s 60m **24M**; pink twr on dwelling with G roof; 49°06'·30N 02°48'·87W. 992271319. (16M NNE of Ile de Bréhat).
Barnouic VQ (3) 5s 15m 7M; 49°01'·64N 02°48'·41W.
Roche Gautier VQ (9) 10s; 49°02'·013N 02°54'·36W.
Les Héaux de Bréhat ☆ Fl (4) WRG 15s 48m, **W15M**, R/G11M; 227°-R-247°-W-270°-G-302°-W-227°; Gy twr; 48°54'·50N 03°05'·18W (4·7M WNW of Ile de Bréhat).

9.19.5 PASSAGE INFORMATION

More passage information is threaded between successive harbours in this Area. **Bibliography:** *The Channel Islands* (Imray/RCC/Carnegie); *N Brittany & Channel Islands CC* (Fernhurst/Cumberlidge); *Channel Pilot* (NP27). *Channel Havens* (ACN/Endean); *Shell Channel Pilot* (Imray/Cunliffe).

THE CHANNEL ISLANDS

In an otherwise delightful cruising area (AC 2669) the main problems include fog and poor visibility, the very big tidal range, strong tidal streams, overfalls and steep seas which get up very quickly. The shoreline is generally rugged with sandy bays and many offlying rks. It is important to use large scale AC, and recognised leading marks (of which there are plenty) when entering or leaving many of the harbours and anchs. Several passages are marked by beacons and perches identified by an alphabetical letter(s) in lieu of topmark. Beware high speed ferries.

From the N, note the Casquets TSS and ITZ. Soundings of Hurd Deep can help navigation. The powerful lights at the Casquets, Alderney, Cap de la Hague, Cap Levi, Barfleur and Les Hanois greatly assist a night or dawn landfall. By day Alderney is relatively high and conspicuous. Sark is often seen before Guernsey which slopes down from S to N. Jersey is low-lying in the SE. The islands are fringed by many rky dangers. In poor visibility stay in harbour.

►*Over a 12hr period tidal streams broadly rotate anti-clockwise around the Islands, particularly in open water and in wider chans. The E-going (flood) stream is of less duration than the W-going, but is stronger. The islands lie across the main direction of the streams, so eddies are common along the shores. The range of tide is greatest in Jersey (9·6m sp, 4·1m np), and least in Alderney (5·3m sp, 2·2m np). Streams run hard through the chans and around headlands and need to be worked carefully; neaps are easier, particularly for a first visit. Strong W'lies cause a heavy sea, usually worst HW ±3.*◄

As well as the main harbours, described in some detail, there are also many attractive minor harbours and anchorages. In the very nature of islands a lee can usually be found somewhere. Boats which can take the ground can better explore the quieter hbrs. Avoid lobster pots and oyster beds.

THE CASQUETS AND ORTAC CHANNEL

Casquets It ho is conspic on the largest island of this group of rks 5·5M W of Alderney (AC 60). Offlying dangers extend 4ca W and WSW (The Ledge and Noire Roque) and 4ca E (Pt Colote). The tide runs very hard around and between these obstructions. A shallow bank, on which are situated Fourquie and l'Equêt rks (dry) lies from 5ca to 1M E of Casquets, and should not be approached. Ortac Rk (24m) is 3·5M E of Casquets. Ortac Chan runs NNW/SSE 5ca W of Ortac.

►*Here the stream starts to run NE at HW St Helier –2½, and SW at HW St Helier +0355; sp rates up to 5½kn (7kn reported).*◄

Ortac Channel should not be used in bad weather due to tremendous overfalls; these and violent eddies also occur over Eight Fathom Ledge (8½ca W of Casquets) and over the SW, SSW and SSE Casquet Banks where least depths of 7·3m occur.

ALDERNEY AND THE SWINGE

Braye Harbour (AC 2845) together with pleasant bays and anchs around the island, offer shelter from different wind/sea directions. The sunken NE extremity of Admiralty Breakwater should only be crossed in calm conditions, outside LW±2 and about 50m off the head of the Breakwater where there is 2·3m.

The **Swinge** lies between Burhou with its bordering rks, and the NW coast of Alderney. It can be a dangerous chan, and should only be used in reasonable vis and fair weather. On the N side of the Swinge the main dangers are Boues des Kaines, almost awash at LW about 7½ca ESE of Ortac, and North Rk 2½ca SE of Burhou. On S side of the Swinge beware Corbet Rk (0·5m high) with drying outliers, 5ca N of Fort Clonque, and Barsier Rk (0·9m) 3½ca NNW of Fort Clonque.

►*The SW-going stream begins at HW St Helier +0340, and the NE stream at HW St Helier –0245, sp rates 7-8kn. On the NE-going stream, beware the very strong northerly set in vicinity of Ortac.*◄

The tide runs very hard, and in strong or gale force winds from S or W there are very heavy overfalls on the SW-going stream between Ortac and Les Etacs (off W end of Alderney).

In strong E winds, on the NE-going stream, overfalls occur between **Burhou** and Braye breakwater. These overfalls can mostly be avoided by choosing the best time and route (see below) but due to the uneven bottom and strong tides broken water may be met even in calm conditions.

►*It is best to pass SW through the Swinge is about HW St Helier +4, when the SW-going stream starts; hold to the SE side of the chan since the stronger stream runs on the Burhou side. But after HW St Helier +5, to clear the worst of the overfalls keep close to Burhou and Ortac, avoiding North Rk and Boues des Kaines.*◄

Pierre au Vraic (dries 1·2m) is an unmarked pinnacle rock at 49°41'·61N 02°16'·94W,1·8M S of Ortac and 1·8M WSW of Les Étacs, almost in the fairway to/from the Swinge. Arriving on a fair tide from Guernsey it will be well covered, but it is a serious hazard if leaving the Swinge on a SW-going spring tide close to local LW. Carefully study the clearing bearings shown on AC 60.

Heading NE at about HW St Helier –2, Great Nannel in transit with E end of Burhou clears Pierre au Vraic to the E, but passes close W of Les Etacs. On this transit, when Roque Tourgis fort is abeam, alter slightly to stbd to pass 1ca NW of Corbet Rk; keep near SE side of the channel.

THE ALDERNEY RACE

This race, characterised by very strong tidal streams, runs SW/NE between Cap de la Hague and Alderney, but its influence extends at least as far SW as 02° 20'W (AC 3653). The fairway, approx 4M wide, is bounded by Race Rk and Alderney S Banks to the NW, and to the SE by rky banks 3M E of Race Rk, and by Milieu and Banc de la Schôle (least depth 2·7m). These dangers which cause breaking seas and heavy overfalls should be carefully avoided. In bad weather and strong wind-against-tide the seas break in all parts of the Race and passage is not advised. Conditions are worst at springs.

►*In mid-chan the SW-going stream starts at HW St Helier +4½ (HW Dover) and the NE-going stream at HW St Helier –2¼ (HW Dover +5½), sp rates both 5·5kn. The times at which the stream turns do not vary much in various places, but the rates do; for example, 1M W of Cap de la Hague sp rates reach 7-8kn.*◄

For optimum conditions, timing is of the essence. As a rule of thumb the Race should be entered on the first of the fair tide so as to avoid peak tidal streams with attendant overfalls/seas.

►*Thus SW-bound, arrrive off Cap de la Hague at around HW St Helier +4½ (HW Dover –½ to HW Dover) when the stream will be slack, whilst just starting to run SW off Alderney. A yacht leaving Cherbourg at HW Dover –3 will achieve the above timing by utilising the inshore W-going tidal eddy.*

Conversely, NE-bound, leave St Peter Port, say, at approx local HW St Helier –4½ (HWD+3) with a foul tide so as to pass Banc de la Schôle as the fair tide starts to make.◄ A later departure should achieve a faster passage, but with potentially less favourable conditions in the Race. On the NE-going stream the worst overfalls are on the French side.

9.19.6 SPECIAL NOTES: CHANNEL ISLANDS

The Channel Islands (Alderney, Guernsey, Sark, Jersey and other smaller islands) lie not in the Channel, but in the Bay of St Malo. Alderney, Herm, Jethou, Sark and Brecqhou are all part of the Bailiwick of Guernsey and the States (Parliament) of Alderney have seats in the States of Guernsey.

The Islands are self-governing with their own laws, judiciary and Customs, but conduct their foreign affairs mostly through the English crown. They are not part of either the UK or the EU. The French call the CI Les Îles Anglo-Normandes (Aurigny, Guernsey, Sercq et Jersey). Standard Time is UT (Zone 0).

Charts Admiralty Leisure folio SC5604 (£44·30, 7th ed. published Feb 2013) contains 17 sheets of the CIs. These and other charts are listed under individual ports.

Ports of entry Braye, Beaucette, St Sampson, St Peter Port, St Helier and Gorey.

Customs British yachts entering the CI, except Jersey, *must* complete and deposit the local Customs declaration form and may have to show the vessel's registration documents; they are no longer expected to fly the Q flag arriving from the UK or France. On arrival back in UK they are subject to Customs formalities. Yachts going to France need usual documents (passports etc).

Speed limits, Jersey, 5kn in all hbrs, and within 200m of water's edge in any bay, inside 10m depth contour, Les Écrehou and Les Dirouilles, inside 5m depth contour, Les Minquiers. **Guernsey**, 6kn within bays, 0·5M of Herm and the Humps, and the area defined by the coastlines of Jethou, Fauconnière and Crevichon. St Peter Port outer hbr 6kn, inner hbr 4kn (see chartlet).

Medical Jersey has reciprocal medical arrangements with the UK, but the other CI do not and visitors will have to pay for costly inpatient / outpatient care. Medical insurance recommended.

Weather forecasts prepared by Jersey Met Office for the CI area and adjacent coasts of Normandy and Brittany are available ☎0900 669 0022 (premium rate) throughout the CI and UK. From France replace the first 0 by 00 44. There are more details in Chapter 6.

SAR operations are co-ordinated by Guernsey Coastguard in the N area and Jersey Coastguard in the S (see Chapter 5). Major incidents are co-ordinated with CROSS Jobourg and Falmouth CGOC. LBs at Braye, St Peter Port, St Helier and St Catherine's Bay (Jersey).

Telephones CI phones are UK integrated but charges, especially on mobiles, may vary. Toll-free and premium numbers may be blocked when roaming with non-CI mobiles. For an online telephone directory visit www.theguernseydirectory.com

Courtesy flags A courtesy flag in CI ports is a mark of politeness but not essential. Local flags are: *Jersey* R ensign with Jersey Royal Arms (three lions passant with gold crown above); see Fig 5(9).

Guernsey R ensign with Duke William's cross in the fly. Vessels owned by Guernsey residents may wear this ensign; see Fig 5(9).

Sark The English (St George's) flag, Normandy arms in the canton.

Alderney The English (St George's) flag and in the centre a green disc charged with a gold lion.

Herm The English (St George's) flag, and in the canton the Arms of Herm (three cowled monks on a gold diagonal stripe between blue triangles containing a silver dolphin).

Cars can be hired in Jersey, Guernsey and Alderney. In Sark cars are prohib, but bikes and horse-drawn carriages can be hired.

Animals may only be landed from boats from the UK, Ireland, Isle of Man or other CI, but not if the boat has visited France. No vessel with an animal on board may lie alongside a pontoon or quay without a Revenue Officer's permission.

UK currency can be used but not vice versa. Postage stamps, issued by Jersey, Guernsey and Alderney, must be used in the appropriate Bailiwick; Guernsey and Alderney stamps are interchangeable.

Gas Some UK Gas retailers may not accept Channel Island bottles.

9.19.7 ALDERNEY

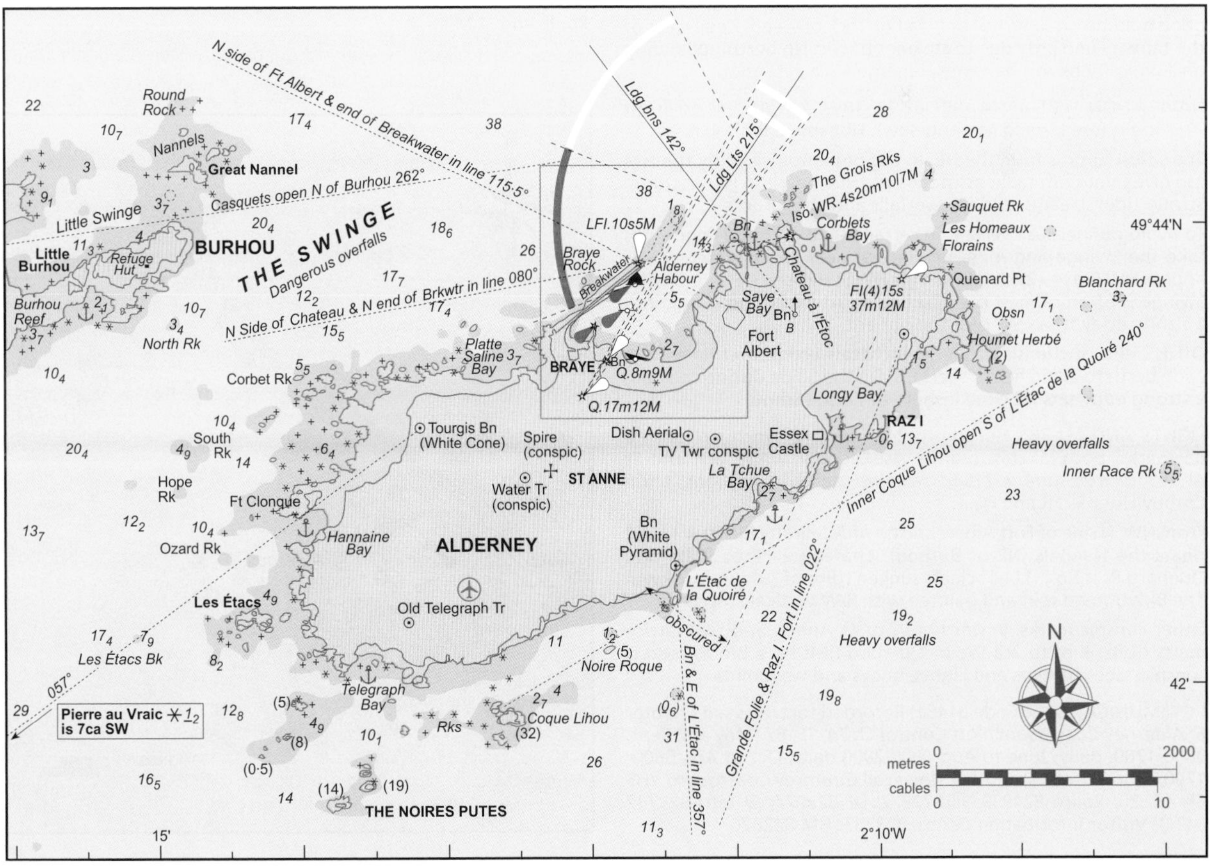

ANCHORAGES AROUND ALDERNEY There are several ⚓s, all picturesque but only safe in settled weather and offshore winds; most are very small and many have offlying rocks. Entry to these anchorages is not advised without local knowledge, advice from the HM, a good Pilot book plus AC 60 and/or preferably 2845. None provide any facilities. Clockwise from Braye they are:

Saye Bay 49°43´·85N 02°10´·87W. Small sandy bay 4ca E of ent to Braye Hbr. Appr on transit 142° of ldg bns; move E to open up the ent. Ent is 100m wide between Homet des Pies and Homet des Agneaux. Exposed to N'lies. Château à l'Étoc ☆ is 300m ENE. Speed limit 4kn.

Longy Bay 49°43´·06N 02°10´·29W. Wide drying bay with good holding on sand. Speed limit 4kn. Appr on N between Queslingue (a 14m high stack) and a rk 0·6m to stbd. ⚓ in 3·5m closer to Essex Castle than to Raz Island to await fair tide in the Race. Whilst the stream is setting SW offshore, a NE-going eddy develops along the island's southern shore and this would assist a straightforward arrival.

La Tchue 49°42´·78N 02°10´·75W. Good holding in small bay surrounded by cliffs. La Rocque Pendante to the E and smoking rubbish tip to the NW are both conspic.

Telegraph Bay 49°42´·01N 02°13´·51W. Pleasant sandy bay on SW tip of the island but ringed by rks. Appr 035° between Noires Putes and Coupé. Old Telegraph Twr (93m) is conspic until obsc'd close inshore, when a pillar on the cliff edge offers brgs, as does the astern transit of Coupé (7m) and and Orbouée (0.5m).

Hannaine Bay 49°42´·73N 02°13´·98W. A good place to await the flood tide. Appr Tourgis Bn △ ≠ 057° SE side of Fort Clonque. Beware rks either side. ⚓ on sand in 3m, 100m S of Fort.

Platte Saline Bay 49°43´·37N 02°12´·65W. Good shelter from E'lies. Les Jumelles and Outer Fourchie guard the ent. Beach is unsafe for swimming.

Burhou 49°43´·64N 02°15´·49W. Temp'y ⚓ in bay SW of Burhou, only on SW stream; exposed at HW on the NE-going stream. Appr on 010° for the gap between Burhou and Little Burhou.

9.19.8 BRAYE HARBOUR

Alderney **49°43'·77N 02°11'·51W** ✪✪✪◊◊◊✿✿✿

CHARTS AC 2669, 3653, 60, 2845, 5604.7/.8; SHOM 7158, 6934; Navi 1014; Imray C33A, 2500

TIDES –0400 Dover; ML 3·5; Duration 0545

Standard Port ST HELIER (⟶)

Times				Height (metres)			
High Water		Low Water		MHWS	MHWN	MLWN	MLWS
0300	0900	0200	0900	11·0	8·1	4·0	1·4
1500	2100	1400	2100				
Differences *BRAYE*							
+0050	*+0040*	*+0025*	*+0105*	*–4·8*	*–3·4*	*–1·5*	*–0·5*

SHELTER Good, but exposed to strong N/NE'lies. ⚓s as charted; good holding on sand, but only fair on rock or weed. Keep clear of the fairway and jetty due to steamer traffic. No berthing/landing on Admiralty bkwtr; beware submerged 3ca extension.

NAVIGATION WPT 49°44´·08N 02°11´·18W, 215°/0.82M to front 215° ldg lt (see Lts and Marks below). Hbr speed limit 4kn.

The safest appr is from the NE. In fog or limited visibility the HM can give small craft radar assistance and RDF bearings HO. Caution: Strong tidal streams, eddies, overfalls and many rocks.

To avoid dangerous overfalls in certain wind and tide conditions take the Swinge and Alderney Race at/near slack water; this is approx HW Braye +2½ & LW +2½ (or HW St Helier +3½ and –3). The Swinge is often calmest near Corbet Rk. At mid-flood (NE-going) a strong eddy flows SW past the hbr ent.

Off NE end of the island give Brinchetais Ledge and Race Rk a wide berth to avoid heavy overfalls. On the S side during the ebb, a strong eddy sets NE close inshore of Coque Lihou.

LIGHTS AND MARKS Hbr ldg lts 215°, both Q synch; co-located daymarks, both W cols, orange △s. Old Hbr white bcn and St Anne's church spire ≠ 210·5° remains useful in daylight. Little Crabby Hbr has FR and FG.

From NW, N side of Fort Albert and hd of Admiralty Bkwtr ≠ 115·5° clears the Nannels (NE of Burhou). Château à l'Etoc lt ho and Quenard Pt lt ho ≠ 111·1° clears sunken ruins of Admiralty Bkwtr. The Bkwtr head is lit and painted with B/W vertical stripes.

Other conspic marks: Water twr W of St Anne's and two lattice masts (R lts) E of it. 2ca SW of Quenard Pt lt ho a blockhouse is conspic. See chartlets and Lights, buoys and waypoints.

COMMUNICATIONS (Code 01481) Recorded forecasts see Chapter 6; *Alderney Coastguard* /Port Control Ch **74**, 16, 67 (May and Sept, 0800-1700, daily; June to Aug 0800-2000 daily; Oct to Apr, 0800-1700, Mon-Fri: all LT) at other times call *Guernsey Coastguard* VHF Ch 16, 20; Police 824999; Ⓗ 822822; Dr 822077; Ⓥ Info 823737 (H24); Visitor Information Centre 823737; HM 822620.

FACILITIES 70 Y 🅥s (£15·00) with pick-up lines lie parallel to the Admiralty bkwtr and in blocks E of Braye Jetty and SW of Toulouse Rock. Orange buoys are for locals only. If >12m LOA, check suitability of 🅥 with HM. ⚓s (£5·00 inc 🚿) as on chartlet.

HM (aka CG & ⊖): ☎822620. mark.gaudion@gov.gg www.sailalderney.com/harbour.html www.alderney.gov.gg

Commercial Quay 🚰 🚿 🗑 ⛴ ⓔ Ⓔ ⚒ (25t).

Little Crabby Hbr Access at the top of the tide only for **Mainbrayce**, VHF Ch 37 *Mainbrayce*, ☎822772, mob 07781 415420: ⛽ 🚰 ⚒ ACA ⛽ ⓟ. Water taxi call *Mainbrayce* Ch M (0800-2359) ☎ as above, £1·50 each way till 2130, £2·50 after 2130.

Alderney SC ☎822758, visitors welcome.

Town (St Anne) ✕ 🛒 ✉ Ⓑ. ✈ direct to Guernsey, Southampton; other connections via Guernsey. **Ferries** via Guernsey to Jersey, Poole and St Malo.

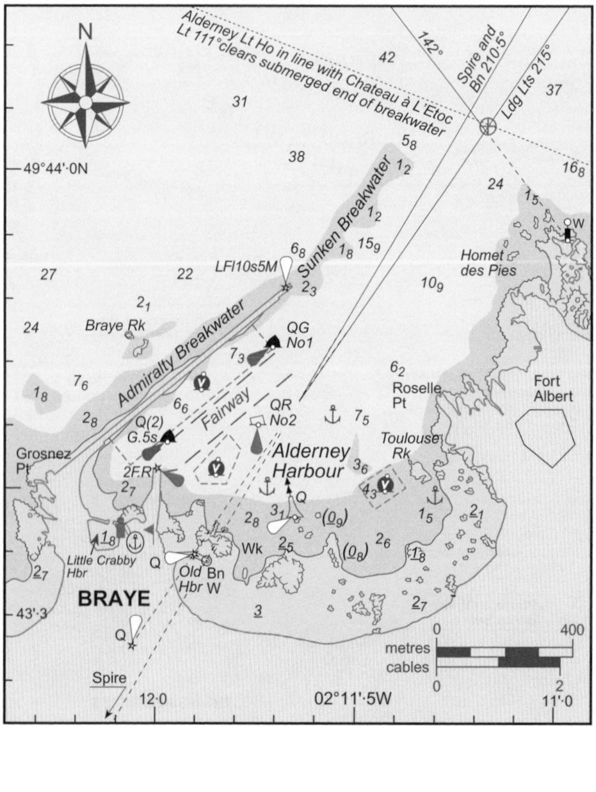

APPROACHES TO GUERNSEY

From the N/NE, The Little Russel Channel (AC 3654, 808) gives the most convenient access to Beaucette Marina and St Peter Port (AC 3140). But it needs care, due to rks which fringe the chan and appr, and the strong tide which sets across the ent.

►*In mid-chan, S of Platte and NW of Bréhon, the NE-going stream begins at HW St Peter Port –0245, and the SW stream at HW St Peter Port +0330, sp rates both 5·25kn which can raise a very steep sea with wind against tide.*◄

With lts on Platte Fougère, Tautenay, Roustel, Platte and Bréhon, plus the 220° ldg lts for St Peter Port, the Little Russel can be navigated day or night in reasonable vis, even at LW.

The Big Russel is wider and easier. In bad weather or poor vis it may be a better approach to St Peter Port, via Lower Heads SCM lt buoy, though may be lumpy on a rising sp tide. From the NW, Doyle Passage, which is aligned 146°/326° off Beaucette, can be used but only by day with local knowledge. From the S or W, the natural route is around St Martin's Pt, keeping 1·5ca ENE of Longue Pierre bcn (LP) and a similar distance off Anfré bcn (A).

In onshore winds keep well clear of the W coast, where in bad weather the sea breaks on dangers up to 4M offshore. But in settled weather it is worth exploring the rock-strewn bays.

9.19.9 LITTLE RUSSEL CHANNEL

See notes above and AC 5604.9/10, 807, 808

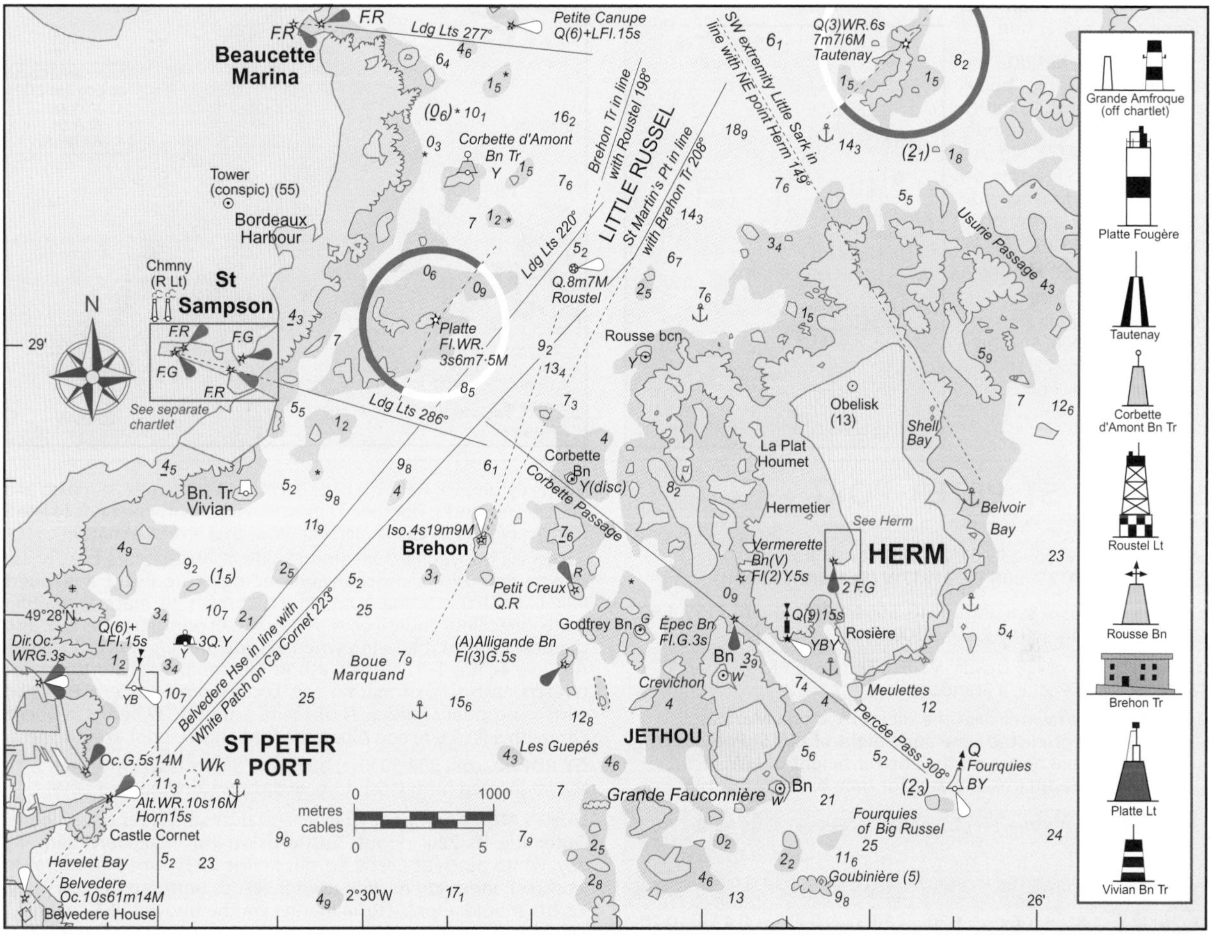

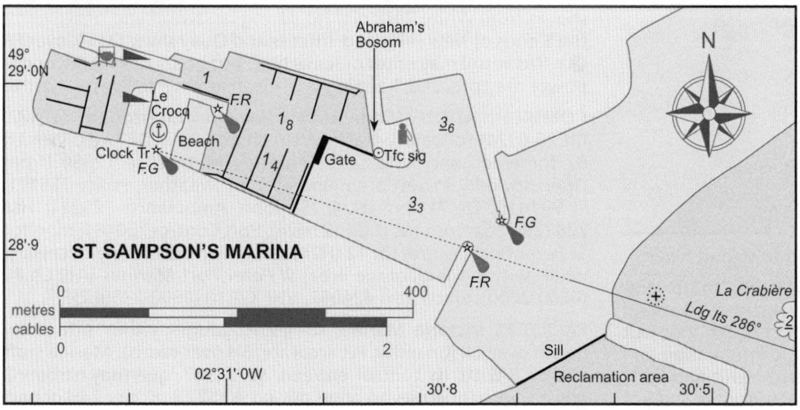

St Sampson's Hbr 49°28'·91N 02°30'·73W. Dries 3·6m. Port of entry. Good shelter but strictly a working hbr. Visit only by prior arrangement for repair work. Entry via lifting flapgate HW -1 to +2. Marina tfc sigs SW cnr Abraham's Bosom: steady ● = ent/exit; Fl ● or steady ● = No ent/exit. WPT 49°28'·70N 02°29'·65W. 2 Chy's NW of hbr conspic. Ldg lts 286°: Front on S Pier, FR; rear on clocktower, FG. Other lts as chartlet and LBW. On S Pier a 360° Fl R above FR (shown landward) = large vessel under way in the hbr; no ent/exit for other craft without Dockmaster's approval on Ch 12 (H24) or ☎01481 720229. Speed limit 6kn. in hbr. Services: (Marine & General 01481 243048, VHF Ch 17) (75t) . by bowser at Abraham's Bosom (E side) must pre-book ☎01481 200800/245858.

9.19.10 BEAUCETTE

Guernsey **49°30'·19N 02°30'·20W**

CHARTS AC 3654, 807, 808, 5604.9; SHOM 7159, 6904, 6903; Navi 1014; Imray C33A, 2500

TIDES –0450 Dover; ML 5·0; Duration 0550. See Facilities and St Peter Port for access times.

SHELTER Excellent in marina. Entry not advised in strong N–SE onshore winds.

NAVIGATION WPT 49°30'·15N 02°28'·85W, 277°/8½ ca to ent. Appr from Little Russel to mid-way between Platte Fougère lt tr (W with B band, 25m) and Roustel lt tr. Pick up the ldg marks/lts, SWM L Fl 10s, a SHM Fl G 5s, 2 PHM buoys Fl R 5s & Fl (3) R 5s, a NCM perch Q and a SHM perch Q (3) G 5s at the ent. Beware stream setting across the appr chan and drying rocks either side.

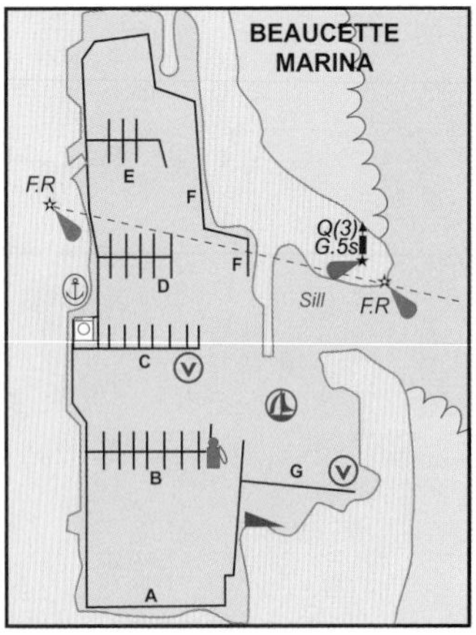

LIGHTS AND MARKS See chartlet and Lights, buoys and waypoints. Petite Canupe is a very spindly SCM lt bcn. 277° ldg lts: both FR. Front, R arrow on W background, stbd side of ent; rear, W arrow on R background, on roof of W bldg, with windsock.

COMMUNICATIONS (Code 01481); Police 725111; ⊜ 245000; St John Ambulance 725211; HM & water taxi VHF Ch 80 (0700-2200).

FACILITIES Marina sill dries $\underline{2}$·37m. 6 Y waiting buoys lie outside and a tide gauge is inside the 8m wide ent channel. For entry sequence and a berth it is essential to pre-call HM with boat details: ☎245000, mob 07781102302. www.beaucettemarina.com info@beaucettemarina.com

115 inc approx 45Ⓥ £2·25, min charge £15·75/boat; £0·75 for <4hrs. on pontoon B, (16t) (12t) ☎247066, bike hire, access ramp is steep @ LW.

Village Basic food shop. Good coastal walks. For further information see St Peter Port; 20 mins by bus 6/6A (but bus stop is nearly a mile away).

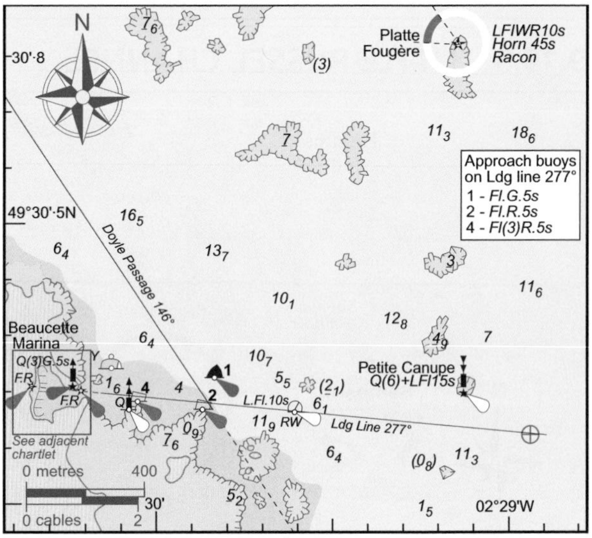

9.19.11 ST PETER PORT

Guernsey

N appr WPT: 49°30'·23N 02°27'·68W (Little Russel)
S appr WPT: 49°25'·00N 02°31'·17W (St Martin's Point)

CHARTS AC 3654, 808, 807, 3140, 5604.10/11; SHOM 7159, 6903, 6904; Navi 1014; Imray C33A, 2500

TIDAL ACCESS –0439 Dover; ML 5·2; Duration 0550
NOTE: St Peter Port is a Standard Port.

To find depth of water over the sill into Victoria Marina:

1. Look up predicted time and height of HW St Peter Port.
2. Enter table below on the line for height of HW.
3. Extract depth (m) of water for time before/after HW.

Ht (m) of HW St Peter Port	Depth of water in metres over the sill (dries $\underline{4}$·2 m)						
	HW	±1hr	±2hrs	±2½hrs	±3hrs	±3½hrs	±4hrs
6·20	1·85	1·67	1·30	1·03	0·75	0·47	0·20
·60	2·25	2·00	1·50	1·13	0·75	0·37	–
7·00	2·65	2·34	1·70	1·23	0·75	0·27	–
·40	3·05	2·67	1·90	1·33	0·75	0·27	–
·80	3·45	3·00	2·10	1·43	0·75	0·07	–
8·20	3·85	3·34	2·30	1·53	0·75	–	–
·60	4·25	3·67	2·50	1·63	0·75	–	–
9·00	4·65	4·00	2·70	1·73	0·75	–	–
·40	5·05	4·34	2·90	1·83	0·75	–	–
·80	5·45	4·67	3·10	1·93	0·75	–	–

SHELTER Good, but Victoria Marina is exposed to strong E'lies.

NAVIGATION WPT 49°27'·82N 02°30'·78W, 227°/0·68M to hbr ent. Offlying dangers, big tidal range and strong tidal streams demand careful navigation. From N the Little Russel is most direct appr, but needs care especially in poor visibility; see Passage Information and Little Russel Channel chartlet. Big Russel between Herm and Sark, passing S of Lower Hds SCM lt buoy, is an easier appr. From W and S of Guernsey, give Les Hanois a wide berth. Beware ferries, shipping and unlit racing marks. Hbr speed limits: 6kn from outer pier hds to line S from New Jetty to Castle pier; 4kn W of that line (see chartlet).

Access via buoyed/lit chan along S side of hbr. Beware busy cruise ship tenders using same chan and landing pontoon at E end Albert Pier (Apr-Oct). Marina boat directs arrivals to marina, waiting pontoon (colour coded) or, N of it, Swan Ⓥ pontoons nos 1–5, also the best options if arriving when marina unmanned (2200-0600). All have , nos 1–4 are walk-ashore (seasonal only). Pontoons for tenders each side of marina ent. Local moorings, centre of hbr, with a secondary fairway N of them. ⚓ prohib. Ⓥ berths in Queen Elizabeth II (in 3·0m) and Albert Marinas only by prior arrangement.

GY RDF beacon, 304·50 kHz, on Castle Bkwtr is synchronised with the co-located horn (15s) to give distance finding; see LBW.

LIGHTS AND MARKS See chartlet and Lights, buoys and waypoints. Outer ldg lts 220°: Front, Castle bkwtr hd; rear, Belvedere. By day, white patch at Castle Cornet in line 223° with Belvedere Ho (conspic). Inner ldg lts 265° are for ferries berthing at New Jetty. Yachts should appr Victoria marina via the buoyed/lit S channel.

Traffic Signals When a large vessel is under way a single FR ● is shown from White Rock pier hd, facing landward and/or seaward; the S ends of New Jetty and Inter-Island Quay show Q Fl Y over FR ● = 'No vessel may enter or leave hbr', but boats <15m LOA under power may proceed, keeping well clear commercial vessel berths.

COMMUNICATIONS (Code 01481) *Guernsey Coastguard* 720672, Ch 20 (H24) for safety traffic, VHF Ch 16/67 for DF brgs, VHF Ch 62 for emergency link calls; Guernsey Met office 12080 (from Guernsey only, lowest premium rate) for weather; Police 725111; ⊜ 741410; Dr 711237 (H24); St John Ambulance 725211; HM 720229; *St Sampson* VHF Ch 12 (H24); Port Control 720481, monitor *St Peter Port Control* Ch **12** (H24) call only if absolutely necessary, when within the pilotage area; *St Peter Port Marinas* VHF Ch 80 (0600-2200); water taxi 424042, VHF Ch 10 (0800-2359LT).

FACILITIES Victoria Marina, sill $\underline{4}$·2m; gauges either side show depth over sill (on entry, PH accurate, SH over-reads). Marina staff and/or R/G tfc lts control ent/exit. ☎725987. guernsey.harbour@gov.gg www.guernseyharbours.gov.gg 400Ⓥ £3·00, per 24H or part

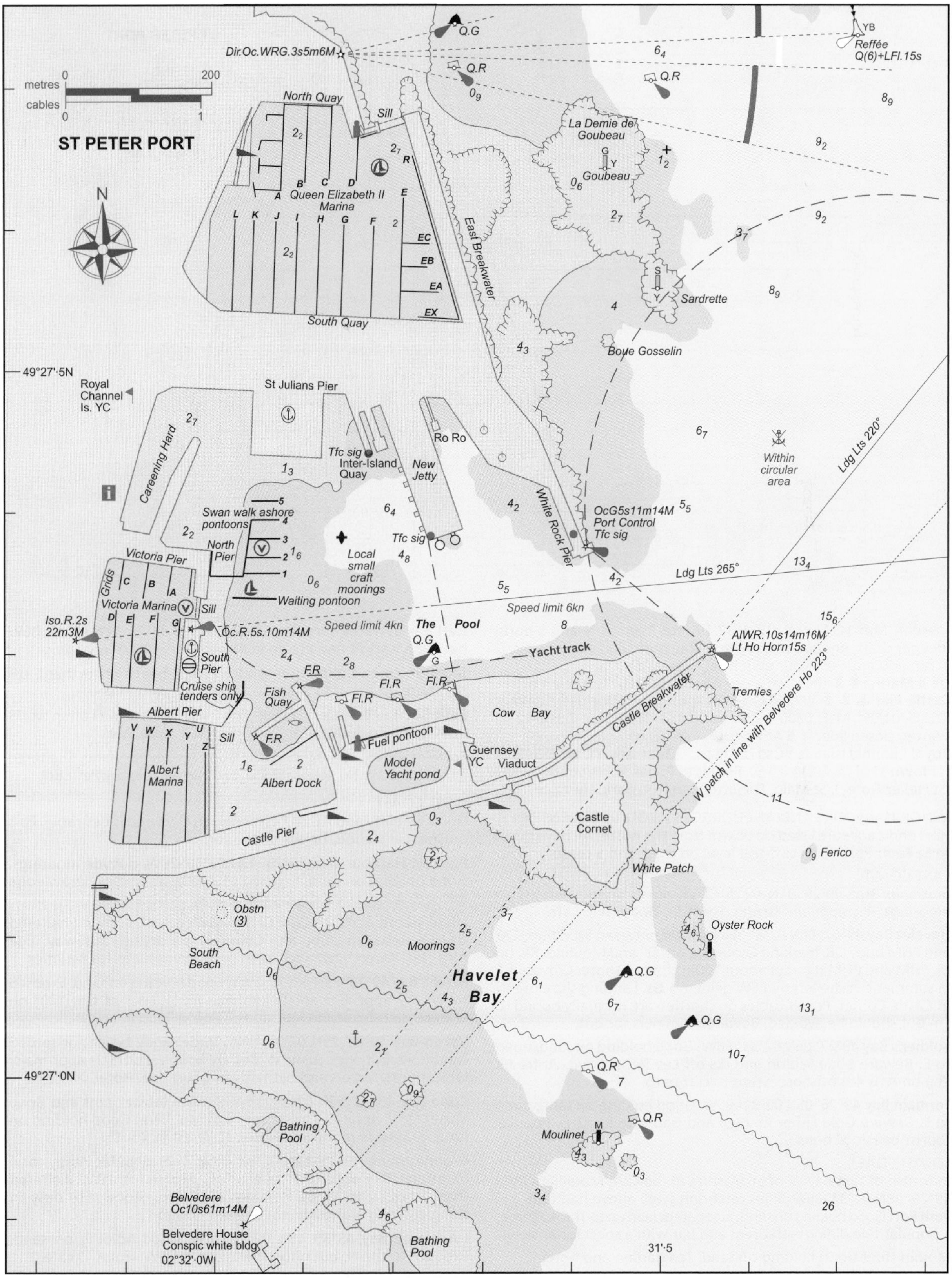
ST PETER PORT
metres 0 200
cables 0 1
N
Dir.Oc.WRG.3s5m6M
Q.G
Q.R
Q.R
Reffée Q(6)+LFl.15s
YB
North Quay
Sill
Queen Elizabeth II Marina
South Quay
East Breakwater
La Demie de Goubeau
Goubeau
Sardrette
Boue Gosseling
49°27'·5N
Royal Channel Is. YC
St Julians Pier
Careening Hard
Tfc sig
Inter-Island Quay
New Jetty
Ro Ro
White Rock Pier
OcG5s11m14M Port Control Tfc sig
Within circular area
Ldg Lts 220°
Ldg Lts 265°
Swan walk ashore pontoons
North Pier
Victoria Pier
Grids
Local small craft moorings
Waiting pontoon
Victoria Marina
Sill
Iso.R.2s 22m3M
Oc.R.5s.10m14M
Speed limit 4kn
The Pool
Speed limit 6kn
Yacht track
AlWR.10s14m16M Lt Ho Horn15s
South Pier
Cruise ship tenders only
Fish Quay
F.R
Fl.R
Cow Bay
Tremies
Castle Breakwater
Albert Pier
Fuel pontoon
Model Yacht pond
Guernsey YC
Viaduct
Albert Marina
Albert Dock
Castle Pier
Castle Cornet
W patch in line with Belvedere Ho 223°
Ferico
White Patch
Obstn (3)
Oyster Rock
South Beach
Moorings
Havelet Bay
49°27'·0N
Bathing Pool
Moulinet
Belvedere Oc10s61m14M
Belvedere House Conspic white bldg
02°32'·0W
31'·5

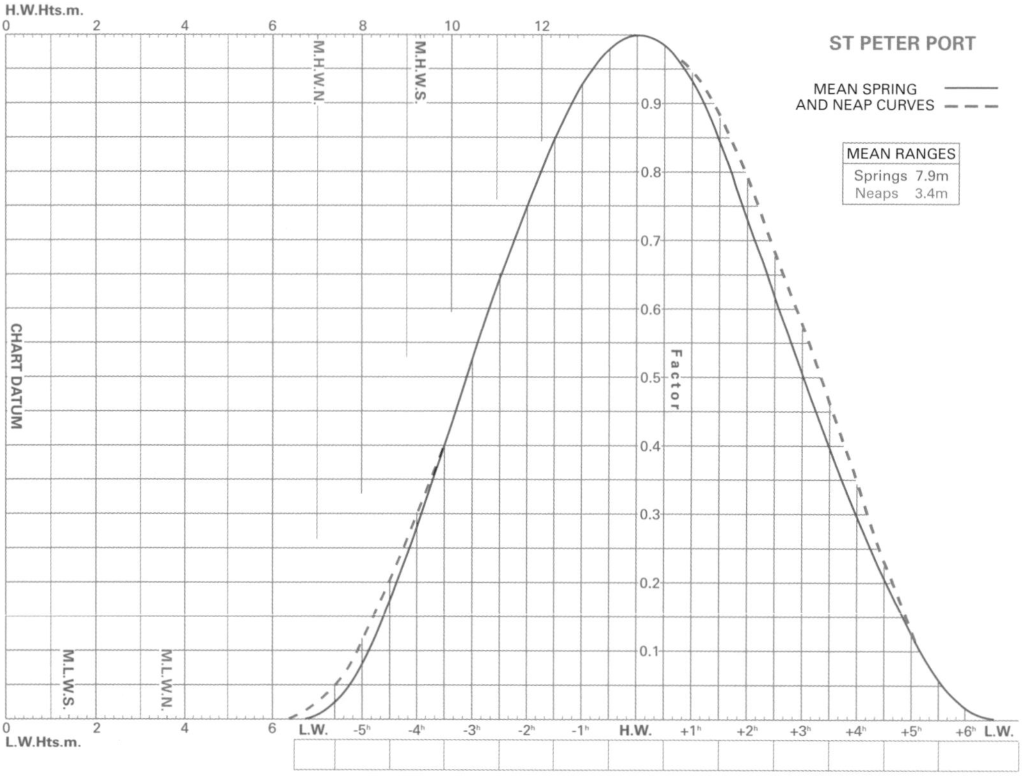

thereof. Max LOA/draft, 12·8m/2.1m but 1·5m at N and S ends, (deeper draft, enquire ahead); max stay normally14 days; ⛴ ♿ ⊡ 🚰 but you must use your own hose; free wi-fi.
QE II Marina 🚹 🚺 times vary, esp Winter, ☎726071, free wi-fi.
Castle Pier 🚰 🚹 🚺 ☎726071 (dries springs, check tides) Summer (01/05–01/09) M–F, 0800–1730. Sat, 0830–1730 Sun, 0830–1230. Winter, closed Sun. ⛽ ACA, 🔧 ⛵ Ⓔ Ⓦ.
Royal Channel Islands YC ☎723154, 🍷. **Guernsey YC** ☎725342, ✕ 🍷. **Town** ✕ 🍷 🛒 ⊡ @ ✉ Ⓑ. Ferries to Poole, Portsmouth, Jersey (St Helier/Gorey), St Malo, Diélette, Carteret, Sark, Herm; ✈.

MINOR HARBOURS AND ANCHORAGES AROUND GUERNSEY

Hbrs and ⚓ages are listed clockwise from the north. All have buses to St Peter Port (from cliff-top level on the E and S coasts).

EAST COAST

Bordeaux Hbr 49°29'·31N 02°30'·37W. Small drying hbr full of moorings. Rky appr and strong crosstide. Open to E. Café.

Havelet Bay 49°27'·06N 02°31'·68W. Enter between SHM buoy QG and PHM buoy QR, marking Oyster Rk, bn 'O', and Moulinet Rk, bn M. SHM and PHM lt buoys about 100m closer inshore. Crowded ⚓ in summer but sheltered in SW gales; no 🅐s. Landing slip close W of Castle Cornet. Power cables on chartlet are normally buried to 1m but should be avoided. Beware swimmers far out.

Soldier's Bay 49°27'·06N 02°31'·68W. Good holding on sand; open to E. Beware Boue Sablon and rks off Les Terres Point. Anfré Rk ($\underline{3}_3$) bn A, is 4ca offshore. Steps to cliff path.

Fermain Bay 49°26'·05N 02°31'·95W. Good holding on sand; open to E. Beware Gold Fisher Rk ($\underline{3{\cdot}6}$) and Gabrielle Rk ($\underline{2{\cdot}1}$). Popular tourist beach. ✕ hotel 🍷.

SOUTH COAST

In centre of first bay W of St Martin's Pt, beware Mouillière ($\underline{8{\cdot}5}$) 49°25'·28N 02°32'·86W. S'lies can bring swell above half tide.

Petit Port Good holding on sand. Steep steps lead up to The Auberge, a popular fine dining restaurant and bar with a spectacular view.

Moulin Huet Good holding on sand. Tea garden and hotel.

Saints Bay Good holding on sand. Below half tide beware uncharted rock in middle and unburied telephone cable on E side. ⚓ outside moorings with trip line. Café, hotel, bar.

Icart Bay Beware Fourquie de la Moye ($\underline{3{\cdot}1}$) 49°25'·28N 02°32'·86W between Icart Pt and Pte de la Moye. Within Icart Bay are:

Jaonnet. Good holding on sand off small beach or further E off rky shore. Exposed to S. No facilities. Cliff path inland.

Petit Bôt Bay Beware drying reef on E side. A short swell often works in. ✕ up hill to hotel, 🍷 ✈ ✉ 🛒. Better ⚓ close W at:

Portelet 49°25'·11N 02°35'·28W. Good holding on sand. Sheltered from N and W. No access inland. Facilities via dinghy/Petit Bôt.

WEST COAST

Good visibility and AC 807 essential; an E'ly wind is desirable. Pass outside Les Hanois, unless bound for:

Portelet Harbour ⚓ at 49°26'·40N 02°40'·26W, outside moorings. Good holding on sand. Exposed to W. Rky appr; local knowledge advised. Avoid small drying stone quay. ✕ hotel 🍷.

Lihou Island ⚓ 49°27'·88N 02°39'·46W, off NE corner. Sheltered from E. Between Lihou and Guernsey is a drying causeway. Tide runs fast. Avoid bird sanctuaries on offlying islets. No facilities.

Perelle Bay 49°28'·23N 02°38'·89W. Good holding on sand. Exposed to W; rky appr. Beware Colombelle Rk ($\underline{1}_5$) NE of brg 128° on cement mill. ⚓ outside moorings. 🍷 hotel Ⓟ Ⓓ.

Vazon Bay 49°28'·29N 02°37'·09W. Wide sandy beach for settled conditions, but open to the W. Beware Boue Vazon ($\underline{3}$) in appr, many lobster pots, surfers and bathers. Long surf line. Hotel, ✕ 🍷.

Cobo Bay 49°28'·66N 02°36'·33W. Beware lobster pots and Boue Vazon ($\underline{3}$) in appr. Rky appr from S of Moulière. Good holding on sand; ⚓ outside moorings. Hotel, ✕ 🍷 ✉ 🛒 Ⓟ Ⓓ.

Grande Havre 49°30'·11N 02°33'·09W. Very popular, many local moorings. Rky appr 171° as charted; exposed to NW, sheltered from S'lies. ⚓ to W of Hommet de Grève. Stone slip, busy in summer; lying alongside not advised. Hotel 🍷.

L'Ancresse Bay 49°30'·45N 02°31'·38W. Good holding on sand. Exposed to the N, but good shelter from S/SW. Hotel 🍷 café.

Fontenelle Bay 49°30'·48N 02°30'·69W. Good holding on sand. Exposed to the N. Beware drying rks on E of ent. No facilities.

STANDARD TIME (UT)
For Summer Time add ONE hour in **non-shaded areas**

ST PETER PORT LAT 49°27′N LONG 2°32′W

TIMES AND HEIGHTS OF HIGH AND LOW WATERS

Dates in red are SPRINGS
Dates in blue are NEAPS

YEAR **2018**

JANUARY

Date	Day	Time	m
1	M	0530	9.1
		1201	1.5
		1800	9.2
2	TU	0024	1.3
		0622	9.6
		1254	1.0
		○ 1851	9.5
3	W	0115	1.0
		0711	9.8
		1344	0.8
		1940	9.6
4	TH	0202	0.9
		0758	9.9
		1431	0.7
		2027	9.6
5	F	0248	1.0
		0844	9.8
		1517	0.9
		2112	9.3
6	SA	0333	1.4
		0928	9.4
		1601	1.4
		2157	8.8
7	SU	0417	1.9
		1013	8.8
		1646	1.9
		2242	8.3
8	M	0502	2.5
		1100	8.2
		1734	2.6
		◑ 2331	7.7
9	TU	0553	3.1
		1153	7.6
		1827	3.1
10	W	0030	7.3
		0653	3.5
		1257	7.2
		1930	3.5
11	TH	0143	7.0
		0806	3.7
		1412	7.0
		2043	3.6
12	F	0256	7.1
		0919	3.6
		1522	7.1
		2149	3.4
13	SA	0355	7.4
		1018	3.2
		1617	7.4
		2242	3.1
14	SU	0443	7.8
		1107	2.9
		1704	7.8
		2327	2.7
15	M	0525	8.2
		1149	2.5
		1746	8.1
16	TU	0006	2.4
		0604	8.6
		1228	2.2
		1825	8.4
17	W	0044	2.2
		0642	8.8
		1305	2.0
		● 1902	8.6
18	TH	0118	2.0
		0718	8.9
		1340	1.9
		1937	8.6
19	F	0152	2.0
		0752	8.9
		1414	1.8
		2011	8.6
20	SA	0224	2.0
		0824	8.8
		1447	1.9
		2043	8.5
21	SU	0256	2.2
		0856	8.6
		1519	2.1
		2115	8.3
22	M	0328	2.4
		0930	8.4
		1553	2.3
		2150	8.1
23	TU	0404	2.7
		1008	8.1
		1631	2.6
		2230	7.8
24	W	0446	2.9
		1054	7.8
		1716	2.9
		◐ 2320	7.6
25	TH	0539	3.2
		1151	7.5
		1815	3.1
26	F	0023	7.4
		0649	3.4
		1304	7.4
		1931	3.2
27	SA	0144	7.3
		0818	3.3
		1429	7.4
		2058	3.0
28	SU	0308	7.7
		0942	2.8
		1547	7.8
		2214	2.6
29	M	0419	8.2
		1051	2.2
		1653	8.4
		2317	2.0
30	TU	0518	8.8
		1151	1.6
		1751	8.9
31	W	0013	1.4
		0611	9.4
		1245	1.0
		○ 1842	9.4

FEBRUARY

Date	Day	Time	m
1	TH	0105	1.0
		0700	9.8
		1334	0.6
		1930	9.7
2	F	0152	0.7
		0746	10.0
		1419	0.5
		2014	9.7
3	SA	0235	0.7
		0830	10.0
		1501	0.6
		2055	9.6
4	SU	0316	0.9
		0910	9.6
		1541	1.0
		2134	9.2
5	M	0354	1.4
		0948	9.1
		1618	1.6
		2211	8.6
6	TU	0431	2.0
		1026	8.4
		1655	2.3
		2248	7.9
7	W	0509	2.7
		1105	7.7
		1734	3.0
		◑ 2330	7.3
8	TH	0554	3.4
		1153	7.1
		1823	3.6
9	F	0026	6.8
		0656	3.8
		1302	6.7
		1930	3.9
10	SA	0151	6.6
		0816	3.9
		1434	6.6
		2055	3.9
11	SU	0318	6.9
		0940	3.7
		1549	6.9
		2210	3.6
12	M	0417	7.3
		1040	3.2
		1642	7.4
		2303	3.1
13	TU	0503	7.8
		1127	2.7
		1726	7.8
		2346	2.6
14	W	0545	8.3
		1208	2.2
		1806	8.3
15	TH	0025	2.2
		0623	8.7
		1247	1.9
		● 1844	8.6
16	F	0102	1.8
		0700	8.9
		1323	1.6
		1920	8.8
17	SA	0136	1.6
		0735	9.1
		1358	1.5
		1954	8.9
18	SU	0210	1.6
		0808	9.1
		1430	1.4
		2026	8.9
19	M	0241	1.6
		0840	9.0
		1502	1.6
		2057	8.8
20	TU	0313	1.8
		0913	8.8
		1533	1.8
		2130	8.5
21	W	0345	2.1
		0948	8.5
		1608	2.1
		2207	8.2
22	TH	0423	2.4
		1030	8.1
		1649	2.6
		2251	7.8
23	F	0510	2.9
		1122	7.6
		1742	3.0
		◐ 2349	7.4
24	SA	0615	3.3
		1232	7.2
		1857	3.3
25	SU	0110	7.2
		0750	3.4
		1408	7.1
		2035	3.3
26	M	0249	7.4
		0929	3.0
		1538	7.5
		2202	2.8
27	TU	0407	7.9
		1042	2.3
		1645	8.2
		2308	2.1
28	W	0508	8.6
		1140	1.6
		1741	8.8

MARCH

Date	Day	Time	m
1	TH	0002	1.5
		0559	9.3
		1232	1.0
		1829	9.3
2	F	0051	0.9
		0646	9.8
		1318	0.5
		○ 1913	9.7
3	SA	0135	0.6
		0729	10.0
		1400	0.4
		1955	9.8
4	SU	0216	0.5
		0810	10.0
		1439	0.5
		2032	9.7
5	M	0253	0.7
		0847	9.7
		1514	0.9
		2107	9.3
6	TU	0327	1.2
		0920	9.2
		1546	1.5
		2138	8.8
7	W	0358	1.8
		0952	8.5
		1616	2.2
		2208	8.1
8	TH	0429	2.5
		1024	7.8
		1646	2.9
		2241	7.5
9	F	0504	3.2
		1102	7.1
		1724	3.6
		◑ 2324	6.9
10	SA	0557	3.8
		1158	6.6
		1826	4.1
11	SU	0035	6.5
		0717	4.1
		1332	6.3
		1954	4.2
12	M	0225	6.5
		0849	3.9
		1513	6.6
		2128	3.9
13	TU	0345	7.0
		1006	3.4
		1614	7.1
		2232	3.3
14	W	0436	7.5
		1058	2.8
		1700	7.7
		2319	2.7
15	TH	0519	8.1
		1141	2.2
		1742	8.2
		2359	2.2
16	F	0559	8.6
		1221	1.8
		1820	8.6
17	SA	0038	1.7
		0637	9.0
		1259	1.4
		● 1857	9.0
18	SU	0115	1.4
		0713	9.2
		1335	1.2
		1931	9.2
19	M	0149	1.2
		0747	9.4
		1409	1.1
		2004	9.2
20	TU	0223	1.2
		0820	9.3
		1441	1.2
		2037	9.1
21	W	0255	1.3
		0854	9.1
		1514	1.4
		2110	8.9
22	TH	0328	1.7
		0931	8.8
		1549	1.9
		2147	8.5
23	F	0406	2.1
		1012	8.2
		1629	2.4
		2231	8.0
24	SA	0452	2.7
		1104	7.6
		1722	3.0
		◐ 2328	7.5
25	SU	0558	3.2
		1216	7.1
		1838	3.4
26	M	0051	7.1
		0738	3.4
		1358	7.0
		2024	3.4
27	TU	0236	7.3
		0920	3.0
		1529	7.5
		2151	2.9
28	W	0354	7.9
		1029	2.3
		1633	8.1
		2253	2.2
29	TH	0452	8.6
		1124	1.6
		1724	8.8
		2344	1.5
30	F	0541	9.2
		1211	1.0
		1809	9.3
31	SA	0030	1.0
		0626	9.6
		1256	0.7
		○ 1851	9.6

APRIL

Date	Day	Time	m
1	SU	0113	0.7
		0707	9.8
		1336	0.6
		1930	9.7
2	M	0152	0.7
		0746	9.7
		1412	0.7
		2005	9.6
3	TU	0227	0.8
		0820	9.5
		1445	1.1
		2037	9.3
4	W	0259	1.2
		0852	9.0
		1514	1.6
		2106	8.8
5	TH	0327	1.8
		0921	8.5
		1541	2.2
		2135	8.2
6	F	0355	2.4
		0951	7.9
		1607	2.9
		2205	7.7
7	SA	0426	3.0
		1026	7.2
		1638	3.5
		2242	7.1
8	SU	0510	3.6
		1114	6.7
		1730	4.0
		◑ 2338	6.6
9	M	0628	4.0
		1234	6.3
		1902	4.3
10	TU	0118	6.4
		0758	4.0
		1420	6.4
		2034	4.0
11	W	0256	6.8
		0918	3.5
		1534	6.9
		2148	3.5
12	TH	0357	7.3
		1017	2.9
		1625	7.5
		2241	2.9
13	F	0444	7.9
		1105	2.3
		1708	8.1
		2325	2.3
14	SA	0526	8.5
		1148	1.8
		1749	8.6
15	SU	0007	1.7
		0606	8.9
		1229	1.3
		1827	9.0
16	M	0047	1.3
		0645	9.3
		1307	1.0
		● 1904	9.3
17	TU	0125	1.0
		0723	9.5
		1344	0.9
		1940	9.4
18	W	0202	1.0
		0800	9.5
		1420	1.0
		2016	9.4
19	TH	0238	1.1
		0838	9.3
		1457	1.3
		2053	9.2
20	F	0315	1.4
		0918	8.9
		1535	1.7
		2134	8.7
21	SA	0356	1.9
		1002	8.3
		1618	2.3
		2220	8.2
22	SU	0447	2.5
		1057	7.7
		1713	2.9
		◐ 2319	7.6
23	M	0556	3.0
		1211	7.2
		1832	3.4
24	TU	0041	7.3
		0731	3.2
		1347	7.1
		2011	3.4
25	W	0217	7.4
		0902	2.9
		1510	7.5
		2131	2.9
26	TH	0332	7.8
		1007	2.3
		1610	8.1
		2231	2.3
27	F	0429	8.4
		1100	1.8
		1700	8.6
		2320	1.7
28	SA	0517	8.9
		1146	1.4
		1744	9.0
29	SU	0005	1.3
		0601	9.2
		1229	1.1
		1824	9.3
30	M	0047	1.1
		0642	9.3
		1308	1.0
		○ 1902	9.4

Chart Datum is 5·06 metres below Ordnance Datum (Local). HAT is 10·3 metres above Chart Datum.

STANDARD TIME (UT)
For Summer Time add ONE hour in **non-shaded areas**

ST PETER PORT LAT 49°27'N LONG 2°32'W

TIMES AND HEIGHTS OF HIGH AND LOW WATERS

Dates in red are SPRINGS
Dates in blue are NEAPS

YEAR **2018**

MAY

Date	Day	Time	m
1	TU	0125	1.1
		0719	9.3
		1344	1.2
		1937	9.3
2	W	0200	1.2
		0754	9.1
		1416	1.4
		2009	9.1
3	TH	0231	1.5
		0825	8.8
		1444	1.8
		2038	8.7
4	F	0300	1.9
		0855	8.4
		1511	2.3
		2107	8.3
5	SA	0329	2.4
		0926	7.9
		1538	2.8
		2138	7.8
6	SU	0400	2.9
		1001	7.4
		1610	3.4
		2215	7.3
7	M	0440	3.4
		1045	6.9
		1656	3.8
		2304	6.9
8	TU	0543	3.7
		1149	6.6
		1810	4.1
		◑	
9	W	0017	6.7
		0707	3.8
		1317	6.6
		1939	4.0
10	TH	0149	6.8
		0824	3.5
		1436	6.9
		2053	3.6
11	F	0302	7.2
		0928	3.0
		1536	7.4
		2154	3.0
12	SA	0358	7.7
		1021	2.5
		1626	8.0
		2245	2.4
13	SU	0447	8.3
		1109	1.9
		1712	8.5
		2332	1.9
14	M	0532	8.8
		1155	1.5
		1755	9.0
15	TU	0017	1.4
		0616	9.2
		1239	1.1
		● 1836	9.3
16	W	0101	1.1
		0659	9.4
		1321	1.0
		1918	9.5
17	TH	0143	0.9
		0742	9.5
		1403	1.0
		1959	9.5
18	F	0225	1.0
		0825	9.3
		1444	1.2
		2041	9.3
19	SA	0308	1.2
		0909	9.0
		1527	1.6
		2126	8.9
20	SU	0354	1.7
		0958	8.5
		1615	2.2
		2215	8.4
21	M	0447	2.2
		1054	7.9
		1711	2.7
		2314	7.9
22	TU	0554	2.7
		1202	7.5
		1823	3.1
		◐	
23	W	0026	7.6
		0713	2.9
		1322	7.4
		1946	3.2
24	TH	0148	7.5
		0832	2.8
		1438	7.6
		2101	2.9
25	F	0301	7.7
		0937	2.5
		1539	7.9
		2201	2.5
26	SA	0359	8.1
		1030	2.2
		1630	8.3
		2252	2.2
27	SU	0450	8.4
		1117	1.9
		1715	8.6
		2338	1.8
28	M	0535	8.6
		1200	1.7
		1757	8.9
29	TU	0019	1.6
		0616	8.8
		1240	1.6
		○ 1835	9.0
30	W	0058	1.6
		0654	8.8
		1316	1.7
		1911	9.0
31	TH	0134	1.6
		0729	8.7
		1349	1.8
		1944	8.9

JUNE

Date	Day	Time	m
1	F	0206	1.8
		0803	8.5
		1419	2.1
		2016	8.6
2	SA	0237	2.0
		0835	8.3
		1448	2.4
		2047	8.3
3	SU	0308	2.4
		0908	7.9
		1518	2.8
		2119	8.0
4	M	0341	2.7
		0942	7.6
		1552	3.1
		2155	7.6
5	TU	0419	3.1
		1023	7.3
		1633	3.5
		2238	7.3
6	W	0508	3.4
		1114	7.0
		1727	3.7
		◑ 2335	7.1
7	TH	0613	3.5
		1218	6.9
		1840	3.8
8	F	0044	7.0
		0726	3.4
		1331	7.0
		1956	3.6
9	SA	0159	7.2
		0834	3.1
		1440	7.4
		2104	3.2
10	SU	0307	7.6
		0936	2.7
		1540	7.8
		2203	2.6
11	M	0405	8.1
		1031	2.2
		1634	8.4
		2258	2.1
12	TU	0459	8.5
		1123	1.7
		1724	8.8
		2350	1.6
13	W	0551	9.0
		1214	1.4
		1813	9.2
		●	
14	TH	0039	1.2
		0640	9.3
		1303	1.1
		1859	9.5
15	F	0128	0.9
		0728	9.4
		1350	1.0
		1946	9.6
16	SA	0216	0.9
		0816	9.4
		1436	1.1
		2032	9.5
17	SU	0303	1.0
		0903	9.2
		1522	1.4
		2119	9.2
18	M	0351	1.3
		0952	8.8
		1611	1.8
		2208	8.8
19	TU	0443	1.8
		1044	8.3
		1703	2.3
		2301	8.3
20	W	0539	2.3
		1142	7.9
		1802	2.8
		◐	
21	TH	0001	7.9
		0642	2.7
		1247	7.5
		1909	3.1
22	F	0110	7.6
		0751	2.9
		1357	7.4
		2021	3.1
23	SA	0222	7.5
		0858	2.9
		1503	7.6
		2126	3.0
24	SU	0326	7.6
		0957	2.7
		1559	7.8
		2222	2.7
25	M	0421	7.8
		1048	2.5
		1647	8.1
		2310	2.4
26	TU	0509	8.1
		1133	2.3
		1731	8.4
		2354	2.2
27	W	0552	8.3
		1214	2.2
		1811	8.6
28	TH	0034	2.0
		0632	8.4
		1252	2.1
		○ 1848	8.7
29	F	0111	1.9
		0709	8.5
		1327	2.1
		1924	8.7
30	SA	0146	1.9
		0745	8.4
		1400	2.1
		1958	8.6

JULY

Date	Day	Time	m
1	SU	0219	2.0
		0819	8.3
		1431	2.3
		2030	8.5
2	M	0252	2.2
		0852	8.1
		1503	2.5
		2102	8.2
3	TU	0325	2.4
		0925	7.9
		1535	2.8
		2136	8.0
4	W	0359	2.7
		1001	7.7
		1611	3.0
		2214	7.7
5	TH	0439	3.0
		1042	7.4
		1654	3.3
		2300	7.5
6	F	0527	3.2
		1133	7.3
		1749	3.4
		◑ 2357	7.3
7	SA	0629	3.3
		1234	7.2
		1857	3.5
8	SU	0104	7.3
		0740	3.2
		1346	7.3
		2014	3.3
9	M	0219	7.5
		0852	2.9
		1457	7.7
		2126	2.8
10	TU	0330	7.8
		0958	2.5
		1602	8.1
		2230	2.3
11	W	0434	8.3
		1059	2.1
		1701	8.6
		2330	1.8
12	TH	0532	8.7
		1156	1.6
		1755	9.1
13	F	0025	1.3
		0626	9.1
		1250	1.2
		● 1846	9.5
14	SA	0118	0.9
		0718	9.4
		1340	0.9
		1936	9.8
15	SU	0208	0.7
		0807	9.5
		1428	0.9
		2023	9.8
16	M	0255	0.7
		0854	9.5
		1514	1.0
		2109	9.6
17	TU	0341	1.0
		0939	9.2
		1559	1.4
		2153	9.2
18	W	0427	1.4
		1024	8.7
		1644	1.9
		2239	8.6
19	TH	0513	2.0
		1112	8.1
		1731	2.5
		◐ 2328	8.0
20	F	0604	2.6
		1204	7.6
		1826	3.0
21	SA	0025	7.5
		0702	3.1
		1308	7.2
		1930	3.4
22	SU	0135	7.1
		0811	3.4
		1420	7.1
		2044	3.5
23	M	0251	7.1
		0921	3.4
		1527	7.3
		2152	3.3
24	TU	0355	7.3
		1021	3.2
		1622	7.6
		2246	3.0
25	W	0447	7.6
		1110	2.9
		1708	8.0
		2332	2.6
26	TH	0532	7.9
		1153	2.6
		1750	8.3
27	F	0014	2.3
		0612	8.2
		1233	2.3
		○ 1829	8.6
28	SA	0052	2.0
		0651	8.4
		1309	2.1
		1906	8.7
29	SU	0128	1.9
		0727	8.5
		1343	2.0
		1941	8.8
30	M	0202	1.9
		0801	8.5
		1415	2.0
		2014	8.7
31	TU	0235	1.9
		0834	8.5
		1446	2.2
		2045	8.6

AUGUST

Date	Day	Time	m
1	W	0306	2.1
		0904	8.3
		1517	2.4
		2116	8.4
2	TH	0337	2.3
		0936	8.1
		1549	2.6
		2150	8.1
3	F	0411	2.6
		1012	7.9
		1625	2.9
		2230	7.9
4	SA	0451	2.8
		1056	7.6
		1710	3.1
		◑ 2319	7.6
5	SU	0543	3.1
		1151	7.4
		1810	3.3
6	M	0023	7.3
		0652	3.3
		1302	7.3
		1931	3.4
7	TU	0143	7.3
		0816	3.2
		1425	7.5
		2059	3.1
8	W	0307	7.6
		0936	2.9
		1541	7.9
		2214	2.6
9	TH	0420	8.1
		1044	2.3
		1646	8.5
		2318	1.9
10	F	0521	8.6
		1144	1.7
		1743	9.1
11	SA	0015	1.3
		0616	9.2
		1239	1.2
		● 1835	9.6
12	SU	0107	0.8
		0706	9.6
		1329	0.8
		1923	10.0
13	M	0155	0.5
		0753	9.8
		1415	0.6
		2008	10.1
14	TU	0240	0.5
		0836	9.7
		1457	0.7
		2051	9.9
15	W	0322	0.7
		0918	9.4
		1538	1.1
		2131	9.4
16	TH	0401	1.3
		0957	8.9
		1617	1.7
		2210	8.8
17	F	0440	2.0
		1036	8.3
		1656	2.4
		2249	8.1
18	SA	0521	2.7
		1117	7.6
		1739	3.1
		◐ 2335	7.3
19	SU	0609	3.4
		1210	7.1
		1836	3.7
20	M	0038	6.8
		0714	3.9
		1328	6.7
		1952	3.9
21	TU	0210	6.6
		0838	4.0
		1455	6.8
		2120	3.8
22	W	0333	6.8
		0956	3.7
		1559	7.2
		2225	3.4
23	TH	0428	7.3
		1049	3.2
		1648	7.7
		2312	2.9
24	F	0512	7.8
		1133	2.8
		1729	8.2
		2353	2.4
25	SA	0552	8.2
		1212	2.3
		1808	8.6
26	SU	0031	2.0
		0630	8.5
		1249	2.0
		○ 1845	8.9
27	M	0108	1.8
		0706	8.8
		1323	1.8
		1920	9.0
28	TU	0142	1.6
		0740	8.8
		1356	1.8
		1953	9.0
29	W	0213	1.6
		0811	8.8
		1426	1.8
		2024	9.0
30	TH	0244	1.7
		0841	8.7
		1456	2.0
		2054	8.8
31	F	0313	2.0
		0911	8.5
		1526	2.2
		2126	8.5

Chart Datum is 5·06 metres below Ordnance Datum (Local). HAT is 10·3 metres above Chart Datum.

STANDARD TIME (UT)
For Summer Time add ONE hour in **non-shaded areas**

ST PETER PORT LAT 49°27′N LONG 2°32′W

TIMES AND HEIGHTS OF HIGH AND LOW WATERS

Dates in red are SPRINGS
Dates in blue are NEAPS

YEAR **2018**

SEPTEMBER

Date	Day	Time	m	Time	m	Time	m	Time	m
1	SA	0345	2.3	0945	8.2	1600	2.5	2203	8.2
2	SU	0422	2.7	1025	7.9	1641	2.9	2250	7.7
3	M	0510	3.1	1118	7.5	1738	3.3	◑ 2352	7.3
4	TU	0618	3.5	1230	7.2	1902	3.6		
5	W	0120	7.1	0754	3.5	1406	7.3	2046	3.3
6	TH	0259	7.4	0926	3.1	1531	7.8	2208	2.7
7	F	0414	8.0	1036	2.5	1637	8.5	2310	1.9
8	SA	0512	8.7	1134	1.7	1732	9.2		
9	SU	0003	1.2	0603	9.3	1225	1.1	● 1820	9.7
10	M	0052	0.7	0649	9.7	1312	0.7	1906	10.1
11	TU	0137	0.4	0733	9.9	1355	0.5	1948	10.1
12	W	0218	0.4	0813	9.9	1435	0.7	2027	9.9
13	TH	0256	0.8	0850	9.6	1512	1.1	2104	9.5
14	F	0331	1.3	0925	9.0	1546	1.7	2137	8.8
15	SA	0404	2.1	0957	8.4	1619	2.4	2210	8.1
16	SU	0436	2.9	1031	7.7	1655	3.2	◐ 2247	7.3
17	M	0515	3.6	1114	7.0	1744	3.8	2340	6.7
18	TU	0616	4.2	1225	6.6	1901	4.2		
19	W	0117	6.3	0747	4.4	1416	6.6	2039	4.1
20	TH	0306	6.6	0925	4.1	1532	7.0	2157	3.6
21	F	0404	7.1	1024	3.5	1622	7.6	2246	3.0
22	SA	0447	7.7	1107	2.9	1704	8.1	2327	2.5
23	SU	0526	8.2	1146	2.4	1743	8.6		
24	M	0005	2.0	0603	8.7	1223	2.0	1819	9.0
25	TU	0041	1.7	0639	9.0	1258	1.7	○ 1855	9.2
26	W	0116	1.4	0713	9.1	1331	1.5	1928	9.3
27	TH	0148	1.4	0745	9.2	1404	1.5	2000	9.3
28	F	0220	1.5	0816	9.1	1435	1.7	2032	9.1
29	SA	0251	1.7	0848	8.9	1506	1.9	2106	8.8
30	SU	0323	2.1	0922	8.5	1541	2.3	2143	8.3

OCTOBER

Date	Day	Time	m	Time	m	Time	m	Time	m
1	M	0400	2.6	1003	8.1	1623	2.8	2230	7.8
2	TU	0449	3.2	1056	7.6	1721	3.3	◑ 2335	7.2
3	W	0559	3.6	1213	7.2	1851	3.6		
4	TH	0112	7.0	0745	3.7	1356	7.3	2042	3.3
5	F	0255	7.4	0919	3.2	1522	7.8	2158	2.6
6	SA	0404	8.1	1024	2.5	1623	8.5	2255	1.9
7	SU	0457	8.8	1117	1.8	1714	9.2	2345	1.3
8	M	0544	9.4	1205	1.2	1801	9.7		
9	TU	0030	0.8	0627	9.7	1250	0.8	● 1844	10.0
10	W	0113	0.7	0708	9.9	1331	0.7	1924	10.0
11	TH	0152	0.7	0746	9.8	1409	0.9	2001	9.7
12	F	0227	1.1	0821	9.5	1444	1.3	2035	9.3
13	SA	0259	1.6	0853	9.0	1516	1.8	2106	8.7
14	SU	0328	2.3	0922	8.4	1545	2.5	2137	8.0
15	M	0356	3.0	0954	7.8	1617	3.2	2211	7.4
16	TU	0427	3.7	1031	7.2	1659	3.8	◐ 2256	6.8
17	W	0519	4.2	1129	6.7	1813	4.2		
18	TH	0017	6.4	0653	4.5	1316	6.5	1946	4.3
19	F	0217	6.5	0832	4.3	1449	6.8	2111	3.8
20	SA	0327	7.0	0944	3.7	1546	7.4	2207	3.2
21	SU	0413	7.6	1031	3.1	1630	8.0	2251	2.6
22	M	0453	8.2	1112	2.6	1710	8.5	2331	2.1
23	TU	0531	8.7	1150	2.1	1749	8.9		
24	W	0009	1.7	0608	9.0	1228	1.7	○ 1826	9.2
25	TH	0046	1.4	0644	9.3	1305	1.5	1902	9.4
26	F	0122	1.3	0719	9.4	1341	1.4	1937	9.4
27	SA	0157	1.4	0753	9.3	1416	1.5	2013	9.3
28	SU	0231	1.6	0829	9.1	1451	1.7	2051	8.9
29	M	0308	2.0	0907	8.8	1530	2.2	2132	8.4
30	TU	0348	2.5	0951	8.3	1616	2.7	2222	7.9
31	W	0440	3.1	1047	7.8	1718	3.2	◑ 2330	7.3

NOVEMBER

Date	Day	Time	m	Time	m	Time	m	Time	m
1	TH	0553	3.6	1204	7.4	1848	3.5		
2	F	0105	7.2	0734	3.6	1341	7.4	2026	3.2
3	SA	0238	7.5	0901	3.2	1501	7.9	2138	2.6
4	SU	0344	8.1	1004	2.6	1602	8.5	2234	2.0
5	M	0435	8.7	1056	2.0	1652	9.0	2322	1.6
6	TU	0520	9.2	1142	1.5	1738	9.3		
7	W	0006	1.3	0602	9.5	1226	1.2	● 1820	9.5
8	TH	0047	1.1	0642	9.6	1306	1.2	1900	9.5
9	F	0125	1.2	0719	9.6	1344	1.3	1936	9.4
10	SA	0200	1.5	0753	9.3	1418	1.6	2010	9.0
11	SU	0230	1.9	0825	9.0	1449	2.0	2041	8.6
12	M	0259	2.4	0855	8.5	1519	2.5	2112	8.1
13	TU	0326	3.0	0926	8.0	1551	3.1	2146	7.5
14	W	0357	3.5	1002	7.4	1629	3.6	2228	7.0
15	TH	0440	4.0	1051	7.0	1727	4.0	◐ 2328	6.6
16	F	0554	4.4	1207	6.7	1849	4.1		
17	SA	0101	6.6	0726	4.3	1341	6.8	2008	3.9
18	SU	0226	6.9	0843	4.0	1452	7.2	2113	3.4
19	M	0325	7.4	0942	3.4	1545	7.7	2206	2.9
20	TU	0412	7.9	1031	2.8	1631	8.2	2252	2.4
21	W	0455	8.5	1115	2.3	1714	8.7	2335	1.9
22	TH	0536	8.9	1158	1.8	1756	9.1		
23	F	0017	1.6	0615	9.3	1240	1.5	○ 1837	9.3
24	SA	0058	1.4	0655	9.5	1321	1.3	1918	9.4
25	SU	0138	1.3	0735	9.5	1402	1.3	2000	9.3
26	M	0219	1.5	0816	9.4	1444	1.5	2042	9.1
27	TU	0300	1.8	0859	9.1	1528	1.8	2128	8.6
28	W	0345	2.3	0947	8.6	1617	2.3	2220	8.1
29	TH	0438	2.8	1043	8.1	1718	2.8	2324	7.7
30	F	0546	3.2	1152	7.7	1833	3.1	◑	

DECEMBER

Date	Day	Time	m	Time	m	Time	m	Time	m
1	SA	0042	7.4	0709	3.4	1313	7.6	1955	3.1
2	SU	0205	7.5	0830	3.2	1430	7.8	2107	2.8
3	M	0313	7.9	0936	2.8	1533	8.1	2206	2.4
4	TU	0408	8.3	1030	2.4	1627	8.5	2256	2.1
5	W	0455	8.7	1118	2.0	1714	8.7	2341	1.9
6	TH	0538	9.0	1202	1.8	1758	8.9		
7	F	0022	1.7	0618	9.2	1244	1.7	● 1838	9.0
8	SA	0101	1.7	0656	9.2	1322	1.7	1915	8.9
9	SU	0136	1.9	0731	9.1	1356	1.8	1950	8.7
10	M	0208	2.1	0804	8.9	1429	2.1	2022	8.5
11	TU	0237	2.4	0835	8.6	1500	2.4	2055	8.1
12	W	0307	2.8	0908	8.2	1532	2.8	2128	7.8
13	TH	0339	3.2	0943	7.8	1608	3.2	2206	7.4
14	F	0416	3.6	1023	7.4	1651	3.5	2251	7.1
15	SA	0505	3.9	1115	7.1	1748	3.7	◐ 2351	6.9
16	SU	0614	4.1	1224	6.9	1900	3.8		
17	M	0107	6.9	0734	4.0	1341	7.0	2010	3.6
18	TU	0222	7.1	0845	3.6	1449	7.4	2115	3.2
19	W	0323	7.6	0946	3.1	1548	7.8	2211	2.7
20	TH	0416	8.1	1040	2.6	1640	8.3	2303	2.2
21	F	0505	8.6	1130	2.0	1730	8.7	2352	1.8
22	SA	0551	9.1	1219	1.6	1818	9.1	○	
23	SU	0039	1.4	0637	9.4	1307	1.3	1905	9.3
24	M	0126	1.2	0723	9.6	1354	1.1	1951	9.4
25	TU	0211	1.2	0808	9.6	1440	1.1	2038	9.3
26	W	0257	1.4	0854	9.5	1526	1.3	2124	9.0
27	TH	0343	1.7	0942	9.1	1615	1.7	2213	8.6
28	F	0432	2.2	1033	8.6	1707	2.2	2307	8.1
29	SA	0528	2.7	1129	8.1	1805	2.6	◑	
30	SU	0008	7.7	0632	3.1	1235	7.7	1912	3.0
31	M	0121	7.5	0746	3.3	1349	7.5	2025	3.1

Chart Datum is 5·06 metres below Ordnance Datum (Local). HAT is 10·3 metres above Chart Datum.

Channel Islands

9.19.12 HERM

Herm **49°28′·22N 02°27′·26W** ❁❁◬✿✿✿

CHARTS and TIDES As for St Peter Port.

SHELTER Good shelter E or W of island depending on winds.

NAVIGATION Access is not difficult, if properly planned. Herm is reached from the Little Russel Channel via any of 7 passages all of which require reasonable visibility and care with tidal streams. AC 807 & 808 list the marks and bearings of all the passages.

The Alligande Passage is the simplest and most direct from St Peter Port. Approach with the Vermerette bcn (topmark 'V') in transit 074° with W patch on Hbr quay. Leave Alligande 'A', Godfrey 'GB' and Epec 'E' bcns to starboard; skirt close N of Vermerette. When its base is awash, there is 1m at hbr ent. The tide will be setting N. Sand build-up W of Vermerette affects craft NW-bound in the Percée Passage.

The appr from the Big Russel is more open and leads easily to pleasant ⚓s at Belvoir Bay and Shell Bay.

LIGHTS AND MARKS Ldg lts, both FW (occas) and W drums at 078°. 2FG (vert) on quay hd. Night appr not advised for visitors.

COMMUNICATIONS (Code 01481) Island Admin ☎750000 for overnight stay in hbr.

FACILITIES

Herm Harbour, options:

- Lie to mooring lines secured to N and S walls inside hbr.
- Dry out on the beach to the E, moored fore/aft to chains.
- 5 🅥s to N and 6 to W of hbr dry out; 6 more to NW: rky bottom to the N; isolated boulders/sand to W.

www.herm.com for navigation details and webcams of hbr & buoys. No fees; donations welcome. ⛽ 🏁 ✕ 🛒 limited 🚌. Can be busy at summer weekends, better mid-week.

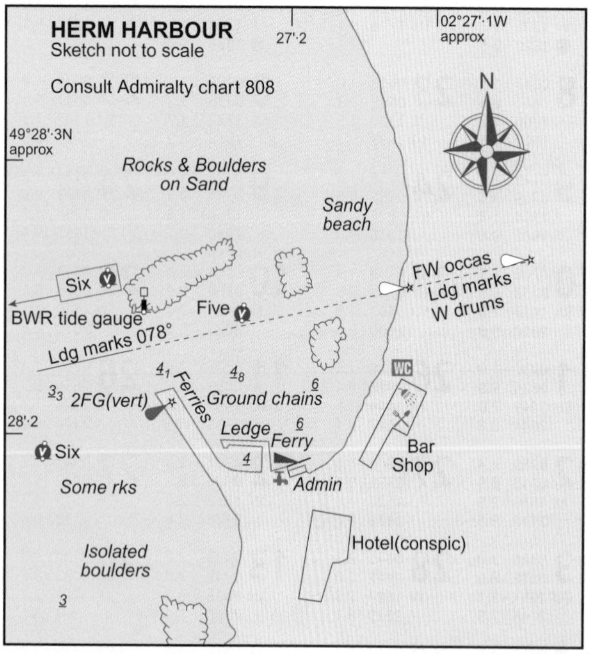
HERM HARBOUR
Sketch not to scale
Consult Admiralty chart 808
27′·2
02°27′·1W approx
N
49°28′·3N approx
Rocks & Boulders on Sand
Sandy beach
FW occas
Ldg marks W drums
Six
BWR tide gauge
Five
Ldg marks 078°
Ferries
Ground chains
2FG(vert)
28′·2
Ledge
Ferry
Six
Bar
Shop
Some rks
Admin
Hotel(conspic)
Isolated boulders
WC

Rosière Steps Easiest appr is from the Big Russel via Percée passage; avoid Fourquies ($\underline{2}_3$, NCM lt buoy) Meulettes ($\underline{1}_7$) and Tinker ($\underline{2}_7$). ⚓ 49°28′·22N 02°27′·22W NW of Rosière steps; good holding on sand, but exposed to S and SW. Access for landing only; do not linger alongside. Buoys are for ferries and Herm-owned boats only; hourly ferries by day. The bottom step is about 1.5m above the seabed which may be inconvenient at LWS. Caution: From just before HW to HW+2 tide sets hard onto the steps.

Belvoir Bay 49°28′·40N 02°26′·34W and **Shell Bay** are good ⚓s on sand, sheltered from W. Easy access from E; from S keep 400m offshore. Beach café or walk 800m to Harbour village. Note: Jethou, Crevichon and Grande Fauconnière are private. No landing.

9.19.13 SARK

Sark **49°25′·81N 02°20′·45W** Creux ❁❁◬✿✿✿

CHARTS AC 808, 5604.12; SHOM 7159, 6904; Navi 1014; Imray C33A, 2500

TIDES –0450 Dover; ML 5·3; Duration 0550

Standard Port ST HELIER (⟶)

Times				Height (metres)			
High Water		Low Water		MHWS	MHWN	MLWN	MLWS
0300	0900	0200	0900	11·0	8·1	4·0	1·4
1500	2100	1400	2100				
Differences SARK (MASELINE PIER)							
+0005	+0015	+0005	+0010	–2·1	–1·5	–0·6	–0·3

Tidal streams *Beware large tidal range, strong streams and many lobster pots. In Gouliot (W coast) and Goulet Passages the streams reach 6-7kn at springs. Note that at about half-tide the streams are slack around Sark. At HW the stream sets hard to the N, ie onto Little Sark. At LW the stream sets hard to the S, ie onto Bec du Nez (N tip). If bound from Guernsey to Sark's E coast, go N-about at HW and S-about at LW; conversely on the return.*

SHELTER Sark is fringed by rocks, but the centres of the bays are mainly clear of dangers. A safe ⚓age or 🅥s can usually be found sheltered from offshore winds. But, depending on wind and tide, they may be uncomfortable, except in settled weather; see also Facilities.

NAVIGATION From the West, WPT 49°25′·27N 02°24′·30W, 070°/1·29M towards the Pilcher monument (Sark mill is obsc'd by trees) for Havre Gosselin or La Grande Grève.
From the N or after rounding Bec du Nez, the WPT is 49°27′·30N 02°21′·42W, on the 153° charted transit (aka the outside passage) towards Grève de la Ville and Maseline. Noire Pierre rk is unlit but marked with a Y post & radar reflector. The inside passage, W of drying Pécheresse, is used by locals but ill advised for visitors.

LIGHTS AND MARKS Point Robert lt ho and Courbée du Nez are the only navigational lights on Sark; see chartlet and Lights, buoys and waypoints.

COMMUNICATIONS (Code 01481) Police (Guernsey) 725111; ⊖ (Guernsey) 726911; Dr 832045; HM 832323, VHF Ch 10; Maseline Hbr VHF Ch 13, season only; Tourist Office 832345.

ANCHORAGES, 🅥s, HARBOURS AND FACILITIES

Anti-clockwise from Bec du Nez, the ⚓s below (all unlit) are safe in offshore winds; in other conditions they can be exposed and sometimes dangerous. Some are only suitable around LW.

🅥s at Havre Gosselin and Grève de la Ville are free (courtesy Sark Moorings ☎832260, 07781 106065). Donations welcome in local boxes or c/o Le Grand Fort, Sark, Channel Islands, GY9 0SF. Water taxi Ch 10. All other moorings are private; use only in emergency.

WEST COAST (all ⚓s are exposed to W'lies)

Saignie Bay 49°26′·53N 02°22′·10W. Sand and shingle with fair holding. Picturesque rock formations.

Port à la Jument 49°26′·17N 02°22′·42W. Sand and shingle with fair holding. Difficult shore access.

Brecqhou Island is strictly private; landing prohibited.

Havre Gosselin 49°25′·77N 02°22′·68W. Popular deep (4-9m) ⚓. 20 Y 🅥s (see above). Beware of drying rk at extreme NW of bay. Crowded in summer. 299 steps to cliff top and panoramic views.

Port és Saies 49°25′·41N 02°22′·28W. Sandy inlet, steep cliff path.

La Grande Grève 49°25′·38N 02°22′·59W. Wide sandy bay, subject to swell, but popular day ⚓age. Beware two rks (drying $\underline{0}$·3m and ✳) in the appr. Temporary steps to cliff-top panoramic views.

LITTLE SARK

Port Gorey 49°24′·60N 02°22′·72W. ⚓ or pick up Y 🅥 (free) in centre of deep, weedy bay over LW only; heavy swell begins near half-flood. Rocky appr from just NW of Grande Bretagne (18m high) then 045° into bay. Rocks must be positively identified. Remains of quay with ladder. Cliff walk past silver mine ruins to hotel.

Rouge Terrier 49°24′·78N 02°21′·87W. Sandy with some local moorings under high cliffs. Exposed to E. Landing with cliff path to hotel. Also ⚓ 49°25′·09N 02°21′·70W, 4ca NNE in Baleine Bay.

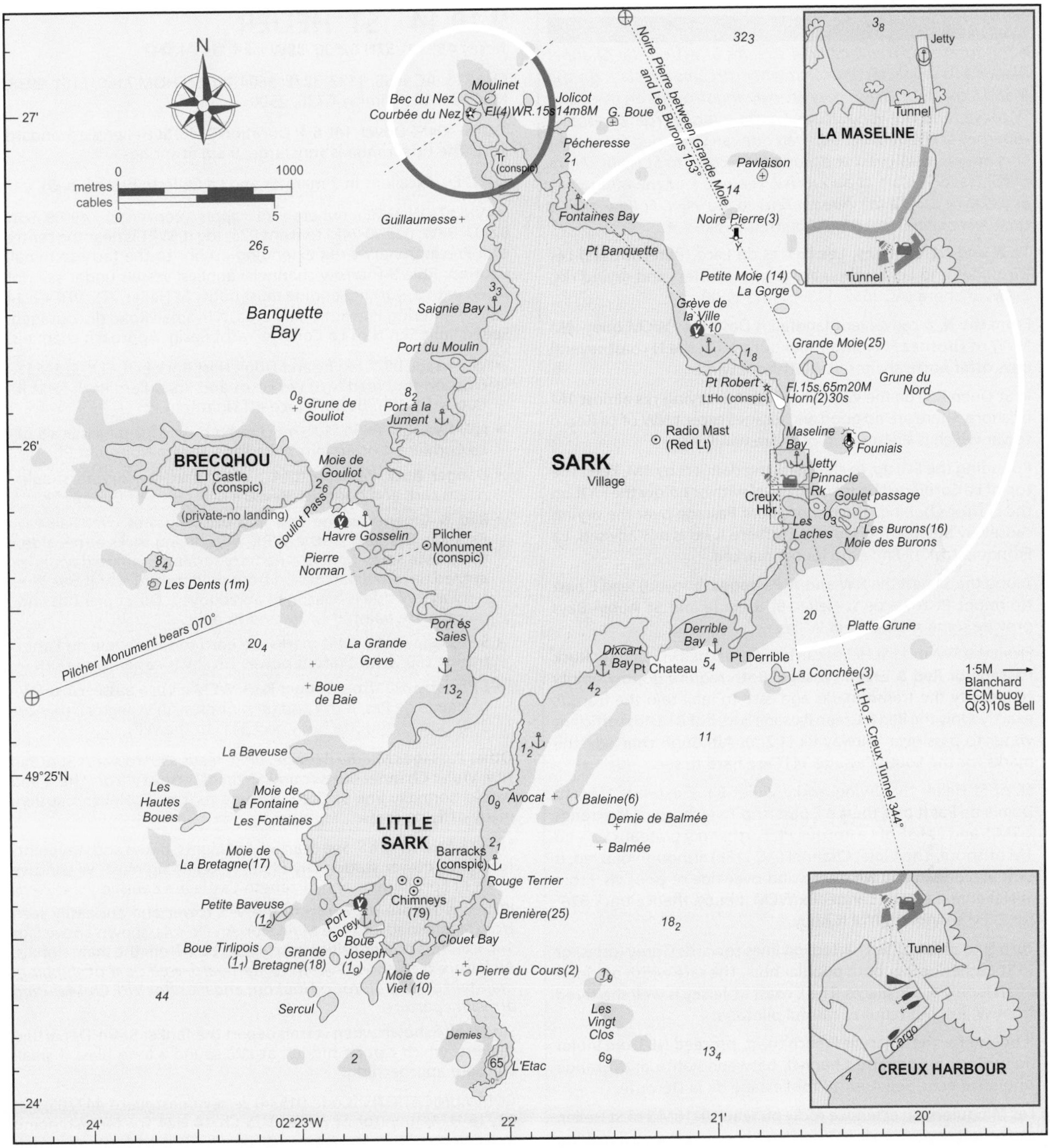

EAST COAST

Dixcart Bay 49°25′·33N 02°21′·48W. Popular sandy bay with good holding, but open to S'lies. Drying rocks either side of the bay but not in the centre. Cliff path and walk to hotels. Beware rockslides.

Derrible Bay 49°25′·41N 02°21′·07W. Sandy bay with good holding. Open to the S. No dangers in the bay, but keep off SW tip of Derrible Pt. Picturesque caves and steep climb ashore.

Creux Harbour 49°25′·80N 02°20′·61W dries completely, fair weather only, prone to surge/swell. Local transits: Pinnacle Rk on with E edge of Grand Moie 001°; or Creux tunnel (white arch) on with Pt Robert lt ho 344°. The lt ho dips behind the cliffs when close inshore. In the Goulet Passage (E of Creux) S-bound navigation is prohibited to commercial vessels (except with HM's permission) but not to yachts in either direction.

Dry out bow to NE wall, stern to ⚓. ⌒ possible only at inner part of the S pier, clear of steps and cargo berth at outer end. ☎832025 (kiosk) ⛽(free) ⛽ ▬ ▬ ⛽ ⛽ via HM; walk or tractor up steep hill to village ✕ ⛽ ⛽ ⛽ ⛽ ⛽ ✉ Ⓑ. Bikes and horse-drawn carriages for hire.

Maseline Harbour 49°25′·96N 02°20′·60W is prone to surge/swell. Busy ferry hbr with no yacht berths (except to land people). Call HM Ch 13 for approval to ⚓. Moorings are private. ☎832070 (kiosk) ⛽(3t). Condor catamaran to Jersey/St Malo.

Grève de la Ville 49°26′·35N 02°21′·06W. ⚓ close in out of tide. Fair holding sand/shingle. Open to E. Seven Y ⛽s (free, see p 838). Easy walk ashore.

Les Fontaines 49°26′·78N 02°21′·62W. Sand and shingle with fair holding. Reef drying 4·5m extends 1ca N from shore. ⚓ between reef and Eperquerie headland. Exposed to the E.

With grateful acknowledgements to John Frankland, author of *Sark, Round the Island*.

JERSEY

▶*The rotatory pattern of tidal streams affecting the Channel Islands as a whole dictates that when streams are slack on the N and S coasts of Jersey, they are running strongly on the E and W coasts; and vice versa. If approaching Jersey from Guernsey/Alderney at HW St Helier +4, a fair tide can be carried for at least 6hrs down the W coast and along the S coast to St Helier. From the S, leave St Malo at about HW, keeping E of the Minquiers, in order to carry a fair tide for 6hrs to St Helier. Follow similar tidal tactics when coasting around the island.*◀

To N and NE of Jersey, Les Pierres de Lecq (Paternosters) Les Dirouilles and Les Écrehou are groups of islets and drying rks, 2–4M offshore (AC *3655*, 1136, 1137, 1138).

From the N, a convenient landfall is Desormes WCM buoy, 4M NNW of Grosnez Pt (conspic lookout tr). On the N coast several bays offer anchs sheltered in offshore winds.

In St Ouen Bay on the W coast, which has drying rks almost 1M offshore, there are no good anchorages except NW of La Rocco tower which is sheltered in offshore winds.

Rounding the SW tip, to clear offlying dangers by 1M, keep the top of La Corbière lt ho (conspic) level with or below the FR lt on the clifftops behind. The inshore Boat Passage over the drying causeway between Jersey and Corbière lt ho is not advised. La Frouquie rock (9·8m) is no longer marked.

Along the S coast the **NW and W Passages** (buoyed) lead E past Noirmont Pt towards St Helier. St Brelade and St Aubin Bays provide some shelter from W'lies.

From the SW and S St Helier can be approached via **Danger Rock Passage** or **Red & Green Passage**. Both require good visibility to identify the transit marks and care to maintain the transits exactly. Only the Red & Green Passage is lit, but it needs sufficient water to pass over Fairway Rk (1·2m). Although charted, the marks for the South Passage 341° are hard to see.

SE of St Helier the drying, rocky Violet Bank extends 1M S to Demie de Pas lt bcn, thence E past Icho Twr (conspic). It extends 1·7M S and 2M SE of La Rocque Pt. Further rky plateaux extend 1M offshore. The **Violet Channel** (AC 1138) although buoyed, is best avoided in bad weather, wind-over-tide or poor vis. From St Helier make good Canger Rk WCM lt buoy, thence track 078° for 2·2M to Violet SWM lt buoy.

Turn N to pick up the charted ldg lines towards Gorey (dries) or to St Catherine Bay, both popular hbrs. The safe width of Violet Chan is only 5ca in places. The E coast of Jersey is well sheltered from W'lies, but requires careful pilotage.

If bound for the adjacent French coast, proceed NE from Violet buoy via the **Anquette Channel**, between Petite and Grande Anquette bcns. See Area 18 for Passage de la Déroute.

Les Minquiers, an extensive rocky plateau 10–18M S of St Helier, can be left to port, ie via NW and SW Minquiers buoys, if making for St Malo; or to stbd via NE and SE Minquiers buoys. A more direct route via N and SE Minquiers buoys requires sufficient height of tide to clear rocks drying 2m in the northern part. For a first visit the plateau should only be entered in settled weather, with exquisite care and a good Pilot book – not to mention *The Wreck of the Mary Deare* by Hammond Innes. The anchorage off Maîtresse Île is the principal attraction. From Jersey approach via the Demie de Vascelin SHM buoy with bcns in transit 167°. See St Helier.

9.19.14 ST HELIER

Jersey **49°10'·57N 02°06'·98W** ✽✽✽◊◊◊✿✿

CHARTS AC 3655, 1137, 3278, 5604.14/15; SHOM 7160, 7161, 6938; Navi 534, 1014; Imray C33B, 2500

TIDES –0455 Dover; ML 6·1; Duration 0545. St Helier is a Standard Port. The tidal range is very large, 9·6m at springs.

SHELTER Excellent in 2 marinas and La Collette basin (no Ⓥ).

NAVIGATION WPT (where all apprs converge) 49°09'·95N 02°07'·38W, 023°/0·74M to front 023° ldg lt. WPT is near the centre of a Precautionary Area extending up-hbr to the ferry terminal. Caution: Rule 9 (narrow channels) applies; vessels under sail not fitted with a working engine must notify St Helier VTS VHF Ch 14 before entering Precautionary area. ⚓ in Small Road discouraged. Speed limit 5kn N of La Collette Yacht Basin. Approach channels:

- **W Passage** 082° ldg lts and Dog's Nest Rock bcn, Fl Y 3s 3M (Y cross on top) lead N of Les Fours and Ruaudière Rock SHM lt buoys, to WPT. Beware race off Noirmont Pt.
- **NW Passage** (095°/110°, much used by yachts) passes 6ca S of La Corbière lt ho to join W Passage abeam Noirmont Pt.
- **Danger Rock Passage** (044°) unlit; past rky, drying shoals; needs care and good vis. Beware overfalls S of Danger Rk.
- **Red & Green Passage** Ldg line 022·7° passes over Fairway Rk 1·2m, 8ca SSW of the WPT, with drying rocks either side; thence via Small Road to the ferry terminal, where daymarks are red dayglow patches on front dolphin and rear lt twr. The fairway's W side is beaconed and buoyed. Outer pier hds and dolphin are painted white and floodlit.
- **S Passage** (341°) unlit marks are hard to see. Demie de Pas in transit 350° with floodlit power stn chy is easier to see D/N.
- **E Passage** 290° from Canger Rock WCM lt buoy passes close SW of Demie de Pas, B tr/Y top (at night stay in W sector); thence 314° past Hinguette buoy and 341° to the WPT.

Other Passages Middle Passage, unlit, leads 339° towards St Aubin Hbr. Violet Channel skirts round SE tip of Jersey to/from the N and would normally link to the E Passage to/from St Helier. Caution: many offlying reefs.

LIGHTS AND MARKS See chartlet and Lights, buoys and waypoints for lights. Power station chy (95m, floodlit) Sig mast, W concave roofs of Fort Regent and Elizabeth Castle are conspic.

IPTS Sigs 1-4 are shown from the VTS tower and are easily seen from Small Road and the Main Hbr. An Oc Y 4s, shown above Sigs 1-4, exempts power-driven craft <25m LOA from the main signals. All leisure craft should: *Keep to starboard, well clear of shipping; maintain a sharp all-round lookout and monitor VHF Ch 14 during arrival/departure.*

Sig 2 is also shown when vessels depart the Tanker Basin. Departing tankers, which can be hidden at LW, sound a long blast if small craft are approaching.

COMMUNICATIONS (Code 01534) *Jersey Coastguard* 447705; Ch **82,** 16 H24; monitor *St Helier VTS* Ch 14 H24 for ferry/shipping movements; *St Helier Pierheads* on Ch 18 broadcasts recorded wind direction and speed; Police 612612; ⊖ 448000; Ⓗ 622000. No marina VHF, but call *VTS* if essential; Marine Leisure Centre (enquiries) 447708.

FACILITIES **Port Control** ☎447708 or 447788, ⚓ ⛴(32t) ⛵ Grids. www.jerseymarinas.je marinas@gov.je

Fuel ⛽ ⛽ at the ent to La Collette (HW ±4; 07700 347313); a fuel barge by ent to Old Hbr (H24, self service, cr/debit card; ☎525247 07829 876543); Elizabeth marina (HW ±3; ☎07797 723090) self service, cr/debit card.

La Collette Basin, good shelter in 1·8m. Access H24. Caution: Ent narrow at LWS, least depth 1·1m; keep close to W side; PHM buoys mark shoal on E side. 130 ⛵ locals only, no Ⓥ berths, access H24. ⛽ ⛽ (at top of tide) ⛴(65t and 25t, ☎447773) ⛵.

St Helier YC ☎721307, ✕ ▭.

Continued on page 842

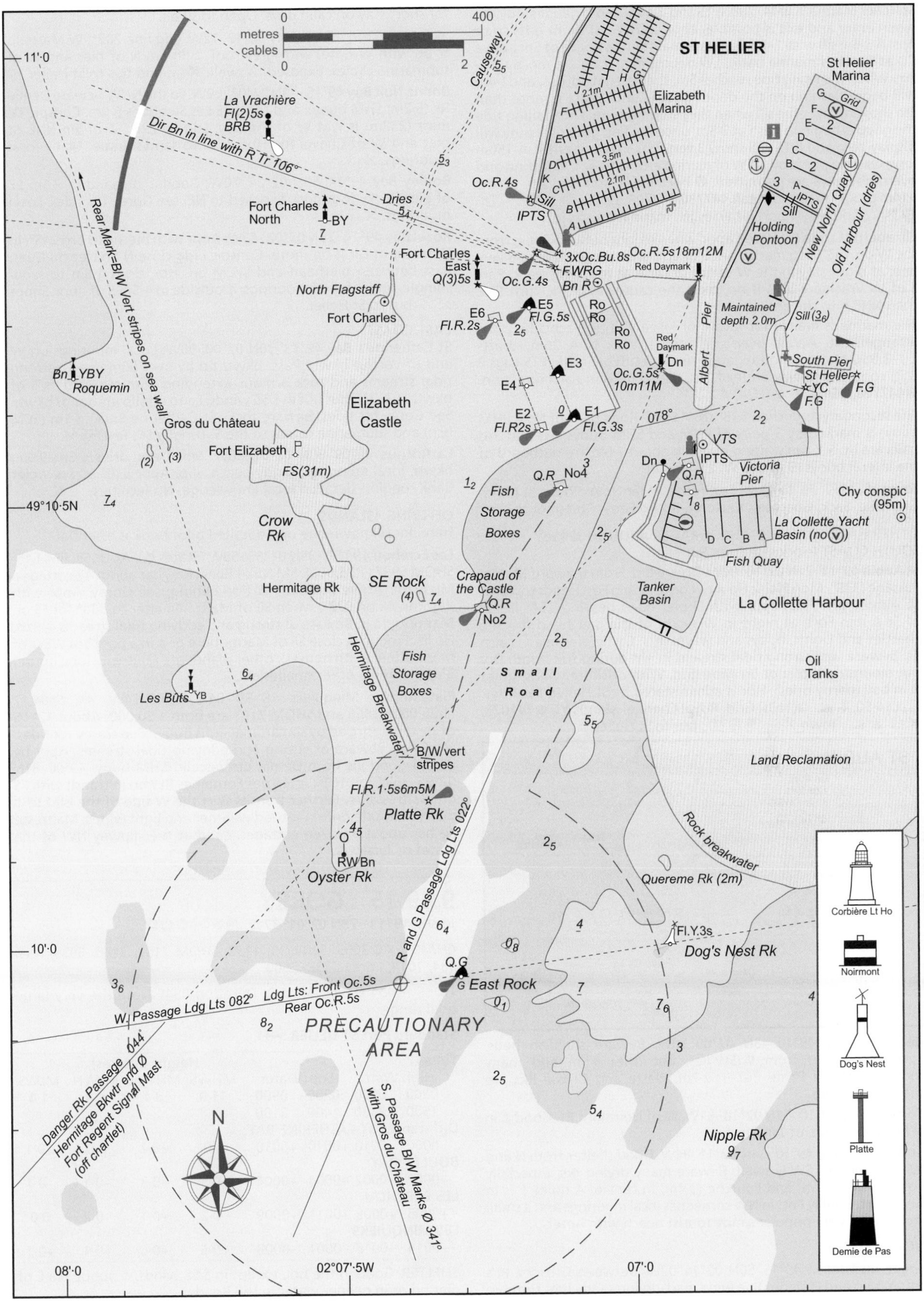
ST HELIER
metres
cables
0
400
2
St Helier Marina
Elizabeth Marina
La Vrachière
Fl(2)5s
BRB
Dir Bn in line with R Tr 106°
Causeway
Dries
Fort Charles North
BY
Fort Charles East
Q(3)5s
North Flagstaff
Fort Charles
Oc.R.4s
Sill
IPTS
3xOc.Bu.8s
F.WRG
Bn R
Oc.G.4s
Oc.R.5s18m12M
Red Daymark
E5
Fl.G.5s
E6
Fl.R.2s
E3
E4
E2
Fl.R2s
E1
Fl.G.3s
Ro Ro
Red Daymark
Dn
Oc.G.5s
10m11M
Albert Pier
078°
Maintained depth 2.0m
Holding Pontoon
New North Quay
Old Harbour (dries)
Grid
Sill
South Pier
St Helier YC
F.G
VTS
IPTS
Victoria Pier
Q.R
Q.R
No4
Fish Storage Boxes
Chy conspic (95m)
La Collette Yacht Basin (no V)
Fish Quay
Tanker Basin
La Collette Harbour
Oil Tanks
Land Reclamation
Rear Mark=B/W Vert stripes on sea wall
Bn YBY
Roquemin
Gros du Château
Fort Elizabeth
FS(31m)
Elizabeth Castle
Crow Rk
Hermitage Rk
SE Rock
Crapaud of the Castle
Q.R
No2
Hermitage Breakwater
Fish Storage Boxes
Small Road
Les Bûts
YB
B/W vert stripes
Fl.R.1·5s6m5M
Platte Rk
RW Bn
Oyster Rk
R and G Passage Ldg Lts 022°
Rock breakwater
Quereme Rk (2m)
Fl.Y.3s
Dog's Nest Rk
Q.G
East Rock
W. Passage Ldg Lts 082°
Ldg Lts: Front Oc.5s
Rear Oc.R.5s
PRECAUTIONARY AREA
Danger Rk Passage 044°
Hermitage Bkwtr end Ø
Fort Regent Signal Mast
(off chartlet)
S. Passage B/W Marks Ø 341°
with Gros du Château
N
Nipple Rk
11'·0
49°10·5N
10'·0
08'·0
02°07'·5W
07'·0
Corbière Lt Ho
Noirmont
Dog's Nest
Platte
Demie de Pas

Channel Islands

St Helier Marina ☎447708. IPTS and digital depth gauges indicate when entry and exit is possible, approx (HW± 3) slight diffs sp or nps. A 3·6m sill with 1·4m flap gate maintains a depth of 5m above CD at S end of marina basin; LW depths in marina are mostly 2m-3m. When the rising tide reaches 5m, the flap gate drops, and 1·4m will begin flashing on the depth gauges until there is more than 2m showing over the sill when they stop flashing. On a falling tide the gauges begin to flash at 2·5m; once the flap gate rises they will display zero and IPTS will show 3 vert R lts = do not enter. A 150m long waiting pontoon is SW of marina ent, with; rafting and overnight stays are permitted. Ⓥ berths: E, F and G in 2m; yachts >14m or >2·1m draught call 447730/447708, £2·85. Grid, www.portsofjersey.je marinas@ports.je

Elizabeth Marina Preferred appr, when height of tide >7m, is from the W on 106°. Ldg marks, just S of ent, are orange □s with B vert line; at night stay in the W sector of Dir lt at front daymark. Pass S of La Vrachière IDM lt bn, cross the causeway 5·3m, turn ENE then NNE into the ent.

The marina is mainly for locals, or large visiting yachts by prior arrangement. Access over sill/flapgate; max LOA 20m, drafts 2·1–3·5m. At ent a digital gauge reads depth over sill. IPTS (sigs 2 & 3) control one-way ent/exit, usually 10 mins in each direction. ☎447708, 564 (H24).

The secondary appr chan 338° from Small Road (ie N of No 4 PHM buoy) is marked by 3 pairs of PHM and SHM buoys, 1st and 3rd pairs are lit. 5 Y can waiting buoys in about 1·0m are outboard of the lateral buoys (3 to the W, 2 to the E).

Town . Fast ferries (Mar-Nov): Poole, St Malo, Granville, Sark, Guernsey, Carteret, Ro Ro Ferry: Portsmouth.

OTHER HARBOURS AND ANCHORAGES AROUND JERSEY

SOUTH COAST (clockwise from St Helier)

St Aubin 49°11′·21N 02°10′·02W. Dries 6·8m. From seaward Middle Passage (339°, Mon Plaisir Ho ≠ twr on St Aubin Fort) leads towards St Aubin Fort. Final appr with N pier head bearing 254° lies N of St Aubin Fort; at night in W sector of the pier head lt – see chartlet and Lights, buoys and waypoints. Castle pier head is also lit. Beware very strong tidal streams in ent during full flood. Dry out alongside N pier or on wide grid. With offshore winds, quiet ⚓ in bay (partly dries). Hbr is administered by St Helier. Facilities: £14·50, (1t 5t) Grid. **Royal Channel Islands YC** ☎741023. **Town**, bus to St Helier.

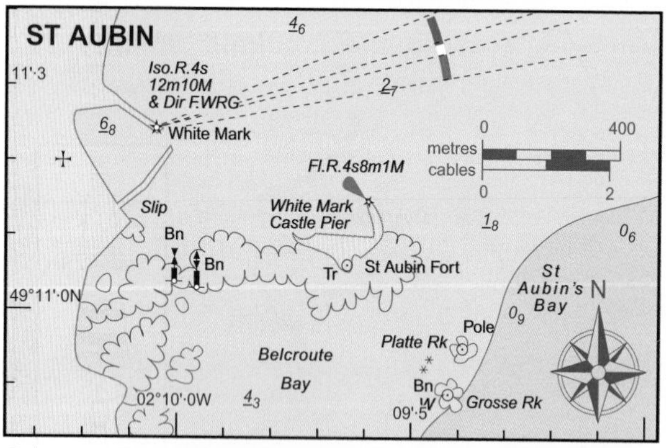

Belcroute Bay 49°10′·43N 02°09′·60W. Beware shellfish beds. Excellent shelter from W/SW'lies, but dries 3·5m and many moorings; ⚓ off Pt de Bût in 2·7m. Platte and Grosse Rks are marked by poles.

Portelet Bay 49°10′·13N 02°10′·61W. W of Noirmont Pt. Good ⚓ in N'lies, either side of Janvrin Twr.

St Brelade's Bay 49°10′·64N 02°11′·84W. Good shelter from N and W, but open to SW'ly swell. Beware many drying rks, especially Fournier Rk (0·9m) and Fourché (3·4m) in centre. A quiet ⚓ is in Beau Port. Bouilly Port in NW corner has local moorings and a small stone jetty. Very popular sandy tourist beach with hotels.

NORTH COAST

Grève au Lancon 49°15′·50N 02°14′·07W. Between Grosnez Pt's squat lt ho and Plémont Pt a wide, part-drying sandy bay, suitable for short stay on calm days. Open to swell.

Grève de Lecq 49°14′·98N 02°12′·12W. Ldg line 202°: W Martello tr on with W hotel with grey roof. ⚓ in 5m N of pier and W of submarine cables. Exposed to swell. , and bus to St Helier.

Bonne Nuit Bay 49°15′·19N 02°07′·09W. To the NNW beware Demie Rk (5·2m; SHM buoy); and to the E Les Sambues 5·5m. Conspic TV mast (232m) is ½M W of the bay. Ldg lts 223°. ⚓ in 5m NNE of pier and W of Chevel Rk. Hbr dries to sand/shingle. Many local moorings.

Bouley Bay 49°14′·50N 02°04′·70W. Good ⚓ on sand in 2·5m SE of pier (rocky footings). Exposed to NE, see Gorey for tides. Local moorings.

Rozel Bay 49°14′·25N 02°02′·43W. Appr with pierhead brg 245°, in W sector of Dir lt on shore. Conspic bldg close N on Nez du Guet. Pass between pierhead and WCM bn. Hbr, dries 1·5m to sand/shingle, and is full of moorings; ⚓ outside in 4-5m S of appr. Shops, bus to St Helier.

EAST COAST

St Catherine's Bay 49°13′·30N 02°00′·90W. Local moorings off W end of Verclut bkwtr. Pass bkwtr hd by over 50m due to strong tidal streams and rock armour extending 15m seaward. ⚓ S of bkwtr in 3–7m, but not in S/SE winds. Land on slip at root of bkwtr. See Gorey for tides, beware rocky St Catherine Bank, 3·1m (ECM bcn) and submarine cables to the S. Dinghy SC, RNLI.

La Rocque 49°09′·80N 02°01′·88W. Small hbr dries 6·5m–9·6m; bkwtr, local moorings, sandy beach, slip. Appr 330° across Violet Bank requires detailed local knowledge. No facilities.

OFFLYING ISLANDS

Here, local knowledge or a detailed pilot book is essential.

Les Écrehou 49°17′·39N 01°55′·58W (States). AC 3655, 5604.15; SHOM 6937 (1:25,000). 5M NE of Rozel Bay, has about 12 cottages. ML 6·2m. Arrive at about ½ tide ebbing; see Gorey. Appr with Bigorne Rk on 022°; when SE of Maître Ile alter to 330° for FS on Marmotière Is. Beware of strong and eddying tidal streams 4–8kn. No lts. Pick up close SE of Marmotière or ⚓ in a pool 3ca WSW of Marmotière (with houses); other islands are Maître Ile (one house) Blanche and 5 other small islets.

Plateau des Minquiers 48°58′·04N 02°03′·74W. AC *5604.17* (1:25,000); 3656 and SHOM 7161 are both 1:50,000. About 12M S of Jersey, encircled by six cardinal light buoys. See Gorey for tides. ML 6·4m. Beware of strong and eddying tidal streams. Appr by day in good vis from Demie de Vascelin SHM buoy, 49°00′·81N 02°05′·15W, on 161°: Jetée des Fontaines RW bn in transit with FS on Maîtresse Ile. Further transits skirt the W side of the islet to ⚓ due S of it; safe only in settled weather and light winds. Maîtresse Ile has about a dozen cottages. Land at the slipway NW of the States of Jersey.

9.19.15 GOREY

Jersey **49°11′·78N 02°01′·37W**

CHARTS AC 3655, 5604./16, 1138; SHOM 7157, 7160, 6939; Navi 534, 1014; Imray C33B, 2500

TIDES –0454 Dover; ML 6·0; Duration 0545 Note the very large tidal range.

Standard Port ST HELIER (⟶)

Times				Height (metres)			
High Water		Low Water		MHWS	MHWN	MLWN	MLWS
0300	0900	0200	0900	11·0	8·1	4·0	1·4
1500	2100	1400	2100				
Differences ST CATHERINE BAY							
0000	+0010	+0010	+0010	0·0	–0·1	0·0	+0·1
BOULEY BAY							
+0002	+0002	+0004	+0004	–0·3	–0·3	–0·1	–0·1
LES ECREHOU							
+0005	+0009	+0011	+0009	–0·2	+0·1	–0·2	0·0
LES MINQUIERS							
–0014	–0018	–0001	–0008	+0·5	+0·6	+0·1	+0·1

SHELTER Good in the hbr, except in S/SE winds. ⚓ about 2ca E of pier hd or in deeper water in the Roads.

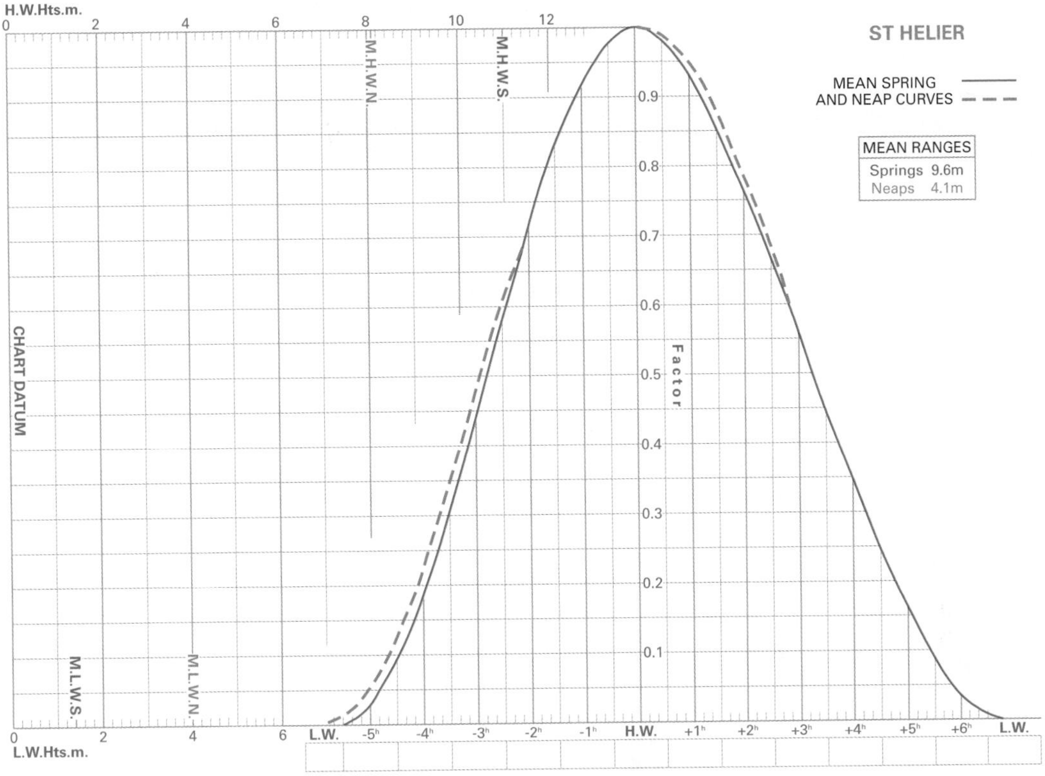
ST HELIER
MEAN SPRING AND NEAP CURVES
MEAN RANGES
Springs 9.6m
Neaps 4.1m
H.W.Hts.m.
L.W.Hts.m.
CHART DATUM
M.H.W.N.
M.H.W.S.
M.L.W.S.
M.L.W.N.
Factor
L.W.
H.W.
L.W.

NAVIGATION WPT 49°11´·18N 01°59´·59W, 298°/1·3M to pier hd lt. On appr, keep well outside all local bcns until the ldg marks are identified, but beware Banc du Chateau (0·4m least depth) 1M offshore NE of 298° ldg line (see below); and Azicot Rk (dries 2·2m) just S of 298° ldg line, 2ca from ent. There are at least 3 approaches:

- Ldg line 298°: Gorey pierhead, W frame-work twr; rear ldg mark House (west gable end). Best for visitors.
- Pierhead ≠ ✠ spire 304° leads close to Road Rk (3·3m) and over Azicot Rk (2·2m).
- Pierhead ≠ white house/R roof 250° leads close to Les Arch bn (B/W with A topmark) and Pacquet Rk (0·3m).

See Passage information for the Violet Chan to St Helier. The Gutters and Boat Passage across Violet Bank are not advised.

LIGHTS AND MARKS See chartlet and Lights, buoys and waypoints. Mont Orgueil Castle (67m) is highly conspic.

COMMUNICATIONS (Code 01534) Marinecall 09068 969656; ⊖ 833833; for Dr contact Port Control St Helier 447788; *Gorey Hbr* Ch 74 (not permanently manned); Info *Jersey Coastguard* Ch 82.

FACILITIES **Hbr** dries to 6·9m. 12 drying ⛵s, 150m W of pier hd, 4 drying against pier hd, all £14·50. Port Control ☎447708. HW ±3 (HO) by hose at pierhead mob 07797 742384, (7t).

Town Ⓑ bus to St Helier. Ferries to Guernsey, Carteret.

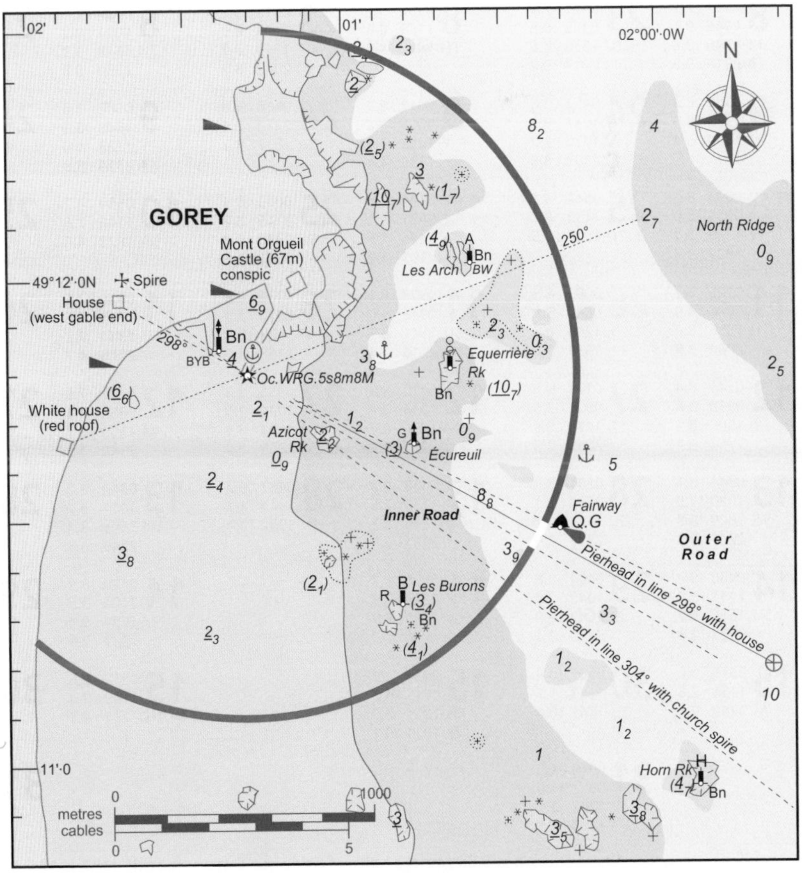

STANDARD TIME (UT)
For Summer Time add ONE hour in **non-shaded areas**

ST HELIER LAT 49°11′N LONG 2°07′W

TIMES AND HEIGHTS OF HIGH AND LOW WATERS

Dates in red are SPRINGS
Dates in blue are NEAPS

YEAR **2018**

JANUARY

Date	Time	m	Date	Time	m
1 M	0519 1205 1751	10.8 1.5 10.9	16 TU	0014 0557 1235 1817	2.6 10.0 2.3 9.9
2 TU	0030 0612 1301 ○ 1843	1.3 11.3 1.1 11.2	17 W	0052 0633 1312 ● 1852	2.3 10.2 2.1 10.1
3 W	0124 0702 1353 1932	1.1 11.6 0.8 11.4	18 TH	0127 0707 1347 1925	2.2 10.4 2.0 10.2
4 TH	0213 0750 1442 2020	1.0 11.6 0.8 11.3	19 F	0200 0740 1420 1958	2.1 10.5 1.9 10.2
5 F	0300 0835 1529 2105	1.1 11.4 1.0 10.9	20 SA	0232 0812 1453 2031	2.1 10.4 2.0 10.2
6 SA	0345 0919 1613 2148	1.5 11.0 1.5 10.3	21 SU	0304 0845 1525 2104	2.2 10.3 2.1 10.0
7 SU	0428 1002 1656 2231	2.0 10.3 2.1 9.7	22 M	0336 0919 1559 2139	2.4 10.0 2.4 9.6
8 M	0511 1046 1740 ◑ 2318	2.7 9.6 2.8 9.0	23 TU	0411 0955 1636 2217	2.8 9.6 2.8 9.2
9 TU	0558 1136 1830	3.3 8.9 3.4	24 W	0451 1037 1720 ◐ 2304	3.2 9.2 3.2 8.8
10 W	0014 0655 1239 1932	8.5 3.8 8.4 3.8	25 TH	0541 1132 1816	3.5 8.7 3.5
11 TH	0126 0806 1356 2044	8.2 4.0 8.2 3.9	26 F	0007 0649 1246 1931	8.5 3.8 8.5 3.6
12 F	0241 0918 1509 2151	8.4 3.8 8.4 3.7	27 SA	0128 0815 1412 2056	8.5 3.6 8.6 3.3
13 SA	0344 1020 1609 2247	8.7 3.5 8.8 3.3	28 SU	0251 0938 1533 2213	8.9 3.1 9.2 2.8
14 SU	0436 1111 1658 2333	9.2 3.0 9.2 2.9	29 M	0404 1049 1642 2319	9.6 2.4 9.9 2.1
15 M	0519 1155 1740	9.6 2.6 9.6	30 TU	0507 1153 1741	10.4 1.7 10.6
			31 W	0019 0602 1252 ○ 1833	1.5 11.0 1.1 11.1

FEBRUARY

Date	Time	m	Date	Time	m
1 TH	0114 0652 1344 1921	1.0 11.5 0.7 11.4	16 F	0112 0650 1332 1908	2.0 10.5 1.7 10.4
2 F	0203 0738 1432 2006	0.8 11.7 0.5 11.5	17 SA	0146 0723 1406 1941	1.8 10.7 1.5 10.6
3 SA	0248 0821 1514 2047	0.8 11.7 0.7 11.2	18 SU	0219 0756 1439 2014	1.7 10.8 1.5 10.6
4 SU	0328 0901 1553 2125	1.0 11.3 1.1 10.7	19 M	0251 0830 1510 2047	1.6 10.8 1.5 10.5
5 M	0405 0938 1627 2201	1.6 10.7 1.8 10.1	20 TU	0322 0903 1543 2120	1.8 10.6 1.8 10.2
6 TU	0439 1013 1700 2237	2.3 9.9 2.6 9.3	21 W	0355 0937 1616 2155	2.1 10.1 2.2 9.8
7 W	0514 1051 1735 ◑ 2318	3.0 9.1 3.3 8.6	22 TH	0431 1015 1655 2236	2.6 9.5 2.8 9.2
8 TH	0555 1139 1822	3.7 8.3 4.0	23 F	0515 1103 1744 ◐ 2332	3.1 8.9 3.3 8.7
9 F	0017 0655 1252 1935	8.0 4.2 7.8 4.4	24 SA	0616 1213 1857	3.6 8.4 3.7
10 SA	0144 0821 1425 2105	7.8 4.4 7.7 4.3	25 SU	0053 0745 1349 2032	8.3 3.7 8.3 3.6
11 SU	0308 0943 1541 2216	8.1 4.0 8.1 3.8	26 M	0231 0920 1523 2159	8.6 3.3 8.8 3.0
12 M	0410 1044 1636 2309	8.6 3.4 8.7 3.2	27 TU	0353 1039 1634 2309	9.3 2.5 9.6 2.2
13 TU	0458 1133 1720 2354	9.2 2.8 9.3 2.7	28 W	0457 1144 1732	10.2 1.7 10.4
14 W	0538 1215 1759	9.7 2.3 9.7			
15 TH	0034 0615 1255 ● 1834	2.3 10.2 2.0 10.1			

MARCH

Date	Time	m	Date	Time	m
1 TH	0009 0550 1241 1821	1.5 10.9 1.0 11.1	16 F	0010 0550 1231 1810	2.3 10.1 1.9 10.2
2 F	0102 0638 1331 ○ 1906	0.9 11.5 0.6 11.4	17 SA	0049 0626 1310 ● 1845	1.8 10.6 1.5 10.6
3 SA	0148 0721 1414 1946	0.6 11.7 0.5 11.5	18 SU	0126 0701 1346 1919	1.5 10.9 1.2 10.9
4 SU	0229 0801 1452 2023	0.6 11.7 0.6 11.4	19 M	0201 0736 1420 1953	1.3 11.1 1.1 11.0
5 M	0305 0837 1525 2057	0.9 11.4 1.0 10.9	20 TU	0234 0811 1452 2027	1.2 11.1 1.2 11.0
6 TU	0337 0910 1555 2128	1.4 10.8 1.7 10.3	21 W	0307 0846 1525 2102	1.3 10.9 1.4 10.6
7 W	0406 0940 1621 2158	2.0 10.0 2.5 9.5	22 TH	0341 0921 1559 2137	1.7 10.4 1.9 10.1
8 TH	0434 1011 1648 2230	2.8 9.2 3.3 8.8	23 F	0417 1000 1638 2218	2.3 9.7 2.6 9.4
9 F	0506 1048 1723 ◑ 2314	3.6 8.3 4.0 8.0	24 SA	0500 1048 1727 ◐ 2313	2.9 9.0 3.3 8.7
10 SA	0554 1146 1823	4.2 7.6 4.6	25 SU	0601 1159 1840	3.5 8.3 3.8
11 SU	0036 0715 1334 2006	7.5 4.6 7.3 4.7	26 M	0036 0732 1341 2020	8.3 3.7 8.1 3.8
12 M	0227 0858 1509 2140	7.6 4.4 7.7 4.3	27 TU	0220 0910 1515 2148	8.5 3.3 8.7 3.1
13 TU	0340 1011 1609 2240	8.2 3.7 8.4 3.5	28 W	0342 1028 1623 2256	9.2 2.5 9.6 2.3
14 W	0430 1104 1654 2327	8.9 3.0 9.1 2.9	29 TH	0443 1130 1716 2353	10.1 1.7 10.4 1.6
15 TH	0512 1149 1734	9.6 2.4 9.7	30 F	0534 1223 1803	10.8 1.1 11.0
			31 SA	0043 0619 1310 ○ 1844	1.1 11.3 0.8 11.3

APRIL

Date	Time	m	Date	Time	m
1 SU	0126 0659 1350 1922	0.8 11.5 0.7 11.4	16 M	0059 0634 1320 ● 1853	1.4 11.0 1.2 11.1
2 M	0204 0736 1424 1956	0.8 11.4 0.9 11.2	17 TU	0138 0713 1357 1930	1.1 11.2 1.0 11.3
3 TU	0237 0810 1454 2027	1.0 11.1 1.3 10.9	18 W	0215 0751 1433 2008	1.0 11.3 1.0 11.2
4 W	0306 0841 1521 2056	1.4 10.6 1.8 10.3	19 TH	0251 0830 1509 2046	1.1 11.0 1.3 10.9
5 TH	0334 0909 1546 2123	2.0 10.0 2.5 9.7	20 F	0328 0910 1547 2125	1.5 10.5 1.8 10.3
6 F	0400 0938 1611 2152	2.7 9.2 3.2 8.9	21 SA	0408 0953 1629 2210	2.0 9.8 2.5 9.6
7 SA	0431 1011 1644 2229	3.4 8.4 3.9 8.2	22 SU	0455 1045 1721 ◐ 2308	2.7 9.0 3.2 8.9
8 SU	0513 1059 1734 ◑ 2333	4.1 7.7 4.5 7.6	23 M	0559 1158 1835	3.3 8.4 3.7
9 M	0621 1232 1901	4.5 7.3 4.8	24 TU	0029 0725 1333 2007	8.5 3.5 8.3 3.6
10 TU	0131 0758 1423 2047	7.4 4.5 7.5 4.5	25 W	0204 0854 1457 2129	8.6 3.2 8.8 3.1
11 W	0257 0924 1529 2158	7.9 4.0 8.2 3.8	26 TH	0321 1007 1601 2234	9.2 2.5 9.5 2.4
12 TH	0352 1023 1617 2250	8.6 3.2 8.9 3.1	27 F	0421 1106 1653 2329	9.9 1.9 10.2 1.8
13 F	0437 1112 1659 2336	9.4 2.5 9.6 2.4	28 SA	0511 1157 1738	10.5 1.5 10.7
14 SA	0517 1157 1738	10.0 1.9 10.2	29 SU	0017 0554 1242 1818	1.4 10.8 1.3 10.9
15 SU	0018 0556 1240 1816	1.8 10.6 1.5 10.7	30 M	0059 0633 1320 ○ 1854	1.3 11.0 1.3 11.0

Chart Datum is 5·88 metres below Ordnance Datum (Local). HAT is 12·2 metres above Chart Datum.

STANDARD TIME (UT)
For Summer Time add ONE hour in **non-shaded areas**

ST HELIER LAT 49°11'N LONG 2°07'W

TIMES AND HEIGHTS OF HIGH AND LOW WATERS

Dates in red are SPRINGS
Dates in blue are NEAPS

YEAR **2018**

MAY

Date	Day	Time	m	Time	m	Time	m	Time	m	Moon
1	TU	0136	1.3	0709	10.9	1353	1.4	1927	10.9	
2	W	0207	1.4	0743	10.7	1422	1.7	1958	10.7	
3	TH	0237	1.7	0814	10.4	1450	2.0	2028	10.3	
4	F	0305	2.1	0843	9.9	1517	2.5	2056	9.7	
5	SA	0335	2.6	0913	9.3	1545	3.1	2125	9.1	
6	SU	0407	3.2	0946	8.6	1618	3.7	2201	8.5	
7	M	0447	3.8	1030	8.0	1703	4.2	2253	7.9	
8	TU	0543	4.2	1139	7.6	1811	4.6			◑
9	W	0020	7.6	0659	4.3	1316	7.6	1939	4.5	
10	TH	0155	7.8	0823	4.0	1433	8.1	2100	4.0	
11	F	0300	8.4	0931	3.4	1529	8.8	2202	3.3	
12	SA	0352	9.1	1027	2.7	1617	9.5	2254	2.6	
13	SU	0438	9.8	1117	2.1	1701	10.1	2342	2.0	
14	M	0523	10.4	1205	1.6	1744	10.7			
15	TU	0028	1.5	0606	10.9	1250	1.2	1826	11.1	●
16	W	0113	1.2	0650	11.2	1333	1.0	1908	11.3	
17	TH	0156	1.0	0733	11.2	1415	1.0	1951	11.3	
18	F	0238	1.0	0817	11.0	1457	1.3	2034	11.0	
19	SA	0321	1.3	0903	10.6	1540	1.7	2119	10.5	
20	SU	0406	1.8	0951	10.0	1626	2.3	2207	9.9	
21	M	0457	2.4	1045	9.3	1720	2.9	2304	9.3	
22	TU	0557	2.9	1151	8.8	1827	3.3			◐
23	W	0015	8.8	0710	3.2	1309	8.6	1944	3.4	
24	TH	0136	8.8	0826	3.1	1425	8.9	2058	3.1	
25	F	0249	9.1	0935	2.7	1529	9.3	2203	2.7	
26	SA	0350	9.5	1034	2.3	1623	9.8	2259	2.3	
27	SU	0442	9.9	1126	2.1	1709	10.2	2347	2.0	
28	M	0527	10.2	1210	1.9	1750	10.4			
29	TU	0029	1.9	0607	10.3	1249	1.9	1827	10.5	○
30	W	0107	1.8	0644	10.4	1323	1.9	1901	10.5	
31	TH	0140	1.8	0718	10.3	1354	2.0	1933	10.4	

JUNE

Date	Day	Time	m	Time	m	Time	m	Time	m	Moon
1	F	0212	2.0	0751	10.1	1424	2.2	2005	10.2	
2	SA	0243	2.2	0823	9.8	1455	2.5	2036	9.8	
3	SU	0315	2.5	0855	9.4	1526	2.9	2107	9.4	
4	M	0349	2.9	0929	9.0	1600	3.4	2143	8.9	
5	TU	0426	3.3	1009	8.5	1640	3.8	2227	8.5	
6	W	0513	3.7	1101	8.1	1733	4.1	2326	8.1	◑
7	TH	0612	3.9	1209	8.0	1841	4.2			
8	F	0042	8.1	0721	3.9	1325	8.1	1956	4.0	
9	SA	0158	8.4	0833	3.5	1432	8.6	2107	3.5	
10	SU	0301	8.9	0938	3.0	1530	9.3	2209	2.9	
11	M	0357	9.6	1036	2.4	1623	9.9	2305	2.2	
12	TU	0449	10.2	1130	1.9	1713	10.5	2358	1.7	
13	W	0541	10.7	1222	1.4	1803	11.0			●
14	TH	0049	1.3	0630	11.0	1313	1.2	1850	11.3	
15	F	0140	1.0	0720	11.2	1401	1.1	1938	11.4	
16	SA	0228	0.9	0808	11.1	1448	1.2	2026	11.2	
17	SU	0316	1.1	0857	10.8	1535	1.5	2113	10.9	
18	M	0404	1.5	0945	10.3	1623	1.9	2201	10.3	
19	TU	0453	1.9	1035	9.7	1713	2.5	2252	9.7	
20	W	0545	2.5	1130	9.2	1808	3.0	2349	9.2	◐
21	TH	0644	2.9	1232	8.8	1911	3.3			
22	F	0056	8.9	0748	3.2	1342	8.7	2019	3.3	
23	SA	0208	8.8	0855	3.2	1450	8.9	2125	3.2	
24	SU	0314	9.0	0957	3.0	1549	9.2	2225	2.9	
25	M	0411	9.2	1052	2.8	1639	9.6	2317	2.6	
26	TU	0500	9.5	1140	2.6	1723	9.9			
27	W	0002	2.4	0543	9.7	1222	2.4	1802	10.1	
28	TH	0042	2.2	0622	9.9	1258	2.3	1839	10.2	○
29	F	0118	2.1	0658	10.0	1332	2.3	1913	10.3	
30	SA	0152	2.1	0732	10.0	1405	2.3	1947	10.2	

JULY

Date	Day	Time	m	Time	m	Time	m	Time	m	Moon
1	SU	0226	2.1	0806	9.9	1438	2.4	2019	10.1	
2	M	0259	2.3	0839	9.7	1510	2.6	2052	9.8	
3	TU	0332	2.5	0912	9.4	1543	2.9	2126	9.5	
4	W	0407	2.8	0948	9.1	1619	3.2	2203	9.1	
5	TH	0446	3.2	1028	8.7	1702	3.6	2247	8.7	
6	F	0532	3.5	1118	8.5	1754	3.8	2345	8.4	◑
7	SA	0629	3.6	1222	8.4	1900	3.9			
8	SU	0055	8.4	0738	3.6	1335	8.5	2015	3.7	
9	M	0211	8.7	0851	3.3	1446	9.0	2128	3.1	
10	TU	0320	9.2	1000	2.7	1550	9.6	2233	2.5	
11	W	0423	9.8	1103	2.2	1649	10.3	2334	1.9	
12	TH	0522	10.4	1202	1.7	1745	10.9			
13	F	0033	1.3	0617	10.9	1258	1.3	1837	11.3	●
14	SA	0129	1.0	0709	11.2	1351	1.0	1928	11.5	
15	SU	0221	0.7	0759	11.3	1440	1.0	2016	11.5	
16	M	0309	0.8	0846	11.1	1527	1.1	2101	11.3	
17	TU	0355	1.0	0931	10.7	1611	1.5	2145	10.8	
18	W	0439	1.5	1014	10.2	1655	2.1	2229	10.1	
19	TH	0522	2.2	1059	9.5	1739	2.7	2315	9.4	◐
20	F	0607	2.9	1149	8.9	1830	3.3			
21	SA	0010	8.8	0701	3.4	1251	8.5	1932	3.7	
22	SU	0120	8.3	0807	3.7	1404	8.4	2043	3.8	
23	M	0236	8.3	0918	3.7	1515	8.6	2152	3.5	
24	TU	0343	8.6	1022	3.4	1613	9.0	2250	3.2	
25	W	0438	9.0	1114	3.1	1701	9.4	2339	2.8	
26	TH	0524	9.4	1159	2.7	1743	9.8			
27	F	0021	2.4	0604	9.7	1239	2.5	1820	10.1	○
28	SA	0100	2.2	0641	9.9	1315	2.3	1856	10.3	
29	SU	0136	2.0	0715	10.1	1349	2.2	1929	10.4	
30	M	0210	2.0	0748	10.1	1422	2.2	2002	10.4	
31	TU	0242	2.0	0820	10.1	1454	2.2	2034	10.3	

AUGUST

Date	Day	Time	m	Time	m	Time	m	Time	m	Moon
1	W	0314	2.1	0852	10.0	1525	2.4	2106	10.0	
2	TH	0347	2.3	0925	9.7	1558	2.7	2139	9.7	
3	F	0421	2.7	0959	9.3	1635	3.1	2216	9.2	
4	SA	0459	3.1	1040	8.9	1718	3.5	2302	8.8	◑
5	SU	0547	3.5	1134	8.6	1815	3.8			
6	M	0007	8.5	0652	3.7	1247	8.4	1932	3.8	
7	TU	0130	8.4	0814	3.6	1411	8.7	2058	3.4	
8	W	0255	8.8	0935	3.1	1528	9.3	2213	2.7	
9	TH	0409	9.5	1045	2.4	1635	10.0	2320	2.0	
10	F	0512	10.2	1148	1.8	1734	10.8			
11	SA	0022	1.3	0607	10.9	1247	1.2	1826	11.4	●
12	SU	0118	0.8	0658	11.3	1339	0.9	1915	11.7	
13	M	0209	0.5	0745	11.5	1427	0.7	2001	11.8	
14	TU	0255	0.5	0828	11.4	1511	0.8	2043	11.6	
15	W	0336	0.8	0908	11.1	1551	1.2	2122	11.0	
16	TH	0414	1.4	0946	10.5	1628	1.9	2159	10.3	
17	F	0449	2.2	1023	9.7	1704	2.7	2237	9.4	
18	SA	0524	3.0	1102	8.9	1744	3.4	2322	8.6	◐
19	SU	0607	3.8	1155	8.2	1838	4.1			
20	M	0025	7.9	0711	4.3	1315	7.9	1956	4.3	
21	TU	0157	7.7	0838	4.4	1444	8.0	2121	4.1	
22	W	0320	8.1	0955	4.0	1551	8.6	2226	3.6	
23	TH	0420	8.6	1052	3.4	1641	9.2	2317	3.0	
24	F	0506	9.2	1138	2.9	1723	9.7			
25	SA	0000	2.5	0545	9.7	1219	2.5	1801	10.1	
26	SU	0040	2.1	0621	10.1	1256	2.2	1835	10.4	○
27	M	0117	1.9	0654	10.3	1331	2.0	1909	10.6	
28	TU	0151	1.7	0726	10.5	1404	1.9	1941	10.7	
29	W	0223	1.7	0758	10.6	1435	1.8	2012	10.7	
30	TH	0254	1.7	0829	10.5	1506	2.0	2044	10.5	
31	F	0325	1.9	0900	10.2	1538	2.3	2116	10.1	

Chart Datum is 5·88 metres below Ordnance Datum (Local). HAT is 12·2 metres above Chart Datum.

STANDARD TIME (UT)
For Summer Time add ONE hour in **non-shaded areas**

ST HELIER LAT 49°11′N LONG 2°07′W

TIMES AND HEIGHTS OF HIGH AND LOW WATERS

Dates in red are SPRINGS
Dates in blue are NEAPS

YEAR **2018**

SEPTEMBER

Date	Day	Time	m	Time	m	Time	m	Time	m
1	SA	0357	2.3	0933	9.8	1611	2.7	2150	9.6
2	SU	0433	2.9	1009	9.3	1650	3.2	2232	9.0
3	M	0516	3.4	1058	8.7	1744	3.7	◑ 2334	8.4
4	TU	0620	3.9	1212	8.3	1905	4.0		
5	W	0106	8.2	0751	3.9	1350	8.4	2042	3.6
6	TH	0246	8.5	0922	3.4	1519	9.1	2204	2.9
7	F	0403	9.4	1035	2.6	1627	10.0	2311	2.0
8	SA	0503	10.3	1137	1.8	1723	10.8		
9	SU	0010	1.2	0555	11.0	1233	1.2	● 1812	11.5
10	M	0104	0.7	0642	11.5	1323	0.8	1858	11.8
11	TU	0151	0.5	0724	11.7	1407	0.6	1940	11.9
12	W	0232	0.6	0804	11.6	1447	0.8	2019	11.6
13	TH	0310	0.9	0840	11.2	1523	1.2	2054	11.1
14	F	0342	1.5	0914	10.6	1555	1.9	2127	10.3
15	SA	0412	2.3	0945	9.8	1625	2.7	2159	9.4
16	SU	0440	3.2	1017	9.0	1658	3.6	◐ 2235	8.5
17	M	0514	4.0	1059	8.2	1744	4.3	2329	7.7
18	TU	0611	4.7	1216	7.6	1903	4.7		
19	W	0115	7.4	0751	4.9	1411	7.6	2045	4.5
20	TH	0256	7.7	0926	4.4	1527	8.2	2159	3.9
21	F	0357	8.4	1027	3.7	1617	9.0	2250	3.2
22	SA	0442	9.1	1112	3.0	1659	9.6	2333	2.5
23	SU	0520	9.7	1152	2.5	1736	10.2		
24	M	0013	2.1	0555	10.2	1231	2.1	1810	10.6
25	TU	0051	1.8	0628	10.6	1307	1.8	○ 1844	10.8
26	W	0127	1.5	0701	10.8	1341	1.6	1917	11.0
27	TH	0200	1.4	0733	10.9	1414	1.6	1949	11.0
28	F	0232	1.5	0805	10.9	1446	1.7	2022	10.8
29	SA	0304	1.7	0838	10.6	1518	2.0	2056	10.4
30	SU	0336	2.2	0911	10.1	1553	2.5	2131	9.8

OCTOBER

Date	Day	Time	m	Time	m	Time	m	Time	m
1	M	0412	2.8	0948	9.5	1633	3.1	2215	9.0
2	TU	0457	3.4	1038	8.8	1728	3.7	◑ 2319	8.4
3	W	0604	4.0	1155	8.3	1853	4.0		
4	TH	0059	8.1	0740	4.1	1341	8.3	2034	3.7
5	F	0242	8.5	0913	3.5	1511	9.1	2154	2.9
6	SA	0354	9.4	1024	2.6	1615	10.0	2258	2.0
7	SU	0449	10.3	1122	1.8	1707	10.8	2353	1.3
8	M	0537	11.0	1214	1.2	1754	11.4		
9	TU	0042	0.9	0620	11.4	1301	0.9	● 1836	11.7
10	W	0126	0.8	0700	11.6	1342	0.9	1916	11.7
11	TH	0204	0.9	0737	11.5	1419	1.1	1952	11.4
12	F	0238	1.3	0811	11.1	1452	1.5	2025	10.9
13	SA	0308	1.8	0841	10.6	1521	2.1	2056	10.2
14	SU	0334	2.5	0910	9.9	1550	2.8	2125	9.4
15	M	0401	3.3	0939	9.1	1620	3.6	2158	8.5
16	TU	0432	4.1	1015	8.3	1701	4.2	◐ 2244	7.8
17	W	0521	4.7	1117	7.6	1810	4.7		
18	TH	0017	7.3	0649	5.1	1321	7.5	1952	4.7
19	F	0215	7.5	0839	4.8	1449	8.0	2116	4.2
20	SA	0321	8.2	0948	4.0	1543	8.7	2212	3.4
21	SU	0407	9.0	1036	3.3	1625	9.4	2257	2.8
22	M	0446	9.6	1119	2.7	1703	10.0	2339	2.2
23	TU	0523	10.2	1159	2.1	1740	10.5		
24	W	0019	1.8	0557	10.6	1238	1.8	○ 1815	10.9
25	TH	0058	1.5	0632	11.0	1315	1.5	1851	11.1
26	F	0134	1.4	0708	11.2	1351	1.4	1927	11.2
27	SA	0209	1.4	0743	11.1	1426	1.5	2004	11.0
28	SU	0244	1.6	0819	10.9	1503	1.8	2042	10.5
29	M	0321	2.1	0857	10.4	1541	2.3	2123	9.9
30	TU	0401	2.7	0939	9.7	1626	2.9	2212	9.2
31	W	0450	3.3	1033	9.0	1725	3.5	◑ 2319	8.5

NOVEMBER

Date	Day	Time	m	Time	m	Time	m	Time	m
1	TH	0559	3.9	1149	8.5	1848	3.8		
2	F	0053	8.3	0730	3.9	1327	8.5	2020	3.5
3	SA	0225	8.7	0855	3.4	1451	9.1	2135	2.8
4	SU	0333	9.4	1003	2.7	1554	9.9	2236	2.1
5	M	0427	10.2	1100	2.0	1645	10.5	2329	1.6
6	TU	0514	10.7	1150	1.6	1731	11.0		
7	W	0016	1.4	0556	11.1	1235	1.4	● 1812	11.2
8	TH	0058	1.3	0634	11.2	1315	1.3	1850	11.2
9	F	0135	1.4	0710	11.1	1350	1.5	1926	11.0
10	SA	0207	1.7	0743	10.9	1422	1.8	1959	10.6
11	SU	0236	2.1	0814	10.5	1452	2.2	2030	10.0
12	M	0304	2.6	0843	9.9	1522	2.7	2101	9.4
13	TU	0332	3.2	0913	9.3	1553	3.4	2133	8.8
14	W	0404	3.9	0948	8.6	1632	3.9	2215	8.1
15	TH	0447	4.4	1037	8.0	1727	4.4	◐ 2321	7.6
16	F	0554	4.8	1201	7.6	1845	4.6		
17	SA	0101	7.5	0725	4.8	1344	7.8	2011	4.4
18	SU	0224	8.0	0849	4.4	1451	8.3	2119	3.8
19	M	0319	8.6	0948	3.7	1540	9.0	2212	3.1
20	TU	0404	9.3	1037	3.0	1624	9.6	2300	2.5
21	W	0445	10.0	1123	2.4	1705	10.2	2344	2.0
22	TH	0525	10.5	1207	1.9	1746	10.7		
23	F	0027	1.6	0604	10.9	1249	1.6	○ 1827	11.0
24	SA	0109	1.4	0645	11.2	1331	1.4	1908	11.1
25	SU	0150	1.4	0725	11.3	1412	1.4	1951	11.0
26	M	0230	1.5	0807	11.1	1453	1.6	2035	10.7
27	TU	0312	1.9	0851	10.7	1537	2.0	2122	10.1
28	W	0357	2.4	0938	10.1	1626	2.5	2213	9.5
29	TH	0448	3.0	1032	9.5	1724	3.0	2315	9.0
30	F	0552	3.4	1138	9.0	1835	3.3	◑	

DECEMBER

Date	Day	Time	m	Time	m	Time	m	Time	m
1	SA	0030	8.7	0707	3.6	1257	8.8	1952	3.3
2	SU	0151	8.8	0825	3.4	1416	9.0	2104	3.0
3	M	0301	9.2	0933	3.0	1523	9.5	2207	2.6
4	TU	0359	9.7	1032	2.5	1619	9.9	2301	2.2
5	W	0448	10.2	1124	2.1	1707	10.2	2349	2.0
6	TH	0531	10.5	1210	1.9	1750	10.4		
7	F	0031	1.9	0610	10.7	1251	1.9	● 1828	10.5
8	SA	0108	2.0	0646	10.7	1326	1.9	1905	10.5
9	SU	0141	2.1	0721	10.6	1359	2.0	1939	10.3
10	M	0212	2.3	0753	10.4	1431	2.2	2011	10.0
11	TU	0242	2.6	0825	10.1	1502	2.6	2044	9.6
12	W	0313	3.0	0856	9.6	1535	3.0	2117	9.1
13	TH	0345	3.4	0930	9.1	1611	3.4	2154	8.6
14	F	0422	3.9	1009	8.6	1654	3.8	2239	8.2
15	SA	0510	4.3	1101	8.2	1748	4.1	◐ 2341	7.9
16	SU	0614	4.5	1213	7.9	1857	4.2		
17	M	0059	7.9	0731	4.4	1335	8.1	2012	4.0
18	TU	0213	8.2	0847	4.0	1442	8.5	2119	3.5
19	W	0312	8.8	0950	3.4	1538	9.1	2217	2.9
20	TH	0404	9.5	1045	2.8	1629	9.8	2310	2.3
21	F	0453	10.2	1136	2.1	1719	10.4		
22	SA	0000	1.8	0540	10.7	1227	1.6	○ 1807	10.8
23	SU	0049	1.5	0627	11.1	1315	1.3	1855	11.1
24	M	0136	1.3	0714	11.4	1403	1.1	1943	11.1
25	TU	0222	1.3	0800	11.4	1450	1.2	2031	11.0
26	W	0308	1.5	0847	11.1	1537	1.4	2118	10.6
27	TH	0355	1.8	0934	10.7	1624	1.8	2206	10.1
28	F	0443	2.3	1022	10.1	1714	2.3	2257	9.5
29	SA	0535	2.8	1116	9.5	1810	2.8	◑ 2355	9.0
30	SU	0635	3.2	1218	9.0	1913	3.2		
31	M	0103	8.7	0744	3.5	1331	8.8	2022	3.3

Chart Datum is 5·88 metres below Ordnance Datum (Local). HAT is 12·2 metres above Chart Datum.

North Brittany

Paimpol to Pointe de Penmarc'h

9.20.1	**Contents**	847
9.20.2	**Area map, Distance table and TSS off Ouessant**	848
9.20.3	**Tidal stream chartlets**	850
9.20.4	**Lights, buoys and waypoints**	852
9.20.5	**Passage information** North Brittany – 855 • Paimpol to Ploumanac'h – 856 • Les Sept Îles to Baie de Morlaix – 856 • Île de Batz to Le Four – 856 • Ouessant (Ushant) – 856 • Chenal du Four – 872 • Chenal de la Helle – 872 • Approaches to Brest – 872 • L'Iroise and Baie de Douarnenez – 872 • Raz de Sein to Pointe de Penmarc'h – 872	855
9.20.6	**Special notes for France; see Area 17**	
9.20.7	**Paimpol**	857
9.20.8	**Île de Bréhat** Passe de la Gaine	857
9.20.9	**Lézardrieux**	859
9.20.10	**Pontrieux**	860
9.20.11	**Tréguier**	860
9.20.12	**Port Blanc**	861
9.20.13	**Perros-Guirec** Les Sept Îles	861
9.20.14	**Ploumanac'h** Trégastel-Plage	863
9.20.15	**Trébeurden**	864
9.20.16	**Léguer River (Lannion)** Locquémeau • Locquirec	864
9.20.17	**Primel-Trégastel**	865
9.20.18	**Morlaix** Penzé River	866
9.20.19	**Roscoff** Île de Batz • Moguériec • Brignogan (Pontusval)	868
9.20.20	**L'Aber Wrac'h**	869
9.20.21	**L'Aber Benoit** Portsall • Argenton	870
9.20.22	**L'Aber-Ildut**	870
9.20.23	**Le Conquet** Anse de Bertheaume	871
9.20.24	**Chenal du Four**	873
9.20.25	**Île d'Ouessant** Île de Molène	874
9.20.26	**Rade de Brest, Brest tide tables/curves** R L'Elorn • R L'Aulne	875
9.20.27	**Brest, tidal coefficients**	879
9.20.28	**Camaret**	882
9.20.29	**Morgat**	882
9.20.30	**Douarnenez**	883
9.20.31/32	**Raz de Sein and Île de Sein**	884
9.20.33	**Audierne** Ste Evette • St Guénolé • Le Guilvinec	885

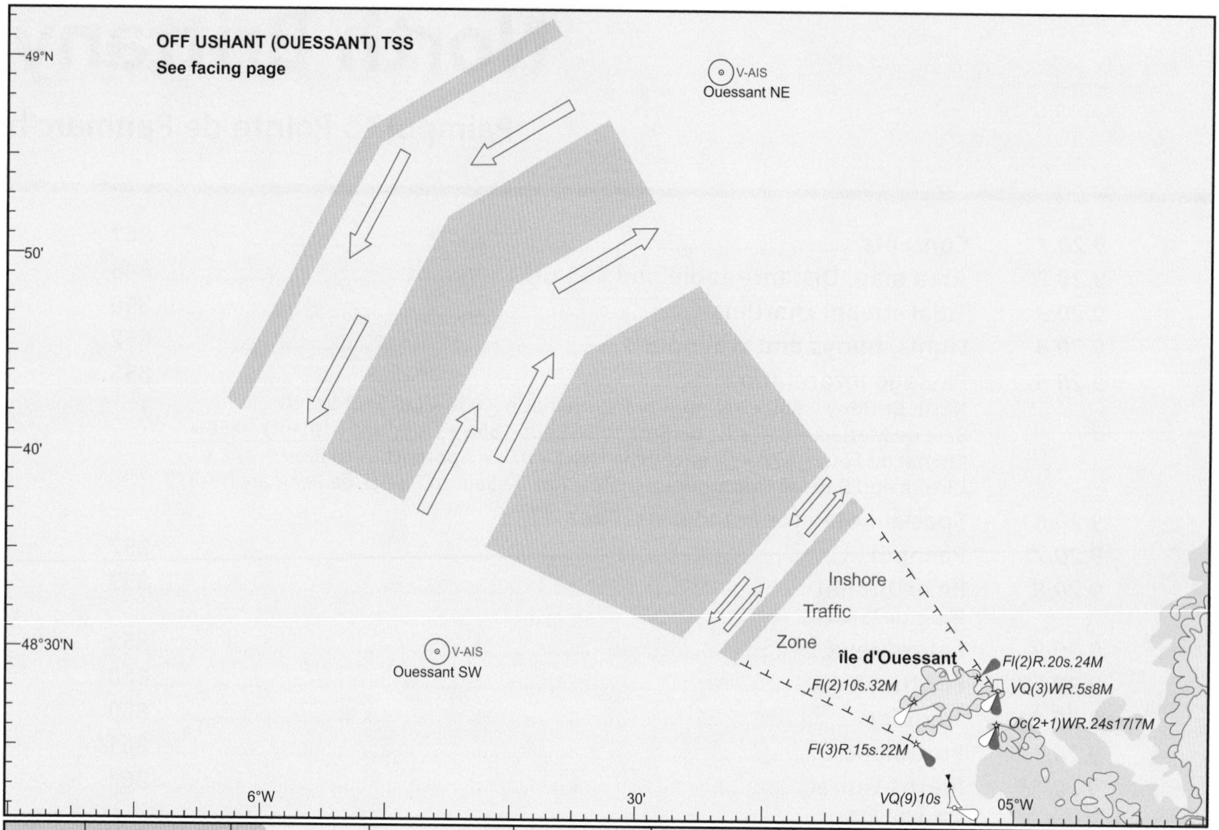
OFF USHANT (OUESSANT) TSS
See facing page
V-AIS
Ouessant NE
49°N
50'
40'
48°30'N
V-AIS
Ouessant SW
Inshore
Traffic
Zone
île d'Ouessant
Fl(2)R.20s.24M
Fl(2)10s.32M
VQ(3)WR.5s8M
Oc(2+1)WR.24s17/7M
Fl(3)R.15s.22M
VQ(9)10s
6°W
30'
05°W

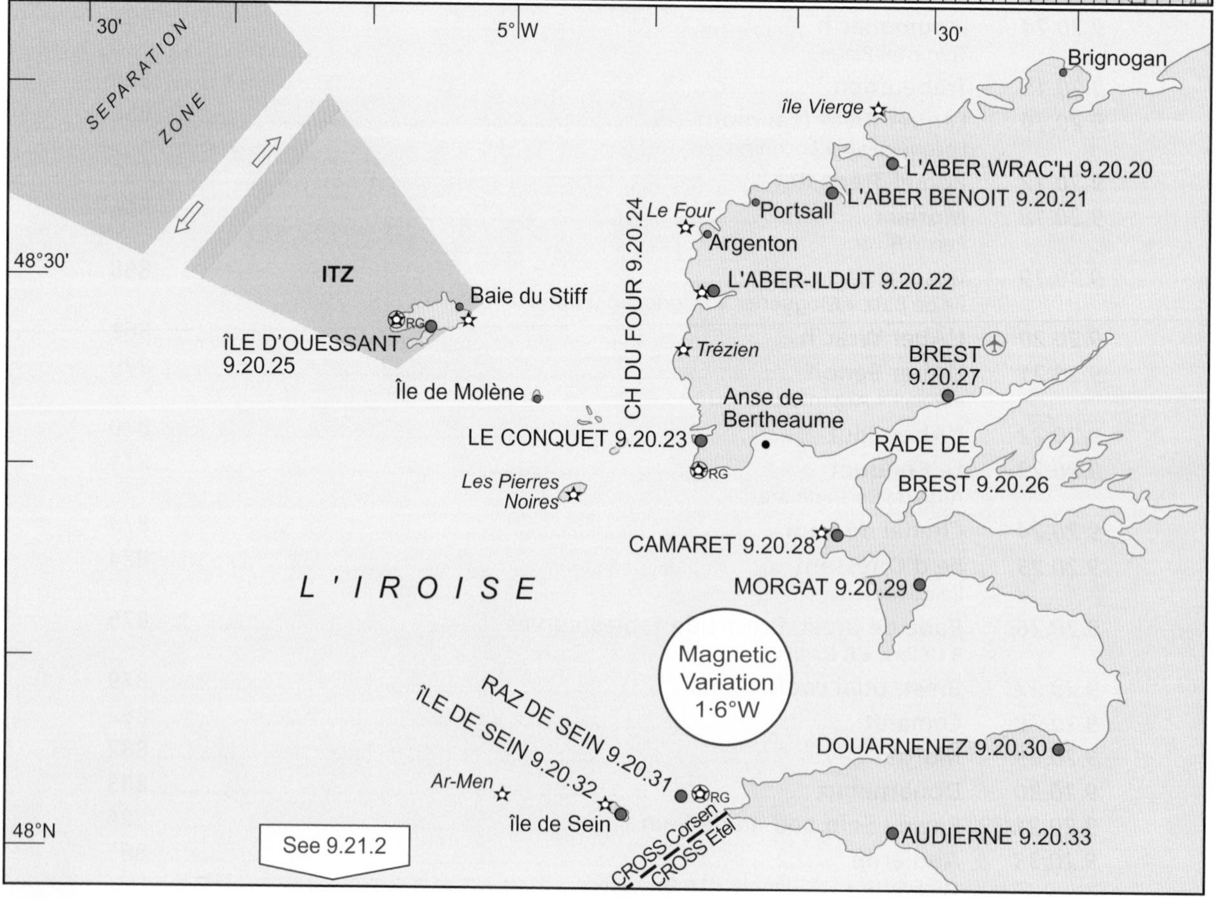
30'
5°W
30'
SEPARATION
ZONE
Brignogan
île Vierge
L'ABER WRAC'H 9.20.20
L'ABER BENOIT 9.20.21
Le Four
Portsall
Argenton
CH DU FOUR 9.20.24
48°30'
ITZ
L'ABER-ILDUT 9.20.22
Baie du Stiff
RG
ÎLE D'OUESSANT
9.20.25
Trézien
BREST
9.20.27
Île de Molène
Anse de
Bertheaume
LE CONQUET 9.20.23
RADE DE
BREST 9.20.26
RG
Les Pierres
Noires
CAMARET 9.20.28
L'IROISE
MORGAT 9.20.29
Magnetic
Variation
1·6°W
RAZ DE SEIN 9.20.31
ÎLE DE SEIN 9.20.32
DOUARNENEZ 9.20.30
Ar-Men
RG
île de Sein
48°N
See 9.21.2
CROSS Corsen
CROSS Etel
AUDIERNE 9.20.33

TRAFFIC SEPARATION SCHEME OFF ÎLE D'OUESSANT

The TSS and ITZ layout is depicted opposite and on AC 2675, 2649, 2655 and 2647. There are 3 lanes NW of Île d'Ouessant and the ITZ:

- A two-way lane, 2M wide (040°-220°) for passenger ships operating regular schedules from/to a Channel port west of 1°W and for vessels sailing from/to ports between Cap de la Hague and Cabo Finisterre
- A NE-bound lane, 4·8M wide (028°-208°; 060°-240°)
- An outer SW-bound lane, 4·8M wide, aligned as above

Yachts are advised to stay out of the TSS, not using any of the lanes. Cross the TSS only if essential. Otherwise they may route:

- To seaward of the TSS
- Through the ITZ, which is approx 8M wide (NW-SE)
- Inshore of Île d'Ouessant by the Passage du Fromveur
- Or, more usually, further inshore by the Chenal du Four.

Ouessant Traffic broadcasts: traffic info, nav warnings and special weather bulletins on Ch 79, in French and English, at H +10 and +40; and routine weather bulletins every 3hrs from 0150 UT, Ch 79.

Ouessant Traffic may provide radar surveillance within 40M of Le Stiff Radar (48°28′·57N 05°03′·18W) H24 on request Ch **13**, 79, 16.

9.20.2

North Brittany

Paimpol to Pointe de Penmarc'h

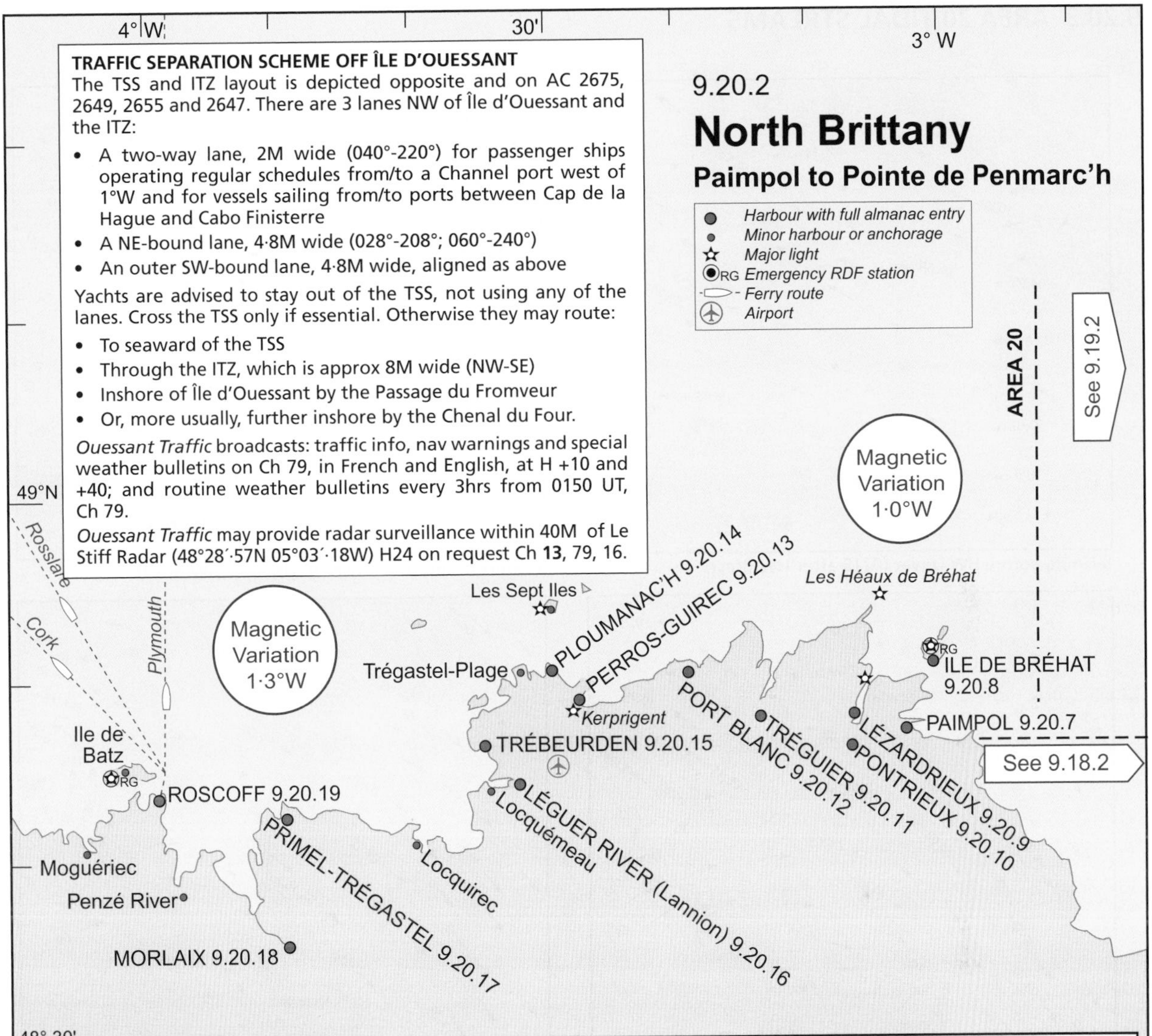
Harbour with full almanac entry
Minor harbour or anchorage
Major light
RG Emergency RDF station
Ferry route
Airport
4°W
30'
3° W
49°N
48° 30'
Magnetic Variation 1·0°W
Magnetic Variation 1·3°W
AREA 20
See 9.19.2
See 9.18.2
Rosslare
Cork
Plymouth
Les Sept Iles
Les Héaux de Bréhat
PLOUMANAC'H 9.20.14
PERROS-GUIREC 9.20.13
Trégastel-Plage
Kerprigent
TRÉBEURDEN 9.20.15
PORT BLANC 9.20.12
TRÉGUIER 9.20.11
LÉZARDRIEUX 9.20.9
PONTRIEUX 9.20.10
ILE DE BRÉHAT 9.20.8
PAIMPOL 9.20.7
Ile de Batz
RG
ROSCOFF 9.20.19
Moguériec
Penzé River
MORLAIX 9.20.18
PRIMEL-TRÉGASTEL 9.20.17
Locquirec
Locquémeau
LÉGUER RIVER (Lannion) 9.20.16

DISTANCE TABLE

Approximate distances in nautical miles are by the most direct route while avoiding dangers and allowing for TSS. Places in *italics* are in adjoining areas; places in **bold** are in 9.0.5, Cross-Channel Distances.

1	***St Quay-Portrieux***	**1**																								
2	Paimpol	15	**2**																							
3	Bréhat (Port Clos)	15	8	**3**																						
4	**Lézardrieux**	21	14	6	**4**																					
5	Pontrieux	28	21	13	11	**5**																				
6	**Tréguier**	30	29	22	22	29	**6**																			
7	Port Blanc	33	31	24	24	31	17	**7**																		
8	Perros-Guirec	37	35	28	28	35	21	4	**8**																	
9	Ploumanac'h	40	33	27	29	36	25	10	6	**9**																
10	Trébeurden	48	44	38	40	47	32	21	17	11	**10**															
11	**Lannion**	52	48	42	44	51	33	25	21	15	6	**11**														
12	Primel-Trégastel	58	52	44	47	54	37	26	22	17	12	16	**12**													
13	Morlaix	67	64	58	60	67	46	40	36	30	23	24	11	**13**												
14	**Roscoff**	59	58	52	54	61	41	32	28	22	17	19	7	12	**14**											
15	**L'Aberwrac'h**	91	88	82	84	91	72	64	60	54	49	51	39	48	32	**15**										
16	L'Aber Benoit	92	89	83	85	92	76	65	61	55	50	52	40	45	33	7	**16**									
17	Lampaul	114	110	104	106	113	98	87	83	77	72	74	62	67	55	29	28	**17**								
18	L'Aber-Ildut	105	101	95	97	104	89	78	74	68	63	62	53	59	46	20	14	8	**18**							
19	**Le Conquet**	114	110	104	106	113	98	87	83	77	72	71	62	68	55	29	23	17	9	**19**						
20	Brest (marina)	125	119	114	114	121	107	96	92	86	83	87	74	79	67	42	41	31	9	18	**20**					
21	Camaret	124	120	114	116	123	108	97	93	87	82	81	72	78	65	39	33	27	4	13	10	**21**				
22	Morgat	134	130	124	126	133	118	107	103	97	92	91	82	88	75	49	43	37	11	20	24	16	**22**			
23	Douarnenez	139	135	129	131	138	123	112	108	102	97	96	87	93	80	54	48	42	16	25	29	21	11	**23**		
24	Audierne	144	139	133	135	142	128	117	113	108	102	101	93	98	86	55	53	40	21	30	34	28	27	30	**24**	
25	*Loctudy*	169	165	159	161	168	153	142	138	132	127	126	117	123	110	84	78	72	46	55	62	55	53	55	30	**25**

9.20.3 AREA 20 TIDAL STREAMS

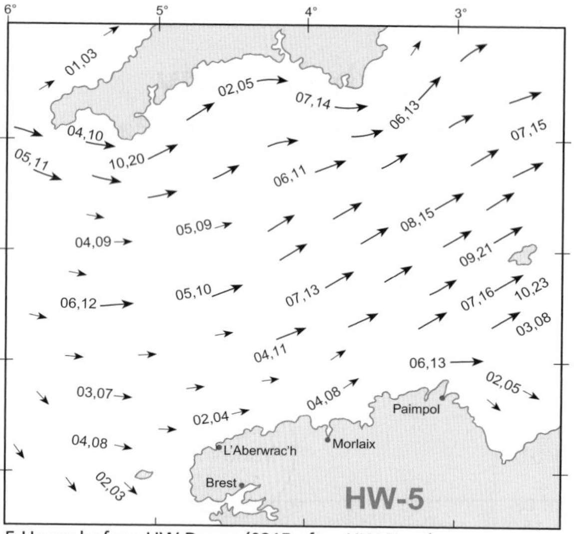

5 Hours before HW Dover (0215 after HW Brest)

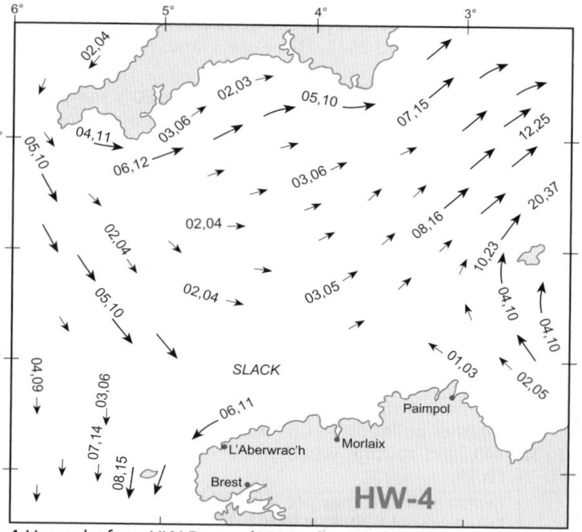

4 Hours before HW Dover (0315 after HW Brest)

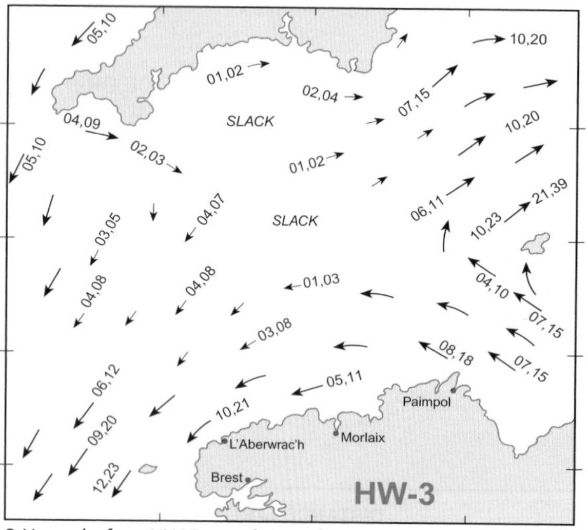

3 Hours before HW Dover (0415 after HW Brest)

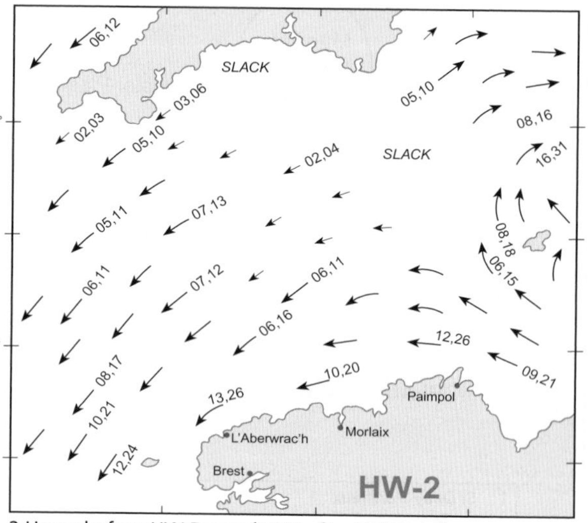

2 Hours before HW Dover (0515 after HW Brest)

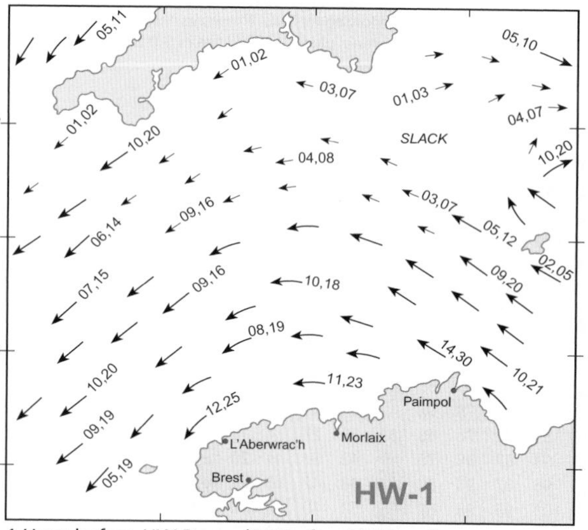

1 Hour before HW Dover (0615 after HW Brest)

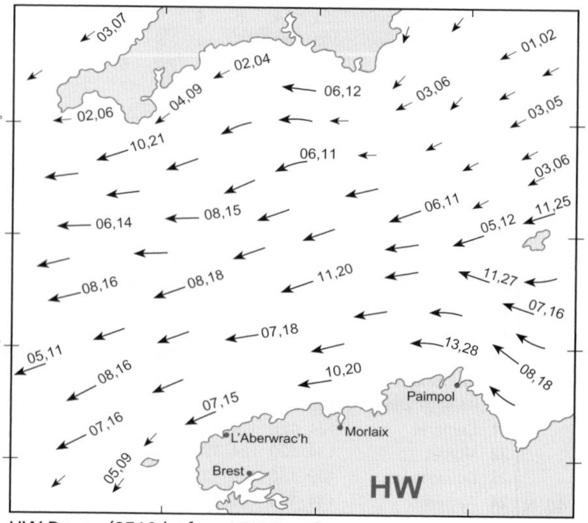

HW Dover (0510 before HW Brest)

Southward 9.21.3 Eastward 9.18.3 Northward 9.1.3

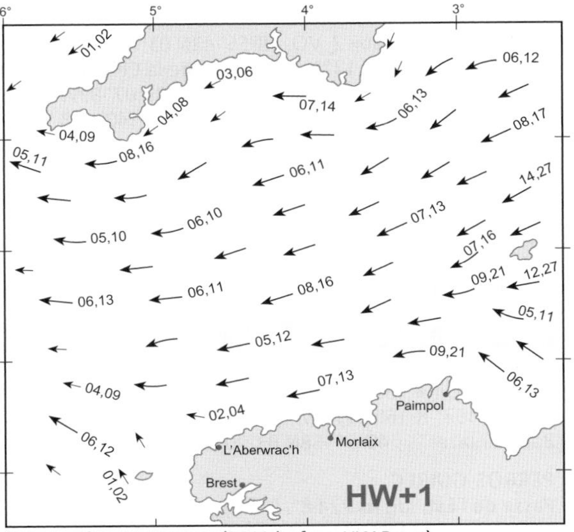

1 Hour after HW Dover (0410 before HW Brest)

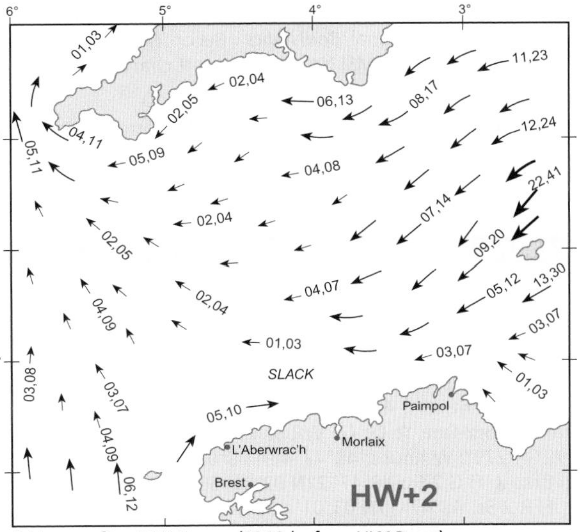

2 Hours after HW Dover (0310 before HW Brest)

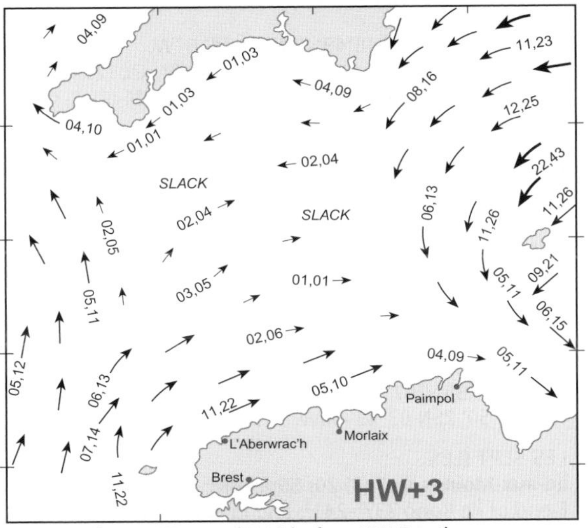

3 Hours after HW Dover (0210 before HW Brest)

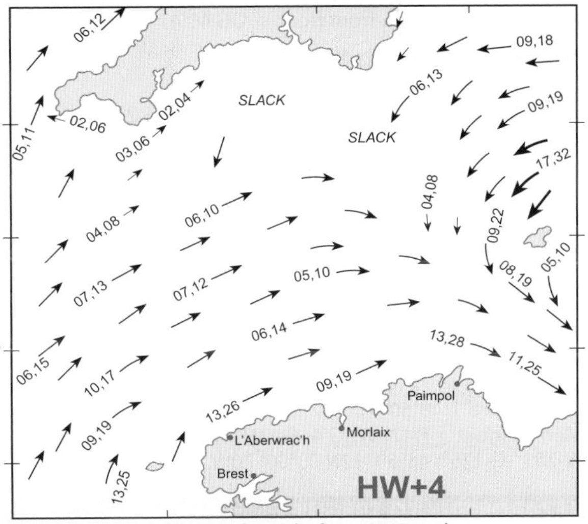

4 Hours after HW Dover (0110 before HW Brest)

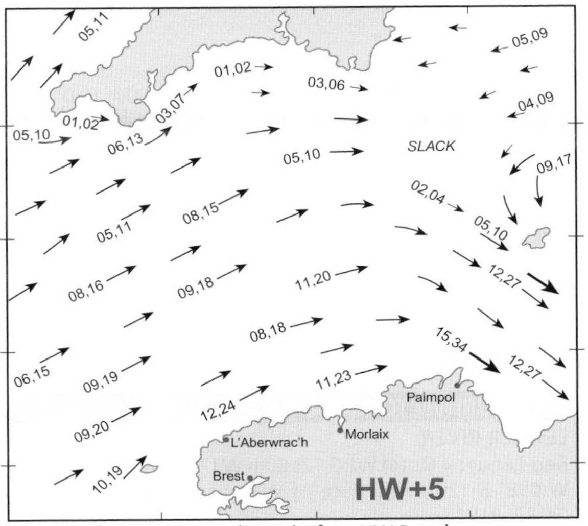

5 Hours after HW Dover (0010 before HW Brest)

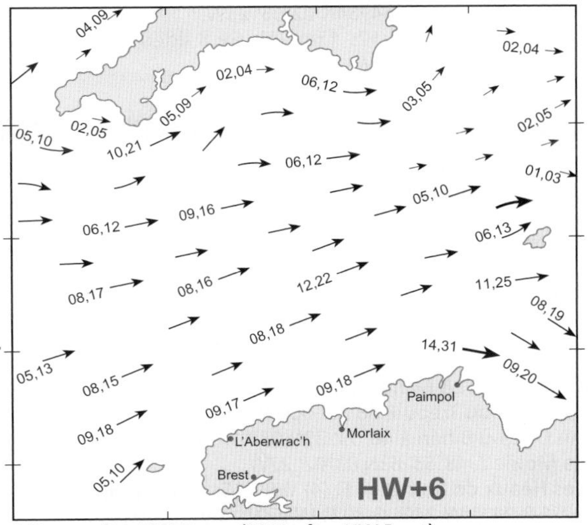

6 Hours after HW Dover (0050 after HW Brest)

N Brittany

9.20.4 LIGHTS, BUOYS AND WAYPOINTS

Bold print = light with a nominal range of 15M or more. CAPITALS = place or feature. *CAPITAL ITALICS* = light-vessel, light float or Lanby. *Italics* = Fog signal. ***Bold italics*** = Racon. Many marks/buoys are fitted with AIS (MMSI No); see relevant charts.

OFFSHORE MARKS

Roches Douvres ☆ Fl 5s 60m **24M**; pink twr on dwelling with G roof; 49°06′·30N 02°48′·87W. 992271319.
Barnouic VQ (3) 5s 15m 7M; 49°01′·63N 02°48′·41W.
Roche Gautier VQ (9) 10s; 49°02′·00N 02°54′·73W.

PAIMPOL TO ÎLE DE BRÉHAT

PAIMPOL

Les Calemarguiers 48°46′·98N 02°54′·84W.
L'Ost Pic Fl(4)WR 15s 20m, W9M, R6M; 105°-W-116°-R-221°-W-253°- R-291°-W-329°; obsc by islets near Bréhat when brg < 162°; W twr/turret, R top; 48°46′·77N 02°56′·42W.
Les Charpentiers 48°47′·89N 02°56′·01W.
Pte de Porz-Don ☆ Oc (2) WR 6s 13m **W15M**, R11M; 269°-W-272°-R-279°; W house; 48°47′·48N 03°01′·55W. 992271327.
El Bras Fl G 2·5s; 48°47′·21N 03°01′·50W.
Fl R 2·5s; 48°47′·17N 03°01′·49W.
Ldg lts 262·2°, both QR 5/12m 7/10M. Front, Kernoa jetty; W & R hut; 48°47′·09N 03°02′·44W. Rear, Dir QR, intens 260·2°-264·2°; W pylon, R top; 360m from front. QG 48°47′·12N 03°02′·47W.

CHENAL DU FERLAS (277°-257°-271°)

Lel Ar Serive 48°49′·98N 02°58′·76W.
Loguivy Dir lt 257°: Q WRG 12m 10/8M; 254°-G-257°-W-257·7°-R-260·7°; Gy twr; 48°49′·37N 03°03′·67W.
Les Piliers 48°49′·77N 02°59′·99W.
Kermouster Dir 271°: Fl WRG 2s 16m, W 10M, R/G 8M; 267°-G-270°-W-272°- R-274°; W col; 48°49′·55N 03°05′·19W (R. Trieux).

ÎLE DE BRÉHAT

Le Paon Oc WRG 4s 22m W11M, R/G8M; 033°-W-078°-G-181°-W-196°- R-307°-W-316°-R-348°; Y twr; 48°51′·92N 02°59′·15W.
Roche Guarine 48°51′·63N 02°57′·63W, Chenal de Bréhat.
Rosédo ☆ Fl 5s 29m **20M**; W twr; vis 006°-340° (334°); 48°51′·45N 03°00′·29W.
La Chambre 48°50′·16N 02°59′·58W.
Men-Joliguet Fl (2) WRG 4s 6m W11M, R/G8M; 255°-R-279°-W-283°-G-175°; 48°50′·12N 03°00′·20W.

LÉZARDRIEUX TO TRÉGUIER

LE TRIEUX RIVER to LÉZARDRIEUX

Nord Horaine 48°54′·54N 02°55′·23W.
La Horaine Fl (3) 12s 13m 7M; Gy 8-sided twr on B hut; 48°53′·50N 02°55′·22W.
Men-Marc'h 48°53′·17N 02°51′·82W.
Ldg lts 224·8°: Front, **La Croix** ☆ Q 15m **18M**; intens 215°-235°; two Gy ○ twrs joined, W on NE side, R tops; 48°50′·23N 03°03′·25W. Rear **Bodic** ☆ Dir Q 55m **22M**; intens 221°-229°; W ho with G gable; 2·1M from front.
Les Sirlots *Whis;* 48°52′·95N 02°59′·58W.
Coatmer ldg lts 218·7°. Front, Q RG 16m R/G7M; 200°-R-250°-G-053°; W gable; 48°48′·26N 03°05′·75W. Rear, QR 50m 7M; vis 197°-242°; W gable; 660m from front.
Les Perdrix Fl (2) WG 6s 5m, W6M, G3M; 165°-G-197°-W-202·5°-G-040°; G twr; 48°47′·74N 03°05′·79W.

CHENAL DE LA MOISIE (339·4°); PASSE DE LA GAINE (241·5°)

La Vieille du Tréou 48°52′·00N 03°01′·09W.
An Ogejou Bihan 48°53′·37N 03°01′·91W.
La Moisie 48°53′·83N 03°02′·22W.
Les Héaux de Bréhat ☆ Fl (4) WRG 15s 48m, **W15M**, R/G11M; 227°-R-247°-W-270°-G-302°-W-227°; Gy ○ twr; 48°54′·50N 03°05′·17W. 992271320.
Basse des Héaux 48°54′·07N 03°05′·28W.
Pont de la Gaine 48°53′·12N 03°07′·40W.

JAUDY RIVER TO TRÉGUIER

La Jument des Héaux VQ; 48°55′·42N 03°08′·04W.
Grande Passe ldg lts 137°. Front, Port de la Chaine, Oc 4s 12m 11M; 042°-232°; W house; 48°51′·55N 03°07′·89W. Rear, **St Antoine** ☆ Dir Oc R 4s 34m **15M**; intens 134°-140°; R & W house; 0·75M from front. (Both marks are hard to see by day.)
Basse Crublent QR; *Whis;* 48°54′·29N 03°11′·16W.
Le Corbeau Fl R 4s; 48°53′·35N 03°10′·26W.
Pierre à l'Anglais Fl G 4s; 48°53′·21N 03°10′·46W.
Petit Pen ar Guézec Fl (2) G 6s; 48°52′·52N 03°09′·44W.
La Corne Fl (3) WRG 12s 14m W8M, R/G6M; 052°-W-059°-R-173°-G-213°-W-220°-R-052°; W twr, R base; 48°51′·35N 03°10′·62W.

TRÉGUIER TO TRÉBEURDEN

PORT BLANC

Le Voleur Dir 150°: Fl WRG 4s 17m, W14M, R/G 11M; 140°-G-148°-W-152°-R-160°; W twr; 48°50′·20N 03°18′·52W.
Basse Guazer ; 48°51′·58N 03°20′·96W.

PERROS-GUIREC

Passe de l'Est, ldg lts 224·8°. Front, Le Colombier Dir Q 28m 14M; intens 214·5°-234·5°; W house; 48°47′·87N 03°26′·66W. Rear, **Kerprigent** ☆, Dir Q 79m **21M**; intens 221°-228°; W twr, 1·5M from front.
Pierre du Chenal 48°49′·29N 03°24′·67W.
Passe de l'Ouest. Kerjean Dir lt 143·6°, Oc (2+1) WRG 12s 78m, W10M, R/G 8M; 133·7°-G-143·2°-W-144·8°- R-154·3°; W twr, B top; 48°47′·79N 03°23′·40W.
Les Couillons de Tomé 48°50′·90N 03°25′·75W.
La Horaine 48°49′·89N 03°27′·26W.
Roche Bernard 48°49′·43N 03°25′·46W.
Gommonénou VQ R 1M; 48°48′·27N 03°25′·83W.
Jetée du Linkin Fl (2) G 6s 4m 6M; W pile, G top; 48°48′·20N 03°26′·31W.

PLOUMANAC'H

Mean-Ruz Oc WR 4s 26m W12M, R9M; 226°-W-242°-R-226°; obsc by Pte de Trégastel when brg <080°; partly obsc by Les Sept-Îles 156°-207° and partly by Île Tomé 264°-278°; pink □ twr; 48°50′·25N 03°29′·00W.

LES SEPT ÎLES

Île-aux-Moines ☆ Fl (3) 20s 59m **24M**; obsc by Îliot Rouzic and E end of Île Bono 237°-241°, and in Baie de Lannion when brg <039°; Gy twr/dwelling; 48°52′·72N 03°29′·40W. 992271326.
Les Dervinis 48°52′·35N 03°27′·32W.

TRÉGASTEL-PLAGE

Île Dhu 48°50′·37N 03°31′·24W.
Les Triagoz Fl (2) WR 6s 31m W14M, R11M; 010°-W-339°-R-010°; obsc in places 258°-268° by Les Sept-Îles; Gy □ twr, R lantern; 48°52′·28N 03°38′·80W. 992271324.
Bar-ar-Gall VQ (9) 10s; 48°49′·79N 03°36′·22W.
Le Crapaud Q (9) 15s; 48°46′·67N 03°40′·59W.

TRÉBEURDEN

Pte de Lan Kerellec Iso WRG 4s; W8M, R/G5M; 058°-G-064°-W-069°-R-130°; Gy twr; 48°46′·74N 03°35′·06W.
Ar Gouredec VQ (6) + L Fl 10s; 48°46′·41N 03°36′·59W.
An Ervennou Fl (2) R 6s; 48°46′·48N 03°35′·96W.
NW bkwtr Fl G 2·5s 8m 2M; IPTS; 48°46′·33N 03°35′·21W.

TRÉBEURDEN TO MORLAIX

LÉGUER RIVER

Beg-Léguer Oc (4) WRG 12s 60m W12M, R/G9M; 007°-G-084°-W-098°-R-129°; west face of W house, R lantern; 48°44′·31N 03°32′·91W.
Kinierbel ; *Bell;* 48°44′·15N 03°35′·18W.

LOCQUÉMEAU
Ldg lts 121°: Front, ✩ QR 21m 7M; 068°-228°; W pylon, R top; 48°43'·41N 03°34'·44W. Rear, ✩ QR 39m 7M; 016°-232°; W gabled house; 484m from front.
Locquémeau ▲ *Whis;* 48°43'·86N 03°35'·93W.
Locquémeau approach ▲ Fl G 2.5s; 48°43'·62N 03°34'·96W.

LOCQUIREC
Gouliat 48°42'·57N 03°38'·97W.

PRIMEL-TRÉGASTEL
Méloine 48°45'·56N 03°50'·68W.
Ldg lts 152°, both ✩ QR 35/56m 7M. Front, 134°-168°; W □, R stripe, on pylon; 48°42'·45N 03°49'·19W. Rear, R vert stripe on W wall; 172m from front.
W bkwtr ✩ Fl G 4s 6m 7M; 48°42'·77N 03°49'·52W.

BAIE DE MORLAIX
Chenal de Tréguier ldg lts 190·5°: Front, ✩ Île Noire Oc (2) WRG 6s 15m, W11M, R/G8M; 051°-G-135°-R-211°-W-051°; obsc in places; W □ twr, R top; 48°40'·35N 03°52'·54W. Common Rear, **La Lande** ☆ Fl 5s 85m **23M**; obsc by Pte Annelouesten when brg >204°; W □ twr, B top; 48°38'·20N 03°53'·14W.
La Pierre Noire 48°42'·56N 03°52'·20W.
La Chambre ▲ 48°40'·74N 03°52'·51W.

Grande Chenal ldg lts 176·4°: Front, **Île Louet** ☆ Oc (3) WG 12s 17m **W15M**,G10M; 305°-W (except where obsc by islands)-244°-G-305°; W □ twr, B top; 48°40'·41N 03°53'·34W. Common Rear, **La Lande** as above.
Pot de Fer *Bell;* 48°44'·23N 03°54'·02W.
Stolvezen 48°42'·64N 03°53'·41W.
Ricard ▲ 48°41'·54N 03°53'·51W.
Vieille ▲ 48°42'·60N 03°54'·11W. (Chenal Ouest de Ricard 188·8°)
La Noire 48°41'·65N 03°54'·06W.
Corbeau ▲ 48°40'·63N 03°53'·33W.

MORLAIX RIVER
Barre de-Flot No 1 ▲ 48°40'·18N 03°52'·95W.
No 2 Fl R 2s; 48°39'·88N 03°52'·53W.
No 3 Fl G 2s; 48°39'·25N 03°52'·32W.
No 4 Fl R 2s; 48°38'·62N 03°51'·62W.
No 5 ▲ Fl G 2s; 48°38'·04N 03°51'·34W.
No 7 ▲ 48°37'·68N 03°51'·03W.

PENZÉ RIVER
Cordonnier 48°42'·93N 03°56'·59W.
Guerhéon ▲ 48°42'·73N 03°57'·18W.
Trousken 48°42'·26N 03°56'·54W.
Pte Fourche ▲ 48°42'·14N 03°56'·76W.
Ar Tourtu 48°41'·99N 03°56'·57W.
An Nehou (Caspari) 48°41'·56N 03°56'·45W.
Le Figuier 48°40'·46N 03°56'·16W.

ROSCOFF TO ÎLE VIERGE

BLOSCON/ROSCOFF
Astan VQ (3) 5s 9m 6M; 48°44'·91N 03°57'·66W.
Le Menk Q (9) WR 15s 6m W5M, R3M; 160°-W-188°-R-160°; 48°43'·28N 03°56'·71W.
Basse de Bloscon VQ; 48°43'·71N 03°57'·55W.
Bloscon pier ✩ Fl WG 4s 9m W10M, G7M (in fog Fl 2s); 200°-W-210°-G-200°; W twr, G top; 48°43'·21N 03°57'·69W.
Roscoff Marina ent, E side, ✩ Fl (2) R 6s 4M; 48°43'·10N 03°57'·90W.
Ar Pourven Q; 48°43'·04N 03°57'·70W.
Ar-Chaden Q (6) + L Fl WR 15s 14m, W8M, R6M; 262°-R-289·5°-W-293°-R-326°- W-110°; YB twr; 48°43'·94N 03°58'·26W.
Men-Guen-Bras Q WRG 14m, W9M, R/ G6M; 068°-W-073°-R-197°-W-257°-G-068°; BY twr; 48°43'·76N 03°58'·07W.
Roscoff ldg lts 209°: Front, N môle ✩ Oc (3) G 12s 7m 7M; synch; 078°-318°; W col, G top; 48°43'·56N 03°58'·67W. **Rear** ☆ Oc (3) 12s 24m **15M**; 062°-242°; Gy □ twr, W on NE side; 430m from front.

CANAL DE L'ÎLE DE BATZ
Roc'h Zu 48°43'·88N 03°58'·59W.
Jetty hd (LW landing) ✩ Q 5m 1M; BY col; 48°43'·92N 03°58'·97W.
Run Oan 48°44'·10N 03°59'·30W.
Perroch 48°44'·10N 03°59'·71W.
Tec'hit Bihan 48°44'·02N 04°00'·88W.
La Croix 48°44'·19N 04°01'·30W.
L'Oignon 48°44'·04N 04°01'·35W.
Basse Plate 48°44'·25N 04°02'·53W.

ÎLE DE BATZ
Île aux Moutons VQ (6)+ L Fl 10s 3m 7M; 48°44'·25N 04°00'·52W; landing stage, S end and ent to hbr.
Malvoch 48°44'·26N 04°00'·67W, W side of ent.
Lt ho ☆ Fl (4) 25s 69m **23M**; Gy twr; 48°44'·71N 04°01'·62W. Same twr, auxiliary lt, FR 65m 7M; 024°-059°. 992271315.

MOGUÉRIEC
Ldg lts 162°: Front ✩ Iso WG 4s 9m W11M, G6M; 158°-W-166°-G-158°; W twr, G top; jetty 48°41'·34N 04°04'·47W. Rear ✩ Iso G 4s 22m 7M, synch; 142°-182°; W col, G top; 440m from front.

PONTUSVAL
Pointe de Pontusval 48°41'·42N 04°19'·32W.
Ar Peich ▲ 48°40'·90N 04°19'·16W.
Pte de Beg-Pol ✩ Oc (3) WR 12s 16m W10M, R7M; Shore-W-056°-R-096°-W-shore; W twr, B top, W dwelling; 48°40'·67N 04°20'·76W. QY and FR lts on towers 2·4M S.
Aman-ar-Ross Q 7M; 48°41'·88N 04°27'·03W.
Lizen Ven Ouest VQ (9) 10s 5M; 48°40'·53N 04°33'·63W.
Île-Vierge ☆ Fl 5s 77m **27M**; 337°-325°; Gy twr; 48°38'·33N 04°34'·05W. 992271317.

ÎLE VIERGE TO L'ABER-ILDUT

L'ABER WRAC'H
Libenter Q (9) 15s 6M; 48°37'·45N 04°38'·46W.
Outer ldg lts 100·1°: Front, Île Wrac'h ✩ QR 20m 7M; W □ twr, Or top; 48°36'·88N 04°34'·56W. Rear, Lanvaon ✩ Q 55m 12M; intens 090°-110°; W □ twr, Or △ on top; 1·63M from front.
Grand Pot de Beurre 48°37'·21N 04°36'·48W.
Petit Pot de Beurre 48°37'·12N 04°36'·23W.
Basse de la Croix ▲ Fl G 2·5s; 48°36'·92N 04°35'·99W.
Breac'h Ver ▲ Fl (2) G 6s 6m 3M; △ on twr; 48°36'·63N 04°35'·38W.
Dir ✩ 128°, Oc (2) WRG 6s 5m W13M, R/G11M; 125·7°-G-127·2°-W-128·7°-R-130·2°; 48°35'·89N 04°33'·82W, root of W bkwtr .
Marina ent: QG 3m 2M; vis 186°-167° (341°); 48°35'·97N 04°33'·64W. QR 3m 2M; vis 244°-226° (342°).

L'ABER BENOÎT
Petite Fourche 48°36'·99N 04°38'·75W.
Rusven Est ▲ 48°36'·30N 04°38'·63W.
Rusven Ouest *Bell;* 48°36'·07N 04°39'·43W.
Basse du Chenal 48°35'·81N 04°38'·53W.
Poul Orvil 48°35'·52N 04°38'·29W.
La Jument 48°35'·10N 04°37'·41W.
Ar Gazel ▲ 48°34'·90N 04°37'·27W.
Le Chien 48°34'·67N 04°36'·88W.

ROCHES DE PORTSALL
Le Relec 48°35'·99N 04°40'·84W.
Corn-Carhai ✩ Fl (3) 12s 19m 9M; W 8-sided twr, B top; 48°35'·19N 04°43'·94W.
Grande Basse de Portsall VQ (9) 10s 9m 4M; 48°36'·70N 04°46'·13W.
Basse Paupian 48°35'·31N 04°46'·27W.
Bosven Aval 48°33'·82N 04°44'·27W.

Men ar Pic 48°33′·65N 04°44′·03W.
Portsall Oc (4) WRG 12s 9m W13M, R/G10M; 058°-G-084°-W-088°-R-058°; W col, R top; 48°33′·84N 04°42′·26W.

ARGENTON to L'ABER-ILDUT

Le Taureau 48°31′·46N 04°47′·34W.
Argenton, Île Dolvez, front ldg bcn 086° 48°31′·25N 04°46′·23W.
Le Four ☆ Fl (5) 15s 28m **22M**; Gy ○ twr; 48°31′·38N 04°48′·32W.
L'Aber-Ildut ☆ Dir Oc (2) WRG 6s 12m W10M, R10M, G10M; 078°-G-081°-W- 085°-R- 088° ; W bldg; 48°28′·26N 04°45′·56W.
Le Lieu Fl R 2.5s 4M; 48°28′·25N 04°46′·66W.

CHENAL DU FOUR AND CHENAL DE LA HELLE

Ldg lts 158·5°. Front, **Kermorvan** ☆ Fl 5s 20m **22M**; obsc'd by Pte de St Mathieu when brg <341°; W □ twr; *Horn 60s*; 48°21′·72N 04°47′·40W. 992271316.
Rear, **Pte de St Mathieu** ☆ Fl 15s 56m **24M**; W twr, R top; 48°19′·79N 04°46′·26W. 992271318. Same twr: Dir F 54m **28M**; intens 157·5°-159·5°.
Q WRG 26m, W12M, R/G 8M; 085°-G-107°-W-116°-R-134°; W twr 54 m WNW of previous entry; 48°19′·80N 04°46′·30W.
Plâtresses N Fl G 2·5s; 48°26′·46N 04°50′·71W.
Valbelle Fl R 2·5s; 48°26′·43N 04°50′·03W.
Plâtresses SE Fl (2) G 6s; 48°25′·96N 04°50′·52W.
Saint Paul Fl (2) R 6s; 48°24′·82N 04°49′·16W.
Pte de Corsen Dir Q WRG 33m W12M, R/G8M; 008°-R-012°-W-015° (ldg sector)- G-021°; W hut; 48°24′·89N 04°47′·61W.

CHENAL DE LA HELLE

Ldg lts 137·9°: Front, **Kermorvan** ☆ see above. Rear, **Lochrist** ☆ Dir Oc (3) 12s 49m **22M**; intens 135°-140°; W 8-sided twr, R top; 48°20′·55N 04°45′·82W. 992271310.
Luronne ; 48°26′·61N 04°53′·78W.
Ldg lts 293·5° astern (to join Ch du Four S of St Paul): Front, Le Faix VQ 16m 8M; 48°25′·73N 04°53′·91W. Rear, **Le Stiff** ☆ (below at Ouessant); 6·9M from front.
Ldg line 142·5°, optional day only (to join Ch du Four SE of St Pierre): Front, **Kermorvan** ☆ see above. Rear, two W gables (Les Pignons de Kéravel, 48m) 48°20′·10N 04°45′·55W
Pourceaux Q; 48°24′·00N 04°51′·31W.
Saint-Pierre Fl (3) G 12s; 48°23′·09N 04°49′·09W.
Rouget Fl G 4s; 48°22′·04N 04°48′·88W (Ch du Four).
Grande Vinotière Fl R 4s 12m 5M; R 8-sided twr; 48°21′·94N 04°48′·42W.
Le Conquet, Môle Ste Barbe Fl G 2·5s 5m 6M; 48°21′·57N 04°46′·98W.
Les Renards 48°21′·00N 04°47′·48W.
Tournant et Lochrist Fl (2) R 6s; 48°20′·64N 04°48′·12W,
Ar Christian Braz 48°20′·68N 04°50′·14W, E of Ile de Béniguet.
Ldg line 325°: Front, Grand Courleau ; rear, La Faix (above).
Ldg lts 007°: Front, **Kermorvan** ☆ above. Rear, **Trézien** ☆ Dir Oc (2) 6s 84m **20M**; intens 003°-011°; Gy twr, W on S side; 48°25′·41N 04°46′·74W. 992271309.
Les Vieux-Moines Fl R 4s 16m 5M; 280°-133°; R 8-sided twr; 48°19′·33N 04°46′·63W, 5ca SSW of Pte de St Mathieu.
La Fourmi Fl G 4s; 48°19′·25N 04°47′·96W.

OUESSANT AND ÎLE MOLÉNE

OFF USHANT TSS

Ouessant NE ⊙; V-AIS; 48°59′·51N 05°24′·00W.
Ouessant SW ⊙; V-AIS 48°30′·00N 05°45′·00W.

ÎLE D'OUESSANT

Le Stiff ☆ Fl (2) R 20s 85m **24M**; two adjoining W twrs; 48°28′·47N 05°03′·41W. Radar twr, conspic, 340m NE, Q (day); FR (night).
Port du Stiff, E môle Dir Q WRG 11m W10M, R/G7M; 251°-G-254°-W-264°-R-267°; W twr, G top; 48°28′·12N 05°03′·25W.
Baie du Stiff: Gorle Vihan 48°28′·32N 05°02′·60W.
Men-Korn VQ (3) WR 5s 21m 8M; 145°-W-040°-R-145°; BYB twr; 48°27′·96N 05°01′·32W.
Men ar Froud 48°26′·62N 05°03′·67W.
La Jument Fl (3) R 12s 36m 10M; 241°-199°; Gy 8-sided twr, R top; 48°25′·33N 05°08′·04W.
Nividic VQ (9) 10s 28m 10M; 290°-225°; Gy 8-sided twr, helicopter platform; 48°26′·74N 05°09′·06W.
Créac'h ☆ Fl (2) 10s 70m **32M**; obsc 247°-255°; W twr, B bands; 48°27′·55N 05°07′·76W.

ÎLE MOLÈNE and ARCHIPELAGO

Kéréon Oc (3) WR 12s 38m 10M; 019°-W-248°- R-019°; Gy twr; 48°26′·24N 05°01′·59W; unreliable.
Les Trois-Pierres Iso WRG 4s 15m W9M, R/G6M; 070°-G-147°-W-185°-R-191°-G-197°-W-213°-R-070°; W col; 48°24′·70N 04°56′·84W.
Molène, Old môle Dir 191°, Fl (3) WRG 12s 6m W9M, R/G7M; 183°-G-190°-W-192°-R-203°; 48°23′·85N 04°57′·29W.
Same structure: Chenal des Laz , Dir 261°: Fl (2) WRG 6s 9m W9M, R/G7M ; 252·5°-G-259·5°-W-262·5°-R-269·5°.
Pierres-Vertes VQ (9) 10s 9m 5M; 48°22′·19N 05°04′·76W.
Pierres Noires ; 48°18′·47N 04°58′·15W.
Les Pierres Noires ☆ Fl R 5s 27m **19M**; W twr, R top; 48°18′·67N 04°54′·88W.

BREST AND APPROACHES

Basse Royale Q (6) + L Fl 15s; 48°17′·45N 04°49′·61W.
Vandrée VQ (9) 10s; *Whis;* 48°15′·21N 04°48′·24W.
Goëmant ; 48°15′·12N 04°46′·34W.
La Parquette Fl RG 4s 17m R6M, G6M; 244°-R-285°-G-244°; W 8-sided twr, B diagonal stripes; 48°15′·90N 04°44′·29W.
Coq Iroise 48°19′·07N 04°43′·99W.
Charles Martel Fl (4) R 15s; 48°18′·95N 04°41′·92W.
Trépied 48°16′·73N 04°41′·50W.
Swansea Vale Fl (2) 6s; *Whis;* 48°18′·27N 04°38′·85W.

GOULET DE BREST

Le Chat 48°20′·29N 04°41′·72W (Anse de Bertheaume).
Le Trez Hir 48°20′·78N 04°41′·96W.
Pte du Petit-Minou ☆ Fl (2) WR 6s 32m **W17M,** R13M; Shore-R-252°-W-260°-R-307°-W(unintens)-015°-W-065·5°; 036·5°-R(intens)-039·5°; 70·5°-W-shore; Gy twr, R top; 48°20′·19N 04°36′·86W. 992271300.
Ldg lts 068°, both Dir Q 30/54m **22M. Front, Pte du Petit-Minou,** intens 067·3°-068·8°. **Rear, Pte du Portzic** ☆, Aux Dir Q 54m; intens 065°-071° (see below).
Fillettes VQ (9) 10s; 48°19′·75N 04°35′·66W.
Kerviniou Fl R 2·5s; 48°19′·77N 04°35′·25W.
Basse Goudron Fl (2) R 6s; 48°20′·03N 04°34′·86W.
Mengam Fl (3) WR 12s 10m W11M, R8M; 034°-R-054°-W-034°; R twr, B bands; 48°20′·32N 04°34′·56W.
Pte du Portzic ☆ Oc (2) WR 12s 56m **W19M, R15M**; 219°-R-259°-W-338°-R-000°-W-065·5° (vis 041°-069° when west of Goulet)-W-219°; Gy twr; 48°21′·49N 04°32′·05W. Same lt ho, Aux Dir Q, rear 068° ldg lt. Aux ☆ Dir Q (6) + L Fl 15s 54m **23M**; intens 045°-050°.

BREST

Pénoupèle Fl R 2·5s; 48°21′·45N 04°30′·53W.
S jetty QR 10m 7M; 094°-048°; W/R twr; 48°22′·10N 04°29′·46W.
E jetty QG 10m 7M; W/G twr; 48°22′·15N 04°29′·22W.
Ldg lts 343.5°: Front Dir Q WRG 24m W9M, R/G6M; 334°-G-342°-W-346°-R-024°; 48°22′·80N 04°29′·62W. Rear Dir Q 32m 9M; intens 342°-346°; 115m from front.
Le Château Marina, S Jetty hd, Fl G 2·5s 8m 4M; 48°22′·66N 04°29′·49W.
Le Château Marina, N Jetty hd, Fl R 2·5s 8m 4M; 48°22′·67N 04°29′·45W.

Port de Commerce, E ent: N jetty Oc (2) G 6s 8m 7M; W/G pylon; 48°22'·76N 04°28'·53W. S jetty Oc (2) R 6s 8m 5M; W pylon, R top; 48°22'·69N 04°28'·48W.
R2 Fl (2) R 6s; 48°22'·01N 04°28'·75W.
R1 Fl G 6s; 48°21'·83N 04°28'·29W.
R4 Fl (3) R 12s; 48°22'·22N 04°28'·06W.
R3 Q (6) + L Fl 15s; 48°22'·48N 04°27'·36W.

LE MOULIN BLANC MARINA
Moulin Blanc Fl (2) R 6s; 48°22'·80N 04°25'·91W
MBA Q(3) 10s 3m 2M; pontoon elbow; 48°23'·54N 04°25'·74W.

CAMARET
N môle Iso WG 4s 7m W12M, G9M; 135°-W-182°-G-027°; W pylon, G top; 48°16'·85N 04°35'·31W.
Port Vauban wavebreak, S end, Fl (2) G 6s 2m 2M; 48°16'·74N 04° 35'·33W.
S môle Fl (2) R 6s 9m 5M; R pylon; 48°16'·63N 04°35'·33W.

POINTE DU TOULINGUET TO RAZ DE SEIN
Pte du Toulinguet ☆ Oc (3) WR 12s 49m **W15M**, R11M; Shore-W-028°-R-090°-W-shore; W □ twr; 48°16'·81N 04°37'·72W.
La Louve 48°16'·76N 04°38'·03W.
Mendufa 48°16'·05N 04°39'·43W.
Basse du Lis Q (6) + L Fl 15s 9m 6M; 48°12'·99N 04°44'·53W.
Le Chevreau 48°13'·30N 04°36'·98W.
Le Bouc Q (9) 15s; 48°11'·51N 04°37'·37W.
Basse Vieille Fl (2) 6s 8m 7M; 48°08'·22N 04°35'·75W.

MORGAT
Pointe de Morgat ☆ Oc (4) WRG 12s 77m **W15M**, R11M, G10M; Shore-W-281°-G-301°-W-021°-R-043°; W □ twr, R top, W dwelling; 48°13'·17N 04°29'·80W.
Hbr approach Q R 1.2s; 48°13'·60N 04°29'·55W.
Hbr ent Fl R 2.5s; 48°13'·58N 04°29'·72W'.

DOUARNENEZ to RAZ DE SEIN
Île Tristan Fl (3) WR 12s 35m, W6M, R6M; Shore-W-138°-R-153°-W-shore; Gy twr, W band, B top; 48°06'·14N 04°20'·24W.

Pointe du Millier ☆ Oc (2) WRG 6s 34m **W16M**, R12M, G11M; 080°-G-087°-W-113°-R-120°-W-129°-G-148°-W-251°-R-258°; W house; 48°05'·92N 04°27'·93W. 992271015.
Basse Jaune 48°04'·70N 04°42'·45W.

RAZ DE SEIN
Tévennec Q WR 28m W9M R6M; 090°-W-345°-R-090°; W □ twr and dwelling; 48°04'·28N 04°47'·73W. Same twr, Dir Fl 4s 24m 12M; intens 324°-332° (through Raz de Sein).

La Vieille ☆ Oc (2+1) WRG 12s 33m **W18M**, R13M, G14M; 290°-W-298°-R-325°-W-355°-G-017°-W-035°-G-105°-W-123°-R-158°-W-205°; Gy □ twr; 48°02'·44N 04°45'·40W.
La Plate Q (9) 15s 19m 6M; 48°02'·37N 04°45'·58W.
Le Chat Fl (2) WRG 6s 27m 6M; 096°-G-215°-W-230°-R-271°-G-286°-R-096°; YB twr; 48°01'·43N 04°48'·86W.

CHAUSSÉE DE SEIN and ÎLE DE SEIN
Cornoc-An-Ar-Braden Fl G 4s; 48°03'·23N 04°50'·84W.
Men-Brial Oc (2) WRG 6s 16m, W12M, R9M, G7M; 149°-G-186°-W-192°-R-221°-W-227°-G-254°; G&W twr; 48°02'·28N 04°50'·97W.
Île de Sein ☆ Fl (4) 25s 49m **29M**; W twr, B top; 48°02'·62N 04°52'·02W. Same twr, Dir Q WRG, W8M, R/G 6M; 267°-G-269°-W-271°-R-275°. 992271043.
Ar-Men ☆ Fl (3) 20s 29m **21M**; W twr, B top; 48°03'·01N 04°59'·87W. 992271044.
Chaussée de Sein VQ (9) 10s 9m 6M; *Whis*; ***Racon O (3cm), 10M***; 48°03'·74N 05°07'·75W.

AUDIERNE
Pointe de Lervily Fl WR 4s 20m W14M, R11M; 236°-W-269°-R-294°-W-087°-R-109°; W twr, R top; 48°00'·04N 04°33'·94W.
Gamelle W , VQ (9) 10s; 47°59'·46N 04°32'·85W.
Jetée de Ste-Évette Fl (2) R 6s 2m 7M; R lantern; 090°-000° (270°); 48°00'·31N 04°33'·07W.
Passe de l'Est ldg lts 331°: Front, Jetée de Raoulic Fl (3) RG 12s 11m, R/G6M; 085°-R-034°-G-085°-R-085°; 48°00'·55N 04°32'·46W.
Kergadec 006°: Dir Q WRG 43m W12M, R/G9M; 000°-G-005·3°-W-006·7°-R-017°; W 8-sided twr, R top; 48°00'·96N 04°32'·78W.
Gamelle E ; 47°59'·46N 04°32'·05W.

POINTE DE PENMARC'H
Eckmühl ☆ Fl 5s 60m **23M**; Gy 8-sided twr; 47°47'·89N 04°22'·36W.
Men-Hir Fl (2) WG 6s 19m, W7M, G4M; G135°-315°, W315°-135°; W twr, B band; 47°47'·74N 04°23'·99W.
Cap Caval Q (9) 15s; 47°46'·47N 04°22'·68W.
Locarec Iso WRG 4s 11m, W9M, R/G6M; 063°-G-068°-R-271°-W-285°-R-298°-G-340°-R-063°; iron col on rk; 47°47'·29N 04°20'·31W.

LE GUILVINEC
Névez Fl G 2·5s; 47°45'·84N 04°20'·08W.
Ldg lts (triple Q) 053°, all synch: **Front**, Q 7m 8M; 233°-066°; W pylon; Môle de Léchiagat, spur; 47°47'·43N 04°17'·07W. Middle, Q WG 12m W14M, G11M; 006°-W-293°-G-006°; synch; R □ on R col; Rocher Le Faoutés, 210m from front. Rear, Q 26m 8M, 051·5°-054·5°, R □ on W twr; 0·58M from front.

9.20.5 PASSAGE INFORMATION
More passage information is threaded between successive harbours in this Area. **Bibliography**: *North Brittany* (Imray/RCC/ Lawson) *North Brittany and Channel Islands CC* (Fernhurst/ Cumberlidge); *Shell Channel Pilot* (Imray/Cunliffe); *Channel Pilot* (NP 27); *Channel Havens* (ACN/Endean); *Secret anchorages of Brittany* (Imray/Cumberlidge).

NORTH BRITTANY
This ever-popular cruising ground (AC 2648, 2647, 2643, 2028) is not one to trifle with, but conversely it is rewarding to navigate into a remote anchorage or small fishing harbour. Here the unique character and appeal of N Brittany is all around you.

Good landfall marks must be carefully identified, as a back-up to GPS, before closing the rock-strewn coast. In rough weather, poor visibility (fog and summer haze are frequent) or if uncertain of position, it may be prudent to lie off and wait for conditions to improve; there are few safe havens. Closer inshore the tidal streams are variable with associated overfalls. Thorough careful planning remains the key to safe pilotage.

In the E of the area the outer approaches to **Paimpol, Île de Bréhat, Lézardrieux** and **Tréguier** may be complicated by strong tidal streams. At times there may be a proliferation of landmarks which must be selectively identified. Concentrate on those which affect your pilotage and discard those which are non-essential and may even distract you from the task.

Once W of **Roscoff** there are few safe hbrs and anchorages until **L'Aberwrac'h** where many British yachts tend to pause and await good conditions for negotiating the Chenal du Four. This is rarely as difficult as it is imagined to be. The Atlantic swell can be a new experience for some, but in moderate winds it is rarely a hazard. It can however much reduce the range at which objects, especially floating marks and other small craft, are seen.

PAIMPOL TO PLOUMANAC'H

In the offing, 11-18M NNE of Île de Bréhat and on a direct track from/to Guernsey, are Plateau de Barnouic (lit) and **Plateau des Roches Douvres** (light house); both with drying and submerged rks, to be given a wide berth in poor vis (AC 2027, 2028, 3673).

Approaching L'Ost-Pic from the SE, keep to seaward of the three ECM marks E of it or enter Baie de **Paimpol** from a point about 1M E of the most N'ly ECM (Les Charpentiers); but it is safe to pass about 300m east of L'Ost Pic in moderate weather.

The Ferlas channel (AC 3673) lies E-W south of **Ile de Bréhat**, and is useful if entering/leaving R. Trieux from/to the E. It is easiest to beacon-hop past the 5 SCM bcns and 1 IDM bcn marking the N side of the chan; the S side is less well marked.

For the many yachts approaching from Guernsey, Les Héaux-de-Bréhat light house is a conspic landfall day/night for either Tréguier or Lézardrieux. Closer in or from the E, La Horaine (lt beacon) is a better landfall for the latter. It marks the Plateaux de la Horaine and des Échaudés and other rocks to the SE. In poor visibility it should be closed with caution and left at least 7ca to the SE, as the flood stream sets strongly onto it.

The Grand Chenal 224·7° is the main, lit channel into the R. de Trieux for **Lézardrieux** and further upriver to **Pontrieux**. From NW the unlit Chenal de La Moisie leads 159° to join the Grand Chenal off Ile de Bréhat.

The **Passe de la Gaine** 241·5° is a useful inshore route between Lézardrieux and Tréguier, avoiding a detour round Les Héaux. If taken at above half tide, it presents no problem in fair weather. But it is unlit and from the NE the distant ldg marks are hard to see in poor visibility or against a low sun. However two SHM beacons to the S and SW of Les Héaux-de-Bréhat lighthouse can be used as a handrail towards Pont de la Gaine.

The Grande Passe 137·3° into **Rivière de Tréguier** is well lit, but ldg marks are hard to see by day. Use the NE Passage with caution.

Between Basse Crublent lt buoy and Port Blanc unmarked rocks extend 2M offshore. **Port Blanc** can be difficult to identify by day until it opens on 150°. **Perros-Guirec** is approached either side of Ile Tomé from NE or NW via well lit/marked channels; take care not to be neaped. **Ploumanac'h** can only be entered by day. It boasts some of the most spectacular pink granite along the North Brittany coast.

LES SEPT ÎLES TO BAIE DE MORLAIX

(AC 2026). **Les Sept Îles** (AC 2027) consist of five main islands and several islets, through which the tide runs strongly. Île aux Moines is lit, and all the islands are bird sanctuaries. Further W, Plateau des Triagoz has offlying dangers WSW and NE of the lt, where the sea breaks heavily.

▶Here the stream turns ENE at HW Brest –0230, and WSW at HW Brest +0330, sp rates both 3·8kn.◀

Trégastel-Plage is a small anchorage W of Ploumanac'h. To the SW the coast as far as **Trébeurden** is not easily approached due to many offlying rks. The radome NE of Trébeurden is conspic. Further S in the Baie de Lannion is Locquémeau and anchorages near the mouth of the drying R. Léguer up to **Lannion**. Locquirec is a pleasant drying harbour 3·5M SW of Locquemeau. **Primel-Trégastel**, at the E ent to Baie de Morlaix, is a useful inlet to await the tide up to Morlaix. To the N Plateau de la Méloine dries.

The Baie de Morlaix (AC 2745) is bestrewn with drying rks and shoals, all marked. Careful pilotage and adequate visibility are needed to negotiate any of the chans which are narrow in parts. Chenal de Tréguier 190·5° and the Grand Chenal 176·4° are both lit. The former should only be used HW ±3 due to shoals at the S end. Grand Chenal passes close E of Île Ricard with Île Louet and La Lande lights in transit; abeam Calhic bn tr alter to port to pass between Château du Taureau (conspic) and Île Louet. Continue SSE and upriver to lock into **Morlaix** Marina in complete shelter. The ⚓age NE of Carantec is reached from Chenal Ouest de Ricard.

ÎLE DE BATZ TO LE FOUR

▶2M N of Île de Batz the E-going stream begins at HW Brest –0400, and the W-going stream at HW Brest +0200, sp rates 3·8kn. The flood and ebb streams deflected N of Ile de Batz may be >5kn, in opposition and violent. Against any existing sea state, the resultant breaking seas can endanger small craft which are therefore strongly advised to pass at least 2-2½M north of Batz. See the French tidal stream atlas 563-UJA.◀

Approaching **Roscoff** from the NE, leave Astan ECM lt buoy to stbd tracking with Men Guen Bras lt bcn in transit 213° with white Chapelle St Barbe, to round Ar Chaden lt bcn for Roscoff's drying harbour. Bound for Roscoff Marina pass E of No1 pillar by and Basse de Bloscon NCM, then S towards Bloscons prominent ferry terminal pier. (AC 2026, 2025, 2745)

S of the island **Canal de L'Île de Batz**, day only and above half tide, requires careful pilotage at its narrower eastern end. From near Ar Chaden steer 275° for the Q bn at end of the conspic LW ferry pier. Pass 30m N of this bn, then alter to 300° for Run Oan SCM. Thence steer 283°, leaving Perroch NCM bcn twrs 100m to port. When clear of this rky, drying shoal alter to 270°, leaving Porz Kernok hbr bkwtrs well to stbd then midway between L'Oignon NCM and La Croix SCM bcns. With these abeam steer 281° for Basse Plate NCM bn; thence West into open waters.

Proceeding W from Île de Batz towards Le Four there are many offlying dangers, in places 3M offshore. Swell may break on shoals even further to seaward. With strong tides, in poor vis or bad weather it is a coast to avoid. But in fair weather enjoy its delightful harbours such as Moguériec, Brignogan, L'Aberwrac'h, L'Aberbenoit, Portsall and Argenton. N of L'Aberwrac'h is the conspic Île Vierge lt ho, reputedly the tallest in the world.

▶N of Le Libenter buoy, off L'Aberwrac'h, the NE-going stream starts at HW Brest –0500, sp rate 3·8kn, and the WSW-going stream at HW Brest +0100.◀

L'Aberwrac'h is accessible at all tides and strategically placed to catch the tide S through Chenal du Four. The marina is also well protected from NW'lies.

W of L'Aberwrac'h a daytime only/good vis chan leads inshore of Roches de Portsall to Le Four lt ho.The distant marks are not easy to identify and it is only 1M shorter than the offshore route via Basse Paupian WCM buoy. AC 1432 or SHOM 7094 and a detailed pilot book essential.

OUESSANT (USHANT)

(AC 2356) Île d'Ouessant lies 10M off NW Brittany, surrounded by five lt ho's. It is a rky island, with dangers extending 5ca to NE, 7½ca to SE, 1·5M to SW and 1M to NW; here Chaussée de Keller is a dangerous chain of unmarked drying and submerged rks running 1M W of Île de Keller and into the ITZ. There are anchorages and moorings at **Lampaul** and **Baie du Stiff**, the former exposed to the SW and the latter to the NE.

Ouessant is an important landfall, but avoid in thick weather. Ideally, stay in harbour until the vis improves. In fair weather and reasonable visibility the pilotage in the well-marked chans between it and the mainland is not too demanding. But the tide runs hard in places, causing overfalls when against wind >F5.

▶Tidal streams are strong around the island, and in the chans between it and the mainland. Off Baie du Stiff (lt, radar twr) the stream turns NW at HW Brest +0400, and SE at HW Brest –0200, max rates 2¾kn.◀

The routes outside Ouessant TSS or via the ITZ add much to the distance and are exposed to sea, swell and shipping. Yachts usually take the inshore chans, ie: Chenal du Four, most direct and popular; Chenal de la Helle, an alternative to N part of Chenal du Four (also gives access to Île Moléne) is less direct but better in bad weather. Passage du Fromveur, SE of Ouessant, is easiest but longer and can be extremely rough. *▶The NE-going stream starts HW Brest –0515, max rates 8-9kn; the SW-going stream starts around HW Brest, max rates 7-8kn.◀*

9.20.6 Special Notes for France: See Area 17.

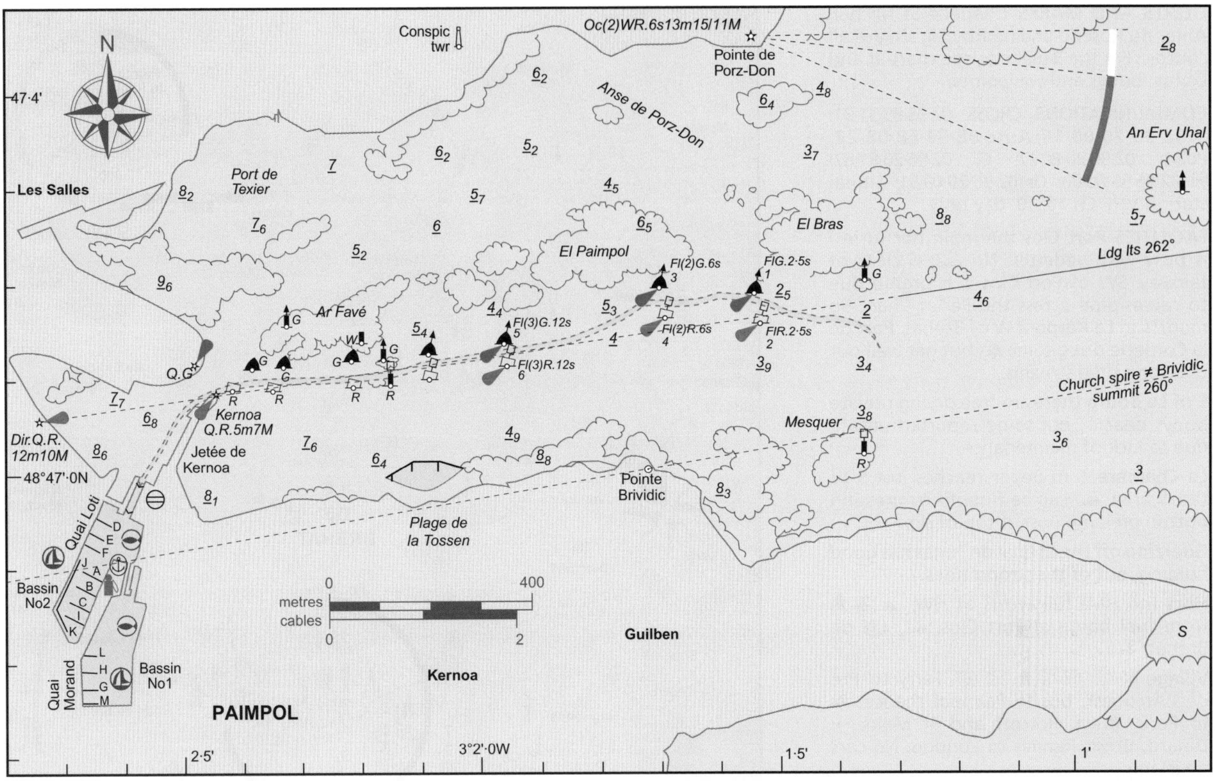

9.20.7 PAIMPOL

Côtes d'Armor **48°47´·00N 03°02´·56W** ❁❁◊◊◊✿✿

CHARTS AC 2648, 2027, 2028, 3673; SHOM 7152, 7154, 7127; Navi 537; Imray C34

TIDES Dover –0525; ML 6·1; Duration 0600

Standard Port ST MALO (⟵)

Times				Height (metres)			
High Water		Low Water		MHWS	MHWN	MLWN	MLWS
0100	0800	0300	0800	12·2	9·3	4·2	1·5
1300	2000	1500	2000				
Differences PAIMPOL							
–0010	–0005	–0035	–0025	–1·4	–0·9	–0·4	–0·1

SHELTER Good shelter from all winds in hbr, but few ⚓s as most of the Anse de Paimpol dries, including the appr chan to hbr.

NAVIGATION Bearing in mind the very large tidal range, there is enough water in the bay for most craft from half-flood.

WPT 48°47´·82N 02°54´·58W, 262°/5·2M to Kernoa jetty hd. Chenal de la Jument 260° is the outer appr. After La Jument PHM bn tr, alter onto 262·2° inner ldg line; or ⚓ in 5m to await the tide. Small buoys/bns in final 1M of chan (dries 6-7m) may be hard to see against a low evening sun. The drying rks (El Paimpol, El Bras and Ar Fav) are close N of the ldg line.

An alternative appr from Île de Bréhat lies E of Les Piliers NCM bn tr, thence S past Pte de la Trinité. Or appr via Cadenenou NCM and Chenal du Denou 193°. SHOM 7127 is essential for these and other inshore passages which should only be attempted towards HW.

LIGHTS AND MARKS From the S L'Ost-Pic lt is a conspic □ W tr 4M E of Paimpol. Pte de Porz-Don, lt ho on a white house, is 7ca ENE of hbr ent; its W sector leads 270° to intercept the inner 262·2° ldg lts at La Jument bcn twr. A conspic twr (52m) is 3ca W of Porz-Don.

Chenal de la Jument, outer ldg marks 260°: Paimpol ✠ spire (the N'ly of two) on with the ill-defined summit of Pte Brividic. Inner ldg lts, both QR, 262·2°: front, Jetée de Kernoa.

COMMUNICATIONS CROSS 02·98·89·31·31; Auto 08·92·68·08·22; Police 02·96·20·80·17; ⊖ 02·96·20·81·87; Brit Consul 01·44·51·31·00; Ⓗ 02·96·55·60·00; Dr 02·96·55·15·15; Port Mgr 02·96·20·80·77; HM and Lock VHF Ch 09 (0800-1200LT and lock opening hrs); Aff Mar 02·96·55·35·00.

FACILITIES Lock opens HW ±2½, 60m x 12m, ☎02·96·20·90·02. **Marina** ☎02·96·20·47·65. port-plaisance.paimpol@wanadoo.fr www.ville-paimpol.fr **Basin No 2** 306+24 Ⓥ, May-Sep €2·62; Ⓥ berths, pontoon A, min depth 3·8m. (hose) @ ♿. **Basin No 1** Yachts up to 40m LOA. (25t, 6t, 4t). **E Quays** ⚒ 🔧 SHOM Ⓔ. **Town** ✕ ⊠ Ⓑ Ⓗ ⇌ ✈ Dinard, Brest, Rennes. **Ferry** Roscoff, St Malo.

9.20.8 ÎLE DE BRÉHAT

Côtes d'Armor 48°51'·00N 03°00'·00W ❁❁❁◊◊✿✿✿

CHARTS AC 2648, 2027, 2028, 3673; SHOM 7152, 7154; Navi 537; Imray C34

TIDES –0525 Dover; ML 5·8; Duration 0605

Standard Port ST MALO (⟵)

Times				Height (metres)			
High Water		Low Water		MHWS	MHWN	MLWN	MLWS
0100	0800	0300	0800	12·2	9·3	4·2	1·5
1300	2000	1500	2000				
Differences LES HEAUX DE BRÉHAT							
–0015	–0010	–0100	–0045	–2·3	–1·6	–0·6	–0·1
ÎLE DE BRÉHAT							
–0015	–0005	–0040	–0030	–1·6	–1·2	–0·5	0·0

SHELTER Good in Port Clos and at Port de la Corderie, except in W-NW'lies. See Facilities for other ⚓s depending on wind direction.

NAVIGATION From the NE use R. Trieux WPT (Lézardrieux) and 224·8° ldg line. From the N use Ch de Bréhat 167·4° (distant ldg marks) then enter Ferlas Chan from the E via WPT 48°49´·39N 02°55´·08W, 277°/3·4M to abm Port Clos. For the R Trieux, follow Ferlas Chan transits Ⓒ – Ⓕ, as shown on AC 3673.

LIGHTS AND MARKS Chapelle St Michel, Amer du Rosedo and nearby Sig stn are all conspic. For the 3 main lts, see chartlet and Lights, buoys and waypoints.

COMMUNICATIONS CROSS 02·98·89·31·31; [LB] 02·96·20·00·14; Auto 08·92·68·08·22; Police 02·96·20·80·17; ⊖ 02·96·20·81·87; [H] 02·96·55·60·00; Dr 02·96·20·09·51; Signal station VHF Ch 16, 10, day only.

FACILITIES **Port Clos** the main hbr (dries) is busy with vedettes. No [mooring buoy]; [anchorage] clear of fairway. SW of Port Clos [anchorage] is prohib due to cables/pipe across the Ferlas Chan. So moor/[anchorage] in **Le Kerpont** W of Bréhat. **Port de la Corderie** dries; some [visitors' buoys] but get well out of strong tidal streams.

E of Le Bourg there are free drying private buoys near [anchorage], but some reported unsafe due to lack of maintenance.

La Chambre [anchorage] in upper reaches just S of the [prohibited anchorage] area. [slipway] can be floodlit by pressing button on lamp post at top of slip.

Guerzido off the Chenal de Ferlas has good holding, out of the strong tides.

Hbrs (no HM) full access at HW, [symbols] from fuel barge at Port Clos, [slipway]; CN de Bréhat, [symbols].

Village [symbols] Ⓑ. Ferry to Pte de l'Arcouest, bus to Paimpol thence [train] to Paris, Brest, Roscoff and St Malo. ✈ Dinard, Brest, Rennes to London. No cars on island.

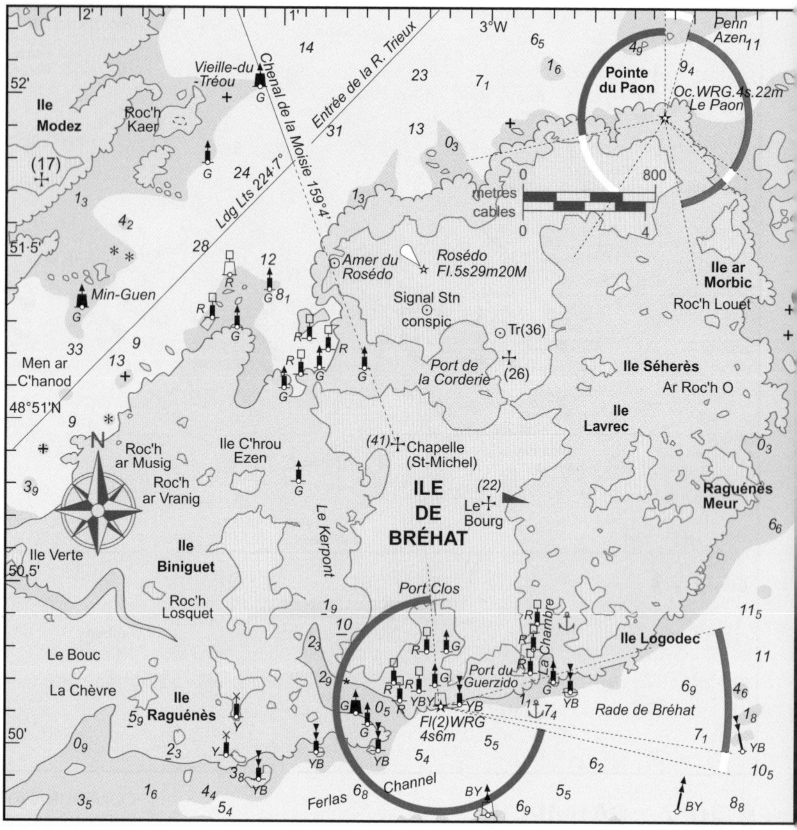

OUTER APPROACHES TO LÉZARDRIEUX AND TRÉGUIER WITH PASSE DE LA GAINE BETWEEN

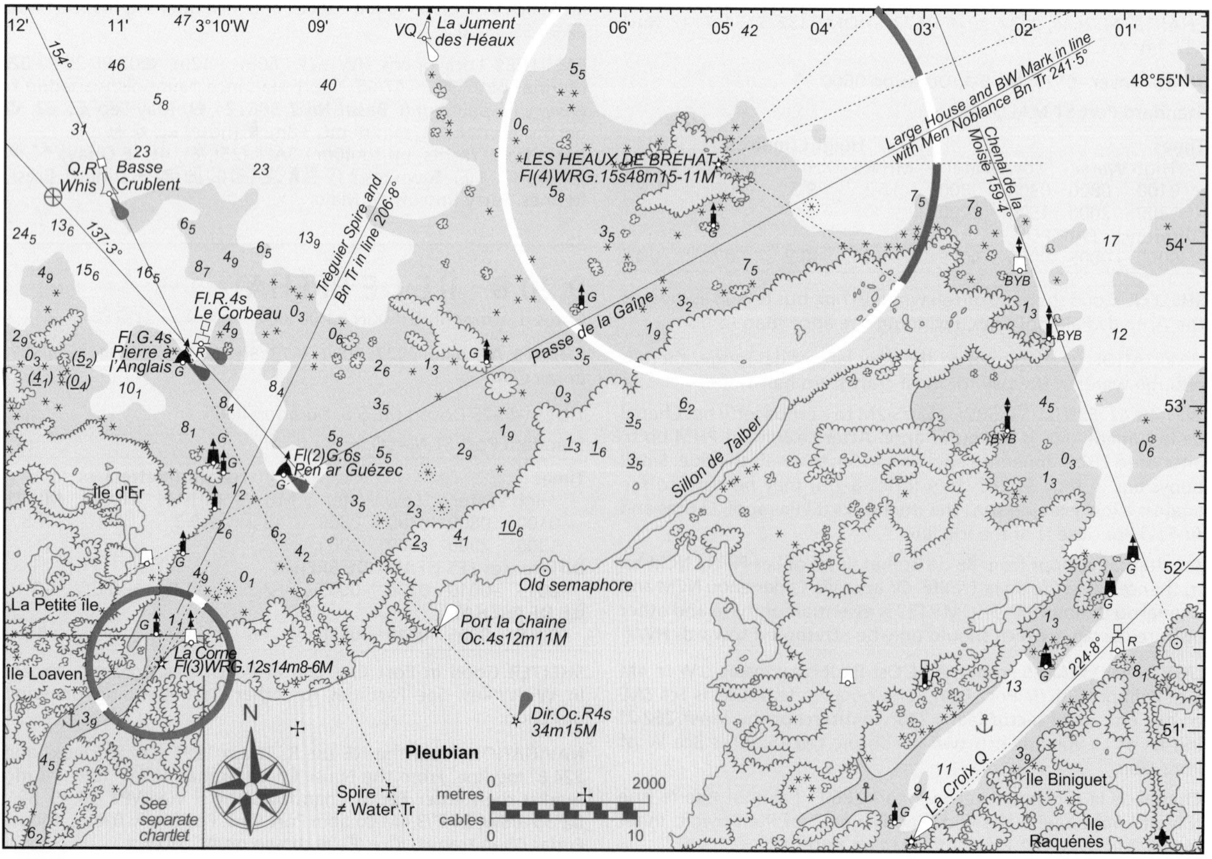

9.20.9 LÉZARDRIEUX

Côtes d'Armor **48°47´·34N 03°05´·89W**

CHARTS AC 2648, 2027, 2028, 3673; SHOM 7152/3, 7126/7; Navi 537; Imray C34

TIDES –0510 Dover; ML 5·9; Duration 0610

Standard Port ST MALO (⟵)

Times				Height (metres)			
High Water		Low Water		MHWS	MHWN	MLWN	MLWS
0100	0800	0300	0800	12·2	9·3	4·2	1·5
1300	2000	1500	2000				
Differences LÉZARDRIEUX							
–0020	–0015	–0055	–0045	–1·7	–1·3	–0·5	–0·2

SHELTER Very good in all weathers. Strong stream at half tide.

NAVIGATION WPT 48°54´·98N 02°56´·07W, 224·7°/6·7M to La Croix, front 224·8° ldg lt. Offshore dangers include Roches Douvres, Barnouic, Plateau de la Horaine and rky shoals to the W in the outer apps. Off the river ent allow for strong cross-streams.

The 3 well-marked approach channels are:

- **Grand Chenal**, main lit chan from NE, best for strangers. Ldg lts 224·7°: Front, La Croix, two double-barrelled trs, W on NE side with R tops. Rear, Bodic (2·1M from front) high up amongst the trees.
- **Ch de la Moisie**, unlit from the NW: Amer du Rosédo, W obelisk on 159·4° with St Michael's chapel (both conspic on Île de Bréhat). It also connects with Passe de la Gaine, short cut from/to Tréguier; see chartlet on previous page.
- **Ferlas Chan** (lit) from E or W, passing S of Île de Bréhat. By day follow the 5 SCM bcns on the N side of the chan. At night: W sector (281°) of Men Joliguet, WCM bcn twr.
  W sector (257°) of Roche Quinonec at Loguivy.
  W sector (271°) of Kermouster joins Coatmer 218·7° ldg line.

Within the Trieux river:

- Coatmer ldg lts 218·7°: front, low down amongst trees; rear, 660m from front, high up almost obsc'd by trees.
- W sector (200°) of Les Perdrix, a stout green bcn twr. Speed limit 5kn from Perdrix to the bridge.

LIGHTS AND MARKS See Lights, buoys and waypoints for offshore lts at Roches Douvres lt ho, Barnouic ECM bn tr, Les Héaux de Bréhat lt ho and, on Île de Bréhat, Pte du Paon and Rosédo. Outer and inner approach marks are described above. There are no navigational lights S of Perdrix.

Beware, at night, the unlit, 16m high Roc'h Donan 400m S of Perdrix. At the tidal marina floodlights on shore may dazzle yachts arriving.

COMMUNICATIONS CROSS 02·98·89·31·31; Auto 08·92·68·08·22; Police 02·96·20·18·17; ⊜ at Paimpol 02·96·20·81·87; Brit Consul 01·44·51·31·00; Dr 02·96·20·18·30; Aff Mar (Paimpol) 02·96·55·35·00; Marina VHF Ch 09 (0730-2200 Jul/Aug; 0800-1200 and 1400-1800 rest of year).

FACILITIES Tidal marina ☎02·96·20·14·22. http://port.3douest.com/lezardrieux/ port-lezardrieux@wanadoo.fr Access H24. 380 + 50 Ⓥ. Berth on the first pontoon (No 3) or as directed by HM. €2·39. €2·00. Multihulls and boats >12·5m LOA should moor on s €1·67 or Ⓥ pontoon. Ⓔ Divers, (50t).

YC de Trieux ☎02·96·20·10·39.

Non-tidal marina (247) has some Ⓥ berths (2·4m inside). The retaining wall is marked by 5 unlit Y SPM perches, the sill by PHM/SHM perches. Access over sill 4·9m with automatic flap. As sill covers on the flood, at CD +6·15m, flap drops to give 1·1m clearance. A depth gauge shows water over sill. The waiting pontoon is as on chartlet. IPTS sigs 2 & 4 control entry/exit.

Town Ⓑ (occas bus to Paimpol & Lannion) ✈ Lannion. **Ferry** Roscoff.

Yachts can continue about 12km upriver (via bridge, clearance 17m) to lock in at Pontrieux in complete shelter.

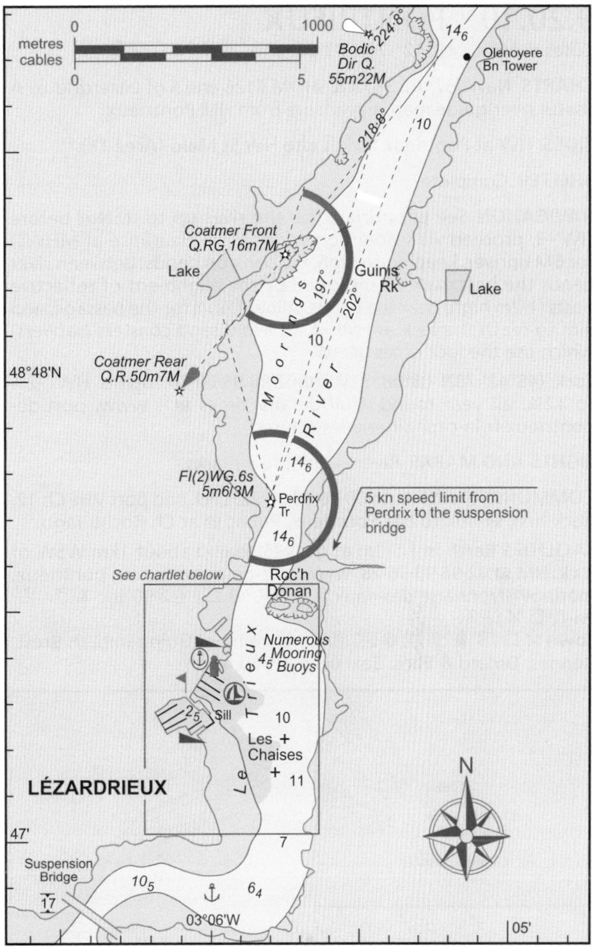

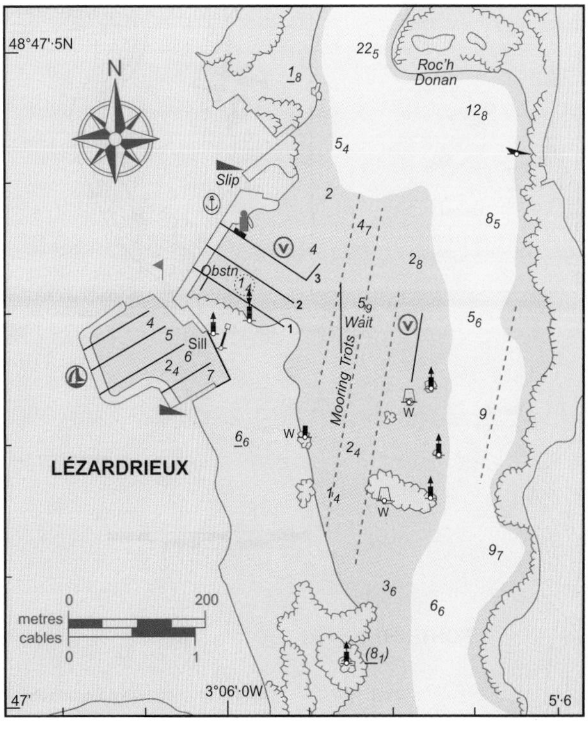

9.20.10 PONTRIEUX

Côtes d'Armor **48°42'·74N 03°08'·98W** ❀❀◊◊✿✿✿

CHARTS Navi 537; AC 3673 & SHOM 7126 end S of Lézardrieux. A useful river guide/map is available from HM Pontrieux.

TIDES HW at Pontrieux lock is also HW St Malo (Area 18).

SHELTER Complete.

NAVIGATION See Lézardrieux for the river up to it. Not before HW –3, proceed via suspension bridge (17m clearance at MHWS) for 6M upriver, keeping to high, rky bank on bends. Between river bends the best water is indicated by the alignment of reflective posts (1-2m high) near the bends. Allow 1½hrs for the passage, and aim to reach the lock at HW –1, to avoid sand coasters *(sabliers)* which use the lock occas at HW.

Lock (48°42'·78N 03°08'·31W) ☎02·96·95·60·70; opens HW –2¼ to +2¼, all year round, (full details/ times at : www. port-de-pontrieux.fr/la-capitainerie/les-ecluses/).

LIGHTS AND MARKS River is unlit; few marks.

COMMUNICATIONS Auto 08·36·68·08·22; Lock and port VHF Ch 12, (lock hrs); ☎ link to HM Pontrieux; Public ☎ at Ch Roche Jagu.

FACILITIES Berth in 1·5-3m at quay (SE bank) about 1km WSW of lock. HM ☎ 02·96·95·36·28; www.port-de-pontrieux.fr; pontrieux.marinov@lyonnaise-des-eaux.fr 80+40 Ⓥ €2·90 inc wi-fi;
Town @ Ⓑ ≹ Paimpol/Guingamp, ✈ Brest, Rennes, Dinard & Paris. Taxi 02·96·95·60·43.

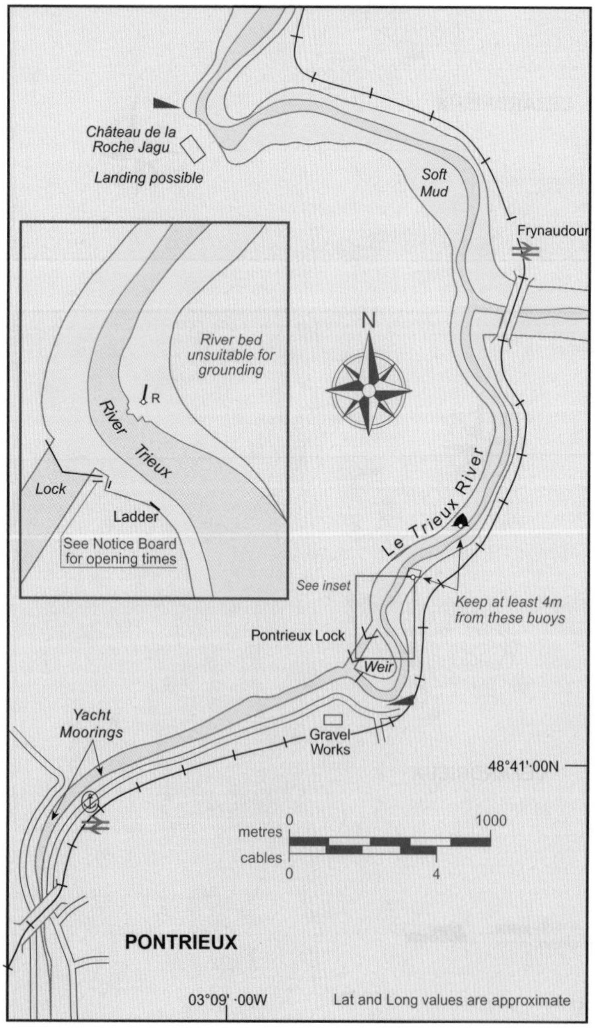

9.20.11 TRÉGUIER

Côtes d'Armor **48°47'·21N 03°13'·27W** ❀❀❀◊◊◊✿✿✿

CHARTS AC 2648, 2027, 2028; SHOM 7152, 7126; Navi 537; Imray C34

TIDES –0540 Dover; ML 5·7; Duration 0600

Standard Port ST MALO (⟵)

Times				Height (metres)			
High Water		Low Water		MHWS	MHWN	MLWN	MLWS
0100	0800	0300	0800	12·2	9·3	4·2	1·5
1300	2000	1500	2000				
Differences TRÉGUIER							
–0020	–0020	–0100	–0045	–2·3	–1·6	–0·6	–0·2
PORT-BÉNI (5ca SSE of La Corne lt twr)							
–0020	–0020	–0105	–0050	–2·4	–1·7	–0·6	–0·2

SHELTER Good. Possible ⚓s, keeping clear of fairway and fish farms. 7ca SW of La Corne lt tr, but exposed to N'lies; N and S of La Roche Jaune village; and in well sheltered pool (6m) 1ca NE of No 10 buoy (8ca N of marina).

NAVIGATION WPT 48°54'·13N 03°11'·50W (abeam Basse Crublent PHM buoy) 137°/2·1M to Pen ar Guézec SHM light buoy, a key turning point. Caution: strong tidal streams across the well-lit chan. The three approach channels, with marks, are:

- **Grande Passe** 137·3°. Ldg marks (hard to see by day): Front, Port de la Chaine, white ho; rear, St Antoine, RW ho. At Pen ar Guézec SHM buoy alter 216° in La Corne's W sector.
  A clearer transit from Basse Crublent is: Pleubian spire (charted) and adj water twr (on skyline) ≠ 154° to pass between Pierre à l'Anglais and Le Corbeau bys (both lit).
- **Passe de la Gaine** Unlit short cut to/from Lézardrieux. See chartlet below Île De Bréhat. Adequately marked, navigable by day with care/sufficient tide, good vis; but marks hard to see from afar in low sun/ poor vis. 241·5° ldg marks: Front, Men Noblance bcn twr, W with B band, ≠ rear mark (W wall with B vert stripe) below the skyline, right of conspic Plougrescant ✠ spire. Stay on transit to hold narrow chan. See Passage info.
- **Passe du Nord-Est** 205°/207°: unlit, dangerous with W-NW winds as sea breaks across the shallowest part of chan. On 205° keep W of La Jument NCM buoy and adjacent rky shoals; jink port onto 207° transit of Tréguier spire and Skeiviec bcn twr, for direct appr to La Corne.

In river, heed buoys and bns, eg keep E of Taureau SHM light buoy, 300m SW of La Corne lt ho, to clear adjacent drying mudbank. Speed limit 5kn south of No 3 SHM lt buoy. Less water reported from No 11 lt by to marina, approx 5M from La Corne lt hse.

LIGHTS AND MARKS See Lights, buoys and waypoints/chartlet. Important marks: La Corne, a stumpy WR lt tr; 6ca to the N is Men Noblance black/white bcn tr (for Passe de la Gaine); and 4ca SW is Skeiviec W bn tr. The spire of Tréguier cathedral is 4·6M SSW of La Corne, but obsc. by high wooded banks entering the estuary.

COMMUNICATIONS CROSS 02·96·89·31·31; Auto 08·92·68·08·22; Police 02·96·20·84·30; ⊖ 02·96·20·81·37; Brit Consul 01·44·51·31·00; Ⓗ 02·96·05·71·11; Dr 02·96·92·32·14; Aff Mar 02·96·92·30·38 (Paimpol); Marina VHF Ch 09, office hrs in season, 7/7: 0700-2145: Winter, M-F 0800-1200 & 1330-1730 (Sat 1630): Sun shut.

FACILITIES A 30m waiting pontoon, least depth 1·2m LWS, 500m N of marina, boats >15m LOA & multihulls can use overnight. **Marina** *Arr/dep at slack water,* tide sets hard N/S diagonally through pontoons. Berth bows to tide on outer part of pontoons C, D, E. F pontoon is exclusively for vessels >14m, max LOA/Wt, 30m/100t, depth 3m LAT on outside, 2.8m inside. HM ☎02·96·92·42·37, mob 06·72·70·70·20 portplaisance.treguier@wanadoo.fr www.ville-treguier.fr/culture-sports-loisirs/port-plaisance.php 260 + 70Ⓥ €2·80 > 20m, €57.00 + €3.00 per/m extra. wi-fi @, (40t) ☎02·96·92·15·15/93·55.

Le Petit Baigneur ☎02·96·11·40·69. **CN de Tréguier** ☎02·96·92·37·49, opposite marina, Sat evenings only. **Town** (small s/market near cathedral delivers) Ⓑ. Market Wed. ≹ via bus to Paimpol, Guingamp, Lannion. ✈ Brest, Rennes, Dinard. **Ferry** Roscoff, St Malo.

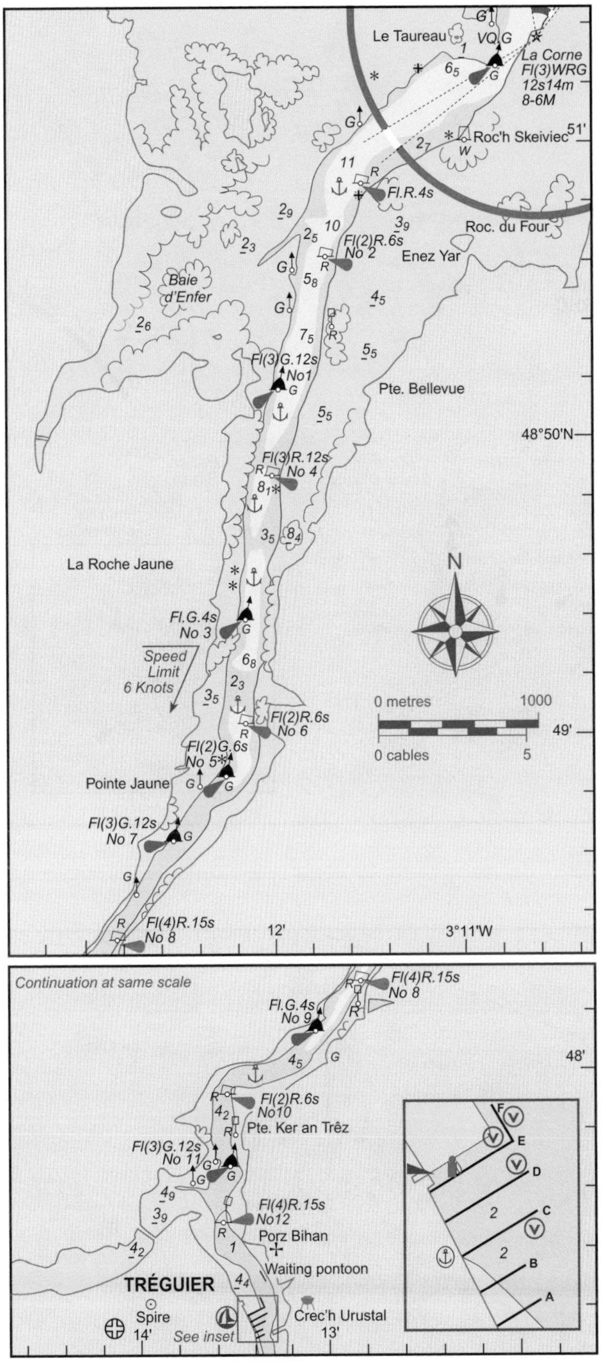

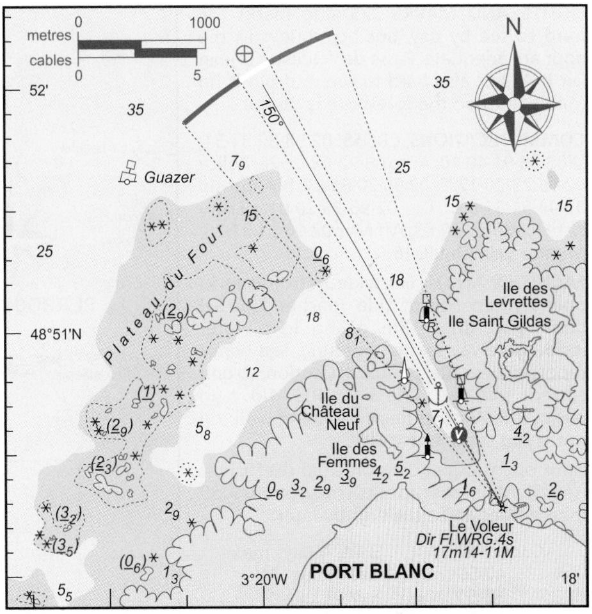

9.20.12 PORT BLANC

Côtes d'Armor **48°50´·54N 03°18´·89W**

CHARTS AC 2648, 2027; SHOM 7152, 7125/6; Navi 537, 538; Imray C34

TIDES –0545 Dover; ML 5·3; Duration 0600. Interpolate between Les Héaux de Bréhat and Perros-Guirec. HW–0040 and ht –2·0m on St Malo. MHWS 9·0m; MHWN 6·8m.

SHELTER Good in natural hbr (aka Port Bago) but very uncomfortable in winds with any N in them.

NAVIGATION WPT 48°52´·24N 03°20´·16W, 150°/1·9M to first Ⓥ. The fairway does not open up until at the WPT. Appr on ldg line 150° towards Le Voleur Dir lt; the rear ldg mark is hard to see amongst trees. From the SW approach via Basse Guazer PHM buoy, 7ca SW of the WPT. Beware ebb tide initially setting hard towards drying Plateau du Four.

LIGHTS AND MARKS 150° ldg marks: Front, Le Voleur Dir lt, low down amongst trees (between white cottage and Grand Hotel, conspic white block); rear, 5ca from front, La Comtesse Mill, unlit and obscured by trees on skyline. A white obelisk (16m) on Île du Château Neuf is conspic to stbd of the fairway. A smaller obelisk to port on Île St Gildas is less obvious.

COMMUNICATIONS CROSS 02·33·52·72·13; Auto 08·92·68·02·22; ⊜ 02·96·20·81·87; Brit Consul 01·44·51·31·00; *Port Blanc* VHF Ch 09, 16; Aff Mar 02·96·92·30·38;.

FACILITIES 5 W Ⓥs, marked VISIT in approx 5m. Safe ⚓ and good holding, where charted in 7m. Or dry out alongside quays, 1·3m; best to pre-recce. HM ☎02·96·92·89·11 in sailing school. or Ⓥ €7·00 all LOA, (16t) .

Town ✕ (basic). Taxi 02·96·92·64·00, ⇌ Lannion. ✈ Brest, Rennes, Dinard. **Ferry** Roscoff.

9.20.13 PERROS-GUIREC

Côtes d'Armor **48° 48´·17N 03° 26´·21W** (Jetty hd)

CHARTS AC 2648, 2027; SHOM 7152, 7125; Navi 537, 538; Imray C34

TIDES –0550 Dover; ML 5·4; Duration 0605

Standard Port ST MALO (⟵)

Times				**Height (metres)**			
High Water		Low Water		MHWS	MHWN	MLWN	MLWS
0100	0800	0300	0800	12·2	9·3	4·2	1·5
1300	2000	1500	2000				
Differences PERROS-GUIREC							
–0035	–0035	–0115	–0100	–2·8	–2·0	–0·7	–0·1

SHELTER Very good in marina. Off Pointe du Chateau safe ⚓, except in NE'lies, in approx 3m good holding; plus 5 small W Ⓥs.

NAVIGATION From the E, WPT 48°49´·86N 03°23´·66W, 224·8°/2·4M to Jetée Linkin. From the W, WPT 48°50´·53N 03°26´·45W, 143·5°/1·8M to join 224·8° ldg line. Caution: Rocks extend 7ca W and 6ca NE of Île Tomé. Local moorings E of Jetée du Linkin are marked by 2 SHM buoys.

LIGHTS AND MARKS 225° ldg marks are hard to see by day, but bcns/buoys in the appr are adequate. Passe de l'Ouest: Kerjean Dir lt 143·6° also hard to see, but old lt ho (gable end) on the foreshore is clearer.

COMMUNICATIONS CROSS 02·98·89·31·31; ⓁⒷ02·96·91·40·10; Auto 08·92·68·02·22; Police 02·96·23·20·17; ⊜02·96·20·81·87; Brit Consul 01·44·51·31·00; Dr 02·96·23·20·01; Entry gate 02·96·23·19·03; Aff Mar 02·96·91·21·28; Marina VHF Ch 09, 16.

FACILITIES Access: 6m wide gate (no lock) opens when rise of tide reaches 7m. Sill under gate dries $\underline{3}$·5m, giving 3·5m water inside gateway on first opening, less water reported near fuel pontoon. Caution: strong current initially. Gate sigs: IPTS. No ⚓ in basin. R & W poles mark retaining wall; do not try to cross it near HW.

Gate opens depending on tidal coefficient (see St Malo coefficients) may open > 30 mins earlier and close slightly later:

Coeff <40	=	Shut, 4 days max
40-50	=	HW –½ to HW
50-60	=	HW –1 to +½
60-70	=	HW ±1
>70	=	approx HW ±1½

Marina ☎02·96·49·80·50. www.port-perros-guirec.com portdeplaisance@perros-guirec.com 720+80Ⓥ €3·30. Ⓥ berth on N'most 2 pontoons in 2·5m. wi-fi, Ⓔ SHOM (7t). **YC** ☎02·96·91·12·65.

Town ✕ ✉ Ⓑ. ⇌ Lannion. ✈ Brest. **Ferry** Roscoff.

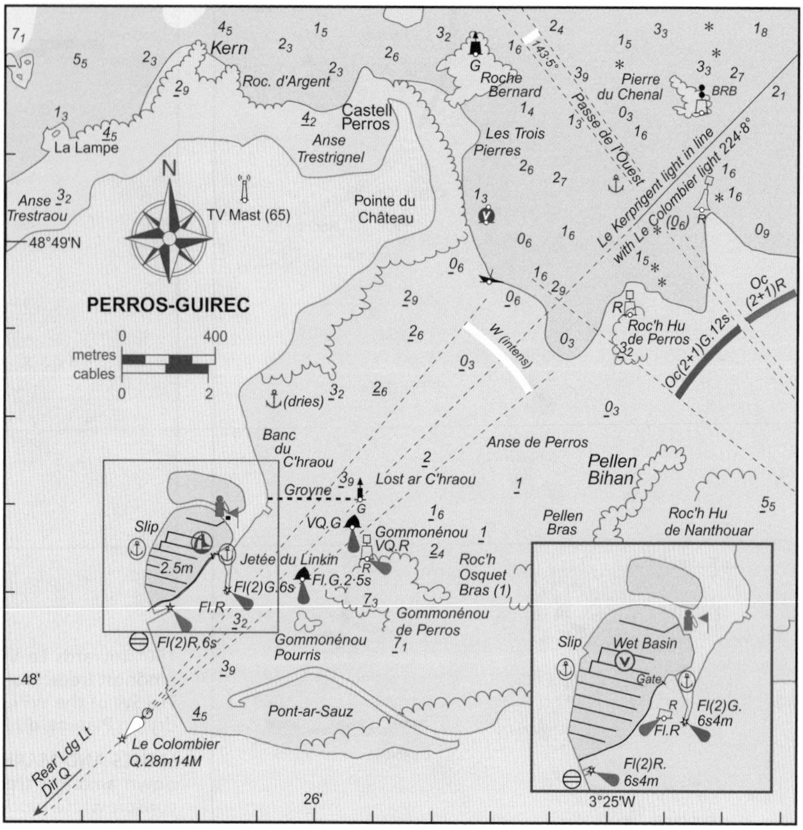

LES SEPT ÎLES *See notes on facing page*

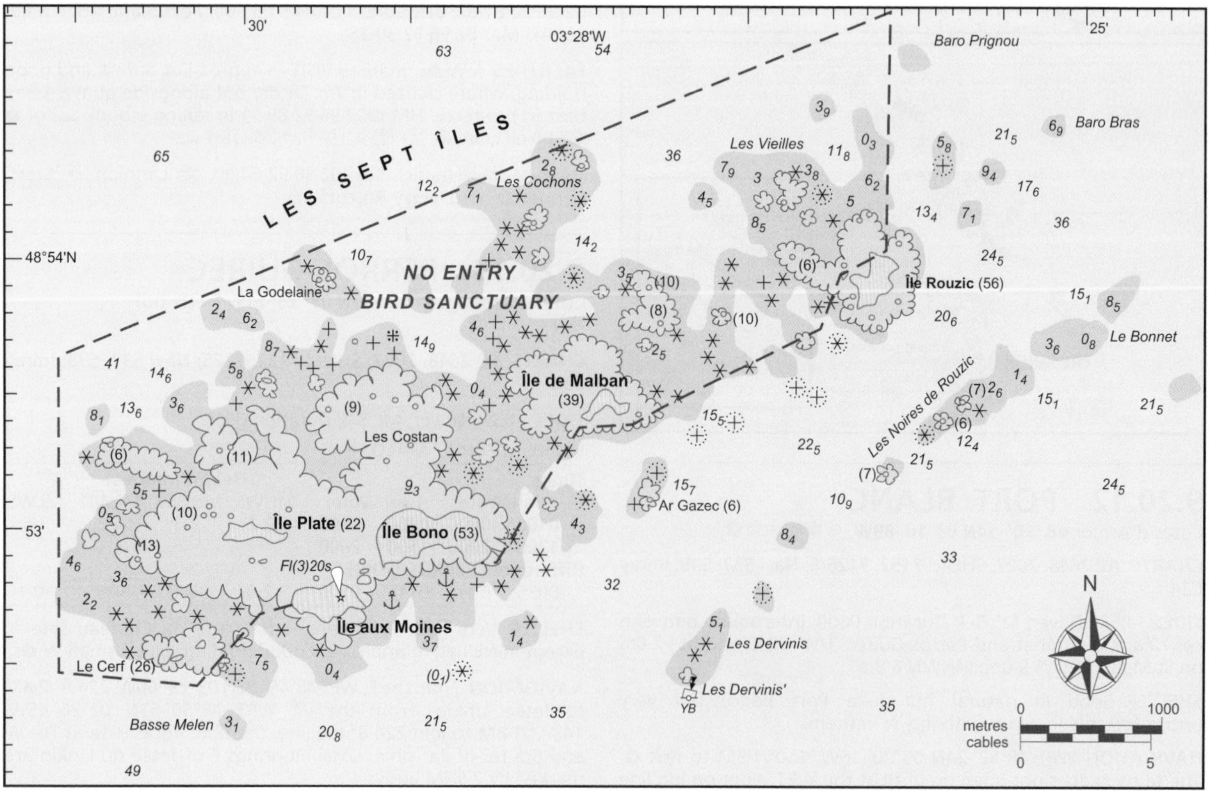

OFFSHORE ISLANDS

LES SEPT ÎLES, Côte d'Armor, **48° 52´·72N 03°29´·16W**. AC 2026, 2027; SHOM 7152 (large scale 1:20,000). See chartlet on previous page. HW-0550 on Dover (UT); +0005 on Brest. HW ht –1·8m on Brest. ML 5·2m. Use Ploumanac'h differences.

The whole archipelago, outlined with a dashed line, is a no-entry bird sanctuary. Île aux Moines is the only one of the 7 islands/islets on which landing is permitted; no shore facilities. It is safe to sail NW of Les Dervinis (SCM buoy) and Les Noires de Rouzic (always visible) a steep-to rocky chain SE of the main group.

Straightforward approach to Île aux Moines, allowing for strong stream. Avoid a rock (0·6m) 300m SE of the island. Best ⚓ (Lat/Long as on line 1) is due E of jetty at E end of Île aux Moines and S of W end of Île Bono; overnight only in calm settled weather. Vedettes use a mooring buoy here. More exposed ⚓s are S of the Old Fort (W end of island) or close S of Île Bono; both require care due to rocks, clearly shown on SHOM 7152. The most dangerous is at 48° 52´·45N 03°28´·68W; it dries 0·1, is rarely seen but often encountered. Only slightly less dangerous is the rock drying 1·4 at 48° 52´·64N 03°28´·28W.

Île aux Moines lt ho is a very conspic grey twr whose 24M beam is obscured by Bono and Rouzic in a 4° arc (237°-241°) and when brg <039°, ie if tucked into the Baie de Lannion.

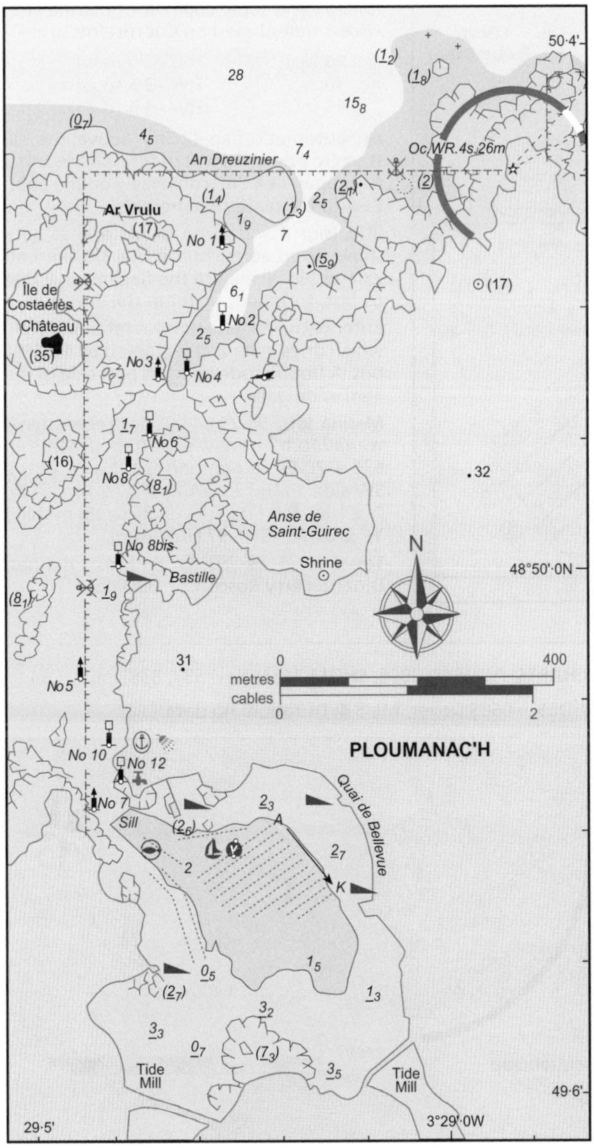

9.20.14 PLOUMANAC'H

Côtes d'Armor **48° 49'·78N 03° 29'·51W** (Sill) ❁❁◊◊✿✿✿

CHARTS AC 2648, 2027 (limited scale 1:48,700); SHOM 7125 (1:10,000 inset); Navi 537, 538; Imray C34

TIDES –0550 Dover; ML 5·5; Duration 0605

Standard Port ST MALO (⟵)

Times				Height (metres)			
High Water		Low Water		MHWS	MHWN	MLWN	MLWS
0100	0800	0300	0800	12·2	9·3	4·2	1·5
1300	2000	1500	2000				
Differences PLOUMANAC'H							
–0035	–0040	–0120	–0100	–2·9	–2·0	–0·7	–0·2

SHELTER Good inside. Appr is uncomfortable against the ebb in strong N'lys, favour the PHMs; dangerous during spring ebb with strong NE winds.

NAVIGATION WPT 48°51´·44N 03°29´·09W, 188°/1·2M to ent between Mean Ruz lt ho and Château Costaérès (conspic). At the entrance beware An Dreuzinier, unmarked rocks (drying 1·4m) 100m N and NE of No 1 SHM perch; not a problem with sufficient rise of tide, but near LW stick to a line 225° through the Nos 2 and 4 PHM perches. 11 unlit perches mark the chan.

Entry is over a sill, drying 2·55m, which retains 1·2m to 2·3m within. If concrete base of No 5 perch (the 3rd SHM) is covered, depth over sill is >1·4m. No 12 PHM perch right next to sill has depth gauge; note: gauge not visible when >3m over sill.

LIGHTS AND MARKS See chartlet and Lights, buoys and waypoints. Mean Ruz lt ho is a reddish square twr. Signal stn, 8ca SSE, is conspic from the E. Night entry not advised.

COMMUNICATIONS Ⓛ 02·96·20·00·45; Auto 08·92·68·08·22; Brit Consul 01·44·51·31·00; Dr 02·96·91·42·00; HM VHF Ch 09.

FACILITIES Between Nos 8 and 8bis perches on the E side of chan are 3 waiting buoys marked VPG in 1·5m least depth.

Port de Plaisance Inside the sill, are moorings for FVs and yachts >12m in a trot to stbd of ent in 3m, with 2 drying trots of small craft outboard. For best water keep to port and approach the yacht moorings from NW. Ⓥs are 1st trot (A) of dumbbell buoys; max LOA 12m. Yachts >12m may be able to tie up to the fishing vessel trots perpendicular to the sill. SE & SW sides of hbr are very shallow.

HM (part time) ☎02·96·91·44·31 or 02·96·49·80·50 (Perros-Guirec). www.port-perros-guirec.com 230 + 20 Ⓥs, €3·30. The full time Perros HM also oversees Ploumanac'h and Anse de Trestraou, a pleasant anchorage on N side of Perros town, well sheltered from S and W winds; exposed to NE'lies.

Quai Bellevue ⌐ ▬ Ⓓ Ⓟ. ✎ ☎02·96·23·05·89. **YC de Perros-Guirec** Bus to Lannion and Perros. **Ferry** see Roscoff.

ANCHORAGE 1M WEST OF PLOUMANAC'H

TRÉGASTEL-PLAGE, Côtes d'Armor, **48°50´·04N 03°31´·29W**, AC 2026, 2027; SHOM 7152, 7125. HW –0550 on Dover (UT); +0005 and –1·8m on Brest HW; ML 5·1m; Duration 0605. Use Ploumanac'h differences.

A large W radome, conspic 3·2M S of the ent, gives general orientation. Enter between PHM bcn on Île Dhu (just W of Île Dé, with dice-shaped Pierre Pendue) and SHM bcn (or buoy if bcn destroyed) off Le Taureau, rk drying 4·5m. A conspic house with □ turret, brg approx 165° leads between Île Dhu and Le Taureau. But it is easier to track 183° leaving the 3 PHM bcns about 60m to port. SHOM 7125 (1: 20,000) is strongly advised.

Beyond SHM bcn, ⚓ or pick up westernmost Ⓥs €10·00/night, S of Île Ronde (nearest the ent). Good ⚓ in 2m, but exposed W to N, with swell near HW springs; more comfortable at neaps.

Facilities: ▬ in E part of hbr. **CN de Trégastel** ☎02·96·23·45·05.

Town (Ste Anne, 0·5M inland) ✕ ▢ ▢ ▢ ▢ ✎ ✉ Ⓑ; Dr 02·96·23·88·08/02·96·15·96·49.

9.20.15 TRÉBEURDEN

Côtes d'Armor **48°46′·29N 03°35′·15W** ❁❁◊◊◊✿✿

TIDES –0605 Dover; ML 5·5; Duration 0605

Standard Port BREST (⟶)

Times				Height (metres)			
High Water		Low Water		MHWS	MHWN	MLWN	MLWS
0000	0600	0000	0600	6·9	5·4	2·6	1·0
1200	1800	1200	1800				
Differences TRÉBEURDEN							
+0100	+0110	+0120	+0100	+2·3	+1·9	+0·9	+0·4

CHARTS AC 2026; SHOM 7151/2, 7125, 7124; Navi 537, 538; Imray C34

SHELTER Good in marina (2–2·6m). ⚓ off NE side of Île Milliau is exposed to W'lies.

NAVIGATION WPT 48°45′·34N 03°40′·00W, 067°/3M to first PHM buoy in white sector of Lan Kerellec Dir lt. From WSW, go direct to ⊕; thence enter the buoyed chan (105°/088°) to marina.

From E and N, round Bar-ar-Gall and Le Crapaud WCM buoys; continue S for 1·4M, before altering 067° towards the ⊕. If properly planned, the short-cut 183° between Le Crapaud reef and reefs N and S of Île Losket is safe in offshore winds.

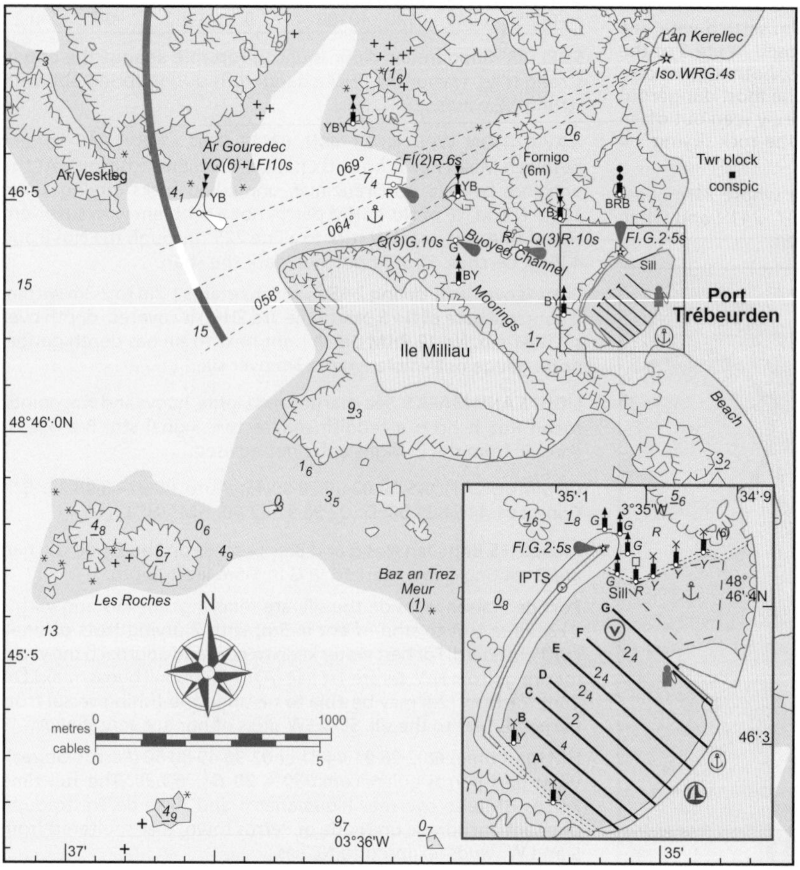

LIGHTS AND MARKS See chartlet and Lights, buoys and waypoints. Lan Kerellec Dir lt leads 067° to the start of buoyed chan, aligned approx 100° with ✠ spire (conspic, 115m).

COMMUNICATIONS CROSS 02·98·89·31·31; Police 02·96·23·51·96 (Jul/Aug); ⊜ 02·96·48·45·32; Brit Consul 01·44·51·31·00; *Port Trébeurden* VHF Ch 09, 16; Aff Mar 02·96·91·21·28.

FACILITIES 10 Y waiting buoys lie S of the fairway and some 600m W of marina ent. Access times based on Coefficients are:

95 (sp)	HW –3½ to +4
70	HW –3¾ to +4¼
45 (np)	HW –4¾ to +5¼

An automatic flap (2·5m) above the sill starts to open when ht of tide is 4·0m and is fully open at 4·3m (conversely on the ebb). Best to calculate tidal heights.

IPTS (sigs 2 and 4) on bkwtr and at gate show when access is possible. Do not ent/exit within 20 mins of the flap moving, due to fast, turbulent water in the entrance.

Enter between gate posts in retaining wall, which dries 3·5m and is marked by 4 Y SPM bns. A floodlit tide gauge is port side of the 15m wide gate.

Marina ☎02·96·23·64·00. portrebeurden@wanadoo.fr www.port-trebeurden.com 625 + 70 Ⓥ on pontoon G (NE side <11m, SW side >11m) July/Aug €3·70, inc ⚡ @, ⛿ €1·00. 🚿🚻 ⊡ ⚒ ⛵ (16t mobile) **YC** ☎02·96·15·45·97 (July-Aug).

Town ✕ ☐ 🛒 ✉ Ⓑ. ✈ Brest, Rennes, Dinard. **Ferry** Roscoff or St Malo.

9.20.16 LÉGUER RIVER (Lannion)

Côtes d'Armor **48°43′·76N 03°33′·28W (2nd G bcn)** ❁❁◊✿✿✿

CHARTS AC 2648, 2026; SHOM 7124; Navi 537, 538; Imray C34

TIDES –0605 Dover; ML 5·4; Duration: no data

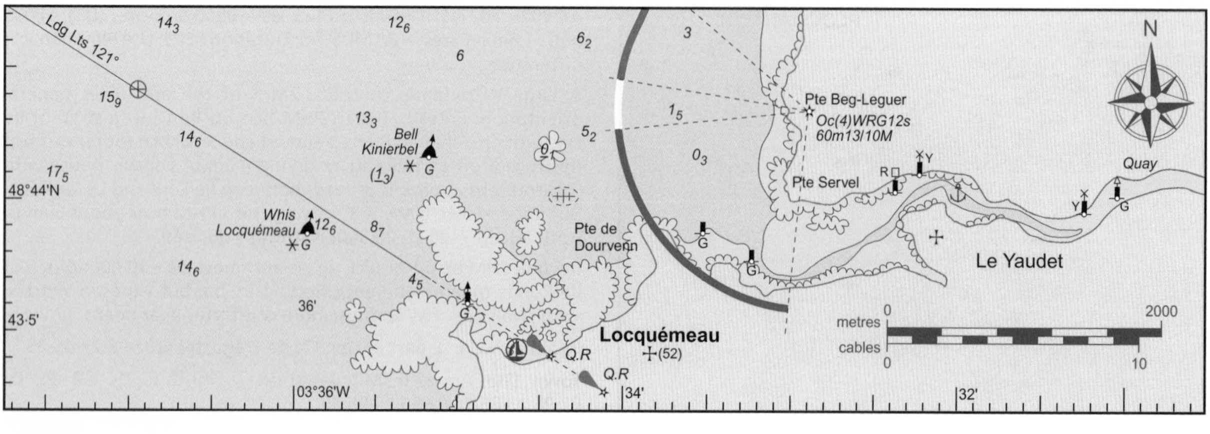

Standard Port BREST (⟶)

Times				Height (metres)			
High Water		Low Water		MHWS	MHWN	MLWN	MLWS
0000	0600	0000	0600	6·9	5·4	2·6	1·0
1200	1800	1200	1800				
Differences LOCQUIREC							
+0100	+0110	+0125	+0100	+2·3	+1·9	+0·9	+0·5

SHELTER Good, except in strong W/NW winds. No access at LW sp, esp in strong NW'lies when seas break on the drying bar. ⚓ in non-drying pools off Le Yaudet and up to the 2nd Y perch, but very little space due to silting and many local moorings; a vacant mooring is possible or ⚓ outside and recce by dinghy.

NAVIGATION WPT 48°44'·38N 03°36'·87W, 091°/2·6M to Pte Beg-Léguer lt (also on Locquémeau ldg lts 121°). Leave Kinierbel SHM buoy close to stbd; stand on until Trébeurden spire bears 004° (to clear a drying patch) then alter 135° for the ent, passing close to two G bcn twrs. Le Yaudet pool is 8ca further E.

Chan upriver to Lannion is narrow, steep-to, dries and is unmarked by bcns; best seen at LW before attempting. Just below Lannion town, opp Quai de Loguivy, drying out on the N bank may be feasible; a recce by dinghy or on foot is advised.

LIGHTS AND MARKS See chartlet and Lights, buoys and waypoints. Pte de Beg-Léguer lt ho is a squat twr, R top, built onto a house and on high cliffs. Le Yaudet spire helps to pinpoint the river ent.

COMMUNICATIONS CROSS 02·98·89·31·31; Auto 08·92·68·08·22; Police 02·96·46·69·50; ⊖ 02·96·48·45·32; Brit Consul 01·44·51·31·00; Dr 02·96·47·23·15; Aff Mar 02·96·55·35·00.

FACILITIES HM ☎02·96·47·29·64, slip (dries) water (1t) only in emergency. ✕ in Le Yaudet, but few supplies.

Lannion, ✕ SHOM Ⓔ ✉ Ⓑ.

ADJACENT HARBOURS IN BAIE DE LANNION

LOCQUÉMEAU, Côtes d'Armor, **48°43'·60N 03°34'·96W** (1st SHM perch). AC 2648, 3669; SHOM 7124. HW –0600 on Dover (UT); +0110 on Brest; HW ht +1·5m on Brest; ML 5·3m. SHOM 7124 is desirable as it shows the various perches. A small drying hbr by ent to Lannion River (above); use the same WPT. Approach leaving Locquémeau SHM buoy close to stbd. There are two quays: the outer is accessible at LW, but open to W winds. Yachts can dry out at inner quay, on S side. Ldg lts 121° to outer quay: front, W pylon + R top; rear, hard-to-see W gable and R gallery. Facilities: **Town** ✕.

LOCQUIREC, Finistère, **48°41'·41N 03°38'·79W**. AC 3669, 2648; SHOM 7124. Tidal data see Lannion. Small drying hbr at mouth of Le Douron R, with good shelter from W'lies. The whole estuary dries to extensive, shifting sandbanks (2·9m to 6·1m). No lights, but Gouliat NCM buoy is 7ca N of Pte du Château and a SHM bcn twr (6ca S of the hbr, marking Roche Rouge) is conspic. E of Pte du Château, off Île Vert, there are 25 W moorings +2 Ⓥ, €6·50p/n, in up to 4m. Beyond, Locquirec harbour and bay has 304 W drying moorings, + 5 Ⓥ, also €6·50, pleasant tempy ⚓, overnight if able to take the ground, or dry on stone quay. Land at slip. A small, laid-back resort, inc some fine trad. hotel-restaurants and Ⓒ. Mairie (Port Authority) ☎02·98·67·42·20.Good LW cockling.

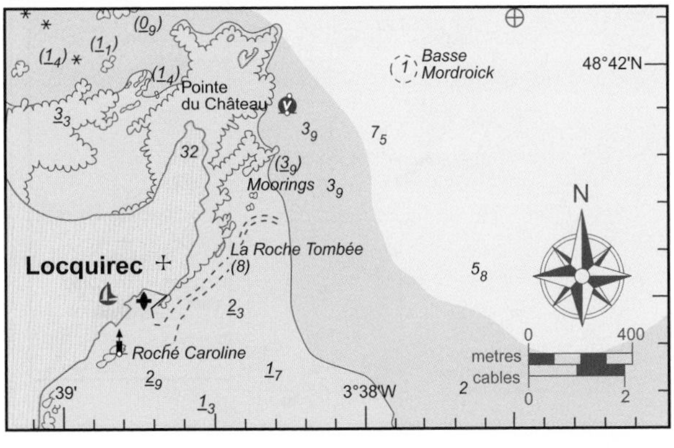

9.20.17 PRIMEL-TRÉGASTEL

Finistère **48°42'·79N 03°49'·46W**

CHARTS AC 2026, 2745; SHOM 7151, 7124, 7095; Navi 538; Imray C34, C35

TIDES See Morlaix for differences ANSE DE PRIMEL. –0610 Dover; ML 5·3; Duration 0600.

SHELTER Access at all tides, but exposed to N/NW'lies; if strong, seas break across ent. Drying upper reaches are well sheltered.

NAVIGATION WPT 48°43'·59N 03°50'·10W, 152°/0·9M to the hbr bkwtr. Beware drying rks NE of Pte de Primel. Enter exactly on 152° ldg marks, past a SHM bcn marking Ar Zammeguez (3m high). The ent, between a PHM and 2nd SHM bcns, is narrow. A useful hbr to await the tide up to Morlaix.

LIGHTS AND MARKS Pte de Primel is a conspic 42m high rky islet NNE of the hbr. 152° ldg marks/lights are clear but precise: three white walls with R vert stripe in serried ranks up the hillside surrounded by small pine trees; ldg lts, both QR, are on the front and rear marks.

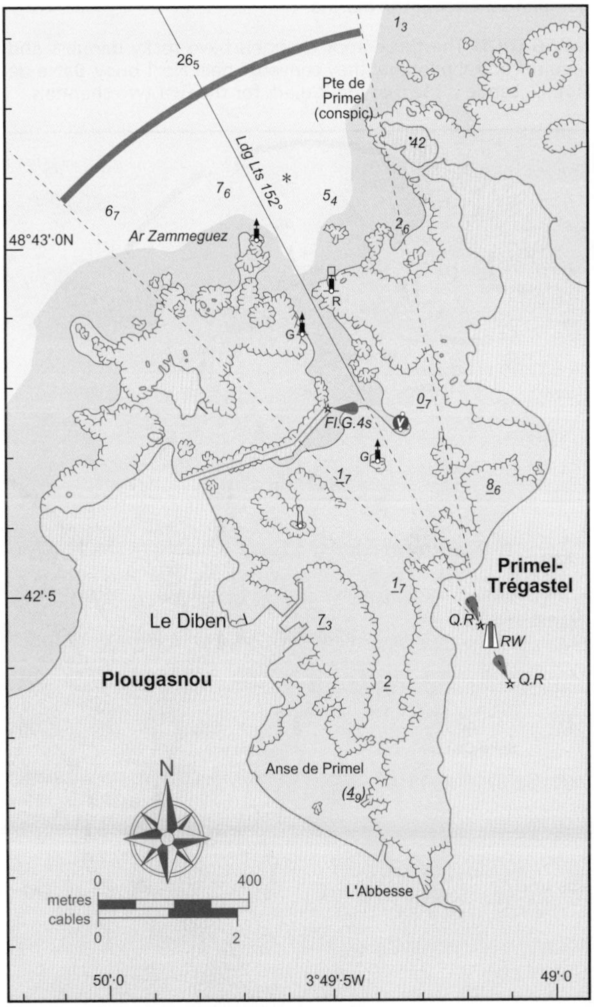

COMMUNICATIONS 06·14·38·26·81; Dr 02·98·67·30·20; Brit Consul 01·44·51·31·00; HM 06·81·79·67·49 (English speaker); VHF Ch 09, 16 (season); Rolland Marine B'yard 02·98·72·30·06.

FACILITIES Le Diben (Plougasnou) on W side is a FV hbr. FVs occupy most of the bkwtr; rafting possible. In summer a line is strung along the quay for yachts to tie on to, the E end is non-drying; not safe in N'lies. A small ⚓age and 16 W Ⓥs in about 1m (13 are drying) are SE of the bkwtr head. Or ⚓ to SE or SW of bkwtr hd in 2·9m. Ⓔ (45t). **Primel-Trégastel** ✕ ✉ Ⓑ. **Ferry** Roscoff.

N Brittany

9.20.18 MORLAIX

Finistère **48°35'·31N 03°50'·30W** (Lock)

CHARTS AC 2026, 2745; SHOM 7151, 7095; Navi 538; Imray C34, C35

TIDES –0610 Dover; ML 5·3; Duration 0610

Standard Port BREST (⟶)

Times				Height (metres)			
High Water		Low Water		MHWS	MHWN	MLWN	MLWS
0000	0600	0000	0600	6·9	5·4	2·6	1·0
1200	1800	1200	1800				
Differences MORLAIX (CHÂTEAU DU TAUREAU)							
+0055	+0105	+0115	+0055	+2·0	+1·7	+0·8	+0·3
ANSE DE PRIMEL							
+0100	+0110	+0120	+0100	+2·1	+1·7	+0·8	+0·3

SHELTER Good in the bay, except in onshore winds. Strong N'lies can raise a steep sea even in the estuary. ⚓ NE of Carantec is exposed, especially to NW; landing stage dries about 4·6m. Complete shelter in the marina.

NAVIGATION The three appr channels have rocky dangers and require careful pilotage; they converge near No 1 buoy, Barre de Flot. La Lande is the rear ldg lt/mark for the first two channels.

- **Chenal de Tréguier** is best at night, but almost dries: WPT 48°42'·55N 03°51'·93W (abm La Pierre Noire SHM bcn) 190·5°/1·84M to La Chambre bcn twr. Ldg lts 190·5°: Front mark, Île Noire lt bcn.
- **Grand Chenal** is shallower but lit: WPT 48°42'·65N 03°53'·53W, (abm Stolvezen PHM buoy) 176°/2·23M to Île Louet lt, passing E of Ile Ricard. Ldg lts 176·4°: Front mark, Île Louet lt ho.
- **Chenal Ouest de Ricard** is the deepest, but unlit. It deviates 188·8° from Grand Chenal, passing W of Ile Ricard. 188·8° ldg marks: Pierres de Carantec and Kergrist, both painted white.

The Morlaix River is buoyed/bcn'd but unlit and prone to silting. ⚓ off Pen al Lann and Dourduff (dries) clear of extensive oyster beds marked by small orange buoys/stakes.

Morlaix lock, marina and town are 5·5M upriver from No 1 SHM buoy.

LIGHTS AND MARKS See Lights, buoys and waypoints and chartlet. Château du Taureau fort is conspic 4ca N of No 1 buoy. Some marks omitted for clarity.

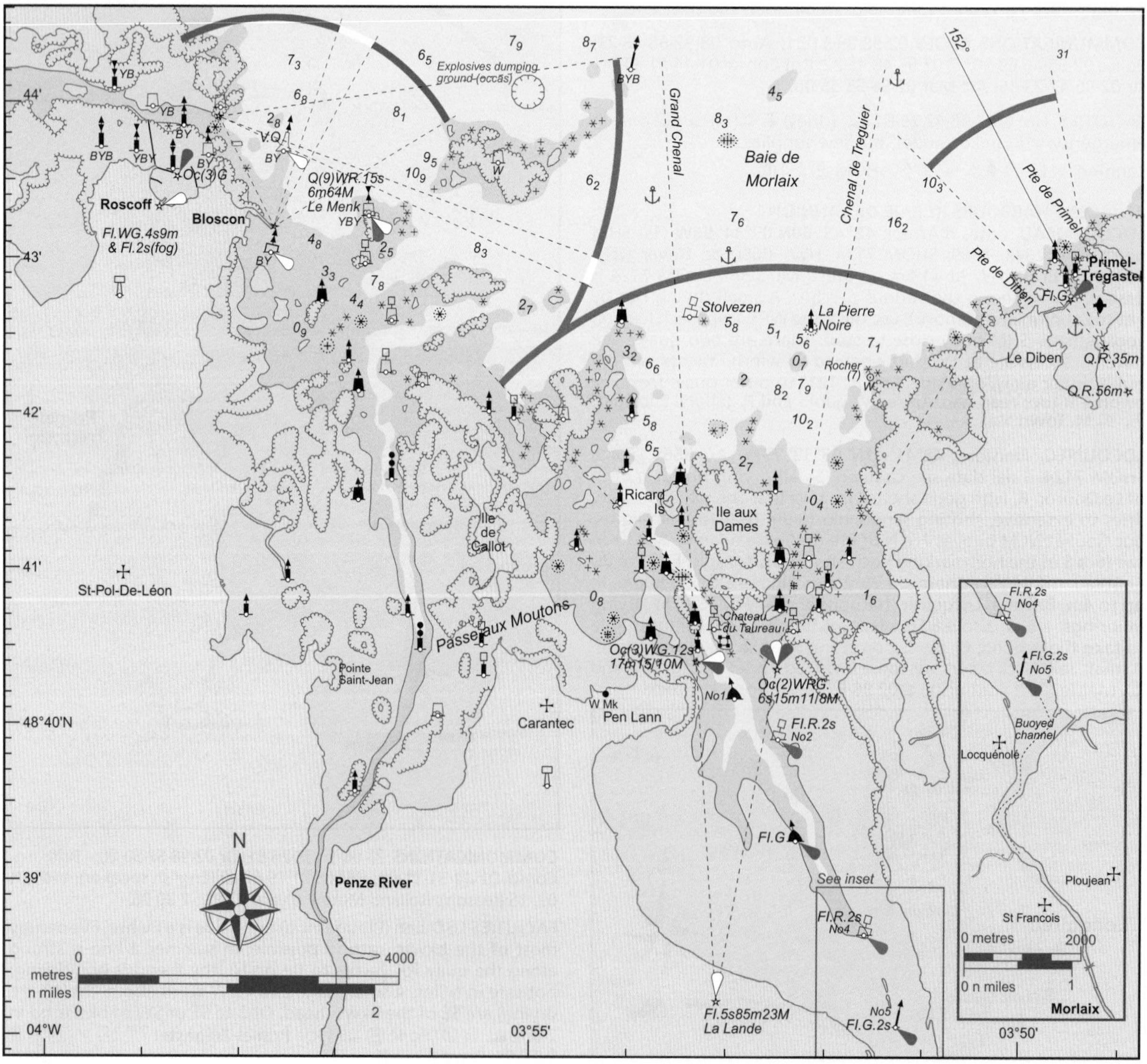

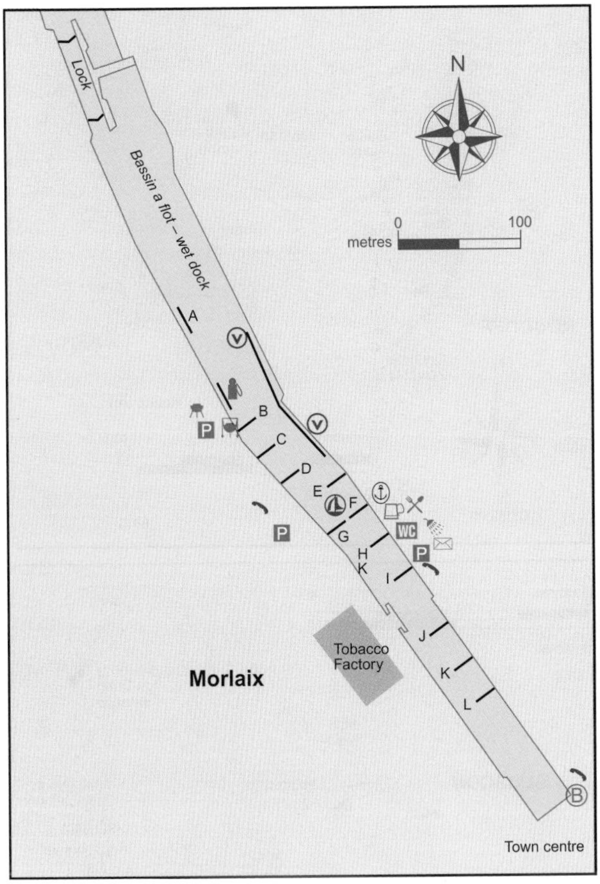
N
Lock
Bassin a flot – wet dock
metres
0
100
A
B
C
D
E
F
G
H
K
I
J
K
L
Tobacco Factory
Morlaix
Town centre

COMMUNICATIONS CROSS 02·98·89·31·31; 02·98·72·35·10; Auto 08·92·68·02·29; Police 02·98·88·17·17; 02·98·69·70·84; British Consul 01·44·51·31·00; 02·98·62·62·45; Port and Marina VHF Ch 09; Aff Mar 02·98·62·10·47.

FACILITIES Morlaix lock ☎02·98·88·15·10/06·77·50·15·90 opens by day only (SR-SS) at HW –1½, HW and HW+1; wait alongside W quay.

Marina ☎02·98·62·13·14 www.plaisancebaiedemorlaix.com plaisance.morlaix@morlaix.cci.fr 150+32Ⓥ Jun-Sep €2·50; multihulls x150%. Ⓥ pontoon (fingers) on E bank, parallel to road. In lock hours a movable footbridge across the marina is usually open. (8t).

Town Ⓔ SHOM Ⓑ. ✈ Brest, ferry Roscoff.

ANCHORAGES W AND NW OF MORLAIX

PENZÉ RIVER, Finistère, Ent **48°42′·24N 03°56′·66W**, AC 2745; SHOM 7095. HW –0610 on Dover (UT) +0105 on Brest; HW ht +1·2m Brest; ML 5·0m; Duration 0605.

The Penzé river lies W of Île Callot. From NNW, appr between Cordonnier and Guerhéon bcn twrs at mid-flood. Or, for deeper water, from the ENE pass between Les Bizeyer reef and Le Paradis bcn twr; thence S via beaconed channel.

Passe aux Moutons, between Carantec and Île Callot, is a drying (6·2m) short cut from the E into the Penzé, with adequate rise.

S of Le Figuier IDM bcn the chan narrows and is scantily marked by small oyster withies, then by mooring trots. Best shelter is SW of Pte de Lingos: moor in 1·2m off St Yves where the old ferry slips provide landing places.

S of Pont de la Corde (10m clearance) the river is buoyed and navigable on the tide for 3M to Penzé. No access 1 Mar–31 Aug to a Nature Reserve at the head of the river.

Facilities at Carantec Ⓔ. **Town** Ⓑ.

Penzé (drying) limited.

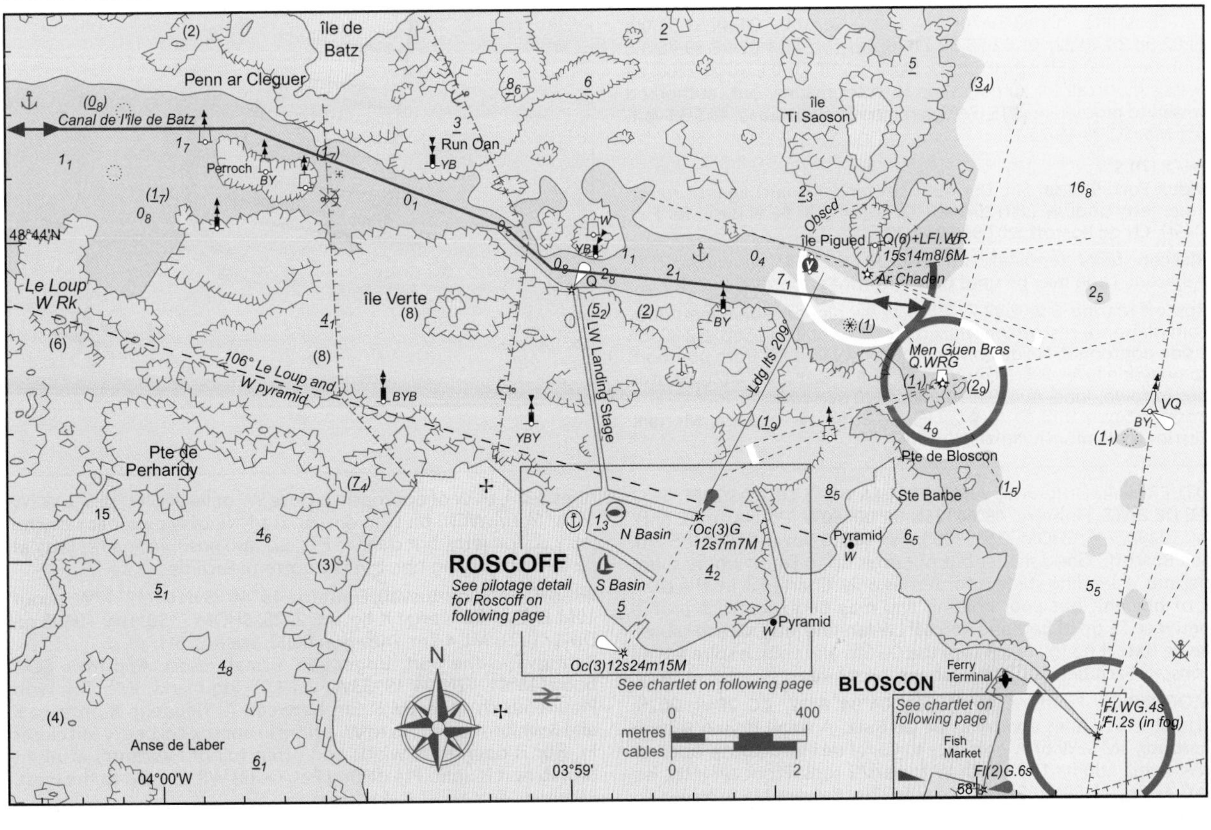
Île de Batz
Penn ar Cleguer
Canal de l'Île de Batz
Perroch
BY
Run Oan
YB
Île Ti Saoson
Île Pigued
Q(6)+LFl.WR.
15s14m8/6M
Obscd
Ar Chaden
Men Guen Bras
Q.WRG
48°44'N
Le Loup
W Rk
Île Verte
106° Le Loup and W pyramid
BYB
YBY
LW Landing Stage
Ldg lts 209°
BY
VQ
Pte de Perharidy
Pte de Bloscon
Ste Barbe
N Basin
Oc(3)G
12s7m7M
Pyramid
W
ROSCOFF
See pilotage detail for Roscoff on following page
S Basin
Oc(3)12s24m15M
See chartlet on following page
BLOSCON
Ferry Terminal
See chartlet on following page
Fish Market
Fl.WG.4s
Fl.2s (in fog)
Fl(2)G.6s
Anse de Laber
04°00'W
03°59'
metres
cables
0
400
2
N

9.20.19 ROSCOFF

Finistère **48°43'·54N 03°58'·59W** ✿✿◊◊✿✿✿

CHARTS AC 2026, 2745; SHOM 7151, 7095; Navi 538; Imray C35

TIDES –0605 Dover; ML 5·2; Duration 0600

Standard Port BREST (⟶)

Times				Height (metres)			
High Water		Low Water		MHWS	MHWN	MLWN	MLWS
0000	0600	0000	0600	6·9	5·4	2·6	1·0
1200	1800	1200	1800				
Differences ROSCOFF							
+0055	+0105	+0115	+0055	+2·0	+1·7	+0·8	+0·3
ÎLE DE BATZ							
+0045	+0100	+0105	+0055	+2·0	+1·6	+0·9	+0·4
BRIGNOGAN (48°40'·6N 04°19'·2W)							
+0040	+0045	+0100	+0040	+1·5	+1·2	+0·6	+0·2

SHELTER Good in drying Vieux Port except in strong N/E'lies. 12 W 🅐s, €8·50 all LOA, in 4-5m close W of Ar Chaden are exposed. Shelter very good in large modern marina.

NAVIGATION **Roscoff Marina** (S of ferry port): Appr H24 on 205° in W sector of mole hd lt. Avoid ferries; do not attempt to enter marina from south. Beware strong tide on all outer berths and close to E bkwtr, also long seaweed fronds if berthing stern to tide. **Vieux Port**: From the N, WPT 48°45'·88N 03°56'·00W, 213°/2·5M to Men Guen Bras lt. From the E approach between Plateau de la Méloine and Plateau des Duons; or pass S of the latter and N of Le Menk bcn lt twr in Ar Chaden's W sector (289·5°-293°). From the W, WPT 48°44'·27N 04°04'·06W, 090°/1M to Basse Plate bcn twr; thence via well-marked Canal de l'Île de Batz; see Passage information. Approach near HW over many large drying rks on 209° ldg line: see Lights, buoys and waypoints. N mole hd has B/W vert stripes.

LIGHTS AND MARKS See chartlet and Lights, buoys and waypoints. Île de Batz lt ho is conspic through 360°. E ent to Canal de l'Île de Batz flanked by bcn twrs: Ar Chaden YB and Men-Guen-Bras BY.

COMMUNICATIONS CROSS 02·98·89·31·31; LB 06·82·18·01·34; Auto 08·92·68·08·29; Police 02·98·69·00·48; ⊖ (Bloscon) 02·98·69·70·84; ⊖ (Roscoff) 02·98·69·70·15; Brit Consul 01·44·51·31·00; H 02·98·88·40·22; Dr 02·98·69·71·18; Roscoff HM 02·98·69·76·37, mob 06·70·50·96·68, VHF Ch 09; *Bloscon* VHF Ch 09, (0700-2200) all vessels must call for authorisation to enter marina, only authorised vessels to proceed on IPTS GWG vert, no vessels to leave, IPTS 3R vert. Aff Mar 02·98·69·70·15.

FACILITIES

Vieux Port, S Basin 5m. Dry out with fender board against rough inner jetty or quay. 280+20🅥 €0·73. Facilities (5t). **CN de Roscoff** ☎02·98·69·72·79.

Bloscon ferry terminal. HM ☎02·98·61·27·84, www.roscoff.fr. Adjacent ⚓age may be used only with HM's approval.

Roscoff Marina ☎02·98·79·79·49, www.plaisancebaiedemorlaix.com plaisance.roscoff@morlaix.cci.fr 625 + 40🅥Jun-Sep, €2·80, on S side pontoon B, N side pontoon D. Convenient lift from pontoons to quayside level. (H24) (50t) (2t). Shuttle bus to town, June–Aug, 0700–1700, or 10 min walk.

Roscoff Town Ⓑ . ⇌ ✈ Brest, Morlaix. Ferries to Plymouth, Rosslare, Cork.

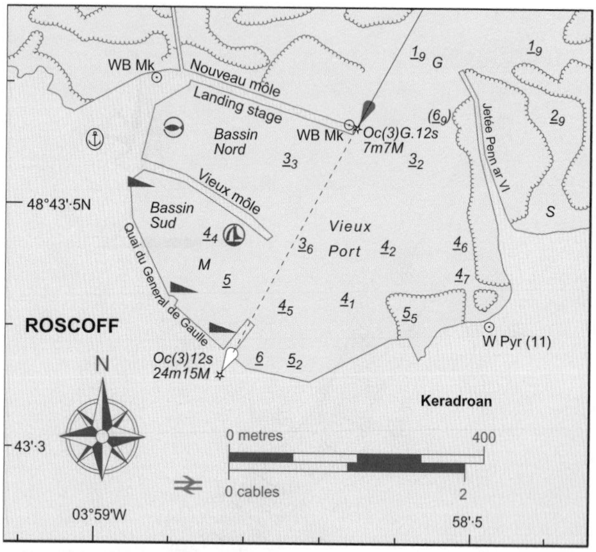

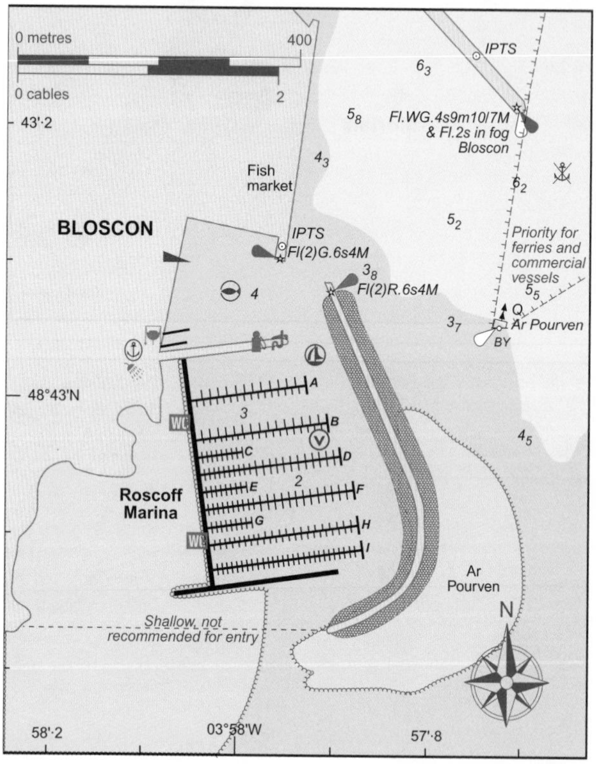

OTHER HARBOURS AND ANCHORAGES WEST OF ROSCOFF

ÎLE DE BATZ, Finistère, **48°44'·26N 04°00'·60W** (Porz-Kernok ent). AC 2026, 2745; SHOM 7151, 7095; HW +0610 Dover (UT); ML 5·2m. See Roscoff. Good shelter but hbr dries up to 5m; ⚓ where space permits. E landing stage is for ferries only. Charted ⚓ in the chan E of hbr ent, but poor holding and may be exposed. ⚓ prohib between SE tip of Batz and Roscoff LW landing jetty, due to cables. Île de Batz lt ho (gy twr, B top) the CG Stn and church spire are all conspic. Facilities: basic shops, bike hire.

MOGUÉRIEC, Finistère, **48°41'·35N 04°04'·41W**, AC 2648, 2026; SHOM 7151. Tides approx as Île de Batz. A small drying fishing harbour, 3M SSW of W entrance to Canal de l'Île de Batz, open to NW swell. Ldg lts 162°, both W towers/G tops: Front on jetty, Iso WG 4s 9m, W158°-166°; rear Iso G 4s 22m. Beware Méan Névez rk, dries 3·3m, to W of approach. ⚓ close SW of Île de Siec, or 3ca WSW of Ar Skeul WCM bn tr in 4m, or 2ca NNE of Moguériec's drying jetty. Dry out on jetty, but clear of FVs. Drying also possible against jetty at Île de Siec's drying hbr, but rky bottom. Facilities:

BRIGNOGAN (Pontusval), Finistère, **48°40'·59N 04°19'·17W**, about 10M ENE of Île Vierge lt ho. AC 2025; SHOM 7150. HW +0605 on Dover (UT); ML 4·7m; Duration 0600; see Roscoff.

Pontusval is the port, Brignogan a small resort. App from ECM buoy (48°41'·42N 04°19'·33W) via 178° ldg marks, W bn on with Plounéour ch spire 1M S. Ent between Ar Neudenn R bn tr to E and 3 white-topped rks to W. ⚓ here in approx 4m or dry out closer in. Hbr is open to N winds and often full of FVs. Entry at night prohib as it is unlit. Pte de Beg Pol, Oc (3) WR 12s, 1M to the west. Facilities: 5 🅐's (free).

9.20.20 L'ABER WRAC'H ❁❁◊◊✿✿✿

Finistère **48°35'·97N 04°33'·62W** (marina ent)

CHARTS AC 2025, 1432; SHOM 7150, 7094; Navi 539; Imray C35

TIDES +0547 Dover; ML 4·5; Duration 0600

Standard Port BREST (⟶)

Times				Height (metres)			
High Water		Low Water		MHWS	MHWN	MLWN	MLWS
0000	0600	0000	0600	6·9	5·4	2·6	1·0
1200	1800	1200	1800				
Differences L'ABER WRAC'H, ÎLE CÉZON							
+0030	+0030	+0040	+0035	+0·8	+0·7	+0·2	0·0

SHELTER Good in marina, but ⚓s uncomfortable in strong NW wind. No ⚓ off the marina. Paluden, 1·5M upriver (unlit/unbuoyed; beware oyster beds) is well sheltered in all winds.

NAVIGATION WPT (Grand Chenal) 48°37'·35N 04°38'·51W, abm Libenter WCM buoy, 100°/1·5M to Petit Pot de Beurre ECM bcn twr. Here pick up the inner appr chan 128°/1·7M, in W sector of Dir Lt Oc (2) WRG 6s, passing a SHM lt buoy, SHM bcn lt twr and a PHM lt buoy, to the last SHM bcn twr; thence visual for 700m to the pool/pontoon at L'Aber Wrac'h. Beware: lge unlit mooring buoys.

Chenal de la Malouine is a narrow short cut from/to N & E, only by day and in good weather: 176·2° transit of Petit Pot de Beurre with Petite Île W obelisk; precise tracking is required. Beware breakers and cross-tides.

Chenal de la Pendante 135·7° is rarely used as it crosses drying rks, saves few miles and the unlit marks are hard to see. Front, B/W 'smiley' on Île Cézon; rear, W obelisk/orange top, 650m S of hbr.

Caution: E side of marina ent, rocks drying $\underline{0}$·8m marked by 4 Y SPM buoys outside the E wavebreak and 5 inside where a W cardinal bn and 2 PHM perches also define this No Entry area. These bys/marks are unlit. Speed limits 5kn in chan, 3kn in marina.

LIGHTS AND MARKS See chartlets and Lights, buoys and waypoints. Grand Chenal 100·1° ldg marks/lts: front on Île Wrac' h, W □ twr orange top, QR; rear, 1·63M E at Lanvaon, W □ twr orange △ top, Q. A Dir lt Oc (2) WRG 6s 128° and two elusive ldg twrs, both W with R tops, mark the inner chan. QG and QR lts mark the marina ent.

COMMUNICATIONS CROSS 02·98·89·31·31; Auto 08·92·68·02·29; Police 02·98·04·00·18 or just 17; ⊜ 02·98·85·07·40; Brit Consul 01·44·51·31·00; Ⓗ 02·98·22·33·33; Dr 02·98·04·91·87; HM 02·98·04·91·62, VHF Ch 09, 16 (0800-2000LT in season); Aff Mar 02·98·04·90·13.

FACILITIES

Marina 70 Ⓥ inside W wavebreak (or outside in good weather and inside E wavebreak (tight space, prepare warps/fenders prior to entry) outer E side for trip boats to Île Vierge and FVs only (see inset). Jun-Sep, €2·88; 20 numbered W ⚓s €2·28 (+ €0.22pp/day tax) multihulls +150%. www.port-aberwrach.com aberwrach@port.cci-brest.fr. (H24 with cr/card) Ⓔ (15t) (1t). **YC des Abers** ☎02·98·04·92·60.

L'Aber Wrac'h ✕.

Landéda (Jul/Aug bus €1·00 rtn: M-Sat 11 times/day; Sun 3 times/day; or 20 mins up-hill walk): ✉ Ⓑ a.m. Tues-Fri. Bus to Brest ⇄ & ✈. **Ferry** Roscoff.

Paluden. HM ☎02·98·04·63·12. 20 dumbbell ⚓s in 5m ✕.

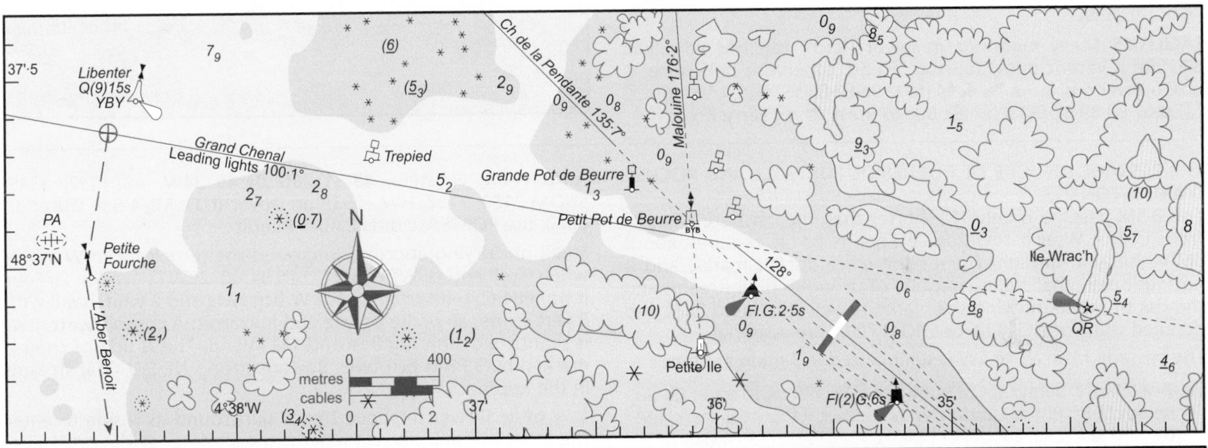

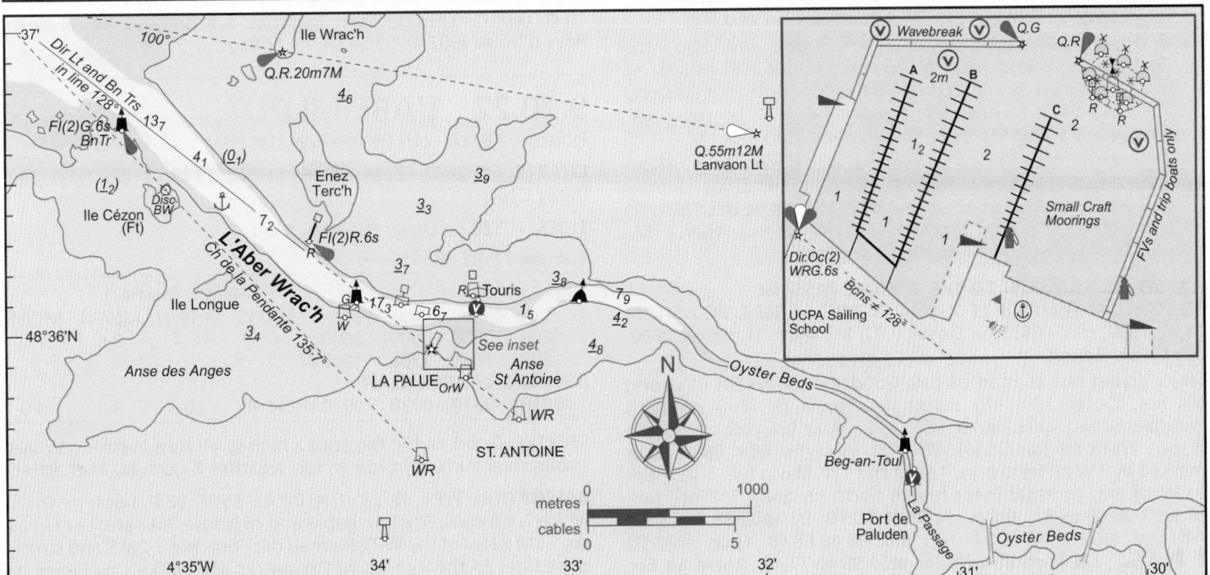

9.20.21 L'ABER BENOIT

Finistère **48°34'·64N 04°36'·89W**

CHARTS AC 2025, 1432; SHOM 7150, 7094; Navi 539, 540; Imray C35

TIDES +0535 Dover; ML 4·7; Duration 0555

Standard Port BREST (⟶)

Times				Height (metres)			
High Water		Low Water		MHWS	MHWN	MLWN	MLWS
0000	0600	0000	0600	6·9	5·4	2·6	1·0
1200	1800	1200	1800				
Differences L'ABER BENOIT							
+0022	+0025	+0035	+0020	+1·0	+0·9	+0·4	+0·2
PORTSALL							
+0015	+0020	+0025	+0015	+0·6	+0·5	+0·1	0·0

SHELTER Excellent, but do not enter at night, in poor vis nor in strong WNW winds; best near LW when dangers can be seen.

NAVIGATION WPT 48°37'·00N 04°38'·84W, close W of Petite Fourche WCM buoy; thence follow the tracks shown on chartlet. Beware oyster beds. Tidal streams up to 3kn at half-tide. River is navigable on the tide to Tréglonou bridge 3M upstream.

LIGHTS AND MARKS Unlit. Vital to identify correctly buoys and beacons in the approach chan.

COMMUNICATIONS CROSS/LB 02·98·89·31·31; Auto 08·92·68·08·29; Police 02·98·48·10·10 or 17; ⊖ 02·98·85·07·40; British Consul 01·44·51·31·00; HM VHF Ch 09, 06·19·87·75·39 (0830–1230, 1500–1830 Jul–Aug).

FACILITIES Many moorings in lower reach, call HM who will allocate a vacant buoy, Jul-Aug, €1·50, otherwise half price. ⚓ poss upriver nps. (☎02·98·89·86·55). **Village** (☎02·98·89·87·06) Ⓑ. Bus to Brest ⇄ ✈. **Ferry** Roscoff.

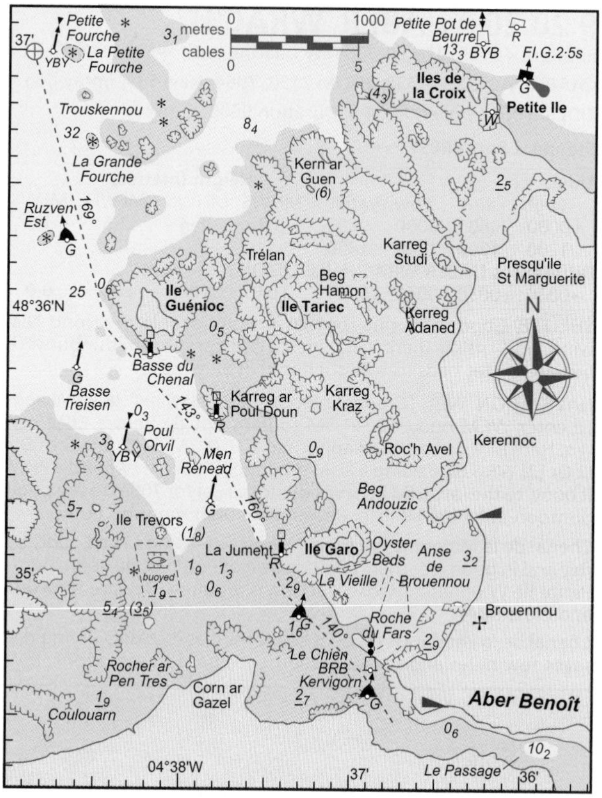

THE PASSAGE INSHORE OF ROCHES DE PORTSALL AND ROCHES D'ARGENTON

This 8·5M passage is only 1M shorter than the offshore passage from L'Aber Wrac'h towards Le Four lt ho. It requires about 6M visibility in daylight (to see the more distant marks) and is navigationally challenging because of strongish tidal streams and the risk of mis-identifying the marks. A well-illustrated Pilot and detailed study of AC 1432, or SHOM 7094, are essential.

The passage from NE to SW is summarised in 3 main sections:

- 7 ca SW of Libenter WCM buoy (see L'Aber Wrac'h) enter Ch du Relec 218·5°: Pte de Landunvez W bcn twr, R top (rear mark, 6M distant) just open left of Petit Men Louet, W bcn twr 4M distant. Leave Le Relec ECM buoy (1.5M distant) close to stbd.
- With Corn Carhai lt ho almost abeam to stbd, alter stbd into Ch du Raous: Bosven Kreiz W bcn twr in transit 249° with rks S of Le Gremm, a 12m high rk. Hold this for 7ca then alter port 228°: Le Four lt ho open left of Bosven Aval W bcn twr. 7ca later jink 7° to port to clear Bosven Aval; then pick up:
- The astern transit 036° of Bosven Aval with Bosven Kreiz. After 1·5M (Pte de Landunvez to port) intercept Chenal Méridional de Portsall, another astern transit 049°: the saddle of Le Yurc'h (7m high rk) on with Grand Men Louet W bcn twr. After 2·2M pass SE of Le Four lt ho into the Ch du Four.

HARBOURS ADJACENT TO THE INSHORE PASSAGE

PORTSALL, Finistère, **48°33'·79N 04°43'·04W**. AC 3688, 1432; SHOM 7150, 7094. HW +0535 on Dover (UT); ML 4·4m; Duration 0600. See L'Aber Benoit.

Small drying hbr at head of bay. Good shelter except in strong NW'lies. Outer 109° ldg marks: Le Yurc'h rk (7m) on with Ploudalmézeau spire. Inner 085° ldg marks (W cols; rear with R top). Front col has Oc (4) WRG 12s, W sector 084°-088°. Appr marked by 3 W bn trs to port, 1 SHM and 1 NCM bcn twr. ⚓ in >10m to W of ent, or enter inner hbr to berth on quay. Tel/Facilities: LB ☎02·98·48·69·17; Police 02·98·48·10·10; Dr ☎02·98·48·75·52; Aff Mar ☎02·98·48·66·54; Taxi ☎02·98·48·68·48. **Quay** (0·5t); **CN Portsall Kersaint** ☎02·98·48·77·49; **Ancre an Eor** ☎02·98·48·73·19. **Town** ✕ ⊠.

ARGENTON, Finistère, **48°31'·26N 04°46'·34W**. AC 1432, 3345; SHOM 7150, 7122. HW +0535 on Dover (UT); ML 4·6m; Duration 0600; use PORTSALL diffs L'Aber Benoit.

Small hbr drying approx 5·5m; good shelter except in W winds when swell enters. WPT 48°31'·14N 04°48'·29W (2½ca S of Le Four lt ho) 084·6°/1·4M to first of 2 W bcn twrs and a white wall with R vert stripe, all on Île Dolvez and in transit. A conspic water twr is slightly S of this ldg line and 1M inland. The N side of chan is marked by 3 PHM bcn twrs. Beware strong NE-SW tidal streams in the approach.

⚓ W of Île Dolvez in about 2m; or skirt round its N side to enter the inner hbr and dry out against the stone quay/slip on N side. 10 Ⓐs reported but not seen. Facilities: on quay. **Nautisme en Pays d'Iroise** ☎02·98·89·54·04. **Village** ✕.

9.20.22 L'ABER-ILDUT

Finistère **48°28'·24N 04°45'·75W** (1st PHM bcn)

CHARTS AC 2647, 2356, 3345; SHOM 7149, 7122; Navi 540; Imray C36

TIDES +0520 on Dover (UT); ML 4·2m

Standard Port BREST (⟶)

Times				Height (metres)			
High Water		Low Water		MHWS	MHWN	MLWN	MLWS
0000	0600	0000	0600	6·9	5·4	2·6	1·0
1200	1800	1200	1800				
Differences L'ABER-ILDUT							
+0010	+0010	+0020	+0010	+0·4	+0·3	0·0	0·0

SHELTER Good, but in the appr a high swell runs in strong W'lies; strong river current inside. In fair weather ⚓ outside, as chartlet.

NAVIGATION WPT 48°28'·07N 04°47'·95W, 083°/1·6M to Dir lt which is on conspic white gable end of house. Beware: Les Liniou rks 1·5M NNW of the WPT, Plateau des Fourches 1·2M S and strong cross tides in the approach. Drying rks are marked by Pierre de l'Aber SHM bcn and Le Lieu PHM bcn twr 5m; the latter is easier to see. At the narrow ent (2m) leave Men Tassin PHM bn and Rocher du Crapaud, a large rounded rock, 30m to port to clear drying spit on S side chan, marked by Beg ar Groas SHM bcn. Drop sails before entering under power alone, max 3kts. Beyond Porscave quay, the channel lies S of of 3 Y bys before turning NNE towards the quay and short-stay pontoon Care needed at LWS (max draft 2m) visit first in daylight. All quays dry at LW. A good hbr to await the tide in the Ch du Four; see Passage information, Chenal du Four.

LIGHTS AND MARKS See chartlet and Lights, buoys and waypoints. Glizit yellow water twr is conspic 6·5ca N of the ent. Dir lt 083° is a good daymark (see above); its 3° R sector and Le Lieu bcn, Fl R 2·5s 4M, mark dangers on N side of chan, the only lit mark on the S side, Beg ar Groas SHM bcn, Fl G 2.5s 1M, is right at the narrowing ent. An inland uncharted water twr is almost on 083°; the 078·5° transit shown on AC 2356 and AC 3345, using Lanildut and Brélès small church spires is very hard to see and obsc'd by trees when close in.

COMMUNICATIONS CROSS 02·98·89·31·31; LB 02·98·89·30·31; Meteo 08·92·68·08·08; Auto 08·36·68·08·08; Police 02·98·48·10·10 (or emergency 17); ⊜ 02·98·44·35·20; Dr 02·98·04·33·08; HM VHF Ch 09, Jun-Sep in office hours; Aff Mar 02·98·48·66·54; Tourism 02·98·48·12·88.

FACILITIES HM ☎02·98·04·36·40 (season) mob 06·31·93·58·71. www.lanildut.fr port.aber-ildut@wanadoo.fr **Hbr** 410 M, inc 16 🅥s; €2·00 (average) multihull +50%; max LOA 11m, draft 2m.1 x 🅥13m. Raft on dumbbells (V trot) just before 2nd PHM bcn or beyond FV quay (landing) on outer dumbbells (G trot). No ⚓ inside hbr. at fuel pontoon, (2m), H24 self service, cr/cards. Limited 🅥 just upstream on new (2017) pontoon (2m) €2·00/m,

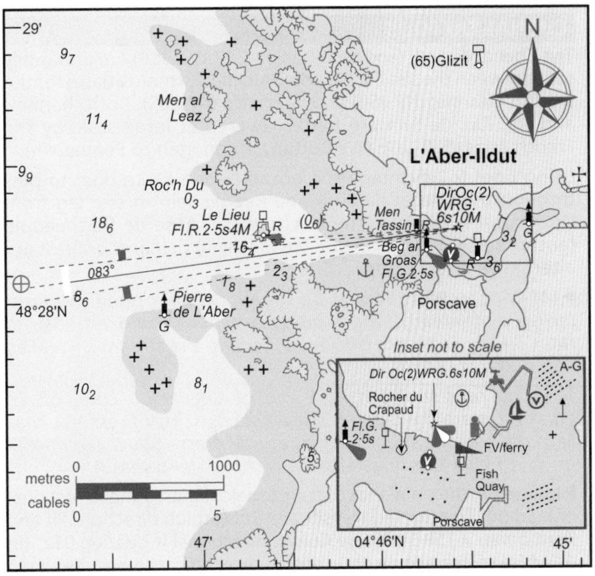

. Short stay (1hr) and also available at Porscave (opp bank) on E side of pontoon.
Village ✕ ⊠. Bus to Brest 25km. Ferries: Ouessant, Molène.

9.20.23 LE CONQUET

Finistère **48°21'·60N 04°47'·00W** (Hbr ent)

CHARTS AC 2356, 3345 with 1:10,000 inset; SHOM 7149, 7148, 7122; Navi 540; Imray C36

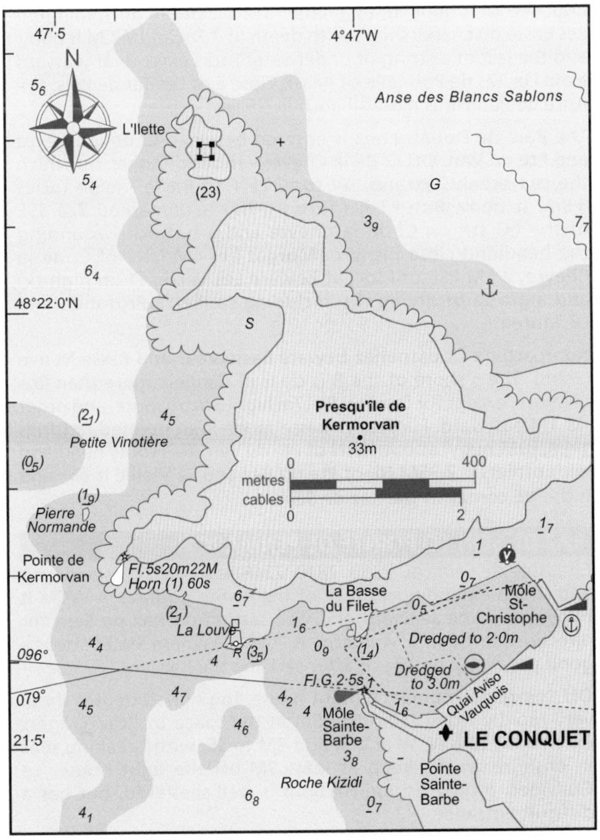

TIDES +0535 Dover; ML 3·9; Duration 0600

Standard Port BREST (⟶)

Times				Height (metres)			
High Water		Low Water		MHWS	MHWN	MLWN	MLWS
0000	0600	0000	0600	6·9	5·4	2·6	1·0
1200	1800	1200	1800				
Differences LE CONQUET							
0000	0000	+0005	+0005	–0·1	–0·1	–0·1	0·0
LE TREZ HIR (Anse de Bertheaume)							
–0005	–0005	–0015	–0010	–0·3	–0·3	–0·1	0·0

SHELTER Good except in strong W'lies. Nearest ⚓ is in Anse des Blancs Sablons, sheltered from W/SW but fair weather only.

NAVIGATION WPT 48°21'·68N 04°48'·50W, 096°/1M to Mole Ste Barbe lt. From the NW, beware Grande and Petite Vinotière rks. From the SSW keep seaward of Les Renards IDM buoy and R bcn twr closer inshore. In hbr ent keep closer to Mole Ste Barbe lt, to avoid La Basse du Filet (1·4m) on N side.

LIGHTS AND MARKS See chartlet and Lights, buoys and waypoints. Mole Ste-Barbe lt in line 096° with church spire leads to hbr ent. 079° transit of La Louve R bn tr and end of Mole St Christophe (inner mole) is only valid outside the hbr.

COMMUNICATIONS CROSS 02·98·89·31·31 and 1616; 02·98·84·60·64; Auto 08·92·68·08·29; Police 02·98·89·00·13; British Consul 01·44·51·31·00; Dr 02·98·89·01·86; *Le Conquet Port* (HM) VHF 08, 16; Aff Mar 02·98·89·00·05.

FACILITIES The Avant Port is reserved for FVs & workboats; ferries use Mole Ste Barbe; ⚓ prohib. Call the HM for a vacant mooring or dry out further ENE on one of 12 🅥s; all LOA €7·00 per day. **HM** ☎02·98·89·18·58, mob 06·71·11·67·41 yann.lagadec@leconquet.fr. **Town** ✕ ⊠ Ⓑ. Bus to Brest. **Ferries** Molène, Brest and Ouessant.

ANCHORAGE EAST OF PTE DE ST MATHIEU

ANSE DE BERTHEAUME, 48°20'·44N 04°41'·84W. AC 2350, 3427. SHOM 7401. A useful passage ⚓ to await the tide E to Brest, N into Ch du Four, or S toward Raz de Sein. ⚓ in 3-5m between slip NNW of the Fort and an ECM bcn 3ca further N. Good shelter in W'lies. 1ca NE of Fort de Bertheaume (32m, conspic) Le Chat rk (6·8m) is marked by an ECM bcn. No lights.

CHENAL DU FOUR

The Chenal du Four (and de la Helle; AC 3345, 2356) are unhappily split between the small scale Admiralty tidal stream atlases for the English Channel (NP 250) and W France (NP 265). Both channels and the Raz de Sein are better covered at large scale by the French atlas (560-UJA: NW Brittany, Brignogan to Penmarc'h).

Using tides to advantage it is possible for a 5½kn boat to pass through the Chenal du Four and Raz de Sein in one leg from L'Aberwrac'h to Audierne or vice versa. Anse de Bertheaume (anchorage 4M east of Pte de Ste Mathieu) Camaret or Brest are alternative interim stops.

►1M W of Le Four the S-going stream begins around HW Brest (arrive a little early); the N-going stream at HW Brest −5¾, sp rates 3·6kn. Further S, off Pte de Corsen, the stream is weaker, max 2·3kn at springs.

The tide runs strongest at S end of Chenal du Four, off Le Conquet. Here the S-going stream starts at HW Brest +¼, max 5kn; the N-going stream begins at HW Brest −5¾, 5·2kn max at sp. Wind-over-tide may raise many short, steep seas.◄

Pilotage. On the mainland coast are 6 major lights, either directional or leading. The charted transits are: St Mathieu directional lt and Kermorvan ≠ 158·5°; Pte de Corsen directional lt bearing 012° (in its white sector and on your port quarter). Thence pass between Rouget SHM lt buoy and Grande Vinotière lt bn. Maintain the 325·5° astern transit of Grand Courleau unlit NCM bcn twr ≠ Le Faix NCM lt bcn twr. Track 145·5° to pass midway between La Fourmi SHM lt buoy and Vieux-Moines lt bcn twr.

Alternatively a simple buoy-hopping sequence (below) can be used by day or night. The 3 legs are short and the speed over the ground is likely to be quite high, but other buoys between the waypoints provide a useful check on progress and any deviation from the planned track.

Leg 1:	From ⊕ 48°31'·5N 04°49'·0W (5ca W of Le Four) track 188°/5M (leaving Les Liniou well to port) to Valbelle PHM buoy.
Leg 2:	Thence track 168°/4·6M to abeam Grande Vinotière lt bn.
Leg 3:	Finally track 172°/2·7M to La Fourmi SHM lt buoy (for Raz de Sein); or
Leg 3A:	156°/2·9M to Vieux-Moines lt bcn (for Brest/ Camaret).

Homeward-bound, or along the N Brittany coast, enter the S end of Chenal du Four at LW Brest; a fair tide can then be carried through the channel and NE past Île Vierge. The reverse sequence of pilotage is followed. Two hours is par for the 12M passage.

L'Aber-Ildut, 3·5M SSE of Le Four lt ho, and **Le Conquet**, 3ca SE of Pte de Kermorvan, are the only ports on the mainland coast: the former is safe if there is no swell or W'lies; the latter has limited facilities for yachts but in offshore winds there are anchorages in Anse de Porsmoguer and Anse des Blancs-Sablons, both between Corsen and Kermorvan.

CHENAL DE LA HELLE

►At N end of Chenal de la Helle the ENE-going stream starts at HW Brest −0520 (sp rate 2·8kn), and the SW-going stream at HW Brest −0045 (sp rate 3·8kn).◄

The Chenal de la Helle converges at a 20° angle with the Chenal du Four and the two meet WSW of Pte de Corsen or just N of Grande Vinotière, depending on which of two track variants you take (AC 3345, 2356).

A simple GPS-based buoy-hopping sequence is as follows:

From close abeam Luronne WCM buoy track 137°/4·7M to St Pierre SHM buoy, passing Le Faix lt twr and Le Pourceau NCM lt buoy. Thence 169°/3·9M to La Fourmi SHM buoy, passing Rouget SHM lt buoy, Grande Vinotière and Tournant et Lochrist PHM lt buoy en route.

APPROACHES TO BREST

The outer approaches lie between Chaussée des Pierres Noires and Pte St Mathieu to the N and Pte du Toulinguet to the S (AC 2350, 3427, 3428). From the W maintain the 068° transit of Petit-Minou and Portzic ldg lts on the N shore; or keep slightly north of this transit to avoid large ships. From the S steer NNE towards Pte du Petit-Minou to pick up the transit, but beware rks 7M W and SW of Pte du Toulinguet. Yachts <25m LOA are exempt from VTS, but should monitor VHF Ch 08 or 16.

Abeam Petit-Minou lt ho the Goulet (Straits) de Brest narrows to 1M. Drying rocks almost in mid-stream may be left to port or starboard; they are marked by a WCM lt buoy, 2 PHM lt buoys and Roche Mengam IDM lt bn. A course of 075° through the Passe Nord leaves the latter 2ca to stbd.

►In Passe Sud a useful back-eddy close inshore sets ENE during the ebb. Tidal streams reach 4·5kn in the Goulet.◄

Beyond Pte du Portzic a buoyed chan leads ENE to **Brest** and the marinas at Le Château and Moulin Blanc. In the **Rade de Brest** (AC 3429) around Île Longue (a peninsula) are DG ranges, no-anchoring and no-entry areas, but there is room to anchor off Roscanvel in the lee of the Quélern peninsula. Further east the beautiful River Aulne can be explored well inland to Port Launay and as far as **Chateaulin**.

L'IROISE AND BAIE DE DOUARNENEZ

L'Iroise is the sea area SW of Chaussée des Pierres Noires and N of Chaussée de Sein (AC 2350, 2349). On the NE side of L'Iroise (AC 3427) a chain of rks extends 7M W from Pte du Toulinguet. There are several chans through these rocks, of which the simplest for Brest and Camaret is the 3ca wide **Chenal du Toulinguet** which runs NNW/SSE between La Louve WCM bcn twr (1ca W of Pte du Toulinguet) on E side and Le Pohen rk on the W side.

►Here the N-going stream begins at HW Brest −0550, and the S-going at HW Brest +0015, sp rates 2·75kn.◄

3·5M SSE of Pte du Toulinguet is Le Chevreau (WCM bcn; dries 5·9m) with La Chèvre 5ca NE of it. 1·9M S of Le Chevreau is Le Bouc (WCM lt buoy; dries 7·4m). 5·7M SW of Pte du Toulinguet lies Basse du Lis, rky shoals with depth of 2·7m and WCM lt buoy, and the last of a string of underwater rocks extending seaward from Les Tas de Pois (Pile of Peas). Close E of Les Tas de Pois, the Anse de Pen-Hir is a useful anch in NE'lies.

The Baie de Douarnenez is entered between C. de la Chèvre and Pte du Van. Off C. de la Chèvre various dangers, on which the sea breaks, extend SW for 2·25M to Basse Vieille (dries 0·8m) lt buoy. Basse Laye (dries 0·7m) is unmarked 7ca SSE of the CG stn on C. de la Chèvre and a hazard if rounding the headland close inshore. **Morgat** lies 4M NNE of C. de la Chèvre. 2·5M ESE of Morgat beware Les Verrès (12m high rk) and a group of drying rks, including La Pierre-Profonde and Le Taureau.

Approaching **Douarnenez** beware Basse Veur and Basse Neuve (2·2m). The S shore of the B is clear of dangers more than 2ca offshore, except for Duellou Rk (7m high) 5ca offshore, and other rks 1M eastward. Further W Basse Jaune is an isolated rk (dries 1·4m; IDM buoy) about 1M N of Pte du Van. This rocky headland with offliers is 2·25M NE of Pte du Raz and La Vieille lt twr and is the NE corner of the Raz de Sein.

RAZ DE SEIN TO POINTE DE PENMARC'H

Chaussée de Sein (AC 2350, 2819, 2348) is a chain of islands, rks and shoals extending 15M W of the Pointe du Raz. A WCM lt buoy marks the seaward end. See section on **Raz de Sein** for directions through it. **Audierne** is 10M ESE where **Ste Evette** is a good passage ⚓ before or after tackling the Raz.

Off Pointe de Penmarc'h (light house, fog signal) depths shoal very rapidly from >60m to <5m in the space of 7ca; dangers extend 1M to NW, W and S, and 3M to SE, with breaking seas in onshore winds; keep at least 3M off the light house. Le Guilvinec, a busy fishing harbour is well sheltered, but has a difficult entrance.

9.20.24 CHENAL DU FOUR

AC 3345. Simple buoy-hopping/GPS track: — — — — — — *See Passage information for notes on this and Chenal de la Helle.*

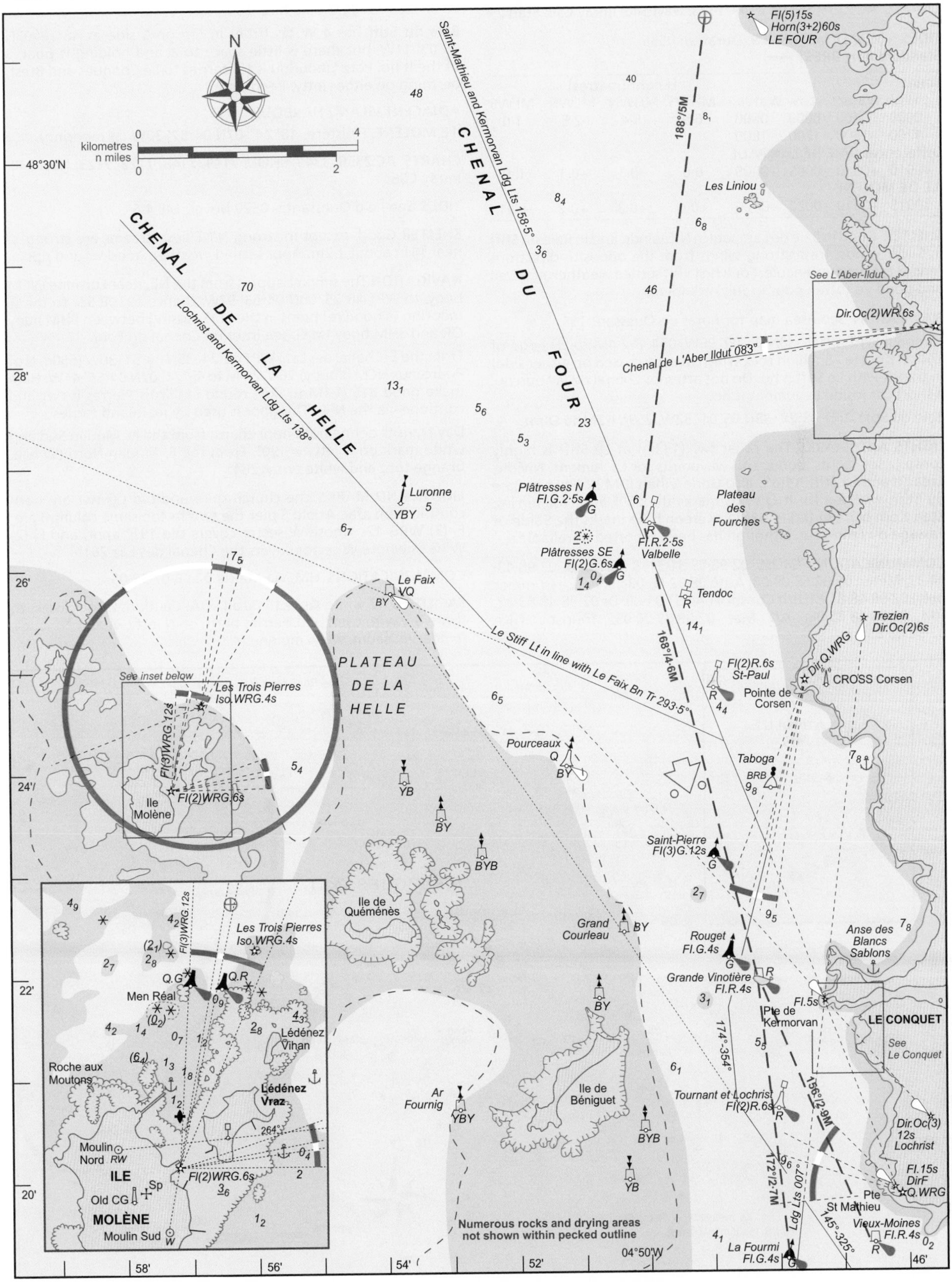
N
kilometres
n miles
48°30'N
28'
26'
24'
22'
20'
58'
56'
54'
52'
04°50'W
46'
Fl(5)15s
Horn(3+2)60s
LE FOUR
188°/5M
Les Liniou
See L'Aber-Ildut
Dir.Oc(2)WR.6s
Chenal de L'Aber Ildut 083°
CHENAL DU FOUR
Saint-Mathieu and Kermorvan Ldg Lts 158·5°
CHENAL DE LA HELLE
Lochrist and Kermorvan Ldg Lts 138°
Luronne
YBY
Plâtresses N
Fl.G.2·5s
Plâtresses SE
Fl(2)G.6s
Fl.R.2·5s
Valbelle
Plateau des Fourches
Tendoc
Le Faix
VQ
BY
Le Stiff Lt in line with Le Faix Bn Tr 293·5°
168°/4·6M
Fl(2)R.6s
St-Paul
Trezien
Dir.Oc(2)6s
Dir.Q.WRG
CROSS Corsen
Pointe de Corsen
PLATEAU DE LA HELLE
See inset below
Les Trois Pierres
Iso.WRG.4s
Fl(3)WRG.12s
Fl(2)WRG.6s
Ile Molène
Pourceaux
Q
BY
YB
BY
BYB
Taboga
BRB
Saint-Pierre
Fl(3)G.12s
Ile de Quéménès
Grand Courleau
BY
Rouget
Fl.G.4s
Grande Vinotière
Fl.R.4s
Anse des Blancs Sablons
Fl.5s
Pte de Kermorvan
LE CONQUET
See Le Conquet
174°-354°
Ile de Béniguet
Ar Fournig
YBY
BYB
YB
Tournant et Lochrist
Fl(2)R.6s
156°/2·9M
Dir.Oc(3)
12s
Lochrist
Fl.15s
DirF
Q.WRG
Pte St Mathieu
172°/2·7M
Ldg Lts 007°
145°-325°
Numerous rocks and drying areas not shown within pecked outline
La Fourmi
Fl.G.4s
Vieux-Moines
Fl.R.4s
Q.G
Q.R
Men Réal
Lédénez Vihan
Roche aux Moutons
Lédénez Vraz
264°
Moulin Nord RW
ILE MOLÈNE
Old CG
Sp
Moulin Sud W

9.20.25 ÎLE D'OUESSANT

Finistère **48°26'·64N 05°07'·49W** (B de Lampaul) ❁❁✿✿✿

CHARTS AC 2356; SHOM 7149, 7123; Navi 540; Imray C36; Stan 2

TIDES +0522 Dover; ML 3·9; Duration 0555
Standard Port BREST (⟶)

Times				Height (metres)			
High Water		Low Water		MHWS	MHWN	MLWN	MLWS
0000	0600	0000	0600	6·9	5·4	2·6	1·0
1200	1800	1200	1800				
Differences BAIE DE LAMPAUL							
+0010	+0010	–0005	+0005	0·0	–0·1	–0·1	0·0
ÎLE DE MOLENE							
+0015	+0010	+0020	+0020	+0·4	+0·3	+0·2	+0·1

SHELTER Good in Baie de Lampaul in N-E winds, and in Baie du Stiff in S-NW winds; fresh/strong winds from the opposite directions render the bays untenable. For a first visit settled weather, no swell and good vis (often poor in July) are ideal.

NAVIGATION See Area map for notes on Ouessant TSS.

Lampaul WPT 48°25´·38N 05°09´·96W, 054.4°/2·4M to LH edge of Youc'h Korz (a 28m high rock which may be passed on either side) in transit with Le Stiff lt ho. Do not attempt Chenal de la Fourche, a short cut inside La Jument lt ho.

Baie du Stiff WPT 48°28´·38N 05°01´·32W, 259°/1·3M to Dir lt.

LIGHTS AND MARKS The radar twr (132m) at Le Stiff is highly conspic. See Lights, buoys and waypoints for La Jument, Nividic, Creac'h and Le Stiff lt ho's; also Gorle Vihan IDM bcn twr in Baie du Stiff, where a Dir lt Q WRG marks the 259° appr for ferries; Men-Korn bcn twr (lit) is 1.3M E. Kéréon lt ho marks the S side of Passage du Fromveur, although has been reported unreliable.

COMMUNICATIONS CROSS 02·98·89·31·31 & 1616; LB 02·98·48·84·33; Meteo 08·92·68·08·08; Auto 08·92·68·08·29; Police (summer only) 02·98·48·81·61; Brit Consul 01·44·51·31·00; Dr 02·98·48·83·22; HM 02·98·48·80·06; Aff Mar 02·98·89·00·05; Tourist Office 02·98·48·85·83.

FACILITIES Lampaul has room to ⚓ in 6-10m and 19 free moorings SE of the PHM/SHM bcn twrs off the narrow drying hbr (not usually accessible to visitors). Ferries no longer use Lampaul. **Village** ✕ ⓑ @ bike hire ✈.

Baie du Stiff has 4 W moorings (free) in 5m on S side at 48°28'·03N 05°03'·11W, but there is little space to ⚓ and holding is poor. S of the lt ho, Porz Liboudou is for ferries to Le Conquet and Brest, berthing on either jetty; keep clear.

ADJACENT ISLAND HARBOUR

ÎLE MOLÈNE, Finistère, **48°24'·07N 04°57'·30W** (LB mooring).

CHARTS AC 2356, 3345; SHOM 7149, 7148, 7122, 7123; Navi 540; Imray C36

TIDES See Île d'Ouessant; +0520 Dover; ML 4·6

SHELTER Good, except in strong N/NE'lies; streams are strong. ⚓ near LB in about 1·2m. Appr settled weather, good vis and nps.

NAVIGATION The simpler appr is from the NE, near Luronne WCM buoy, to WPT 48°25´·00N 04°56´·97W; thence 191°/8·5ca to the LB mooring (a good ref point in the hbr) passing between PHM buoy QR and SHM buoy Iso G; see inset on Chenal du Four.

From the E (Chenal des Laz) WPT 48°24´·35N 04°51´·30W (650m N of Pourceaux NCM lt buoy) 264°/2·7M to 48°24´·07N 04°55´·41W. Here make good 315°/1·1M to skirt round Les Trois Pierres lt twr and continue via the N ⊕. This appr is used by mainland ferries.

Day transits define both appr chans: from the N, Moulin Sud and white mark on N jetty ≠ 190°. From the E, Moulin Nord (W bcn, orange top) and white twr ≠ 264°.

LIGHTS AND MARKS The church spire and old CG twr are both conspic from afar. At old S pier the two lts (on same column) are: Fl (3) WRG 12s whose W sector covers the 191° appr; and Fl (2) WRG 6s whose W sector covers the Chenal des Laz 261°.

COMMUNICATIONS HM, via Mairie 02·98·07·39·05.

FACILITIES 12 white moorings, €15·00 all LOA. Caution: those closest to shore dry with coeff >90. Ferries berth on N jetty. ✕ ✉; near museum. www.molene.fr

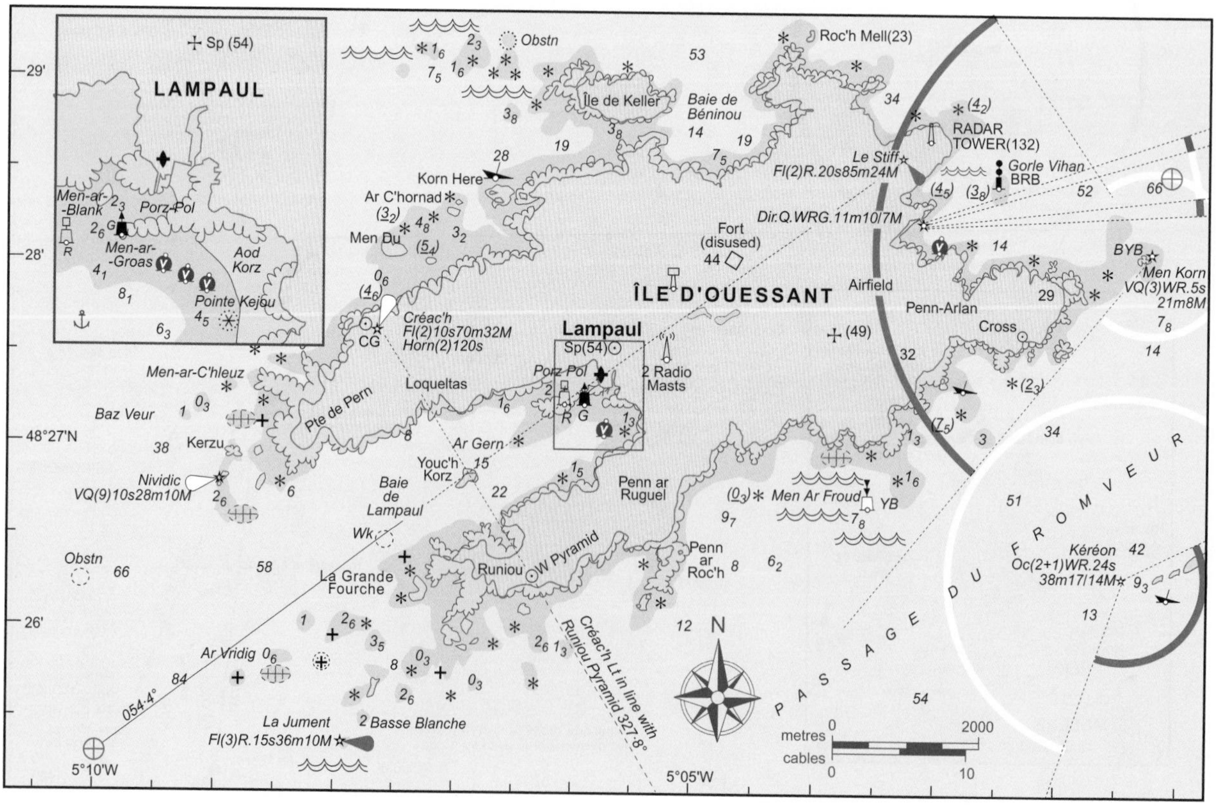

9.20.26 RADE DE BREST

Finistère **48°20'·75N 04°32'·10W** (Goulet de Brest, E end)

CHARTS AC 3427, 3428, 3429; SHOM 7401, 7400, 7397, 7398, 7399; Navi 542; Imray C36. Beyond the N and E edges of AC 3429 & SHOM 7400, the Rivers Elorn and Aulne are usefully covered on IGN land maps 0516, 0517 & 0518 (1:25,000). These maps show some depths, Lat/Long values, much valuable topographical data and are readily available.

TIDES

Standard Port BREST (⟶)

Times				Height (metres)			
High Water		Low Water		MHWS	MHWN	MLWN	MLWS
0000	0600	0000	0600	6·9	5·4	2·6	1·0
1200	1800	1200	1800				
Differences TINDUFF (48°20´·2N 04°21´·9W)							
+0005	+0005	+0005	+0005	+0·4	+0·3	+0·2	+0·2
PONT DE TERENEZ (48°16´·1N 04°15´·7W)							
+0005	+0005	+0010	+0005	+0·5	+0·4	+0·3	+0·3

In most of the bays in the Rade de Brest tidal streams are weak, but in the main rivers they can exceed 2kn at sp.

SHELTER The Rade (50 sq miles) is a sheltered cruising ground when the weather offshore is bad. There are attractive ⚓s in the SE part of the Rade and up the Rivers Elorn and Aulne.

NAVIGATION WPT 48°18´·20N 04°44´·26W, 068°/5·3M to front ldg lt (Pte du Petit Minou); thence through the Goulet de Brest. See Lights, buoys & waypoints for light details. Tidal streams run hard, max 4·6kn on the spring ebb and 3·5kn on the flood.

Pass either side of Plateau des Fillettes, rks well marked by 3 lt buoys and Mengam IDM lt bcn twr. Keep well inshore to avoid warships and commercial vessels and to cheat any foul tide.

The area S and SW from the Moulin Blanc Marina is very shoal, and yachts should head WSW from the marina to R1 buoy and Basse du Renard WCM buoy or Pte de l'Armorique.

In the SW part of Rade de Brest are various naval sites with no ⚓, prohib zones and DG ranges around Île Longue. There are however ⚓s at Le Fret (SE of Île Longue) whence a ferry runs to Brest; and off Roscanvel in the lee of the Quélern Peninsula. There are 2 free 🅥s at both Roscanvel and Quélern and 3 white 🅥s, €10·00, at Lanveoc, marked 'Accuil'.

E of Pte de l'Armorique there are ⚓s and W 🅥s in 3m in Anse de L'Auberlac'h, Baie de Daoulas and its inlets/creeks (very shoal) at the mouth of the River de l'Hôpital and up the drying/buoyed River de Faou. S of here the much larger River Aulne (see below) can easily be explored 18M upriver from Landévennec to Châteaulin.

RIVERS FLOWING INTO THE RADE DE BREST

RIVER ÉLORN, entered 1·2M E of Moulin Blanc Marina, is navigable to Landerneau, 6M upriver. From Pont Albert-Louppe (29m) and Pont de l'Iroise (25m clearance) the river is buoyed/lit for 2M. Further up it is marked by smaller unlit buoys and perches, some of which may well be some distance outboard of navigable water. Good ⚓s are at Le Passage, 8ca above the bridges, or further NE in Anse St Nicolas.

The drying port of Landerneau can be reached on the tide via a lifting bridge, ☎06·11·03·31·20. Dry out against the N quay. Few nautical facilities, but a pleasant town.

RIVER AULNE To the SE of Rade de Brest, L'Aulne is a lovely river with steep wooded banks. There are ⚓s off Landévennec, below both Térénez bridges (27m) and also 🅥s 1½M above the E bridge. Charted depths are optimistic.

At Guily-Glaz, 14M above Landévennec, a lock (operating HW Brest –2 to +1½, but not between 2100 and 0730; ☎02·98·86·03·21) gives access to the canalised river (2·7m) and Port Launay on a U-bend. Port Launay is a popular place to winter against the attractive stone quays in complete shelter. Facilities: 🔌 on quay, ⛽ (apply to Town Hall, weekdays only before 1700 ☎02·98·86·09·63) 🚰 ✕. Easy access to the N165 motorway.

2·25M further on is Châteaulin, a charming country town and head of the navigable river. Beware shallow spots mid-river. Facilities: small Ⓥ pontoon, no ⛽ ☎02·98·86·10·05; 🚰 🛒 100m from quay.

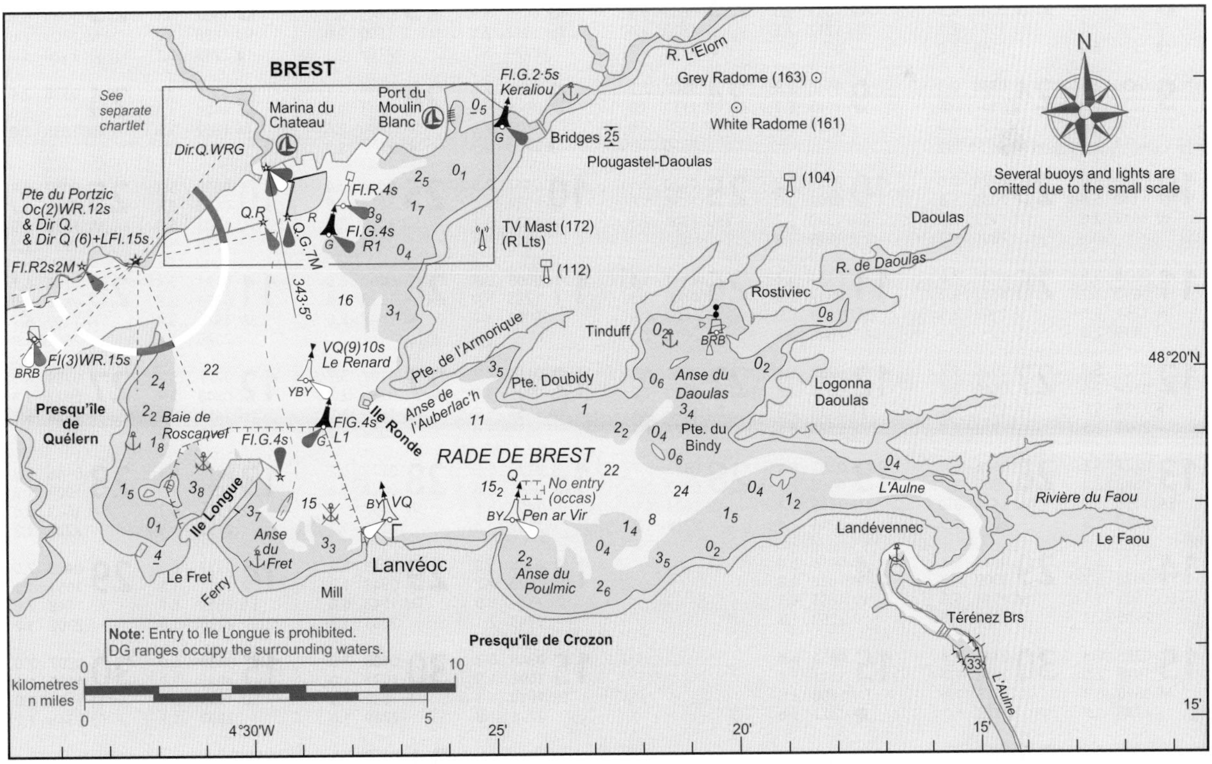

STANDARD TIME UT –01
Subtract 1 hour for UT
For French Summer Time add ONE hour in **non-shaded areas**

BREST LAT 48°23′N LONG 4°30′W

TIMES AND HEIGHTS OF HIGH AND LOW WATERS

Dates in red are SPRINGS
Dates in blue are NEAPS

YEAR **2018**

JANUARY

Date	Time	m	Date	Time	m
1 M	0356 1020 1624 2242	7.1 1.1 7.2 1.0	16 TU	0436 1056 1653 2312	6.5 1.8 6.4 1.8
2 TU	0447 1111 1714 ○ 2332	7.4 0.8 7.4 0.8	17 W	0511 1131 1727 ● 2346	6.7 1.6 6.5 1.7
3 W	0536 1201 1803	7.6 0.6 7.4	18 TH	0545 1205 1800	6.8 1.5 6.6
4 TH	0021 0624 1250 1851	0.8 7.6 0.7 7.3	19 F	0020 0618 1239 1833	1.7 6.8 1.5 6.5
5 F	0109 0712 1338 1939	0.9 7.4 0.9 7.0	20 SA	0054 0651 1312 1906	1.7 6.8 1.6 6.5
6 SA	0157 0759 1427 2027	1.2 7.1 1.2 6.7	21 SU	0128 0726 1347 1941	1.7 6.7 1.7 6.3
7 SU	0245 0847 1517 2116	1.6 6.7 1.6 6.3	22 M	0204 0802 1425 2020	1.9 6.5 1.8 6.2
8 M	0336 0938 1610 ◑ 2210	2.0 6.3 2.1 5.9	23 TU	0244 0842 1507 2105	2.1 6.3 2.1 6.0
9 TU	0430 1035 1708 2311	2.3 5.9 2.4 5.6	24 W	0330 0931 1557 ◐ 2200	2.3 6.0 2.3 5.8
10 W	0532 1140 1812	2.6 5.6 2.6	25 TH	0424 1030 1657 2306	2.5 5.8 2.4 5.7
11 TH	0018 0640 1251 1919	5.5 2.7 5.5 2.6	26 F	0531 1142 1808	2.6 5.7 2.5
12 F	0126 0749 1358 2022	5.6 2.6 5.6 2.5	27 SA	0020 0646 1300 1923	5.7 2.5 5.8 2.3
13 SA	0227 0849 1453 2114	5.8 2.4 5.8 2.3	28 SU	0136 0802 1414 2033	6.0 2.2 6.2 1.9
14 SU	0316 0938 1539 2158	6.1 2.2 6.1 2.1	29 M	0244 0909 1518 2134	6.4 1.7 6.6 1.5
15 M	0358 1019 1618 2236	6.3 2.0 6.3 1.9	30 TU	0344 1008 1613 2229	6.9 1.2 7.0 1.1
			31 W	0437 1100 1704 ○ 2320	7.3 0.8 7.3 0.8

FEBRUARY

Date	Time	m	Date	Time	m
1 TH	0526 1149 1751	7.5 0.6 7.4	16 F	0525 1145 1741	6.8 1.4 6.7
2 F	0008 0612 1236 1836	0.7 7.6 0.5 7.4	17 SA	0000 0559 1218 1813	1.4 7.0 1.3 6.8
3 SA	0053 0656 1321 1919	0.8 7.5 0.7 7.2	18 SU	0034 0632 1251 1846	1.4 7.0 1.2 6.8
4 SU	0137 0738 1404 2000	1.0 7.3 1.0 6.9	19 M	0108 0705 1326 1920	1.4 7.0 1.3 6.7
5 M	0220 0818 1446 2041	1.3 6.9 1.5 6.4	20 TU	0143 0740 1402 1956	1.5 6.8 1.5 6.5
6 TU	0303 0859 1530 2124	1.7 6.4 2.0 6.0	21 W	0222 0819 1443 2037	1.7 6.6 1.7 6.3
7 W	0349 0945 1619 ◑ 2216	2.2 5.9 2.4 5.6	22 TH	0305 0903 1529 2128	1.9 6.2 2.1 6.0
8 TH	0442 1041 1717 2321	2.6 5.5 2.8 5.3	23 F	0357 0959 1626 ◐ 2232	2.2 5.9 2.4 5.7
9 F	0546 1155 1829	2.9 5.2 3.0	24 SA	0501 1111 1737 2350	2.5 5.6 2.6 5.6
10 SA	0039 0703 1319 1945	5.3 3.0 5.2 2.9	25 SU	0620 1238 1901	2.5 5.6 2.5
11 SU	0154 0817 1429 2048	5.4 2.8 5.5 2.6	26 M	0117 0746 1404 2019	5.8 2.3 5.9 2.1
12 M	0252 0914 1519 2136	5.8 2.5 5.8 2.3	27 TU	0233 0859 1509 2123	6.2 1.8 6.4 1.7
13 TU	0337 0958 1559 2216	6.1 2.1 6.1 2.0	28 W	0333 0957 1603 2218	6.7 1.3 6.9 1.2
14 W	0416 1036 1635 2252	6.4 1.8 6.3 1.8			
15 TH	0451 1111 1708 ● 2327	6.6 1.6 6.6 1.6			

MARCH

Date	Time	m	Date	Time	m
1 TH	0425 1048 1651 2306	7.2 0.9 7.2 0.9	16 F	0425 1045 1644 2301	6.6 1.5 6.6 1.5
2 F	0511 1135 1734 ○ 2351	7.5 0.6 7.4 0.7	17 SA	0500 1119 1717 ● 2336	6.9 1.3 6.8 1.3
3 SA	0554 1217 1815	7.6 0.6 7.4	18 SU	0535 1154 1750	7.1 1.1 7.0
4 SU	0034 0634 1258 1853	0.7 7.5 0.7 7.2	19 M	0010 0609 1228 1823	1.1 7.2 1.0 7.0
5 M	0113 0711 1336 1929	0.9 7.3 1.0 6.9	20 TU	0046 0643 1303 1858	1.1 7.2 1.1 7.0
6 TU	0152 0746 1413 2004	1.2 6.9 1.5 6.6	21 W	0122 0720 1341 1935	1.2 7.0 1.3 6.8
7 W	0230 0821 1450 2041	1.6 6.4 2.0 6.1	22 TH	0202 0759 1422 2017	1.4 6.7 1.6 6.5
8 TH	0310 0859 1532 2124	2.1 5.9 2.5 5.7	23 F	0247 0845 1509 2107	1.7 6.3 2.0 6.1
9 F	0356 0946 1623 ◑ 2223	2.6 5.4 2.9 5.3	24 SA	0339 0941 1606 ◐ 2212	2.1 5.9 2.4 5.7
10 SA	0453 1054 1732 2344	2.9 5.1 3.2 5.1	25 SU	0444 1055 1719 2334	2.4 5.6 2.6 5.6
11 SU	0609 1228 1900	3.1 5.0 3.2	26 M	0607 1228 1847	2.5 5.5 2.6
12 M	0111 0735 1357 2015	5.2 3.0 5.2 2.9	27 TU	0107 0736 1355 2008	5.7 2.3 5.9 2.2
13 TU	0220 0841 1453 2107	5.5 2.6 5.6 2.5	28 W	0222 0848 1457 2111	6.2 1.8 6.3 1.7
14 W	0308 0929 1534 2148	5.9 2.2 5.9 2.1	29 TH	0319 0943 1548 2203	6.7 1.3 6.8 1.3
15 TH	0348 1008 1610 2226	6.3 1.9 6.3 1.8	30 F	0408 1031 1632 2249	7.0 1.0 7.1 1.0
			31 SA	0452 1115 1713 ○ 2331	7.3 0.8 7.3 0.9

APRIL

Date	Time	m	Date	Time	m
1 SU	0532 1154 1750	7.4 0.8 7.3	16 M	0507 1126 1724 ● 2345	7.1 1.0 7.1 1.0
2 M	0010 0608 1231 1825	0.9 7.3 0.9 7.1	17 TU	0544 1204 1800	7.2 0.9 7.2
3 TU	0047 0642 1306 1858	1.0 7.1 1.2 6.9	18 W	0023 0622 1242 1838	1.0 7.2 1.0 7.1
4 W	0123 0715 1340 1930	1.3 6.8 1.6 6.6	19 TH	0104 0702 1323 1918	1.0 7.1 1.2 6.9
5 TH	0158 0748 1415 2005	1.7 6.4 2.0 6.2	20 F	0147 0746 1407 2003	1.3 6.8 1.5 6.6
6 F	0235 0823 1452 2044	2.1 5.9 2.4 5.8	21 SA	0235 0835 1456 2057	1.6 6.4 1.9 6.2
7 SA	0317 0904 1536 2135	2.5 5.5 2.9 5.4	22 SU	0330 0935 1555 ◐ 2203	2.0 5.9 2.3 5.9
8 SU	0408 1002 1638 ◑ 2249	2.9 5.1 3.2 5.1	23 M	0437 1049 1709 2326	2.3 5.6 2.6 5.7
9 M	0516 1129 1802	3.1 4.9 3.3	24 TU	0558 1217 1835	2.4 5.6 2.6
10 TU	0016 0638 1303 1926	5.1 3.1 5.0 3.1	25 W	0052 0721 1336 1951	5.8 2.2 5.9 2.2
11 W	0131 0753 1410 2026	5.4 2.8 5.4 2.7	26 TH	0203 0828 1437 2052	6.1 1.9 6.2 1.8
12 TH	0227 0848 1457 2112	5.7 2.4 5.8 2.2	27 F	0259 0922 1526 2142	6.5 1.5 6.6 1.5
13 F	0311 0931 1536 2152	6.1 1.9 6.2 1.8	28 SA	0346 1009 1609 2227	6.8 1.3 6.9 1.3
14 SA	0352 1011 1613 2230	6.5 1.5 6.6 1.5	29 SU	0428 1051 1648 2308	7.0 1.1 7.0 1.2
15 SU	0430 1049 1648 2308	6.9 1.2 6.9 1.2	30 M	0507 1129 1724 ○ 2345	7.0 1.1 7.0 1.2

Chart Datum is 3·64 metres below IGN Datum. HAT is 7·9 metres above Chart Datum.

STANDARD TIME UT –01
Subtract 1 hour for UT
For French Summer Time add ONE hour in **non-shaded areas**

BREST LAT 48°23′N LONG 4°30′W

TIMES AND HEIGHTS OF HIGH AND LOW WATERS

Dates in red are SPRINGS
Dates in blue are NEAPS

YEAR **2018**

MAY

Date	Day	Time	m	Time	m	Time	m	Time	m
1	TU	0542	6.9	1204	1.2	1757	7.0		
2	W	0021	1.3	0615	6.8	1238	1.4	1830	6.8
3	TH	0055	1.5	0647	6.6	1311	1.7	1903	6.6
4	F	0130	1.7	0720	6.3	1345	2.0	1937	6.2
5	SA	0207	2.1	0755	5.9	1421	2.4	2014	5.9
6	SU	0246	2.4	0834	5.6	1502	2.7	2100	5.6
7	M	0332	2.7	0925	5.2	1554	3.0	2202	5.3
8	TU	0429	2.9	1036	5.0	1704	3.2	◑ 2318	5.2
9	W	0540	2.9	1158	5.1	1824	3.1		
10	TH	0032	5.3	0654	2.8	1311	5.3	1932	2.8
11	F	0134	5.6	0756	2.4	1408	5.7	2026	2.3
12	SA	0227	6.0	0847	2.0	1455	6.1	2113	1.9
13	SU	0313	6.4	0933	1.6	1537	6.5	2156	1.5
14	M	0356	6.8	1016	1.3	1618	6.9	2238	1.2
15	TU	0439	7.0	1059	1.1	1658	7.1	● 2321	1.0
16	W	0521	7.2	1141	0.9	1739	7.2		
17	TH	0004	0.9	0604	7.2	1224	1.0	1822	7.2
18	F	0049	0.9	0649	7.1	1308	1.1	1907	7.1
19	SA	0136	1.1	0737	6.8	1356	1.4	1956	6.8
20	SU	0227	1.4	0830	6.4	1448	1.8	2052	6.4
21	M	0324	1.8	0930	6.1	1548	2.1	2157	6.1
22	TU	0429	2.1	1039	5.8	1657	2.4	◐ 2310	5.9
23	W	0542	2.2	1154	5.7	1812	2.4		
24	TH	0026	5.9	0654	2.2	1306	5.8	1924	2.3
25	F	0134	6.0	0759	2.0	1407	6.1	2025	2.0
26	SA	0231	6.2	0855	1.8	1459	6.3	2117	1.8
27	SU	0320	6.4	0943	1.6	1544	6.5	2203	1.6
28	M	0403	6.5	1025	1.5	1623	6.7	2244	1.5
29	TU	0442	6.6	1104	1.5	1700	6.7	○ 2322	1.5
30	W	0517	6.6	1139	1.6	1734	6.7	2357	1.5
31	TH	0551	6.5	1213	1.7	1807	6.6		

JUNE

Date	Day	Time	m	Time	m	Time	m	Time	m
1	F	0032	1.6	0624	6.4	1247	1.8	1841	6.5
2	SA	0107	1.8	0658	6.2	1321	2.0	1915	6.3
3	SU	0143	2.0	0733	6.0	1357	2.3	1952	6.1
4	M	0220	2.2	0811	5.7	1435	2.5	2033	5.8
5	TU	0302	2.4	0855	5.5	1521	2.7	2124	5.6
6	W	0350	2.6	0951	5.3	1616	2.9	◑ 2225	5.4
7	TH	0449	2.7	1059	5.2	1723	2.9	2333	5.4
8	F	0556	2.7	1209	5.4	1833	2.7		
9	SA	0039	5.6	0701	2.5	1313	5.6	1936	2.4
10	SU	0139	5.9	0801	2.1	1410	6.0	2031	2.1
11	M	0234	6.2	0855	1.8	1501	6.4	2123	1.7
12	TU	0325	6.6	0945	1.4	1549	6.8	2212	1.3
13	W	0414	6.9	1034	1.2	1636	7.1	● 2300	1.0
14	TH	0502	7.1	1121	1.0	1723	7.2	2348	0.9
15	F	0550	7.2	1209	0.9	1810	7.3		
16	SA	0037	0.8	0639	7.1	1257	1.0	1859	7.2
17	SU	0127	0.9	0729	6.9	1346	1.2	1949	7.0
18	M	0218	1.2	0821	6.6	1438	1.5	2043	6.7
19	TU	0313	1.5	0916	6.3	1534	1.9	2140	6.3
20	W	0411	1.8	1016	6.0	1635	2.2	◐ 2243	6.0
21	TH	0514	2.1	1121	5.8	1741	2.3	2350	5.8
22	F	0620	2.2	1228	5.7	1848	2.4		
23	SA	0057	5.8	0724	2.2	1332	5.8	1952	2.3
24	SU	0159	5.9	0824	2.1	1429	6.0	2050	2.1
25	M	0253	6.0	0916	2.0	1518	6.2	2139	2.0
26	TU	0339	6.1	1001	1.9	1601	6.3	2222	1.8
27	W	0420	6.2	1041	1.8	1639	6.5	2301	1.7
28	TH	0457	6.3	1118	1.8	1715	6.5	○ 2337	1.7
29	F	0532	6.3	1153	1.8	1749	6.6		
30	SA	0012	1.7	0606	6.3	1227	1.8	1823	6.5

JULY

Date	Day	Time	m	Time	m	Time	m	Time	m
1	SU	0046	1.7	0639	6.2	1301	1.9	1857	6.4
2	M	0121	1.8	0713	6.1	1335	2.0	1932	6.3
3	TU	0156	1.9	0749	6.0	1411	2.2	2009	6.1
4	W	0234	2.1	0828	5.8	1451	2.4	2051	5.9
5	TH	0316	2.3	0913	5.6	1537	2.5	2141	5.7
6	F	0406	2.4	1009	5.5	1633	2.6	◑ 2240	5.6
7	SA	0504	2.5	1114	5.5	1738	2.7	2347	5.6
8	SU	0610	2.5	1222	5.6	1847	2.5		
9	M	0054	5.8	0718	2.3	1328	5.9	1953	2.2
10	TU	0159	6.0	0821	2.0	1429	6.2	2055	1.8
11	W	0300	6.4	0919	1.6	1526	6.6	2151	1.4
12	TH	0356	6.7	1014	1.3	1620	7.0	2244	1.0
13	F	0449	7.0	1106	1.0	1711	7.3	● 2336	0.8
14	SA	0539	7.2	1156	0.9	1800	7.4		
15	SU	0026	0.7	0628	7.2	1245	0.9	1849	7.4
16	M	0115	0.7	0717	7.1	1333	1.0	1937	7.2
17	TU	0204	0.9	0804	6.8	1422	1.3	2025	6.9
18	W	0253	1.3	0853	6.5	1512	1.6	2114	6.5
19	TH	0344	1.7	0944	6.1	1605	2.0	◐ 2208	6.1
20	F	0439	2.1	1040	5.8	1703	2.3	2308	5.7
21	SA	0539	2.4	1144	5.6	1808	2.5		
22	SU	0015	5.5	0645	2.6	1252	5.5	1916	2.6
23	M	0125	5.5	0751	2.5	1358	5.7	2022	2.5
24	TU	0228	5.6	0851	2.4	1455	5.9	2117	2.3
25	W	0320	5.8	0940	2.2	1541	6.1	2203	2.0
26	TH	0403	6.0	1022	2.0	1621	6.3	2243	1.9
27	F	0440	6.2	1059	1.9	1657	6.5	○ 2318	1.7
28	SA	0515	6.3	1134	1.8	1731	6.6	2352	1.6
29	SU	0548	6.4	1207	1.7	1804	6.6		
30	M	0026	1.6	0620	6.4	1240	1.7	1837	6.6
31	TU	0059	1.6	0652	6.4	1313	1.8	1910	6.6

AUGUST

Date	Day	Time	m	Time	m	Time	m	Time	m
1	W	0132	1.7	0725	6.3	1347	1.9	1944	6.4
2	TH	0207	1.8	0800	6.1	1424	2.0	2021	6.2
3	F	0245	2.0	0840	5.9	1505	2.2	2104	6.0
4	SA	0330	2.2	0928	5.8	1554	2.4	◑ 2157	5.8
5	SU	0423	2.4	1028	5.6	1655	2.6	2303	5.6
6	M	0528	2.5	1140	5.6	1807	2.6		
7	TU	0018	5.6	0642	2.5	1255	5.7	1924	2.4
8	W	0135	5.9	0756	2.2	1408	6.1	2035	2.0
9	TH	0244	6.2	0902	1.8	1512	6.6	2137	1.5
10	F	0344	6.7	1000	1.4	1608	7.0	2232	1.0
11	SA	0437	7.0	1053	1.0	1659	7.4	● 2323	0.7
12	SU	0526	7.3	1142	0.8	1747	7.6		
13	M	0012	0.5	0613	7.4	1230	0.7	1833	7.6
14	TU	0058	0.6	0657	7.3	1315	0.8	1916	7.4
15	W	0142	0.8	0740	7.0	1400	1.1	1959	7.0
16	TH	0226	1.2	0822	6.6	1444	1.5	2041	6.6
17	F	0311	1.7	0906	6.2	1530	2.0	2126	6.1
18	SA	0358	2.2	0955	5.8	1622	2.4	◐ 2220	5.6
19	SU	0454	2.6	1057	5.5	1724	2.8	2329	5.3
20	M	0602	2.9	1212	5.3	1838	2.9		
21	TU	0051	5.2	0719	2.9	1329	5.4	1954	2.8
22	W	0206	5.4	0827	2.7	1433	5.7	2056	2.5
23	TH	0302	5.7	0919	2.4	1521	6.0	2142	2.2
24	F	0345	6.0	1001	2.1	1601	6.3	2222	1.9
25	SA	0421	6.2	1038	1.9	1636	6.5	2257	1.7
26	SU	0454	6.4	1112	1.7	1709	6.7	○ 2330	1.5
27	M	0526	6.6	1145	1.6	1742	6.8		
28	TU	0002	1.4	0557	6.6	1217	1.5	1814	6.9
29	W	0034	1.4	0628	6.7	1249	1.5	1846	6.8
30	TH	0107	1.4	0700	6.6	1322	1.6	1918	6.7
31	F	0141	1.6	0733	6.5	1358	1.8	1954	6.5

Chart Datum is 3·64 metres below IGN Datum. HAT is 7·9 metres above Chart Datum.

STANDARD TIME UT –01
Subtract 1 hour for UT
For French Summer Time add ONE hour in **non-shaded areas**

BREST LAT 48°23′N LONG 4°30′W

TIMES AND HEIGHTS OF HIGH AND LOW WATERS

Dates in red are SPRINGS
Dates in blue are NEAPS

YEAR **2018**

SEPTEMBER

Date	Day	Time	m	Time	m	Time	m	Time	m
1	SA	0218	1.8	0811	6.2	1438	2.0	2035	6.2
2	SU	0301	2.1	0856	6.0	1526	2.3	2126	5.9
3	M	0352	2.4	0955	5.7	1625	2.6	◑ 2233	5.6
4	TU	0458	2.6	1110	5.6	1740	2.7	2356	5.5
5	W	0618	2.6	1236	5.7	1907	2.5		
6	TH	0123	5.7	0741	2.4	1357	6.1	2024	2.0
7	F	0236	6.2	0850	1.9	1501	6.6	2126	1.5
8	SA	0333	6.7	0948	1.4	1556	7.1	2220	1.0
9	SU	0423	7.1	1039	1.0	1644	7.5	● 2308	0.6
10	M	0509	7.4	1126	0.7	1729	7.6	2353	0.5
11	TU	0552	7.5	1210	0.7	1811	7.6		
12	W	0036	0.6	0633	7.4	1252	0.8	1851	7.4
13	TH	0116	0.9	0711	7.1	1333	1.1	1929	7.0
14	F	0155	1.3	0748	6.7	1413	1.6	2006	6.6
15	SA	0235	1.8	0826	6.3	1455	2.0	2045	6.0
16	SU	0317	2.4	0910	5.8	1541	2.5	2132	5.5
17	M	0407	2.8	1008	5.4	1640	2.9	◐ 2240	5.1
18	TU	0515	3.1	1128	5.2	1755	3.1		
19	W	0012	5.0	0641	3.2	1255	5.3	1921	3.0
20	TH	0140	5.2	0759	2.9	1405	5.6	2027	2.7
21	F	0238	5.6	0853	2.6	1454	5.9	2115	2.3
22	SA	0319	5.9	0934	2.2	1533	6.3	2154	1.9
23	SU	0355	6.3	1011	1.9	1609	6.6	2229	1.7
24	M	0428	6.5	1045	1.6	1643	6.8	2303	1.4
25	TU	0500	6.8	1119	1.4	1716	7.0	○ 2336	1.3
26	W	0532	6.9	1151	1.3	1748	7.1		
27	TH	0009	1.2	0603	6.9	1225	1.3	1821	7.1
28	F	0042	1.3	0635	6.9	1259	1.4	1855	6.9
29	SA	0117	1.4	0710	6.7	1336	1.6	1932	6.7
30	SU	0156	1.7	0748	6.5	1418	1.9	2014	6.3

OCTOBER

Date	Day	Time	m	Time	m	Time	m	Time	m
1	M	0239	2.0	0834	6.1	1508	2.2	2107	5.9
2	TU	0332	2.4	0934	5.8	1609	2.5	◑ 2218	5.6
3	W	0440	2.7	1054	5.6	1728	2.7	2347	5.5
4	TH	0605	2.8	1227	5.7	1858	2.5		
5	F	0117	5.8	0731	2.4	1348	6.1	2014	2.0
6	SA	0225	6.3	0839	1.9	1449	6.7	2113	1.5
7	SU	0319	6.8	0933	1.4	1540	7.1	2203	1.0
8	M	0406	7.1	1022	1.1	1626	7.4	2249	0.8
9	TU	0449	7.4	1106	0.8	1708	7.5	● 2331	0.7
10	W	0529	7.4	1148	0.8	1747	7.5		
11	TH	0011	0.8	0606	7.3	1227	1.0	1824	7.3
12	F	0048	1.1	0641	7.1	1305	1.3	1859	6.9
13	SA	0124	1.5	0716	6.8	1343	1.7	1933	6.5
14	SU	0201	2.0	0751	6.3	1422	2.1	2009	6.0
15	M	0240	2.4	0831	5.9	1505	2.6	2052	5.6
16	TU	0325	2.9	0922	5.5	1558	2.9	◐ 2152	5.2
17	W	0426	3.2	1038	5.2	1707	3.2	2321	5.0
18	TH	0550	3.3	1206	5.2	1831	3.1		
19	F	0054	5.1	0714	3.1	1321	5.4	1944	2.8
20	SA	0159	5.5	0814	2.8	1415	5.8	2036	2.5
21	SU	0244	5.9	0858	2.4	1458	6.2	2118	2.1
22	M	0321	6.2	0937	2.0	1536	6.6	2155	1.7
23	TU	0357	6.6	1014	1.6	1612	6.9	2232	1.4
24	W	0431	6.9	1050	1.4	1648	7.1	○ 2307	1.2
25	TH	0505	7.0	1125	1.3	1723	7.2	2343	1.2
26	F	0539	7.1	1202	1.2	1759	7.2		
27	SA	0019	1.2	0614	7.1	1239	1.3	1836	7.0
28	SU	0058	1.3	0652	7.0	1320	1.5	1917	6.8
29	M	0140	1.6	0734	6.7	1406	1.7	2004	6.4
30	TU	0227	2.0	0824	6.3	1458	2.1	2101	6.0
31	W	0322	2.4	0927	6.0	1602	2.4	◑ 2213	5.7

NOVEMBER

Date	Day	Time	m	Time	m	Time	m	Time	m
1	TH	0430	2.7	1046	5.8	1720	2.5	2339	5.6
2	F	0554	2.7	1215	5.9	1845	2.4		
3	SA	0101	5.9	0715	2.4	1330	6.2	1956	2.0
4	SU	0206	6.3	0821	2.0	1430	6.6	2053	1.6
5	M	0258	6.7	0914	1.6	1520	6.9	2142	1.3
6	TU	0344	7.0	1002	1.3	1604	7.2	2227	1.1
7	W	0426	7.2	1045	1.1	1645	7.2	● 2308	1.1
8	TH	0505	7.2	1125	1.1	1723	7.2	2346	1.2
9	F	0541	7.2	1203	1.2	1758	7.0		
10	SA	0022	1.4	0616	7.0	1240	1.4	1833	6.8
11	SU	0057	1.7	0650	6.8	1317	1.7	1907	6.4
12	M	0133	2.0	0725	6.4	1354	2.1	1943	6.0
13	TU	0210	2.4	0803	6.1	1434	2.4	2023	5.7
14	W	0252	2.8	0848	5.7	1521	2.8	2113	5.3
15	TH	0343	3.1	0947	5.4	1618	3.0	◐ 2224	5.1
16	F	0450	3.3	1104	5.3	1730	3.1	2347	5.1
17	SA	0609	3.2	1220	5.4	1843	2.9		
18	SU	0059	5.3	0719	2.9	1323	5.7	1944	2.6
19	M	0155	5.7	0813	2.6	1414	6.0	2034	2.2
20	TU	0240	6.1	0858	2.2	1458	6.4	2118	1.9
21	W	0321	6.5	0940	1.8	1540	6.7	2159	1.5
22	TH	0401	6.8	1021	1.5	1620	7.0	2239	1.3
23	F	0439	7.1	1101	1.2	1700	7.2	○ 2320	1.2
24	SA	0518	7.2	1142	1.1	1741	7.2		
25	SU	0001	1.1	0559	7.3	1225	1.1	1824	7.1
26	M	0044	1.2	0642	7.1	1310	1.3	1910	6.9
27	TU	0129	1.5	0729	6.9	1359	1.5	2000	6.6
28	W	0219	1.8	0821	6.6	1453	1.8	2057	6.2
29	TH	0315	2.1	0922	6.3	1555	2.1	2204	5.9
30	F	0420	2.4	1033	6.0	1706	2.3	◑ 2318	5.8

DECEMBER

Date	Day	Time	m	Time	m	Time	m	Time	m
1	SA	0534	2.5	1150	6.0	1820	2.3		
2	SU	0032	5.9	0649	2.4	1302	6.1	1929	2.1
3	M	0138	6.1	0755	2.1	1404	6.4	2028	1.9
4	TU	0233	6.4	0851	1.9	1457	6.6	2119	1.6
5	W	0322	6.7	0941	1.6	1543	6.7	2205	1.5
6	TH	0405	6.8	1025	1.5	1624	6.8	2246	1.5
7	F	0444	6.9	1106	1.4	1702	6.8	● 2324	1.5
8	SA	0521	6.9	1143	1.5	1738	6.7		
9	SU	0000	1.6	0556	6.9	1220	1.6	1813	6.6
10	M	0036	1.8	0631	6.7	1255	1.7	1847	6.4
11	TU	0111	2.0	0705	6.5	1331	1.9	1922	6.1
12	W	0147	2.2	0742	6.3	1409	2.2	1959	5.9
13	TH	0225	2.5	0821	6.0	1449	2.5	2041	5.6
14	F	0307	2.7	0906	5.7	1535	2.7	2133	5.4
15	SA	0358	2.9	1003	5.5	1630	2.9	◐ 2238	5.3
16	SU	0500	3.0	1111	5.4	1736	2.9	2349	5.3
17	M	0611	3.0	1220	5.5	1843	2.7		
18	TU	0055	5.5	0717	2.7	1323	5.8	1944	2.4
19	W	0153	5.9	0814	2.4	1418	6.1	2038	2.1
20	TH	0244	6.3	0906	2.0	1508	6.5	2127	1.7
21	F	0331	6.6	0954	1.6	1556	6.8	2214	1.4
22	SA	0417	7.0	1041	1.3	1642	7.1	○ 2300	1.2
23	SU	0502	7.2	1127	1.0	1728	7.2	2346	1.1
24	M	0548	7.4	1214	0.9	1815	7.2		
25	TU	0033	1.1	0635	7.4	1301	0.9	1903	7.1
26	W	0121	1.2	0724	7.2	1351	1.1	1953	6.9
27	TH	0211	1.4	0814	7.0	1443	1.4	2046	6.5
28	F	0304	1.7	0908	6.6	1539	1.7	2143	6.2
29	SA	0401	2.0	1008	6.3	1640	2.0	◑ 2246	5.9
30	SU	0504	2.3	1114	6.0	1746	2.3	2354	5.8
31	M	0613	2.4	1225	5.9	1854	2.3		

Chart Datum is 3·64 metres below IGN Datum. HAT is 7·9 metres above Chart Datum.

BREST TIDAL COEFFICIENTS 2018

Date	Jan		Feb		Mar		Apr		May		June		July		Aug		Sept		Oct		Nov		Dec	
	am	pm	am	pm	am	pm	am	pm	am	pm	am	pm	am	pm	am	pm	am	pm	am	pm	am	pm	am	pm
1	92	97	107	109	97	102	105	105	94	92	77	74	73	72	74	72	70	65	63	57	48	49	56	
2	101	104	109	108	106	109	103	100	89	86	71	68	70	67	69	66	60	55	52	47	52		58	61
3	106	107	106	103	110	109	96	92	82	77	64	60	64	62	62	59	51	47	44		57	63	64	69
4	106	104	98	92	108	104	86	80	72	67	56	52	59	56	55	52	45		45	48	69	76	73	77
5	101	96	85	78	100	94	74	67	61	56	49	45	53	50	49		45	48	54	62	82	87	80	83
6	91	85	71	63	88	81	60	53	50	45	43	41	48	47	48	47	54	61	70	78	92	95	85	86
7	79	72	56	49	74	66	46	40	40	37	41		46		49	52	69	77	85	92	97	99	87	87
8	65	59	43	39	58	51	35	31	34		41	44	47	50	57	64	85	93	98	103	99	97	86	85
9	54	49	36		44	38	29		34	35	47	52	53	58	70	78	99	105	106	107	95	93	83	80
10	46		35	37	33	30	30	34	39	43	57	63	63	69	85	92	108	111	108	106	89	84	78	74
11	44	44	40	45	30		39	45	49	55	69	76	75	82	97	103	111	110	104	100	79	74	71	67
12	46	49	50	55	33	37	52	59	62	68	81	87	87	93	106	109	108	104	95	89	68	62	63	58
13	52	55	60	65	43	49	65	72	75	81	92	96	97	101	109	109	99	92	83	75	56	50	54	50
14	59	63	69	74	55	62	78	84	86	91	99	101	103	104	107	103	85	77	68	61	45	40	46	42
15	66	69	78	81	68	74	89	93	96	99	102	101	105	103	98	92	69	61	53	46	35	33	40	38
16	72	75	84	87	79	84	97	100	101	102	100	98	101	97	85	78	53	46	40	34	32	33	37	39
17	77	79	88	90	88	92	101	102	102	100	94	90	93	88	70	62	39	34	30		36		41	
18	80	81	90	90	94	96	101	99	98	94	85	80	82	75	55	48	31		29	30	40	45	45	50
19	81	81	89	87	98	98	96	92	90	84	75	69	69	63	43		31	33	34	39	51	57	55	61
20	80	79	84	81	97	95	87	81	79	72	65	61	57		39	37	38	43	45	51	63	69	67	73
21	77	75	77	72	92	88	75	68	67	62	58		52	49	38	40	49	55	57	63	75	81	79	85
22	72	69	67	62	84	78	62	56	58		56	55	47	47	44	48	61	66	69	75	85	90	89	93
23	66	62	57	52	72	66	52		56	55	56	57	48	50	53	58	71	76	80	84	93	95	97	99
24	58	55	49	48	59	53	50	51	57	59	59	62	53	56	63	67	80	84	88	91	97	98	100	100
25	52	50	49		49		55	59	62	66	64	67	60	63	71	75	87	89	94	95	97	95	99	97
26	50		54	60	47	48	65	71	70	73	69	71	66	69	78	80	91	92	96	96	93	89	94	90
27	51	54	67	75	52	58	77	82	77	79	73	74	71	74	83	84	92	91	94	92	85	80	86	81
28	59	65	83	90	66	73	87	91	81	83	75	76	75	77	85	86	90	87	88	84	74	69	75	70
28	72	79			81	88	93	95	84	84	76	76	78	78	85	85	84	80	79	73	64	60	65	61
30	86	93			94	98	96	95	84	83	76	75	78	78	83	81	75	69	67	61	57	55	58	56
31	99	103			102	104			81	80			77	76	77	74			55	51			55	

Tidal coefficients indicate the magnitude of the tide on any particular day, without having to look up and calculate the range, and thus determine whether it is springs, neaps or somewhere in between. This table is valid for all areas covered by this Almanac. Typical values are:

120	Very big spring tide
95	**Mean spring tide**
70	Average tide
45	**Mean neap tide**
20	Very small neap tide

See also coefficients for Calais (p 765), Cherbourg (p 792), St Malo (p 811) and Pointe de Grave (p 942).

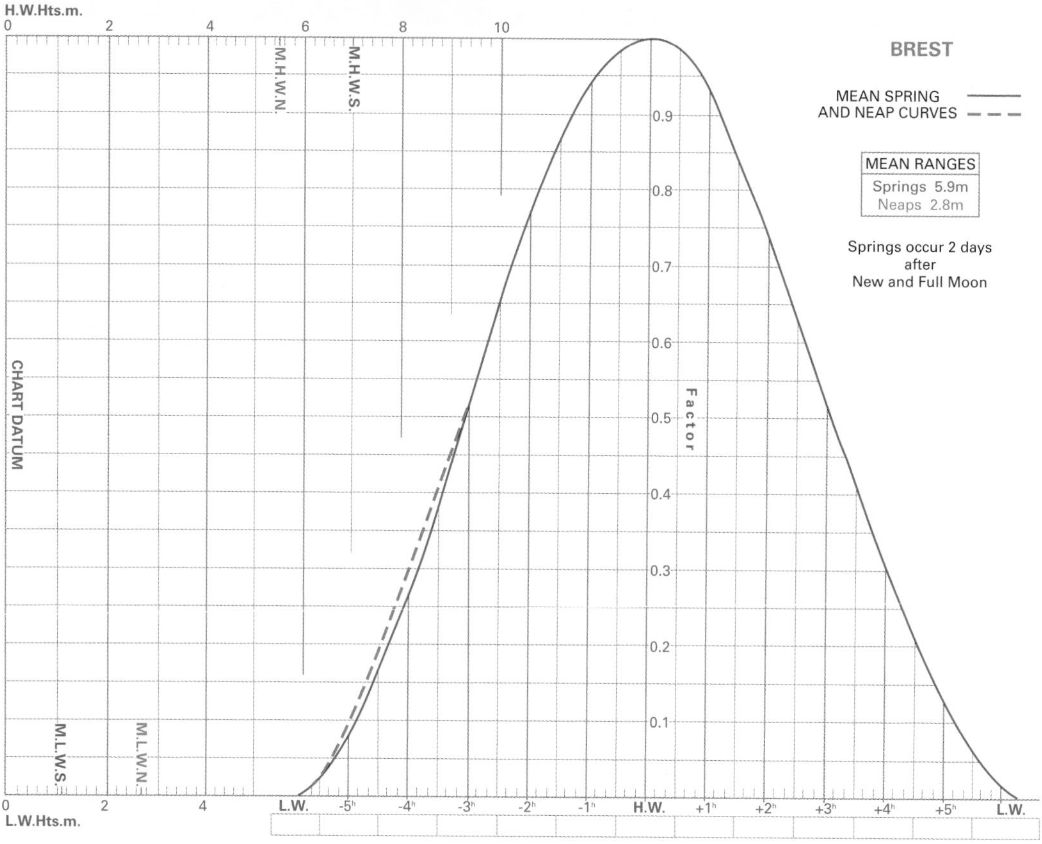

9.20.27 BREST

Finistère **48°22'·00N 04°28'·28W** (Port centre) ❁❁❁◊◊◊✿✿

CHARTS See under Rade de Brest.

TIDES +0520 Dover; ML 4·0; Duration 0605. Note: Brest is a Standard Port (⟵). Tidal coefficients are in Chapter 9.

SHELTER Excellent in both Moulin Blanc marina and Marina du Château. Access all tides H24. Brest is a busy naval, commercial and fishing port.

NAVIGATION See Rade de Brest for the outer approaches. Ldg lts 068° at Pte du Petit Minou and Pte du Portzic. Navigation within the Naval Port and the River Penfeld is strictly prohibited; see AC 3428 and chartlet. Keep clear of all warships.

For **Marina du Château** from S WPT 48°21'·70N 04°29'·15W, 344°/1M to marina ent via Passe Sud, leaving the Naval Base to port; or from E via S part of the Port de Commerce using Passe de l'Est and Passe de la Santé. Le Château and the American Monument are conspic.

For **Port du Mouin Blanc** marina WPT 48°22'·80N 04°25'·88W 007°/7ca via MB1/MB2 chan buoys to Q (3) 10s in centre of Port du Moulin Blanc marina, thence as directed into N or basins. The large W roof of the Océanopolis Marine Life Centre, is conspic except near LW.

COMMUNICATIONS CROSS 02·98·89·31·31; Monitor *Brest Port* (at Pte du Portzic) VHF Ch **08** (controls apprs to Brest); ⛆ 02·98·32·55·55; Auto 08·92·68·08·29; Police 02·98·43·77·77; ⊖ 02·98·44·35·20; Brit Consul 01·44·51·31·00; Ⓗ 02·98·22·33·33; Dr 02·98·44·38·70; HM Brest 02·98·33·41·41; Aff Mar 02·98·80·62·25; Marinas VHF Ch 09 (HO).

FACILITIES **Sté des Régates de Brest** ☎02·98·02·53·36, ✕. **YC Rade de Brest** ☎02·98·44·63·32. **CN Municipal** ☎02·98·34·64·64.

Marina du Château ⓐ ent 48°22'·68N 04°29'·48W. ☎02·98·33·12·50 (0800-2200 Jul-Aug) www.marinasbrest.fr chateau@marinasbrest.fr 650 ⊆ + 120 ⓥ €2·90, multihulls +150%, pontoon A, and S side of pontoon PC. English spoken. ♞ ♞ (H24) ✕ ⊡ 🛒. ⊡ ♂ ▲ ⊡ (short walk from marina), ♿ free wi-fi. ⚑(25t) 5 mins to city centre by bus/tram.

Port du Moulin Blanc ⓐ ☎02·98·02·20·02. www.marinasbrest.fr moulinblanc@marinasbrest.fr. Excellent facilities, and very helpful bi-lingual staff. 1340⊆ + 120ⓥ €2·40, no surcharge for multihulls, ♞ ♞ H24 (French cr/card or pre-arrange with HM) ✕ ⊡ 🛒 ⊡ ▲ ♂ ♿ ⊡ SHOM ✎ ⊡ Ⓔ ⚒ ⚑(14t,40t) ⊡(18t) ⟋. No 3 bus, 20 mins to city centre. Océanopolis, 55 aquariums, just minutes away!

City All facilities: ✉ Ⓑ ⥂ Guipavas ✈. **Ferry** Roscoff. Brest Festival of the Sea, 2nd wk July every 4 years, 2020 is the next festival year.

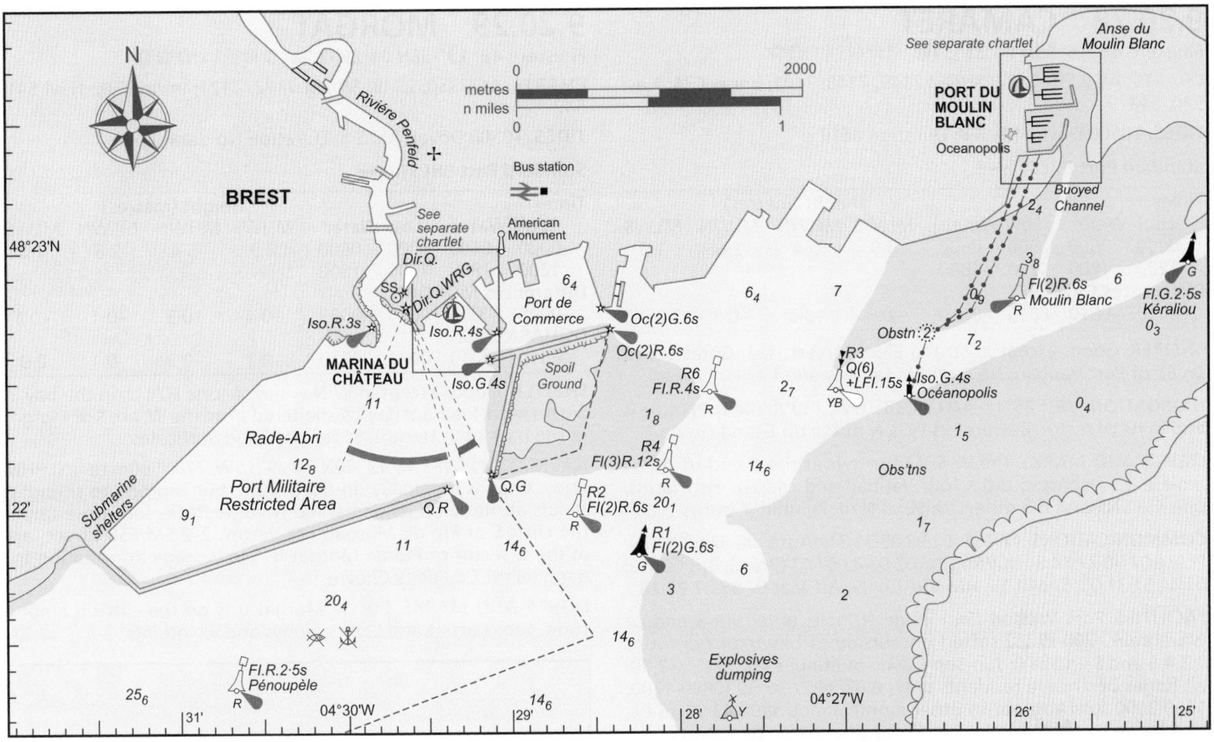
BREST
Rivière Penfeld
Bus station
American Monument
See separate chartlet
Port de Commerce
Spoil Ground
MARINA DU CHÂTEAU
Rade-Abri
Port Militaire Restricted Area
Submarine shelters
PORT DU MOULIN BLANC
Oceanopolis
Anse du Moulin Blanc
Buoyed Channel
Explosives dumping
Iso.R.3s
Iso.R.4s
Iso.G.4s
Oc(2)G.6s
Oc(2)R.6s
Fl.R.4s
Fl(3)R.12s
Fl(2)R.6s
Fl(2)G.6s
Q.G
Q.R
Fl.R.2·5s
Pénoupèle
Q(6) +LFl.15s
Iso.G.4s
Océanopolis
Fl(2)R.6s
Moulin Blanc
Fl.G.2·5s
Kéraliou
Obstn
Obs'tns
48°23'N
22'
04°30'W
04°27'W

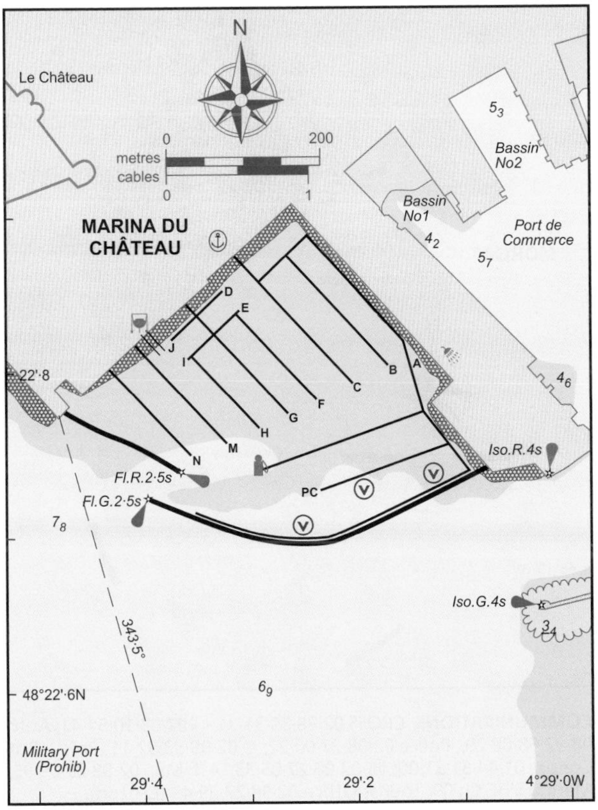
Le Château
MARINA DU CHÂTEAU
Bassin No1
Bassin No2
Port de Commerce
Fl.R.2·5s
Fl.G.2·5s
Iso.R.4s
Iso.G.4s
343·5°
Military Port (Prohib)
48°22'·6N

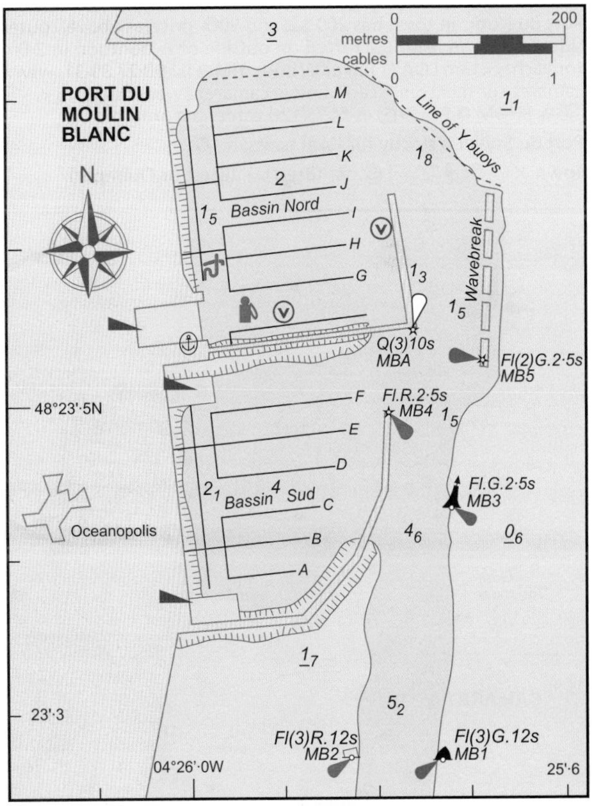
PORT DU MOULIN BLANC
Bassin Nord
Bassin Sud
Oceanopolis
Line of Y buoys
Wavebreak
Q(3)10s MBA
Fl(2)G.2·5s MB5
Fl.R.2·5s MB4
Fl.G.2·5s MB3
Fl(3)R.12s MB2
Fl(3)G.12s MB1
48°23'·5N
04°26'·0W

9.20.28 CAMARET

Finistère **48°16'·85N 04°35'·31W** ✽✽✽◊◊◊✿✿

CHARTS AC 2350, 3427; SHOM 7149, 7148, 7401; Imray C36; Navi 540, 542

TIDES +0500 Dover; ML 3·8; Duration 0610

Standard Port BREST (⟵)

Times				Height (metres)			
High Water		Low Water		MHWS	MHWN	MLWN	MLWS
0000	0600	0000	0600	6·9	5·4	2·6	1·0
1200	1800	1200	1800				
Differences CAMARET							
–0010	–0010	–0015	–0010	–0·3	–0·3	–0·1	0·0

SHELTER Good, except in strong E'lies. Access H24. Good ⚓ and Ⓥs SE of Port Vauban. No ⚓ within fairway and hbr.

NAVIGATION WPT 48°17'·44N 04°36'·09W, 139°/0·8M to N mole lt and in its W sector. Beware rks W & N of Pte du Grand Gouin.

LIGHTS AND MARKS The W SHM bcn twr at the E end of the N mole is very conspic; ditto Tour Vauban and chapel. Fish farms, one 3ca ENE and the other 3ca SE of N mole, unlit Y buoys.

COMMUNICATIONS CROSS 02·98·89·31·31; Auto 08·92·68·08·29; Police 02·98·27·84·94 (Jul/Aug); ⊖ 02·98·33·97·11 (Brest); Brit Consul 01·44·51·31·00; SAMU 15; HM VHF Ch 09; Aff Mar 02·98·27·93·28.

FACILITIES **Port Vauban** (5m) inside N mole; enter via S end of wavebreak. 200 Ⓥ ⊆ rafted on outside of bkwtr or pontoons 2,3,4,5 and S end of 6; Jun-Sep €2·46; multihulls +50%; ⚑ €2·00; all finger berths are residents only; ☎02·98·27·95·99 (0830-1200; 1600-2000 July/Aug, varies other months) mob ☎06·43·09·26·83, in emergency. ♞ ⚓ local wi-fi €5·00 p/w. 20 W Ⓥs marina rate –50%.

Port du Notic, in town has 200 ⊆ and 50Ⓥ price as above, outer side E pontoon. Also ⊆ rafted on outside of A pontoon in 2·0m for yachts <13m LOA (1·0m at W end). **HM☎** 02·98·27·89·31. www.camaret-sur-mer.com capitainerie.camaret@wanadoo.fr ⊡ ♿ ⓟ ⓓ ⚐ SHOM @ ⚒ ⊞ Ⓔ ⚠ ⚒ ⛴(12t) careening area.

Port du Styvel is strictly for local boats; no Ⓥ.

Town ✕ ⊡ ⛟ ♞ ⓟ ✉ Ⓑ. ⇌ (Brest) ✈ (Brest or Quimper).

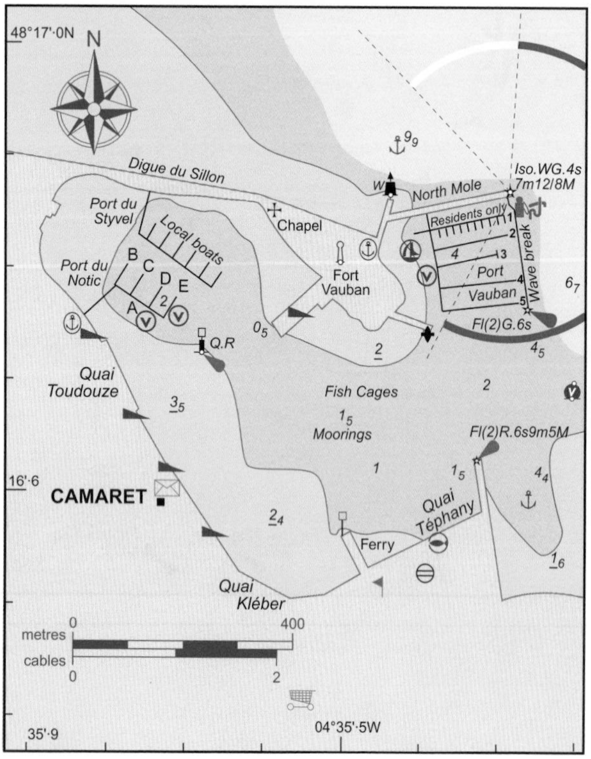

9.20.29 MORGAT

Finistère **48°13'·56N 04°29'·76W** ✽✽✽◊◊✿✿✿

CHARTS AC 2350, 2349; SHOM 7172, 7121; Imray C36; Navi 541, 542

TIDES +0500 Dover; ML 3·8; Duration No data

Standard Port BREST (⟵)

Times				Height (metres)			
High Water		Low Water		MHWS	MHWN	MLWN	MLWS
0000	0600	0000	0600	6·9	5·4	2·6	1·0
1200	1800	1200	1800				
Differences MORGAT							
–0005	–0010	–0020	–0005	–0·4	–0·3	–0·1	+0·1
DOUARNENEZ							
–0010	–0010	–0020	–0010	–0·3	–0·3	–0·1	0·0

SHELTER Good, except in W-N winds. Access H24. ⚓ in the bay in 2m on sand. Pleasant day ⚓s, sheltered from the W, are S of Morgat in the bays of St Hernot, St Norgard and St Nicolas.

NAVIGATION WPT 48°13'·60N 04°29'·15W, 270°/500m to first PHM buoy. Chan is nominally dredged 1·5m, but is prone to silting; it shoals abruptly on its unmarked N edge. Rocks lurk close under the cliffs S of Pte de Morgat. Les Verrès, 2–2·5M ESE of ent, are in the G sector of Pte de Morgat lt. See Passage information for dangers off Cap de la Chèvre.

LIGHTS AND MARKS Pte de Morgat lt is on the clifftop among trees. See chartlet and Lights, buoys and waypoints.

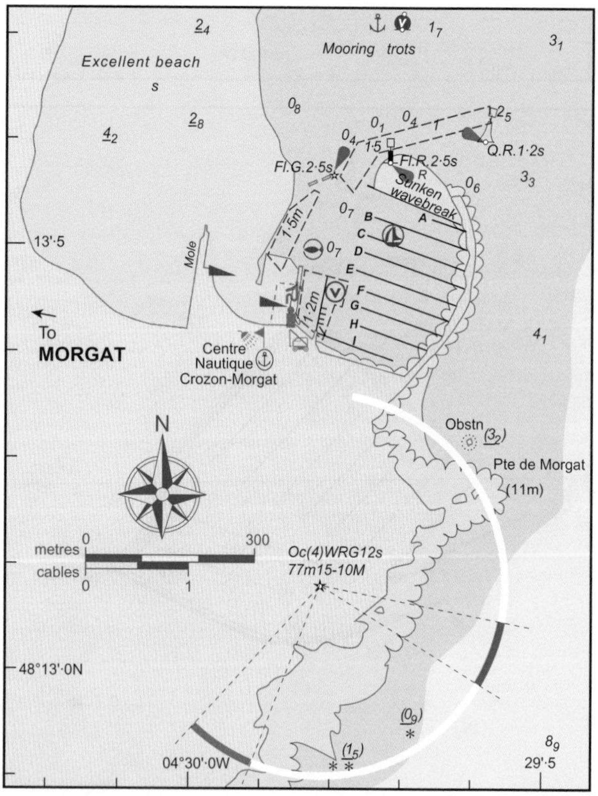

COMMUNICATIONS CROSS 02·98·89·31·31; ⓛ 02·98·10·51·41; Auto 08·92·68·08·29; Police 02·98·27·00·22; ⊖ 02·98·33·97·11 (Brest); Brit Consul 01·44·51·31·00; Ⓗ 02·98·27·05·33; Aff Mar 02·98·27·09·95; Marina VHF Ch 09; Tourist Office 02·98·27·29·49 (Crozon).

FACILITIES **Marina** ☎02·98·27·01·97 ports@mairie-crozon.fr www.mairie-crozon.fr 646 + 35Ⓥ €1·90, on small pontoon parallel to fuel dock: fingers on E side or ⊆ on W side for larger yachts. 40 unmarked Ⓥs, €0·95, ⛴ ⚐ ♞ ♞ ⚒ ⊞ ⚒ Ⓔ ⊡ ♿ ⛴(6t).

YC ☎02·98·16·00·01. **Town** (Crozon) ✕ ⊡ ⛟ ♞ ✉ Ⓑ ⇌ ✈ (Brest or Quimper). **Ferry** Roscoff.

9.20.30 DOUARNENEZ

Finistère **48°05'·98N 04°20'·35W**

CHARTS AC 2349; SHOM 7121; Imray C36; Navi 542.

TIDES Differences Morgat. +0500 Dover; ML 3·7; Duration 0615

SHELTER In strong NW'lies due to seas/swell the outer Grande Passe Ⓥ pontoons can be uncomfortable. Rade de Guet ⚓ areas in 1·5-3m are exposed to N/NE'lies. Good shelter in Port Rhu.

NAVIGATION WPT 48°06'·71N 04°20'·83W, 157°/0·8M to abeam outer Ⓥ pontoon. Basse Veur (4·8m) and Basse Neuve (2·2m) are 8 and 4ca NNW of Île Tristan lt and in its R sector. 5ca NW of Tréboul jetty, QG, keep well NE of Rochers Le Coulinec and La Tête de Pierre, a rocky ledge, both off chartlet.

LIGHTS AND MARKS Daymarks: Two conspic spires and Île Tristan lt twr are in transit 147°. Île Tristan is a cliffy, wooded island. See chartlet and Lights, buoys and waypoints for details.

COMMUNICATIONS CROSS 02·98·89·31·31; 02·98·84·60·64; Auto 08·92·68·08·29; 02·98·33·97·11 (Brest); Brit Consul 01·44·51·31·00; Ⓗ 02·98·92·25·00; Port HM 02·98·92·14·85; Port Rhu VHF Ch 09; FV Port VHF Ch 12; Aff Mar 02·98·75·31·30; Marina VHF Ch 09.

FACILITIES from seaward: Grande Passe 60Ⓥ Apr-Sep, €2·50; the southerly pontoons project slightly into the fairway. access H24. Other facilities as per Tréboul.

Tréboul Marina (1·5m) is full of local boats. ☎02·98·74·02·56. www.inet-bretagne.fr 463 Apr-Sep, €2·50; N of berth, Ⓔ (12t) (6t) . **YC** ☎02·98·92·02·03.

Port Rhu ☎02·98·92·00·67. 30Ⓥ Apr-Sep, €2·50; If conditions are bad in Grande Passe pre-arrange a berth at Port Rhu's non-tidal basin (3·2m); or at pontoons S of the bridge (16·5m clnce at HW, coeff 80) in 2·2m. Enter over a sill (1·1m) via 10m wide gate which opens approx HW ±2 when Coeff >70.

Port Neuf is for FVs only. **Port de Rosmeur** is full of moorings, but ⚓ S of it, as charted, in about 1·5m; convenient for town.

Town @ Ⓑ ✈ (Quimper). **Ferry** Roscoff.

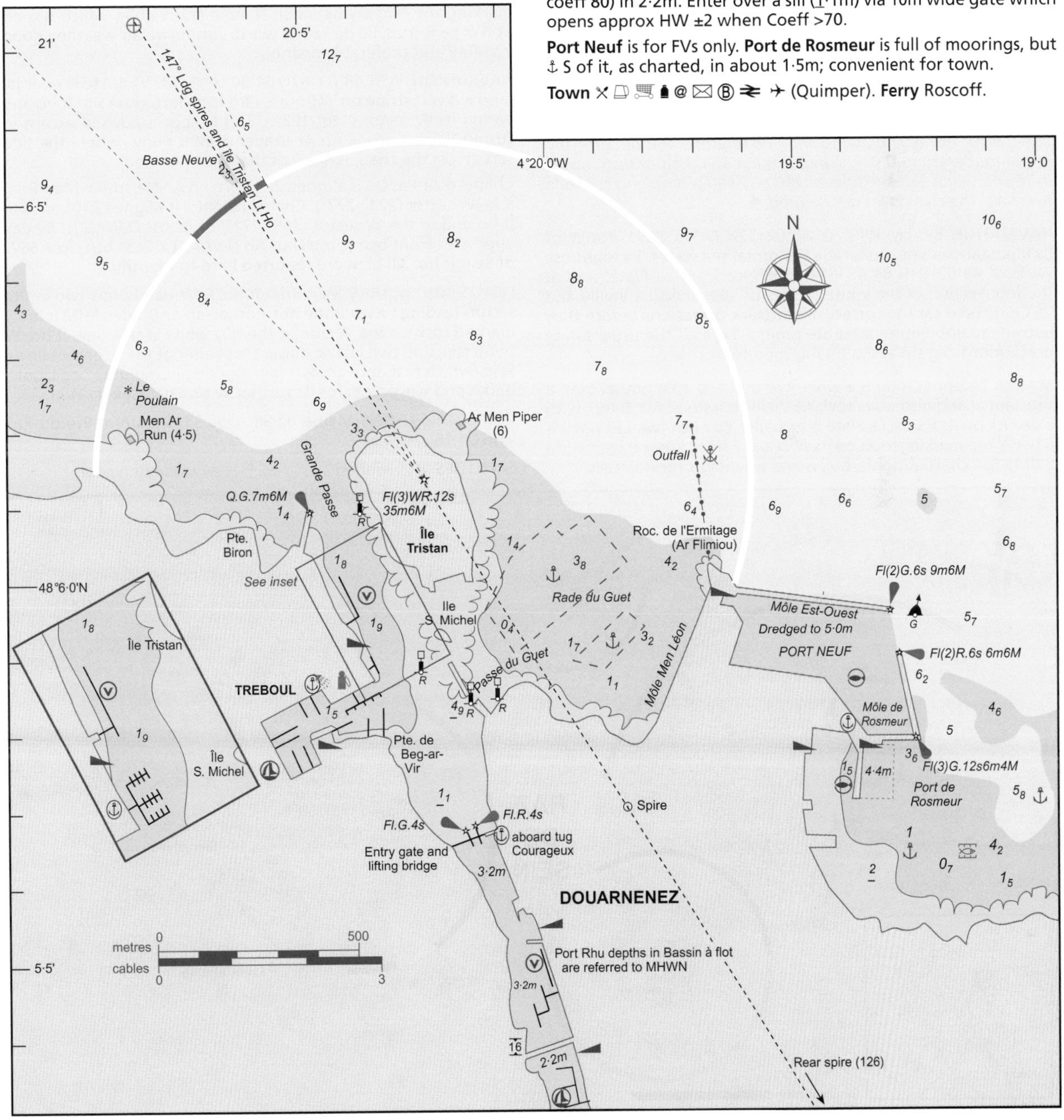

9.20.31 THE RAZ DE SEIN

GEOGRAPHY The Raz (pronounced *Raah*) is bounded by Le Chat bcn twr to the W (at E end of Chaussée de Sein) and to the E by La Vieille lt ho which with La Plate lt tr marks the dangers extending 8ca off Pte du Raz. Plateau de Tévennec, 2·9M NNE of Le Chat, consists of islets, drying rks and shoals which extend 5ca in all directions from the lt ho thereon. Other dangers on the N side of the Raz are rks and shoals extending nearly 1M W and WSW from Pte du Van, and Basse Jaune (1·4m) 1M to N.

On the S side the main dangers, all 1·5M off La Vieille, are: to the SW, Kornog Bras, a 3·7m deep rk; to the S, Masklou Greiz, rky shoals (7·6m) on which sea can break heavily; and to the SE, Roche Moulleg (5·2m).

TIDAL STREAMS ▶*In the middle (48°02'·88N 04°46'·76W) of the Raz the NE-going (flood) stream begins at HW Brest +0550, sp rate 6·5kn; the SW-going (ebb) stream begins at HW Brest –½, sp rate 5·5kn. Slack water, as the N-going flood expires, occurs between about HW Brest –1 and –½; if S-bound aim for the middle of that window, ±15 mins. If N-bound, slack water is about HW Brest +5½. Study tidal diamond 'D' on chart 2348. There are eddies near La Vieille on both streams.*

As a rule the Raz should always be taken at slack water to ensure the least uncomfortable conditions. Precise timing is vital: even an hour early or late on slack water can greatly affect the sea state. In good weather, near nps, wind and tide together, it is not difficult. But in moderate to strong winds it ***must*** *be taken at slack water. In strong winds-against-tide which raise steep breaking seas and overfalls, the chan* ***must not*** *be used.*◀

NAVIGATION By day, WPT 'D' 48°02'·37N 04°45'·88W, 2ca W of La Plate, allows visual pilotage in normal sea states. By night use WPT 'N' 48°02'·91N 04°46'·61W, 308°/9ca from La Plate, and at the intersection of the white sectors of Tévennec, La Vieille and Le Chat. Take care to correct minor track deviations before they become major. Ensure accurate timing. Take all the usual safety precautions. Sig stn at Pte du Raz monitors Ch 16.

MARKS Tévennec lt ho is a white twr perched on a house, atop a substantial and distinctive rock. La Vieille is a stone twr, B top, with a derrick on its E side. La Plate is a smaller YBY bcn twr. Le Chat is a B twr, Y top marking rocks on its W, N and E sides; keep at least 0·5M E of it. See chartlet/Lights, buoys and waypoints for lt details.

9.20.32 ÎLE DE SEIN

Finistere **48°02'·34N 04°50'·89W**

CHARTS AC 2348*; SHOM 7147, 7148, 7423*; Imray C36, C37; Navi 541. *Both have 1:10,000 insets of the island.

TIDES ML 3·6

Standard Port BREST (⟵)

Times				Height (metres)			
High Water		Low Water		MHWS	MHWN	MLWN	MLWS
0000	0600	0000	0600	6·9	5·4	2·6	1·0
1200	1800	1200	1800				
Differences ÎLE DE SEIN							
–0005	–0005	–0015	–0010	–0·8	–0·6	–0·3	–0·1

SHELTER The non-drying N part of the hbr is open to N and E winds; the drying S part of the hbr is protected from E and S by two large bkwtrs. The island itself affords some shelter from W'lies. ⚓ near the LB, but clear of 3 pairs of small lateral buoys (Apr-Oct) marking the fairway between N mole and S quay, which is used at HW by ferries. Île de Sein is worth visiting in fair weather, good visibility and preferably near nps.

NAVIGATION WPT 48°03'·67N 04°50'·71W, 187°/1·4M to Men-Brial lt ho ≠ B vert stripe on W house, (3rd from left, close S of lt ho and within its W sector (186°-192°)). This N appr is advised except in strong N'lies. Cornoc-An-Ar-Braden SHM lt buoy, where the tide sets across the chan, is 4ca S of the ⊕.

Chenal d'Ar Vas Du is aligned 224°: bcn on An Nerroth ≠ Men-Brial lt ho W sector (221°-227°). Chenal Oriental is aligned 270° on Sein lt ho and in the W sector (269°-271°) of its Dir Q WRG lt. By day appr with front bcn (close N of An Nerroth) ≠ 265° bcn close SSW of Sein lt ho. All bcns are reported hard-to-identify.

LIGHTS AND MARKS Men-Brial lt ho, G/W bands, has two white sectors leading towards the hbr. Cornoc-an-ar-Braden SHM lt buoy marks a rock on the W side of the N'ly white sector. Sein lt ho, W twr/B top, and two lattice masts are conspic at the W end of Île de Sein (which first appears as a low rounded hummock). See Lights, buoys and waypoints for lts further W on Chaussée de Sein.

COMMUNICATIONS Mairie 02·98·70·90·35; Sig stn at Pte du Raz VHF Ch 16.

FACILITIES ✕ limited, ✉. www.enezsun.com

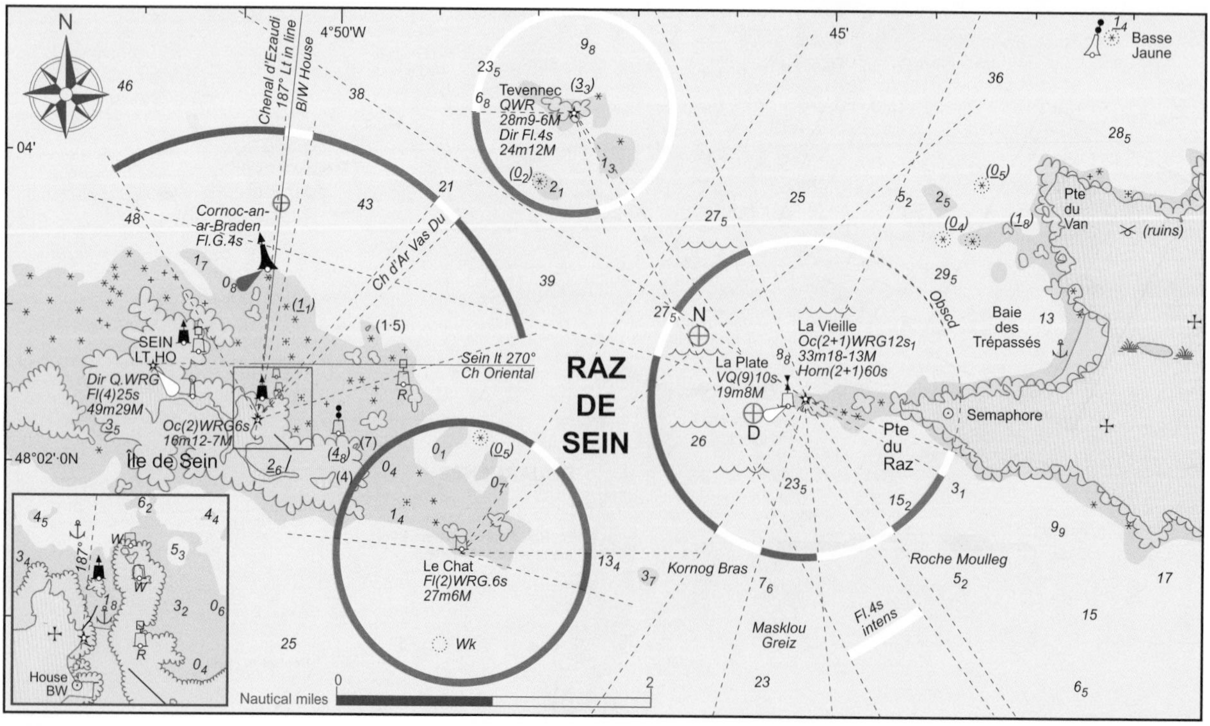

9.20.33 AUDIERNE

Finistere **48°00'·55N 04°32'·42W**

CHARTS AC 2819 inc inset; SHOM 7147, 7148; Imray C36, C37; Navi 541

TIDES +0440 Dover; ML 3·1; Duration 0605

Standard Port BREST (⟵)

Times				Height (metres)			
High Water		Low Water		MHWS	MHWN	MLWN	MLWS
0000	0600	0000	0600	6·9	5·4	2·6	1·0
1200	1800	1200	1800				
Differences AUDIERNE							
–0035	–0030	–0035	–0030	–1·7	–1·3	–0·6	–0·2
ANSE DE FEUNTEUN AOD (6M WNW Audierne)							
–0030	–0040	–0035	–0025	–1·3	–1·1	–0·5	–0·1
LE GUILVINEC							
–0010	–0025	–0025	–0015	–1·8	–1·4	–0·6	–0·1
LESCONIL							
–0010	–0030	–0030	–0020	–1·9	–1·4	–0·6	–0·1

SHELTER Good in marina; see also Ste Evette below. There is limited room to ⚓ in the bight N of La Petite Gamelle SCM bcn.

NAVIGATION From the W, WPT 47°59'·47N 04°33'·01W (abeam Gamelle Ouest WCM buoy) 006°/1·5M to Kergadec Dir lt. Appr between La Gamelle, rks drying 0·9m in the middle of the bay, and Le Sillon de Galets rks to the W. Appr is difficult in strong S'lies, when seas break at the ent.

From the SE, WPT 47°59'·46N 04°31'·56W (3ca E of Gamelle Est SCM buoy) 331°/1·2M to bkwtr lt. This track leaves La Gamelle reef 300m to port. If bound for Ste Evette, do not turn WNW until well clear N of La Gamelle and Pte de Lervily's R sector.

Bar at ent; inside, dredged chan initially lies about 25m off the bkwtr. Leave R bcn close to port then pick up the 359° ldg marks, vert R/W chevrons, to avoid rocks at foot of bkwtr and banks to stbd drying 1·1m to 2·1m.

At root of bkwtr pick up 2nd set of R/W chevrons on corner of fish market bldg ≠ 045°; leave the fish market close (15m) to stbd, then alter 90° port towards the marina.

Leave the FV quays and yacht pontoons close to port to clear the bank to stbd, drying 1·9m and more. On departure there are 225° ldg chevrons by the roadside at root of W bkwtr.

LIGHTS AND MARKS See chartlet and Lights, buoys and waypoints. By day from the W WPT, Kergadec, W 8-sided lt tr, R top, ≠ old lt ho (hard to see) leads 006°. At night stay in the W sector (005°-007°) of Kergadec. From SE WPT, 331° ldg marks (no longer lit) are: Front, conspic white twr on Jetée du Raoulic (long W bkwtr); rear Kergadec. Fish market is a conspic B/W bldg.

COMMUNICATIONS CROSS 02·98·89·31·31; LB 02·98·70·07·54; Auto 08·92·68·08·29; Police 02·98·70·04·38; ⊖ 02·98·33·97·11 (Brest); Brit Consul 01·44·51·31·00; H 02·98·75·10·10; Aff Mar 02·98·70·03·33; HM VHF Ch 09.

FACILITIES **Marina** Access HW –2 to +1 for 2m draft. Quays reserved for FVs. Berth initially on any hammerhead. Pontoons A-C are dredged 2m at the outer end, but 1·6m will be found between dredgings. Pontoons D-G are dredged 2m; avoid F & G as the flood sets strongly towards the bridge. HM ☎02·98·75·04·93, mob 06·72 ·91·70·52. www.audierne.info 100 + 30Ⓥ €2·50. **Poulgoazec** (15t) s.

Town Ⓔ Ⓑ. Most shops close Mon outside Jul/Aug. Bus to Quimper for ⇄ ✈. **Ferry** Roscoff.

SAINTE ÉVETTE The long bkwtr gives good shelter, but in strong SE-SW winds it is very uncomfortable and swell intrudes. Access H24. 30 W Ⓥs (€1·29) in 1-2m, some very close together. Or ⚓ free in 3-4m close to seaward of Ⓥs in moderate holding on sand. Avoid the S side of N pier/slip used by vedettes.

HM ☎02·98.70.00.28. by hose from N side of N jetty (approx HW ±3) limited victuals.

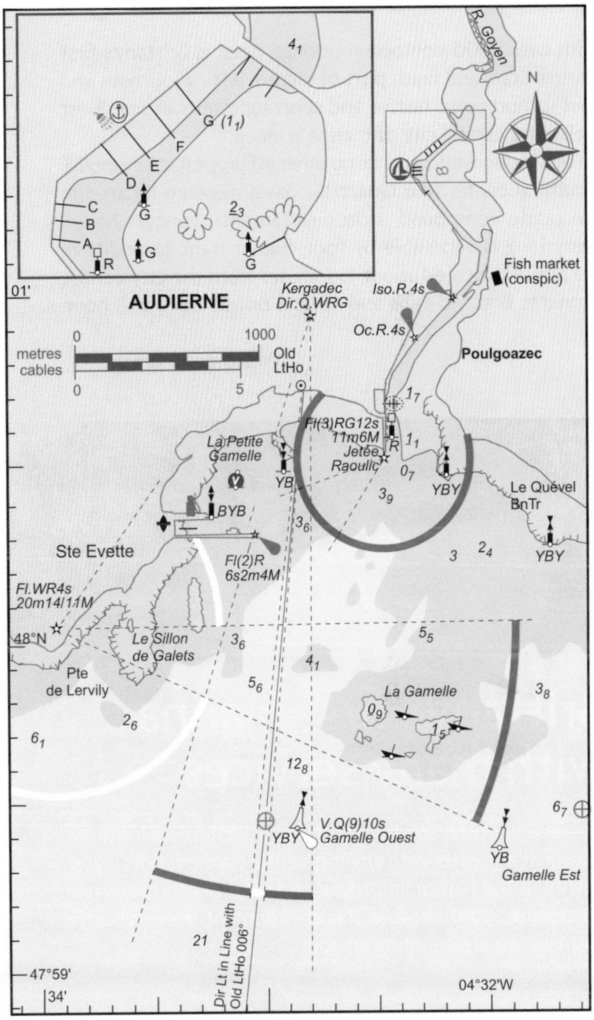

FISHING HARBOURS N AND E OF THE POINTE DE PENMARC'H

ST GUÉNOLÉ, Finistere, **47°48'·68N 04°22'·93W**. AC 2819, 2820; SHOM 7146/7, 6645; Navi 543. Strictly a fishing port; yachts only in emergency/force majeure. Narrow ent difficult in fresh W'lies, impossible in heavy weather. 3 sets of ldg marks/lts (see SHOM 6645). Pilot book essential. HM ☎02·98·58·60·43/ 06·78·85·38·85.

LE GUILVINEC, Finistere, **47°47'·46N 04°17'·17W**. AC 2819, 2820, 3640; SHOM 7146/7, 6646. HW + 0447 on Dover (UT); ML 3·0m. See Bénodet. Good shelter and useful passage port (3m) but total priority to FVs; no ent/exit 1600-1830. Access H24 for <2·5m draft. Start from Névez SHM buoy. Appr is easy if able to see 053° triple ldg lts or the large, conspic dayglo red daymarks. Close in, beware Lost Moan rocks, SE of ent, marked by RW bcn lt twr. Good ⚓ SE of hbr ent in 7·7m staying clear of fairway. Three 053° ldg lts, all Q synch (see Area 21): front, W pylon; middle, 210m from front, R □ on W pylon; rear, 0·58M from front, R □ on W pylon with R stripe. VHF Ch 12. HM (Plaisance) ☎02·98·58·14·47; www.leguilvinec.com Facilities: 4 Ⓥs, 4 at NE end of hbr, €1·56, ⊖ Ⓔ.

South Brittany

Loctudy to St Nazaire

9.21.1 Contents 887
9.21.2 Area map and Distance table 888
9.21.3 Tidal stream chartlets 890
9.21.4 Lights, buoys and waypoints 892
9.21.5 Passage information 896
South Brittany – 896 • Loctudy to Concarneau – 900 • Concarneau to Lorient – 900 • Île de Groix, Lorient and Belle Île – 902 • Baie de Quiberon – 909 • Crouesty to Le Croisic – 911 • Le Croisic to the River Loire and to Nantes – 914
9.21.6 Special notes for France, see Area 17
9.21.7 Loctudy 896
Lesconil
9.21.8 Bénodet 897
9.21.9 Port-la-Forêt 897
9.21.10 Îles de Glénan 898
9.21.11 Concarneau 899
9.21.12 Minor harbours between Concarneau and Lorient 900
Aven and Bélon Rivers • Brigneau • Merrien • Doëlan • Le Pouldu
9.21.13 Port Tudy (Île de Groix) 901
Loc Maria
9.21.14 Lorient 902
9.21.15 River Étel 904
9.21.16 Sauzon (Belle Île) 904
Ster Wenn
9.21.17 Le Palais (Belle Île) 905
9.21.18 Passage de la Teignouse 905
9.21.19 Houat and Hoëdic 905
9.21.20 Port Haliguen 907
Port Maria
9.21.21 La Trinité-sur-Mer 907
9.21.22 Golfe du Morbihan 908
9.21.23 Vannes 910
9.21.24 Crouesty 911
Pénerf
9.21.25 Vilaine River 912
Arzal • La Roche Bernard
9.21.26 Piriac 913
9.21.27 La Turballe 913
9.21.28 Le Croisic 914
9.21.29 Le Pouliguen 915
9.21.30 Pornichet 915
9.21.31 Saint-Nazaire (R. Loire) 916
Nantes • Port de Comberge • Port de la Gravette • St Gildas

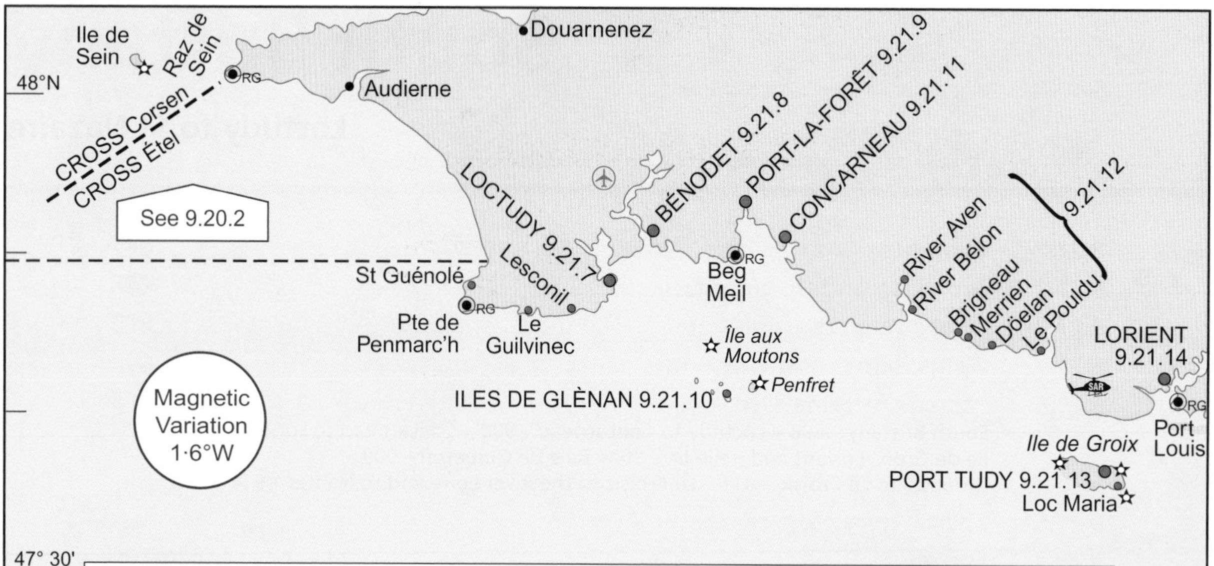
Ile de Sein
Raz de Sein
RG
48°N
Douarnenez
Audierne
CROSS Corsen
CROSS Étel
See 9.20.2
LOCTUDY 9.21.7
BÉNODET 9.21.8
PORT-LA-FORÊT 9.21.9
CONCARNEAU 9.21.11
9.21.12
River Aven
River Bélon
Brigneau
Merrien
Döelan
Le Pouldu
St Guénolé
Lesconil
Pte de Penmarc'h
Le Guilvinec
Beg Meil
Île aux Moutons
Penfret
ILES DE GLÈNAN 9.21.10
LORIENT 9.21.14
Port Louis
Ile de Groix
PORT TUDY 9.21.13
Loc Maria
SAR
Magnetic Variation 1·6°W
47° 30'
47°N
5°W
4°30'
4°W
3°30'

DISTANCE TABLE

Approximate distances in nautical miles are by the most direct route while avoiding dangers and allowing for TSS. Places in *italics* are in adjoining areas; places in **bold** are in 9.0.5, Cross-Channel Distances.

		1	2	3	4	5	6	7	8	9	10	11	12	13	14	15	16	17	18	19	20
1	*Le Conquet*	1																			
2	*Camaret*	13	2																		
3	*Morgat*	22	16	3																	
4	*Douarnenez*	29	21	11	4																
5	Audierne	30	28	27	30	5															
6	Loctudy	55	55	53	55	30	6														
7	Bénodet	58	58	57	60	33	4	7													
8	Port-la-Forêt	65	64	63	66	36	12	12	8												
9	Concarneau	63	62	61	64	37	12	11	4	9											
10	Lorient	84	86	85	88	61	38	36	33	32	10										
11	Le Palais (Belle Ile)	95	99	98	101	74	54	52	48	47	26	11									
12	Port Haliguen	100	105	104	107	80	59	57	55	53	32	11	12								
13	La Trinité	108	110	109	112	85	64	62	60	58	37	16	8	13							
14	Crouesty	108	110	109	112	85	64	62	60	58	37	16	9	8	14						
15	Vannes	120	121	120	123	96	75	73	71	69	48	27	20	19	12	15					
16	*Arzal/Camöel*	131	130	129	132	105	84	82	80	78	57	36	31	31	28	37	16				
17	Le Croisic	124	125	124	127	100	79	77	75	73	48	27	26	26	22	33	18	17			
18	La Baule/Pornichet	134	131	130	133	106	85	82	80	78	55	34	35	36	30	40	30	13	18		
19	St Nazaire	145	138	137	140	113	95	91	90	87	66	41	42	45	40	50	39	24	12	19	
20	*Pornic*	146	149	148	151	124	105	101	100	97	72	45	47	49	43	55	42	24	18	16	20

TABLE OF BUDGET AIRLINE ROUTES

The table below shows direct flights by 5 budget airlines from 6 coastal airports (Nantes and Bordeaux are only 45 minutes by train to/from the coast) to no less than 10 UK regional and 3 London airports.

UK: A – Z / FRANCE: N – S	Birmingham	Bristol	East Midlands	Edinburgh	Exeter	Gatwick	Glasgow	Leeds/Bradford	Liverpool	Luton	Manchester	Southampton	Stansted
Brest	FB			FB		EJ	FB	FB			FB	FB	
Nantes				FB	FB	EJ	FB		EJ		FB		
La Rochelle	FB	EJ	RY	FB		EJ	FB				FB	FB	RY
Bordeaux		EJ		RY		BA/EJ			EJ	EJ		FB	
Biarritz													RY
Rennes				FB	FB		FB	FB			FB	FB	

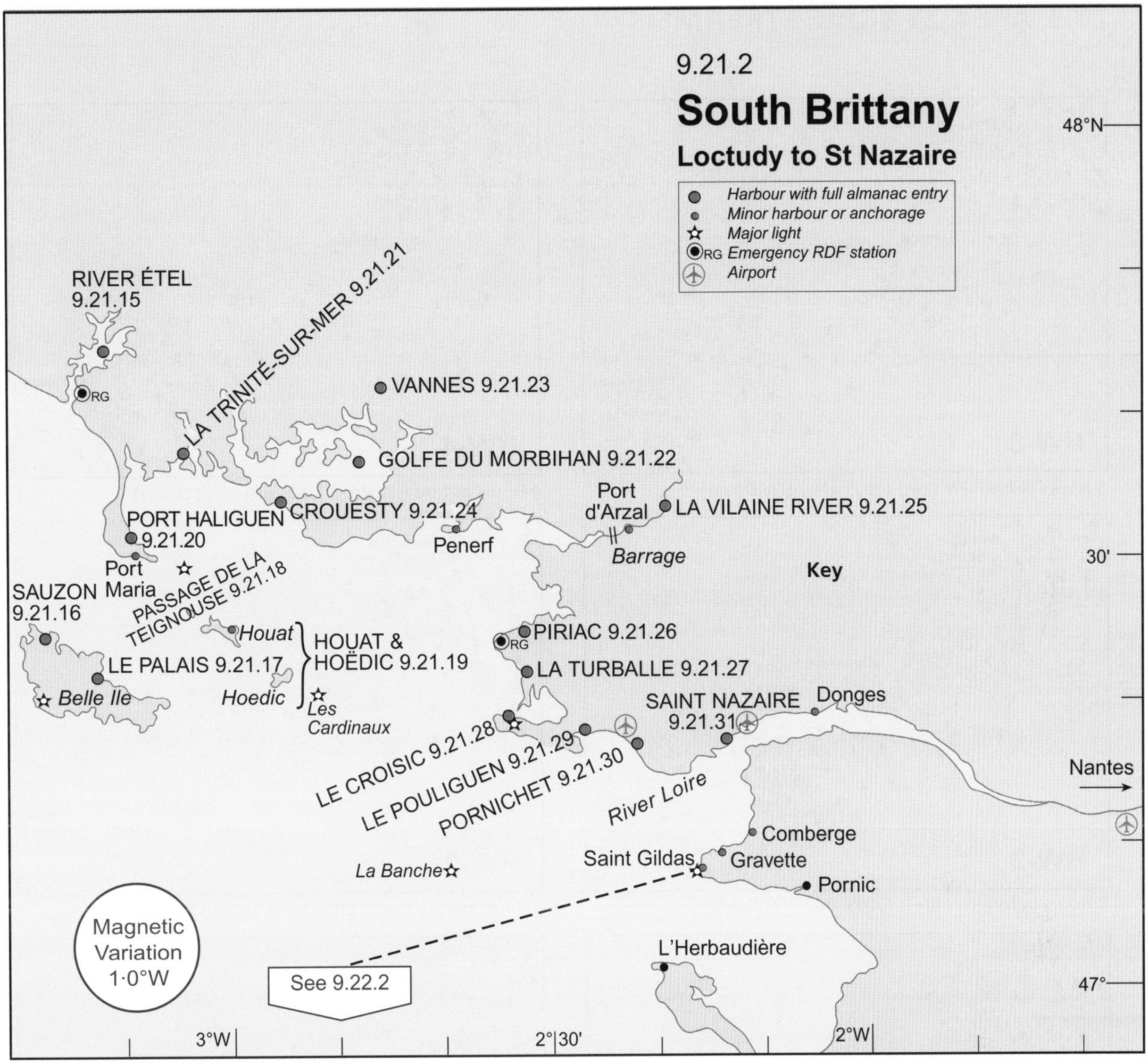
9.21.2
South Brittany
Loctudy to St Nazaire
Harbour with full almanac entry
Minor harbour or anchorage
Major light
RG Emergency RDF station
Airport
48°N
30'
47°
3°W
2°|30'
2°W
RIVER ÉTEL
9.21.15
RG
LA TRINITÉ-SUR-MER 9.21.21
VANNES 9.21.23
GOLFE DU MORBIHAN 9.21.22
PORT HALIGUEN
9.21.20
CROUESTY 9.21.24
Penerf
Port
d'Arzal
LA VILAINE RIVER 9.21.25
Barrage
Key
Port
Maria
SAUZON
9.21.16
PASSAGE DE LA
TEIGNOUSE 9.21.18
Houat
HOUAT &
HOËDIC 9.21.19
LE PALAIS 9.21.17
Belle Ile
Hoedic
Les
Cardinaux
PIRIAC 9.21.26
LA TURBALLE 9.21.27
SAINT NAZAIRE
9.21.31
Donges
LE CROISIC 9.21.28
LE POULIGUEN 9.21.29
PORNICHET 9.21.30
River Loire
Nantes
Comberge
Saint Gildas
Gravette
Pornic
La Banche
Magnetic
Variation
1·0°W
L'Herbaudière
See 9.22.2

KEY AND CONTACT DETAILS OF BUDGET AIRLINES

Key	Airline	Website	UK	France
BA	British Airways	www.ba.com	0844 493 0787	08·25·82·54·00
EJ	EasyJet	www.easyjet.com	0913 232 3636	08·99·70·00·41
FB	Flybe	www.flybe.com	0871 700 2000	+44 1392 268529
RY	Ryanair	www.ryanair.com	0871 246 0000	08·92·56·21·50*

* French only

9.21.3 AREA 21 TIDAL STREAMS

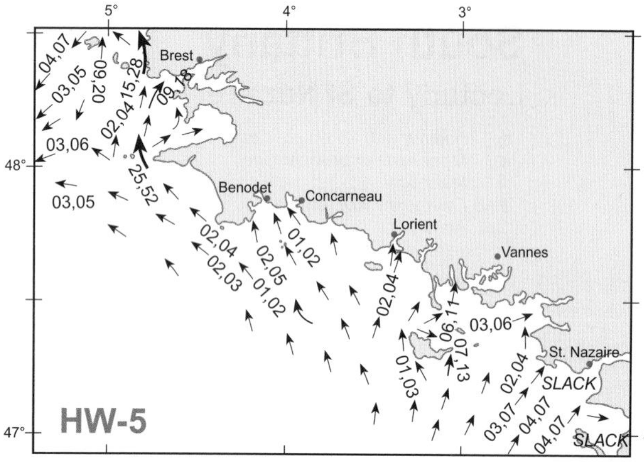

5 Hours before HW Brest (0005 after HW Dover)

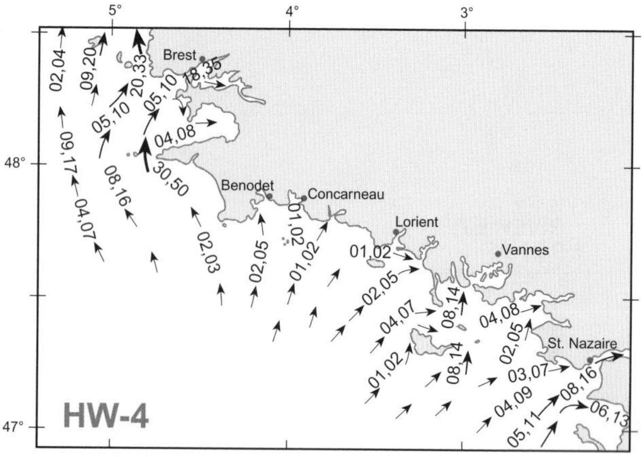

4 Hours before HW Brest (0105 after HW Dover)

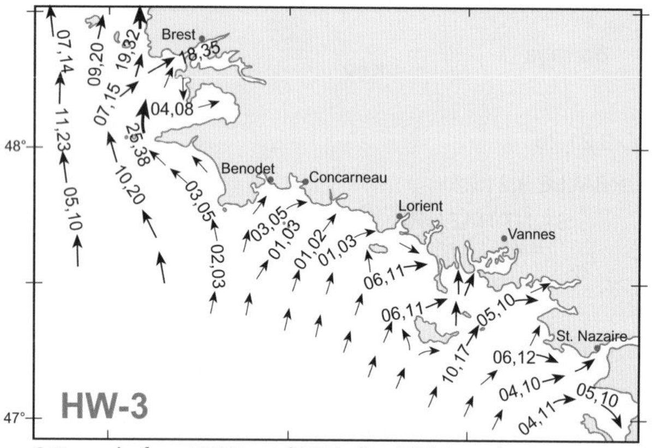

3 Hours before HW Brest (0205 after HW Dover)

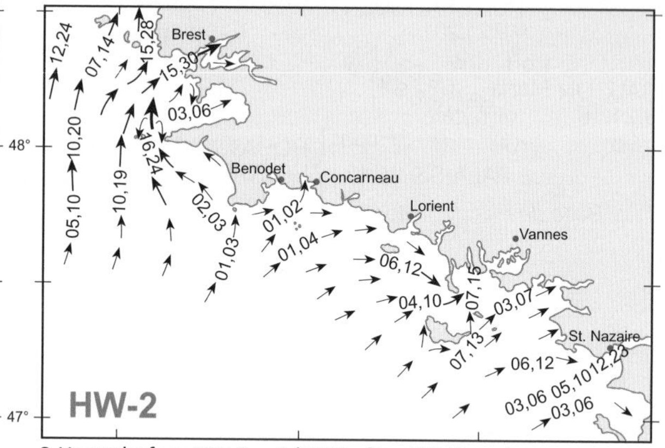

2 Hours before HW Brest (0305 after HW Dover)

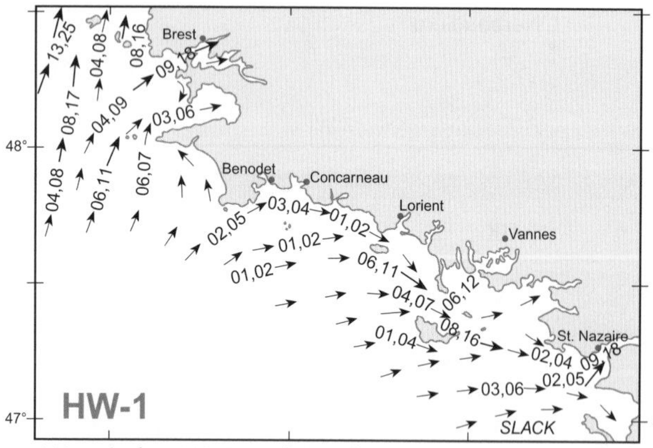

1 Hour before HW Brest (0405 after HW Dover)

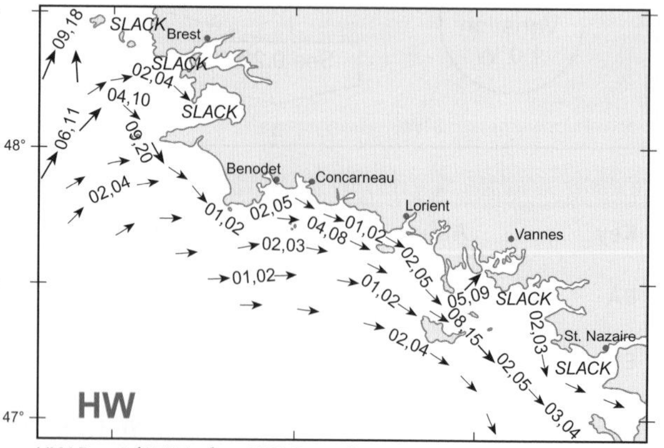

HW Brest (0505 after HW Dover)

CAUTION: Due to the very strong rates of the tidal streams in some of the areas covered by these chartlets, many eddies and overfalls may occur. Where possible some indication of these eddies has been included. In many areas there is either insufficient information or the eddies are unstable. Tidal streams are generally weak offshore.

Strong winds may also have a great effect on the rate and direction of the tidal streams in all these chartlets.

Note: These chartlets are based on the Admiralty tidal stream atlas for France, W coast (NP 265, 2nd edition 2005) which uses data from actual observations out to 20-35M offshore.

The comparable French atlas (558-UJA; 2005) gives data for further offshore, based on computer predictions. It covers from Audierne to Le Croisic and contains large scale chartlets of the areas from Loctudy to Concarneau inc Iles de Glénan; Lorient and Ile de Groix; Belle Ile and the west part of Quiberon Bay.

560-UJA (1994) is recommended for large scale coverage of the Chenal du Four and Raz de Sein.

Northward 9.20.3   Southward 9.22.3

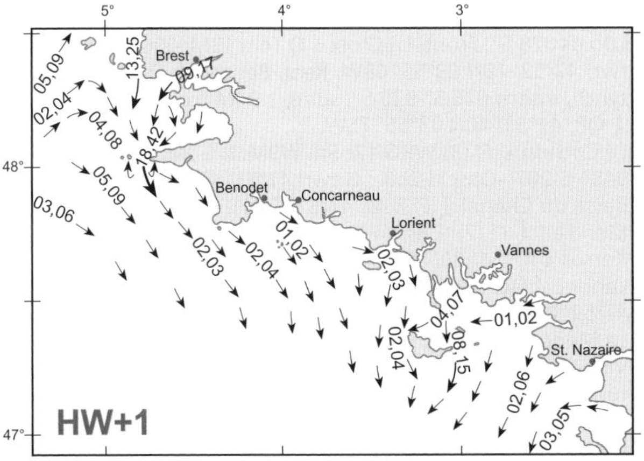

1 Hour after HW Brest (0605 after HW Dover)

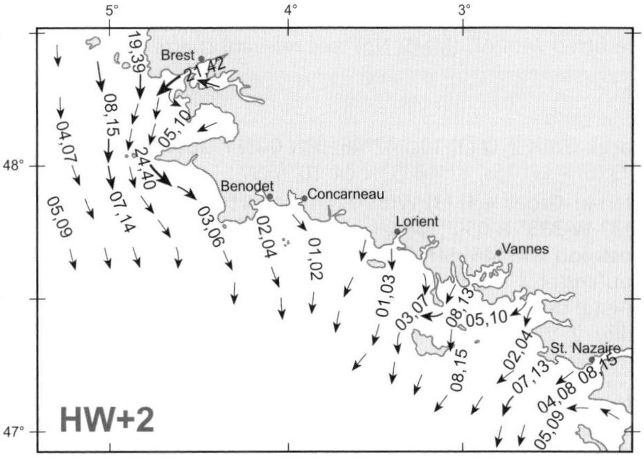

2 Hours after HW Brest (0515 before HW Dover)

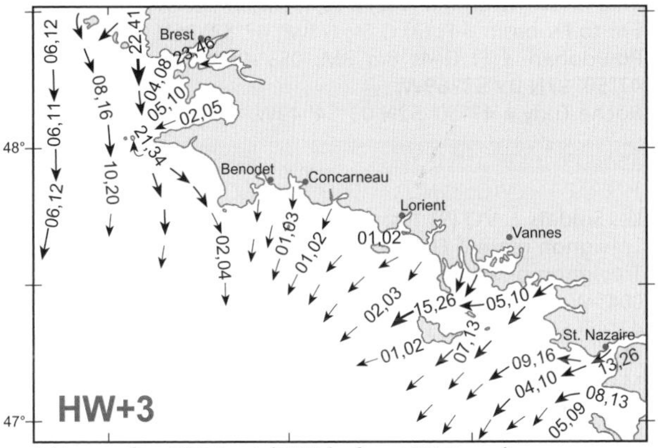

3 Hours after HW Brest (0415 before HW Dover)

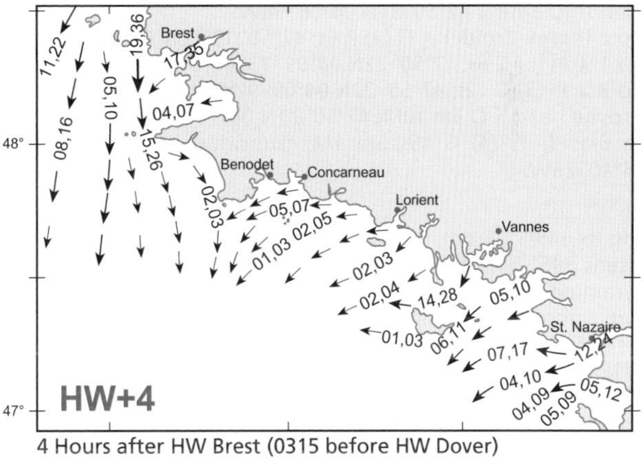

4 Hours after HW Brest (0315 before HW Dover)

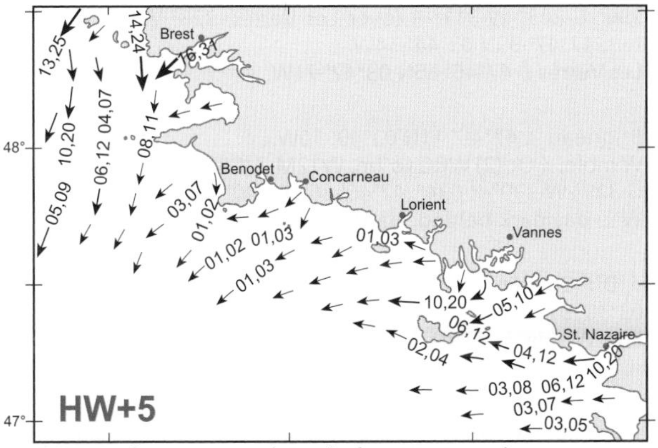

5 Hours after HW Brest (0215 before HW Dover)

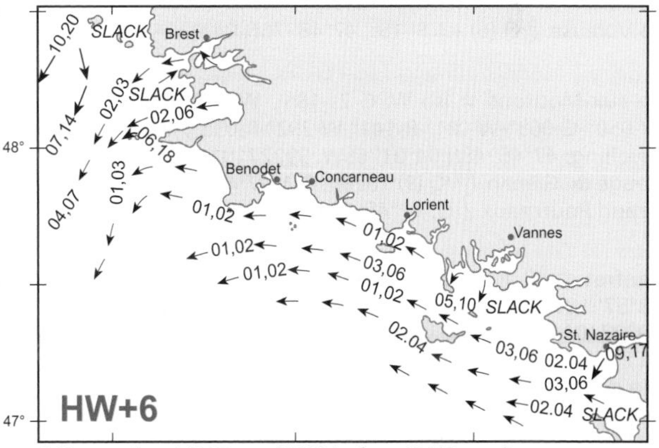

6 Hours after HW Brest (0115 before HW Dover)

CAUTION: Due to the very strong rates of the tidal streams in some of the areas covered by these chartlets, many eddies and overfalls may occur. Where possible some indication of these eddies has been included. In many areas there is either insufficient information or the eddies are unstable. Tidal streams are generally weak offshore.

Strong winds may also have a great effect on the rate and direction of the tidal streams in all these chartlets.

Note: These chartlets are based on the Admiralty tidal stream atlas for France, W coast (NP 265, 2nd edition 2005) which uses data from actual observations out to 20-35M offshore.

The comparable French atlas (558-UJA; 2005) gives data for further offshore, based on computer predictions. It covers from Audierne to Le Croisic and contains large scale chartlets of the areas from Loctudy to Concarneau inc Iles de Glénan; Lorient and Ile de Groix; Belle Ile and the west part of Quiberon Bay.

560-UJA (1994) is recommended for large scale coverage of the Chenal du Four and Raz de Sein.

9.21.4 LIGHTS, BUOYS AND WAYPOINTS

Bold print = light with a nominal range of 15M or more. CAPITALS = place or feature. *CAPITAL ITALICS* = light-vessel, light float or Lanby. *Italics* = Fog signal. ***Bold italics*** = Racon. Many marks/buoys are fitted with AIS (MMSI No); see relevant charts.

LOCTUDY TO CONCARNEAU

LESCONIL

Karek Greis Q (3) 10s; 47°46'·03N 04°11'·36W.
Q (6) + LFl 15s; 47°46'·53N 04°10'·63W
Men-ar-Groas Fl (3) WRG 12s 14m, W10M, R/G7M; 268°-G-313°-W-333°-R-050°; W lt ho, G top; 47°47'·79N 04°12'·68W.
Rostolou 47°46'·64N 04°07'·29W.
Boulanger VQ (6) + L Fl 10s;47°47'·38N 04°09'·13W.
Chenal de Bénodet 47°48'·53N 04°07'·04W.
Bilien VQ (3) 5s; 47°49'·10N 04°08'·09W.

LOCTUDY

Pte de Langoz ☆ Fl (4) WRG 15s 12m, **W15M**, R11M G12M; 115°-G-243°-W-257°-G-284°-W-295°-R-318°-W-328°-R-025°; W twr, R top; 47°49'·88N 04°09'·55W.
Karek-Saoz Fl R 2·5s 3m 1M; R twr; 47°50'·02N 04°09'·38W.
Men Audierne 47°50'·34N 04°08'·94W.
No 2 (Karek-Croisic) Fl (2) R 6s; 47°50'·19N 04°09'·49W.
No 1 Fl (2) G 6s; 47°50'·22N 04°09'·73W.
No 3 Fl (3) G 12s; 47°50'·22N 04°09'·99W.
Groyne head Q 3m 10M; 47°50'·21N 04°10'·34W.
Le Blas Fl (4) G 15s 5m 1M; truncated col; 47°50'·28N 04°10'·23W.

BENODET

Ldg lts 345·5°: Front, Pte du Coq Dir Oc (3) G 12s 11m 10M; intens 345°-347°; W ○ twr, G stripe; 47°52'·31N 04°06'·70W.
Pyramide Oc (3) 12s 48m 14M; 338°-016°, synch; W twr, G top; common rear, 348m from front.
Lts in line 000·5°: Front, Pte de Combrit Oc (2) WR 6s 19m, W12M, R9M; 325°-W-017°-R-325°; W □ twr, Gy corners 47°51'·86N 04°06'·78W. Common rear, Pyramide; see above.
Rousse 47°51'·55N 04°06'·47W. La Potée 47°51'·78N 04°06'·55W.
Pte du Toulgoët Fl R 2·5s 2m 1M; 47°52'·30N 04°06'·86W.
Le Taro 47°50'·51N 04°04'·83W.
La Voleuse Q (6) + L Fl 15s; 47°48'·76N 04°02'·49W.

ILE AUX MOUTONS and LES POURCEAUX

Île-aux-Moutons ☆ Iso WRG 2s 18m, **W15M**, R/G11M; 035°-W-050°-G-063°-W-081°-R-141°-W-292°-R-035°; W □ twr and dwelling; 47°46'·48N 04°01'·66W. 992271013.
Rouge de Glénan VQ (9) 10s 8m 8M; 47°45'·48N 04°03'·95W.
Grand Pourceaux Q; 47°45'·98N 04°00'·80W.

ÎLES DE GLÉNAN

Penfret ☆ Fl R 5s 36m **21M**; W □ twr, R top; 47°43'·26N 03°57'·18W. Same twr: auxiliary Dir Q 34m 12M; 295°-315°. 992271014.
La Pie Fl (2) 6s 9m 3M; 47°43'·75N 03°59'·76W.
Pte de la Baleine VQ (3) 5s 2M; 47°43'·26N 03°59'·20W.
Les Bluiniers 47°43'·35N 04°03'·81W.
Offlying marks, anticlockwise from the west:
Basse Pérennès Q (9) 15s 8m 5M; 47°41'·06N 04°06'·14W.
Jument de Glénan Q (6) + L Fl 15s 10m 4M; 47°38'·76N 04°01'·41W.
Laoennou 47°39'·65N 03°54'·70W.
Jaune de Glénan Q (3) 10s; 47°42'·56N 03°49'·83W.

PORT-LA-FORÊT

Linuen Q (3) 10s; 47°50'·76N 03°57'·31W.
Laouen Pod 47°51'·23N 03°58'·00W.
Cap Coz mole Fl (2) WRG 6s 5m, W7M, R/G5M; Shore-R-335°-G-340°-W-346°-R-shore; 47°53'·49N 03°58'·28W.
Le Scoré 47°52'·75N 03°57'·56W.
Les Ormeaux 47°53'·27N 03°58'·34W.
Entry channel Fl G 2·5s; 47°53'·39N 03°58'·12W.
Fl R 2·5s; 47°53'·39N 03°58'·22W.
Kerleven mole Fl G 4s 8m 6M; 47°53'·60N 03°58'·37W.

CONCARNEAU

Ldg lts 028·5°: Front, La Croix Q 14m 13M; 006·5°-093°; R&W twr; 47°52'·16N 03°55'·08W. **Rear, Beuzec** ☆ Dir Q 87m **23M**; synch, intens 026·5°-030·5°; spire, 1·34M from front.
QR; 47°51'·40N 03°55'·75W.
Le Cochon Fl (3) WRG 12s 5m W9M, R/G6M; 230°-R-352°-W-048°-G-207°-Obsc'd-230°; G twr; 47°51'·47N 03°55'·55W.
Basse du Chenal Fl R 4s; 47°51'·54N 03°55'·66W.
Men Fall Fl (2) G 6s; 47°51'·76N 03°55'·28W.
Kersos 47°51'·80N 03°54'·93W (Anse de Kersos).
Lanriec QG 13m 8M; 063°-078°; G window on W gable end; 47°52'·01N 03°54'·64W.
La Medée Fl (3) R 12s 9m 4M; 47°52'·07N 03°54'·80W.
Ville-Close Q WR, W9M, R6M; 209°-R-354°-W-007°-R-018°; R turret; 47°52'·27N 03°54'·76W.
No 1 Fl (4) G 15s 4m 5M; G turret; 47°52'·16N 03°54'·72W.
Marina wavescreen Fl (4) R 15s 3m 1M; 47°52'·23N 03°54'·79W.
No 2 Fl R 4s 4m 5M; G turret; 47°52'·31N 03°54'·71W.
Ville-Close (NE end) Fl (2) R 6s; R twr; 47°52'·37N 03°54'·68W.
Ent to FV basin Fl (2) G 6s; G twr; 47°52'·36N 03°54'·63W.
Pouldohan Fl G 4s 6m 8M; 053°-065°; W □ twr, G top; 47°50'·97N 03°53'·69W.
Roché Tudy 47°50'·52N 03°54'·49W.

CONCARNEAU TO ÎLE DE GROIX

PTE DE TRÉVIGNON TO PORT MANEC'H

Les Soldats VQ (9) 10s; 47°47'·86N 03°53'·42W.
Trévignon mole Fl G 4s 5m 6M; 47°47'·69N 03°51'·30W.
Trévignon bkwtr root Fl (2) WRG 6s 11m, W10/7M, R/G7M; 004°-W-051°-G-085°-W-092°-R-127°; 322°-R-351°; W □ twr, G top; 47°47'·59N 03°51'·33W.
Men Du 47°46'·41N 03°50'·50W.
Men an Tréas 47°45'·77N 03°49'·66W.

PORT MANEC'H (Aven and Bélon rivers)

Port Manech Oc (4) WRG 12s 38m, W10M, R/G7M; obscd by Pte de Beg-Morg when brg <299°; 050°-W (unintens)-140°-W-296°-G-303°-W-311°-R (over Les Verrès)-328°-W-050°; W & R twr; 47°47'·99N 03°44'·34W.
Les Verrès 47°46'·65N 03°42'·71W.

BRIGNEAU

Brigneau 47°46'·11N 03°40'·10W.
W mole, Oc (2) WRG 6s 7m, W12M, R/G9M; R col, W top; 280°-G-329°-W-339°-R-034°; 47°46'·86N 03°40'·18W. In line 331° with W □ daymark behind, Hard to see, rear beacon unlit.

MERRIEN

Dir QR 26m 7M; 004°-009°; W □ twr, R top; 47°47'·04N 03°38'·97W.
Ent, W side . E side 47°46'·45N 03°38'·89W.

DOËLAN

Ldg lts 013·8°: Front Oc (3) WG 12s 20m, W13M, G10M; W shore-305°, G305°-314°, W314°-shore; W lt ho, G band and top; 47°46'·32N 03°36'·51W. Rear Oc (3)R 12s 27m 9M; W lt ho, R band & top; 326m from front.

LE POULDU

Ent 47°45'·74N 03°32'·25W.
Grand Cochon 47°43'·03N 03°30'·81W.
Pte de Kerroc'h Oc (2) WRG 6s 22m W11M, R/G8M; 096·5°-R-112°·5-G-132°-R-302°-W-096·5°; W twr, R top; 47°41'·97N 03°27'·66W. 992271009.

ÎLE DE GROIX

Pen Men ☆ Fl (4) 25s 60m **29M**; 309°-275°; W □ twr, B top; 47°38'·84N 03°30'·56W.
Speerbrecker, 47°39'·10N 03°26'·33W.

Port Tudy, N môle ☆ Fl (2) G 6s 12m 7M; W twr, G top; 47°38′·72N 03°26′·73W.
E môle ☆ Fl (2) R 6s 11m 6M; 112°-226°; W twr R top; 47°38′·68N 03°26′·78W.
Basse Melité 47°38′·84N 03°25′·54W.
Pte de la Croix ☆ Oc WR 4s 16m, W12M, R9M; 169°-W-336°-R-345°-W-353°; W pedestal, R lantern; 47°38′·05N 03°25′·02W.
Edouard de Cougy 47°37′·93N 03°23′·90W.
Pointe des Chats ☆ Fl R 5s 16m **19M**; W □ twr and dwelling; 47°37′·24N 03°25′·30W.
Les Chats Q (6) + L Fl 15s; 47°35′·70N 03°23′·57W.

LORIENT AND RIVER ÉTEL

LORIENT, PASSE DE L'OUEST

Passe de l'Ouest ldg lts 057°: both Dir Q 11/22m 13/**18M**. Front, Les Sœurs; intens 042·5°-058·5°, 058·5°-042·5°, 4M range only; R twr, W bands; 47°42′·13N 03°21′·84W. Rear **Port Louis** ☆, 740m from front (see below).
Banc des Truies Q (9) 15s; 47°40′·76N 03°24′·48W.
Loméner, Anse de Stole, Dir ☆ 357·2°: Q WRG 13m, W10M, R/G8M; 349·2°-G-355·2°-W-359·2°-R-005·2°; W twr, R top; 47°42′·30N 03°25′·54W.
A2 Fl R 2·5s; 47°40′·94N 03°24′·98W.
Les Trois Pierres Q RG 11m R/G6M; 060°-G-196°-R-002°; B twr, W bands; 47°41′·53N 03°22′·47W.
A8 Fl R 2·5s; 47°41′·90N 03°22′·52W.

PASSE DU SUD

Bastresses Sud QG; 47°40′·77N 03°22′·09W.
Les Errants Fl (2) R 6s; 47°41′·10N 03°22′·38W.
Bastresses Nord Fl (2) G 6s; 47°41′·11N 03°22′·20W.
Locmalo Fl (3) G 12s; 47°41′·67N 03°22′·13W.

SOUTH OF PORT LOUIS

La Paix ; 47°41′·97N 03°21′·84W.
Île aux Souris ☆ Dir Q WG 6m, W3M, G2M; 041·5°-W-043·5°-G-041·5°; G twr; 47°42′·15N 03°21′·52W.
Fl G 2·5s; 47°42′·13N 03°21′·21W.
Ban-Gâvres FV/yacht hbr, W jetty ☆ Fl (2) G 6s 3M; 47°42′·06N 03°21′·11W. E jetty ☆ Fl (2) R 6s 3M; 47°42′·06N 03°21′·06W.

ENTRANCE CHANNEL

Ldg lts 016·5°, both Dir QG 8/14m 13M; intens 014·5°-017·5°; synch; W twrs, G tops. Front ☆, 47°43′·47N 03°21′·63W (Île St Michel). Rear ☆, 306m from front.
La Citadelle Oc G 4s 6m 6M; 012°-192°; 47°42′·59N 03°21′·94W.
Secondary yacht chan, RGR, 47°42′·49N 03°22′·12W.
La Petite Jument Oc R 4s 5m 6M; 182°-024°; R twr; 47°42′·58N 03°22′·07W.
Le Cochon Fl R 4s 5m 5M; RGR twr; 47°42′·80N 03°22′·00W.
No 1 47°42′·80N 03°21′·84W.

PORT LOUIS (Port de la Pointe)

D 1 47°42′·76N 03°21′·52W.
Jetty ☆ Fl G 2·5s 7m 6M; W twr, G top; 47°42′·71N 03°21′·37W.
Anse du Driasker Stage Head Fl R 2·5s 2M, metal mast.

KERNEVEL

Kéroman ldg lts 350°, both Dir Oc (2) R 6s 25/31m **15M**; synch; intens 349°-351°: **Front** ☆, 47°43′·60N 03°22′·02W, R ho, W bands. **Rear** ☆ R&W topmark on Gy pylon, R top; 91m from front.
Banc du Turc Fl G 2·5s; 47°43′·33N 03°21′·85W.
Kernével marina, entrance: ☆ QR 1M; 47°43′·39N 03°22′·10W.
Ldg lts 217°, both Dir QR 10/18m **15M**; intens 215°-219°; synch: **Front, Kernével** ☆ R&W twr; 47°43′·02N 03°22′·32W. **Rear** ☆ W □ twr, R top; 290m from front.
Q (3) 10s; marks wreck; 47°43′·49N 03°22′·05W.

NORTHERN PART OF LORIENT HARBOUR

Grand Bassin (FV hbr) E side of ent, ☆ Fl RG 4s 7m 6M; 000°-G-235°-R-000°; W twr, G top; 47°43′·63N 03°21′·87W.
Ste Catherine marina ent ☆ QG 5m 3M; 47°43′·52N 03°21′·12W.
N side of marina ent ☆ QR 2m 2M 47°43′·53N 03°21′·10W.
Pengarne Fl G 2·5s 3m 3M; G twr; 47°43′·88N 03°21′·23W.
No 9 Fl (2) G 6s; 47°43′·95N 03°21′·16W.
No 11 Fl (3) G 12s; 47°44′·04N 03°21′·01W.
Pen-Mané marina, bkwtr elbow ☆ Fl (2) G 6s 4M; 47°44′·11N 03°20′·86W.
Blavet River, No 1 Fl (2+1)G 10s; 47°44′·20N 03°20′·78W.
No 2 Fl R 2·5s; 47°44′·26N 03°20′·74W.
Pointe de l'Espérance, Dir ☆ 037°, Q WRG 8m W10M, R/G8M; 034·2°-G-036·7°-W-037·2°-R-047·2°; W twr, G top; 47°44′·51N 03°20′·66W.
Ro-Ro jetty ☆ QR 7m 2M; 47°44′·42N 03°20′·96W.
No 8 Fl R 2·5s; 47°44′·56N 03°20′·98W, ent to Lorient marina.

RIVIÈRE D'ÉTEL

Roheu 47°38′·54N 03°14′·70W.
Épi de Plouhinec ☆ Fl R 2·5s 7m 2M; 47°38′·59N 03°12′·86W.
W side ent ☆ Oc (2) WRG 6s 13m W9M, R/G6M; 022°-W-064°-R-123°-W-330°-G-022°; R twr; 47°38′·69N 03°12′·83W.
Conspic R/W radio mast (CROSS Étel) 47°39′·73N 03°12′·11W.
Les Pierres Noires 47°35′·53N 03°13′·29W.

BELLE ÎLE AND QUIBERON BAY (W OF 2° 50′W)

PLATEAU DES BIRVIDEAUX (6M NNW of Belle Île)

Fl (2) 6s 24m 10M; BRB twr; 47°29′·15N 03°17′·46W. 992271028.

BELLE ÎLE

Pte des Poulains ☆ Fl 5s 34m **23M**; 023°-291°; W □ twr and dwelling; 47°23′·31N 03°15′·11W.
Les Poulains 47°23′·44N 03°16′·68W.
N Poulains 47°23′·68N 03°14′·88W.
Sauzon, NW jetty ☆ Fl G 4s 8m 8M; 47°22′·49N 03°13′·04W.
SE jetty ☆ Fl R 4s 8m 8M; 315°-272°; W twr, R top; 47°22′·45N 03°13′·00W. Inner hbr, W jetty ☆, QG 9m 5M; 194°-045°; W twr, G top; 47°22′·37N 03°13′·13W.
Le Palais, N jetty ☆ QG 11m 7M; obsc 298°-170° by Ptes de Kerdonis and Taillefer; W twr, G top; 47°20′·84N 03°09′·04W.
No 1 Fl (2) G 6s; 47°20′·82N 03°08′·96W;
No 2 Fl R 4s; 47°20′·71N 03°08′·89W;
No 4 Fl (2) R 6s; 47°20′·78N 03°09′·01W.
S jetty ☆ QR 11m 7M; obsc'd 298°-170° (see N jetty); W twr, R lantern; 47°20′·82N 03°09′·07W.
Pointe de Kerdonis ☆ Fl (3) R 15s 49m **15M**; obsc'd 225°-320° (095°) by vegetation, 004°-155° (151°) by land. W □ twr, R top and W dwelling; 47°18′·60N 03°03′·58W.
Les Galères 47°18′·77N 03°02′·76W.
SW coast of Belle Île: La Truie 47°17′·11N 03°11′·79W.
Goulphar ☆ Fl (2) 10s 87m **27M**; Gy twr; 47°18′·65N 03°13′·63W.

PORT MARIA (Quiberon ferry port)

Light ho ☆ Q WRG 28m W14M, R/ G10M; 246°-W-252°-W-297°-G-340°-W-017°-R-051°-W-081°-G-098°-W-143°; W twr, G lantern; 47°28′·78N 03°07′·45W.
Le Pouilloux 47°27′·88N 03°08′·01W.
Ldg lts 006·5°, both Dir QG 5/13m **16/17M**; intens 005°-008°; W twrs, B bands: **Front**, 47°28′·63N 03°07′·18W. 992271029. **Rear**, 230m north; 992271030.
Les Deux Frères Fl R 2·5s; 175°-047°;47°28′·34N 03°07′·29W.
S bkwtr ☆ Oc (2) R 6s 9m 7M; W twr, R top; 47°28′·54N 03°07′·31W.

CHAUSSÉE and PASSAGE DE LA TEIGNOUSE

Le Four 47°27′·78N 03°06′·54W.
Les Trois Pierres 47°27′·46N 03°05′·24W.
Roc er Vy 47°27′·70N 03°04′·40W; Chenal en Toull Bras.
Roc er Vy 47°27′·86N 03°04′·35W.
Basse Cariou 47°26′·94N 03°06′·38W.
Basse du Chenal 47°26′·66N 03°05′·77W.
Goué Vaz S Q (6) + L Fl 15s; 47°25′·76N 03°04′·93W.
La Teignouse ☆ Fl WR 4s 20m **W15M**, R11M; 033°-W-039°-R-033°; W ○ twr, R top; 47°27′·44N 03°02′·75W. 992271007.
Basse du Milieu Fl (2) G 6s 9m 2M; 47°25′·91N 03°04′·12W.

Goué Vaz E Fl (3) R 12s; 47°26'·23N 03°04'·28W.
NE Teignouse Fl (3) G 12s; 47°26'·55N 03°01'·87W.
Basse Nouvelle Fl R 2·5s; 47°26'·98N 03°01'·99W.

CHAUSSÉE and PASSAGE DU BÉNIGUET

Les Esclassiers 47°25'·68N 03°03'·05W.
Le Grand Coin 47°24'·45N 03°00'·26W.
Bonen Bras 47°24'·26N 02°59'·88W.

ÎLE DE HOUAT

Le Rouleau 47°23'·67N 03°00'·31W.
Port St-Gildas N môle ☆ Fl (2) WG 6s 8m W9M, G6M; 168°-W-198°-G-210°-W-240°-G-168°; W twr, G top; 47°23'·57N 02°57'·34W.
Mussel beds, 1-1.5M NNE of above ☆ and in its G sector (198°-210°) marked by 2 at S end, and VQ (3) 5s & VQ at N end.
Bcns SE and S of Houat: Men Groise 47°22'·77N 02°55'·00W.
Er Spernec Bras 47°22'·09N 02°55'·23W.
Men er Houteliguet 47°22'·54N 02°56'·38W.

ÎLE DE HOËDIC

Les Sœurs 47°21'·14N 02°54'·74W.
La Chèvre 47°21'·08N 02°52'·55W.
Port de l'Argol bkwtr ☆ Fl WG 4s 10m W9M, G6M; 143°-W-163°-G-183°-W-194°-G-143°; W twr, G top; 47°20'·66N 02°52'·48W.
Er Gurranic'h 47°20'·51N 02°50'·44W.
Cohfournik 47°19'·49N 02°49'·69W.
Grands Cardinaux ☆ Fl (4) 15s 28m 13M; R and W twr; 47°19'·27N 02°50'·10W. 992271025; 2·1M SE of Argol.
Le Chariot 47°18'·76N 02°52'·95W.
Er Palaire 47°20'·16N 02°55'·01W.

PORT HALIGUEN

Banc de Quiberon S Q (6) + L Fl 15s; 47°28'·04N 03°02'·34W.
Banc de Quiberon N 47°29'·65N 03°02'·58W.
E bkwtr hd ☆ Oc (2) WR 6s 10m, W11M, R8M; 233°-W-240·5°-R-299°-W-306°-R-233°; W twr, R top; 47°29'·36N 03°05'·94W.
Port Haliguen 47°29'·38N 03°05'·55W; marks 1·7m patch.
NW bkwtr hd ☆ Fl G 2·5s 9m 6M; 47°29'·34N 03°06'·02W.
Bugalet wreck 47°31'·19N 03°05'·45W.
Men er Roué 47°32'·25N 03°06'·06W.

LA TRINITÉ-SUR-MER

Rivière de Crac'h ☆ Q WRG 11m W10M, R/G7M; 321°-G-345°-W-013·5°-R-080°; W twr, G top; 47°34'·09N 03°00'·37W.
Buissons de Méaban 47°31'·66N 02°58'·49W.
Le Petit Buisson 47°32'·14N 02°58'·57W.
Roche Révision 47°32'·63N 02°59'·36W.
Petit Trého Fl R 2·5s; 47°33'·47N 03°00'·71W.
R. de Crac'h Dir ☆ 347°: Oc WRG 4s 9m W13M, R/G 11M; 345°-G-346°-W-348°-R-349°; W twr; 47°35'·03N 03°00'·98W.
S pier ☆ Q WR 6s 6m, W9M, R6M; 090°-R-293·5°-W-300·5°-R-329°; W twr, R top; 47°35'·09N 03°01'·50W.
Marina wavebreak/pier ☆ Iso R 4s 8m 5M; 47°35'·28N 03°01'·46W.

GOLFE DU MORBIHAN

Méaban 47°30'·77N 02°56'·23W.
Outer ldg marks 001°: Front, Petit Vezid ; W obelisk; 47°34'·17N 02°55'·23W. Rear, Baden ch spire (83m) 47°37'·20N 02°55'·14W.
Pointe de Port-Navalo ☆ Oc (3) WRG 12s 32m, **W15M**, R/G11M; 155°-W-220°; 317°-G-359°-W-015°-R-105°; W twr and dwelling; 47°32'·87N 02°55'·11W.
Ldg marks 359°: Front, Grégan Q (6) + L Fl 15s 3m 8M; 47°33'·91N 02°55'·05W. Rear, Baden ch spire (5 lines above).
Auray river: Catis 47°36'·14N 02°57'·23W.
César 47°38'·36N 02°58'·22W.
No 13 47°39'·48N 02°58'·64W (last bcn before 14m bridge).
Morbihan: Grand Mouton QG; 47°33'·71N 02°54'·85W.
Gavrinis 47°34'·21N 02°54'·05W.
Jument 47°34'·29N 02°53'·43W.
Creizic S 47°34'·63N 02°52'·84W.
Creizic N 47°34'·93N 02°52'·20W.
Les Rechauds, two 47°36'·18N 02°51'·30W.
Truie d'Arradon 47°36'·58N 02°50'·27W.
Logoden 47°36'·70N 02°49'·91W.
Drenec 47°36'·84N 02°48'·39W.
Bœdic 47°36'·85N 02°47'·59W.
Roguédas Fl G 2·5s 4m 4M; G twr; 47°37'·12N 02°47'·28W.

CROUESTY

Ldg lts 058°, both Dir Q 10/27m 8M; intens 056·5°-059·5°: Front ☆ R panel, W stripe; 47°32'·53N 02°53'·95W. Rear ☆, W twr; 315m from front.
No 1 QG; 47°32'·26N 02°54'·76W.
No 2 47°32'·26N 02°54'·76W.
N jetty ☆ Fl R 4s 9m 7M; R&W □ twr; 47°32'·47N 02°54'·14W.
S jetty ☆ Fl G 4s 9m 7M; G&W □ twr; 47°32'·45N 02°54'·10W.

PLATEAU DU GRAND MONT

Chimère 47°28'·83N 02°53'·98W.
L'Epieu 47°29'·51N 02°52'·91W.
St Gildas 47°29'·78N 02°52'·87W.
Grand Mont 47°28'·98N 02°51'·12W.

QUIBERON BAY (E OF 2° 50'W) TO PTE DU CROISIC

PLATEAU DE SAINT JACQUES

Le Bauzec 47°28'·90N 02°49'·40W.
St Jacques 47°28'·17N 02°47'·52W.
Port St Jacques, jetty ☆ Oc (2) R 6s 5m 6M; W 8-sided twr, R top; 47°29'·24N 02°47'·41W.

PLATEAU DE LA RECHERCHE

Recherche Q (9) 15s; 47°25'·56N 02°50'·39W.
Locmariaquer 47°25'·82N 02°47'·36W.

PÉNERF

Outer Rade Fl (5) Y 20s; 47°27'·58N 02°39'·56W.
Penvins 47°28'·93N 02°40'·09W.
Borenis 47°29'·21N 02°38'·35W.
Tour des Anglais W bcn; 47°30'·21N 02°37'·94W; appr brg 031·4°.
Pignon Fl (3) WR 12s 6m W9M, R6M; 028·5°-R-167°-W-175°-R-349·5°-W-028·5°; R twr; 47°30'·03N 02°38'·89W.

VILAINE RIVER

Pte de Penlan ☆ Oc (2) WRG 6s 26m, **W15M**, R/G11M; 292·5°-R-025°-G-052°-W-060°-R-138°-G-180°; W sector defines Passe de la Grande Accroche; W twr, R bands; 47°30'·97N 02°30'·11W.
Bertrand Iso WG 4s 6m, W9M, G6M; 040°-W-054°-G-227°-W-234°-G-040°; G twr; 47°31'·06N 02°30'·72W.
Basse de Kervoyal Dir Q WR W8M, R5M; 269°-W-271°-R-269°; W sector leads to/from Nos 1 & 2 buoys; 47°30'·37N 02°32'·62W.
No 1 Fl G 2·5s; 47°30'·32N 02°28'·73W.
No 2 Fl R 2·5s; 47°30'·41N 02°28'·71W.
Pointe du Scal ☆ QG 8m 4M; 47°29'·67N 02°26'·87W.

ÎLE DUMET

Fort ☆ Fl (3) WRG 15s 14m, W7M, R/G4M; 090°-G-272°-W-285°-R-335°-W-090°; W col, G top; 47°24'·69N 02°37'·21W.
Basse-Est Île Dumet Q (3) 10s; 47°25'·20N 02°34'·93W.
Île Dumet Q; 47°25'·90N 02°36'·05W.

MESQUER

Laronesse 47°25'·96N 02°29'·50W.
Basse Normande 47°25'·47N 02°29'·80W.
Jetty ☆ Oc WRG 4s 7m W10M, R/G7M; 067°-W-072°-R-102°-W-118°-R-293°-W-325°-G-067°; W col & bldg; 47°25'·31N 02°28'·05W.

PIRIAC-SUR-MER

Grand Norven Q; 47°23'·55N 02°32'·89W.
Inner mole ☆ Oc (2) WRG 6s 8m, W10M, R/G7M; 066°-R-148°-G-194°-W-201°-R-221°; W col; 47°22'·93N 02°32'·71W. *Siren 120s (occas), 35m SW.* E bkwtr ☆ Fl R 4s 4m 5M; W pylon, R top; 47°23'·00N 02°32'·67W.
Les Bayonnelles Q (9) 15s;47°22'·56N 02°35'·23W.

LA TURBALLE
Ldg lts 006·5°, both Dir Iso R 4s 11/19m 3M; intens 004°-009°: Front, 47°20′·70N 02°30′·87W. Rear, 275m N of the front lt.
Ouest Jetée de Garlahy ☆ Fl (4) WR 12s 13m, W10M, R7M; 060°-R-315°-W-060°; W pylon, R top; 47°20′·70N 02°30′·93W.
Digue Tourlandroux ☆ Fl G 4s 4m 2M; G post, E side of access chan; 47°20′·75N 02°30′·88W.

LE CROISIC
Basse Hergo Fl G 2·5s 5m 3M; 47°18′·62N 02°31′·69W.
Jetée du Tréhic ☆ Iso WG 4s 12m W14M, G11M; 042°-G-093°-W-137°-G-345°; Gy twr, G top; 47°18′·49N 02°31′·42W. F Bu fog det lt, 100m SE.
Outer ldg lts 155·5°, both Dir Q 10/14m 13M; intens 154°-158°: Front ☆ 47°17′·96N 02°30′·99W . Rear ☆, 116m from front.
Middle ldg lts 174°, both QG 5/8m 11M; 170·5°-177·5°: Front 47°18′·06N 02°31′·07W. Rear, 48m from front.
Le Grand Mabon Fl (3) R 12s 6m 2M; 47°18′·05N 02°31′·03W.
Inner ldg lts 134·7°, both QR 6/10m 8M; intens 132·5°-143·5°; synch.
Basse Castouillet Q (9) 15s; 47°18′·12N 02°34′·37W.
Basse Lovre 47°15′·87N 02°29′·58W, Chenal du Nord.

PLATEAU DU FOUR/BANC DE GUÉRANDE
Bonen du Four Q; 47°18′·53N 02°39′·29W.
Le Four ☆ Fl 5s 23m **18M**; W twr, B diagonal stripes; 47°17′·87N 02°38′·05W. 992271016.
Ouest Basse Capella Q (9) 15s; *Whis;* 47°15′·66N 02°42′·78W.
Goué-Vas-du-Four Q (6) + L Fl 15s; 47°14′·91N 02°38′·20W.
Sud Banc Guérande VQ (6) + L Fl 10s; 47°08′·80N 02°42′·81W.
Restricted Area centred on 47°14′·37N 2°46′·65W, limits marked by 4 Fl Y 4s, enclosing 2 Fl (5) Y 20s ODAS bys.

POINTE DU CROISIC TO POINTE DE ST GILDAS

PLATEAU DE LA BANCHE
NW Banche Q 8m 4M; 47°12′·86N 02°31′·02W.
W Banche VQ (9) 10s; 47°11′·64N 02°32′·41W.
La Banche ☆ Fl (2) WR 6s 22m **W15M**, R11M; 266°-R-280°-W-266°; B twr, W bands; 47°10′·62N 02°28′·08W. 992271020.
SE Banche 47°10′·40N 02°26′·10W.

PLATEAU DE LA LAMBARDE
NW Lambarde 47°10′·84N 02°22′·93W.
SE Lambarde Q (6) + L Fl 15s; 47°10′·04N 02°20·80W.

BAIE DU POULIGUEN (or Baie de la Baule)
Penchateau Fl R 2·5s; 47°15′·24N 02°24′·35W.
Les Guérandaises Fl G 2·5s; 47°15′·03N 02°24′·29W.
47°15′·24N 02°23′·50W.
Les Evens 47°14′·32N 02°22′·55W.
Les Troves 47°14′·23N 02°22′·41W.
NNW Pierre Percée 47°13′·63N 02°20′·63W.
La Vieille 47°14′·03N 02°19′·51W.
Sud de la Vieille 47°13′·75N 02°19′·54W.
Le Caillou 47°13′·65N 02°19′·18W.
Le Petit Charpentier 47°13′·34N 02°18′·95W.
Le Grand Charpentier ☆ Q WRG 22m, W14M, R/G10M; 020°-G-054°-W-062°-R-092°-W-111°-R-310°-W-020°; Gy lt ho, G lantern; 47°12′·83N 02°19′·13W. 992271026.

LE POULIGUEN
Basse Martineau 47°15′·54N 02°24′·34W.
La Vieille ,Fl (2) G 6s 2M, 47°15′· 83N 02°24′·43W.
Petits Impairs Fl (3) G 12s 6m 2M; 47°15′·99N 02°24′·61W.
SW jetty ☆ QR 13m 9M; 171°-081°; W col; 47°16′·39N 02°25′·39W.

PORNICHET (La Baule)
S bkwtr ☆ Iso WRG 4s 11m, W10M, R/G7M; 303°-G-081°-W-084°-R-180°; W twr, G top; 47°15′·49N 02°21′·14W.
Ent,W side ☆ QG 3m 1M; B perch, G top; 47°15′·51N 02°21′·12W.
E side ☆ QR 4m 1M; B perch, R top; 47°15′·50N 02°21′·10W.

ST NAZAIRE APPROACH (Chenal du Sud)
S-N1 L Fl 10s 8m 5M; ***Racon Z (3cm), 3–8M***; 47°00′·07N 02°39′·84W.
S-N2 Iso 4s 8m 5M; 47°02′·08N 02°33′·47W.
Les Chevaux Fl G 2·5s; 47°03′·53N 02°26′·37W.
Thérèsia Fl R 2·5s; 47°04′·84N 02°27′·27W.
La Couronnée Fl (2) G 6s; ***Racon T, 3–5M***; 47°07′·60N 02°20′·05W.
Lancastria Fl (2) R 6s;47°08′·88N 02°20′·37W.

PASSE DES CHARPENTIERS
Portcé ☆ ldg lts 025·5°, both Dir Q 6/36m **22/24M**: **Front**, intens 024·7°-026·2°; synch; W col; 47°14′·57N 02°15′·44W. 992271021.
Rear ☆ (H24); intens 024°-027°; W twr; 0·75M from front. 992271023.
Wreck (Y) Fl (3) R 12s; 47°09′·87N 02°19′·46W.
No 1 VQ G; 47°09′·94N 02°18′·40W.
No 2 VQ R; 47°10′·06N 02°18′·72W.
No 6 Fl (3) R 12s; 47°12′·05N 02°17′·31W.
No 5 Fl (4) G 15s; 47°12′·65N 02°16′·57W.
No 8 Fl (4) R 15s; 47°12′·75N 02°16′·86W.
No 7 VQ G; 47°13′·30N 02°16′·11W.
No 10 VQ R; 47°13′·62N 02°16′·16W. (Buoys 9 - 18 not listed).
Pointe d'Aiguillon ☆ Oc (3) WR 12s 27m, W13M, R10M; 207°-R-233°-W-293°; 297°-W-300°-R-327°-W-023°; 027°-R-089°; W lt ho, conspic; 47°14′·54N 02°15′·79W. 992271018.
Ville-ès-Martin jetty ☆ Fl (2) 6s 10m 10M; W twr, R top; 47°15′·33N 02°13′·66W.
Morées Fl (3) WR 12s 12m, W6M, R4M; W058°-224°, R300°-058°; G twr; 47°15′·00N 02°13′·02W.

SAINT NAZAIRE
W jetty ☆ Oc (4) R 12s 11m 8M; W twr, R top; 47°15′·97N 02°12′·25W.
E jetty ☆ Oc (4) G 12s 11m 11M; W twr, G top; 47°15′·99N 02°12′·14W. (Ent lock for big ships into Bassin St Nazaire)
No 20 QR; 47°16′·19N 02°11′·37W.
Sud Basse Nazaire Q (6) + L Fl 15s; 47°16′·21N 02°11′·51W.
Basse Nazaire Fl G 2·5s; 47°16′·24N 02°11′·63W.
SE Old mole Fl R 2·5s; 47°16′·24N 02°11′·73W.
Old Môle ☆ Q (3) 10s 18m 11M; 153·5°-063·5°; W twr, R top; weather signals; 47°16′·27N 02°11′·82W.
Fl (2) R 6s 5m 1M; R dolphin ; 47°16′·37N 02°11′·80W.
Entrée Est ☆ Fl (3) R 12s 9m 9M; R pylon; 47°16′·47N 02°11′·85W.
Ldg lts 280° (into E lock) 2 VQ Vi; front 47°16′·49N 02°11′·92W.

EAST SIDE OF RIVER, SOUTH TO PTE DE ST GILDAS
Le Pointeau, Digue S ☆ Fl WG 4s 4m, W10M, G7M; 050°-G-074°-W-149°-G-345°-W-050°; G&W ○ hut; 47°14′·02N 02°10′·96W.
Port de Comberge La Truie 47°12′·06N 00°13′·36W.
S jetty ☆ Oc WG 4s 7m W9M, G6M; 123°-W-140°-G-123°; W twr, G top; 47°10′·70N 02°09′·90W.
Port de la Gravette La Gravette 47°09′·81N 02°13′·06W.
Bkwtr hd ☆ Fl (3) WG 12s 7m, W8M, G5M; 183°-W-188°-G-124°-W-138°-G-183°; W structure, G top; 47°09′·64N 02°12′·70W.
Anse du Boucau bkwtr ☆ Fl (2) G 6s 3M; 47°08′·41N 02°14′·80W.
Pte de Saint Gildas ☆ Q WRG 20m, W14M, R/G10M; 264°-R-308°-G-078°-W-088°-R-174°-W-180°-G-264°; col on W house, G top; 47°08′·02N 02°14′·74W. 992271017.
Nord Couronnée Q; 47°07′·34N 02°17′·78W.

RIVER LOIRE TO NANTES
Well buoyed/lit to Île de Bois, thence G lts, S side; R lts N side.
No 21 VQ G; 47°16′·96N 02°10′·25W.
Suspension bridge, mid-span ☆ Iso 4s 55m, vis up/down stream; 47°17′·10N 02°10′·24W; between 2 conspic R/W twrs.
MA Fl (2) G 6s; 47°17′·50N 02°09′·22W.
MB Fl (3) G 12s; 47°17′·95N 02°07′·53W.
Fernais-25 Fl (4) G 15s; 47°18′·10N 02°06′·60W.
Paimboeuf, môle root ☆ Oc (3) WG 12s 9m, W10M, G7M; Shore-G-123°-W-shore; W twr, G top; 47°17′·42N 02°01′·95W.
Île de Bois (upstream) Fl (2) G 6s; 47°12′·79N 01°48′·27W.
Ldg lts 064° Rear Dir VQ R; 47°12′·00N 01°34′·35W, Y-junction with Bras de la Madeleine.

9.21.5 PASSAGE INFORMATION

More passage information is threaded between ports. **Bibliography:** *Atlantic France* (Imray/RCC/Parkinson); NP 22 *Bay of Biscay Pilot*.

SOUTH BRITTANY

▶*Tidal streams are weak offshore, but can be strong in estuaries, channels and around headlands, especially in the north of the Area. The Admiralty tidal stream atlas for W France uses data from actual observations. The French equivalent gives much more computer-based data.*◀

Mist and haze are quite common in the summer, fog less so. Winds are predominantly from SW to NW, often light and variable in summer, but in early and late season N or NE winds are common.

Summer gales are rare and usually related to passing fronts; the sea is often calm or slight, but swell, usually from W or NW, can severely affect exposed anchorages.

In summer the sea/land breeze cycle, known locally as the *vent solaire*, can disrupt moorings and anchorages open to the NE: After a quiet forenoon, a W'ly sea breeze sets in about midday, blowing onshore. It slowly veers to the NW, almost parallel to the coast, reaching Force 4 by late afternoon; it then veers further to the N, expiring at dusk. Around midnight a land breeze may pipe up from the NE and freshen sufficiently to kick up rough seas. By morning the wind has abated.

9.21.6 SPECIAL NOTES FOR FRANCE: See Area 17.

HARBOUR 11·8M EAST OF POINTE DE PENMARC'H

LESCONIL, Finistere, **47°47'·70N 04°12'·64W**. AC 2820, 3640; SHOM 7146, 6646; Navi 543. Tides, see Bénodet; ML 3m. Former fishing port 7·8M SW of Loctudy, increasingly popular with leisure craft. Well sheltered in winds W-N-E, appr is difficult in strong S'lys and not advised. Appr from Karek Greis ECM buoy, on ldg line 325°, church spire just open W of Men ar Groas lt ho, W twr/G top; at night in W sector 313°-333°. Bkwtr lts are QG and Oc R 4s.

Yachts are welcomed Apr/May-Sept only, with 22 Ⓥ on seasonal walk ashore pontoon €3·10; the old fish quay €2·00, (max LOA 15m/draught 2·5m) or fore/aft on 6 x 's €2·00 (in 1·5-3·0m) multihulls x 1·5. Call ahead, HM VHF Ch 09, ☎06·72·04·55·80/ 02·98·82·20·22 (0800-1000; 1700-2000) www.plobannalec-lesconil.com port@plobannalec-lesconil.fr Facilities: © ✉ wi-fi, limited or supermarket (2km) inc. Buses to Quimper (1hr) for ✈.

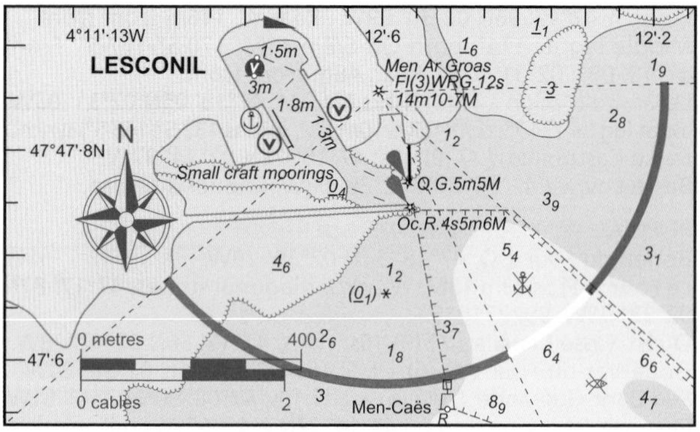

9.21.7 LOCTUDY

Finistere **47°50'·34N 04°10'·55W**

CHARTS AC 2820, 3641; SHOM 7146, 6649; Navi 543; Imray C37, 38

TIDES +0505 Dover (UT); ML 3·0; Duration 0615. See Bénodet.

SHELTER Excellent in marina and hbr, except in strong ESE'lies. Little space to ⚓ due many s/moorings in the river.

NAVIGATION WPT 47°50'·21N 04°09'·06W, 270°/0·8M to abeam the SHM bcn Fl (4) G 15s; thence alter stbd 305° to marina. Stay on the N side of buoyed chan (2 SHM lt buoys). Karek Croisic PHM lt buoy marks a 1·1m rock. Beware shoals and drying patches from W to ENE of Men Audierne SHM unlit spar buoy. From S and W, appr via Bilien ECM buoy to WPT. Sp ebb runs at 3½kn.

Yachts must enter/leave hbr under power. Keep clear of FVs, esp 1630-1830LT daily when yachts should NOT enter/exit hbr.

Pont l'Abbé (3M upriver; 2m) is accessible to shoal draft boats on the flood; chan marked by perches.

LIGHTS AND MARKS Perdrix twr, N of appr chan, B/W chequers.

COMMUNICATIONS CROSS 02·97·55·35·35; 02·98·87·41·12; 08·36·68·08·29; Auto 08·92·68·08·29; 02·98·58·28·80; Ⓗ (6km) 02·98·82·40·40; Dr 02·98·87·41·80; Port VHF Ch 12; Aff Mar 02·98·87·41·79; Marina Ch 09 (Office hrs).

FACILITIES **Marina** ☎02·98·87·51·36. www.loctudy.frport.plaisance .loctudy@wanadoo.fr 592 + 65 Ⓥ pontoon A, >13m LOA inside wavebreak PL, €2·52; 50 s €1·90. (9t). **Town** ½ mile, free bikes at marina. (1mile) Ⓑ.

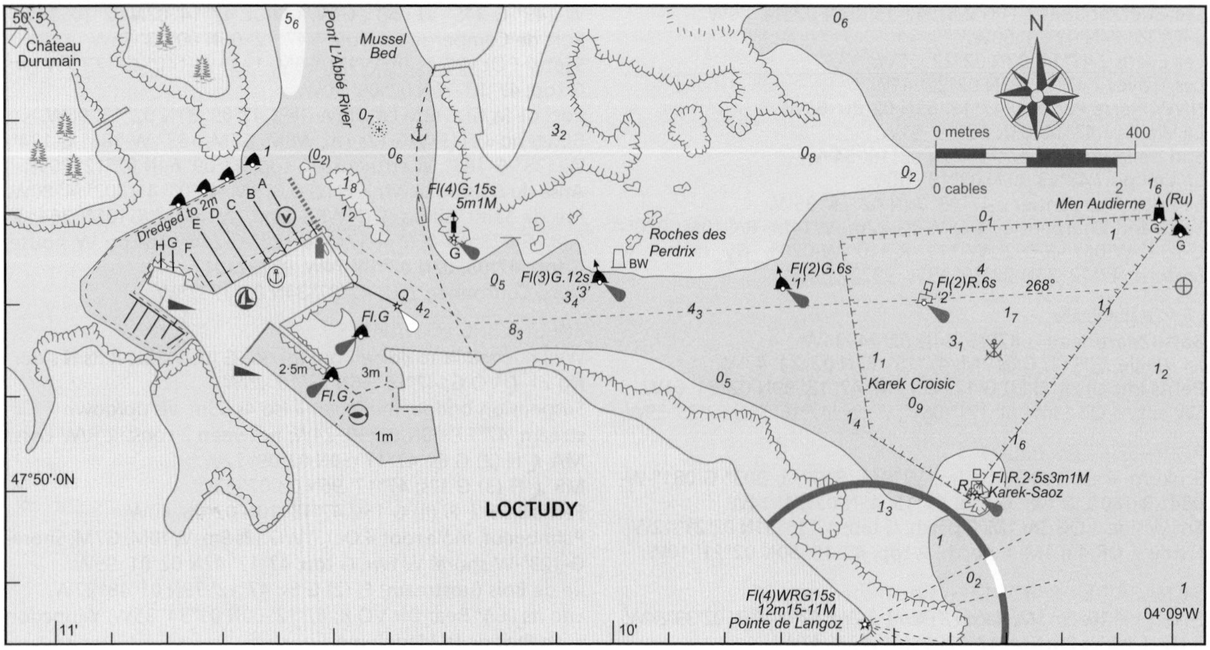

9.21.8 BÉNODET

Finistere **47°51'·56N 04°06'·42W**

CHARTS AC 2820, 3641; SHOM 6649, 6679; Navi 543; Imray C37

TIDES +0450 Dover; ML 3·1; Duration 0610

Standard Port BREST (⟵)

Times				**Height (metres)**			
High Water		Low Water		MHWS	MHWN	MLWN	MLWS
0000	0600	0000	0600	6·9	5·4	2·6	1·0
1200	1800	1200	1800				
Differences BÉNODET							
–0010	–0025	–0030	–0020	–1·6	–1·3	–0·5	0·0
PORT DU CORNIGUEL							
+0015	+0010	–0015	–0010	–2·0	–1·6	–1·0	–0·7
LOCTUDY							
–0010	–0030	–0035	–0020	–2·0	–1·6	–0·8	–0·3

SHELTER Good in Sainte-Marine (W bank) and Penfoul (E bank) marinas; see Facilities for note about strong tidal streams. ⚓ in Anse du Trez in offshore winds or N of Cornouaille bridge. Between these two points ⚓ in the fairway is prohib.

NAVIGATION WPT 47°51′·25N 04°06′·30W, 345·5°/1·1M to front ldg lt. The centre of the bay is clear for small craft, but beware Roches de Mousterlin at the SE end of the bay (La Voleuse SCM lt buoy) and various rks off Loctudy to the SW.

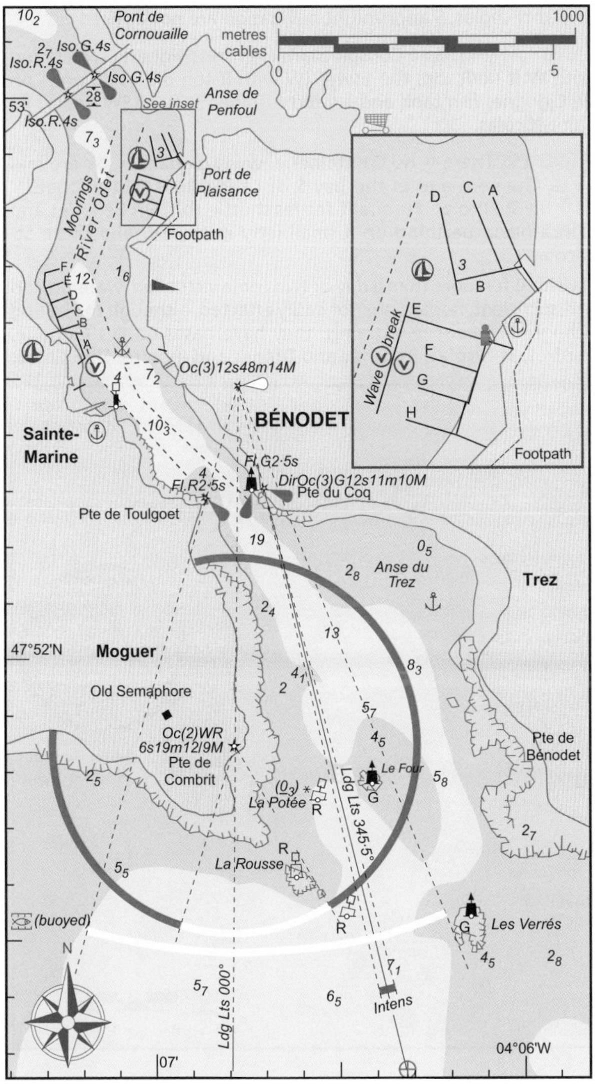

The 000° ldg line has no special merit and must be vacated early to avoid grounding on Pte de Combrit. Beware drying ledges around Les Verrès, La Rousse and Le Four unlit bcn twrs. Speed limit 3kn in hbr.

LIGHTS AND MARKS 345·5° ldg lts, synch/daymarks: Front, W ○ tr, G vert stripe, G top (elusive until close); rear, conspic W tr, G top.

COMMUNICATIONS CROSS 02·97·55·35·35; LB 02·98·57·02·00; 02·98·94·03·43; ⊖ 02·98·55·04·19 (Quimper); Brit Consul 01·44·51·31·00; Dr 02·98·57·22·21; Aff Mar 02·98·58·13·13; Marinas Ch 09 (0800-2000LT in season).

FACILITIES Both marinas accessible H24 at any tide, but it is best to arr/dep near slack water to avoid the strong stream, esp 4kn ebb, through the pontoons with risk of damage. At Ste-Marine the hammerheads are like trampolines at their outer ends, do not jump ashore. At Penfoul berths on both inside and outside of the wavebreak are best avoided except by larger vessels.

SAINTE-MARINE: **Marina** ☎02·98·56·38·72. port.plaisance@combrit-saintemarine.fr www.combrit-saintemarine.fr 670+100Ⓥ €2·64; or €1·87 for €2·00. **Town** ✕ Ⓔ ✉ Ⓑ. Pedestrian ferry to Bénodet, Apr-Sept, (note: stops for lunch!).

BÉNODET: **Penfoul Marina** ☎02·98·57·05·78. www.benodet.fr 510+40Ⓥ €2·70(multihulls x 1·5); also 175 buoys +15 €1·77. (0600-2300 cr/card) ✕ free wi-fi Ⓔ (10t).

Town All facilities, ✉ Ⓑ. Bus to Quimper for ⇄ ✈.

Above the Cornouaille Bridge (28m) the charming R Odet is navigable on the tide for some 7M. Beware vedettes. There are pleasant ⚓s at Anse de Combrit, Anse de Kérautren, Porz Keraign, Porz Meilou, Anse de Toulven (a hidden creek) and SW of Lanroz. Beware marine farms. SHOM 6679 is advised.

N of Lanroz the river shoals progressively to 0·5m in places and is less interesting. Quimper is the limit of navigation for Bridge (5·8m clearance) 0·5M below the city.

9.21.9 PORT-LA-FORÊT

Finistere **47°53'·49N 03°58'·24W**

CHARTS AC 2820, 3641; SHOM 7146, 6650; Navi 543, 544; Imray C38

TIDES +0450 Dover; ML 2·9; Duration 0615
Use Differences CONCARNEAU.

SHELTER Very good in marina (2m). Restricted ⚓ inside Cap Coz; or to seaward on the W side of the Bay N'ward from Beg-Meil.

NAVIGATION WPT 47°52′·53N 03°57′·85W, 343°/1·0M to Cap Coz lt. Beware: Basse Rouge 0·8m, 6·5ca S of Cap Coz; Le Scoré (unlit SCM perch) and buoyed oyster farms in apprs. At sp a shoal patch 0·8m just S of the ent denies access around LW; but there are 12 W waiting buoys close SSW of ent. Shoaling reported in the inner chan, dredged 1·2m to marina and flanked by local moorings along W side.

LIGHTS AND MARKS Cap Coz, Dir lt, leads 343° into chan marked with buoys and bns; the first pair of chan buoys are lit, Fl R 2·5s and Fl G 2·5s. The only conspic landmarks are Beg-Meil sig stn, 2·2M S of Cap Coz; the bldgs of Concarneau to the E and a forest of masts at PLF marina.

COMMUNICATIONS CROSS-Etel/LB 02·97·55·35·35; (Beg Meil); Auto 08·92·68·08·29; Police 02·98·50·15·00 (Concarneau); ⊖ and H see Concarneau; British Consul 01·44·51·31·00; HM VHF Ch 09; Aff Mar 02·98·60·51·42.

FACILITIES **Marina** ☎02·98·56·98·45. capitainerie@port-la-foret.fr www.port-la-foret.fr. 1069 inc Ⓥ €3·23 (multihulls x 1·5). Ⓥ pontoon opp inner end E bkwtr on N side of largest boat hoist basin. 240m pontoon berthing for larger vessels, dredged 5m, lies along the inner W side of ent. (H24/cr/card) ✕ (delivers ☎02·98·56·97·44) defib Ⓒ (70t,25t) (3t)
YC ANPLF ☎02·98·56·84·13.

Town ✕ ✉ Ⓑ. ⇄ ✈ Quimper. **Ferry** Roscoff.

See chartlet overleaf

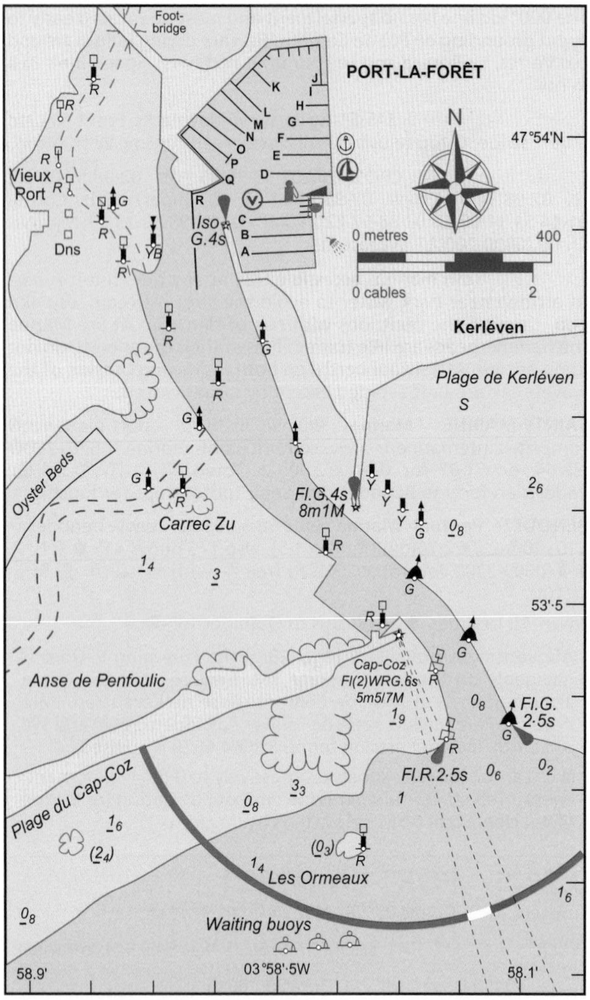
PORT-LA-FORÊT
Foot-bridge
Vieux Port
Dns
Iso G.4s
0 metres 400
0 cables 2
47°54'N
Kerléven
Plage de Kerléven
Oyster Beds
Carrec Zu
Fl.G.4s 8m1M
53'·5
Anse de Penfoulic
Cap-Coz Fl(2)WRG.6s 5m5/7M
Fl.G. 2·5s
Fl.R.2·5s
Plage du Cap-Coz
Les Ormeaux
Waiting buoys
58.9'
03°58'·5W
58.1'

9.21.10 ÎLES DE GLÉNAN

Finistere **47°42'·98N 03°59'·60W** (Île Cignone)

CHARTS AC 2820, 3640; SHOM 7146, 6648; Navi 243; Imray C38

TIDES ML 3·0. See Concarneau for differences.

SHELTER Visit in settled weather as ⚓s can be exposed, especially near HW. The more popular are close W of N tip of Île de Penfret or La Chambre on E side; close E of Île Cigogne or S in La Bombe; N of Île du Loc'h; and NW of Île de Bananec. Other ⚓s can be found.

NAVIGATION Cardinal buoys mark the S and SW limits of the islands; and Basse Jaune, a large, offlying shoal to the SE. Les Pourceaux (rocks) and Île aux Moutons are close N.

WPT 47°44′·15N 03°57′·04W, 186°/0·9M to Penfret lt ho, is the easiest entry point to Glénan. There is enough water HW±3 for most boats, but below half-tide careful pilotage is needed and a constant awareness of the state of the tide. Boats of the Glénan Sailing School abound and are best avoided. Speed limit is 8kn mid-Jun to mid-Sept.

Other approaches: Also from N, Cigogne twr in transit 182° with chimney on Île du Loc'h leads close E of La Pie IDM lt bcn; avoiding the drying Pierres-Noires further E.

From the W, broad Chenal des Bluiniers, 095°/088°, used by Bénodet-St-Nicolas ferries, passes S of Les Bluiniers SCM, and close N of Broc'h NCM, (NW of Île Drénec) drying 0·7m between Îles Drénec and St-Nicholas. S apprs/night navigation are not advised.

LIGHTS AND MARKS Conspic marks: Penfret, highest (17m) island with W lt ho/R top; the tower (W with B top on E side only) on Île Cigogne; fish tank and a wind turbine (5 FR) at SW end of Île Saint-Nicolas.

FACILITIES There is no Capitainerie. www.glenans.fr ⚓s are laid in La Chambre and in the bay S of La Pie; fees €14·50/boat. ✕ in St-Nicolas. Frequent ferries shuttle to/from Bénodet and Concarneau, berthing on a small jetty at the SW end of Île St-Nicolas.

If visiting for more than a day or two come victualled, watered and self-sufficient. Repairs are not easily effected, although the Sailing School may assist in extremis; they have bases on Îles Cignone, Penfret, St-Nicolas, Bananec and Drénec and monitor VHF Ch 16.

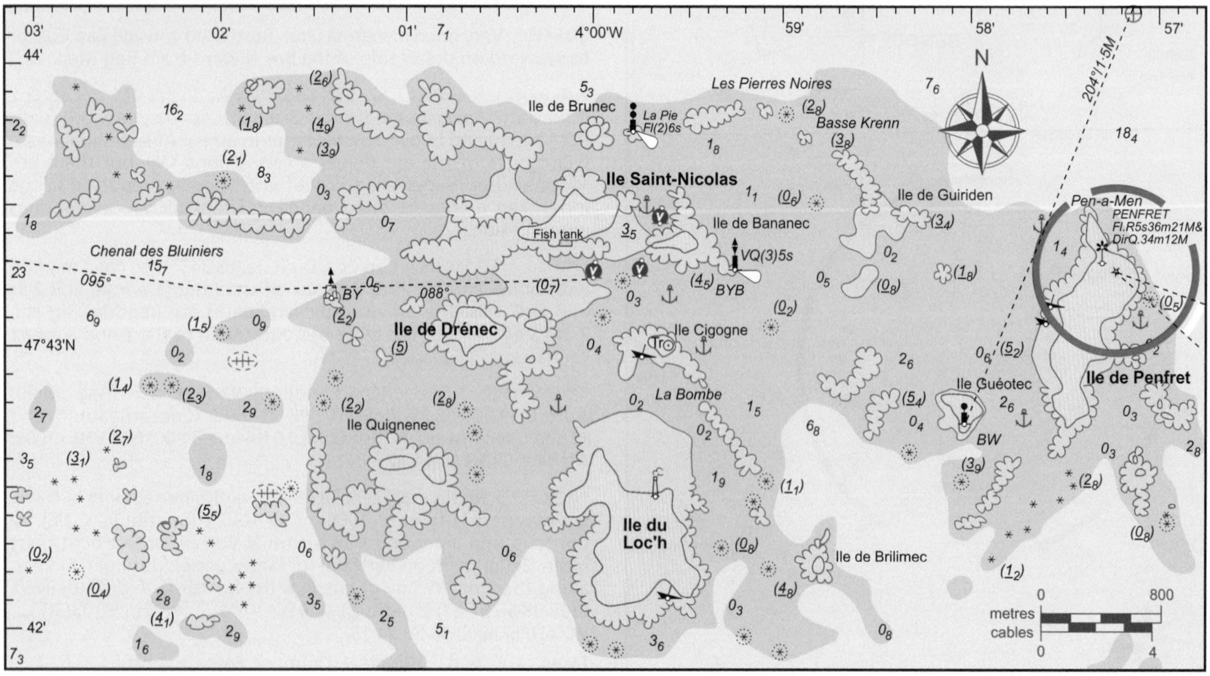
03'
02'
01'
4°00'W
59'
58'
57'
44'
47°43'N
42'
Les Pierres Noires
Ile de Brunec
La Pie Fl(2)6s
Basse Krenn
204°/1·5M
Ile Saint-Nicolas
Ile de Guiriden
Ile de Bananec
Fish tank
VQ(3)5s
BYB
Chenal des Bluiniers
095°
088°
BY
Pen-a-Men
PENFRET Fl.R5s36m21M& DirQ.34m12M
Ile de Drénec
Ile Cigogne
La Bombe
Ile Guéotec
Ile de Penfret
BW
Ile Quignenec
Ile du Loc'h
Ile de Brilimec
metres 0 800
cables 0 4

9.21.11 CONCARNEAU

Finistere **47°52'·15N 03°54'·77W** ❁❁❁◊◊◊✿✿✿

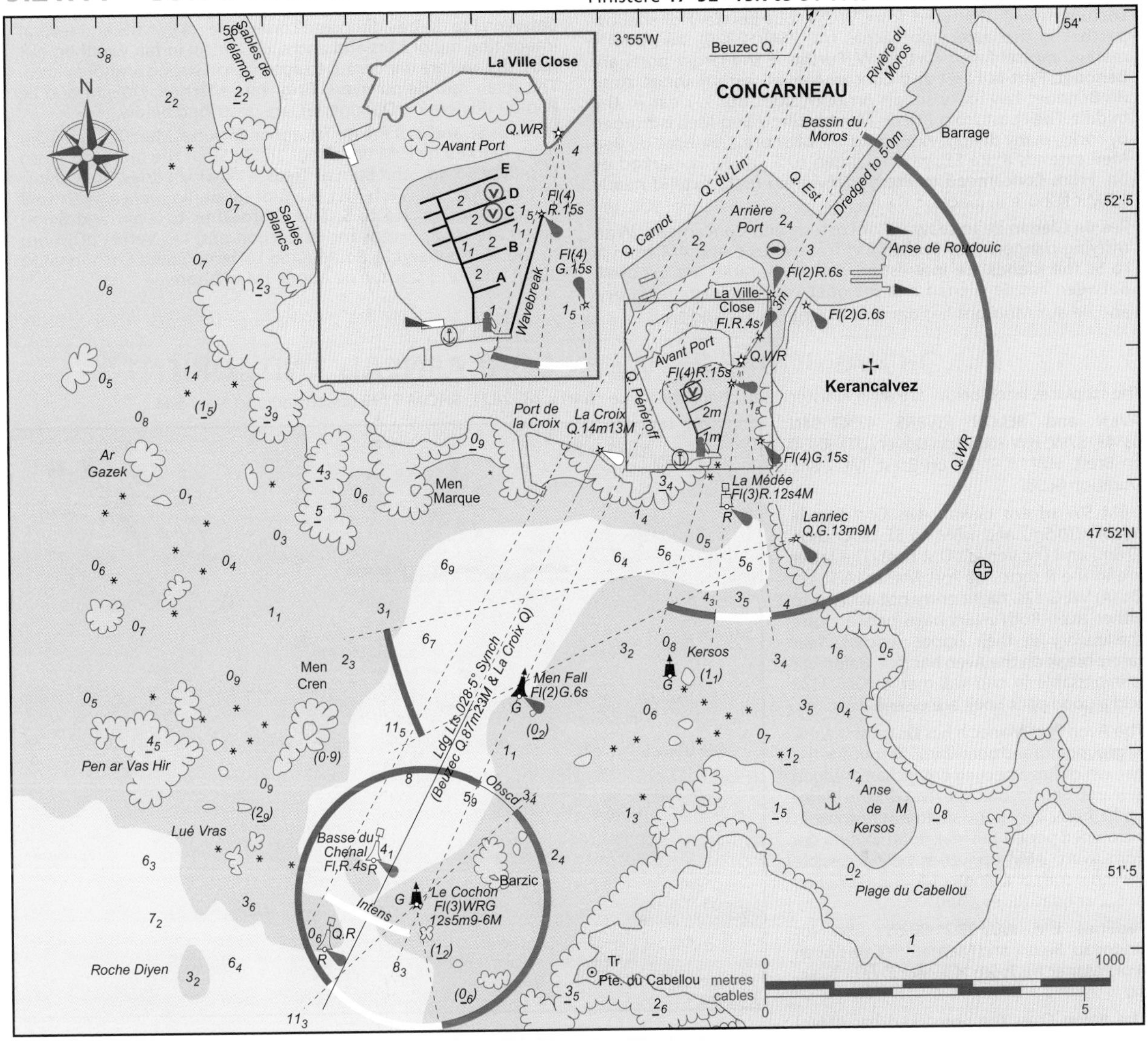

CHARTS AC 2820, 3641; SHOM 7146, 6650; Navi 543/4; Imray C38

TIDES +0455 Dover; ML 3·0; Duration 0615

Standard Port BREST (⟵)

Times				Height (metres)			
High Water		Low Water		MHWS	MHWN	MLWN	MLWS
0000	0600	0000	0600	6·9	5·4	2·6	1·0
1200	1800	1200	1800				
Differences CONCARNEAU							
–0010	–0030	–0030	–0020	–1·8	–1·4	–0·6	–0·1
ÎLE DE PENFRET (Îles de Glénan)							
–0005	–0030	–0030	–0020	–1·9	–1·5	–0·7	–0·2

SHELTER Good, except in strong S'lies; not ideal for wintering.

NAVIGATION WPT 47°50'·62N 03°56'·33W, 028·5°/1·0M to abm Le Cochon SHM bcn twr. Beware large FVs and rks around Men Cren and Le Cochon. Speed limits: 5kn between le Cochon and Men Fall; 4kn inshore of Men Fall SHM lt buoy.

LIGHTS AND MARKS See chartlet and Lights, buoys and waypoints. Ldg lts 028·5°: front, small RW twr, very hard to see against bldgs behind; rear, Beuzec spire on skyline, 1·34M from front. Pass between Le Cochon G bcn twr (easier to see than the ldg marks) and Basse du Chenal PHM buoy, QR. After Men Fall SHM buoy, track 070° toward Lanriec lt, in a G window on W gable end. It is better to lower sail here as there is little room to do so further up-chan. Note the 0·5m depth close SSW of La Médée PHM bcn twr.

COMMUNICATIONS CROSS 02·97·55·35·35; Police 17; ⊖ 02·98·97· 01·73; Brit Consul 01·44·51·31·00; Ⓗ 02·98·52·60·60; Dr 02·98·97·85·95; Fire 18; HM (Port) 02·98·97·57·96, VHF Ch 12 (H24); Aff Mar 02·98·60·55·56; Marina Ch 09 (0700-2100LT in season).

FACILITIES

Marina ☎02·98·60·51·10 port-de-plaisance@concarneau.fr is very crowded in high season. 290 + 52Ⓥ €3.25 (first two hrs free) on both sides of pontoon D (2m). D and E pontoons very busy Fridays, sailing school changeover day. Yachts can also berth on inside of anti-wash barrier but around LW beware two rocks off hammerhead C, one close E (least depth 1_5), the other SE (mid-chan, least depth 1_1). Fuel berth in about 1m is only accessible near HW, depending on draft. SHOM ACA (17t).

Yacht pontoon on NE corner of La Ville Close, locals only; Arrière Port solely for FVs. It has good heavy maintenance/repair facilities; or go to Port-la-Forêt or Bénodet. ⚓ in Anse de Kersos may now be subject to charges. **Town** Ⓔ ✉ Ⓑ bus to Quimper ⇌ and ✈. **Ferry** via Roscoff.

LOCTUDY TO CONCARNEAU

Loctudy is well sheltered from W/SW, but be wary of shallow patches in the outer approaches (AC 2646, 2820), and poorly marked mussel farms further W. Further E the larger ports are **Bénodet, Port-la-Forêt** and **Concarneau**, all with marinas. Anse de Bénodet has rocky shoals on both sides but is clear in the middle.The coast from Pte de Mousterlin to Beg Meil is fringed by rocks, many drying, extending 1M offshore. Chaussée de Beg Meil extends 8½ca SE, where Linuen rock (dries) is marked by bn. From Concarneau to Pte de Trévignon rocks extend nearly 1·5M offshore in places.

Îles de Glénan lie to seaward of Loctudy and Concarneau. With offlying dangers they stretch 5M from W to E and 4M from N to S. The islands are interesting, but anchorages are exposed. Between Îles de Glénan and Bénodet Les Pourceaux reefs dry, and Île aux Moutons has dangers extending SW and NW.

CONCARNEAU TO LORIENT

Between Pte de Trévignon and Lorient are rocky cliffs and several interesting minor hbrs and anchs, delightful in fair weather; but most dry and are dangerous to approach in strong onshore winds. The Aven and Bélon rivers, Brigneau, Merrien, Doëlan and Le Pouldu (Rivière de Quimperlé), are described below.

Hazards SE and E of Pte de Trévignon include: Men Du, a rk 0·3m high, marked by IDM bn, about 1·25M SE of the same Pte. Corn Vas, depth 1·8m, and Men ar Tréas, a rk which dries, are close S, both buoyed. Île Verte lies 6ca S of Île de Raguénès, with foul ground another 2ca to S. The approaches to Aven and Bélon Rivers are clear, except for Le Cochon and Les Verrés (IDM bn) to the SE. Between Le Pouldu and Lorient, Grand Cochon (SCM buoy) and Petit Cochon lie about 1M offshore.

9.21.12 MINOR HARBOURS BETWEEN CONCARNEAU AND LORIENT

The six places listed below are all in Finistere and share the same charts: AC 2821, SHOM 7138 (essential) and Navi 544.

AVEN and BELON RIVERS 47°47′·94N 03°43′·87W, HW +0450 on Dover (UT) –0030 on Brest. HW ht –1·9m on Brest; ML 2·8m; Duration 0608.

1·6M SW of ent beware Les Cochons de Rospico (0·5m) and 1·6M to SE Le Cochon (0·8m) and Les Verrès (IDM bcn). The latter are in the R sector of Port Manec'h's lt ho, Oc (4) WRG 12s. Night entry not advised to either river. Both rivers have bars and are shallow/dry in their upper reaches. Seas rarely break on the Aven bar, but Belon bar is impassable in bad weather. SHOM 7138 and a good pilot book are essential.

The Aven Port Manec'h has Ⓥs (possible risk of grounding) and good ⚓ in 2·5m outside the bar, which has a buoyed entry chan dredged at least 0·6m. Beyond, the river dries in places up to 1·6m. Very good shelter at Rosbraz in a crowded pool, 1·6m max depth but no Ⓥs. Pont-Aven, 3·6M upriver, is only accessible for shoal craft or a dinghy. Moorings in 2·5m; or ⌓ at quay (dries 2·5m).

Facilities HM ☎02·98·71·08·65 (also for Brigneau, Belon, and Merrien); **YC de l'Aven** (Port Manec'h). **Town** ✕ ⌑ ⚒ Ⓓ Ⓟ 🔧 ⛵ ✉.

The Bélon Cross the unmarked bar (0·6m) HW –1 in mid-river. After about 700m the chan S-bends; take care to avoid drying banks. 1M upriver off NW bank poss ⚓ in pool up to 12·4m deep, unreliable holding. Beware 3kn streams. ✕ ⌑ ⛵ ✉.

BRIGNEAU, 47°46′·87N 03°40′·13W. HW –0020 on Brest; ML 2·8m. Small drying, fair weather hbr. In strong onshore winds ent is dangerous, with hbr untenable due to swell. WPT 47°46′·25N 03°39′·67W, 331°/7ca to front leading mark ☆ Oc (2) WRG 6s 331° ldg line: bkwtr Dir lt, W twr/R top, ≠ rear W panel (hard to see); at night the white sector (329°-339°) leads to ent; see Lights, buoys and waypoints for details. Some Ⓥs (€1·10/m) or ⚓ E side of ent or ⌓ on drying W quay. ⚒ ✕ ⌑ 🛒 ⛽.

MERRIEN, 47°46′·77N 03°39′·02W. Tides as Brigneau. Small drying inlet, rky ledges either side of appr; sandbar 0·1m. Appr with W□ lt twr/R top (on skyline above trees) brg 005°; at night (not advised) QR, vis 004°-009°. ⚓ or moor to 2 W Ⓥs outside ent (€1·10/m) or ⌓ drying quay SE side; avoid oyster beds. ⚒ ✕ ⌑.

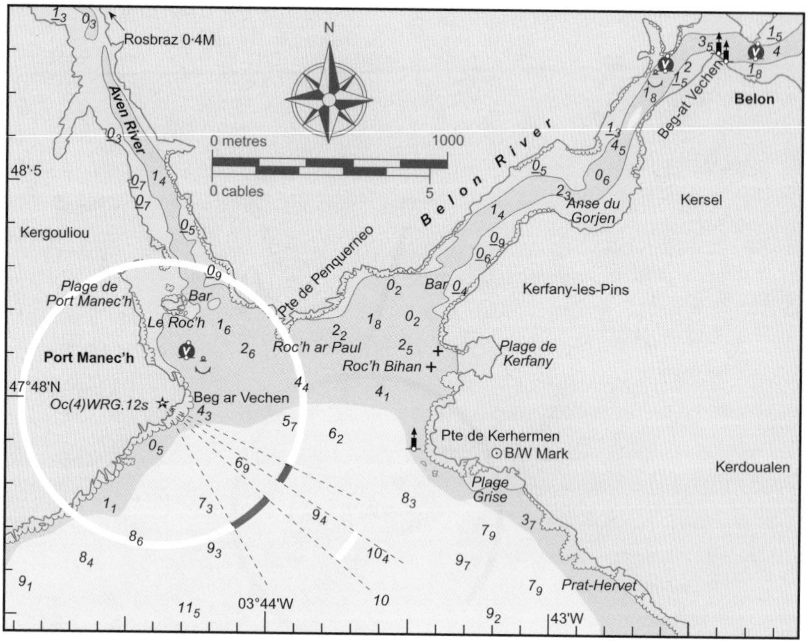

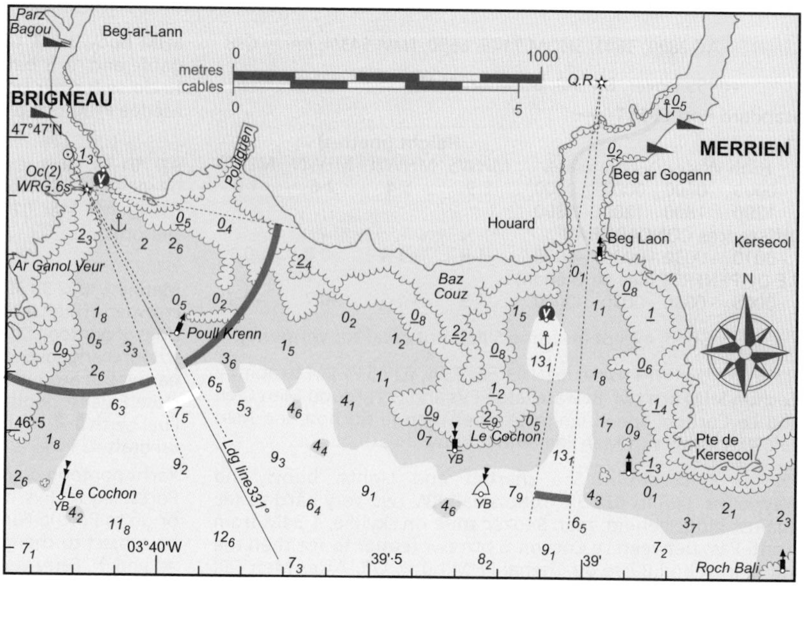

DOËLAN, 47°46´·21N 03°36´·55W. HW +0450 on Dover (UT) –0035 on Brest; HW ht –2·2m on Brest; ML 3·1m; Duration 0607. Fair weather only, open to onshore winds. 6 large W round buoys (€1·10/m) just N and S of bkwtr are for temp/short stay. 4 small dayglo red s (€1·10/m) afloat in outer hbr. Drying at W quay or raft on FV upriver. Daymarks: Two outsize lt ho's in transit 013·8°: front (*aval*) W twr/G band & top; rear (*amont*) W twr/R band & top. Conspic factory chy E of front ldg lt. Facilities: HM ☎02·98·71·53·98. **Village** Dr.

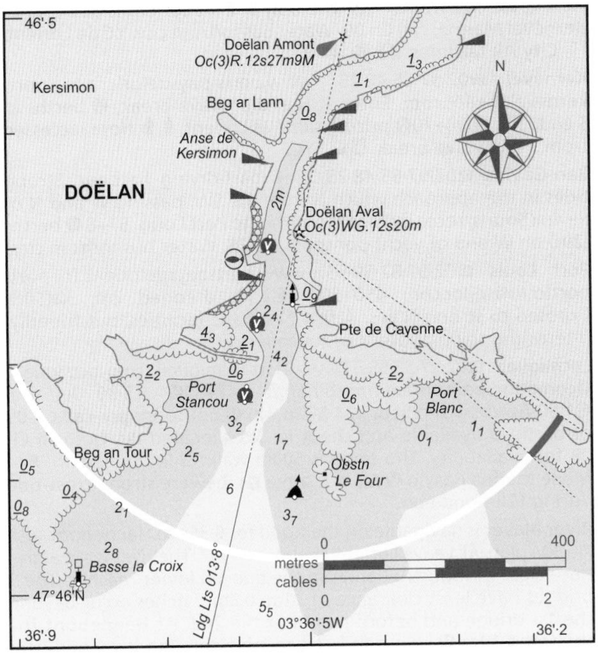

LE POULDU, 47°45'·70N 03°32'·23W. Tides as Brigneau. Strictly fair weather HW appr, close to W side of the wide Quimperlé estuary, marked by low cliffs and 2 unlit PHM bcns; chan shifts. In onshore winds the bar is dangerous on the ebb, up to 6kn sp. Guidel marina (E bank): adequate shelter for boats <9·5m/1·5m draft, 99+3 , €1·70. HM ☎02·97·05·99·92/06·07·18·11·54. Ch 09. www.sellor.com Bus. Otherwise ⚓ 300m NW in 2·8m pool.

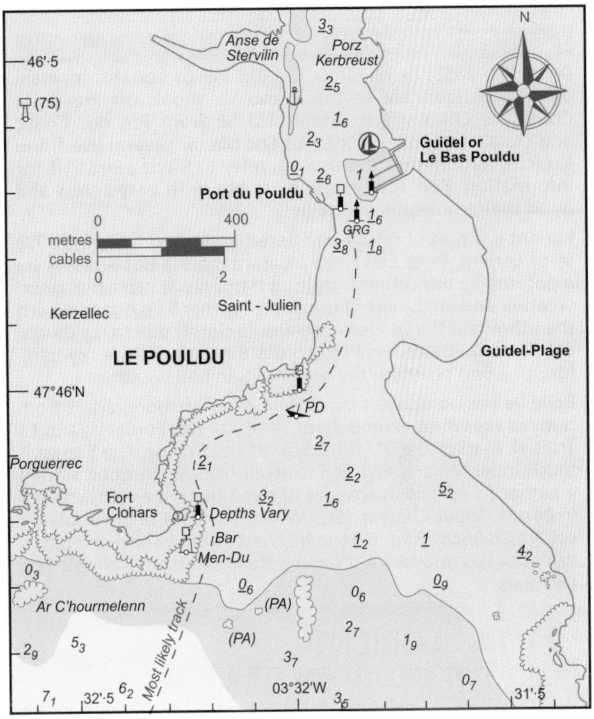

9.21.13 PORT TUDY (Île de Groix)

Morbihan **47°38'·72N 03°26'·73W**

CHARTS AC 2821, 2822; SHOM 7031, 7032, 7139; Navi 544; Imray C38

TIDES +0505 Dover; ML 3·1; Duration 0610

Standard Port BREST (⟵)

Times				**Height (metres)**			
High Water		Low Water		MHWS	MHWN	MLWN	MLWS
0000	0600	0000	0600	6·9	5·4	2·6	1·0
1200	1800	1200	1800				
Differences PORT TUDY (Île de Groix)							
0000	–0025	–0025	–0015	–1·7	–1·3	–0·5	–0·1

SHELTER Good, but in strong N/NE'lies swell enters outer hbr.

NAVIGATION WPT 47°39'·11N 03°26'·29W (100m E of Speerbrecker ECM buoy) 218°/0·5M to N mole hd lt, just in R sector of E mole hd lt. Beware rks SE of appr, and ferries. From E or SE pass N of Basse Mélite NCM buoy.

Use SHOM 7139 (1:20,000) for exploring the island, including Locmaria (below) Port St Nicolas and Port Lay.

LIGHTS AND MARKS The three principal lts on Groix are: Pen-Men lt ho at NW end of island, W □ tr, B top; Pte de la Croix lt at NE end; and Pte des Chats at SE end. There are no ldg lts, although the mole head lts in transit 219° clear offlying rks to the E. By day the N mole lt ho and conspic water twr (1M SW of hbr) ≠ 220° lead close W of Speerbrecker to ent.

COMMUNICATIONS CROSS 02·97·55·35·35; Auto 08·92·68·08·56; Police 02·97·86·81·17; 02·97·86·80·93; Brit Consul 01·44·51·31·00; Ⓗ (Lorient) 02·97·83·04·02; HM VHF Ch 09 during opening hours for gate into wet basin; Aff Mar 02·97·37·16·22.

FACILITIES HM ☎02·97·86·54·62. Access H24. **Outer hbr**, moor F&A; 120 s in 2-4m, <10M €11·00, >10M €14·50. No ⚓ in hbr, often full in season, tight space, prepare long lines and fenders prior to entry, and dinghy to get ashore. Prone to ferry wash/noise.

Marina 43 €2·53, first 2 pontoons inside E mole, dredged 2·0-2·5m, no pre-booking, berths at a premium in season.

Wet basin (104 mostly locals) access via gate HW±2 (0630–2200) but less at small neaps. No opening if swell/backwash.

Quay (0800–1200 & 1400–1900, ☎02·97·86·80·96) (3t). **Town** . Ferry to Lorient.

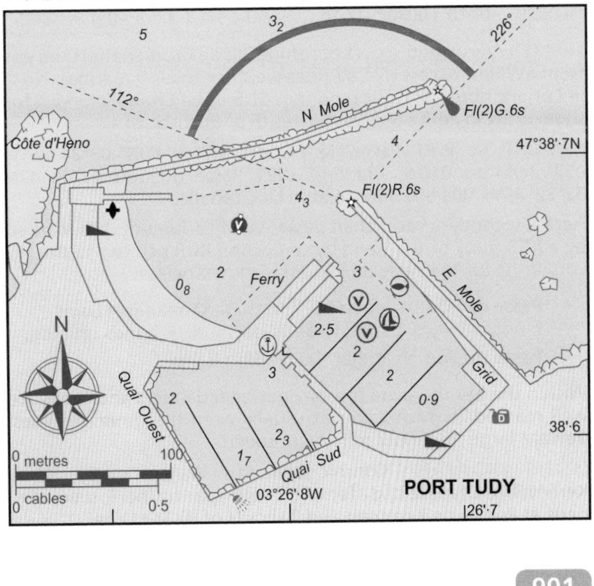

DRYING HARBOUR NEAR SE END OF ÎLE DE GROIX

LOCMARIA, Morbihan, **47°37'·40N 03°26'·42W**. AC 2820/1, SHOM 7139; –0020 Brest; ML 2·8m. Appr is open to the S, but in offshore winds tiny drying hbr gives shelter. Steer N initially for G bcn twr; then pick up 350° ldg line, W bcn ≠ conspic Ho. Enter between PHM/SHM bcns; a SCM and NCM bcn drying reef. Limited space inside to dry out; or ⚓ outside the hbr either side of the ldg line. Facilities in village, ✕ 🛒 . Le Bourg is approx 1 mile walk.

ÎLE DE GROIX, LORIENT AND BELLE ÎLE

(AC 2352, 2353) Île de Groix lies 4M SW of Lorient. Its main offlying dangers are to the E and SE: shoals off Pte de la Croix; Les Chats which extend 1M SE from Pte des Chats; and shoals extending 7½ca S of Loc Maria. Several live firing exercise stations exist in this area, refer to Navtex and VHF for information. **Port Tudy** is the main hbr with easy access and good shelter except from NE'lies.

Lorient is a port of refuge, sheltered apprs and 5 marinas. 7M SE of Lorient, **River Étel** has a pleasant marina but access is via a potentially difficult ent, shifting bar; only approach in good weather and on the last of the flood. Further S do not approach the isthmus of the Quiberon peninsula closely due to rky shoals. 6M W of Quiberon lies Plateau des Birvideaux (lt) a rky bank (depth 4·6m) on which the sea breaks in bad weather.

Belle Île has no dangers more than 2½ca offshore, apart from buoyed rks which extend 7½ca W of Pte des Poulains, and La Truie rk marked by IDM bn tr 5ca off the S coast. The S coast is much indented and exposed to swell from W. In good settled weather (only) and in absence of swell there is an attractive ⚓ in Port du Vieux Château (Ster Wenn) 1M S of Pte des Poulains; see *North Biscay Pilot*. On the NE coast lie **Sauzon**, which partly dries but has good anch off and is sheltered from S and W, and **Le Palais**.

9.21.14 LORIENT

Morbihan **47°42'·60N 03°22'·00W** ✿✿✿◊◊◊✿✿

CHARTS AC 2821, 304; SHOM 7031, 7032, 7139, 7140; Navi 544, 545; Imray C38

TIDES +0455 Dover; ML 3·1; Duration 0620

Standard Port BREST (⟵)

Times				Height (metres)			
High Water		Low Water		MHWS	MHWN	MLWN	MLWS
0000	0600	0000	0600	6·9	5·4	2·6	1·0
1200	1800	1200	1800				
Differences *LORIENT and PORT LOUIS*							
+0005	*–0020*	*–0020*	*–0010*	*–1·9*	*–1·5*	*–0·7*	*–0·2*
HENNEBONT (Blavet River)							
+0015	–0015	+0005	+0005	–1·9	–1·5	–0·8	–0·2
PORT D'ETEL							
+0020	–0010	+0030	+0010	–2·0	–1·3	–0·4	+0·5

SHELTER Very good, a port of refuge. Île de Groix shelters the ent from SW'lies. Access H24 all tides/weather to all 5 marinas. No ⚓ in Lorient hbr/chans, but moorings ENE of La Citadelle and ⚓ for shoal draft in Petite Mer de Gâvres (E of Port Louis).

NAVIGATION WPT Passe de l'Ouest, 47°40'·80N 03°24'·85W, 057°/2·0M to 016·5° ldg line. WPT Passe du Sud 47°40'·47N 03°22'·46W, 008·5°/2·15M to abm La Citadelle.

Here a secondary yacht chan passes W of La Jument. It is marked by a RGR buoy to the S and by Le Cochon RGR bcn twr to the N. Ldg/dir lts for the Passe de l'Ouest is shown below:

- **Passe de l'Ouest**: ldg lts 057°, both Dir Q near Port Louis. Front, R twr, W bands. Rear, W daymark, R bands on bldg.
- **Passe du Sud** no longer has leading lights.

Within the hbr there are few navigational dangers and chans are well marked/lit. Yachts do not usually need the inner ldg lines. Beware large multihulls moving at speed.

LIGHTS AND MARKS Conspic daymarks: Water twr 8ca W of Kernével; La Citadelle stbd of ent; Port-Louis spire further E, submarine pens at Pointe de Kéroman and 2 silos N of Île St Michel.

COMMUNICATIONS CROSS 02·97·55·35·35; 🄻🄱 02·97·86·29·62; ⊖ 02·97·37·34·66; Auto 08·92·68·08·56; Police 02·97·64·27·17; Sea Police 02·97·12·12·12; Brit Consul 01·44·51·31·00; 🄷 02·97·64·81·58; Port HM 02·97·37·11·86; VHF Ch 11 *Lorient Port* (H24); Aff Mar 02·97·37·16·22; Marinas VHF Ch 09 (in season: 0800-1230, 1330-2000, out of season: 0830-1200, 1400-1800).

FACILITIES **Lorient Marina**, inset on the main chartlet. ☎02·97·21·10·14. www.ports-paysdelorient.fr port-lorient@sellor.com ⊆ in Avant Port 2·5-3m, crowded in season. 320+50Ⓥ €3·50 Jul/Aug; €1·40 Apr/May/Jun/Sep. Wet Basin 2·5m. ⊡ ✎ ⊡ Ⓔ ✗ ⊡ SHOM ACA ⚠ ▬ ⊡(25t) ⊡(1½t). The only 🚹🚺 in Lorient is at S end of Kernével Marina; call Ch 09. Water bus to/from city. **YC de Lorient**, ⊡. **City** All facilities, ✉ Ⓑ ⇌ ✈.

Kernével ☎02·97·65·48·25. www.ports-paysdelorient.fr port-kernevel@sellor.com. Enter at N end of wave-break, Ⓥ berths at S end, 3m. 1000+70Ⓥ pricing same as Lorient, 🚹🚺 Note: accessed from S end wave-break. ⊡ ▬ YC.

Ban-Gâvres ☎02·97·65·48·25. Tiny, part-drying harbour. Strong tides in the approach which is from the SW, passing W and N of Île aux Souris; recce by foot ferry from/to Port Louis. 57+8 Ⓥ berths (2m) on W end of yacht pontoon, €1·75. Water bus to/from city.

Port Louis ☎02·97·82·59·55. www.portspaysdelorient.fr port-portlouis@sellor.com 450+50Ⓥ €2·90, dredged 2m, ⊡(50t). Exposed to strong N'lies. A few FVs; basic facilities, but friendly; interesting town. Water bus to/from city.

Locmiquélic ☎02·97·33·59·51 www.port-locmiquelic.com locmiquelic @compagniedesportsdumorbihan.fr 447+30Ⓥ €3·30 Jul/Aug; €1·50 Apr/May/Jun/Sep, in 1·5-3m. No Ⓥ pontoon: pre-call Ch 09 or berth as available and check in. No allocated ⊡s, but call Ch 09 for availability. The town is 500m walk. ⊡ ⊡ (limited) ⊡. **Pen Mané Marina** has no Ⓥ ⊆ but some ⊡s, beware strong cross-tide during full flood/ebb.

River Blavet is navigable on the flood for 6·3M to Hennebont. Use AC 304 plan Ⓐ. Leave Lorient at about HW–2. The river is attractive once clear of industrial areas in the buoyed lower reaches. The 3 bridges have least clearance of 21m. 0·3m patches occur beyond the 1st bridge and before and after the 2nd. At **Hennebont** the sheltered 14m Ⓥ pontoon is 1st to stbd; the 2nd is for vedettes only. No ⊡ ⊡; 12hrs max stay. Good facilities in town. See also Area 18 for the Canal du Blavet to Pontivy.

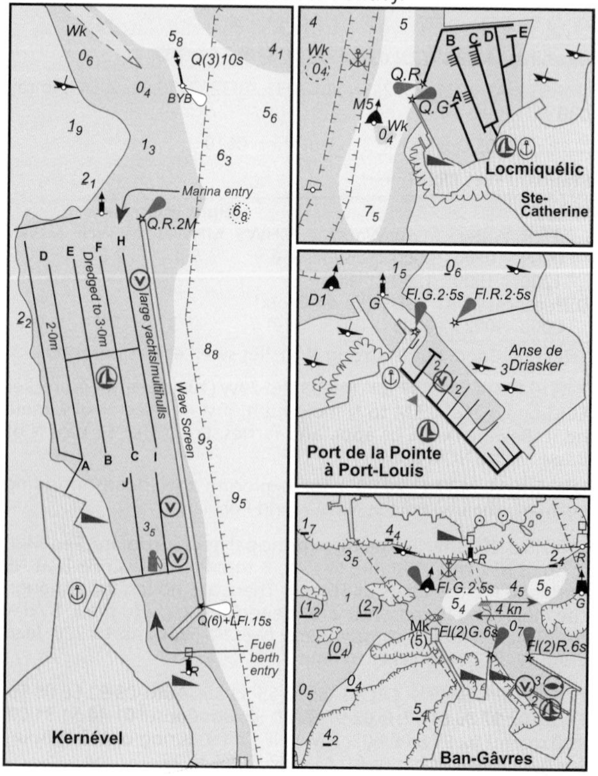

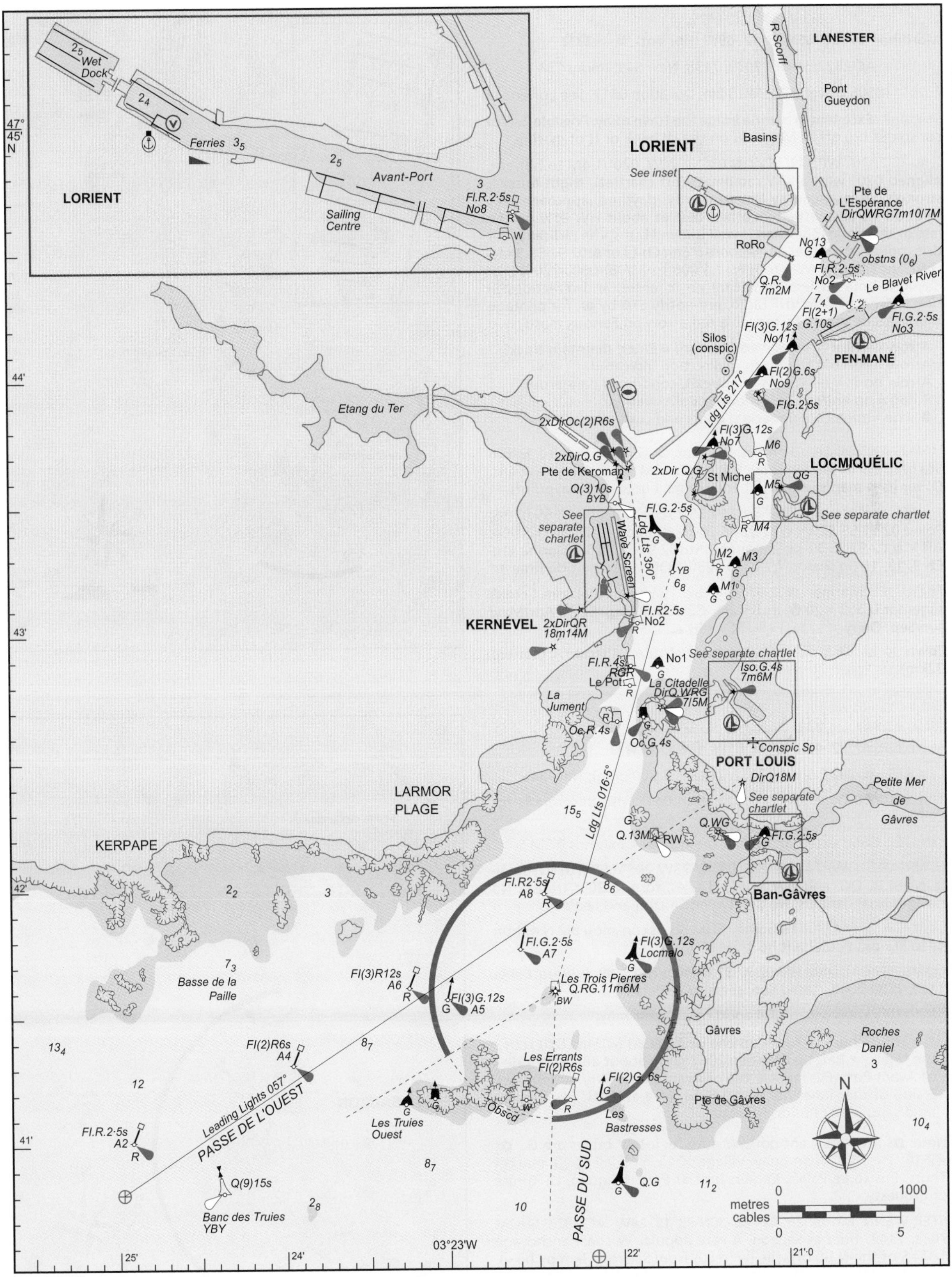
LORIENT
Wet Dock
Ferries
Avant-Port
Sailing Centre
Fl.R.2·5s
No8
LANESTER
R Scorff
Pont Gueydon
Basins
LORIENT
See inset
Pte de L'Espérance
DirQWRG7m10/7M
RoRo
No13
Q.R.
7m2M
Fl.R.2·5s
No2
obstns
Le Blavet River
Fl(2+1)G.10s
Fl.G.2·5s
No3
Fl(3)G.12s
No11
Silos (conspic)
PEN-MANÉ
Fl(2)G.6s
No9
Ldg Lts 217°
FlG.2·5s
Etang du Ter
2xDirOc(2)R6s
2xDirQ.G
Pte de Keroman
Fl(3)G.12s
No7
M6
LOCMIQUÉLIC
2xDir Q.G
St Michel
Q(3)10s
BYB
M5
QG
See separate chartlet
Fl.G.2·5s
M4
See separate chartlet
Wave Screen
Ldg Lts 350°
YB
M2
M3
M1
KERNÉVEL
2xDirQR
18m14M
Fl.R2·5s
No2
Fl.R.4s
RGR
Le Pot
No1
See separate chartlet
Iso.G.4s
7m6M
La Citadelle
DirQ.WRG
7/5M
La Jument
Oc.R.4s
Oc.G.4s
Conspic Sp
PORT LOUIS
DirQ18M
See separate chartlet
Petite Mer de Gâvres
LARMOR PLAGE
Ldg Lts 016·5°
Q.13M
RW
Q.WG
Fl.G.2·5s
KERPAPE
Ban-Gâvres
Fl.R2·5s
A8
Fl.G.2·5s
A7
Fl(3)G.12s
Locmalo
Basse de la Paille
Fl(3)R12s
A6
Fl(3)G.12s
A5
Les Trois Pierres
Q.RG.11m6M
BW
Gâvres
Roches Daniel
Fl(2)R6s
A4
Les Errants
Fl(2)R6s
Fl(2)G.6s
Les Truies Ouest
Obscd
Les Bastresses
Pte de Gâvres
Leading Lights 057°
PASSE DE L'OUEST
Fl.R.2·5s
A2
Q(9)15s
Banc des Truies
YBY
PASSE DU SUD
Q.G
metres
cables
1000
03°23'W
25'
24'
22'
21'·0
47°
45'
N
44'
43'
42'
41'

9.21.15 RIVER ÉTEL

Morbihan **47°38′·65N 03°12′·69W** (Hbr ent)

CHARTS AC 2822; SHOM 7032, 7138; Navi 545; Imray C38

TIDES +0505 Dover (UT); ML 3·2m; Duration 0617. See Lorient.

SHELTER Excellent in marina inside the town quay. Possible ⚓s S of conspic LB ho, off Le Magouër on the W bank or N of marina.

NAVIGATION WPT 47°37′·31N 03°13′·44W, 020°/1·4M to hbr ent, aligned 020° with a R/W radiomast (off chartlet). Night entry is strongly discouraged by Hbr Authority; daytime, approach only in good vis and settled weather; best at about HW –1½ on the last of the flood. The chan is well buoyed but shifts radically; bar dries approx 0·4m. Call *Semaphore d'Etel* Ch 13 or ☎02·97·55·35·59 HW-3 to HW+2 (HW-4 to HW+2 15/06 to 31/08) 0600-2200LT, or daylight hours if less, for clearance to enter, and directions in simple French. If no VHF radio, pre-notify ETA by ☎, for pilotage signals to be shown by movable red arrow on Fenoux mast:

> Arrow vertical (also stowed position) = Enter, maintain track.
> Arrow deflected L/R = turn in direction indicated.
> Arrow horiz = no vessels to ent/exit, conditions dangerous.
> R flag = no ent/exit, insufficient depth over bar.
> ● = no ent/exit for undecked boats and craft <8m LOA.

LIGHTS AND MARKS Dir lt W side of ent, Oc (2) WRG 6s; no ⚓ within 5ca of it. Épi de Plouhinic bn, Fl R 2·5s 7m 2M, marks groyne at ent. Other lts & marks as chartlet and Lights, buoys and waypoints.

COMMUNICATIONS CROSS 02·97·55·35·35; Auto 08·92·65·02·56; Police 02·97·55·32·11; ⊜ 02·97·36·20·76; Brit Consul 01·44·51·31·00; Aff Mar 02·97·55·30·32; Semaphore Stn 02·97·55·35·59; Marina VHF Ch 9, 13, 16 (in season 7/7 0830-1230/1330-1900 and tide times).

FACILITIES **Marina** ☎02·97·55·46·62. www.ria-etel.com etel@sagemor.fr 383 + 20 Ⓥ in 1·5-2m, €2·90 Jul/Aug; €2·30 Apr/May/Jun/Sep. **Quay** (6t).

Town . Bus to ⇌ (Auray 15km) ✈ (Lorient 32km).

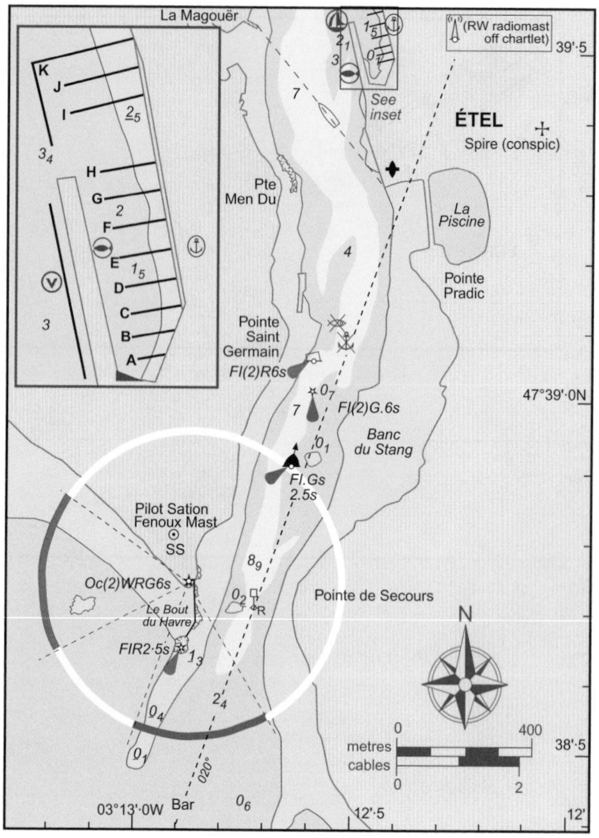

9.21.16 SAUZON (Belle Île)

Morbihan **47°22′·47N 03°13′·01W**

CHARTS AC 2822; SHOM 7032, 7142 (1:7,500 plan); Navi 545

TIDES +0450 Dover; ML 3·0; Duration 0615. Use differences for Le Palais.

SHELTER Good except in NE'lies. Drying creek extends 0·5M S.

NAVIGATION WPT 47°22′·88N 03°12′·73W, 205°/685m to NW Jetée lt. Main lt, QG, and NW Jetée, Fl G 4s, form a 205° transit. No navigational dangers. No ⚓ between Sauzon and Le Palais.

LIGHTS AND MARKS Le Gareau SHM bcn is conspic 0·9M N of hbr; ditto Pte des Poulains lt ho 1·6M NW.

COMMUNICATIONS HM 02·97·31·63·40, VHF Ch 09, Jul/Aug: 0900-1230, 1700-2000; closed Sun; see also Le Palais.

FACILITIES www.sauzon.fr/Leport.htm Yachts may:

> • ⚓ ENE of hbr ent • Pick up one of 22 W Ⓥs (<15m LOA) N of the N jetty • Raft up between 20 W Ⓥs in about 2m on W side of Avant Port (FVs moor E side of Avant Port) • Dry out on the E side of the inner hbr on 50 R Ⓥs, fore and aft; firm, level mud/sand. Inner hbr dries about 1·6–2m.

Note: Ⓥs are R in avant port, W outside; locals' buoys are G. Ⓥs €2·10, ⚓ €1·05. on quay. **Village** Ⓑ ©; market Thurs. Bus to Le Palais. Repairs best at Port Haliguen, La Trinité or Crouesty.

STER WENN, Morbihan, **47°22′·30N 03°15′·24W**. AC 2822; SHOM 7032, 7142. Tides as Sauzon. A very popular W coast anchorage 1·1M S of the N tip of Belle Île (recce from Sauzon, 3km by bike). From the NW enter Ster-Vraz, the outer inlet. When abeam the 5th hole of the golf course to the N, Ster Wenn opens to stbd. ⚓ where space permits, stern line ashore. Shelter is good in all winds. Facilities: None, other than relative peace.

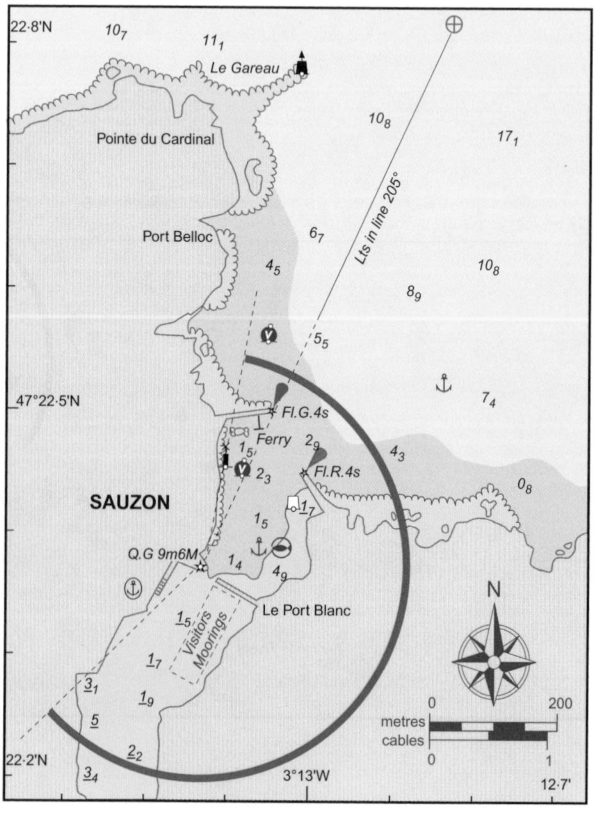

9.21.17 LE PALAIS (Belle Île)

Morbihan **47°20'·84N 03°08'·98W** ❁❁❁◊◊◊✿✿✿

CHARTS AC 2822, 2823; Imray C39; SHOM 7032, 7142; Navi 545

TIDES +0458 Dover; ML 3·1; Duration 0615

Standard Port BREST (⟵)

Times				Height (metres)			
High Water		Low Water		MHWS	MHWN	MLWN	MLWS
0000	0600	0000	0600	6·9	5·4	2·6	1·0
1200	1800	1200	1800				
Differences LE PALAIS							
–0005	–0025	–0025	–0010	–1·8	–1·3	–0·7	–0·2

SHELTER Good, but strong E'lies cause heavy swell in Avant Port. No ⚓ between Le Palais and Sauzon, nor in hbr.

NAVIGATION WPT 47°21'·20N 03°08'·39W, 231°/6ca to N Pier lt. Enter close to SHM, fast ferries sound horn outside hbr and expect it to be clear as they enter.

LIGHTS AND MARKS Lts as chartlet. La Citadelle is conspic.

COMMUNICATIONS CROSS 02·97·55·35·35; Auto 08·92·68·08·56; Police 02·97·31·80·22; ⊖ 02·97·31·85·95; Brit Consul 01·44·51·31·00; Ⓗ 02·97·31·48·48; Dr 02·97·31·40·90; HM 02·97·31·42·90, VHF Ch 09 (Season: 0800-1200, 1400-2000. Out of season 0800-1200, 1500-1800); Aff Mar 02·97·31·47·08.

FACILITIES www.belle-ile.com **Avant Port** 70 Ⓥs (€2·00) in 3 trots inside Mole Bourdelle for <18m LOA. Need dinghy to get ashore, hbr staff help secure to mole and bys, have long lines ready and fenders both sides; shallow draft on Ⓥs to port. Multihulls +150%, +200% Jul/Aug. (10t,5t) . Packed in season. **Inner hbr** dries. Poss berthing on stbd quay.

Bassin à Flot Enter via gate/ lifting bridge, opens HW –1½ to +1 (0600-2200LT) Ⓥ (90) €2·50 rafting on either side in 2·5m, multihulls +150%, +200% Jul/Aug; max LOA 30m.

Marina (Bassin de la Saline, 1·7–2m) (24hrs notice req'd) if finger berths vacant; max LOA 13m. Enter via lifting bridge beyond Bassin à Flot. 8 Ⓥ €2·50. **YC** ☎02·97·31·55·85.

Town ✕ ⊠ Ⓑ. Ferry to Quiberon ⇄ ✈.

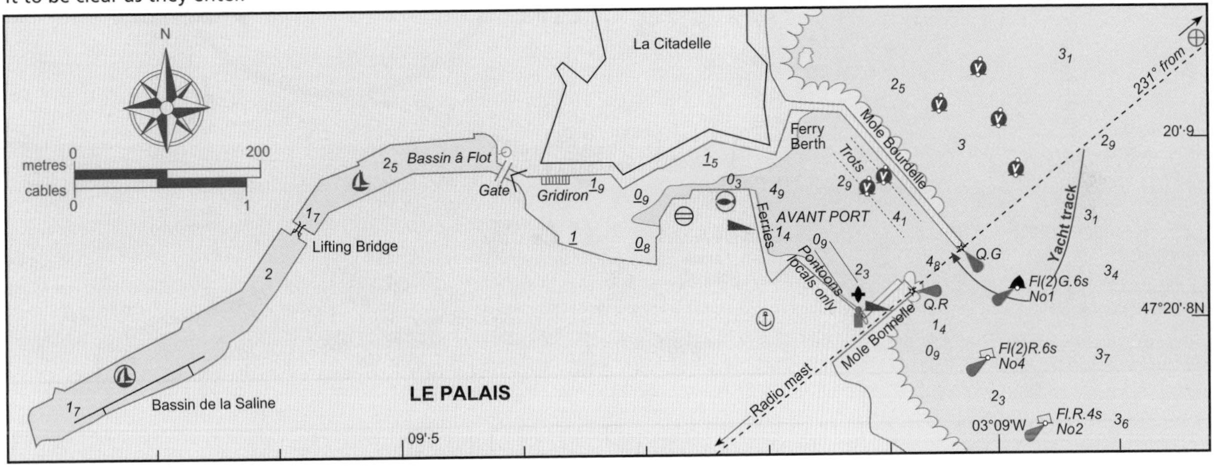

9.21.18 PASSAGE DE LA TEIGNOUSE

See the upper chartlet on the next page

This is the easiest route through the Chaussée de La Teignouse being deep, wide, well buoyed and lit. See AC 2357; SHOM 7141. From WPT 47°25'·35N 03°05'·00W appr with La Teignouse lt ho brg 036° (by night in its W sector 033°-039°). The chan is marked by Goué Vas Sud SCM, Basse du Milieu SHM and Goué Vas Est PHM lt buoys. Abeam Goué Vas Est, turn stbd 068°, passing between Basse Nouvelle PHM and NE Teignouse SHM lt buoys, into open waters. Minor variations on this route can be used. Further SE, **Passage du Béniguet** 044° lies NW of Houat and **Passage des Soeurs** 016° between Houat and Hoëdic, both unlit.

The **shortest passage**, saving 3M if to/from Port Haliguen, lies between Le Four SCM and Les Trois Pierres NCM bcn twrs with La Teignouse lt ho brg 094°. Turn N as the rocky chan opens between Iniz en Toull Bras to stbd and a SCM and 2 ECM perches to port; see pecked line. Only for experienced navigators by day, exercising caution at LW; pre-study SHOM 7141 carefully; expect strong cross-streams.

9.21.19 HOUAT and HOËDIC

❁❁◊✿✿✿

CHARTS AC 2823, 2835; Imray C39; SHOM 7033, 7143; Navi 545

TIDES +0505 Dover; ML 3·1; Duration 0605

Standard Port BREST (⟵)

Times				Height (metres)			
High Water		Low Water		MHWS	MHWN	MLWN	MLWS
0000	0600	0000	0600	6·9	5·4	2·6	1·0
1200	1800	1200	1800				
Differences HOUAT							
+0005	–0025	–0025	–0010	–1·7	–1·3	–0·6	–0·3
HOËDIC							
+0010	–0035	–0025	–0020	–1·8	–1·4	–0·7	–0·3

HOUAT 47°23'·57N 02°57'·34W (Port St Gildas). Appr from N or NE passing abeam La Vieille rk (conspic 17m) NNE of which mussel beds are marked by 4 buoys: NCM VQ, ECM VQ(3) 5s and 2 unlit SPM. The only lt on the island is on the hbr bkwtr head, Fl (2) WG 6s; the G sector covers La Vieille and buoyed mussel beds. At night appr in W sectors on either side; details in Lts, bys & waypoints.

Good shelter, except from N/NE'lies, at Port St Gildas, near E end of the N coast. Moor fore & aft on two dumbbell Ⓥ trots in centre hbr and along N wall; no ⚓ in hbr. S part of hbr dries. Keep clear of ferries on W quay and FVs on N quay. E of the hbr are 15 W Ⓥs and space to ⚓.

Tréach er Gourhed, aka Rade de Houat, is a 7 cables wide, crab-shaped bay at the ESE end of Houat, designated a No-anch area due to cables. Other ⚓s at Tréach er Béniguet, Portz Ler and Portz Navallo, all at NW end of Houat. No ent (15/4-31/8) to Nature reserves at Er Yoc'h and Ile Guric and Séniz at NW end. Facilities: Mairie 02·97·30·68·04, ✕ ⊠ Dr. Ferries to Quiberon, Lorient, La Turballe, Le Croisic.

HOËDIC 47°20'·67N 02°52'·45W (Port de L'Argol). Appr from NNW or NNE passing abeam La Chèvre rk (unlit IDM bcn) and W sectors of bkwtr lt, Fl WG 4s; its G sector (163°-183°) covers La Chèvre.

Good shelter, except in N/NE'lies, at Port de L'Argol, on N coast. Ferries berth at the W end hbr wall; a 72m walk ashore pontoon with finger berths lies inside the E end, a trot of 4 large Ⓥ in hbr centre, or ⚓ outside to NNE. On the S coast, Port de la Croix, dries but ⚓ outside in 2-4m. Other ⚓s in the island's lee. 1·5M SE of Hoëdic, Grands Cardinaux lt ho, R twr/W band Fl (4) 15s, marks the outer reefs. Facilities: ✕ limited. Ferries as for Houat.

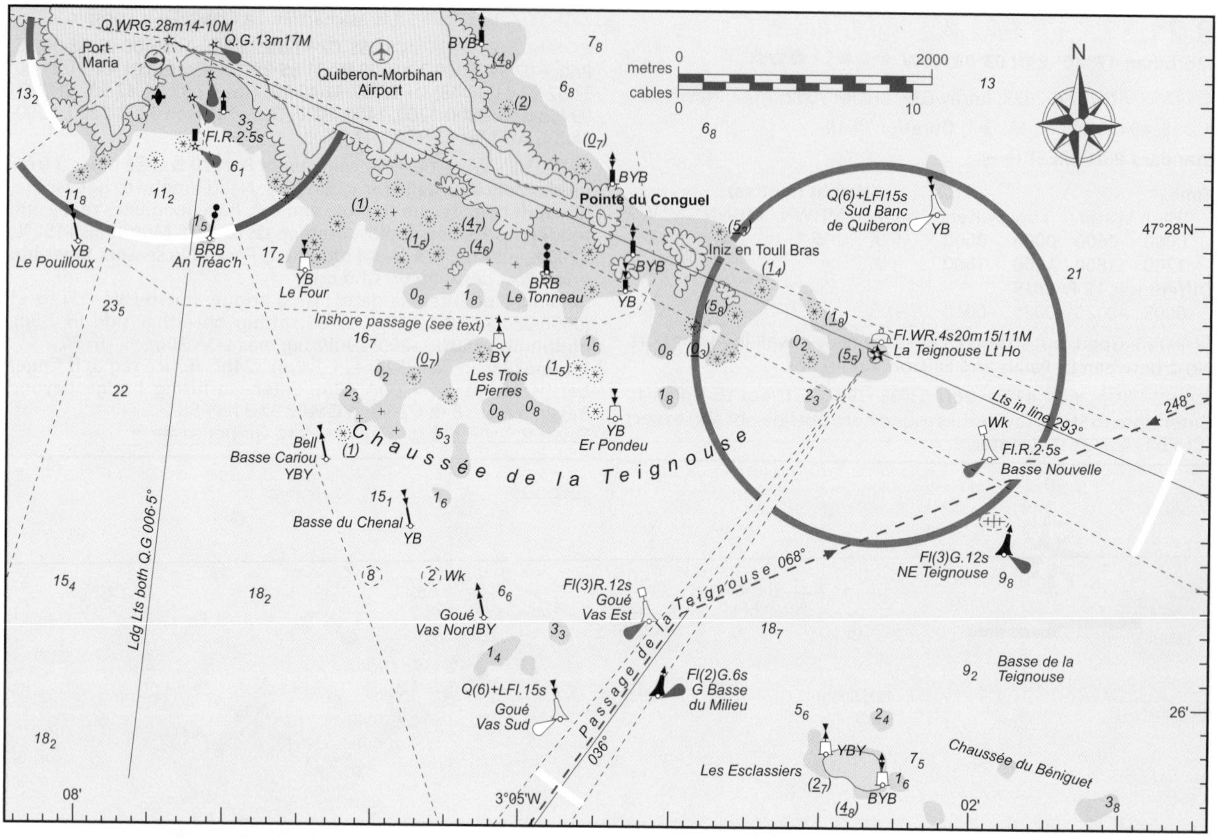
Q.WRG.28m14-10M
Q.G.13m17M
Port Maria
Quiberon-Morbihan Airport
metres
cables
2000
10
N
Fl.R.2·5s
Le Pouilloux
An Tréac'h
Le Four
Le Tonneau
Pointe du Conguel
BYB
Q(6)+LFl15s
Sud Banc de Quiberon
YB
47°28'N
Iniz en Toull Bras
Inshore passage (see text)
Les Trois Pierres
Fl.WR.4s20m15/11M
La Teignouse Lt Ho
Lts in line 293°
248°
Wk
Fl.R.2·5s
Basse Nouvelle
Bell
Basse Cariou
YBY
Er Pondeu
Chaussée de la Teignouse
Basse du Chenal
Ldg Lts both Q.G 006·5°
Fl(3)G.12s
NE Teignouse
Fl(3)R.12s
Goué Vas Est
Goué Vas Nord BY
Passage de la Teignouse 068°
Basse de la Teignouse
Q(6)+LFl.15s
Goué Vas Sud
Fl(2)G.6s
G Basse du Milieu
26'
036°
Les Esclassiers
Chaussée du Béniguet
08'
3°05'W
02'

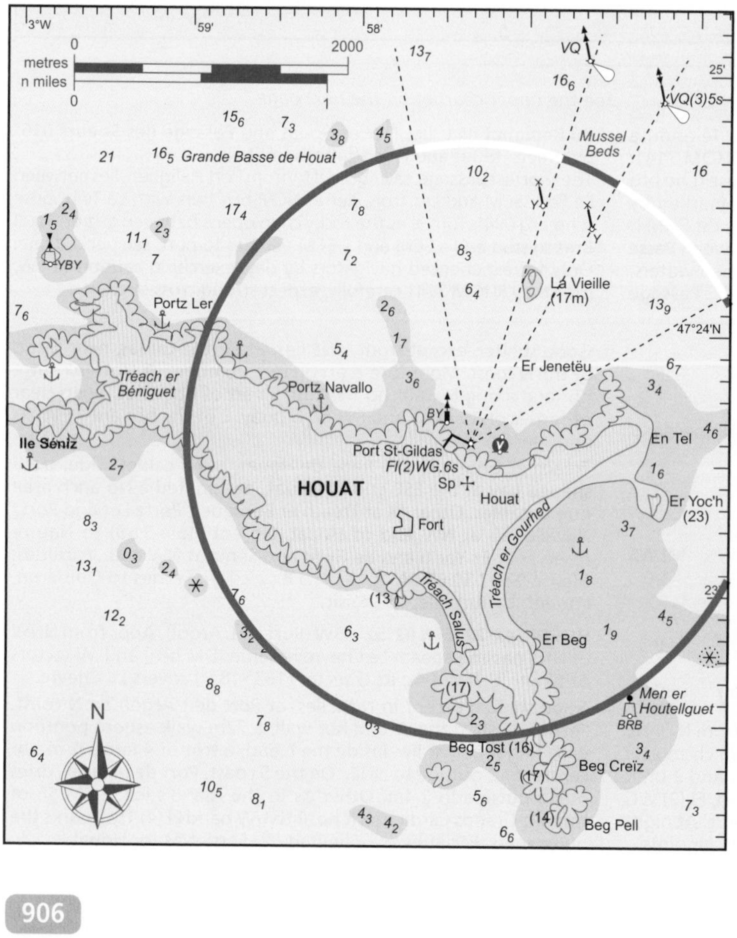
3°W
59'
58'
metres
n miles
2000
VQ
VQ(3)5s
25'
Mussel Beds
Grande Basse de Houat
La Vieille (17m)
47°24'N
Portz Ler
Tréach er Béniguet
Portz Navallo
Er Jenetëu
Ile Séniz
Port St-Gildas
Fl(2)WG.6s
Sp
Houat
HOUAT
Fort
En Tel
Er Yoc'h (23)
Tréach er Gourhed
Tréach Salus
Er Beg
23'
Men er Houtellguet
BRB
Beg Tost (16)
Beg Creïz
Beg Pell
N

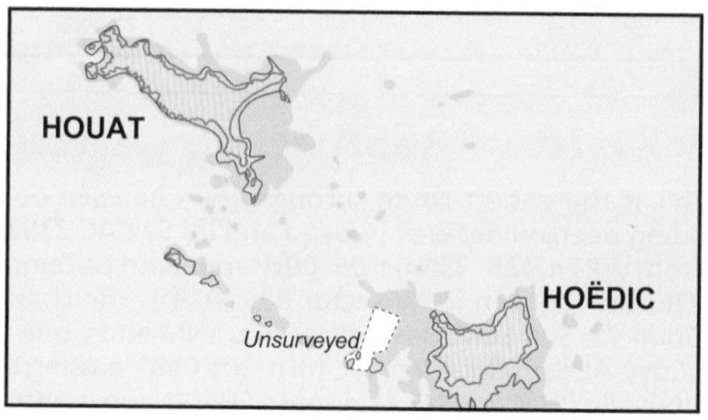
HOUAT
HOËDIC
Unsurveyed

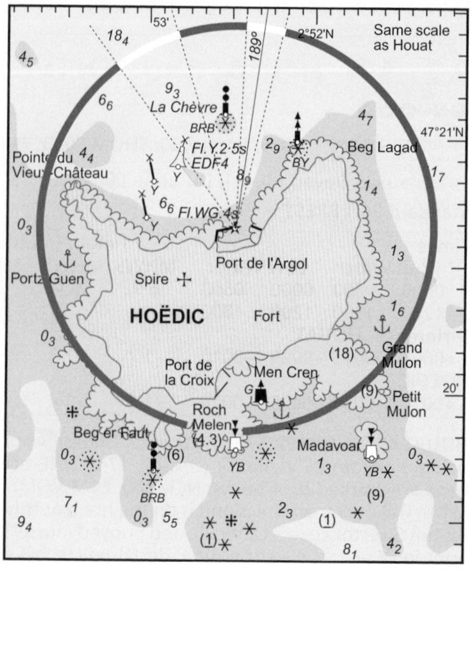
53'
2°52'N
Same scale as Houat
189°
La Chèvre
BRB
Fl.Y.2·5s
EDF4
47°21'N
Beg Lagad
Pointe du Vieux-Château
Fl.WG.4s
Port de l'Argol
Portz Guen
Spire
HOËDIC
Fort
Grand Mulon
Port de la Croix
Men Cren
Petit Mulon
20'
Roch Melen (4.3)
Beg er Faut
Madavoar
YB
BRB

9.21.20 PORT HALIGUEN

Morbihan **47°29′·35N 03°05′·97W** ❁❁❁◊◊◊✿✿

CHARTS AC 2357; Imray C38, 39; SHOM 7141, 7032, 7033; Navi 545

TIDES +0500 Dover; ML 3·1; Duration 0615

Standard Port BREST (⟵)

Times				Height (metres)			
High Water		Low Water		MHWS	MHWN	MLWN	MLWS
0000	0600	0000	0600	6·9	5·4	2·6	1·0
1200	1800	1200	1800				
Differences PORT HALIGUEN							
+0010	–0020	–0015	–0010	–1·6	–1·2	–0·6	–0·2
PORT MARIA							
+0010	–0025	–0025	–0015	–1·6	–1·3	–0·6	–0·1
LA TRINITÉ							
+0025	–0020	–0015	–0010	–1·6	–1·1	–0·5	–0·2

SHELTER Good, but uncomfortable in strong NW to NE winds.

NAVIGATION WPT 47°29′·80N 03°05′·00W, 237°/7ca to bkwtr lt. From W or S, appr via Passage de la Teignouse.

LIGHTS AND MARKS Hazards: Banc de Quiberon (2·7m at S end) marked by an unlit NCM and a lit SCM buoy. The W sector (299°-306°) of bkwtr lt, Oc (2) WR 6s, clears its S end. A 1·7m shoal marked by an unlit SCM buoy 'Port Haliguen', is avoided by approaching in the other W sector (233°-240·5°) of the bkwtr lt.

COMMUNICATIONS CROSS 02·97·55· 35·35; ☼ 02·97·64·34·86; Auto 08·92·68·08·56; Police 02·97·50·07·39; Dr 02·97·50·13·94; Marina Ch 09.

FACILITIES **Marina** Access H24. ☎02·97·50·20·56. www.sagemor.com port-haliguen@sagemor.fr 970 + 100Ⓥ €3·60. Ⓥ berths alongside/rafted both sides of pontoon V, with 10 finger berths on the NW end arm. Ice (13t) (2t). **Town** (Quiberon) Ⓑ ✈.

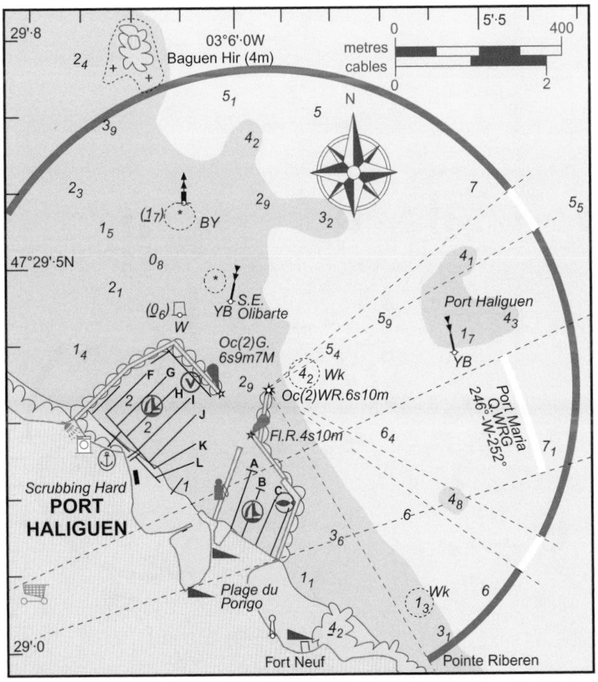

PORT MARIA, Morbihan, **47°28′·54N 03°07′·31W**. AC 2357; SHOM 7032, 7141. See Port Haliguen. Shelter good in all winds, but access dangerous in strong SE–SW winds. It is a very busy ferry/FV port, only feasible for yachts in emergency. ⚓ in SW of hbr in approx 2m. HM ☎02·97·50·08·71. Facilities: at E quay, SHOM (6t).

9.21.21 LA TRINITÉ-SUR-MER

Morbihan **47°35′·28N 03°01′·46W** ❁❁❁◊◊◊✿✿

CHARTS AC 2371, 2357; Imray C39; SHOM 7033, 7141,7034; Navi 545, 546

TIDES +0455 Dover; ML 3·2; Duration 0610

Standard Port BREST (⟵). Differences see Port Haliguen.

SHELTER Very good, except in strong SE/S winds near HW when La Vaneresse sandbank is covered. No ⚓/fishing in river.

NAVIGATION WPT 47°33′·38N 03°00′·42W, 347·2°/1·0M to No 2 PHM buoy. No navigational dangers; the Rivière de Crac'h is well marked by buoys and perches. Best water close to E bank. Beware many oyster beds, marked with perches. The channel is buoyed on both W sectors. Speed limit 5kn.

LIGHTS AND MARKS Daymarks include: Mousker, a 4·5m rk, off-white paint; and ✠ spire at La Trinité. See chartlet and Lights, buoys & waypoints. Rivière de Crac'h Q WRG, W twr/G top, but amid trees. 1M upriver: Dir lt 347°, Oc WRG 4s, W twr. S Pier, Q WR 6s 9/6M, W twr/R top, W 293·5°-300·5°.

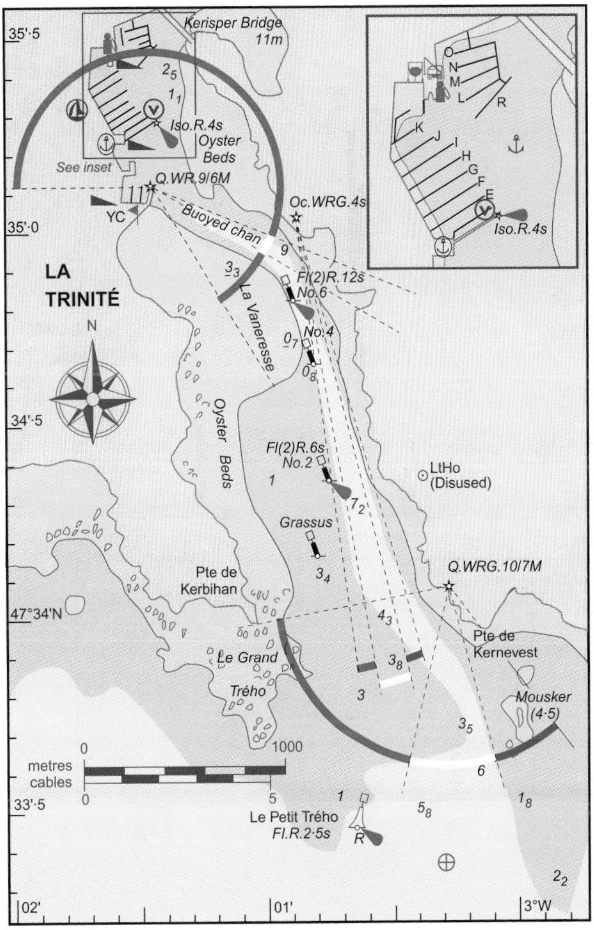

COMMUNICATIONS CROSS 02·97·55·35·35; 02·97·55·01·15; ☼ 02·97·64·34·86; Auto 08·92·68·08·56; Police 02·97·55·71·62; ⊖ 02·97·55·73·46; Brit Consul 01·44·51·31·00; Dr 02·97·55·74·03; Marina VHF Ch 09; Aff Mar 02·97·24·01·43.

FACILITIES **Marina** ☎02·97·55·71·49. www.baie-de-quiberon.com access H24 at all tides. Marina boat will meet. Ⓥ pontoon (fingers) is first N of ☆ Iso R 4s. 1030 +120Ⓥ €3·60. SHOM, Ⓔ Ice (36t) Grid.

CN ☎02·97·55·73·48.

Town Ⓑ. Auray. ✈ Lorient, Rennes. UK Ferry: via Roscoff, St Malo.

9.21.22 GOLFE DU MORBIHAN

Morbihan **47°32'·87N 02°55'·28W** (Ent) ❁❁◊◊◊✿✿✿

CHARTS AC 2823, 2371; SHOM 7033, 6992, 7034; Imray C39; Navi 546. Road map N° 0921 (IGN TOP 25 series, 1:25,000) is most useful in the Morbihan as a shoreside complement to charts.

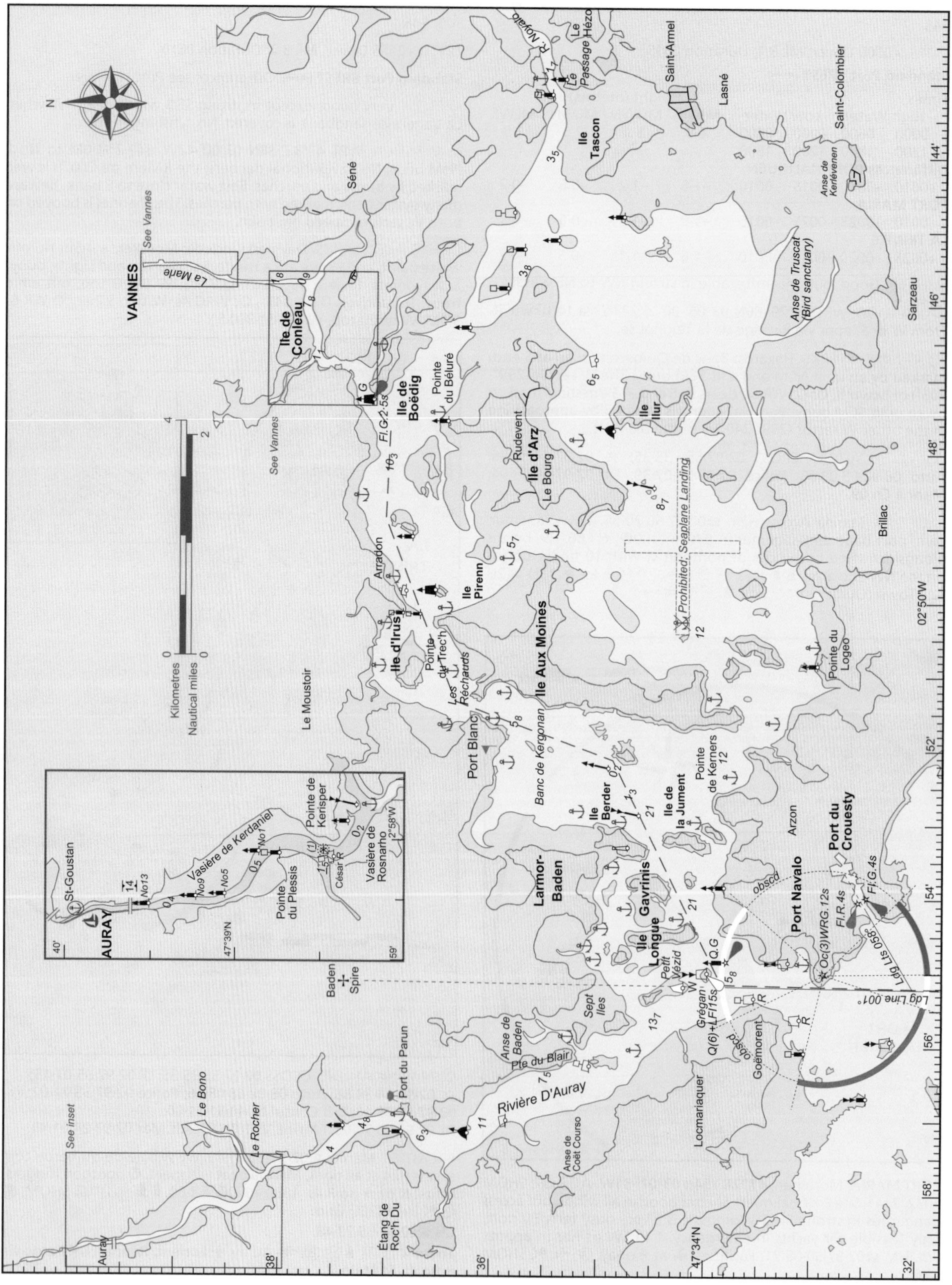
VANNES
See Vannes
La Marle
Ile de Conleau
Séné
Ile de Boëdig
Fl.G.2·5s
Pointe du Béluré
R. Noyalo
Le Passage
Le Hézo
Saint-Armel
Lasné
Ile Tascon
Saint-Colombier
Anse de Kerlévenen
Anse de Truscat (Bird sanctuary)
Sarzeau
Rudevent
Ile d'Arz
Le Bourg
Ile Ilur
Prohibited; Seaplane Landing
Brillac
Arradon
Ile Pirenn
Ile d'Irus
Pointe du Trec'h
Les Réchauds
Ile Aux Moines
Pointe du Logeo
Le Moustoir
Port Blanc
Banc de Kergonan
Ile Berder
Ile de la Jument
Pointe de Kerners
Arzon
Port du Crouesty
Port Navalo
Larmor-Baden
Gavrinis
Ile Longue
Petit Vézid
Grégan
Q(6)+LFl15s
Q.G
Oc(3)WRG.12s
Fl.R.4s
Fl.G.4s
Ldg Lts 058°
Ldg Line 001°
obscd
Baden Spire
Sept Iles
Anse de Baden
Pte du Blair
Goëmorent
Locmariaquer
Port du Parun
Rivière D'Auray
Anse de Coët Courso
Étang de Roc'h Du
Le Bono
Le Rocher
See inset
Auray
AURAY
St-Goustan
Vasière de Kerdaniel
Pointe de Kerisper
Pointe du Plessis
César R
Vasière de Rosnarho
Kilometres
Nautical miles
02°50'W
47°34'N

TIDES +0515 Dover; ML 3·0
Standard Port BREST (⟵)

Times				Height (metres)			
High Water		Low Water		MHWS	MHWN	MLWN	MLWS
0000	0600	0000	0600	6·9	5·4	2·6	1·0
1200	1800	1200	1800				
Differences PORT NAVALO							
+0030	–0005	–0010	–0005	–2·0	–1·5	–0·8	–0·3
AURAY							
+0035	0000	+0015	–0005	–2·2	–1·8	–1·1	–0·4
ARRADON							
+0135	+0145	+0140	+0115	–3·8	–3·0	–1·8	–0·7
VANNES							
+0200	+0150	+0140	+0120	–3·7	–2·9	–2·0	–0·8
LE PASSAGE (47°35´·4N 02°43´·1W)							
+0200	+0200	+0210	+0135	–3·7	–2·0	–1·9	–0·8
LE LOGEO							
+0140	+0140	+0145	+0115	–4·0	–3·1	–2·0	–0·8

SHELTER The Golfe du Morbihan is a large, inland tidal sea with deep apprs and entrance. A significant sea state is rare, except for tide rips in the ent. Shelter can usually be found from all winds, but the many ⚓s (see chartlet and Facilities) are increasingly restricted by extensive local moorings. It is essential to use chain when ⚓ing, unless well out of the tide. Île aux Moines and Île d'Arz are the only public islands. Vannes is the only marina.

NAVIGATION WPT 47°31´·97N= 02°55´·29W (as for Crouesty) 001°/1·7M to abeam Grand Mouton lt bcn. Pilotage is not difficult and the strong streams are not inherently dangerous, it's worth pre-plotting the desired tracks/distances within the channels. Marks can then be more readily identified and track adjusted with ease, especially if beating. Night navigation is not advised.

Caution: Many vedettes in season. Frequent ferries cross from Port Blanc to Île aux Moines, at times with scant regard for IRPCS; keep well clear of them. Avoid numerous bird sanctuaries in SE, and oyster beds marked by withies. Much of the E & SE dries.

TIDAL STREAMS *The very strong tidal streams which reach 9·1kn between Île Berder and Île de la Jument dictate ent/exit times.*

On AC 2371 study tidal diamonds ◊ B (off Port Navalo lt ho), ◊ D at Grand/Petit Mouton and ◊ G at the S tip of Ile Berder. These give a good idea of when the flood and ebb should start, hence earliest times to ent/exit. At ◊ B the flood starts at about HW Brest –4½. At ◊ G the ebb starts at about HWB +2¼. Their rates however may be conservative. At ◊ D for example the max rate is 5·2kn whereas the tidal vectors here show 6·9 to 8kn.

For a first visit avoid springs; entry at night with a tide running is hazardous. Off Grand Mouton sp rates reach 8kn and in the ent can exceed 4kn. Flood starts HW Brest – 0400 and turns at HW Brest + 0200. Here the flood divides: the weaker flow enters the R. Auray; whilst the major stream sets strongly toward Petit & Grand Mouton rks before setting into the main chan. Maintain 001° until Grand Mouton lt bcn is abaft the beam, but beware shoals E of Goémorent R bcn twr.

The streams ease in the upper reaches except between Pte de Toulindag and Port Blanc where ◊ K indicates >5kn. HW times become later further E, eg HW Vannes is 2 hrs after HW Pt Navalo. HW Auray is only 25 mins after HW Port Navalo.

LIGHTS AND MARKS The 001° appr ldg daymarks are: front, Petit Vézid W obelisk (from afar looks like a yacht sail); rear, Baden ✠ spire (3·3M). Chans and dangers are well marked. The only lts are: Port Navalo lt ho at the ent. Inside ent: Grand Mouton SHM bcn and Le Grégan, a squat SCM bcn. Roguédas, a large SHM bcn is near the appr chan to Vannes.

FACILITIES, clockwise from **AURAY RIVER**

LOCMARIAQUER 47°34´·19N 02°55´·81W. Two drying quays 500m apart: To S, ferries use the buoyed chan to Cale du Guilvin, ⌓ (S side only, max 30 mins) ⛴ fuel 06.03.09.15.06; drying ⚓ to W. To N, Cale de Locmariaquer (used by ferries) slip. **Village** ✕ 🛒 © ✉ bike hire, buses.

SEPT ÎLES 47°35´·09N 02°56´·18W: Small, quiet ⚓. Enter Anse de Baden, mostly dries, between mainland and W end of island.

PORT DU PARUN 47°36´·76N 02°56´·96W: Drying inlet: no moorings but ⚓ with quay, slip & all facilities. ☎02·97·57·00·15.

LE ROCHER 47°38´·17N 02°57´·75W: Sheltered, but full of moorings.

LE BONO 47°38´·43N 02°57´·21W: Moor or ⚓ (rky bottom) off Banc de la Sarcelle. ⌓ in drying basin, ☎02·97·57·88·98. **Village** ✕ 🛒 © 🔧 ⛽ ✉.

AURAY 47°39´·84N 02°58´·73W: The river shoals to 0·2m, but St Goustan is accessible at mid-flood via a bridge with 14m MSL and 0·4m depth; gauge shows air clearance. Calculate tides carefully for a safe passage. 12 dumbbell 🅥s in a pool upriver; drying ⌓ at St Goustan; or 🅥s S of 14m bridge. HM ☎02.97.56.29.08. ⛴ 🔧 ⚒. **Town** ✕ 🛒 © ✉ ⇌.

NW AND CENTRAL AREAS

ÎLE LONGUE 47°34´·17N 02°54´·44W: ⚓ out of the stream. No landing.

LARMOR BADEN 47°34´·82N 02°53´·62W: good ⚓s to S and further W, but many moorings, HM ☎02·97·57·20·86; 06·14·19·12·76. Village: ✕ 🛒 ✉ ⛴ (4t). Ferry to Île Gavrinis all year.

ÎLE BERDER 47°34´·81N 02°53´·05W: pleasant ⚓ E of the island.

PORT BLANC 47°36´·32N 02°51´·66W: HM ☎02·97·26·30·57, mob 06·11·07·56·89. Ch 09, 0845-1230; many moorings €2·40. Quay, ⛴ ✕ 🚿 © ✉ free seasonal water taxi, Ch 09 *Service de Rade*. Ferry ½hrly to Île aux Moines.

ÎLE AUX MOINES: a popular public island. The narrows between Pte de Toulindag and Port Blanc can be rough; beware Les Réchauds drying rks. ⚓ 47°36´·22N 02°51´·11W; or 🅥 pontoon (🚿) the W'ly of two; land at small marina. Free seasonal water taxi, VHF Ch 09 *Service de Rade* or sound horn. HM ☎02·97·26·30·57, 0845-1230, 🚿. Quieter ⚓s S & E of Pte du Trec'h and SE tip of island.

ARRADON: limited ⚓ 47°36´·84N 02°50´·24W, exposed to S. HM ☎ 02·97·44·01·23. Ch 09. Apr-Sep 1400-1700. Many local moorings, €2·40. ⛴ 🚿. Free seasonal water taxi, Ch 09 *Service de Rade*. Pier, depth gauge/disabled access, max 15 mins stay on W side only.

ÎLE PIRENN: exposed ⚓ 47°35´·79N 02°49´·42W in tidal stream.

ÎLE D'ARZ, a public island. ⚓ 47°36´·45N 02°47´·43W NE of Pte du Béluré (ferry landing); E of Le Bourg (good shelter); or to the W, depending on winds. Rudevent village: 🔧 ⚒.

ÎLE DE BOËDIG: sheltered ⚓ 47°37´·00N 02°46´·53W, if moorings permit, in Chenal de Badel N of the island.

ÎLE DE CONLEAU 47°37´·62N 02°46´·73W: ⚓ or moor in bight just S of village, as space permits. ✕ 🔧 ⚒ in village.

EAST AND SOUTH AREAS

SÉNÉ 47°37´·19N 02°44´·49W: dry out in traditional hbr at head of inlet; 🔧. Easy bike recce 2M SSE from Vannes.

LE PASSAGE: ⚓ 47°35´·43N 02°42´·93W off Pte du Passage (depths upriver not charted). Village: (St Armel): ☕. Seasonal ferry.

KERNERS: ⚓ 47°33´·65N 02°52´·44W in 3-6m off Anse de Kerners or further SE off Anse de Pen Castel. Ferry to Île aux Moines.

ÎLE DE LA JUMENT 47°34´·20N 02°53´·15W: good shelter E of island out of the tide; handy for leaving the gulf on the tide.

PORT NAVALO 47°33´·00N 02°54´·86W: ⚓ in bay, but full of moorings, and open to W/NW winds. Convenient to await the tide. HM ☎02·97·53·82·12. All facilities at Crouesty (½ mile by road).

BAIE DE QUIBERON

Open to the E and SE, this is an important and attractive cruising area with centres at **Port Haliguen, La Trinité**, the **Morbihan** and **Crouesty** (AC 2823). The S side of the bay is enclosed by a long chain of islands, islets, rocks and shoals from Presqu'île de Quiberon to Les Grands Cardinaux 13M SE. The islands of **Houat** and **Hoëdic** are well worth visiting, ideally mid-week. From W or S, enter the Bay via Passage de la Teignouse in W sector (033°-039°) of La Teignouse lt ho; thence 068° between Basse Nouvelle lt buoy and NE Teignouse lt buoy.

▶*In this channel the NE-going flood starts at HW Brest –6¼, and the SW-going at HW Brest, sp rates 3·75kn; in strong winds it is best to pass at slack water.*◀

Passage du Béniguet and Passage des Soeurs are alternatives.

9.21.23 VANNES

Morbihan **47°38′·45N 02°45′·62W**

CHARTS AC 2823, 2371; Imray C39; SHOM 7034; Navi 546

TIDES See GOLFE DU MORBIHAN. ML 2·0m

SHELTER Excellent in all winds.

ACCESS by day only, no earlier than 0730 and no later than 2130 and depending on HW times, the entry gate and the Kérino swing bridge (VHF Ch 09) both remain open for free-flow (HW±2½). Waiting pontoons (partly drying) are up-/downstream of the bridge; intercom to HM is on the downstream pontoon. The Bridgemaster may occasionally speak by loudhailer.

Traffic signals (3 vert lts) on the bridge's western pier are:
F ●●● = no passage; F ●●● = proceed;
Oc ●●● = No passage unless committed, but unmasted boats may transit.

The **entry gate** (not a lock) approx 250m N of the bridge is remotely controlled by the HM. HW Vannes –2½, when the gate opens, is the same as HW Port Tudy (a French Standard Port). The sill retains 2·1m in the wet basin. F ●●●●● = NO GO; F ●●● = GO.

The *Guide pratique du Port* (a free annual schedule of gate hrs etc) is very useful and available from Port de Plaisance, La Rabine, 56019 Vannes or download as a pdf at www.mairie-vannes.fr/uploads/media/GuidePortVannes2017 01.pdf.

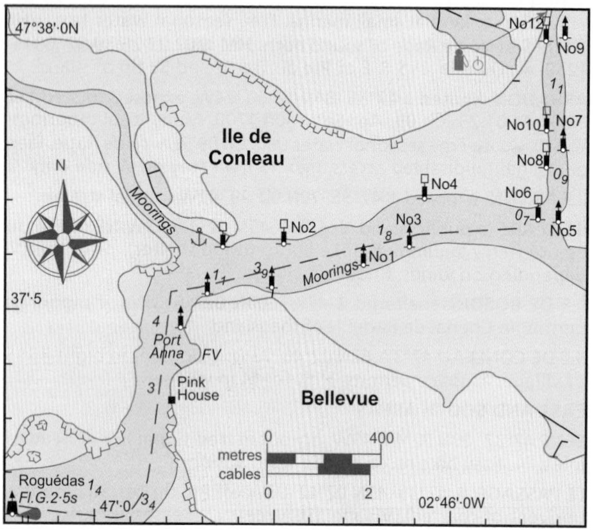

NAVIGATION WPT: see Golfe du Morbihan. After Roguédas SHM lt bcn do not cut the shallow corner to port; if anything head ESE until the chan opens up. Turn N'wards when a pink house on its E bank bears 020°. Passage upstream past Île de Conleau is easy and well marked. Beacon'd appr chan to Vannes is narrow, least charted depth 0·7m, but dredged 2·1m from No 6 bcn to the bridge.

LIGHTS AND MARKS No navigation lts N of Roguédas, Fl G 2.5s.

COMMUNICATIONS CROSS 02·97·55·35·35; 02·97·42·49·49; Police 02·97·47·19·20; 02·97·01·36·00; Brit Consul 01·44·51·31·00; 02·97·01·41·41; HM VHF Ch 09 (0800-1200, 1500-1900 Jul-Aug); Aff Mar 02·97·63·40·95.

FACILITIES **Marina** 02·97·01·55·20. www.mairie-vannes.fr port.plaisance@mairie-vannes.fr 214+70 €2·64, multihulls +50%. Marina launch may allot a finger berth. If not, visitors berth/raft N/S on pontoons D and G, just S of mobile foot-bridge (*passerelle*).
(10t); nearest fuel by hose is at Crouesty.

City SHOM .

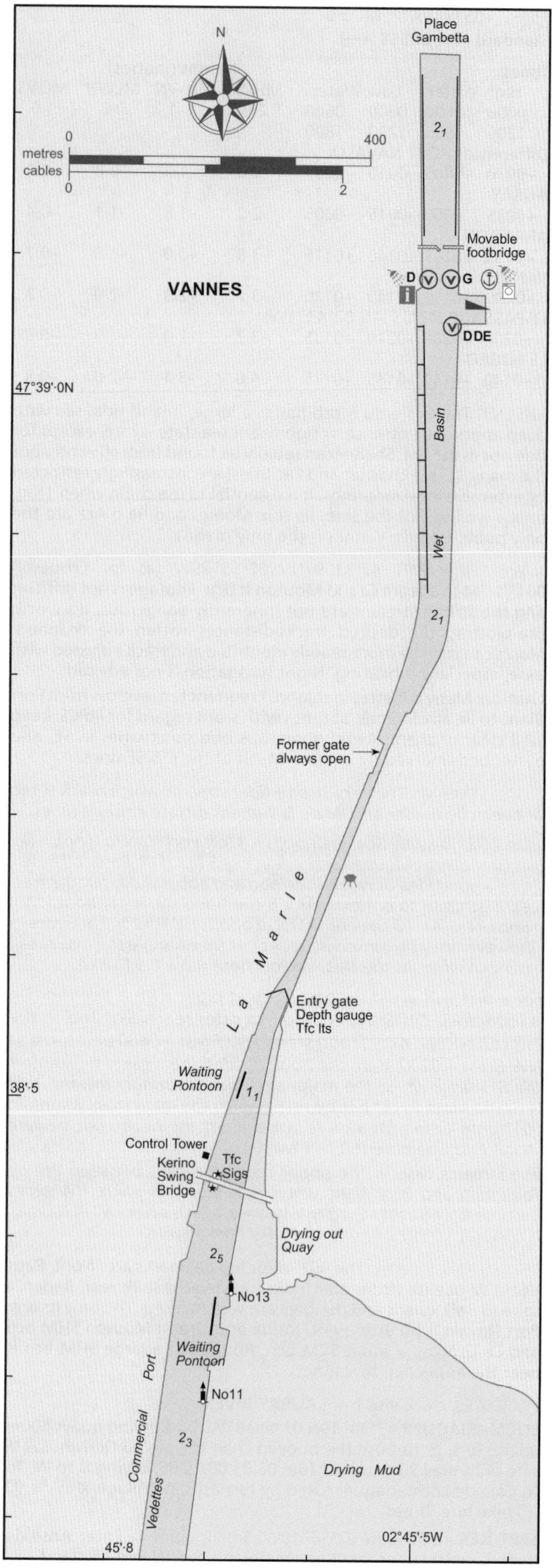

CROUESTY TO LE CROISIC

East of the Morbihan entrance, dangers extend 1M seaward of Pte de St Jacques (where a small hbr dries). 3M offshore Plateau de la Recherche has depths of 1·8m (AC 2823). SE of **Pénerf,** which provides good anchorage, Plateau des Mats is a rocky bank, drying in places, extending up to 1·75M offshore.

Across the ent to the **Vilaine River** beware La Grande Accroche, a large shoal with least depth 1m. The main lit chan leads NW of La Grande Accroche, to the bar on N side.

►*Here the flood begins at HW Brest –0515, and the ebb at HW Brest +0035, sp rates 2·5kn.*◄

In SW winds against tide the sea breaks heavily; the Passe de la Varlingue, 5ca W of Pte du Halguen, is then better, but beware La Varlingue (dries 0·3). At **Arzal/Camoël** yachts can lock into the non-tidal Vilaine River for **La Roche Bernard** (6km) and **Redon** (29km) to access the **Ille et Rance Canal** to Dinan/St Malo.

South of Pte du Halguen in a little frequented corner of Quiberon Bay, other dangers include the rocky shoals, both 0·6m, of Basse de Loscolo and Basse du Bile, close inshore. Off Pte du Castelli, the Plateau de Piriac extends about 1·75M NW with depths of 2·3m and drying rocks closer inshore. The small hbr and marina at **Piriac** lies on the N side of Pointe du Castelli and Les Bayonelles (dry) extend 5ca W. A chan runs between Plateau de Piriac and Île Dumet (lt) which is fringed by drying rocks and shoals particularly on N and E sides.

In the Rade du Croisic are the fishing harbours of **La Turballe** and **Le Croisic**, the former with a marina. Off Pointe du Croisic dangers extend 1M to N and W. Plateau du Four, a dangerous drying bank of rocks, lies about 4M W and WSW of Pointe du Croisic, marked by buoys and lt ho near N end. Approx 3M SW of Ouest Basse Capella WCM, a Restricted Area centred on 47° 14'· 37N 02° 46'· 65W, with limits marked by 4 SPM Fl Y 4s, encloses 2 ODAS bys, Fl (5) Y 20s. 2.8M ESE of Pointe du Croisic, Basse Lovre is a rocky shoal with depths of 0.7m, 5ca offshore, marked by a SCM buoy.

9.21.24 CROUESTY

Morbihan **47°32'·46N 02°54'·13W** ❀❀❀◊◊◊✿✿

CHARTS AC 2823, 2371; Imray C39; SHOM 6992, 7034, 7033; Navi 546

TIDES +0505 Dover; ML 3·0; Duration 0555

Standard Port BREST (⟵)

Times				Height (metres)			
High Water		Low Water		MHWS	MHWN	MLWN	MLWS
0000	0600	0000	0600	6·9	5·4	2·6	1·0
1200	1800	1200	1800				
Differences CROUESTY							
+0010	–0025	–0015	–0010	–1·5	–1·1	–0·6	–0·2

SHELTER Very good, but strong onshore winds can raise dangerous seas in the ent. Quiberon peninsula gives some shelter from W'lies.

NAVIGATION WPT 47°31'·97N 02°55'·30W, 058°/0·9M to hbr ent. Access chan is dredged 1·8m and buoyed. Caution: drying shoal close NW of ldg line between Nos 6 and 8 buoys; stay in the chan especially near LW.

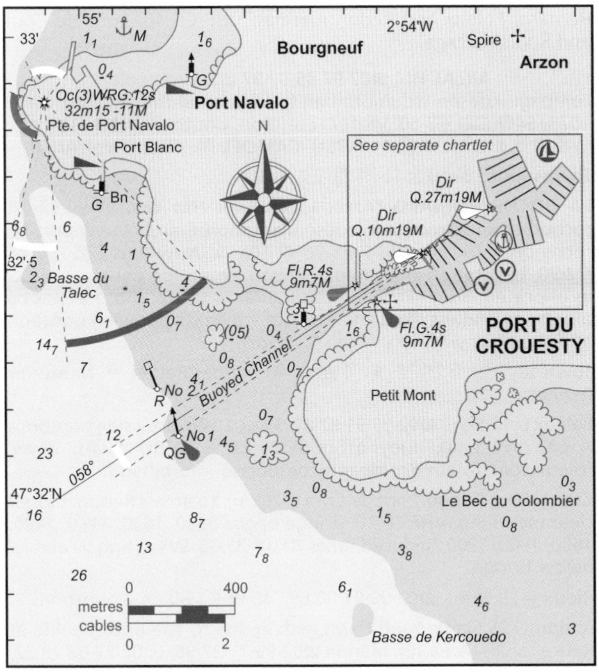

LIGHTS AND MARKS Ldg marks/lts 058°: Front W vert stripe on R panel; rear the tall grey lt ho. Only No 1 SHM lead-in buoy is lit, QG. See chartlet and Lights, buoys and waypoints for details.

COMMUNICATIONS CROSS 02·97·55·35·35; LB 02·97·41·35·35; Auto 08·92·68·08·56; Police 02·97·53·71·65; ⊖ 02·97·01·36·00; Brit Consul 01·44·51·31·00; Dr 02·97·53·71·61; HM VHF Ch 09; Aff Mar 02·97·41·84·10.

FACILITIES The enormous **Port du Crouesty Marina** has 6 large separate basins; see large-scale chartlet below. HM ☎02·97·53·73·33. www.baie-de-quiberon.com 1432+130Ⓥ €3·60. On pontoons V1, V2 and V3 in Ⓥ basin on S side of fairway; boats >12m LOA can berth on the wall between V1 and V2. During peak season additional Ⓥ berthing on N side, rafting on pontoons W and U, with nearby. For free water taxi call VHF Ch 09. (H24 with cr/card) Ⓔ ✗ (45t) (10t) wi-fi.

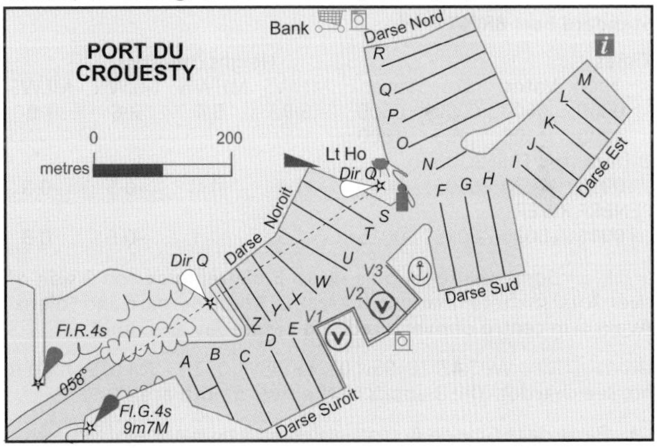

Town (Arzon) ✗ ⊠ Ⓑ. ⇄ Vannes. ✈ Vannes, Lorient, St Nazaire, Rennes.

MINOR HARBOUR, approx 13 track miles east of Crouesty

PÉNERF RIVER, Morbihan, **47°30'·03N 02°38'·89W,** AC 2823; SHOM 7033, 7135 (advised, plus good Pilot). HW +0515 on Dover (UT); Duration 0610; ML 3·3m. See Vilaine River. Shelter good, except in fresh W'lies. The 3 ents require careful planning & pilotage:

Passe de l'Ouest is shoal and poorly marked. **Passe du Centre** is the widest and easiest, least depth 0·7m. Appr on 359° ldg line, Le Pignon red lt bcn ≠ Le Tour du Parc spire, passing between Penvins PHM buoy and Borénis SHM buoy. Leave a SHM bcn (marking a drying reef) 150m to the E; thence pass 40m E of Le Pignon, whose white sector covers the appr, but night entry is not advised for a first visit. **Passe de l'Est** has 4m, but is narrower and rks are close to stbd. It joins Passe du Centre E of Le Pignon bcn. Once in the river, head ENE for 1M to ⚓ off Pénerf quay. Beware oyster beds.

Facilities . **Village** ✗ (at Damgan).

9.21.25 VILAINE RIVER

Morbihan **47°30′·38N 02°28′·71W** (1st lt buoys)

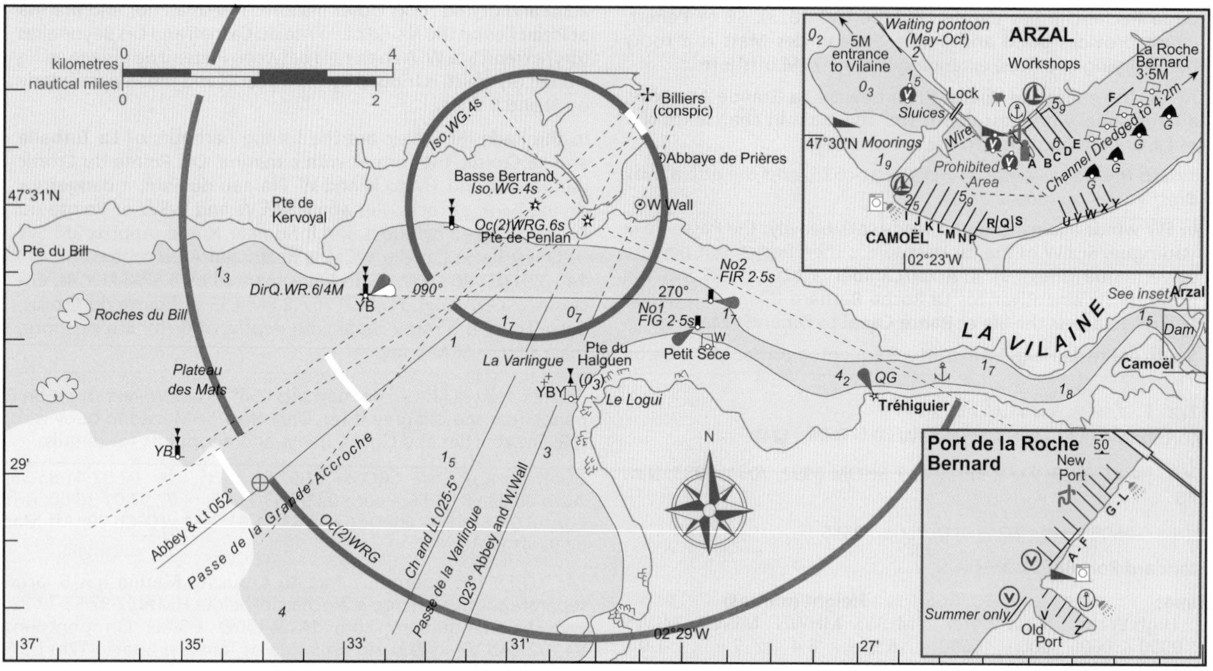

CHARTS AC 2823; SHOM 7033, 7144; Navi 546; Imray C39. Note: 2823 ends at river mouth. 7144 continues to La Roche-Bernard.

TIDES +0500 Dover; ML (Pénerf) 3·3; Duration 0610

Standard Port BREST (⟵)

Times				Height (metres)			
High Water		Low Water		MHWS	MHWN	MLWN	MLWS
0000	0600	0000	0600	6·9	5·4	2·6	1·0
1200	1800	1200	1800				
Differences TRÉHIGUIER							
+0035	−0020	−0005	−0010	−1·4	−1·0	−0·5	−0·3
PÉNERF RIVER							
+0015	−0025	−0015	−0015	−1·5	−1·1	−0·6	−0·3

SHELTER Some shelter, 4 blue ⚓s to E of Tréhiguier on S side of river. Total shelter in marinas at Arzal, La Roche Bernard and Foleux. Avoid ⚓ in centre of river, dredging occurs day and night.

NAVIGATION WPT 47°28′·95N 02°33′·96W, 052°/3·3M to Penlan lt ho; see chartlet. The 3 appr's to the river mouth are:

- Passe de la Grande Accroche: Penlan lt ho ≠ Abbey de Prières 052°. Marks are reportedly conspic by day.
- Penlan lt ≠ Billiers ch tr 025·5°, leaving La Varlingue Rk (0·3m) close to stbd.
- Passe de la Varlingue (unlit): W wall ≠ Abbey Tr 023°, passing close to WCM bcn and oyster poles off Le Logui.

In strong onshore winds, especially at sp ebb, seas can break in shallow ent to La Vilaine (min 0·5m). Best enter/leave near HW. River well byd to Tréhiguier, adequate beyond, keep to chan.

Arzal lock usually opens hourly up to 9 times per day, 0700–2100 (LT) Jul/Aug; rest of year, 0800, 0900, 1100,1200, 1400, 1600, 1800, 2000 (LT) but times can vary, see: www.lavilaine.com/index.php/en/ for current lock and Cran bridge times, call HM Ch 11, or ☎09·69·32·22·97 for recorded info. Avoid prohib areas (Y bys) below/above barrage. Below lock wait on large W by or use 200m pontoon with access to N bank. Follow lock-keeper's instructions in lock; secure to vertical chains or raft alongside other vessels; anticipate surge when upper gates open. Above lock, wait on 2 lge W bys SW Arzal. Speed limit above Arzal is 5·5kn, marked port areas 3·0kn and nav works 2·0kn.

LIGHTS AND MARKS See chartlet. Two Dir lts in approaches are:

- Basse Bertrand, 14m G twr. The W sector (040°-054°) overlaps the W sector of Penlan in Passe de la Grande Accroche.
- Pte de Penlan, 18m W twr, R bands; W sector 052°-060°.

At river ent Petit Sécé W bcn twr is easier to see than Nos 1 & 2 buoys. On S side of lock the control twr is conspic.

COMMUNICATIONS CROSS 02·97·55·35·35; Auto 08·92·68·08·56; ⊜ 02·97·63·18·71 (Vannes); Brit Consul 01·44·51·31·00; Ⓗ 02·99·90·61·20; Dr 02·97·45·01·21; Pont de Cran 02·99·90·11·31; Aff Mar 02·99·90·32·62; VHF Ch 09: Arzal-Camoël, La Roche Bernard, Foleux and Redon marinas; VHF Ch 10: Pont de Cran and R Vilaine/canal.

FACILITIES **ARZAL** HM ☎02·97·45·02·97 arzal-cameol@compagniedesportsdumorbihan.fr www.arzal-cameol.com 1078+54Ⓥ €3·60. Visitor reception, pontoon A H24. Ⓔ (35t). **CAMOËL**. Check in at Arzal.

Towns (both 3km) Ⓑ.

LA ROCHE BERNARD (Arzal lock+6km): HM ☎02·99·90·62·17. roche-bernard@compagniedesportsdumorbihan.fr www.port-la-roche-bernard.com **Old Port** 96 Ⓥ 108 ⚓. **New Port** 335+56 Ⓥ, €2·90, best to call HM to book ahead, reception pontoon A, as allocated. Summer Ⓥ pontoon an alternative, shore access by dinghy on endless fixed line – do not navigate between pontoon and shore. wi-fi Ⓔ (13t).

Town Ⓑ. Vannes/Redon. ✈ Nantes or Rennes.

Foleux (+12·5km) ☎02·99·91·87·87. 321 + 20Ⓥ (outer side pontoons A & C) on N bank; buoys off both banks. (30t) wi-fi. www.foleux.com foleux@compagniedesportsdumorbihan.fr

Cran Swing Bridge/Pont de Cran (+26km), to access Redon. Closed clearance 5.8m. VHF Ch 10. Bridge opens 0930, 1030, 1130, 1400, 1600, 1800, 1900. Reduced times 01/10-31/03. W waiting by above/below bridge.

Rieux (+29.5km), ☎02·99·91·90·69, 40 Ⓥ €1·80 on 2 pontoons.

Redon (+35.5km): good town,with access to the Brittany/ Ille et Rance canals (Area 18). **Marina** ☎02·99·71·22·96, or 07·77·88·23·22, cepredon@yahoo.fr. 128 +10Ⓥ €2·20 in 2·5m; mast (500kg).

9.21.26 PIRIAC

Loire Atlantique **47°23´·02N 02°32´·67W** ❁❁◊◊✿✿

CHARTS AC 2823; Imray C39, 40; SHOM 7033, 7136; Navi 546

TIDES Interpolate between Vilaine River (Penerf) and Le Croisic. HW +0505 on Dover (UT); ML 3·3m; Duration 0605. Locals use predictions for Le Croisic.

SHELTER Good in marina, near HW can be exposed to N'lies.

NAVIGATION WPT 47°23´·69N 02°32´·38W, 197°/7ca to hbr ent in the W sector (194°-201°) of Piriac lt, Oc (2) WRG 6s.

Plateau de Piriac extends about 1M W and N from the hbr; to the SW it is marked by a WCM buoy, Q (9) 15s, and to the NNW by Le Rohtrès NCM bcn twr and by Grand Norven NCM lt bcn, Q. Shoals extend, do not attempt to pass S of these bcns even near HW.

At night the W sectors of Île Dumet lt (272°-285°) and of Pte de Mesquer lt (067°-072°) help to position within the W sector of Piriac lt, as well as bns, lit QG to N and QR to NE of hbr ent.

LIGHTS AND MARKS Piriac church belfry is a conspic daymark, aligned approx 197° with chan. The Sig stn at Pte de Castelli, 8ca SW of the hbr, is a conspic white, prow-shaped structure.

COMMUNICATIONS CROSS 02·97·55·35·35; LB 02·40·23·55·74 (Jul-Aug only); Auto 08·92·68·08·44; ⊜ 02·40·23·32·51 (Turballe); Brit Consul 01·44·51·31·00; HM VHF Ch 09; Aff Mar 02·40·11·77·50.

FACILITIES **Marina** ☎02·40·23·52·32. www.portpiriacsurmer.fr portpiriacsurmer@sainte-nazaire.cci.fr. Sill into marina is at CD+0·7m, but drop gate (marked by PHM and SHM perches) does not open until tide reaches CD+2·2M, when 1·3–1·5m over the sill shows on large digital depth indicator and IPTS sigs 2 or 4. Beware strong inflow, best when >1·5m depth showing. Avoid retaining wall marked by Y SPM perches. 750+70Ⓥ on pontoon E, €3·40. ⛽ pontoon D, ▬ Ⓔ ✂ ⚒(12t).

Town The attractive small town has ✕ ▭ 🛒 ✉ Ⓑ market.

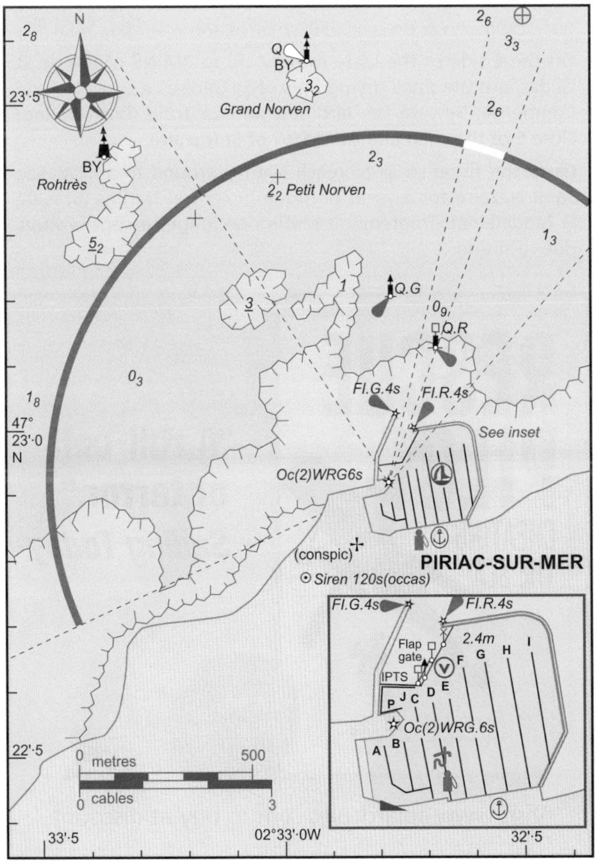

9.21.27 LA TURBALLE

Loire Atlantique **47°20´·70N 02°30´·89W** ❁❁◊◊◊✿✿

CHARTS AC 2823; Imray C39, 40; SHOM 6826, 7033; Navi 546

TIDES Approx as for Le Croisic

SHELTER Good in all winds, but in strong SSW'lies heavy swell can close the hbr. In N to E winds it is possible to ⚓ S of the hbr.

NAVIGATION WPT 47°20´·19N 02°30´·99W, 006·5°/5ca to W bkwtr lt. The ent is not easily seen until S of the hbr. Appr in W sector (315°-060°) of W bkwtr lt to pick up the 006·5° ldg lts. A number of small unlit R and G bys close to the ldg transit may be ignored. Jun-Sep a buoyed No ⚓ area lies between 060° and 090° 8 cables to the west bkwtr lt. From the SW avoid Plateau du Four and shoals off Le Croisic. There is an active fleet of 80 FVs.

LIGHTS AND MARKS By day Trescalan ✠ and water tr (conspic) 1M ENE of hbr, lead 070° to just S of ent. R bcn twr is 80m off W bkwtr.

COMMUNICATIONS CROSS 02·97·55·35·35; Auto 08·92·68·08·44; ⊜ 02·40·23·37·51; HM call VHF Ch 09 before entering. If in Jul/Aug the marina is full and closed to new arrivals, it is announced on Ch 09; Aff Mar 02·40·23·33·35.

FACILITIES **Marina** ☎02·40·23·41·65. www.port-peche-turballe.fr plaisance.turballe@wanadoo.fr 315+30Ⓥ €2·10.

Access H24. Inside ent, turn 110° stbd round a blind corner into the marina (1·5-2m). There are shoal patches between A–G and B–F pontoons, therefore craft >1·5m draught should not enter LW springs ±2 to avoid grounding.

Visitors are rafted tight into the rectangular box off B pontoon; if staying a few days a vacant finger berth may be allotted on request. Call before entering; see R/T.

⛽(min 10 ltrs); pay by French cr/card or at Coopérative Maritime ☎02·40·62·80·05 (facing hbr); Ⓓ Ⓟ at garage 500m. ▬ ✂ Ⓔ ⚒ (32t) ☎02·40·62·80·40, in Capitainerie, YC SHOM Ice @ in Capitainerie and the Municipal library.

Town ✕ 🛒 ▭ ✉ Ⓑ Dr. Buses to St Nazaire and Nantes.

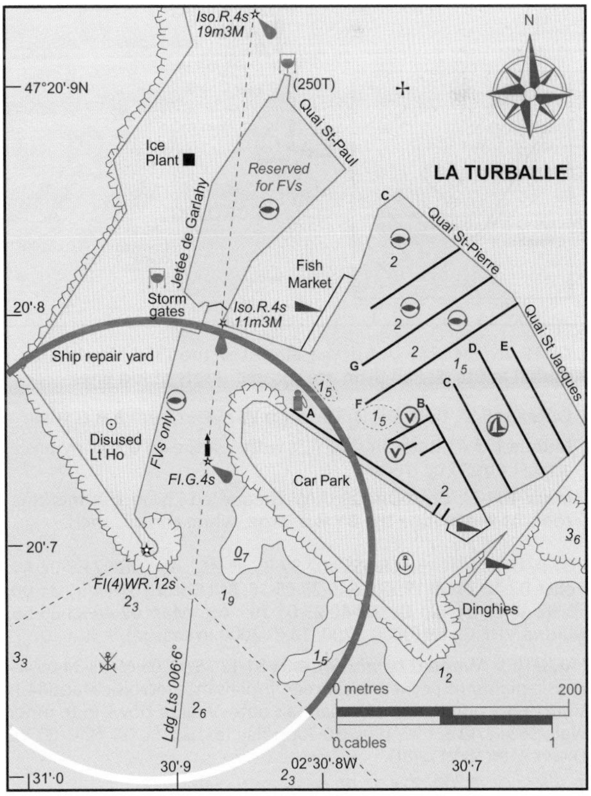

9.21.28 LE CROISIC

Loire Atlantique **47°18'·52N 02°31'·35W** ✵✵◊◊◊✿✿✿

CHARTS AC 2646, 2986, 2823; Imray C39; SHOM 7033, 7395, 7145 (the preferred large scale chart); Navi 546, 547

TIDES +0450 Dover; ML 3·3; Duration 0605

Standard Port BREST (⟵)

Times				Height (metres)			
High Water		Low Water		MHWS	MHWN	MLWN	MLWS
0000	0600	0000	0600	6·9	5·4	2·6	1·0
1200	1800	1200	1800				
Differences LE CROISIC							
+0015	–0040	–0020	–0015	–1·5	–1·1	–0·6	–0·3

SHELTER Good. No ⚓ in Le Poul; full of moorings, very strong ebb.

NAVIGATION WPT 47°18'·97N 02°31'·65W, 155·5°/5ca to Tréhic bkwtr hd. Beware rks and shoals close in to Hergo SHM bcn twr in Tréhic's W sector (093°-137°). In its SW G sector dangers extend 2M W to Basse Castouillet WCM buoy. Keep strictly on the ldg lines as appr and hbr dry extensively; chan is dredged 2m at first, then 1·6m and 1·2m. Sp tides reach 4kn. 4 drying basins (*Chambres*) are formed by islets (*Jonchères*).

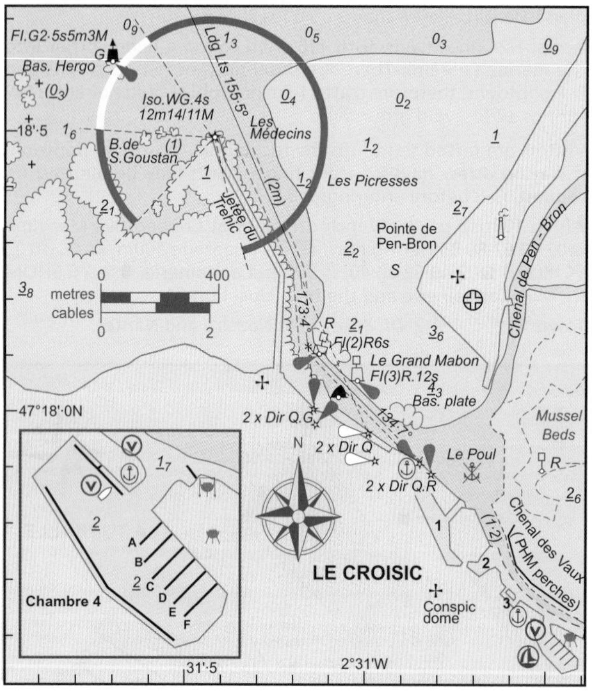

LIGHTS AND MARKS A ✠ dome, almost on the 155·5° ldg line, and hospital at Pte de Pen Bron are conspic. 3 sets of ldg lines:

Outer 155·5°: both Dir Q; Or □s on W pylons, rear has G top

Middle 173·4°: both Dir QG; Y □s with G stripe on G & W pylons, almost obsc'd by trees.

Inner 134·7°: both Dir QR; R/W chequered □s on fish market roof. At the marina the BY is a large, white conspic shed.

COMMUNICATIONS CROSS 02·97·55·35·35; ☼ 08·92·68·02·44; Police 02·40·23·00·19; ⊖ 02·40·23·05·38; Brit Consul 01·44·51·31·00; Ⓗ 02·40·23·01·12; Dr 02·40·23·01·70; Aff Mar 02·40·23·06·56; Marina VHF Ch 09 (0800-1200; 1330-2000 in season).

FACILITIES **Marina** (*Chambre 4*). ☎09·81·12·75·92, 06·65·93·34·05. le-croisic-plaisance.peche-plaisance44.fr/plaisance.lecroisic@lapp44.fr Visitors dry out against the marina's outer wall or bows-in to inner wall. 360+27Ⓥ €1·90, plus €0·20pp/day tax. ⛴ ⚒ ⊡ ✖ ⛽ Ⓔ YC Divers ♿ ⛽(180t) ⛽(8t).

Town ✕ ⊡ ⊡ ⊡ ⊡ ▮ ✉ Ⓑ ⇄ ✈ (St Nazaire).

LE CROISIC TO THE RIVER LOIRE AND TO NANTES

From Chenal du Nord, the **Baie du Pouliguen** is entered between Pte de Penchâteau and Pte du Bec, 3M to E (AC 2986). **Pornichet** marina is in the SE corner of the bay which is partly sheltered from the S by reefs extending SE from Pte de Penchâteau to Le Grand Charpentier, but a heavy sea develops in strong S-SW winds. The W approach chan through these reefs lies between Penchâteau and Les Guérandaises lateral buoys. From S the easiest channel through the reefs, esp if bound for Pornichet, is between Les Evens and Les Troves, buoyed but unlit.

The **River Loire** is France's longest river (1000km) rising in the Massif Central a mere 160km north of the Med. It flows north towards Never and Orleans and then west past Tours, Angers and Nantes to the Atlantic at St Nazaire.

Its estuary (AC 2986, 2989), with much commercial traffic, is entered from seaward via either the Chenal du Nord or the Chenal du Sud. The former, used by yachts and coastal traffic, runs ESE between the mainland and two shoals, Plateau de la Banche and Plateau de la Lambarde.

Chenal du Sud, the main deepwater channel, leads NE between Plateau de la Lambarde and Pte de St Gildas.

A secondary chan, which yachts should use to avoid large ships in the main chan, lies close NW of and parallel to the main chan. It extends 4·5M NE from abeam Pte d'Aiguillon to St Nazaire suspension bridge and is marked by seven SCM lt buoys, ZD1-7, all Q(6) + L Fl 15s; stay between these and the main channel PHM buoys.

The 35M passage from St Nazaire to Nantes (AC 2985, SHOM 7396) is well marked. Contact *Loire Port Control* on Ch 14 and subsequently monitor Ch 14/16.

▶*Here the in-going stream begins at HW Brest –0500, and the out-going at HW Brest +0050, sp rates about 2·75kn.*◀

On the E side of the Loire estuary, up to 4M NE of Pte de St Gildas, are the small drying hbrs of St Gildas, La Gravette and Comberge. Beware Les Jardinets and La Truie (both drying) close E of the chan and 4·5M SSW of St Nazaire.

Carry the flood so as to reach Nantes around local HW. See Saint-Nazaire for a yacht pontoon in central Nantes (Bras de la Madeleine). Trentemoult Marina no longer accepts visitors due to silting.

9.21.29 LE POULIGUEN

Loire Atlantique **47°16'·42N 02°25'·33W** ❀❀◊◊✿✿✿

CHARTS AC 2646, 2986; Imray C39; SHOM 7395, 7145; Navi 547

TIDES Sp +0435 Dover, Nps +0530 Dover; ML 3·3; Duration Sp 0530, Nps 0645

Standard Port BREST (⟵)

Times				Height (metres)			
High Water		Low Water		MHWS	MHWN	MLWN	MLWS
0000	0600	0000	0600	6·9	5·4	2·6	1·0
1200	1800	1200	1800				
Differences LE POULIGUEN							
+0020	−0025	−0020	−0025	−1·5	−1·1	−0·6	−0·3

SHELTER Very good, except in SE winds. In strong S'lies, beware swell and breakers in the approach chan. Pornichet, 3M to the E, has a much easier approach and ent.

NAVIGATION WPT 47°15'·54N 02°24'·34W, Basse Martineau unlit PHM buoy, 321°/1.1M to hbr ent. Reefs running 4M ESE towards Grand Charpentier lt ho, Q WRG, form a barrier across the Baie du Pouliguen which may be entered via any of 4 passes; see AC 2986 or the larger scale SHOM 7145.

Best appr at HW –1 from W/SW between Pte de Penchâteau and Les Evens (drying reef). From Basse Martineau, leave La Vieille SHM perch and Petits Impairs bcn twr, Fl (2) G 6s, well to stbd, and 3 PHM bns closer to port. The inner access chan shifts, dries approx 1·5m and is marked by one PHM and 5 SHM poles.

LIGHTS AND MARKS See chartlet/Lights, buoys and waypoints for lt details. W jetty, QR, is a slim, conspic white column, R top. The final SHM pole marks the narrowing chan and E training wall which covers. Navigational lights are very hard to see against shore lts of La Baule and night appr is not advised without a prior day visit.

COMMUNICATIONS Ⓛ 02·40·61·03·20; CROSS 02·97·55·35·35; Auto 08·92·68·08·44; Police 02·40·24·48·17; ⊜ 02·40·61·32·04; Brit Consul 01·44·51·31·00; Dr 08·36·69·12·34; HM VHF Ch 09, 0900-2000 in season; Aff Mar 02·40·23·06·56.

FACILITIES 30 ⓥ berths on pontoon A, to stbd at ent. Here yachts up to 2m draft can stay afloat but further N will be aground. First fixed bridge has 2·5m clearance. Beware strong ebb tide.

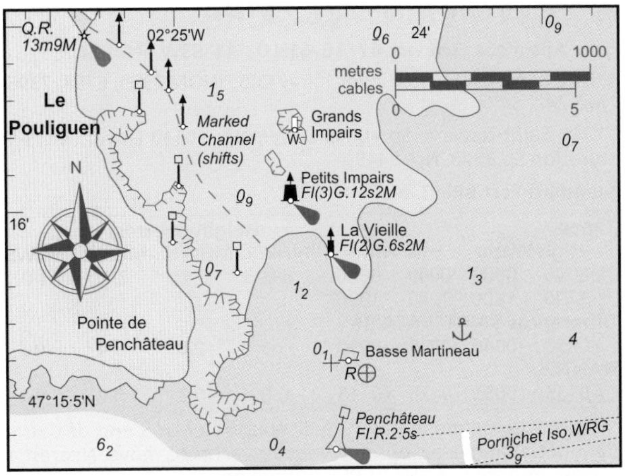

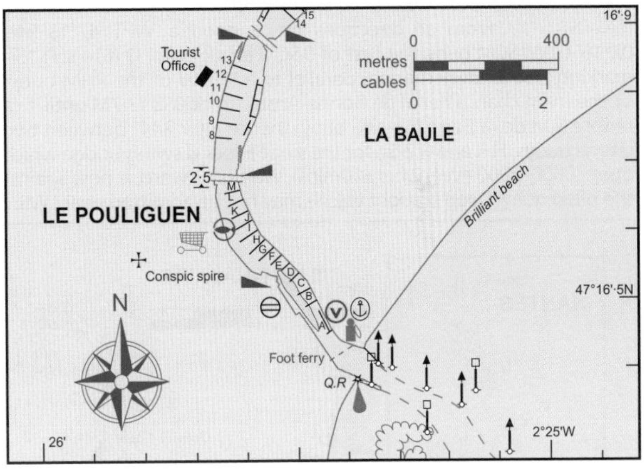

HM (E Quay) ☎02·40·11·97·97. port.labaulelepouliguen@saint-nazaire.cci.fr www.lepouliguen.fr 720+30ⓥ max LOA 11·5m, €3·20. Divers (17t) (Mast 500kg) YC ☎02·40·60·57·87.

Town (W bank) Ⓑ ⇌. ✈ St Nazaire.

9.21.30 PORNICHET

Loire Atlantique **47°15'·51N 02°21'·11W** ❀❀❀◊◊◊✿✿✿

CHARTS AC 2986, 2989; Imray C39; SHOM 7395, 6797, 7145; Navi 547

TIDES Sp +0435 Dover, Nps +0530 Dover; ML 3·3; Duration Sp 0530, Nps 0645

Standard Port BREST (⟵)

Times				Height (metres)			
High Water		Low Water		MHWS	MHWN	MLWN	MLWS
0000	0600	0000	0600	7·0	5·5	2·7	1·1
1200	1800	1200	1800				
Differences PORNICHET							
+0020	−0045	−0022	−0022	−1·5	−1·1	−0·6	−0·3
LE GRAND CHARPENTIER							
+0015	−0045	−0025	−0020	−1·6	−1·2	−0·7	−0·4

SHELTER Very good in large man-made marina; full facilities.

NAVIGATION WPT 47°15'·41N 02°22'·15W, 082·5°/0·7M to N-facing ent in W sector (081°-084°) of bkwtr lt. From SW, track 037°/1·5M between Les Evens PHM and Les Troves SHM unlit buoys. From SSE track 333°/3M from Le Grand Charpentier lt ho.

LIGHTS AND MARKS Navigational lts are very hard to see against shore lts of La Baule. Masts in the marina are conspicuous.

COMMUNICATIONS CROSS 02·97·55·35·35; 02·40·90·08·80; Auto 08·92·68·08·44; ⊜ 02·40·45·88·78; Brit Consul 01·44·51·31·00; Ⓗ 02·40·90·60·60; Dr 02·40·60·17·20; HM VHF Ch 09; Aff Mar 02·40·23·06·56.

FACILITIES **Marina** ☎02·40·61·61·06. portechouagepornichet@nantesstnazaire.cci.fr Access H24 for <2·5m draft. Best to pre-call, or tempy berth on hammerheads A, B, D, F, G, L, M and N. 1000+150ⓥ €1·70. SHOM Ⓔ (25t).

Town Dr, Ⓑ ⇌. ✈ St Nazaire (Montoir).

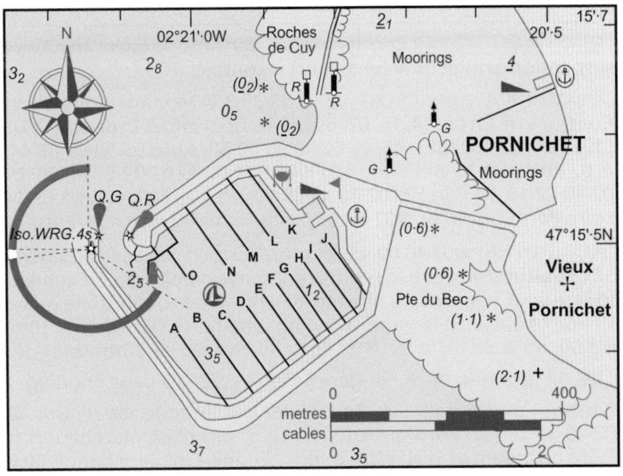

9.21.31 SAINT-NAZAIRE

Loire Atlantique **East lock 47°16′·51N 02°11′·93W** ✿✿✿✿.

CHARTS AC 2986, 2989, 2985; Imray C40; SHOM 7395, 6797, 7396; Navi 248, 547

TIDES Saint-Nazaire: Sp +0445 Dover, Nps –0540 Dover; ML 3·6; Duration Sp 0640, Nps 0445.

Standard Port BREST (⟵)

Times				Height (metres)			
High Water		Low Water		MHWS	MHWN	MLWN	MLWS
0000	0600	0000	0600	6·9	5·4	2·6	1·0
1200	1800	1200	1800				
Differences SAINT- NAZAIRE							
+0030	–0040	–0010	–0010	–1·1	–0·8	–0·4	–0·2
NANTES							
+0135	+0055	+0125	+0215	–0·6	–0·3	–0·8	–0·1

SHELTER Complete in Bassin de St-Nazaire or at S end of Bassin Penhoët. Commercial ops may require yachts to move. Nearest ⚓ is close inshore 5ca NNE of Pte d'Aiguillon.

NAVIGATION From all directions make good a WPT 47°13′·94N 02°16′·01W: SCM buoy, the first of 6 SCM lt buoys (all Q (6) + L Fl 15s) marking a secondary channel parallel to and NW of the PHM buoys of the main chan (Chenal de Bonne-Anse). Track 053°/3·7M until 1 ca before Sud de la Basse Nazaire buoy; thence alter 344° between two lateral buoys, Fl R and G 2·5s, for the small E lock & swing bridge which open (0800–2000 every 2 hrs ±10mins). Waiting, s'ward, is poss against the piled quay. Deep draught vessels may not be admitted near LWS.

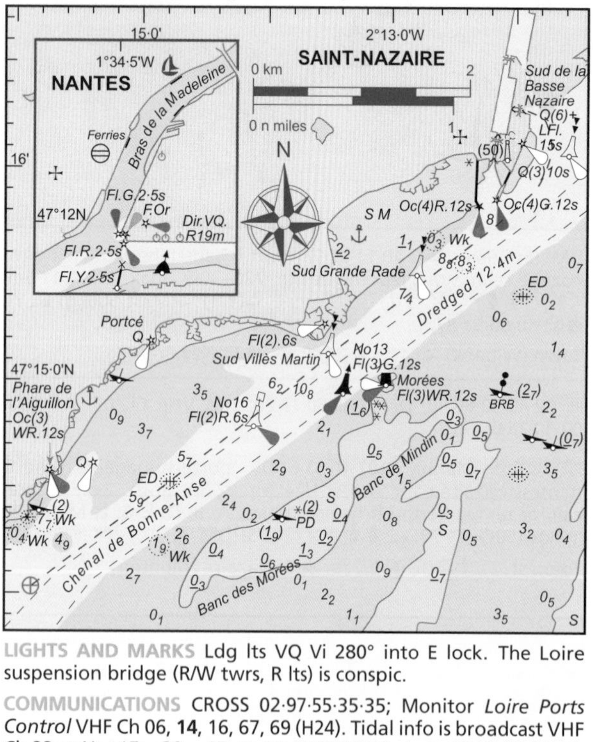

LIGHTS AND MARKS Ldg lts VQ Vi 280° into E lock. The Loire suspension bridge (R/W twrs, R lts) is conspic.

COMMUNICATIONS CROSS 02·97·55·35·35; Monitor *Loire Ports Control* VHF Ch 06, **14**, 16, 67, 69 (H24). Tidal info is broadcast VHF Ch 23 at H, +15, +30, +45; Météo 02·40·90·00·80; Auto 08·92·68·08·44; Customs 02·40·45·88·70; Brit Consul 01·44·51·31·00; Ⓗ 02·72·27·80·00; Dr 02·40·22·15·32; Port HM 02·40·45·39·00; pre-call lock on VHF Ch 14 *Loire Port Control* or ☎02·40·66·09·26 for entry into lock/Bassins.

FACILITIES HM ☎02·40·00·45·89, once berthed call at Capitainerie SE of Bassin St-Nazaire to register and leave mobile phone number in case your vessel needs moving. Berth/raft on rough stone quays W side of Bassin St-Nazaire, avoiding ferry berth (Y stripes); <10m, €3·00, no water or fuel; Ⓔ. www.mairie-saintnazaire.fr

City All facilities; ⇌ ✈. Re-generation WW2 sub pens ongoing.

Passage to Nantes: Les Portes de L'Atlantique boatyard, ☎ 02·40·27·10·10, www.placedeport.com nicholas@placedeport.fr 7.5M upstream of St-Nazaire bridge, S bank, E of Paimboeuf, 60m

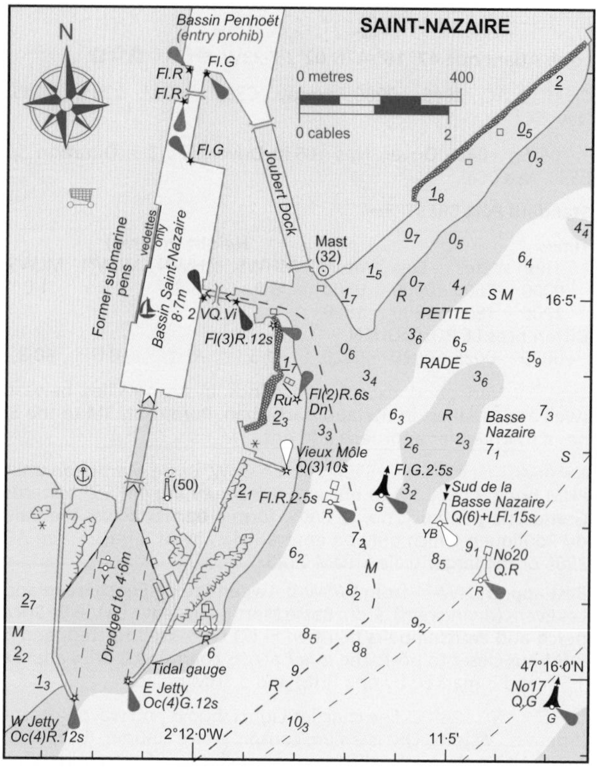

pontoon, Ⓥ welcome, €3·00, showers (H24) water fuel, wi-fi, (50t) courtesy cars/bicycles to access **Town** 2M ✕ ✉.

NANTES see chartlet left, AC 2985 Ⓓ, SHOM 6797, 7396. Ponton des Chantiers (SE bank of Bras de la Madeleine) mainly for ferries; €2·30 (but no yachts 15/06–31/08); water fuel no WCs. Ponton Bélem (NW bank downstream of Anne de Bretagne bridge) 20 Ⓥ; €2·60, water fuel. Call Bureau de Port du Ponton Bélem, VHF Ch 09. (Daily in season 0900-1230, 1400-1900.) ☎02·40·37·04·62 for les3ports@nge-nantes.fr. Both pontoons are exposed to ferry wash and tide (4+kn). Trentemoult marina is badly silted; no visitors.

MINOR HARBOURS FROM ST-NAZAIRE TO PTE ST GILDAS

Three small drying hbrs (below, from N to S) are NE of Pte de St-Gildas, on the E side of the R. Loire. Flanked by shellfish beds on rky ledges drying up to 4ca offshore, bkwtrs shelter from W'lies but the hbrs are exposed to N/NE.

Charts: AC 2986, 2981, 2989; SHOM 7395, 6797; Navi 547.

Tides: Interpolate Le Grand Charpentier, St-Nazaire and Pornic.

PORT DE COMBERGE, Loire Atlantique, **47°10′·52N 02°09′·96W.** 2·7M NW is La Truie rk, 3m marked by unlit IDM bn; 1·5M W of it are rocks drying 1·2m. Appr with bkwtr lt in transit with the old lt ho beyond, or night, 136° in the W sector. Beware Les Moutons, rk drying 0·7m, 7½ca NW of the bkwtr lt near approach track. Narrow ent; tiny hbr dries 2m, access half-flood. HM ☎02·40·27·82·85. Facilities: YC and at St Michel-Chef-Chef.

PORT DE LA GRAVETTE, Loire Atlantique, **47°09′·64N 02°12′·71W**, 2·2M NE of Pte de St Gildas. Daymarks, bkwtr lt in transit 130° with La Treille water tr, 2M inland. Unlit NCM bns mark shellfish beds, beyond 600m bkwtr, turn stbd between lateral buoys; the N part of the hbr has about 1·2m water, but dries inshore.

ST GILDAS (Anse du Boucau) Loire Atlantique, **47°08′·47N 02°14′·74W**. The hbr is 5ca N of Pte de St Gildas lt ho, Q WRG. The hbr bkwtr extends 3ca N, with a large tide gauge and ☆ at its N end. An unlit SHM bn, and a SHM buoy, Fl G 2·5s (May-Sept) lie 150m and 300m NNW of bkwtr hd. Appr from 1M N of Pte de St Gildas on brg 177°, or night, in the W sector 174°-180° of St Gildas lt ho. L'Ilot rky ledge is marked by a PHM bn. Use a mooring in 1·5m N part of the hbr or dry out further S. HM ☎02·40·21·60·07. VHF Ch 09. Facilities: YC (5t) at Préfailles 1M to E.

South Biscay

River Loire to the Spanish border

9.22.1 **Contents** ... 917

9.22.2 **Area map and Distance table** ... 918

9.22.3 **Tidal stream charts** ... 920

9.22.4 **Lights, buoys and waypoints** ... 922

9.22.5 **Passage information** ... 925
The Bay of Biscay and West Coast of France – 925 • Baie de Bourgneuf – 926 • Ile d'Yeu to Pertuis Breton – 930 • Pertuis Breton – 930 • Pertuis d'Antioche – 930 • Île d'Oléron – 934 • Pointe de Grave to Arcachon – 946 • Arcachon to the Spanish Border – 947

9.22.6 **Special notes for France. See Area 17**

9.22.7 **Pornic** ... 925

9.22.8 **L'Herbaudière (Île de Noirmoutier)** ... 926
Noirmoutier-en-l'Ile • Fromentine

9.22.9 **Port Joinville (Île d'Yeu)** ... 927
Port de la Meule

9.22.10 **St Gilles-Croix-de-Vie** ... 928

9.22.11 **Les Sables d'Olonne** ... 929

9.22.12 **Bourgenay** ... 930
Jard-sur-Mer • L'Aiguillon/La Faute-sur-Mer • Marans • La Flotte, Ile de Ré

9.22.13 **Ars-en-Ré** ... 932

9.22.14 **St Martin-de-Ré** ... 932

9.22.15 **La Rochelle** ... 933

9.22.16 **Île d'Oléron: Port St Denis, Le Douhet, Boyardville** ... 934
Île d'Aix (La Charente River)

9.22.17 **Rochefort** ... 936
La Seudre River (Marennes, La Tremblade)

Pointe de Grave, tidal coefficients, tide tables/curves ... 937

9.22.18 **The Gironde Estuary** ... 940

9.22.19 **Royan** ... 941

9.22.20 **Port Bloc** ... 943

9.22.21 **Port Médoc** ... 943

9.22.22 **The River Gironde** ... 944
Meschers • Mortagne • Bourg

9.22.23 **Pauillac** ... 944

9.22.24 **Bordeaux** ... 945

9.22.25 **Canals to the Mediterranean** ... 945

9.22.26 **Landes range** ... 946

9.22.27 **Bassin d'Arcachon** ... 947
La Vigne • Andernos • Fontainevieille • Audenge

9.22.28 **Capbreton** ... 949

9.22.29 **Anglet/Bayonne** ... 949

9.22.30 **St Jean de Luz** ... 950

9.22.31 **Hendaye** ... 951

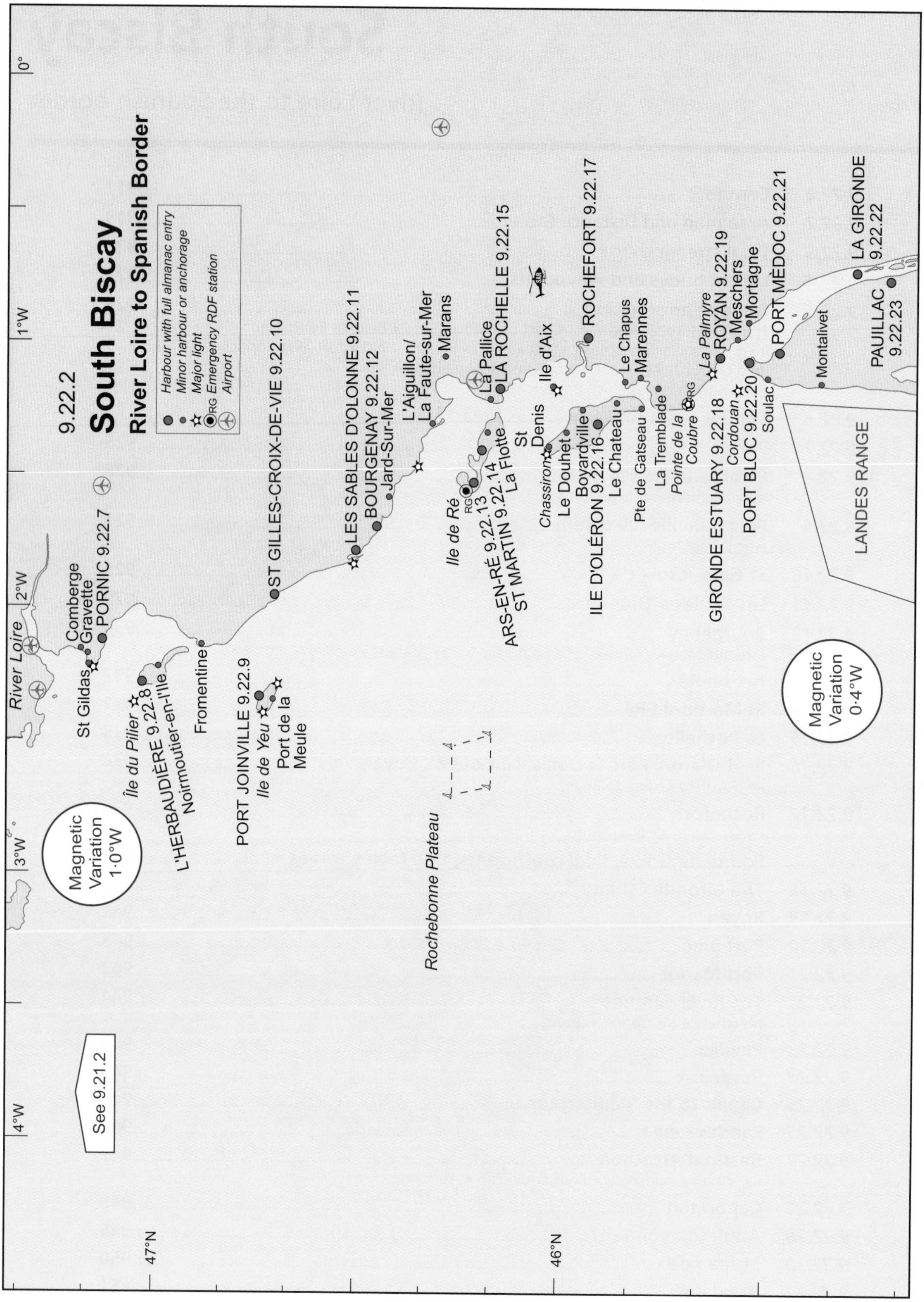
9.22.2
South Biscay
River Loire to Spanish Border
Harbour with full almanac entry
Minor harbour or anchorage
Major light
RG Emergency RDF station
Airport
0°
1°W
2°W
3°W
4°W
47°N
46°N
See 9.21.2
Magnetic Variation 1·0°W
Magnetic Variation 0·4°W
River Loire
St Gildas
Comberge
Gravette
PORNIC 9.22.7
Île du Pilier
L'HERBAUDIÈRE 9.22.8
Noirmoutier-en-l'Ile
Fromentine
PORT JOINVILLE 9.22.9
Ile de Yeu
Port de la Meule
ST GILLES-CROIX-DE-VIE 9.22.10
LES SABLES D'OLONNE 9.22.11
BOURGENAY 9.22.12
Jard-Sur-Mer
L'Aiguillon/
La Faute-sur-Mer
Marans
Rochebonne Plateau
Ile de Ré
RG
ARS-EN-RÉ 9.22.13
ST MARTIN 9.22.14
La Flotte
La Pallice
LA ROCHELLE 9.22.15
St Denis
Ile d'Aix
Chassiron
Le Douhet
Boyardville
ILE D'OLÉRON 9.22.16
Le Chateau
ROCHEFORT 9.22.17
Le Chapus
Marennes
Pte de Gatseau
La Tremblade
Pointe de la Coubre
RG
GIRONDE ESTUARY 9.22.18
La Palmyre
ROYAN 9.22.19
Cordouan
PORT BLOC 9.22.20
Soulac
Meschers
Mortagne
PORT MÈDOC 9.22.21
Montalivet
PAUILLAC 9.22.23
LA GIRONDE 9.22.22
LANDES RANGE

1	***Le Conquet***	1																								
2	*St Nazaire*	145	2																							
3	Pornic	146	16	3																						
4	L'Herbaudière	144	16	10	4																					
5	Port Joinville	147	35	30	20	5																				
6	St Gilles-C-de-Vie	166	45	40	29	18	6																			
7	Sables d'Olonne	181	65	55	40	31	16	7																		
8	Bourgenay	190	74	64	49	40	25	9	8																	
9	Ars-en-Ré	204	88	71	63	51	41	23	17	9																
10	St Martin (I de Ré)	208	92	75	67	55	44	27	20	8	10															
11	La Rochelle	218	101	92	76	66	51	36	29	17	12	11														
12	Boyardville	227	110	101	85	66	55	40	37	25	20	15	12													
13	Rochefort	242	126	116	102	84	75	61	54	40	36	26	21	13												
14	R La Seudre	242	125	116	100	89	71	58	52	49	33	24	36	30	14											
15	Port St Denis	220	103	94	78	59	48	33	30	22	21	13	7	26	22	15										
16	Port Bloc/Royan	234	122	115	107	97	85	71	60	60	56	51	51	65	29	44	16									
17	Pauillac	266	154	147	139	129	117	103	92	92	88	84	81	100	59	74	32	17								
18	Bordeaux	289	177	170	162	152	140	126	115	115	111	107	104	123	82	97	55	23	18							
19	Cap Ferret	274	168	160	153	138	130	113	110	111	102	98	95	114	75	88	70	100	123	19						
20	Capbreton	316	220	215	211	192	186	169	166	168	165	156	152	172	131	145	124	156	179	58	20					
21	Anglet/Bayonne	328	232	223	223	200	195	181	178	176	177	168	164	184	143	157	133	164	187	70	12	21				
22	St Jean de Luz	338	242	233	233	210	205	191	188	183	187	178	174	194	153	167	143	174	197	80	22	31	22			
23	Hendaye	341	245	236	236	213	208	194	191	185	190	181	177	197	156	170	145	177	200	83	25	34	8	23		
24	*Santander*	300	243	237	229	212	210	204	204	207	206	202	199	218	184	192	179	212	235	133	106	103	88	94	24	
25	*Cabo Finisterre*	382	404	399	390	377	395	393	394	407	406	407	404	423	399	397	403	433	456	376	370	373	354	360	274	25

DISTANCE TABLE
Approximate distances in nautical miles are by the most direct route while avoiding dangers and allowing for TSS. Places in *italics* are in adjoining areas; places in **bold** are in 9.0.5, Cross-Channel Distances.

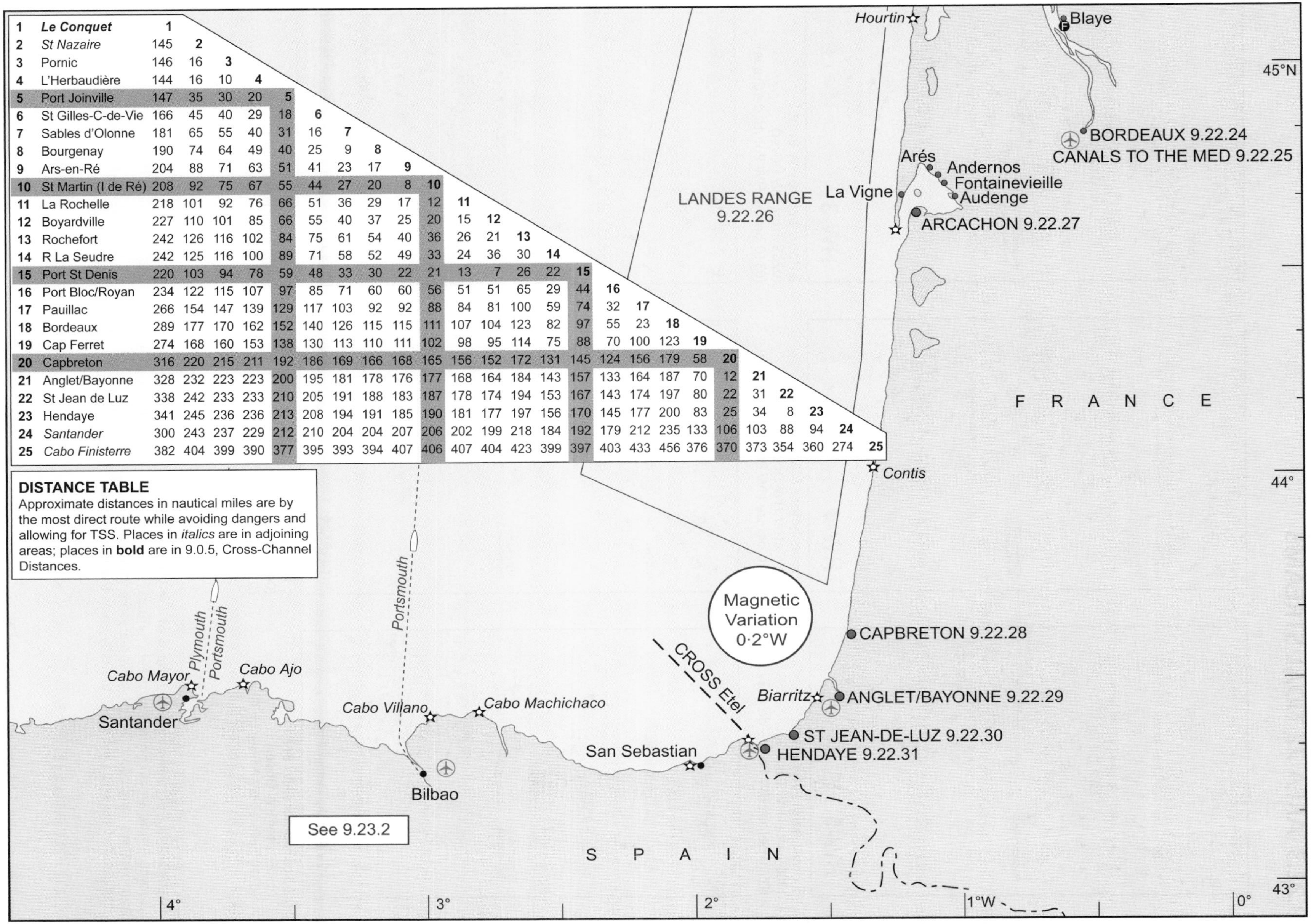

Hourtin
Blaye
45°N
BORDEAUX 9.22.24
CANALS TO THE MED 9.22.25
Arés
Andernos
Fontainevieille
Audenge
La Vigne
LANDES RANGE 9.22.26
ARCACHON 9.22.27
F R A N C E
Contis
44°
Magnetic Variation 0·2°W
CAPBRETON 9.22.28
CROSS Etel
Biarritz
ANGLET/BAYONNE 9.22.29
ST JEAN-DE-LUZ 9.22.30
HENDAYE 9.22.31
San Sebastian
Cabo Machichaco
Cabo Villano
Bilbao
Portsmouth
Plymouth
Portsmouth
Cabo Mayor
Cabo Ajo
Santander
See 9.23.2
S P A I N
4°
3°
2°
1°W
0°
43°

9.22.3 AREA 22 TIDAL STREAMS

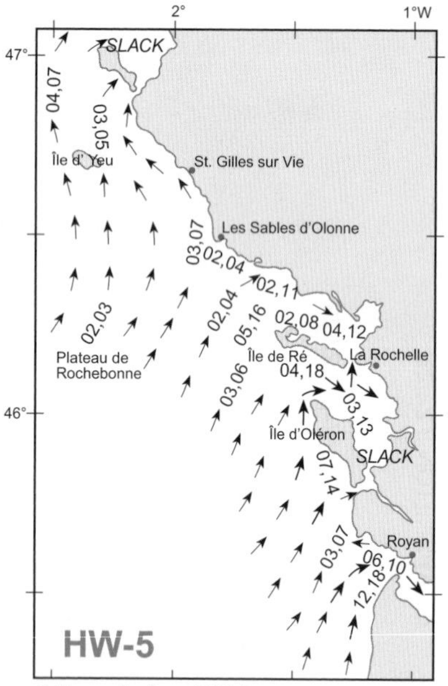

5 Hours before HW Brest
(0005 after HW Dover)
(0510 before HW Pointe de Grave)

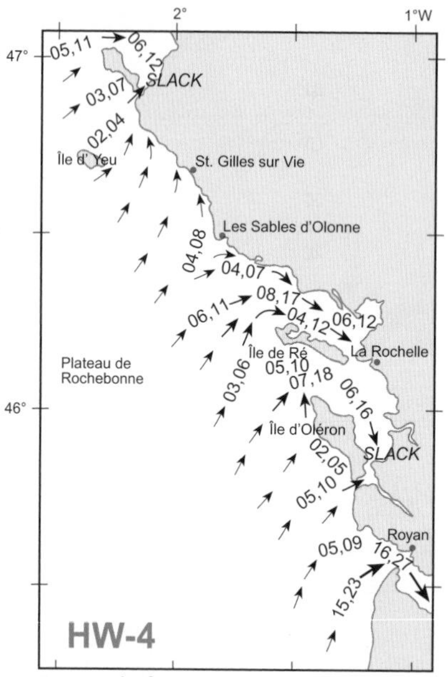

4 Hours before HW Brest
(0105 after HW Dover)
(0410 before HW Pointe de Grave)

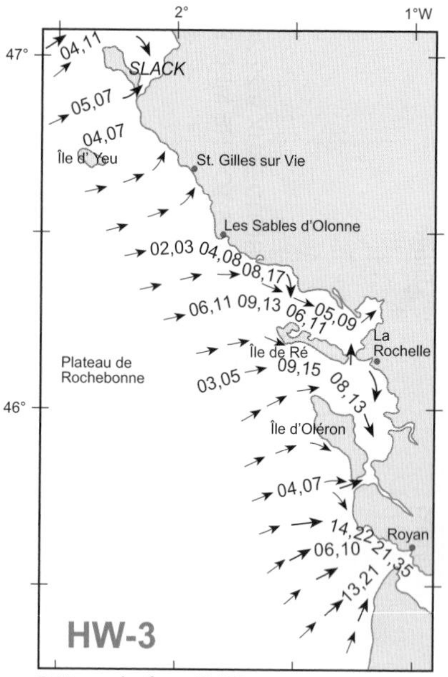

3 Hours before HW Brest
(0205 after HW Dover)
(0310 before HW Pointe de Grave)

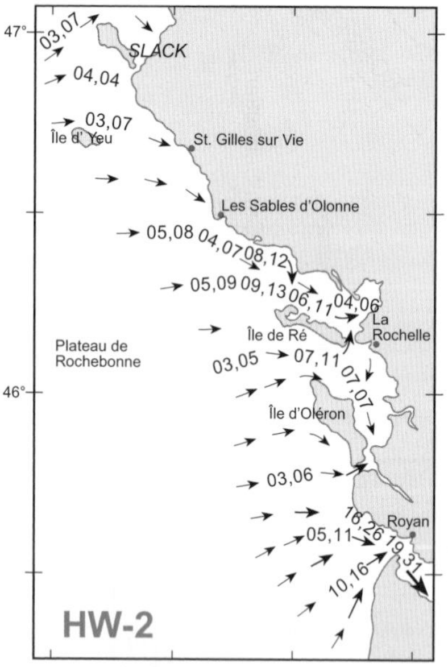

2 Hours before HW Brest
(0305 after HW Dover)
(0310 before HW Pointe de Grave)

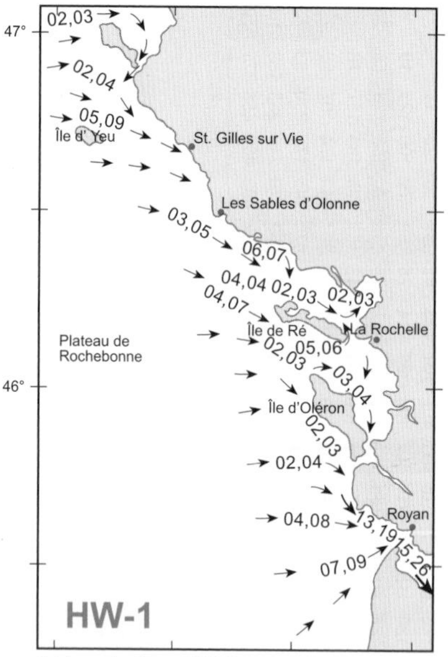

1 Hour before HW Brest
(0405 after HW Dover)
(0110 before HW Pointe de Grave)

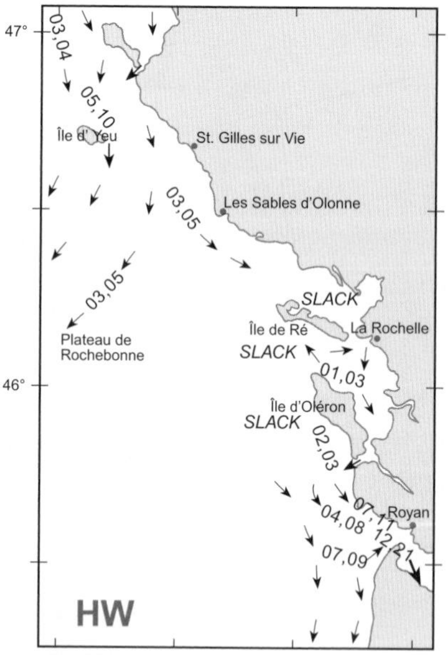

HW Brest
(0505 after HW Dover)
(0010 before HW Pointe de Grave)

CAUTION: Due to the very strong rates of the tidal streams in some of the areas covered by these chartlets, many eddies and overfalls may occur. Where possible some indication of these eddies has been included. In many areas there is either insufficient information or the eddies are unstable. Tidal streams are generally weak offshore.

Strong winds may also have a great effect on the rate and direction of the tidal streams in all these chartlets.

Northward 9.21.3

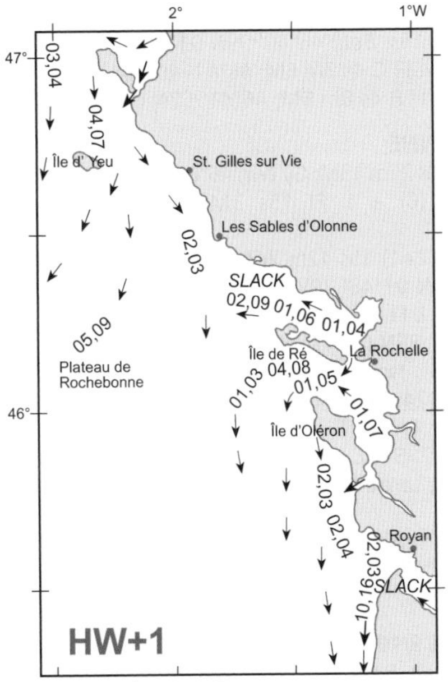

1 Hour after HW Brest
(0605 after HW Dover)
(0050 after HW Pointe de Grave)

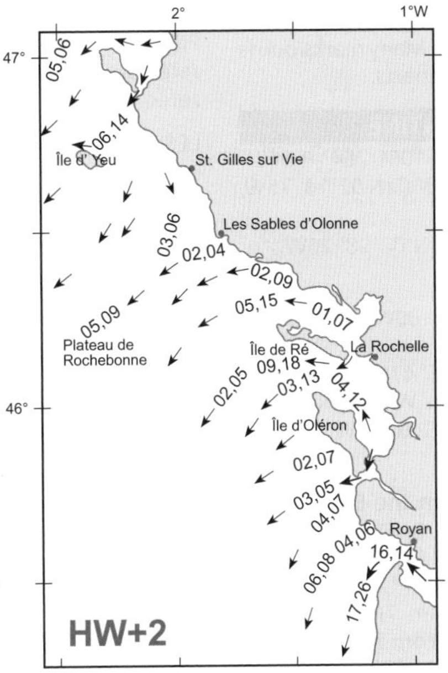

2 Hours after HW Brest
(0515 before HW Dover)
(0150 after HW Pointe de Grave)

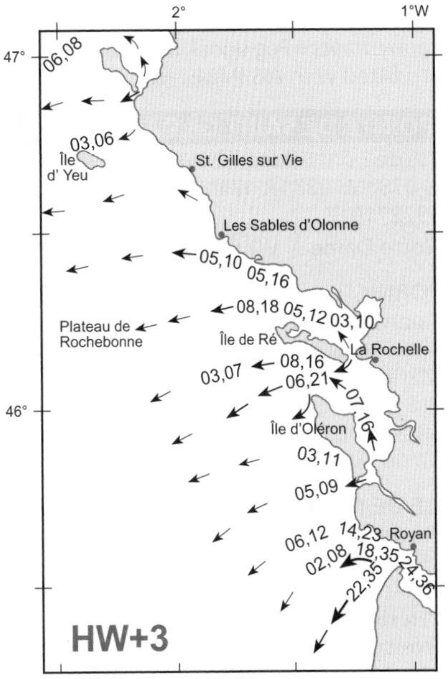

3 Hours after HW Brest
(0415 before HW Dover)
(0250 after HW Pointe de Grave)

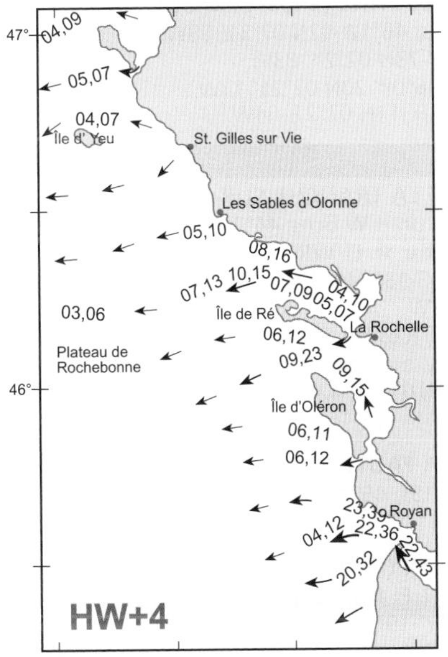

4 Hours after HW Brest
(0315 before HW Dover)
(0350 after HW Pointe de Grave)

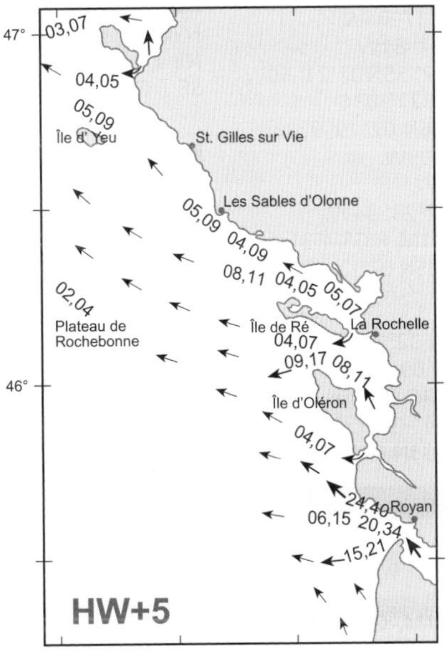

5 Hours after HW Brest
(0215 before HW Dover)
(0450 after HW Pointe de Grave)

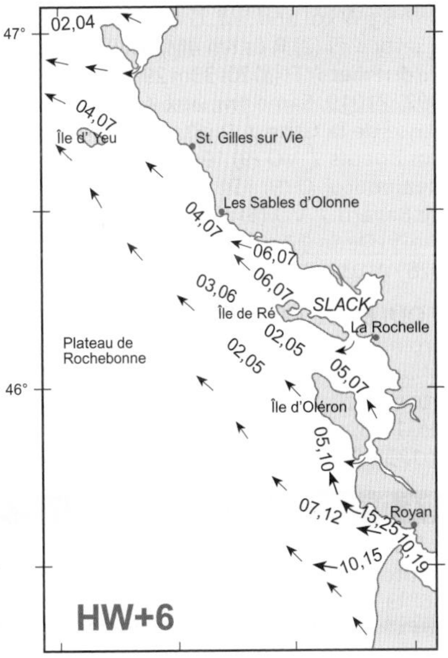

6 Hours after HW Brest
(0115 before HW Dover)
(0550 after HW Pointe de Grave)

Note: These chartlets are based on the Admiralty tidal stream atlas for France, W coast (NP 265, 2nd edition 2005) which uses data from actual observations out to 20-35M offshore.

The comparable French atlas (559-UJA; 2001) gives data for further offshore, based on computer predictions. It covers at large scale the approaches to St Nazaire; Les Sables d'Olonne to Pertuis de Maumusson; and the mouth of the Gironde.

No tidal stream atlas is published by either the French or UK Hydrographic Offices for the waters southward to the Spanish border.

9.22.4 LIGHTS, BUOYS AND WAYPOINTS

Bold print = light with a nominal range of 15M or more. CAPITALS = place or feature. *CAPITAL ITALICS* = light-vessel, light float or Lanby. *Italics* = Fog signal. ***Bold italics*** = Racon. Many marks/buoys are fitted with AIS (MMSI No); see relevant charts.

POINTE DE SAINT GILDAS TO FROMENTINE

Pte de Saint Gildas Q WRG 20m, W14M, R/G10M; 264°-R-308°-G-078°-W-088°-R-174°-W-180°-G-264°; 47°08'·02N 02°14'·75W. 992271017.

Notre Dame VQ (9) 10s 7m 3M; 47°05'·42N 02°08'·26W.

PORNIC

Approaches Fl G 4s; 47°06'·39N 02°06'·60W; Fl R 4s; 47°06'·40N 02°06'·64W

Marina ent, S side Fl (2) R 6s 4m 2M; 47°06'·47N 02°06'·67W.

Pte de Noëveillard Oc (4) WRG 12s 22m W13M, R/G10M; Shore-G-051°-W-079°-R-shore; W □ twr, G top, W house; 47°06'·62N 02°06'·92W.

ÎLE DE NOIRMOUTIER anti-clockwise from the East

Pte des Dames ☆ Oc (3) WRG 12s 34m, **W19M, R/G15M**; 016·5°-G-057°-R-124°-G-165°-W-191°-R191°-267°-W-357°-R-016·5°; W □ twr; 47°00'·67N 02°13'·26W. La Chaise 47°01'·21N 02°12'·64W.

L'Herbaudière, ldg lts 187·5°, both Q 5/21m 7M, Gy masts. Front, 47°01'·59N 02°17'·84W. Rear, 310m from front.

Martroger, Q WRG 11m W9M, R/G6M; 033°-G-055°-W-060°-R-095°-G-124°-W-153°-R-201°-W-240°-R-033°; 47°02'·61N 02°17'·11W.

W jetty Oc (2+1) WG 12s 9m W10M, G7M; 187·5°-W-190°-G-187·5°; W col and hut, G top; 47°01'·63N 02°17'·84W.

E jetty Fl (2) R 6s 8m 4M; 47°01'·61N 02°17'·81W.

Île du Pilier ☆ Fl (3) 20s 33m **29M**; Gy twr; 47°02'·55N 02°21'·60W. 992271019. Same twr, aux QR 10m 11M, 321°-034°.

Passe de la Grise Q (6) + L Fl 15s; 47°01'·66N 02°19'·97W.

Les Boeufs VQ (9) 10s; 46°55'·04N 02°27'·99W.

Réaumur Q (9) 15s; 46°57'·46N 02°24'·22W.

Le Bavard VQ (6) + L Fl 10s; 46°56'·79N 02°23'·34W.

Pte du Devin (Morin) Oc (4) WRG 12s 10m W11M, R/G8M; 314°-G-028°-W-035°-R-134°; W col & hut, G top; 46°59'·15N 02°17'·60W.

GOULET DE FROMENTINE

Fromentine L Fl (3) 10s 3m 6M; 46°53'·10N 02°11'·40W

Milieu Fl (4) R 15 s 6m 5M; 46°53'·59N 02°09'·63W.

Pte de Notre Dame-de-Monts Dir Oc (2) WRG 6s 21m, W13M, R/G10M; 000°-G-043°-W-063°-R-073°-W-094°-G-113°-W-116°-R-175°-G-196°-R-230°; W twr, B top; 46°53'·33N 02°08'·54W.

ÎLE D'YEU TO BOURGENAY

ÎLE D'YEU

Petite Foule (main lt) ☆ Fl 5s 56m **24M**; W □ twr, G lantern; 46°43'·04N 02°22'·91W. 992271031.

Les Chiens Perrins Q (9) WG 15s 16m W7M, G4M; 330°-G-350°-W-200°; 46°43'·60N 02°24'·58W.

Pont d'Yeu 46°45'·81N 02°13'·81W.

La Sablaire Q (6) + L Fl 15s; 46°43'·62N 02°19'·49W.

Port Joinville ldg lts 219°, both QR 11/16m 6M, 169°-269°: Front, Quai du Canada 46°43'·61N 02°20'·94W. Rear, 85m from front.

NW jetty Oc (3) WG 12s 7m, W11M, G8M; Shore-G-150°-W-232°-G-279°-W-285°-G-shore; W 8-sided twr, G top; 46°43'·77N 02°20'·82W. La Galiote 46°43'·73N 02°20'·71W.

Pte des Corbeaux ☆ Fl (2+1) R 15s 25m **20M**; 083°-143° obsc by Île de Yeu; W □ twr, R top; 46°41'·41N 02°17'·08W.

Port de la Meule Oc WRG 4s 9m, W9M, R/G6M; 007·5°-G-018°-W-027·5°-R-041·5°; Gy twr, R top; 46°41'·62N 02°20'·72W.

SAINT GILLES-CROIX-DE-VIE

Pte de Grosse Terre ☆ Fl (4) WR 12s 25m, **W18M, R15M**; 290°-R-339°-W-125°-R-145°; W truncated twr; 46°41'·54N 01°57'·92W.

Ldg lts 043·7°, both Q 7/28m **15M**; 033·5°-053·5°; synch; W □ twrs, R tops: Front, 46°41'·86N 01°56'·75W. 992271027. Rear, 260m NE. 992271034.

Pilours Q (6) + L Fl 15s; *Bell;* 46°40'·99N 01°58'·09W.

Jetée de la Garenne Fl G 4s 8m 6M; 46°41'·46N 01°57'·25W.

Jetée de Boisvinet Fl R 4s 8m 6M; 46°41'·62N 01°57'·16W.

LES SABLES D'OLONNE

Les Barges Fl (2) R 10s 25m 13M; Gy twr; 46°29'·70N 01°50'·50W.

Petite Barge Q (6) + L Fl 15s 3M; *Whis;* 46°28'·90N 01°50'·61W.

L'Armandèche ☆ Fl (2+1) 15s 42m **24M**; 295°-130°; W 6-sided twr, R top; 46°29'·39N 01°48'·29W. 992271035.

Nouch Sud Q (6) + L Fl 15s; 46°28'·55N 01°47'·41W.

Nouch Nord 46°28'·88N 01°47'·36W.

SW Pass, ldg lts 032·5°, Iso 4s 12/33m **16M, Front** ☆, 46°29'·42N 01°46'·37W. 992271024. **Rear** ☆, **La Potence**, W □ twr.

SE Pass, ldg lts 320°: Front, E jetty QG 11m 8M; W twr, G top; 46°29'·44N 01°47'·51W. 992271032. Rear, Tour d'Arundel Q 33m 13M, synch; large Gy □ twr; 46°29'·63N 01°47'·74W. 992271022.

Jetée St Nicolas (W jetty) QR 1·2s 16m 8M; 143°-094°; W twr, R top; 46°29'·23N 01°47'·52W.

BOURGENAY

Ldg lts 040°, both QG 9/19m 7M. Front, 020°-060°; on S bkwtr; 46°26'·34N 01°40'·62W. Rear, 010°-070°; 162m from front.

Landfall L Fl 10s; 46°25'·26N 01°41'·93W.

Ent Fl R 4s 8m 9M & Iso G 4s 6m 5M; 46°26'·29N 01°40'·75W.

PLATEAU DE ROCHEBONNE (Shoal 32M offshore)

NW Q (9) 15s; *Whis;* 46°12'·92N 02°31'·58W.

NE Iso G 4s; 46°12'·73N 02°24'·83W.

SE Q (3) 10s; *Bell;* 46°09'·20N 02°21'·13W.

SW Fl (2) R 6s; 46°10'·11N 02°27'·04W.

PERTUIS BRETON

JARD-SUR-MER and LA TRANCHE-SUR-MER

Ldg marks 036°, two unlit W bcns; 46°24'·47N 01°34'·16W.

Pte du Grouin du Cou ☆ Fl WRG 5s 29m, **W20M, R/G16M**; 034°-R-061°-W-117°-G-138°-W-034°; W 8-sided twr, B top; 46°20'·67N 01°27'·83W.

La Tranche pier Fl (2) R 6s 6m 6M; R col; 46°20'·55N 01°25'·63W.

Mussel farm, No entry, marked by: Q, 46°17'·17N 01°22'·19W. Q (3) 10s, 46°15'·73N 01°18'·42W. Q (6) + L Fl 15s, 46°15'·16N 01°19'·98W. Q (9) 15s, 46°16'·28N 01°22'·88W.

L'AIGUILLON and LA FAUTE-SUR-MER

Le Lay Q (6) + L Fl 15s; 46°16'·10N 01°16'·53W.

No 1 46°16'·65N 01°16'·25W. Many mussel beds.

ANSE DE L'AIGUILLON (for La Sèvre Niortaise & Marans)

ATT de L'Aiguillon L Fl 10s; 46°15'·33N 01°11'·50W.

Inner fairway 46°17'·19N 01°09'·65W.

Port du Pavé Fl G 4s 9m 7M; W col, G top; 46°18'·15N 01°08'·01W.

ÎLE DE RÉ

Les Baleineaux VQ 23m 7M; pink twr, R top; 46°15'·81N 01°35'·22W.

Les Baleines ☆ Fl (4) 15s 53m **27M**; conspic Gy 8-sided twr, R lantern; 46°14'·64N 01°33'·69W.

ARS-EN-RÉ

Dir 268° Oc WRG 4s, W10M, R/G 7M, 275·5°-G-267·5°-W-268·5°-R-274·5°; W hut with W □ topmark; 46°14'·05N 01°28'·60W.

Les Islattes Q 13m 3M; NCM bcn twr 46°14'·03N 01°23'·32W.

Bûcheron No 1 Fl G 2·5s; 46°14'·21N 01°25'·98W.

Bûcheron No 3 Fl (2) G 6s; 46°14'·14N 01°26'·94W.

Le Fier d'Ars, inner ldg lts 232·5°, both Q 5/13m 9/11M: Front

R/W frame on W col; 46°12'·75N 01°30'·59W. Rear ✧ 142°-322°; B vert rectangle on W mast, 370m from front.

ST MARTIN DE RÉ

Lt ho, E of ent ✧ Oc (2) WR 6s 18m W10M, R7M; Shore-W-245°-R-281°-W-shore; W twr, R top; 46°12'·44N 01°21'·89W.
W mole ✧ Fl G 2·5s 10m 5M; obsc'd by Pte du Grouin when brg <124°; W post, G top; 46°12'·49N 01°21'·91W.

LA FLOTTE

N bkwtr ✧ Fl WG 4s 10m W12M, G9M; 130°-G-205°-W-220°-G-257°; W ○ twr, G top; 46°11'·33N 01°19'·30W.
Dir lt 212·5°, Moiré effect, is next to the main lt twr.
ÎLE DE RÉ (South coast, from the W, inc bridge)
Chanchardon ✧ Fl WR 4s 15m W11M, R8M; 118°-R-290°-W-118°; B 8-sided twr, W base; 46°09'·71N 01°28'·41W.
Chauveau ☆ Oc (3) WR 12s 27m **W15M**, R11M; 057°-W-094°-R-104°-W-342°-R-057°; W ○ twr, R top; 46°08'·03N 01°16'·42W.
Bridge span (30m cl'nce) for SE-bound vessels, ✧ Iso 4s 34m 8M; 46°10'·18N 01°14'·75W . Span (30m cl'nce) for NW-bound vessels, ✧ Iso 4s 34m 8M; 46°10'·26N 01°14'·52W.
La Pallice, W mole, ✧ Fl G 4s 5m 6M; 46°09'·78N 01°14'·45W.
S end, ✧ Q (6) + L Fl 15s 6m 9M; 46°09'·36N 01°14'·52W.

LA ROCHELLE AND LA CHARENTE TO ROCHEFORT

LA ROCHELLE

Chauveau VQ (6) + L Fl 10s; 46°06'·56N 01°16'·06W.
Roche du Sud Q (9) 15s; 46°06'·37N 01°15'·22W.
La Rochelle ldg lts 059°, both Dir Q 15/25m 13/14M; synch; by day Fl 4s. Front; intens 056°-062°; R ○ twr, W bands; 46°09'·35N 01°09'·16W. Rear, 044°-074°, obsc'd 061°-065°; W 8-sided twr, G top, 235m from front.
Lavardin Fl (2) 6s 14m 7M; BRB IDM twr; 46°08'·09N 01°14'·52W.
Les Minimes Q (9) 15s; 46°08'·01N 01°11'·60W.
Pte des Minimes ✧ Fl (3) WG 12s 8m; W8M, G5M; 059°-W-213°; 313°-G-059°; 8-sided twr on piles; 46°08'·27N 01°10'·76W.
Chan buoy QG; 46°08'·53N 01°10'·87W; marking hbr limit.
Tour Richelieu Fl (2)R 6s 0m 6M; R twr; 46°08'·90N 01°10'·34W.
Port des Minimes, W bkwtr ✧ Fl G 2·5s; W twr, G top; 46°08'·88N 01°10'·18W.
E bkwtr ✧ VQ(9) 10s 3M; Y/B band, 46°08'·92N 01°10'·09W.

LA CHARENTE

Fort Boyard twr ✧ Q (9) 15s; 45°59'·96N 01°12'·85W.
Ldg lts 115°, both Dir QR 8/21m **19/20M**; intens 113°-117°; W □ twr, R top: **Front** ☆, 45°57'·96N 01°04'·38W. **Rear, Soumard** ☆, 600m from front. Same twr: ✧ QR 21m 8M; vis 322°-067°.
Île d'Aix ☆ Fl WR 5s 24m **W24M, R20M**; 103°-R-118°-W-103°; two conspic W ○ twrs, R top; 46°00'·60N 01°10'·67W.
Pte Ste Catherine, jetty hd Q (6) + L Fl 15s 5m 4M; 45°59'·05N 01°07'·85W. Les Palles Q; 45°59'·54N 01°09'·56W.
Fouras, Port Sud bkwtr ✧ Fl WR 4s 6m 9/6M; 115°-R-177°-W-115°; 45°58'·97N 01°05'·72W. Rear 75m from front.

ROCHEFORT

Night passage by yachts is not advised.
✧ Fl (2) G 6s; bcn 45°55'·21N 00°56'·98W, 1·4M S of Rochefort.

ÎLE D'OLÉRON

Pte de Chassiron ☆ Fl 10s 50m, **28M**; conspic W twr, B bands; 46°02'·80N 01°24'·62W, NW tip of island.
Antioche Q 20m 11M; 46°03'·94N 01°23'·71W.

ST DENIS

Dir ✧ 205°, Iso WRG 4s 14m, W11M, R/G8M; 190°-G-204°-W-206°-R-220°; 46°01'·61N 01°21'·92W.
E jetty ✧ Fl (2) WG 6s 6m, W9M, G6M; 205°-G-277°-W-292°-G-165°; □ hut; 46°02'·10N 01°22'·06W.

PORT DU DOUHET and PASSAGE DE L'OUEST

Seaweed farm VQ; 46°00'·65N 01°17'·38W.
N ent 46°00'·10N 01°19'·20W.
Fish farm Q; 46°00'·24N 01°15'·34W. Q (3) 10s; 45°59'·84N 01°14'·79W.

BOYARDVILLE

Mole ✧ Fl (2) R 6s 8m 5M; obsc'd by Pte des Saumonards when brg <150°; W twr, R top; 45°58'·24N 01°13'·83W.

COUREAU D'OLÉRON and LE CHÂTEAU D'OLÉRON

Juliar Q (3) WG 10s 12m, W11M; G8M; 147°-W-336°-G-147°; 45°54'·11N 01°09'·48W.
Chateau d'Oléron, ldg lts 318·5°, both QR 11/24m 7M; synch. Front, 191°-087°; R line on W twr; 45°53'·03N 01°11'·45W. Rear, W twr, R top; 240m from front.
St Trojan-les-Bains bridge (limits of nav width, 18m clearance) Fl G 4s 4M, 45°51'·42N 01°11'·20W; Fl R 4s 4M, 45°51'·40N 01°11'·7W.

LA SEUDRE RIVER

Pte du Mus de Loup ✧ Oc G 4s 8m 6M; 118°-147°; 45°47'·70N 01°08'·60W.
Pertuis de Maumusson. Depths & buoys subject to change.
ATT Maumusson L Fl 10s; 45°45'·73N 01°18'·05W.
La Barre 45°46'·59N 01°16'·25W.
Tabouret 45°46'·93N 01°16'·15W.
Mattes 45°46'·93N 01°15'·29W.
Gatseau 45°47'·36N 01°14'·70W.

LA COTINIÈRE (SW side of island)

Ent ldg lts 339°, both ✧ Dir Oc (2) 6s 6/14m 13/12M; synch: Front, 329°-349°; W twr, R top; 45°54'·72N 01°19'·79W. Rear, intens 329°-349°; W twr, R bands; 425m from front on W bkwtr.
W bkwtr head ✧ Fl (2) R 6s 11m 8M; 45°54'·81N 01°19'·70W.

GIRONDE APPROACHES AND TO BORDEAUX

GRANDE PASSE DE L'OUEST

Pte de la Coubre ☆ Fl (2) 10s 64m **28M**; W twr, R top; 45°41'·78N 01°13'·99W. Same twr, Q R 42m10M; 030°-R-110°.
BXA Iso 4s 8m 7M; ***Racon B***; 45°34'·10N 01°26'·63W. 992271005.
La Palmyre Wtr Twr Dir ☆ 056·7°, WRG 54m **W25M R/G20M**; 055·25°-FG-055·95°-AlWG-056·58°-FW-057·42°-AlWR-058·02-FR-058·72°; Gy Wtr Twr; 45°41'·65N 01°10'·18W.
Duc d'Albe ✧ Fl(2) 6s 10m 2M; W pylon on dolphin; 45°39'·56N 01°08'·77W.
No 1 QG; 45°36'·17N 01°21'·70W; 992271036.
No 6 VQ (6) + L Fl 10s; 45°38'·27N 01°17'·91W.
No 7a Fl G 4s; 45°38'·96N 01°14'·85W.
No 9 Q; 45°39'·43N 01°12'·79W.
No 11 Iso G 4s; 45°39'·06N 01°10'·60W.
No 11A Fl G 2·5s; 45°38'·37N 01°07'·90W.
No 13 Fl (2) G 6s; 45°37'·34N 01°06'·41W.
No 13A Fl (3) G 12s; 45°35'·68N 01°04'·19W.
No 13B QG; 45°34'·65N 01°02'·99W.
Ldg lts 327° (down-river): Front, Terre-Nègre ✧, Oc (3) WRG 12s 39m W14M, R/G11M; 304°-R-319°-W-327°-G-000°-W-004°-G-097°-W-104°-R-116°; W twr, R top on W side; 45°38'·77N 01°06'·39W. Rear, **La Palmyre** Oc (3) R 12s 57m 17M; W radar Twr; 45°39'·72N 01° 07'·25W. 1.1M from front (Terre Nègre) above.
Cordouan ☆ Oc (2+1) WRG 12s 60m, **W19M, R16M, G15M**; 014°-W-126°-G-178·5°-W-250°-W (unintens) -267°-R (unintens)-294·5°-R-014°; obsc'd in estuary when brg >285°; W twr, Gy band; 45°35'·18N 01°10'·40W.

PASSE SUD (or DE GRAVE)

Ldg lts 063°: **Front, St Nicolas** ☆ Dir QG 22m **16M**; intens 061·5°-064·5°; W □ twr; 45°33'·73N 01°05'·01W.
Rear, Pte de Grave ☆ Oc WRG 4s 26m, **W17M, R/G13M**; 033°-W(unintens)-054°-W-233·5°-R-303°-W-312°-G-330°-W-341°-W(unintens)-025°; W □ twr, B corners and top, 0·84M from front.
G 45°30'·33N 01°15'·55W. G3 45°32'·79N 01°07'·72W.

Ldg lts 041°, both Dir QR 33/61m **18M**. **Front, Le Chay** ☆ 45°37'·31N 01°02'·43W. **Rear, St Pierre** ☆, 0·97M from front. G4 45°34'·70N 01°05'·80W. G6 45°34'·88N 01°04'·80W.

ROYAN
R1 Iso G 4s; 45°36'·56N 01°01'·96W.
S jetty Fl (2) R 10s 11m 12M; 199°-116°; 45°37'·00N 01°01'·81W.
Hbr ent, W jetty Fl (3) R 12s 8m 6M; 45°37'·12N 01°01'·53W.

PORT BLOC and PORT-MÉDOC
Pte de Grave, jetty Q 6m 2M; 45°34'·42N 01°03'·68W.
Port Bloc, ent N side Fl G 4s 9m 3M; 45°34'·14N 01°03'·74W.
Port-Médoc, N bkwtr head QG 4M; 45°33'·40N 01°03'·39W.

MESCHERS, MORTAGNE, PORT MAUBERT, PAUILLAC and BLAYE
Meschers ldg lts 354·4°: QG (privately maintained). Front 45°33'·20N 00°56'·63W, on E bkwtr head. Rear, 130m from front.
Mortagne ent VQ (9) 10s; 45°28'·24N 00°49'·02W.
Port Maubert, ldg lts 024·5°, both QR 5/9m 5M; 45°25'·56N 00°45'·47W.
Pauillac, No 43 Fl (2) G 6s; 45°12'·44N 00°44'·27W.
NE elbow Fl G 4s 7m 5M; 45°11'·95N 00°44'·59W.
Ent E side QG 7m 4M; 45°11'·83N 00°44'·59W.
Blaye, No S9 45°09'·35N 00°40'·27W; 1·8M N of Blaye.
N quay Q (3) R 5s 6m 3M; 45°07'·49N 00°39'·99W.
D6 Fl (2) R 6s; 45°06'·91N 00°39'·93W, 0.6M S of Blaye.
Bec d'Ambés QG 5m 5M; 45°02'·53N 00°36'·47W (here Rivers Dordogne and Garonne flow into River Gironde).

BORDEAUX
Pont d'Aquitaine 4 F Vi; 44°52'·82N 00°32'·28W.
No 73 Iso G 4s; 44°52'·72N 00°32'·24W.
Lormont Iso R 4s, S end of Ⓥ pontoon; 44°52'·62N 00°32'·12W.
Lock ent to Bassins Nos 1 and 2, 44°51'·72N 00°33'·07W.
Pont de Pierre, 44°50'·30N 00°33'·78W, Km 0.

POINTE DE GRAVE TO THE SPANISH BORDER

Hourtin ☆ Fl 5s 55m **23M**; R □ twr; 45°08'·51N 01°09'·63W.
Cap Ferret ☆ Fl R 5s 53m **22M**; W ○ twr, R top; 44°38'·72N 01°14'·90W. Same twr, Oc (3) 12s 46m 11M; 045°-135°.

ARCACHON, PASSE NORD
Buoys may be moved, or added, as the chan shifts. Positions shown here are approximate and should be used with caution. Nos 10 &12 buoys do not exist; 11, 13, 14 lie btwn nos 9N &15.
ATT-ARC SWM L Fl 10s 8m 5M; 44°34'·046N 01°18'·75W.
Outer/entrance channel inward to Cap Ferret:

1N	44°34'·571N 01°17'·81W.
2N	44°34'·681N 01°17'·84W.
3N	44°34'·49N 01°16'·43W.
4N	44°34'·61N 01°16'·57W.
5N	44°34'·78N 01°15'·92W.
7N	44°35'·12N 01°15'·33W.
6N	44°35'·87N 01°14'·66W.
8N	44°36'·53N 01°14'·39W.
9N	44°36'·96N 01°14'·34W.
15	44°39'·85N 01°12'·04W.

Marina W bkwtr QG 6m 6M; 44°39'·77N 01°09'·14W.
E bkwtr QR 6m 6M; 44°39'·76N 01°09'·07W.
Port de La Vigne Iso R 4s 7m 5M, occas; 44°40'·43N 01°14'·36W.
La Salie Fl (2) 6s; 44°30'·43N 01°17'·75W.
Contis ☆ Fl (4) 25s 50m **23M**; W ○ twr, B diagonal stripes; 44°05'·59N 01°18'·99W.

CAPBRETON
Digue Nord Fl (2) R 6s 13m 12M; W ○ twr, R top; 43°39'·36N 01°26'·90W.
Estacade Sud Fl (2) G 6s 9m 8M; 43°39'·27N 01°26'·83W.

ANGLET and BAYONNE
BA L Fl 10s; 43°32'·59N 01°32'·85W, 144°/0·93M to hbr ent.
Outer ldg lts 090°, both Dir Q 9/15m **19M**; intens 086·5°-093·5°; synch; W twrs, R tops. Front, **Boucau** ☆ 43°31'·81N 01°31'·23W. Rear, 250m from front.
Outer N bkwtr QR 11m 8M; W/R twr; 43°31'·88N 01°31'·99W.
Outer S bkwtr Q (9) 15s 15m 6M; 43°31'·53N 01°31'·76W.
Inner ldg lts 111·5°, both Dir QG 6/10m 14M; intens 109°-114° Front, W/G hut; 43°31'·63N 01°30'·94W. Rear, 149m from front.
Inner N jetty Iso R 4s 12m 8M; 43°31'·82N 01°31'·42W.
Inner S jetty Iso G 4s 9m 10M; W □ twr, G top; 43°31'·73N 01°31'·48W. IPTS from twr 260m ESE.
N training wall Fl (2) R 6s 9m 8M; 43°31'·76N 01°31'·25W.
N training wall Fl (3) R 12s 9m 3M, 43°31'·75N 01°31'·18W.
N training wall Fl (4) R 15s 9m 3M, 43°31'·73N 01°30'·97W.
S training wall Fl (3) G 12s 9m 3M, 43°31'·67N 01°31'·21W.
S training wall Fl (4) G 15s 9m 3M, 43°31'·64N 01°30'·96W.
S training wall QG 7m 8M; 43°31'·63N 01°30'·90W.
Anglet marina ent Fl G 2·5s 6m 2M; 43°31'·57N 01°30'·51W.

Upriver toward Bayonne fixed bridge, 5·2m clearance:
Digue Basse Fl G 4s 3m 4M, 43°31'·54N 01°30'·08W.
Ldg lts 322·4°: Front, Forges QR 14m 8M; vis 188°-098°; 43°31'·61N 01°29'·92W. Rear, Dir Iso R 4s 18m 13M; intens 312·4°-332·4°.
No 1 Iso G 4s; 43°31'·34N 01°29'·72W.
No 2 QR; 43°30'·89N 01°29'·46W.
Pte de Blanc-Pignon Fl (2) G 6s 8m 9M; 43°30'·92N 01°29'·61W.
No 10 VQR; 43°30'·11N 01°29'·39W.
Pont de l'Aveugle Dir Q WRG W10M, R/G7M; 165°-G-170°-W-175°-R-195°; 43°30'·05N 01°29'·53W.

BIARRITZ
Pointe Saint-Martin ☆ Fl (2) 10s 73m **27M**; W twr, B top; 43°29'·62N 01°33'·24W.

ST JEAN DE LUZ
Outer ldg lts 138·5° (Passe d'Illarguita): Front, Socoa Q WR 36m W12M, R8M; shore-W-264°-R-282°-W-shore; W □ twr, B stripe; 43°23'·70N 01°41'·20W.

Rear, Bordagain, Dir Q 67m **20M**; intens 134·5°-141·5°; B/W panel, B/W pylon; 43°23'·12N 01°40'·50W.

Middle ldg lts 101°, both Oc (4) R 12s 30/47m **18M**; intens 095°-107°; synch. **Front, Ste Barbe** ☆, W △ on W hut; 43°23'·96N 01°39'·88W. **Rear** ☆, B △ on W □ twr, 340m from front.

Inner ldg lts 150·7°, both Dir QG 18/27m **16M**; intens 149·5°-152·2°. **Front, E jetty** ☆ W□twr, R stripe; 43°23'·25N 01°40'·15W.
Rear ☆, W □ twr, G stripe; 410m from front, S of marina.
Digue des Criquas (W bkwtr) Iso G 4s 11m 6M; G □ twr; 43°23'·84N 01°40'·67W.
East Groyne Fl R 4s 7m 2M; 43°23'·29N 01°40'·18W.

HENDAYE
Cabo Higuer ☆ Fl (2) 10s 63m **23M**; 072°-340°; □ twr, R cupola; 43°23'·52N 01°47'·52W (in Spain).
Refuge port ent, Fl (2) G 7s 7m 5M; 43°23'·13N 01°47'·35W.
W training wall Fl (3) G 9s 9m 5M; 43°22'·82N 01°47'·34W.
E training wall hd Fl (3) R 9s 8m 5M; 43°22'·67N 01°47'·23W.
E training wall root, Pte des Dunes Fl R 5s 7m 2M; 43°22'·38N 01°47'·34W.
Fl G 5s; 43°22'·31N 01°47'·45W.
VQ (3) G 5s 3m 3M; G bent mast; 43°22'·10N 01°47'·27W.
Marina, W bkwtr, elbow Fl (2) R 6s 6m 2M; 294°-114°; 43°22'·08N 01°47'·16W.
S jetty Q (9) 15s 5m 3M; Y col; 43°22'·05N 01°47'·05W.
L Fl G 10s 3m 4M; G mast; 43°21'·99N 01°47'·07W.

9.22.5 PASSAGE INFORMATION

More passage information is threaded between successive harbours in this Area. **Bibliography**: *Atlantic France* (Imray/RCC/Parkinson); *South Biscay* (Imray/RCC/Pickard); The *Bay of Biscay Pilot* NP22. AC 1104, 20, 2664, 1102; carry also large-scale French charts for inshore waters.

THE BAY OF BISCAY AND WEST COAST OF FRANCE

Despite its reputation, weather in the southern part of the Bay is often warm and settled in summer when the Azores high and Spanish heat low are the dominant weather features.

NE'lies prevail in sea area Fitzroy in summer and gales may occur twice monthly, although forecast more frequently. Atlantic lows can bring W'ly spells at any time together with long swells which are dangerous inshore. SE or S winds are rare, but wind direction and speed often vary from day to day. Sea and land breezes can be well developed in the summer. Off N Spain *Galernas* are dangerous squally NW winds which blow with little warning. Visit www.franksingleton.clara.net/biscay.html for useful Met and routeing information.

Rainfall is moderate, increasing in the SE, where thunder is more frequent. Sea fog occurs May-Oct, but is less common in winter. Japanese seaweed has been reported as a nuisance.

►*Tidal streams are weak offshore, but can be strong in estuaries and channels, and around headlands. The tidal stream chartlets at 9.22.3 are based on NP 265 (Admiralty tidal stream atlas for France, W Coast) which uses data from actual observations out to 15-25M offshore. The equivalent French Atlas gives more data, based on computer predictions.*◄

The general direction and rate of the surface current much depends on wind: in summer it is SE, towards the SE corner of B of Biscay, where it swings W along the N coast of Spain. In winter with W gales, the current runs E along N coast of Spain, sometimes at 3kn or more. When crossing the Bay of Biscay, allow for a likely set to the E, particularly after strong W winds.

The Continental Shelf with mean depths of 130m is a major feature of the Bay of Biscay. From 75M SW of Pointe du Raz it closes the French coast near Capbreton. AC 1104 shows depths plummeting to 4000m in the space of 20M. This steep slope allied to Atlantic swell can cause severe sea states.

9.22.6 Special Notes for France See Area 17.

9.22.7 PORNIC

Loire Atlantique **47°06'·54N 02°06'·59W** ❀❀❀◊◊◊✿✿✿

CHARTS AC 2646, 2986, 2981; Imray C40; SHOM 7395, 7394; Navi 547, 549

TIDES +0515 Dover; ML 3·6; Duration 0540

Standard Port BREST (⟵)

Times				**Height (metres)**			
High Water		Low Water		MHWS	MHWN	MLWN	MLWS
0500	1100	0500	1100	6·9	5·4	2·6	1·0
1700	2300	1700	2300				
Differences PORNIC							
–0050	+0030	–0010	–0010	–1·1	–0·8	–0·4	–0·2
POINTE DE SAINT GILDAS							
–0030	+0025	–0005	–0020	–1·3	–0·9	–0·5	–0·2

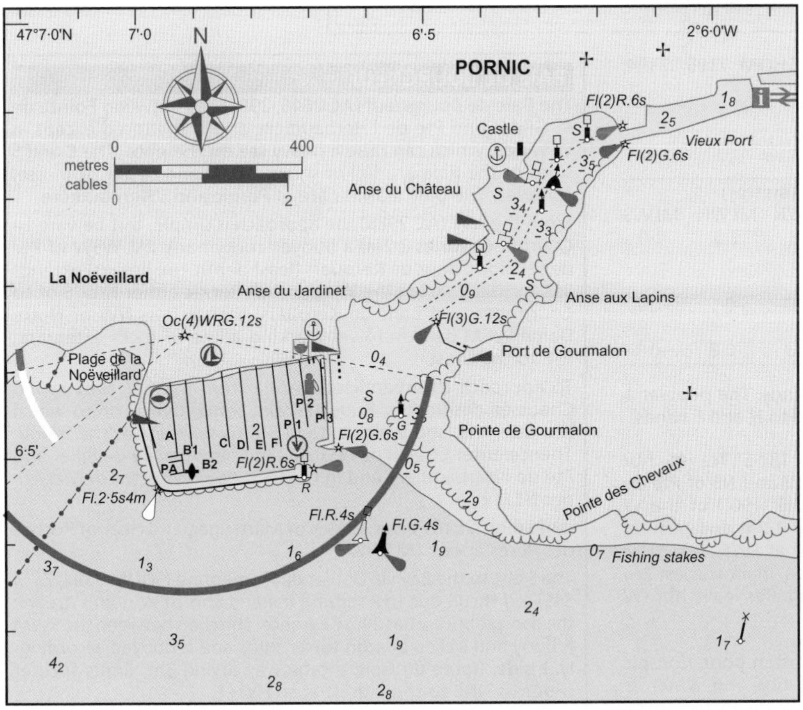

SHELTER Very good in the large marina.

NAVIGATION WPT 47°05'·98N 02°08'·86W, 073°/1·6M to hbr ent, is in the W sector of Pte de Noëveillard lt ho. A SPM buoy, Fl Y 2·5s, at 47°06'·17N 02°07'·40W marks the seaward end of an outfall.

Beware Banc de Kerouars 4-6M WSW of harbour, least depth 0·7m, on which seas break; it is unmarked, but the W sector of Pte de Noëveillard lt clears it by night.

From the NW pass between this bank and the mainland. All other hazards are well marked. The S end of B de Bourgneuf is full of oyster beds, and many obstructions.

Do not attempt entry at LWS. Approach to marina reported silting, best depths close to west side of channel. Two sets of PHM and SHM beacons avoid rocky spurs close to E and S bkwtrs.

LIGHTS AND MARKS See chartlet and Lights, buoys and waypoints. The W sector (051°-079°) of Pte de Noëveillard lt ho lies between Notre-Dame WCM bcn twr VQ (9) 10s, and the E end of Banc de Kerouars 0·7m. The lt ho and trees behind are not easily seen.

COMMUNICATIONS CROSS/LB 02·97·55·35·35 or 196; Auto 02·40·82·60·60; Police 02·40·82·00·29; Brit Consul 01·44·51·31·00; Dr 02·40·82·01·80; HM VHF Ch 09 (H24); Taxi 02·40·82·17·13 or 02·40·82·87·62.

FACILITIES Marina ☎02·40·82·05·40 accueil.portdepornic@gmail.com www.portdepornic.com. Depth 2m, no access LW±2 for draft >1·7m when Coeff >75, nor in SE–SW winds >F7. Call ahead VHF Ch 09 or berth temp'y on 'Ponton d'accueil' at marina ent for berth allocation, ⓥ berths are at S ends of pontoons P3 (1st to stbd, LOA <8m) P2 (<10m) or where directed. ☎02·40·82·05·40. 754+40ⓥ €3·00. H24 cr/debit card, on small pontoon (<2m LW) with drying ledge inshore, order artisan bread/croissants in evening for delivery (am). Ⓔ (50t).

CN de Pornic ☎02·40·82·34·72.

Old hbr dries 2·5m; access via marked, lit drying channel. Locals only.

Town Market Thurs & Sun am. ✕ ✉ Ⓑ ⥂ ✈ (Nantes). **Ferry** via Roscoff/St Malo.

9.22.8 L'HERBAUDIÈRE Loire Atlantique **47°06'·54N 02°06'·59W**

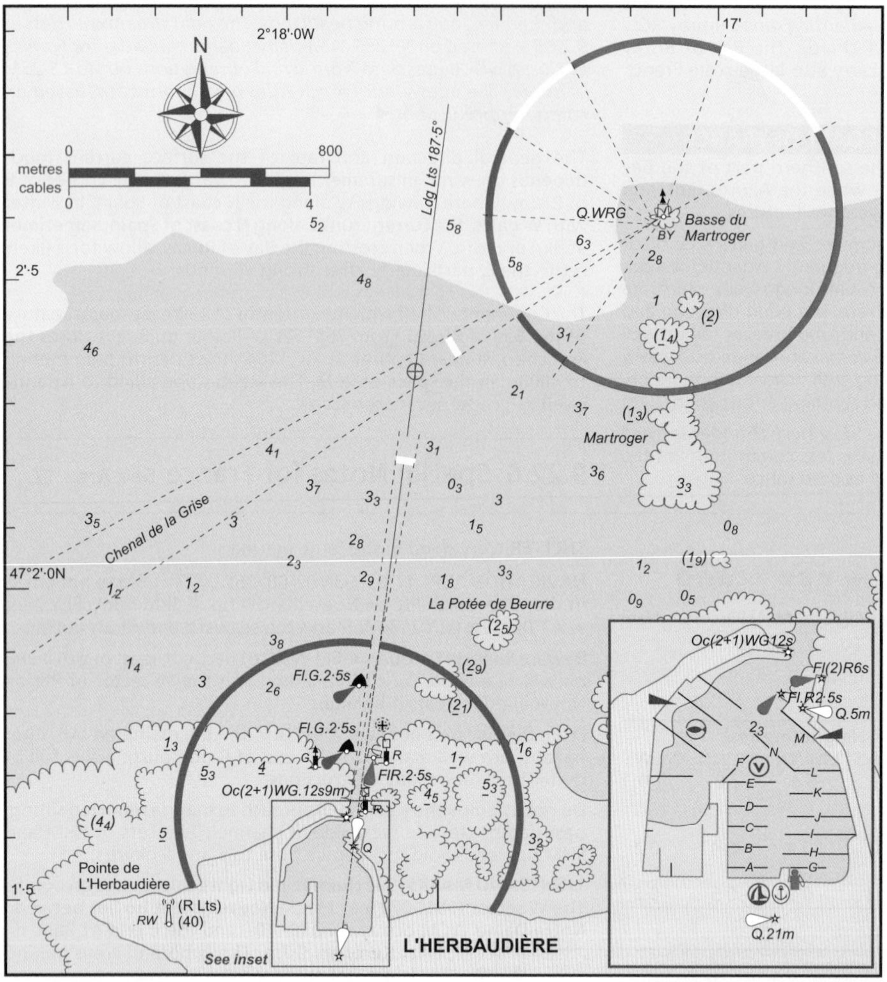

is 2·7M WNW of hbr. Other lts/marks as chartlet and Lights, buoys and waypoints.

At night initial positioning is assisted by any of the 3 W sectors (see Lights, buoys and waypoints) of Basse de Martroger, NCM bcn twr. Ldg lts 187·5°, both hard-to-see-by-day grey masts, Q, lead over Banc de la Blanche (1·5m) approx 2M N of hbr.

COMMUNICATIONS
LB 02·51·39·33·90; CROSS 02·97·55·35·35; 02·40·84·80·19; Auto 08·92·68·08·85; Police 02·51·39·04·36; ⊖ 02·51·39·06·80; British Consul 01·44·51·31·00; Dr 02·51·39·05·64; HM VHF Ch 09 (HO); Aff Mar 02·51·39·94·03.

FACILITIES
Marina ☎02·51·39·05·05 herbaudiere.port@wanadoo.fr www.portdeplaisance-herbaudiere.com. Dredged 1·5m. Ⓥs berth on pontoon F or as directed. 572 + 50Ⓥ €3·06. (Jul/Aug) Ⓔ (30t) SC.

Town Ⓑ (Nantes). **Ferry** via Roscoff/St Malo.

CHARTS AC 2646, 2986, 2981; Imray C40; SHOM 7395, 7394; Navi 547, 549

TIDES +0500 Dover; ML 3·4

Standard Port BREST (⟵)

Times				Height (metres)			
High Water		Low Water		MHWS	MHWN	MLWN	MLWS
0500	1100	0500	1100	6·9	5·4	2·6	1·0
1700	2300	1700	2300				
Differences L'HERBAUDIÈRE							
–0045	+0025	–0020	–0020	–1·4	–1·0	–0·5	–0·2
FROMENTINE							
–0045	+0020	–0015	+0005	–1·7	–1·3	–0·8	–0·1

SHELTER Good in marina, except in N to E winds. The popular ⚓ off Pte des Dames lt, 4+M to the E, is exposed to N and E winds.

NAVIGATION WPT 47°02'·32N 02°17'·70W, 187·5°/7ca to hbr ent. There are rocks and banks to the SW, NW and NE of Pte de l'Herbaudière. Ldg lts and white sector (187·5°-190°) of the W jetty lt both lead into ent chan, dredged to 1·2m and passing close W of two 0·3m patches; care is needed at LWS. Two SHM buoys, both Fl G 2·5s, and a PHM buoy, Fl R 2·5s, mark the last 2ca of the chan. W bkwtr obscures vessels leaving. FVs leave hbr (W side) early morning.

LIGHTS AND MARKS Visibility in summer is often poor. Conspic daymarks are R/W radio mast 500m W of hbr and water tr about 1M SE. Ile du Pilier lt ho, with two distinctive twrs,

BAIE DE BOURGNEUF

The Baie de Bourgneuf (AC 2646, 2981) lies between Pointe de St Gildas and Pte de l'Herbaudière and is sheltered except in W winds, which can raise a heavy sea on the ebb. The E and S sides of the Baie are full of shoals, rocks and oyster or mussel fisheries. The only marinas are at Pornic and L'Herbaudière.

From the NW (AC 2986) the approach is simple, but beware La Couronnée (dries 2·2m) a buoyed rocky bank 2M WSW of Pte de St Gildas. Banc de Kerouars (least depth 1m; breaks) extends 3M further E. From the W approach **Pornic** either N or S of La Couronnée and Banc de Kerouars; thence pass NW of Notre Dame WCM beacon tower marking a line of rocks extending ESE to the coast.

To approach **L'Herbaudière** Marina from the SW, skirt round Chaussée des Boeufs, buoyed rocks, some drying, on to which the tide sets; and which extend 6M to seaward of the island. Thence enter Chenal de la Grise (3m) between Île du Pilier and Pte de l'Herbaudière and in the 055°-060° W sector of Martroger NCM bcn.

If heading NE to Pornic, pass N of Martroger, and clear of Roches des Pères about 1M ENE.

The S ent to the Bay via Goulet de Fromentine (SHOM 7394; ECM 549) is difficult due to a shifting bar and 8hrs of W-going stream; the conspic bridge has 24m clearance. The chan between the SWM lt buoy and Milieu beacon tower shifts and is buoyed accordingly. Inside, Route du Gois, a causeway drying 3m, limits further progress NNE to shoal draft at sp HW±1.

MINOR HARBOUR ON NE CORNER OF ÎLE DE NOIRMOUTIER

NOIRMOUTIER-EN-L'ÎLE 46°59′·33N 02°13′·17W. AC 2981; SHOM 7394. Tides as opposite. Good shelter and 4M SE of L'Herbaudière, but this FV hbr dries up to $\underline{3}$·6m on mud/gravel. Appr across drying rock ledges to the N and E of ent. The E'ly of 2 chans runs SSW from approx 47°00′·70N 02°11′·10W, then doglegs WNW to the ent. It is marked by 5 unlit PHM bns. There are some council visitors moorings off Pte de Dames, €13·00 p/day, (good beach, poss a bit rolly), and from the lt ho, Oc (3)WRG 12s, an inshore chan runs S which is more easily followed keeping about 400m off 5 unlit SHM bns along the shore. Both chans meet at the ent where the flood tide sets S. S jetty hd has ☆ Oc (2) R 6s. Follow the jetty on N side for about 1M to hbr. A recce is advised (3M overland from L'Herbaudière).

HM ☎02·51·39·08·39. **Quay** Ⓔ (4t).

Town Ⓑ at Nantes, via ferry to Pornic and bus. **Ferry** via Roscoff or St Malo.

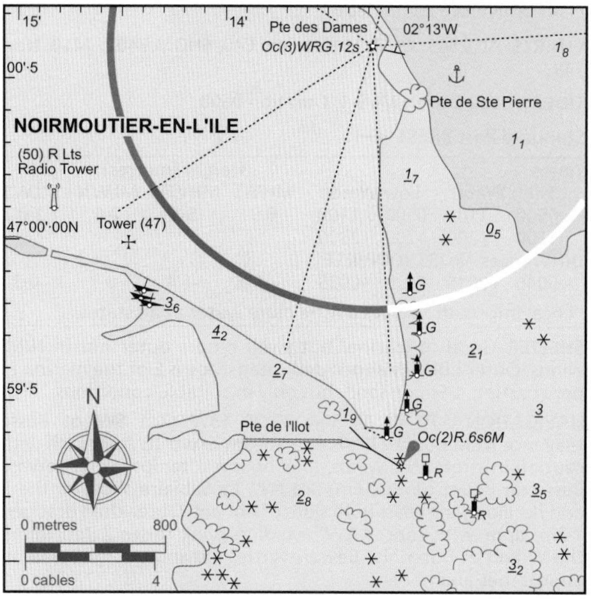

MINOR HARBOUR AT SOUTH END OF ÎLE DE NOIRMOUTIER

FROMENTINE, Vendée, 46°53′·60N 02°08′·60W. AC 2981, SHOM 7394. HW +0550 on Dover (UT); ML 3·2m; Duration 0540. Tides L'Herbaudière. Do not appr from Baie de Bourgneuf as there is a road causeway (Le Gois) dries $\underline{3}$m, from Île de Noirmoutier to the mainland.

From Fromentine SWM lt buoy, L Fl 10s, 46°53′·10N 02°11′·40W, track 072°/1·4M via Goulet de Fromentine to Tourelle Milieu, Fl (4) R 15s, R twr, and Boisvinet W bcn twr. The chan is buoyed, moved as necessary, but is very shallow, so dangerous in bad weather. At sp the ebb can reach 8kn, the flood 5kn. Do not attempt night entry. Pass under the bridge (clearance 24m, two x Iso 4s 32m 18M). ⚓ W of pier near PHM buoy Fl R 2s. At Pte du Notre Dames-de-Monts, there is a Dir lt, Oc (2) WRG 6s; see Lights, buoys and waypoints for sector details.

Facilities: **Quay** (3t).

9.22.9 PORT JOINVILLE (Île d'Yeu)

Vendée **46°43′·75N 02°20′·77W**

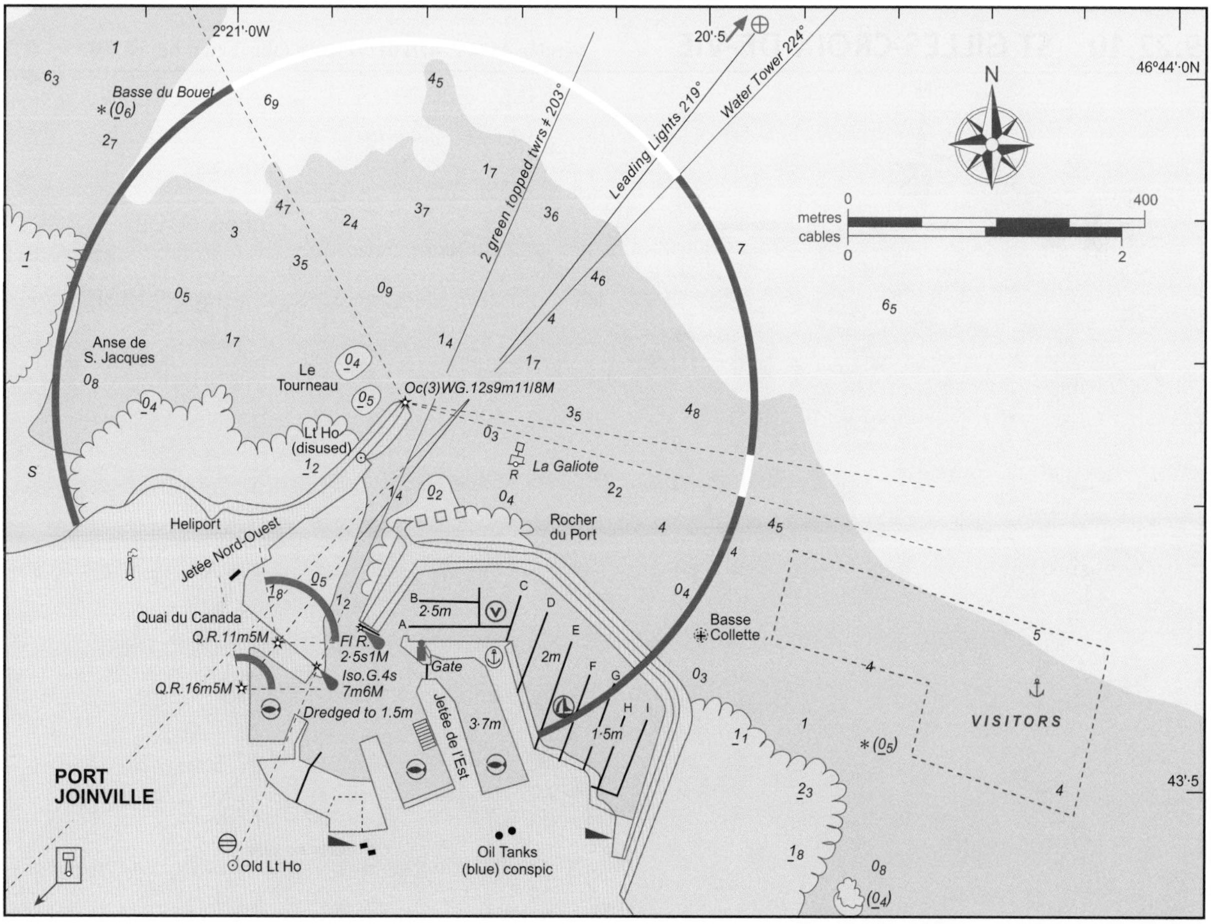

Continued overleaf

PORT JOINVILLE *continued*

CHARTS AC 2663, 2997, 3640; Imray C40; SHOM 7402, 7410; Navi 549

TIDES +0550 Dover; ML 3·1; Duration 0600

Standard Port BREST (⟵)

Times				Height (metres)			
High Water		Low Water		MHWS	MHWN	MLWN	MLWS
0500	1100	0500	1100	6·9	5·4	2·6	1·0
1700	2300	1700	2300				
Differences *PORT JOINVILLE							
−0040	+0015	−0030	−0035	−1·9	−1·4	−0·7	−0·3

*Local information gives a little more water at all states.

SHELTER Good in marina, but swell enters outer hbr in N/NE winds. Outer hbr ⚓̸. Visitors' dedicated ⚓age is E of the marina as per chartlet; 4-5m on sand, but only in suitable conditions.

NAVIGATION WPT 46°44′·30N 02°20′·13W (7ca SW of Basse Mayence NCM buoy) 219°/7ca to abeam bkwtr lt. Approach with caution in strong N-E winds; if F8 do not attempt entry. Beware Basse du Bouet (dries 0·6m) 3ca NW, La Sablaire shoal to the E and rks along the coast both sides of hbr ent. Outer chan dredged 1·2m; appr with care at LW, avoiding bank (dries 2·3m) filling the W half of outer hbr. Beware ferries moving at high speed in approaches and hbr ent.

LIGHTS AND MARKS Daymarks: Very conspic water twr leads 224° to hbr. Two green-topped white twrs (front, Quai du Canada Iso G 4s; rear, Old lt ho) ≠ 203° also lead into hbr. Conspic chimney W of hbr ent. Ldg lts 219°, both QR. Other lts: see Lts, buoys and waypoints.

IPTS sigs at ent to marina on E pierhead are not visible from seaward but control movements of vessels departing marina.

COMMUNICATIONS CROSS 02·97·55·35·35; LB 02·51·58·32·01; ☼ 02·51·36·10·78; Auto 08·92·68·08·85; Police 02·51·58·30·05; ⊖ 02·51·39·06·80; Brit Consul 01·44·51·31·00; H 02·51·68·30·23; Dr 02·51·59·30·00/02·51·58·30·58; Aff Mar 02·51·59·42·60; Marina VHF Ch 09, 16 (HO).

FACILITIES Marina Very crowded in season; best to pre-book as it is the only secure hbr on Yeu. Ⓥ at E end of pontoons A & B. ☎02·51·58·38·11. plaisance.iledyeu@vendee.cci.fr 330+170Ⓥ €3·30. (15t). **CN Ile d'Yeu** ☎02·51·58·31·50.

The wet basin (3·7m) access HW±1½ via entry gate 02·51·58·37·01, is mainly for FVs, but possible overflow for yachts in high season; no pontoons; R/G tfc lts at the gate.

Town ✕ Ⓑ ⇌ (St Gilles-Croix-de-Vie) ✈ (Nantes). Helicopter from hbr to mainland, La Barre de Monts. Flights from airfield 2M west of hbr to Nantes and (summers only) to Les Sables d'Olonne. **Ferry** via Roscoff or St Malo, then Fromentine, St Gilles and Les Sables d'Olonne.

ANCHORAGES ON S COAST OF ILE D'YEU

PORT DE LA MEULE, 46°41′·68N 02°20′·75W. AC 2663; SHOM 7410. −0050 sp and −0020 nps on Brest; ML 3·0m. Small, drying fishing hbr on S side of Ile d'Yeu, only safe in settled offshore weather; untenable in S winds. Many little FVs inside hbr; best to ⚓ outside and W of the ent.

Between Pte de la Père to the W and Pte de la Tranche to the SE, appr on 023° towards W square patch on Gy □ lt tr, R top, Oc WRG 4s; at night in W sector (018°-027·5°) but night ent not advised. Within 1ca of ent beware rks, first to port, then to stbd. Few facilities: s, 1½ miles to ✕.

ANSE DES VIEILLES, 46°41′·53N 02°18′·70W; 1M W of Pte des Corbeaux. Use SHOM 7410. Good shelter from N'lies. ⚓ clear of bathing area in 8-9m N or NE of Ours des Vieilles rks drying 3·5m.

9.22.10 ST GILLES-CROIX-DE-VIE

Vendée **46°41′·47N 01°57′·29W** (abm bkwtr hd)

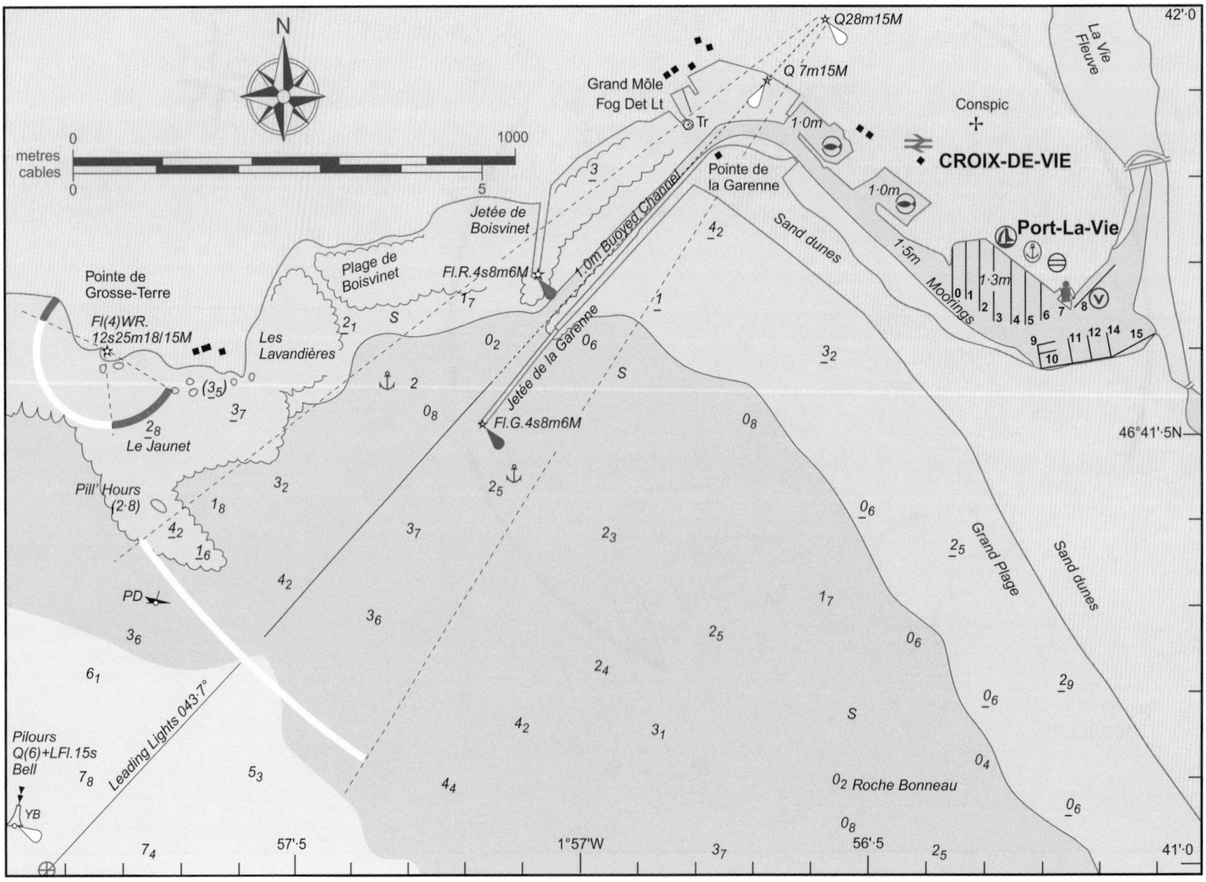

CHARTS AC 2663, 2997; Imray C40; SHOM 7402; Navi 1022, 549

TIDES +0500 Dover; ML 3·2; Duration 0600

Standard Port BREST (⟵)

Times				Height (metres)			
High Water		Low Water		MHWS	MHWN	MLWN	MLWS
0500	1100	0500	1100	7·0	5·5	2·7	1·1
1700	2300	1700	2300				
Differences ST GILLES-CROIX-DE-VIE							
–0030	+0015	–0030	–0030	–1·8	–1·3	–0·6	–0·3

SHELTER Good in marina and easy access except in strong SW'lies or swell when breakers form off ent. Waiting ⚓ off ent, NW or SE of ldg line in 2·0–3·5m.

NAVIGATION WPT 46°40'·94N 01°58'·02W, on the 043·7° ldg line and abeam Pilours SCM lt buoy, 043·7°/0·72M to Jetée de la Garenne lt. From W & NW, beware Rocher Pill'Hours (2·8m) and drying reefs extending 1ca SE.

Ent chan (⚓ prohib) is dredged 1·0m, but narrow and very shallow near bkwtr hds due to silting which persists despite dredging; depths may be further reduced. Keep well off the first two chan buoys which are laid outboard of drying rks; and, tfc permitting, keep slightly W of 043·7° ldg line.

Best arr/dep HW –2 to HW to avoid strong ebb, up to 6kn in ent at springs which may complicate berthing on outer ends of pontoons. Do not arr/dep LW±2 if >1·5m draft.

LIGHTS AND MARKS Daymarks are Pte de Grosse-Terre (rky hdland) with lt ho, W truncated conical tr; and two spires NE of the marina. The front ldg mark is initially hard to see against bldgs behind.

COMMUNICATIONS CROSS 02·97·55·35·35; LB 02·51·55·01·19; ☼ 02·51·36·10·78; Auto 08·92·68·08·85; Police 02·51·55·01·19; ⊖ 02·51·55·10·18; Brit Consul 01·44·51·31·00; Dr 02·51·55·11·93; HM VHF Ch 09 (season 0600-2200; out of season 0800-1200, 1400-1800LT); Aff Mar 02·51·55·10·58.

FACILITIES **Marina** ☎02·51·55·30·83. port.la.vie@wanadoo.fr www.semvie.com Dredged 1·3–1·5m. Ⓥ berth/raft on pontoon No 8 or as directed, or pick up Ⓥ S of marina. 900+100Ⓥ €2·67. SHOM Ⓔ (35t) (2·2t). **CN** ☎02·51·54·09·31.

Town Ⓑ. A ferry runs to Ile d'Yeu. **Ferry** Roscoff or St Malo.

9.22.11 LES SABLES D'OLONNE

Vendée **46°29'·42N 01°47'·54W**

CHARTS AC 2663, 2998, 3638; Imray C40, C41; SHOM 7402, 7403, 7411; Navi 1022

TIDES +0530 Dover; ML 3·2; Duration 0640

Standard Port BREST (⟵)

Times				Height (metres)			
High Water		Low Water		MHWS	MHWN	MLWN	MLWS
0500	1100	0500	1100	6·9	5·4	2·6	1·0
1700	2300	1700	2300				
Differences LES SABLES D'OLONNE							
–0030	+0015	–0035	–0035	–1·7	–1·2	–0·6	–0·3

SHELTER Very good in Quai Garnier and Port Olona Marinas.

NAVIGATION WPT 46°28'·49N 01°47'·23W (abeam Nouch Sud SCM buoy, Q (6)+L Fl 15s) 032·5°/5ca to intersection with 320° ldg line; thence 7ca to the hbr ent. To the W, beware Les Barges d'Olonne, extending 1·3M W of Pte de Aiguille.

The 2 appr chans are: the SW chan with La Potence ldg lts 032·5°, which lead into SE chan on ldg line 320°. In bad weather use the SE chan. Le Noura (1·3m) and Le Nouch (0·7m) are isolated rks on shoals S of Jetée St Nicolas. Further SE, Barre Marine breaks, even in moderate weather. A buoyed wk (dries) lies off hbr ent, to E of 320° ldg line.

Access at all tides; entry is easy except in strong winds from SE to SW when apprs get very rough. Sailing is prohib in the narrow dredged chan (2m). Best water initially is on the E side, then mid-chan. Caution: oncoming vessels passing very close.

LIGHTS AND MARKS See Lights, buoys and waypoints and chartlet for lt details. Les Barges lt ho, 2M W of ent. L'Armandèche lt ho, conspic 6ca W of ent. SW Chan ldg lts 032·5°: both Iso 4s H24. SE Chan ldg lts 320°: front QG on E bkwtr; rear, Q on Tour d'Arundel a large grey twr. St Nicolas jetty hd, QR. Inner ldg lts 328·1°, both Iso R 4s; R/W vert stripes, hard to see by day but not essential for yachts.

COMMUNICATIONS CROSS 02·97·55·35·35; ☼ 02·51·36·10·78; Auto 08·92·68·08·85; Police 02·51·33·69·91; ⊖ 02·51·23·58·00; Brit Consul 01·44·51·31·00; H 02·51·21·06·33; Dr 02·51·95·14·47; Port HM 02·51·95·11·79, VHF Ch 12 (0800-1800); Aff Mar 02·51·28·81·91; Marinas VHF Ch 09 *Plaisance Quai Garnier* or *Port Olona* (0600-2400LT in season).

Continued overleaf

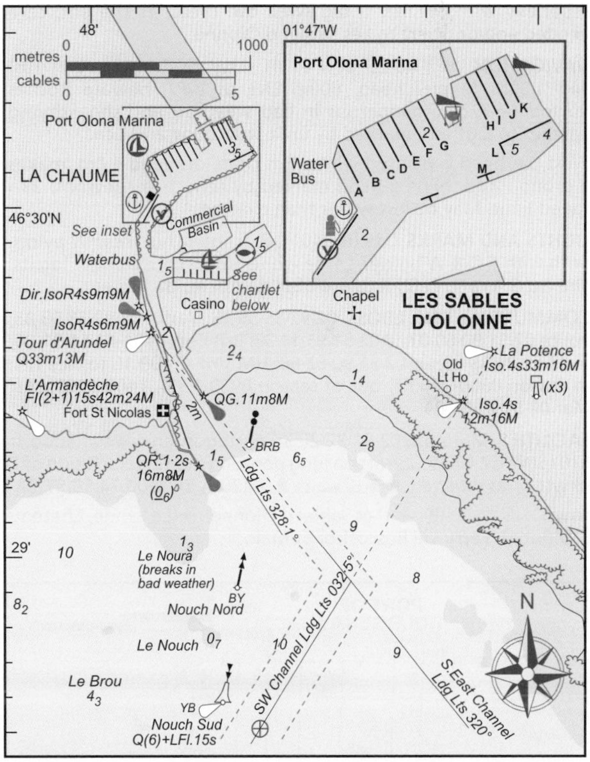

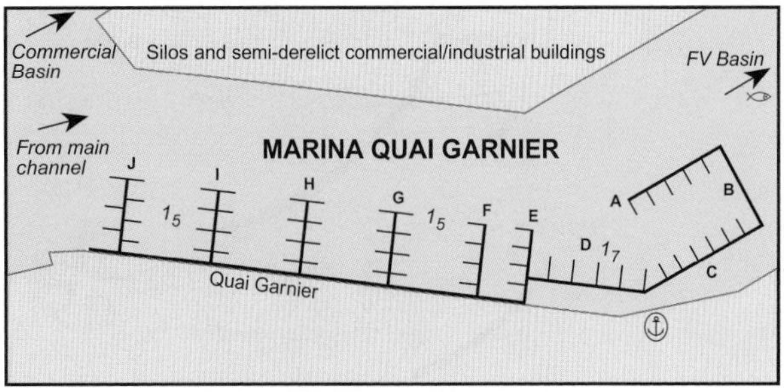

LES SABLES D'OLONNE *continued*

FACILITIES Marina Quai Garnier ☎06·78·07·15·15/ 06·73·76·94·65. www.vendee.cci.fr 119 inc Ⓥ on 10 pontoons (J-A); berthing prohibited on hammerheads; €3·00; Occas wash from FVs. N of pontoon J at the gate into the Commercial basin an Oc Y lt shows when a vessel is entering/leaving (HW ±2); keep clear. Readers report good facilities and helpful staff. Very close to town centre, shops and many restaurants.

Port Olona Marina ☎02·51·32·51·16. www.portolona.fr portolona@wanadoo.fr (1·5–3·5m). Access H24. Visitors check in at accueil/fuel pontoon port side, by Capitainerie. Distant pontoon, at NE end, is for Ⓥ and multihulls, but on request a berth may be found in pontoons A-C. 990+110Ⓥ €2·95. (0800-2000) Ⓔ SHOM Divers (28t).

Town ✕ Ⓑ ✈. **Ferry** Roscoff or St Malo.

9.22.12 BOURGENAY

Vendée **46° 26′·27N 01° 40′·70W**

CHARTS AC 2663, 2998; Imray C41; SHOM 7069, 7403; Navi 1022

TIDES +0600 Dover; ML 3·1; Duration 0640. Use Differences Les Sables d'Olonne, 5·5M NW.

SHELTER Good in marina (2m). Even in moderate weather, and especially with SW'lies, a big swell can break at the ent; care needed and/or divert to Les Sables d'Olonne.

NAVIGATION WPT 46°25′·27N 01°41′·93W (SWM buoy, L Fl 10s) 040°/1·32M to pier head. 600m ENE of WPT, beware Roches du Joanne (2·9m; dangerous in bad weather) and shoal/drying patches to E of ent, marked by unlit SHM buoy and bcn.

West pierhead is painted white. Ent chan, dredged 1·0m, makes a pronounced, blind S-bend marked by reflective chevrons; 3kn speed limit. May be less water than charted.

LIGHTS AND MARKS Ldg lts 040° QG; front W hut; rear W pylon, both with G □ & W border. Large white bldg is conspic near ldg lts. The Iso G 4s and Fl (2) R 6s are obsc'd until inside hbr ent.

COMMUNICATIONS CROSS 02·97·55·35·35; Auto 08·92·68·08·85; Police 02·51·90·60·07; ⊜ 02·51·95·11·33; Brit Consul 01·44·51·31·00; Ⓗ 02·51·21·85·85; Dr 02·51·90·62·68; HM VHF Ch 09 16 (office hrs: in season 0800-2100LT, out of season 0900-1200, 1400-1800); Aff Mar 02·51·21·81·81.

FACILITIES Marina ☎02·51·22·20·36 portbourgenay@wanadoo.fr 610+50Ⓥ €2·67. Ⓥ/raft on long pontoon (no fingers) N side of E bkwtr or as directed. (20t). **YC** ☎08.74.50.57.57.

Town ✕ Ⓑ. (Les Sables d'Olonne). ✈(La Lande, Chateau d'Olonne). **Ferry** via Roscoff or St Malo.

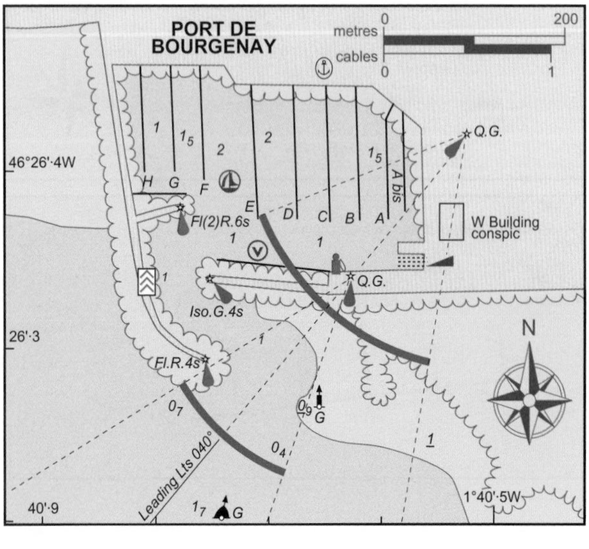

ILE D'YEU TO PERTUIS BRETON

Île d'Yeu, 30m high, has its main lt ho near the NW end where Les Chiens Perrins lt bcn marks offliers. On the NE coast a very conspicuous water twr gives a good lead into **Port Joinville**, crowded in season. The passage along the NE of the island carries 6-7m nearer to the island. Pte des Courbeaux lt ho is at the low SE end of the island. The passage along the NE of the island carries 6-7m nearer to the island. ►*Here the E-going stream starts at HW Brest –5¾ and the W-going at HWB –¼.*◄ The SW coast is steep-to and rky, with a tiny drying hbr at Port de la Meule (best to anch outside) and, further E, anch at Anse des Vieilles, both only tenable in settled conditions.

Les Marguerites, rky shoals, lie SSW of Goulet de Fromentine, with the part-drying reef, Pont d'Yeu (SCM buoy) extending midway between the mainland and the Île d'Yeu; here anch is prohibited in a 2·2M wide strip due to underwater cables (AC 2663, 2997, 2998).

The low-lying, wooded Côte de la Vendée continues 40M SE to Pte du Grouin-du-Cou with few dangers more than 1·5M offshore, except near Les Sables d'Olonne. 17M E of Port Joinville is **St Gilles-Croix-de-Vie**. Thence 17M SSE is **Les Sables d'Olonne**, with Les Barges drying reef (lt) extending 2·5M W of the entrance. **Bourgenay** is 6M further SE. The approaches to these secure hbrs, all with marinas, are exposed to onshore winds from SE to NW, and susceptible to swell. **Jard-sur-Mer** is a small drying harbour midway between Bourgenay and Pte du Grouin-du-Cou.

PERTUIS BRETON

Pertuis Breton is entered between Pte du Grouin-du-Cou and Pointe des Baleines (both lit) on **Île de Ré**, which is surrounded by shallows and drying areas (AC 2999). Beware rocky ledges (dry) extending 2·5M NW from Les Baleines. Pertuis Breton gives access to the harbours of **Ars-en-Ré, St Martin** and **La Flotte** on the N shore of Île de Ré. From St Martin to Pte de Sablanceaux (SE tip) there are extensive oyster beds.

On the mainland side, in fresh NW winds against tide a bad sea builds on the bank which extends 8M W of Pointe du Grouin du Cou. 1M SSE of the Pointe is the unmarked Roche de l'Aunis (depth 0·8m). SE of the Pte the coast is fronted by sand dunes and mussel beds, whose seaward limits are marked by unlit buoys. 8M ESE is the drying ent to Rivière Le Lay, with a bar (dries 1m) dangerous in bad weather. Thence the channel to L'Aiguillon and La Faute-sur-Mer is marked by bcns and buoys. Offshore a large mussel farm (3M x 1M) is marked by 4 cardinal and 2 SPM light buoys.

5M further E is the entrance to Anse de l'Aiguillon, in which there are extensive mussel beds. Here the Sèvre Niortaise estuary, after 3·5M, leads via a canal into the port of **Marans**. Further S the main route continues SE and E, passing under the fine road bridge (30m clearance) between the mainland and Île de Ré and into Rade de la Pallice; thence to La Rochelle or the Pertuis d'Antioche.

PERTUIS D'ANTIOCHE

The low-lying shores of the Pertuis d'Antioche (AC 2999) converge eastwards to **La Rochelle, Ile d'Aix**, La Charente River and **Rochefort**. Île de Ré forms the N side, fringed by rocky ledges extending 2·5M SE from Pte de Chanchardon (lt) and nearly 1M from Pte de Chauveau (marked by lt twr and two bcns).

Île d'Oléron lies SE of Pertuis d'Antioche. At its N tip, off Pte de Chassiron (light house and signal station), reefs extend 5ca W, 1·5M N to Rocher d'Antioche (lit) and 1·5M E; here there is often a nasty sea.

Well offshore, 43M WNW of Pointe de Chassiron, The Plateau de Rochebonne is a chain of rocks on which the sea breaks dangerously. It has least depth 3·3m, is marked by 2 cardinal and 2 lateral light buoys and is enclosed by a circular 'Area to be avoided', radius 7M centred on 46°10′·00N 02°25′·60W – although the rocks only occupy the NNE half of the circle.

MINOR HARBOURS ON THE N SHORE OF PERTUIS BRETON

JARD-SUR-MER, Vendée, **46°24′·43N 01°34′·78W**. AC 2663, 2998 (1:10,000 inset); SHOM 7403. HW +0600 on Dover (UT); HW–0010 & ht –2·0m on Brest; ML 3·1m; Duration 0640. 2 W bcns 4ca E of hbr ent lead 036° between the drying Roches de l'Islatte and Roches de la Brunette, marked by buoys (May-Sep). Inner RW bcns at W end of hbr lead 293° into small drying unlit hbr, 4·5m max at HW.

Moorings inside bkwtr, inc 7 Y Ⓥs. HM's office with blue roof and adjacent bldgs are conspic. HM (occas) ☎02·51·33·90·61; ⊜ ☎02·51·95·11·33. Facilities: Jetty Divers (5t).

L'AIGUILLON/LA-FAUTE-SUR-MER, Vendée, **46°19′·95N 01°18′·78W**. AC 2663, 2999; SHOM 7404. HW +0535 on Dover (UT) HW –0030, ht +0·6m on Pte de Grave (Zone –0100); ML 3·4m. The bar dries and is dangerous in bad weather; avoid in strong S or W winds. The ent is only safe in fine weather with offshore winds. A transformer at 46°18′·20N 01°14′·90W is conspic on a hill NE of Pte d'Arcay. Beware mussel beds with steel piles which cover at HW; also oyster beds.

Access HW±3, max 1·5m draft; not suitable for keel boats. Appr from Le Lay SCM buoy, 46°16′·15N 01°16′·49W, with transformer brg 033°. The drying berths at both hbrs are small enclosures made of rough timber framing; no facilities for visitors. Upriver the low bridge has 3m clearance. HM L'Aiguillon ☎05·51·97·06·57; HM La Faute ☎05·51·56·45·02.

MARANS, Vendée, approx **46°18′·70N 01°00′·00W**. AC 2663, 2999; SHOM 7404; Navi 551. Tides: see L'Aiguillon above; HW at Brault lock = HW La Rochelle + 0020. From SWM buoy, L Fl 10s, (46° 15′·45N 01°11′·39W) appx 2·5M c. 035° to beginning of the buoyed chan (dries 1·0m) which leads NE past Pavé jetty, Fl G 4s. In the estuary and lower chan beware mussel beds with many posts which cover at HW.

Waiting buoys below Brault bridge, which lifts at between HW±1 when the lock opens, day only. Pre-check times ☎06·64·49·29·60 before entering the river. The vast lock (104 x 45m wide, with sloping sides) contains a waiting pontoon and small swing bridge at the far end.

A straight 3M long canal (4·7m) leads to good shelter in non-tidal hbr, max LOA 16m. Beyond new finger pontoons raft on other yachts. HM ☎05·46·01·02·99/06·25·79·16·35, portdemarans@orange.fr; (40+10 Ⓥ) €1·20, (wood) (8t). **Town** Market (Tues & Sat). ☎05·46·01·53·33, 0·5M below Brault bridge, has for larger yachts.

MINOR HARBOUR ON ÎLE DE RÉ

LA FLOTTE, Charente Maritime, **46°11′·34N 01°19′·30W**. AC 2999; SHOM 7404, 7412. HW +0535 on Dover (UT). From NW keep clear of Le Couronneau; from E, keep N of bcn off Pte des Barres. Appr on 212·5° in W sector (205°-220°) of La Flotte lt ho, W tr + G top, Fl WG 4s. Alongside it a Moiré indicator shows vert B line when on track 212·5°, or chevrons pointing in the direction to regain track. 5 waiting buoys outside; or ⚓ off in 3m, sheltered from S & W.

Outer hbr is sheltered by mole and dries 2·0m. 3 pontoons (6 Ⓥ berths, max LOA 10m, on mole, €2·60) in outer hbr: pre-booking advised. Inner hbr dries 2·8m. HM ☎05·46·09·67·66. **Quay** Grid . **CN de la Flotte-en-Ré** ☎05·46·09·97·34, (Jul-15 Sep).

ILE DE RÉ (9.22.13 and 9.22.14) *See overleaf*

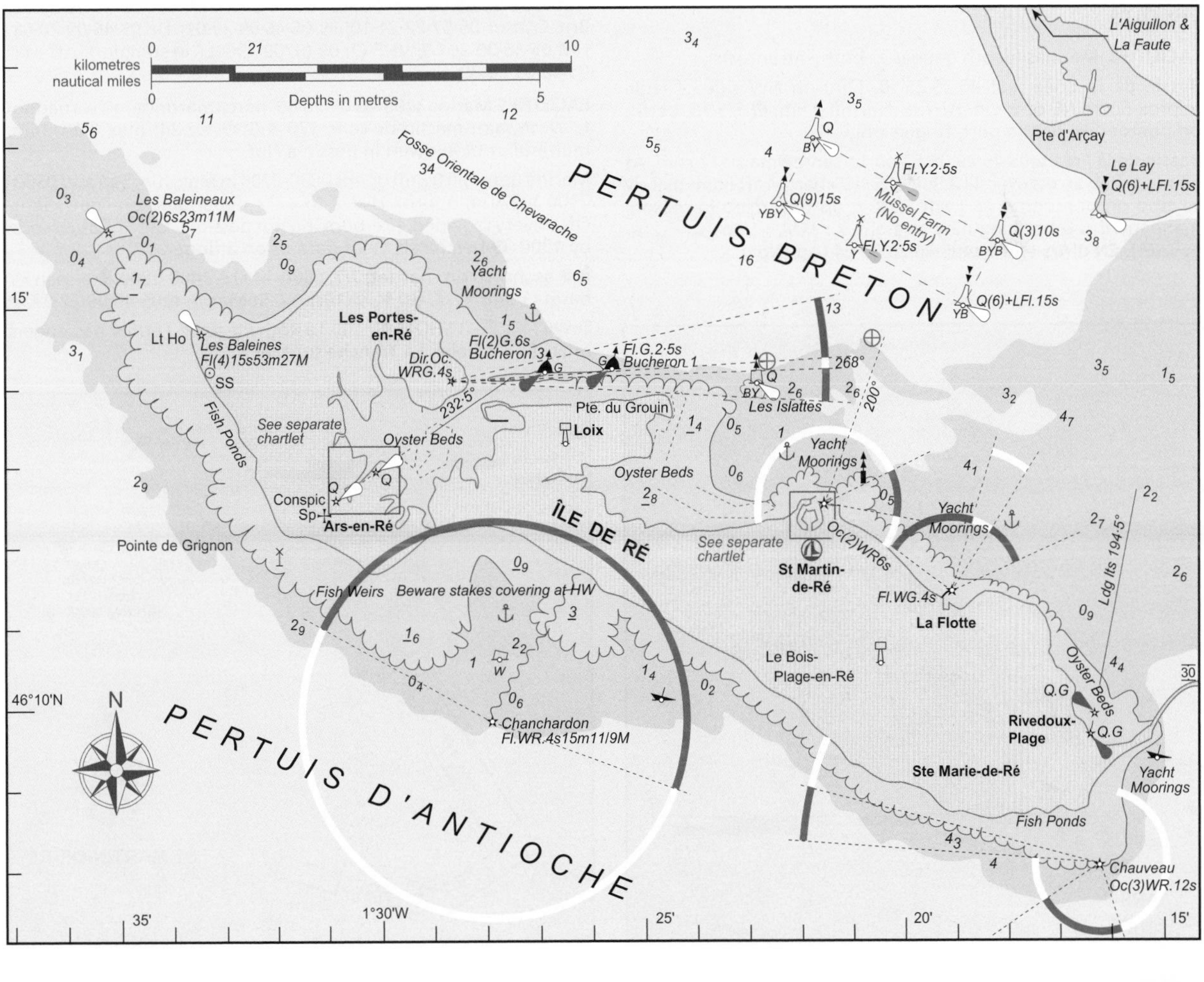

9.22.13 ARS-EN-RÉ

Charente Maritime **46°12'·64N 01°30'·71W**

CHARTS AC 2998, 2999; Imray C41; SHOM 7404, 7412; Navi 1022

TIDES +0540 Dover; ML 3·7m; See St Martin-de-Ré.

SHELTER ⚓ clear of channel in a pool (2m) close S of Pte du Fier. Both small marinas are sheltered, but in the confined space with strong NE'lies manoeuvring may be difficult for LOA >13m.

NAVIGATION WPT 46°14'·18N 01°23'·25W, 268°/1·8M to first SHM chan buoy, Bûcheron 1. Beware shoal ground 0·8m to 2·5m both sides of the outer appr chan. Continue to the inner, buoyed and beaconed 232·5° ldg line, where buoys are moved to mark new sand/mudbanks. Port d'Ars is at the head of a dog-legged chan in the SW corner of the bay, Le Fier d'Ars, which dries to salt pans & oyster beds. Night appr not advised without prior day visit. HW –1 is best time to arr/dep the basins. Times vary with draft (max 1·8m) coefficient, wind and barometer.

LIGHTS AND MARKS Les Islattes NCM bcn lt twr is conspic S of the ⊕. Loix water twr is conspic S of the 268° appr chan.

Dir ⚡, Oc WRG 4s (hard to see by day) covers the 268° outer appr chan. To the right of it and 3M west, Les Baleines lt ho may be seen.

Inner 232·5° ldg lts, hard to see by day, lead across Fiers d'Ars into Port d'Ars: front, W □ with R lantern; rear, B □ on W framework tr, G top. See Lights, buoys and waypoints and chartlet for light details. In the town the ✠ spire, white with black top, is conspic about 330m SSW of the rear 232·5° ldg lt.

COMMUNICATIONS CROSS 02·97·55·35·35; Auto 08·92·68·08·17; Police 05·46·84·32·67; ⊖ 05·46·41·11·73; Brit Consul 05·57·22·21·10; Dr 05·46·29·44·19; Aff Mar 05·46·09·68·89 (at La Flotte); Marinas VHF Ch 09.

FACILITIES Marinas (depth gauges at both entrances):

Bassin de la Criée ☎05·46·29·25·10. (2m) on NW side of chan approx 600m NE of town. Access over sill 2·5m. ⓥ €3·16, berth, on pontoon H, first to port, fingers only.

Bassin de la Prée ☎05·46.29.08.52 portarsenre@mairie17.com. At head of chan access over sill 2·9m. ⓥ €3·16, berth/raft immediately to stbd on pontoon D in 1·8m. Rafted up to 5 deep in season; manoeuvring & berthing may be tight for LOA >13m. (6t). **CN d'Ars-en-Ré** ☎05·46·29·23·04 (Apr-Nov).

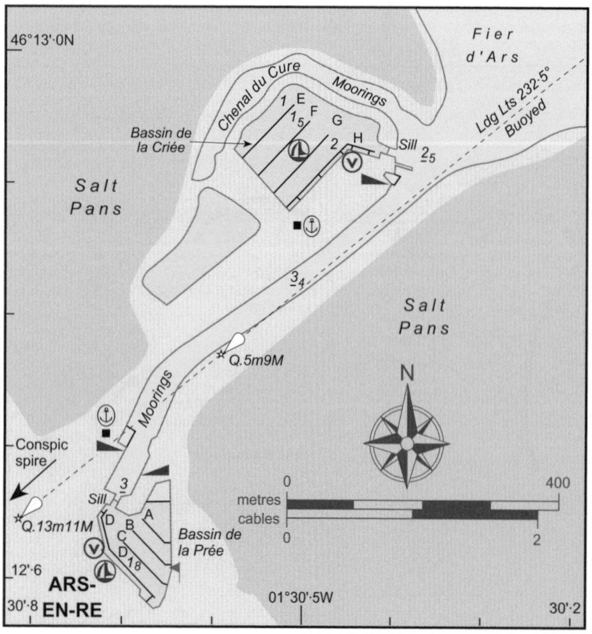

9.22.14 ST MARTIN-DE-RÉ

Charente Maritime **46°12'·50N 01°21'·93W**

CHARTS AC 2998, 2999; Imray C41; SHOM 7404, 7412; Navi 551, 1022

TIDES +0535 Dover; ML 3·7

Standard Port POINTE DE GRAVE (⟶)

Times				Height (metres)			
High Water		Low Water		MHWS	MHWN	MLWN	MLWS
0000	0600	0000	0500	5·3	4·4	2·1	1·0
1200	1800	1200	1700				
Differences ST MARTIN, Ile de Ré							
+0005	–0030	–0025	–0030	+0·7	+0·5	+0·3	–0·1

SHELTER 4 W waiting buoys or ⚓ off ent which is difficult in strong NW-NE winds. These winds also render untenable a waiting pontoon (in season; prev dredged 2m, but now dries, very soft mud) inside NW mole. Complete shelter in marina (depth 3m).

NAVIGATION WPT 46°14'·68N 01°20'·74W, 200°/2·3M to St Martin mole hd. From the NW, keep N and E of Banc du Rocha (1·2m) extending 2½M ENE from Pte du Grouin. From SE, pass well N of unlit NCM bcn, about ¾M NE of ent, marking Le Couronneau drying ledge in R sector (245°-281°) of St Martin lt ho. By day appr 210·5° lt ho ≠ □ ✠ tr; or 202° mole hd ≠ ✠ tr; the lt ho is far easier to see than the mole head.

LIGHTS AND MARKS Conspic daymarks: La Citadelle 3ca E of hbr ent; Lt ho, Oc (2) WR 6s, W twr/R top, on ramparts SE of ent; and the □ ✠ tr and nearby ruins. Mole hd, Fl G 2·5s, is obsc'd by Pte du Grouin when brg <124°. See chartlet and Lights, buoys and waypoints for details.

COMMUNICATIONS CROSS 02·97·55·35·35; 05·46·41·29·14; Auto 08·92·68·08·17; Police 05·46·09·21·17; ⊖ 05·46·09·21·78; Brit Consul 05·57·22·21·10; Ⓗ 05·46·09·20·01; Dr 05·46·09·20·08; HM 05·46·09·26·69, VHF Ch 09 (0700-1900LT in summer); Aff Mar 05·46·09·68·89.

FACILITIES Marina ☎05·46·09·26·69. portstmartindere@wanadoo.fr www.saint-martin-de-re.fr 170 + 50ⓥ €3·24; max LOA 16m, multihulls not allowed in Bassin à Flot.

Marina gate (sill 0·8m) opens 0630-2200 in May, Jun, Sep and 0500-2300 Jul/Aug; approx HW–2 to +2½, depending on coefficient. Often very crowded, pre-booking not possible. Get WC key code by 1900. ⓥ berth/raft W of gate or on a finger.

as shown on chartlet; 7/7, 0800-1200 & 1400-1800. also in FV basin (1·5m) Ⓔ (10t). **YC St Martin** ☎05·46·09·22·07.

Town SHOM Ⓑ. La Rochelle ⇌ ✈. Ferries: passengers only, La Rochelle, La Tranche sur Mer.

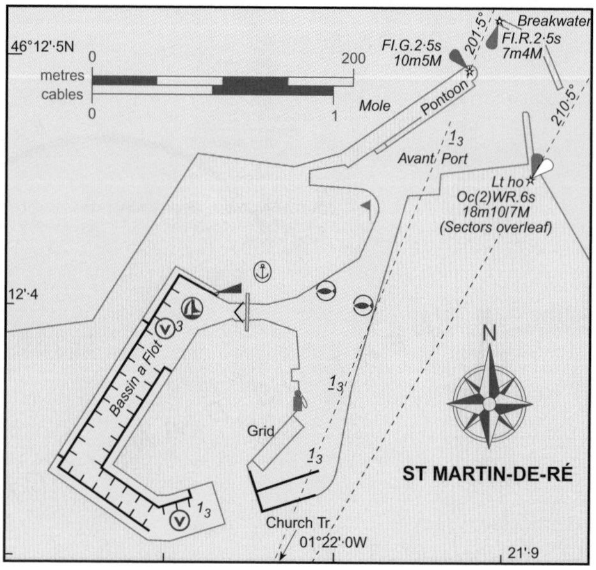

9.22.15 LA ROCHELLE

Charente Maritime **46°08'·83N 01°10'·11W** ✿✿✿◊◊◊✿✿✿

CHARTS AC 2999, 3000, 2743; Imray C41; SHOM 7404, 7413; Navi 551, 1022

TIDES +0515 Dover; ML 3·8

Standard Port POINTE DE GRAVE (⟶)

Times				Height (metres)			
High Water		Low Water		MHWS	MHWN	MLWN	MLWS
0000	0600	0000	0500	5·3	4·4	2·1	1·0
1200	1800	1200	1700				
Differences *LA ROCHELLE and LA PALLICE*							
+0015	*–0030*	*–0020*	*–0025*	*+0·7*	*+0·5*	*+0·3*	*–0·1*

SHELTER Very good in Port des Minimes, the largest marina on the western Atlantic coast; excellent in Vieux Port.

NAVIGATION WPT 46°08´·41N 01°11´·40W, 059°/0·9M to abm Tour Richelieu (with tide gauge) marking a drying rky spit N of the chan. Appr from N or S of Plateau du Lavardin to pick up 059° ldg line. Pte des Minimes lt bcn (aka Bout du Monde) and a WCM lt buoy mark drying rks extending 4ca SW of the marina.

The appr chan is narrow and shallow (0·5m) and care must be taken at MLWS; speed limit 5kn, yachts should stow/make sail west of the Harbour Limit (Nos1and 2 lateral bys). Ent to Port des Minimes 1ca past Tour Richelieu Fl (2) R 6s, NW side of marina's W bkwtr is fringed by 4 G bcns, with ▲ topmarks, the last one lit QG, and a Fl G 2·5s lt at bkwtr hd. Speed limit 3kn in marina.

For Vieux Port stay on 059° ldg line in chan (35m narrow) leaving 4 small PHM buoys well to port. Caution: Vedettes run all hours. The unlit chan is not advised at night.

LIGHTS AND MARKS See chartlet/Lights, buoys & waypoints. The rear 059° ldg lt, Q, is briefly obscured by Tour St Nicolas between 061°-065°, ie when approaching between La Pallice and Lavardin plateau. Tour St Nicolas, Tour de la Chaine and Tour de la Lanterne, near the Vieux Port, are conspic by day and floodlit at night.

COMMUNICATIONS CROSS 02·97·55·35·35; ☼ 05·46·50·86·00; Auto 08·92·68·08·17; Police 05·46·00·50·99; ⊖ 05·46·41·11·73; Brit Consul 05·57·22·21·10; Ⓗ 05·46·27·33·33; Dr 05·46·42·19·22; Port des Minimes VHF Ch 09 (H24); Vieux Port VHF Ch 09; Aff Mar 05·46·28·07·28.

FACILITIES Port des Minimes Marina ☎05·46·44·41·20. www.portlarochelle.com capitainerie@portlarochelle.com. 4,500, inc 400 Ⓥ. From marina ent, continue 100m SSE and berth on acceuil pontoon to obtain berth allocation. Max LOA 25m. €3·00 (pay 2 nights, 3rd free). pontoon de service, W end of Digue du Bout Blanc (0800-1800/ 2000 in season) or self service H24 (cr/debit card) at berth adjacent to Capitainerie. SHOM ⊠ Ⓑ Ⓔ (50t) (10t). Water bus to town (Bassin d'Echouage) every H (except 1300) 1000-2000; Jul/Aug H and H+30, 0900-2330.

Vieux Port comprises 3 separate basins, call ☎05·46·41·32·05, mob ☎06·03·54·00·57. From S to N:

Bassin des Chalutiers (5m). Access by prior arrangement. Entry gate ☎ 05·46·52·14·56, mob 06·16·46·60·26. Mainly used for events and by long-stay and mega-yachts.

Bassin d'Echouage (part-dredged 1·3m) is entered between the twin twrs of St Nicolas and La Chaine. It is an atmospheric tidal basin, but it can be noisy at night. vieuxport@portlarochelle.com 75 + 40Ⓥ €2·40. First 2 pontoons for Ⓥ.

Bassin des Yachts (3m). Access HW –2 to +½ via entry gate with sill 1·2m; gate ☎05·46·52·14·56, mob 06·16·46·60·26. Night ent by prior arrangement. 100 €2·40; 15m max LOA. (150t) (10t).

Town @ ⊠ Ⓑ Laleu ✈ direct flts to London, Birmingham, So'ton etc; see Area 21. Ferries: via Roscoff, St Malo.

La Pallice, 3M W, is a commercial/FV port with no yacht facilities.

Note: The adjacent bridge to Ile de Ré is lit/buoyed for big ships: N-bound between piers Nos 13/14; S-bound Nos 10/11; 30m air clearance. Yachts may transit other spans, subject to suitable air and water clearance.

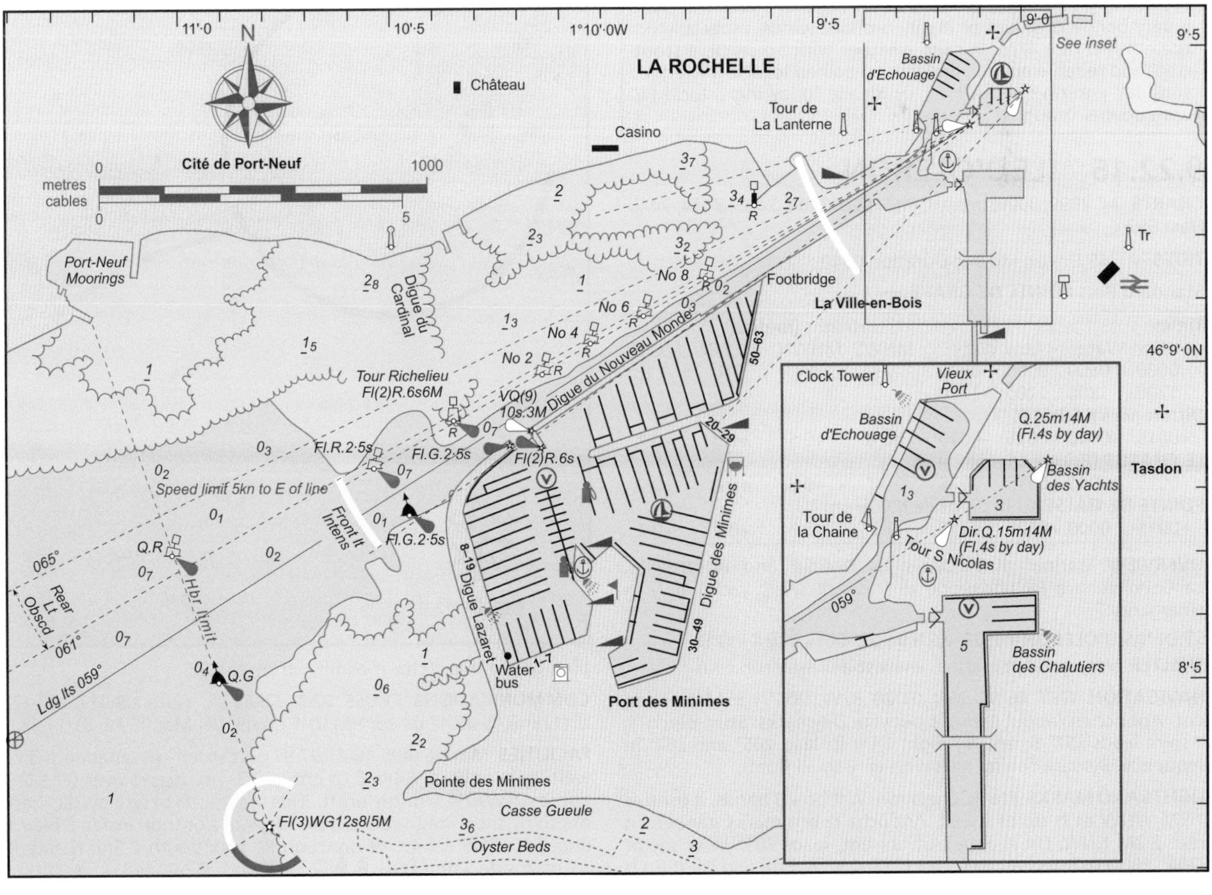

ÎLE D'OLÉRON

On the NE coast of Ile d'Oléron (AC 2663, 2999, 3000) there are marinas at **Port St Denis** and **Le Douhet** at the N end; further S is a yacht basin at **Boyardville** and a fishing harbour at Le Château. All are sheltered from the prevailing W'lies.

From Pertuis d'Antioche, Grande Rade des Trousses is entered via either Passage de l'Est close to Île d'Aix or Passage de l'Ouest, which run each side of La Longe and Le Boyard, an extensive sandbank on which stands Fort Boyard with light tower. From Grande Rade, where good anch is found except in fresh NW winds, the narrow and shallow Coureau d'Oléron winds between ledges, oyster beds and constantly shifting shoals, with buoys moved to conform. About 2M SE of Le Chateau it is crossed by a bridge, clearance 18m; the bridge arch for the navigable chan is marked at road level by W □ boards, with ▲ or ■ superimposed, illuminated at night. Just N of bridge is Fort-Louvois (32m) connected to mainland by causeway. SHOM 7414 is needed.

▶*S-going stream starts at HW Pte de Grave –2½; N-going at HW Pte de Grave +5, sp rates 2kn.*◀ Up the Seudre River there are anchs and yacht facilities at **Marennes** and **La Tremblade**.

The W coast, from Pointe de Chassiron 15M SSE to Pte de Gatseau, is bounded by drying rks and shoals. In bad weather the sea breaks 4 or 5M offshore. La Cotinière, the only hbr, is almost exclusively a fishing port, exposed to the Atlantic.

▶*Tidal streams are weak, sp rate 1kn, starting NW at HW Pte de Grave +0300 and SE at HW Pte de Grave –0505, but often overcome by current due to prevailing wind. The rate, however, increases towards Pte de Gatseau.*◀

Here **Pertuis de Maumusson** separates the island from the mainland. A SWM lt buoy 'ATT Maumusson' just over 3½M WSW of Pointe de Gatseau marks the approach. Banc de Gatseau and Banc des Mattes, both of which dry up to 3.9m, lie N and S of the chan; the sand bar usually has a depth of about 1·5m. Depth and position vary, and unlit lateral buoys are moved accordingly. Any swell speedily forms breakers, and the chan is very dangerous then or in any onshore winds, especially on the ebb (sp rate 4kn). In calm weather with no swell, a stout craft and reliable engine, and having gained local knowledge, consider entering about HW –1; ideally following a local FV with deeper draught.

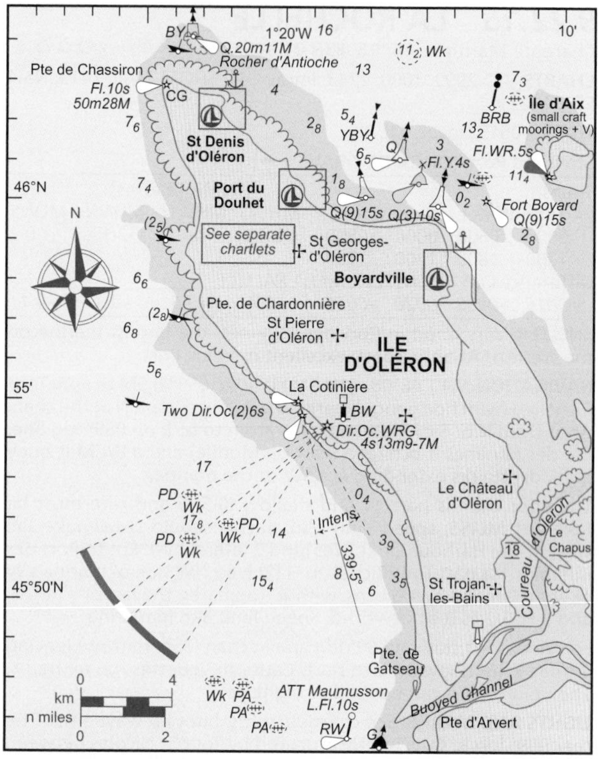

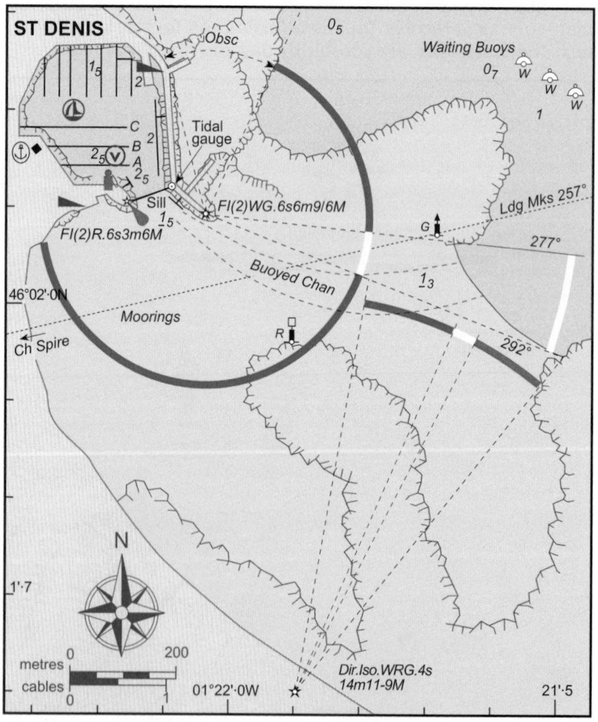

9.22.16 ÎLE D'OLÉRON

CHARTS AC 2999, 3000; Imray C41; SHOM 7404, 7405, 7414, 7415; Navi 552

TIDES +0545 Dover; ML 3·9; Duration 0540

Standard Port POINTE DE GRAVE (⟶)

Times				Height (metres)			
High Water		Low Water		MHWS	MHWN	MLWN	MLWS
0000	0600	0000	0500	5·3	4·4	2·1	1·0
1200	1800	1200	1700				
Differences ILE D'AIX							
+0015	–0040	–0025	–0030	+0·8	+0·5	+0·3	–0·1
LE CHAPUS (Bridge to mainland)							
+0015	–0040	–0015	–0025	+0·7	+0·6	+0·4	+0·2
POINTE DE GATSEAU (S tip of Île d'Oléron)							
+0015	0000	–0020	–0015	0·0	–0·1	+0·2	+0·1

OVERVIEW Marinas at St Denis, Le Douhet and Boyardville. La Cotinière is a FV hbr prone to frequent swell; yachts only in emergency.

ST DENIS D'OLÉRON 46°02'·07N 01°22'·06W ❁❁◊◊✿✿

SHELTER Very good in marina. www.st-denis-oleron.com

NAVIGATION WPT 46°03'·26N 01°20'·82W, 205°/1·35M to chan ent. Appr chan (about 1·1m) is buoyed. Daymarks: SHM perch ≠ ✠ spire leads 257° to ent. By night 2 Dir lts lead 205° and 284° in sequence. Beware fishing nets with very small floats.

LIGHTS AND MARKS Pte de Chassiron, W lt ho + B bands, is conspic 1·9M WNW at N tip of island. Antioche lt bcn marks dangerous reef 2·2M NNW. Dir lt, ½M S of hbr ent, leads 205° in W sector (204°-206°) to intercept W sector (277°-292°) of second Dir lt on N pier; or use this sector if coming from the SE.

COMMUNICATIONS CROSS 02·97·55·35·35; Auto 08·92·68·08·17; Ⓗ (12km) 05·46·47·00·86; HM VHF Ch 09; Aff Mar 05·46· 85·14·33.

FACILITIES Marina ☎05·46·47·97·97 port.stdenis@wanadoo.fr 3 W waiting bys about 700m E of ent in 0·7–1m. Access over sill 1·5m approx HW±2½ for 2m draft. Tide gauge, E bkwtr by sill, best depth by short stay, walk ashore (drying) pontoon inside E bkwtr end. 600+70Ⓥ €2·47. Ⓥ pontoon A, max depth 2·5m: N side if <10m, S side >10m LOA. wi-fi €2·00 p/d (10t).

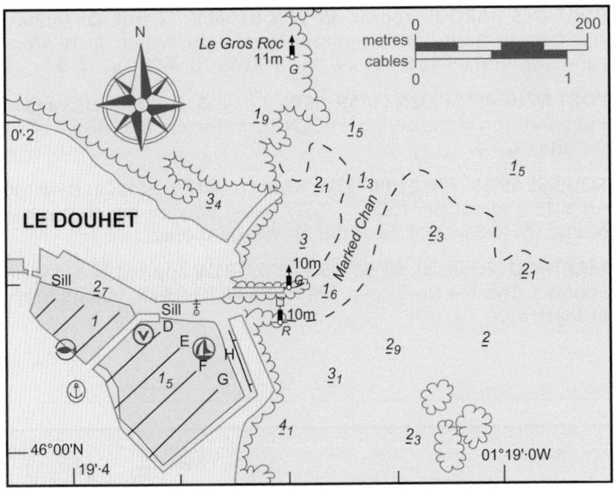

LE DOUHET 46°00'·09N 01°19'·20W

SHELTER Very good in marina, SE part of hbr; FVs use NW part.

NAVIGATION WPT 46°00'·65N 01°17'·38W, NCM buoy VQ, 246°/1·4M to ent. Unlit, buoyed appr chan dries about 1·6m to approx 0·35M offshore. Ent difficult in fresh NE'lies against ebb; beware swell, oyster beds and overfalls.

LIGHTS AND MARKS The WPT buoy is 1·4M W of another NCM lt buoy Q; the latter plus an ECM buoy, Q (3) 10s, mark a fish farm in Passage de l'Ouest (toward Boyardville). La Longe and Le Boyard, rocky/sandy shoals, are marked by an unlit WCM buoy and by Fort Boyard, conspic twr 29m, Q (9) 15s. The Capitainerie and yacht masts are the only conspic features; no lts at marina.

COMMUNICATIONS Ch 09; port-plaisancedudouhet@wanadoo.fr

FACILITIES Marina ☎05·46·76·71·13. Access over a sill marked by tide gauge, 1·8m CD. Caution: sandbanks encroach on approach channel, reduce access times and need frequent dredging, sometimes closing hbr completely. Not advised for draft >1.5m. 326 + 30Ⓥ €1·96; max LOA 15m. at St Georges d'Oléron and La Brée.

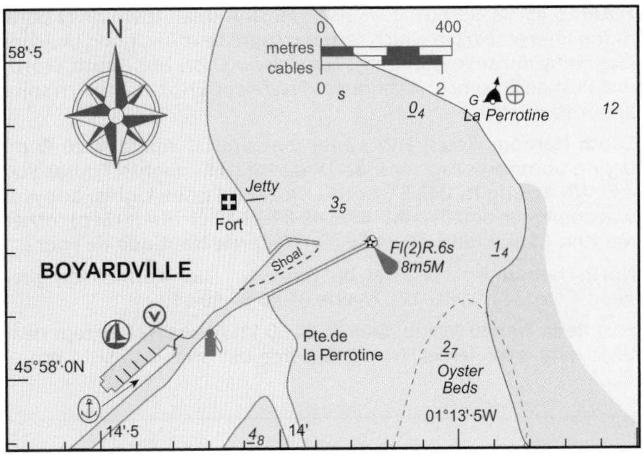

BOYARDVILLE 45°58'·25N 01°13'·83W

TIDES HW +0545 on Dover (UT); use Ile d'Aix.

SHELTER Very good in non-tidal marina (2·2m). 3 W waiting buoys are 7ca N of bkwtr hd, or ⚓ there in 3m.

NAVIGATION WPT 45°58'·44N 01°13'·36W, La Perrotine SHM buoy, 239°/3ca between sandbanks to S bkwtr head; in the ent chan hug the S bkwtr for best water. Strong river current, 2kn @ sp. Stand on beyond the ent to avoid a bank to stbd, then turn stbd onto about 350° for the gate; allow departures to leave first.

LIGHTS AND MARKS Le Boyard, a sandy shoal, is marked by Fort Boyard, conspic twr 29m, Q (9) 15s. A fish farm in the Passage de l'Ouest is marked by an ECM buoy, Q (3) 10s and NCM buoy Q.

COMMUNICATIONS Auto 08·92·68·08·17; Brit Consul 05·57·22·21·10; Gatemaster 05·46·47·23·71; HM VHF Ch 09; Aff Mar 05·46·47·00·18.

FACILITIES Marina ☎05·46·76·48·56. port-plaisance.boyardville@wanadoo.fr Drying appr chan. Waiting pontoon on NW bank is 50m SW of automatic gate which opens H24, when level reaches CD+4.3M, approx HW±1½ nps and HW±3 sp. ● = ent gate is shut. Ⓥ berths/rafting against NE quay to stbd. 190+60Ⓥ €1·96. on SE bank ☎05·46·47·01·36; 0800-1230, 1400-1830. (14t). **YCB** ☎05·46·47·10·28.

LA CHARENTE RIVER

CHARTS AC 3000, 2747; SHOM 7414, 7415

TIDES See Île d'Oléron/Rochefort; interpolate between Ile d'Aix and Rochefort. Ile d'Aix, HW + 0545 (UT) on Dover; ML 3.9m.

NAVIGATION See notes under Rochefort. Fort Boyard, 1·6M WSW of Pte St Catherine's, is conspic and lit Q (9) 15s 29m; ringed by a No entry area, radius 200m. Upriver expect to meet sea-going cargo ships which have priority. Night navigation by yachts is prohibited because the banks cannot be seen.

MINOR HARBOURS & ANCHORAGES

ILE D'AIX Charente Maritime, **46°00'·60N 01°10'·45W**. Fair weather ⚓s are charted SW, S and NE of the island. On W side of island, near LW keep 3ca off the two WCM perches. St Catherine's Pt (S tip of d'Aix) Fl WR 5s, two conspic white lt twrs, R tops; 103°-R-118°-W-103° (345°). R sector (15°) covers rks off NW tip of Ile d'Oléron.

Off Pte St Catherine are 25 drying Ⓥs (W with dayglo G band, €10); buoys with R band = locals only; Blu band = with HM's approval. HM 06·17·80·38·07.

Facilities: . Ferry to Fouras. **CNIA** ☎05·46·84·69·89.

Continued overleaf

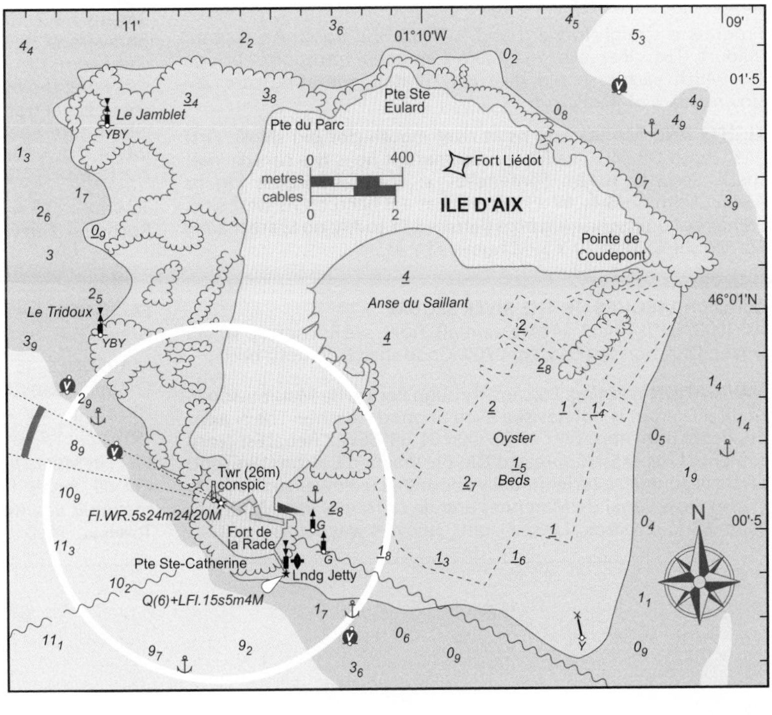

FOURAS 45°58′·99N 01°05′·69W (S Hbr). A small town on N bank of the Charente from which ferries cross to Ile d'Aix; good beaches and many mussel/oyster beds. The 3 drying hbrs are: South, North and Port de la Fumée. A chequered twr near S Hbr and the ch spire are both conspic.

South Harbour Access HW ±2 for max draft 1·5m. 55 + 20 Ⓥ on drying pontoons. Facilities: (3t). Lights: Fouras Sud Fl WR 4s. Ldg lts 042·5°, both Oc (2) R 6s; see Lights, buoys & waypoints for details. HM ☎05·46·84·23·10 (1 Jun-30 Sep); other months, Mairie ☎05·46·84·66·09. **YC** Cercle Nautique de Fouras.

North Harbour No 3 is free but dries. . Fouras Nord pier head Oc (3+1) WRG 12s. Mairie 05·46·84·60·11.

Port de la Fumée Mairie ☎05·46·84·60·11. Access H24, except near LWS. Jetty is for ferries. No 53 is free but dries, . SHM bcn, QG.

PORT DES BARQUE approx **45°57′N 01°04′W**. 2 free s (afloat) Apr-Oct; shift to afloat pontoon overnight (when ferry stops running). HM 05·46·84·51·24/ 06·78·90·45·10, .

PORT NEUF 45°57′·02N 00°59′·80W. 2 free s (afloat); also a 64m long pontoon at the drying line. **CN Rochefortais** ☎05·46·87·34·61 (on site), .

SOUBISE 45°55′·75N 01°00′·32W, 8 berths (€17, pay at Capitanerie) on a 48m afloat pontoon, SW bank. Beware big ship wash. Mairie 05·46·84·92·04. Facilities: village shops.

MARTROU (Echillais), 45°54′·95N 00°57′·85W approx; 10·5M from Fouras S. This is a No ⚓ Area. Mairie 05·46·83·03·74. Village shops at Martrou.

9.22.17 ROCHEFORT

Charente Maritime **45°56′·55N 00°57′·29W**

CHARTS AC 3000, 2747; Imray C41; SHOM 7414, 7415; Navi 552

TIDES +0610 Dover

Standard Port POINTE DE GRAVE (⟶)

Times				Height (metres)			
High Water		Low Water		MHWS	MHWN	MLWN	MLWS
0000	0600	0000	0500	5·3	4·4	2·1	1·0
1200	1800	1200	1700				
Differences ROCHEFORT							
+0035	−0015	+0125	+0030	+1·2	+0·9	+0·1	−0·2
LA CAYENNE (R. Seudre)							
+0030	−0015	−0005	−0010	+0·3	+0·2	+0·3	0·0

SHELTER Excellent in the marina, popular for over-wintering.

NAVIGATION WPT 45°59′·63N 01°09′·51W (N-abeam Les Palles NCM buoy, Q) 115°/2·1M to next ldg line 134·5°. Beware drying wreck just S of WPT. The bar, 1M S of Fouras, carries least depth 0·9m. Beware very strong currents here, except at HW or LW. Stream in river runs about 2kn (4kn in narrows) and at sp there is a small bore. Check tide range carefully before visit, there are several days a month when there is insufficient rise to access the marina, otherwise leave Fort Boyard/Ile d'Aix approx HW −3 to reach Rochefort (about 13M from the WPT) near HW while the ent gate is open. The river is navigable 3·5M on to Tonnay-Charente.

Progress is straightforward and swift on the flood. An elegant viaduct, 32m clearance, and 400m E an aerial transporter bridge (to which yachts should give way if it is operating) are 2M downstream of Rochefort.

LIGHTS AND MARKS Ldg lts at river mouth (for big ships): First 115°, both QR, W □ trs/R tops; Soumard lt ho is the conspic rear mark. Second, abeam Fontenelles : Port-des-Barques ldg lts 134·5°, both Iso G 4s, W □ trs; rear has a B band on its west side. 19 pairs of unlit white ldg bcns (lettered TT to AA; no S) are mainly for big ships; ditto 10 Y SPM buoys, Fl Y 4s.

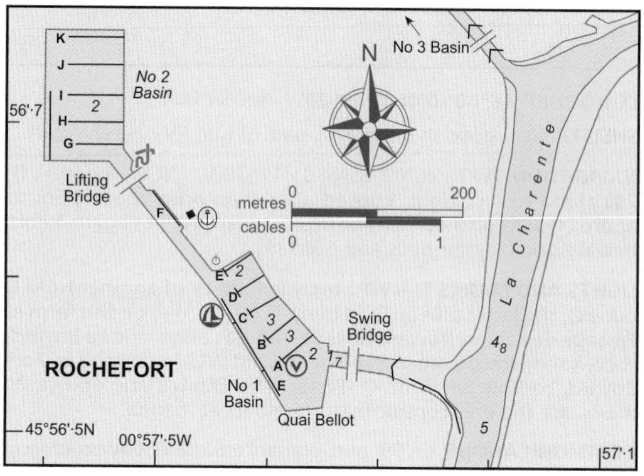

COMMUNICATIONS CROSS 02·97·55·35·35; 05·46·41·11·11; Auto 08.92.68.08.17; Police 05·46·87·26·12; 05·46·99·03·90; Brit Consul 05·57·22·21·10; Dr 05·46·99·61·11; Commercial port VHF Ch 12; Aff Mar 05·46·84·22·67; Marina VHF Ch 09 (HW±1).

FACILITIES Marina ☎05·46·83·99·96, mob 06·86·01·64·29, port.plaisance@ville-rochefort.fr www.ville-rochefort.fr 300+40 Ⓥ in Bassins 1 & 2, €1·98 + €0·20 pp/day tax. Marina Entry gate opens on average HW La Rochelle −½ to +1 0530-2230 in season; pre-check with HM. Two waiting pontoons outside the gate both dry, soft mud, the most S'ly suffers badly from wash from fast moving commercial traffic. Road bridge between Bassins Nos 1 and 2 lifts when gate open; berth as directed by HM. Ⓔ (16t, 7t). A 36m pontoon, 120m S of ent to Bassin 1, is short stay €2·10/m + .

Town Ⓑ (Rochefort, winter only, and La Rochelle). **Ferry** via Roscoff or St Malo.

MINOR HARBOURS ON THE RIVER SEUDRE

AC 3000; SHOM 7405, 7414 (essential). Tides, see Rochefort. +0545 Dover; Duration Sp 0545, Np 0700. Good shelter in both hbrs.

NAVIGATION Warning: Passage through Pertuis de Maumusson (S of Ile d'Oléron) is not advised even in good weather. The N appr applies to both hbrs. WPT 45°56′·00N 01°08′·56W, Chenal Est-Nord *i*, thence Chenal Est, Coureau d'Oléron, Viaduc d'Oléron (18m) and Ch de la Soumaille (dries initially about 0·7m). Power cables (16m cl'nce) cross Canal de Marennes and de la Tremblade. Marennes spire (88m) is conspic. Lts see Lights, buoys & waypoints.

FACILITIES There are ⚓s off La Cayenne village (very crowded) La Grève (½M upstream) and at the ent to Chenal de la Tremblade.

MARENNES, 45°49′·17N 01°06′·67W. **Yacht basin** ☎05·46·85·02·68 (2·5m). Access via automatic ent gate, opens about HW±2 sp, HW±1 np. (6t).
Town (La Rochelle).

LA TREMBLADE 45°46′·07N 01°08′·17W. HM ☎05·46·76·47·97. Ch 09 Small hbr (3m) in the town centre; yachts dry on soft mud against stone quay. (5t).
Town Ⓑ.

STANDARD TIME UT –01
Subtract 1 hour for UT
For French Summer Time add ONE hour in **non-shaded areas**

POINTE DE GRAVE LAT 45°34′N LONG 1°04′W

TIMES AND HEIGHTS OF HIGH AND LOW WATERS

Dates in red are SPRINGS
Dates in blue are NEAPS

YEAR **2018**

JANUARY

Day	Time	m	Time	m	Time	m	Time	m
1 M	0410	5.4	1006	1.1	1639	5.5	2228	1.0
2 TU	0500	5.6	1059	0.9	1729	5.6	○ 2319	0.9
3 W	0550	5.7	1150	0.8	1819	5.6		
4 TH	0007	0.9	0639	5.7	1238	0.8	1908	5.4
5 F	0054	1.0	0729	5.5	1325	0.9	1957	5.2
6 SA	0140	1.1	0819	5.3	1412	1.1	2048	5.0
7 SU	0227	1.3	0911	5.1	1500	1.4	2141	4.7
8 M	0318	1.6	1007	4.8	1553	1.7	◑ 2240	4.5
9 TU	0414	1.8	1109	4.5	1652	1.9	2346	4.3
10 W	0519	2.0	1218	4.4	1800	2.0		
11 TH	0055	4.3	0629	2.1	1328	4.4	1910	2.1
12 F	0157	4.4	0738	2.1	1429	4.4	2011	2.0
13 SA	0248	4.6	0836	1.9	1517	4.6	2102	1.8
14 SU	0331	4.7	0924	1.8	1557	4.7	2145	1.7
15 M	0409	4.9	1005	1.7	1633	4.8	2223	1.6
16 TU	0444	5.0	1043	1.5	1707	4.9	2258	1.5
17 W	0519	5.1	1118	1.4	1740	4.9	● 2332	1.4
18 TH	0552	5.2	1152	1.4	1812	5.0		
19 F	0007	1.4	0625	5.2	1227	1.4	1843	4.9
20 SA	0041	1.4	0659	5.1	1301	1.4	1916	4.9
21 SU	0115	1.5	0734	5.1	1336	1.5	1951	4.8
22 M	0151	1.6	0813	5.0	1413	1.6	2032	4.7
23 TU	0230	1.7	0857	4.8	1454	1.7	2121	4.5
24 W	0316	1.8	0950	4.7	1543	1.8	◐ 2222	4.4
25 TH	0412	1.9	1053	4.6	1645	1.9	2334	4.4
26 F	0521	2.0	1208	4.5	1757	1.9		
27 SA	0052	4.5	0635	1.9	1328	4.6	1910	1.8
28 SU	0203	4.7	0747	1.7	1437	4.9	2019	1.6
29 M	0304	5.0	0855	1.4	1536	5.1	2121	1.3
30 TU	0359	5.3	0955	1.1	1629	5.3	2217	1.1
31 W	0450	5.5	1049	0.9	1719	5.5	○ 2308	0.9

FEBRUARY

Day	Time	m	Time	m	Time	m	Time	m
1 TH	0539	5.7	1139	0.7	1806	5.5	2355	0.8
2 F	0626	5.7	1225	0.7	1851	5.5		
3 SA	0040	0.8	0711	5.6	1309	0.8	1935	5.3
4 SU	0122	1.0	0755	5.4	1350	1.0	2016	5.1
5 M	0204	1.2	0837	5.1	1432	1.3	2056	4.8
6 TU	0247	1.4	0919	4.8	1515	1.6	2141	4.5
7 W	0335	1.7	1009	4.5	1606	1.9	◑ 2238	4.3
8 TH	0431	2.0	1113	4.2	1708	2.2	2353	4.1
9 F	0541	2.2	1237	4.1	1824	2.3		
10 SA	0115	4.2	0658	2.2	1357	4.2	1938	2.2
11 SU	0219	4.3	0807	2.1	1455	4.3	2038	2.0
12 M	0308	4.5	0901	1.9	1539	4.5	2124	1.8
13 TU	0349	4.8	0945	1.7	1616	4.7	2204	1.6
14 W	0425	4.9	1023	1.5	1649	4.9	2240	1.5
15 TH	0459	5.1	1059	1.4	1721	5.0	● 2314	1.4
16 F	0532	5.2	1133	1.3	1752	5.1	2349	1.3
17 SA	0605	5.3	1208	1.2	1823	5.1		
18 SU	0023	1.2	0638	5.3	1241	1.2	1855	5.1
19 M	0056	1.2	0712	5.3	1315	1.2	1929	5.0
20 TU	0130	1.3	0749	5.1	1350	1.3	2006	4.9
21 W	0207	1.4	0831	5.0	1428	1.5	2051	4.7
22 TH	0249	1.6	0921	4.8	1513	1.7	2146	4.5
23 F	0341	1.8	1023	4.5	1611	1.9	◐ 2257	4.4
24 SA	0449	1.9	1143	4.4	1726	2.0		
25 SU	0026	4.4	0611	2.0	1313	4.5	1848	2.0
26 M	0148	4.6	0734	1.8	1426	4.7	2005	1.8
27 TU	0253	4.9	0847	1.5	1526	5.0	2111	1.4
28 W	0348	5.2	0946	1.2	1618	5.2	2206	1.1

MARCH

Day	Time	m	Time	m	Time	m	Time	m
1 TH	0438	5.5	1038	0.9	1705	5.4	2255	0.9
2 F	0524	5.6	1124	0.7	1748	5.5	○ 2340	0.8
3 SA	0607	5.7	1207	0.7	1828	5.5		
4 SU	0021	0.8	0647	5.6	1246	0.8	1906	5.3
5 M	0100	0.9	0724	5.4	1324	1.0	1940	5.1
6 TU	0138	1.1	0759	5.1	1400	1.3	2013	4.9
7 W	0215	1.4	0833	4.8	1437	1.6	2049	4.6
8 TH	0256	1.7	0913	4.5	1520	1.9	2137	4.3
9 F	0344	2.0	1009	4.2	1614	2.2	◑ 2246	4.1
10 SA	0448	2.3	1135	3.9	1732	2.4		
11 SU	0017	4.0	0612	2.4	1315	4.0	1857	2.4
12 M	0139	4.2	0731	2.3	1424	4.2	2005	2.2
13 TU	0237	4.4	0830	2.0	1512	4.4	2056	2.0
14 W	0320	4.6	0916	1.8	1550	4.6	2137	1.7
15 TH	0358	4.9	0956	1.5	1623	4.8	2214	1.5
16 F	0433	5.1	1033	1.3	1655	5.0	2250	1.3
17 SA	0506	5.3	1108	1.2	1727	5.2	● 2325	1.2
18 SU	0540	5.4	1143	1.1	1759	5.2		
19 M	0000	1.1	0615	5.4	1218	1.1	1832	5.2
20 TU	0035	1.1	0650	5.4	1252	1.1	1907	5.2
21 W	0110	1.1	0728	5.3	1328	1.2	1945	5.1
22 TH	0147	1.2	0811	5.1	1407	1.4	2030	4.9
23 F	0230	1.4	0902	4.8	1452	1.6	2124	4.7
24 SA	0322	1.7	1005	4.5	1550	1.9	◐ 2235	4.4
25 SU	0431	1.9	1131	4.4	1706	2.1		
26 M	0011	4.4	0559	1.9	1304	4.4	1833	2.0
27 TU	0136	4.6	0726	1.8	1415	4.7	1954	1.8
28 W	0241	4.9	0836	1.5	1513	4.9	2058	1.5
29 TH	0335	5.2	0932	1.2	1602	5.2	2150	1.2
30 F	0422	5.4	1019	1.0	1645	5.3	2237	1.0
31 SA	0504	5.5	1103	0.9	1725	5.4	○ 2319	0.9

APRIL

Day	Time	m	Time	m	Time	m	Time	m
1 SU	0543	5.5	1143	0.9	1801	5.4	2359	0.9
2 M	0619	5.4	1220	1.0	1835	5.3		
3 TU	0035	1.0	0652	5.2	1254	1.1	1906	5.1
4 W	0110	1.2	0723	5.0	1327	1.3	1937	4.9
5 TH	0144	1.4	0755	4.8	1401	1.6	2012	4.7
6 F	0220	1.6	0832	4.5	1439	1.9	2055	4.4
7 SA	0302	1.9	0920	4.2	1525	2.2	2153	4.2
8 SU	0356	2.2	1037	3.9	1634	2.5	◑ 2316	4.1
9 M	0516	2.4	1217	3.9	1804	2.5		
10 TU	0041	4.1	0640	2.3	1337	4.1	1918	2.3
11 W	0149	4.3	0746	2.1	1431	4.3	2014	2.1
12 TH	0240	4.5	0837	1.8	1512	4.6	2100	1.8
13 F	0322	4.8	0920	1.6	1548	4.8	2141	1.5
14 SA	0400	5.1	1000	1.4	1623	5.0	2219	1.3
15 SU	0437	5.3	1038	1.2	1658	5.2	2257	1.1
16 M	0514	5.4	1115	1.0	1733	5.3	● 2335	1.0
17 TU	0552	5.4	1152	1.0	1810	5.4		
18 W	0013	1.0	0631	5.4	1230	1.0	1848	5.3
19 TH	0051	1.0	0713	5.3	1309	1.1	1930	5.2
20 F	0132	1.1	0759	5.1	1351	1.3	2018	5.0
21 SA	0218	1.3	0852	4.8	1439	1.5	2114	4.8
22 SU	0313	1.6	0958	4.5	1538	1.8	◐ 2227	4.5
23 M	0422	1.8	1126	4.4	1653	2.0		
24 TU	0000	4.5	0547	1.8	1251	4.5	1818	2.0
25 W	0119	4.6	0709	1.7	1358	4.6	1934	1.8
26 TH	0223	4.8	0816	1.5	1454	4.9	2037	1.5
27 F	0316	5.0	0909	1.3	1540	5.0	2128	1.3
28 SA	0401	5.2	0955	1.1	1621	5.1	2214	1.2
29 SU	0441	5.2	1037	1.1	1658	5.2	2255	1.1
30 M	0517	5.3	1116	1.1	1732	5.2	○ 2333	1.1

Chart Datum is 2·83 metres below IGN Datum. HAT is 6·1 metres above Chart Datum.

STANDARD TIME UT –01
Subtract 1 hour for UT
For French Summer Time add ONE hour in **non-shaded areas**

POINTE DE GRAVE LAT 45°34′N LONG 1°04′W

TIMES AND HEIGHTS OF HIGH AND LOW WATERS

Dates in red are SPRINGS
Dates in blue are NEAPS

YEAR **2018**

MAY

Date	Time	m	Time	m	Time	m	Time	m
1 TU	0551	5.2	1151	1.1	1805	5.2		
2 W	0008	1.1	0623	5.1	1224	1.3	1837	5.1
3 TH	0042	1.2	0654	4.9	1257	1.4	1909	4.9
4 F	0115	1.4	0727	4.7	1330	1.6	1945	4.8
5 SA	0150	1.6	0803	4.5	1406	1.8	2026	4.6
6 SU	0229	1.8	0847	4.2	1448	2.1	2116	4.3
7 M	0316	2.0	0948	4.0	1544	2.3	2222	4.2
8 TU	0420	2.2	1112	4.0	1703	2.4	◑ 2338	4.2
9 W	0539	2.2	1232	4.0	1819	2.3		
10 TH	0048	4.3	0649	2.1	1335	4.2	1920	2.1
11 F	0147	4.5	0747	1.9	1424	4.5	2013	1.9
12 SA	0237	4.7	0836	1.6	1507	4.8	2100	1.6
13 SU	0323	5.0	0921	1.4	1548	5.0	2144	1.4
14 M	0406	5.2	1004	1.2	1628	5.2	2227	1.1
15 TU	0449	5.3	1046	1.0	1708	5.3	● 2310	1.0
16 W	0532	5.4	1128	1.0	1750	5.4	2353	0.9
17 TH	0616	5.4	1210	1.0	1834	5.4		
18 F	0036	0.9	0703	5.3	1254	1.0	1921	5.3
19 SA	0122	1.0	0752	5.1	1339	1.2	2012	5.1
20 SU	0210	1.2	0848	4.8	1430	1.4	2111	4.9
21 M	0306	1.4	0954	4.6	1528	1.7	2222	4.7
22 TU	0411	1.6	1112	4.5	1637	1.8	◐ 2342	4.6
23 W	0525	1.7	1227	4.5	1753	1.9		
24 TH	0054	4.6	0640	1.7	1332	4.6	1906	1.8
25 F	0157	4.7	0746	1.6	1428	4.7	2009	1.6
26 SA	0251	4.8	0841	1.4	1514	4.8	2102	1.5
27 SU	0337	4.9	0929	1.3	1555	4.9	2148	1.4
28 M	0416	4.9	1011	1.3	1631	5.0	2230	1.3
29 TU	0453	5.0	1049	1.3	1706	5.1	○ 2308	1.3
30 W	0527	5.0	1124	1.3	1741	5.1	2343	1.3
31 TH	0601	4.9	1158	1.4	1815	5.0		

JUNE

Date	Time	m	Time	m	Time	m	Time	m
1 F	0018	1.3	0633	4.8	1231	1.5	1849	4.9
2 SA	0052	1.4	0706	4.7	1305	1.6	1924	4.8
3 SU	0127	1.5	0742	4.5	1341	1.7	2003	4.7
4 M	0204	1.7	0822	4.4	1421	1.9	2047	4.5
5 TU	0246	1.8	0911	4.2	1508	2.1	2140	4.4
6 W	0337	2.0	1014	4.1	1608	2.2	◑ 2242	4.3
7 TH	0440	2.1	1126	4.1	1717	2.2	2348	4.3
8 F	0548	2.0	1234	4.2	1823	2.1		
9 SA	0052	4.4	0652	1.9	1333	4.4	1921	1.9
10 SU	0151	4.6	0749	1.7	1426	4.7	2016	1.6
11 M	0246	4.8	0842	1.5	1514	4.9	2108	1.4
12 TU	0338	5.1	0932	1.2	1601	5.1	2159	1.2
13 W	0427	5.2	1020	1.1	1648	5.3	● 2248	1.0
14 TH	0516	5.3	1108	0.9	1735	5.4	2337	0.8
15 F	0604	5.4	1155	0.9	1824	5.4		
16 SA	0025	0.8	0654	5.3	1242	1.0	1914	5.4
17 SU	0113	0.9	0745	5.1	1329	1.1	2007	5.2
18 M	0202	1.0	0839	4.9	1419	1.3	2104	5.0
19 TU	0254	1.2	0939	4.7	1514	1.5	2206	4.8
20 W	0351	1.4	1045	4.5	1614	1.7	◐ 2313	4.6
21 TH	0455	1.6	1153	4.4	1721	1.8		
22 F	0021	4.5	0603	1.7	1259	4.4	1831	1.8
23 SA	0125	4.5	0710	1.7	1357	4.5	1937	1.8
24 SU	0223	4.5	0811	1.7	1448	4.6	2034	1.7
25 M	0312	4.6	0902	1.6	1530	4.7	2124	1.6
26 TU	0355	4.7	0947	1.5	1609	4.8	2208	1.5
27 W	0433	4.7	1026	1.4	1646	4.9	2247	1.4
28 TH	0509	4.8	1103	1.4	1721	5.0	○ 2323	1.4
29 F	0544	4.8	1137	1.4	1756	5.0	2358	1.4
30 SA	0617	4.7	1211	1.4	1831	4.9		

JULY

Date	Time	m	Time	m	Time	m	Time	m
1 SU	0032	1.4	0649	4.7	1246	1.5	1905	4.9
2 M	0107	1.4	0722	4.6	1321	1.6	1941	4.8
3 TU	0143	1.5	0758	4.5	1357	1.7	2020	4.7
4 W	0220	1.6	0839	4.4	1438	1.8	2105	4.6
5 TH	0303	1.7	0929	4.3	1525	1.9	2157	4.5
6 F	0353	1.8	1029	4.2	1623	2.0	◑ 2257	4.4
7 SA	0453	1.9	1137	4.2	1728	2.0		
8 SU	0003	4.4	0600	1.9	1245	4.4	1835	1.9
9 M	0111	4.5	0705	1.7	1349	4.6	1938	1.7
10 TU	0216	4.7	0807	1.5	1447	4.8	2038	1.4
11 W	0316	4.9	0905	1.3	1541	5.1	2137	1.2
12 TH	0411	5.1	1000	1.1	1632	5.3	2232	1.0
13 F	0503	5.3	1053	0.9	1723	5.5	● 2325	0.8
14 SA	0553	5.4	1143	0.9	1813	5.5		
15 SU	0014	0.7	0643	5.3	1231	0.9	1904	5.5
16 M	0102	0.7	0732	5.2	1317	0.9	1954	5.4
17 TU	0149	0.9	0822	5.0	1404	1.1	2045	5.1
18 W	0236	1.1	0913	4.8	1453	1.3	2138	4.9
19 TH	0325	1.3	1007	4.5	1545	1.5	◐ 2235	4.6
20 F	0419	1.6	1109	4.3	1645	1.8	2339	4.4
21 SA	0522	1.8	1217	4.3	1753	1.9		
22 SU	0048	4.3	0632	1.9	1324	4.3	1904	1.9
23 M	0155	4.3	0740	1.9	1423	4.4	2009	1.9
24 TU	0252	4.3	0838	1.8	1510	4.5	2103	1.7
25 W	0338	4.5	0927	1.7	1551	4.7	2149	1.6
26 TH	0417	4.6	1008	1.6	1628	4.8	2229	1.5
27 F	0453	4.7	1045	1.5	1703	4.9	○ 2305	1.4
28 SA	0527	4.8	1120	1.4	1737	5.0	2340	1.3
29 SU	0558	4.8	1154	1.4	1810	5.0		
30 M	0014	1.3	0629	4.8	1227	1.4	1843	5.0
31 TU	0047	1.3	0700	4.8	1301	1.4	1916	5.0

AUGUST

Date	Time	m	Time	m	Time	m	Time	m
1 W	0121	1.4	0732	4.7	1334	1.5	1952	4.9
2 TH	0155	1.4	0808	4.6	1410	1.6	2032	4.8
3 F	0232	1.6	0851	4.5	1450	1.7	2120	4.6
4 SA	0315	1.7	0944	4.4	1540	1.8	◑ 2217	4.5
5 SU	0408	1.8	1050	4.3	1643	1.9	2325	4.4
6 M	0515	1.9	1205	4.3	1757	1.9		
7 TU	0042	4.4	0629	1.9	1323	4.5	1910	1.8
8 W	0157	4.6	0740	1.7	1429	4.8	2020	1.5
9 TH	0302	4.8	0847	1.5	1527	5.1	2124	1.2
10 F	0358	5.1	0947	1.2	1620	5.3	2221	0.9
11 SA	0450	5.3	1041	1.0	1710	5.5	● 2313	0.7
12 SU	0540	5.4	1130	0.8	1759	5.6		
13 M	0001	0.6	0627	5.4	1217	0.8	1847	5.6
14 TU	0046	0.7	0712	5.3	1301	0.8	1932	5.5
15 W	0129	0.8	0755	5.1	1344	1.0	2017	5.2
16 TH	0211	1.1	0838	4.9	1427	1.2	2101	4.9
17 F	0254	1.4	0922	4.6	1513	1.5	2150	4.5
18 SA	0342	1.7	1015	4.3	1606	1.8	◐ 2249	4.3
19 SU	0439	2.0	1126	4.1	1713	2.1		
20 M	0006	4.1	0551	2.2	1248	4.1	1831	2.2
21 TU	0128	4.1	0710	2.2	1357	4.3	1945	2.1
22 W	0232	4.2	0816	2.0	1450	4.5	2043	1.9
23 TH	0321	4.4	0907	1.8	1532	4.7	2129	1.7
24 F	0359	4.6	0949	1.7	1608	4.8	2208	1.5
25 SA	0433	4.7	1026	1.5	1642	5.0	2244	1.4
26 SU	0505	4.8	1100	1.4	1714	5.1	○ 2318	1.3
27 M	0535	4.9	1133	1.3	1746	5.2	2352	1.2
28 TU	0605	5.0	1206	1.3	1818	5.2		
29 W	0025	1.2	0635	5.0	1238	1.3	1851	5.1
30 TH	0057	1.3	0706	4.9	1310	1.4	1925	5.0
31 F	0129	1.4	0740	4.8	1344	1.5	2004	4.9

Chart Datum is 2·83 metres below IGN Datum. HAT is 6·1 metres above Chart Datum.

STANDARD TIME UT –01
Subtract 1 hour for UT
For French Summer Time add ONE hour in **non-shaded areas**

POINTE DE GRAVE LAT 45°34'N LONG 1°04'W

TIMES AND HEIGHTS OF HIGH AND LOW WATERS

Dates in red are SPRINGS
Dates in blue are NEAPS

YEAR **2018**

SEPTEMBER

Date	Time	m	Date	Time	m
1	0204	1.5	16	0303	1.8
	0820	4.7		0923	4.4
	SA 1422	1.6		SU 1527	1.9
	2050	4.7		2157	4.2
2	0245	1.6	17	0355	2.1
	0910	4.5		1031	4.2
	SU 1509	1.8		M 1630	2.2
	2147	4.5		◐ 2321	4.0
3	0335	1.8	18	0508	2.4
	1015	4.4		1202	4.1
	M 1610	2.0		TU 1754	2.4
	◑ 2300	4.4			
4	0443	2.0	19	0057	4.0
	1138	4.3		0636	2.4
	TU 1731	2.0		W 1324	4.2
				1915	2.3
5	0028	4.4	20	0207	4.1
	0604	2.0		0747	2.2
	W 1308	4.5		TH 1422	4.4
	1855	1.9		2016	2.0
6	0148	4.6	21	0256	4.4
	0725	1.9		0840	2.0
	TH 1419	4.8		F 1506	4.6
	2011	1.6		2102	1.8
7	0252	4.8	22	0334	4.6
	0836	1.6		0922	1.8
	F 1517	5.1		SA 1542	4.9
	2115	1.2		2141	1.6
8	0347	5.1	23	0407	4.8
	0936	1.2		0959	1.6
	SA 1608	5.4		SU 1616	5.1
	2209	0.9		2217	1.4
9	0436	5.3	24	0437	5.0
	1028	1.0		1034	1.4
	SU 1656	5.6		M 1648	5.2
	● 2258	0.7		2251	1.3
10	0521	5.5	25	0508	5.1
	1115	0.8		1108	1.3
	M 1741	5.7		TU 1720	5.3
	2343	0.7		○ 2325	1.2
11	0604	5.5	26	0538	5.1
	1159	0.8		1141	1.2
	TU 1824	5.6		W 1753	5.3
				2358	1.2
12	0025	0.8	27	0610	5.2
	0645	5.4		1214	1.2
	W 1240	0.9		TH 1826	5.3
	1904	5.5			
13	0104	0.9	28	0031	1.2
	0723	5.2		0642	5.1
	TH 1319	1.0		F 1248	1.3
	1943	5.2		1902	5.2
14	0142	1.2	29	0105	1.3
	0759	4.9		0717	5.0
	F 1358	1.3		SA 1323	1.4
	2020	4.9		1942	5.0
15	0221	1.5	30	0142	1.4
	0836	4.7		0758	4.9
	SA 1439	1.6		SU 1402	1.5
	2101	4.5		2030	4.8

OCTOBER

Date	Time	m	Date	Time	m
1	0223	1.6	16	0313	2.2
	0850	4.7		0943	4.3
	M 1450	1.8		TU 1545	2.3
	2130	4.5		◐ 2233	4.0
2	0315	1.9	17	0420	2.5
	0956	4.5		1108	4.1
	TU 1553	2.0		W 1705	2.4
	◑ 2249	4.4			
3	0424	2.1	18	0011	4.0
	1126	4.4		0549	2.5
	W 1718	2.1		TH 1234	4.2
				1830	2.4
4	0024	4.4	19	0127	4.1
	0551	2.1		0704	2.4
	TH 1300	4.6		F 1340	4.4
	1848	1.9		1935	2.2
5	0140	4.6	20	0219	4.4
	0714	1.9		0800	2.2
	F 1409	4.9		SA 1429	4.6
	2002	1.6		2024	1.9
6	0240	4.9	21	0259	4.6
	0824	1.6		0845	1.9
	SA 1504	5.2		SU 1508	4.9
	2101	1.3		2106	1.7
7	0332	5.2	22	0333	4.8
	0921	1.3		0925	1.7
	SU 1553	5.4		M 1544	5.1
	2152	1.0		2144	1.5
8	0417	5.4	23	0406	5.0
	1010	1.1		1002	1.5
	M 1638	5.6		TU 1619	5.3
	2237	0.9		2220	1.3
9	0459	5.5	24	0438	5.2
	1055	0.9		1039	1.3
	TU 1719	5.6		W 1654	5.4
	● 2320	0.8		○ 2256	1.2
10	0539	5.5	25	0512	5.3
	1137	0.9		1115	1.2
	W 1758	5.6		TH 1730	5.4
	2359	0.9		2331	1.2
11	0616	5.4	26	0546	5.3
	1216	1.0		1151	1.2
	TH 1835	5.4		F 1807	5.4
12	0036	1.1	27	0008	1.2
	0651	5.2		0623	5.3
	F 1253	1.2		SA 1228	1.2
	1909	5.1		1846	5.3
13	0112	1.3	28	0045	1.3
	0724	5.0		0702	5.2
	SA 1329	1.4		SU 1308	1.3
	1943	4.8		1931	5.1
14	0147	1.6	29	0125	1.4
	0800	4.8		0748	5.0
	SU 1407	1.7		M 1351	1.5
	2021	4.5		2022	4.8
15	0226	1.9	30	0211	1.6
	0843	4.5		0842	4.8
	M 1450	2.0		TU 1442	1.7
	2112	4.2		2125	4.6
			31	0305	1.9
				0950	4.6
				W 1547	1.9
				◑ 2247	4.4

NOVEMBER

Date	Time	m	Date	Time	m
1	0415	2.1	16	0450	2.5
	1122	4.6		1131	4.2
	TH 1709	2.0		F 1729	2.4
2	0016	4.5	17	0025	4.1
	0538	2.1		0605	2.5
	F 1246	4.7		SA 1240	4.3
	1833	1.9		1838	2.3
3	0126	4.7	18	0127	4.3
	0658	1.9		0707	2.3
	SA 1352	4.9		SU 1339	4.5
	1944	1.6		1935	2.1
4	0223	4.9	19	0214	4.5
	0805	1.7		0759	2.0
	SU 1448	5.2		M 1427	4.8
	2041	1.4		2023	1.8
5	0313	5.1	20	0254	4.8
	0900	1.4		0844	1.8
	M 1535	5.3		TU 1510	5.0
	2130	1.2		2106	1.6
6	0356	5.3	21	0332	5.0
	0949	1.2		0927	1.6
	TU 1618	5.4		W 1550	5.2
	2214	1.1		2146	1.4
7	0436	5.4	22	0410	5.2
	1033	1.1		1008	1.4
	W 1657	5.4		TH 1630	5.3
	● 2255	1.1		2226	1.2
8	0514	5.4	23	0448	5.3
	1113	1.1		1049	1.2
	TH 1734	5.4		F 1710	5.4
	2333	1.1		○ 2307	1.2
9	0549	5.3	24	0528	5.4
	1151	1.2		1131	1.1
	F 1809	5.2		SA 1753	5.4
				2348	1.1
10	0009	1.3	25	0610	5.4
	0624	5.2		1214	1.1
	SA 1228	1.3		SU 1837	5.3
	1843	5.0			
11	0043	1.5	26	0030	1.2
	0658	5.1		0655	5.3
	SU 1303	1.5		M 1258	1.2
	1917	4.8		1925	5.2
12	0119	1.7	27	0115	1.3
	0734	4.9		0744	5.2
	M 1340	1.7		TU 1345	1.3
	1954	4.6		2018	5.0
13	0156	1.9	28	0203	1.5
	0815	4.7		0840	5.0
	TU 1420	1.9		W 1438	1.5
	2039	4.3		2121	4.7
14	0239	2.2	29	0258	1.7
	0907	4.4		0947	4.8
	W 1507	2.2		TH 1539	1.7
	2144	4.1		2236	4.6
15	0335	2.4	30	0403	1.9
	1014	4.3		1107	4.7
	TH 1610	2.4		F 1651	1.8
	◐ 2308	4.0		◑ 2354	4.6

DECEMBER

Date	Time	m	Date	Time	m
1	0517	2.0	16	0459	2.4
	1223	4.8		1134	4.3
	SA 1806	1.8		SU 1733	2.2
2	0102	4.7	17	0020	4.2
	0631	1.9		0605	2.3
	SU 1329	4.9		M 1239	4.4
	1916	1.7		1837	2.1
3	0201	4.8	18	0120	4.4
	0738	1.8		0705	2.1
	M 1427	5.0		TU 1339	4.6
	2015	1.6		1934	1.9
4	0251	5.0	19	0212	4.6
	0836	1.6		0800	1.9
	TU 1516	5.1		W 1433	4.8
	2106	1.4		2025	1.7
5	0336	5.1	20	0259	4.9
	0926	1.4		0851	1.7
	W 1559	5.1		TH 1523	5.0
	2151	1.3		2114	1.5
6	0415	5.2	21	0344	5.1
	1011	1.3		0940	1.4
	TH 1638	5.2		F 1610	5.2
	2232	1.3		2200	1.3
7	0453	5.2	22	0429	5.3
	1052	1.3		1028	1.2
	F 1715	5.1		SA 1656	5.4
	● 2310	1.3		○ 2247	1.1
8	0529	5.2	23	0514	5.5
	1130	1.3		1115	1.1
	SA 1751	5.1		SU 1742	5.4
	2346	1.4		2333	1.1
9	0605	5.2	24	0601	5.5
	1207	1.4		1203	1.0
	SU 1825	5.0		M 1830	5.4
10	0021	1.5	25	0020	1.1
	0640	5.1		0649	5.5
	M 1242	1.5		TU 1250	1.0
	1859	4.8		1919	5.3
11	0056	1.6	26	0107	1.1
	0715	5.0		0740	5.4
	TU 1318	1.6		W 1339	1.1
	1934	4.7		2011	5.1
12	0133	1.8	27	0155	1.3
	0753	4.8		0834	5.3
	W 1355	1.8		TH 1429	1.2
	2013	4.5		2108	4.9
13	0212	2.0	28	0247	1.5
	0836	4.6		0934	5.1
	TH 1436	2.0		F 1523	1.4
	2101	4.3		2211	4.7
14	0257	2.2	29	0343	1.7
	0927	4.5		1040	4.9
	F 1525	2.1		SA 1623	1.7
	2202	4.2		◑ 2320	4.6
15	0352	2.3	30	0447	1.8
	1027	4.4		1150	4.7
	SA 1624	2.2		SU 1730	1.8
	◐ 2312	4.1			
			31	0029	4.5
				0557	1.9
				M 1300	4.7
				1841	1.9

Chart Datum is 2·83 metres below IGN Datum. HAT is 6·1 metres above Chart Datum.

S Biscay

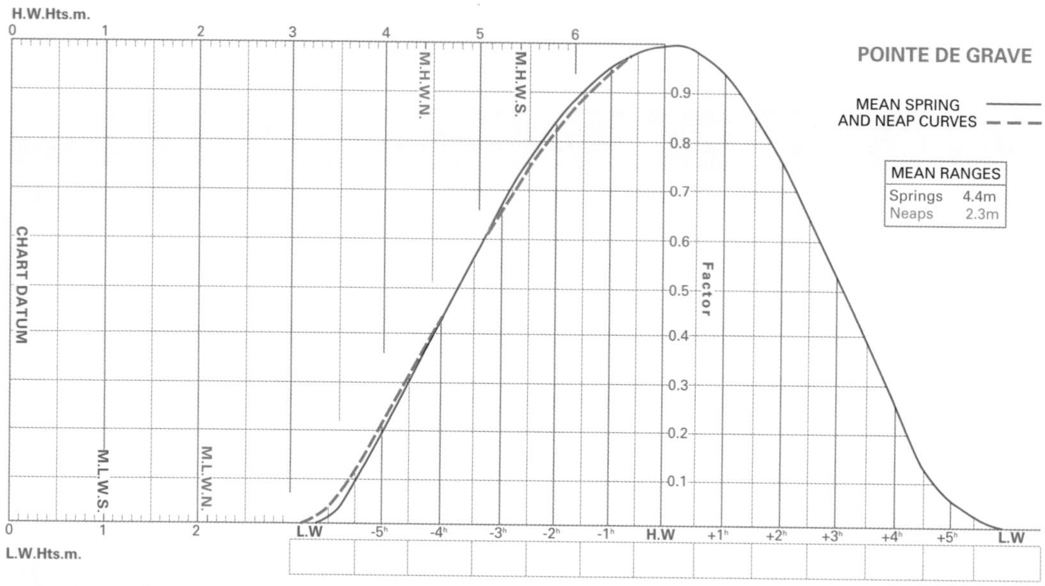

H.W.Hts.m.
L.W.Hts.m.
CHART DATUM
M.L.W.S.
M.L.W.N.
M.H.W.N.
M.H.W.S.
Factor
L.W
H.W
POINTE DE GRAVE
MEAN SPRING AND NEAP CURVES
MEAN RANGES
Springs 4.4m
Neaps 2.3m

9.22.18 THE GIRONDE ESTUARY

CHARTS AC 3057/8, 3068; SHOM 7425/6/7: all these are essential.

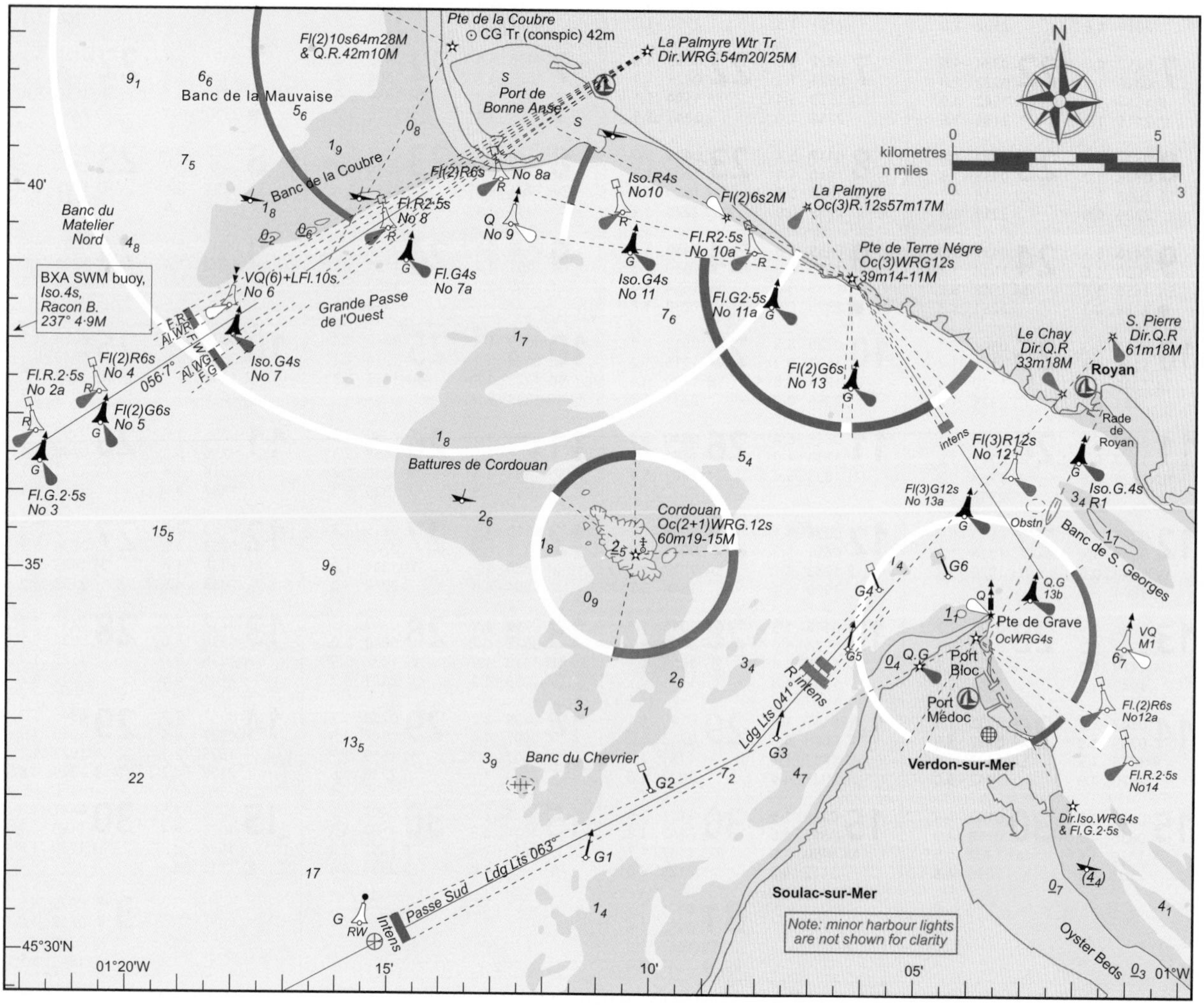

Pte de la Coubre
CG Tr (conspic) 42m
Fl(2)10s64m28M & Q.R.42m10M
La Palmyre Wtr Tr Dir.WRG.54m20/25M
Banc de la Mauvaise
Port de Bonne Anse
Banc de la Coubre
Banc du Matelier Nord
BXA SWM buoy, Iso.4s, Racon B. 237° 4·9M
Fl(2)R6s No 8a
Fl.R2·5s No 8
Iso.R4s No10
Q No 9
Fl.G4s No 7a
Iso.G4s No 11
Fl(2)6s2M
La Palmyre Oc(3)R.12s57m17M
Fl.R2·5s No 10a
Pte de Terre Négre Oc(3)WRG12s 39m14-11M
Fl.G2·5s No 11a
VQ(6)+LFl.10s. No 6
Grande Passe de l'Ouest
Iso.G4s No 7
Fl(2)R6s No 4
Fl.R.2·5s No 2a
Fl(2)G6s No 5
Fl.G.2·5s No 3
056·7°
Fl(2)G6s No 13
Le Chay Dir.Q.R 33m18M
S. Pierre Dir.Q.R 61m18M
Royan
Rade de Royan
Fl(3)R12s No 12
Iso.G.4s R1
Battures de Cordouan
Cordouan Oc(2+1)WRG.12s 60m19-15M
Fl(3)G12s No 13a
Obstn
Banc de S. Georges
G6
G4
Q.G 13b
Pte de Grave OcWRG4s
VQ M1
Port Bloc
Port Médoc
Verdon-sur-Mer
R intens
Ldg Lts 041°
G5
G3
Fl.(2)R6s No12a
Fl.R.2·5s No14
Dir.Iso.WRG4s & Fl.G.2·5s
Banc du Chevrier
G2
G1
Passe Sud
Ldg Lts 063°
Intens
Soulac-sur-Mer
Note: minor harbour lights are not shown for clarity
Oyster Beds
kilometres
n miles
40'
35'
45°30'N
01°20'W
15'
10'
05'
01°W

TIDES
Standard Port POINTE DE GRAVE (⟵)

Times				Height (metres)			
High Water		Low Water		MHWS	MHWN	MLWN	MLWS
0000	0600	0000	0500	5·3	4·4	2·1	1·0
1200	1800	1200	1700				
Differences CORDOUAN							
–0010	–0010	–0025	–0015	–0·4	–0·4	–0·1	–0·2
RICHARD							
+0020	+0020	+0035	+0030	0·0	–0·1	–0·4	–0·5
LAMENA							
+0035	+0045	+0125	+0100	+0·3	+0·1	–0·5	–0·3
LA REUILLE							
+0135	+0145	+0305	+0230	–0·1	–0·3	–1·3	–0·7
LE MARQUIS							
+0145	+0150	+0320	+0245	–0·2	–0·4	–1·5	–0·9
LIBOURNE (La Dordogne)							
+0250	+0305	+0540	+0525	–0·6	–0·9	–2·0	–0·4

In the Gironde and the R Dordogne the sp flood reaches 3kn and the ebb 4kn, continuing for 1½hrs after predicted LW time. In the Garonne the sp flood starts with a small bore and runs at 3kn, ebb reaches 5kn. *The Annuaire des Marées Estuaire de la Gironde*, downloadable from www.bordeaux-port.fr, is full of useful tidal information for the Gironde and also Arcachon.

▶*Off Terre-Nègre lt the SE-going stream begins at HW –0500 (sp 1·5kn), and the NW-going at HW+0130 (sp 2·5kn).*◀

Between Pte de Grave and Bordeaux the height of water at Verdon, Richard, Lamena, Pauillac, Fort Médoc, Bec d'Ambes, Le Marquis and Bordeaux (see R Gironde chartlet) is automatically broadcast H24 on Ch 17 every 5 mins. From these read-outs it is possible to deduce, for example, when the flood starts to make.

SHELTER See Royan to Bordeaux.

NAVIGATION La Gironde is a substantial waterway. The mouth of the estuary is 9M wide between Pte de la Coubre and Pte de Grave and narrows from 6M wide off Royan to 2.5M at Pauillac. The Garonne and Dordogne flow into the Gironde at Bec d'Ambes (45°02'N). Be alert for ferries and shipping.

The outer apprs can be dangerous due to Atlantic swell, very strong tidal streams and currents, extensive shoals and shifting sandbanks. Swell, strong W'lies and an ebb tide raise dangerous, breaking seas some 5m high; in such conditions do not attempt entry. Nevertheless at the right time and in the right weather both entrances are straightforward by day and night.

The two approach channels are:

- **Grande Passe de l'Ouest** WPT BXA SWM buoy, Iso 4s, 45°37'·53N 01°28'·68W, 057°/4·0M to Nos 1 & 2 buoys. The chan is deep and well marked/lit. Keep well clear of La Mauvaise and Matelier Nord banks (overfalls) the drying Banc de la Coubre and Battures de Cordouan.

  Leave No 1 buoy at LW on 057° Dir lt WRG, La Palmyre Wtr Tr. Hold to stbd side of buoyed channel, gradually swinging eastward to No 7a SHM, Fl G 4s, and once past No 9 NCM, Q, head south eastwards in W sector (097°-104°) of Tèrre Negre lt. Using stern transit 327° (Tèrre Negre Oc W / La Palmyre Oc R) enter R Gironde past No 13b SHM QG, off Pointe de Grave.
- **Passe du Sud** is a useful short cut if arriving from the S. It carries approx 5m through shoals, but Platin de Grave, N of G4 and G6 buoys, has only 1·4m or less. Not advised in poor vis or heavy swell. The six lateral buoys are unlit.

  WPT 45°30'·00N 01°15'·33W, abeam 'G' unlit SWM buoy, 063°/5·5M (063° ldg lts: Front, QG; rear, Oc WRG 4s) to G3 buoy. Here pick up the 041° ldg lts (both QR) to G4 buoy where alter stbd to G6 buoy passing S of Platin de Grave. Thence track direct to Royan or via No 13b buoy to Port-Médoc.

LIGHTS AND MARKS See chartlet and Lights, buoys & waypoints for details of lts mentioned above. **Other major lts in estuary**: La Coubre lt ho, W twr, top third R. 2M NNE is a R/W CG twr. Cordouan lt ho is an elegant, W sculpted twr on a drying plateau in mid-estuary.

COMMUNICATIONS *Bordeaux Port Control* Ch 12 (H24) provides radar surveillance from BXA buoy to Bordeaux, plus MSI on request.

9.22.19 ROYAN

Charente Maritime **45°37'·12N 01°01'·50W**

CHARTS AC 3057, 3058; Imray C42; SHOM 7426, 7425; Navi 553, 554

TIDES +0530 Dover; ML 3·2; Duration Sp 0615, Np 0655

Standard Port POINTE DE GRAVE (⟵)

Times				Height (metres)			
High Water		Low Water		MHWS	MHWN	MLWN	MLWS
0000	0600	0000	0500	5·3	4·4	2·1	1·0
1200	1800	1200	1700				
Differences ROYAN							
0000	–0005	0000	0000	–0·1	–0·1	0·0	0·0

SHELTER Good in marina. Access difficult in strong W/NW'lies.

NAVIGATION WPT 45°36'·56N 01°01'·96W (R1 SHM buoy, Iso G 4s; marks wk (3m) 260m E) 030°/0·64M to hbr ent. The Gironde apprs can be dangerous; see The Gironde Estuary for details; allow about 2hrs from Pte de la Coubre to Royan. Beware Banc de St Georges (0·4m) 1M S of WPT. Off hbr ent, there is an eddy, running S at about 1kn on the flood and 3kn on the ebb. Caution: FVs and fast ferries.

LIGHTS AND MARKS Cathedral spire is conspic modern 'spike'. See chartlet and Lights, buoys & waypoints for lt details.

COMMUNICATIONS CROSS 02·97·55·35·35; Auto 08.92.68.08.17; 05·56·34·20·11; Police 05·46·38·34·22; ⊖ 05·46·23·10·24; Brit Consul 05·57·22·21·10; Ⓗ 05·46·38·01·77; HM VHF Ch 09, 16 (season 0800-2000; otherwise 0900-1800LT); Aff Mar 05·46·39·26·30.

FACILITIES Marina Care needed near LW sp. Ent chan, least depth 0·1m, silts but is regularly dredged to at least 0·8m; it narrows markedly off New Jetty hd. Accueil pontoon is dead ahead, W of the ent.

Marina ☎05·46·38·72·22 (Jul/Aug 7/7 0800-2000) www.port-royan.com port.royan@wanadoo.fr 900 + 100Ⓥ €2·12. (☎ 05·46·38·53·39. 0830-1200, 1430-1830, 7/7 in season) SHOM Grid Ice Ⓔ de-mast (1·5t) (26t). **Base Nautique (YC)** ☎05·46·05·44·13.

Town Ⓑ (Bordeaux). Ferry via Roscoff or St Malo; fast ferries to Port Bloc.

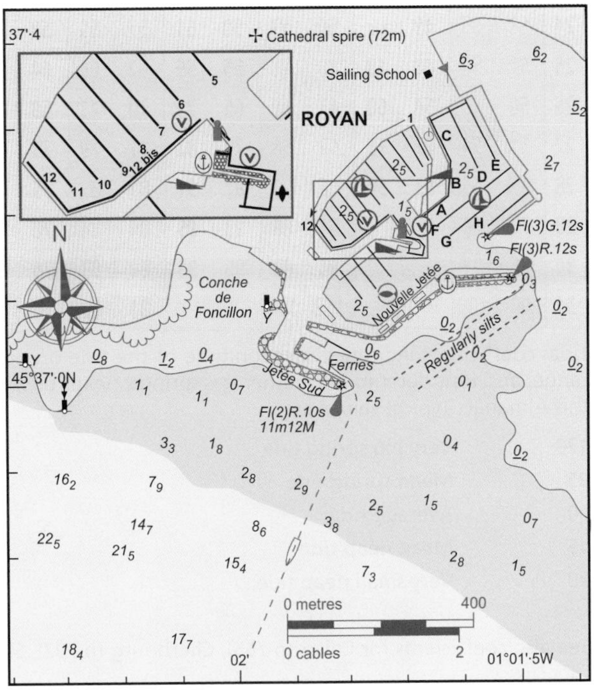

POINTE DE GRAVE TIDAL COEFFICIENTS 2018

Date	Jan		Feb		Mar		Apr		May		June		July		Aug		Sept		Oct		Nov		Dec	
	am	pm	am	pm	am	pm	am	pm	am	pm	am	pm	am	pm	am	pm	am	pm	am	pm	am	pm	am	pm
1	92	97	107	109	97	102	105	105	94	92	77	74	73	72	74	72	70	65	63	57	48		56	
2	101	104	109	108	106	109	103	100	89	86	71	68	70	67	69	66	60	55	52	47	49	52	58	61
3	106	107	106	103	110	109	96	92	82	77	64	60	64	62	62	59	51		44		57	63	64	69
4	106	104	98	92	108	104	86	80	72	67	56	52	59	56	55	52	47	45	45	48	69	76	73	77
5	101	96	85	78	100	94	74	67	61	56	49	45	53	50	49		45	48	54	62	82	87	80	83
6	91	85	71	63	88	81	60	53	50	45	43	41	48	47	48	47	54	61	70	78	92	95	85	86
7	79	72	56	49	74	66	46	40	40	37	41		46		49	52	69	77	85	92	97	99	87	87
8	65	59	43	39	58	51	35		34		41	44	47	50	57	64	85	93	98	103	99	97	86	85
9	54	49	36		44	38	31	29	34	35	47	52	53	58	70	78	99	105	106	107	95	93	83	80
10	46		35	37	33		30	34	39	43	57	63	63	69	85	92	108	111	108	106	89	84	78	74
11	44	44	40	45	30	30	39	45	49	55	69	76	75	82	97	103	111	110	104	100	79	74	71	67
12	46	49	50	55	33	37	52	59	62	68	81	87	87	93	106	109	108	104	95	89	68	62	63	58
13	52	55	60	65	43	49	65	72	75	81	92	96	97	101	109	109	99	92	83	75	56	50	54	50
14	59	63	69	74	55	62	78	84	86	91	99	101	103	104	107	103	85	77	68	61	45	40	46	42
15	66	69	78	81	68	74	89	93	96	99	102	101	105	103	98	92	69	61	53	46	35	33	40	38
16	72	75	84	87	79	84	97	100	101	102	100	98	101	97	85	78	53	46	40	34	32		37	
17	77	79	88	90	88	92	101	102	102	100	94	90	93	88	70	62	39		30		33	36	39	41
18	80	81	90	90	94	96	101	99	98	94	85	80	82	75	55	48	34	31	29	30	40	45	45	50
19	81	81	89	87	98	98	96	92	90	84	75	69	69	63	43		31	33	34	39	51	57	55	61
20	80	79	84	81	97	95	87	81	79	72	65		57		39	37	38	43	45	51	63	69	67	73
21	77	75	77	72	92	88	75	68	67	62	61	58	52	49	38	40	49	55	57	63	75	81	79	85
22	72	69	67	62	84	78	62	56	58		56	55	47	47	44	48	61	66	69	75	85	90	89	93
23	66	62	57	52	72	66	52		56	55	56	57	48	50	53	58	71	76	80	84	93	95	97	99
24	58	55	49		59	53	50	51	57	59	59	62	53	56	63	67	80	84	88	91	97	98	100	100
25	52	50	48	49	49		55	59	62	66	64	67	60	63	71	75	87	89	94	95	97	95	99	97
26	50		54	60	47	48	65	71	70	73	69	71	66	69	78	80	91	92	96	96	93	89	94	90
27	51	54	67	75	52	58	77	82	77	79	73	74	71	74	83	84	92	91	94	92	85	80	86	81
28	59	65	83	90	66	73	87	91	81	83	75	76	75	77	85	86	90	87	88	84	74	69	75	70
28	72	79			81	88	93	95	84	84	76	76	78	78	85	85	84	80	79	73	64	60	65	61
30	86	93			94	98	96	95	84	83	76	75	78	78	83	81	75	69	67	61	57	55	58	
31	99	103			102	104			81	80			77	76	77	74			55	51			56	55

Tidal coefficients indicate the magnitude of the tide on any particular day, without having to look up and calculate the range, and thus determine whether it is springs, neaps or somewhere in between. This table is valid for all areas covered by this Almanac. Typical values are:

120	Very big spring tide
95	**Mean spring tide**
70	Average tide
45	**Mean neap tide**
20	Very small neap tide

See also coefficients for Calais (p 765), Cherbourg (p 792), St Malo (p 811) and Brest (p 879).

9.22.20 PORT BLOC

Gironde **45°34'·12N 01°03'·72W**

CHARTS AC 3057, 3058; Imray C42; Navi 553, 554; SHOM 7426, 7425

TIDES Use predictions for Pointe de Grave (←) 4ca N. Caution strong tidal streams.

SHELTER Good, but primarily a ferry harbour (caution: wash) and Service station for Bordeaux port authority and pilot boats, plus some fishing vessels. Swell enters in bad weather.

NAVIGATION WPT 45°34'·66N 01°02'·98W (13b SHM buoy, QG) 224°/7ca to harbour ent. Ent is 30m wide and is effectively fully used by ferries which have priority. Pauillac 25M; Bordeaux 53M.

LIGHTS AND MARKS Pte de Grave lt ho, W □ twr, B corners and top. Woods behind the hbr. See chartlet and Lights, buoys and waypoints.

COMMUNICATIONS CROSS 02·97·55·35·35; Radar Verdon VHF Ch 12, 11 (H24); 05·56·34·20·11; Auto 08·92·68·08·17; Police 05·56·09·80·29; ⊖ 05·56·09·65·14; Brit Consul 05·57·22·21·10; Dr 05·56·09·60·04; HM 05·56·09·63·91; Aff Mar 05·56·09·60·23.

FACILITIES Space for yachts is very limited; possible on pontoons W side of the hbr dredged 3m. Visitor berthing requires prior approval from AUPB (Port Bloc Users' Association). No or 's. Royan (3·4M NNE) or Port-Médoc 7ca S are far better options.

AUPB ☎05·56·09·72·64. **Moto YC de la Pointe de Grave** ☎05·56·09·84·02, good (10t).

Town ✕ (Verdon) ⇄ ✈ Bordeaux. Fast local ferries to Royan every 45 mins.

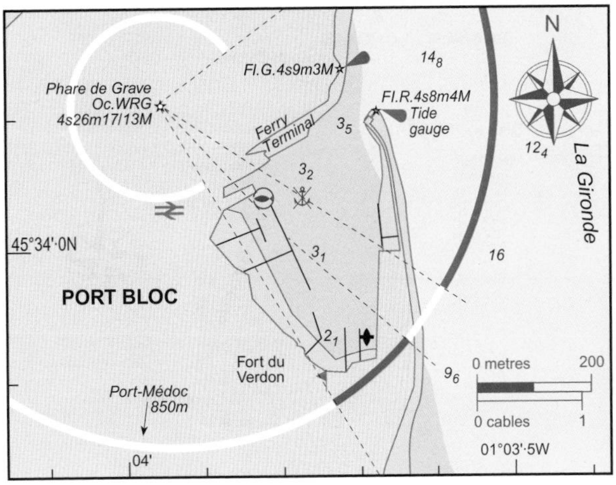

9.22.21 PORT MÉDOC

Gironde **45°33'·40N 01°03'·46W**

CHARTS AC 3057, 3058; SHOM 7426, 7425; Imray C42; Navi 553, 554

TIDES Pointe de Grave is a Standard Port whose predictions (←) apply to Port Bloc and Port Médoc; no tidal constraints.

SHELTER Good, in depths 2-3m. It is approx 1M S of Pte de Grave and 0·7ca S of Port Bloc on the W bank of the R Gironde.

NAVIGATION WPT 45°34'·66N 01°02'·97W (13b SHM buoy, QG) about 195°/1·3M to hbr ent, dredged 3m. Access H24 at all states of the tide. Le Verdon oil jetty, about 8ca SE, is dangerous and in a prohib area; no landing. Caution: strong tidal streams.

LIGHTS AND MARKS Marina's N and S bkwtr heads are lit QG and QR respectively. Pte de Grave lt ho (see Lights, buoys and waypoints) is 8ca NNW of the marina ent. Just N of the lt ho a 51m high red radio mast is marked by R lts. At Le Verdon cranes adj to the oil jetty are conspic. The oil jetty is marked by: Fl (3) G 12s at its N end and Fl G 2·5s at the S end, no landing. 9 ca further S is a Dir lt 171·5°, Iso WRG 4s.

COMMUNICATIONS CROSS 02·97·55·35·35; *Radar de Bordeaux* (VTS) Ch 12 (H24); Auto 08·92·68·02·17; Police 05·56·09·80·29; ⊖ 05·56·09·65·14; Brit Consul 05·57·22·21·10; Dr 05·56·09·60·04; Aff Mar 05·56·09·60·23; Marina VHF Ch 09.

FACILITIES Marina ☎05·56·09·69·75. www.port-medoc.com capitainerie@port-medoc.com 740 + 60, max LOA 25m, €2·42. The reception pontoon is at the N end of marina. 150 new berths were created for summer 2016, with a further 250 planned for 2017. ✕ some shops, (45t) bike hire. Footpath to town starts near pontoon N. 10m wide free public just N of hbr, W of ECM.

Le Verdon (1·3km S) ✕ good ⇄ ✈ (Bordeaux). Fast ferry Port Bloc to Royan every 45 mins €3·00; info ☎05·56·73·37·73.

Soulac-sur-Mer is 7·5km SW.

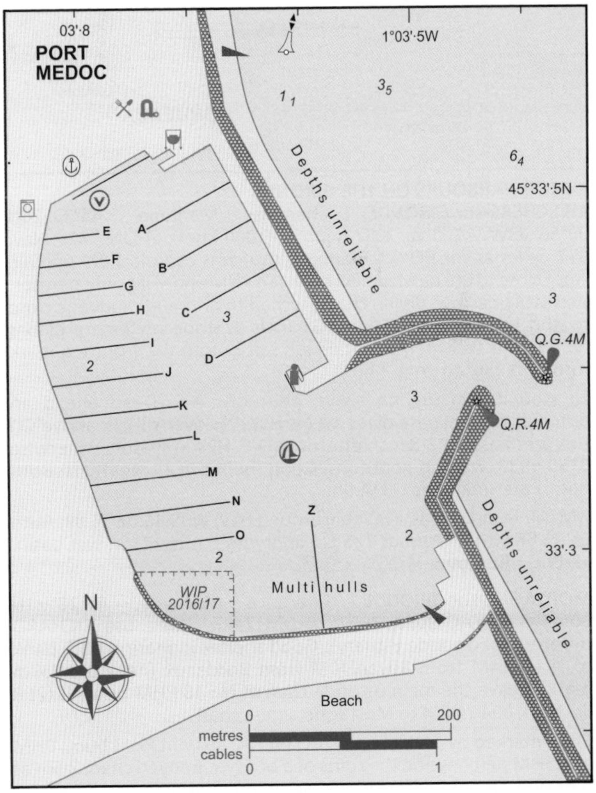

9.22.22 THE RIVER GIRONDE

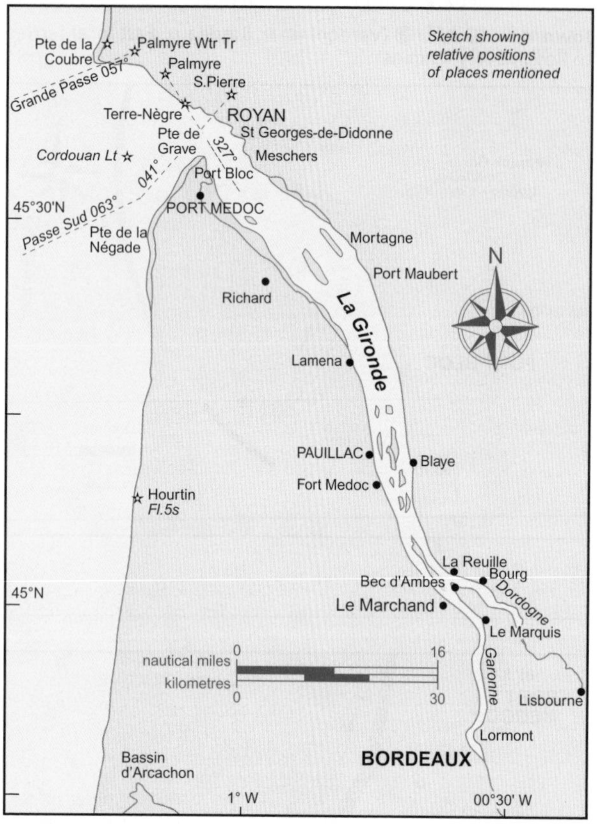

MINOR HARBOURS ON THE GIRONDE

MESCHERS-sur-GIRONDE, Charente Maritime, **45°33'·20N 00°56'·63W**. AC 3058, 3057 (with 1:10,000 inset); SHOM 7426; Navi 554. Tides as for ROYAN. Talmont church is conspic 1·8M upriver. Appr close to Pte de Meschers between PHM and SHM unlit perches. Access via narrow, drying chan perched to port and mudbank close to stbd. Ldg marks/lts 354·4°, 2 G panels, W stripe, on G metal pylons with QG lts (privately maintained); just before the front ldg mark turn port 330° to enter hbr.

To stbd drying marina basin, pontoons A-C. Dead ahead an automatic entry gate gives access HW±2½ over sill 2m above CD to a wet basin in 2·5m on pontoons D-F; H24 in season, otherwise 0730-1930; waiting pontoons. Good shelter in all weathers. Both basins are small; max LOA 9m.

HM (M. Jean-Luc Rat, available around HW) ☎05.46.02.56.89; Auto 05.36.68.08.17. **Marinas** 125 ⊆ in drying basin, 123 in wet basin: 18 Ⓥ €1·80. **Town** ✕ ⊐ 🛒 Ⓟ Ⓓ.

MORTAGNE-sur-GIRONDE, Charente Maritime, **45°28'·21N 00°48'·81W**. AC 3058, 3057; SHOM 7426. Tides, use RICHARD differences (Gironde Estuary). Good shelter in marina on E bank of river, 14M from Royan/40M from Bordeaux (near the 75km mark). Leave the main Gironde chan at No 18 PHM buoy, Fl (2) R 6s; track 094°/4·6M to Mortagne access chan.

Ent is marked by a WCM buoy, VQ (9) 10s, an unlit PHM buoy, PHM and SHM perches and the ruins of a bcn twr. Buoyed chan, 2·5m at half tide, trends 063°/0·9M across drying mudbanks to entry gate which opens HW–1 to HW (give 48hrs notice out of season). VHF Ch 09. HM ☎05.46.90.63.15. Facilities: **Marina** 130+20 Ⓥ in 4·5m €1·65, 🚹 🚺 ⛴ 🔧 ⛺ ⛽(10t) 🛒 Ice Aff Mar, ⊖ and Ⓛ at Royan; Auto 05.36.68.08.17.

BOURG-sur-GIRONDE (Actually on the Dordogne) **45°02'·28N 00°33'·61W**. AC 3068, 3069; SHOM 7030. Tides, use LA REUILLE (Gironde Estuary). 18 ⊆ + 2 Ⓥ <12m LOA, no rafting, on the W'ly of 2 long pontoons (parallel to shore); in strong W'lies very choppy against the ebb. HM ☎05.57.68.40.06. 🚰 ⚡ ⛺ (9T) ⛴.

9.22.23 PAUILLAC

Gironde **45°11'·83N 00°44'·59W** ❀❀◊◊◊✿✿✿

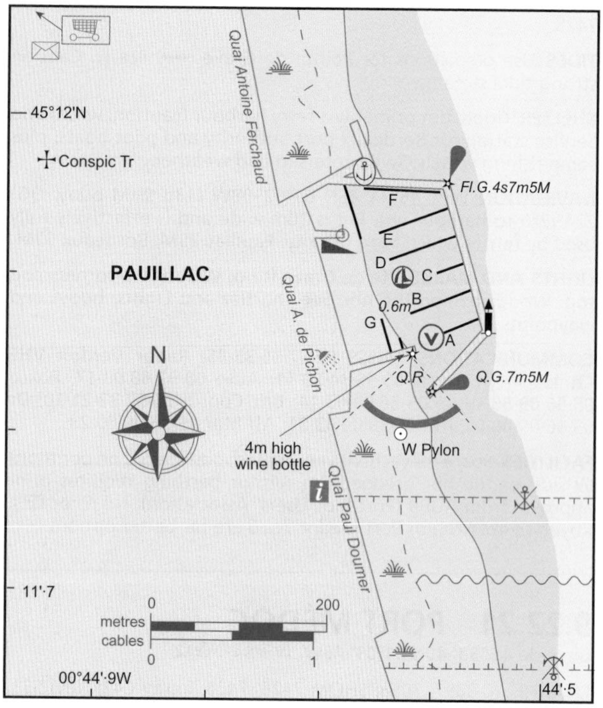

CHARTS AC 3058, 3068 (Inset D; 1: 20,000); SHOM 7427

TIDES HW +0620 on Dover (UT); ML 3·0m

Standard Port POINTE DE GRAVE (⟵)

Times				Height (metres)			
High Water		Low Water		MHWS	MHWN	MLWN	MLWS
0000	0600	0000	0500	5·3	4·4	2·1	1·0
1200	1800	1200	1700				
Differences PAUILLAC							
+0100	+0100	+0205	+0135	+0·2	0·0	−1·0	−0·5
BORDEAUX							
+0200	+0225	+0405	+0330	0·0	−0·2	−1·7	−1·0

SHELTER Excellent in marina. ⚓ possible close E of marina; or 500m further S clear of a 250m wide No-anch area (due to underwater cables).

NAVIGATION WPT 45°12'·45N 00°44'·27W [No 43 SHM buoy, Fl (2) G 6s], 196°/0·65M to hbr ent. Depths 2·0-4·5m; at LW hug the E side of entrance, due to silting. Do NOT arrive on the ebb; only manoeuvre in Marina at HW, approx HW Pte de Grave −3 and +2; see tidal diamond 'C' (45°13'·80N, 2M N). Strong current in approach, from S leave channel at No 43 buoy only; from N leave at No 45. Avoid the Airbus delivery ship depot, 1·2-1·7M north.

LIGHTS AND MARKS See chartlet and Lights, buoys and waypoints for lt details. The church twr, NW of the marina ent is conspic. So too is a 4m high bottle of Pauillac on the W side of the ent.

COMMUNICATIONS CROSS 02·97·55·35·35; ⛅ 05·36·68·08·33; ⊖ 05·56·59·04·01; Brit Consul 05·57·22·21·10; Marina VHF Ch 09 (0800–1200 & 1400-1800LT).

FACILITIES Marina ☎05·56·59·12·16. 130+20Ⓥ €2·50; max LOA 15m. Ⓥ berth on W end of pontoons A or B or any hammerhead; see HM for vacant berth. ⛴ (haul-out on trailer, max 12m/15t) 🔧 ⚡ ⚒ de-masting ⛺(15m max) Ⓓ Ⓟ(0800-1800) from local garage only.

CN de Pauillac ☎05·56·59·12·58.

Town ✕ ⊐ 🛒 ⊚ ✉ Ⓑ.

9.22.24 BORDEAUX

Gironde, **44°52´·79N 00°32´·18W** (Pont d'Aquitaine) ❁❁❁✿✿✿

CHARTS AC 3068, 3069; SHOM 7030

TIDES HW +0715 on Dover (UT); ML 2·4m. Slack water is at approx HW Pte de Grave –2 and +2½; see tidal ◊s C and D.

SHELTER Good. Both Lormont and the Halte Nautique may be exposed to wash and flotsam. Do not berth on city quays.

NAVIGATION The chan is well marked/lit. Beware big ships, strong currents (up to 5kn if river in spate) and possibly large bits of flotsam. At No 62 WCM buoy (close NW of Bec d'Ambès) keep to stbd into the R Garonne, with 12M to run to Bordeaux. De-mast before the Pont de Pierre (4·2m). Impressive vertical lift bridge, Pont Chaban-Delmas.

LIGHTS AND MARKS Pont d'Aquitaine (49m) and the new Pont Chaban-Delmas (53m) are good landmarks. Lts as on chartlet.

COMMUNICATIONS *Bordeaux Traffic* VHF Ch 12; ⊜ 05·57·81·03·60; Brit Consul 05·57·22·21·10; Bordeaux Port (PAB) 05·56·90·59·57, postoffice@bordeaux-port.fr www.bordeaux-port.fr; Aff Mar 05·56·00·83·00; Bègles marina VHF Ch 09.

FACILITIES from seaward: **Lormont YC** ☎05·56·31·50·10 is almost under Pont d'Aquitaine on E bank: limited space on S pontoon; de-masting crane; Clubhouse. FVs/ferries use the N pontoon. (The marina on the opposite bank is private, no Ⓥ.)
Bassin No 2 (1·5M S of bridge). Pre-arrange with HM ☎05·56·90·59·57 mob 06·13·79·10·75, or Ch 12. A waiting pontoon is just S of the lock; ☎05·56·90·59·85 for latest info. No ⛽ or security. Facilities await development. ▬ SHOM ✎ Ⓔ (mobile, 5t de-masting).
Halte Nautique, E bank close SE of Pont de Pierre. ⛽.
Bègles Marina (Port Garonne), W bank, Km 66. 4km S of Pont de Pierre. ☎05·56·85·76·04. 60+ 20 Ⓥ at N end of the wave-break.

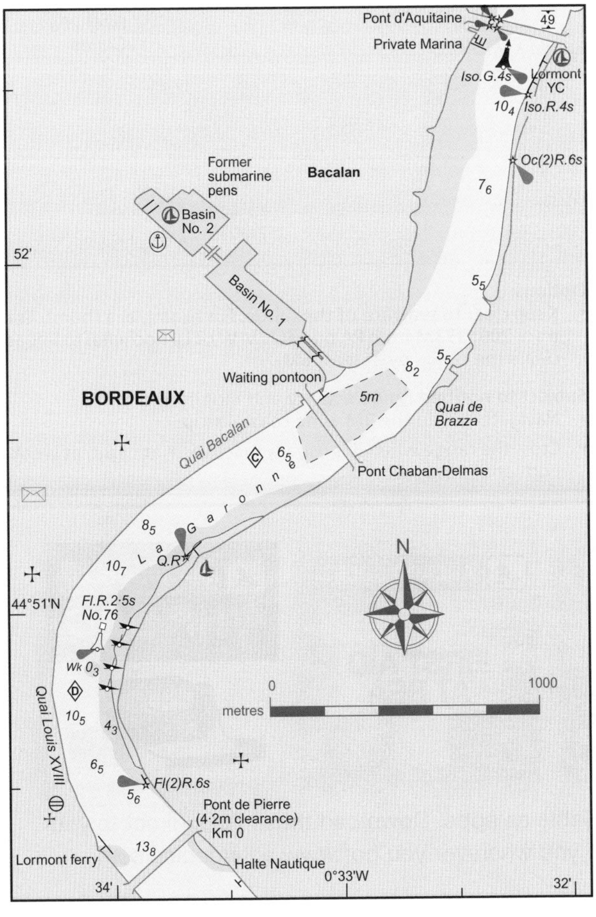

9.22.25 CANALS TO THE MEDITERRANEAN

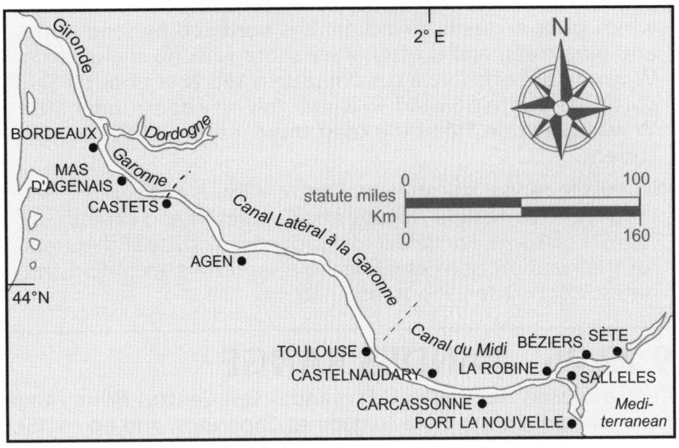

The Canal Latéral à la Garonne and **Canal du Midi** form a popular route to the Mediterranean, despite some 120 locks. The transit can be done in about a week, but 2-3 weeks is more relaxed. Masts can be lowered at Royan, Port-Médoc, Pauillac or Bordeaux.

Leave Bordeaux at LW Pointe de Grave for the 30M leg upriver to the first lock at Castets. Commercial traffic and W-bound boats have right of way. Most of the locks on the Canal Latéral à la Garonne are automatic. On the older and more interesting Canal du Midi there are many hire cruisers in summer. Depths vary with winter rainfall, summer drought and silting/dredging.

⛽ is available by hose at Bordeaux (Bègles) Mas d'Agenais, Agen, Toulouse (Port Sud), Castelnaudary, Port la Robine and by can elsewhere. 🛒 and 🚰 are readily obtainable. Tolls are listed in Special Notes for France Area 17. *Guide Vagnon No 7* or *Navicarte No 11* are advised. Further info from: Service de la Navigation de Toulouse, 8 Port St Etienne, 31079 Toulouse Cedex, ☎05·61·36·24·38, www.sn-sud-ouest.equipement.gouv.fr/en. See also *The Canal du Midi* (ACN).

SUMMARY Canal	From	To	Km/ Locks	Min Depth(m)	Min Ht(m)
Canal Latéral à la Garonne	Castets	Toulouse	193/53	2·2	3·5
Canal du Midi	Toulouse	Sète	240/65	1·6	3·0
Canal de la Nouvelle	Salleles	Port la Nouvelle	37/14	1·5	3·1

Dimensions: Max LOA 30m; draft 1·5m (varies with season); max beam 5·5m. Headroom of 3·3m is to centre of arch; over a width of 4m, clearance is about 2·4m.

Speed limits: 8km/hr (about 4½kn) but 3km/hr under bridges and over aqueducts.

POINTE DE GRAVE TO ARCACHON

(AC 2664, 1102) From Pte de la Négade to Capbreton, the coast is a featureless stretch of 107M broken only by the estuary which gives access to Arcachon. It is bordered by sand dunes and pine trees, and is often a lee shore with no shelter from W winds. 5M offshore a current usually sets N at about 0·5kn, particularly with a S wind; in winter this may be stronger after W winds. Within 1M of the coast there may be a S'ly counter-current.

A missile range, operated by Centre d'Essais des Landes, lies between Pointe de la Négade and Capbreton and extends up to 45M offshore. For details of boundaries, activity and sources of information, see below. Make every effort to obtain the latest information about range activity.

9.22.26 LANDES RANGE

Centre d'Essais des Landes (CEL: Landes Test Centre) firing range extends from Pointe de la Negade to Capbreton and up to 45M offshore. It is bounded by 45°27'N 01°13'W (inshore N) 45°12'N 02°00'W (NW corner) 44°00'N 02°25'W (SW corner) and 43°41'N 01°30'W (inshore S). The inshore boundary lies parallel to and about 3M off the coast. See chartlet, AC 1104 & 2664. CEL Range Control is at 44°26'N 01°15'W.

Sectors: The range is in two blocks, N and S of an 8M wide, 39M long, safe access corridor to Arcachon, orientated E-W from ATT-ARC buoy to the range boundary at 44°34'·05N 02°12'·91W. Within the two blocks those sectors which are active, or are planned to be, are referred to by their Lat/Long co-ordinates in all radio broadcasts, telephone recordings and enquiries.

Range activity: Sectors may be active Mon-Fri from 0800 LT, but are usually inactive Sat/Sun, at night and in August. **However there can be exceptions to the above.** Navigation may be prohibited in active sectors inside the 12M territorial limit. Beyond 12M it *'is strongly discouraged due to the particularly dangerous tests carried out'*. A No-entry box (1·6M x 1M) is centred on 44°22'·70N 01°25'·50W, 13M SSW of ATT-ARC buoy. **You must check range activity before entering the range.**

Information on Range activity is available from:

- ☎+33 (0)5·58·82·22·58 recorded info H24, inc daily activity.
- Semaphore stations at Chassiron (Île d'Oléron) Pte de Grave, Cap Ferret, Messanges and Socoa (St Jean-de-Luz): on request Ch 16 for advance notice of activity. See also Chapter 5 for ☎ Nos. Some English spoken.
- CROSS Etel broadcasts 0703, 0715, 0733, 0745 and 0803LT or ☎+33 (0)2·97·55·35·35.
- CEL, after announcement on Ch 16, broadcasts Ch 06, 10: Mon-Thu, 0815 & 1615, and Fri 0815 & 1615 (when firing); all LT.
- CEL on request Ch 06, Mon-Thu 0800-1700 (1100 Fri).
- CEL ☎+33 (0)5·58·78·18·00; same hrs as previous line.
- Local NMs (AvUrNavs) at HMs' offices and Affaires Maritimes in Arcachon.

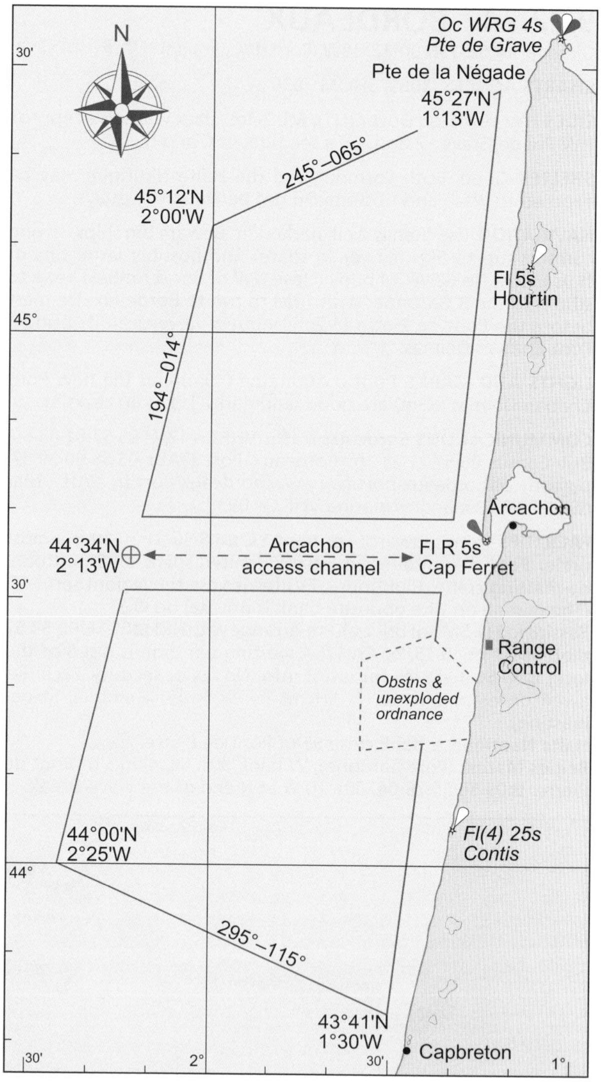

Options:

- Keep clear to seaward of the range. For example, a rhumb line track 200°/173M from PA buoy (22M W of La Rochelle) to Bilbao clears the range by at least 6M.

Subject to notified range activity and monitoring Ch 16:

- Navigate within the 3M wide coastal strip.
- Cross the range when it is usually inactive, ie at night, at weekends and in August.

ARCACHON TO THE SPANISH BORDER

Arcachon is accessible from offshore via an E-W corridor (not normally active) through the Landes range. The entrance to Bassin d'Arcachon and the marina is via the well buoyed, but unlit, Passe Nord between extensive, shifting sandbanks on which the sea breaks even in calm conditions. Study the text for optimum timing, swell and weather conditions before attempting entry (AC 1102, 1343).

▶ *The times of HW and LW occur progressively later from the seaward to the inner ends of the access channel. HW at Arcachon np is 10 mins and at sp is 25 mins after HW Pointe de Grave. LW at np is 20 mins after, and at sp the same as LW Pointe de Grave. Tidal streams in the appr can attain in excess of 4kn on the ebb at sp. N of the town, streams can reach in excess of 3·5kn sp.*◀

It is worth inserting in your GPS the Lat/Long of the key buoys as waypoints; see Lights, buoys and waypoints and also get the latest update from Cap Ferret sig station on Ch 13 or ☎05·56·60·60·03. Positively identify each buoy as you pass it; do not cut corners. Passe Sud is closed to navigation and most of the buoys have been lifted.

Strong N or W winds and swell make the narrow approach chan to the large marina at **Capbreton** impassable. Anglet/Bayonne may then be a safer option; or stay at sea. The Fosse (or Gouf) de Capbreton, a submarine canyon, lies at right angles to the coast. The 50m depth contour is 3ca W of Capbreton hbr bkwtr and the 100m line is 4ca further W. In strong W winds a dangerous sea breaks along the N and S edges of it, but within the very deep waters of the Fosse the sea is relatively calm.

Anglet has a marina, but there are few if any facilities for yachts further up the R. Adour at Bayonne.

▶*At L'Adour entrance the flood runs E and SE from HW Pointe de Grave (PdG) –6½, sp rate 2-4kn. The ebb runs W from HW PdG –½, sp rate 3-5kn. Slack water lasts for a mere 15 mins, after which the rate increases rapidly.*◀

S of Pte St Martin the coast has mostly sandy beaches and rocky cliffs, with offlying rocky shoals and the Pyrenees visible as a backdrop.

St Jean-de-Luz (AC 1343) is best approached for the first time or in bad weather through Passe d'Illarguita (between Illarguita and Belhara Perdun shoals): follow the 138° transit (Le Socoa lt on with Bordagain lt) until the Ste Barbe ldg lts (101°) are in transit; thence enter by Passe de l'Ouest on the 151° transit of the inner hbr ldg lts. In strong W winds the sea breaks on Plateau de St Jean-de-Luz, a chain of rky shoals lying 1-4M offshore.

▶*On the rising tide the incoming stream sets more strongly through the East entrance, then follows the E shore of the Bay to where the R Nivelle enters. In the yacht anchorages in the NW part of the Bay an eddy sets N at about 0·5kn.*

During the falling tide the outgoing flow from La Nivelle sets through the West entrance; the rate in the yacht anchorages is 1kn. Heavy seas in the entrance can stop the flow from leaving the Bay and it continues clockwise around the eastern part of the Bay.◀

Baie de Fontarabie (Rada de Higuer in Spanish) lies on the border of France and Spain and is entered between Pte Ste Anne and Cabo Higuer (a bare, rugged cape with lt ho) 1·75M WNW. In the middle of the bay a neutral area is marked by beacons as shown on AC 1171. To seaward of this area the boundary line (approximately 01°46'·2W) runs N from a white pyramid on the S shore, about 1M SW of Pte Ste Anne.

Les Briquets (dry) lie 1M N of Pte Ste Anne. Keep to W of Banc Chicharvel and Bajo Iruarri in ent to B. Entry should not be attempted with strong onshore winds or heavy swell. R La Bidassoa (Ría de Fuenterrabía in Spanish) is entered between breakwaters in SW corner of the B, giving access to the marina at **Hendaye-Plage**. See Area 23 for the Spanish part of the harbour and the marina at Fuenterrabía.

9.22.27 BASSIN D'ARCACHON

Gironde **44°39'·77N 01°09'·11W** (marina ent) ❀◊◊◊✿✿✿

CHARTS AC 2664; Imray C42; SHOM 6766, 7428; Navi 255, 1024

TIDES +0620 Dover; ML 2·5

Standard Port POINTE DE GRAVE (⟵)

Times				Height (metres)			
High Water		Low Water		MHWS	MHWN	MLWN	MLWS
0000	0600	0000	0500	5·3	4·4	2·1	1·0
1200	1800	1200	1700				
Differences ARCACHON (7 cables WNW of marina)							
+0005	+0020	+0030	+0005	–1·0	–1·0	–0·8	–0·6
CAP FERRET							
–0005	0000	+0020	–0005	–1·1	–1·1	–0·7	–0·4

SHELTER Good in marina. If full, ⚓ N of it, except in strong N'lies. No access to Bassin d'Arcachon in strong SW-N winds or at night.

NAVIGATION WPT 44°33'·048N 01°18'·714W (ATT-ARC SWM buoy) 088°/0·64M to nos 1N & 2N buoys in the well marked N Passe channel. However, **none of these buoys are lit**; a night entry is **not** recommended for first visit. Buoys may at times be off station or missing and are only re-laid annually.

Prior to approach, visitors are urged to make contact with English-speaking *Cap Ferret Semaphore* Ch 16, 13 (HJ) ☎05·56·60·60·03 for a buoyage and navigational updates.

N Passe trends NE then N between Banc d'Arguin and Banc du Toulinguet towards Cap Ferret. The longer S Passe is un-marked and closed to navigation, although some local FVs may still use it. In any wind the sea breaks on the shifting sand banks between Cap Ferret and Wharf de la Salie, but the chan buoys can be seen between the breakers (not as fearsome as it sounds).

Start appr ideally at HW–1 and no later than HW+1. Due to the very strong ebb (6kn sp) the chan bar (mean depth 3·7-4·5m) is impassable from HW+1 until LW, better to wait until LW+3. Best to leave on the last of the flood. When swell is higher than 1m, bar may be dangerous. If in doubt, stay out.

Be aware of any activity in firing ranges between Pte de la Negade and Capbreton, out to 40M offshore; see Landes Range.

LIGHTS AND MARKS ATT-ARC (SWM lt buoy) is moved to show approach to N Passe. See Lights, buoys and waypoints and website Updates for the most recent positions of appr buoys for use as waypoints.

Cap Ferret is low-lying but its white/red lt ho is conspic, as are a water twr close N and the white Sig stn close S. The Dune de Pyla (103m high) on E shore is very conspic, unless hidden in haze.

COMMUNICATIONS Ⓛ 05·56·22·36·75; CROSS 02·97·55·35·35; Auto 08·92·68·08·33; Police 05·56·83·04·63; ⊜ 05·56·72·29·24; Brit Consul 05·57·22·21·10; Ⓗ 05·56·83·39·50; Dr 05·56·83·04·72; HM VHF Ch 09, 16 (H24); Aff Mar 05·57·52·57·07; Sig Stn 05·56·60·60·03.

FACILITIES Marina ☎05·56·22·36·75. plaisance@port-arcachon.com www.arcachon.com 2350+250 Ⓥ; €4·22, 2nd night free. Very crowded in season. Berth/raft on accueil pontoon (35m long); 2 days max stay. There are *very few* Ⓥ berths in Jul/Aug and on any public holiday in summer. Waiting list: 9,000+ applicants and 25+ years!

Extensive moorings (Areas U-Z) along the S shore west of the marina are not for daily use. They are patrolled by police launches.

☎05·56·22·36·74 (0800-1845 Aug; OT 0815-1845) SHOM Ⓔ (45t) (20t).

YC du Bassin d'Arcachon ☎05·56·83·22·11, ✕.

Town ✕ Ⓑ ⇄. Electric minibus into town approx every 20 mins. ✈ Bordeaux. **Ferry** Roscoff/St Malo.

MINOR HARBOURS IN THE ARCACHON BASIN

Around the Basin are many small hbrs which dry LW ±2 or 3hrs, but are worth exploring by shoal draft boats: To the W, La Vigne*, Le Canon, Piquey and Claouey; to the NE, Port de Lège, Arès, Andernos*, Fontainevieille*, Lanton (Cassy) and Audenge*; and to the S, La Teste and Gujan. *See next page. Secondary chans in the Bassin d'Arcachon are marked by piles lettered A to K, clockwise from the N, plus pile number.

LA VIGNE, 44°40′·44N 01°14′·35W. HW time & ht approx as Cap Ferret above; ML 2·4m. See Bassin d'Arcachon. Good shelter, but crowded; beware strong currents across hbr ent. 2 perches mark the ent and on the SW point, a lt Iso R 4s 7m 5M. A small bkwtr (unlit) protrudes into the ent from the NE side. Aff Mar ☎05·56·60·52·76. Facilities: **Marina** ☎05·56·60·54·36. 268 + 2, max LOA 8·5m. (2t).

ANDERNOS, 44°44′·53N 01°06′·54W. HW time & ht approx as Arcachon 9.22.27. Dredged chan to Bétey is marked by lateral poles D0 to D14; thence side chan to Andernos. Ent Fl G 4s and Fl R 4s. Jetty + pontoon for yachts able to dry out, max LOA 12m. Bad silting may occur despite dredging. Also ⚓ on flat drying foreshore. HM ☎05·56·82·00·12. Few facilities.

FONTAINEVIEILLE, 44°43′·30N 01°04′·63W. Tides as Bassin D'Arcachon. Drying marina on NE side of Bassin d'Arcachon, access via Chenal de Mouchtalette. Proceed from E0 PHM pile to E8, where fork left onto NNE for 7ca to hbr ent. No lts. Boats dry out on pontoons. Auto 05·36·65·08·33.

Facilities: **Marina** ☎05·56·82·17·31. 178+ 2.

AUDENGE, 44°40′·58N 01°01′·57W. Tides as 9.22.27. Drying marina and oyster port 5·5M E of Arcachon. Appr from G0 PHM pile via drying Chenal d'Audenge to G8 pile, 5ca short of the ent. Mairie ☎05·56·03·81·50. The Old Port (84 berths) is to the N; the New Port has 130 pontoon berths, YC.

Other drying hbrs: to the NE, Port du Bétey & de Cassy; and E of Arcachon, Ports de La Teste & de La Hume and Port du Teich.

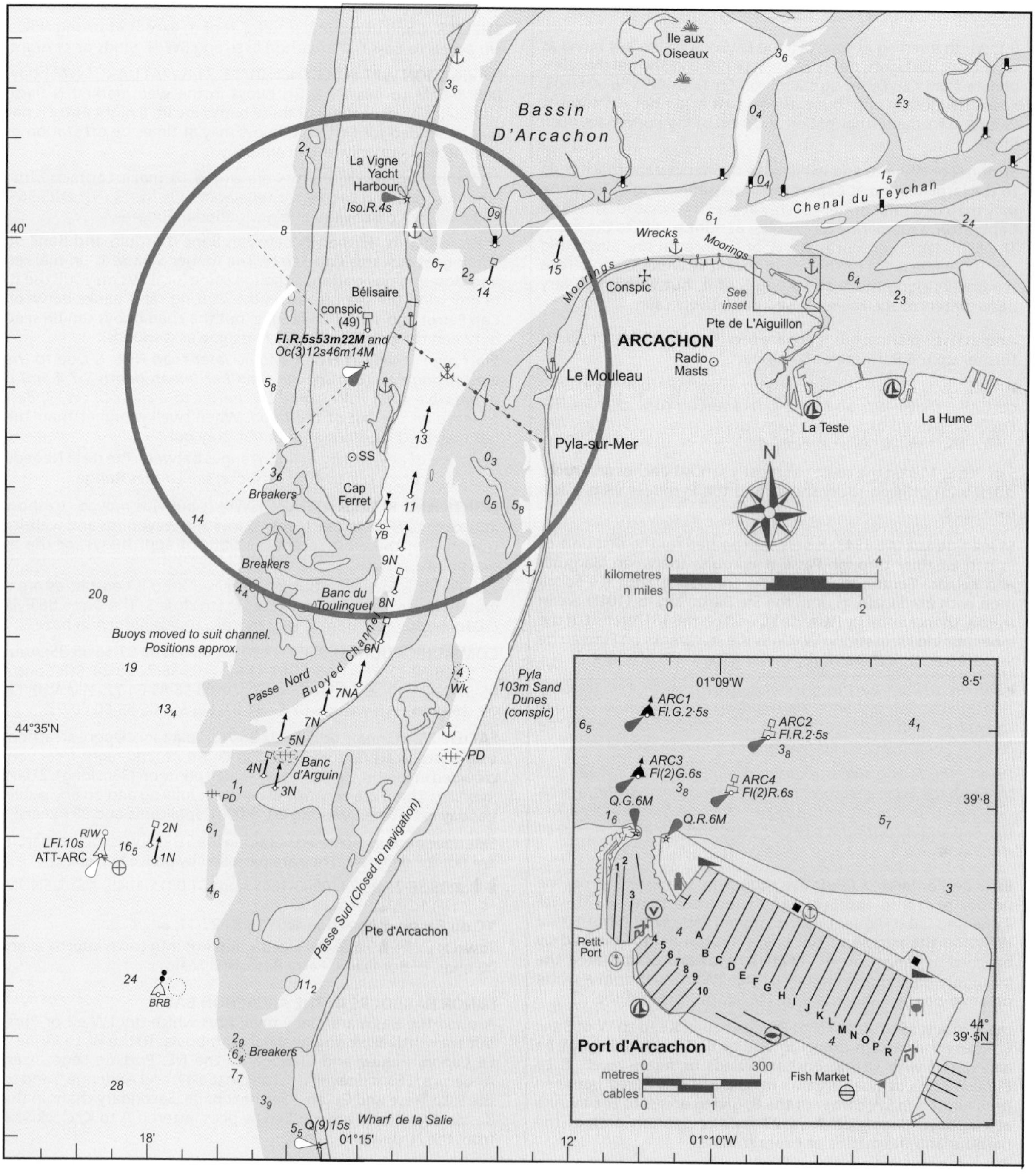

9.22.28 CAPBRETON

Landes **43°39'·34N 01°27'·00W**

CHARTS AC 1102; SHOM 7440; Navi 555, 1024

TIDES +0450 Dover; ML 2·3. Use differences for St Jean de Luz.

SHELTER Good, but the narrow canalised ent (Canal du Boucarot) is dangerous in strong winds from W to N. Do not enter if swell or seas are seen to be breaking in mid-chan, although they often break either side. No ⚓ outside the entrance.

NAVIGATION WPT 43°39'·63N 01°27'·49W, 123°/5ca to N pier lt. Bkwtr lts in line 123° lead to hbr ent. Gouf de Capbreton is a submarine canyon off the hbr ent where in last 3ca depths shoal rapidly from 50m to 3m; see Passage information. Access ±2hr for 2m draft. Silting occurs around head of S jetty, a wooden *estacade* which should be given a wide berth. An obstn 255° S jetty lt 300m is dangerous at LW; take great care.

Inside Canal du Boucarot best water is close to N jetty initially; from abeam small statue of Virgin Mary, move to mid-chan or just S of mid-chan. Marina entrance is via the obvious gap in training wall on SE side of chan, abeam conspic Capitainerie.

LIGHTS AND MARKS A casino and red-roofed sanatorium are conspic S of ent and a water twr 1M ENE. Lts as chartlet and 9.22.4. S jetty lt is on an extension close W of the former lt bcn.

COMMUNICATIONS CROSS 02·97·55·35·35; Auto 08·92·68·08·40; Police 05·59·50·31·52; ⊖ 05·59·46·68·80; Brit Consul 05·57·22·21·10; Ⓗ (Bayonne) 05·59·44·35·35; HM VHF Ch 09 (0700-2100 in season); Aff Mar 05·58·72·10·43.

FACILITIES Marina ☎05·58·72·21·23. www.port-capbreton.com info@port-capbreton.com. The 3 basins are in an inverted Y-shape. Chan and basins dredged 1·5m. 890+60Ⓥ €2·47. Ⓥ pontoon B (2nd to stbd of marina ent). (☎05·58·72·15·66, 0830-1300, 1400-2000) Ⓔ (30t) (1·5t).

CNCP ☎05·58·72·67·09.

Town Ⓑ Bayonne (17km); ✈ Biarritz (25km).

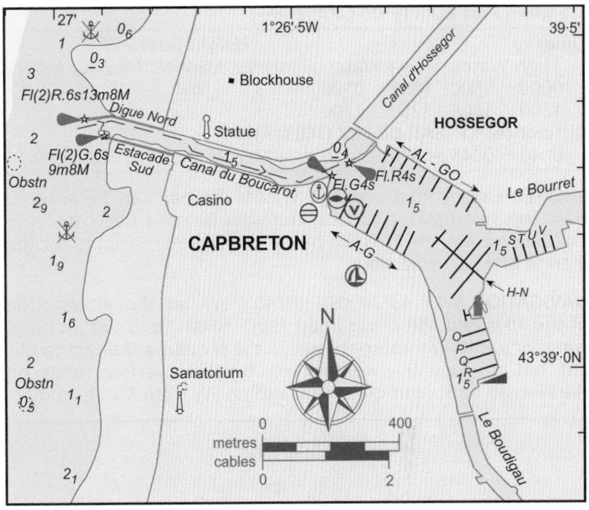

9.22.29 ANGLET/BAYONNE

Pyrénées Atlantique **43°31'·81N 01°31'·95W**

CHARTS AC 1102, 1175; SHOM 7440, 7430; Navi 555

TIDES +0450 Dover (UT); ML 2·5

Standard Port POINTE DE GRAVE (⟵)

Times				Height (metres)			
High Water		Low Water		MHWS	MHWN	MLWN	MLWS
0000	0600	0000	0500	5·3	4·4	2·1	1·0
1200	1800	1200	1700				
Differences L'ADOUR (BOUCAU)							
–0030	–0035	–0040	–0025	–1·1	–1·1	–0·4	–0·3

SHELTER Very good in Anglet Marina, 7ca E of ent on S bank of R Adour, but in NE winds cement dust from the industrial N bank may be a problem. No ⚓ due to commercial ships to which yachts must give way.

NAVIGATION WPT 43°32'·59N 01°32'·76W (BA SWM buoy, L Fl 10s) 142°/0·9M to N bkwtr lt. Easy access except in strong W winds. Strong tidal streams: 1·5-4kn flood, 2·4-5kn at sp ebb.

At Bayonne no passage for masted craft beyond bridge (9·5m clearance); interesting old quarter, 3M upriver on S bank.

LIGHTS AND MARKS Outer ldg lts 090°, both Q, W pylons/R tops. Inner ldg lts 111°, both QG, lit when chan is practicable. 3 more sets of ldg lts upriver to Bayonne. Other lts as chartlet and 9.22.4. Pte St Martin lt ho is 2·45M SSW of hbr.

IPTS (full code) from conspic Sig twr (W, B stripe) S side of ent.

COMMUNICATIONS CROSS 02·97·55·35·35; 05·59·23·84·15; Auto 08·92·65·08·64; ⊖ 05·59·59·08·29; Brit Consul 05·57·22·21·10; Ⓗ 05·59·44·35·35; HM Port 05·59·63·11·57; Port/pilots VHF 12, 16 (0800-1200, 1400-1800LT); Aff Mar 05·59·55·06·68; Marina VHF Ch 09.

FACILITIES Marina ☎05·59·63·05·45, 05·59·63·22·12. portdeplaisance@agglo-bab.fr www.agglo-bab.fr (Port du Brise-Lames; 1·7–3·5m) 367+58Ⓥ €2·38, SHOM Ⓔ (25t) (1·3t).

YC Adour Atlantique ☎05·59·63·16·22.

Bayonne Ⓑ ✈ (Biarritz). **Ferry** Bilbao.

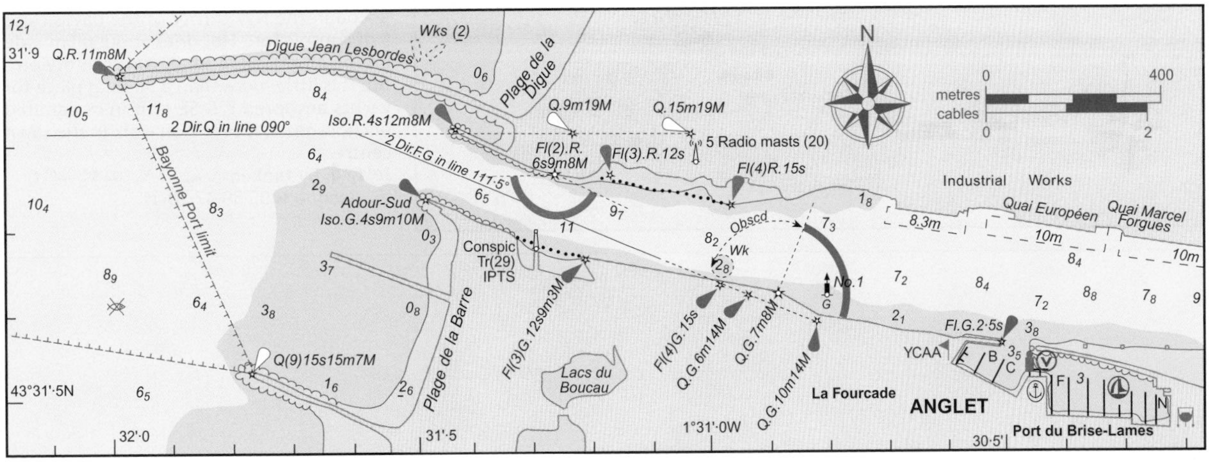

9.22.30 ST JEAN DE LUZ
(Basque name: Donibane Lohizune)

Pyrénées Atlantique, **43°23´·85N 01°40´·61W** ❁❁◊◊✿✿✿

CHARTS AC 1102, 1170; SHOM 7440, 7431; Navi 555

TIDES HW +0435 on Dover (UT); ML 2·5m

Standard Port POINTE DE GRAVE (⟵)

Times				Height (metres)			
High Water		Low Water		MHWS	MHWN	MLWN	MLWS
0000	0600	0000	0500	5·3	4·4	2·1	1·0
1200	1800	1200	1700				
Differences ST JEAN DE LUZ (SOCOA)							
–0040	–0045	–0045	–0030	–1·0	–1·0	–0·5	–0·4

SHELTER Except in strong NW winds, the bay can be entered H24. The 3 designated yacht anchorages (see chartlet) offer safe holding in 2-4m; the SE is less prone to swell. See Facilities for the marina and Socoa harbour.

NAVIGATION WPT 43°24´·09N 01°40´·79W (at the intersection of the 101° and 150·7° ldg lines) 150·7°/500m to W ent. In good weather yachts can approach within the N quadrant direct to hbr ent, but in heavy W'ly weather seas break on various shoals on the Plateau de St Jean-de-Luz, extending SW from Biarritz almost to Hendaye. 3M W of hbr ent and 2M NE of Hendaye, beware Les Briquets rks, drying 0·4m.

The 3 appr chans (outer, middle, inner) are for big ships or smaller craft in bad weather and should be taken in sequence:

Outer chan leads 138° between Illarguita and Belhara Perdun banks. It is the main and only safe approach at night and in bad weather. Ldg lts: Front, Socoa QWR, 12m; W □ twr, B stripes (R sector covers Socoa hbr ent). Rear Q; B ■/W bands on W pylon/B bands, hard to see by day, but the nearby Bordagain twr, 100m, is more readily visible.

Middle chan 101° is intercepted at 43°24´·23N 01°41´·90W. Thence, or if arriving direct from the W, it leads past the hbr's W bkwtr, to the WPT. Ldg lts at Ste Barbe: Both Oc (4) R 12s; front, W △ on W bldg; rear, B ▲ on W twr.

Inner chan leads 150·7° from the WPT through the W ent into the bay and via a buoyed chan to St Jean de Luz hbr. Ldg lts: Both Dir QG, conspic white twrs: front has a R vert stripe; rear, a G vert stripe.

The unmarked E ent to the bay is used by locals, but is not recommended. Beware: a large unlit mooring buoy S of Digue d'Artha, antipollution booms off the SW and SE beaches and an unmarked submerged jetty in the SE corner of bay.

Speed limits: in the bay 7kn; port area 5kn. Ent/exit the port only under power. FVs tend to ent/exit the FV hbr at speed and with much wash in the narrow access channel.

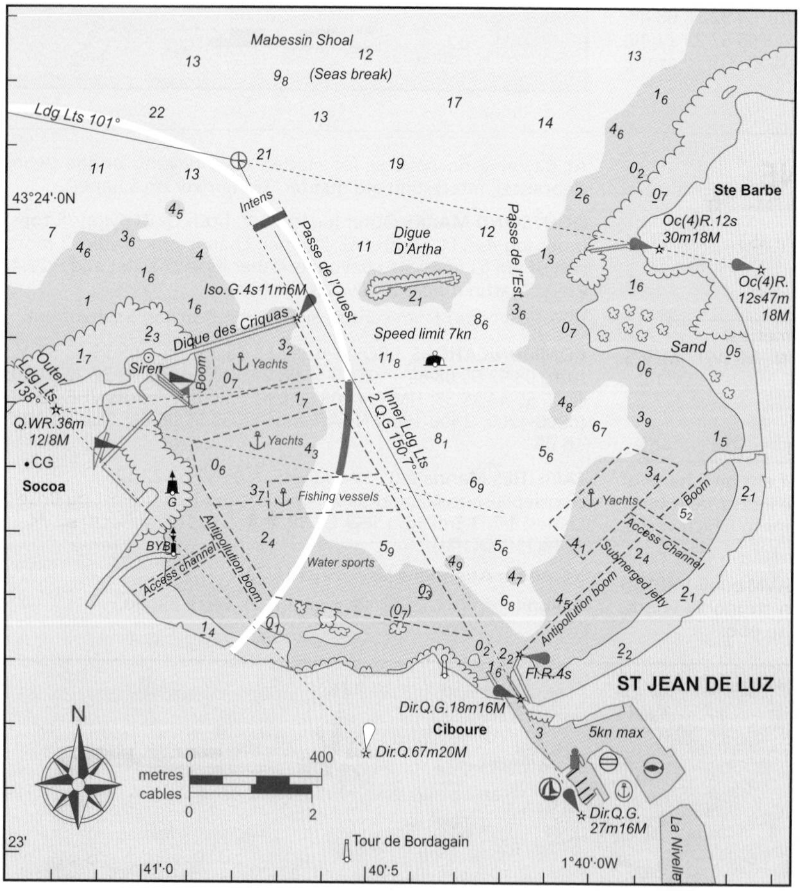

Mabessin Shoal
(Seas break)
Ldg Lts 101°
43°24'·0N
Intens
Passe de l'Ouest
Digue D'Artha
Passe de l'Est
Ste Barbe
Oc(4)R.12s 30m18M
Oc(4)R. 12s47m 18M
Iso.G.4s11m6M
Digue des Criquas
Speed limit 7kn
Sand
Outer Ldg Lts 138°
Siren
Boom
Yachts
Q.WR.36m 12/8M
•CG
Socoa
Inner Ldg Lts 2 Q.G 150·7°
Fishing vessels
Antipollution boom
Access channel
BYB
Water sports
Access Channel
Submerged jetty
Antipollution boom
Fl.R.4s
ST JEAN DE LUZ
Dir.Q.G.18m16M
Ciboure
5kn max
Dir.Q.67m20M
N
metres
cables
0
400
2
Dir.Q.G. 27m16M
La Nivelle
Tour de Bordagain
23'
41'·0
40'·5
1°40'·0W

LIGHTS AND MARKS La Rhune, an 898m high conical mountain bears 160°/5·5M from the W ent; conspic in good visibility. Digue des Criquas (the W bkwtr) is lit, Iso G 4s. Digue d'Artha is a detached unlit bkwtr across the middle of the bay. See chartlet and Lights, buoys and waypoints for details.

COMMUNICATIONS CROSS 02·97·55·35·35; LB 05·59·47·22·98; ☼ 05·59·22·03·30; Auto 08·92·68·08·64; Police 05·59·26·01·55; Brit Consul 05.57.22.21.10; Aff Mar 05·59·47·14·55; Marina Ch 09, 16; 0700-1230 & 1400-2000 in season.

FACILITIES

ST JEAN DE LUZ Marina ☎05·59·47·26·81, 05·59·47·86·11. Small facility (2·5m) 73+8Ⓥ max LOA 16m; €3·03. at Ciboure, in Bassin de Larraldénia, close to rear 150·7° ldg lt and W and SW of the FV hbr. Berth/raft on hammerheads of the first 2 pontoons, or as directed. East of the pontoons beware the long slipway marked by 2 PHM bcns. by tanker, Ⓔ (6t).

Town Ⓑ.

Socoa in the NW corner of the bay is close S of conspic fort. Hbr dries about 0·5m; tide gauge at ent. Here small craft can dry out, but it is little more than a landing place for yachts anchored E & SE of it in designated anchorages. It is over 2km walk to the town centre.

Jetty by tanker, (1t).

YC Basque ☎05·59·47·18·31.

9.22.31 HENDAYE

Pyrénées Atlantique **43°22′·75N 01°47′·28W**

CHARTS AC 1102, 1170; SHOM 7440, 7431; Navi 555

TIDES HW +0450 on Dover (UT); ML 2·3m
Use differences ST JEAN DE LUZ (SOCOA).

SHELTER Excellent in marina. Access H24, but exposed to N/NE and S/SW gales. Possible ⚓ in river or the Baie de Chingoudy but both are overcrowded. A Spanish port of refuge (2-3m) lies S of C Higuer, for FVs rather than for yachts. Note: Fuenterrabía (Hondarrabia, Area 23) is Spanish. See chartlet for neutral zone.

NAVIGATION WPT 43°23′·81N 01°46′·51W, 212°/1·15M to W bkwtr hd. Beware Les Briquets 8ca N of Pte Ste Anne at E end of the Baie; near centre of B, keep clear of Bajo Iruarri. River ent 6·5-1·3m is easy except in heavy N'ly swell; sp ebb is very strong. Inshore of Pte des Dunes, Fl R 2·5s, hug the E training wall for best water. A spit drying 1·3m (SHM bn, VQ (3) G 5s) off Fuenterrabía narrows the chan to about 100m wide before the marina ent opens.

LIGHTS AND MARKS La Rhune, a 900m high conical mountain, is conspic in good vis 8M ESE of hbr. Cabo Higuer lt ho is conspic at W side of bay on a rugged headland.

COMMUNICATIONS CROSS 02·97·55·35·35; 05·59·24·58·80; Auto 08·92·68·08·64; Police 05·59·50·31·52; ⊖ 05·59·48·10·68; Brit Consul 05·57·22·21·10; Ⓗ 05·59·20·08·22; Aff Mar 05·59·47·14·55; Marina VHF Ch 09 (H24).

FACILITIES

Marina ☎05·59·48·06·10. www.hendaye-tourisme.fr station.littorale@hendaye.com (2·5-3m) 803 + 50Ⓥ €3·10 (3rd night free) is entered close W of a Fl Y 4s and a conspic RW TV relay mast (40m). Accueil pontoon A in NW corner. (H24) Ⓔ @ (30t).

YC ☎05·59·20·03·02.

Town ✕ Ⓑ ⇌ (TGV Paris-Madrid) ✈ Fuenterrabía, or for UK flights Biarritz (☎05·59·43·83·83). Local ferry from Hendaye to Fuenterrabía every 15 mins. UK ferry from Bilbao or Santander.

Fuenterrabía Marina, see Area 23.

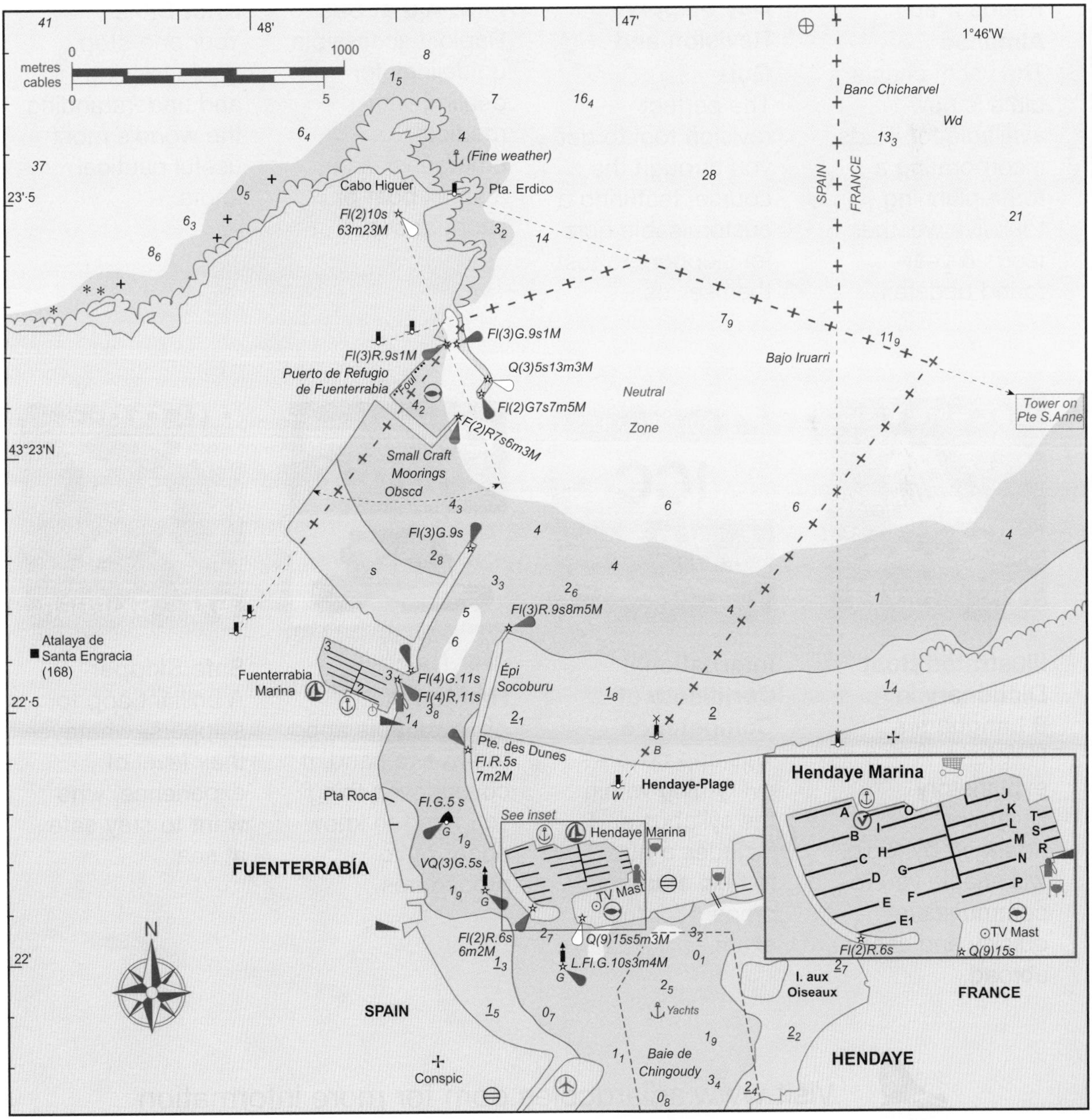

N & NW Spain

Fuenterrabía to Bayona

9.23.1 Contents ... 953
9.23.2 Area map and Distance table ... 954
9.23.3 Lights, buoys and waypoints ... 956
9.23.4 Passage information ... 959
Bay of Biscay: Wind, Weather and Sea – 959 • Crossing the Bay of Biscay – 959 • French Border to Santander – 959 • Santander to Cabo Ortegal – 966 • Cabo Ortegal to Cabo Finisterre – 971 • Cabo Finisterre to the Portuguese Border – 979
9.23.5 Special notes for Spain ... 959
9.23.6 Fuenterrabía ... 960
9.23.7 Pasajes ... 960
9.23.8 San Sebastián ... 961
Ría de Orio
9.23.9 Guetaria ... 961
9.23.10 Zumaya ... 962
Motrico
9.23.11 Lequeitio ... 962
9.23.12 Elanchove ... 963
Bermeo
9.23.13 Bilbao ... 963
9.23.14 Castro Urdiales ... 964
9.23.15 Laredo ... 965
Santoña
9.23.16 Santander ... 965
Suances
9.23.17 San Vicente de la Barquera ... 967
9.23.18 Ribadesella ... 967
Llanes
9.23.19 Lastres ... 968
9.23.20 Gijón ... 968
Avilés • San Esteban de Pravia
9.23.21 Cudillero ... 969
9.23.22 Luarca ... 969
9.23.23 Ría de Ribadeo ... 970
9.23.24 Ría de Viveiro ... 970
9.23.25 Ría de Cedeira ... 971
Ría del Barquero • Ensenada de Santa Marta de Ortigueira
9.23.26 Ferrol ... 972
9.23.27 Ría de Ares ... 972
9.23.28 Ría de Betanzos ... 973
9.23.29 La Coruña, tide tables/curves ... 974
9.23.30 Ría de Corme y Laxe ... 978
9.23.31 Ría de Camariñas ... 978
Finisterre • Ensenada del Sardineiro • Ría de Corcubión
9.23.32 Ría de Muros ... 981
9.23.33 Ría de Arosa ... 981
9.23.34 Ría de Pontevedra ... 983
9.23.35 Ría de Vigo ... 984
9.23.36 Bayona ... 986

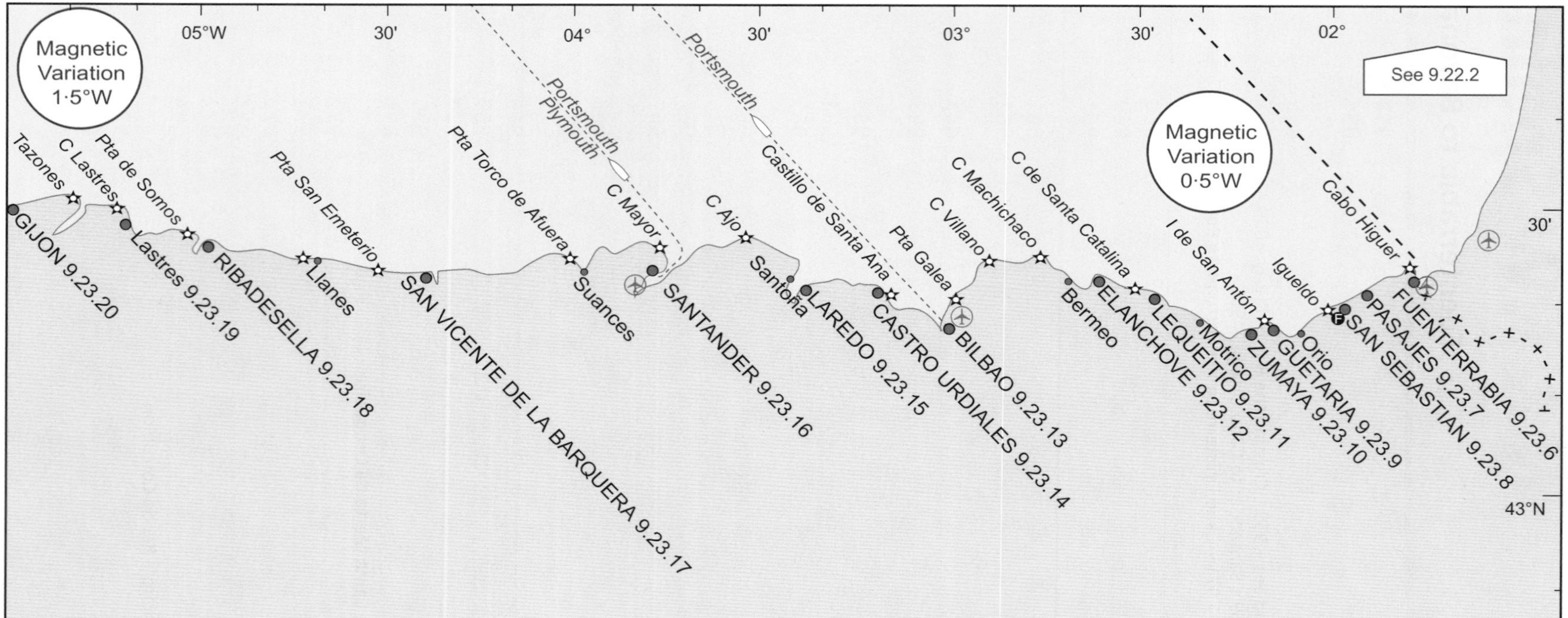
Magnetic Variation 1·5°W
Magnetic Variation 0·5°W
See 9.22.2
05°W
30'
04°
30'
03°
30'
02°
30'
43°N
30'
42°N
Portsmouth
Plymouth
Portsmouth
Tazones
GIJON 9.23.20
C Lastres
Lastres 9.23.19
Pta de Somos
RIBADESELLA 9.23.18
Pta San Emeterio
Llanes
SAN VICENTE DE LA BARQUERA 9.23.17
Pta Torco de Afuera
Suances
C Mayor
SANTANDER 9.23.16
C Ajo
Santoña
Castillo de Santa Ana
LAREDO 9.23.15
CASTRO URDIALES 9.23.14
Pta Galea
BILBAO 9.23.13
C Villano
C Machichaco
Bermeo
C de Santa Catalina
ELANCHOVE 9.23.12
LEQUEITIO 9.23.11
Motrico
I de San Antón
ZUMAYA 9.23.10
GUETARIA 9.23.9
Orio
Igueldo
SAN SEBASTIAN 9.23.8
PASAJES 9.23.7
Cabo Higuer
FUENTERRABIA 9.23.6

		1	2	3	4	5	6	7	8	9	10	11	12	13	14	15	16	17	18	19	20
1	*Le Conquet*	**1**																			
2	*Fuenterrabia*	330	**2**																		
3	San Sebastian	326	13	**3**																	
4	Zumaya	322	23	13	**4**																
5	C. Machichaco	308	44	34	20	**5**															
6	Bilbao (ent)	311	63	58	39	19	**6**														
7	Santander	300	92	82	63	48	39	**7**													
8	S. Vicente de la B	300	116	108	93	77	63	38	**8**												
9	Gijon	293	171	160	147	128	115	90	56	**9**											
10	Cabo Penas	286	179	168	154	135	123	97	63	12	**10**										
11	Ribadeo	306	224	213	199	180	176	150	128	65	53	**11**									
12	Vivero	308	250	239	225	206	202	176	143	92	80	33	**12**								
13	C. Ortegal	305	267	256	242	215	211	185	151	100	88	41	18	**13**							
14	La Coruña	340	305	294	280	253	249	223	189	138	126	79	56	38	**14**						
15	Cabo Villano	380	342	337	317	290	286	260	226	213	163	116	93	75	45	**15**					
16	Muros	402	380	369	355	328	324	298	264	251	201	154	131	113	83	38	**16**				
17	Vilagarcia	442	420	409	395	368	364	338	304	291	241	194	171	153	123	78	40	**17**			
18	Sanxenxo	449	427	416	402	375	371	345	311	298	248	201	178	160	130	85	42	26	**18**		
19	Vigo	453	434	423	409	382	378	352	318	305	255	208	185	167	137	92	35	35	18	**19**	
20.	Bayona	453	434	423	409	382	378	352	318	305	255	208	185	167	137	92	35	36	19	11	**20**

DISTANCE TABLE

Approximate distances in nautical miles are by the most direct route, whilst avoiding dangers and allowing for Traffic Separation Schemes. See also Distance Table at 9.24.2.

9.23.2

North & West Spain

Fuenterrabia to Bayona

- ● *Harbour with full almanac entry*
- • *Minor harbour or anchorage*
- ☆ *Major light*
- ◉RG *Emergency RDF station*
- *Ferry route*
- *Airport*

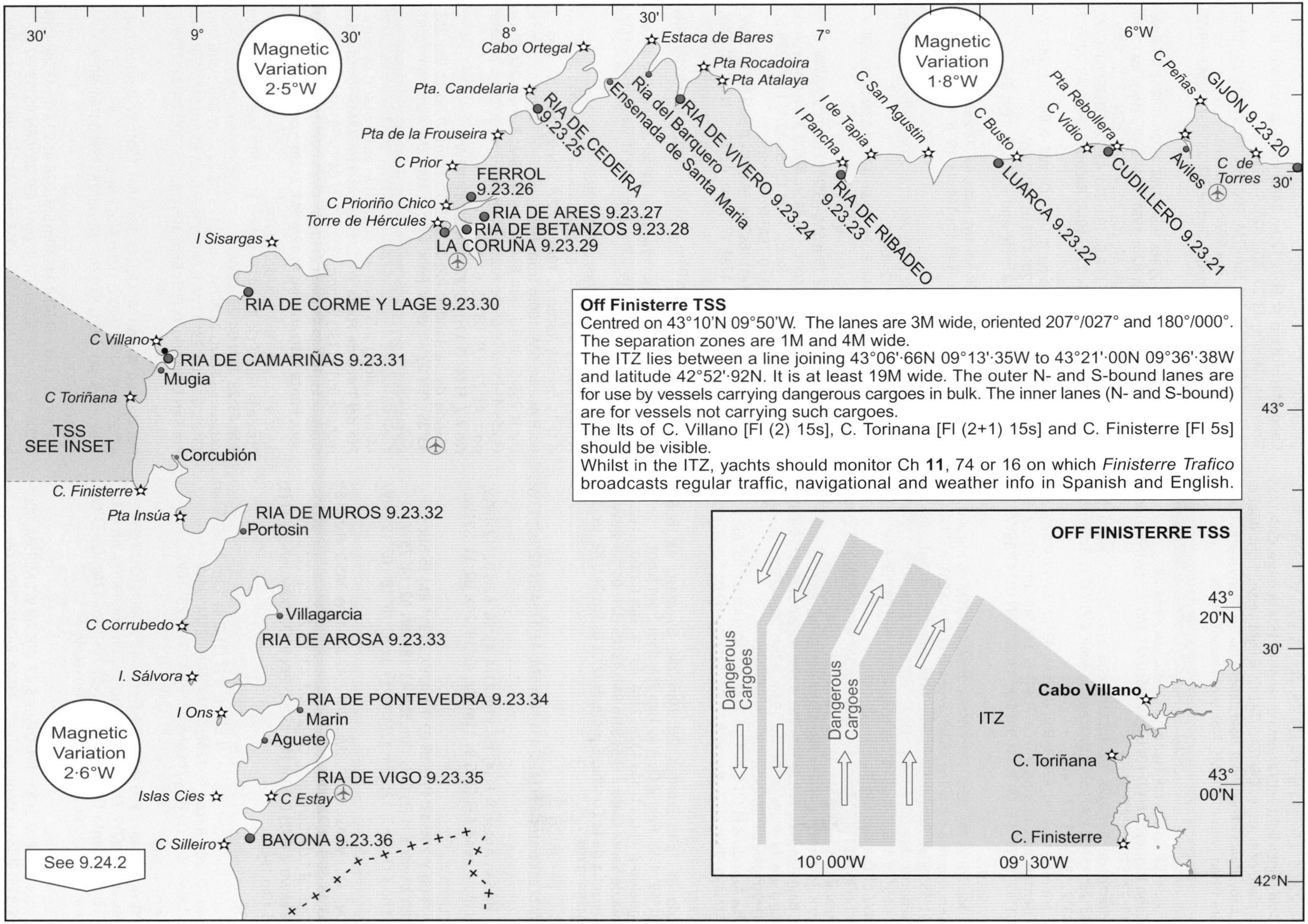
30'
9°
30'
8°
30'
7°
6°W
30'
43°
30'
42°N
Magnetic Variation 2·5°W
Magnetic Variation 1·8°W
Magnetic Variation 2·6°W
Cabo Ortegal
Estaca de Bares
Pta Rocadoira
Pta Atalaya
Pta. Candelaria
RIA DE CEDEIRA 9.23.25
Ensenada de Santa Maria
Ria del Barquero
RIA DE VIVERO 9.23.24
I de Tapia
I Pancha
RIA DE RIBADEO 9.23.23
C San Agustin
C Busto
LUARCA 9.23.22
C Vidio
Pta Rebollera
CUDILLERO 9.23.21
C Peñas
GIJON 9.23.20
Aviles
C de Torres
Pta de la Frouseira
C Prior
FERROL 9.23.26
C Prioriño Chico
Torre de Hércules
RIA DE ARES 9.23.27
RIA DE BETANZOS 9.23.28
LA CORUÑA 9.23.29
I Sisargas
RIA DE CORME Y LAGE 9.23.30
C Villano
RIA DE CAMARIÑAS 9.23.31
Mugia
C Toriñana
TSS SEE INSET
Corcubión
C. Finisterre
Pta Insúa
RIA DE MUROS 9.23.32
Portosin
Villagarcia
C Corrubedo
RIA DE AROSA 9.23.33
I. Sálvora
RIA DE PONTEVEDRA 9.23.34
I Ons
Marin
Aguete
RIA DE VIGO 9.23.35
Islas Cies
C Estay
C Silleiro
BAYONA 9.23.36
See 9.24.2

Off Finisterre TSS

Centred on 43°10'N 09°50'W. The lanes are 3M wide, oriented 207°/027° and 180°/000°. The separation zones are 1M and 4M wide.

The ITZ lies between a line joining 43°06'·66N 09°13'·35W to 43°21'·00N 09°36'·38W and latitude 42°52'·92N. It is at least 19M wide. The outer N- and S-bound lanes are for use by vessels carrying dangerous cargoes in bulk. The inner lanes (N- and S-bound) are for vessels not carrying such cargoes.

The lts of C. Villano [Fl (2) 15s], C. Torinana [Fl (2+1) 15s] and C. Finisterre [Fl 5s] should be visible.

Whilst in the ITZ, yachts should monitor Ch **11**, 74 or 16 on which *Finisterre Trafico* broadcasts regular traffic, navigational and weather info in Spanish and English.

OFF FINISTERRE TSS
Dangerous Cargoes
Dangerous Cargoes
ITZ
Cabo Villano
C. Toriñana
C. Finisterre
43° 20'N
43° 00'N
10° 00'W
09° 30'W

9.23.3 LIGHTS, BUOYS AND WAYPOINTS

Bold print = light with a nominal range of 15M or more. CAPITALS = place or feature. *CAPITAL ITALICS* = light-vessel, light float or Lanby. *Italics* = Fog signal. ***Bold italics*** = Racon. Many marks/buoys are fitted with AIS (MMSI No); see relevant charts.

FUENTERRABÍA TO SANTANDER

FUENTERRABÍA For Hendaye lts etc, see Area 22.
Cabo Higuer ☆ Fl (2) 10s 63m **23M**; 072°-340°; □ twr, R cupola; 43°23'·52N 01°47'·52W.
Puerto de Refugio, NE bkwtr head ✧ Fl (2) G 7s 7m 5M; 43°23'·13N 01°47'·35W.W training wall ✧ Fl (3) G 9s 9m 5M; 43°22'·83N 01°47'·34W.
E training wall hd ✧ Fl (3) R 9s 8m 5M; 43°22'·67N 01°47'·23W.
Fuenterrabía marina ent, ✧ Fl (4) G 11s 9m 3m; 43°22'·59N 01°47'·51W. ✧ Fl (4) R 11s 9m 1M; 43°22'·56N 01°47'56W.

PASAJES
Mo (A) 7s 7M; 43°21'·31N 01°56'·28W; 166°/1M to hbr ent.
Senocozulúa lts in line 154·8° **Front** ☆ Q 67m **18M**; 43°19'·89N 01°55'·60W. **Rear** ☆ Oc 3s 86m **18M**, 40m from front.
Senocozulúa Dir ✧ 154·5°: Oc (2) WRG 12s 50m 10M; 152·5°-G-154·5°-W-156·5°-R-161·5°; W twr; 43°19'·90N 01°55'·61W, close NW of the two ldg lts.
Inner ldg lts 114·3°: Front ✧ Iso R 4s 13m 5M; 43°19'·70N 01°55'·30W. Rear ✧ Q R 1s 34m 5M; 43°19'·55N 01°55'·16W.
W Bajo Bancha Fl G 5s 7M; 43°20'·24N 01°55'·88W.
E Bajo Bancha Fl R 5s 16m 7M; R twr; 43°20'·22N 01°55'·65W.
Faro de la Plata ✧ Oc 4s 153m 13M; 285°-250°; W bldg; 43°20'·08N 01°56'·04W (W side of ent).
Pta Arando ✧ Fl (2) R 7s 12m 11M; 43°20'·14N 01°55'·68W
Atalaya, 96m; IPTS; ***Racon K, 20M***; 43°20'·11N 01°55'·47W.

SAN SEBASTIÁN
Ldg lts 158°: Front ✧ QR 10m 7M; Gy mast; 43°18'·85N 01°59'·45W. Rear ✧ Oc R 4s 16m 7M; 25m from front.
Igueldo ☆ Fl (2+1) 15s 132m **26M**; 43°19'·36N 02°00'·61W.
Isla de Santa Clara ✧ Fl 5s 51m 9M; 43°19'·32N 01°59'·89W.
Dársena de la Concha, E mole, Fl (2) G 8s 9m 3M; 43°19'·34N 01°59'·37W.

RÍO DE ORIO
W breakwater ✧ Fl (4) G 11s 18m 5M; 43°17'·49N 02°08'·13W.

GUETARIA
I. de San Antón ☆ Fl (4) 15s 91m **21M**; 43°18'·62N 02°12'·08W.
N mole head ✧ Fl (3) G 9s 11m 5M; 43°18'·24N 02°11'·891W.

ZUMAYA
Fl (5) Y 20s; 43°19'·83N 02°13'·47W, 213°/1·8M to hbr ent.
NW bkwtr ✧ Fl (2) G 7s 18m 5M; 43°18'·38N 02°14'·75W.
Lt ho ✧ Oc (1+3) 12s 39m 12M; Port sigs; 43°18'·18N 02°15'·08W.

MOTRICO
Dir Oc WRG 12m 3M; 241.2°-G-244·1°-W-245·9°-R-248·8°; 43°18'·50N 02°22'·80W.
Central Tidal Barrage Q 18m 3M; 43°18'·75N 02°22'·60W.
N bkwtr ✧ Fl (2) G 10m 1M; 43°18'·59N 02°22'·80W. Inner ✧ Fl (3) G 10m 1M.

ONDÁRROA
Punta Barracomuturra, N bkwtr ✧ Fl (3) G 8s 13m 12M; *Siren Mo (O) 20s*; ***Racon G, 12M***; 43°19'·54N 02°24'·94W.
S bkwtr ✧ Fl (2) R 6s 7m 6M; 43°19'·49N 02°25'·10W.

LEQUEITIO
Pta Amandarri ✧ Fl G 4s 8m 5M; Gy twr; 43°22'·00N 02°29'·93W.
Aislado, Fl (2) R 8s 5m 4M; Gy bcn. Basin ent: FR/FG 7m 4M.
Cabo de Santa Catalina ☆ Fl (1+3) 20s 44m **17M**; Gy ○ twr; *Horn Mo (L) 20s;* 43°22'·63N 02°30'·60W.

ELANCHOVE
Digue N ✧ Fl G 3s 8m 4M. Digue S ✧ F WR 7m W8M,R5M; 000°-W-315°-R (over dangers)-000°; 43°24'·24N 02°38'·23W.

BERMEO
Cabo Machichaco ☆ Fl 7s 120m **24M**; lookout twr and bldg; *Siren Mo (M) 60s;* 43°27'·30N 02°45'·19W.
Rosape ✧ Fl (2) WR 10s 36m 7M; 108°-R-204°-W-232°; W bldg; 43°25'·07N 02°42'·76W, 3ca SSW of hbr ent.
N bkwtr ✧ Fl G 4·5s 16m 4M; Gy twr; 43°25'·39N 02°42'·59W.

BILBAO
C. Villano (Gorliz) ☆ Fl (1+2) 16s 163m **22M**; 43°26'·03N 02°56'·63W.
Punta Galea ☆ Fl (3) 8s 82m **19M**; 011°-227°; stone twr with dwelling, Gy cupola; *Siren Mo (G) 30s;* 43°22'·30N 03°02'·13W.
E bkwtr hd (detached) ✧ Fl R 5s 19m 7M; 43°22'·77N 03°04'·67W.
W bkwtr head ✧ Fl G 5s 21m 10M; ***Racon X, 20M***; 43°22'·67N 03°05'·04W.
Contradique de Algorta dir lt 142°, Oc WR 4s 9m 3M; 134°-W-149°-R-174°; Gy col; 43°20'·47N 03°01'·21W.
Contradique de Algorta mole end ✧ Fl R 5s 18m 3M, W twr; 43°20'·51N 03°01'·67W.
Getxo marina bkwtr ✧ QR 5m 1M, R col; 43°20'·23N 03°01'·03W.
Las Arenas marina ✧ Oc G 4s 1m 1M; 43°19'·83N 03°00'·98W.

CASTRO URDIALES
Castillo de Santa Ana ☆ Fl (4) 24s 47m **20M**; W twr; *Siren Mo (C) 60s;* 43°23'·07N 03°12'·88W.
N bkwtr ✧ Fl G 3s 12m 6M; 8-sided twr; 43°22'·87N 03°12'·54W.

LAREDO and RIA DE SANTOÑA
Laredo N bkwtr ✧ Fl R 5s 15m 5M; 43°25'·11N 03°25'·17W.
Santoña ldg lts 283·5°: Front, ✧ Fl 2s 5m 8M; B ▼ on framework; 43°26'·34N 03°27'·60W. Rear, ✧ Oc (2) 5s 12m 11M; 279·5°-287·5°; ○ on framework; 0·75M from front.
Pta Pescador lt ho ✧ Fl (3+1) 18s 37m 9M;43°27'·90N 03°26'·17W.
C. Ajo ☆ Oc (3) 16s 69m **17M**; W ○ twr; 43°30'·67N 03°35'·73W.

SANTANDER
Cabo Mayor ☆ Fl (2) 10s 89m **21M**; W ○ twr; *Horn Mo (M) 40s;* 43°29'·42N 03°47'·45W.
Isla de Mouro ✧ Fl (3) 16s 37m 11M; 43°28'·40N 03°45'·35W.
La Cerda ✧ Fl (1+4) 20s 22m 7M; obsc'd when brg <160°; 43°28'·01N 03°45'·83W.
No 1 Fl G 5s; 43°27'·73N 03°46'·22W.
Punta Rabiosa ldg lts 235·8°, both intens 231·8°-239·8°: Front ✧ Q 1s 7m 6M; ***Racon K, 10M***; 43°27'·52N 03°46'·43W. Rear ✧ Iso R 4s 10m 6M, 100m from front.
Dir lt 259·5°, WRG 18m 6M; 257·8°-Fl G-258·3°-FG-258·8°-Oc G-259·4°-FW-259·6°-Oc R-260·2°-FR-260·7°-Fl R-261·2°; metal post; 43°27'·33N 03°48'·61W.
No 7 Fl (4) G 11s; 43°27'·46N 03°47'·98W.
Marina de Santander, ldg lts 235·6°: Front ✧ Iso 2s 9m 2M; 43°25'·75N 03°48'·84W. Rear ✧ Oc 5s 10m 2M; 46m from front.

SANTANDER TO CABO PEÑAS

Many lts along this coast are so high as to be obsc'd by mist.
Pta del Torco de Fuera ☆ Fl (1+2) 24s 33m **22M**; obsc'd close inshore 091°-113°; W twr; 43°26'·51N 04°02'·61W.
Suances ldg lts 149·5°: Front ✧ Fl 2s 8m 5M; 43°26'·19N 04°02'·08W. Rear, Punta Marzán ✧ Iso 4s 12m 5M; 212m from front.

SAN VICENTE DE LA BARQUERA
Pta de la Silla ✧ Oc 3·5s 41m 13M; 115°-250°; twr; *Horn Mo (V) 30s;* 43°23'·58N 04°23'·56W.
W bkwtr ✧ Fl WG 2s W7M, G6M; 175°-G-225°-W-045°; W/G twr; 43°23'·71N 04°23'·11W. E bkwtr ✧ Fl (2) R 8s 6m 5M; W/R twr.
Pta San Emeterio ☆ Fl 5s 66m **20M**; 43°23'·90N 04°32'·20W.

LLANES
Pta de San Antón ☆ Oc (4) 30s 16m **15M**; W 8-sided twr; 43°25'·21N 04°44'·88W, 150m S of hbr ent.
N bkwtr (Osa) ✧ Fl G 5s 13m 5M; 43°25'·18N 04°44'·90W.

RIBADESELLA
Pta del Caballo ✧ Fl (4) R 11s 10m 5M; 278·4°-212·9°; 43°28'·08N 05°03'·98W. Fl R 5s 7m 3M; R post; 43° 28'·06N 05°03'·92W.
Somos ☆ Fl (2+1) 12s 113m **25M**; twr; 43°28'·36N 05°04'·97W.

LASTRES

E bkwtr ☆ Fl (3) G 9s 13m 4M; 43°30'·89N 05°15'·90W.
C. Lastres ☆ Fl (5) 25s 116m **23M**. W ○ twr; 43°32'·04N 05°18'·02W.
Tazones ☆ Fl 7·5s 127m **20M**; W 8-sided twr; 43°32'·87N 05°23'·94W. Bkwtr head, ☆ Fl (2) G 7s 10m 5M.

GIJÓN

El Musel, NE mole ☆ Fl (2+1) G 10s 22m 7M; 43°34'·26N 05°40'·58W.
Piedra Sacramento ▲ Fl (2) G 6s 11m 5M; 8-sided twr; 43°32'·83N 05°40'·30W. Marina ent ☆ Fl (2) R 6s 9m 3M; 43°32'·79N 05°40'·21W.
Cabo de Torres ☆ Fl (2) 10s 80m **18M**; 43°34'·31N 05°41'·96W.
Puerto de Candás ☆ Oc (2)10s 38m **15M**; R twr, W ho; *Horn Mo (C) 60s;* 43°35'·66N 05°45'·65W.
Punta del Cuerno ☆ Dir Fl WRG 4s 20m 3M; 284°-R-286°-W-288°-G-290°; R/W col; 43°35'·69N 05°45'·61W
N bkwtr hd ☆ Fl (3) G 9s 11m 3M.
Luanco ldg lts 255°: Front, inner bkwtr ☆ Fl G 5s 3m 5M; 43°36'·91N 05°47'·36W. Rear ☆ Oc G 4s 6m 5M, 200m from front.
Cabo Peñas ☆ Fl (3) 15s 115m **35M**; Gy 8-sided twr; 43°39'·33N 05°50'·92W.

CABO PEÑAS TO PUNTA DE LA ESTACA DE BARES

Avilés, Pta de la Forcada ☆ Fl R 5s 23m 7M; R mast on W truncated twr; 43°35'·82N 05°56'·84W.
Pta del Castillo ☆ Oc WR 5s 38m **W20, R17M**; 091·5°-R-113°-W-091·5°; W □ twr; 43°35'·72N 05°56'·72W. ☆ Fl (2) R 7s is 30m SW.
Ent chan, S side ☆ Fl (2) G 7s 12m 5M; 106°-280°; W ○ twr, G band; 43°35'·57N 05°56'·49W. ☆ Fl G 5s 15m 5M is 390m west.
San Estaban de Pravia, W bkwtr ☆ Fl (2) 12s 19m **15M**; W ○ twr, B bands; *Siren Mo (N) 30s;* 43°34'·21N 06°04'·64W.
Ldg lts 206·2°: Front, Q 7m 1M; W twr, R bands; 43°34'·05N 06°04'·71W. Rear, Iso 4s 28m 1M; W pylon, R bands; 206·2°/360m.
Cudillero, Pta Rebollera ☆ Oc (4) 16s 42m **16M**; W 8-sided twr; *Siren Mo (D) 30s;* 43°33'·96N 06°08'·68W. N bkwtr ☆ Fl (3) G 9s.
Cabo Vidio ☆ Fl 5s 99m **25M;** ○ twr; 43°35'·62N 06°14'·61W.
Cabo Busto ☆ Fl (4) 20s 84m **25M**; 43°34'·15N 06°28'·17W.

LUARCA

Punta Altaya ☆ Oc (3) 15s 63m 14M; W □ twr; *Siren Mo (L) 30s;* 43°32'·98N 06°31'·95W.
Ldg lts 170°, both W cols, R bands: Front ☆ Fl 5s 19m 3M; 43°32'·78N 06°32'·11W. Rear ☆ Oc 4s 26m 3M; 41m from front.
W Dique ☆ Fl (3) G 9s 6m 3M; 43°32'·96N 06°32'·24W.
Cabo de San Agustín ☆ Oc (2) 12s 70m **25M**; W ○ twr, B bands; 43°33'·81N 06°44'·05W.
C. San Sebastían ☆ Fl (2+1) 19s 22m **18M**; 43°34'·43N 06°56'·75W.

RÍA DE RIBADEO

Punta de la Cruz ☆ Fl (4) R 11s 16m 7M; 43°33'·39N 07°01'·74W.
Isla Pancha ☆ Fl (3+1) 20s 26m **21M**; W ○ twr, B bands; 43°33'·39N 07°02'·52W, W side of entrance.
1st ldg lts 140°, both R ◇s, W twrs. Front, Pta Arroxo ☆ Iso R 18m 5M; 43°32'·81N 07°01'·52W. Rear ☆ Oc R 4s 24m 5M; 228m SE.
2nd ldg lts 205°. Front, Muelle de García ☆ VQ R 8m 3M; R ◇, W twr; 43°32'·49N 07°02'·23W. Rear ☆ Oc R 2s 18m 3M.
Marina, ☆ Fl G 5s 9m 3M; 43°32'·45N 07°02'·16W. ☆ Fl R 5s 9m 1M.
Punta Atalya (San Ciprian) ☆ Fl (5) 20s 39m **20M**; W ○ twr, B band; 43°42'·03N 07°26'·20W. Alúmina Port, N bkwtr Fl (2) WG 8s 17m 4M; 110°-W-180°-G-110°; 43°42'·98N 07°27'·58W.

RÍA DE VIVEIRO

Pta Roncadoira ☆ Fl 7·5s 92m **21M**; W twr; 43°44'·15N 07°31'·58W.
Pta de Faro ☆ Fl R 5s 18m 7M; W twr; 43°42'·74N 07°35'·03W.
Pta Socastro ☆ Fl G 5s 18m 7M; G twr; 43°43'·08N 07°36'·42W.
Cillero, outer bkwtr ☆ Fl (2) R 7s 8m 5M; 43°40'·93N 07°36'·16W.
Marina ent ☆ Fl (2+1) G 15s 7m 1M; 43°40'·15N 07°35'·71W.

RÍA DEL BARQUERO

Isla Coelleira ☆ Fl (4) 16s 87m 7M; 43°45'·52N 07°37'·77W.
Pta de la Barra ☆ Fl WRG 3s 15m 5M; 198°-G-213°-W-240°-R-255°-G-213°; W twr; 43°44'·51N 07°41'·31W.
Pta del Castro ☆ Fl (2) 7s 14m 5M; 43°44'·46N 07°40'·48W.

PTA DE LA ESTACA DE BARES TO CABO VILLANO

Pta de la Estaca de Bares ☆ Fl (2) 7·5s 99m **25M**; obsc'd when brg >291°; 8-sided twr, R roof; 43°47'·17N 07°41'·06W.
Espasante, W bkwtr ☆ Fl R 5s 11m 3M; 43°43'·22N 07°48'·84W.
Cariño bkwtr ☆ Fl (3) G 9s 12m 5M; 43°44'·05N 07°51'·75W.
Cabo Ortegal (Pta de los Aguillones) ☆ Fl (2+1) 15s 122m **18M**; W ○ twr, R band; 43°46'·26N 07°52'·18W.
Punta Candelaria ☆ Fl (3+1) 24s 87m **21M**; 43°42'·67N 08°02'·95W.

RÍA DE CEDEIRA

Punta del Sarridal ☆ Oc WR 6s 39m 10M; Shore-R -145°-W-172°-R-145°; R ○ twr; 43°39'·61N 08°04'·52W.
Pta Promontorio ☆ Oc (4) 10s 24m 11M; 43°39'·05N 08°04'·20W.
Piedras de Media Mar ♙ Fl (2) 7s 14m 4M; BRB twr; 43°39'·44N 08°04'·71W.
Bkwtr hd ☆ Fl (2) R 7s 10m 5M; R post; 43°39'·30N 08°04'·20W.
Punta Frouxeira ☆ Fl (5) 15s 73m **20M**; 43°37'·05N 08°11'·25W.
Cabo Prior ☆ Fl (1+2) 15s 105m **22M**; 055·5°-310°; 6-sided twr; 43°34'·06N 08°18'·86W.
Punta del Castro ☆ Fl (2) 7s 42m 8M; W 6-sided twr; 43°30'·47N 08°19'·73W.

RÍA DE FERROL

Cabo Prioriño Chico ☆ Fl 5s 35m **23M**; 225°-129·5°; W 8-sided twr; 43°27'·53N 08°20'·40W.
Ent bkwtr head ☆ Fl R 5s 21m 7M; ***Racon N 12M***; 43°27'·23N 08°19'·80W. Bkwtr spur on NE side Fl (2) R 7s 12m 3M.
Batería de San Cristóbal ☆ 042° Dir WRG 33m 5M, 038·2°-FG-040°-AlWG-041·5°-W-042·5°-AlWR-044°-FR-045·7°; white □ twr; 43°28'·07N 08°18'·39W. 992241085.
Ldg lts 085·2°: Front, Pta de San Martín ☆ Q 1s 10m 3M; 43°27'·58N 08°17'·07W. 992241086. Rear ☆ Oc 4s 5M; 701m from front. 992241087.

RÍA DE ARES and RÍA DE BETANZOS

Ares bkwtr ☆ Fl (4) R 11s 10m 5M; R twr; 43°25'·35N 08°14'·29W.
Sada N pier ☆ Fl (4) G 11s 13m 5M; G twr; 43°21'·77N 08°14'·53W.

LA CORUÑA

Torre de Hércules ☆ Fl (4) 20s 104m **23M**; □ twr, 8-sided top; 43°23'·15N 08°24'·39W.
Canal del Oeste ldg lts 108·5°, both W 8-sided twrs: Front, Pta de Mera ☆ Oc WR 4s 54m, W8M R3M; 000°-R-023°; 100·5°-R-105·5°-W-114·5°-R-153°; ***Racon M, 18M; 020°-196°***; 43°23'·00N 08°21'·27W.
Rear ☆ LFl 8s 80m 8M; 357·5°-177·5°; 300m from front.
Canal del Este ldg lts 182°, both R/W chequered □ twrs: Front, Pta Fiaiteira ☆ Iso WRG 2s 28m, W10M, R/G7M; 146·4°-G-180°-W-184°-R-217·6°; ***Racon X, 11-21M***; 43°20'·59N 08°22'·25W.
Rear ☆ Oc R 4s 52m 5M; 380m from front.
Dique Barrié de la Maza ☆ Fl G 3s 18m 7M; 43°21'·90N 08°22'·48W.
Dársena de la Marina ☆ Fl (3) G 9s 8m 2M; 43°22'·01N 08°23'·66W.
Pta Langosteira bkwtr hd ☆ Fl (4) R 12s 7M; 43°20'·75N 08°32'·00W. 992242179.
Islas Sisargas ☆ Fl (3) 15s 108m **23M**; W 8-sided twr and W bldg; *Siren Mo (S) 30s;* 43°21'·60N 08°50'·78W. AIS, 992242125.
Punta Nariga ☆ Fl (3+1) 20s 53m **22M**; W ○ twr; 43°19'·24N 08°54'·69W.

RÍA DE CORME Y LAXE

Pta del Roncudo ☆ Fl 6s 36m10M; 43°16'·50N 08°59'·47W.
Pta de Laxe ☆ Fl (5) 20s 64m **20M**; W twr; 43°13'·84N 09°00'·65W.
Corme, mole ☆ Fl (2) R 5s 12m 3M; 43°15'·64N 08°57'·80W.
Laxe, N mole ☆ Fl G 3s 15m 4M; G ○ twr; 43°13'·37N 08°59'·96W.

CABO VILLANO TO THE PORTUGUESE BORDER

RÍA DE CAMARIÑAS and to PUNTA INSUA

C. Villano ☆ Fl (2) 15s 103m **28M**; 031·5°-228·5°; 8-sided twr, Gy cupola; ***Racon M, 35M***; 43°09'·63N 09°12'·69W.

Camariñas ldg lts 081°: Front, Pta Villueira Fl 5s 13m 9M; W ○ twr; 43°07′·38N 09°11′·56W. Rear, Pta del Castillo, Iso 4s 26m 11M; 079·5°-082·5° (3°); W twr, 612m from front.
Camariñas, outer bkwtr Fl R 5s 7m 3M; 43°07′·45N 09°10′·69W.
Pta de la Barca Oc 4s 11m 10M; 43°06′·79N 09°13′·19W.
Muxia bkwtr hd Fl (4) G 11s 14m 5M; ○ twr with G △ topmark; 43°06′·36N 09°12′·73W; obscured 146°-175° over El Carreiro
Pta de Lago Oc (2) WRG 6s 13m, W6M, R/G4M; 029·5°-W-093°-G-107·8°-W-109·1°-R-139·3°-W-213·5°; W twr; 43°06′·60N 09°10′·01W.
Cabo Toriñana ☆ Fl (2+1) 15s 63m **24M**; W ○ twr; *(1·7M SE of ☆)*; 43°03′·19N 09°17′·84W. 992242179 .
Cabo Finisterre ☆ Fl 5s 142m **23M**; *Siren (2) 60s*; 8-sided twr; obscd when brg >149°; ***Racon O, 35M***; 42°52′·94N 09°16′·31W. 992242141.

SENO DE CORCUBIÓN

Lobeira Grande Fl (3) 15s 16m 9M; 42°52′·84N 09°11′·12W.
Carrumeiro Chico Fl (2) 7s 7m 6M; 42°54′·37N 09°10′·76W.
Cabo Cée Fl (5) 13s 25m 7M; Gy twr; 42°54′·98N 09°11′·02W.
Corcubión bkwtr Fl (2) R 7s 10m 5M; 42°56′·70N 09°11·39W.
Pta Insúa ☆ Fl (3) WR 9s 26m; **W15M**, R14M; 020°-R-045°-W-070°-R-090°-W-125°-R-152°-W-020°; 42°46′·28N 09°07′·55W.

RÍA DE MUROS

Pta Queixal Fl (2+1) 12s 25m 9M; 42°44′·36N 09°04′·73W.
C. Rebordiño Fl (2) R 7s 17m 10M; 42°46′·20N 09°02′·90W.
Muros Fl (4) G 11s 9m 3M; G/W bcn; 42°46′·64N 09°03′·29W.
Portosin bkwtr Fl (3) G 9s 8m 5M; 42°45′·94N 08°56′·93W.
Pta Cabeiro Oc WR 3s 35m W9M, R6M; 050°-R-054·5°-W-058·5°-R-099·5°-W-189·5°; Gy twr; 42°44′·36N 08°59′·44W.
O Son outer bkwtr Fl (2) G 7s 7m 3M; G/W banded ○ twr; 42°43′·72N 09°00′·06W.
Pta Focha Fl 5s 27m 4M; ○ twr; 42°41′·98N 09°01′·59W.

RÍA DE AROSA (Selected lights only)

C. Corrubedo ☆ Fl (2+3) WR 20s 31m **15M**; dangerous sector 347°-R-040°; ***Racon K***; ○ twr, W cupola; 42°34′·57N 09°05′·39W. 992241092.
Isla Sálvora ☆ Fl (3+1) 20s 38m **21M**; vis 217°-126°; 42°27′·97N 09°00′·80W. Same twr, ☆ Fl (3) 12·7s **16M**; ☆ Fl R 7·3s **18M**, both covering 126° -160° danger sector. 992242126.
Santa Uxia Marina bkwtr knuckle Fl (2+1) G 15s 8m 3M; G ○ twr +R band; 42°33′·76N 08°59′·27W. 1ca NW Fl (2) R 7s 8m 3M.
Isla Rúa Fl (2) WR 7s 25m 12M; 121·5°-R-211·5°-W-121·5°; ***Racon G***; 42°32′·96N 08°56′·38W.
Pobra do Caramiñal Marina bkwtr Fl (2+1) R 15s 3M; R post, G band; 42°36′·33N 08°56′·04W.
Puerto Cabo de Cruz S bkwtr head Fl (2) G 7s 3M; G post, W band; 42°36′·87N 08°53′·56W
Rianxo NW bkwtr hd Fl (3) G 9s 3M; 42°39′·00N 08°49′·54W.
Vilagarcia, Dir lt 070·5° Fl WRG 6s, **W15M** R/G12M; 0608-G-070°-W-071°-R-073°; 42°36′·41N 08°46′·07W.
N mole Fl (3) R 9s 7m 3M; ○ twr; 42°36′·14N 08°46′·37W. I Arosa Pta Caballo Fl (4) 11s 12m 10M; 42°34′·34N 08°53′·04W.

PENINSULA DEL GROVE

Roca Pombeiriño Fl (2) G 12s 13m 8M; WGW bcn twr; 42°28′·93N 08°56′·83W.
Piedras Negras marina, bkwtr hd Fl (4) WR 11s 6m, W4M R3M; 305°-W-315°-R-305; R ○ twr; 42°27′·47N 08°55′·09W.
Bajo Piedra Seca Fl (3) R 9s 4m 5M; 42°27′·00N 08°54′·62W.

RÍA DE PONTEVEDRA

Bajo Fagilda QR 1s 16M; 42°24′·76N 08°53′·76W. 992241102.
Bajo Los Camoucos Fl (3) R 9s 12m 8M; 42°23′·71N 08°54′·75W.
Isla Ons ☆ Fl (4) 24s 126m **25M**; 8-sided twr; 42°22′·95N 08°56′·19W.
Portonovo mole Fl(2) R 7s 10m 5M; 42°23′·65N 08°49′·13W.
Sangenjo marina, Fl R 5s 5m 3M; 42°23′·81N 08°48′·06W. NE side Fl G 5s 5m 3M; 42°23′·83N 08°48′·03W.
Cabezo de Morranzán Iso R 5s; 42°22′·37N 08°47′·04W.
Raxó mole Fl (4) R 11s 8m 5M; R ○ twr; 42°24′·12N 08°45′·26W.
Isla Tambo Fl (3) 8s 35m 11M; W ○ twr; 42°24′·48N 08°42′·47W.
Combarro S jetty hd Fl (3) R 9s 3M; 42°25′·62N 08°42′·22W.
Rio Lérez mouth Fl R 5s, Fl G 5s; 42°24′·84N 08°41′·22W.
Aguete Fl (4) G 11s 3M, 42°22′·66N 08°44′·20W.
Marina, E end Fl (2) G 7s 1M; 42°22′·55N 08°44′·16W.
Bueu N bkwtr Fl G 5s 9m 5M; G twr; 42°19′·79N 08°47′·02W.
Beluso N bkwtr Fl (4) G 11s 7m 5M; 42°20′·02N 08°47′·90W.
Cabeza de la Mourisca Fl (2) G 7s 10m 5M; 42°20′·90N 08°49′·17W.
Aldán jetty Fl (3) R 9s 7m 5M; R twr; 42°16′·95N 08°49′·38W.
Punta Couso Fl (3) WG 10·5s 18m, W10M, G8M; 060°-G-096°-W-190°-G-000°; 42°18′·56N 08°51′·33W.

ISLAS CÍES

Isla del Norte, Pta de Monte Agudo Fl G 5s 24m 10M; 42°14′·60N 08°54′·19W.
Monte Faro ☆ Fl (2) 8s 186m **22M**; obsc'd 315°-016·5° over Bajos de Los Castros and Forcados; ○ twr; 42°12′·85N 08°54′·90W. 992242128.
Isla del Faro, Pta Canabal Fl (3) 20s 63m 9M; W twr; 42°12′·73N 08°54′·77W.
Isla de San Martin, Cabo Vicos Fl (3) R 9s 93m 10M; obsc'd 108°-210·5°; W twr; 42°11′·51N 08°53′·48W.
Islote Boeiro Fl (2) R 8s 22m 5M; W twr; 42°10′·75N 08°54′·61W.

RÍA DE VIGO

N Chan, outer ldg lts 129°, both 090°-180°; W ○ twrs: Front, Cabo del Home Fl 3s 36m 9M; 42°15′·20N 08°52′·39W. 992241104. Rear, Pta Subrido Oc 6s 53m 11M; 815m from front,.
Punta Robaleira Fl (2) WR 7·5s 25m, W11M, R9M; 300·5°-W-321·5°-R-090°; 115·5°-R-170·5°; R twr; ***Racon C***; 42°15′·00N 08°52′·38W (285m S of Cabo del Home ldg lt).
Cangas NE mole Fl R 5s 8m 5M; R ○ twr; 42°15′·61N 08°46′·83W.
Cabo Estay (S chan) ldg lts 069·3°, both R twrs, W bands; vis 066·3°-072·3°. **Front** ☆ Iso 2s 16m **18M**; ***Racon B, 22M***; 42°11′·13N 08°52′·39W. 992241105. **Rear** Oc 4s 48m **18M**, 660m from front.
Bouzas, NE head Fl (2+1) G 15s 9m 5M; 42°14′·07N 08°44′·67W.
Marina Dávila Sport Fl (2) G 7s 10m 5M; 42°13′·99N 08°44′·42W.
Muelle del Berbés, N head Fl (3) G 9s 9m 5M; G twr; 42°14′·43N 08°44′·01W.
Muelle de Transatlánticos, NE head Fl (4) G 11s 5M; G post; 42°14′·59N 08°43′·56W.
Vigo marina ent, QG and QR 9m 5M; 42°14′·57N 08°43′·41W.
Pta Lagoa marina, bkwtr hd, QG 1s 1m 2M, 42°15′·50N 08°42′·30W.
La Guia ☆ Oc (2+1) 20s 37m **15M**; W twr; 42°15′·57N 08°42′·14W.

BAYONA to the PORTUGUESE BORDER

Las Serralleiras Q (9) 15s 4M; 42°09′·23N 08°53′·35W.
Pta Lameda Fl (2) G 8s 27m 5M; W twr; 42°09′·39N 08°50′·98W.
Ldg/Dir lts 084°, both W twrs: Front, Cabezo de San Juan Fl 6s 8m 10M; 42°08′·13N 08°50′·10W. Rear, **Panjón Dir** ☆ 084°, Oc WRG 4s **W18M, R15M**, G14M; 079°-G-083°-W-085°-R-088°; 42°08′·33N 08°48′·95W.
Dique de Abrigo QG 10m 5M; G/W twr; 42°07′·49N 08°50′·58W.
C. Silleiro ☆ Fl (2+1) 15s 83m **24M**; W 8-sided twr, R bands; 42°06′·26N 08°53′·75W. 992242119.
C. Silleiro Lt by Q; 42°07′·26N 08°54′·72W. 992241106.
La Guardia N bkwtr Fl (2) R 7s 11m 5M; R twr; *Siren Mo (L) 30s*; 41°54′·07N 08°52′·90W. S bkwtr Fl (2) G 7s 11m 5M; G/W twr.

9.23.4 PASSAGE INFORMATION

More passage information is threaded between successive hbrs in this Area. **Bibliography**: *NW Spain & Portugal* (Fernhurst/Jens); *South Biscay* (Imray/RCC/Pickard); *Cruising Galicia* (Imray/Rojas/Bailey); *Atlantic Spain and Portugal* (Imray/RCC/Buchanan); *Bay of Biscay Pilot* (NP 22); *W Coasts of Spain and Portugal Pilot* (NP 67).

BAY OF BISCAY: WIND, WEATHER AND SEA

NE'lies prevail in sea area Finisterre in summer and gales may occur twice monthly, although forecast more frequently. Atlantic lows can bring W'ly spells at any time. Wind direction and speed often varies daily, but SE or S winds are rare. Sea and land breezes can be well developed in the summer. Off N Spain *Galernas,* dangerous squally NW winds, can blow with little warning. Coastal winds are intensified by the Cordillera Cantábrica (2615m mountains).

Despite its reputation, the S part of the Bay is often warm and settled in summer when the Azores high and Spanish heat low are the dominant weather features. Rainfall is moderate, increasing in the SE, with thunder more frequent. Sea fog, which often precedes strong winds, occurs May-Oct, but is less common in winter.

▶*There are no tidal stream atlases. Streams are weak offshore, but can be strong in narrow channels and off headlands.*◀

Surface current much depends on wind: in summer it sets SE ½–¾kn, towards the SE corner of Bay of Biscay, thence W along N coast of Spain. When crossing the Bay, allow for some set to the E, particularly after strong west winds.

CROSSING THE BAY OF BISCAY

Distances across the Bay are tabulated at 9.0.8. Leaving the English Channel, the track (208°/362M) from Ushant ITZ to Cabo Villano (AC 1104) lies undesirably close to busy shipping lanes, but a track (213°/287M) from, say, harbours between **Loctudy** and **Concarneau**, to Cabo Ortegal is substantially offset to the SE of the shipping route. Cabo Ortegal as a landfall permits onward passage to **La Coruña**. Or, if conditions for rounding Ortegal are bad (as is not unknown) **Ría de Viveiro** is a safe refuge. From Scilly or Ireland the direct track lies in about 7°-8°W.

Within the Bay itself, sailing down the French coast is attractive and allows a 200M passage from **La Rochelle** to **Santander**. Landes missile range between Pointe de Grave and Capbreton extends up to 45M offshore. It may inhibit coastal passages, but is usually inactive at night, w/ends and August.

The Continental Shelf, where depths plummet from 150m to over 4000m in only 30M, can cause dangerous seas in swell and bad weather. From a position about 60M SW of Ile de Sein it trends SE to the Franco/Spanish border as shown on AC 1104.

Atlantic swell runs in mainly from W or NW. It is not a problem well offshore, except over the Continental Shelf in bad weather. Considerable rolling is probable; other yachts or even small ships may be lost to view in the troughs. Closer inshore swell will exacerbate the sea state and render entry to, and exit from, lee shore harbours dangerous. With a 2m swell running, crossing a bar with 4m depth over it and breaking seas would be foolhardy. In winter some harbours may be closed for long periods.

FRENCH BORDER TO SANTANDER

The N coast of Spain is bold and rocky (AC 1290, 1291, 1292). In clear visibility the peaks of the **Cordillera Cantábrica** may be seen from well offshore. The coast is mostly steep-to, but it is best to keep 2-3M offshore (beyond the 50m contour) to avoid short, steep seas breaking on isolated shoals. Many major lights are sited high, and often obscured by low cloud/mist in onshore weather. Most small rivers have bars and none are navigable far inland.

From Hendaye to Santander harbours are closely spaced compared with further west. Ports of refuge in NW gales are: **Pasajes** (no yacht facilities), **Guetaria**, **Bermeo**, **Bilbao**, **Castro Urdiales** and **Santander**. **San Sebastián** is an attractive ⚓ but exposed to the NW. **Bilbao** and **Santander** are ferry ports and major cities with marinas. Fishing hbrs with ⛵ or ⚓ include: **Guetaria**, **Motrico**, **Bermeo**, **Lequeitio**, **Elanchove** and **Laredo.**

9.23.5 SPECIAL NOTES FOR SPAIN

Regions/Provinces: Spain is divided into 17 autonomous regions, ie in Area 23, Guipuzcoa (Basque Country) Cantábrica, Asturias and Galicia. Most regions are sub-divided into provinces, eg in Galicia: Lugo, La Coruña, Pontevedra and Orense (inland). The province is shown below the name of each main port.

Language: This Almanac recognises regional differences (eg Basque, Gallego) but in the interests of standardisation uses the spelling of Castilian Spanish where practicable.

Spanish charts (SC). Contact Instituto Hidrográfico de la Marina, Plaza San Severiano 3, 11007 Cádiz, ☎(956) 599 414; www.armada.mde.es/ihm or order from chart agents in Madrid, Bilbao, Santander, Gijon, La Coruña, Villagarcia de Arosa and Vigo.

Currency is the Euro €. VAT (IVA) is 21%.

Courtesy ensign: E of Bilbao it may be politic to fly the Basque flag, Fig 5 (9) or none at all. The Spanish ensign may give offence, especially if flown above the autonomous Basque flag.

Fuel: Diesel (*Gasoleo*) is of two types: *Gasoleo A* is taxed and supplied to yachts from marina pumps or by cans from a filling station ashore. *Gasoleo B* is untaxed and usually only available to FVs from a pump on the fish quay.

Standard Time in Spain is UT –1, but in Portugal it is UT.

Spanish secondary ports referenced to Lisboa. Time differences for those Spanish ports which are referenced to Lisboa (all south of Ría de Muros) when applied to the printed times of HW and LW for Lisboa, give HW and LW times in Spanish Standard Time. DST is the only correction required.

Telephone: To call Spain from UK dial 00 34, then the area code, followed by the 6 digit ☎ number. Internally dial the area code plus the ☎ number. To call UK from Spain, dial 07 44, then area code less the initial 0, plus the ☎ number.

Emergencies: ☎900 202 202 for Maritime Rescue. Fire, Police and Ambulance call 112. *Rioja Cruz* (Red Cross) operate LBs.

Public Holidays: Jan 1, 6; Good Friday; 1 May (Labour Day); June 11 (Corpus Christi); Aug 15 (Assumption); Oct 12 (National Day); Nov 1 (All Saints Day); Dec 6, 8 (Immaculate Conception) 25.

Representation: Spanish Tourist Office, 64 North Row, London W1K 7DE; ☎020 7317 2011. info.londres@tourspain.es www.spain.info

British Embassy, Paseo de la Castellana 259D, 28046 Madrid; ☎(91) 334 2194. Consular Section ☎(902) 109 356.

Buoyage: Preferred channel buoys [RGR, Fl (2+1) R and GRG, Fl (2+1) G] are quite widely used; see Chapter 3.

Documents: (See Chapter 2 Cruising Formalities) Spain, although an EU member, still checks papers. This can be a time-consuming, repetitive and inescapable process. The only palliatives are courtesy, patience and good humour. Organise your documents to include:

Personal – Passports; crew list, ideally on headed paper with the yacht's rubber stamp, giving DoB, passport nos, where joined/intended departure. Certificate of Competence (Yachtmaster Offshore, ICC/HOCC etc). Radio Operator's certificate. EHIC is advised for medical treatment.

Yacht – Registration certificate, Part 1 or SSR. Proof of VAT status. Marine insurance. Ship's Radio licence. Itinerary and ship's log.

Access: Ferries from UK to Santander and Bilbao. Flights from UK to Bilbao, Santiago de Compostela and Madrid. Internal flights via Madrid to Asturias, La Coruña and Vigo. Buses are mostly good and trains adequate, except in more remote regions.

SAR: A Spanish Government agency SASEMAR is responsible for the all-weather lifeboats, tugs, search helicopters and aircraft. Irrespective of value, assisted vessels <20m LOA are charged €350/hour including towing; 20m-30m LOA €749/hour (2016).

9.23.6 FUENTERRABÍA (Hondarribia)

Guipúzcoa **43°22'·56N 01°47'·52W**

CHARTS AC 1292, 1170; SC 391, 3910; SHOM 6556, 6558, 6786; Navi 555. *Spanish* and French names for the same feature: *Rada de Higuer* = Baie de Fontarabie or de Figuier; *Ría de Fuenterrabía* = La Bidassaoa (river).

TIDES HW +0450 on Dover (UT); ML 2·3m
Interpolate between **SOCOA** (St Jean de Luz) and **PASAJES**.

SHELTER Excellent in marina, access H24. S of Cabo Higuer, a FV hbr, 2-3m, is a port of refuge. Good ⚓ in river off Pta Roca.

NAVIGATION WPT 43°23'·87N 01°46'·44W, 212°/1·15M to W bkwtr hd. Beware Les Briquets 8ca N of Pte Ste Anne at E end of the Baie. Near centre of B, keep clear of Bajo Iruarri. River ent (6·5-1·3m) is easy except in heavy N'ly swell; sp ebb is very strong.

The neutral zone between France and Spain is delineated by the alignment of 4 pairs of beacons; see Hendaye (Area 22).

LIGHTS AND MARKS Cabo Higuer lt ho, a square stone twr with R top, is conspic at W side of bay, as is the high dorsal ridge which runs down to the headland. A red-roofed castle is prominent 2 cables SSE of Cabo Higuer lt ho. La Rhune, an 898m high conical peak, bears 120°/8M from the marina.

COMMUNICATIONS (Code 943) MRSC (942) 213030; Emergency 112; Marina VHF Ch 09 (H24); Club Nautico ☎642788.

FACILITIES **Marina** ☎641711 (3m) 595 + 25 Ⓥ; berth on pontoon G (1st to port). Pontoons A-E are NW of the central pontoon F; G-J are to the SE. €2.50 (30 days pa max); max LOA 16m. Boats > 16m LOA should ⚓ in the Bay or in Baie de Chingoudy. (UK cr/cards) (35t) (3t).

Town (Fuenterrabía or Biarritz). Ferries, local: Fuenterrabía to Hendaye. UK: Santander, Bilbao.

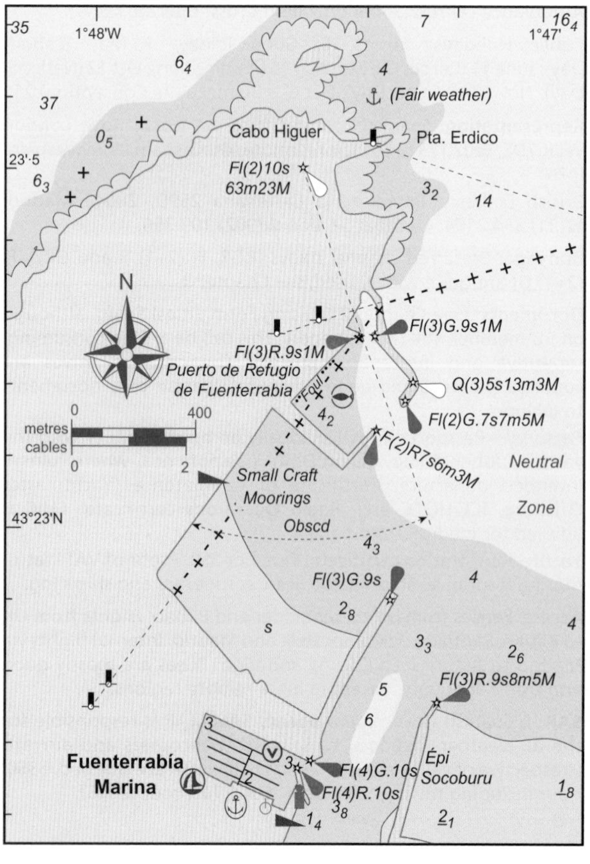

9.23.7 PASAJES (Pasaia)

Guipúzcoa **43°20'·23N 01°55'·82W**

CHARTS AC 1292, 1171, 1157; SC 391/2, 3911; SHOM 6375, 6558

TIDES See San Sebastian.

SHELTER A port of refuge (3·5M E of San Sebastián, 7M from France). Yachts may ⚓ as shown on the chartlet: the bay NE of Dir lt is fair weather only; the other two ⚓s are outside local small craft moorings, as space allows; the N'ly is subject to wash.

NAVIGATION WPT 43°21'·31N 01°56'·28W , SWM buoy [Mo (A) 7s], 166°/1·0M to hbr ent, a 200m wide cleft in spectacular cliffs. Appr on 154·8° transit of Dir lt, Oc (2) WRG 12s (Racon M) with ldg lts: front Q, rear Oc 3s; all on the W cliff. Inner ldg line 144·3° on Iso 4s, Rear Q 1s on E shore.

Shoals (1·5m) E of ent marked by conspic 16m high R lt twr, shoal (3·4m) W of ent, marked by lit SHM. Inner chan, dredged 10m, is only 100m wide, but well marked/lit; do not impede large vessels/FVs; be alert for departing ships.

LIGHTS AND MARKS Observe and obey IPTS located high on the E cliff at Atalya de Pasajes (Racon K). Sigs 1, 2 and 3 are shown to seaward and inwards; the ent is blind and narrow for big ships.

COMMUNICATIONS (Code 943) MRSC (942) 213030; Emergency 112; Brit Consul (902)109356; HM 351816 ppasajes@sarenet.es; Port VHF Ch 09 (H24).

FACILITIES Pasajes is a busy FV and commercial hbr with no yacht facilities. Ⓔ. **Town** Ⓑ.

9.23.8 SAN SEBASTIÁN (Donostia)

Guipúzcoa **43°19′·48N 01°59′·79W**

CHARTS AC 1292, 1171; SC 391, 392, 3910; SHOM 6558, 6786

TIDES

Standard Port POINTE DE GRAVE (⟵)

Times				**Height (metres)**			
High Water		Low Water		MHWS	MHWN	MLWN	MLWS
0000	0600	0000	0500	5·3	4·4	2·1	1·0
1200	1800	1200	1700				
Differences SAN SEBASTIÁN							
–0110	–0030	–0040	–0020	–1·1	–1·2	–0·5	–0·4
PASAJES							
–0050	–0030	–0045	–0015	–1·1	–1·3	–0·5	–0·5

SHELTER Fair; the ⚓ becomes lively or dangerous in any NW/N′lies when heavy swell enters. ⚓ S of Isla Santa Clara or SW of YC, in both cases clear of moorings and with ⚓ buoyed.

NAVIGATION WPT 43°19′·85N 02°00′·00W, 158°/0·4M to hbr ent (between Isla de Santa Clara and Monte Urgull). Avoid La Bancha on which the sea breaks in swell and heavy weather. Open up the bay before standing in.

LIGHTS AND MARKS Monte Urgull (huge statue of Virgin Mary) is prominent from all directions; from E it looks like an island. Monte Igueldo on W side of ent is only slightly less obvious. Isla de Santa Clara is lower and inconspicuous; not seen until the nearer appr. Ldg marks (grey masts) are hard to see, but a large R and W Palladian-styled villa is conspic on 158°. Ldg lts, although intense, may be masked by shore lts.

COMMUNICATIONS (Code 943) MRSC (942) 213030; Emergency 112; Met 274030; Auto 906 365320; Brit Consul (902)109356; Real Club Nautico VHF Ch 09 (H24).

FACILITIES for visiting boats do not match the city's elegance. **Real Club Náutico** ☎423574, www.rcnss.com; ⚓(best to pre-arrange) ✕ ⊡ Ice. YC launch will meet and direct (Ch 09) to a vacant ⚓.

Dársena de la Concha is overcrowded, with limited space on Ⓥ pontoon dead ahead of ent; W part shelves quite steeply; inner basins are locals/FVs only.

City ✕ ⊡ 🛒 ⛽ ✉ Ⓑ Ⓗ. ⇌ & ✈ Fuenterrabía (25km). ✈ also at Bilbao (92km) and ferry to UK.

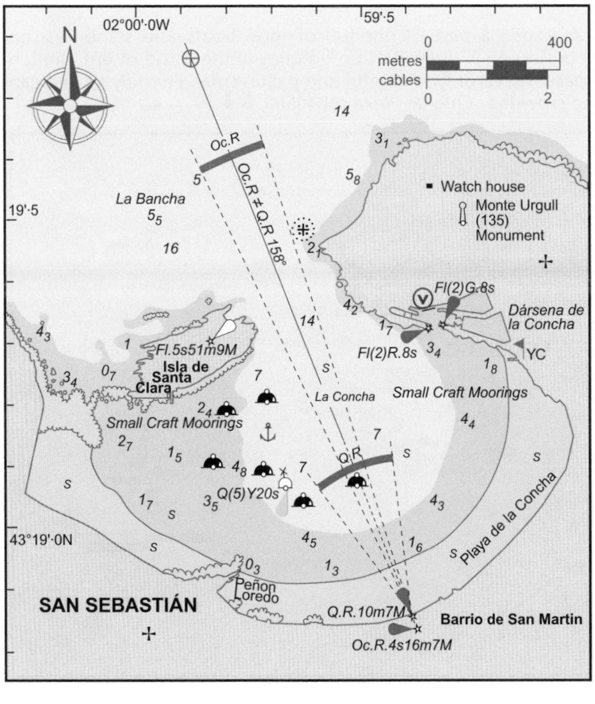

MINOR HARBOUR 3M ESE OF GUETARIA

RÍA DE ORIO Guipúzcoa **43°17′·49N 02°07′·98W**. AC 1292; SC 944, 303A; SHOM 6786, 6379. Tides: MHWS 4·1m, MLWS 0·5m; MHWN 3·2m, MLWN 1·4m. Interpolate between San Sebastián & Guetaria.

WPT 43°17′·97N 02°07′·95W, 180°/5ca to W bkwtr between Mte Talai (360m) to the E and Mte Amesti (188m) to the W. Small marina (2-3m) 5ca upriver from the ent, on the east bank and just N of the road bridge, 17·5m clearance. Best water to the E. Good shelter, but exposed to N′lies when swell may work in. Fair weather tempy ⚓ outside to the E off San Juan beach in 5m.

Best appr just before HW. See Lights, buoys and waypoints for the two entrance lts. A first visit at night is not advised despite a total of 17 nav lts.

HM ☎(943) 249400. www.ekpsa.com VHF 09. kirolportua@ekpsa.com 300 ⊆ €0.71 x LOA x beam (m)/per day (30 days max); max LOA 12m. Facilities: ⛽ ⊡ (H24) ⊡ (32t) ⟋. **Town** 800m south. ✕ ⊡ 🛒.

9.23.9 GUETARIA (Getaria)

Guipúzcoa **43°18′·23N 02°11′·93W**

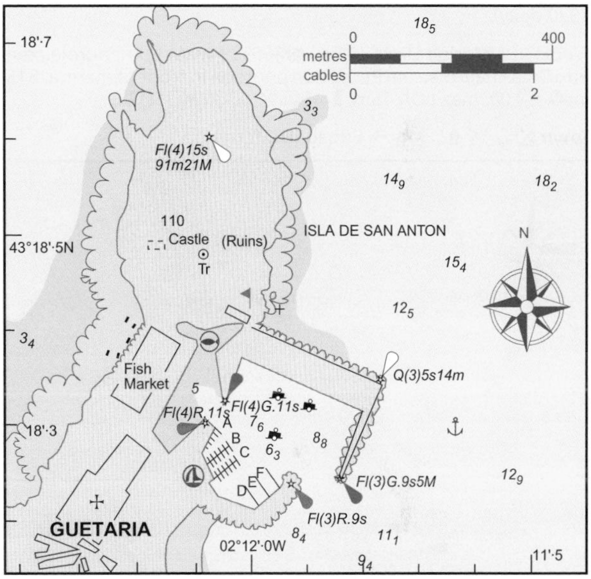

CHARTS AC 1292, 1171; SC 392, 3921; SHOM 6379, 6786

TIDES

Standard Port POINTE DE GRAVE (⟵)

Times				**Height (metres)**			
High Water		Low Water		MHWS	MHWN	MLWN	MLWS
0000	0600	0000	0500	5·3	4·4	2·1	1·0
1200	1800	1200	1700				
Differences GUETARIA							
–0110	–0030	–0040	–0020	–0·9	–1·0	–0·5	–0·4

SHELTER The only good shelter in S-NW winds between Pasajes and Bilbao. No ⚓ in hbr which is generally foul. In fair weather ⚓ on sand or pick up a buoy close S of hbr ent, but exposed to E′lies.

NAVIGATION WPT 43°18′·90N 02°11′·00W, 225°/9½ca to hbr ent. Appr is straightforward day/night in fair visibility.

LIGHTS AND MARKS Lts as chartlet and Lts, bys & wypts. The mouse-like profile of Isla de San Anton is distinctive; lt ho on its N side.

COMMUNICATIONS (Code 943) MRSC (942) 213030; Emergency 112; Met 906 365 320; Auto 906 365365; ⊖ via Marina; Brit Consul (902)109356; HM VHF Ch 09 (H24).

FACILITIES **Marina** ☎580959 thage@infonegocio.com pontoons A-F, Ⓥ welcome but space limited, no rafting allowed, 300 ⊆; €2.40. max LOA 14m. (30t) (5t) ⟋. FVs use N side of outer hbr and all the inner hbr.

Club Náutico y Pesca ☎140201, ✕ ⊡. **Town** ✕ ⊡ 🛒 ⛽ ✉ ⇌ ✈ Bilbao (UK ferry).

9.23.10 ZUMAYA (Zumaia)

Guipúzcoa **43°18'·36N 02°14'·92W** (Hbr ent)

CHARTS AC 1292; SC 392, 3921; SHOM 6379, 6786

TIDES As for Guetaria.

SHELTER Good in the marina, but in strong onshore winds the appr could be difficult. In E'lies a fair weather ⚓ off Pta Izustarri, clear of rks at sandy beach 3ca NE of hbr ent. No ⚓ in hbr.

NAVIGATION WPT 43°19'·85N 02°14'·51W (8ca W of ODAS buoy, Fl (5) Y 20s) 190°/1·5M to hbr ent. Easy appr from NNE, but keep clear of rocks W of Pta Iruarriaundieta and S of Pta Izustarri. The access chan, least depth 0·1m as shown on SC 3921, is said to be dredged 3m. Best water is to stbd; near LW keep 10m off the NW bkwtr and river bank. The Rio Urola flows through the hbr.

LIGHTS AND MARKS Lt ho, Oc (1+3) 12s, is a white 8-sided tower with blue cupola. Lts as chartlet and Lights, buoys & waypoints.

COMMUNICATIONS (Code 943) MRSC (942) 213030; Emergency112; Brit Consul (902)109356; Marina VHF Ch 09 (0900-1300 & 1400-1930 daily)

FACILITIES **Marina Urola** (2·5m) ☎860938 www.marinaurola.com info@marinaurola.com Reception pontoon in front of marina. 515 incⓋ €3.00; max LOA 15m. (35t).

Town Bilbao (UK ferry).

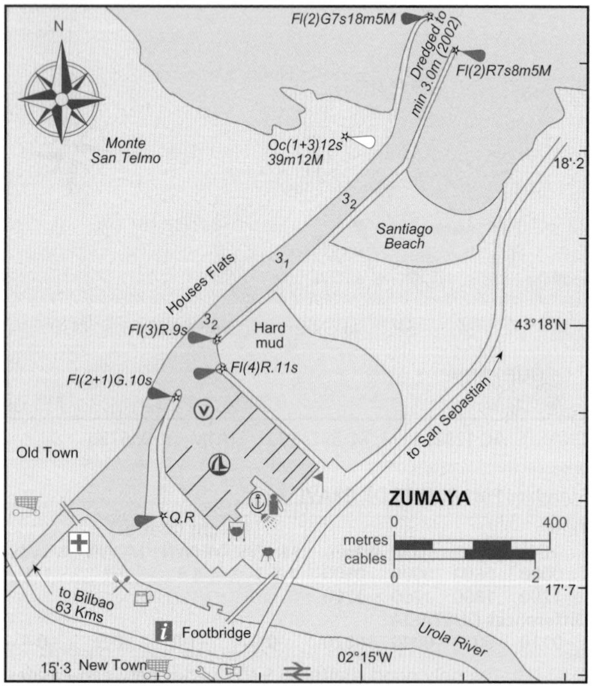

MINOR HARBOUR 6M W OF ZUMAYA

MOTRICO (Mutriku) Guipúzcoa **43°18'·5N 02°22'·9W**. Tides: interpolate between Guetaria & Lequeitio. AC 1292; SC 392, 3922; SHOM 6379. Small FV hbr (4m) in rky inlet. Well sheltered in NE winds by large new outer bkwtr, but swell may still work in. WPT 43°18'·76N 02°21'·99W, lies on the 245° WRG Oc. dir lt, 7ca from outer bkwtr, which must be left to stbd. The ent is easily seen from E, but from W open hbr & town before approaching. Lts as chartlet.

Either ⚓ inside the bkwtr in 5m or berth in inner harbour at new (2015) **Marina Mutriku** (3m) HM ☎(943) 603326 VHF Ch09 (0900-1300,1500-2200),www.ekpsa.eus/es/nuestros-puertos/ mutriku1@ekpsa.com 301 inc Ⓥ €0·63 m² day, max14m; (5t).

Town.

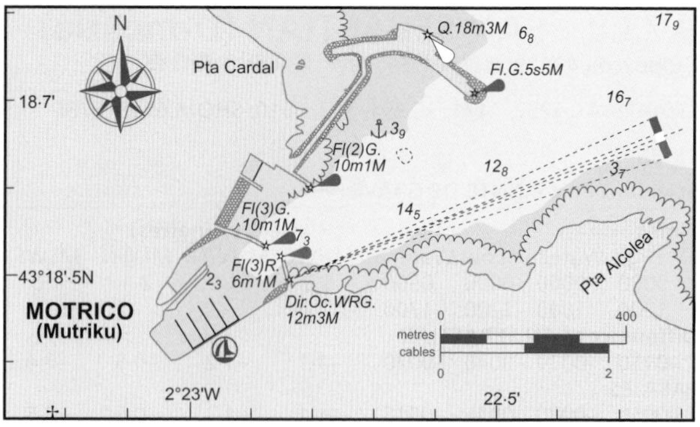

9.23.11 LEQUEITIO (Lekeitio)

Vizcaya **43°22'·00N 02°29'·91W**

CHARTS AC 1292, 1171; SC 392, 393; SHOM 6379, 5009

TIDES

Standard Port POINTE DE GRAVE (⟵)

Times				Height (metres)			
High Water		Low Water		MHWS	MHWN	MLWN	MLWS
0000	0600	0000	0500	5·3	4·4	2·1	1·0
1200	1800	1200	1700				
Differences LEQUEITIO							
−0115	−0035	−0045	−0025	−1·1	−1·2	−0·5	−0·4

SHELTER Good. ⚓ in about 3m or pick up a vacant buoy at the S end of basin where there are extensive small craft trots. In settled weather ⚓ further out, to E or W of Isla de San Nicolas.

NAVIGATION WPT 43°22'·25N 02°29'·68W, 214°/3ca to abeam Pta Amandarri lt. Avoid rky shoals close E of 213·8° ldg line and ruins of old bkwtr (Fl (2) R 8s) further S.

LIGHTS AND MARKS Conspic daymarks: Cabo de Santa Catalina 0·8M to the NW. Isla de San Nicolas is rky, steep-sided, wooded and linked to mainland by a part-drying causeway. Church dome SSW of hbr. Palacio Uribarren, the rear 213·8° ldg mark.

COMMUNICATIONS (Code 946) MRSC (942) 213030; Emergency 112; Brit Consul (902)109356; HM 243324, VHF Ch 09.

FACILITIES S part of hbr full of local boats and some FVs, no mooring on N quay. Raft up on quay immed stbd of ent, limited space. No WC or showers. Peaceful and picturesque. Friendly YC but can be crowded. Club de Pesca ☎840500.

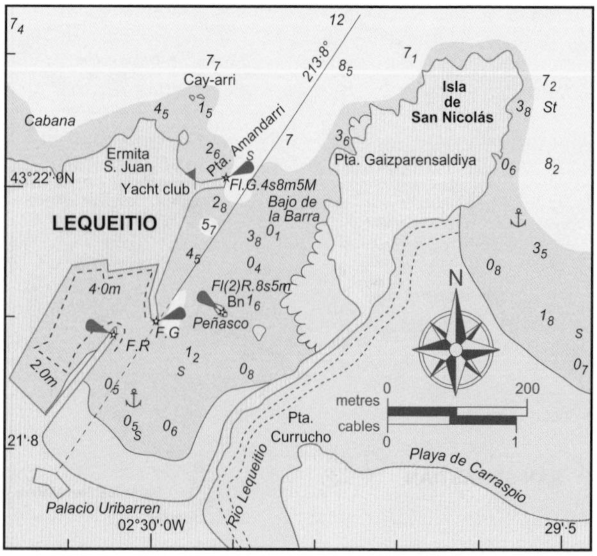

9.23.12 ELANCHOVE (Elantxobe)

Vizcaya **43°24'·23N 02°38'·21W** ✿✿✿

CHARTS AC 1292, 1171; SC 393; SHOM 6380, 6991

TIDES Interpolate between Lequeitio and Bermeo.
Standard Port POINTE DE GRAVE (⟵)

Times				Height (metres)			
High Water		Low Water		MHWS	MHWN	MLWN	MLWS
0000	0600	0000	0500	5·3	4·4	2·1	1·0
1200	1800	1200	1700				
Differences BERMEO							
–0055	–0015	–0025	–0005	–0·7	–0·7	–0·5	–0·4

SHELTER Sheltered from W in lee of Cabo Ogoño, but exposed to N/E. In calm weather temporary ⚓ to E of hbr ent in 5m.

NAVIGATION WPT 43°24'·67N 02°37'·61W, 225°/6ca to N mole hd. From the W, hbr is not visible until bearing >205°.

LIGHTS AND MARKS The S Mole, F WR lt shows Red (315°-000°) over inshore dangers to the SE. Cabo Machichaco, Fl 7s, is 6M WNW.

COMMUNICATIONS (Code 944) MRSC (942) 213030; Emergency 112; Brit Consul (902)109356; HM 881323.

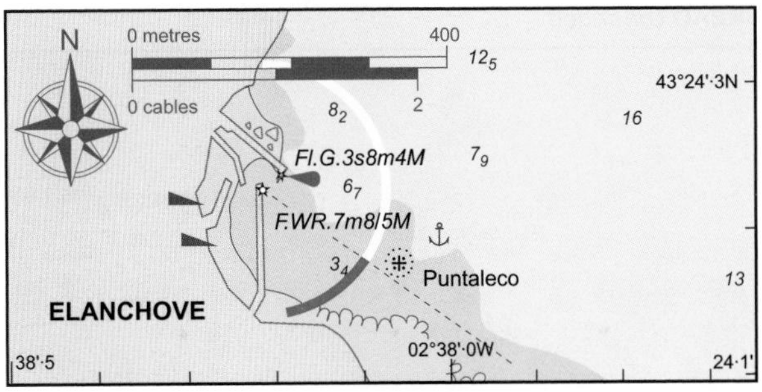

FACILITIES Tiny hbr in spectacular setting at foot of steep 100m cliffs. The N part of outer hbr and all the inner hbr dry. At ent turn hard port into S part of outer hbr to pick up buoy in about 3m or ⚓ with tripping line as the bottom may well be foul. On S mole is feasible, but a 1m wide underwater ledge requires a holding-off line to kedge ⚓.

Village Basic; Bus to Bilbao for ⇄ ✈. 15km south by road is Guernica, the ancient sacred city of the Basques.

HARBOUR 2·7M SE OF CABO MACHICHACO

BERMEO 43°25'·35N 02°42'·57W. Tides: see Elanchove. AC 1292, 1172; SC 393, 3931; SHOM 6380, 6991. A busy commercial & FV port, well sheltered from N, but swell enters in E'lies.

Hbr is between the wide drying estuary of Rio Mundaca and conspic Cabo Machichaco to NW. Appr on 218° in W sector (204°-232°) of Rosape Dir lt to clear unlit Isla de Izaro, 1M ENE of hbr and the N mole. NW corner of outer harbour taken up with fore/aft moorings for locals between buoys and piles.

Inner harbour, **Marina Bermeo** locals only, Ⓥ limited to 7 €0.76m² on walk ashore pontoon in 3-4m SW side inner harbour outer N pier. No; reported very uncomfortable in strong wind/swell. Best visited only in settled offshore weather.

VHF Ch 09,16. HM ☎(946) 18 64 45 mob 908 87 33 30. www.ekpsa.eus/es/nuestros-puertos/ bermeo1@ekpsa.com (12t). **Town** Ⓔ Ⓑ. ⇄ to Guernica.

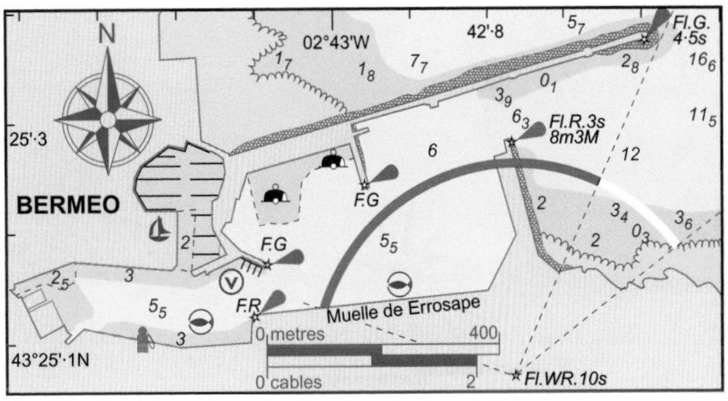

9.23.13 BILBAO (Bilbo)

Vizcaya **43°22'·73N 03°04'·87W** (outer ent) ✿✿✿

CHARTS AC 1292, 1174, 1173; SC 394, 394A, 3941; SHOM 6774, 6991

TIDES

Standard Port POINTE DE GRAVE (⟵); ML 2·4.

Times				Height (metres)			
High Water		Low Water		MHWS	MHWN	MLWN	MLWS
0000	0600	0000	0500	5·3	4·4	2·1	1·0
1200	1800	1200	1700				
Differences ABRA DE BILBAO							
–0125	–0045	–0055	–0035	–1·1	–1·2	–0·5	–0·4
PORTUGALETE (INNER HARBOUR)							
–0100	*–0020*	*–0030*	*–0010*	*–0·6*	*–1·2*	*–0·2*	*–0·6*

SHELTER Excellent in both marinas. ⚓ in 3-5m between these two havens which are adjacent to a pleasant suburb.

NAVIGATION WPT 43°23'·17N 03°05'·21W, 150°/5ca to outer hbr ent. This is formed by a W bkwtr extending 1·25M NE from Punta Lucero, a 308m high unlit headland on the W side. The submerged E bkwtr extends WNW for almost 2M from Punta Galea, Fl (3) 8s, on the E side of El Abra. It is marked by 3 SPM lt buoys, but can be crossed with caution; approx 7m depth was found close off Pta Galea. A mini-TSS is aligned 150°/330° 1·6M towards the outer hbr ent.

From the outer ent follow the buoyed fairway/TSS 120°/2M and 143°/1M across El Abra (= outer hbr/roads) to Dique de Santurtzi. thence 195°/3 cables to the inner hbr. Yachts should stay just outside the fairway buoys and keep clear of ships using the TSS.

After passing Contradique de Algorta, Fl R 5s, round the head, Fl (2+1) R 10s, of a new jetty (for cruise liners) extending W from Getxo bkwtr. When clear turn SE for Getxo Marina and SSE across the inner hbr to Las Arenas yacht hbr.

LIGHTS AND MARKS 5 wind turbines (inc 3 lit) near the head of W bkwtr are prominent. The Port Control bldg/twr is conspic at the SE end of Dique de Santurtzi. 2 power stn chimneys (200m high) with R/W bands are conspic 1M SW of Port Control. Glare from industrial plants may be seen from afar at night. Caution: Flood lights on the beach at Algorta (43°21'·34N 03°01'·08W) shine seaward and are very distracting when inbound at night, up to 0100LT.

COMMUNICATIONS (Code 944) MRCC 839411; Met via YC; Emergency 112; ⊜ 234700; Brit Consul (902)109356; Ⓗ 903100; Port HM 241416; Port Control VHF Ch 05, **12**, 16; Marinas VHF Ch 09.

FACILITIES **Getxo Marina** ☎912367 www.getxokaia.com getxokaia@getxokaia.com (1·9-2·9m) on S side of Contramuelle de Algorta. 827 incⓋ €5.00; max LOA 18m, southern pontoon J only, prone to wash, (H24) Ⓔ (45t) (5t). Metro line 1 for downtown, board at Gobela/Neguri stations.

Las Arenas Yacht hbr ☎637600; www.rcmarsc.es puerto@rcmarsc.es, near the mouth of R. Bilbao in 1-3m, is prone to wash at HW, run jointly by **Real Club Maritimo del Abra** and **Real Sporting Club**. 250 + 50Ⓥ €3.00 + €3.44/day. Ⓔ (35t) (5t). Metro line 1 for downtown, board at Areeta station.

City centre is 10km SE of marinas. There are no yacht berths up-river. Bilbao is a major industrial city, but also a leading cultural and commercial centre. The Guggenheim museum is close to the Old Quarter. Main tourist office ☎910800.

All facilities; ⇄ Sondika ✈ is 10km NE of the city centre. P&O ferry to/from Portsmouth, approx 33hrs, every 3 days.

BILBAO *continued*

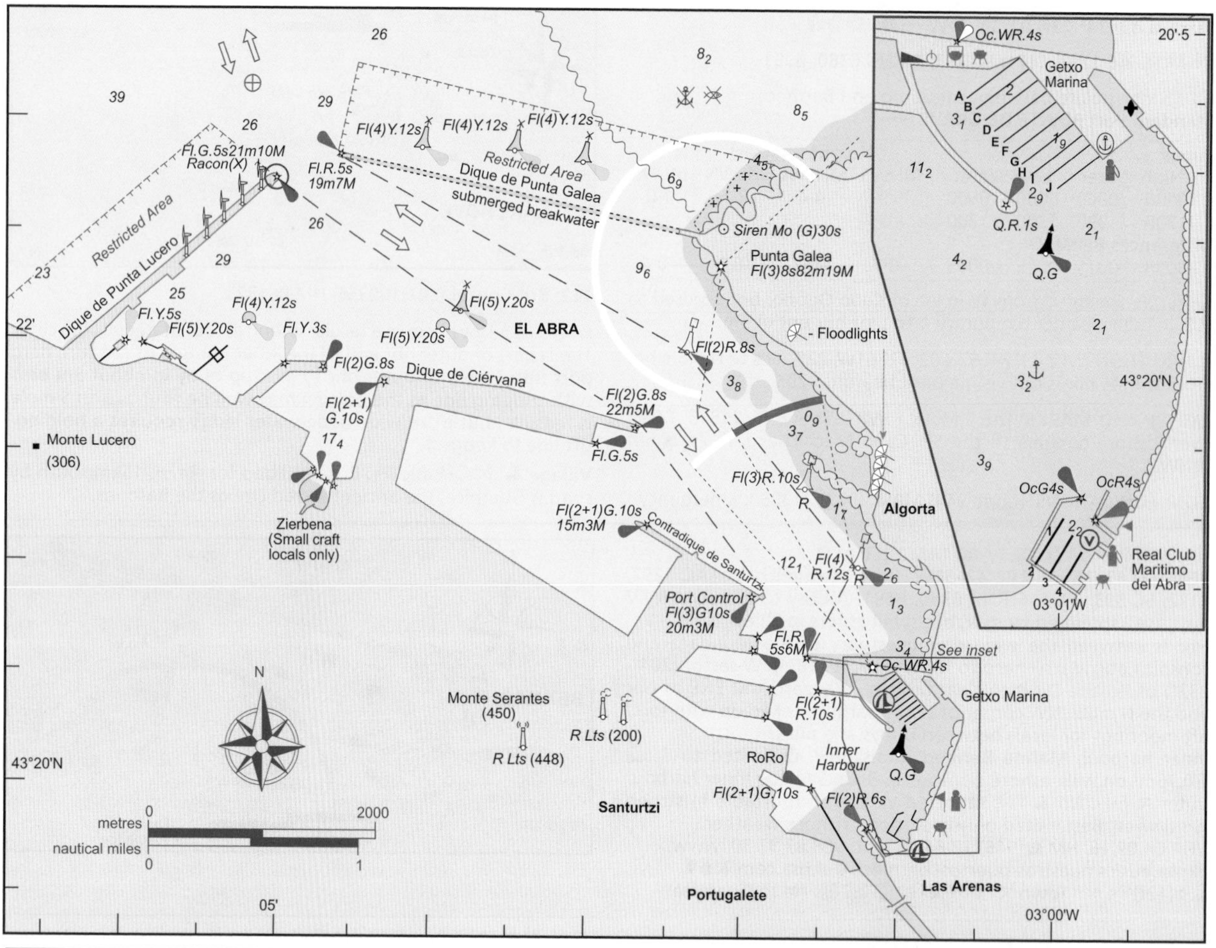

Fl.G.5s21m10M
Racon(X)
Restricted Area
Dique de Punta Lucero
Fl.Y.5s
Fl(5)Y.20s
Fl(4)Y.12s
Fl.Y.3s
Fl.R.5s
19m7M
Fl(4)Y.12s
Fl(4)Y.12s
Fl(4)Y.12s
Restricted Area
Dique de Punta Galea
submerged breakwater
Siren Mo (G)30s
Punta Galea
Fl(3)8s82m19M
Fl(5)Y.20s
Fl(5)Y.20s
EL ABRA
Floodlights
Fl(2)R.8s
Fl(2)G.8s
Dique de Ciérvana
Fl(2+1)
G.10s
Fl(2)G.8s
22m5M
Fl.G.5s
Monte Lucero
(306)
Zierbena
(Small craft
locals only)
Fl(3)R.10s
Algorta
Fl(2+1)G.10s
15m3M
Contradique de Santurtzi
Fl(4)
R.12s
Port Control
Fl(3)G10s
20m3M
Fl.R.
5s6M
See inset
Oc.WR.4s
Getxo Marina
Fl(2+1)
R.10s
Monte Serantes
(450)
R Lts (200)
R Lts (448)
RoRo
Inner
Harbour
Q.G
Fl(2+1)G.10s
Fl(2)R.6s
Santurtzi
Portugalete
Las Arenas
43°20'N
metres
0
2000
nautical miles
0
1
05'
03°00'W
Oc.WR.4s
Getxo
Marina
Q.R.1s
Q.G
OcG4s
OcR4s
Real Club
Maritimo
del Abra
03°01'W
20'·5
43°20'N

9.23.14 CASTRO URDIALES

Cantabria **43°22'·80N 03°12'·60W**

CHARTS AC 1292, 1174; SC 394, 394A; SHOM 3542, 6991

TIDES Differences, see Laredo facing page.

SHELTER Good, except in N-E winds when swell enters. A few Ⓐs or ⚓ in 9m on mud to seaward of the 6 lines of mooring trots which fill the NE part of hbr.

NAVIGATION WPT 43°23'·55N 03°11'·69W, 222°/1·0M to hbr ent, as under title. N mole lt ≠ S mole lt form an approx 222° ldg line. The approach is straightforward with no hazards. In the hbr use the fairway to avoid extensive mooring trots.

LIGHTS AND MARKS From the NW, town and hbr are obsc'd until rounding Pta del Rabanal with its conspic cemetery. The ✠, lt ho and castle are easily identified on Santa Ana which dominates the hbr. Lts as chartlet and Lights, buoys and waypoints.

COMMUNICATIONS (Code 942) MRCC (944) 839411; Emergency 112; CG/LB 900 202 202; Met via HM (below); ⊖861146; Brit Consul (902)109356; HM 861585; YC VHF Ch 09, call *Club Náutico*.

FACILITIES 150+ private moorings in the outer hbr; FVs fill inner hbr. ⌒ on N mole possible if calm and no swell. Club ☎861585. www.cncu.es cnautico@cncu.es; ask at club for any available moorings; ⚓ free, but €15.00 YC fee includes use of YC launch *Blancona* (Ch 09) & club facilities. Space for tenders at YC limited; . **YC** ✕ ☎861234 to reserve a table.

Town ✕, ✈ Bilbao.

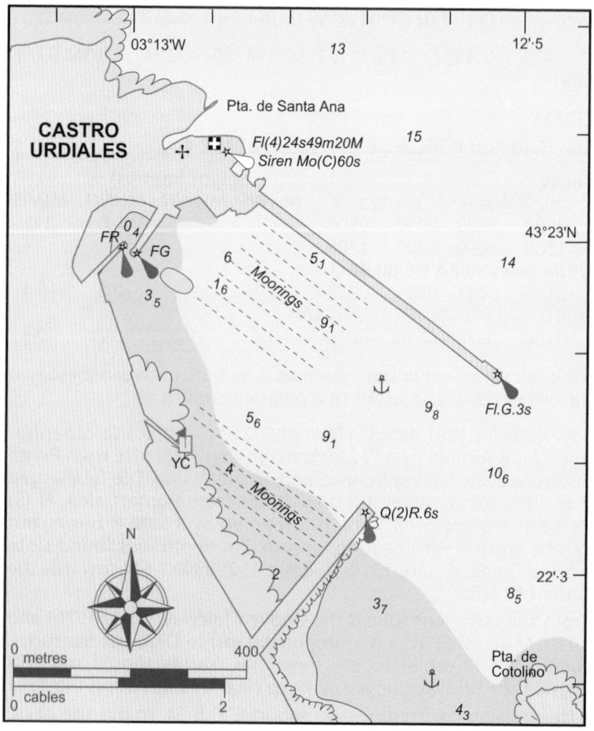

03°13'W
12'·5
CASTRO
URDIALES
Pta. de Santa Ana
Fl(4)24s49m20M
Siren Mo(C)60s
FR
FG
Moorings
43°23'N
Fl.G.3s
YC
Moorings
Q(2)R.6s
22'·3
metres
0
400
cables
0
2
Pta. de
Cotolino

9.23.15 LAREDO

Cantabria **43°25'·08N 03°25'·25W (ent)**

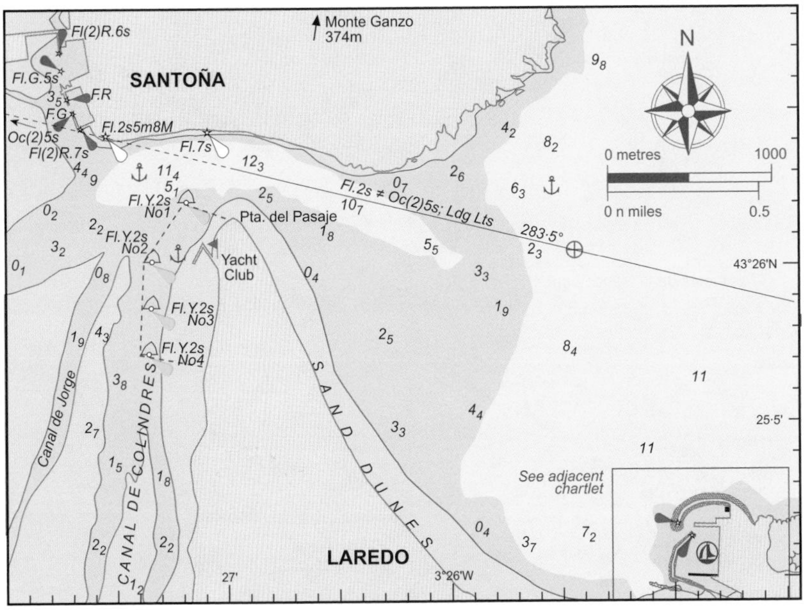

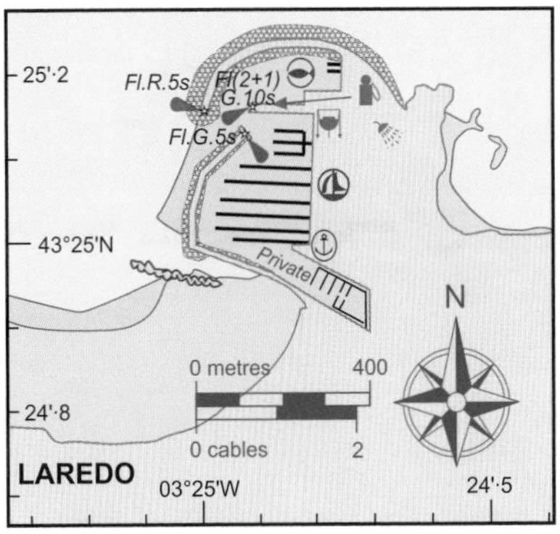

For Santoña 283·5°/1·3M to the narrows N abeam of Pta del Pasaje. The least charted depth on the ldg line is 3·5m, but expect less due to silting. The sandy estuary is exposed to E and S. A shallow chan runs 2·3M S to Colindres.

LIGHTS AND MARKS Santoña 283·5° ldg marks are hard to see. Monte Ganzo, 374m conspic mountain on N side is 1.2M NW of the Wpt. Pta del Pescador lt ho is 1M N of Monte Ganzo.

CHARTS AC 1292, 1171; SC 394, 3942; SHOM 3542

TIDES **Standard Port POINTE DE GRAVE (⟵)**

Times				Height (metres)			
High Water		Low Water		MHWS	MHWN	MLWN	MLWS
0000	0600	0000	0500	5·3	4·4	2·1	1·0
1200	1800	1200	1700				
Differences CASTRO URDIALES							
–0040	–0120	–0110	–0020	–1·3	–1·5	–0·6	–0·6
RIA DE SANTOÑA (03°28'W)							
–0005	–0045	–0035	+0015	–0·6	–1·2	–0·3	–0·7

SHELTER Good in marina, also W of Pta del Pasaje (CN de Laredo has ⚓ sheltered from E'lies).

NAVIGATION WPT 43°25'·97N 03°25'·47W. For Laredo, 170°/9ca to ent. Caution due to extensive fish havens N of Laredo ent.

COMMUNICATIONS (Code 942) MRCC (944) 839411; Emergency 112; Brit Consul (902)109356. Marina, VHF Ch 09.

FACILITIES **Puerto Deportivo de Laredo;** ☎605592. www.puertodeportivodelaredo.es puertos@cantabria Access 24H, all weather and tides, 857 berths inc 45 visitors €3·50/m inc, berths allocated by LOA (max 20m). (50t). Marina under new management 2017, reports welcome.

Laredo YC, ☎605812/16, www.rcnlaredo.es info@rcnlaredo.es W of Pta del Pasaje, a few buoys or ⚓ in 2m in area marked by 4 Y buoys, Fl Y 2s. LW landing on jetty/pontoons. (6t).

Village Several on outskirts, 5 mins walk from marina, ✈ Bilbao/Santander, bus station. Colindres for large.

Santoña has 2 basins; 5 visitors, max LOA 8·5m, lots of FVs. Reports of yachts being made unwelcome. at the SE corner;

9.23.16 SANTANDER

Cantabria **43°27'·66N 03°46'·13W** (between Nos 1 & 2 chan buoys)

CHARTS AC 1291/2, 1145; SC 401, 4011; SHOM 7365, 6991

TIDES **Standard Port POINTE DE GRAVE (⟵); ML 2·5**

Times				Height (metres)			
High Water		Low Water		MHWS	MHWN	MLWN	MLWS
0000	0600	0000	0500	5·3	4·4	2·1	1·0
1200	1800	1200	1700				
Differences *SANTANDER*							
–0020	*–0100*	*–0050*	*0000*	*–0·6*	*–1·2*	*–0·3*	*–0·7*
RÍA DE SUANCES (04°03'W)							
0000	–0030	–0020	+0020	–1·4	–1·5	–0·6	–0·6

SHELTER Access H24, all weather/tides. Fair shelter off the city but subject to wash; very good shelter upriver at marina.

NAVIGATION From the E, WPT 43°28'·45N 03°44'·54W (E of Isla de Mouro) 236°/1·4M to Nos 1/2 buoys.

From the W, WPT 43°29'·49N 03°46'·57W (4ca E of Cabo Mayor). Thence in fair weather head SE between Isla de Mouro and Peninsula de la Mágdalena (min depth 7·3m). In heavy weather keep NE of Isla de Mouro. Punta Rabiosa ldg lts lead 235·8° into the well-buoyed/lit DW chan, defined by a Dir WRG lt 259·5°.

For Marina Santander (see chartlet inset) follow the buoyed chan to No 17 small GRG buoy, Fl (2+1) G 10s; here turn WSW for marina ent. Caution: the hard-to-see 235·6° ldg marks to marina lead close to or over a shifting, drying sandbank. Night entry not advised unless already visited by day.

LIGHTS AND MARKS The university, formerly a Royal Palace, is conspic on Peninsula de la Mágdalena. City buildings are prominent. Long oil jetty is conspic N of Marina Santander; 400m westward a glazed pyramid-shaped building is a good daymark.

COMMUNICATIONS (Code 942) MRSC 213030; Emergency 112; Local weather broadcast VHF Ch 11 every 4hrs, 0245-2245 and via HM; ⊜ via HM; HM 223900; Port Authority *Santander Prácticos* VHF Ch **14**, 16; Marinas VHF Ch 09; Airport 202120.

FACILITIES Four options, from seaward:

- **Club Nautico de La Horadada** (CNH) ☎280402. www.horadada.es. ⚓ for 7–10m LOA craft NW of Nos 1 & 3 buoys, in 5m on rock; bay is almost full of local moorings. Tripping line essential.
- **Pedreña Marina,** 8ca SSE of Pta Rabiosa and the main channel. Access from No 4 buoy via PHM marked/lit chan with least depth 1·4m. Limited visitors (vessels <10m only) access is tight, reports would be welcomed. www.marinapedrena.com
- **Darsena de Molnedo**: Real Club Marítimo de Santander (RCMS; near city) ☎214050 www.rcmsantander.com. 108 berths max LOA 12m in 1·7m but few if any visitors. €3.10/m. RCMS

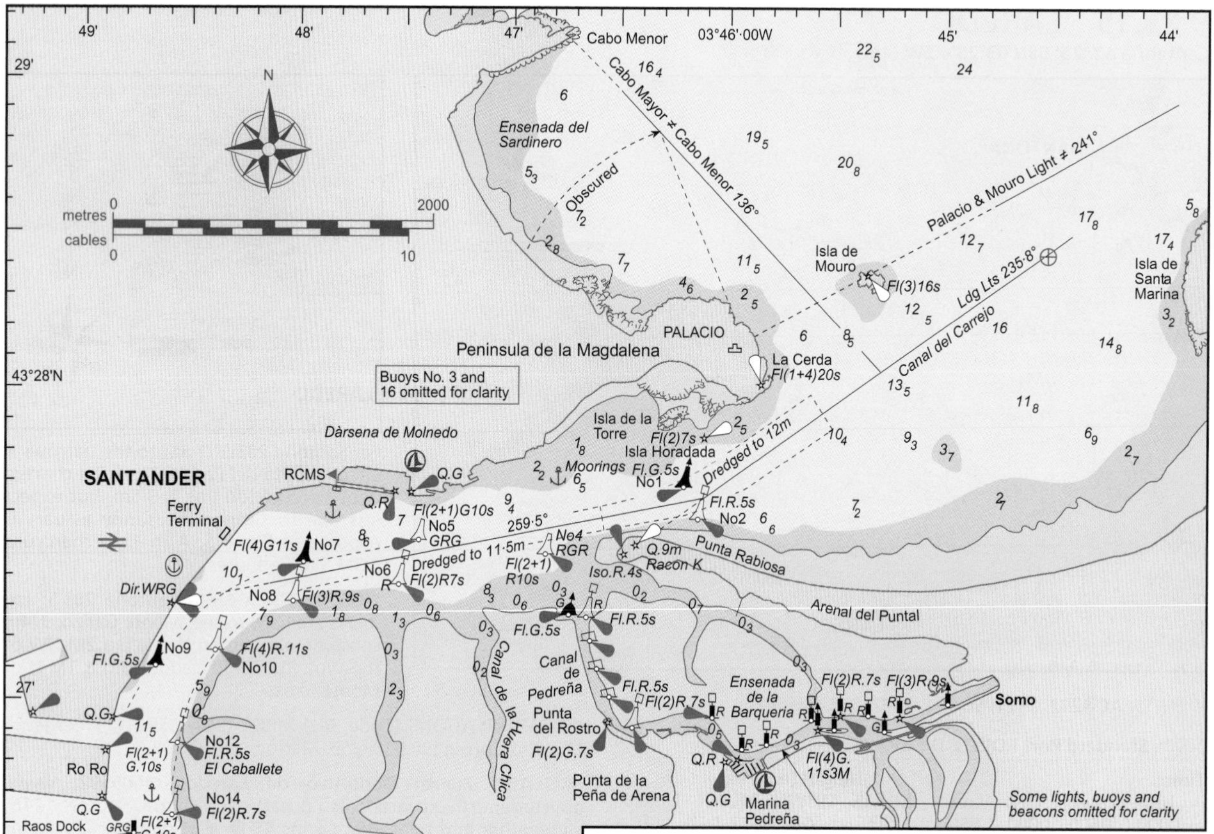
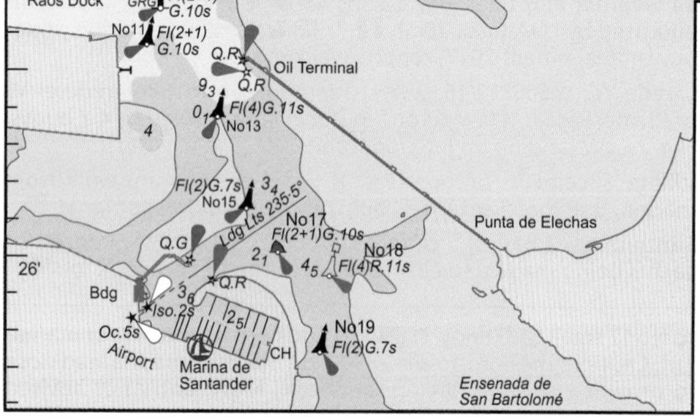

Cabo Menor
03°46'·00W
Cabo Mayor ≠ Cabo Menor 136°
Ensenada del Sardinero
Obscured
metres 0 2000
cables 0 10
Palacio & Mouro Light ≠ 241°
Isla de Mouro
Fl(3)16s
Ldg Lts 235·8°
Isla de Santa Marina
Canal del Carrejo
PALACIO
Peninsula de la Magdalena
La Cerda
Fl(1+4)20s
43°28'N
Buoys No. 3 and 16 omitted for clarity
Dàrsena de Molnedo
Isla de la Torre
Fl(2)7s
Isla Horadada
Fl.G.5s
No1
Dredged to 12m
Moorings
SANTANDER
RCMS
Q.G
Q.R
Fl(2+1)G10s
No5
GRG
259·5°
Ferry Terminal
Fl(4)G11s
No7
No4
RGR
Fl.R.5s
No2
Q.9m
Racon K
Punta Rabiosa
Dredged to 11·5m
No6
Fl(2)R7s
Fl(2+1) R10s
Iso.R.4s
Dir.WRG
No8
Fl(3)R.9s
Arenal del Puntal
Fl.G.5s
Fl.R.5s
No9
Fl(4)R.11s
No10
Canal de Pedreña
Canal de la Hoya Chica
Ensenada de la Barqueria
Fl(2)R.7s
Fl(3)R.9s
Somo
Punta del Rostro
Fl(2)G.7s
No12
Fl.R.5s
El Caballete
Ro Ro
Fl(2+1) G.10s
Q.R
Fl(4)G. 11s3M
Punta de la Peña de Arena
Q.G
Marina Pedreña
Some lights, buoys and beacons omitted for clarity
Raos Dock
GRG
No14
Fl(2)R.7s
No11
Oil Terminal
Fl(4)G.11s
No13
Fl(2)G.7s
No15
Ldg Lts 235·5°
No17
Fl(2+1)G.10s
No18
Fl(4)R.11s
Punta de Elechas
Bdg
Iso.2s
Oc.5s
Airport
Marina de Santander
CH
No19
Fl(2)G.7s
Ensenada de San Bartolomé

berths S side, misc N side. (27t) (1·5t). ⚓s and ⚓ S of the dock are exposed to wash.

- **Marina de Santander** ☎369298 is approx 2·7M further upriver, but 20 mins bus/taxi ride to the city. 1400 inc Ⓥ in 2·2-3·1m, max LOA 23m, €4.43, max 15 days. (taxi req'd) Ⓔ (27t). Security adequate to leave a yacht. Little noise from adjacent Parayas airport. marinasantander@marinasantander.com www.marinasantander.com

City www.puertosantander.com All amenities; ⇌ & bus; Brittany ferry terminal ☎360611 is 6ca W of Darsena de Molnedo; ✈.

SUANCES, Cantabria. **43°25'·78N 04°02'·08W** (marina). AC 1291, 1150; SC 4012; SHOM 2042. Tidal differences overleaf. No access in N'lies or when swell breaking over bar, 1m; not advised at night. On late flood from ⊕ 43°25'·78N 04°02'·08W track 149·5°/8ca on ldg bcns (Q & Iso 4s) to Fl(4)R 11s bcn at hd of trng wall. Best water E side of chan. Marina (Fl (4) R & G 11s) has small craft pontoon. If >8m LOA, on piled N or W walls. Basics in village, ✕.

SANTANDER TO CABO ORTEGAL

Harbours west of Santander (AC 1290, 1291) are increasingly far apart compared with those to the east. 28M W of Santander, San Vicente de la Barquera is a well sheltered estuary, with limited anchoring possibilities but no alongside berths. 32M further W, Ribadesella's marina has visitor berthing for boats <12m. The magnificent backdrop to this section of coast are the **Picos de Europa** mountains (2648m), the peaks often visible 15M offshore while cloud obscures their lower slopes.

Further west a heavy NW swell, known as a *Vaga de Mar*, breaks over banks and closes any ports which have bars. It can occur quite suddenly in calm weather, but is usually associated with strong NW'lies. In summer NE winds predominate and fog occurs fairly often especially in late June to early July.

Gijón with a modern marina offers refuge; it lies close SE of, but quite distinct from, El Musel, the very large commercial harbour whose northerly extension, under construction may be a trap for unwary yachts cruising close inshore.

Cudillero and **Luarca** are small fishing hbrs worth visiting, but beware swell especially off Cudillero. **Ría de Ribadeo** (with a much improved marina) is the first of the *Rías altas* (ie upper or northern) sunken estuaries not unlike a Scottish sea loch. **San Ciprian**'s aluminium port (AC 1122) offers within its long bkwtrs a sheltered ⚓ of refuge close to its W shore.

Ría de Viveiro has a well sheltered marina and several anchorages to await fair winds around Cabo Ortegal. **Ría del Barquero** and the **Ensenada de Santa Marta**, to E and W of Pta de la Estaca de Bares, offer many attractive ⚓s exposed only to N/NE winds; but beware S/SW winds off the mountains being accelerated through the valleys. This stretch of steep, rocky coast is deeply indented and rises to over 500m a few miles inland.

►*From Pta de la Estaca de Bares to Cabo Ortegal (8M) the tidal stream sets E or NE on a rising tide and W or SW when falling, rates up to 2kn inshore and perceptible for a considerable distance offshore.*◄

9.23.17
SAN VICENTE DE LA BARQUERA

Cantabria. **43°23'·69N 04°23'·06W** ❁❁◌◌✿✿✿

CHARTS AC 1291; SC 402, 4021; SHOM 6381, 6991

TIDES

Standard Port POINTE DE GRAVE (⟵)

Times				**Height (metres)**			
High Water		Low Water		MHWS	MHWN	MLWN	MLWS
0000	0600	0000	0500	5·3	4·4	2·1	1·0
1200	1800	1200	1700				
Differences SAN VICENTE DE LA BARQUERA							
–0020	–0100	–0050	0000	–1·4	–1·5	–0·6	–0·6
RÍA DE TINA MAYOR (04°31'W, 6M W of San Vicente)							
–0020	–0100	–0050	0000	–1·3	–1·5	–0·6	–0·6

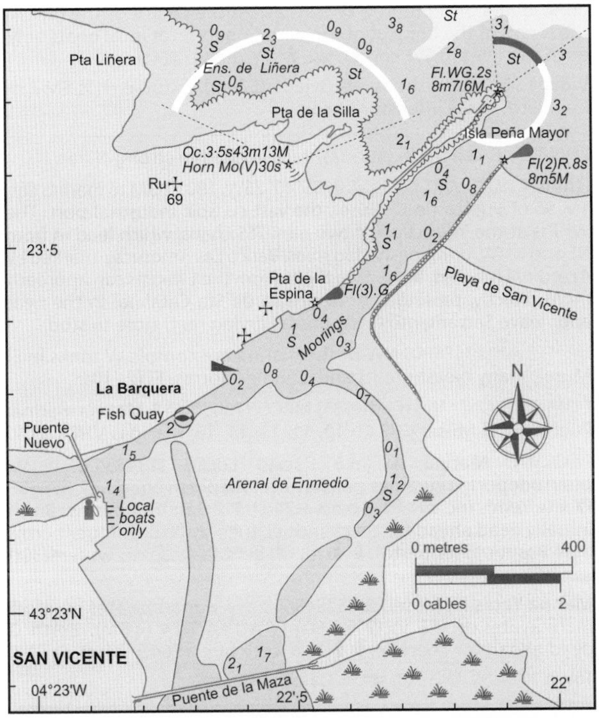

SHELTER Well protected large shallow estuary. An active FV hbr with virtually no yacht berth availability. ⚓ing very difficult due to local moorings and FV's on mid-stream pontoons. Berthing on the fish quay at La Barquera is not feasible, it is busy and also lacks steps and ladders for access. Only poss. ⚓ in chan E of Arenal de Enmedio, landing poss. at steps just S of small local marina.

NAVIGATION WPT 43°24'·39N 04°22'·16W, 223°/1M to hbr ent (abeam Isla Peña Menor). Beware shallow bar and tidal streams 3-4kn. Avoid access near LW if there is any swell at all. Depths are as per SC 4021 but may be more water.

LIGHTS AND MARKS Pta de la Silla lt ho and hbr lts. Beach E of ent, castle & church upriver are conspic.

COMMUNICATIONS (Code 942) MRCC 326050; Emergency 112; Brit Consul (902)109356; HM 710004.

FACILITIES **Town** About 41km NExE of the Picos de Europa. ✉ ⓑ ✈ (Santander). www.sanvicentedelabarquera.org

HARBOUR 16M WEST OF SAN VICENTE DE LA BARQUERA

LLANES, Asturias. **43°25'·15N 04°44'·92W**. AC 1291; SC 403; SHOM 5009. Tides: Interpolate between San Vicente and Ribadesella. The small FV hbr faces E. Do not enter in strong N to E winds or heavy swell, or below half-tide. The N pierhead, ☆ Fl G 5s, is conspic due to brilliantly coloured concrete rock armour. The S side of the ent is marked by ☆ Fl R 5s and San Anton lt ho, easily seen from the E. Approx 150m further W a ☆ Fl (3) G 9s marks a small basin to stbd; berth/raft in 2m where space permits (very limited due to FVs) on smooth N or E walls or as directed. No room to ⚓. ✕ good shops. turismo@ayuntiamentodellanes.com www.llanes.com **Marina** ☎985 401421, ent via a lock. 140, €0·15/m²/day, max LOA <10m, limited Ⓥ on 20m pontoon, port hand side of basin. Lock traffic signals: 3 G (vert) for open and 3 R (vert) for closed.

9.23.18 RIBADESELLA

Asturias 43°28'·06N 05°03'·99W ❁❁◌◌✿✿✿

CHARTS AC 1291, 1150; SC 403, 4031; SHOM 6381, 6691

TIDES

Standard Port POINTE DE GRAVE (⟵)

Times				**Height (metres)**			
High Water		Low Water		MHWS	MHWN	MLWN	MLWS
0000	0600	0000	0500	5·3	4·4	2·1	1·0
1200	1800	1200	1700				
Differences RIBADESELLA							
+0005	–0020	–0020	+0020	–1·3	–1·3	–0·6	–0·4

SHELTER Good. No space within the hbr to ⚓.

NAVIGATION WPT 43°28'·59N 05°04'·02W, 180°/5ca to Pta del Caballo. Bajo Serropio, 7ca NNE of ent, breaks in heavy seas. Easy appr at HW, do not attempt in strong onshore winds when swell breaks on bar, reported 2m, but less after NW gales. Hug the N bank 25m off the promenade to clear drying, buoyed sandbanks to stbd, turn 90° to stbd at last SHM, then steer SW towards marina, only turning to port when abeam of the long visitors' pontoon.

LIGHTS AND MARKS E of hbr ent smooth, dark cliffs and a chapel are distinctive. To the W a white beach is distinct. The channel up-river is now well lit and buoyed; see chartlet.

COMMUNICATIONS (Code 985) MRCC 326050; Emergency 112; Brit Consul (902)109356; HM 860038, VHF Ch 09 occasionally.

FACILITIES **Marina** on W bank in 3m, ent dredged 2·5m, has Ⓥ pontoon, max 12m LOA €15·00/night + €50·00 refundable deposit for gate key. free wi-fi at marina office, (8t).

Town ✕ ✉ ⓑ Ⓔ YC ✈ Oviedo (78km).

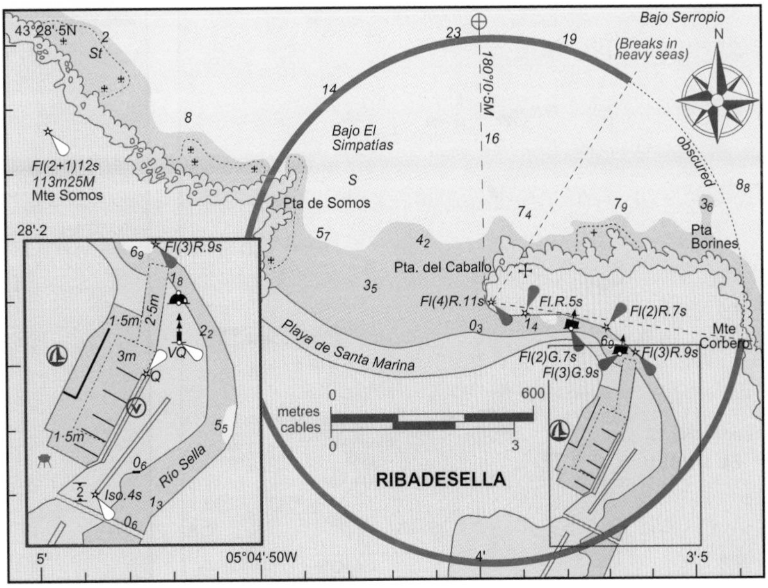

9.23.19 LASTRES

Asturias 43°30'·90N 05°15'·93W

CHARTS AC 1291, 1153, 1150; SC 403, 4041; SHOM 6991, 5009

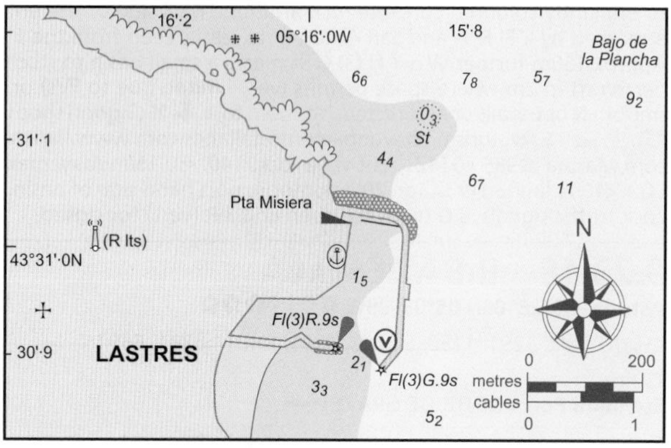

TIDES Interpolate between Ribadesella and Gijon.

SHELTER Well protected from W'lies by steep hillside, but in strong E'lies it becomes uncomfortable despite a substantial E bkwtr. ⚓ about 1ca S of the hbr in 5m on sand, clear of a fish farm marked by Fl Y 2·5s.

NAVIGATION WPT 43°31'·16N 05°15'·35W, 235°/5ca to hbr ent. Access H24. Easy approach in all but strong E'lies, avoiding Bajo de la Plancha (5·7m) 3ca NNE of ent, breaks in heavy seas; also a pinnacle rk (0·3m) close NNE of the E bkwtr.

LIGHTS AND MARKS A 118m high, R/W TV mast (R lts) is conspic close W of the hbr. Cabo Lastres lt ho is 1·9M NW.

COMMUNICATIONS (Code 985) MRCC 326050; Emergency 112; Brit Consul (902)109356; HM 850003; FV President 850075; Tourist office (Colunga) 852200.

FACILITIES Berth/raft at the S end of the E bkwtr in 4-7m. FVs berth on W quays or moor in E-W trots across the centre of the hbr. At the N end of the hbr a pontoon with fingers is for local boats only, ditto the inlet in SW corner. (FV quay) (4t).

Village Basic shops, Oviedo (62km). Asturias ✈ is 5M E of Cudillero. www.infoasturias.com

9.23.20 GIJÓN

Asturias **43°32'·78N 05°40'·26W**

CHARTS AC 1290, 1291, 1153, 1154; SC 404, 404A, 4042; SHOM 6381, 5009

TIDES

Standard Port POINTE DE GRAVE (⟵); ML 2·3

Times				Height (metres)			
High Water		Low Water		MHWS	MHWN	MLWN	MLWS
0000	0600	0000	0500	5·3	4·4	2·1	1·0
1200	1800	1200	1700				
Differences *GIJON*							
−0005	*−0030*	*−0030*	*+0010*	*−0·9*	*−1·4*	*−0·4*	*−0·7*
LUANCO (05°47'W)							
−0010	−0035	−0035	+0005	−1·3	−1·3	−0·6	−0·4
AVILÉS (05°56'W)							
−0100	−0040	−0050	−0015	−1·1	−1·6	−0·5	−0·7
SAN ESTABAN DE PRAVIA (06°05'W)							
−0005	−0030	−0030	+0010	−1·3	−1·3	−0·6	−0·4

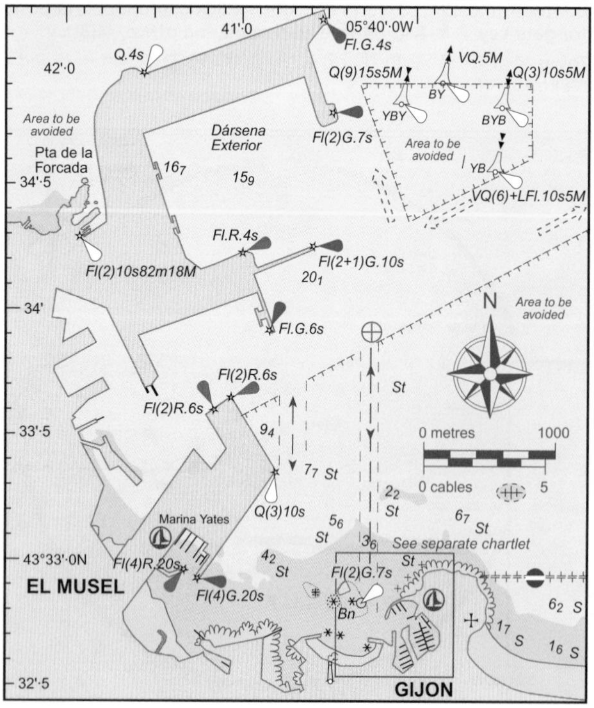

SHELTER Excellent in marinas; care needed in strong N'lies.

NAVIGATION WPT 43°33'·78N 05°40'·26W, 180°/1·3M to marina ent, 1M SE of Puerto de El Musel, the vast conspic industrial port. The WPT is at the Y-junction of two mini-TSS chans, which lead in from NE and NNW, primarily for big ships. Banco Las Amosucas, marked by 4 cardinal lt buoys, lies within the Y. From the E yachts can approach more directly, passing N of Peninsula de Sta Catalina. In the near appr leave Sacramento G twr (marks drying reef) close to stbd.

LIGHTS AND MARKS NW of the marina are conspic W tanks in El Musel, many nav/shore lts and Cabo de Torres, Fl (2) 10s.

COMMUNICATIONS (Code 985) MRCC 326050; & Met via marina; Puerto de El Musel VHF Ch 10, 11, 12, **14**, 16; Marinas VHF Ch 09.

FACILITIES **Marina** (aka Puerto Local) ☎344543. www.puertodeportivogijon.es info@puertodeportivogijon.es 658+88 €0.70/m², inc . Access H24 (1·2–2·5m) in 4 basins. Berth initially dead ahead for check-in/fuel, then shift to finger berths in N Basin (Antepuerto). no wi-fi (30t) . YC.

Marina Yates (El Musel) ☎687549658. www.marinayates.es info@marinayates.es 156 inc €0.50/m². Access H24 (4·5m). Berth G dead ahead for check/in. bike hire (64t) (5t).

Town @ Ⓑ ⇌ ✈ Oviedo (42km).

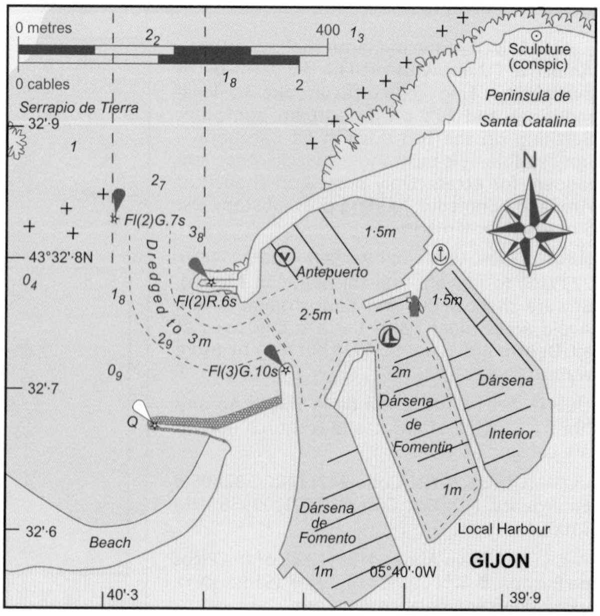

HARBOUR 6M SOUTH WEST OF CABO PEÑAS

AVILÉS, Asturias. **43°35'·65N 05°56'·77W**. AC 1290, 1142; SC 405A, 4052; SHOM 5009, 7361. Tides: 9.23.20. A port of refuge, except in W/NW'lies >F9, but also heavily industrialised and a FV hbr. Port VHF Ch **12** 16. HM ☎(985) 541 111, paviles@paviles.com. The ent, S of Pta del Castillo lt ho and N of conspic white beach, is open to W/NW but well sheltered from N'lies. The well-marked/lit ent chan runs E x S for 7ca then turns S for 2M to **Club Náutico Marina de Avilés** pontoons at 43°33'·66N 05°55'·28W, W side of chan; max LOA about 12m, ☎ +34 607 811525 (for marina gate access code and to pay) Ⓥ €1.18/m. Beware FV wash. YC at Salinas, 2M NW. Old town is close SW and very picturesque. ✈ Asturias (14km).

HARBOUR 3M EAST OF CUDILLERO

SAN ESTEBAN DE PRAVIA, Asturias. **43°34'·21N 06°04'·54W**. AC 1290, 1133; SC 405, 405A, 4041; SHOM 5009. Tides: Gijón. A former coaling port, now only a few FVs berth on E bank at San Juan de la Arena quay, 90m long. The 206·2° ldg lts lead very close to the W bkwtr hd. Appr near HW due to silting in the ent. Possible on FV quay or on facing quays on W bank. Or ⚓ in river on sand in 2·2m just S of ent to town quays.

9.23.21 CUDILLERO

Asturias **43°33'·96N 06°08'·80W** (W bkwtr hd)

CHARTS AC 1290; SC 934, 405, 405A; SHOM 5009

TIDES Use San Estaban de Pravia, 3M W; see Gijón.

SHELTER Good in large modern basin, NW of hbr ent, but N'ly swell can make entry/exit difficult and may work into the basin.

NAVIGATION WPT 43°34'·33N 06°08'·71W, 190°/3½ca to W bkwtr hd. From the W keep at least 5ca offshore until clear of Piedras las Colinas, tall islets/reefs NW of ent. From the E appr with Pta Rebollera lt ho on initial bearing of 200°. The rocky ent opens up only when close to. Narrow chan skirts the W bkwtr into basin. Before leaving look over the bkwtr to assess swell.

LIGHTS AND MARKS Pta Rebollera lt ho is conspic W 8-sided twr.

COMMUNICATIONS (Code 985) MRCC 326050; Emergency 112; Brit Consul (902)109356; HM VHF Ch 27.

FACILITIES Hammerhead N pontoon if space permits or SW of pontoons on 12 yellow/red fore/aft pick up buoys. (Note: reptd in poor condition and most taken by local small craft, 2016; aft pick up buoy held underwater by a weight.) €15·00/night. FVs moor/berth at NW end of the basin. The old drying hbr, S of ent, is exposed to swell, but handy for dinghies; yachts can dry out on slip. HM ☎591114, (gasoleo B) from FV quay, small shipyard.

Village 5 mins by dinghy, 25 mins on foot.

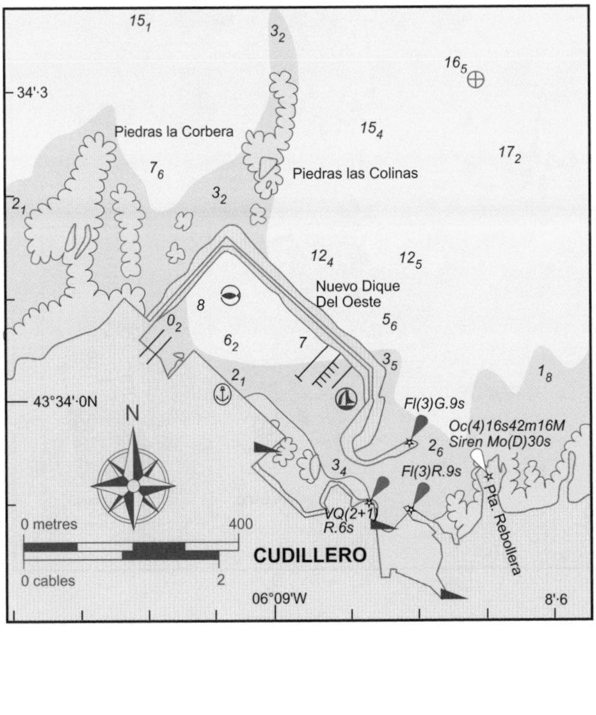

9.23.22 LUARCA

Asturias **43°32'·95N 06°32'·20W**

CHARTS AC 1290, 1133; SC 933, 934, 4061; SHOM 6381, 5009

TIDES

Standard Port POINTE DE GRAVE (⟵)

Times				Height (metres)			
High Water		Low Water		MHWS	MHWN	MLWN	MLWS
0000	0600	0000	0500	5·3	4·4	2·1	1·0
1200	1800	1200	1700				
Differences LUARCA							
+0010	–0015	–0015	+0025	–1·1	–1·1	–0·5	–0·3

SHELTER The outer hbr is protected from all but N'lies, but swell can intrude (reported to badly affect the Ⓐs). No room to ⚓ inside the hbr.

NAVIGATION WPT 43°33'·51N 06°32'·29W, 170°/6ca to E bkwtr hd lt ho which is conspic and almost in transit with the ldg marks. Appr on the ldg lts/marks 170° to clear rky shoals either side.

LIGHTS AND MARKS Cabo Busto is 3M ENE of hbr ent. Pta Blanca (or Focicón) lt ho is W □ tr and house on prominent headland 300m ENE of hbr ent; conspic ✠ close by. 170° ldg lts are on thin W lattice pylons, R bands; not easy to see until close in.

COMMUNICATIONS (Code 985) MRCC 326050; Emergency 112; Brit Consul (902)109356; HM 640176/640083.

FACILITIES Moor fore-and-aft to the E bkwtr, stern to 2 x steel Ⓐs which are close together, plus 3 small plastic Ⓐs. Underwater obst'ns of 1·3m, close bkwtr reported, so caution at springs, but in calm conditions it is possible to lie alongside the bkwtr.

Narrow chan leads SE to inner hbr dredged 2m (prone to silting). Pontoons in SE corner are full of local craft, little chance of a berth. Temp'y on NW side may be possible. from FV quay, (8t).

Town Friendly YC next to front ldg lt.

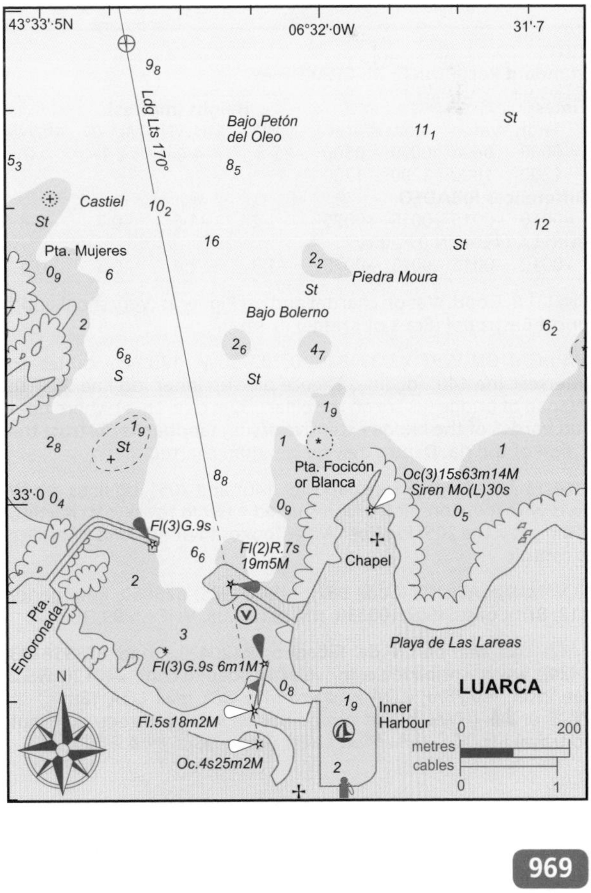

9.23.23 RÍA DE RIBADEO

Lugo **43°32'·44N 07°02'·16W** (Marina ent)

CHARTS AC 1290, 1096; SC 932, 4071; SHOM 5009

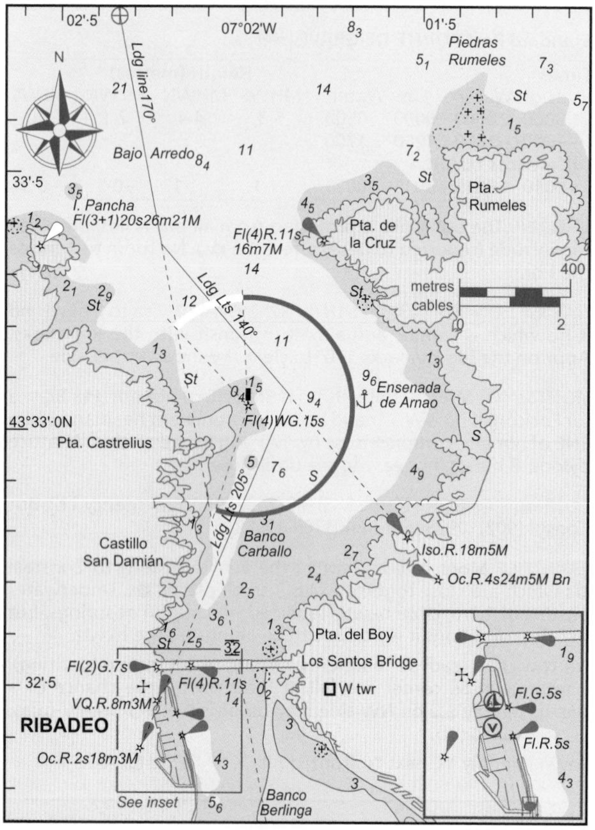

TIDES

Standard Port POINTE DE GRAVE (⟵)

Times				Height (metres)			
High Water		Low Water		MHWS	MHWN	MLWN	MLWS
0000	0600	0000	0500	5·3	4·4	2·1	1·0
1200	1800	1200	1700				
Differences RIBADEO							
+0010	–0015	–0015	+0025	–1·2	–1·5	–0·7	–0·8
BURELA (43°40'N 07°20'W)							
+0010	–0015	–0015	+0025	–1·3	–1·4	–0·5	–0·4

SHELTER Good. ⚓ as on chartlet and off Figueras (very shoal appr) or off Castropol (8ca S of bridge) in 4m.

NAVIGATION WPT 43°33'·84N 07°02'·30W, 170°/4½ cables to intersect the 140° ldg line. Thence pick-up inner ldg line 205° to W span of bridge (lts are on the pillars; 32m clearance) where tides run hard. S of the bridge extensive drying sandbanks obstruct the E side of the ría. Depths may be less than charted.

LIGHTS AND MARKS Daymarks for 140° and 205° ldg lines are W twrs with R ◊. Conspic R onion-shaped twr in town (off chartlet) is almost ≠ the 205° ldg line. White lookout twr at E end of bridge is conspic.

COMMUNICATIONS (Code 982); MRCC (985) 326050; Emergency 112; Brit Consul (902)109356; HM ☎128005, VHF Ch 09, 16.

FACILITIES **Marina/CN de Ribadeo** ☎120428, mob 648958143 (H24); www. cnribadeo.com vela@cnribadeo.com; 240+20 Ⓥ see inset, €0·78m² (LOA x beam) May-Oct, max LOA 18m or (HW±1hr), in fishing hbr on small pontoon adjacent to travel lift. (8t). **Town** Ⓑ.

9.23.24 RÍA DE VIVEIRO

Lugo **43°40'·93N 07°36'·16W** (Celeiro bkwtr hd)

CHARTS AC 1290, 1122; SC 931, 4082; SHOM 5009, 6383

TIDES

Standard Port POINTE DE GRAVE (⟵)

Times				Height (metres)			
High Water		Low Water		MHWS	MHWN	MLWN	MLWS
0000	0600	0000	0500	5·3	4·4	2·1	1·0
1200	1800	1200	1700				
Differences RÍA DE VIVEIRO							
+0010	–0015	–0015	+0025	–1·3	–1·3	–0·6	–0·4

SHELTER Good, except in N'lies. ⚓ in E'lies inside Isla Insua d'Area, 1·3M NE of Celeiro. In S-W winds ⚓ at the head of the ría off Playa de Covas in 6-7m.

NAVIGATION Easy ent, 7ca wide, between Isla Gabeira and Pta de Faro. WPT 43°43'·25N 07°35'·30W (mouth of the ria) 195°/2·4M to round Celeiro bkwtr hd. Keep clear of this major FV hbr.

LIGHTS AND MARKS Mte Faro Juances, is a distinctive conical peak (193m) close SE of Pta de Faro.

COMMUNICATIONS (Code 982) MRCC (985) 326050; Emergency 112; Celeiro HM 560074; Celeiro Port VHF Ch 16; Marina VHF Ch 09.

FACILITIES **Marina Viveiro** ☎mob 690604452; www.www.northwestmarinas.com/en/marina-viveiro/the-marina/marina viveiro@marinaviveiro.com 243 inc Ⓥ €2·80, max 18m LOA on fingers, 30m LOA on quayside S pontoon, (N pontoon Guardia Civil del Mar only), multihulls +50%. by tanker/hose from nearby fuel depot. (New fuel berth completion due 2017.) wi-fi (35t) (8t). **Town** Ⓑ.

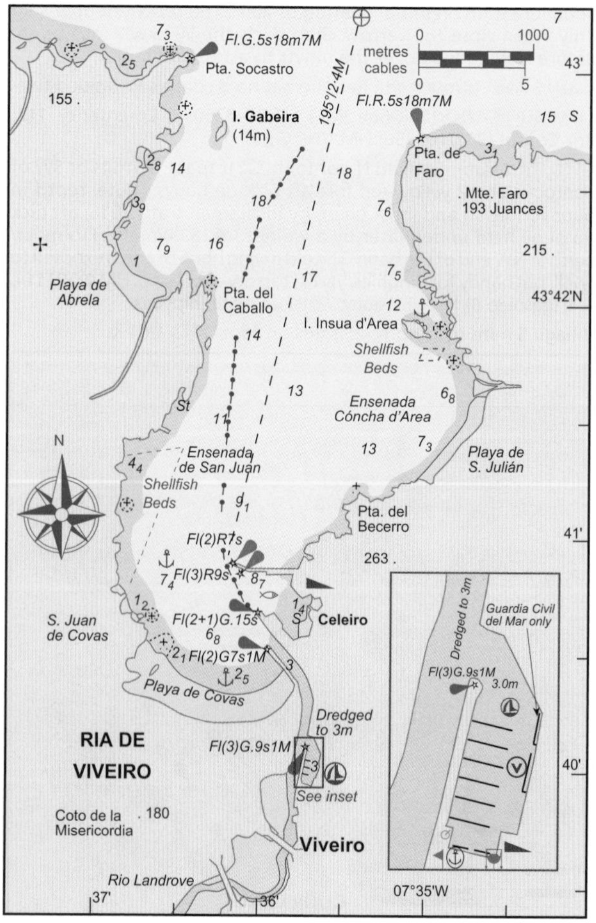

RÍA DEL BARQUERO. 43°45'·00N 07°40'·70W. AC 1290, 1122; SC 931, 4082; SHOM 6383. Tides: Ría de Viveiro. A delightful ría, exposed only to NE'lies. There is an ⚓ at Bares below the steep, high W bank and 2·5M SSW a shallow access channel leads to a tiny hbr at El Barquero in depths 1·5-2·5m.

On the E side of the ría, yachts may ⚓ N of Pta del Castro, clear of an outfall; or a berth may be found in the modern FV port at Vicedo on the S or W quays.

See Lights, buoys and waypoints for lts at: Isla Coelleira (an islet between this ría and Ría de Viveiro); Pta de la Estaca de Barra; Pta de la Barra; Pta del Castro; and Vicedo.

MINOR HARBOURS SOUTH OF CABO ORTEGAL

CARIÑO. 43°44'·21N 07°52'·14W is 2M S of Cabo Ortegal (AC 1122) and well sheltered from all W'lies. After rounding the outer commercial jetty, ⚓ in 5-6m on sand within the bay. Dinghies can be left on an extended pontoon in the NW corner of the hbr; Ashore: shops. In E'lies, ⚓ off **Espasante** FV hbr, 2·3M ESE of Cariño (AC 1111).

RÍA DE SANTA MARTA DE ORTIGUEIRA. 43°42'·78N 07°50'·60W. Tides: +0050 La Coruña (⟶); MHWS –0·1; MHWN +0·4; MLWN –0·1; MLWS +0·3; streams reach 5kn sp. SC 4083 (1:20,000) is essential for pilotage. WPT 43°45'·00N 07°50'·60W, 180°/2·4M to the Ría ent (L/L above) to arrive (or leave) HW-1. ⚓s in 3 pools off Pta Postina (11·4m) Pta Sismundi (11·1m) and Pta Redonda (5·2m).

The access chan crosses the 0·4m bar on a S'ly track with Isla de San Vicente 50m to port. Silting can occur on the bar, due caution is recommended, but inside the ría the chan is dredged to 3m. It turns W, SW and S in three legs each about 1M long and is marked by small lateral buoys and occas perches/withies. The eponymous town will be seen when 7ca WNW of it. In sequence, first pass a quay with blue crane, a small private jetty, and finally reach the marina ent. Rewarding pilotage to an elegant town.

Facilities: ❤ welcome; 3 YC pontoons (2m max) max LOA 12m. ✕ Ⓑ; coast road & ⇄ to La Coruña ✈.

CABO ORTEGAL TO CABO FINISTERRE

Cabo Ortegal should be rounded at least 2M off due to the offlying needle rocks, Los Aguillones. Most of the major headlands should be given a good offing to avoid fluky winds and, in some cases, pinnacle rocks. The deeply indented coast (AC 1111, 3633, 3764) begins to trend WSW, with 600m high mountains rising only 5M inland. Coastal features are often hard to identify against this background. Here many major lights are sited so high as to be obscured by low cloud/mist in onshore weather.

▶*Tidal streams set SW on the ebb and NE on the flood. Any current tends to run SW, then S.*◀

The **Ría de Cedeira** is entered 3M SSW of Pta Candelaria lt ho. This small attractively wooded ría offers refuge by day/night to yachts unable to round Cabo Ortegal in strong NE'lies. Several banks along this stretch break in heavy weather when they should be passed well to seaward.

About 20M further SW, having passed Pta de la Frouxeira, Cabo Prior, Pta de Castro and Cabo Prioriño Chico, all lit, is the entrance to **Ría de Ferrol**, a well-sheltered commercial and naval port, but with limited yacht facilities. The adjacent **Ría de Ares** and **Ría de Betanzos** are attractive alternatives, both with easy access to their marinas.

La Coruña is a port of refuge, accessible in all weathers and has excellent yacht facilities with two marinas near the city centre and another to the south.

5M W of Torre de Hércules lt ho, a huge new commercial port at La Coruña is nearing completion (2017) at Punta Langosteira and must be avoided by small craft. The direct course across the 19M bight W to the Islas Sisargas will keep you clear of this and other inshore hazards; passage between Islas Sisargas and the mainland is not advised. 8M SW of Pta Nariga, between Pta del Roncudo and Pta de Lage, is the unspoiled **Ría de Corme y Laxe** with two small fishing hbrs in the NNE and SSW corners of the bay.

Cabo Villano, a rocky headland with lighthouse, siren and conspicuous wind turbines, is a possible landfall after crossing Biscay. 4ca NW of it El Bufardo (43°10'·00N 09°13'·28W) is a dangerous pinnacle rock awash at CD.

20M NW of Cabo Villano and 22M NW of Punta de la Barca is the **Off Finisterre TSS**; see Area Map. Yachts have more than adequate searoom within the ITZ whose southern boundary lies due west of Cabo Finisterre. *Finisterre Tráfico* (VTS) on VHF **11**, 74, 16 broadcasts regular information about Navwarnings, weather and traffic in Spanish and English. On request it can also provide the vessel's position, course and speed and the identity of other vessels in the vicinity.

The entrance to **Ría de Camariñas**, the last of the rías altas and a safe refuge, is 2·4M S of Cabo VillaNo There is a small, friendly marina at Camariñas, and on the SW side of the ria a new 224 berth marina at Mugia, and a sheltered anchorage just S.

Cabo Toriñana and **Cabo Finisterre** both have charted dangers, mostly pinnacle rocks, lying up to 1M offshore; hence the popular name *Costa del Morte* for this wild, magnificent and sometimes forbidding coast.

9.23.25 RÍA DE CEDEIRA

La Coruña **43°39'·38N 08°03'·86W** (⚓) ❄❄❄◇◇✿✿✿

CHARTS AC 1290, 1111, 1122; SC 411; SHOM 5009, 3007

TIDES Interpolate between Santa Marta de Ortigueira (Ría de Viveiro) and Ferrol. ML no data.

SHELTER Very good; handy for awaiting a fair wind to round Cabo Ortegal. ⚓ in 3-4m about 500m SE of the modern FV port, excellent holding on sand. Although the whole ría is a marine reserve (see chartlet) there are no constraints on visitors who can ⚓ anywhere for free.

NAVIGATION WPT 43°41'·00N 08°05'·41W, 155°/1·7M to Pta del Sarridal. From N keep > 1M off Pta Candelaria until the ría opens. From the S a similar offing clears rks N/NW of Pta Chirlateira.

155° ldg line Pta Promontorio lt ho ≠ Pta del Sarridal. Abeam Pta Chirlateira with Pta Xian brg 161°, track midway between Pta del Sarridal and Piedras de Media Mar. When the bkwtr hd bears 060° turn toward the anchorage. The E end of the bay shoals rapidly toward the drying mouth of Rio de Cedeira.

LIGHTS AND MARKS Piedras de Media Mar, BRB lt twr conspic in centre of ría, can be passed on either side. A chapel is conspic 4ca N of the hbr. Lts as chartlet and Lights, buoys and waypoints.

COMMUNICATIONS (Code 981) MRSC 209541; Emergency 112; Brit Consul (902)109356; Fishermen Cofradia ☎480389, No VHF, MF *Cedeira Cofradia* 1800kHz, 2182.

FACILITIES Hbr (110t) ☎492212.

Town ✕ Ⓔ Ⓑ; ⇄ & ✈ La Coruña.

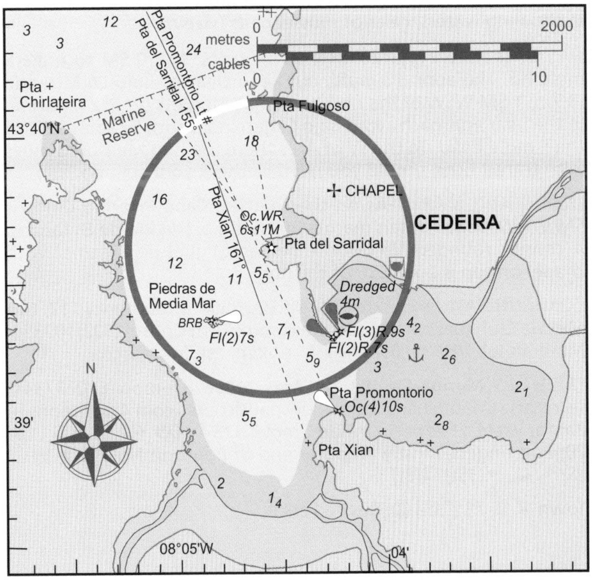

9.23.26 FERROL

La Coruña 43°28'·56N 08°14'·61W (Curuxeiras dock) ❁❁❁◊✿✿

CHARTS AC 1111, 1094, 1118, 1117; SC 412, 412A, 4122, 4123; SHOM 3007

TIDES

Standard Port LA CORUÑA (⟶); ML 2·2.

Times				Height (metres)			
High Water		Low Water		MHWS	MHWN	MLWN	MLWS
0000	0600	0000	0500	4·2	2·8	1·6	0·3
1200	1800	1200	1700				
Differences *FERROL (La Grana)*							
–0002	*–0002*	*+0001*	*+0001*	*0·0*	*0·0*	*0·0*	*0·0*

SHELTER Very good inside ría, but be aware of strong tides and occasional squalls in the narrows.

⚓s, from seaward, N shore of appr chan: Ensenada de Cariño (poor holding, good shelter except in S'lies); inshore of Pereiro PHM buoy in 5-6m. Inside the ría (see chartlet) S shore: Ensenada de el Baño and off Mugardos; on N shore off Pta de Caranza, ESE of chapel and near No 2 PHM buoy (off chartlet).

NAVIGATION WPT 43°26'·59N 08°20'·17W (close to WCM lt buoy and in the white sector (041·5°-042·5°) of Batería de San Cristóbal Dir lt) 042°/1·3M to pick up the 085·2° ldg line. Caution: From near Cabo Prioriño Chico lt ho a substantial bkwtr extends 145°/0·5M, halfway across the ent to the Ria. Chan is deep and adequately buoyed/lit. In bad weather avoid the outer banks (Tarracidos, Cabaleiro and Leixiñas) to the N and W.

LIGHTS AND MARKS C. Prioriño Chico bkwtr head, Fl R 5s 21m 7M; adjacent T-jetty Fl (2) R 7s 10m 3M. Ldg lts 085·2° through the narrows.

COMMUNICATIONS (Code 981) MRSC 209541; Emergency 112; Brit Consul (902)109356; HM 364055.

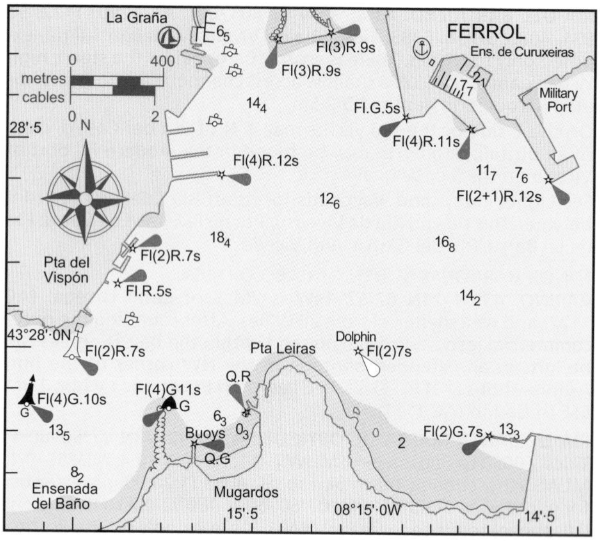

FACILITIES Limited yacht facilities in this naval, commercial and ship-building port. **Marina Terramar** at La Graña: approx 50 berths a few visitors' berths or ⚓. ⊖ ⛽ Ⓓ Ⓟ ▬ ⚒ ✕ (1·5t) YC. Bus every ½hr to the city (20 mins).

Dársena de Curuxeiras is central, but berths in 2m on NE side is against stone walls and prone to ferry wash. The 3 pontoons at the head of this inlet are not available to visitors. ☎321594, ▬ Ⓓ Ⓟ ⚒ (8t).

Other options: Ría de Ares has yacht pontoons in the small FV hbr. Sada (Ría de Betanzos) has two marinas and good bus links to La Coruña.

City All facilities.

9.23.27 RÍA DE ARES

Marina **43°25'·34N 08°14'·38W** ❁❁❁◊✿✿✿

CHARTS AC 1111, 1094; SC 412, 412A; SHOM 3007, 7598, 6665

TIDES Use differences for La Coruña.

SHELTER Good in the marina/fishing hbr at the W end of the 1M wide, sheltered bay (Ensenada de Ares) but the ría is exposed to strong NW'lies and swell. ⚓ NE of the hbr in 3-5m, good holding on muddy sand. The ambience is peaceful and relaxed. The ría extends E past Redes toward Puentedeume, where there is day ⚓ in shoaling waters, clear of mussel beds (*viveiros*).

NAVIGATION WPT 43°24'·88N 08°14'·03W, 340°/0·5M to hbr's E mole hd. The appr is simple, but keep clear of Bajo La Miranda (3·7m; 1·5M WSW of the hbr) and adjacent islets off Pta Miranda. In the near approach avoid Bajo Cagarroso (2·1m) 5 cables SSW of the E mole head. To the W of Ares there are two Measured miles with transit bcns, should you need to check your speedo.

LIGHTS AND MARKS As on the chartlet. Cabo Prioriño Chico is 5M WNW. Sada/Fontan marina/hbr is 4M S; see Ría de Betanzos. A conspic rounded hill (Monte de San Miguel de Breamo) with chapel on top is 2·7M ESE of the hbr.

COMMUNICATIONS (Code 981) MRSC 209541;Emergency 112; ⊖ & Met via Club (below) which is welcoming; Brit Consul (902)109356; Marina/Club VHF Ch 09, English spoken, ask for Marco.

FACILITIES **Marina/CN Ría de Ares** ☎468787 mob 610737344. secretaria@nauticoares.com www.nauticoares.com 4 pontoons in 2m for yachts; FVs berth inside E mole. 325 + 16Ⓥ €2.79 max LOA 20m on fingers, mostly on outer end of pontoon No 1. ✕ ⚒ ▬ (35t) (8t).

Town ✕ ⊠ Ⓑ. Bus to Ferrol.

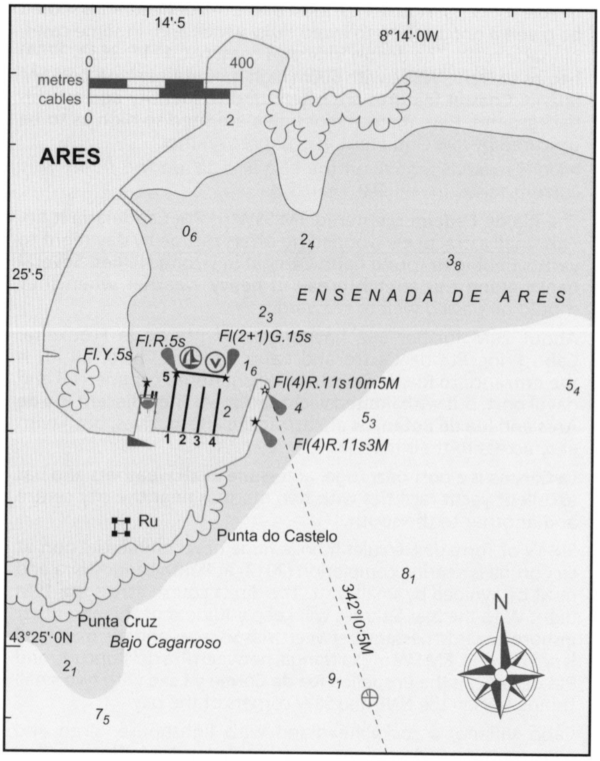

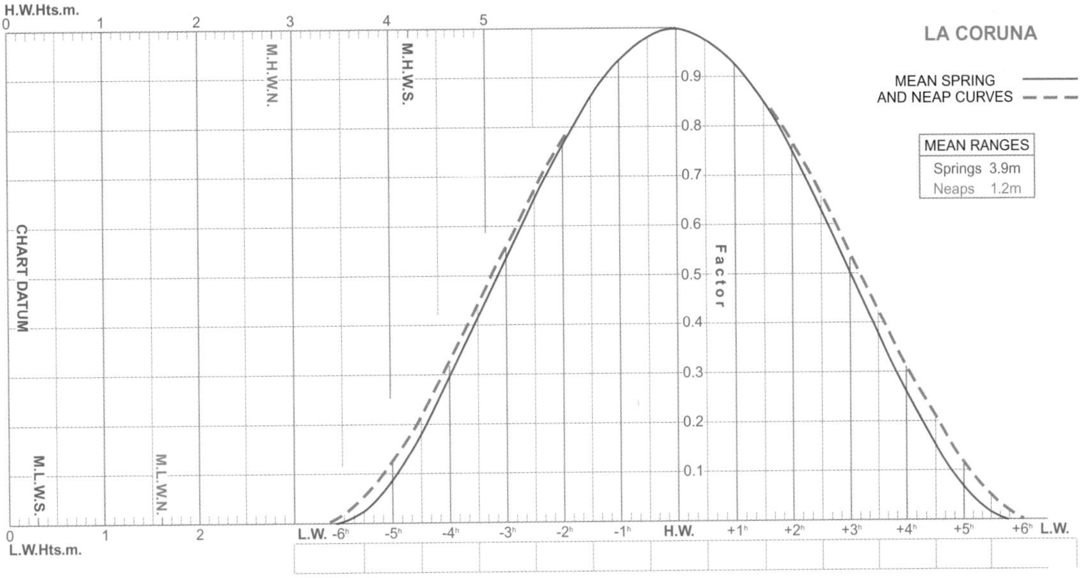

9.23.28 RÍA DE BETANZOS

La Coruña **43°21'·73N 08°14'·45W**

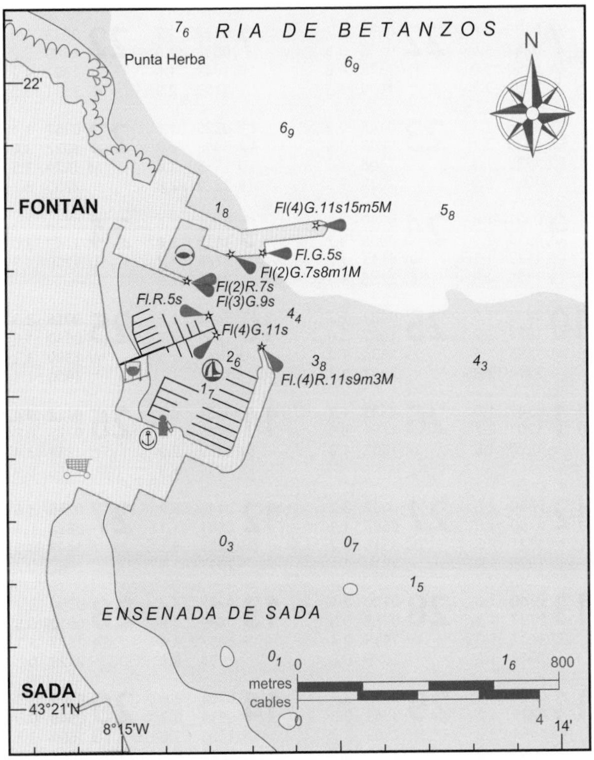

CHARTS AC 1111, 1094; SC 412, 412A; SHOM 3007, 7598, 6665

TIDES Use differences for La Coruña.

SHELTER Very good in two marinas in Fontán hbr, Marina Sada, S side of hbr and Club Náutico de Sada, NW side. Keep close to the eastern hammerheads on arrival. Visitors are very welcome at this well-run fully-equipped marina, a safe haven for a longer stay or winter lay-up. Alternatively, ⚓ N or E of the hbr in 4-7m, but beware holding on weedy bottom.

NAVIGATION WPT 43°24'·34N 08°15'·07W, 171°/2·6M to Fontán hbr's N mole hd. Appr the WPT on an ESE track midway between Pta Miranda to the NE and Pta Redonda* to the SW; Bajo La Miranda (3·7m) lies 6ca SW of the former. The Ria is wide and easy to enter, but shoals steadily S of the hbr. There are shellfish beds visible close to the shore from 2M NW of Fontán.

*Note: a second Pta Redonda is 4M ESE of the first mentioned, opposite Fontán.

LIGHTS AND MARKS Hbr lts proliferate, as on the chartlet, mostly marking FV quays on the N and W side of the hbr. 1·4M NE of the hbr Pta de San Pedro lt (off chartlet) is listed as Perbes pierhd, Dir Fl (2) WR 7s. At the head of the ría a bridge across the Río Mandeo is clearly visible.

COMMUNICATIONS (Code 981) MRSC 209541; Emergency 112; Brit Consul (902)109356; HM 620005; Marinas VHF Ch 09.

FACILITIES **Marina Sada** ☎619015, mob 661356269, (1000-1400, 1600-1900) www. marinasada.com marinasada@marinasada.com 630+ Ⓥ €2·72, max 20m LOA, max stay 6 months. (1000-2000) Ⓔ (32t). Safe over-wintering.

Club Náutico de Sada ☎619018, mob 653469579, www. nauticodesada.es info@clubnauticodesada.com 313 inc Ⓥ, €2·50, in 2-3m, max 20m LOA, facilities same as Marina Sada, except (50t).

Town Facilities at Sada (10 mins walk) are better than Fontán: Ⓑ Ⓗ. La Coruña by taxi 20 mins, by hourly bus 30 mins.

STANDARD TIME UT –01
Subtract 1 hour for UT
For French Summer Time add ONE hour in **non-shaded areas**

LA CORUÑA LAT 43°22′N LONG 8°24′W

TIMES AND HEIGHTS OF HIGH AND LOW WATERS

Dates in red are SPRINGS
Dates in blue are NEAPS

YEAR **2018**

JANUARY

Day	Time	m	Day	Time	m
1	0309	3.9	16	0351	3.6
	0921	0.5		1001	0.9
M	1535	3.9	TU	1609	3.4
	2139	0.5		2210	0.9
2	0358	4.1	17	0424	3.6
	1011	0.3		1035	0.8
TU	1625	4.0	W	1642	3.4
	○ 2227	0.4		● 2243	0.8
3	0446	4.2	18	0457	3.7
	1101	0.2		1107	0.8
W	1715	4.0	TH	1714	3.5
	2315	0.4		2315	0.8
4	0535	4.2	19	0529	3.7
	1150	0.2		1140	0.7
TH	1804	3.9	F	1747	3.5
				2348	0.8
5	0003	0.4	20	0603	3.7
	0624	4.1		1214	0.8
F	1240	0.4	SA	1821	3.4
	1854	3.7			
6	0051	0.6	21	0022	0.9
	0714	3.9		0639	3.6
SA	1331	0.6	SU	1249	0.8
	1945	3.5		1858	3.4
7	0142	0.8	22	0059	0.9
	0807	3.7		0718	3.6
SU	1424	0.8	M	1328	0.9
	2040	3.3		1938	3.3
8	0236	1.0	23	0141	1.1
	0902	3.4		0801	3.4
M	1521	1.0	TU	1412	1.1
	◑ 2139	3.1		2026	3.2
9	0337	1.2	24	0230	1.2
	1004	3.2		0851	3.3
TU	1624	1.2	W	1504	1.2
	2246	3.0		◐ 2123	3.1
10	0445	1.4	25	0330	1.3
	1113	3.0		0952	3.2
W	1732	1.3	TH	1608	1.3
	2355	3.0		2233	3.1
11	0558	1.4	26	0443	1.4
	1223	3.0		1105	3.1
TH	1838	1.3	F	1722	1.3
				2349	3.1
12	0059	3.0	27	0602	1.3
	0704	1.4		1222	3.2
F	1325	3.0	SA	1835	1.1
	1934	1.3			
13	0152	3.2	28	0101	3.3
	0800	1.3		0715	1.1
SA	1416	3.1	SU	1332	3.4
	2021	1.2		1941	0.9
14	0237	3.3	29	0203	3.6
	0845	1.1		0817	0.8
SU	1458	3.2	M	1433	3.6
	2101	1.0		2037	0.7
15	0316	3.4	30	0258	3.8
	0925	1.0		0912	0.5
M	1535	3.3	TU	1526	3.8
	2137	0.9		2128	0.5
			31	0348	4.0
				1002	0.3
			W	1616	3.9
				○ 2216	0.3

FEBRUARY

Day	Time	m	Day	Time	m
1	0436	4.2	16	0437	3.7
	1050	0.2		1046	0.6
TH	1703	4.0	F	1654	3.5
	2302	0.3		2256	0.6
2	0522	4.2	17	0509	3.8
	1136	0.1		1118	0.6
F	1748	3.9	SA	1726	3.6
	2347	0.3		2328	0.6
3	0607	4.2	18	0542	3.8
	1220	0.3		1150	0.6
SA	1832	3.8	SU	1759	3.6
4	0030	0.4	19	0001	0.6
	0651	4.0		0617	3.8
SU	1304	0.5	M	1224	0.6
	1916	3.6		1834	3.6
5	0114	0.6	20	0037	0.7
	0735	3.7		0654	3.7
M	1348	0.7	TU	1301	0.7
	2000	3.4		1912	3.5
6	0200	0.9	21	0117	0.8
	0821	3.4		0734	3.6
TU	1434	1.0	W	1342	0.9
	2049	3.1		1955	3.3
7	0250	1.2	22	0203	1.0
	0912	3.1		0822	3.4
W	1527	1.3	TH	1431	1.1
	◑ 2146	3.0		2049	3.2
8	0350	1.4	23	0259	1.2
	1014	2.9		0921	3.2
TH	1633	1.4	F	1532	1.2
	2257	2.8		◐ 2157	3.1
9	0506	1.5	24	0413	1.3
	1132	2.8		1038	3.1
F	1750	1.5	SA	1651	1.3
				2322	3.1
10	0014	2.8	25	0542	1.3
	0627	1.5		1206	3.1
SA	1251	2.8	SU	1816	1.2
	1902	1.4			
11	0121	3.0	26	0045	3.2
	0735	1.4		0704	1.1
SU	1353	2.9	M	1323	3.2
	1957	1.3		1929	1.0
12	0213	3.1	27	0152	3.5
	0826	1.2		0809	0.8
M	1439	3.0	TU	1425	3.5
	2041	1.1		2028	0.8
13	0255	3.3	28	0248	3.7
	0907	1.0		0903	0.5
TU	1517	3.2	W	1517	3.7
	2118	1.0		2118	0.5
14	0331	3.5			
	0942	0.9			
W	1551	3.3			
	2152	0.8			
15	0404	3.6			
	1015	0.7			
TH	1623	3.5			
	● 2224	0.7			

MARCH

Day	Time	m	Day	Time	m
1	0337	4.0	16	0338	3.6
	0950	0.3		0948	0.7
TH	1604	3.9	F	1557	3.5
	2203	0.4		2159	0.7
2	0422	4.1	17	0411	3.8
	1034	0.2		1019	0.5
F	1646	4.0	SA	1629	3.7
	○ 2245	0.3		● 2231	0.6
3	0504	4.2	18	0444	3.9
	1115	0.2		1051	0.5
SA	1727	3.9	SU	1701	3.8
	2326	0.3		2304	0.5
4	0544	4.1	19	0518	3.9
	1154	0.3		1124	0.4
SU	1805	3.8	M	1735	3.8
				2339	0.5
5	0005	0.4	20	0553	3.9
	0624	3.9		1159	0.5
M	1232	0.5	TU	1810	3.8
	1843	3.7			
6	0045	0.6	21	0016	0.5
	0702	3.7		0632	3.8
TU	1310	0.7	W	1236	0.6
	1922	3.5		1849	3.7
7	0125	0.8	22	0057	0.7
	0742	3.4		0714	3.6
W	1350	1.0	TH	1318	0.8
	2003	3.2		1934	3.5
8	0208	1.1	23	0145	0.9
	0825	3.1		0803	3.4
TH	1435	1.3	F	1408	1.0
	2051	3.0		2028	3.3
9	0301	1.4	24	0243	1.1
	0918	2.9		0905	3.2
F	1532	1.5	SA	1511	1.2
	◑ 2155	2.8		◐ 2139	3.1
10	0411	1.5	25	0401	1.2
	1034	2.7		1027	3.0
SA	1653	1.6	SU	1634	1.4
	2318	2.8		2307	3.1
11	0541	1.6	26	0533	1.2
	1207	2.7		1159	3.0
SU	1820	1.6	M	1805	1.3
12	0040	2.8	27	0032	3.2
	0700	1.5		0655	1.1
M	1321	2.8	TU	1316	3.2
	1926	1.4		1918	1.1
13	0140	3.0	28	0140	3.4
	0757	1.3		0758	0.8
TU	1412	3.0	W	1415	3.4
	2014	1.2		2015	0.8
14	0226	3.2	29	0234	3.7
	0839	1.1		0849	0.5
W	1451	3.2	TH	1503	3.7
	2052	1.0		2102	0.6
15	0304	3.4	30	0320	3.9
	0915	0.9		0932	0.4
TH	1525	3.3	F	1546	3.8
	2127	0.8		2145	0.4
			31	0402	4.0
				1012	0.3
			SA	1625	3.9
				○ 2224	0.4

APRIL

Day	Time	m	Day	Time	m
1	0442	4.1	16	0416	3.9
	1050	0.3		1022	0.4
SU	1701	3.9	M	1634	3.9
	2302	0.4		● 2240	0.4
2	0519	4.0	17	0453	4.0
	1126	0.4		1058	0.4
M	1737	3.9	TU	1711	3.9
	2340	0.5		2318	0.4
3	0555	3.8	18	0532	4.0
	1201	0.6		1135	0.4
TU	1812	3.7	W	1750	3.9
				2359	0.5
4	0016	0.6	19	0614	3.8
	0631	3.6		1216	0.6
W	1236	0.8	TH	1833	3.8
	1847	3.6			
5	0054	0.9	20	0044	0.6
	0707	3.4		0701	3.7
TH	1312	1.0	F	1302	0.8
	1925	3.3		1921	3.6
6	0135	1.1	21	0136	0.8
	0747	3.1		0754	3.4
F	1352	1.3	SA	1355	1.0
	2009	3.1		2019	3.4
7	0222	1.3	22	0238	1.0
	0835	2.9		0900	3.2
SA	1443	1.5	SU	1501	1.2
	2105	2.9		◐ 2131	3.2
8	0325	1.5	23	0357	1.1
	0942	2.7		1022	3.0
SU	1555	1.6	M	1624	1.3
	◑ 2220	2.8		2255	3.2
9	0449	1.6	24	0524	1.1
	1113	2.6		1149	3.0
M	1726	1.7	TU	1750	1.3
	2345	2.8			
10	0612	1.5	25	0016	3.3
	1235	2.7		0640	1.0
TU	1841	1.5	W	1300	3.2
				1900	1.1
11	0054	3.0	26	0122	3.4
	0715	1.3		0739	0.8
W	1332	2.9	TH	1357	3.4
	1935	1.3		1956	0.9
12	0146	3.2	27	0215	3.6
	0801	1.1		0828	0.7
TH	1415	3.1	F	1443	3.6
	2017	1.1		2042	0.7
13	0227	3.4	28	0300	3.7
	0839	0.9		0910	0.5
F	1452	3.4	SA	1523	3.7
	2054	0.9		2123	0.6
14	0304	3.6	29	0340	3.8
	0914	0.7		0948	0.5
SA	1526	3.6	SU	1600	3.8
	2129	0.7		2202	0.5
15	0340	3.8	30	0418	3.8
	0948	0.5		1024	0.5
SU	1600	3.8	M	1636	3.8
	2204	0.5		○ 2239	0.5

Chart Datum is 1·86 metres below NMMA Datum. HAT is 4·5 metres above Chart Datum.

STANDARD TIME UT –01
Subtract 1 hour for UT
For French Summer Time add ONE hour in **non-shaded areas**

LA CORUÑA LAT 43°22′N LONG 8°24′W

TIMES AND HEIGHTS OF HIGH AND LOW WATERS

Dates in red are SPRINGS
Dates in blue are NEAPS

YEAR **2018**

MAY

Day	Time	m	Day	Time	m
1 TU	0454 1058 1710 2316	3.8 0.6 3.8 0.6	16 W	0430 1034 1650 2300	4.0 0.4 4.0 0.4
2 W	0529 1132 1744 2352	3.7 0.7 3.7 0.7	17 TH	0514 1117 1734 2346	3.9 0.4 4.0 0.4
3 TH	0603 1206 1819	3.5 0.9 3.6	18 F	0601 1202 1821	3.8 0.5 3.9
4 F	0029 0639 1242 1856	0.9 3.3 1.1 3.4	19 SA	0036 0652 1252 1914	0.5 3.7 0.7 3.7
5 SA	0109 0718 1321 1938	1.1 3.1 1.3 3.2	20 SU	0131 0750 1348 2013	0.7 3.4 0.9 3.5
6 SU	0153 0803 1407 2028	1.3 3.0 1.4 3.1	21 M	0235 0855 1453 2122	0.9 3.2 1.1 3.4
7 M	0248 0901 1508 2132	1.4 2.8 1.6 2.9	22 TU	0347 1010 1609 ◐ 2238	1.0 3.1 1.2 3.3
8 TU	0358 1017 1626 ◑ 2246	1.5 2.7 1.6 2.9	23 W	0504 1127 1726 2352	1.0 3.1 1.2 3.3
9 W	0514 1136 1743 2358	1.5 2.8 1.6 3.0	24 TH	0614 1235 1834	1.0 3.2 1.1
10 TH	0621 1241 1845	1.4 2.9 1.4	25 F	0057 0713 1331 1931	3.3 0.9 3.3 1.0
11 F	0056 0714 1330 1934	3.1 1.2 3.1 1.2	26 SA	0151 0803 1418 2019	3.4 0.8 3.4 0.9
12 SA	0145 0757 1413 2017	3.3 1.0 3.4 1.0	27 SU	0237 0845 1459 2102	3.5 0.8 3.6 0.8
13 SU	0227 0837 1452 2057	3.5 0.8 3.6 0.8	28 M	0318 0923 1537 2141	3.6 0.7 3.6 0.7
14 M	0308 0915 1530 2136	3.7 0.6 3.8 0.6	29 TU	0356 0959 1613 ○ 2219	3.6 0.7 3.7 0.7
15 TU	0348 0954 1609 ● 2217	3.9 0.4 3.9 0.4	30 W	0432 1034 1648 2256	3.6 0.8 3.7 0.7
			31 TH	0507 1108 1722 2332	3.5 0.8 3.7 0.8

JUNE

Day	Time	m	Day	Time	m
1 F	0542 1143 1757	3.4 0.9 3.6	16 SA	0552 1151 1812	3.8 0.5 4.0
2 SA	0009 0617 1218 1834	0.9 3.3 1.0 3.5	17 SU	0028 0645 1243 1905	0.4 3.7 0.6 3.9
3 SU	0047 0655 1256 1914	1.0 3.2 1.2 3.3	18 M	0123 0740 1338 2003	0.5 3.5 0.8 3.7
4 M	0128 0737 1339 1959	1.1 3.0 1.3 3.2	19 TU	0222 0841 1437 2104	0.7 3.3 0.9 3.5
5 TU	0216 0827 1430 2052	1.3 2.9 1.4 3.1	20 W	0326 0946 1543 ◐ 2211	0.9 3.2 1.1 3.3
6 W	0312 0927 1531 ◑ 2153	1.3 2.8 1.5 3.0	21 TH	0433 1054 1653 2320	1.0 3.1 1.2 3.2
7 TH	0416 1035 1641 2300	1.4 2.8 1.5 3.0	22 F	0540 1201 1802	1.1 3.1 1.2
8 F	0521 1142 1748	1.3 2.9 1.4	23 SA	0026 0642 1301 1903	3.2 1.1 3.2 1.2
9 SA	0003 0621 1241 1847	3.1 1.2 3.1 1.3	24 SU	0124 0735 1352 1956	3.2 1.0 3.3 1.1
10 SU	0100 0713 1332 1938	3.3 1.0 3.3 1.0	25 M	0215 0821 1437 2043	3.3 1.0 3.4 1.0
11 M	0150 0800 1418 2026	3.5 0.8 3.5 0.8	26 TU	0259 0902 1517 2125	3.3 0.9 3.5 0.9
12 TU	0238 0846 1503 2112	3.6 0.7 3.7 0.6	27 W	0338 0939 1554 2203	3.4 0.9 3.6 0.8
13 W	0325 0930 1548 ● 2159	3.8 0.5 3.9 0.4	28 TH	0415 1015 1630 ○ 2240	3.4 0.9 3.6 0.8
14 TH	0413 1016 1634 2247	3.9 0.4 4.0 0.3	29 F	0449 1050 1704 2315	3.4 0.9 3.6 0.8
15 F	0501 1103 1722 2336	3.9 0.4 4.1 0.3	30 SA	0523 1124 1738 2350	3.4 0.9 3.6 0.8

JULY

Day	Time	m	Day	Time	m
1 SU	0557 1158 1814	3.3 0.9 3.5	16 M	0016 0631 1229 1851	0.2 3.8 0.4 4.0
2 M	0026 0633 1234 1851	0.9 3.2 1.0 3.4	17 TU	0107 0722 1319 1943	0.4 3.6 0.6 3.8
3 TU	0103 0711 1312 1931	1.0 3.2 1.1 3.4	18 W	0159 0815 1412 2037	0.6 3.4 0.8 3.6
4 W	0144 0754 1356 2016	1.1 3.1 1.2 3.3	19 TH	0254 0911 1509 ◐ 2135	0.8 3.2 1.0 3.3
5 TH	0230 0843 1446 2107	1.2 3.0 1.3 3.2	20 F	0353 1013 1614 2240	1.0 3.1 1.2 3.1
6 F	0323 0941 1546 ◑ 2207	1.3 2.9 1.4 3.1	21 SA	0458 1121 1724 2350	1.2 3.0 1.3 3.0
7 SA	0424 1046 1653 2312	1.3 3.0 1.4 3.1	22 SU	0606 1227 1835	1.3 3.0 1.3
8 SU	0529 1152 1801	1.2 3.1 1.3	23 M	0058 0707 1327 1936	3.0 1.2 3.1 1.2
9 M	0018 0631 1254 1904	3.2 1.1 3.2 1.1	24 TU	0155 0759 1417 2027	3.0 1.2 3.2 1.1
10 TU	0119 0729 1350 2001	3.3 0.9 3.5 0.9	25 W	0242 0844 1500 2110	3.1 1.1 3.3 1.0
11 W	0215 0822 1442 2054	3.5 0.7 3.7 0.6	26 TH	0322 0922 1537 2148	3.2 1.0 3.5 0.9
12 TH	0309 0913 1532 2146	3.7 0.6 3.9 0.4	27 F	0358 0958 1612 ○ 2223	3.3 0.9 3.6 0.8
13 F	0400 1002 1621 ● 2236	3.8 0.4 4.0 0.2	28 SA	0432 1032 1645 2257	3.3 0.8 3.6 0.8
14 SA	0451 1051 1711 2326	3.9 0.3 4.1 0.2	29 SU	0504 1104 1718 2329	3.4 0.8 3.6 0.7
15 SU	0541 1140 1800	3.9 0.3 4.1	30 M	0536 1137 1751	3.4 0.8 3.6
			31 TU	0002 0609 1210 1825	0.8 3.4 0.8 3.6

AUGUST

Day	Time	m	Day	Time	m
1 W	0035 0644 1245 1902	0.8 3.3 0.9 3.5	16 TH	0127 0741 1341 2003	0.6 3.5 0.8 3.6
2 TH	0112 0721 1324 1942	0.9 3.2 1.0 3.4	17 F	0215 0831 1431 2054	0.9 3.3 1.0 3.3
3 F	0152 0804 1408 2028	1.0 3.2 1.2 3.3	18 SA	0307 0927 1531 ◐ 2155	1.1 3.1 1.3 3.0
4 SA	0239 0855 1502 ◑ 2123	1.2 3.1 1.3 3.2	19 SU	0410 1035 1644 2310	1.4 2.9 1.4 2.8
5 SU	0336 0958 1608 2230	1.3 3.0 1.4 3.1	20 M	0525 1151 1805	1.5 2.9 1.5
6 M	0444 1111 1725 2345	1.3 3.0 1.3 3.1	21 TU	0030 0639 1301 1916	2.8 1.4 3.0 1.4
7 TU	0559 1225 1840	1.2 3.2 1.2	22 W	0135 0738 1356 2010	2.9 1.3 3.1 1.2
8 W	0058 0707 1331 1946	3.2 1.1 3.4 0.9	23 TH	0225 0825 1440 2053	3.0 1.2 3.3 1.0
9 TH	0202 0807 1428 2043	3.4 0.8 3.7 0.6	24 F	0304 0903 1517 2129	3.2 1.0 3.4 0.9
10 F	0258 0901 1520 2135	3.6 0.6 3.9 0.4	25 SA	0338 0938 1551 2202	3.3 0.9 3.6 0.8
11 SA	0350 0950 1609 ● 2224	3.8 0.4 4.1 0.2	26 SU	0410 1010 1622 ○ 2233	3.4 0.8 3.7 0.7
12 SU	0438 1037 1656 2311	3.9 0.3 4.2 0.1	27 M	0440 1041 1654 2303	3.5 0.7 3.7 0.6
13 M	0525 1123 1743 2357	4.0 0.3 4.2 0.2	28 TU	0511 1112 1726 2334	3.5 0.7 3.8 0.6
14 TU	0610 1208 1829	3.9 0.3 4.1	29 W	0542 1144 1759	3.6 0.7 3.7
15 W	0042 0655 1254 1915	0.3 3.7 0.5 3.8	30 TH	0006 0615 1218 1834	0.7 3.5 0.8 3.7
			31 F	0040 0651 1255 1912	0.8 3.5 0.9 3.5

Chart Datum is 1·86 metres below NMMA Datum. HAT is 4·5 metres above Chart Datum.

STANDARD TIME UT –01
Subtract 1 hour for UT
For French Summer Time add ONE hour in **non-shaded areas**

LA CORUÑA LAT 43°22′N LONG 8°24′W

TIMES AND HEIGHTS OF HIGH AND LOW WATERS

Dates in red are SPRINGS
Dates in blue are NEAPS

YEAR **2018**

SEPTEMBER

Date	Day	Time m	Time m	Time m	Time m
1	SA	0119 0.9	0732 3.3	1338 1.0	1956 3.4
2	SU	0203 1.1	0820 3.2	1430 1.2	2050 3.2
3	M	0259 1.3	0923 3.1	1538 1.4	◑ 2201 3.0
4	TU	0412 1.4	1043 3.1	1704 1.4	2328 3.0
5	W	0538 1.3	1207 3.2	1829 1.2	
6	TH	0049 3.2	0655 1.2	1319 3.4	1938 0.9
7	F	0154 3.4	0757 0.9	1417 3.7	2034 0.6
8	SA	0249 3.7	0849 0.6	1508 4.0	2123 0.4
9	SU	0336 3.9	0936 0.4	1554 4.2	● 2208 0.2
10	M	0421 4.0	1020 0.3	1638 4.3	2251 0.1
11	TU	0503 4.0	1102 0.3	1721 4.2	2332 0.2
12	W	0544 4.0	1144 0.4	1803 4.1	
13	TH	0012 0.4	0624 3.8	1226 0.5	1844 3.8
14	F	0052 0.7	0705 3.6	1308 0.8	1926 3.5
15	SA	0134 1.0	0749 3.4	1354 1.1	2012 3.2
16	SU	0220 1.2	0840 3.1	1449 1.3	2108 2.9
17	M	0319 1.5	0945 2.9	1601 1.5	◐ 2224 2.7
18	TU	0438 1.6	1107 2.9	1730 1.6	2356 2.7
19	W	0605 1.6	1226 2.9	1849 1.5	
20	TH	0110 2.8	0711 1.5	1327 3.1	1945 1.3
21	F	0200 3.0	0759 1.3	1412 3.3	2027 1.1
22	SA	0239 3.2	0838 1.1	1450 3.4	2102 0.9
23	SU	0312 3.3	0912 0.9	1523 3.6	2134 0.8
24	M	0343 3.5	0944 0.8	1555 3.7	2204 0.7
25	TU	0413 3.6	1015 0.7	1626 3.8	○ 2234 0.6
26	W	0443 3.7	1046 0.6	1658 3.9	2305 0.6
27	TH	0515 3.8	1119 0.6	1732 3.9	2337 0.6
28	F	0549 3.7	1154 0.7	1808 3.8	
29	SA	0013 0.7	0625 3.7	1233 0.8	1848 3.6
30	SU	0052 0.9	0707 3.5	1317 1.0	1934 3.4

OCTOBER

Date	Day	Time m	Time m	Time m	Time m
1	M	0137 1.1	0757 3.4	1411 1.2	2032 3.2
2	TU	0236 1.3	0903 3.2	1524 1.3	◑ 2149 3.0
3	W	0354 1.4	1028 3.1	1655 1.4	2321 3.0
4	TH	0526 1.4	1156 3.2	1821 1.2	
5	F	0043 3.2	0645 1.2	1307 3.5	1927 0.9
6	SA	0145 3.4	0745 1.0	1404 3.7	2020 0.6
7	SU	0235 3.7	0834 0.7	1452 4.0	2106 0.4
8	M	0319 3.9	0919 0.5	1536 4.1	2147 0.3
9	TU	0400 4.0	1000 0.4	1617 4.2	● 2227 0.3
10	W	0439 4.1	1040 0.4	1657 4.1	2305 0.4
11	TH	0517 4.0	1119 0.5	1736 4.0	2342 0.6
12	F	0554 3.9	1159 0.6	1814 3.8	
13	SA	0019 0.8	0632 3.7	1239 0.9	1853 3.5
14	SU	0057 1.1	0712 3.5	1322 1.1	1935 3.2
15	M	0139 1.3	0758 3.2	1412 1.4	2025 2.9
16	TU	0231 1.6	0856 3.0	1517 1.6	◐ 2135 2.8
17	W	0345 1.7	1013 2.9	1643 1.6	2308 2.7
18	TH	0516 1.7	1137 2.9	1805 1.6	
19	F	0028 2.8	0630 1.6	1244 3.0	1906 1.4
20	SA	0123 3.0	0723 1.4	1334 3.2	1950 1.2
21	SU	0204 3.2	0805 1.2	1415 3.4	2027 1.0
22	M	0239 3.4	0841 1.0	1450 3.6	2100 0.8
23	TU	0311 3.6	0914 0.8	1524 3.8	2132 0.7
24	W	0343 3.7	0947 0.7	1557 3.9	○ 2204 0.6
25	TH	0416 3.9	1021 0.6	1632 3.9	2237 0.6
26	F	0450 3.9	1056 0.6	1709 3.9	2312 0.6
27	SA	0526 3.9	1135 0.6	1748 3.9	2350 0.7
28	SU	0606 3.8	1217 0.7	1832 3.7	
29	M	0033 0.8	0651 3.7	1306 0.9	1923 3.5
30	TU	0122 1.1	0745 3.5	1404 1.1	2025 3.2
31	W	0224 1.3	0853 3.3	1519 1.2	◑ 2143 3.1

NOVEMBER

Date	Day	Time m	Time m	Time m	Time m
1	TH	0343 1.4	1016 3.2	1646 1.3	2312 3.1
2	F	0512 1.4	1140 3.3	1807 1.1	
3	SA	0028 3.2	0628 1.2	1250 3.5	1910 0.9
4	SU	0128 3.4	0727 1.0	1346 3.7	2001 0.7
5	M	0217 3.7	0816 0.8	1434 3.9	2045 0.6
6	TU	0300 3.8	0900 0.7	1517 4.0	2125 0.5
7	W	0339 3.9	0941 0.6	1557 4.0	● 2203 0.5
8	TH	0416 4.0	1020 0.6	1635 3.9	2239 0.6
9	F	0452 4.0	1058 0.6	1712 3.8	2315 0.7
10	SA	0528 3.9	1136 0.7	1748 3.6	2350 0.9
11	SU	0605 3.7	1215 0.9	1826 3.4	
12	M	0027 1.1	0643 3.5	1256 1.1	1905 3.2
13	TU	0107 1.3	0726 3.3	1342 1.3	1951 3.0
14	W	0154 1.5	0816 3.1	1437 1.5	2049 2.8
15	TH	0254 1.7	0919 3.0	1546 1.6	◐ 2205 2.7
16	F	0412 1.7	1034 3.0	1704 1.6	2326 2.8
17	SA	0531 1.7	1146 3.0	1811 1.5	
18	SU	0031 2.9	0634 1.5	1245 3.2	1903 1.3
19	M	0120 3.1	0723 1.3	1332 3.3	1946 1.1
20	TU	0201 3.3	0804 1.1	1414 3.5	2024 0.9
21	W	0238 3.6	0842 0.9	1452 3.7	2100 0.8
22	TH	0314 3.8	0920 0.8	1530 3.8	2136 0.6
23	F	0350 3.9	0958 0.6	1609 3.9	○ 2213 0.6
24	SA	0429 4.0	1038 0.5	1651 3.9	2253 0.5
25	SU	0509 4.0	1121 0.5	1735 3.9	2336 0.6
26	M	0554 4.0	1208 0.6	1823 3.7	
27	TU	0022 0.8	0643 3.8	1300 0.7	1917 3.5
28	W	0115 0.9	0739 3.7	1400 0.9	2019 3.3
29	TH	0216 1.1	0844 3.5	1509 1.0	2131 3.2
30	F	0328 1.3	0958 3.4	1626 1.1	◑ 2249 3.1

DECEMBER

Date	Day	Time m	Time m	Time m	Time m
1	SA	0447 1.3	1115 3.4	1740 1.1	
2	SU	0003 3.2	0601 1.2	1225 3.4	1845 1.0
3	M	0104 3.4	0704 1.1	1324 3.5	1938 0.9
4	TU	0155 3.5	0756 1.0	1414 3.6	2024 0.8
5	W	0240 3.6	0842 0.9	1459 3.7	2105 0.8
6	TH	0320 3.8	0924 0.8	1539 3.7	2143 0.7
7	F	0358 3.8	1004 0.7	1617 3.7	● 2219 0.8
8	SA	0434 3.8	1042 0.7	1654 3.6	2254 0.8
9	SU	0509 3.8	1120 0.8	1729 3.5	2330 0.9
10	M	0545 3.7	1157 0.9	1805 3.4	
11	TU	0005 1.0	0621 3.6	1235 1.0	1842 3.3
12	W	0043 1.2	0700 3.5	1315 1.2	1922 3.1
13	TH	0123 1.3	0743 3.3	1400 1.3	2009 3.0
14	F	0211 1.5	0832 3.2	1453 1.4	2105 2.9
15	SA	0309 1.6	0931 3.1	1555 1.5	◐ 2213 2.8
16	SU	0418 1.6	1038 3.0	1702 1.5	2324 2.9
17	M	0529 1.6	1144 3.1	1805 1.4	
18	TU	0026 3.0	0631 1.4	1244 3.2	1859 1.2
19	W	0118 3.2	0724 1.3	1335 3.4	1946 1.0
20	TH	0204 3.4	0811 1.0	1422 3.5	2030 0.9
21	F	0247 3.7	0856 0.8	1507 3.7	2112 0.7
22	SA	0330 3.9	0940 0.6	1552 3.8	○ 2155 0.5
23	SU	0413 4.0	1025 0.5	1638 3.9	2240 0.5
24	M	0458 4.1	1112 0.4	1726 3.9	2326 0.5
25	TU	0545 4.1	1201 0.4	1816 3.8	
26	W	0014 0.6	0636 4.0	1253 0.5	1909 3.6
27	TH	0106 0.7	0729 3.9	1348 0.6	2005 3.5
28	F	0202 0.9	0828 3.7	1449 0.8	2107 3.3
29	SA	0304 1.1	0932 3.5	1554 1.0	◑ 2216 3.2
30	SU	0413 1.2	1041 3.3	1704 1.1	2327 3.1
31	M	0527 1.3	1153 3.2	1812 1.1	

Chart Datum is 1·86 metres below NMMA Datum. HAT is 4·5 metres above Chart Datum.

9.23.29 LA CORUÑA (A Coruña)

La Coruña **43°22'·01N 08°23'·69W** (Marina) ❁❁❁◊◊◊✿✿✿

CHARTS AC 1111, 1094, 1110; SC 412, 412A, 4126; SHOM 3007, 7598, 6665

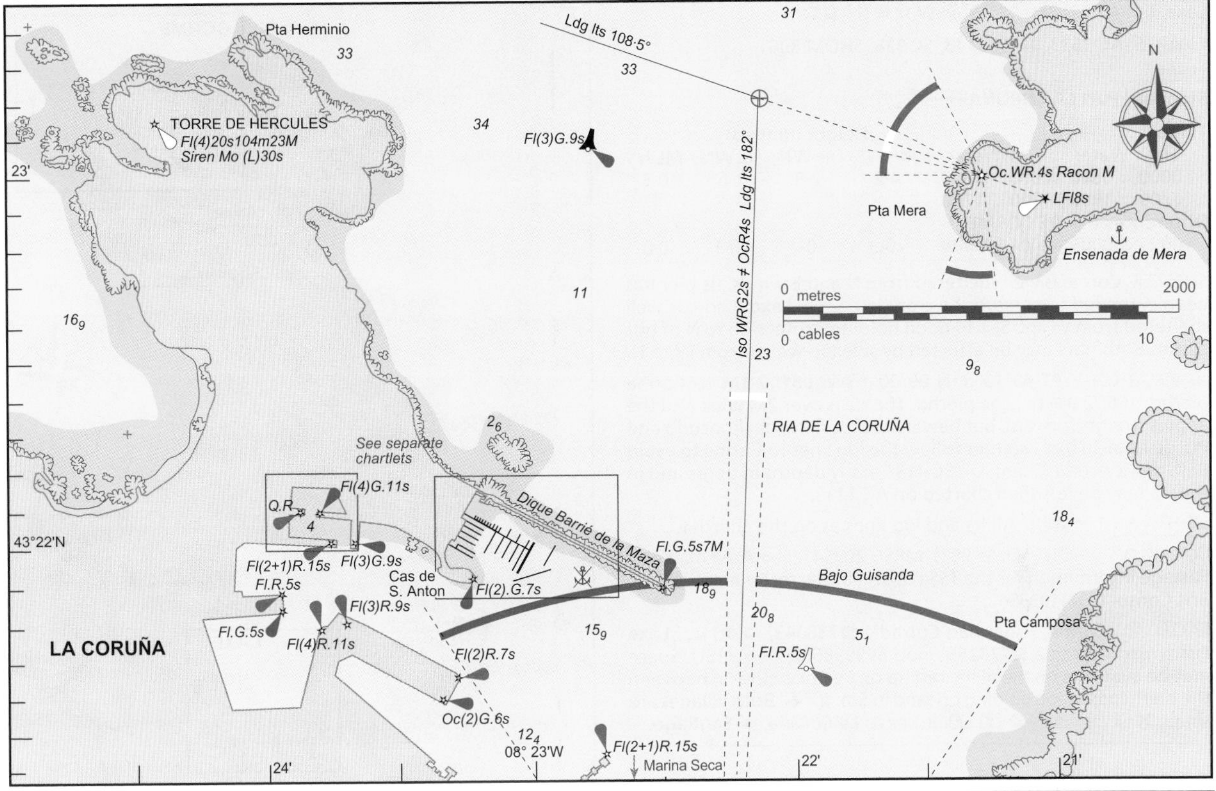

TIDES ML 2·2. Note: La Coruña is a Standard Port (⟵).

SHELTER from seaward: Marina Coruña, close N of Castillo de San Antón, is sheltered from wash/swell by two wavebreaks. Note: ⚓ prohibited SE of wavebreaks and within hbr limits, you will be moved by Maritime Police; no ⚓s. Marina Real in 3-4m is well sheltered. Possible ⚓s in the Ria de la Coruna include NE corner, Ensenada de Mera, in NW/NE winds, and S corner, E end Playa de Santa Christina in W/S winds.

NAVIGATION WPT 43°23'·21N 08°22'·12W, 189°/1·3M to head of Dique de Abrigo; thence 6-9ca west to marina. The WPT is where the 108·5° & 182° ldg lines intersect. Avoid Banco Yacentes, about 1M NW of WPT (off chartlet). Speed limit 3kn in hbr.

LIGHTS AND MARKS Conspic marks: Torre de Hércules lt ho; 5·3M SW of which is power stn chy (218m).

COMMUNICATIONS (Code 981 or 881) MRSC 209541; Emergency 112; VTS VHF Ch 13; ⊜ & Met via YCs; Brit Consul (902)109356; HM 216161; Port Control VHF Ch 12; Marinas VHF Ch 09.

FACILITIES **Marina Coruña** ☎881920482; www.northwestmarinas.com jesusga@marinacoruna.es or marinacoruna@marinacoruna.es 700 +100Ⓥ €2.95, Jun-Sep, max 50m LOA, multihulls + 50%, discounts for longer stays. (note: pontoon, 4m LW); wi-fi @ (50t). For repairs go to **Marina Seca** 1·5M S at 43°20'·92N 08°22'·97W; ☎ as above; (50t).

Marina Real (Real Club Nautico de La Coruna) ☎226880 (ext 3) mob 650053130 www.marinarealcoruna.com marina@rcncoruna.com 350 inc 40 Ⓥ €2.67, Jun-Sep, max 30m LOA, multihulls + 50%. Ⓔ wi-fi (32t) just N of Castillio de San Antón, see **Marina Coruña** inset.

City All amenities. Larger quantities duty free available for registered (non private) commercially run vessels/charter yachts from Bunoil S.L. ☎136248 (HO), or mob 639186552, in Dársena de Oza, inside outer end bkwtr, opposite Marina Seca. Bus, ⇌ ✈.

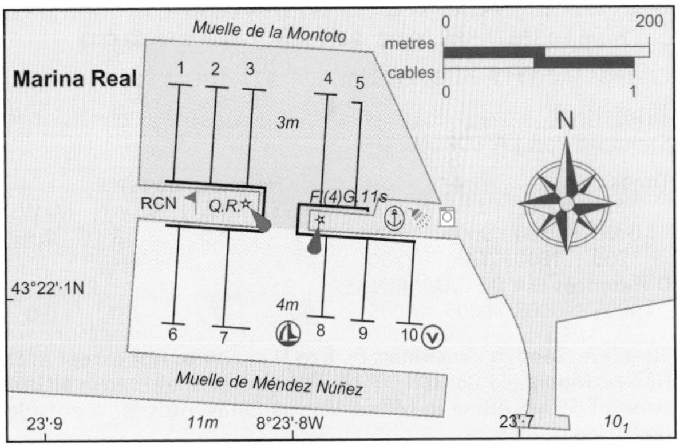

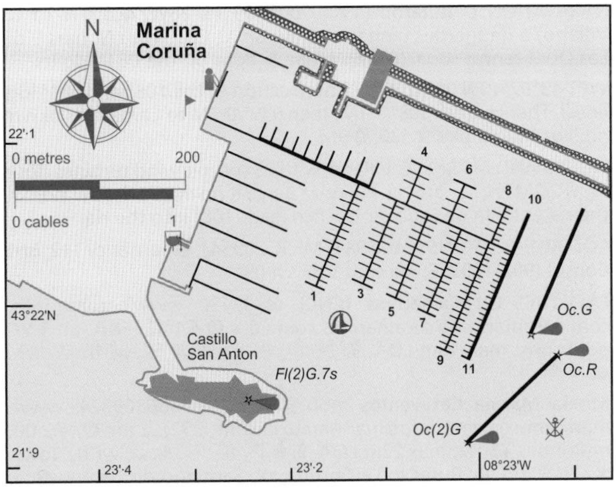

N & NW Spain

9.23.30 RÍA DE CORME Y LAXE

La Coruña. Corme lt **43°15′·63N 08°57′·83W** ❁❁❁◊✿✿
Laxe, E lt **43°13′·35N 08°59′·95W** ❁❁❁◊✿✿

CHARTS AC 3633, 1111, 1113; SC 928; SHOM 3007

TIDES
Standard Port LA CORUÑA (⟵)

Times				Height (metres)			
High Water		Low Water		MHWS	MHWN	MLWN	MLWS
0000	0600	0000	0500	4·2	2·8	1·6	0·3
1200	1800	1200	1700				
Differences RÍA DE CORME							
–0005	–0005	–0004	–0004	–0·3	–0·2	–0·1	0·0

SHELTER **Corme** is well sheltered from N and E winds. Its pier has been extended to enlarge the crowded ⚓age. **Laxe** (Lage) is well sheltered from W and S, ⚓ in good holding/protection to N of hbr bkwtr. Both hbrs may be affected by swell in winds from W to N.

NAVIGATION WPT 43°15′·31N 09°00′·63W: 081°/2·1M to Corme pierhd; 166°/2·0M to Lage pierhd. The ría is over 2M wide and the appr is straightforward, but beware rocks off Pta del Roncudo and Pta de Laxe. In bad weather follow the ldg lines to Corme to avoid Bajo de La Averia (5·6m). On SC 4131 many depths in apprs and in the ría may be less than charted on AC 1113.

LIGHTS AND MARKS All lts and ldg lines as on the chartlet.

COMMUNICATIONS (Code 981). MRSC 209541; See Area map and Passage information for the TSS/ITZ off Finisterre; Emergency 112; Brit Consul (902)109356.

FACILITIES **Corme,** Fisherman Cofradia ☎738043, (crane)(4t) (slip). **Laxe** Fisherman Cofradia ☎728255 mob 699998686, (crane)(16t). Space may be available on the piers, raft up on FVs or ⚓ close in between the pierheads, good holding on sand in 5m. **Both villages** are small: ✕ ⛟ 🛒 ✉ Ⓑ @. Buses to La Coruña, ✈ Santiago.

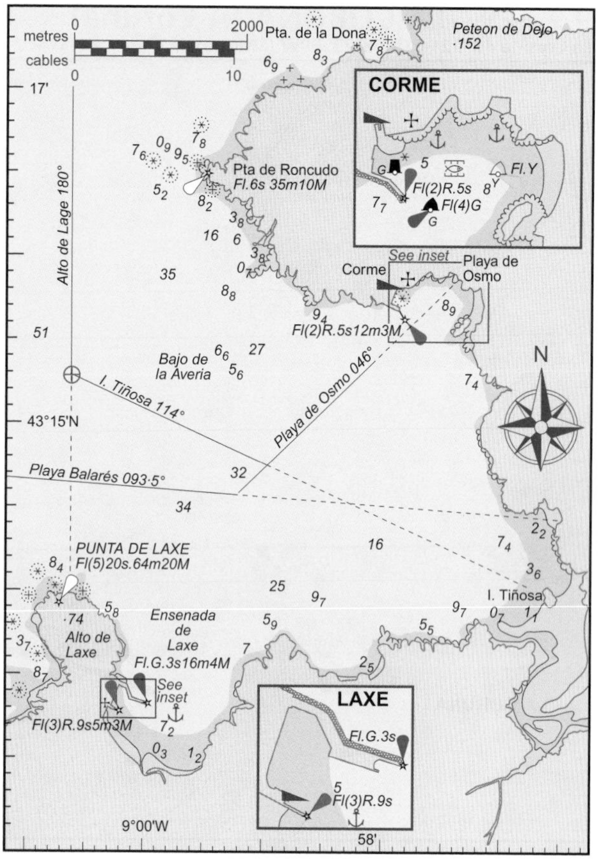

9.23.31 RÍA DE CAMARIÑAS

La Coruña **43°07′·58N 09°10′·94W** (CNC) ❁❁❁◊◊✿✿✿

CHARTS AC 1111, 3633, 1113; SC 928, 927; SHOM 3007

TIDES
Standard Port LA CORUÑA (⟵)

Times				Height (metres)			
High Water		Low Water		MHWS	MHWN	MLWN	MLWS
0000	0600	0000	0500	4·2	2·8	1·6	0·3
1200	1800	1200	1700				
Differences RÍA DE CAMARIÑAS							
–0005	–0005	–0005	–0005	–0·2	–0·2	–0·1	0·0

SHELTER Good in **Camariñas**, or ⚓ to N or NW of hbr except in E/NE′lies, **Mugia** (43°06′·36N 09°12′·73W) is well sheltered in all but strong E/SE′lies either in Muxia Marina Cataventos, or ⚓ outside hbr in lee of bkwtr.

NAVIGATION El Bufardo (43°10′·00N 09°13′·28W, 4ca NW of C. Villano) a dangerous pinnacle rk awash at CD. From N pass E of Las Quebrantas shoal (0·6m). From S appr on the 081° ldg lts.

WPT 43°07′·27N 09°12′·65W (intersection of the 108° and 081° ldg lines). Thence track 108°/1·1M, then 039°/0·7M to Camariñas bkwtr hd. For Mugia bkwtr 180°/0·9M.

LIGHTS AND MARKS C. Villano, with 23 conspic wind turbines close SE, is 2·2M N of ent to ría. Pta de la Barca lt ho marks the SW side of the ría ent. Pta de Lago dir lt ≠ bcn leads 108° into the ría.

COMMUNICATIONS (Code 981) MRSC 209541; Emergency 112; Brit Consul (902)109356; Marinas VHF Ch 09.

FACILITIES **CN Camariñas** (CNC) ☎737130 www.cncamarinas.com cncamarinas@cncamarinas.com 60 + Ⓥ €1·82 F&A, on 3 YC pontoons. max 18m LOA. wi-fi.

Muxia Marina Cataventos mob 673168199/ 666369324; www.marinamuxia.com info@marinamuxia.com 232 inc Ⓥ, €2·00, multihulls +50%, max 22m LOA. wi-fi. **Town** ✕ ⛟ 🛒 ✉ Ⓑ. Buses to La Coruña, ✈, Santiago de Compostela.

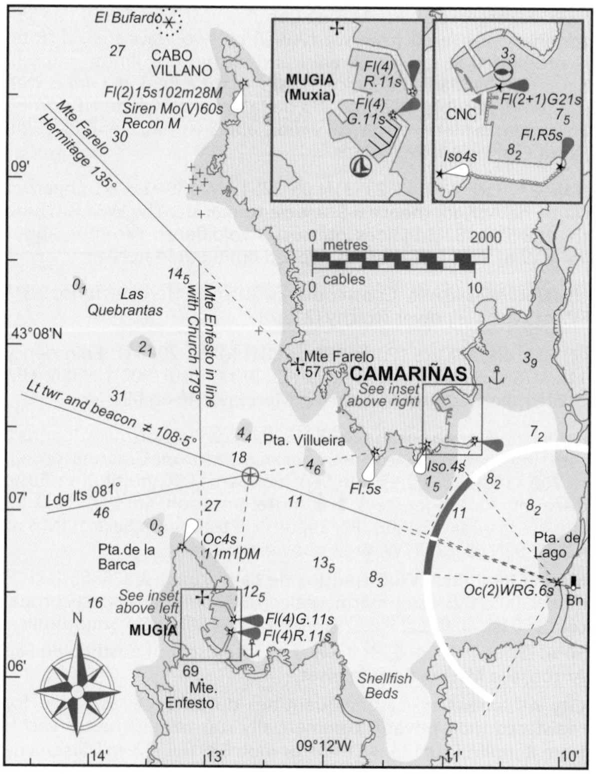

CABO FINISTERRE TO THE PORTUGUESE BORDER

NE of Cabo Finisterre (AC 3674) the Ensenada del Sardineiro and Ría de Corcubión are sheltered ⚓s except in S'lies and despite fish farms. From 5 to 11M south, beware various islets, reefs and shoals N and NW of Pta Insua, notably the unmarked Las Arrosas and Bajo de los Meixidos; the latter is in the red sector (070°-090°) of Pta Insua and can be passed inshore if bound to/from Ría de Muros.

The 40M stretch (AC 3633) from Pta Queixal to Cabo Silleiro makes an impressive cruising ground, encompassing the four major rías bajas (lower or southern) from N to S: Muros, Arosa, Pontevedra and Vigo. All resemble large and scenic Scottish sea lochs with interesting pilotage to fishing hbrs and the many sheltered anchorages. In summer NE winds can blow strongly down all rías, usually without raising any significant sea. The last three rías are sheltered from onshore winds by the coastal islands at their mouth. These Galician islands have protected National Park status, with restrictions on pleasure craft, anchoring, fishing and diving, see: www.iatlanticas.es.

Ría de Muros (AC 1756) is the smallest and easiest to enter. Monte Louro at the N side of the entrance is a distinctive, 239m high, conical hill. The ancient town of Muros itself is worth visiting and the 212 berth **Marina Muros** usually has plenty of space for visitors. The anchorage off the harbour is renowned for poor holding in weed. Most of the bays and inlets are occupied by fish farms, often unlit and unmarked, so night pilotage is not advised. On the eastern shore **Portosin** is a very well run, modern marina with every facility.

Ría de Arosa (AC 1764) the largest ría, runs 14M inland and is up to 6M wide. Isla Sagres and Isla Salvora at the western side of the entrance provide shelter from SW'lies and are within the National Park. **Villagarcia** is the principal hbr and marina, but there are other marinas at **Santa Uxia de Ribeira, Caramiñal, Puerto Cabo de Cruz, Rianxo, Vilanova** and **Piedras Negras**. There are many anchorages, mostly good holding on mud, several active fishing fleets and numerous fish farms and nets. Isla de Arosa and Peninsula del Grove, both in the SE part of the Ria, provide intricate pilotage and secluded anchorages.

Ría de Pontevedra (AC 1732) can be entered from the NW by one of two minor channels (Canals de la Fagilda and de Los Camoucos) between the mainland and Isla Ons. The main entrance, Boca del Sudoeste, is from the SW where the channel is unobstructed and 3·5M wide. On the N shore **Sanxenxo** is a modern marina whilst near the N end (AC 1733) **Combarro** has a marina and is a popular tourist spot. The naval base at Marin has nothing for yachts, but **Aguete** has a small marina and **Beluso** caters for yachts and FVs. Isla Ons and Isla Onzas are protected by National Park rules.

Ría de Vigo (AC 1730) is notable for the large busy port of **Vigo** and, to the S, Bayona's pleasant hbr with 2 marinas. The beautiful Islas Cies, comprising Isla del Norte and the smaller Isla de San Martin, are within the National Park and also provide considerable shelter to the ría against onshore winds. The two approach channels, from NW and SW, have been formalised into 2 mini-TSS which meet in a Precautionary area where the ría narrows down and the docks begin. **Marina Davila Sport** in the Bouzas area has first class BY, 1M SW of the long-established but rather small marina near central Vigo. 1M NE **Punta Lagoa** Marina is on the W side of Monte de la Guia which is topped by a conspic chapel. Several lesser marinas are on the N bank and within the Ensenada de San Simón beyond the Rande bridge (38·8m clearance).

Bayona AC 3633 is too small a scale, 1:200,000, for pilotage. AC 1730, 1:25,000, subject to bilateral agreement with Spain, will hopefully include Bayona which is usually approached from seaward on the 084° leading line, passing between Las Serralleiras, rky islets to the N, and to the S Cabo Silleiro and its offshore reefs marked by a NCM buoy. The long-established Monte Real YC marina has been supplemented by Bayona marina close S; there is still space to anchor.

The Río Miño, 15M S of Cabo Silleiro, is the Spanish/Portuguese border. The river ent is difficult and best not attempted.

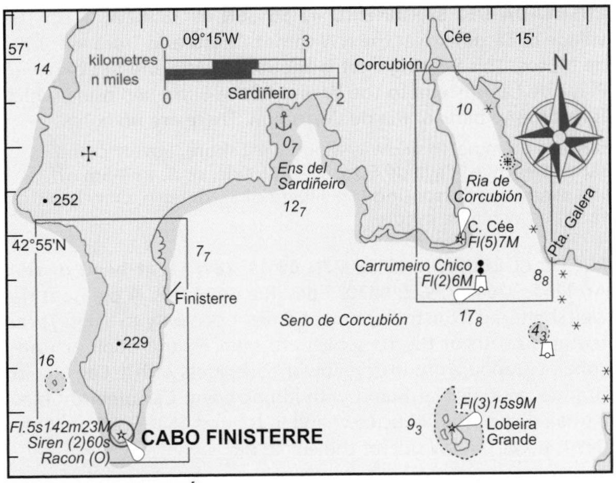

SENO DE CORCUBIÓN

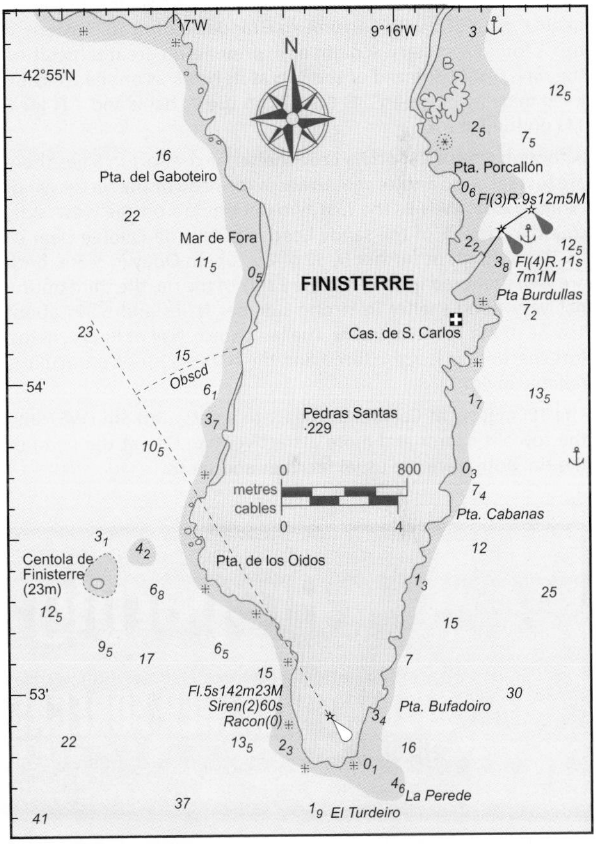

MINOR HARBOURS IN SENO DE CORCUBIÓN

FINISTERRE. 42°54'·59N 09°15'·36W (hbr ent). AC 1111, 3764; SC 927, 9270. Tides: Ría de Muros, Corcubión. Finisterre (or Fisterra, the end of the Ancient World) is famous and imposingly massive. The touristy town has no yacht facilities. But it is worth walking 1·5M from the hbr to the granite lt ho for the views and ambience. Quickly forming dense fog is frequent on this coast. From the N, Centolo de Finisterre is a 23m high pinnacle rock 9ca WNW of the lt ho. Beware La Carraca with 2·1m over it (42°53'·93N 09°18'·53W) less obvious therefore more dangerous. El Turdeiro (1·9m) is 300m due S of the cape, with a sprinkling of lesser rocks closer inshore where small FVs cluster; keep well clear. The E side is mostly steep-to.

The hbr (see chartlet) is usually full of small FVs, but in settled weather it is safe to ⚓ outside in 5-10m, either close S of the bkwtr or to the N off the Playa de Langosteira.

ENSENADA DEL SARDIÑEIRO 42°56'·36N 09°13'·82W, ⚓ off the village of Sardineiro at the NW corner. Charts and Tides as for Ría de Muros. This S-facing inlet is about 6ca wide and lies between Playa de Langosteira to the W and to the E the peninsula which forms the W bank of Ría de Corcubión. There are no lights.

Beware 0.7m patch midway along west shore. Lovely ⚓ and sandy beach at Playa de Estorde, on E side, or ⚓, in 4-5m off the sandy beach fronting the village of Sardiñeiro. Only basic facilities available ashore.

RÍA DE CORCUBIÓN 42°56'·77N 09°11'·28W (⚓ at head of ria). AC 1111, 3764; SC 927, 9270. Tides: Ría de Muros. A pleasant ría, well sheltered from the summer NE'lies, open only to S'lies. Three features south of the ría which are seen on the approach are: Lobeira Grande, a group of yellowish rocky islets with lt; Carrumeiro Grande, a single flat island with ldg bcn; and Carrumeiro Chico, a small rock with IDM bcn twr and lt. It bears 162°/6ca from Cabo Cée lt ho at the SW side of the ent to ría.

The simplest approach for yachts is to pass between Cabo Cée and Carrumeiro Chico on a NE'ly heading, thence straight up the ría on 342° for 1·5M, with Carrumeiro Grande bearing 162° astern, if this is found necessary. A night appr presents no great difficulties: the ría is 0·5M wide and of the 3 lts at its head, as on the chartlet, keep midway between ☆ Fl (2) R 7s on the W bank and ☆ Fl (4) G 11s on the E bank.

Although Corcubión offers little shelter or comfort in S'lies there are several good anchorages towards the head of the ría for winds ranging from W-N-E. The first two options are on the west side, sound in close E of the sandy beach at Playa de Quenje clear of local moorings, or further N, SE of Corcubión Quay in 5-8m, both are well sheltered from W. On the E side of the ría, the third option has very good shelter in strong summer N'lies and E'lies about 1ca SE of Pta Fornelos in 6m. The last choice, NW of Pta Fornelos, (off chartlet), is less sheltered and the holding is not particularly reliable in 4m.

The 100m jetty at Corcubión is easy to access with 4m LWS, and the town is nearer and more attractive than Cée at the head of the ría; both have the usual facilities and shops.

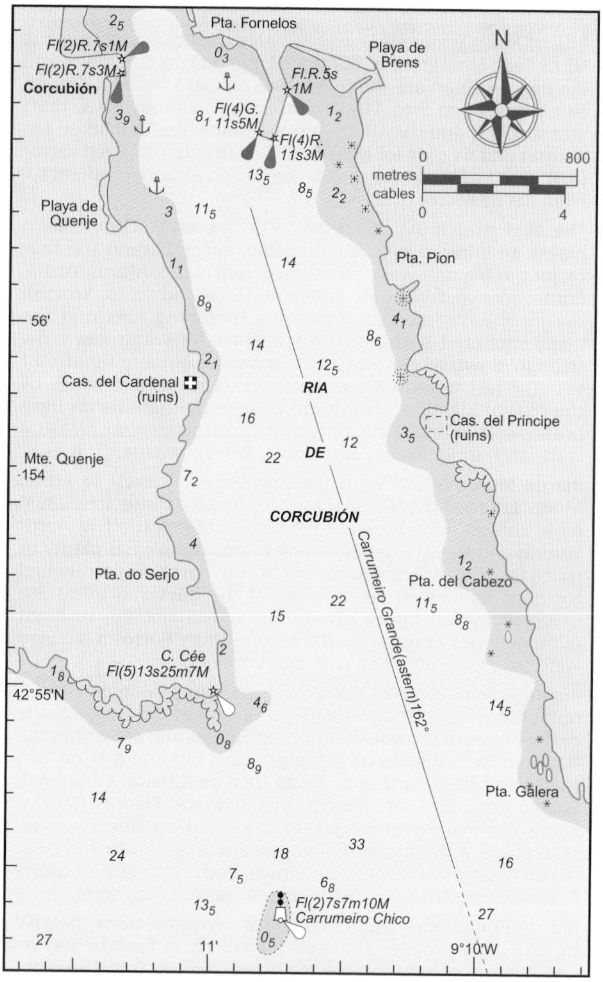

9.23.32 RÍA DE MUROS

La Coruña **42°46'·56N 09°03'·41W** (Muros) ❁❁❁◊◊✿✿✿

CHARTS AC 1756; SC 415, 415A; SHOM 3007

TIDES

Standard Port LISBOA (⟶)

Times				**Height (metres)**			
High Water		Low Water		MHWS	MHWN	MLWN	MLWS
0500	1000	0300	0800	3·8	3·0	1·5	0·6
1700	2200	1500	2000				
Differences CORCUBION							
+0055	+0110	+0120	+0135	–0·5	–0·4	–0·3	–0·1
MUROS							
+0050	+0105	+0115	+0130	–0·3	–0·3	–0·2	–0·1

SHELTER Excellent in Marina Muros. ⚓ off harbour (but beware poor holding in weed) or at Ensenada de San Francisco to the SSW. Noya, at the head of the ría, is only accessible to shoal draft. CN Portosín on the E shore is sheltered, efficient and welcoming – a real pleasure; see Facilities.

NAVIGATION WPT 42°43'·60N 09°03'·36W, 1·25M SE of Punta Queixal lt and 2·0M NW of Punta Focha lt (off chartlet). From the N, the Canal de los Meixidos (between the mainland and Bajo de los Meixidos and Los Bruyos, where its least width is 1.1M) is usable with care. From the S avoid Bajos la Baya. The ría is mostly deep and clear, but beware mussel rafts (*bateas*) off the N shore.

LIGHTS AND MARKS Mte Louro is a conspic conical hill (239m) N of Pta Queixal. Isla Creba is a good mark NW of Portosin. Principal lts: Pta Queixal, C. Reburdino, Pta Cabeiro, Pta Focha.

COMMUNICATIONS (Code 981) MRCC 767320; Emergency 112; Brit Consul (902) 109356; HM 826005; *Marina Muros* VHF Ch 09, H24. *Real Club Náutico Portosín* VHF Ch 09.

FACILITIES **Marina Muros** 42°46'·64N 09°03'·29W ☎827660; www.muport.es info@muport.es 212 inc Ⓥ €3·00, in outer hbr, inner hbr only for locals/FVs. ✕ ⛽ (not near LW) Ⓑ wi-fi; ⇌ and ✈ Santiago de Compostela (40km by bus).

RCN Portosín 42°45'·94N 08°56'·92W. ☎766598 mob618609061 info@rcnportosin.com www.rcnportosin.com 220 inc Ⓥ €2·72 F&A/fingers in 3·5-8m; ✕ @ (32t) (3t).

Village 2km: ✕ Ⓑ car hire. ✈ Santiago, 1hr drive.

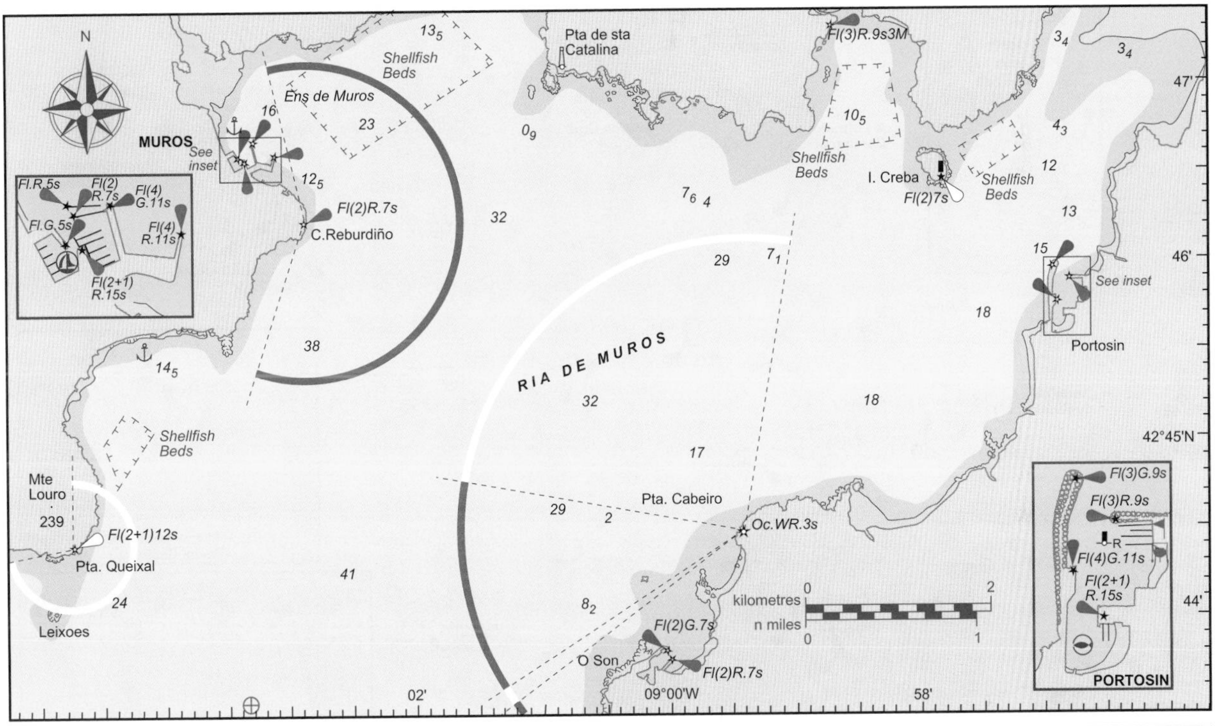

9.23.33 RÍA DE AROSA

La Coruña (NW shore) Pontevedra (SE shore).
42°34'·58N 08°54'·15W (mid-Ría) ❁❁❁◊◊◊✿✿✿

CHARTS AC 1734, 1764, 1762, 1755; SC 415, 415B/C

TIDES

Standard Port LISBOA (⟶); ML 2·05

Times				**Height (metres)**			
High Water		Low Water		MHWS	MHWN	MLWN	MLWS
0500	1000	0300	0800	3·8	3·0	1·5	0·6
1700	2200	1500	2000				
Differences VILAGARCIA							
+0040	+0100	+0110	+0120	+0·2	–0·3	0·0	–0·4

SHELTER Shelter can be found from most winds. Many ⚓ages await exploration with large scale charts and a Pilot book.

NAVIGATION WPT 42°27'·00N 08°59'·50W, 025°/6·6M to 5ca E of Is Rua (lt) 42°32'·96N 08°56'·38W. Isla Sálvora (lt) is usually left to port; the inshore passage to NW between Isla Sagres and Pta Falcoeiro, Canal de Sagres, is rock bordered but viable in daylight with good weather and AC 1734 or SC 4152/3, essential for cruising Ría de Arosa, the largest ría (approx 14M x 7M). The fairway to Vilagarcia is buoyed/lit, but the many mussel rafts (*bateas*) on either side are either unlit, or marked by Y lt buoys. The low bridge from Isla de Arosa to the mainland prevents passage.

LIGHTS AND MARKS Principal lts/marks are on the chartlet as scale permits. Isla Rúa is a prominent rky islet with lt ho.

COMMUNICATIONS (Codes: 981 La Coruna, NW shore. 986 Pontevedra, SE shore). MRCC (981) 767320; Emergency 112; Brit Consul (902) 109356; Santa Uxia, Caramiñal, Cabo de Cruz, Rianxo, Vilagarcia and Vilanova, VHF Ch 09, 16.

FACILITIES Marinas (see insets)

Santa Uxia 42°33'·80N 08°59'·34W. ☎981874739, mob 648187171 www.nauticoriveira.com secretariaclub@nauticoriveira.com. 70 Ⓥ max LOA 14m F & A on 4 pontoons in 4m. **Town** All facilities.

Marina a Pobra do Caramiñal 42°36'·27N08°56'·10W. ☎608174395, www.muport.es info@muport.es 305 in 3·5m inc 30 Ⓥ, €3·00 inc WC. by taxi.

Marina Cabo de Cruz 42°36'·60N 08°53'·30W, VHF Ch 09, ☎

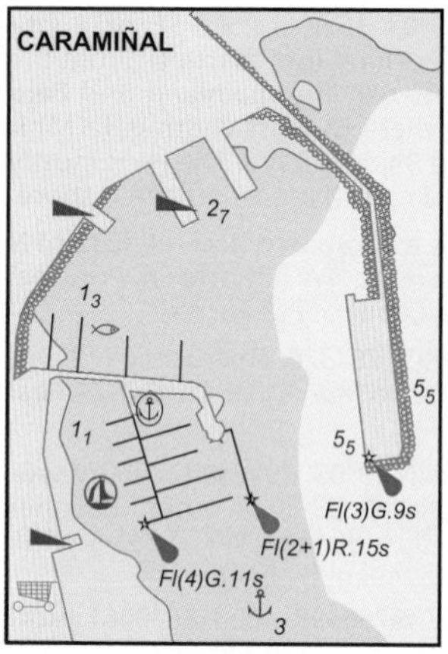
CARAMIÑAL
Fl(3)G.9s
Fl(2+1)R.15s
Fl(4)G.11s

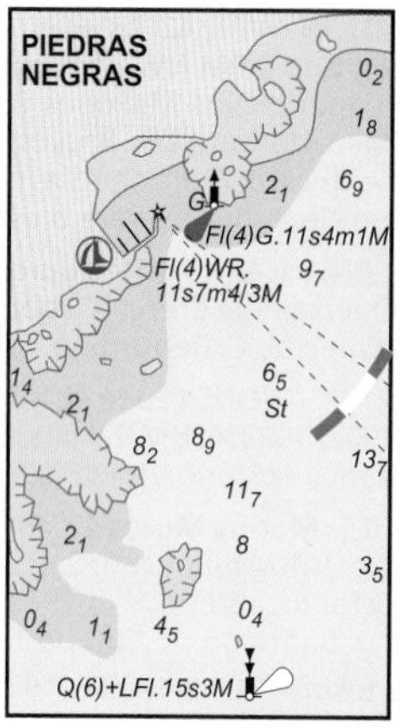
PIEDRAS NEGRAS
Fl(4)G.11s4m1M
Fl(4)WR. 11s7m4/3M
Q(6)+LFl.15s3M

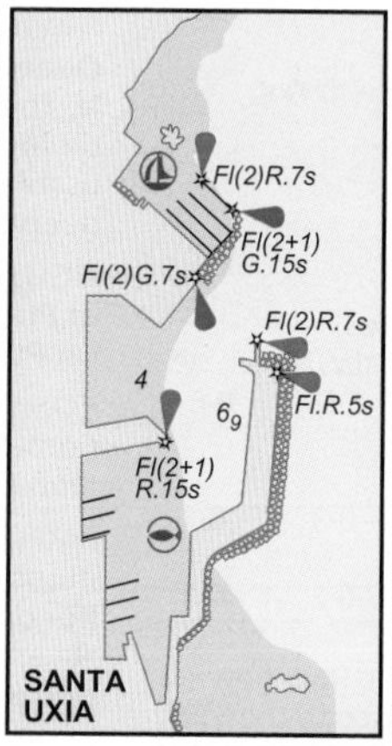
Fl(2)R.7s
Fl(2+1) G.15s
Fl(2)G.7s
Fl(2)R.7s
Fl.R.5s
Fl(2+1) R.15s
SANTA UXIA

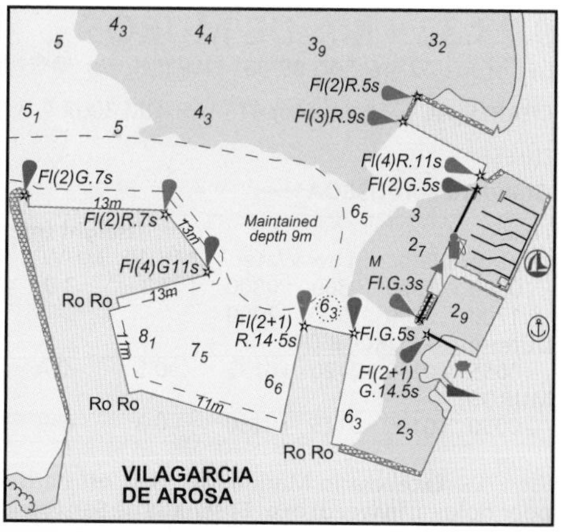
Fl(2)R.5s
Fl(3)R.9s
Fl(4)R.11s
Fl(2)G.5s
Fl(2)G.7s
Fl(2)R.7s
Maintained depth 9m
Fl(4)G11s
Ro Ro
Fl.G.3s
Fl(2+1) R.14·5s
Fl.G.5s
Fl(2+1) G.14.5s
VILAGARCIA DE AROSA

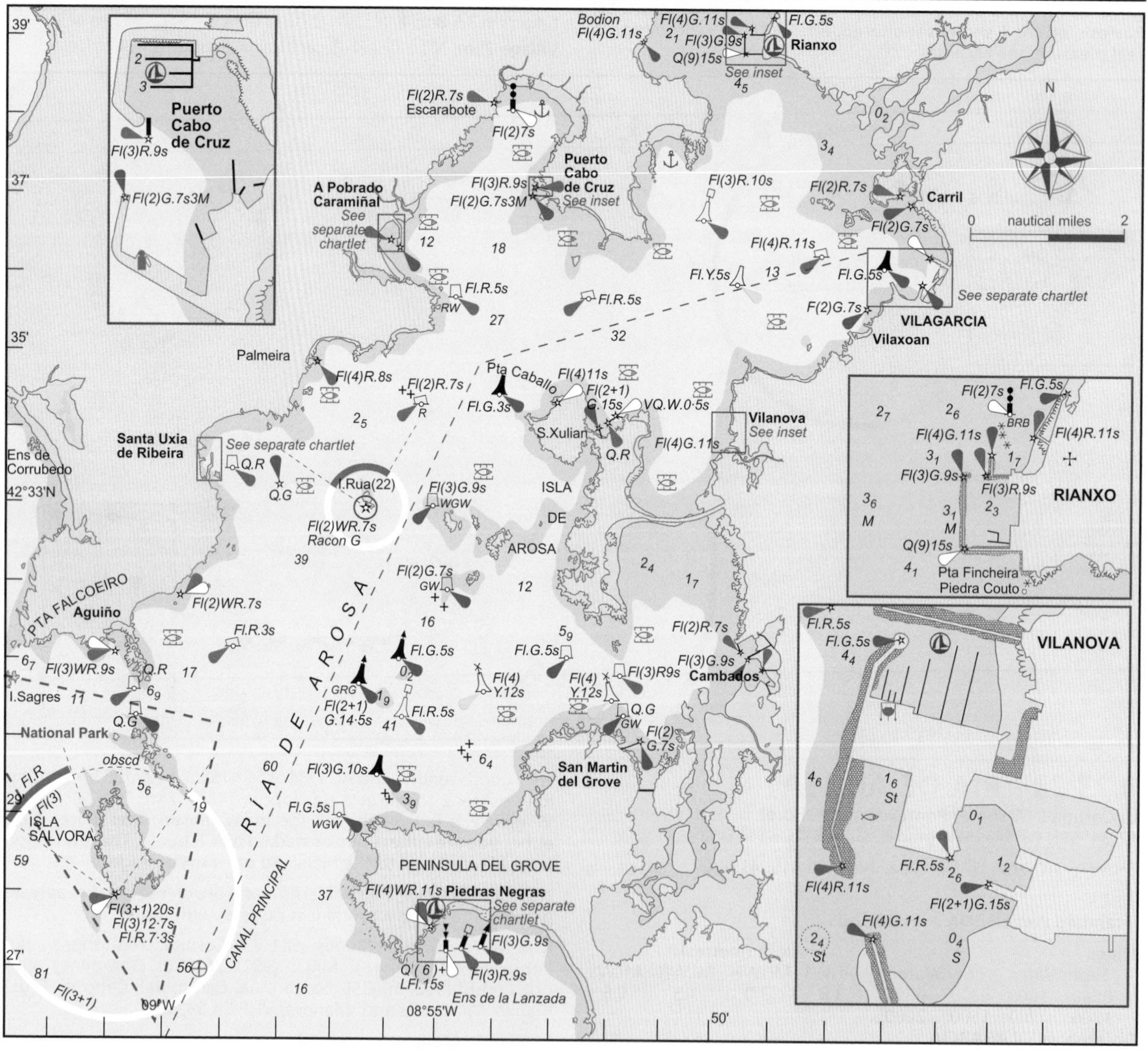
Puerto Cabo de Cruz
Rianxo
See inset
Escarabote
A Pobrado Caramiñal
See separate chartlet
Carril
nautical miles
VILAGARCIA
Vilaxoan
Palmeira
Pta Caballo
Vilanova
Santa Uxia de Ribeira
S.Xulian
Ens de Corrubedo
I.Rua(22)
Racon G
ISLA DE AROSA
PTA FALCOEIRO
Aguiño
I.Sagres
National Park
Cambados
San Martin del Grove
ISLA SALVORA
RÍA DE AROSA
CANAL PRINCIPAL
PENINSULA DEL GROVE
Piedras Negras
Ens de la Lanzada
RIANXO
Pta Fincheira
Piedra Couto
VILANOVA

(622)884846, info@nauticoboiro.com www.nauticoboiro.com 200&+30 Ⓥ, 6m-max 22m LOA in 2m-5m, €2·10, inc wi-fi. **Town** Boiro, 4km/10 mins taxi, shops.

Rianxo 42°39'·00N 08°49'·51W. ☎866107. 2 pontoons at SE corner in 1·4m; 80 or ⚓ just SE of the town off the beach.

Vilagarcia 42°36'·04N 08°46'·21W. ☎986 511175. marinavilagarcia @marinavilagarcia.com 450 inc Ⓥ €2·00 as directed or on 1st pontoon to stbd in 3-5m; Ⓔ (70t) (50t) YC. **Town** nearby (unmanned, Spanish cr/cards). Ⓑ (service only) ⇄ Vigo, Santiago, La Coruna ✈ Santiago.

Vilanova Marina 42°33'·98N 08°50'·05W. ☎ 986561420 - mob 24H 670623084 marinaarousa@marinaarousa.es www.marinaarousa.com. €2·32/m. Due to extensive *viveros* the only appr is from the N: WPT at 42°35'·09N 08°50'·87W (Fl (3) G 10s); thence 179°/1·2M to 0·5M abm Vilanova. ⛽ ⛵ ⚑(35t) ⛴ in FV basin to the S.

Piedras Negras 42°27'·50N 08°55'·09W. ☎986 738430. www.cnsvicente.org administracion@cnsvicente.org ⊕42°26'·97N 08°54'·28W, 310°/8ca to ent in W sector (305°-315°) of Fl (4) WR 11s. 134 berths inc ⓥ €2·95; 2 pontoons + fingers, 12m max LOA; depths 4-6m. ⛽ ⛽ ⚓ ⛽ wi-fi, ⚑(35t). **CN** ☎738325, ✕ ⛵ ☎738435.

FV harbours with yacht facilities or ⚓s include: **San Xulian** (Isla Arosa, N Bay) 42°33'·94N 08°52'·14W; ⚓ 1ca NW of the S' most pier which has 4 pontoons for small craft on W side. ⚓ in S Bay at 42°33'·36N 08°52'·57W in 5-8m; restricted by many moorings. ⛴ at head of the bay.

Cambados 42°30'·69N 08°49'·11W, S of Tragove FV hbr. Very shallow, 0·3m; only advised for multihulls and bilge-keelers.

9.23.34 RÍA DE PONTEVEDRA

Pontevedra **42°22'·00N 08°50'·00W** (mid-Ría) ❁❁❁◇◇◇✿✿✿

CHARTS AC 3633, 1732/3; SC 416A/B; SHOM 3007

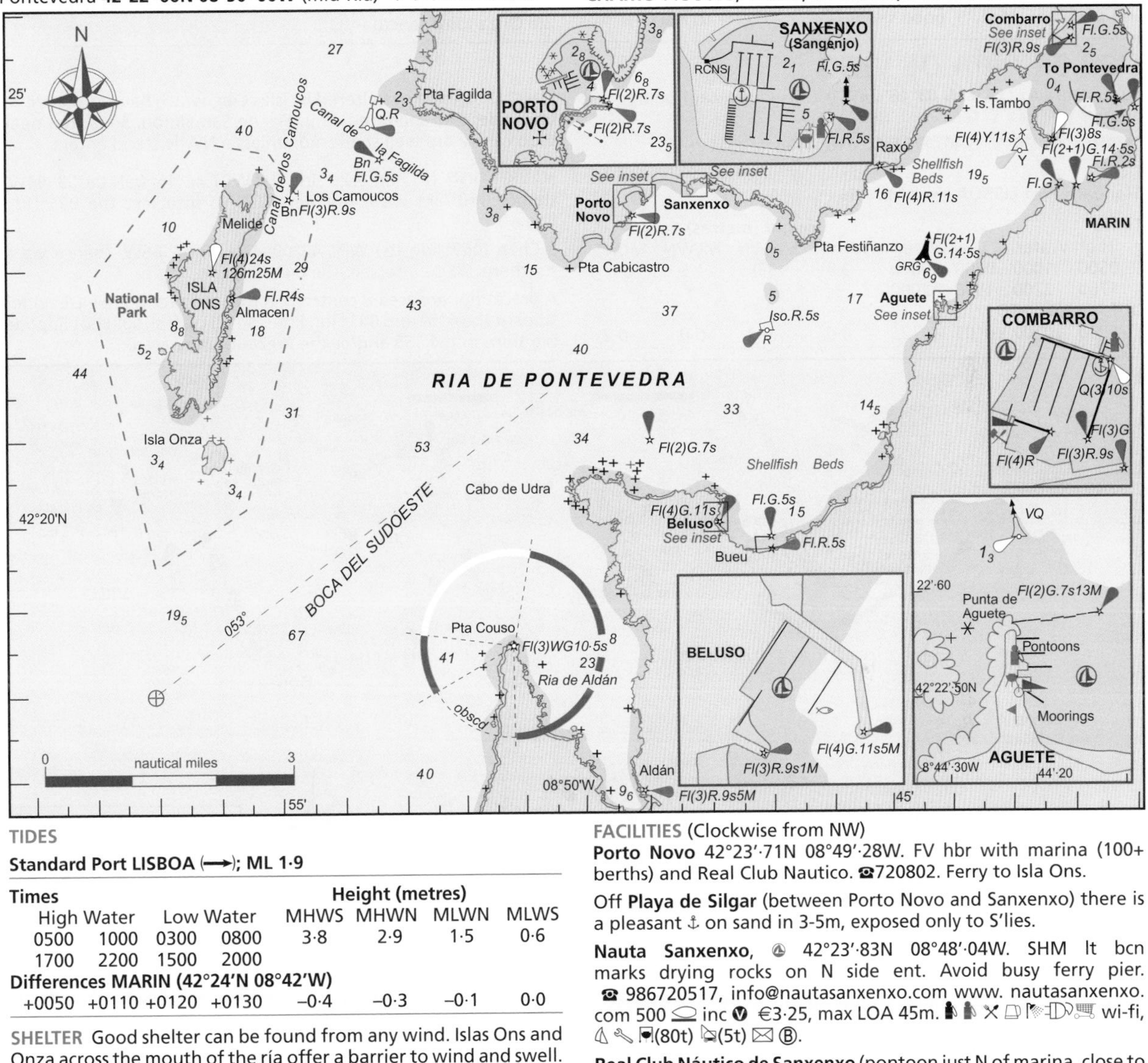

TIDES

Standard Port LISBOA (⟶); ML 1·9

Times				Height (metres)			
High Water		Low Water		MHWS	MHWN	MLWN	MLWS
0500	1000	0300	0800	3·8	2·9	1·5	0·6
1700	2200	1500	2000				
Differences MARIN (42°24'N 08°42'W)							
+0050	+0110	+0120	+0130	−0·4	−0·3	−0·1	0·0

SHELTER Good shelter can be found from any wind. Islas Ons and Onza across the mouth of the ría offer a barrier to wind and swell. Marinas, hbrs and ⚓s are listed under Facilities.

NAVIGATION From WPT 42°18'·00N 08°57'·16W, (which also lies on the 129° ldg lts for Ria de Vigo) track 053° to enter via the main chan, Boca del Sudoeste, into centre of ria between Cabo de Udra and Pta Cabicastro.

From the NW small craft normally transit the Canal de la Figilda on 125° or the Canal de Los Camoucos on 180°; both are approx 3ca wide and viable in rougher weather with due care.

LIGHTS AND MARKS As chartlet. Isla Ons is a steep, cliffy, rocky island with conspic octagonal lt ho.

COMMUNICATIONS (Code 986). MRCC (981) 767320; Emergency 112; Marin VHF Ch 12, 16; Marinas VHF Ch 09.

FACILITIES (Clockwise from NW)

Porto Novo 42°23'·71N 08°49'·28W. FV hbr with marina (100+ berths) and Real Club Nautico. ☎720802. Ferry to Isla Ons.

Off **Playa de Silgar** (between Porto Novo and Sanxenxo) there is a pleasant ⚓ on sand in 3-5m, exposed only to S'lies.

Nauta Sanxenxo, ⓦ 42°23'·83N 08°48'·04W. SHM lt bcn marks drying rocks on N side ent. Avoid busy ferry pier. ☎ 986720517, info@nautasanxenxo.com www.nautasanxenxo.com 500 berths inc ⓥ €3·25, max LOA 45m. ⛽ ⛽ ✕ ⛵ wi-fi, ⚑(80t) (5t) ✉ Ⓑ.

Real Club Náutico de Sanxenxo (pontoon just N of marina, close to beach) ☎986803400, info@rcnsanxenxo.com www.rcnsanxenxo.com 62 berths inc ⓥ €3·05, max LOA 12m. ✕ ⛵.

Raxó 42°24'·06N 08°45'·34W. Temp'y ⚓ in about 5m off bkwtr hd.

Combarro 42°25'·38N 08°42'·12W. AC 1733. 287 + 45 ⓥ <12m & 2 ⓥ max 20m LOA, €2.80/m. Good depths in marina and channel but do not pass north of Isla Tambo; leave mussel rafts to port in final approach. ☎(986) 778415, www.combarromar.com comercial@combarromar.com; ⛽ ⛽ ✕ ⛵ ⚑(50t) (6t) ⛴.

Pontevedra 42°24'·86N 08°41'·35W, mouth of Rio Lérez. A LW dinghy recce of shallow chan between training walls is advised; least depth 1·3m. Access restricted by overhead cables (19m clearance) and motorway bridge (12m clearance). **Town** The provincial capital has all domestic facilities and good road links.

Continued overleaf

N & NW Spain

Marin 42°23'·94N 08°42'·21W, a naval, commercial and FV port, with no yacht facilities (tiny marina in W basin, private). Isla Tambo, NW, is a restricted military area; landing prohib.

Aguete 42°22'·55N 08°44'·16W. **Marina** ☎702373 www.rcmaguete.com N'most fragmented pontoon is a wavebreak, inner pontoons approx 100 little space for ⓥ but many ⚓s. To clear offlying rks, round the SHM buoy before turning S. (28t) (8t). **Real Club de Mar** ✕ . **Village** Few shops.

Bueu 42°19'·79N 08°47'·02W. A FV hbr, no ⓥ; ⚓ to W of hbr in about 5m. Mussel rafts to NNW and NNE. Hbr ent lit as chartlet. HM ☎320042, ✕ good shops . Ferry to Isla Ons.

Beluso 42°20'·01N 08°47'·90W. Mussel beds (*viveiros*) are E/NE of the hbr. 2nd pontoon to stbd is for yachts, F & A berths, but access to shore may be difficult due to coded gates. HM ☎400870 if he can be found. Excellent ✕. 20 mins walk to Bueu.

Ria de Aldán Punta del Con at 42°20'·01N 08°47'·90W, head of Ria. Worth exploring in settled weather; beware mussel rafts on W side. Temp'y ⚓s may be found on E side and at head of ría.

Isla Ons Almost uninhabited, but very popular with tourists in season. At Almacen jetty (Fl R 4s) ferry wash detracts from the ⚓ or possible ⚓s; ✕ . Fair weather ⚓ in 5m off Melide beach 42°23'·37N 08°55'·50W, but within National Park. No landing on Isla Onza (bird sanctuary).

9.23.35 RÍA DE VIGO

Pontevedra **42°13'·85N 08°48'·26W** (centre of precautionary area) ❁❁❁◊◊◊✿✿✿

CHARTS AC 3633, 1730, 1731; SC 416, 416B; SHOM 7595

TIDES

Standard Port LISBOA (⟶); ML 1·96

Times				Height (metres)			
High Water		Low Water		MHWS	MHWN	MLWN	MLWS
0500	1000	0300	0800	3·8	3·0	1·5	0·6
1700	2200	1500	2000				
Differences *VIGO*							
+0040	*+0100*	*+0105*	*+0125*	*0·0*	*–0·3*	*0·0*	*–0·2*

SHELTER The ría is sheltered by Islas Cies, which have attractive ⚓s on E side; also sheltered ⚓s in Ens de San Simon. 3 marinas near Vigo centre are well sheltered, unless a NW'ly scend enters.

NAVIGATION N Chan (129° ldg lts) WPT 42°16'·09N 08°53'·94W, thence 160°/2M via a northern TSS to intersect the 095° ldg line.

S Chan (069° ldg lts) WPT 42°09'·42N 08°54'·86W, thence via a southern TSS to intersect the 041° ldg line.

A precautionary area is centred on the intersection (see L/L under title) of the 095° and 041° ldg lines. Small craft should not impede big ships in the TSS and/or the Precautionary area.

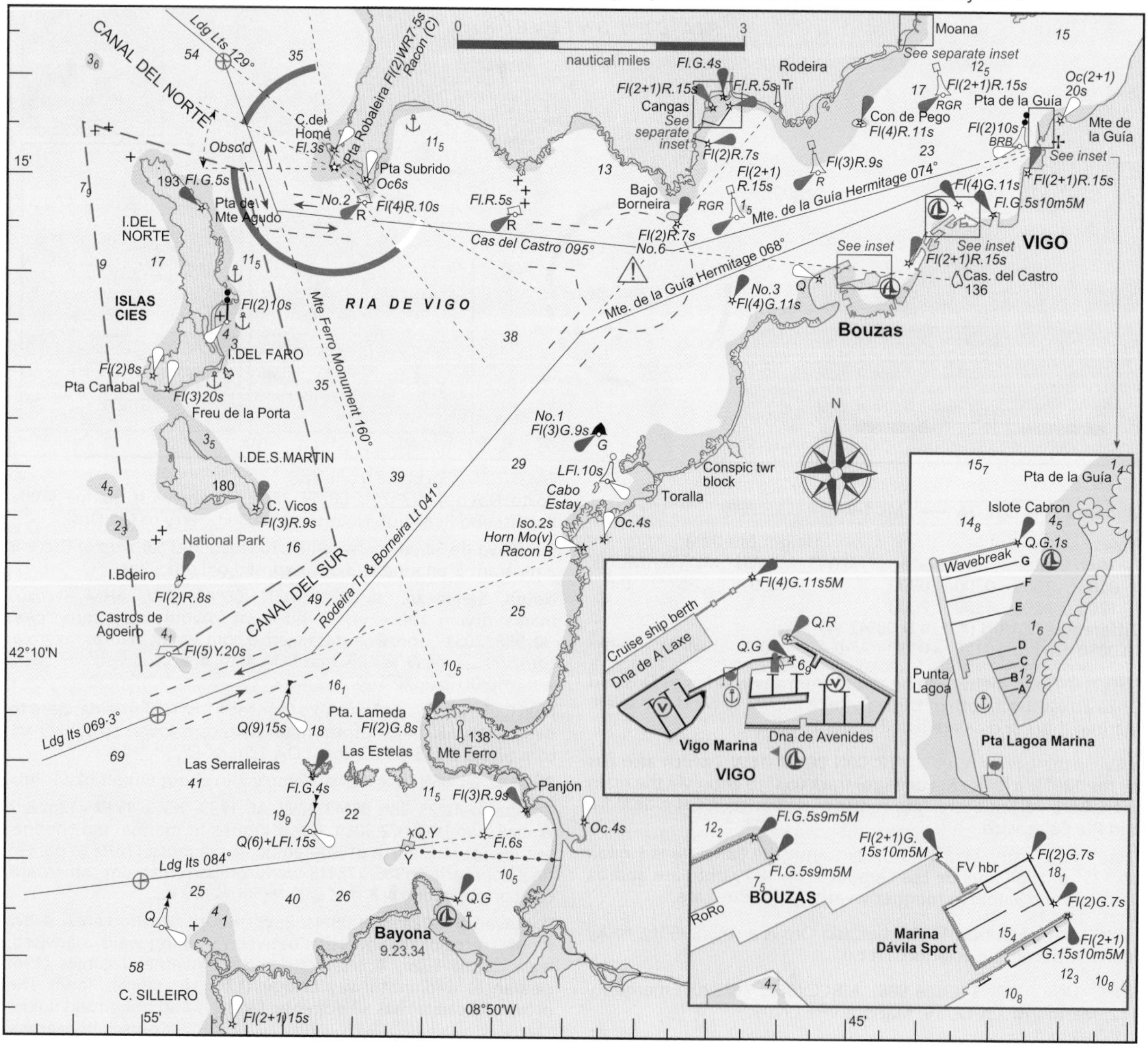

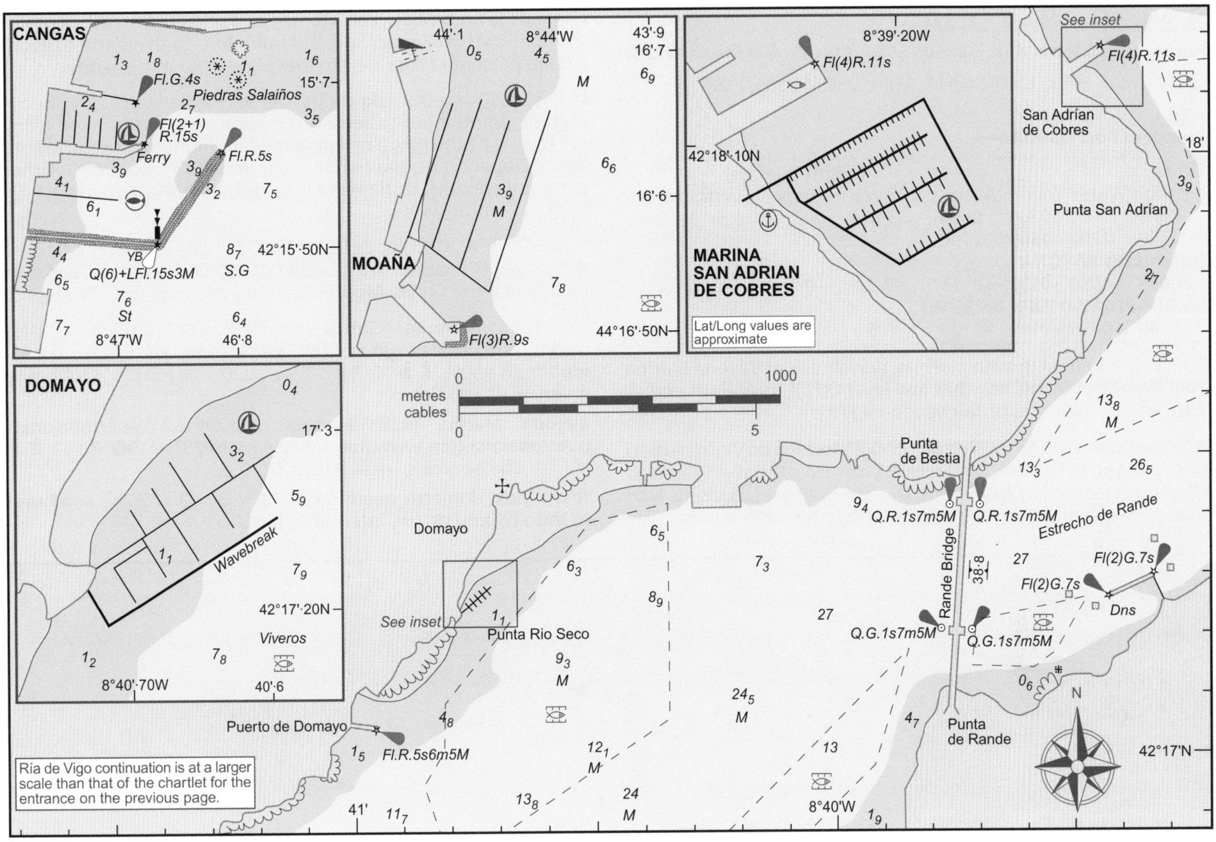
CANGAS
Fl.G.4s
Piedras Salaiños
Fl(2+1) R.15s
Ferry
Fl.R.5s
YB
Q(6)+LFl.15s3M
S.G
St
42°15'·50N
8°47'W
46'·8
15'·7
44'·1
8°44'W
43'·9
16'·7
16'·6
MOAÑA
Fl(3)R.9s
44°16'·50N
8°39'·20W
Fl(4)R.11s
42°18'·10N
MARINA SAN ADRIAN DE COBRES
Lat/Long values are approximate
See inset
San Adrían de Cobres
Punta San Adrían
18'
DOMAYO
17'·3
Wavebreak
42°17'·20N
Viveros
8°40'·70W
40'·6
metres
cables
1000
Domayo
See inset
Punta Rio Seco
Puerto de Domayo
Fl.R.5s6m5M
Ría de Vigo continuation is at a larger scale than that of the chartlet for the entrance on the previous page.
Punta de Bestia
Q.R.1s7m5M
Q.R.1s7m5M
Estrecho de Rande
Rande Bridge
38·8
Fl(2)G.7s
Fl(2)G.7s
Dns
Q.G.1s7m5M
Q.G.1s7m5M
Punta de Rande
42°17'N
8°40'W
41'

The buoyed inner fairway is defined by brgs of 068° and 074° on the conspic Hermitage (chapel) tower on Monte de la Guía. Beware extensive unlit mussel rafts (*bateas*) along the N shore.

LIGHTS AND MARKS Islas Cies are easily identified by their high, rugged bare slopes and white beaches on the E side. Ldg lts/marks for the appr chans are as per the chartlet and Lights, buoys and waypoints.

COMMUNICATIONS (Code 986); MRCC 222230; Emergency 112; ⊖ & Met at marinas; Brit Consul (902)109356; Port Control *Vigo Prácticos* VHF Ch 14, 16; Marinas Ch 09; Club Náutico de Rodiera (Cangas) Ch 06; ⇄269414; ✈ 268200; Turismo 224757.

FACILITIES heading NE up the Ria:

NW shore

Cangas 42°15'·66N 08°46'·97W. Rodeira is a small friendly YC marina in the NW corner of Ensenada de Cangas. ☎986304246; portodeportivo@nauticorodeira.com www. nauticorodeira.com ♥ on fingers as directed; approx €2·50. ⛽ ⛴ (64t) ⛴(8t). **YC** (English spoken) ⛴ ⛴. Good security, 24hrs guard. If full, ⚓ ESE of marina clear of ferries and FVs. **Town** Usual facilities, ⛴ ⛴. Ferry to Vigo ½ hourly.

Moaña Marina 42°16'·66N 08°44'·00W. ☎311140. www.moanamar.es; Appr from S, passing El Con hbr. Avoid *viveros* to NE and E. €1·37. Limited ♥ on fingers at N end of 1st pontoon (other fingers too short) telephone before arrival. ⛴.

Domayo Marina 42°17'·26N 08°40'·60W, 7ca W of suspension bridge between Domayo hbr Fl R 5s and conspic factory quay to NE. Best approach from SW, close inshore of fish farms (*viveros*).

NE of Rande suspension bridge (38.8m clearance)

Ensenada de San Simón, 42°17'·29N 08°39'·63W (AC 1730) has peaceful ⚓s in 3-4m mud off W, E and S sides, clear of *viveros*. €2.50; ✕ (lunch only) ⛴.

San Adrián de Cobres 42°18'·08N 08°39'·20W. **Marina** ☎874007, contacto@acimutnorte.com www.acimutnorte.com. Skirt a large *vivero* S and E of the marina to appr from the NE. Pierhead lt Fl (4) R 11s is the only lt, close NW of the marina. 204 on fingers inc♥ max LOA 18m, €1.25 ✕ @.

SE shore (Vigo city)

Marina Dávila Sport ⛵ 42°13'·97N 08°44'·42W, ☎244612 www.davilasport.es recepcion@davilasport.es. In Darsena de Bouzas, staff speak good English. €3.20. Many ♥. ⛽ ⛴ ⛴ ⛴ Ⓔ ⛴ modern repair facilities for all yacht sizes, highly recommended. ⛴(70t). **CN** ☎232442, ✕ ⛴.

Vigo Marina 42°14'·56N 08°43'·42W. Narrow ent, between PHM/SHM lt twrs. ☎449694, mob 638037201/ VHF Ch 09 (both H24); www.rcnauticovigo.com puertodeportivo@rcnauticovigo.com 436 F&A, fingers ♥ €2.65, in west basin (Dársena de A Laxe) max 10m LOA; east basin (Dársena de AS Avenidas) >10m to max 35m LOA. ⛽ ⛴ (0900-2100) ⛴ ⛴ ⛴ Ⓔ ⛴ ⛴ ⛴ wi-fi security H24, key card access, ⛴ ⛴ (32t) ⛴(3t). **RCN** clubhouse ☎433588, ✕ ⛴ ⛴ WC.

Pta Lagoa Marina 42°15'·51N 08°42'·46W. ☎410096. www.yatesport.es lagoa@yatesport.es VHF 09. 250 + 100♥ €3.40, max LOA 24m, draft 3·5m. ⛽ ⛴ ⛴ ⛴ ⛴ Ⓔ ⛴ ⛴(70t); 2½km N of city.

City of Vigo All amenities, ⇄ ✈ (internal flights).

9.23.36 BAYONA

Pontevedra **42°07'·45N 08°50'·55W** (MRCY) ❀❀❀◊◊◊✿✿✿

CHARTS AC 3633, 1730; SC 417, 416B; SHOM 7596, 7595

TIDES

Standard Port LISBOA (⟶)

Times				**Height (metres)**			
High Water		Low Water		MHWS	MHWN	MLWN	MLWS
0500	1000	0300	0800	3·8	3·0	1·5	0·6
1700	2200	1500	2000				
Differences BAYONA							
+0035	+0050	+0100	+0115	−0·3	−0·3	−0·2	−0·1
LA GUARDIA (41°54'N 08°53'W)							
+0040	+0055	+0105	+0120	−0·5	−0·4	−0·3	−0·2

SHELTER Excellent in both marinas; wavebreak at Bayona Marina 20m NE of pontoons, now has low level Q.Fl.Y lts at each end. ⚓ E/NE of marinas, clear of fairway to FV jetty.

NAVIGATION WPT 42°07'·78N 08°55'·06W (see Ría de Vigo chartlet) 084°/2·8M to SPM buoy QY. From S keep 1M off Cabo Silleiro to clear reefs marked by NCM buoy, Q. Las Serralleiras, rks/islets N of ldg line, are marked by SCM & WCM lt buoys and by a lt bcn. The Canal de la Porta, between Monte Ferro and Las Estelas is a useful shortcut to/from Ría de Vigo, but hold close to the island to avoid a 0.9m patch and rock which dries close W of mid-channel.

LIGHTS AND MARKS Ldg/Dir lts 084° as chartlet and Lights, buoys and waypoints, hard-to-see white conical twrs, the front on a tiny rky islet. N of the bay, a prominent white monument is on Monte Ferro. Dique de Abrigo (white wall) has a G/W tower QG. Other conspic daymarks: castle walls (parador) and MRCY flag-mast. FV jetty has white crane.

COMMUNICATIONS (Code 986) MRCC 222230; Emergency112; ⊖ & Met via YC/marina; Brit Consul (902)109356; *Puerto Deportivo de Bayona* VHF Ch 09; *Monte Real Club de Yates* VHF Ch 71.

FACILITIES **Monte Real Club de Yates (MRCY)** ☎385000. secretaria@mrcyb.com www.mrcyb.es 200 F&A + some Ⓥs in 6m, €2.95, multihulls +50%, Ice (20t) (1·5t). Clubhouse is very well appointed.

Bayona Marina ☎385107, mob 626299162. puertobaiona@puertobaiona.com www.puertobaiona.com 297 + 19Ⓥ €3.00. WC key access, Ice (35t) (6t).

Town Most domestic needs inc Ⓔ; and buses to Vigo (21km) ⇄ (✈, internal flights).

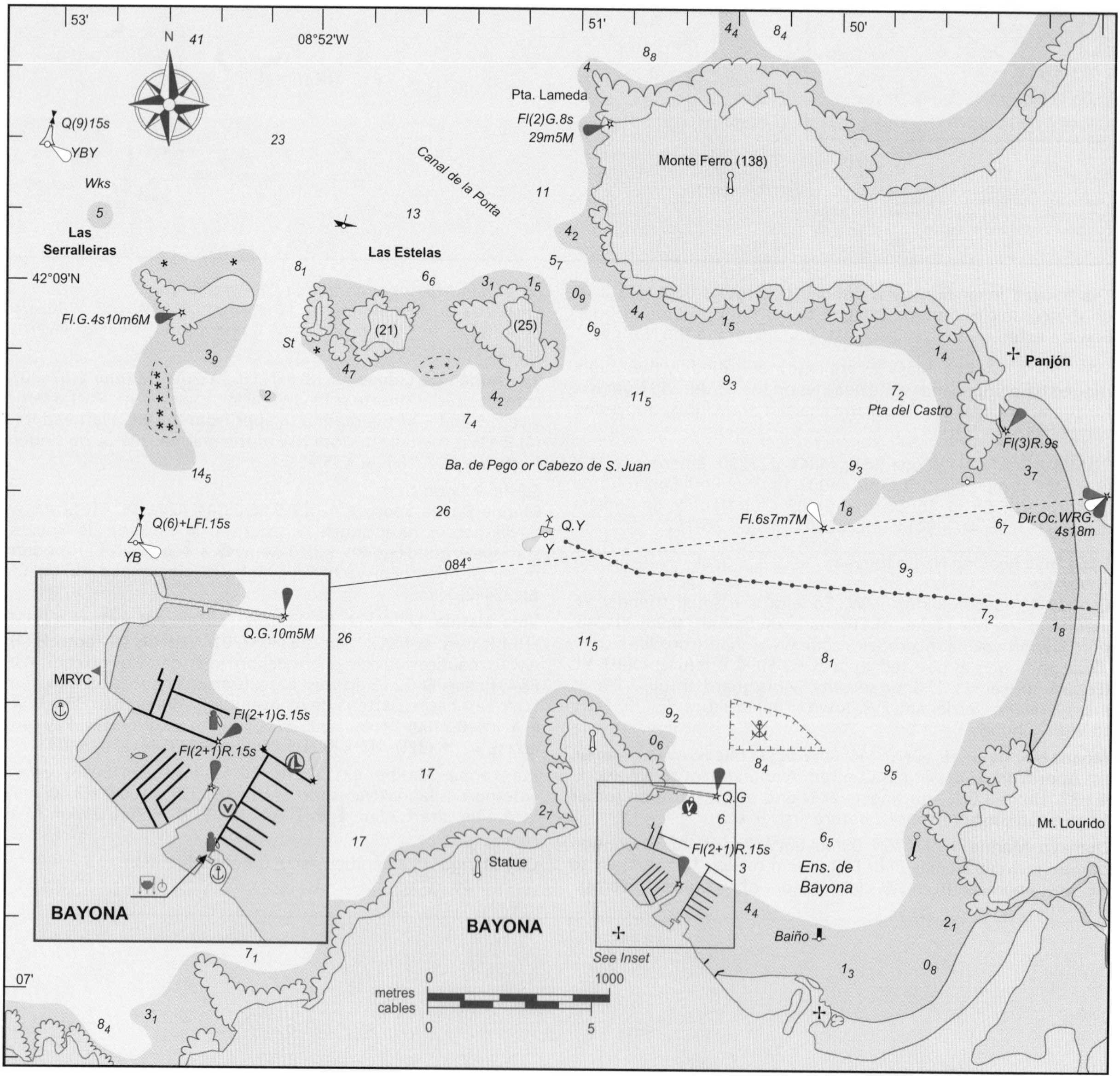

Portugal

Viana do Castelo to Vila Real de Santo António

9.24.1 Contents 987

9.24.2 Area map and Distance table 988

9.24.3 Lights, buoys and waypoints 990

9.24.4 Passage information 992
Wind and Weather – 992 • The Spanish Border to Cabo Raso – 992 •
Cabo Raso to Cape St Vincent – 999 • Southern Portugal: the Algarve – 1005

9.24.5 Special notes for Portugal 992

9.24.6 Viana do Castelo 993

9.24.7 Póvoa de Varzim 993

9.24.8 Leixões 994
Rio Douro • Porto

9.24.9 Porto (Oporto) 994

9.24.10 Aveiro 995

9.24.11 Figueira da Foz 995

9.24.12 Nazaré 996

9.24.13 Peniche 996

9.24.14 Cascais 997

9.24.15 Lisboa (Standard port, tide tables/curves) 997

9.24.16 Sesimbra 1003

9.24.17 Setúbal 1003
Arrábida

9.24.18 Sines 1004
Baleeira

9.24.19 Lagos 1004
Alvor

9.24.20 Portimão 1005

9.24.21 Albufeira 1006

9.24.22 Vilamoura 1006

9.24.23 Faro and Olhão 1007
Tavira

9.24.24 Vila Real de Santo António 1008

9.24.2 Portugal

Viana do Castelo to Vila Real de Santo Antonio
The Azores

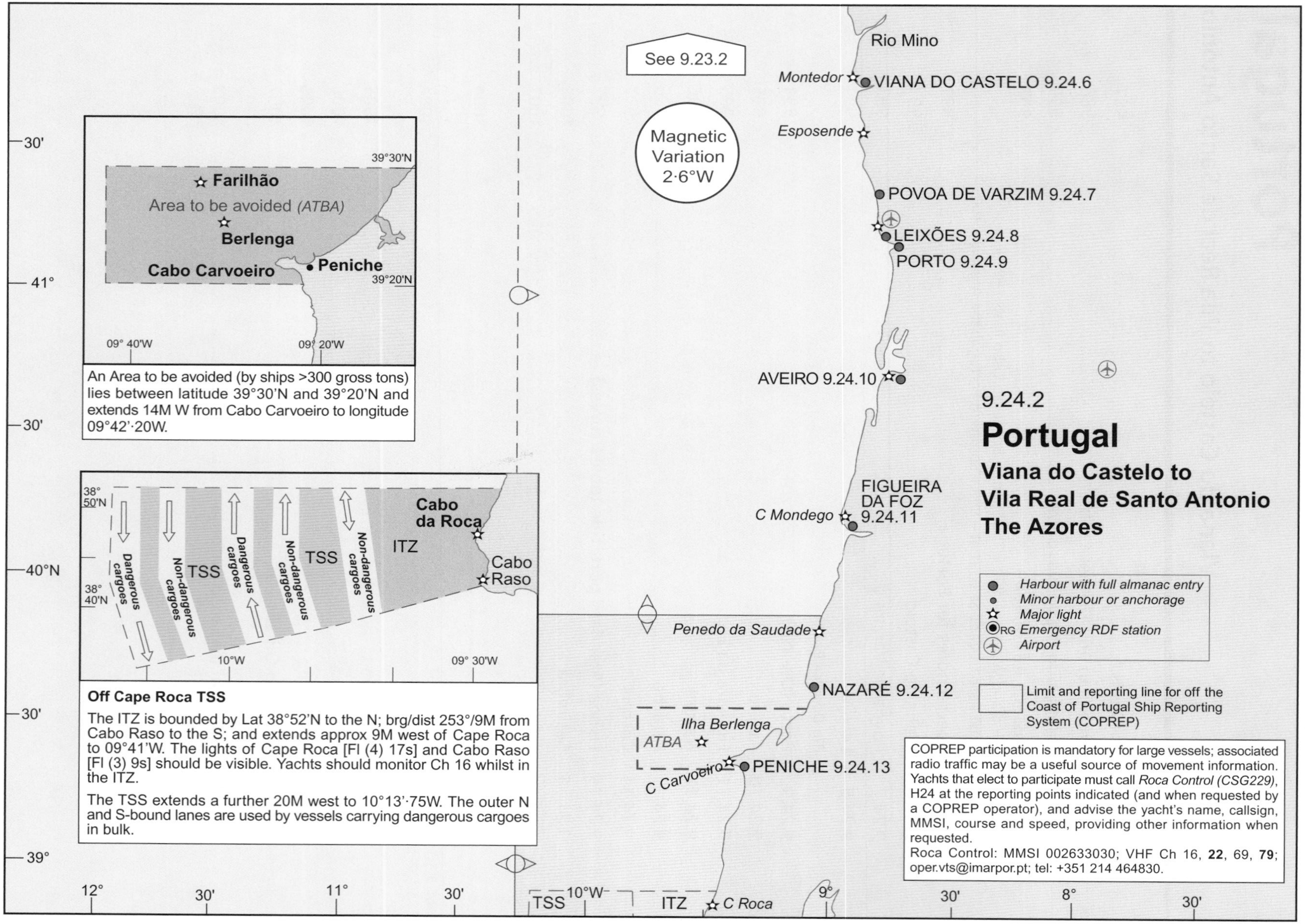

Rio Mino
Montedor
VIANA DO CASTELO 9.24.6
Esposende
POVOA DE VARZIM 9.24.7
LEIXÕES 9.24.8
PORTO 9.24.9
AVEIRO 9.24.10
C Mondego
FIGUEIRA DA FOZ 9.24.11
Penedo da Saudade
NAZARÉ 9.24.12
Ilha Berlenga
ATBA
C Carvoeiro
PENICHE 9.24.13
C Roca
TSS
10°W
ITZ
See 9.23.2
Magnetic Variation 2·6°W
Harbour with full almanac entry
Minor harbour or anchorage
Major light
RG Emergency RDF station
Airport
Limit and reporting line for off the Coast of Portugal Ship Reporting System (COPREP)
Farilhão
Area to be avoided (ATBA)
Berlenga
Cabo Carvoeiro
Peniche
39°30'N
39°20'N
09° 40'W
09° 20'W
Cabo da Roca
Cabo Raso
ITZ
TSS
Dangerous cargoes
Non-dangerous cargoes
38° 50'N
38° 40'N
10°W
09° 30'W
30'
41°
30'
40°N
30'
39°
12°
30'
11°
30'
9°
30'
8°
30'

An Area to be avoided (by ships >300 gross tons) lies between latitude 39°30'N and 39°20'N and extends 14M W from Cabo Carvoeiro to longitude 09°42'·20W.

Off Cape Roca TSS

The ITZ is bounded by Lat 38°52'N to the N; brg/dist 253°/9M from Cabo Raso to the S; and extends approx 9M west of Cape Roca to 09°41'W. The lights of Cape Roca [Fl (4) 17s] and Cabo Raso [Fl (3) 9s] should be visible. Yachts should monitor Ch 16 whilst in the ITZ.

The TSS extends a further 20M west to 10°13'·75W. The outer N and S-bound lanes are used by vessels carrying dangerous cargoes in bulk.

COPREP participation is mandatory for large vessels; associated radio traffic may be a useful source of movement information. Yachts that elect to participate must call *Roca Control (CSG229)*, H24 at the reporting points indicated (and when requested by a COPREP operator), and advise the yacht's name, callsign, MMSI, course and speed, providing other information when requested.
Roca Control: MMSI 002633030; VHF Ch 16, **22**, 69, **79**; oper.vts@imarpor.pt; tel: +351 214 464830.

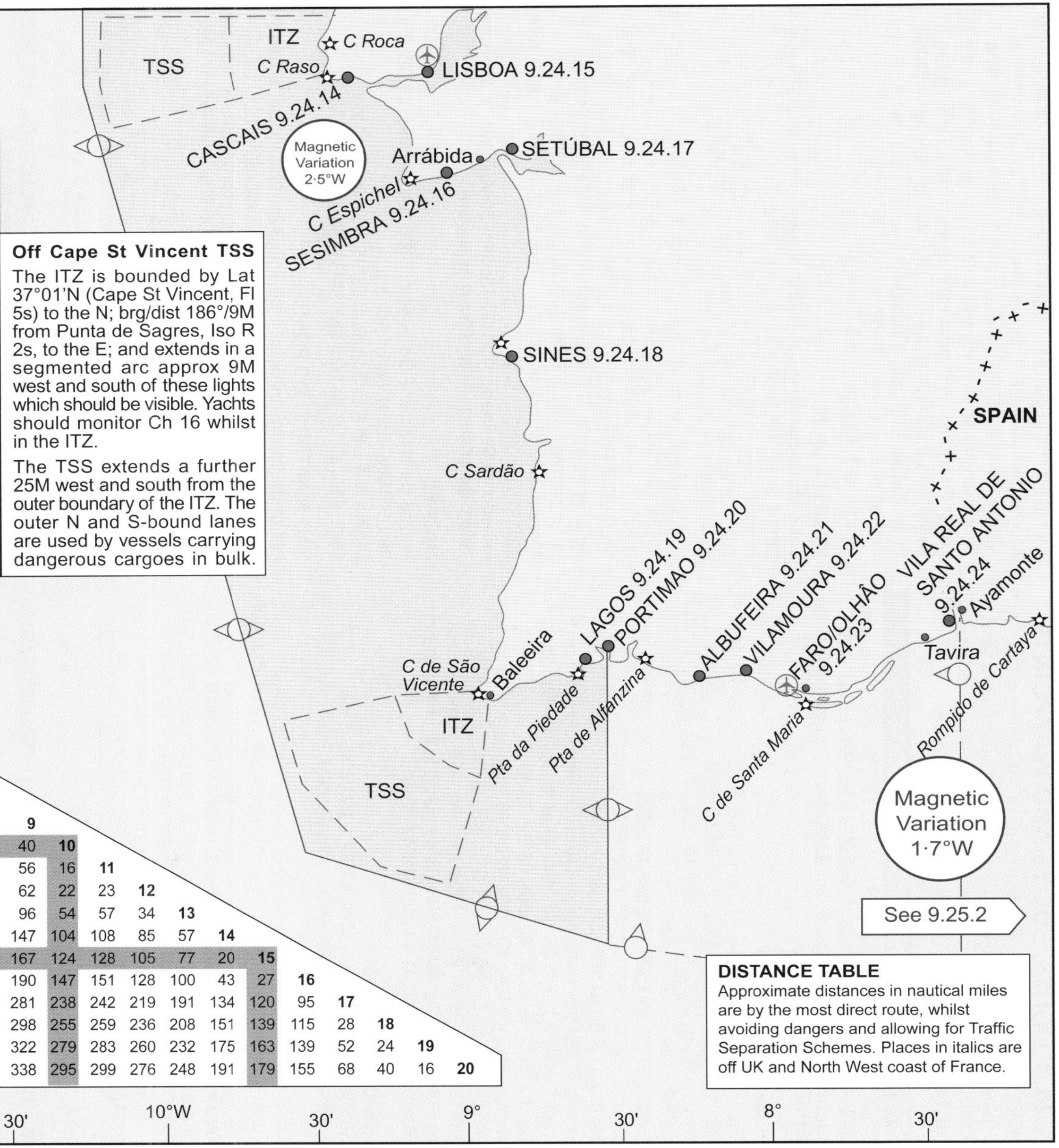
TSS
ITZ
C Roca
C Raso
LISBOA 9.24.15
CASCAIS 9.24.14
Magnetic Variation 2·5°W
Arrábida
SETÚBAL 9.24.17
C Espichel
SESIMBRA 9.24.16
SINES 9.24.18
C Sardão
SPAIN
C de São Vicente
Baleeira
LAGOS 9.24.19
PORTIMAO 9.24.20
Pta da Piedade
Pta de Alfanzina
ALBUFEIRA 9.24.21
VILAMOURA 9.24.22
FARO/OLHÂO 9.24.23
C de Santa Maria
VILA REAL DE SANTO ANTONIO 9.24.24
Ayamonte
Tavira
Rompido de Cartaya
ITZ
TSS
Magnetic Variation 1·7°W
See 9.25.2
30'
38°
30'
37°
30'
36°N
12°
30'
11°
30'
10°W
30'
9°
30'
8°
30'

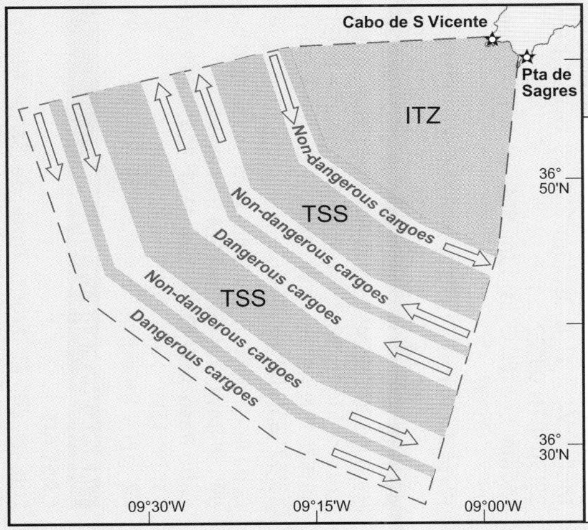
Cabo de S Vicente
Pta de Sagres
ITZ
TSS
TSS
Non-dangerous cargoes
Non-dangerous cargoes
Dangerous cargoes
Non-dangerous cargoes
Dangerous cargoes
36° 50'N
36° 30'N
09°30'W
09°15'W
09°00'W

Off Cape St Vincent TSS

The ITZ is bounded by Lat 37°01'N (Cape St Vincent, Fl 5s) to the N; brg/dist 186°/9M from Punta de Sagres, Iso R 2s, to the E; and extends in a segmented arc approx 9M west and south of these lights which should be visible. Yachts should monitor Ch 16 whilst in the ITZ.

The TSS extends a further 25M west and south from the outer boundary of the ITZ. The outer N and S-bound lanes are used by vessels carrying dangerous cargoes in bulk.

1	*Longships*	1																			
2	*Ushant (Créac'h)*	100	2																		
3	La Coruña	418	338	3																	
4	Cabo Villano	439	365	43	4																
5	Bayona	510	436	114	71	5															
6	Viana do Castelo	537	468	141	98	32	6														
7	Leixões (Pôrto)	565	491	169	126	63	33	7													
8	Nazaré	659	585	263	220	156	127	97	8												
9	Cabo Carvoeiro	670	596	274	231	171	143	114	22	9											
10	Cabo Raso	710	636	314	271	211	183	154	62	40	10										
11	Lisboa (bridge)	686	652	330	287	227	199	170	78	56	16	11									
12	Cabo Espichel	692	658	336	293	233	205	176	84	62	22	23	12								
13	Sines	726	692	370	327	267	239	210	118	96	54	57	34	13							
14	Cabo São Vicente	777	743	421	378	318	290	261	169	147	104	108	85	57	14						
15	Lagos	797	763	441	398	338	310	281	189	167	124	128	105	77	20	15					
16	Vilamoura	820	786	464	421	361	333	304	212	190	147	151	128	100	43	27	16				
17	Cádiz	911	877	555	512	452	424	395	303	281	238	242	219	191	134	120	95	17			
18	Cabo Trafalgar	928	894	572	529	469	441	412	320	298	255	259	236	208	151	139	115	28	18		
19	Tarifa	952	918	596	553	493	465	436	344	322	279	283	260	232	175	163	139	52	24	19	
20	Gibraltar	968	934	612	569	509	481	450	360	338	295	299	276	248	191	179	155	68	40	16	20

DISTANCE TABLE

Approximate distances in nautical miles are by the most direct route, whilst avoiding dangers and allowing for Traffic Separation Schemes. Places in italics are off UK and North West coast of France.

9.24.3 LIGHTS, BUOYS AND WAYPOINTS

Bold print = light with a nominal range of 15M or more. CAPITALS = place or feature. *CAPITAL ITALICS* = light-vessel, light float or Lanby. *Italics* = Fog signal. ***Bold italics*** = Racon. Many marks/buoys are fitted with AIS (MMSI No); see relevant charts.

RIO MIÑO (SPANISH BORDER) TO LISBOA

Río Miño ent, Fort Ínsua ☆ Fl WRG 4s 16m W12M, R8M, G9M; 204°-G-270°-R-357°-W-204°; W col; 41°51'·57N 08°52'·48W.
Montedor ☆ Fl (2) 9·5s 102m **22M**; Twr, R cupola and bldg; 41°45'·07N 08°52'·41W.

VIANA DO CASTELO

Dir lt Barra ☆ Oc WRG 4s 14m 8/6M; 350°-G-005°-W-010°-R-025°; on Pilots' twr; 41°41'·05N 08°50'·30W.
Outer mole ☆ Fl R 3s 9M; W col, R bands; 41°40'·46N 08°50'·66W.
No 2 Fl R 3s; 41°40'·53N 08°50'·48W.
E mole ☆ Fl G 3s 9M; 41°40'·67N 08°50'·25W.
No 1 Fl G 3s; 41°40'·68N 08°50'·29W.
Ldg lts 012·5° (for docks only); R twrs, W stripes: **Front** ☆ Iso R 4s 14m 5M; 41°41'·33N 08° 50'·35W. **Rear** ☆ Oc R 6s 32m 5M.
No 3 Fl (2) G 3s; 41°40'·86N 08°50'·24W.
No 4 Fl (2+1) R 5s; 41°40'·89N 08°50'·36W.
Rio Lima: Nos. 5-13 s are Fl G 3s. Nos. 6-14 s are Fl R 3s.
No 13 Fl G 3s; 41°41'·49N 08°49'·27W, SSE of marina ent.
No 14 Fl R 3s; 41°41'·56N 08°49'·33W, SSE of marina ent.
Marina ent, unlit; 41°41'·60N 08°49'·33W.

PÓVOA DE VARZIM

Molhe N ☆ Fl R 3s 14m 12M; 41°22'·23N 08°46'·28W.
Molhe S ☆ L Fl G 6s 4M; 41°22'·27N 08°46'·07W.

LEIXÕES

Tanker mooring Fl (3) 15s 6M; *Horn (U) 30s;* 41°12'·10N 08°45'·06W. Oil refinery 2M E of this buoy is conspic D/N.
Leça ☆ Fl (3) 14s 56m **28M**; W twr, B bands; 41°12'·08N 08°42'·73W.
Outer N mole, Quebra-Mar ☆ Fl WR 5s 24m W12M, R9M; 001°-R-180°-W-001°; Gy twr; *Horn 20s;* 41°10'·37N 08°42'·49W.
S mole ☆ Fl G 4s 17m 7M; 328°-285°; *Horn 30s;* 41°10'·68N 08°42'·34W.
Inner N mole ☆ Fl R 4s 9m 6M; 173°-353°; 41°10'·70N 08°42'·51W.
No 2 Fl (3) R 8s; 41°10'·77N 08°42'·51W.
No 4 Fl (2) R 5s; 41°10'·86N 08°42'·60W .
Marina bkwtr ☆ L Fl (2) R 12s 4m 2M; 41°11'·08N 08°42'·25W.

RIO DOURO/PORTO

N mole head Fl R 5s 16m 9M; W twr, R stripes; 41°08'·73N 08°40'·72W.
S mole head Fl G 5s 14m 6M; W col, G stripes; 41°08'·67N 08°40'·53W.
Up-river buoys in sequence:
No 1 Fl G 3s; 41°08'·74N 08°40'·29W.
No 2 Fl R 3s; 41°08'·72N 08°39'·77W.
No 3 Fl (2) G 5s; 41°08'·65N 08°39'·52W.
No 4 Fl (2) R 5s; 41°08'·80N 08°39'·12W.
No 5 Fl (3) G 6s; 41°08'·78N 08°38'·85W.
No 6A Fl (3) R 6s; 41°08'·44N 08°37'·26W.
No 8 Fl R 4s; 41°08'·39N 08°37'·12W; 4 ca W of bridge, 8·8m.

AVEIRO

Boia Aveiro, , Fl(3)G 7s; 40°·37'·86N 08° 46'·98W.
Lt ho Aero ☆ Fl (4) 13s 65m **23M**; R/W twr; 40°38'·57N 08°44'·87W.
Ldg lts 060·6°; both Or posts, G bands: Front ☆, Oc R 3s 10m 9M (4M day); 40°38'·81N 08°45'·04W. Rear ☆ Oc R 6s 15m 9M (4M day) 440m from front; vis 05° each side of Ldg line.
Molhe N, SW extension, outer end, Mohle ☆ Fl Y 1.5s 12m 2M, W col, R bands; 40° 38'·57N 08° 45'·87W.
Molhe N ☆ Fl R 3s 15m 8M; W twr, R bands; 40°38'·54N 08°45'·92W.
Molhe S ☆ Fl G 3s 15m 9M; W col, G bands; 40°38'·53N 08°45'·47W
Molhe Central ☆ L Fl G 5s 8m 3M; 40°38'·64N 08°44'·95W.
Monte Farinha ☆ Fl (2+1) R 6s 6m 4M; 40°39'·48N 08°43'·51W; Y-junction of Canal Principal and Canal de San Jacinto, to the N. Canal Principal is well buoyed and defined by 3 sets of ldg lts.
Terminal Sul ☆ Q (2+1) G 6s 6m 3M; 40°38'·26N 08°41'·33W.
Inner Canal Principal: 2 lateral lt buoys, 1 lt bcn and 7 unlit lateral buoys. Lock, 40°38'·75N 08°39'·74W, into Canal das Piramides for yacht berths.

FIGUEIRA DA FOZ

Cabo Mondego ☆ Fl 5s 96m **28M**; W twr and house; 40°11'·46N 08°54'·31W, 3M NNW of Figueira da Foz.
Hbr ent ldg lts 046·5°, both W strucs, R bands: Front ☆ Oc R 3s 6m 2M; 40°08'·83N 08°52'·21W. Rear, ☆ Oc R 3s 15m 6M; vis 039° - 055°.
Ldg lts 081·5°, both W cols, R bands: Front ☆ Iso R 5s 6m 4M; 40°08'·83N 08°51'·23W. Rear, ☆ Oc R 6s 10m 4M; 081·5°/239m.
Molhe N ☆ Fl R 6s 13m 9M; *Horn 35s;* 40°08'·60N 08°52'·70W.
Molhe S ☆ Fl G 6s 13m 7M; 40°08'·59N 08°52'·41W.
Inner N bkwtr ☆ Fl R 3s 8m 4M; 40°08'·78N 08°52'·10W.
Inner S bkwtr ☆ Fl G 3s 8m 4M; 40°08'·69N 08°52'·08W.
Marina ent, Fl (2) G 8s & Fl (2) R 8s, 6m 2M; G & R twrs; 40°08'·81N 08°51'·52W.
Penedo da Saudade ☆ Fl (2) 15s 54m **30M**; □ twr, and house; 39°45'·84N 09°01'·86W, 10M N of Nazaré.

NAZARÉ

Pontal da Nazaré ☆ Oc 3s 49m 14M; twr & bldg; 39°36'·25N 09°05'·15W, 9ca NNW of hbr ent.
Molhe N ☆ L Fl R 5s 14m 9M; 39°35'·45N 09°04'·59W.
Molhe S ☆ L Fl G 5s 14m 8M; 39°35'·36N 09°04'·70W.

SÃO MARTINHO DO PORTO

Ponta de Santo António ☆ Iso R 6s 32m 9M; W col, R bands; *Siren 60s;* 39°30'·61N 09°08'·61W (NE side of ent).
Ldg lts 145·1°, both W cols, R bands: Front ☆ Iso R 1·5s 9m 9M; 39°30'·14N 09°08'·39W. Rear ☆ Oc R 6s 11m 9·5M, 129m from front.

LOS FARILHÕES/ILHA DA BERLENGA

Farilhão Grande ☆ Fl (2) 5s 99m 13M; 39°28'·73N 09°32'·72W.
Ilha da Berlenga ☆ Fl 10s 120m **16M**; W □ twr and houses; *Horn 28s;* 39°24'·90N 09°30'·60W (5·7M NW of C. Carvoeiro).

PENICHE

Cabo Carvoeiro ☆ Fl R 6s 56m **15M**; W □ twr; *Horn 35s;* 39°21'·63N 09°24'·47W, on the W tip of the Peniche peninsula.
Molhe W ☆ Fl R 3s 13m 9M; W twr, R bands; *Siren 120s;* 39°20'·87N 09°22'·53W.
Molhe E ☆ Fl G 3s 13m 9M; W twr, G bands; 39°20'·98N 09°22'·39W.

Porto das Barcas ☆ L Fl R 6s 29m 6M; post; 39°13'·81N 09°20'·47W.
Porto Dineiro ☆ Oc 3s 19m 8M; 39°12'·83N 09°20'·55W.
Assenta ☆ L Fl 5s 74m 13M; W structure on conical base; 39°03'·53N 09°24'·85W (17M N of Cabo da Roca).
Ericeira ldg lts 083°; Front, N Pier Head ☆ Fl (3) R 12s 11m 6M; 38°57'·79N 09°25'·41W. Rear, ☆ Oc R 13s 34m 6M; *Siren 70s;* 38°57'·85N 09°25'·06W.

C. da Roca ☆ Fl (4) 17s 164m **26M**; W twr and bldgs; 38°46'·90N 09°29'·84W. R lt (527m) 5M E at Pena.
Cabo Raso ☆ Fl (3) 9s 22m **15M**; 324°-189°; R twr; 38°42'·57N 09°29'·15W, 3·2M WNW of Cascais.
C2 Fl Y 5s; outfall buoy; 38°39'·99N 09°27'·97W.

LISBOA TO CAPE ST VINCENT

CASCAIS

Ldg lts 284·7°: Front, **Forte de Santa Marta** ☆ Oc WR 6s 24m **W18M**, R14M; 233°-R-334°-W-098°; W □ twr, Bu bands; 38°41'·42N 09°25'·25W. Rear, **Guia** ☆ Iso WR 2s **W19M, R16M**; 326°-W-092°; 278°-R-292°; W twr; 38°41'·74N 09°26'·78W.

MC1, 2 & 3 all ⚓s, VQ (6) + L Fl 10s, mark the SE side of marina.
CC2 ⚓ Fl R 4s; NE of bkwtr hd; 38°41′·63N 09°24′·80W.
No 2 ⚓ Fl R 10s (May-Oct); 38°41′·69N 09°24′·99W.
Marina Molhe Sul ☆ Fl (3) R 4s 8m 6M; 38°41′·59N 09°24′·84W.
Molhe Norte ☆ Fl (2) G 4s 8m 3M; 38°41′·60N 09°24′·90W.

RIO TEJO, N BANK

Marconi ☆ Iso WR 3s 17m 9M; 048°-R-058°-W-068°; Y twr; 38°40′·86N 09°20′·78W, on Ponta da Rana 3·25M ESE of Cascais.
Forte de São Julião ☆ Oc R 5s 38m 14M; 38°40′·47N 09°19′·52W.
Oeiras marina, S pier hd ☆ Fl R 3s 9m 5M; 38°40′·56N 09°19′·00W.
N pier hd ☆ Fl G 3s 9m 5M; 38°40′·62N 09°18′·99W.
Doca de Paço de Arcos, W pier ☆ Fl R 5s 9m 4M; 38°41′·43N 09°17′·61W. E pier ☆ Fl G 5s; 38°41′·46N 09°17′·59W.

LISBOA

Triple ldg lts 047·1°: Front, **Gibalta** ☆ Oc R 6s 30m **21M**; 039·5°-054·5°; twr & cupola, R stripes; 38°41′·95N 09°15′·97W.
Middle, **Esteiro** ☆ Oc R 6s 81m **21M**; 039·5°-054·5°; W twr, R bands; ***Racon Q, 15M***; 38°42′·23N 09°15′·59W.
Rear, **Mama** ☆ Oc R 6s 153m **21M**; 045·5°-048·5°; platform; 38°43′·65N 09°13′·63W.
No 2 ⚓ Fl R 10s; 38°37′·29N 09°23′·28W.
No 1 ⚓ Fl G 2s; 38°39′·55N 09°18′·79W.
Forte Bugio ☆ Fl G 5s 27m 12M; ○ twr on fortress; *Horn Mo (B) 30s*; 38°39′·63N 09°17′·93W.
No 3 ⚓ Fl G 3s; 38°40′·04N 09°18′·26W.
No 5 ⚓ Fl G 4s; 38°40′·43N 09°17′·65W.
No 7 ⚓ Fl G 5s; 38°40′·74N 09°16′·90W.
No 9 ⚓ Fl G 6s; 38°40′·55N 09°14′·57W.
Bridge (Ponte 25 de Abril). Fl (3) G 9s and Fl (3) R 9s on the N (38°41′·64N 09°10′·69W) and S (38°41′·10N 09°10′·56W) pillars; vis up- and downstream, covering main (70m) and inshore spans.
Lisnave ☆ Fl G 2s 4m 3M; 38°41′·29N 09°08′·63W, S bank. Docks & industrial areas lie S and E of this lt.

Cabo Espichel ☆ Fl 4s 167m **26M**; W 6-sided twr; *Horn 31s;* 38°24′·92N 09°12′·97W.

SESIMBRA

Cavalo Fort ☆ Oc 5s 34m 14M; R ○ twr; 38°26′·01N 09°07′·01W.
Ldg lts 003·5°, both ☆ L Fl R 5s 9/21m 7/6M: Front, 38°26′·51N 09°06′·09W. Rear 34m from front. Pierhead ☆ Fl R 3s 8M.

SETÚBAL

Ldg lts 039·7°, both ☆ Iso Y 6s 12/60m **22M** (by day 5/6M). Front, R structure, W stripes; 38°31′·08N 08°54′·00W (fish dock). Rear, **Azêda**, vis 038·3°-041·3°; R hut on piles; 1·7M from front.
No 1 ⚓ Fl G 3s 5M; 38°26′·99N 08°58′·17W.
No 2 ⚓ Fl (2) R 10s 13m 9M; ***Racon B, 15M***; 38°27′·22N 08°58′·45W.
No 4 ⚓ Fl R 4s 13m 4M; 38°27′·92N 08°57′·71W.
No 3 ⚓ Fl G 5s; 38°28′·33N 08°56′·78W.
No 5 ⚓ Fl G 4s 13m 4M; 38°29′·20N 08°55′·36W.
Forte de Outão ☆ Oc R 6s 33m 12M; 38°29′·31N 08°56′·05W.
João Farto ⚓ Q (9) 15s; 38°30′·33N 08°54′·44W.
Forte de Albarquel ☆ Iso R 2s 16m 6M; 38°30′·65N 08°54′·79W.
Commercial dock (yachts in W half); 38°31′·22N 08°53′·13W.
Pinheiro da Cruz ☆ Fl 3s 66m 11M; W ○ col, R stripes; 38°15′·47N 08°46′·28W. Firing area extends 6M offshore.

SINES

Cabo de Sines ☆ Fl (2) 15s 55m **26M**; W twr & house; obsc 001°-003° (2°) & 004°- 007° (3°); 37°57′·57N 08°52′·82W.
⚓ Fl (5) Y 20s; 37°55′·36N 08°55′·80W, 2·2M WSW of W mole hd.
W mole hd ☆ Fl 3s 20m 12M; 37°56′·48N 08°53′·33W.
Sines W ⚓ Fl R 3s 6M; 37°56′·12N 08°53′·25W, 4ca S of W mole hd.
E mole, NW head ☆ L Fl G 8s 16m 6M; 37°56′·32N 08°51′·95W.
Borboleta ⚓ VQ (3) 5s; 37°55′·18N 08°50′·89W.

Marina mole ☆ Fl G 4s 4M; W twr, G bands; 37°57′·03N 08°52′·03W.
FV bkwtr ☆ Fl R 6s 6M; W twr, R bands; 37°57′·06N 08°52′·19W.
Ponta da Gaivota ☆ L Fl 7s 19m 13M; 37°51′·10N 08°47′·78W.
Rio Mira, ent ☆ Fl 3s 22m 12M; 37°43′·12N 08°47′·40W.
Cabo Sardão ☆ Fl (3) 15s 67m **23M**; 37°35′·93N 08°49′·01W.

CAPE ST VINCENT TO THE SPANISH BORDER

CAPE ST VINCENT/SAGRES

Cabo de São Vicente ☆ Fl 5s 84m **32M**; W twr and bldg; *Horn Mo (I) 30s;* 37°01′·36N 08°59′·78W.
Ponta de Sagres ☆ Iso R 2s 51m 11M; 36°59′·67N 08°56′·95W.
Baleeira mole ☆ Fl WR 4s 12m, W14M, R11M; 254°-W-355°-R-254°; W twr; 37°00′·67N 08°55′·43W.

LAGOS

Pta da Piedade ☆ Fl 7s 50m **20M**; 37°04′·81N 08°40′·14W.
W bkwtr ☆ Fl R 4s 7M; W col, R bands; 37°05′·93N 08°39′·83W.
E bkwtr ☆ Fl (2) G 6s 6M; W col, G bands; 37°05′·91N 08°39′·92W.
Alvor ent, ☆ Fl R/G 4s; W twrs, R/G bands; 37°07′·10N 08°37′·11W.

PORTIMÃO

Ponta do Altar ☆ L Fl 5s 31m **16M**; vis 290°-170°; W twr and bldg; 37°06′·34N 08°31′·17W.
Ldg lts 019·1°: Both ☆ Iso R 6s 18/30m 6M, W cols, R bands. Front; 37°07′·35N 08°31′·31W. Rear ☆ 54m from front.
Outer E mole ☆ Fl G 5s 9m 7M; 37°06′·50N 08°31′·59W.
Outer W mole ☆ Fl R 5s 9m 7M; 37°06′·52N 08°31′·76W.
Marina S end ☆ Iso R 2s 6m 3M; 37°06′·90N 08°31′·62W.
No 2 ⚓ Fl R 4s; 37°07′·04N 08°31′·46W.
Marina ent, S side ☆ Fl R 6s 3M; 37°07′·10N 08°31′·58W.
N side ☆ Fl G 6s 3M; 37°07′·14N 08°31′·58W.
Marina N end ☆ Iso R 4s 8m 3M; 37°07′·33N 08°31′·58W.

Pta de Alfanzina ☆ Fl (2) 14s 62m **29M**; 37°05′·19N 08°26′·54W.
Armacão de Pera ☆ Oc R 5s 24m 6M; 37°06′·00N 08°21′·36W.

ALBUFEIRA

Ponta da Baleeira ☆ Oc 6s 30m 11M; 37°04′·81N 08°15′·80W.
N bkwtr ☆, Fl (2) G 5s 9m 4M, approx 37°04′·81N 08°15′·57W.
S bkwtr ☆, Fl (2) R 5s 9m 4M, approx 37°04′·76N 08°15′·57W.
Olhos de Água ☆ L Fl 5s 29m 7M; 37°05′·42N 08°11′·35W.

VILAMOURA

Vilamoura ☆, Fl 5s 17m **19M**; 37°04′·460N 08°07′·37W.
Marina, W mole ☆ Fl R 4s 13m 5M; 37°04′·08N 08°07′·38W.
E mole ☆ Fl G 4s 13m 5M; 37°04′·12N 08°07′·30W.

FARO, OLHÃO and TAVIRA

Ent from sea: E mole ☆ Fl G 4s 9m 6M; 36°57′·79N 07°52′·14W.
W mole ☆ Fl R 4s 9m 6M; 37°57′·84N 08°52′·25W, appr on 352°.
Access ldg lts 020·9°: Front, Barra Nova ☆ Oc 4s 8m 6M; 37°58′·22N 07°52′·00W. Rear, **Cabo de Santa Maria** ☆ Fl (4) 17s 49m **25M**; W ○ twr; 36°58′·48N 07°51′·88W.
No 6 ⚓ Fl R 6s; 36°58′·40N 07°52′·20W (NW to Faro; NE to Olhão).
No 20 ⚓ Fl R 6s, 37°00′·05N 07°55′·1W (approx 2M to **Faro**).
No 8 ⚓ Fl R 3s; 36°59′·82N 07°51′·16W; 2·2M N & ENE to **Olhão**.
Tavira ldg lts 325·9°: Front, ☆ Fl R 3s 9m 4M. Rear, Fl R 3s 10m 5M; sync'd with front.
E mole ☆ Fl G 2·5s 5m 6M; 37°06′·82N 07°37′·03W.

VILA REAL DE SANTO ANTONIO

Lt ho ☆ Fl 6·5s 51m **26M**; W twr, B bands; 37°11′·20N 07°24′·91W.
Bar, No 1 buoy ⚓ Q (3) G 6s; approx 37°08′·90N 07°23′·44W.
No 2 ⚓ Fl R 4s; 37°08′·83N 07°23′·74W.
W bkwtr ☆ Fl R 5s 4M; 37°09′·75N 07°24′·03W.
Marina, QR at S end; QR/QG at ent; QR at N end.

9.24.4 PASSAGE INFORMATION

More passage information is threaded between successive harbours in this Area. **Bibliography**: *SW Spain & Portugal CC* (Fernhurst/ Jens); *Atlantic Spain and Portugal* (Imray/RCC/Buchanan); *W coasts of Spain and Portugal Pilot* (NP 67).

WIND AND WEATHER

In summer the Portuguese Trades (*Nortada*) are N'ly F4-6 and the Portugal Current runs S at ½-¾kn. Summer gales are rare; coastal fog is common in the mornings. If N-bound, especially if lightly crewed, try making daily passages between about 0400 and 1200 to avoid the stronger afternoon winds, possibly augmented by a fresh onshore sea breeze.

►*Tidal streams appear to set N on the flood and S on the ebb, but are poorly documented.*◄

PORT CLOSURES Some hbrs, especially on this coast, may be closed for weather reasons, ie strong to gale force onshore winds and/or heavy swell causing dangerous breaking seas at the hbr ent or over the bar. Closures may be promulgated by radio and Navtex. At Leixões, Aveiro and Figueira da Foz the following signals, with minor variations = port closed:

By day: cylinder/ball hoisted close up; at half-mast = enter with caution. By night: ●●●(vertical) steady or flashing.

THE SPANISH BORDER TO CABO RASO

The Río Miño (*Minho* in Portuguese) 15M S of Cabo Silleiro, forms the northern border with Spain. The river ent is difficult and best not attempted.

The 150M long coastline is hilly as far S as **Porto**, then generally low and sandy, backed by pine forests, to Cabo Carvoeiro; there are few prominent features (AC 3633, 3634, 3635). Coasting yachts should keep at least 3M offshore; see **Viana do Castelo**, a commercial and fishing port, with a marina at the NE end. **Povoa de Varzim** has a marina.

6.45M NNW of Póvoa de Vazim, 3M offshore, and previously the site of a floating wind turbine; the undersea power line to the shore remains marked by three SPM buoys, (Y), the two most westerly Fl Y 2·5s, as shown on AC 3634.

Seaplane Operating Areas are used for landing, take-off and drawing water to fight forest fires along this, and the rest of the Portuguese coast. They are approx 1.5M long x 0.5M wide and must be avoided when in use, usually in summer.

Leixões is an industrial port 2M N of the mouth of the R Douro; it may be closed in bad weather due to heavy swell breaking on the bar. There is a seaplane operating area with an associated no entry zone N of Leixões which requires caution. The R Douro is not easily entered, but two substantial bkwtrs at the river mouth have improved access; there is a new marina 3M upriver. Oporto can easily be visited by road from Leixões to recce the latest situation.

Aveiro (⚓) and **Figueira da Foz** (marina) are exposed to the W and can be closed in bad weather; the latter can be identified from N or S by the higher ground (257m) of Cabo Mondego. 34M further SSW **Nazaré** is an artificial fishing harbour and port of refuge with easy entrance and a marina.

Cabo Carvoeiro, the W tip of Peniche peninsula, looks like an island from afar (do not confuse with Ilha Berlenga). Ilha da Berlenga and Os Farilhões, both lit, are respectively 5 and 9·5M NW of Cabo Carvoeiro, and within an '**Area to be avoided**' (by big ships) formerly an ITZ; see Area map.

The normal coastal route is between Cabo Carvoeiro and Berlenga; this chan is deep, clear and 5M wide, although it appears narrower until opened up. **Peniche** fishing port/marina on the S side of the peninsula is well sheltered from N'lies, but open to SW swell. The coastline rises steadily to the 527m high ridge of Sintra, inland of Cabo da Roca, S of which it drops steeply to the low headland of Cabo Raso. The **Off Cabo da Roca Traffic Separation Scheme** is 14M to seaward of that cape and extends a further 20M W with extra lanes for dangerous cargoes. The ITZ is 14M wide; see Area map.

9.24.5 SPECIAL NOTES FOR PORTUGAL

Districts/Provinces: Portugal is divided into 18 administrative districts. The names of the former coastal provinces (N-S: Minho, Douro, Beira Litoral, Estremadura, Alentejo and Algarve) are still used and appear below the name of each hbr.

Charts: The 2 folios are: FA, old (*antigo*) only a few charts, with 2 digit chart nos; and F94. F94 charts (5 digit nos) include: 4 offshore charts 23201-04; 6 coastal charts 24201-06; 12 hbr charts 26301-12; 8 hbr appr charts 26401-08; and 3 charts of hbr plans 27501-03. 12 Leisure (*recreio*) charts at 1:150,000 scale, Nos 25R01-12, cover the whole coast N-S. Some long-established marinas are not yet charted at large scale.

Portuguese charts and publications are available from Chart agents, one of the largest : J Garraio & Ca Lda, ave 24 de Julho, 2 - 1st Dto, 1200-478 Lisboa; ☎213 473 081. info@jgarraio.pt www. jgarraio. For Portuguese Hydrographic Office, see Ch 1.

Standard Time is UT (**NOT** UT –1); add 1hr for DST, in force from the last Sun in Mar until the Sat before the last Sun in Oct.

Representation: Portuguese Tourist Office, 11 Belgrave Square, London SW1X 8PP; ☎020 7201 6666.

Tourist Office, Ave António Augusto de Aguiar 86, P-1000 Lisboa; ☎213 425 231.

British Embassy, Rua de S. Bernardo 33, 1249-082 Lisboa; ☎21 359 4082.

There are Consulates in Lisbon/Portimão & Hon Consuls at Oporto and Ponta Delgada (Azores) ☎808 203537 (all same number).

Telephone: To call Portugal from UK dial +351, the area code, then the ☎ number. To call UK from Portugal, dial +44, the area code less the initial 0, then the ☎ number. The area code is mandatory, even within the same area; ie nine numbers in all. National emergency ☎112; National SAR ☎214 401 919.

R/T: VHF Ch 09 is the recreational craft channel; it is used by all Portuguese marinas, in addition to any Port VHF channels.

Access: There are daily flights in season to/from the UK via Porto, Lisboa and Faro with connections by bus and/or train to other towns. See also Area 25 for Spanish flights.

Currency is the Euro €. VAT (IVA) is 23%. Credit cards are widely accepted; cash dispensers are in all towns.

Public Holidays: Jan 1; Shrove Tues; Good Friday; April 25 (Liberation Day); May 1 (Labour Day); Jun 10 (Camões Day); Aug 15 (Assumption); Dec 8 (Immaculate Conception) 25 (Christmas). Also every town has a local *festa*.

Documents: (See Ch 2 Cruising Formalities) Portugal observes EU regulations but formalities may be lengthy. Papers needed: *Personal* – Passports; crew list, ideally on headed paper with the yacht's rubber stamp, giving DoB, passport nos, where joined/ intended departure. Certificate of Competence (Yachtmaster Offshore, ICC/HOCC etc). Radio Operator's certificate. EHIC.

Yacht – Registration certificate. Proof of VAT status. Marine insurance. Ship's Radio licence. Itinerary, backed up by ship's log.

9.24.6 VIANA DO CASTELO

Minho **41°41'·68N 08°49'·21W** (Marina ent)

CHARTS AC 3633/4, 3257; PC 24201, 26401; SC 41B

TIDES

Standard Port LISBOA (⟶); ML 2·0

Times				Height (metres)			
High Water		Low Water		MHWS	MHWN	MLWN	MLWS
0400	0900	0400	0900	3·8	3·0	1·5	0·6
1600	2100	1600	2100				
Differences VIANA DO CASTELO							
–0020	0000	+0010	+0015	–0·3	–0·3	–0·2	–0·1
ESPOSENDE (41°32'N)							
–0020	0000	+0010	+0015	–0·6	–0·5	–0·2	–0·1

SHELTER Excellent in marina; possible strong current across its ent. No ⚓ in river. Night entry not advised if any swell.

NAVIGATION WPT 41°40'·18N 08°50'·37W, 007·5°/7ca in the W sector of dir lt Oc WRG 4s to abeam No 3 SHM lt buoy. Ignore the 012·5° ldg line which applies solely to the shipyard/FV area.

The outer mole hd (Fl R 3s) should be given a wide clearance; best water lies E of No 2 buoy. The flood reaches 2kn max; the ebb 3kn, but 6kn if river in spate. Entry to the hbr prohibited during seaplane firefighting operations, 3.3M SSW of Outer Mole.

Caution 1: 13M S of Viana 3 SPM buoys, the 2 outer buoys Fl Y 2.5s, mark a wave-generated power trial. Keep well seaward of the floating equipment which may be hard to see. See opposite.

LIGHTS AND MARKS Montedor lt ho is a R twr 4M NNW. ⛪ dome on Monte Santa Luzia is conspic, almost aligned with 007·5° dir lt. Storm sigs are displayed close SE of dir lt Oc WRG 4s. See Lights, buoys and waypoints for details. Nos 5 to 14 buoys are Fl R 3s or Fl G 3s.

COMMUNICATIONS (Code 258) MRCC (21) 4401919; Police 822345; ⊜ 823346; Brit Consul 808 203 537; Port HM 829096, Call *Porto de Viana* Ch 16; 11 (0900-1200; 1400-1700LT); Yacht Club and Marina Ch 09.

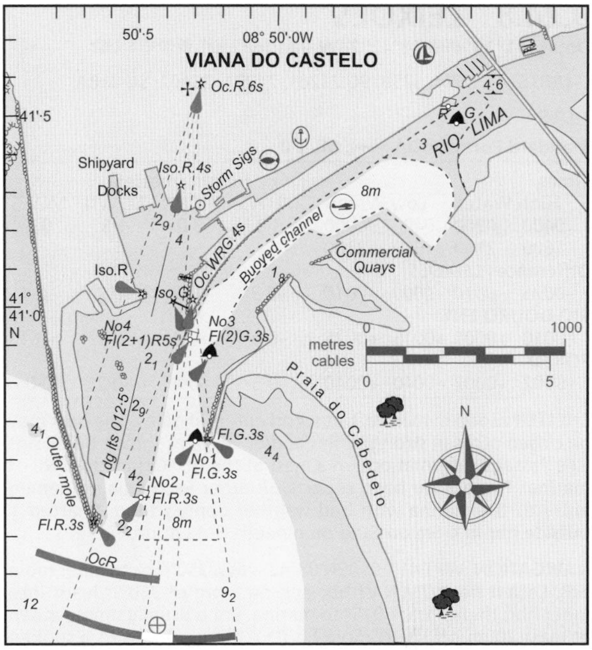

FACILITIES Marina ☎359500. www.apvc.pt apvc@apvc.pt (3m) 200 incⓋ €2·60 up to 12m LOA is abeam Nos 13 & 14 buoys and 200m short of low (4·6m) and noisy road/rail bridge. A small pedestrian bridge across the marina ent lifts on request, if shut berth on waiting pontoon, bridge remains open 0000–0800. Limited Ⓥ berths F&A on W side of first pontoon D. Ⓔ Ⓑ (20t). YC. No sign of a marina planned in the long FV basin (41°41'·34N 08°50'W).

Town ✕ Ⓑ Ⓗ ⇌ (1km). ✈ Porto (50km).

9.24.7 PÓVOA DE VARZIM

Minho **41°22'·20N 08°46'·00W** (Marina ent)

CHARTS AC 3634 (too small scale, 1:200,000, to be of much practical value); PC 24201

TIDES

Standard Port LISBOA (⟶)

Times				Height (metres)			
High Water		Low Water		MHWS	MHWN	MLWN	MLWS
0400	0900	0400	0900	3·8	3·0	1·5	0·6
1600	2100	1600	2100				
Differences PÓVOA DE VARZIM							
–0020	0000	+0010	+0015	–0·3	–0·3	–0·1	–0·1

SHELTER Good in all winds, but ent is rough in heavy swell and becomes impracticable when wave height >3m. In particular give a wide berth to the head of the N mole where there may be broken water. Reports of larger yachts being denied entry to the marina with bad weather approaching.

NAVIGATION WPT 41°21'·48N 08°46'·73W, 030°/1M to hbr ent. Follow SHM buoys (marking a shoal near the S bkwtr) round to the marina. Tidal streams are weak but there is an appreciable current, mainly S-going, along the coast.

LIGHTS AND MARKS Mole hd lts are on R and G posts with W bands. High rise blocks/hotels and sandy beaches are conspic. Monte São Félix is an isolated rounded hill (209m) 4·5M NNE.

COMMUNICATIONS (Code 252) MRCC (21) 4401919; Police 620026; Brit Consul 808 203 537; Ⓗ 690600; Hbr VHF Ch 11, 16 (M-F 0900-1200, 1400-1700); Marina VHF Ch 09; Tourist office 298120.

FACILITIES FVs use the N part of hbr; the friendly marina is to the SE. Ⓥ berth on the N'most reception/fuel pontoon in 2·4 to 3m.

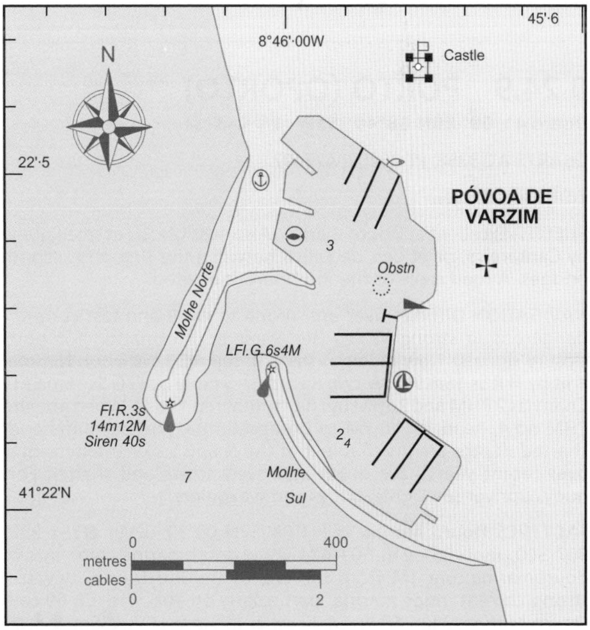

Marina ☎688121. www.clubenavalpovoense.com 241, inc some Ⓥ €1·65; 18m max LOA. Good facilities, many yachts lay up here: (at the FV hbr) Ⓔ (35t).

Town ✕ Ⓑ Ⓗ ⇌ (15 mins walk; trains to Porto, 30km and ✈ 18km).

9.24.8 LEIXÕES

Douro **41°11'·08N 08°42'·24W** (Marina ent) ❀❀❀◊◊✿

CHARTS AC 3634, 3258; PC 23201, 24201, 26402; SC 418A

TIDES

Standard Port LISBOA (⟶); ML 2·0

Times				Height (metres)			
High Water		Low Water		MHWS	MHWN	MLWN	MLWS
0400	0900	0400	0900	3·8	3·0	1·5	0·6
1600	2100	1600	2100				
Differences *LEIXÕES*							
–0025	*–0010*	*0000*	*+0010*	*–0·3*	*–0·3*	*–0·2*	*–0·1*
RIO DOURO ENT							
–0010	+0005	+0015	+0025	–0·6	–0·4	–0·1	+0·1
PORTO							
+0002	+0002	+0040	+0040	–0·5	–0·4	–0·2	0·0

SHELTER Good in marina, but scend enters in gales. The port may be closed occas in strong W'lies and/or swell, as shown by tfc sigs (see Passage information) on a mast at the Hbr Office close NE of marina. There have been reports of larger yachts being denied entry to the marina with bad weather approaching. Charted ⚓ outside hbr in 4-6m on sand/mud needs HM's approval.

NAVIGATION WPT 41°10'·09N 08°42'·26W, 350°/6ca to inner mole hds. Leça lt ho, 1·7M N of hbr ent, on a brg of 350·5° leads into inner hbr; thence track 015° to marina. Ent is usually simple. Keep at least 200m off the N mole hd (Quebra-mar) due to a sunken bkwtr (2·5m) and a wreck (8m) 100m SW and S of it.

LIGHTS AND MARKS N of Leça lt are many R/W banded chy's at the oil refinery. From the S, bldgs of Porto are conspic.

COMMUNICATIONS (Code 229) MRCC (21) 4401919; LB 226. 170091; Met 484527 (Porto airport); Police 383649; ⊖ 951476; Brit Consul 808 203 537; Fire 380018; H 391000; HM 953000; Marina *Porto Atlântico* VHF Ch 09 (0900-1230; 1400-1800).

FACILITIES Marina Porto Atlântico ☎964895 www.marinaportoatlantico.net (2·9-1·5m) is rather oily with limited facilities onsite. 200 F&A + 40Ⓥ €1·64; reception W quay. ✕ ⊐ ⊡ ⊡ @ ⊡ ⊡ ⊡ ⊡ ⊡ Ⓔ ⚒ ⊡(6t). **Clube de Vela Atlântico** ✕ ☎963547. **Clube Naval de Leça** Bar ☎951700. **Sport Club do Porto** ☎952225.

Town ✕ ⊐ ⊡ ✉ Ⓑ. Bus & Metro to Porto (5km); ⇌ and ✈.

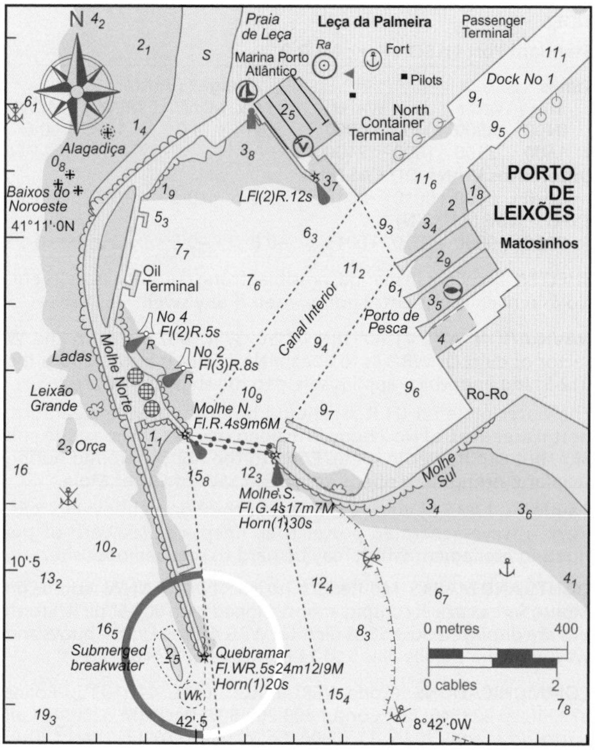

9.24.9 PORTO (OPORTO)

Douro **41°08'·80N 08°40'·55W** ❀❀◊◊✿✿

CHARTS AC 3258; PT 26402; 426402

TIDES see above.

SHELTER Excellent at Douro marina. Also possible ⊆ at small quay by Cantareira, or at Cais de Estiva between the first and second bridges. A road recce of the Rio Douro is advised.

NAVIGATION Difficult river ent, prone to swell and fast current; dangerous in strong W'lies (see Passage information for port closure signals). New moles at the ent; see AC 3258 inset. N mole is lit by Fl R 5s 16m 9M (W twr, R stripes); S mole by Fl G 5s 15m 6M. Chan has 2 PHM and 2 SHM bys (lit, numbered 1 to 4). When abeam PHM no 4, head 161°/0·3M to Douro Marina. The bar shifts and charted depths are unreliable, but the N and S bkwtr extensions over recent years have much improved access and shelter. For buoys upriver see Lights, buoys and waypoints.

FACILITIES Douro Marina ⊕ (41°08'·57N 08°39'·02W) ☎351 220 907 300, mob 351 918 501 474 www.douromarina.com info@douromarina.com 1M from the ent to the Rio Douro, beware strong current inside marina, particularly on ebb. VHF Ch 09 call *Douro Marina*. 240 + 60 Ⓥ €4·30 inc ⊡ ⊡, max LOA <50m. ⊡ ⊡ ⊡ ⊡ © ⊡(50t) ⊡(3t). Friendly staff, English, French & Spanish spoken. Free shuttle bus to large shopping complex; buses to centre of Porto, car/cycle hire available. Many good reports received.

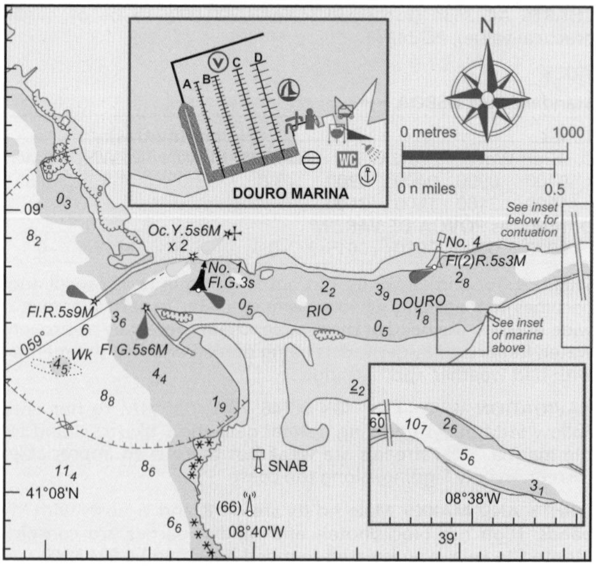

9.24.10 AVEIRO

Beira Litoral **40°38'·51N 08°45'·86W** (Hbr ent)

CHARTS AC 3634, 3227; PC 24201, 24202, 26403, 59; SC 4219

TIDES

Standard Port LISBOA (⟶); ML 2·0

Times				Height (metres)			
High Water		Low Water		MHWS	MHWN	MLWN	MLWS
0400	0900	0400	0900	3·8	3·0	1·5	0·6
1600	2100	1600	2100				
Differences AVEIRO							
+0005	+0010	+0010	+0015	–0·5	–0·4	–0·1	0·0
SAN JACINTO (40°40'N 08°44'W)							
+0025	+0030	+0030	+0045	–0·7	–0·5	–0·1	+0·2
FIGUEIRA DA FOZ							
–0015	0000	+0010	+0020	–0·5	–0·4	–0·2	0·0

SHELTER Good, but the bar (Rptd 10m LWN 2015) becomes impassable in strong onshore winds and the port is often one of the first on this coast to be closed by bad weather or swell, even if there is no wind.

Two small marinas usually have space (see Facilities) or ⚓ at the N end of Baia de San Jacinto in about 7m avoiding the large drying sandbank (buoyed) inside the outer end of the bay's N bkwtr.

NAVIGATION WPT (off chartlet) Boia Aveiro buoy, 40°37'·86N 08°46'·98W, 056°/1·1M to hbr ent. Caution: strong tidal streams. From abeam the lt ho the ent to B de San Jacinto is about 9 ca NE. Do not proceed further E.

LIGHTS AND MARKS Hbr lts as chartlet/Lights, buoys and waypoints. The R/W banded lt ho and R/W Aero lt ho twr are conspic on either side of ent. Tfc sigs (Passage information) are shown from a mast close N of the lt ho. The 060·6° ldg line (marks hard to see) leads between the moles. A military airfield with conspic control twr is NE of the hbr ent.

Caution: changes to depths S of main appr reported: an area liable to change exists centred 40°37'·69N 08°46'·00W.

COMMUNICATIONS (Code 234) ☎393300; Brit Consul 808 203 537; HM 393300, www.portodeaveiro.pt geral@portodeaveiro.pt; Port VHF Ch 11, 16 (M-F, 0900-1200 & 1400-1700).

FACILITIES A helpful, English/French-speaking contact in Aveiro is Senhor Cala Barras, Avela YC. A ferry reported to run from near the ⚓ in Baia de San Jacinto to Aveiro.

CVCN YC marina, Ⓥ via Mira Canal (2m) and road bridge (14m air draught) www.cvcn.pt

Avela YC marina 3/4Ⓥ ☎422142 www.avela.pt near electrical cable (21m air draught)

Town The attractive old town, with its *moliceiros* (mussel boats) fine buildings and a network of canals, is reminiscent of a mini-Venice. S to Figueira da Foz and Coimbra (worth a visit) and N to Porto. ✈ Põrto and Lisboa (77km and 256km) by motorway.

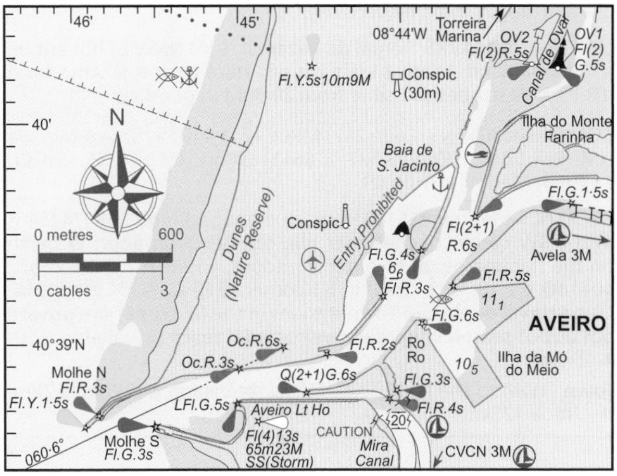

9.24.11 FIGUEIRA DA FOZ

Beira Litoral **40°08'·68N 08°52'·48W** (Hbr ent)

CHARTS AC 3634, 3635, 3228; PC 24201/2, 26404, 34, 64; SC 42A

TIDES See under Aveiro; ML 2·0

SHELTER Excellent in marina on N bank, 0·75M from hbr ent. **Bar** at ent has charted depth of 4·1m, but this cannot be relied upon. It shifts/shoals constantly and can be highly dangerous in swell, especially Nov-Mar with strong W/NW winds. Conditions on the bar are signalled from mast at Forte de Santa Catarina (N of inner moles) and may be broadcast on VHF Ch 11.

NAVIGATION WPT 40°08'·61N 08°53'·12W (off chartlet) 081°/5ca to hbr ent. The bar in bad weather is the only offshore danger.

LIGHTS AND MARKS Cabo Mondego lt ho is 3M NW of hbr ent. Buarcos light is on the beach 1·1M N of hbr ent. Ldg lts lead 081·5° past marina ent. Lts as chartlet and Lights, buoys and waypoints. Extensive beaches N and S of hbr ent and a white suspension bridge (39m cl'nce) 1·5M E of ent are conspic from seaward.

COMMUNICATIONS (Code 233) Maritime Police 916 352629; Port VHF Ch 11, 422955; Marina VHF Ch 08 (call *Capmarfoz*).

FACILITIES **Marina** ☎402910, ipc.gap@mail.telepac.pt (2-2·8m). Strong ebb tide can affect pontoons nearest marina ent. Reception/fuel berth is dead ahead of ent. 200 incⓋ €2·65, plus possible surcharge for beam, multihulls +50%.

Town ✈ Põrto.

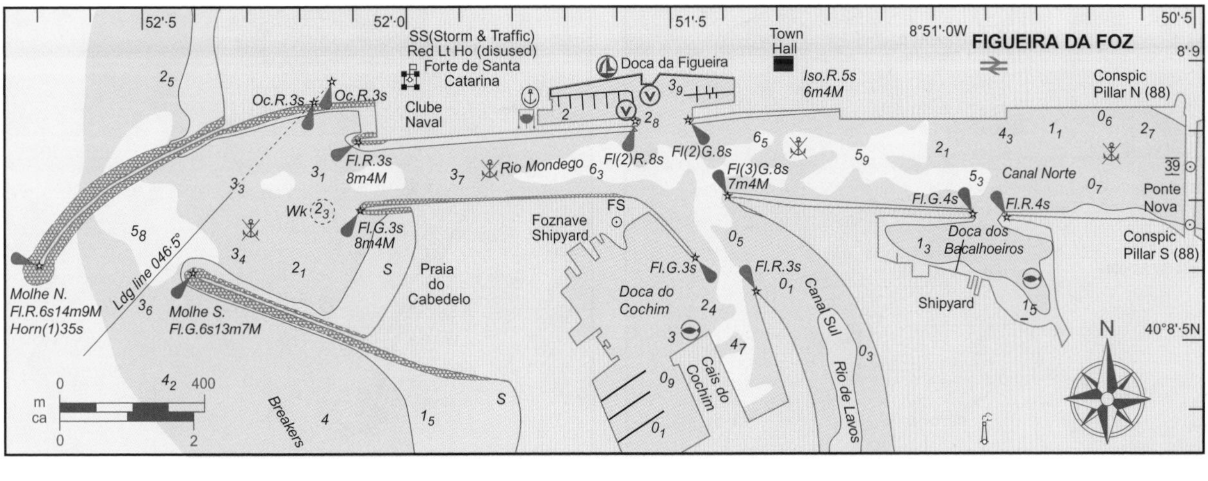

Portugal

9.24.12 NAZARÉ

Estremadura **39°35'·42N 09°04'·63W** ❀❀❀👍👍✿✿

CHARTS AC 3635; PC 24203, 26302, 34, 65

TIDES

Standard Port LISBOA (⟶); ML 2·0

Times				Height (metres)			
High Water		Low Water		MHWS	MHWN	MLWN	MLWS
0400	0900	0400	0900	3·8	3·0	1·5	0·6
1600	2100	1600	2100				
Differences NAZARÉ (Pederneira)							
–0030	–0015	–0005	+0005	–0·5	–0·4	–0·1	0·0

SHELTER Good with all-weather access. No ⚓ in outer harbour.

NAVIGATION WPT 39°35'·69N 09°05'·95W, 106°/1M to hbr ent. Due to an underwater canyon there are depths of 452m and 152m 5M and 7ca offshore respectively.

LIGHTS AND MARKS Pontal da Nazaré lt is 1M NNW of hbr ent on a low headland; keep at least 2ca off. Here a conspic wind farm (FR lts & W strobes) is visible from 20-30M in good vis.

COMMUNICATIONS (Code 262) MRCC (21) 4401919; ⊜ & Met via HM; Brit Consul 808 203 537; Ⓗ 561116; Port HM 561255, CHF Ch 11 (HO); Marina VHF Ch 09.

FACILITIES **Marina** ☎561401 (British manager) mob 968074254 is in the SW corner of the inner hbr, call (VHF) on appr; Ⓥ berth on the hammerheads or outer pontoons, <15m and 3·5m draft. 40+14Ⓥ €2·15. 🚿🚻 (H24) in NE corner, ⊡ Ⓒ ⛴ 🔧 ⚒ ⛽(80t) ⛵. **Clube Naval de Nazaré** The pontoons in the NE corner are private but out-of-season visitors are welcomed if space is available, with ⚓ ⛽, wi-fi.

Town (1½M to the N) ✕ 🛒 ✉ Ⓑ. ⇌ Valado dos Frades 7km. ✈ Lisboa 125km.

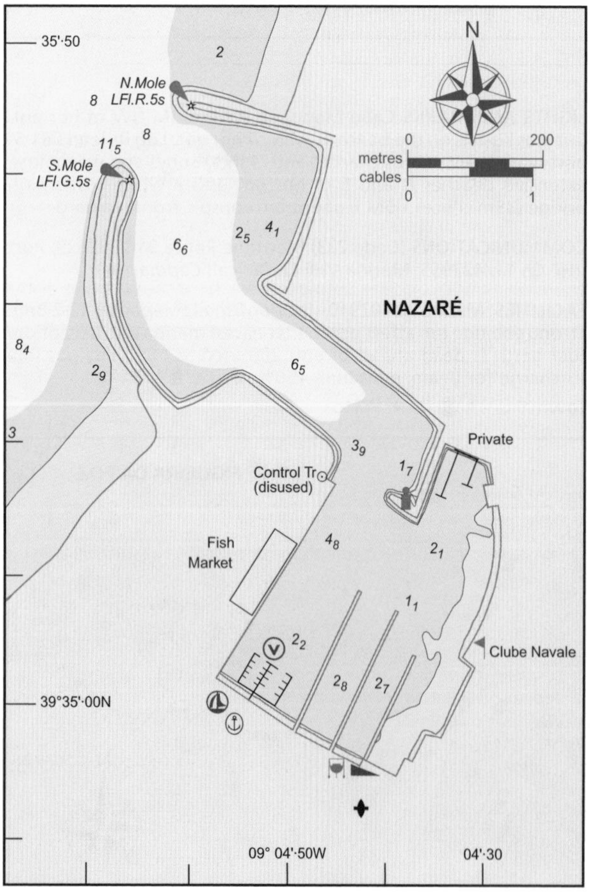

9.24.13 PENICHE

Estremadura **39°20'·82N 09°22'·48W** ❀❀👍👍✿✿

CHARTS AC 3635; PC 24203, 26405, 36

TIDES

Standard Port LISBOA (⟶); ML 2·0

Times				Height (metres)			
High Water		Low Water		MHWS	MHWN	MLWN	MLWS
0400	0900	0400	0900	3·8	3·0	1·5	0·6
1600	2100	1600	2100				
Differences PENICHE							
–0035	–0015	–0005	0000	–0·3	–0·3	–0·1	–0·1
ERICEIRA (38°58'N, 24M S)							
–0040	–0025	–0010	–0010	–0·4	–0·3	–0·1	0·0

SHELTER Good all-weather hbr, but uncomfortable if SW swell works in; also noisy and prone to FV wash. Possible moorings or ⚓ in SE part of hbr; holding is good, but ground may be foul. The ⚓ in 4m on N side of peninsula is open to swell, even in S'lies.

NAVIGATION WPT 39°20'·42N 09°22'·53W, 000°/5ca to W mole hd. 3kn speed limit in hbr. The coastal route, a 5M wide chan between Cabo Carvoeiro and Ilha da Berlenga, is often rough.

Peniche and the offshore islands are in an 'Area to be avoided', only by ships >300t (for environmental reasons); see Area map.

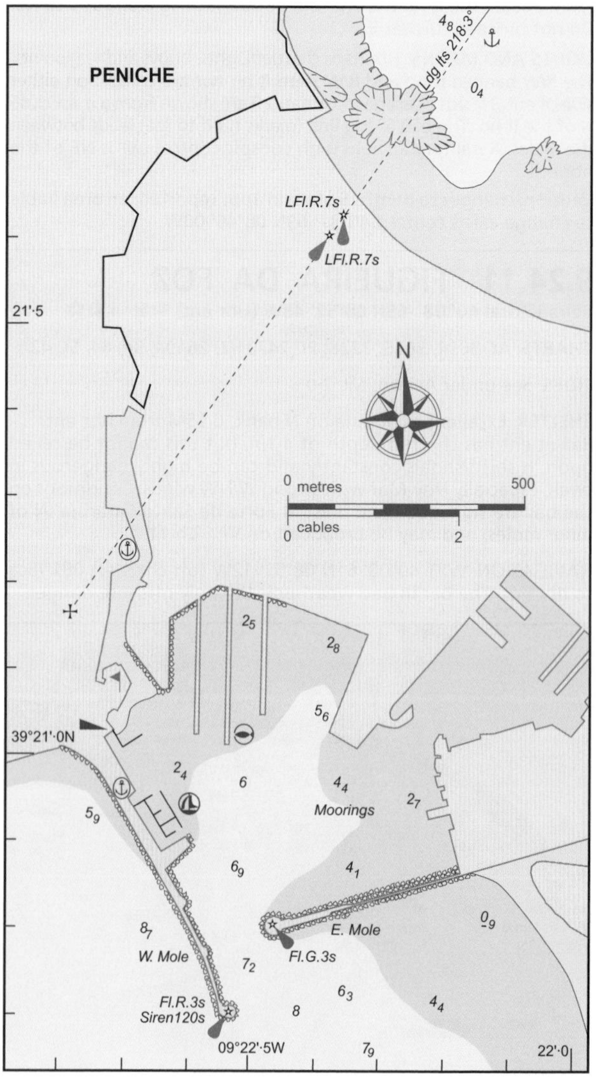

On the SE side of Ilha Berlenga ⚓ below the lt ho. Os Farilhões lies 4·5M further NW. These islands lie within a Nature Reserve.

LIGHTS AND MARKS Peniche looks like an island from afar, not to be confused in poor vis with Berlenga. An isolated square tower block is conspic about 2ca NNE of the harbour. Cabo Carvoeiro is 2M WNW of hbr ent and steep-to apart from Nau dos Carvos, a conspic high rk close-in. Other lts as chartlet and Lights, buoys and waypoints. Storm sigs are shown from the root of W mole.

COMMUNICATIONS (Code 262) MRCC (21) 4401919; LB 789629; Brit Consul 808 203 537; H 781702; Port HM 781153, VHF Ch 16 (H24); Marina VHF Ch 09.

FACILITIES Berth on outer pontoon (2·4-3·5m) of small marina ☎ 783331. 130+ 20Ⓥ €1·60. (or tanker) YC.

Town ✕ ≷ Obidos (30km) ✈ Lisboa (80km).

9.24.14 CASCAIS

Estremadura **38°41'·59N 09°24'·88W**

CHARTS AC 3635, 3220; PC 27504, 26303; SC 4310

TIDES

Standard Port LISBOA (⟶); ML 2·0

Times				Height (metres)			
High Water		Low Water		MHWS	MHWN	MLWN	MLWS
0400	0900	0400	0900	3·8	3·0	1·5	0·6
1600	2100	1600	2100				
Differences CASCAIS							
–0040	–0025	–0015	–0010	–0·3	–0·2	0·0	+0·1

SHELTER Good in marina or on outer pontoons. ⚓ N of marina in designated area 3-5m, sheltered from all but E winds.

NAVIGATION WPT 38°41'·28N 09°24'·57W, 334°/4ca to CC2 and on the 285° ldg line. MC1-3 SCM buoys mark no-entry area.

LIGHTS AND MARKS Guia, rear 285° ldg lt, is 1·2M from the front, Santa Marta. Other lts as chartlet.

COMMUNICATIONS (Code 21) MRCC 4401919; Brit Consul 808 203 537; Marina VHF Ch 09 (0900-2000).

FACILITIES Marina ☎(21)4824857. www.mymarinacascais.com reception@marinacascais.pt 638 inc 125Ⓥ €3·00, (in 6m) multihulls +50%. (0900-2000) Ⓒ Ⓑ (70t) (2t). Mail pickup: Casa de S° Bernardo, Marina de Cascais, 2750-800 Cascais.

Town All amenities. ≷ to Lisboa (½hr) every ¼hr, 0530-0230.

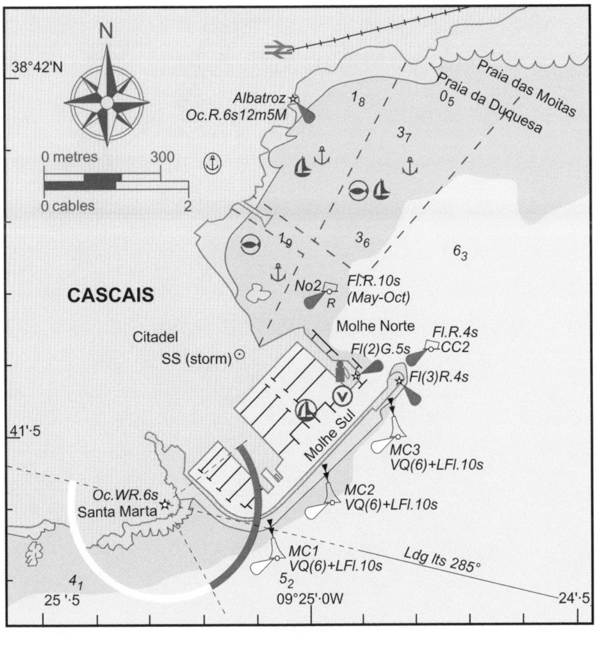

9.24.15 LISBOA

Estremadura **38°41'·75N 09°10'·71W** (N span of Ponte 25 de Abril)

CHARTS AC 3635, 3220, 3221, 3222; PC 26406, 26303, 26304, 26305, 26306, 26307, 24204, 24203, 25R07; SC 4310

TIDES

Standard Port LISBOA (⟶); ML 2·0

TimesHeight (metres)							
High Water		Low Water		MHWS	MHWN	MLWN	MLWS
0400	0900	0400	0900	3·8	3·0	1·5	0·6
1600	2100	1600	2100				
Differences PACO DE ARCOS (5·5M W of Tejo bridge)							
–0020	–0030	–0005	–0005	–0·4	–0·4	–0·2	–0·1
PEDROUCOS (2·2M W of Tejo bridge)							
–0010	–0015	0000	0000	–0·3	–0·2	–0·1	0·0

SHELTER is good in the marinas along the N bank of R Tejo.

NAVIGATION From N/NW keep at least 5ca off Cabo da Roca (see Area map for TSS) and Cabo Raso. Magnetic anomalies 3M SSE of Cabo Raso can alter local variation by +5° to –3°.

WPT 38°36'·90N 09°22'·90W (5ca SE of No 2 buoy) 047°/5·4M to abeam No 5 buoy. This is the main DW chan, Barra Sul, into R Tejo proper; shoals lie on either side and break in bad weather. Tidal streams reach 5kn in the river and the ebb sets towards the shoals E of Forte Bugio. Caution: cross-current at the ent to marinas. Speed limit E of Torre de Belém: 10kn, but 5kn within 300m of shore.

Barra Norte, a lesser chan carrying 5·2m, is a short cut for yachts between Cascais and R Tejo in fair weather; it passes close S of Forte de S. Julião and is orientated 285°/105° on ldg lts at Forte de Sta Marta and Guia (obscured by trees from the east by day).

LIGHTS AND MARKS See Lts, buoys and waypoints, chartlets and hbr text. Conspic features, W-E, include: Torre de Belém, Padrao dos Descobrimentos, Ponte 25 de Abril and statue of Cristo Rei.

COMMUNICATIONS (Code 21) MRCC 4401919; Monitor *Lisboa Port Control* (VTS, applies to yachts >20m LOA) Ch 12, 13 - **74** broadcasts MSI as required; Brit Consul 808 203 537; Port HM **12**, 01, 05, 60; Marinas VHF Ch 09.

FACILITIES

Oeiras Marina 38°40'·59N 09°18'·99W. ☎(21)4401510. Ch 09. www.portoderecreio.oeirasviva.pt porto.recreio@oeirasviva.pt 275 €2·91, multihulls +100%. (0800-2200) Ⓒ @ (8t). Fast trains to Lisboa 16km; see Cascais.

Marinas Ⓐ-Ⓓ are run by Lisboa port authority (www.portodelisboa.pt ☎(3611000). In all these marinas average cost is €2·25.

Ⓐ **Doca de Bom Sucesso** 38°41'·55N 09°12'·70W. ☎(21)3922080. doca.bomsucesso@portodelisboa.pt 163 mostly local yachts, F&A in 3m. ✕ ≷ bus to Lisboa.

Ⓑ **Doca de Belém** 38°41'·64N 09°13'·24W. ☎(21)3922203. doca.belem@portodelisboa.pt 194 yachts, v few Ⓥ; F&A in 3m. ✕ ≷ bus to Lisboa.

Ⓒ **Doca de Santo Amaro** 38°41'·92N 09°12'·65W, almost below suspension bridge (noise from road and night life). ☎(21)3922011. doca.stamaro@portodelisboa.pt 287 (few Ⓥ) in 4m. ✕ ≷ bus 2M to city centre.

Ⓓ **Doca de Alcântara** 38°42'·15N 09°09'·42W). Chan turns W into marina at dock end, swing bridge open 1900-0700, then every H and H+½; doca.alcantara@portodelisboa.pt ☎ (21)3922048, 440 F&A inc Ⓥ in 8m. ✕ ≷ bus 2M to city.

Ⓔ **Marina Parque das Nações** 38°45'·37N 09°05'·92W 1·35M S of Vasco de Gama bridge. ☎(218) 949066. www.marinaparquedasnacoes.pt info@marinaparquedasnacoes.pt 400 (inc Ⓥ) €2.50 (pay 5 days, stay 7) multihulls +50%. ✕ Ⓒ (35t) (3t). Marina reptd well over 50% silted (2017) inc part of ent/ some areas drying at sp: call Ch 09 for guidance to berth.

Centro Náutico de Algés Boatyard, between Oeiras and Torre de Belem, 38°41'·47N 09°14'·07, ☎(21)3032440; www.cnalges.pt geral@cnalges.pt 300+ (50t).

Tagus Yacht Centre, Amora, Seixal Bay 38°38'·07N 09°06'·77W. ☎(21)2276400. www.tagusyachtcenter.com info@tagusyachtcenter.com. (70t). Ferries: Seixal to Lisboa.

City All amenities; ≷ ✈.

Portugal

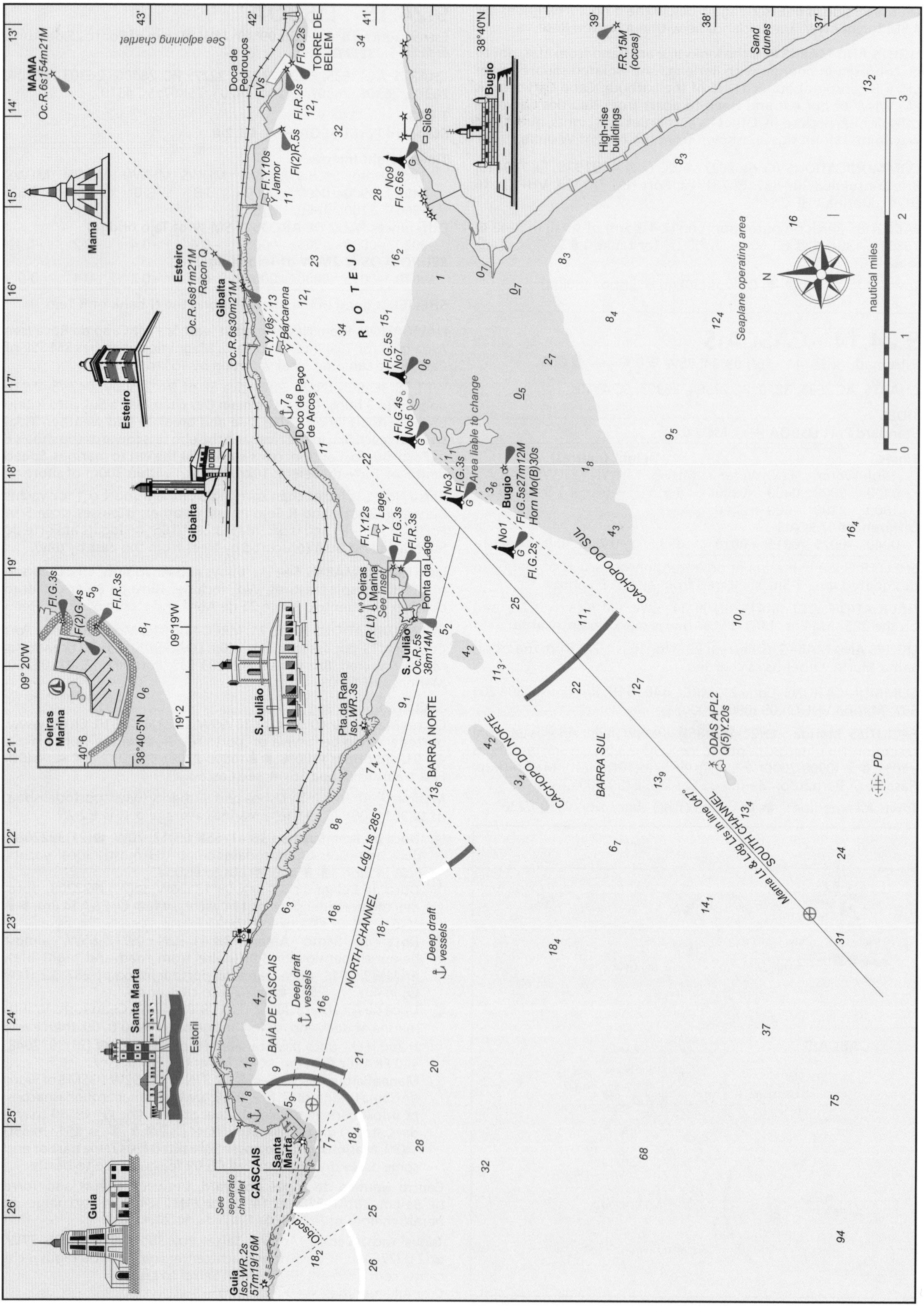

MAMA
Oc.R.6s154m21M
See adjoining chartlet
Doca de Pedrouços
TORRE DE BELEM
Fl.G.2s
Fl.R.2s
FVs
Fl(2)R.5s
Fl.Y.10s
Jamor
Mama
Esteiro
Oc.R.6s81m21M
Racon Q
Gibalta
Oc.R.6s30m21M
Fl.Y.10s
Barcarena
R I O T E J O
Doco de Paço de Arcos
Gibalta
Esteiro
No9
Fl.G.6s
Silos
Bugio
Fl.G.5s
No7
Fl.G.4s
No5
Area liable to change
No3
Fl.G.3s
Bugio
Fl.G.5s27m12M
Horn Mo(B)30s
No1
Fl.G.2s
38°40'N
F.R.15M
(occas)
Sand dunes
High-rise buildings
Seaplane operating area
nautical miles
Oeiras Marina
Fl.G.3s
F(2)G.4s
Fl.R.3s
38°40'5N
09°19'W
09° 20'W
Fl.Y.12s
Lage
Fl.G.3s
Fl.R.3s
Oeiras Marina
(R Lt)
See inset
Ponta da Lage
S. Julião
Oc.R.5s
38m14M
S. Julião
CACHOPO DO SUL
CACHOPO DO NORTE
Pta.da Rana
Iso.WR.3s
BARRA NORTE
BARRA SUL
ODAS APL2
Q(5)Y.20s
PD
Ldg Lts 285°
SOUTH CHANNEL
Mama Lt & Ldg Lts in line 047°
NORTH CHANNEL
Deep draft vessels
BAÍA DE CASCAIS
Estoril
Santa Marta
Guia
See separate chartlet
CASCAIS
Santa Marta
Guia
Iso.WR.2s
57m19/16M
Obscd

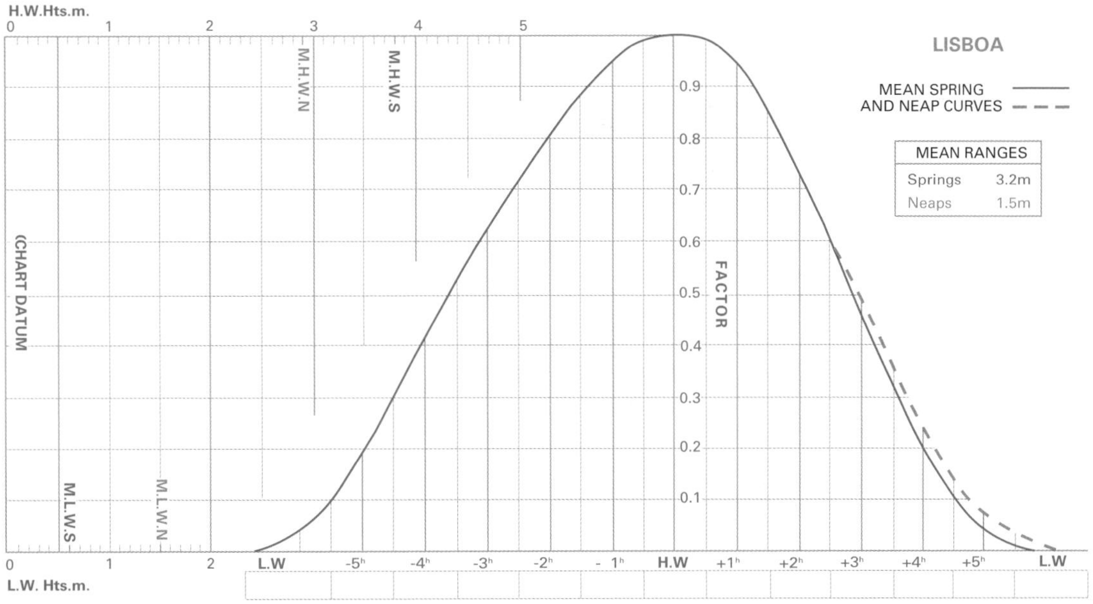

CABO RASO TO CAPE ST VINCENT

Cascais is an expensive stop for yachts on passage or not wishing to go 12M E to Lisboa. **Oeiras Marina**, 5M E of Cascais, is also a good stop. From Cascais to the Rio Tejo (Tagus) use the Barra Norte (least depth 5m) which joins the main Barra Sul abeam São Julião lt. In **Lisboa** 5 marinas line the N bank of the R Tejo. If S-bound, stand on 1M beyond Forte Bugio before turning for flat-topped Cabo Espichel (AC 3635, 3636).

Eastward the coast rises to 500m high cliffs. **Sesimbra** is well sheltered from N'lies. Near the ent to R Sado, Arrábida's shallow bay offers temp'y ⚓. **Setúbal** has few yacht facilities. Thence unbroken beaches stretch 35M to Cabo de Sines, light house and conspicuous chimneys. **Sines** is a strategically placed commercial port 56M N of Cabo São Vicente; its small marina has limited facilities. A tiny bay (37°17'·51N 08°52'·08W) below the high cliffs of Punta da Arrifana gives shelter from N'lies.

STANDARD TIME (UT)
For Summer Time add ONE hour in **non-shaded areas**

LISBOA LAT 38°43′N LONG 9°07′W

TIMES AND HEIGHTS OF HIGH AND LOW WATERS

Dates in red are SPRINGS
Dates in blue are NEAPS

YEAR **2018**

JANUARY

Date	Day	Time	m	Time	m	Time	m	Time	m
1	M	0214	3.8	0810	0.5	1441	3.8	2029	0.5
2	TU	0304	4.0	0901	0.4	1532	3.8	○ 2118	0.4
3	W	0354	4.1	0950	0.3	1621	3.9	2205	0.5
4	TH	0441	4.1	1038	0.3	1709	3.8	2252	0.5
5	F	0528	4.0	1125	0.4	1756	3.7	2338	0.7
6	SA	0616	3.8	1213	0.6	1844	3.5		
7	SU	0026	0.9	0705	3.6	1302	0.8	1936	3.3
8	M	0118	1.1	0758	3.4	1357	1.1	◑ 2034	3.1
9	TU	0218	1.3	0858	3.2	1500	1.2	2139	3.0
10	W	0327	1.4	1006	3.0	1608	1.3	2248	3.0
11	TH	0440	1.4	1115	3.0	1715	1.3	2350	3.1
12	F	0547	1.3	1215	3.0	1812	1.2		
13	SA	0044	3.2	0642	1.2	1306	3.1	1859	1.1
14	SU	0129	3.3	0728	1.1	1350	3.2	1940	1.0
15	M	0209	3.4	0808	1.0	1429	3.3	2017	0.9
16	TU	0246	3.5	0844	0.9	1505	3.3	2052	0.9
17	W	0321	3.6	0918	0.8	1540	3.4	● 2125	0.8
18	TH	0355	3.6	0951	0.8	1614	3.4	2158	0.8
19	F	0428	3.6	1024	0.7	1648	3.4	2231	0.8
20	SA	0502	3.6	1057	0.8	1722	3.3	2305	0.9
21	SU	0537	3.5	1131	0.8	1758	3.3	2341	0.9
22	M	0615	3.5	1209	0.9	1838	3.2		
23	TU	0021	1.0	0656	3.3	1252	1.0	1924	3.1
24	W	0110	1.1	0746	3.2	1344	1.1	◐ 2021	3.0
25	TH	0211	1.2	0848	3.1	1450	1.2	2131	3.0
26	F	0326	1.3	1004	3.1	1606	1.2	2248	3.1
27	SA	0446	1.2	1123	3.1	1720	1.1		
28	SU	0001	3.3	0600	1.0	1234	3.3	1827	0.9
29	M	0104	3.5	0704	0.8	1336	3.5	1926	0.7
30	TU	0201	3.7	0801	0.5	1431	3.7	2019	0.6
31	W	0253	3.9	0852	0.4	1521	3.8	○ 2107	0.4

FEBRUARY

Date	Day	Time	m	Time	m	Time	m	Time	m
1	TH	0342	4.1	0939	0.3	1608	3.8	2152	0.4
2	F	0428	4.1	1023	0.3	1653	3.8	2236	0.4
3	SA	0512	4.1	1106	0.3	1736	3.7	2318	0.5
4	SU	0554	3.9	1147	0.5	1818	3.5		
5	M	0000	0.7	0637	3.7	1229	0.8	1901	3.3
6	TU	0044	0.9	0721	3.4	1314	1.0	1947	3.1
7	W	0133	1.2	0810	3.1	1407	1.3	◑ 2043	2.9
8	TH	0235	1.4	0912	2.9	1512	1.4	2154	2.8
9	F	0352	1.5	1028	2.8	1629	1.5	2309	2.8
10	SA	0513	1.5	1143	2.8	1740	1.4		
11	SU	0014	3.0	0619	1.4	1243	2.9	1837	1.3
12	M	0105	3.1	0710	1.2	1331	3.0	1921	1.1
13	TU	0148	3.3	0750	1.0	1411	3.2	1959	1.0
14	W	0226	3.4	0826	0.9	1447	3.3	2034	0.9
15	TH	0302	3.6	0859	0.8	1522	3.4	● 2107	0.8
16	F	0336	3.7	0931	0.7	1555	3.5	2140	0.7
17	SA	0410	3.7	1003	0.6	1629	3.5	2212	0.7
18	SU	0445	3.7	1035	0.6	1703	3.5	2246	0.7
19	M	0520	3.7	1109	0.6	1739	3.5	2321	0.7
20	TU	0556	3.6	1145	0.7	1817	3.4		
21	W	0000	0.8	0636	3.5	1225	0.8	1859	3.3
22	TH	0045	1.0	0722	3.3	1314	1.0	1951	3.1
23	F	0142	1.1	0822	3.1	1417	1.2	◐ 2059	3.0
24	SA	0258	1.3	0940	3.0	1538	1.3	2223	3.0
25	SU	0427	1.2	1108	3.0	1703	1.2	2344	3.2
26	M	0549	1.1	1224	3.2	1816	1.0		
27	TU	0052	3.4	0656	0.8	1326	3.4	1916	0.8
28	W	0149	3.7	0751	0.6	1419	3.7	2007	0.6

MARCH

Date	Day	Time	m	Time	m	Time	m	Time	m
1	TH	0240	3.9	0838	0.4	1507	3.8	2052	0.4
2	F	0326	4.1	0922	0.3	1550	3.9	○ 2135	0.3
3	SA	0409	4.1	1002	0.3	1631	3.9	2215	0.4
4	SU	0450	4.0	1041	0.4	1710	3.8	2254	0.5
5	M	0529	3.9	1118	0.5	1748	3.6	2331	0.6
6	TU	0606	3.6	1155	0.8	1824	3.4		
7	W	0010	0.9	0643	3.4	1232	1.0	1902	3.2
8	TH	0052	1.1	0722	3.1	1315	1.3	1946	3.0
9	F	0144	1.4	0813	2.8	1413	1.5	◑ 2048	2.8
10	SA	0258	1.5	0930	2.7	1535	1.6	2214	2.8
11	SU	0430	1.6	1103	2.7	1701	1.6	2335	2.8
12	M	0548	1.5	1215	2.8	1807	1.4		
13	TU	0034	3.0	0643	1.3	1305	3.0	1855	1.3
14	W	0120	3.2	0724	1.1	1346	3.2	1934	1.1
15	TH	0159	3.4	0759	0.9	1422	3.3	2009	0.9
16	F	0236	3.6	0832	0.7	1457	3.5	2043	0.8
17	SA	0312	3.7	0905	0.6	1532	3.6	● 2116	0.6
18	SU	0347	3.8	0938	0.5	1607	3.7	2151	0.6
19	M	0423	3.8	1011	0.5	1642	3.7	2226	0.6
20	TU	0500	3.8	1046	0.5	1719	3.7	2302	0.6
21	W	0538	3.7	1123	0.6	1758	3.6	2342	0.7
22	TH	0619	3.5	1204	0.8	1840	3.4		
23	F	0028	0.9	0707	3.3	1253	1.0	1932	3.2
24	SA	0126	1.1	0807	3.1	1357	1.3	◐ 2040	3.1
25	SU	0245	1.3	0929	3.0	1522	1.4	2207	3.1
26	M	0417	1.3	1059	3.0	1651	1.3	2330	3.2
27	TU	0539	1.1	1214	3.2	1804	1.1		
28	W	0038	3.5	0643	0.9	1312	3.5	1901	0.9
29	TH	0133	3.7	0734	0.6	1402	3.7	1950	0.7
30	F	0222	3.9	0819	0.5	1447	3.8	2033	0.5
31	SA	0306	4.0	0900	0.4	1528	3.9	○ 2113	0.4

APRIL

Date	Day	Time	m	Time	m	Time	m	Time	m
1	SU	0347	4.0	0937	0.4	1607	3.9	2151	0.4
2	M	0425	3.9	1013	0.5	1643	3.8	2228	0.6
3	TU	0501	3.8	1047	0.6	1717	3.7	2303	0.7
4	W	0534	3.6	1120	0.8	1749	3.5	2338	0.9
5	TH	0607	3.3	1154	1.0	1822	3.3		
6	F	0016	1.1	0642	3.1	1232	1.3	1900	3.1
7	SA	0102	1.4	0725	2.9	1321	1.5	1951	2.9
8	SU	0207	1.5	0829	2.7	1436	1.7	◑ 2107	2.8
9	M	0336	1.6	1008	2.6	1609	1.7	2239	2.8
10	TU	0459	1.5	1131	2.8	1722	1.6	2349	3.0
11	W	0559	1.4	1227	3.0	1816	1.4		
12	TH	0040	3.2	0644	1.1	1310	3.2	1858	1.2
13	F	0123	3.4	0722	0.9	1349	3.4	1936	0.9
14	SA	0203	3.6	0758	0.8	1426	3.6	2013	0.8
15	SU	0242	3.7	0834	0.6	1504	3.7	2050	0.6
16	M	0321	3.8	0910	0.5	1542	3.8	● 2127	0.5
17	TU	0400	3.9	0947	0.5	1620	3.9	2206	0.5
18	W	0441	3.9	1025	0.5	1700	3.8	2247	0.6
19	TH	0522	3.8	1106	0.6	1742	3.7	2330	0.7
20	F	0607	3.6	1150	0.8	1827	3.5		
21	SA	0020	0.9	0658	3.3	1241	1.1	1921	3.4
22	SU	0121	1.1	0801	3.1	1347	1.3	◐ 2030	3.2
23	M	0238	1.2	0921	3.0	1510	1.4	2153	3.2
24	TU	0405	1.2	1045	3.1	1634	1.3	2311	3.3
25	W	0521	1.1	1155	3.2	1744	1.2		
26	TH	0017	3.5	0622	0.9	1251	3.5	1840	1.0
27	F	0111	3.7	0712	0.7	1340	3.6	1928	0.8
28	SA	0159	3.8	0755	0.6	1423	3.8	2011	0.6
29	SU	0242	3.8	0834	0.6	1503	3.8	2050	0.6
30	M	0322	3.8	0910	0.6	1540	3.8	○ 2127	0.6

HAT is 4·3 metres above Chart Datum.

STANDARD TIME (UT)
For Summer Time add ONE hour in **non-shaded areas**

LISBOA LAT 38°43′N LONG 9°07′W

TIMES AND HEIGHTS OF HIGH AND LOW WATERS

Dates in red are SPRINGS
Dates in blue are NEAPS

YEAR **2018**

MAY

Day	Time	m	Time	m	Time	m	Time	m
1 TU	0359	3.8	0945	0.6	1615	3.8	2202	0.7
2 W	0433	3.6	1017	0.8	1648	3.7	2237	0.8
3 TH	0505	3.5	1050	0.9	1719	3.5	2312	0.9
4 F	0537	3.3	1123	1.1	1751	3.4	2349	1.1
5 SA	0610	3.1	1159	1.3	1827	3.2		
6 SU	0032	1.3	0651	2.9	1244	1.5	1913	3.0
7 M	0126	1.5	0746	2.8	1345	1.6	2014	2.9
8 TU	0238	1.5	0904	2.7	1506	1.7	◑ 2132	2.9
9 W	0356	1.5	1029	2.8	1623	1.6	2248	3.0
10 TH	0501	1.4	1134	2.9	1724	1.4	2349	3.1
11 F	0554	1.2	1225	3.2	1814	1.2		
12 SA	0039	3.3	0639	1.0	1309	3.4	1858	1.0
13 SU	0125	3.5	0721	0.8	1352	3.6	1941	0.8
14 M	0210	3.7	0802	0.6	1434	3.8	2023	0.6
15 TU	0254	3.8	0843	0.5	1517	3.9	● 2106	0.5
16 W	0339	3.9	0925	0.5	1600	3.9	2149	0.5
17 TH	0424	3.9	1008	0.5	1644	3.9	2235	0.5
18 F	0510	3.8	1052	0.6	1730	3.8	2323	0.6
19 SA	0558	3.6	1140	0.8	1819	3.7		
20 SU	0015	0.8	0651	3.4	1234	1.0	1914	3.5
21 M	0116	1.0	0753	3.2	1337	1.2	2019	3.4
22 TU	0226	1.1	0905	3.1	1451	1.3	◐ 2132	3.3
23 W	0342	1.1	1020	3.1	1607	1.3	2245	3.3
24 TH	0453	1.1	1127	3.2	1716	1.2	2350	3.4
25 F	0554	1.0	1224	3.4	1814	1.0		
26 SA	0045	3.5	0644	0.9	1314	3.5	1904	0.9
27 SU	0134	3.6	0728	0.8	1358	3.6	1948	0.8
28 M	0217	3.6	0808	0.8	1438	3.7	2027	0.8
29 TU	0257	3.6	0844	0.8	1515	3.7	○ 2105	0.8
30 W	0334	3.5	0919	0.8	1550	3.7	2141	0.8
31 TH	0408	3.5	0952	0.9	1623	3.6	2216	0.9

JUNE

Day	Time	m	Time	m	Time	m	Time	m
1 F	0441	3.4	1025	0.9	1655	3.5	2251	0.9
2 SA	0513	3.3	1059	1.0	1728	3.4	2327	1.0
3 SU	0548	3.2	1135	1.2	1804	3.3		
4 M	0007	1.2	0626	3.0	1216	1.3	1845	3.2
5 TU	0052	1.3	0714	2.9	1305	1.5	1935	3.1
6 W	0148	1.4	0813	2.8	1408	1.5	◑ 2037	3.0
7 TH	0253	1.4	0924	2.8	1519	1.5	2147	3.0
8 F	0359	1.3	1034	2.9	1627	1.4	2254	3.1
9 SA	0500	1.2	1135	3.1	1726	1.2	2354	3.3
10 SU	0554	1.0	1229	3.3	1820	1.0		
11 M	0049	3.4	0645	0.8	1319	3.5	1911	0.8
12 TU	0141	3.6	0733	0.7	1407	3.7	2000	0.6
13 W	0232	3.7	0820	0.6	1456	3.9	● 2048	0.5
14 TH	0321	3.8	0907	0.5	1543	4.0	2137	0.4
15 F	0410	3.8	0954	0.5	1631	4.0	2226	0.4
16 SA	0459	3.8	1042	0.6	1719	3.9	2315	0.5
17 SU	0548	3.7	1131	0.7	1809	3.8		
18 M	0007	0.6	0640	3.5	1223	0.9	1902	3.7
19 TU	0102	0.8	0737	3.3	1320	1.0	2000	3.5
20 W	0203	1.0	0839	3.2	1424	1.2	◐ 2105	3.3
21 TH	0309	1.1	0947	3.1	1534	1.3	2213	3.3
22 F	0417	1.2	1054	3.2	1644	1.2	2319	3.3
23 SA	0521	1.1	1154	3.2	1746	1.2		
24 SU	0018	3.3	0615	1.1	1246	3.3	1840	1.1
25 M	0109	3.3	0702	1.0	1333	3.4	1927	1.0
26 TU	0154	3.3	0744	0.9	1414	3.5	2009	0.9
27 W	0235	3.4	0822	0.9	1453	3.5	2047	0.9
28 TH	0313	3.4	0858	0.9	1529	3.6	○ 2123	0.9
29 F	0348	3.4	0932	0.9	1603	3.6	2158	0.9
30 SA	0421	3.3	1006	0.9	1636	3.5	2232	0.9

JULY

Day	Time	m	Time	m	Time	m	Time	m
1 SU	0455	3.3	1039	1.0	1709	3.5	2307	0.9
2 M	0529	3.2	1114	1.0	1744	3.4	2343	1.0
3 TU	0605	3.2	1151	1.1	1822	3.3		
4 W	0021	1.1	0646	3.1	1232	1.3	1904	3.2
5 TH	0106	1.2	0734	3.0	1322	1.3	1955	3.1
6 F	0200	1.3	0832	2.9	1424	1.4	◑ 2056	3.1
7 SA	0303	1.3	0939	3.0	1534	1.4	2205	3.1
8 SU	0410	1.2	1048	3.1	1643	1.3	2314	3.2
9 M	0515	1.1	1152	3.3	1748	1.1		
10 TU	0019	3.3	0615	0.9	1251	3.5	1848	0.9
11 W	0119	3.5	0711	0.8	1346	3.7	1943	0.7
12 TH	0215	3.7	0804	0.6	1439	3.8	2036	0.5
13 F	0308	3.8	0854	0.5	1530	4.0	● 2126	0.4
14 SA	0358	3.8	0943	0.5	1619	4.1	2215	0.3
15 SU	0447	3.8	1030	0.5	1707	4.1	2303	0.4
16 M	0534	3.8	1117	0.6	1754	4.0	2350	0.5
17 TU	0622	3.6	1204	0.7	1843	3.8		
18 W	0039	0.7	0712	3.4	1255	0.9	1934	3.6
19 TH	0131	0.9	0806	3.3	1351	1.1	◐ 2031	3.3
20 F	0230	1.1	0908	3.1	1456	1.3	2136	3.2
21 SA	0336	1.3	1015	3.0	1608	1.4	2245	3.0
22 SU	0445	1.3	1121	3.1	1719	1.3	2350	3.0
23 M	0548	1.3	1220	3.2	1820	1.3		
24 TU	0047	3.1	0640	1.2	1310	3.3	1911	1.1
25 W	0135	3.2	0725	1.1	1354	3.4	1954	1.0
26 TH	0217	3.3	0804	1.0	1433	3.5	2032	0.9
27 F	0255	3.3	0841	0.9	1510	3.6	○ 2107	0.9
28 SA	0330	3.4	0915	0.9	1544	3.6	2140	0.8
29 SU	0403	3.4	0947	0.9	1617	3.6	2212	0.8
30 M	0436	3.4	1020	0.9	1650	3.6	2244	0.8
31 TU	0509	3.4	1052	0.9	1724	3.6	2317	0.9

AUGUST

Day	Time	m	Time	m	Time	m	Time	m
1 W	0543	3.3	1126	1.0	1759	3.5	2352	0.9
2 TH	0620	3.3	1203	1.1	1837	3.4		
3 F	0030	1.0	0702	3.2	1247	1.2	1922	3.3
4 SA	0117	1.1	0752	3.1	1341	1.3	◑ 2018	3.1
5 SU	0216	1.3	0855	3.0	1450	1.4	2127	3.1
6 M	0329	1.3	1009	3.1	1610	1.3	2245	3.1
7 TU	0445	1.2	1124	3.2	1726	1.2		
8 W	0000	3.2	0555	1.1	1232	3.4	1834	0.9
9 TH	0106	3.4	0657	0.9	1332	3.7	1933	0.7
10 F	0203	3.6	0752	0.7	1426	3.9	2025	0.5
11 SA	0255	3.8	0842	0.5	1516	4.1	● 2114	0.3
12 SU	0344	3.9	0929	0.4	1604	4.2	2200	0.3
13 M	0430	3.9	1013	0.4	1649	4.2	2244	0.3
14 TU	0514	3.9	1057	0.5	1734	4.1	2326	0.5
15 W	0558	3.7	1140	0.6	1818	3.8		
16 TH	0009	0.7	0642	3.5	1225	0.9	1903	3.6
17 F	0055	1.0	0728	3.3	1314	1.1	1953	3.3
18 SA	0146	1.2	0823	3.1	1414	1.4	◐ 2053	3.0
19 SU	0249	1.4	0930	3.0	1529	1.5	2207	2.9
20 M	0406	1.5	1045	3.0	1651	1.5	2324	2.9
21 TU	0520	1.5	1154	3.0	1802	1.4		
22 W	0027	3.0	0620	1.4	1249	3.2	1855	1.3
23 TH	0117	3.1	0707	1.2	1333	3.4	1937	1.1
24 F	0158	3.3	0746	1.1	1412	3.5	2013	1.0
25 SA	0234	3.4	0821	1.0	1448	3.6	2046	0.9
26 SU	0308	3.5	0854	0.9	1522	3.7	○ 2117	0.8
27 M	0341	3.5	0925	0.8	1555	3.7	2148	0.7
28 TU	0413	3.6	0957	0.8	1628	3.7	2219	0.7
29 W	0446	3.6	1029	0.8	1701	3.7	2250	0.8
30 TH	0520	3.5	1102	0.9	1736	3.6	2324	0.9
31 F	0555	3.5	1138	1.0	1814	3.5		

HAT is 4·3 metres above Chart Datum.

Portugal

STANDARD TIME (UT)
For Summer Time add ONE hour in **non-shaded areas**

LISBOA LAT 38°43′N LONG 9°07′W

TIMES AND HEIGHTS OF HIGH AND LOW WATERS

Dates in red are SPRINGS
Dates in blue are NEAPS

YEAR **2018**

SEPTEMBER

Date	Day	Time	m	Time	m	Time	m	Time	m
1	SA	0000	1.0	0635	3.3	1219	1.1	1856	3.3
2	SU	0044	1.1	0722	3.2	1311	1.2	1950	3.2
3	M	0141	1.3	0823	3.1	1420	1.4	◑ 2102	3.0
4	TU	0258	1.4	0943	3.1	1549	1.4	2229	3.1
5	W	0426	1.4	1106	3.2	1714	1.2	2350	3.2
6	TH	0543	1.2	1219	3.5	1824	1.0		
7	F	0056	3.5	0645	1.0	1319	3.7	1921	0.7
8	SA	0151	3.7	0739	0.7	1411	4.0	2011	0.5
9	SU	0240	3.9	0826	0.6	1500	4.2	● 2056	0.4
10	M	0325	4.0	0910	0.4	1545	4.2	2139	0.3
11	TU	0408	4.0	0952	0.4	1628	4.2	2219	0.4
12	W	0450	4.0	1033	0.5	1709	4.1	2258	0.6
13	TH	0529	3.8	1113	0.7	1749	3.8	2337	0.8
14	F	0608	3.6	1153	0.9	1829	3.5		
15	SA	0016	1.1	0649	3.4	1237	1.2	1912	3.3
16	SU	0100	1.3	0734	3.2	1330	1.4	◐ 2004	3.0
17	M	0158	1.6	0836	3.0	1444	1.6	2120	2.8
18	TU	0320	1.7	1000	2.9	1616	1.7	2251	2.8
19	W	0448	1.7	1120	3.0	1735	1.5		
20	TH	0002	2.9	0554	1.5	1220	3.2	1830	1.4
21	F	0053	3.1	0642	1.4	1306	3.3	1911	1.2
22	SA	0133	3.3	0721	1.2	1345	3.5	1945	1.0
23	SU	0208	3.4	0755	1.0	1420	3.7	2017	0.9
24	M	0241	3.6	0827	0.9	1454	3.8	2048	0.8
25	TU	0314	3.7	0859	0.8	1528	3.8	○ 2119	0.7
26	W	0347	3.7	0932	0.7	1603	3.9	2151	0.7
27	TH	0421	3.8	1005	0.7	1638	3.8	2224	0.7
28	F	0456	3.7	1040	0.8	1715	3.7	2259	0.8
29	SA	0533	3.7	1117	0.9	1754	3.6	2337	1.0
30	SU	0613	3.5	1200	1.0	1838	3.4		

OCTOBER

Date	Day	Time	m	Time	m	Time	m	Time	m
1	M	0022	1.2	0701	3.3	1253	1.2	1934	3.2
2	TU	0120	1.4	0803	3.2	1405	1.4	◑ 2049	3.1
3	W	0241	1.5	0926	3.2	1538	1.4	2221	3.1
4	TH	0413	1.5	1053	3.3	1704	1.3	2340	3.3
5	F	0530	1.3	1204	3.5	1811	1.0		
6	SA	0042	3.5	0631	1.0	1302	3.8	1905	0.8
7	SU	0134	3.8	0722	0.8	1353	4.0	1952	0.6
8	M	0220	3.9	0807	0.6	1439	4.1	2034	0.4
9	TU	0303	4.0	0850	0.5	1523	4.2	● 2114	0.4
10	W	0344	4.1	0930	0.5	1604	4.1	2152	0.5
11	TH	0423	4.0	1008	0.6	1642	4.0	2229	0.7
12	F	0500	3.8	1046	0.7	1719	3.7	2304	0.9
13	SA	0535	3.7	1123	0.9	1755	3.5	2339	1.1
14	SU	0611	3.5	1203	1.2	1832	3.2		
15	M	0018	1.4	0650	3.2	1250	1.4	1916	3.0
16	TU	0108	1.6	0741	3.0	1356	1.6	◐ 2023	2.8
17	W	0224	1.8	0858	2.9	1525	1.7	2201	2.7
18	TH	0358	1.8	1029	2.9	1649	1.6	2322	2.9
19	F	0512	1.7	1137	3.1	1748	1.5		
20	SA	0016	3.1	0605	1.5	1227	3.3	1832	1.3
21	SU	0057	3.3	0646	1.3	1308	3.5	1909	1.1
22	M	0134	3.5	0722	1.1	1346	3.6	1942	0.9
23	TU	0209	3.6	0756	0.9	1423	3.8	2016	0.8
24	W	0244	3.8	0831	0.8	1500	3.8	○ 2050	0.7
25	TH	0320	3.8	0907	0.7	1538	3.9	2125	0.6
26	F	0357	3.9	0944	0.7	1617	3.9	2201	0.7
27	SA	0435	3.9	1022	0.7	1657	3.8	2239	0.8
28	SU	0515	3.8	1104	0.8	1740	3.6	2321	0.9
29	M	0559	3.6	1150	1.0	1828	3.4		
30	TU	0009	1.1	0649	3.5	1246	1.1	1926	3.2
31	W	0109	1.4	0752	3.3	1358	1.3	◑ 2041	3.1

NOVEMBER

Date	Day	Time	m	Time	m	Time	m	Time	m
1	TH	0228	1.5	0912	3.3	1524	1.3	2207	3.1
2	F	0355	1.5	1034	3.3	1645	1.2	2321	3.3
3	SA	0510	1.3	1143	3.5	1750	1.0		
4	SU	0021	3.5	0610	1.1	1241	3.7	1843	0.8
5	M	0112	3.7	0701	0.9	1332	3.9	1929	0.7
6	TU	0158	3.9	0746	0.7	1417	4.0	2011	0.6
7	W	0240	4.0	0828	0.6	1500	4.0	● 2049	0.6
8	TH	0320	4.0	0908	0.6	1540	3.9	2126	0.7
9	F	0357	3.9	0945	0.7	1617	3.8	2201	0.8
10	SA	0432	3.8	1022	0.8	1652	3.6	2235	0.9
11	SU	0506	3.7	1058	1.0	1725	3.4	2309	1.1
12	M	0539	3.5	1136	1.1	1800	3.2	2346	1.3
13	TU	0615	3.3	1219	1.3	1840	3.0		
14	W	0030	1.5	0659	3.1	1312	1.5	1933	2.8
15	TH	0129	1.7	0758	3.0	1423	1.6	◐ 2050	2.8
16	F	0250	1.8	0917	2.9	1541	1.6	2217	2.8
17	SA	0409	1.7	1034	3.0	1648	1.5	2322	3.0
18	SU	0511	1.6	1134	3.1	1741	1.3		
19	M	0011	3.2	0600	1.4	1223	3.3	1824	1.1
20	TU	0054	3.4	0643	1.1	1308	3.5	1904	0.9
21	W	0134	3.6	0724	0.9	1350	3.7	1943	0.8
22	TH	0214	3.7	0804	0.8	1433	3.8	2022	0.7
23	F	0254	3.9	0845	0.7	1516	3.8	○ 2102	0.6
24	SA	0336	3.9	0927	0.6	1559	3.8	2143	0.6
25	SU	0419	3.9	1010	0.6	1644	3.8	2226	0.7
26	M	0503	3.9	1056	0.7	1730	3.7	2311	0.9
27	TU	0550	3.8	1146	0.8	1821	3.5		
28	W	0002	1.0	0642	3.6	1242	1.0	1919	3.3
29	TH	0101	1.2	0742	3.5	1347	1.1	2027	3.2
30	F	0211	1.3	0853	3.4	1501	1.2	◑ 2142	3.2

DECEMBER

Date	Day	Time	m	Time	m	Time	m	Time	m
1	SA	0328	1.4	1007	3.3	1615	1.1	2253	3.2
2	SU	0441	1.3	1116	3.4	1722	1.1	2355	3.4
3	M	0545	1.1	1217	3.5	1817	0.9		
4	TU	0048	3.5	0639	1.0	1309	3.6	1905	0.9
5	W	0135	3.7	0727	0.9	1356	3.7	1948	0.8
6	TH	0218	3.8	0810	0.8	1439	3.7	2027	0.8
7	F	0258	3.8	0850	0.8	1518	3.6	● 2104	0.8
8	SA	0335	3.8	0927	0.8	1555	3.5	2139	0.8
9	SU	0410	3.7	1004	0.8	1630	3.5	2213	0.9
10	M	0444	3.6	1040	0.9	1703	3.3	2247	1.0
11	TU	0516	3.5	1116	1.0	1736	3.2	2322	1.2
12	W	0551	3.4	1154	1.1	1813	3.1		
13	TH	0001	1.3	0629	3.3	1237	1.3	1856	2.9
14	F	0047	1.5	0715	3.1	1328	1.4	1951	2.8
15	SA	0145	1.6	0813	3.0	1429	1.5	◐ 2100	2.8
16	SU	0255	1.6	0921	3.0	1537	1.4	2212	2.9
17	M	0406	1.5	1031	3.0	1640	1.3	2316	3.0
18	TU	0508	1.4	1133	3.1	1735	1.2		
19	W	0010	3.2	0602	1.2	1228	3.3	1825	1.0
20	TH	0059	3.4	0652	1.0	1320	3.5	1913	0.8
21	F	0146	3.6	0740	0.8	1410	3.6	1959	0.7
22	SA	0233	3.8	0828	0.6	1458	3.7	○ 2045	0.6
23	SU	0320	3.9	0915	0.5	1546	3.8	2131	0.6
24	M	0407	4.0	1002	0.4	1634	3.8	2217	0.6
25	TU	0454	4.0	1050	0.5	1722	3.7	2304	0.6
26	W	0542	3.9	1139	0.6	1812	3.6	2353	0.8
27	TH	0632	3.8	1231	0.7	1905	3.4		
28	F	0046	0.9	0726	3.6	1327	0.9	2003	3.3
29	SA	0146	1.1	0827	3.4	1430	1.0	◑ 2109	3.2
30	SU	0254	1.2	0935	3.3	1539	1.1	2218	3.1
31	M	0407	1.3	1045	3.2	1648	1.2	2324	3.2

HAT is 4·3 metres above Chart Datum.

9.24.16 SESIMBRA

Baixo Alentejo **38°26'·30N 09°06'·49W** (Mole hd) ❁❁◊◊✿✿

CHARTS AC 3635, 3636; PC 24204, 26407; SC42B

TIDES Standard Port LISBOA (⟵); ML 2·0

Times				Height (metres)			
High Water		Low Water		MHWS	MHWN	MLWN	MLWS
0400	0900	0400	0900	3·8	3·0	1·5	0·6
1600	2100	1600	2100				
Differences SESIMBRA							
−0045	−0030	−0020	−0010	−0·4	−0·4	−0·1	0·0

SHELTER Good in marina. Or ⚓ in about 5m to N or E of ent and clear of fairway, local moorings and underwater cables. Strong N'ly gusts blow down from high ground late pm/evening.

NAVIGATION WPT 38°25'·86N 09°06'·15W, 333°/0·5M to breakwater head, which is 475m W of the ldg line; and on the 003·5° ldg line.

LIGHTS AND MARKS 003·5° ldg lts/marks (NE of the hbr) are hard to see by day and night. Bkwtr hd lt, W twr, R bands, and Forte do Cavalo lt, R ○ twr are both conspic. See Lights, buoys and waypoints.

COMMUNICATIONS (Code 212) Brit Consul 808 203 537; Port VHF Ch 11; Marina VHF Ch 09.

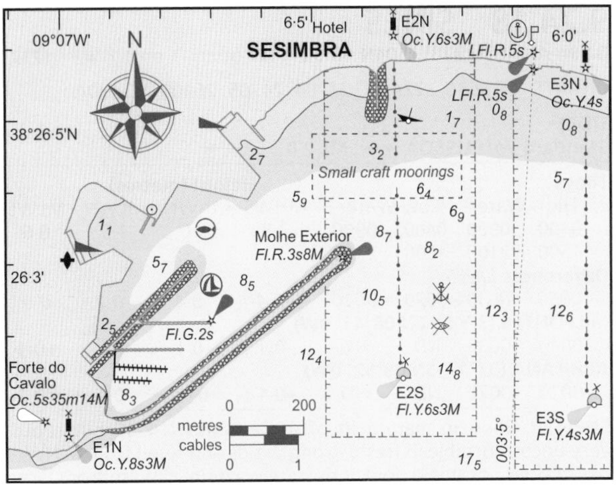

FACILITIES YC Marina ☎233451, 130 berths but often full in summer, €2·60, multihulls +50%. (fish market). www.naval-sesimbra.pt

Town (1½M to the NE) ✕ ⊠ Ⓑ. Bus into town. ⇄ Seixal. ✈ Lisboa. Tourist amenities. 30 mins bus to Lisboa or, to avoid traffic jams, local bus to Cacilhas and ferry across the Tejo.

9.24.17 SETÚBAL

Baixo Alentejo **38°31'·22N 08°53'·14W** (Marina) ❁❁◊◊✿✿

CHARTS AC 3635, 3636, 3259; PC 24204, 26308/09; SC42B

TIDES
Standard Port LISBOA (⟵); ML 2·0

Times				Height (metres)			
High Water		Low Water		MHWS	MHWN	MLWN	MLWS
0400	0900	0400	0900	3·8	3·0	1·5	0·6
1600	2100	1600	2100				
Differences *SETÚBAL*							
−0020	*−0015*	*−0005*	*+0005*	*−0·3*	*−0·3*	*−0·2*	*−0·1*

SHELTER Good in marina, but almost always full. A new marina is at Troia; see Facilities. ⚓ SW of the FV basin in up to 13m.

NAVIGATION WPT 38°27'·06N 08°58'·26W (abm No 1 buoy & No 2 bcn, Racon B) 040°/5·2M to front ldg lt. The 10m bar is dangerous only in strong SW'lies against a spring ebb. R Sado is shoal either side until N of Forte de Outão; heed the ldg line/buoys/bcns.

LIGHTS AND MARKS As Lights, buoys and waypoints/chartlet.

COMMUNICATIONS (Code 265) VTS *Setúbal Port Control* VHF Ch 73 (mandatory for yachts >15m LOA; MSI broadcasts on request) Brit Consul 808 203 537; Ⓗ 561116; Port VHf Ch 11; Marina VHF Ch 09.

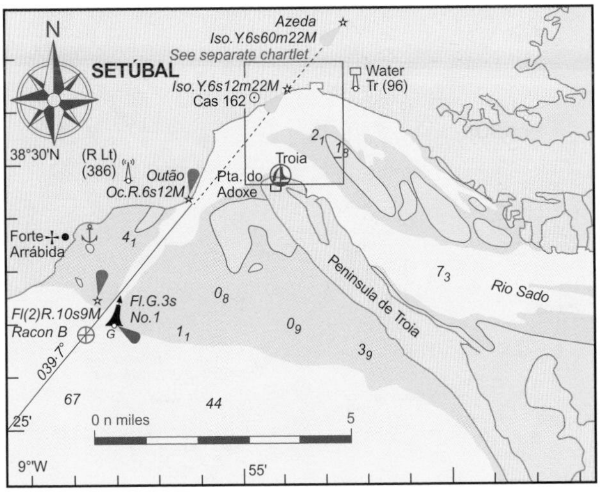

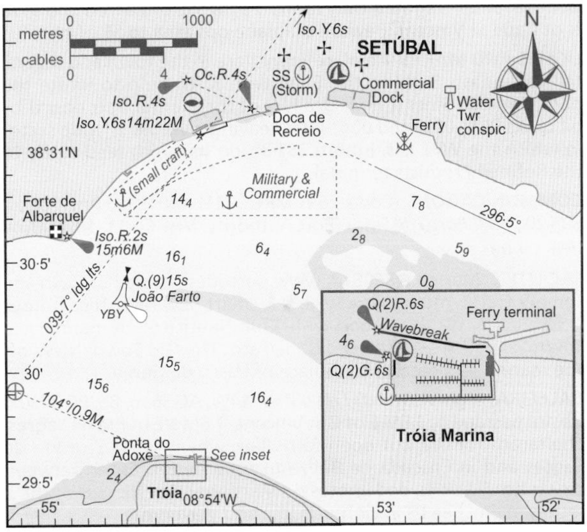

FACILITIES Setúbal's so-called marina is crowded with small FVs and local boats and most unlikely to accommodate visiting yachts. ☎542076, 155 berths.

Doca de Recreio at Setúbal is even smaller; local boats only. Industrial quays extend 6M upriver to the ESE.

Town ✕ ⊠ Ⓑ good train/bus to Lisboa ⇄ ✈.

ADJACENT ANCHORAGE

ARRÁBIDA 38°28'·52N 08°58'·77W, 1·5M NNW of ent to Rio Sado (AC 3259). Popular but shallow day ⚓ in 2·5m at SW end of the bay, sheltered from N by high ground, but also prone to katabatic gusts. Appr from SSW, 1-2ca offshore to avoid Baixo de Alpertuche (0·6m). Caution: rocky reef at NE end of bay.

HARBOUR ACROSS THE RIO SADA

Tróia Marina at 38°29'·66N 08°54'·14W has modern facilities and is part of an up-market development. From Setúbal it bears 207°/1·75M.

From a WPT at 38°29'·88N 08°55'·28W (on the 039·7° leading line) make good 104°/9 cables to the marina ent; lights as chartlet. 187 berths (fingers) inc Ⓥ in 2·5-4·0m, max LOA 18m.

☎499333, mob 933 389847. May-Sep 0830-2100. VHF Ch 09. marina@troiaresort.pt; reported quite expensive; ✕ 4 mins walk, @.

9.24.18 SINES

Baixo Alentejo **37°57'·04N 08°52'·11W** (marina ent)

CHARTS AC 3636, 3224; PC 24204, 24205, 26408; SC 430A

TIDES

Standard Port LISBOA (⟵); ML 2·0

Times				Height (metres)			
High Water		Low Water		MHWS	MHWN	MLWN	MLWS
0400	0900	0400	0900	3·8	3·0	1·5	0·6
1600	2100	1600	2100				
Differences *SINES*							
−0050	*−0030*	*−0020*	*−0010*	*−0·4*	*−0·4*	*−0·1*	*0·0*
MILFONTES (37°43'·0N 08°47'·0W)							
−0040	−0030	ND	ND	−0·1	−0·1	0·0	+0·1
ARRIFANA (37°17'·5N 08°52'·0W)							
−0030	−0020	ND	ND	−0·1	0·0	−0·1	+0·1

SHELTER Good in marina in offshore winds N-E-SE but reptd. very uncomfortable in fresh/strong winds and swell from S- NW. S bkwtr does not shield pontoons from waves/backwash from large bay to N. ⚓ NW of the marina in 4m; holding is reportedly poor E of 08°52'·00W.

NAVIGATION WPT 37°55'·70N 08°52'·97W, 027°/1·5M to ent to the marina bay. The outer ent, between W and E moles, is 1M wide. From the NW, caution: derelict outer 400m section of the W mole dries 0·6m. A PHM buoy, Fl R 3s, 680m S of the mole hd ☆ (Fl 3s) *must* be rounded. In strong S'lies swell may cause turbulence off W mole. Sines is strategically located 51M SSE of Cascais and 57M N of Cape St Vincent. Beware seaplane ops area to SE of hbr.

LIGHTS AND MARKS An oil refinery flare in the town and several tall chy's/masts 3-4M to the E (all with R lts) help to locate the port. Cabo de Sines lt ho is 9ca NW of the marina; it is obsc'd by oil tanks 001°-003° and 004°-007°, leaving a visible 1° wide sector in which the WPT lies. Ignore 357·3° ldg lts which lead solely to the Refined Products terminal.

COMMUNICATIONS (Code 269) MRCC (21) 4401919; Brit Consul 808 203 537; *Porto de Sines* (Port Authority) VHF Ch 11, 13; Marina VHF Ch 09.

FACILITIES Marina ☎860612. www.portodesines.pt 250 pontoon berths in 4m, some Ⓥ €2·11, multihulls +50%. smart new HM office houses facilities; v.good wi-fi. **Club Náutico** SE of marina. **Town** ✕ Ⓑ ⇄ ✈ Lisboa/Faro. The Old Town, NNW of the marina, is pleasant; birthplace of Vasco da Gama.

BALEEIRA, Algarve 37°00'·72N 08°55'·44W. AC 3636, 89. PC 27502. Useful passage ⚓, 3·5M E of C St Vincent, 1·6M NE of Pta de Sagres. Sheltered from W, but open to NE'lies, when the ⚓s E of Pta de Sagres and in Enseada de Belixe may be better. Enter between bkwtr hd, Fl WR 4s, and Ilhotes do Martinhal, 4ca NE. ⚓ N of the 2 jetties in 6m. See lts in Lights, buoys and waypoints.

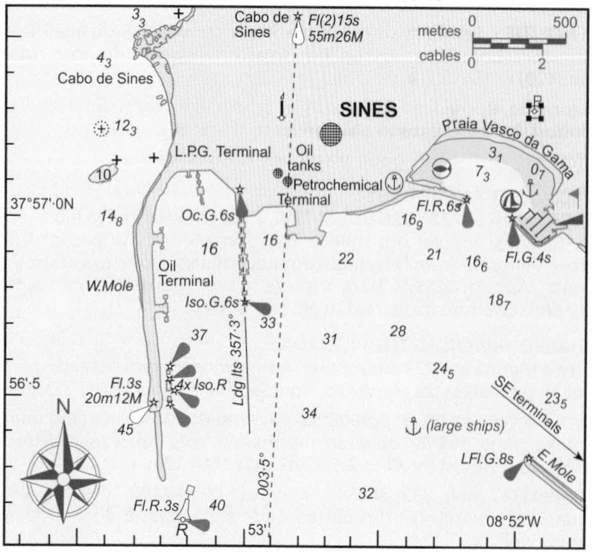

9.24.19 LAGOS

Algarve **37°05'·93N 08°39'·94W** (Hbr ent)

CHARTS AC 3636, 89; PC 24206, 25R11

TIDES

Standard Port LISBOA (⟵); ML 2·0

Times				Height (metres)			
High Water		Low Water		MHWS	MHWN	MLWN	MLWS
0400	0900	0400	0900	3·8	3·0	1·5	0·6
1600	2100	1600	2100				
Differences LAGOS							
−0100	−0040	−0030	−0025	−0·4	−0·4	−0·1	−0·1
ENSEADA DE BELIXE (Cape St Vincent)							
−0050	−0030	−0020	−0015	+0·3	+0·2	+0·2	+0·2

SHELTER Very good in marina; access H24 all tides. Swell possible at ent in strong SE winds. The ⚓ close NE of the E mole in 3-5m is exposed only to E and S winds and possible SW swell.

NAVIGATION WPT 37°05'·75N 08°39'·06W, 284°/7ca to hbr ent. Fishing nets may extend up to 1M offshore. Beware fish farms SW of Ponta de Piedade, marked by 4 Y SPM bys, Fl(4)Y12s. From Ponta da Piedade keep 5ca offshore to clear rocks; otherwise there are no offshore dangers. Final appr is on 282°, W mole head lt ≠ Santo António church. Shoaling in ent; care needed at LW if draft >1·5m. Note, small craft moor W of chan. 3kn hbr speed limit.

Berth at arrival pontoon stbd side close SE of lifting foot-bridge which opens on request 0800-2200, 1/6-15/9; 0900-1800 16/9-31/5, except for some ¼hr spells for train passengers. Unmasted craft may transit when bridge is down.

LIGHTS AND MARKS Lts as chartlet and Lights, buoys and waypoints. The river chan is unlit, except by shore lts. Pta da Piedade is 1·2M S, with conspic. 20m lattice radio/radar mast close behind Lt Ho. Pta do Altar (Portimão) is 7M E.

COMMUNICATIONS (Code 282) MRCC (21) 4401919; 461406; Met (218) 447000; VHF Ch 12 at 1000 and 1400 LT in season; Police 762930; Brit Consul 808 203 537; Ⓗ 770100; Fire 770790; HM 769161; *Marina de Lagos* VHF Ch 09 for bridge, pump-out and fuel.

FACILITIES Marina ☎770210 marina@marlagos.pt www.marinadelagos.pt. 462+Ⓥ €4·61,(multihulls +100% high season, +50% med and low). Short stay €8·61/hr. ✕ Ⓒ @ (35t) **Club de Vela** ☎762256. **Town** all usual amenities, ⇄ ✈ Faro (75km).

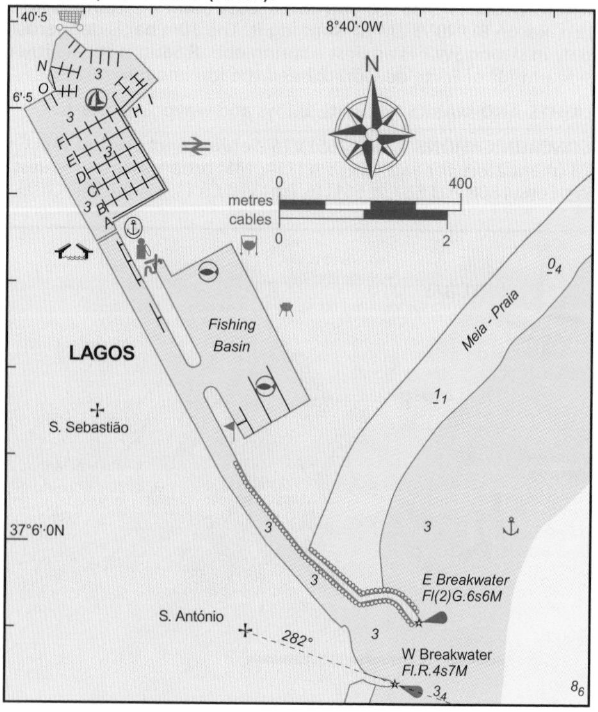

ANCHORAGE 2·6M ENE OF LAGOS

ALVOR 37°07'·06N 08°37'·16W. PC 27502. Beware of an Aquatic Revival Park S of Alvor, centred on 37°05'·75N 08°35'·09W, marked with 4 Y special marks. A peaceful but shallow lagoon entered between moles Fl R 4s & G 4s, but not in strong onshore winds nor at night. ⚓ just inside the ent to port in about 2·2m or off Alvor (1·2M E) in about 1·6m. The channel is buoyed, but the sandbanks frequently move, best to enter on the young flood whilst the drying banks can be seen. While not geared for yachtsmen, it is a lively tourist spot, not devoid of charm.

SOUTHERN PORTUGAL: THE ALGARVE

An ITZ extends 15M W/SW of Cape St Vincent and the TSS 20M further west; see Area map & AC 89, 93. Passage ⚓s, sheltered from N'lies, are at Enseada de Belixe (E of Cabo São Vicente) and at Enseadas de Sagres and da Baleeira (NE of Pta de Sagres).

The direct route to Gibraltar is 110°/175M (Cabo São Vicente to Tarifa). Alternatively make a series of coastal legs using the good marinas at Lagos, Portimão, Albufeira and Vilamoura.

E of Cabo São Vicente the summer climate becomes more Mediterranean, ie hotter, clearer, winds more from NW to SW. Swell may decrease, tidal streams are slight and the current runs SE. Hbrs along the coasts of the Algarve and SW Andalucía are sheltered from all but S'lies (infrequent). The 'Nortada', which comes in most afternoons from the NW, can inc to F5 or 6.

Nets around tuna farms can be a problem NE of Ponta de Sagres and 4M SSW of the entrance to Faro/Olhão at Cabo de Santa Maria. These are charted (AC 93) but dimly lit and hard to see against shore lights. Ideally, stay outside the 50m contour and keep a careful lookout. More nets lie S and E of Ilha de Armona. Numerous lobster pot markers are a hazard all along the Algarve coast.

At Cabo de Santa Maria a gap in the low-lying dunes gives access to the lagoons and chans leading to Faro and Olhão, where a marina has been built (but may not be open to visitors); there are also some peaceful anchorages, notably Culatra Is (ferries to Olhão).

The marina at Vila Real de Santo António is on the Portuguese bank of the Rio Guadiana, which forms the Spanish border.

9.24.20 PORTIMÃO

Algarve **37°06'·51N 08°31'·71W** (Hbr ent) ❁❁❁◊◊◊✿✿

CHARTS AC 91, 3636, 89, 83; PC 24206, 26310

TIDES

Standard Port LISBOA (⟵); ML 2·0

Times				Height (metres)			
High Water		Low Water		MHWS	MHWN	MLWN	MLWS
0400	0900	0400	0900	3·8	3·0	1·5	0·6
1600	2100	1600	2100				
Differences PORTIMÃO							
–0100	–0040	–0030	–0025	–0·5	–0·4	–0·1	+0·1
PONTA DO ALTAR (Lt ho E of ent)							
–0100	–0040	–0030	–0025	–0·3	–0·3	–0·1	0·0
ENSEADA DE ALBUFEIRA							
–0035	+0015	–0005	0000	–0·2	–0·2	0·0	+0·1

SHELTER Good in marina on W bank. Good ⚓ off Ferragudo. ⚓ inside E molhe in about 4m is prone to swell and FV wash.

NAVIGATION WPT 37°06'·04N 08°31'·94W, 021°/5ca to hbr ent. Beware an artificial reef W of Portimão, approx 1M SSW of Ponta do Faco (marked by four Y lit bys). Seaplane operating area approx 1.5M SW of hbr ent. Beyond W molhe stay on ldg line until past No 2 by, due to shifting sandbank just inside ent. River is straightforward, but flood & ebb streams run hard; berth bows to the stream. Caution: 2 low (1.4m cl'nce) fixed road/rail bridges N of Portimão centre.

LIGHTS AND MARKS Ponta do Altar lt ho is on low cliffs to E of ent. The R-roofed church at Ferragudo is conspic by day, almost on the 019° ldg line. Ldg lts as chartlet and Lights, buoys and waypoints; both on R/W banded columns, moved when chan changes.

COMMUNICATIONS (Code 282) MRCC;417714; Police 470734; Brit Consul 808 203537; Port VHF Ch 11; Marina VHF Ch 09.

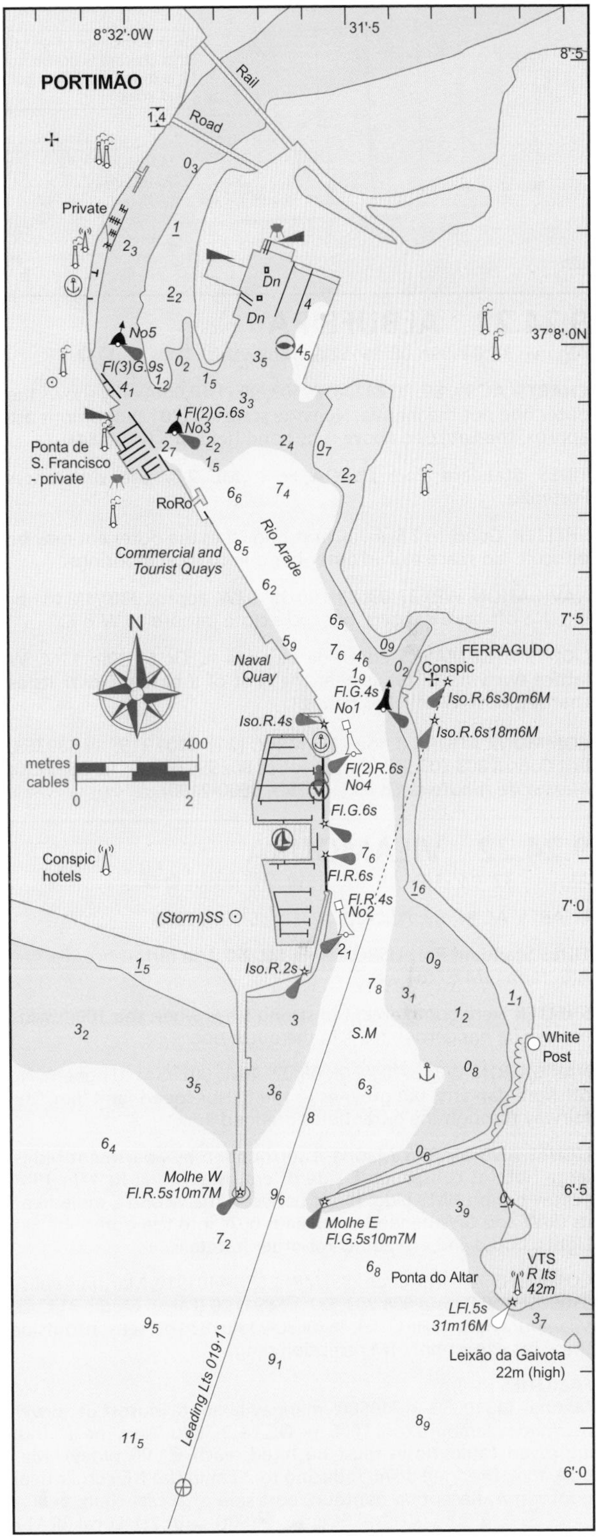

FACILITIES **Marina de Portimão** ☎400680, www.marinadeportimao.com.pt info@marinadeportimao.com.pt 620 inc Ⓥ €3·75; max LOA 50m, draft 4.5m, multihulls +50% (root N bkwtr), wi-fi.

Fishing Hbr (300t /9m beam) (20t).

Town 20 mins walk, bus every 10 mins summer, taxis/car hire at marina. Wide choice of ; Ⓑ Ⓗ ✈ Faro (65km).

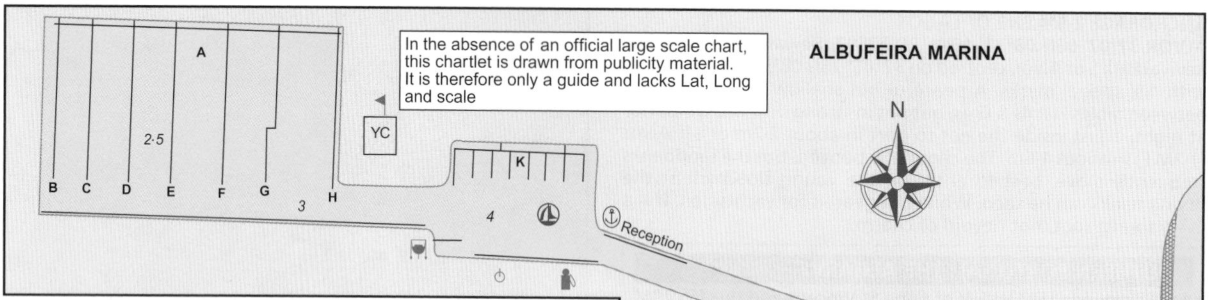
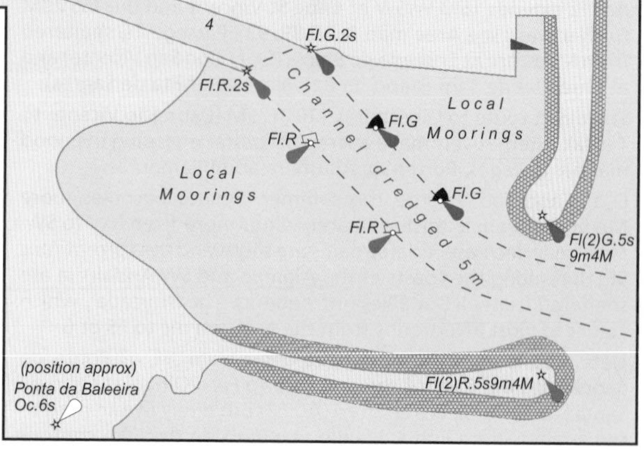

9.24.21 ALBUFEIRA

Algarve **37°04'·90N 08°15'·52W** (N bkwtr lt)

CHARTS AC 91, 89; PC 24206, 27503, 90 (1:10,000) only shows the outer hbr, not the marina. No large scale AC (2012). Positions are approx; the Lat/Long above is by hand-held GPS (WGS 84).

TIDES Standard Port LISBOA (⟵); **ML 2·0.** See differences Portimão.

SHELTER Good, in 2·5–4·0m. In strong E'lies the outer ent may be difficult. No space to ⚓ in outer hbr due to local moorings.

NAVIGATION WPT 37°03'·88N 08°15'·02W, approx 338°/1M to hbr ent. No offshore dangers, but rocks close inshore to W & E.

LIGHTS AND MARKS Ponta de Baleeira lt, Oc 6s 30m 11M, W lattice twr with R top, is near the root of S bkwtr. Bkwtr lts as chartlet, both W cols, R/G bands.

COMMUNICATIONS (Code 289) MRCC (21) 4401919; ⊜ 589363; Brit Consul 808 203 537 (Portimão); Ⓗ 802555 (Faro); Taxi 583230; *Marina de Albufeira* Ch 09 (1/6-15/9: 0900-2100).

FACILITIES Marina ☎289 514282, mob 964249596, 475 +Ⓥ €4·28. info@marinadealbufeira.com www.marinadealbufeira.com mob 962079546, (70t) (6t) YC. **Town** Most facilities; Ⓑ ⇌. ✈ Faro 30km.

9.24.22 VILAMOURA

Algarve **37°04'·10N 08°07'·35W**

CHARTS AC 91, 89; PC 24206, 27503; SHOM 7300

TIDES Standard Port LISBOA (⟵); **ML 2·0.** Use differences for Albufeira (6M to the west).

SHELTER Very good, except in strong S'lies when the 100m wide ent can be dangerous. No ⚓ in the outer hbr.

NAVIGATION WPT 37°03'·60N 08°07'·40W, 007°/5ca to hbr ent. No offshore dangers, but groynes to the E. Hbr speed limit 3kn. The fairway through the outer hbr is dredged 4m.

LIGHTS AND MARKS Marina is surrounded by apartment bldgs; large hotel is conspic on E side of ent. Main lt, Fl 5s 17m 19M, yellow twr on HM's bldg; this lt between the W and E mole head lts (R/W and G/W banded twrs) leads 007° into the outer hbr. See Lights, buoys and waypoints for other lt details.

COMMUNICATIONS (Code 289) MRCC (21) 4401919; Maritime Police 310575; Brit Consul 808 203 537; Ⓗ 891100 (Faro); Medic 314243; *Vilamoura Radio* VHF Ch 09, 16 (0830-2130/1830 off season) outside these hrs expect only 1M reception range.

FACILITIES

Marina ☎310560 310580 marinavilamoura@lusort.pt www.marinadevilamoura.com 1000 inc Ⓥ €3·78 Jul/Aug, inc ,(but approved cables/hoses must be hired, each €1·00 p/day). Max LOA 40m. Dredged 3·3m, reducing to 2·0m in the NE corner near pontoon A. Reception pontoon, port side of access chan. @ Ⓔ (60t) (6t,2t). Local Ⓑ M-F 0830-1445, plus ©s. Free by sludge boat comes to your yacht. Mail pick-up, if addressed to: Marina de Vilamoura, 8125-409 Quarteira, Portugal.

Clube Náutico (by reception area) welcomes visitors: lounge, @.

Faro (20km) has most facilities, inc ⇌ ✈ ☎800800.

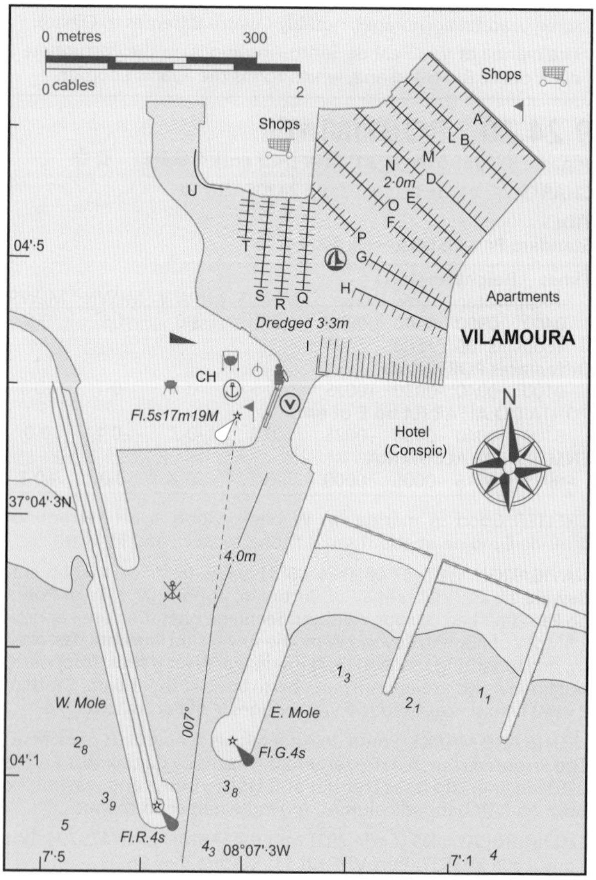

9.24.23 FARO and OLHÃO

Algarve **36°57'·81N 07°52'·19W** (Hbr entrance)

CHARTS AC 91, 89, 83; PC 24206, 26311; SC 44B

TIDES Standard Port LISBOA (⟵); ML 2·0

Times				Height (metres)			
High Water		Low Water		MHWS	MHWN	MLWN	MLWS
0400	0900	0400	0900	3·8	3·0	1·5	0·6
1600	2100	1600	2100				
Differences PORTO DE FARO-OLHÃO							
−0050	−0030	−0015	+0005	−0·4	−0·4	−0·1	−0·1

SHELTER Generally good in the lee of coastal dunes. Popular ⚓s in 3-5m are inside Ilha da Culatra, abm lt Fl 5s or off jetty Oc G 4s.

NAVIGATION WPT 36°57'·04N 07°52'·12W, 352°/7ca to narrow ent (dangerous in strong S'lies); extensive shoals to the W. Seaplane operating area 1.4M E of ent. Enter near HW between moles, Fl R 4s & G 4s, and training walls. Abeam Cabo de Santa Maria lt ho, chan forks into salt marshes: WNW to Faro or NE to Olhão.

The **Faro** chan carries 5·4m for the buoyed/lit 4M to the Commercial quay (not for yachts); but beyond depths vary.

The **Olhão** buoyed/lit chan (5M) is narrower and carries 2·1m least depth. From N of No 5 buoy enter the marina by an E-W chan, depth approx 2m, marked by 3 PHM buoys.

LIGHTS AND MARKS Cabo de Santa Maria lt ho near root of long E trng wall and adjacent VTS twr (42m) are conspic. Lt ho is also rear 021° ldg lt to abeam front ldg lt; see chartlet/Lights, buoys and waypoints.

COMMUNICATIONS (Code 289) IPTM (Institute of Ports & Shipping) Olhão 715912; Brit Consul 808 203 537; both ports VHF Ch 11, 09: Faro H24; Olhão, M-F office hrs.

FACILITIES

Faro HM ☎822025. ⚓ in 3m, 3ca SW of Doca de Recreio, small craft only; low bridge across ent, clearance 0.5m W sp; 0.5m depth LW sp. Some noise from airport, but not after 2100LT.

Olhão HM ☎703160. Marina, W end; max LOA 17m, draft 3m, rarely Ⓥ space, call, if available, keep N of PHM bys, berth on wavebreak. No ⛽ or WC. ⚓ in fairways but ⚓ poss E of wavebreak in 2-3m, good holding, mud; poss outer wall Puerto deportivo.

Upstream, Marina Formosa ☎702162, (20t, 2m draft); secure winter lay up ashore.

Towns Both are sizeable, all amenities inc @ ⇄ ✈.

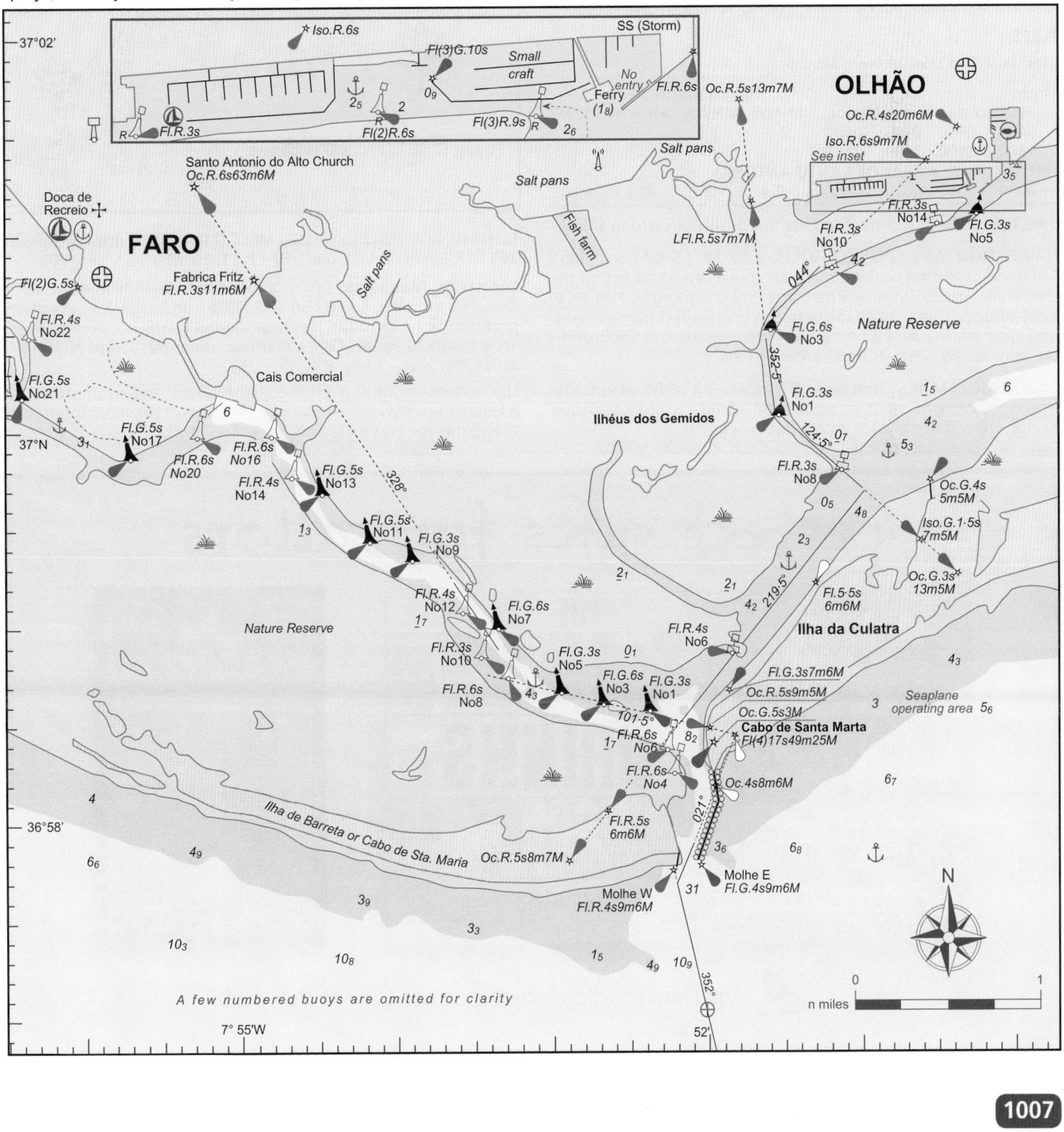

MINOR PORT 11M W OF VILA REAL DE SANTO ANTÓNIO

TAVIRA. 37°06'·69N 07°37'·01W. AC 89, 93; PC 24206, 27503; SC 44A/B. Tide, interpolate between Faro/Olhão and Vila Real de San António. The narrow (about 70m) ent between I de Tavira and sand dunes to the E is lit by Fl G and R lts 2·5s and ldg lts 325·9° over the bar, front Fl R 3s, front & rear sync'd. ⚓ in about 3m on sand SW of the entrance in the Rio Formosa and SE of the small community of Quatro Aguas (a planned marina is on hold). Show an ⚓ lt, due to FVs.

Town is 1M (20 mins walk or dinghy) NW of the ⚓ and, apart from a small craft BY and diesel supply, has little to offer a visiting yacht, being essentially a working FV port. Access is not possible for masted boats due to a low road bridge. Facilities: YC ☎281 326 858, ✕ 🛒 ✉ Ⓑ Ⓗ ⇌ ✈ (Faro).

9.24.24

VILA REAL DE SANTO ANTÓNIO

Algarve **37°10'·80N 07°24'·49W** (Marina) ❁❁◊◊✿✿

CHARTS AC 91, 89, 93; PC 24206, 26312; SC 440, 440A

TIDES

Standard Port LISBOA (⟵); ML 2·0

Times				Height (metres)			
High Water		Low Water		MHWS	MHWN	MLWN	MLWS
0400	0900	0400	0900	3·8	3·0	1·5	0·6
1600	2100	1600	2100				
Differences VILA REAL DE SANTO ANTÓNIO							
–0050	–0015	–0010	0000	–0·4	–0·4	–0·1	+0·1

SHELTER Good in marina, but river ent difficult in strong S'lies.

NAVIGATION WPT 37°09'·00N 07°23'·35W (No 1 SHM buoy) 340°/9ca to hd of W trng wall. Caution: Extensive drying areas E of the trng walls stretch 2M east. The bar (1·0m) is marked by Nos 3/4 P/SHM lt buoys. Hug the W bank between trng walls (E partly covers) and up to marina. Access best at slack water as streams and current are very strong: 2½kn (up to 6kn in winter).

LIGHTS AND MARKS High bldgs, FR lts, are 3M WNW of ent. Vila Real lt ho, W twr/B bands, is conspic. 2M inland a white suspension bridge (18m cl'nce MSL) is visible from seaward.

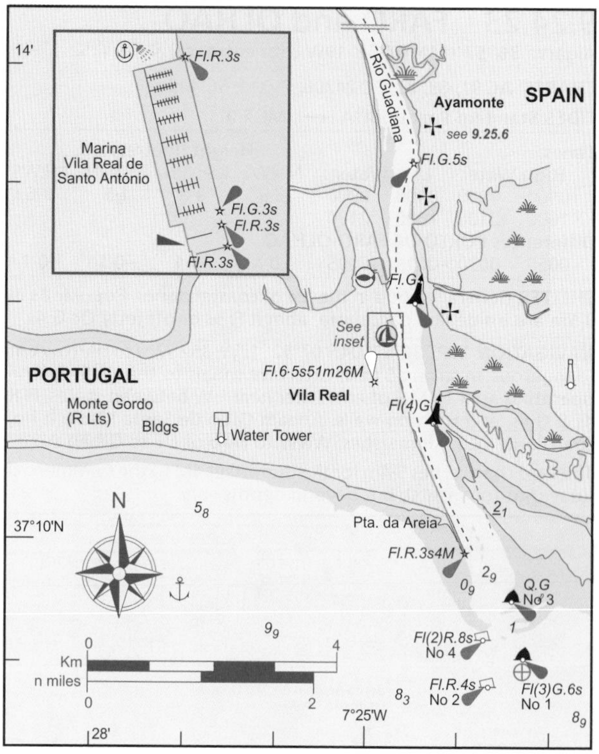

COMMUNICATIONS (Code 281) MRCC (21) 4401919; Brit Consul 808 203 537; *Porto de Vila Real* VHF Ch 11, 16; Marina VHF Ch 09.

FACILITIES Marina ☎513769 anguadiana@mail.telepac.pt (2m) Ⓥ €2·60 p/m, ⚡+€2·50 p/d; 25% surcharge for reception pontoon. ⛽ on pontoon just N of marina (cards not accepted); 1NM downstream ☎542069, marinaguadiana@sapo.pt (70t). **YC** ☎511306, ✕ ⛵. **Town** ✕ 🛒 ✉ Ⓑ.

Upriver better water is off the Spanish bank and Ayamonte. The R Guadiana is navigable for about 20M to ⚓ off Alcoutim (pontoons €7·50/day for 1st week) and Pomerão (27M).

South West Spain, Gibraltar & Morocco

Ayamonte to Europa Point and Ceuta

9.25.1 Contents 1009

9.25.2 Area map 1010

9.25.3 Lights, buoys and waypoints 1010

9.25.4 Passage information 1012
Portuguese Border to Rio Guadalquivir – 1012 •
Chipiona to Cape Trafalgar – 1016 • Strait of Gibraltar – 1021 • Morocco – 1026

9.25.5 Special notes for SW Spain 1012

9.25.6 Ayamonte 1013

9.25.7 Isla Canela 1013

9.25.8 Isla Cristina 1014

9.25.9 El Rompido (Rio de las Piedras) 1014

9.25.10 Punta Umbria 1015

9.25.11 Mazagón (Huelva River) 1015

9.25.12 Chipiona 1016

9.25.13 Rio Guadalquivir 1016

9.25.14 Sevilla 1017

9.25.15 Bay of Cádiz 1017
Rota • Puerto Sherry • Puerto Santa Maria • Puerto America

9.25.16 Sancti-Petri 1019

9.25.17 Barbate 1019

9.25.18 Tarifa 1021

9.25.19 Algeciras 1021

UNITED KINGDOM

9.25.20 Gibraltar, Special notes, tide tables/curves 1022
La Linea

MOROCCO

9.25.21 Tangier 1026

9.25.22 Ceuta (to Spain) 1026

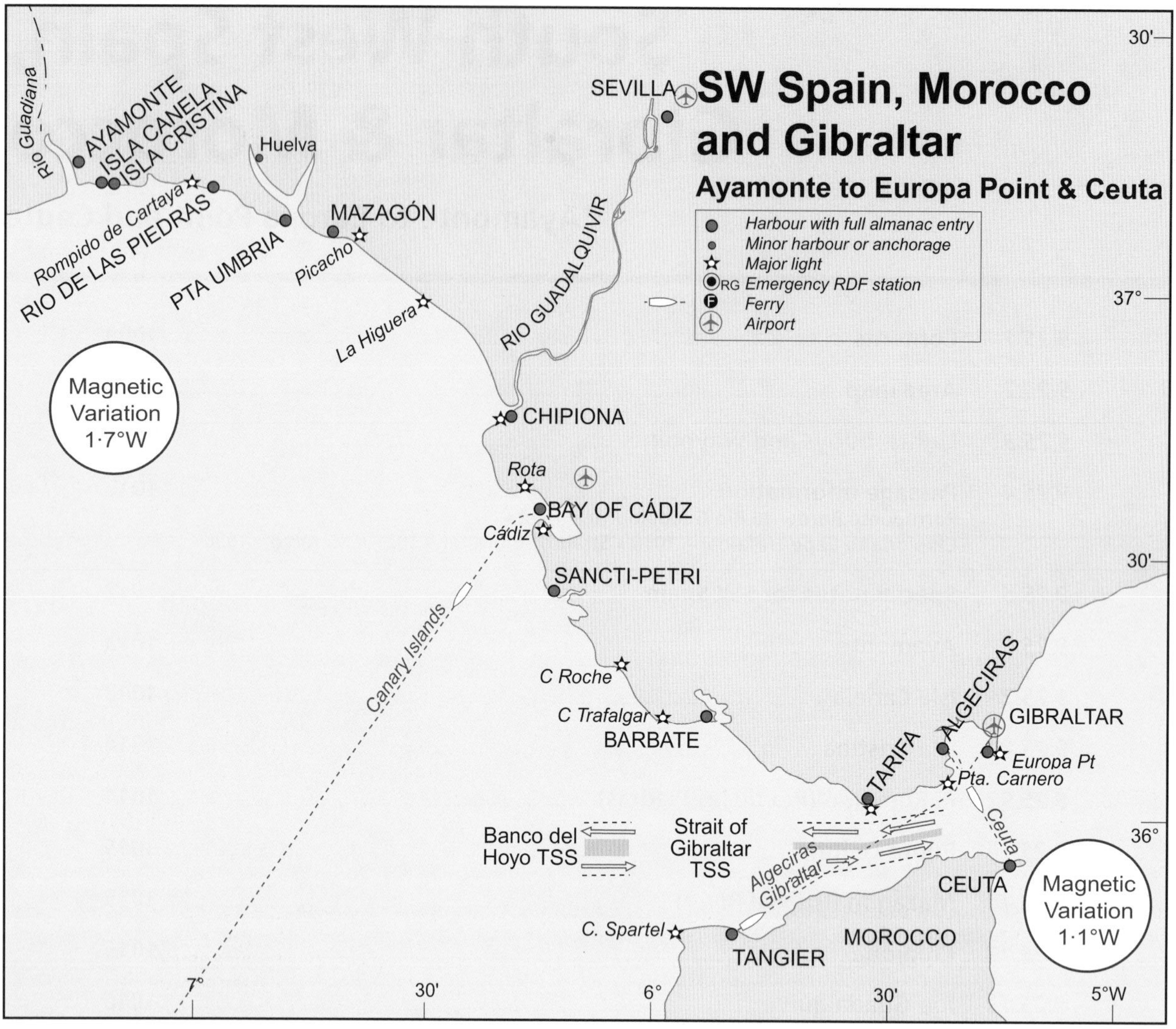
SW Spain, Morocco and Gibraltar
Ayamonte to Europa Point & Ceuta
Harbour with full almanac entry
Minor harbour or anchorage
Major light
RG Emergency RDF station
Ferry
Airport
Rio Guadiana
AYAMONTE
ISLA CANELA
ISLA CRISTINA
Huelva
Rompido de Cartaya
RIO DE LAS PIEDRAS
PTA UMBRIA
Picacho
MAZAGÓN
La Higuera
RIO GUADALQUIVIR
SEVILLA
Magnetic Variation 1·7°W
CHIPIONA
Rota
BAY OF CÁDIZ
Cádiz
SANCTI-PETRI
Canary Islands
C Roche
C Trafalgar
BARBATE
TARIFA
ALGECIRAS
GIBRALTAR
Europa Pt
Pta. Carnero
Ceuta
Banco del Hoyo TSS
Strait of Gibraltar TSS
Algeciras Gibraltar
CEUTA
C. Spartel
TANGIER
MOROCCO
Magnetic Variation 1·1°W
30'
37°
30'
36°
7°
30'
6°
30'
5°W

9.25.3 LIGHTS, BUOYS AND WAYPOINTS

Bold print = light with a nominal range of 15M or more. CAPITALS = place or feature. *CAPITAL ITALICS* = light-vessel, light float or Lanby. *Italics* = Fog signal. ***Bold italics*** = Racon. Many marks/buoys are fitted with AIS (MMSI No); see relevant charts.

RÍO GUADIANA TO SEVILLA

AYAMONTE (E side of Río Guadiana)

No 1 Fl (3) G 6s; 37°09′·00N 07°23′·35W.
No 2 Fl R 4s; 37°08′·63N 07°23′·23W.
E trng wall ☆ Fl (2) 5s 2M; 37°09′·97N 07°23′·69W.
W trng wall ☆ Fl R 3s 4M; 37°09′·77N 07°23′·93W (Portugal).
Vila Real de Santo Antònio ☆ Fl 6·5s 51m **26M**; W ○ twr, B bands; 37°11′·20N 07°24′·91W (Portugal).
Marina ent, ☆ QR and ☆ QG; 37°12′·70N 07°24′·54W.
Baluarte (ferry landing) Fl (2) G 5s 1M; G ○ twr; 37°12′·78N 07°24′·63W.

ISLA CANELA and ISLA CRISTINA

Appr Fl 10s 5M; 37°10′·51N 07°19′·49W.
W mole hd ☆ VQ (2) R 5s 9m 4M; 37°10′·83N 07°19′·60W.
Ldg lts 312·8°; framework twrs. Front ☆ Q 8m 5M; 37°11′·50N 07°20′·30W approx. Rear ☆ Fl 4s 13m 5M, 100m from front.
Isla Canela marina ent, QR and QG; 37°11′·40N 07°20′·26W.
Isla Cristina marina ent, QR and QG; 37°11′·89N 07°19′·65W.

RÍO DE LAS PIEDRAS

El Rompido ☆ Fl (2) 10s 41m **24M**; W & R ○ twr; 37°13′·12N 07°07′·72W, 4M WNW of the bar buoy.

RÍA DE HUELVA

Punta Umbria, LFl10s 5M, 37°09′·53N 06°57′·18W.
Punta Umbria bkwtr hd ☆ VQ(6)+L Fl 10s 10m 5M: Y framework twr/B base; 37°09′·85N 06°53′·93W.
Ent chan lateral buoys are moved frequently as the chan shifts.
Real Club Maritimo S hd ☆ Fl 3 R 3M; 37°10′·53N 06°57′·02W.
Punta Umbria Marina S hd ☆ Fl(2)R 10s 3M; 37°10′·82N 06°57′·36W.
Punta Umbria ent S'wards, tanker Fl (4) Y 20s 8M; *Siren Mo (E) 30s*; 37°04′·79N 06°55′·59W. 992241108.
Huelva, main chan, Dir ☆ 339·2°, WRG 59m 8M; 337·2°-Fl G-337·8°-FG-338·3°-OcWG-338·9°-FW-339·1°-OcWR-339·7°-FR-340·2°-Fl R-340·7°; W twr; 37°08′·57N 06°50′·67W, 8ca NW of marina ent.
Q (9) 15s; 37°05′·55N 06°49′·11W.
No 1 Fl G 5s; 37°06′·34N 06°49′·49W.
No 2 Fl R 5s; 37°06′·22N 06°49′·65W.
Juan Carlos I bkwtr hd ☆ Fl (3+1) WR 20s 29m, W12M, R9M; 165°-W-100°-R-125°; ***Racon K, 12M***; 37°06′·49N 06°49′·94W. 992241107.
No 3 Fl (2) G 10s; 37°06′·90N 06°49′·75W.
No 4 Fl (2) R 10s; 37°06′·85N 06°49′·94W.
No 5 Fl (3) G 15s; 37°07′·54N 06°50′·06W.

No 6 Fl (3) R 15s; 37°07′·51N 06°50′·27W.
No 7 Fl (4) G 20s; 37°07′·79N 06°50′·27W.
No 8 Fl (4) R 20s; 37°07′·78N 06°50′·52W.

MAZAGÓN

Picacho lt ho ☆ Fl (2+4) 30s 50m **25M**; 37°08′·11N 06°49′·56W.
Marina, S bkwtr ☆ QG 7m 2M; 37°07′·89N 06°50′·18W.
N bkwtr ☆ QR 5m 2M; 37°07′·95N 06°50′·08W.
Inner ent, Fl G 5s 3m 1M and Fl R 5s 3m 1M.
Fl (2) 10s; 37°04′·30N 06°43′·71W, off Torre del Loro (ruins).
La Higuera ☆ Fl (3) 20s 45m **20M**; 37°00′·51N 06°34′·18W.

CHIPIONA

Bajo Salmedina Q (9) 15s 9m 5M; 36°44′·46N 06°28′·35W.
Pta de Chipiona ☆ Fl 10s 67m **25M**; 36°44′·26N 06°26′·52W.
Marina, No 2 Fl (2) R 7s; 36°45′·14N 06°25′·58W.
No 4 Fl (3) R 11s; 36°45′·05N 06°25′·51W.
N bkwtr head ☆ Fl (2) G 7s 6m 5M; 36°44′·96N 06°25′·71W.
N inner jetty ☆ Fl (3) G 9s 2m 1M; 36°44′·89N 06°25′·77W.
SE side of ent ☆ Fl (4) R 11s 3m 3M; 36°44′·89N 06°25′·70W.

RÍO GUADALQUIVIR

No 1 L Fl 10s; ***Racon M, 10M***; 36°45′·85N 06°26′·85W. 992241110 .
No 2 Q (9) 15s; 36°47′·35N 06°26′·76W (1·6M N of No 1). 992241109 .
Ldg lts 069°, Y □ on metal towers. Front ☆ Q 28m 5M; 36°47′·85N 06°20′·25W. Rear, ☆ Iso 4s 61m 10M; 5ca from front.
Selected buoys in sequence as far as Bonanza:
No 3 Fl G 5s; 36°46′·20N 06°25′·45W.
No 4 Fl R 5s; 36°46′·27N 06°25′·60W.
No 7 Fl (3) G 10s; 36°46′·58N 06°24′·14W.
No 8 Fl (3) R 10s; 36°46′·68N 06°24′·19W.
No 11 Fl G 5s; 36°46′·95N 06°22′·94W.
No 12 Fl R 5s; 36°47′·05N 06°22′·93W.
No 13 Fl (2) G 6s; 36°47′·10N 06°22′·47W.
No 14 Fl (2) R 6s; 36°47′·19N 06°22′·45W.
No 17 Fl (4) G 12s; 36°47′·51N 06°21′·18W.
No 20 Fl R 5s; 36°47′·81N 06°20′·70W.
Bonanza Dir ☆ 146° Iso 4s 21m 7M(142°-W-150°); R twr/W top/ W building; 36°48′·17N 06°20′·16W.
Upstream the river is marked by lt bcns, lt buoys and a few ldg lts.

SEVILLA

Esclusa Beacon C ☆ Fl (2+1) R 14·5s 9m 5M; 37°18′·92N 06°00′·83W, G ○ twr, R band. Fork stbd to city centre via lock, or port for Gelves marina, ent Fl R 5s (37°20′·43N 06°01′·40W) and Fl G 3s.

CADIZ TO CABO TRAFALGAR

ROTA (Clockwise around the Bay of Cadiz)

Bajo El Quemado Fl (2) R 9s; 36°35′·99N 06°23′·27W. 992241090 .
Rota Aero ☆ Alt Fl WG 9s 79m **17M**; R/W chequered water twr on 8 cols, conspic; 36°38′·13N 06°20′·834W.
Rota ☆ Oc 4s 33m 13M; W ○ lt ho, R band; 36°36′·95N 06°21′·43W.
Marina, S pier ☆ Fl (3) R 10s 8m 3M; 36°36′·86N 06°21′·04W.
N pier ☆ Q (6) G 12s; G post; 36°36′·91N 06°21′·10W.
Bajo Las Cabezuelas Fl (4) R 10s; 36°35′·21N 06°19′·95W. 992241091 .

PUERTO SHERRY and PUERTO DE SANTA MARIA

La Galera Q; 36°34′·53N 06°17′·64W.
Puerto Sherry marina, S bkwtr ☆ Oc R 4s 4M; 36°34′·64N 06°15′·25W. N bkwtr ☆ Oc G 5s 3M. Basin ent, QR and QG.
Santa María ldg lts 040°: Front ☆ QG 16m 4M; 36°35′·77N 06°13′·35W. Rear ☆ Iso G 4s 20m 4M; 253m from front.
W trng wall head ☆ Fl R 5s 10m 3M; 36°34′·35N 06°14′·95W.
W trng wall root Fl (2) R 5s 1M; 36°35′·07N 06°14′·12W.
E trng wall ☆ Fl (2) G 7s 9m 3M; 36°34′·68N 06°14′·39W.
E bkwtr ☆ Q (9) 15s 3M; 36°34′·46N 06°14′·35W.

CÁDIZ CITY and PUERTO AMERICA

Castillo de San Sebastián ☆ Fl (2) 10s 38m **25M**; metal ○ twr; 36°31′·70N 06°18′·97W.
Bajos de San Sebastián Q (9) 15s; 36°31′·30N 06°20′·36W.
L Fl 10s; for Canal Principal; 36°33′·84N 06°19′·90W.
No 1 Fl G 3s; 36°33′·12N 06°19′·07W.
No 3 Fl (2) G 4s; 36°33′·15N 06°18′·31W.
No 4 Fl (2) R 4s; 36°33′·57N 06°17′·88W.
No 5 Fl (3) G 13s; 36°33′·08N 06°17′·31W.
No 6 Fl (3) R 10s; 36°33′·39N 06°17′·19W.
Spur N of S. Felipe ☆ Fl (4) G 10s 10m 3M; 36°32′·72N 06°16′·79W.
San Felipe mole ☆ Fl G 3s 10m 5M; G twr; 36°32′·57N 06°16′·77W.
E mole ☆ Fl R 2s 11m 5M; 36°32′·44N 06°16′·63W.
Puerto America, NE bkwtr, ☆ Fl (2+1) G 6s 1M; G twr; 36°32′·41N 06°17′·03W.
Real Club Nautico pier ☆ FG; 36°32′·35N 06°17′·13W.
International Free Zone hbr: No 1 Fl (3) G 9s; 36°30′·66N 06°15′·45W. **Puerto Elcano** marina ent 36°30′·08N 06°15′·45W.

SANCTI PETRI

Punta del Arrecife ☆ Q (9) 15s 7m 3M; 36°23′·73N 06°13′·51W.
Sancti Petri castle ☆ Fl 3s 18m 9M; twr; 36°22′·76N 06°13′·29W.
Ldg lts 050°: Front ☆ Fl 5s 12m 6M; 36°22′·91N 06°12′·24W. Rear ☆ Oc (2) 6s 16m 6M.
No 1 Fl (3) G 9s 5M; 36°22′·45N 06°12′·93W.
No 2 Fl (3) R 9s 5M; 36°22′·46N 06°12′·98W.
No 3 Fl (4) G 11s 3M; 36°22′·64N 06° 12′·71W.
No 4 Fl (4) R 11s 3M; 36°22′·66N 06°12′·71W.
Inner ldg lts 346·5°: Front ☆ Fl 5s 11m 6M. Rear ☆ Oc (2) 6s 21m.
Piedra Larga Fl G 5s 8m 2M; 36°23′·02N 06°12′·74W.
Bajo de Poniente Fl R 5s 8m 2M, 36°23′·02N 06°12′·79W.
Cabo Roche ☆ Fl (4) 24s 44m **20M**; 36°17′·74N 06°08′·41W.
Puerto de Conil W bkwtr hd ☆ Fl (2) R 8s 9m 5M; R round twr; 36°17′·57N 06°08′·08W.
Cabo Trafalgar ☆ Fl (2+1) 15s 50m **22M**; 36°10′·97N 06°02′·09W.

THE GIBRALTAR STRAIT

BARBATE

Barbate lt ho ☆ Fl (2) WR 7s 22m, W10M, R7M; 281°-W-015°-R -095°; W ○ twr, R bands; 36°11′·22N 05°55′·42W.
SW mole ☆ Fl R 4s 11m 5M; 36°10′·79N 05°55′·55W.
Inner NE mole ☆ Fl G 3s 8m 2M; 36°10′·95N 05°55′·79W.
Marina ent, Fl (2+1) R 21s 2M, 7 Fl (4) Y 20s (anti-oil boom) and Fl R 4s 2M.
△-shaped tunny net, N end, Q (Mar-Sep); 36°10′·72N 05°55′·39W (1ca E of hbr ent). Other marks clockwise:
Q (3) 10s (Mar-Sep); 36°08′·89N 05°55′·39W.
VQ (6) + L Fl 12s (Jul-Sep); 36°08′·07N 05°55′·07W.
VQ (6) + L Fl 12s (Mar-Jun); 36°08′·82N 05°57′·12W.
VQ (9) 10s (Mar-Sep); 36°09′·20N 05°56′·00W, centre of net.
Punta de Gracia ☆ Oc (2) 5s 74m13M; 36°05′·39N 05°48′·57W.
Pta Paloma ☆ Oc WR 5s 44m, W10M, R7M; 010°-W-340°-R-010°, over Bajo de Los Cabezos; 36°03′·84N 05°43′·19W.

TARIFA

Tarifa ☆ Fl (3) WR 10s 40m **W26M, R18M**; 113°-W-089°-R-113°; W twr; ***Racon C, 20M***; 36°00′·07N 05°36′·58W. 992242147.
Lado E ☆ Fl R 5s 12m 3M; 36°00′·23N 05°36′·38W.
Outer SE mole ☆ Fl G 5s 11m 5M; vis 249°-045°; G twr with statue of Virgin Mary; 36°00′·39N 05°36′·21W.
Inner S mole ☆ Fl (2) R 6s 7m 1M; 36°00′·51N 05°36′·16W.

ALGECIRAS

Pta Carnero ☆ Fl (4) WR 20s 42m, **W16M**, R13M; 018°-W -325°-R-018°; W ○ twr; 36°04′·62N 05°25′·58W.
Algeciras Fl (2) 7s; 36°06′·73N 05°24′·97W, 1·2M ESE of marina ent. 992241112 .
Darsena del Saladillo (marina) outer approach buoys: Fl(2)G 7s; 36°07′·18N 05°25′·83W. Fl (3) G 9s; 36°07′·19N 05°25′·97W. Fl (2) R 7s; 36°07′·07N 05°25′·73W.
Marina, off outer S jetty Fl (3) R 9s, 36°07′·13N 05°26′·10W.

N jetty ⚝ Fl (4) G 11s 5m 1M; 36°07'·13N 05°26'·22W.
Inner S jetty ⚝ Fl (4) R 11s 4m 1M; 36°07'·14N 05°26'·28W.

LA LÍNEA and ALCAIDESA MARINA,

Dique de Abrigo hd ⚝ Fl G 5s 8m 5M; G post, 30°09'·51N 05°22'·04W.
Alcaidesa Marina N Muelle hd ⚝ Fl (2+1)R 14·5s 5m 1M; R col G band; 36°09'·56N 05°21'·54W.
E pier N hd ⚝ Fl (3) G 9s 5m 1M; G col; 36°09'·54N 05°21'· 53W.
E pier S hd ⚝ Fl (2) R 7s 5m 1M; R col; 36°09'·51N 05°21'·51W.
Dique de Capitania hd ⚝ Fl (2) G 7s 5m 3M; G post; 36°09'·49N 05°21'·57W.

GIBRALTAR

Aero ☆ Mo (GB) R 10s 405m **30M**; 36°08'·57N 05°20'·59W.
Europa Pt ☆ Iso 10s 49m **18M**; W vis 197°-125°; W ○ twr, R band; 36°06'·58N 05°20'·69W.
A head ⚝ Fl 2s 10m 5M; *Horn 10s;* 36°08'·04N 05°21'·85W.
Queensway Quay marina, N ent ⚝ FR/FG, 36°08'·16N 05°21'·39W.
Coaling Island, SW corner ⚝ 2 FR (vert); 36°08'·19N 05°21'·46W.
B head ⚝ QR 9m 5M; 36°08'·14N 05°21'·84W.
C head ⚝ QG 10m 5M; 36°08'·54N 05°22'·04W.
D head ⚝ QR 18m 5M; 36°08'·65N 05°21'·95W.
E Head ⚝ QG 6m 5M; 36°08'·98N 05°21'·96W.
Runway threshold, both sides, VQ occas; 36°09'·01N 05°21'·59W.

MOROCCO (WEST TO EAST)

Cap Spartel ☆ Fl (4) 20s 92m **30M**; Y □ twr; *Dia (4) 90s;* 35°47'·47N 05°55'·43W.

TANGIER

Monte Dirección (Le Charf) ☆ Oc (3) WRG 12s 88m **W16M**, R12M, G11M; 140°-G-174·5°-W-200°-R-225°; 35°45'·98N 05°47'·35W.
N bkwtr ⚝ Fl (3) 12s 20m 14M; 35°47'·47N 05°47'·60W.
SE mole ⚝ Oc R 4s 7m 6M; 35°47'·29N 05°47'·87W.
Jetée des Yachts ⚝ Iso G 4s 6m 6M; 35°47'·23N 05°48'·14W.
Pta Malabata ☆ Fl 5s 77m **22M**. W □ twr; 35°48'·99N 05°44'·92W.
Basses des Almirantes ⚝ VQ; 35° 49'· 72N 5° 45'· 75W.
Ksar es Srhir ⚝ Fl (4) 12s 16m 8M; 35°50'·91N 05°33'·67W.
Pta Círes ☆ Fl (3) 12s 44m **18M**; 060°-330°; 35°54'·42N 05°28'·89W.

CEUTA (Spanish enclave)

Punta Almina ⚝ Fl (2) 10s 148m 22M; 35°53'·90N 05°16'·85W.
W pier ⚝ Fl G 5s 13m 5M; ***Racon O, 12M;*** 35°53'·75N 05°18'·68W;
E pier ⚝ Fl R 5s 13m 5M; vis 245°-210°; 35°53'·74N 05°18'·47W. 992241114.
Marina ent, S bkwtr elbow and S bkwtr head: two synchronised ⚝ Fl (4) G 11s 6/5m 1M; 35°53'·42N 05°18'·94W and 65m ESE.

9.25.4 PASSAGE INFORMATION

More passage information lies between harbours in this Area.

Bibliography: *Atlantic Spain and Portugal* (Imray/RCC/Buchanan); *SW Spain and Portugal Cruising Companion* (Fernhurst/Jens)*; W Coasts of Spain and Portugal Pilot* (Admiralty, NP 67) covers Cabo Ortegal to Gibraltar.

The Straits Handbook by Colin Thomas of Straits Sailing (☎+35051372) covers Gibraltar, Spanish ports from Chipiona to Benalmadena in the Med, Ceuta and Marina Smir in Morocco.

PORTUGUESE BORDER TO RÍO GUADALQUIVIR

(AC 93) On the Spanish bank of the Rio Guadiana **Ayamonte** has a marina, the most W'ly of 16 modern marinas in SW Andalucía; 4M to the E, **Isla Canela** W bank and **Isla Cristina** E bank of Ria de la Higuerita both have marinas. 13M further E, Rio de las Piedras requires care on entry due to shifting shoals and bar, but is a peaceful river with a marina at **El Rompido**. S of Huelva there are marinas at **Punta Umbria** and **Mazagón** (AC 73). Keep clear of commercial ships going to/from **Huelva**.

About 30M SE is the mouth of the **Río Guadalquivir** (AC 85) navigable 54M to **Sevilla**. Caution: NW of the estuary large fish havens in shoal waters extend 5M offshore. **Chipiona** marina is a good place to check the latest info for the passage to and lock times at Sevilla; and to time your departure so as to carry a fair tide and synchronise your arrival with lock and bridge opening hours.

9.25.5 SPECIAL NOTES FOR SW SPAIN

Regions/Provinces: Spain is divided into 17 autonomous regions, eg Andalucía. Most regions are sub-divided into provinces, eg in Atlantic Andalucía: Huelva, Sevilla and Cadiz. The province is shown below the name of each main port.

Language: This Almanac recognises regional differences, but in the interests of standardisation uses the spelling of Castilian Spanish where practicable.

Spanish Charts (SC): Contact Instituto Hidrográfico de la Marina, Plaza San Severiano 3, 11007 Cádiz, ☎(956) 599 414; www.armada.mde.es/ihm Or order from chart agents in Madrid, Huelva, Sevilla, Cadiz and Algeciras, also larger UK chart agents.

Standard Time in Spain is UT –1, but in Portugal it is UT.

Spanish secondary ports referenced to Lisboa: Time differences for these Spanish ports (all down to Barbate) when applied to the printed times of HW and LW for Lisboa (UT) give HW and LW times in Spanish Standard Time. Add DST, when applicable.

Telephone: To call Spain from UK dial 00-34, then the area code, followed by the ☎ number. To call UK from Spain, dial 07-44, then area code, less the initial 0, then the ☎ number.

Emergencies: ☎900 202 202 for Fire, Police and Ambulance. *Rioja Cruz* (Red Cross) operate LBs.

Public Holidays: Jan 1, 6; Good Friday; 1 May (Labour Day); June 11 (Corpus Christi); Aug 15 (Assumption); Oct 12 (National Day); Nov 1 (All Saints Day); Dec 6, 8 (Immaculate Conception) 25.

Representation: Spanish Tourist Office, 64 North Row, London W1K 7DE; ☎020 7317 2011. info.londres@tourspain.es www.spain.info

British Embassy, Paseo de la Castellana 259D, 28046 Madrid; ☎917 146 301. There are British Consuls at Malaga ☎902 109 356.

Buoyage: IALA Region A system is used. Preferred chan buoys (RGR, Fl (2+1) R and GRG, Fl (2+1) G) are quite widely used.

Documents: (See Chap 2 Cruising Formalities) Spain, although an EU member, still checks papers. This can be a time-consuming, repetitive and inescapable process. The only palliatives are courtesy, patience and good humour. Organise your papers to include:

Personal – Passports; crew list, ideally on headed paper with the yacht's rubber stamp, giving DoB, passport nos, where joined/intended departure. Certificate of Competence (Yachtmaster Offshore, ICC/HOCC etc). Radio Operator's certificate. EHIC (advised for medical treatment).

Yacht – Registration certificate, Part 1 or SSR. Proof of VAT status. Marine insurance. Ship's Radio licence. Itinerary, backed up by ship's log.

Currency is the Euro €. VAT (IVA) 21%.

Marina fees: Marinas run by or linked to the Andalucían Junta (www.eppa.es) ie all but Algeciras, charge on average €2.45/m LOA inc 21% VAT in season (1/6-30/9); low season 50% less.

Fuel: Diesel (*Gasoleo*) is of two types: *Gasoleo A* is taxed and available from marina pumps or by cans from a filling station ashore. *Gasoleo B* is untaxed and usually only available to FVs.

Travel: UK ferries from/to Santander and Bilbao.

Direct UK flights from Jerez, Sevilla, Madrid, Malaga & Gibraltar.

Internal flights via Madrid to Jerez, Sevilla and Malaga.

Buses are usually good and trains adequate, except in the more remote regions.

9.25.6 AYAMONTE

Huelva **37°12'·70N 07°24'·50W**

CHARTS AC 93; SC 440, 440A; PC 24206, 26312

TIDES

Standard Port LISBOA (⟵); ML 1·8

Times				Height (metres)			
High Water		Low Water		MHWS	MHWN	MLWN	MLWS
0500	1000	0500	1100	3·8	3·0	1·5	0·6
1700	2200	1700	2300				
Differences AYAMONTE							
+0005	+0015	+0025	+0045	–0·7	–0·6	–0·1	–0·2
RÍA DE HUELVA, BAR							
0000	*+0015*	*+0035*	*+0030*	*–0·1*	*–0·6*	*–0·1*	*–0·4*

SHELTER Good in Vila Real Marina on W bank of Rio Guadiana.

NAVIGATION WPT 37°08'·51N 07°23'·09W (No 1 SHM buoy, Q (3) G 6s) 340°/9ca to hd of W trng wall. Least depth over bar 2·0m, avoid near low water. See Vila Real de Santo Antonio for chartlet, lts and directions upriver. Sanlucar, 20M up Rio Guadiana, is accessible on the flood. Ayamonte Marina, strong cross current across narrow ent chan, ideally only enter after half flood. At night, beware unlit former fuel pontoon to port just inside ent.

LIGHTS AND MARKS High bldgs, FR lts, are 3M WNW of ent. White suspension bridge 2M inland is visible from seaward. Vila Real lt ho, ☆ Fl 6·5s 51m **26M** W ○ tr, B bands, is 1·5M S. ☆ Fl G 5s, 350m N of marina, marks ferry berths.

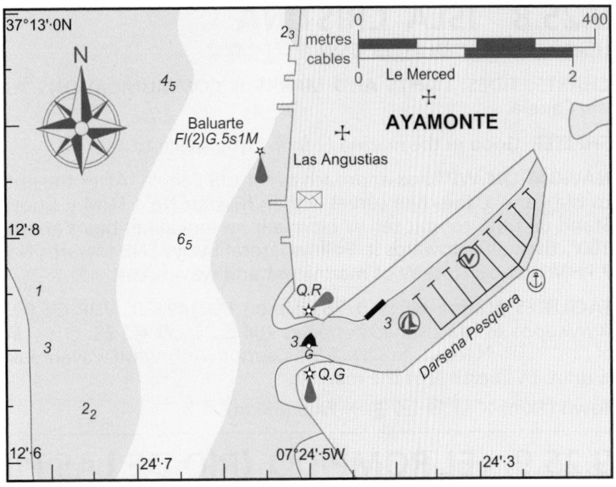

COMMUNICATIONS (Code 959). Huelva MRSC 243000; Brit Consul 902 109356; HM 471407; Marina VHF Ch 09 (H24).

FACILITIES **Marina** (0.6m-1·5m) ☎034498, mob 6001491 is W'most of 13 marinas run by Junta de Andalucía, www.eppa.es. ayamonted@eppa.es 317 inc Ⓥ €3·12 on outer 4 pontoons in 3m;

Town YC. Ferries to Vila Real de Santo António. Bus Huelva (60km); ✈ Faro (48km).

9.25.7 ISLA CANELA

Huelva **37°11'·24N 07°20'·45W**

CHARTS AC 93; SC 440, 440A

TIDES Use Differences Ayamonte

SHELTER Good in the marina (2·5m) but little room to ⚓. The appr is open to SE'lies.

NAVIGATION Isla Canela and Isla Cristina share a common outer approach into Ría de la Higuerita. Best appr at half-flood, when drying sand banks can be seen.

WPT 37°10'·51N 07°19'·46W (SWM buoy, Fl 10s, off chartlet) 000°/4ca to W mole head, where depth is 1·2m. Pick up the 312·8° ldg lts. After 7ca between trng walls, for Isla Canela marina turn 90° port between QR and QG lights.

See Isla Cristina for continuation.

LIGHTS AND MARKS Ldg lts (front Q 7m 5M; rear Fl 4s 12m 5M) aligned 312·8° between the W mole head VQ (2) R 5s 9m 4M, and the covering trng wall to stbd. The powerful lt Fl 6·5s 51m **26M** at Vila Real de Santo António is 4M to the W.

COMMUNICATIONS (Code 959) Huelva MRSC 243000; Brit Consul 902 109356; Marina VHF Ch 09.

FACILITIES **Marina** ☎4790000 www.marina-islacanela.com marina@islacanela.es 231 inc Ⓥ, €2·90, max LOA 12m, in 2.5m. (32t) (2t).

Town Infrequent bus Ayamonte (17km); ✈ Faro (65km).

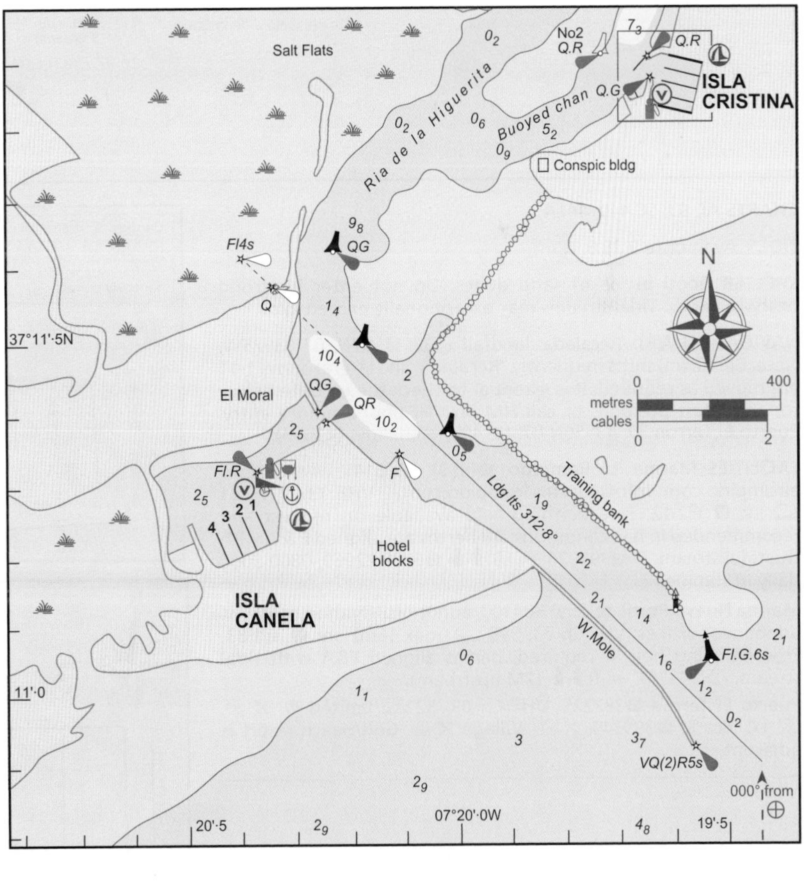

9.25.8 ISLA CRISTINA

Huelva **37°11'·88N 07°19'·65W**

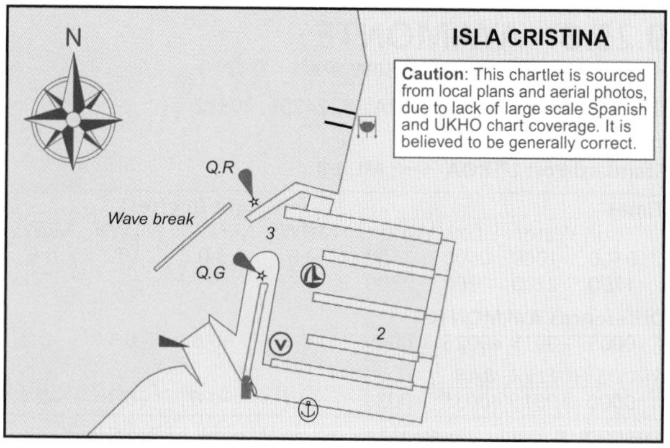
ISLA CRISTINA
Caution: This chartlet is sourced from local plans and aerial photos, due to lack of large scale Spanish and UKHO chart coverage. It is believed to be generally correct.
N
Q.R
Wave break
3
Q.G
2

CHARTS, TIDES, LIGHTS AND MARKS & COMMUNICATIONS As Isla Canela.

SHELTER Good in the marina (2·0m). Little space to ⚓.

NAVIGATION WPT and approach as for Isla Canela. After the ent to Isla Canela, the chan curves N then NE past No 1 SHM lt buoy. Stand on until conspic tall W bldg (a lt ho lookalike) bears about 100°, then alter towards it. Follow lateral buoys ENE towards No 2 PHM lt buoy, close W of marina ent and wavebreak.

FACILITIES **Marina** ☎959 077613; mob 600149130. VHF Ch 09. www.eppa.es islacristinad@eppa.es 204 inc **V** €2·23. Ice (32t) (5t). Caution: Anti-wash wavebreak is unlit. FVs berth N of the marina.

Town (1km) Ⓑ ✈ Faro (65km).

9.25.9 EL ROMPIDO (RIO DE LAS PIEDRAS)

Huelva **37°13'·00N 07°07'·72W** (Marina)

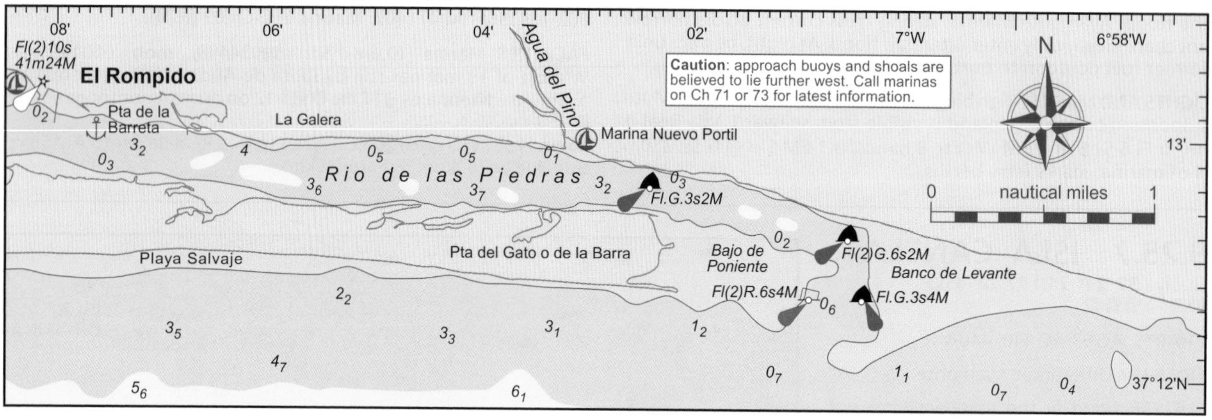
08'
06'
04'
02'
7°W
6°58'W
13'
37°12'N
Fl(2)10s 41m24M
El Rompido
Pta de la Barreta
La Galera
Agua del Pino
Marina Nuevo Portil
Caution: approach buoys and shoals are believed to lie further west. Call marinas on Ch 71 or 73 for latest information.
Rio de las Piedras
Fl.G.3s2M
0 nautical miles 1
Playa Salvaje
Pta del Gato o de la Barra
Bajo de Poniente
Fl(2)G.6s2M
Banco de Levante
Fl(2)R.6s4M
Fl.G.3s4M
N

CHARTS AC 93; SC 440, 441A

TIDES Ayamonte 9.25.6.

SHELTER Good in lee of sand dunes. Do not enter in strong onshore winds. Tidal streams may exceptionally exceed 2kn.

NAVIGATION WPT: 'Recalada' landfall 37°11'·67N 07°03'·25W. Note: Bar (0·4m) shifts frequently, 'Recalada' and lateral buoys 1-11 are moved as required. It is essential to check the website below for the latest positions or call HM on VHF/phone before entry. Puerto El Terron 37°13'·50N 07°10'·49W is shallow (<1·2m).

FACILITIES **Marina El Rompido** ☎(959) 399614. www.puertoelrompido.com info@puertoelrompido.com. VHF Ch 71. 331 inc **V** €2·12. Free berthing help available on request and recommended in bad conditions. All berths are aligned F & A with the tidal stream. ☎399026, ☎6209 22969, 0800-2000 daily in summer.

Marina Nuevo Portil, ☎(359) 504100, adnnportil@yahoo.es www.adnneuvoportil.es; VHF Ch 73, 395 (max 16m) inc **V**, €1·83. Free berthing help if required, berths aligned F&A with tidal stream. wi-fi (2M upstream).

Puerto El Terron ☎382225. VHF Ch 09. 32 limited **V**. **YC**, 6ca E, ☎399349. **Village**. Golf/beach resort is adjacent.

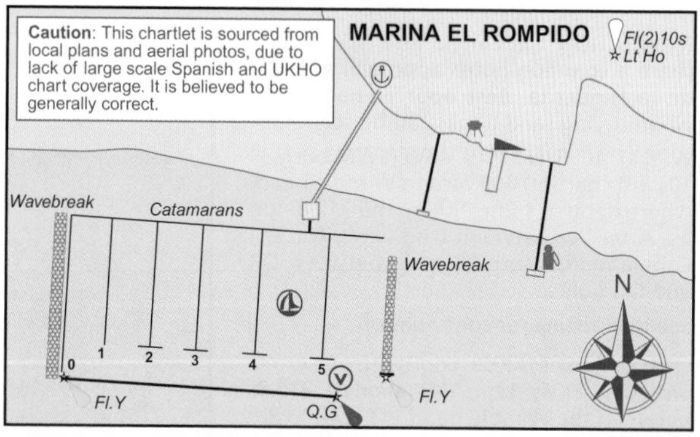
Caution: This chartlet is sourced from local plans and aerial photos, due to lack of large scale Spanish and UKHO chart coverage. It is believed to be generally correct.
MARINA EL ROMPIDO
Fl(2)10s Lt Ho
Wavebreak
Catamarans
Wavebreak
0
1
2
3
4
5
Fl.Y
Q.G
Fl.Y
N

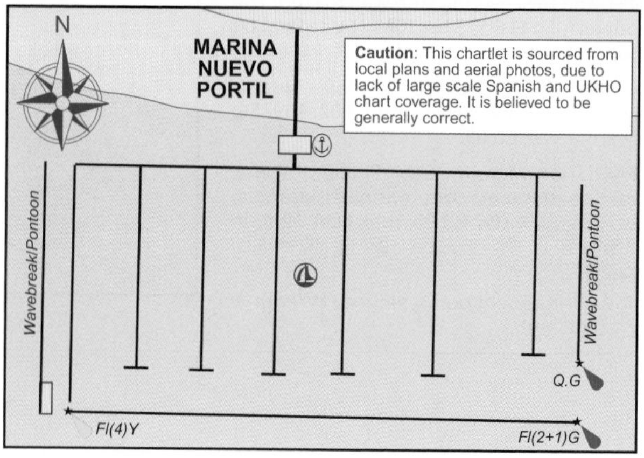
N
MARINA NUEVO PORTIL
Caution: This chartlet is sourced from local plans and aerial photos, due to lack of large scale Spanish and UKHO chart coverage. It is believed to be generally correct.
Wavebreak/Pontoon
Wavebreak/Pontoon
Q.G
Fl(4)Y
Fl(2+1)G

9.25.10 PUNTA UMBRIA

Huelva **37°10′·89N 06°57′·48W**

CHARTS As for Mazagón. TIDES As for Special Notes. Tidal streams are strong and arrival near slack water will assist berthing.

SHELTER Good within wavebreak at Punta Umbria Marina.

NAVIGATION WPT 37°09′·53N 06°57′·18W Punta Umbria, LFl10s 5M, then NE'wards to ent chan, (lateral buoys, moved frequently). 5M SSE of ent a tanker discharge mooring Fl (4)Y is centred in a 0.5M prohib area, the pipeline ashore marked by 3 Y SPM, Fl (4) Y and 2 Y SPM, QY.

LIGHTS AND MARKS See Lights, buoys and waypoints.

COMMUNICATIONS Marina VHF Ch 06.

FACILITIES from seaward: **Real Club Maritimo** ☎(959) 311899, www.remtpu.com remtpu@remtpu.com 200+60 Ⓥ. **Punta Umbria Marina** ☎314304. www.eppa.es puntaumbriad@eppa.es 267 inc Ⓥ in 6m, max LOA 12m, €2·06. **Punta Umbria RCN Marina** is 5ca further upriver. Privately run, limited space for Ⓥ but more peaceful than downstream. **Town**

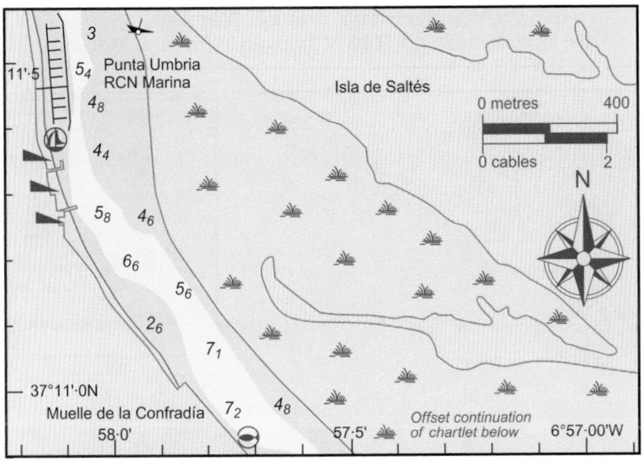

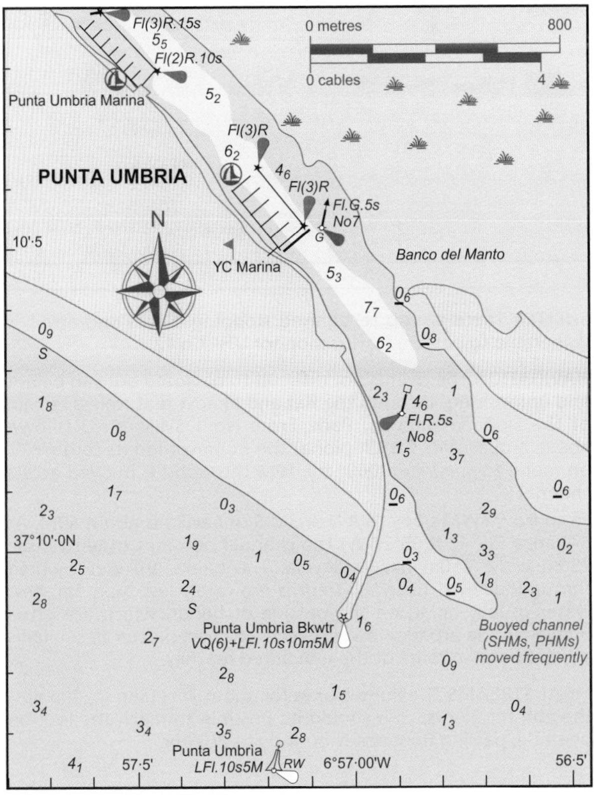

9.25.11 MAZAGÓN

Huelva **37°07′·92N 06°50′·13W** (Marina ent)

CHARTS AC 91, 93, 73; SC 441, 4411, 4413; SHOM 6862, 7300

TIDES See Ayamonte, 9.25.6, Ría de Huelva, Bar; ML 1.8.

SHELTER Good in marina (overleaf) entered hdg ESE downriver.

NAVIGATION WPT 37°05′·55N 06°49′·11W, abm WCM buoy, Q (9) 15s (off chartlet) 339°/2·5M to marina. After the first pair of chan buoys (off chartlet) the straightforward appr is sheltered by a 7M long bkwtr.

At No 7 SHM buoy turn stbd to the marina ent; the deep, well lit, buoyed 339·2° channel diverges WNW into Huelva's industrial complex. Keep clear of large ships.

About 5M W of the WPT an oil pipe line runs N to a refinery. It is marked by an SBM and 3 SPM buoys, all Fl (4) Y 20s; keep 500m clear. ⚓ prohib within 500m either side of the line of buoys.

LIGHTS AND MARKS Dir lt 339·2° (off chartlet); W twr. The bkwtr hd has a W twr, R band. Picacho lt ho, W twr with R corners/R roofed bldg, is 5ca NE of marina (off chartlet). See Lights, buoys and waypoints.

COMMUNICATIONS (Code 959) MRCC (956) 684740; Brit Consul Malaga 902 109356; Huelva Port VHF Ch 06, 11, 12, **14;** Marina VHF Ch 09.

FACILITIES in large, modern **Marina** (4m): ☎536251. mazagon@eppa.es 647 incⓋ €2·06. Ice YC (32t). Huelva (24km); ✈ Sevilla (130km).

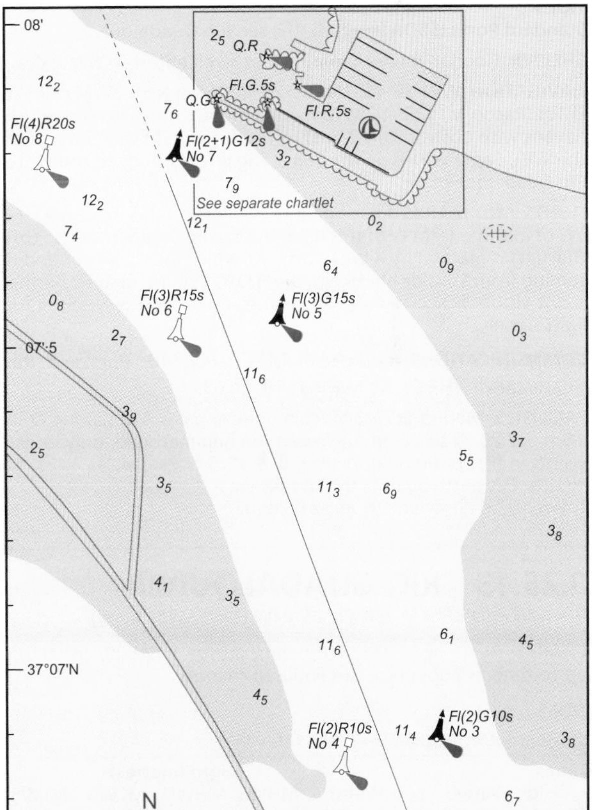

MAZAGÓN MARINA

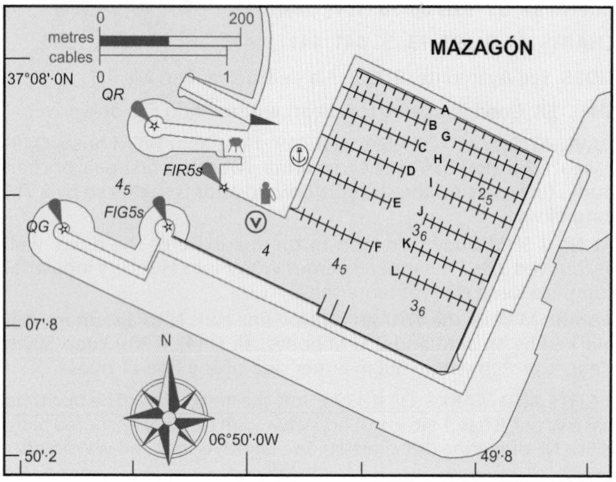

CHIPIONA TO CAPE TRAFALGAR

Around **Cadiz Bay** (AC 86, 88) there are marinas at **Rota**, **Puerto Sherry**, **Santa Maria** and two in the hbr of Cádiz itself. S of Cádiz keep about 4M offshore to clear inshore banks. **Sancti-Petri** marina lies on a remote and interesting river with a slightly tricky approach. **Puerto de Conil**, a small fishing hbr 7M SSE of Sancti-Petri, is just S of Cabo Roche. Local boats only and few facilities except water and diesel, but in winds W-N-E, a handy passage anchorage, 3-4m, just E of hbr ent off a sandy beach.

Artificial reefs, reducing charted depths by approx 2·5m, are common from Cadiz to C. Trafalgar; see AC 93 & 142. Cabo Trafalgar may be rounded within 100m of the lt ho, inshore of a tidal race, or about 4M off to clear shoals lying from SW to NW of the cape. Plans for a wind farm (up to 500 turbines) about 2·5M off Cabo Trafalgar remain stalled in the face of strong opposition from local fishermen.

Tunny nets set up to 7M offshore, and usually marked by cardinal lt buoys, include:

- Close off Barbate hbr, extending 2·7M S, Mar–Aug.
- Off Zahara beach (5M SE of Barbate) extending 1·7M SW to two WCM and one SCM lt buoys, Mar–Sep.
- 1M NW of Tarifa, to 1M SW, buoyed as Zahara, Mar–Jul.

9.25.12 CHIPIONA

Cádiz **36°44'·96N 06°25'·69W** (W bkwtr hd)

CHARTS AC 85; SC 4421, 4422 (Sheets 2 and 3)

TIDES
Standard Port LISBOA (⟵); ML 1·9; see Rio Guadalquivir.

SHELTER Good in modern marina, but swell enters in NW gales.

NAVIGATION WPT 36°45'·75N 06°26'·82W, adj No 1 SWM buoy, L Fl 10s (Racon M) 125°/1·2M to marina ent. Caution: extensive fish havens with obstructions 2·5m high lie from 3·5M to 7·5M NW of the WPT. Same WPT is on the 068·9° ldg line for buoyed chan into Río Guadalquivir.

LIGHTS AND MARKS Chipiona (Pta del Perro) lt ho is conspic 1M SW of marina. 1·7M W of this lt ho, the drying Bajo Salmedina (off chartlet) is marked by a WCM bcn twr which must be rounded if coming from S. Inside hbr bkwtr, the Fl (3) G 9s light, near FV berths, is not visible from seaward. See Lights, buoys and waypoints for light details.

COMMUNICATIONS (Code 956) MRCC 684740; Port and Río Guadalquivir VHF Ch 12; Marina VHF Ch 09.

FACILITIES **Marina** ☎373844, chipiona@eppa.es 412 berths inc Ⓥ in 3·5m, €2.20. Ⓥ berth on fuel/reception hammerhead; only larger yachts in first basin on port side. (32t). FVs berth against the NW bkwtr.
Town Ⓑ and ✈ Jerez (32km).

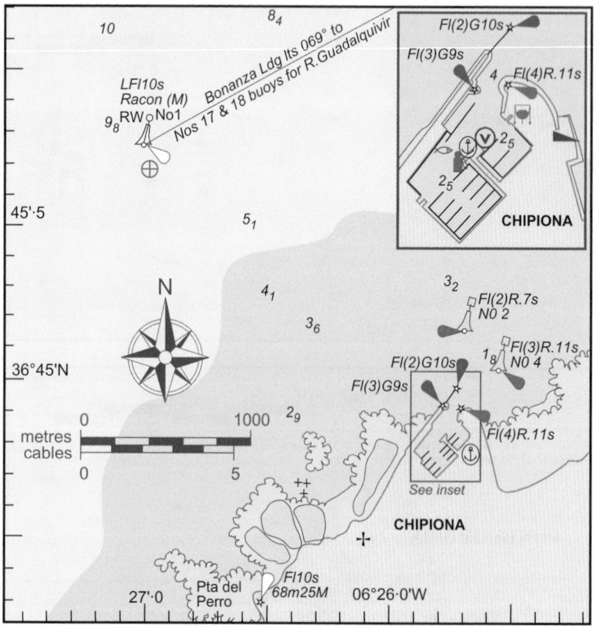

9.25.13 RÍO GUADALQUIVIR

Huelva/Cádiz **36°45'·73N 06°27'·03W** (No 1 SWM buoy)

CHARTS AC 85 or SC 4422 (18 sheets, mostly 1:12,500) corrected up-to-date as buoys/bcns are liable to change.

TIDES

Standard Port LISBOA (⟵); ML 1·9

Times				Height (metres)			
High Water		Low Water		MHWS	MHWN	MLWN	MLWS
0500	1000	0500	1100	3·8	3·0	1·5	0·6
1700	2200	1700	2300				
Differences RÍO GUADALQUIVIR, BAR (36°45'N 06°26'W)							
–0005	+0005	+0020	+0030	–0·7	–0·5	–0·2	–0·1
BONANZA (36°48'N 06°20'W)							
+0025	+0040	+0100	+0120	–1·0	–0·9	–0·7	–0·3
CORTA DE LOS JERONIMOS (37° 08'N 06°05'W, 16M S of Sevilla)							
+0210	+0230	+0255	+0345	–1·2	–0·9	–0·5	–0·1
SEVILLA							
+0400	+0430	+0510	+0545	–1·8	–1·3	–0·7	–0·2

SHELTER There are no recognised stopping places and any ⚓ is vulnerable to passing traffic; monitor VHF Ch 12.

NAVIGATION The river is not difficult to navigate but can be hot and uninspiring, through the flat and almost featureless terrain of the Doñana National Park. From No 1 SWM buoy (shown above and as WPT for Chipiona) the Bonanza ldg lts (both Y □, on metal towers) lead 069° for 10M through lit, buoyed access channel.

From No 1 SWM buoy to a lock 3M S of Sevilla is about 49M. At Bonanza (36°48'N 06°20'W) the channel becomes truly riverine, 750m wide; 250m nearer Sevilla. The banks are well marked throughout by lt beacons. Depths are rarely less than 5m, best water usually being on the outside of bends, which are often buoyed in the broader lower reaches. A chart plotter or similar is a great boon in some of the unmarked reaches.

TIDAL STREAMS The flood makes for about 7hrs (3kn sp, 1kn nps) the ebb for 5½hrs; so it should be possible to reach the lock on one tide, passing Bonanza N-bound at LW –½hr.

9.25.14 SEVILLA

Sevilla **37°19'·86N 05°59'·74W** (Lock) ❁❁❁◊◊◊✿✿✿

CHARTS & TIDES AC 85; SC 4422 (sheets 17/18). ML Sevilla 1·3M

SHELTER Good; safe to over-winter. Very hot 40°C+ in summer.

NAVIGATION A new lock, S of Pta del Verde, ☎(954) 454196, opens 0100, 0400, 0700, 0900, 1100, 1300, 1600, 1900 & 2100LT daily; secure to ladders or diagonal rubber strips.

Delicias bridge (10·1m; ☎ 954) 247630) lifts Mon, Wed, Fri 2200; Sat/Sun/Hols 2000. 1hr before ETA request passage Ch 12. R lts at lock & bridge = no go; Lock, Intens Fl W = enter; Bridge, G = pass.

COMMUNICATIONS (Codes 954, 955) Brit Consul 902 109 356; Lock, Port, Delicias bridge VHF Ch 12; marinas Ch 09.

FACILITIES **Gelves** 37°20'·43N 06°01'·39W on the river, ie **not** accessed via the lock, therefore tidal; may silt. Overhead cables (16·5m) downriver; approx 3M from the city centre. ☎(955) 761212. www.puertogelves.com 133+Ⓥ €0.93, in about 3m, waiting pontoon. ✕ 🛒 ⛽ 🔧 (25t).

Sun Sails Marina 37°19'·90N 05°59'·49W, 300m E of the old lock almost below HT cables; a long pontoon in a quiet creek 3M from city; useful stop if waiting to transit Delicias bridge 2M N. ☎(954) 184848 www.sunsails.es. 150 ⊆ inc Ⓥ in 6m, ⛽ 🔧.

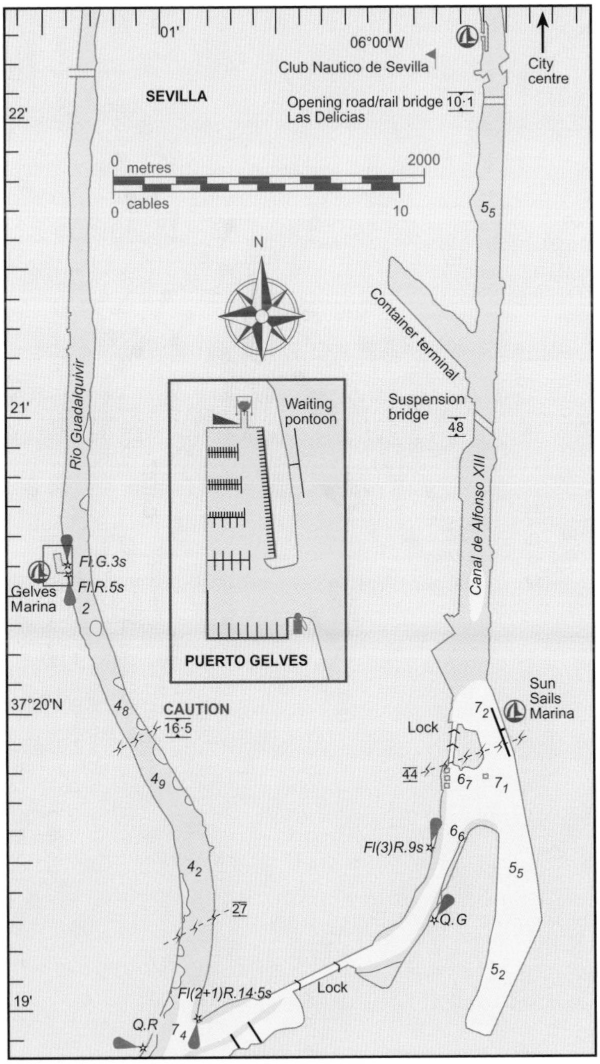

Club Náutico de Sevilla 37°22'·18N 05°59'·60W, excellent facilities close to city centre; also possible ⊆ on E quay. ☎(954)454777. www.nauticosevilla.com 100+Ⓥ in 3m; pre-book €0.52/m²/day. ✕ Ice. **City** All amenities, ⇌ ✈ 10km.

9.25.15 BAY OF CÁDIZ

Cádiz **36°33'·91N 06°19'·88W** (SWM buoy) ❁❁❁◊◊◊✿✿✿

CHARTS AC 93, 86, 88; SC 443, 443A, 443B, 4430, 4431, 4437

TIDES

Standard Port LISBOA (⟵); ML 1·8

Times				Height (metres)			
High Water		Low Water		MHWS	MHWN	MLWN	MLWS
0500	1000	0500	1100	3·8	3·0	1·5	0·5
1700	2200	1700	2300				
Differences ROTA							
–0010	+0010	+0025	+0015	–0·7	–0·7	–0·4	–0·1
PUERTO DE SANTA MARIA							
+0006	+0006	+0027	+0027	–0·6	–0·5	–0·4	–0·1
PUERTO CÁDIZ							
0000	*+0020*	*+0040*	*+0025*	*–0·5*	*–0·6*	*–0·3*	*0·0*

SHELTER is good in the 4 marinas listed below, clockwise from N.

NAVIGATION **Rota** WPT 36°35'·97N 06°21'·01W, 000°/9ca to marina ent. Airfield lt (Al Fl WG 9s) and conspic water tank bear 004°/2·1M from WPT. From W/NW keep 1·5M offshore to clear shoals. Naval vessels may be at ⚓ S of Rota Naval base. Significant shoaling reported; keep to stbd (N bkwtr) side of ent chan.

Puerto Sherry WPT 36°33'·98N 06°15'·22W, 000°/7ca to marina entrance. Modern bldgs around the marina are conspic.

Puerto de Santa Maria same WPT as P. Sherry, follow the W sector of Dir Fl WRG 6s to marina in canalised Rio Guadalete, dredged 4·5m. Ldg lts 040°: front, QG; rear Iso G 4s. From W, the N Chan trends ESE, inshore of shoals toward both marinas.

Puerto América (at N tip of Cádiz). WPT 36°32'·75N 06°16'·36W, 238°/0·5M to marina ent passing close S of Dique de San Felipe head. From S, keep to seaward of extensive shoals N & W of Cádiz. The S Chan (Canal del Sur) is not navigable for draft >2·5m. The shore is low-lying, but next to the marina a W bldg on Dique de San Felipe is conspic.

LIGHTS AND MARKS Lts/buoys as chartlets and Lights, buoys and waypoints. Conspic daymarks: Rota lt ho 33m, W twr/R band, at marina. Puerto Sherry, W bkwtr hd ○ twr. Cádiz city, golden-domed cathedral and radio twr (113m) close SE. Further SSE: Two power cable pylons (155m) dockyard cranes and two long bridges to mainland, vertical clearance 66m and 17.9m.

COMMUNICATIONS (Code 956) Cádiz Trafico VHF Ch **74;** ⊜ & Met via marinas (see below); Brit Consul 902 109 356; Port HM 224011; Marinas VHF Ch 09.

FACILITIES **Rota Marina** ☎840069, rota@eppa.es 509 ⊆ inc Ⓥ in 4·5m, €2.06. 🔧 (32t) (5t).

Puerto Sherry ☎870103. www.puertosherry.com 753 ⊆ incⓋ €2.31; 3·0-4·5m. (50t) 🔧 Ⓔ ✕ YC ☎ 858751. Arrivals berth as chartlet.

Puerto de Santa Maria (RCN) ☎852527. rcnpuerto@oNo com www.rcnpsm.com Very pleasant Real Club Náutico has 250 ⊆ + a few Ⓥ berths in 3·0-8·0m; €2.98, pre-booking is not essential. 10 hammerhead pontoons (A-J) on NW bank plus two mid-stream pontoons. 🔧 (5t) (25t) ✕. FVs berth upriver. Ferry to Cádiz.

Puerto América ☎223666. puertoamerica@eppa.es 253 ⊆ inc Ⓥ in 7·5m, €2·06. 🔧 (10t).

Real Club Náutico de Cádiz A private basin close SW of Puerto America. ☎213262. www.cherrytel.com 160 ⊆ in 3m. Ⓥ berths unlikely. good ✕.

Cadiz City All amenities, ⇌; ✈ Jerez (25km). Spanish Hydrographic Office (IHM) is at 36°31'·38N 06°17'·04W (1·5M from Puerto America): Plaza San Severiano 3, 11007 Cádiz; ☎599414. www.armada.mde.es/ihm

BAY OF CÁDIZ including marinas at: ROTA, PUERTO SHERRY, PUERTO DE SANTA MARIA and PUERTO AMERICA

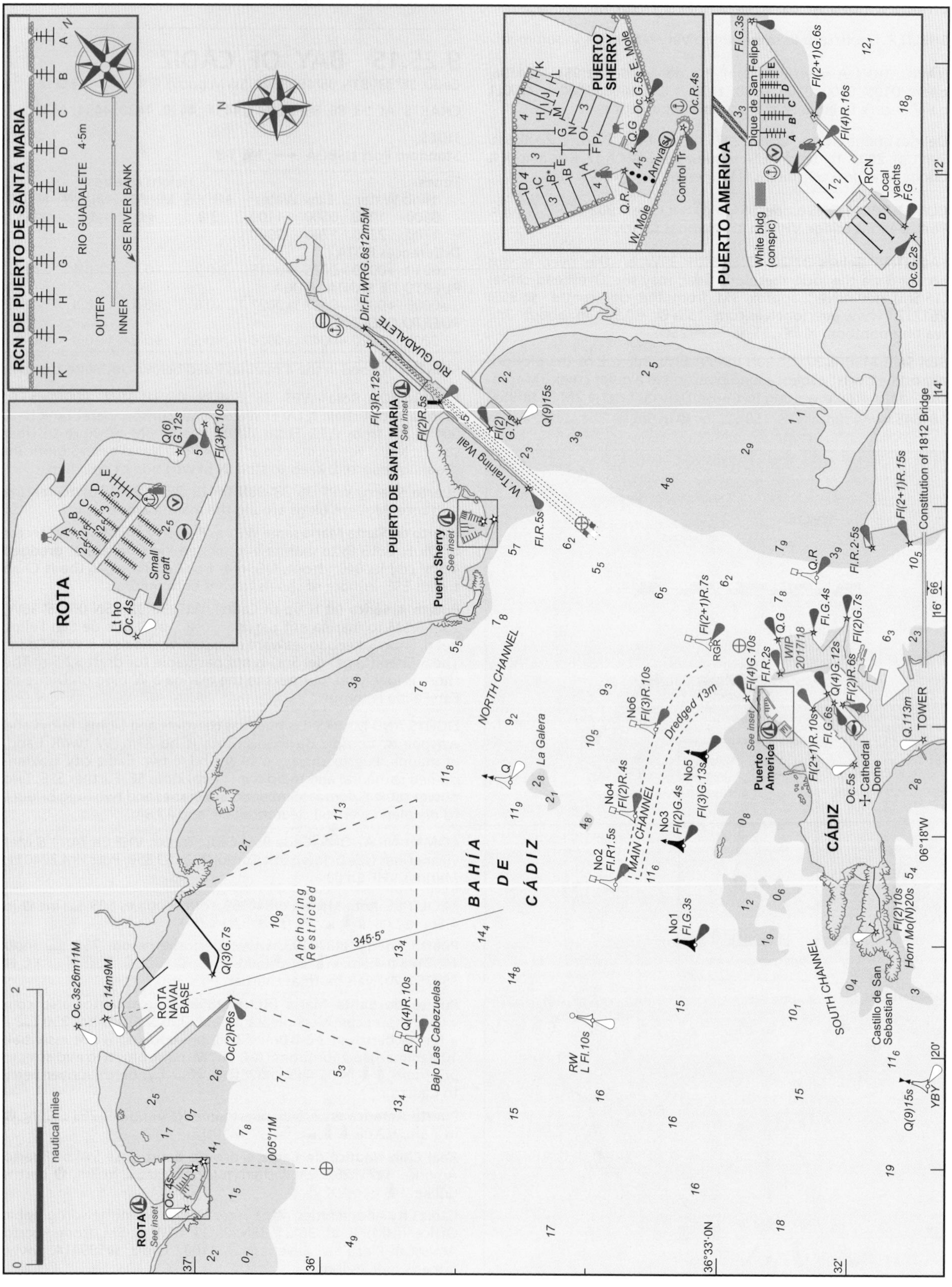
RCN DE PUERTO DE SANTA MARIA
OUTER
INNER
RIO GUADALETE 4·5m
SE RIVER BANK
ROTA
Lt ho Oc.4s
Small craft
Q(6) G.12s
Fl(3)R.10s
PUERTO SHERRY
Oc.G.5s E. Mole
Oc.R.4s
Control Tr
W. Mole
Arrivals
Q.R
Q.G
PUERTO AMERICA
White bldg (conspic)
Dique de San Felipe
Fl.G.3s
Fl(2+1)G.6s
Fl(4)R.16s
RCN
Local yachts
F.G
Oc.G.2s
Dir.Fl.WRG.6s12m5M
RIO GUADALETE
Fl(3)R.12s
Fl(2)R.5s
PUERTO DE SANTA MARIA
See inset
W. Training Wall
Fl(2) G.15
Q(9)15s
Fl.R.5s
Puerto Sherry
See inset
NORTH CHANNEL
Fl(2+1)R.7s
RGR
Q.R
Fl.R.2·5s
Fl(2+1)R.15s
Constitution of 1812 Bridge
Q.G
WIP 2017/18
Fl.G.4s
Fl(2)G.7s
Fl(4)G.10s
Fl.R.2s
Q(4)G.12s
Fl(2)R.6s
Puerto America
See inset
Fl(2+1)R.10s
Fl.G.6s
Q.113m TOWER
Cathedral Dome
Oc.5s
CÁDIZ
No6 Fl(3)R.10s
Dredged 13m
No5 Fl(3)G.13s
La Galera
Q
No4 Fl(2)R.4s
MAIN CHANNEL
No3 Fl(2)G.4s
No2 Fl.R1.5s
No1 Fl.G.3s
BAHÍA DE CÁDIZ
Anchoring Restricted
345·5°
Q(3)G.7s
ROTA NAVAL BASE
Oc.3s26m11M
Q.14m9M
Oc(2)R6s
R Q(4)R.10s
Bajo Las Cabezuelas
RW L Fl.10s
SOUTH CHANNEL
Castillo de San Sebastian
Fl(2)10s Horn Mo(N)20s
Q(9)15s
YBY
005°1M
ROTA See inset
Oc.4s
nautical miles
36°33'·0N
06°18'W
N

9.25.16 SANCTI-PETRI

Cádiz **36°23′·80N 06°12′·55W**

CHARTS AC 93; SC 443B, 4438

TIDES Interpolate between differences Puerto Cádiz and Cabo Trafalgar (Barbate); ML No data

SHELTER Good, except with swell and in S'lies. ⚓ or moor in stream, W of marina.

NAVIGATION WPT 36°22′·32N 06°13′·15W 050°/5ca to intercept 346·5° ldg line which leads between 4 lateral lt beacons, R/G with topmarks. From the 2nd pair of beacons track onto the 346·5° ldg line for 6ca to the gateway formed by the last pair of beacons (Fl R/G 5s 7m 2M). A night appr is not advised first-time.

Best appr at half-flood in fair vis; least charted depth 2·2m, but silting occurs. Sp ebb can be >4kn. Swell and/or strong S'lies render the appr dangerous. El Arrecife, a long drying reef, and other shoals prevent a direct appr from W/NW. 9M SSE, large tunny nets (N, S and W cardinal bys) may be encountered 2-4M SW of the beach resort town of Conil.

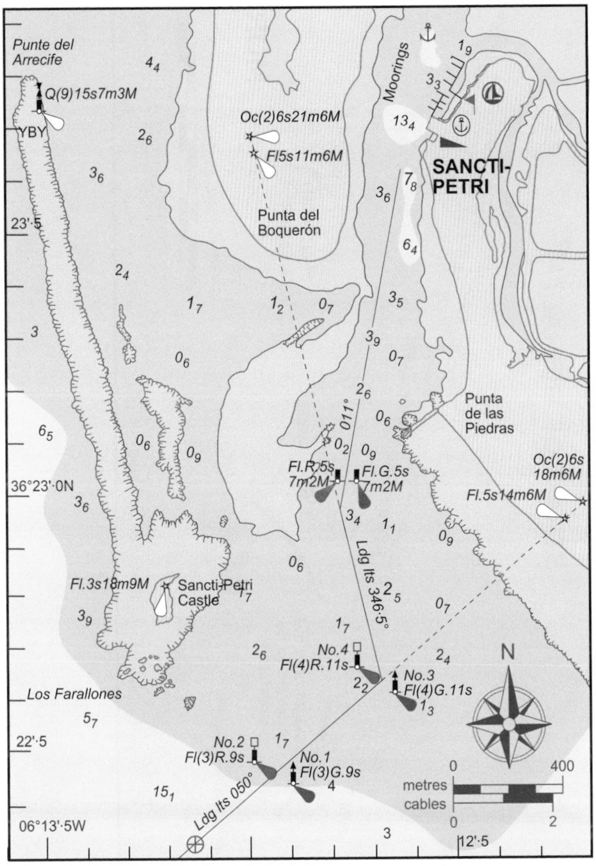

LIGHTS AND MARKS See chartlet and Lights, buoys and waypoints. The castle's 16m square twr, Fl 3s, is conspic. 050° and 346·5° ldg marks are hard-to-see lattice twrs. 4 lateral beacons define the 050° ldg line.

COMMUNICATIONS (Code 956) MRCC ☎684740; Brit Consul 902 109356; Marina *Puerto Sancti-Petri VHF* Ch 09.

FACILITIES **Marina** ☎496169. sanctipetri@eppa.es Arrival pontoon in front of marina office, beware tidal stream over 3kn. 90 in 5m, inc 2 Ⓥ on pontoons in 2–5m, €3·20; see HM. ⚓s €1.56. limited and in season. **Club Náutico**.

Village Few facilities in abandoned 'ghost town' at mouth of sandy, peaceful lagoon; ⇌ San Fernando (18km); ✈ Jerez (50km).

9.25.17 BARBATE

Cádiz **36°10′·79N 05°55′·54W**

CHARTS AC 91, 142; SC 444, 4441

TIDES

Standard Port LISBOA (⟵); ML 1·2

Times				Height (metres)			
High Water		Low Water		MHWS	MHWN	MLWN	MLWS
0500	1000	0500	1100	3·8	3·0	1·5	0·5
1700	2200	1700	2300				
Differences CABO TRAFALGAR							
−0003	−0003	+0026	+0026	−1·4	−1·2	−0·6	−0·1
RIO BARBATE							
+0016	+0016	+0045	+0045	−1·9	−1·6	−0·5	+0·1
PUNTA CAMARINAL (36°05′N 05°48′W)							
−0007	−0007	+0013	+0013	−1·7	−1·5	−0·7	−0·2

SHELTER Good. FVs berth in the large outer basin.

NAVIGATION WPT 36°10′·81N 05°55′·38W, 270°/200m to abeam SW mole hd. From the W there is room to enter between the SW mole hd and the NCM lt buoy (see below) but do not wander S of the buoy, especially at night. From the SE keep 2M offshore to avoid tunny nets NW of Cabo Plata (36°06′·15N 05°49′·50W).

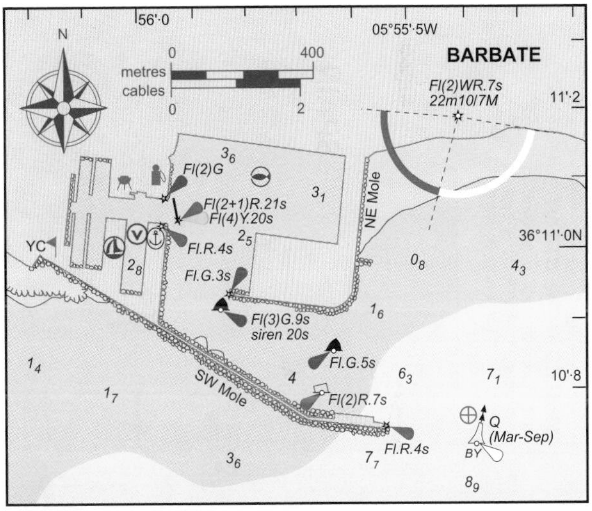

Near the WPT a NCM lt buoy marks the apex of a triangular tunny net, which extends 2·7M S and is marked by 2 SCM lt buoys at its base, an ECM lt buoy on its E side and a WCM lt buoy near its centre; see chartlet overleaf, Lights, buoys and waypoints and AC 142. A guard vessel, showing ●● (vert) and listening Ch 70, may be on station. Tunny nets, Mar-Sep, are a real hazard, especially at night. Nets may be laid E of Pta Camarinal and NW of Tarifa.

LIGHTS AND MARKS Barbate lt ho, Fl (2) WR 7s, W twr + R bands, is 4ca N of hbr ent, on edge of town. Other lights as chartlet and Lights, buoys and waypoints. Orange sodium lts in the hbr make navigational lts hard to discern.

COMMUNICATIONS (Code 956) MRCC ☎684740; Barbate is at W end of Gibraltar Strait VTS, monitor *Tarifa Traffic* VHF Ch 10 on passage; Brit Consul 902 109356; Marina VHF Ch 09.

FACILITIES

Marina ☎431907. barbated@eppa.es in the 3 inner basins (2·8m). A movable anti-pollution boom lies E of the marina ent; its SSE end is lit Fl (4) Y 20s 1M. 314 inc Ⓥ in 3m, €1·93. Ice (45t). **Club Náutico** ☎433905.

Town is about 2M away, although is closer; Ⓑ. Bus to Cádiz (61km). ✈ Jerez, Gibraltar or Malaga.

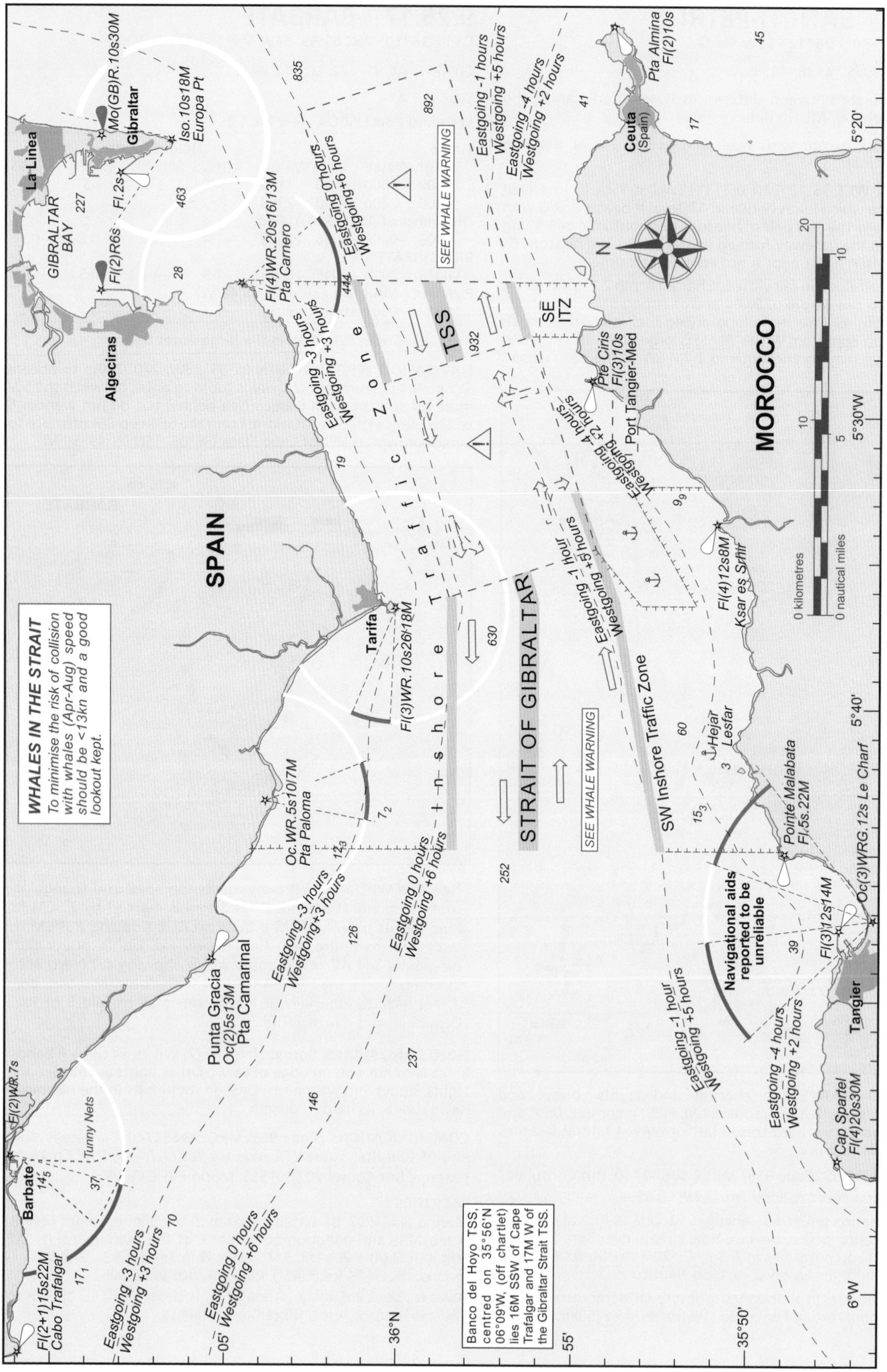
WHALES IN THE STRAIT
To minimise the risk of collision with whales (Apr-Aug) speed should be <13kn and a good lookout kept.
SPAIN
MOROCCO
STRAIT OF GIBRALTAR
GIBRALTAR BAY
La Linea
Gibraltar
Algeciras
Tarifa
Barbate
Ceuta (Spain)
Tangier
Inshore Traffic Zone
TSS
SE ITZ
SW Inshore Traffic Zone
SEE WHALE WARNING
SEE WHALE WARNING
Banco del Hoyo TSS, centred on 35°56'N 06°09'W, (off chartlet) lies 16M SSW of Cape Trafalgar and 17M W of the Gibraltar Strait TSS.
Navigational aids reported to be unreliable
Fl(2+1)15s22M Cabo Trafalgar
Fl(2)WR.7s
Tunny Nets
Punta Gracia Oc(2)5s13M Pta Camarinal
Oc.WR.5s10/7M Pta Paloma
Fl(3)WR.10s26/18M
Fl(4)WR.20s16/13M Pta Carnero
Fl(2)R6s
Fl.2s
Mo(GB)R.10s30M
Iso.10s18M Europa Pt
Pta Almina Fl(2)10s
Pte Ciris Fl(3)10s
Port Tangier-Med
Fl(4)12s8M Ksar es Srhir
Hejar Lesfar
Pointe Malabata Fl.5s.22M
Oc(3)WRG.12s Le Charf
Fl(3)12s14M
Cap Spartel Fl(4)20s30M
Eastgoing -3 hours Westgoing +3 hours
Eastgoing 0 hours Westgoing +6 hours
Eastgoing -1 hours Westgoing +5 hours
Eastgoing -4 hours Westgoing +2 hours
Eastgoing -1 hour Westgoing +5 hours
Eastgoing -4 hours Westgoing +2 hours
0 kilometres 10 20
0 nautical miles 5 10
N
36°N
55'
35°50'
05'
6°W
5°40'
5°30'W
5°20'

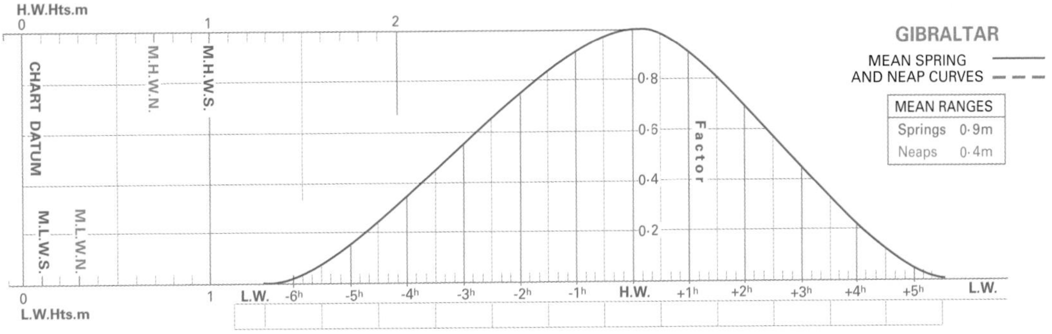

STRAIT OF GIBRALTAR

▶*Tidal streams: Near the middle of the Strait the stream sets east from HW Gib and west from HWG –6. Closer inshore, streams start progressively earlier as shown on the chartlet opposite. To find when (approx) the tidal stream turns, apply the time intervals on the pecked lines to the time of HW Gib. Max rates, about 3kn in both directions, are usually found close inshore off headlands, decreasing offshore to <1·5kn.*◀

A surface current, as distinct from a tidal stream, always flows east in the centre of the Strait reaching about 2kn at the eastern end. Its speed decreases from the centre of the Strait towards the shore where the tidal stream influence increases.

Surface flow is the combined effect of tidal streams and the constant surface current into the Med. The resultant max surface flow is about 2kn W-going and 5kn E-going (further influenced by recent E or W winds). W-bound yachts should hug the Spanish coast.

Tidal races on the Spanish side form: off Cape Trafalgar, usually up to 2M SW, but 5-12M in heavy weather; near Bajo de Los Cabezos (2-4M S of Pta Paloma); and NW of **Tarifa**. The position and violence of these races depends on wind (especially over tide) springs/neaps and the state of the tide. For more information, see *W Coasts of Spain and Portugal* Pilot.

TSS is aligned 090°/270° and 073°/253°s in mid-strait. Yachts bound to/from **Gibraltar** usually use the northern ITZ. Traffic from/to the Moroccan port of Tangier-Med joins/leaves the TSS north of Punta Ciris.

Tarifa VTS, c/s *Tarifa Trafico* Ch **10**, 16, 67 gives radar surveillance on request and offers a reporting system (voluntary for yachts) between 05°58′W and 05°15′W. MSI is broadcast routinely and on request in Spanish and English Ch 67.

9.25.18 TARIFA

Cádiz **36°00′·35N 05°36′·26W** (Outer hbr)

CHARTS AC 142; SC 445, 445B, 4450; SHOM 1619, 7042

TIDES See Gibraltar for differences.

SHELTER A bolt-hole in bad conditions. In W'lies ⚓ off hbr ent in 5m. In a *levanter* ⚓ NW of the causeway as on the chartlet.

NAVIGATION WPT 36°00′·07N 05°35′·91W, 315°/4ca to hbr ent. S of Tarifa lt the ITZ is only 1·5M wide. A SCM lt buoy, 1M NNW of Tarifa lt, marks a tunny net (Mar-Jul) extending WNW to 2 WCM lt buoys thence to shore; care needed if approaching the NW ⚓.

LIGHTS AND MARKS See chartlet and Lts, buoys and waypoints.

COMMUNICATIONS HM 956 585400; no port VHF. See Passage information above for Tarifa VTS.

FACILITIES Only ⛽. No specific berths for yachts; space on the dog-legged SE mole, clear of ferries, may be possible.

Inner basin: Ferries berth at the terminal in the NE corner and on S side. FVs on the S and W sides; *Guardia Civil* vessels and small naval craft use pens on N side.

Town ✕ ⊠ Ⓑ ⇌ ✈ Jerez, Gibraltar, Malaga.

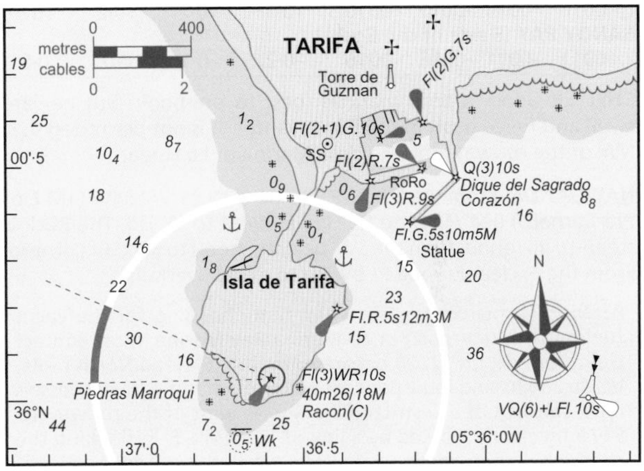

9.25.19 ALGECIRAS

Cádiz **36°07′·12N 05°26′·16W** (Marina ent)

CHARTS AC 3578, 142, 1448, 1455; SC 445, 445A, 4451, 4452

TIDES

Standard Port GIBRALTAR (⟶); ML 0·66; differences overleaf.

SHELTER Good in marina, except perhaps in strong SE'lies.

NAVIGATION WPT 36°06′·73N 05°24′·97W (Algeciras Isolated Danger Mark, Fl (2) 7s, off chartlet) 295°/0·97M to first appr buoys. From S, keep 5ca off Pta de San García and beware drying reefs S of hbr ent. From N/E, beware big ships at ⚓, high-speed ferries.

LIGHTS AND MARKS The Hbr Control twr is conspic by day, close WNW of the marina.

COMMUNICATIONS (Code 956) MRCC 684740; Brit Consul 902 109356; HM 572620, VHF Ch 09, 12; Port Authority 585400; Marina VHF Ch 09 16.

FACILITIES Marina/Real Club Náutico de Algeciras ☎600666; info@realclubnauticoalgeciras.es www.realclubnauticoalgeciras.es Max LOA 16m. (25t).

Town ✕ ⊠ Ⓑ ⇌ ✈ Jerez, Gibraltar, Malaga.

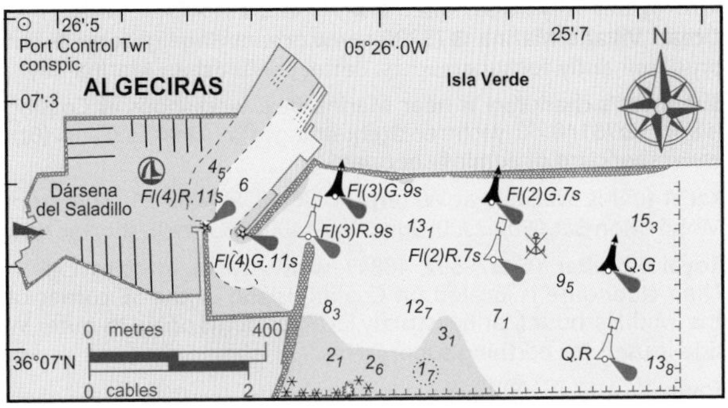

9.25.20 GIBRALTAR

36°08'·96N 05°22'·00W (100m off 'E' Hd)

CHARTS AC 142, 3578, 1448, 144, 45 (Note: these charts do not accurately depict the layout of Marina Bay and Queensway Quay Marinas); SC 445, 445A, 4452.

TIDES **Standard Port GIBRALTAR (⟶); ML 0·5**

Times				Height (metres)			
High Water		Low Water		MHWS	MHWN	MLWN	MLWS
0000	0700	0100	0600	1·0	0·7	0·3	0·1
1200	1900	1300	1800	Note the very small range			
Differences TARIFA							
–0038	–0038	–0042	–0042	+0·3	+0·3	+0·2	+0·1
PUNTA CARNERO							
–0010	–0010	0000	0000	0·0	+0·1	+0·1	+0·1
ALGECIRAS							
–0010	–0010	–0010	–0010	+0·1	+0·2	+0·2	+0·2
SANDY BAY (E side of the Rock)							
–0011	–0011	–0016	–0016	–0·2	–0·1	0·0	0·0

SHELTER Good in both marinas (best to pre-book) but beware swell and fierce gusts in the E'ly *Levanter*. It is not permitted to ⚓ NW of the runway, off Alcaidesa Marina or La Línea.

NAVIGATION From the SW, WPT 36°04'·62N 05°24'·34W (1M E of Pta Carnero) 024°/4·7M to 'E' Hd; 030°/4M to 'A' Hd. The Rock is steep-to all round; from the SW, beware shoals to S of Pta Carnero. From the E, clear Europa Pt by 3ca to avoid overfalls.

Arriving yachts with masts >10m high, heading for the yacht fuel berth (Waterport) or to Marina Bay Marina, must contact *Gibraltar Port* Ch **12**, 20 **before** rounding 'E' Head/North mole. VQ strobe lts and loudspeakers warn of aircraft activity; vessels must stay out of a Restricted Entry area west of the runway, its S'ly limit clearly marked by a line of 10 PHM's, Fl R, flanking the channel; do not transit while W lts are flashing. See chartlet. All yachts now clear Customs in/out at their chosen marina.

LIGHTS AND MARKS The Rock (423m) is easily seen, but from the W not until rounding Pta Carnero, 5M to SW. The Aero lt atop the Rock is obsc'd when within 2M W of it. Europa Pt, near sea level, has 3 sectored lts; see Lights, buoys and waypoints. At N end of bay, industrial plants are conspic day/night. Shore lts may mask commercial vessels at ⚓ and navigational lights.

COMMUNICATIONS International code +350 (Area code 200) ⊜ 72901; Met 53416; Ambulance/Police 199; Fire 190; Ⓗ 79700; Port Captain (HM) 77254, VHF Ch 06; QHM 55901, VHF Ch 08; Gibraltar Bay VHF Ch 12, 71; Queensway Quay and Marina Bay Marinas: VHF Ch 71; ✈ 73026.

FACILITIES **Queensway Quay Marina** ☎44700, info@queenswayquay.com www.queenswayquay.com 160 inc**V** mostly F&A, and some ⌓ <12m £17·00, 12-15m £24·00 1 Mar-31 Oct. ⛽ 1·25p/ltr ⚡17p/kwh. At its NW corner the marina entrance (least depth 3·5m) is closed by an anti-wash boom 2100-0830. wi-fi, no fuel. Close to town centre.

Marina Bay ☎73300 pieroffice@marinabay.gi www.marinabay.gi. 209 ⌓ mostly F&A, in 1·8–3·7m, inc 29 **V**: <12m £15·50, 12-15m £23·50 1 Mar-31 Oct. ⛽ 1·25p/ltr ⚡17p/kwh. Close to airport runway but only occas noise. ✕ ACA wi-fi.

Ocean Village Marina ☎73300 www.oceanvillage.gi some**V** but predominantly for superyachts. Better shelter than Marina Bay

Sheppard's chandlery is near Marina Bay; workshops at Coaling Island; ☎75148. yachtrep@gibraltar.gi Ⓔ (6t). www.sheppard.gi admin@sheppard.gi

Yacht fuel is available at Waterport, 36°08'·90N 05°21'·37W from Mobil (Mon-Sat 0900-2300; Sun 0900-1400; also Shell, shorter hrs).

Royal Gibraltar YC ☎78897, 48847. www.rgyc.gi. info@rgyc.gi Their clubhouse is located on Coaling Island at the SE corner of the Mid-Harbour Marina (strictly local residents only). Its outer W side is used for berthing superyachts.

Town ✕ ✉ Ⓑ Ⓗ, ✈.

SPECIAL NOTES FOR GIBRALTAR

Standard time is UT –1, as in Spain. DST (UT –2) is kept from the last Sun in Mar until the Sat before the last Sun in Oct.

Telephone The international dial code is +350 (this includes calling from Spain) then 200, then the 5 digit number.

Customs Visiting RIBs must obtain prior written permission to enter from Collector of Customs, Customs House, Waterport, Gibraltar, ☎78879; VHF Ch 14 – or entry may be refused.

Local winds Levanters are E'lies, common with high pressure to the N and low to the S. A persistent Levanter produces the roughest seas in the Strait, severe squalls (violent in a F8) and eddies in the lee of the Rock. The Poniente is a frequent W'ly, slightly less common in summer. The Vendaval is a strong SW'ly associated with lows, with rain/drizzle near coasts. In light summer conditions, a strong daytime sea breeze (SSW) may affect Europa Point.

MARINA 1M N OF GIBRALTAR

LA LÍNEA, 36°09'·49N 05°21'·60W, Alcaidesa Marina ☎+34 (956) 021660 mob +34690339636; marina@alcaidesa.com www.alcaidesamarina.com 624 inc 60**V** in 3m to 5m, €1·55 (+ taxes). (75t) ✕. **La Línea**, town, ✕.

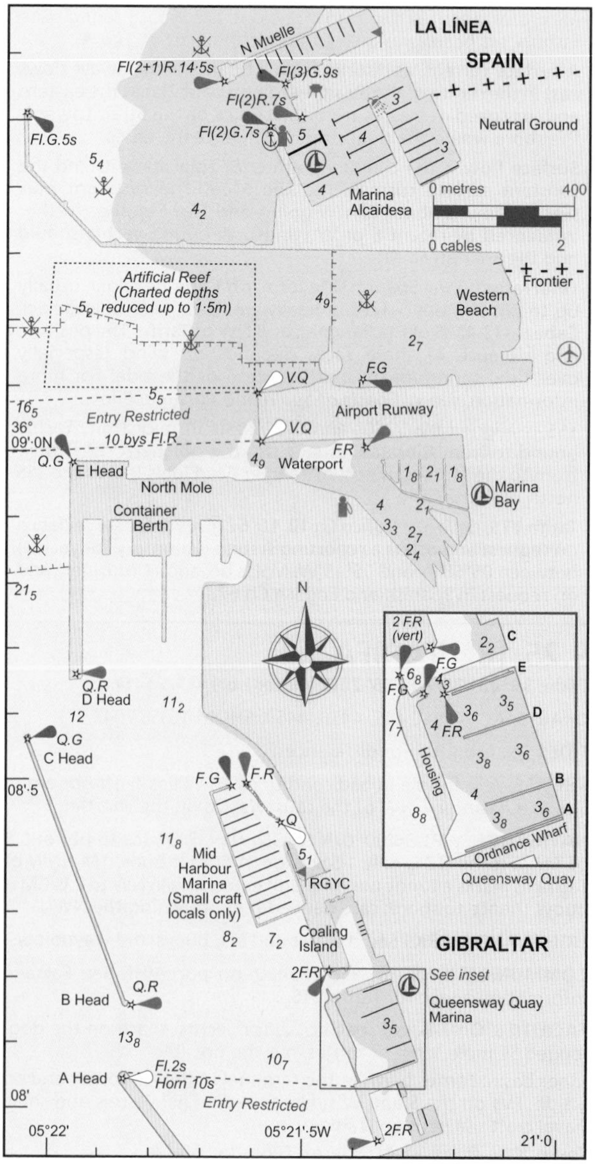

STANDARD TIME UT –01
Subtract 1 hour for UT
For Gibraltar Summer Time add ONE hour in **non-shaded areas**

GIBRALTAR LAT 36°08′N LONG 5°21′W

TIMES AND HEIGHTS OF HIGH AND LOW WATERS

Dates in red are SPRINGS
Dates in blue are NEAPS

YEAR **2018**

JANUARY

Date	Day	Time	m	Time	m	Time	m	Time	m
1	M	0212	0.9	0751	0.1	1428	1.0	2021	0.0
2	TU	0302	1.0	0838	0.0	1518	1.0	○ 2108	0.0
3	W	0350	1.0	0926	0.0	1608	1.0	2154	0.0
4	TH	0438	1.0	1013	0.0	1657	1.0	2239	0.0
5	F	0525	1.0	1101	0.1	1746	1.0	2324	0.1
6	SA	0615	1.0	1150	0.1	1837	0.9		
7	SU	0011	0.1	0707	0.9	1245	0.2	1930	0.8
8	M	0104	0.2	0803	0.8	1345	0.2	◑ 2026	0.8
9	TU	0205	0.2	0903	0.8	1453	0.3	2129	0.7
10	W	0317	0.3	1009	0.8	1608	0.3	2240	0.7
11	TH	0437	0.3	1116	0.8	1720	0.3	2353	0.7
12	F	0544	0.3	1216	0.8	1816	0.2		
13	SA	0050	0.7	0633	0.2	1305	0.8	1900	0.2
14	SU	0137	0.8	0713	0.2	1348	0.8	1939	0.1
15	M	0216	0.8	0750	0.2	1427	0.8	2016	0.1
16	TU	0252	0.8	0825	0.2	1504	0.9	2051	0.1
17	W	0325	0.9	0859	0.1	1539	0.9	● 2125	0.1
18	TH	0356	0.9	0933	0.1	1613	0.9	2157	0.1
19	F	0428	0.9	1005	0.1	1646	0.9	2228	0.1
20	SA	0500	0.9	1038	0.1	1719	0.9	2259	0.1
21	SU	0535	0.9	1112	0.2	1756	0.8	2332	0.1
22	M	0614	0.8	1151	0.2	1836	0.8		
23	TU	0010	0.2	0659	0.8	1238	0.2	1924	0.7
24	W	0059	0.2	0752	0.8	1338	0.2	◐ 2021	0.7
25	TH	0203	0.2	0854	0.8	1453	0.2	2130	0.7
26	F	0328	0.2	1005	0.8	1620	0.2	2252	0.7
27	SA	0456	0.2	1122	0.8	1739	0.2		
28	SU	0008	0.7	0603	0.2	1229	0.8	1839	0.1
29	M	0110	0.8	0657	0.1	1326	0.9	1930	0.0
30	TU	0203	0.9	0747	0.0	1419	0.9	2018	0.0
31	W	0253	0.9	0834	0.0	1510	1.0	○ 2104	-0.1

FEBRUARY

Date	Day	Time	m	Time	m	Time	m	Time	m
1	TH	0341	1.0	0921	0.0	1558	1.0	2148	-0.1
2	F	0426	1.0	1005	0.0	1645	1.0	2228	0.0
3	SA	0511	1.0	1048	0.0	1730	0.9	2308	0.0
4	SU	0555	0.9	1131	0.0	1816	0.9	2347	0.0
5	M	0641	0.9	1215	0.1	1903	0.8		
6	TU	0028	0.1	0729	0.8	1304	0.2	1952	0.8
7	W	0115	0.2	0821	0.8	1400	0.2	◑ 2045	0.7
8	TH	0215	0.3	0920	0.7	1512	0.3	2148	0.6
9	F	0338	0.3	1030	0.7	1643	0.3	2309	0.6
10	SA	0515	0.3	1145	0.7	1756	0.3		
11	SU	0025	0.7	0616	0.3	1245	0.7	1845	0.2
12	M	0119	0.7	0700	0.2	1332	0.8	1925	0.2
13	TU	0200	0.8	0736	0.2	1411	0.8	2001	0.1
14	W	0234	0.8	0811	0.1	1448	0.8	2035	0.1
15	TH	0306	0.8	0844	0.1	1522	0.9	● 2107	0.1
16	F	0338	0.9	0916	0.1	1556	0.9	2139	0.0
17	SA	0409	0.9	0948	0.1	1629	0.9	2209	0.0
18	SU	0442	0.9	1021	0.1	1703	0.9	2240	0.1
19	M	0516	0.9	1054	0.1	1738	0.9	2312	0.1
20	TU	0553	0.9	1131	0.1	1818	0.8	2348	0.1
21	W	0635	0.9	1213	0.1	1904	0.8		
22	TH	0031	0.2	0725	0.8	1306	0.2	1958	0.7
23	F	0129	0.2	0825	0.8	1418	0.2	◐ 2104	0.7
24	SA	0254	0.3	0938	0.7	1559	0.2	2228	0.7
25	SU	0441	0.2	1104	0.7	1734	0.2	2355	0.7
26	M	0559	0.2	1219	0.8	1838	0.1		
27	TU	0101	0.8	0655	0.1	1319	0.8	1927	0.0
28	W	0155	0.9	0743	0.0	1411	0.9	2012	0.0

MARCH

Date	Day	Time	m	Time	m	Time	m	Time	m
1	TH	0242	0.9	0828	0.0	1500	0.9	2054	-0.1
2	F	0327	1.0	0911	-0.1	1545	1.0	○ 2133	-0.1
3	SA	0410	1.0	0951	-0.1	1628	1.0	2210	-0.1
4	SU	0451	1.0	1030	0.0	1710	0.9	2245	0.0
5	M	0531	0.9	1107	0.0	1752	0.9	2320	0.0
6	TU	0612	0.9	1144	0.1	1834	0.8	2355	0.1
7	W	0654	0.8	1224	0.1	1918	0.8		
8	TH	0033	0.2	0740	0.7	1310	0.2	2006	0.7
9	F	0122	0.3	0832	0.7	1413	0.3	◑ 2101	0.6
10	SA	0235	0.3	0938	0.6	1550	0.3	2213	0.6
11	SU	0434	0.3	1104	0.6	1726	0.3	2344	0.6
12	M	0554	0.3	1218	0.7	1821	0.2		
13	TU	0047	0.7	0639	0.2	1308	0.7	1901	0.2
14	W	0130	0.7	0715	0.2	1348	0.8	1936	0.1
15	TH	0205	0.8	0748	0.1	1424	0.8	2009	0.1
16	F	0238	0.9	0821	0.1	1459	0.9	2041	0.1
17	SA	0311	0.9	0853	0.1	1533	0.9	● 2113	0.0
18	SU	0345	0.9	0927	0.0	1608	0.9	2145	0.0
19	M	0420	1.0	1000	0.0	1644	0.9	2218	0.0
20	TU	0456	1.0	1035	0.0	1721	0.9	2253	0.1
21	W	0534	0.9	1113	0.1	1802	0.9	2330	0.1
22	TH	0617	0.9	1154	0.1	1849	0.8		
23	F	0014	0.2	0706	0.8	1245	0.2	1944	0.8
24	SA	0112	0.2	0806	0.8	1358	0.2	◐ 2050	0.7
25	SU	0239	0.3	0921	0.7	1548	0.3	2214	0.7
26	M	0433	0.3	1052	0.7	1726	0.2	2343	0.7
27	TU	0553	0.2	1211	0.8	1827	0.1		
28	W	0048	0.8	0647	0.1	1310	0.8	1914	0.1
29	TH	0140	0.9	0732	0.0	1359	0.9	1955	0.0
30	F	0225	0.9	0814	0.0	1444	0.9	2034	0.0
31	SA	0307	1.0	0853	0.0	1527	0.9	○ 2111	0.0

APRIL

Date	Day	Time	m	Time	m	Time	m	Time	m
1	SU	0347	1.0	0931	0.0	1607	0.9	2145	0.0
2	M	0426	1.0	1007	0.0	1647	0.9	2218	0.0
3	TU	0503	0.9	1041	0.0	1725	0.9	2251	0.1
4	W	0541	0.9	1115	0.1	1805	0.8	2324	0.1
5	TH	0619	0.8	1150	0.1	1846	0.8		
6	F	0000	0.2	0701	0.7	1230	0.2	1930	0.7
7	SA	0043	0.3	0750	0.7	1324	0.3	2022	0.7
8	SU	0145	0.3	0850	0.6	1453	0.3	◑ 2123	0.6
9	M	0331	0.4	1008	0.6	1635	0.3	2242	0.6
10	TU	0511	0.3	1133	0.6	1740	0.3	2356	0.7
11	W	0605	0.3	1231	0.7	1824	0.2		
12	TH	0045	0.7	0643	0.2	1314	0.8	1900	0.2
13	F	0125	0.8	0717	0.2	1351	0.8	1934	0.1
14	SA	0202	0.9	0751	0.1	1428	0.9	2007	0.1
15	SU	0239	0.9	0825	0.1	1506	0.9	2042	0.1
16	M	0317	1.0	0901	0.0	1544	1.0	● 2118	0.1
17	TU	0356	1.0	0939	0.0	1624	1.0	2155	0.1
18	W	0435	1.0	1017	0.0	1705	1.0	2233	0.1
19	TH	0517	1.0	1057	0.1	1748	0.9	2315	0.1
20	F	0602	0.9	1140	0.1	1838	0.9		
21	SA	0002	0.2	0653	0.9	1234	0.2	1934	0.8
22	SU	0104	0.3	0755	0.8	1349	0.2	◐ 2041	0.8
23	M	0231	0.3	0909	0.7	1531	0.3	2200	0.8
24	TU	0415	0.3	1037	0.7	1701	0.2	2322	0.8
25	W	0534	0.2	1155	0.8	1803	0.2		
26	TH	0026	0.8	0628	0.1	1252	0.8	1849	0.1
27	F	0117	0.9	0712	0.1	1340	0.9	1929	0.1
28	SA	0200	0.9	0752	0.0	1423	0.9	2006	0.1
29	SU	0241	0.9	0830	0.0	1504	0.9	2042	0.1
30	M	0321	0.9	0907	0.0	1543	0.9	○ 2117	0.1

Chart Datum is 0·25 metres below Alicante Datum (ie Mean Sea Level, Alicante). HAT is 1·2 metres above Chart Datum.

STANDARD TIME UT –01
Subtract 1 hour for UT
For Gibraltar Summer Time add ONE hour in **non-shaded areas**

GIBRALTAR LAT 36°08′N LONG 5°21′W

TIMES AND HEIGHTS OF HIGH AND LOW WATERS

Dates in red are SPRINGS
Dates in blue are NEAPS

YEAR **2018**

MAY

Date	Day	Time	m	Time	m	Time	m	Time	m
1	TU	0359	0.9	0942	0.0	1621	0.9	2151	0.1
2	W	0435	0.9	1016	0.1	1659	0.9	2224	0.1
3	TH	0511	0.9	1049	0.1	1736	0.8	2258	0.2
4	F	0548	0.8	1123	0.2	1815	0.8	2333	0.2
5	SA	0628	0.7	1201	0.2	1858	0.7		
6	SU	0014	0.3	0714	0.7	1250	0.3	1947	0.7
7	M	0109	0.3	0809	0.7	1402	0.3	2042	0.7
8	TU	0229	0.4	0914	0.6	1531	0.3	◑ 2145	0.7
9	W	0402	0.3	1030	0.6	1643	0.3	2253	0.7
10	TH	0511	0.3	1139	0.7	1736	0.3	2352	0.8
11	F	0559	0.2	1230	0.8	1817	0.2		
12	SA	0039	0.8	0639	0.2	1314	0.8	1854	0.2
13	SU	0123	0.9	0717	0.1	1355	0.9	1931	0.1
14	M	0205	0.9	0756	0.1	1437	0.9	2010	0.1
15	TU	0248	1.0	0836	0.0	1520	1.0	● 2051	0.1
16	W	0331	1.0	0917	0.0	1603	1.0	2133	0.1
17	TH	0416	1.0	1000	0.0	1648	1.0	2217	0.1
18	F	0501	1.0	1044	0.1	1735	1.0	2303	0.1
19	SA	0550	1.0	1131	0.1	1827	0.9	2354	0.2
20	SU	0644	0.9	1226	0.2	1925	0.9		
21	M	0056	0.2	0745	0.8	1336	0.2	2028	0.8
22	TU	0215	0.3	0854	0.8	1500	0.3	◐ 2139	0.8
23	W	0342	0.3	1012	0.8	1621	0.3	2252	0.8
24	TH	0501	0.2	1126	0.8	1727	0.2	2355	0.8
25	F	0601	0.2	1226	0.8	1817	0.2		
26	SA	0047	0.9	0647	0.1	1315	0.8	1859	0.2
27	SU	0133	0.9	0728	0.1	1359	0.9	1938	0.1
28	M	0214	0.9	0806	0.1	1440	0.9	2015	0.1
29	TU	0254	0.9	0843	0.1	1520	0.9	○ 2051	0.1
30	W	0332	0.9	0919	0.1	1558	0.9	2126	0.1
31	TH	0409	0.9	0954	0.1	1634	0.9	2201	0.2

JUNE

Date	Day	Time	m	Time	m	Time	m	Time	m
1	F	0446	0.9	1028	0.1	1710	0.8	2236	0.2
2	SA	0522	0.8	1102	0.2	1747	0.8	2312	0.2
3	SU	0559	0.8	1138	0.2	1827	0.8	2350	0.3
4	M	0641	0.7	1219	0.2	1911	0.8		
5	TU	0036	0.3	0729	0.7	1313	0.3	2000	0.7
6	W	0136	0.3	0825	0.7	1421	0.3	◑ 2054	0.7
7	TH	0247	0.3	0927	0.7	1532	0.3	2153	0.7
8	F	0400	0.3	1037	0.7	1636	0.3	2256	0.8
9	SA	0505	0.2	1141	0.7	1730	0.2	2354	0.8
10	SU	0558	0.2	1234	0.8	1816	0.2		
11	M	0045	0.9	0644	0.1	1323	0.9	1900	0.1
12	TU	0133	0.9	0729	0.1	1410	0.9	1944	0.1
13	W	0221	1.0	0814	0.0	1457	1.0	● 2029	0.1
14	TH	0310	1.0	0900	0.0	1545	1.0	2116	0.1
15	F	0359	1.0	0947	0.0	1633	1.0	2204	0.1
16	SA	0448	1.0	1033	0.0	1722	1.0	2253	0.1
17	SU	0538	1.0	1121	0.1	1813	1.0	2345	0.1
18	M	0632	0.9	1212	0.1	1909	0.9		
19	TU	0042	0.2	0730	0.9	1312	0.2	2007	0.9
20	W	0148	0.2	0832	0.8	1419	0.2	◐ 2109	0.9
21	TH	0300	0.3	0939	0.8	1530	0.3	2214	0.8
22	F	0416	0.3	1050	0.8	1642	0.3	2319	0.8
23	SA	0527	0.2	1156	0.8	1743	0.3		
24	SU	0016	0.8	0621	0.2	1250	0.8	1832	0.2
25	M	0106	0.9	0706	0.2	1337	0.8	1913	0.2
26	TU	0149	0.9	0745	0.1	1420	0.8	1952	0.2
27	W	0231	0.9	0823	0.1	1500	0.9	2030	0.2
28	TH	0310	0.9	0859	0.1	1537	0.9	○ 2106	0.2
29	F	0347	0.9	0934	0.1	1612	0.9	2142	0.2
30	SA	0423	0.9	1008	0.1	1646	0.9	2216	0.2

JULY

Date	Day	Time	m	Time	m	Time	m	Time	m
1	SU	0457	0.8	1040	0.1	1719	0.9	2251	0.2
2	M	0532	0.8	1113	0.2	1754	0.8	2326	0.2
3	TU	0609	0.8	1148	0.2	1832	0.8		
4	W	0005	0.2	0650	0.8	1229	0.2	1916	0.8
5	TH	0051	0.3	0739	0.7	1319	0.3	2005	0.8
6	F	0148	0.3	0836	0.7	1422	0.3	◑ 2101	0.8
7	SA	0256	0.3	0941	0.7	1533	0.3	2204	0.8
8	SU	0410	0.3	1054	0.7	1644	0.3	2311	0.8
9	M	0522	0.2	1200	0.8	1745	0.2		
10	TU	0013	0.9	0620	0.1	1257	0.8	1838	0.2
11	W	0109	0.9	0711	0.1	1350	0.9	1927	0.1
12	TH	0202	1.0	0759	0.0	1440	1.0	2016	0.1
13	F	0254	1.0	0847	0.0	1530	1.0	● 2105	0.1
14	SA	0345	1.0	0935	0.0	1618	1.0	2154	0.0
15	SU	0434	1.0	1020	0.0	1706	1.0	2241	0.1
16	M	0524	1.0	1105	0.1	1755	1.0	2329	0.1
17	TU	0614	1.0	1151	0.1	1846	1.0		
18	W	0019	0.1	0707	0.9	1240	0.2	1938	0.9
19	TH	0114	0.2	0803	0.8	1335	0.2	◐ 2034	0.9
20	F	0215	0.2	0903	0.8	1438	0.3	2133	0.8
21	SA	0326	0.3	1010	0.8	1551	0.3	2239	0.8
22	SU	0448	0.3	1122	0.7	1709	0.3	2345	0.8
23	M	0557	0.3	1226	0.8	1809	0.3		
24	TU	0042	0.8	0646	0.2	1319	0.8	1854	0.3
25	W	0130	0.8	0726	0.2	1402	0.8	1934	0.2
26	TH	0212	0.8	0803	0.2	1441	0.9	2011	0.2
27	F	0250	0.9	0838	0.1	1516	0.9	○ 2047	0.2
28	SA	0326	0.9	0912	0.1	1548	0.9	2121	0.2
29	SU	0400	0.9	0944	0.1	1619	0.9	2155	0.2
30	M	0432	0.9	1015	0.1	1650	0.9	2227	0.2
31	TU	0505	0.9	1046	0.2	1722	0.9	2300	0.2

AUGUST

Date	Day	Time	m	Time	m	Time	m	Time	m
1	W	0539	0.9	1117	0.2	1757	0.9	2335	0.2
2	TH	0617	0.8	1152	0.2	1837	0.9		
3	F	0015	0.2	0701	0.8	1234	0.2	1923	0.8
4	SA	0104	0.2	0755	0.8	1328	0.3	◑ 2017	0.8
5	SU	0207	0.3	0859	0.7	1441	0.3	2121	0.8
6	M	0327	0.3	1015	0.7	1609	0.3	2235	0.8
7	TU	0457	0.2	1134	0.8	1727	0.3	2349	0.9
8	W	0607	0.2	1240	0.8	1827	0.2		
9	TH	0052	0.9	0701	0.1	1335	0.9	1918	0.1
10	F	0148	1.0	0749	0.1	1426	1.0	2006	0.1
11	SA	0241	1.0	0835	0.0	1515	1.1	● 2054	0.0
12	SU	0331	1.0	0920	0.0	1601	1.1	2140	0.0
13	M	0418	1.1	1002	0.0	1647	1.1	2224	0.0
14	TU	0505	1.0	1043	0.0	1731	1.1	2307	0.1
15	W	0551	1.0	1123	0.1	1817	1.0	2351	0.1
16	TH	0639	0.9	1204	0.2	1904	0.9		
17	F	0036	0.2	0730	0.9	1250	0.2	1954	0.9
18	SA	0128	0.3	0825	0.8	1344	0.3	◐ 2049	0.8
19	SU	0233	0.3	0927	0.7	1457	0.4	2153	0.8
20	M	0401	0.4	1043	0.7	1633	0.4	2311	0.7
21	TU	0531	0.3	1201	0.8	1748	0.4		
22	W	0020	0.8	0625	0.3	1259	0.8	1836	0.3
23	TH	0112	0.8	0705	0.3	1341	0.8	1914	0.3
24	F	0153	0.9	0740	0.2	1417	0.9	1950	0.2
25	SA	0229	0.9	0813	0.2	1449	0.9	2023	0.2
26	SU	0302	0.9	0845	0.1	1520	1.0	○ 2057	0.2
27	M	0334	1.0	0916	0.1	1550	1.0	2129	0.1
28	TU	0406	1.0	0947	0.1	1621	1.0	2201	0.1
29	W	0438	1.0	1017	0.1	1653	1.0	2234	0.1
30	TH	0512	1.0	1048	0.2	1727	1.0	2307	0.2
31	F	0549	0.9	1122	0.2	1805	1.0	2345	0.2

Chart Datum is 0·25 metres below Alicante Datum (ie Mean Sea Level, Alicante). HAT is 1·2 metres above Chart Datum.

STANDARD TIME UT –01
Subtract 1 hour for UT
For Gibraltar Summer Time add ONE hour in **non-shaded areas**

GIBRALTAR LAT 36°08'N LONG 5°21'W

TIMES AND HEIGHTS OF HIGH AND LOW WATERS

Dates in red are SPRINGS
Dates in blue are NEAPS

YEAR **2018**

SEPTEMBER

Date	Day	Time	m	Time	m	Time	m	Time	m
1	SA	0632	0.9	1201	0.3	1850	0.9		
2	SU	0030	0.2	0725	0.8	1252	0.3	1944	0.9
3	M	0130	0.3	0829	0.8	1406	0.4	◑ 2049	0.8
4	TU	0300	0.3	0948	0.8	1549	0.4	2210	0.8
5	W	0448	0.3	1117	0.8	1718	0.3	2336	0.8
6	TH	0601	0.2	1227	0.9	1819	0.2		
7	F	0043	0.9	0652	0.1	1323	1.0	1909	0.1
8	SA	0138	1.0	0737	0.1	1411	1.0	1954	0.1
9	SU	0227	1.0	0819	0.0	1457	1.1	● 2039	0.0
10	M	0314	1.1	0900	0.0	1540	1.1	2121	0.0
11	TU	0358	1.1	0939	0.0	1622	1.1	2202	0.0
12	W	0441	1.1	1016	0.1	1704	1.1	2240	0.1
13	TH	0523	1.0	1052	0.1	1744	1.0	2319	0.1
14	F	0606	1.0	1129	0.2	1826	1.0	2357	0.2
15	SA	0652	0.9	1208	0.3	1912	0.9		
16	SU	0041	0.3	0742	0.8	1255	0.4	2002	0.8
17	M	0138	0.4	0841	0.8	1404	0.4	◐ 2104	0.7
18	TU	0308	0.4	0954	0.7	1549	0.5	2227	0.7
19	W	0455	0.4	1123	0.7	1720	0.4	2353	0.8
20	TH	0556	0.4	1227	0.8	1811	0.4		
21	F	0047	0.8	0637	0.3	1310	0.9	1848	0.3
22	SA	0127	0.9	0711	0.2	1344	0.9	1922	0.2
23	SU	0201	0.9	0743	0.2	1416	1.0	1955	0.2
24	M	0234	1.0	0815	0.2	1447	1.0	2028	0.2
25	TU	0306	1.0	0846	0.2	1519	1.1	○ 2101	0.1
26	W	0339	1.0	0917	0.1	1553	1.1	2134	0.1
27	TH	0413	1.0	0949	0.2	1627	1.1	2208	0.1
28	F	0448	1.0	1022	0.2	1703	1.1	2243	0.2
29	SA	0527	1.0	1058	0.2	1742	1.0	2320	0.2
30	SU	0611	0.9	1138	0.3	1827	1.0		

OCTOBER

Date	Day	Time	m	Time	m	Time	m	Time	m
1	M	0004	0.3	0703	0.9	1230	0.3	1921	0.9
2	TU	0105	0.3	0809	0.8	1349	0.4	◑ 2029	0.8
3	W	0246	0.4	0930	0.8	1540	0.4	2155	0.8
4	TH	0440	0.3	1102	0.8	1708	0.3	2327	0.8
5	F	0550	0.3	1213	0.9	1807	0.2		
6	SA	0034	0.9	0638	0.2	1307	1.0	1854	0.2
7	SU	0125	1.0	0720	0.1	1352	1.1	1937	0.1
8	M	0211	1.0	0758	0.1	1435	1.1	2018	0.1
9	TU	0253	1.1	0836	0.1	1516	1.1	● 2058	0.0
10	W	0335	1.1	0912	0.1	1556	1.1	2136	0.1
11	TH	0415	1.1	0947	0.1	1634	1.1	2212	0.1
12	F	0454	1.0	1022	0.2	1712	1.0	2247	0.1
13	SA	0533	1.0	1056	0.2	1750	0.9	2323	0.2
14	SU	0614	0.9	1133	0.3	1831	0.9		
15	M	0001	0.3	0700	0.8	1216	0.4	1919	0.8
16	TU	0051	0.4	0755	0.8	1318	0.4	◐ 2018	0.7
17	W	0215	0.4	0902	0.7	1500	0.5	2134	0.7
18	TH	0406	0.4	1024	0.7	1637	0.4	2307	0.7
19	F	0517	0.4	1139	0.8	1735	0.4		
20	SA	0011	0.8	0602	0.3	1228	0.9	1815	0.3
21	SU	0054	0.9	0638	0.3	1305	0.9	1850	0.2
22	M	0129	0.9	0711	0.2	1339	1.0	1924	0.2
23	TU	0203	1.0	0743	0.2	1413	1.0	1958	0.2
24	W	0237	1.0	0815	0.2	1449	1.1	○ 2032	0.1
25	TH	0313	1.1	0848	0.2	1526	1.1	2108	0.1
26	F	0350	1.1	0923	0.2	1604	1.1	2144	0.1
27	SA	0428	1.1	1000	0.2	1644	1.1	2222	0.2
28	SU	0510	1.0	1039	0.2	1726	1.0	2303	0.2
29	M	0555	1.0	1124	0.3	1813	1.0	2349	0.3
30	TU	0649	0.9	1219	0.3	1909	0.9		
31	W	0052	0.3	0755	0.9	1342	0.4	◑ 2017	0.8

NOVEMBER

Date	Day	Time	m	Time	m	Time	m	Time	m
1	TH	0234	0.4	0913	0.8	1526	0.4	2141	0.8
2	F	0418	0.3	1041	0.9	1648	0.3	2311	0.8
3	SA	0527	0.3	1152	0.9	1748	0.2		
4	SU	0018	0.9	0616	0.2	1245	1.0	1835	0.2
5	M	0108	1.0	0657	0.2	1329	1.0	1917	0.1
6	TU	0151	1.0	0735	0.1	1410	1.0	1956	0.1
7	W	0232	1.0	0811	0.1	1450	1.1	● 2034	0.1
8	TH	0311	1.0	0847	0.1	1529	1.0	2111	0.1
9	F	0350	1.0	0922	0.1	1607	1.0	2147	0.1
10	SA	0427	1.0	0956	0.2	1644	1.0	2222	0.2
11	SU	0504	0.9	1031	0.2	1721	0.9	2256	0.2
12	M	0542	0.9	1108	0.3	1800	0.8	2333	0.3
13	TU	0625	0.8	1149	0.3	1845	0.8		
14	W	0018	0.3	0715	0.8	1244	0.4	1938	0.7
15	TH	0126	0.4	0815	0.8	1408	0.4	◐ 2043	0.7
16	F	0304	0.4	0922	0.7	1539	0.4	2159	0.7
17	SA	0424	0.4	1034	0.8	1647	0.4	2316	0.8
18	SU	0520	0.3	1135	0.8	1736	0.3		
19	M	0011	0.8	0601	0.3	1222	0.9	1816	0.2
20	TU	0053	0.9	0637	0.2	1302	0.9	1853	0.2
21	W	0131	0.9	0711	0.2	1341	1.0	1929	0.1
22	TH	0210	1.0	0746	0.2	1421	1.0	2007	0.1
23	F	0249	1.0	0823	0.1	1503	1.1	○ 2046	0.1
24	SA	0331	1.0	0903	0.1	1546	1.1	2127	0.1
25	SU	0413	1.1	0944	0.2	1630	1.1	2209	0.1
26	M	0458	1.0	1028	0.2	1715	1.0	2253	0.2
27	TU	0545	1.0	1117	0.2	1805	1.0	2342	0.2
28	W	0639	0.9	1215	0.3	1901	0.9		
29	TH	0044	0.3	0742	0.9	1332	0.3	2006	0.8
30	F	0209	0.3	0854	0.9	1459	0.3	◑ 2121	0.8

DECEMBER

Date	Day	Time	m	Time	m	Time	m	Time	m
1	SA	0339	0.3	1011	0.9	1618	0.3	2243	0.8
2	SU	0453	0.3	1122	0.9	1723	0.2	2353	0.8
3	M	0550	0.2	1219	0.9	1814	0.2		
4	TU	0046	0.9	0634	0.2	1306	1.0	1858	0.1
5	W	0132	0.9	0714	0.2	1348	1.0	1938	0.1
6	TH	0213	0.9	0751	0.1	1429	1.0	2016	0.1
7	F	0253	0.9	0827	0.1	1508	1.0	● 2054	0.1
8	SA	0331	0.9	0904	0.1	1547	0.9	2130	0.1
9	SU	0408	0.9	0939	0.2	1625	0.9	2205	0.1
10	M	0444	0.9	1015	0.2	1701	0.9	2240	0.2
11	TU	0520	0.9	1051	0.2	1739	0.8	2316	0.2
12	W	0558	0.8	1130	0.3	1819	0.8	2355	0.3
13	TH	0641	0.8	1215	0.3	1904	0.7		
14	F	0043	0.3	0731	0.8	1315	0.3	1956	0.7
15	SA	0152	0.3	0827	0.7	1429	0.4	◐ 2055	0.7
16	SU	0311	0.3	0929	0.7	1542	0.3	2204	0.7
17	M	0421	0.3	1034	0.8	1646	0.3	2315	0.7
18	TU	0518	0.3	1134	0.8	1739	0.2		
19	W	0013	0.8	0603	0.2	1226	0.9	1824	0.2
20	TH	0101	0.8	0644	0.2	1313	0.9	1907	0.1
21	F	0146	0.9	0724	0.1	1359	1.0	1949	0.1
22	SA	0231	1.0	0806	0.1	1445	1.0	○ 2033	0.0
23	SU	0317	1.0	0850	0.1	1533	1.0	2117	0.0
24	M	0403	1.0	0936	0.1	1620	1.0	2203	0.0
25	TU	0449	1.0	1023	0.1	1708	1.0	2249	0.1
26	W	0537	1.0	1113	0.1	1758	1.0	2337	0.1
27	TH	0629	1.0	1208	0.2	1852	0.9		
28	F	0031	0.2	0726	0.9	1312	0.2	1950	0.8
29	SA	0137	0.2	0829	0.9	1424	0.2	◑ 2054	0.8
30	SU	0251	0.3	0937	0.8	1539	0.3	2206	0.8
31	M	0409	0.3	1048	0.8	1653	0.2	2322	0.8

Chart Datum is 0·25 metres below Alicante Datum (ie Mean Sea Level, Alicante). HAT is 1·2 metres above Chart Datum.

MOROCCO

From Cap Spartel eastward for some 35M to Punta Almina the coast is generally rugged with mountains rising progressively higher to the east. Jbel Musa (one of the ancient Pillars of Hercules) towers 848m/2782ft high, only 8ca from the coast.

If using the SW and/or SE ITZs, be aware of the large commercial port of Tanger-Med which extends 2·7M SW of Pta Ciris and connects into the Gibraltar TSS.

The Spanish enclave of **Ceuta** (AC 2742) and, 10M further south, Marina Smir are popular day trips from Gib. Be aware of frequent high-speed ferries crossing the Strait and warships.

9.25.21 TANGIER

Morocco **35°47'·42N 05°47'·45W**

CHARTS AC 142, 1912; SC 445, 446, 4461

TIDES **Standard Port GIBRALTAR (⟶); ML 0·5**

Times **Height (metres)**

High Water		Low Water		MHWS	MHWN	MLWN	MLWS
0000	0700	0100	0600	1·0	0·7	0·3	0·1
1200	1900	1300	1800	Note the very small tidal range.			
Differences *TANGIER**				***Moroccan Zone Time is 0 (UT)**			
–0030	*–0030*	*–0020*	*–0020*	*+1·3*	*+1·0*	*+0·5*	*+0·3*
HEJAR LESFAR*							
–0035	–0035	–0005	–0005	+0·8	+0·6	+0·4	+0·2
PUNTA CIRIS*							
–0110	–0110	–0110	–0110	+0·2	+0·2	+0·2	+0·1
*CEUTA**							
–0045	*–0045*	*–0050*	*–0050*	*0·0*	*+0·1*	*+0·1*	*+0·1*

SHELTER Good, except in N to E winds to which the bay and hbr are exposed. In E winds ⚓ in 6m 4ca SSW of Pte Malabata lt ho in the lee of high ground. Very good within new marina SE of the Old Harbour.

NAVIGATION WPT 35°48'·33N 05°46'·94W, 205°/1M to N mole hd, within the white sector of El Charf Dir lt, passing W of an IDM lt buoy. The approach is straightforward, but from W, beware vessels emerging from the new fishing hbr in the approach to the old hbr and also ferries using the port.

LIGHTS AND MARKS Caution: Local navigational aids are reported

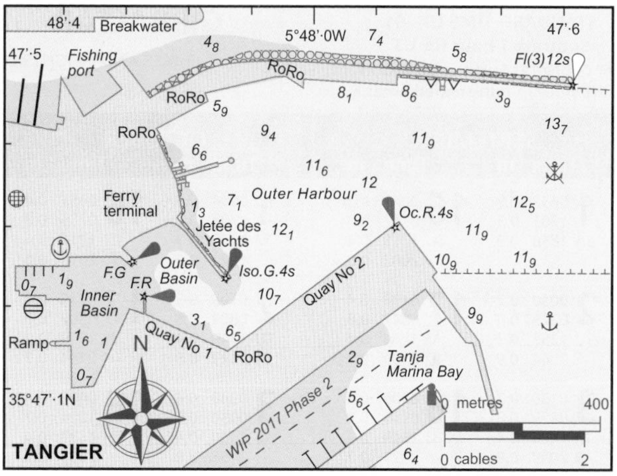

to be unreliable, missing, unlit or out of position.

Brg/dist of lights and conspic landmarks from the N: bkwtr hd 14m high W lt twr. Cap Spartel, 270°/6·4M. Conspic W water twr, 265°/1·6M. El Charf (Monte Dirección) 172°/1·5M, a 100m high conical hill with bldg/minaret; below the summit is a Dir lt whose WRG sectors cover the bay. IDM lt buoy, 067°/0·5M. Pte Malabata lt ho 055°/2·6M. Other lights as chartlet and Lights, buoys and waypoints.

Hbr signals may be flown from the HM's office: R flag = Hbr open; Y flag = Hbr closed; Blue flag = Bad weather expected.

COMMUNICATIONS (Code +212) Port (0)53993 7495. Arabic, French and Spanish spoken, call Ch 16 for a working channel.

FACILITIES **Tanja Marina Bay,** pontoon berths, S side of new 626 berth facility. ☎(0)539331717; info@tanjabaymarina.ma www. tanjabaymarina.ma. (Note: WIP ongoing 2017/18 to complete pontoon berthing N side hbr and shoreside infrastructure, reports welcome.)

Royal Yacht Club Tanger ☎(0)539938575; ryct1925@gmail.com www.ryct.ma

Town All services, ferries to Tarifa, ✈ Tangier Battouta 14km.

9.25.22 CEUTA

Spanish enclave **35°53'·75N 05°18'·62W**

CHARTS AC 3578, 142, 2742; SC 44C, 445, 451, 4511

TIDES **Standard Port GIBRALTAR (⟶); ML 0·5**; see Tangier.

SHELTER Good in marina. The harbour ent is exposed to the *levanter* and NE winds. Fresh SE'lies raise heavy seas in the Bay of Ceuta. In strong W'lies heavy squalls blow down from the mountains. No ⚓ to N and NE of the E pier. Ensenada de la Almadraba (S of the marina isthmus) is a sheltered ⚓ in W or N winds.

NAVIGATION WPT 35°54'·75N 05°18'·62W, 180°/1·0M to W side of hbr ent. From there make good 222° to the marina ent. From the E give a wide berth to the N side of the Almina Peninsula from which islets and Bajo Isabel (3·6m) extend about 4ca N. Beware high-speed ferries at the hbr ent.

LIGHTS AND MARKS Jbel Musa 848m (one of the ancient Pillars of Hercules) is 4·7M W of the hbr. Monte Hacho fort 204m is 1·1M E of the hbr, with Punta Almina lt ho a further 0.5M east. At the N end of Muelle Espana the Port Control twr is conspic by day; leave it to stbd for the marina ent.

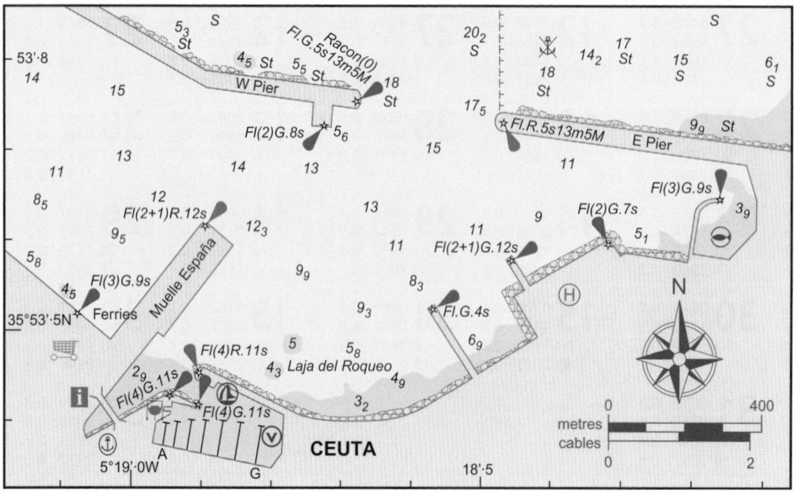

COMMUNICATIONS (Code +34 956, as if on the Spanish mainland); Port VHF Ch 09, **12;** *Banda Marina* VHF Ch 09; Tourist info 506275.

FACILITIES **Marina Hércules** ☎525001 (0800-1330 and 1700-2000) www.mahersa.es info@mahersa.es 300 max LOA 20m. Expect to berth on fingers at pontoon G (furthest east). Depths vary from 4m to 2m. €0·62m²/day, €2·90/day, €4·36/day; wi-fi. Heliport – Malaga and Algeciras.

Real Club Náutico ✕.

Town ✕ Good local market, ✉ Ⓑ. Frequent ferries to Algeciras. ✈ Tangier, Gibraltar, Malaga.

Portuguese Islands

Flores, Faial, Pico, São Jorge, Graciosa, Terceira, Santa Maria and São Miguel; Porto Santo and Madeira

9.26.1 Contents 1027

9.26.2 Area map and Distance table 1028

9.26.3 Special notes for the Portuguese Islands 1029

THE AZORES ARCHIPELAGO

9.26.4 Lights, buoys and waypoints 1030

9.26.5 Porto das Lajes (Flores) 1032

9.26.6 Horta (Faial) 1032

9.26.7 Madalena (Pico) 1033

9.26.8 Cais (São Roque) do Pico (Pico) 1034

9.26.9 Velas (São Jorge) 1034

9.26.10 Calheta (São Jorge) 1034

9.26.11 Vila da Praia (Graciosa) 1035

9.26.12 Angra do Heroísmo (Terceira) 1035

9.26.13 Praia da Vitória (Terceira) 1036

9.26.14 Vila do Porto (Santa Maria) 1036

9.26.15 Ponta Delgada (São Miguel) 1037

9.26.16 Vila Franca do Campo (São Miguel) 1037

Ponta Delgada (Standard port, tide tables) 1038

THE MADEIRA ARCHIPELAGO

9.26.17 Lights, buoys and waypoints 1041

9.26.18 Porto do Porto Santo 1042

9.26.19 Quinta do Lorde (Madeira) 1042
Baía de Abra • Caniçal • Machico

9.26.20 Funchal (Madeira) 1043

9.26.21 Calheta (Madeira) 1043
Madalena do Mar • Porto Moniz •

Casablanca (Standard port, tide tables/curves) 1044

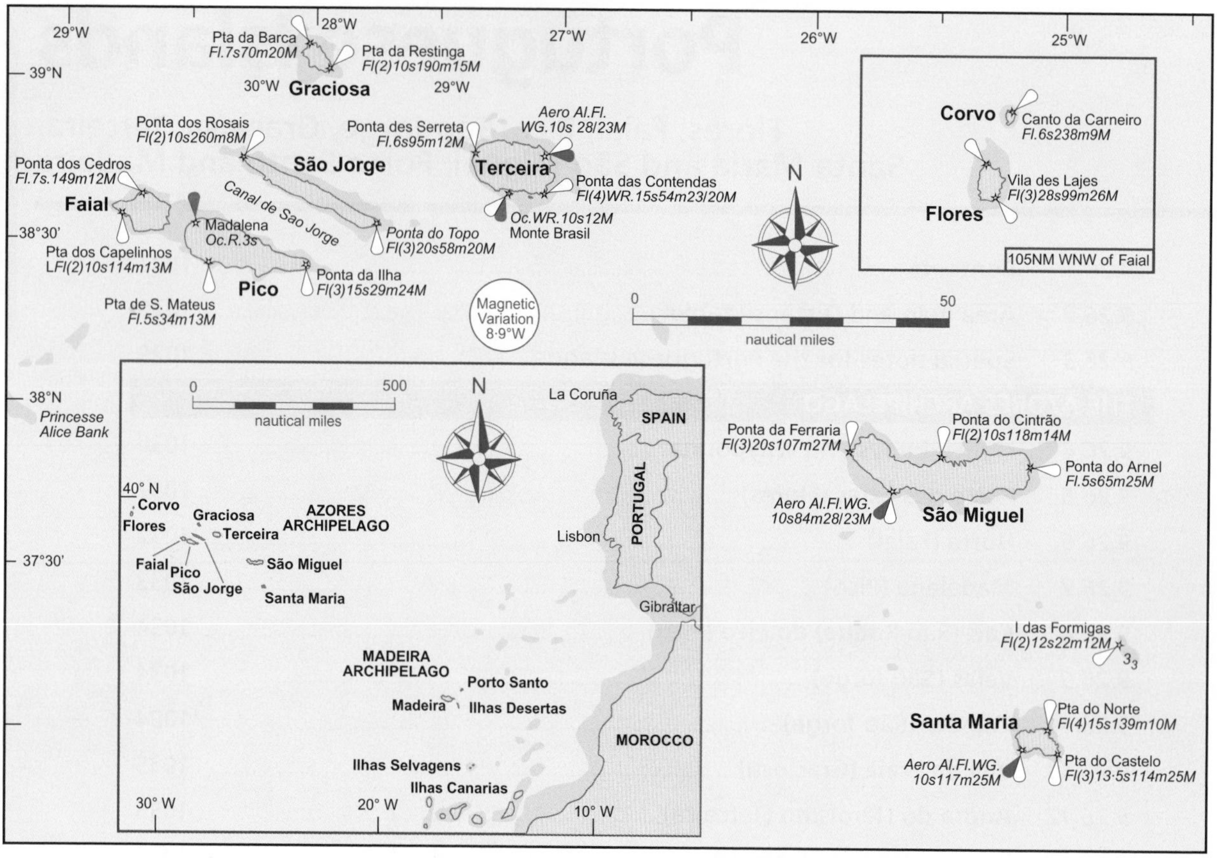
29°W
28°W
27°W
26°W
25°W
39°N
38°30'
38°N
37°30'
Pta da Barca
Fl.7s70m20M
Pta da Restinga
Fl(2)10s190m15M
30°W Graciosa 29°W
Ponta dos Rosais
Fl(2)10s260m8M
São Jorge
Ponta des Serreta
Fl.6s95m12M
Aero Al.Fl.
WG.10s 28/23M
Terceira
Ponta das Contendas
Fl(4)WR.15s54m23/20M
Oc.WR.10s12M
Monte Brasil
Ponta dos Cedros
Fl.7s.149m12M
Faial
Canal de Sao Jorge
Madalena
Oc.R.3s
Ponta do Topo
Fl(3)20s58m20M
Pta dos Capelinhos
LFl(2)10s114m13M
Ponta da Ilha
Fl(3)15s29m24M
Pico
Pta de S. Mateus
Fl.5s34m13M
Magnetic Variation 8·9°W
N
0
50
nautical miles
Corvo
Canto da Carneiro
Fl.6s238m9M
Vila des Lajes
Fl(3)28s99m26M
Flores
105NM WNW of Faial
Princesse Alice Bank
0
500
nautical miles
N
La Coruña
SPAIN
PORTUGAL
Lisbon
Gibraltar
MOROCCO
40° N
Corvo
Flores
Graciosa
Terceira
AZORES ARCHIPELAGO
Faial
Pico
São Jorge
São Miguel
Santa Maria
MADEIRA ARCHIPELAGO
Porto Santo
Madeira
Ilhas Desertas
Ilhas Selvagens
Ilhas Canarias
30° W
20° W
10° W
Ponta da Ferraria
Fl(3)20s107m27M
Ponta do Cintrão
Fl(2)10s118m14M
Ponta do Arnel
Fl.5s65m25M
Aero Al.Fl.WG.
10s84m28/23M
São Miguel
I das Formigas
Fl(2)12s22m12M
Santa Maria
Pta do Norte
Fl(4)15s139m10M
Aero Al.Fl.WG.
10s117m25M
Pta do Castelo
Fl(3)13·5s114m25M

PORTUGUESE ISLANDS DISTANCE TABLE

Approximate rhumb line distances in nautical miles between selected harbours/ anchorages in the Madeira and Azores archipelagos. Distances shown are by the most direct route, considering likely dangers and typical currents/weather.

1	Porto das Lajes (Flores)	1																
2	Horta (Faial)	131	2															
3	Madalena (Pico)	135	5	3														
4	Cais/São Roque (Pico)	143	16	12	4													
5	Velas (São Jorge)	144	22	15	11	5												
6	Vila da Praia (Graciosa)	152	48	45	42	37	6											
7	Angra de Heroismo (Terceira)	190	69	65	54	52	44	7										
8	Praia do Vitoria (Terceira)	199	81	78	66	63	49	14	8									
9	Ponta Delgada (São Miguel)	277	150	147	135	135	138	93	91	9								
10	Vila do Porto (Santa Maria)	320	192	191	179	179	185	143	142	54	10							
11	Porto (Porto Santo)	817	691	691	677	676	679	636	634	544	500	11						
12	Quinta do Lorde (Madeira)	817	689	689	672	673	674	631	629	540	494	31	12					
13	Funchal (Madeira)	828	699	699	683	684	663	620	618	529	483	41	12	13				
14	Calheta (Madeira)	787	659	659	646	645	648	605	602	514	467	56	27	16	14			
15	Ilha Deserta Grande											38	18	22	36	15		
16	Ilha Selvagem Grande											179	165	162	172	148	16	
17	Ilha Selvagem Pequena											183	168	165	173	152	10	17

Ilhas Selvagens and Ilhas Desertas may not be visited without a permit, only obtainable ***in advance*** from Madeira/Porto Santo.

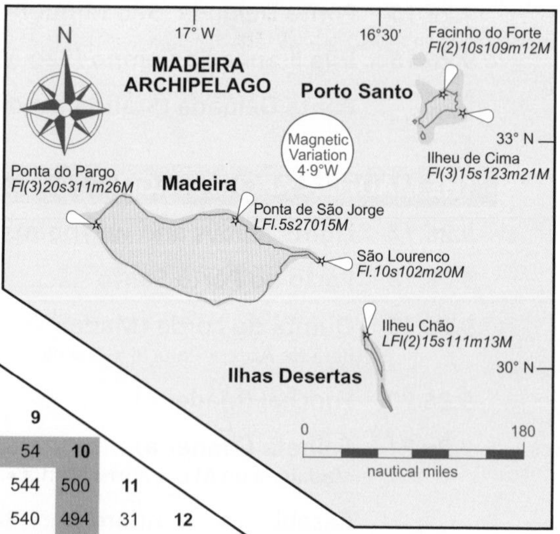
N
17° W
16°30'
MADEIRA ARCHIPELAGO
Porto Santo
Facinho do Forte
Fl(2)10s109m12M
Magnetic Variation 4·9°W
33° N
Ilheu de Cima
Fl(3)15s123m21M
Ponta do Pargo
Fl(3)20s311m26M
Madeira
Ponta de São Jorge
LFl.5s27015M
São Lourenco
Fl.10s102m20M
Ilheu Chão
LFl(2)15s111m13M
Ilhas Desertas
30° N
0
180
nautical miles

OCEANIC DISTANCE TABLE

Approximate distances in nautical miles are by the most direct route while avoiding dangers and allowing for TSS and common shipping concentrations. Oceanic legs over 60 miles have been calculated as great circles

1	English Harbour (Antigua)	**1**																
2	Road Town (Tortola)	186	**2**															
3	St Georges (Bermuda)	945	847	**3**														
4	Cork	3280	3313	2697	**4**													
5	Falmouth	3368	3409	2819	189	**5**												
6	Brest	3346	3404	2835	286	136	**6**											
7	La Coruña	3132	3197	2695	504	440	350	**7**										
8	Lisboa	3026	3115	2700	836	780	658	327	**8**									
9	Vilamoura	3065	3178	2771	969	928	853	464	151	**9**								
10	Porto (Porto Santo)	2630	2738	2423	1180	1144	1068	751	492	472	**10**							
11	Funchal (Madeira)	2595	2704	2397	1217	1186	1110	793	528	511	41	**11**						
12	Europa Point (Gibraltar)	3178	3291	2910	1114	1087	960	618	294	155	577	617	**12**					
13	Casablanca	3061	3174	2835	1135	1114	978	637	313	208	438	472	188	**13**				
14	Ponta Delgada (São Miguel)	2270	2349	1930	1133	1183	1145	862	771	839	544	529	984	918	**14**			
15	Horta (Faial)	2165	2235	1791	1169	1235	1202	966	904	979	691	699	1125	1065	150	**15**		
16	Las Palmas (Gran Canaria)	2662	2785	2552	1458	1410	1334	1016	705	651	301	283	705	527	775	911	**16**	
17	Mindelo (Cape Verdes)	2109	2263	2342	2242	2218	2145	1840	1553	1505	1078	1042	1563	1386	1252	1314	869	**17**

9.26.3 PORTUGUESE ISLANDS: SPECIAL NOTES

Geography The Azores comprises 9 islands in 3 groups:

- Western group: Corvo and Flores
- Central group: Faial, Pico, São Jorge, Graciosa and Terceira
- Eastern group: São Miguel and Santa Maria

The Madeira archipelago comprises:

- Porto Santo
- Madeira
- Islas Desertas – three islands: Ilhéu Chão, Ilha Deserta Grande and Ilhéu Bugio
- Islas Selvagens – three small islands: Selvagem Grande, Selvagem Pequena, Ilhéu de Fora, plus a group of rocks, Ilhéus do Norte

Both in the Azores and Madeira the islands are well spread out. See the Distance table.

Harbours

Azores – The largest and most visited harbours are Horta (Faial) Angra do Heroísmo (Terceira) and Ponta Delgada (São Miguel). Lajes on Flores is oft-visited because it is closest to the USA and to the E-bound transatlantic track. At least one harbour suitable for yachts, for each of the rest of the islands, is shown.

Madeira – The largest and most visited yacht harbours are Porto de Porto Santo, which is the closest to mainland Portugal, and Quinta do Lorde (E Madeira). Other yacht harbours include Funchal and Calheta, both on Madeira's south coast.

Standard Time

Azores – is UT +1, ie 1hr behind UT.

Madeira – is UT, i.e. the same time as the UK.

In both island groups 1hr is added in March for summer time and removed in October, the same as the rest of Europe.

Tides

Azores – Ponta Delgada is the Standard Port with a regular, semi-diurnal regime. In summer HWS is usually around 0200 and 1400 LT, and HWN 0700 and 2000 LT. Tidal range is small: 1·4m sp and 0·6m np. Secondary port differences are <8 mins and <0·2m, thus interpolation is not really necessary. The rising tide sets E-NE, the ebb W-SW. Rates are at their greatest at mid-tide springs and are influenced by strong winds.

Madeira – Casablanca is the Standard Port with a regular, semidiurnal regime. Tidal range is < 2·2m; HWS = HW Dover +3, HWN = HW Dover +3·5. Spring rates max 1·25kn (neaps 0·5kn) floods NE/ENE, ebb is reciprocal.

Currents

Azores – <1kn and variable, but tending towards S or SE-going; locally influenced by each island's topography.

Madeira – the around 0·5kn ambient S or SW-going current is influenced by an inshore current flowing NW-SW from Pta do Pargo to Funchal, causing eddies offshore.

Navigation

Azores – Jul-Aug is a good time for UK-based yachts to visit, after trans-Atlantic boats have passed through in May-Jun. It is best to get back to the UK by end Aug to avoid autumnal gales.

A DGPS station on Horta at 38°32'N 28°37'W is operational on 308 kHz out to a range of 295M. W variation as area map, decreasing 9' annually.

Madeira – June-Sept is a good time for UK-based yachts to visit, before boats heading for a transatlantic circuit have passed through in the autum/winter. W variation as area map, decreasing 8' annually.

Lights, buoys, daymarks All islands are well lit (see area maps) but some higher lts may be obscured by low cloud. In the Azores, Pico (a 2351m/7713ft dormant volcano) is visible from 50M in good visibility. Pico Ruivo de Santana (Madeira) is lower (1862m/6109ft) but will still be raised earlier than Porto Santo (516m/1693ft) on approach from the NE.

The buoyage system is IALA 'A' (reverse of IALA 'B' as used in the Americas). Thus red can buoys are to be left to PORT and green conical buoys to STARBOARD, whilst following the general direction of buoyage. There are few buoys.

Weather Jetstream migrations-permitting, the Azores High usually predominates from June to mid-Sept with light winds/calms and warm settled conditions in the Azores group. If it is not established, windier more variable European conditions may prevail. In summer winds are usually NE'ly over the Central and Eastern groups and visibility is good; fog is rare. Humidity may be high but not uncomfortable. Summers average about 22°C and winters 14°C.

Being SE of the Azores High, for the main part of the year the Madeira archipelago experiences N to NE'ly winds, rarely more than 25kn, often with patches of calm. The temperature remains fairly constant in the summer at about 24°C and about 16°C in winter.

In the winter both island groups may be affected by depressions tracking across the Atlantic and this can produce very strong SW'ly winds.

NAVTEX – São Miguel, Cencomaraçores (F) transmits a 24hr forecast in English on 518 kHz for sea areas Altair, Açores, Irving, Milne and Marsala every 4hrs from 0050 UT; see Chapter 6 and Fig 6(14). São Miguel, Cencomaraçores (J) transmits the forecast on 490 kHz in Portuguese every four hours from 0130.

Porto Santo – Cencomarmadeira (P) transmits a 24hr forecast in English on 518 kHz, for sea areas Josephine, Madeira, Casablanca, Canaries, Meteor, every 4hrs from 0230, including nav warnings within a 20M radius of Madeira and Porto Santo. Covering the same information, Porto Santo, Cencomarmadeira (M) transmits in Portuguese on 490 kHz, every 4hrs from 0100.

See Chapter 6 for forecasts on VHF Ch 11.

Books – *W Coasts of Spain & Portugal* (Admiralty NP67). *The Atlantic Crossing Guide* (Jane Russell RCC/ACN). The detailed *Atlantic Islands* (Anne Hammick/Hilary Keatinge, RCC/Imray) is essential and gives thorough treatment to these Portuguese islands as well as the Canaries and Cape Verdes.

Charts – are listed under each harbour.

Azores – AC 1950 and PC 41101 cover the whole archipelago. PC 43101 covers the western island group, 43102 the central group and 43103 the eastern.

Madeira – AC 4104 and PC 33101 (both 1:350,00) cover the whole archipelago. AC1831 and PC 36201 cover Porto Santo, Madeira and Islas Desertas. PC 36407 covers Ilhas Selvagens.

Formalities

Brit Hon Consul is at Ponta Delgada (São Miguel) or ☎808 203 537 (Lisbon).

Madeira and the Azores are in the EU, but arr/dep procedures can differ for each island group. For E-bound yachts the Azores may be the first port of entry into Europe, so the process is important. Fly flag 'Q' on arrival. Well organised ship's and personal papers, plus courtesy, good humour and patience are a great help. Expect to be processed by Immigration (*Serviço Estrangeiros e Fronteiras (SEF)* Customs (*Alfândega*) and *Policia Maritima*; plus *Guarda Nacional Republicana* (tax authority) and the local HM (*Capitão do Porto*) all of whom may (not) be in the same building.

It is acceptable to fly the Azorean/Madeiran flags on the stbd halyard *below* the Portuguese courtesy ensign. Departure clearance, valid for 24hrs, is also required, even between islands. If you cancel, the process must re-start. In Madeira, all 4 marinas are licensed to process yacht clearance paperwork and may be treated as ports of entry.

Foreign yachts staying in Portuguese waters (or hauled ashore) for more than 183 days may be subject to a 'long stay tax'. Long stay yachts from other EU countries will need to provide evidence that VAT has been paid within the EU. Otherwise VAT will be claimed by the authorities as part of the temporary importation process.

Ilhas Desertas and Ilhas Selvagens – permits must be obtained before visiting these islands. There are officials stationed on them who **will not** allow you to land if you do not have the correct documents. The permits are FOC and can be obtained in Funchal at the National Parks Department, or via any of the four Madeiran marinas (though allow 2 days for them to arrange this). Ship's papers and passports are required to obtain a permit.

Telephone – International dialling code for both groups is 351. Area codes are: 291 for Madeira and Porto Santo; 292 for Flores, Corvo, Faial and Pico; 295 for São Jorge, Graciosa and Terceira; and 296 for São Miguel and Santa Maria.

On all islands the area code must be dialled even within the same island, 9 digits in all. Faxes and e-mail are easy to send/receive.

In both the Azores and Madeira archipelago mobile voice and data coverage is good in populated areas, patchy elsewhere.

Public Holidays – For both groups they are mostly the same as Portugal, see Area 24. Every town has a local festa.

Azores – Local festas are: Ponta Delgada 1 April; Velas 23 April; Porto das Lajes 1 June; Praia da Vítoria 20 June; Horta / Angra de Heroismo / Vila Franca do Campo 24 June; Madalena 22 July; Vila da Praia 12 August; Calheta 25 November.

Madeira – An additional public holiday, Madeira Day, is on 1 July. Porto Santo and Calheta's festa is 24 June and Funchal's is 21 August.

Flights, Azores – Most European airlines, eg TAP, route via Lisboa to São Miguel, Faial and Terceira, but Sata (Air Azores; ☎00 351 296 209720; www.sata.pt) flies direct from Gatwick (London) to São Miguel every Tues. Sata also shuttles between all 9 islands. There are direct flights from/to Boston, USA and Canada.

Madeira – There are two scheduled airlines, TAP and Easyjet. TAP route via Lisboa to Porto Santo & Funchal and Easyjet route via London Gatwick and Bristol to Funchal, and Transavia with regular weekly flights to Paris. Several other airlines fly into Funchal on a less regular basis, these include Thomas Cook, Thomson Flights, Monarch and Jet2. A car ferry runs between Porto Santo and Funchal daily during the summer, see www.portosantoline.pt

Value Added Tax (IVA) – is 22% Madeira and 18% Azores.

AZAB – The Azores and Back race (Falmouth–Ponta Delgada) is held every 4 years. It continues to be a true corinthian event, open to all comers, with limited sponsorship. The next race will be in 2019, see: www.azab.co.uk.

THE AZORES ARCHIPELAGO

9.26.4 AZORES: SELECTED LIGHTS

Bold print = light with a nominal range of 15M or more. CAPITALS = place or feature. *CAPITAL ITALICS* = light-vessel, light float or Lanby. *Italics* = Fog signal. ***Bold italics*** = Racon. All positions are WGS 84 Datum. Sequence is from WNW to ESE.

ILHA DO CORVO

Canto de Carneira ☆ Fl 6s 238m 9M; W twr/R bands; 39°43'·04N 31°05'·35W.

Pta Negra Fl 5s 22m 6M; col on W building; 39°40'·18N 31°06'·86W.

Pta Negra, Cabos Boqueirão ☆, Fl (2) R 8s 11m 3M RW post, marks submarine cables, 39°40'·21N 31°06'·73W.

ILHA DAS FLORES

Ponta do Albarnaz ☆, Fl 5s 103m **22M**, 035°-258°; W twr, R cupola; 39°31'·10N 31°13'·90W.

Santa Cruz, Canto de San Pedro ☆, Fl (2) R 8s 15m 4M RW post, marks submarine cables, 39°27'·38N 31°07'·72W.

Santa Cruz, Pedra Açucareiro ☆, Fl R 5s 13m 4M; 39°27'·27N 31°07'·48W.

PORTO VELHO (SANTA CRUZ), ldg lts 261·6°: Front, L Fl G 5s 13m 4M, 39°27'·24N 31°07'·53W; rear L Fl G 5s 15m 4M, 17m from front.

PORTO DAS POÇAS (SANTA CRUZ), ldg lts 284·6°: Front, Fl R 3s 8m 5M, 39°27'·08N 31°07'·62W; rear Fl R 3s 17m 5M, 40m from front.

PORTO DAS LAJES, ldg lts 270°: Dir Iso WRG 6s 9m W9M R/G6M; 265·5°-G-268·5°-W-271·5°-R-274·5°; R ◇ on W column, R bands; 39°22'·81N 31°10'·27W.

Bkwtr hd ☆ Fl (2) R 12s 14m 9M; 39°22'·75N 31°09'·95W.

Ponta das Lajes ☆, Fl (3) 28s 98m **26M**, 263°-054°; W twr, R cupola; 39°22'·53N 31°10'·60W, SE corner of island.

Faja Grande ☆, Fl 5s 13m 4M; W post, R bands; 39°27'·56N 31°15'·78W

ILHA DO FAIAL

Ponta dos Cedros ☆, Fl 7s 148m 12M; 38°38'·29N 28°43'·29W.

Ponta da Ribeirinha ☆, Fl (3) 20s 135m 12M; Post; 38°35'·74N 28°36'·15W, E end of island.

HORTA

Boa Viagem, ldg Lt 285° ☆ Dir Iso WRG 6s 12m W9M R/G6M; 276°-G-282°-W-288°-R-294°; R ◇ on W post; 38°32′·23N 28°37′·54W.
Bkwtr hd ☆ Fl R 3s 20m 11M; W structure; 38°32′·03N 28°37′·27W.
Ldg lts 195·3°: both Iso G 2s 13/15m 2M; Red X on W posts, R bands. Front 38°31′·67N 28°37′·51W; rear 12m from front.

ILHA DO PICO

MADALENA

N Bkwtr ☆ Oc R 3s 11m 10M; W twr, R bands; 38° 32′·17N 28° 32·0W.
W Bkwtr Fl(3) G 8s 5m 5M, W col, G bands; 38° 32′·13N 28°32′·12W.
Ldg lts 138·9°: both Fl G 6s 16/20m 5M; W posts, R bands. Front 38°31′·99N 28°31′·84W; rear 128m from front.
Ponta da Ilha ☆ Fl (3) 15s 28m **24M**, 166°-070°; W twr, R cupola and bldg; 38°24′·75N 28°01′·84W, E tip of island.

CAIS DO PICO

Cais do Pico ☆ Oc R 6s 10m 6M; R lantern on W structure, 5m; 38° 31′·62N 28° 19·20W.
Mole hd ☆ Fl G 3s 11m 2M; W twr, G bands; 38° 31′·85N 28° 19·15W.
Cabos Galeão ☆ Fl (2) R 8s 8m 9M; 38°25′·50N 28°25′·38W.
Ponta de São Mateus ☆ Fl 5s 33m 13M; 284°-118°; W twr; 38°25′·37N 28°26′·91W.

ILHA DE SÃO JORGE

Ponta dos Rosais ☆ Fl (2) 10s 282m 8M; 38°45′·22N 28°18′·73W.
Ponta do Norte Grande ☆ Fl 6s 34m 12M; R col, W bands; 38°40′·83N 28°03′·03W.
Ponta do Topo ☆ Fl (3) 20s 60m **20M**, 133°-033°; W twr, R cupola and bldg; 38°32′·92N 27°45′·28W, E tip of island.
Ponta do Junçal Fl 3s 64m 6M; R col, W bands; 38° 35′·66N 27° 58·77W.

CALHETA

Pier ☆ Fl R 3s 12m 10M; W twr, R bands; 38° 36′·04N 28° 00·61W.
Ponta da Queimada Fl 5s 37m 10M; W column, R bands; 38° 40′·15N 28° 11·58W.

VELAS

Quay Pier Head ☆ Fl R 5s 14m 7M, W twr, R bands; 38° 40′·68N 28° 12·18W.
Marina Pier Head ☆ Fl(3)G 9s 8m 3M, G twr, W bands; 38° 40′·78N 28° 12·18W.
Mole Pier Head ☆ Fl(3) R 9s 4m 3M, R post, W bands; 38° 40′·78N 28° 12·21W.
Cabos Velas ☆ Fl(2) R 8s 12m 9M, W post, R bands; 38° 40′·71N 28° 12·22W; marks submarine cable area.

ILHA GRACIOSA

Ponta da Barca ☆ Fl 7s 71m **20M**; vis 029°-031°, 035°-251°, 267°-287°; W twr, R cupola & B bands; 39°05′·61N 28°02′·98W.

VILA DA PRAIA

Ldg lts 306·9°: Front, Fl R 2s 8m 6M vis 293°-321°; W twr, R bands; 39°03′·21N 27°58′·16W. Rear, Iso R 4s 13m 6M vis 293°-321°; W column, R bands; 39°03′·24N 27°58′·19W.
Mole hd ☆ Fl G 3s 15m 9M, W twr, G bands; 39°03′·16N 27°57′·96W.
Cabos Praia ☆ Fl(2) R 8s 5m 9M, R lantern on building; 39°03′·07N 27°58′·26W; marks submarine cable area.
Ponta da Restinga ☆ Fl (2) 10s 188m **15M**; 165°-098°; R twr & cupola; 39°00′·84N 27°57′·29W.

ILHA TERCEIRA

Ponta da Serreta ☆ Fl 6s 99m 12M; W twr, R bands; 38°45′·95N 27°22′·45W, NW end of island.
Lajes ☆ Aero Al Fl WG 10s 132m **W28M**, **G23M**; 38°45′·59N 27°04′·84W.

PRAIA DA VITORIA

N mole ☆ Fl 5s 19m 10M; W post, Bk bands; 38°43′·59N 27°03′·06W. Marina in NW corner of hbr.
S mole Fl R 3s 22m 8M; W twr, R bands; 38°43′·24N 27°02′·92W.
Pta das Contendas ☆ Fl (4) WR 15s 53m **W23M**, **R20M**; 220°-W-020°-R-044°-W-072°-R-093°; W twr, R top; 38°38′·62N 27°05′·07W.

ANGRA DO HEROÍSMO

Ldg lts 340·9°: front, Fl R 4s 20m 7M, R post; 38°39′·25N 27°13′·09W. Rear, Oc R 6s 54m 7M, R lantern on Y structure; 505m from front.
Porto Pipas (marina ent, S side) ☆ Fl G 3s 13m 6M.
N mole, ☆ Fl (2) R 6s 8m 3M; 38°39′·12N 27°12′·95W.
Monte Brasil ☆ Oc WR 10s 27m 12M; 191°-R-295°-W-057°; W col, R bands; 38°38′·60N 27°13′·04W.

ILHA DE SÃO MIGUEL

Ferraria ☆ Fl (3) 20s 106m **27M**; 339°-174°; W twr, R cupola; 37°51′·21N 25°51′·02W, NW end of island.
Ponta do Arnel ☆ Aeromarine Fl 5s 65m **25M**; 157°-355°; W twr, R cupola; 37°49′·45N 25°08′·14W, E end of island.
Ponta Garça ☆ Oc WR 5s 100m **W16M**, R13M; 240°-W-080-R-100°; twr and house; 37°42′·86N 25°22′·19W, S side of island.

VILAFRANCA DO CAMPO

Marina N pier head: Fl G 4s 11m 9M; W twr, G bands; 37° 42′·82N 25° 25′·77W.
Marina S pier head: Fl R 4s 11m 9M; W col, R bands; 37°42′·79N 25°25′·71W.

PONTA DELGADA

Bkwtr head ☆ L Fl R 6s 16m 10M; W twr, R bands; 37°44′·18N 25°39′·40W, 450m SSE of marina ent.
Naval Club Dir lt 309°: Fl (2) WRG 5s 24m 10M (H24); 301·5°-G-306·5°-W-311·5°-R-316·5°; 37°44′·45N 25°39′·39W.
Terminal pier E hd ☆ Fl(2)R 5s 2m 3M; W col, R bands; 37°44′·35N 25°39′·61W.
Terminal pier W hd ☆ Fl(3)G 15s 2m 3M; W col, G bands; 37°44′·24N 25°39′·83W.
Quebra floating bkwtr S end ☆ Q(6)+LFl W 15s 3M; 2 ▼ (vert) on Bk bcn, Y top; 37°44′·26N 25°39′·97W.
Marina mole hd ☆ Fl G 3s 12m 10M; W twr, G bands; 37°44′·32N 25°39′·57W, 450m NNW of bkwtr head.
Forte S. Bras ☆ Fl (4) WRG 8s 13m 10M (H24); 259°-G-261°-W-263°-R-265°; 37°44′·13N 25°40′·37W.
Santa Clara ☆ L Fl 5s 26m **15M**; 282°-102°; R lantern; 37°44′·00N 25°41′·16W, between airport and Ponta Delgada.
Airport ☆ Aero Al Fl WG 10s 83m **W28M, G23M**; 282°-124°; control twr; 37°44′·62N 25°42′·46W, 2·5M W of Ponta Delgada.
Ilhéus das Formigas ☆ Fl 5s 22m 9M; W twr; 37°16′·26N 24°46′·83W (islet 20M NE of Ilha de Santa Maria).

ILHA DE SANTA MARIA

Pta do Norte ☆ Fl (4) 15s 138m 12M; W structure, R bands. 37°00′·77N 25°03′·55W.
Pta do Castelo ☆ Aeromarine Fl (3) 13·5s 113m **25M**; 181°-089°; W twr, R cupola and bldg. 36°55′·77N 25°00′·97W, SE corner of island.

VILA DO PORTO

Control twr mole head ☆ L Fl R 5s 14m 5M; R trunc twr, W stripes; 36°56′·49N 25°08′·92W.
Naval Club, ☆ Fl (2) WRG 8s 24m 10M; 346°-G-351°-W-354°-R-359°; 36°56′·80N 25°08′·86W.
Pta do Malmerendo ☆ Fl (2) 10s 49m 12M; W bldg, R bands; vis 282°-091°; 36°56′·43N 25°09′·42W.
Airport ☆ Aero Al Fl WG 10s 116m **WG25M**; 021°-121°; shown by day in poor vis; control twr. 36°58′·37N 25°09′·90W, W end of Is.

9.26.5 PORTO DAS LAJES (FLORES)

Flores **39°22'·82N 31°09'·96W (Hbr ent)**

CHARTS AC 1950, 1959; PC 41101, 43101, 46401

TIDES MHWS 1·5M; MHWN 1·2M; MLWN 0·7M; MLWS 0·4M

SHELTER is good, and the new bkwtr gives good protection against NE'lies in the marina, though there may be a scend. ⚓ where indicated on sand; elsewhere patches of gravel and rock offer poor holding and uncomfortable in N-NE'lies.

Lajes has supplanted the much smaller and more difficult hbr at Santa Cruz, 5M NNE.

NAVIGATION WPT 39°22'·81N 31°09'·00W, 270·0°/9ca to hbr ent. The approach is straightforward by day, but Flores is fringed by rocks; keep at least 1M off. The 9M wide passage between Flores and Corvo can be choppy at sp; deepest water is in the N half.

LIGHTS AND MARKS See Azores Selected Lts for details. The bkwtr lt is often destroyed in winter and is not wholly reliable in summer. The 270° ldg lts lead clear of inshore rocks to stbd and the bkwtr to port. By day the church, water tower and lt ho are all conspic; the latter's light is obscured N of a brg of 263°.

COMMUNICATIONS (Code 292). Brit Consul 808 203 537; Medical emergency 112. Ⓗ 592294; HM 593437, Ch 14,16; Tourist Info 592369 (Santa Cruz).

FACILITIES lajes.flores@aptosa.com, €1·25/m (up to 500 ltrs) ☎ 292 593813, (12t,40t) . Mail pick-up via Café Beira Mar, Lajes das Flores 9960, Azores. Internet access foc at library.

Clube Naval welcomes/helps visitors: ☎292 593145. info@cnlflores.com www.cnlflores.com

Town ✕ ✉ Ⓑ Ⓒ Ⓗ ✈ at Santa Cruz, 12km.

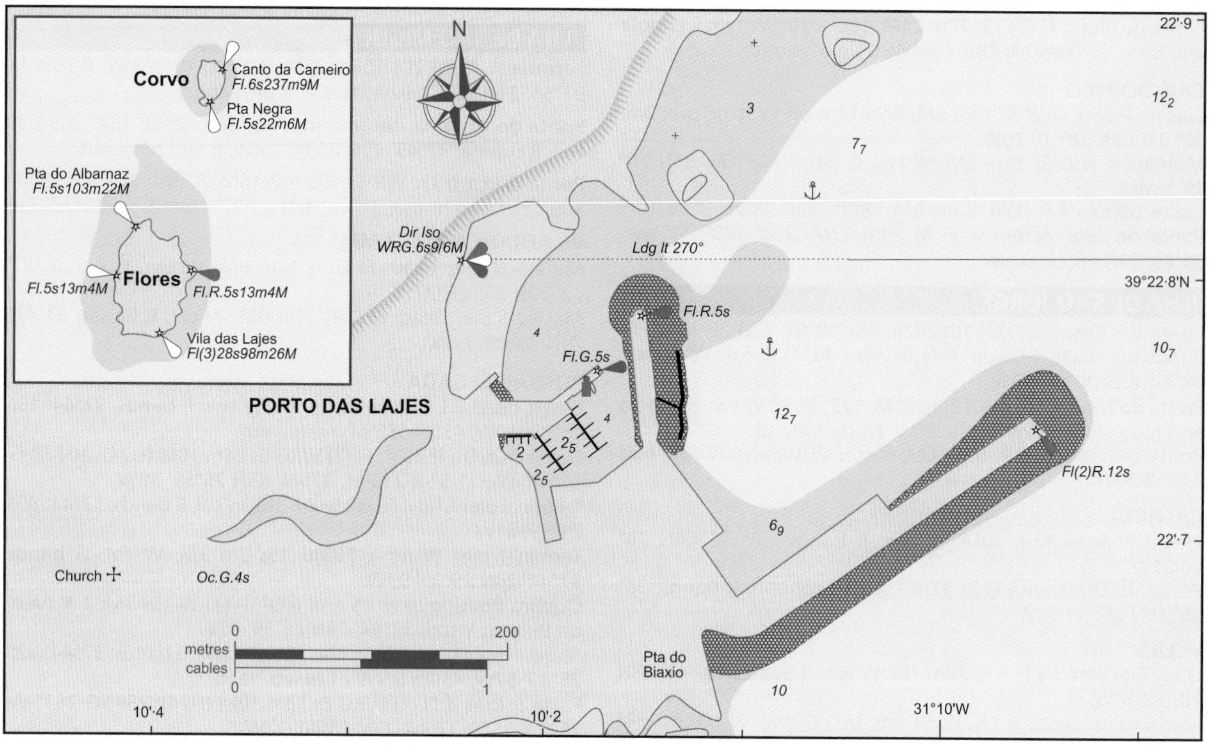

MINOR HARBOUR 9M N OF ILHA DO FLORES

CORVO 39°40'·30N 31°06'·00W. PC 43101, 46401. A small hbr approx 3ca N of Punta Negra. The hbr is exposed to N/NE and suffers badly from swell much of the time; it is unwise to berth alongside, the ⚓ is unreliable: yachts should not be left unattended.

9.26.6 HORTA (FAIAL)

Faial **38°32'·05N 28°37'·38W (Hbr ent)**

CHARTS AC 1950, 1956, 1957; PC 43102, 46403; SHOM 7605

TIDES MHWS 1·6M; MHWN 1·2M; MLWN 0·7M; MLWS 0·4M

SHELTER Good, except in strong SW-SE winds which raise a steep, confused sea in the hbr. ⚓ in hbr allowed (patchy holding). No ⚓ at Porto Pim, an inlet S of the hbr.

NAVIGATION WPT 38°32'·04N 28°36'·00W 270°/1M to bkwtr hd. The 195° ldg line is not for yachts. Streams in the 2·6M wide Canal do Faial between Faial and Pico reach 2½kn eddying SSW towards Horta. Beware many ferries, Baixa do Sul rk (7·1m) in mid-chan which breaks in SW gales. The modern cruise ship terminal lies north of the marina.

LIGHTS AND MARKS See Azores Selected Lts for details. Near the W end of Faial, Vale Formoso, L Fl (2) 10s 113m 13M, is reported to have a range of only about 5M. Monte da Guia, 1M S of the harbour, is a steep, rounded extinct volcano with conspic radio mast. SSW of the marina the Observatory and a hotel tower block are conspic.

COMMUNICATIONS (Code 292) Brit Consul 808 203 537; Medical emergency 112; Ⓗ 200200; APTO (Port Authority) 208300, call *Capimarhorta* VHF Ch 11, 16; Call *Marina da Horta* VHF Ch 10/16 (0800-2000 daily); Portuguese, English, French and Spanish spoken; MAYS *Mid-Atlantic* VHF Ch 77 (HO); Tourist Info 292237.

FACILITIES Marina ☎292391693, 📠292 293986. www.marinasazores.com/horta hortamarina@aptosa.com 300 inc Ⓥ €1·25/m, multihull +50%. In 2 basins: the long-established N basin (2-3m, for locals and smaller visitors) and a new S basin mainly for mega yachts (but <35m LOA, 6m draft). Reception/fuel pontoon is between the basins. Private yacht moorings lie outside the marina. (cash only) via MAYS Ⓔ (20t). Mail pick-up via marina, Av'da Gago Sacadura Cabral 7, 9900 Horta, Faial, Açores; or via Café Sport or MAYS.

Long-term plans envisage a new bkwtr extending SSE from a point about 250m NNE of Boa Viagem lt, giving better shelter and more room to ⚓.

Mid-Atlantic Yacht Services (MAYS) at N end of marina is the key company for visiting yachts, for all repairs, advice, handling mail, fax and email. Helpful and friendly. ☎292 391616. mays@mail.telepac.pt

Clube Naval da Horta ☎292 391719/ 200680 (S of marina) Ch 16 during office hours. secretariado@cnhorta.org Welcomes visitors for racing. Small ✕ .

Café Sport ☎292 292327 www.petercafesport.com welcoming yachtsmen since about 1975, no sailing trip to Horta is considered complete without a stop at this famous bar. There is also a scrimshaw museum upstairs.

Town ✕ ✉ Ⓑ Ⓒ ACA Ⓗ ✈ (UK direct).

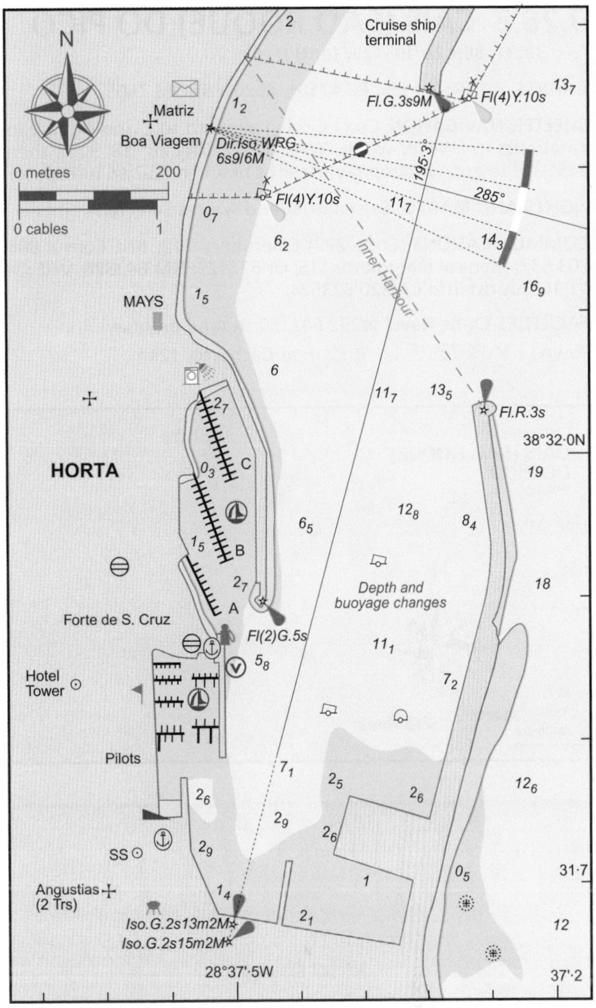

9.26.7 MADALENA (PICO)

Pico **38°32'·15N 28°32'·00W (Ent)**

CHARTS AC 1950,1956,1957; PC 43102, 46403; SHOM 7605

TIDES Use Horta, see Azores Special notes.

SHELTER Reasonable in harbour, though some swell finds its way in and wash from ferries can be troublesome. Alongside space may be at a premium, so ⚓ is usually the best option.

NAVIGATION WPT 38°32·'46N 28°32·'33W thence 139°/4ca to ent. Beware ferry traffic manoeuvring in hbr and WIP 2014.

LIGHTS AND MARKS Madalena N Bkwtr Oc R 3s 11m 10M; W twr, R bands; 38° 32'·2N 28°32'·0W.

W Bkwtr Fl (3) G 8s 5m 5M, W col, G bands; 38°32'·13N °32'·12W.

Ldg lts 138°·9 Front Fl G 6s 15m 5M; W post R bands; 38° 32'·0N 28° 31'·9W.

COMMUNICATIONS (Code 292) Brit Consul 808 203 537; Emergency 112; Medical Emergency 115; Dr 622241; Hbr Auth VHF Ch 11, 16; Tourist Info 623345/623524.

FACILITIES Poss Ⓥ N pier. ☎292 622365/623303. marina@azores.com €1·23/m, no .

Clube Naval do Madalena welcomes visitors: ☎292 623042. cnmpico@hotmail.com.

Town ✕ ✉ Ⓑ Ⓒ. ✈ Cachorro (5km) or via ferry to Horta. Reports welcome.

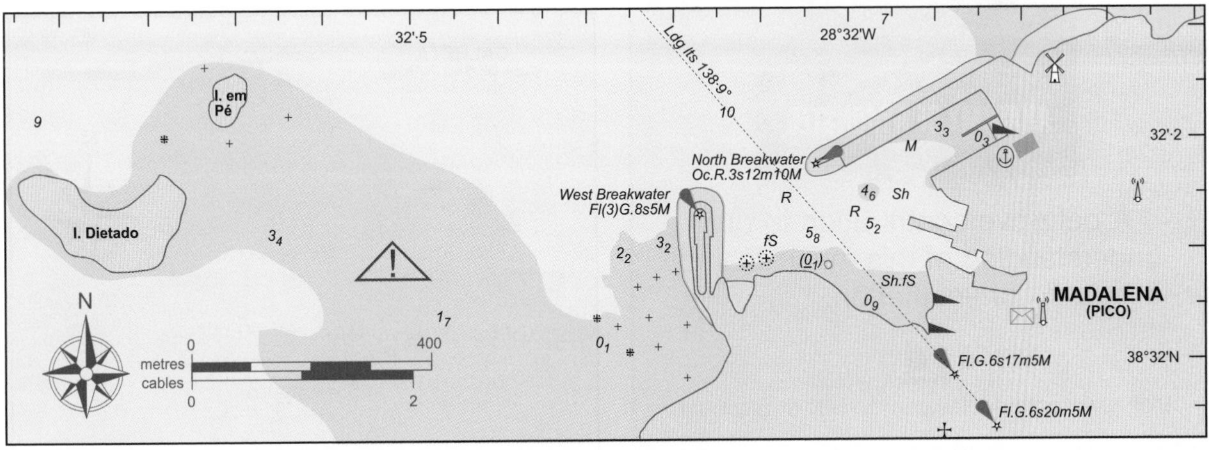

9.26.8 CAIS (SÃO ROQUE) DO PICO

Pico **38°31'·80N 28°19'·12W (ent)**

CHARTS AC 1950, 1956; PC 47501, 46201; SHOM 7605

SHELTER/NAVIGATION Can be rolly: exposed to E and subject to katabatics in SW-NW winds. WPT 38° 32'·04N 28° 18'·90W, then 215°/3ca to ent. ⚓ (deep/rky) clear of bkwtr, or on it if space.

LIGHTS AND MARKS See chartlet and Azores Selected Lights.

COMMUNICATIONS (Code 292) Emergency 112; Brit Consul 808 203 537; Medical emergency 115; Dr 672123; HM 642326, VHF Ch 11,16; Tourist Info 679320/623524.

FACILITIES Clube Naval ☎292 642150, (and on quay).
Town Ⓑ Ⓒ ✈ at Cachorro, 12km.

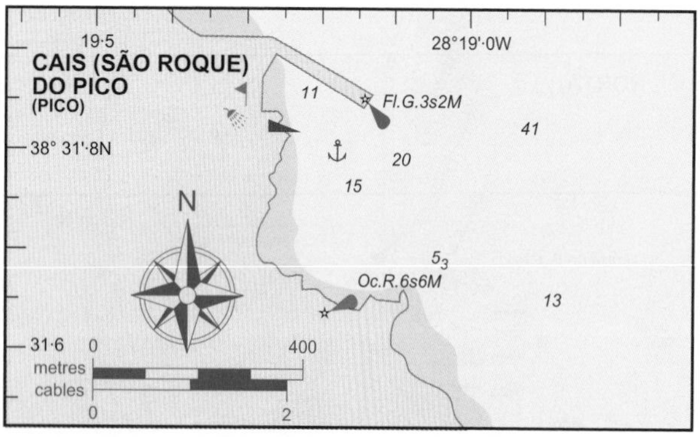

9.26.9 VELAS (SÃO JORGE)

São Jorge **38°40'·61N 28°12'·14W (bkwtr)**

CHARTS AC 1950, 1956; PC 43102, 178; SHOM 7605

SHELTER/NAVIGATION Well protected, but very small. Keep clear of ferry traffic.

LIGHTS AND MARKS Marina Pier Head Fl(3)G 9s 8m 3M G tr, W bands.Mole Pier Head Fl(3) R 9s 4m 3M R post, W bands.

COMMUNICATIONS (Code 295) Maritime Police 432388; Emergency 112; Brit Consul 808 203 537; Medical emergency 115; Dr 412122; HM 412336, VHF Ch 11; *Velas Marina* VHF Ch 16/10 (0800-2000 mid May-mid Aug); Tourist Info 432395/412440.

FACILITIES Marina ☎295 698900 saojorge@aptosa.com www.marinasazores.com 76 inc€1·25/m, multihull +50%. no wi-fi . **Clube Naval das Velas** ☎295 432169.
Town Ⓑ Ⓒ Ⓗ.

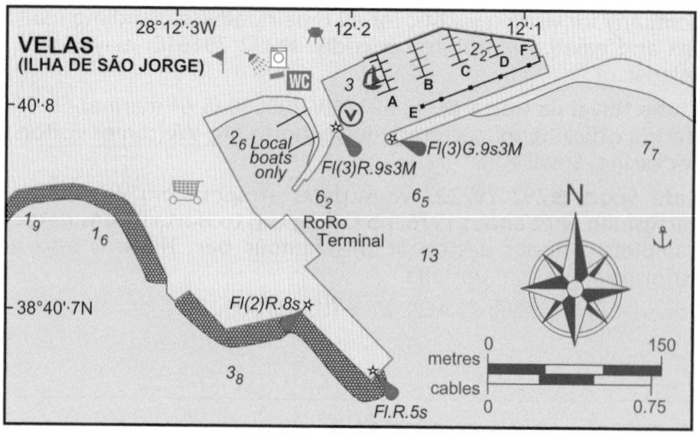

9.26.10 CALHETA (SÃO JORGE)

São Jorge **38°35'·96N 28°0'·54W (bkwtr)**

CHARTS AC 1950, 1956; PC 43102, 178; SHOM 7605

NAVIGATION/SHELTER/LIGHTS WPT 38°35'·77N 28°0'·65W, then 025°/2 ca to bkwtr. Keep close in to bkwtr and quay, rocky shallows close E. Bkwtr lt uncertain. Shelter better than it looks.

LIGHTS AND MARKS New bkwtr Fl R 3s 9m 10M; W twr, R bands; 38° 36'·0N 28° 00'·6W.

COMMUNICATIONS (Code 295) Emergency 112; Brit Consul 808 203 537; Medical emergency 115; Dr 416498; Tourist Info 416252/ 412440.

FACILITIES HM ☎295 416142, €1·25/m, only.
Town Ⓑ Ⓒ ✈ at Velas, 16km.

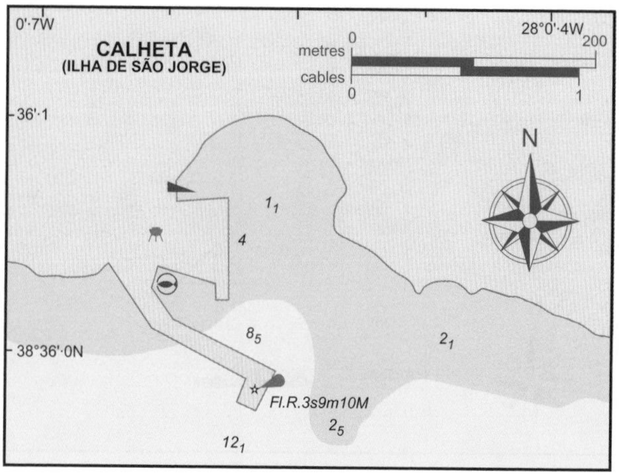

9.26.11 VILA DA PRAIA (GRACIOSA)

Graciosa **39°03'·18N 27°58'·11W** ❀◊✿✿

CHARTS AC 1950, 1956, 1957; PC 43102, 113; SHOM 7605

TIDES Santa Cruz MHWS 1·6M; MHWN 1·3M; MLWN 0·7M; MLWS 0·3M, see Azores Special notes.

SHELTER ⚓ can be rolly, afforded some protection by Ilhéu da Praia, but exposed E to S. Fishing hbr, very crowded, Ⓥ not encouraged.

NAVIGATION WPT 39°03'·05N 27°57'·88W then 1.5ca along 306·9° to ⚓.

LIGHTS AND MARKS Ldg lts 306·9° Front: Fl R 2s 8m 6M vis 293°-321°; W twr, R bands; Rear: Iso R 4s 14m 6M vis 293°-321°; W col, R bands. N Mole, Fl G 3s 15m 9M; W mast. Hbr ent, S pier Fl R 3s 10m 6M, N quay, Fl (2) G 6s 5m3M. Submarine cables warning lt, Fl (2) R 8s 13m 9M, vis 264°-292°.

COMMUNICATIONS (Code 295) Emergency 112; Brit Consul 808 203 537; Medical emergency 115; HM 712128, VHF Ch 11,14,16; Tourist Info 712888/712059.

FACILITIES Town ✕ Ⓑ Ⓒ Ⓗ and small ✈ at Santa Cruz, 7km. Ferries to Faial, Horta.

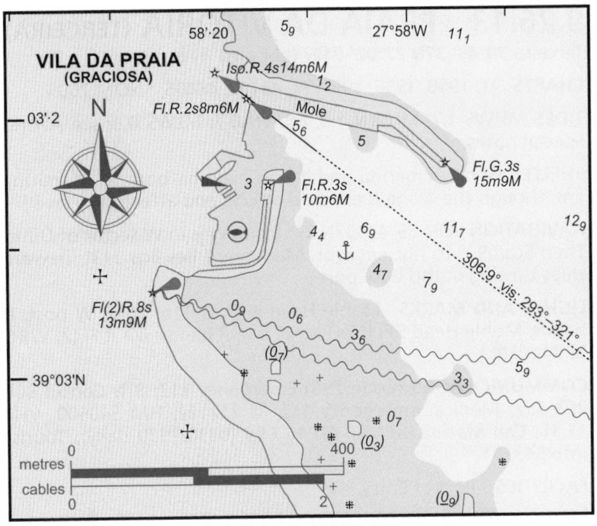

9.26.12 ANGRA DO HEROÍSMO (TERCEIRA)

Terceira **38°39'·10N 27°12'·93W (Marina ent)** ❀❀❀◊◊✿✿✿

CHARTS AC 1950, 1956, 1957; PC 43102, 46405; SHOM 7605

TIDES MHWS 1·6M; MHWN 1·3M; MLWN 0·7M; MLWS 0·4M

SHELTER Good. Exposed only to strong S/SE winds and, if any S in the wind, swell may enter.

A bkwtr extending 1ca W from Porto Pipas ☆ Fl G 3s is planned.

⚓ SW of the marina off the YC, but clear of Baixa da Prainha, a rock awash at CD. Private moorings are laid NE of this rock.

NAVIGATION WPT 38°38'·00N 27°12'·54W, 341°/1·1M to abeam marina ent and on 341° ldg line. Beware unlit Ilhéus das Cabras (146m high islets) 3·3M ESE of the hbr and 9ca offshore.

2M SE of these islets is Ilhéus Fradinhos 8m high pinnacle rks. Both are in the R sectors of Pta das Contendas lt ho.

Monte Brasil has a marine reserve extending about 1M off the coast around it, starting from S Benedicto castle on the E side and continuing round to Ponta de S Diogo on the W side. No ⚓'ing or fishing permitted in the reserve.

LIGHTS AND MARKS See Azores Selected lights for details. Front ldg lt is on a R mast at a conspic twin-towered church; rear is a yellow structure, R top. Monte Brasil, a 205m high peninsula with wooded slopes, is close SW of the marina. Ponta do Farol lt on its SE flank is on a W col, R bands.

COMMUNICATIONS (Code 295) Maritime Police via HM; Brit Consul 808 203 537; Medical emergency 112; Ⓗ 212122 @ Praia da Vitória; HM 540500, VHF Ch 11, 16; Marina VHF Ch 09, 16 (0800-2000 daily); Taxi 212004; Tourist Info 213393.

FACILITIES Angra do Heroísmo (Angra) is a handsome city, a fine natural hbr and a UNESCO World Heritage Site since 1983.

Marina ☎295 540000. www.marinasazores.com/angra marina. angra@aptg.pt 260 inc 60 Ⓥ (18m max LOA) €1·25/m, multihull +50%; Ⓥ finger berths usually on adjacent pontoon G. Depths 3·4m, but less at the NW end. From the ent, reception is due N. (reception pontoon) ✕ Ⓔ (50t). Mail pick-up from Marina, Código Postal 9700-154, Angra do Heroísmo, Terceira, Açores, Portugal.

Angra YC (Porto Pipas mole) welcomes visitors, ☎295 216530.

Town ✕ Ⓑ Ⓒ Ⓗ. ✈ Lajes (24km) direct to UK.

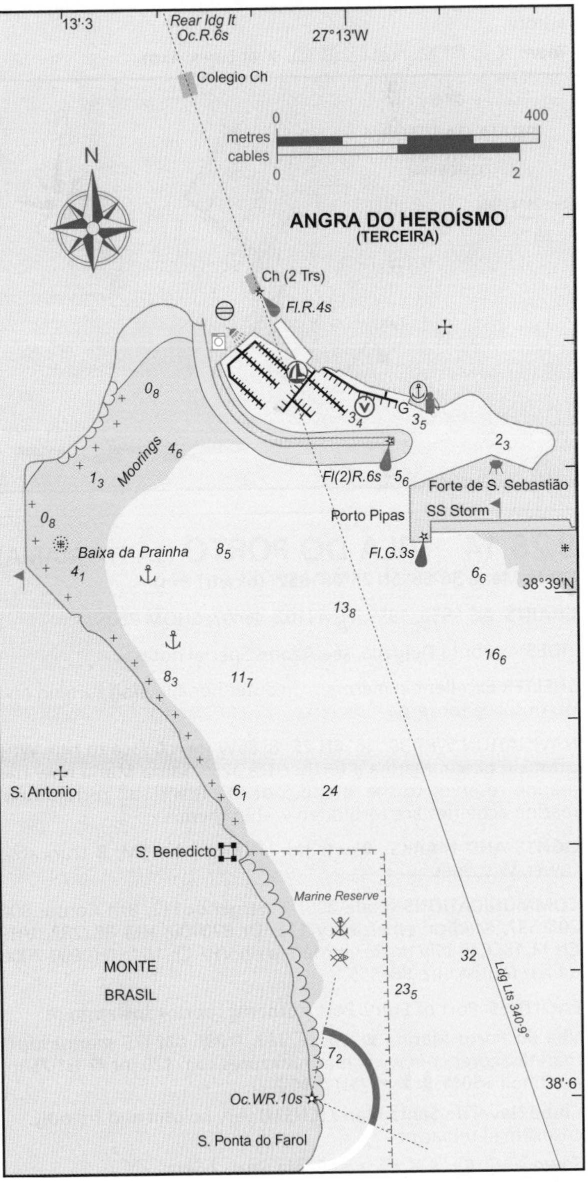

9.26.13 PRAIA DA VITÓRIA (TERCEIRA)

Terceira **38°43'·37N 27°02'·91W (hbr ent)**

CHARTS AC 1950, 1956, 1957; PC 43102, 46405; SHOM 7605

TIDES MHWS 1.7; MHWN 1.3; MLWN 0.7; MLWS 0.3; see Azores Special notes.

SHELTER Good in marina and if ⚓ in main harbour SE of marina ent, though the ⚓'age is exposed to E/SE and affected by swell.

NAVIGATION WPT 38°43'·37N 27° 02'·27W is in W sector of Dir lt. Then 5ca/090° to hbr ent wpt. Marina ent lies 6ca 313°, beware ships turning in this busy port.

LIGHTS AND MARKS Mohle Head N Fl 5s 11m 10M; W post, B bands. Mohle Head S Fl R 3s 8M; W twr, R bands; Dir lt Fl (2) WRG 5s 24m 10M.

COMMUNICATIONS (Code 295) Emergency 112; Brit Consul 808 203 537; Medical emergency 115; Ⓗ 212122; HM 540500, VHF 11,16; **Call** *Marina* on VHF Ch 16 / 09 (0830-1930 daily); Tourist info 543251.

FACILITIES Port of Entry.

Marina ☎295 512082/540019, €1·25/m, 210 inc Ⓥ; (tanker 24hrs notice) (48hrs notice) (35t). Popular for laying up ashore.

Town Market Ⓑ Ⓒ. ✈ at Lajes, 4km.

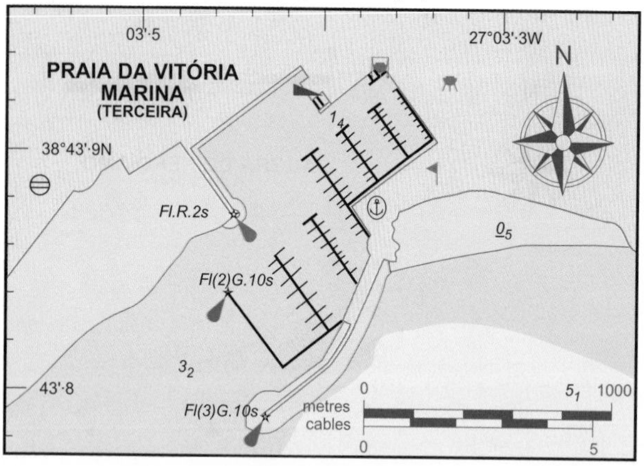

9.26.14 VILA DO PORTO (SANTA MARIA)

Santa Maria **36°56'·5N 25°08'·85W (bkwtr)**

CHARTS AC 1950, 1959; PC 43102, 46407; SHOM 7605

TIDES As Ponta Delgada, see Azores Special notes.

SHELTER Excellent in marina. ⚓ in outer hbr allowing turning and berth space for ferry.

NAVIGATION WPT 36° 56'·0N 25° 8'·85W then 0°/5ca to title WPT off main bkwtr. Marina a further 1ca 325°. Santa Maria now has marine reserves to the N and S of the island, all recreational marine activities are forbidden within them.

LIGHTS AND MARKS Bkwtr hd: LFl R 5s 14m 5M; R truncated tower, W stripes.

COMMUNICATIONS (Code 296). Emergency 112; Brit Consul 808 203 537; Medical emergency 115; Dr 820100; HM 882282, VHF Ch 11,16; Call *Vila do Porto Marina* on VHF Ch 16 / 10 (0800-2000 daily); Tourist Info 886355.

FACILITIES Port of Entry. Port Authority: portovdp@apsm.pt

Vila do Porto Marina ☎296 882282. 296 882176 marinavdp@marinasazores.com www.marinasazores.com 120 inc Ⓥ €1·25/m, multihull +50%. (75t).

Clube Naval de Santa Maria (CNSM) very helpful and friendly. cnsm@mail.telpac.pt

Town Ⓑ Ⓒ ✈ at Santa Cruz, 2·5km.

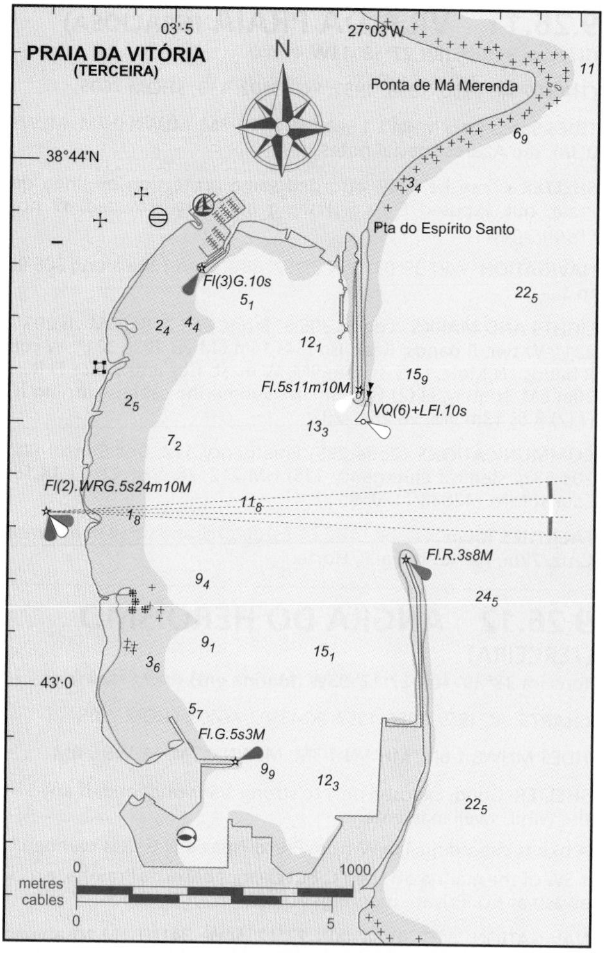

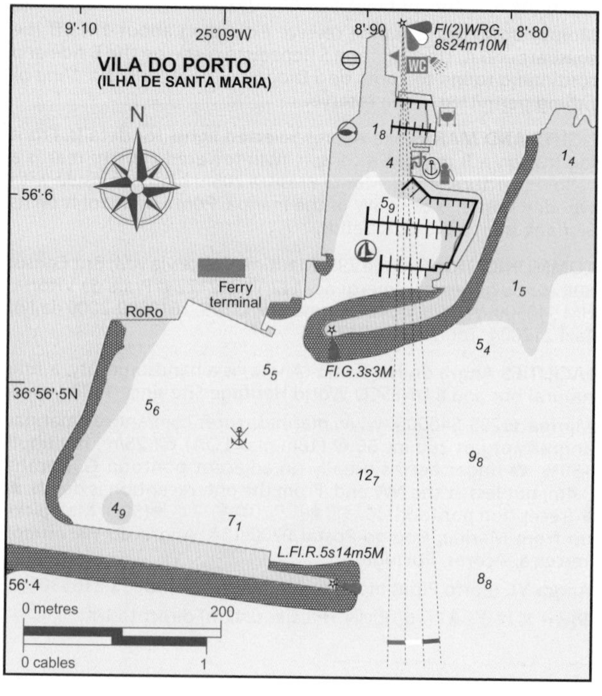

9.26.15 PONTA DELGADA
(SÃO MIGUEL)

São Miguel **37°44'·23N 25°39'·24W**

CHARTS AC 1950, 1895; PC 43103, 46406; SHOM 7432

TIDES MHWS 1·7M; MHWN 1·3M; MLWN 0·7M; MLWS 0·3M

SHELTER Good inside the high and substantial bkwtr, but in strong E-S winds a heavy swell enters. ⚓ is allowed, but not encouraged, at the W end of the hbr in 8-10m on sand and well clear of any ship operations.

NAVIGATION WPT 37°44'·27N 25°39'·12W, where the W sectors of the 309° and 262° Dir lts intersect; thence 284°/4ca to marina.

LIGHTS AND MARKS See Azores Selected lights for details of directional lts. The 300-1100m high island is easily seen from afar. Conspic marks include the W twr + R bands on bkwtr head and the Solmar bldg, a white 22 storey hotel, close W of the marina.

COMMUNICATIONS (Code 296) MRCC Ponta Delgada 281777 – only accepts safety and distress calls, mrcc.delgada@mail.telepac.pt; and nav bulletins VHF Ch 11 in Portuguese; see Chapters 5 & 6 for times and content; Police/Fire/Ambulance 112; Brit Consul 808 203 537; Rua Domingos Rebelo 43A, 9500-234 Ponta Delgada; Ⓗ 203000, ask at marina for doctor or dentist; Port HM 205240, VHF 11, 16; *Marina* VHF Ch **9**/16 (0900-1830 M-Fri; 0900-1730 Sat/Sun).

FACILITIES Marina, East and West basins, (3·5m-8m) ☎296 281510/11/12. marinapdl@apsm.pt www.marinasazores.com 670 inc Ⓥ €1·25/m, multihull +50% mostly in newer W basin, but essential to visit reception pontoon first, N side of ent to E basin, along with via HM Ⓔ Diver (25t).

Mail pick-up: c/o Marina de Ponta Delgada, Aptdo 3 – Calheta, 9500 Ponta Delgada, São Miguel, Açores, Portugal.

Clube Naval de Ponta Delgada (E of marina) welcomes visitors: (3t). ☎296 308380. atendimento@cnpdl.pt www.cnpdl.pt

City Market Ⓑ Ⓒ Ⓗ. ✈ 4km W: flights direct to Gatwick, UK every Tues and daily via Lisboa to European destinations.

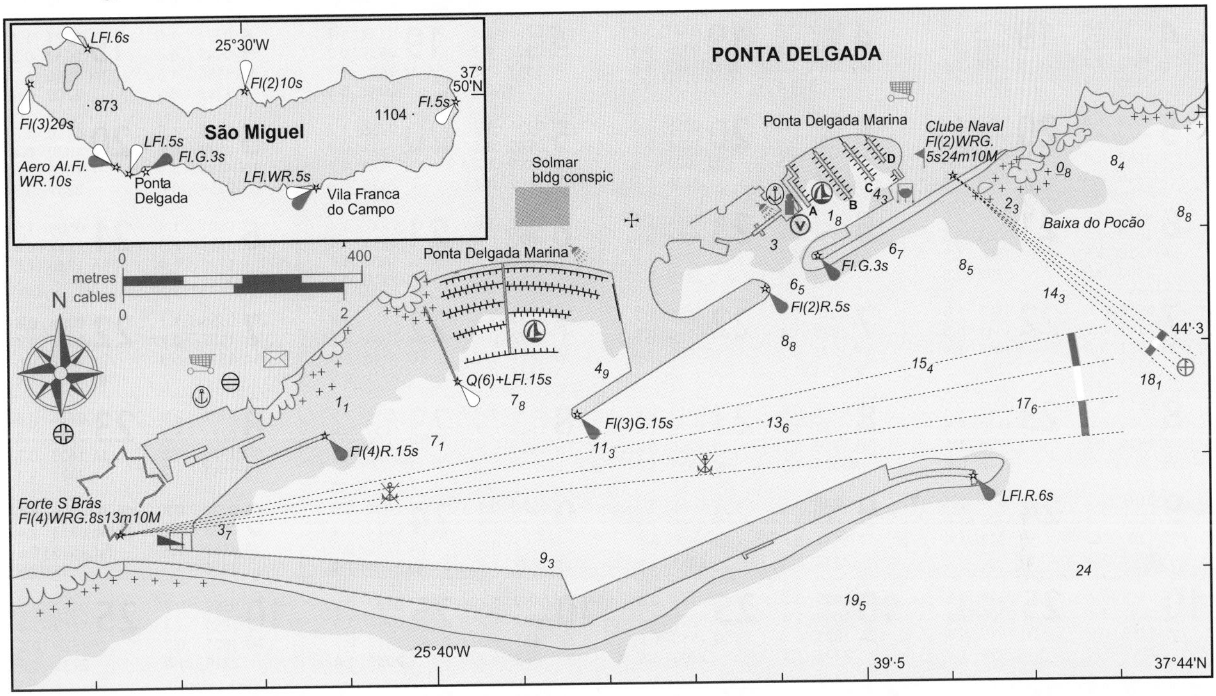

9.26.16 VILA FRANCA DO CAMPO
(SÃO MIGUEL)

São Miguel **37°42'·79N 25°25'·78W (marina ent)**

CHARTS AC 1950, 1895; PC 43103, 46406, 165; SHOM 7432

TIDES As Ponta Delgada **SHELTER** Excellent in marina.

NAVIGATION Pass inside or outside Ilhéu da Vila to WPT 37° 42'·54N 25° 25'·56W then 325°/3ca to marina ent (title wpt). Caution necessary due to construction works.

LIGHTS AND MARKS Marina Pier Head: Fl G 4s 11m 9M; W twr, G bands; 37° 42'·80N 25° 25'·80W. 2 x Y marks (B pole, Y stripes) indicate works area.

COMMUNICATIONS (Code 296). Emergency 112; Brit Consul 808 203 537; Ⓗ 203000; Dr 582117; *APTO* VHF Ch 09/16.

FACILITIES Marina ☎296 581488 (0830-1230 & 1330-1630). marinaem@sapo.pt; 156 limited Ⓥ, €1·70/m. Ⓒ (6t).

Clube Naval de Vila Franca do Campo welcomes visitors ☎296 582333. cnvfc@mail.telepac.pt / cnvfc@clix.pt;.

Town Ⓑ Ⓒ Ⓗ ✈ 23km W, flights direct to UK.

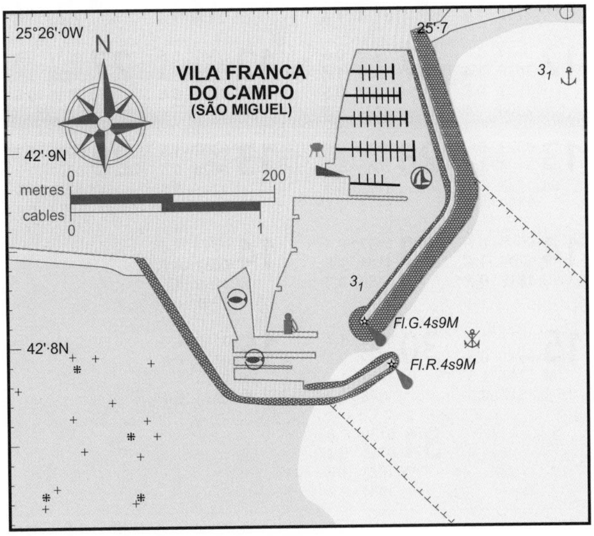

STANDARD TIME UT +01
Add 1 hour for UT
For Azores Summer Time add ONE hour in **non-shaded areas**

PONTA DELGADA LAT 37°44′N LONG 25°40′W

TIMES AND HEIGHTS OF HIGH AND LOW WATERS

Dates in red are **SPRINGS**
Dates in blue are **NEAPS**

YEAR **2018**

JANUARY

Date	Day	Time	m	Time	m	Time	m	Time	m	Moon
1	M	0023	1.8	0637	0.3	1244	1.7	1857	0.2	
2	TU	0111	1.8	0728	0.2	1334	1.7	1945	0.2	○
3	W	0159	1.9	0817	0.2	1424	1.7	2032	0.2	
4	TH	0247	1.9	0907	0.2	1513	1.7	2120	0.3	
5	F	0336	1.8	0958	0.3	1603	1.6	2209	0.4	
6	SA	0426	1.7	1050	0.4	1655	1.5	2300	0.5	
7	SU	0519	1.6	1144	0.5	1751	1.4	2357	0.6	
8	M	0617	1.5	1244	0.6	1854	1.3			◑
9	TU	0103	0.6	0721	1.4	1350	0.6	2005	1.3	
10	W	0218	0.7	0831	1.4	1459	0.6	2117	1.3	
11	TH	0332	0.7	0939	1.3	1601	0.6	2218	1.4	
12	F	0434	0.7	1036	1.4	1652	0.6	2308	1.4	
13	SA	0523	0.6	1124	1.4	1735	0.6	2350	1.5	
14	SU	0605	0.6	1205	1.4	1812	0.5			
15	M	0027	1.5	0641	0.5	1242	1.5	1847	0.5	
16	TU	0101	1.6	0715	0.5	1316	1.5	1919	0.4	
17	W	0133	1.6	0748	0.4	1349	1.5	1951	0.4	●
18	TH	0204	1.6	0820	0.4	1421	1.5	2023	0.4	
19	F	0236	1.6	0853	0.4	1454	1.5	2055	0.4	
20	SA	0309	1.6	0927	0.4	1529	1.5	2129	0.4	
21	SU	0344	1.6	1003	0.5	1606	1.5	2207	0.5	
22	M	0423	1.6	1043	0.5	1649	1.4	2250	0.5	
23	TU	0508	1.5	1130	0.6	1739	1.4	2342	0.6	
24	W	0601	1.5	1226	0.6	1842	1.4			◐
25	TH	0048	0.6	0706	1.4	1336	0.6	1956	1.4	
26	F	0208	0.7	0822	1.4	1452	0.6	2113	1.4	
27	SA	0328	0.6	0939	1.4	1603	0.5	2221	1.5	
28	SU	0438	0.5	1046	1.5	1705	0.4	2320	1.6	
29	M	0537	0.4	1144	1.6	1759	0.3			
30	TU	0012	1.7	0630	0.3	1237	1.7	1848	0.3	
31	W	0100	1.8	0719	0.2	1325	1.7	1934	0.2	○

FEBRUARY

Date	Day	Time	m	Time	m	Time	m	Time	m	Moon
1	TH	0147	1.9	0806	0.2	1411	1.8	2019	0.2	
2	F	0232	1.9	0851	0.2	1456	1.7	2102	0.2	
3	SA	0316	1.9	0935	0.2	1540	1.7	2145	0.3	
4	SU	0400	1.8	1019	0.3	1624	1.6	2229	0.4	
5	M	0445	1.6	1103	0.4	1709	1.5	2315	0.5	
6	TU	0533	1.5	1151	0.6	1801	1.4			
7	W	0010	0.6	0629	1.4	1248	0.7	1904	1.3	◑
8	TH	0120	0.7	0737	1.3	1359	0.7	2023	1.3	
9	F	0246	0.8	0857	1.3	1517	0.7	2142	1.3	
10	SA	0405	0.7	1009	1.3	1623	0.7	2243	1.4	
11	SU	0503	0.7	1104	1.3	1713	0.6	2330	1.4	
12	M	0547	0.6	1148	1.4	1754	0.6			
13	TU	0008	1.5	0624	0.5	1225	1.5	1829	0.5	
14	W	0041	1.6	0657	0.5	1259	1.5	1901	0.4	
15	TH	0113	1.6	0729	0.4	1330	1.5	1932	0.4	●
16	F	0144	1.7	0759	0.4	1401	1.6	2003	0.4	
17	SA	0214	1.7	0830	0.4	1433	1.6	2035	0.4	
18	SU	0247	1.7	0902	0.4	1506	1.6	2108	0.4	
19	M	0321	1.7	0936	0.4	1542	1.6	2145	0.4	
20	TU	0358	1.6	1014	0.4	1622	1.5	2226	0.5	
21	W	0441	1.6	1057	0.5	1709	1.5	2315	0.5	
22	TH	0531	1.5	1150	0.6	1807	1.4			
23	F	0019	0.6	0636	1.4	1259	0.6	1923	1.4	◐
24	SA	0143	0.7	0759	1.3	1426	0.6	2051	1.4	
25	SU	0315	0.6	0927	1.4	1550	0.6	2208	1.5	
26	M	0432	0.5	1040	1.5	1656	0.5	2309	1.6	
27	TU	0531	0.4	1138	1.5	1750	0.4			
28	W	0001	1.7	0621	0.3	1228	1.6	1837	0.3	

MARCH

Date	Day	Time	m	Time	m	Time	m	Time	m	Moon
1	TH	0047	1.8	0706	0.2	1312	1.7	1920	0.2	○
2	F	0130	1.9	0748	0.2	1354	1.8	2001	0.2	
3	SA	0211	1.9	0828	0.2	1434	1.7	2040	0.2	
4	SU	0252	1.8	0907	0.2	1513	1.7	2119	0.3	
5	M	0331	1.7	0945	0.3	1551	1.6	2158	0.4	
6	TU	0411	1.6	1022	0.4	1630	1.5	2238	0.5	
7	W	0453	1.5	1102	0.6	1713	1.4	2324	0.6	
8	TH	0540	1.4	1149	0.7	1806	1.3			
9	F	0025	0.7	0642	1.3	1253	0.8	1921	1.3	◑
10	SA	0153	0.8	0807	1.2	1421	0.8	2053	1.3	
11	SU	0327	0.8	0935	1.2	1545	0.8	2208	1.3	
12	M	0434	0.7	1039	1.3	1644	0.7	2300	1.4	
13	TU	0521	0.6	1124	1.4	1728	0.6	2340	1.5	
14	W	0558	0.5	1201	1.4	1804	0.5			
15	TH	0014	1.5	0631	0.5	1234	1.5	1836	0.4	
16	F	0046	1.6	0702	0.4	1305	1.6	1908	0.4	
17	SA	0117	1.7	0732	0.3	1336	1.6	1939	0.3	●
18	SU	0149	1.7	0803	0.3	1408	1.7	2013	0.3	
19	M	0222	1.7	0836	0.3	1443	1.7	2048	0.3	
20	TU	0258	1.7	0911	0.3	1520	1.7	2126	0.3	
21	W	0337	1.7	0950	0.4	1601	1.6	2210	0.4	
22	TH	0421	1.6	1034	0.4	1649	1.5	2301	0.5	
23	F	0514	1.5	1127	0.6	1748	1.5			
24	SA	0007	0.6	0622	1.4	1239	0.6	1906	1.4	◐
25	SU	0137	0.6	0752	1.3	1413	0.7	2037	1.4	
26	M	0310	0.6	0923	1.3	1540	0.6	2155	1.5	
27	TU	0424	0.5	1034	1.4	1646	0.5	2255	1.6	
28	W	0520	0.4	1128	1.5	1737	0.4	2345	1.7	
29	TH	0606	0.3	1213	1.6	1821	0.3			
30	F	0028	1.8	0647	0.3	1254	1.7	1901	0.3	
31	SA	0109	1.8	0725	0.2	1332	1.7	1940	0.3	○

APRIL

Date	Day	Time	m	Time	m	Time	m	Time	m	Moon
1	SU	0148	1.8	0802	0.2	1409	1.7	2017	0.3	
2	M	0226	1.8	0837	0.3	1445	1.7	2053	0.3	
3	TU	0303	1.7	0911	0.3	1520	1.6	2129	0.4	
4	W	0339	1.6	0945	0.4	1556	1.5	2207	0.5	
5	TH	0418	1.5	1021	0.6	1635	1.5	2250	0.6	
6	F	0501	1.4	1103	0.6	1722	1.4	2344	0.7	
7	SA	0556	1.3	1158	0.7	1826	1.3			
8	SU	0102	0.8	0716	1.2	1320	0.8	1953	1.3	◑
9	M	0235	0.8	0848	1.2	1452	0.8	2116	1.3	
10	TU	0350	0.7	0959	1.3	1601	0.7	2216	1.4	
11	W	0441	0.6	1049	1.3	1650	0.6	2300	1.4	
12	TH	0521	0.5	1128	1.4	1729	0.6	2337	1.5	
13	F	0556	0.5	1202	1.5	1804	0.5			
14	SA	0012	1.6	0628	0.4	1235	1.6	1838	0.4	
15	SU	0046	1.7	0701	0.3	1308	1.7	1913	0.3	
16	M	0121	1.7	0735	0.3	1343	1.7	1950	0.3	●
17	TU	0158	1.8	0811	0.3	1421	1.8	2029	0.3	
18	W	0238	1.7	0850	0.3	1502	1.7	2112	0.3	
19	TH	0321	1.7	0932	0.3	1546	1.7	2200	0.4	
20	F	0410	1.6	1020	0.4	1638	1.6	2257	0.5	
21	SA	0508	1.5	1117	0.6	1740	1.5			
22	SU	0008	0.6	0620	1.4	1232	0.6	1857	1.4	◐
23	M	0134	0.6	0748	1.3	1403	0.7	2022	1.4	
24	TU	0259	0.6	0913	1.4	1525	0.6	2136	1.5	
25	W	0407	0.5	1019	1.4	1628	0.6	2235	1.6	
26	TH	0500	0.4	1110	1.5	1718	0.5	2324	1.6	
27	F	0544	0.4	1153	1.6	1801	0.4			
28	SA	0007	1.7	0624	0.3	1232	1.6	1841	0.4	
29	SU	0046	1.7	0700	0.3	1309	1.7	1918	0.3	○
30	M	0124	1.7	0735	0.3	1344	1.7	1954	0.3	

HAT is 1·9 metres above Chart Datum.

STANDARD TIME UT +01
Add 1 hour for UT
For Azores Summer Time add ONE hour in **non-shaded areas**

PONTA DELGADA

LAT 37°44'N LONG 25°40'W

TIMES AND HEIGHTS OF HIGH AND LOW WATERS

Dates in red are SPRINGS
Dates in blue are NEAPS

YEAR **2018**

MAY

Date	Day	Time	m	Time	m	Time	m	Time	m
1	TU	0200	1.7	0808	0.3	1419	1.7	2030	0.4
2	W	0236	1.6	0841	0.4	1454	1.6	2106	0.4
3	TH	0312	1.5	0915	0.5	1529	1.6	2143	0.5
4	F	0350	1.4	0951	0.5	1607	1.5	2225	0.6
5	SA	0432	1.4	1031	0.6	1650	1.4	2314	0.7
6	SU	0522	1.3	1120	0.7	1744	1.3		
7	M	0019	0.7	0629	1.2	1227	0.8	1855	1.3
8	TU	0137	0.7	0750	1.2	1350	0.8	◑ 2013	1.3
9	W	0252	0.7	0904	1.2	1504	0.7	2119	1.4
10	TH	0349	0.6	1000	1.3	1601	0.7	2211	1.4
11	F	0435	0.6	1045	1.4	1647	0.6	2254	1.5
12	SA	0514	0.5	1124	1.5	1728	0.5	2334	1.6
13	SU	0552	0.4	1202	1.6	1808	0.4		
14	M	0014	1.7	0629	0.3	1240	1.7	1848	0.3
15	TU	0055	1.7	0709	0.3	1320	1.8	● 1930	0.3
16	W	0137	1.7	0750	0.2	1402	1.8	2015	0.3
17	TH	0222	1.7	0833	0.3	1447	1.8	2103	0.3
18	F	0311	1.7	0920	0.3	1536	1.7	2155	0.3
19	SA	0404	1.6	1012	0.4	1631	1.7	2255	0.4
20	SU	0504	1.5	1112	0.5	1733	1.6		
21	M	0004	0.5	0614	1.4	1223	0.6	1844	1.5
22	TU	0120	0.5	0732	1.4	1343	0.6	◐ 1959	1.5
23	W	0235	0.5	0849	1.4	1459	0.6	2109	1.5
24	TH	0340	0.5	0953	1.4	1603	0.6	2209	1.5
25	F	0434	0.5	1046	1.5	1655	0.5	2259	1.5
26	SA	0519	0.4	1130	1.5	1740	0.5	2344	1.6
27	SU	0559	0.4	1210	1.6	1821	0.4		
28	M	0024	1.6	0635	0.4	1247	1.6	1859	0.4
29	TU	0102	1.6	0710	0.4	1322	1.6	○ 1935	0.4
30	W	0139	1.6	0744	0.4	1357	1.6	2011	0.4
31	TH	0215	1.5	0817	0.4	1432	1.6	2046	0.5

JUNE

Date	Day	Time	m	Time	m	Time	m	Time	m
1	F	0251	1.5	0852	0.5	1507	1.6	2123	0.5
2	SA	0328	1.4	0927	0.5	1544	1.5	2203	0.6
3	SU	0408	1.4	1006	0.6	1624	1.5	2248	0.6
4	M	0453	1.3	1050	0.6	1711	1.4	2340	0.6
5	TU	0547	1.3	1144	0.7	1806	1.4		
6	W	0042	0.7	0651	1.2	1250	0.7	◑ 1911	1.3
7	TH	0148	0.7	0800	1.3	1402	0.7	2017	1.4
8	F	0250	0.6	0903	1.3	1507	0.7	2117	1.4
9	SA	0344	0.6	0957	1.4	1602	0.6	2210	1.5
10	SU	0432	0.5	1045	1.5	1652	0.5	2259	1.5
11	M	0517	0.4	1130	1.6	1739	0.4	2346	1.6
12	TU	0602	0.3	1215	1.7	1826	0.3		
13	W	0033	1.7	0647	0.3	1301	1.8	● 1914	0.3
14	TH	0121	1.7	0733	0.3	1347	1.8	2004	0.2
15	F	0211	1.7	0821	0.3	1436	1.8	2055	0.2
16	SA	0302	1.7	0911	0.3	1527	1.8	2149	0.3
17	SU	0356	1.6	1003	0.4	1620	1.7	2246	0.3
18	M	0454	1.5	1100	0.5	1718	1.6	2347	0.4
19	TU	0556	1.5	1203	0.5	1821	1.6		
20	W	0053	0.5	0703	1.4	1312	0.6	◐ 1929	1.5
21	TH	0201	0.5	0814	1.4	1425	0.6	2037	1.5
22	F	0306	0.6	0920	1.4	1533	0.6	2140	1.4
23	SA	0403	0.6	1018	1.4	1631	0.6	2235	1.5
24	SU	0453	0.5	1107	1.5	1721	0.6	2322	1.5
25	M	0535	0.5	1149	1.5	1804	0.5		
26	TU	0005	1.5	0614	0.5	1228	1.6	1843	0.5
27	W	0044	1.5	0650	0.5	1304	1.6	1919	0.5
28	TH	0121	1.5	0724	0.4	1339	1.6	○ 1954	0.5
29	F	0156	1.5	0758	0.4	1413	1.6	2029	0.5
30	SA	0232	1.5	0832	0.5	1447	1.6	2104	0.5

JULY

Date	Day	Time	m	Time	m	Time	m	Time	m
1	SU	0307	1.5	0906	0.5	1522	1.6	2141	0.5
2	M	0343	1.4	0942	0.5	1558	1.5	2220	0.6
3	TU	0423	1.4	1021	0.6	1639	1.5	2303	0.6
4	W	0507	1.3	1106	0.6	1725	1.4	2352	0.6
5	TH	0559	1.3	1200	0.7	1819	1.4		
6	F	0049	0.6	0700	1.3	1304	0.7	◑ 1920	1.4
7	SA	0151	0.6	0807	1.3	1414	0.7	2026	1.4
8	SU	0255	0.6	0912	1.4	1521	0.6	2130	1.4
9	M	0354	0.5	1011	1.5	1623	0.6	2230	1.5
10	TU	0450	0.4	1106	1.6	1719	0.4	2325	1.6
11	W	0542	0.4	1157	1.7	1812	0.3		
12	TH	0018	1.6	0632	0.3	1246	1.8	1903	0.3
13	F	0110	1.7	0721	0.3	1335	1.8	● 1953	0.2
14	SA	0200	1.7	0809	0.2	1423	1.9	2044	0.2
15	SU	0251	1.7	0858	0.3	1513	1.9	2134	0.2
16	M	0341	1.7	0947	0.3	1603	1.8	2226	0.3
17	TU	0432	1.6	1038	0.4	1655	1.7	2319	0.4
18	W	0526	1.5	1133	0.5	1750	1.6		
19	TH	0016	0.5	0625	1.4	1234	0.6	◐ 1851	1.5
20	F	0118	0.6	0731	1.4	1345	0.7	1959	1.4
21	SA	0225	0.6	0842	1.3	1500	0.7	2108	1.4
22	SU	0330	0.6	0949	1.4	1608	0.7	2211	1.4
23	M	0428	0.6	1045	1.4	1704	0.6	2304	1.4
24	TU	0515	0.6	1131	1.5	1749	0.6	2349	1.4
25	W	0556	0.5	1211	1.5	1828	0.5		
26	TH	0028	1.5	0632	0.5	1247	1.6	1903	0.5
27	F	0104	1.5	0707	0.5	1321	1.6	○ 1937	0.5
28	SA	0138	1.5	0739	0.4	1353	1.6	2009	0.4
29	SU	0211	1.5	0811	0.4	1425	1.6	2042	0.4
30	M	0244	1.5	0843	0.4	1457	1.6	2115	0.4
31	TU	0317	1.5	0917	0.5	1531	1.6	2149	0.5

AUGUST

Date	Day	Time	m	Time	m	Time	m	Time	m
1	W	0352	1.5	0952	0.5	1607	1.6	2226	0.5
2	TH	0431	1.4	1032	0.6	1648	1.5	2308	0.6
3	F	0517	1.4	1119	0.6	1736	1.5	2359	0.6
4	SA	0612	1.4	1218	0.6	1834	1.4	◑	
5	SU	0101	0.6	0720	1.3	1331	0.7	1946	1.4
6	M	0214	0.6	0836	1.4	1451	0.6	2102	1.4
7	TU	0327	0.6	0947	1.5	1605	0.6	2213	1.5
8	W	0432	0.5	1049	1.6	1707	0.5	2314	1.5
9	TH	0529	0.4	1143	1.7	1802	0.3		
10	F	0009	1.6	0620	0.3	1233	1.8	1852	0.2
11	SA	0059	1.7	0708	0.3	1321	1.9	● 1940	0.2
12	SU	0147	1.8	0754	0.2	1407	1.9	2027	0.2
13	M	0233	1.8	0839	0.2	1452	1.9	2112	0.2
14	TU	0318	1.7	0924	0.3	1538	1.8	2158	0.3
15	W	0403	1.6	1009	0.4	1625	1.7	2244	0.4
16	TH	0451	1.5	1058	0.5	1714	1.6	2333	0.5
17	F	0542	1.4	1153	0.6	1810	1.4		
18	SA	0029	0.6	0644	1.3	1301	0.7	◐ 1916	1.3
19	SU	0137	0.7	0759	1.3	1425	0.7	2034	1.3
20	M	0254	0.7	0918	1.3	1546	0.7	2149	1.3
21	TU	0402	0.7	1023	1.4	1647	0.7	2247	1.3
22	W	0455	0.6	1112	1.4	1732	0.6	2332	1.4
23	TH	0537	0.6	1152	1.5	1810	0.5		
24	F	0010	1.4	0613	0.5	1226	1.6	1843	0.5
25	SA	0044	1.5	0646	0.5	1258	1.6	1914	0.4
26	SU	0116	1.5	0717	0.4	1329	1.6	○ 1945	0.4
27	M	0147	1.5	0747	0.4	1359	1.7	2015	0.4
28	TU	0217	1.6	0818	0.4	1430	1.7	2045	0.4
29	W	0249	1.6	0850	0.4	1502	1.6	2118	0.4
30	TH	0322	1.5	0925	0.4	1537	1.6	2152	0.4
31	F	0400	1.5	1003	0.5	1617	1.5	2232	0.5

HAT is 1·9 metres above Chart Datum.

STANDARD TIME UT +01
Add 1 hour for UT
For Azores Summer Time add ONE hour in **non-shaded areas**

PONTA DELGADA LAT 37°44′N LONG 25°40′W

TIMES AND HEIGHTS OF HIGH AND LOW WATERS

Dates in red are SPRINGS
Dates in blue are NEAPS

YEAR **2018**

SEPTEMBER

Date	Day	Time	m	Time	m	Time	m	Time	m	Moon
1	SA	0443	1.5	1049	0.6	1703	1.5	2320	0.6	
2	SU	0537	1.4	1147	0.6	1802	1.4			
3	M	0023	0.6	0647	1.4	1305	0.7	1920	1.3	◑
4	TU	0146	0.7	0813	1.4	1438	0.7	2049	1.3	
5	W	0313	0.6	0933	1.4	1557	0.6	2206	1.4	
6	TH	0423	0.5	1037	1.6	1700	0.4	2307	1.5	
7	F	0519	0.4	1131	1.7	1752	0.3	2359	1.6	
8	SA	0608	0.3	1218	1.8	1838	0.2			
9	SU	0045	1.7	0652	0.3	1303	1.9	1922	0.2	●
10	M	0128	1.8	0735	0.2	1346	1.9	2004	0.2	
11	TU	0210	1.8	0817	0.2	1428	1.9	2045	0.2	
12	W	0251	1.7	0858	0.3	1510	1.8	2125	0.3	
13	TH	0332	1.6	0939	0.4	1552	1.7	2205	0.4	
14	F	0414	1.5	1023	0.5	1637	1.5	2248	0.5	
15	SA	0459	1.4	1112	0.6	1727	1.4	2336	0.6	
16	SU	0555	1.3	1216	0.7	1831	1.3			◐
17	M	0041	0.7	0710	1.3	1344	0.8	1955	1.2	
18	TU	0208	0.8	0840	1.3	1516	0.8	2121	1.2	
19	W	0330	0.7	0953	1.3	1621	0.7	2224	1.3	
20	TH	0429	0.7	1045	1.4	1707	0.6	2310	1.4	
21	F	0512	0.6	1125	1.5	1744	0.5	2347	1.4	
22	SA	0548	0.5	1159	1.5	1816	0.5			
23	SU	0019	1.5	0620	0.5	1230	1.6	1846	0.4	
24	M	0049	1.6	0651	0.4	1300	1.7	1915	0.4	
25	TU	0119	1.6	0721	0.4	1330	1.7	1945	0.3	○
26	W	0149	1.6	0752	0.3	1402	1.7	2015	0.3	
27	TH	0221	1.6	0825	0.3	1435	1.7	2048	0.3	
28	F	0256	1.6	0901	0.4	1512	1.6	2124	0.4	
29	SA	0335	1.6	0942	0.4	1553	1.6	2205	0.5	
30	SU	0420	1.5	1030	0.5	1642	1.5	2255	0.6	

OCTOBER

Date	Day	Time	m	Time	m	Time	m	Time	m	Moon
1	M	0515	1.5	1132	0.6	1746	1.4			
2	TU	0001	0.6	0629	1.4	1257	0.7	1911	1.3	◑
3	W	0133	0.7	0759	1.4	1433	0.6	2046	1.3	
4	TH	0304	0.6	0921	1.5	1551	0.5	2201	1.4	
5	F	0413	0.6	1024	1.6	1649	0.4	2258	1.5	
6	SA	0507	0.4	1115	1.7	1737	0.3	2345	1.6	
7	SU	0552	0.3	1201	1.8	1820	0.2			
8	M	0027	1.7	0635	0.3	1243	1.8	1900	0.2	
9	TU	0107	1.8	0715	0.2	1323	1.8	1938	0.2	●
10	W	0146	1.8	0754	0.3	1403	1.8	2016	0.2	
11	TH	0224	1.7	0833	0.3	1442	1.7	2052	0.3	
12	F	0302	1.7	0912	0.4	1522	1.6	2129	0.4	
13	SA	0340	1.6	0952	0.5	1602	1.5	2207	0.5	
14	SU	0422	1.5	1038	0.6	1648	1.4	2250	0.6	
15	M	0511	1.4	1135	0.7	1746	1.3	2348	0.7	
16	TU	0617	1.3	1256	0.8	1908	1.2			◐
17	W	0111	0.8	0746	1.3	1429	0.8	2039	1.2	
18	TH	0242	0.8	0907	1.3	1541	0.7	2148	1.3	
19	F	0349	0.7	1005	1.4	1630	0.6	2237	1.3	
20	SA	0437	0.6	1048	1.5	1709	0.5	2315	1.4	
21	SU	0515	0.6	1124	1.5	1742	0.5	2348	1.5	
22	M	0549	0.5	1157	1.6	1813	0.4			
23	TU	0019	1.6	0622	0.4	1229	1.6	1844	0.3	
24	W	0050	1.6	0654	0.3	1301	1.7	1915	0.3	○
25	TH	0123	1.7	0728	0.3	1336	1.7	1948	0.3	
26	F	0157	1.7	0805	0.3	1413	1.7	2024	0.3	
27	SA	0236	1.7	0845	0.3	1453	1.6	2104	0.3	
28	SU	0318	1.7	0930	0.4	1539	1.6	2148	0.4	
29	M	0406	1.6	1023	0.5	1633	1.5	2242	0.5	
30	TU	0505	1.5	1130	0.6	1741	1.4	2352	0.6	
31	W	0619	1.4	1254	0.6	1907	1.3			◑

NOVEMBER

Date	Day	Time	m	Time	m	Time	m	Time	m	Moon
1	TH	0122	0.7	0744	1.4	1422	0.6	2035	1.3	
2	F	0248	0.6	0902	1.5	1535	0.5	2146	1.4	
3	SA	0356	0.6	1005	1.6	1631	0.4	2241	1.5	
4	SU	0449	0.5	1056	1.6	1717	0.3	2327	1.6	
5	M	0535	0.4	1141	1.7	1759	0.3			
6	TU	0008	1.7	0617	0.3	1222	1.7	1837	0.3	
7	W	0046	1.7	0656	0.3	1302	1.7	1914	0.3	●
8	TH	0124	1.7	0734	0.3	1340	1.7	1949	0.3	
9	F	0200	1.7	0812	0.3	1418	1.6	2024	0.4	
10	SA	0237	1.6	0849	0.4	1456	1.5	2059	0.4	
11	SU	0314	1.6	0928	0.5	1535	1.5	2135	0.5	
12	M	0353	1.5	1011	0.6	1617	1.4	2215	0.6	
13	TU	0437	1.4	1101	0.7	1708	1.3	2305	0.7	
14	W	0531	1.4	1206	0.7	1814	1.2			
15	TH	0011	0.8	0642	1.3	1326	0.7	1937	1.2	◐
16	F	0135	0.8	0802	1.3	1441	0.7	2053	1.2	
17	SA	0252	0.8	0909	1.3	1540	0.6	2150	1.3	
18	SU	0350	0.7	1001	1.4	1625	0.6	2234	1.4	
19	M	0435	0.6	1043	1.5	1703	0.5	2312	1.5	
20	TU	0514	0.5	1120	1.5	1738	0.4	2347	1.6	
21	W	0551	0.4	1157	1.6	1813	0.4			
22	TH	0022	1.6	0629	0.4	1235	1.7	1848	0.3	
23	F	0059	1.7	0708	0.3	1314	1.7	1926	0.3	○
24	SA	0139	1.8	0750	0.3	1357	1.7	2007	0.3	
25	SU	0221	1.8	0835	0.3	1442	1.7	2051	0.3	
26	M	0308	1.7	0925	0.3	1532	1.6	2140	0.4	
27	TU	0359	1.7	1021	0.4	1629	1.5	2236	0.5	
28	W	0457	1.6	1126	0.5	1734	1.4	2342	0.6	
29	TH	0605	1.5	1240	0.5	1851	1.4			◑
30	F	0101	0.6	0721	1.5	1357	0.5	2010	1.4	

DECEMBER

Date	Day	Time	m	Time	m	Time	m	Time	m	Moon
1	SA	0221	0.6	0835	1.5	1508	0.5	2121	1.4	
2	SU	0331	0.6	0939	1.5	1606	0.5	2219	1.5	
3	M	0429	0.5	1034	1.5	1656	0.4	2307	1.5	
4	TU	0518	0.5	1122	1.6	1738	0.4	2350	1.6	
5	W	0601	0.4	1204	1.6	1817	0.4			
6	TH	0029	1.6	0641	0.4	1244	1.6	1854	0.4	
7	F	0106	1.7	0720	0.4	1323	1.6	1929	0.4	●
8	SA	0142	1.7	0756	0.4	1400	1.6	2003	0.4	
9	SU	0218	1.6	0833	0.4	1436	1.5	2038	0.4	
10	M	0254	1.6	0910	0.5	1513	1.5	2113	0.5	
11	TU	0330	1.5	0949	0.5	1552	1.4	2150	0.6	
12	W	0409	1.5	1032	0.6	1635	1.3	2231	0.6	
13	TH	0453	1.4	1121	0.6	1725	1.3	2322	0.7	
14	F	0546	1.4	1220	0.7	1827	1.2			
15	SA	0024	0.7	0649	1.3	1328	0.7	1938	1.2	◐
16	SU	0138	0.8	0758	1.3	1434	0.7	2047	1.3	
17	M	0248	0.7	0901	1.4	1531	0.6	2144	1.3	
18	TU	0347	0.7	0955	1.4	1619	0.6	2232	1.4	
19	W	0437	0.6	1043	1.5	1703	0.5	2315	1.5	
20	TH	0523	0.5	1128	1.6	1745	0.4	2358	1.6	
21	F	0608	0.4	1213	1.6	1828	0.3			
22	SA	0041	1.7	0653	0.3	1259	1.7	1911	0.3	○
23	SU	0125	1.8	0740	0.3	1346	1.7	1956	0.3	
24	M	0211	1.8	0828	0.3	1435	1.7	2043	0.3	
25	TU	0259	1.8	0919	0.3	1526	1.6	2133	0.3	
26	W	0350	1.8	1013	0.3	1619	1.6	2225	0.4	
27	TH	0444	1.7	1111	0.4	1718	1.5	2324	0.5	
28	F	0544	1.6	1213	0.5	1822	1.4			
29	SA	0030	0.6	0649	1.5	1321	0.5	1933	1.4	◑
30	SU	0144	0.6	0800	1.5	1431	0.6	2046	1.4	
31	M	0259	0.6	0909	1.4	1537	0.6	2152	1.4	

HAT is 1·9 metres above Chart Datum.

THE MADEIRA ARCHIPELAGO

9.26.17 LIGHTS, BUOYS AND WAYPOINTS

Bold print = light with a nominal range of 15M or more. CAPITALS = place or feature. *CAPITAL ITALICS* = light-vessel, light float or Lanby. *Italics* = Fog signal. ***Bold italics*** = Racon. Many marks/buoys are fitted with AIS (MMSI No); see relevant charts.

ILHA DO PORTO SANTO

Ilhéu de Cima ☆ Fl (3) 15s 123m **21M**; aeromarine; W □ twr and dwelling; 33°03'·28N 16°16'·75W.
Ilhéu de Ferro ✶ LFl 15s 129m 13M; W twr, R lantern with building; 33°02'·3N 16°24'·4W.
N Coast ✶ Fl (2) 10s 109m 12M; vis 064°-243° (179°); W twr with R bands; 33°05'·79N 16°20'·42W.

PORTO DO PORTO SANTO
S mole head ✶ Fl G 4s 16m 6M; W col, G bands; 33°03'·5N 16°18'·9W.
N mole head ✶ Fl R 4s 12m 7M; W col, R bands; 33°03'·58N 16°18'·91W.
Cabos Cabeço ✶ Fl (2) R 8s 9m 9M; W post, R bands; vis 308°-328° (20°) marks submarine cable; 33°02'·0N 16°21'·4W.

ILHA MADEIRA

E Point, **Ilhéu de Fora** ☆ Fl 10s 102m **20M**; W twr, R cupola, W building; 32°43'·82N 16°39'·41W.
W Point, **Ponta do Pargo** ☆ Fl (3) 20s 311m **26M**; W twr, R cupola; 32°48'·6N 17°15'·5W.
N Point, **Porto de São Jorge** ☆ LFl 5s 270m **15M**; twr and dwelling; 32°49'·9N 16°54'·1W.
Porto do Moniz ✶ Fl WR 5s; twr; 116°-R-127°-W-116° (349°); 32°52'·2N 17°09'·8W.

QUINTA DO LORDE
S mole head✶ Fl (2) G 5s 8m 6M; W post, G bands; 32°44'·4N 16°42'·9W.
N mole head ✶ Fl (2) R 5s 8m 3M; W post, R bands; 32°44'·5N 16°42'·8W.

QUINTA DO LORDE TO FUNCHAL
Caniçal Pier Head ✶ Fl G 5s 12m 9M; W twr, G bands; 32°43'·97N 16°44'14W.
Machico, São Roque ✶ LFl WR 5s 16m W9M, R7M; W twr, G bands; 32°43'·97N 16°44'14W.
Santa Catarina Airport ✶ Aero AlFl WG 10s 72m; control twr; 32°41'·62N 16°46'·53W.

FUNCHAL
Funchal mole head ✶ Fl R 5s 14m 8M; W col, R bands; vis 275°-075° (160°); 32°38'·5N 16°54'·4W.
Funchal marina E mole ✶ F G 9m 2M; W col, G bands; 32°38'·7N 16°54'·6W.
Funchal marina W mole ✶ F R 10m 3M; W col, R bands; 32°38'·69N 16°54'·66W.

FUNCHAL TO CALHETA
Cabos Gorgulho ✶ Fl (2) R 8s 8m 9M; lantern with R bands; vis 330°-025° (55°); marks submarine cable; 32°38'·2N 16°56'·1W.
Camara de Lobos ✶ Oc R 6s 22m 9M; W structure; 32°38'·8N 16°58'·5W.
Ribeira Brava ✶ Fl R 5s 6m 6M; W twr, R bands; 32°40'·07N 17°03'·8W.

CALHETA
E pier head ✶ Fl G 5s 9m 6M; G/W twr; 32°43'·0N 17°10'·3W.
W pier head ✶ Fl R 5s 9m 6M; R/W twr; 32°42'·99N 17°10'·3W.
E pier root ✶ Fl (2) G 5s 7m 2M; G/W twr on wall; vis 002°-042° (40°) & vis 075°-125° (50°); 32°43'·0N 17°10'·3W.
W pier root ✶ Fl (2) R 5s 7m 2M; lantern on wall; vis 130°-320° (190°); 32°43'·0N 17°10'·3W.
Inner bkwtr ✶ Fl (3) G 5s 7m 2M; lantern on wall; 32°42'·8N 17°10'·1W.

ILHAS DESERTAS

Ilhéu Chão (Farilhão) ✶ LFl (2) 15s 111m 13M; twr and building; 32°35'·2N 16°32'·5W.
Ilhéu Bugio (Ponta da Agulha) ✶ Fl 4s 71m 13M; 163°-100°; twr; 32°24'·0N 16°27'·6W.

ILHAS SELVAGENS

Selvagem Grande ✶ Fl 4s 162m 13M; W col R bands; 30°08'·73N 15°52'·27W. (Can often be extinguished due to storms.)
Selvagem Pequena ✶ Fl (2) 6s 49m 12M; R lantern on col; 30°02'·16N 16°01'·66W. (Can often be extinguished due to storms.)

9.26.18 PORTO DO PORTO SANTO

33°03'·45N 16°18'·80W (Hbr ent)

CHARTS AC 1689; PC 36401; Imray E3

TIDES

Standard Port CASABLANCA (⟶)

Times				Height (metres)			
High Water		Low Water		MHWS	MHWN	MLWN	MLWS
ND	ND	ND	ND	3·7	2·9	1·5	0·8
Differences PORTO SANTO							
–0014	ND	–0011	ND	–1·3	–1·1	–0·6	–0·5

SHELTER Good but can be a strong surge.

NAVIGATION Ilha do Porto Santo lies approx 440M SW of Portugal. Porto do Porto Santo is the only destination for yachts on the island. If approaching from the NE head for WPT 33°08N 16°13W to avoid Ilhéu de Fora (note there is one of these near Madeira too). Then proceed round the E side of Ilhéu de Cima, looking out for the lighthouse Fl(3) 15s 123m 21M. The passage between this island and Porto Santo island is very rocky. WPT 33°02·80N 16°16·00W, then 285° for 2·6M to reach close SW of the hbr ent. The marina is in the NW corner of the harbour.

LIGHTS AND MARKS See chartlet and Lights, buoys and waypoints.

COMMUNICATIONS Emergency 112; Police 291 208 400; British Consul 808 20 35 37; Hospital 291 705 600; GNR (Customs) 291 982 328; Polícia Maritima 291 980 076; HM 291 980 070, VHF Ch 11; Marina VHF Ch 09; Tourist Office 291 982 361.

FACILITIES Visitors should call ahead on Ch 09 (0800-1800) and then go to the arrivals pontoon on the end of the concrete wall, even if wanting to take one of the moorings.

Marina and Boatyard ☎291 980 080, www.portosdamadeira.com portosdamadeira@apram.pt. 140 (inc Ⓥ) + 40; €2·35 (pontoon inc and) max LOA 25m and draught <3·5m; multihull +50%; €1·35/m discount for 7+ days. (cash only) in the Commercial hbr (HW only), book through the marina. (basic) Ⓔ (25t).

Town ©. Ferry to Funchal (in Commercial hbr) ✈ 5km (to Funchal).

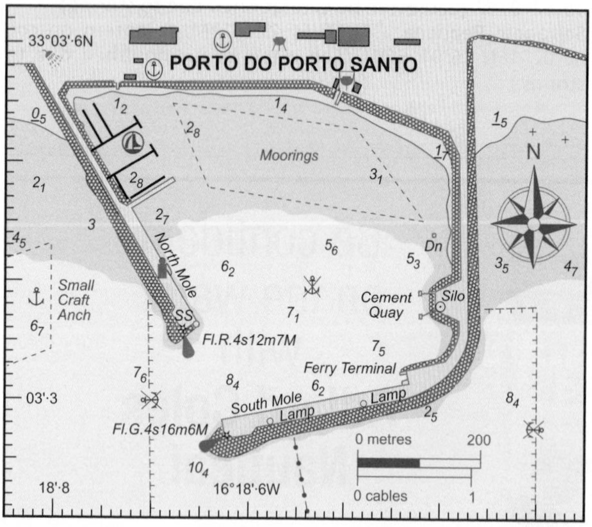

ANCHORAGE W OF PORTO SANTO MARINA

When the weather is fair it is possible to ⚓ off the beach at Baia do Porto Santo in the small craft ⚓age. However, this is not free, approx €6·00 per vessel <15m which is payable to the Harbour Authority, and no facilities are supplied. There can be some katabatic gusts down the valley from Pico do Facho.

9.26.19 QUINTA DO LORDE

32°44'·43N 16°42'·86W (S mole)

CHARTS AC 1831, 1684, 1685; PC 36402; Imray E3

TIDES See Funchal.

SHELTER Good in the marina. However, Quinta do Lorde often experiences light winds even if the weather is strong offshore, due to the shelter of high cliffs, although they can sometimes also create localised windy conditions, when down draughts are accelerated by the hills.

NAVIGATION Ilhéu de Fora/São Lourenço lthο is conspic. WPT 32°43'·32N 16°38'·95W is 0·5M SW of Ilhéu de Fora; then 0·5M W and 290°/3·95M to the marina ent. Maintain 0·5M offing when rounding the island to avoid underwater rocks, esp if going twds Baia de Abra ⚓age 3·5M E of Quinta do Lorde.

LIGHTS AND MARKS Ilhéu de Fora lighthouse, Fl 10s 103m 20M, a W twr with red cupola on top of a W building. See also chartlet and Lights, buoys and waypoints.

COMMUNICATIONS Lifeboat (SANAS) 291 230112; Emergency 112; Police 291 208400; British Consul 808 20 35 37; Hospital 291 705 600; Marina VHF 09, 16; Boatyard VHF Ch 09.

FACILITIES Quinta do Lorde Marina ☎291 969607, marina@quintadolorde.pt www.quintadolorde.pt. Call ahead prior to arrival, daytime staff will meet you in boat and direct to berth. At night, take the first available berth you find on entry. 264 (inc 150 Ⓥ) €3.15, draught <4·5m; multihulls +50%. (extra charge for card payment) © Car hire. Swimming pool in 5 star resort nearby.

Boatyard (3·7M SW of the marina, beneath the airport runway) ☎291 969 800, www.repmaritima.com Ⓔ (35t). ✈ Madeira International (10km).

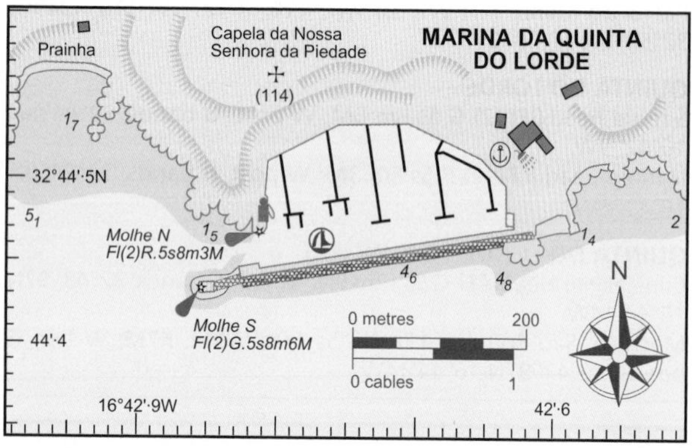

ANCHORAGE 3·5M E OF QUINTA DO LORDE MARINA

Baía de Abra 32°44·60N 16°41·60W. Approx 3·5M E of Quinta do Lorde marina. Good protection from N'lies but NE'lies can occasionally make it a bit choppy. Peaceful. No facilities ashore, but some good walking.

MINOR HARBOURS W OF QUINTA DO LORDE MARINA

Caniçal 32°44·00N 16°44·21W. Approx 1·25M SW of Quinta do Lorde Marina. Commercial hbr with no facilities for yachts. The ⚓age is off the small beach W of the hbr, near the Yacht Club. This area is also popular with local fishermen. Most facilities ashore including a BY.

Machico 32°42·94N 16°45·68W. Approx 3M SW of Quinta do Lorde marina. When coming from the E, give a wide berth to Baixa da Cruz, a rock with 1·2M clearance which is very hard to locate visually. There is a small marina here, but only for local boats. ⚓ off the beach. In W to SW winds, ⚓ing below the São Roque light may give better shelter. There may be the possibility of rafting up on the extended E mole. Entry at night is not recommended due to many unlit moorings and difficulty identifying navigation lights.

9.26.20 FUNCHAL

32°38'·30N 16°54'·20W (0·3M SE of bkwtr head)

CHARTS AC 1831, 1685, 1689; PC 36402; Imray E3

TIDES

Standard Port CASABLANCA (⟶)

Times				**Height (metres)**			
High Water		Low Water		MHWS	MHWN	MLWN	MLWS
ND	ND	ND	ND	3·5	2·8	1·5	0·8
Differences FUNCHAL							
–0023	*ND*	*–0019*	*ND*	*–1·1*	*–1·0*	*–0·5*	*–0·4*

SHELTER The hbr is open to the E and S and unlike the rest of the island, Funchal often experiences S to SW'ly winds, dying at night. This can leave an onshore swell overnight which makes the hbr uncomfortable.

The marina is completely sheltered, but is often overcrowded. The permitted ⚓age is a small area E of the marina off the beach which can be very exposed and is partly cordoned off by six lit Y buoys.

A large new marina just E of the existing one was due to open 2017 (WIP 2016/17) N of the new cruise ship terminal. The future of the small craft anchorage remains uncertain (2017). Yachts are not permitted to ⚓ S of the 10M contour.

NAVIGATION No hazards when appr from E or W. Watch out for high speed vessels when close-in and at night, beware of large unlit mooring buoys in the anchorage.

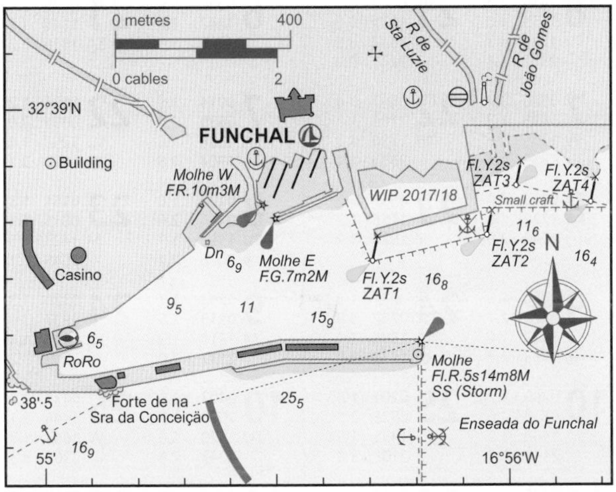

LIGHTS AND MARKS In daylight from the E, Ponta do Garajau, (3·5M E of Funchal) is very visible due to a large floodlit statue of Christ on top. From the W, the oil terminal at Praia Formosa is visible by day and at night the lt at Camara de Lobos, Oc R 6s 22m 9M, acts as a guide. For hbr lts see the chartlet and Lights, buoys and waypoints.

COMMUNICATIONS Lifeboat (SANAS) 291 230112; Guarda Nacional Republicana (Customs) 291 214460; Polícia Maritima 291 213110; Brit Consul 808 20 35 37; HM 291 225281/225288 (Capimarfunchal) VHF Ch 11, 12, 13; Marina VHF Ch 09; Tourist Office 291 211902.

FACILITIES Marina ☎291 232717 geral@marina-funchal.com www.marina-funchal.com 210, €2·50, draught <3m. Full of local boats, very limited space for Ⓥ. The reception dock/fuel berth is immed st'bd as you enter the hbr. Ⓔ.

Town Ⓑ.

Ferries Porto Santo. ✈ Madeira International 18km.

9.26.21 CALHETA

32°42'·85N 17°10'·60W (0·3M SW of bkwtr head)

CHARTS AC 1831; PC 36403; Imray E3

TIDES See Funchal.

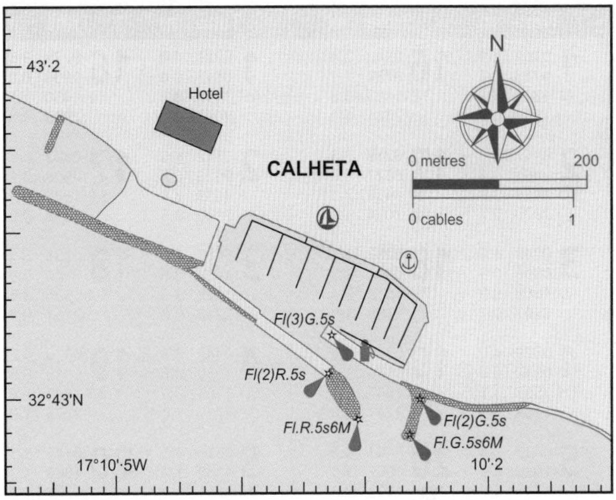

SHELTER Despite the addition of outer moles, swell still seems to enter the marina and is more of an issue at the W end.

NAVIGATION Best to avoid entry at night on your first visit. At low tide, deeper draught yachts should keep to mid-channel (reports of concrete debris on S side of ent chan).

COMMUNICATIONS Lifeboat (SANAS) 291 230 112; Brit Consul 808 20 35 37; Marina VHF Ch 09, 16.

FACILITIES Marina ☎291 824 003 info@portoderecreiodacalheta.com www.portoderecreiodacalheta.com 339 inc Ⓥ €2·50, draught <3·5m; multihulls +70%. Call ahead on VHF for a berth. Otherwise tie up to the pontoon on the W end of the W bkwtr. (cr/cards accepted) Ⓒ.

Clube Naval do Calheta ☎291 823675, ✈ Madeira International 40km.

Town (1·25M away) Ⓑ.

ANCHORAGE 2M E OF CALHETA MARINA

Madalena do Mar 32°41·90N 017°08·30W. Fair weather ⚓age only, with village supplying basic facilities.

STANDARD TIME (UT)
For Moroccan Summer Time add ONE hour in **non-shaded areas**

CASABLANCA LAT 33°36′N LONG 07°37′W

TIMES AND HEIGHTS OF HIGH AND LOW WATERS

Dates in red are SPRINGS
Dates in blue are NEAPS

YEAR **2018**

JANUARY

Date	Time	m	Date	Time	m
1 M	0102 0715 1329 1932	3.7 0.7 3.7 0.7	16 TU	0142 0754 1403 2001	3.4 1.1 3.3 1.1
2 TU	0152 0805 1419 ○ 2020	3.9 0.6 3.8 0.7	17 W	0217 0827 1438 ● 2034	3.5 1.0 3.3 1.0
3 W	0240 0854 1509 2107	4.0 0.5 3.8 0.7	18 TH	0252 0901 1513 2108	3.6 1.0 3.4 1.0
4 TH	0329 0942 1557 2154	4.0 0.6 3.7 0.7	19 F	0326 0934 1547 2141	3.6 1.0 3.4 1.0
5 F	0417 1030 1645 2240	3.9 0.7 3.6 0.9	20 SA	0401 1007 1622 2214	3.6 1.0 3.3 1.1
6 SA	0506 1119 1735 2328	3.8 0.9 3.4 1.1	21 SU	0436 1041 1657 2249	3.5 1.1 3.3 1.2
7 SU	0556 1209 1828	3.5 1.1 3.2	22 M	0512 1117 1735 2329	3.4 1.2 3.2 1.3
8 M	0021 0652 1307 ◑ 1928	1.3 3.3 1.3 3.0	23 TU	0553 1158 1820	3.3 1.3 3.1
9 TU	0124 0755 1414 2037	1.5 3.1 1.5 2.9	24 W	0017 0642 1251 ◐ 1917	1.4 3.1 1.4 3.0
10 W	0240 0907 1526 2149	1.6 2.9 1.6 2.9	25 TH	0120 0745 1400 2028	1.5 3.0 1.5 2.9
11 TH	0358 1018 1633 2253	1.6 2.9 1.5 2.9	26 F	0240 0901 1520 2145	1.5 3.0 1.4 3.0
12 F	0505 1119 1727 2345	1.6 2.9 1.5 3.1	27 SA	0401 1017 1634 2255	1.4 3.1 1.3 3.2
13 SA	0558 1208 1812	1.4 3.0 1.4	28 SU	0512 1126 1738 2356	1.2 3.2 1.1 3.4
14 SU	0028 0641 1250 1851	3.2 1.3 3.1 1.2	29 M	0612 1226 1833	1.0 3.4 0.9
15 M	0107 0719 1328 1927	3.3 1.2 3.2 1.1	30 TU	0049 0705 1319 1922	3.6 0.7 3.6 0.7
			31 W	0139 0754 1408 ○ 2009	3.9 0.5 3.7 0.6

FEBRUARY

Date	Time	m	Date	Time	m
1 TH	0227 0841 1454 2053	4.0 0.4 3.8 0.6	16 F	0228 0836 1450 2045	3.6 0.9 3.5 0.9
2 F	0312 0925 1539 2136	4.0 0.5 3.8 0.6	17 SA	0302 0908 1523 2118	3.7 0.8 3.5 0.9
3 SA	0357 1008 1623 2218	4.0 0.6 3.6 0.8	18 SU	0336 0940 1556 2151	3.7 0.9 3.5 0.9
4 SU	0442 1050 1706 2259	3.8 0.8 3.5 1.0	19 M	0410 1013 1631 2226	3.6 0.9 3.4 1.0
5 M	0526 1132 1751 2344	3.5 1.1 3.2 1.2	20 TU	0446 1048 1708 2304	3.5 1.0 3.3 1.1
6 TU	0612 1219 1841	3.3 1.3 3.0	21 W	0526 1128 1751 2350	3.4 1.1 3.2 1.2
7 W	0035 0706 1314 ◑ 1941	1.4 3.0 1.5 2.8	22 TH	0614 1218 1845	3.2 1.3 3.1
8 TH	0141 0813 1425 2054	1.6 2.8 1.6 2.8	23 F	0050 0716 1324 ◐ 1955	1.4 3.0 1.4 3.0
9 F	0306 0932 1545 2210	1.7 2.7 1.7 2.8	24 SA	0212 0836 1451 2118	1.4 2.9 1.5 3.0
10 SA	0429 1046 1655 2314	1.6 2.7 1.6 2.9	25 SU	0343 1001 1617 2237	1.4 2.9 1.4 3.1
11 SU	0532 1144 1748	1.5 2.8 1.5	26 M	0501 1115 1726 2342	1.2 3.1 1.2 3.3
12 M	0003 0618 1229 1830	3.0 1.4 3.0 1.3	27 TU	0602 1215 1822	0.9 3.3 1.0
13 TU	0044 0657 1307 1906	3.2 1.2 3.1 1.2	28 W	0036 0653 1306 1909	3.6 0.7 3.5 0.7
14 W	0120 0731 1342 1940	3.3 1.1 3.3 1.0			
15 TH	0154 0804 1416 ● 2013	3.5 1.0 3.4 0.9			

MARCH

Date	Time	m	Date	Time	m
1 TH	0124 0738 1352 1953	3.8 0.5 3.7 0.6	16 F	0126 0733 1348 1946	3.5 0.9 3.4 0.9
2 F	0210 0821 1435 ○ 2034	3.9 0.5 3.8 0.5	17 SA	0159 0805 1421 ● 2019	3.6 0.8 3.5 0.8
3 SA	0253 0902 1517 2114	4.0 0.5 3.8 0.6	18 SU	0234 0837 1455 2053	3.7 0.8 3.6 0.8
4 SU	0334 0940 1557 2153	3.9 0.6 3.7 0.7	19 M	0308 0911 1530 2128	3.7 0.7 3.6 0.8
5 M	0415 1018 1636 2231	3.7 0.8 3.5 0.9	20 TU	0345 0946 1606 2205	3.7 0.8 3.6 0.8
6 TU	0454 1055 1716 2311	3.5 1.0 3.3 1.1	21 W	0423 1024 1646 2247	3.6 0.9 3.5 0.9
7 W	0536 1135 1759 2355	3.2 1.3 3.1 1.3	22 TH	0507 1106 1731 2335	3.4 1.1 3.3 1.1
8 TH	0623 1222 1849	3.0 1.5 2.9	23 F	0557 1158 1826	3.2 1.2 3.2
9 F	0050 0720 1323 ◑ 1953	1.5 2.7 1.6 2.7	24 SA	0037 0702 1305 ◐ 1935	1.3 3.0 1.4 3.0
10 SA	0209 0838 1448 2114	1.7 2.6 1.7 2.7	25 SU	0201 0823 1435 2100	1.4 2.9 1.5 3.0
11 SU	0342 1004 1612 2231	1.7 2.6 1.7 2.8	26 M	0333 0951 1604 2221	1.3 2.9 1.4 3.1
12 M	0455 1112 1714 2329	1.6 2.7 1.6 2.9	27 TU	0449 1104 1712 2327	1.2 3.1 1.2 3.3
13 TU	0546 1201 1800	1.4 2.9 1.4	28 W	0548 1201 1806	1.0 3.3 1.0
14 W	0013 0626 1240 1839	3.1 1.2 3.1 1.2	29 TH	0020 0635 1249 1852	3.5 0.8 3.5 0.8
15 TH	0051 0701 1314 1913	3.3 1.1 3.3 1.0	30 F	0107 0718 1333 1934	3.7 0.6 3.6 0.7
			31 SA	0150 0758 1414 ○ 2013	3.8 0.6 3.7 0.6

APRIL

Date	Time	m	Date	Time	m
1 SU	0231 0835 1453 2051	3.8 0.6 3.7 0.7	16 M	0204 0807 1426 ● 2028	3.7 0.7 3.7 0.7
2 M	0309 0911 1530 2128	3.7 0.7 3.6 0.8	17 TU	0242 0844 1505 2108	3.7 0.7 3.7 0.7
3 TU	0348 0946 1607 2205	3.6 0.9 3.5 0.9	18 W	0323 0923 1546 2150	3.7 0.7 3.7 0.7
4 W	0425 1022 1645 2243	3.4 1.0 3.3 1.1	19 TH	0406 1006 1630 2236	3.6 0.8 3.6 0.9
5 TH	0504 1059 1724 2324	3.2 1.2 3.2 1.3	20 F	0454 1053 1719 2330	3.4 1.0 3.5 1.0
6 F	0547 1142 1809	3.0 1.4 3.0	21 SA	0549 1148 1816	3.2 1.2 3.3
7 SA	0014 0639 1236 1904	1.5 2.8 1.6 2.8	22 SU	0034 0655 1257 ◐ 1925	1.2 3.0 1.4 3.1
8 SU	0120 0746 1352 ◑ 2016	1.6 2.6 1.7 2.7	23 M	0154 0815 1423 2045	1.3 2.9 1.5 3.1
9 M	0248 0913 1519 2137	1.7 2.6 1.7 2.8	24 TU	0320 0937 1546 2203	1.3 3.0 1.4 3.2
10 TU	0407 1028 1629 2243	1.6 2.7 1.6 2.9	25 W	0431 1046 1653 2308	1.2 3.1 1.3 3.3
11 W	0503 1121 1721 2333	1.5 2.9 1.5 3.1	26 TH	0528 1142 1747	1.0 3.3 1.1
12 TH	0547 1203 1803	1.3 3.1 1.3	27 F	0001 0614 1229 1832	3.4 0.9 3.4 1.0
13 F	0015 0624 1240 1840	3.3 1.1 3.3 1.1	28 SA	0047 0655 1312 1914	3.5 0.8 3.5 0.8
14 SA	0052 0658 1315 1915	3.4 0.9 3.4 0.9	29 SU	0130 0733 1352 1953	3.6 0.8 3.6 0.8
15 SU	0128 0732 1350 1951	3.6 0.8 3.6 0.8	30 M	0209 0809 1429 ○ 2031	3.6 0.8 3.6 0.8

HAT is 4·0 metres above Chart Datum.

STANDARD TIME (UT)
For Moroccan Summer Time add ONE hour in **non-shaded areas**

CASABLANCA LAT 33°36'N LONG 07°37'W

TIMES AND HEIGHTS OF HIGH AND LOW WATERS

Dates in red are SPRINGS
Dates in blue are NEAPS

YEAR **2018**

MAY

Day	Time	m	Day	Time	m
1	0246	3.5	16	0221	3.7
	0844	0.9		0822	0.7
TU	1506	3.6	W	1444	3.8
	2107	0.9		2052	0.6
2	0323	3.4	17	0307	3.7
	0919	1.0		0907	0.7
W	1541	3.5	TH	1530	3.8
	2143	1.0		2140	0.7
3	0400	3.3	18	0355	3.6
	0954	1.1		0954	0.8
TH	1618	3.4	F	1619	3.7
	2221	1.1		2230	0.7
4	0438	3.2	19	0447	3.5
	1032	1.2		1045	1.0
F	1657	3.2	SA	1711	3.6
	2302	1.2		2325	0.9
5	0520	3.0	20	0543	3.3
	1114	1.4		1141	1.2
SA	1740	3.1	SU	1808	3.4
	2348	1.4			
6	0608	2.8	21	0027	1.1
	1203	1.6		0647	3.1
SU	1829	3.0	M	1247	1.3
				1913	3.3
7	0044	1.5	22	0140	1.2
	0706	2.7		0800	3.0
M	1306	1.7	TU	1404	1.4
	1929	2.9	◐	2026	3.2
8	0155	1.6	23	0257	1.2
	0820	2.7		0915	3.0
TU	1423	1.7	W	1521	1.4
◑	2040	2.8		2139	3.2
9	0310	1.6	24	0406	1.2
	0933	2.7		1022	3.1
W	1536	1.7	TH	1628	1.3
	2149	2.9		2244	3.2
10	0412	1.5	25	0504	1.1
	1032	2.9		1119	3.2
TH	1634	1.5	F	1725	1.2
	2246	3.0		2340	3.3
11	0502	1.3	26	0551	1.1
	1120	3.1		1207	3.3
F	1722	1.4	SA	1813	1.1
	2334	3.2			
12	0544	1.2	27	0028	3.3
	1202	3.3		0633	1.0
SA	1804	1.2	SU	1251	3.4
				1857	1.0
13	0016	3.4	28	0110	3.4
	0622	1.0		0711	1.0
SU	1241	3.4	M	1330	3.5
	1844	1.0		1936	1.0
14	0057	3.5	29	0150	3.4
	0701	0.8		0747	1.0
M	1320	3.6	TU	1408	3.5
	1925	0.8	○	2014	0.9
15	0138	3.6	30	0227	3.3
	0740	0.7		0822	1.0
TU	1401	3.7	W	1444	3.5
●	2008	0.7		2049	1.0
			31	0303	3.3
				0857	1.0
			TH	1519	3.4
				2125	1.0

JUNE

Day	Time	m	Day	Time	m
1	0340	3.2	16	0345	3.7
	0933	1.1		0943	0.7
F	1556	3.4	SA	1607	3.8
	2203	1.1		2221	0.6
2	0417	3.2	17	0437	3.6
	1010	1.2		1034	0.9
SA	1635	3.3	SU	1659	3.7
	2242	1.2		2314	0.8
3	0458	3.1	18	0531	3.4
	1051	1.3		1127	1.0
SU	1716	3.2	M	1753	3.6
	2324	1.3			
4	0541	2.9	19	0010	0.9
	1135	1.5		0629	3.2
M	1800	3.1	TU	1227	1.2
				1853	3.4
5	0011	1.4	20	0114	1.1
	0631	2.8		0734	3.1
TU	1226	1.6	W	1335	1.3
	1850	3.0	◐	1959	3.2
6	0105	1.5	21	0224	1.3
	0729	2.8		0844	3.0
W	1328	1.6	TH	1449	1.4
◑	1949	2.9		2110	3.1
7	0210	1.5	22	0334	1.3
	0836	2.8		0952	3.0
TH	1438	1.6	F	1601	1.4
	2054	2.9		2218	3.1
8	0316	1.5	23	0436	1.3
	0939	2.9		1053	3.1
F	1543	1.5	SA	1704	1.3
	2156	3.0		2318	3.1
9	0414	1.4	24	0528	1.2
	1035	3.0		1146	3.2
SA	1640	1.4	SU	1757	1.2
	2252	3.1			
10	0504	1.2	25	0009	3.1
	1124	3.2		0613	1.2
SU	1730	1.2	M	1231	3.3
	2343	3.3		1842	1.1
11	0550	1.1	26	0053	3.2
	1210	3.4		0653	1.1
M	1817	1.0	TU	1311	3.3
				1922	1.1
12	0030	3.4	27	0133	3.2
	0635	0.9		0729	1.1
TU	1255	3.6	W	1348	3.4
	1904	0.8		1959	1.0
13	0118	3.6	28	0209	3.2
	0720	0.8		0804	1.0
W	1341	3.7	TH	1424	3.4
●	1952	0.7	○	2034	1.0
14	0206	3.7	29	0245	3.2
	0806	0.7		0839	1.0
TH	1429	3.8	F	1459	3.4
	2041	0.6		2108	1.0
15	0255	3.7	30	0321	3.2
	0854	0.7		0914	1.1
F	1517	3.9	SA	1535	3.4
	2130	0.5		2143	1.0

JULY

Day	Time	m	Day	Time	m
1	0357	3.2	16	0420	3.6
	0950	1.1		1017	0.7
SU	1612	3.4	M	1641	3.8
	2219	1.1		2253	0.7
2	0434	3.2	17	0510	3.5
	1027	1.2		1105	0.9
M	1650	3.3	TU	1731	3.6
	2257	1.2		2343	0.9
3	0513	3.1	18	0602	3.3
	1106	1.3		1158	1.1
TU	1730	3.2	W	1825	3.4
	2336	1.3			
4	0555	3.0	19	0038	1.1
	1148	1.4		0659	3.1
W	1812	3.1	TH	1258	1.3
			◐	1925	3.1
5	0020	1.4	20	0141	1.3
	0642	2.9		0806	3.0
TH	1239	1.5	F	1411	1.4
	1902	3.0		2036	3.0
6	0113	1.4	21	0253	1.4
	0739	2.9		0918	2.9
F	1342	1.6	SA	1530	1.5
◑	2002	2.9		2149	2.9
7	0218	1.5	22	0404	1.4
	0845	2.9		1026	2.9
SA	1453	1.5	SU	1643	1.4
	2109	2.9		2256	2.9
8	0327	1.4	23	0505	1.4
	0952	3.0		1124	3.0
SU	1601	1.4	M	1741	1.3
	2215	3.0		2352	2.9
9	0429	1.3	24	0555	1.3
	1051	3.1		1212	3.1
M	1702	1.2	TU	1828	1.2
	2316	3.1			
10	0525	1.1	25	0037	3.0
	1145	3.3		0636	1.2
TU	1758	1.0	W	1252	3.2
				1907	1.1
11	0011	3.3	26	0116	3.1
	0617	0.9		0713	1.1
W	1236	3.5	TH	1329	3.3
	1850	0.8		1942	1.0
12	0104	3.5	27	0152	3.2
	0706	0.8		0747	1.1
TH	1326	3.7	F	1404	3.4
	1940	0.6	○	2015	1.0
13	0154	3.6	28	0225	3.2
	0754	0.7		0820	1.0
F	1415	3.9	SA	1437	3.5
●	2029	0.5		2047	0.9
14	0243	3.7	29	0259	3.3
	0842	0.6		0853	1.0
SA	1503	4.0	SU	1512	3.5
	2118	0.4		2120	0.9
15	0332	3.7	30	0333	3.3
	0929	0.6		0926	1.0
SU	1552	3.9	M	1546	3.5
	2205	0.5		2152	1.0
			31	0408	3.3
				1000	1.1
			TU	1621	3.4
				2225	1.0

AUGUST

Day	Time	m	Day	Time	m
1	0442	3.2	16	0529	3.3
	1034	1.2		1124	1.1
W	1657	3.3	TH	1751	3.3
	2300	1.1		2357	1.2
2	0519	3.1	17	0620	3.1
	1112	1.3		1217	1.3
TH	1735	3.2	F	1846	3.1
	2338	1.2			
3	0600	3.0	18	0052	1.4
	1156	1.4		0721	2.9
F	1820	3.1	SA	1326	1.5
			◐	1953	2.8
4	0025	1.4	19	0203	1.6
	0652	2.9		0835	2.8
SA	1254	1.5	SU	1453	1.6
◑	1917	3.0		2114	2.7
5	0126	1.4	20	0327	1.6
	0758	2.9		0953	2.8
SU	1409	1.5	M	1618	1.6
	2029	2.9		2232	2.7
6	0244	1.5	21	0440	1.5
	0913	2.9		1100	2.9
M	1532	1.4	TU	1722	1.5
	2146	2.9		2333	2.8
7	0402	1.4	22	0534	1.4
	1025	3.1		1151	3.0
TU	1645	1.2	W	1809	1.3
	2258	3.1			
8	0508	1.2	23	0019	2.9
	1128	3.3		0617	1.3
W	1746	1.0	TH	1231	3.2
	2359	3.3		1846	1.2
9	0605	1.0	24	0056	3.1
	1222	3.5		0653	1.2
TH	1840	0.8	F	1307	3.3
				1919	1.1
10	0052	3.5	25	0130	3.2
	0655	0.8		0726	1.1
F	1312	3.8	SA	1340	3.4
	1928	0.5		1951	1.0
11	0141	3.7	26	0202	3.3
	0742	0.6		0757	1.0
SA	1400	3.9	SU	1412	3.5
●	2015	0.4	○	2021	0.9
12	0228	3.8	27	0234	3.4
	0827	0.5		0828	0.9
SU	1446	4.0	M	1445	3.6
	2059	0.4		2051	0.9
13	0314	3.8	28	0306	3.4
	0911	0.6		0900	0.9
M	1532	4.0	TU	1518	3.6
	2143	0.5		2121	0.9
14	0358	3.7	29	0338	3.4
	0954	0.7		0931	1.0
TU	1617	3.8	W	1551	3.5
	2226	0.7		2153	0.9
15	0443	3.5	30	0411	3.4
	1038	0.8		1005	1.0
W	1703	3.6	TH	1625	3.4
	2310	0.9		2225	1.0
			31	0446	3.3
				1041	1.2
			F	1702	3.3
				2302	1.2

HAT is 4·0 metres above Chart Datum.

STANDARD TIME (UT)
For Moroccan Summer Time add ONE hour in **non-shaded areas**

CASABLANCA LAT 33°36'N LONG 07°37'W

TIMES AND HEIGHTS OF HIGH AND LOW WATERS

Dates in red are SPRINGS
Dates in blue are NEAPS

YEAR **2018**

SEPTEMBER

Date	Time	m	Date	Time	m
1 SA	0526 1123 1747 2347	3.2 1.3 3.1 1.3	16 SU	0003 0634 1238 1907	1.5 2.9 1.6 2.8
2 SU	0615 1219 1844	3.0 1.4 3.0	17 M	0107 0743 1405 ◐ 2031	1.7 2.8 1.7 2.6
3 M	0047 0721 1338 ◑ 2001	1.4 2.9 1.5 2.9	18 TU	0239 0909 1543 2200	1.8 2.7 1.7 2.6
4 TU	0212 0844 1513 2128	1.5 2.9 1.5 2.9	19 W	0405 1026 1653 2307	1.7 2.8 1.6 2.8
5 W	0344 1006 1634 2246	1.5 3.0 1.3 3.0	20 TH	0506 1122 1740 2353	1.6 3.0 1.4 2.9
6 TH	0457 1113 1736 2348	1.3 3.3 1.0 3.3	21 F	0550 1204 1817	1.4 3.2 1.3
7 F	0554 1208 1827	1.0 3.5 0.8	22 SA	0030 0626 1239 1850	3.1 1.3 3.3 1.1
8 SA	0039 0642 1257 1913	3.5 0.8 3.8 0.6	23 SU	0103 0659 1312 1921	3.3 1.1 3.5 1.0
9 SU	0126 0726 1343 ● 1956	3.7 0.6 4.0 0.4	24 M	0134 0731 1344 1950	3.4 1.0 3.6 0.9
10 M	0209 0808 1426 2037	3.8 0.6 4.0 0.4	25 TU	0205 0801 1416 ○ 2020	3.5 0.9 3.6 0.9
11 TU	0252 0849 1509 2117	3.8 0.6 4.0 0.6	26 W	0236 0833 1449 2050	3.6 0.9 3.7 0.9
12 W	0333 0930 1552 2156	3.7 0.7 3.8 0.7	27 TH	0308 0905 1522 2122	3.6 0.9 3.6 0.9
13 TH	0415 1010 1633 2235	3.6 0.9 3.5 1.0	28 F	0342 0940 1558 2157	3.5 1.0 3.5 1.0
14 F	0456 1052 1717 2316	3.4 1.1 3.3 1.2	29 SA	0419 1018 1638 2235	3.5 1.1 3.4 1.1
15 SA	0541 1139 1806	3.1 1.3 3.0	30 SU	0501 1103 1725 2322	3.3 1.2 3.2 1.3

OCTOBER

Date	Time	m	Date	Time	m
1 M	0552 1201 1825	3.2 1.4 3.0	16 TU	0018 0652 1311 ◐ 1939	1.7 2.9 1.7 2.6
2 TU	0024 0659 1322 ◑ 1945	1.5 3.0 1.5 2.9	17 W	0139 0811 1448 2111	1.8 2.8 1.8 2.6
3 W	0153 0824 1501 2117	1.6 3.0 1.5 2.9	18 TH	0314 0935 1607 2225	1.8 2.8 1.7 2.7
4 TH	0330 0950 1621 2235	1.5 3.1 1.3 3.1	19 F	0424 1039 1700 2316	1.7 2.9 1.5 2.9
5 F	0444 1058 1722 2334	1.4 3.3 1.0 3.3	20 SA	0513 1126 1740 2355	1.6 3.1 1.4 3.1
6 SA	0539 1153 1811	1.1 3.6 0.8	21 SU	0553 1205 1815	1.4 3.3 1.2
7 SU	0023 0626 1241 1854	3.5 0.9 3.8 0.7	22 M	0029 0628 1240 1847	3.3 1.2 3.5 1.1
8 M	0107 0709 1325 1935	3.7 0.7 3.9 0.6	23 TU	0102 0701 1314 1918	3.5 1.1 3.6 1.0
9 TU	0149 0750 1407 ● 2013	3.8 0.7 3.9 0.6	24 W	0134 0734 1347 ○ 1950	3.6 1.0 3.7 0.9
10 W	0230 0829 1447 2051	3.8 0.7 3.8 0.7	25 TH	0208 0808 1422 2023	3.7 0.9 3.7 0.9
11 TH	0309 0908 1528 2127	3.7 0.8 3.7 0.9	26 F	0242 0844 1459 2059	3.7 0.9 3.7 0.9
12 F	0348 0946 1607 2203	3.6 0.9 3.5 1.1	27 SA	0320 0923 1540 2137	3.7 0.9 3.6 1.0
13 SA	0426 1025 1647 2240	3.4 1.1 3.2 1.3	28 SU	0401 1006 1624 2220	3.6 1.0 3.4 1.1
14 SU	0507 1108 1732 2323	3.2 1.4 3.0 1.5	29 M	0447 1056 1715 2311	3.5 1.2 3.3 1.3
15 M	0554 1159 1825	3.0 1.6 2.8	30 TU	0540 1156 1817	3.3 1.3 3.1
			31 W	0015 0646 1314 ◑ 1935	1.5 3.2 1.4 3.0

NOVEMBER

Date	Time	m	Date	Time	m
1 TH	0140 0808 1444 2101	1.6 3.1 1.4 3.0	16 F	0205 0829 1501 2124	1.9 2.9 1.7 2.7
2 F	0311 0930 1602 2216	1.6 3.2 1.3 3.1	17 SA	0324 0940 1605 2224	1.8 2.9 1.6 2.9
3 SA	0424 1039 1702 2315	1.4 3.3 1.1 3.3	18 SU	0424 1037 1654 2311	1.7 3.1 1.5 3.1
4 SU	0520 1135 1751	1.2 3.5 1.0	19 M	0512 1123 1735 2351	1.5 3.2 1.3 3.2
5 M	0004 0608 1223 1834	3.5 1.0 3.6 0.9	20 TU	0553 1204 1811	1.3 3.4 1.2
6 TU	0048 0652 1308 1914	3.6 0.9 3.7 0.8	21 W	0028 0631 1243 1847	3.4 1.2 3.5 1.0
7 W	0130 0733 1350 ● 1952	3.7 0.8 3.7 0.8	22 TH	0105 0709 1322 1924	3.6 1.0 3.6 0.9
8 TH	0210 0813 1429 2028	3.7 0.8 3.7 0.9	23 F	0143 0748 1402 ○ 2002	3.7 0.9 3.7 0.9
9 F	0248 0851 1507 2103	3.7 0.9 3.5 1.0	24 SA	0222 0830 1444 2043	3.8 0.8 3.7 0.9
10 SA	0325 0928 1546 2138	3.6 1.0 3.4 1.2	25 SU	0305 0914 1529 2127	3.8 0.8 3.6 0.9
11 SU	0402 1006 1624 2215	3.4 1.2 3.2 1.3	26 M	0350 1002 1618 2214	3.8 0.9 3.5 1.1
12 M	0441 1046 1705 2255	3.3 1.3 3.0 1.5	27 TU	0439 1053 1710 2306	3.7 1.0 3.4 1.2
13 TU	0523 1131 1752 2343	3.2 1.5 2.9 1.7	28 W	0533 1151 1810	3.5 1.2 3.2
14 W	0613 1227 1850	3.0 1.7 2.8	29 TH	0006 0635 1259 1919	1.4 3.4 1.3 3.1
15 TH	0044 0714 1340 ◐ 2006	1.8 2.9 1.8 2.7	30 F	0119 0747 1418 ◑ 2036	1.5 3.3 1.4 3.0

DECEMBER

Date	Time	m	Date	Time	m
1 SA	0241 0903 1534 2149	1.5 3.2 1.3 3.1	16 SU	0209 0832 1455 2119	1.8 2.9 1.7 2.8
2 SU	0356 1014 1637 2251	1.5 3.3 1.3 3.2	17 M	0321 0937 1557 2218	1.7 3.0 1.6 3.0
3 M	0459 1114 1730 2344	1.3 3.3 1.2 3.4	18 TU	0422 1035 1650 2309	1.6 3.1 1.4 3.1
4 TU	0552 1206 1815	1.2 3.4 1.1	19 W	0514 1127 1736 2355	1.4 3.2 1.3 3.3
5 W	0031 0638 1252 1856	3.5 1.1 3.5 1.0	20 TH	0602 1214 1820	1.2 3.4 1.1
6 TH	0113 0721 1335 1935	3.6 1.0 3.5 1.0	21 F	0039 0647 1300 1903	3.5 1.0 3.5 1.0
7 F	0153 0800 1414 ● 2011	3.6 1.0 3.5 1.0	22 SA	0123 0733 1346 ○ 1947	3.7 0.9 3.6 0.8
8 SA	0231 0838 1452 2046	3.6 1.0 3.4 1.1	23 SU	0208 0819 1433 2032	3.8 0.7 3.7 0.8
9 SU	0307 0914 1528 2121	3.6 1.1 3.3 1.1	24 M	0254 0907 1521 2119	3.9 0.7 3.7 0.8
10 M	0343 0950 1605 2156	3.5 1.1 3.2 1.2	25 TU	0341 0955 1610 2206	3.9 0.7 3.7 0.9
11 TU	0420 1027 1643 2234	3.4 1.2 3.1 1.4	26 W	0430 1045 1700 2256	3.8 0.8 3.5 1.0
12 W	0459 1107 1724 2315	3.3 1.4 3.0 1.5	27 TH	0521 1137 1754 2349	3.7 1.0 3.4 1.2
13 TH	0542 1152 1810	3.2 1.5 2.9	28 F	0616 1236 1854	3.5 1.2 3.2
14 F	0002 0629 1243 1905	1.6 3.1 1.6 2.8	29 SA	0051 0720 1343 ◑ 2002	1.4 3.3 1.3 3.1
15 SA	0059 0726 1346 ◐ 2011	1.8 3.0 1.7 2.8	30 SU	0204 0831 1457 2115	1.5 3.2 1.4 3.0
			31 M	0323 0945 1607 2224	1.5 3.1 1.4 3.1

HAT is 4·0 metres above Chart Datum.

A

Abandon ship ... 113
Abbreviations and symbols ... 7
Abdominal pain ... 121
Accidents and injuries ... 122
Acute illness ... 121
Admiralty chart symbols ... 6
Agents ... 2
Allergies ... 121
Automatic Identification System (AIS) ... 42

B

BBC World Service ... 12
Beaufort scale ... 82
Belgium
- Coast radio stations ... 100
- Special notes ... 740

Bites and stings ... 122
Bleeding
- Internal ... 122
- Nosebleed ... 125
- Open wound ... 122

Budget flights ... 888
Buoyage, direction of ... 39
Burgee ... 79
Burns and scalds ... 122

C

Cardinal marks ... 38
Certificate of Competence, International ... 22
Channel crossing
- Central part ... 198
- Eastern part ... 262
- from SW England ... 179

Channel Islands
- Coast Radio Stations ... 70
- SAR operations ... 829
- Special notes ... 829
- Weather forecasts ... 96

Chart
- Admiralty symbols ... 6
- Datum (CD) ... 54
- Datum (horizontal) ... 40
- Electronic
  - Raster ... 40
  - Vector ... 40
- Plotters ... 41

Chest injury ... 122
Childbirth ... 125
Children
- Acute illness ... 121
- Resuscitation ... 119

Choking ... 120
Coastguard, HM ... 114
- MSI broadcasts ... 89
- Remote stations ... 91

Coast radio stations ... 68
- Belgium ... 100
- Channel Islands ... 70
- Denmark ... 71
- Germany ... 72, 98
- Ireland ... 70, 96
- Spain ... 76, 102

Collision regulations ... 24
Communications (Chapter 5) ... 63
- Coast radio stations ... 68
- Flag etiquette ... 79
- International code of signals ... 64
- International Port Traffic Signals (IPTS) ... 78
- Vessel Traffic Services (VTS) ... 68, 78

Constipation ... 121
Conversion tables ... 11
CROSS, VHF broadcasts ... 101
Cruising formalities ... 22
Crush injuries ... 122
Customs, Foreign ... 23
Customs, HM ... 22
- Arrival from an EU country ... 22
- Arrival from a non-EU country ... 23
- Notice of departure ... 22

Cuts ... 122

D

Dead reckoning ... 35
Declination, sun ... 47
Denmark
- Coast radio stations ... 71
- Special notes ... 653
- Weather forecasts ... 97

Dental problems ... 123
Diabetes ... 121
Diarrhoea ... 121
Digital Selective Calling (DSC) ... 109
Directing signals by aircraft ... 113
Disabled facilities information ... 131
Dislocations ... 123
Distances
- Across the Bay of Biscay ... 135
- Across the English Channel ... 132
- Across the Irish Sea ... 133
- Across the North Sea ... 134

Distress ... 108
- Alerting ... 108
- Mobile telephones ... 110
- Raising the alarm ... 114
- Signals and emergencies ... 110

Documents, personal ... 22
Double lift ... 113
Drowning ... 120
Drugs and medication ... 125
Drug smuggling ... 23
Dutchman's log ... 36
Duty free stores ... 22

E

EasyTide ... 59
Eclipses ... 10
EGNOS ... 39
Emergency, definitions of ... 108
Emergency resuscitation (ABC) ... 118
Ensigns ... 79, 80
Environmental guidance ... 132
EPIRB, Registration and false alerts ... 107
Exercise areas, Submarine
- NW Scotland ... 451
- SW Scotland ... 484

Eye problems ... 123

F

Ferries, Scotland, west coast ... 466
Fever ... 121
Firing ranges
- Castlemartin Range ... 546
- Landes Range ... 946
- Lulworth Ranges ... 188
- Manorbier Range ... 546
- Pembrey Range ... 546
- Penally Range ... 546
- Pendine Range ... 546

First Aid (Chapter 8) ... 117
- Abdominal pain ... 121
- Acute (sudden) illness ... 121
- Allergies ... 121
- Bites and stings ... 122
- Bleeding ... 122
- Books on first aid ... 126
- Burns and scalds ... 122
- Chest injury ... 122
- Childbirth ... 125
- Children ... 121
- Choking ... 120
- Constipation ... 121
- Crush injuries ... 122
- Cuts and wounds ... 122
- Dental problems ... 123
- Diabetes ... 121
- Diarrhoea ... 121
- Drowning ... 120
- Drugs and medication ... 125
- Emergency resuscitation ... 118
- Eye problems ... 123
- Fever ... 121
- First aid kit ... 125
- First aid objectives ... 118
- Fish hook injury ... 122
- Fractures and dislocations ... 123
- Frostbite ... 124
- Head injury ... 124
- Heart attack ... 121
- Hypothermia ... 120
- Injections ... 126
- Medical advice by R/T ... 118
- Medical care abroad ... 118
- Nail injuries ... 124
- Nosebleed ... 125
- Observation form ... 127
- Poisoning ... 125
- Seasickness ... 121
- Shock ... 120
- Strains and sprains ... 125

First aid kit ... 125
Fish hook injuries ... 122
Flags
- Code ... 64
- Ensigns ... 79, 80
- Etiquette ... 79

Fractures ... 123
France, Special notes ... 757
Frostbite ... 124

G

Gale warnings ... 85
Geostrophic scales ... 85
Germany
- Coast radio stations ... 72, 98
- Special notes ... 672
- Weather forecasts ... 98

Gibraltar
- Special notes ... 1022
- Weather forecasts ... 104

GMDSS ... 107
GPS ... 39
Gunfacts ... 68

H

Harbour information ... 131
Harbours, Coasts and Tides (Chapter 9) ... 129
Hazards ... 43
Head injury ... 124
Health regulations ... 22
Heart attack ... 121
Helicopter rescue ... 113
HF radio ... 66
HF radio facsimile broadcasts ... 91
Highest Astronomical Tide (HAT) ... 54
High seas bulletins ... 89
HM Coastguard ... 69, 89, 114
Horizontal datums ... 40
Hydrographic surveys ... 40
Hypothermia ... 120

I

IALA buoyage ... 38
- Cardinal marks ... 38
- Isolated danger marks ... 39
- Lateral marks ... 38
- Preferred channel marks ... 38
- Safe water marks ... 39
- Special marks ... 39

Immigration ... 23
Importation, Temporary (TI) ... 23
Injections ... 126
Injury
- Chest ... 122
- Crush ... 122
- Fish hook ... 122
- Head ... 124
- Nail ... 124

Inland waterways
- Belgium ... 740
- Brittany ... 816
- Caledonian Canal ... 396, 410, 458
- France ... 758
- Netherlands ... 710
- To the Mediterranean ... 945

Insurance....22
Inter-ship VHF channels....65
Introduction....1
IPTS....78
Ireland
Coast radio stations....96
Special notes....572
Weather forecasts....96

L

Lateral marks....38
Lifeboats....75
Light(s)
Characteristics....36, 37
Lights and shapes....31
Navigation....29, 30
Rising or dipping distance....49
Sectors, arcs of visibility....36
Link calls
MF....68
Paying for....68
VHF....68
Lowest Astronomical Tide (LAT)....54

M

Map of Almanac areas....130
MAYDAY calls....108, 109
Medical care abroad....118
Medical help by R/T....110
Medical observation form....127
MF link calls....68
MF radio....66
MHWS, MHWN, MLWS, MLWN....54
Mines, explosive....43
Moon
Phases....52
Rise/set tables....51
MSI broadcasts by HM Coastguard....89

N

Nail injuries....124
National Coastwatch Institution (NCI)....69, 115
Naval exercise areas, SW England....165, 451, 484
Navareas....43
Navigational tables
Distance off by vertical sextant angle....46
Distance off when rising or dipping....49
Distance of horizon....44
Distance, speed and time....45
Moonrise/set....51
Sunrise/set....49
Sun's declination....47
Navigation (Chapter 3)....33
Automatic Identification System (AIS)....42
Chart plotters....41
Dead reckoning....35
Electronic charts....40
Hazards....43
IALA buoyage....38
Lights....36, 37, 49
Navigational Tables....44
Offshore energy installations....44
Passage planning....35
Radar....41
Satellite navigation
EGNOS....39
GPS....39
SOLAS V....35
Warnings....43
Waypoints....40
Navigation lights....30
Navtex....86
Netherlands
Coastguard (IJmuiden)....99
Weather forecasts....96, 99
North Sea, crossing to UK
from Denmark....658
from German Bight....676
from Netherlands....710
Nosebleed....125

O

Offshore energy installations....44
Oil and gas installations....338

P

PAN-PAN, Urgency signal....109
Passage planning....35
Plotters, chart....41
Poisoning....125
Port operations VHF channels....65
Portugal
Special notes....992
Weather forecasts....103
Wind and weather....992
Portuguese Islands, Special notes....1029
Prowords....65
Public holidays, UK....10

R

Racons (radar beacons)....43
Radar
Collision avoidance....42
Navigation aid....42
Radio
Broadcasts....85, 86
Licences....65
Radio silence, cancelling/relaxing....109
R/T procedures....65
Time signals....12
Radio: Weather information....96
Reference Data (Chapter 1)....5
Abbreviations and symbols....7
Admiralty chart symbols....6
Conversion tables....11
Eclipses....10
E-mail addresses....9
Postal addresses....9
Public holidays, UK....10
Radio time signals....12
Time, UT and DST....12
Vocabularies....12
Websites....9
Regulations (Chapter 2)....21
Collision regulations....24
Cruising formalities....22
Customs....22, 23
Lights and shapes....31
Navigation lights....30
Part A: General....24
Part B: Steering and sailing rules....24
Part C: Lights and shapes....29
Part D: Sound and light signals....29
Red deisel....23
Travelling with pets....23
Resuscitation
Children....119
Emergency (ABC)....118
Problems....120
Problems during; drowning and hypothermia....120

S

Safety....105
Equipment recommended....107
Signals....108, 109
Satellite communications....67
Satellite navigation....39
EGNOS....39
GPS....39
Schengen Treaty....23
Sea Areas (GMDSS)....108
Search and Rescue (SAR): Resources....71
Search and Rescue (SAR): UK....114
Seasickness....121
Sea states....83
Secondary ports....54, 55, 56, 58
SÉCURITÉ, Safety signal....110
Semaphore (Signal) stations....75
Shipping forecast, BBC Radio 4....94
Shock....120
Signals, international
Code of signals....64
Port Traffic Signals (IPTS)....78
Storm warning signals....86
SOLAS V....35
Sound signals....32
Spain
Coast radio stations....76, 102
Special notes....959, 1012
Special notes
Belgium....740
Channel Islands....828, 829
Denmark....653
France....757
Germany....672
Gibraltar....1022
Ireland....572
Portugal....992
Portuguese Islands....1029
Spain....959, 1012
Standard ports....54, 55, 56
Storm warnings....61
Storm warning signals, International....86
Strains and sprains....125
Stroke....122
Strong wind warnings....85
Subfacts....68, 451, 484
Submarines....43
Sun
Declination....47
Rise/set tables....49
True bearing....47, 48
Survival times....110
Swell....82
Symbols, Abbreviations and....7

T

Tidal coefficients
Brest....879
Calais....765
Cherbourg....792
Pointe de Grave....942
St Malo....811
Tidal curves
Aberdeen....386
Avonmouth....556
Belfast....640
Brest....880
Burnham-on-Crouch....306
Cherbourg....796
Chichester Harbour....243
Christchurch to Selsey, special curves....218
Cobh....592
Cuxhaven....682
Dartmouth....173
Dieppe....773
Dover....264
Dublin....576
Dunkerque....754
Esbjerg....664
Falmouth....152
Galway....621
Gibraltar....1021
Greenock....488
Harwich....319
Helgoland....676
Hoek van Holland....728
Holyhead....523
Immingham....342
Invergordon....405
La Coruña....973
Le Havre....775
Leith....381
Lerwick....424
Lisboa....999
Liverpool....515
London Bridge....299
Lowestoft....326
Margate....286
Milford Haven....542

Oban 463
Plymouth 165
Pointe de Grave 940
Poole 201
Heights at Town Quay 204
Portland 185
Portsmouth 233
River Foyle 630
River Tees 351
River Tyne/North Shields 361
Sheerness 289
Shoreham 255
Special curves, Christchurch to Selsey 218
Southampton 228
St Helier 843
St Malo 812
St Peter Port 834
Stornoway 438
Tarbert Island 606
Ullapool 445
Vlissingen 736
Walton-on-the-Naze 313
Wick 413
Wilhelmshaven 692
Zeebrugge 742
Tidal streams
Belgium 704
Biscay, S 920
Brittany, N 850
Brittany, S 890
Channel Islands 824
England, Central S 194
England, E 274
England, NE 334
England, NW 500
England, SE 250
England, SW 140
France, Central N 800
France, N 752
Germany 668
Ireland, N 614
Ireland, S 568
Isle of Wight and Solent 216
Isles of Scilly 140
Mull of Kintyre 479
Netherlands 704
Portland 180
Rathlin Island 636
Scotland, NE 394
Scotland, NW 432
Scotland, SE 368
Scotland, SW 470
Thames Estuary 280
Wales, S and Bristol Channel 530
Tide tables
Aberdeen 387
Avonmouth 553
Belfast 641
Brest 876
Burnham-on-Crouch 307
Casablanca 1044
Cherbourg 793
Chichester Harbour 244
Cobh 589
Cowes 223
Cuxhaven 683
Dartmouth 170
Dieppe 770
Dover 266
Dublin 577
Dunkerque 759
Esbjerg 661
Falmouth 153
Galway 622
Gibraltar 1023
Greenock 489
Harwich 320
Helgoland 677
Hoek van Holland 725
Holyhead 524
Immingham 343
Invergordon 406
La Coruña 974
Le Havre 776
Leith 378
Lerwick 425
Lisboa 1000
Liverpool 512
London Bridge 300
Lowestoft 327
Margate 283
Milford Haven 543
Oban 459
Plymouth 162
Pointe de Grave 937
Ponta Delgada 1038
Poole 206
Portland 182
Portsmouth 234
River Foyle 631
River Tees 352
River Tyne/North Shields 358
Sheerness 292
Shoreham 256
Southampton 225
St Helier 844
St Malo 812
St Peter Port 835
Stornoway 439
Tarbert Island 607
Ullapool 446
Vlissingen 736
Walton-on-the-Naze 314
Wick 414
Wilhelmshaven 692
Zeebrugge 742, 743
Tides (Chapter 4) 53
Barometric pressure effects 61
Calculations 55, 56
Clearances under bridges 58
Coefficients 54
Computation of stream rates 61, 62
Computer predictions 58
EasyTide 59
TotalTide 59
Definitions 54
Duration 54
Factors 58
Interval 54
Meteorological effects 61
MHWS, MHWN, MLWS, MLWN 54
Range 54
Rise/Fall 54
Secondary ports 54, 55, 56, 58
Standard Ports 55
Storm warnings 61
Streams, diamonds & atlases 59, 60
Streams in rivers 61
Twelfths rule 58
Wind, effect on tides 61
Time, UT and DST 12
TotalTide 59
Traffic Separation
Banco del Hoyo 1010
Botney Ground, off 702, 710, 711
Brown Ridge, off 702, 711
Cape Roca, off 988, 992
Cape St Vincent, off 989, 1005
Casquets, off 139, 798, 822, 828
Dover Strait 252, 262, 751
Fastnet Rock, off 566, 594
Finisterre, off 955, 971
Friesland, East 711
Friesland, West 710, 711
German Bight, western approaches 690, 711
Gibraltar Strait 1010, 1021
Harwich approaches 317, 318
Hinder, West 724
Holyhead 523
Humber approaches 333
Jade approach 673, 690
Land's End, off 138, 144, 145
Maas 728
Maas, North 702, 728
Maas, West Inner and Outer 728
Neist Point, off 430
Netherlands, North, off 667, 702, 711
Netherlands, South, and Belgium 703
Netherlands, South, off 724
Noord Hinder North 702, 724, 728
Noord Hinder off 724
Noord Hinder South 724
North Channel 469, 629
Ouessant (Ushant), off 848, 849, 856
Scilly, South of 138, 144, 145
Scilly, West of 138, 144, 145
Skerries, off 613, 618
Smalls, off 528, 534
Terschelling-German Bight 673, 690, 700, 711
Texel, off 710, 711
Tuskar Rock, off 567, 575, 582, 584
Vigo approaches 979, 984
Vlieland North 711
Vlieland, off 710
Twelfths rule 58

U

Updates 2
Urgency 108, 109

V

Vent solaire 896
Vessel Traffic Service (VTS) 78, 681
Elbe, River 681
Ems, River 700
Nieuwe Waterweg 729
Noordzeekanaal 721
Weser, River 690
VHF
CROSS broadcasts 100, 101
Inter-ship channels 65
Link calls 68
Port operations channels 65
Radio 65
Visual signals, shore to ships 113
Vocabularies 12
Breton 892
Danish 653
Gaelic 573
Volmet 96
Voluntary Separation Scheme (VSS), Dover 262

W

Waypoints 40
Weather (Chapter 6) 81
Actual weather reporting stations 95
Beaufort scale 82
Douglas Sea State scale 83
Fax forecasts, HF radio broadcasts 91
High seas bulletins 89
Inshore waters forecast 94
Land forecasts 94
MSI broadcasts by HM Coastguard 89
Navtex 86
Press forecasts 96
Sea states 83
Sources abroad
Channel Islands 96
Denmark 97
France 100
Germany 98
Gibraltar 104
Ireland 96
Netherlands 96, 99
Portugal & the Azores 103
Spain 102
Telephone forecasts, Météo 102
Television forecasts 96
Terminology 86
Wind farms 44
Wireless internet 66
Wounds 122

A

Abbenfleth ... 680
Aberaeron ... 538
Aberdaron ... 523
Aberdeen ... 386
Aberdour ... 370, 376
Aberdovey ... 538
Aberporth ... 538
Abersoch ... 535
Aberystwyth ... 538
A'bhodaich ... 482
Acairseid Mhór ... 442
Accumersiel ... 697
Achillbeg Island (South Point) ... 616
Adrigole ... 599
Ailsa Craig ... 473
Albert Bridge ... 295
Albufeira ... 991, 1006
Aldeburgh ... 325
Alde, River ... 324
Alderney ... 826, 828, 829, 830
Algeciras ... 1011, 1021, 1022
Allington Lock ... 291
Altacarry Head (Rathlin East) ... 617
Alte Mellum ... 695
Alte Weser light house ... 689
Althorne ... 305
Alt, River ... 516
Alum Bay ... 211
Alvor ... 1005, 1032
Amble ... 362
Ameland ... 713
Amlwch ... 523
Amrum-Hafen ... 673, 674
Amsterdam ... 712, 721
Andernos ... 948
Andijk ... 719
Anglesey ... 518
Anglet ... 924, 949
Angra do Heroísmo ... 1031, 1035
Annalong ... 646
Annan Waterfoot ... 496
Anse de Bertheaume ... 871
Anse de Feunteun Aod ... 885
Anse de Penfoul ... 897
Anse de Primel ... 866
Anse de St Martin ... 796
Anse des Vieilles ... 928
Anstey's Cove ... 174
Anstruther ... 381
Antwerpen ... 729, 740
Anvil Point ... 143
Aran Islands ... 620
Aranmore light house ... 617
Arbroath ... 384
Arcachon ... 924, 947
Ardglass ... 645
Ardgroom ... 601
Ardinamar ... 463
Ardnakinna Point ... 571
Ardnamurchan ... 435
Ardnave Point ... 475
Ardrishaig ... 477
Ardrossan ... 473, 492
Argenton ... , 870
Arinagour ... 455
Arisaig ... 452
Arklow ... 582
Arklow Roadstone Harbour ... 582
Armadale Bay ... 450
Ar-Men ... 855
Arnish Point ... 434
Arnside ... 509
Arrábida ... 1003
Arradon ... 909
Arrifana ... 1004
Arrochar ... 486
Arromanches ... , 786
Ars-en-Ré ... 922, 932
Arun, River ... 254
Ashlett Creek ... 209, 231
Audenge ... 948
Audierne ... 885, 889
Aulne, River ... 875
Aultbea ... 449
Ault light house ... 755
Auray ... 894, 909
Auskerry ... 397, 419
Aust ... 552
Aveiro ... 990, 995
Aven, River ... 892
Aveton Gifford ... 166
Avilés ... 957, 967, 968, 969
Avoch ... 409
Avonmouth ... 558
Avon, River (Devon) ... 166
Avon, River (Dorset) ... 210
Ayamonte ... 1010, 1013
Ayr ... 473, 492, 493
Azores
- Angra do Heroísmo ... 1031, 1035
- Cais (São Roque) do Pico ... 1031, 1034
- Calheta ... 1031, 1034
- Ferraria ... 1031
- Horta ... 1031, 1032
- Madalena ... 1031, 1033
- Ponta da Barca ... 1031
- Ponta da Sereta ... 1031
- Ponta das Lajes (Flores) ... 1030
- Ponta Delgada ... 1031, 1037
- Ponta do Albarnaz ... 1030
- Ponta do Arnel ... 1031
- Ponta do Castelo ... 1031
- Ponta do Topo ... 1031
- Ponta Garça ... 1031
- Porto das Lajes ... 1030, 1032
- Praia de Vitória ... 1031, 1036
- Santa Clara ... 1031
- Santa Maria ... 1031
- Velas ... 1031, 1034
- Vila da Praia ... 1031
- Vila do Porto ... 1031, 1036
- Vila Franca do Campo ... 1031

B

Babbacombe Bay ... 174
Backaland Bay ... 419
Badachro ... 449
Badcall Bay ... 445
Badentarbat Bay ... 449
Baginbun Head ... 585
Baie de Bourgneuf ... 922, 926, 1041
Baie de Lampaul ... 874, 875
Baie de Morlaix ... 856
Baily ... 570
Balbriggan ... 647
Ballinskelligs Bay ... 601
Ballycastle ... 637
Ballycotton ... 571, 588
Ballycrovane ... 601
Ballyholme Bay ... 639
Ballysadare Bay ... 626
Balta Sound ... 398, 423
Baltimore ... 571, 597
Baltrum ... 671, 698
Banff ... 396, 401
Bangor (Belfast Lough) ... 617, 640
Bangor (Menai) ... 503, 518, 520
Banjo Pier (Looe) ... 142, 158
Bann, River ... 634
Bantham ... 166
Bantry Bay ... 571, 599, 600
Barbate ... 1011, 1019
Bardsey Island ... 503, 518, 523, 532
Barfleur ... 756, 789
Barmouth ... 537
Barnstaple ... 561
Barra ... 442
Barra Head ... 434, 442
Barrow-in-Furness ... 502, 506, 509
Barry ... 550
Bartlett Creek ... 291
Basta Voe ... 423
Bath (Westerschelde) ... 733
Battlesbridge ... 305
Bay of Biscay ... 925, 959
Bay of Cádiz ... 1011, 1017, 1018
Bay of Laig ... 454
Bayona ... 958, 986
Bayonne ... 947, 949
Beachley ... 552
Beachy Head ... 252, 253, 262
Beadnell Bay ... 362
Bear (Bere) Island ... 600
Beaucette ... 832
Beaulieu, River ... 196, 215
Beaumaris ... 520
Bee Ness ... 291
Beidenfleth ... 680
Belcroute Bay ... 842
Belfast Harbour ... 639
Belfast Lough ... 618, 639
Belle Île ... 893, 904, 905
Beluso ... 984
Belvoir Bay ... 838
Bembridge ... 198, 233
Bénodet ... 872 , 892, 896, 897, 900
Bensersiel ... 671, 697
Berck ... 766
Berghaven ... 729
Berkeley ... 552
Bermeo ... 956, 963
Berwick-upon-Tweed ... 337, 363, 364
Beuzec ... 892
Bideford ... 561
Bilbao (Bilbo) ... 956, 963
Binic ... 803, 819
Bishop Rock ... 142
Bishops, the ... 534
Black Ball Harbour ... 599, 600
Black Nore Point ... 533
Blackpool ... 502, 510
Black Rock (Falmouth) ... 142, 150
Black Rock (North Ireland) ... 616
Black Rock (Yarmouth, IoW) ... 196, 212
Blacksod Bay ... 625
Blacktoft ... 346
Blackwater, River ... 277, 310
Blakeney ... 338
Blankenberge ... 709, 746
Blavands Huk ... 652
Blue Mull ... 423
Blue Mull Sound ... 424
Blyth ... 361
Boddam ... 400
Bodic ... 852
Bognor Regis ... 254
Bonanza ... 1016
Bonawe ... 462
Bonne Nuit Bay ... 842
Boontjes ... 706
Bordeaux (France) ... 924, 944, 945
Bordeaux (Guernsey) ... 834
Borkum ... 699
Borsfleth ... 680
Boscastle ... 562, 563
Bosham ... 242
Boston ... 336, 341
Bouley Bay ... 842
Boulmer ... 362
Boulogne ... 754, 766
Bound Skerry ... 397
Bourgenay ... 922, 930
Bourg-sur-Gironde ... 944
Bovisand Pier ... 159
Boyardville ... 923
Boyne, River Bar ... 646
Bradwell ... 310
Brake ... 688
Brancaster Staithe ... 336, 339
Brandaris light tower ... 706, 715
Brandon Bay ... 572, 603
Braye ... 826, 830
Brehon ... 826
Bremen ... 688
Bremerhaven ... 671, 688
Brentford Dock Marina ... 299
Breskens ... 739
Bressay ... 397
Brest ... 872, 880
Bridgwater ... 559
Bridlington ... 349
Brightlingsea ... 277, 311

Brighton 252, 259
Brigneau 892, 900
Brignogan 868
Bristol 556
Bristol Channel 532
Brixham 173
Broad Haven 625
Brodick 481
Broekerhaven 719
Brough Haven 347
Brough of Birsay 397
Brownsea Island 196, 200
Bruichladdich 475
Brunsbüttel 670, 686
Bryher 146
Buckie 396, 402
Bucklers Hard 215
Bude 562, 563
Bueu 984
Bull Point 533
Bull Rock 572
Bull Sand Fort 346
Bunbeg 627
Burela 970
Burghead 396, 403
Burhou 830
Burnham-on-Crouch 305
Burnham-on-Sea 559
Burnmouth 370, 373
Burntisland 370, 374
Burnt Islands 481
Burra Voe 424
Burray Ness 420
Burry Port 548
Bursledon 231
Burton Stather 346
Bur Wick 420
Busum 670, 675
Bute 483
Butt of Lewis 434

C

Cabo Ajo 956
Cabo Busto 957
Cabo Carvoeiro 990
Cabo Corrubedo 958
Cabo da Roca 990
Cabo de Cruz 958, 981
Cabo de San Agustín 957
Cabo de Santa Catalina 956
Cabo de Santa Maria 991, 1007
Cabo de São Vicente 991
Cabo de Sines 991
Cabo de Torres 957
Cabo Espichel 991
Cabo Finisterre 958, 979
Cabo Higuer 924, 956
Cabo Lastres 957
Cabo Machichaco 956
Cabo Mayor 956
Cabo Mondego 990
Cabo Ortegal 957, 971
Cabo Peñas 957
Cabo Prior 957
Cabo Prioriño Chico 957
Cabo Raso 990, 992
Cabo Roche 1011
Cabo San Sebastían 957
Cabo Sardão 991
Cabo Silleiro 958
Cabo Spartel 1012
Cabo Trafalgar 1011, 1016, 1019
Cabo Vidio 957
Cabo Villano (Bilbao) 956
Cabo Villano, (Camariñas) 957, 978
Cadgwith 149
Cádiz 1018
Cadzand-Bad 735
Caen 755, 785
Caernarfon 520, 521
Caernarfon Bar 521
Cahersiveen Marina 602
Cais (São Roque) do Pico 1031, 1034
Caister-on-Sea 330
Caladh Harbour 481
Calais 754, 764
Caledonian Canal 396, 410, 436, 458
Calf of Man 502
Calf Sound 507
Calheta (Madeira) 1041, 1043
Calheta (São Jorge) 1031, 1034
Calshot Spit 197
Camaret 855, 882
Cambados 983
Campbeltown 480
Camusnagaul 449
Cancale 802, 806, 808
Cangas 985
Canna 435, 454
Cantick Head 397
Canvey Island 295, 303
Capbreton 924, 949
Cap d'Alprech 754
Cap d'Antifer 769
Cap de Carteret 802, 826
Cap de la Hague 787, 826
Cap de la Hève 755
Cape Cornwall 563
Cape Wrath 396, 418, 434, 437
Cap Ferret 947
Cap Fréhel 803
Cap Gris-Nez 754
Cap Lévi 756
Caramiñal 958
Cardiff 532, 546, 550
Cardigan 539
Cardigan Bay 532
Carentan 756, 788
Cargreen 159
Cariño 957, 971
Carlingford Lough 646
Carloway 443
Carmarthen 547, 548
Carna 570
Carnlough Harbour 617, 637
Carnsore Point 585
Carradale Bay 480
Carreg-y-Chwislen 523
Carrickarory 629
Carrickfergus 618, 639
Carrigaholt Bay 605
Carsaig Bay 456, 476
Carteret 802, 805
Cascais 990, 997
Cashla Bay 620
Casquets 826, 828
Castillo de San Sebastián 1011
Castillo de Santa Ana 956
Castlebay 442, 443
Castlemartin Range 546
Castletown 502, 505
Castletown Bay 505
Castletown (Bearhaven) 599, 600
Castletownshend 596
Castro Urdiales 956, 964
Cat Firth 422
Caudebec 780
Cayeux-sur-Mer 754, 767
Cemaes Bay 523
Ceuta 1012, 1026
Channel Light Vessel 826
Chanonry 396
Chapman's Pool 189
Charlestown 156
Chatham 291
Chauveau 923
Cheek Point 586
Chelsea Harbour 299
Chenal de la Helle 872
Chenal du Four 872, 873
Chepstow 550
Cherbourg 756, 790
Chesil Beach/Cove 178
Chester 515
Chichester Harbour 198, 241
Chipiona 1011, 1016
Christchurch 210
Church Ope Cove 189
Clacton-on-Sea 311
Clare Island 625
Cleanderry 601
Clear Island 597
Cleavel Point 200
Clevedon 558
Clew Bay 625
Clifden Bay 625
Clonakilty Bay 595, 596
Clovelly 561
Clyde, River 487
Clyth Ness 396
Cobo Bay 834
Cockenzie 375
Codling Lanby 570
Colchester 311
Coleraine 634
Colne, River 277, 303, 311
Colonsay 472, 475
Colwyn Bay 515
Combarro 983
Concarneau 892, 899, 900
Coningbeg 570
Connah's Quay 502, 515
Connel 462
Contis 924
Conwy 506, 517
Conyer Creek 288
Copinsay 397
Coquet Island 337, 348
Cordouan 923, 941
Cork 571, 592
Corpach 436, 457
Corran Narrows 456
Corryvreckan 474
Corta de Los Jeronimos 1016
Coryton 303
Cotehele Quay 159
Cotentin Peninsula 804
Courseulles-sur-Mer 755, 785
Courtmacsherry 571, 595
Courtown 582
Coverack 149
Covesea Skerries 396
Cowes/River Medina 196, 221
Crac'h, River 894
Craighouse 475
Craignure 457
Crail 381
Cramond 376
Cranfield Point 646
Craobh Marina 465
Craster 362
Créac'h 854
Creux Hbr 839
Criccieth 536
Crinan 474
Crinan Canal 476
Cromarty 409, 411
Cromer 338
Crouch, River 277, 305
Crouesty 909, 911
Crowlin Islands 450
Cuan Sound 463
Cudillero 957, 969
Cullen 401
Cullercoats 357
Culmore Bay 629
Cultra 639
Cumberland Basin 556
Cumbrae 482
Cushendall 637
Cushendun Bay 638
Cuxhaven 670, 682

D

Dagebüll 670, 673
Dahouet 803, 817
Dale Roads 540
Darnett Ness 291
Darrynane 601
Dartmouth 168
Deal 252, 265
Deauville 755, 782
Deben, River 323

De Block van Kuffeler 719
Dee, River 502, 515
Deer Sound 420
Deganwy 506, 517
Delfzijl 712, 713
Dell Quay 242
Den Helder 717, 724
Den Oever 706, 718, 719
Derby Haven 507
Déroute de Terre 804
Derrible Bay 839
Derwent, River 504
Diélette 802, 804
Dieppe 755, 768
Dinan 815
Dinard 808, 810
Dingle Bay 572, 602, 604
Dingwall 409
Dirk Bay 595
Dittisham 168
Dives-sur-Mer 755, 783
Dixcart Bay 839
Dodman Point Firing Range 156
Doel 734
Doëlan 892, 901
Donaghadee 639, 640
Donegal Harbour 627
Donostia (San Sebastián) 956, 961
Doove Balg 706
Dornie Bridge 452
Dornoch Firth 396, 411
Douarnenez 855, 872, 882, 883
Douglas 508
Douglas Head 502
Dover 252, 265
Dover Strait 269
Drummore 488, 495, 496
Dubh Artach 436
Dublin 570, 576
Duclair 780
Duddon Bar 505
Dunany Point 646
Dunbar 373
Dunbeacon Harbour 599
Duncansby Head 396, 412
Dundalk 646
Dundee 383
Dundrum Bay 646
Dungarvan Bay 588
Dungarvan Harbour 587
Dungeness 253, 262
Dunkerque 754, 762, 763
Dunkerron Harbour 601
Dun Laoghaire 570, 580
Dunmanus Bay 598
Dunmanus Harbour 598
Dunmore East 571, 587
Dunnet Head 396
Dunoon 485
Dunstaffnage 463
Durdle Door 189
Durgerdam 719
Dury Voe 424

E

Eastbourne 252, 261
East Channel light buoy 826
East Frisian Islands 695
East Loch Tarbert 478, 442
East Pier Head 571
East Wangerooge 696
Eckmühl 855
Edam 719
Eday 419
Eddystone 142
Eemshaven 712
Eeragh (Rock Island) 616
Egmond-aan-Zee 707
Eidersperrwerk 675
Eigg Harbour 454
Eilean a' Cheo (Skye) 435, 449, 450, 452
Eilean Glas 434
Elanchove (Elantxobe) 956, 963
Elbe, River 680
Elberry Cove 173
Elie 371, 376
Ellewoutsdijk 709, 733
Élorn, River 875
El Rompido 1010, 1014
Elsfleth 688
Emden 671, 700
Emshorn 700
Ems, River 671
Emsworth 198, 242
English and Welsh Grounds 558
Enkhuizen 719
Enseada da Baleeira 1004
Enseada de Belixe 1004
Ensenada del Sardiñeiro 980
Ensenada de San Simón 985
Ericeira 996
Erme, River 166
Erquy 803, 817
Esbjerg 652, 660
Esha Ness 398
Esposende 993
Esteiro 991
Étaples 766
Étel, River 893, 902, 904
Etretat 774
Europa Point 1012, 1022
Europlatform 730
Exe, River 175
Exeter, Exmouth Dock 177
Exmouth 175
Eyemouth 370, 372

F

Fair Isle 397, 423, 424
Fairlie Quay 483
Falaise des Fonds 755
Falmouth and River Fal 150
Fambridge 305
Fanad Bay 628
Fanad Head 617
Fanø 664
Farne Islands 363
Faro 991, 1007
Faslane 486
Fastnet 571
Faversham 288
Fawley 230
Fécamp 755, 774
Felixstowe Ferry 323
Felixstowe Pier 323
Fermain Bay 834
Ferraria 1031
Ferrol 957, 972
Ferryside 548
Fiddler's Ferry 515
Fidra 373
Fife Ness 371
Figueira da Foz 990, 995
Filey Bay 349
Findhorn 396, 404
Findochty 396, 402
Finisterre 979
Firth of Clyde 483
Firth of Forth 375
Firths Voe 397
Fischerbalje 671
Fishbourne Channel 242
Fishcombe Cove 173
Fisherrow 376
Fishguard 539
Flamborough Head 337
Flannan Isles 435, 443
Flat Holm 532, 550
Fleetwood 510
Flotta 419
Flowerdale Bay 449
Föhr 673
Folkestone 252, 264
Folly Inn 221
Folly Reach 221
Fontainevieille 948
Fontenelle Bay 834
Formby 511
Fort Belan 520
Fort (Cromwell) Point 572
Fort de l'Ouest 756
Forte de Santa Marta 990
Forth and Clyde Canal 377
Forth, River 370
Fortrose 409
Fort William 436, 457
Foula 398, 423, 424
Fouras 936
Fowey 157
Fraserburgh 396, 400
Freiburg 680
Fremington 561
Freshwater Bay 210, 211
Fromentine 922, 926, 927
Fuenterrabía (Hondarribia) 956, 960
Funchal 1041, 1043

G

Galley Head 571
Gallions Point Marina 298
Galway Bay 616, 619
Galway Harbour 620
Gardenstown 400
Gareloch, Garelochhead 472, 486
Garlieston 495, 496
Garnish Bay 601
Getaria (Guetaria) 956
Gibalta 991
Gibraltar 1012, 1022
Gibraltar Strait 1011, 1020, 1021
Gigha 474, 475
Gijón 957, 968
Gills Bay 417
Girvan 473, 493
Gladstone Dock 515
Glandore (Unionhall) 595
Glasson Dock 509
Glenarm 637
Glengariff 599
Glengarrisdale Bay 475
Glin 605
Gluckstadt 680
Gluss Island 398
Goeree light tower 707
Goleen 598
Golfe du Morbihan 894, 908
Golspie 411
Gometra 456
Goole 346
Gorey 842
Gorleston 278, 330
Gorran Haven 152
Gosport 238, 239
Gott Bay 454, 455
Goulphar 893
Gourdon 385
Gourock 485
Goury 802, 804
Grådyb 659, 664
Grandcamp 756, 787
Grande Havre 834
Grande Île 802
Grand Léjon 803
Grangemouth 371, 376
Granton 370, 376
Granville 806
Gravelines 754, 763
Gravesend 276, 295
Greatman Bay 620
Great Yarmouth 278, 312, 330, 336
Greenway Quay 168
Greetsiel 671, 699
Grève au Lancon 842
Grève de la Ville 839
Grève de Lecq 842
Greystones 576, 581
Gribbin Head 156, 157
Griminish 434
Grimsby 347

Grosnez Point 827
Grosser Vogelsand 680
Grunna Voe 422
Gruting Voe 422
Grutness Voe 422
Guernsey 826, 831
Guetaria (Getaria) 956, 961
Gugh 145
Gull Stream 252

H

Hale Head 515
Hamble, River 197, 230, 231
Hamburg 680, 687
Hammersmith Bridge 295
Hamna Voe 422
Hamworthy 200
Hannaine Bay 830
Hanstholm 651, 655
Hansweert 733, 734
Haringvliet 707, 724
Harlesiel 671, 696, 697
Harlingen 706, 716
Harrington 504
Hartland Point 533, 558
Hartlepool 337, 348, 355
Harwich 278, 312
Haseldorf 680
Haskeir Island 435
Hastings 252, 261, 263
Haulbowline 618
Havelet Bay 826, 834
Havengore 304
Haverfordwest 540
Havre Gosselin 838
Hayle 533, 563
Hayling Island 242
Hejar Lesfar 1026
Helford River 149
Helgoland 670, 675
Helmsdale 412
Hendaye 924, 951
Hengistbury Head 210
Hennebont 902
Herm 826, 838
Herne Bay 276, 287
Hestan Islet 496
Het Vlie 714
Heugh (Hartlepool) 337
Heugh (Holy Island) 337, 363
Heurteauville 780
Hever, River 670
Heysham 509
Hilbre Island 515
Hillswick 424
Hindeloopen 719
Hinkley Point 559
Hirtshals 651, 655
Hoedekenskerke 733
Hojer 664
Holehaven 295
Holliwell Point 305
Holyhead 522
Holy Island 337, 363
Holy Loch 485
Hondarribia (Fuenterrabía) 956, 960
Honfleur 779
Hook Head 570
Hooksiel 671, 689
Hoorn 719
Hope Cove 166
Hopeman 396, 403
Horne 680
Horns Rev 659
Hörnum 670, 673, 674
Horse Sand Fort 197, 239
Horseshoe Harbour 581, 597
Horta 1031, 1032
Hourtin 924
Houton Bay 419
Howth 575
Hoy 419
Hugh Town 145
Huibert Gat 712
Hull 346
Hullbridge 305
Humber Bridge 337, 342, 346
Hunstanton 339
Hurst Point 196, 210
Husum 670, 673, 674
Hvide Sande 652, 658
Hyskeir 435
Hythe firing ranges 262
Hythe (Southampton) 197, 228

I

Icart Bay 834
Igueldo 956
IJmuiden 707, 720
IJsselmeer 718
Île-aux-Moines 909
Île-aux-Moines light house 852
Île-aux-Moutons 892
Île Berder 909
Île Cézon 869
Île d'Aix 923, 934, 935
Île d'Arz 909
Île de Batz 853, 856, 868
Île de Boëdig 909
Île de Bréhat 852, 857
Île de Conleau 909, 910
Île de Groix 892
Île de Hoëdic 894, 905
Île de Houat 894, 905
Île de la Jument 909
Île de Molène 854, 874
Île de Noirmoutier 922, 927
Île de Penfret 892, 898, 899
Île de Ré 922, 931
Île de Sein 855, 884
Île des Hébihens 817
Île d'Oléron 923, 934
Île d'Ouessant 854, 856, 874
Île Dumet 894
Île du Pilier 922
Île d'Yeu 922, 930
Île Harbour 803
Île Longue 909
Île Louet 853, 866
Île Pirenn 909
Îles Chausey 807
Îles de Glénan 892, 898
Îles Saint-Marcouf 756, 787, 788
Île-Vierge light house 853
Ilfracombe 533, 560
Ilha da Berlenga 990
Ilha de Porto Santo 1041
Ilha Madeira 1041
Ilhas Desertas 1041
Ilhas Selvagen 1041
Immingham 343
Inchcolm 376
Inishbofin 625
Inisheer 616
Inishowen 617
Inishtrahull 617
Inner Dowsing light tower 341
Instow 533
Inveraray 477
Inverewe Gardens 449
Invergordon 396, 409
Inverie Bay 454
Inverkip 485
Inverness 396, 409
Inverness Firth 396, 411
Inward Rocks 552
Iona 456
Ipswich 278
Irvine 492
Isigny-sur-Mer 756
Isla Canela 1010, 1013
Isla Cristina 1010, 1014
Isla de San Antón 956
Isla de Tapia 957
Isla Ons 958, 984
Isla Pancha 957
Isla Sálvora 958
Islas Cíes 958, 984
Isla Sisargas 957
Islay 472, 474
Isle Martin 445
Isle of Man 502, 505, 506
Isle of May 371, 381
Isle of Walney 502
Isle of Whithorn 495, 496
Isle Ristol 449
Isles of Scilly 142, 144, 145

J

Jade, River 690
Jaonnet 834
Jard-sur-Mer 922, 931
Jaudy, River 852
Jersey 827, 840, 842
Johnshaven 385
Juist 671, 698, 699
Jupiter Point 159
Jura 475

K

Kallin 442
Kenmare 601
Kenmare River 601
Kéréon 854
Kerjean 852
Kermorvan 854
Kerners 909
Kerprigent 852
Ketelhaven 719
Kettletoft Pier 397, 419, 421
Kew Bridge 295
Keyhaven 210
Kiel Canal 686
Kiel-Holtenau 687
Kiggaul Bay 616, 620
Kildalloig Bay 480
Kilkeel 645, 646
Kilkieran Bay 620
Kilkieran Cove 619
Killadysert 605
Killala Bay 626
Killard Point 645
Killary Harbour 625
Killeany Bay 619
Killough Harbour 645
Killybegs 627
Killyleagh 645
Kilmakilloge 601
Kilmokea Point 586
Kilmore Quay 570, 585
Kilrush 572, 606
Kingsbridge 167
King's Lynn 340
Kinlochbervie 434, 444
Kinnaird Head 396
Kinsale 571, 594
Kippford 496
Kirkaldy 381
Kirkcaldy 371
Kirkcudbright 496
Kirk Sound 419
Kirkwall 397, 420
Kish Bank 570
Knock 671
Knude 652
Kornwerderzand 718
Kruckaumundung 680
Kyle Akin 452
Kyle of Durness 417
Kyle of Lochalsh 452
Kyle of Tongue 417

L

La Balue 802
La Banche 895
Labasheeda 605
L'Aber Benoît 853, 870

Gazetteer

L'Aber-Ildut....854, 870
L'Aberwrac'h....853, 869
La Cayenne....936
La Chambre....858
La Charente, River....923, 935, 936
La Collette....840
La Corbière....827
La Coruña....957, 977
La Cotinière....923
La Croix....852
La Dordogne, River....941
L'Adour, River....924, 949
La Flotte....923, 931
La Garonne, River....924, 944, 945
La Gironde, River....940, 945
Lagos....991, 1004
La Grande Grève....838
La Guardia....986
La Guia....958
La Higuera....1011
L'Aiguillon/La-Faute-sur-Mer....922, 931
La Jouvente....815
La Jument....854
La Lande....853
Lambay Island....570, 617, 635
Lamena....941
Lamlash....481
Lampaul....874
Lancaster....509
L'Ancresse Bay....834
Landes Range....946
Land's End....561
Langeoog....671, 698
Langstone Harbour....198, 240
Lannion (Léguer River)....864
La Pallice....933
La Pierre-de-Herpin....802
La Pommeraie....815
La Rance, Barrage and River....802, 803, 815
Laredo....956, 965
La Reuille....941
Largs....483
La Richardais....815
L'Armandèche....922
Larmor Baden....909
Larne....618, 638
La Roche Bernard....912
La Rochelle....923, 933
La Rocque....842
La Seudre, River....936
Lastres....968
La Tchue....830
La Teignouse....894
La Tremblade....936
La Trinité-sur-Mer....894, 907
La Turballe....895, 913
Lauwersoog....706, 712, 716
La Vieille....855
La Vigne....948
Lawrence Cove....600
Laxey....502, 505
Le Bono....909
Leça....990, 1030
Le Chapus....934
Le Colombier....852
Le Conquet....854, 871
Le Croisic....895, 911, 914
Le Crotoy....767
Leeds & Liverpool Canal....515
Lee-on-The-Solent....238
Le Four light house....854, 856
Le Four (Loire Atlantique)....895
Le Grand Jardin....802, 803
Le Guilvinec....855, 885
Le Havre....755, 774, 779
Le Hourdel....767
Leigh-on-Sea....276, 303
Leith....370, 375
Leixões....990, 994
Le Légué....803, 818
Le Logeo....909
Lelystad....719
Le Marquis....941
Le Minihic....815
Lemmer....719
Lemvig....651, 656, 657
Leopold II mole head....709
Le Palais....893, 905
Le Passage....909
Le Pointeau....895
Le Pouldu....901
Le Pouliguen....895, 915
Lequeitio (Lekeitio)....956, 962
Le Rocher....909
Lerwick....424
Les Ardentes....807
Les Baleines....922
Les Bas Sablons....803
Lesconil....892, 896
Les Ecrehou....842
Le Sénéquet....805
Les Fontaines....839
Les Hanois....826
Les Héaux de Bréhat....827, 852, 857
Les Minquiers....842
Les Pierres Noires....854
Les Sables d'Olonne....922, 929
Les Sept Îles....852, 856, 862, 863
Le Stiff....854
Le Touquet....754, 766
Le Tréport....755, 768
Le Trez Hir....871
Lézardrieux....852, 858, 859
L'Herbaudière....922, 926
Libourne....941
Lihou Island....834
Lild Strand....651
Lillo....734
Limehouse Basin....298
Limfjord....651, 657
Linklet Bay....419
Linnenplate....675
L'Iroise....872
Lisboa....991, 997
Liscannor....618, 619
Lismore....436
List....670, 673, 674
Little Bernera....438
Littlehampton....254
Little Haven....539
Little Killary Bay....625
Little Loch Broom....449
Little Russel Channel....831
Little Samphire Island....572
Liverpool....515
Lizard Point....142, 148
Llanddwyn Island....520
Llandudno....515
Llanelli....548
Llanes....956, 967
Llangwm....540
Loch A'bhraige....450
Loch Aline....457
Loch Alsh....452
Loch Beag....465
Loch Bervie....444
Loch Boisdale....434, 442
Loch Carnan....434, 442
Loch Carron....451
Loch Craignish....436, 465
Loch Creran....456
Loch Dunvegan....450
Loch Eatharna....454, 455
Loch Eil....457
Loch Eport....442
Loch Eriboll....417
Loch Ewe....445, 449
Loch Eynort....442
Loch Feochan....463
Loch Gairloch....445
Lochgoilhead....486
Loch Harport....450
Loch Hourn....452
Loch Inver....434, 444, 445
Loch Lathaich....456
Loch Laxford....444, 445
Loch Leven....456
Loch Linnhe....436, 457
Loch Long....487
Loch Maddy....442
Loch Melfort....436, 464
Loch Moidart....454
Loch Na Keal....456
Loch Nedd....445
Loch Nevis....435, 452
Loch Ranza....481
Loch Riddon....481
Lochrist....854
Loch Shell....442
Loch Shieldaig....449
Loch Shuna....465
Loch Skipport....442
Loch Snizort....450
Loch Spelve....456
Loch Sunart....455
Loch Sween....475
Loch Tarbert....475
Loch Thurnaig....449
Loch Torridon....437, 450
Locmaria....902
Locquemeau....865
Locquirec....865
Loctudy....892, 896
Loire, River....914, 916
London Bridge....279, 299
Londonderry....629
Lonehort Harbour....599
Long Hope....419
Longships....142
Longy Bay....830
Looe....158
Looe Channel....239
Loop Head....572
Lopwell....159
Lorient....893, 902
Lossiemouth....396, 402
L'Ost Pic....808
Lostwithiel....157
Loth....419, 421
Lough Foyle....617, 629
Lough Swilly....628
Lowestoft....278, 326
Luanco....968
Luarca....957, 969
Luce Bay firing ranges....488
Luhe....680
Lulworth Cove....185, 189
Lulworth firing ranges....188
Lundy Island....533, 560, 562
Lune, River....502
Lybster....396, 411
Lydd firing ranges....262
Lyme Bay....175
Lyme Regis....178
Lymington....196, 213
Lyness....419
Lyngvig....652
Lynher, River....161, 165
Lynmouth....559, 560
Lynmouth Foreland....533
Lynn of Lorn....436, 456
Lyvet....815

M

Maassluis....729, 730
Maasvlakte light house....707
MacDuff....396, 401
Machrihanish....475
Madalena....1031, 1033
Madeira
    Calheta....1041, 1043
    Funchal....1041, 1043
    Ilha de Porto Santo....1041
    Ilha Madeira....1041
    Ilhas Desertas....1041
    Ilhas Selvagen....1041
    Porto de Porto Santo....1042
    Porto de Porto Santo....1041
    Quinta do Lorde....1041, 1042
Makkum....719
Malahide....570, 574
Maldon....310

Mallaig 435, 454
Mama 991
Manchester Ship Canal 515
Marans 931
Marazion 148
Marchwood 228
Marennes 936
Margate 276, 287
Marin 983, 984
Marino Point 592
Marken 719
Markermeer 719
Marsdiep 707
Martin's Haven 539
Martrou 936
Maryport 502, 504
Maseline Harbour 839
Maughold Head 502
Mazagón 1011, 1015
McDermott Base 404
Medemblik 719
Medina, River/Cowes 196, 221
Medway 276
Medway, River 290
Meikle Ferry 411
Memmert 698
Menai Bridge 520
Menai Strait 503, 518, 520
Merrien 892, 900
Mersey and Dee, Rivers 502
Mersey, River 516
Meschers-sur-Gironde 944
Methil 381
Mevagissey 156
Mew Island 617
Middlesbrough 350, 355
Mid Yell Voe 423
Milfontes 1004
Milford Haven 540
Mill Cove 595
Millport 482
Milton Creek 288
Minehead (Bristol Channel) 533, 559
Mine Head (South Ireland) 571
Minsener Oog 695
Minsmere 325
Mizen Head 571, 594
Mochras 536
Moclett 419
Moelfre 523
Moguériec 868
Monach Islands 443
Monnickendam 719
Monte Dirección (Le Charf) 1012
Montedor 990
Monte Faro 958
Montrose 371, 384
Moray Firth 399, 409
Mordreuc 815
Morecambe 502, 509
Morgat 855, 882
Morlaix 853, 866
Morocco 1026
Mortagne 944
Mostyn Quay 515
Motrico (Mutriku) 956, 961, 962
Moulin Huet 834
Mousehole 147
Mouth 376
Moville 629
Muck 451
Muckle Flugga 398
Muckle Skerry 420
Mugia (Muxia) 971
Mühlenberg 687
Muiden 719
Muiderzand 719
Mullaghmore 626
Mullion Cove 148
Mull of Galloway 488
Mull of Kintyre 472, 477
Mulroy Bay 617, 627, 628
Mumbles 532, 549
Mumbles Head 546
Munkmarsch 673
Mupe Bay 185
Muxia (Mugia) 971

N

Naarden 719
Nab Deep Water Channel 193
Nab Tower 197
Nairn 396, 404
Narlwood Rocks 552
Nash 532
Nazaré 990, 996
Neath, River 549
Needles 196
Needles Channel 196, 211
Neist Point 435
Nes (Ameland) 706, 713, 716
Ness 396
Nessmersiel 671, 698
Netley 228
Neuharlingersiel 671, 697, 698
Neuwerk 672
Newarp 336
Newbiggin 361
Newburgh 383
Newcastle 645
Newcastle-upon-Tyne 357
New Grimsby Sound 145
Newhaven 252, 260
New Hythe 291
Newlyn 147
Newport 221, 550, 551
Newquay (Cornwall) 563
New Quay (Wales) 532, 538
New Ross 586
Newry 646
Newton Haven 362
Newtown River 214
Neyland 540
Nieblum 670
Nieuwe Waterweg 707, 729
Nieuwpoort 709, 748
Noirmoutier-en-l'Île 927
No Man's Land Fort 232, 239
Noodzeekanaal 721
Noordwijk-aan-Zee 707
Noordzeekanaal 707
Nordby (Fanø) 664
Norddeich 671, 698, 699
Nordenham 688
Norderney 671, 698
Nord-Ostsee Kanal 686
Norfolk Broads 330
North Bank 570
North Bay 442
North Berwick 370, 373
North Bull 570
North Channel (East Solent) 197
North Channel (Hurst Point) 196
North Channel (Poole) 196
North Fambridge 305
North Foreland 253, 262
North Frisian Islands 673
North Harbour 597
North Kessock Pier 409
Northney 242
North Rona 396
North Ronaldsay 397
North Shields 357
North Sunderland (Seahouses) 337, 362
North Uist 434
Noss Head 396
Noup Head 397
Nuevo Portil 1014

O

Oban 436, 462
Odet, River 897
Oeiras 997
Old Grimsby Sound 145
Old Head of Kinsale 570, 571, 584
Olhão 991
Olna Firth 422
Omonville-la-Rogue 756, 796
Oostende 709, 746
Oosterschelde 732
Oostmahoorn 713
Oporto (Porto) 990, 994
Ore, River 324
Orford Ness 278, 312, 325
Orkney Islands 397, 418
Ormond's Harbour 601
Ornsay 435
Orsay Island 475
Ortac Rock 828
Orwell, River 278, 319
Osea Island 310
Otterndorf 680, 682
Oudeschild 706, 716
Ouessant SW Lanby 854
Ouistreham 755, 784
Outer Hebrides 435, 437, 442, 443
Out Skerries 423
Owers 252, 253
Oyster Haven 594

P

Paal 734
Paco de Arcos 997
Padstow 563
Pagham 254
Paignton 173
Paimpol 852, 856, 857
Papa Westray 419
Par 156
Paris 781
Pasajes (Pasaia) 956, 960
Passage de la Déroute 804
Passage de la Teignouse 893, 905
Passe de la Gaine 858
Pauillac 924, 944
Pedroucos 997
Peel 507
Pegal 419
Pellworm 674
Penarth 533, 550
Pendeen 533
Penedo da Saudade 990
Pénerf, River 894, 911, 912
Peniche 990, 996
Peninnis Head 142, 145
Pen Men (Île de Groix) 892
Pennan Bay 400
Penryn 150
Pentland Firth 413
Penzance 148
Penzé River 867
Perelle Bay 834
Perranporth 563
Perros-Guirec 852, 861
Perth 383
Pertuis Breton 922, 930
Pertuis d'Antioche 930
Peterhead 399
Petit Bôt Bay 834
Petite Foule 922
Petit Port 834
Picacho 1011
Piedras Negras 983
Pierowall 419, 421
Pierre de Herpin 802
Pierres Noires 854
Pile light (Dundalk) 618
Pinnaumundung 680
Pinnau-Neuendeich 680
Piriac 894, 913
Pittenweem 381
Pladda 473
Plateau de Rochebonne 922
Plateau des Minquiers 827, 842
Platte 826
Platte Fougère 826
Platte Saline Bay 830
Plockton 450, 451
Plouër 815

Ploumanac'h 856, 863
Plymouth 142, 159
Pointe de Barfleur 756, 787
Pointe de Chassiron 923
Pointe de Gatseau 934
Pointe de Grave 923, 924, 937
Pointe de Grosse Terre 922
Pointe de Kerdonis 893
Pointe de la Coubre 923
Pointe de Langoz 892
Pointe de Penlan 894, 912
Pointe de Porz-Don 852
Pointe de Saint-Gildas 916, 922
Pointe des Chats 893
Pointe des Corbeaux 922
Pointe des Dames 922
Pointe des Poulains 893
Pointe de St Mathieu 854
Pointe de Ver light house 755, 785
Pointe du Grouin du Cou 922
Pointe du Haut-Blanc 754
Pointe du Millier 855
Pointe du Petit-Minou 854
Pointe du Portzic 854, 872
Pointe du Roc 802
Pointe du Toulinguet 855, 872
Pointe St Martin 924
Point Lynas 503
Point of Ayre 502
Point of Fethaland 398
Point Robert light house 827
Polduff Pier 582
Polperro 158
Ponta da Barca 1031
Ponta da Sereta 1031
Ponta das Lajes (Flores) 1030
Ponta Delgada 1031, 1037
Ponta do Albarnaz 1030
Ponta do Altar 991, 1005
Ponta do Arnel 1031
Ponta do Castelo 1031
Ponta do Topo 1031
Ponta Garça 1031
Pont de Térénez 875
Pontevedra 983
Pontrieux 860
Pontusval 853
Poolbeg 570
Poole Harbour 196, 200
Poolewe Bay 449
Poplar Dock Marina 298
Porlock Weir 559
Pornic 922, 925
Pornichet 895, 915
Portaferry 645
Port à la Jument 838
Port Askaig 475
Portavadie 478
Portavogie 618, 640, 645
Portbail 802, 806
Port Bannatyne 482
Port-Béni 860
Port Blanc (Brittany) 861
Port Blanc (Morbihan) 909
Port Bloc 924, 943
Port Cardigan 539
Portcé 895
Portchester Lake 238
Port Clos 857
Port Crannaich 480
Port de Comberge 916
Port de la Corderie 857
Port de la Gravette 916
Port de la Meule 928
Port de Lévi 756, 791
Port des Barques 936
Port des Minimes 933
Port d'Etel 902
Port Dinorwic 520
Port du Becquet 756, 791
Port du Corniguel 897
Port du Douhet 923, 935
Port du Havre-Antifer 755, 769, 779
Port du Parun 909
Port Edgar 375
Portelet Bay (Jersey) 842
Portelet Harbour (Guernsey) 826, 834
Port Ellen 472, 475
Port-en-Bessin 755, 784, 786
Port Erin 505, 507
Port és Saies 838
Port Glasgow 487
Port Gorey 838
Port Haliguen 894, 907
Porthcawl 532, 549
Porth Conger 145
Porth Cressa 145
Porth Dinllaen 523
Porthgain 539
Porthleven 148
Porthmadog 537
Porth Mellin 148
Porth Trecastell 523
Porth Ysgaden 523
Portimão 991, 1005
Port Isaac 563
Portishead 558
Portishead Point 533
Port Joinville 922, 927, 928
Portknockie 401
Port-la-Forêt 892, 897
Portland Bill/Harbour 143, 179
Portland Race 179
Port Louis 893, 902
Portmagee 603
Portmahomack 411
Port Manec'h 892, 900
Port Maria 898, 907
Port-Médoc 924, 943
Portmellon 152
Portmore 629
Port Navalo 894, 909
Port Neuf 936
Porto das Lajes 1030, 1032
Porto do Porto Santo 1041, 1042
Porto Novo 983
Porto (Oporto) 990, 994
Portosín 981
Portpatrick 494, 495
Portreath 563
Portree 450
Portrush 635
Portsall 870
Portscatho 152
Portsmouth 197, 237
Portsoy 401
Port St Mary (Isle of Man) 507
Port Talbot 549
Port Tudy 893, 901
Portugalete (Bilbao) 963
Port William 496
Pottery Pier (Poole) 200
Póvoa de Varzim 990, 993
Praia de Vitória 1031, 1036
Preston 511
Primel-Trégastel 853, 865
Puerto America 1011, 1017, 1018
Puerto Cabo de Cruz 981
Puerto Cádiz 1017, 1018
Puerto de Conil 1011, 1016
Puerto de San Estaban 957
Puerto de San Esteban de Pravia 969
Puerto de Santa Maria 1011, 1017, 1018
Puerto Sherry 1011, 1017, 1018
Puilladobhrain 463
Punta Atalya 957
Punta Candelaria 957
Punta Caraminal 1019
Punta Carnero 1011, 1022
Punta Círes 1012, 1026
Punta da Piedade 991
Punta de Alfanzina 991
Punta de la Estaca de Bares 957
Punta de la Frouxeira 957
Punta del Castillo 957
Punta del Cuerno 957
Punta del Torco de Fuera 956
Punta de San Antón 956
Punta Galea 956
Punta Insúa 958
Punta Langosteira 957, 971
Punta Malabata 1012
Punta Nariga 957
Punta Rebollera 957
Punta Roncadoira 957
Punta San Emeterio 956
Punta Umbria 1010, 1015
Pwllheli 536

Q

Queenborough 289
Quenard Point light house 826
Quiberon 907
Quillebeuf 780
Quimper 897
Quinta do Lorde 1041, 1042
Quiole Barrier 645

R

Rabbit Island 595
Rade de Brest 875
Rade de la Capelle 787
Ramsey Sound 534, 539
Ramsgate 253, 270
Ramsholt 323
Rantum 673
Rapness 419
Rathlin Island 637
Rathlin O'Birne, west side 616
Rathmullan 628
Rattray Head 396
Ravenglass 505
Raxó 983
Raz de Sein 855, 884
Red Bay 617, 637
Redbridge 228
Redkirk 496
Regnéville-sur-Mer 802, 806
Renfrew 487
Restronguet 150
Rhinns of Islay 472
Rhu 486
Rhubh' a Mháil 475
Rhubh' a Mháil (Ruvaal) 472
Ría de Aldán 984
Ría de Ares 957, 972
Ría de Arosa 958, 981
Ría de Betanzos 957, 973
Ría de Camariñas 957, 978
Ría de Cedeira 957, 971
Ría de Corcubión 980, 981
Ría de Corme y Laxe 957, 978
Ría de Huelva 1010
Ría de Huelva Bar 1013
Ría del Barquero 957, 971
Ría de Muros 958, 981
Ría de Pontevedra 958, 983
Ría de Ribadeo 957, 970
Ría de Santa Marta de Ortigueira 970, 971
Ría de Suances 965, 966
Ría de Tina Mayor 967
Ría de Vigo 958, 984
Ría de Vivero 957, 970
Rianxo 958, 982
Ribadesella 956, 967
Ribble, River 502, 511
Richard 941
Richborough 270
Richmond Lock 295
Ringaskiddy 592
Ringstead Bay 189
Río de Las Piedras 1010, 1014
Río de Orio 956, 961
Rio Douro entrance 994
Río Guadalquivir 1011, 1012, 1016
Río Guadiana 1010, 1013
Río Miño 979, 992
Roach, River 304
Roancarrigmore 571

Roaringwater Bay....597
Roberts Cove....592
Rochebonne....803
Rochefort....923, 936
Roches Douvres....827, 852
Roche's Point....571
Rochester....291
Rochford....304
Rockabill....617
Rockall....443
Rømø (Havneby)....652, 664
Rona....417, 435
Roompotsluis....732
Roscoff....853, 868
Rosédo light house....852
Rosehearty....400
Rosière Steps....838
Rosneath....486
Rosslare....570, 584
Rota....1011, 1017
Rotheneuf....808
Rother, River....263
Rothesay....482
Rotten Island....616
Rotterdam....729, 730
Rouen....779, 780
Rouge Terrier....838
Round Island....142
Roundstone Bay....620
Rousay....419
Roustel....826
Royan....924, 941
Rozel Bay....842
Rubha nan Gall....436
Rubha Reidh....434
Rum....454
Runswick Bay....350
Rüschkanal....687
Ruthenstrom....680
Ryde....197, 232
Ryde Sand....232
Rye....252, 263

S

Sagres....991
Saignie Bay....838
Saints Bay....834
Salcombe....167
Salen455, 457
Saltash....159
Sancti Petri....1011, 1019
Sanday....419
Sandend Bay....401
Sandettie Bank....764
Sandown....233
Sandwich....270
Sandy Bay....1022
San Estaban de Pravia....957, 968, 969
San Jacinto....995
San Sebastián (Donostia)....956, 961
Santa Clara....1031
Santa Maria (Azores)....1031
Santander....956, 965
Santoña....956, 965
San Vicente de la Barquera....956, 967
Sanxenxo....983
San Xulian....983
Sark....838
Saundersfoot....547
Sauzon....893, 904
Saye Bay....830
Scalasaig....475
Scalloway....398, 424
Scapa Bay....397, 418
Scarborough....337, 349
Scarinish....435
Scharhorn....680
Scheveningen....707, 723, 724
Schiermonnikoog....712, 713
Schillig....689
Schleswig-Holstein....672
Schulau....680, 687
Schull....571, 598
Schulpengat....707
Schwinge, River....680
Scolpaig....443
Scoraig....449
Scrabster....417
Seaham....337, 356
Seahouses (North Sunderland)....362
Sea Mills....556
Seemannshöft....680
Seil Sound....464
Seine, River....775, 780
Sella Ness....398
Selsey Bill....252, 253
Séné....909
Sept Îles....909
Sesimbra....991, 1003
Setubal....991, 1003
Seven Stones....142
Severn Bridges....552
Severn Estuary....546
Sevilla....1011, 1016, 1017
Shaldon Bridge....174
Shambles Bank....179
Shannon Estuary, River....572, 605
Shapinsay....419
Sharfleet Creek....291
Sharpness....552
Sheep Haven....627, 628
Sheep's Head....571
Sheerness....276
Shell Bay....838
Shetland Islands....397, 421, 422
Shiant Islands....442
Shieldaig....450
Shingles Bank....209
Shirehampton....556
Shoeburyness....303
Shoreham....252, 255
Silloth....502, 504
Sines....1004
Skadan South....397
Skagen....651, 654
Skegness....341
Skeld....423
Skelligs Rock....572
Skerries....503, 647
Skerries Bank....143, 168
Skerryvore....435
Skokholm Island....532
Skomer Island....539
Skroo....397
Skye (Eilean a' Cheo)....435, 449, 450, 452
Sligo....626
Slyne Head....616
Small Isles....454
Smalls....532
Smerwick Harbour....603
Sneem....601
Soay....450
Socoa....950
Soldier's Bay....834
Solent....209, 220
  Central....197
  Eastern....197, 239
  Marks....196
  Precautionary Area....220
  Western....196
Solva....539
Solway Firth....502, 503
Somos....956
Sorel Point light house....827
Soubise....936
Sound of Harris....434, 442
Sound of Iona....456
Sound of Jura....474
Sound of Mull....436, 456
Sound of Raasay....435
Sound of Sleat....435
Southampton....197, 209, 228
South Bishop....532
South Dock Marina....298
Southend (Mull of Kintyre)....480
Southend-on-Sea....276, 303
Southerness Point....496
South Ferriby....347
South Ness....398
Southport....515
South Queensferry....376
South Rock....645
South Ronaldsay....419
Southsea....238
South Stack....503
South Wick....419
Southwold....278, 325
Sovereign Harbour....252, 261
Spiekeroog....697, 698
Spit Sand Fort....197, 238
Spurn Head....336, 342, 346
Squince Harbour....595
St Abb's....373
St Abb's Head....370
Stackpole Quay....547
Stade....670
Stadersand....680
Staffa....456
St Agnes....145
St Alban's Head....179, 188
St Andrew's....383
St Ann's Head....532
Stansore Point....215
St Anthony Head....142, 150
St Antoine....852
Starcross....175
Start Point (Devon)....143, 156, 167
Start Point (Orkney)....397
St Aubin....827, 842
Stavoren....719
St Bees Head....502
St Brelade Bay....842
St Briac....803, 817
St Brides Bay....539
St Brieuc....803, 818
St Cast Le Guildo....803, 817
St Catherine Bay (Jersey)....842
St Catherine's Point (Fowey)....142
St Catherine's Point (IoW)....198, 209
St Denis d'Oléron....923, 934
Steep Holm....550
Stellendam....708
Ster Wenn....904
St Evette....885
St Germain-sur-Ay....805
St German's River....159, 165
St Gilles-Croix-de-Vie....922, 928, 929
St Guénolé....885
St Helen's Fort....198, 233
St Helen's Pool....145
St Helier....827, 840
St Hernot Bay....882
St Ives....533, 563
St Jean de Luz....924, 950
St Jean de Monts....922
St Katharine Haven....298
St Kilda....435, 443
St Malo....802, 804, 808
St Martin de Ré....923, 932
St Mary's....147
St Mawes....150
St Michael's Mount....148
St Monans....371, 376
St Nazaire....895, 916
St Nicolas Bay (Morgat)....882
St Nicolas (Les Sables d'Olonne)....929
St Nicolas (Pointe de Grave)....923
St Ninian's Bay....481
St Norgard Bay....882
Stoer Head....434
Stokes Bay....209
Stonehaven....371, 385
Stor....680
Storloch....680
Stornoway....434, 437
Stour, River (Dorset)....210
Stour, River (Essex/Suffolk)....278, 318
Stour, River (Kent)....270
St Peter (Eider, River)....670
St Peter Port....826, 832

Gazetteer

St Quay-Portrieux ... 803, 820
Straight Point ... 168, 176
Strangford Lough ... 644, 645
Stranraer ... 494
Strathy Point ... 396
Straw Island ... 616
Stroma ... 396, 417
Stromness ... 397, 420
Stronsay ... 421
Strumble Head ... 532
St Sampson's Harbour ... 834
St Suliac ... 815
St Thomas Head ... 558
St Tudwall's Roads ... 535
Studland Bay ... 200, 233
St Vaast-la-Hougue ... 756, 789
St Valéry-en-Caux ... 755, 773
St Valéry-sur-Somme ... 754, 767
Sudbrook ... 552
Süderhöft ... 675
Suderoogsand ... 673
Sule Skerry ... 396, 417
Sullom Voe ... 398, 422, 424
Sumburgh ... 424
Sumburgh Head ... 397
Summer Isles ... 445
Sunderland ... 337, 356
Sunk Head ... 310
Sunk Inner Precautionary Area ... 273
Swale, River ... 276, 288
Swanage ... 196, 199
Swanwick ... 231
Swarbacks Minn ... 422
Swellies, The ... 520
Swinge ... 828
Sylt ... 673

T

Tabs Head ... 341
Tamar, River ... 165
Tancarville Bridge ... 780
Tanera Beg ... 449
Tanera Mor ... 449
Tangier ... 1012, 1026
Tarbat Ness ... 396
Tarbert Island (Shannon) ... 605
Tarbert (Loch Fyne) ... 478
Tarifa ... 1011, 1021, 1022
Tarn Point ... 505
Tater-du ... 142
Tautenay ... 826
Tavira ... 991, 1008
Tavy, River ... 159
Taw and Torridge, Rivers ... 533, 561
Tay, River ... 383
Tazones ... 957
Tean Sound ... 145
Teddington Lock ... 297
Tees, River ... 350
Teignmouth ... 174
Telegraph Bay ... 830
Tenby ... 547
Termunterzijl ... 712
Terneuzen ... 739
Terre-Nègre ... 923
Terschelling ... 714, 715
Teüfelsbruck ... 687
Thames Estuary/River ... 276, 279, 282, 295
Thames Tidal Barrier ... 277, 297
Thisted Havn ... 651
Thorney Channel ... 198, 242
Thorsminde ... 656, 658
Thurso ... 396
Thyborøn ... , 651, 656
Tighnabruaich ... 482
Tilbury ... 295
Tinduff ... 875
Tingwall ... 420
Tinker's Hole ... 456
Tiumpan Head ... 434
Tobermory ... 456
Tollesbury ... 310
Tonning ... 675
Topsham ... 175
Torduff Point ... 496
Torquay ... 174
Torre de Hércules ... 957
Torridge, River ... 561
Tory Island ... 617
Totland Bay ... 210, 211
Totnes ... 168
Tralong Bay ... 595
Trawbreaga Bay ... 629
Trearddur Bay ... 523
Trébeurden ... 852, 864
Tréboul ... 883
Trefor ... 523
Trégastel-Plage ... 852, 863
Tréguier ... 852, 858, 860
Tréhiguier ... 912
Tresco ... 145, 146
Treshnish Isles ... 456
Trévignon ... 892
Trevose Head ... 533
Trézien ... 854
Troon ... 473, 493
Trouville ... 755, 782
Truro ... 150
Trwyn Dinmor ... 523
Tuckton Bridge ... 210, 218
Turf Lock ... 175
Turnberry Point ... 473
Turnchapel ... 159
Tuskar Rock ... 570, 575, 582
Tyne, River ... 337, 357

U

Ullapool ... 437, 445
Ulva Sound ... 456
Ulverston ... 509
Unionhall (Glandore) ... 595
Upnor ... 291
Ura Firth ... 422
Urk ... 719
Ushenish ... 434

V

Vaila Sound ... 422, 423
Val-André ... 817
Valentia Harbour ... 602
Vannes ... 909, 910
Vatersay Sound ... 434
Vatteville ... 780
Vazon Bay ... 834
Vegesack ... 688
Velas ... 1031, 1034
Ventnor ... 233
Viana do Castello ... 990, 993
Vila da Praia ... 1031
Vila do Porto ... 1031, 1036
Vila Franca do Campo ... 1031
Vilagarcia ... 958, 981, 982
Vilaine, River ... 894, 912
Vilamoura ... 991, 1006
Vilanova ... 982
Vila Real de Santo Antònio ... 991, 1008, 1010
Village Bay (St Kilda) ... 443
Vlaardingen ... 730
Vlieland ... 715
Vlissingen ... 734
Volendam ... 719

W

Wadebridge ... 563
Wainfleet ... 341
Waldringfield ... 323
Wallasea ... 305
Walsoorden ... 734
Walton Backwaters ... 278, 313
Wangerooge ... 689, 696
Wareham ... 200, 202
Warrenpoint (Carlingford Lough) ... 646
Warren Point (R Exe) ... 175
Warren Point (R Yealm) ... 166
Warsash ... 230, 231
Wash ... 336, 339
Watchet ... 559
Waterfoot ... 637
Waterford ... 586
Watermill Cove ... 145
Watermouth ... 560
Watwick Point ... 532
Welland, River ... 341
Wellhouse Rock ... 552
Wells-next-the-Sea ... 336, 339
Wemyss Bay ... 485
Weser, River ... 681, 689
West Bay (Bridport) ... 178
West Burra Firth Inner ... 398
West Cove ... 601
Westerheversand ... 670
Westerschelde ... 724, 733
West Frisian Islands ... 713
Westhoofd light house ... 707
Westkapelle ... 708, 733
West Kyle ... 481
West Loch Tarbert ... 438, 475
West Mersea ... 310
Weston ... 228
Weston-super-Mare ... 558
Westport ... 625
West Schouwen light house ... 708
West Stones ... 339
West Terschelling ... 714, 715
West Wangerooge ... 696
Wexford ... 582, 583
Weymouth ... 187
Whalsay ... 397, 422
Whitaker Beacon ... 305
Whitby ... 337, 350
Whitehaven ... 502, 505
White House ... 552
Whitsand Bay ... 158
Whitstable ... 276, 287
Wick ... 396, 412
Wicklow ... 570, 581
Wicklow Head ... 570
Widewall Bay ... 420
Widnes ... 515
Wielingen Channel ... 708
Wilhelmshaven ... 671, 691
Winteringham Haven ... 347
Winterton-on-Sea ... 330
Wisbech ... 336, 340
Wischhafen ... 680
Wolf Rock ... 142
Woolwich ... 295
Wootton Creek ... 197, 232
Worbarrow Bay ... 189
Worhden ... 680
Workington ... 502, 504
Workum ... 719
Worthing ... 252, 255
Wouldham ... 291
Wyk ... 674
Wyre light house ... 510
Wyre Sound (Orkney) ... 419

Y

Yare, River ... 330
Yarmouth (Isle of Wight) ... 196, 212
Yealm, River ... 166
Yelland Marsh ... 561
Yell Sound ... 397, 398, 422
Youghal ... 587

Z

Zeebrugge ... 730, 741
Zeegat van Terschelling ... 706, 714
Zoutkamp ... 713
Zumaya (Zumaia) ... 956, 962